THE
INTERNATIONAL
AUTHORS AND WRITERS
WHO'S WHO

THE INTERNATIONAL AUTHORS AND WRITERS WHO'S WHO

EDITORIAL DIRECTOR:

Ernest Kay, D.litt., F.R.S.A., F.R.G.S.

Sales Director:

Roger W. G. Curtis M. A. (Cantab.)

Production Director:

Nicholas S. Law

Assistant Editors:

Diane Hobbs

Angela Bridgeman

Deborah Fitchett

Researcher:

Joy Dean

All communications to: International Biographical Centre,
Cambridge CB2 3QP, England

THE INTERNATIONAL AUTHORS AND WRITERS WHO'S WHO

TENTH EDITION

EDITORIAL DIRECTOR

ERNEST KAY

93714

International Biographical Centre
Cambridge England

First published 1934
Second Edition 1935
Third Edition 1948
Fourth Edition 1960
Fifth Edition 1963
Sixth Edition 1972
Reprinted 1972
Seventh Edition 1976
Eighth Edition 1977
Ninth Edition 1982
Tenth Edition 1986

ISBN 0 900332 88 3

Computer typesetting by SB Datagraphics, Wyncolls Road, Colchester, Essex, England
Printed and bound in the United Kingdom by The Bath Press, Lower Bristol Road, Bath BA2 3BL.

INTERNATIONAL BIOGRAPHICAL CENTRE

The IBC group publishes one of the widest ranges of contemporary biographical reference works under any one imprint; some titles date back to the 1930's.

Current titles include:
Dictionary of International Biography
Men of Achievement (Illustrated)
The World Who's Who of Women (Illustrated)
International Authors and Writers Who's Who*
International Businessmen's Who's Who
International Who's Who in Art and Antiques
International Who's Who in Community Service
International Who's Who in Education
International Who's Who in Engineering
International Who's Who in Medicine
International Who's Who in Music
International Who's Who in Poetry*
International Youth in Achievement
The World Who's Who of Women in Education
Who's Who in the Commonwealth
Who's Who in Western Europe
Dictionary of Latin American and Caribbean Biography
Dictionary of Scandinavian Biography
Foremost Women of the Twentieth Century

* recently published in combined volumes.

All enquiries to:
International Biographical Centre
Cambridge CB2 3QP
England

FOREWORD BY THE EDITORIAL DIRECTOR

I am extremely pleased to introduce this Tenth Edition of the *International Authors and Writers Who's Who*. This volume has taken many months to compile and is, I believe, a worthy successor to previous editions which have proved so popular with librarians and readers.

When I wrote my Foreword to the Ninth Edition, I announced that it had been decided to issue the *International Authors and Writers Who's Who* every three years in future; several unfortunate delays have meant that we are a few months behind schedule but my colleagues and I have already decided to begin work on an Eleventh Edition and we will do all we can to publish editions on a regular basis.

The Ninth Edition incorporated the Sixth Edition of the *International Who's Who in Poetry*; it seemed unnecessary as well as economically unrealistic to publish two separate titles and this Tenth Edition completes the process of merger. This Edition lists poets of distinction from all over the world together with novelists, critics, essayists, technical and professional writers and all those formally sought and found in the *International Authors and Writers Who's Who*. In this Edition we have also bowed to numerous requests (and a few complaints) for the inclusion of magazine and publishers' editors and leading journalists. Indeed we have been extremely pleased with the response from these individuals who have not only been eager to provide biographical information but who have also shown the importance of the role they play in preparing and presenting words that are read immediately by millions of avid readers and which affect the social and political lives of most countries.

I know that my editors would wish me to thank the many authors' organizations, book publishers, literary agents and individuals in every continent who have advised and assisted us in the preparation of this Edition. Many of them obviously wish to ensure that we do as good a job as possible; we deeply appreciate their co-operation. As always, we try to include as many writers as we can, given that our policy is to publish only that information which has been verified and checked by the individuals themselves. Since many writers and authors are difficult to contact by mail as their addresses are rarely made public, we regret their omission from these pages as a result.

We emphasize that there is no charge or fee of any kind for biographical inclusion, nor is there any obligation to purchase. With this in mind, those who feel that they should be included in future editions are warmly invited to sent their names and addresses to the International Biographical Centre; in the same way, readers are encouraged to nominate their favourite writers for future inclusion and, while names are always useful reminders, addresses of individuals or their agents are most valuable.

To bring writers of all persuasions together, the International Biographical Centre has founded *The World Literary Academy*. This incorporates *The International Academy of Poets* and the *Academy's* aim is to promote the work of its Fellows and to encourage literature and literacy. Fellowship is offered to all writers of prose and poetry, to encourage best-selling authors and popular journalists as well as those who have had few works published but who have shown a literary ability. *The World Literary Academy* was formally launched in 1985 as part of the Silver Jubilee celebrations of the International Biographical Centre to mark twenty-five years of Who's Who publishing. Those wishing to receive details concerning Fellowship are invited to write to The Secretary, *The World Literary Academy*, International Biographical Centre, Cambridge CB2 3QP, England.

Having mentioned the 1985 Silver Jubilee of the IBC, I should remind readers of this volume that this title was originally published by Burke's Peerage in London as *The Authors and Writers Who's Who* in 1934. While this is the fourth edition published by the IBC since we purchased the title in the mid-1970s, the title itself has already celebrated its Golden Jubilee.

Every writer included in this Tenth Edition was sent a typescript of his or her entry for correction and, although some typescripts were not returned, every care has been taken to ensure the accuracy of each biography. It may be, however, that the occasional error has crept in and, if so, I apologize in advance.

It is my great personal pleasure to send best wishes to those who appear in, and use, this Edition all over the world.

International Biographical Centre
Cambridge CB2 3QP, England
June 1986

A

AALTONEN, Ilta Annikki Tyyne, b. 21 May 1911, Pori, Finland. Author. m. Erkki Aaltonen, 1 Sep. 1934, Helsinki, 2 sons, 1 daughter. *Education:* Studied, University of Helsinki, 1932–35, 1946–47; Examination in Swedish Language, 1955. *Publications:* A Senseless Caprice, 1946; A Storm, 1948; Human Beings in a Critical Period, short stories, 1951; Plays: The Hands, 1960; The Death of Klaus Fleming, 1963; Restless Young People and a Testament, 1970. *Honours:* 3rd Prize, Historical Drama Competition, 1963; Artist Pension of the State, 1975. *Memberships:* Union of Finnish Authors; Union of Finnish Dramatists; Union of the Finnish Defenders of Peace; Society Finland-Soviet Union; PAND-Artists for Peace. *Address:* Ohjaajantie 3A3, 00400 Helsinki, Finland.

AALTONEN, Ulla-Maija, b. 28 Aug. 1940, Vihti, Finland. Writer. *Education:* BA, USA. *Publications:* Uma's Book, 1977; Books on, Mostly Minx, a filly, a horse and a jumper, 1976, 1979, 1985; Colette – A Little Black Dog, 1978; Rabbits Don't Cry, 1978; Goats March In, 1979; Books for adolescents on, manners, 1979, sex, 1980, alcohol, 1983; Mr Andersson's Travels, 1980; Mr Andersson Gets Ill, 1981, etc, 20 in all. *Contributions to:* Anna, 1974–79; Uusi Suomi, 1979–85; 11 major local dailies. *Honour:* State Information Award, 1980. *Membership:* Finnish Writers Association. *Address:* 08500 Lohja, Finland.

AARON, Bernard Alan, b. 30 Aug. 1939, Newcastle-on-Tyne, England. Performing Artist/Teacher/Composer. *Education:* Royal Conservatory of Music, Toronto (classical guitar) 1982. *Publications:* Compositions: Peppercorn's Magic, (music score for children's play by Florence Novelli), 1975; Guitar Dictation Book, 1978; Christmas Variations, 1979; Five Variations on Greensleeves, 1980; Seven Variations on Coventry Carol, 1980; Music scores for Florence Novelli's children's plays: Itchy, Snitchy and Boo, 1981, 1983, Misty, the Little Lost Cloud, 1981, 1983; Mrs Perriwinkle's Cosmic Dream, 1981; Mrs Oodle-Noodle and Crumdum, 1982; Mrs Oodle-Noodle and Santa, 1982; Santa and the King, 1982; Spindlerion and the Princess, 1983; Queen Cat of Furbit, 1983; Freeky the Pretty Witch, 1984; Twinkle and the Cosmic Pirate, 1984; Spanish Essay No 1, 1981; La Guitare Enchantee (student arrangements) 1982; Hungarian Dance, 1985; Unicef Lullaby, 1985. *Contributor to:* Classical Guitar Magazine (UK), Feature and music publication – April 1985, Review – December 1985; Guitar International, Feature, music publication and letter to editor – Feb. 1985. *Membership:* Playwrights Union of Canada, 1980–84. *Address:* 18A Gloucester Street, Clifton Village, Bristol BS8 4JF, England.

ABBOTT, Gertrude Webster, b. 31 Jan. 1897. Instructor/Professor of Art. *Education:* Honours Graduate, Chicago School of Applied and Normal Art; Cambridge, Massachusetts, School of Architecture; Lowthorpe School of Landscape Architecture, Groton, Massachusetts; University of Illinois; University of Colorado; Special Study, Europe and USA. m. Howard Clinton Abbott, PhD. *Appointments include:* Instructor in Art, Milwaukee-Downer College, Wisconsin; Supervisor of Art, Andover, Massachusetts, Public Schools; Instructor in Art, Washington High School, Sioux Falls; Professor of Art and Head of Department, Sioux Falls College, 1934–49. *Contributor to:* Various anthologies including Anthology of South Dakota Poetry, 1935; Prarie Poets III, 1966; Voices of South Dakota, 1977. Various newspapers and periodicals especially Pasque Petals, official organ of South Dakota Society; PEO Record; The Mayflower Quarterly. *Honours include:* Editor Emeritus for serving as Interim Editor, Pasque Petals, 1971–74; Honorary DLitt, Sioux Falls College, 1975. *Memberships include:* South Dakota State Poetry Society; National Federation of State Poetry Societies; Academy of American Poets.

Address: 2708 Wood Drive, Sioux Falls, SD 57105, USA.

ABBOTT, James Edward, b. 24 Oct. 1956, Amersham, England. Journalist. *Education:* BA Honours, Philosophy, Politics and Economics. *Contributions to:* Modern Railways; The Times; Marketing Week; Metal Bulletin. *Address:* 24 Rothesay Avenue, London SW20, England.

ABELA, Joseph M, b. 23 Nov. 1931. Lecturer, Philosophy & Multicultural Education. m. Carol Lee Parkes. *Education:* Corpus Christi College, Melbourne, Australia; University of Papua New Guinea; Louvain University, Belgium; BPhil; Lic. en Phil.; PhD. *Appointments include:* Research fellow, Academy of Social Sciences, Monash University, Australia; Lecturer, State College of Victoria. *Publications include:* Tlitt Iqlub, in Maltese, 1952; Driegh ma Driegh, in Maltese, 1971; Maltese Poems, 1980. *Contributor to:* Blacksmith, 1975; The Poets Choice, 1968; 'SCOPP', 1977, 1978, 1979; in Maltese: Il-Malti; Lehen il Malti; Forum; numerous anthologies. *Honours include:* Member, Malta Academy for Contribution to Maltese Literature; 2nd Prize, Eucharist Competition 1948; 1st Prize, Malta Literature Society International Competition, 1957. *Memberships:* Australasian Association of Philosophers; The Malta Academy; Poets Union of Australia; Fellowship of Australian Writers. *Address:* 34 Park Avenue, Caves Beach, Swansea, NSW 2281, Australia.

ABELL, Carol Louise, b. 25 Sep. 1940. Secretary; Editor; Poet; Writer; Lecturer. *Education:* DLitt, University of New York, USA; PhD, University L.Asia. *Appointments include:* Secretary, Federation of International Poetry Association of UNESCO; Editor, New Muses, Washington DC. *Publications include:* Morning Glory World, 1977; Five-Leaf Clover, 1981; reviews; prefaces etc. *Contributor to:* Numerous magazines, anthologies etc, including: Indianapolis Star; Indianapolis Herald; Independent; Evansville Courier; New Voices of American Poetry; Verbeia; Poet; Eclipse; Young Published Newsletters; Year Book of Modern Poetry; Adventures in Poetry Magazine; An Anthology of Texan Poems; Nouvelle Europe; etc. *Honours include:* Poet Laureatships; Golden Diplomas; Trophies; numerous other awards. *Memberships include:* International Literature Society; Poets International Organisation; International Poetry Society; New York Poetry Forum; American Poetry Society; Centro Studi E Scambi Internazionali. *Address:* PO Box 39072, Washington, DC 20016, USA.

ABELLAN, José[r] Luis, b. 19 May 1933, Madrid Spain. University Professor. *Education:* MA, PhD, University Complutense, Madrid. *Publications include:* La idea de América, 1972; Sociologia del 98' 1974; La industria cultural en Espana, 1975; El erasmismo español, 1976; El exicio espanol de 1939, 6 vols 1976–78; Historias de posguerra, 1979; Historia critica del pensamiento espanol, 4 vols 1979–81; Anthologies including: Los espanôles vistos por si mismos, 1977; Editor of several textbooks and editor of collections, Biblioteca de Pensamiento. *Contributions to:* Numerous national and foreign journals. *Honours:* Essay Prize, El Europeo, Madrid, 1975; Grant, Juan March Foundations for a study of 18th century thought; National Prize for Literature, 1981; Member of Executive Board, UNESCO, 1983. *Memberships include:* Asociaction Internacional de Hispanistas; Ateneo de Madrid; PEN Club (Spain); Sociedad Española de Filosofia; Ed Comm of Espasa-Calpe (Madrid). *Address:* Gravina 7, 28004 Madrid, Spain.

ABERCROMBIE, Virginia Townsend, 24 Dec. 1927, Houston, Texas, USA. Author. m. John B Abercrombie, 1 Apr. 1950, 2 sons, 1 daughter. *Education:* BA, University of Texas, Austin. *Publications:* Catering in Houston co-author, 1977; Places to Take a Crowd, co-author, 1979; Christmas in Texas anthology of poems, co-editor, 1979; Catering To Houston, 1981. *Contributions* *include:* Texas Traveler; Riversedge; Journal Vignette; Gusto; The Bluegrass Literary Review; Rising Star; The Cathartic; The White Rock Review; Poet. *Honours:* 3rd place 1977, Honorable mention 1978, Writer's Digest Poetry Contest; Selected to read in the Houston Festival, 1982. *Address:* 3 Smithdale Court, Houston, TX 77024, USA.

ABERNATHY, David Myles, b. 27 June 1933, Connelly Springs, North Carolina, USA. m. Kathryn Lynn Fordham, 16 Oct. 1971, 2 sons. *Education:* AB, High Point College, 1955; M.Div., Emory University, 1962; STM, Union Theological Seminary, New York, 1964. *Appointments:* Instructor, English, University of Maryland, 1957–59; Visiting Instructor, Communications, Interdenominational Theological Center, Atlanta University, 1961–63; Tutor Assistant, 1963–64, Tutor, 1965, Union Theological Seminary, New York; Instructor, Massey College, 1969–70; Instructor, Speech, 1969–70, Adjunct Professor, Communications, 1965–72, Emory University; Guest Professor, Columbia Theological Seminary, 1965–72; Churchman in Residence, Candler School of Theology, 1985. *Publications include:* Hello, Japan, 1957; A Child's Guidebook to Rome, 1964; Life is for Growing, 1967; Reflections, 1969; Keystone for Education, 1969; Ideas, Inventions and Patents, with Wayne Knipe, 1975; Oneness in Christ, Editor, Contributor, 1981; Understanding the Teaching of Jesus, with Norman Perrin, 1983; Four Gospels to Modern English, in preparation. *Contributor to:* Numerous professional journals and magazines. *Honours:* Litt.D. Rust College, 1974; L.H.D., Texas Wesleyan College, 1980. *Memberships include:* Authors League of America; National Academy of Television Arts & Sciences; American Society of Composers, Authors and Publishers; National Academy of Recording Arts and Sciences, Board of Governors; Broadcast Pioneers, Life Member; American Film Institute; International Communication Association; Public Relations Society of America, Accredited Member; American Academy of Religion; etc. *Address:* 935 Bream Court, NE, Marietta, GA 30067, USA.

ABRAMS, Meyer Howard, b. 23 July 1912, Long Branch, New Jersey, USA. Educator. m. Ruth Gaynes, 1 Sep. 1937, New York City, USA, 2 daughters. *Education:* AB, 1934, MA, 1937, PhD, 1940, Harvard University; Henry Fellow, University of Cambridge, England, 1934–35. *Literary Appointments:* Advisory Editor, W W Norton & Co Inc, 1961–. *Major Publications:* The Milk of Paradise, 1934, 2nd edition 1970; The Mirror & The Lamp: Romantic Theory & the Critical Tradition, 1953; A Glossary of Literary Terms, 1957, 4th edition 1981; Natural Supernaturalism: Tradition & Revolution in Romantic Literature, 1971; The Correspondent Breeze: Essays on English Romanticism, 1984; Editor: The Norton Anthology of English Literature, 1962, 5th edition 1986. *Contributor to:* Various literary periodicals of essays on literature and critical theory. *Honours:* Christian Gauss Prize, 1954; James Russell Lowell Prize, 1975; American Academy Award in Humanistic Studies, 1984; Honorary Doctorates, University of Rochester, 1978, Northwestern University, 1981, University of Chicago, 1982. *Memberships:* Modern Language Association, Executive Council 1961–64; American Academy of Arts & Sciences, 1940–; American Philosophical Society, 1950–; Founders Group, National Humanities Center. *Address:* Department of English, Cornell University, Ithaca, NY 14853, USA.

ABRAMSON, Martin, b. 25 Jan. 1921, Brooklyn, New York, USA. Journalist; Author. m. Marcia Zagon, 9 May 1949, 1 son, 1 daughter. *Education:* BA, City College of New York; Graduate study, Columbia School of Journalism; MA, University of California. *Publications:* The Real Al Jolson, 1956; The Barney Ross Story (Monkey on my Back), 1959; The Padre of Guadalcanal Story, 1964; Hollywood Surgeon, 1969; Forgotten Fortunes, 1973; The Trial of Chaplain Jensen, 1976; Consumer's Guide to Travel Agencies, 1980. *Contributions to:* Major US magazines including:

Readers Digest; Cosmopolitan; Better Homes and Gardens; Playboy; Esquire; Sport; American Legion Magazine; Travel & airline magazines; United Feature Syndicate; etc. *Honours include:* Bronze Star Medal, US Army, as Stars & Stripes, correspondent, World War II; Best Magazine Article Award, Writers Alliance, 1975; Best Sports Story, Citadel Press, 1971; Community Service Award, Kiwanis Clubs of America, 1978. *Memberships:* Charter member, American Society of Journalists & Authors; Overseas Press Club; US Tennis Writers Association; CCNY Communications Alumni; President, Peninsula Public Library, Lawrence, New York. *Literary Agent:* Bertha Klausner International Literary Agency. *Address:* 827 Peninsula Boulevard, Woodmere, NY 11598, USA.

ACCROCCA, Elio Filippo, b. 17 Apr. 1923, Cori, Italy. Writer. *Education:* Lic in Lit, University of Rome, Italy. *Publications:* Portonaccio, 1949; Ritorno a Portonaccio, 1959; Innestogramme-Correspondenze, 1965; Europa Inquieta, 1972; Siamo, non Siamo, 1974; Il Superfluo, 1980; Bagage, 1984; Videogrammi della Prolunga, 1984; Esercizi Radicali, 1984. *Contributions to:* La Fiera letteraria; Europa letteraria; La Gazzettadel Mezzagiorno, and others. *Honours include:* Premi Letterari di poesia, Chianciano, 1965; Tagliacozno, 1974. *Membership:* Director, Accademia Bellw Arti, Foggia. *Address:* Via Canino 22, Rome, Italy.

ACHTERLAND, Gerrit, b. 7 Dec. 1953, Geraardsbergen, Belgium. Writer; Editor. m. Sonia Sergooris, 6 Sep. 1974, Roosdaal, 1 son, 1 daughter. *Education:* Koninkiljk Atheneum. *Literary Appointments:* Former Chief Editor, several literary reviews; Poetry Editor. *Publications:* Poetry: Sigaar als oude wijn, 1973; Clitoris, 1975; Gedichten 1973–1978, 1978; Als de eenvoud uit je ogen straalt, 1979; De warmte van een verloren einder, 1980; De parfumeur-créateur, 1986. *Contributions to:* Numerous journals. *Honours:* Poetry Awards, City of Halle, 1976, 1984. *Memberships include:* Literary Society Kofschip-Kring VZW; etc. *Literary Agent:* De Backer Ivo, Belgium. *Address:* Editions Gerrit Achterland, c/o De Backer Ivo Kelistraat 47C, 1760 Roosdaal, Belgium.

ADAIR, Virginia H, b. 28 Feb. 1913. University Professor. m. Douglas Adair, (deceased), 2 sons, 1 daughter. *Education:* BA, Mount Holyoke College; MA, Radcliffe; TA, University of Wisconsin, 1935–37; further graduate work, University of Washington, Harvard, Claremont Graduate School. *Appointments:* Instructor, English, Miss Fine's School, College of William & Mary, Pomona College, La Verne College; Assistant, Associate & Full Professor, California State Polytechnic University, 1957–80. *Honours:* 1st Prize, Katherine Irene Glascock, 1932, 1933; Special Category Prize, Poet Lore, 1972; Best Poems of 1974; Car Poly, founded V H Adair Poetry Award. *Memberships:* Poetry Society of America. *Contributor to:* Christian Science Monitor; Atlantic; New Republic; Saturday Review; Poetry; Poetry Northwest; Poet Lore; NY Quarterly; Massachusetts Review; Colorado Quarterly; Michigan Quarterly; Epos; Lyric; Wormwood; Snowy Egret; Janus-SCTH; Poets West. *Address:* 489 West 6th, Claremont, CA 91711, USA.

ADAMS, Alger LeRoy, b. 1 Aug. 1910, Omaha, Nebraska, USA. Clergyman; Journalist. m. Jessie Wells Adams, 31 May 1937, Orange, 1 daughter. *Education:* MA, Teachers College, Columbia University, 1968; Columbia Graduate School of Journalism, 1969; STB, General Theological Seminary, 1937; Hobart College, DD, 1983. *Appointments:* Assistant to Editor & Publisher, New York Amsterdam News, 1941–45; Managing Editor, Episcopal Diocese of New York Bulletin, 1947–56; Associate Editor, Ebony Magazine, 1956–57; Owner, Editor, Publisher, Westchester County Press, 1950–; Managing Editor, Teamsters Local 445 Dispatch, 1960–75. *Publications:* Taffy, 1949; With My Eyes Wide Open, 1951. *Contributor to:* The Witness, 1950; Various travel pieces on Caribbean, Around the World, Spain, Portugal, Africa. *Honours:* Phi Beta Kappa; White English Prize, 1932; Phi Delta Kappa.

Memberships: Society of Professional Journalists; Association of Travel Editors; National Megrp Publishers Association. *Literary Agent:* Anne Elmo, New York City. *Address:* 61 Pinecrest Drive, Hastings on Hudson, NY 10706, USA.

ADAMS, Anna Theresa, b. 9 Mar. 1926, London, England. Writer; Artist; Teacher. m. Norman Adams, 18 Jan. 1947, Burnt Oak, 2 sons. *Education:* NDD, Painting, Harrow School of Art, 1945; NDD Sculpture, Hornsey College of Art, 1950. *Literary Appointments:* Part-time Teacher, Various schools; Designer, Chelsea Pottery, 1953–56; Art Teacher, Comprehensive schools, Manchester and Settle, 1966–73; Poet-in-Residence, Loughborough University of Technology, 1978. *Publications:* Journey Through Winter, 1969; A Rainbow Plantation, 1971; Memorial Tree, 1972; Parabola, 1975; Unchanging Seas, 1978; A Reply to Intercepted Mail, 1979; An Island Chapter, 1983; Brother Fox, 1984; Dear Vincent, 1986. *Contributions to:* Guardian; Countryman; Scottish Field; Encounter; PN Review; Stand; Country Life; Poetry Review; Outposts; Poetry Durham; The Green Back; The Dalesman; Orbis; Acumen. Poetry Now, programmes, Radio 3, Schools broadcasts, radio, British Broadcasting Corporation. *Honours:* 1st Prize, Yorkshire Poets, 1973, 75, 76; Arnold Vincent Bowen Award, 1976; Bursary, Yorkshire Arts Association, 1978. *Memberships:* Poetry Society. *Address:* Butts Hill House, Horton-in-Ribblesdale, Settle, North Yorkshire BD24 OHD, England.

ADAMS, Howard Digby, 3 Apr. 1922, Australia, Deceased 15 Aug. 1985. Cartoonist and Artist. m. Wendy Poulton, 15 June 1963. *Literary Appointments:* Senior lecturer/co-ordinator, of Drawing, School of Art and Design, Chisholm Institute of Technology, Caulfield, Melbourne, Australia, 1971–79. *Contributions include:* Australasian Post; Daily Telegraph, Napier, New Zealand; National Australia Bank; Parkes Champion Post; Your Garden; Engadine District News; G J Coles and Co Ltd; Advocate, Coffs Harbour; Prime Time; 'Australasian Office News; Mobil Oil Australia Limited; Several other newspapers, periodicals and company bulletins use his cartoons.

ADAMS, Julia Davis, b. 23 July 1900, Clarksburg, West Virginia, USA. Writer. m. William McMillan Adams, 30 Mar. 1974, Charles Town. *Education:* BA, Barnard, 1922. *Publications:* Swords of the Vikings, 1928; Vaino, 1929; Mountains Are Free, 1930; Stonewall Jackson, 1932; Remember & Forget, 1932; No Other White Men, 1937; Peter Hale, 1939; The Sun Climbs Slow, 1942; The Wind and the Grass, 1943; The Shenandoah, 1945; Cloud on the Land, 1951; Bridle on the Wind, 1953; Eagle on the Sun, 1956; Legacy of Love, 1961; Ride with the Eagle, 1963; A Valley & A Song, 1963; Mount Up, 1967; Never Say Die, 1980. *Contributor to:* Smithsonian Magazine; American Bar Association Journal. *Honours:* LLD, Salem College, 1984. *Address:* 115 Brookstone Drive, Princeton, NJ 08540, USA.

ADAMS, Lillian Loyce, b. 10 Jan. 1912, Cadiz, Texas, USA. Professor of Business Administration. *Education:* BBA, Texas Arts & Industry University, Kingsville, 1931; MBA, University of Texas, Austin, 1935; PhD, University of Texas, 1959. *Publications:* (Poetry) Quaking Leaves, 1940; Three Wishes, 1947; (Professional) Secretary's Business Review, Contributing Author, 1959; Managerial Psychology, 1965; (Travel) The Three T's – Teach, Travel & Tell, 1960; Harp Beyond the Wall, 1979; Heritage Poems and Others, 1982. *Contributor to:* Numerous Anthologies, Journals, etc. *Honours:* Sigma Iota Epsilon (MGT); Beta Gamma Sigma; Delta Pi Epsilon; Alpha Chi; Pi Omega Pi; Phi Chi Theta; NSA; Golden Key Scholarship; Teacher of the Year, 6th District TBEA, 1972; etc. *Memberships include:* President, 1961–62, Various Other Offices, Texas Business Education Association; AAUW, President Local Chapter, 3 yrs; Texas State Teachers Association, President, Walker County Unit. *Address:* 216 Elmwood, Huntsville, TX 77340, USA.

ADAMS, Wilfried M G, b. 23 Nov. 1947, Louvain, Flanders (Belgium). Poet; Literary Critic; Journalist; Translator; Lyricist of rock songs. Divorced, 1 son. *Education:* Candidate in law; Licentiate Germanic philology cum laude, Catholic University, Louvain. *Publications:* Poetry: Uit de Brand, III, 1968; Eleven Sic! for a Lady, 1969; Graafschap, 1970; Geen Vogelkreet de Roos, 1975; Aanspraak, 1981; Dicta Dura, 1985; Afwezigheid, 1986. Essays: Hugues C Pernath: Mijn gegeven, woord, 1972. *Contributions to:* Dietsche Warande & Belfort; Diogenes, De Nieuwe; Ons Erfdeel; Poeziekrant. *Honours:* Prijs Vlaamse Poëziedagen, 1971; Premie Knokke-Heist, 1976; Prijs Francine Urbin-Choffray, 1980. *Memberships:* Comité van de Vlaamse Poëziedagen; Vereniging van Vlaamse Letterkundigen; Maatschappij der Nederlandse Letterkunde, Leiden, Holland; Co-founder, Working Member and 1st Secretary, Confrèrie de Recherches, 1984. *Literary Agent:* KMB, Antwerp. *Address:* Lange Vlierstraat 25, B-2000 Antwerp, Belgium.

ADAMSON, Iain, b. 22 Aug. 1928, Westerton, Dunbartonshire, Scotland. Author/Director of Studies, London Art College. *Education:* Glasgow Academy, Scotland; Goethe Institute, Munich, Federal Republic of Germany; University of Vienna, Austria; University of Paris, France. *Publications include:* The Old Fox; The Forgotten Men; A Man of Quality; The Great Detective. *Contributor to:* Numerous papers and magazines in UK, USA, Canada, Austria; TV Spokesman, Reporter, Farming News; Scottish Daily Express; Sunday Express; Daily Mirror; Daily Express; Santa Monica Outlook, Los Angeles, USA; Foreign Correspondent in France, Spain and Germany for Daily Express. *Address:* Iain Adamson and Partners, 11 Bolt Court, Fleet Street, London, England.

ADE, Walter Frank Charles, b. 24 Oct. 1910, Ottawa, Canada. University Professor. *Education:* BA, Queens University, 1933; MA, University of Toronto, 1939; PhD, Northwestern University, 1949; Ed.D. Indiana University, USA, 1960. *Publications include:* Animal Fiction in European Literature, 1939; The Mermaid of Fiction and Fact: History and Deception, 1948; Das Sprichtwort in den Werkens Andreas Gryphilivs, 1949; Les Sirènes á travers les Siècles, 1954; Voltaire on Education, 1960; Le Chant du Cygne dans la Mythologie et le Folklore: eesai d'une explication, 1964; Franz Grillparzer as a Literary Critic, 1970; Thomas Lodge's Rosalynde as the Source of William Shakespeare's As You Like It: a comparison, 1970; Lessing's Nathan The Wise, 1972; Merimée's Carmen, 1973; Das Lehrbuch von der Sinnbild-Kunst, 1973; Molière's The Physician in Spite of Himself, 1975; Molière's The School for Husbands, 1975; Proverbs in Thomas Lodge's Rosalynde, 1975; Biographies of Early American Educators, 1977; Outstanding and Colourful American Women: Famous and Infamous, 1978; Jacques Offenbach's Opera The Tales of Hoffman and E.T.A. Hoffman's Original German Tales: a comparison, 1980; Ricarda Huch's The Deruga Case, 1981; 12 biographies; 88 monographs and articles. *Contributions to:* Numerous Literary journals. *Honours:* Recipient of several literary and research awards. *Memberships:* Several literary and academic organisations. *Address:* 8021 Schreiber Drive, Munster, IN 43621, USA.

ADELMAN, George, b. 17 Sep. 1926, Boston, Massachusetts, USA. Editor, Librarian. m. Sandra Cohen, 17 July 1957, Boston, 2 daughters. *Education:* BA Psychology, Dartmouth College USA, 1947; MA Psychology, University of Boston, 1949; SM, Library Science, Simmons College, 1950. *Literary Appointments:* Boston Public Library, 1950; Technical Information Officer, US Office of Naval Research, 1954; Editor & Publisher, Neurosciences Research Program, Massachusetts Institute of Technology, 1964. *Major Publications:* Editor, The Encyclopedia of Neuroscience, 1986; Co-editor, Neurosciences Research Symposium Summaries, 1965–78; Associate Editor, The Neurosciences Study Program, 1966–79; Co-editor, The Neurosciences Paths of Discovery, 1975; Co-editor, The Organisation of the Cerebral Cortex, 1982.

Contributor to: The Library Journal; Subscription Books Bulletin; World Book Encyclopaedia; Science Year; Psychology Review; Parapsychology Review. *Address:* 1904 Beacon Street, Brookline, MA 02146, USA.

ADERMAN, Ralph Merl, b. 27 May 1919, Malinta, Ohio, USA. University Professor, American & English Literature. m. Alice C Rath, 26 Nov. 1942, Toledo, 1 son. *Education:* BE, 1941, MA, 1945, University of Toledo, PhD, University of Wisconsin. *Publications:* The Letters of James Kirke Paulding, 1962; Aspects of American English, with E.M. Kerr, 1963, revised edition 1971; Washington Irving Reconsidered, 1969; The Letters of Washington Irving, with H L Kleinfeld & J S Banks, 4 volumes; The Quest for Social Justice, Editor, 1982; The History of Milwaukee County 1835–1985, Editor, 1986. *Contributor to:* Various literary journals. *Honours:* Recipient, Award of Merit, Milwaukee Co. Historical Society, 1964. *Memberships:* MLA; National Council of Teachers of English; MS Society. *Address:* 2302 E Newberry Blvd, Milwaukee, WI 53211, USA.

ADHIKARI, Santosh Kumar, b. 24 Nov. 1923. Writer; Author; Retired College Principal. m. Sadhona. *Education:* Calcutta University, India; Associate, Indian Institute of Bankers; Diplomas in Industrial Finance and Management. *Literary Appointment:* Vidyasager Lecturer, The University of Calcutta. *Publications include:* Ekla Chalo Re (Go Thou Alone), 1948; Clouds on the Horizon, 1960; At Some Other Domain, 1973; Blossoms in the Dust, 1980. (Novels): Rakta Kamal, 1967; Nirjan Sikhar, 1971; 4 Books of Essays: (in Bengali); Adhunik Manasikata D Vidyasagar, 1984; Vidyasagar; Saheed Jatin Vas O Bharater Biplab Andolan; Santrasbad and Bhagat Singh (in English): Vidyasagar and the Regeneration of Bengal; Banking Law and Practice; Lending Banker; Editor, Spark, anthology of Indian Poetry in English. *Contributions to:* Major journals of Calcutta and All India Radio, Calcutta. *Memberships:* Honorary Secretary, PEN, West Bengal Branch; Honorary General Secretary, The Vidyasagar Research Centre; The Asiatic Society, Calcutta. *Address:* 81 Raja Basanta Roy Road, Calcutta 700 029, India.

ADKINS, Arthur William Hope, b. 17 Oct. 1929, Leicester, England. University Teacher. m. Elizabeth Mary Cullingford, 16 Sep. 1961, Bradford, Yorkshire, England, 1 son, 1 daughter. *Education:* BA 1952, MA 1955, D Phil, 1957, University of Oxford, England. *Major Publications:* Merit & Responsibility: A Study in Greek Values, 1960; From the Many to the One, 1970; Moral Values & Political Behaviour in Ancient Greece, 1972; Poetic Craft in the Early Greek Elegists, 1985. *Contributor to:* Classical Quarterly; Phoenix; Harvard Studies in Classical Philology; Greek, Roman & Byzantine Studies; Antike und Abendland; and others. *Address:* Department of Classics, University of Chicago, 1050 East 59th Street, Chicago, IL 60637, USA.

ADLER, Lawrence Joel, b. 10 July 1939, White Plains, New York, USA. Writer. *Education:* BS, University of Wisconsin, 1961; Graduate Studies, Diploma in Business Administration, London School of Economics, England, 1964. *Publications:* Man With a Mission: Pele, 1975; Young Woman in the World of Race Horses, 1978; Famous Horses in America, 1979; The Texas Rangers, 1979; Heroes of Soccer, 1980. *Literary Agent:* Writers House, New York. *Address:* 324 East 74th Street, New York City, NY 10021, USA.

ADLER, Margot Susanna, b. 16 Apr. 1946, Little Rock, Arkansas, USA. Journalist; Radio Producer; Talk Show Host. *Education:* BA, University of California, Berkeley, 1968; MS, Columbia School of Journalism, 1970; Nieman Fellow, Harvard University, 1982. *Publication:* Drawing Down the Moon, Witches, Druids, Goddess-worshippers and other Pagans in America Today, 1979, paperback 1981; revised edition, 1986. *Memberships:* Authors Guild; Womens INK; National Writers Union. *Literary Agent:* Jane Rotrosen. *Address:* 333 Central Park West, New York, NY 10025, USA.

ADSTOFTE, Flemming Krone Haugsted, b. 8 May 1937, Copenhagen, Denmark. Director General, Board of Wholesalers Organisation and of Board of Recycling Industries, Denmark; Manager, Danish Business Radio; Former Television and Radio Reporter. *Education:* Studied Political science, Universities of Copenhagen and Munster, 1957–62; Political Institutions and language, Cambridge University, England, 1960–61. *Publications:* Denmark and NATO, 1959, 11, 1965; Books on politics and communications, 1965–75, farming, 1976–85. *Contributions to:* Danish radio and television; Chief Editor, Frit Erhverv. *Membership:* Danish Journalists Association. *Address:* Stengards Alle 31a, 2800 Lyngby, Denmark.

AERTS, Huib Maria, b. 24 Apr. 1908, Belgium. Journalist; Publisher. m. Emily Gierts, Grimbergen, 8 June 1938, 1 son, 2 daughters. *Education:* Philosophical & Theological studies, Seminary; Bachelor, Historical Sciences. *Publications:* Nachtelyke Gaarde, poems, 1932; Heimwee, novel, 1941; De Magische Overzyde, novel with pen-name: Elmar Borg, 1960. *Contributions to:* Journals: De Standaard, Het Algemeen een Nieuws; Periodicals: De Vlaamse Pluimvee-industrie; Pluimree. *Honours:* Provincial Literary Premium, Brabant, 1932; Prize, Royal Academy, best literary performance, biennial period 1960–61, Flanders. *Membership:* Society of Flemish Authors. *Address:* Stokkelstraat 26, 1950 Kraainem, Belgium.

AFRICANO, Lillian, b. 7 June 1935, USA. Author; Columnist. m. Arthur L Africano, 28 June 1958, New Jersey (divorced 1977), 2 sons, 1 daughter. *Education:* BA, summa cum laude, Barnard College, 1957; Columbia University Graduate School, 1958. *Literary Appointments:* Editor, Critic, The Villager; Editor, Journal of the National Acupuncture Society; Critic, Writer, Asbury Park Press; News Editor, Penthouse/Forum; Columnist: One Woman's Voice and Woman's World. *Publications:* The Businessman's Guide to the Middle East; The Doctor's Walking Book (co-author); Something Old, Something New; Passions; Gone From Breezy Hill. *Contributions to:* National newspapers and magazines. *Memberships:* Phi Beta Kappa; National Press Club; Outer Critics Circle; Drama Desk (Past Vice-President, Secretary); American Society of Journalists and Authors (Past Program Chairman). *Literary Agent:* Elaine Markson. *Address:* 45 West 10th Street, New York, NY 10011, USA.

AGAWA, Hiroyuki, b. 24 Dec. 1920, Hiroshima, Japan. Author. m. Miyo Masuda, 16 Oct. 1949, Tokyo, 3 sons, 1 daughter. *Education:* MA, Japanese Literature, Tokyo Imperial University. *Publication:* The Reluctant Admiral – Yamamoto and the Imperial Navy 1979 (English translation only). *Membership:* Royal Art Academy of Japan. *Address:* 2-31-5, Utsukushiga-oka, Midori-ku, Yokohama, Japan 227.

AGLIETTI, Susan L Burke, b. 11 Feb. 1945, Binghamton, New York, USA. Editor; Publisher. m. Jean-Pierre Aglietti, 10 Apr. 1972, Binghamton, 2 sons, 1 daughter. *Education:* BA, University of Rochester, 1966; University of Neuchatel, Switzerland; MA, San Francisco, State University, California, USA, 1970. *Literary Appointments:* Publisher, Editor, Vintage '45 Press (Quarterly journal for women). *Publication:* Maternal Legacy, 1985. *Contributions to:* Various newspapers and magazines of over 100 articles. *Address:* PO Box 266, Orinda, CA 94563, USA.

AGO, Roberto, b. 26 May 1907, Vigevano, Pavia, Italy. Judge, International Courts of Justice, 1979; University Professor. *Education:* PhD, University of Naples; PSD, University of Rome. *Publications include:* Regles generales des Cornflits de lois, 1936; Le Delit international, 1934; Positive Law and International Law, 1957; Protection internationale des personnes morales, 1964, 1969; Codification du droit international, 1969; Droit des traites a la lumiere de la Convention de Vienne, 1971; Cours general de droit international public, 1973; State Responsibility, up UN, 1970–79; Pluralism and the Origins of International Community, 1978; The First

International Communities in the Mediterranean World, 1983; Le droit international dans la conception de grotius, 1983; I quarante armi delle N. U., 1985. *Honours include:* Hon. sausa Dr., Paris, Geneva, Nice, Nancy, Toulouse; Grand Croix, Order of Merit, Italy; CBE; Leg. Honners. *Memberships include:* President, Italian Society for International Organisation; Italian Delegate, ILO Conference, 1945–; International Law Committee, UN, 1957–; Former President. *Address:* Via della Mendola 143, Rome, Italy.

AGOSTINI, Franchino b. 12 July 1927, Viganello, Switzerland. Dentist. *Education:* Laurea, Medical Dentist, 1956. *Publications:* Angolo d'Astro, 1967. co-translator, Antologia Poetica Europea, 1973; Columnist, Giornale del Popolo (Lugano Switzerland); La Colonnina E...Altro, (Corsivetti), 1981; Quando Saro Lontano, (Poesie Ed. Edleweiss-Lugano), 1985. *Honours:* Cavaliere Nuova Europa; Legione d'Oro; Accademia Tiberina. *Memberships:* Association Medici Scrittori Italiani; PEN Club (Ticino-Grigioni). *Address:* Via Giacometti 1, 6900 Lugano, Switzerland.

AGRAWAL, S P, b. 30 Jan. 1928, Gowan, District Budaun, Uttar Pradesh, India. Director of Social Science Documentation Centre. *Education:* BA 1952, BSc (Prev), Agra University; MA (Prev) 1954, Certificate in Library Science 1952, Aligarh Muslim University; French Course, School of Foreign Languages, Government of India, 1966. *Literary Appointments include:* Librarian, Central Secretariat Library, 1960–64 and 1968–70; Deputy Director Documentation 1972–77, Division Head Documentation 1977–79, Indian Council of Social Science Research, New Delhi; Director, Social Science Documentation Centre, ICSSR, New Delhi, 1980–; Editor, Shree Hari Katha, 1975–. *Publications include:* Pustak Sankya Praveshikya, (with Md. Zubair). 1954; Indian Educational Documents Since Independence, (with A Biswas), 1971; Mohandas Karamchand Gandhi, 4 volumes, 1974–82; Role and Functions of National Commissions for Unesco, 1975; Role of Unesco in Education, (with J C Aggrawal), 1981; Festivals: National International, 1985. *Contributions to:* Publications including: ILA Bulletin; The Hawk; ICSSR Newsletter; The Serials Librarian; Journal of M S University of Baroda. *Honour:* Freedom Fighters Samman Pension. *Memberships include:* Life member, Association of Writers and Illustrators for Children; FID National Committee; Government of India Librarians Association. *Address:* Social Science Documentation Centre, ICSSR, 35 Ferozshah Road, New Delhi 110001, India.

AHERN, Thomas Francis, b. 3 Aug. 1947, Holbrook, Massachusetts, USA. Writer. m. Simone Joyaux, 3 Aug. 1984, Providence, Rhode Island, USA. *Education:* BA, Brown University, 1970; MA, Brown University, 1973. *Publications:* The Capture of Trieste, 1978; Superbounce, 1982; Hecatombs of Lake, 1984. *Honour:* National Endowment for the Arts Fellowship, 1979. *Address:* 23 No. Fair Street, Warwick, RI 02888, USA.

AHERN, Tim(othy James), b. 27 July 1952, Renton, Washington, USA. Biochemist. m. Gabriele Friederike Koch, 30 Oct. 1982, Seattle, Washington. *Education:* BA, Slavic Languages and Literature, 1975; BS, Molecular Biology, Biological Oceanography, 1975; PhD, Enzymology and Natural Products Chemistry, University of Washington, 1980. *Publication:* The Illnesstraited Colossick Idition of James Joyce's Finnegans Wake, Chapter One, 1983. *Contributor to:* James Joyce Broadsheet, 1978–79; Mainichi Daily News, Japan, 1981–82. *Memberships:* Amnesty International (Group Leader, 1979–80); American Association for the Advancement of Science; American Chemical Society. *Address:* 18218 58th NE, Seattle, WA 98155, USA.

AHL, David H, b. 17 May 1939, New York City, USA. Editor; Writer. 1 son, 2 daughters. *Education:* BEE, Cornell University, 1961; MSIA, Carnegie-Mellon University, 1963. *Publications include:* Basic Computer Games, 1st million-selling computer book, 1972; More Basic Computer Games, 1979; Big Computer Games, 1984; The Computer Idebook Series, 1983; etc. *Contributions to:* Creative Computing; New York Times; Ladies Home Journal; National Geographic; Parent's Choice; Mathematics Teacher; Journal of Market Research; Computer Education; etc. *Honours:* Recognition & achievement awards: SE Asia Computer Society, 1978, 1984; DPMA, 1977; University of Wisconsin, 1979; AFIPS, 1979, 1982; ACGNJ, 1981. *Address:* Creative Computing, 12 Indian Head Road, Morristown, NJ 07960, USA.

AHL, Frederick Michael, b. 5 Sep. 1941, Barrow-in-Furness, England. Professor of Classics. m. Mary Elaine McAninch, 30 Aug. 1969, Dallas, Texas, 1 son, 1 daughter. *Education:* BA, 1962; PhD, 1966. *Literary Appointments:* Assistant Professor of Classics: University of Utah, USA, 1966, University of Texas, 1968; Assistant Professor, 1971, Associate Professor, 1974, Professor, 1978–, Department of Classics, Cornell University, Ithaca, New York. *Major Publications:* To Read Greek (with R D Armstrong), 1969; Lucan: An Introduction, 1976; Metaformations: Soundplay and Wordplay in Ovid and Other Classical Poets, 1985; Seneca: Three Tragedies, 1986. *Contributor to:* American Journal of Philology; Aufstieg and Niedergang der römischen Welt (papers on Statius, Silius Italicus and Silver Age Poetry). *Honour:* William Evans Fellowship, University of Otago, New Zealand, 1982. *Address:* 305 Mitchell Street, Ithaca, NY 14850, USA.

AHLO, Börje Walter, b. 19 Nov. 1932, Jakobstad, Finland. Writer. *Publications:* i debutdiktantologin Tre, 1968; I Skuggen av ditt leende, 1972; Det är inte alla dagar, 1974; Nattens barn, 1977; Utsikt fran Mitt fönster, 1979; Sifferism, 1981; I pausen mellan regnen, 1982; Dikter i urval, 1984; Spegling, 1985. *Contributions include:* Horizon; Hembygden; Capital News; Jacobstad's News. *Honours include:* Numerous grants including: 5 grants, Jacobstad Culture Committee, 1969–82; 3 author grants, Swedish Culture Fund, 1970, 1973 and 1981; Ministry of Education Library Grant, 1973. *Address:* Lindskogsgatan 26, 68620 Jakobstad 2, Finland.

AHNSTROM, Doris Newell, b. 4 Aug. 1915, Muskegon, Michigan, USA. Writer, Editor, Association Executive. *Education:* Brenau College; New York University; Columbia University. *Publications:* Complete Book of Helicopters, 1954, 2nd edition 1968; Complete Book of Jets and Rockets, 1957, 2nd edition 1970. *Contributions to:* Various aviation publications. *Memberships:* Authors Guild, Aviation/Space Writers Association; American Institute of Aeronautics and Astronautics; American Helicopter Society; Society of Air Safety Investigators. *Literary Agent:* Evelyn Singer. *Address:* 705 Americana Drive, Annapolis, MD 21403, USA.

AHO, James Alfred, b. 29 Oct 1942, Aberdeen, Washington, USA. Sociologist. m. Margaret McMahan, 6 Aug 1966, Albuquerque, New Mexico, 3 sons. *Education:* PhD, Sociology, Washington State University, 1971. *Publications:* German Realpolitik and American Sociology, 1975; Religious Mythology and the Art of War, 1981. *Contributions to:* Eight articles in magazines and newspapers on Wilderness and the Outdoors, Contemporary Movies and Warfare; Four book reviews in professional journals; Six articles in professional journals mostly on Violence and War; Chapter in book on Religious Dimensions of Nuclear Weaponry. *Address:* 206 South 17th, Pocatello, ID 83201, USA.

AHONEN, Erkki Paavali, b. 8 Jan. 1932, Kiuruvesi, Finland. Writer. m. 1956, divorced 1977, 2 sons, 3 daughters. *Education:* HuK, Turku University, 1958; Studied Theoretical Philosophy and Theoretical Physics, 1973–83. *Publications include:* Hyppy (poetry), 1960; Novels: Tanaan ei paljon tapahdu, 1961; Kyyditys, 1962; Kivia vuoret, 1965; Paperihanskat, 1967;

Kuumatka, 1969; Kylma paikka, 1970; Science Fiction: Paikka nimelta Plaston, 1968; Tietokonelapsi, 1972; Syva matka, 1976; Kappaleen liikkeen kuvaaminen x, t – tasolla, 1983 (mechanics); Runot, 1983 (poetry). *Contributions to:* several publications (philosophy and physics). *Honour:* State Prize, 1968. *Membership:* Finnish Society of Authors. *Address:* Wiurila, 24910 Halikko as, Finland.

AIGNER, Alexander, b. 18 May 1909, Graz, Austria. University Professor of Mathematics. *Education:* PhD, 1936. *Publications:* (lyric poems) Einsamer Weg, 1958; Zwischendurch zugeschaut, 1966; (humorous mathematical poems), Tangenten an den Frohsinn, 1978. *Membership:* Member, Styrian Federation of Writers. *Address:* Humboldtstrasse 17, 8010 Graz, Austria.

AITKEN, Robert Baker, b. 19 June 1917, Philadelphia, Pennsylvania, USA. Teacher at Diamond Sangha, a Zen Buddhist Society. m. Anne Hopkins, 23 Feb. 1957, San Francisco, 1 son by previous marriage. *Education:* BA, English Literature, 1947, MA, Japanese Studies, 1950, University of Hawaii. *Publications:* A Zen Wave: Basho's Haiku and Zen, 1978; Taking the Path of Zen, 1982; The Mind of Clover: Essays in Zen Buddhist Ethics, 1984. *Contributions to:* Buddhist Christian Studies; Co-Evolution Quarterly; Coyote's Journal; The Eastern Buddhist; Journal of Transpersonal Psychology; Parabola; The Middle Way; Ten Directions; Wallace Stevens Journal; Zero. Also in-house journals: Blind Donkey; Kahawai; Diamond Sangha. *Address:* 2119 Kaloa Way, Honolulu, HI 96822, USA.

AJALSTEINSSON, Ragnar Ingi, b. 15 Jan. 1944, Vajbrekka, Iceland. Teacher. m. Sigurlina Davijsdottir, 20 Apr. 1981, Stajarfell, 2 sons. *Education:* BEd. *Publications:* Hrafnkela, poems, 1974; Undir Holmatindi, poems, 1977; Eg er alkoholisti, poems, 1981; Dalavisur, poems, 1982. *Contributions to:* Editor, Dalablajij, monthly magazine. *Membership:* Writers Union of Iceland. *Address:* Laugaland, 371 Bujardal, Iceland.

AJIBADE, Adeyemi Olanrewaju, b. 28 July 1939, Otta, Nigeria. Actor; Playwright; Director. m. Gwendoline Augusta Ebonywhite, May 1973, St Marylebone, London, 2 daughters. *Education:* Diplomas, Dramatic Arts, Film Technique; British Drama League Diploma, Theatre Production; Associate of Drama Board. *Appointments:* Tutor & Producer of Drama, Panel of Inner London Education Authority; Visiting Director, Actors Workshop, London; Artistic Director, Pan-African Players, Keskidee Centre (London); Assistant Advisor to Earl of Snowdon on Mary Kingsley; Senior Arts Fellow & Artistic Director, Unibadan Masques, Acting Company of Ibadan University, Nigeria. *Major Works:* Lagos, Yes Lagos, BBC Radio (Heinemann in collection); Award (Keskidee Centre); The Black Knives (ORTF, Paris); The Big One, Parcel Post (Royal Court, London); Behind the Mountain, Mokai, The Girl from Bulawayo (Arts Theatre, Ibadan University); Fingers Only (Black Theatre Cooperative, London); Para Ginto (black version, Peer Gynt), commissioned by Birmingham Repertory Theatre; Waiting for Hannibal, Africans in arms struggle against Roman invasion, 204 BC. *Honours:* Four times recipient of British Arts Council Bursary Award for Playwriting, 1976, 1977, 1981, 1984. *Memberships:* Fellow, Royal Society of Arts; British Kinematographic Society; Theatre Writers Union; Black Writers Association. *Literary Agent:* Dr Jan Van Loewan, Michael Imison, London. *Address:* 29 Seymour House, Churchway, London NW1, England.

AKAVIA, Mirjam, b. 20 Nov. 1927, Krakow, Poland. Novelist. m. Hanan Akavia, 3 Dec. 1946, 2 daughters. *Literary Appointments:* Member, Control-Committee, Hebrew Writers Association; Member, Juri-Committee for CFAT; Delegate to Federation of Writers in Israel. *Publications:* Childhood at Fall, in Hebrew 1975, in Dutch 1981, in Swedish 1982, in German 1983; The Price, in Hebrew 1978; Galia and Miklosh, 1982; My Own Vineyard, 1984; Collection of Short Stories, 1985.

Contributor to: Moznaim, Literary Monthly of Hebrew Writers Association; Iton 77, Literary Monthly, and others. *Honours:* Dvorzecki Prize – Yad Vashem 1979; Massuah Prize, 1982; Amicus Poloniae, 1984; Gracovians Prize, 1985; Preis der Deutschen Korczak Gesellschaft 1985. *Memberships:* Hebrew Writers Association; The PEN Centre in Israel. *Address:* Repidim Str 4/a Tel-Aviv 69982, Israel.

AKERMAN, Anthony, b. 12 Aug. 1949, Durban, Republic of South Africa. Theatrical Director, Writer. *Education:* Study of Law, University of Natal, Pietermaritzburg, RSA, 1968; BA English Literature, Speech & Drama, Rhodes University, Grahamstown, RSA, 1969–71; Post-graduate Honours Degree, English Literature, 1971–72; Directors Course, Bristol Old Vic Theatre School, 1973–74; Post-graduate Diploma in Theatre Studies, Sherman Theatre, University of Cardiff, Wales, 1974–75. *Literary Appointments:* Director of various theatrical productions in theatres in Britain, France & The Netherlands. *Major Publications:* Somewhere on the Border, 1983; A Man out of the Country, 1984; (translated) A Snow, by Willem Jan Otten, 1984. *Address:* Barndesteeg 15/I, 1012 BV Amsterdam, The Netherlands.

ÅKERMAN, (Erik) Nordal, b. 9 Dec. 1941, Lund, Sweden. Managing Director, Swedish Institute of International Affairs. m. Sigrid Combüchen (novelist), 1 daughter. *Education:* Associate Professor in History & National Security. *Literary Appointments:* Editor-in-Chief, Allt om Böcker, (All on Books), leading Scandinavian literary magazine. *Major publications:* 25 books in Swedish on strategy, development models, the US, City Planning, Culture, since 1964; On the Doctrine of Limited War, (in English), 1973. *Contributor to:* Hammarskjöld Foundation, Uppsala (Can Sweden be Shrunk? Development Dialogue 1981–82). *Membership:* Swedish Union of Writers. *Address:* Swedish Institute of International Affairs, Box 1253, 111 82 Stockholm, Sweden.

AKHTAR, Hoshiarpuri, b. 20 Apr. 1918, Hoshiarpur, E. Punjab, India. Advocate. *Education:* BA; LLB. *Literary Appointments:* Editor, Urdu Section, Crescent, Islamia College Lahore Magazine, 1936–37. *Publications:* Alaamat, 1979; Aeena-o-Chiragh, 1985 (Urdu Poetry), 1985. *Contributor to:* Humayun; Adabi Dunya; Adab-i-Latif; Auraq; Fanoon; Seep; Naya Daur; Afkar; Saqi; Zamana; Nadeem; Sahifa. *Memberships:* Assistant Secretary, Halqua-i-Arbab-i-zauq, Delhi, India, 1946–47. *Address:* 0/548 Kartarpura, Rawalpindi, Pakistan.

AKINS, Terese Margaret, b. Chicago, Illinois, USA. Poet. m. Herbert V Akins, 14 May 1938, Chicago, 2 sons. *Education:* Compton College; LB Poetry, Institute of Lifetime Learning. *Appointments:* Resource Person in Poetry, Long Beach Schools, California, 1973–; Recording Secretary, Lakewood Cultural Arts Council, 1975–76; Editor, Weingart Sr. Newsletter; Poetry Judge National Conference of Christians and Jews; Poetry Judge, Monterey Park; Essay Judge, Santa Monica Historical Society; Secretary (Correspondence) LKWD Pan American Association; Community Resource Speaker on Poetry for Long Beach Schools, *Publications:* Not as Candles 1975; Tomkin Tanka and Haiku 1976; *Contributor to:* Not as Candles 1975; Sea to Sea in Song l965-66; Velvet Paws in Print 1967; Yearbook of Modern Poetry 1971; Lyrics of Love 1972; Outstanding Contemporary Poetry 1972, 73; Apollo Anthology 1972, 75; Fireflower; Haiku Highlights; Poet India and numerous other journals and anthologies. *Honours:* Recipient of various diplomas and certificates from poetry associations. *Memberships* include: American Poetry League; Long Beach Writers Club (Poetry Director); Founder, Orpheus Chapter, Vice President and Membership Chairman, Californian Federation of Chaparral Poets (Founder and 1st President, Apollo Chapter, 2nd Vice President State Board, JR–Sr Contest Chairman 1974–77); World Poetry Society. *Address:* 4748 Oliva Avenue, Lakewood, CA 90712, USA.

AKUFFO, Ferdinand William Bekoe, b. 5 Mar. 1946, Accra, Ghana. Teacher, Researcher. m. Melian Shalubala Akuffo, Lusaka, 25 Feb. 1984, 1 daughter. *Education:* BA (Legon), Accra, Ghana; D Phil (Oxon), Oxford, England; Post-doctoral work, St Edmunds House, Cambridge, 1975–76. *Publications:* Indiginization of Christianity: A Study in Ghanaian Pentecostalism. *Contribution to:* Issues in Zambia's Development. *Memberships:* Section of Social Science Libraries, International Federation of Library Associations and Institutions; United States African Studies Association; Fellow, The Royal Anthropological Institute of Great Britain and Northern Ireland. 1979; International Commission of Anthropological Documentation, 1981; Society of Authors, London. *Address:* The Department of African Development Studies, School of Humanities and Social Sciences, University of Zambia, P O Box 32379, Lusaka, Zambia.

ALANDER, Rainer, b. 2 June 1937. Harbour Pilot, Turku, Finland. m. Siw Alander, 1962, 1 son, 1 daughter. *Publications:* Ansiktet, 1963; Sandkornet, 1964; Personerna, 1969; Lastmarket, 1972; En sorts frihet, 1974; Barlast, 1980; Halsningar fran San Francisco, 1986. *Address:* Furuvaagen 13, 20540 Turku 54, Finland.

ALANDER, Siw Verna Birgitta, b. 15 June 1940, Vasa. Teacher, Author. m. Nils Rainer Alander, 30 Aug. 1962, Abo, Finland, 1 son, 1 daughter. *Publications:* Bandet, 1979; Tunneln, 1982; Blå Duvan, 1985. *Honour:* Literary Award of the Finnish State, 1984. *Membership:* Society of Swedish Authors in Finland. *Literary Agent:* Soderstrom & Co. *Address:* Furuvägen 13, 20540 Abo 54, Finland.

ALBERS, Frank, b. 2 Mar. 1960, Schoten, Belgium. Writer. *Education:* Licence diplome, Philosophy, State University of Ghent, Belgium; MLitt, Hertford College, Oxford University, 1986. *Publications:* Poetry: Amfibie, 1978; Broedgebied, 1980; Chronos, 1984. Fiction: Angst van een sneeuwman, 1982. *Contributions to:* Various Flemish magazines and periodicals such as: Diogenes, Standaard, NVT, De nieuwe. *Honours:* Several minor awards for poetry; Yang Prize for fiction, for Angst van een sneeuwman. *Memberships:* Founding member, Plusjke Society. *Address:* Acacialaan 34, 2020 Antwerp, Belgium.

ALBERT, Burton, b. 25 Sep. 1936, Pittsfield, Massachusetts, USA. Writer; Communications Consultant. *Education:* BS, N Adams (Mass) State College; MA, Duke University. *Publications include:* Codes for Kids, 1976; Mine, Yours, Ours, 1977; More Codes for Kids, 1979; Reader's Digest Reading Skill Buildings, 1977; Write to Communicate the Language Arts in Process, with D M Murray, levels 3-6, 1973–74; Sharkes & Whales, 1979; Code Busters!, 1985. *Contributor to:* Various educational publications including, Instructor; Early years; The Reading Teacher; Language Arts. *Honours:* Recipient, Nomination, Educational Press Award, 1977–78. *Memberships:* National Council of Teachers of English. *Address:* 3 Narrow Brook Road, Weston, CT 06883, USA.

ALBERT, Linda I, b. 15 Nov. 1939, New York City, USA. Writer. Divorced, 2 sons, 1 daughter. *Education:* BS, 1968, MS, 1972, Education, State University of New York; PhD, Psychology, Lyon International University, 1984. *Publications:* Coping With Kids, 1982; Coping with Kids & Schools, 1985. *Contributor to:* Syndicated Columnist: Coping with Kids, Gannett News Service, Washington DC, 1980–. *Membership:* American Society of Journalists & Authors. *Literary Agent:* Pam Bernstein, William Morris Agency. *Address:* 5238 Bon Vivant Dr #74, Tampa, FL 33603, USA.

ALBINO, Joseph Xavier, b. 19 Mar. 1937, Syracuse, New York, USA. Writer; Photographer. m. Mary Louise Burdick, 30 July 1960, Clinton, 5 daughters. *Education:* BA, Le Moyne College, 1959; MS, Syracuse University, 1982. *Literary Appointments include:* Technical Editor, Writer, Heavy Military Electronics Department, General Electric Company, Syracuse, New York, 1960–62; Freelance Editorial and Photographic work, 1962–85. *Contributions to:* Numerous publications including: American Agriculturist; Better Camping and Hiking; Catholic Sun; Constructioneer; Drug Topics; Farm Journal; Flooring; Focus; Hospital Topics; Housewares Review; Industrial Bulletin; The Jesuit; Manage; National Livestock Producer; National Surveyor; Personnel Journal; Power Parade; Private Pilot; Rural New Yorker; Spiritual Life; Successful Farming; Today's Family; Turkey World; Western Fruit Grower; West Texas Livestock Weekly; Woodworking Digest; Writers Digest. As an On-Site Assignment Photographer has worked for numerous national agencies, corporations and publications. *Address:* 221 Hillbrook Road, Syracuse, NY 13219, USA.

ALCOCK, (Garfield) Vivien, b. 23 Sep. 1924, Worthing, England. Author. m. Leon Garfield, 23 Oct. 1948, London, 1 daughter. *Education:* Oxford School of Art. *Publications:* The Haunting of Cassie Palmer, 1980; The Stonewalkers, 1981; The Sylvia Game, 1982; Travellers by Night, 1983; Ghostly Companions, 1984. *Membership:* Authors Society. *Literary Agent:* John Johnson. *Address:* 59 Wood Lane, London N6, England.

ALDAN, Daisy, b. 16 Sep. 1923, New York City, USA. Writer. *Education:* BA, Hunter College; MA, Speech and Education, Brooklyn College; Doctorate Degree, Free University of Pakistan, Karachi; Graduate Courses, City University. *Appointments include:* Teacher, various Universities and Schools; Editor, Magazines; Currently, Freelance Poetry Workshops, Schools, Libraries, etc. *Publications:* The Destruction of Cathedrals and other Poems, 1964; Journey, 1970; 1 plus 1 equals 1, with Elaine Mendlowitz, 1970; Or Learn to Walk on Water, 1970, 2nd edition 1980; Seven:Seven, 1970; The Masks Are Becoming Faces; Breakthrough, 1971; Love Poems of Daisy Aldan, 1978; Stones, 1974; Verses for the Zodiac, 1975; Between High Tides, 1978; A Golden Story, 1979; Poetry and Consciousness, 1979; Contemporary Poetry and the Evolution of Consciousness, 1981; The Art and Craft of Poetry, 1982; Numerous Translations; Poetry in many anthologies; Editor: Folders 1,2,3,4; A New Folder; Poems from India; etc. *Contributor to:* Publish it Yourself; A One Woman Press; Magic Circles Weekend; Books as art; etc; Criticle Articles include: The Words of the Tribe, Poetry; On Beat Poetry, Wagner Literary Magazine; etc. *Honours:* Recipient numerous honours and awards including Herman Ritter Award; National Foundation for the Arts Poetry Prize; Hunter College Hall of Fame. *Memberships include:* PEN; Poetry Society of America, Board Member, 3 years; World Congress of Poets; Ecole Libre des Hautes Etudes; English Teachers Association. *Address:* 103-26 68th Road, Forest Hills, NY 11375, USA.

ALDRIDGE, A Owen, b. 16 Dec. 1915, Buffalo, New York, USA. Professor; Editor. *Education:* BS, Indiana University, 1937; MA, University of Georgia, 1938; PhD, Duke University, 1942; DUP, University of Paris (Sorbonne), 1955. *Major Publications:* Franklin & his French Contemporaries, 1957; Man of Reason: Life of Thomas Paine, 1959; Jonathan Edwards, 1964; Benjamin Franklin – Philosopher & Man, 1965; Benjamin Franklin & Nature's God, 1967; Comparative Literature – Matter & Method, 1965; The Iberi-American Enlightenment, 1971; Voltaire & the Century of Light, 1975; Comparative Literature Japan & the West, 1979 (in Japanese translation); Early American Literature: A Comparatist Approach, 1982; Thomas Paine's American Ideology, 1984; Fiction in Japan & the West, (in Japanese Translation), 1985. *Contributor to:* Professional journals. *Address:* University of Illinois Department of Comparative Literature, 2070 Foreign Language Building, Urbana, IL 61801, USA.

ALDRIDGE, John Watson, b. 26 Sep. 1922, Sioux City, Iowa, USA. Literary Critic; Educator. m. Patricia McGuire Eby, 16 July 1983, Ann Arbor, Michigan, 5 sons by previous marriages. *Education:* BA, University of California at Berkeley, 1947. *Literary Appointments:*

Lecturer, Christian Gauss Seminars in Criticism, Princeton University, 1953–54; Lecturer, Breadloaf Writers Conference, 1966–69; Rockefeller Humanities Fellowship, 1976; Book Critic, MacNeil/Lehrer Television News, 1983–84. *Major Publications:* After the lost Generation, (criticism), 1951; In Search of Heresy (criticism), 1956; The Party at Cranton (novel), 1960; Time to Murder and Create (criticism), 1966: In the Country of the Young (social commentary), 1970; The Devil in the Fire (criticism), 1972; The American Novel and the way We Live Now, (criticism), 1983. *Contributor to:* Harper's; Saturday Review; New York Times Book Review; New York Herald Tribune Book Week; Chicago Tribune Book World. *Honours:* Fulbright Senior Lectureships, 1958–59, 1962–63; Berg Professorship, New York University, 1958; Writer-in-Residence, Hollins College, 1960–62. *Memberships:* PEN Club; Authors' League of America; National Book Critics Circle. *Literary Agent:* Gerard F McCauley. *Address:* 1050 Wall Street, #4-C, Ann Arbor, MI 48105, USA.

ALEDZKA-FRYBESOWA, Aleksandra, b. 25 Nov. 1923, Kaweczyn, Poland. Translator. *Education:* AB, Warsaw University. *Publications:* Poems, 1963; Poems, 1970; Poems, 1977; Essays on Art, 1973; Essays on Art, 1979; Translations include: E Zola's, Son Excellence Rougon, 1955; G Greene's, The Burnt-Out Case, 1962; R Caillois's, Essays, 1967; P Valery's, Essays, 1971; G Painter's, M Proust, 1972; E Guillevic's, Poems, 1979; A Saint-Exupery, Citadelle, 1985; S Weil, Thoughts, 1985; Poems, 1982. *Contributions to:* Wiez; Znak; Tygodnik Powszechny; Tworcrosz; Poezja; Literature na swiecie. *Memberships:* Polish Writers Association; PEN. *Address:* Orzechowska 3 m. 6, 02068 Warsaw, Poland.

ALENIER, Karren LaLonde, b. 7 May 1947, Cheverly, Maryland, USA. Office Automation Analyst. 1 son. *Education:* National Honor Society, Northwood High School, 1965; Honours French, University of Maryland, 1969. *Publications:* Wandering on the Outside, 1975, 2nd Edition, 1978; The Dancer's Muse, 1981; Whose Woods These Are, 1983. *Contributions to:* Calvert Review; George Washington Review; Princeton Spectrum; Gargoyle; Washington Review; Telephone; Sulphur River Review. *Honours:* The Dellbrook Award, 1978 & 1979; The Billee Murray Denny Award (S1000), 1981. *Memberships:* Poetry Society of America; Word Works, Board Member 1984, Secretary; Poetry Committee of Greater Washington DC, Board Member, 1985. *Address:* PO Box 42164, Washington, DC 20015, USA.

ALEXANDER, Charles Robert, b. 5 Dec. 1936, Detroit, Michigan, USA. Editor; Writer; Lecturer. *Education:* BA, Wayne State University; MA, PhD, Principia University. *Literary Appointments:* Fellow, Bridgeport Writers Conclave; Guest Lecturer, Annual, East/West Mantra Society; Laureate Oblate, Orpheus Club. *Publications:* Collected Sayings of Sri Ram Dass, 1974, Five Years Among the Christadelphians, 1976; Side Issues of Mesmerism, 1979; Guardian Guilt: A History of the Shriners, 1981; Morphine and Mrs Eddy, 1981; Tourist Guide to India Ashrams, 1982; Handbook of Avatars, 1982; Cults of Transcendence, 1985; Footnotes to the Mother Church Manual (to be published); Wit and Wisdom of Jehovah's Witnesses (to be published); Shorthand Diaries of Charles Taze Russell (to be published). *Contributor to:* Sphinx, 1984; India Journal, 1984; Statesman, 1985; Fortune and Commerce, 1985; 32nd Degree, 1985; Indian Journal, 1986. *Honours:* First Prize, Bridgeport Writers Conclave; Prometheus Award, Cambridge Authors Association; Honorary Mention, American Mime Association; Second Prize, Mystery Writers Confab. *Literary Agent:* Arthur & Keith Associates, Pontiac, Michigan. *Address:* 15 East Kirby #531, Detroit, MI 48202, USA.

ALEXANDER, Eugenie Mary, b. 2 Sep. 1919, Wallasey, Cheshire, England. Writer; Artist. *Education:* NDD; ATD; Chelsea School of Art; Goldsmiths' College of Art; St Anne's College, Sanderstead; Demonstration School for Froebel Educational Institute. *Publications:* Art for Young People, 1958; Fabric Pictures, 1959; Museums and How to Use Them, 1974. *Contributions to:* Observer Colour Supplement; Daily Telegraph; Guardian; House and Garden; She; Art and Craft; The Teacher; Woman's Own; Woman's Realm, (features, art exhibitions and book reviews). 10 one-man exhibitions of fabric collages. *Membership:* Hurlingham Club. *Address:* 56 King George Street, Greenwich, London SE10 8QD, England.

ALEXANDER, Janet, b. 14 Sep. 1907, Dublin, Republic of Ireland. *Education:* MA, St Andrew's University, Scotland. *Publications include:* A Child in the House, 1955; A Furnished Room, 1958; As Strangers Here, 1960; The Maiden Dinosaur, 1964; Talk to Me, 1965. Children's Books include: My Friend Specs McCann, 1955; This Happy Morning, 1959; The Battle of St George Without, 1966; Tom's Tower, 1965; Switch On, Switch Off (one act plays), 1968; Dragons Come Home, 1969; The Prisoner in the Park, 1971; The Other People, 1972; We, Three Kings, 1974; Little Nipper, books for Macmillan, 1975; Wait for It, (collected stories for children) 1979. *Contributor to:* Punch; Homes & Gardens; The Horn Book; etc. *Honours:* Recipient, Honorary Book Award for, The Battle of St George Without; Book World Childrens Spring Festival, 1968. *Address:* St Monica Home, Cote Lane, Westbury-on-Trym, Bristol BS9 3UN, England.

ALEXANDER, Stella, b. 14 June 1912, Shanghai, China. Writer & Researcher. m. John Alexis Alexander, 7 July 1933, London, 1 son, 1 daughter, marriage dissolved. *Education:* BA Oxford University, England, 1933, MA, 1969. *Major Publications:* Church & State in Yugoslavia since 1945; Chapter on The Catholic Church in Croatia in Catholics, the State & the European Radical Right, (to be published); The Triple Myth – a Life of Cardinal Aloyzijc Stepenac (in preparation). *Contributor to:* South Slav Journal; Religion in Communist Lands; The Friend. *Address:* 10A Shooters Hill Road, London SE3 7BD, England.

ALEXIADIS, George, b. 18 Dec. 1911, Athens, Greece. Lawyer. m. Katherine Tsarpalis, 13 Dec. 1967, Athens. *Education:* Doctor, Summa cum laude, Athens University. *Literary Appointments:* Editor: Political review, Perspective, 1961–66; Daily newspaper, Hestia (Vesta), 1974–. *Publications:* Legal and Sociological Aspects of the Idea of the Nation, 1939; Geoeconomy and Geopolicy of Greek Countries, 1945, 46; The Reform of Criminal Law in Soviet Russia, 1957; Political History of Modern Greece, 1960–63; The First Balkan Alliance of 1867–1868, 1971; A Strange Theory About the French Revolution, 1975; Territorial Sea – Continental Shelf and the Turkish Pretensions on the Aegean, 1976; NATO Without Metaphysics, 1976; The Revelation of a Myth – The Greek-Turkish Friendship, 1976; The Panslavism, 1980; The Origins of Greek-Italian War of 1940–1941, 1982; The First Greek Legislator, 1982. *Contributions to:* French political magazines: Express; Figaro; Revue des Deux Mondes. *Honours:* Medal of National Resistance. *Memberships:* Board of Directors, Greek Association for the Advancement of Science, 1966. *Address:* 41 Levidou Street, Kiphissia 14563, Greece.

ALI, Ahmed, b. 1 July 1910, Delhi, India. Novelist, Poet, Scholar, Diplomat. m. Bilqees Jehan Begam (deceased), 19 Oct. 1950, Karachi, 3 sons, 1 daughter. *Education:* BA Honours, MA. *Literary Appointments:* Lecturer in English, Universities of Lucknow, Agra, Allahabad, 1932–41; Professor, Head of Department of English, Presidency College, Calcutta, 1944–46; Visiting Professor, National Central University of China, 1947–48; Michigan State University USA, 1975; Senior Posts, Pakistan Foreign Service, 1950–60; Fulbright Professor, Western Kentucky University, Bowling Green, Kentucky, Southern Illinois University, Carbondale, 1978–79. *Major Publications:* 5 volumes of short stories in Urdu, 1932–45; Twilight in Delhi, (novel), 1940; Ocean of Night (novel), 1964; Of Rats and Diplomats (novel), 1985; The Golden Tradition, (anthology of

Urdu Poetry in English), 1973; Selections from Ghalib, (translated), 1969; Purple Gold Mountain (verse), 1960; Al-Qur'an (translation in English), 1984; The Prison-House (short stories), 1985; Mr Eliot's Pennyworld of Dreams, 1941. *Contributor to:* New Writing; Penguin New Writing; Atlantic Monthly; New Directions; L'Orient; International Poetry Review; New Quarterly; Eastern Horizon; Journal of Commonwealth Literature; Journal of South Asian Studies; and others. *Honours:* Fulbright Visiting Professor, 1978–79; Sitara-i-Imtiaz (Star of Distinction), Government of Pakistan, 1983; Honorary Citizen of Nebraska, USA, 1979. *Memberships:* Founder-Member, All-India Progressive Writers' Association; Founding Member, Pakistan Academy of Letters. *Address:* 21-A Faran Society, Hyder Ali Road, Karachi, Pakistan.

ALIANAK, Hrant, b. 5 Feb. 1950, Khartoum, Sudan. Writer, Actor, Director. m. Sheila McComb, 7 Aug. 1985, Toronto, Canada. *Education:* 2 years at university; McGill University, Montreal, Canada; York University, Toronto. *Literary Appointments:* Dramaturge, Theatre Passe Muraille, Toronto, Canada, 1981–82. *Publications include:* As writer/Director: Lucky Strike; Night; The Blues; Passion and Sin; Christmas; Brandy; Mathematics; Western; Tantrums; As Director: Lady in the Night, opera, 1977; Kiss, television 1975. *Honours include:* Canada Council Awards; Ontario Arts Council Awards. *Membership:* Playwrights Union of Canada. *Literary Agent:* Great North Artists' Management, 345 Adelaide Street W 500, Toronto, Ontario M5V-1R5, Canada. *Address:* 629 Broadview Avenue, Toronto, Ontario M4K 2HG, Canada.

ALIESAN, Jody, b. 22 Apr. 1943, Kansas City, Missouri, USA. Poet. *Education:* BA English Literature, Occidental College, 1965; MA English & American Literature, Brandeis University, 1966; 2 years additional graduate study, 1966–68. *Major Publications:* Soul Claiming, 1975; as if it will matter, 1978; Desire, 1985. *Contributor to:* Wall Street Journal; Contemporary Quarterly; Studia Mystica; Portland Review; In Anthologies: Leaving the Bough: 50 American Poets of the 80s; Pioneer Letters: The Letter as Literature, 1981; and others. *Honours:* Various awards, including National Endowment for the Arts Writing Fellowship, 1978; National Merit Scholarship, Occidental College, 1965; Woodrow Wilson Fellowship, 1966. *Memberships:* Feminist Writers Guild. *Address:* Waldron, WA 98297, USA.

ALKAAOUD, Elizabeth Ann Furlong, b. 3 Oct. 1945, Montreal, Quebec, Canada. Teacher; Scholar. m. Ali Hassan Alkaaoud, 1965, 1 son. *Education:* BA, University of Arizona, 1972; MA, Rice University, Houston, 1982; PhD, Rice University, 1984. *Literary Appointment:* Editorial Assistant, Studies in English Literature 1500–1900, Editor, Robert L Patten, 1979–80. *Publication:* Doctoral Dissertation: What the Lion Ment! (Conography of the Lion in the Poetry of Edmund Spenser, 1984). *Contributor to:* Stone Country; New Jersey Northwoods Journal, Michigan; Hyperion, North Carolina; Berkeley Poetry Review, California; Care, Caritas and the Role of the Samaritan, in, Piers Plowman, Proceedings of the Seventh Annual International Conference on Patristic, Medieval and Renaissance Studies, The Augustinian Institute, 1985; Una's Lion, in, The Spenser Encyclopedia, 1986. *Honours:* Poetry Readings, Rica University, 1979, BD; Poetry Reading, The Houston Festival, 1982. *Memberships:* The Medieval Institute; Modern Language Association; The Renaissance Society of America; The Spenser Society. *Address:* 3123 University Boulevard, Houston, TX 77005, USA.

ALLAN, Philip, b. 24 Oct. 1944, Cheshire, England. Publisher. m. Suzanne Sewell, 10 Oct. 1970, Shoreham-by-Sea, Sussex, 4 sons. *Education:* MA Honours, Cambridge University. *Literary Appointments:* Publisher, Philip Allan Publishers Limited, Deddington, Oxford. *Contributions to:* Times Higher Education Supplement; The Bookseller. *Address:* Philip Allan Publishers Limited, Market Place, Deddington, Oxford OX5 4SE, England.

ALLAN, Roger Glenmor, b. 21 Mar. 1951, Enfield, Middlesex, England. Writer; Editor; Actor. *Education:* Combined Honours History and Philosophy, 1974, Undergraduate biological sciences, 1976–78, University of Guelph, Canada. *Literary Appointments:* Contributing Editor, Electronics Today International; Editor, Computers in Education. *Contributions to:* Forces Magazine; Insearch Magazine; Electronics Today International; Computing Now!; Software Now!; Computers in Education; Bridges Magazines. *Membership:* Canadian Science Writers Association. *Address:* Computers in Education, c/o Moorshead Publications, Suite 601, 25 Overlea Boulevard, Toronto, Ontario, Canada M4H 1B1.

ALLAN, Ted, b. 25 Jan. 1916, Montreal, Canada. Writer. m. Kate Lenthier, 1940, Boston, USA, divorced, 1 son, 1 daughter. *Publications:* This Time a Better Earth, 1939; The Scalpel, The Sword, The Story of Dr Bethune, co-author, 1954; Willie The Squowse, 1980; Love is a Long Shot, 1984; Don't You Know Anybody Else?, 1985; Stage Plays: Oh What a Lovely War; Gog and Magog, (with Roger MacDougal); The Secret of the World; I've Seen You Cut Lemons. *Contributor to:* Short Stories in: Colliers; Harpers; Readers Digest; The Canadian; New Masses; New Yorker; Madamoiselle. *Honours:* Academy Award Nomination, Best Original Screenplay, Lies My Father Told, 1976. *Memberships:* Dramatists League, England; Writers Guild of America; Authors League, USA; Playwright's Union, Canada. *Literary Agent:* Max Becker, 115 East 82nd Street, New York, NY 10028, USA. *Address:* c/o Mike Zimring, William Morris Agency, 151 El Camino, Beverly Hills, CA 90212, USA.

ALLEN, Arly Harrison, b. 23 Aug. 1938, Lawrence, Kansas, USA. Vice-President and General Manager of Allen Press Incorporated. m. Constance Huested, 23 June 1962, Lawrence, Kansas, 1 son, 1 daughter. *Education:* BA, English, University of Kansas, 1960; Italian Language, Univeresita per gli Stranieri, Perugia, Italy, French Language, Sorbonne, Paris, France, 1960–61; MA, Medieval History, University of Kansas, 1963; Medieval History, Universita del Sacro Cuore, Milan, Italy, 1963–64; PhD, Medieval History (incomplete), University of Toronto, Canada, 1964–66. *Publications:* Steps Toward Better Scientific Illustrations, 1976; Steps Toward Better Scientific Illustrations, 3rd Edition, 1982; The Family of Archbishop Guido da Velate, 1968. *Contributor to:* Illustrating Science, 1980–85; Handbook of the Guild of Natural Science Illustrators, 1985; CBE Views, 1985. *Memberships:* Board of Directors, Council of Biology Editors; Association of Earth Science Editors; European Association of Scientific Editors; Society for Scholarly Publishing; Medieval Academy of America; Society of Architectural Historians. *Honours:* Italian Government Study Grant, Fulbright Travel Grant, 1963–64; Province of Ontario Scholarships, 1964–66; Max Brodel Memorial Lecturer, Association of Medical Illustrators, 1984. *Address:* 1101 West 21st Street, Lawrence, KS 66044, USA.

ALLEN, Douglas Malcolm, b. 15 June 1941, New York, USA. Professor. *Education:* BA, Yale University, 1963; Banaras Hindu University, 1963–64; MA, 1966, PhD, 1971, Vanderbilt University. *Appointments:* Southern Illinois University, 1967–72; Vanderbilt University, 1972–73; Central Connecticut State College, 1973–74; University of Maine, 1974–. *Publications:* Structure and Creativity in Religion, 1978; Mircea Eliade: An Annotated Bibliography, with Dennis Doeing, 1980; Mircea Eliade et le phenomene religieux, 1982. *Contributor to:* Journal of Religion; Bulletin of Concerned Asian Scholars; Imagination and Meaning. *Honours:* Editorial Board, Bulletin of Concerned Asian Scholars, 1976–; Editorial Board, Philosophy and Social Criticism, 1976–; American council of Learned Societies, shared 1st Prize for best first book in history of religions, 1982. *Address:* Dept. of Philosophy, The Maples, University of Maine, Orono, ME 04469, USA.

ALLEN, Frank Charles, b. 22 Mar. 1939, Evanston, Illinois, USA. *Education:* BA, 1961, PhD, 1969, English,

University of Maryland; MA, English, New York University, 1963. *Publications:* A Critical Edition of Robert Browning's Bishop Blougram's Apology, 1976; Magna Mater, 1981; Seeds of Recognition, 1984. *Contributor to:* American Book Review; Common Ground; Gargoyle; Library Journal; Literature East and West; Parnassus; Poet Lore; Chandrabhaga; Connecticut Fireside; The DeKalb Literary Arts Journal; Insight; Men V; Mickle Street Review; The Other Side; Snowy Egret. *Honour:* Poetry in, Dear Winter, Anthology. *Address:* 1546 C–1 Catasauqua Road, Bethlehem, PA 18018, USA.

ALLEN, Jeffrey, b. 9 Mar. 1948, Detroit, Michigan, USA. Author. *Education:* BA, University of Michigan. *Publications:* Mary Alice, Operator Number Nine, 1975; Bonzini! The Tattooed Man, 1976; The Secret Life of Mr Weird, 1983; Nosey Mrs Rat, 1985. *Honours:* Showcase book selection for, Bonzini! The Tattooed Man, Children's Book Council Inc New York. *Literary Agent:* Little, Brown and Co., Boston, Massachusetts; Viking Penguin Inc, New York, New York. *Address:* 140 Missouri Street, San Francisco, CA 94107, USA.

ALLEN, Louis, b. 22 Dec. 1922, Redcar, Yorkshire, England. University Teacher and Military Historian. m. Margaret Wilson (deceased), 4 June 1949, Manchester, 4 sons, 2 daughters (1 deceased). *Education:* BA, MA, University of Manchester; Studies, Universities of London and Paris. *Literary Appointments:* Formerly: Northern Arts Literature and Drama Panel; BBC General Advisory Council; Chairman, BBC Northeast Region Advisory Council, -1975. *Publications:* Le Barbier de Seville, 1951; Le Mariage de Figaro, 1952; Sittang, The Last Battle, 1971; Japan, The Years of Triumph, 1971; The End of the War in Asia, 1976; John Henry Newman and the abbé Jager, 1976; Singapore, 1977; Burma, The Longest War, 1984. *Contributions to:* Decisive Battles of the 20th Century, (book), 1976; Numerous journals including: Sunday Times; Observer; Tablet; Literary Review; Commonwealth; Journal of Asian Studies. *Memberships:* President 1979–80, British Association for Japanese Studies. *Address:* Dun Cow Cottage, Durham, DH1 3ES, England.

ALLEN, Robert Day, b. 28 Aug 1927, Providence, Rhode Island, USA. University Professor. m. Suzanne T Allen, five children. *Education:* AB, Brown University, Providence, Rhode Island, 1949; PhD, University of Pennsylvania, Philadelphia, 1953; Postdoctoral trainee, Wenner Gren Institute, University of Stockholm, 1953–54. *Literary Appointments:* Assistant Instructor of Zoology, University of Pennsylvania, 1950–51; Instructor of Zoology, University of Michigan, 1954–56; Assistant Professor of Biology, 1956–61, Associate Professor of Biology, 1961–66, Princeton University; Professor of Biology, 1966–75, Chairman, Department of Biological Sciences, 1966–72, State University of New York at Albany; Professor of Biology, 1975–, Chairman, Department of Biological Sciences, 1975–79, Ira Allen Eastman Professor, 1979–, Dartmouth College, Hanover, New Hampshire; Associate Editor, Journal of Mechanochemistry and Cell Motility, 1971–75; Editor, Microscopica Acta, 1978–82; Editor and Founder, Cell Motility, 1980–85; Cell Motility and the Cytoskeleton, 1986–; Initiator, Videodisc Supplement; Reviewer (ad hoc), Journal of Cell Biology; Journal of Biophysics; Science; Nature; Cell Motility; Exp Cell Research; Journal Cell Science; Journal of Protozoology. *Publications:* Primitive Motile Systems in Cell Biology, co-editor with N Kamiya; Science of Life 1977. *Contributions to:* Numerous scientific journals including Journal of Biophysical and Biochemical Cytology; Nature; Journal of Cell Biology; Scientific American; Science; Journal of Histochemistry and Cytochemistry; Journal of Cell Science Cell Motility and many more. Author of numerous chapters in scientific books and lecturer to numerous universities and scientific institutions. *Honours:* Recipient of numerous honours and awards including Guggenheim Fellowships: Faculty of Science, Osaka University 1961, University of Cambridge 1966. *Memberships include:* American Association for the Advancement of Science;

American Society for Cell Biology; Biophysical Society; Sigma Xi; Royal Microscopical Society of London. *Address:* Department of Biological Sciences, Dartmouth College, Hanover, NH 03755, USA.

ALLEN, Roger Michael Ashley, b. 24 Jan. 1942, Tavistock, Devon, England. Professor. m. 25 Nov. 1972, Philadelphia, USA. 1 son, 1 daughter. *Education:* BA, Oriental Studies, 1965, MA, 1968, D Phil 1968, University of Oxford, England; Honorary AM, University of Pennsylvania, 1973. *Literary Appointments:* Assistant Professor, 1968–73, Associate Professor, 1973–84, Professor of Arabic Language and Literature, University of Pennsylvania, 1985–. *Major Publications:* Al-Muwaylihi's Hadith Isa ibn Hisham: A Study of Egypt during the British Occupation, 1974; The Arabic Novel: an Historical & Critical Introduction, 1982; Modern Arabic Literature, 1985. *Contributor to:* Journal of Arabic Literature; International Journal of Middle East Studies; Middle East Journal; Edebiyat; Mundus artium; Muslim World; Journal of the American Research Center in Egypt; World Literature Today; and others. *Honour:* Lindback Foundation Award for distinguished teaching, 1972. *Memberships:* Middle East Studies Association (Research & Training Committee, 1971–74); American Oriental Society; American Association of Teachers of Arabic (President, 1977). *Address:* Department of Oriental Studies, University of Pennsylvania, Philadelphia, PA 19104, USA.

ALLEN, Samuel Washington, b. 9 Dec. 1917, Columbus, Ohio, USA. Retired Professor. div. 1 daughter. *Education:* AB, Fisk University, 1938; JD, Harvard Law School, 1941. *Literary Appointments:* Avalon Professor of Humanities, Tuskegee University, 1968–70; Visiting Professor, English, Wesleyan University, 1970–71; Professor, English & Afro-American Literature, Boston University, 1971–81. *Publications:* Poetry includes: Ivory Tusks & Other Poems, 1968; Paul Vessey's Ledger, 1975; Editor, Poems from Africa, 1973; etc. Translations: Orphée Noir, Jean-Paul Sartre, 1951; etc. Essays: Tendencies in African Poetry, 1958; Negritude & its Relevance to the American Negro Writer, 1959; Two Writers: Senghor & Soyinka, 1967; The Civil Rights Struggle, 1970; A Personal Interview with W E B DuBois, 1971; The African Heritage, 1970; etc. Reviews. *Contributions to:* Numerous academic & professional journals including: African Heritage; Negro Digest; Journal of Afro-American Studies. Books: The Ideology of Blackness, ed. Raymond F. Betts, 1971; Background to Black American Literature, ed. Ruth Miller, 1971; What Black Educators Are Saying, ed. Nathan Wright, 1970; etc. Work translated into French, German & Italian. *Memberships:* New England Poetry Club, Board of Directors. *Address:* 145 Cliff Avenue, Winthrop, MA 02152, USA.

ALLEN, Walter Ernest, b. 23 Feb. 1911, Birmingham, England. Author. m. Peggy Yorke Joy, 8 Apr. 1944, Hampstead, 2 sons, 2 daughters. *Education:* BA (Hons), University of Birmingham, 1932. *Literary Appointments:* Literary Adviser, Michael Joseph Limited, 1945–59; Literary Editor, New Statesman, 1959–61. *Publications:* Innocence is Browned, 1938; Blind Man's Ditch, 1939; Arnold Bennett, 1948; Dead Man Over All, 1950; English Novel, 1954; All In a Lifetime, 1959; Tradition and Dream, 1964; George Eliot, 1964; Short Story in English, 1981; As I Walked Down New Grub Street, 1981. *Contributions to:* New Statesman; Spectator; Listener; Times Literary Supplement; Encounter; London Magazine; New York Times Book Review; Nation; New Republic, etc. *Memberships:* Fellow, Royal Literary Society; Society of Authors. *Literary Agent:* David Higham Associates. *Address:* 4B Alwyne Road, London N1 2HH, England.

ALLEY, Henry Melton, b. 27 Jan. 1945, Seattle, Washington, USA. Assistant Professor. m. Patricia Mary Grimm, 21 Dec. 1967, Seattle, Washington, 1 daughter. *Education:* BA (Hons), English, Stanford University, 1967; MFA, Creative Writing, 1969, PhD, Prose Fiction, 1971, Cornell University. *Literary Appointments:*

Teaching Assistant, Cornell University, 1967–70; Associate Professor, English, College of the School of the Ozarks, 1972–75; Associate Professor, English, University of Idaho, 1975–82; Assistant Professor, Literature, University of Oregon Honors College, 1982–. *Publications:* The York Handbook for the Teaching of College Creative Writing, 1979; Through Glass, (novel), Second Printing 1981; The Lattice, (novel), 1986. *Contributions to:* University Review; Webster Review; The New Infinity Review; Cimarron Review; River Bottom Magazine; The Slackwater Review; The Lake Superior Review; Sawtooth; Snapdragon; The Virginia Woolf Quarterly; The Pikestaff Forum; Outerbridge; The Pale Fire Review; Kansas Quarterly; Iowa English Bulletin; The Midwest Quarterly; The Rocky Mountain Review of Language and Literature; The Journal of Narrative Technique; Twentieth Century Literature, etc. *Honours:* Cornell Senior Graduate Fellowship, 1971; Semifinalist, Associated Writing Program Series in the Novel, 1981. *Memberships:* MLA; Associated Writing Programs; National Conference on British Studies; Phi Beta Kappa. *Address:* Honors College, University of Oregon, Eugene, OR 97403, USA.

ALLINSON, Sidney, b. 20 Oct. 1930, Durham, England. Communications Consultant. m. Alice Beverley née Collins, 5 Mar. 1955, Toronto, Canada, 3 sons. *Literary Appointments:* Editor, Yearbook, Royal Canadian Military Institute; Assistant Editor, SITREP Newsletter, RCMI. *Major Publications:* Season for Homicide, 1969; How to Survive when the Money Crash Comes, 1974; How to make money fast as a Ghost Writer, 1976; The Bantams: The Untold Story of World War I, 1981; Jeremy Kane, 1986. *Contributor to:* Various publications, of articles on military history, business topics, short stories. *Memberships:* Ontario Vice-President, Canadian Authors Association; Chairman, Selection Committee, Bowker Award for Military History. *Address:* 24 Ravencliff Crescent, Scarborough, Ontario, M1T 1R8, Canada.

ALLISON, Gay Delores, b. 7 Aug. 1948, Saskatchewan, Canada. English Teacher, Editor, Poet. m. Geoff Hancock, 6 Aug. 1983, Toronto, Canada, 1 daughter. *Education:* BA, B Ed, University of British Columbia, Canada; MA, University of Toronto. *Literary Appointments:* Co-founder, Woman's Writing Collective, 1975; Poetry Editor, Landscape, 1976; Founding Editor, Fireweed, Feminist journal, 1977; Poetry Editor, Waves, literary journal, 1983; Fiction Editor, The Canadian Forum, literary and political magazine, 1984. *Publications:* Women and Their Writing I and II, anthology, 1975, 1976; Landscape, anthology (Editor), 1977; Life: Still, poetry, 1982; The Unravelling, poetry, 1985; Transformations, poetry, forthcoming 1986. *Contributions to:* Landscape; Fireweed; Island; The Canadian Forum; Women and Their Writing I and II; PCR; Quarry; Writer's Quarterly; other Canadian journals. *Honour:* Poetry Award, Ontario Teacher's Federation, 1981–82. *Membership:* The League of Canadian Poets: Amnesty International. *Address:* Fiction Editor, The Canadian Forum, 70 The Esplanade, 3rd Floor, Toronto, Ontario M5E IR2, Canada.

ALLMAN, Edwin Christian, b. 7 July 1954, Harrisburg, Pennsylvania, USA. Journalist; Music Critic. *Education:* BS, MS, Experimental Psychology & English Education. *Literary Appointments:* Mardi Gras Film & Literary Advisory Board, 1982; Allentown Consultant, 1983. *Publications:* The Great River Road – Kill Recipe Conspiracy; Messiah; Mayhem's Angel. *Contributions to:* Gris-Gris; Billboard; New Orleans Magazine; Baton Rouge State Times & Morning Advocate; Upstate; Facing South; Enterprise; More; Entree; Light Labour; Vieux Carre Courier. *Honours:* 2nd Place, Rural Revitalization Award, 1972; Commendation, Louisiana Music Commission, 1984. *Membership:* The Hellion. *Address:* PO Box 3456, Baton Rouge, LA 70821, USA.

ALLOTT, Miriam, b. 16 June 1920. University Lecturer. m. Kenneth Allott, 2 June 1951 (deceased 1973). *Education:* MA, Liverpool, 1946; PhD, 1949.

Literary Appointments: William Noble Fellowship in English Literature, 1946–48; Lecturer, Senior Lecturer, Reader, English Literature, Liverpool, 1948–70; Andrew Cecil Bradley Professor of Modern English Literature, 1973–81; Professor of English, Birkbeck College, London University, 1981–85. *Publications:* The Art of Graham Greene, with Kenneth Allott, 1951; Novelists on the Novel, 1959; The Complete Poems of John Keats, 1970; The Complete Poems of Matthew Arnold, Second Edition, 1979, first edition Kenneth Allott, 1965; Matthew Arnold, 1986 (with R H Super): Numerous essays and articles on nineteenth century and twentieth century novelists and poets, notably Keats, Shelley, Arnold, Clough, the Brontes, George Eliot, Henry James, James Joyce, Graham Greene, Iris Murdoch, William Golding. *Membership:* English Association (Executive and Publications Committees). *Address:* 21 Mersey Avenue, Liverpool 19, England.

ALLOWAY, David Nelson, b. 1927, Emmaus, Pennsylvania, USA. College Professor. *Education:* BA, Muhlenberg College; MA, Columbia University; PhD, New York University. *Publications:* Economic History of the United States, 1965; Minorities and the American City, 1971; Urban Problems and the Suburban Perspective, 1978; Survey of the Crime Problem in America, 1981. Co-Author: Agony of the Cities, 1970; Education Information Guide, series, Biology of Education, 1978; History of American Education, Medical Education in the United States; American Ethnic Groups: The European Heritage, 47 volumes, 1980, 81; Crime in America: Historical Patterns and Contemporary Realities – An Annotated Bibliography, 1985. *Contributions to:* Encyclopedia Britannica, 1964; Choice; International Migration Review; Social Education; Intellect School and Society; Phi Delta Kappan. *Honours include:* Medaglia d'Oro per le Scienze, 1980, Il Grande Collare Croce d'Onore al Merito, 1980, Accademia delle Scienze di Roma, Italy; Medaille d'Or en Science, Academie Internationale de Lutec de Paris, France, 1980; Grand Croix de Valeur Civisme, Civisme et Renovation Francias, 1980; Medaille Argent, Academie Universelle de Lausanne, Switzerland, 1984. *Address:* 1303–B Troy Towers, Bloomfield, NJ 07003, USA.

ALLWOOD, Martin Samuel, b. 13 Apr. 1916, Jönköping, Sweden. Author; Professor. m. Enelia Paz Gomez, 20 Dec. 1976, Jönköping, 2 sons, 3 daughters by previous marriage. *Education:* MA Cantab; MA Columbia, 1949; Dr.rer.pol, Technische Hochschule, Darmstadt, 1953. *Appointments:* President, Anglo American Centre, Sweden; Professor, Mass Media, Nordic College of Journalism, Sweden. *Publications:* More than 80 books in Swedish and English including: Middlevillage, 1943; The Cemetery of the Cathedrals, 1945; Scandinavian Songs and Ballards, 1953; Eilert Sundt, 1957; Toward a New Sociology, 1964; The Swedish Crime, Play, 1976; The Collected Poems of Edith Södergran, Translations, 1980; New English Poems, 1981; Modern Scandinavian Poetry, 1982; Valda Svenska dikter, 1982; A Dream of Poland, 1982; The Academy, a Play, 1984; Meet Will Shakespeare, Nine Scenes from the life of Shakespeare, 1985. *Contributor to:* Numerous articles in professional journals. *Memberships:* Founding Member, Gothenburg Society of Authors; Swedish Society of Immigrant Authors; Life Member, Plesse Academy, Bovenden West Germany. *Address:* Anglo-American Center, 565 00 Mullsjö, Sweden.

ALMARIO, Virgilio S, b. 9 Mar. 1944, San Miguel, Bulacan, Philippines. Teacher. m. Emelina B Soriano, 1 Jan. 1973, 2 daughters. *Education:* BA Political Science 1963, MA Pilipino 1974, University of the Philippines. *Literary Appointments include:* Senior Editor, Research and Analysis Centre, Department of Public Information, 1975; Executive Director, Children's Communication Center, 1981; Columnist, Observer, 1981–82; Columnist, Philippines Daily Express, 1981–. *Publications include:* Makinasyon at Ibang Tula, 1968; Ang Makata sa Panahon ng Makina, 1972; Poktrinang Anakpawis, 1979; Balagtasismo vs Modernismo, 1984;

Mga Retrato at Rekwerdo, 1984; Palipad-Hangin, 1985; Taludtod at Talinghaga, 1985. *Contributions to:* Essays, stories, poems and translations in Magazines and journals including: Dawn; Trends; Philippine Studies; Asia-Philippines Leader; Graphic; Bulaklak; Liwayway; Parnasong Tagalog; Manlilikha; Philippine Contemporary Literature. *Honours include:* Essay 1st prize 1979, Poetry 1st prize 1970, Palanca Memorial Awards; Grand Prize, Cultural Centre Literary Awards, 1984; Poet of the Year, Institute of National Language, 1984; Ten Outstanding Young Men for Literature, 1984. *Memberships include:* Vice-Chairman 1981, Chairman 1984 Writers Union of the Philippines; Secretary-General, Philippine Board on Books for Young People, 1984–. *Address:* 52 Sampaquita Avenue, Mapayapa Village, Quezon City, Metro Manila, Philippines.

ALMEIDA, Marcia de, b. 21 Apr. 1952, Rio de Janeiro, Brazil. Journalist, Producer, Scriptwriter. *Education:* New York University, USA. *Literary Appointments:* Sindicato dos Jornalistas do Rio Grande do Sul, Universidade Federal do Rio Grande do Norte, 1980; New Mexico University, Albuquerque, USA, 1982. *Major Publications:* Collections: Cacos, 1977; Cacos II, 1978; Te Quero Verde, 1982; Short Stories: Fios Y Navios, 1978; Sob O Signo da Chuva, 1979; Poetry: De Cunhatã pra Cunhã, 1981; Novels: Casulo das Aguas, 1983; Nos Quintais do Mundo, 1986. *Contributor to:* Journals: Jornal do Brasil; O Globo; Reporter; Critica; Ultima Hora; O Dia; Semana Sul; Flagrante Livre; Leia Livros; Eolha de Sao Paolo; Tribuna da Imprensa; Magazines: Radice; Anima; Ele e Ela; Casa Viva; Pais Modernos; Ficcao. *Honour:* 3rd Award VI Concurso Nacional de Contos do Estado do Paraná, 1974. *Memberships:* Writers' Union of Rio de Janeiro; Brazilian Writers' Union; Sindicato dos Artistas e Técnicos em Espetáculos de Diversão de Rio de Janeiro. *Literary Agent:* Agência Literária Carmen Balcells, Brazil. *Address:* Avenue Nossa Senhora de Copacabana 252 flat 901, Copacabana, Rio de Janeiro, Brazil 22020.

ALSEN, Eberhard, b. 26 Oct. 1939, Nuremberg, Germany. Professor of Literature. *Education:* BA (equivalent), University of Bonn, Germany, 1962; MA, Indiana University, Bloomington, USA, 1965; PhD, 1967. *Literary Appointments:* Teaching Associate, Indiana University, 1963–65; Assistant Professor, University of Minnesota, 1966–69; Professor, State University of New York at Cortland, 1969–; Fulbright Professor, University of Tubingen, Germany, 1975, 76, 81, 82. *Publications:* Salinger's Glass Stories as a Composite Novel, 1983; American Short Stories on Film; Herman Melville's Bartleby, 1985. *Contributions to:* American Literature; Anglia 91; Studies in Short Fiction; Transition. *Memberships:* Modern Language Association; German Society for American Studies. *Address:* Department of English, State University of New York, College at Cortland, Cortland, NY 13045, USA.

ALSTEIN, Marc Van, b. 18 Mar. 1947, Antwerp, Belgium. Writer. m. Anne-Marie Cevlemans, 29 Dec. 1972, Antwerp, 2 sons. *Major Publications:* De Opstand (The Revolt), 1975; Het Vertrer Naar Amerika (Leaving for America), 1981; Een Stel Voorname Heren (Those Distinguished Gentlemen), 1982; Het Vitzicht op de Wereld (The View of the World), 1984. *Contributor to:* Dietsche Warande en Belfort; De Nieuwe; Elsevier Magazine; De Standaard; and others. *Honour:* Honorary Fellow, University of Iowa, USA. *Membership:* PEN Club. *Address:* Heideland 52, B–2510 Mortsel, Antwerp, Belgium.

ALSTON, Anthony John, b. 19 Dec. 1919, London, England. Oriental Linguist; Author. *Education:* New College, Oxford; PhD (Indian Philosophy), Banaras Hindu University, India, 1964. *Publications:* The Realization of the Absolute, 1959, 2nd edition 1971; Panchadashi (Editor of Translation from Sanskrit, by Hari Prasad Shastri), 1965; That Thou Art, 1967; Devotional Poems of Mirabai, 1980; Samkara on the Absolute, 1980; Samkara on Creation, 1980; Samkara on the Soul, 1981; Yoga and the Supreme Bliss (Urdu

and Persian Poems of Swami Rama Tirthal), 1982. *Contributor to:* Selfknowledge; The Hindi Review; Hibbert Journal; etc. *Memberships:* Society of Authors. *Address:* 31 Northumberland Place, London W2 5OS, England.

ALTMAN, Philip L, b. 6 Jan. 1924, Kansas City, Missouri, USA. Editor; Administrator. m. Lillian Berlinsky, 1 Sep. 1946, Kansas City, Missouri, 1 son 1 daughter. *Education:* BA, University of Southern California, 1948; MSc, Western Reserve University, 1949. *Literary Appointments:* Director and Editor, Office of Biological Handbooks 1959–79; Executive Editor, Biology Databook Series, 1983–. *Publications:* Handbook of Respiration, 1958; Handbook of Circulation, 1959; Blood and Other Body Fluids, 1961; Growth, 1962; Biology Data Book, 1st edition 1964; Environmental Biology, 1966; Metabolism, 1968; Respiration and Circulation, 1971; Biology Data Book, 2nd Edition Volume I 1972, Volume II 1973, Volume III 1974; Cell Biology, 1976; Human Health and Disease, 1977; Inbred and Genetically Defined Strains of Laboratory Animals, 1979; Pathology of Laboratory Mice and Rats, 1985. *Contributor to:* Contributions to scientific journals and edited volumes including (most recent), First International Conference of Scientific Editors, Israel 1977, in CBE Newsletter, June 1977; Zoology CODATA Directory of Data Sources for Science and Technology, in CODATA Bulletin No. 38, 1980; The Council of Biology Editors: A 25-Year Chronology of Events, in CBE Views, Vol 4 1981; Publications of the Council of Biology Editors, in CBE Views Vol 6, 1983. *Address:* Federation of American Societies for Experimental Biology, 9650 Rockville Pike, Bethesda, MD 20814, USA.

ALVAREZ, Alfred, b. 5 Aug. 1929, London, England. Author. m. Anne Adams, 7 Apr. 1966, Toronto, 2 sons, 1 daughter. *Education:* BA, 1952, MA, 1956, Corpus Christie College, Oxford. *Publications:* The Shaping Spirit, 1958; The School of Donne, 1961; The New Poetry, Editor, Introduction, 1962; Under Pressure, 1965; Beyond All This Fiddle, 1968; Lost, Poems, 1968; Penguin Modern Poets, No. 18, 1970; Apparition, poems, 1971; The Savage God, 1971; Beckett, 1973; Hers, 1974; Hunt, 1978; Autumn to Autumn and selected Poems, 1978; Life After Marriage, 1982; The Biggest Game in Town, 1983; Offshore, 1986. *Honours:* Vachel Lindsay Prize for Poetry, Poetry Chicago, 1961. *Agent:* Deborah Rogers, London. *Address:* c/o Deborah Rogers, 44 Blenheim Crescent, London W9, England.

AMANSHAUSER, Gerhard, b. 2 Jan. 1928, Salzburg, Austria. Writer. *Education:* Technical University of Graz, Austria; Universities of Vienna and Marburg/Lahn. *Publications:* Aus der Leben der Quaden, (novel), 1968; Der Deserteur, (short stories), 1970; Satz und Gegensatz (essays), 1972; Argenisse eines Zauberers (satires and marginalia), 1973; Schloss mit spaten Gasten (novel), 1975; Grenzen (essays), 1977; Aufzeichnungen einer Sonde (parodies), 1979; List der Illusionen (remarks), 1985; Gedichte, 1986. *Contributions to:* Literatur und Kritik; Neues Forum; Protokolle; Neue Rundschau. *Honours:* Georg Trakl Promotion Prize, 1952; Theodor Korner Prize, 1970; Rauriser Literaturpreis, 1973; Forderungspreis der Stadt Salzburg, 1975; Preis der Salzburger Wirtschaft, 1985. *Address:* Brunnhausgasse 10, 5020 Salzburg, Austria.

AMARO, Kenneth Angel, b. 27 Mar. 1952, Christiansted, St Croix. Journalist. m. Rosalyn Vanessa, 29 Apr. 1979, Jacksonville, Florida, USA, 1 daughter. *Education:* BA, Jones College, Jacksonville; Diploma, R-E-I Engineering School, Sarasota, Florida; Diploma, St Croix Central High School. *Honours:* Award of Excellence in Medical Journalism, 1983; Newsmaker Award for Coverage of Public Education, 1984. *Memberships:* Sigma Delta Chi; Association of Black Journalists. *Address:* 5501 University Club Blvd, Jacksonville, FL 32211, USA.

AMBATSIS, Jannis, b. 2 Jan. 1926, Athens, Greece. Senior Administrative Officer, Library of the Central

Board of National Antiquities of Sweden; Author. m. Inga-Maria Lindmar, 19 July 1959, 1 daughter. *Education:* University of Stockholm. *Major Publications:* Grekisk Mat, 1963; Grekland, 1964; Grekland i fickan, 1965; Levande Grekland, 1966; Citronträdets dotter, 1964; Nygrekiska sägner och legender, 1967; Grekiska folkvisor, 1968; Nygrekisk litteratur, 1970; Grekiska folksagor, 1975; The Published Writings of Agnes Geijer 1928–78, 1978; Greklands tredje ansikte, 1980; Translations of Swedish Poetry into Greek, 1976; Contributions to various works. *Contributor to:* Fornvännen, Journal of the Royal Academy of Letters, History & Antiquities of Sweden. *Honour:* Recipient, Swedish Authors' Fund Prize. *Memberships:* Swedish Society of Authors; Minerva; Swedish Society of Translators; PEN; The Swedish Archaeological Society. *Address:* Bollhusgränd 6, ltr, S–111 31 Stockholm, Sweden.

AMBJÖRNSSON, (Elsa) Gunila, b. 12 Mar. 1938, Kalmar, Sweden. Writer, Director. m. 1958–72, 1 son. *Education:* BA Literature, German/Scandinavian Languages, History of Science; Film Education, tv. *Major publications:* Truls (childrens book), 1967; Skräkpkultur at barnen (culture), 1968; Barnteater en klassfraga (childrens theatre); Ville Valle och Viktor (parts 1-2, childrens books), 1971; Läsning för barn, 1974; More important: Film scripts, drama for stage and television. *Contributor to:* Chronicles in Arbetaren; BIM; Ord och Bild; Dagens Nyheter Expressen; other daily papers & magazines, on film, media & literature, politics. *Memberships:* PEN; Swedish Writers Guild. *Address:* Rörsträndsgatan 31, S–11340 Stockholm, Sweden.

AMERY (Right Hon) H Julian, b. 27 Mar. 1919. Member of Parliament, UK (Conservative, Preston North, 1950–66, Brighton Pavilion 1969–). *Education:* Balliol College, University of Oxford, England. *Publications:* Sons of the Eagle, 1948; The Life of Joseph Chamberlain: Vol IV 1901–03, At the Height of His Power, 1951, Volumes V & VI, Joseph Chamberlain & The Tariff Reform Campaign 1901–14, 1969; Approach March (autobiography), 1973. *Contributor to:* Various newspapers & journals. *Honours include:* Privy Councillor, 1960; Knight Commander of the Order of the Phoenix; Order of Oman 1st Class. *Address:* 112 Eaton Square, London SW1, England.

AMIR, Aharon, b. 17 May, 1923, Israel. Writer; Translator. m. 6 Mar. 1969, Tel Aviv, 2 sons, 1 daughter. *Education:* Oriental Studies, Hebrew University, Jerusalem. *Appointments:* Editor, Aleph Monthly, 1948–53; Secretary General, Centre of Young Hebrews, 1951–53; Literary Director, Am. Hassefer Publishers Ltd Tel Aviv, 1957–65; Chief Editor Keshet Quarterly, 1958–76; Editorial Council, Ariel International Quarterly, 1982–. *Publications Include:* Qadim, 1949, Love (short stories), 1950; And Death Shall Have No Dominion, 1955; Saraph, 1956; Nun (part I), novel, 1969; Yated, 1970; Prose (short stories), 1978; Shalom Nifrad, 1979; A Better World, novel, 1979; Heres, 1984; Nun (part II), 1985; Aphrodite, novella, 1986. *Contributor to:* Ha'aretz; Davar; Ma'ariv; Yedioth Aharonoth (dailies); Moznayim (monthly); Keshet (quarterly). *Memberships:* Member, Acadamy of Hebrew Languages, Jerusalem; President, Club for Hebrew Thinking, 1965–67. *Address:* 41 Tagore Street, Tel-Aviv, Israel.

AMLÔT, Robin André, b. 18 Aug. 1958, The Wirral, Cheshire, England. Journalist. *Education:* BA (Politics), University of Lancaster, England. *Literary Appointments:* Editor, Tin International, 1983. *Contributor to:* Business Times (Malaysia), Business Review (Thailand); The Guardian; The Daily Mail; Brentford, Chiswick & Isleworth Times; Ealing & Chiswick Guardian; Chiswick Gazette; British Book Review. *Address:* 7, High Road, London, W4 2NE, England.

AMOR, Anne Clark, b. 4 Feb. 1933, London. Author. m. Abdallah Amor, 23 Feb. 1982, 1 son, 1 daughter. *Education:* Honours degree in English, London University. *Publications:* Beasts and Bawdy, 1975; Lewis Carroll: A Biography, 1979; The Real Alice, 1981;

Mrs Oscar Wilde: A Woman of Some Importance, 1983. *Membership:* Lewis Carroll Society. *Literary Agent:* A M Heath, 40-42 William IV Street, London WC2N 4DD. *Address:* 16 Parkfields Avenue, London NW9 7PE, England.

ANAND, Mulk Raj, b. 12 Dec. 1905, Peshawar, India. Author, Novelist, Art Critic. m (1) Kathleen Van Gelder, 1 daughter, (2) Shirin Vajifdar, 26 Jan. 1950, Bombay. *Education:* BA Honours, Punjab; PhD, London, England. *Literary Appointments:* Lecturer, School of Intellectual Cooperation, Geneva, Switzerland; Visiting Professor, several universities, India; Tagore Professor, University of Punjab. *Publications:* Hindu View of Art, 1929; Persian Painting, 1930; Untouchable, 1932; Coolie, 1933; Two Leaves and a Bud, 1937. *Contributions to:* New Statesman, London; Tribune, London; Marc magazine, Bombay. *Honours:* Laureate, International Peace of World Peace Council Prize, 1950; Padma Bhushan, President of India, 1965; D Litt Honoris Causa, Universities of Delhi, Andhra, Benares, Shanti-Niketan and Pantiala. *Membership:* Chairman, National Akademi of Art, India. *Address:* 25 Cuffe Parade, Bombay 5, India.

ANAND, Valerie May Florence, b. 6 July 1937, London, England. Industrial Editor. m. Dalip Singh Anand, 26 Mar. 1970, Croydon, Surrey, England. *Major Publications:* Historical Trilogy: Gildenford, 1977; The Norman Pretender, 1979; The Disputed Crown, 1981; To a Native Shore (contemporary novel), 1984. *Contributor to:* Accountancy; The Evening News. *Literary Agent:* Scribner's Sons, USA. *Address:* 53 Melrose Avenue, Mitcham, Surrey CR4 2EH, England.

ANASTASSOV, Petar, b. 27 Oct. 1942, Markovo, Bulgaria. Writer. *Literary Appointment:* Director, The State Publishing House, Hristo G Danov. *Publications:* Winter Tenderness 1968; No Special Peculiarities 1971; A Triple Mirror 1972; A Square on the Hill 1977; As I love You 1982; An Undying Love Only 1984. *Contributor to:* All main Bulgarian Literary editions. *Honour:* An Honoured Worker of Culture, 1974. *Membership:* Union of Bulgarian Writers. *Address:* 101 General D Nikolaev Street, Plovdiv, Bulgaria.

ANDELSON, Robert Vernon, b. 19 Feb. 1931, Los Angeles, California, USA. Educator; Social Philosopher. m. Bonny von Orange Johnson, 7 June 1964. *Education:* AA, Los Angeles City College, 1949–50; California State University, Los Angeles, 1950–51; AB equivalent, University of Chicago, 1952; AM 1954, PhD, 1960, University of Southern California. *Literary Appointments:* Editorial Board, The American Journal of Economics and Sociology 1969–; Editorial Board, The Personalist 1975-80; Referee, The Pacific Philosophical Quarterly, 1981–. *Publications:* Imputed Rights: An Essay in Christian Social Theory 1971; Editor and co-author: Critics of Henry George: A Centenary Appraisal of Their Strictures on Progress and Poverty, 1979. *Contributor to:* The Concept of Creativity in the Thought of Rilke and Berdyaev, in The Personalist, 1962; Some Fundamental Inconsistencies in Fletcher's Situation Ethics, in The Personalist, 1970; Black Reparations: A Study in Gray, in The Personalist, 1978; Rousseau and the Rights of Man, in Modern Age, 1984 plus 16 additional articles. *Honours:* Recipient of George Washington Honor Medals (for public addresses), Freedoms Foundation, 1970, 1972. *Address:* Department of Philosophy, Auburn University, AL 36849, USA.

ANDERSEN, Benny Allan, b. 7 Nov. 1929, Copenhagen. Author. m. Cynthia La Touche Andersen, 28 Dec. 1981, Lyngby. *Publications:* Den musikalske al, 1960; Kamera med Kokkenadgang, 1962; Den indre bowlerhat, 1964; Portraetgalleri, 1966; Det sidste Oh, 1969; Her i reservatet, 1971; Svantes viser, 1972; Personlige papirer, 1974; Under beg ojne, 1978; Himmelspraet, 1979; Tiden og storken, 1985; Pa broen, 1981; Puderne, 1965; Tykke-Olsen M.fl., 1968; Over Skulderen, 1983; Contributor to Anthologies: Niet noodzakelijk met insteeming, Dutch, 1967; Poesia moderna danese, Italian, 1971; Norraen Ljod, Icelandic 1972; Anthologie de la poesie danoise contemporaine, French, 1975; Anegdoty Losu, Polish, 1976; Skumju Druva, Latvian, 1977; Dan Elbeszelok, 1978, Hungarian; N3 Cobpemehhonoatckon Mo33NN, Russian, 1983. *Contributor to:* Malahat Review; Mundus Artium; Contemporary Literature in Translation; Poetry Now; Prism International; West Coast Review; Literary Review; Scandinavian Review; Liberté; Svetova Literatura; Complete works translated: Kuddarna, 1969; Selected Poems, 1975; Vissa Dagar, 1976; Das Leben ist schmal und hoch, 1977; The Pillows, 1983; Selected Prose, 1983; etc. *Address:* Kaerparken 11, 2800 Lyngby, Denmark.

ANDERSON, Alfred George, b. 30 May 1925, Collie, Western Australia, Australia. Journalist. m. Joyce Margaret Nielsen, 14 Jan. 1956, Cootamundra, New South Wales, 2 sons. *Literary Appointments:* Cadet Journalist, The West Australian, 1941; Managing Editor, Cootamundra Daily Herald, 1957–61; North West Newspapers, Nudgee, 1961–64; Group Editor, *Publications:* Shipping News Limited, Sydney, 1957–59; Editor, Bowls in New South Wales, Sydney, 1969–73, Maryborough-Bervey Bay Chronicle, Queensland, 1973–. *Honours:* Mayor, Cootamundra, New South Wales, 1960–61, *Address:* 20 Errol Street, Maryborough, Queensland 4650, Australia.

ANDERSON, Barbara Gallatin, b. 13 May 1927, San Francisco, California, USA. Anthropologist. divorced, 1 son, 2 daughters. *Education:* BA, San Francisco College for Women, 1947; University of California, 1955–56; Doctorat de l'Universite de Paris, Sorbonne, France, 1959. *Publications:* The Aging Game: Success, Sanity and Sex After 60, 1979; Don't Follow Mother: The Misadventures of an Anthropologist, Co-Author: The Vanishing Villages, 1964; Bus Stop for Paris, 1965; Culture and Aging, 1964; Medical Anthropology, 1978. *Contributions to:* Marriage and the Family, 1973; Many Sisters, 1974; Coping with Aging, 1982; Clinically Applied Anthropology, 1982; American Anthropologist, 1971, *Honours:* Research Award, California State University, 1971; Faculty Research Abroad Award, US Office of Education, 1972; Distinguished Author Award, Southern Methodist University, 1981; Flora Stone Mather Visiting Professor, Case Western Reserve University, 1979; University Distinguished Professor of Anthropology, Southern Methodist University, Dallas, Texas, 1983–. *Membership:* American Medical Writers Association. *Literary Agent:* Charles Neighbors, San Antonio, Texas. *Address:* Department of Anthropology, Southern Methodist University, Dallas, TX 75275, USA.

ANDERSON, Jessica, b. Queensland, Australia. Writer. *Publications:* An Ordinary Lunacy, 1963; The Last Man's Head, 1970; The Commandant, 1975; Tirra Lirra by the River, 1978; The Impersonators, 1980, published in US as, The Only Daughter, 1975. *Honours:* Miles Franklin Award, 1978; Joint Winner, Australian Natives' Award, 1978; Miles Franklin Award, 1981; New South Wales Premier's Literary Award, 1981. *Membership:* The Australian Society of Authors. *Literary Agent:* Elaine Markson, New York, USA. *Address:* PO Box 1030, Pott's Point, Sydney, NSW 2011, Australia.

ANDERSON, Margaret Anna, b. 23 Sep. 1948, New York, USA. Writer. *Education:* AB, 1970, MA, 1972, MSW, 1979, West Virginia University; Post-graduate, University of Southern California, Santa Cruz, 1979. *Appointments:* Poet-in-Residence, West Virginia Arts and Humanities Commission, 1979–81; Visiting Poet, University of Pittsburgh, 1981–84; Visiting Lecturer, Hamilton College, Clinton, New York, 1985; Visiting Poet, The Pennsylvania State University, 1986. *Publications:* The Great Horned Owl, 1979; Years Than Answer, 1980. *Contributor to:* Quarterly West; American Poetry Review; Poetry East; Anthology of Contemporary Poetry & Magazine Verse; Appalachian Regional Anthology. *Honours:* Recipient, Grants, Poets, National Endowment for the Arts, 1984, Pennsylvania Arts Council, 1982; Grant, Individual Artists, West Virginia Arts and Humanities Commission, 1980.

Memberships: Poetry Society of America; Associated Writing Programmes. *Address:* 353 North Porter Street, Waynesburg, PA 15370, USA.

ANDERSON, Marjorie Ogilvie, b. 9 Feb. 1909, St Andrews, Scotland. Historian. m. A O Anderson, 10 Oct. 1932, St Andrews. *Education:* BA, University of Oxford. *Major Publications:* (co-editor) 'Chronicle of Melrose, 1936; (editor) 'Chronicle of Holyrood, 1938; (editor & translator with A O Anderson), Adomnan's Life of Columba, 1961; Kings & Kingship in early Scotland, 1973; 2nd edition 1981; Chapter in, The Scottish Tradition, 1974; Chapter in The Medieval Church of St Andrews, edited by D McRoberts, 1976; Chapter in, Ireland in Early Medieval Europe, edited D Whitelock, 1982. *Contributor to:* Scottish Historical Review; Historical Studies. *Memberships:* Fellow, Society of Antiquaries of Scotland. *Honours:* D Litt, University of St Andrews, 1973; Agnes Mure Mackenzie Prize, Saltire Society, 1974. *Address:* W View Cottage, Lade Braes Lane, St Andrews, Fife, KY16 9EP, Scotland.

ANDERSON, Nathan Ruth, b. 28 Jan. 1934, NYC, USA. Syndicated Columnist; TV News Host/Writer/Co-Producer, Cablenet. *Education:* George Washington University; New York University. *Contributor to:* Parents; Pageant; Readers Digest; Science Digest; TV Guide; Mademoiselle; Contributing Writer to Medical Insights; Sunday Magazine Supplement; Chicago Sunday Times. *Honours:* Recipient of Numerous Honours. *Memberships:* International Platform Association; Chicago Press Club; Lake Company Association of Journalists; Chicago Women in Broadcasting; American Medical Writers Association; Press Veterans Association; National Museum of Women in the Arts; Chicago Unlimited; National Association of Female Executives; Honorary Member, Future Physicians of America; Elected Trustee, Round Lake Area Public Library; Co-Writer, Beth Fonda Award for Excellence in Medical Feature Writing, 1984. *Address:* VIP Medical Grapevine, 161 Nasa Circle, Round Lake, IL 60073, USA.

ANDERSON, Peter, b. 30 Mar. 1950, Detroit, Michigan, USA. Playwright; Actor. m. Melody Anderson, 23 Apr. 1983, Vancouver, British Columbia, Canada. *Education:* BA, Honours, University of Michigan, USA; Dell'Arte School of Mime and Comedy. *Literary Appointments:* Artistic Director, Writer, Performer, Peachy Cream Productions, Ann Arbor, Michigan, USA. 1973–76; Editor, Street Fiction Press, 1973–76; Writer and performer. Green Thumb Company, City Stage, Theatre Sports Vancouver, Western Canada Theatre Company, New Play Centre and Axis Mime Theatre; Playwright in Residence, Caravan Stage Company, 1977–. *Publications:* Horseplay, with Phil Savath, 1983; Law of the Land, 1983; Only Birds and Fools Fly, co-author, 1985. Plays produced: Animal Farm; The Coyotes; Sweethearts. *Contributions to:* Anon; The Periodical Lunch. *Honours:* Poetry, 1968, Fiction, 1969, Poetry, 1971, Hopwood Award for Creative Writing; Runner Up, Seattle Comedy Contest, 1980; Commissioned to complete play, Rattle in the Dash, Arts Club Theatre, Playwrights 86 Programme, 1982; Canada Council Grant for playwriting, 1984; Jesse Award Nominee for best childrens play and for best actor, 1984. *Memberships:* Playwrights Union of Canada. *Address:* RR2, Invermuir Road, Sooke British Columbia, Canada VOS INO.

ANDERSON, Poul William, b. 25 Nov. 1926, Bristol, Pennsylvania, USA. Writer. m. Karen Kruse, 12 Dec. 1953, Berkeley, California, USA, 1 daughter. *Education:* BSc, University of Minnesota, 1948. *Major Publications:* Brain Wave, 1954; The High Crusade, 1960; Guardians of Time, 1961; Three Hearts & Three Lions, 1961; Tau Zero, 1971; The Broken Sword (revised edition), 1971; Hrolf Kraki's Saga, 1973; A Midsummer's Tempest, 1974; The Atavar, 1978; The Merman's Children, 1979; Orion Shall Rise, 1983. *Contributor to:* Analog; Magazine of Fantasy & Science Fiction; Destinies; National Review; Boy's Life; and others (several hundred contributions). *Honours:* Hugo

Awards, 1961, 1964, 1968, 1971, 1973, 1978, 1982; Nebula Awards, 1971, 1972, 1981; J R R Toikien Memorial Award, 1978; Mythopoeic Award, 1975; Knight of Mark Twain, 1971. *Memberships:* Science Fiction Writers of America (President 1972-73); Baker Street Irregulars. *Literary Agent:* Scott Meredith, New York. *Address:* 3 Las Palomas, Orinda, CA 94563, USA.

ANDERSON, Robert Woodruff, b. 28 Apr. 1917, NYC, USA. Playwright; Screenwriter; Novelist. *Education:* AB, (Magna cum laude), 1939, MA 1941, Harvard University. *Publications:* Tea and Sympathy, 1953; All Summer Long, 1954; Silent Night Lonely Night, 1959; The Days Between, 1965; You Know I Can't Hear When the Water's Running, 1967; Solitaire/Double Solitaire, 1971; Free and Clear, 1983; (novels) After, 1973; Getting Up and Going Home, 1978; (screenplays), The Nun's Story, 1959; The Sand Pebbles, 1966; etc. *Honours:* Recipient, Awards for, I Never Sang for My Father, Writers' Guild, 1970. *Memberships:* President, Dramatists Guild, 1971-73; Authors League Coun; Writers Guild of America; W. Am. Playwrights Theatre, Board of Trustees; UCLA, 1973. *Literary Agent:* ICM. *Address:* Bacon Road, Roxbury, CT 06783, USA.

ANDERSON, Vivienne, b. Philadelphia, Pennsylvania, USA. Educator: Author. *Education:* EdD, Teachers College, Columbia University. *Publications include:* Patterns of Educational Leadership; Your America; Editor, Paperbacks in Education; The School Administrator and His Publications. *Honours include:* Freedoms Foundation Award; Shattuck Centennial Award for Outstanding Service to Education. *Memberships include:* President, Citizens Planning Committee for Greater Albany; President, Co-Founder and Board Member, Very Special Arts, USA; President, New York State Committee on Arts for the Handicapped; President, New York State Alliance for Arts Education (affiliate of John F Kennedy Center for Performing Arts).

ANDERSON, Walter Truett, b. 27 Feb. 1933, Oakland, California, USA. Writer. m. Maurica Osborne, 10 Feb. 1968, San Francisco, USA, 1 son. *Education:* AB Political Science, University of California, Berkeley; MA Political Science, California State University, Northridge; PhD, Political Science & Social Psychology, University of Southern California. *Major Publications:* The Age of Protest, 1969; Campaigns, Politics & Environment, 1970; Politics & The New Humanism, 1973; Evaluating Democracy (with J Allman), 1974; A Place of Power, 1976; Therapy & the Arts, 1977; Open Secrets, 1979; The Upstart Spring, Rethinking Liberalism, 1983; To Govern Evolution, 1986. *Contributor to:* Pacific News Service, New Age (as Editor); Journal of Humanistic Psycology (Member, Board of Editors). *Honour:* Political Book Award, New Options 1984 for, Rethinking Liberalism. *Literary Agent:* Barbara Lowenstein Associates, New York, USA. *Address:* 1112 Curtis Street, Albany, CA 94706, USA.

ANDERSON, William Gary, b. 13 Mar. 1945, Rockville Centre, New York, USA. History Professor. m. Frances Corace, 1 son, 1 daughter. *Education:* AB cum laude, University of Notre Dame, 1967; MA, Hofstra University, 1968; PhD, State University of New York at Stony Brook, 1975. *Publications:* John Adams and the Creation of the American Navy, 1975; The Price of Liberty. The Public Debt of the American Revolution, 1983. *Contributions to:* The American Neptune; The History Teacher; The Numismatist; Friends of Financial History; *Honour:* 1st Prize, American Numismatic Association Heath Literary Award, 1975. *Address:* History Department, Suffolk County Community College, Selden, NY 11784, USA.

ANDREASEN, Uffe, b. 9 June 1943, Grindsted, Denmark. Counselor for Cultural Affairs. *Education:* MA, History of Literature. *Publications:* Poul Moller, 1973; Romantismen, 1974; Dansk Litteratur Historie Vol. III, 1976; Corsaren I-VII, (Editor), 1977-81; Kjebenhauus flyvende Post I-IV, (Editor), 1981-84. *Honours:*

Recipient, Schwanenflugel Ed. Prize, 1977. *Memberships:* Det Danske Sprog og Litteraturselskab; Bakkehuse. *Address:* Ministry of Foreign Affairs, Asiatisk Plads 2, OK-1448, Copenhagen K, Denmark.

ANDRESKI, Stanislav Leonard, b. 8 May 1919, Czestochowa, Poland. Writer, Professor Emeritus since 1984. *Education:* BSc, MSc, PhD, University of London, England. *Publications include:* Military Organisation & Society, 1954; 2nd edition, 1968; The Uses of Comparative Sociology, 1965, paperback 1969, Spanish Translation 1973; Parasitism & Subversion: The Case of Latin America, 1966, Spanish Translation 1967; Social Sciences as Sorcery, 1972; Spanish, German, French, Italian and Japanese translations, 1973-75; The Prospects of a Revolution in the USA, 1973; Max Weber's Insights & Errors, 1984. *Contributor to:* Various professional journals. *Honour:* Recipient of Alfred Jurzykowski Foundation Award, New York, 1974. *Memberships:* Editorial Board, Journal of Strategic Studies; The Institute of Patentees and Inventors, London. Honorary Member, Greek Institute of Criminology; Writers' Guild of US. *Literary Agent:* Curtis Brown. *Address:* Farriers, Village Green, Upper Basildon, RG8 8LS, England.

ANDREW, Malcolm Ross, b. 27 Jan. 1945, England. Academic. m. Lena Margareta Bernström, 17 Aug. 1968, Cambridge, 1 son, 1 daughter. *Education:* BA 1967, MA 1970, St Catharine's College, Cambridge; MA, Simon Fraser University, British Columbia, Canada, 1969; D Phil, York University, England, 1972. *Literary Appointments:* Lecturer in English 1974, Senior Lecturer 1984, University of East Anglia, Norwich: Professor of English Language and Literature, The Queen's University, Belfast, Northern Ireland, 1985. *Publications:* On the Properties of Things, book VII, 1975; The Poems of the Pearl Manuscript (with Ronald Waldron), 1978; The Gawain-Poet: An Annotated Bibliography 1839-1977, 1979; Two Early Renaissance Bird Poems, 1984. *Contributions to:* Articles and reviews on English literature in learned journals including: Modern Philology; The Review of English Studies; English Language Notes; English Studies. *Honour:* Canada Council Doctoral Fellowship, 1969-72. *Memberships:* Early English Text Society: New Chaucer Society: International Arthurian Society; Medieval Academy of America; Modern Language Association of America. *Address:* 39 Cranmore Gardens, Belfast BT9 6JL, Northern Ireland.

ANDREWS, Edgar Harold, b. 16 Dec. 1932, Didcot, Berkshire, England. University Professor. m. Thelma Doris Walker, 16 Sep. 1961, Welwyn, 1 son, 1 daughter. *Education:* BSc, PhD, DSc, University College, London; FIP; FIM; C Phys; C Eng. *Publications:* Fracture in Polymers, 1968; From Nothing to Nature, 1978; God, Science and Evolution, 1980; The Promise of the Spirit, 1982; Christ and the Cosmos, 1986. *Contributions to:* Nearly 100 scientific articles in scientific journals including: Proceedings of the Royal Society; Journal of Materials Science. *Honour:* A A Griffith Silver Medal, 1977. *Address:* Redcroft, 87 Harmer Green Lane, Welwyn, Hertfordshire, England.

ANDREWS, Lyman, b. 2 April 1938. Lecturer in American Studies, The University, Leicester; Editor. *Education:* Bradeis University, 1956-60; King's College, London 1960-61; University of California, Berkeley, 1961-63. *Literary Appointments:* Fulbright Scholar, 1960-61; Woodrow Wilson Fellow, 1961-62; Tchng Fellow, University of California, 1962-63; Phelan Fellow, University of California, 1963-64; Temporary Lecturer, University of Wales, 1964-65; Visiting Professor, Poetry, Indiana University, Bloomington, 1978-79. *Publications:* Ash Flowers, 1958; Fugitive Visions, 1962; The Death of Mayakovsky and Other Poems, 1968; Kaleidoscope: New and Selected Poems, 1973; Anthologised in UK, USA, France and Jugoslavia. *Contributor to:* Sunday Times (regular poetry critic); Poems appear in: Encounter; Partisan Review; Transatlantic Review; Minnesota Review; British Book News; Times Higher Ed Supplement. *Honours:* Warren

Poetry Prize, 1959, 1960; Brandeis Lyric Poetry Prize, 1960. *Memberships:* PEN; National Poetry Centre, London. *Address:* Department of English, The University, Leicester LE1 7RH, England.

ANDREWS, Marcia Stephanie, b. 7 Aug. 1947, Portland, Oregon, USA. Writer. *Education:* BA, English, Portland State University, 1970; MA, Creative Writing, San Francisco State University, 1984. *Publications:* Poetry: Lullaby, in Mothers and Fathers: Being Parents, Remembering Parents, 1979; The Hollyhock Girl, in Antenna, 1980; Two of a Kind, in Undinal Songs, 1982; How My Love for Her is Like a Fugue, Coming into My Own, in New Lesbian Writing, 1984; Flowering, in Dreaming of Wings: Women's Poems for Peace, 1984; The Total Solar Eclipse Viewed in Eastern Oregon, February 26, 1979, in State of Peace: The Women Speak, 1985. Short fiction: The Bride, in Immaculata, 1966; The Company Party, in So's Your Old Lady, 1979; Going Crazy, in Common Lives, 1982; Aqua Marine, in Southern Humanities Review, 1984; Satori, in Ceilidh, 1985; The Survivor, Newstories Magazine, 1986. Nonfiction: When Silence Has Its Way With You: Hazel Hall, in Women and Literature: Gender and the Literary Voice, 1980; Novel, A Summer's Tale, 1986. *Contributor to:* The Review Magazine; Dretch Exsibilate Magazine; The Atlanta Quarterly; Mendocino Review; The Coe Review; New Mexico Humanities Review; The Hoodoo Times, Odessa Poetry Review, etc. *Honours:* Honorable Mention, Crosscurrents Fiction Awards for Aqua Marine 1982; Honorable Mention, Crosscurrents Fiction Awards for, The Survivor 1983; Second Prize, UCLA's Gertrude Stein Awards, 1984 for, Pink Roses; Literary Fellowship, Ludwig Vogelstein Foundation, New York, 1985. *Membership:* National Writers Union. *Address:* 390 Bartlett Street #12, San Francisco, CA 94110, USA.

ANDREY, Goulyashki, b. 7 May 1914, Sofia. Writer. m. Emilia Kostova Petrova, 1 son, 1 daughter. *Education:* Degree in Social Sciences. *Literary Appointment:* Chief Editor of the Literary magazine Savremennik. *Publications:* Novels: The Fleece of Gold, 1958; The Seven Days of Our Life, 1966; The Adventures of Avakoum Zakhov, 1961–85. *Contributor to:* All main Bulgarian Literary editions. *Honours:* The Dimitrov Prize (three times); A Hero of the Socialist Labour (twice). *Membership:* Union of Bulgarian Writers, Vice President. *Address:* 59 boul. Biryuzov, Sofia, Bulgaria.

ANDROLA, Ronald H, b. 7 Aug. 1954, Pennsylvania, USA. Writer; Editor; Publisher. m. Diane C Shied, 2 Mar. 1980, Seattle, 1 daughter. *Publications:* 14 Poems, 1981; The Spirituality of Husbands, 1982; The Kiss, 1984; Curls Thru the Language, 1984; T'n A, 1984; Steam & Garlic, 1984; The Taste of Pain, 1984. *Contributor to:* Gargoyle; Bogg; Abbey; Planet; Thunder Sandwich; Impetus; Gypsy; Random Weirdness; Poetry Motel; Raw Bone; Slipstream; Rolling Stone; Outlaw, etc. *Address:* 1547 W 24th Erie, PA 16502, USA.

ANGEL, Leonard Jay, b. 20 Sep. 1945, Montreal, Canada. Playwright. *Education:* BA, McGill University, 1966; MA 1968, MA 1970, PhD 1974, University of British Columbia. *Publications:* After Antietam/Isadora & G.B., 1978; The Unveiling, 1983; The Silence of the Mystic, 1983; Eleanor Marx, 1985. *Contributions to:* Religious Studies; Capilano Review. *Honours:* Doctoral Fellowship 1972–74, Artist B Grant 1979 and 1982, Canada Council. *Memberships:* Chairman British Columbia Region, 1978. Chair External Affairs Committee 1980–81, Guild of Canada Playwrights; Playwrights Union of Canada. *Address:* 865 Durward Avenue, Vancouver, BC V5V 2Z1, Canada.

ANGLESEY, (The Marquess of), Henry, b. 8 Oct. 1922, London, England. Peer of the Realm. *Publications:* (Editor) The Capel Letters, 1814–1817, 1955; One-Leg: The Life & Letters of 1st Marquess of Anglesey, 1961; (Editor) Sergeant Pearman's Memoirs, 1968; (Editor) Little Hodge, 1971; A History of the Britsh Cavalry, 1816–1919, Volume I, 1973; Volume II,

1975, Volume III, 1981. *Contributions to:* Sunday Telegraph, (reviews). *Honour:* FRSL. *Literary Agent:* Curtis Brown. *Address:* Plas Newydd, Anglesey, North Wales.

ANSCOMBE, Isabelle, b. 4 Oct. 1954, London, England. Writer. m. Howard Grey, 17 Dec. 1981, London, 1 daughter. *Education:* MA, English, Newnham College, Cambridge. *Publications:* Not Another Punk Book, 1978; Arts and Crafts in Britain and America with Charlotte Gere, 1978; Omega and After: Bloomsbury and the Decorative Arts, 1981; A Woman's Touch: Women in Design from 1860 to the Present Day, 1984. *Contributions to:* The Times; Harpers & Queens; The Connoisseur; Vogue; Cosmopolitan; Crafts Magazine; The Guardian; Antique Dealer–Collectors Guide. *Literary Agent:* Sheila Watson. *Address:* Watson and Little, Suite 8, 26 Charing Cross Road, London WC2H OOG, England.

ANSELL, Sydney Thomas, b. 29 Dec. 1907, London, England. Literary Journalist. *Publications:* In Sleep a King, (London): The Many Coloured Mantel and A String of Pearls, (Calcutta); With This Key – Sonnets, (Dacca); Three Hands, (Dacca), (Co-author); A Time for Singing, (Dhaka), 1984; The Birds Began to Sing, Children's verse, (Dacca). *Contributor to:* Magazines and journals including: Bangladesh Observer; Chambers Journal; English Life Publications; Irish Monthly; Poetry Review; Rann (UK); Lantern; Kaleidoscope; Wings; Chromatones (USA); Enterprise; Outlook; Orient Lit; Vision (Pakistan); Illustrated Weekly of India; Pekan (India). *Address:* Sylhet House, 119/A Segun Bagan, Dacca 2, Bangladesh.

ANTLER, b. 29 Jan. 1946. Poet. *Education:* BS, Anthropology, MA, English University of Wisconsin, Milwaukee, Wisconsin, USA; Iowa Writers Workshop, Iowa City, Iowa. *Publications:* Factory, 1980; Last Words: Selected Poems 1967–1984, 1986. *Contributions to:* American Poetry Review; Earth First!; Passaic Review; Mickle Street Review; Gay Sunshine; Changing Men; Sing Heavenly Muse!; Co-Evolution Quarterly; City Lights Journal; New Directions Anthology; Bugle America; Chelsea; Zerox. *Honour:* Walt Whitman Award, 1985. *Memberships:* Wilderness; The Ultimate Literary Society. *Address:* c/o City Lights Books, 261 Columbus Avenue, San Francisco, CA 94133, USA.

ANTONAZZI, Frank J, Jr b. 5 Oct. 1950, New York City, USA. Public Relations Consultant. m. Theresa Sue LaVelle, 17 Nov. 1982, Monticello, Indiana, USA, 1 son. *Education:* BA English, State University of New York at Buffalo, 1972. *Literary Appointments:* Regnery Publishing, Indiana, 1978–79; Instructor, Indiana Vocational Technical Institute, 1978–81; Public Relations Consultant, Society of Underprivileged & Handicapped Children, Alexandria, Virginia, 1983–. *Major Publication:* Free Hope (novel) to be published. *Contributor to:* Rapport; Choice; Green's Magazine; Various anthologies and literary magazines. *Address:* 6621 Berkshire Drive, Alexandria, VA 22310, USA.

ap ROBERTS, Ruth, b. 14 Nov. 1919, Vancouver, British Columbia, Canada. Professor of English. m. Robert R apRoberts, 11 June 1941, Vancouver, 1 son, 3 daughters. *Education:* BA, 1st class honours, University of British Columbia; MA, PhD, University of California, Berkeley and Los Angeles. *Literary Appointments:* Chairman, Department of English, Riverside, California, USA. *Publications:* The Moral Trollope, 1971; Arnold and God, 1984. *Contributions to:* Eire-Ireland, 1971; Language, Logic and Genre, 1974; Nineteenth Century Fiction, 1975; PMLA, 1977. *Honours:* Guggenheim Fellowship, 1978–79. *Memberships:* Modern Language Association; President, Philological Association of the Pacific Coast. *Address:* Department of English, University of California, Riverside, CA 92521, USA.

APFEL, Necia H, b. 31 July 1930, Mount Vernon, New York, USA. Science Writer. m. Dr Donald A Apfel, 7 Sep. 1952, Mount Vernon, 1 son, 1 daughter. *Education:* BA,

Tufts University, 1952; Radcliffe College Graduate School, 1953; Northwestern University Graduate School, 1968. *Publications:* It's All Elementary: From Atoms to the Quantum World of Quarks, Leptons and Gluons, 1985; Calendars: A First Book, 1985; Astronomy and Planetology, 1983, 84; Stars and Galaxies: A First Book, 1982; The Moon and Its Exploration: A First Book, 1982; It's All Relative: Einstien's Theory of Relativity, 1981, 85; Architecture of the Universe, co-author, 1979; Astronomy One, co-author, 1972. *Contributions to:* Odyssey Magazine, columnist and contributor. *Memberships:* Childrens Reading Round Table; Society of Childrens Book Writers. *Literary Agent:* Ray Peekner Literary Agency, Wisconsin. *Address:* 3461 University Avenue, Highland Park, IL 60035, USA.

APOSTOLOS-CAPPADONA, Diane Pan, b. 10 May 1948, Trenton, New Jersey, USA. University Lecturer; Researcher; Writer. m. Joseph B. Cappadona, 24 Apr. 1971, Falls Church, Virginia. *Education:* BA, 1970, MA, 1973, The George Washington University; MA, The Catholic University of America, 1979; PhD Candidate, The George Washington University. *Literary Appointments:* Editorial Assistant, The George Washington University, 1970–73; Art Editor, The Hill Rag, 1984–; General Art Editor, World Spirituality: An Encyclopedic History of the Religious Quest, 1985–90. *Publications:* Editor, The Sacred Play of Children, 1983; Art, Creativity and the Sacred: An Anthology in Religion and Art (Editor and Contributor), 1984; The History of Religious Ideas, Volume III: From Muhammad to the Reformers (Co-translator with Alf Hiltebeitel), 1985; Symbolism, The Sacred and the Arts: Essays by Mircea Eliade (Editor and Translator), 1985. *Contributions to:* Art International; Cross Currents; GW Forum; Horizons; International Symposium on Asian Studies; Journal of Pre-Raphaelite Studies, etc. Chapters in collected volumes: Interpreting the Tradition, The Art of Theological Reflection; Modern Secular Spirituality. *Honours:* Alden B Dow Creativity Center, Residential Fellow, 1982; Edward F Albee Foundation, Residential Fellow, 1983; The Society for the Arts, Religion and Contemporary Culture Fellow, 1985. *Address:* Department of Religion, The George Washington University, Washington, DC 20052, USA.

APPEL, Maria Magdalena Helene Eugenie, b. 30 Apr. 1906, Vienna, Austria. Professor (retired); Author; Writer. m. Dr Gustav Dichler, 6 July 1933, Vienna. *Education:* PhD, University of Vienna, 1930; Mag.Phil, 1972. *Publications:* Englisch fur den Kaufmann, 3 volumes, 5th edition, 1972, reprint, 1976; English, Gate to the World, 2 volumes, 3rd edition, 1970, reprint, 1973; Englische Sprachubungen, 7th edition, 1981; Englische Stilubungen, 1966; Die Erde kust ich (Haiku), 1976; Blutenzweige (stories), 1976; Solange die Kerze brennt (stories), 1977; Schuhu Mandrill (fairy tales), 1978; Und deswegen! (stories), 1981. *Contributions to:* Englische Studien, and several other publications. *Honour:* Renewal of Doctor of Philosophy by University of Vienna, 1980. *Memberships:* Member of Several literary associations including: Osterreichischer Autorenverband; Ost. Schriftstellerverband; Katholischer Schriftstellerverband; Verein der Schriftstellerinnen und Kunstlerinnen. *Address:* Johann Strauss-Gasse 28/18, A–1040 Vienna, Austria.

APPENZELLER, Otto, b. 11 Dec. 1927, Czernowitz, Romania. Professor of Neurology and Medicine. m. Judith Bryce, 11 Dec. 1956, Sydney, Australia, 3 sons. *Education:* MB, BS, MD, Sydney; PhD, London; FRACP, FACP, FAAN. *Literary Appointments:* Council of Biology Editors. *Publications:* The Autonomic Nervous System. An Introduction to Basic and Clinical Concepts, 3rd Edition, 1982; Headache, Major Problems in Internal Medicine, 1980; Sports Medicine: Fitness Training Injuries, 2nd Edition, 2nd Printing, 1984; Neurologic Differential Diagnosis, 1985; Le Cefalee, 1984. *Contributions to:* Annals of Sports Medicine, Founding Editor; Functional Neurology, Editor; Handbook of Clinical Neurology; Neurology; Medical and Health Annual 1983; Encyclopaedia

Britannica. *Address:* University of New Mexico School of Medicine, Department of Neurology, Albuquerque, NM 87131, USA.

APPLETON, (Rt Rev) George, b. 20 Feb. 1902, Windsor, England. Ecclesiastic. *Education:* MA, Selwyn College, University of Cambridge; St Augustine's College, Canterbury. *Major Publications:* John's Witness to Jesus, 1955; In His Name, 1956; Glad Encounter, 1959; On the Eightfold Path, 1961; Daily Prayer & Praise, 1962; Acts of Devotion, 1963; One Man's Prayers, 1967; Jerusalem Prayers for the World Today, 1973; Journey for a Soul, 1974; Way of a Disciple, 1979; Practice of Prayer, 1980; The Quiet Heart, 1983; Entry into Life, 1984; Hour of Glory, 1985; Heart of the Bible, 1986; General Editor, The Oxford Book of Prayer, 1985. *Address:* 112A St Mary's Road, Oxford OX4 1QF, England.

APPLEWHITE, Philip Boatman, b. 14 Sep. 1938, USA. Biologist. m. Harriet V. Branson, 10 Aug. 1963, Cleveland, Ohio, 1 son, 2 daughters. *Education:* BA, Pomona College, 1960; MIA, Yale University, 1962; PhD, Stanford University, 1965. *Publications:* Organizational Behavior, 1965; Studies in Organizational Behavior and Management, 1971; Focus Biology, 1975; Understanding Biology, 1978; Molecular Gods, 1981. *Contributions to:* Over 55 papers in journals such as, Nature; Plant Physiology; Journal of General Physiology; Physiology and Behavior. *Address:* Biology Department, Yale University, PO Box 6666, New Haven, CT 06511, USA.

APTER, Howard, b. 16 Feb. 1922, Vienna, Austria. Author; Editor; Journalist. *Education:* BS, MA, Columbia University, New York, USA. *Publications in progress:* Winterstrike, history, World War II; Confessions of a Travel Writer, reminiscence. *Contributions to:* Numerous magazines & newspapers. Contributing Editor, Travel Agent Magazine, New York; News Editor, Travel Trade Magazine, New York. *Membership:* American Association of Travel Editors. *Literary Agent:* Maximilian Becker, 115 E 82nd Street, New York, NY 10028, USA. *Address:* PO Box 543, FDR Station, New York, NY 10022, USA.

APTHEKER, Bettina, b. 12 Sep. 1944, North Carolina. Writer; Teacher. 1 son, 1 daughter. *Education:* BA, 1967, University of California at Berkeley; MA, 1976 San Jose State University; PhD, 1983, University of California, Santa Cruz. *Publications:* The Academic Rebellion in the United States: A Marxist Appraisal, 1972; The Morning Breaks: The Trial of Angela Dairs, 1975; Woman's Legacy: Essays on Race, Sex and Class in American History, 1982; A Labor of Love: Women's Work, Women's Consciousness and the Meaning of Daily Life, in progress, 1987. *Contributions to:* numerous publications including The Nation, Women's Studies Quarterly. *Honour:* Most Distinguished Alumni, Speech Communication, San Jose State University, 1982. *Address:* Women's Studies, Kresge College, University of California, Santa Cruz, CA 95064, USA.

ARCHER, Peter James George, b. 7 Mar. 1951, Romford, Essex, England. Journalist. m. Teresa Mary Greening, 1 Jan. 1977, St Albans. *Education:* BA (History), University of Newcastle, England. *Honour:* South Atlantic Medal (for coverage of the Falklands War). *Address:* Press Association, 85 Fleet Street, London EC4, England.

ARCHER, Peter Kingsley, b. 20 Nov. 1926, Wednesbury, England. Member of Parliament, Warley, West Midlands; Shadow Cabinet Minister of Northern Ireland. m. Margaret Irene Smith, 7 Aug. 1954, 1 son. *Education:* LLD, University of London, 1946, LLB, London School of Economics, 1950; BA, University College, London, 1952. *Publications:* The Queen's Courts, 1956; Communism and the Law, 1963; Freedom at Stake (co-author), 1966; Human Rights, 1969; Purpose in Socialism, 1973; The Role of Law Officers, 1979. *Contributor to:* Contemporary Review; Socialist Commentary; Editor, Social Welfare and the

Citizen, 1957. *Memberships:* Bencher, Gray's Inn; Amnesty International. *Address:* c/o House of Commons, London SW1, England.

ARCHER, Robyn, b. 18 June 1948, Adelaide, Australia. Entertainer. *Education:* BA Honours English; Diploma of Education. *Publications:* The Robyn Archer Songbook, 1980; Mrs Bottle Burps, 1983; A Star is Torn (co-author with Diana Simmonds), 1986. *Productions:* Plays produced: The Live-Could-Possibly-Be-True-One Day Adventures of Superwoman, 1972; A Star is Torn, (co-author with Rodney Fisher) Australia 1979, 1980 and 1983, London 1982–83; The Conquest of Carmen Miranda, 1984–85; The Three Legends of Kra, 1984–85; Il Magnifico, 1984; Songs From Sideshow Alley, 1978 and 1984; Cabarets devised: Kold Komfort Kaffee, 1978; The Pack of Women, London 1981, Australia 1983; Cut and Thrust, London 1983; The 1985 Scandals, Australia 1985; Television Adaptations: The Conquest of Carmen Miranda, 1984; The Pack of Women, 1985. *Contributions to:* Australasian Drama Studies; Australia Fair?; The All Australian Ha Ha Book. *Honours:* Sydney Critics Circle Award. 1980; Henry Lawson Award for Contributions to the Arts, 1980. *Membership:* Actors Equity Aust/UK; Australian Society of Authors; Australian Writers Guild; The Directors Guild of Great Britain. *Literary Agent:* Black and Blue Inc Pty Ltd. *Address:* 10 Belgrave Street, Petersham, New South Wales 2049, Australia.

ARDLEY, Neil Richard, b. 26 May 1937, Wallington, Surrey. Writer. m. Bridget Mary Gantley, 3 Sep. 1960, Marnhull, Dorset, 1 daughter. *Education:* BSc Bristol University, 1959. *Publications include:* How Birds Behave, 1971; Atoms and Energy, 1975; Birds Of Towns, 1975; Birds Of The Country, 1975; Birds of Coasts, Lakes and Rivers, 1976; Birdwatching, 1978; Man and Space, 1978; Birds, 1978; Birds of Britain and Europe, 1978; Birds and Birdwatching, 1980; 1001 Questions and Answers (with Bridget Ardley) 1981; In The World of Tomorrow Series 1981–82; Transport On Earth, 1981; Out Into Space, 1981; Tomorrow's Home, 1981; School, Work and Play, 1981; Our Future Needs, 1982; Health and Medicine, 1982; Future War and Weapons, 1982; Fact or Fantasy? 1982; Computers, 1983. Action Science Series 1983–84; Working With Water, 1983; Using the Computer, 1983; Hot and Cold, 1983; Sun and Light, 1983; Making Measurements, 1983; Exploring Magnetism, 1983; Making Things Move, 1984; Discovering Electricity, 1984; Air and Flight, 1984; Sound and Music, 1984; Simple Chemistry, 1984; Force and Strength, 1984.; My Favourite Science Encyclopeadia, 1984; Just Look At ... Flight, 1984; Sinclair ZX Spectrum User Guide, 1984; Just Look At ... The Universe, 1985; The Science of Energy, 1985. *Contributor to:* Caxton Yearbook (Caxton); Our World Encyclopedia (Macmillan); Collins Music Dictionary; Joy of Knowledge Encyclopedia (Mitchel Beazley). *Honour:* Fellow, Royal Society of Arts, 1981. *Address:* 13a Priory Avenue, Bedford Park, London W4, England.

ARDMORE, Jane Kesner, b. 12 Sep. 1915, Chicago, Illinois, USA. Author; Journalist. m. Albert Ardmore, 10 Nov. 1951, Los Angeles, California, 1 daughter. *Education:* PhB, University of Chicago, Illinois. *Publications:* Novels: Women Inc, 1946; Julie, 1952; To Love is To Listen, 1967. Biographies: Take My Life, Eddie Cantor, 1957; The Self Enchanted, Mae Murray, 1959; The Dress Doctor, Edith Head, 1959; Portrait of Joan, Joan Crawford, 1962. *Contributions to:* Good Housekeeping; McCall's; King Features; Sunday Women; Woman's Own, England; Ladies Home Journal; Redbook. *Honours:* Fiction Prize, Indiana Writers Conference, 1942; Fiction Award, California Press Women, 1967; Headliner Award, Women In Communications, 1968. *Membership:* Hollywood Women's Press Club. *Literary Agent:* McIntosh and Otis, New York; Heath and Company, London, England. *Address:* 10469 Dunleer Drive, Los Angeles, CA 90064, USA.

ARIDAS, Chris, b. 12 Nov. 1947, USA. Roman Catholic Priest. *Education:* PhD candidate, Theology. *Publications:* Discernment, 1979; Your Catholic Wedding, 1981; Soundings, 1983. *Contribution to:* Powerlessness: Sign of an Evangelist, Catholic Evangelist. *Address:* 40 Grove Place, Babylon, NY 11702, USA.

ARIYOSHI, Rita Clare Gormley, b. 12 Feb. 1939, New York, USA. Journalist; Editor; Photographer. m. (2) James Masaji Ariyoshi, 9 Dec. 1984, Honolulu, 2 sons, 4 daughters, 2nd Marriage. *Publications:* Hawaii's Great Festival of Restaurants, 1982; Maui on My Mind, 1985. *Contributor to:* A Day in the Life of Hawaii, 1984; Editor in Chief, Aloha, RSVP Magazine; Articles in, Los Angeles Magazine; Texas Monthly; Weight Watchers Magazine; inflight publications of Singapore Airlines, Philippine, Western American Airlines; Consumers Digest; Modern Bride; Australian Women's Weekly; etc. *Honours:* Pacific Area Travel Association Special Commendation, Photo-essay on Baguio, Philippines, appearing in, Mabuhay, Philippine Air's inflight Magazine, 1983; Best Photo, Best Feature, National Federation of Press Women, Hawaii, 1982. *Membership:* National Federation of Press Women, Hawaii Chapter, Vice President, 1984; Society of American Travel Writers. *Address:* 828 Fort Street Mall, Honolulu, HI 96813, USA.

ARJATSALO, Arvi Ensio, b. 27 Jan. 1927, Viipuri, Finland, School Teacher. m. Anni Ainikki Ranta, 14 July 1951, 2 sons, 1 daughter. *Publications:* Textbooks and other books including: Viltsi ja muut, 1971; Kovikset, 1976; Mohkamammutti, 1977; Varastettu enkeli, 1980; Ma oon Maukka, 1981; Sammatin Elias, 1982; Lonnrot, 1985; Pumminmerkit, 1985. *Contributor to:* Apu, Seura, Kotiposti, Koululainen. *Memberships:* Association of Finnish Writers for Children and Youth; Finnish Society of Authors; Society of Finnish Literature. *Honours:* Tauno Karilas Prize, Association of Finnish Writers for Children and Youth, 1977; The Finnish State Prize, 1978, 81; H C Andersen Certificate of Honour. The International Board on Books for Young People, 1980; Topelius Prize, Association of Finnish Writers for Children and Youth, 1983. *Literary Agent:* Otava Publishing Company Limited. *Address:* Lukupuronrinne 1 J, 02200 Espoo, Finland.

ÄRLEMALM, Inger, b. 13 Nov. 1937, Strömstad, Sweden. Writer. m. Gunnar Wärdig, 23 May 1985, 1 son, 1 daughter. *Education:* Fil Kand. *Publications:* The Labour Environment and the Unborn Children, 1980; Sisters, Comrades, 1981; Equality in Labour Unions, 1985. *Contributor to:* Columnist: Morgonbris. *Membership:* Swedish Authors Union. *Address:* Bergspringen 5, 17540 Jartalla, Sweden.

ARLETT, Vera Isabel, b. 18 Aug. 1896. Retired Author and Lecturer. *Publications:* Poems, 1927; Permanence, 1929; The Road to Assissi, 1935; The Wind Rider, 1937; Christmas Carols and Winter Poems, 1944; England 1940, 1958; Give me Not Lethe, 1962; Wait for Me, Daybreak, 1964. *Contributions to:* Past contributor to publications including: The Observer; Sunday Times; Time and Tide; Western Morning News; Country Life; Sussex County Magazine; The Poetry Review. *Honours Include:* Medal from John Drinkwater for best unpublished volume of verse, 1926; Medal for Lyric Poetry, University of Liverpool, 1931. *Memberships:* Life Fellow, International PEN; Society of Women Writers and Journalists; Life Fellow, International Institute of Arts and Letters; Poetry Society, London; Past Committee member Sussex branch, Radius Religious Drama Society. *Address:* 92 Lavington Road, Worthing, Sussex, England.

ARMAS MARCELO, J J, b. 22 July 1946, Las Palmas, Gran Canaria, Spain. Novelist. *Education:* Licenciate, Philosophy and Letters, University of Madrid. *Literary Appointments:* Founder, Inventarios Provisionales, Las Palmas, Director, Ediciones Cabildo Insular de Gran Canaria, Las Palmas, 1974–78; Director, Argos Vergara Ediciones, 1980–83; Literary critic, Plaza y Janés,

1983–. *Publications:* El camaléon sobre la alfombra, 1974; Estado de coma, 1976; Calima, 1978; Las naves quemadas, 1982; El árbol del bien y del mal, 1985. *Contributions to:* Inventarios Provisionales; Ediciones Cabildo Insular de Gran Canaria; Diario 16; LID Agencia de Noticias; Nueva Frontera; Firmas Agencia de Noticias. *Honours:* Galdós Prize for, El camaléon sobre la alfombra, 1975. *Membership:* Spanish PEN Club. *Address:* Residencial El Reloj 7, Las Rozas, Madrid, Spain.

ARMSTRONG, Diane Julie, b. 18 July 1939, Krakow, Poland. Freelance Writer. m. Michael Lawrence Armstrong, 20 Dec. 1959, 1 son, 1 daughter. *Education:* BA, Sydney University, Australia. *Contributions to:* Reader's Digest; Playboy; Vogue; Harper's Bazaar; Good Housekeeping; Cosmopolitan; Cleo; The Australian; The Sydney Morning Herald; National Times; Financial Review; Melbourne Age; Sun-Herald; Pol. *Honour:* Pluma de Plata, Award given by Mexican Government, 1983, for the best travel article written about Mexico, 1982. *Address:* 181 Military Road, Dover Heights, Sydney 2030, Australia.

ARMSTRONG, Patrick Hamilton, b. 10 Oct. 1941, Leeds, Yorkshire, England. University Lecturer. m. Moyra E J Irvine, 8 Aug. 1964, Altcar (Lancs), 2 sons. *Education:* BSc (Honours) 1963, Dip Ed1964, MA 1966, University of Durham, England; PhD (CNAA), 1970. *Major Publications:* Discovering Ecology, 1973; Discovering Geology, 1974; The Changing Landscape, 1975; a series of childrens' books for Ladybird Books, 1976–; Ecology, 1977; Reading & Interpretation of Australian & NZ Maps, 1981; Living in the Environment (with L T Miller), 1982; The Earth: Home of Humanity (with N Jarvis), 1984; Charles Darwin in Western Australia, 1985. *Contributor to:* New Scientist; Geographical Magazine; East Anglian Magazine; Geography; Cambridgeshire Life; Eastern Daily Press; Hemisphere; Journal of Biography; The Expatriate; Work & Travel Abroad; West Australian Newspaper; and others. *Memberships:* Australian Society of Authors; Geographical Association; British Ecological Society; Institute of Australian Geographers. *Literary Agent:* Curtis Brown. *Address:* Department of Geography, University of Western Australia, Nedlands, WA 6009, Australia.

ARNADE, Charles W, b. 11 May 1927, Goerlitz, Germany. Professor of International Studies and History. *Education:* AA, Colegio La Salle, Cochabamba, Bolivia, 1945; BA, 1950, MA, 1952, University of Michigan, USA; PhD, University of Florida, 1955. *Publications:* The Emergence of the Republic of Bolivia, 1957, 70; Florida on Trial, 1553–1602, 1959; The Siege of St Augustine, 1959; El Humanista Tadeo Haenke, 1959, 60; La Insurgencia de la Nacion Boliviana, 1964, 72; Vicente Pazos Kanki, Compendio de la Historiadelos Estados Unidos de 1825, 1976; Bolivian History, 1984. *Contributions to:* Various journals. *Honours:* Recipient of various honours. *Memberships include:* Phi Beta Kappa. *Address:* 219 Main Street, Box 2381, San Antonio, FL 34266, USA.

ARNOLD, Bob, b. 5 Aug. 1952, Adams, Massachusetts, USA. Poet; Stonemason. m. Susan Eileen Paules, 1974. *Publications:* Rope of Bells, 1974; Along the Way, 1979; Habitat, 1979; Thread, 1980; Self-Employed, 1984; Go West, 1984; Back Road Caller, 1985; Where Rivers Meet, 1986. *Contributions to:* Harpers; New Letters, Ploughshares; Spoor; Country Journal; Smoot; Aspect. *Address:* Green River, VT 05301, USA.

ARNOLD, Denis Midgley, b. 15 Dec. 1926, Sheffield, Yorkshire, England. Professor of Music. *Education:* BA 1947, BMus 1948, ARCM 1948, MA by thesis 1950. *Major Publications:* Monteverdi, 1963; Marenzio, 1965; Giovanni Gabrieli, 1974; (editor) Giovanni Gabrieli: Opera Omnia (6 volumes), 1957–74; (editor with N Fortune) The Monteverdi Companion, 1968; (editor with N Fortune) The Beethoven Companion, 1971; (joint editor) Music & Letters, 1976–80; Giovanni

Gabrieli & The Venetian School of the late Renaissance; The New Oxford Companion to Music, 1983; Bach (Past Masters), 1984. *Contributor to:* Musical Quarterly; Monthly Musical Record; Musica Disciplina; The Musical Times; Rivista Musicale Italiana; The Listener; The Gramaphone; Early Music. *Honours:* CBE; Fellow, Royal College of Science; Honorary Member, Royal Academy of Music. *Memberships:* Royal Musical Association; International Musicological Society; Gesellschaft für Musikforschung; Italian Musicological Society. *Address:* Faculty of Music, University of Oxford, St Aldates, Oxford OX1 1DB, England.

ARNOLD, Harry John Philip, b. 3 Oct. 1932, Portsmouth, England. Company Director. m. Audrey Cox, 27 Apr. 1957, Portsmouth, 1 daughter. *Education:* MA, University of Oxford, England; Dip. Cam; FRAS; FBIS. *Major Publications:* Aid to Developing Countries (Bodley Head), 1961; Aid for Development (Bodley Head), 1966; Photographer of the World: A Biography of Herbert Ponting, 1969; Another World: The Pictures of Herbert Ponting, 1975; William Henry Fox Talbot, 1977; Images from Space: The Camera in Orbit 1979. *Contributor to:* British Journal of Photography (Space Correspondent). *Honour:* Annual Prize for Distinguished Achievement in Photographic History (Photographic Society of New York), 1978. *ADDRESS:* 30 Fifth Avenue, Havant, Hampshire, PO9 2PL, England.

ARNOLD, Heinz Ludwig, b. 29 Mar. 1940, Essen/Ruhr, Federal Republic of Germany. Writer; Critic; Editor. *Education:* Studied Literary science, University of Göttingen. *Literary Appointments:* Editor; Text und Kritik, 1963; Kritisches Lexikon zur deutschsprachigen Gegenwartsliteratur, 1978–; Kritisches Lexikon zur Fremdsprachigen Gegenwartsliteratur, 1983–. *Publications:* Brauchen wir noch die Literatur?, 1972; Gespräche mit Schriftstellern, 1975; Gesprach mit F Durrenmatt, 1976; Deutsche über die Deutschen, 1975; Handbuch der deutschen Arbeiterliteratur, 1977; Tagebuch eine Chinareise, 1978; Als Schriftsteller leben, 1979; Literaturbetrieb in der Bundesrepublik Deutschland, 1981. *Contributions to:* Die Zeit; Deutsches Allgemeines Sonntagblatt. Various radio stations in Federal Republic of Germany. *Memberships:* Association of German Writers; PEN Centre, Federal Republic of Germany; Ohio Tuplip Order. *Address:* Tuckermannweg 10, 3400 Göttingen, Federal Republic of Germany.

ARNOLD, Janet, b. 6 Oct. 1932, Bristol, England. Writer, Lecturer. *Education:* NDD, 1953, ATD, 1954, West of England College of Art, Bristol. *Literary Appointments:* Jubilee Research Fellowship, 1978–81; Leverhulme Research Fellowship, 1982–. *Major Publications:* Patterns of Fashion 1660–1860, 1964, 1972; Patterns of Fashion 1860–1940, 1965, 1972; Perukes & Periwigs, 1970; A Handbook of Costume, 1973; Lost from Her Majesties Back, 1980; Patterns of Fashion 1560–1620, 1985; Queen Elizabeth's Wardrobe Unlock'd, (in proof) 1986. *Contributor to:* Waffen- und Kostümjunde; The Times Educational Supplement; Costume; the Burlington Magazine; Sweet England's Jewels, & catalogue entries for portraits in, Princely Magnificence (catalogue of the exhibition of European Court Jewels of the Renaissance 1500–1630; Victoria & Albert Museum, 1980; Contributor to series of Six 15-minute programmes for BBC2 Television and others. *Memberships:* Society of Authors; Costume Society; Fellow of the Society of Antiquaries, 1984; Honorary Advisor, International Association of Costume, 1983–. *Honour:* Recipient, Winston Churchill Travelling Fellowship, 1973. *Address:* Department of Drama, Royal Holloway College, University of London, Egham Hill, Egham, Surrey TW20 OEX, England.

ARNOLD-GULIKERS, Marie-Madeleine Elisabeth Eugenia Laura, b. 1 Oct. 1919, Liege, Belgium. Freelance Journalist. m. Arnold Max, 2 Nov. 1940, Liege, 3 sons. *Education:* Commercial Studies. *Appointments:* Co-founder, Contributor, L'Horizon Nouveau, 3 years; Contributor, Centre Afrique, 3 years,

Co-Founder, Contributor, La Presse Africaine, Bukavu, Zaire, 10 years. *Contributor to:* Major Reports in Zaire, Rwanda, Tanzania, Kenya, Seychelles, Mauritius, Reunion, Malagasy, Peru, Chile, Argentina, Iran, Turkey, Polynesia, Philippines, Far East; USA, Italy, Spain, Portugal, Denmark, Norway, Lapland, Ireland, Great Britain, Austria, Israel, Tunisia, Canada, Taiwan; Editor, General Interest articles, interviews, investigations, critiques, art news, etc. *Memberships:* General Association of Journalists of the Belgian Press; International Federation of Journalists; Association of European Journalists; French Speaking Union of Belgians Abroad; International Union of Journalists & of French Speaking Press. *Address:* 1 Rue des Bruyeres, 5870 Mont-St-Guibert, Belgium.

ARNOT, Michelle, b. 3 Feb. 1953, New York City, USA. Publisher. m. Roger Brown, 30 June 1978 at New York City. *Education:* MA French and Romance Philology, Columbia University, USA; BA Comparative Literature, Beloit College, USA. *Major Publications:* Foot Notes, Doubleday, 1980, Sphere 1981; England; What's Gnu: A History of the Crossword Puzzle, Random House, 1981, Papermac 1982, England. *Contributor to:* Vogue (US); McCalls; The Washington Woman; Gentleman's Quarterly. *Memberships:* Authors Guild; American Society of Journalists and Authors. *Literary Agent:* Gloria Loomis, Watkins Loomis Agency. *Address:* 58 MacDougal Street, New York City, NY 10012, USA.

ARNOTT, Margaret Anne, b. 8 Sep. 1916, Bath, England. Teacher (retired). m. Thomas Grenfell Arnott, 16 Feb. 1942, Bath, 2 sons, 1 daughter. *Education:* Honours degree in English Language & Literature, University of London. *Major Publications:* The Brethren, 1969; Journey into Understanding, 1971; The Secret Country of C S Lewis, 1974; Life to the Archbishop: Life of Jean Coggan, 1977; Fruits of the Earth, 1979; The Unexpected Call, 1981; He shall with Giants Fight: The Story of John Bunyan, 1985. *Contributor to:* The Sign (Woman's page 1970–84). *Honour:* 1st Prize Youth Section for all Religious Publishers awards, USA for, The Secret Country of C S Lewis, 1975. *Literary Agent:* Edward England Books. *Address:* Hall Barn, Levisham, Pickering, North Yorkshire YO18 7NL, England.

ARONSON, Linda Jane, b. 20 Mar. 1950, London, England. Writer. m. Mark Aronson, 7 Oct. 1972, Oxford, 1 son, 1 daughter. *Education:* BA (1st Class Hons), New University of Ulster, 1971. *Literary Appointments:* Script Consultant at Australian Film and TV School, 1982. *Publications:* Stage Plays, The Fall Guy, 1977; Redinka's Lesson, 1985; Dinkum Assorted, (under Commission); Three Winters in Arcadia West, 1986; Film Scripts: Kostas, 1979; TV Scripts: The Young Wife (adaptation of the novel by David Martin), 1983; Stefan, 1984. *Honours:* Australia Council Junior Fellowship, 1979; Australian Writers' Guild AWGIE Award (Television Series), 1983; Winner of the Sydney Theatre Company's Short Play Commission, 1984; Australian Writers' Guild AWGIE Award (Television Series), 1985; South Australian AETT 3rd Biennial Play Award, 1986; Australia Council Writer's Fellowship, 1986. *Memberships:* Australian Writers' Theatre (Founder Member); International Theatre Institute's Australian Committee; Australian Writers' Guild. *Literary Agent:* Curtis Brown (Australia). *Address:* c/o Curtis Brown (Australia) Pty Ltd, P O Box 19, Paddington, Sydney 2021, New South Wales, Australia.

ARONSON, Virginia, b. 30 Mar. 1954, Brighton, Massachusetts, USA. Nutritionist, Writer. *Education:* BA Nutrition, 1975; Registered Dietitian, 1976; MA Nutrition 1977. *Major Publications:* Guidebook for Nutrition Counselors, 1980; Dear Dr Stare: What Should I eat?, 1982; Your Basic Guide to Nutrition, 1983; Practical Guide to Optimal Nutrition, 1983; 30 Days to Better Nutrition, 1984; RX Executive Diet, 1985; Food After 50, Food, for Fun & Fitness, 1985; Dietetic Technician: Effective Nutrition Counseling, 1985. *Contributor to:* The First Aider (AT the Training Table, column); Consuming Passions (Consuming Concerns, column); Nutrition Today (Looking Back, column); Runner's World; Fit; Health; Shape; New England Journal of Medicine, (reviews); Journal of the American Medical Association; Journal of Nutrition Education; FDA Consumer; Nutrition Forum; Environmental Nutrition. *Membership:* American Medical Writers Association. *Address:* Nutrition Counselors Associates, 5 Diehl Road, Lexington, MA 02173, USA.

AROPALTIO, Kirsi Helena Susanna, b. 14 May 1945, Helsinki, Finland. Theatre Director; Author. m. Markku Aropaltio, 23 May 1968, Helsinki, 2 sons, 1 daughter. *Education:* Graduated from The Theatre School of Finland, 1970. *Literary Appointments:* Several plays and adaptations for childrens' theatre, 1970–85, 5 performed in the National Theatre of Finland. *Publications:* Puppet Theatre & Maskplays, (Aropaltio – Gronholm – Kauppinen), 1979. *Contributions to:* Several articles and critiques of puppet theatre in Finnish newspapers. *Honour:* Art Prize of the City of Espoo, 1982. *Memberships:* UNIMA, Finland; Finnish Theatre Directors' Union; Finnish Playwrights' Union. *Literary Agent:* Finnish Playwrights' Union. *Address:* Särkitie 7 B, 02170 Espoo, Finland.

ARORA, Ramesh K, b. 28 Nov. 1940, Lahore, India. Teacher; Researcher. m. Usha, 5 Feb. 1969, Jaipur, 2 sons. *Education:* B Com, MA, MPA, MPh, PhD. *Literary Appointments:* Editor: Administrative Change, biannual journal, 1973–; Prashasnika, quarterly, 1977–80. *Publications:* Comparative Public Administration, 1972; Administrative Change in India, 1974; Public Enterprises in India, 1975; Jaipur Profile of a Changing City, 1977; The Indian Administrative System, 1978; Bureaucracy and Development: Indian Perspectives, 1978; People's Participation in Development Process, 1979; Training and Administrative Development, 1979; Perspectives in Administrative Theory, 1979; Administrative Theory, 1984; Development Policy and Administration in India, 1985. *Contributions to:* Hong Kong Journal of Public Administration; Chinese Journal of Public Administration; Politics, Administration and Change; Indian Journal of Public Administration; The Economic Times; and many others. *Honours:* Best Student Gold Medal, University of Rajasthan, 1960–61; Fulbright Fellowship, 1969–70; Joseph Harris Fellowship, 1971; Kansas University Summer Fellowship, 1971; Pi Sigma Alpha, 1971. *Memberships include:* Past Honorary Secretary, Indian Public Administration Association; Vice Chairman Jaipur chapter, Indian Society for Training and Development; Academic Committee, Indian Institute of Public Administration; Raja Rammohan Roy Library Foundation; Secretary, Centre for Administrative Change; Past Director, Adult and Continuing Education, University of Rajasthan; Director, Social Sciences Research Centre, University of Rasthan. *Address:* Department of Public Administration, University of Rajasthan, B–56 Janata Colony, Jaipur 302004, India.

ARRILLAGA, Maria, b. 18 Apr. 1940. Associate Professor of Spanish. *Education:* BS, St Louis University, Missouri, USA, 1961; MA, New York University, 1966; PhD Candidate, University of Puerto Rico. *Literary Appointments:* Instructor Puerto Rican Art & Music, New York City Community College, Brooklyn, 1970–71; Writer for Escuela, 1971–73; Associate Professor of Spanish, Faculty of General Studies, University of Puerto Rico, 1973–. *Publications:* Vida en el tiempo, 1974; New York in the Sixties, 1976; Cascada de sol, 1977; Poemas 747, 1977; Frescura, 1981. *Contributions to:* Now, Jamaica; Communidad, Mexico; The Puerto Rican Poets, New York City; El Mundo; Guajana; Review Interamericana; Atenea; Sin Nombre, Puerto Rico; various anthologies including: Poemario de la mujer puertorriguena, 1976; Melanthika (an anthology of Pan-Caribbean writing), 1977; Literatura puertorriquena: su processo en el tiempo, 1983; Antologia de la mujer puertorriguena, 1981. *Honours include:* First Prize, Poetry, Institute of Puerto Rican Literature for Frescura, 1981, 1981; First Prizes, Essays, ICPRJr. College, Mayaquez, 1982, 83; First

Prize, Short Story, ICPR Jr. College, Mayaquez, 1984. *Memberships:* Ateneo Puertorriqueno; PEN Club of Puerto Rico, Board of Directors, 1980–83. *Address:* Calle Acuario 747, Urbanizacion Venus Gardens, Rio Piedras, PR 00926 USA.

ARTHUR, Elizabeth Ann, b. 15 Nov. 1953, New York. Writer/University Professor. m. Steven Bauer, 19 June 1982, Dorset, Vermont, USA. *Education:* BA, English, 1978, Diploma in Education, 1979, University of Victoria, Victoria, British Columbia. *Literary Appointments:* Visiting Instructor of Creative Writing, University of Cincinnati, Cincinnati OH, 1983–84; Assistant Professor of Creative Writing, Miami University, Oxford OH, 1984–85; Assistant Professor of English, Indiana University, Indianapolis, 1985–. *Publications:* Island Sojourn (non-fiction) 1980; Beyond the Mountain (novel) 1983. *Contributor to:* A Vision of the True West; The New York Times, 1983. Articles with outdoor subjects in Backpacker, Outside, Ski X-C. *Honours:* William Sloane Fellowship in Prose, Bread Loaf Writers Conference, Middlebury VT, 1980; Writing Fellowship, The Ossabaw Island Project, Savannah GA, 1981; Grant-in-Aid, Vermont Council on the Arts, 1981–82; Fellowship in Prose, National Endowment for the Arts, 1982–83. *Membership:* Poets and Writers Inc, New York. *Literary Agent:* Jean Naggar. *Address:* Bath, Indiana, USA.

ARVOLA, Oiva Väinö, b. 1 July 1935, Kolari, Finland. 2 sons, 1 daughter. *Literary Appointments:* State's of Literature committee 1977–82; State's of Art Centre committee 1983–85. *Publications:* Kesäpäivän seisaus, 1972; Vieraat ajat, 1973; Neliapila/Viisikymmenta askelta, 1974; Taivaan painamat, 1975; Kaamosmaa, 1976; Linnustajan maa, 1977; Kampsuherrain saagat, Maa Maakunta Martti Miettunen, 1981; Satavuotiaan saaga, 1982; Talvisilmut, Tornio, 1983; Neljan tuulen saagat, 1985. *Contributions to:* Kaleva, Kaltio, Kellokas, Keskisuomalainen, Lapin Kansa, Parnasso, Pohjolan Sanomat. *Honours:* Prize of State, 1968; Prize of Maakuntakirjailijat, 1981; Prize of Province's Art, 1981. *Memberships:* Kirjailijaliitto ry; Arvostelijain Liito ry; Näytelmäkirjailijaliitto ry; Maakuntakirjailijat ry. *Literary Agent:* Kirjayhtymä Oy Pohjoinen Oy. *Address:* Kolpeneentie 1 B, 96400 Rovaniemi 40, Finland.

ASH, Allan Howard, b. 12 Jan. 1926, Parramatta, New South Wales, Australia. Writer. m. Freda Mary Oliver, 20 Aug. 1960, Parramatta, 3 daughters. *Education:* Diploma, Advertising; Certificates, Marketing, Theology. *Appointments:* Editor, 1951–61, 1981–, Australian Gliding; Editor, Airsport, 1959–61; Editor, Victorian Baptist Witness, 1966–67; Group Editor, Thomson Publicatons, 1971–75. *Contributor to:* Regular Monthly Contributor, Aircraft, 1953–57, 1981–; Occasional Articles Sydney Morning Herald; Melbourne Age; North Australian Monthly; Modern Motor; Australian Flying; Australian Baptist; Australian Evangelical; New Life; etc. *Memberships:* Australian Religious Press Association, Executive Council member, Editor, Quarterly Journal. *Address:* 2 Heath Avenue, Frankston, Victoria 3199, Australia.

ASHDOWN, Dulcie Margaret, b. 24 Feb. 1946, London, England. Writer; Editor. *Education:* BA (Hons), Bristol University. *Publications:* Ten books including: Ladies in Waiting, 1976; Princess of Wales, 1978; Royal Children and Royal Weddings 1000 year histories, 1980, 81. *Contributions to:* Majesty; The Lady; British Heritage, USA; Heritage.

ASHE, Geoffrey Thomas, b. 29 Mar. 1923, London, England. Writer; Lecturer. *Education:* BA, University of British Columbia, Canada; BA, Trinity College, Cambridge University, England. *Publications:* The Tale of the Tub, 1950; King Arthur's Avalon, 1957; From Caesar to Arthur, 1960; Land to the West, 1962; The Land & the Book, 1965; Gandhi, 1968; The Quest for Arthur's Britain, 1969; All About King Arthur, 1969; Camelot & the Vision of Albion, 1971; The Art of Writing Made Simple, 1972; The Finger & the Moon, 1973; Do What You Will, 1974; The Virgin, 1976; The Ancient Wisdom, 1977; Miracles, 1978; A Guidebook to Arthurian Britain, 1980; Kings and Queens of Early Britain, 1982; Avalonian Quest, 1982; The Discovery of King Arthur, 1985. *Memberships:* FRSL; Camelot Research Committee, Co-Founder, Secretary; International Arthurian Society. *Address:* Chalice Orchard, Well House Lane, Glastonbury, Somerset BA6 8BJ, England.

ASHE, John Harold, b. 4 Sep. 1907. Retired Accountant. m. Joan Margaret. *Education:* Fellow, Australian Society of Accountants; Associate, Institute of Chartered Accountants, Australia; Associate, Chartered Institute of Secretaries and Administrators. *Appointments include:* Taxation Officer, Townsville Branch, Union Fidelity Trustee Co of Australia Ltd, 1945–71. *Publications:* Songs of Sentiment, 1968; Highlights of History, 1980; numerous songs (mainly comedy about Australia) including: Game As Ned Kelly; Harry the Breaker; I Lost My Heart on Hayman Islands; (LP's): Island Songs of the Great Barrier Reef; Aussie Songs with a Laugh; Songs with an Aussie Slant; Fair Dinkum Aussie Fun; Fair Dinkum Mate; Advance Australia Fair Dinkum; How Are Ya Mate?; Australia for Me; over 80 songs published in Sydney, Australia; also several songs recorded by Slim Dusty and by Chad Morgan. *Membership:* Foundation fellow, International Academy of Poets. *Address:* 409 Walker St, Townsville, Queensland 4810, Australia.

ASHER, Jane, b. 5 Apr. 1946, London, England. Actress. m. Gerald Scarfe, 2 sons, 1 daughter. *Publications:* Jane Asher's Party Cakes, 1982; Jane Asher's Fancy Dress, 1983; Silent Nights for You and Your Baby, 1984; Jane Asher's Quick Party Cakes, 1986. *Contributor to:* Various articles. *Literary Agent:* Mark Lucas, Fraser & Dunlop. *Address:* c/o Chatto & Linnit, Globe Theatre, Shaftesbury Avenue, London W1, England.

ASHER, Sandy, b. 16 Oct. 1942, Pennsylvania, USA. Writer. m. Harvey Asher, 31 Jan. 1965, Philadelphia, 1 son, 1 daughter. *Education:* AB, 1964. Indiana University. *Publications:* Summer Begins, 1980; Daughters of the Law, 1980; Just Like Jenny, 1982; Things are Seldom What They Seem, 1983; Missing Pieces, 1984; Teddy Teabury's Fabulous Fact, 1985; Everything is Not Enough, under contract. *Contributions to:* various professional journals. *Honours:* National Endowment for the Arts Creative Writing Fellowship Grant, 1978; Mark Twain Award Master List, 1984. *Memberships:* Dramatists' Guild; Society of Children's Book Writers; Children's Reading Roundtable of Chicago. *Literary Agent:* Mrs Claire M Smith, Harold Ober Associates. *Address:* c/o Mrs Claire M Smith, Harold Ober Associates, 40 East 47th Street, New York City, NY 10017, USA.

ASHLEY, Bernard, b. 2 Apr. 1935, London, England. Teacher. *Education:* Teacher's Certificate; Advanced Diploma in Education, Cambridge Institute of Education. *Major Publications:* The Trouble with Donovan Croft, 1974; Terry on the Fence, 1975; All my Men, 1977; A Kind of Wild Justice, 1978; Break in the Sun, 1980; Dodgem, 1982; High Pavement Blues, 1983; Janey, 1985; Running Scared, 1986. *Contributor to:* Books for Your Children; Junior Education; Books for Keeps. *Memberships:* Writers' Guild; Int. Board of Books for Young People. *Honours:* The, Other, Award, 1976; Runner-up, Carnegie Medal, 1979. *Address:* 128 Heathwood Gardens, London SE7 8ER, England.

ASHLEY, Jack, b. 6 Dec. 1922, Widnes, England. Member of Parliament. m. Pauline Crispin, 15 Dec. 1951, London, 3 daughters. *Education:* Diploma, Ruskin College, Oxford; MA, Cambridge University. *Publication:* Journey Into Silence, 1973. *Address:* House of Commons, London, SW1A OAA, England.

ASHMOLE, Bernard, b. 22 June 1894, Ilford, England. University Professor. m. Dorothy Irene de Peyer, 1920, 1 son, 2 daughters. *Education:* Classical scholar, Hertford College, Oxford; 11th Royal Fusiliers,

1914–18; Craven Fellow, & Student, British Schools, Athens & Rome, 1920–22. *Appointments Include:* Yates Professor of Archaeology, University of London, 1929–48; Keeper of Greek & Roman Antiquities, British Museum, 1939–56; Lincoln Professor of Classical Archaeology, University of Oxford, 1956–61; Fellow of Lincoln College, Oxford, 1956–80; Geddes-Harrower Professor, Greek Art & Archaeology, University of Aberdeen, 1961–63. *Publications:* Catalogue of Ancient Marbles at Ince Blundell, 1929; Greek Sculpture & Painting (with Beazley), 1932, 1966; The Ancient World (with Groenewegen-Frankfurt), 1967; Olympia: Sculptures of the Temple of Zeus (with Yalouris & Frantz), 1967; Architect & Sculptor in Classical Greece, 1972. *Contributions to:* Journal of Hellenic Studies; etc. *Honours Include:* FRIBA; FBA; Honorary Fellow, Lincoln College, Oxford, 1980; Honorary Fellow, University College, London 1974; Honorary Fellow, Archaeological Society of Athens, 1978; Kenyon Medal, British Academy, 1979; Cassano Medal, Taranto, 1980. *Address:* 5 Tweed Green, Peebles, EH45 8AP, Scotland.

ASIMOV, Isaac, b. 2 Jan. 1920, USSR. Writer. m. Janet Opal Jeppson, 30 Nov. 1973, New York City, USA, 1 son, 1 daughter (previous marriage). *Education:* BSc, Chemistry, 1939, MA, 1941, PhD, 1948, Columbia University, USA. *Publications:* Author of 322 Books. *Contributions to:* About 3,000 publications. *Honours:* Recipient of numerous honours and awards. *Memberships:* Science Fiction Writers of America; Mystery Writers of America, etc. *Address:* 10 West 66th Street, New York, NY 10023, USA.

ASKEW, William Clarence, b. 23 Nov. 1910, Hamilton, Georgia, USA. Emeritus Professor of History, Colgate University. *Education:* BA, Mercer University, 1931; MA, 1934, PhD, 1936, Duke University. *Publications:* Europe, and Italy's Acquisition of Libya, 1911–12, 1942; Power, Public Opinion and Diplomacy, Co-editor and Contributor 1959; Modern Italy: A Topical History since 1861, Contributing Author, 1974. *Contributions to:* American Historical Review; Journal of Modern History; Slavonic and East European Review, and others. *Honours:* John Simon Guggenheim Memorial Fellow, 1952; Fulbright Scholar, Italy, 1952–54. *Memberships include:* American Historical Association; Society for Italian Historical Studies; President, New York State Association of European Historians, 1970–71. *Address:* 9 East Kendrick Avenue, Hamilton, NY 13346, USA.

ASLET, Clive William, b. 15 Feb. 1955, London, England. Writer. m. 27 Sep. 1980, Cambridge. *Education:* MA, Peterhouse, Cambridge. *Publications:* The Last Country Houses, 1982; The National Trust Book of the English House (with Alan Powers), 1985. *Contributions to:* Numerous publications. *Membership:* Founding Secretary, The Thirties Society, 1979–. *Literary Agent:* Curtis Brown. *Address:* Flat 5, 19 Gloucester Street, London, SW1V 2DB, England.

ASNA, M Alaeddin, b. 24 Apr. 1940, Istanbul, Turkey. Public Relations Consultant. m. Sibel Asna, 6 Jan. 1982. *Education:* BA Political Sciences, Ankara University; MA PublicRelations and Journalism, Michigan State University, USA. *Literary Appointments:* General Secretary, Turkish Pen Club. *Publications:* Halkla Iliskiler, 1969 (5 editions); Beseri Iliskiler, 1972 (4 editions); Sandaldaki Adam, 1974; Public Relations, 1983. *Contributions to:* Varlik; Cumhuriyet; Milliyet. *Honour:* Poet of the Year, Ankara Art Club, 1976. *Membership:* Turkish Pen Club. *Address:* Vali Konagi Cad 31, Istanbul, Turkey.

ASPLER, Tony, b. 12 May 1939, London, England. Writer. m. Brenda Lisle, 11 July 1971, London, 1 son, 1 daughter. *Education:* BA, English & Philosophy, McGill University, Canada, 1959. *Publications include:* The Streets of Askelon, 1972; One of my Marionettes, 1973; Co-author with Gordon Pape, Chain Reaction 1978, The Scorpion Sanction, 1980, The Music Wars, 1981, Vintage Canada, 1982. *Membership:* Founding Chairman, Crime Writers of Canada. *Literary Agent:*

Colbert Agency, Toronto. *Address:* 202 Keewatin Avenue, Toronto, Ontario, Canada.

ASSELINEAU, Roger Maurice, b. 24 Mar. 1915, Orleans, France. Professor of American Literature. *Education:* Lic es Lettres, English, Sorbonne; Agregation in English, 1938; Doct es Lettres, Sorbonne, 1953. *Publications include:* L'Evolution de Walt Whitman, 1954; The Literary Reputation of Mark Twain, 1964, USA, 1971; Poesies Incompletes, 1959; The Evolution of Walt Whitman, 1960–62; E A Poe, 1970; The Transcendentalist Constant in American Literature, 1980; Incomplete Poems, 1984. *Contributor to:* Etudes Anglaises; Revue de Litterature Comparee; Forum; Dialogue; Calamus; Walt Whitman Review. *Honours:* Walt Whitman Prize, Poetry Society of America; Honorary Doctorate, University of Poznan. *Memberships include:* Honorary President, French Association for American Studies; MLA Vice President, FILLM; Hemingway Society; International Association, University Professors in English; Society des Gens de Lettres. *Address:* 114 Avenue Leon Blum, 92160 Antony, France.

ASSINIWI, Bernard, b. 31 July 1935, Montréal, Québec, Canada. Communicator, Health and Welfare Canada; Medical Services. m. Marina Desrochers, 3 Sep. 1955, 3 sons. *Education:* BA Agriculture; MA Biology. *Appointment:* Judge-in-Chief, Literary Contest of Abitibi-Témiscamingu, 1972. *Publications:* Author of 25 books on History, Culture and Life of Indians of North America; Ananish-Nah-Be, 1971; Sagana, 1972; Indian Recipes, 1972; Survival in the Bush, 1973; History of Indians, 3 vols, 1974; Lexique des Noms Indiens, 2 vols, 1975; A l'Indienne, 1973; 7 books for children, 1973–74; Contes Adultes du Pays Algonquin, 1985; Il n'y a Plus D'Indiens' (Théâtre); Le Bras Coupé, Roman, 1976. *Contributor to:* Numerous magazines, etc. *Memberships:* Union des Écrivains Québécois; Association des Écrivains de Langue Française, Paris, France; Union des Artistes de Montréal. *Honour:* Finalist at Montreal Literary Contest, with Anish-Nah-Be, 1971. *Address:* c/o Les Editions Leméac Incorporated, 5111 Rue Durocher, Montréal, Québec, Canada.

ASTOR, Susan, b. 2 April 1946, New York City, New York, USA. Poet; Teacher. 2 daughters. *Education:* BA, Adelphi University. *Publication:* Dame, 1980. *Contributions to:* Croton Review; Confrontation; Poet Lore; West Hills Review; Wisconsin Review. *Honours:* 1st Prize: C W Post Poet in the Community Award, 1980; Schuylkill County Council for the Arts, 1983; California Quarterly, 1985. *Memberships:* Poetry Society of America; Poets and Writers. *Address:* 113 Princeton Street, Roslyn Heights, NY 11577, USA.

ASTRACHAN, Samuel, b. 4 Jan. 1934, New York City, USA. Professor, Novelist. m. Claude Jeanneau, 25 Mar. 1960, New York, 1 son. *Education:* BA, Columbia College, 1955. *Literary Appointments:* Professor of Creative Writing, Wayne State University, Detroit, Michigan. *Publications:* An End to Dying, 1956; The Game of Dostoevsky, 1965; Rejoice, 1970; Katz-Cohen, 1978. *Honour:* Rockefeller Foundation Partisan Review Fellowship. *Membership:* PEN. *Address:* La Juverde, 84220 Gordes, France.

ATKINS, Arthur Harold. b. 27 Mar. 1910, Nottingham, England. Journalist. m. Lily Buxton, 17 Sep. 1938, London. *Education:* BA, 1938, MA, 1942, Balliol College, University of Oxford, England; Postgraduate Study, London School of Economics & Political Science, 1946–47. *Literary Appointments:* Reporter, Scientific Correspondent, Assistant Theatre Critic, Nottingham Journal, 1928–35; Sub-Editor, General News Desk, Reuters, London, 1938–39; Sub-editor, Daily Dispatch, Manchester 1940–41; Foreign Sub-editor, Manchester Guardian, 1941–44; Special Writer, The Evening News, London, 1944–49; Political (Lobby) Correspondent, 1944–45; News & Diary Writer, The Star, London, 1949–51; Headquarters Press & Public Relations Officer, Ministry of National Insurance and National Assistance Board, 1951–53;

Foreign Sub-editor, Daily Telegraph, 1954–55; Features Sub-editor, 1955–56, Arts and Leader-page Sub-editor, and Peterborough Diary Contributor etc, 1956–76; Book reviewer, 1956–85, Assistant Theatre Critic, 1962–85. Freelance Writer, 1976–. *Major Publications:* Sinister Smith (novel), 1938; Beecham Stories (jointly), 1978; The Barbirollis: A Musical Marriage (jointly), 1983. *Contributor to:* The Manchester Guardian; Contemporary Review; Socialist Commentory; Manchester Guardian Weekly; British Weekly; The Observer; The Sunday Dispatch; The News Chronicle; The Glasgow Herald; Birmingham Despatch; The Oxford Mail; and to BBC Radio. *Address:* 16, Hallgate, Blackheath Park, London SE3, England.

ATKINS, John Alfred, b. 26 May 1916, Carshalton, Surrey, England. Author. m. 1940, Hammersmith, London, 2 daughters. *Education:* BA Honours, History. *Literary Appointment:* Docent in English Literature, University of Lodz, Poland, 1970–76. *Publications:* Rain and the River, novel, 1953; George Orwell, 1954, 71; Six Novelists Look at Society, 1977; J B Priestley: Last of the Sages, 1981; Sex in Literature, 4 volumes, 1970, 73, 78, 82. *Contributions to:* Penguin New Writing; Life and Letters Today; Bananas; English Story; Windmill; various others. *Honour:* Arts Council Award, 1970. *Address:* Braeside Cottage, Birch Green, Birch, Colchester, Essex CO2 ONH, England.

ATOJI, Cynthia Ann, b. 28 June 1960, Amas, Iowa, USA. Editor. *Education:* BSc, University of Illinois, Champaign. *Contributions to:* Seventeen; Young Ambassador; Power for Living; Group; His; Christian Reader; Pacific Garden Mission Newsletter; Westchester-Rockland Newspapers. *Honours:* Robert Stain Memorial Scholarship; Golden Key Honor Society; Dow Jones Newspaper Fund Scholarship. *Memberships:* Kappa Tau Alpha; Phi Kappa Phi; Alpha Lambda Delta. *Address:* 702 86th Place, Downers Grove, IL 60516, USA.

ATSUMI, Ikuko, b. 28 May 1940, Japan. Professor, Writer, Editor. *Education:* BA 1964, MA 1967, Aoyamagakuin University, Japan; Creative Writing Courses, USA and Canada. *Literary Appointments:* Poet-in-Residence, University of Iowa, USA, 1976; Bunting Fellow, Radcliffe College, Cambridge, Massachusetts, 1980–81. *Publications:* Betrayal, 1973; The Burning Heart, Anthology of Japanese Women Poets (translator and co-editor with Kenneth Hexroth), 1977; What Parachute Soldiers Don't See, 1981. *Contributions to:* New Directions; Feminist International; Rekitei; Iowa Review. *Honours include:* Fellowship, Bunting Institute, American Council of Learned Societies, 1980–81. *Memberships:* Reketei, Japan. *Address:* 19 Birch Hill Road, Stow, MA 01775, USA.

ATWOOD, Ann Margaret, *Education:* BA, University of Redlands, California, USA; Art Center School, Los Angeles. *Publications:* The Little Circle, 1967; New Moon Cove, 1969; The Wild Young Desert, 1970; Haiku, The Mood of Earth, 1971; The Kingdom of the Forest, 1972; My Own Rhythm, 1973; Haiku-Vision, 1977; For All that Lives, 1979; Fly With the Wind, 1979. Publisher: Chas Scribner's Sons: Drifting with the Moon, adaptations of German Haiku by Gunther Klinge, 1978. *Honours:* Including: Annual Book Award, University of California, Irvine, 1967, 70, 72. *Memberships:* Jacques Cousteau Society; Sierra Club. *Address:* 32013 Point Place, South Laguna, CA 92677, USA.

ATWOOD, Margaret, b. Nov. 1939, Ottawa, Canada. Writer. *Education:* BA, Victoria College, University of Toronto, 1961; MA, Radcliffe College, Harvard University, USA, 1962. *Literary Appointments:* Writer-in-Residence, University of Toronto, 1972–73; Film Script Writer; Writer for Market Research Firm. *Publications:* Poetry Includes: The Circle Game, 1966, 67; The Animals in That Country, 1969, 68; You Are Happy, 1974, 75; Selected Poems, 1976, 78; Two-Headed Poems, 1976, 78; True Stories, 1981; Interlunar, 1984. Fiction includes: The Edible Woman,

1969, 70; Surfacing, 1972, 73; Lady Oracle, 1976; Dancing Girls, short stories, 1977; Life Before Man, 1979, 80; Bodily Harm, 1981; Murder in the Dark, 1983; Bluebeard's Egg, short stories, 1983; The Handmaid's Tale, 1985. Childrens Books: Up In the Tree, 1978; Anna's Pet, 1980. Non-Fiction: Survival: A Thematic Guide to Canadian Literature, 1972; Second Worlds: Selected Critical Prose, 1982; Editor: The Oxford Book of Canadian Verse in English, 1982. *Contributions to:* Poetry: Tamarack Review; Canadian Forum; New Yorker; Atlantic Monthly; Poetry, USA; Kayak; Quarry; Prism; Numerous anthologies in Canada and USA. Short Stories: Tamarack Review; Alphabet; Harpers; CBC Anthology and others. Reviews and Critical Articles: Quarry; Canadian Literature; Macleans and others. *Honours include:* Presidents Medal, University of Western Ontario, 1965; Governor General's Award, 1966; Union Poetry Prize, 1969, Bess Hoskins Prize, 1974, Poetry, Chicago, Illinois, USA; City of Toronto Book Award, 1977; Canadian Booksellers Association Award, 1977; St Lawrence Award for Fiction, 1978; Radcliffe Graduate Medal, 1980; Molson Award, 1981; Guggenheim Fellowship, 1981; Companion of Order of Canada, 1981; Honorary degrees, Trent University, Queens University and Concordia. *Address:* c/o McClelland and Stewart, 25 Hollinger Road, Toronto Ontario, Canada.

AUBERT, Rosemary Proe, b. 4 May 1946, USA. Freelance Writer. *Education:* BA, St Bonaventure University, Olean,New York, USA; MA, York University, Toronto, Canada. *Literary Appointments:* Senior Editor, Harlequin Romance; Teacher (part-time), Seneca College; Workshop Lecturer, Canadian Authors' Association; Workshop Leader, Clarke Institute of Psychiatry. *Major Publications:* Two Kinds of Honey, (poems) 1977; Novels: Sons of Eden, 1983; A Red Bird in Winter, 1984; Garden of Lions, 1985. *Contributor to:* Numerous periodicals, including: Canadian Literature; Canadian Forum; Poetry Canada Review; Prism; Cross-Canada Writers' Quarterly. *Honour:* Alberta Poetry Contest, 1974. *Memberships:* Canadian Poets' Association; Phoenix (Poets' Workshop). *Address:* 3 Condor Avenue, Toronto, M4J 3M5, Canada.

AUDERSKA, Halina, b. 3 July 1904, Odessa, Poland. Writer. *Education:* Studies of Polish philology, philosophy, University of Warsaw. *Publications:* Author of 7 historical plays, novels, 110 radio plays. Works include: Fugitives, 1952; The Republic Will Pay, 1954; Pomegranate, 1971, 3rd edition, 1978; Birds' Highway, 1973, 5th edition, 1979; Indian Summer, 1974, 5th editon, 1979; Smaragdine Eyes, 1977, 2nd edition, 1978; Just a Man, 1980; The Mermaid's Sword, 1980, 3rd edition, 1981; The Queen Bona, 2nd edition, 1983; To Kill Fear, 1985. *Honours include:* 1st class: Special Prize for Literary Output, 1985; National Prize for Literary Output, 1984; Prize, Minister of Culture and Art, 1977. Prize, Warsaw City, 1971, Chairman of Ministers Council, 1977. *Memberships include:* Past Vice Chairman, current Chairman, Polish Union of Writers; International Theatre Institute; PEN; SEC. *Address:* Kopernika 11/11, 00359 Warsaw, Poland.

AUERBACH, Jessica, b. 15 Mar. 1947, Newark, New Jersey, USA. Writer. m. Joshua Auerbach, 15 June 1969, Maplewood, New Jersey, 2 daughters. *Education:* AB, Vassar College, 1969; MAT, Wesleyan University, 1972. *Major Publication:* Winter Wife, 1983. *Contributor to:* Vassar Quarterly, 1982 (Bird in the Basement). *Honour:* National Endowment for the Arts Fellowship in Creative Writing, 1985. *Membership:* Authors' Guild. *Literary Agent:* Jean V Naggar. *Address:* 20 Rolling Ridge Road, Ridgefield, CT 06877, USA.

AUGER, Pierre Victor, b. 1899, Paris, France. Professor, University of Paris; formerly Director General, European Space Research Organisation. *Education:* DCS, University of Paris., *Publications:* What Are Cosmic Rays?, (Chicago University Press); Les Rayons Cosmiques, (Press Universitaire de France); L'Homme Microscopique, (Flammarion, Paris); Main Trends in Scientific Research, UN-ESCO-UNO, 1961.

Contributions to: Deogene-Revue Philosophique (Paris); Les Recontres de Geneve (La Baconiere, Neuchatel); Impact (UNESCO). Memberships: French Academy of Sciences, Great Officer Legion of Honour; FRSA; Fellow, AM Physics Society Recipient, Feltrinelli Prize, 1961; Kalinga International Prize, 1972; Gaute Langmuir, 1978. Address: 12 Rue Emile Faguet, Paris 14, France.

AUGUSTIN, Elisabeth, b. 13 June 1903, Berlin. Writer. Publications include: Het had erger kunnen zyn, 1979; Der Gartch, 1982; Ja, mein Engel, 1981; Jakob und der Andre, 1982; meine sprache deine sprache, 1985. Honours: Georg Mackensen Prize for the best German 1977 short story; Adolf Georg Bartels-Ehrung. Memberships: PEN; Verenging van Letterkundigen; Die Kogge; Autorenkreis Plesse; Regensburger Schriftsteller-Gruppe. Address: Schrijvershuis, Huddestraat 7, 1018 HB Amsterdam, Netherland.

AUKERMAN, Dale H b. 16 June 1930, West Alexandria, Ohio. Writer. m. Ruth Seebass, 24 July 1965, Kassel, West Germany, 1 son, 2 daughters. Education: AB, University of Chicago, 1949; 3 years graduate work, University of Chicago; 1 year graduate work, Glasgow University. Publications: On the Ground Floor of Heaven (with Reuel B Pritchett) 1980; Darkening Valley: A Biblical Perspective on Nuclear War, 1981. Contributions to: Many articles in Sojourners; Messenger; Baptist Peacemaker etc. Address: 191, Stem Road, Union Bridge, MD 21791, USA.

AURA, Erkki Olavi, b. 18 Nov. 1942, Tampere, Finland. Theatre Director. 1 son, 1 daughter. Education: MA, University of Tampere, 1981. Publications: The Planet of Nonsense, 1975; The Golden Spinning Wheel, 1976; Thieves of Aurora Borealis, 1977; A Happy Creature, 1979, (plays for children); The Man Who Was Searching for the Last Sentence, 1982, (radioplay); a Master of Warkho-Riwer, 1982, (poems); RAMI, 1985, (rock-play); Win Gambling on!' 1986, (musical); True Friend, 1986, (radioplay). Contributions to: Theatre and literary critiques and essays in numerous Finnish newspapers. Membership: Finnish Dramatists' Society. Literary Agent: Finnish Dramatists' Society. Address: Seinájoki City Theatre, Finland.

AUSTICK, David, b. 8 Mar. 1920, Leeds, England. Master Bookseller & Publisher. Address: 25 Cookridge Street, Leeds, LS1 3AN, England.

AVERY, Gillian Elise, b. 1926. Writer. Education: Dunottar School, Reigate, Surrey, England. Major Publications: Fiction: The Warden's Niece, 1957; Trespassers at Charlcote, 1958; James Without Thomas, 1959; The Elephant War, 1960; To Tame a Sister, 1961; The Greatest Gresham, 1962; The Peacock House, 1963; The Italian Spring, 1964; The Call of the Valley, 1966; A Likely Lad (Guardian Award 1972), 1971; Huck & her Time Machine, 1977; The Lost Railway, 1980; Onlookers, 1983. Non-fiction: 19th Century Children: Heroes & Heroines in English Children's Stories, (with Angela Bull), 1965; Victorian People in Life & Literature, 1970; The Echoing Green: Memories of Regency & Victorian Youth, 1974; Children's books, 1967–70; anthologies of stories & extracts from early children's books. Literary Agent: A D Peters. Address: 32 Charlbury Road, Oxford OX2 6UU, England.

AVERY, Martin, b. 23 June 1955, Canada. Writer; Editor; Publisher; Publicist. m. Batsheva Paul, 6 Nov. 1982, Toronto. Education: BA Honours, Individualized Studies in folklore, literature and creative writing, York University, Toronto, 1979; MFA Writing, Vermont College, Norwich University, Montpelier, Vermont, USA, 1985. Publications: First Impressions, compendium, editor John Metcalf, 1980; Cottage Country Stories, 1981; Cottage Gothic, 1982; The Singing Rabbi, 1983; Northern Comfort, 1985; Metro Media Directory, 1985. Contributions to: Toronto Star; Toronto Sun; The Globe and Mail; Best Canadian Stories; Grain; Impulse; Descant; Capilano Review; English Quarterly; Free Fall; Boreal; Directions; Only Paper Today; OPT, Writing etc. Memberships: Periodical Writers Association of Canada; Writers Union of Canada; Associated Writing Programs, USA, International Association of Business Communicators (ABC). Literary Agent: Stan Colbert, Toronto, Canada. Address: Avery Communications, 660 Briar Hill Avenue, Toronto, Ontario, M6B 4B7, Canada.

AVEY, Ruby Doreen, b. 29 Jan. 1927, Hove, Sussex, England. Author, Lecturer & Broadcaster. Education: St Mary's Convent, Portslade; Hove Secretarial College, Hove. Literary Appointments: Part-time Tutor in Creative Writing at Hove Adult Further Education Centre, 1971–82, Ford Open Prison, 1974–76. Major Publications: The House of Harron, 1977; Shadows on the Snow, 1978; A Wedding in Winter, 1978; Love is for Tomorrow, 1979; Lord of the Watchtower, 1980; Call for Nurse Hope, 1980; Bracelet for a Bride, 1980; Portrait of a Woman, 1980; Nurse in Deep Water, 1981; Love & Nurse Jeni, 1981; Arabian Love Story, 1981; Nurse at Tye Towers, 1982; As one small Candle, 1982; Because I Loved You, 1982; Jo Lane – Store Nurse, 1983; Miranda, 1983; and others. Contributor to: Newspapers, Local Radio & numerous magazines. Membership: Romantic Novelists' Association. Address: 53 Norway Street, Portslade, Brighton, Sussex BN4 1AE, England.

AVI-SHAUL, Mordechay, b. 17 May 1898. Poet; Novelist; Translator of Classical Literature; Writer. m. 3 children. Education: Teachers Training College; Hebrew University; Institute for Jewish Studies. Literary Appointments: Associate with Ketubim, Literary weekly, 1928–33; Founding Member, Levant Publishing Company & Associate Editor of KEDEN, literary bulletin, 1943–44; Editor, Thmurot (The Turning Tide) for problems of art and society, 1951; Joint Editor, Shalom, periodical of Israeli Peace Movement. Publications: Ba'azikim, 1932; Juggernaut, 1945; Ballad on Peace, 1966; Israel Landscape (prose poems), 1956; The Necklace, 1928; Poems of Impatience, 1982; Swiss Metamorphoses, 1963; King Karadash and Other Profane Stories, 1965; The Graves are Ready, 1968; Jew Suss, 1932, Habima theatre, Volpone (adapted 1934 from Ben Jonson Obel Theatre); Numerous translations including J W Goethe: Die Leiden des jungen Werther, The Entailed Estate. Contributor to: Literary supplements of newspapers, magazines and periodicals including: Orlogin; Moznaim, Proza Literary and Art Magazine. Honours include: Tchernichowsky Prize for classical translation, 1957; ACUM Prize for belles-lettres, 1966; Order of the Flag of the Hungarian People's Republic for cultural relations, 1979; L'Insigna Honorifique of Association of Friendship Societies of USSR, 1980. Memberships include: PEN Centre in Israel; Founder Member, Israel League for Human and Civil Rights, President; World Peace Council; Hebrew Writers Association. Address: Beth Avot 12/41, 52960 Ramat Efal, Ramat Gan, Israel.

AWDRY, Wilbert Vere, b. 15 June 1911, Ampfield, Romsey, Hampshire, England. Clergyman, Author. Education: MA, St Peter's College, University of Oxford; Diploma in Theology, Wycliffe Hall, Oxford. Major Publications: Three Railway Engines; Thomas the Tank Engine; James the Red Engine, and 23 other titles in this childrens' series; Industrial Archaeology in Gloucestershire, 1974; (joint editor) A Guide to the Steam Railways of Great Britain, 1979. Memberships: Society of Authors; National Book League. Address: Sodor, 30 Rodborough Avenue, Stroud, Gloucestershire GL5 3RS, England.

AYCKBOURN, Alan, b. 1939, London, England. Theatre Director; Playwright. Plays: Mr Whatnot, 1963; Relatively Speaking, 1968; How the Other Half Loves, 1972; Time and Time Again, 1973; Absurd Person Singular, 1974; The Norman Conquests, Trilogy, 1975; Absent Friends, 1976; Confusions, 1976; Bedroom Farce, 1975; Bedroom Farce, Absurd Person Singular and Absent Friends, published as one volume, 1976; Just Between Ourselves, 1976; Ten Times Table, 1977;

Joking Apart, 1978; Sisterly Feelings, 1979; Taking Steps, 1979; Season's Greetings, 1980; Lay Upstream, 1981; Intimate Exchanges, 1982; A Chorus of Disapproval, 1984; Woman in Mind, 1985. Joking Apart and Other Plays, hardback, 1969, Radio Drama Productions, British Broadcasting Corporation Leeds, 1965–70. *Membership:* Garrick Club. *Literary Agent:* Margaret Ramsay Limited. *Address:* c/o Margaret Ramsay Limited, 14a Goodwin's Court, St Martin's Lane, London WC2N 4LL, England.

AYERST, David George Ogilvy, b. 24 July 1904, London, England. Writer. m. Larema Fisher, 29 Dec. 1936, London, 1 son, 4 daughters. *Education:* Scholar, Senior Scholar, Christ Church, Oxford University; Scholarship in Modern History, Gibbs University; 1st class Modern history, 1926. *Literary Appointments:* Editorial staff, Manchester Guardian, 1929–34; Historian, The Guardian, 1964–74; Member, The Scott Trust, 1969–78. *Publications:* Understanding Schools, 1967; Records of Christianity, with A S T Fisher, 1970; Guardian: Biography of a Newspaper, 1971; Guardian Omnibus, editor, 1973; Garvin of the Observer, 1985. *Contribution to:* Chambers Encyclopedia. *Honour:* CBE, 1964. *Address:* Littlecote, Church Green, Burford, Oxford OX8 4RY, England.

AYGUESPARSE, Albert, b. 1 Apr. 1900, Brussels, Belgium. Writer. m. Rachel Tielemans, 27 Dec. 1924, 1 daughter. *Education:* Ecole Normale, Brussels. *Literary Appointments:* Member, Royal Academy of French Language and Literature, Belgium; Director, Review, Marginales. *Publications:* L'Heure de la Verite, 1947; Notre ombre nous precede, 1952; Simon-la-Bonte, 1965; Les Mal-Pensants, 1979. Poems: Le Vin noir de Cahors, 1957; Arpenteur de l'ombre, 1980; Les Armes de la guerison, 1973; Pour saluer le jour qui nait, 1975. Short Stories: Le Partage des jours, 1972; La Nuit de Polastri, 1985. *Contributions to:* Le Journal des Poetes; Le Spantole; Marginales; La Boite a Poemes. *Honours:* Grand Officer: Order of Leopold, Belgium; Order of the Crown, Belgium. Grand Prix, Triennial of the Novel, 1954; Victor Rossel Prize, 1952; Emile Bernheim Prize, 1983; Chatrian Prize, 1967; Mount Saint Michel Grand Prix, 1975; Charles Van Lerberghe Prize, 1977. *Memberships:* Committee member: Pen Club; Association of Belgian Writers; International Poetry Biennials. Society of Men of Letters. *Address:* Rue Marconi 118, 1180 Brussels, Belgium.

AYITTAH, Sampson Na, b. 13 July 1933, Ada Foah, Ghana. Journalist. m. Gloria Abaya-Teye, 4 Mar. 1972, Big Ada, 1 son, 3 daughters. *Education includes:* Diploma, Journalism, London School of Journalism, London, England; Diploma, French, Alliance Francaise, Paris, France; Diploma, Book Writing, United Nations. *Literary Appointments:* Assistant Librarian, Accra Central Library, Accra, Ghana, 1960–61; Translator, Journalist, Librarian, Ghana News Agency, Accra, 1961–; Overseas News Editor, Agence France Presse, Paris, France, 1970. *Publications:* Your Life Guide, 1977; Enrich Your Life, 1985; Witch versus Wizard,

1986. *Contributions to:* Ghana News Agency; The Newsman; African Press Service. *Memberships:* Ghana Association of Writers; Ghana Journalists Association, Past member, British Library Association. *Address:* Ghana News Agency, PO Box 2118, Accra, Ghana.

AYLEN, Leo, b. Vryheid, Zululand, South Africa. Poet; Author; Film Director; m. Annette Battam. *Education:* MA (1st Class Honours), New College, Oxford University; PhD, Bristol University. *Appointment:* Television Producer for British Broadcasting Corporation, 1965–70; Writer. *Publications:* Books (Poetry): Discontinued Design; I, Odysseus; Sunflower; Return to Zululand; Red Alert: This is a God Warning; Jumping-Shoes; Books (Non-fiction): Greek Tragedy and the Modern World; Greece for Everyone; The Greek Theater; Children's Opera: The Apples of Youth. Films for TV include: The Drinking Party; 1065 and All That; Dynamo;' Who'll Buy a Bubble?; Steel, Be My Sister; Soul of a Nation. *Honours:* Nominated for British Television Awards, 1966; Poet-in-Residence, Fairleigh Dickinson University, New Jersey, 1972–74; Cecil Day Lewis Fellowship, London, 1979–80; Hooker Distinguished Visiting Professor, McMaster University, Ontario, 1982. *Memberships:* Poetry Society of Britain; Poetry Society of USA; Writers' Guild of Great Britain; Writers' Guild of USA; British Actors Equity; Association of Cinema and Television Technicians. *Address:* 71 Chelsham Road, London SW4 6NN, England.

AYLING, Stanley Edward, b. 15 Mar. 1909. Schoolmaster, Biographer. m. Gwendoline Annette Hawkins, 17 Dec. 1936, London, 2 sons. *Education:* MA, Emmanuel College, University of Cambridge. *Major publications:* Portraits of Power, 1963; The Georgian Century, 1966; Nineteenth-Century Gallery, 1970; George the Third, 1972; The Elder Pitt, Earl of Chatham, 1976; John Wesley, 1979; A Portrait of Sheridan, 1985. *Honour:* Fellow, Royal Society of Literature, 1980. *Literary Agent:* Anthony Sheil Associates. *Address:* The Beeches, Middle Winterslow, Salisbury, Wiltshire, England.

AZRAEL, Judith Anne, b. 28 July 1938, Baltimore, Maryland, USA. Writer. divorced. 1 son, 1 daughter. *Education:* BA, University of Wisconsin; MFA with honours, University of Oregon. *Literary Appointments:* Visiting Writer, Western Washington University; Instructor, College of the Redwoods, Whatcom Community College. *Publications:* Fire in August, 1969; Fields of Light, 1974; Antelope are Running, 1978; Apple Tree poems, 1984. *Contributions to:* The Nation; Western Humanities Review; Southern Poetry Review; The Christian Science Monitor; Minnesota Review; Confrontation; Calliope; Mendocino Review; Works; December; Lillabulero; Ghost Dance; Red Cedar Review; Footprint; Sunstone Review; Jeopardy; Stone County; Wormwood Review; Black Bear Review; Laurel Review. *Memberships:* Associated Writer's Program; Poets and Writers. *Address:* PO Box 45, Lummi Island, WA 98262, USA.

B

BABINGTON SMITH, Constance, b. 15 Oct. 1912, Puttenham, Surrey, England. Writer. *Major Publications:* Evidence in Camera, 1958, 3rd edition 1974; Air Spy, 1957; Testing Time, 1961; (editor) Letters to a Friend by Rose Macaulay, 1961, 2nd edition, 1968; (editor) Last Letters to a Friend by Rose Macaulay, 1962; (editor) Letters to a Sister by Rose Macaulay, 1964; (editor) Pleasures of Ruins by Rose Macaulay & Roloff Beny, 1964; Amy Johnson, 1967; Rose Macaulay: A Biography, 1972; John Masefield: A Life, 1978, paperback 1985; Julia de Beausobre: A Russian Christian in the West, 1983. *Contributor to:* Aeroplane; The Sunday Times; Sunday Telegraph, and others. *Honours:* MBE (Mil), 1945; Legion of Merit, USA, 1945. *Memberships:* Fellow, Royal Society of Literature; Authors' Club. *Literary Agent:* A D Peters. *Address:* c/o A D Peters, 10 Buckingham Street, London WC2, England.

BABULA, William, b. 19 May 1943, Stamford, Connecticut, USA. University Professor of English and Dean. m. Karen Gemi, 19 June 1965, 1 son, 1 daughter. *Education:* BA, Rutgers University, 1965; MA 1967, PhD 1969, University of California, Berkeley. *Literary Appointments:* Assistant Professor 1969–75, Associate Professor 1975–77, Professor 1977–81, Acting Chairman 1975–76, Chairman 1976–81, English Department, University of Miami, Coral Gables, Florida; Professor of English, Dean of School of Arts and Humanities, Sonoma State University, Rohnert Park, California, 1981–. *Publications:* Shakespeare and the Tragicomic Archetype, 1975; Shakespeare in Production, 1981; The Fragging of Lt Jones, play, 1983; The Bombing of Berkeley and Other Pranks, novel; The Winter of Mrs Levy, play; Creatures, play. *Contributions to:* Mike Shayne Mystery Magazine; The Texas Review; Gem; Fiction 83 Anthology; The Mendocino Review; Fiction 84 Anthology; Articles in professional journals. *Honours:* Gualala Arts 1st Prize Award, 1983; 1st Prize, 24th Annual Deep South Writers' Conference, 1984. *Memberships:* Dramatists Guild; Authors League of America; Associated Writing Programs; Phi Beta Kappa. *Address:* Sonoma State University, Rohnert Park, CA 94928, USA.

BACHE, Ellyn, b. 22 Jan. 1942, Washington DC, USA. Writer. m. Terry Bache, 5 July 1969, 3 sons, 1 daughter. *Education:* BA, University of North Carolina, 1964; MA, English Literature, University of Maryland, 1967. *Literary Appointment:* Editor-in-Chief, Antietam Review, 1983–85. *Publication:* As Ellen Matthews, Culture Clash, 1982. *Contributions to:* McCall's; Yale Magazine; Southern Humanities Review; Virginia Country; Ascent; New Southern Literary Messenger; Woman's World. *Memberships:* Director, Washington Council, Maryland, Arts Council; Literary Advisory Panel, Maryland State Arts Council. *Literary Agent:* J Sanford Greenburger. *Address:* 2314 Waverley Drive, Wilmington, NC 28403, USA.

BACHMAN, William David, b. 30 July 1952, Philadelphia, USA. Freelance Photojournalism. m. 25 Feb. 1984, Melbourne, Australia. *Education:* BA, Asian Studies, Australian National University, 1974. *Appointments:* Managing Editor, 1978–79, Photographic Editor, 1982–, Fall-Line Ski Magazine, Melbourne. *Publication:* Wellsboro – Faces and Places, 1981. *Contributor to:* Numerous Editorial and Photographic Contributions to Fall-Line; Australian Ski Yearbook; Australian Ski Business; Powder, (USA); Australian Playboy; Australasian Post; The AGE; Transair; Signature; Wild. *Membership:* Fellowship, Australian Writers, Victoria. *Address:* 55 Mayston St, East Hawthorn, Victoria 3123, Australia.

BÄCK, Tomas Mikael, b. 18 Feb. 1946, Vasa. Poet, Critic. m. Anita Hilda Marguerite Savonius, 27 Dec. 1971, Helsingfors, 1 son, 1 daughter. *Education:* Librarian, Svenska Social-och Kömmunalhogskolan, Helsingfors; BA Helsingfors University. *Appointments:* Vice-Chairman, Chairman, Board, Boklaget for södra Finland; Board Member, Finlands svenska författareförening. *Publications:* Andhämtning, 1972; Och hastigt förstaå, 1975; Början av ett Är, 1977; Tills vi äger våra liv, 1980; Denna dag, 1982; Regnljus och snö, 1984; Språngmarsch på stället, 1985. *Contributor to:* Café Existens, Gothenburg; Boklagets Litterära Ársmagasin; Svenskbygden; Folktidningen Ny Tid; etc. *Honours:* Svenska Litteratursällskapet, Helsingfors, 1978, 1985. *Address:* Borgågatan 47-49 B 13, SF 00520 Helsingfors.

BACKSTRÖM, Lars David, b. 18 Feb. 1925. Writer. *Education:* Fil mag, 1951, Fil lic, 1955, Uppsala University. *Literary Appointments:* Editor, Ord's Bild mag, 1962–70; Editor, Forfattarforlagets Tidskrift (Writers Co-op), 1970–73; Visiting Lecturer in Scandinavian Studies, University of Wisconsin, Madison, USA, 1968. *Publications* include: K D Logrens dikter, (K D Logren's Poems) 1955; Världen omkring oss, (The World Around Us) 1962; Oppen stad, (Open City) 1967; Hjärnskakning, (Concussion of the Brain) 1976; Författarliv (Author's Life), short stories and diary, 1982; Gröna dikter (Green Poems), 1982; Vad är poesi? essays (What is Poetry?), 1985; Det trenkantiga päronet (The Triangular Pear) translation of poems by various authors, 1965 etc. *Memberships:* Writers' Centre; Swedish Writers' Union. *Address:* Osterplan 15B, S–753 31 Uppsala, Sweden.

BAGG, Charles Ernest, b. 7 May 1920, London, England. Retired Consultant Psychiatrist. *Education:* Downing College, Cambridge University; Westminster Hospital, London; MA; MRCS; LRCP; DPM; FRC Psych, 1983; Fellow, International Biographical Association, 1980; Fellow, World Literary Academy, 1985. *Publications:* Handbook of Psychiatry for Social Workers & Health Visitors, 1977; Contributing Author: The Samaritans in the 70's, 1973; Answers to Suicide, 1978; The Samaritans in the 80's, 1980. *Contributor to:* Journal of Neurology, Neurosurgery & Psychiatry; Medical Press; British Journal of Psychiatry; Development Medicine & Child Neurology; British Medicine; British Journal of Occupational Therapy. *Honour:* Silver Medal, International Biographical Centre, 1985. *Address:* Little Broomfield, Broomfield Hill, Great Missenden, Buckinghamshire, England.

BAGLEY, John Joseph, b. 1908, St Helens, Lancashire, England. Reader in History (retired). *Education:* MA, University of Liverpool. *Major Publications include:* History of Lancashire, 1956; Life in Medieval England, 1960; Henry VIII & his Times, 1962; Historical Interpretation (2 volumes), 1965 & 1971; Poor Law (with A J Bagley) 1966; Lancashire Diarists, 1975; Medieval People, 1978; The Earls of Derby 1485–1985, 1985. *Contributor to:* Historical Society of Lancashire & Cheshire; Lancashire Life. *Memberships:* Association of University Teachers; Tutors Association; Vice-President, Historic Society of Lancashire & Cheshire. *Address:* 10 Beach Priory Gardens, Southport, Merseyside PR8 1RT, England.

BAGLEY, Mary Carol, b. 11 Mar. 1958, St Louis, Missouri, USA. Writer; University Instructor. *Education:* BA 1980, MA 1982, University of Missouri, St Louis, USA. *Literary Appointments:* Features Editor, Current Newspaper; Managing Editor, Watermark Literary Magazine; Stringer, Suburban News Journals; Contributing Editor, Metro Bride Magazine; Editor, Guide to St Louis Theatres. *Major Publications:* The Front Row, Missouri's Grand Theatres, 1984; The Light Bearers of Doom, 1985; The St Louis Fox; Advisor, business writing text: Business Writing: Concepts and Applications. *Contributor to:* Marquee Magazine; Outlook; Missouri Life; St Louis Magazine; Midwest Motorist; Post-Dispatch; Globe-Democrat; St Louis Journalism Review; The Times; The Weekly; Construction News and Review; West End Word; Metro Bride; Watermark; and others. *Honours:* Latin Honours, 1980; Graduate Essay Prize, 1982. *Membership:*

Writer's Guild. *Address:* St Louis University, St Louis, MO 63103, USA.

BAGRYANA, Elisaveta, b. 29 Apr. 1893, Sofia, Bulgaria. Writer. m. Alexander Likov, 1941, 1 son, 1 daughter. *Education:* Bulgarian Philology, Sofia University. *Literary Appointment:* An editor at the Septemvry literary magazine. *Publications:* The Eternal and Saint One, 1927; Star of the Saylor, 1932; Miraculous Dream, 1952; Coastwards, 1963; Poems, 1968. *Contributor to:* All main Bulgarian literary editions. *Honours:* People's Worker of Culture; A Hero of Socialist Labour; A Hero of People's Republic of Bulgaria. *Membership:* Union of Bulgarian Writers. *Address:* 58 Neofit Rilski Street, Sofia, Bulgaria.

BAIGELL, Matthew E, b. 27 Apr. 1933, New York City, USA. Art Historian. m. Renee, 2 daughters. *Education:* BA, University of Vermont, 1954; MA, Columbia University, 1955; PhD, University of Pennsylvania, 1965. *Publications:* A History of American Painting, 1971; Thomas Hart Benton, 1974; The American Scene: American Painting During the 1930's, 1974; Charles Burchfield, 1976; Dictionary of American Art, 1979; Thomas Cole, 1981; Albert Bierstadt, 1981; A Concise History of American Painting and Sculpture, 1984. *Contributions to:* Art Journal; Arts Magazine; Art in America; Artists Proof; Arts Canada; Art Criticism; Architectural Review; Journal of the Society of Architectural Historians; Art and Artists; Studio International; Kansas Quarterly. *Address:* Art History Department, Voorhees Hall, Rutgers University, New Brunswick, NJ 08903, USA.

BAIGENT, Beryl, b. 16 Dec. 1937, Wales. Teacher. m. Alan H Baigent, 19 Jan 1963, Leicester, 3 daughters. *Education:* BA; MA, to be completed in 1987. *Literary Appointments:* Editorial Staff, POMSEED; judge, UAPA Laureate Award; judge, Woodstock Public Library, National Book Week, Poetry Contest. *Publications:* The Sacred Beech and other Poems of Wales, 1985; The Shape that Haunts Thought's Wilderness, forthcoming. *Contributor to:* Alter Year Book 1981, 82, 85; Poetry Toronto. *Honours:* Add to ninth edition – June Fritch Memorial Award Canadian Authors Association, 1983. *Memberships:* As Before. *Address:* 137 Byron Avenue, Thamesford, Ontario NOMZ MO, Canada.

BAILEY, Gordon Keith, b. 22 Feb. 1936, Stockport, Cheshire, England. Schools' Counsellor. m. Corrine, 2 Aug. 1958, Stockport, 1 son, 3 daughters. *Education:* BA (honours), Theology. *Publications:* Plastic World, 1971; Mothballed Religion, 1972; Patchwork Quill, 1975; Can A Man Change?, 1979; 100 Contemporary Christian Poets, 1983; I Want To Tell You How I Feel, God, 1983. *Contributions to:* Today; People Magazine, (USA); Reach Out, (NZ). *Address:* Maple Cottage, 198 Hole Lane, Northfield, Birmingham B31 2DB, England.

BAILEY, Harold Walter, b. 16 Dec. 1899, Devizes, Wiltshire, England. University Professor. *Education:* BA, MA, University of Western Australia; BA, MA, DPh, University of Oxford, England. *Publications include:* Zoroastrian Problems in the Ninth Century Books, Khotanese Texts, Volumes I-VIII; Khotanese Buddhist Texts; Saka Documents, 4 Portfolios; 1 Text Volume; Dictionary of Khotan Saka, 1979. *Contributor to:* Journal of Royal Asiatic Society; Bulletin of School of Oriental & African Society; various periodicals; Festschriften. *Memberships include:* President, Philological Society, 1948–52; President, Royal Asiatic Society, 1964–67; President, Society of Afghan Studies, 1972; President, Society of Mithraic Studies, 1975. *Honours:* Recipient, Triennial Gold Medal, Royal Asiatic Society, 1971; Honorary D Litt, Oxford, 1976. *Address:* Queen's College, Cambridge, England.

BAILEY, Peter Harry, b. 16 Feb. 1937, London, England. Writer. *Education:* Central School of Speech and Drama, 1953–56. *Literary Appointments:* Literary Fellow, Universities of Durham and Newcastle upon Tyne, 1972–74; Visiting Lecturer, English Literature, North Dakota State University, USA, 1977–79.

Publications: At The Jerusalem, 1967; Trespasses 1970; A Distant Likeness, 1973; Peter Smart's Confessions, 1977; Old Soldiers, 1980; An English Madam, 1982; Gabriel's Lament, 1986. *Contributions to:* Reviews: The Observer; The Times; The London Standard; The Listener and others. *Honours:* Somerset Maugham Award, 1968; Arts Council Award for best first novel published 1965–67, 1968; Authors Club, 1970; E M Forster Award, 1974; Bicentennial Fellowship, 1976; George Orwell Memorial Prize, 1978. *Literary Agent:* Deborah Rogers. *Address:* 79 Davisville Road, London W12 9SH, England.

BAIRD, Susan Barker, b. 28 Dec. 1942, Rahway, New Jersey, USA. Nursing Editor. 1 daughter. *Education:* Diploma, Johns Hopkins Hospital; BA, New England College; MPH, Boston University. *Appointments:* Editorial Board Member, Oncology Nursing Forum, 1977; Editor, Oncology Nursing Forum, 1979; Editor-in-Chief, Oncology Nursing Forum, 1985; Advisory Board Member, Springhouse Corporation, 1983, Community Nursing Newsletter, 1984. *Contributor to:* Oncology Nursing Forum; ASCO Proceedings; RN; Clinical Cancer Trials; Clinical Research; Topics in Clinical Nursing; Journal of the National Intravenous Therapy Association; Seminars in Oncology; European Journal of Cancer and Clinical Oncology. *Memberships:* Council of Biology Editors; International Academy of Nursing Editors. *Address:* 617 Ivy League Lane, Rockville, MD 20850, USA.

BAIRDEN, Andrew White, b. 15 Feb. 1930, Glasgow, Scotland. Mechanical Engineer. m. Jean Emond at Niagara Falls, Canada, 27 Oct. 1951, 2 daughters. *Education:* British Ordinary Certificate, Mechanical Engineering, Royal Technical College. *Contributions to:* British Digest Illustrated, UK Magazine, The Scottish Banner, The British Observer, British Weekly, Union Jack (West Coast correspondent & feature writer). *Memberships:* British Amateur Press; Greater Los Angeles Press Club; Foreign Press Centre, Los Angeles. *Address:* 5409 Michelle Drive, Torrance, CA 90503, USA.

BAKER, Carlos Heard, b. 5 May 1909, Biddeford, Maine, USA. Teacher; Writer. m. 22 Aug. 1932, Asheville, North Carolina, USA, 1 son, 2 daughters. *Education:* AB, Dartmouth College, AM, Harvard University, PhD, Princeton University. *Major Publications include:* Shelley's Major Poetry, 1948; Hemingway: The Writer as Artist, 1952, 4th edition 1974; A Friend in Power (novel), 1958; The Land of Rumbelow (novel), 1963; A Year and a Day (poems), 1963; Ernest Hemingway: A Life Story (biography), 1969; The Gay Head Consipiracy (novel), 1973; The Talismans & Other Stories, 1976; Selected Letters of Ernest Hemingway (editor), 1981; The Echoing Green: Romantic & Modern Poetry, 1984. *Honour:* Recipient Guggenheim Fellowship, 1965–66; Honorary degrees. *Memberships:* American Philosophical Society, 1982. *Address:* 34 Allison Road, Princeton, NJ 08540, USA.

BAKER, Carole, Wallsend, England. Writer; Technical Author; Photo-Journalist. *Education:* BA, Hons, English and Philosophy, Hull University, England. NCTJ First Photo-Journalism, Press Photography, Computer Studies Certificate, Newcastle-on-Tyne. *Literary Appointments:* Senior Author, Technical Writing Association, Nottingham, 1985–; Editor, Start Magazine of Literature and the Arts, 1986–. *Publication:* CENTAR – Leisure Centre User's Guide, 1986. *Contributor to:* Literary journalism for Start Magazine; Photo-Journalism for Dec User, Computing, Tractor and Farm Machinery Trader, Far Eastern Agriculture, Bedfordshire Journal. *Literary Agent:* Start Magazine. *Address:* Technical Writing Associates, Queen's Chambers, King Street, Nottingham, England.

BAKER, Claire J, b. 27 Sep. 1927, Berkeley, California, USA. Poet; Playwright. *Education:* Currently working on AA at Contra Costa College, San Pablo, California. *Literary Appointments:* Secretary, Diablo-Alameda Branch, National League of American Pen

Women, 1983–84; Secretary, Poetry Organization for Women, 1983; Board of Directors, Ina Coolorith Circle and Alameda Poets, 1984–85. *Publications:* 4 books of Poetry: Touchings, 1976; Dear Mother, 1979; Space on Church Lane, 1982; Collage of Wild Leaves, 1983; Kim (play) performed in 1983 and televised in 1984, shown over Channel 32. Author of five plays; Special Ongoing Project: Promotion of Poetry Landmarks (Poets Corner), 12 to date, Northern California; Editorship, 'Current', Creative Arts Collection of Contra Costa College, 1985–86. *Contributions:* approximately 1017 poems published in magazines, journals, newspapers, anthologies such as: The Writer; Bulletin of Poetry Society of America; Blue Unicorn; Portland Oregonian; Alameda Times-Star; Pen Woman, etc. *Honours:* Recipient of 201 prizes and Honorary Mention Awards including: Triton Medallion for poem, Old Man; Reader in International Womens Poetry Festival, 1976. *Memberships:* National League American Pen Women; California Writers Club; California State Poetry Society; Bay Area Poets Coalition; Alameda Poets. *Address:* 2451 Church Lane #47, San Pablo, CA 94806, USA.

BAKER, Eleanor Elizabeth, b. 21 Aug. 1944, Pretoria, South Africa. Writer. m. Walter Baker, 3 Apr. 1969, 1 son, 1 daughter. *Education:* BA; BA (Hons); MA, Literature (cum laude); Pretoria University. *Publications:* Wereld Sonder Einde, 1973; Splinterspel, 1974; Morketiden, 1975; Monica, 1978; As'n Pou Kon Vlieg, 1980; Weerkaatsings, 1984; Dossier van'v Gyseling, 1985; Reflections (planned for summer 1986). *Contributor to:* 10 Plus (youth magazine); SABC. *Honours:* Finalist, Perskor Prize, twice; FAK Literary Prize, (for Weekaafsings), 1984. *Membership:* South African Writers Guild. *Literary Agent:* Dinah Wiener, London, England. *Address:* c/o Dinah Wiener, 59 Kentish Town Road, London NW1 8NY, England.

BAKER, Lillian, b. 12 Dec. 1921, New York, USA. Author; Historian. m. Roscoe Albert Baker, 1 son, 1 daughter. *Education:* Certificate, Famous Writers School; Credit course, University of California; Numerous writing courses, seminars, various colleges. *Major Publications:* The Collector's Encyclopaedia of Hatpins & Hatpin Holders, 1975; 100 Years of Collectable Jewellery; 1850–1950, 1978 (into 5th edition); Art Nouveau & Art Deco Jewellery, 1980; Creative & Collectable Miniatures, 1984; Hatpins & Hatpin Holders: An Identification & Value Guide, 1983; The Concentration Camp Conspiracy: A Second Pearl Harbour, 1981; Fifty Years of Collectable Fashion Jewellery: 1925–1975, 1985. *Contributions to:* Gardens Valley News, weekly column, 1964–76; New American Poets, 1969; Poetry publication, El Camino College, California; Trunkline Style & Stamina, Antique Trader Weekly, American Collector, Miniature Collector, Antiques Journal, Yesteryear, Collectors News etc. 1976–83; Editor, Points (newsletter, collectors of hatpins), 1977–; US Government Publication, Japanese American Evacuation Redress, 1984. *Honours:* Honorable mention, anthology, New American Poets, 1969; Freedoms Foundation, Valley Forge; 10th Place, National Contest, article award, 1977; Award of Merit (scholarship category), The Concentration Camp Conspiracy, Conference of California Historical Societies, 1983; Grant, Hoover Institution on War, Revolution and Peace, Stanford University, 1985; Many TV, Radio and public appearances. *Address:* 15237 Chanera Avenue, Gardena, CA 90249, USA.

BAKER, Samm Sinclair, b. 29 July 1909, USA. Writer. m. Natalie Bachrach, 12 June 1937, Paterson, New Jersey, 1 son, 1 daughter. *Education:* University of Pennsylvania, 1929. *Literary Appointments:* Lecturer, Writing, Columbia University, New York University, University of Pennsylvania, Drexel University, Iona College. *Publications include:* Over 30 books including 3 best-sellers: The Complete Scarsdale Medical Diet, with Dr Herman Tarnower; The Doctor's Quick Weight Loss Diet, with Dr Irwin Stillman; The Doctor's Quick Inches-Off Diet. Other titles include: Family Treasury of Art, with Natalie Baker; Conscious Happiness; Lifetime Fitness, with Jane Boutelle; Your Key to Creative

Thinking; How to be an Optimist; 5 gardening books; Erotic Focus: The New Way to Enhance Your Sexual Pleasure, with Dr Barbara De Betz, 1985; Make Money Writing: Writing Nonfiction that SELLS, 1986. etc. *Contributions include:* 100's of articles, stories, book excerpts, short features etc, in many leading magazines. *Honours include:* Awards, wartime & charities writing. *Membership:* Writers Guild. *Literary Agent:* Curtis Brown, NYC & London. *Address:* 1027 Constable Drive South, Mamaroneck, NY 10543, USA.

BAKER, Vera Lee, b. 10 Dec. 1925, Faculty Secretary. *Education:* Claremore College, 1974–76. *Literary Appointments:* Stenographer, Oklahoma Department of Public Welfare, 1946–51; Co-owner, Officer Manager, Book-keeper, Baker's Plumbing, Claremore College, 1972–77; Secretary National Hydro Hoist Company Incorporated, 1979–. *Contributor to:* Egress (Claremore College Anthology), 1975, 1977; Cherokee Recollections (book by Maude Du Priest), 1976; Poem in Unicorn, 1979; Poem in literary magazine Arulo!, 1981: etc. *Honours Include:* Tied for 1st Place, Egress, Claremore College, 1977; Award, Writer's Digest Magazine, (poem), 1979; First Place Award, Poetry Society of Oklahoma, 1985. *Memberships:* Poetry Society of Oklahoma; Secretary, Literary Lunch Bunch, Claremore College, 1976–77; National Federation of State Poetry Societies. *Address:* 1005 North Sioux, Claremore, OK 74017, USA.

BAKER, Victor Richard, b. 19 Feb. 1945, Waterbury, Connecticut, USA. Professor. m. Pauline Marie, 10 June 1967, Livingston Manor, New York, 2 sons. *Education:* BS, Rensselaer Polytechnic Institute, Troy, New York, 1967; PhD, University of Colorado, Boulder, 1971. *Literary Appointments:* Editorial Board: Geology, 1975–83; Geomorphology, 1985–1988, Springer Series in Physical Environment, 1985–88. *Publications:* The Channeled Scabland (co-editor), 1978; Surficial Geology: Building With the Earth (co-author), 1981; Catastrophic Flooding (Editor), 1981; The Channels of Mars, 1982. *Contributions to:* Quarternary Research; Journal of Geological Education; Science; American Scientist; Geology; Nature; American Journal of Science; Journal of Geology; Environmental Geology; Geological Society of America Bulletin; Water Resources Research; Journal of Geophysical Research; Icarus; Progress in Physical Geography; Journal of Sedimentary Petrology. *Honours:* Fellow, The Geological Society of America, 1976; Fulbright-Hays Senior Research Scholar, 1979–80. *Address:* Department of Geosciences, University of Arizona, Tucson, AZ 85721, USA.

BAKER WHITE, John, b. 12 Aug. 1902, West Malling, Kent, England. Journalist. *Major Publications:* Red Russia Arms; Dover – Nuremberg Return; The Red Network, Nationalisation; Chaos or Cure; The Soviet Spy System; The Big Lie; Pattern for Conquest; Sabotage is Suspected; True Blue. *Contributor to:* Central Press (features); Soviet Analyst. *Honours:* Justice of the Peace; Territorial Decoration. *Memberships:* Canterbury Society; Royal United Services Institution; Stour Valley Society; President, East Kent Fruit Society; Jacob Sheep Society. *Address:* Street End Place, Street End, Nr Canterbury, Kent, England.

BAKKEN, Dick, b. 24 Aug. 1941, Montana, USA. Poet. *Education:* BA, English, Pacific Lutheran University, Tacoma, 1963; MA, English, Washington State University, 1966. *Literary Appointments include:* Associate Faculty, Creative Writing, Cochise College, Douglas and Sierra Vista, Arizona, 1981–; Artist in Education, Arizona Commission on the Arts, 1985–; Editor-Publisher, Salted Feathers, poetry magazine and books, 1964–; Poetry Co-Editor, Bisbee Times, Arizona, 1982; Co-Editor, Weed-Free, 1983. *Publications include:* Hungry!, 1967; Miracle Finger, 1975; Here I Am, 1979; True History of the Eruption, 1980; Feet with the Jesus (poems), forthcoming; Grand Opening (7 short poems), forthcoming. *Contributions to:* Poetry Now; Poetry Northwest; Colorado State Review; St

Andrews Review; Red Hand Book; Mississippi Mud; Iron Country; Human Voice; Abraxes; Artspace; Poetry Flash; The Only Journal of the Tibetan Kite Society; Matrix; Poetry on the Buses. Poetry readings, workshops, lectures, writing conferences, arts commissions, poetry festivals, etc. *Address:* PO Box BT, Bisbee, AZ 85603, USA.

BALAGUE SALVIA, Miguel, b. 21 Jan. 1910, Bellvis, Lerida, Spain. Professor of Greek, Hebrew & Holy Scriptures. *Education:* Studies of Theology & Bible, Institutim Biblicim Romanum; Bach & Master Degrees. *Publications include:* Evangelio de San Lucas, 1944; Diccionario Griego-Espanol, 15 volumes, 1945; Gramitica Griega, 2 volumes, 1954; Jesucristo, Vida y Luz, 1963; La Senal del Templo, 1963; Prehistoria de la Salvacion, 1967; Historia de la Salvacion, 1968; El Testamento de Iesus, 1976; El Espirutu Santa Teresa Jounet Ibars, 1976. *Contributor to:* Numerous publications including: La Biblia de Catalunya, 1936, 1968; El Diccionario del Mundo Clasico; Enciclopedia Biblica; Cultura Biblica; Revista Biblica; Estudios Biblicos; Roca Viva; Teologia Espiritual; Ephemerides Mariologicae; Studia Papyrologica; La Vida Sobrenatural; El Cruzado Espanol; Que pasa? *Address:* Fuentes de Bejar, Salamanca, Spain.

BALDVINSSON, Sveinbjörn Ingvar, b. 27 Aug. 1957, Reykjavík, Iceland. Writer. m. Jóna Finnsdóttir, 1 son, 1 daughter. *Education:* BA, Literature, University of Iceland. *Publications:* I skugga mannsins (poetry), 1976; Stjörnur í skónum (Cyclus of songs, poetry and additional music on an LP), 1978; Ljóo handa hinum og pessum (poetry), 1981; Ietta verdur allt í lagi (TV play, Icelandic television), 1984; Lífdagatal (poetry), 1984; Translations: Sláturhús Fimm (Slaughterhouse Five) by Kurt Vonnegut, 1982; Gudlaun hr Rosewater (God Bless You Mr Rosewater, by K Vonnegut, 1985. *Contributions to:* Daily Morgunbladid (literary criticism since 1978); jazz reviews and articles. *Memberships:* The Writers Association of Iceland; Member of Selection Committee, Writers Association of Iceland, 1984–. *Address:* Sóleyjargata 19, 101 Reykjavík, Iceland.

BALDWIN, Bertha Marjorie, b. Faygate, Horsham, West Sussex, England. Poet; Lay Psychotherapist. *Education:* BA, Honours, Philosophy, University College, London; Guy's Hospital, London. *Appointments:* Poetry Board, Manifold, 1963–69. *Publications:* To Early White Narcissi, 1953; Poems and Translations, 1961; The Slain Unicorn, 1965; English Summer, 1981. *Contributor to:* Numerous Anthologies including: Without Adam, 1968; Doyes for the Seventies, 1969; Look Through a Diamond, 1971; Nine O'Clock Bell, 1985; Contributor to 4 of 6 Anthologies of the Camden Poetry Group; Periodical Contributions include, Poetry Review; Outposts; Manifold; Country Life; North American Mentor; etc. *Honours:* 1st Prize, Poetry Contest, Association of Ukrainians in Great Britain, 1966; 2nd Prize, Poetry Contest, Shelley Society of New York, USA, 1977; Exchange Fellowship, Philosophy, University of Louvain, 1940. *Memberships:* Poetry Society of America; Shelley Society of New York; Founder Fellow, International Academy of Poets; International Poetry Society; Camden Poetry Group; Fellow, Trinity College of Music Speech & Drama. *Address:* Old School Cottage, Colgate, Horsham, West Sussex RH12 4SY, England.

BALES, James Edward, 1 Nov. 1951, Milwaukee, USA. Librarian. m. Lisa Dodd Kelly, 28 Dec. 1984, Fredericksburg. *Education:* BA, English, Illinois College, 1973; MS, Literary Science, University of Illinois, Urbana, 1974. *Appointments:* Assistant Librarian, Eureka College, 1974–76; Public Service Librarian, Illinois College, 1976–80; Readers Services Librarian, Mary Washington College, 1980–. *Publications:* Horatio Alger, JR: An Annotated Bibliography of Comment and Criticism, co-author, 1981; The Lost Life of Horatio Alger, JR, co-author, 1985. *Contributor to:* Editor, Horatio Alger Society Newsboy, 1974–. *Honours:* Horatio Alger Society Newsboy Award, 1983; Horatio

Alger Society President's Award, 1982. *Memberships:* Virginia Library Association; American Library Association; Horatio Alger Society. *Address:* Mary Washington College Library, 1301 College Ave, Fredericksburg, VA 22401, USA.

BALK, Alfred W, b. 24 July 1930, Oskaloosa, Iowa, USA. Journalist. m. Phyllis L Munter, 7 June 1952, Moline, Illinois, 2 daughters. *Education:* BS, MS, Medill School of Journalism. Northwestern University, Evanston, Illinois. *Literary Appointments:* Reporter, Chicago Sun-Times; Freelance Writer for National Magazines; Feature Editor, Editor at Large, Saturday Review; Visiting Editor, Editor, Columbia Journalism Review; Editor and Publisher, Editorial Director, World Press Review. *Publications:* The Religious Business, The Free List: Property without Taxes; Our Troubled Press, (co-editor); A Free and Responsive Press. *Contributions to:* Magazines and Journals including: Harper's; Saturday Evening Post; Saturday Review; New York Times Magazine; The Nation; Columbia Journalism Review; McCall's; National Civic Review; Reader's Digest. *Honours:* Wells Memorial Key, Society of Professional Journalists/Sigma Delta Chi, 1966; Alumni Merit Award, Northwestern University, 1984. *Memberships:* President, American Society of Professional Authors and Journalists; Treasurer, Member of Executive Committee, American Society of Magazine Editors. *Address:* Room 1610, 230 Park Avenue, New York, NY 10169, USA.

BALL, John Bradley, b. 21 Aug. 1932, Nottingham, England. Journalist, Publisher, Broadcaster. m. Virginia Hooley, 26 May 1956, 1 son, 1 daughter. *Contributor to:* Womens Journal; Holiday Magazine (US); High Life; Holiday Inn Magazine; Manchester Evening News; Motoring and Travel Editor, Topic Magazine Group. *Honour:* PATA Magazine Travel Writer of the Year, 1979. *Memberships:* Guild of Motoring Writers (1957); British Guild of Travel Writers (1960); British Association of Travel Editors. *Address:* Clumber Lodge, Newstead Abbey Park, Nottinghamshire, England.

BALL, John Dudley, Junior, b. 8 July 1911, Schenectady, New York, USA. Author. m. Patricia Hamilton, 22 Aug. 1942, 1 son. *Education:* BA, Carroll College, Waukesha, Wisconsin, 1934. *Literary Appointments:* Member, Editorial Staff, Fortune Magazine, 1937–40; Music Editor, Brooklyn Eagle, 1946–51; Columnist, Music and Records, New York World Telegram, 1951–52; Editor-in-Chief, DMS Incorporated, 1961–62; Full-time writing, 1963–; Chairman, Mystery Library, University of California, San Diego Extension. *Publications:* Records for Pleasure, 1947; Operation Springboard, 1958; Spacemaster I, 1960; Edwards: USAF Flight Test Center, 1962; Judo Boy (Junior Literary Guild selection), 1964; In the Heat of the Night (Edgar Award, 1966; Critics Award, London; Academy Award Best Picture of Year, 1968), 1965; Arctic Showdown, 1966; Rescue Mission, 1966; The Cool Cottontail (Mystery Guild selection), 1966; Dragon Hotel, 1968; Miss 1000 Spring Blossoms, 1968; Johnny Get Your Gun, 1969; Last Plane Out, 1969; The First Team, 1971; Five Pieces of Jade (Detective Book Club selection), 1972; The Fourteenth Point, 1973; Mark One-The Dummy (Detective Book Club selection), 1974; The Winds of Mitamura, 1975; Police Chief (Detective Book Club selection), 1977; The Killing in the Market (Detective Book Club selection), 1978; Then Came Violence (Detective Book Club selection), 1980; Editor: Cope Cade; The Mystery Story, 1976. *Memberships:* Aviation and Space Writers Association; Mystery Writers America; British Crime Writers Association; Baker Street Irregulars; All-American Karate Federation; Mensa; Civil Air Patrol. *Address:* 16401 Otsego Street, Encino, CA 91436, USA.

BALLARD, Juliet Lyle Brooke (Mrs Lyttleton W), b. 6 Feb. 1913. Poet, Editor, Prose Writer. *Education:* AB, Randolph-Macon Woman's College, 1934; Certificate of Social Case Work, Richmond Professional Institute, 1938. *Literary Appointments:* Associate Editor, Association for Research and Enlightenment Journal,

1966–70; Associate Editor, Association for Research and Englightenment Children's Magazine, 1970; Editor, Treasure Trove (Association for Research and Enlightenment Children's quarterly), 1971–73. *Major Publications:* Under a Tropic Sun, 1945; Winter Has Come, 1945; The Ballad of the Widow's Flag (official poem of The Star-Spangled Flag House Association, Baltimore, Maryland), 1956; Prose Works: The Hidden Laws of Earth, 1979; Treasures from Earth's Storehouse, 1980; The Art of Living, 1982. *Contributor to:* Composers, Authors and Artists of America; Wings; Nature Magazine; Canadian Poetry; Poems for our Time; Moccasin; Driftwind; The Raven; The Lantern; Blue Moon; Kaleidograph; L'Alouette; Silver Star; The Searchlight; With Rhyme and Reason; American Poet; Greetings; ARE Journal; Coronet; and others. *Honours:* Participant in various radio programmes; Library exhibitions of books and poems; Winner of literary organisation contests; 1st prize, Saucier Lyric Award, National Federation of State Poetry Societies; 1965; Syracuse University Library manuscript collection, 1964. *Memberships:* Composers, Authors and Artists of America. *Address:* 2217 Wake Forest Street, Virginia Beach, VA 23451, USA.

BALLOU, H B, b. 12 Feb. 1938, New Haven, Connecticut, USA. Divorced, 2 sons, 1 daughter. *Education:* Associates Degree, Construction Management; Numerous Correspondence Diplomas: Engineering, Aeronautics, Meteorology, Air Navigation, Police Science, Writing. *Literary Appointments:* Conference Founder, First Annual Writers Conference, Texas Woman's University, Denton, 1986. *Publications:* Expose' of the Connecticut Superior Court, 1974; Drafting Profession; Plumbing. *Contributor to:* Columnist, Contractor Magazine, 1984–85; New England Builder; Plumbing Engineer Magazine. *Memberships:* The Authors Guild Inc; Authors League of America Inc; National Writers Club; North Texas Chapter, National Writers Club, Founding President, 1984–85. *Address:* 7418 Courtside Drive, Garland, TX 75042, USA.

BALON, Eugene Kornel, b. 1 Aug. 1930, Orlova. University Professor. m. Christine Flegler, 1 Aug. 1980, 1 son. *Education:* MSc, 1952, PhD, 1962, Charles University, Prague, Czechoslovakia. *Literary Appointments:* Editor in Chief, Founder, Environmental Biology of Fishes, international journal, 1976–; Series Editor and Founder, Perspectives in Vertebrate Science and Developments in Environmental Biology of Fishes. *Publications:* Expedition Cayo Largo, in Slovak, 1967; Lake Kariba; A Man-Made Tropical Ecosystem in Central Africa, 1974; Charrs: Salmonid Fishes of the Genus Salvelinus, 1980; Early Life Histories: New Ecological, Developmental and Evolutionary Perspectives, 1985 and others. *Contributions to:* Various scientific journals, proceedings and magazines over 231 articles and chapters. *Address:* RR 3, Rockwood, Ontario, Canada NOB 2KO.

BALTENSPERGER, Peter, b. 30 May 1938, Winterthur, CH. Teacher. 2 daughters, 1 granddaughter. *Education:* BSc, Chemistry, Technikum, Winterthur, Switzerland; BA, English, Carleton University, Ottawa, Canada; BA(Hons), English, Brock University, St Catharines, Canada; Specialist Certificate, University of Toronto, Faculty of Education. *Publications:* Lost Seasons (poetry), 1981; This Place (poetry), 1982; Saints and Sinners of Niagara (historical), 1982; Inner Journeys (instructional), 1983; Moonfires (poetry), 1984; Mirror Mirror (poetry), 1984; Guardians of Time (science fiction novel), 1984. *Contributor to:* Canadian Literature; Dalhousie Review; Antigonish Review; Descant; Quarry; Poetry Canada Review; Chelsea Journal; Origins; Pierian Spring; Writers' Quarterly; Germination; The New Quarterly; CV/II; Brick; English Quarterly; Waves; Gamut; West Coast Review; Prairie Journal; Northern Light; Squatchberry Journal; Nebula; Poetry Toronto; Alchemist. *Honours:* Hilroy Fellowship Award for Innovative Teaching, 1982; Pierian Spring Editor's Prize, 1982, 83. *Memberships:* Niagara Writers Group; Canadian Poets' Association; Canadian

Publishers' Association. *Address:* 11 Dundas Crescent, St Catharines, Ontario, L2T IT4, Canada.

BALTHAZAR, Robert Louis Marie, b. 21 Aug 1940, Antwerp. Writer. *Publications:* Poetry: Monnik Tee, 1961; Jaden Boek Jaspis, 1962; Jonathan Drinkt Weer, 1963; Alchimie, Een Toverboek, 1965; Geharnaste Kwetsbaarheid, 1968. Essay: Walkie Talkie 1, 1961. *Contributions to:* Gazet Van Antwerpen, Wij (art critic and columnist); Sinteze, Baal, Stuip, TNT (also co-editor); Nul; Kontrast; Tafelronde; Nouvelles a la main (poetry); Lecture, US-Literature, radio (BRT 3). *Membership:* Vereniging van Vlaamse Letterkundigen (VVL). *Address:* Goudbloemstraat 19, 2008 Antwerp, Belgium.

BALTZAR, Veijo Oskari, b. 9 June 1942, Kuopio, Finland. Author. *Major Publications:* The Burning Road, 1968; (Swedish Translation, 1969); The Blood Engagement, 1972; Mari, 1974; The Black Sarah's Cutglass Ball, 1978, childrens book dramatized for radio in Sweden and Finland; Dramas: The Black Whip, 1981; The Road, 1981; The Hungry Cranes, 1982; I Forge a Horse from a Stone, 1983; The Iron Nights, 1984. *Contributor to:* Helsingin Sanomat; Suomen Kuvalehti; Nya Pressen; and others. *Honour:* Theatre Prize, 1982 with Gypsy Theatre Drom. *Memberships:* Finnish Authors' Society; Finnish Playwriters' Society. *Address:* Juhaninkatu 18, 05830 Hyvinkää, Finland.

BALY, Lindsay Gordon, b. 4 Mar. 1927, Sydney, Australia. Editor. *Publication:* Ironbottom Sound, historical novel, World War II, in press. *Contributions to:* Melbourne Age, newspaper; Australian Veterinary Journal. *Membership:* Australian Society of Authors. *Literary Agent:* C Harold, Tapelk Ltd, Malvern, Worcestershire, England. *Address:* Moonlight Road, Kangaroo Ground, Victoria, Australia 3097.

BANCE, Alan Frederick, b. 7 Mar. 1939, London, England. University Professor of German Language and Literature. m. Sandra Davis, 31 Aug. 1964, London, 2 daughters. *Education:* BA Honours, University College, London; PhD, Selwyn College, Cambridge. *Publications:* The German Novel 1945–1960, 1980; Weimar Germany: Writers and Politics (Editor). 1982; Theodor Fontane: The Major Novels, 1982. *Contributions to:* Chapter in, The Second World War in Fiction (Editors H Klein, J Flower and E Homberger), 1984; Reviews for journals including: Times Literary Supplement; Germanistik; Modern Language Review; Articles in academic journals including: Forum For Modern Language Studies; Seminar; German Life and Letters; Festschriften. *Memberships:* Committee member 1982, Modern Humanities Research Association. *Address:* 8 Oakmount Avenue, Highfield, Southampton SO2 1DR, England.

BANGS, Carol Jane, b. 22 June 1949, Portland, Oregon, USA. Writer. m. James A Heynen, 1 Aug. 1973, Eugene, Oregon, 1 son, 1 daughter. *Education:* BA, Portland State University, 1970; MA 1972, PhD 1977, University of Oregon. *Literary Appointments:* Assistant Editor, Portland State Review, 1968–70; Assistant Editor, Northwest Review, 1971–75; Instructor, University of Oregon 1975, Boise State University 1976; Adjunct Professor, Western Washington University 1976–80, Peninsula College 1976–81, University of Washington 1983–84; Instructor, Bellevue College, 1980. *Publications:* Irreconcilable Differences, 1978; The Bones of the Earth, 1983. *Contributions to:* Northwest Review; College English; New Directions Annuals; University of Windsor Review; Malahat Review; Seattle Review; Concerning Poetry; Bellingham Review; Northwest America; The Fiddlehead; Modern Fiction Studies. *Honours:* NDEA Fellowship for Graduate Studies, 1971–74. *Memberships:* Modern Language Association; Philological Association of the Pacific Coast; Associated Writing Programs. *Address:* c/o Centrum Foundation, Box 1158, Port Townsend, WA 98368, USA.

BANKS, Lynne Reid, b. 1929, London, England. Writer. m. Chaim Stephenson, 1965, Nicosia, Cyprus, 3 sons. *Education:* Royal Academy of Dramatic Art. *Publications include:* The L-Shaped Room, 1960; An End to Running, 1962; Children at the Gate, 1968; The Backward Shadow, 1970; Two Is Lonely, 1974; Dark Quartet, 1976; My Darling Villain, for young adults, 1977; The Indian in the Cupboard, for children, 1980; Defy The Wilderness, 1981; The Warning Bell, 1984; 10 other books. *Contributions to:* Sunday Telegraph; Guardian; Times Educational Supplement; Times; Observer; The Spectator; Jewish Chronicle; McCalls; Ladies Home Journal; Good Housekeeping; etc. Plays for stage, radio and TV. *Honours:* Yorkshire Arts Literary Award, 1977; Western Australia Young Librarians Award; California Young Readers Medal, 1985. *Literary Agent:* Watson, Little Ltd. *Address:* c/o Watson, Little Limited, 26 Charing Cross Road, London WC2, England.

BANKS, Oliver Talcott, b. 14 Jan. 1941, Cambridge, Massachusetts, USA. Writer. m. Elaine M Arment, 28 Aug. 1971, Lincoln, Massachusetts. *Education:* MA, Boston University; MFA, Princeton University, 1966; PhD, Princeton University, 1975. *Publications:* Watteau and the North, 1977; The Rembrandt Panel, 1979; The Caravaggio Obsession, 1984. *Contributions:* of book reviews to, The Washington Post's Book World; Art and Auction; Art and Antiques. *Honour:* Nominated for Edgar Award for The Rembrandt Panel, 1979. *Membership:* The Writers Guild. *Literary Agent:* J Randall Williams III. *Address:* 195 Adams Street, Brooklyn, NY 11201, USA.

BANKS, Russell, b. 28 Mar. 1940, Newton, Massachusetts, USA. Novelist. m. (3) Kathy Walton Banks, 13 Mar. 1982, 4 daughters. *Education:* BA, English, Highest Honours, University of North Carolina. *Publications include:* Searching for Survivors, 1975; Family Life, 1975; Hamilton Stark, 1978; The New World, 1978; The Book of Jamaica, 1980; Trailerpark, 1982; The Relation of my Imprisonment, 1984; Continental Drift, 1985. *Contributions to:* New York Times Book Review; Washington Post; American Review; Vanity Fair; Antaeus; Partisan Review; New England Review; Fiction International; Boston Globe Magazine; etc. *Honours:* Best American Short Stories, 1971, 1985; Fels Award for Fiction, 1974; Prize Story, O Henry Awards, 1975; Guggenheim Fellow, 1976; NEA Fellowships, 1977, 1983; St Lawrence Award for Fiction, 1976; Others, 1976–85. *Memberships:* PEN; Authors Guild; Board of Directors 1968–71, Secretary 1970–71, Coordinating Council of Literary Magazines. *Literary Agent:* Ellen Levine Literary Agency. *Address:* c/o Ellen Levine Literary Agency, 432 Park Avenue South, Suite 1205, New York, NY 10016, USA.

BANKSON, Douglas Henneck, b. 13 May 1920, Valley, Washington, USA. Playwright; Teacher; Director. m. Beverly Olga Carlson, 12 June 1943, Tacoma, Washington, 2 sons, 1 daughter. *Education:* BA, 1943, MA, 1948, PhD, 1954, University of Washington. *Literary Appointments:* Instructor, Humanities, University of Idaho, 1955; Assistant professor, English, 1957, Associate professor, Drama, 1959, University of Montana; Professor, Creative writing, 1966–85, Head, Department of Creative Writing, 1978–83, Professor Emeritus, 1985–, University of British Columbia, Canada. *Publications:* Plays produced: Shellgame, 1960; Fallout, 1963; Resthome, 1965; Lenore Nevermore, 1972; Signore Lizard, 1974; Ella, 1981; Felicity, 1982; Mr Poe, 1985; author of numerous short works for stage and radio. *Honours:* Lifetime Achievement Award, Vancouver Professional Theatre Alliance, 1984. *Address:* 4722 West Second Avenue, Vancouver, British Columbia, Canada V6T 1B9.

BANNER, Bob, b. 9 Aug. 1951, Detroit, Michigan, USA. Publisher; Writer. *Education:* BA Political Psychology, Oakland University, USA; Publisher's Certificate, University of California, Berkeley. *Literary Appointments:* Publisher of Critique. *Contributor to:* Critique; Conspiracy Digest; New Age Journal. *Address:* P O Box 11451, Santa Rosa, CA 95406, USA.

BANNISTER, Patricia Valeria, b.21 Nov. 1923, London, England. Writer. Widow, 1 son, 1 daughter. *Education:* Business College. *Publications:* The Lord & The Gypsy (UK, Debt of Honour), 1978; Love's Duet (UK, A Perfect Match), 1979; Mistress of Willowvale, 1980; Nanette, 1981; Some Brief Folly, 1981; Feather Castles, 1982; Married Past Redemption, 1983; Noblest Frailty, 1983; The Wagered Widow, 1984; Sanguinet's Crown, 1985; Golden Chronicles Saga, Book 1, Practice to Deceive, 1985. *Contributions:* Biographical articles, trade papers. *Honours:* Barbara Cartland Loving Cup for idealising romance, 1983; Romantic Times Award, best Regency novel, 1983. *Membership:* Authors Guild, USA. *Literary Agent:* Patrick Delahunt, John Schaffner Associates Inc, New York. *Address:* c/o Patrick Delahunt, John Schaffner Association Inc, 114 E 28th Street, New York, NY 10016, USA.

BANTING, Peter Myles, b. 17 Mar. 1936, Hamilton, Canada. Professor. m. Wendy Sharon Papple, 24 Apr. 1981, Burlington, 1 son, 1 daughter. *Education:* BA, 1958, MBA, 1965, McMaster University; PhD, Michigan State University, 1971. *Publications:* Canadian Cases in Marketing, 1968; Marketing in Canada, 1973; Canadian Marketing, 1977. Numerous contributions to various journals. *Address:* KTH 238, Faculty of Business, McMaster University, Hamilton, Ontario, Canada, L8S 4M4.

BANTOCK, Gavin Marcus August, b. Apr. 1939. University Teacher. *Education:* New College, Oxford University, 1960–63. m. *Appointments include:* English Chair and Head of Department, 3 secondary schools in UK, 1964–69; Professor of English, Reitaku University, Kashiwa-shi, Chiba-ken, Japan. *Publications:* Christ (epic poem), 1965; Juggernaut, 1968; A New Thing Breathing, 1969; Anglo-Saxon Translations (Anhaga) 1971; Eirenikon, 1973; Faber Book of 29th Century Verse, poems, 1975; Dragons, 1979; Pioneers of English Poetry, 1979; Towards Humanity, 1985. *Contributor to:* Spectator; Punch; Isis; Poetry Review; New Measure; Second Aeon; Pembroke Magazine, USA; Tri-quarterly, USA; Oxford Book of 20th Century English Verse. *Honours:* Richard Hillary Award, 1964; Alice Hunt-Bartlett Award, 1966; Eric Gregory Award, 1969. *Memberships:* Advst to University Shakespeare Association, Tokyo; Founder and Director, Fests English Speaking Theatre, Tokyo, 1982–. *Address:* Reitaku University, Kashiwa-shi, Chiba-ken, Japan.

BARASH, Samuel Theodore, b. 16 Apr 1921, Brooklyn, New York, USA. Real Estate Appraiser/Author. m. Selma Silber, 1 Sep. 1946, Richmond Hill, New York, 1 daughter. *Education:* BSS, College of City of New York, 1943. *Literary Appointments:* Technical Editor, Consumers Digest and Moneymaker Magazines, 1979–83; Technical Editor, Prentice Hall Inc, Publishers, 1980–83. *Publications:* Standard Real Estate Appraising Manual, 1979; How to Reduce Your Real Estate Fakes, 1979; How to Cash-in on Little-Known Local Real Estate Profit Opportunities, 1981; Complete Guide to Appraising Condominiums and Co-operatives, 1982; Encyclopedia of Appraisal Forms and Model Reports, 1983. *Contributions to:* Consumers Digest Magazine; Moneymaker Magazine and various other publications. *Membership:* Authors' Guild. *Address:* RD 1, Box 130, Lakes Road, Monroe, NY 10950, USA.

BARBA, Harry, b. 17 June, 1922, Bristol, Connecticut, USA. Educator; Writer; Publisher; University Professor; Director of Writer. *Education:* AB, Bates, 1944; MA, Harvard University, USA, 1951; MFA, University of Iowa, 1960; PhD, ibid. 1963. *Publications:* For the Grape Season, 1960; The Bulbuls, 1963; 3 by Harry Barba, 1967; One of a Kind–the Many Faces and Voices of America, 1976; The Day the World Went Sane, 1979; What's Cooking in Congress, 1979; The Gospel According to Everyman, 1981; What;'s Cooking in Congress II, 1985; Trip to Byzantium (novel), 1985.

Contributor to: Univ Review; S W Review; Quartet, etc. *Honours Include:* Various fellowships and grants. *Memberships Include:* Authors Guild Inc; Authors League of America, Inc; PEN; Poets and Writers; MLA. *Address:* 47 Hyde Boulevarde, Ballston Spa, NY 12020, USA.

BARBER, James Geoffrey, b. 4 Jan. 1952, Washington DC, USA. Historian, National Portrait Gallery, Smithsonian Institution. *Education:* BA History, St Francis College, Loretto, Pennsylvania, 1973; MA History, Virginia Polytechnic Institute & State University, 1977. *Major Publications:* We Never Sleep: The First 50 Years of the Pinkertons, 1981; The Godlike Black Dan, 1982; Portraits from the New Deal, 1983; Blessed are the Peacemakers, 1983. *Contributor to:* Guide to Alexandria, 1978; Alexandria History, 1981; Smithsonian, 1981. *Address:* 6609 East Wakefield Drive C-1, Alexandria, VA 22307, USA.

BARBER, Laurie Ernest, b. 13 Sep. 1940, Newcastle, New South Wales, Australia. Newspaper Publisher. m. Glenda Joy Parfitt, 15 Feb. 1964, Inverell, NSW, 2 sons, 2 daughters. *Major Publication:* World of its own (editor), 1981. *Honours:* Member of Golden Dozen, International Society of Weekly Newspaper Editors, 1980; Runner-up, Graham Perkin Memorial Australian Journalist of the Year, 1980. *Memberships:* International Society of Weekly Newspaper Editors; Central processing unit; International Press Institute; Vice-President, New South Wales Country Press Association. *Address:* 9 Marsden Crescent, Port Macquarie, 2444, New South Wales, Australia.

BARBER, Lynda Graham, b. 12 Dec. 1944, Pittsburgh, Pennsylvania, USA. Writer. m. Ray C Barber, 3 June 1967, Washington, Pennsylvania, USA. *Education:* BA, Indiana University of Pennsylvania. *Major Publications:* Who Lives Inside? (Juvenile), 1976; The Kit Furniture Book, 1982; Round Fish, Flatish & Other Animal Changes (Juvenile), 1983; Personality Decorating, 1986. *Contributor to:* Redbook; Mademoiselle; Ms; Savvy; Country Journal; Travel & Leisure; Family Circle; and other. *Honour:* AIGA Award 1983 for, The Kit Furniture Book. *Literary Agent:* Edite Kroll. *Address:* 295 Washington Avenue, Brooklyn, NY 11205, USA.

BARBER, Richard William, b. 30 Oct. 1941, Dunmow, Essex, England. Publisher. *Education:* History, Corpus Christi College, University of Cambridge (Trevelyan Scholar). *Major Publications include:* Arthur of Albion, 1961, 1972; Henry Plantagenet, 1964, 1974; The Knight of Chivalry, 1970, 1974; King Arthur in Legend & History, 1972; Dictionary of Fabulous Beasts, 1973, 1976; The Figure of Arthur, 1973, 1977; Edward Prince of Wales & Aquitaine, 1978; The Devil's Crown, 1978; The Arthurian Legends, 1979; A Dictionary of Mythology, 1979; A Strong Land and A Sturdy (childrens) 1977; Tournaments, 1978; The Penguin Guide to Medieval England, 1984; The Pasrons, 1984. *Honours:* Somerset Maugham Award, 1971; Times Educational Supplement Junior Information Book Award, 1978; several Book Club Choices/alternatives; Fellowships: Royal Society of Literature, Society of Antiquaries, Royal Historical Society. *Address:* Stangrove Hall, Alderton, Nr Woodbridge, Suffolk IP12 2BL, England.

BARBOSA, Miguel, b. 22 Nov. 1925, Lisbon, Portugal. Writer, Painter. *Education:* Economics & Finance, University of Lisbon. *Major Publications:* (short stories:) Retalhos de Vida, 1955; Manta de Trapos, 1962; (plays:) O Palheiro, 1963; Os Carnivoros, 1964, 1973; O Piquenique, 1964, 1973; O Insecticida, 1965, 1974; A Mulher que Pariu a France, 1971; Los Profetas de la Paja, 1973; How New York was destroyed by Rats, 1977; The Materialisation of Love, 1978; (novels:) Rineu do Morro, 1972, 1975; Mulher Macumba, 1973; A Pileca no Poleiro, 1976; As Confissoes de Vom Cacadon de Dinossauros, 1981; Esta Louca Profissao de Escritor, 1983; Cantas a Vom Fogo-Fatuo, 1985. *Contributor to:* Various Publications,

including: Mester (University College of Los Angeles). *Honours:* Recipient, 1st Prize, Maria Tereza Alves Viana Theatre, Sao Paulo, Brazil; Prix 'Nu', Jubilé Mondial d'arts Plastiques, Nice, France, 1984; Honorable Mention, ler Quadriennale Mondiale des Beaux Arts, Lyon, France, 1985. *Memberships include:* Portuguese Society of Writers; Portuguese Society of Authors; International Platform Association; International Biographical Association. *Address:* Avenue Jao Crisostomo 9–12, Lisbon 1000, Portugal.

BARBOUR, Douglas Fleming, b. 21 Mar. 1940, Winnipeg, Manitoba, Canada. Professor of English Literature, University of Alberta. m. Sharon Nicoll, 21 May 1966, Toronto. *Education:* BA, Acadia University, 1962; MA, Dalhousie University, 1964; PhD, Queens University, Kingston, Ontario, 1976. *Publications include:* Poetry: Land Fall, 2nd edition 1973; White, 1972; he. & she. &.., 1974; Shore Lines, 1979; The Harbingers, 1984; Visible Visions: Selected Poems, 1984; etc. Editorial: The Story So Far Five, 1978; The Maple Laugh Forever: Anthology of Canadian Comic Poetry, with Stephen Scobie, 1981; Writing Right: Poetry by Canadian Women, with Marni Stanley, 1982; Three Times Five: Short Stories by Harris, Sawai, Stenson, 1983: Richard Sommer: Selected & New Poems, 1984. *Criticism:* Worlds Out of Words: The SF Novels of Samuel R Delany, 1979; Over 25 articles on Canadian literature, science fiction & fantasy, contemporary writing, in various literary journals. Poetry Editor, Canadian Forum, 1978–80. Member, Editorial Boards, Quarry, 1966–68, White Pelican, 1971–76, NeWest Press, Longspoon Press. Poetry Readings, all over Canada, New York, Europe. *Address:* 10808 75th Avenue, Edmonton, Alberta, Canada T6E 1K2.

BARCLAY, John Bruce, b. 30 Nov. 1909, Edinburgh, Scotland. University Lecturer; Author; Producer for Educational Films. *Education:* MA, PhD, Edinburgh University. *Publications:* Edinburgh, 1965; The Tounis Scule, 1974; When Work is Done, 1971; Children's Cinema Clubs, 1951; Children's Film Tastes, 1956; Viewing Tastes of Adolescents, 1961; Editor, Looking At Lothian, 1979 (for Royal Geological Society); The SSC Story 1784–1984; Pill Box and Service Cap, 1985. *Contributor to:* Scottish Educational Journal; Scottish Adult Education; Times Educational Supplements; Lo Spettacolo; National Press; Honorary Editor, Scottish Journal of Adult Education, 1973–75. *Memberships:* President, Rotary Club of Edinburgh; Royal Overseas Club. *Address:* 25 Gardiner Road, Edinburgh EH4 3RP, Scotland.

BARESOVA, Vera, b. Czechoslovakia. Actress; Director. *Major Publications:* Stage adaptations of, Platero and I (Juan Ramon Jiménez), Edgar Allan Poe: Poetic One-Man Theatre, François Villon: Poetic One-Man Theatre, White Nights (by Dostojevski). *Address:* Utrechtsedwarsstraat 93/III, 1017 WD Amsterdam, Netherlands.

BARHAM, Patte, b. Los Angeles, California, USA. Author; Columnist. *Education:* University of Southern California; University of Arizona. *Major Publications:* Pin-Up Poems; Operation Nightmare, 1952; Rasputin, Man Behind the Myth, (with Maria Rasputin), 1978. *Contributor to:* Society West, (publisher), 1975–78; Syndicated Columnist, Meredith Newspapers, Herald Community Newspapers, Los Angeles; Sterling Newspapers, Canada. *Address:* 100 Fremont Place, Los Angeles, CA 90005, USA.

BARKER, A L, b. 13 Apr. 1918, Kent, England. Retired Journalist. *Literary Appointments:* Member of panel of judges, Katherine Mansfield Prize, 1984. *Publications:* Innocents, 1947; A Case Examined, 1965; The Middling, 1967; John Brown's Body, 1969; Femina Real, 1971; A Source of Embarassment, 1974; Life Stories, 1981; Relative Successes, 1984; No Word of Love, 1985. *Contributions to:* New Statesman; Quarto; Harper's Bazaar; Bonnier's Literary magazine; Botteghe Oscure; Harper's magazine; Good Housekeeping; Pick of Today's Short Stories; Woman and Beauty; Penguin

Modern Stories; Nova; Fiction Magazine; Short Story Monthly; Cosmopolitan; Vole; Woman; English Story; Women's Journal. *Honours:* Atlantic Award in Literature, 1945; Somerset Maugham Award, 1947; Cheltenham Festival of Literature Award, 1963; Arts Council Award, 1970; South East Arts Creative Book Award, 1981. *Memberships:* Fellow, Royal Society of Literature; Executive Committee, PEN English Centre. *Address:* 103 Harrow Road, Carshalton, Surrey, England.

BARKER, (Antony) Revel, b. 10 Dec. 1944, Leeds, England Journalist. m. Angela M. Pearce Greenshields, 1977, 1 son, 1 daughter. *Literary Appointments:* Reporter, Pudsey and Stanningley News, 1961–62; Reporter, Yorkshire Evening Post, 1962–65; Reporter, Daily Mirror, 1965–76; Reporter, Sunday Mirror, 1976–78; Defence Correspondent and Foreign Editor, Sunday Mirror, 1978–85; Group Editorial Manager, 1985–. *Address:* 33 Holborn, London EC1P 1DQ, England.

BARKER, Dennis, b. 21 June 1929, Lowestoft, England. Journalist; Novelist. *Publications:* (novels): Candidate of Promise, 1969; The Scandalisers, 1974; (non-fiction): Soldiering On, 1981; One Man's Estate, 1983; Parian Ware, 1985. *Contributions to:* Suffolk Chronicle and Mercury, Ipswich (Reporter, 1947–48); East Anglian Daily Times (Reporter, Feature Writer, Theatre and Film Critic, 1948–58); Express & Star, Wolverhampton (Estates and Property Editor, Feature Writer, Theatre Critic, Columnist, 1958–63); The Guardian (Midlands Corespondent, 1963–67; Reporter, Feature Writer, Columnist, 1967–); Punch; BBC. *Memberships:* National Union of Journalists, Secretary, Suffolk Branch, 1953–58, Chairman, 1958, Home Counties District Council, 1956–57; Life Member, Newspaper Press Fund; Writers Guild of Great Britain; Broadcasting Press Guild. *Literary Agent:* David Higham Associates Limited. *Address:* c/o David Higham Associates Limited, 5-8 Lower John Street, Golden Square, London, W1R 4HA, England.

BARKER, Paul, b. 24 Aug, 1935, Halifax, Yorkshire, England. Magazine Editor/Editor, New Society. m. Sally Huddleston, 3 sons, 1 daughter. *Education:* MA, Oxford University. *Literary Appointment:* Director 1982–85, Advisory Editor 1985–, The Fiction Magazine. *Publications:* Editor: A Sociological Portrait 1972; Editor: One for Sorrow, Two for Joy, 1972; Editor: The Social Sciences Today, 1975; Editor: Arts in Society, 1977; Editor: The Other Britain, 1982; Editor: Founders of the Welfare State, 1985. *Contributor to:* Various magazines, newspapers, radio and TV programmes. *Address:* 15 Dartmouth Park Avenue, London NW5.

BARKSDALE, William Evans, b. 9 May 1937, Fort Smith, Arkansas, USA. Agricultural Journalist; Photographer. m. Sandra May Ramsey, 19 June 1959, Fort Smith, 2 sons. *Education:* BSc, Agriculture, University of Arkansas. *Literary Appointments:* Associate Editor, Progressive Farmer, 1959–65; Senior Editor, Editor-in-Chief, Farm Quarterly, 1965–73; Freelance agricultural journalist. 1975–. *Contributions to:* Progressive Farmer; Farm Quarterly; Cotton Farming; Successful Farming; Southern Farm & Ranch. *Address:* PO Box 17726, Memphis, TN 38117, USA.

BARLING, Thomas F R, b. 30 Dec. 1936, London, England. Author; Film Director. m. 21 Mar. 1985, London. *Education:* National Diploma in Design, London School of Printing and Graphic Arts. *Publications:* Bergman's Blitz, 1973; The Shooter Man, 1974; The Snowdon Labyrinth, 1975; The Olympic Sleeper, 1979; Goodbye Piccadilly, 1980; Bikini Red North, 1981; The Pagan Land, 1981; Terminate with Prejudice, 1982; The Sirens of Autumn, 1983; The Smoke, 1986; God Is an Executioner, 1987. *Literary Agent:* Mark Lucas, Frazer & Dunlop. *Address:* c/o Fraser and Dunlop, 91 Regent Street, London W1R 8RU, England.

BARLOW, Derrick, b. 29 Apr. 1921, Stoke-on-Trent, England. Fellow, Jesus College, Oxford, England.

Education: M Litt, MA, Queen's College, Oxford University. *Publications:* F Hebbel, Selected Essays, 1962; C Zuckmayer, Three Stories, 1963; C Zuckmayer, Die Fastnachtbeicht, 1966; C Sternheim, Bürger Schippel, 1969; Hebbel & Hauptmann, Makers of 19th Century Culture, 1982. *Contributions to:* German Life & Letters; Modern German Studies; Modern Language Review; Times Educational Supplement; Times Higher Educational Supplement; Journal of English & Germanic Philol. *Memberships:* English Goethe Society; Modern Humanities Research Association; Institute of Germanic Studies; Conference of University Teachers of German. *Address:* 77 Mill Street, Kidlington, Oxford, England.

BARNABY, Charles Frank, b. 27 Sep. 1927. Consultant; Writer. m. Wendy Elizabeth, 19 Dec. 1972, Stockholm, Sweden, 1 son, 1 daughter. *Education:* MSc, PhD, University of London. *Major Publications:* Radionuclides in Medicine, 1970; Man and the Atom, 1971; Preventing the Spread of Nuclear Weapons (editor), 1971; Anti-ballistic Missile Systems (co-editor), 1971; Arms Uncontrolled (co-author), 1975; Nuclear Energy, 1980; Future Warfare (editor and co-author), 1982; Prospects for Peace, 1983; The Automated Battlefield, 1986. *Contributor to:* New Scientist. *Honour:* Honorary Doctorate, Free University, Amersterdam, Netherlands. *Literary Agent:* Judith Hall, London. *Address:* Brandreth, Chilbolton, Stockbridge, Hampshire SO20 6AW, England.

BARNES, James John, b. 16 Nov. 1931, St Paul, Minnesota, USA. Professor of History. m. Patience Rogers Plummer, 9 July 1955, Bronxville, New York, 1 son, 1 daughter. *Education:* BA magna cum laude, Amherst College, 1954; BA 1956, MA Oxon 1961, New College, Oxford; PhD, Harvard University, 1960; DHL, College of Wooster, 1976. *Publications:* Free Trade in Books: A Study of the London Book Trade since 1800, 1964; Authors, Publishers and Politicians: The Quest for an Anglo-American Copyright Agreement 1815–54, 1974; Hitler's Mein Kampf in Britain and America, 1930–39 (with Patience P Barnes), 1980. *Contributions to:* Articles, reviews and papers to publications including: American Literature; The American Oxonian; Literature and History; Papers of the Bibliographical Society of America. *Honours include:* Rhodes Scholarship, New College, Oxford, 1954–56; Woodrow Wilson Fellowship, Harvard University, 1956–57; Fulbright Scholarship, 1978; Several research grants. *Memberships include:* Phi Beta Kappa; American Historical Association; Conference on British Studies; Society for Values in Higher Education; The United Oxford & Cambridge Club, London; Dominion Students, London; The Bibliographical Society, UK; National Book League, UK. *Address:* 7 Locust Hill, Crawfordsville, IN 47933, USA.

BARNES, Jim Weaver, b. 22 Dec. 1933, Summerfield, Oklahoma, USA. Editor, Professor of Comparative Literature. m. Carolyn Louise Turpin, 23 Nov. 1973, Kirksville, Missouri, USA, 2 sons. *Education:* BA, Southeastern Oklahoma State University, 1964; MA 1966, PhD 1972, Comparative Literature, University of Arkansas. *Literary Appointments:* Editor, The Chariton Review, 1975; Member, Literature Panel, Coordinating Council of Literary Magazines, 1981; Professor of Comparative Literature, NE Missouri State University. *Major Publications:* The American Book of the Dead, 1982; Summons & Signs: Poems by Dagmar Nick (translation from German), 1980; The Fish on Poteau Mountain (poems), 1980; Work included in Carriers of the Dream Wheel: Contemporary Native American Poetry, 1975. *Contributor to:* The Chicago Review; The Nation; Mundus Artium; Southwest Review; Laurel Review; Panache; Poetry Now; New Letters; and over 100 others. *Honours:* National Endowment for the Arts Fellowship in Poetry, 1978; Translation Prize, Columbia University, 1980; Faculty Enrichment Grant, Canadian Government. *Memberships:* Modern Language Association; Delegate-at-Large in Ethnic Studies, 1980–82; Co-ordinating Council of Literary Magazines. *Literary Agent:* The

Chariton Review. *Address:* The Chariton Review, NE Missouri State University, Kirksville, MO 63501, USA.

BARNES, John (Sir), b. 22 June 1917, London, England. H.M. Diplomatic Service (retired). m. Cynthia Stewart, 1 May 1948, London, 2 sons, 3 daughters. *Education:* Classical Tripos I & II First Class, Porson Scholar, Trinity College, Cambridge, 1939. *Publication:* Ahead of His Age: Bishop Barnes of Birmingham, 1979. *Contributions to:* Encounter; Survival; Modern Churchman; Asian Affairs; Cambridge Review; Studia Diplomatica, (Belgium); Christian News From Israel. *Address:* Hampton Lodge, Hurstpierpoint, Sussex BN6 9QN, England.

BARNES, Kenneth Charles, b. 17 Sep. 1903, London, England. Headmaster. m. (1) Frances Jackson, 27 Aug. 1927, Brighton, died 1969, 1 son, 1 daughter; (2) Eleanor Spray, 29 Nov. 1969, Croydon. *Education:* BSC, Hons, London MRST. *Publications:* Sex, Friendship and Marriage, 1938; He and She, 1958; The Creative Imagination, 1960; The Involved Man, 1966; Making Judgements and Decisions, 1971; A Vast Bundle of Opportunities, 1975; Has Science Exploded God?, 1976; Energy Unbound, 1980; Integrity in the Arts, 1984. *Contributions to:* Listener; New Scientist; Quaker Periodicals. *Address:* Ingsway, Bolton Percy, York, England.

BARNES, Richard Gordon, b. 5 Nov. 1932. Poet; Professor of English. *Education:* BA, Pomona College, USA, 1954; MA, Harvard University, 1955; PhD, Claremont Graduate School, Riverside, 1958–59; Freelance, 1959–61; Professor of English, Director of Creative Writing, Pomona College, Claremont, California. *Publications:* Plays and Fugitive Essays 1963–66, 1966; The Complete Poems of R G Barnes, 1972; Thirty One Views of San Bernardino, 1975; Hungry Again for Next Day, 1978; Lyrical Ballads, 1979; A Lake on the Earth, 1981. *Contributions to:* Paris Review; Ironwood; Buttons; Stooge; Green House; Beloit Poetry Journal; Momentum; Loon; Fat Point; The Pacific Circle; Byzzyva; Light Year; Field. *Address:* Department of English, Pomona College, Claremont, CA 91711, USA.

BARNSTONE, Willis, b. 13 Nov. 1927, Lewiston, Maine, USA. Poet; Professor. m. Helle Tzalopoulou, 1 June 1949, Paris, France, 2 sons, 1 daughter. *Education:* BA, Bowdoin College, 1948; MA, Columbia University, 1956; PhD, Yale University, 1960. *Publications:* From This White Island, 1959; Greek Lyric Poetry, 1962; Sappho, 1965; Modern European Poetry, 1967; China Poems, 1976; Borges at Eighty, 1982; The Poetics of Ecstasy, 1982; The Other Bible, 1984. *Contributions to:* Magazines and Journals, including: The New Yorker; Times Literary Supplement; New York Times; New York Review of Books; The Nation; Kenyon Review; Partisan Review. *Honours:* Nomination, Pulitzer Prize 1960 and 1976, National Book Award 1977; Lucille Medwick Memorial Award, Poetry Society of America, 1978. *Memberships:* American Pen Club; Poetry Society of America. *Literary Agent:* Sallie Gouverneur. *Address:* Comparative Literature, BH 402, Indiana University, Bloomington, IN 47405, USA.

BARON, Alec, b. Leeds, England. Playwright. m. Judith Sally Edelston, 1 son, 3 daughters. *Publications:* Many plays performed on radio, television and in the theatre. *Contributions to:* Arts Yorkshire, Theatre Correspondent, etc. *Honour:* Joint Winner, BBC/YAA Playwriting Competition, 1977. *Membership:* Writers Guild of Great Britain. *Address:* 19 Park View Crescent, Leeds LS8 2ES, England.

BARON, Dennis E, b. 9 May 1944, New York City, USA. Professor of English and Linguistics. m. Iryce White, 21 Oct. 1979, 2 daughters. *Education:* AB, Brandeis University, 1965; MA, Columbia University, 1968; PhD, University of Michigan, 1971. *Literary Appointments:* Professor of English and Linguistics, University of Illinois, 1975–; Director of Rhetoric, University of Illinois, 1985–; Editor, Publication of the American Dialect Society, 1985–. *Publications:* Case Grammar and Diachronic English Syntax, 1974; Grammar and Good Taste, Reforming the American Language, 1982; Going Native: The Regeneration of Saxon English, 1982; Grammar and Gender, 1986. *Contributions to:* American Speech; College English. *Honours:* Fulbright Lecturer, University de Poitiers, France, 1978–79; Associate, Center for Advanced Study, Université of Illinois, 1984–85. *Memberships:* American Dialect Society; National Council of Teachers of English (Member, Commission on the English Language); Modern Language Association; Linguistic Society of America. *Address:* Department of English, University of Illinois, 608 S Wright Street, Urbana, IL 61801, USA.

BARONE, Dennis, b. 11 Mar. 1955, Teaneck, New Jersey, USA. Teacher; Writer. m. Deborah Ducoff, 21 Aug. 1977, Rahway, New Jersey. *Education:* BA, Bard College; MA, PhD, University of Pennsylvania. *Major Publications:* Echo of the Imperfect, 1981; The House of Land, 1985. *Contributor to:* Boundary 2; American Book Review; Partisan Review; Credences; and others. *Memberships:* Coordinating Council of Literary Magazines; Library Company of Philadelphia; Modern Language Association. *Address:* c/o 1200 Farrell Terrace, Rahway, NJ 07065, USA.

BARONI, Christophe, b. 2 Sep. 1934, Villars, Vaud, Switzerland. Writer. *Education:* License en Classics, Doctor in Educational Science. University of Lausanne; Trained as Psychoanalyst, Geneva. *Publications:* Nietzsche educateur, 1961; Introduction à la psychologie des profondeurs, 1966; Les Parents, ces inconnus, 1969; L'infidélité, pourquoi?, 1970; Mais avec amour, 1971; Mieux que la pilule: la vasectomie, 1972; Le sexe fort serait-il, inconsciemment, le sexe faible?, 1973; Ce que Nietzsche a vraiment dit, 1975. *Contributions to:* Swiss radio and television; Construire; Ouverture, Founder Editor. *Honours:* Prize for doctoral thesis, Lausanne University. *Memberships:* Swiss Society of Writers; Geneva Society of Writers; Vaud Association of Writers. *Address:* Tattes-d'Oie 85, CH–1260 Nyon, Switzerland.

BARR, Densil, b. Harrogate, Yorkshire, England. Author. *Major Publications:* The Man With Only One Head (novel), 1955; Radio Plays broadcast: The Clapham Lamp-post Saga, 1967, 1968, 1969, 1981; Gladys on the Warddrobe, 1970, 1971, 1972, 1983; But Petrovsky Goes on for Ever, 1971, 1972, 1973, 1975, 1985; The Last Tramp, 1972, 1973; The Square at Bastogne, 1973, 1974; The Battle of Brighton Beach, 1974; To a Green World Far Away, 1975, 1976, 1977; With Puffins for Pawns, 1976, 1979; Anatomy of an Alibi, 1978, 1982; The Speech, 1979; Two Gaps in the Curtain, 1979, 1982; Klemp's Diary, 1980; Who was Karl Raeder?, 1980; The Boy in the Cellar, 1981; The Glory Hallelujah Microchip, 1982; The Dog that was only a Prophet, 1982, 1983; The Mythical Isles, 1983; St Paul Transferred, 1983. *Contributor to:* Transatlantic Review; International Storyteller; Kolokon. *Membership:* Fellow PEN. *Address:* 15 Churchfields, Broxbourne, Hertfordshire EN10 7JU, England.

BARR, Patricia Miriam, b. 25 Apr. 1934, Norwich, Norfolk, England. Writer. *Education:* BA, English Literature, University of Birmingham; MA, English, University College, London. *Major Publications:* The Coming of the Barbarians, 1967; The Deer Cry Pavilion, 1968; A Curious Life for a Lady 1970; To China with Love 1972; The Menyahills 1976; Taming the Jungle 1978; Chinese Alice 1981; Uncut Jade 1983; Kenjiro 1985. *Honour:* Winston Churchill Fellowship for Historical Biography, 1972. *Membership:* Society of Authors. *Literary Agent:* Carol Smith, 25 Hornton Court, London W8. *Address:* Flat 2, 25 Montpelier Row, Blackheath, London SE3, England.

BARR, Robert R, b. 20 Dec. 1931, Peoria, Illinois, USA. Writer & Translator. m. Marilyn Fish, 7 Dec. 1974, 1 daughter. *Education:* Marquette University, 1948–49; AB 1954, MA, 1955. University of St Louis, USA;

Graduate study, 1959–63; STD, Institute Catholique de Paris, France, 1967. *Literary Appointments:* Teacher, Kapaun High School, Wichita, Kansas, 1956–59; Vice-Rector, Russian Papal College, Rome, Italy, 1969–70; Assistant Professor of Theology, St Anselm's College, Manchester, New Hampshire, 1970–71; Religious Editor, Silver Burdett Co, Publisher, Morristown, New Jersey, 1974–79; Editor, Today's Parish, 1979–80; Lecturer in Philosophy, University of Connecticut, 1980–; Entered Society of Jesus 1949, ordained Byzantine Catholic Priest, 1962. *Major Publications:* Main Currents in Early Christian Thought, 1966; To Remember Jesus: The Meaning of Mass for Children, 1972; Breve Patrologia, 1982; What is The Bible?, (juvenile), 1983; numerous translations from 9 modern & ancient languages. *Contributor to:* Modern Schoolman; New Catholic World; Laval Theologique et Philosophique. *Memberships:* Religious Education Association of USA & Canada. *Address:* 7 Old Colony Road, North Stonington, CT 06359, USA.

BARREAU, Jean-Claude, b. 10 May 1933, Paris, France. Counseller a la Presidence de la Republique. m. Lefebure Segolene, 23 Oct. 1971, Paris, 1 son, 1 daughter. *Education:* Lic-Law; Lic.Hol. *Publications include:* What is the Trouble?, 1969; Who is God, 1971; The Prayer and the Drug, 1974; The Right Way to Deal with Religion, 1976; Les Memoires de Jesus, 1978; La Traversée de l'islande Roman, 1979; Le Vent du Desert, 1981; Les Innocent, de Pigalle, 1983; Essay, Que Vive La France, 1985. *Contributor to:* Express; Literary Critic; Le Monde. *Honours:* Prize Noel, 1967; Recipient, various other honours and awards including Director, Edition Belfond, Edition Nathan. *Membership:* Literary Society. *Address:* Palais De L'Elysee, Rue du Fl St Honore, 75008, Paris, France.

BARRETT, Charles Peter, b. 30 June 1939, London, England. Journalist. m. Raye Elizabeth Marshall, 30 Nov. 1967, at Sydney, New South Wales, 2 sons, 1 daughter. *Education:* Diploma of Physical Education, Loughborough, England. *Literary Appointments Include:* News Editor, The Financial Times; Editor: Timber Trades Yearbook; Fire Protection Year Book; Shipping Marks on Timber; Australian and NZ General Practitioner; Australasian Weekly Manufacturer; Australian Mining; Editor and Publisher, What's On Video. *Publications:* The Award Winning Book of the Award Winning Film, 1970; The Australian Video Movie Book. *Contributions include:* Thousands of contributions to various publications on a very diverse range of subjects. *Memberships:* National Union of Journalists; Australian Journalists Association. *Address:* P O Box 12, Rockdale, NSW 2216, Australia.

BARRETT, Evelyn Mary, b.24 July 1928, Northolt, Middlesex, England. Magazine Editor. m. Charles Barrett, 4 June 1949, Ewell, Surrey, 1 son. *Literary Appointments:* Editor, Gemcraft; Editor, Popular Crafts; Editor, Homebrew Supplier (continuing); Editor, Model Hobby Trader (continuing). *Publications:* Guide to Good Craft Suppliers, 1982; Guide to Good Craft Suppliers, 1984; Guide to Special Interest Holidays, 1984; Craft and Hobby Breaks, 1985. *Contributor to:* Gemcraft; Popular Crafts; Golden Hands; Homebrew Supplier; Model Hobby Trader. *Address:* ACE Publishing Ltd, Liberty House, 222 Regent Street, London W1R 6AH.

BARRETT, Harry Bemister, b. 29 May 1922, Port Dover, Ontario, Canada. Teacher; Farmer. *Education:* BSA, University of Toronto, 1949. *Publications:* Nineteenth Century Journals and Paintings of William Pope, (M F Feheley), 1976; Burning of Dover, 1814, (Cine Press), 1976; Lore & Legends of Long Point, (Burns & MacEachern), 1978. *Contributions to:* Treasures of Canada; Nature Canada; Ontario Naturalist; Past Editor, Ontario Agricultural Sci, etc. *Memberships:* include Agricultural Institute of Canada; Soil Conservation Society of America; Past Local President, Ontario Institute of Agrologists. *Honours:* Combat Medals, World War II. *Address:* 21 Bridge Street, Port Dover, Ontario NOA INO, Canada.

BARRETT, Helen Elizabeth-Anne, b. 20 Aug. 1942, Adelaide, Australia. Writer, Publisher. *Literary Appointments:* Publisher, D'Artagnan Publishing, Adelaide, Australia, 1982. *Publications:* A Good Year For Riding, 1982; Waminda, 1982; A Good Christmas for Riding, 1985. *Contributions to:* Go-Set and Juke, Rock and Roll magazines, 1969–75; Hoofs and Horn, National Rider and The Australian Horse and Rider, Australian equestrian magazines, 1977–; Lifestyle Garden series. *Memberships:* Australian Society of Authors; Australian Book Publishers' Association; Australian Journalists' Association. *Address:* 10 Burton Avenue, Beaumont, South Australia 5066, Australia.

BARRETT, Jeffrey William, b. 17 Oct. 1944, Boston, Massachusetts, USA. Consultancy Company President. m. Shirley Zamora. *Education:* BA, University of Notre Dame; MA, Johns Hopkins School of Advanced International Studies. *Publications:* Impulse to Revolution in Latin America, 1985. *Contributions to:* Survey; Foreign Service Journal. *Address:* 1419 East Capitol Street South East, Washington, DC 20003, USA.

BARRETT, Peter, b. 30 June 1934, London, England. Journalist; Broadcaster. m. Raye, 30 Nov. 1968, 2 sons, 1 daughter. *Education:* Diploma, Physical Education (Lough). *Appointments:* President, Clive Cussler Pitt Society, 1970; President, Robert Ludlum Appreciation Club, 1975; Vice-Marshall, Alida Baxter Lovers Association, 1980. *Publications:* The Award Winning Book of the Award Winning Film, 1970; Australian Mining Year book, 1980, 1981, 1982, 1983, 1984, 1985; Typical Day in the Office, 1984. *Contributor to:* Numerous publications including General Practitioner; Freight News Weekly; What's on Video; etc. *Address:* P O Box 12, Rockdale, New South Wales 2216, Australia.

BARRICELLI, Jean-Pierre, b. 5 June 1924, Cleveland, Ohio, USA. Professor. m. Norma Gaeta, 19 Oct. 1957, Boston, Massachusetts, 1 son, 2 daughters. *Education:* BA, 1947, MA, 1948, PhD, 1953, Harvard University. *Literary Appointments:* Assistant Professor, Brandeis University, 1953–62; Visiting Professor, Norwegian School of Business Administration, Bergen, Norway, 1962–63; Associate Professor, Professor, University of California, Riverside, California, USA, 1963–; Visiting Professor, New York University, 1978; Kenan Distinguished Professor of Humanities, College of William and Mary, 1988–89. *Publications:* Ernest Chansson: His Life and Works, 1955; Demonic Souls: Three Essays on Balzac, 1964; Machiavelli's Prince: Analysis of Treatise on Power Politics, 1975; Alessandro Manzoni, 1976; Chekhov's Great Plays, 1981; Interrelations of Literature, 1982; Giacomo Leopardi, 1986. *Contributions to:* Various publications in his field. Editor: The Heliconian; Modern Philology; Italian Quarterly, former. Associate Editor, The Comparatist; Fantasy Studies; Bibliography; Selecta. *Honours include:* Phi Beta Kappa, 1947, Humanities Award, 1947, Harvard University; Fulbright Fellowships, 1950–51, 1962–63; Humanities Institute Awards, 1968, 69, Distinguished Teaching Award, 1974, University of California; Outstanding Educator of America, 1973; Kenan Distinguished Professor of Humanities, William and Mary, 1988–89. *Memberships include:* International and American Comparative Literature Associations; Division Chair, Modern Language Association; Dante Association of America; Southern Comparative Literature Association. *Address:* 5984 Windemere Way, Riverside, CA 92506, USA.

BARRIE, Alexander, b. 1923, Barnsley, England. Author. m. Anne C L Pitt, 3 Dec. 1955, 3 sons, 1 daughter. *Education:* Diploma, Architectural Association School of Architecture. *Publications:* War Underground, UK and USA, 1961, 81; Jonathan Kane Series: Fly for Three Lives; Operation Midnight; Let Them All Starve; Jonathan Kane's Jungle Run; Jonathan Kane Climbs High, 1975–79, 1985–86. *Contributions to:* Daily Telegraph Magazine; Reader's Digest (Director). *Memberships:* Steering Wheel Club; Medway Yacht Club. *Literary Agent:* Watson Little

Limited. *Address:* 33 Manor Way, London SE3 9XG, England.

BARRIE, Shirley Grace, b. 30 Sep. 1945, Tillsonburg, Ontario, Canada. Playwright. m. Kenneth Richard Chubb, 28 May 1966, Tillsonburg, 1 son, 1 daughter. *Education:* BA, University of Western Ontario, London, 1966; MA, Carleton University, Ottawa, 1970. *Literary Appointments:* Teacher of English, Ottawa Board of Education, 1966–69, 1970–71; Co-founder (with Kenneth Chubb) and Associate Director, Wakefield Tricycle Company (alternate theatre company producing new plays), 1972–84; Leader, Playwriting Workshops, City Literary Institute, London, 1974–; Teacher, Summer Course, Creative Writing, Carleton University, Ottawa, 1975. *Publications:* Stage Plays include: Riders of the Sea, 1982; Jack Sheppard's Back, 1982; Shusha and the Story Snatcher, 1984; The Pear is Ripe, 1984; Sawdust, 1984; Topsy Turvy, 1984. Radio/TV: When Wings Have Roots, BBC Radio 4, 1969. Currently working on two series ideas for television. *Honours:* Bursary from Arts Council of Great Britain to research history of Saint Simonians, source of material for, The Pear is Ripe, 1981. *Memberships:* Theatre Writers Union; Playwrights Union of Canada; Women in Entertainment; Conference of Women Theatre Directors and Administrators. *Literary Agent:* Janet Fillingham, Anthony Sheil Associates, London. *Address:* 462 Clendenan Avenue, Toronto, M6P 2X6, Ontario, Canada.

BARRON, Gregory Joseph, b. 1 Dec. 1952, Cleveland, Ohio, USA. Writer. m. Sarah Curtis Murphy, 5 Nov. 1983, New Haven, Connecticut. *Education:* BA, University of Pennsylvania. *Literary Appointments:* Creative Writing Fellow, Syracuse University, 1976–77; Instructor, Creative Writing, 1977–78; Writer-in-Residence, Phillips Exeter Academy, 1980–81; Instructor, Creative Writing, Phillips Exeter Academy, Summer School, 1981, 82, 83; Breadloaf Creative Writing Fellow, 1982. *Publication:* Groundrush, 1982. *Contributions to:* Taking on Air (Book Review); Sportstyle Magazine, 1983. *Honours:* Creative Writing Fellowship, Syracuse University, 1976–77; George Bennett Memorial Fellowship, Phillips Exeter Academy, 1980–81; Bread Loaf Creative Writing Fellowship, 1982; Literary Arts Fellowship, New Jersey State Council on the Arts, 1985. *Literary Agent:* Liz Darhansoff. *Address:* 253 6th Street, Hoboken, NJ 07030, USA.

BARROS PARDO, Tomas, b. 3 Feb. 1922, Toledo, Spain. University Professor. *Education:* Graduate, Higher School of Fine Arts, San Fernando of Madrid. *Publications include:* Poetry: A imagen y semejanza, 1973; Los Orjos de la Colina, 1963; Berro diante da morte, 1964; Abraio, 1978; Essays including: Los procesos abstractivos del arte contemporaneo, Prolongo del Dr Domingo Garcia Sabell, 1965; Sobre el origen de la corteza en los astros, 1973; El simbolo de la sombre a en Rosalia y en la poesia. Books: Theater; Panteon Familiar, 1975; O Dragon, 1972; O Veo de Maya; Cos ollos do morto and A Raina e o seu Bufon, in O home que gabeou o cume, 1984. *Contributions to:* La Noche, numerous ciritiques and essays; Le Voz de Galicia; Numerous anthologies; Most Spainish poetry reviews. Former Editor and Founder, Aturuxo, and Revista Nordes. *Honours include:* 1st International Poetry Prize, New York Circle of Iberoamerican Writers and Poets (for A Imagen y Semajanza), 1972. *Memberships include:* Corresponding member, Royal Academy of Gallega. *Address:* Calle Ronda de Nelle 125–8o F, La Coruna, Spain.

BARROS PARDO, Tomás, b. 3 Feb. 1922, Toledo, Spain. University Professor. *Education:* Graduated Higher School of Fine Arts, San Fernando of Madrid. *Publications include:* Poetry: A imagen y semejanza, 1973; Los Ojos de la Colina, 1963; Berro diante da morte, 1964; Abrajo, 1978; Essays include: Los procesos abstractivos del arte contemporaneo; Prólogo del Dr Domingo Garcia Sabell, 1965; Sobre el origen de la corteza en los astros, 1973; El simbolo de la sombra en

Rosalia y en la poesia. Theatre: O Dragón, 1972; Panteón familiar, 1975; O Veo de Maya, Cosollos do mor, A Raina e o seu Bufón (in same volume), 1978; O Home que gabeou ó cume, 1978. *Contributions to:* La Noche (numerous critiques & essays); La Voz de Galicia; Numerous anthologies, most Spanish poetry reviews; Aturuo (former editor, founder); Revista Nordés (former editor, founder). *Memberships include:* Correspondent, Royal Academy, Gallega. *Honours include:* 1st International poetry prize, New York Circle of Iberoamerican Writers & Poets (for A Imagen y semejanza), 1972. *Address:* Ronda de Nelle 125–80F, la Caruña 15010, Spain.

BARROSO, Eleonora Beatriz de Azevedo, b. 4 Feb. 1935, Leopoldina, Minas, Brazil. Education Specialist, Ministry of Education and Culture. *Education:* Degree in Education, Federal University of Rio de Janeiro; Postgraduate Studies in Anthropology. *Contributions to:* Bolteetim Informativo da FNLIJ-IBBY; Revista Brasileira de Estudos Pedagogicos, Instituto Nacional de Estudos e Pesquisas Educacionais, INEP/MEC; Bibliografia Brasileira de Educacao, INEP/MEC. *Address:* Rua Siqueira Campos 143, Bl E Apto 1237, Copacabana, Rio de Janeiro 22031, Brazil.

BARROW, Geoffrey Eric, b. 27 Jan. 1936, Snodland, Kent, England. Technical Writer and Editor of Training Material. m. 1960, 3 children. *Education:* Diploma in Training Management. *Literary Appointment:* R Pollard Associates, Technical Publishers, 1979–82; OTS Training Projects, Singapore, 1982–83; Vocational Analyst/Technical Editor and Writer/Project Team Leader, Dynarabia Training projects, Al Khobar, Saudi Arabia, 1984–85. *Publications include:* Numerous training manuals and textbooks. *Memberships:* Institute of Scientific and Technical Communicators. *Address:* 51 Turpins Way, Baldock, Hertfordshire SG7 6LW, England.

BARRY, James P, b. 23 Oct. 1918, Alton, Illinois, USA. Writer; Editor; Photographer; Association Executive. m. Anne Elizabeth Jackson, 16 Apr. 1966, Columbus, Ohio. *Education:* BA cum laude, Ohio State University, 1940. *Publications:* Georgian Bay: The Sixth Great Lake, 1968, revised, 1978; The Battle of Lake Erie, 1970; Bloody Kansas, 1972; The Noble Experiment, 1972; The Fate of the Lakes, 1972; The Louisiana Purchase, 1973; Henry Ford and Mass Production, 1973; Ships of the Great Lakes, 1973; The Berlin Olympics 1936, 1975; The Great Lakes: A First Book, 1976; Wrecks and Rescues of the Great Lakes, 1981. *Honours:* Award, for Ships of the Great Lakes, American Society for State and Local History, 1974; Nonfiction History Award, for Wrecks and Rescues of the Great Lakes, Society of Midland Authors, 1982. *Memberships:* Phi Beta Kappa; Royal Canadian Yacht Blub; Great Lakes Historical Society; World Ship Society; Marine Historical Society. *Address:* 353 Fairway Boulevard, Columbus, PH 43213, USA.

BARRY, Joseph Amber, b. 13 June 1917, Scranton, Pennsylvania, USA. Writer. m. Naomi Jolles, 1946, Paris, France (div. 1965), 2 sons. *Education:* AB 1939, AB in LS 1940, University of Michigan, USA; Doctoral study, Sorbonne University of Paris, France. *Publications:* Left Bank, Right Bank, 1951; Architecture As Space, editor, 1957; Contemporary American Architecture, 1958; France, 1965; The People of Paris, 1966; Passions and Politics: A Biography of Versailles, 1972; Infamous Woman: The Life of George Sand, English, French, Italian and Spanish editions, 1976; Couples-France, French edition 1985; Versailles, French editon, 1986. *Contributions to:* Horizon; New Republic; Smithsonian; Holiday; The New York Times Magazine; L'Express; L'Histoire; and others. *Honours:* Versailles – American Library Association Notable Book of 1972; George Sand biography was 3 times chosen as a book club selection. *Memberships:* PEN Club; Author's Guild; Anglo-American Press Association, Paris; Phi Beta Kappa. *Literary Agent:* Robert Lescher, 155 East 71st Street, New York, NY 10021, USA. *Address:* 107 rue Lauriston, 75116 Paris, France.

BARRY, Paul b. 27 May 1952, Upper Darby, Pennsylvania, USA. Editor; Writer. m. Beth Kaufman, 15 Sep. 1984, Danbury, Connecticut. *Education:* BA English, Carnegie-Mellon University, Pittsburgh, Pennsylvania. *Contributions to:* Poetry: Kansas Quarterly; The Ohio Review; Poetry and others. Interviews: The College Board Review. *Honours:* Award for Excellence in Educational Journalism, for interview in The College Board Review, Educational Press Association of America, 1985. *Address:* 235 West 102nd Street, Apt 4-I, New York City, NY 10025, USA.

BARRY, Richard Hugh, b. 9 Nov. 1908, London, England. Translator; Army Officer (retired). *Education:* Royal Military College, Sandhurst, 1927–28; Staff College, Camberley, 1938; Imperial Defence College, 1957. *Publications:* (Translations): Inside Hitler's Headquarters, 1964; Strategy Series, 1965–67; Stauffenberg, 1967; The Orders of the Death's Head, 1969; Twice Through the Lines, 1972; The Goebbels Diaries, 1978. *Contributions to:* Encounter. *Honours:* Schlegel-Tieck Prize, (German Translation), 1968 & 1972; Scott-Moncrieff Prize, (French Translation), 1970. *Membership:* Translators' Association. *Address:* Little Place, Farringdon, Alton, Hampshire GU34 3EH, England.

BARSTOW, Stan, b. 28 June 1928, Horbury, Yorkshire, England. Novelist; Scriptwriter. m. Constance Mary Kershaw, 8 Sep. 1951, Ossett, 1 son, 1 daughter. *Education:* Ossett Grammar School. *Publications:* A Kind of Loving, 1960; The Desperadoes, 1961; Ask Me Tomorrow, 1962; Joby, 1964; The Watchers on the Shore, 1966; A Raging Calm, 1968; A Season with Eros, 1971; The Right True End, 1976; A Brother's Tale, 1980; The Glad Eye, 1984; Just You Wait and See, 1986. *Honours:* Hon MA, Open University, 1982; Royal Television Society Writer's Award, 1975. *Memberships:* Writers' Guild of Great Britain; Society of Authors; PEN, England. *Literary Agent:* Harvey Unna and Stephen Durbridge Ltd. *Address:* Goring House, Goring Park Avenue, Ossett, West Yorks WF5 OHK, England.

BART, Benjamin F, b. 21 Dec. 1917, Chicago, Illinois, USA. Director of Comparative Literature Programme; Professor of French. *Education:* BA 1938, MA 1946, PhD 1947, Harvard University. *Publications:* La France, Carrefour des Civilisations europeennes, 1950; Flaubert's Landscape Descriptions, 1956; Edition of Albert Camus, l'Exil et le Royaume, 1965; Madame Bovary and the Critics, 1966; Flaubert, 1967; The Legendary Sources of Flaubert's Saint-Julien, 1976. *Contributions to:* Numerous literary journals and reviews. *Honours include:* Grant, American Philosophy Society, 1960, 63; Senior Research Fellow, National Endowment for the Humanities, 1974. *Memberships include:* Phi Beta Kappa. *Address:* 407 South Highland Avenue, Pittsburgh, PA 15206, USA.

BARTELSKI, Leslaw, b. 8 Sep. 1920, Warsaw, Poland. Writer. m. Maria Zembrzuska, 29 June 1947, 1 son, 1 daughter. *Education:* Master of Law, Warsaw University, 1948. *Literary Appointments:* Co-editor, Sztuka i Narod, 1942–44; Co-editor, Nowiny Literackie, 1947–48; Co-editor, Nowa Kultura, 1953–63. *Publications:* Against Annihilation, narrative poem, 1948; A Twice Seen Landscapes, novel, 1958; Genealogy of the Survivors, sketches about the years 1939–44, 1963; The Rider of Madara, sketches about Bulgaria, 1963; Seaweed, novel, 1964; Warsaw Rising, historical essay, 1965; Fighting Warsaw, 1968, Mokotow 1944, monograph, 1971; Bloodstained Wings, novel, 2 volumes, 1975; The Shadow of War, sketches, 1983. *Contributions to:* Gazetta Krakowska. *Honours:* Cross of Valour, 1944; Cavaler 1966, Officer 1972, Commander 1960, Cross of Polonia Restituta; Cross of the Home Guard, London 1966; Bulgarian Order Ciril and Methody 1st class, 1966; Cross of Warsaw Rising, 1981, State Prize 1951, Warsaw Prize, Pietrzaks Prize and Prize of Minister of Defense, 1969; Prize of Minister of Culture, 1977; Pietrzaks Prize, 1985. *Memberships:* Chairman of Warsaw Branch 1972–76,

Polish Writers Union; PEN. *Address:* Fr Joliot Curie 17 m I, 02–646 Warsaw, Poland.

BARTHOLOMEW, Paul Jason, b. 12 Sep. 1936, Hudson Falls, New York, USA. Publicist; Administrator. m. Christine Kartsonakis, 25 Apr. 1959, New York City, 4 sons, 1 daughter. *Education:* New England Bible Institute, Framingham, Massachusetts, 1957; Diploma, Valley Forge College, Pennsylvania, 1958; BS, Central Bible College and Seminary, Missouri, 1960; MS, State University of New York, Brockport, 1963; Certificate, School Administrator; Russel Sage College; Siena College; Hofstra University; Princeton Theological Seminary; PhD, University of Beverly Hills, 1986. *Publications:* Shadows of Turning (first of series of six volumes), 1985; 3 non-published non-fictions; 3 volumes of Messages From an Old Country Church; Ghost writer for several well-known public figures. *Contributor to:* Washington County Post (poetry); Our Western World's Greatest Poems, 1983; The American Poetry Anthology, 1983; Our World's Best Loved Poems, 1984; Hearts of Fire, Volume II, 1985; Publisher and Recorder Lyrics and Musicals including; Eternal Love; Trust Him; Love is a Symphony; Praise the Lord; A Christmas Gift; Serenade of Love; Regal Reign. *Honours:* Numerous honours and awards. *Address:* 6 Drakes Bay, Corona del Mar, CA 92625, USA.

BARTLETT, Christopher John, b. 12 Oct. 1931. Bournemouth, England. University Professor. *Education:* BA, University of London (external), 1953; PhD, London, 1956. *Major Publications:* Great Britain & Sea Power 1815–53, 1963; Castlereagh, 1966; The Long Retreat 1945–70, 1971; The Rise & Fall of the Pax Americana, 1974; History of Post-war Britain 1945–74, 1977; The Global Conflict 1880–1970, 1984. *Contributor to:* History; English Historical Review; American Historical Review. *Memberships:* Fellow, Royal Historical Society. *Address:* Department of History, The University, Dundee DD1 4HN, Scotland.

BARTLETT, Elizabeth, b. New York City, USA. Poet & Editor. m. Paul Bartlett, 19 Apr. 1943, 1 son. *Education:* BS Education, Teachers College, New York City, USA; Graduate non-degree studies, Columbia University. *Literary Appointments:* Poetry Editor, ETC (Review of General Semantics), 1963–76; Professor of Creative Writing, San Diego State University, 1979–81; Poetry Editor, Crosscurrents (Literary Review), 1984–; Teaching, English: University of California at Santa Barbara, San José State University; Speech & Drama, Southern Methodist University. *Major Publications:* Poems of Yes & No, 1952; Behold This Dreamer, 1959; Poetry Concerto, 1961; It Takes Practice Not to Die, 1964; Threads, Twelve-tone Poems, 1968; Selected Poems, 1970; The House of Sleep, 1975; In Search of Identity, Dialogue of Dust, 1977; Address in Time, A Zodiac of Poems, 1979; Memory is No Stranger, 1981; The Gemini Poems, 1984. *Contributor to:* Harper's; National Forum; New York Times; Poetry Review; Virginia Quarterly; The Literary Review; Canadian Forum; Queen's Quarterly; and many others (over 800 poems). *Honours:* Various Foundation awards; National Endowment for the Arts Award, 1970; Short Story Award, PEN/NEA, 1983, 1985; Travel Grant, 1985. *Memberships:* Poetry Society of America; Authors Guild; Authors League; Society for General Semantics; PEN American Center. *Address:* 2875 Cowley Way-1302, San Diego, CA 92110, USA.

BARTLETT, Eric George, b. 25 Aug. 1920, Llanbradach, Wales. Retired Postal Officer. m. Pauline Nancy Lewis, 9 Feb. 1974, Cardiff. *Education:* 2nd Dan and Doshi Teaching Certificate in Judo of Sekai Butokukwai and International Budo Council. *Publications:* The Case of the 13th Coach, 1958; The Complete Body Builder, 1961; Judo and Self Defence, 1962; Self Defence in the Home, 1967; Basic Judo, 1974; Basic Fitness, 1976; Smoking Flax, 1977; Summer Day at Ajaccio, 1979; Basic Karate, 1980; Weight Training, 1984; Healing Without Harm, 1985. *Contributions to:* Christian Herald: Judo Bulletin; Judoka; Ringsport; International Budo Council Bulletin.

Memberships: Society of Authors; Chairman 1960–62, Vice Chairman 1985–, Cardiff Writer Circle. *Address:* 5 Bryngwyn Road, Cyncoed, Cardiff CF2 6PQ, Wales.

BARTON, John Bernard Adie, b. 26 Nov. 1928, London, England. Theatre Director; Dramatic Adapter; Fight Director. m. Anne Righter. *Education:* BA, MA, King's College, Cambridge. *Publications:* The Hollow Crown (Samuel French), 1962; The Hollow Crown (expanded in version), (Hamish Hamilton Ltd), 1971; The Wars of the Roses, 1970; The Greeks, with Kenneth Cavander, 1981; Playing Shakespeare, 1982; Director, numerous plays including: The Greeks, Aldwych Theatre, 1979/80; The Vikings, 1983; Life's A Dream, RSC The Other Place, 1983; The Devils, RSC The Pit, 1984; Waste, Lyric, 1984; Dreamplay, RSC, The Pit, 1985. *Agent:* Margaret Ramsey Ltd. *Address:* 14 De Walden Court, 85 Cavendish St, London W1, England.

BARTOSZEWSKI, Wladyslaw, b. 19 Feb. 1922, Warsaw, Poland. Writer; Historian. *Education:* Doctor honoris causa, Polish University in Exile, London, 1981; Doctor h.c. Baltimore Hebrew College, USA, 1984; *Literary Appointments:* Vice President, Institute for Polish Jewish Studies, Oxford, England; Visiting Professor, Munich, Eichstätt, 1983–87. *Publications include:* Warsaw Death Ring, 1939–44, 2nd edition, 1970; The Samaritans, Heroes of the Holocaust with Z Lewin USA, 1970; 1859 Days ofWarsaw 1974; The Warsaw Ghetto As It Really Was, 1983; Days of the Fighting Capital: A Chronicle of the Warsaw Uprising, 1984. *Contributor to:* Various Catholic magazines and papers. *Honours include:* Polish Military Cross, 1944; Medal and Title of The Righteous Among the Nations, The Martyrs and Heroes Remembrance Yad Washem, Jerusalem, 1963; Prize, Alfred Jurzykowski Foundation, New York, 1967; Prize, Polish Pen, Warsaw, 1975; Herder Prize, Vienna, 1983; Commander, Polonia Restituta (with Star), London, 1986. *Memberships:* Polish PEN, Secretary General 1972; Associate Member, French PEN. *Address:* Karolin-ki 12; 02-635 Warsaw, Poland.

BARUCH, Izak Zacharias, b. 3 Nov. 1917, Amsterdam, The Netherlands. Physician. m. Hanny Birnbaum, 27 May 1960, Amsterdam, 2 sons, 1 daughter. *Education:* University of Amsterdam. *Appointments:* Member, Penaescula. *Publications:* The Schoolchild, 1952; Man & Woman in Marriage, 1954; Medicine in Ancient Israel, 1961; Guillaume de Baillou and his Importance for Reumatology, 1961; Life & Work of Vesalius, 1963; Say Yes to Love, 1957. *Contributor to:* Journal of American Medical Association; Journal of Canadian Medical Association; Dutch Journal of Medicine; Editor, Monthly Reconstruction; New.Isr. Weekly. *Honours:* Med.de la Reconnaissance francaise, 1947; Officer of Orange-Nassau, 1975; Cross for Resistence Activities, 1983. *Membership:* Literary Society of Physicians. *Address:* Gerrit van der Veenstr. 141, 1077 DX Amsterdam, The Netherlands.

BARUSKE, Heinz, b. 6 Mar. 1915, Kolberg, then German Republic, now Poland. Scientific Author. *Education:* Universities Greifswald, Kiel and Copenhagen; Studies of Scandinavian Lit, Lang and Eskimology. *Publications:* Gronland, grosste Insel der Erde 1968; Eskino-Machen, 1969; Skandinavische Volksmadchen, 1972; Das Nordmeer und die Freiheit der See, 1974; Die Nordischen Literaturen, 1974; Island (Moderne Erzahler der Welt), 1974; Marchen der Eskimo, 1975; Skandinavische Marchen, 1976; Danemark (Moderne Erzahler der Welt), 1977; Gronland, Wunderland der Arktis, 1977; Aus H C Andersens Tagebuchern, 1980; Land ansdem Meer (Zur Kultur Islands und der Faroer-In-seln), 1980; FmLand der Meer-jungfrau. Reisch in Danemark, 1982; Kunst- und Reisefuhrer, Norwegen, 1986; Hans Egene. Die Heiden im Eis, 1986. *Contributor to:* Various articles. *Honours:* Kogge Study Prize, 1971; Knight Cross, Icelandic Falcon Order, 1975; Honorary Professor, 1975; Knight Cross, 1st degree, Danish Order of Dannebrog, 1977; Bundesverdienstkreuf, 1985.

Memberships: Correspondent, Danish Writers' Association; Die Kogge, European Writers' Association; Association German Writers. *Address:* Wittstocker Strasse 8, D-1000 Berlin 21, Federal Republic of Germany,

BARZILAY, E Isaac, b. 31 Mar. 1915. Teacher. *Education:* MA, Hebrew University, Jerusalem, Israel, 1939–40; PhD, Columbia University, New York, USA, 1955. *Literary Appointments:* Instructor, Hebrew Teachers Seminary, Herzliyah, 1947–58; Assistant Professor, Brooklyn College, New York City, 1955; Assistant Professor, Queen's College, New York, 1956–57; Assistant Professor, Wayne State University, Detroit, Michigan, 1957–58; Associate Professor, 1959–67, Professor, 1967–85, Columbia University. *Major Publications:* Between Reason & Faith: Certi-Rationalization in Italian Jewish Thought 1250–1650, 1967; Shlomo Yehudah Rapoport (Shia) 1790–1867 & His Contemporaries, 1969; Yoseph Shlomo Delmedigo (Yashar of Candia), 1974. *Contributor to:* Proceedings of the American Academy for Jewish Research; Jewish Social Studies; Jewish Quarterly Review; and others. *Honour:* Honorary Doctorate of Hebrew Letters, Jewish Theological Seminary of America. *Memberships:* President, American Academy of Jewish Research, 1982–85; Editorial Board, Paalir, Jewish Hebrew Annual Review. *Address:* 258 Riverside Drive 5B, New York, NY 10025, USA.

BASHAM, Richard Dalton, b. 21 Sep. 1945, Hollywood, California, USA. University Senior Lecturer. m. Charoen Riwthong, 28 Sep. 1977, Honolulu, 1 son. *Education:* BA, George Washington University; MA, PhD, University of California. *Publications:* Urban Anthropology : The Cross Cultural Study of Complex Societies, 1978; Crisis in Blanc and White: Urbanization and Ethnic Identity in French Canada, 1978. *Contributor to:* International Journal of Symbology; Fronteirs; Exploring Total Institutions. *Address:* Dept of Anthropology, University of Sydney, Sydney, NSW 2006, Australia.

BASILE, Leon Edmund, b. 12 Dec. 1955, Woburn, Massachusetts, USA. Die-cutting Pressman. *Education:* BA English and History, University of Massachusetts at Boston, 1977; Archives Institute, Emory University & Georgia Department of Archives and History, 1978; MA History, University of Georgia, USA, 1979. *Major Publications:* The Civil War Diary of Amos E Stearns, a Prisoner at Andersonville (editor), Fairleigh Dickinson University Press, 1981; Adventures Afloat and Ashore: The Civil War Reminiscences of Henry Grant, US Navy and First New Hampshire Light Battery (editor), in progress. *Contributor to:* Civil War History; Lincoln Herald; The Journal of Mississippi History; The United Daughters of the Confederacy Magazine; North-South Trader; The Antiques Journal; The Georgia Historical Quarterly. *Honours:* Jefferson Davis Medal in Gold, awarded by the United Daughters of the Confederacy for Outstanding Research in Southern History, 1976. *Address:* 9 Colonial Road, Woburn, MA 01801, USA.

BASMAJIAN, Shaunt (Shant), b. 30 Sep. 1950. Poet; Driver. *Appointments:* Co-Founder, Editor, Old Nun Publication, 1972–75; Co-Founder, Writer, Old Nun Magazine, 1974–75. *Publications include:* On My Face, 1970; Spare Change, 1972; Quote Unquote, 1973; The Resurrection of the Third Happening, 1976; Source Poem, 1976; Boundaries Limits and Space, 1980; Surplus Waste and Other Poems, 1982; 8 Irritations, 1983; Anthologies include: House Poets Anthology, 1974; New Bohemian Embassy Anthology, 1975; North American Armenian Poets, 1976; Anthology of experimental Poetry, 1978; Sound Poetry Catalogue, 1978; Here is A Poem; Other Channels, 1984; Anti-War Poems Anthology, 1984; Records include: Afraid To Touch/Always Sixteen, 1980. *Contributor to:* Numerous professional journals and magazines. *Memberships include:* The House of Poets; League of Canadian Poets; Composers Authors and Publishers Association of Canada; Canadian Haiku

Society; etc. *Address:* PO Box 822, Adelaide St PO, Toronto, Ontario M5C 2K1, Canada.

BASS, Brian John, b. 5 July 1933, Strood, Kent, England. Journalist. m. Edna Glynn, 6 Aug. 1956, 2 sons, 1 daughter. *Literary Appointments:* Peterborough Advertiser; Boston Guardian; Ilkeston Pioneer; Birmingham Mercury; Daily Express; Daily Mail; Daily Mirror. *Address:* 58 Eden Rd, Elmers End, Beckenham, Kent, England.

BASS, Clara May Overy, b. 11 May 1911, Grimsby, England. Authoress; Poetess. m. Donald Leslie Bass, 27 Aug. 1937, 1 son. *Appointments:* International Committee Member, Centro Studi e Scambi, Rome, Italy; Founder Fellow, International Poetry Society. *Publications include:* Dreams of a Singer, 1963; Living Poetry, 1968; Major & Minor, 1970; Trio, 1973; Quintet, 1974; Major & Minor, paperback, 1975; Reflections, 1985. *Contributor to:* Collected Poems Anthology; Masters of Modern Poetry, Rome; Anthologies Centro Di Cultura; SS Croce, Taranto, Italy, Religious Poetry, 1974, 1977, 1978, 1979; Ipso Facto; Quaderni di Poesia; Mosaic; Twist; City & machine Age Poetry; Orbis; Expression One; Village Review; Nature Poetry, 1, 2; Love Poetry; headland; Parnassus; Breakthru; Grimsby Evening Telegraph; Grimsby News; Evening Telegraph. *Memberships include:* Writers Guild of Great Britain. *Honours:* Diploma Di Premiazione Targa, Shield, Holy Cross, 1977, 1978, 1979; Long Service Silver Medal, Operatic Society; Diplomas, Piano, Singing; First Prize Trophy, Premiazione Diploma, Targa Silver Medals. *Address:* 68 Lestrange St, Cleethorpes, South Humberside DN35 7HL, England.

BASS, Ellen, b. 16 June 1947, Philadelphia, Pennsylvania, USA. Writer; Teacher. 1 daughter. *Education:* BA, English Literature, Goucher College, 1968; MA, Creative Writing, Boston University, 1970. *Literary Appointments:* Teacher, Writing Workshops for Women. *Publications include:* No More Masks! An Anthology of Poems by Women, co-editor with Florence Howe, 1973; I'm Not Your Laughing Daughter, 1973; Of Separateness & Merging, 1977; For Earthly Survival, 1980; I Never Told Anyone : Writings by Women; Survivors of Child Sexual Abuse, 1983; Our Stunning Harvest, 1985. *Contributions to:* Atlantic Monthly; Ms; Calyx; etc. *Honour:* Elliston Book Award. *Memberships:* National Writers Guild; Feminist Writers Guild; International Women Writers Guild. *Literary Agent:* Charlotte Raymond. *Address:* 426 36th Avenue, Santa Cruz, CA 95062, USA.

BASS, Howard, b. 28 Oct. 1923, Waltham Cross, England. Author; Journalist. *Appointments:* Sports Writer, Programme Publications Limited, London, England, 1947–48; Managing Director, Howard Bass Publications Limited, London, 1948–69; Editor, Winter Sports magazine, 1948–69; Winter Sports Correspondent, Evening News, London, 1960–61; Daily Telegraph, 1961–; Sunday Telegraph, 1961–; London Standard, 1973–. *Publications:* The Sense in Sport, 1941; This Skating Age, 1958; The Magic of Ski-ing, 1959; Winter Sports, 1966; American edition, 1968; Success in Ice Skating, 1970; International Encyclopaedia of Winter Sports, 1971; Let's Go Skating, 1974, American edition, 1976; Tackle Skating, 1978; Ice Skating for Pleasure, 1979; Ice Skating, 1980; The Love of Skating, 1980, American edition, 1980; Elegance on Ice, 1980, American edition, 1980; Skating for Gold, 1980; Glorious Wembley, 1982. *Contributor to:* Sport and Recreation, London; Ski Racing, Denver, USA; Skating, Boston, USA; Canadian Skater, Ottawa, Canada; Daily Telegraph; Sunday Telegraph; Toronto Star, Canada; Ski Racing, USA; Ski, London; London Standard; Winter Sports text authority; Encyclopaedia Britannica; Guinness Book of Records. *Memberships:* International Sports Press Association (committee member); Sports Writers Association of Great Britain. *Address:* 256 Willow Road, Enfield, Middlesex EN1 3AT, England.

BASTÉ, Joan G (Mr), b. 29 Aug. 1920, Barcelona, Spain. Writer; Translator. m. Rosalind Hazel Manning. *Education:* General Certificate, Independent Courses, Philosophy. *Publications:* Poetry: Tú, com un arbre, 1938; La inútil aventura, 1985. Guide books: incl. Barcelona, 1949. Drama: incl. Quasi un Paradis (with Joan Oliver), Multiplicando por Cero. Adaptations: incl. El tesoro de Juan Sin Tierra (by R C Sherriff), 1956. Novels: incl. El Rio en Llamas, 1954; Espartaco, 1961; El Evangelio segun Joan Basté, 1977; La pell del pit, 1984; La pau del camp, 1985. Other works incl: Lexicographies, 12 volumes (co-author, director), 1952; 3 chapters, translation, La Epopeya de las Grandes Construcciones, 1965; Short stories, La maquina de pensar, Consultorio sentimental, 1984; 100 radio talks. *Contributions to:* Various publications incl. Destino; Ritmo; La Vanguardia. *Honours Include:* 1st Prize, Villa de Bilbao, novel; 1st Prize, Ignacio Aldecoa, short stories (Tiempo circular), 1980. *Address:* Mas El Solanot, Apartado de Correos 250, Olot, Gerona, Spain.

BATARSE, Guillermo Feliciano, b. 1 May 1948, Matamoros, Mexico, Psychotherapist. *Education:* BS Social Sciences; Certified Psychotherapist; Certified Humanist Senior Counselor, American Humanist Association; International Academy of Professional Counseling and Psychotherapy. *Contributions to:* Daily contributions and commentaries on international politics, world events and social sciences, El Siglo De Torreon. *Memberships:* National Writers Club; Newspaper Institute of America. *Address:* Calle Durango number 319 Oriente, Gomez Palacio, Durango, 35000 Mexico.

BATCHELOR, John Barham, b, 15 Mar. 1942, Farnborough, Hampshire, England. Fellow, New College, Oxford. m. Henrietta Jane Letts, 14 Sep. 1968, Cowden, Kent, 2 sons, 1 daughter. *Education:* MA, PhD, Magdalene College, University of Cambridge. *Major Publications:* Mervyn Peake: A Biographical & Critical Exploration, 1974; Breathless Hush (novel), 1974; The Edwardian Novelists, 1982; H G Wells, 1985. *Contributor to:* The Tablet; The Month; Yearbook of English Studies; Times Literary Supplement; The Observer; Essays in Criticism; Review of English Studies. *Memberships:* Society of Authors. *Address:* New College, Oxford, England.

BATCHELOR, John Dennis, b. 22 Aug. 1947, London, England. Company Director. m. Julie Frances Elizabeth Clarke, 3 Aug. 1973, Lagos, Nigeria. *Publications:* The Congo, 1980; The Euphrates, 1981. *Contributions to:* Backpacker's Africa, 1983; Globetrotters Handbook, 1983; Wexas Travellers Handbook, 1985; Geographical Magazine! *Address:* 52 Thorndon Court, Eagle Way, Brentwood, Essex, England.

BATCHELOR, Julie Frances Elizabeth, b. 30 Jan. 1947, Manchester, England. Teacher. m. John Dennis Batchelor, 3 Aug. 1973, Lagos, Nigeria. *Education:* BA (Hons), French and Russian, University of Leeds; Postgraduate Certificate in Education, Homerton College, Cambridge. *Publications:* The Congo, 1980; The Euphrates, 1981. *Contributions to:* Backpackers' Africa, 1983; Wexas Travellers Handbook, 1985. *Address:* 52 Thorndon Court, Eagle Way, Brentwood, Essex, England.

BATES, (Sir) David Robert, b. 18 Nov. 1916, Omagh, Northern Ireland. University Teacher. *Education:* BSc, MSc, Queen's University, Belfast; DSc, University College, London. *Major Publication:* (editor) The Planet Earth, 1957, 2nd edition 1964. *Memberships:* Fellow of the Royal Society; Honorary Foreign Member, American Academy of Arts & Sciences; Associate, Royal Academy of Belgium; Royal Irish Academy; Foreign Associate, National Academy of Science of the US; Senior Member, International Academy of Quantum Molecular Science. *Honours:* Knight, 1978; Hughes Medal, Royal Society, 1970; Chree Medal, Institute of Physics, 1973; Gold Medal, Royal Astronomic Society, 1977; Honorary Doctorates,

Universities of Ulster, National University of Ireland, Dublin, Glasgow, York (England), York (Canada), Belfast & Stirling. *Address:* 1 Newforge Grange, Belfast BT9 5QB, Northern Ireland.

BATES, Susannah Vacella Church, b. 23 Feb. 1941, New Orleans, Louisiana, USA. Buyer/Manager of Bookstore. m. Albert David Bates, 14 Oct. 1968, at Windsor, Connecticut, 3 daughters. *Publications:* The Pendex, an index of pen and house names in fantastic, thriller and series literature, 1981. *Contributions to:* Putnam Observer-Patriot, 1978–80; Weirdbook 5; Year's Best Horror Stories Number 3, 1973; Weirdbook 20; 1985; Book reviews to East-West Journal, 1977–79; Collecting Paperbacks?. *Honours:* Scholastic National Award, Best Short Story, 1956; Scholastic Regional Award, Opera Set, 1956. *Memberships:* Paperback Collectors Guild, 1977–83; Co-editor 1978–84, Pulp Heroes Amateur Press Association; August Derleth Society, 1981–83. *Address:* 355 Kennedy Drive, Putnam, CT 06260, USA.

BATHO, Edith Clara, b. 1895, London, England, deceased 21 Jan. 1986. *Education:* MA, DLitt, University of London; D de l'Université Poitiers, France. *Major Publications:* The Ettrick Shepherd, 1927; The Later Wordsworth, 1934; (with B Dobree, The Victorians & After, 1938; Chronicles of Scotland, by Hector Boerce (edited for Scottish Text Society), Volume 1 with W W Seton & R W Chambers 1936, Volume 2 with H W Husbands 1941; A Wordsworth Selection, 1962. *Address:* Coxhill Manor, Chobham, Surrey, England.

BATTIN, B W, b. 15 Nov. 1941, Ridgewood, New Jersey, USA. Writer. m. Sandra McCraw, 14 Feb. 1976, Shreveport, Louisiana. *Education:* BA, University of New Mexico, 1969. *Publications:* Angel of the Night, 1983; The Boogeyman, 1984; Mary, Mary, 1985; Satan's Servant, 1985; Programmed for Terror, 1985. *Literary Agent:* Dominick Abel, New York. *Address:* Rt 1, Box 419-H, Belen, NM 87002, USA.

BATTLE, Allen Overton, b. 19 Nov. 1927, Memphis, Tennessee, USA. Clinical Psychologist. *Education:* BS, Siena College, Memphis, 1949; MA, 1953, PhD, 1961, Catholic University of America; Board of Professional Psychologists, 1971. *Publications:* Status Personality in a Negro Holiness Sect, 1961; The Research Process as Applied to Nursing, 1967; Clinical Psychology for Physical Therapists, 1975; The Psychology of Patient Care: A Humanistic Approach, 1979. *Contributor to:* Various professional journals. *Honours include:* Res. Appreciation Award for Outstanding Contributions to the Training of Residents in Psychology, 1973. *Address:* 2220 Washington Avenue, Memphis, TN 38104, USA.

BATTLE, Lois, b. West Australia. Writer. *Education:* BA, University of California, Los Angeles, USA. *Publications include:* Season of Change, 1980; War Brides, 1982; Southern Women, 1984. *Membership:* Authors Guild. *Literary Agent:* Jane Rotrosen, New York, USA. *Address:* c/o St Martin's Press, 175 Fifth Avenue, New York, NY 10010, USA.

BATTS, Michael S, b. 2 Aug. 1929, Mitcham, Surrey, England. Lecturer; Writer. *Education:* BA, 1952, BA (Hons) 1953, London University, England; PhD, University of Freiburg, 1957; DLitt, University of London, 1973. *Publications:* Die Form der Aventiuren in Nibelungenlied, 1961; Editor, Essays on German Literature in Honour of G Joyce Hallamore, 1968; Gottfried von Strassburg, 1971; Das Nibelungenlied; Parelleldruck der Hss A B und C nebst Lesarten der uebrigen Handschiften, 1971; The Bibliography of German Literature, 1978. *Contributor to:* Various books; Articles and reviews in professional journals. *Honours include:* Alexander von Humboldt Foundation senior Fellowship 1964–65; Fellow the Royal Society of Canada, 1973; Various Fellowships and grants. *Memberships:* MLA: Medieval Academy of America; Canadian Association of University Teachers of German; Educational Seminar, 1971–81. *Address:*

Department of German, University of British Columbia, Vancouver V6T 1W5, Canada.

BAUER, Nancy, b. 7 July 1934, Massachusetts, USA. Writer. m. William Bauer, 9 June 1956, 2 sons, 1 daughter. *Education:* BA, Mount Holyoke College, 1956. *Literary Appointment:* Writer-in-Residence, Cape Cod Writers Conference, 1983. *Publications:* Flora, Write This Down, 1982; Wise-Ears, 1985. *Contributions to:* (10 Articles), Arts Atlantic; Fate Atlantic; Fiddlehead; Canadian Fiction Magazine; Abba. *Honour:* Second Prize, Short Story, CBC Literary Competition, 1982. *Membership:* Writers Federation of New Brunswick, Member, Founding Committee. *Address:* 252 Stanley Street, Fredericton, NB, Canada E3B 3A3.

BAUMGARTEN, Sylvia (Rosen), b. 12 Nov. 1933, Toronto, Canada. Writer. m. Sidney Baumgarten, 26 June 1955, at Springfield, Massachusetts, 3 sons, 1 daughter. *Education:* AB, Brown University, USA, 1955. *Major Publications:* Marielle, 1982; Lysette, 1983; Delphine, 1983; Pocket Books, Coronet Books, England; Dreams so Fleeting, Warner Books, 1985. *Membership:* Authors Guild. *Literary Agent:* Writers House, Inc, New York City. *Address:* 307 East 12th Street, New York, NY 10003, USA.

BAUWENS, Marcel François Maximilien, b. 6 Mar. 1928, Brussels, Belgium. Journalist. *Education:* Licencié en Journalisme, University of Brussels, 1952. *Publication:* Jusqu'au bout de la démocratie, 1982. *Contributions to:* Le Soir, newspaper, Brussels; Contributor for Belgium, Journal de l'année, 1970–82. *Membership:* Editorial Board, Poetry Review, European Association for the Promotion of Poetry. *Address:* Rue des Francs 13, 1040 Brussels, Belgium.

BAWDEN, Nina, b. 1925, London, England. Author. *Education:* MA, Somerville College, Oxford. *Publications include:* Who Calls the Tune, 1953; Change Here for Babylon, 1955; The Solitary Child, 1956; Devil by the Sea, 1958; Just Like a Lady, 1960; Tortoise by Candlelight, 1963; A Woman of My Age, 1967; The Grain of Truth, 1969; The Birds on the Trees, 1970; Anna Apparent, 1972; George Beneath a Paper Moon, 1974; Walking Naked, 1981; The Ice House, 1983; Princess Alice, 1985; (for Children) The Secret Passage; The Witch's Daughter; A Handful of Thieves; The Runaway Summer; Squib; Carrie's War, 1973; The Peppermint Pig, 1975; Afternoon of a Good Woman; Familiar Passions, 1978; The Robbers, 1978; The Finding, 1985. *Contributor to:* Daily Telegraph, (fiction review). *Honours:* Recipient, Guardian Award for The Peppermint Pig; Yorkshire Post Novel of the Year Award for Afternoon of a Good Woman, 1976. *Memberships include:* PEN; Society of Authors; FRSL. *Literary Agent:* Curtis Brown Ltd. *Address:* 22 Noel Road, London N1, England.

BAXTER, Christopher Raymond, b. 4 Feb. 1946, Melbourne, Australia. Publisher. m. Maureen Susan Baxter, 19 Nov. 1983, Melbourne. *Education:* BA, Diploma of Education, Monash University. *Literary Appointments:* Editor and Publisher, Wild Magazine, Rock Magazine. *Publications:* Various rockclimbing guidebooks. *Contributions to:* Several mountaineering magazines. *Address:* PO Box 415, Prahran, Victoria 3181, Australia.

BAXTER, Patricia Edith Wilson, b. Hull, England. Teacher. *Education:* Teacher's Certificate; BA (Hons). *Publications:* Puppet Plays for Junior Range, 1965; Soltan in the Sandwiches, 1974. *Contributions to:* Contemporary Review; World Medicine; The Lady; Community Care; Teaching and Training; The Teacher; 85 Dorset Poets; Popular Caravan. *Memberships:* Havant and District Arts Society. *Address:* 4 Willow Close, Havant, Hants PO9 2SX, England.

BAXTER, Raymond Frederic, b. 25 Jan. 1922, London, England. Broadcaster; Writer. m. Sylvia Kathryn née Johnson, 20 Sep. 1945, Mulhouse, France, 1 son, 1 daughter. *Literary Appointments:* BBC Staff Commentator, Writer & Producer for Radio & TV, 1947–65, thereafter freelance. *Major Publications:* Tomorrow's World. Volumes 1 & 2 (with James Burke & Michael Latham), 1970, 1971; Farnborough Commentary, 1980. *Contributor to:* Numerous publications, including: Aeroplane; Flight; Autocar; Motor Boat & Yachting; Punch; Daily Telegraph; Radio Times; film commentaries, various radio & television programmes. *Honours:* Fellow, Royal Society of Arts, 1966; Harold Pemberton Trophy, 1966; Honorary Freeman of the City of London, 1968; Liveryman, Guild of Air Pilots, 1982. *Membership:* Guild of Motoring Writers (Committee 1961–65). *Address:* The Green Cottage, Wargrave Road, Henley-on-Thames, Oxfordshire RG9 3HX, England.

BAXTER, Trevor Walter, b. 18 Nov. 1932, London, England. Writer. *Education:* Diploma, RADA, London. *Literary Appointments:* Mellon Visiting Distinguished Professor, Rice University, Houston, Texas, 1985. *Publications:* Plays: Lies, 1976; The Undertaking, 1979; The Last Evensong (BBCTV) 1985. *Literary Agent:* Fraser & Dunlop. *Address:* c/o Fraser & Dunlop, 91 Regent Street, London, England.

BAYBARS, Taner, b. 18 June, 1936, Nicosia, Cyprus. Book Promotions Officer, British Council. *Major Publications:* A Trap for the Burglar, 1965; Selected Poems of Nazim Hikmet, 1967; Plucked in a Far-off Land, 1970; The Moscow Symphony, 1970; The Day Before Tomorrow, 1972; Narcissus in a Dry Pool, 1978; To Catch a Falling Man, 1963; Pregnant Shadows, 1981. *Contributor to:* Critical Quarterly; The Listener; Ambit; The Tablet; Poetry Review; Artrage; Dalhouse Review; Outposts. *Membership:* Poetry Society (London). *Literary Agent:* David Higham Associates. *Address:* 69 Onslow Gardens, London N10 3JY, England.

BAYLEY, Barrington John, b. 9 Apr. 1937, Birmingham, England. Science Fiction Author. *Publications:* (Novels) The Star Virus, 1970; Annihilation Factor, 1972; Empire of Two Worlds, 1972; Collision Course, 1973; The Fall of Chronopolis, 1974; The Soul of the Robot, 1974; The Garments of Caen, 1976; The Grand Wheel, 1977; Star Winds, 1978; The Pillars of Eter Ity, 1982; The Zen Gun, 1983; The Forest of Peldain, 1985; The Rod of Light, 1985; (story collections) The Knights of the Limits, 1978; The Seed of Evil, 1979. *Memberships:* Science Fiction Foundation. *Agents:* E J Carnell Literary Agency, England. Scott Meredith Agency (Foreign). *Address:* 48 Turreff Avenue, Donnington, Telford, Shropshire TF2 8HE, England.

BAZLEY, Rosemary, b. 15 July 1900. Housewife; Teacher. m. *Appointments include:* ATS, 2 years; Part-time Lecturer, German, Kidderminster College of Further Education, 6 years; Private Teacher of German. *Publications include:* (Poetry Booklets) Shadow Pantomime, 1960; Pride of the Evening, 1963; Turn of the Year, 1968; Run of the Mill, 1972; (Poems) Peacock Parade, 1966; Resurgent, 1968; Cats on my Coffin, 1970; (Broadcasts BBC Midland Poets Series) Flying Swan, 1960; To a Deaf Friend, 1964; Unrest, 1965l (British Forces Broadcasting Service) Shepherds Delight, 1976; Interviewed Cologne, 1968 & 1970; All Things to Enjoy, 28 poems, 1979; Seedtime and Harvest, 1982; Beyond Winter, 1985. *Contributor to:* Numerous magazines, journals, including Homes & Garden; The Lady. *Honours:* Prize, Envoi Magazine, 1965; Prize, Anglo-Welsh Competition, 1969; Orbis; Has Taken part in various public readings of her own work. *Memberships:* Writers Guild; Worcester Writers Guild; International Poetry Society; Girl Guide Movement, 1921–, as District & Divisional Commissioner, Co Ranger Adviser, Co Trefoil Guild Recorder. *Address:* 32 Chaddesley Road, Kidderminster, Worcestershire, England.

BEACHCROFT, Thomas Owen, b. 3 Sep. 1902, Bristol, England. Service with BBC. *Education:* BA, Balliol College, University of Oxford, 1924. *Major Publications:* A Young Man in a Hurry, 1934; You Must Break Out Some Times, 1936; The Parents Left Alone, 1940; Collected Stories, 1946; Malice Bites Back, 1948; Asking for Trouble, 1948; Goodbye Aunt Hesther, 1955; The Modest Art, 1968; Five Hide Village: A History of Datchworth in Hertfordshire (with W B Emms), 1985. *Contributor to:* Criterion; Various magazines & broadcasting organisations throughout the world. *Memberships:* Authors Society; PEN. *Literary Agent:* Curtis Brown. *Address:* c/o Curtis Brown, 1 Craven Hill, London W2 3EP, England.

BEAGLE, Peter Soyer, b. 20 Apr. 1939, New York City, USA. Novelist; Screenwriter. *Education:* BA, University of Pittsburgh, 1959. *Publications:* A Fine and Private Place, 1960; I See By My Outfit, 1965; The Last Unicorn, 1968; The California Felling, 1969; The Lady and Her Tiger, 1976; The Garden of Earthly Delights, 1982. *Contributor to:* Holiday; Saturday Evening Post; Ladies Home Journal; Parabola; Oui; Town and Country; Atlantic Monthly; Mademoiselle; Seventeen; New York Times Book Review; etc. *Honours:* O Henry Award, 1965; Guggenheim Award, 1972; National Endowment for the Arts Award, 1977. *Memberships:* Authors Guild; PEN; National Endowment for the Arts Award, 1977. *Memberships:* Authors Guild; PEN; Dramatists Guild; Writers Guild of America, West. *Literary Agents:* McIntosh & Otis, New York City; Robinson-Weintraub, Los Angeles. *Address:* c/o McIntosh & Otis, 475 5th Avenue, New York City, NY 10017, USA.

BEAN, Kenneth Walter, b. 21 Sep. 1931, Coulsdon, Surrey, England. Journalist. m. Pamela Anne Bentley Standen, Crondall, Hampshire, 1956, 1 son, 1 daughter. *Literary Appointments:* Assistant Editor, Food Processing and Packaging, 1956–62; Editor, Food Industries Weekly, 1962–63; Editor, Westminster Review, 1963–67; Editor, World Crops, 1963–; Editor, Livestock International, 1977–. *Address:* Yew Tree House, Horne, Horley, Surrey RH6 9JP, England.

BEARDSLEY, John M, b. 28 Oct. 1952, New York, USA. Art Critic and Curator. m. Stephanie Ridder, 1 son, 1 daughter. *Education:* AB, Harvard University, 1974; MA, University of Virginia 1985. *Publications:* Art in Public Places, 1981; Black Folk Art in America, 1930–1980, with Jane Livingston, 1982; Earthworks and Beyond: Contemporary Art in the Landscape, 1984; A Landscape for Modern Sculpture: Storm King Art Center, 1985. *Contributions to:* Art Forum; Art International; Art Journal; The Public Interest; and others. *Honours:* Art Critics Fellowship, National Endowment for the Arts, 1984. *Address:* c/o Corcoran Gallery of Art, 17th Street at New York Avenue NW, Washington, DC 20006, USA.

BEARE, Geraldine, b. 29 Feb. 1948, Middlesex, England. Writer; Indexer. m. Geoffrey Beare, 4 Sep. 1971, Brondesbury, 2 sons. *Education:* Business Studies. *Publications:* Index, Strand Magazine 1891–1950, 1982. *Contributions to:* Antiquarian Book Monthly Review; Folio Magazine; The Indexer; Journal of Newspaper & Periodical History; Popular Archaeology. *Membership:* Programme Organiser, Vice-Chairman, Society of Indexers. *Address:* 39 Victoria Road, Knaphill, Woking, Surrey GU21 2AH, England.

BEAUCHEMIN, Yves, b. 26 June 1941, Noranda, Quebec, Canada. Journalist. m. Viviane Saint-Onge, Montreal, 2 sons. *Education:* Arts Degree, University of Montreal, 1965. *Publications:* L'Enfirouapé, novel, 1974, 1985; Le Matou, novel, 1981, 1982; Sueurs, in Fuites et poursuites, short story, 1982; Cybèle, short story, 1982. *Contributions to:* Sept-Jours, 1966–67; Dimensions, 1969; Liberté, 1977; L'Actualité, 1978; Le Devoir, 1978–79; Longueur d'onde, 1980. *Honours:* France-Quebec Prize, Paris, 1975; Young Authors Prize, Journal de Montreal, 1981; Literary Grand Prix, Urban Community of Montreal, 1982; Summer Novel Prize, Cannes, 1982. *Memberships:* Union of Quebec Writers; Association of French-Speaking Writers. *Literary Agent:*

Claude Choquette, 340 Neuve-France, Saint-Jean, Quebec, Canada J3B 1A1. *ADDRESS:* 247 Saint-Jacques, Longueuil, Quebec, Canada J4H 3B8.

BEAVER, Paul Eli, b. 3 Apr. 1953, Winchester, England. Author; Editorial Consultant. m. Ann Middleton, 20 May 1978, Corby, Northants. *Education:* Professional Associate, Royal Institution of Chartered Surveyors; Associate Degree, Mining Surveying, Sheffield City Polytechnic. *Literary Appointments:* Editor, IPMS Magazine, 1976–80; Editor, Helicopter World, 1982; Editor, Defence Helicopter World, 1982–; Associate Editor, Commuter World, 1984–; Associate Editor, Space, 1985–86. *Publications:* Ark Royal, 1979; The British Aircraft Carrier, 1982, 1984; The Encyclopaedia of the Modern Royal Navy, 1982, 1985; The Invincible Class, 1984; Missile Systems (With Philip Birtles), 1985; various Warships Illustrated, 1985, 1986; Encyclopaedia of Aviation (General Editor), 1986. *Contributor to:* Navy International; Avieanews International, Belgium; Armed Forces; Aero (Federal Germany); Warplane; Warship World; Ships Monthly; Chartered Surveyor; Chartered Minerals and Land Surveyor; Air Pictorial; Defenders of Wildlife USA. *Honour:* Nominated PPA Editor of the Year, 1985. *Membership:* Aerospace Writers Association, USA. *Address:* 19 Bexmoor Way, Old Basing, near Basingstoke, Hampshire RG24 0BL, England.

BEC, Pierre, b. 11 Dec. 1921, Paris, France. Professor at University of Poitiers. *Literary Appointments:* Professor of German, Medieval Language and Literature, University of Poitiers; Director, Higher Study Center for Medieval Civilizations, University of Poitiers. *Publications:* Au Briu de l'Estona: Poems in Provencal, 1955; The Hand of Dawn, 1966; La Quista de l'Aute: Poems in Provencal, 1971; Sonets barrocs enta Iseut: Poems occitans, 1979. *Contributions to:* Cahiers de Civilisation Medievale, University of Poitiers. *Memberships:* Institute of Studies of the Langue d'Oc, President; International PEN Club (Langue d'Oc). *Address:* Nanteuil, 86440 Migne Auxances, France.

BECHERVAISE, John Mayston, b. 11 May 1910, Malvern, Victoria, Australia. Writer. *Education:* Private Tutors; Royal Melbourne Institute of Technology; Melbourne Teachers College; University of London. *Publications include:* The Far South, 1961; Blizzard & Fire, 1963; World of Difference, Australia, 1966; Sketchbook Series: Victorian Goldfields, 2 volumes; Blue Mountains, 1971; Old Victorian Pubs, 1973; Ballarat, 1977; Castlemaine, 1979; University of Melbourne, 1977; Sketchbooks illustrated, various artists; Wilson's Promontory, 1976; Antarctica, the Last Horizon, 1979; The Bendigo Book, 1982; Rediscovering Victoria's Goldfields, 1980. *Contributor to:* Literary Magazines. *Memberships:* Australian Society of Authors; PEN; Fellowship of Australian Writers English Association. *Honours include:* Weickhardt Award for Australian Literature, 1968; Hon DLitt, Deakin University. *Address:* 185 Roslyn Road, Belmont, Victoria 3216, Australia.

BECHTEL, Helmut, b. 2 Sep. 1929, Dusseldorf, Germany. Author; Photographer; Composer. m. Ute Schaffter, 30 May 1958, Dusseldorf, 1 son, 2 daughters. *Publications:* Author of over 42 books with own colourphotos on wildflowers and indoor plants; orchids; animals; geography and nature; photography; including, Insekten Mitteleuropas, 1982; Perfekle Telegotos, 1982; Perfekle Weitwinkelfotos, 1984; Mein farloiger Pflanzen fuhrer, 1984; Orchideeutas (with Ph. Cribb, E Launert), 1980, 2nd editon 1985; Composer of chamber, sacred and orchestra music, 8 compositions printed. *Contributor to:* More than 60 compositions contributed to various Magazines and journals. *Address:* Haus Steinbach, 5169 Heimbach/Eifel, Federal Republic of Germany.

BECKER, Jurek, b. 30 Sep. 1937, Lodz, Poland. Writer. *Education:* Studies of Philosophy, 1957–61. *Major Publications:* Jakob der Lügner, 1969; Irreführung der Behörden, 1974; Der Boxer, 1976; Schlafloser Tag,

1978; Nach der ersten Zukunft, 1980; Aller Welt Freund, 1982. *Honours:* Stadtschreiber von Bergen-Enkheim, 1982; Heinrich Mann Prize, German Democratic Republic, 1971; Charles Veillon Prize, Switzerland, 1971; Literary Prize, Bremen, Federal Republic of Germany, 1974; National Prize, German Democratic Republic, 1975. *Memberships:* Former Member, Writers' Association, German Democratic Republic; PEN; Akademie für Sprache und Dichtung, Darmstadt, Federal Republic of Germany. *Literary Agent:* Suhrkamp Verlag. *Address:* c/o Suhrkamp Verlag, Lindenstraße, D–6000 Frankfurt/Main 1, Federal Republic of Germany.

BECKETT, Gillian, b. 18 Jan. 1935, Westminster, London, England. Former Teacher. *Education:* BA, Honours, University of London, 1972. *Major Publications include:* (co-author) Illustrated Encyclopaedia of Indoor Plants; Planting Native Trees & Shrubs (with husband), 1979. *Contributor to:* Which Book of Houseplants, 1979; The Lady; Country Life. *Address:* Bramley Cottage, Stanhoe, King's Lynn, Norfolk PE31 8QF, England.

BECKETT, Kenneth Albert, b. 12 Jan. 1929, Brighton, Sussex, England. Horticulturalist; Technical Advisor; Editor. m. Gillian Tuck, 1 Aug. 1973, King's Lynn, 1 son. *Education:* Diploma in Horticulture, Royal Horticultural Society. *Literary Appointments:* Technical Editor, Gardeners' Chronicle, Reader's Digest; Editor, International Dendrological Society. *Major Publications:* The Love of Trees, 1975; Illustrated Dictionary of Botany, 1977; Concise Encyclopaedia of Garden Plants, 1978; Amateur Greenhouse Gardening, 1979; Growing Under Glass, 1981; Complete Book of Evergreens, 1981; Growing Hardy Perennials, 1981; Climbing Plants, 1983. *Contributor to:* The Garden; The Plantsman. *Address:* Bramley Cottage, Stanhoe, King's Lynn, Norfolk PE31 8QF, England.

BECKMAN, Delores, b. 12 Aug. 1914, Ohio, USA. Author. m. Jack E Beckman, 1 Sep. 1935, Mexico, 1 son. *Education:* Chaffey Junior College, Upland, California. *Publications:* My Own Private Sky, 1980; Who Loves Sam Grant?, 1983; Who Loves Same Grant?, paper, 1984. *Contributions to:* Dell Publishing and MacFadden Bartell, short and teenager stories and articles. *Honours:* Childrens Book Award, for My Own Private Sky, International Reading Association, 1981. *Memberships:* CRRT; SCBW; Authors League; Authors Guild. *Literary Agent:* Dorothy Markinko, McIntosh and Otis, New York. *Address:* PO Box 98, Rimrock, AZ 86335, USA.

BECKMAN, Erik, b. 23 Apr. 1935, Vänersborg, Sweden. Writer. m. Lena Jacobson, 30 Mar. 1961, 1 son, 2 daughters. *Education:* Filosofie magister (Philosophy, Literature, Nordic Language), 1962. *Major Publications:* Farstu (poetry), 1963; Någon Något (novel), 1964; Hertigens kartonger (novel), 1965; Varifrån dom observeras (poetry), 1966; Inlandsbanan (novel), 1967; Kyss er! (poetry), 1969; Kameler dricker vatten (novel) 1971; Sakernas tillstånd (miscellaneous), 1973; Tumme (poetry), 1974; Jag känner igen mej (novel), 1977; Den kommunala kroppen (poetry), 1979; Kärleksgubbar! Herdedikter (Poetry), 1981; Kommunalrådet cyklar förbi (short stories), 1982; Katt och sten (prose), 1984; 10 plays for Radio, 1971–82. *Contributions to:* Critical reviews & articles in Dagens Nyheter, Stockholm, 1977–85. *Honours include:* Aftonbladet Prize, 1966; Dobloug Prize, Swedish Academy, 1972; Nordic Radio Drama Prize, 1977; Läkerol Prize, 1985. *Memberships:* Swedish Writers' Union; Swedish Union of Playwrights; PEN. *Address:* Vadarvägen 46, S–731 42 Köping, Sweden.

BECKWITH-COMBER, Lillian, b. 25 Apr. 1916, Ellesmere Port, England. Author. *Major Publications:* The Hills is Lonely, 1959; The Sea for Breakfast, 1961; The Loud Halo, 1964; Green Hand, 1967; A Rope in Case, 1968; About my Father's Business, 1971; Lightly Poached, 1973; The Spuddy, 1974; Beautiful Just, 1975; Hebridean Cookbook, 1976; Bruach Blend,

1978; A Shine of Rainbows, 1984. *Contributor to:* Various Womens' magazines (short stories). *Memberships:* Society of Authors; Mark Twain Society (US); Women of the Year Association. *Literary Agent:* Curtis Brown. *Address:* c/o Curtis Brown Ltd, 162-168 Regent Street, London W1R 5TA, England.

BECLEANU-IANCU, Adela, b. 16 Jan. 1935, Albeşti-Ialomita, Romania. Researcher; Editor. m. Beniamin Iancu, 28 Aug 1954, Bucharest. *Education:* PhD. *Major Publications:* Genesis of Romanian Culturology, 1974; Short Philosophical Dictionary (co-author), 1973; Philosophical Dictionary (co-author), 1978; The Socialist Civilisation (co-author), 1979; Romanian Spirituality, 1980; Interdisciplinarity in the Contemporary Science (co-author), 1980; Studies on the History of World Philosophy IX (co-author), 1984. *Contributor to:* Revişta de Filosofie; Contemporanul; Forum; Era Socialista; Ateneu; Cronica; Romanian Review. *Memberships:* Romanian Scientific Association; Scientific Interdisciplinary Committee of Romania. *Address:* Str 13 Decembrie No 29C, Bucharest 70707, Romania.

BEDARD, Patrick Joseph, b. 20 Aug. 1941, Waterloo, Iowa, USA. Journalist. *Education:* BS, Mechanical Engineering, Iowa State University, 1963; Master of Automotive Engineering, Chrysler Institute of Engineering, 1965. *Literary Appointments:* Various appointments on Car and Driver magazines since 1967, currently Editor At Large. *Contributions to:* Regular contributions to Sports Illustrated and Esquire; occasional contributions to more specialised publications. *Honour:* Ken W Purdy Award, 1982. *Address:* 165 E 32 Street, New York, NY 10016, USA.

BEDFORD, Bruce Leonard, b. 17 Oct. 1942, Leeds, Yorkshire, England. Writer. m. Jennifer Mary Ball, 1 son, 3 daughters. *Publications:* Challenge Underground, 1975; Underground Britain, 1985; Two radio plays broadcast. *Contributions to:* Numerous publications. *Membership:* Playwrights Company. *Address:* Cleeve House, Theale, Near Wedmore, Somerset, England.

BEDFORD, Sybille, OBE, b. 16 Mar. 1911, Berlin, Germany. Author. *Publications:* A Visit to Don Otavio, 1953, 1984; A Legacy,1956, 1984; The Best We Can Do: The Trial of Dr Bodkin Adams, 1958; The Faces of Justice, 1961; A Favourite of the Gods, 1963, 1984; A Compass Error, 1968, 1984; Aldous Huxley: A Biography, Volume I 1973, Volume II 1974. *Contributions to:* UK: Horizon; Spectator; Encounter; Times Literary Supplement; Guardian; Times; Vogue; Harpers & Queen; etc. USA: Life; Saturday Evening Post; Esquire; New York Book Review; New York Times; etc. Numerous book reviews. *Memberships:* Vice President, English Centre, PEN; Royal Society of Literature; Society of Authors. *Address:* c/o Messrs Coutts, 1 Park Lane, London W1Y 4BS.

BEECHING, Jack, b. 8 May 1922, Hastings, Sussex, England. Writer. *Publications:* Poetry: Aspects of Love, 1950; The Polythene Maidenhead in, Penguin Modern Poets, 1969; Twenty Five Short Poems, 1982. Novels: Let Me See Your Face, 1958; The Daceta Project, 1967; Death of a Terrorist, 1982. History: The Chinese Opium Wars, 1975; An Open Path: Christian Missionaries 1515–1914, 1979; The Galleys at Lepanto, 1982. *Literary Agent:* Tessa Sayle, London. *Address:* c/o Tessa Sayle, 11 Jubilee Place, London SW3 3CE, England.

BEECHING-PRIETO, Marian Train, b. 6 Aug. 1912. Teacher; Free-lance Writer. Widow, 1 daughter. *Education:* Colegio Laguarda Coroyon, Havana, Cuba; University of Miami, USA; University of Florida, Gainesville. *Literary Appointments:* Miami Dade Community College; Literary Consultant, University of Miami. *Publications include:* 18 books including: The Wise Rooster; A Kite For Carlos; Johnny Lost; Peter Pelican; Play It In Spanish; Raimundo; Fun Jewelry; All Uco and Itzo; Pablo's Petunias; Tomato Boy. *Contributions to:* New York Times; Mademoiselle; Harpers'; Orion; Exploring The Unknown; Inter Years;

800 articles and stories. *Honours:* Outstanding Juvenile of the Year, 1969; Books for Brotherhood, National Council of Christians and Jews, 1972. *Memberships:* Miami Writers Club; Friends of the Everglades; Marja Institute. *Address:* 2499 SW 34 Avenue, Miami, FL 33145, USA.

BEERMAN, Herman, b. 13 Oct. 1901, Johnstown, Pennsylvania, USA. Medical Doctor. m. Emma N Segal, 13 May 1924. *Education:* BA 1923, MD 1927, Sc D (Med) 1935, University of Pennsylvania. *Publications:* Numerous papers. *Contributions to:* Numerous learned journals including: Pennsylvania Medical Journal; American Journal of Medical Science; British Journal of Venereal Disease; Psychosomatic Medicine; American Journal of Syphilis, Gonorrhoea and Venereal Disease. *Honours:* Annual Herman Beerman Lecture, Society for Investigative Dermatology, 1960; Festschrift Journal of Investigative Dermatology, 1969; Thomas A Parran Award, American Venereal Disease Association, 1974; Citation form Governor of Pennsylvania for service on his Venereal Disease Committee, 1974; Several honorary and Life memberships. *Memberships include:* Philadelphia Art Alliance; Philadelphia Museum of Art; Sigma Xi, Phi Lambda Kappa; Pennsylvania Academy of Fine Arts; The Athenaeum of Philadelphia. *Address:* 2422 Pine Street, Philadelphia, PA 19103, USA.

BEESLEY, Patrick, b. 13 June 1913, Barnt Green, Worcester, England. Author. *Education:* BA, Trinity College, Cambridge University. *Publications:* Very Special Intelligence: The Story of the Admiralty's Operational Intelligence Centre 1939–45, 1977, USSR, 1981, Paperback, 1980; latest edition, Ballantine Books, 1981; Very Special Admiral: The Life of Admiral John Godfrey CB, 1980; Room 40, British Naval Intelligence 1914–1918, Paperback, 1984. *Contributions to:* Naval Review; Royal United Services Institution Journal; Navy International; Marine Rundschau, Federal Republic of Germany; Proceedings of US Naval Institute, USA. *Literary Agent:* Campbell Thomson and McLaughlin Limited. *Address:* 17 Clarendon Park, Lymington, Hampshire SO4 8AX, England.

BEGIN, Luc A, b. 7 Oct. 1943, Montreal, Canada. Editor. m. Lorraine Bayard, 7 Aug. 1965, Montreal, Canada. *Education:* MA. *Publications:* Vertiges, 1972; Depuis Silence, 1977; D'Après-Nous, 1984. *Membership:* Union des Ecrivains Quebecois. *Honour:* Prix Air Canada, 1984 Societe des Ecrivains Canadiens. *Address:* 3752 Parc La Fontaine, Montreal, Quebec, Canada H2L 3M4.

BEGUIN, Louis-Paul, b. 31 Mar. 1923, Amiens, France. Linguist, Writer, Columnist. *Education:* BA, Amiens-Lille; Master Degree, Sorbonne University, Paris; Management Diploma, New York; Terminology Diploma, Montréal, Canada. *Literary Appointment:* Cultural Agent (French Language Board, Québec). *Major Publications:* Miroir de Janus, 1966; Un Homme et son langage, 1977; Problèmes de Langage, 1978; Vocabulaire des Assurances, 1979; Impromptu de Québec, 1974; Idoles et Paraboles, 1982; Poêmes et Pastiches, 1985; and others. *Contributor to:* French Language daily newspapers in Québec and Montréal (more than 4000 articles). *Honours:* Poetry Award, Paris, 1967; Prix Montcalm Award (for Impromptu de Québec), 1974. *Memberships:* PEN Club of Canada; Québec Writers Union. *Address:* 165 Rue de la Gauchetière ouest app. 502, Montréal H2Z 1X6, Québec, Canada.

BEHME, Robert Lee, b. 15 May 1924, Seattle, Washington, USA. Writer; Editor. m. Geraldine Camilleri, 16 July 1982, San Jose, California. 2 sons, previous marriage. *Education:* Arts degree, Art Center School, Los Angeles. *Publications include:* Plastic Automobiles, 1955; Custom Cars, 1955; Custom Car Annual, 1957; Snowmobiles, 1973; Recreational Vehicles, 1975; Bonsai & Bonkei, 1979; Garden How To Do It, 1981; Shasta & M, Rogue, 1982. *Contributions:* Department Editor, Field & Stream, 1975–80; Camping Journal, 1971–75; Publisher, Pet Business, 1973–85; Freelance writer, major US magazines including, Better Homes & Gardens, True, Coronet, etc. *Honour:* Achievement Award, RVI Association, 1978. *Literary Agent:* Blassingame, McCauley & Wood, New York City. *Address:* 337 Bella Vista, Los Gatos, CA 95030, USA.

BEHR, Edward, b. 7 May 1926, Paris, France. Journalist. m. Christiane Wagrez, 7 Jan. 1967. *Education:* MA (Cantab). *Publications:* The Algerian Problem, 1962; The 36th Way, with Sydney Liu, 1968; Anyone Here Been Raped and Speaks English?, 1981; Getting Even, 1982. *Contributor to:* Sunday Times; Observer; New York Times; L'Express; Le Nouvel Observateur; Liberation, etc. *Literary Agent:* Ed Victor. *Address:* C/o Newsweek, 162 Faubourg St Honore, Paris 75008, France.

BEHRENS, Roy R, b. 27 June 1946, Independence, Iowa, USA. University Professor. m. Mary Elizabeth Snyder, 6 Nov. 1982, Milwaukee. *Education:* BA, University of Northern Iowa, 1968; MA Art Education, Rhode Island School of Design, 1972. *Literary Appointments:* Design Editor, The North American Review, 1972–85; Editor, Ballast Quarterly Review, 1985. *Publications:* The Life of Fiction, (with J Klinkowitz), 1976; Art and Camouflage: Concealment and Deception in Nature, Art and War, 1981; Design in the Visual Arts, 1984; Illustration as an Art, 1986. *Contributions to:* Journals and magazines including: Leonardo; Journal of Aesthetic Education; Art Education. *Honour:* Certificate of Merit, Society of Publication Designers, New York, 1973. *Address:* Department of Art, University of Wisconsin-Milwaukee, Milwaukee, WI 53201, USA.

BEHRENS-GIEGL Erna (Sylvia J), b. 26 Oct. 1917, Odrau, Silesia. English Teacher. *Education:* Language Studies, Examination for English Teaching. *Publications include:* Translation, Almerico Ribera Mariarosa, 1944; Translator, English Authors for Magazines, 1945–47; Der Reisegefaehrte, 1946; Die Bruecke in den Tag, 1947; Zur Erinnerung, 1948, 2nd edition, 1956; 99% ist wahr I 1929–45, 1969; 99% ist wahr II 1945–73; Short stories, essays & fairy tales. *Contributor to:* Der Bauernbuendler; cultural magazines; anthologies; Serial Flucht aus der Vergangenheit, 1983–84; some contributions in English, The Travelling Companion, in press. *Honours:* Lyric Prize, Die Umwelt, 1982. *Memberships:* Austrian Writers Association; Der Kreis; Lower Austrian Cultural & Native Studies Working Group; Honorary Member, European-American Cultural Society Eurafok, 1973; Verband der Geistig Schaffenden; Wiener Frauenklub; etc. *Literary Agent:* Vienna Press, Vienna. *Address:* Kerngasse 19, A–1238 Vienna, Austria.

BEIM, Norman, b. 2 Oct. 1923, Newark, New Jersey, USA. Playwright/Actor. *Education:* Ohio State University; Institute of Contemporary Art, Washington DC; Hedgerow Theatre School, Philadelphia, Pennsylvania. *Publications:* Plays: The Deserter. *Productions:* Pygmalion and Galatea; Success; The Costume Ball; The Battle of Valor; Guess Who's Not Coming to Dinner; The World of Dracula; Marvelous Party; A Marriage of Convenience; The Professor Graduates; etc. *Honours:* Second Prize, New England Theatre Conference 1942 for Inside; First Prize, Samuel French Competition, 1978 for The Deserter. *Literary Agent:* Francis Lonnee, Amsterdam, Holland. *Address:* 425 West 57 Street, New York City, NY 10019, USA.

BEISSEL, Henry Eric, b. 12 Apr. 1929, Cologne, Federal Republic of Germany. Professor of English. m. Arlette Franciere, 3 Apr. 1981, 1 daughter. *Education:* MA, English Literature, University of Toronto, Canada. *Literary Appointments:* Editor, Edge, political and literary journal, 1963–69, Edmonton and Montreal, Canada. *Publications include:* Poetry includes: Witness the Heart, 1963; New Wings For Icarus, 1966; Face On The Dark, 1970; The Salt I Taste, 1975; Cantos North, 1978; Season of Blood, 1984; Poems New and Selected, 1985; Translations of works of other poets; Poetry for children including: The World Is A Rainbow, 1968; The Adventures of Sting-a-lot Kitty, book length poem; Verses For a Children's Zoo, collection; Drama including: Inook and the Sun, 1973; Under Coyote's Eye, 1979; Improvisations for Mr X, 1980; Translations of drama: Fiction and non-fiction. *Contributions to:* Anthologies and journals including: Athanor; Annals; English Literature of the Dominions; Modern Canadian Verse; Poetry of the Committed Individual; Poets of Canada; Tamarack Review; Canadian Poetry; Quarry. *Honours include:* Epstein Award, 1958; Davidson Award, 1959; DAAD Fellowship, 1977; Several awards and grants from Canada Council and Ministère des Affaires culturelles du Quebec. *Memberships include:* President 1980–81, League of Canadian Poets; International Academy of Poets; Guild of Canadian Playwrights; Playwrights Canada; PEN Club; Canadian Authors and Composers Association. *Literary Agent:* Arlette Franciere. *Address:* P O Box 339, Alexandria, KOC 1AO, Canada.

BELINKI, Karmela, b. 19 May 1947, Helsinki, Finland. Journalist; Writer. *Education:* BA, MA, PhD, Trinity College, Cambridge University, England; University of Helsinki, Finland; Swedish University of Abo; Studied music, Finland, Salzburg Seminar in American Studies. *Literary Appointments:* Journalist, several newspapers, 1965–73, Ministry of Labour, OECD, 1973–75, Finnish Foreign Trade Association, 1976–78, Association of Language Teachers in Finland, 1978–79; Senior programme Producer, Radio documentaries, Cy Yleisradio Ab, 1979–. *Publications:* Ge jamlikheten en chans, essays, 1972; Trettioett, essays, 1979; Women's Suffrage and Fiction in England 1905–1914, thesis; Manpower Policy in Finland, editor, 1977. *Contributions to:* Hundreds of articles, radio and television programmes. *Memberships:* Swedish Writers Society of Finland; honorary positions, National and International womens organisations. *Literary Agent:* Schildts, Helsinki. *Address:* Helsinki, Finland.

BELL, Barbara H, b. 7 May 1920. Journalist; Radio Commentator. m. David L Bell, 7 May 1939, Watkins Glen, New York, 1 son, 1 daughter. *Appointments include:* News editor, Schuyler County, 1978–; Feature Writer, Reporter, Photographer, Freelance, 1954–62; Feature Writer, Reporter, Photographer, Ithica Journal, 1962–78; Editor, Schuyler County Historical Social Journal, 1964–. *Publications include:* Little Tales from Little Schuyler, 1962; More Tales from Little Schuyler, 1967; Glance Backward, 1970; Ballard of Bertie, 1966; To My Grandson and Other Poems, 1969. *Contributions to:* Mid Western Chaparral Poets; Blue River Poetry Magazine; The American Bard; Hoosier Challenge; Sunday Telegram; Chemung Valley Reporter; Hartford Times; Glance Backward, weekly History column, Ithaca Journal, 1967–78. *Honours:* B M Heith Award, 1958. *Address:* RD1, Irelandville Road, Watkins Glen, NY 14891, USA.

BELL, Charles Greenleaf, b. 31 Oct. 1916, Greenville, Mississippi, USA. Author; Educator. *Education:* BS, University of Virginia, 1936; BA 1938, LittB, 1939, University of Oxford, England; MA, 1966. *Major Publications:* Verse: Songs for a New America, 1953; revised 1966; Delta Return, 1956, revised 1969; Five Chambered Heart, 1985; Novels: The Married Land, 1962; The Half Gods, 1968; (film) The Spirit of Rome, 1965; Symbolic History (38 slide-tape shows) forthcoming. *Contributor to:* Harper's Magazine; New Yorker; Atlantic Monthly. *Honours include:* Rhodes Scholarship; Ford Foundation Fellowship; Rockefeller Grant, 1948. *Address:* 1260 Canyon Road, Santa Fé, NM 87501, USA.

BELL, Marvin Hartley, b. 3 Aug. 1937, New York City, USA. Poet; Teacher. m. Dorothy Murphy, 2 sons. *Education:* BA, Alfred University, 1958; Graduate Journalism, Syracuse University, 1959; MA Literature, University of Chicago, 1961; MFA Literature, University of Iowa, 1963. *Literary Appointments:* Professor, University of Iowa, 1965–; Visiting Lecturer, Goddard College, 1970; Visiting Professor, University of Hawaii, 1981–82. *Publications:* A Probable Volume of Dreams, poems, 1969; The Escape Into You, a sequence of poems, 1971; Residue of Songs, poems, 1974; Stars Which See, Stars Which Do Not Sea, poems, 1977; These Green-Going-To-Yellow, poems, 1981; Segues: A Correspondence in Poetry, (with William Stafford), poems, 1983; Old Snow Just Melting: Essays and Interviews, 1983; Drawn by Stones, by Earth, by Things That Have Been in the Fire, poems, 1984. *Contributions to:* Magazines and journals including: The New Yorker; The Atlantic Monthly; The Nation; Poetry: The American Poetry Review; The Virginia Quarterly Review; Antaeus; Triquarterly; Ploughshares; Field; Stand. *Honours include:* Lamont Award, Academy of American Poets, 1969; Bess Hokin Award, Poetry, 1969; National Book Award Finalist, 1977; National Endowment for the Arts Fellowships, 1978 and 1984; American Poetry Review Prize, 1982. *Address:* Writer's Workshop: EPB; The University of Iowa, Iowa City, IA 52242, USA.

BELL, Robert Charles, b. 22 Nov. 1917, Sudbury, Ontario, Canada. Retired Plastic Surgeon. *Education:* MB, BS, St Bartholomew's Hospital, London, England; FRCS; LRCP; LMC (Canada). *Publications include:* Diaries from the Days of Sail, 1971; Tyneside Pottery, 1971; The Use of Skin Grafts, 1973; Unofficial Farthings 1820–70, 1975; The Building Medalets of Kempson & Skidmore, 1978; The Board Game Book, 1979. *Contributor to:* Monthly feature article in, Coin, 1979; Games of the World, 1975; Consultant, Games & Puzzles; Editorial Board, British Journal Plastic Surgery, 1972–75. *Honours:* Premier Award, Drs Hobbies Exhibition, 1959; Prize Award, Numismatic Literary Guild, 1970–71, 1972–73. *Address:* 20 Linden Road, Gosfort, Newcastle upon Tyne 3, NE3 4EY, England.

BELLAIRS, John, b. 17 Jan. 1938, Marshall, Michigan, USA. Writer. *Education:* AB, Notre Dame University, 1959; AM, University of Chicago, 1960. *Major Publications:* The Face in the Frost, 1969; The House with a Clock in its Walls, 1973; The Figure in the Shadows, 1975; The Letter, the Witch & the Ring, 1976; The Treasure of Alpheus Winterborn, 1978; The Curse of the Blue Figurine, 1983; The Mummy, the Will & the Crypt, 1983; The Dark Secret of Weatherend, 1984; The Spell of the Sorcerer's Skull, 1984; The Revenge of the Wizard's Ghost, 1985. *Memberships:* Authors Guild; Authors League. *Honours:* Recipient, Woodrow Wilson Fellowship, 1959. *Literary Agent:* Richard Curtis. *Address:* 28 Hamilton Avenue, Haverhill, MA 01830, USA.

BELLANCOURT, Max Edmond Henri, b. 3 May 1920, Amiens, France. University Lecturer; Linguistic Adviser; Author; Radio & Television Broadcaster. *Education:* L ès L DES, Toulouse University; Diplomas in English and French Phonetics, University College, London, England, DLitt. *Publications include:* Guerres, Révolutions et Mouvements Littéraires 1815–1945, 1951; The Living Language Course, 1949–50; Notre Ville, 1961–67; En Route, 1966–67; French for Fun (2 volumes), 1968; Linguaphone English Manual, 1970; RSVP, BBC French Course (3 volumes; 3 records), 1969–70; Eurotone French Course (2 volumes), 1975; Linguaphone Intermediate French Course (3 volumes), 1979; Linguaphone English Manual (3 volumes), 1985. *Contributions to:* French review, USA; numerous BBC Schools and Further Education Programs, 1946–; ITV Schools Programs, 1962–. *Honours:* Knight, Palmes Académiques, 1963, Officer, 1975; Knight of the Order of Merit, France, 1980. *Memberships:* Societies of Authors, Radio Authors; Association for Literary and linguistic Computing. *Literary Agent:* David Highams Associates. *Address:* Au Vieux Port, 33148 Taussat, France.

BELLE, Charles Earl, b. 2 Sep. 1940, Chicago, Illinois, USA. Journalist. m. Rita Cummings, 11 May 1981, Dundee, Scotland, 1 son, 1 daughter. *Education:* BS BA, Roosevelt University; MBA, Harvard Graduate School of Business Administration. *Contributions to:* Black Enterprise Magazine, Energy Crisis. *Honours:* Economics for Journalist, Brookings Institution, 1978;

Journalist, National Endowment for the Humanities, 1979. *Memberships:* Past President, San Francisco African American Historical and Cultural Society Incorporated. *Literary Agent:* Rita Cummings, Cummings and Associates, California. *Address:* 270 Francisco Street, San Francisco, CA 94133, USA.

BELLVILLE, Cheryl Walsh, b. 27 Aug. 1944, Deming, New Hampshire, USA. Photographer. m. Rod Bellville, 28 July 1972, 1 son, 1 daughter. *Education:* BFA Photography, University of Minnesota. *Publications:* Round-Up, 1982; Large Animal Veterinarians, (with Rod Bellville), 1983; Stockyards, (with Rod Bellville), 1984; Farming Today, Yesterday's Way, 1984; All Things Bright and Beautiful, Photo essay illustrated, 1984; Rodeo, 1985. *Honours:* Large Animal Veterinarians, Outstanding Science Trade Book for Children, NSTA-CBC. *Address:* 2823 8th St S, Minneapolis, MN 55454, USA.

BELOFF, Max (Lord), b. 1913, London, England. *Education:* Corpus Christi and Magdalen Colleges, University of Oxford, MA, D Litt. *Major Publications include:* Europe & the Europeans, 1957; The Great Powers, 1959; American Federal Government, 1959; New Dimensions in Foreign Policy, 1961; The United States & the Unity of Europe, 1963; The Balance of Power, 1968; The Future of British Foreign Policy, 1969; Imperial Sunset, Volume 1, 1969; The Intellectual in Politics, 1970; The Government of the United Kingdom, (with G R Peele), 1980; 2nd edition 1985; Wars and Welfare: Britain 1914–1945, 1984. *Contributor to:* Various journals & newspapers. *Honours:* LLD; D Litt; DCL; Knighted, 1980; Life Peer, 1981. *Memberships:* Fellow of the British Academy; Fellow, Royal Historical Society; Fellow, Royal Society of Arts. *Address:* Flat 9, 22 Lewes Crescent, Brighton, West Sussex, England.

BELOFF, Nora, b. 24 Jan. 1919, London, England. Writer. m. Clifford Makins, 9 Mar. 1976, London, England. *Education:* BA History, Lady Margaret Hall, University of Oxford. *Literary Appointments:* Journalism with Reuters News Agency, The Economist, The Observer, freelance writing. *Major Publications:* The General says No; The Transit of Britain, 1973; Freedom Under Foot, 1977; No Travel like Russian Travel, 1978; Tito's Flawed Legacy. Yugoslavia & the West 1938–84, 1985. *Contributor to:* Numerous periodicals. *Address:* 11 Belsize Road, London NW6 4RX, England.

BEMBERG, George, b. 30 Sep. 1915, Buenos Aires, Argentina. Author. *Education:* BA, Paris University, France, 1934; MA, Harvard University, USA, 1941. *Publications:* La Vie Absente, 1944; L'Innocence Americaine, 1948; Fils du Pays, 1948; Quatre Mains, 1953; The American Abel & His Brother Cain, 1966; New York, 1973; Tripletale, (3 one-act plays), 1979; Knitters In The Sun, (2 act plays), 1980; Le Retour Au Pays, (Nouveau Commerce), 1985. *Contributions to:* American, French journals. *Address:* 20 rue de Dragon, Paris 75006, France.

BEN-ARI, Dani, b. Forest Hills, New York, USA. Editor; Writer. *Literary Appointments:* Editor, Long Island Magazine, 1975–78; Freelance Editor, Writer, 1978–80; Associate Editor, Auto Trim News, 1980–; *Regular Contributor,* Recognition Magazine, 1984. *Publications:* Ghost Author, Book on Fireplace & Woodstove Cooking, 1980. *Contributor to:* Long Island Magazine; Westchester Magazine; Long Island Journal; Sunstorm; New York Times; Newsday; Long Island Heritage; Auto Trim News; etc. *Membership:* Volunteer Critic, National Writers Club. *Address:* 1550 N Grand Avenue, Baldwin, NY 11510, USA.

BENATAR, Stephen Royce, b. 26 Mar. 1937, London, England. Novelist. m. Eileen Dorothy Bird, 23 Jan. 1965, Dulwich, London, 2 sons, 2 daughters. *Education:* King's College, London; Teaching Diploma, Sittingbourne College of Education. *Publications:* The Man on the Bridge, 1981; Wish Her Safe At Home, 1982; When I Was Otherwise, 1983; Such Men Are

Dangerous, 1985. *Honour:* #7,000 Award from Arts Council of Great Britain, 1983. *Literary Agent:* Curtis Brown. *Address:* 72 Berkeley Street, Scunthorpe, South Humberside, England.

BENCE-JONES, Mark, b. 29 May, 1930, London, England. Writer. m. Gillian Pretyman, 2 Feb. 1965, London, England, 1 son, 2 daughters. MA, Hons, Pembroke College, Cambridge, England; MRIAC, Royal Agricultural College, Cirencester, England. *Publications:* All a Nonsense, 1957; Paradise Escaped, 1958; Nothing in the City, 1965; The Remarkable Irish, 1966; Palaces of the Raj, 1973; The Cavaliers, 1976; Clive of India, 1977; Burke's Guide to the Country Houses of Ireland, 1978; The British Aristocracy (with H M Massinguerd), 1979; The Viceroys of India, 1982; Ancestral Houses, 1985. *Contributions to:* Country Life; Irish Times; Holiday; Vogue; Introductory Articles in Burke's Peerage, etc. *Membership:* Royal Society of Arts. *Literary Agent:* Anthony Sheil Associates. *Address:* c/o Anthony Sheil Associates Ltd, 43 Doughty Street, London WC1N 2LF, England.

BENDERLY, Beryl Lieff. b. 25 Dec. 1943, Chicago, Illinois, USA. Author. m. Jordan Paul Benderly, 22 May 1964, Newark, New Jersey. 1 son, 1 daughter. *Education:* BA 1964, MA 1966, University of Pennsylvania; Certificate in Spanish, Universidad de los Andes, Bogota, Columbia, 1964; Doctoral study. Washington University, St Louis, Missouri. *Publications:* Discovering Culture: An Introduction to Anthropology, (co-author), 1977; Dancing Without Music: Deafness in America, 1980; Thinking About Abortion, 1984. *Contributions to:* Family Circle; Psychology Today; Redbook; Science 81,82 and 83; Washington Post Book World; Smithsonian; and others. *Honours:* Woodrow Wilson Fellowship, 1964; National Media Award, American Psychological Association, 1981; Honourable mention, Odyssey Institute Media Award, 1981; Exceptional Achievement Citation, Council for Advancement and Support of Education, 1984. *Memberships:* Phi Beta Kappa; Member Board of Directors, American Society of Journalists and Authors; Authors Guild; National Association of Science Writers; National Book Critics Circle; Vice-President, Member of Board of Directors, Washington Independent Writers. *Literary Agent:* Mary Evans, Virginia Barber Agency. *Address:* c/o Virginia Barber Literary Agency, 353 West 21st Street, New York, NY 10011, USA.

BENEDETTI, Quentin J, b. 21 April 1926, Mt Vernon, Ohio, USA. Public Relations, Theatre, Recording. m. 24 Jan. 1948, 3 sons, 1 daughter. *Education:* BA Arts & Communication. *Major Publications:* My Travels with Agnes Moorehead – The Lavendar Lady (in preparation), 1985. Topsy or Sorry About That Harriett, an original all black musical fable about, The Underdog Who Wins, Book, Music and Lyrics, 1984; Co-Author of Book, Co-Producer, Chocolonia, an original musical fantasy about impotence of the Potentate on a Futuristic Planet of Chocolonia in 2100. *Literary Agent:* Larry Suglio & Associates. *Address:* P O Box 2388, Toluca Lake, CA 91602, USA.

BENEDICT, Burton, b. 20 May 1923, Baltimore, Maryland, USA. Social Anthropologist. m. Marion Steuber, 23 Sep. 1950, London, England, 2 daughters. *Education:* AB, Harvard University, Cambridge, Massachusetts, 1949; PhD Social Anthropology, University of London, England, 1954. *Appointments:* Senior Research Fellow, McGill University, Montreal, Canada, 1954–55; Sociological Research Officer, Colonial Social Science, 1955–58; Lecturer, London School of Economics, 1958–68; Professor of Anthropology, University of California at Berkeley, 1968–; Dean of Social Sciences, University of California at Berkeley, 1971–74; Associate Director, Lowie Museum of Anthropology, 1984–. *Major Publications:* Indians in a Plural Society, 1961; Mauritius: Problems of a Plural Society 1965; People of Seychelles, 1966; Problems of Smaller Territories, 1967; Men, Women & Money in Seychelles, 1982; The Anthropology of World's Fairs, 1983. *Contributor to:* Human Relations;

Amereican Anthropologist; Southwestern Journal of Anthropology; more than 60 others. *Honours:* Various Research Fellowships, 1958–83. *Memberships:* Royal Anthropological Institute, Member of Council 1962–68; Fellow, American Anthropological Association; Association of Social Anthropologists of the British Commonwealth; Scientific Fellow, London Zoological Society. *Address:* Department of Anthropology, University of California at Berkeley, Berkeley, CA 94720, USA.

BENEDIKTSSON, Jakob, b. 20 July 1907, Fjall, Iceland. Philologist. *Education:* MA, PhD, University of Copenhagen, Denmark. *Publications include:* Two Treatises on Iceland, 1943; Veraldar Saga, 1944; Ferdabok Tomasar Saemundssonar, 1947; Ole Worm's Correspondence with Icelands, 1948; G Andresson, Deilurit, 1948; Persius rimur, 1949; Arngrimi Jonae Opera I-IV, 1950–57; Arngrimur Jonsson & His Works, 1957; Skardsarook, 1958; Sturlunga Saga (Early Icelandic Manuscripts I), 1958; Islenzka-donsk ordabok Vidbaetir, 1963; Islendingabok Landanamabok, 1968; Landnamabok, 1974; Romverja Saga, 1980; Hugtok ogy heiti i bokmentafraedi, 1983. *Contributor to:* Assistant editor, Old Icelandic Dictionary, 1939–46; Editor in Chief, Icelandic Dictionary, 1948–77. *Memberships:* Various professional organisations. *Address:* 2 Stigahlid, Reykjavik, Iceland.

BENFIELD, Derek, b. 11 Mar. 1926, Bradford, Yorkshire, England. Writer; Actor. m. Susan Elspeth Lyall Grant, 17 July 1953, Savoy Chapel, London, 1 son, 1 daughter. *Education:* Royal Academy of Dramatic Art. *Publications:* (Plays) In for The Kill, 1981; Look Who's Talking, 1984; Touch and Go, 1985. *Membership:* Society of Authors. *Agent:* Harvey Unna & Stephen Durbridge Ltd. *Address:* 4 Berkeley Road, London SW13 9LZ, England.

BENGTSON, John Erik Robert, b. 21 July 1938, Degerfors, Sweden. Teacher. *Education:* MA, Uppsala University, 1964. *Publications:* Ikaros (novel) 1967; Hur jag slutade som adjunkt och gick in vid Scotland Yarks flygande polis (novel) 1969; Fotboll pa lördag (novel) 1971; Hejaröda vita laget (novel) 1975; Pep Talk (poems) 1977; Marathon, 1979; California Here I Come (novel) 1980; Hurra för de gossar som till Trossnäshea ga (novel) 1983. *Honours:* Bonniers Travel Grant, 1971; Cultural Prize, 1974; Cultural Grant, Karlstad, 1978. *Literary Agent:* Författa-förkaget, Stockholm, Sweden. *Address:* Vasagatan 17 A, 652 22 Karlstad, Sweden.

BENNETT, Gordon Clowe James Joseph, b. 17 Dec. 1922, New York, USA. Writer; Writing Instructor; Supervisory Education Specialist. m. Lois Florence Monahan, 16 June 1948, New York, 3 sons, 5 daughters. *Education:* Studied College, Military Evaluation, 2 years. *Literary Appointments:* Writing Instructor, Christopher Newport College, Newport News, Virginia; John Tyler Community College, Chester, Virginia. *Publications:* Short stories published in Anthologies; Contributor, Chapters to books on Home-Study Education; Author, Pamphlets, Circulars, etc, on educational subjects. *Contributor to:* Mystery Short Stories in: 'Ellery Queen's Mystery Magazine'; 'Alfred Hitchcock's Mystery Magazine'; Mike Shayne Mystery Magazine'; 'Espionage Magazine'; etc. *Honours:* Honour Roll of the Yearbook of the Detective Story, 1977, 1978; Honour Roll of the Yearbook of the Mystery and Suspense Story, 1982, 1983. *Memberships:* National Writers Club; Mystery Writers of America; Virginia Writers Club; Education Writers Association. *Address:* PO box 627, Waverly, VA 23890, USA.

BENNETT, Jobitharaj Joseph, b. 23 June 1931, Rangoon, Burma. Management Consultant. m. Adeline Dhanaraj, 11 June 1956, Madras, India, 2 sons. *Education:* B Com, MA, PhD. *Literary Appointments:* Editorship of Technical Magazines. *Contributor to:* Various technical publications. *Honour:* Honorary Doctorate in Literature, World University, Tucson,

Arizona, USA, 1985. *Memberships:* Fellow, United Writers Association of India. *Address:* President, Bennett & Associates, St Thomas Mount, Madras 600 016, India.

BENNETT, John (Frederic), b. 12 Mar. 1920. Educator: Poet. *Education:* BA, Oberlin College, USA, 1942; MA 1950, PhD 1956, Adams Fellow in English, University of Wisconsin. *Appointments include:* Associate Professor, to Professor, 1959–63, Chairman, English, 1960–68, Rockford College; Professor, 1968–70, Pennings Distinguished Professor, 1970–, Poet-in-Res, 1979–, St Norbert College. *Publications:* The Zoo Manuscript, 1968; Griefs and Exultations, 1970; The Struck Leviathan: Poems on Moby Dick, 1970; Knights and Squires: More Poems on Moby Dick, 1972; Echoes from the Peaceable Kingdom, 1978; Seeds of Mustard, Seeds of Tare, 1979; Fire in the Dust, 1980. *Contributor to:* The Beloit Poetry Journal; The New Yorker; The NY Times; The Wisconsin Academy Review; Chicago Tribune Magazine; Wind; Prairie Schooner; Urthkin; The Reformed Journal; Various others. *Honours include:* Mid Western Book of the Year, 1970; Midland Authors Poetry Award, 1971, 1978; Numerous others. *Address:* 526 Karen Lane, Green Bay, WI 54301, USA.

BENNETT, John M, b. 12 Oct. 1942, Chicago, USA. Poet. m. C.Mehrl Bennett, 4 July 1980, Ohio, 2 sons. *Education:* PhD, University of California, Los Angeles, 1970; Certified Poetry Therapist, 1985. *Publications:* Over 30 books and chapbooks including: White Screen, 1976; Found Objects, 1973; Meat Watch, 1977; Nips Poems, 1980; Puking Horse, 1980; Time Release, 1978; Jerks, 1980; Some Blood, with C.Mehrl Bennett, 1982; Blender, 1983; Burning Dog, 1983; Antpath, 1984; Nose Death, 1984. *Films:* E Z Sleep, 1978; Time's T-Bone, 1979; Mail Art Romance, 1982 with John McClintock. *Exhibitions:* One-man shows, readings, participation, various galleries USA and overseas, 1974–. *Contributions:* Graphics, word art, articles, reviews, translations in over 1975 magazines, journals, anthologies. Editor, Lost and Found Times, journal of experimental and avant-garde art and writing, 1974; Publisher/Editor, Luna Bisonte Prods, producer of artists' books, broadsides, other art and poetry products, 1974–. *Honours include:* Awards, San Francisco Poetry Film Festival and Ann Arbor Film Festival, 1979; Ohio Arts Council Awards, 1979, 1980, 1982, 1985. *Address:* Luna Bisonte Prods, 137 Leland Avenue, Columbus, OH 43214, USA.

BENNETT, Ray, b. 31 Mar. 1944, Wilson, North Carolina, USA. Journalist. *Education:* Virginia State College (University). *Publication:* Us All (publication pending). *Honours:* Associated Press Best Feature Reporter, 1982, 1983; Outstanding Young American; Distinguished American. *Address:* 1111 Park Avenue, Baltimore, MD 21201, USA.

BENNETT; Stephen, b. 29 Nov. 1952, Newcastle, New South Wales, Australia. Full-time Free-lance Writer; Photographer. m. *Education:* BA, English and Drama (almost completed), University of Newcastle, New South Wales; Diploma, Teaching, English, History. *Literary Appointment:* Tutor, Creative Writing, Adult Education. *Contributions to:* Most major Australian Magazines in outdoors, recreation and tourism fields. *Membership:* Australian Outdoor Writers Association (Organizing Committee Member several years). *Address:* P O Box 326, Castle Hill, New South Wales, Australia 2154.

BENOIT, Jacques, b. 28 Nov. 1941, Saint Jean, Quebec, Canada. Journalist; Wine Writer. m. Michelle Gelinas, 5 May 1962, 2 daughters. *Publication:* Jos Carbone, 1967; Les Voleurs, 1969; Patience et Firlipon, 1970; Les Princes, 1973; Gisele et Le Serpent, 1981; Les Plaisirs du vin, 1985. *Contributor to:* Weekly Columnist, La Presse, 1982–. *Honours:* Literary Prize of Quebec, 1968. *Memberships:* Union Des Ecrivains Quebecois; Sardec. *Address:* 4139 St Old Orchard, Montreal, Quebec H4A 3B3, Canada.

BENSON, Kathleen, b. 10 Feb. 1947, Keene, NH, USA. Museum Educator. *Education:* BA, University of Connecticut, Storrs. *Publications:* Scott Joplin: The Man Who Made Ragtime (with Jim Haskins), 1978; The Stevie Wonder Scrapbook (with Jim Haskin), 1978: A Man Called Martin Luther, 1980; Picture Book for Children: Joseph on the Subway Trains (Addison-Wesley), 1981, Illustrated by Emily Arnold McCully; Lena, a personal and professional biography of Lena Horne, (with Jim Haskins), 1984; Nat King Cole, an intimate biography, (with Jim Haskins), 1985. *Honours:* Recipient, Deems Taylor Award for excellence in writing in the field of music. *Memberships:* Phi Beta Kappa; Phi Kappa Phi. *Address:* 325 West End Avenue, 7D, New York, NY 10023, USA.

BENSON, Mary, b. 9 Dec. 1919, Pretoria, South Africa. Writer. *Publications:* Tshekedi Khama, 1960; The African Patriots, 1963, 1964; At the Still Point, 1969, 1971; South Africa: the Struggle for a Birthright, 1969 (International Defence & Aid), 1985; Nelson Mandela, 1986; Editor, Athol Fugard Notebooks, 1983. *Contributor to:* London Magazine; Observer; Yale Theatre; Theatre Quarterly; Botswana Notes & Records; etc; BBC Radio Drama & Documentaries. *Literary Agent:* Curtis Brown. *Address:* 34 Langford Court, London NW8 9DN, England.

BENSTEAD, Steven Cecil, b. 29 Oct. 1951, London, England. Bookseller. *Education:* BA, English & History. *Publication:* The Wooing of a Lady, 1978. *Contributions to:* Pierian Spring, short stories. *Memberships:* Writers Union of Canada; Workshop Chairman, Canadian Authors Association; Manitoba Writers Guild. *Address:* 467 Inkster Blvd, Winnipeg, Manitoba, Canada R2W OK6.

BENSTOCK, Bernard, b. 23 Mar. 1930, NYC, USA. Professor. *Education:* BA, Brooklyn College; MA Columbia University; PhD, Florida State University. *Publications include:* Sean O'Casey, (Bucknell University Press), 1970; Paycocks and Others: Sean O'Casey's World, (Gill and Macmillan), 1976; James Joyce: The Undiscovered Country (Gill and Macmillan), 1977; Who's He When He's at Home: A James Joyce Directory, (with S Benstock), 1980; James Joyce (Ungar), 1985; 3 books co-edited; edited: Essays in Detective Fiction (Macmillan), 1983; Critical Essays on James Joyce, (G K Hall), 1985; The Seventh of Joyce (Indiana), 1982. *Contributor to:* Various reviews and quarterlies; Co-editor, 2 literary publications. *Memberships include:* Board of Trustees, 1967–, President, James Joyce Federation, 1971–77; MLA. *Literary Agent:* John Hassel. *Address:* University of Tulsa, Tulsa, OK 74104, USA.

BENTHALL, Jonathan Charles Mackenzie, b. 12 Sep. 1941, Calcutta, India. Institute Director. *Education:* MA, King's College, University of Cambridge, *Major Publications:* Science & Technology in Art Today, 1972; The Body Electric: Patterns of Western Industrial Culture, 1976. *Contributor to:* Various journals, including, Anthropology Today, 1985 (formerly Royal Anthropological Institute News 1974–84). *Honour:* Chevalier de l'Ordre dea Arts et des Lettres, France, 1973. *Address:* Royal Anthropological Institute, 56 Queen Anne Street, London W1M 9LA, England.

BENTLEY, Eric, b. 14 Sep. 1916, Bolton, Lancashire, England. Writer. *Education:* BA 1938, BLitt, 1939, University of Oxford, England. *Major Publications:* Drama: Orpheus in the Underworld; A Time to Die and a Time to Live; The Red, White and Black; Are you or Have you Ever Been?; The Recantation of Galileo Galilei; From the Memoirs of Pontius Pilate; Lord Alfred's Lover; Wannsee; Fall of the Amazons; Concord; Criticism: A Century of Hero Worship: The Playwright as Thinker; Bernard Shaw; In Search of the Theatre; The Dramatic Event; What is Theatre?' The Life of the Drama; The Theatre of Commitment; Theatre of War; The Bentley Variations; (editor, translator) Seven Plays by Brecht; Naked Masks – Five Plays by Pirandello; The Wire Harp: Wolf Biermann; The Brecht Commentaries; Monstrous

Martyrdoms, book consisting of 3 plays including, German Requiem; The Pirandello Commentaries; The Brecht Memoir; also Recordings of songs, especially Brecht and Biermann. *Contributor to:* Innumerable periodicals. *Honours:* Honorary Doctorates, University of Wisconsin, 1974, University of East Anglia, 1979. *Membership:* PEN Club. *Address:* 194 Riverside Drive, New York, NY 10025, USA.

BENTLEY, Gerald Eades, b. 23 Aug. 1930, Chicago, USA. Teacher. m. Anne Elizabeth Kathryne Louise Budd, 22 June 1952, Hayward, 2 daughters. *Education:* BA, Princeton University, 1952; BLitt, 1954, D Phil, 1956, D Litt, 1985, Oxford University, England. *Appointments:* Instructor, University of Chicago, 1956–60; Assistant Professor to Professor, University of Toronto, 1960–; Fulbright Lecturer, Algeria, 1967–68, India 1975–76, China 1982–83. *Publications:* Editor, William Blake, The Vala or The Four Zoas, 1963; The Early Editions of Flaxman's Classical Designs, 1964; Editor, William Blake, Tiriel, 1969; Blake Records, 1969; Blake Books, 1977; A Bibliography of George Cumberland, 1975; Editor, William Blake's Writing, 2 volumes, 1978. *Contributor to:* Times Literary Supplement; Review of English Studies; University of Toronto Quarterly; etc. *Honours:* Fellow, Guggenheim Foundation, 1958–59; Fellow, Canada Council, and its successor, Social Sciences and Humanities Research Council of Canada, 1963–64, 1970–71, 1977–78, 1984–85; Jenkins Award for Bibliography. *Memberships:* Modern Language Association, Life Member; Oxford Bibliographical Society, North American Representative; Conference on Editorial Problems, Occasional Chairman; Bibliographical Society. *Address:* 246 MacPherson Avenue, Toronto, Ontario M4V 1A2, Canada.

BENTLEY, Judith McBride, b. 8 Apr. 1945, Beech Grove, Indiana, USA. Writer; Teacher. m. Allen R Bentley, 6 June 1970, Wyomissing Hills, Pennsylvania, 1 son, 1 daughter. *Education:* BA, Oberlin College, 1967; MA, Graduate School of Arts and Sciences, 1969, MA, School of Education, New York University, 1975. *Literary Appointments:* Editorial Assistant, Assistant Editor, Saturday Review, 1970–72; Copy Editor, Newsweek Books, 1973–74. *Publications:* State Government, 1978; The National Health Care Controversy, 1981; American Immigration Today: Pressures, Problems, Policies, 1981; Busing: the Continuing Controversy, 1982; Justice Sandra Day O'Connor, 1983; The Nuclear Freeze Movement, 1984. *Contributions to:* Seattle's Child. *Membership:* Pacific Northwest Writers Conference. *Address:* 4747 132nd Ave S E, Bellevue, WA 98006, USA.

BENTON, Kenneth Carter, b. 4 Mar. 1909, Sutton Coldfield, England. Diplomatic Service (retired), Novelist. *Education:* BA, University of London. *Major Publications:* Twenty-Fourth Level, 1969; Sole Agent, 1970; Spy in Chancery, 1972; Death on the Appian Way. 1972; Craig & the Jaguar, 1973; Craig & the Tunisian Tangle, 1974; Craig & the Midas Touch, 1975; A Single Monstrous Act, 1976; The Red Hen Conspiracy, 1977. *Contributor to:* Conflict Studies. *Honours:* Companion of the Order of St Michael & St George. *Memberships:* Crime Writers Association (Chairman 1974–75); Detection Club. *Address:* 2 Jubilee Terrace, Chichester, West Sussex PO19 1XL, England.

BENVENISTE, Asa, b. 25 Aug. 1925, Writer; Publisher. *Education:* BA, New School for Social Research, New York City, New York, USA. French Language and Literature, Sorbonne, Paris, France. *Appointments include:* Editor: Zero Quarterly, Paris, France and London, England, 1948–56; Paul Hamlyn, London, England, 1958–60; Studio Vista, London, 1960–62; Trigram Press, London, 1965–. *Publications:* Poems of the Mouth, 1966; Count Three, 1969; The Atoz Formula, 1969; Edge, 1975; Dense Lens, 1975; Listen, 1975; Apart Again, 1976; Throw Out the Life Line, 1983. *Contributions to:* Ambit; Transatlantic Review; New Departures; European Judaism; South West Review; The Atlantic Review; Ant's Forefoot.

Radio 3, Poetry, British Broadcasting Corporation. *Memberships:* National Poetry Secretariat. *Address:* 68 Bridge Lanes, Hebden Bridge, West Yorkshire HX7 6AT, England.

BEREANO, Nancy K, b. 17 Aug. 1942, New York, USA. Publisher and Editor, 1 son. *Education:* BA, Queens College, City University of New York, 1963. *Literary Appointments:* Edited Feminist Series, Crossing Press, 1980–84; Owner, Firebrand Books, 1984–. *Address:* Firebrand Books, 141 The Commons, Ithaca, NY 14850, USA.

BERESFORD-HOWE, Constance Elizabeth, b. 10 Nov. 1922, Montreal, Canada. Professor of English. m. Christopher W Pressnell, 30 Dec. 1960, 1 son. *Education:* BA, 1945, MA, 1946, McGill University; PhD, Brown University, 1950. *Publications:* The Unreasoning Heart, 1945; Of This Day's Journey, 1946; The Invisible Gate, 1949; My Lady Greensleeves, 1955; The Book of Eve, 1970; A Population of One, 1974; The Marriage Bed, 1980; Night Studies, 1985. *Contributor to:* Short Stories: Saturday Night; Chatelaine; Maclean's Magazine; Articles, The Writer; The Montrealer. *Honours:* Dodd Mead Intercollegiate Literary Fellowship, 1948; Canadian Bookseller's Annual Award, 1971. *Memberships:* Canadian Writers' Union; International PEN, Past President, Canadian Centre. *Literary Agent:* Bella Pomer. *Address:* 16 Cameron Crescent, Toronto M49 1Z8, Canada.

BERGE, Hans Cornelis ten, b. 24 Dec. 1938; Writer; Poet. *Appointments include:* Lecturer, Art Academy, Arnham, The Netherlands; Writer-in-Residence, University of Texas, Austin, TX, USA; Editor, Literary Journal, Raster, Grid, Amsterdam, The Netherlands. *Publications:* Gedichten, poems, a collection of 3 poetrybooks, 1969; The White Shaman, 1973; Poetry of the Aztecs, 1972; Va-banque, 1977; A Semblace of Reality, 1981; Texan Elegies, 1983; (novels) Zelfportret met witte muts, 1985; Het geheim van een opgewekt humeur, 1986; numerous poetry translations, Pound, Ekelof, Tarn, White, Villaurrutia; 3 prose books; 3 books of myths and fables of Artic peoples; 1 book of essays. *Contributor to:* Raster; De Gids; Vrij Nederland; New Directions in Poetry and Prose; Chicago Review; Plural; Dimension; Les Lettres Nouvelles. *Honours include:* Prize for Prose, City of Amsterdam, 1971; Van der Hoogt Prize, 1968. *Memberships:* Maatschappij der Nederlandse Letterkunde (Society of Dutch Literature); PEN. *Literary Agent:* Van Splunteren, Amsterdam. *Address:* c/o Meulenhoff Publishers, PO Box 100, 1000 AC Amsterdam, The Netherlands.

BERGEL, Hans, b. 26 July 1925, Kronstadt, Romania. Author. *Education:* History of Arts, University Cluj-Napoca, Bucharest. *Publications:* Rumanien, Portrait einer Nation, 1969; Ten Southern European Short Stores, 1972; Die Sachsen in Siebenburgen nach dreissig Jahren Kommunismus, 1976; Der Tanz in Ketten, 1977; Gestalten und Gewalten, 1982; A Picture Book of Transkylvania, 1983; Hermann Uberth oder Der Mythische Traum vom Fliegen, 1984, Der Tod des Hirten, 1985, etc. *Contributor to:* Kulturpolitische Korrespondenz, Bonn; Rhein-Neckar Zeitung, Heidelberg; Sudost-deutsche Vierteljahresblatter, Munchen; Zeitbuhne, Munchen; Der Gemeinsame Weg, Bonn, etc. *Honours:* Short Story Prize, Bonn, 1972; Georg Dehio Prize, Esslingen, 1972; Goethe Foundation Prize, Basel, 1972; Medien Prize, Bavarian Broadcasting Company, 1983, etc. *Memberships:* Kunstlergilde e V. Esslingen; PEN International, Bonn, *Address:* Rabensteinstrasse 28, D-8000 München 60, Federal German Republic.

BERGER, Bruce, b. 21 Aug. 1938, Evanston, Illinois, USA. Writer. *Education:* BA, English, Yale University, 1961. *Literary Appointment:* Poetry Editor, Aspen Anthology. *Publications:* There was a River, 1979; Hangin' On, 1980. *Contributions to:* Americana; The New York Times; Commonweal; The Yale Review; Adventure Travel; Rocky Mountain Magazine; Mountain Gazette; Poetry; Western Humanities

Review; Westways; Aspen Magazine. *Honour:* Nathan Haskell Dole Award, The Lyric, 1973. *Address:* Box 482, Aspen, CO 81612, USA.

BERGER, François, b. 16 May 1950, Neuchâtel, Switzerland. Barrister. *Education:* Licence degree in Law, Neuchâtel University. *Publications:* Mémoire d'anges, poetry, 1981, éditions La Baconnière, Switzerland; Gestes du Veilleur, poetry, 1984, éditions L'Age d'Homme, Switzerland. *Honours:* Louise Labé Prize, Paris, France, 1982; Distinction of Schiller Foundation, Zürich, Switzerland, 1985. *Memberships:* Société suisse des écrivains, Association des écrivains de langue française. *Address:* Rebatte 28, 2068 Hauterive (Neuchâtel), Switzerland.

BERGER, Ivan Bennett, b. 9 July 1939, Brooklyn, New York, USA. Editor; Writer. m. Roberta Thumim, 8 Sep. 1985, New York. *Education:* Yale University. *Literary Appointments:* Editor, Electronics and Photography, Popular Mechanics, 1972–77; Senior Editor, Popular Electronics, 1977–79; Technical Editor, Audio, 1982–. *Publications:* The True Sound of Music (ghosted half), 1973; The New Sound of Stereo, 1985 (in press). *Contributions to:* Saturday Review; Esquire; The New York Times; Washington Post; Los Angeles Times; High Fidelity; Audio; Popular Mechanics; Popular Science; Penthouse; Science Digest; Technology Illustrated; Newsday; Working Women and over 100 other periodicals. *Honour:* The True Sound of Music, chosen among the 100 best scientific and technical books of 1973 by Library Journal. *Memberships:* American Society of Journalists and Authors; Computer Press Association. *Literary Agent:* Theron Raines, Raines & Raines, New York. *Address:* 161 West 75th Street, New York, NY 10023, USA.

BERGER, Nomi, b. 11 Jan. 1945, Montreal, Quebec, Canada. Author. *Education:* BA, American University, Washington, District of Columbia, USA. *Publications:* Echoes of Yesterday, 1981; Love's Proud Masquerade, 1982; Devotions, 1983; Dragon Flower, 1984; The Best of Friends, 1984. *Memberships:* Canadian Authors Association; Romance Writers of America; Authors Guild, USA. *Literary Agent:* Howard Morhaim, New York, USA. *Address:* 545 Sherbourne Street, 1704, Toronto, Ontario, Canada M4X 1W5.

BERGHAHN, Volker Rolf, b. 15 Feb. 1938, Berlin, Germany. University Teacher. *Education:* MA, University of North Carolina, USA; PhD, University of London; Habilitation, University of Mannheim, Federal Republic of Germany. *Major Publications:* Der Stahlhelm 1918–1935, 1966; Der Tirpitz-Plan, 1971; Rstung und Machtpolitik, 1973; Germany & the Approach of War in 1914, 1973; Militarismus, 1975; Militarism, 1981; Modern Germany, 1982; Unternehmer und Politik in der Bundesrepublik, 1985. *Contributor to:* Various journals. *Memberships:* of various organisations. *Address:* Department of History, University of Warwick, Coventry CV4 7AL, England.

BERGMAN, Ellen Anna, b. 23 Apr. 1919, Gothenberg, Sweden. Stage Director. m. Ingmar Bergman, 1946, 2 sons, 2 daughters. Goteborgs Stads Fortjansttecken, 1982. *Publications:* Drama ABC, 1971, 1976; several plays produced in Theatre and on Radio. *Memberships:* Sveriges Dramatikerforbund. *Address:* Teatergatan 17, 41135 Goteborg, Sweden.

BERGQUIST, Lois Marie, b. 10 Sep. 1925, Jamestown, New York, USA. Professor of Microbiology. *Education:* AB, MS, University of Southern California; PhD, Loma Linda University. *Publications:* Lipoproteins in Health and Disease, 1962; Microbiology for the Hospital Environment, 1981; Laboratory Exercises in Microbiology (co-author), 1981; Changing Patterns of Infectious Disease, 1985. *Contributions:* 130 papers in clinical chemistry and microbiology journals, many co-authored with R L Searcy. *Honours:* Recipient Outstanding Educator Award of America, 1973; Recipient National Science Foundation Faculty Grants

for Advanced Study, 1970, 75. *Address:* 6210 Riverton Avenue, North Hollywood, CA 91606, USA.

BERGSTEN, Gunilla, b. 11 Apr. 1933, Norrköping, Sweden. University Lecturer;Theatre Critic. m. Staffan Bergsten, 30 July 1957, Copenhagen, 1 son, 2 daughters. *Education:* Doctor in Literary History (Comparative Literature) 1963. *Publications:* Thomas Mann's Doctor Faustus. Untersuchungen zu den Quellen und zur Struktur des Romans, (Studia Litterarum Upsaliensia, 3), Lund 1963; English translation: Thomas Mann's Doctor Faustus. The sources and structure of the novel, Chicago University Press, 1969; Contributions to The World History of Literature (Norstedts), 1973. *Contributor to:* Upsala Nya Tidning; Artes; Studia Neophilologica; Samlaren; Orbis Litterarum. *Membership:* The Swedish PEN club. *Address:* Folkungagatan 22 B, S–753 36 Uppsala, Sweden.

BERGSTEN, Staffan, b. 12 Nov. 1932, Orebro, Sweden. University Lecturer. *Education:* Fil dr, University of Uppsala. *Publications:* Time & Eternity, A Study in the Structure & Symbolism of T S Eliot's Four Quartets, 1960; Erotiken Stagnelius, 1966; Jaget och varlden Kosmiska analogier i svensk, 1900–talslyrik, 1971; Osten Sjostrand, 1974; Mary Poppins & Myth, 1978; Gamie Kant, 1979; Olyckan, 1982; Omvagen hem, 1985. *Contributor to:* Swedish Broadcasting Corp. *Membership:* PEN, Stockholm. *Address:* Uppsala Universitet, S–75105, Uppsala, Sweden.

BERGSTRÖM, Berit Eva Maria, b. 11 Apr. 1942, Solvesborg, Sweden. Writer; Psychoanalyst. *Education:* MA; BA; Clinical Psychologist; Psychoanalytic Training. *Publications:* (Poetry) Dimensioner, dissektioner, 1967; (Novels) Exekutionen, 1968; En svensk drom, 1970; Brodet och stenarna, 1973; Stackars Karl, 1977; Det gatfulla barnet, 1980. *Honours:* Grant, Bonniers Publishing House, 1969–70; Grant, Swedish Union of Authors, 1971–79, 1980–; Appearance in Book of the Month Club, 1977, 1980. *Memberships:* Swedish Union of Authors; Swedish PEN. *Address:* Riddargatan 68, 11457 Stockholm, Sweden.

BERISTAIN, Antonio, b. 4 Apr. 1924, Medina Rioseco, Spain. Head of Department of Criminal Law; University Lecturer and Professor of Penal Law. *Education:* MA, Burgos, 1950; LLB, Valadolid, 1953; BD, Frankfurt, 1957; LLD, Madrid, 1961. *Publications:* The Delinquent and the Rule of Law, 1971; Drugs (co-author), 1974; Measures and Prevention and Treatment in Criminal Law, 1974; The Fine in Spanish Criminal Law, 1976; Crisis of Criminal Law, 1977; Estudios Penales (co-author), 2nd edition, 1977; Cuestiones Penales y Criminologicas, 1979; Fuentes de Derecho Penal Vasco, Siglos XI-XVI, (co-author), Bilbao, Gran Enciclopedia Vasca, 1980; La pena-retribucion y las actuales concepciones Criminologicas, Buenos Aires, Depalmo, 1982; Estudios Vascos de Criminologia, (co-author), Bilbao Mensajero, 1982; Desbideraketa, Bazterketa eta Gizarte Kontrola, Onate Institute Vasco Administracion Publica, 1984; Reformas penales en el mundo de hoy (co-author), Madrid, Edersa, 1984; El delincuente en la democracia, Buenos Aires, Editor Universidad, 1985; Ciencia penal y Criminologica, Madrid, Tecnos, 1985; Jornadas de estudio de la legislacion del Menor, (co-author), Madrid, Mº de Justicia, 1985; La droga en la sociedad actual, (co-author), San Sebastian, Cap, 1985; Problemas criminologicos, Mexico, Institute National Ciencias Penales, 1985. *Contributor to:* Professional journals including International Journal for the Sociol. of Law, London, (Mbr. of Bd.); corres, Belgian and French legal journals. *Honours:* 1st Prize, Institute of Young persons Award for Study on Juvenile Delinquency and Society, 1968. Honorary Doctorate, University of Pau, France. *Memberships include:* International Society of Criminology; Secretary, Spanish Section, International Association of Criminal Law; Basque Institute of Criminology, Founder and Director. *Address:* Facultad de Derecho, Barrio Ibaeta, San Sebastian 9, Spain.

BERKE, Roberta Ann Elzey, b. 16 Mar. 1943, Elyria, Ohio, USA. Freelance Author; Broadcaster. m. Joseph H Berke, 18 May 1968, London, England, 1 son, 1 daughter. *Education:* BA, Bennington College, 1965. *Publications:* Sphere of Light, poems and graphics, 1972; Bounds Out of Bounds, a critical overview of modern American and British poetry, 1981. *Contributions to:* Various British Broadcasting Corporation radio of poetry readings and poetry adaptations. Various poetry readings in colleges and educational institutions, USA and England. *Honours:* Glascock Memorial Prize for Poetry, 1965; Fellow, Regent's College, London. *Memberships:* Poetry Society; Society of Authors. *Literary Agent:* Elaine Markson, New York, USA. *Address:* 9 Regent's Park Terrace, London NW1 7EE, England.

BERKELEY, Ellen Perry, b. 10 May 1931, New Rochelle, New York, USA. Writer. m. Roy Berkeley, 9 Sep. 1966, New York. *Education:* BA, Smith College, 1952; Architectural Studies, Harvard University, Graduate School of Design, 1952–55. *Appointments:* Senior Editor, The Architectural Forum, 1967–72; Senior Editor, Architecture Plus, 1972–75. *Publications:* Maverick Cats: Encounters with Feral Cats, 1982. *Contributor to:* Numerous articles, Architectural Forum; Architectural Plus; The Village Voice; New York Times; Architecture; Vermont Life; etc. *Honours:* John L Loeb Fellowship, Advanced Environmental Studies, Harvard University Graduate School of Design, 1972; 3rd Prize, National League of American Pen Women, for Maverick Cats, 1984. *Memberships:* American Society of Journalists and Authors; Authors Guild; League of Vermont Writers; National League of American Pen Women. *Address:* Box 311, Shaftesbury, VT 05262, USA.

BERKOFF, Steven, b. 3 Aug. 1937, London, England. Actor. m. 24 Aug. 1976, London. *Publications:* East and Other Plays, 1976; Gross Intrusion, short stories, 1978; The Trial and Metamorphosis, plays from Kafka's novels, 1980; Decadence and Greek, 2 plays, 1983; West and Other Plays, 1984. *Honours:* Distinguished achievement award for play Greek, Los Angeles Drama Critics Circle; Distinguished Achievement Award for play Decadence, Los Angeles Weekly. *Literary Agent:* Joanna Morston. *Address:* c/o 1 Clairville Grove, London SW7, England.

BERKOVITCH, Israel, b. 10 Dec. 1917, Manchester, England. Science Writer. m. June Mary Williams, 1 Nov. 1942, London, 1 son, 2 daughters. *Education:* PhD, London; Fellow, Royal Society of Chemistry; Member, Institution of Chemical Engineers. *Publications:* Coal on the Switchback, 1977; Coal: Energy and Chemical Storehouse, 1978; World Energy : Looking Ahead to 2020, Editor, 1978. *Contributor to:* Annual Coal Review in, Encyclopaedia Britannica Year Book; frequent contributions to a variety of chemical and engineering technical magazines. *Address:* 35 Wrensfield, Hemel Hempstead, Hertfordshire HP1 1RN, England.

BERKOW, Robert, b. 5 Mar. 1929, Baltimore, Maryland, USA. Physician; Editor; Teacher. m. Esther Berkow, 1 July 1951, Baltimore, 1 son, 2 daughters. *Education:* BS, 1949, MD, 1953, University of Maryland. *Publications:* Psychologic Aspects of Back Pain in Orthopaedic Surgery, 1964; Editor, The Merck Manual, Edition 13, 1977. *Contributor to:* Patient Care 2; Merck Manual; etc. *Honours:* Phi Delta Epsilon; Alpha Omega Alpha; Graduated with Honour, University of Maryland, 1949. *Memberships:* Council of Biology Editors; Society for Scholarly Publishing. *Address:* Merck Sharp and Dohme Research Laboratories, West Point, PA 19486, USA.

BERKOWITZ, Gerald Martin, b. 11 Jan. 1942, New York City, USA. Professor of English. *Education:* AB 1963, MA 1964, Columbia University; MA 1967, PhD 1969, Indiana University. *Literary Appointments:* Assistant Professor, University of Southern California, 1967–71; Assistant Professor 1971–77, Associate 1977–84, Professor 1984–, Department of English, Northern Illinois University; Associate Editor, Players, 1971–78; Editorial Board, Genre, 1984–. *Publications:* David Garrick: A Reference Guide, 1980; Editor, The Plays of David Garrick, 1980; Sir John Vanbrugh & the End of Restoration Comedy, 1981; New Broadways: Theatre Across America, 1950–80, 1982. *Contributions:* Frequent scholarly & critical articles, Shakespeare Quarterly, Theatre Journal, Players, etc. *Address:* English Department, Northern Illinois University, Dekalb, IL 60115, USA.

BERKOWITZ, William R, b. 21 Sep. 1939, Albany, New York, USA. Psychologist; Writer. m. Madelon Helfer, 3 Sep. 1962, Tarrytown, New York, 1 son, 1 daughter. *Education:* BA, Honours, Cornell University, 1961; PhD, Stanford University, 1965. *Publications include:* Community Impact: Creating Grass-Roots Change in Hard Times, 1982; Community Dreams: Ideas for Enriching Neighbourhood & Community Life, 1984. *Contributions include:* 12 articles in professional psychology journals; Various short pieces & book excerpts. *Honour:* Phi Beta Kappa, 1961. *Literary Agent:* Bleecker Street Associates, 88 Bleecker Street, Suite 6P, New York, NY 10012. *Address:* 12 Pelham Terrace, Arlington, MA 02174, USA.

BERKSON, Bill, b. 30 Aug. 1939. Poet. *Education:* Brown University, USA. 1957–59; The New School, 1959–60; Columbia College, 1959–60. *Appointments include:* Associate Producer, WNDT-TV, 1964–65; Guest Editor, The Museum of Modern Art, 1965–69; Visiting Fellow, Ezra Stiles College, Yale University, 1969–70; Resident Poet, Poets in the Schools Programmes, 1974–; Adjunct Professor, Southampton College, New York, 1979–80; Editor & Publisher, Big Sky, 1971–. *Publications include:* Saturday Night Poems 1960–61, 1961, 2nd edition 1975; Shining Leaves, 1969; Recent Visitors, 1973; Hymns of St Bridget, with F O'Hara, 1974; Visitors, 1973; Enigma Variations, 1975; 100 Women, 1975; Blue is the Hero, selected Poems, 1960–75, 1976; Lush Life, 1984; Start Over, 1983. *Contributor to:* Paris Review; The World; Poetry; The Floating Bear; Big Table; Art & Literature; Chicago; One; Telephone; Art in America; Yale Literary Magazine; etc. *Honours include:* Dylan Thomas Memorial Poetry Award, 1959; National Endowment for Arts, Creative Writing Fellowship in poetry, 1980; Briarcombe Fellow, 1983. *Address:* Box 389 Bolinas, CA 94924, USA.

BERLANS, Theodore, b. 26 Mar. 1929, Chicago, Illinois, USA. Author. m. Cynthia Rich, 23 Dec. 1956, Chicago, 1 son, 2 daughters. *Education:* BA, University of Illinois, Urbana, 1950; AM, University of Chicago, 1972. *Publications:* Author of sixteen books, most recent: After the diet...Then What?, with Henry A Jordan MD, 1980; Fitness Fact Book, 1980; The Doctor's Calories-Plus Diet, with Henry A Jordan MD, 1981; Living with your Allergies and Asthma, with Lucia Fischer-Pap MD, 1983; The Dieter's Almanac, 1984. *Contributions to:* Contributor of more than 200 articles to major magazines including: Time; Reader's Digest; Politics Today; Harper's Bazaar; Woman's Day; Shape; Fit; Vital; Chicago; Vogue; Mademoiselle; Ladies Home Journal; Family Circle, to numerous newspapers and to professional journals e.g. Humanitas; New England Journal of Medicine; Western Medicine; National Journal of Education; Modern Health Care. *Honours:* Recipient of 15 professional awards including: The Distinguished Achievement in Medical Writng Award, Greater Chicago Area Chapter, American Medical Writers Association, 1973; Public Service Award in Journalism, Magazine Category, American Optometric Association, 1973; Certificate of Appreciation, Vision Conservation Institute, 1973; Two Beth Fonder Memorial Awards for Excellence in Medical Feature Writing, Greater Chicago Chapter, American Writers Association, 1975 and 1978; Fellow, American Medical Writers Association, 1976; Certificate of Excellence, Chicago '78 Communications Award. *Memberships:* President, Society of Midland Authors; President/Fellow, American Medical Writers Association; National Association of Science Writers; Society of Professional Journalists; Authors Guild; American Association for the Advancement of Science. *Literary Agents:* Julian Bach Jr, New York City. *Address:* PO Box 59170, Chicago, IL 60659–0170, USA.

BERLIND, Bruce (Peter), b. 17 July 1926, New York, New York, USA. University Professor. m. (1) Doris Lidz, divorced (2) Mary Dirlam, 5 children, divorced, (3) Jo Anne Pagano. *Education:* Graduate, The Mercersburg Academy, Pennsylvania, 1943; AB, Princeton University, 1947; MA 1950, PhD 1958, The Johns Hopkins University. *Literary Appointments:* Junior Instructor of English, The Johns Hopkins University, 1948–50 and 1952–54; Instructor of English 1954–58, Assistant Professor 1958–63, Associate Professor 1963–66, Professor 1966–, Chairman of the Department 1967–72, Charles A Dana Professor of English 1980–, Colgate University. *Publications:* Three Larks for a Loony, 1957; Ways of Happening, 1959; Companion Pieces, 1971 and 1980–; Selected Poems of Agnes Nemes Nagy, (translator), 1980; Birds and Other Relations: Selected Poetry of Dezsö Tandori, (translator), 1986. *Contributions to:* Publications including: The Beloit Poetry Journal; Chicago Review; Epoch; The Hopkins Review; Poetry, Chicago; The New York Herald Tribune; Massachusetts Review; Blue Grass; Quarterly Review of Literature; Transatlantic Review; Iowa Review; Encounter; Stand; New Letters. *Honours:* Grants, Lucius N Littauer Foundation, 1958 and 1959; Grant, Colgate University Research Council, 1970; Hungarian PEN Translation Programme, 1977 and 1979; Fulbright Research Award, Budapest, 1984. *Memberships:* Poetry Society of America; American Literary Translators Association. *Address:* Box 237, Hamilton, NY 13346, USA.

BERLINER, Don, b. 3 July 1930, Columbus, Ohio, USA. Writer. *Education:* BSc, Business Administration, Ohio State University, 1953. *Publications:* Aviation Juveniles, a series of aviation juveniles published by Lerner Publications, Home Airplanes, Air Racing, Aerobatics, Yesterday's Airplanes, Personal Planes, Helicopters, Scale Model Planes, Flying Model Planes, Record-Breaking Airplanes, and Unusual Airplanes, 1979–85; World War II Jet and Rocket Planes, 1982; Victory Over the Wind – the Story of the World Air Speed Record, 1983. *Contributor to:* 200 + articles to aviation and science magazines in the USA, Europe and Japan. *Address:* 1202 S Washington St, Alexandria, VA 22314, USA.

BERMAN, Claire Gallant, b. 4 July 1936, New York, USA. Writer. m. Noel B Berman, 19 July 1959, New York, 3 sons. *Education:* BA, Barnard College. *Literary Appointments:* Senior Editor, Cosmopolitan, 1958–63; Contributing Editor, New York magazine, 1973–78; Editor, Permanency Report, 1976–; Editorial Board, Remarriage, 1984–. *Publications:* A Great City For Kids, 1969; We Take This Child: A Candid Look at Modern Adoption, 1974; Making It As a Stepparent, 1980, 1986; What Am I Doing In A Stepfamily?, 1982. *Contributions to:* Major newspapers and magazines including: New York; Readers Digest; Woman's Day; Working Mother; Parents; MS; New York Times. *Memberships:* Past Program Chair, Past member Executive Committee, Nominating Committee member, American Society of Journalists and Authors; Author's League. *Literary Agent:* Julian Bach. *Address:* 52 Riverside Drive, New York, NY 10024, USA.

BERMAN, Claire Ruth, b. 26 Mar. 1953, Boston, Massachusetts, USA. Medical/Technical Editor. *Education:* BA, Williams College, 1975; MS, Boston University, 1977; Science Communication, School of Public Communication. *Publications:* Copy Editor: Abrams Angiography: Vascular and Interventional Radiology, 1983; Cardiovascular and Interventional Radiology, Volume 5-8, 1982–85. *Contributor to:* Book Reviews: Clinical Lab Products, 1976; Medical Communications, 1980; Articles: Meetings & Conventions, 1977–79; Microwave Journal, 1979–81; Nursing Pulse of New England, 1978. *Honours:* 2nd Prize, Award of Excellence, Copy Editing, for Digital Subtraction Angiography: A Special Issue, Cardiovascular and Interventional Radiology, Volume 6, Nos 3-4, 1983. *Memberships:* American Medical Writers Association; Society for Technical Communications; Council for Biology Editors; Society for Scholarly Publishing. *Address:* 260 Mason Terrace, Brookline, MA 02146, USA.

BERMANGE, Barry, b. 7 Nov. 1933, London, England. Playwright-Director; Composer of Works for Voices and Process Music; Film & TV Director. m. Maggie Ross, 10 Mar. 1961, London, 1 step-daughter. *Education:* Student, Fine Arts/Theatre Science, Essex 1947–52. *Appointments:* Freelance Director, BBC Radio and TV, Radio and TV Stations in The Netherlands, Federal Republic of Germany; Freelance Film Director, International. *Publications:* No Quarter, 1968; Nathan and Tabileth, 1967; Oldenberg, 1967; No Quarter, 1969; The Interview, 1969; Invasion, 1969; Scenes from Family Life, 1972. *Contributor to:* Numerous professional journals, magazines, radio, tv etc. *Honours:* British Arts Council Drama Bursary, 1964; Ohio State Award, for Amor Dei, Acoustic Work No. 2, 1967; German Critics Prize, for Tramp, 1968; Karl-Sczuka-Preis Nomination for SOS, Acoustic Work No. 6, 1979; Karl Sczuka-Preis for Warcries, Acoustic Work No 7, 1981; Play of the Month Award, for The Soldiers, Acoustic Work No 9, 1985, presented by Deutsche Akademie der Darstellende Kunste, Schaupielhaus, Frankfurt-am-Main; Karl-Sczuka-Preis Nomination for: Nathan and Tabileth (Rehearsed), The Soldiers, Acoustic Work No 9, Testament, Acoustic Work No 10, 1985. *Literary Agent:* Ms L Bright; Worldwide Literary Agencies. *Address:* 35 Alexandra Park Road, London N10 2DD, England.

BERMANT, Chaim Icyk, b. 26 Feb. 1929, Poland. Author. m. Judith Weil, 16 Dec. 1962, 2 sons, 2 daughters. *Education:* MA (Hons) MLitt, Glasgow University; LSE; MSc. *Publications:* Troubled Eden, 1967; The Cousinhood, 1970; Coming Home, 1976; The Jews, 1977; The Patriarch, 1981. *Contributions to:* Innumerable publications. *Honour:* Wingate Prize for Coming Home, 1977. *Literary Agent:* A P Watt, London. *Address:* c/o A P Watt, 26-28 Bedford Row, London, WC1, England.

BERNAYS, Anne Fleischman, b. 14 Sep. 1930, New York, USA. Writer; Teacher. m. Justin Kaplan, 29 July 1954, New York City, 3 daughters. *Education:* BA, Barnard College, 1952. *Appointments:* Writer-in-Residence, Emerson College, 1978, 1980; Visiting Writer, University of Massachusetts, 1985; Staff, Harvard University Extension Programme, 1985–86. *Publications:* Short Pleasures, 1962; The New York Ride, 1965; Prudence, Indeed, 1966; The First to Know, 1975; Growing Up Rich, 1975; The School Book, 1980; The Address Book, 1983. *Contributor to:* Atlantic Monthly; New York Times; Washington Post; Christian Science Monitor; New Republic; Harvard Magazine; Sports Illustrated; Travel & Leisure; Ploughshares; etc. *Honours:* Edward Lewis Wallant Award, 1976; Matrix Award, 1981. *Memberships:* Co-Chairman, PEN, New England; Executive Board. *Literary Agent:* Russell & Volkening. *Address:* 16 Francis Ave, Cambridge, MA 02138, USA.

BERNE, Stanley, b. 8 June 1923, Staten Island, NY, USA. Writer; Professor; Producer and Co Host, TV Series. *Education:* BA, Rutgers University; MA, NY University. *Publications:* (with Arlene Zekowski) A First Book of the Neo-Narrative (Wittenborn), 1954; (with A Zedowski), Cardinals and Saints, (Wittenborn), 1958; The Dialogues, (Wittenborn), 1962; The Multiple Modern Gods and Other Stories, (Wittenborn), 1964; The Unconscious Victorious and Other Stoires, (Horizon Press), 1969, 1973; The New Rubaiyat, (Am-Can), 1973; Future Language, (Horizon Press), 1976; The Great American Empire, (Horizon Press), 1982. *Memberships:* COSMEP; Rio Grande Writers Association; PEN; The Santa Fe Writers Coop. *Address:* American-Canadian Publishers Inc, Box 4595, Santa Fe, NM 87502, USA.

BERNSTEIN, Charles, b. 4 Apr. 1950. Poet. *Education:* AB, Harvard College, USA, 1972. m. Susan B Laufer. *Literary Appointments:* William Lyon McKenzie King Fellow, Simon Fraser University, Editor & Founder (with B Andrews) L = A = N- = G = U = A = G = E; Editor, Asylum's Press; Coordinator, Ear Inn Reading Series, New York. *Major Publications include:* Parsing, 1976; Shade, 1978; Disfrutes, 1979; Poetic Justice, 1979; Senses of Responsibility, 1979; Legend, 1980; Controlling Interests, 1980; The Occurrence of Tunes, 1981; Stigma, 1981; Islets/Irritations, 1983; Resistance, 1983; The L = A = N = G = U = A = G = E Book, 1984; Content's Dream: Essays 1975-84, 1986; The Sophist, 1986. *Contributor to:* This; Roof; A Hundred Posters; Reality Studios; Hills; The Difficulties; Sun & Moon; La Bas; The World; American Book Review; Sulfur; Paris Review; Temblor; numerous similar journals. *Honours:* National Endowment for the Arts Creative Writing Fellowship, 1980; Phi Beta Kappa; John Simon Guggenheim Memorial Fellowship, 1985; University of Auckland Foundation Visiting Fellowship, New Zealand, 1986. *Memberships:* Editor 43 Poets (1984) in boundary 2, 1986; Language Sampler, in Paris Review 1982. *Address:* 464 Amsterdam Avenue, New York, NY 10024, USA.

BERRINGTON, Hugh Bayard, b. 12 Dec. 1928, Surbiton, England. University Teacher. *Education:* BSc, Economics, London University, 1954; Nuffield College, Oxford, 1954-56. *Publications:* Backbench Opinion in the House of Commons 1955-59, with S E Finer and D J Bartholomew, 1961; Backbend Opinion in the House of Commons 1945-55, 1973. *Contributor to:* British Journal of Political Science; Parliamentary Affairs; Political Quarterly. *Memberships:* Political Studies Association of the United Kingdom, Secretary/Treasurer, 1958-61, Treasurer, 1961-64, Chairman, 1977-80; Political Studies Association. *Address:* Dept of Politics, The University, Newcastle Upon Tyne NE1 7RU, England.

BERRY, Adrian Michael, b. 15 June 1937, London, England. Journalist; Author. m. Marina Sulzberger, 1967, 1 son, 1 daughter. *Education:* BA, Oxford University. *Publications:* The Next Ten Thousand Years, 1974; The Iron Sun, 1977; From Apes to Astronauts, 1981; The Super Intelligent Machine, 1983; High Skies and Yellow Rain, 1983; Koyama's Diamond, 1984; Labyrinth of Lies, 1985. Computer Software: Stars and Planets; The Wedgwood Benn Machine; Kings and Queens of England; Secret Key, with Keith Malcom. *Contributions to:* The Spectator; The Literary Review; Sunday Telegraph Magazine. *Literary Agent:* Gillon Aitken. *Address:* 11 Cottesmore Gardens, Kensington, London W8, England.

BERRY, Don George, 23 Jan. 1932, USA. Writer. m. Winifrid Shirley, 11 Dec. 1957, Gearhart, 2 sons, 1 daughter. *Education:* BA, Reed College, 1953. *Publications:* Trask, 1960; Majority of Scoundrels, 1961, 2nd edition 1969; Moontrap, 1962, 1969, 2nd edition; Mountain Men, 1962; To Build a Ship, 1963; Guide to Flyfishing, 1985; Guide to Mountaineering, 1985. *Contributor to:* Several hundred works of fiction & non-fiction in various US and Commonwealth Publications, 1956-. *Honours:* Burien Library Guild Award, Best Novel, 1960, 1962; Golden Spur Award, Best Novel, 1962; Gold Medal, New York International Film Festival, 1969, Chicago International Film Festival, 1970, Atlanta International Film Festival, 1969. *Address:* 500 5th Ave W, #55, Seattle, WA 98119, USA.

BERRY, Francis, b. 23 Mar. 1915. *Education:* BA, London University; MA, Exeter University. *Publications:* Gospel of Fire, 1933; Snake in the Moon, 1936; The Iron Christ, 1938; Fall of a Tower, 1943; Murdock and Other Poems, 1947; The Galloping Centaur, 1952, 70; Poet's Grammar, 1958; Morant Bay and Other Poems, 1961; Poetry and the Physical Voice, 1962; The Shakespeare Inset, 1966; Ghosts of Greenland, 1966; I Tell of Greenland, 1977; From the Red Fort, 1984.

Contributions to: Times Literary Supplement; The Listener; New Statesman; The Observer; Critical Quarterly. *Memberships:* Fellow, Royal Society of Literature. *Address:* 4 Eastgate Street, Winchester, Hampshire SO23 8EB, England.

BERRY, Herbert, b. 9 May 1922, New York City. University Professor. m. Elizabeth McHenry, 3 Sep. 1948, Plainview, Nebraska, 1 son, 3 daughters. *Education:* BA, magna cum laude, Furman University, Greenville, South Carolina, 1947; MA, 1948, PhD, English, 1953, University of Nebraska. *Literary Appointments:* Instructor in English, University of Nebraska, 1950-51; Assistant Professor of English, University of Omaha, 1951-55; Associate Professor and Head of English, Doane College, 1955-58; Assistant Professor of English, 1959-62, Associate Professor of English, 1962-67, University of Western Ontario; Professor of English, University of Saskatchewan, 1967-. *Publications:* Sir John Suckling's Poems and Letters from Manuscript, 1960; The First Public Playhouse, editor, 1979. *Contributions to:* The Globe Bewitched and El Hombre Fiel, Medieval and Renaissance Drama in England, 1984; The Globe: Documents and Ownership, The Third Globe, 1981; Americans in the Playhouses, Shakespeare Studies, 1976; Sir John Denham at Law, Modern Philology, 1974, and many others. *Honours:* Editorial Advisory Board, Records of Early English Drama; Editorial Advisory Board, Essays in Theatre; Advisory Board for the Building of Globe III in Detroit. *Memberships:* Shakespeare Association of America; Renaissance Society of America; Association of Canadian University Teachers of English; International Shakespeare Society. *Address:* Department of English, University of Saskatchewan, Saskatoon, Saskatchewan, Canada S7N OWO.

BERRY, Ila F, b. 9 June 1922, Freelance Writer; Poet; Student of Creative Writing. *Education:* AA, Fullerton College, USA; BA, John F Kennedy University; MA, English and Creative Writing, San Francisco State University, 1985. *Appointments:* Long Distance Operator and Supervisor, Pacific Telephone Co, Los Angeles, California; Investigator, International Department, Bank of America, San Francisco, California. *Publications:* Poetry: Come Walk with Me, 1979; Rearranging the Landscape, March 1986. *Contributor to:* The Los Angeles Times; Oakland Tribune; Blue Unicorns; Attention Please; Ideals; Haiku Highlights; Communicating Through Word and Image; Tunnel Road; The Sandpiper; Torchlight. *Honours include:* Jessamyn W Creative Writing Award, 1969; Woman of Distinction, Fullerton College, 1969; Grand Prize, Poetry, Poets Dinner, 1974. *Memberships:* Ina Coolbrith Circle, President 1977-79; California State Poetry Society; Robert Frost Chapter, Californian Federation of Chaparral Poets; Co-ordinator, 1981, Writers Conference, Mills College, Oakland, California, The Californian Writers Club; The National League of American Pen Women. *Address:* 761 Sequoia Woods Pl, Concord, CA 94518, USA.

BERRY, Jim, b. 24 Sep. 1946, Brentford, England. Journalist, Photographer, Editor. *Education:* City & Guilds, Photography; Institute of Incorporated Photographers; London College of Printing, Magazine Production. *Major Publications:* The Moon Stallion, 1982; New Poetry, 1983; Contributor to World Wildlife Fund Volume of Stories for Children, 1985. *Contributor to:* Sunday Telegraph; Los Angeles Times; New York Times; Look & Learn; Bild-Zeitung; Adventure Travel; Living in Thailand; Scope; Editor of In Flight magazines, Humsafar (PIA), Royal Wings (ALIA), Jatres (BIMAN), Travel Review; and others. *Literary Agent:* Carolyn Whitaker, London Independent Books; Al Zuckerman, Writers House, New York, USA. *Address:* 10 Arkley Park, Barnet Road, Barnet, Herts, EN5 3JQ, England.

BERRY, Joan Carol (née Potts), b. 21 Jan. 1933, Hudson, New York, USA. Administrative Assistant. m. Revd Dr Philip John Berry, 8 Oct. 1952, Wollaston, Massachusetts, USA, 3 sons, 1 daughter. *Education:* BA

English, Creative Writing, University of Texas at El Paso, 1985. *Literary Appointments:* Freelance Writing Staff, Fortress Press, Philadelphia, Pennsylvania. *Major Publications:* For Everything A Season, 1970; Faith in the Center Ring: An Elephantine Question, 1978; Chancel Dramas: Reflections in a Shop Window, 1984; Sweet Innocence, 1986; What if? 1985. *Contributor to:* Juvenile Magazines, various periodicals of Church Publishing Houses, newspapers, Christian Monthly Magazines; Decisions; 1985; Meditations for the Religious. *Memberships:* National Writers Club. *Address:* 5422 Wellesley Street West, La Mesa, CA 92806, USA.

BERSSENBRUGGE, Mei-mei, b. 10 May 1947, Beijing, China. Poet. *Education:* BA, Reed College, USA, 1969; MFA, Columbia University, 1973. *Publications:* Summits Move With the Tide, 1974; Random Possessions, 1979; The Heat Bird, 1984. *Contributions to:* Partisan Review; Yardbird Reader; Conjunctions. *Honours:* National Endowment for the Arts, 1976, 1981; American Book Awards, 1979, 84. *Memberships:* Poetry Society of America; Segue Foundation (Treasurer). *Address:* PO Box 685, El Rito, NM 87530, USA.

BERTIN, Eddy C, b. 26 Dec. 1944, Hamburg. Clerk/Writer. m. Yvette van Renterghem, 29 July 1967, Ghent, 1 daughter. *Education:* A6/A2 Languages and Commerce. *Publications:* Over 30 books since 1969. Most recent: De Schadow van de Raaf, 1983; De Griezelgste Verhalen van Eddy Bertin, 1984; Xenon, 1984; Powrot Donikad, 1985. *Contributions to:* More than 100 magazines and journals all over the world. *Honours:* SFAN Award for Best Science Fiction Story, 1970; SFAN Award for Best Science Fiction Book, 1972; Europe SF Special Award for Best Science Fiction Story, 1972; SFAN Award for Best Critical Works and Best Magazine, 1973; Beneluxcon Award for Best Science Fiction Story, 1976; BNA Award for Best Science Fiction Story, 1978; Eurocon Award for Best Story Collection, 1978. *Memberships:* British Fantasy Society; British Science Fiction Society; World Science Fiction; Belgian Science Fiction Association (SFAN); Ned. Contact Center, for SF (NCSF). *Address:* Dunwich House, Maurits Sabbestraat 69, B-9219 Gent (Gentbrugge), Belgium.

BESSBOROUGH, (10th Earl of), Frederick Edward Neuflize Ponsonby, b. 29 Mar. 1913. Vice President of European Parliament & Deputy Leader of European Conservative Group, 1972-79; Led Missions to the Peoples' Republic of China, 1977 and 1984. *Education:* MA, Trinity College, Cambridge. *Publications:* (with Muriel Jenkins), Nebuchadnezzar, 1939; (after H Belloc), The Four Men, 1951; Like Stars Appearing, 1953; The Noon is Night, 1954; Darker the Sky, 1955; Typtich, 1957; A Place in the Forest, 1958; Return to the Forest, 1962; Enchanted Forest, 1984. *Contributor to:* Articles and review to various publications. *Memberships include:* Theatre Association; Chichester Festival Theatre Trust; Roxburghe Club. *Honours:* Chevalier, Legion of Honour; MRI; FRGS. *Address:* 4 Westminster Gardens, London SW1, England.

BETHELL, Brian, b. 20 Mar. 1950, London, England. Writer; Theatrical Producer. m. Heather Jane Marshall, 7 Sep. 1972, 2 daughters. *Education:* BA, Law and Industrial Relations, University of Kent, Canterbury. *Publications:* The Defence Diaries of W Morgan Petty, 1984; European Entries, 1985. *Contributions to:* Numerous publications. *Literary Agent:* Fraser & Dunlop Scripts (Mark Lucas). *Address:* c/o Viking Books, 536 Kings Road, London, SW10, England.

BETSKO, Kathleen Selina, b. 6 May 1939, Coventry, England, Playwright. Div. 1 son, 1 daughter. *Education:* BA Summa cum laude, Theatre department, University of New Hampshire, USA. *Productions:* Beggars Choice, 1 act play, Eugene O'Neill Theatre Centre 1978; Earplay National Public Radio drama project 1980; Australian Public Radio 1983; Johnny Bull, full length play,

Eugene O'Neill Theatre Centre 1981; Mark Taper Forum, Los Angeles, 1981; Yale Repertory Theatre, New Haven, 1982; Stitchers and Starlight Talkers, full length play, Eugene O'Neill Theatre Center, 1982; Johnny Bull adapted for television, teleplay by author, 1985. *Publications Include:* Johnny Bull, play, 1985; Interviews with Contemporary Women Playwrights (editor with Rachel Koenig), 1986. *Honours:* New York State CAPS Grant, 1982; Eugene O'Neill National Playwrights Conference Fellow, 1978, 1981 and 1982. *Memberships:* The Dramatists Guild Inc; The Authors League of America Inc; Writers Guild of America East Inc; The Actors Studio Playwrights Unit; The Writers Bloc. *Literary Agents:* Jonathan Sand and Carol Reich, Writers and Artists Agency Inc. *Address:* Manhattan Playa, 400 West 43rd Street Number 19F, New York, NY 10036, USA.

BETTS, James Winston, b. 7 Apr. 1949, Toronto, Canada. Playwright, Lyricist, Composer. m. Catherine Ellen Knights, Toronto, 21 Jan. 1984, 1 daughter. *Education:* MA, University of Toronto, Canada. *Major Plays Produced:* On a Summer's Night, 1978; The Mystery of the Oak Island Treasure, 1983; The Last Voyage of the Devil's Wheel, 1984; Thin Ice, 1985; The Treehouse at the Edge of the World, 1986. *Honours:* Chalmers Children's Play Award, 1983; Dora Mavor Moore Award, 1983. *Memberships:* President, Guild of Canadian Musical Theatre Writers; Playwrights Union of Canada. *Literary Agent:* Ron Francis. *Address:* c/o Ron Francis, 12 Birch Avenue, Suite 205, Toronto, Ontario, M4V IC8, Canada.

BETTS, Richard Kevin, b. 15 Aug, 1947, Easton, Pennsylvania, USA. Foreign Policy Analyst, Brookings Institution. *Education:* BA, Harvard University, USA, 1969, MA, 1971, PhD 1975. *Publications:* Soldiers, Statesmen and Cold War Crises, 1977; co-author, The Irony of Vietnam: The System Worked, 1980; co-author, Nuclear Non-Proliferation and US Foreign Policy, 1980; Cruise Missiles: Technology, Strategy, Politics, (editor) 1981; Surprise Attack: Lessons for Defense Planning, 1982. *Contributions to:* World Politics; Foreign Policy; Orbis Political Science Quarterly; Journal of Strategic Studies (ed board). *Honours:* Sumner Prize, Harvard University, 1976; National Intelligence Study Centre Award for Best Article, 1978 and 1980; Woodrow Wilson Award, 1980; Harold D Lasswell Award, 1979. *Memberships:* Council on Foreign Relations; American Political Science Association; International Studies for Strategic Association; Arms Control Association; International Institute for Strategic Studies; Consortium for the Study of Intelligence. *Address:* 4740 Connecticut Avenue NW, Apartment 303, Washington, DC 20008, USA.

BEUKENKAMP, Ger, b. 31 July 1946, Amsterdam, The Netherlands. Playwright. *Appointment:* Teacher, Playwrighting, School of Stage Directing, Amsterdam. *Publications:* Plays: Several TV plays; Als de Lente komt; Oma brengt iets moois uit Holland; Er Waren twee Koningskinderen; Stage Plays: Weiland; De Wisselwoing, Het College, Domela Nieuwenhuis. *Honours:* G Van der Viesprijs Prize for Weiland, 1976; Visser Neerlandeiaprijs, for De Wisselwoning. *Literary Agent:* International Drama Agency, Amsterdam. *Address:* Amstel 330 hs, 1017 Ar Amsterdam, The Netherlands.

BEUKES, Gerhard Johannes, b. 21 Nov. 1913, Upington, South Africa. University Professor, Afrikaans Literature. *Education:* BA, STD, University of Stellenbosch; MA, University of South Africa; Litt D, University of Pretoria. *Publications:* Die Moderne Eenbedryf, 1947; Skrywers en Rigtings, 1952; 7 Drama, 1947-61; 20 One Act Plays, 1945-69. *Memberships:* Past Chairman, South Africa Akademie vir Wetenskap en Kuns; De Maatschappy der Nederlandsche, Leiden; South African Authors Guild, Honorary Member; Performing Arts Council, OFS. *Honours:* Hertzog Prize for Drama, 1952; 1st Prize for Drama, Tercentenary Celebration, Dept of Arts & Science, 1952. *Address:* 24

Peter Cresc, Bloemfontein 9301, Republic of South Africa.

BEVERIDGE, William Ian Beardmore, b. 23 Apr. 1908, Junee, Australia. University Professor. m. Patricia Dorothy Thomson, 31 May 1935, Melbourne, Australia, 1 son. *Education:* BVSc, 1931, DVSc, 1940, Sydney University; DSc, Cambridge University, 1974. *Publications:* The Art of Scientific Investigation, 1950; Frontiers in Comparative Medicine, 1972; Influenza: the last great plague, 1977; Seeds of Discovery 1980; Viral Diseases of Farm Livestock, 1981; Bacterial Diseases of Cattle, Sheep and Goats, 1983. *Contributions to:* Numerous contributions to scientific journals mainly on infectious diseases of man and animals. *Honours:* D V M (h c) Hannover; Gamgee Gold Medal of World Veterinary Association; Honorary membership of many professional associations in seven countries. *Address:* University House, GPO Box 1535, Canberra 2601, Australia.

BEYNON, Daniel Islwyn, b. 12 June 1920, Gwynfa Pontyates, Wales. Baptist Minister; Writer. m. Margaret Mary Onwy, Meinciau, 1 son. *Education:* Myrdin College, Carmarthen; Swansea University; Presbyterian College, Carmarthen; Diploma in Theology, University of Wales. *Publications:* Cyrchu At Y Sêr, 1963; Llwybrau'r Gorlan, 1964; Gwersi'r Gorlan, 1967; Hen Bentrefwyr, 1968; Mersydd Y Gorlan, 1969; Talcen Caled, 1971; Eseia Williams, Aberteifi, 1973; Mewn Trwbwl O Hyd, 1974; Pedol Yn Lludw, 1974. *Contributions to:* Seren Cymru Antur; Editor, Welsh Baptist Year Book, 1974. *Address:* Maesgwyn, Carmel, Llanelli SA14 7TL, Dyfed, Wales.

BEZRUCHKA, Stephen Anthony, b. 9 May 1943, Toronto, Canada. Medical Doctor. *Education:* BSc, University of Toronto, 1966; AM, Harvard University, USA, 1967; MD, Stanford University, USA, 1973. *Publications:* A Guide to Trekking in Nepal, 1972, 5th edition, 1985. *Contributor to:* Field Correspondent, Photographer, Equinox; Technical Photography. *Address:* 5 West Harrison Street, Seattle, WA 98119, USA.

BHANDARI, M C, b. 19 Nov. 1935, Chhotikhatu, Rajasthan, India. Chartered Accountant; Social Worker. m. Champadevi Bhandari, 7 May 1951, Chhotikhatu, 2 sons, 5 daughters. *Education:* BComm, Calcutta University, 1955; Chartered Accountant, Institute of Chartered Accountants of India, 1956. *Literary Appointments:* Editor: Finance and Commerce, 1958–70; Quill, 1972–80; Chartered Accountant, 1970–71. *Publications:* Guide to Company Law Procedures, 1964; Company Formation Encyclopedia, 1965; Corporate Law and Management Encyclopedia, 1968; Memorandum and Articles of Association of Companies, 1984. *Contributing to:* Statesman; Economic Times; Financial Express; Hindustan Standard; Chartered Accountant; Amritz Bahar Patrika; Company Law Journal; Lok Udyag; Commerce; Capital, and others. *Honours:* Doctoral Membership, World University Round Table, Arizona, USA, 1982; President, Institute of Chartered Accountants of India, 1970–71. *Memberships:* President, Society of Intellectuals and Social Workers of India; Chairman, Young Writers Workshop; Convener, BHARAT NIRMAN; President, National Forum of Shareholders. *Address:* 4 Synagogue Street, Calcutta 700001, India.

BHARATI, Agehananda, b. 20 Apr. 1923, Vienna, Austria. (US Citizen). Professor of Anthropology. *Education:* AB, Vienna, 1948; PhD, Sannyasi Mahavidyalaya Varanasi, India 1951. *Publications include:* The Ochre Robe, 1961; The Asiana in East Africa: Jayhind & Uhuru, 1972; The Light at the Centre: Context and Pretext of Modern Mysticism, 1976; Great Traditions & Little Traditions: Indological Studies in Anthropology, 1976; Hindu Views and Ways and the Hindu Muslim Interface, 1982. *Contributor to:* Various professional journals. *Memberships:* Fellow, American Anthropological Association; Fellow, Anthropological Society; Fellow, Society of Applied Anthropology;

Fellow, Royal Asiatic Society, UK; Editor; Tibet Society Bulletin, 1973–. *Address:* 500 Univesity Pl, Syracuse, NY 13210, USA.

BHATIA, Jamunadevi (June), b. 6 June 1919, England, Writer. *Appointments:* Writer in Residence, Lethbridge Community College, Alberta, Canada. *Publications:* Alien There is None, 1959; The Latchkey Kid, 1971; Twopence to Cross the Mersey, 1974; Most Precious Employee, 1976; Minerva's Stepchild, 1979; Liverpool Daisy, 1979; Anthology 80, 1979; By the Waters of Liverpool, 1981; Three Women of Liverpool, 1984; The Suicide Tower, 1981; Lime Street at Two, 1985; Thursday's Child, 1985; The Moneylenders of Shahpur, 1987. *Contributor to:* Government of Alberta Heritage Magazine; Book Reviews: Canadian Author and Bookman, Edmonton Journal. *Honours:* Hudson's Bay Beaver Award, best unpublished manuscript, 1970, 1977; Edmonton Journal Literary Competition Honourable Mention; Honoured by City of Edmonton for distinguished contribution to Literature and to life of the City, 1977; Government of Alberta Achievement Award for Literature, 1979; Nominated for YWCA Woman of the Arts in 1985. *Memberships:* Writers' Union of Canada; Society of Authors, London; Canadian Association of Children's Authors, Illustrators and Performers; Authors' lending and copyright Society Ltd, London. *Agent:* Richard Simon, Richard Scott Simon Ltd. *Address:* c/o The Writers' Union of Canada, 24 Ryerson Street, Toronto, Ontario, Canada.

BIAGI, Shirley Anne, b. 21 June 1944, San Francisco, California, USA. Professor of Journalism. m. Victor J Biondi, 1964, San Francisco, 3 sons. *Education:* Masters Degree in English Literature. *Literary Appointment:* Professor of Journalism, California State University, Sacramento, 1975–. *Publications:* How to Write and Sell Magazine Articles, 1981; A Writer's Guide to the Word Processors, 1984; Interviews that Work, 1986. *Contributions to:* Parade; Writers Digest; Christian Science Monitor; Antioch Review. *Honours:* Poynter Institute for Media Studies Fellow, 1983; Danforth Associate, 1983–. *Memberships:* American Society of Journalists and Authors; Authors Guild. *Address:* California State University, Sacramento, Journalism Department, 6000 J Street CTR 302, Sacramento, CA 95819, USA.

BIANCHI, Robert Steven, b. 30 November, 1943, New York, USA. Museum Curator. *Education:* BA, Rutgers University, 1965; MA 1969, PhD 1976, Institute of Fine Arts, University of New York, USA. *Literary Appointments:* Executive Board Member, Corpus Antiquitatum Augyptiacarum (English Language Editor), 1978; Contributor for Egypt, Archaeological News, 1982; Book Review Editor, Journal of the American Research Centre in Egypt, 1984. *Major Publications:* Egyptian Treasures, 1979; Ancient Egyptian Sculpture, 1979; Treasures of the Nile/Museums of Egypt, 1960; The Vatican Collections: Papacy & Art, 1982; Neferut Net Kemit, 1983. *Contributor to:* Various journals, including: Apollo; The Art Gallery; Archaeology; New Orleans Opera Magazine, (An Egyptologist looks at Aida). *Address:* Department of Egyptian Art, The Brooklyn Museum, Brooklyn, NY 11238, USA.

BIBERGER, Erich Ludwig, b. Passau, Bavaria, Germany. Editor; Writer. *Education:* Exam. Städt, Wirtschafsaufbauschule Passau, 1944; Volkshochschule Passau. *Publications Include:* Dreiklang der Stille (Poems), 1955; Rungang uber dem Nordlicht (Philosophy, fairy tales of atomic age), 1958; Die Traumwelle (novel), 1962; Denn im Allsein der Welt (poems), 1966; Daudu oder der Mann im Mond (radio plays), 1967; Gar mancher (satircal verses), 1967; Anthology 3 (in 47 languages), 1979; Andere Wege bis Zitterluft (Poems), 1982; Was ist hier Schilf, was Reiher (Haiku), 1984; Nichts als das Meer; (Poems), 1984. *Memberships Include:* Chairman, Regensburger Schriftslellerqruppe International, Joint Association of Authors in 16 Countries of the World, 1960– ; Founder, Director, International Regensburger Literaturtage,

1967– : Internationationale Jungautoren-Wettbewerbe, 1972–. Recipient several honours. *Address:* Reichsstrasse 5, D–8400 Regensburg, Federal Republic of Germany.

BIDDIX, Edith Mae, b. 17 Mar. 1941, McDowell County, North Carolina, USA. Reading Aide in Public Schools. *Education:* Diploma, Business Administration, Marion College of Commerce; Diploma, Business and Secretarial Education, Western Piedmont Community College; Secretarial Education, McDowell Technical College. *Publication:* Why Over-Population Is A Sin, 1971. *Contributions of:* Articles and poems to magazines and journals. Articles: Faith and Hope; Poems: Contemporary Literature Press; The Gifts of Art; Springtime; Friendship; Happy Mother's Day; The Touch and God; Love Is; The Touch of His Hand; Thank God For; God's Love Is There; Articles include: Use Your Talents for God; Others Discovering Love. *Honour:* First Place for, The Gifts of Art in McDowell Poetry Contest, 1979. *Memberships:* North Carolina Poetry Society; Christian Writers Club of America; Former Member, National Writers Club. *Address:* 407 Veterans Drive, Marion, NC 28752, USA.

BIDGOOD, Ruth, b. 20 July 1922, Writer. *Education:* BA, 1943, MA, 1947, St Hugh's College, Oxford University, England. *Appointments:* Coder, WRNS; Sub-editor, Chamber's Encyclopedia. *Publications:* The Given Time, 1972; Not Without Homage, 1975; The Print of Miracle, 1978; Lighting Candles, 1982. Radio Poem: Hymn to Saint Efraed. *Contributions to:* Poetry Wales; Anglo-Welsh Review; Planet; Aquarius; Country Life; Countryman; Various others. Featured in various anthologies including: Borestone Mnton. *Honours:* Award for, Not Without Homage, Welsh Arts Council, 1976. *Membership:* English Language Section, Aeademi Gymreig. *Address:* Tyhaearn, Abergwesyn, Llanwrtyd Wells, Powys, LD5 4TP, Wales.

BIEGEL, Paul Johannes, b. 25 Mar. 1925, Bussum, The Netherlands. Author. *Publications:* The King of the Copper Mountains, 1969; The Seven Times Search, 1971; The Little Captain, 1971; The Twelve Robbers, 1974; The Gardens of Dorr, 1975; Far Beyond & Back Again, 1977; The Elephant Party, 1977; Letters from the General, 1979; The Looking-Glass Castle, 1979; The Dwarfs of Nosegay, 1978; Robber Hopsika, 1978; The Fattest Dwarf of Nosegay, 1980; The Tin Can Beast, 1980; The Curse of the Werewolf, 1981; Virgil Nosegay and the Cake Hunt, 1981; Crocodile Man, 1982; Virgil Nosegay and the Wellington Boots, 1984. *Honours:* Best Children's Book of the Year, 1965; Golden Pencil Award, 1972; Silver Pencil Award, 1972, 1974, 1981; Nienke van Hichtum prize for Children's Literature, 1973, State Prize, 1974. *Memberships:* Vereninging van Letterkundigen; Maatschappij van Letterkunde. *Address:* Keizersgracht 227, Amsterdam, The Netherlands.

BIEN, Peter A, b. 28 May 1930, New York City, USA. Professor of English. m. Chrysanthi Yiannakou, 17 July 1955, Thesalonika, Greece, 2 sons, 1 daughter. *Education:* BA, Haverford College, 1952; MA, 1957, PhD, 1961, Columbia University; Bristol University, England; Woodbrooke College, England; Harvard College. *Literary Appointment:* Associate Editor, Journal of Modern Greek Studies, 1984–. *Publications include:* Translations of 3 Nikoa Kazantzakis works into English; L P Hartley, 1963; Constantine Cavafy, 1964; Nikoa Kazantzakis, 1972; Kazantzakis and the Linguistic Revolution in Greek Literature, 1972; Demotic Greek (with J Rassias and C Bien), 1972; Translation of: Life in the Tomb (by Stratis Myrivilis), 1976; Antithesis and Synthesis in the Poetry of Yannis Ritsos, 1980; Demotic Greek II (with J Rassias, C Bien and C Alexion), 1983; Three Generations of Greek Writers, 1983. *Contributor to:* Byzantine and Modern Greek Studies (Associate Editor); World Literature Today! *Honours:* E Harris Harbison Award for Distinguished Teaching, Danforth Foundation, 1968; Fulbright Fellowship to Australia, 1983. *Memberships:* MLA: Modern Greek Studies Association, President, 1982–84. *Address:* Department

of English, Dartmouth College, Hanover, NH 03755, USA.

BIERMAN, Jack Victor, b. 15 Oct. 1942, New York City, New York, USA. Editor. m. Susan Owaki, 11 Aug. 1983, Los Angeles, California, 1 daughter. *Education:* BA, Journalism. *Publications:* Los Angeles Parent Magazine; Parenting of Orange County. *Address:* 3025 Brand Boulevard, Glendale, CA 91204, USA.

BIESANZ, Richard John, b. 5 Mar. 1944, Winona, Minnesota, USA. Sociologist. m. Karen Ann Zubris, 3 July 1965, Detroit, 2 daughters. *Education:* BA, Oakland University, 1964; MA, University of Toledo, 1968. *Publications:* The Costa Ricans, with Mavis Hiltunen Biesanz & Karen Zubris Biesanz, 1982. *Contributions:* Costa Rica: The People, with John Biesanz, Encyclopaedia Britannica, 1970; Numerous reviews, anthropological documentary films, Choice, magazine 1983–. *Address:* 37 West 4th Street, Corning, NY 14830, USA.

BIESIADECKI, Roman Jerome, b. 6 Apr. 1925, Chicopee, Massachusetts, USA. Senior Project Engineering Writer (Aerospace). m. Adelle, 27 Aug. 1957, Las Vegas, USA, 2 daughters. *Education:* BS, University of Detroit, 1949; Certificate, University of Michigan, 1952; BA, Columbia College, Los Angeles, 1958. *Major Publications:* Howard Hughes & The Spruce Goose, Flying the Helicopter, 1980; Howard Hughes – the Best Dam Pilot (in his time); I Believed Him; The Year of the LAMdal Factor – DNA/2183; The Disappearance of Vance Gordon; Detective, Last Case for Roman Jerome. *Memberships:* Aviation/Space Writers Association; American Society of Writers; Science Fiction Writers of America. *Address:* 1003 Stichman Avenue, La Puente, CA 91746, USA.

BIGSBY, Christopher William Edgar, b. 27 June 1941, Dundee, Scotland. University Professor. *Education:* BA, MA, Sheffield University; PhD, Nottingham University. *Publications:* Confrontation & Commitment: A Study of Contemporary American Drama, 1967; Edward Albee, 1969; Dada & Surealism, 1972; Tom Stoppard, 1976; The Second Black Renaissance, 1980; Joe Orton, 1982, 1984, 1985; David Mamet, 1985; Editor, The Black American Writer, 1969; Approaches to Popular Culture, 1975; Superculture, 1976; Edward Albee, 1976; Contemporery English Drama, 1981; The Radical Imagination and the Liberal Tradition, 1982. *Contributor to:* BBC TV & Radio. *Literary Agent:* Curtis Brown; Anthony Sheil. *Address:* 3 Church Farm, Colney, Norwich, England.

BIGUENET, John Joseph, b. 9 Mar. 1949, New Orleans, Louisiana, USA. Teacher; Writer. *Education:* BA, Loyola University, 1971; MFA, University of Arkansas, 1976. *Literary Appointments include:* Poet-in-Residence, University of Arkansas at Little Rock, 1974–76; Freelance Writer, 1976–77; Associate Professor, Loyola University, 1977–; Editor, New Orleans Review, 1979–; Visiting Poet-in-Residence, University of Texas, Dallas, 1980; Literature Panel, National Endowment for the Arts, 1983–85. *Publications:* Foreign Fictions 1978. Contributions in anthologies: Contemporary Poetry in America, 1973; Eating the Menu: Contemporary American Poetry, 1974; Intro 5, 1974; Life as We Know It, 1975. *Contributor to:* Various journals including: The North American Review; Ploughshares; The Georgia Review; Poetry Now; The New Orleans Review; Rhetoric Review; Contemporary Literature in Translation; Mundus Artium; Translation Review; The Lowlands Review and others. *Honours include:* Harpers Magazine Writing Award, 1971; Felix C McKean Award, 1972, 73 and 74; Master Poet Grant, 1974; House of Books Award for Literary Achievement, 1974. *Memberships:* American Literary Translators Association, President; Associated Writing Programs. *Address:* Department of English, Loyola University, New Orleans, LA 70118, USA.

BIHAILJI-MERIN, Oto, b. 3 Jan. 1904, Zemun, Belgrade, Yugoslavia. Art Critic; Author; Essayist. m. Lise Ascher, 1938, 1 daughter. *Education:* Academy of Fine Arts, Belgrade & Berlin. *Publications:* Conquest of Skies, 1936; Spain between Death & Birth, 1937; Modern German Art, 1938; Jugoslavia, a Small Country between Worlds, 1954, 1955, 1956; Primitive Artists in Yugoslavia, 1959; Masks of the Worlds, 1954, 1955, 1956; Primitive Artists in Yugoslavia, 1959; Masks of the World, 1969; End of Art in the Age of Science, 1969; Modern Primitives, Masters of Naive Art? 1971, 1974; Image and Imagination, 1974; Advantures of Modern Art, with N Tomasevic, 1984. *Contributor to:* Various magazines and Journals. *Honours:* Gottfried v Herder Prize, University of Vienna, 1964; Nolit Prize, Belgrade, 1974; AVNOJ Prize, Yugoslavia, 1984. *Memberships:* Yugoslavian Writers Association; Academy of Arts, Brussels. *Address:* Nemanjina 3/111, 11000 Belgrade, Yugoslavia.

BILDERBACK, Diane Elizabeth (Letsom), b. 3 Apr. 1951, Medford, Oregon, USA. Freelance Writer. m. David Earl Bilderback, 27 June 1970, Eugene, Oregon, 2 sons. *Education:* BS, University of Montana, 1974. *Publications:* Garden Secrets (co-author), 1982; Bacckyard Fruits and Berries (co-author), 1984. *Contributions to:* Garden Calendar for Organic Gardening (writer of Zone 1 portion); Organic Gardening; American Journal of Botany (two research articles with husband). *Literary Agent:* Janet Chenery, Chenery Associates. *Address:* 5220 Larch, Missoula, MT 59802, USA.

BILLINGS, Robert, b. 2 June 1949, Niagara Falls, Ontario, Canada. Poet; Editor; Critic. m. Anne Vaughan-Evans, 3 June 1978, Windsor, 1 son. *Education:* BA, History/German, 1971, BA, English, 1974, MA, English, 1976, Queen's University; MA English, Creative Writing, University of Windsor, 1978. *Appointments:* Assistant Editor, Quarry, 1974–77; Associate Editor, Poetry Windsor Poesie, 1977–78; Revies Editor, General Editor, Waves, 1980–83; Editor, Poetry Canada Review, 1984–; Editor, Poetry Toronto, 1983–. *Publications:* Blue Negatives, 1977; The Elizabeth Trinities, 1981; A Heart of Names, 1983; Trying to Dream for My Son, 1984; The Revels, 1986; Anthology Credits include: Here Is a Poem, 1983; The Inner Ear, 1982; The Toronto Collection, 1983. *Contributor to:* Numerous Journals, Canada and Abroad. *Honours:* James H Stitt Prize for Poetry, 1974; Ontario Arts Council and Canada Council Grants, 1977–85. *Memberships:* League of Canadian Poets, Toronto Representative, 1984–85, Treasurer, 1984–85, Gerald Lampert Memorial Award Committee, 1983–84, 2nd Vice President, Chair, Membership Committee, 1985–86. *Address:* 319 St Germain Avenue, Toronto, Ontario M5M 1W4, Canada.

BILLINGS, William Dwight, b. 29 Dec. 1910, Washington DC, USA. University Professor. m. Shirley Ann Miller, 29 July 1958. *Education:* BA, Butler University, 1933; MA 1935, PhD 1936, Duke University. *Literary Appointments:* Editor, Ecology, 1952–57; Editor, Ecological Monographs, 1969–70; Editorial Board, Arctic and Alpine Research, 1975–82; Editorial Board, Ecological Studies, 1975–. *Publications:* Plants and the Ecosystem 1964; Plants, Man and the Ecosystem, 1970; Vegetation and the Environment (with B R Strain) 1974; Plants and the Ecosystem, 3rd edition, 1978; Vegetation of North America (with M G Barbour) 1986. *Contributions to:* More than 100 articles in scientific journals and magazines. *Honours:* Mercer Award, Ecological Society of America, 1962; American Academy Arts and Sciences 1978–; President, Ecological Society of America 1978–79; Honorary Foreign Member, British Ecological Society, 1982–; Fellow, Arctic Institute of North America, 1979–. *Address:* Department of Botany, Duke University, Durham, NC 27706, USA.

BILSON, Geoffrey, b. 27 Jan. 1938, Cardiff, Wales. Professor. m. Beth McLeod, Saskatoon, Canada, 6 Mar. 1971, 1 son, 1 daughter. *Education:* BA, University of Wales; MA, PhD, Stanford University, California, USA.

Publications: A Darkened House; Cholera in 19th Century Canada, 1980; Goodbye Sarah, 1981; Death Over Montreal, 1982; Hockey Bat Harris, 1984. *Contributions to:* Numerous professional & historical journals, articles & reviews. *Memberships:* Writers Union of Canada; Canscaip; Saskatchewan Writers Guild. *Address:* Department of History, University of Saskatchewan, Saskatoon, Saskatchewan, Canada S7N OWO.

BIRCH, Anthony Harold, b. 17 Feb. 1924, Ventnor, Isle of Wight, England. Professor of Political Science. *Education:* BSc (Econ), PhD, University of London. *Major Publications include:* Federation, Finance & Social Legislation, 1955; Small-town Politics, 1959; Representative & Responsible Government, 1964; The British System of Government, 1967, revised 1973, 1980, 1986; Representation, 1971; Political Integration & Disintegration in the British Isles, 1977. *Contributor to:* Political Studies; Journal of Political Sciences; World Politics; and others. *Address:* Department of Political Science, University of Victoria, Victoria, British Columbia, Canada.

BIRCH, Edith, b. Morecambe, England. Teacher; Lecturer; Examiner; Play Producer; Retired Headmistress. *Education:* MA, Oxford University. *Appointments include:* Senior English Lecturer, Homerton College, Cambridge; Vice Principal, Collegiate School, Winterbourne, Bristol; Head Mistress, Moorfield School, Plymouth, Devon. *Contributor to:* Spring Anthol; Mitre Press: Dartington Hall News; Scrip; Breakthru; London Lit Eds; Keats Prize Poems; Dock Leaves; Poet, USA; Westward TV, Plymouth; Plymouth Radio; etc. *Honours include:* Armitage Hargreave's Poetry Trophy and Edith Wheeler Prize, Torbay and South West of England Arts Festival, 1972–76, 1979, 1980, 1981; 1st Place, Slough Arts Festival; 1st Place, 3 act Play, ibid; 3rd Prize, Drake 400 National Poetry Contest, 1980; Festival Poetry Trophy, 1983; Rhyme Revival Recognition Prize, 1982; Three Voices (Selected Poems, with Dorothy and Hugh Birch), 1983; various others. *Memberships include:* International Poetry Society; West Country Writers Association; National Council of Women Arts Rep., Plymouth Evening Branch; Plymouth Athenaeum. *Address:* 5 Elliott Terrace, The Hoe, Plymouth, Devon PL1 2PL, England.

BIRCHAM, Deric Neale, b. 16 Dec. 1934, Wellington, New Zealand. Professional Photographer. m. Patricia Frances Simkin, 18 Apr. 1960, Wellington, 2 daughters. *Education:* PhD (hc); FBIPP; FNZPPA; FRPS; FRSA; FABI; Hon. FIIPP; ANZIM. *Publications:* Seeing New Zealand, 1971, 5th edition, 1975; Waitomo Tourist Caves, 1973; New Zealanders of Destiny, 1978; Old St Paul's, 1982; Rhapsody, 1984; I Shall Pass This Way But Once, 1985; Co-author: Towards a More Just World, 1973; Table Tennis, 1978; Major contributor: Thirteen Facets, 1977; A Day in the Life of New Zealand, 1983; Dunedin: New Zealand's Best Kept Secret, 1984; St Joseph's Cathedral, 1986. Proposed publications: This Is New Zealand, 1986; Great New Zealand Artists, 1986; Other publications: Brochures, Booklets etc. for publicity purposes. Reviewer of 17 books for International Publishing Houses. *Honours:* bestowed by the following organizations: Royal Photographic Society, London, England; Royal Society of Arts, London; St James Press, London; International Institute of Professional Photography, London; British Institute of Professional Photography, Ware, England; Gail Research Institute, Detroit, USA; Universal Intelligence Data Bank of America; Soka Gakkai University, Tokyo, Japan; Albert Einstein International Academy Foundation, Missouri, USA; Marquis Guiseppe Scicluna, International University Foundation, Malta. *Literary Agent:* Richards Literary Agency. *Address:* 130 Easther Crescent, Kew, Dunedin, New Zealand.

BIRD, James Harold, b. 9 June 1923, London, England. University Professor. m. Olwen Joyce, 6 Sep. 1955, Birmingham. *Education:* BA, 1951, PhD, 1953, London. *Publications:* The Geography of the Port of London, 1957; The Major Seaports of the United

Kingdom, 1963; Seaport Gateways of Australia, 1968; Seaports and Seaport Terminals, 1971; Centrality and Cities, 1977. *Contributor to:* Numerous geographical journals. *Memberships:* Royal Geographical Society; President, Institute of British Geographers, 1980–81. *Address:* Dept of Geography, University of Southampton, Southampton SO9 5NH, England.

BIRD, Paul Francis Hughes, b. 17 Oct. 1952, Lytham St Annes, England. Journalist (print & radio). m. Christine Margaret Ibbs, 30 Apr. 1977, Gannawarra, 1 son. *Education:* Diploma of Arts (Media Studies). *Contributor to:* World Vision News in various countries, including England, USA and Kenya; Newspapers, periodicals, Journals dealing with Third World issues; on radio: Political comment throughout Australia, MacQuarrie National Network. *Address:* 19, Lenehan Street, Giralang, ACT 2617, Australia.

BIRD, Sarah McCabe, b. 26 Dec. 1949, Ann Arbor, Michigan, USA. Novelist. m. George Roger Jones, 23 Nov. 1981, Austin, Texas. *Education:* MA Journalism, University of Texas at Austin. *Literary Appointments:* Associate Editor & Columnist for, Third Coast, magazine; Columnist, Campus Voice, magazine. *Major Publications:* Handful of Sky, 1981; Do Evil Cheerfully, 1982; Where Aspens Quake, 1983; Cloud Waltzer, 1984. *Contributor to:* Cosmopolitan; New Time; National Observer. *Honours:* Western Interstate Commission on Education Grant, 1973; Fellowship for Graduate Study in Journalism, 1975–76; Best of Austin Feature Award, 1983, 1984. Burkhardt Parsons Award, 1984. *Membership:* Austin Writers League, Founder. *Literary Agent:* Iris Dahl. *Address:* 1203 Alegria, Austin, TX 78757, USA.

BIRKS, Tony, b. 1 Nov. 1937, Manchester, England. Publisher. m. Margaret Leslie Hay, 14 July 1972, 2 sons. *Education:* MA 2nd class honours, Oxford University; DFA, Commended, Slade School of Fine Art, University of London; ler degree, University of Grenoble. *Literary Appointments:* Art Editor, Isis (Oxford University magazine), 1960. *Publications:* Art of the Modern Potter, 1967; Building the New Universities, 1972; The Potters Companion, 1974; Pottery, a Complete Guide, 1979; Hans Coper biography, 1983. *Contributions to:* Ceramic Review, Crafts Magazine, American Ceramics, Revue de la Ceramique. *Address:* Marston House, Marston Magna, Yeovil, Somerset, England.

BIRNEY, Earle, b. 13 May 1904, Calgary, Alberta, Canada. Writer. divorced, 1 son. *Education:* BA, University of British Columbia; MA, PhD, University of Toronto. *Literary Appointments:* Leonard Graduate Scholar, University of Toronto, 1926–27; Teaching Fellow, University of California, Berkeley, 1927–30; Instructor in English, University of Utah, 1930–34; Royal Society of Canada Research Fellow to University of London, 1934–35; Lecturer in English, University of Toronto, 1936–41; Assistant Professor, 1941–45; Professor of English, University of British Columbia, 1946–62; Head, Department of Creative Writing, 1962–65. *Publications:* David and Other Poems, 1942; Turvey (novel), 1949; Trial of a City (verse drama), 1952; Down the Long Table (novel), 1955; Collected Poems, 2 volumes, 1975; Big Bird in the Bush (stories and sketches), 1978; Spreading Time, Volume 1, 1980, Fall by Fury (new poems), 1978, Words on Waves (radio dramas), 1985; Essays on Chaucesion Irony (lit. criticism), 1985. *Contributions to:* Poems, articles, stories, etc. to several hundred periodicals, anthologies, etc. in Canada, USA, British Commonwealth and translations in Latin America, Italy, Hungary, Russia, Finland, France, Greece, China and India. Magazines include: Harpers, Atlantic Monthly, Times Literary Supplement. *Honours:* Honorary Degrees: LLD, University of Calgary, 1979; DLitt, McGill University, 1981; DLitt, University of Western Ontario, 1984. Numerous other honours including: Officer of the Order of Canada; Lorne Pierce Gold Medal for Poetry, 1953; Nuffield Research Fellowship, British Museum, 1958–59. *Literary Agent:* McClelland and Stewart, Toronto.

Address: Suite 414, 484 Church Street, Toronto, Canada M4Y 2C7.

BIRO, Yvette, b. Budapest, Hungary. Screenwriter; Critic; Professor. m. Dr J Biro, Budapest, deceased 1969. *Education:* PhD, Hungarian Academy of Sciences, 1968. *Literary Appointments:* Hunnia Studio, Budapest; Hungarian Film Academy; Teacher, Universities of Paris, Berkeley, Stanford, New York, USA, Jerusalem; Associate Professor, New York University, Graduate School of Film. *Publications:* The Language of Film, 1964; The dramatic Structure of Film, 1968; Jancso (A Monograph), 1977; Mythobgie Profane, 1982; Profane Mythology, 1982; Co-Author, Screenplays: Winterwind; Confrontation; Agnus Dei; Red Psalm; Twenty Hours; Late Season; Execution for Four Voices. *Contributor to:* Filmkultura, Budapest; Cahiers du Cinema, Paris; Etudes Cinematographiques, Paris; Cinema Sessanta, Rome; Telos, New York; Milleneum, New York; Village Voice, New York. *Memberships:* Federation Internationale de la Presse Cinematographique, Vice President 1970–77. *Address:* 10 Christopher Street, New York, NY 10014, USA.

BISEGGER, Arthur Carl, b. 10 June 1918, Gossau, Switzerland. Journalist; Writer. m. Waltrudis Wildi, 29 Sep. 1942, Einsiedeln, 2 sons, 2 daughters. *Education:* Studied philology and law, Zurich and Paris Universities. *Publications:* Mein Steckenpferd heisst Mode, prose, 1955; Eine Art Venus, prose, 1968; Und danach ward ich, poem, 1977; Wegzeichen, prose, 1978; Im Zeichen der Zwillinge, poem, 1981; Morcoteser und andere Geschichten, prose, 1984. *Memberships:* Schweiz Schriftsteller Verband. *Address:* Postfach 2027, CH–5042 Baden, Switzerland.

BISHOP, Michael, b. 12 Nov. 1945, Lincoln, Nebraska, USA. Writer. *Education:* BA 1967, MA, University of Ga, Athens, 1968. *Publications:* A Funeral for the Eyes of Fire, (Ballantine), 1975; And Strange at Ecbatan the Trees, (Harper and Row), 1976; Stolen Faces, (Harper and Row), 1977; A Little Knowledge, (Berkley/Putnam), 1977; Catacomb Years, (Berkley/Putnam), 1979; Transfigurations, (Berkley/Putman), 1979; Eyes of Fire, revision of, A Funeral for the Eyes of Fire, (Timescape/Pocket Books), 1980; Blooded on Arachne, (short stories), (Arkham House), 1981; Under Heaven's Bridge, with Ian Watson, (Ace), 1982; No Enemy But Time, (Timescape/Simon and Schuster), 1982; paperback Timescape/Pocket Books, 1983, serialized in SF Digest, 1982; One Winter in Eden (Arkham House), 1984; Who Made Stevie Crye?, (Arkham House), 1984; Ancient of Days, (Arbor House), 1985; (Editor anthologies) Changes, with Ian Watson, (Ace), 1982; Light Years and Dark, (Berkley), 1984. *Contributor to:* Short Fiction in Playboy; Alfred Hitchcock's; Ellery Queen's; Isaac Asimov's; Analog; Fantasy and Science Fiction; Omni; Galazy; If; The Missouri Review; Pulpsmith; Interzone; Orbit; Universe; New Dimensions; Shadows; Chrysalis. *Honours:* Houghton Mifflin's Best American Short Stories 1985 for story, Dogs Lives; 2 Nebula Awards; Rhysling Award for poetry; other regional and speciality awards. *Memberships:* Science Fiction Writers of America. *Address:* Box 646, Pine Mountain, GA 31822, USA.

BISIGNANI, Joseph Daniel, b. 9 Nov. 1947, Scranton, Pennsylvania, USA. Travel Guide Writer. m. Mariane Susan Marron, 15 May 1969, Philadelphia, Pennsylvania, 1 daughter. *Education:* BA, Pennsylvania State University, 1965. *Publication:* Japan Handbook, 1983. *Address:* c/o Moon Publications, PO Box 1696, Chico, CA 95926, USA.

BISSOONDOYAL, Basdeo, b. 15 Apr. 1906, Tyack, Riviere des Anguilles, Mauritius. Author. *Education:* BA, Punjab University, 1937; MA, Calcutta University, 1939. *Publications:* Hindu Scriptures, 1961; India in French Literature, 1967; Ved Bhagwan Bole (Hindu), 1972; The Message of the Four Vedas, 1973; Le Rig Veda, 1974; Mahatma Gandhi: A New Approach, 1975; India in World Literature, 1976; Gita ka Adbhoot Gyan,

Hindi, 1978; Life in Greater India, 1984. *Contributor to:* Contemporary Review, London; Le Lotus Bleu, Paris; etc. *Honours:* Recipient, Sahitya Vachaspati Hindi Sahitya Sammelan, 1969; Arya Rattan Dayanand; Death Centenary Award, 1983. *Address:* 14 Sookdeo Bissoondoyal St, Port Louis, Mauritius.

BITA, Lili, b. Zanta, Greece. Author; Actress. *Education:* Fine Arts Degrees, Greek Conservatory of Music, Athens, 1954, Athens School of Drama, 1956; MA, University of Miami, USA, 1978. *Publications:* Steps on the Earth, 1955; Lightning in the Flesh, 1968; Erotes, 1969; Furies, 1969; Zero Hour, 1971; Blood Sketches, 1973; (translation) Anais Nin, A Spy in the House of Love; Sacrifice Exile, Night, 1976; I Crave the Bitter Sea, 1978; Fleshfire, 1979. *Contributor to:* Various journals and anthologies. *Honours:* Malvern Festival Award, 1967; Circle in the Square Fellowship, 1967–68; Performers Award, Austin Theatre Group, 1978. *Address:* 5901 SW 51 St, Miami, FL 33155, USA.

BITTNER, Wolfgang, b. 29 July 1941, Gleiwitz, Germany. Author. m. Angelika Nugel, 14 Aug. 1968, Wilhelmshaven, 2 sons, 1 daughter. *Education:* Abitur, 1966; Studied, Law, Philosophy, Sociology, Universities of Gottingen and Munich, 1966–70; 1st Juridical Diploma, 1970, Dr Jur, 1972, 2nd Juridical Diploma, 1973. Author, 1974–. *Publications:* Rechts-Spruche – Texte Zum Thema Justiz, 1975; Der Aufsteiger oder Ein Versuch Zu leben, 1978; Bis an die Grenze, 1980; Nachkriegsgedichte, poems, 1980; Abhauen, 1980; Weg vom Fenster, 1982; Der Riese braucht Zahnersatz, 1983; Kopfsprunge, 1984; Von Beruf Schriftsteller, 1985. *Contributor to:* Numerous professional journals including, Deutsches Allgemeines Sonntagsblatt; Die Zeit; Vorwarts; etc. *Honours:* Egon-Erwin-Kisch Award, 1978; Cultural Award Schlesien, State of Niedersachsen, 1979; several medals and premiums. *Membership:* Verband Deutscher Schriftsteller, Stuttgart. *Address:* Hilsweg 128, D–3400 Gottingen, Federal Republic of Germany.

BIVONA, Francesco, b. 23 Nov. 1908, New York City, New York, USA. Retired Senior Clerk; Writer. *Education:* AA, Manhattan Community College, 1973; BA, Baruch College, 1975. *Publications:* Booklets Include: Bloom in Fire, 1944; Reason Unbound, 1946; Hill 609, 1947; First Alarm, 1948; Spiritual Return, 1948; To My Judge, 1952; Farewell Muse, 1952; The World of Never, 1953; The Answer, 1958; Abandoned Poems, 1959; Moon Wash, 1960; Thought Parade, 1963; Paper World, 1963; Sonnets from a Sicilian, clothbound, 1967; Seeds in the Desert, soft cover, 1967; Samara, Poems in the Greek Manner, 1969; The Torch Bearer, 1971; When Dreams Endure, 1973; The Astro Men, 1975. Short Stories include: Enemies, 1942; Dancing Belle, 1944; Four stories, 1950; Stolen Laughter, 1954; Running Mouse. 1964; The Captain's Wife, 1972; Stories for the Road, 1985. One-Act Plays include: Guard Detail, 1953; Wedding Gown, 1955; The Family, 1977. Full-length Plays: The Agony of Faust, 4 act poetic drama; Faust on a String, prose comedy in 4 acts. Anthology Editor including: Gypsy Ship, 1959; Determined Dust, 1961; The Road to the Pierian Spring, 1968; Another Gathering, 1972. Co-Editor, America Anthology, 1956. Several songs published. *Contributions to:* Various newspapers, anthologies and journals including: American Courier; American Weave; Boston Globe; Denver Post; Hartford Times; Hobnob; Hoosier Challenger; The Messenger; New York Journal American; Pungolo Verde; Quickenings; Guardino's Gazette; Living Quill; Scimitar and Song; Westminster Magazine; Sunspot. *Memberships:* Dramatists Guild. *Address:* PO Box 612, New York City, NY 10113, USA.

BJÖRKLUND, Kristina Margareta, b. 16 Jan. 1941, Helsinki, Finland. University Lecturer. *Education:* Doctor of Philosophy, 1982. *Publications:* De andras röster, short stories, 1975; Festen, short stories, 1980; Riki och den förtrollade vägen. Studier i Oscar Parlands berättarkonst, doctoral dissertation, 1982; Månens tid, novel, 1985. *Memberships:* Finlands Svenska

Författareförening r f; Finlands PEN. *Address:* Topeliusgatan 21 B 32, 00250 Helsinki, Finland.

BJORNSSON, Jón, b. 12 Mar. 1907, Holt in Siöa, Skaftafellssysla, Iceland. Writer. *Publications:* The Earth's Power, 1942; Family Honor, 1944; The King's Friend, 1946; The Buddha Idol, 1948; Beauteous Day Brightens the Whole World, 1950; Valryr in the Green Coat, 1951; The Fiery Test, 1952; Bergljot, 1954; All These Things Will I Give Thee, 1955; The Virgin Thordis, 1964; The Judge Who Betrayed the Justice, 1977. *Contributor to:* Short stories and criticism to various magazines. *Honours include:* Literary Prize, Icelandic Writers Federation, 1970; Icelandic Radio Federation, 1976. *Memberships include:* Writer's Association of Iceland. *Address:* Karastigur 9, Reykjavik, Iceland.

BLACK, Albert George, b. 22 Aug. 1928, Northville, Michigan, USA. Professor. m. Mary Elizabeth Fared, 1950, 2 sons, 1 daughter. *Education:* MA, University of Michigan, Ann Arbor, 1956; Teaching Fellow 1960–62, ibid. *Major Publications:* The Michigan Novel, 1963; The Vigilant Balance. *Contributions to:* The Asterisk; Journal of English Traditions (editor). *Memberships:* American Medical Writers Association; Modern Language Association; California Association of Technical & Professional Writers (Executive Board); Jane Austen Society, South West (President). *Address:* English Department, California State University, Long Beach, CA 90840, USA.

BLACK, David Macleod, b. 8 Nov. 1941, Cape Town, South Africa. Psychotherapist. m. Jeanne Magagna, 28 Jan. 1984, London. *Education:* MA, Philosophy, Edinburgh University, Scotland, 1966; MA, Eastern Religions, Lancaster University, 1970. *Appointments:* Editor, Extra Verse, 1963–66. *Publications:* With Decorum, 1967; Penguin Modern Poets 11, co-author, 1968; The Educators, 1969; The Happy Crow, 1974; Gravitations, 1979. *Contributor to:* Lines Review, 23, 1967; Scottish International 3, 1968; Akros 10, 1975; Chapman, 1981/82, etc. *Honours:* Scottish Arts Council Awards, 1968, 1969. *Address:* 5a Stock Orchard Crescent, London N7, England.

BLACK, Dorothy, b. 30 Apr. 1914, Johannesburg, South Africa. Playwright; Author; Translator. *Publications:* Stage Play Adaptations include: Landslide, with David Peel, (from Julien Luchaire), 1943; Men Without Shadows, 1947, The Respectable Prostitute, 1947; Crime Passionnel, 1948, (all from Jean-Paul Sartre); Point of Departure, (from Jean Anouilh), 1950; Lucifer and the Lord, (from Sartre) published, 1952; The Public Prosecutor, (from Fritz Hochwaelder) BBC Television, 1953; The Snow Was Black, (from Simenon), 1953; Kean, (from Sartre) published, 1954; Three Sisters, with Miko Iveria (from Chekov), 1955; Wings of The Wind, (from Alexandre Rivemale) 1957; The Innocent Man, (from Fritz Hochwaelder), BBC Radio; The Singing Dolphin, with Beverley Cross, 1958; The Rehearsal, with Pamela Hansford, Johnson, (from Jean Anouilh), 1961; Bonne Soupe, (from Félicien Marceau), 1961; Isabelle, (from Jaques Deval), 1964; Maxiubules, (from Marcel Aymé), 1964; Sword of Vengeance, (from Fritz Hochwaedler), TV and BBC Radio, 1975. A Ballet: The Soldier's Tale, with Michael Flanders, (from Stravinsky-Ramuz), 1955. Books: Flying Mannequin, (memoirs by Freddy); De Gaulle And His France, (from Jacques de Launay), Biography; Julie, (from the Comtesse Felicité de Choiseul Meuse), 1970; Riding To Jerusalem, (from Evelyn Coquet), 1978, For BBC Radio: I'll Never Be Seven, (from Gilbert Léautier), 1982; Upper Circle, (a theatrical Chronicle), 1985; of simultaneous translations for World Theatre Seasons at the Aldwych Theatre, 1963–75. *Apppointments:* Secretary, Apollo Society; Front of House Manager, London Academy of Music and Drama's MacOwan Theatre, 1977–. *Membership:* Society of Authors; PEN. *Address:* 16 Brunswick Gardens, London W8 4AJ, England.

BLACKBURN, Alexander Lambert, b. 6 Sep. 1929, Durham, North Carolina, USA. Professor of

English/Creative Writing. m. 15 Oct. 1975, Colorado Springs, 2 sons, 1 daughter. *Education:* BA, Yale University, 1951; MA, North Carolina University, 1956; PhD, Cambridge University, 1963. *Literary Appointments:* Instructor of English, Hampden – Sydney College, Virginia, 1959–60; Instructor of English, University of Pensylvania, 1963–65; Lecturer of American Literature, University of Maryland European Division, 1967–73; Assistant Professor of English 1973–78, Associate Professor of English 1978–82, Professor of English 1982–, University of Colorado, Colorado Springs, Founding Editor, Writer's Forum, 1974–. *Publications:* The Myth of the Picaro, 1979; The Cold War of Kitty Pentecost, novel, 1979. *Contributions to:* Faulkner and the Southern Renaissance, 1982; Dictionary of Literary Biography Yearbook 1985; Crosscurrents. *Address:* 6030 Twin Rock Ct, Colorado Springs, CO 80907, USA.

BLACKING, John Anthony Randoll, b. 22 Oct. 1928, Guildford, Surrey, England. Social Anthropologist. m. (1) Brenda Gebers, 29 Oct. 1955, Eshowe, Zululand, 1 son, 7 daughters (2 deceased), (2) Zureena R Desai, 3 Jan. 1978, Salisbury, Wiltshire, England. *Education:* BA Honours, 1953, MA, 1957, King's College, Cambridge University, England; PhD, 1965, DLitt, 1972, University of the Witwatersrand. *Publications:* Black Background, 1964; Vendachilden's Songs: A Study in ethnomusicological Analysis, 1967; Process and Product in Human Society, 1969; How Musical is Man? 1973, 76, also in French, Japanese and Italian editions; Man and Fellowman, 1974; The Anthropology of the Body, Editor, 1977; The Anthropology of the Performing Arts, co-editor, 1980. *Contributions to:* Numerous articles and reviews in scientific journals and in some encyclopedias. *Honour:* Member, Royal Irish Academy, 1984. *Literary Agent:* Curtis Brown. *Address:* 18 Cleaver Park, Belfast BT9 5HX, Northern Ireland.

BLACKMORE, Howard Loftus, b. 27 Oct. 1917, Mitcham, Surrey, England. Author. *Publications:* British Military Firearms 1650–1850, 1961; Firearms, 1964; Arms and Armour, 1965; Guns and Rifles of the World, 1965; Royal Sporting Guns at Windsor, 1968; Hunting Weapons, 1971; The Armouries of the Tower of London, Volume I, Ordnance, 1976; English Pistols, 1985. *Contributions to:* Connoisseur; Country Life; Saturday Book; British History Illustrated; American Rifleman; Gun Digest; Gazette des Armes; Times Literary Supplement; British Book News. *Memberships include:* Arms and Armour Society; Society of Antiquaries of London; Gemmological Association. *Address:* Wildwood, Harestone Hill, Caterham, Surrey CR3 6BN, England.

BLACKWOOD, Alan William, b. 23 Nov. 1932, Croydon, England. Writer. Divorced. *Publications:* The Pageant of Music: Barrie and Jenkins, 1977; Ward Lock's Encyclopedia of Music, 1979; New Encyclopedia of Music, 1983; The Performing World of the Singer, 1981. *Contribuitons:* Reviews in Times Literary Supplement. *Address:* 18 Shelburne Court, Carlton Drive, London SW15 2DQ, England.

BLAIR, Ron, b. 14 Oct. 1942, Sydney, Australia. Writer. *Education:* BA, Sydney University. *Publications:* President Wilson in Paris, 1974; The Christian Brothers, 1976; Marx, 1983; Last Day in Woolloomooloo, 1983. *Contributor to:* Theatre; Australia. *Membership:* Australian Writers Guild. *Literary Agent:* Hilary Linstead & Associates. *Address:* 223 Commonwealth St, Surrey Hills, NSW 2010, Australia.

BLAKE, Leslie James, b. 5 Mar. 1913, Bendigo, Victoria, Australia. Author; Historian. *Education:* BA, MEd, Melbourne University. *Publications include:* Geelong Sketchbook, 1971; Gold Escort, 1971; Wimmera: A Regional History, 1973; Land of the Lowan, 1976; Place Names of Victoria, 1977; Pioneer Schools of Australia, 1977; Gold Escorts in Australia, 1978; Covered Wagons in Australia, 1979; Tales from Old Geelong, 1979; Peter Lalor – the man from Eureka,

1979; Tattyara: A History of Kaniva District, 1981; Schools of the Tattyara, 1981; Captain Dana and the Native Police, 1982; Co-Author & Editor: Letters of Charles Joseph La Trobe, 1975; Green Days and Cherries, 1981; A Gold Digger's Diaries, by Ned Peters, 1981; Aunt Spencer's Diaries, by Mary Read and Mary Spencer, 1981; etc. *Contributor to:* Various journals. *Honours:* Recipient, OBE 1974. *Memberships:* President, Royal Historical Society of Victoria, 1966–71; Fellow, 1970; Vice President PEN, Melbourne, 1971–72. *Address:* 4 Anton Ct, Karingal, Victoria, Australia.

BLAKE, Stephen Charles, b. 25 May 1955, Bungay, England. Journalist. *Literary Appointments:* Editor, Harpers Sports and Leisure. *Contributions to:* Harpers Sports and Leisure, Regular contributions to international sports trade press including Eurosport und Freizeitmode. *Address:* 58 Chesterfield Drive, Riverhead, Sevenoaks, Kent TN13 3EQ, England.

BLAKELEY, Denis, b. 5 Aug. 1931, Dewsbury, Yorkshire, England. Journalist. m. 28 Oct. 1971, Moscow, USSR. *Education:* BA Honours Foreign Languages, London. *Literary Appointments:* Journalism in Bonn, Munich, Vienna, Paris, Moscow; British Broadcasting Corporation; Economist. *Contributions to:* Times Literary Supplement; The Economist; International Management; Christian Science Monitor; Guardian. *Address:* 47 Quai D'Orsay, 75007 Paris, France.

BLAKELEY, William Paul, b. 18 Nov. 1924. Professor Emeritus of Education. m. Velma Vittitoe, 24 Feb. 1953, Modale, Iowa, 1 son, 1 daughter. *Education:* BS Education, University of Nebraska, 1949; MA, University of Minnesota, 1951; PhD, University of Iowa, 1957. *Appointments include:* Teacher, various Junior High Schools, Iowa and Nebraska 1945–55; Assistant Professor of Education, Westmor College, LeMars, Iowa, 1957–58; Assistant Professor, 1958–61, Associate Professor, 1961–68, Professor, 1968–85, Professor Emeritus, 1985–, Drake University. *Contributions to:* Lyrical Iowa, Associate Editor, 1973–; Omaha Sunday World Herald; Oakwood; The Target; Ball State University Forum, Articles and reviews in various educational journals. *Honours:* Various poetry awards. *Memberships:* Iowa Poetry Association; National Council of Teachers of English. *Address:* 1335 39th Street, Des Moines, IA 50311, USA.

BLANK, Franklin, b. 19 Oct. 1921, Philadelphia, Pennsylvania, USA. Writer. m. Annette Evelyn née Chotin, 25 Dec. 1952, Washington DC, USA, 1 daughter. *Education:* BA, Southeastern University, Washington DC, 1956; AA, University of Baltimore, 1966; Graduate work, Mass Communciations, Towson University, 1984–85. *Literary Appointments:* Stringer, Washington-based, National Enquirer, 1979; Jewish Post & Opinion, 1979; Frequent Writer on labour matters, American Federation of Government Employees, 1970–85. *Major Publication:* Allegory (in preparation). *Contributor to:* Journal of Irish Literature; Emergency; People in Action; Grit; Southern Jewish Weekly; VFW Magazine; Police Product News; Government Purchasing; Voyager; Volunteer Fireman; Catholic Life; Dog Fancy; Jewish Times Outlook; People on Parade. *Honours:* Honorable mention, Writers Digest Writing Competitions (International), 1980, 1985. *Memberships:* Authors Guild; National Writers' Club; Corresponding Member, European Academy of Arts, Sciences & Humanities, Antibes, France; World Literary Academy, Cambridge, England. *Address:* 5477 Cedonia Avenue, Baltimore, MD 21206, USA.

BLANK, George W, (III), b. 1 June 1945, Philadelphia, Pennsylvania, USA. Software Entrepreneur. m. Linday Kay Cotton, 19 Aug. 1967, Killeen, Texas, USA, 2 sons. *Education:* AB, Eastern College; M Div Princeton Theological; MSCS, New Jersey Institute of Technology. *Literary Appointments:* Editor in Chief, Softside Publications; Editorial Director, Creative Computing. *Publications:* Pathways through ROM, 1979; The Creative Atari, 1981. *Contributor to:* Creative

Computing; Practical Computing; Popular Computing; Basic Computing; Softside; Prog 80; Microcomputing. *Address:* 239 Fox Hill Road, Denville, NJ 07834, USA.

BLANKOFF, Jean Désiré, b. 21 May 1931, Bredene, Belgium. University Professor. m. Goldie Scarr, 1956, Brussels, 1 son, 1 daughter. *Education:* MA, Slavonic Languages, Literatures, Harvard University, USA. 1959; PhD, Slavonic Philology, History, University of Brussels, 1970. *Publications:* L'art de la Russie ancienne, 1963; La société russe de la seconde moitié du XIXe s vue à travers les ouevres de Saltykov-Ščedrin, Pisemskij et G Uspenskij, 1972. *Contributor to:* 70 articles in 14 journals. *Memberships:* Belgian Society Byzantine Studies; French Society for 18th Century Studies; National Association of Belgium of Teachers of Russian Language and Literature, Vice President; Belgian Centre for Slavic Studies, Treasurer; Société Européene de Culture; Société Internationale d'Etudes du XVIIIe s; Acad[c]emic Européenne des Sciences, des Arts et des Lettres, Paris. *Address:* 13 Avenue Calypso, 1170 Brussels, Belgium.

BLASHFORD-SNELL, John Nicholas, b. 22 Oct. 1936, Hereford, England. Soldier; Colonel and Commander Operation Raleigh; Explorer. *Education:* Victoria College, Jersey Channel Islands; Royal Military Academy, Sandhurst. *Publications include:* Where the Trail Runs Out; In The Steps of Stanley; Expeditions The Experts Way, co-author; A Taste for Adventure, 1978; Operation Drake, with M Cable, 1981; Mysteries – Encounters with the Unexplained, 1983. *Contributor to:* Expedition; The Field; British Army Review; Guns Digest; The Spectator; Yorks Post; Scotsman; Explorers Journal; Daily Telegraph. *Memberships:* Scientific Exploration Society, Chairman; Fellow, Royal Scottish Geographical Society; Chairman British Chapter, Explorers Club. *Honours:* MBE, 1969; Livingstone Medal, 1975; Segrave Trophy, 1975; Freeman, City of Hereford, 1984. *Literary Agent:* June Hall, England. *Address;* c/o Lloyds Bank Ltd, 9 Broad St, St Helier, Jersey, Channel Islands.

BLATE, Samuel Robert, b. 20 July 1944, Brooklyn, New York, USA. Writer; Editor; Professor of English. m. Toni Lee Bress, 25 July 1976, Washington DC, 2 sons. *Education:* AB, University of North Carolina, Chapel Hill, 1965; MA, Goddard College, 1984. *Appointments:* Fiction Staff, The Carolina Quarterly, 1963–65; Poetry Editor, Kaleidescope, Radio Programme, WAMU-FM, 1968–70; Editorial Staff, Potomac Appalachian Magazine, 1973–76; Sponsor, Montgomery College Literary Magazine, 1968–76, 1981–83. *Publications:* Assistant Editor, My Roosevelt Years, by Norman N Littell, 1985; Editor, Introducer, The Felble, 1975, Self-Portrait, 1977, Turning Thirty, 1984, by Tom Barrer; Author, Spirals, 1986. *Contributor to:* Various magazines and newspapers including: The Fairfax County Sun-Echo; The Spur; Potomac Appalachian Magazine; etc. *Honours:* Superior Teaching Awards, Montgomery College, 1968, 1972, 1977. *Memberships:* Washington Independent Writers; Washington Area Writers; National Writers Union; MLA; SAMLA; Mid-Atlantic Group, College English Association, President 1984–85; College English Association; Former Member, Secretary, Association of Editorial Businesses. *Address:* 10331 Watkins Mill Dr, Gaithersburg, MD 20879, USA.

BLAUWERS, Frank Jean, b. 22 Jan. 1933, Antwerp, Belgium. Author. m. 20 Nov. 1952, 1 son, 1 daughter. *Publications:* Tulle Curtains, 1956; The Cesspool, 1958; The Death-Sowers, 1961; Bonanza, Ivanhoe and Father Knows Best, series, 1960–62; The Last Err, 1962; The Temple of Huanapec/A Day in Mexico, 1962; Maya, Maya, 1964; The Wonders of Our Planet, 1965; The Book of Famous Inventions, 1966; Wovoka of the Silverlands, 1970; The White Papuan, 1972; Sons of Heaven, 1975; The Buck-Riders of the Bush, 1974. *Contributions to:* Numerous publications. *Honours:* Prize, Province of Antwerp, for literature, 1972. *Membership:* Society of Flemish Authors. *Address:* Bacchuslaan 78, 2200 Borgerhout – Antwerp, Belgium.

BLAZEK, Ronald, b. 13 June 1936, Chicago, Illinois, USA. Professor of Library Science. m. Genevieve Kanape, 20 Aug. 1960, Chicago, 2 sons. *Education:* BEd, 1958, MEd, 1961, Chicago Teachers College; MS, 1965, PhD, 1971, University of Illinois. *Publications:* Influencing Students Toward Media Center Use, 1975; The Black Experience: A Bibliography of Bibliographies, 1978; Achieving Accountability: Readings on the Evaluation of Media Centers, 1981. *Contributions to:* Illinois Libraries; Journal of Library History; Journal of Education for Librarianship; Southeastern Librarian; The Reference Librarian; R Q Collection Management; Florida Libraries, book reviewer; American Reference Book Annual, 1979, 80, 81, 82, 83; Numerous invited presentations. *Honours:* Outstanding Senior, Chicago Teachers College, 1958; Beta Phi Mu, 1965; Higher Education Act Fellowship, 1968–89, Shapiro Fellow, 1970, University of Illinois; Commendation as Runner Up, Provost's Teaching Award, Florida State University, 1977. *Memberships:* Various offices, American Library Association. *Address:* School of Library and Information Studies, Florida State University, Tallahassee, FL 32308, USA.

BLEY, Deborah Lang, b. 3 Mar. 1952, Washington, District of Columbia, USA. Writer; Editor. m. David Bruce Bley, 11 Feb. 1973, Phoenix, Maryland, 1 daughter. *Education:* Diploma in Nursing; Undergraduate Degree Candidate, English. *Literary Appointments:* Editorial Board, 1982–, Assistant Editor, 1982–, Child's Way (changed name to Brilliant Star, 1983–); Editor-in-Chief, Brilian Star, 1985–. *Contributions to:* Child's Way; Brilliant Star; World Order. *Membership:* Society of Children's Book Writers, USA. *Address:* Suburban Office Park, 5010 Austin Road, Hixson, TN 37343, USA.

BLOCH, Barbara Joyce, b. 26 May 1925, New York, USA. Cookbook Writer and Editor. m Theodore Benjamin, 20 Sep. 1964, New York City, 2 daughters. *Education:* University of New York. *Literary Appointments:* President, International Cookbook Services. *Major Publications:* Anyone can Quilt, 1975; Meat Board Meat Book, 1977; If it Doesn't Pan Out, 1981; All Beef Cookbook, 1973; In Glass Naturally (author/editor), 1974; Fresh Ideas with Mushrooms, 1977; American adaptations of some 25 European Cookbooks for major US publishers. *Contributor to:* Monthly Column, House Beautiful; Westchester Magazine. *Address:* 21 Dupont Avenue, White Plains, NY 10605, USA.

BLOCH, Robert, b. 5 Apr. 1917, Chicago, Illinois, USA. Writer. *Publications include:* Psycho, 1959; The Best of Robert Bloch, 1977; Cold Chills, 1977; The King of Terrors, 1977; Out of the Mouths of Graves, 1979; Such Stuff as Screams Are Made Of, 1979; There Is A Serpent in Eden, 1979; Psycho II, 1982; The Mystery of the Worm, 1983; The Night of the Ripper, 1984. *Contributions to:* Playboy; Penthouse; Gall; Cosmopolitan; Red Book; Blue Book; Ellery Queen Mystery Magazine, and various others. *Honours:* Life Career Awards: 1st World Fantasy Convention, 1975; Atlanta Science Fiction Convention, 1984; World Science Fiction Convention, 1984. *Memberships:* Past President, Mystery Writers of America; Science Fiction Writers of America; Writers Guild of America. *Literary Agent:* Kirby McCauley Limited. *Address:* 2111 Sunset Crest Drive, Los Angeles, CA 90046, USA.

BLODGETT, Edward Dickinson, b. 26 Feb. 1935, Philadelphia, Pennsylvania, USA. Professor. m. Elke Kruger, 11 Sep. 1960, Haddonfield, New Jersey, 1 son, 2 daughters. *Education:* BA, Amherst College, 1956; MA, University of Minnesota, 1961; PhD, Rutgers, 1969. *Publications:* Take Away the Names, 1975; Sounding, 1977; Beast Gate, 1980; Configuration: Essays in the Canadian Literatures, 1982; Arche/Elegies, 1983. *Contributions to:* Speculum; The Minnesota Review; Boundary 2; The Sixties; Carolina Quarterly; Arion; Modern Poetry Studies; The Classical Journal; Canadian Literature; Canadian Fiction Magazine; Canadian Review of Comparative Literature;

Canadian Forum; Concerning Poetry; Capilano Review; The Malahat Review; Ariel. *Honours:* Anna von Helmholtz-Phelan Scholarship for Creative Writing, 1961; President's Medal, University of Western Ontario for Cold Pastorals, 1980; Social Science and Humanities Research Council Leave Grant, 1980–81; Writers Guild of Alberta Award for Poetry for Arche/Elegies, 1984. *Memberships:* Writers League of Alberta, President, 1981–83; The League of Canadian Poets. *Literary Agent:* J Kellock. *Address:* 12 Grantham Place, St Albert, Alberta, Canada T6G 2E6.

BLOM, Anita, b. 15 Mar. 1929, Kobe, Japan. Actress; Director. m. Palle Granditsky, 23 Jan. 1959, Sweden, 2 sons, 1 daughter. *Education:* Royal Dramatic Theatre, Stockholm, 1948. *Publications:* Childrens Plays: Thin Air, 1963; Jonte, 1974; Kurre & Kompis, 1975; The First Time Eva Died, 1976' The Bird of Joy, 1980; The Biting Machine, 1978. *Memberships:* Svenska Dramatiker Forbundet. *Address:* Ringvagan 49, 181 33 Lidingo, Sweden.

BLOM, Karl Arne, b. 22 Jan, 1946, Nassjo, Sweden. Author. m. Karin Gyllen, 29 June 1969, 1 son, 2 daughters. *Education:* BA, 1972. *Publications:* The Moment of Truth, 1974; Limits of Pain, 1978. *Contributor to:* The Armchair Detective; The Mystery Fancier; Pinkerton; Jury. *Honours:* The Sherlock Award, 1974; Lund Cultural Prize, 1980; The Spangen Award, 1983; The Marten Award, 1984. *Memberships:* Mystery Writers of America; Crime Writers Association; Poe Club, Denmark; Society of Crime Writers of Scania, Honorary Chairman; Swedish Academy of Detection. *Literary Agent:* Lennart Sane Agency. *Address:* Smaskolevagan 22, S 223 67 Lund, Sweden.

BLOMERUS, Helene Marié, b. 24 Dec. 1931, Keetmanshoop, Namibia. TV Scriptwriter. *Publications:* Fosforblom, 1968; Blou As Beginsel van Duisternis, 1975; Soo-oo-oopwa, 1975; Ithaka, 1985. *Contributor to:* Tydskrif vir Letterkunde; Izwe; Ophir; Poet; Labris; De Arte; Yang; New Nation; Sestiger; Wurm; etc; Former Co-Editor, Avant-Garde SA Magazine – Wurm. *Memberships:* Afrikaanse Skrywersgilde; International Women's Writing Guild. *Address:* Mossiestreet 990, Silverton X5 Pretoria, 0184, Republic of South Africa.

BLOOM, Joseph Harris, b. 11 Feb. 1938, Brooklyn, New York, USA. Freelance Medical Writer. m. Adrienne Tufts Welch, 23 June 1985, Lumberville, Pennsylvania, 2 sons by previous marriage, 1 stepson, 1 stepdaughter. *Education:* BS, Philadelphia College of Textiles and Science, 1959; MS, Rensselaer Polytechnic Institute, 1960. *Literary Appointments:* Editor: Gwynnews, 1982–; Newsearch, 1984–. *Publications:* Copyrighted Plays: Contrary to Order, with William Barnett, 1972; Scott Joplin: King of Ragtime, 1976; Murder in Group, 1984; The Magician, 1985. *Contributions to:* Product Engineering; Camping Magazine; Jewish Digest; Catholic Boy; Startling Mystery Stories; New Haven Journal Courier; New Haven Evening Register. *Honours:* Addy Award, Philadelphia Council of Advertising, 1978. *Memberships:* American Medical Writers Association. *Address:* Suite 208, Gwynedd Plaza 1, Spring House, PA 19477, USA.

BLOOM, Murray Teigh, b. 19 May 1916, New York City, USA. Author. m. Sydelle Cohen, 20 Apr. 1944, New York, 2 daughters. *Education:* BA, Columbia College, 1937; MS, Graduate School of Journalism, Columbia University, 1938. *Literary Appointments:* Head and Teacher, Magazine Writing section, Biarritz-American University, France, 1945; Chairman, Editor Writer Relations Committee, American Society of Journalists and Authors, 1960–. *Publications:* Money of Their Own, 1958; The Man Who Stole Portugal, 1966; The Trouble With Lawyers, 1969; Rogues to Riches, 1972; The 13th Man, 1977; The Brotherhood of Money, 1984; The White Crow, play, 1984. *Contributions to:* Major US periodicals of over 600 articles. *Honours:* 50th Anniversary Medal, Graduate School of Journalism, Columbia University; Gavel Award, American Bar Association. *Memberships:* Founder and Former

President, American Society of Journalists and Authors; Dramatists Guild of New York; Authors Guild, New York. *Literary Agent:* Julian Bach, New York. *Address:* 40 Hemlock Drive, Kings Point, NY 11024, USA.

BLOOMFIELD, Anthony John Westgate, b. 8 Sep. 1922, London, England. Writer. m. Anneliese Hubner, 31 July 1954, 1 son. *Publications:* Russian Roulette, 1955; The Delinquents, 1958; The Tempter, 1961; Throw, 1965; Life for a Life, 1971. *Contributions to:* Contributor to various journals including, Ellery Queen's Magazine. *Literary Agent:* David Higham Associates. *Address:* 22 Hendon Street, Brighton BN2 2EG, England.

BLOOMFIELD, Norman Owen, b. 20 Aug. 1920, London, England. Journalist. m. Evaline Todd, 19 Jan. 1946, Leeds, 1 daughter. *Appointments:* Editor, Hairdressers Journal, 1976; Hair, 1977; Managing Editor, Hairdressers Journal International, Hair, Black Beauty and Hair, Beauty Salon, 1980. *Publications:* How to Blow Style, instructional, 1976; Fashion Geniuses of the World, 1978. *Contributor to:* Hair; Black Beauty & Hair; Hairdressers Journal International; Peluquerias, Spain. *Address:* 6 Gales Close, Merrow Park, Guildford, Surrey, England.

BLOUIN, Claude R, b. 30 Jan. 1944, Sorel, Canada. Teacher. m. Gisèle Trudeau, 16 June 1973, Ste-Emelie-de-l'energie, 1 son. *Education:* BA, CAPES, MA, University of Montréal; Credits on Japanese Art & Theatre, Sophia University, Tokyo, Japan. *Major Publications:* Du Japon et D'ici (essays, short stories), 1975; Le dragon blessé (short novel), 1979; Le Chemin Détourné (essay on Kobayashi and Japanese films), 1982; Dire L'éphémère (essay/fiction), 1984. *Contributor to:* Sequences; Cinéma Québec; Kinema Jumpo (Japan); Contemporanul (Romania); Ecran (France); Trajectoires; Ecrits du Canada Francais; APLF. *Memberships:* Québec Writers' Union. *Address:* 687 St-Viatuer, Joliette, P Quebec, Canada.

BLUM, David, b. 7 Sep. 1935, Los Angeles, California, USA. Author; Orchestra Conductor. m. Sarah Sally Teitelbaum, 23 July 1956, Los Angeles, 1 son, 1 daughter. *Education:* Juilliard School of Music. *Publications:* Casals & the Art of Interpretation, 1977; Paul Tortelier: A Self-Portrait in Conversation with David Blum, 1983; The Art of Quartet Playing: The Guarneri Quartet in Conversation with David Blum, 1986. *Membership:* Society of Authors, UK. *Literary Agent:* A P Watt Ltd, London, UK. *Address:* 15 chemin de la Sapinière, 1253 Vandoeuvres, Switzerland.

BLUM, Richard A, b. 28 July 1943, Brooklyn, New York, USA. Television Programme Development Executive; Writer; Educator. *Education:* BA, Fairleigh Dickinson University, 1965; MS, Boston University; PhD, University of Southern California, 1977. *Literary Appointments:* Professor of Screenwriting, University of Maryland, 1983–. Visiting Professor of Screenwriting: Harvard University Summer School, 1984, 85, 86; American Film Institute, 1983, 84. *Publications:* Television Writing: From Concept to Contract, 1980, 84; American Film Acting, 1984. *Contributions to:* The Writer; The Scriptwriter; Educational Editor; Journal of Performing Arts Review; Western Speech Journal; Central Speech Journal; Cinema Canada; Audio-Visual Communication; Resources in Education. Television Writer – Producer: PBS; NBC-TV; Universal Studios; Columbia Pictures–TV. *Honours include:* Best Playwright, FDU, 1964, 65; Media Programme Supervisor, National Endowment for the Humanities, Washington, District of Columbia, 1978–81. *Memberships:* Writers Guild of America; Academy of Television Arts and Sciences; National Association of Educational Broadcasters; American Theatre Association; Washington Independent Writers; The Writers Center. *Address:* 2208 Washington Avenue, Silver Spring, MD 20910, USA.

BLUMBERG, Richard E, b. 22 June 1944, New York, USA. Attorney; Author. m. Barbara C Seidner, 3 Oct.

1968, Teaneck, 2 sons. *Education:* BA, BS, American University; LLB, JD, Rutgers University. *Publication:* The Rights of Tenants, 1978. *Contributor to:* Over 100 articles to professional journals & magazines including: Harvard Civil Rights–Civil Liberties Law Review; Housing and Development Reporter; Clearinghouse Review; Municipal Attorney, 1974; Housing Law Bulletin; etc. *Literary Agent:* Ellen Levine, New York City. *Address:* 1950 Addison Street, Berkeley, CA 94704, USA.

BLUSTEIN, Joseph Edward, b. 16 July 1936, Montreal, Canada. Psychiatrist. m. Benita Cransky, 3 Dec. 1964, at Montreal, 1 son, 1 daughter. *Education:* BSc Honours in Biochemistry, McGill University, 1953–57; MDCM, McGill University, 1957–61; Associate Professor of Psychiatry, School of Medicine, Faculty of Health Sciences, University of Ottawa. *Major Publications:* Haematological Aspects, in Toxic and Adverse Reaction Studies with Neuroleptics and Antidepressant, H E Lehmann and T A Ban Eds, 1968; Brain Tumours Presenting as Functional Psychiatric Illnesses (with M V Seeman), Canadian Psychiatric Association Journal, 1962; Further Observations on Brain Tumours Presenting as Functional Psychiatric Conditions, Psychiatric Journal of the University of Ottawa, volume 1-2; A Pilot Study of Injectable Valium in a General Hospital Setting (with S Rheaume & J M Sendbuehler), Laval Medical, 1970. *Contributor to:* Book Review Editor, The Psychiatric Journal of the University of Ottawa. *Memberships:* Director, Adult Psychiatry Outpatient Clinics, Ottawa General Hospital; Member Library Committee, Canadian Psychoanalytical Society; Pharmacology and Therapeutics Committee, Ottawa General Hospital; Pharmacokinetics Sub-Committee, Ottawa General Hospital; Member, Board of Directors and Advisor on Programmes, Gateway House for Recovering Alcoholics. *Address:* Ottawa General Hospital, 501 Smyth Road – Room 4424, Ottawa, Ontario K1H 8L6, Canada.

BLY, Carol McLean, b. 16 Apr. 1930, Duluth, USA. Writer. 2 sons, 2 daughters. *Education:* BA, Wellesley College; University of Minnesota. *Publications:* Letters from the Country, 1981; Backbone, 1984. *Contributions to:* Various publications including Minnesota Public radio magazine; Milkweed Chronicle; Nation; The New Yorker; Ploughshares; Triquarterly; Twin Cities Magazine; biography in Ariadne's Thread; translation from Danish of novel, One Down. *Honours:* Minnesota State Arts Board Fellowship, 1980; Bush Foundation Fellowship, 1981. *Memberships:* Member, The Loft; Member, The Authors' Guild. *Literary Agent:* George Borchardt. *Address:* Rt 2 Box 546, Sturgeon Lake, MN 55783, USA.

BLYTH, Myrna, b. 22 Mar. 1939, New York City, New York, USA. Editor. m. Jeffrey Blyth, 25 Nov. 1962, New York City, 2 sons. *Education:* BA, Bennington College, Vermont, 1960. *Literary Appointments:* Senior Editor: Ingenue Magazine, New York, 1963–68; Family Health Magazine, New York, 1968–71. Executive Editor, Family Circle, New York, 1972–81; Editor-in-Chief, Ladies' Home Journal, New York, 1981–. *Publications:* Cousin Suzanne, 1975; For Better and For Worse, 1978. *Contributions to:* The New Yorker; New York; Reader's Digest; McCall's; Redbook. *Memberships:* American Society of Magazine Editors; Women's Media Group; Child Care Action Campaign; The Author's Guild. *Literary Agent:* Arthur Pine, New York. *Address:* 90 Riverside Drive, New York, NY 10024, USA.

BLYTHE, Ronald George, b. 6 Nov. 1922. Author. *Appointments:* Literature Panel, Eastern Arts Association; Management Committee, Society of Authors; Local History Faculty, University of East Anglia; Chairman, Essex Arts Festival; President, John Clare Society. *Publications:* A Treasonable Growth, 1960; The Age of Illusion, 1963; William Hazlitt: Selected Writings, 1970; Akenfield, 1969; Aldeburgh Anthology, 1972; The View in Winter, 1979; From the Headlands, 1983; Collected Short Stories, 1985; Divine Landscapes, 1986; Edited, with introductions works by Tolstoy, Jane Austen, Thomas Hardy, T E Powys. *Contributor to:* New Statesman; Observer; Sunday Times; Listener; Times Literary Supplement; Country Life; New York Times; etc; BBC Films: A Painter in the Country; Constable Observed; Writers and Places; Akenfield. *Honours:* Fellow, Royal Society of Literature, 1969; Heineman Award, 1969; Society of Author's Travel Scholarship, 1970. *Literary Agent:* Deborah Rogers Ltd. *Address:* Bottengom's Farm, Wormingford, Colchester, Essex, England.

BOADT, Lawrence Edward, b. 26 Oct. 1942, Los Angeles, California, USA. Professor of Biblical Studies, Roman Catholic Priest. *Education:* MA Religious Studies, St Paul's College, Washington DC, 1968; MA Semitic Languages, Catholic University of America, Washington DC, 1972; Licentiate in Biblical Studies 1973, Doctorate in Biblical Studies 1976, Pontifical Institute, Rome, Italy. *Literary Appointments:* Associate Editor, Paulist Press, 1976. *Publications:* Ezekiel's Oracles Against Egypt, 1980; Biblical Studies: Meeting Ground of Jews and Catholics, 1981; Jeremiah 1-25: A Commentary, 1982; Jeremiah 26-52, Zephaniah, Habakkok and Nahum, 1983; Reading of the Old Testament: An Introduction, 1984; Introduction to Wisdom Literature and the Book of Proverbs, 1985. *Contributions to:* CBQ; Vetus Testamentum; JBL; Academe. *Address:* St Paul's College, 3015 4th Street NE, Washington, DC 20017, USA.

BOASE, Roger Abdul Wahhab, b. 3 Apr. 1946, Glasgow, Scotland. Lecturer. m. Dr Aisha Ahmad, 13 June 1969, London, 2 sons. *Education:* BA, Double Honours, French, Spanish, Pembroke College, Cambridge University; MA, PhD, Spanish, Westfield College, University of London. *Publications:* The Origin & Meaning of Courtly Love – A critical study of European scholarship, 1977; The Troubadour Revival – A study of social change & traditionalism in late medieval Spain, 1978, Spanish Translation, 1981. *Contributor to:* Dictionary of the Middle Ages, 1980; Bulletin of Hispanic Studies; Iberoromania; Journal of Hispanic Philology; Islamic Quarterly; Muslim World Book Review. *Honours:* Honorary Research Associate, Westfield College, University of London, 1984. *Memberships:* Fellow, Islamic Academy; International Courtly Literature Society; Association of British Hispanists; International Arthurian Society; Research into Lost Knowledge Organisation. *Address:* 53 Hamilton Terrace, London NW8 9RG, England.

BOATMAN, Diana Penelope Elizabeth, b. 3 July 1940, St Albans, England. Freelance Copy Editor; Indexer. m. M G C Boatman, 21 Sep. 1963, St Albans, 2 daughters. *Education:* MA, Cambridge University. *Literary Appointments:* Assistant to Editor, Royal Institute of Chemistry, 1964–66; Honorary Editor, The Marshlander, Journal, Romney Hythe & Dymchurch Railway Association, 1982–85. *Indexes for:* The Labour Party, 1979; Poet's London, 1980; Solvent Problems in Industry, 1984; Techniques for High Temperature Fatigue Testing, 1984; etc. Annual Index for: International Journal of Cement Composites & Lightweight Concrete, Volumes II-VII, 1981–86; International Journal of Ambient Energy, Volumes I-II, 1981. *Contributions to:* The Marshlander, 1982–86. *Address:* 61 Halkingcroft, Slough, Berkshire SL3 7AZ, England.

BOBANGO, Gerald James, b. 15 Sep. 1942, Erie, Pennsylvania, USA. Writer. m. Janet Christine Weibel, 8 June 1968, Erie, Pennsylvania, 2 daughters. *Education:* AB, Gannon College; MEd, Edinboro State College; PhD, Pennsylvania State University. *Appointment:* Founder and Editor, Bibliophilos Quarterly Journal of Research and Fiction, 1982. *Publications:* The Emergence of the Romanian National State, 1979; The Romanian Orthodox Episcopate of America: The First Half-Century, 1979; Religion and Politics: Archbishop Valerian Trife and His Times, 1981; Romanian Orthodoxy in Youngstown, 1906–1981, 1981; Historical Anniversary Album of the ROEA, 1979. *Contributor to:* Colonel Alexandru Ioan Cuza: The

Making of a Hospodar; in Southeastern Europe, 1975; The Union and League of Romanian Societies in America: An Assimilative Force Reviewed, East European Quarterly, 1978; Romanians, entry in Harvard Encyclopedia of American Ethnic Groups, 1980. *Memberships:* Romanian-American Academy of Arts and Sciences. *Honours:* Fulbright Fellow, Romania, 1970; International Research and Exchange Board Fellow, 1970–71; Immigration History Research Center Fellow, 1975–76. *Address:* West Virginia University, College of Law, Morgantown, WV 26506, USA.

BOCCIO, Karen Corinne, b. 18 Nov. 1954, New York City, New York, USA. Poet. m. Paul Alexander Boccio, 4 Dec. 1978, New York City, 2 sons. *Education:* BA, Columbia University, 1982. *Publications:* Inner Sanctions, 1980; Co-author of screen play. *Contributions to:* Poets Celebrate America; Carousel; Valhalla; Mati; New Scribes; New Worlds Unlimited 10th Annual Anthology; Small Press Magazine; New Leaves. *Honours:* Graduate Magna Cum Laude with honours in French and English, Columbia University, 1982. *Memberships:* Columbia Alumni Association; Poets and Writers Incorporated; Co-Founder and Editor of a small press. *Address:* 88-01 80th Street, Woodhaven, NY 11421, USA.

BOCZKOWSKI, Krzysztof, b. 2 May 1936, Warsaw, Poland. Professor of Genetics, Medical Academy of Warsaw. *Education:* Professor, dr hab, Medicine. *Publications:* Otwarte usta losu, 1975; Swiatlo dnia, 1977; Dawny i Obecny, 1978; W niewoli w sniegu w cieplym czolnie krwi, 1981; Twarze czekaja na wiecznosc, 1984; Dusza z ciala wyleciaia, 1985; Clinical Cytogentics, 1970, 1980; Intersexuality, 1970, 1980, 1985; Sex Determination and Differentiation, 1975, 1983; Human Sex, 1970, 1973, 1985, etc. *Contributor to:* Literatura na Swiecie; Tworczosc; Kultura; Literature; Nurt; Odra; Integracje; Pismo literacko-artystyczne, etc. *Honours:* Red Rose, Best First Book of Poetry, 1972; Pegaz Prize, for translations of poetry, especially T S Eliot, 1975. *Membership:* Polish Writers Union. *Literary Agent:* Authors Agency, Warsaw. *Address:* Dept of Genetics, Medical Academy of Warsaw, Starynkiewicza 1, 02-015 Warsaw, Poland.

BODART, Joni, b. 16 Dec. 1947, Windchester, Virginia, USA. University Professor. *Education:* BA, 1969, BS, 1969, MLS, 1971, MA, 1984, PhD, 1985, Texas Womens University. *Literary Appointments include:* Young Adult Librarian, Fremont Main Library, Alameda County Library, California, 1973–78; Young Adult Coordinator, Stanislaus Co. Free Library, California, 1978–79; Library Consultant, Pergamon Press, New York, 1981–82; Counselor Business Manager. Survival House, Texas, 1982–83; Instructor, School of Library and Information Management, Emporia State University, Emporia, Kansas, 1983–. *Publications:* Booktalk ! Booktalking and School Visiting for Young Adult Audiences, 1980; Booktalk ! 2, Booktalking Presentations for All Ages and Audiences, 1985. *Contributions to:* Top of the News; Texas Libraries; School Library Journal. Various lectures and workshops. Book reviewer: School Library Journal, 1971–76; Top of the News, 1984; Voice of Youth Advocates, 1984, Columnist 1984–; Editor, Top of the News, 1985–. *Memberships:* American Library Association; Association for Library and Information Science Education; Kansas Library Association; Past President, Bay Area Young Adult Librarians. *Address:* Emporia State University, School of Library and Information Management, 1200 Commercial, Emporia, KS 66801, USA.

BODDINGTON, Craig Thornton, b. 12 Nov. 1952, Kansas City, Kansas, USA. Magazine Editor. m. Paula Lynn Merriman, 3 Mar. 1984, Los Angeles. *Education:* BA English, University of Kansas, 1974. *Literary Appointments:* Staff, Petersen's 'Hunting' magazine, 1979–. *Publications:* America – The Men and Their Guns That Made Her Great (editor), 1981; Campfires and Game Trials – Hunting North American Big Game, 1985. *Contributions to:* Outdoor Life, Sports Afield, Guns and Ammo and other outdoor/hunting periodicals, 1972–79; Hunting magazine and annuals; Chapters in various anthologies. *Memberships:* Outdoor Writers Association of America. *Address:* 16044 Knapp Street, Sepulveda, CA 91343, USA.

BODDY, William Charles, b. 22 Feb. 1913, London, England. Editor. m. Winifred Holbrook, London, 3 daughters. *Literary Appointments:* Freelance Motoring and Aviation Writer; Acting Editor, Motor Sport, 1939–; Full-time Editor, Motor Sport, 1945–. *Publications:* Continental Sports Cars, 1946; History of Brooklands Motor Course, 1950; World's Land Speed Record, 1951; 200 Mile Race, 1948; Montlhéry, Paris, Autodrome, 1961; Sportscar Pocket Book, 1961. *Contributions to:* Almost every English Motoring Magazine; The Aeroplane, etc. *Membership:* Guild of Motoring Writers. *Address:* Llwynbarried Hall, Nantmel, Powys LD1 6EW, Wales.

BODE, Carl, b. 14 Mar. 1911, Milwaukee, Wisconsin, USA. m. (1) Margaret Lutze, (dec), 1938, 3 daughters, (2) Charlotte Watkins Smith, 1972. *Education:* PhB, University of Chicago, 1933; MA, 1938, PhD, Northwestern University, 1941. *Literary Appointments include:* Teacher, Milwaukee Vocational School, 1933–37; Assistant Professor of English, University of California, Los Angeles, 1946–47; Professor of English, University of Maryland, 1947–81; Executive Secretary, American Studies Program, University of Maryland, 1950–57; Cultural Attache, American Embassy to GB, 1957–59; Chairman, USA Educational Commission (Fulbright). UK, 1957–59; Visiting Professor, California Institute of Technology; Claremont Colleges; Northwestern University; Stanford University, University of Wisconsin. *Publications include:* (cultural hist) The American Lyceum; Antebellum Culture; The Half-World of American Culture; (poems) The Sacred Seasons; The Man Behind You; Practical Magic; (biog) Mencken; (newspaper essays) Highly Irregular; The New Mencken Letters (Ed); Maryland; A History. *Memberships include:* President, Popular Culture Association of America; President, American Studies Association; FRSL. *Address:* Department of English, Univesity of Maryland, College Park, MD 20742, USA.

BOECKMAN, Charles, b. 9 Nov. 1920, San Antonio, Texas, USA. Author. m. Patricia Ellen Kennelly, 25 July 1965, Corpus Christi, Texas, 1 daughter. *Publications:* Maveric Brand, 1961; Unsolved Riddles of the Ages, 1965; Our Regional Industries, 1966; Cool, Hot and Blue, 1968; And the Beat Goes On, 1972; Surviving Your Parents' Divorce, 1980. *Contributions to:* Over 1,000 short stories and articles to national publications since 1942. *Honour:* Best Detective Stories of the Year Anthology, 1976. *Membership:* American Society of Authors and Journalists. *Address:* 322 Del Mar Boulevard, Corpus Christi, TX 78404, USA.

BOEHM, George A W, b. 3 Aug. 1922, New York City, New York, USA. Science Writer. m. Alexandra Sarno, 1 Apr. 1944, New York, 2 sons, 3 daughters. *Education:* BA, Columbia College, New York. *Publications:* The New World of Maths, 1959, published, USA, UK, Sweden, Netherlands, USSR, Spain, Japan and Federal Republic of Germany. *Contributions to:* Fortune; Newsweek; Scientific American; Reader's Digest; New York Times Magazine; and numerous others. *Memberships:* National Association of Science Writers; American Mathematical Society. *Address:* 330 East 79th Street, New York, NY 10021, USA.

BOESCHE, Mathilde, b. 31 Jan. 1928, Elbing, Germany. Writer. m. 7 July 1950, Berlin, divorced 1964, 2 sons, 1 daughter. *Publications:* 4 childrens books; (Lyrical Works include) Metamorphische Variation, Nimm an damit du reiner wirst, Blue is the Colour of the Sky; My Foot Gropes for a Bridge, 1951–68; 300 Romantical Romances. *Contributor to:* Revue; Israel Chadaschot; German World in USA; etc. *Honours:* Dr Litt, World University, USA, 1981; Diploma d'Onore, Accademia Leonardo da Vinci, Rome, 1982; Studiosis Humanitas, 1984; European Banner of Arts, Accademia

Europea, 1984. *Memberships:* World Poetry Society International; Verband deutschsprachiger Schriftsteller in Israel; Plesse-Kreis. *Address:* Laurinsteig 14A, 1000 Berlin 28, Federal Republic of Germany.

BOGNER, Franz Josef, b. 19 June 1934, Limburg, Federal Republic of Germany. Actor; Author. *Publications:* Die Maus mit dem Sparbuch, fables, 1970; DAS arabische SYSTEM, poetry, 1971; ich bin. so?!; prose, 1972; goethes V'st, composition of quotations, 1973, 2nd edition, 1974; Die Maus, die den Halt verlor, spoken fables on Long-playing record, 1974; F J Bogner's Fabel-Haftes Lesebuch, fables, 1986. Various radio and stage plays. *Address:* Wichernweg 40, 6250 Limburg, Federal Republic of Germany.

BOGUE, Lucile Maxfield, b. 21 Apr. 1911, Salt Lake City, Utah, USA. Author; Educator. m. Arthur E Bogue, 25 Dec. 1935, Colorado, 2 sons. *Education:* AA, Colorado College; BA, University of Northern Colorado; MA, San Francisco State University; Post Graduate, San Miguel de Allende, College Internationale, Sophia University and University of California, Berkeley. *Literary Appointments include:* Professor of English, Colegio Amereicano, Guayaguil; Professor of Comparative Literature, Foreign Study Tour, London, Versailles, Vienna and Rome. *Publications:* Typhoon! Typhoon!, 1970; Eye of the Condor, 1975; Salt Lake, 1982; Bloodstones, 1980; Windbells on the Bay, 1983; Dancers on Horseback: The Perry Mansfield Story, 1984. *Contribution to:* Blue Unicorn; Instructor; Grade Teacher; Country Poet; Cambric Press; International Womens Place Anthology; New Worlds Unlimited; Tecolote. *Honours include:* Colorado Poet of the Year, 1941; Browning Society of San Francisco Award, 1966; Bogue Library and Lucy Bogue Hall named, Yampa Valley College, 1967; Nominee, Colorado Woman of Achievement, 1967; World of Poetry Prize, 1976; National Writers Club Awards, 1979, 81, 84; Writers West Award, 1984; Woman of the Year, League of American Penwomen, 1983. *Memberships:* President, California Writers Club; California Federation of Chapparral Poets; California State Poetry Society; Academy of American Poets; Dramatists Guild; Authors League of America; National League of American Pen Women; Ina Coolbrith Circle; National Writers Club; Playwrights Center; Womens National Book Association; Poetry Society of America. *Literary Agent:* Bertha Klausner. *Address:* 2611 Brooks, El Cerrito, CA 94530, USA.

BOHIGIAN, Valerie, b. New York City, New York, USA. Writer, Author. m. Haig Bohigian, 4 Aug. 1970, 2 daughters. *Education:* BA English; MA English. *Literary Appointments:* Editorial Consultant: Self Reliant, Trader's Journal, Tradeworld News. *Publications:* Successful Flea Market Selling, 1981; How To Make Your Home-Based Business Grow, 1984; 'Real' Money From Home, 1985. *Contributions to:* Woman's Day; American Way; Redbook; Self-Reliant; New Woman; Trader's Journal; Fifty Plus; Tradeworld News; The Writer; and others. *Membership:* American Society of Journalists and Authors. *Literary Agent:* Mr Dominick Abel. *Address:* 225 Hunter Avenue, North Tarry Town, NY 10591, USA.

BÖHNING, Wolf-Rüdiger, b. 29 Sep. 1942, Braunschweig, Federal Republic of Germany. Official, International Labour Office, Geneva. m. Margaret-Jill Ratcliffe, 5 Oct. 1968, Bournemouth, England, 1 son, 1 daughter. *Education:* Diplom-Politologe, Political Science, Free University of Berlin. *Publications:* The Migration of Workers in the United Kingdom and the European Community, 1972; Studies in International Labour Migration, 1984. *Contributor to:* International Migration and the Western World: past, present, future, International Migration, Volume 16, 1978; International Migration in Western Europe: Reflections on the Past Five Years, International Labour Review, Volume 118, 1979; Regularising the Irregular, International Migration, volume 21, 1983. *Address:* 37a Chemin du Grand Voiret, 1228 Geneva, Switzerland.

BOKOR, Pierre, b. 24 May 1940, Cluj, Romania. Artistic Director; French-Canadian Writer. m. Maria Mitrache, 17 Sep. 1975, Bucharest, Romania, 1 son, 1 daughter. *Education:* Master of Arts. *Appointments:* Literary Appointments began in 1956. *Publications:* Somersault in the Street, 1971; Stop the Century, 1976; Don't Lean Outside!, 1975; My Little Toreador!, 1976; Exit at the Page 201, 1979; Book About Toma Caragiu, 1984 and several theatrical plays including Amoooor, 1984. *Memberships:* SACD, France; SARDEC, Canada; Playwrights Union of Canada; CEAD, Canada. *Honours:* Cultural Achievement Award, City of Edmonton, 1982; Creative Arts Award, City of Edmonton, 1984; Alberta Achievement Award, Excellence Category for Outstanding Contribution to the Arts, 1984; Playwrights Award, Metz, France, 1985. *Address:* 9309 96 Street, Edmonton, T6C 3Y6, Alberta, Canada.

BOLAY, Karl H, b. 23 Nov. 1914, Saarbruecken, Federal German Republic. Author; Literary Critic; Editor; Translator. *Education:* Abitur, 1934, Socionom, 1955; Libn, 1955; Dr Lit, 1977. *Publications include:* Auf der Flucht vor uns selber, 1976; Auf der suche nach mir selber, 1979; Harrisburg ar overallt, 1979; Non-fiction; Att lana ut konst, 1967; Riv Kulturbarriarerna, 1970; Svenskarna och deras Immigranter, 1975; Translations include: The Unknown Soldier, from Finnish to German. *Contributor to:* Numerous journals and magazines. *Honours:* Recipient of several awards from Swedish Authors Foundation. *Memberships:* German Authors Union; Swedish Authors Association. *Literary Agent:* Graphikum. *Address:* Pilvägen 15, S–260 40 Viken, Sweden.

BOLDEMANN, Karin, b. 13 July 1928, Lübeck, Germany. Writer; Librettist. *Lyrics include:* Libretto for Second of Eternity (première, Opera of Stockholm, 1974); Libretto for Joseph (première, Opera of Stockholm, 1979); Libretto for The Hour of Madness (Theatre, Milmö, 1968, TV, 1968), with L Boldemann, T Lundqvist, B-W Hallberg (composers); Drama Whiteflower, Isak, (Royal Dramatic Theatre, Stockholm, 1985). *Contributor to:* Artes (of essays) published by The Musical Academy, The Academy of Arts, The Swedish Academy. *Honours:* National Scholarship of Arts, 1975, 1978, 1980. *Memberships:* Swedish Union of Authors; Swedish Union of Dramatists. *Address:* Bergv 11, 131 50 Saltsjo-Duvnas, Stockholm, Sweden.

BOLLINGER, Armin, b. 1 Nov. 1913, Zurich, Switzerland. University Professor. *Education:* D Phil, University of Zurich; Dr hc, University of Cuzco. *Publications:* Die Inka, 1974; 3 Körner von gelbem Mais, 1981; Speilball der Machtigen, 1982; Einführung in die Welt der Indios, 1982; Die Indiovölker Altmexikos, 1982; El Curandero, 1982; Die tanzenden Krokodile, 1983; Die Maya, 1984; Die Kette des Häuptlings, 1985. *Contributions to:* Die Indianische Tragödie, July 1985. *Honours:* Honorary Prize fo the Kanton Zurich 1983. *Memberships:* PEN International, London; PEN-Zentrum Schweiz; Schweiz Schriftsteller-Verband. *Address:* Hofwiesenstrasse 296, 8050 Zurich, Switzerland.

BOLTON, Frederic James, b. 12 June 1908, Research Chemist. *Education:* BSc, Birkbeck College, London University, 1934; FRIC. *Publications:* A View From Ben More, 1972; Glasgow Central Station, 1972; The Wild Uncharted Country, A Scientific Pilgrimage, 1973. *Contributions to:* Akros; Elders; Glasgow Herald; Nature; New Athenian Broadsheet; Outposts; Poetry of Today; Rotary; Scotsman; Scottish Poetry IV; Lines; British Broadcasting Corporation Scottish Life and Letters, radio. *Honour:* 2nd prize, Scottish Association for the Speaking of Verse, Poetry Competition, Edinburgh, Scotland, 1965. *Address:* 17 Wester Coates Avenue, Edinburgh, Scotland EH12 5LS.

BOND, Edward, b. 1934, London, England. Playwright. *Publications:* (Plays) The Pope's Wedding, 1962; Saved, 1965; Early Morning, 1968; Narrow Road to the Deep North, 1968; Black Mass, (one act), 1970; Lear, 1971; Passion, (one act), 1971; The Sea, 1973;

Bingo, 1974; The Foot, 1976; We Come to the River (Opera libretto, Music by Hans Werner Henze), 1976; A-A-Americal, 1976; (Translation) The Three Sisters; Chekov; Spring Awakening (Wedekind); The Woman, 1979; The Bundle, 1979; The Worlds, 1980; Restoration and the Cat, 1982; Summer, 1983; Human Cannon, 1984; The War Plays, (Trilogy), 1985; After the Assasinations, 1983. *Contributor to:* Sunday Times; Guardian. *Agent:* Margaret Ramsay. *Address:* 14a Goodwins Court, St Martin's Lane, London WC2, England.

BOND, Harold, b. 2 Dec. 1939, Boston, Massachusetts, USA. Poet; Editor; Teacher. *Education:* BA, Northeastern University, Boston, 1962; MFA, University of Iowa, 1967. *Appointments include:* Instructor, Poetry Workshops, Center for Adult Education, Cambridge, 1968–; Editor, Akarat Magazine, 1969-70 (currently on Editorial Board); Instructor Poets-in-Schools Programme, Massachusetts, 1971–74, 1977–79, New Hampshire, 1973–76, Poets Who Teach Incorporated. *Publications include:* Co-Author, 3x3, 1969; The Northern Wall, 1969; Dancing on Water, 1970; The Way it Happens to You, 1979. *Contributions to:* Numerous magazines and anthologies including: The Young American Poets, 1968; Speaking for Ourselves: American Ethnic Writing, 1969; The New Yorker Book of Poems, 1969; A Decade of Armenian-American Writing, 1969; Eleven Boston Poets, 1970; East Coast Poets, 1971; Getting Into Poetry, 1972; New Voices in American Poetry, 1973; Outside/Inside, 1973; Shake the Kaleidoscope, 1973; Writing a Poem, 1975; Armenian-American Poets: Bilingual Anthology, 1976; I Sing the Song of Myself: Autobiographical Poems, 1978; Traveling American with Today's Poets, 1977; Anthology of Magazine Verse, 1981; The Aspect Anthology, 1981; Poems: A Celebration, 1982; Despite This Flesh, 1985; Toward Solomon's Mountain, 1986; Ararat; New Yorker; Harper's Magazine; Saturday Review; New Republic; North American Review; Iowa Review; Carleton Miscellany; Choice; Boston Review. *Honours include:* 1st Prize, Armenian Allied Arts Association Poetry Competition, 1963, 64, 65; 1st Prize, Kansas City Star Awards, 1967, 68; Creative Writing Fellowship Grant, National Endowment for the Arts, 1976. *Address:* 11 Chestnut Street, Melrose, MA 02176, USA.

BOND, Michael. *Publications:* A Bear Called Paddington, 1958; More About Paddington, 1959; Paddington Helps Out, 1960; Paddington Abroad, 1961; Paddington at Large, 1962; Paddington Marches on, 1964; Paddington at Work, 1966; Here Comes Thursday, 1966; Thursday Rides Again, 1968; Paddington Goes to Town, 1968; Thursday Ahoy, 1969; Parsley's Tail, 1969; Parsley's Good Deed, 1969; Parsley's Problem Present, 1970; Parsley's Last Stand, 1970; Paddington Takes the Air, 1970; Thursday in Paris, 1970; Michael Bond's Book of Bears, 1971; Michael Bond's Book of Mice, 1971; The Day the Animals Went on Strike, 1972; Paddington Bear, 1972; Paddington's Garden, 1972; Parsley Parade, 1972; The Tales of Olga de Polga, 1972; Olga Meets her Match, 1973; Paddington's Blue Peter Story Book, 1973; Paddington at the Circus, 1973; Paddington Goes Shopping, 1973; Paddington at the Seaside, 1974; Paddington at the Tower 1974; Paddington on Top, 1974; Windmill, 1975; How to Make Flying Things, 1975; Eight Olga Readers, 1975; Paddington's Cartoon Book, 1979; J D Polson and the Liberty-Head Dime, 1980; J D Polson and the Dillogate Affair, 1981; Paddington on Screen, 1981; Olga Takes Charge, 1982; The Caravan Puppets, 1983; Paddington at the Zoo, 1984; Paddington and the Knickerbocker Rainbow, 1984; Paddington's Painting Exhibition, 1985; Paddington at the Fair, 1985; Oliver the Greedy Elephant, 1985; (Adult Books) Monsieur Pamplemousse on the Spot, 1986. *Literary Agent:* Harvey Unna, London. *Address:* c/o Harvey Unna & Stephen Durbridge Ltd, 24 Pottery Lane, Holland Park, London W11 4LZ, England.

BOND, Ruskin, b. 19 May. 1934, Kasauli, India. Author, Childrens Books. *Publications:* Angry River, 1972; The Blue Umbrella, 1974; Big Busines, 1979; Night of the Leopard, 1979; The Cherry Tree, 1980; Flames in the Forest, 1981; Tigers Forever, 1983; Earthquake, 1984; Getting Granny's Glasses, 1985; Cricket for the Crocodile, 1986. *Contributor to:* The Lady, London; Cricket, USA; School, Australia; Short Story International, New York. *Honours:* Recipient, John Llewellyn Rhys Prize, 1957. *Membership:* Authors Guild of India. *Address:* Ivy Cottage, Mussoorie, India.

BOND, William Joseph, b. 23 Oct. 1941, Winchester, Massachusetts, USA. College Professor; Author; Lecturer. m. Janet A Lupico, 18 Nov. 1967, Haverhill, 1 son, 1 daughter. *Education:* AA, Burdett College, BS, MAT, Salem State College. *Publications:* Secrets to Success in Your Job, 1977; 1001 Ways to Beat The Time Trap, 1982. *Contributor to:* B Lack Enterprise Magazine; National Public Accountant; Burroughs Clearing House Magazine; etc. *Honours:* Book of the Month, Fortune Book Club, 1982; Nominated, Achiever of Year, USA Today Newspaper; Nominated, Leavey Awards for Excellence in Private Enterprise Education. *Literary Agent:* Attorney Scott Gleason. *Address:* 67 Melrose Avenue, Haverhill, MA 01830, USA.

BONDI, (Sir) Hermann, b. 1 Nov. 1919, Vienna, Austria. Master, Churchill College, Cambridge, England, 1984–. *Education:* MA, Trinity College, Cambridge. *Publications:* Cosmology, 1952, 2nd edition 1960; The Universe at Large, 1961; Relativity & Commonsense, 1964; Assumption & Myth in Physical Theory, 1968; numerous scientific papers. *Contributor to:* Various scientific journals. *Honours:* KCB, 1973; FRS, 1959; Fellow, Royal Astronomical Society. *Membership:* Association of British Scientific Writers. *Address:* Churchill College, Cambridge CB3 0DS, England.

BONENFANT, Rejean, b. 21 Dec. 1945, St Narcisse, Canada. Teacher. m. Danièle Bourassa, 27 July 1968 at Grand-Mère, Canada, 1 son, 1 daughter. *Education:* Master in French Literature; License in Pedagogy and Literature. *Publications:* Un Amour de Papier; L'Ecriveule. *Contributor to:* Hobo-Quebec, Ecrits Du Canada, APLF, Make-Up and Terminus. Director of Le Sabord. *Membership:* UNEQ. *Address:* 2225 Rue des Chenaux, Trois-Rivières, Province of Quebec, Canada G9A 1B1.

BONESSIO di TERZET, Ettore, b. 4 Feb. 1944, La Spezia, Italy. Professor at University of Genoa. m. Bianchi Giampiera, 27 Aug. 1967, La Spezia, 1 son. *Education:* MA; PhD. *Literary Apointment:* Editor, Poetry and Art Magazine, Il Cobold. *Publications:* Solitudine e commission estetica, 1974; Hegel e la poesia moderna, 1975; Arte ed espercieruzd estetica, 1978; L'esperienza dell'arte, 1980; Il Principio della Parola (anthology of distinguished poetry after 1874), 1986. *Contributor to:* Dulfur, USA; International Poetry USA; Tracce; Stilb; Spirali; Symbola; Il Farone; Altri Termini; Nuova Corrente; Artivisive; Studio Marconi; Filasofie Oggi, Italy; Vertice, Portugal; XUL, Argentina; Differentia, USA; Anterem, Italy; Alfabeta, Italy; Effects, USA. *Address:* CP 707, 16100 Genova AD, Italy.

BONGARTZ, Roy, b. 8 Dec. 1924, Providence, Rhode Island, USA. Writer. m. Cecilia Leigh, 6 June 1955, London, deceased, 1 son. *Education:* BA, MA, Miami University; Certificat, University of Paris. *Publications:* The Applicant, play, 1961; Twelve Chases on West Ninety-ninth Street, 1965; New England Records, 1978; Dollarwise Guide to the Southwest, 1985. *Contributor to:* Horizon; The New Yorker; Saturday Evening Post; New Statesman; New York Times; Esquire; The Nation; Argosy; True; Saturday Review; Sports Illustrated; Popular Science; American Heritage; Publishers Weekly; Travel & Leisure; Travel/Holiday; Early American Life; US Air; McCall's; Good Housekeeping; etc. *Honour:* Mary Roberts Rinehart Novel Award, 1960. *Address:* Route 1, Foster, RI 02825, USA.

BONINE, Vivian Way, b. 28 Sep. 1912, Texas, USA. Film Technician; Poetry Editor; Critic. m. (1) Morris W Small, (2) Arvel Earl Bonine, 2 daughters. *Education:* Texas Woman's University, 1929–30; West Texas State University, 1931–43. *Literary Appointments:* Poetry Editor, Critic, Judge, 1966–. *Publications:* Sparks, 1958; Silver Ashes, 1971; California, Land of the Chaparral, 1981; Editor, Scriptorium Arboretum (workshop magazine), 1963–68. *Contributions to:* Numerous journals, magazines and anthologies including: California State Poetry Quarterly, 1979; US in Clover, 1976; Great American World Poets; Poets, India; Pasque Petals, South Dakota; This is Chaparral, 1977. *Honours include:* Doctor, World University, Great China Arts College, Hong Kong, 1970; Various awards: United Poets Laureate International; CFCP; Pasadena Writers Club; Laurel Leaves, Roll of Honour, Poetry, 1978; Blue Ribbon Award at Los Angeles County Fair for Poetry, 1982. *Memberships include:* California State Poetry Society (Monthly Poetry Contest Chairman 1982–85); Pasadena Writers Club (President, 1963–66); Poetry Society of Texas; California Federation of Chaparral Poets; National Federation State Poetry Societies (Publicity Chairman, 1974–75). *Address:* 2556 La Presa Avenue, Rosemead, CA 91770, USA.

BÓNIS Ferenc, b. 17 May 1932, Miskolc, Hungary. Musicologist. m. Terézia Csajbók. *Education:* Liszt Ferenc Academy of Music, Budapest. *Publications:* Erkel Ferenc, 1953; Mosonyi Mihály, 1960; Kadosa Pál, 1965; Béla Bartók. His Life in Pictures & Documents, 1972, 1981; Igy Láttuk Kodályt (Zoltán Kodály as we saw him), 1979, 1982; Igy Láttuk Bartkot (Bartók – as we saw him), 1981; Tizenhárom találkozas Ferencsik Jánossal (13 Meeting with János Ferencsik), 1984; Ein Wendepunkt in Bartóks kompositorischer Laufbahn, 1985. *Contributor to:* Magyar Zenetudomany, Editor, 1959–; Magyar Zenetudomány, Editor, 1959–; Magyar Zenetörténeti Tanulmányok, editor, 1968–. *Memberships:* International Society for Musicology; Society for Music Research; The Bayreuth International Arts Centre, Advisory Board; Hungarian Kodly Society Praesidium. *Honour:* Recipient, Ferenc Erkel Prize, 1973. *Address:* Belgrad Rakpart 27 1 5, H–1056 Budapest, Hungary.

BONNER, Thomas, b. 19 Sep. 1942, New Orleans, USA. Professor; Writer. m. Judith Ann Hopkins, 27 Aug. 1966, New Orleans, 2 daughters. *Education:* BA, Southeastern LA University; MA, PhD, Tulane University. *Appointments:* Editor, Xavier Review; Book Critic, Times-Picayune. *Publication:* William Faulkner: William B Wisdom Collection, 1980; A Kate Chopin Dictionary, forthcoming. *Contributor to:* Mississippi Quarterly; Southern Quarterly; Resources for American Literary Scholarship; New Laurel Review; Bulletin of Bibliography; Notes on American Literature; Negative Capability; Markham Review. *Honours:* Andrew W Mellon Postdoctoral Fellowship for Literary Research, 1982. *Memberships:* Society for the Study of Southern Literature, Executive Council member, 1982–85; MLA, SCMLA Conference on Christianity and Literature. *Address:* 6202 Marshal Foch, New Orleans, LA 70124, USA.

BONNEY, Lorraine Gagnon, b. 28 Nov. 1922, Edmonton, Alberta, Canada. Author. m. Orrin H Bonney, 5 June 1955, Dallas, Texas, Deceased. *Education:* BA, University of Alberta. *Publications:* Guide to the Wyoming Mountains and Wilderness Areas, 1960, 3rd edition 1970; Field Book Teton Range and Gros Ventre Range, 1970; Field Book Big Horn Range, 1970; Field Book Yellowstone Park and Absaroka Range, 1970; Field Book Wind River Range, 1970; Field Book – Grand Teton National Park and Jacksons Hole, 1983; Battle Drums & Geysers, 1970. *Contributor to:* Alaska; Teton Magazines; Appalachia. *Honours:* Recipient various honours and awards including Guide to Wyoming Mountains, Best Book, Wyoming Historical Society, 1965; Field Book Wind River Range, Best Camping Book, 1968; Battle Drums, Best Book, Wyoming Historical Society, 1970, Wyoming Literary Map of 1984. *Memberships:* Outdoor Writers Association of

America; American Society of Journalists and Authors. *Address:* P O Box 129, Kelly (Jackson Hole), WY 83011, USA.

BOONE, Bruce, b. 16 Mar. 1940, Portland, Oregon, USA. Writer. *Education:* BA, English, St Mary's College, California, 1962; MA, English, 1966, PhD, English, 1976, University of California, Berkeley. *Literary Appointments:* Teacher, Freshman Composition and World Classics, St Mary's College, Morega, California; Teacher, Marxist Theory for Writers, Small Press Traffic Bookstore. *Publications:* Veins of Earth (poetry), 1970; My Walk with Bob (stories), 1979; LaFontaine (translations) (with Robert Gluck), 1981; Karate Flower (chapbook), 1973; Century of Clouds (novel), 1980. *Contributions to:* The Language Book, 1984; Poetry Flash No. 76, 1979; Panjandrum, 1973; Social Text; The Advocate; Poetics Journal; American Book Review, etc. *Honour:* Briarcombe Residency, Bolinas, California, 1981–82. *Memberships:* Modern Language Association; Marxist Literary Group. *Address:* 1016 Noe Street, San Francisco, CA 94114, USA.

BOONE, Gene, b. 26 Dec. 1962, South Carolina, USA. Editor; Writer. *Appointments:* Editor, RSVP Press, 1983–; Editor, The World's A Poet Anthology; Editor, Poetry Collection, Echoes of the Heart & Mind, 1986. *Publications:* Writing to be Published, 1984; Crocodile Tears, 1985; Markets for Writers, 1985; Practical Solutions for Writers, 1985 (pen name San Chaplan); Promotion for The Writer, 1985 (pen name San Chaplan). *Contributor to:* Fate Magazine; Poet; Writer's Lifeline; Published; Professional Poet; Anti-War Poems; Writer's Journal; The Writer and Poet's Market. *Address:* RSVP Press, Box 394, Society Hill, SC 29593, USA.

BOORSTIN, Daniel J, b. 1 Oct. 1914, Atlanta, Georgia, USA. Author; Historian. m. Ruth Carolyn Frankel, 9 Apr. 1941, New York, 3 sons. *Education:* AB, Harvard College, 1934; BA, Jurisprudence, Honours (Rhodes Scholar) 1936, BCL, Honours, 1937, Bailliol College, Oxford University, England; Student, Inner Temple, London 1934–37; JSD (Sterling Fellow), Yale, 1940. *Publications:* The Mysterious Science of the Law, 1941; The Lost World of Thomas Jefferson, 1948; The Genius of American Politics, 1953; America and the Image of Europe, 1960; The Decline of Radicalism, 1969; The Sociology of the Absurd, 1970; Democracy and Its Discontents, 1974; The exploring Spirit: America and the World, Then and Now, 1976; The Republic of Technology, 1978; The American: The Colonial Experience, 1958, The American: The National Experience, 1965, The Americans: The Colonial Experience, 1958, The Discoverers, 1983; Editor: Delaware Cases 1792–1830, 3 volumes, 1943; A Lady's Life in the Rocky Mountains, 1960; An American Primer, 2 volumes, 1966–68; American Civilization, 1972; The Chicago History of American Civilization, 30 volumes, 1972; Co-Editor, Textbook, A History of the United States, 1980; etc. *Contributor to:* Numerous periodicals. *Honours include:* D Litt, Cambridge University, 1968, University of Sheffield, England, 1979; numerous other honorary degrees; Bowdoin Prize, Harvard, 1934; Jenkins Prize, Balliol College, 1935; Yonger Prize, Balliol College, 1936; Bancroft Prize, Columbia University, 1959; Pulitzer Prize for History and Dexter Prize for, The Americans: The Democratic Experience, 1974; etc. *Memberships:* Past President, American Studies Association; Colonial Society of Massachusetts; Antiquarian Society; American Academy of Arts and Sciences; American Historical Association; American Philosophical Society; Royal Historical Society. *Address:* 3541 Ordway St, NW, Washington DC 20016, USA.

BOOTHROYD, Basil, b. 4 Mar. 1910. Author; Journalist. *Publications:* Motor if You Must, 1959; The Whole Thing's Laughable, 1961; You Can't Be Serious, 1965; Let's Stay Married, 1966; Philip, Life of Duke of Edinburgh, 1971; Accustomed As I Am, 1975; Let's Move House, 1976. *Contributor to:* Punch; Homes & Gardens; Journal of Institute of Bankers; etc. *Honours:* Kt of Mark Twain, USA, 1971; Imperial Tobacco Radio

Award, Best Comedy Writer, 1976; Freeman, City of London. *Memberships:* Society of Authors; Savage Club. *Agent:* A P Watt Ltd. *Address:* c/o A P Watt Ltd, 26-8 Bedford Square, London WC1R 4HL, England.

BOREL, Jacques, b. 17 Dec. 1925, Paris France. Literary Adviser; Writer. *Education:* Lic ès Lettres, University Paris, Sorbonne; Diploma d'Etudes Superieures. *Literary Appointments:* Cultural Attache, French Embassy, Belgium, 1984–. *Publications:* L'adoration (novel), 1965; Tata ou de l'education (play), 1967; Le retour (novel), 1970; Marcel Proust (essay), 1972; La depossession (diary), 1973; Commentaires (essays), 1974; Un voyage ordinaire (diary), 1975; Poesie et nostalgie (essays), 1979; Histoire de mes vieux habits (novel), 1979; Petite Histoire de mes Reves (Essay), 1981; Editor, Verlaine's Complete Works, 1958–59, Poetical Works, 1961 and Complete Works in Prose, 1972; translation of James Joyce's The Cat and the Devil, 1966; Collected Poems, 1967. *Contributor to:* Various magazines and journals. *Honours:* Prix Concourt, 1965; Chevalier Ordre des Arts et Lettres, 1971. *Memberships:* PEN Club. *Address:* Editions Gallimard, 5 rue Sébastien Bottin, 75007 Paris, France.

BORENSTEIN, Emily Ruth Schwartz, b. 6 May 1923, Elizabeth, New Jersey, USA. Poet; Lecturer; Psychiatric Social Work/Clinical Therapist. m. Morris Borenstein, 27 June 1942, Montgomery, Alabama, 1 son, 2 daughters. *Education:* BS Comparative Literature 1964, MS Social Work 1984, Columbia University; MA English, New York University, 1972. *Publications:* Woman Chopping, 1978; Cancer Queen, 1979; Finding My Face, 1979; Night of the Broken Glass, 1981; Anthologies: Voices Within The Ark, 1980; Phoenix Rising: An Anthology of Contemporary Jewish Voices, 1981; Anthology of Magazine Verse, 1981; Blood to Remember: American Poets on the Holocaust, 1986. *Contributions to:* Webster Review; Voices Israel; One Generation After; Jewish Spectator; Jewish Currents; European Judaism; Response; En/Passant; Studia Mystica; Twigs; Voices of the Seventies; Zahir; Mundus Artium; Poet Lotre; Bitterroot; Croton Review; Pivot; Greenfield Review; Epos; Cymberlands; Remington Review; Glassworks; Mikrokosmos; Tree; Waves; Cyclo-Flame; Pontchartrain Review; Rufus. *Honour:* Poetry Award, Jewish Currents, 1978. *Memberships:* Poetry Society of America; Poets and Writers. *Address:* 189 Highland Avenue, Middletown, NY 10940, USA.

BORER, Mary Cathcart, b. 3 Feb. 1906, London, England. Writer. *Education:* BSc, London. *Publications:* Britain: 20th Century; Africa; What Became of the Mamelukes; Famous Rogues; Tabitha (play with Arnold Ridley), 1956; Two Villages, 1973; Willingly to School, 1976; Hampstead & Highgate: Two Hilltop Villages, 1976; The City of London, 1977; London Walks and Legends, 1981; The Story of Covent Garden, 1984; various radio and TV scripts. *Address:* Robin Hill, 4 Station Road, Tring, Hertfordshire HP23 5NG, England.

BORGEAUD, Georges, b. 27 July 1914, Lausanne, Switzerland. Writer; Journalist. *Education:* High School. *Publications:* Le Mean, 1952; La Vaisselle des Eveques, 1960; Le Voyage a l'estranger, 1974; I fali pres, 1962. *Contributor to:* Le Figaro; Le Point; La Parissienne; Ecriture; Le Journal de Geneve; Gazette de Lausanne. *Honours:* Critics Award, 1952; Journalists Prize, City of Rome, 1961; Renaudot Prize, 1974. *Memberships:* PEN; Society of Swiss Writers; Society of French Authors. *Address:* 59 Rue Floidevaus, 75014 Paris, France.

BOROS, Attila, b. 5 Apr. 1934, Budapest, Hungary. Music Editor; Radio Reporter. *Publications:* Klemperer in Hungary, 1973, 2nd edition 1984; Music and Microphone – 40 Years of the Budapest Symphony Orchestra, 1985; Hungarian Translation of Karl Bohms Autobiography: Ich erinnere mich ganz genau, 1977; The 30 Years of Hungarian Opera, 1945–75, 1979. *Contributor to:* Muzsika. *Address:* Paulay Ede u 14, Budapest 1061, Hungary.

BOROWITZ, Albert, b. 27 June 1930, Chicago, Illinois, USA. Lawyer; Writer. *Education:* BA, 1951, MA, 1953, Harvard University; JD, 1956. *Publications:* Fiction in Communist China, 1954; Innocence and Arsenic: Studies in Crime and Literature, 1977; The Woman Who Murdered Black Satin: The Bermondsey Horror, 1981; A Gallery of Sinister Perspectives: Ten Crimes and a Scandal, 1982; The Jack the Ripper Walking Tour Murder, 1986. *Contributions to:* American Scholar; Musical Quarterly; 19th Century French Studies; American Bar Association Journal; Victorian Newsletter; Armchair Detective and others. *Memberships:* Rowland Club, Cleveland; Former member, Council of Fellows. *Literary Agent:* Laurence Pollinger, London, England. *Address:* 2561 Coventry Road, Shaker Heights, OH 44120, USA.

BORSON, Roo, b. 20 Jan. 1952, Berkeley, California, USA. Writer. *Education:* BA, Goddard College; MFA, Creative Writing, University of British Columbia, Canada, 1977. *Publications:* Landfall, 1977; In the Smoky Light of the Fields, 1980; Rain, 1980; A Sad Device, 1981; The Whole Night, Coming Home, 1984. *Contributor to:* Numerous journals including: American Poetry Review; New Orleans Review; California Quarterly; Poetry Australia; Canadian Literature; Canadian Forum; Queen's Quarterly; Saturday Night; The Malahat Review; Anthologies Include: The New Oxford Book of Canadian Verse, 1982; An Anthology of Canadian Literature in English, Volume II, 1983; Canadian Poetry Now: 20 Poets of the Eighties, 1984. *Honours:* MacMillan Poetry Prize, University of British Columbia, 1977; 1st Prize, Poetry, CBC Literary Competition, 1982; Canada Council Junior Arts Grants, 1983–84, 1984–85; Nominated, Governor General's Award for, The Whole Night, Coming Home, 1984. *Membership:* League of Canadian Poets. *Address:* 244 Alvarado Road, Berkeley, CA 94705, USA.

BORTIN, Virginia, b. 19 June 1936, Philadelphia, Pennsylvania, USA. Writer. m. George Bortin, 18 Feb. 1967, Philadelphia, PA, USA. *Education:* BA, University of Pennsylvania. *Publications:* Publicity for Volunteers, 1981; Image of a Man, (with George Bortin), 1984. *Contributions to:* Articles in, Biblical Archaeologist Magazine, Woman's World Magazine, various newspapers; Poems in, New York Quarterly; syndicated colunm, Newspaper Enterprise Association. *Literary Agent:* Ellen Levine. *Address:* Beverly Hills, CA, USA.

BOSE, Dakshina Ranjan, b. 26 Dec. 1912, Barrajogini, Bangladesh, Journalist; Novelist; Poet; Essayist. m. Sobha, 8 May 1942, Dacca, 3 sons. *Education:* Graduate, Calcutta University, 1935. *Literary Appointments:* Assistant Editor, Bande Mataram; Night Editor, Kesari; News Editor, Jugantar (all Bengali dailies); Lecturer, Department of Journalism, University of Calcutta; Chief Editor: daily Uttar Banga Sangbad (North Bengal News) and Paschim Banga Sangbad (West Bengal News). Toured USA as Leader Grantee, (Journalism and Literature) as guest of State Department, 1956. Presided over sections of All India Bengali Literary Conference in different years from 1957, Vice President for many years; Special Guest, West German Tagore Centenary Celebrations, 1961. *Publications:* Satabdir Suya (Sun of the Century on Tagore) 1941; Bidesh Bibhui (Foreign Lands) travel stories 1958; Ekti Prithibi Ekti Hriday (One World, One Heart) collection of stories, 1962; Sagar Ranir Deshe (In the Sea Queen's Empire) novel for children, 1963; Sanskritir Dharma (Image of Culture) essays 1971; Padma Aamar Ganga Aumar Poems on New Bangladesh 1971; Sandhyarati (Offerings of the Evening) collection of songs, 1977. *Contributions to:* Many poems, stories, novels and essays on art, culture, education and politics published in various magazines and journals and many translated and printed in different Indian and foreign language newspapers and periodicals. *Honours:* Soviet Land Nehru Award, 1966; Ultorath Literary Prize as Best Bengali Poet of the Year, 1967; Award for writing children's literature for many years, 1969. *Memberships:* Life Member and Vice President for several terms, All India Bengali Literary

Conference; Bangiya Shahitya Parisad (Calcutta); Past President, Suhrid Sangha Pathagar (Friends' Reading Library). *Literary Agent:* Rabin Baul, Saibya Prakashani (Publishers) 86/1 Mahatma Gandhi Road, Calcutta. *Address:* 64/13 Belgachia Road, Calcutta 700 037, India.

BOSLOUGH, John Irvan, b. 18 June 1942, Charlotte, North Carolina, USA. Journalist; Author. 1 daughter. *Education:* AB cum laude, History of Science, Princeton University, 1967. *Literary Appointments:* Reporter, Associated Press; Editor, Salida (Colorado) Mountain Mail; Science/Medical writer, Washington correspondent, The Denver Post; Science Editor, US News & World Report. *Publications:* Stephen Hawking's Universe, New York 1984, also as Beyond the Black Hole, London 1985. *Contributions to:* National Geographic; Smithsonian; Reader's Digest; Psychology Today; The Washington Post; Time Magazine; Historic Preservation; Science 81/82; US News & World Report. *Honours:* News coverage award, Associated Press, 1972; Feature writing award, Colorado Press Association, 1972; Best article, non-geographic journal, National Council for Geographic Education, 1982. *Literary Agent:* John Brockman Associates Inc, New York. *Address:* Arlington, VA 22207, USA.

BOSQUET, Alain, b. 28 Mar. 1919, Odessa, Russia. Writer. *Education:* Free University of Brussels, Belgium, 1938–40; MA, University of Paris, Sorbonne, France. *Publications include:* (Poems) Un 1945–67, 1979; 100 Notes Pour Une Solitude, 1970; Notes Pour Un Amour, 1972; Notes Pour Un pluriel, 1974; Le Livre du Doute et de la Grace, 1977; Sonnets pour une fun de siecle, 1980; Poems Deux (1970–74), 1982; Un jour apres la vie, 1985; (Novels) La Grande Eclipse, 1952; Un Besoin de malheur, 1963; La Confession Mexicaine, 1965; Les Bonnes intentions, 1976; Une Mere Russe, 1978; Jean-Louis Trabart Medecin, 1980; L'Enfant que tu etais, 1982; Ni Guerre Ni Paix, 1983; Les Fetes Cruelles, 1984; (Short Story) Un homme pour un autre, 1985. *Contributor to:* Le Monde; Le Quotidien De Paris; Magazine Litteraire; Le Figaro; etc. *Honours include:* Grand Prix de Poesio of French Academy, 1967; Grand Prix du Roman of French Academy, 1978; etc. *Memberships include:* Vice President, Academy Mallarme. *Address:* c/o Gallimard, 5 rue Sebastien-Bottin, 75007 Paris, France.

BOSSCHER, Lucien Stanislas de, b. 16 Jan. 1909, Kooigem, West-Flanders, Belgium. Novelist. m. Gabrielle Demedts, 11 June 1957, Waregem. *Publications:* Student Jefke (serial story), 1928–29; De 7 Flesschen van de Kanunnik, 1945; De Laatste Flessen Van de Kanunnik, 1947; Radio Plays for INR-West-Vlaanderen, 1951–52; De vinger in de champagne, 1952; Eva onder de leeuwen, 1958; Niet zonder blozen, jongedame, 1971; Alle liefde is extra, 1973; In ons paradijs stond een pruimeboom, 1974; Anna-Bella en de speelvogel, 1977. *Contributor to:* Hooger leven; Ons land; Astrid; Boekengids; Dietsche Warande & Belfort; Handen. *Address:* Marie-José-residentie, Sint-Jansplein 14/26, 8500 – Kortrijk, West-Flanders, Belgium.

BOSTON, Bruce David, b. 16 July 1943, Chicago, Illinois, USA. Editor; Writer; Teacher. *Education:* BA, 1965, MA, 1967, University of California. *Publications:* Jackbird, 1976; She Comes When You're Leaving, 1982; All The Clocks are Melting, Poetry, 1984; Alchemical Texts, Poetry, 1985. *Contributions to:* New York Times Magazine; Fiction; Pushcart Prize Anthology; Isaac Asimov's SF Magazine; New Worlds; The Twilight Zone; 100 Great Fantasy Short Stories; Tomorrows Voices; Burning With a Vision. *Honours:* Milford Science Fiction Fellow, 1973; Yaddo Colony Fellow, 1974; Puchcart Prize for Fiction, 1976; Rhysling Award, 1985. *Memberships:* Fiction Editor, Berkeley Poets Workshop and Press; Secretary, Science Fiction Poetry Association. *Literary Agents:* Uto Prop, Germany. *Address:* 1819 9th Street Apt B, Berkeley, CA 94710, USA.

BOSTON, Bruce Ormand, b. 11 Aug. 1940, New Castle, Pennsylvania, USA. Writer. Divorced, 3 sons. *Education:* AB. Muskingum College, 1962; BD, 1968, PhD, 1973, Princeton Theological Seminary. *Publications:* A Resource Manual of Information on Educating the Gifted and Talented, 1975; Gifted and Talented: Developing Elementary and Secondary School Programmes, 1975; The Sorcerer's Apprentice, 1976; Testing the Gifted Child: An Interpretation in Lay Language, 1976; Education Policy and the Education for All Handicapped Children Act (PL 94-142), 1977; Individualized Assessment Reports in Special Education, 1978; Education Policy and Hispanic American Educational Leadership, 1980; Speeking Common Ground: The Dialogue Between the Educator and the Politician, 1981; The American High School: Time for Reform, 1982; Educating Able Learners, 1985. *Contributor to:* Numerous commissioned and freelance articles in newspapers and journals; 30 scripts produced. *Honours:* Scripts written by him have won 2 Cine Golden Eagle Awards, 1977, 1985. *Address:* 11433 Valley Road, Fairfax, VA 22033, USA.

BOSWORTH, David, b. 4 Mar. 1947, Northampton, Massachusetts, USA. m. Jacqueline Wayne Bosworth, 19 Sep. 1970, 2 sons. *Education:* BA, Brown University. *Appointments:* Senior Lecturer, English, University of Maine, 1983; Assistant Professor, English, University of Washington, 1984–. *Publications:* The Death of Descartes, collection of short fiction, 1980; From My Father, Singing, 1985. *Contributor to:* Ohio Review; Antioch Review; Aqui Review; Ploughshares; Boston Review; Boston Globe; Pushcart Prize. *Honours:* National Endowment for Arts Fellowship, 1980; Dave Heinz Prize, 1980; Special Citation, Hemmingway Award, 1981; Ingram Merrill Foundation, 1983; Editors' Book Award, 1984. *Memberships:* PEN; Writers Poets Inc. *Literary Agent:* Georges Borchardt. *Address:* Dept of English, University of Washington, Seattle, WA 98195, USA.

BOSWORTH, David Anthony, b. 23 Feb. 1958, Middlesbrough, England. Journalist. *Literary Appointments:* Reporter, Celtic Press Newspapers, South Wales, 1977–80; Staffwriter, What Car? magazine, 1980–82; Editor, Which Car?, 1982–. *Address:* Which Car?, Haymarket Publishing, 55 Heath Road, Twickenham, Middlesex TW1 4JW, England.

BOSWORTH, Richard James Boon, b. 7 Dec. 1943, Sydney, New South Wales, Australia. University Professor. m. Michal Gwyn Newell, 23 Sep. 1965, Sydney, 1 son, 1 daughter. *Education:* BA, 1st class honours, 1965, MA 1st class honours, 1969, University of Sydney; PhD, Cambridge University, England, 1971. *Publications:* Italy, The Least of the Great Powers, 1979; Italy and the Approach of the 1st World War, 1983; Old Worlds and New Australia, co-author, 1984. *Contributions to:* Historical Journal; Journal of Contemporary History; European Studies Review; Italian Quarterly; Australian Journal of Politics and History; Nuova Rivista Storica; various others. *Membership:* Deputy Director, F May Foundation of Italian Studies. *Address:* History Department, University of Sydney, Sydney, NSW 2006, Australia.

BOTTRALL, Margaret, b. 27 June 1909, Sydney, Australia. University Lecturer (retired). *Education:* MA, Lady Margaret Hall, Oxford University, Oxford, England; MA, Cambridge University, Cambridge. *Publications:* George Herbert, 1954; Every Man a Phoenix, 1958; Macmillan Casebooks on Blake: Songs of Innocence and Experience, 1970; G M Hopkins: Poems, 1975. *Contributions to:* The Economist; Critical Quarterly; Christian. *Address:* 72 Cavendish Avenue, Cambridge, CB1 4UT, England.

BOTTRALL, Francis James Ronald, b. 2 Sep. 1906, Camborne, Cornwall, England. Retired Diplomat. m. Margot Pamela Samuel, 10 July 1954, London, 1 son by previous marriage. *Education:* MA, Cantab 1933. *Appointments:* Principal Reviewer, RS, 9 years. *Publications:* (poetry) The Lossening, 1931; Festivals of

Fire, 1934; The Turning Path, 1939; Farewell and Welcome, 1945; Selected Poems, 1946; The Palisades of Fear, 1949; Adam Umparadised, 1954; Collected Poems, 1961; Day and Night, 1974; Poems 1955–73, 1974; Reflections on the Nile, 1980; Against a Setting Sun, 1984; Anthologies with Gunnar Ekelof: T S Eliots Dikter i Urval, 1942; with Margaret Bottrall, The Zephyr Book of English Verse, 1945; Collected English Verse, 1946; Art History, Rome Art Centres of the World, 1968. *Contributor to:* Numerous professional journals & magazines. *Honours:* OBE, 1949; Coronation medal, 1953; Theocritus International Poetry Prize, Syracuse, Sicily, 1954; FRSL, 1955; Grand Officer, Order of Merit, Republic of Italy, 1973; Knight Commander of the Order of St John of Jerusalem, Malta, 1977.

BOTWIN, Carol, b. New York City, New York, USA. Writer. 1 son, 1 daughter. *Education:* BA, New York University. *Publications:* Sir and the Teenage Girl, 1972; The Love Crisis, 1979, 80; Love Lives: Why Women Behave the Way They Do in Relationships, 1983; Is There Sex After Marriage?, 1985. *Address:* 645 West End Avenue, New York City, NY 10025, USA.

BOUCHER, Denise, b. 12 Dec. 1935, Victoriaville, Quebec, Canada. Writer. *Publications:* Retailles, poetry, 1977; Lyprine, poetry, 1978; Lesfeesontsoif, theatre play, 1978; La Liberte n'est pas Libre, theatre play, 1985. *Address:* 3675 rue Drohet, Montreal, Quebec H2X 3H7, Canada.

BOUCHIER, Lady Isabella Dorothy Guyver, b. 14 Feb. 1922, Yokohama, Japan. Author, Poet, Composer. m. Air Vice Marshal Sir Cecil Bouchier KBE CB DFC, 14 Aug. 1968, Worthing, England. 1 Stepson. *Education:* Mills College, California; San Francisco Conservatory of Music. *Literary Appointments:* Publications Officer, British Embassy, Tokyo 1949–52; Librarian, British Council, Tokyo, 1953–56; Senior Writer, Radio Japan, Japan Broadcasting Corporation, 1960–80. *Publications:* Japan, 1966; Tu Tse-Chun, 1967; A Haiku Journey, 1974. 5th Printing, 1984; National Parks of Japan, (with Mary Sutherland), 1980, 3rd Printing, 1985; The Japanese Crane, 1981, 3rd Printing, 1985; Totto Chan: The Little Girl at the Window, 1982, 14th Printing, 1985. *Contributions to:* Numerous Japanese, European, and American journals. *Honour:* Foreign Language Prize, Mills College, 1944.d *Membership:* Japan Society of Rights of Authors and Composers. *Literary Agent:* Kodansha International. *Address:* 2275 Isshiki, Hayama, Kanagawa-ken 240–01, Japan.

BOUHIER, Jean Georges Alfred Leon, b. 24 Feb. 1912. Writer; Journalist. *Education:* Study of Pharmacy and Natural Sciences. *Literary Appointments:* Founder, Rochefort School; Literary Critic, Journalist; Mayor, Fay-aux-Loges, etc. *Publications:* Hallucinations, 1937; Homme mon Frere, 1939; Pensee des Actes, 1941; Dompter le Fleuve, 1942; Trois Pasumes, 1943; Creation, 1943; Calcaire, 1945; Pour l'Amour de Colette, 1950; De Mille Endroits, 1952; Croire a la Vie, 1954; La Paix du Coeur, 1959; Tercets de la Vie Simple, 1963; Poemes de la Mer, 1975; Pourcontre, 1976; Le Jeu d'Autant, 1976; Rade Foraine, 1977; Fortune de Ler, 1980; l'Enfant de l'Orage, 1982; Les Poets de l'ecole De Rodiefort (Anthology), 1983; Quand le Soleil Efface i'Ouebre, 1985. *Contributor to:* Numerous French poetry journals, and translations in journals in USA, Spain, Egypt, Romania, Greece, India, Tunisia, etc. *Honours:* Knight of Academy of Palms, 1967; Knight of Arts and Letters, 1972. *Memberships include:* Society of Men of Letters of France; Union of Writers. *Address:* 189 Rocade du Belvédère, 83140 Six Fours les Plages, France.

BOULTING, Sydney, b. Maidenhead, Berkshire, England. Theatrical Director, Producer and Writer. m. Joan Miller, 19 May 1948, Kensington. *Appointments:* Lecturer on Theatre, Film and Television; Producer, Director, Senior Drama Director, ARTC, 1955–58; Producer and Director, ABPC, 1959–61. *Publications:* No Star Nonsense, 1949; The Little Fellow, 1951; Handbook for Amateur Theatre, 1957; George Robey, 1972; Charlie Chaplin, 1965; JP, 1978. Collaborator: Circus, 1976; Elvira Barney, 1977; The Barbirollis, 1983. *Contributions to:* 20th Century and After; The Stage; Plays and Players; The Free Thinker; The Guardian; What's On; The Times. *Honours:* Fellow, Royal Society of Authors; Knight of Mark Twain. *Membership:* Society of Authors, Associate, Cine-Technicians; Savage Club. *Address:* 15 Herons Lea, Sheldon Avenue, London, N6 4NB, England.

BOULTON, Marjorie, b. 7 May 1924, Teddington, England. Writer. *Education:* DPhil, MA, BLitt, Somerville College, Oxford; Licenciate, British Esperanto Association. *Publications:* The Anatomy of Poetry, 1953; The Anatomy of Prose, 1954; Kontralte, 1955; Saying What We Mean, 1959; Eroj: Virino ĉe la Landlimo; The Anatomy of Drama, 1960; Zamenhof, 1960; Okuloj, 1967; The Anatomy of the Novel, 1975; The Anatomy of Literary Studies, 1980; Poeto Fajrakora, 1983; Faktoj Kaj Kantazioj, 1984; etc. *Contributor to:* Regular Contributor to: Monato; Reviews, Notes and Queries; Articles, reviews, translations, poems, short stories etc. *Honours:* Matthew Arnold Prize, Oxford University, 1947; John Buchanan Prize, Liverpool University, 1958; Antoni Grabowski Prize, Universal Esperanto Association, 1984; Elected to Academy of Esperanto, 1967. *Memberships:* Society of Authors; Esperantista Verkista Asocio, Committee Member. *Literary Agent:* John Johnson, London. *Address:* 36 Stockmore Street, Oxford OX4 1JT, England.

BOUMELHA, Penelope Ann, b. 10 May 1950, London, England. Researcher; Tutor. m. Abdelkrim, 1974, 1 daughter. *Education:* BA, Lady Margaret Hall, Oxford University, 1972; PhD, 1981; MA, 1982. *Literary Appointments:* Various part-time tutoring and freelance writing appointments, 1981–; Compiler of, The Index of English Literary Manuscripts for Mansell Publishing Limited; Temporary full-time Lecturer in English, Christ Church, Oxford University, 1984–; Lecturer in English, University of Western Australia, 1985–. *Publications:* Thomas Hardy and Women: Sexual Ideology and Narrative Form, 1982; Charlotte Bronte, 1985; Co-author: In the Shadow of His Language: Gender and Nationality in 19th Century Irish Fiction, 1986, etc. *Honour:* E G Thackeray Scholarship at Lady Margaret Hall, 1969–72.

BOURAOUI, Hedi, b. 16 July 1932, Sfax, Tunisia. University Professor; Master, Stong College. *Education:* Degree in Arts, English Literature, University of Toulouse, 1958; MA, English and American Literature, Indiana University, USA, 1960; PhD, Romance Studies, 1966, Cornell University. *Appointments:* Editor, Poetry Canada Review, 1980–84; Permanent Canadian Correspondant, Sindbad, Maroc, 1983; Elected Editorial Consultant, Casil, Nigeria, 1985. *Publications:* (Poetry) Musocktail, 1966; Tremble, 1969; Eclate Module, 1972; Vesuviade, 1976; Sans Frontieres, 1979; Haituvois Suivi de Antillades, 1980; Tales of Heritage, 1981; Vers et l'Envers, 1982; Ignescent, 1982; Investiture; Poetic Drama; Essays; Language Instruction Text: Parole et action, 1971; Short Story, Seul, 1984; (Novel) L'Icônaison, 1985. *Contributor to:* Numerous professional journals including, Journal of Popular Culture; Reseach Studies; Etudes francaises; French Review; Waves; Pro-Culture; Research in African Literature; Civilisation and Culture; York Gazette; etc. *Honours:* Cyrille et Methode Medal on 1300th Anniversary of Bulgarian State, 1982; Silver Medal, Poesiades, Academic Institute of Paris, 1982; France-Canada Prize, 14th International Salon of the Foundation Michel-Ange, 1984; Prix Montaigne, 15th International Salon of the Foundation Michel-Ange, 1985. *Memberships:* President: Maghreb Studies Association, London, England; African Literature Association, USA, Canadian Society for Comparative Study of Civilizations for a Period of 3 years; Member, Union of Quebecois Writers; Canadian League of Poets. *Address:* 314A Stong College, York University, 4700 Keele Street, North York, Ontario, Canada M3J 1P3.

BOURDEAUX, Michael Alan, b. 19 Mar. 1934, Praze, Cornwall, England. Director of Research Institute. *Education:* BA (Hons) Russian and French, Oxford University, England, 1957, Theology, 1959, MA, 1960. *Publications:* Opium of the People, 1965, 1977; Religious Ferment in Russia, 1968; Patriarch and Prophets, 1970, 1976; Faith on Trial in Russia, 1971; Aida of Leningrad, (editor with Xenia Howard-Johnston), 1972, paperback, 1976; Land of Crosses: The Catholic Church in Lithuania Today, 1979; Risen Indeed: Lessons in Faith from USSR, 1983. *Contributor to:* Church Times. *Honour:* Recipient Templeton Prize for Progress in Religion, 1984. *Literary Agent:* Edward England. *Address:* 34 Lubbock Road, Chislehurst, Kent BR7 5JJ, England.

BOURGEOIS, Faye Emily Anne, b. 31 July 1947, Marvelville, Ontario, Canada. Editor and Writer. m. Richard A G Bourgeois, 20 Aug. 1977, Vernon, Ontario. *Education:* BA Honours English, Carleton University. *Literary Appointments:* Associate Editor, Canadian Grocer Magazine, Maclean Hunter Limited, 1978–81; Editor, Modern Purchasing Magazine, Maclean Hunter Limited, 1981–. *Honours:* 1st prize for best merchandising article, Kenneth H Wilson Memorial Awards, 1979; 1st prize for best single article, graphics, Kenneth R Wilson Memorial Awards, 1981. *Membership:* National Editors and Writers Society. *Address:* Maclean Hunter Building, 777 Bay Street, Toronto, Ontario M5W 1A7, Canada.

BOURNE, Daniel Carter, b. 2 Mar. 1955, Olney, Illinois, USA. Poet; Translator; Editor. m. Karen Kovacik, 10 Dec. 1983, Bloomington, Indiana. *Education:* BA, with honours, 1979, MFA candidate, Indiana University. *Literary Appointment:* Editor, Artful Dodge, 1979–. *Publication:* Boys Who Go Aloft, 1986. *Contributions to:* Poetry contributed to various journals including: Poetry Northwest; Minnesota Review; Milkweed Chronicle; Indiana Review; Kansas Quarterly; Images; Spoon River Quarterly; Great River Review; Blue Unicorn; Paintbrush; Cottonwood; Stone Country; Embers; Northeast; Sou'wester; Sun Dog; Alaska Quarterly Review, and others. Translations of Polish poets Tomasz Jastrun and Marek Bienkowski contributed to various publications; Various interviews have been featured in Artful Dodge. *Honours:* Outstanding Undergraduate in Comparative Literature, 1978, Translation Fellowship to Warsaw University, Poland, 1982–83, Indiana University; Fulbright Fellowship to Warsaw University, 1985–86. *Address:* PO Box 1473, Bloomington, IN 47402, USA.

BOURNE, Geoffrey, b. 17 Nov. 1909, Australia. Medical Educator and Researcher. m. Maria Nelly Golarz, 31 Oct. 1964, Grand Bahama, Bahamas, West Indies, 2 sons. *Education:* BSc honours, MSc, DSc, University of Western Australia, Australia, D Phil, University of Oxford, England. *Literary Appointments:* Co-editor 1950, Editor in Chief 1985, International Review of Cytology, Academic Press; Editor, World Review of Nutrition and Dietetics, Karger Medical Publishers, Basel, Switzerland, 1955–. *Publications:* The Mammalian Adrenal Gland, 1949; The Ape People, 1975; Primate Odyssey, 1976; The Gentle Giants (The Gorilla Story), 1979; Starvation in Europe. *Contributions to:* Scientific and other journals. *Address:* St Georges University School of Medicine, Grenada, West Indies.

BOUVARD, Marguerite, b. 1 Oct. 1937, Trieste, Italy. Professor; Writer. m. Jacques Bouvard, 25 Nov. 1959, New York City, 1 son, 1 daughter. *Education:* BA, Northwestern University; MA, Boston University, Radcliffe College; PhD, Harvard University. *Appointments:* Professor, Creative Writing, Regis College, 1977–. *Publicatioans:* The Labor Movement in the Common Market Countries, 1972; The Intentional Community Movement, 1975; Journeys Over Water, 1982; Landscape and Exile, 1985; Voices from an Island, 1985. *Contributor to:* Numerous journals and magazines including, Seattle Review; Literary Review; West Branch; Ohio Journal; etc. *Honours:* Scholarship

Bread Loaf Writers' Contest, 1976; Winner, All Nations Poetry Contest, 1975; Winner, Quarterly Review of Literature Contest, 1982; Residencies at MacDowell Colony, Ragdale Foundation, Yaddo, Virginia Center for the Creative Arts, 1978–84. *Memberships:* Poetry Society of America; New England Poetry Club, Board of Directors; Poets and Writers Inc. *Address:* Regis College, Weston, MA 02193, USA.

BOVE, Anthony, 5 Feb. 1955, Philadelphia, USA. Author and Editor. *Education:* AB English, Tufts University, USA. *Major Publications:* The TRS-80 Model 3 User's Guide, 1982; Wordstar Pocket Reference, 1983; User's Guide to CP/M, 1984; Infoworld's Essential Guide to CP/M, 1984; Free Software, 1985. *Contributor to:* User's Guide (Editor); The Portable Companion (Editor); Datacast (Editor); Whole Earth Software Catalog & Review (Contributing Editor); Guest Editor, Infoworld. *Honour:* 1st prize awarded by the Society for Technical Communications for the Business BASIC Reference Manual (Data General) in the Handbook category, 1979. *Membership:* Computer Press Association. *Address:* 117 Ware Road, Woodside, CA 94062, USA.

BOVEY, John, b. 17 Apr. 1913, Minneapolis, Minnesota, USA. Retired Diplomat; Writer of Fiction. m. Marcia Peterson Palmer, 28 July 1943, Annapolis, Maryland, 1 daughter. *Education:* BA, 1935, MA, 1938, Harvard University. *Publication:* Desirable Aliens, 1980. *Contributions to:* Magazines and journals in USA, UK and France of stories (some 25) and articles; Kansas Quarterly; Colorado Quarterly; Prairie Schooner; Foreign Service Journal; Carleton Miscellany; The Literary Review; The Virginia Quarterly Review; Gothic; New England Review; Four Quarters; Canto; New Orleans Review; Confrontation; Blackwood's Magazine; Cornhill Magazine; Adam; Paris Voices; Iron; London Magazine; International Herald Tribune; International Spectator; Le Monde; Studia Diplomatica; Town and Country; Christian Science Monitor. *Honours:* David Bruce Fiction Prize (2nd Prize); Emily Green Balch, Fiction Award, 1981, 83, 84; First Prize, Kansas Quarterly Fiction, 1985. *Address:* 19 Chauncy Street, Cambridge, MA 02138, USA.

BOWDEN, Betsy Ann, b. 30 Jan. 1948, Grove City, Pennsylvania, USA. English Professor. *Education:* BA, University of Wisconsin, Madison, 1970; PhD, University of California, Berkeley, 1978. *Literary Appointments:* Pennsylvania State University at State College, 1978–81; Rutgers University, Camden, 1981–. *Publications:* Performed Literature: Words and Music by Bob Dylan, 1982; Chaucer Aloud (The Chaucer Tapes): Varying Interpretations of Written Text, forthcoming 1986. *Contributions to:* Medievalia et Humanistica, 1979; Blake: An Illustrated Quarterly, 1980; Southwest Folklore, 1980 and others. *Memberships:* Modern Language Association; New Chaucer Society; Medieval Academy of America; Philadelphia Writers' Organization. *Address:* Department of English, Rutgers University, Camden, NJ 08102, USA.

BOWDEN, Gregory Andrew Houston, b. 1 July 1948, London, England. Author. m. Michaela Figgess, 6 May 1978, Burghfield, England, 2 daughters. *Education:* MA Modern History, Mansfield College, University of Oxford, England. *Major Publications:* Morgan – First & Last of the Real Sports Cars, 1971; British Gastronomy, 1975; Story of the Raleigh Cycle, 1975; More Morgan, 1976; Two Wheels to the Top (Reg Harris), 1976. *Literary Agent:* Campbell Thomson & McLaughlin (John McLaughlin). *Address:* c/o Campbell Thomson & McLaughlin Ltd, 31 Newington Green, London N16 9PU, England.

BOWDER, Diana Ruth, b. 14 May 1942, Oxford, England. Solicitor; Author. m. John Michael Bowder, 6 Aug. 1966, Oxford, 2 daughters. *Education:* BA, Lady Margaret Hall, Oxford, 1965; MA, 1969; D.Phil, 1977. *Publications:* The Age of Constantine and Julian. 1978; Editor and Contributor, Who Was Who in the Roman World, 1980; Who Was Who in the Greek World, 1982.

Contributor of: West Hanney House: The Old Rectory in The Blowing Stone (local History), 1984. *Honours:* Barclay-Head Prize for Ancient Numismatics, Oxford University, 1968; Pelham Studentship for Study at British School at Rome, Oxford University, 1968. *Address:* c/o Phaidon Press Limited, Littlegate House, St Ebbe's Street, Oxford, England.

BOWEN, Desmond, b. 25 July 1921, Ottawa, Ontario, Canada. Professor. m. Jean Fraser, 25 Dec. 1942, Ottawa, 2 sons, 3 daughters. *Education:* BA, Carleton University, 1950; MA 1954, PhD, Queen's University, Kingston, Ontario, 1963. *Publications:* Idea of the Victorian Church, 1968; Souperism: Myth of Reality, 1971; Protestant Crusade in Ireland, 1978; Paul Cardinal Cullen and the Shaping of Modern Irish Catholicism, 1983. *Contributions to:* View from the Pulpit, Alexander R C Dallas, The Warrior Saint, 1978; Journal of the Irish Christian Study Centre, History and the Shaping of Irish Protestantism, 1984. *Honours:* Fellow, Royal Society of Antiquaries of Ireland, 1967; Fellow, Institute of Irish Studies, Queen's University, Belfast, Northern Ireland, 1983. *Literary Agent:* Gill and Macmillan, Dublin, Eire. *Address:* Institute of Irish Studies, Queen's University, Belfast, Northern Ireland.

BOWEN, Jill, b. 19 May 1943, New South Wales, Australia. Journalaist. Divorced. 1 daughter. *Education:* University of New England. *Literary Appointments:* Sydney Morning Herald, 1961–64; Editor, Stockman's Hall of Fame. *Publication:* The Biography of Cattle King, Sir Sydney Kidman. (1857–1935), published 1985. *Contributions to:* Numerous magazines and journals. *Honour:* Australian ARRA Sportswriter of the Year, 1981. *Memberships:* Australian Society of Authors; Australian Journalists' Association. *Address:* 3 Landscape Avenue, Forestville, New South Wales, Australia 2087.

BOWEN, John Griffith, b. 5 Nov. 1924, Calcutta, India. Writer; Television Producer. *Education:* MA, Oxford University. *Publications include:* The Truth Will Not Help Us; After the Rain; The Centre of the Green; Storyboard; The Birdcage; A World Elsewhere; Squeak; The McGuffin; The Girls. Plays: I Love You Mrs Patterson; After the Rain; The Fall & Redemption of Man; Little Boxes; The Disorderly Women; The Corsican Brothers; Heil, Caesar; Singles; Which Way Are You Facing; The Inconstant Couple; Uncle Jeremy. *Contributions to:* London Magazine; Times Literary Supplement; New York Times Book Review; New Statesman; Gambit; Journal of Royal Asiatic Society; Times Educational Supplement; Listener. *Honour:* Tokyo Prize, 1974. *Memberships:* Executive Committee, PEN; Committee of Management, Society of Authors; Executive Committee, Writers Guild of Great Britain. *Literary Agent:* Elaine Greene Ltd. *Address:* Old Lodge Farm, Sugarswell Lane, Edgehill, Banbury, OX15 6HP, England.

BOWER, Donald E(dward) b. 19 July 1920, Lockport, New York, USA. Executive Director, The National Writers Club. 1 son. *Education:* BA, University of Nebraska. *Publications:* Roaming the American West, 1970; Ghost Towns and Back Road, 1972; The Magnificent Rockies, 1973; The Great Northwest, 1973; Fred Rosenstock: A Legend in Books and Art, 1976; The Professional Writers Guide, 1983. *Contributions to:* Colorado Magazine; American West Magazine; Empire Magazine; Contemporary Magazine; Journal of the West; Writers West. *Honours:* Top Hand Award (Best article by a Colorado author) 1969; Top Hand Award (Best non-fiction book by a Colorado author) 1976. *Memberships:* Board Secretary, National Writers Club; Western Writers of America; American Society of Journalists and Authors; Authors Guild. *Address:* 15087 E Radcliff Drive, Aurora, CO 80015, USA.

BOWERING, George Harry, b. 1 Dec. 1937, Penticton, Canada. University Professor of English. *Publications:* (novel) Mirror on the Floor, 1967; Burning Water, 1980; (poem-suite), Rocky Mountain Foot, 1969; (selected poems) Touch, 1971; (poems) In the Flesh, 1974; Kerrisdale Elegies, 1984; Seventy-One Poems for People, 1985; (poems and prose) The Catch, 1976; (poems) Allophanes, 1977; (stories) Flycatcher, 1974; A Short Sad Book, 1977; Protective Footwear, 1979; Another Mouth, 1979; A Place to Die, 1984; (criticism) A Way With Words, 1982; The Mask in Place, 1983; Craft Slices, 1985; Sheila Watson (ed) 1985. *Contributions to:* Essays and reviews, Open Letter, Associate Editor, Canadian Literature. *Honours:* Governor-General's award in Poetry, 1970; Canadian Council Award, 1971, 1977; Governor-General's award in fiction, 1980. *Address:* 2499 W 37th Ave, Vancouver, BC, V6M 1P4, Canada. .

BOWERS, Edgar, b. 2 Mar. 1924. Teacher, *Education:* BA, University of NC; MA, PhD, Stanford University; Princeton University; University of Paris, France. *Literary Appointments:* Instructor, English, Duke University, 1952–55; Assistant Professor, English, University of California at Santa Barbara, 1958–. *Publications:* The Form of Loss, 1956; Living Together, 1973; The Astronomers, 1965; Witnesses, 1982. *Contributor to:* Hudson Review; Sewanee Review; Southern Review; Poetry Chicago; Virginia Quarterly; Paris Review; Spectator; London Magazine; Western Review, etc. *Honours:* Rockefeller Award, Sewanee Review, 1954; Ingram Merrill Award, 1974; Brandeis Univ Award in Creative Arts, 1980. *Address:* 1502 Miramar Beach, Santa Barbara, CA 93108, USA.

BOWERS, Neal, b. 3 Aug. 1948, Clarksville, Tennessee, USA. Poet; Teacher. m. Nancy Brooker, 21 Oct. 1979, Columbia, Missouri, USA. *Education:* PhD, University of Florida, 1976. *Literary Appointments:* Associate Professor of English & Chair of Creative Writing Department of English, Iowa State University. *Publications:* Theodore Roethke: The Journey from I to Otherwise, 1982; The Golf Ball Diver, 1983; James Dickey: The Poet as Pitchman, 1985. *Contributions to:* Over 100 poems & articles published in over 50 different magazines & journals including, The American Poetry Review; Harvard Magazine; Georgia Review; Modern Poetry Studies. *Honours:* Winner in 3rd Annual Minnesota Voices Project Competition, 1983. *Memberships:* Associated Writing Programs; Poets & Writers; Academy of American Poets. *Address:* Department of English, 203 Ross Hall, Iowa State University, Ames, IA 50011, USA.

BOWETT, Derek Williams, b. 1927, Manchester, England. Whewell Professor, Queens College, Cambridge University. *Education:* CBE, LLD, QC, FBA, Downing College, Cambridge University. *Publicatioans:* Self-Defence in International Law, 1958; Law of International Institutions, 1964; United Nations Forces, 1964; The Law of the Sea, 1968; The Search for Peace, 1972; Legal Régime of Islands, 1978. *Contributor to:* Various legal periodicals. *Address:* Queens College, Cambridge, England.

BOWLES, Paul, b. 30 Dec. 1910, New York City, USA. Writer. *Publications include:* The Sheltering Sky, 1949; Let it Come Down, 1952; Their Heads are Green, 1963; Collected Stories, 1979; The Spider's House; Up Above the World; Points in Time; Midnight Mass (short stories), 1985. *Contributor to:* London Magazine; Harper's Bazaar; Encounter; Partison Review; Harper's Magazine; Esquire; Vogue; Holiday; Rolling Stone; Mademoiselle; Transatlantic Review, etc. *Honours:* Guggenheim Fellowship, 1941; Academy of Arts and Letters, 1950; Rockefeller Grant, 1959; National Endowment for Arts, 1977; National Endowment for Arts Senior Fellowship 1980. *Literary Agent:* William Morris Agency Inc. *Address:* 2117 Tanger Socco, Tangier, Morocco.

BOWLEY, Rex Lyon, b. 27 July 1925, Exeter, England. Schoolmaster. m. Joan Miles, 20 Apr. 1950, Isles of Scilly, 2 daughters. *Education:* MA, Trinity College, Dublin University, Republic of Ireland. *Publications:* Teaching Without Tears, 1961, 4th edition, 1976; The Fortunate Islands: The Story of the Isles of Scilly, 7th edition, 1980; The Isles of Scilly Standard Guidebook, 6th edition, 1986; Readings for Assembly, 1976. *Memberships:* Society of Authors. *Address:* PO Box No 1, St Mary's, Isles of Scilly, Cornwall TR21 OPR, England.

BOWLING, Ann Patricia, b. 7 May 1951, England. Senior Research Fellow; Medical Sociologist. *Education:* BSc, Honours, Sociology; MSc, Sociology as Applied to Medicine; PhD, Sociology of Medicine. *Appointment:* Senior Research Fellow, Centre for Study of Primary Care, North East Thames Regional Health Authority, and Department of Clinical Epidemiology, London Hospital Medical School. *Publications:* Delegation in General Practice, 1981; Life After a Death: A Study of the Elderly Widowed. *Contributor to:* Chapters in 3 books; Articles in World Medicine; Nursing Mirror; Nursing Times; Mims Magazine; Times Health Supplement; Lancet; Community Care; etc; Book Reviews for Journals. *Address:* 10 Talbot Avenue, London N2, England.

BOYD, Doris-Regina, b. 17 Jan. 1952, Birmingham, Alabama, USA. Journalist. 1 daughter. *Education:* BA, Television Radio & Film, Stephens College, 1975. *Contributor to:* The Street Speaker; Essence Magazine; Poetry Anthology, 1984. *Honours:* Award, Investigative Reporting, Gannett Co Inc; V I Advertising Club Award of Excellence. *Memberships:* Virgin Island Press Association, President; National Association of Black Journalists. *Literary Agent:* Attorney Daniel Muse. *Address:* 35 BBB Dronigens Gade, St Thomas, US Virgin Islands.

BOYD, Hugh Alexander, b. 17 Jan. 1907, Ballycastle, Northern Ireland. Retired Grammar School Vice Principal. m. Margaret Boyd McClure (BA, Dip Ed), 4 Nov. 1939, Ballycastle, 2 sons, 1 daughter. *Education:* BA, 1927, H Dip Ed, 1928, MA, 1933, Queen's University of Belfast; Hon MA (Ed), Queen's University of Belfast, 1980; M Litt, Trinity College, Dublin, 1950; M Phil, New University of Ulster, 1983; Deputy Chairman, Convocation, Life Member, Ex President, Queen's University Association, Queen's University, Belfast, 1976–77. *Appointments:* Fellow, Society of Antiquaries, Scotland; Honorary Member, Glens of Antrim Historical Society; Fellow, Royal Society of Antiquaries of Ireland. *Publications:* History of the Church of Ireland in Roman Parish, 1932; History of the Church of Ireland in Dunluce Parish, 1934; History of Rathlin Island, 1947; Old Ballycastle and Marconi at Ballycastle, 1968; Notes on the Following Parishes – Culfeightrin, Tickmacrevan (Glenarm), Ardclinis (Carnlough), Dunaghy (Clough), Drummaul (Randalstown), Craigs (Cullybackey), Ballintoy, Finvoy, Rasharkin, Kilconriola (Ballymena), Christ Church Cathedral, Dublin. *Contributor to:* The Glynns. *Honours:* MA (ED) Honoris Causa, Quwen's University of Belfast, 1980. *Address:* Mowbray House, Ballycastle BT54 6BH, Northern Ireland.

BOYD, Joseph Ian, b. 23 Jan. 1935, Blaine Lake, Saskatchewan, Canada. Catholic Priest, University Professor. *Education:* MA, University of Toronto; PhD, University of Aberdeen. *Literary Appointments:* Editor, Chesterton Review, 1974–86. *Publication:* The Novels of G K Chesterton, 1975. *Contributions to:* Various journals including: Tablet; New Blackfriars; Seven. *Address:* St Thomas More College, 1437 College Drive, Saskatoon, Saskatchewan S7N OW6, Canada.

BOYD, Malcolm, b. 8 June 1923, Buffalo, New York, USA. Writer; Episcopal Priest. *Education:* BA, University of Arizona, 1944; BD, Church Divinity School of the Pacific, Berkeley, California, 1954; STM, Union Theological Seminary, New York, 1957. *Publications include:* Are You Running With Me, Jesus?, 1965; Free to Live, Free to Die, 1967; The Fantasy Worlds of Peter Stone, 1969; As I Live & Breathe: Stages of an Autobiography, 1970; Take Off the Masks, 1978; Look Back in Joy, 1981; Half Laughing/Half Crying: Songs for Myself, 1986. *Contributions to:* New York Times; Los Angeles Times: Washington Post; Esquire; Ms;

Parade; Playboy; Ladies Home Journal. *Honours:* Malcolm Boyd Collection, archive of papers & letters, Boston University, 1968; Writer-in-residence, Mishkenot Sha'ahanim, Jerusalem, 1974; Guest Fellow, Yale University, 1968–69, 1971–72. *Memberships:* PEN, American Centre; Authors Guild; President, Los Angeles Centre of PEN, 1984–. *Literary Agent:* Florence Feiler, 1524 Sunset Plaza Drive, Los Angeles, CA 90069, USA. *Address:* 1227 4th Street, Santa Monica, CA 90401, USA.

BOYD MAUNSELL, Nevill Francis Wray, b. 22 Dec. 1930, London, England. Financial Journalist. m. Lyghia Peterson, 5 Oct. 1957, Worcester, 1 son, 1 daughter. *Education:* BA, University College, Oxford. *Literary Appointments:* Reuters; Financial Times; Time and Tide; Daily Sketch; The Birmingham Post. *Contributions to:* Daily Mail; Sunday Times; Evening Standard; numerous magazine articles. *Address:* 2 Leopold Avenue, Wimbledon, London SW19 7ET, England.

BOYER, Ruth Eleanor Gasink, b. 18 May 1913, Minneapolis, Minnesota, USA. Professor of Social Work. m. Welch Hall Boyer, 20 Dec. 1943, Naples, Italy. *Education:* BA; MSS; DSW. *Publications:* Monograph, The Boyer Measure of Field Performance, 1967; An Approach to Human Services, 1975; The Happy Adolescent, 1982; Be Gentle With Yourself: You Have A Right To Be Happy, 1982; Be Gentle With Yourself: Your Feelings And The Bad Guys, 1982. *Contributions to:* Contributor to various journals including, Minnesota Journal of Education, Indian Journal of Social Research, Rocky Mountain Social Science Journal, Smith College for Social Work Journal; The Hard to Reach Child, in, The Unusual Child, (editor Joseph Roucek); Poetry, The Georgia Impression, 1967, Smith College Journal, 1974. *Honours:* Personal Representative, Governor of Arkansas, White House Conference on Aging, 1971; Dr Ruth G Boyer Day, City of North Little Rock Arkansas; Professor Emeritus, University of Arkansas, 1977. *Address:* #6 Yaqui Place, Sherwood, AR 72116, USA.

BOYNE, Walter James, b. 2 Feb. 1929, East St Louis, Illinois, USA. Retired Military Officer; Museum Director. m. Elizabeth Jeanne Quigley, 26 Dec. 1952, St Louis, Missouri, 1 son, 3 daughters. *Education:* BSBA, with Honors, University of California, 1959; MBA, with Honors, University of Pittsburgh, 1963; PhD, Aeronautical Sciences, Salem College, West Virginia, 1984. *Literary Appointments:* Associate Editor, Wings and Airpower Magazines, 1969; Columnist, Air Line Pilots Association Magazine, 1982; Columnist, AOPA Pilot Magazine, 1984. *Publications:* The Jet Age, 1979; Flying, 1980; Messerschmidt Me 262, 1981; Boeing B-52, 1981; Vertical Flight, 1983; Aircraft Treasures of Silver Hill, 1983; de Havilland DH-4, 1984; Phantom in Combat, 1985; The Learning Edge, 1986; Novel: Blue Nomad, publication 1986. *Contributions:* of over 300 articles on air and space subjects to more than 20 different magazines and journals; monthly columnist in Airline Pilot and AOPA Pilot. *Honour:* Best Foreign Book of the Year, Aero Club of France, for Messerschmitt Me 262, 1982. *Literary Agent:* Jaques de Spoelberch, Norfolk, Connecticut. *Address:* 9134 Continental Drive, Alexandria, VA 22309, USA.

BOZARSLAN, Mehmet Emin, b. 15 Sep. 1934, Lice, Kurdistan, Turkey. Writer, Poet. *Publications:* ABC in Kurdish, 1968; Mem û Zin by Ahmedi Khani, translation from Kurdish toTurkish and transcription from Arabic to Latin alphabet, 1968; Serefname, translation from Arabic to Turkish, 1971; Içerdekiler ve Disardakiler, short stories, 1974; Kurdish-Turkish Dictionary, transcription, 1978; Meyro, short stories, 1979; Mîr Zoro, Kurdish Fables, 1980; Gurê Bilûrvan, Kurdish Fables, 1982; Kêz Xatün, Kurdish Fables, 1982; Serketina Misken, Kirdish Fables, 1984; 'Jîn, Kurdish magazine from 1918–19, volume 1, transcription from Arabic to Latin alphabet and written introduction, 1985. *Honours:* Honorary diploma and silver medal, Universal Academy of Lausanne, 1984. *Memberships:* Swedish Union of Writers; Center of Swedish Writers; Union of

Writers in Turkey; Universal Academy of Lausanne. *Address:* Box 3050, 750 03 Uppsala 3, Sweden.

BRACEWELL-MILNES, John Barry, b. 29 Dec. 1931, Wallington, Surrey, England. Author; Economic Consultant. m. Ann Jacqueline Cowley, 25 June 1977, Banstead, 1 son, 1 daughter. *Education:* BA 1956, MA 1958, New College, Oxford; PhD, Kings College, Cambridge, 1959. *Publications:* The Measurement of Fiscal Policy, 1971; Is Capital Taxation Fair? 1974; Economic Integration of East & West, 1976; The Camel's Back: An International Comparison of Tax Burdens, 1976; Investment Incentives, 1977; Tax Avoidance & Evasion, 1979; The Economics of International Tax Avoidance, 1980; The Taxation of Industry: Fiscal Barriers to the Creation of Wealth, 1981; Land and Heritage: The Public Interest in Personal Ownership, 1982. *Contributor to:* Intertax; British Tax Review; European Taxation; Bulletin for International Fiscal Documentation; etc. *Membership:* Society of Authors. *Address:* 26 Lancaster Court, Banstead, Surrey SM7 1RR, England.

BRACHER, Karl Dietrich, b. 13 Mar. 1922, Stuttgart, Germany. University Professor. *Education:* PhD, University of Tubingen, 1948; Harvard University, USA, 1949–1950. *Literary Appointments:* University Professor, Bonn (formerly Berlin, Stanford, Princeton, Oxford, Tel Aviv). *Publications:* The Dissolution of the Weimar Republic, 1955; The Nazi Seizure of Power, 1960; The German Dictatorship, 1969; The German Dilemma, 1974; The Crisis of Europe 1917–1975, 1976 & 1979; History and Violence, 1981; The Age of Ideologies, 1984. *Contributions to:* Editor, Co-editor & contributor to several German, English & American journals. *Honours:* Hon DHL, Florida State University, USA; Hon Dr jur, University Graz, Austria. *Memberships:* PEN, Federal Republic of Germany; For Hon Mbr, American Academy of Arts & Science; Corres Fellow, British Academy; Am Philosl Soc; Austrian Academy of Sciences; German Academy of Language & Poetry. *Address:* Stationsweg 17, Bonn, Federal Republic of Germany.

BRADBURY, Malcolm Stanley, b. 7 Sep. 1932, Sheffield, England. Writer; Professor. *Education:* BA, University College of Leicester, 1953; MA, Queen Mary College, University of London, 1955; PhD, Manchester University, 1959. *Publications:* What is a Novel, 1969; The Social Context of Modern English Literature, 1971; Possibilities: Essays on the State of the Novel, 1972; Editor, contributor, E M Foster's, A Passage to India, 1970; Co-editor, major contributor, The Penguin Companion to Literature, Volume 3; American & Latin-American, 1971; (novels), Eating People is Wrong, 1960; Stepping Westward, 1965; The History Man, 1975; (stories) Who Do You Think You Are?, 1976; numerous critical & scholarly articles; 2 stage reviews; radio & television plays including, The After Dinner Game, (with C Bigsby), 1975; Love on a Gunboat, 1977. *Contributions to:* Various books & professional journals. *Honours:* Royal Society of Literature Award, 1976. *Membership:* Literary Panel, Eastern Arts Association. *Literary Agent:* Curtis Brown Ltd, England; John Cushman, USA. *Address:* School of English & American Studies, University of East Anglia, Norwich, Norfolk NR4 7TJ, England.

BRADDON, Russell Reading, b. 26 Jan. 1921, Sydney, Australia. Author. *Education:* BA, University of Sydney. *Publications:* (some 28 books including) The Naked Island, 1951; Those in Peril, 1954; Cheshire, VC, 1954; Nancy Wake, 1956; Joan Sutherland, 1962; Roy Thomson of Fleet Street, 1965; The Inseperables, 1968; Will You Walk a Little Faster, 1969; Prelude & Fugue for Lovers, 1971; The Progress of Private Lilyworth, 1971; End Play, 1972; Suez: Splitting of a Nation, 1973; The Hundred Days of Darien, 1974; All the Queen's Men, 1977; The Finalist, 1977; The Predator, 1980; TV Script Writer and Presenter, ABC TV Sydney, BBC TV London, 1981–85. *Address:* c/o John Farquharson Ltd, 162-168 Regent Street, London W1R 5B, England.

BRADFORD, James Chapin, b. 7 Apr. 1945, Detroit, Michigan, USA. College Professor. m. Judith Ann Robinson, 21 Mar. 1964, Traverse City, Michigan, 2 sons. *Education:* BA, MA, Michigan State University; PhD, University of Virginia. *Literary Appointment:* Book Review Editor, The Journal of the Early Republic, 1978–. *Publications:* Anne Arundel County, Maryland: A Bicentennial History, 1978; Command Under Sail: Makers of the American Naval Tradition, 1985; The Papers of John Paul Jones (due out 1985); Commanders of the Old Steam Navy: Makers of the American Naval Tradition (due out 1986). *Memberships:* Member of several historical societies. *Address:* Department of History, Texas A & M University, College Station, TX 77843, USA.

BRADFORD, Karleen, b. 16 Dec. 1936, Toronto, Canada. Writer. m. James Creighton Bradford, 22 Aug. 1959, Toronto, 2 sons, 1 daughter. *Education:* BA, University of Toronto, 1959. *Publications:* A Year for Growing, 1977, (Reprinted as Wrong Again, Robbie, 1983); The Other Elizabeth, 1982; I Wish There Were Unicorns, 1983; The Stone in the Meadow, 1984; The Haunting at Cliff House, 1985. *Contributor to:* Short stories and articles to school readers and magazines in USA and Canada including Ginn and Company, Nelson Canada, Holt, Rinehart and Winston, Laidlaw Brothers; Cricket Magazine; Cricket and Company, England; Canadian Children's Annual; The Instructor; Canadian Aviation etc. *Honours:* Ontario Arts Council Grant, 1977; First Prize, CommCept KidLit Contest, 1979; First Prize 1978, Second Prize 1984, Short Story, Juvenile Division, Canadian Authors' Association Ottawa Branch Prose Contest; Canada Council Grants 1983 and 1985. *Memberships:* The Writers' Union of Canada, Chairman, Curriculum Committee, 1984/85; Canadian Society of Children's Authors, Illustrators and Performers; Canadian Authors' Association, Newsletter Editor, 1984/85; Ottawa Independent Writers. *Address:* c/o Writers' Union of Canada, 24 Ryerson Avenue, Toronto, Ontario, Canada M5T 2P3.

BRADLEY, Jerry, b. 24 Aug. 1948, Jacksboro, Texas, USA. Associate Professor of Humanities. *Education:* BA English, Midwestern University, 1969; MA 1973, PhD 1975, English, Texas Christian University. *Literary Appointments:* Assistant Professor, Rhetoric, Boston University, 1975–76; Assistant Professor 1976–81, Associate Professor 1981–, Humanities, New Mexico Tech; Editor, New Mexico Humanities Review, 1978–; Editor, Saurian Press,1980–.*Contributions to:* Poetry to: New England Review; Charlton Review; Descant; Southwestern Review; Scree; Colorado State Review; Vanderbilt Review; Modern Poetry Studies; Latitudes 30°18; Rocky Mountain Review; El Nahuatzen; Third Eye; Back Bay View; Pearl; Vega; Gathering Stars; Newsletter Inago; Essays in: Western American Literature; Literary Magazine Review; New Mexico Humanities Review. *Honour:* Boswell Poetry Prize, 1979 and 1984. *Memberships:* Texas Association of Creative Writing Teachers; Rocky Mountain Modern Language Association; Associated Writing Programs; American Academy of Poets. *Address:* Box A, New Mexico Tech, Socorro, NM 87801, USA.

BRADY, Frank, b. 15 Mar. 1934, Brooklyn, New York, USA. Professor. m. Maxine L Kalfus, 31 Mar. 1963, New York City, USA. *Education:* BS, State University of New York; MA, New York University; MFA, Columbia University; PhD Candidate, New York University. *Literary Appointments:* Associate Publisher, Documentary Books; Editorial Director, Drake Publishing Co, Hammond, Inc. *Major Publications:* Profile of a Prodigy, 1964; Hefner, 1973; Onassis, 1975; Barbra, 1976; Orson Wallis, 1986. *Contributor to:* New York Times; Saturday Evening Post; Stern; Paris Match; and others. *Honour:* Nominated for Luther Mott Award for Outstanding Research, 1975. *Memberships:* PEN; Bernard Shaw Society; Authors' Guild; Authors' League. *Literary Agent:* James Seligmann. *Address:* 175 West 72nd Street, New York, NY 10023, USA.

BRADY, Holly W, 28 Apr. 1947, Evanston, Illinois, USA. Writer, Magazine Editor. *Education:* BA English, Stanford University; MAT English & Education, Miami University at Oxford, Ohio. *Contributor to:* Classroom Computer Learning; Learning Magazine; Curriculum Product Review; Mademoiselle; and others. *Honours:* First Place, Ad Campaign, Advertising Executives Association of Ohio Daily Newspapers; 1975; Distinguished Achievement Award, Educational Press Association of America, 1984. *Membership:* Education Writers Association. *Address:* 384 Riviera Drive, San Rafael, CA 94901, USA.

BRADY, Terence Joseph, b. 13 Mar. 1939, London, England. Playwright; Actor; Novelist. m. The Honourable Charlotte Bingham, 15 Jan. 1964, Warwick Street, 1 son, 1 daughter. *Education:* Moderatorship in History & Political Science, Trinity College, Dublin. *Publications:* Rehearsal, novel, 1973; The Fight Against Slavery, 1975; Rose's Story, 1973; Yes Honestly, 1977, with Charlotte Bingham. *Contributions to:* Punch; Living; Daily Mail; Country Homes; etc. *Honours:* Writers Guild Award, best radio comedy. *Memberships:* Writers Guild; BAFTA. *Literary Agent:* A D Peters & Co. *Address:* c/o A D Peters, Literary Agents, 10 Buckingham Street, London WC2, England.

BRAITHWAITE, Brian, b. 15 May 1927, London, England. Publishing Director. m. Gwendoline Everson, 7 Nov. 1962, London, 2 sons, 1 daughter. *Literary Appointments:* Advertisement Representative, Associate Newspapers, 1948–53; Hulton Press, 1953–56; New Scientist, 1956–62; Advertisement Manager, New Society, 1962–64; Advertisement Director, Director, Queen, 1964–69; National Magazine Company, 1969– ; Publisher, Harpers Bazaar, Harpers & Queen, Cosmopolitan; Publishing Director, National Magazine Company (Good Housekeeping). *Publications:* Business of Womens Magazines, (with Joan Barrell), 1978. *Membership:* Past Chairman, Publicity Club of London, 1983–84. *Address:* 1 Narbonne Avenue, London SW4 9JR, England.

BRAITHWAITE, Max, b. 7 Dec. 1911, Nokomis, Saskatchewan, Canada. Novelist. m. Aileen Treleaven, 12 Oct. 1935, Saskatoon, 2 sons, 3 daughter. *Publications:* Why Shoot the Teacter, 1965 (Feature Film 1975); Never Sleep Three in a Bed, 1967; The Night We Stole The Mounties Car, 1971; A Privilege and a Pleasure, 1973; Lusty Winter, 1978; Mr Gruber's Folly, 1981; All The Way Home, 1986. *Contributor to:* Numerous articles in: Liberty; Maclean's; Chatelaine; Canadian Home Journal; Saturday Night, etc; Radio & TV Plays; Film Scripts. *Honour:* Leacock Medal for Humour, 1972. *Memberships:* Writers' Union of Canada; ACTRA. *Address:* Box 163, Port Carling, Ontario, Canada.

BRALEY, Bernard Arthur, b. 26 June 1924, Highbury, London, England. Publisher/Chartered Secretary. m. Joan Veronica Frost, 30 Apr. 1949, Coulsdon, Surrey, 1 son, 1 daughter. *Education:* Associate of the Chartered Institute of Secretaries. *Literary Appointments:* Managing Director, Galliard Ltd; Managing Director, Stainer and Bell Ltd. *Publications:* Benjamin the Bus, Pause for 1982, Pause for 1983; Pause for 1984; co-editor: New Horizons; co-editor; Galliard Book of Carols. *Contributor to:* Worship and Preaching. *Address:* Lornehurst, 191 Creighton Avenue, London N2 9BZ, England.

BRAMANN, Jorn K, b. 21 Dec. 1938, Wuppertal, Germany. Professor of Philosophy; Independent Video Producer. *Education:* PhD, University of Oregon, 1971; Staatsexamen in Philosophy, German Literature, University of Cologne, Germany. *Publications:* Self Determination, Editor anthology, 1984; Capital as Power, 1984; Unemployment and Social Values, Editor anthology, 1984; Wittgenstein's Tractatus and the Modern Arts, 1985. Translations: Climb, But Downward, by Wolfdietrich Schunuvve, 1983; Uprising in East Germany, Stories by Jochen Biem, 1985. *Contributions to:* Numerous professional journals.

Honours: Stipends, National Endowment for the Humanities, 1975–76, 1981, 84. *Memberships:* President, Allegany Video Society. *Literary Agent:* Jeanette Axelrod, Fairport, New York. *Address:* 2156 Carter Road, Fairport, NY 14450, USA.

BRAMESCO, Norton Jay, b. 2 Mar. 1924, New York City, USA. Advertising Executive. m. (2) Ronnie Zolondek, 12 May 1979, East Hampton, 1 son, 1 daughter, by previous marriage. *Education:* BSc, Columbia University, 1949. *Publications:* The Crossword Puzzle Compendium, with Jordan Lasher, 1980; Radiation, with Martin D Ecker, 1981; The Illustrated Encyclopedia of Crossword Words, with Michael Donner, 1982. *Contributor to:* Numerous professional journals, magazines & newspapers. *Literary Agent:* John Boswell. *Address:* 120 E 34th St, New York, NY 10016, USA.

BRANDAO, Ignacio de Loyola, b. 31 July 1936, Araraquara, Brazil. Writer. 2 sons. *Publications:* Zero, 1974; Dentes ao Sol, 1976; Nao Veras Pais Nenhum, 1981; O Verde Violentou O Muro, 1984; O Beijo Nao Vem Da Boca, 1985; Bebel Que A Cidade Comeu, 1968; Cadeiras Proibidas, 1977. *Contributions to:* Folha de Sao Paulo, Brazilian newspaper; Brazilian version of Playboy magazine. *Honours:* Prize, Institute Italo Latino Americano, Italy. *Literary Agent:* Thomas Colchie, 700 Fort Washington Avenue, New York, 10040, USA. *Address:* Avenida Djalma Dutra 695, Araraquara SP, 14.800 Brazil.

BRANDENBERG, Aliki, b. Wildwood Crest, New Jersey, USA. Writer & Illustrator, Children's Books. *Education:* Graduate, Philadelphia College of Art. *Publications:* Keep Your Mouth Closed Dear, 1966; Three Gold Pieces, 1968; At Mary Bloom's 1976; The Two of Them, 1979; Mummies Made in Egypt, 1979; How a Book is Made, 1986; Diggin Up Dinosaurs, 1981; We Are Best Friends, 1982; A Medieval Feast, 1983; Use Your Head, Dear, 1983; Feelings, 1984; Jack and Jake, 1986. *Honours:* 1st Prize, Children's Book Award, New York Academy of Sciences, 1977; Junior Book Award, Boys Club of America, 1968. *Address:* 17 Regent's Park Terrace, London NW1 7ED, England.

BRANDEWYNE, Rebecca, b. 4 Mar. 1955, Knoxville, Tennessee, USA. Author. m. Gary D Brock, 14 Nov. 1983, Wichita, Kansas, USA. *Education:* BA Journalism, 1975, MA Communications, 1979, Wichita State University. *Major Publications:* No Gentle Love, 1980; Forever My Love, 1982; Love, Cherish Me, 1983; Rose of Rapture, 1984; And Gold was Ours, 1984. *Memberships:* Charter Member, Romance Writers of America; Western Writers of America. *Literary Agent:* Maxwell J Lillienstein. *Address:* PO Box 18036, Wichita, KS 67218, USA.

BRANDI, John, b. 5 Nov. 1943, Poet; Painter. *Education:* BA, University of California, Northridge, USA, 1965. *Appointments include:* Writer-in-Residence, Carlsbad, NM, USA, 1977–78; Poet-in-Residence, Carlsbad Caverns National Park, 1978; Artist-in-Residence, Socorro, NM, 1979–80. *Publications include:* Rite for the Beautification of All Beings, 1981; Andean Town Circa, 1980; 1978; Poems From Four Corners, 1978; Looking for Minerals, 1975; Firebook, 1974; The Phoenix Gas Slam, 1973; In a December Storm, 1973; Emptylots, 1971; Poet Afternoon in A Square of Guadalajara, 1970; The Crow That Visited Was Flying Backwards, 1984; That Back Road W, 1985; Poems at the Edge of Day, 1985; Zuleikha's Book, 1986; Chimborazo: Life on the Haciendas of Highland Ecuador, 1976; Narrowguage to Riobamba, 1976; Y Aun Hay Mas, 1975; Desde Alla, 1971; Diary from a Journey to the Middle of the World, 1978. *Contributor to:* LA Free Press; Denver Post; NM Humanities Review; Zero; Atlantic Monthly; Handbook; Tree; Kayak; Puerto del Sol; Chelsea; Kuksu; El Palacio. *Honours include:* National Endowment for the Arts Fellowship for Individual Writers, 1980; PEN America Writes Grant, 1973; Portland State Poetry Award, 1971. *Address:* Star Rt Box 760, Corrales, NM 87048, USA.

BRANDON-COX, Hugh, b. 14 June 1917, Elmstead, Essex, England. Author; Naturalist; Artist. *Publications:* Hovran – Swedish Bird Lake, 1968; Trail of the Arctic Nomads, 1969; Summer of a Million Wings, 1974. *Contributor to:* Former Editor, The West-Countryman; Swedish & Norwegian Magazines. *Memberships:* FZS; President, North Norfolk Naturalists. *Address:* Studio Cottage, Suffield, Norwich, Norfolk NR11 7EQ, England.

BRANDT, Anthony, b. 21 Nov. 1936, New Jersey, USA. Free-lance Writer. m. Lorraine Dusky, 21 Sep. 1981, Sag Harbour, NY. *Education:* AB, Princeton University, 1958; MA, Columbia University, 1961. *Major Publications:* Reality Police: The Experience of Insanity in America, 1975; The First Sex: American Men After Twenty Years of Feminism, forthcoming. *Contributor to:* Esquire (columnist), 1983–84; The Atlantic; American Heritage; Psychology Today; Connoisseur; Go; and others. *Literary Agent:* Brandt & Brandt, New York. *Address:* Box 968, Sag Harbor, NY 11963, USA.

BRANICK, Vincent Patrick, b. 26 Apr. 1941, San Francisco, USA. Educator. m. Marie Elizabeth Spellacy, 27 Aug. 1984, Columbus, 1 son, 1 daughter. *Education:* Phil D, University of Freiburg; SS.D. Pontifical Biblical Institute; MBA, University of Dayton. *Publications:* An Ontology of Understanding: Karl Rahner's Metaphysics of Knowledge in the Context of Modern German Hermeneutics, 1974; Wonder in a Technical World: An Introduction to the Method and Writers of Philosophy, 1980; Mary, The Spirit, and the Church, Editor, 1981. *Contributor to:* Numerous professional journals including, Catholic Biblical Quarterly; Journal of Biblical Literature, etc. *Honours:* Woodrow Wilson Fellow, 1963. *Memberships:* Academic Affairs Administrators; Catholic Biblical Association; Society of Biblical Literature; American Catholic Philosophical Association. *Address:* 605 Kling Drive, Dayton, OH 45419, USA.

BRANNIGAN, Colin Thomas, b. 16 May 1937, Denton, Manchester, England. Journalist. m. Joyce Roe, 17 May 1958, West Hartlepool, 1 son, 2 daughters. *Literary Appointments:* Editor, The Star, Sheffield, 1968–78; Editorial Director, Essex County Newspapers, 1978–. *Honours:* Campaigning Journalist of the Year, 1971. *Memberships:* National President, Guild of British Newspaper Editors, 1979–80. *Address:* Culver Street West, Colchester, Essex, England.

BRASHER, Christopher William, b. 21 Aug. 1928, Guyana. Journalist. m. Shirley Bloomer, 28 Aug. 1959, Chelsea, 1 son, 2 daughters. *Education:* MA, St John's College, Cambridge. *Appointments:* Columnist, Olympic Corespondent, The Observer, 1961–; Race Director, London Marathon; Managing Director, Fleetfoot Ltd, Brasher Leisure Ltd. *Publications:* The Red Snows, with Sir John Hunt, 1960; Sportsman of our Time, 1962; A Diary of the XVIIIth Olympiad, 1964; Mexico, 1968; Munich, 1971. *Contributor to:* Numerous professional journals and magazines. *Honours:* Sportswriter of the Year, 1968, 1976; National Medal of Honour, Finland, 1975. *Address:* The Navigator's House, River Lane, Richmond, Surrey TW10 7AG, England.

BRASHERS, Howard Charles, b. 11 Dec. 1930, Knott, Martin County, Texas, USA. Professor of English. m. Kerstin Brorson, 13 June 1959, 3 sons. *Education:* BA, University of California, 1956; MA, San Francisco State University, 1960; PhD, University of Denver, Colorado, 1962. *Literary Appointments:* Fulbright Lecturer in American Studies, Royal University of Stockholm, Sweden, 1962–65; Assistant Professor, English, University of Michigan, USA, 1965–68; Assistant Professor, 1968–70, Associate Professor, 1970–73, Professor, 1973–, English, San Diego State University, California. *Publications include:* The Other Side of Love, 2 novellas, 1963; The Life of America, 1965; Introduction to American Literature, 1965; Creative Writing: Fiction, Drama, Poetry, The Essay, 1968; Creative Writing for High School Students, 1968;

The Structure of Essays, 1972; Whatta Ya Mean, Get Out O' That Dirty Hole? I Live Here!, poems and cartoons, 1974; Developing Creativity, 1974; A Snug Little Purchase, 1979; Creative Writing Handbook, 1984. *Contributions to:* South Dakota Quarterly; Michigan Quarterly Review; Eight Stories; Blue Cloud Quarterly; American Indian Quarterly; Four Quarters; Denver Quarterly; Sewanee Review; Moderna Sprak; American-Scandinavian Review; College Composition and Communication; Discovering Literature; various others. *Honours:* Fullbright Teaching Award, English Institute, University of Stockholm Sweden, 1962–65; Outstanding Faculty Award, College of Arts and Letters, San Diego State University, 1980. *Address:* 9231 Molly Woods Avenue, La Mesa, CA 92041, USA.

BRASS, Alister John Douglas, b. 24 Aug. 1937, Australia. Medical Editor/Writer. *Education:* MA, BM, BCh, Oxford University; LRCP (London), MRCS (England) Royal Colleges Conjoint Board. *Literary Appointments:* Editor, St Mary's Hospital Gazette (UK); Assistant Editor, Medical Journal of Australia; Senior Editor, Journal of the American Medical Association; Directing Editor, CIBA Medical Education (USA); Editor-in-Chief, Annual Reviews Inc, Palo Alto, USA; Editor, Medical Journal of Australia. *Publications:* Bleeding Earth – A Doctor Looks at Vietnam, 1968; Aids and Australia 1985. *Contributor to:* The Observer (London); The Month (London); New England Journal of Medicine; Quadrant (Australia); The Australian (Sydney); Medical Journal of Australia; Journal of American Medical Association. *Membership:* Chicago Literary Club. *Address:* 77 Arundel Street, Glebe, New South Wales 2037, Australia.

BRASWELL, George Wilbur Junior, b. 30 May 1936, Emporia, Virginia, USA. Teacher. m. Margaret Joan Owen, 14 June 1958, Canton, North Carolina, 2 sons, 2 daughters. *Education:* BA, Wake Forest University; BD, Yale University Divinity School; Doctor of Ministry, Southeastern Baptist Theological Seminary; MA, PhD, University of North Carolina, Chapel Hill. *Publications:* To Ride a Magic Carpet, 1976; Understanding World Religions, 1983. *Contributions to:* Educating for Christian Missions; Journal of Church and State; Missiology; The Christian Century; Faith and Mission; Perspectives in Religious Studies. *Honours:* Phi Beta Kappa, 1958; Omicron Delta Kappa, 1958. *Address:* PO Box 892, 339 North Main Street, Wake Forest, NC 27587, USA.

BRATHWAITE, Errol Freeman, b. 3 Apr. 1924, Clive, Hawkes Bay, New Zealand. Writer. m. Alison Irene Whyte, 20 Mar. 1948, Christchurch, 1 son, 1 daughter. *Publications include:* Fear in the Night, novel, 1959; Long Way Home, novel, 1964; The Flying Fish, The Needle's Eye, The Evil Day, novel trilogy, 1964, 1965, 1967; The Companion Guide to the North/South Island of New Zealand, 2 volumes, 1970, 1972; New Zealand & Its People, 1974; Sixty Red Nightcaps, non-fiction, 1980; New Zealand, 1980; Morning Flight, non-fiction, 1970; Beautiful New Zealand, 1985; etc. *Contributions to:* New Zealand Weekly; Country Life; Military Modelling. *Honours:* Otago Daily Times Centennial Novel Prize, 1961; New Zealand Literary Fund Award for merit, 1962. *Memberships:* Patron, South Island Writers Association; PEN. *Literary Agent:* Richards Literary Agency, PO Box 31240, Milford, Auckland 9, New Zealand. *Address:* 12 Fulton Avenue, Christchurch 1, New Zealand.

BRATTMAN, Steven Ronald, b. 17 Mar. 1948, Playwright; Poet. *Education:* BA, UCLA, USA. *Contributor to:* Envoi, England; Scrip, England; Message, France; Crucible, New Zealand; Two Tone, Zimbabwe; Cardinal USA; Zahir, USA; Major Poets Quarterly, USA; Cycloflame, USA; Fireflower, Canada; The Poet, USA; The Kindred Spirit; Archer; Mockersatz; Earthwise; The Yellow Butterfly; Thirteen; Anthologies include, Yearbook of Modern Poetry and Contemporary American Poetry. *Address:* 1664 South Crescent Heights Boulevard, Los Angeles, CA 90035, USA.

BRAY, Andrew, b. 5 June 1947, England. Editor, Yachting Monthly. m. Margaret Cartwright, 12 Apr. 1975, Ilminster, 1 son, 3 daughters. *Address:* Yachting Monthly, Kings Reach Tower, Stamford Street, London SE1 9LS, England.

BRAY, Nicholas Paul, b. 22 Apr. 1948, Kingswood, England. Journalist. m. Josette Dacosta, 18 Mar. 1971, Bombay, India, 1 son, 2 daughters. *Education:* BA Honours, Oxford, England; University of Vienna, Austria; School of Oriental and African Studies, London, England. *Literary Appointments:* Chief Correspondent, Reuters, Brussels, Belgium, 1981–82; Bureau Chief, Wall Street Journal/Europe, Paris, France, 1983– . *Address:* 3 rue du Faubourg Saint Honoré, 75008 Paris, France.

BREE, Germaine, b. 2 Oct. 1907, Lasalle, Gard, France. College Professor. *Education:* Licence-ès-Lettres d'Anglais, 1930; Ag[c]egation d'Anglais, 1932, Sorbonne University, Paris; Diplome d'Études Supérieures, 1931. *Major Publications:* Du Temps perdu au Temps retrouvé: Introduction à l'oeuvre de Marcel Proust, 1950; André Gide: i'insaisissable Protée: Etude Critique de l'ouevre d'André Gide, 1953; An Age of Fiction: The French Novel from Gide to Camus, 1957; Camus, 1959; The World of Marcel Proust, 1966; Women Writers in France: Variations on a Theme, 1973; Litterature Française: le XXᵉ Siècle II 1920–70, 1978; (with Ed Morot-Sir) Du Surrealisme àl'Empire de la critique Arthaud, 1984. *Contributor to:* Romanic Review; French Review; Yale French Studies; and other professional journals. *Honours:* Recipient of several honorary degrees. *Memberships:* Several professional organisations. *Address:* 2135 Royall Drive, Winston-Salem, NC 27106, USA.

BREHM, Sharon S, b. 18 Apr. 1945, USA. Professor of Psychology. *Education:* BA 1957, PhD 1973, Duke University; MA, Harvard University, 1968. *Publications:* The Application of Social Psychology to Clinical Practice, 1976; Help for your Child: A Parent's Guide to Mental Health Services, 1978; Developmental Social Psychology, edited with S Kassin & F Gibbons, 1981; Psychological Reactance: A Theory of Freedom & Control, with Jack W Brehm, 1981; Intimate Relationships, 1985. *Contributions to:* Numerous scholarly journals; Chapters in scholarly collections. *Address:* 2401 Massachusetts Street, Lawrence, KS 66044, USA.

BRENDON, Piers George Rundle, b. 21 Dec. 1940, Stratton, Cornwall, England. Writer. m. Vyvyen Davis, 1968, 2 sons. *Education:* MA, PhD, Magdelene College, Cambridge, *Publications:* Hurrell Froude and the Oxford Movement, 1974; Hawker of Morwenstow, 1975; Eminent Edwardians, 1979; The Life and Death of a Press Baron, 1982; Winston Churchill: A Brief Life, 1984; Ike: The Life and Times of Dwight D Eisenhower, 1986. *Contributor to:* Reviews for many paper & journals including: The Times; The Observer; The Mail on Sunday; etc. *Literary Agent:* Curtis Brown Ltd. *Address:* 4B Millington Road, Cambridge CB3 9HP, England.

BRENNAN, John Christopher, b. 17 June 1949, Nottingham, England. Financial Journalist. m. Holly Johnston, 10 July 1971, University of Lancaster, 2 daughters. *Education:* BSc Economics Honours, University College of Wales, Aberystwyth; MA, University of Lancaster. *Literary Appointments:* Financial Journalist, Investors Guardian; Financial Correspondent, Investors Chronicle; Insurance Correspondent, The Times; Property Correspondent, The Financial Times; New Editor, Financial Weekly; Editor, Executive World, Moneycare, Homes and Savings; Contributing Editor, World Investor. *Publications:* The Political Pound – Study of Exchange Control, 1982. *Contributions to:* Daily Telegraph; Sunday Telegraph; Marketing; Banking World; Financial Weekly. *Address:* Headway Publications, 47 Whitcomb Street, London WC2, England.

BRENNAN, Joseph Payne, b. 20 Dec. 1918, Bridgeport, Connecticut, USA. Library Assistant. m. Doris M Philbrick, New Haven, Connecticut, USA, 24 Oct. 1970. *Major Publications:* Heart of Earth, 1950; Nine Horrors & a Dream (stories), 1958; The Wind of Time, 1962; Nightmare Need, 1964 (poems); Casebook of Lucius Leffing (stories), 1973; Stories of Darkness & Dread, 1973; Chronicles of Lucius Leffing, 1977; Shapes of Midnight, (stories), 1980; Creep to Death (poems), 1981; Evil Always Ends (novella), 1982; 60 Selected Poems, 1985. *Contributor to:* The American Scholar; Chicago Review; Commonweal; Esquire; New York Times; London Evening Standard; Georgia Review; Southern Poetry Review; Twilight Zone; New England Review; Yale Literary Magazine; and many others. *Membership:* Poetry Society of America. *Literary Agent:* Kirby McCauley Ltd. *Address:* 26 Fowler Street, New Haven, CT 06515, USA.

BRESLOW, Maurice Allen, b. 12 May 1935, Boston, Massachusetts, USA. Writer; University Teacher. m. Margaret Joan Cheesman, 31 Dec. 1980. Brewer's Mills, Ontario, Canada, 1 son, 1 daughter. *Education:* BA, Cornell University; MA, Tufts University; DFA MFA, Yale University. *Literary Appointments:* Assistant Professor, University of Montana, 1966–67; Associate Artistic Director, Long Wharf Theatre, New Haven, Connecticut, 1968–70; Associate Professor of Drama, Queen's University, Kingston, Canada, 1973–. *Publications:* Silver Bird and Scarlet Feather and Adam and Eve and After, 2 plays in 1 volume, 1982; When The World Was Young and Pinocchio, 2 plays in 1 volume, 1982; The Odyssey play, 1986. *Contributions to:* Short Stories and articles to: New York Herald-Tribune, Paris edition; Queen's Quarterly; Whig-Standard Macazibel Quadrille Magazine. *Honour:* Herbert and Patricia Brookin Scholarship, Yale University. 1965–66. *Memberships:* Association for Canadian Theatre History; Playwrights Union of Canada. *Address:* Cedarpoint Farm, RR # 1, Seeley's Bay, Ontario, KOH 2N0, Canada.

BRETT, David, b. 30 Dec. 1937, Leeds, England. University Lecturer. m. Barbara Freeman, 1 Nov. 1962, 1 son, 1 daughter. *Education:* BA, PhD (RCA). *Literary Appointments:* Resident Playwright, Nottingham Playhouse, 1963–64; Artist in Residence, American University of Washington DC, 1966–67. *Publications:* Ultramarin (12 plays) 1972; Black Folder (novel) 1976; High Level (travel) 1983. Numerous plays performed. *Contributions to:* Reviews in The Listener; Circa; Muveszet (Budapest); Artscribe etc. Numerous radio scripts etc. *Honours:* Arts Council Bursary (Traverse Theatre) 1972; Herbert Read Prize, 1982. *Literary Agent:* Rosica Colin Ltd. *Address:* 1 Fairview, Saintfield, Co Down, Northern Ireland BT24 7AD.

BREWER, Kenneth Wayne, b. 28 Nov. 1941, Indianapolis, Indiana, USA. Teacher. *Education:* BA, Western New Mexico University, 1965; MA, New Mexico State University, 1967; PhD, University of Utah, 1973. *Literary Appointments:* Literary Arts Advisory Panel, Utah Arts Council, 1981–85; Director, Western Writing Conference, 1984, Utah State University. *Publications:* Places, Shadows, Dancing People, 1969; Sum of Accidents, 1977; Round Again, 1980; The Collected Poems of Mongrel, 1981; To Remember What is Lost, 1982. *Contributions to:* River Styx; Poetry Northwest; Wind Literary Journal; Blue Unicorn; Green's Magazine; The Spirit That Moves Us; Pembroke; Stone Country; Contemporary Quarterly; Westigan Review; Western Humanities Review; Hanging Loose; Utah Holiday; South Dakota Review and many others. *Honour:* First Place Award, Long Poem Division, Original Writing Competition, Utah Institute of Fine Arts, 1978. *Memberships:* Rocky Mountain Modern Language Association; Western American Literature Association. *Address:* English Department, UMC 32, Utah State University, Logan, UT 84321, USA.

BREWER, Lucie Elisabeth, b. 16 Jan. 1923, London, England. Teacher in College of Education. m. Derek

Stanley Brewer, 17 Aug. 1951, Patshull, 3 sons, 2 daughters. *Education:* Honours Degree in English, Diploma in Education, MA, Birmingham University. *Appointments:* Senior Lecturer in English, Homerton College, Cambridge. *Publications:* From Cuchulain to Gawain, 1973; The Return of King Arthur, (with Beverly Taylor), 1983. *Contributions to:* William Morris Journal; VII. *Membership:* William Morris Society. *Address:* The Master's Lodge, Emmanuel College, Cambridge, England.

BREZAN, Jurij, b. 9 June 1916, Rackclwitz, Germany. Author. *Publications include:* 52 Wochen sind ein Jahr, Novel, 1954; Der Gymnasiast, novel, 1958; Semester der Verlorenen Zeit, novel, 1959; Maunesjahre, novel, 1963; Krabat oder die Verwandlung der Welt, novel, 1976; Bild der Vaters, novel, 1982; 6 volumes of stories, poetry, drama, children's books. *Contributor to:* Sinn und Form; Neue Deutsche Literatur; Weimarer Beitrage; Rozhlad. *Honours include:* National Prize, Democratic Republic, 1951, 1964, 1976; Karl Marx Order, 1971. *Memberships:* Academy of Arts, Democratic German Republic; Writers Association of German Democratic Republic, Vice President; PEN, Democratic German Republic. *Address:* Parkstrasse 18, DDR Bauken, Democratic Republic of Germany.

BREŽNA (Geerk), Irena, b. 26 Feb. 1950, Bratislava, CSSR. Journalist/Psychologist. m. Frank Geerk, 28 May 1976, Basel, Switzerland, 1 son. *Education:* Diploma of Faculty in Philosophy, University of Basel, Switzerland. *Publications:* Comme un serpent sous une pierre, in Voix de femmes en russie, edited in Paris by Denoel/Gonthier, 1982; Translator from Russian into German of Frau und Russland, 1983. *Contributions to:* Poesie, Swiss literary journal; Transatlantik, German journal; Der Alltag, Swiss journal; Kontinent, Russian exile magazine; Swiss Radio. *Honour:* First Prize for Literature, Linguistic Department, University of Bern, Switzerland, 1984. *Address:* Friedensgasse 13, 4056 Basel, Switzerland.

BRIDGEMAN, (Victoria) Harriet (Lucy) (Viscountess), b. 30 Mar. 1942. Director of Picture Library, Author. *Education:* MA, Trinity College, Dublin, Republic of Ireland. *Publications:* The Masters, executive editor, 1965–68; Discovering Antiques, editor, 1970–71; The British Eccentric, 1974; An Encyclopedia of Victoriana, 1975; Society Scandals, 1976; Beside The Seaside, 1976; Needlework: An Illustrated History, 1978; A Guide to Gardens of Europe, 1979. *Literary Agent:* Abner Stein. *Address:* 19 Chepstow Road, London W2 5BP, England.

BRIDGES, Herb, b. 19 Oct. 1929, USA. US Postal Service. m. Eleanor Witcher, 18 Nov. 1961, Newnan, Georgia, USA, 2 sons, 1 daughter. *Education:* AB, University of Georgia. *Major Publications:* Scarlett Fever, 1977; Favorite Scenes from Gone with the Wind, 1981; The Filming of Gone with the Wind, 1984. *Contributor to:* Antique Journal; Collector's Showcase; Antique Trader; The Big Reel. *Address:* P O Box 192, Sharpsburg, GA 30277, USA.

BRIERLEY, David, b. 30 July 1936, Durban, South Africa. Author. m. Caroline Gordon Walker, 23 Apr. 1960, St Stevens, Palace of Westminster, 1 daughter. *Education:* BA, Honours, Oxon. *Publications:* Cold War, 1979; Blood Group O, 1980; Big Bear, Little Bear, 1981; Shooting Star, 1983; Czechmate, 1984; Skorpion's Death, 1985. *Membership:* Crime Writers Association. *Literary Agent:* Curtis Brown Ltd. *Address:* Old Farm, Harthall Lane, Kings Langley, Hertfordshire WD4 8JW, England.

BRIFFAZ-LOVELAND, Laure, b. 7 Sep. 1953, Nancy, France. m. Gérard Briffaz de Larmoud, 7 June 1975, 1 son. *Education:* Associate in Arts, American College in Paris, France, 1973. *Major Publication:* Le Chemin du Lieu. *Contributor to:* Les Elytres du Hanneton. *Membership:* Grenier Jane Tony – Brussels. *Address:* 27 Avenue W Churchill, 1180 Brussels, Belgium.

BRIGGINSHAW, James Francis (Jim), b. 28 Jan. 1926, Ipswich, Queensland, Australia. Newspaper Editor. m 1 son. *Literary Appointments:* Journalist, Queensland Times, Ipswich, Queensland; Journalist, The Telegraph, Brisbane, Queensland; Sub Editor, Sydney Morning Herald, Sydney, New South Wales; Sub Editor, The Sun, Sydney; Chief Sub Editor, The Courier-Mail, Brisbane; Chief Sub Editor, The Australian, Brisbane; Sub Editor, West Australian, Perth, Western Australia; Editor, The Northern Star, Lismore, New South Wales. *Major Publications:* Fishing the New South Wales North Coast, 2nd edition 1982. *Contributor to:* (TV Critic); TV Times; Fishing News (Queensland Editor); Seacraft (Queensland writer). *Honours:* W G Walkley National Award for Journalism, 1975; A J A Prodi Award for Journalism, 1981; Sir Harry Budd Memorial Award for Journalism, 1981; Highly Commended, Australian Journalist of the Year (Graham Perkin Award), 1981. *Address:* The Northern Star, Lismore, New South Wales, Australia 2480.

BRIGGS, Anasa P, b. San Bernardino, California, USA. Producer; Writer; Host of Anasa Briggs Series. *Education:* BA, Drama, University of California, Santa Barbara. *Contributor to:* One Method of Developing Local Community Support, SECA Newsletter. *Honours:* Best Actress, Civic Light Opera, San Bernadino, 1968; Lompoc Federal Prison Afro-American Society for Performance and Instruction, 1972; Nominee, Best Actress, Supporting Lead Role, Old Globe Theatre, San Diego, 1973–74; 1st Runner Up, Model of the Year, San Diego, 1976; Semi-Finalist, State Model of the Year Pageant, 1976; Bronze Medal, International Film and TV Festival of New York, 1983; Nancy Wilson Foundation's Outstanding Achievement Award, 1983; San Diego Emmy Nominee, Producer Category, 1984; Press and Publicity Award, San Diego Chapter of the NAACF, 1984; Reading is Fundamental Award, 1985; many other honours and awards. *Memberships:* Fellow, Media Institute, University of Southern California Midsummer Institute in Broadcast Management for Minorities Employed in Radio and TV; California Public Broadcasting Commission, Fellow; San Diego Association of black journalists Executive Board; National Academy of TV Arts and Sciences, San Diego Chapter Member, etc. *Address:* KPBS/TV 15 San Diego State University, San Diego, CA 92182, USA.

BRIGGS, Asa, b. 7 May 1921, Keighley, Yorkshire, England. Historian; University Administrator. m. 1 Sep. 1955, 2 sons, 2 daughters. *Education:* BA, Sidney Sussex College, Cambridge, 1941; BSc, London University, 1941. *Publications:* Victorian People, 1954; Age of Improvement, 1959; History of Broadcasting in the United Kingdom, Volume I 1961, Volume 2 1965, Volume 3 1970, Volume 4 1979; Victorian Cities, 1963; They Saw It Happen 1897–1940, 1960; How They Lived 1700–1815, 1969; Editor, The Nineteenth Century, 1970; A Social History of England, 1983; The BBC, The First Fifty Years, 1985. *Contributor to:* Various newspapers; journals; encyclopedias; etc. *Honours:* Marconi Award for Broadcasting History; many honorary doctorates. *Memberships:* President, British Social History Society; President, Ephemera Society; Member, Society of Authors; Life Peer, 1976. *Address:* The Caprons, Koere Street, Lewes, Sussex, England.

BRILLANT, Jacques, b. 17 Sep. 1924, Rimouski, Canada. Writer. m. at Rimouski, Louise Casgrain, 12 May, 1956, 3 sons. *Education:* BA, University of Moncton; Licence in Political & Social Studies, University of Louvain. *Literary Appointment:* Union des [a]ecrivains québecois (Canada). *Major Publications:* Le Jardin de Nuit, poems, Japan, 1960; Soeur Jeanne (satirical), Montréal, 1967; L'Impossible Québec (essay), 1968; Le Soleil (novel), Montréal, Leméac, 1979; 1967; L'anti-monde (novel), Montréal Leméac, 1985. *Contributor to:* Various Québec weeklies. *Honours:* Order of St John; Order of Malta. *Memberships:* Pen Club (Monaco); Fellow, Royal Society of Arts, London, England. *Address:* 43 Boulevard des Moulins, MC 98000, Monaco.

BRINGHURST, Robert, b. 16 Oct. 1946, Los Angeles, California, USA. Poet. m. Miki Cannon Sheffield, 1974 (divorced 1981), 1 daughter. *Education:* BA, Indiana University, Bloomington, 1973; MFA, Creative Writing, University of British Columbia, Vancouver, 1975; Undergraduate study: Massachusetts Institute of Technology; University of Utah and Indiana University. *Literary Appointments:* Visiting Lecturer, Department of Creative Writing, University of British Columbia, 1975–77; Lecturer, Department of English, 1979–80; Part-time Lecturer, Simon Fraser University, Burnaby, 1983–84; Poet-in-Residence, School of Fine Arts, The Banff Centre, Fall 1983; Writer-in-Residence, Writers Federation of Nova Scotia, Fall 1984; Guest Editor various publications; Reviews Editor, Canadian Fiction Magazine, 1974–75; General Editor, Kanchenjunga Poetry Series, 1973–79; Freelance commercial editor, typographer and book designer, 1975–78; President, Robert Bringhurst Limited, 1978–. *Publications:* Books include: Ocean/Paper/Stone, 1984; The Raven Steals the Light, 1984. *Contributions to:* Canadian Literature, American Poetry Review and several other publications; Essays and Articles, also translations from Greek, Arabic, Italian, Spanish and French. *Honours:* Poetry Prizes, Grants and Awards including Canada Council Arts Grant A, 1984. *Memberships:* Sierra Club; Alpine Club of Canada; Writers Union of Canada; League of Canadian Poets; Western Literature Association; Association Typographique Internationale. *Address:* c/o The Writers Union of Canada, 24 Ryerson Avenue, Toronto, Ontario M5T 2P3, Canada.

BRINK, Alijd, b. 28 Aug. 1911, Amsterdam, The Netherlands. Paintress; Poetess; Essayist. *Education:* Courses at Hendrik de Keyser School, Amsterdam. *Appointments include:* 2 years, Studio of painter, Piet van Wijngaardt, Amsterdam; Assistant, setting up & running, Institute of Medical Psychology, Amsterdam. *Publications:* Stenen Stromen ook, 1959; Het onbekommerd zwijgen, 1961; Het grote varen, 1965; Met Stenen ogen in het park, 1973; Een kwestie van tijd, 1980; De kleur van het uur, 1982; en de novellen an ander proza, Een gat in de zon, 1966; De ijsvogel, 1972; Groeien naar een onderdak, 1977; Vaawel Adje – en nu voorgoed, 1979; Nu de huid van de dag is weggeworpen, 1982; In d-ademende klok van de wereld, 1983; De Goldflengte van het licht, 1985. *Contributor to:* Anthologies, Poems About Old Age, 1978, poem Gerontologisch, broadcast by Netherlands Christian Radio Association, 1978, Nieuw Viaams Tijdschrift, Belgium; Nieuwe Stemmen, Belgium; Margreit, Holland; various essays & stories. *Honours include:* Essay Award, Nieuwe Stemmen for easy Dichten uit Zelfbehoud, 1961; various pieces broadcast; various other honours. *Agent:* Wim J Simons, Foundation for Literary Publications, Amsterdam. *Address:* Hazenpad 12, 7581 BG Losser, The Netherlands.

BRINK, Andre Philippus, b. 29 May 1935, Vrede, South Africa. Professor. *Education:* DLitt, Rhodes University; DLitt (honoris causa) University of the Witwatersrand. *Publications:* Lobola vir die Lewe, 1962; Die Ambaddadeur, 1963; File on a Diplomat, 1966; Kennis van die Aand, 1973; Looking on Darkness, 1974; An Instant in The Wind, 1976; Rumours of Rain, 1978; A Dry White Season, 1978; A Chain of Voices, 1982; The Wall of the Plague, 1984. *Contributor to:* Books Abroad; Asahi Journal; Theatre Quarterly; Standpunte. *Honours:* Reina Prinsen Geerligs Prize, 1964; CNA Award, 1965, 1978, 1982; Academy Prize for Prose Translation, 1970; Martin Luther King Memorial Prize, 1980; Prix Medicis Etranger, 1980. *Address:* Rhodes University, Grahamstown, Republic of South Africa.

BRINKLEY, Alan, b. 2 June 1949, Washington DC, USA. Historian. *Education:* AB, Princeton University, 1971; AM History, 1975, PhD History, 1979, Harvard University, USA. *Major Publications:* America in the Twentieth Century (co-author), 1982; Voices of Protest: Huey Long, Father Coughlin & the Great Depression, 1982; American History: A Survey (co-author), 1983. *Contributor to:* Harper's; The Atlantic; London Review of Books; Wilson Quarterly; New York Times; Washington Post; Boston Globe; The New Republic; Journal of American History; Reviews in American History; and others. *Honours:* American Book Award for History, 1982; Guggenheim Fellowship, 1984–85; Woodrow Wilson International Centre for Scholars Fellowship, 1985. *Address:* Department of History, Harvard University, Cambridge, MA 02138, USA.

BRISBY, Stewart, b. 3 Feb. 1945, Bronx, New York, USA. Writer; Television Producer/Director. *Education:* New York University; Onondaga Community College, Auburn Community College. *Publications:* A Death in America, 1968; Urinating in the Pool, 1974; Born into a Felony (Anthology), Co-Editor and Publisher, 1978. *Contributions to:* Berkeley Barb; Blow; Callaloo; Eccentric; Margins Magazine; Minetta Review; Midwest Poetry; Nickel Review; One Shot Deal; Passages North; Poetry Magazine; 70 on the 70's Anthology; South Dakota Review; Tandava; Urthkin; Greenfield Review. *Honours:* Creative Artists Program Service Fellowship Grant Recipient, 1981; National Endowment on the Arts Grant to produce 'Born into a Felony', 1978; Semi-Finalist for CAPS Grant, 1976. *Address:* 430 East 105 Street #2C, New York, NY 10029, USA.

BRISK, Rita, b. 18 Oct. 1925, Journalist. *Literary Appointments:* Reporter, Evening Gazette, Middlesbrough, 1939–; Feature Writer, Sunderland Echo, 1946–56; Feature Writer and verse Contributor with Cheshire Independent Newspapers, 1956–. *Publications:* Jenny Wren, a D-Day memoire, accepted by Royal Navy Museum, Portsmouth; The Anvil of the Heart; Contemplation, 1967; Lifelines, 1979; (lyricist) Premier performance of, Images of Love, Manchester Royal Northern College of Music: Dawn and Dusk, A collaborated collection of Poetry, with Hari Haryarock, edited by Rita Brisk, also Hebrew translation; A Selected Work on the Stocks, 1986. *Contributor to:* Manchester Sketch; Jewish Life Magazine. *Memberships:* Founder Fellow, International Poetry Society; Manchester Poetical Society. *Address:* 40 Broadway, Cheadle, Cheshire.

BRITTAN, Samuel, b. 29 Dec. 1933, England. Journalist. *Education:* BA, Jesus College, Cambridge, 1955; MA. *Publications:* Steering the Economy, 3rd edition, 1971; Left or Right: The Bogus Dilemma, 1968; Capitalism & the Permissive Society, 1973; The Delusion of Incomes Policy, with Peter Lilley, Temple Smith, 1977; The Economy Consequences of Democracy, 1977; How to End the Monetarist Controversy, 1981; Role and Limits of Government: Essays in Political Economy, 1983. *Contributor to:* Various Journals. *Honours:* 1st Winner, Sr Wincott Award for Financial Journalists, 1971; George Orwell Prize, 1980; Honorary DLitt, Heriot-Watt University, 1985. *Memberships:* Political Economy Club. *Address:* The Financial Times, Bracken House, 10 Cannon Street, London EC4, England.

BRITTON, Julia, b. 27 June 1924, Cheshire, England. Writer; Journalist, 1 son, 2 daughters. *Education:* BA Hons, Victoria University. *Literary Appointments:* Writer in Residence, Stage Company, South Australia, 1984. *Productions:* A Cage in the Country, 1982; A Ritual Killing, 1982; Miles Franklin and the Rainbow's End, 1984; Exits and Entrances, 1983; Listening to Shells, 1983. *Contributions:* of Poetry to various publications. *Honours:* Best Radio Play (McGregor Award) 1981; Australian Writers' Guild Award for Best Unproduced Script, 1982. *Memberships:* Australian Writers' Guild; South Australian Writers' Theatre. *Address:* 287 Esplanade, Henley Beach, South Australia 5022.

BROCK, Michael George, b. 9 Mar. 1920, Bromley, Kent, England. University Teacher. *Education:* Corpus Christi College, Oxford, BA, 1943, MA, 1948, Oxford University. *Publications:* The Great Reform Act, 1973; Editor with Eleanor H Brock, H H Asquith: Letters to

Venetia Stanley, 1982. *Contributor to:* American Oxonian; The Guardian; English Historical Review; Economic History Review; History Today; Oxford Review of Education; Oxford Magazine; Political Studies; Past & Present; Times Educational Supplement; Victorian Studies; Welsh Historical Review; Times Higher Educational Supplement. *Honours:* Honorary Fellowship, Wolfson College, Oxford, 1977; CBE, 1981; Honorary Fellowship, Corpus Christi, Oxford, 1982; Hon D Litt, University of Exeter, 1982; Fellow, Royal Society of Literature, 1983. *Address:* 186 Woodstock Road, Oxford OX2 7NQ, England.

BROCK, Peter de Beauvoir, b. 30 Jan. 1920, Guernsey, Channel Islands. University Professor; Historian. *Education:* MA, 1948, DPhil, 1954, Oxford University; PhD, University of Cracow, Poland, 1950. *Publications:* The Political & Social Doctrines of the Unity of Czech Brethern, 1957; Pacifism in the United States, 1968; Twentieth Century Pacifism, 1970; Pacifism in Europe to 1914, 1972; The Slovak National Awakening, 1976; Polish Revolutionary Populism, 1977; The Mahatma and Mother India, 1983. *Honours:* Recipient, John Simon Guggenheim Fellowship, 1961. *Address:* Dept of History, University of Toronto, Toronto, Ontario M5S 1A1, Canada.

BROCK, Randall J, b. 24 Nov. 1943, Colfax, Washington, USA. Poet. *Education:* BA History, BA Education, Eastern Washington State University; Master of Fine Arts, University of Oregon. *Major Publications:* Mouse Poems, 1971; Poems & Photographs, 1979; I Am Poems, 1982; Pockets of Origin, 1983; Shadows of Seclusion, 1983; Goat Poems, 1984; Solid Blue, 1985. *Contributor to:* The Nantucket Review; Gypsy; Charas; Wind; Chimera; and others. *Memberships:* Piedmont Literary Society. *Address:* 1214 Sprague Apt 25, Spokane, WA 99204, USA.

BROCKETT, Oscar Gross, b. 18 Mar. 1923, Hartsville, Tennessee, USA. University Professor; Author. m. Lenyth Spenker, 4 Sep. 1951, Stanford, deceased, 1 daughter. *Education:* BA, Peabody College, 1947; MA, 1949; PhD, 1953; Stanford University. *Appointments:* Editor, Educational Theatre Journal, 1959–62; Series Editor, Theatre and Dramatic Studies, 1984–. *Publications:* Bibliographical Guide to Research in Speech & Dramatic Art, 1963; The Theatre an Introduction, 1964. 4th edition, 1979; Plays for the Theatre, 1967, 4th edition 1984; History of the Theatre, 1971; Studies in Theatre and Drama, 1972; Century of Innovation, 1973; The Essential Theatre, 1976, 3rd edition, 1984; World Drama, 1984. *Contributor to:* 50 articles in scholarly journals. *Honours:* Fulbright Award, 1963–64; Guggenheim Fellowship, 1970–71; Fellow, American Society for Theatre Research; International Federation for Theatre Research; Modern Language Association; Speech Communications Association. *Address:* Dept of Drama, University of Texas, Austin, TX 78712, USA.

BRODERICK, Damien Francis, b. 22 Apr. 1944, Melbourne, Australia. Writer. *Education:* BA, Monash. *Publications:* A Man Returned, 1965; Sorcerers World, 1970; The Zeitgeist Machine, 1977; The Dreaming Dragons, 1980; The Judas Mandala, 1982; Transmitters, 1984; The Black Grail (in press); Strange Attractors (in press). *Honour:* Ditmar Award (Australian SF Achievement Award) for, The Dreaming Dragons, 1981. *Address:* 19 Croft Crescent, Reservoir, Victoria, Australia.

BRODIE, Malcolm, b. 27 Sep. 1926, Glasgow, Scotland. Journalist. m. Margaret Stevenson, 14 Sep. 1949, Belfast, Northern Ireland, 3 sons. *Literary Appointments:* Sports Editor, Belfast Telegraph, 1952–. *Publications:* History of Irish Football, 1962; Centenary History of the Irish Football Association, 1980; The Story of Glentoran, 1982; Official History of Linfield, 1985. *Contributor to:* Daily Telegraph; Sunday Telegraph; Glasgow Herald; News of the World; Sunday Mail; Radio Times. *Honours:* MBE, 1979; Rothmans Sportswriter of the Year, Northern Ireland, 1979; Highly Commended, Provincial Sports Writer, British Sports Journalism Awards, 1982. *Address:* Belfast Telegraph, 124 Royal Avenue, Belfast, Northern Ireland.

BRODY, Robert Leon, b. 5 Apr. 1952, Bronx, New York, USA. Writer. m. Elvira Storab, 11 Mar. 1979, Fresh Meadows, New York, 1 son. *Education:* BA. *Contributions to:* Esquire; Omni; New York; GQ; New York Times; Family Circle; Cosmopolitan; Glamour; Self; Harper's Bazaar; Newsday Magazine; Science Digest; American Health; New York Daily News. *Membership:* American Society of Journalists and Authors. *Literary Agent:* Denise Marcil. *Address:* 104-20 Queens Boulevard 6U, Forest Hills, NY 11375, USA.

BROG, Molly Jane, b. 2 July 1950, La Grande, Oregon, USA. Professor. *Education:* BS Health Education, Brigham Young University, 1975; MA Health Education, Oregon State University, 1975; EdD, Secondary Education Curriculum & Instruction, Brigham Young University, 1983. *Literary Appointments:* Assistant Professor of Education, Eastern Oregon State College. *Major Publications:* The Self-Health Handbook (with B Q Hafen), 1980; Health Management Promotion & Self-Care (contributor), 1981; Emotional Survival (with B Q Hafen), 1983; Medical Self-Care & Assessment (with B Q Hafen), 1983; Alcohol (with B Q Hafen), 1983; Prehospital Emergency Care & Crisis Intervention (contributor), 1983. *Contributor to:* Life & Health; Perceptual & Motor Skills. *Memberships:* Phi Delta Kappa; Phi Kappa Phi; Eta Sigma Gamma. *Address:* 910 B Avenue, La Grande, OR 97850, USA.

BROMHEAD, Peter Alexander, b. 27 Jan. 1919, Madras, India. Professor. *Education:* MA, DPhil, Exeter College, Oxford, England. *Publications:* Private Members; Bills in the British Parliament, 1956; The House of Lords and Contemporary Politics, 1958; Life in Modern Britain, 1962, 6th edition, 1984; Life in Modern America, 1970, 2nd edition, 1978; The Great White Elephant of Maplin Sands, 1973; The American Experience Now, 1974; Britain's Developing Constitution, 1975; Politics in Britain, 1979. *Contributor to:* Parliamentary Affairs; Political Studies; Public Administration; Political Quarterly; New Society; New Europe; Town & Country Planning; etc. *Literary Agent:* Curtis Brown Acad. *Address:* Department of Politics, University of Bristol, 12 Priory Road, Bristol 8, England.

BRONNER, Stephen Eric, b. 19 Aug. 1949, New York City, USA. Professor of Political Science. *Education:* BA, City College of New York, 1971; MA, 1972, PhD, 1975, University of California, Berkeley. *Appointment:* Professor of Political Science, Rutgers University, 1976–. *Publications:* A Beggar's Tales (novel), 1978; A Revolutionary for Our Times: Rosa Luxemburg, 1981; Passion and Rebellion: The Expressionist Heritage (with Douglas Kellner), 1983; Socialism in History: Political Essays of Henry Pachter (Editor), 1984. *Contributions to:* Politics and Society; Minnesota Review; The Boston University Journal; Salmagundi; New German Critique; Telos; Social Research; Socialtext; Political Theory; Coloquia Germanica. *Honours:* Bennett Essay Prize, City College of New York, 1971; Department Scholarship, University of California, Berkeley, 1972; Fulbright-Hays Grant, University of Tubingen, BRD, 1973; Dean's Fellowship, University of California, Berkeley, 1974; Merit Awards, Rutgers University, 1979, 81. *Address:* 200 Cabrini Boulevard, New York, NY 10033, USA.

BROOK, David, b. 1 Apr. 1932, New York City, USA. Professor. *Education:* BA, Johns Hopkins University, 1954; MA 1955; PhD, Columbia University, 1961. *Publications:* The UN and the China Dilemma, 1955; Preface to Peace, 1964; Search for Peace, 1970. *Contributor to:* American Political Science Review; Journal of E Asiatic Studies. *Honours:* Wilton Park Fellow, 1972. 1973. *Memberships:* Executive Committee, International Studies Association, Middle Atlantic Region, 1976–; Member, Executive Board of Non-governmental Organization, United Nations Comm on Youth, 1985–; Representative, International Studies Association, 1981–; Chairman, United Nations Non-governmental Organization Sub-committee on Global Education of the Committee on Youth, 1984–; American Political Science Assn; American Society of International Law; American Association of University Professors. *Address:* 135 Hawthorne Street, Apartment 6–H, Brooklyn, NY 11225, USA.

BROOKE, Christopher Nugent Lawrence, b. 23 June 1927, Cambridge, England. University Professor of History. m. Rosalind Beckford Clark, 1951, 3 sons. *Education:* BA 1945, MA 1952, Litt D 1973, Gonville and Caius College, Cambridge. *Publications include:* From Alfred to Henry III, 1961; The Saxon and Norman Kings, 1963; Europe in the Central Middle Ages, 1964; Time the Archsatirist, 1968; The 12th Century Renaissance, 1970; The Structure of Medieval Society, 1971; The Heads of Religious Houses, England and Wales 940-1216, (with D Knowles and V London), 1972; The Monastic World, 1000–1300, (with W Swaan), 1974; London 800-1216; The Shaping of a City, (with G Keir), 1975; Popular Religion in the Middle Ages, (with R Brooke), 1984; A History of Gonville and Caius College, 1985. *Contributions to:* Numerous books and historical journals. *Honour:* Honorary Doctorate, University of York, 1984. *Memberships include:* Fellow, British Academy; Fellow, Royal Historical Society; Fellow, President 1981–84, Society of Antiquaries; Corresponding Fellow, Medieval Academy of America; Fellow, Societa Internazionale di Studi Francescani. *Address:* Faculty of History, West Road, Cambridge CB3 9EF, England.

BROOKE, Michael Zachary, b. 5 Nov. 1921, Cambridge, England. Author and Consultant. m. Hilda Gillatt, 25 July 1953, at Attercliffe, Sheffield, 2 sons, 1 daughter. *Education:* BA History (1st Class Honours), 1943, MA, 1945, University of Cambridge, England; MA, 1964, PhD, 1969, University of Manchester, England. *Major Publications:* Frédéric Le Play: Engineer and Social Scientist, Longmans, 1970; The Strategy of Multinational Enterprise (with HL Remmers), 1st edition, Longmans, 1970, 2nd edition, Pitman, 1978; US edition, American Elsevier, 1971, French translation, Editions Sirey, 1973, Japanese translation, Sangyo Nohritsu Tanki Daigaku, 1974, Spanish translation, Aguilar, 1981; The Multinational Company in Europe (with HL Remmers & others), Longmans, 1972, US editon, University of Michigan Press, 1974, French translation Forces et Faiblesses des Entreprises Multinationales, Les éditions d'organisation, Paris 1974; The Schoolmaster in the EEC, (editor, with D Gilling-Smith, H J Ruff and A J Meyrick), National Association of Schoolmasters, 1973; A Bibliography of International Businesses (with M Black & P Neville), Macmillan, 1977; The International Firm (with H L Remmers), Pitman, 1977; US edition, Houghton Mifflin, 1978; International Corporate Planning (with M van Beusekom), Pitman, 1979; Handbook of International Trade (with P J Buckley, 2 volumes), Kluwer 1982; International Financial Management Handbook (with P Goodman & J MacArthur, 2 volumes), Kluwer, 1983; Centralisation and Autonomy, Holt, Rinehurt & Winston, 1984; Selling Management Service Contracts in International Business, Holt, Rinehart & Winston, 1985. *Contributor to:* Management Decision; Revue Internationalede Sociologie; Sociologia Internationalis; Indian Administrative Management Review; Omega; International Studies of Management and Organisation; Futures; Planned Innovation; The London Quarterly; Etudes Sociales; *Honour:* Fellow, Academy of International Business, 1982. *Membership:* Society of Authors, Chairman of Authors North, 1978–80. *Literary Agent:* Curtis Brown Ltd, *Address:* 21 Barnfield, Urmston, Manchester M31 1EW, England.

BROOKS, Douglas Lee, b. 5 Aug. 1916, New Haven, Connecticut, USA. Environmental Scientist. m. Elizabeth Blakey Thatcher, 27 Dec. 1941, Philadelphia, Pennsylvania, 4 sons. *Education:* BS, Yale University; MS, DSc, Massachusetts Institute of Technology. *Publications:* America Looks to the Sea: Ocean Use and

the National Interest, 1984; The Summer Place and other Poems, 1982, 85; Scenarios for My Old Age – Poems, Fantasies, Dreams, 1984. *Contributions to:* Journal of Meteorology; Ops Res; BioScience,; Hartford Courant. *Address:* 40 Loeffler Road, Apt 303P, Bloomfield, CT 06002, USA.

BROOKS, Jeremy, b. 17 Dec. 1926, Southampton, England. Writer. *Education:* Magdalen College, Oxford; Camberwell School of Art. *Publications:* Novels: The Water Carnival, 1957; Jampot Smith, 1960; Henry's War, 1962; Smith, as Hero, 1965; Doing The Voices, 1986; English stage adaptations include: Brecht's, Puntila; 5 plays by Gorky; Chekhov's Ivanov; Ostrovsky's, The Forest; Euripedes', Medea; Dylan Thomas's, A Child's Christmas in Wales; Screenplays, dramatisations etc. Our Mother's House; Work...is a Four-letter Word; An Artist's Story; The Grand Inquisitor. *Contributions to:* Sunday Times; The Observer; Various reviews and anthologies. *Honours:* OBIE Special citation for English stage adaptation of Gorky's, Summerfolk, 1975; Best Translation Award, British Theatre Association, 1982. *Memberships:* Theatre Writers Union; Writers Guild. *Literary Agent:* Deborah Rogers Limited. *Address:* 12 Bartholomew Road, London NW5 2AJ, England.

BROOKS, Lester James, b. 8 Nov. 1924, Des Moines, Iowa, USA. Writer. m. Patricia Kersten, 10 Sep. 1950, New York, USA, 3 sons. *Education:* BA & Certificate in Journalism, State University of Iowa; MA, Columbia University. *Major Publications:* Behind Japan's Surrender; Great Civilisations of Ancient Africa; Blacks in the City; How to Buy Property Abroad; How to Buy a Condominium; Fisher Guide to Spain & Portugal 1984–86. *Contributor to:* Several major magazines in USA. *Honours:* Various literary awards. *Memberships:* Authors Guild; Society of American Travel Writers; Travel Journalists Guild; National Association of Business Economists. *Address:* New Canaan, Connecticut, USA.

BROOKS, Patricia K, b. 17 December 1926, Chicago, Illinois, USA. Writer. m. Lester J Brooks, 10 Sep. 1950, New York, 3 sons. *Education:* BA, Vassar College; MA, University of Minnesota. *Publications:* The Presidents' Cookbook, 1968; Meals that Can Wait, 1970; How to Buy Property Afloat, 1974; How to Buy a Condominium, 1975; Best Restaurants New England, 1980; Country Inns of New England, 1984; Fisher Guide to Spain & Portugal, 1983, 1985. *Contributor to:* Regular articles for: Bon Appetit; Vogue; House Beautiful; Travel & Leisure; Travel/Holiday; House and Garden; Modern Bride; New York Times; IBM's Think; Newsday. *Honours:* PATA Travel Award, 1969; Venture Travel Award, 1970. *Memberships:* American Society of Journalists & Authors; Society of American Travel Writers; New York Travel Writers, former Treasurer. *Address:* 43 Marshall Ridge Road, New Canaan, CT 06840, USA.

BROOKS, Terry, b. 8 Jan. 1944, Sterling, Illinois, USA. Attorney; Novelist. *Education:* BA, Hamilton College, 1966; LLB, Washington & Lee University School of Law. *Publications:* The Sword of Shannara, 1977; The Elfstones of Shannara, 1982; The Wishsong of Shannara, 1985; Magic Kingdom for Sale, 1986. *Address:* 1310 Sinnissippi Road, Sterling, IL 61081, USA.

BROPHY, Brigid, b. 12 June 1929, London, England. Writer. m. Sir Michael Levey, 12 June 1954, London, 1 daughter. *Education:* St Hugh's College, Oxford. *Literary Appointments:* Vice-Chairman, British Copy-right Council, 1976–80. *Publications Include:* Hackenfeller's Ape, 1953; The King of a Rainy Country, 1956; Black Ship to Hell, 1962; Flesh, 1962; The Finishing Touch, 1963; The Snow Ball, 1964; Mozart the Dramatist, 1964; Don't Never Forget, 1966; Fifty Works of English Literature We Could Do Without, with Michael Levey & Charles Osborne, 1967; Black & White: A Portrait of Aubrey Beardsley, 1968; In Transit, 1969; Prancing Novelist, 1973; The Adventures of God in his Search for the Black Girl, & Other Fables, 1973; Pussy Owl, 1976; Beardsley & His World, 1976; Palace Without Chairs, 1978; The Prince & the Wild Geese, 1983; A Guide to Public Lending Rights 1983. Plays include: The Burglar, 1967; The Waste Disposal Unit, radio, 1968. *Contributions to:* London Review of Books; Times Literary Supplement. *Honours:* Cheltenham Literary Festival 1st Prize, first novel, 1954; London Magazine prize for prose, 1962. *Membership:* Executive Council 1975–78, Writers Guild of Great Britain. *Literary Agent:* Giles Gordon, Anthony Sheil Associates. *Address:* Flat 3, 185 Old Brompton Road, London SW5 OAN, England.

BROSMAN, Catherine (Hill), b. 7 June 1934, Professor of French. m. (2) 1970, 1 daughter. *Education:* BA, 1955, MA, 1957, PhD, 1960, Rice University, Houston, Texas; postgraduate study University of Grenoble, France, 1957–58. *Appointments:* Instructor in French, Rice University, 1960–62; Assistant Professor of French, Sweet Briar College, 1962–63; Assistant Professor of French, University of Florida, 1963–66; Associate Professor of French, Mary Baldwin College, 1966–68; Associate Professor, Professor of French, Tulane University, 1968–. *Publications:* Watering, 1972; Critical works: Andre Gide: l'evolution de sa pensee religieuse, 1962; Malraux, Sartre and Aragon as Political Novelists, 1964; Roger Martin du Gard, 1968; Jean-Paul Sartre, 1983. Poems: Abiding Winter, 1983. *Contributor to:* Sewanee Review; Texas Quarterly; Southern Review; Southwest Revies; Critical Quarterly; Shenandoah; Virginia Quarterly Review; Colorado Quarterly; Southern Poetry Review; Prairie Schooner; Kansas Quarterly etc. *Address:* 7834 Willow Street, New Orleans, LA 70118, USA.

BROSSARD, Nicole, b. 27 Nov. 1943, Montreal, Canada. Writer. 1 daughter. *Education:* Licence es Lettres, University of Montreal. *Appointments:* Co-Director, Co-Founder, La Barre du Jour, 1965–75, Les têtes de Pioche, 1976–79, NBJ, 1977–79; Member, President, Jury for the Emile Nelligan Poetry Awards, 1979–82; Visiting Professor, Queens University, Kingston, 1982. *Publications:* Le centre blanc, 1978; Amantes, 1980; Double Impression, 1984; Un livre, 1970; French Kiss, 1974; L'amèr ou le Chapitre effrité, 1977; Le sens apparent, 1980; La Picture Theory, 1982; Journal intime, 1984. *Contributor to:* Les Herbes Rouges; La Barre du Jour; Etudes francaises; Estuaire; Possibles; La vie en rose; Journal of Canadian Fiction; Prism International; Ethos International; Rampike; Canadian Fiction Magazine; Canadian Literature; Dalhousie French Studies Review; Fireweed; Opus International; Masques; etc. *Honours:* Governor General Awards, Poetry, Mécanique jongleuse, 1975, Double impression, 1985. *Memberships:* Union des ecrivains quibicois (UNEQ) Board of Directors, 1977–79, Vice-President, 1983–85. *Address:* 34 Ave. Robert, Outremont, Quebec H3S 2P2, Canada.

BROUGHTON, James, b. 10 Nov. 1913, California, USA. Poet; Film Writer; Director; Playwright. *Education:* BA, Stanford University, California. 1936. *Literary Appointments:* Resident Playwrite, Playhouse Repertory Theater, San Francisco, 1958–64; Playwrite Fellow, Eugene O'Neil Theater Foundation, Waterford, Conn, 1969; Teacher, School of Creative Arts, San Francisco State University, San Francisco, Art Institute. *Publications include:* High Kukus, 1968; A Long Undressing, 1971; Seeing the Light, 1977; The Androgyne Journal, 1977; Ecstasies, 1983; (films) Mothers Day, 1948; The Pleasure Garden, 1953; The Bed, 1968; Dreamwood, 1973; Testament, 1974; Devotions, 1983; This Is It, 1971; The Golden Postions; Ergogeny; (anthol) Mark In Time, 1971; (play) Bedlam, 1969. *Honours include:* James D Phelan Award in Literature, 1948; Prix du fantaisie poetique, Cannes, 1954; Grand Prize, Bellevue Festival, 1970; Film Culture's 12th Independent Film Award, 1975; Cited as Grand Classic Master of Independent Cinema; Guggenheim Fellowships, 1971, 1973; Grants, National Endowment for the Arts, 1976, 1982; Doctor of Fine Arts, San Francisco Art Institute. *Address:* PO Box 183, Mill Valley, CA 94942, USA.

BROUGHTON, T Alan, b. 9 June 1936. Professor of English. *Education:* BA, Swarthmore College, 1962; MA, University of Washington, 1964. *Literary Appointments:* Teaching Assistant, University of Washington, 1962–64; Instructor, Sweet Briar College, 1964–66; Assistant, Associate and Full Professor, University of Vermont, 1966–. *Publications:* The Skin and All, poems with prints by Bill Davison, 1972; In the Face of Descent, 1975; Adam's Dream, 1975; The Man on the Moon, 1979; A Family Gathering, novel, 1977; The Horsemaster, novel, 1984; Hob's Daughter, novel, 1984; Preparing to be Happy, poems, 1986; Dreams Before Sleep, 1982. *Contributions to:* American Weave; Beloit Poetry Journal; Christian Science Monitor; Commonweal; Confrontation; Descant; Poetry Northwest; Prairie Schooner and others. *Honours:* 2nd Prize, Yankee 1971 Annual Poetry Awards; Best Poem of 1972, Borestone Mountain Poetry Awards, 1972, 73, 74; Family Clark Balch Award, Virginia Quartely Review, 1974; National Endowment for the Arts, 1976–77; Guggenheim, 1982–83. *Memberships:* Phi Beta Kappa; Poetry Society of America; Authors Guild; PEN. *Literary Agent:* Allen Levine, New York. *Address:* English Department, University of Vermont, 315 Old Mill, Burlington, VT 05401, USA.

BROUWERS, Toon, b. 4 Apr. 1943, Antwerp, Belgium. Dramaturg, Professor. m. Mart Hermans, 6 Apr. 1974, Antwerp, 3 daughters. *Education:* Doctor in Law, University of Louvain, 1966; 1st prize Speech and Drama, Koninklijk Conservatorium Antwerpen, 1970. *Literary Appointments:* Editor 1970, General Editor 1982, De Scene, monthly theatre review, Antwerp. *Publications:* De Lange Wandeling, poems, 1974; Landelijke Gedichten, poems, 1977; About 15 translations and adaptations of theatre plays. *Contributions to:* Several journals and magazines. *Honours:* Basiel de Craene-prijs, for poetry, 1972. *Memberships:* Board of Direction, Vereniging van Vlaamse Toneelauteurs (Association of Flemish Dramatists). *Literary Agent:* SABAM, Brussels; ALMO, Antwerp. *Address:* Arthur Goemaerelei 99, B 2018 Antwerpen, Belgium.

BROWN, Cheryl Renee Minter, b. 11 Feb. 1944, Aire, Massachusetts, USA. Editor and Publisher. m. at San Bernardino 26 Jan. 1963 to Hardy L Brown, 1 son, 3 daughters. *Education:* Associate Arts degree, San Bernardino Valley College; BA, San Bernardino California State University. *Major Publications:* Black History, 1968. *Contributor to:* Weekly newspaper with feature articles. *Honours:* International Leadership Conference, World Association of Girl Scouts, representing the Western Hemisphere, Curevaca, Mexico; Alumnus of the Year, 1982; Kiwanis Division 36 Family of the Year 1985. *Membership:* Journalism Society; Society of Professional Journalists Sigma Delta Chi. *Address:* P O Box 1581, Riverside, CA 92502, USA.

BROWN, Eloise Metcalf, b. 3 Feb. 1913. Homemaker. m. *Publications:* Bicentennial Patriotic Song. *Contributor to:* The World's Fair Anthology of Verse; Anthology of Alaska Poets; The Sampler, Volumes 1-X; Chattanooga Times; Chattanooga News; Free Press; Fort Payne Journal; The Laurellian; The Lookout; Dade Company Times; Creative Expressions; Church Bulletins; etc. *Honours:* in demand for poetry readings at clubs. *Memberships:* Worthy Matron, Order of Eastern Star; Office Board, United Methodist Church; Teacher, Wesley Fellowship Class; Chairperson, Christian Global Concerns; Charter Member, Alaska State Poetry Society; Dekalb Poets; Academy of American Poets; National Federation of Poetry Societies. *Address:* R 1 Box 650, Valley Head, AL 35989, USA.

BROWN, George Mackay, b. 17 Oct. 1921, Stromness, Orkney, Scotland. Writer. *Education:* MA, Edinburgh University. *Publications:* Calender of Love, 1967; An Orkney Tapestry, 1969; A Spell for Green

Corn, 1970; Greenvoe, 1972; Magnus, 1973; The Two Fiddlers, 1974; Selected Poems, 1977; Three Plays, 1984; Time in a Red Coat, 1984; Christmas Poems, 1984; Christmas Stories, 1985. *Contributor to:* Scotsman; Glasgow Herald; Atlantic Monthly; Harper's Bazaar; Encounter; etc. *Honours:* Several Awards, Scottish Arts Council; MA, Copen University; LLD, Dundee University; DLitt, Glasgow University; FRSL; OBE. *Address:* 3 Mayburn Court, Stromness, Orkney KW16 3DH, Scotland.

BROWN, Ian James Morris, b. 28 Feb. 1945, Barnet, England. Playwright; Drama Lecturer. m. Judith Sideway, 8 June 1968, London, 1 son, 1 daughter. *Education:* MA(Hons), English Literature and Language, Edinburgh University, 1967; DipEd, 1970; MLitt, 1975. *Literary Appointments:* Committee Member, Pool Theatre Club, 1974–76; Member, Drama Panel, North West Arts, 1980–83; Director, Theatre Exchange Theatre Company, 1982–; Member, General Arts Panel, North West Arts, 1983–. *Publications:* Plays: Mother Earth, 1970; The Bacchas, 1972; Carnegie, 1973; The Knife, 1973; The Fork, 1976; New Reekie, 1977; Mary, 1977; Runners, 1978; Mary Queen and the Loch Tower, 1979; Joker in the Pack, 1983 (all produced in London or Edinburgh); Pottersville, readings, Victoria Theatre, Stoke, 1982; Poems, Alsager Gallery Visual Arts and Poetry Exhibition, 1981; Rune, choral text, John Currie Singers, 1973; Rabelais, readings, Edinburgh Festival, 1973; Positively the Last Final Farewell Performance, ballet scenario, Scottish Ballet, 1972. *Contributions to:* New Writing and the Theatre, Manchester University; Interface; Scottish Theatre News; Education Bulletin, Arts Council of Great Britain; Papers presented at conferences, Reports, etc. *Honours:* Grierson Verse Prize, 1966; Scottish Arts Council Bursary, 1973, 77. *Memberships:* Scottish Society of Playwrights, Chairman, 1973–75, 1984–; Theatre Writers Union. *Literary Agent:* Margaret Ramsay Limited. *Address:* 4 Beechwood Drive, Alsager, Stoke-on-Trent, ST7 2HG, England.

BROWN, Jerry Earl, b. 24 June, 1940, Palestine, Texas, USA. Novelist & Freelance Writer. m. Frances Alicia Plank, 4 Apr. 1971, Boulder, Colorado, USA. *Major Publications:* Under the City of Angels, 1981; Darkhold, 1985. *Contributor to:* Canoe Magazine; Marathoner; The Runner; Denver Post; This Week in Denver; Colorado Monthly; Empire Magazine; Sunday Camera; and others. *Membership:* National Writers' Club (Assistant Director 1977–81). *Literary Agent:* Phyllis Westberg (Harold Ober Associates, New York). *Address:* 2950 Washington Street, Boulder, CO 80302, USA.

BROWN, John Gracen, b. 8 Oct. 1936. Poet; Dramatist. *Education:* BS, MS, Education, West Virginia University Engineering School; Illinois University, Psychology, Philosophy, Educational University of Colorado, Literature, Maths; High School Guidance Teacher; History, Geography, English Literature, Maths; High School Guidance Director. *Publications:* Variation in Verse, 1975; A Sojourn of the Spirit, 1981; Passages in the Wind, 1986; (Dramas) The Judgement, 1978; The Mission, 1984. *Contributor to:* North American Mentor Magazine; The Prairie Post; Scimatar & Song; S–B Gazette; Voices International; Journeys; Adventure World; Junior World; Cardinal Poetry Quarterly. *Honours:* Much work in Variation in Verse, A Sojourn of the Spirit, and Passages in the Wind, put to music; 1st Prize, International Society of Bassists, for Voices. *Address:* 430 Virginia Ave, Martinsburg, WV 25401, USA.

BROWN, Marel, b. 17 Dec. 1899, Carroll County, Georgia, USA. Freelance Writer. m. Alex Brown, 8 Oct. 1919, Atlanta, Georgia, USA. *Literary Appointments:* Secretary & Assistant to Editor, 1924–30; Chairman, Books for Russia, for Atlanta in World War II. *Major Publications:* Red Hills, 1941; Hearth-Fire, 1943; Fence Corners, 1952; The Shape of a Song, 1968; Three Wise Women of the East, 1970; Presenting Georgia Poets, 1979; Children's Books: Lilly May & Dan, 1946; The

Greshams of Greenway, 1950; The Cherry Children, 1956. *Contributor to:* Christian Herald; Christian Science Monitor; Home Life; New York Times; and many others. *Honours:* Poet of the Year, Dixie Council of Authors & Journalists, 1968; Writer of the Year, Atlanta Writers Club, 1968. *Memberships:* National League of American PEN-Women Atlanta Branch; Poetry Society of America; Poetry Society of Georgia; Atlanta Writers Club; International Biographical Association; International Academy of Poets; and others. *Address:* 1938 North Decatur Road NE, Atlanta GA 30307, USA.

BROWN, Marie James (Sister), OP, b. 12 Mar. 1907, Saulte Ste. Marie, Ontario, Canada. Business Education Teacher. *Education:* BS, Siena Heights College; MA, Education, DePaul University, Chicago; Gregg teacher's Diploma, Gregg Institute, Chicago; MA, Library Science, Toledo University; Diploma, Nonfiction Writing, Christian Writers Institute. *Publications:* Currently working on a book, Women in Ministries. *Contributor to:* Pastoral Life; Sisters Today; Parish Family Digest; Living Message; NAMRP Quarterly Publication. *Honours:* Roland Johnson Memorial Award for Outstanding Professional Writing, Mississippi Valley Writers Conference, 1977; Award of Merit, Outstanding Achievement in Non-Fiction Skills, Mississippi Writers Conference, 1978. *Memberships:* Professional Member, National Writers Club, Aurora, Colorado. *Address:* 235 Madden Hall, 1257E. Siena Heights Drive, Adrian, MI 49221, USA.

BROWN, Marlene, b. 5 Apr. 1952, Madras, India, Editor, Journalist, Author. *Education:* BSc Mathematics Honours, Madras and London University. *Literary Appointments:* Editor, ICP Journal, United Kingdom; Editor, Software News International (Europe); Editor, International Computer Products. *Publications Include:* Poetry books; Children's books; Relational Databases. *Contributions to:* Wall Street Journal; The Sunday Observer; The Financial Times; The Accountant and Accountancy; Computer Weekly, Australasia; Software News, USA; Systems User; Government News; Fortune, USA; Computer Decisions, USA; Computer-Asia, Hong Kong; Nikkei, Japan; Computer Graphics World, USA; Modern Office, Australia; Computing, UK; Data Processing, UK; Computer Systems, UK; Ace publications; New Scientist's; Irish Computer; Middle East Hospital; Ergonomics; Computer Zeitung, Germany; Mach Shevim, Israel; Datamytt Computer Scandinavia, De Automatiscng, The Netherlands. *Honours:* Journalist of the Year Award, for technical publishing, Features, 1983. *Memberships:* Pen UK; Press Club UK. *Address:* 26 Redcliffe Close, Old Brompton Road, London SW5 9HX, England.

BROWN, Richard George Bolney, b. 15 Sep. 1935, Wolverhampton, England. Wildlife Biologist, *Education;* BA (Hons) Zoology, Oxford University, England, 1957, D Phil, Zoology, 1962. *Publications:* Voyage of the Iceberg, published Toronto, 1983, New York, 1984, London, 1985; French Translation, 1984. *Contributions to:* Newsday (monthly colomn Observations), New York; popular articles in Canadian publications such as Equinox and Nature Canada; over 90 assorted scientific papers, reviews and translations. *Honour:* Kortright Prize, 1983 (Canadian National Sportsmen's Shows/Outdoor Writers of Canada) for Voyage of the Iceberg. *Address:* c/o Canadian Wildlife Service, Bedford Institute of Oceanography, PO Box 1006, Dartmouth, Nova Scotia, Canada B2Y 4A2.

BROWNE, William Paul, b. 15 May 1945, Cherokee, Iowa, USA. Professor of Political Science. m. Linda Sue Thomas, 1968, Cherokee, Iowa. *Education:* BS, 1967, MS, 1969, Iowa State University; PhD, Washington University, St Louis, 1971. *Literary Appointment:* Department of Political Science, Central Michigan University. *Publications:* The New Politics of Food, 1978; The Role of U.S. Agriculture in Foreign Policy, 1979; Politics, Programs and Bureaucrats, 1980; Rural Policy Problems, 1982; Aging and Public Policy, 1983; World Food Partners, 1986. *Contributions:* of articles on interest groups, agriculture policy and bureaucracy in

Proceedings of the Amereican Academy of Political Science; Journal of Politics; Western Political Quarterly; Policy Social Science Quarterly; Public Administration Review (3); Policy Studies Review; Policy Studies Journal; Midwest Review of Public Administration; Ethnicity; Education, State and Local Government Review; Urban Affairs Annual; Yearbook in Politics and Public Policy; Police Chief; Michigan Municipal Review. *Honours:* Fellow, American Political Science Association, 1968, 1969–71; Central Michigan University Achievement Award, 1974; Research Awards: Farm Foundation, U.S. Department of Agriculture, Resources for the Future. *Memberships:* American Political Science Association; Midwest Political Science Association, (Chair, Pi Sigma Alpha Committee, 1977); Michigan Conference of Political Scientists (President-elect, 1984); American Society of Public Administration; Policy Studies Organization (Editorial Board, 1980–81). *Address:* 8085 Essex Drive, Lake Isabella, Weidman, MI 48893, USA.

BROWNING, Christopher Robert, b. 22 May 1944, Durham, North Carolina, USA. University Professor. m. Jennifer Jane Horn, 19 Sep. 1970, Oberlin, Ohio, 2 daughters. *Education:* BA, 1967, Oberlin College, Oberlin, Ohio; MA 1967, PhD, 1975, University of Wisconsin – Madison. *Publications:* The Final Solution and the German Foreign Office, 1978; Fateful Solution: Essays on the Emergence of the Final Solution, 1985. *Contributions to:* Journal of Contemporary History; Yad Vashem Studies; Annual of the Simon Wiesenthal Center; Vierteljahrshefte fuer Zeitgeschichte; Militeargeschichtliche Mitteilungen, also chapters contributed to various anthologies. *Address:* Department of History, Pacific Lutheran University, Tacoma, WA 98447, USA.

BROWNING, William Abell, b. 12 June 1921, Lebanon, Kentucky, USA. Roman Catholic Priest. *Education:* Bachelor of Theology, Angelicum University, Rome; Diploma in Spiritual Theology, Dominican House of Studies, River Forest, Illinois, USA. *Publications:* Woman's Highest Fulfillment; God Really Loves Us. *Contributions to:* Review for Religious; Sisters Today. *Address:* 1924 Newburg Road, Louisville, KY 40205, USA.

BROWNJOHN, Alan Charles, Author; Poet. *Education:* Merton College, Oxford. *Publications include:* Editor of anthologies, New Poems 1970–71, with S Heaney and J Stallworthy; First I Say This, 1969; booklet of Philip Larkin, British Council series, Writers and Their Work, 1975; Arts Council anthology, New Poetry 3 with Maureen Duffy, 1977; Seven collections of verse including: The Railings, 1961; The Lions' Mouths, 1967; Sandgrains on a Tray, 1969; Brownjohn's Beasts (for Children) 1970; Warrior's Career, 1972; A Song of Good Life, 1975; A Night in the Gazebo, 1980; Collected Poems, 1983; Translation of Goethe's play Torquato Tasso with Sandy Brownjohn, 1985. *Contributor to:* Leading journals of poems, articles and reviews; New Statesman; Ambit; Encounter; The Observer; The London Magazine; The New Review etc; Work featured on Radio 3 BBC in, Poetry Now series and individual programmes. *Honours:* Cholmondeley Award for Poetry, 1979; Society for Authors Travelling Scholarships, 1985. *Address:* 2 Belsize Park, London NW3, England.

BROWNJOHN, John Nevil Maxwell, b. Rickmansworth England. Literary Translator; Screenwriter. *Education:* MA, Lincoln College, Oxford. *Publications:* Night of the Generals, 1962; Memories of Teilhard de Chardin, 1964; Klemperer Recollections, 1964; Brothers in Arms, 1965; Goya, 1965; Rodin, 1967; The Interpreter 1967; Alexander the Great, 1968; The Poisoned Stream, 1969; The Human Animal, 1971; Here in the Tower, 1972; Strength through Joy, 1973; Madam Kitty, 1973; A Time for Truth, 1974; The Boat, 1974; A Direct Flight to Allah, 1975; The Manipulation Game, The Night of the Long Knives, 1976; The Hittites;, 1977; Willie Brandt Memoirs, 1978; Canaris, 1979; Life with the Enemy, 1979; A German Love Story,

1980; Richard Wagner, 1983; The Middle Kingdom, 1983; Solo Run, 1984; Momo, 1985; The Last Spring in Paris, 1985; Invisible Walls, 1986; Mirror in the Mirror, 1986. Screen Credits: Tess (with Roman Polanski), 1979; The Boat, 1981; Pirates, 1986; The Name of the Rose, 1986. *Honours:* Schlegel Tieck Special Award, 1979; US PEN Prize, 1981. *Memberships:* Past Chairman, Translators Association; Society of Authors. *Address:* The Vine House, Nether Compton, Sherborne, Dorset DY9 4QA, England.

BROWNSTEIN, Ronald J, b. 4 June 1958, New York City, New York, USA. Journalist. m. Nina Easton, 27 May 1983, Los Angeles, California. *Education:* Honours, State University of New York, Binghamton, 1979. *Publications:* Who's Poisoning America?, editor, 1981; Reagan's Ruling Class, co-author, 1982, 83. *Contributions to:* Esquire; New Republic; Parade; Reader's Digest; Washington Monthly; New York Times; Los Angeles Times; Christian Science Monitor; Boston Gobe; Baltimore Sun; National Journal, White House correspondent. *Address:* National Journal, 1730 M Street North West, Washington, DC 20036, USA.

BROXON, Mildred 'Bubbles' Downey, b. 7 June 1944, Atlanta, Georgia, USA. Writer. m. William David Broxon, 15 Sep. 1969, Seattle, Washington (dec.). *Education:* BA, Psychology 1965, BS, Nursing 1970, Seattle University. *Publications include:* Novels: Eric Brighteyes 2: A Witch's Welcome (as Sigfriour Skaldaspillir), 1979; The Demon of Scattery, with Poul Anderson, 1979; Too Long a Sacrifice, 1981. Novelettes: Glass Beads, Vertex Magazine, 1975; Singularity, Isaac Asimov's Science Fiction Magazine, 1978 & others; Strength, with Poul Anderson, in, The Magic May Return, ed. Larry Niven, 1981; Sea Changeling, in Isaac Asimov's Science Fiction Magazine, 1981. *Contributions:* Short stories, numerous magazines, anthologies. *Memberships:* Vice President, Science Fiction Writers of America, 1976–78; Mystery Writers of America. *Literary Agent:* Jarvis, Braff Ltd, 260 Willard Avenue, Staten Island, NY 10314, USA.

BROZEN, Yale, b. 6 July 1917, Kansas City, Missouri, USA. Economist. *Education:* AS, Kansas City Junior College; BA, University of Chicago; PhD, University of Chicago. *Literary Appointments:* Editor, American Enterprise Institute Evaluative Studies Series. *Major Publications:* Workbook for Economics, 1946; Textbook for Economics, 1948; Automation: The Impact of Technological Change, 1963; Advertising & Society, 1974; Is Government the Source of Monopoly?, 1980; Mergers in Perspective, 1982; Concentration, Mergers & Public Policy, 1982. *Contributor to:* Journal of World Trade Law; Journal of Law & Economics; Antitrust Bulletin; Private Practice; Regulation. *Honour:* Emory University Prize for Outstanding Contribution to Scholarship on Law & Economics, 1982. *Address:* 1101 East 58th Street, Chicago, IL 60637, USA.

BRUALDI, Margaret Higbie, b. 3 Mar. 1924, Eveleth, Minnesota, USA. Editor. m. (1) Charles E Higbie, 21 Feb. 1948, London, England, (2) Richard Brualdi, 26 Aug. 1978, Madison, Wisconsin, USA; 3 sons, 1 daughter. *Education:* BA French, BA Linguistics, MA Linguistics, University of Wisconsin, USA. *Literary Appointments:* Editor, Business Manager, Ba Shiru (Journal of African Languages & Literature), 1980–. *Memberships:* African Literature Association; Co-ordinating Council of Literary Magazines. *Address:* 866 Van Hise Hall, University of Wisconsin, Madison, WI 53706, USA.

BRUBACH, Holly, b. 7 Dec. 1953, Pittsburgh, Pennsylvania, USA. Writer. *Education:* BA, English & History, Duke University, 1975. *Literary Appointments:* Staff Writer, Vogue Magazine, 1978–82; Staff Writer, The Atlantic Monthly, 1982; Contributing Editor, Vogue Magazine, 1982. *Contributions to:* Ballet News; Ballet Review; Vogue; Horizon; Saturday Review; New York Times Book Review. *Honour:* National Magazine Award in Essays & Criticism, 1982. *Literary Agent:* Amanda Urban, ICM. *Address:* c/o Amanda Urban, ICM, 40 West 57th Street, New York, NY 10019, USA.

BRUCE LOCKHART, Robin, b. 13 Apr. 1920, London, England. Stockbroker; Writer. *Education:* Royal Naval College, Dartmouth; Economics, Cambridge University. *Publications:* Ace of Spies, 1967; Halfway to Heaven – The Story of the Carthusian Order, 1985. *Contributor to:* Various newspapers including, Financial Times, (For Manager, 1946–52); Beaverbrook newspapers (various senior appointments, 1953–59). *Memberships:* Society of Sussex Authors. *Literary Agent:* Campbell Thomson & McLaughlin Ltd. *Address:* 37 Adelaide Crescent, Hove, Sussex BN3 2JL, England.

BRUCHAC, Joseph Edward III, b. 16 Oct. 1942, Saratoga Springs, NY, USA. Teacher; Writer. *Education:* BA, Cornell University, 1965; MA, Syracuse University, 1966; PhD, Union Graduate School, 1975. *Publications:* Indian Mountain (poetry), 1971; Entering Onondage (poetry), 1978; Translator's Son (poetry), 1983; Remembering the Dawn (poetry), 1983; The Dreams of Jesse Brown (novel), 1978; The Good Message of Handsome Lake (poems and Transls), 1979; Iroquois Stories (folklore), 1985; The Wind Eagle (folklore), 1985; Translator's Son (poetry), 1980; Remembering the Dawn (poetry), 1983. *Contributor to:* Hudson Review; Paris Review; Nation; American Poetry Review; etc. *Honours:* Writing Fellowship, Syracuse University, 1965–66; CAPS Grant, NY State, 1973; Grant, National Endowment for the Arts, 1974; Rockefeller Foundation Fellowship, 1982; NY State CAPS Grant, 1982; NEA/PEN Syndicated Fiction Award, 1983. *Memberships include:* American Branch PEN; Poetry Society of America. *Literary Agent:* McIntosh and Otis Agency. *Address:* PO Box 80, Greenfield Centre, NY 12833, USA.

BRUDNICKI, Jan Zdzislaw, b. 2 Nov. 1936, Ursynów, Poland. Editor; Critic. m. Maria Brudnicki, 26 July 1962, 1 daughter. *Education:* Warsaw University. *Literary Appointments:* Proxy of Head Editor, Nowy Wyraz, 1970–75; Secretary, Editorial Office, Poezja, 1975–. *Publications:* Zofia Nalkowska, 1969; Tadeusz Nowak, 1978; Weik Prozy, Century of Prose, 1979; Jerzy Zawieyski, 1985; Anthology of essays Pogranicza poezji, 1983; Elaboration, J. Zawieyski Memoir, Drama v. 1 – 1983, 1985. *Contributor to:* Poezja; Nowy Wyraz; Rocznik Literacki; Miesiecznik Literacki; Kierunki; Tygodnik Kulturalny; Kultura; Nowe Ksiazki; etc. *Honours:* Miesiecznik Literacki, 1979; Students of Red Rose, Czerwonejrozy, 1984. *Memberships:* Zwiazek Literatow Polskich; Society Polish Writers; International Association of Literary Critics; AICL. *Address:* Panstwowy Instytut Wydawniczy, 'Iskry', 'PAX', Ludowa Spóldzielnia Wydawnicza, Poland.

BRÜGMANN-EBERHARDT, Lotte, b. 1 Feb. 1921, Dortmund, Federal Republic of Germany. Journalist. m. Hans Brügmann, 9 July 1971, 3 daughters. *Publications:* Das zerstörte Gesicht, 1954; Die Halligfriesin, 1956; Ein Grab in fremder Erde, 1957; Das unselige Erbe derer von Waldern, 1958; Bedenk, was du versprichst, 1963; Liebe ist kin Unglück, 1965; Ein Licht entzünden, 1984; Ein bunter Kranz, 1985. *Contributions to:* Numerous German-speaking newspapers and other publications including: Städte in Schleswig-Holstein; Schriftsteller in Schleswig-Holstein-Heute, 1980; Musik-Ein Lesebuch Schleswig-Holsteinischer Autoren, 1981; Soli Deo Gloria Lyrik Anthologie, 1985. *Memberships:* Writers in Schleswig-Holstein; Eutiner Literary Circle. *Address:* Schillerstrasse 3, 23 Kiel, Federal Republic of Germany.

BRULOTTE, Gaetan, b. 8 Apr. 1945, Levis, Quebec, Canada. Writer. m. Dominique Rieuf, 16 Oct. 1982, France. *Education:* Certificate of Education, BA, Education, BA, Modern Languages & Literature, Diplome Ecole Normale Superience MA, French Studies, Laval University, Quebec; PhD, French Literature, La Sorbonne, Paris. *Appointments:* Member, several Literary Juries; Guest Speaker, USA, Canada, Europe; Director, several conferences on Literature; Founder, Director, Editor, Books Review Section, Trois-Rivieres's Daily newspaper, Le Nouvelliste; Founder, Director, Editor, Literary Review, Pretestes; Founder,

Director, Editor, En vrac; Direction, Production, Literary Programmes for CFCQFM; Plays, Scrips, CBC Radio, TV, Cinema, etc. *Publications:* L'Emprise, 1979; Le Surveillant, 1982; Les Messagers de l'Ascenseur, Le Client, 1983; Le colloque de Tanger, 1976; The Imaginary and the Writing, 1972; The Aspects of Erotic Literature, 1978. *Contributor to:* Numerous professional journals, magazines and newspapers. *Honours:* Laureat De l'Anlam, France, 1979; Prix Robert-Cliche, 1979; Prix Adrienne-Choquette, 1981; Prix France-Quebec, Paris, 1983; 1st Prize, Radio Drama Contest, CBC, 1983; The Book of the Month, Nos Livres. *Memberships:* International PEN Club; UNEQ, Montreal; Adelf, Paris; Sardec, Montreal; AQPF, Quebec; Canadian Writers Association, Board of Directors; Counsellor, Mauricie's Writers Society, President 1980–81, Director, 1982–83; etc. *Literary Agent:* Louise Myette, Montreal, Canada. *Address:* 17 Rue Larrey, 75005 Paris, France.

BRUNILA, Kai Daniel, b. 3 Apr. 1919, Helsinki, Finland. Author. m. (2) May-Britt Lindroos, 4 Aug. 1965, 1 son, 3 daughters. *Appointments:* Journalist, Hufvudstadsbladet, 1945–54, Nya Pressen, 1954–57; Managing Director, Publisher, Oy Williams Ab, 1957–76. *Publications:* Kaveringar, 1942; 100 ar pa boljan, 1956; Porkala ar vart, 1956; Finlands krig, 1983; Musical, Lyckosparken, 1959; revues, hundreds of Radio & TV programmes. *Contributor to:* Numerous magazines, journals and newspapers. *Address:* Ekeberga, 02550 Evitskog, Finland.

BRUNNER, Lillian Sholtis, b. Freeland, Pennsylvania, USA. Professional Nurse; Author. m. Mathias J Brunner, 6 Sep. 1951, New Haven, 1 son, 2 daughters. *Education:* Diploma, School of Nursing; BSc, University of Pennsylvania; MSN, Case Western Reserve University. *Appointments:* Editor, News Bulletin, Pennsylvania League for Nursing; Editor, Nursing Alumni Newsletter, School of Nursing, University of Pennsylvania Hospital; Editorial Boards: Five Nursing Periodicals; Nursing Life; Nursing and Health Care; Nursing '86; Nursing Reference Library; Topics in Clinical Nursing; Nursing Author, 1950–. *Publications:* Co-Author: Surgical Nursing, 2 editions, 1950, 1955; Eliason's Surgical Nursing, 11th edition 1959; Art of Clinical Instruction, 1959; Manual of Operating Room Technology, 1966; Textbook of Medical and Surgical Nursing, 5 editions, 1964–84; Lippincott Manual of Nursing Practice, 4 editions, 1974–86. *Contributor to:* Numerous professional journals. *Honours:* Recipient various honours and awards. *Memberships:* American Medical Writers' Association; Secretary, Vice President, Philadelphia Branch, National League of American Pen Women; National Secretary, National League of American Pen Women, 1984–86. *Address:* 1247 Berwyn-Paoli Road, Berwyn, PA 19312, USA.

BRUNSKILL, Ronald William, b. 3 Jan. 1929, Lowton, England. Architect; University Lecturer. *Education:* BA, Honours, Architecture, 1951, MA, 1952, PhD, 1963. Manchester University. *Publications:* Illustrated Handbook of Vernacular Architecture, 1971, 2nd edition 1978; Vernacular Architecture of the Lake Counties, 1974; English Brickwork, with Alec Clifton-Taylor, 1977; Houses, 1982; Traditional Building of Britain, 1982; Traditional Farm Buildings of Britain, 1982; Timber Building in Britain, 1985. *Contributor to:* Various architectural & archaeological journals. *Address:* School of Architecture, University of Manchester, Manchester M13 9PL, England.

BRUNSON, Dorothy E, President, Brunson Communications Inc. 2 sons. *Appointments:* Rodless Decorators, 1960–62; Assistant General Manager, Radio Station WWRL, 1964–68; Vice President, Marketing & Media Director, Howard Sanders Advertising Ltd, 1968–70; Vice President, Marketing & Media Director, Eden Advertising and communications Inc, 1970–72; General Manager, Radio Stations WLIB/WBLS, 1973–79; President, Brunson Communications Inc, 1979–. *Publications:* New York State Women's Commission – 15 Outstanding Women

Booklet, 1985; Black Woman's Career Guide, 1983; Baltimore Business & Living Journal, 1984; Glamour Magazine, 1985; etc. *Contributor to:* Metropolitan Magazine; Essence Magazine; PACE, 1984. *Honours:* Kizzy Award, 1982; Woman of the Year, Bio-Africa Inc; 1st Black Woman General Manager, Sation Owner, American Women in Radio & TV; Mayors Recognition Award; new York Women's SpecialCommission Recognition Award; Black Citizens for Fair Media, Pioneer Award, 1981; etc. *Memberships:* Park Heights Advisory Board, Baltimore; Harlem Commonwealth Council, New York City; John Hopkins Metro Centre, Baltimore, Chairman, Minority Committee; Kennedy Institute for Handicapped Children, etc. *Address:* 1922 W Peachtree St, Atlanta, GA 30309, USA.

BRUSEWITZ, Gunnar (Kurt), b. 7 Oct. 1924, Stockholm, Sweden, Author/Artist. m. Ingrid Andersson, 21 Oct. 1946, Irsta, 2 daughters. *Education:* Royal Academy of Art, Dr Phil. *Publications:* Include: Arstidsbockerna I – IV, Jakt, 1967; Bjornjagare Och Fjärilsmålare, 1968; Stockholm – Staden PÅ Landet, 1969; Skissbok, 1970; Sjö, 1972; Skog, 1974; Lång Vår, 1977; Strandspegling, 1979; Wings and Seasons, 1980; Arktisk sommar, 1981; Den Nöjsamma Nyttigheten, 1982; Solvarvets Tecken, 1983; Sveriges Natur – En Resa I Tid Och Rum, 1984. *Contributions to:* Stockholms – Tidningen 1947–60; Svenska Dagbladet 1961–; Several Swedish magazines and publications. *Honours include:* Stockholm City Presentation Prize, 1970; Dag Hammarskjold Medal, 1975; Phil Dr h c, University of Stockholm, 1982. *Memberships include:* Publicistklubben; PEN; Sv Förf.förbundet World Wildlife Fund, Swedish Section, 1976–; Royal Society of Science in Uppsala. *Literary Agent:* Wahlstrom and Widstrand forlag, Stockholm. *Address:* Lisinge, 762 00 Rimbo, Sweden.

BRUSSEL, Gust van, b. 12 Sep. 1924, Antwerp, Belgium. Public Relations Officer, Generale Bank, Antwerp. m. Guinée Monique 3 Feb. 1948, 8 sons, 4 daughters. *Major Publications:* De Visioenen van Jacques Weiniger, 1960; Het Labyrint, 1966; Cassandra en de Kalebas, 1967; Voor een Plymouth Belvedere, 1967; De Ring, 1969; Een Nacht met Aphrodite, 1979; Verlaten Landschag, 1980; Vader van Huwbare Dochters, 1983; De Waanzinnige Stad, 1984; De Abortus, 1985. Poetry and Fairy Tales. *Contributor to:* Magazines: Topics; Diogenes; Nieuw Vlaams Tÿdschrift; and others. SFAN Award, SF Novel, 1970. *Memberships:* Vereniging der Vlaamse Letterkundigen; Vereniging van de Schrijvers Voor de Jeugd; Literair Salon; Hendrik Consciencestichtung. *Address:* Quellinstraat 13 B 4, 2018 Antwerp, Belgium.

BRUST, Steven Karl Zoltan, b. 23 Nov. 1955, St Paul, Minnesota, USA. Writer. m. Reen M Kostamo, 29 Dec. 1974, St Paul, Minnesota, 1 son, 3 daughters. *Publications:* Thereg, 1983; To Reign in Hell, 1984 and 1985; Yendi, 1984; Brokedown Palace, 1986. *Memberships:* Science Fiction Writers of America; Executive Vice-President, Minnesota Science Fiction Society. *Literary Agent:* Valerie Smith. *Address:* 4880 106th Avenue NE, Circle Pines, MN 55014, USA.

BRUSTAT, Fritz Wilheilm Karl, b. 25 Nov. 1907, Stettin, Pomerania, Germany. Retired Civil Servant. *Education:* Captain, Master Mariner; Studies of Political Sciences, State University, Kiel. *Publications include:* Lichter uber dem Meer, 1950; Unternehmen Rettung, 1970; Windjammer auf grosser Fahrt, 1973; Kap Hoorn Saga, 1975; Leb wohl, Vineta, 1967; Fischer vor Island, 1953; Funfmal 100,000 Tonnen, 1973; China-Unterwegs im Reich der Mitte, 1976; Segel, Silber and Kanonen, (Anson-Story), 1978; Im Wind der Ozeane, 1980; Ali Cremer: U 333, 1982; Um Kopf und Kragen, 1982; Nasses Eichenlaub, 1983; 16 Books; documentary films; radio commentaries. *Contributor to:* Schiff und Zeit; Kohlers Flotten-Kalender; Schiff and Hafen/Kommandobrucke. *Honour:* Medaille Hommage de Amicale International des Capitaines au long Cours Cap Horniers, Saint Malo. *Memberships:* Schriftsteller in Schleswig-Holstein und Eutiner Kreis e V, Assn German

Writers; Recipient of Study Grant, Office for Foreign Affairs, 1968. *Literary Agent:* Literatur-Agentur Axel Poldner Munchen. *Address:* Blocksberg 8, 2300 Kiel 1, Federal German Republic.

BRUTON, Eric Moore, b. London, England. Publisher; Retailer. *Publications:* 11 Crime Novels, 1957–67; True Book about Clocks, 1957; True Books about Diamonds, 1961; Automation, 1962; Dictionary of Clocks & Watches, 1962; The Longcase Clock, 1964; Clocks & Watches 1400–1900, 1967; Clocks & Watches, 1968; Diamonds, 1970; Antique Clocks and Clock Collecting, 1974; History of Clocks & Watches, 1979; The Wetherfield Collection, 1980; Legendary Gems, 1986. *Honours:* Hanneman Award for Contribution to Gemmological Literature, USA, 1982. *Memberships:* Fellow, Counsellor, Gemmological Association of Great Britain; Fellow, Counsellor, British Horological Institute; Liveryman, Worshipful Company of Clockmakers; Liveryman, Worshipful Company of Turners; Freeman, Worshipful Company of Goldsmiths; President, National Association of Goldsmiths. *Literary Agent:* Elaine Greene Ltd, London. *Address:* Bentley Old Hall, Bentley, Ipswich, Suffolk IP8 3JX, England.

BRYAN, Evelyn McDaniel Frazier, b. 2 Apr. 1911, Hampton, South Carolina, USA. Writer. *Education:* AB, Winthrop College, South Carolina, USA, 1933; Various Postgraduate institutions. *Major Publications Include:* Hunting your Ancestors in South Carolina 2nd edition, 1974; Cemeteries of Upper Colleton County, South Carolina, 1975. *Contributor to:* Various magazines and newspapers, including The News & Courier, 1965–69; The State, Special Correspondent, 1965–72; Florida Times-Union. *Honours Include:* Lila Moore Stanton Awards, 1963, 1971, 1972; Numerous Prizes for Poetry, History, Musical composition etc; Numerous literary awards. *Memberships include:* Charter Member & Various offices, The Tea & Topics Literary Club; Various offices, Colonel Joseph Glover Chapter, Daughters of the American Revolution; National League of American Penwomen; General Federation of Women's Clubs; Numerous genealogical, literary and historical societies and associations; Jacksonville Art Museum. *Address:* Broadview Towers 3-B, 1596 Lancaster Terrace, Jacksonville, FL 32204, USA.

BRYANT, James Cecil, b. 21 Oct. 1931, Lake Wales, Florida, USA. College Professor. m. Marion Lois Carnett, 19 June 1955, Winter Haven, 2 sons. *Education:* BA, Stetson University; BD, MDiv, Southern Baptist Theological Seminary; MA, University of Miami; PhD, University of Kentucky. *Appointments:* Assistant Professor, Florida State University, Tallahassee; Associate, Professor, Mercer University, Atlanta; Editor, Basharat Magazine, 1977–. *Publications:* New Columbus, 1965; Indian Springs, 1971; Smooth Runs the Water, 1973; The Morningside Man, 1975; Charlie Brown Rembers Atlanta, 1982; Tudor Drama and Religious Controversy, 1984; The Atlanta Baptist Association, 1984; The Capital City Club, 1985. *Contributor to:* Over 100 articles in magazines, journals, newspapers. *Honours:* Georgia Author of the Year, 1973; Georgia Author of the Year in Biographical Writing, 1975; Special Award by Dixie Council of Authors and Journalists, 1983. *Memberships:* Atlanta Writers Club, President, 1976; Dixie Council of Authors and Journalists, Chairman, Board of Trustees, 1984–; Southeastern Renaissance Conference; Atlanta Press Club. *Address:* 1470 Leafmore Place, Decatur, GA 30033, USA.

BRYANT, Sylvia Leigh, b. 8 May 1947, Lynchburg, Virginia, USA. Editor; Publisher; Poet; Freelance Writer. *Education:* DLit, World University, 1981. *Appointment:* Editor/Publisher, Anthology Society. *Contributions:* Poetry in, Adventures in Poetry, anthology; The Poet; Adventures in Poetry Magazine; Modern Images; Hoosier Challenger; Animal World; etc. *Honours include:* International Poet Laureate, United Poets Laureate International 1979; Certificate of Merit, Accademia Leonardo da Vinci, 1980; Distinguished Service Citation, World Poetry Society, 1981; Gold

Medal, Accademia Leonardo da Vinci, 1980; Poet Laureate Programme, State of Virginia, 1981; etc. *Memberships:* International Academy of Poets; United Poets Laureate International; Dr Stella Woodall Poetry Society; World Poetry Society; Centro Studi e Scambi Internazionali-Accademia Leonardo da Vinci; National Trust for Historic Preservation; International Platform Association; etc. *Address:* 106 Garford Road, Madison Heights, VA 24572, USA.

BRYCE, (Mobley) James, b. 29 Aug. 1934, Arkansas, USA. Writer. m. Isabel Bryce, 15 Apr. 1984, Toronto, Canada, 3 sons. *Education:* AA, English, Valley College, Southern California. *Publications:* Reincarnation Now, 1979; Power Basics of Basketball, 1984; Power Basics of Soccer, 1984; Power Basics of Football, 1985; Power Basics of Auto Racing, 1985. *Contributor to:* Associate Editor, Expansion Magazine, USA Edition; Articles for Expansion Magazine, England. *Memberships:* Washington DC Independent Writers Guild; Writers Guild of America. *Literary Agent:* James Heacock, Santa Monica, California. *Address:* Heacock Literary Agency, 1523 Sixth Street # 14, Santa Monica, CA 90401, USA.

BRYCE-SMITH, Gillian, b. 28 Jan. 1935, Cambridge, England. Journalist. m. B H Bryce-Smith, 8 Sep. 1962, Cambridge, 1 son, 1 daughter. *Literary Appointments:* Editor, 'Sailplane and Gliding'. *Address:* 281 Queen Edith's Way, Cambridge, CB1 4NH, England.

BRYER, Alastair Robin Mornington, b. 13 May 1944, Mombasa, Kenya. Chartered Town Planner. m. Jennifer Sheridan Moir Skelton, Winchester, 19 Sep. 1976, 1 son. *Education:* BA, Honours, Dunelm; MRTPI. *Literary Appointments:* Honorary Editor, Royal Cruising Club Journal. *Major Publications:* Jolie Brise; A Tall Ship's Tale, 1982; Living in a Country House; Edinburgh, both in preparation. *Contributions to:* BBC Talks; The Planner; Hampshire; Swans Hellenic Cruises (lecturer). *Honour:* 2nd place, Book of the Sea Award, 1982. *Literary Agent:* Toby Eady & Associates. *Address:* Princes Place, Closworth, Yeovil, Somerset, England.

BRYNJULFSDOTTIR, Anna Kristin, b. 23 Dec. 1938, Reykjavik, Iceland. Writer. m. Elias Snaeland Jonsson, 24 June 1967, Arbaer Church, 3 sons. *Education:* Degrees, Reykjavik College, 1958. Teachers University, 1960; Courses in Latin and Greek, University of Iceland, 1983–. *Publications:* Books for children including, Tiny Miny, 1976; Gliding down the Rainbow, 1978; Julia and Snorri, 1979. *Membership:* Writers Union of Iceland. *Address:* Brekkutun 18, Box 24, 200 Kopavogur, Iceland.

BRYSON, William Hamilton, b. 29 July 1941, Richmond, Virginia, USA. Law Teacher. *Education:* BA, Hampden-Sydney College, 1963; LL B, Harvard University, 1967; LL M, University of Virginia, 1968; Christs College, Clare College, PhD, Cambridge University, England, 1972. *Appointment:* Professor, Law, University of Richmond, 1973–. *Publications:* Interrogatories and Depositions in Virginia, Charlottesville, 1969; Dictionary of Sigla and Abbreviations to and in Law Books before 1607, 1975; The Equity Side of the Exchequer, 1975; The Virginia Law Reporters Before 1880, 1977; A Census of Law Books in Colonial Virginia, 1978; Discovery in Virginia, 1978; Notes on Virginia Civil Procedure, 1979; A Bibliography of Virginia Legal History Before 1900, 1979; Legal Education in Virginia 1779-1979: A Biographical Approach, 1982; Handbook on Virginia Civil Procedure, 1983; Editor, Virginia Circuit Court Opinions, Volumes 1, 2, 1985. *Contributor to:* Numerous professional journals including: American Journal Legal History; University of Richmond Law Review. *Honours:* Phi Beta Kappa, 1963; Yorke Prize, Cambridge University Faculty of Law, 1973. *Memberships:* Fellow, Royal Historical Society; Selden Society, Correspondent for Virginia; American Society for Legal History, Board of Directors, 1981–84; Virginia Historical Society. *Address:* School of Law, University of Richmond, VA 23173, USA.

BUCHANAN, Robert Angus, b. 5 June 1930, Sheffield, England. University Reader. m, Brenda June Wade, 10 Aug. 1955, Sheffield, 2 sons. *Education:* BA, 1953, MA, 1957, PhD, 1957, St Catherine's College, Cambridge. *Publications:* Technology and Social Progress, 1965; Industrial Archaeology in Britain, 1972; History and Industrial Civilization, 1979; Brunel's Bristol, 1982; Industrial Archaeology of the Bristol Region, with Neil George Watkins, 1976. *Contributor to:* Transactions of the Newcomen Society; Victorian Studies, volume 26, 1983; Economic History Review, volume 38, 1985. *Address:* Centre for the History of Technology, University of Bath, Claverton Down, Bath BA2 7AY, England.

BUCHMAN, Marion, b. USA. Poet. Div. *Education:* PhD in Letters. *Literary Appointments:* Instructor in Prosody, Universities and colleges in Washington, DC, Pippa Passes, Kentucky and in Baltimore, Maryland. *Publications include:* A Voice in Ramah, poems, 1959; America, 1976. *Contributions include:* Cheltenham Anthology of Prize Poems; Arizona Review; Redbook; Poetry Review; Maryland English Journal; Stroud Festival Anthology Award Poems. *Honours Include:* Over 100 international poetry awards including Cheltenham Prize of Great Britain, 1969. *Memberships:* Poetry Society of America; London Poetry Secretariat. *Address:* 5955 D Pimlico Road, Baltimore, MD 21209, USA.

BUCHWALD-PELC, Paulina Maria, b. 4 June 1934, Poznan, Poland. Professor, Polish Literature. *Education:* Studies of Polish Philosophy. University of Poznan; PhD, 1970. *Publications:* Malpaczlowiek Anonimowa satyra z XVIII w, 1966; Satyra czasow saskich, 1969; Aleksander Augezdecki, 1972; Stare i nowe w czasach saskich, 1978; Polskie druki emblematyczne, 1981. *Contributor to:* Pamietnik Literacki. *Memberships:* Literary Society of Adam Michiewiez; Society of Friends, of Books. *Address:* ul Baleya 7m 61, 02-132 Warsaw, Poland.

BUCK, Paul Francis, b. 10 Aug 1946, Woolwich, London, England. Poet. 1 son. *Literary Appointments:* Member, Literary Advisory Panel, Yorkshire Arts Association, 1973–77; Editor of Curtains Magazine; Guest Editor of Spectacular Diseases Magazine. *Publications:* Pimot, 1968; The Honeymoon Killers, 1970; RE/QUI/RE(QUI)RE, 1976; Lust, 1976; Studies towards a Portrait, 1979; XXXX5, 1980; Violations, 1980; Turkish Delight, 1982; Editor of Anthologies: Voix-Off/Angleterre, Matières d'Angleterre, Violent Silence. *Contributor to:* Curtains; Spanner; Change; Temblor; Obliques; Poetry Review; Spectacular Diseases, Exit; In'Hui; Ear in a Wheatfield, etc. *Honours:* YAA Writer's Bursary; SEA Writer's Bursary. *Membership:* Association of Little Presses; SET International. *Literary Agent:* Valerie Hoskins. *Address:* 4 Bower Street, Maidstone, Kent ME16 8SD, England.

BUCKLEY, Peter Martin, b. 23 May 1938, Connecticut, USA. Writer/Editor. *Education:* BA, Duke University. *Literary Appointments:* Editor, Plays and Players (UK), 1972; Editor, East/West Network (Publishers of Magazines) 1973–80; Associate/Contributing Editor, Vanity Fair, 1983–. *Publication:* No Time Lost, 1982. *Contributions to:* UK: Plays and Players; Films and Filming; Sight and Sound; Time Out; The Observer. US: Rolling Stone; Vogue; Gentleman's Quarterly; Vanity Fair; Horizon; Historical Preservation; Travel and Leisure etc. *Literary Agent:* Lynn Seligman, Julian Bach Ltd, New York City. *Address:* 160 Bleecker Street, New York, NY 10012, USA.

BUCZACKI, Stefan Tadeusz, b. 16 Oct. 1945, Derby, England. Writer; Broadcaster. m. Beverley Ann Charman, 8 Aug. 1970, Ampfield, Hampshire, 2 sons. *Education:* BSc (1st Class Hons), Botany, Southampton University; D.Phil, Forestry, Oxford University. *Publications:* Collins Guide to the Pests, Diseases and Disorders of Garden Plants, 1981; Collins Gem Guide to Mushrooms and Toadstools, 1982; Collins Shorter

Guide to the Pests, Diseases and Disorders of Garden Plants, 1983; Zoosporic Plant Pathogens, 1983; Best Garden Pests and Diseases, 1985; Gardeners Questions Answered, 1985. *Contributions to:* The Times; Financial Times; Country Life; Sunday Telegraph; Geographical Magazine; Countryman; House and Garden; Vogue; Woman; Amateur Gardening; Practical Gardening; Horticulture Industry; Big Farm Management, etc. Over 70 scientific papers to major journals. *Memberships:* Institute of Biology; Institute of Horticulture; Associate, Royal Photographic Society; Fellow, Linnean Society. *Literary Agent:* Carol Smith, London. *Address:* c/o Carol Smith Literary Agency, 25 Hornton Court, Kensington High Street, London W8 7RT, England.

BUDDEE, Paul Edgar, b. 12 Mar. 1913, Perth, Western Australia, Australia. Author. *Publications include:* Stand To and Other War Poems, 1943; Osca and Olga Trilogy, 1955; Unwilling Adventurers, 1967, 79; Mystery of Moma Island, 1969; Escape of Fenians, 1972; Opal, series, 12 books, 1972; Escape of John O'Reilly, 1973; Call of Sky, 1978; What Happened to the Artful Dodger?, 1984; Jud Mudbury–Parkhurst Boy, 1986. *Contributions to:* All Australian newspapers and publications, literary journals and educational magazines. *Honours:* Citizen of the Year Award for outstanding service to State in art, culture and entertainment, 1977; Grants, Literary Board of Australia, 1977, 78, 84. *Memberships:* Past President, Fellowship of Writers, Western Australia; Australian Society of Authors. *Address:* 11 The Parapet, Willetton, WA 6155, Australia.

BUDOFF, Penny Wise, b. 7 July 1939, Albany, New York, USA. Physician; Researcher; Author. m. Seymour L Budoff, 24 June 1962, 1 son, 1 daughter. *Education:* BA, Syracuse University and University of Wisconsin, 1959; MD, State University of New York Upstate Medical Center, 1963. *Publications:* No More Menstrual Cramps and Other Good News, 1980; No More Hot Flushes and Other Good News, 1983. *Contributor to:* Numerous professional journals, magazines, newspapers including, Ladies Home Journal; Bazaar; Mademoiselle; Ladies Circle; Ms; McCalls; Womens Day; Journal of the American Medical Association; Journal of Reproductive Medicine; New England Journal of Medicine; Female Patient; Sexual Medicine Today; etc. *Honours:* New York Times Best Sellers List, 4 weeks for, No More Hot Flashes and Other Good News; Woman of the Year, C W Post College, Greenvale, New York, Ford Foundation Early Admissions 4-year College Scholarship. *Literary Agent:* Sandra Elkin, New York. *Address:* 11 Fairbanks Blvd, Woodbury, NY 11797, USA.

BUENO DE MESQUITA, Bruce James, b. 24 Nov. 1946, New York City. University Professor. m. Arlene Carol Steiner, 11 Aug. 1968, New York, 1 son, 2 daughters. *Education:* BA, Queens College, 1967; MA, 1968, PhD, 1971, University of Michigan. *Publications:* Strategy, Risk and Personality in Coalition Politics, 1975; India's Political System, with Richard Park, 1979; The War Trap, 1981; Forecasting Political Events: The Future of Hong Kong, with David Newman and Alvin Rabushka, 1985. *Contributions to:* International Studies Quarterly; American Political Science Review; Review of International Studies; Journal of Conflict Resolution; Chicago Tribune; Comparative Strategy; Social Science Review etc. *Honours:* Dag Hammarskjold Memorial Award, 1966; Guggenheim Fellow, 1977; Karl Deutsch Award, 1985. *Address:* Department of Political Science, University of Rochester, Rochester, NY 17627, USA.

BUERO-VALLEJO, Antonio, b. 29 Sep. 1916, Guadalajara. Playwright. m. Victoria Rodriquez, 5 Mar. 1959, Madrid, Spain, 2 sons. *Education:* BA, Fine Arts Studies. *Publications:* Story of a Stairway; The Words in the Sand; In the Burning Darkness; The Dream Weaver; The Awaited Sign; Almost a Fairytale; Dawn; Irene or the Treasure; Today's a holiday; The Cards Face Down; A Dreamer for a People; The Ladies in Waiting; Concert a Saint Ovide; Adventure in Gray; The Basement Window; Myth (Libreto for an Opera); The Sleep of Reason; The Foundation; God's Arrival; The Double Case History of Doctor Valmy; Three Masters Before the Public (Essays); The Shot; Judges in the Night; The Immovable Terror; Alligator; Secret Dialogue. *Honours:* Prizes: Lope de Vega, 1949; Amigos de los Quintero, 1949; Maria Rolland, 1956, 58, 60; Fundacion March, 1956; Nacional de Teatro, 1957, 58, 59, 60; Critica de Barcelona, 1958; ElEspectador y la Critica, 1967, 70, 74, 76, 77, 81, 84; Leopoldo Cano, 1967, 70, 73, 74, 76; Mayte, 1974; Poro Teatral, 1974; Officer des Palmes Academiques Prancaises, 1980. *Memberships:* The Real Academia Espanola; The Hispanic Society of America; International Committee of the Theatre of Nations; Honorary Fellow: The American Association of Teachers of Spanish and Portuguese; Society of Spanish and Spanish-American Studies, Modern Language Association of America; Member, Deutscher Hispanisten-Verband, Circulo de Bellas Artes de Madrid; Fellow, Sociedad General de Autores de Espana; Ateneo de Madrid. *Address:* General Diaz Porlier 36, 28001 Madrid, Spain.

BUFORD, William Holmes, b. 6 Oct. 1954, USA. Editor, Journalist. *Education:* BA Highest Honours, University of California, Berkeley, USA; MA Cantab, University of Cambridge, England. *Literary Appointments:* Editor, Granta, 1979. *Contributions to:* New Statesman; Times Literary Supplement; Sunday Times; Harpers. *Memberships:* Society of British Editors. *Literary Agent:* Gillon Aitken. *Address:* Granta, 44a Hobson Street, Cambridge CB1 1NL, England.

BULA, Allan, b. 28 July 1931, Southwest London, England. Freelance Writer. m. Angela Finch, 15 June 1957, Ewell, Surrey, 1 son, 2 daughters. *Education:* BSc, Economics. *Publications:* Aphorisms in, 1,001 Logical Laws, 1979; What is a Wife?, 1982. *Contributions:* Essay, Quartet, 1964, British Journal of Aesthetics, 1964; Reflections, The Indexer, 1981, 1982, Sunrise, USA, 1954; etc. *Memberships:* Honorary Secretary 1978–82, British Amateur Press Association; Chairman 1973–80, Guildford Writers Circle; Media Network; The Fossils, USA; Thoreau Society, USA. *Address:* 73 Wickham Avenue, Bexhill-on-Sea, East Sussex, TN39 3ES, England.

BULMER-THOMAS, Ivor, b. 30 Nov. 1905, Cwmbran, Wales. *Education:* St John's & Magdalen Colleges (Hon Fellow 1985), Oxford; MA Oxon. *Publications:* Coal in the New Era, 1934; Greek Mathematics, 1939–42; The Party System in Great Britain, 1953; Growth of the British Party System, 1965. *Contributor to:* Dictionary of Scientific Biography; Classical Review; Times Literary Supplement; Editorial Staff, The Times, 1930–37; Chief Leader Writer, News Chronicle, 1937–39; Leader Writer, Acting Deputy Editor, Daily Telegraph, 1952–56. *Honours:* DSc, University of Warwick; Stella della Solidarieta, Italiana, 1948; CBE, 1984. *Memberships:* FSA, London; Athenaeum; International Institute of Differing Civilizations; Societe Europeenne de Culture. *Address:* 12 Edwardes Square, London W8 6HG, England.

BULPIN, Thomas Victor, b. 31 Mar. 1918, Umkomaas, Natal, South Africa. Author; Publisher. *Education:* St Johns College, Johannesburg. *Publications:* Lost Trails on the Lowveld, 1950; Shaka's Country, 1952; The Ivory Trail, 1954; Islands in a Forgotten Sea, 1958; Trail of the Cooper King, 1959; The White Whirlwind, 1961; The Hunter is Death, 1968; To the Banks of the Zambezi, 1965; Lost Trails of the Transvaal, 1965; Natal & the Zulu Country, 1966; Discovering Southern Africa, 1970; Tickey, the Story of a Clown, 1976; Southern Africa, Land of Beauty, 1976; Illustrated Guide to Southern Africa, 1978; Senic Wonders of Southern Africa, 1985. *Contributor to:* Cape Times; Geographical Journal; Cape Argus; Spotlight. *Address:* Box 1516, Cape Town 8000, Republic of South Africa.

BUNCE, Linda Susan, b. 13 Mar. 1956, Enfield, England. Writer. m. James Mortimer Bunce, 25 Mar 1972, Divorced 1979, 1 son 1 daughter. *Publications:*

Honesty, 1980, 1981; Pretties 1981, 1982; Sisters 1983. *Literary Agent:* Imogen Parker, Curtis Brown, 162-68 Regent Street, London. *Address:* 48 Kynaston Road, Enfield, Middlesex, England.

BUNTING, John Reginald, b. 12 Nov. 1916, Mansfield, England. Educator; Chief Federal Adviser on Education, Federation of Nigeria; Former Director General, Centre for Educational Development Overseas & Former Adviser, Education, The British Council. m. May Hope Sturdy, 7 Dec. 1940, Munro College, Jamaica, West Indies. *Education:* MA, University of Oxford; Diploma, Education. *Publications:* Civics for Self Government, 1956; For East Africa, 1961, For Caribbean, 1960; Books 5 & 6 Primary English Course, Nigeria, 1960, Ghana, 1962, Sierra Leone, 1969, West Cameroon, 1971; Civics, A Course in Citizenship & Character Training, 1973; To Light a Candle – Problems of Education in the Developing Commonwealth & Britain, 1976. *Contributor to:* Honorary Joint Editor, West African Journal of Education, 1957–60; Consultant Editor, Books for All, Britains Contribution, UK National Commission for UNESCO, 1972. *Honours:* Coronation Medal, 1953; CBE 1965. *Address:* 8 Springhill Gardens, Lyme Regis, Dorset DT7 3HL, England.

BUNYAN, Hector, b. 8 Oct. 1947, Georgetown, Guyana. Playwright; Letter Carrier (part-time). m. Brenda Chin Chan, 26 July 1969, Toronto, Canada, 1 son, 1 daughter. *Education:* BTech Business Management, Ryerson Polytechnic Institute; MA, Educational Planning, Ontario Institute for Studies in Education. *Literary Appointments:* Writer-in-Residence, Theatre Passe Muraille, Toronto, 1981–82; Writer-in-Residence, June 1984 to August 1984. *Publications:* Plays produced: Prodigals in a Promised Land, 1981; Three Beats to a Bar, 1984; This One For You (planed production May 1986). *Honour:* Canada Council Awardee, 1985–86. *Membership:* Playwrights Union of Canada. *Address:* 1509 Davenport Road, Unit 2, Toronto, Ontario, Canada M6H 2H9.

BURCHARD, Peter Duncan, b. 1 Mar. 1921, Washington DC, USA. Writer. m. Elizabeth R Chamberlain, 23 Mar. 1946, New York, New York, 1 son, 2 daughters. *Education:* Diploma, Philadelphia College of Art, 1947. *Literary Appointments:* Guggenheim Fellowship, 1966. *Publications:* The River Queen, 1958; The Carol Moran, 1959; Jed, 1960; Balloons: From Paper Bags to Skyhooks, 1960; North by Night, 1962; One Gallant Rush: Robert Gould Shaw and His Brave Black Regiment, 1965; Stranded: A Story of New York in 1875, 1967; Bimby, 1968; Chito, 1969; Pioneers of Flight, 1970; Rat Hell, 1971; A Quiet Place, 1972; The Deserter, 1973; Harbor Tug, 1974; Whaleboat Raid, 1977; Ocean Race: A Sea Venture, 1978; Chinwe, 1979; Digger, 1980; First Affair, 1981; Sea Change, 1984; Venturing: An Introduction to Sailing, 1986. *Contributions to:* Interplay; Connoisseur; Small Boat Journal. *Honours:* William Allen White Award, 1961; Lewis Carroll Shelf Award, 1961. *Memberships:* Author's Guild; American Chapter, International PEN. *Address:* 943 Boston Post Road, Madison, CT 06443, USA.

BURCHFIELD, Robert William, b. 27 Jan. 1923, Wanganui, New Zealand. Lexicographer; Grammarian. m. (1) Ethel May Yates, 2 July 1949, Palmerston North, New Zealand, 1 son, 2 daughters. Divorced 1976, (2) Elizabeth Austen Knight, 5 Nov. 1976, London. *Education:* MA, Victoria University of Wellington, 1948; BA, 1951, MA, 1955, Magdalen College, Oxford, England. *Appointments:* Lecturer, English, Christ Church, Oxford, 1953–57; Editor, A Supplement to the Oxford English Dictionary, 1957–86. *Publications:* The Oxford Dictionary of English Etymology, co-author, 1966; A Supplement to the Oxford English Dictionary, Volume I, 1972, II 1976, III 1982, IV 1986; The Spoken Word, 1981; The English Language, 1985; The New Zealand Pocket Oxford Dictionary, 1986. *Contributor to:* Times Literary Supplement; Encounter; Translations Philological Society; etc. *Honours:* CBE, 1975; Hon D

Litt, Liverpool, 1978; Hon D Lit, Wellington, New Zealand, 1983. *Membership:* Early English Text Society, Secretary 1955–62, Member of Council, 1968–80. *Address:* 14 The Green, Sutton Courtenay, Oxfordshire OX14 4AE, England.

BURGESS, Anthony, b. 25 Feb. 1917, Manchester, England. Novelist; Critic. m. Liliana Macellari, 9 Oct. 1968, 1 son. *Education:* BA, Honours, LLD, Manchester. *Appointments:* Professor, University of North Carolina, 1970; Princeton University, 1971; Distinguished Professor, City College, New York, 1972–75; Literary Adviser, Tyrone Guthrie Theatre, Minneapolis, 1972–75; Literary Critic, Observer. *Publications:* (TV Scripts include) Moses the Lawgiver and Jesus of Nazareth (series), 1977; Blooms of Dublin, 1983; (Books) Time for a Tiger, 1956; The Enemy in the Blanket, 1958; Beds in the East, 1959; The Right to an Answer, 1960; The Doctor is Sick, 1960; The Worm and the Ring, 1961; Devil of a State, 1961; A Clockwork Orange, 1962 (filmed 1971); The Wanting Seed, 1962; Honey for the Bears, 1963; The Novel Today, 1963; Language Made Plain, 1964; Nothing Like the Sun, 1964; The Eve of Saint Venus, 1964; A Vision of Battlements, 1965; Here Comes Everybody – an Introduction to James Joyce, 1965; Tremor of Intent, 1966; A Shorter Finnegans Wake, 1966; The Novel Now, 1967; Urgent Copy, 1968; Shakespeare, 1970; MF, 1971; Napoleon Symphony, 1974; Moses, 1976; Abba Abba, 1977; New York, 1977; Ernest Hemingway and His World, 1978; Where the Ice Cream Grows, 1979; Earthly Powers, 1980; On Going to Bed, 1982; This Man and Music, 1982; The End of World News, 1982; Ninety-Nine Novels, 1984; (TV Scripts) translated Rostand, Cyrano de Bergerac, 1971; translated Sophocles, Oedipus the King, 1973; as Joseph Kell: One Hand Clapping, 1961; Inside Mr Enderby, 1963; As John Burgess Wilson, English Literature; A Survey for Students, 1958. *Contributor to:* Observer; Spectator; Listener; Encounter; Queen; Times Literary Supplement; Hudson Review; Holiday; Playboy; American Scholar; etc. *Honours:* Premio Branca, 1981; Critic's Award, UK, 1979; US Gold Medal, 1971; Christopher Award, 1975. *Address:* 44 rue Grimaldi, Principality of Monaco.

BURGESS, Lorraine Marshall, b. 13 May 1913, Chicago, Illinois, USA. Garden Writer and Photographer. m. Guy Burgess, 1 Dec. 1945, Elko, Nevada, 2 sons. *Education:* BFA, University of Illinois; MFA, Colorado College. *Publications:* Garden Makers Answer Book, 1975; Garden Art, 1981. Editor: Garden Ideas Annual, 1974, 75. *Contributions to:* American Horticulturist, 10 years; Horticulture; House and Garden; Gardens for All; Womans Day. *Honour:* US National Garden Bureau, 1984. *Membership:* Fellow, Garden Writers of America. *Literary Agent:* Fran Collin, New York. *Address:* 202 Old Broadmoor Road, Colorado Springs, CO 80906, USA.

BURGETT, Gordon Lee, b. 17 June 1938, Chicago, USA. Lecturer; Writer; Publisher. m. Judith Anne Litsinger, 22 Jan. 1961, Park Ridge, 2 daughters. *Education:* MA, Latin American Studies, University of Illinois, 1960; MA, Luso-Brazilian Studies, University of Wisconsin, 1962; MFT, L A Foreign Trade, Thunderbird Graduate School of International Management, 1962; MA, Latin American History, Northern Illinois University, 1970. *Publications:* The Query Book, 1980; Ten Sales From One Article Idea, 1982; How to Sell 75% of Your Freelance Writing, 1984; Speaking for Money, with Mike Frank, 1985; Query Letters/Cover Letters: How They Sell Your Writing, 1985. *Contributor to:* Over 900 articles in various journals including, Better Homes and Gardens; Travel; Dynamic Years; Modern Bride; The Runner; The Lion; Jack and Jill; Better Camping; etc.; most major Newspapers in USA; Hundreds of Comedy Greeting Cards. *Membership:* American Society of Journalists and Authors; National Speakers' Assocation. *Address:* 537 Arbol Verde St, Carpinteria, CA 93013, USA.

BURGHARDT, Walter John, b. 10 July 1914, New York City, USA. Priest; Theologian. *Education:* MA

1937, PhL 1938, Ordained 1941, STL 1941. Woodstock College, Maryland; STD, The Catholic University of America, 1957. *Literary Appointments:* Managing Editor, 1946–67, Editor 1967–, Theological Studies; Co-editor, Woodstock Papers, 1957–67; Co-editor, Ancient Christian Writers', 1958–. *Publications:* The Image of God in Man According to Cyril of Alexandria, 1957; The Testimony of the Patristic Age Concerning Mary's Death, 1957; All Lost in Wonder: Sermons on Theology and Life, 1960; Saints and Sanctity, 1965; Towards Reconciliation, booklet, 1974; Seven Hungers of the Human Family, booklet, 1977; Tell The Next Generation: Homiliesand Near Homilies, 1980; Sir, We Would Like to See Jesus: Homilies From a Hilltop, 1982; Seasons That Laugh or Weep: Musings on the Human Journey, 1983; The Charter of Maryland; 1632, 1965, 1983, booklet, 1983; He Can Deal Gently: The Catholic Priest 23 to 83, booklet; Still Proclaiming Your Wonders: Homilies for The Eighties, 1984; As Editor: The Idea of Catholicism, (with William F Lynch), 1960; Woman: New Dimensions, 1977; Religious Freedom: 1965 and 1975. A Symposium on a Historic Document, 1977; Why The Church?, (with William G Thompson), 1977. *Contributions to:* Numerous varied magazines and journals. *Honours include:* 12 Honorary Degrees. *Memberships include:* The Association Internationale d'Etudes Patristiques; The Catholic Commission on Intellectual and Cultural Affairs; The North American Patristic Society; The Mariological Society of America; North American Academy of Ecumenists; The Catholic Theological Society of America; The American Theological Society. *Address:* Jesuit Community, Georgetown Unversity, Washington, DC 20057, USA.

BURKE, A E Bricard, b. 4 Mar. 1951, Montreal, Canada. Writer. *Education:* BA English, Magna cum laude; MA, BEd, Diplomas in elementary and secondary school teaching; PhD Candidate, Canadian Literature. *Literary Appointments:* Prairie Correspondent, Poetry Canada; Feature Writer, Cross-Canada Writers' Quarterly; Literary Editor, The Prairie Journal; In-House Editor, Prairie Journal Press. *Major Publications:* The Beginning of the Sky, 1986; Matricide, 1986; Three sections, ABCMA (vols. 3,4 and to appear). *Contributor to:* The Prairie Journal of Canadian Literature (Literary editor); Canadian Poetry; The Canadian Review; Essays on Canadian Writing; Dandelion; Blue Buffalo; Poetry Canada Review; Cross-Canada Writers Quarterly; The Calgary Herald; Prairie Fire. *Honours:* Loyola Scholar, 1972; Ontario Government Scholarships and Quebec Government Scholarships, York University Scholarship, 1972–73; Humanities Research Council Fellowship, 1978. *Memberships:* Canadian Studies Association; Humanities Association; Association of Canadian & Quebec Literatures; Association for Canadian Theatre History; Alberta Writers' Association; and others. *Address:* Prairie Journal Press, c/o PO Box G997, Station G, Calgary, Alberta T3A 3G2, Canada.

BURKE, John Frederick, b. 8 Mar. 1922, Rye, Sussex, England. Freelance Writer. *Publications include:* Swift Summer, 1949; Echo of Barbara, 1959; Suffolk, 1971; Sussex, 1974; The Eye Stones, 1975; English Villages, 1975; The Devil's Footsteps, 1976; Czechoslovakia, 1976; The Florian Signet, 1977; Lady Grove, 1978; The Figurehead, 1979; Look Back on England, 1980; Musical Landscapes, 1983; Roman England, 1984; Editor, Tales of Unease, Series; Film Novelisation of Look Back in Anger and numerous other titles. *Contributor to:* New Frontiers; New Worlds; Science Fantasy; Country Life. *Honour:* Atlantic Award in Literature, Rockefeller Foundation, 1948–49. *Literary Agent:* David Higham Associates. *Address:* 8 North Parade, Southwold, Suffolk, England.

BURKE, John Joseph, b. 4 May 1942, Buffalo, New York, USA. Professor. m. Mary Katherine Koob, 9 Aug. 1969, Shawnee Mission, 1 son, 3 daughters. *Education:* AB, Boston College, 1967; MA, Northwestern University, 1968; PhD, UCLA, 1974. *Appointments:* Acting Assistant Professor, 1974–79, Associate Professor, 1979–85, Professor, 1985–, University of Alabama. *Publications:* Signs and Symbols on Chaucer's Poetry, 1981; The Unknown Samuel Johnson, 1983. *Contributor:* Albion; South Atlantic Review: Studies in the Novel; Eighteenth-Century Studies; ECCB; Studies in Eighteenth-Century Culture; Philological Quarterly; Clio. *Memberships:* American Society for Eighteenth-Century Studies; Southeastern American Society for Eighteenth-Century Studies, Executive Board, 1985–88; Modern Language Association. *Address:* Department of English, Drawer AL, Unviersity of Alabama, University, AL 35486, USA.

BURKE, Martyn John, b. 4 June 1951, Limerick, Ireland. Hospital Worker; Freelance Lecturer. m. Petra van Ierssel, 18 Apr. 1983, St Niklaas, Belgium. *Literary Appointments:* Editor, The Green Door, 1981; Belgian Editor Poet/India, 1982. *Publications:* Hellas, 1984; Zanjan, 1985; Ko, 1986,. *Contributor to:* Poems, stories and essays in New Irish Writing, Deus Ex Machina (Belgium); Bitterroot (USA) and many others. *Honour:* Doctorate in Literature (honorary) The World University, Arizona, USA, 1982. *Membership:* World Poetry Society. *Address:* Walburgstraat 1, 2700 St Niklaas, Belgium.

BURKHART, Paul Logan, b. 30 Sep. 1945, USA. Editor, Publisher. m. Leslie Johnson, 18 Nov. 1982, Vancouver, 1 son. *Education:* BA, Yale/Kenyon: Professional Teaching Certificate, University of British Columbia; MA, Guelph. *Literary Appointments:* Editor/Publisher, Pacific Yachting magazine, 1982; Editor in Chief, Canadian Yachting magazine, 1985; Editorial Director, Special Interest Publications, Maclean Hunter, 1985. *Publications:* Publisher: Pacific Yachting Cruising Guide to British Columbia, Volume III 1983, Volume IV 1984. *Memberships:* Outdoor Writers Association of America. *Address:* Special Interest Publications, 202 1132 Hamilton Street, Vancouver, British Columbia, V6B 2S2, Canada.

BURKITT, Denis Parsons, b. 28 Feb. 1911, Northern Ireland. Surgeon, Cancer Epidemiology. m. Olive Rogers, 28 July 1943, 3 daughters. *Education:* MB, B CH, BAC, 1935; FRCS Ed, 1938; MD, 1946; Postgraduate Surgical Training, 1935–41; Surgeon, RAMC, 1941–46; Joined HM Colonial Service, Uganda, 1946. *Appointments:* Government Surgeon, Uganda, Lecturer, Surgery, Makerere University College Medical School, 1946–64; Senior Consultant Surgeon, Ministry of Health, Uganda, 1961–64; Medical Research Council, External Scientific Staff, Uganda, 1964–66, London, 1966–76; Honorary Senior Research Fellow, St Thomas's Hospital Medical School, London, 1976–. *Publications:* Co-Editor, Treatment of Burkitt's Lymphoma, 1967; Burkitt's Lymphoma, 1970; Refined Carbohydrate Foods and Disease, 1975; Don't Forget the Fibre in Your Diet, 1979; Western Diseases: Their Emergence and Prevention, 1981; Dietary Fibre, Fibre-Depleted Foods and Disease, 1985. *Contributor to:* Over 300 Scientific articles in various journals and magazines. *Honours:* Harrison Prize, Royal Society of Medicine, 1964; Stuart Prize, British Medical Association, 1966; Walker Prize, Royal College of Surgeons, 1971; Gold Medals, Society of Apothecaries, London, 1972, British Medical Association, 1978; Arnott Gold Medal, Irish Hospitals and Medical Schools Association, 1968; Recipient, several awards from USA including Bristol-Myers Award for Distinguished Achievement on Cancer Research, 1982; The Charles Mott General Motors Award for Cancer Research, 1982; Gairdner Foundation Award, Canada, 1973; Paul Ehrlich-Ludwig Darmstaedter Gold Medal, 1972; Diplome de Medaille d'or, Academie de Medecine, France, 1982; Beaumont Bonelli Award, Italy, 1983; Recipient, numerous Honorary Degrees & Fellowships. *Memberships include:* East African Association of Surgeons; Brazilian Society of Surgery; Sudan Association of Surgeons; etc. *Address:* The Old House, Buslage, Stroud, Gloucestershire GL6 8AX, England.

BURLAND, Brian Berkeley, b. 23 Apr. 1931, Paget, Bermuda. Novelist; Poet; Scenarist. m. Edwina Ann Trentham, 7 July 1962, Somerset, Bermuda, 2 sons, 2 daughters. *Education:* Aldenham School; Oxford and

Cambridge Joint Board School Certificate, 1948; Graduate English, the Novel and Drama, University of Western Ontario, London, 1948–51. *Literary Appointments:* Seminars on the Novel, University College, London, 1971; Seminar on the Novel, Washington and Lee, Virginia, 1973; Writer-in-Residence, Southern Seminary, Virginia, 1973; Seminars on the Novel, American School, London, 1974; Conductor, writing workshop, 3 weeks, Bermuda Writers Conference, 1978; Teacher, Creative Writing Workshop, University of Hartford, 1981–82; Guest Fellow, Sillimen & Calhoun Colleges, Workshop on Novel, Yale, 1982–83. *Publicatons:* A Fall from Aloft, 1968; A Few Flowers for St George, 1970; Undertow, 1971; The Sailor and the Fox, 1973; Surprise, 1974; Stephen Decatur, The Devil and the Endymion, 1975; The Flight of the Cavalier, 1980; Love is a Durable Fire, 1985. Poetry: To Celebrate a Happiness That is America, 1971; (For children): St Nicholas and the Tub, 1984. *Contributions to:*Vogue, London. *Honour:* Individual Artist Grant, Connecticut Committee on the Arts, 1984. *Memberships:* Fellow, Royal Society of Literature; The Authors Guild Inc; The Authors League of America, Inc. *Literary Agent:* Murray Pollinger, 4 Garrick Street, London WC2E 4BH. *Address:* Book Hill, Essex, CT 06426, USA.

BURN, Andrew Robert, b. 25 Sep. 1902, Kynnersley, Shropshire, England. Teacher. *Education:* BA, Christ Church, Oxford, 1925; MA, ibid, 1928. *Publications include:* Minoans, Philistines & Greeks, 1400–900 BC, 1930; The Romans in Britain: An Anthology of Inscriptions, 1932, revised 1969; The Modern Greeks, 1942; Pericles & Athens, 1948; Agricola & Roman Britain, 1953; The Lyric Age of Greece, 1960; Persia & the Greeks, 1962; A Traveller's History of Greece, 1965, reprinted as, The Pelican History of Greece, 1966, revised 1978; The Warring States of Greece, 1968; The Living Past of Greece, with Mary W Burn, 1980, UK & USA; 2nd edition, Persia & the Greeks (to 449 BC), with Postscript by D M Lewis, 1984. *Contributions include:* Persia & the Greeks, 546-334 BC, in Volume II, Cambridge History of Iran, 1984; Articles, various journals. *Honours include:* Various academic prizes; Silver Cross of the Phoenix, Greece; Fellow, Society of Antiquaries, London, 1981; Doctor of Letters, University of Oxford, 1982. *Address:* 23 Ritchie Court, 380 Banbury Road, Oxford OX2 7PW, England.

BURNHAM, R P(eter), b. 29 June 1944, Biddeford, Maine, USA. University Professor. m. Kathleen A FitzPatrick, 4 Aug 1973, Madison, Wisconsin. *Education:* BA, English Literature, University of Maine – Portland, 1971; MA, English Literature, 1972, PhD, English Literature, 1977, University of Wisconsin. *Literary Appointment:* Editor, The Long Story, 1982–. *Contributions to:* Critical articles on Matthew Arnold in Arnoldian 8, 1981, and 12, 1984, and on Mackenzie's Man of Feeling in Studies in Scottish Literature 18, 1983; Prose pieces: Guest Editorial in Small Press Review vol 15 no 12, 1983 and short piece in Pikestaff Forum No. 6. *Honours:* Woodrow Wilson Fellow, 1971; Phi Kappa Phi, 1979. *Membership:* Co-ordinating Council of Literary Magazines. *Address:* 11 Kingston St, North Andover, MA 01845, USA.

BURNHAM, Sophy, b. 12 Dec. 1936, Baltimore, Maryland, USA. Writer. *Education:* BA, Smith College, 1958. *Publications:* The Art Crowd, (David McKay Inc) 1973; (editor) Threat to Licensed Nuclear Facilities (Mitre Corp), 1975; The Landed Gentry, (G P Putnam Sons), 1978; Buccaneer, (Frederick Warne), 1977; The Dogwalker (Warne), 1979; Plays: Penelope, 1976; The Study, 1979; The Witch's Tale, 1978, others. Films: The Smithsonian's Whale, 1963; The Leaf Magazine; Town and Country; Esquire etc. *Awards:* Best Magazine Feature, National Steeplechase and Hunt Association, 1974; Best Childrens Radio Play, National Association Community Broadcaster, 1980; Award of Excellence, Communications Arts Magazine, 1980; 1st Prize, Women's Theatre Award, Seattle, Washington, 1981. *Memberships include:* Authors' Guild Inc; Washington Independent Writers; Named Daughter of Mark Twain Society, 1974. *Literary Agent:* Brandt and Brandt,

Address: 1405 31st St NW, Washington, DC 20007, USA.

BURNS, Alan, b. 29 Dec. 1929, London, England. Author; Professor of English. m. (1) Carol Lynn, 1954, London, (2) Jean Illien, 1980, Minneapolis, USA, 1 son, 2 daughters. *Appointments:* Henfield Writing Fellow, University of East Anglia, 1971; C Day Lewis Writing Fellow, Woodberry Down School, London, 1973; Arts Council Writing Fellow, City Literary Institute, London, 1976–77; Professor, English, University of Minnesota, 1977–; Writer-in-Residence, Associated Colleges of the Twin Cities, Minneapolis St Paul, 1980; Bush Foundation of Minnesota Writing Fellow, 1984–85. *Publications include:* Buster, 1961; Europe After the Rain, 1965; Celebrations, 1967; Babel, 1969; Dreamerika!, 1972; The Angry Brigade, 1973; The Day Daddy Died, 1981; Revolutions of the Night, 1986; Play: Palach, 1970; To Deprive and Corrupt, 1972; The Imagination on Trial, 1981. *Contributor to:* Kenyon Review, 1967; Books & Bookmen; New Statesman; Minnesota Daily, 1981, 1982; Times Higher Education Supplement, 1982. *Honours:* Arts Council Maintenance Grant, 1967; Arts Council Bursaries, 1969, 1973. *Membership:* Poets & Writers, New York. *Literary Agent:* Deborah Rogers, London W11. *Address:* English Dept, University of Minnesota, Lind Hall, Church Street S E, Minneapolis, MN 55455, USA.

BURNS, Carol, b. 27 Oct. 1934, London, England. Writer; Painter; Designer; Lecturer. m. Alan Burns, (div) 2 children. *Education:* Slade Diploma & Postgraduate Scholarship, Slade School of Fine Art, London University, 1955–59. *Publications:* Infatuation, (New Writers 6), 1967; The Narcissist, 1967; (Publisher, Calder). *Contributions to:* Books & Bookmen; Tribune; Resurgence; Matrix-City Lit Magazine, (Editor); More-Morley College Magazine, (Editor). *Honours:* Arts Council Award, 1975; C Day Lewis Fellowship, Greater London Arts Association, 1978. *Memberships:* include City Lit Association, (Lecturer in Creative Writing). *Literary Agent:* Deborah Rogers. *Address:* 26A Ladbroke Gardens, London W11 2PY, England.

BURNS, Robert Grant, b. 3 Oct. 1938, Jacksonville, Texas, USA. Musician/Writer. *Education:* Juilliard School of Music, 1956–57; BA, Baylor University, 1960; M Mus, 1966, Doctoral Work, 1973, University of Texas at Austin. *Literary Appointment:* Master Poet, Texas Commission on the Arts and Humanities, 1973–75. *Publications:* Nettie Petty's Recollections, 1966; Quiet World, 1967; Poems and Stories from Pecan Springs, two volumes, 1974; Music for a Winter Morning, 1974. *Contributions to:* Miscellaneous articles published in various books, newspapers and magazines. Poems published in The New Yorker; Poetry; Chelsea; The Carolina Quarterly; The Carleton Miscellany; Voices and other magazines, also in Travois, The American Literary Anthology and 3 other anthologies. *Honours:* First Prize, Poetry Contest, Seventeen Magazine, 1958; Poetry Award, Baylor University, 1960; First Prize for Graduate Poetry, The University of Texas, 1966; Poetry Award, National Endowments for the Arts, 1969; Dobie Paisano Fellowship, Texas Institute of Letters, 1970, and many others. *Address:* 1408 Mohle Drive, Austin, TX 78703, USA.

BURNS, Robert Ignatius, b. 16 Aug. 1921, San Francisco, California, USA. Priest; Historian; Author; University Professor. *Education:* BA, 1945, MA, 1947, Gonzaga University; MA, Fordham University, 1949; PhB 1946, Phil Lic 1947, Jesuit Pontifical Faculty, Spokane, Washington; SThB 1951, SThLic, 1953, Jesuit Pontifical Faculty, Alma, California; PhD, Johns Hopkins University, 1958; D és Sc Hist, Fribourg University, Switzerland, 1961. *Publications include:* Jesuits and Indian Wars, 1966, Revised 1985; The Crusader Kingdom of Valencia, 2 volumes, 1967; Islam Under The Crusaders, 1973; Medieval Colonialism, 1975; Moors and Crusaders in Mediterranean Spain, 1978; Jaume I, 1981; El Reino de Valencia en el siglo XIII 2 volumes, 1982; Muslims, Christians and Jews in Crusader Valencia, 1985; The Worlds of Alfonso the

Learned and James the Conqueror, 1985. *Contributions to:* Various journals, encyclopedias etc. *Honours include:* Trustee 1975–77, Executive 1977–78, Life Fellow, 1978, Medieval Academy of America; President 1976, American Catholic History Association; President 1976–78, Academy Research History Medieval Spain. *Address:* University of California, Los Angeles, CA 90024, USA.

BURSK, Christopher, b. 23 Apr. 1943, Cambridge, Massachusetts, USA. Teacher. m. 19 June 1966, Haverhill, Massachusetts, 2 sons, 1 daughter. *Education:* PhD, Boston University, 1975. *Major Publications:* Standing Watch, 1978; Little Harbor, 1982; Place of Residence, 1983; Making Wings, 1983. *Contributor to:* Argo; Encounter; Poetry Chicago; American Poetry Review; Paris Review; and others. *Honour:* Guggenheim Fellowship, 1984. *Address:* 704 Hulmeville Avenue, Langhorne Manor, PA 19047, USA.

BURTON, Hester, b. 6 Dec. 1913, Beccles, England. *Education:* BA, Oxford University. *Publications:* Castors Away!, 1962; Time of Trial, 1963; In Spite of All Terror, 1968; To Ravensrigg, 1976. *Honours:* Carnegie Medal, 1963; ALA Notable Book, 1971; Runner Up, Boston Globe/Horn Book Award. *Membership:* Society of Authors. *Address:* Mill House, Kidlington, Oxford, England.

BURTON, Maurice, b. 28 Mar. 1898, London, England. Zoologist. m. Margaret Rosalie Maclean, 13 Apr. 1930, Twickenham, 2 sons, 1 daughter. *Education:* DSc; Diploma, Pedagogy. *Publications:* The Story of Animal Life, 1949; Animal Courtship, 1953; Phoenix Reborn, 1959; Systematic Dictionary of Mammals, 1962; Sixth Sense of Animals, 1972. *Contributor to:* Illustrated London News (Science Editor 1946–54); Daily Telegraph (Nature Correspondent, 1949–); Various scientific journals (publications on sponges). *Literary Agent:* Murray Polinger, London. *Address:* Weston House, Albury, Guildford, Surrey GU5 9AE, England.

BURY, John Patrick Tuer, b. 30 July 1908, Trumpington, Cambridge, England. Historian; Editor; Author. *Education:* MA, LittD, Corpus Christi College, Cambridge. *Publications:* Gambetta & the National Defence, 1936; France 1814–1940, 1949; The College of Corpus Christi BVM 1822–1952, 1952; Editor, New Cambridge Modern History, volume X, 1960; Napoleon III & the Second Empire, 1964; Editor, Romilly's Cambridge Diary 1932–42, 1967; France: The Insecure Peace, 1972; Gambetta & the Making of the Third Republic, 1973; Gambetta's Final Years, 1877–1882, 1982. *Contributor to:* Theology; Revue Historique; Annales de Normandie; French Historical Studies; Historical Journal; English Historical Review. *Membership:* Fellow, Royal Historical Society. *Address:* 71 Grange Road, Cambridge, England.

BUSCH, Frederick, b. 1 Aug. 1941, Brooklyn, New York, USA. Writer; Teacher. m. Judith Burroughs, 29 Nov. 1963, Allentown, 2 sons. *Education:* AB, Muhlenberg, 1962; MA, Columbia, 1967; Litt D, Muhlenberg, 1980. *Appointments:* Professor, English, Colgate University. *Publications:* I Wanted a Year Without Fall, 1971; Breathing Trouble, 1973; Hawkes, 1973; Manual Labour, 1974; Domestic Particulars, 1976; The Mutual Friend, 1978; Rounds, 1979; Harwater Country, 1979; Take This Man, 1981; Invisible Mending, 1984; Too Late American Boyhood Blues, 1984; When People Publish, 1986; Sometimes I Live in the Country, 1986. *Contributor to:* Paris Review; Harper's; Esquire; New Yorker; Georgia Review; Stand; Triquarterly; Essays in New York Times; Book Review, Modern Fiction Studies, etc. *Honours:* National Endowment for the Arts Fellowship, 1976; Guggenheim Fellowship, 1980; Ingram Merrill Fellowship, 1981; Inclusion in various O'Henry, & Best American Short Story Volumes. *Literary Agent:* Elaine Markson, New York. *Address:* Box 31A RD1, New Turnpike Road, Sherburne, NY 13460, USA.

BUSH, Alan, b. 22 Dec. 1900, London, England. Composer; Concert Pianist; Music Writer. m. Nancy Rachel Head, 31 March 1931, Paddington, London, 3 daughters. *Education:* London Matriculation; DMus, London; DMus Honoris Causa, Dunelm. *Publications:* In My Eighth Decade and Other Essays, 1980. Composer of 4 full length grand operas and 107 orchestral, chamber music, solo songs, choral works and solo instrumental works. *Honours:* Prize for full length opera, Wat Tyler, Arts Council Opera Competition, 1951. *Address:* 25 Christchurch Crescent, Radlett, Hertfordshire WD7 8AQ, England.

BUSH, Anthony James, b. 14 Jan. 1948, Tiverton, Devon, England. Journalist. m. June Caroline Florence Wills, 7 June 1969, Exeter, Devon, 2 sons. *Literary Appointments:* Regional Press, 1965–74; Sub-Editor, Fleet Street, 1974–77; Assistant Editor, Export Direction, 1977–79; Editor, Export Direction, 1979–81; Founder Editor, World Grain International Commodity Magazine, 1981–83; Founder Editor, Overseas Trade, British Overseas Trade Board Publication, 1984; Editor, Part-owner, Export Times, 1985–. *Publications:* The Business Travel Planner, 1980. *Contributor to:* The Traveller; Executive Travel; International Trade Finance; a number of Country Life Magazines. *Address:* Export Times, 4 New Bridge Street, London EC4, England.

BUSH, George Franklin, b. 1 July 1909, Philadelphia, Pennsylvania, USA. Writer, Writers' Workshop Director; Retired Professor. m. 12 June 1939, Philadelphia, 1 son, 3 daughters. *Literary Appointments:* Director, Maine Writers Workshop, 1968–; Publisher, Letters Magazine. *Publications:* Born to Die; Chinese Countdown; The Rhythm Within; Joshua of Jericho Bay; The Truth Fairy; Technical: Kinematics; Reading Engineering Drawings; History of the U S Virgin Islands Part I: to 1916, 1985; The Truth Fairy (Weird Tales of an eleeomosyrian) 1985; Pearls from my Oyster (Contributions to Letters by E B White, Richard Eberhart, Kay Boyle, Buclminster Fuller, Carlos Baker, etc), 1985; 42 articles including: Helicopter Blade Geometry; Geometry and Assembly of Viruses. *Contributions to:* Saturday Review; Yankee; Maine Digest; Old Farmer's Almanac; Organic Gardening; Aerospace Historian; Princeton Engineer; Poetry; National Humane Review; Yearbook of American Poetry (anthology); Windfall Poems; Texas Review. *Address:* Box 905, RDI, Stonington, ME 04681, USA.

BUSK, Birgit Nyemann, b. 4 Dec. 1928, Aarhus, Denmark. Freelance Writer and Journalist. *Education:* Marselisborg Gymnasium, Aarhus; Proficiency Certificate, University of Cambridge, England, 1948; Social and Philosophical studies; Woodbrooke College, Birmingham, England, 1949; Peace Studies, Freundschaftsheim, Buc eburg, German Federal Republic, 1950; Peace Seminar, Berlin, 1951; Participant in social experiment, Chateau de Bouron, Champcevrais, Yonne, France, 1952; Degree, Danish School of Journalism, Aarhus, Denmark, 1979; Journalist, Seminar, Hamburg, 1980; Journalist, Seminar, Berlin, 1985. *Address:* Skovfaldet 2Q,8200 Aarhus,N, Denmark.

BUSSEM, Eberhard, b. 23 Nov. 1941, Stettin, West Germany. Television Journalist. *Education:* Studies of History & Political Science, Universities of Freiburg, Vienna, Istanbul, Cologne & Munich. *Publications:* Die Karlsbader Beschlusse von 1819 (Gerstenberg Buchverlag), 1974; Repetitorium der deutschen Geschichte Mittelalter, 1968; Neuzeit 1, 1969; Neuzeit 3, 1972; Mittelalter Quellen, 1977; Kalenderrechner Mittelalter und Neuzeit, 1971 (new editions Verlag KG Saur). *Address:* Böcklinstr. 7, D-8000 Munich 79, Federal Republic of Germany.

BUSSIÈRES, Simone, b. 8 June 1918, Quebec City, Quebec, Canada. Publisher. m. Rosaire Bussières, 27 July 1945, Quebec, (dec.) *Education:* Higher Education Diploma. *Literary Appointments:* Secretary and Chairman, Society of Canadian Writers; Director, French-Speaking Centre of Pen International.

Publications: L'Heritier, novel, 1951; Les Fables des trois commeres, 1963; Methode de lecture spontanee, 1963, 65, 66; Joies de lire, 1965; Le Petit Sapin qui a pousse sur une etoile, 1971; C'est la fete, 1981; Dans mon petit violon, 1985. *Contribution to:* Le Jeudi, 1942. *Honour:* Medal, Canadian Library Association for Children, 1973. *Memberships:* Society of Canadian Writers; Union of Quebecois Writers; French-Speaking Centre of PEN International. *Address:* 1645 av Notre-Dame, Charlesbourg, Quebec, Canada G2N 1S6.

BUTLER, David Edgeworth, b. 1924. m. Marilyn Butler, 1962, 3 sons. *Education:* MA, PhD, St Paul's New College, Oxford. *Literary Appointments:* JE Proctor, Visiting Fellow, Princeton University, 1947–48; Student, Nuffield College, 1949–51; Resident Fellow, 1951–54; Dean, Senior Tutor, 1956–64; Personal Assistant, HM Ambassador, Washington, 1955–56; Co-Editor, Electoral Studies, 1982. *Publications include:* The British General Election of 1951, 1952; The Electoral System of Britain, 1918–51; The British General Election of 1955, 1955; The Study of Political Behaviour, 1958; (ed) Elections Abroad, 1959; The British General Election of 1959, 1960 (with R Rose); British Political Facts 1900–1960, 1963, (with J Freeman); The British General Election of 1964, 1965, (with A King); The British General Election of 1966, 1966; Political Change in Britain, 1969, (with D Stokes); The British General Election of 1970, 1971, (with M Pinto-Duschinsky); The Canberra Model, 1973; The British General Election of 1974, 1974, (with D Kavanagh). *Memberships:* United Oxford and Cambridge United Club. *Honours:* Honorary Doctorate, University Paris, 1978; Queen's University, Belfast, 1985. *Address:* Nuffield College, Oxford, Oxon, England.

BUTLER, Jack Armand, b. 8 May 1944, Alligator, Mississippi, USA. Mathematician. m. Jayne Tull, 20 Feb. 1983, Eureka Springs, Arkansas. 2 daughters. *Education:* BS, Mathematics; BA, English Literature; MFA. *Publications:* West of Hollywood, poems, 1980; Hawk Gumbo and Other Stories, 1982; The Kid Who Wanted to be a Spaceman, poems, 1984; Jui-Jitsu for Christ, novel, 1986. *Contributions to:* Anthologies: Best Poems of 1976; Ozark, Ozark; Intro 2; Intro 3; Arkansas Voices; Mississippi Writers: Reflections of Childhood and Youth. Magazines and Journals including: The New Yorker; Atlantic Monthly; Poetry; Poetry Northwest; Southern Poetry Review; Black Warrior Review; New Orleans Review; Texas Quarterly; Mississippi Review; Barataria Review; Pebble; Stone Drum; Lucille; Cotton; Arkansas Times; Cedar Rock; Arkansas Gazette. *Honours:* Award for best book of poems. Voices, Boatwright Literary Festival, 1971; Fiction Contest 1st Prizes, 1980, 81, 2nd prize, 1978, Black Warrior Review. *Memberships:* Organisation Committee, Arkansas Literary Society; Chairman, Porter Fund. *Literary Agents:* Ted Parkhurst and Liz Parkhurst. *Address:* 5820 Hawthorne, Little Rock, AR 72207, USA.

BUTLER, Michael Gregory, b. 1 Nov. 1935, England. University Lecturer. *Education:* Fitzwilliam College, Cambridge University, 1954–59; Trinity College, Oxford University, 1957–58; MA, Cambridge; Diploma of Education, Oxford; PhD, CNAA. *Appointments include:* Head of German, Ipswich School; Lecturer, 1970, Senior Lecturer, Head, Department of German, 1984–, University of Birmingham. *Publications:* Nails and Other Poems, 1964; The Novels of Max Frisch, 1976; Englische Lyrik der Gegenwart, Editor, 1981; Samphire New Poetry, Co-Editor with K Williams, 1968–81; The Plays of Max Frisch, 1985; Frisch: Andorra, 1985. *Contributions to:* Times Literary Supplement; Times Higher Education Supplement; Samphire; Migrant; Mica; The Poetry Review; Vagabond; various others. British Broadcasting Corporation. *Honours:* Taras Schevchenko Memorial Prize, 1962; Visiting Fellowship, Humanities Research Centre, Australian National University, 1979. *Address:* 45 Westfields, Catshill, Bromsgrove, England.

BUTT, Robyn-Marie, b. 17 Jan. 1959, Woodstock, Ontario, Canada. Playwright; Culture Critic. *Education:* BFA, Honours, York University; Banff School of Fine Arts, Writing Workshop Phase II. *Appointments include:* Writing for CBC Television. *Publication:* Play, Bad Taste, 1985. *Contributor to:* Canadian children's Annual; T O Magazine; York Excalibur; York Theatre Journal; Canadian Theatre Review; etc. *Honours:* Mavor Moore Award for most promising new playwright, York University, 1982; Canada Council Playwright Residency Award, Theatre Passe Muraille, 1983; Ontario Arts Council Residency Award, 1984; Canada Council of Arts Grant B for Literature, 1985–86. *Memberships:* Founding Member, PM3 Writers Group, Theatre Passe Muraille; Six Playwrights, Unit, 1984–85. Tarragon Theatre; Playwrights Union of Canada. *Address:* 678 Broadview Avenue, Apt. 105, Toronto M4K 2P2, Canada.

BUTTACI, Salvatore M, b. 12 June 1941. Marketing. m. Susan Linda Buttaci. *Education:* BA Communications & Arts, Seton Hall University, New Jersey, USA; Master of Business Administration (marketing), Rutgers University, New Jersey. *Literary Appointments include:* High School English Teacher, 1978–80; Marketing Analyst, 1980–; Editor, New Worlds Unlimited, 19784–. *Major publications:* Coming Home Poems: Stops and Pauses on the Scrapbook Express, 1974; In Praise of Grandpa: Memory Poems, 1976; Co-editor (with Susan Linda Gerstle) of annual poetry anthologies including: Echoes of the Unlocked Odyssey, 1974; Shadows of the Elusive Dream, 1975; Reflections of the Inward Silence, 1976; Whispers of the Unchained Heart, 1977; Tracings of the Valiant Soul, 1978; Visions of the Enchanted Spirit, 1979; Mirrors of the Wistful Dreamer, 1980; Images of the Mystic Truth, 1981; Dreams of the Heroic Muse, 1982; Journeys of the Poet/Prophet, 1983; Voices of the Majestic Sage, 1984. *Contributor to:* Numerous literary magazines and journals. *Honours* include: 1st prize, Poetry, 1977; 2nd prize, 1979, Journey into Fantasy Creative Writer Contest. *Memberships:* New Jersey Poetry Society; Committee of Small Magazine Editors and Publishers, Inc; New York Poetry Forum; American Society of Composers, Authors and Publishers; International Platform Association; Songwriters Guild; Association of MBA Executives. *Address:* P O Box 556, Saddle Brook, NJ 07662, USA.

BUTTERFIELD, Sir (William) John (Hughes), b. 28 Mar. 1920, Birmingham, England. Physician; Educator; Regius Professor of Physics, Cambridge University. *Education:* BM, 1945, DM, 1967; Oxford University; MD, Johns Hopkins University, USA, 1951; MA, MD, Cambridge University, 1975; Honorary LLD, Nottingham University, 1977; Hon D Med Sci, Keio University. *Publications:* Priorities in Medicine, 1968; Tolbutamide after 10 years, 1970; Health & Sickness in an Urban Community, 1973. *Contributor to:* Numerous medical journals. *Honours:* OBE, 1953; Rock Carling Lecturer, 1968; Osler Lecturer, 1971; Linacre Lecturer, 1979. *Memberships:* Editor, Committee, Journal of Chronic Diseases; Editor, Committee, Wiley's International Dictionary of Medicine & Biology, 1986; Executive Committee, Byron Society; Fellow, Royal Society of Arts. *Address:* Master's Lodge, Downing College, Cambridge, England.

BUTTERICK, George F, b. 7 Oct. 1942, Yonkers, New York, USA. Scholar; Poet. m. Colette Marie Hetzel, 1965, 2 sons. *Education:* BA, Manhattan College, 1964; PhD, State University of New York, Buffalo, 1970. *Appointments:* Curator, Literary Archives, University of Connecticut. *Publications:* The Norse, 1973; Reading Genesis, 1976; A Guide to the Maximus Poems, 1978; The Postmoderns: The New American Poetry Revised, Co-Editor, 1982; The Maximus Poems of Charles Olson, Editor, 1983; Rune Power, 1983; The Three-Percent Stranger. *Contributor to:* Sulfur; Exquisite Corpse; Credences; Temblor; Sagetrieb; Conjunctions. *Address:* 194 North Street, Willimantic, CT 06226, USA.

BUTTERY, Douglas Norton, b. Harrogate, England. Author. *Education:* MSc, University of London. *Publications:* (as D N Buttrey) Cellulose Plastics, 1947; Plasticizers, 1950; Plastics in the Furniture Industry, 1964; Plastics in Furniture, Editor, 1976; (as Densil Barr) The Man With Only One Head, Novel, 1955, 1962; radio plays. *Contributor to:* Plastics & Polymers; SCI Annual Reports; Times Review of Industry; Plastics Today; Packaging Technology; British Plastics; Forest Society Journal; etc. *Memberships:* PEN; Chairman, Player Playwrights, London; FRSC; FPRI. *Address:* 15 Churchfields, Broxbourne, Hertfordshire EN10 7JU, England.

BUTTITTA, Anthony (Tony), b. 26 July 1907, Chicago, Illinois, USA. Writer, Journalist; Theatrical Press Representative. *Education:* Teacher's Certificate, Louisiana State Normal College, Natchitoches; BA, University of Texas, 1929; Graduate work on MA, University of North Carolina. *Publications:* Singing Piedmont (One-Act Play), 1937; After the Good Gay Times, a memoir of F Scott Fitzgerald, Asheville Summer of 1935, 1974; Uncle Sam Presents: A Memoir of the Federal Theatre Project, 1936–39; with Barry Witham. *Contributor to:* Saturday Review of Literature; Hollands Magazine of the South; Readers Digest. *Honours:* Recipient of Prizes for Plays. *Memberships include:* Association of Theatrical Press Agents and Managers; Authors Guild. *Literary Agent:* International Creative Management. *Address:* 28 Jones Street, New York, NY 10014, USA.

BUTTNER, Ludwig, b. 20 Aug. 1909, Pegnitz, German Federal Republic. Professor. *Education:* Universities of Konigsberg; Berlin; Erlangen-Nuremberg; Munich; London, England. *Publications include:* Thoughts on the Ethnological Aspects of Literary Science, 1939; A History of the Town of Pegnitz, 1355–1955, 1955; Neuchner's Image of Man, 1967; From Benn to Enzensberger: An Introduction to the Contemporary German Lyric Poetry 1945–70, 1971; The Tragedy of a Writer, Robert Grriepenkerl, Life and Work 1810–68, 1977; Many essays. *Contributions to:* Various magazines and journals. *Honour:* Stipend of the Deutsche Forschungsgemeinschaft, International Platform Association, USA. *Memberships include:* MLA; AAUP; Bavarian Philological Society; German Philological Society. *Address:* Schachenstre 7, 81 Garmisch-Partenkirchen, German Federal Republic.

BUXBAUM, Martin, b. 27 June 1912. Writer; Poet. *Education:* Master in Journalism, Cranston University, USA; Art Scholarship, Columbia Technical University. *Literary Appointments include:* Manager of Communications, Sealtest Corporation, Washington, District of Columbia, 1947–53; Director of Communications, Marriott Corporation, Washington, 1953–76 (Retired). *Publications:* Rivers of Thought, 1958; The Underside of Heaven, 1963; Table Talk, 2 Volumes, 1964, 73; The Unsung, volume I, 1964, Volume II, 1965; Whispers in the Wind, 1966; Around Our House, 1968; Once Upon a Dream, 1970; The Warm World of Martin Buxbaum, 1974. *Contributions to:* Reader's Digest; National Enquirer; Guideposts; Sunshine Magazine; Congressional Record. *Honours include:* Poet of the Year, State of Maryland, 1967; George Washington Medal of Honour, 1964, 70-73, 76; Kentucky Colonel, 1971. *Address:* 7819 Custer Road, Bethesda, MD 20814, USA.

BUZO, Alexander John, b. 23 July 1944, Sydney, New South Wales, Australia. Playwright. m. Merelyn Elizabeth Johnson, 21 Dec. 1968, Sydney, 2 daughters. *Education:* BA, University of New South Wales. *Literary Appointments:* Resident Playwright, Melbourne Theatre Company, 1972–73; Management Committee, Australian Writers Club, 1984–85. *Publications:* Plays: The Front Room Boys, 1970; MacQuarie, 1972; 3 Plays, 1978; Coralie Lansdowne Says No, 1974; Tom, 1975; Martello Towers, 1976; Makassar Reef, 1979; Big River/The Marginal Farm, 1985. Non-Fiction: Tautology, 1981; Meet the New Class, 1981. Fiction: The Search for Harry Allway, 1985. *Contributions to:*

Sydney Morning Herald; The Financial Review; pol; Pacific Islands Monthly; Playboy; The Bulletin; The National Times; Theatre Quarterly; Theatre Australia; Southerly; Overland. *Honours:* Gold Medal, Australian Literature Society, 1972. *Membership:* Stage Convenor, Australian Writers' Guild. *Literary Agent:* June Cann Management. *Address:* 14 Rawson Avenue, Bondi Junction, Sydney, NSW 2022, Australia.

BYATT, Antonia Susan, b. 24 Aug. 1936, Sheffield, England. Writer. m. Peter John Duffy, 26 Nov. 1969, Brixton, 1 son, deceased, 3 daughters. *Education:* BA, Honours, English, (Cantab); 1957; Fellowship, Bryn Mawr College, USA, 1957–58; BLitt, 1959. *Publications:* Shadow of a Sun, 1964; The Game, 1967; The Virgin in the Garden, 1978; The July Ghost, 1980; Still Life, 1985. *Contributor to:* Numerous professional journals and magazines; 4 Broadcasts on Personal View; Series on words, 1978. *Memberships:* Judge, Booker Prize, 1973; Member, Panel of Judges, Hawthornden Prize; Judge, David Higham Memorial Prize; Fellow, Royal Society of Literature; Deputy Chairman, Committee of Management, Society of Authors, 1985–; International PEN. *Literary Agent:* A D Peters. *Address:* 37 Rucholme Road, London SW15 3LF, England.

BYERS-PEVITTS, Beverley, b. 15 Aug. 1939, Ohio County, Kentucky, USA. Professor, Theatre/Speech; Playwright. m. Robert Richard Pevitts, 12 June 1966, Chicago, 1 son. *Education:* BA, English, Kentucky Wesleyan College, 1961; MA, Theatre, Southern Illinois University, 1968; PhD, Southern Illinois University. *Appointments:* Guest Editor, Theatre Annual, 1985; Addressed Conference on Women Playwrights, Stanford University, 1984. *Publications:* An Exploration of Fefu and Her Friends, Women in American Theatre, 1981; Anthology of Plays by Contemporary American Women Playwrights, in progress; Reflections in a Window, The Best Short Plays of 1982. *Contributor to:* Chrysalis; Southern Theatre; American Theatre Association. *Honours:* Distinguished Woman of the American Theatre Association, 1977; National Endowment for Humanities Grant Recipient, New York University, 1977; Dissertation Research Award, Fellowship, Graduate School, Southern Illinois University, 1977; NEH Grant Recipient, University of Wisconsin, 1983. *Memberships:* American Theatre Association, University and College Theatre Association, Executive Vice President (President Elect), 1984–85; ATA, Women's Programme President, 1982–84; American College Theatre Festival, National and Executive Committee, 1984–85. *Address:* Division of Theatre/Speech, Dept of Communication and Fine Arts, Kentucky Wesleyan College, Owensboro, KY 42301, USA.

BYRD, Odell Richard, b. 22 Sep. 1943, USA. Antique Dealer. *Education:* AA; BA. *Literary Appointments:* Fellow, International Academy of Poets, 1981–82. *Publications:* A Voice Within, poetry, 1979; Love Poems, 1981. *Contributions to:* The New Rennaissance; New World Anthology; Black Books Bulletin; International Black Writer. *Honours:* Outstanding Contribution to Literature, 1979; Appreciation in the Field of Poetry, 1983. *Address:* 2310 Gordon Avenue, Richmond, VA 23224, USA.

BYRNE, John F, b. 18 June 1934, Chicago, Illinois, USA. Writer, Translator, Public Relations Consultant. *Education:* BA, St John's University, Collegeville, Minnesota, USA; subsequently New York University, Universidad de Madrid, Escuela Oficial de Periodismo, Madrid, Spain. *Literary Appointments:* Editor-in-Chief, Common Market Business Reports, Spanish Business Reports. *Major Publications:* On China & Cuba, 1963; The Parish, 1965; Vaticano, 1980; all translated. *Contributor to:* Current Biography. *Memberships:* Chicago Press Club; Asociación de Corresponsales de Prensa Iberoamericana; American Translators Association; Asociación Profesional Español de Traductores e Intérpretes; Ateneo Científico, Literario y Artístico (Madrid); Fellow of the International Biographical

Association. *Address:* Genl. Diaz Porlier, 45, 28001 Madrid, Spain.

BYSTRZYCKI, Przemystaw, b. 23 May 1923, Przemysl, Poland. Writer/Novelist. *Education:* MA, Political Economics; MA, Sociology. *Publications:* Smieré nad Agfar-wadi, 1960; Szkockie potzegnania, 1963; Strumien, 1964; Anujka, 1968; Wyspa Wniebowstapienis, 1974; Wtoskie kartki, 1977; Niessie i inne Opowiadania, 1976; Plynie Rzeka, plynie ... 1982, 2 volumes; Kamienne lwy, 1983; Znak cichociemnych, 1984, 1985; Ponar i inne opowiadania, 1985. *Memberships:* Polish PEN Club; Polish Literary Association; Soc Scientiarum ac Litterarun Premisliensis; Adam Mickiewicz Asociation. *Address;* Poznan 60-750, ul Wyspianskiego 12 m 11, Poland.

C

CABLE James (Sir), b. 15 Nov. 1920, London, England. Writer; Lecturer. m. 6 Sep. 1954, 1 son. *Education:* PhD, Cambridge University. *Publications:* As Grant Hugo: Britain in Tomorrow's World, 1969; Appearance and Reality in International Relations. 1970. Gunboat Diplomacy, 1971; The Royal Navy and the Siege of Bilbao, 1979; Gunboat Diplomacy 1919-1979, 1981; Britain's Naval Future, 1983; Diplomacy at Sea, 1985; The Geneva Conference of 1954 on Indo-China, 1986. *Contributions to:* Numerous professional publications. *Honour:* CMG. *Membership:* International Institute for Strategic Studies. *Address:* c/o Lloyds's Bank Limited, 16 St James Street, London SW1A 1EY, England.

CACCIATORE, Vera, b. 9 Nov. 1911, Rome, Italy. Writer. m. Edoardo Cacciatore, 24 Feb. 1941, Sienna. *Education:* D Litt, University of Rome. *Publications:* La Vendita all'Asta, 1953; La Palestra, 1961; La Forza Motrice, 1968; The Swing, 1959: Shelley and Byron in Pisa, 1961; La Forza Motrice, 1968; A Room in Rome, 1970; La Scalinata, 1984. *Honours:* MBE, 1958; Honorary Member, Poetry Society of America, Keats-Shelley Association of America. *Address:* 12 Largo Cristina di Svezia, 00165 Rome, Italy.

CADDEL, Richard Ivo, b. 13 July, 1949, Bedford, England. Librarian. m. Ann Barker, 31 Aug. 1971, Heaton, Tyne and Wear, England, 1 son, 1 daughter. *Education:* BA, Newcastle upon Tyne, England, 1971. *Appointment:* Director/Literary Editor, PIG Press, 1973-. *Publications:* Quiet Alchemy, 1976; Shelter, 1979; Sweet Cicely, 1983; Deadly Sins, 1984. *Contributor to:* A Poem in its Place in Orono, 1984; Lee Harwood in Dictionary of Literary Biography, 1985. *Memberships:* Association of Little Presses; John Clare Society. *Address:* 7 Cross View Terrace, Durham DH1 4JY, England.

CADIEUX, Pauline Marie A A, b. Quebec Province, Canada. Newspaperwoman; Writer. m. 31 May 1941, Widow, Sydney, 1 son, 2 daughters. *Education:* Certificate in History, University of Montreal. *Appointments:* Invited to 60 radio and television programs, 40 towns meetings and 20 schools organizations, 1976-84; Presidents d'honneur of 1980 Rimouski Salon du livre; Presidente d'honneur for launching of encyclopedic book Églises et Croix d'église du Diocese de Rimouski. *Publications:* La Lampe dans la Fenetre, 1976, chosen for film Cordelia, 1977; Bigame, 1977; Nouvelliste serial story, 1978, republished as Flara la rouquine. Chosen as Librarians Choice, 1978; Violences...un climat social, 1981. *Contributor to:* magazines and journals. *Memberships:* Union des ecrivains Quebecois; Societe des auteurs canadiens; Le regroupement des auteurs de l'Est du Quebec. *Honours include:* Guest of Honour, Federation Franco-Colombienne, Vancouver, 1980. *Address:* 116 Ulric Tessier, St Ulric de Riviere Blanche, Quebec, Canada GOJ 3HO.

CADY, Jack, b. 20 Mar. 1932, Columbus, Ohio, USA. Writer. *Education:* BSc, University of Louisville. *Appointments:* University of Washington, 1968-73; Knox College, 1973-74; Clarion College, 1974; University of Alaska SE, 1977-78; University of Washington Extension, 1978-; Pacific Lutheran University, 1984. *Publications:* Tattoo, 1978; The Well, 1982; The Burning, 1982; The Jonah Watch, 1982; Singleton, 1982; McDowell's Ghost, 1983; The Man Who Could Make Things Vanish, 1984. *Contributor to:* Seattle Post Intelligencer; Daily News; etc. *Honours:* Atlantic Monthly First Award, 1965; Iowa Prize for short fiction, 1972; Washington State Governor's Award, 1972; National Literary Anthology Award, 1970; Washington Distinguished Writer Award, 1978. *Memberships:* PEN International; Author's Guild; Society of Professional Journalists. *Literary Agent:*

Clyde Taylor, Curtis Brown Ltd. *Address:* 315 Logan St, Port Townsend, WA 98368, USA.

CAGGIANO, Philip, b. 11 Aug. 1949, Northport, Long Island, New York, USA. Director; Writer. *Education:* BS, New York University. *Literary Appointments:* Teacher of Playwriting, Eugene O'Neill Center; Lecturer, Opera America, American Theater Association; National Opera Association; and numerous universities. Assistant to Curator, Met's Centennial exhibit, The Metropolitan Opera; The First Hundred Years; Member, Metropolitan Opera's Press Department. *Publications:* The Ring, 4 plays for Children, Avon Books, 1982. Productions throughout the US and Europe. Written, Directed and Designed for Opera, Film and Theatre. *Address:* Press Department, Metropolitan Opera, Lincoln Center, New York, NY 10023, USA.

CAILLIAU, Philippe, b. 18 July 1954, Elisabethtown, Belgian Congo. Teacher, Dutch & Verbal Expression, Brussels, Belgium. m. Anne Vandenbroucke, 12 Jan. 1984, Brussels. *Education:* Licentiate German Philology & Theory of Literature, Qualified & Graduated to teach Dutch, Free University of Brussels, 1976. *Literary Appointments:* Poet; Reviewer; Essayist; Maker of visual & concrete poetry. *Publications include:* The Murdered and His Accoucheuse, poetry, 1975; The Expedition to Cloaca, poetry, 1976; Jef Geeraerts, monograph, 1978; Reconstruction, poetry, 1981; About Ben Bruid in de Morgen van Hugo Claus, instruction booklet, 1981; Company of Amnesty International, poetry for 4 voices, 1982; Dirk de Witte, monograph, 1984; Hugo Claus, The Duck Hunt, essay, 1985. *Contribution include:* Numerous Dutch magazines & journals; Yearbook concerning Gerard Reve; Critical Lexicon of Dutch Literature After 1945. *Honours:* A few, since 1975. *Memberships:* Association of Dutch Writers; International Association of Poets, Essayists & Novelists. *Literary Agent:* SABAM (Belgian Association of Authors, Composers & Editors), Aarlenstraat 75-77, B-1040 Brussels, Belgium. *Address:* Margaretha van Oostenrijkplein 17/bus 11, B-1080 Brussels, Belgium.

CAIRNCROSS, John, b. 25 July 1913, Lesmahagow, Lanarkshire, Scotland. Writer. *Education:* L és L, Sorbonne, Paris, France; BA, Cambridge University, England. *Literary Appointments:* Rome Correspondent, Economist, Observer and CBC, 1952-54. *Publications:* Translator of Racine's, Iphigenia, Phaedra, Athaliah, 1963; Andromache and other plays, 1967; Translator of Corneille's, The Cid, Cinna, The Theatrical Illusion, 1975; Molière Bourgeois et Libertin, 1963; After Polygamy Was Made a Sin, 1974; Things To Come: An Approach To Food/Population Planning; La Fontaine Fables, and Other Poems, 1982. *Contributions to:* Revue d'Histoire Litteraire de la France; Le XVII Siécle; Chief editor, Bangkok, Registered United Nations Economic Commission. *Address:* Via Armando Spadini 16, 00197 Rome, Italy.

CAIRNEY, John, b. 16 Feb. 1930, Bailleston, Glasgow, Scotland. Actor, Writer, Director. m. (1) Sheila Cowan, 29 May 1954, div. 1980, 1 son, 4 daughters. (2) Alannah O'Sullivan, 27 Sep. 1980, Oxford, New Zealand. *Education:* Diploma of Drama, RSAMD, 1953; Certificate of Dramatic Studies 1953, BA 1984, Student M Litt currently, Glasgow University. *Literary Appointments:* Director, Shanter Productions, Glasgow, 1974-; Managing Director, John Cairney and Company Limited, 1984-; Director, Theatre Consultants (Scotland), 1974-. *Publications include:* Pantomime Script, play, 1953; An Actor's Life (A Series), articles, 1962; The Women in my Life, poems, 1967; Another School of Thought, play, 1968; The Robert Burns Story, solo play, 1969; McGonagall, solo play, 1970; The Scotland Story, pageant, 1972; The Ivor Novello Story, musical, 1973; An Edinburgh Salon, revue, 1974; Robert Service, duologue, 1977; As Others Saw Him, documentary, 1979; Knox and Mary, duologue, 1980; Have Scripts Will Travel, article, 1981; The Chopin Affair, recital with pianist, 1982; Football Crazy, duologue, 1982; A Wilde Fancy, duologue, 1983; Rab, musical, 1984. *Contributions to:* Scotsman; Annabelle magazine; Drama Magazine; Scottish Theatre News. *Honours:* Art Gold Medal, 1943; RSAMD Silver Medal, 1953; James Bridie Award and Alec Guiness Award, 1953; Jubilee Medal, 1977; Scottish Tourist Board Citation for Burns Festival, 1977. *Memberships:* Writer's Guild; Scottish Society of Playwrights. *Literary Agent:* Shanter Productions, 44 St Vincent Crescent, Glasgow. *Address:* 44 St Vincent Crescent, Glasgow G3 8NG, Scotland.

CAIRNS, David, b. 11 June 1904, Ayton, Berwickshire, Scotland. Emeritus Professor of Practical Theology. *Education:* BA, 1928, MA, 1938, Oxford University, England; Aberdeen, Tubingen, Zurich & Montpelier. *Publications include:* The Image of God in Man, (SCM Press), 1953; enlarged and revised edition, (Collins, Fontana Press), 1973; A Gospel Without Myth? – Bultmann's Challenge to the Preacher, (SCM Press), 1960; God Up There – A Study in Divine Transcendence, (St Andrew Press), 1967; In Remembrance of Me – Aspects of the Lord's Supper, (Bles), 1967; various translations from German. *Contributions to:* Scottish Journal of Theology; etc. *Honours:* include DD, Edinburgh University, 1953. *Membership:* Faith and Order Commission, World Council of Churches, 1956–66. *Address:* 29 Viewfield Gardens, Aberdeen AB1 7XN, Scotland.

CAITLIN, Elise, b. 18 May 1952, New York City, USA. Playwright. *Education:* BA, MFA, Brandeis University. *Literary Appointments:* Four commissions to write plays for the Actors Theatre of Louisville, Kentucky, 1984, 85, 86. *Publication:* The Complete Spy (co-author Robert McGarvey), 1984. *Contributions to:* Playboy; Success; Business to Business; Genesis; California Living; Boys Life. *Address:* c/o Allen & McGarvey, 4482 Barranca Parkway #260, Irvine, CA 92714, USA.

CALABRIA, Mary Anne Hayes, b. 4 Sep. 1956, Jersey City, New Jersey, USA. Editor; Writer. m. James J Hayes, 14 Dec. 1974, 1 son, 2 daughters. *Literary Appointments:* Editor, Dollars Daily. *Publication:* Ask the Coupon Queen, Pocket book, 1979. *Contributions to:* Woman's Day; Family Circle. *Address:* P O Box 302, Englishtown, NJ 07726, USA.

CALDECOTT, Moyra, b. 1 June 1927. Author. m. Oliver Zerffi Stratford Caldecott, 5 Apr. 1951, London, 2 sons, 1 daughter. *Education:* BA, MA, University of Natal. *Publications:* Novels: Weapons of the Wolfhound, 1976; Guardians of the Tall Stones, 1977 and 1986; The Lily and The Bull, 1979; The King of Shadows, 1981; Child of the Dark Star, 1984; The Tower and the Emerald, 1985; The Son of the Sun, 1986. Short books: Adventures by Leaflight, 1978; The Twins of the Tylwyth Teg, 1983; Taliesin and Avagddu, 1984; Bran, son of Llyr, 1985. *Contributor to:* Poems: Anthologies: Reading Aloud, 1961; Rhyme and Rhythm, 1965; Gallery, 1988, Magazines: Outposts; Ambit. *Literary Agent:* Deborah Rogers, 49 Blenheim Crescent, London W11 2EF. *Address:* 19 Turney Road, London SE21 8LX, England.

CALDER, David Lewis Scott, b. 22 Oct. 1946. *Education:* LLB, Liverpool University, England. *Literary Appointments:* Jointly runs the Windows Project and the Merseyside Dial-a-Poem Service. *Publications:* Dealers and Dancers, 1972; Cube, 1972; Me, Jane and Kong, 1974; Fingerbook of Thumb, 1975; Leaf of Mouth, 1976; Spaced, 1978; Batik, 1980; A Handbook for Adventure Playgrounds, 1979; Buchan, 1982; Theorems of Violence, 1984; Islands, 1984; Arts Council mixed Media theatre events. *Contributor to:* Journals including: Ambit; PN Review; New Departures; Poetry Review. *Memberships:* Poets Conference. *Address:* PO Box 2, Merseyside Arts Association, Bluecoat Chambers, Liverpool 1, England.

CALDER, Simon Peter Ritchie, b. 25 Dec. 1955, Crawley, England. Writer. *Education:* BSc, University of Warwick; BA, Open University. *Publications:* Hitchhikers Manual: Britain, 1979, 1985; Europe: A Manual for Hitch-hikers, 1980, 1985; Travellers

Survival Kit: USA & Canada, 1985; Travellers Survival Kit: Europe, 1986; Adventure Holidays, 1986. *Contributor to:* The Guardian; Transitions (USA). *Membership:* Registered Indexer, Society of Indexers. *Address:* Vacation Work Publications, 9 Park End Street, Oxford OX1 1HJ, England.

CALDWELL, Erskine, b. 17 Dec. 1903, Moreland, Georgia, USA. Author. *Education:* University of Virginia. *Publications:* 52 fiction & non-fiction books including: Deep South, 1968; Annette, 1973. *Memberships:* San Francisco Press Club; Phoenix (Arizona) Press Club; American Academy of Arts & Letters. *Agent:* L Pollinger Ltd, England; McIntosh & Otis Inc, USA. *Address:* PO Box 4550 Hopi Stn, Scottsdale, AZ 85258, USA.

CALHOUN, Richard James, b. 5 Sep, 1926, Jackson, Tennessee, USA. University Professor and Editor. m. Doris Marie Somerville, 5 June 1954, Erie, Pennsylvania, 1 son, 2 daughters. *Education:* BA, George Peabody College of Vanderbilt University, 1948; MA, Johns Hopkins University, 1950; PhD, University of North Carolina, Chapel Hill, 1959. *Literary Appointments:* Assistant Professor, Davidson College, North Carolina, 1958–61; Assistant Professor – Professor 1961–; Alumni Professor of English 1968–; Clemson University; Fulbright Senior Lecturer, University of Ljubljana, University of Sarayevo, Yugoslavia, 1969–70; Contributing Editor, South Carolina Review, 1973–; University of Aarhus, Odense University, Denmark, 1976. *Publications:* Tricentennial Anthology of South Carolina Literature, 1970; James Dickey, The Expansive Imagination, 1973; The South: Two Decades of Change, 1975; James Dickey, 1983. *Contributions to:* Publications including: Southern Literary Journal; Southern Review; South Atlantic Bulletin; South Carolina Review. *Honours:* Southern Fellowship, Carnegie Foundation for Advancement of Teaching, 1957–58; Cooperative Programme in the Humanities Fellowship, Ford Foundation, 1964–65. *Memberships:* South Atlantic Modern Language Association; Modern Language Association; Vice President, Society for the Study of Southern Literature; President, Philological Association of the Carolinas. *Address:* Department of English, Clemson University, Clemson, SC 29631, USA.

CALLAHAN, Dorothy M, b. 24 Dec. 1934, Bronx, NY, USA. Learning Disabilities Teacher Consultant. m. Robert Callahan, 3 May 1958, 1 son, 1 daughter. *Education:* BA (magna cum laude), English, Education, Journalism; MSc, Reading Education. *Publications:* Under Christopher's Hat, 1972, Jimmy: The Story of the Young Jimmy Carter, 1978; Ruffian, 1983; Thoroughbreds, 1983. *Contributor to:* New York Times; New York Daily News; Seventeen Magazine; Lady's Circle; Modern Maturity; Thoroughbred Record' American Turf Monthly; Backstretch; Florida Horse; Racing Digest. *Address:* 45 Summit Road, Hamburg, NJ 07419, USA.

CALLIHAN, Harriet K, b. 8 Feb. 1930, USA. Executive Director/Editor, medical publication, The Proceedings. m. Clair C Callihan, Chicago, Illinois, 17 Dec. 1955, 1 daughter. *Education:* MBA, University of Chicago. *Literary Appointments:* Managing Editor, official medical publication, Proceedings, 1975–. *Memberships:* President, American Medical Writers Association; National Science Writers Association. *Address:* 422 Central Avenue, Wilmette, IL 60091, USA.

CALLOW, Philip, b. 26 Oct. 1924, Birmingham, England. Writer. m. Penelope Newman, 2 Mar. 1974, Yeovil. *Education:* Teaching Certificate, St Luke's College, Exeter, Devon. *Literary Appointments:* Writer in Residence, Sheffield City Polytechnic. *Publications:* Son and Lover: the young D H Lawrence, 1975; The Story of my Desire, 1976; Janine, 1977; The Subway To New York, 1979; Cave Light, 1981; Woman With a Poet, 1983; New York Insumnia, 1984. *Honours:* Arts Council bursary, 1966; C Day Lewis Fellowship, Richmond, 1973; Southern Arts Fellowship, Reading, 1974; Arts Council Fellowship, Falmouth, 1977; Arts

Council Fellowship, Sheffield, 1980. *Literary Agent:* MBA Literary Agents, 45 Fitzroy Street, London W1. *Address:* Flat 3, Highfield Hall, Totley Hall Lane, Sheffield 17, South Yorkshire, England.

CALMENSON, Stephanie Lyn, b. 28 Nov. 1952, Brooklyn, New York, USA. Writer. *Education:* BA, Brooklyn College; MA, New York University. *Publications:* Never Take a Pig to Lunch, anthology, 1982; One Little Monkey, 1982, 4th edition, 1983, produced by British Broadcasting Corporation television, 1984; My Book of the Seasons, 1982; Where Will the Animals Stay?, 1983; That's Not Fair!, 1983; Where is Grandma Potamus?, 1983; The Birthday Hat: A Grandma Potamus Story, 1983; The Kindergarten Book, 1983; Barney's Sand Castle, 1983; Bambi and the Butterfly, 1983; Ten Furry Monsters, 1984; The Afterschool Book, 1984; All Aboard the Goodnight Train, 1984; Waggleby of Fraggle Rock, 1985; Ten Items or Less, 1985; Happy Birthday, Buddy Blue, 1985; The Laugh Book, anthology with Joanna Cole, 1986; Gobo and The Prize From Outer Space, 1986; The Sesame Street ABC Book, 1986; The Sesame Street Book of First Times, 1986; Little Duck's Moving Day, 1986; The Read-Aloud Treasury, anthology with Joanna Cole, 1987. *Contributions to:* Parents Magazine; Millimeter Magazine. *Memberships:* Mystery Writers of America; Society of Childrens Book Writers. *Address:* 150 East 18th Street, New York City, NY 10003, USA.

CAMERON, Bella, b. 8 Aug. 1918. Retired Secretary, Poet; Freelance Journalist. *Major Publications:* Bitter Honey, 1975; Contrary Winds, 1976; Open Air Seance, 1977; Desire & Wisdom, 1978; Love Letters, 1978; Human Flutes, 1979; Sardonic Taskmaster, 1981. *Contributor to:* North American Mentor Magazine; Poet India; Haiku Journal; Cyclo-Flame Anthologies; Orbis; The Record; Tell Tale; Poetry Notts Magazine; The New Earth; Canvas; Bedsitter; and others. *Memberships include:* United Poet Laureates; International Avalon Foundation, USA; Overseas Editor, American Mosaic Magazine & Twist; Fellow, Associate Editor, International Society of Literature, Lancashire, England; Titular Member, Centro Studi E Scambi, Italy; Fellow, International Who's Who of Poetry; World Poetry Society International; Lancashire Authors Association; North American Mentor Poetry; and others. *Honours include:* International Woman, 1975 with Laureate Honours & Gold Laurel Crown; Doctor of Humane Letters, Université Libre, 1976; Honorary Life Member, Avalon Foundation, 1978; Diploma for Poetics, Academia Leonardo Da Vinci, 1979; and others. *Address:* Flat 2, 22 York Road, St Annes on Sea, Lancashire FY8 1HP, England.

CAMERON, Elspeth Macgregor, b. 10 Jan. 1943. Toronto, Canada. University Professor, Writer. m. Paul F Lovejoy, 15 Apr. 1977, Montreal, Canada, 2 sons, 1 daughter. *Education:* BA Honours English, University of British Columbia, 1964; MA, University of New Brunswick, 1965; PhD, McGill University, 1970. *Literary Appointments:* Professor of English, Loyola College, Concordia University, 1970–77; Senior tutor, University of Toronto, 1980–86. *Publications:* Hugh Maclennan: A Writer's Life, 1981; Irving Layton: A Portrait, 1985. *Contributions to:* Saturday Night. *Honours:* Biography Award, University of British Columbia, 1981; Finalist, Governor General's Award, Non-fiction, 1981; Fiona Mee Literary Journalism Award, 1982; Honourable mention, Fiona Mee Literary Award, 1983. *Memberships:* PEN; PWAC; ACUTE; ACOL; The Writer's Union. *Literary Agent:* Colbert Agency Ltd, Toronto. *Address:* 28 Oriole Gardens, Toronto, Ontario M4V IV7, Canada.

CAMERON, Kim Sterling, b. 30 Sep. 1946, Utah, USA. Professor of Organizational Behaviour and Higher Education. m. Melinda Cummings, 24 Aug. 1970, Salt Lake City, Utah, 2 sons, 4 daughters. *Education:* BS, MS, Brigham Young University; MA, PhD, Yale University. *Publications:* Interpersonal Skill Development for Managers, 1981; Coffin Nails and Corporate Strategies, 1982; Organizational Effectiveness, 1983; Developing Management Skills, 1984. *Contributions to:* Professional journals in the fields of organizational behaviour, management and higher education. *Honour:* Fulbright Distinguished Scholar to Brazil, 1984. *Address:* Graduate School of Business Administration, University of Michigan, Ann Arbor, MI 48109, USA.

CAMERON WATT, Donald, b. 17 May 1928, Rugby, England. University Professor; Historian. *Education:* MA, Oxford University, England. *Publications:* Britain Looks to Germany, 1965; Personalities and Policies, 1965; A History of the World in the 20th Century, Part 1, 1890–1919, 1967; Hitler's Mein Kampf, 1969; Survey of International Affairs for 1961, published 1965; for 1962, published 1963; for 1963 published 1972 (Editor 1962–71); Too Serious a Business, 1975; Succeeding John Bull. America in Britain's Place, 1900–1975, 1984. *Contributor to:* Numerous historical and political books and journals, newspapers etc. including, Documents on German Foreign Policy 1918–45 (Assistant Editor 1951–54); Bulletin of European Association of American Studies (Editor 1962–66); Political Quarterly, (member of Ed Board); Marine Policy; (Member of Ed Board). *Memberships:* Several British and foreign professional organisations including Association of Contemporary Historians (Chairman); Royal Historical Society (Fellow); International Commission for the History of International History; Greenwich Forum; Royal Institute of International Affairs. *Literary Agent:* A D Peters and Company. *Address:* c/o London School of Economics, Aldwych, London WC2, England.

CAMPBELL, Alistair Robert Macbrair, b. 9 May 1946, Cardiff, Wales. Publisher. m. Frances, 10 Sep. 1968, Oxford, 1 son, 2 daughters. *Education:* BSc (Hons), Zoology, Aberdeen University. *Literary Appointment:* Editorial Director, Blackwell Scientific Publications Limited, 1979–. *Publications:* A Guide to the Birds of the Coast, Second Edition, 1976 with Dr Bruce Campbell; Microform Publishing, with Peter Ashby, 1979; Journal Publishing with J Meadows and Gillian Page (in press). *Contributions to:* New Scientist; Nature and other periodicals connected with publishing and science. *Address:* Old School, School Lane, Stadhampton, Oxford, England.

CAMPBELL, Alistair Te Ariki, b. 25 June 1925, Rarotonga. m. (1) Fleur Adcock, 2 sons; (2) Meg Andesen, 1 son, 2 daughters. *Education:* BA, Diploma of Teaching. *Literary Appointments:* Founder, Poetry Programme, New Zealand Broadcasting Service, 1958. *Publications:* (Verse) Mine Eyes Dazzle, 1950; Sanctuary of Spirits, 1963; Wild Honey, 1964; Kapiti, 1972; Collected Poems, 1981; Soul Traps; 1985; (memoirs) Island to Island, 1984; (drama) When the Bough Breaks, 1974; (Children's story) The Happy Summer, 1961. *Contributor to:* Numerous contributions to magazines and journals. *Honours:* Gold Medal, La Spezia International Film Festival, 1974; New Zealand Book Award for Poetry, 1982. *Memberships:* President, Treasurer, PEN New Zealand; Patron of Poetry Society; Member, Writers Guild. *Address:* 4 Rawhiti Road, Pukerua Bay, New Zealand.

CAMPBELL, Ewing, b. 26 Dec. 1940, Alice, Texas, USA. Writer. *Education:* BBA, North Texas State University; MA, University of Southern Mississippi; PhD, Oklahoma State University. *Literary Appointment:* Assistant Professor, Texas A & M University, 1984. *Publications:* Novels: Weave It Like Nightfall, 1977; The Way of Sequestered Places, 1982; The Rincon Triptych, 1984; Tic Douloureaux (forthcoming); Stories: Piranesi's Dream (forthcoming). *Contributions to:* Kenyon Review; Chicago Review; Pax. *Address:* Department of English, Texas A & M University, College Station, TX 77843, USA.

CAMPBELL, Ian, b. 25 Aug. 1942, Lausanne, Switzerland. Reader, English, University of Edinburgh. *Education:* MA, Aberdeen, 1964; PhD, Edinburgh, 1970. *Appointments:* Member, English Literature Dept, University of Edinburgh, 1967–; Guest Appointments,

Guelph, Duke, UCLA; British Council Appointments, France, Germany. *Publications:* Co-Editor, McLellan's Jamie the Saxt; Editor: Carlyle's Reminiscences & Selected Essays, Critical Essays in Nineteenth Century Scottish Fiction; Thomas Carlyle, 1974, 1975, 1978; Carlyle Letters, 12 volumes, 1970–85; Thomas Carlyle, 1974; Nineteenth Century Scottish Fiction: Critical Essays, 1978; Thomas and Jane, 1980; Lewis Grassic Gibbon, 1984. *Contributor to:* Numerous papers to learned journals. *Honour:* British Academy Research Fellowship, 1980. *Memberships:* President, Carlyle Society; Past President, Scottish Association for the Speaking of Verse; Council Member, Association for Scottish Literary Studies. *Address:* Dept of English, University of Edinburgh, David Hume Tower, George Square, Edinburgh EH8 9JX, Scotland.

CAMPBELL, James Howard, b. 1928, Detroit, Michigan, USA. Artist. m. Sarah Joanne Dohse, 1 June 1948, at Ansonia, Ohio, 3 daughters. *Literary Appointments:* Weekly columnist, Ansonian weekly newspaper; San Jose Mercury-News, San Francisco Examiner. *Publications:* Two Willing and More, illustrations of verse by Paul C Imschuriler, 1973; Hold Fast, writer and illustrator, ill strated history of sail. *Honours:* Artist of the Year, 1976 and 1984, SCAA. *Memberships:* Society of Western Artist; Santa Clara Art Association; International Society of Marine Painters. *Address:* 335 Rosemary Street West, San Jose, CA 95110, USA.

CAMPBELL, John (Malcolm), b. 2 Sep. 1947. Writer. m. Alison Macracken, 5 Aug. 1972, Edinburgh, 1 son, 1 daughter. *Education:* BA, Edinburgh, 1970; PhD, Edinburgh, 1975. *Publications:* Lloyd George: The Goat in the Wilderness, 1977; Roy Jenkins: A Biography, 1983; F E Smith, First Earl of Birkenhead, 1983. *Contributor to:* Book Reviews: The Times; Times Literary Supplement; Times Higher Educational Supplement; London Review of Books; New Statesman; Spectator; Listener; Scotsman; Sunday Times; History Today; Political Quarterly. *Honours:* 2nd Prize, Yorkshire Post, Award for Best First Book of 1977. *Memberships:* Society of Authors; London Library. *Agent:* Bruce Hunter, David Higham Associates. *Address:* 35 Ladbroke Square, London W11 3NB, England.

CAMPBELL, Josephine (Anne), b. 31 Jan. 1927, Evansville, Indiana, USA. Writer; Editor. m. Donald H Campbell, 15 Mar. 1947, Washington DC, 3 daughters. *Appointments include:* Daytona Beach, Florida, News-Journal; Washington Post, World Report; Freelance: New York Times, North American Newspaper Alliance, Associated Press, Washington Star, Manchester Guardian, others; Own News Bureau covering Washington & UN, daily Nawa-i-Waqt, Weekly Qindeel, Lahore, Pakistan; Special USIA Assignments include: NAACP Convention, Miami, 1980; Kenya, Tanzania, Somalia for Topic Magazine, 1981; Olympic Summer Games, Los Angeles, 1984; Congressional Tour in Gabon, Cameroon, Mozambique, 1985; World Conference on Food and Water, Texas, 1985; Professional & Community involvements include: Delegate, International Feminists' Planning Conference, Harvard, 1973; Participant, Wilhelm Weinberg Labour/Management/Public Interest Seminar, 1976; Invited Participant 25th Anniversary Seminar, 1984; Jefferson Scholar, George Washington University, 1980–81; Participant Briefings on National Security for 50 US media women; Sponsor, Johnson Foundation, Wingspread, Wisconsin, 1985; Commissioner, Prince George's County Human Relations Commission, 1975–80; Chair, White House/Justice Department Task Force, Sex Discrimination; Board, American Civil Liberties Union, Prince George's County. *Memberships include:* National Press Club; Society for International Development; World Affairs Council; Coalition of Labour Union Women; National Women's Political Caucus; Women's Institute for Freedom of the Press; Dog Writers Association of America. *Address:* 3723 36th Street, Mount Rainier, MD 20712, USA.

CAMPBELL, Katharine Margaret, b. 23 Aug. 1959, Redhill, Surrey, England. Financial Journalist. *Education:* Congratulatory First Class BA, Joint Hons, German and Ancient Greek, St Hilda's College, Oxford. *Literary Appointment:* Editorial Staff Writer, The Banker, 1984–. *Contributions to:* The Banker, Investors Chronicle, etc. Articles on Euromarket, financial futures and options, Hong Kong capital market, securities industry. *Address:* 38 Balcombe Street, London NW1 6ND, England.

CAMPBELL, Keith Oliver, b. 15 May 1920, Lakemba, New South Wales, Australia. Emeritus Professor of Agricultural Economics, University of Sydney. m. Christiana McFadyen, 17 Sep. 1949, Raeford, North Carolina, USA, 1 son, 2 daughters. *Education:* BSc Agr (Hon 1), University of Sydney, 1943; MA, PhD, University of Chicago, Illinois, USA, 1946–49; MPA, Harvard University, 1949. *Publications:* Agricultural Marketing and Prices, 1973; The Agricultural Sector in the Australian Economy, 1977; Food for the Future, 1978; Australian Agriculture – Reconciling Change and Tradition, 1980; The Scientific Basis of Modern Agriculture (Editor), 1986. *Contributions to:* Numerous professional journals, magazines and newspapers; Chapters in books. *Honours:* Littauer Fellow, Harvard University, 1948–49; Fellow, Australian Institute of Agricultural Science, 1963; Academy of the Social Sciences in Australia, 1964; Elmhirst Memorial Lecturer, International Association of Agricultural Economists, 1982. *Address:* 188 Beecroft Road, Cheltenham, NSW 2119, Australia.

CAMPBELL, Ramsey, b. 4 Jan. 1946, Liverpool, England. Author. m. Jenny Chandler, 1 Jan. 1971, Cheltenham, 1 son, 1 daughter. *Publications:* Demons by Daylight, 1973; The Height of the Scream, 1976; The Doll Who Ate His Mother, 1976; The Parasite, 1980; The Nameless, 1981; Dark Companions, 1981; Incarnate, 1983; The Face That Must Die, first unabridged edition, 1983; Obsession, 1985; Cold Print, 1985. *Contributions to:* Fantasy Review, USA, Columnist. *Honours:* British Fantasy Award, Best Short Story, In the Bag, 1978; World Fantasy Award, Best Short Story, The Chimney, 1978; British Fantasy Award, Best Novel, The Parasite, 1980; World Fantasy Award, Best Short Story, Mackintosh Willy, 1980. *Memberships:* British Fantasy Society, President; Mystery Writers of America. *Literary Agents:* Kirby McCauley, USA; Carol Smith, UK. *Address:* 31 Penkett Road, Wallasey L45 7QF, Merseyside, England.

CAMPBELL-SMITH, Duncan J, b. 21 Nov. 1950, England. Management Consultant and Writer on Business Affairs. m. Anne-Catherine Phillips, 14 May 1983, 1 son. *Education:* 1st class honours, Modern history, Merton College, Oxford University, 1972; Diploma in Arabic, Middle East Center for Arab Studies, Lebanon, 1978. *Publications:* Struggle For Take-Off: The Story of British Airways 1979–86, 1986. *Honours:* British Press Awards Commendation for International Reporting, 1982. *Literary Agent:* Felicity Bryan, Curtis Brown Group. *Address:* 3 Northolme Road, London N5 2UZ, England.

CAMPELLO, Myriam, b. 4 Sep. 1940, Rio de Janeiro, Brazil. Fiction Writer. *Education:* Graduated, Journalism, 1964. *Literary Appointments:* Resident Fiction Writer, Bernardine Scherman Fellow, MacDowell Colony for Creative Artists, New Hampshire, USA, 1982, 1985. *Publications:* Novels; Cerimonia da Noite 1973, Sortilegiu 1981. Short stories in collections: Antologia de Contistas Novos, 1971; O Conto da Mulher Brasileira, 1978; Muito Prazer, 1982; O Prazer é Todo Meu, 1984. *Contributions to:* Numerous magazines, journals, collections, Brazil and abroad, translations into French, English, Polish (short stories). *Honour:* Fernando Chinaglia Award, Best Unpublished Novel, 1972 (published 1973). *Membership:* Sindicato dos Escritores do Rio de Janeiro. *Address:* Avenida Sao Sebastiao 111 Ap. S.103, Urca 22291, Rio de Janeiro, RJ, Brazil.

CAMUS, Jean-Renaud-Gabriel, b. 10 Aug. 1946, Chamalieres, France. Writer. *Education:* Diploma of Higher Studies of History of Law; Diploma of Higher Studies in Political Science; Diploma, Institute of Political Studies, Paris; Licence degree in Arts; MPh. *Publications:* Passage, 1975; Travers, 1978; Tricks, 1979; Buena Vista Park, 1980; Journal d'un Voyage en France, 1981; Ete, Travers II, 1982; Notes Achriennes, 1982; Roman Roi, 1983; Chroniques Achriennes, 1984; Notes sur les Manieres du Temps, 1985. *Honours:* Chevalier, French Order of Arts and Letters, 1984; Pensionnaire, Academy of France in Rome, Villa Médicis, 1985–. *Memberships:* Association for Support and Illustration of Contemporary Literature, France. *Address:* 76 Rue du Bac, 75007 Paris, France.

CANDLER, Julie J, b. 28 Dec. 1919, Illinois, USA. Freelance Writer. 1 son, 2 daughters. *Literary Appointments:* Publicity writer, Grant Advertising, 1953–55; Reporter/photographer/editor, Birmingham Eccentric, 1955–60; Director, Cranbrook Writers Guild & Camp Oakland Youth Programs Inc. *Publication:* Woman at the Wheel, 1967. *Contributions to:* Womans Day, 18 years; Various trade publications, magazines, articles on automobiles, travel, camping, boating, etc; Newsletters, brochures. press releases; Numerous television appearances including, Today Show, To Tell The Truth. *Honours include:* Headliner Award, Women in Communications, 1967; Public Service Award, National Safety Council, 1967; Deep Woods Award, Outdoor Writers Association,. 1974; Writers Award, Recreational Vehicle Industry Association, 1974; Uniroyal Journalism Safety Award, 1974; Writers Award, National Foundation for Highway Safety, 1973; Woman of the Year, New York Auto Show, 1975. *Memberships include:* Detroit Auto Writers Group; Vice President, Cranbrook Writers Guild; Detroit Chapter, Women in Communications; American Society of Journalists & Authors; Society of Professional Journalists; Authors League. *Literary Agent:* Emilie Jacobsen. *Address:* 430 North Woodward, Birmingham, MI 48011, USA.

CANFIELD, Gae Whitney, b. 4 May 1931, Kingman, Kansas, USA. Librarian. m. Robert L Canfield, 22 Aug. 1954, at Manhattan, Kansas, 1 son, 1 daughter. *Education:* Master of Library Science. *Publication:* Sarah Winnemucca of the Northern Paiutes, 1983. *Address:* 166 Hillcrest Road, Berkeley, CA 94705, USA.

CANO-BALLESTA, Juan, b. 12 Mar. 1932, Murcia, Spain. Professor of Spanish Literature. *Education:* Philosophy Studies in Comillas and Paderborn, 1950–56; PhD, Romance Philology, University Munich, 1961. *Publications include:* La poesia espanola entre pureza y revolucion 1930–36, 1972; La poseia de Miguel Hernandez, 1962; Maestros del cuento espanol moderno, 1974; Miguel Hernandez-El hombre y su poesi, 1974; Miguel Hernandez: Poesia y prosa de guerre, 1977; En torno a Miguel Hernandez, 1978; Literatura y technologia; Las letras elspanolas ante la revolucion industrial. *Contributor to:* Numerous publications including: Romanische Forschungen; La Torre; Insula; Symposium; Papeles de Son Armadans. *Honours include:* Morse Research Fellow, Yale University, 1968–69; Fellowship, American Council Learned Societies, 1975–76. *Memberships include:* Modern Language Association; American Association Teachers of Spanish and Portuguese; International Association Hispanists. *Address:* Department of Spanish, 402 Cabell Hall, University of Virginia, Charlottesville, VA 22903, USA.

CANTONI, Louis Joseph, b. 22 May 1919, Detroit, Michigan, USA. Professor; Psychologist; Poet. *Education:* AB, University of California, Berkeley, 1946; MSW, University of Michigan, 1949; PhD, ibid, 1953. *Publications include:* Placement of the Handicapped in Competitive Employment, 1957; Counselling Your Friends, co-author, 1961; With Joy I Called To You, poetry, 1969; Supervised Practice in Rehabilitation Counselling, 1978; Gradually the Dreams Change, poetry, 1979; Golden Song Anthology, poetry (principal editor), 1985. *Contributions to:* American Psychologist; Journal of Rehabilitation; Poet; etc. *Honour:* Certificate of Honour, outstanding service, Poetry Society of Michigan, 1984. *Memberships include:* Fellow, American Association for the Advancement of Science; Chairman, National Association of Rehabilitation Counsellor Educators, 1965–66. *Address:* Wayne State University, Detroit, MI 48202, USA.

CAPRA, Fritjof, b. 1 Feb. 1939, Vienna, Austria. Writer. *Education:* PhD, Theoretical Physics, University of Vienna, 1966. *Major Publications:* The Tao of Physics, 1975; The Turning Point, 1982; Green Politics, 1984. *Contributor to:* Numerous scientific publications, including: New Society; American Journal of Physics; ReVISION; The American Theosophist; Acta Physica Austriaca. *Literary Agent:* John Brockman, New York. *Address:* P O Box 5805, Berkeley, CA 94705, USA.

CARAMELLO, Charles Anthony, b. 29 Feb. 1948, Plymouth, Massachusetts, USA. Professor. m. Anne Olszewski, 30 Apr. 1979, Annapolis, Maryland, USA. *Education:* BA English & Religion, Wesleyan University, 1970; MA English, University of Wisconsin at Milwaukee, 1973; PhD English, University of Wisconsin, Milwaukee, 1978. *Literary Appointments:* Lecteur, Université de la Sorbonne Nouvelle, 1976–76; Publications Coordinator, Center for 20th Century Studies, University of Wisconsin at Milwaukee, 1976–78; Assistant Professor of English, 1978–83, Associate Professor of English, 1983–, University of Maryland at College Park. *Major Publications:* Performance in Postmodern Culture (co-editor), 1977; Silverless Mirrors: Book, Self & Postmodern American Fiction, 1983. *Contributor to:* Descant; Dalhousie Review; Southern Humanities Review; Sun & Moon. *Honours include:* Frederick J Hoffman Award, 1972, 1978; Andrew W Mellon Postdoctoral Fellowship in the Humanities, Center for Humanities, Wesleyan University, 1982–83; Fellow, National Humanities Center, North Carolina, 1984–85. *Memberships:* Modern Language Association; Henry James Society; Samuel Beckett Society. *Address:* 3726 Connecticut Avenue NW, Washington, DC 20008, USA.

CARAS, Roger Andrew, b. 24 May 1928, Massachusetts, USA. Author; Television Correspondent. m. Jill Langdon Barclay, 5 Sep. 1954, at Boston, 1 son, 1 daughter. *Education:* BA, Northeastern University, Western Reserve University, University of Southern California; DLit (Hon), Rio Grande College; DLaws (Hon) University of Pennsylvania. *Literary Appointment:* Adjunct Professor of English, Southampton College. *Major Publications include:* Antarctica: Land of Frozen Time, 1962; Dangerous to Man, 1964; Wings of Gold, 1965; The Custer Wolf, Last Chance on Earth, 1966; North American Mammals, 1967; Sarang, 1968; Monarch of Deadman Bay, Panther!, 1969; Source of the Thunder, 1970; The Private Lives of Animals, Venomous Animals of the World, 1974; A Zoo in Your Room, Sockeye, 1975; The Forest, Yankee, 1979; The Roger Caras Dog Book, 1980; A Celebration of Dogs, 1982; The Endless Migration, Mara Simba, 1985. *Contributor to:* Audubon; New York Times; Ladies Home Journal; National Wildlife; Science Digest; National Observer; Financial Times; Texas Quarterly; Harper's Bazaar; New York; Family Health; Physician's World; The Dial; Family Circle and others. *Honours:* Numerous awards for television writing and reporting, Humane work etc. Fellow of the Royal Society of Arts. *Memberships:* Outdoor Writers' Association of America; Dog Writers Association. *Literary Agent:* Roberta Pryor. *Address:* 46 Fenmarsh Road, East Hampton, NY 11937, USA.

CARDELL, Margaret Timothea (Kim), b. 19 Mar. 1941, Newquay, Cornwall, England. Agricultural Journalist. m. Ron Harrison, 16 Jan. 1975, Truro, 3 stepsons. *Education:* Dip Ed, 1963; Dip Ag (NZ), 1970. *Appointments:* Reporter, Taranaki Herald, 1966; Nelson Evening Mail, 1968; Associate Editor, 1970–77, Contributing Editor, 1977–81, Livestock Farming; Editor, The Sheep Farmer, 1981–. *Contributor to:*

Articles to all farming press; Reports to BBC & TV. *Honours:* Fison Award, Outstanding Contributions to Agricultural Journalism, 1st Woman Winner, 1974. *Membership:* Guild of Agricultural Journalists. *Address:* Little Hendra, Ashton, Helston, Cornwall TR13 9TX, England.

CARDOZA, Anne, b. 18 Nov. 1941, New York City, New York, USA. Author; Film Script Writer. *Education:* BS, New York University, 1964; MA, San Diego State College, 1979. *Publications:* Author of 33 books including: Psyche Squad, 1979; High Paying Jobs in Six Months or Less, 1984; In the Chips – How to Use Your Computer to Make Money, 1985; Robotics, 1985; Careers in Robotics, 1985; Careers in Aerospace, 1985. Filmscripts include: Otherhood, 1979. *Contributions to:* Various professional publications of over 300 articles of fiction or non-fiction. Grant proposal writer and publicist. *Honours:* Merit Award, Achievers International, 1979; Scholarship, Graduate work in journalism, KFMB-TV, 1977; Mensa Scholarship, 1977. *Address:* P O Box 4333, San Diego, CA 92104, USA.

CARETTE, Hendrik B, b. 17 Dec. 1946, Bruges, Belgium. Journalist. *Literary Appointments:* Editor of literary review Diogenes, 1984–. *Major Publications:* Winter te Damme (poetical work), 1974; Ik leef dus ik zweef nog, 1978; Klacht van een grootgrondbezitter, 1985. *Contributor to:* Gedicht, (Netherlands); Kreatief, De Nieuwe, (Belgium). *Honour:* Trap-prijs, 1979. *Address:* Zeedijk 148, bus 242, 8400 Oostende, Belgium.

CAREY, Mary Virginia, b. 19 May 1925, New Brighton, Cheshire, England. Writer. *Education:* BSc, College of Mount St Vincent, New York City, New York, USA, 1946. *Publications include:* Novelizations of Walt Disney Motion Pictures – Juveniles; Grandmothers are Very Special People, Editor and Compiler, 1977; The Owl Who Loved Sunshine, juvenile, 1977; The Mystery of the Magic Circle, 1978; The Mystery of the Sinister Scarecrow, 1979; A Compendium of Bunk, or How to Spot a Con Artist, co-author, 1976; A Place for Allie, 1985; Mystery of the Creep Show Crooks, 1985. *Contributions to:* Coronet; Walt Disney's Mickey Mouse Club Magazine. *Memberships:* Authors Guild; PEN; Society of Children's Book Writers. *Address:* 645 Hampshire Road 137, Westlake Village, CA 91361, USA.

CARLEN, Claudia, b. 24 July 1906, Detroit, Michigan, USA. Librarian. *Education:* BLS, High distinction, 1928, MLS, 1938, Post graduate, 1938, University of Michigan; University of Chicago, Illinois, 1953; Archives course and Certificate, Case Western Reserve University, 1977; Universities of Maryland and Montana. *Literary Appointments:* Librarian, Marygrove College, Detroit, Michigan, 1944–69; Index Editor, New Catholic Encyclopedia, Washington, 1963–67; Managing Editor, Corpus Dictionary Programme, 1968–70; Vice President, Corpus Instrumentorum Incorporated, 1969–70; Library Consultant, North American College Graduate Division, Rome, Italy, 1971–72; Librarian, St Johns Seminary, Plymouth, Michigan, 1972–79; Scholar in Residence, 1982–. *Publications:* Guide to the Encyclicals, 1939; Guide to the Documents of Pius XII, 1951; Dictionary of Papal Pronouncements, 1958; The Papal Encyclicals: 1740–1981, 5 volumes, 1982. *Contributions to:* Festschriften; Wilson Library Bulletin; Library Journal; American Archivist; Catholic Library World; Library Trends; Thomist; Catholic Historical Review; Various multi-authored volumes. *Honours:* Phi Beta Kappa, 1928; Phi Kappa Phi, 1928; Beta Phi Mu, 1955; Distinguished Alumna Award, University of Michigan, 1974; LittD, Catholic University of America, 1983. LHD: Marygrove College, 1981; Loyola University of Chicago, Illinois, 1983. *Address:* 44011 Five Mile Road, Plymouth, MI 48170, USA.

CARLILE, Henry, b. 6 May 1934, San Francisco, California, USA. Professor of Literature & Creative Writing. m. Sandra McPherson, 22 July 1966, Seattle, Washington, divorced 1985, 1 daughter. *Education:* AA Grays Harbor College, 1960; BA 1962, MA 1967, University of Washington. *Literary Appointments:* Instructor of English, Portland State University, 1967; Guest Editor, Poetry Northwest, Sept-Dec, 1971; Guest Poetry Editor, Iowa Review, Winter 1979; Visiting Lecturer, University of Iowa Program in Creative Writing, 1978–80; Professor of Literature & Creative Writing, Portland State University. *Major Publications:* The Rough-hewn Table, 1971; Running Lights, 1981. *Contributor to:* American Poetry Review; The Nation; New Yorker; Parnassus; Poetry Now; and others. *Honours:* National Endowment for the Arts Discovery Grant, 1970; also Fellowship in poetry, 1976; PEN Syndicated Fiction Award, 1983; Ingram Merrill Fellowship in Poetry, 1985. *Membership:* Associated Writing Programs. *Address:* Department of English, Portland State University, P O Box 751, Portland, OR 97207, USA.

CARLSON, Ronald Frank, b. 15 Sep. 1947, Logan, Utah, USA. Writer. m. Georgia Elaine Craig, 14 June 1969, Salt Lake City, 2 sons. *Education:* BA, MA, University of Utah, 1972. *Literary Appointments:* Writer in Residence, Hotchkiss School, Lakeville, Connecticut, 1983; Novelist in Residence, Sundance Playwrights Institute, Sundance, Utah, 1984; Visiting Writer, Writers at Work Conference, Park City, Utah, 1985. *Publications:* Betrayed by F Scott Fitzgerald, 1977; Truants, 1981, 82; News of the World, 1986. *Contributions to:* Carolina Quarterly; TriQuarterly; Coda; Sports Illustrated; McCall's; and others. *Honours:* Connecticut Commission of the Arts Grant, 1978; Sabbatical, Hotchkiss School, Lakeville, Connecticut, 1979; Alan Collins Fellowship, Bread Loaf Writers Conference, 1983; National Endowment for the Arts, Fiction Fellowship, 1985. *Memberships:* Authors Guild. *Literary Agent:* Brandt and Brandt, New York. *Address:* 1272 East 500 South, Salt Lake City, UT 84102, USA.

CARMAN, William Young, b. 1909, Ottawa, Ontario, Canada. Retired Deputy Director, National Army Museum, 1965–74. *Publications include:* A History of Firearms, 1955; Indian Army Uniform (Cavalry), 1961; British Military Uniform, 1962; Headdress of the British Army (Yeomanry), 1970; Indian Army Uniforms (Infantry), 1969; Model Soldiers, 1972; Royal Artillery, 1973; Badges & Insignia of the Armed Forces, with Commander May, 1974; Dictionary of Military Uniform, 1977; Uniforms of the British Army (Cavalry), 1982; Uniforms of the British Army (Infantry), 1985. *Contributor to:* Society for Army Historical Research; Military History Society; Encyclopedia Britannica; etc. *Memberships:* FSA; Fellow, Royal Historical Society; Vice President, Military Historical Society; Life Vice President, British Model Soldier Society. *Address:* 94 Mulgrave Road, Sutton, Surrey, England.

CARNEY, Matthew, b. 27 Dec. 1922, New York City, USA. Writer. 2 sons, 2 daughters. *Education:* BA Letters, University of Southern California; Candidate, Doctorat d'Université, Sorbonne, Paris. *Publications:* The Drifter, 1960; Peripheral American, 1981; Run out of Time, 1982; Love Versed in Life, 1983. *Contributor to:* Newsletters of: American Taurine Clubs; La Busca; Pases Y Lances; Las Noticias; La de La; On Jurisprudence: The Recorder; San Francisco, USA. *Address:* 4 Impasse Astrolabe, Paris 75015, France.

CARONE, Pasquale A, b. 26 June 1914, New York City, USA. Psychiatrist. m. Jacqueline Bruno, 9 June 1940, New York City, 1 son, 1 daughter. *Education:* BA, New York University; MD, Creighton University School of Medicine. *Publications:* Drug Abuse In Industry (co-author), 1973; Absenteeism In Industry (co-author), 1975; The Emotionally Troubled Employee (co-author), 1976; Women In Industry (co-author), 1977; Misfits In Industry (co-author), 1978. *Contributions:* Co-author, A New Method of Treatment of Affective Psychoses and Psychoses with Depressive Features, The Journal of Nervous and Mental Diseases, 1950; co-author, The Drug Abuse Crisis: A Report to the Illinois Crime Investigating Commission, The Journal of Asthma

Research, Sep. 1971. *Address:* 400 Sunrise Highway, Amityville, NY 11701, USA.

CARPENTER, John Randell, b. 14 Apr. 1936, Cambridge, Massachusetts, USA. Writer; Editor; Translator; Teacher. m. Bogdana Maria-Magdalena Chętkowska, 15 Apr. 1963, Warsaw, Poland, 1 son, 1 daughter. *Education:* Ba, cum laude, Harvard College, 1958; Sorbonne, University of Paris, 1962–66; Doctorat d'université, 1966. *Literary appointments:* Translator and Editor, 1966–74; Poet-in-Residence, Teacher, 1975–76; Fellow, National Endowment for the Arts (in poetry), 1976–77; Fellow, National Endowment for the Arts (in translation), 1980–81; Poet-in-Residence and Teacher, 1977–80; Lecturer, University of Washington, 1980; University of Michigan, 1984, 1985. *Publications:* Gathering Water, 1976; Egret, 1977; Pebble, Needle and Star, 1978; Poetry, Space and Children, 1985; Selected Poems of Zbigniew Herbert (translation), 1977; Report from the Besieged City by Z Herbert (translation), 1985. *Contributions:* of poems, translations and articles to journals such as: Poetry (Chicago); Quarterly Review of Literature: Times Literary Supplement; Encounter, etc. *Honours:* Witter Bynner Poetry Translation Award, Poetry Society of America, 1979; Islands and Continents Translation Award, Second Prize, 1979. *Memberships:* American Literary Translators Association; Poets and Writers Incorporated. *Address:* 1606 Granger Avenue, Ann Arbor, MI 48104, USA.

CARR, John Francis, b. 25 Dec. 1944, Philadelphia, Pennsylvania, USA. Writer. m. Victoria Alexander Carr, 14 May 1983, Northridge, 1 son, 1 daughter. *Education:* BA, Psychology and History. *Publications:* Ophidian Conspiracy, 1975; Pain Gain, 1976; Carnifex Mardi Gras, 1981; Great Kings , with Roland Green, 1985. *Contributor to:* Fiction Editor, Popular Computing, 1984–; Managing Editor, Far Frontiers, 1984–; Associate Editor, There Will be War, The Science Fiction Year Book. *Memberships:* Science Fiction Writers of America, Editor, Bulletin, 1978–80, Treasurer, 1982–. *Literary Agent:* Cherry Winer Literary Agency. *Address:* 10512 Yarmouth Avenue, Granada Hills, CA 91344, USA.

CARR, Roger Vaughan, b. 6 Nov. 1937, Melbourne, Australia, Author. m. Patricia Adele Butler, 14 Apr. 1971, Brighton, Victoria, 3 sons, 1 daughter. *Publications:* Surfie, 1966; 22 Children's Novels including Firestorm !, 1985. *Contributor to:* The Bulletin, Sydney; Pony Magazine & Annual, England; The Weekly Times; Victorian Education Department School Magazines. *Honours:* Commonwealth Literary Fund Grant, 1965; 2 Year Australia Council Writing Fellowship, 1973–75. *Membership:* Australian Writer's Guild Ltd. *Literary Agent:* Ann Elmo Agency Inc, New York, USA. *Address:* Aireys Inlet, Victoria 3221, Australia.

CARRIER, Constance, b. 29 July 1908. Teacher. *Education:* BA, Smith College; MA, Trinity College. *Publications include:* The Middle Voice, 1954; Poems of Properties, 1961; Poems of Tibullus, 1964; Aesopus Hodie, co-author, 1985. *Contributions to:* Numerous anthologies, journals and magazines including: Atlantic Monthly; New Yorker; American Scholar; Christian Science Monitor; Yankee; Poetry; Harper's; Chicago Tribune. *Honours:* Golden Rose Award, New England Poetry Society, 1971; Tribune Prizes, 1969, 70; Lamont Award, 1954; various other awards and several fellowships. *Address:* 225 West Main, New Britain, CT 06052, USA.

CARROLL, Eliot, b. 31 Jan. 1947, Montreal, Canada. Interior Landscaper; Playwright. m. Barbara Vuk, 19 Aug. 1977, Toronto, 1 son, 1 daughter. *Education:* Distinction, Honours Philosophy, McGill University, Sir George Williams University. *Publication:* Birth Rite, 1982. *Contributions to:* Montreal Star, music critic, 1975–77. *Memberships:* Former Treasurer, Board member, Playwrights Workshop, Montreal; Playwrights Canada. *Address:* 295 St Louis, Dorval, Quebec, Canada H9S 2S3.

CARROLL, Robert Peter, b. 18 Jan. 1941, Dublin, Republic of Ireland. University Lecturer, Glasgow. m. Mary Anne Alice Stevens, 30 Mar. 1968, Edinburgh, 2 sons, 1 daughter. *Education:* BA 1962, MA 1967, Trinity College, Dublin: PhD, University of Edinburgh, Scotland, 1967. *Publications:* When Prophecy Failed, 1979; From Chaos to Covenant, 1981; Jeremiah: A Commentary, 1986. *Contributions to:* The Biblical Translator: Expository Times: Journal for the Study of the OT: Numen: Oudtestamentische Studien; Scottish Journal of Theology; Studia Theologica; Vetus Testamentum; Zeitschrift für die alttestamentliche Wissenschaft. *Membership:* Committee member, Society for Old Testament Study. *Address:* 5 Marchmont Terrace, Dowanhill, Glasgow G12 9LT, Scotland.

CARSON, Herbert L, b. 3 Oct. 1929. Teacher; Writer. *Education:* BA, University of Pittsburgh, USA, 1953; MA, Columbia University, 1955; PhD, University of Minnesota, 1959. *Literary Appointments include:* Instructor, University of Minnesota, 1955–59; Instructor, University of Nebraska, 1959–60; Assistant Professor to Professor, Ferris State College, 1960–; Book Reviewer, Grand Rapids Press; Visiting Professor, Youngstown State University, 1966. *Publication:* Editor, 45th Anniversary Volume, Poetry Society of Michigan, 1980. *Contributor to:* North American Mentor Magazine; Grand Rapids Press; Classical Outlook; Classical Bulletin; Kansas Quarterly; Forum; Carolina Quarterly; Personalist; Quarterly Journal Communication; various books including: Steps in Successful Speaking, 1968; The Impact of Fiction (with A L Carson), 1970; Royal Tyler: A Critical Biography (with A L Carson), 1979; Domestic Tragedy (with Ada Lou Carson), 1982. *Honours include:* Grant, National Endowment for Humanities and Ford Foundation; Distinguished Teacher Award, Michigan Association of State Universities; Distinguished Faculty Award, Ferris State College. *Membership:* Member, Board of Directors, Michigan Humanities Council. *Address:* J-4 Humanities, Ferris State College, Big Rapids, MI 49307, USA.

CARTER, Anne Elizabeth, b. 8 July 1944, East St Louis, Illinois, USA. Newspaper Editor. *Education:* BA, Maryville College, St Louis, Missouri; MA, St Mary's University, San Antonio, Texas. *Literary Appointment:* Editor, RSCJ Newsletter. *Publication:* God Loved the Muddle, 1978. *Contributions to:* Catholic Charismatic; RSCJ Newsletter. Mary's Song of Praise, Hymn, 1977. *Membership:* Catholic Press Association. *Address:* 801 South Spoede Road, St Louis, MO 63131, USA.

CARTER, Frances Larraine Tunnell. College Professor/President, Carter Craft Inc. *Education:* BS, University of Southern Mississippi, USA, 1946; MS, University of Tennessee, 1947; PhD, University of Illinois, 1954; numerous other universities. *Literary Appointments include:* Consultant to various schools etc including Reading Cores, Talladega City Schools, 1978–79, 1979–80; Assistant Professor 1956–57, Associate Professor 1957–63, Professor 1963–, Samford University, School of Education; Visiting Professor, Hong Kong Baptist College, 1965–66; Instructor of Charm Classes, Ricky Ridge Community School, 1976; Editor, Woman's Missionary Union (National Office) 1983–85. *Publications include:* Books for children include: Sammy in the Country, 1960; Tween-Age Ambassador, 1970; Sharing Times Seven, 1971; Ching Fu and Jim, 1978. *Contributor to:* Numerous guide books, programmes and study units for under privileged children; 54 articles; 28 poems. *Honours include:* Birmingham's Women of the Year, 1977; Birmingham's Vol of the Year, 1980; offs various other organisations; Personal Development Chairman, 1980–82; Delta Kappa Gamma; Kappa Omicron Phi; Pi Mu; Phi Delta Kappa; President, Sanford University Faculty Women's Club, 1980–81; Various Literary prizes. *Memberships:* President, Alabama State Poetry Society, 1972–82; Vice President 1978–79; National President, Kappa Delta Epsilon (Education) 1980–85;

President, Woman of the Year Ltd. 1984–86. *Address:* 2561 Rocky Ridge Road, Birmingham, AL 35243, USA.

CARTER, (His Eminence) Gerald Emmett, b. 1 Mar. 1912, Montreal, Canada. Bishop; Cardinal of Roman Catholic Church; Archbishop of Toronto. *Education:* Grand Seminary of Montreal; University of Montreal. *Publications:* The Catholic Public Schools of Quebec, (W J Gage Ltd), 1957; Psychology and the Cross, (The Bruce Publishing Company), 1959; The Modern Challenge to Religious Education, (William H Sadlier Inc), 1961. *Honours include:* Honorary Canon Cathedral Basilica Montreal, 1952–61; Honorary Doctor of Laws, McGill University, 1980; Notre Dame University, 1981; Companion of the Order of Canada, 1983. *Membership Include:* Montreal Cathedral School Commission, 1948–61; Chairman, International Committee for English in the Liturgy, 1971–76; Member, Council on Economic Affairs of the Holy See, 1981. *Address:* Archdiocese of Toronto, 355 Church Street, Toronto, Ontario, M5B 1ZB, Canada.

CARTER, Walter Horace, b. 20 Jan. 1921, Albemarle, North Carolina, USA. Newspaper Publisher; Author; Magazine Writer. m. (1) Lucille Miller Carter, (dec); (2) Brenda C Strickland, 29 Oct. 1983, Tabor City, NC, 1 son, 2 daughters. *Education:* AB Journalism, University of North Carolina. *Publications:* Land That I Love, 1978; Creatures and Chronicles From Cross Creek, 1980; Wild and Wonderful Santer-Cooper Country, 1982; Nature's Masterpiece, A Homosassa, 1984; Return to Cross Creek, 1985. *Contributions to:* Various magazines; over 1000 stories published. *Honours:* Pulitzer Prize for Meritorious Public Service, 1953; Sidney Hillman Award, One of Ten Most Outstanding Young Men in America, 1954. *Memberships:* President, Outdoor Writers Association, 1981, 82, 83; President, Southeastern Outdoor Press Association, 1984–85. *Address:* 101 Crescent Street, Tabor City, NC 28463, USA.

CARTLAND, Barbara, b. England. Author. *Publications include:* Approximately 180 books including (Novels) Jigsaw; Passionate Attainment; Open Wings; No Heart is Free; Love is an Eagle; Blue Heather; Love is Dangerous; Love in Hiding; The Fire of Love; The Enchanting Evil; The Irrisistible Buck; Fire on the Snow; Bewitched; As Eagles Fly; Passions in the Sand; Conquered by Love; The Disgraceful Duke; Vote for Love; The Magic of Love; A King in Love; Lies for Love; Love Rules; Winged Victory; Love and the Marquis; A World of Love; Starlight; True Love; Love and Kisses; Sapphires in Siam; A Caretaker of Love; Secrets of the Heart; (Philosophical), Touch the Stars; (Biography), Ronald Cartland; (Historical) Bewitching Women; The Private Life of Charles II; Empress of Austria; Metternich – The Passionate Diplomate; (Sociology), You in the Home; Love Life & Sex; (Cookery Book) Food for Thought; Men are Wonderful; Editor, The Common Problem, by R Cartland; various dramas, radio plays, verses & autobiography; TV, The Frost Programme, 1968. *Contributor to:* Worldwide TV & Radio. *Honours include:* Dame of Grace of St John of Jerusalem. *Memberships include:* Vice President, St John Ambulance Brigade; Hertfordshire President, National Association for Health. *Address:* Camfield Place, Hatfield, Hertfordshire, England.

CARUBA, Alan, b. 9 Oct. 1937, Newark, New Jersey, USA. Public Relations Counsellor. *Education:* BA, University of Miami, Florida. *Publications:* People Touch, 1972; The Boring Book, in progress. *Contributions to:* Complete Guide to Writing Non-Fiction, 1984; Leading business journals, USA & UK; Former contributor, New York Times. *Honours:* Literary Luminary, New Jersey, 1977; Author Award, Newark College of Engineering, 1974. *Memberships:* American Society of Journalists & Authors; International Association of Business Communicators; The Society of Professional Journalists; American Society of Business & Economic Writers; National Association of Science Writers; National Book Critics Circle. *Address:* P O Box 40, Maplewood, NJ 07040, USA.

CARUS, Marianne, b. 16 June 1928, Germany. Editor in Chief and General Manager. m. Milton Blouke Carus, 3 Mar. 1951, Gummersbach, 1 son, 2 daughters. *Education:* Abitur, Gymnasium Gummersbach, 1948; Masters equivalent, Freiburg University; Additional Studies, Sorbonne, Paris, France; Additional studies, University of Chicago, Illinois, USA. *Literary Appointments:* Editor in Chief and General Manager, Cricket Magazine. *Publications:* Cricket's Choice, editor and compiler with Clifton Fadlman, 1974. *Contributions to:* Children's Literature in Education, volume II, 1980. *Memberships:* ALSC Division, ALA; Director, ALSC Board, 1982–85; Magazine Publishers Association; Children's Reading Roundtable, Chicago; Friends of USBBY; Society of Children's Book Writers; Friends of CCBC Inc. *Address:* Cricket Magazine, P O Box 300, Peru, IL 61354, USA.

CARVALHO ASSUMPCÃO, Vera, b. 25 Aug. 1947, São Paulo, Brazil. Writer. m. Elsio Vinicius Mattos de Assumpcão, 4 Sep. 1968, Sao Paulo, 2 sons, 1 daughter. *Publications:* Maria Eugenia, 1982; Querpuayú, 1985. *Honours:* Prizes for Short Stories; 1979, 1981, 1982, 1984; Scholarship, University of Evora, Portugal, 1985. *Membership:* Uniao Brasileira de Escritores. *Literary Agent:* Agencia Literaria CB LTDA. *Address:* Rua Tomé Portes 656, 04623 São Paulo, Brazil.

CARVALHO-NETO, Paulo de, b. 1 Sep. 1923, Brazil. Author: Writer. m. Ivolina Rosa, 1949, Brazil, 4 sons, 1 daughter. *Education:* PhD, Literature, University of Sao Paulo, Brazil; Master in Social Sciences, University of Brazil at Rio de Janeiro; Board Certified Hypotherapist (Professional Hypnotist), California, USA. *Publications:* Concepto de Folklore, 1956; Folklore y Psicoanelisis, 1956; Folklore del Paraquay, 1961; Diccionario del Folklore Ecuatoriano, 1964; 'Historia del Folklore Iberoamericano, 1969; Mi Tio Atahualpa (novel), 1972; Los Ilustres Maestros, (novel), 1975. *Membership:* PEN International Association of Writers, California, USA. *Honours:* International Folklore Prize, Guiseppe Pitrè, Italy, 1969; Chicago University Prize in Folklore, 1972; Honorable Mention Casa de las Americas Prize (novel), 1975; Keynote Speaker, International Meeting of Writers, Lahti, Finland, 1981. *Literary Agent:* Carmen Balcalls Literary Agency, Spain and Brazil. *Address:* Rua Raul Pompeia 149, Ed. La Rochelle, Ap. 1004, 20.000 Rio de Janeiro, RJ, Brazil.

CARVER, (Lord) (Richard) Michael (Power), b. 24 Apr. 1915, Bletchingley, England. Field Marshall. m. Edith Lowry-Corry, 22 Nov. 1947, Edwardstone, 2 sons, 2 daughters. *Education:* Winchester College; Royal Military College, Sandhurst (King's Gold Medal). *Publications:* Second to None, 1952; El Alamein, 1962; Tobruk, 1964; The War Lords, Editor, 1976; Harding of Petherton, 1978; War Since 1945, 1980; A Policy for Peace, 1982; The Seven Ages of the British Army, 1984. *Contributor to:* Times Literary Supplement; New York Times – Sunday Book Reviews. *Honours:* MC, 1942; DSO, 1943; CBE, 1945; GCB, 1971; Life Peer, 1977. *Literary Agent:* David Higham Associates, London. *Address:* Wood End House, Wickham, Fareham, Hants PO17 6JZ, England.

CARVER, Raymond, 25 May 1938, Oregon, USA. Writer. Divorced, 1 son, 1 daughter. *Education:* AB, Humboldt State University. *Appointments:* Teacher, Universities of California, Berkeley and Santa Cruz, Iowa, Texas, Syracuse. *Publications:* Noa-Klamath, 1968; Winter Insomnia, 1970; Will You Please Be Quiet, Please?' 1976; At Night the Salmon Move, 1976; What We Talk About When We Talk About Love, 1981; Cathedral Fiction, 1983; Fires, Essays, Poems, Stories, 1984; Where Water Comes Together with Other Water, 1985; Ultramarine, 1986. *Contributor to:* New Yorker; Atlantic Monthly; Paris Review; Artaeus; Harper's; Tri-Quarterly; etc. *Honours:* Guggenheim Memorial Award, 1978–79; National Endowment in the Arts Award in Poetry, 1970, and in Fiction, 1978; Strauss Living Award, 1983. *Memberships:* PEN; Authors Guild. *Agent:* Amanda Urban, New York City. *Address:* 832 Maryland Avenue, Syracuse, NY 13210, USA.

CARVILL, Barbara M, b. 6 Sep. 1940, Jimenau, Germany. Professor of German. *Education:* Universities of Freiburg, Paris, Hamburg and Toronto. *Publication:* Der Verfuhrte Leser: Johann Karl August Musaus Romane und Romankritiken, 1984. *Address:* German Department, Calvin College, Grand Rapids, MI 49506, USA.

CASADA, James Allen, b. 28 Jan, 1942, Sylva, North Carolina, USA. Historian. m. Ann Fox, 3 June 1967, Chatham, Virginia, 1 daughter. *Education:* BA, King College, Bristol, Tennessee, 1964; MA, VPI and State University, Blacksburg, Virginia, 1967; PhD, Vanderbilt University, 1972. *Literary Appointments:* Guest Editor, Conch Review of Books, 1976; General Editor, Themes in European Expansions, Garland Publishing Company, 1979–; Editor-at-Large, Sporting Classics Magazine, 1983–; Advisory Editor, Premier Press, 1983–. *Publications:* Dr David Livingstone and Sir Henry Morton Stanley, 1976; Sir Harry H Johnston: A Bio-Bibliographical Study, 1977; African and Afro-American History: A Review of Recent Trends, 1978; Major contributor on history to The Discoverers, 1980; Editor of five volumes in Hunting Reprint Series, 1980–83; General Editor of ongoing series of reference volumes, Themes in European Expansion, 1979–, plus others. *Contributions to:* Sporting Classics Magazine; The Scottish Merchant; Geographical Journal; The Historian; Southern Quarterly; History in Africa; Southern History, etc. Author of some 200 articles in popular and scholarly publications. *Honours:* John Hay Whitney Opportunity Fellow, 1970–71; Research Grant from American Philosophical Society, 1973, 77, 83; Research Grant from National Geographic Society, 1976; Fellow, Institute for Advanced Studies in the Humanities, University of Edinburgh, 1977; Winthrop Distinguished Professor, 1983. *Memberships:* Phi Kappa Phi; Phi Alpha Theta; Fellow, Royal Geographical Society; Hakluyt Society; Conference on British Studies; African Studies Association of the UK and others. *Address:* 1250 Yorkdale Drive, Rock Hill, SC 29730, USA.

CASADO, Demetrio, b. 20 July 1934, Navares de Enmedio, Spain. Sociologist. *Education:* Doctor of Pharmacology; Diploma of Psychology. *Publications:* Perfiles del hambre, 1967; La Prbreza en la estructura social de Espana, 1976; Castilla como necesidad, Editor, 1980; Por Una Accion Socialy cultural alternativa, 1984. *Memberships:* Collegiate Association of Spanish Writers; Castilian Association of Sociology. *Address:* Av Reina Victoria 70 8eE, Madrid, 28003 Spain.

CASADY, Cort, b. 22 Apr. 1947, McAllen, Texas. Writer-Producer. m. Barbara Mercer Kellard, 28 Dec. 1972, Oahu, Hawaii. *Education:* BA (cum laude), 1968, Harvard University. *Publication:* The Singing Entertainer: A Contemporary Study of the Art and Business of Being a Professional, (with John Davidson) 1979. *Contributions to:* New West; Los Angeles Magazine; San Diego Magazine; Chatsworth Evening News. *Memberships:* The Signet Society; Writers Guild of America. *Literary Agent:* Steve Weiss, William Morris Agency Inc. *Address:* c/o William Morris Agency, 151 El Camino Drive, Beverly Hills, CA 90212, USA.

CASEY, W Wilson, b. 20 July 1954, Woodruff, South Carolina, USA. Direct Mail Marketing Specialist. *Education:* BS, Education, University of South Carolina, 1977. *Appointments:* Freelance Writer, Spartanburg-Herald-Journal Newspaper. *Publications:* How to Beat Speeding Tickets, 1980; Hangover Remedies, 1979; How Ladies Can Meet Mr Right, 1978; How to Lose Weight Despite Yourself, 1977 Beer Can Poles, 1976; Tu Trivia Teasers, 1984. *Contributor to:* Nationally Syndicated Newspaper Columnist, Wire Service, Copley News Service, San Diego, 1981–. *Honour:* Distinguished Writer Award, University of South Carolina Spartanburg Alumni Association, 1984. *Address:* PO Box 268, Lyman, SC, 29365, USA.

CASOLARO, J Daniel, b. 16 June 1947, Fort Meade, Maryland, USA. Author. m. Terrill Pace, 12 Dec. 1968, Stonington, Connecticut, 1 son. *Education:* St Leo College, 1964–65; Providence College, Rhode Island 1965–68; University of Paris, Sorbonne, Paris, France, 1966. *Publications:* Makes Me Think of Tall Green Grass, a collection of short stories, 1973; 2 plays and 20 stories, 1976; The Ice King, 1982. *Contributions to:* Rhode Island Review; Providence Journal; Washington Star; Best Medium Publications; National Enquirer; Globe Newspapers; Globe Communications (Montreal); World News; National Star; National Geographic; Home and Auto; El Dorado News-Times; American Contractor; Journal; Retailer; Russian Report; Medical News Digest; Computer Daily; Software Digest; Mini-Micro Computer Report; Computer Age; Crime Control Digest; Corrections Digest; Court Systems Digest; Computer Crime Digest; Defense Policy Report; EFTS-Industry Report; Data Communications. *Honour:* Short Story Award, Rhode Island Review. *Memberships:* Author's Guild; Authors League of America, Society of Professional Journalists; Business Writers of America; United States Congressional Press Gallery. *Literary Agent:* Joshua Kaufman, Washington, District of Columbia, USA. *Address:* 11626 Pine Tree Drive, Fairfax, WA 22033, USA.

CASS, Ronald Andrew, b. 12 Aug. 1949, Washington DC, USA. Professor of Law. m. Valerie Christina Swanson, 24 Aug. 1969, Tarzana, California, 1 son, 1 daughter. *Education:* BA, University of Virginia, 1970; JD, Honours, University of Chicago, 1973. *Appointments:* Assistant Professor, Law, University of Virginia, 1976–81; Associate, Center for Advanced Studies, Charlottesville, 1980–81; Associate Professor, 1981–83; Professor, 1983–, Law, Boston University. *Publications:* Revolution in the Wasteland: Value and Diversity in Television, 1981; Administrative Law, with Colin S Diver, forthcoming. *Contributor to:* Journal of Law, Ethics and Public Policy; Duke Law Journal; Boston University Law Review; University of Pennsylvania Law Review; Virginia Law Review; University of Chicago Law Review; etc. *Memberships:* Phi Beta Kappa; Order of the Coif; Phi Eta Sigma. *Address:* Boston University School of Law, 765 Commonwealth Avenue, Boston, MA 02215, USA.

CASSEL, Don, b. 4 Apr. 1942, Canada. College Professor. m. Barbara J Winger, 20 May 1967, Toronto, Canada, 2 daughters. *Education:* BA, Computer Science, York University, 1975. *Publications:* Programming Language One, 1972; Basic Programming in Real Time, 1975; PL/1: A Structured Approach, 1978; Introduction to Computers and Information Processing, 1980; Basic Made Easy, 1980; Introduction to Computers and Information Processing: Language Free Edition, 1981; Introduction to Computers and Information Processing: BASIC, COBOL, FORTRAN, Pascal, 1981; The Structured Alternative: An Introduction to Program Design Coding, Style, Debugging and Testing, 1983; An Introduction to Microcomputers: Audio-Visual Presentation, 1983; FORTRAN Made Easy, 1983; BASIC 4.0 Programming for the PET/CBM, 1983; BASIC Programming for the Commodore VIC-2[s0], 1984; BASIC Programming for the Commodore 64, 1984; Computers Made Easy, 1984; WordStar Simplified for the IBM Personal Computer, 1984; Easywriter Simplified for the IBM Personal Computer, 1984; BASIC Made Easy 2nd Edition, 1985; Introduction to Computers and Information Processing; BASIC, COBOL, FORTRAN, Pascal, 2nd Edition, 1985; Commodore 64 Graphics, Sound and Music, 1985; DBASE II Simplified for the IBM Personal Computer, 1985; WordStar Simplified, 1985. *Address:* Humber College, 205 Humber College Boulevard, Rexdale, Ontario M9W 5L7, Canada.

CASSELL, Dana Kay, b. 12 Dec. 1941, Hornell, New York, USA. Author, Consultant, Lecturer. m. Don Cuddy, 2 July 1983, 2 sons, 2 daughters. *Publications:* How To Advertise and Promote Your Retail Store, 1983; Making Money With Your Home Computer, 1984. *Contributions to:* 150 publications including: Working

Woman; American Legion Magazine; Modern Bride; Income Opportunities; Barron's Weekly; Mechanix Illustrated; Guest Informant; The Writer; Mother Earth News; Exploring; Executive Digest. *Memberships:* Founder and Executive Director, Florida Freelance Writers Association; American Society of Journalists and Authors; The Authors Guild; Newsletter Editor, Florida Publishers Group; Board of Advisors, National Association of Independent Publishers. *Literary Agent:* Meg Ruley, Jane Rotrosen Agency. *Address:* PO Box 9844, Fort Lauderdale, FL 33310, USA.

CASSELLS, Cyrus Curtis, b. 16 May 1957, Dover, Delaware, USA. Writer/Poet/Translator. *Education:* BA, Communications (Film and Broadcasting), Stanford University, 1979. *Literary Appointment:* Poetry Judge, Arizona State Poetry Society, 1985. *Publications:* The Mud Actor (Holt, Rinehart and Winston, The National Poetry Series,) 1982. *Contributions to:* Atlantic Window, The Southern Review, 1985; Sally Hemings to Thomas Jefferson, and Strange Fruit, Callaloo, 1984; The Blind Boy, The Boy of Leaves, and Travellers for a Time, Shankpainter, 1983; Ojiisama, Tokyo, Quilt, 1981 etc. *Honours:* Academy of American Poets Prize, Stanford University, 1979; Winner of the 1982 National Poetry Series for, The Mud Actor; Nominee for the 1982 Bay Area Book Reviewer's Award in Poetry for, The Mud Actor; 1983 Callaloo Creative Writing Award for the poem, Sally Hemings to Thomas Jefferson; Creative Writing Fellowships from the Fine Arts Work Center in Provincetown, Massachusetts, YADDO, The Mallay Colony and the Helene Wurlitzer Foundation. *Memberships:* Poetry Society of America; PEN; PEN Freedom to Write Committee. *Address:* c/o 1142 East Avenue J-1, Lancaster, CA 93535, USA.

CASSIDY, John, b. 29 Oct. 1928, England. College Lecturer. m. Marion Cutler, 25 July 1955, Halifax, Yorkshire, 2 sons, 1 daughter. *Education:* BA, 1952, MA, 1953, University of Manchester. *Literary Appointment:* Literature Advisory Panel, North West Arts, 1983–. *Publications:* The Dancing Man, 1977; An Attitude of Mind, 1978; Night Cries, 1982. *Contributions to:* Stand; Iowa Review; Poetry Review; Poems featured in various publications. *Honours:* Poet's Yearbook Award, 1977; Recommendation for Night Cries, Poetry Book Society, 1982. *Address:* 53 Bryn Lea Terrace, Barrow Bridge, Bolton, Lancashire BL1 7NB, England.

CASSILL, Kay, b. Iowa, USA. m. R V Cassill, 2 sons, 1 daughter. *Education:* BA, English, University of Iowa; Graduate study in communications management, photo-journalism, news, feature writing, printmaking, drawing, painting; Member, Iowa Writers Workshop. *Literary Appointments:* Research Assistant, Ford Foundation, Education and Arts Division, New York; Executive Secretary and Member, Board of Directors, Associated Writing Program; Lecturer, Providence College, University of Rhode Island; Correspondent, New York Times Syndicate, FAN, NANA, TWNS. *Publications:* Twins: Nature's Amazing Mystery, 1982; The Complete Handbook for Freelance Writers, 1981. *Contributions to:* People; McCalls; Us; Better Homes & Gardens; Viva; Physician's World; Smithsonian; Saturday Review; Kiwanis; Marathon World, etc. *Honours:* Distinctive Short Stories, 1976; Penney-Missouri Journalism Award, Expanding Opportunities, 1975; Judge, Virginia Commonwealth University National Poetry Contest, 1974. *Memberships:* American Society of Journalists and Authors; Author's Guild; Overseas Press Club. *Address:* 22 Boylston Avenue, Providence, RI 02906, USA.

CASSILL, Ronald Verlin, b. Iowa, USA. Author. m. Kay, 2 sons, 1 daughter. *Education:* BA, University of Iowa, 1939; MA, 1947. *Literary Appointments:* Teacher, Writers Workshop, University of Iowa, 1948–52, 1960–66; Professor, Brown University, 1966–83; Reviewer for New York Times. *Publications:* Eagle on the Coin, 1950; Clem Anderson, 1961; Pretty Leslie, 1963; The President, 1964; The Father, 1965; The Happy Marriage, 1966; LaVie Passionnee of Rodney Buckthorne, 1968; In An Iron Time, 1969; Doctor

Cobb's Game, 1970; The Goss Women, 1974; Hoyt's Child, 1976; Editor, Norton Anthology of Short Fiction, 1977; Labors of Love, 1980; Flame, 1980; After Goliath, 1985 and several short stories. *Contributions to:* Atlantic Monthly; Esquire; Holiday; Saturday Evening Post, Horizon. *Honours:* Atlantic First Prize, Atlantic Monthly, 1947; Rockefeller Grant Fiction Writing, 1954; O. Henry Prize Stories, 1956; Third Prize, Guggenheim Grant Fiction Writing, 1968. *Memberships:* Associated Writing Programs (Organizer; President 3 years); Phi Beta Kappa. *Address:* 22 Boylston Avenue, Providence, RI 02906, USA.

CASSIN-SCOTT, Marion Doret, b. 15 Aug. 1928, Berlin, Germany. Writer. m. Jack Cassin-Scott, 24 Jan. 1954, London, England, 1 son, 1 daughter. *Publications:* Costume Reference Series, 14 volumes, 1977–84. *Membership:* Society of Authors. *Address:* 108 Melrose Avenue, London NW2 4JX, England.

CASSUTT, Michael, b. 13 Apr. 1954, Minnesota, USA. Writer and Broadcaster. m. Cynthia Lee Stratton, 19 Aug. 1978 at Hudson, Wisconsin. *Education:* BA (radio & television), University of Arizona, Tucson, USA, 1975. *Literary Appointment:* Currently, Director of Children's Programmes, CBS Television, Los Angeles, California, USA. *Major Publication:* The Star Country (novel), forthcoming, Doubleday, 1986. *Contributor to:* (fiction) The Magazine of Fantasy & Science Fiction; Isaac Asimov's Science Fiction Magazine; (anthologies) Universe 8 (Doubleday 1978); The Best of Omni #7 (Omni, 1983); Shadows 7 (Doubleday, 1984); (non-fiction) Spaceflight (Journal of the British Interplanetary Society); Space World; Omni; L-5 News; Future Life; Starlog; (television scripts) Alice; The Twilight Zone. *Memberships:* Science Fiction Writers of America (member of Nebula Awards Jury); Writers Guild of America West; British Interplanetary Society; National Space Institute; L-5 Society; Planetary Society. *Literary Agent:* Richard Curtis, New York City. *Address:* 5523 Ranchito Avenue, Van Nuys, CA 91401, USA.

CASTLE, Anthony Percy, b. 24 May 1938, Dover, Kent, England. Writer/Publishing Consultant. m. Elizabeth Ann Herrington, 2 Sep. 1973, Euston, London, 3 daughters, 1 son. *Education:* Ordained R C Priest June 1963, Secular Priest, South-East London, 1963–72; Teacher's Certificate, Coloma Education College, West Wickham, Kent. *Literary Appointments:* Editor, Christian Celebration International Liturgy Journal, 1973–76; Co-editor, New Sower Religious Education Journal, 1976–78. *Publications:* Tuesday Again 1977; Quotes and Anecdotes for Preachers and Teachers, 1979; Assemble Together, 1981; Through the Year with Pope John Paul II, 1981; Hodder Book of Christian Quotations, 1983; Treasury of the Holy Spirit editor, 1984; Let's Celebrate, 1984; Hodder Book of Christian Prayers, 1986; Perfection of Love, 1986; More Quotes and Anecdotes, 1986; Editor, Basil Hume – A Portrait, 1986. *Contributions to:* Christian Celebration; The New Sower; The Furrow; New Life; Faith; The New Blackfriars; Liturgy and Life. *Membership:* The Keys – Catholic Writers Guild. *Literary Agent:* Edward England, Edward England Books, Crowborough, Sussex. *Address:* 87 North Street, Great Wakering, Essex SS3 0EL, England.

CASTO, Robert Clayton, b. 31 May 1932. Associate Professor of English Literature. *Education:* BA, Yale University, USA, 1954, MA, 1965; MFA, University of Iowa, 1966; MLitt, Oxford University, England, 1968. *Appointments include:* Assistant Professor of English, State University College, Oneonta, New York, USA, 1968–70; Assistant Professor, York University, Toronto, Canada, 1970–74; Associate Professor, 1974–present. *Publications:* A Strange and Fitful Land, 1959; The Arrivals, 1980. *Contributor to:* Numerous anthologies, USA, and periodicals, including, Yale Review; Va Quarterly Review; Literary Review; Commonweal; Beloit Poetry Journal; The Lyric; Chelsea; Yankee; Poet Lore; De Kalb Literary Arts Journal; magazines and journals in Canada include: Waves; Quarry; First

Encounter; Impulse; Journals in UK include: Isis; University Poetry. *Honours:* Recorded work for the Archives of the Library of Congress, 1961; 1st Prize, Academy of American Poets Competition, 1965. *Memberships:* Poetry Society of America; Poets and Writers Inc NYC; Elizabethan Club, Yale University. *Address:* 67 Forman Avenue, Toronto, Ontario M4S 2R4, Canada.

CASTRONOVO, David, b. 30 Oct. 1945, Brooklyn, New York City, USA. Writer; Professor. *Education:* BA, 1967; Brooklyn College; MA, 1968; PhD, 1975, Columbia University. *Publications:* Edmund Wilson, 1985; Thornton Wilder, 1986. *Contributions to:* Colliers Encyclopedia; Ungar Encyclopedia of World Literature in 20th Century; America; Guide to Contemporary American Essays. *Address:* 1619-1 Third Avenue, New York, NY 10128, USA.

CATE, Robert L, b. 11 Aug. 1932, Nashville, Tennessee, USA. Dean of Academic Affairs. m. Dorothy Wright, 17 Aug. 1951, 2 sons, 1 daughter. *Education:* BE, Vanderbilt University, 1953; BD, 1956, PhD, 1960, Southern Baptist Theological Seminary, Louisville, Kentucky. *Publications:* Exodus, 1979; Old Testament Roots for New Testament Faith, 1982; How to Interpret the Bible 1983; Help in Ages Past, Hope for Years to Come, 1983. *Contributions to:* Numerous articles and reviews to journals and magazines. *Address:* Golden Gate Baptist Theological Seminary, Mill Valley, CA, 94941, USA.

CATHCART, Helen. b. Author; Biographer. *Publications:* Her Majesty, 1962; The Queen Mother, 1965; The Married Life of the Queen, 1970; Anne and the Princesses Royal, 1973; Princess Margaret, 1974; Prince Charles, 1976; The Queen in Her Circle, 1977; The Queen Mother Herself, 1979; The Queen Herself, 1981. *Contributions to:* Several journals including the Strand. *Membership:* Member, Society of Authors. *Literary Agent:* Rupert Crew Limited. *Address:* c/o 44 Hill Street, London W1, England.

CATHERS, Kenneth Allen, b. 21 Sep. 1951, Ladysmith, British Columbia, Canada. Pulp Mill Worker. m. Inge Margrethe Hjort, 15 May 1971, Nanaimo, British Columbia, 2 sons. *Education:* BA, University of Victoria, 1973; MA, York University, Toronto, 1975. *Publications:* Images on Water, 1976; Outward Voyage, 1980. *Contributions to:* Event; Prism; Malahat; Tamarack; Wascana; Island, 10 poems; Whale Sound; Skookum Wawa; Waves; Grain; Quarry. *Honours:* Ontario Arts Grant, 1975; Canada Council Grant, 1976. *Address:* Box 1394, Ladysmith, British Columbia, Canada V0R 2E0.

CATHERWOOD, Henry Frederick Ross, (Sir), b. 30 Jan. 1925, Londonderry, Ireland. Member of the European Parliament. m. Elizabeth Lloyd Jones, 2 sons, 1 daughter. *Education:* BA, *Honours:* Clare College, Cambridge, England. *Publications:* The Christian in Industrial Society, 1964; The Christian Citizen, 1969; A Better Way, 1976; First Things First, 1979. *Contributions to:* numerous publications. *Honours:* Honorary Doctorates from Aston, Birmingham, Queens, Belfast, Surrey Universities. *Literary Agent:* Edward England. *Address:* Shire Hall, Castle Hill, Cambridge CB3 0AW, England.

CATLING, Darrel Charles, b. 10 Jan. 1909, London, England. Film Director; Writer. m. Helen Cowie, 10 Oct. 1936, Digswell, 1 son, 3 daughters. *Publications:* The Independent Frame, 1949; Worse Verse, co-author, 1971. *Contributions to:* Sight and Sound; British Journal of Photography; Photographic Journal; International Photographer, USA; Amateur Photographer; Sunday Times. *Memberships:* Honorary Member, British Academy of Film and Television Arts; Directors Guild of Great Britain; Cinema and Television Veterans; Fellow, Royal Photographic Society; Association of Cinematograph Television and Allied Technicians; British Film Institute. *Address:* Travellers Rest, Church Street, Old Hatfield, Hertfordshire, England.

CATRON, Louis E, b. Springfield, Illinois, USA. College Professor of Theatre. m. Joyce Anne Ferrell, 19 Dec. 1977, Norfolk, Virginia. *Education:* BA, Millikin University; MA, PhD, Southern Illinois University. *Publications:* Where Have All The Lightning Bugs Gone? 1973; At A Beetle's Pace, 1973; Touch The Bluebird's Song, 1973; Writing, Producing and Selling Your Play, 1984. *Contributions to:* Dramatics Magazine; The Writer Magazine. *Honours:* Woodrow Wilson Fellow; John Golden Fellow; John Golden Fellow (twice awarded); Outstanding Educators of America (twice awarded). *Address:* Department of Theatre, College of William and Mary, Williamsburg, VA 23185, USA.

CATTAROSSI ARANA, Nelida Maria, b. 23 Feb. 1926, Buenos Aires, Argentina. University Professor in Spanish Literature; Writer; Poet. *Education:* Degrees, Philosophy & Literature, University National of Cuyo.Mendoza, Argentina, 1955; PhD candidate, Spanish Literature, University of Illinois, USA, 1961–63; Doctoral thesis, University of Madrid, Spain, 1964. *Literary Appointments include:* Assistant Professor, Medieval Spanish Literature, University of Madrid, 1964; Research Professor, Modern Languages, University de Cuyo, Argentina, 1966–. *Publications include:* Books of poetry, 1966, 1967, 1969, 1983; Biography, Fausto Burgos, 1978; History of the Literature of the Mendoza Country 1820–1980, 2 volumes, 1982; First Dictionary of Argentine Writers & Women Painters, 1985; Children & Young People in Argentine Poetry, book of essays, 1985. *Contributions include:* Numerous articles in magazines and newspapers, 1959–; Founder Director, Enet Review; Founder Director, Bulletin of the Centre of Idiomatic Actualization & Argentine Culture, 1970–75; Founder Director, Bulletin International of the Information Decade for Women, etc. *Honours include:* SADE (Argentinian), 1963; Scholarships, Illinois, Madrid; Special invitation, Westfield College, University of London, 1965; Scholarship, Organisation of American States, 1975; Ministry of Education Cultural Prizes, 1983, 1984. *Memberships include:* Board, Cuyo American Institute; President, Centre of Idiomatic & Cultural Actualization, 1971–; International Federation of University Women, 1966–; Director, Investigation Literary Office, 1982–; SADE (Argentinian Society of the Writers); Founder Director, MAYAM 85, Bulletin International Decade for Women, 1982. *Literary Agent:* Inca Editorial, Mendoza Argentina. *Address:* Av. Gutierrez 650-4° piso. Dto 29, (5500) Mendoza, Republic of Argentina.

CAUGHEY, John, b. 3 July 1921, Belfast, Northern Ireland. Journalist. m. Viola McConville, 19 May 1952, Belfast, 2 daughters. *Literary Appointments:* Editor, Farmers' Journal, 1952–60; Managing Editor, Farmweek, 1960–61; Sub-editor, Belfast News Letter, 1974–75; Editor, Carrickfergus Advertiser, 1975–77; Northern Ireland Group Editor, Jemma Publications, 1977–; Currently Editor, Ulster Grocer, Ulster Hardware and DIY and Catering and Licensing Review. *Publications:* The Ulster Farmers' Union Story, 1957; Seize Then the Hour, biography, 1974. *Contributions to:* Travel and historical articles and short stories. *Memberships:* Chairman 1966, Publicity Association of Northern Ireland. *Address:* Baronscourt, Alexandra Gardens, Belfast BT15, Northern Ireland.

CAVALIERI, Grace, b. 3 Oct. 1932, Trenton, New Jersey, USA. Writer; Poet; Playwright. m. Kenneth Clegg Flynn, 31 Oct. 1953, Bristol, Pennyslvania, 4 daughters. *Education:* MA, Creative Writing & Education. *Literary Appointments:* Writer-in-Residence, Antioch College, 1969–75; Director, Drama & Literature, WPFW-FM, Washington DC, 1976–78; Associate Director, Childrens & Educational Programming, Public Broadcasting Service, 1978–82; President, Washington Writers Publishing House, 1975–77; Program Officer, Media, National Endowment for the Humanities, 1982–86. *Publications:* Why I Cannot Take a Lover, 1975; Body Fluids, 1977; Swan Research, 1979; Creature Comforts, 1982. *Contributions include:*

Book Reviews: The Falcon, Human Rights a Quarterly, Washington Review of the Arts; Poetry, numerous magazines including, Kauri, New England Review, Discovery, Washingtonian, Soliloquy, Falcon, etc. *Honours:* Playwrighting Awards, 1969–75 (18 plays produced); Writing Fellowship, DC Commission on the Arts, 1970; Grant, Radio Development, National Endowment for the Arts, 1976; The Pen-Fiction Award, prose, The National Commission on Working Women Award for radio series, The Poet and the Peom, 1985; Finalist, The Mayor's Award for Excellence in an artistic discipline; Reader, poetry, The Library of Congress. *Memberships:* Poetry Board, Folger Shakespeare Library, Washington DC; Theatre Board, Commonwealth Theatre, Baltimore, Maryland; Advisory Board, Watershed Foundation; Advisory Board, Living Stage. *Address:* 1813 16th Street NW (1-A), Washington DC 20009, USA.

CAWS, Ian, b. 19 Mar. 1945, Bramshott, Hampshire, England. Senior Social Worker with the Deaf. m. Hilary Walsh, 20 June 1970, Fareham, 3 sons, 2 daughters. *Education:* Certificate, Social Work, 1970; Certificate, Social Workers with the Deaf, 1973, North Western Polytechnic. *Publications:* Looking for Bonfies, 1975; Bruised Madonna, 1979; Boy with a Kite, 1981. *Contributor to:* Critical Quarterly; Dalhousie Review; Honest Ulsterman; Literary Review; London Magazine; Malshat Review; New Edinburgh Review; New Statesman; Thames Poetry; Tribune; Wascana Review; etc. *Honours:* Erie Gregory Award, 1973; Southern Arts Literature Bursary, 1977. Sussex Poet of the Year, 1985. *Membership:* Poetry Society. *Address:* 9 Tennyson Avenue, Rustington, West Sussex BN16 2PB, England.

CEBULA, Richard J, b. 24 Mar. 1944, New York City, USA. Economist. 1 son, 1 daughter. *Education:* BA, Fordham College, 1966; MA, University of Georgia, 1968; PhD, Georgia State University, 1971. *Publications:* The Determinants of Human Migration, 1979; Geographic Living Cost Differentials, 1983. *Contributor to:* Approximately 200 journals including: The Tiebout-Tullock Hypothesis: An Empirical Note; Quarterly Journal of Economics, 1978; Journal of the American Statistical Association; Kyklos; Psychology Today; Southern Economic Journal; Journal of Regional Science; Land Economics; Regional Studies; Metroecomica; Public Choice. *Honours:* Beta Gamma Sigma, 1984; Phi Kappa Phi, 1968; Omicron Delta Epsilon, 1965. *Address:* Emory University, Economics Department, Atlanta, GA 30322, USA.

CEPEDA CALZADA, Pablo, b. 18 July 1926, Cevico de la Torre, Palencia, Spain. Technical Education Administrator. m. Laura Mena Trejo, 6 Dec. 1952. *Education:* Liv.Law; LLD; Dip, Contemporary Problems, Europe & World. *Publications include:* Sombras en la Aurora de la Razon Vital, 1949; Donoso Cortes y Carl Schmitt, 1954; Escila y Caribdis de la razón vital, 1956; El retorno del alma en la vía mística, 1958; La Vida Como Sueno Reflexiones Sobre la Conciencia Espanola, 1964; La Doctrina de la Sociedad en Ortega y Gasset, 1968; Las Ideas Politicas de Ortega y Gasset, 1968; Evocacion de Jorge Manrique, 1968; UN tema palentino en la obra de Unamuno: El Cristo de las Claras, 1968; Reflexiones Sobre la Estabilidad Politica, 1969; El Problema de la Justicia en Job, 1975; Los Caprichos de Goya, 1979; El tormento de Goya-Diálogo, 1979; El filósofo palentino Vicente Fernandez Valcarce, Crísico de Des-cartes, 1982; Baltanás, Capital del Cerrato, 1983; El político de Amusco, Eugenio García Ruiz, 1985. *Contributor to:* Numerous periodicals, local and national & reviews including: Punta Europea; La Estafeta Literaria; Ateneo; Cuadernos Hispanoamericanos. *Honours:* Corres, Institute Political Studies. *Memberships:* Numerous including Tello Tellez de Meneses Institution; Literary Appointment, El Filosofopalentino, Vincente Fernandez Valcarce, Critico de Descartes, Notas sobre el cerrato (comarca Palentina). *Address:* Calle Salvino Sierra No. 4, 3°, Drha, Palencia, Spain.

CERKEZ, Vladimir, b. 26 Nov. 1923, Sarajevo, Yugoslavia. Poet; Novelist. *Education:* Technical High School, 1949. *Publications include:* Novels: Arena; Orlovi i vuci, Eagles and Wolves; Sunce u dimu, Sun in the Smoke; Bez povratka, With no Return; Hrabri vojnik, A Brave Soldier; Suncana zemlja, Country of Sunshine; Spijuni, Spies; Voc strepnje, Night of Fear; Pakao i snovi, Hell and Dreams; Savjest, Consciousness. Short Stories: San i zivot, Dreams and Life; Sjaj zivota, sjena smrti, Shine of Life and Shadow of Death. Childrens Television Plays: Zbjeg, Refuge; Izgubljena torba, Lost Bag; Carobni sesir, Magic Hat. Verse: Stihovi. *Contributions to:* Anthologies: World Poetry, Paris, 1962; Warsaw, Poland, 1968; Moscow, USSR, 1969 and others. *Honours include:* Decoration of the Republic; Decoration of the People; Prize, Union of Writers of Bosnia and Hercegovina, 1959; 27th July Prize for Literature, 1984. *Memberships include:* Past Secretary, Writers of Bosnia and Hercegovina; PEN. *Address:* Djure Djakovica 1.11, 71000 Sarajevo, Yugoslavia.

CHADWICK, Owen, b. 20 May 1916, Bromley, Kent, England. Historian. m. Ruth Hallward, 28 Dec. 1949, Nottingham, 2 sons, 2 daughters. *Education:* Cambridge University. *Appointments:* Professor, Church History, 1953–68, Regius Professor, Modern History, 1968–83, Cambridge. *Publications:* John Cassian, 1950; From Bossuet to Newman, 1957; The Victorian Church, 2 volumes, 1966–70; The Secularization of the European Mind, 1976; The Popes and European Revolution, 1981. *Contributor to:* Learned journals. *Honours:* Wolfson History Prize, 1981; KBE, 1982; Order of Merit, 1983. *Memberships:* British Academy, President, 1981–85. *Address:* Selwyn College, Cambridge University, Cambridge, England.

CHAIR, Somerset de, b. 22 Aug. 1911. Writer;Landowner. *Education:* King's School, New South Wales; Balliol College, Oxford. m. (1) Thelma Arbuthnot, divorced, 2 sons, 1 deceased; (2) Carmen Appleton, divorced, 2 sons; (3) Margaret Patricia Manlove, 1 daughter; (4) Juliet, Marchioness of Bristol (nee Fitzwilliam) 1 daughter. *Appointments include:* MP, Nat C for South West Norfolk, 1935–45; MP, C, South Paddington, 1950–51; Served with Household Cavalry in Middle East during Iraqi and Syrian campaigns, World War II; Chairman, National Appeals Committee of UN Association and Member of National Executive, 1947–50. *Publications include:* The Millennium (poems) 1949; The Story of a Lifetime (novel) 1954; The Waterloo Campaign 1957; Editor of Admiral de Chair's Memoirs, The Sea is Stong, 1961; Collected Verse, 1970; Friends, Romans, Concubines (novel) 1971; Legend of the Yellow River (novel) 1979; Buried Pleasure (autobiography) 1985. *Address:* St Osyth Priory, St Osyth, Essex, England.

CHAKRAVARTI, Subodh Kumar, b. 25 Mar. 1919, Cooch Behar, Bengal, India. Personnel Officer. *Education:* BA, Honours, Calcutta University. *Publications include:* Ramyani Beekshya, 24 volumes, 1957–85; Saswata Bharet, 6 volumes, 1963–84; Amader Desh, 5 volumes, 1964–84; 40 books on travel, novels, short stories in Bengali including adaptations and translations from the Vedas, Upanishads and Puranas of Sanskrit Literature; Editor, Susama Chakrararrti, Sata Barser Pattayatra. *Honours:* Rabuidra Memorial Award, 1963; Susu Sahitya Panshad Award, 1967; Kannu Parampil P. Punnoos. *Address:* Ramyani BF 77, Salt Lake City, Calcutta 700064, India.

CHALLIS, Chris, b. 11 Feb. 1952, Ingatestone, Essex, England. Writer; Lecturer. *Education:* BA Honours, 1973, MA Distinction, 1974, PhD, 1979, Leicester University. *Literary Appointments:* Writer in Residence, Northampton College Arts Center, 1982–83; Arts Council of Great Britain Writing Fellow, BBC Radio, Northampton, Derby, Nottingham, Leicester, 1985. *Publications:* Plays: 8 published or performed. Poetry: Highfields Landscape, 1979; William of Cloudeslee, 1980; Jack Kerouac, Charles Bukowski and Me, 1984; The Wild Thing Went From Side to Side, 1984. Literary Studies: Quest for Kerouac, 1984. *Contributions to:* Numerous publications, UK, USA and Europe; Six Anthologies: British, Belgian, German, 1984 and 1985.

Honour: Bursary, East Midlands Arts Association, 1979. *Memberships:* Past member of Literature and Drama panels, East Midlands Arts Association. *Address:* c/o 65 High Street, Ingatestone, Essex CM4 0AT, England.

CHALMERS PARRY, Shedden, b. 23 Apr. 1900, Youlgreave, Derbyshire, England. Retired Medical Officer of Health. m. Awdry Sybil Williams, 10 Jan. 1936, Wimbledon, 1 daughter. *Education:* BA 1921, MA 1926, Caius College, Cambridge; MRCS; LRCP 1926, DPH 1935, Middlesex Hospital, London. *Publications:* Lascar Hindustani for Ship Surgeons, 1930; Polyglot Medical Questionnaire, with digital system of communication in 27 languages, 9 translations in script-form, Yiddish, Hebrew, Persian, Arabic and Urdu, 1972. *Contributions to:* British Medical Journal; Public Health. *Memberships:* Life Member, President Southern branch 1952, Society of Community Medicine; Fellow, Royal Society of Health. *Address:* St George's, Soberton, Southampton SO3 1QU, England.

CHAMBERLAIN, Kent Clair, b. 22 Jan. 1943, Abilene, Kansas, USA, Author. *Literary Appointments:* Founding Parnassian, Of Parnassus, Poets, 1976; Proprietor, Aquarius Enterprises, 1981; President, United Amateur Press Association of America, 1980–81. *Publications Include:* Ship Bound for Where, 1971; Slant-Lined, Sight-Patterned, Sometimey; Winter's Bird, 1975; Rarely Published, 1977. Appeared in: Beau-Cocoa; Wide Open; Null and Void; Silk Screen; Creative Urge; Sparks of Fire; Blow; Inner Well; Poets on Parade; Circular Causation (Canada); Graffiti; Poet and Lava, (India); Bouquets of Poems, (Italy); 4 Seasons; American Poet; Brotherhood and Peace, (Philippines); Ashland, Boyd County, Kentucky, Daily Independent, (1896); Hartford Connecticut Courant; Slick Press; Encore; Bachaet, etc. *Honours include:* Prizes from Spencer Book Company; Trophy from American Poets Fellowship Society. *Membership:* Life Member, Oregon State Poetry Society. *Address:* 625 Holly Street, Ashland, OR 97520, USA.

CHAMBERLAIN, Mary Christina, b. 3 Sep. 1947, London, England. Lecturer in Cultural Studies. London College of Printing (London Institute). m. Peter Lane, 12 Apr. 1980, London England, 3 daughters. *Education:* MA, Hons. University of Edinburgh, Scotland; MSc (Econ) London School of Economics and Political Science. *Publications:* Fenwomen (Virago/Quartet, 1975, Routledge, Kegan Paul, 1983, History Workshop Series); Old Wives Tales (Virago), 1981; Translations: Paysannes des Marais edition des femmes, 1967; Histoire des Guerisseuses, editions du Rocher, 1983. *Contributor to:* Oral History Journal (reviews editor); New Society; New Socialist (Occasional book reviews). *Honour:* Twenty-Seven Foundation. *Literary Agent:* Anne McDermid, Curtis Brown. *Address:* 21 Onslow Road, Richmond, Surrey TW10 6QH, England.

CHAMBERS, Aidan, b. 1934, Chester-le-Street, County Durham, England. Writer. *Publications include:* The Vase, 1968; Topliner Ghosts, co-editor, 1969; The Reluctant Reader, 1969; Haunted Houses, 1971; Introducing Books to Children, 1973; Ghosts & Hauntings, 1973; More Haunted Houses, 1973; Great British Ghosts, 1974; Great Ghosts of the World, 1974; Flyers & Flying, 1976; Funny Folk, 1976; Ghost Carnival, 1977; Breaktime, 1978; Seal Secret, 1980; Dance on my Grave, 1982; The Present Takers, 1983; Booktalk, 1985. *Contributor to:* Times Educational Supplement; Guardian; Books & Bookmen; Teachers World; Children's Book News; Horn Book; etc; Publisher, Signal Magazine. *Honours:* Children's Literature Association Award for excellence in literary criticism, 1978; Eleanor Farjeon Award for services to children's books, 1982. *Membership:* Society of Authors. *Address:* Lockwood, Station Road, South Woodchester, Gloucestershire GL5 5EQ, England.

CHAMBERT, (Bo Axel) Christian, b. 8 Jan. 1940, Norrköping, Sweden. Art Critic; Teacher of Art History. *Education:* Fil.kand, University of Uppsala, 1963.

Publications: Kultur i Östergotland, with Thomas Millroth, 1976; Drömmen Verkligheten Upporet Texter om bilder, 1977. *Contributor to:* Paletten. *Memberships:* Swedish Section, Association Internationale des Critiques d'Art, President 1978–; Bildförlaget Oppna Ogon, president, 1978–80; Swedish Union of Authors; Swedish National Committee, Contemporary Art Exhibitions Abroad (NUNSKU), 1985–. *Address:* Ringgatan 37A, 752 27 Uppsala, Sweden.

CHAMIEL, Haim Itzchak, b. 18 Jan. 1917. Lecturer; Educator; Author; Poet. m. Hava. *Education:* MA, 1949, PhD, 1953, Hebrew University, Jerusalem, Israel. *Literary Appointments include:* Teacher, Youth Leader, Youth Village, Israel, 1939–44; Editor Educational Material, Pedagogical Adviser, 1945–50; Director, General Education Department, Jewish Agency, Jerusalem, 1950–; Lecturer, Hebrew Literature, 1956, Senior Lecturer, Education, 1968–, Bar Ilan University. *Publications:* Meofeck of Oafck, 1952; Avivim, Poetry for Children, 1958; Moked Venir, 1960; Neroth Moledeth, poetry for children, 1966; Benofe Hayom, 1967; Strains of Homage and Delight, 1978; Researches in Bible Literature and Education. *Contributions to:* Hazhofeh; Bamishor; Maariv; Mabua; Turey Jeshuran; Zeraim; Ishey Israel; various others. *Honours:* Prizes, Hebrew University, 1953; Shapira Prize in Poetry, 1978; Study Prize, Tel Aviv Municipality, 1951. *Memberships:* Association of Composers and Musicians; Association of Editors. *Address:* 7 Fichman, Jerusalem, Israel.

CHAN, Stephen, b. 11 May 1949, New Zealand. University Lecturer. *Education:* BA, English; MA, Political Studies; Auckland; MA, War Studies, London. *Publications;* Postcards from Paradise, 1971; Arden's Summer, 1975; The Commonwealth Observer Group in Zimbabwe, 1985; Songs of the Maori King, 1986. *Contributions;* Poetry and literary crticism in publications throughout New Zealand and North America; scholarly articles in several British journals. *Address:* Queen Elizabeth House, Oxford, England.

CHANCE, Jane, b. 26 Oct. 1945, Neosho, Missouri, USA. Professor of English. m. Paolo Passaro, 30 Apr. 1981, Scorze, Italy, 1 son, 1 daughter. *Education:* BA, English (Hons), Purdue University, Ind, 1967; AM, English, 1968., PhD, English, 1971, University of Illinois, Urbana. *Literary Appointments:* University of Saskatchewan, Saskatoon, Canada, 1971–73; Rice University, 1973–. *Publications:* The Genius Figure in Antiquity and the Middle Ages, 1975; Tolkien's Art: A Mythology for England, 1979, 1980; Woman as Hero in Old English Literature, 1986; Co-Editor, Mapping the Cosmos, 1986; Co-Editor, Approaches to Teaching Sir Gawain and the Green Knight, 1985. *Contributions:* of essays, reviews and poems in Studies in Philology; JEGP; Papers on Language and Literature; Texas Studies in Literature and Language; Chaucer Review; Mittellateinisches Jahrbuch; Antigonish Review; Dalhousie Review. *Honours:* National Endowment for the Humanities Fellowship, 1977–78; John Simon Guggenheim Memorial Foundation Fellowship, 1980–81; Director, NEH Summer Seminar for College Teachers, 1985. *Memberships:* PEN American Center; Author's Guild. *Address:* Department of English, Rice University, Houston, TX 77251, USA.

CHANDLER, S Bernard, b. 31 May 1921, Canterbury, England. Professor. *Education:* BA, University of London, 1947; PhD, 1953. *Publications:* Alessandro Manzoni, 1974; The World of Dante (Editor with J A Molinaro), 1966; Italian Culture: Mediaeval to Modern, (Editor with J A Molinaro), 1979. *Contributor to:* Italian and North American Journals. *Memberships:* Vice President, International Association for the Study of Italian Language & Literature, 1973–82; MLA; 2nd Vice President, AAUP of Italian, 1978–79; Dante Society of America. *Address:* Dept of Italian Studies, University of Toronto, Toronto, Ontario M5S IA1, Canada.

CHANG, Isabelle, b. 20 Feb. 1924, Boston, USA. Librarian; Media Co-ordinator; m. Dr Min Chueh Chang,

28 May, 1948, 1 son, 2 daughters. *Education:* BSLS, Simmons College, USA; AM, Clark University; MA, Anna Maria College. *Publications:* What's Cooking at Chang's, 1959, 1971; Chinese Fairy Tales, 1965; Tales from Old China, 1969; Gourmet on the Go, 1971; The Magic Pole, 1978. *Contributions to:* Massachussetts Teachers; Worcester Sunday Telegram; Parade. *Honour:* John Chandler Greene Award, 1965. *Membership:* Trustee, Shrewsbury Public Library. *Address:* Shrewsbury School System, 45 Oak Street, Shrewsbury, MA 01545, USA.

CHAPLIN, Sidney, b. 1916, Shildon, Co Durham, England, deceased 10 Jan. 1986. Author. *Education:* Fircroft College for Working Men. *Publications include:* The Leaping Lad, 1947; My Fate Cries Out, 1949; The Thin Seam, 1950; The Big Room, 1960; The Day of the Sardine, 1961; The Watchers & the Watched, 1969; Sam in the Morning, 1965; The Mines of Alabaster, 1971; The Smell of Sunday Dinner, 1971; A Tree With Rosy Apples, 1972; On Christmas Day in the Morning, 1978; The Bachelor Uncle, 1980. *Contributor to:* Guardian; Sunday Times; etc. *Honours:* Recipient, OBE. *Memberships:* Literary & Philosophical Society, Newcastle-upon-Tyne; Society of Authors. *Address:* 11 Kimberley Gardens, Newcastle-upon-Tyne NE2 1HJ, England.

CHAPMAN, Raymond, b. 10 Jan. 1924, Cardiff, Wales. University Teacher. m. Patricia McCarthy, 1964, 1 son, 1 daughter. *Education:* BA, 1945, MA 1959, Jesus College, Oxford; MA, King's College, London University, 1947; PhD, London, 1978. *Publications:* A Short Way to Better English, 1956; The Ruined Tower, 1961; Killed by Scandal, 1962; The Loneliness of Man, 1963; Unhallowed Murder, 1966; The Victorian debate, 1968; Faith & Revolt, 1970; Linguistics & Literature, 1973; Letters to an Actress, co-author, 1974; The Language of English Literature, 1982; The Treatment of Sounds in Language and Literature, 1984; The Sense of the Past in Victorian Literature, 1984. *Contributor to:* Modern Language Review; Review of English Studies; English; Poetica; Notes & Queries; Theology; Higher Education Journal; System; Oxford. *Memberships:* Executive Committee, English Association; University Teachers; Sion College. *Address:* 6 Kitson Road, Barnes, London SW13, England.

CHAPMAN, Richard Arnold, b. 15 Aug. 1937, Bexleyheath, Kent, England. University Professor. *Education:* BA, PhD, Leicester University; MA, Carleton University; FBIM. *Publications:* Decision Making, 1968; The Higher Civil Service in Britain, 1970; The Role of Commisions in Policy Making, 1973; Teaching Public Administration, 1973; Style in Administration, Editor with A Dunsire, 1971; The Dynamics of Administrative Reform, with J R Greenaway, 1980; Leadership in the British Civil Service, 1984; Public Policy Studies: the North East of England, 1985. *Contributor to:* Public Administration; Administration; International Review of Administrative Science; Parliamentary Affairs; Review of Politics; International Review of History & Political Science. *Memberships:* Chairman, Public Administration Committee, Joint University Council for Social and Public Administration, 1978–81; Chairman, Joint University Council, 1983–86. *Address:* University of Durham, Dept of Politics, 23–26 Old Elvet, Durham DH1 3HY, England.

CHAPPELL, Barbara Elizabeth, b. 10 Aug. 1926, Rayleigh, Essex, England. Journalism. m. (1) William Phillips, 24 Dec. 1947, Holborn, (2) Harvey Chappell, 12 July 1982, Rayleigh, 1 son, 2 daughters. *Education:* State Registered Nurse. *Appointments:* Editor, Kenya Dairy Farmer, Nairobi, 1960–63; Editor, The Farmer, Zimbabwe, 1978–81; Editor, AgriTrade, London, England, 1981–. *Publications:* Tourist Guide to Harare, 1983; Contributor to: Guide to Aden, 1963; Farmer at War, 1979. *Contributor to:* Weekly Children's Page, Sunday Nation, Kenya, 1964–72; Agony Aunt Columnist, East African Edition, Drum, 1972–74; Fiction to East & Central African Magazines, 1960–84. *Memberships:* Associate Member, Zimbabwe Institute

of Public Relations; Guild of Agricultural Journalists, England. *Address:* 46 Cherry Orchard, Southminster, Essex, CM0 7HE, England.

CHAPPLE, Clement Gerald, b. 15 Nov. 1937, Montreal, Quebec, Canada. Associate Professor, German. m. Josephine Hastings Perkins, 12 Sep. 1964, Hartford, USA, 1 son, 1 daughter. *Education:* BA, Honours, French, German, McMaster University, 1960; AM, German, 1962, PhD, German, 1967, Harvard University. *Appointments:* Translation Consultant, Current Soviet Leaders, 1976–; Co-Editor, McMaster Colloquim on German Literature, 1978–; Editorial Consultant, Houghton Mifflin Company, Boston 1981–; Member, Editorial Advisory Board, Modern German Studies, 1983–; Associate Editor, German Literture, Art and Thought, 1984–. *Publications:* Co-Editor: Thomas Mann: Ein Kolloquium, 1978; The Turn of the Century: German Literature and Art, 1890–1925, 1981; Co-Translator, Co-Editor, Heinrich Zimmer, Artistic Form and Yoga in the Sacred Images of India, 1984; Co-Editor, The Romantic Tradition: German Literature and Music in the Nineteenth Century, 1986. *Contributor to:* articles, translations and review in 'Parabola; Current Soviet Leaders; Denver Quarterly; Modern Austrian Literature. *Honours:* German Academic Exchange Scholarship, Munich, 1958–59; Woodrow Wilson Fellowship, 1960–61, Canada Council Pre-doctoral Fellowships, 1961–63, Harvard. *Memberships:* American Literary Translators Association; Modern Language Association of America; Hugo-von-Hofmannsthal-Gesellschaft; International Arthur Schnitzler Research Association; Canadian Comparative Literature Association. *Address:* Dept of German, McMaster University, Hamilton, Ontario, Canada L8S 4M2.

CHAR, Carlene M, b. 21 Oct. 1954, Honolulu, Hawaii, USA. Editor, Freelance Writer, Illustrator. *Education:* BA Economics, University of Hawaii, 1977; MBA, Columbia Pacific University, 1984; PhD Journalism, Columbia Pacific University, 1985; BGS Computer Science, Roosevelt University, 1986. *Literary Appointments:* Publisher Comber Press, 1983; Editor, Computer Book Review, 1983. *Contributor to:* Popular Computing; Microcomputing; Software Supermarket; Word Processing News; Time-Life Access. *Memberships:* American Society of Journalists & Authors; Authors' Guild; Society of Professional Journalists; Computer Press Association; Society for Technical Communication. *Literary Agent:* Michael Larsen, San Francisco. *Address:* Comber Press, PO Box 37127, Honolulu, HI 96837, USA.

CHARD, Dorothy Doreen, b. 8 May 1916, Tuffley, Gloucestershire, England. Magazine Editor; Freelance Journalist; Author. m. Maurice Noel Chard, 26 July 1941, Tottenhall, Staffordshire. *Appointments:* Editor, Devon Life County Magazine; Tutor, Creative Writing, Devon County Council. *Publications:* 20 fiction; 8 non-fiction. *Contributor to:* Womens' Magazines; Western Morning News; etc; Regular Broadcaster with BBC; Author, Sound Documentaries for BBC. *Memberships:* Society of Authors; Society of Women Writers and Journalists; Crime Writers Association; Westcountry Writers Association. *Address:* Morley, Morley Road, Newton Abbot, Devon TQ12 6NS, England.

CHARNEY, Ann, b. Poland. Writer. *Education:* BA, McGill University; License de Lettres, Sorbonne, Paris; MA French Literature, McGill University. *Publications:* Dobryd, 1973; Eine Polnische Kindheit, 1979. *Contributions to:* Various publications. *Honours:* 1st Prize, Chatelaine Fiction Contest, 1982; National Magazine Award, Gold Medal in Non-Fiction, 1983. *Memberships:* Writers' Union of Canada; PEN; Union des Ecrivaux Quebecois. *Literary Agent:* Sallie Gouverneur. *Address:* 3620 Marlowe Avenue, Montreal, Canada H4A 3L7.

CHARTERIS, Leslie, b. 12 May 1907, Singapore. Writer. *Education:* King's College, Cambridge University. *Publications:* The Saint Meets the Tiger (original title, Meet the Tiger), & 49 other titles in the

Saint series, 1928–79. *Contributor to:* Saint Magazine, Editor, 1953–67; Gourmet, USA; major fiction magazines; many newspapers. *Memberships:* MENSA; FRSA; Savage Club. *Address:* B-12 St James's Court, Serpentine Avenue, Dublin 4, Republic of Ireland.

CHASE, Elaine, b. 31 Aug. 1949, Schenectody, New York, USA. Author. m. Gary Dale Chase, 26 Oct. 1969, 1 son, 1 daughter. *Education:* Study of Journalism, College of General Studies, State University of New York at Albany, USA, 1968; Albany Business College, 1968. *Appointment:* President, Florida Chapter, Romance Writers of America, 1981–85. *Publications:* Rules of the Game, 1980; Tender Yearnings, 1981; A Dream Come True, 1982; Double Occupancy, 1982; Designing Woman, 1983; No Easy Way Out, 1983; Best Laid Plans, 1983; Video Vixen, 1983; Calculated Risk, 1983; Special Delivery, 1984; Lady Be Bad, 1984. *Contributions to:* Books: So You Want A Career in Radio and TV (author T E Hollingsworth); How to Write a Romance and Get it Published (author K Falk); Love's Leading Ladies (author K Falk); Lovelines (author R Guiley). *Honours:* Walden Books Bestseller Award for 1984 for Special Delivery, Dell Publishers top seller for year; Listed as fifth bestselling category author at Waldens for 1984. *Memberships:* Romance Writers of America; Mystery Writers of America; Poets and Writers. *Literary Agent:* Denise Marcil Literary Agency. *Address:* 15703 Cavendish Road, Houston, TX 77059, USA.

CHASE, Otta Louise, b. 8 July 1909. Town Clerk, Sweden, Maine, USA. *Appointments include:* Dictaphone Operator; Housewife and Mother; Town Treasurer, Clerk to Board of Selectman and Town Clerk, 1959–. *Publications:* November Violets, 1973; Tender Vines, 1986. *Contributor to:* Boston Globe; Manchester Union Leader; Nantucket Mirror and Enquirer; Carroll Co Independent; Bridgton News; Norway Advt–Dem; American Legion Magazine; Bittersweet. *Honours include:* George Washington Honorary Medal, Freedoms Foundation at Valley Forge, 1963, 65 and 67; 1st Prize, Poetry Society of New Hampshire, 1969, 1973; 1st Prize, California Federation of Chaparral Poets, 1971; 1st Prize, Kentucky State Poetry Society, 1973, 75; 1st Prize, Driftwood E, 1974; Chosen one of the Golden Poets of 1985 by World of Poetry. *Memberships:* Former Secretary, Poetry Fellowship of Maine; Round Robin Secretary, Poetry Society of New Hampshire; Poetry Society of America; Massachussetts State, Kentucky State, Florida State, Poetry Societies; California Federation of Chaparral Poets. *Address:* RFD 2, Box 1502, Harrison, ME 04040, USA.

CHATOV, Robert, b. 6 Nov. 1927, New York, USA. University Teacher and Researcher. m. Sophia F Cohen, 22 Oct. 1971, Berkeley, California, USA, 2 sons. *Education:* BS, New York University, 1949; MA, Northwestern University, 1951; JD, Wayne State University Law School, 1957; PhD, University of California, Berkeley, 1973. *Appointments:* Various positions in Ford Motor Company 1951–68; Adjunct Faculty, Economics Department, 1958–63, Lecturer, Management Program 1963, Wayne State University; lecturer 1970–71, Visiting Associate Professor, Summer 1981, 1977–78, School of Business Administration, University of California, Berkeley; Assistant Professor, 1972–75, Associate Professor 1975, School of Management, State University of New York at Buffalo; Member of State Bar of Michigan, 1958–; US National Defense Executive Reserve, Department of Commerce, 1967–.*Publications include:* Corporate Financial Reporting: Public or Private Control? 1975; An Analysis of Corporate Statements on Ethics and Behavior (monograph) 1979. *Contributor to:* Numerous articles and book reviews in professional journals. *Memberships:* Academy of Management; State Bar of Michigan; American Business Law Association; Academy of Accounting Historians etc. *Address:* School of Management, State University of New York at Buffalo, Jacobs Management Center, Amherst, NY 14260, USA.

CHAVASSE, Claud Geoffrey Rowden, b. 4 Mar. 1920, Oxford, England. Forester/Scientist (retired). m. Shirley Ray Fisher, at Invercargill, New Zealand, 19 Dec. 1953, 3 daughters. *Education:* MA, Forestry, MA History, Oxford University, England. *Major Publicatons:* Westland's Wealth (with J H Johns), 1959; The Forest World of New Zealand (with J H Johns), 1975; Forestry Handbook (ed.), 1977; New Zealand's Forest Parks (with J H Johns), 1983. *Contributions:* Numerous. *Honours:* Order of the British Empire for Services to Forestry, Conservation and the Community, 1984. *Membership:* PEN, New Zealand. *Address:* 57 McDowell Street, Roturua, New Zealand.

CHEATHAM, Donald D, b. 25 Apr. 1944, St Louis, Missouri, USA. Writer. m. Lois Mueller, 8 Dec. 1980, Nassau, Bahamas, 1 daughter. *Education:* BA. *Publication:* Riptide, 1984. *Contributions to:* The Floridian Magazine; Bay Life Magazine; Tampa Bay Monthly Magazine; Friday Extra Magazine; Playboy Magazine; WLPL Radio; KEGL Radio; St Petersburg Times; Tampa Tribune; Clearwater Sun. *Address:* 7 Elgin Place #802, Honeymoon Island, Dunedin, FL 33528, USA.

CHEETHAM, Erika, b. 7 July 1939, London, England. Author. *Education:* MA, University of Oxford, England, 1961; Diplôme, Sorbonne University, Paris, France, 1957. *Literary Appointments:* Contributor for Nova, Vogue and Readers Digest before first book: Rainbow; The Guardian; Encyclopaedia of the Paranormal, and others; Editor, Carmelite House Group of Newspapers, 1975–78. *Major Publications:* The Prophecies of Nostradamus 1971, 1972, revised 1981; The Further Prophecies of Nostradamus 1985 and beyond, 1985; The Man who saw Tomorrow, television series (US); The Apocalypse, television series (Australia), 1986. *Memberships:* Society of Authors; Lending Rights Society; Société du Bibliothéque Nationale; PEN; Grancho Club. *Literary Agents:* US, Harold Ober Associates; England, Brian Stone of Aitken Stone Hughes Massie. *Address:* 164 Rue du Faubourg Saint Honoré 75008, Paris, France.

CHEN, Ching-chih, b. 3 Sep. 1937, Fukien, China. Professor & Associate Dean, Graduate School of Library & Information Science, Simmons College, Massachusetts, USA. m. Dr Sow-Hsin Chen, 19 Aug. 1961, Ann Arbor, Michigan, 1 son, 2 daughters. *Education:* BA, National Taiwan University, 1959; AMLS, University of Michigan, 1961; PhD, Case Western Reserve University, 1974. *Literary Appointments Include:* Board, Legal Abstracts, 1977–79; Technical Review Panel, National Library of Medicine, 1978; Referee, Special Libraries, etc, 1979–; Board, Progress in Communication Science, 1979–; Editor, book series, Applications in Information Management & Technology, Neal-Schuman Publishers, 1980–; Editor-in-Chief, International quarterly journal, microcomputers for information management; Advisory Boards, various journals; etc. *Publications include:* Books: Application of Operations Research Models to Libraries, 1976; Biomedical, Scientific & Technical Book Reviewing, 1976; Sourcebook on Health Sciences Librarianship, 1977; Quantitative Measurement & Dynamic Library Service, 1978; Library Management Without Bias, 1980; Health Sciences Information Sources, 1981; Microcomputers in Libraries, co-editor, 1982; Numeric Databases, 1984; MicroUse Directory: Software, 1984; Integrating Micro-Based DBMS in Libraries (series, Practical guide to Microcomputers), with Barbara DeYoung, 1984; etc. Numerous book chapters, reports, journal articles, etc. *Honours include:* Scholarships, Fellowships, Grants Awards including: Distinguished Alumnus, University of Michigan, 1980; Distinguished Service, Chinese-American Librarians Association 1982, National Taiwan University 1983, Chinese Library Association 1983; Outstanding Information Science Teacher, American Society for Information Science, 1983; Fellow American Association for the Advancement of Science, 1985. *Memberships Include:* Various professional bodies. *Address:* Graduate School of Library & Information

Science, Simmons College, 300 The Fenway, Boston, MA 02115, USA.

CHEN, Jack, b. 2 July 1908, Port-of-Spain, Trinidad. Writer (Historian); Artist; Educator. m. Yuan-tsung Chen, 3 sons. *Literary Appointments:* Consultant, Chinese Studies, New York State Education Department, New York, USA, 1972; Senior Research Associate, Chinese Studies, Cornell University, 1975; Senior Researcher, Chinese American History, Chinese Culture Center, San Francisco, California, 1978; Project Director, 1981, President, San Francisco American Chinese Opera and Performing Arts Center, 1986–, Pear Garden in the West. *Publications include:* Soviet Art and Artists, 1944; Folk Arts of New China, 1954; New Earth, 1957, revised, 1973; A Year in Upper Felicity, 1974; Inside the Cultural Revolution, 1975; The Sinkiang Story, 1977; The Chinese of America, 1980; Pear Garden in the West: America's Chinese Theater 1852–1985, forthcoming. *Contributions to:* Numerous professional publications including: New York Times; Journal of American Ethnic History; Washington Post; China Daily, Beijing, China; China Reconstructs. *Membership:* Authors Guild. *Address:* 937 Liberty Street, El Cerrito, CA 94530, USA.

CHEN, Jo-hsi (Lucy H C Tuann), b. 15 Nov. 1938, Taipei, Taiwan, Republic of China. Writer. *Education:* BA, Taiwan University, 1961; MA, Johns Hopkins University, USA, 1965. *Publications:* In English: Spirit Calling, 1962; Mayor Yin, 1978; Ethics and Rhetoric of Chinese Cultural Revolution, 1981; Democracy Wall and Unofficial Journals, 1982. In Chinese: Mayor Yin, 1976, 26th edition, 1983; Old Man, 1978; Memoirs of Cultural Revolution, 1979; Another Fortress Besieged, 1981; Random Notes, 1981; Break Siege, 1983; Far-Sighted, 1984; The Two Hus, 1985; Works translated into French, German, Dutch, Japanese, Danish and Swedish. *Contributions to:* China Times; United Daily News, Taipei; China Daily; Center Daily, USA; Shin Min Daily, Singapore; Friendship Publications, China. *Address:* 428 Boynton Avenue, Berkeley, CA 94707, USA.

CHENEY, Theodore A Rees, b. 1 Jan. 1928, Milton, Massachusetts, USA. Professor, Communication & English. *Education:* BA, MA, Boston University, Massachusetts; MA, Fairfield University, Connecticut. *Publications:* Land of the Hibernating Rivers, 1969; Camping By Backpack & Canoe, 1970; Day of Fate, 1980; Getting the Words Right: How to Rewrite Revise & Edit, 1983; Living In Polar Regions, 1986. *Address:* 399 Round Hill Road, Fairfield, CT 06430, USA.

CHÉNIER, Maurice J E, b. 28 Feb. 1938, Sudbury, Ontario, Canada. Journalist. m. Dorothy Joyce McLeod, 4 July 1964, Toronto, Ontario, 1 daughter. *Education:* Diploma, Electrical Technician; Diploma, Architectural Technician; Journalism (Ryerson). *Publications:* Research towards series, 12 books, in progress. *Contributions to:* Reader's Digest (English); Drum, South Africa (English); Wine & Dine Magazine (English); Revue à Table! (French). *Membership:* Presse Gastronomique Internationale. *Address:* 580 Nun's Island, P Q, Canada H3E 1G7.

CHERNIN, Eli, b. 12 Sep. 1924, New York City, New York, USA. Professor of Tropical Public Health. m. June 1956, ex-wife deceased 1984, 2 sons, 1 daughter. *Education:* BS, College City of New York, 1944; MA, University of Michigan, 1948; ScD, Johns Hopkins University, 1952. *Literary Appointments:* Teacher of courses in biomedical writing, 1968–. *Publications:* Tropical Medicine at Harvard, 1954–81. *Contributions to:* 100 scientific papers on tropical medicine. *Honours:* Honorary AM, Harvard University, 1970. *Memberships:* President, Council of Biology Editors; President, International Federation of Scientific Editors. *Address:* Department of Tropical Public Health, Harvard School of Public Health, 665 Huntington Avenue, Boston, MA 02115, USA.

CHERNOW, Burt, b. 28 July 1933, New York City, USA. Writer. m. Ann, 12 Dec. 1970, 3 sons, 2 daughters. *Education:* BS, Art Education, 1958, MA, Higher Art Education, 1960, New York University. *Publications:* Paper, Paint & Stuff, Volumes I and II, 1969; Milton Avery Drawings, 1973; Lester Johnson, 1975; Lester Johnson Paintings: The Kaleidoscopic Crowd, 1975; Contemporary Graphics, 1977; Francisco Zuniga, 1978; Christo, 1978; Will Barnet, 1979–80; Francisco Zuniga, 1980; Richard Lindner Graphics, 1981; Gabor Peterdi Paintings, 1982; The Drawings of Milton Avery, 1984; The Complete Graphics of Francisco Zuniga, 1984. *Contributor to:* 40 articles in, Arts; Arts News; Craft Horizons; Art Education Journal; etc. *Memberships:* International Association of Art Critics; Appraisers Association of America; Silvermine Guild of Artists, Co-Chairman, Board of Directors; Westport Center for the Arts; Connecticut Humanities Council. *Address:* 2 Gorham Avenue, Westport, CT 06880, USA.

CHERRY, Kelly, Writer. *Education:* Dupont Fellow in Philosophy, University of Virginia; MFA, UNC-G. *Publications:* Sick and Full of Burning, 1974; Lovers and Agnostics, 1975; Relativity, 1977; Augusta Played, 1979; In the Wink of An Eye, 1983; The Lost Traveller's Dream, 1984. *Honours:* NEA; Bread Loaf; Yaddo; Romnes; Chancellor's Award; Wisconsin Arts Council; Best American Short Stories; Pushcart Prize. *Address:* English Department, University of Wisconsin, Madison, WI 53706, USA.

CHESTER, (Sir) (Daniel) Norman, b. 27 Oct. 1907, Chorlton-cum-Hardy, Manchester, England. Academic. *Education:* BA, 1930, MA, 1933, DLitt hon, 1968, Manchester University; MA, Oxon, 1946. *Publications include:* Public Control of Road Passenger Transport, 1936; British Government since 1918 (Editor and co-author), 1950; The Nationalised Industries, 1941; Questions in Parliament (Co-author), 1962; Nationalisation of British Industry 1945–51, 1975; English Administrative System 1780–1870, 1981. *Contributor to:* Public Administration; other journals; Editor, Journal of Public Administration, 1943–66.. *Honours:* CBE, 1951; Knighted, 1974; Chevalier de la Legion d'Honneur, 1976. *Membership:* Reform Club. *Address:* 136 Woodstock Road, Oxford OX2 7NG, England.

CHESTERFIELD-EVANS, Janet Lyndall, b. 14 May, 1957, Wollongong, Australia. Journalist. *Education:* BA, MA, Sydney University; Diploma, Secretarial Studies, Honours. *Publication:* The Pot Belly Bear Book, 1986. *Contributor to:* Orana, 1983. *Literary Agent:* Hodder & Stoughton (Aust) P/L. *Address:* 58/11 Yarranabbe Rd, Darling Point, NSW 2027, Australia.

CHESTERMAN, Jean, b. 10 May 1920, Pangbourne, Berkshire, England. Writer. m. David Chesterman, 5 Sep. 1945. Amersham, Buckinghamshire, 2 sons, 1 daughter. *Education:* Diploma of Speech and Drama, London University. *Literary Appointment:* Lecturer, Complementary Studies, Harrow School of Art. *Publications:* A Flight of Words; The Forest, 1971; Old Mr Hotchpotch, 1974; Theme and Variations, 1981; Clutterby Hogg, 1980; Ragdolly Anna, 1979; Three Cheers for Ragdolly Anna, 1985. *Contributions to:* Country Life; The Countryman; Scrip; Poetry Review; The Middle Way; Child Education; Liberal Education, etc. *Honours:* Poetry Review Premium Prize (3 times), 1940. *Address:* 15 Shire Lane, Chorleywood, Hertfordshire, England.

CHEUSE, Alan, b. 23 Jan. 1940, Perth Amboy, New Jersey, USA. Writer. divorced, 1 son, 2 daughters. *Education:* BA, Rutgers University, 1961; PhD, Comparative Literature, Rutgers University, 1974. *Appointments:* Writer-in-Residence, University of the South, 1984, University of Michigan, 1984–86. *Publications:* Candace & Other Stories, 1980; The Bohemians, novel, 1982; The Grandmothers' Club, novel, 1986. *Contributor to:* New Yorker; Boston Globe; Bennington Review; Black Warrior Review; New York Times; Los Angeles Times; Ms; TV Guide; Ladies Home

Journal' Los Angeles Herald Examiner; USA Today; etc. *Honours:* National Endowment for the Arts Writing Fellowship, 1979–80. *Membership:* National Book Critics Circle. *Literary Agent:* Liz Darhansoff, New York. *Address:* c/o English Dept, University of Michigan, Ann Arbor, MI 48109, USA.

CHIAPPELLI, Fredi, b. 24 Jan. 1921, Florence, Italy. University Professor. *Education:* DLitt, University of Florence, Italy; DLitt Hon causa, McGill University, Canada. *Publications include:* Language traditionnel et language personnel dans la peosie italienne contemporaine, 1951; Studi sul Lingusaggio del Tasso epico, 1957; Studi sul Linguaggio del Petrarca, 1973; Machiavelli e la Lingua Florentina, 1974; La vis abdita nel Tasso, 1979; Machiavelli, Legazioni, 111, 1984, IV, 1985; Il Legame Musaico, 1985. *Contributions to:* Major reviews and journals, Italy, Switzerland and USA. Member, Editorial Boards of several journals. *Honours include:* Honorary Member, Phi Beta Kappa, USA; Knight, Order of Civil Merit, Spain; Grand Officer, Order of Merit, Italy; Presidential Gold Medal, Cultural Merits, Italy; various other awards. *Memberships include:* Poets, Playwrights, Editors, Essayists and Novelists; Medieval Academy of America; Ateneo di Science Lettre d'Arti; Dante Alighiere Society; Renaissance Society of America. *Address:* 600 North Kenter Avenue, Los Angeles, CA 90049, USA.

CHIARELOTTO, Antonio, b. 6 Mar. 1908, Montebelluna, Treviso, Italy. Retired Bank Manager. m. Mary Masi, 17 May 1934, 1 son, 1 daughter. *Education:* Studied Accounting, Instituto Tecnico, Treviso; Diploma, Accounting, University of Venice. *Literary Appointments:* President, Treviso Committee of Societa Dante Alighieri, 1980–84, Honorary President, 1984–. *Publications:* Memoria di giorni, 1952; La domenica bianca, 1958; Fiume del Sereno, 1970, 3rd edition, 1980; Mon fumo, 1975, 2nd editon 1977; Sempre piu nitidi i segni, 1977; Mon fumo: My being Nothing, 1982. *Contributor to:* Many Italian and International Magazines and Journals including: Persona; Realta; Cenobio (Switzerland) La Parola del Popolo (USA); Antologia di poesia contemporanea. *Honours include:* Premio Nazionale di Poesia Camposampiero, Padua, 1972; Premio Nazionale Pisa di Poesia e Narrative, 1975; Premio Nazionale Poesia Bergamo, Premio Orobico, 1979; Honorable Mention, Concorso Internazionale di Poesia A Giovannitti, New York, 1981; Qui Aggiungere: Premio Nazion di Poesia, Guido Gozzano P.del Centenario, Belgirate, 1983, Cavaliere, Ministry of Finance, Rome, 1950; Premio di Cultura, from Italian Prime Minister, Rome, 1983; Merit Award, President, Societa Dante Alighieri, Rome, 1984. *Memberships:* Ateneo Veneto, Venice; Associazione Scrittori Veneti, Venice; Centro Internazional Eugenio Montale, Rome; Centro Studi di Poesia e Storia delle Poetiche; Gruppo Internazional di Lettura, Pisa; Association Internazionale des Critiques Litteraires, Paris. *Address:* 16 Via Giacomelli, 31100 Treviso, Italy.

CHIBEAU, Edmond Victor Peter, b. 20 Oct. 1947. Writer. *Education:* Long Island University, USA; University of California, Santa Barbara. *Publications:* The Old Songs, 1977; Portrait of an Artist, 1977; The Prisoners of Hope, 1978; Twelve Poems, 1981. *Contributions to:* Magpie; Shuttle; Nation; Fresh Tracks; Gall; Fly; California State Quarterly; Santa Barbara News Press; Santa Barbara News and Review; Quicksilver Messenger Service; Cardinal; Producer and Editor, Poets on Video. *Honours:* Transcendental Award for Being Born a Poet, 1969. *Memberships:* Dramatists Guild; Playwrights Circle. *Address:* 200 West 81st Street, New York City, NY 10024, USA.

CHIEGER, Bob, b. 12 Sep. 1945, Detroit, Michigan, USA. Writer. *Education:* BA, Finance & Management, University of Hawaii 1981; The GDR Moscow's German Ally, 1983; Honecker's Germany, Editor, 1985. *Address:* Dept of Politics, University of Nottingham, University Park, Nottingham NG7 2RD, England.

CHILDS, James E, b. 31 Mar. 1937, Hyanis, Massachusetts, USA. Professor. 1 son, 1 daughter. *Education:* BA Honours English 1965, MA English 1967, Southern Connecticut State University. *Literary Appointments:* Playwright-in-Residence, Central Connecticut State University, 1984; Plays produced: All Runners, Come, 1976; Chieftains, 1979; Darkness, Fierce Winds, 1980; Michael/Paula, 1982; Thunderbuddies, 1983. *Contributions to:* The Fair; Poet Hope; North American Mentor; New York Times Book Reviews; Charlatan; Film Comment; Sight and Sound; New Haven Register; Village Voice; Literature/Film. *Honours:* National Endowment for the Humanities Fellow, 1972–73; National Endowment for the Humanities Summer Fellowship, Yale University, 1981. *Memberships:* Dramatists Guild; National Book Critics Circle. *Literary Agent:* Joyce Ketay. *Address:* 551 East Main Street, Middletown, CT 06457, USA.

CHIMET, Iordan, b. 18 Nov. 1924, Galatzi, Romania. Freelance Writer. *Education:* BA, University of Bucharest, 1949; LLB, Bucharest Faculty of Law, 1957. *Publications:* Lamento for Little Balthazar, the Fish, 1968; Close Your Eyes and You Will See the City, 1970; Heroes, Ghosts, Little Mice, 1970; An Anthology of Innocence, 1972; Ballad for the Ancient Road, 1976; American Graphics, an Autobiography of the United States, 1976. *Contributor to:* American Review; Contemporanil; Romanian Literary Magazine; Romanian Radio and TV. *Honours include:* Fiction Prize, Writers Union, 1970; Award, Los Angeles National Book Fair, 1973. *Memberships:* Writers Union of Romania; National Cinematography Association of Romania. *Address* 18 Blvd Leontin Salajan, B1 B3bis Sc.2 apt 58, 74613, Bucharest, Romania.

CHISLETT, (Margaret) Anne, b. 22 Dec. 1942, Newfoundland, Canada. Playwright. m. James G Roy, 23 Apr. 1974, Toronto. *Education:* BA Honours English, Memorial University of Newfoundland; Theatre, University of British Columbia. *Publications:* The Tomorrow Box, 1980; Quiet in the Land, 1983. *Honours:* Chalmers Canadian Play Award, 1982; Governor General's Literary Award (Drama), 1984. *Memberships:* Playwrights Union of Canada; Manitoba Association of Playwrights. *Literary Agent:* Robert A Freedman, New York, USA. *Address:* c/o Robert A Freedman Dramatic Agency Incorporated, 1501 Broadway, Suite 2310, New York City, NY 10036, USA.

CHISSELL, Crystal Robbie, b. 11 Apr. 1962, Baltimore, Maryland, USA. Writer; Lawyer. *Education:* BA, Journalism, Howard University; JD Candidate, University of Maryland, current. *Address:* 2300 Bayleaf Court, Baltimore, MD 21209, USA.

CHITTICK, John, b. 29 May 1928, London, England. Writer; Producer. m. Joyce Kate Winter, Bromley. *Education:* Southwest Essex Technical College. *Literary Appointments:* Executive Editor, Focal Press Ltd; Editor, Industrial Screen; Video & Film Correspondent, Financial Times; Chairman, Screen Digest; Consultant Editor, Royal Television Society. *Publications include:* Executive Editor, 1st Edition, Focal Encyclopaedia of Photography; Minor books, How to Produce Megnetic Sound for Films, Film & Effect. *Contributions:* Financial Times; Television, (journal, Royal Television Society); Video & Film Communication; New Education; Campaign; Sight & Sound; etc. *Honours:* Fellow: Royal Photographic Society of Great Britain; British Kinematograph Sound & Television Society; Royal Television Society. Hood Medal, Royal Photographic Society; Queens Silver Jubilee Medal; Presidents Award, Institute of British Photographers; Video Writer of the Year, 1983. Officer, Order of the British Empire (OBE), 1982. *Memberships:* President, Film and Video Press Group; Arts Club, London. *Address:* 37 Gower Street, London WC1E 6HH, England.

CHITTLEBURGH, Michael John, b. 6 Aug, 1930, Great Yarmouth, England. Marketing Director, Publishing Company. m. Caroline Elizabeth Scupham, 2 July 1955; Hutton Rudby, 1 son, 2 daughters.

Education: BSc, Economics; F Inst M. *Publication:* Salesmans Handbook, 1972. *Contributions to:* Institute of Marketing Magazine; National Newsagent; The Bookseller; B Sopf Manual, etc. *Address:* 7 Midmar Avenue, Edinburgh EH10 6BS, Scotland.

CHOATE, Alec Herbert, b. 5 Apr. 1915. Former Surveyor, Writer. m. Shirley Joan Arundel Choate. *Appointments include:* Soldier, 1940–45; Surveyor, Permanent Public Servant, Western Australian Government, 1945–75; Freelance Writer, 1975–. *Major Publications:* Gifts upon the Water, 1978; Poetry Editor, Summerland, Western Australian Sesquicentenary Anthology of Poetry & Prose, 1979. *Contributor to:* Australian Literary Magazines: Poetry; Southerly; Westerly; Saturday Club Book of Poetry; Patterns; Artlook; Australian Anthologies, including the Jindyworobak Anthologies for 1948–53; Dimensions; Lip Service; Poets Australia; Soundings; Memories of Childhood; Summerland; Wide Domain; North of the 26th. *Honours:* Tom Collins Poetry Prize, 1976. *Membership:* Western Australian Branch, Fellowship of Australian Writers. *Address:* 158 Harborne Street, Wembley 6014, WA, Australia.

CHOBOT, Manfred, b. 3 May 1947, Vienna, Austria. Author. m. Dagmar, 17 Aug. 1968. *Education:* 5 years University Studies to Final Examination. *Publications include:* Neue Autoren, 1972; Projekte, 1973; Edlich was Neues, 1973; Reibflachenmultiple: Hrdlicka und die Offentlichkeit, 1977; Der Gruftspion, 1978; Waunst in Wean, 1978; Die Briefe der Kolecek, 1978; Radio plays including: Sonntag nach der mess, 1975; Inventur, 1977; TV Impulse: Schoner wohnen in Wien, 1972; (books) Reform-Projekte, 1980; i wuu net alaane sei, 1983; Krokodile haben keine Tranen 1985; Lesebuch, 1986: (Radio plays) Duell auf der Brucke, 1980; Vom Geben und vom Nehmen, 1981; Auf der Suche nach den verlorenen Sekunden, 1983; Lebenslanglich Wichtelgesse, 1982; Schlussmachen zu dritt, 1986. *Contributor to:* Numerous publications including: Protokolle; Manuskripte; Das Pult; Podium; Sterz; Litfass; Lesezirkel; Kurkiskern; Die horen; Wespennest; Rampe. *Honours include:* Working Scholarship, Region of Lower Austria, 1979; Dramatists Scholarship, 1979; TV Scholarship, 1979; Dramatists Scholarships, 1982, 1985–86; Preis der Arbeiterkammer Oberosterreich, 1981; Scholarship of the Community of Vienna, 1982. *Memberships:* Graz Authors Association, Board Member, Treasurer; Podium Literary Circle, Board Member; Die Kogge; Internationales Dialektinstitut. *Address:* Yppengasse 5/5, A–1160 Vienna, Austria.

CHODES, John Jay, b. 23 Feb. 1939, New York City, USA. Writer. *Education:* Commercial Photography Certificate. *Publications:* Corbitt, (Biography), 1974; Bruce Jenner, (Biography), 1976; The Myth of America's Military Power, 1972. Plays: Molineaux, 1979; Avenue A Anthology, 1969. *Honour:* Journalistic Excellence Award, 1974. *Membership:* Dramatists' Guild. *Literary Agent:* Charles Ryweck. *Address:* 411 East 10th Street, New York, NY 10009, USA.

CHORLEY, Desmond Mason, b. 21 June 1924, Liverpool, England. Writer. m. Edith Marie Leichnitz, 18 Dec. 1952, Ottawa, Canada, 1 son, 1 daughter. *Contributor to:* Saturday Evening Post; Time; Interavia; Flight International; Atlantic Advocate; Canadian Aviation; Private Pilot; Canadian Flight; Aeroplane; Canadian Aircraft Operator; Northern Miner; Aviation Yearbook 1980 (Jeppeson Sanderson); CBC; Montreal Standard; Legion. *Literary Agent:* Meredith Scott, New York. *Address:* 83 Wishing Well Drive, Agincourt, Ontario, M1T 1J2, Canada.

CHRISP, Peter Richard, b. 18 Sep. 1957, Grantham, Lincolnshire, England. Journalist. *Education:* HND, Communications; NCTJ Pre-Entry Certificate; Journalism. *Literary Appointments:* Feature Writer, Custom Car, 1979–82; Associate Editor, 1982–83, Editor 1983–85, Auto Performance; Freelance, 1985–. *Contributions to:* Custom Car; Sporting Cars International; Off Road and 4 Wheel Drive; Superbike;

Breaker; TV & Home Video; Video Retailer; TV & Video Answers; Audio Visual; Television Production; Professional Photographer; Video The Magazine. *Membership:* National Union of Journalists. *Address:* 15 West Street, Croydon, Surrey CR0 1DG, England.

CHRISPIJN, Rob, Lyricist. *Publications:* 80 Lyrics for Herman Van Veen; Songwriter for Liesbeth List, Peter Faber, Heddy Lester; (Books) Dinges; 15 Years of Songwriting; (Photographic Books) Herman, with Gerard Jongerius; Carré, with Jan Swinkels. *Honour:* Best Song of the Year, Conamus Foundation, 1982. *Address:* Jodenweg 1, 8385 GP VledderVeen, The Netherlands.

CHRISTEN, Yves, b. 18 Feb. 1948, Marseillechem and Animal Biology; Licentiate Psychology. *Publications:* L'Heure de la Sociobiologie, 1979; L'Homme, 1980; Mar et Darwin, 1981; Le Stress Vaincu? (with A Soubiran), 1981; Le Dossier Darwin, 1982; Biologie de l'Ideologie, 1985; Alexis Carrel, l'Ouverture de l'Homme, 1986. *Contributor to:* Figaro Magazine: La Recherche (Past Editor); Science d'aujourd'hui, (Director). *Memberships:* Association of Science Writers of France; Association of Science Journalists of the Information Press. *Address:* 27 Avenue Marceau, 75116, Paris, France.

CHRISTEN-DORIZZI, Irma, b. 28 July 1918, St Gall, Switzerland. Publisher. m. Christen Roland, 26 Feb. 1959, St Gall, 3 sons, 2 daughters. *Publications:* Ertraumtes, 1963; Negerli, 1967; Leben Lieben, 1968; Waldkonigin, 1970; Pyramide d.Z., 1972; Im Herzen trag ich, 1977; Der Silsersee erz, 1978; Zauberreich, 1983; Gschrebe isch au gschwatzt, 1985. *Memberships:* Schweiz Schriftstellerverband; Schweiz Bund fur Jugendliteratur; Hebelbund d-Lorrach; Europaische Marchengessellschaft D-Rheint. *Address:* Verlag Irma Christen-Dorizzi, Laupenring 137, CH–4054 Basel, Switzerland.

CHRISTENSEN, Paul, b. 18 Mar. 1943, West Reading, Pennsylvania, USA. Professor of English/American literature and custom. m. Catherine Ann, 20 Aug. 1969, 2 sons, 2 daughters. *Education:* BA, College of William and Mary, 1967; MA, University of Cincinnati, 1970; PhD, University of Pennsylvania, 1975. *Literary Appointments:* Instructor 1974, Assistant Professor 1976, Associate Professor 1980, Full Professor 1984, Texas A and M University. *Publications:* Charles Olson: Call Him Ishmael, criticism, 1979; Old and Lost Rivers, poems, 1977; The Vectory, poems, 1981; Signs of the Whelming, poems, 1983; Weights and Measures, poems, 1985. *Contributions to:* Southern Review; Parnassus: Poetry in Review; Sulfur; Twentieth Century Literature; Pawn Review; Blue Fish; Affinities; Texas Books in Review; The Texas Humanist; Texas Observer; Pebble; The Bloomsbury Review; The Washington Post; American Book Review; and others. *Memberships:* MLA; Poets and Writers Inc. *Address:* Department of English. Texas A and M University, College Station, TX 77843, USA.

CHRISTENSEN, Virginia April, b. 23 Apr. 1952, Mineola, New York, USA. Editorial Director. m. William Allen Kowalsky, 14 Feb. 1985, Northport, New York. *Education:* BA, New College, Hofstra University; Graduate Studies, Law, Adelphi University. *Literary Appointments:* Senior Editor, Billboard Publications, 1977–79; Senior Editor, General Editor, Barron's, 1980–83; Editorial Director, Asher-Gallant Press, 1983–; Teacher, Book Editing, New York Institute of Technology. *Contributor to:* Numerous articles for US Newspaper Newsday. *Honours:* Associate Editor, 14 Volume Encyclopedia of Practical Photography, a work nominated for Carey-Thomas Award. *Address:* New York, USA.

CHRISTIAENS, Andre, b. 24 Mar. 1905. Writer. *Literary Appointments include:* Teacher, Foreign Languages. *Publications:* De Algemene Regel, 1934; Uit de Toren, 1937; Irrequietum, 1937; Onvindbaar Land, 1968; A fscheid van de zondagsschool, 1976;

Verzamelde Gedichten, 1981; In vreemde voetsporen, 1981; Op versvoeten door Brussel, 1983. *Contributor to:* Dietse Warande en Belfort; Nieuw Vlaams Tijdschrift; Groot Nederland; Podium; Tafelronde; De Vlaamse Toeristenbond; Nieuw vlaanderen; Spectator. *Honours:* European Festival of Poetry, Prize, Louvain, 1979; Scriptores Christiani Prize, 1981. *Memberships:* PEN Flanders. *Address:* Blauwe-Vogellaan, 27, 1150 Brussels, England.

CHRISTIAN, Roy Cloberry, b. 8 Oct. 1914, Riddings, Derbyshire, England. Author; Broadcaster; Lecturer. *Education:* Certificate of Education, Daneshill College of Education. *Publications:* Old English Customs, 1966; Ghosts & Legends, 1972; Nottinghamshire, 1974; Peak District, 1976; Vanishing Britain, 1977; Nature-Lovers Companion, Editor, 1972; (for Children) Ships & the Sea, 1962; Factories, Forges, Foundaries, 1974; Derbyshire, 1978. *Contributor to:* Country Life; Listener; Lady; BBC. *Honour:* Recipient, MBE, 1976. *Literary Agent:* David Higham Associates. *Address:* 53 Littleover Lane, Littleover, Derby DE3 6JH, England.

CHRISTIE, (Ann) Philippa. Writer of Children's fiction. *Education:* MA, Girton College, Cambridge, England. *Publications include:* Minnows on the Say, 1955, 3rd edition, 1974; Tom's Midnight Garden, 1956; 3rd edition, 1976 (Carnegie Medal, 1959); Mrs Cockle's Cat, 1961, 2nd edition, 1974; A Dog So Small, 1962, 2nd edition, 1964; (with Sir Harold Scott) From Inside Scotland Yard, 1963; (with Sir Brian Fairfax-Lucy), The Children of the House, 1968, 2nd edition, 1970; The Elm Street Lot, 1969, enlarged edition, 1979; What the Neighbours Did and Other Stories, 1972, 2nd edition, 1974; The Shadow Cage and other Stories of the Supernatural, 1977; The Battle of Bubble and Squeak, 1978 (Whitbread Award, 1978); The Way to Sattin Shore, 2nd edition, 1985; Lion at School and Other Stories, 1985. *Contributor to:* Times Literary Supplement; The Guardian. *Honours:* Carnegie Medal, 1959; Whitbread Award, 1978. *Address:* c/o Kestrel Books, 536 Kings Road, London SW10 OUH, England.

CHRISTIE, Anne, b. 18 Mar. 1939, Scotland. Artist; Writer. m. Jack Ronder (deceased 1979), 29 July 1959, Edinburgh, 1 son, 2 daughters. *Education:* DA, Drawing, Painting, Edinburgh College of Art. *Publications:* My Secret Gorilla, 1981; First Act, 1983; An Honest Woman, 1985. *Contributor to:* Short stories in Womens Magazines, UK, Sweden, Australia. *Literary Agent:* Carol Smith, London. *Address:* c/o Piatkus Books, 5 Windmill Street, London W1P 1HS, England.

CHRISTIE Ian Ralph, b. 11 May. 1919, Preston, Lancashire, England. Professor Emeritus, University College, London. *Education:* Magdalen College, Oxford, 1938–40, 1946–48, Robert Herbert Prize, 1947, BA, MA, 1948. *Appointments:* Assistant Lecturer, History, 1948, Lecturer, 1951, Reader, 1960, Professor, Modern British History, 1966–79, Dean of Arts, 1971–73, Chairman, History Department, 1975–79, Astor Professor, British History, 1979–84. *Publications:* The End of North's Ministry, 1780–1782, 1958; Wilkes, Wyvill and Reform, 1962; Crisis of Empire: Great Britain and the American Colonies, 1754–1783, 1966; Editor, Essays in Modern History Selected from the Transactions of the Royal Historical Society, 1968; Myth and Reality in late Eighteenth-century British Politics and Other Papers, 1970; Editor, The Correspondence of Jeremy Bentham, volume 3, January 1781–October 1788, 1971; Empire or Independence 1760–1766, with B W Labaree, 1976; Bibliography of British History 1789–1851, with Lucy M Brown, 1977; Wars and Revolutions: Britain 1760–1815, 1982; Stress and Stability in late Eighteenth-Century Britain: Reflections on the British avoidance of revolution, The Ford Lectures, 1984. *Contributor to:* various professional journals. *Memberships:* Fellow, British Academy, 1977; Fellow, Royal Historical Society; Joint Literary Director, 1964–70, Council Member 1970–74; Member Editorial Board, History of Parliament Trust, 1973–. *Address:* 10 Green Lane, Croxley Green, Herts WD3 3HR, England.

CHRISTOPHER, Georgia B, b. 13 Oct. 1932, Barnesville, Georgia, USA. Professor of English. *Education:* BA, Agnes Scott College; PhD, Yale University. *Literary Appointments:* Mercer University, Macon, Georgia, 1959–62; University of North Carolina, 1966–71; University of Richmond, 1971–81; (Visiting Professor), Bryn Mawr College, 1977; Emory University, 1981–. *Publication:* Milton and the Science of the Saints, 1982. *Contributions to:* Studies in Philology, 1970; The Verbal Gate to Paradise: Adam's Literary Experience in Book X of Paradise Lost, PMLA, 1975; The Secret Agent in Paradise Regained, Modern Language Quarterly, 1980. *Honours:* Honorary Woodrow Wilson Fellowship, 1955; Fulbright Scholarship to University of Southampton, 1955; Ford Foundation Fellowship, 1957; Fellow, Folger Shakespeare Library, 1976; ACLS Fellowship, 1976; James Holly Hanford Award, 1983. *Memberships:* Renaissance Society of America; Modern Language Association; Milton Society of America; Shakespeare Association; Southeast Renaissance Conference. *Address:* English Department, Emory University, Atlanta, GA 30322, USA.

CHRISTOPHER, Matthew F, b. 16 Aug. 1917, Bath. Pennsylvania, USA. *Publications include:* Shortstop from Tokyo, 1970; Lucky Seven, 1970; Johnny Long Legs, 1970; Look Who's Playing First Base, 1971; Tough to Tackle, 1971; The Kid Who Only Hit Homers, 1972; Face-Off, 1972; Mystery Coach, 1973; Ice Magic, 1973; Desperate Search, 1973; Stranded, 1974; Earthquake, 1975; Devil Pony, 1978; Publisher, Little Brown, Soccer Halfback, 1978; Dirt Bike Racer, 1979; Run Billy Run, 1980; Favor For A Ghost, 1983; The Great Quarterback Switch, 1984; Supercharged Infield, 1985; The Hockey Machine, 1986. *Contributor to:* over 60 magazines including, Sprint; Christian Science Monitors; Readers Digest Educational Services; Imperial Learning Inc; *Honour:* Recipient, Junior Book Award Certificate, Boys Club of America, 1957. *Membership:* Member, Author's Guild. *Address:* 533 Vasto Drive, Venice, FL 33595, USA.

CHRÖSCIELEWSKI, Jadeusz, b. 3 June 1920, Minsk, Marowiecki. Poet; Writer; Translator. m. 2 Aug. 1947, 1 son, 1 daughter. *Education:* Polish & Russian Philology, Warsaw University, 1945. *Publications include:* Poetry: Uczta Aureliana, 1944; Najmilsze strony, 1956; Italia, 1958; Miesiac utajony, 1960; Puste krzeslo, 1966; Hipokrene warminska, 1969; Karta powolania, 1973; Trzy wdzieczne damy i aniol, 1978; Na sliadach maigo doma, 1977; Tozsamosc, 1980; Gwiazdobiory czworbarwne ze snow wystrazygane, 1982; Koncert we Fromborku, 1983; Lgenda Nigra, 1984; Poezje wybrane, 1984; (Novels & Short Stories), Rodzina Jednorozcow, 1960; Szkola dwoch dziewczat, 1965, 1966, 1976; Szkarlatna godzina, 1968, 1970; Aurelian albo zjazd kolezenski, 1971, 1984; Srebrana i odloty, 1974; Laska Matuzalema, 1974; Dzbanek zycia, 1977; Moj ozenek w krainie Feakow, 1979; Podroze staroswieckie, 1982; Pejzaz z Baskai paniutkami, 1984; Editor, Anthologies; Translator of Russian and Soviet poetry. *Contributor to:* Poezja; Literatura na Swiecie; Prsmo; Krontrasty; etc. *Honours:* Honorary Citizen of Minsk Marowiecki, Recipient, honorary diploma, Chairman, USSR Council of Ministers as Translator, 1969; Lodz Vsiv Award, 1973; Minister of Culture and Art Award 1st Class, 1984; Silver 1954, Gold 1970 Crosses of Merit; Knights Cross, Polonia Restituta Order, 1975; Medal, 1980; Officers Crosonia Restituta, 1984. *Memberships:* various professional organisations. *Address:* Al Kosciuszki 98 m5, 90-442 Lodz, Poland.

CHRZANOWSKI, Tadeusz, b. 14 May 1926, Cracow, Poland. Art Historian; Writer. m. Teresa Lewicka, 12 Jan. 1952, Cracow, 2 daughters. *Education:* Graduate of Academy of Economy, Cracow, 1947; MA, 1952, PhD, 1971, Jagiellonian University, Cracow; Dissertation for Assistant Professor, Institute of Art, Polish Academy of Sciences, Warsaw, 1983. *Literary Appointments:* Board Member, Polish Writers Association, Cracow Branch, 1975–82. *Publications:* Farewell to Summer Volume of Poetry, 1957; Living and Dead Boundaries, essays,

1974; Peregrinations in the European Sarmatia essays, 1986; Scholarly works on Art History in edited books and periodicals. *Contributor to:* Constant contributor from 1948 to Catholic weekly Tygodnik Powszechny of poetry, essays, reviews and reports. Essays also published in monthlies Tworczosc; Wiez; Teksty and others. *Honour:* Literary Award in Honour of Stanislaw Vinvenz, 1983. *Address:* ul. Michalowskiego 9/4, 31-126 Kraków, Poland.

CHUBB, Mary Alford, b. 22 Mar. 1903, London, England. Assistant, Archaeological Digs. *Publications:* Nefertiti Lived Here, 1954; City in the Sand, 1957; An Alphabet of Ancient Egypt, 1966; An Alphabet of Ancient Greece (Early Days), 1967; An Alphabet of Ancient Greece (The Golden Years), 1968; An Alphabet of Assyria & Babylonia, 1969; An Alphabet of Ancient Rome, 1971; An Alphabet of the Holy Land, 1973. *Contributor to:* Punch; Ladies magazines; BBC; The Listener. *Address:* Greens, Weston Patrick, Basingstoke, Hants, England.

CHURCH, Albert M III, b. 14 Aug. 1940, Milwaukee, Wisconsin, USA. Economist, 2 sons. *Education:* BA, 1963, Colorado College; PhD, 1971 Claremont Graduate School. *Publications:* Statistics and Computers in the Appraisal Process, (with R Gustafson), 1976; The Taxation of Non-Renewable Resources, 1981; The Sophisticated Investor, 1981; Conflicts Over Resource Use, 1982. *Contributions to:* Numerous Economic publications. *Address:* Department of Economics, University of New Mexico, Albuquerque, NM 87102, USA.

CHUTKOW, Paul, b. 12 July 1947, Chicago, Illinois, USA. Writer; Journalist. m. Eda Jane Cole, 15 Sep. 1976, New Delhi, India, 2 sons. *Education:* BA, Honours, MA, The Writing Seminars, Johns Hopkins University, Baltimore. *Literary Appointments:* Correspondent for: The Baltimore Sun; The Associated Press, Baltimore, New York, India, Paris; Independent Correspondent and Correspondent for The Statesman of India. *Contributor to:* Frequent contributor to: Connoisseur Magazine; New York Times; L'Express; British Broadcasting Corporation, etc. *Literary Agent:* Michael V Carlisle. *Address:* c/o Michael Carlisle, William Morris Agency, 1350 Avenue of the Americas, New York, NY 10019, USA.

CIABATTARI, Jane Dotson, b. 27 Mar. 1946, Emporia, Kansas, USA. Editor in Chief. m. G Mark Ciabattari, 7 Jan. 1967, Palo Alto. *Education:* BA, Stanford University, 1968; MA, Creative Writing, San Francisco State University, 1984. *Appointment:* Editor in Chief, 'Dial', Magazine for Public TV. *Publications:* Included in Anthology, Kansas Women Writers, 1980. *Contributor to:* North American Review; Short Stories and Novella in Redbook; Threepenny Review; The Progressive; Glamour; California Living; Dial; etc. *Honours:* MacDowell Colony Fellow, Summers, 1982, 1983, 1984. *Memberhips:* Authors Guild; Poets and Writers Inc; Advisory Board, Fiction Network. *Literary Agent:* Ellen Levine. *Address:* 36 West 75th Street, New York, NY 10023, USA.

CIRONE, Bettina, b. 19 Aug. 1933, Manhattan, New York City, USA. Photographer; Journalist. *Contributions to:* American Photographer; Photo Methods; Photo District News; Hot Shoe International; Bunte, Quick, Germany; Yomuro Shimbun, Japan; New York Daily News, New York Post, New York Times, USA Today, People, USA; The Star, Match, VSD, France; Numerous other periodicals in USA, Switzerland, South Africa, Italy, UK, South America, Spain, etc. *Honours:* 1st Prize, newspaper category, photography & journalism, Boy Scouts of America, 1984. *Address:* 57 West 58th Street, New York, NY 10019, USA.

CIVASAQUI, Jose, b. 2 Jan. 1916, Saitama, Japan. Poet; Translator. m. Setusko Hirose, 18 Sep. 1940, 2 sons, 1 daughter. *Education:* Saitama School of Commerce, Japan, 1935. *Literary Appointments:* President, Japan Song Translators Society; Managing Director, Japan League of Poets; Managing Director, Japan Guild of Authors & Composers; President 1983–85, Honorary President 1985–, United Poets Laureate International. *Publications:* Living Water, 1948; In His Bosom, 1950; In Thy Grace, 1971; Doshin Shien (translation of A Child's Garden of Verses by R L Stevenson), 1973; Beyond Seeing, 1977. *Contributor to:* Nippon Times; Mainichi; Come Come Club; New Age; Study of Current English; Poetry Nippon; Laurel Leaves, Philippines; Verbeia, UK; Ocarina, India. *Honours include:* Excellence in Poetry, Third World Congress of Poets, 1976; Honorary LHD, L'University Lible d'Asie, Karachi, Pakistan, 1977; HHD, World University, Tucson, Arizona, USA, 1977; Diploma of Merit, International Society of Literature, 1977; Plaque of Distinction, 4th World Congress of Poets, 1979; Jnana Ratna, Honorary Life Fellow, The World Jnana Sadhak Society, India; International Poet Laureate, 8th World Congress of Poets; Honorary President, United Poets Laureate International; Recognition, Outstanding Christian Poetry, with Gerald L K Smith Award, Elna M Smith Foundation; Certificate of Recognition, Platformers USA; Certificate of Appointment, Chief Delegate and Chairman, Japanese National Delegation, World University; Centro Nazionale Culturale 'Pell di luna' Italia : un Premio Speciale per Opera omnia e per la grande dedizone che offre alla cultura mondiale. *Memberships:* Life Fellow, Tagore Institute of Creative Writing International, Madras, India. *Address:* Honcho 2-12-11 Ikebukuro, Toshima-ku, Tokyo 170, Japan.

CIVIL, Jean, b. 5 June 1932, Haiti. Professor. m. 13 Sep. 1960, 1 son, 3 daughters. *Education:* License ès Lettres, MA, Sherbrooke University, Canada. *Literary Appointments:* Editor-in-Chief, Grimoire (Revue), 1976–82; Editor-in-Chief, Passages (Revue), 1982–. *Major Publications:* Entre Deux Pays (Poems), 1979; Le petit Album des Auteurs des Cantons de l'Est, 1980. *Contributor to:* Grimoire; Passages; Présence Francophone. *Honour:* Prix Littéraire 'Jules Lemay', Society St-Jean Baptiste de Sherbrooke, 1984. *Membership:* Former President, currently Vice-President, Association des Auteurs des Cantons de l'Est. *Address:* 515 Fortin Street, Sherbrooke, Quebec J1E 2Z1, Canada.

CLAIRE, William, b. 4 Oct, 1935, Massachusetts, USA, Consultant: Educational and Cultural. m. Sedgley Mellon Schmidt, 22 Nov. 1973, Ottawa, Canada. 1 son. *Education:* BA, Columbia University, New York City; MLS, Georgetown University, Washington, DC. *Literary Appointments:* Founding Editor and Publisher, Voyages, 1967–73; Board of Editors, Literature and Medicine. *Publications:* Publishing in the West, 1974; Essays of Mark Van Doren, 1924–72, 1980; Literature and Medicine, 1984. *Contributions to:* Smithsonian Magazine; American Scholar; Nation; New Republic; New York Times; Antioch Review; Change; New York Quartely, etc. *Honours:* Yaddo Fellowship, 1974; MacDowell Fellowship, 1976; Rockefeller Foundation Residency, Bellagio, Italy, 1979–80. *Memberships:* PEN; Poetry Society of America. *Literary Agent:* Gloria Stern, New York City. *Address:* 3734 R Street NW, Washington, DC 20007, USA.

CLARK, Christine May, b. 25 Apr. 1957, Peoria, Illinois, USA. Childrens Magazine Editor. m. Terry Randolph Clark, 28 Aug. 1982, Indianapolis, Indiana. *Education:* BA, Judson College, Elgin, Illinois, 1978. *Literary Apointments:* News Reporter, Judson College, Elgin, Illinois, 1978; Stringer Countryside Press, Barrington, 1978; Associate Editor, David Cook Publishing Company, Elgin, 1978–80. Editor: Humpty Dumpty Magazine, 1980–; Children's Digest Magazine, 1980–83; Jack and Jill Magazine, 1983–. *Contributions to:* Turtle Magazine; Humpty Dumpty; Jack and Jill; Childrens Digest; Bible-in-Life Stories; The Quiet Hour; The Saints Herald; The Church Herald. Author of religious curriculum, Come Follow Me, 1983 and Living in Covenant, 1985. *Memberships:* Central Indiana Writers Association; Guild of Christian Writers and Poets; Educational Press Association. *Address:* 8345 East 41st Street, Indianapolis, IN 46226, USA.

CLARK, Christopher David, b. 24 Jan. 1951, Normanby, Teesside, England. Author. *Publications:* The Test Match Career of Freddie Trueman, 1980; The Record Breaking Sunil Gavaskar, 1980. *Contributions to:* Sportsweek, Bombay, India. *Literary Agent:* B Ridsdale-Tombling. *Address:* c/o B Ridsdale-Tombling, 32 Jubilee Road, Eston, Cleveland TS6 9HB, England.

CLARK, David R, b. 1920, Seymour Connecticut, USA. University Professor. Writer. *Education:* BA, MA, PhD, Wesleyan University, Yale University, USA. *Publications:* (Co-author) A Curious Quire, 1962; Author, William Butler Yeats and the Theatre of Desolate Reality, 1965; Co-Editor, Irish Renaissance, 1965; Author of Dry Tree, 1966; Co-Editor, Reading Poetry, 1968; A Tower of Polished Black Stones, 1971; Druid Craft, 1971; Author, Lyric Resonance, 1972; Editor, Critical Essays on Hart Crabe, 1982; Author, Yeats at Songs and Choruses, 1983. *Contributions to:* Numerous Literary journals. *Memberships include:* MLA: Am. Comm. Irish Studies; International Society for the Advancement of Irish Literature. Canadian Association for Irish Studies. *Address:* English Department, University of Massachussetts, Amherst, MA 01002, USA.1950, DSc, 1975, Christs College, Cambridge University. *Publications include:* The Prehistory of Southern Africa, 1959; The Atlas of African Prehistory, 1967; The Prehistory of Africa, 1970; The Kalambo Falls Prehistoric Site, volume 1, 1969, volume 2, 1974. *Contributions to:* Various scientific journals. *Honours include:* OBE, 1956; CBE, 1960; Commander, National Order of Senegal, 1969. *Memberships include:* Fellow, British Academy; American Academy of Arts and Sciences; Royal Society of South Africa. *Address:* Department of Anthropology, University of California, Berkeley, CA 94720, USA.

CLARK, Eleanor, b. Los Angeles, California, USA. Author. m. Robert Penn Warren, 7 Dec. 1952, 1 son, 1 daughter. *Education:* BA, Vassar College, 1934. *Literary Appointments:* Editorial work, W W Norton, 1936–39, OSS, Washington, 1943–45; Ghost writer, Translator, Editor, freelance. *Publications:* The Bitter Box, 1946; Rome and A Villa, expanded edition, 1975; The Oysters of Locwauaquer, 1964; Baldui's Gate, novel, 1971; Dr Heart and other stories, 1974; Eyes Etc, a Memoir, 1977; Gloria Mundi, 1979; Camping Out, novel, 1986. *Contributions to:* Atlantic; Partisan Review; Georgia Review; New England Review; Yale Review; New Yorker and others. *Honours:* Guggenheim Fellowship, 1946, 49; North Institute of Arts and Letters award, 1946; National Book Award, Arts and Letters, 1965. *Memberships:* Board of Directors, Yaddo Colony. *Literary Agent:* Harriet Wasserman. *Address:* 2495 Kedding Road, Fairfield, CT 06430, USA.

CLARK, John Howard, b. 6 June 1929, Middlesex, England. Senior Lecturer in Psychology. *Education:* MA, MB, Gonville & Caius College, Cambridge; Westminster Hospital Medical School, London; DPM. *Literary Appointment:* Editor, The Cambridge University Medical Society Magazine, 1951. *Publications:* Medicine, Mind and Men (with John Cohen), 1979; A Map of Mental States, 1983. *Contributor to:* New Worlds, 1967; The Varieties of Ineffability in Proceedings of the First Symposium of the European Psychologists of Religion, Nijmegen, The Netherlands, 1979. *Honour:* Fellow, The Cybernetics Society, London 1984. *Address:* Department of Psychology, University of Manchester, Manchester, M13 9PL, England.

CLARK, Marie Catherine Audrey, b. London, England. Writer. m. Clifton Clark, 16 Feb. 1938, Chiswick. *Publications:* (novels) The Running Tide, 1963; Sparrow's Yard, 1964; (Historical novels) The Echoing Silence, 1967; Castle for Comedy, 1970; The Sapphire and the Pearl, 1970; Cry of the Heart, 1971; A Quarter of the Moon, 1972; Shadows on the Grass, 1973; Enthusiasts in Love, 1975; Publisher: Hurst and Blackett; (Biography) The Young Thackeray, (Max Parrish), 1966. *Contributor to:* Home and Gardens; Woman's Own; Woman; Woman's Realm; The Lady. *Honour:* Theodora Roscoe Award, 1978. *Memberships:*

Society of Authors; Institute of Journalists; Romantic Novelists Association. *Address:* 35 Hadley Gardens, Chiswick, London W4 4NU, England.

CLARK, Michael Dorsey, b. 5 Nov. 1937, Baltimore, Maryland, USA. Professor of History. m. Mary Margaret Dugan, 31 July 1965, New Orleans, Louisiana, 1 son, 1 daughter. *Education:* BA, Yale University, 1959; MA, 1962, PhD, 1965, University of North Carolina. *Publications:* Wordly Theologians: The Persistence of Religion in 19th Century American Thought, 1981; Coherent Variety: The Idea of Diversity in British and American Conservative Thought, 1983. *Contributions to:* Modern Age, 1969; The Huntington Library Quarterly, 1969; Maryland Historical Magazine, 1972. *Membership:* Secretary-Treasurer, Lower Mississippi Chapter, American Studies Association. *Address:* Department of History, University of New Orleans, New Orleans, LA 70148, USA.

CLARK, Neal Cornwell, b. 5 Dec. 1950, Boston, Massachusetts, USA. Nature Writer. *Education:* BS Wildlife Management, University of New Hampshire, Durham, 1973. *Publications:* Eastern Birds of Prey, 1983. *Contributions to:* Boston Globe; Boston Magazine; Boston Phoenix; New England Outdoors' magazine; Appalachia; New Hampshire Profiles; New Hampshire Times; Bird Observer; Bird Watcher's. *Education:* Swiss Institute; Munich University. *Appointments:* Sub-editor, Woman's Illustrated, 1937–39. *Publications:* 60 novels, sundry children's books, 1946–76, as Patricia Robins; (as Claire Lorrimer), The Shadow Falls, 1974; The Secret of Quts Council, 1982, 1983 and 1984; Canada Arts Council B Grant, 1985–86. *Membership:* Playwrights Union of Canada. *Literary Agent:* Mr Ralph Zimmerman, Great North Artists Inc, 345 Adelaide Street West #500, Toronto, Ontario. *Address:* 5087 Connaught Drive, Vancouver, British Columbia V6M IG2, Canada.

CLARKE, Anna, b. 28 Apr. 1919, Cape Town, South Africa. Novelist. *Education:* BSc, Economics, London, England, 1945; BA, Open University, 1974; MA, Sussex University, 1975. *Publications:* The Darkened Room, 1968; A Mind to Murder, 1971; The End of a Shadow, 1972; Plot Counter-Plot, 1974; My Search for Ruth, 1975; Legacy of Evil, 1976; The Deathless & the Dead, 1976; The Lady in Black, 1977; Letter from the Dead, 1977; One of Us Must Die, 1978; The Poisoned Web, 1979; Poison Parsley, 1979; Last Voyage, 1980; Game Set and Danger, 1981; Desire to Kill, 1982; We the Bereaved, 1982; Soon She Must Die, 1983; Last Judgement, 1985. *Memberships:* Crime Writers Association; Society of Authors. *Address:* 12 Franklin Road, Brighton BN2 3AD, Sussex, England.

CLARKE, Anthony Frederick Neville, b. 4 Nov. 1948, Kowloon, Hong Kong. Writer; Author. (div.), 3 daughters. *Publications:* Contact, Secker & Warburg, 1983, filmed for television 1985; Collisions, Secker & Warburg, in press. *Memberships:* Society of Authors: Writers Guild. *Address:* 8 Myddelton Square, London EC1, England.

CLARKE, Arthur C, b. 16 Dec. 1917, Minehead, England. Author. m. Marilyn Mayfield, 1953–64. *Education:* First Class Honours, Physics, Pure and Applied Mathematics, King's College, London, 1946–48. *Literary Appointments:* Assistant Editor, Science Abstracts, Institution of Electrical Engineers, 1949–50; With Walter Cronkite CBS-TV on Apollo, 1968–70; Played Leonard Woolf in Lester James Peries' movie, Beddagama, 1979; Wrote and hosted YTV Series, Arthur Clarke's Mysterious World, 1980 and World of Strange Powers, 1984; Director, Rocket Publishing Company, UK; Underwater Safaris, Sri Lanka, Serendib b.v, Netherlands; Originated communication satellites, Wireless World, 1945; Lunar Mass-driver, Journal of British Interplanetary Society, 1950. *Publications include:* Non-fiction includes: Ascent to Orbit; Boy Beneath the Sea; The Exploration of the Moon; Going Into Space; Voices from the Sky; Fiction includes: Across the Sea of Stars; From the Oceans, From the

Stars; The Nine Billion Names of God; Prelude to Mars; The Sentinel (all anthologies); 2001: A Space Odyssey; The Sands of Mars; Editor: The Coming of the Space Age, etc. *Honours include:* Several Fellowships, honorary degrees and awards. *Memberships include:* Board Member, National Space Institute, USA; Chancellor, University of Moratuwa, Sri Lanka, 1979–. *Address:* "Leslie's House", 25 Barnes Place, Colombo 7, Sri Lanka.

CLARKE, Austin Chesterfield, b. 26 July 1934, Barbados, West Indies. Novelist/Professor. *Education:* Trinity College of Toronto, Canada. *Literary Appointment:* Vice Chairman, Board of Censors, Ontario, 1984–. *Publications:* The Survivors of the Crossing, 1964; Amongst Thistles and Thorns, 1965; The Meeting Point, 1967; Storm of Fortune, 1972; The Bigger Light, 1974; When He Was Free and Young, 1975; The Prime Minister, 1977; Growing Up Stupid Under the Union Jack, 1980; When Women Rule, 1985; Nine Men Who Laughed, 1986; Proud Empires, 1986. *Contributor to:* Tamarack Review, Canada; Bim Literary Review, Barbados; Yale Review, USA; Works in Progress, USA. *Honours include:* Belmont-Saturday Night Short Story Award, 1967; Canada Council Literary Awards 1967, 72, 76; Casa De Las Americas Literary Prize, 1980. *Literary Agent:* Harold Ober Associates Ltd. *Address:* 432 Brunswick Avenue, Toronto, Canada M5R 2Z4.

CLARKE, Peter Edward, b. 2 June 1929, Simon's Town, CP, South Africa. Painter; Graphic Artist; Book Illustrator. *Education:* Informal Art Groups, Cape Town, South Africa, 1947–52; Michelis School of Art, University of Cape Town, 1961; Art Universities in the Netherlands, 1962–63; Norway, 1978–79. *Literary Appointments:* Fulltime Painter, Graphic Artist and Designer, Book Illustrator. *Publications:* Soul Motion III: Peter Clarke South African Artist Poet, (30 poems and a catalogue, Graphic Art Exhibition in the Carl van Vechten Gallery, Fisk University, Tennessee, USA, 1973–74). *Contributor to:* Drum Magazine; Africa Magazine; Contrast; An African Treasury, 1960; Poems from Black Africa, 1963; Junior Voices, 1971; South African Outlook, 1973; New Nation, 1973; Poetry South; Mundus Artium; Living Language; Wietie; Vakalisa; Calendars; Research in African Literature; Cosmopolitan; The Gar; Classic; Reality; First World, etc. *Honours:* DRUM International Short Story Award, 1955; Elected Accademico Onorario of the Accademia Fiorentina delle Arti del Disegno, Florence, Italy, 1965; Honorary Fellow in Writing, University of Iowa, USA, 1975; Diploma of Merit (Lit), Universita delle Arti, Salsomeggiore, Italy, 1982; Diploma of Merit, Accademia Italia, 1983; Honorary Doctor of Literature, World Academy of Arts and Culture, Taipei, Taiwan, 1984. *Address:* 14 Alpha Way, Ocean View CP 7975, Republic of South Africa.

CLARKE, Thomas Ernest Bennett, b. 1907, Watford, England. Journalist, 1927–43; Screenwriter, 1943–. *Education:* Charterhouse School; Clare College, Cambridge. *Publications include:* Go South – Go West; Jeremy's England; Two & Two Makes Five; Cartwright was a Cad; Mr Spirket Reforms; What's Yours?' The World Was Mine; The Wide Open Door; The Trail of the Serpent; This Is Where I Came In, autobiography; The Man Who Seduced a Bank; Murder at Buckingham Palace; Grim Discovery; (Screenplays), Passport to Pimlico; The Blue Lamp; The Magnet; The Lavender Hill Mob; The Titfield Thunderbolt; Gideon's Day; The Horse Without a Head; The Rainbow Jacket; Who Done It?; Sons & Lovers; A Tale of Two Cities; various TV Scripts. *Honour:* Recipient, Academy Award for, The Lavender Hill Mob. *Address:* 13 Oakleigh Court, Oxted, Surrey, England.

CLARKE-McKENNA, Neva Yvonne, b. Gisborne, New Zealand. Author; Artist. m. (1) Edward Alexander Clarke, 18 Jan. 1949, Gisborne, (2) Leonard Woodrow McKenna, 20 Dec. 1975, 1 son, 1 daughter. *Appointments:* Committee, Women Writers Society, New Zealand; President, PEN, New Zealand Centre,

1969–71; New Zealand Book Council, 1971–72; Founder Doubtless Bay Society of Arts. *Publication:* Behind Closed Doors, 1964. *Contributor to:* Short Stories Worldwide; Book Review Panel, New Zealand Broadcasting Corporation, 1965–; New Zealand Drama Panel, 1960–70. *Memberships:* New Zealand Writers Guild; New Zealand Booksellers Association; New Zealand Women Writers Society. *Address:* Coopers Beach, Northland, New Zealand.

CLARY, Sydney Ann, b. 13 Feb. 1948, Auburn, Alaska, USA. Romance Writer. m. Bishop David Clary, 26 Sep. 1967, Baxley, Georgia, 2 daughters. *Publications:* Her Golden Eyes, 1983; Let Passion Soar, 1983; Home at Last, 1983; This Wildfire Magic, 1983; A Touch of Passion, 1985; Look Beyond Tomorrow, 1985. *Contributions to:* Romantic Times; Romantic Times Newsletter. *Honours:* Best Book Nominations, Romantic Times Reviewer, 1983 and 1985. *Memberships:* National Writers Club; Romance Writers of America. *Literary Agent:* Robin Kaigh Literary Agency. *Address:* 104 Eganfuskee Street, Jupiter, FL 33458, USA.

CLAVIEN, Germain, b. 4 Oct. 1933, Sion. Teacher. m. Madeleine Biderbost, 24 Aug. 1984, Sion. *Education:* Degree of literature, Universities of Geneva and Fribourg, Switzerland. *Publications:* Novels: Les Moineaux del'Arveche, 1974; Le Partage, 1974. Poetry: Amour, 1975; La Montagne et la Mer, 1976; Le Soir Finit Toujours par Venir, 1980; Au Nom du Coeur, 1984. *Contributions to:* Gazette de Lausanne; Journal de Geneve; Alliance culturelle romande, review. *Honours:* Hentsch prize of french literature, Geneva, 1957; Prix des libraires Payot, for Les Moineaux de l'Arveche, 1974. *Memberships:* Swiss Writers Society; Association of Writers of French Tongue. *Address:* Ch–1962 Pont-de-la-Morge, Switzerland.

CLAWSON, Robert Wayne, b. 21 Dec. 1939, Glendale, California, USA. Professor. m. Judith Louise Lisy, 25 June 1961, Orange Village, Ohio, 1 son, 1 daughter. *Education:* AB, 1961, MA, Political Science, 1964, University of California, Los Angeles; Certificate of Training, US Defence Language Institute, 1964; Exchange Scholarship, Moscow State University, Russia, 1966; PhD, Political Science, University of California Los Angeles, 1969. *Publications:* Co-Editor, Contributing Author, Nato After Thirty Years, 1981, The Warsaw Pact: Political Purpose and Military Means, 1982; Co-Editor, Nato and the Mediterranean, 1984. *Contributor to:* Numerous scholarly articles in journals in fields of political science, international relations, economics and business affairs. *Address:* 7336 Westview Road, Kent, OH 44240, USA.

CLAYPOOL-MINER, Jane, b. 22 Apr. 1933, McAllen, Texas, USA. Writer. m. (1) Dennis A Shelley, 1951, Las Vegas, Nevada; (2) Richard Yale Miner, 1962, Pennsylvania, 1 daughter. *Education:* BA, Art Education, California State University, Long Beach, 1956; Graduate Work: California State University Los Angeles and University of California, Los Angeles. *Publications:* 50 books for young people including: Why Did You Leave Me? 1980; Dreams Can Come True, 1981; Senior Class, 1981; Alcohol and You, 1981; Flowers for Lisa, 1982; Crisis Series (10 books), 1982; The Boy For Me, 1982; Unemployment, 1982; Joanna, 1984; Senior Dreams Can Come True, 1984. *Contributions to:* Writers Magazine; New England Fashion Digest; Catholic Digest; Berkshire Sample. *Honour:* Writer of the Year, Society of Childrens Book Writers, 1981. *Memberships:* Society of Childrens Book Writers; Association of Authors and Journalists. *Address:* 2883 Lone Jack Road, Olivenhain, CA 92024, USA.

CLAYTON, Peter Arthur, b. 27 Apr. 1937, London, England. Publications Director, Lecturer, Writer. m. Janet Frances Manning, 5 Sep. 1964, London, 2 sons. *Education:* Fellow of the Library Association; Diploma in Archaeology, University of London. *Literary Appointments:* Archaeology Editor, Thames & Hudson Ltd,

1963–73; Humanities Publisher, Longman Group, 1973; Managing Editor, British Museum Publications, 1974–79; Publications Director, B A Seaby Ltd, 1980–. *Major Publications:* Archaeological Sites of Britain, 1976; Companion to Roman Britain, 1980; The Rediscovery of Ancient Egypt, 1982; Das wiederentdeckte alte Ägypten, 1983; L'Egypte retrouvée, 1984; Redescubrimiento del Antiguo Egipto, 1985; Treasures of Ancient Rome (in press). *Contributor to:* Journal of Egyptian Archaeology; Antiquaries Journal; Numismatic Chronicle; Seaby Coin & Medal Bulletin; Coin & Medal News; Iraq. *Honours:* Fellow of the Society of Antiquaries, 1969; Honorary Member, Institute of Archaeology, University of London, 1977. *Memberships:* Council Member, Egypt Exploration Society; Council Member, Royal Numismatic Society; Chairman, Antiquities Dealers Association; various Committees of the Council for British Archaeology. *Address:* 41 Cardy Road, Boxmoor, Hemel Hempstead, Hertfordshire HP1 1RL, England.

CLEALL, Charles, b. 1 June 1927, Heston, Middlesex, England. Her Majesty's Inspector of Schools. *Education:* B Mus, University of London; MA, University of Wales; Scottish Teacher's Certificate, Jordanhill College of Education, Glasgow. *Publications include:* The Selection & Training of Mixed Choirs in Churches, 1960; Music & Holiness, 1964; Sixty Songs From Sankey, 1966; Authentic Chanting (Part 2 of, Reading Hymn Tunes and Singing Psalms, with Dr Francis B Westbrook), 1969; Plainsong for Pleasure, 1969; Voice Production in Choral Technique, 1955, revised & enlarged edition, 1970; A Guide to, Vanity Fair, 1982. *Contributor to:* Musical Times; Music Teacher; Child Education; The Diapason, Chicago; Organists' Review; Columnist, Musical Opinion, (The Master of the Choir), 1957–60; Music Critic, Church of England Newspaper, 1963–73; Editor, Journal of The Ernest George White Society, 1983–. *Address:* Scottish Education Department, 10 Carronhall, Stonehaven, Kincardineshire AB3 2HF, Scotland.

CLEARY, Jon, b. 22 Nov. 1917, Sydney, Australia. Novelist. *Publications:* 34 Novels including, You Can't See Round Corners, 1947; The Sundowners, 1952; Climate of Courage, 1953; A Flight of Chariots, 1964; The High Commissioner, 1966; Mask of the Andes, 1971; Peter's Pence, 1974; High Road to China, 1977; The Beaufort Sisters, 1979; A Very Private War, 1980; The Phoenix Tree, 1984; The City of Fading Light, 1985. *Honours:* Co-Winner, Australian Broadcasting National Radio Play Competition, 1945; 2nd Prize, Sydney Morning Herald Novel Competition, 1946; Australian Literary Society Gold Medal, 1951; Edgar Allen Poe Award, 1974. *Agent:* John Farquharson Ltd, England. *Address:* 71 Upper Pitt Street, Kirribilli, NSW, Australia.

CLEARY, Marion E, b. 7 July 1935, Groton, Massachusetts, USA. Teacher. 2 daughters. *Education:* BS, Education, Bridgewater State College, Massachusetts; MALS, Wesleyan University, Connecticut; Litt D, World University. *Literary Appointments include:* Teacher, HS, Massachusetts, 1962–63, 1967–81; Administrative Intern 1976; Team Leader, 1976; Copy Editor, John Wright PSG Publishers, London, Bristol, Boston, 1980; Instructor, Fisher Junior College, Massachusetts, USA. *Publications:* Study America, co-author, 1976; A Social History of the United States, film guides, Learning Corporation of America, 1975; Cancelled Reservations, Madras, India, 1985. *Contributions to:* North American Mentor Magazine; Poet Lore; The Poet; Driftwood E; Wings Anthology; Bardic Echoes; These Are My Jewels; The Chelmsford Writers' Series, Dartmouth College, 1982; A Teaching Model, English Journal, 1983. *Honours:* National Science Foundation Fellowship, Boston University, 1979; National Humanities Council Fellowship, Dartmouth College, 1982; Fulbright Scholar in India, 1985. *Memberships:* American Academy of Poets; World Poetry Society; Massachusetts Poetry Society. *Address:* 17 Lovers Lane, Groton, MA 01450, USA.

CLEMENT, Wallace, b. 1 Mar. 1949, Niagara, Canada. Professor. m. Elsie Andres, 14 Sep. 1968, Niagara, 2 sons. *Education:* Hon. BA, McMaster University, 1971; MA, 1973, PhD, 1978, Carleton University. *Literary Appointments:* Assistant Professor, McMaster University, 1975–80; Associate Professor, 1980–84, Professor, 1984–, Carleton University; Visiting Research Fellow, Arbetslivscentum, Stockholm, Sweden, 1984–85. *Publicatons:* The Canadian Corporate Elite, 1975; Continental Corporate Power, 1977; Hardrock Mining, 1981; Class, Power and Property, 1983. *Contributor to:* Over 25 articles in journals and collections. *Honours:* Canada Council fellowships, 1973–75; Social Sciences and Humanities Leave Fellowship, 1984–85. *Address:* Department of Sociology and Anthropology, Carleton University, Ottawa, Canada K1S 5B6.

CLEMENTS, Wilma H, b. 12 Feb. 1906, Decatur County, Iowa, USA. Teacher; Poet. m. Albert James Clements, 24 Apr. 1929, Boone County, Iowa, 1 son, 2 daughters. *Education:* BA, Drake University, Des Moines, Iowa, Graduate work, University of Iowa Writer's Workshop, Iowa City, Iowa. *Publication:* Canny W, The Sugar, 1984. *Contributions to:* Bicentennial Edition of Iowa Poetry Day Association, 1975 and 1976; Panorama; A Bicentennial Anthology, 1976; Poems of the Heartland, An Anthology of Iowa Poets, 1979; Songs of the Chaparral, 1980; Winter Song, 1981; Lyrical Iowa; Midwest Chaparral Magazine; Iowa Poetry Day's Annual; Encore Magazine; The Journal-Reporter; Leon; PEO Record; North American Mentor Magazine. *Honours include:* First Place, Midwest Chaparral Magazine Contest in Serious Verse, 1977 and 1979; First Prize, Midwest Chaparral Poets, Light Verse, 1980. *Memberships:* Writer's Workshop, University of Iowa, 1967–68; Iowa Chapter, Midwest Federation of Chaparral Poets, Area Representative, Iowa Poetry Association. *Address:* 807 North Church Street, Leon, IA 50144, USA.

CLEMO, Jack (Reginald John), b. 11 Mar. 1916, Goonamarris, Cornwall, England. Writer. m. Ruth Grace Peaty, 26 Oct. 1968, Trethosa Chapel. *Publications:* Wilding Graft, 1948; Confession of a Rebel, 1949; The Invading Gospel, 1958; The Map of Clay, 1961; Cactus on Carmel, 1967; The Echoing Tip, 1971; Broad Autumn, 1975; Marriage of a Rebel, 1980; The Shadowed Red, 1986. *Contributor to:* Anglo-Welsh Review; Outposts; Meridian; South West Review; Transatlantic Review; PN Review; Dorset Year Book; Christian Woman; Poetry Ireland; New Poetry. *Honours:* Atlantic Award in Literature, 1948; Arts Council Festival Poetry Prize, 1951; Civil List Pension 1961; Cornish Gorsedd Bardship, 1970; Honorary D Litt, Exeter University, 1981. *Membership:* Honorary member, Arts Centre Group, West Country Writers Association. *Address:* 24 Southlands Road, Rodwell, Weymouth, Dorset DT4 9LQ, England.

CLEW, Jeffrey Robert, b. 26 Jan. 1928, London, England. Editorial Director. m. 5 May 1953, 2 daughters. *Publicatons:* Always in the Picture, 1971; The Best Twin, 1974; The Scott Motorcycle, 1974; British Racing Motorcycles, 1976; The Restoration of Vintage & Thoroughbred Motorcycles, 1976; Sammy Miller: The Will to Win, 1976; Frances Beart–A Single Purpose, 1978; Lucky All My Life, 1979; Suzuki, 1980; JAP: The Vintage Years, 1985; Haynes Publishing: The First 25 Years, 1985; plus 19 Motorcycle Owners Workshop Manuals. *Contributor to:* Classic Motor Cycle; Classic Bike; Motorcycle Enthusiast; Motorcycle Sport; Motorcycle Industry Business Journal, USA; On Two Wheels, (Orbis part-work). *Memberships:* Guild of Motoring Writers; South Western Writers Association. *Address:* Sulby, Sparkford Hill Lane, Sparkford, Nr. Yeovil, Somerset BA22 7JF, England.

CLIFTON, Merritt Robin, b. 18 Sep. 1953, Oakland, California, USA. Writer; Editor. m. Pamela June Kemp, 29 Nov. 1976, Reno, Nevada. *Education:* BA, San Jose State University, 1974. *Literary Appointments:* Editor-in-Chief, Samisdat literary magazine and book series, 1973–; Contributing Editor, Small Press Review, 1975–.

Publications: Novels: 24x12, 1975, 80; A Baseball Classic, 1978, 83; Betrayal, 1980. Critical Studies: The Pillory Poetics, 1975, 81; On Small Press as Class Struggle, 1976, 4th edition, 1981; Poems: From An Age of Cars, 1980; Live Free or Die!, 1982; The White Man Problem, 1985. The Samisdat Method: A Do-It-Yourself Guide to Offset Printing, 1978, 81. Freedom Comes From Human Beings, essays, 1980. Relative Baseball, statistical study, 1979, 3rd edition, 1985. Those Who Were There, bibliography, 1985. Numerous other titles. *Contributions to:* Several hundred publications including: The National Pastime; SABR Research Journal; Format; Gypsy; Impetus; Planet Detroit; The Mitre. *Honours:* Phelan scholarships for creative writing, SJSU, 1971–75; Centre for Investigative Journalism, 1980; 2nd, Dumont-Frenette Journalism Award, 1983; Premier, Environment Quebec Concours de Reportage, 1984. *Address:* Box 129, Richford, VT 05476, USA.

CLINE, Beverly Marilyn, b. 27 June 1951, London, Ontario, Canada. Writer. m. Leigh Cline, 18 Jan. 1976, London, Ontario, Canada. *Education:* Specialised honours English degree, York University, Toronto, Canada. *Publications:* Louisa Clark's Annual 1841, 1976; Louisa Clark's Annual 1842, 1977; Louisa Clark's Annual 1843, 1978; The Lombardo Story, 1979; The Terrific Toronto Trivia Book, 1979; Ghostwriter of a non-fiction book and others. *Contributions to:* Toronto Star; Canadian Press; Canada and The World; Toronto Life; Ontario Craft; Resourcebook; The Athenian. *Honours:* Grants, The Canada Council, Ottawa; Grants, The Ontario Arts Council, Toronto. *Memberships:* Writers' Union of Canada; Chairperson Benefits Committee, Toronto Chapter, The Periodical Writers' Association of Canada. *Address:* P O Box 3171, Station D, Willowdale, Ontario, M2R 3G6, Canada.

CLINE, Charles William, b. 1 Mar. 1937, Waleska, Georgia, USA. Professor of English; Poet. m. Sandra Lee Williamson, 11 June 1966, Decatur, Georgia, 1 son. *Education:* AA, Reinhardt College, 1957; Studies Music, College-Conservatory of Music, University of Cincinnati, 1957–58; BA, Peabody College, 1960; MA, Vanderbilt University, 1963; Litt.D, World University, 1981. *Literary Appointments:* Manuscript Procurement Editor, The Fideler Company, 1958; Resident Poet, Kellogg Community College, 1975–. *Publications:* Forty Salutes to Michigan Poets, editor, 1975; Crossing the Ohio, 1976; Questions for the Snow, 1979; Ultima Thule (chapbook), 1984. *Contributor to:* Poet; Voices International; New Laurel Review; Great Lakes Review; Green River Review; Wind Literary Journal; Sou'Wester; Orbis; and many others. *Honours include:* Gold Medal, International Belles Lettres Society, 1975; 2 1st Places, Poetry Society of Michigan, 1975; Certificates of Merit, North American Mentor, 1977, 1978; Diploma di Merito, Università delle Arti, 1982; International Academy of Poets Award, 1983; Star of Contemporary Poetry, Centre Studi e Scambi Internazionali Accademia Leonardo da Vinci, 1984; Silver Medal, International Biographical Centre, 1985. *Memberships:* World Poetry Society; International Society of Literature; International Academy of Poets; World Literary Academy; Tagore Institute of Creative Writing International; Poetry Society of America; Poets & Writers Inc; Associated Writing Programmes; Academy of American Poets; Centro Studi e Scambi Internazionali. *Address:* 9866 South Westnedge Avenue, Kalamazoo, MI 49002, USA.

CLINTON, Lloyd DeWitt, b. 29 Aug. 1946, Topeka, Kansas, USA. Assistant Professor in English. m. Jacqueline F Sobin, 11 July 1973, Wichita, Kansas, 1 step-daughter. *Education:* BA, Southwestern College, Winfield, Kansas, 1968; MA, Wichita State University, Wichita, 1972; MFA 1975, PhD English and Creative Writing, 1981, Bowling Green State University, Bowling Green, Ohio. *Literary Appointments:* Editor, Southwestern Collegian, 1966–67; Teaching Assistant, Wichita State University, 1970–72; Teaching Fellow, Bowling Green State University, 1973–75 and 1978–81; Staff, Kansas Arts Commission, 1972–73; Poet in secondary school systems of Kansas, Montana, South Carolina,

Ohio and Michigan, 1973–81; Instuctor, Wayne State University, 1975–77; Lecturer 1981–85, Assistant Professor 1985–, University of Wisconsin-Whitewater. *Publications:* The Conquistador Dog Texts, 1976; The Rand McNally Poems, 1977; The Coyot. Inca Texts, 1979; Das Illustrite Mississippithal Revisited, 1983; Night Jungle Bird Life, 1983; Furnace, 1985. *Contributions to:* Magazines and journals including: Great Lakes Review; Wisconsin English Journal, Mid-American Review; Contact II; Literary Magazines Review; Abraxas; Salthouse; Cream City Review. *Honours include:* Honourable mention, Elliston Book Award, University of Cincinnati, 1976; Creative Artist Grant, Michigan Council for the Arts, 1981. *Memberships:* Associated Writing Programs; Coordinating Council of Literary Magazines; Modern Language Association; Poetry Society of America. *Address:* 3567 N Murray Avenue, Shorewood, WI 53211, USA.

CLOSS, August, b. 9 Aug. 1898, Neumarkt, Austria, University Professor Emeritus; Author. *Education:* MA, Bristol University, England; DPhil, Graz, Austria. *Publications:* Medieval Exempla, 1934; The Genius of the German Lyric, 1938; Tristan & Isolt, 1944, 3rd edition 1974; Medusa's Mirror, 1957; Reality & Creative Vision, 1963; 20th Century German Literature, 2nd edition 1971; Briefwechsel: R Priebsch, -v Steinmeyer, 1979; Bristol – Hannover: Wie es Begann, 1984. *Contributor to:* Modern Language Review; Times Higher Education Supplement; Germanistik; Universitas; German-Studies; various academic journals in Europe & USA. *Honours:* Austrian Cross of Honour, Science & Arts, 1st Class; Grand Cross for the West German Order of Merit. *Memberships:* FRSL; PEN. *Address:* 40 Stoke Hill, Bristol 9, England.

CLOUDSLEY-THOMPSON, John Leonard, b. 23 May 1921, Murree, India. Professor, Zoology. *Education:* MA, PhD, DSc, Hon DSc, Pembroke College, Cambridge, England. *Publications include:* Spiders, Scorpions, Centipedes & Mites, 1958; Animal Behaviour, 1960; Rhythmic Activity in Animal Physiology & Behaviour, 1961; Animal Conflict & Adaptation, 1965; Animal Twilight, 1967; The Zoology of Tropical Africa, 1969; The Temperature & Water Relations of Reptiles, 1971; Desert Life, 1974; Terrestrial Environments, 1975; Insects & History, 1976; Man & the Biology of Arid Zones, 1977; The Desert, 1977; Animal Migration, 1978; Biological Clocks, Their Functions in Nature, 1980; Tooth and Claw, 1980; Guide to Woodlands, 1985. *Contributor to:* Numerous professional journals and encyclopaedias. *Honours:* Recipient, Medal, Royal African Society, 1969; University of Khartoum Gold Medal, 1981; Biological Council Medal, 1984. *Memberships include:* Fellow, Institute of Biology; Linnean Society; Royal Entomological Society; World Academy of Art and Sciences. *Address:* 4 Craven Hill, London W2 3DS, England.

CLUBB, O Edmund, b. 16 Feb. 1901, South Park, Minnesota, USA. Retired US Foreign Service Officer, Writer. *Education:* University of Washington; BA, University of Minnesota, 1927; George Washington University; MA, California College in China, 1940. US Foreign Service, 1928–52. *Literary Appointments:* Consulting Editor, Atlas magazine, 1961–65; Contributing Editor, Current History magazine, 1976–. *Publications:* 20th Century China, 1964, 3rd revised edition 1978; Communism in China, As Reported From Hankow in 1932, 1968; China and Russia; The Great Game, 1971; The Witness and I, 1974. *Contributions to:* Numerous Periodicals; Staff editor and contributor, Biographical Dictionary of Republican China, 4 volumes, editor Howard L Boorman, 1967–71; Advisory editor, New York Times Great Contemporary Issues Series, China, 1972; Consultant, Time Life Books, WWII Series, Prelude to War, 1977, China-Burma-India 1978. *Memberships:* Diplomatic and Consular Officers, Retired; Academy of Political Science; Authors League; Mongolia Society. *Address:* 276 Riverside Drive, New York, NY 10025, USA.

CLUTTERBUCK, David Ashley, b. 4 June 1947, London, England. Journalist; Company Director. m. Pauline Sandra Neudegg, 16 May 1970, Dunstable, 3 sons. *Education:* BA English Language and Literature, London, 1968. *Literary Appointments:* Editor, Journal of British Nuclear Energy Society, 1969; Technology News Editor 1970, International Management and Managing Editor 1973, New Scientist; Editor of various publications including Issues, Sound Business and Decision Maker, 1983–. *Publications:* How To Be A Good Corporate Citizen, 1981; The Remaking of Work, 1982; Gribble The Goblin, 1982; The Winning Streak (with Walter Goldsmith), 1984; Everybody Needs a Mentor, 1985; New Patterns of Work, 1985; The Winning Streak Work-Out Book, 1985. *Contributions to:* The Times; Management Today; Chief Executive and others. *Literary Agent:* Vivienne Schuster, John Farqharson (Curtis Brown) Limited. *Address:* c/o The Item Group, Burnham House, Burnham, Buckinghamshire, England.

CLYMER, Eleanor, b. 7 Jan. 1906, NYC, USA. Writer of Books for Young People. m. Kinsey Clymer, 1 son. *Education:* BA, University of Wisconsin, 1928. *Publications:* The Trolley Car Family, 1947; Case of the Missing Link, 1962; Search for a Living Fossil, 1963; Second Greatest Invention, 1969; My Brother Stevie, 1967; The Spider, the Cave and the Pottery Bowl, 1971; Me and the Eggman, 1972; Luke Was There, 1973; The Get-Away Car, 1978; My Mother is the Smartest Woman in the World, 1982; The Horse in the Attic, 1983. *Honours:* Regional Library Association Award, 1971; Child Study Association Children's Book Award, 1975; Sequoyah Book Award, 1980. *Memberships:* Authors League of America; Former Chairman, Children's Book Committee, Authors Guild; Children's Literary Association. *Address:* 11 Nightingale Road, Katonah, NY 10536, USA.

COAKLEY, Mary Lewis, b. Baltimore, Maryland, USA. Writer. *Education:* Dominican College of San Rafael, California. *Publications:* Fitting God Into the Picture, 1950, reissued as, A Woman's Way; Our Child – God's Child, 1954; Mister Music Make, 1958; Temptations of the Bible, 1961; Children of the Old Testament, 1961; Children of the New Testament, 1960; Women of the New Testament, 1960; Never Date Women, 1964; Rated-X: The Moral Case Against TV, 1978; Not Alone, 1981; How to Live Life to the Fullest: Handbook for Seasoned Citizens, 1984. *Contributions to:* Philadelphia Bulletin; Catholic World; Catholic Digest; Sign. *Honours include:* 1st Prizes, Contests, National League of American Pen Women. *Memberships:* Past President, Bucks County Writers Guild; Past Treasurer. *Address:* 110 Hewett Road, Wyncote, PA 19095, USA.

COAN, Eugene Victor, b. 26 Mar. 1943, Los Angeles, California, USA. Environmental Politician. *Education:* City College, Los Angeles, 1960–62; AB, University of California at Santa Barbara, 1962–64; PhD, Stanford University, 1964–69. *Major Publications:* Marine Molluscan Genera of Western North America, with Myra Keen, 2nd edition, 1974; The Sierra Club's World Directory of Environmental Organisations (edited with Thaddeus Trzyna), 1976; James Graham Cooper: Pioneer Western Naturalist, 1982. *Contributor to:* Various scientific journals on systematic malacology and environmental issues. *Address:* 891 San Jude Avenue, Palo Alto, CA 94306, USA.

COATES, Doreen Frances, b. 5 July 1912, Plymouth, England. Teacher. *Education:* Teacher's Certificate, Avery Hill Training College, London, 1933. *Publications:* Yellow Door Stories, 1965; Red and Blue Door Stories, 1969; Number Cards, 1969; Stories about Numbers, 1970; Jacko and Delilah Stories, 1978; Whatever Next Stories, 1978; Books in the 360 Reading Scheme, 1979–84. *Contributions to:* Word Puzzles for Quality Puzzle Magazines pub BEAP; Stories for BBC Radio, Listen with Mother; Material for Schools Programmes. BBC TV. *Address:* 42 Deanhill Court, London SW14 7DL, England.

COBERLY, Lenore McComas, b. 23 Feb. 1925, Hamlin, WVA, USA. Writer; Teacher; Editor. m. Camden A Coberly, 14 June 1946, 2 sons, 2 daughters. *Education* MBA, University of Pittsburgh, USA; BS, West Virginia University; Bachelor Degree, Business Administration, West Vancouver University. *Literary Appointments:* Teacher, Creative Arts Over Sixty; Green Lake Writers Conference; Green Lake Elderhostel. *Publications:* Drink from a Sulphur Well, 1973; One Hundred Years of Caring, 1982; Becoming, 1983; Writers Have No Age, 1984. *Contributor to:* Christian Science Monitor; Wisconsin Academy Review; Madison Capital Times; Madison Magazine; Wisconsin Regional Magazine; Nanjing Dacua journal; From the Hills; Editor, Heartland journal. *Memberships:* Credentials Chairman, President, Wisconsin Fellowship of Poets; Wiscon Regional Writers; American Federation of Poetry Societies; National Federation State Poetry Societies; Academy of American Poets. *Address:* 4114 North Sunset Court, Madison, WI 53705, USA.

CODLIN, Ellen Mabel, b. 4 Sep. 1911, London, England. Librarian. m. Ronald D Codlin, 3 Feb. 1945, 1 daughter. *Education:* Fellow, Library Association. *Literary Appointments:* Chelmsford Public Library, 1929–33; Watford Central Library, 1933–35, 1940–45; USA Air Force, 1949–55; General Electric Co, 1955–63; British Oxygen Co, 1963–75; British Insurance Association. 1975–78. *Publications:* Cryogenics and Refrigeration: A Bibliographical Guide, Volume 1, 1968, Volume 2, 1970; Aslib Directory of Information Sources in the UK, 6th edition in preparation. *Address:* 146 Oxhey Avenue, Watford WD1 4HA, Hertfordshire, England.

CODY, Judith Ann, b. 29 Aug. 1946. Poet; Composer. *Education:* Literature major, Foothill College, California, USA. 1975; Private education, oriental language, music and culture, Japan, 1968–70. *Literary Apointments include:* Publisher, Kikimora Publishing Company, Los Altos, California. USA; Officer, San Francisco Bay Area Congress on Women in Music; Lecturer, Foothill College Creative Writing Conference. *Publications:* Vivian Fine, Composer, Bio-Bibliography, 1987; Resource Guide on Women in Music (Editor), Kikimora, 1982; Topics Over Tea, Thermos, One Cup, poetry play, 1979 and 1986. *Contributions to:* Poetry Project 4: World of Poetry; Foreground Magazine; Stonecloud; Sequoia; Foothill Sentinel; Androgyne; The Miniature Anthology; Palo Alto Times; Amphicoria; Atlantic Monthly. *Honours include:* Winner, Atlantic Monthly Writing Contest, 1973; Women's Year poem, on permanent exhibition by Smithsonian Institute, 1977; Golden Poet Award, 1986. *Memberships include:* Author's Guild; Author's League of America; Poets and Writers Inc; International League of Women Composers; American Music Centre. *Address:* Kikimira Publishing Company, PO Box 1107, Los Altos, CA 94022, USA.

COFFMAN, Kimberley Ann, b. 7 July 1956, California, USA. Editor. Writer. *Contributor to:* Canadian Doctor; Flare; Computer Data; Canadian Office; Bath & Kitchen Marketer; Good Health. *Honours:* Kenneth R Wilson Memorial Award, Canadian Business Press, 1980, 1981, 1983. *Memberships:* Canadian Business Press. *Address:* 1450 Don Mills Road, Don Mills, Ontario, M3B 2X7, Canada.

COHAN, Anthony Robert, b. 28 Dec. 1939, New York City, USA. Author. m. Masako Takahashi, 1 June 1974, 1 daughter. *Education:* BA, University of California. *Publications:* Opium, 1984; Canary, 1981. *Contributions:* Book Reviews, Los Angeles Times. *Honour:* Notable Book of the Year, New York Times, 1981. *Membership:* Authors Guild. *Literary Agent:* Don Congdon Associates. *Address:* c/o Don Congdon Associates, 177 East 70th Street, New York, NY 10021, USA.

COHEN, Harry, b. 8 Apr. 1936, Brooklyn, New York, USA. Professor of Sociology. *Education:* BBA, 1956,

MA, 1959, City College of New York; PhD, University of Illinois, 1962. *Publications:* The Demonics of Bureaucracy, 1965; Connections: Understanding Social Relationships, 1981. *Contributor to:* British Journal of Sociology; Personnel; Journal; Western Sociological Review; Humanity and Society; Contemporary Philosophy; most recent being, The Principle of Balances of Differences: Lessons for Humane Living, 1981, The Victim Aggressor Bond, 1984, both in, Contemporary Philosophy. *Honours:* 1st Place, most significant book manuscript, Demonics of Bureaucracy, Iowa State Faculty member, Iowa State University Press, 1964; National Advisory Board of the Institute for Advanced Philosophic Research, 1979–. *Address:* Dept of Sociology, 103 East Hall, Iowa State University, Ames, IA 50011, USA.

COHEN, Ira, b. 3 Feb. 1935. Poet. *Education:* BS, Columbia University. *Appointments:* Editor/Publisher, Gnaoua Press, Tangier, Morocco, 1961–66; Universal Mutant Prods, New York, 1966–70; Starstreams-Bardo Matrix Press, Kathmandu, 1971–78; Contributing Editor, Ins and Outs Press, Amsterdam, 1978–81; San Francisco Ganeshian Synthesis Inc 1981–. 7 Marvels, 1974; From the Divan of Petra Vogt, 1976; Poems from the Cosmic Crypt, 1976; Gilded Splinters, 1977; The Stauffenberg Cycle and Other Poems, 1981; Golden Tortoise Overalls. *Contributor to:* Ins and Outs, Dream Helmet, USA; Bres, Holland; Bastard Angel, USA; Contributing Editor, Thirdrail Magazine, Los Angeles. *Address:* 225 W 106 Street, New York City, NY 10025, USA.

COHEN, Jonathan, b. 4 May 1949, Baltimore, Maryland, USA. Writer. Editor. m. Terry Jean Rosenberg, 4 May 1980, Spring Valley, New York, USA, 1 son. *Education:* BA English, State University of New York at Stony Brook, 1972; MFA Creative Writing, Columbia University, 1976; MA English, PhD English, 1980, State University of New York at Stony Brook, USA. *Literary Appointments:* Assistant Professor of English, Ohio Wesleyan University, Delaware, Ohio, 1981–83. *Major Publications:* H R Hays & Spanish America (editor) 1977; The Dark Room & Other Poems (translator of Enrique Lihn), 1978; Poems from the Island, 1979; Zero Hour & Other Documentary Poems (translator of Ernesto Cardenal), 1980; With Walker in Nicaragua & Other Early Poems 1949–54 (editor & translator of Ernesto Cardenal), 1984. *Contributor to:* New York Times; The Nation; American Poetry Review; Missouri Review; New Directions in Prose & Poetry; and others. *Honours:* Fellowship for Translators Grant, National Endowment for the Arts, 1981; Summer Seminar Award, National Endowment for the Humanities, 1983. *Memberships:* American Literary Translators Association, 1978–; PEN, 1985; Founding Director, Islands & Continents, 1976–80. *Address:* 209 Thompson Street, Port Jefferson, NY 11777, USA.

COHEN, Lysbeth Rose, b. 6 June 1920, London, England. Freelance Writer. m. Dr Douglas Harry Cohen, 15 Feb. 1943, Sydney, Australia, 1 son, 1 daughter. *Education:* BSc, University of Sydney. *Publications:* Dr Margaret Harper, 1971; Rachel Forster Hospital, 1972; Coronary Wife, 1972; Elizabeth Macquarie, 1979; The Tabernacle – Then and Now, 1983; Coronary Caring Without Tears, 1985. *Contributor to:* Several hundred feature articles, profile stories, short stories, music, theatre & book reviews; including: Blackwood's Magazine; Australia Women's Weekly; Women's Day; etc; ABC Radio Scripts. *Honours:* Australia Council Literature Board Grant, 1977; Ian Mudi Prize, 1980; New South Wales Government Cultural Affairs Grant, 1981. *Memberships:* Australian Society of Authors; Australian Writers' Guild; Committee Member, International PEN, Sydney, 1973–78; Society of Women Writers, Committee Member, 1966–72; National Book Council, Committee Member, New South Wales, 1982–. *Address:* 84 Milray Ave, Wollstonecraft, Sydney, NSW 2065, Australia.

COHEN, Marion Deutsche, b. 2 Jan. 1943, Perth Amboy, New Jersey, USA. Writer. m. Jeffrey M Cohen,

9 Aug. 1964, 2 sons, 1 daughter. *Education:* BA, New York University, 1964; MA, 1966; PhD, 1970, Wesleyan University. *Appointments:* Contributing Editor, Mothering Magazine. *Publications:* Tuesday Nights, 1977; The Weirdest is the Sphere, 1979; The Temper Tantrum Book, 1983; An Ambitious Sort of Grief, 1983; Co-Editor, Mother/Poet; She Was Born She Died, 1984; The Limits of Miracles, 1985. *Contributor to:* 7 Mathematics Papers, in Scientific Journals; Over 400 poems in various journals including, Waterways; 10 Articles, 10 Stories various journals. *Memberships:* Feminist Writers Guild. *Address:* 2203 Spruce Street, Philadelphia, PA 19103, USA.

COHEN, Richard Anthony, b. 9 May 1947, Birmingham, England. Publishing Director. m. Caroline Mary Phyllis Moore, 15 Oct. 1982, 1 son. *Education:* BA, Honours, English, Magdalene College, Cambridge, 1969. *Publication:* Biography of Charles de Beaumont, 1984. *Contributions to:* Observer; Sunday Times; Guardian; London Standard; Tablet; New Society. *Literary Agent:* Jacqueline Korn at David Higham Agency. *Address:* 19 Almeric Road, Clapham, London, SW11, England.

COHEN, Zivia, b. 12 Feb. 1930, Israel. Journalist. m. David Cohen, 2 Sep. 1952, 1 son, 1 daughter. *Education:* BA, Rehabilitation; MA, Education. *Literary Appointments:* Editor, Women's Page, Lamerchar; Editor, Naamat. *Publications:* 2 books on Israel's women's unit in the army. *Contributions to:* Naamat. *Honours:* 2 Journalist prizes for the best articles of the year. *Membership:* Israel's Journalist Association. *Address:* Naamat Magazine, P O Box 303, 61002, Tel Aviv, Israel.

COLAABAVALA, Firooze Darashaw, b. 1 Apr. 1924, Bombay, India. Exporter; Writer. m. Shiren K Spencer, 14 May 1963, Bombay, 1 son, 1 daughter. *Education:* N Wadia College. *Publications:* Around the World With Guts and Wits, 1969; Hatchet Man; Adventures of an Indian Tramp, 1974; Hippie Dharma, 1974; Indian Mafia in Action, 1975; Tantra: The Erotic Cult, 1976; Witchcraft: Forbidden World of the Devil, 1977; Sex Slaves of India, 1976; Sinful Cities of the World, 1976; Bombay After Dark, 1976. *Contributor to:* Times of Oman; Arab Times; Kuwait Times; Blitz; Sunday Standard; Free Press; Janayougam; Midday; Afternoon; Times of India, etc. *Address:* Puran Nivas, Arthur Bunder Road, Colaba, Bombay 400005, India.

COLDSMITH, Donald Charles, b. 28 Feb. 1926, Iola, Kansas, USA. Physician; Freelance Writer. m. Edna E Howell, 6 Nov. 1960, Baldwin, 5 daughters. *Education:* BS, Baker University, 1949; MD, University of Kansas, 1958. *Appointments:* Lecturer, English, Emporia State University. *Publications:* Horsin' Around, 1975; Trail of the Spanish Bit, 1980; Horsin' Around Again, 1981; Buffalo Medicine, 1981; The Elk-Dog Heritage, 1982; Follow the Wind, 1983; Man of the Shadows, 1983; Daughter of the Eagle, 1984; Moon of Thunder, 1985; The Sacred Hills, 1985; Pale Star, 1986; River of Swans, 1986. *Contributor to:* Self-syndicated weekly column, Horsin' Around, 1971–; Articles for Western Horseman; Horseman; Horse and Rider; etc. *Memberships:* Western Writers of America, President, 1983–84. *Literary Agent:* Ray Peekner Agency, Milwaukee. *Address:* Emporia, KS 66801, USA.

COLDWELL, Joan, b. 3 Nov. 1936. Huddersfield, England. Professor of English. *Education:* BA Honours 1958; MA with Distinction 1960, University of London; PhD, Harvard University, 1967. *Literary Appointments:* Professor of English, McMaster University, 1972–. *Publications:* Charles Lamb on Shakespeare, 1978. *Contributions to:* Oxford Companion to Canadian Literature, 1983; Articles in: Canadian Literature; Journal of Canadian Fiction; Keats-Shelley Memorial Bulletin; Shakespeare Quarterly; English Studies in Canada; Canadian Journal of Irish Studies; Atlantis. *Honours:* Social Sciences and Humanities Research Council of Canada Leave Fellowship, 1969, 1977 and 1984. *Memberships:* International Shakespeare

Association; Shakespeare Association of America; Charles Lamb Society: Secretary-Treasurer 1976–77; Canadian Association for Irish Studies. *Address:* Department of English, McMaster University, Hamilton, Ontario L8S 4L9, Canada.

COLE, Barry, b. 13 Nov. 1936, England. Writer. 3 daughters. *Education:* Fellow in Literature, Universities of Durham and Newcastle-upon-Tyne, 1970–72. *Publications:* Blood Ties, 1968; A Run Across the Islands, 1968; Moon Search, 1968; Joseph Winter's Patronage, 1969; The Search for Rita, 1970; The Visitors, 1970; The Giver, 1972; Pathetic Fallacies, 1972; Vanessa in the City, 1970; Ulysses in The Town of Coloured Glass, 1970; Dedications, 1976. *Contributions to:* New Statesman; The Spectator; Times Literary Supplement; The Listener; BBC; The Observer, etc. (Poems and Reviews). *Address:* 68 Myddelton Square, London EC1R 1XP, England.

COLE, Eddie-Lou, b. 2 Feb. 1909. Poet; Poetry Editor; Illustrator. m. (1) Laurence A. Cole (2) Ray Wehrman Howard. *Education:* BA, Livingston, Montana, USA; Sacramento City College; University of California, Berkeley; Hon Doctor, Literature Degree, World University, Tucson, Arizona. *Literary Appointments:* Editor and Feature Writer, State Employee Chapt 58 Magazine, Sacramento, California; Poetry Column, Harlequin Press; Illustrator, Promethian Lamp; Currently Poetry Editor, World of Poetry. *Publications:* Of Winter, 1962; Pinions to the Sun, 1963; The Great Wall (self illustrated with Sumi E), 1968; Strange, 1972; Now Technique for Today's Poets, 1977; Ballads and Story Poems (with Katherine Larson), 1978; To India With Love, 1983. *Contributions to:* Numerous anthologies and journals. *Honours:* 155 Poetry Awards; Statue of Victory World Culture Prize, 1985. *Memberships:* Member numerous poetry and literature societies. *Address:* World of Poetry, 1841 Garden Highway, Sacramento, CA 95833, USA.

COLE, Eugene Roger, b. 14 Nov. 1930, Cleveland, Ohio, USA. Clergyman, Author. *Education:* BA, St Edward's Seminary, 1954; M Div, Sulpician Seminary of the Northwest, 1958; AB, Central Washington University, 1960; MA, Seattle University, 1970. *Literary Appointments:* Freelance writer, editor, researcher, 1958–; Poetry critic, The National Writers Club, Denver, 1969–72; Judge, The Poetry Society of America, 1970; Poet-in-service, Poets and Writers Inc, 1974–; Associate Editor, The Harvester, 1955; Guest editor, Experiment: An International Review, 1961; Editorial participant, This is my Best, 1970. *Publications:* Which End, the Empyrean?, play, 1959; April is the Cruelest Month, play, Grand Slam: 13 Great Short Stories About Bridge, 1975; Falling Up: haiku and senryu, 1979; Act and Potency, poems, 1980; Ding an sich: ana poems, 1985; Uneasy Camber: Early Poems and Diversions, 1986. *Contributions include:* Saturday Review; Western Humanities Review; Dalhousie Review; New Mexico Quarterly; Northwest Review; Southern Humanities Review; Beloit Poetry Journal. *Honours:* Poetry Broadcast Award, 1968; Musical Expertise Award, 1970; Lorraine Harr Haiku Award, 1974; Annual Mentor Poetry Award, 1974; Pro Mundi Beneficio Award, 1975; Diploma Di Merito, 1982; Honorary Litt D, 1983. *Memberships include:* Authors Guild; Poetry Society of America; Academy of American Poets; World-Wide Academy of Scholars; Experiment Group; Eighteen Nineties Society, London. *Address:* P O Box 91277, Cleveland, OH 44101, USA.

COLE, Gerald Anthony, b. 20 Jan. 1936, London, England. Lecturer. m. Judith Shipman, 1966, 2 sons, 2 daughters. *Education:* BA, University of Durham, 1959, MA, University of Sussex, 1983. *Major Publications:* Management Principles & Practice, 1979; Management: Theory & Practice, 1982, DP Publications. Presently working on 2nd edition of Management: Theory & Practice for 1986, and Personnel Management: Theory & Practice (for DP Publications). *Memberships:* Society of Authors, 1980; Examiner for Association of Business Executives,

London 1984–. *Address:* The Friary, 49 Charles Street, Berkhamsted, Hertfordshire, HP4 3DH, England.

COLE, Henri Roger, b. 9 May 1956, Fukuoka, Japan. Executive Director, Academy of American Poets. *Education:* BA, College of William and Mary, USA, 1978; MA, University of Wisconsin, 1980; MFA, Columbia University, 1982. *Appointments:* Executive Director, Academy of American Poets, 1982–. *Publications:* The Marble Queen, 1986. *Contributor to:* Poetry; Antaeus; Hudson Review; Grand Street; Shenandoah; etc. *Honour:* Ingram Merrill Foundation Award, 1985. *Address:* The Academy of American Poets, 177 East 87th Street, New York, NY 10128, USA.

COLE, John Reece, b. 28 Jan. 1916, Palmerston, New Zealand. Librarian; Writer. m. Evelyn Joyce Waldin Laing, 30 Aug 1941, Feilding, New Zealand, divorced 1948; Christine McKelvie Bull, 19 Nov. 1948, Wellington, New Zealand, divorced 1972, 1 son, 2 daughters. *Education:* BA; Diploma, Journalism; Diploma, NZLS; ANZLA. *Publications:* It Was so Late & Other Stories, 1949, revised edition, 1978; Pompallier, the House & The Mission, 1957. *Contributor to:* New Zealand Short Stories, 1953–73, 1976–; short story anthologies, Germany, Russia, Poland; Landfall; Australia and New Zealand Literary & Library Journals; Great Short Stories of Australia and New Zealand, Reader's Digest, 1980; New Zealand Writing Since 1945, Oxford University Press, 1984. *Memberships:* International PEN, New Zealand Centre (offices include President 1963–64); NZLA (Council, 1954, 1960–64); Singapore Library Association. *Honours:* International Arts Fellowship, USA, 1952; UNESCO Library Advisor to Government of Indonesia, 1956–58; Director, National Library, Singapore (Colombo Plan); 1962; Chief Librarian, Alexander Turnbull Library, Wellington, 1963–65. *Address:* 26 Napier Street, Karaka Bay Heights, Wellington 3, New Zealand.

COLE, Malcolm Ronald, b. 6 Aug. 1938, Harrow, England. Data Processing Editor. m. Janet Frewin, 20 Mar. 1963, Eastcote, 1 daughter. *Education:* BA, Open University. *Literary Appointments:* Data Processing Consultant, 1983, Data Processing Editor, Accountancy. *Contributions to:* Accountancy, regular monthly reviews of computer software and hardware, occasional general articles; BIM Quarterly; Which Computer. *Address:* 48 Paddenswick Road, Hammersmith, London W6 0UB, England.

COLEMAN, Jane, b. 9 Jan. 1939, Pittsburgh, Pennsylvania, USA. Writer. m. Professor Bernard D Coleman, 27 Mar. 1965, Pittsburgh, 2 sons. *Education:* BA, Creative Writing, University of Pittsburgh, 1960; *Literary Appointments:* Technical Writer, Biophysical Research Laboratory, University of Pittsburgh, 1961–65; Feature Writer and Critic, The Pittsburgh New Sun, 1979–81; Part-time Teacher of English, University of Pittsburgh, 1980; Writer-in-Residence, Carlow College, 1981–; Director of Women's Creative Writing Center, Carlow College, Pittsburgh, 1984–. *Contributions to:* Poetry; Yankee; Tar River Poetry; Xanadu; Hyperion; Backcountry; Cottonwood; Porch; Scree; West Branch; Creeping Bent; Pittsburgh Center for the Arts Magazine; The Plainswoman. Fiction: The Chowder Review, The Plainswoman, Crosscurrents, The Pennsylvania Review and The Gila Review. *Honours:* Third place, Atlantic College Fiction Contest, 1959; Honorable Mention, Poetry, Atlantic College Contest, 1959; First place, The Plainswoman Short Fiction Award, 1983; Second place, The Pendragon Fiction Contest, 1984; First place, Sewickley Magazine, 1985. *Membership:* Board of Directors, International Poetry Forum. *Address:* 400 Devonshire Street, Pittsburgh, PA 15213, USA.

COLEMAN, Mary Ann, b. 31 Jan. 1928, Marion, Indiana, USA. Poet. m. Oliver McCarter Coleman, Jr. 4 Mar, 1955, Atlanta, Georgia, USA. 2 sons. *Education:* Indiana University, 1945–48; BS, 1950, Auburn University; Creative Writing Workshops: University of Iowa, Emory University, University of Gerogia, Hofstra University. Breadloaf. *Literary Appointments:* Poetry

Workshops; Dixie Council of Authors and Journalists, 1970, 71, 74; Dekalb College, 1970; Emory at Oxford, 1973; University of Georgia Continuing Education Center, 1972, 73, 81-85. *Publications:* Disappearances, 1978. *Contributions to:* Southern Poetry Review; Kansas Quarterly; Georgia Review; Literary Review; National Forum; Educational Forum; Commonweal, and others. *Honours:* Georgia Writers' Association, First Prizes in Lyric Contest, 1968; Best Poem Contest, 1969; Book Manuscript of Poetry, 1971; Poetry Society of America's Consuelo Ford Memorial Award for Lyric Poem, 1974. *Memberships:* Poetry Society of America; Georgia State Poetry Society. *Address:* 205 Sherwood Drive, Athens, GA 30606, USA.

COLEMAN, Mary Garland, b. 15 Dec. 1918, Vancouver, Canada. Poet. m. Michael Edward Colemen, 11 June, 1938, Vancouver, 2 sons, 2 daughters. *Education:* Faculty of Arts, University of British Columbia, Vancouver. *Major Publications:* Tapestry, 1947; Duet (with N M Bettesworth), 1953; Evensong, 1974; Driftwood, 1977. *Contributor to:* Regina Leader Post, 1950-60; Saskatchewan Poetry Book; Alberta Poetry Book; Canadian Author & Bookman; Weekly Newspapers in British Columbia. *Memberships:* Canadian Authors Association; Saskatchewan Poetry Association (President 1957-60). *Honours:* 1st Prize, Saskatchewan Poetry Contest, 1963; Honorable Mention, Alberta Poetry Contests, 1963 & 1966; 3rd Prize, British Columbia Womens' Institute Contests, 1967 & 1975. *Address:* 3-1111 Jervis Street, Vancouver, British Columbia, V6E 2C5, Canada.

COLEMAN, Patricia Register, b. 1 Nov. 1936, Orlando, Florida, USA. Writer; Editor. m. William V Coleman, 27 Nov. 1974, Talahassee, 1 son, 2 daughters. *Education:* AB, Florida State University. *Appointments:* Creative Director, Growth Associates, Weston; Editor, Catholic Youth Ministry; Editor, Parish Communication. *Publications:* Mine is the Morning, 10 volumes, 1974; Daybreak, 10 volumes, 1977; The Mustard Seed People, 1984; over 125 books with husband. *Address:* P O Box 215, Weston, VT 05161, USA.

COLEMAN, Susan Mary, b. 10 Oct. 1945, Sydney, Australia. Computer Journalist. m. Dr Grahame Coleman, 25 Jan. 1969, Sydney, 2 daughters. *Education:* Bachelor of Science, Sydney; Diploma of Education, New England. *Literary Appointments:* Editor, Victorian Computer Bulletin, 1976-77; Journalist, 1978-81, Editor, 1981-84, Computerworld Australia; Publisher, Computerworld, 1984-. *Contributions to:* Computerworld Newspaper and other computer-related special publications including Computerworld USA. *Memberships:* Australian Computer Society; Association for Computing Machinery, USA. *Address:* Computerworld Pty Ltd, 74-76 Eastern Road, South Melbourne, Victoria 3205, Australia.

COLEMAN, Terry, b. 13 Feb. 1931, Bournemouth, England. Journalist/Author. *Education:* LLB, London University. *Publications:* A Girl for the Afternoons, (novel) 1965; The Railway Navvies (history) 1965; Providence and Mr Hardy, co-author (biography) 1966; The Only True History (collected journalism) 1969; Passage to America, (history) 1972; The Liners, (history) 1976; The Scented Brawl, (collected journalism) 1978; Southern Cross, (novel) 1979; Editor: An Indiscretion in the Life of an Heiress, (Hardy's lost first novel) 1976; Thanksgiving, (novel) 1982; Formerly Special Writer, Daily Mail; Chief Feature Writer, Guardian. *Contributor to:* Sunday Times; Observer etc. *Honours include:* Yorkshire Post prize for best first book of the year, 1965 for, Railway Navvies; Commended Descriptive Writer of the Year, IPC Awards, London 1972; Feature Writer of the Year, British Press Awards, 1982. *Literary Agent:* A D Peters, London. *Address:* c/o A D Peters, 10 Buckingham Street, London WC2, England.

COLEMAN, William Vincent, b. 27 Jan. 1932, Waterbury, Connecticut, USA. Writer; Publisher. m. Patricia Register, 27 Nov. 1974, TaLlahassee, 1 son, 2 daughters. *Education:* AB; MA; PhD; M Div. *Appointments:* Section Editor, Today's Parish Magazine, 1974-81; Publisher, Growth Associates, 1981-; Editor, Synthesis, 1981-; Editor, The Radical Option, 1985. *Publications:* Mine is the Morning, 10 volumes, 1974; Only Love Can Make It Easy, 1976; God's Own Child, 1978; Daybreak, 10 volumes, 1977; Special Days, 1985; Prayer Talk, 1983; over 200 books with his wife as co-author. *Contributor to:* Professional journals. *Address:* P O Box 215, Weston, VT 05161, USA.

COLES, John Morton, b. 25 Mar. 1930, Woodstock, Ontario, Canada. Professor, European Prehistory; FBA. *Education:* BA, Toronto University; MA, ScD, Cambridge University, England; PhD, Edinburgh University. *Publications:* Archaeology of Early Man, with E Higgs, 1969; Field Archaeology in Britain, 1972; Archaeology by Experiment, 1973; Bronze Age in Europe, with A Harding, 1979; Experimental Archaeology, 1979; Prehistory of the Somerset Levels, with B Orme, 1980; The Archaeology of Wetlands, 1984; Sweet Track to Glastonbury, with B Coles, 1986. *Contributor to:* Various journals. *Address:* Department of Archaeology, University of Cambridge, Cambridge, England.

COLLEDGE, Malcolm Andrew Richard, b. 12 Oct. 1939, Guildford, Surrey, England. University Teacher. *Education:* BA, 1961, MA, 1964, PhD, 1965, St John's College, Cambridge. *Publications:* The Parthians, 1967; The Art of Palmyra, 1976; Parthian Art, 1977; How to Recognise Roman Art, 1979; Co-Editor, Acta of the XI International Congress of Classical Archaeology, 1979; L'impero dei Parti. *Contributor to:* E & W, Rome, Italy; Sumer, Baghdad, Iraq. *Honour:* Recipient, Walston Studentship, University of Cambridge, 1961-62. *Memberships:* Council Society for Promotion of Hellenic Studies, 1971-74; Society for Promotion of Roman Studies, 1974-77; Archaeology, British Institute, Amman, 1983. *Address:* Westfield College, Kidderpore Avenue, London NW3 7ST, England.

COLLEY, Ann Cheetham, b. 9 Jan. 1940, Bury, England. Professor of English. 1 daughter. *Education:* AB, College of William and Mary, USA; MA, University of Virginia; PhD English Literature, University of Chicago. *Publications:* Starting With Poetry, (with Judith K Moore), 1973; Tennyson and Madness, 1983. *Contributions to:* Victorian Poetry; The Journal of Pre-Raphaelite Studies; The Tennyson Research Bulletin; The Bucknell Review; Concerning Poetry. *Address:* 332 Ashland Avenue, Buffalo, NY 14222, USA.

COLLIER, Louise Wilbourn, b. 7 Mar. 1925, Memphis, Tennessee, USA. Wife; Mother. m. John Stuart Collier, 12 Dec. 1953, Memphis, 1 son, 3 daughters. *Education:* BA, Political Science, Rhodes College, Memphis. *Publications:* Pilgrimage: A Tale of Old Natchez, 1983. *Literary Agent:* Phyllis Tickle, St Luke's Press. *Address:* 588 Club Walk, Memphis, TN 38111, USA.

COLLIER, Phyllis K, b. 13 Oct. 1939, Tulsa, Oklahoma, USA. Writer. m. Robert E Collier, 3 Feb. 1978, Seattle, Washington, 1 son, 2 daughters. *Education:* BA, Highline Community College, 1977; BA, University of Washington, 1980. *Publication:* How to Marry a Winner, 1982. *Contributions to:* Mirror Northwest, 1974; Saturday's Women, 1982; Nimrod, 1983; The Windless Orchard, 1984; Cumberland Poetry Review, 1984; New Woman, 1983; Complete Woman, 1984. *Honours:* Best Poem, Highline College, 1974; Top Ten, Nonfiction Book, Pacific N W Writers Conference, 1980; Top Ten, Poetry, Pacific NLW. Writers Conference, 1983; Second Place, Pablo Neruda Poetry Competition, 1983. *Memberships:* Poetry Society of America; Pacific Northwest Writers Conference. *Address:* 11803 S.E. 251st, Kent, WA 98031, USA.

COLLIER, Richard Hughesdon, b. 8 Mar. 1924, London. Author. m. Patricia Eveline Russell, 24 July 1953, Epsom. *Literary Appointments:* Associate Editor,

Phoenix Magazine for the Forces, SE Asia, 1945–46; Editor, Town and Country Magazine, 1946–48; Features Staff, Daily Mail, 1948–49. *Publications:* Captain of the Queens, (Co-author), 1956; Ten Thousand Eyes, 1958; The City That Wouldn't Die, 1959; A House Called Memory, 1960; The Sands of Dunkirk, 1961; Duce, 1971; The Great Indian Mutiny, 1963; The General Next To God, 1965; Bridge Across The Sky, 1978; 1940: The World In Flames, 1979; 1941: Armageddon, 1981; The War That Stalin Won, 1983; The Rainbow People, 1984. *Contributor to:* Readers Digest; Holiday; The Times; etc. *Honour:* Knight of Mark Twain, 1972. *Memberships:* British Film Institute; Royal Horticultural Society; Society for Theatre Research. *Literary Agent:* Curtis Brown. *Address:* c/o Curtis Brown Limited, 162/168 Regent Street, London W1R 5TB, England.

COLLINGS, Rebecca, b. 19 June 1951, London, England. Journalist. *Education:* Journalism Diploma, London College of Printing. *Contributions to:* Variety of specialist business and trade journals. *Address:* 17 Willow Road, London NW3, England.

COLLINS, Neil Adam, b. 20 Jan. 1947, England. Financial Journalist. m. Vivien Goldsmith, 1 daughter. *Education:* MA, Selwyn College, University of Cambridge, England. *Literary Appointments:* City Editor, The Standard, 1979–84; City Editor, The Sunday Times, 1984; Contributor to, The Business Programme, Channel 4 TV. *Address:* c/o The Sunday Times, 200 Gray's Inn Road, London WC1X 8EZ, England.

COLLINS, Raymond Francis, b. 12 May 1935, Providence, Rhode Island, USA. Professor of New Testament Studies. *Education:* PhB, 1955, STB, 1969, MA, 1961, STL, 1961, STD, 1963, Catholic University of Louvian, Belgium. *Publications:* Introduction to the New Testament, 1983; Models of Theological Reflection, 1984; Studies on the First Letter to the Thessalonians, 1984. *Contributions to:* Editorial Board: Louvain Studies; Revue theologique de Louvian. Contributing Editor: Actualidad Pastoral; Canon Law Digest; Emphemerides Theologicae Louvanienses. *Contributions:* Actualidad Pastoral; American College Bulletin; American Ecclesiastical Review; Andover Newton Quarterly; The Bible Today; Biblical Theology Bulletin; Catholic Biblical Quarterly; Church Alert; Downside Review; Emmanuel; Chicago Studies; Irish Theological Quarterly; Laval theologique et philosophique; Listening; The Living Light; Melita Theologica; New Testament Studies. *Address:* Schapenstraat 41, B–3000 Leuven, Belgium.

COLLINS, Robert George, b. 6 June 1926, Danbury, Connecticut, USA. Writer; University Professor. m. May Collins, 1981. *Education:* BA, Honours, English, 1950, MA, English, American Literature, 1952, Miami University; PhD, English & Comparative Literature, University of Denver, 1959. *Appointments:* Numerous teaching positions, Professor, English, University of Ottawa, Canada, 1976–. *Publications include:* Effective Business Writing, co-author, 1953; Spectre in the Fantastic Laboratory, 1956; The Mosaic Reader, co-editor, 1970; New Views of Franz Kafka, Editor, 1970; co-Editor: Sociological Perspectives on Literature, 1971; Scandinavian Literature: Reality & Vision, 1971; Editor, The New Views of the European Novel, 1972; The Novels of William Faulkner, 1973; Author: The Creative Process in Literature: A Symposium, 1974; Tolerable Levels of Violence, 1983; Critical Essays on John Cheever, 1982; etc. *Contributor to:* Numerous professional journals and magazines including Wascana Review; Dalhousie Review; Studies in American Fiction; Twentieth Century Literature; Mosaic; James Joyce Quarterly; etc. *Honours:* Recipient numerous grants. *Memberships:* Modern Language Association of America; Kafka Society; Bronte Society. *Address:* P O Box 276, Kars, Ontario, KOA 2EO, Canada.

COLLIS, Kevin Francis, b. 18 Feb. 1930, Cordelia, Queensland, Australia. Professor of Education. m. Beryl O'Shea, 5 May 1951, Brisbane, 2 sons, 2 daughters. *Education:* BA 1956, B Ed 1964, M Ed 1967, University of Queensland; PhD, University of Newcastle, New South Wales, 1973. *Publications:* A Study of Concrete and Formal Operations in School Mathematics: A Piagetian Viewpoint, 1975; On Children's Reasoning, 1978; Cognitive Development – Research Based on a Neo-Piagetian Approach (with J A Keats and G S Halford, Editors), 1978; Evaluating the Quality of Learning: The Solo Taxonomy (with J B Biggs), 1982. *Contributions to:* The Australian Journal of Education; The Australian Mathematics Teacher; Journal for Research in Mathematics Education; Australian Journal of Psychology; Child Development; Advances in Educational Psychology; Journal of Science and Mathematics in South East Asia; Language Development and Intellectual Functioning; and others. *Honours:* Grants: Australian Research Grants Committee, 1973, 1986; Social Science Research Council of Great Britain, 1974; Education Research and Development Committee, 1976–81; Ian Potter Foundation, 1972 and 1984. *Memberships Include:* Australian Association for Research in Education; Fellow, Australian College of Education; Institute for Educational Research; Mathematical Association of Tasmania; Australian Association of Mathematics Teachers. *Address:* Department of Educational Studies, University of Tasmania, Box 2520, GPO Hobart, Tasmania 7001, Australia.

COLLIS, Roger Bruce, b. 4 Feb. 1935, London, England. Writer; Journalist; Broadcaster. m. Erdmuthe Wischnath, 29 May 1971, London, 1 daughter. *Education:* Liverpool University; Imede Business School, Lausanne. *Publication:* If My Boss Calls...Make Sure You Get His Name, 1984. *Contributions to:* International Herald-Tribune, Weekly Columnist; Chief Executive, Monthly Columnist; Harper's; Queens; The Wall Street Journal; The Washington Post, etc. *Membership:* Institute of Journalists. *Literary Agent:* Reeves Leese & Partners. *Address:* B P 121, 06603 Antibes Cedex.

COLMER, John Anthony, b. 2 Oct. 1921, Plymouth, England. Professor of English. *Education:* BA, 1949, MA, 1953, Keble College, Oxford; PhD, London University, 1955. *Publications include:* Coleridge, Critic of Society, 1959, 1967; Henry IV Part I, 1965; E M Forster: The Personal Voice, 1975; Coleridge to Catch 22: Images of Society, 1978; Patrick White: Riders in the Chariot, 1978; Patrick White, 1984; Co-Editor, New Choice, 1967; Mainly Modern, 1969; Pattern & Voice, 1981; Through Australian Eyes, 1984. *Contributor to:* Modern Language Review; Writers of the English Language Series; Yearbook of English Studies; etc. *Memberships include:* Fellow, Australian Academy of the Humanities, 1971; English Association. *Address:* 4 Everard Street, Glen Osmond, SA 5064, Australia.

COLOMBO, Furio Marco, b. 1 Jan. 1931, Chatillon, Italy. Journalist Writer. m. Alice Oxman, New York, 16 Aug. 1969, 1 daughter. *Education:* Law degree, University of Turin. *Literary Appointments:* Editor, Communicazione Visiva. University of Bologna, 1970–77 Comunicazioni di Massa, Milan, 1979–84. *Major Publications include:* Nuovo Teatro Americano, Milan, 1963; L'America di Kennedy, Milan, 1964; Le Donne Matte, novel, Milan, 1964; Il Prigioniero della Torre Velasca, Racconti, Turin, 1965; Invece della Violenza, Milan, 1967; Le Condizioni del Conflitto, Milan 1969; Italy Two, Catalogue of Italian Contemporary Art, Museum of Philadelphia 1972; The Chinese, New York 1971; Arte e Violenza, Florence 1972; Televisione: La Realta' Come Spettacolo, Milan 1972; Comunicazioni Nelle Societa' Industriali, Bologna 1973; Ipertelevision, Milan 1975; Agenti Segreti, Racconti, Milan 1976; I Prossimi Americani, Milan 1976; In Italy – Postwar Political Life, New York 1981; Passaggio a Occidente, Milan 1982; Il Dio d'America, Milan 1983 (in English, God in America, New York 1984). *Contributions to:* Il Mondo, Rome, 1962–66; E'Espresso, Rome 1966–70; Tempo Presente, Rome 1966, 1970; Ulisse, Rome 1964, 1975; Il Caffe, Rome 1965, 1973; Bianco e Nero, Rome 1972; Il Menabo', Turin 1964–74; Rivista di Estetica, University of Turin 1955–56; Il Verri, Milan 1960–69;

Tuttolibri, Turin 1970; L'editore, Turin 1970; L'Economico, Turin 1970; New York Review of Books, 1979; Enciclopedia Garzanti 1978; Atlante Geografico 1979; Enciclopedia Europea Garzanti 1980. *Honours:* Trumbull Lecturer, Yale University, USA, 1964; Chair of Italian Culture, University of California, Berkeley, 1975. *Memberships:* Executive Committee, Centre for Internationala Scholarly Exchange; Centre for Italian Studies, Columbia University. Istituto di Studi Americani, Rome; Century Association, New York. *Literary Agent:* Marion Young, Nat Sobel Associates, 146 E.19th Street, New York, NY 10003, USA. *Address:* 29 East 64th Street, New York, NY 10021, USA.

COLOMBO, John Robert, b. 24 March 1936, Kitchener, Ontario, Canada. Author & Editor. m. 11 May 1959, 2 sons, 1 daughter. *Education:* University of Toronto. *Literary Appointments:* The Ryerson Press; McClelland & Stewart; The Tamarack Review; Free-lance editor since 1963. *Major Publications:* Over 70 books, including: Colombo's Canadian Quotations; Colombo's Canadian References; Canadian Literary Landmarks; and others. *Contributions to:* Atlantic Monthly; Canadian Literature; Globe & Mail; Maclean's; Graphis International; and others. *Honours:* Centennial Medal, 1967; Order of Cyril & Methodius (First Class); Esteemed Knight of Mark Twain; Philips Information Systems Literary Prize, 1986; and others. *Memberships:* PEN International; Science Fiction Research Associates. *Address:* 42 Dell Park Avenue, Toronto, Ontario, M6B 2T6, Canada.

COLTON, Joel, b. 23 Aug. 1918, New York City, USA. Professor. m. Shirley L Baron, 8 May 1942, New York, 1 son, 1 daughter. *Education:* BA, City College of NY, Magna Cum Laude, 1937; MA 1940, PhD, Columbia University, 1950. *Appointments:* Instructor to Professor of History, 1947–, Chairman, Department of History, Duke University, 1967–74; Director for Humanities, The Rockefeller Foundation, 1974–81. *Publications:* Compulsory Labor Arbitration in France, 1936–39, 1951; Leon Blum: Humanist in Politics, 1966, French Edition, 1968; Twentieth Century, 1968, revised edition, 1980; A History of the Modern World, (with R R Palmer), 1956, sixth edition, 1984, translated into Swedish, Finnish, Arabic, Persian and Spanish. *Contributor to:* Articles and book reviews in American Historical Review; Journal of Modern History; Journal of Politics; Gala Review; South Atlantic Quarterly etc. *Honours:* Phi Beta Kappa, 1936; Guggenheim Fellowship, 1957–58; Rockefeller Foundation Fellowship, 1961–62; Mayflower Book Award, 1967; National Endowment for the Humanities S...Fell..., 1970–71; Fellow, American Academy of Arts and Sciences, 1979; Phi Beta Kappa, Visiting Scholar, 1983–84. *Memberships:* Committee on International Historical Activities, American Historical Assoc, 1980–; Vice President, Society for French Historical Studies, 1972–73; Chairman, European History Section, Southern Historical Assoc, 1975–76; Co President, International Commission on History of Social Movements and Social Structures, 1985–; Boards of Editors, Journal of Modern History, 1968–71; Board of Editors, French Historical Studies, 1985–; Advisory Board, Historical Abstracts, 1982–. *Address:* 6 Stoneridge Circle, Durham, NC 27705, USA.

COLVILLE, John Rupert (Sir) b. 28 Jan. 1915, London, England. Banker. m. Lady Margaret Egerton, 20 Oct. 1948, St Margaret's Westminster, 2 sons, 1 daughter. *Education:* MA, 1st class honours History, Trinity College, Cambridge. *Publications:* Pools Pleasure, 1935; Action This Day, (part author), 1968; Man of Valour, 1972; Footprints in Time, 1976 and 1984; The New Elizabethans, 1977; The Portrait of a General, 1980; The Churchillians, 1981; Strange Inheritance, 1983; The Fringes of Power: Downing Street Diaries 1939–55, 1985. *Contributions to:* Numerous magazines and journals. *Honours:* CVO, 1984; CB, 1955; Knight Bachelor, 1974; Honorary Fellow, Churchill College, Cambridge, 1970; Doctor of Letters, Westminster College, Fulton, 1985. *Address:*

The Close, Broughton, Nr Stockbridge, Hampshire, England.

COMFORT, Iris Tracy, b. Racine, Wisconsin, USA. Writer. *Education:* University Minnesota; University Wisconsin. *Publications:* Earth Treasures: Rocks and Minerals, 1964; Let's Grow Things, 1968; Let's Read About Rocks, 1969; Joey Tigertail, 1972; Shadow Masque, 1980; Echoes of Evil (paperback ed), 1978; Echoes of Evil (Double Day Hardback Edition), 1977; EE-A Gopher, anthology, (Harcourt Brace Jov), 1984. *Contributor to:* Parents' Magazine; Charm Magazine; McCall's Success; Seventeen; Together; Better Homes and Gardens; NY Daily News. *Memberships:* President, Orlando Branch National League American Penwomen, 1974–76; Mystery Writers of America, Incorporated. *Literary Agent:* Larry Sternig Literary Agency. *Address:* 2902 Oxford Street, Orlando, FL 32803, USA.

COMPTON-HALL, Patrick Richard, b, 12 July 1929, Reigate, England. Submarine Museum Director. m. Eve Cameron, 27 Dec. 1962, HMS Dolphin, Gosport, Hants, 3 sons, 2 daughters. *Education:* PSC, JSSC, Naval and Joint Staff Courses UK and USA. *Publications:* Submarines, 1982; The Underwater War 1939–1945, 1982; Submarine Boats, 1983; The Submariners' World, 1983; Naval Warfare Today and Tomorrow, translation from French, 1984; Submarine Warfare – Monsters and Midgets, 1985. *Contributions to:* About 1,200 articles to journals and magazines in UK, USA and Commonwealth. Several BBC Radio comedy series – notably, Bootle. *Honour:* MBE, 1964. *Memberships:* Society of Authors; Society of Translators. *Literary Agent:* A M Heath and Co Ltd. *Address:* Submarine Museum, HMS Dolphin, Gosport, Hants PO12 2AB, England.

CONCANNON, Alan, b. 19 June 1940, Stockport, England. Engineer, Writer. m. Carole Power, 19 Feb. 1966, Stockport, 1 son, 1 daughter. *Education:* Diploma in Journalism (Australia); Higher National Certificate in Electrical Engineering; Member of the Institute of Electrical and Electronic Engineers (USA); Member of the Institution of Electrical and Electronic Incorporated Engineers (UK). *Literary Appointments:* New Zealand Correspondent for International Wood Trade Publications; New Zealand Correspondent for Australian Forest Industries Journal; New Zealand Correspondent for World Wood (USA); Contributing Editor for a number of international magazines. *Contributor to:* Reader's Digest, Science Digest (USA); Australasian Post (Australia); People with Pix (Australia); New Scientist (UK); Prime Time; St Anthony Messenger (Italy); Energy Journal (New Zealand); Scanorama (Sweden); World Farming (USA); Australian Electrical World; NZ Listener; Skyway (New Zealand); Electronics Today International; Consulting Engineer (Canada); Better Business; and other international magazines. *Memberships:* Member of the American Society of Journalists and Authors Inc. (USA); Member of the Associated Business Writers of America. *Address:* 97 Lauderdale Road, Birkdale, Auckland 10, New Zealand.

CONDÉ, Abdurrahman Bruce Alfonso de Bourbon (Prince), b. 5 Dec. 1913, Oakland, California, USA. Major-General, Royal Yemen Army; Former Major, US Army & Air Force. m. HR & IH Olga Beata Nicolaevna Romanov Dolgorukiy, Princess of Ukrania-Ruthenia, Dowager Duchess of Durazzo, 6 Aug. 1984, Tetuan, Morocco, 1 adopted son. *Education:* AA, Santa Ana Junior College, California, 1933; BA 1935, MA 1937, University of California, Los Angeles; 5 yearss graduate study, Islamic, American University of Beirut, Lebanon, 1950–55. *Publications:* Byways of Byblos, 4 editions 1951–60; See Lebanon, 2 editions 1955, 1960; Tripoli of Lebanon, 1961. In preparation: Yemen, South Arabia's Mountain Wonderland; Moorish Spain in Morocco: The Andalucians of Xauen & Tetuan. *Contributions to:* Philatelic press since 1940's, including McKeel's, Stamp Collector etc, USA; Gibbon's Stamp Magazine etc. UK; Westways, California; Los Angeles Times Sunday Supplement; Armenian Review;

The Monarchist, etc. *Memberships:* Association Internationale des Journalistes Philateliques; Society of Philaticians. *Literary Agent:* Taylor Coffman, Cambria, California, USA. *Address:* 'Casa del Rey Aben Humeya', Pajares 5, Narila de Cadiar, Granada, Spain.

CONDON, George Hudson, b. 30 Mar. 1944, Nova Scotia, Canada. Editor, Publisher, Writer, Broadcaster. m. Diderica De Bruyn, 16 Nov. 1982, St Thomas, US Virgin Isles, 3 sons. *Education:* Diploma, Kings County Academy; Diploma, Radio College of Canada; Certificate, York University Continuing Education. *Literary Appointments:* Provincial Editor 1963, Entertainment Editor 1963, The Guardian, Charlottetown, Prince Edward Island; City Editor, The Evening Patriot, Charlottetown, 1965; City Editor, The Chronicle Herald, Halifax, Nova Scotia, 1966; Editor in Chief, The Free Press, Dartmouth, 1968; Editor and Publisher, Canadian Grocer, Toronto, Ontario, 1977. *Publications:* Articles and recordings. *Contributions to:* Canadian Grocer; Atlantic Advocate; Toronto Star; Star Weekly; Maclean's Magazine; CBC Television and Radio. *Honours:* Kenneth R Wilson Memorial Award for Business Writing, 1979 and 1981. *Memberships:* Alliance of Canadian Cinema, Television and Radio Artists; Performing Rights Organization of Canada Limited; Composers, Authors and Publishers Association of Canada Limited. *Address:* The Maclean Hunter Building, 777 Bay Street, Toronto, Ontario, M5W 1A7, Canada.

CONDRY, Dorothea June Douglass, b. 20 June 1935. Writer; Poet. *Education:* BA, MA, Central State University, Edmond; Post MA Education, Oklahoma State University. *Literary Appointments:* Elementary Educator, 1960's; Secondary Educator, 1970's; College Educator in Language Arts, 1978–80. *Publications:* Impressions, 1972; Four Phases of the Moon, 1977; The Latter Days, 1980; The Sign, 1980–81; The Dramatic Pageant, Firebird of Unlimited Happiness, 1981; Corporate Security, 1982. *Contributor to:* Poetry and poetry reviews to: Samisdat, Vermont; Jump River Review; Wisconsin: Poetry of the Great Plains, (anthologies); Stony Hills Review, Maine; Passages, New Jersey; Merging Media; Oklahoma Poetry; Numerous other publications and anthologies during 1985. *Memberships:* Kappa Delta Phi Honorary Society in Education: Independent Artists of Oklahoma; American Institute of Discussion; Contributing Member, Academy of American Poets; International Platform Association. *Address:* Route 2, Calumet, OK 73014, USA.

CONE, Ferne Geller, b. Portland, Oregon, USA. Fiber Artist; Author. m. J Morton Cone, 21 Mar. 1948, Portland, Oregon, 2 daughters. *Education:* University of Washington. *Publications:* Knit Art, 1975; Knutty Knitting for Kids, 1977; Knit With Style, 1979; Crazy Crocheting, 1981; Classy Knitting: A Guide to Easy Sweatering for Beginners, 1984; Classy Knitting, Book II (to be published 1986). *Contributions to:* The Flying Needle; To Cast On (Quarterly contributor). *Honours:* Third Place, Society of Technical Writers, 1979; Honorable Mention, Society of Technical Writers, 1980, 82. *Memberships:* Pacific Northwest Writers Conference (Board of Trustees, Program Chair); Seattle Freelances (Vice-President, President); Society of Childrens Book Writers; Women in Communication (Honors Chair). *Literary Agent:* Jane Jordan Browne. *Address:* 6401 Sand Point Way, NE, Seattle, WA 98115, USA.

CONN, Walter Eugene, b. 11 July 1940, Providence, Rhode Island, USA. University Professor of Religious Studies. m. Joann Wolski, 14 Oct. 1972, Columbia, Missouri. *Education:* BA, Providence College, 1962; MA, Boston College, 1966; Ph L, Weston College, 1966; PhD, Columbia University, 1973. *Literary Appointments:* Book Review Editor 1978–80, Editor 1980–, Horizons. *Publications:* Conversion, edited collection, 1978; Conscience: Development and Self-Transcendence, 1981; Mainstreaming: Feminist Research for Teaching Religious Studies, co-editor with

Arlene Swidler, 1985; Christian Conversion, 1986. *Contributions to:* Reviews and articles in philosophical, psychological and theological scholarly journals. *Honours:* Best Article Award 1977, Best Book Award 1981, College Theology Society. *Memberships:* American Academy of Religion; Catholic Theological Society of America; Board of Directors, College Theology Society; Society for Christian Ethics. *Address:* Religious Studies Department, Villanova University, Villanova, PA 19085, USA.

CONNER, Patrick Rearden, b. 19 Feb. 1907. Writer. *Major Publications include:* Shake Hands with the Devil (Lit Guild selection, USA), 1933, filmed 1958; Rude Earth, 1934; I am Death, 1936; Men must Live, 1937; The Sword of Love, 1938; The Devil among the Tailers, 1947; My Love to the Gallows, 1949; Hunger of the Heart, 1950; The Singing Stone, 1951; The House of Cain, 1952. (under name of Peter Malin) To Kill is my Vocation, 1939; River, Sing me a Song, 1939; Kobo the Brave, 1950. *Contributor to:* Several anthologies of short stories, various newspapers & periodicals, USA, UK & Eire. *Honour:* MBE, 1967. *Address:* 79 Balsdean Road, Woodingdean, Brighton BN2 6PG, Sussex, England.

CONNER, Patrick Roy Mountifort, b. 18 Sep. 1947, London, England. Museum Curator. m. 15 July 1973, London, 1 daughter. *Education:* BA, Worcester College, Oxford; D Phil, University of Sussex. *Publications:* Savage Ruskin, 1979; Oriental Architecture in the West, 1979; Michael 'Angelo' Rooker, 1984. *Contributions to:* Apollo; Art History; The Burlington Magazine; Country Life and many others. *Address:* Brighton, England.

CONNOR, John Anthony, b. 16 March, 1930, Salford, England. Teacher. m. Frances Foad, June, 1961, Kensington, England (divorced 1974), 2 sons, 1 daughter. *Education:* MA, University of Manchester, England, 1968. *Appointments:* Visiting Writer, Amherst College, Massachusetts, 1967–68; Professor of Literature, Wesleyan University, Connecticut, 1971–present. *Publications:* With Love Somehow, 1962; Lodgers, 1965; Kon in Springtime, 1968; In the Happy Valley, 1971; Memoirs of Uncle Harry, 1974; New and Selected Poems, 1982; Spirits of the Place, 1986. *Honour:* Elected Fellow of Royal Society of Literature, 1973. *Address:* 44 Brainerd Avenue, Middletown, CT 06457, USA.

CONRAD, Nancy Lu, b. 26 June 1927, Chillicothe, Ohio, USA. Podiatrist. *Publications:* (Contributing Author): Principles & Practice of Podiatry, 1968; Sports Medicine, 1980. *Contributor to:* Journal of American Podiatry Association; Ohio Valley Chapter Newsletter, American Medical Writers Association; Pickaway County Historical Society Quarterly; Current Podiatry; Circleville Herald; Canadian Podiatrist; British Journal of Chiropody; Good Housekeeping; Podiatry Quarterly; Chiropody Record; etc. *Membership:* American Medical Writers Association. *Honours:* Recipient, Dr Maxwell N Cupshan Award, 1977. *Address:* 1106 S Court St, Circleville, OH 43113, USA.

CONRADI-BLEIBTREU, Ellen, b. 11 June 1929, Heidelberg, Germany. Writer. m. Bruno Schmidt-Bleibtreu, 1956, 1 son, 1 daughter. *Education:* Studied: Agricultural School, Business College; Studied English, Spanish, Philosophy, History, Law, Translators Examination, University of Germersheim-Mainz. *Literary Appointments:* Student, BASF Advertising Department. *Publications:* Klinge durch unser Taubsein. 1950; Jahre mit F.J. (poems), 1951; Schillers Sohn Ernst, 1966; Kraniche, 1970; Fragments, 1973; Ruhestörung (short stories), 1975; Unter dem Windsegel, (poetry), 1978; In Schatten des Genius-Schillers Familie in Rheinland (Prose), 1981; Zeitzeichen (Poetry), 1983; Die Schillers, Biography, 1986; Co-Author, Anthologie de la Poesie feminine mondiale, 1973; Sie schreiben zw. Goch u.Bonn, 1976; Mauern, 1978; Prisma Minden, 1978; Authoresses of the Federal Republic of Germany 1950–80, 1980; Europa in Lyrik u.Prosa, 1984; Das Bildgedicht, 1981. *Contributor to:* Westermanns

Monatsheften; Pazifische Rundschau Vancouver; Co-Editor: Side by Side, 1980; Children's Stories, 1985; Women Composers, 1984. *Honours:* Zwei Menschen Prize, 1976; Hon. Prize, Prose Competition, Mauern, 1977; Companion of Western Europe Diploma, Cambridge, 1980; Medal, Poetry Competition, 1981; World Prize, Literature, Accademia Italia, 1984; Statua della Vittoria, 1984. *Memberships:* Gedok 1965, Professional Advisor for Literature, 5 years; Federation Culture Feminine Paris, 1970, VS 1970–84; Delegate to Commission Arts Letters Music and Regional Consultant for Europe, German Womens Delegation, ICW, 1973, 1978; Die Kogge; European Authors Association; etc. *Address:* Pregelstrasse 5, D–5300 Bonn 1, Federal Republic of Germany.

CONROY, John Wesley (Jack), b. 5 Dec. 1899, Moberly, Missouri. Author. m. Gladys Kelly, 30 June 1922, Moberly, Missouri, 2 sons, 1 daughter. *Education:* University of Missouri, Columbus, 1920. *Literary Appointments:* The Rebel Post, 1929–32; Editor, The Anvil, 1933–35; The New Anvil, 1939–42. *Publications:* The Disinherited, 1933; The Fast Sooner Hound, (with Arna Bontemps), 1942; They Seek a City, 1945; Midland Humour, (Editor), 1947; Slappy Hooper the Wonderful Sign Painter, 1948; Sam Patch, 1951; Anyplace But Here, (with Arna Bontemps), 1960; Writers In Revolt: The Anvil Anthology, 1973; The Jack Conroy Reader, (edited by Jack Salzman and David Ray), 1979; The Weed King and Other Stories, 1985. *Contributions to:* The American Mercury; The Fool Killer; Pagany. *Honours:* John Simon Guggenheim Foundation Grant, 1935; Louis Rabonowitz Award, 1967; National Endowment for the Arts Grant, 1978; Mark Twain Award Society for the Study of Midwestern Literature, 1980. *Membership:* Vice-President, (Missouri), Society of Midland Authors. *Address:* 701 Fisk Avenue, Moberly, MO 65270, USA.

CONSOLIN, Aercio Flavio, b. 10 Jan. Morungaba, Sao Paulo, Brazil. Portuguese Teacher. *Publications:* O Cabide, stories, 1974; Fadário, novel, 1977; A Dança das Auras, stories, 1980; Mancha de Sol, stories, 1985. *Honours:* Fernando Chinaglia Prize, 1975; Guimarães Rosa Prize, 1976; Status of Literature Prize, 1977; Walter Auada Prize, Ribeirão-Pretana Academy of Letters. *Literary Agent:* José Reinaldo Pontes. *Address:* Caixa Postal 12, 13. 260 Morungaba, SP, Brazil.

CONSTANT, Clinton, b. 20 Mar. 1912, Nelson, British Columbia, Canada. US Citizen. Chemical Engineer; Author. *Education:* BSc, Alberta University, 1935; Doctorate, Western Reserve University, USA, 1939; Registered Professional Engineer. *Publications:* The War of the Universe, 1931; The Martian Menace, 1934; O and M Manual for Industrial Waste Treatment Plant, 1975. *Contributions to:* Numerous technical publications and reports on astronomy, chemistry and rocketry. *Memberships include:* American Chemical Society; Royal Astronomical Society, Canada; American Water Works Association; Fellow, New York Academy of Science; American Astronomical Society; Fellow, American Institute Chemical Engineers, Fellow, American Institute of Chemists; Fellow, American Association for the Advancement of Science; Associate Fellow, American Institute Aeronautics and Astronautics. *Address:* PO Box 1217, Hesperia, CA 92345, USA.

CONYERS, Paul Gregory, b. 25 Mar. 1955, Christchurch, New Zealand. Journalist; Public Relations Consultant. Divorced, 1 son, 1 daughter. *Education:* Chamber of Commerce English, Stages 1-11, English & Communications. *Major Publications:* Dining Out 1980 (Sydney Metropolitan Area, Australia); The Proverbial Cricket Book; The Proverbial Golf Book (both national and international). *Contributor to:* Sundowner International Woman's Day; The Sun-Herald; The Sun; The Daily Mirror; Challenge Cup '87 Souvenir Book; The Christchurch Star; The Auckland Star; House & Garden. *Membership:* Australian Society of Authors. *Address:* 63/1-3 Dalley Street, Bondi Junction 2022, Sydney, New South Wales, Australia.

COOK, Albert, b. 28 Oct. 1925. *Education:* AB, 1946, MA, 1947, Classics, Harvard University; Graduate School, 1947–48, Junior Fellow, Society of Fellows, 1948–51, Harvard University; Fulbright Fellow, University of Paris, 1952–53. *Appointments:* Assistant Professor, English, University of California, Berkeley, 1953–56; Associate Professor, 1957–61, Professor, 1961–63, English & Comparative Literature, 1964–71, Professor, Director, 1971–78, State University of New York, Buffalo; Professor, Comparative Literature, 1978–, Professor, Comparative Literature & Classics, 1980–, Professor, Comparative Literature, English & Classics, 1984–, Brown University. *Publications:* The Dark Voyage and the Golden Mean, 1949; The Meaning of Fiction, 1960; The Classic Line: A Study of Epic Poetry, 1967; Prisms, 1967; The Root of the Thing, 1968; Enactment: Greek Tragedy, 1971; French Tragedy: The Power of Enactment, 1981; Shakespeare's Enactment, 1976; Myth and Language, 1980; Changing the Signs, in press, etc. *Contributor to:* Numerous professional journals. *Honours:* Recipient, various honours and awards including Guggenheim Fellow, Paris, 1969–70; Fellow, Classical Studies Foundation Hardt, Geneva, 1968, 1975, CAMARGO Foundation, 1977, Clare Hall, Cambridge University, England, 1982. *Address:* 92 Elmgrove Avenue, Providence, RI 02906, USA.

COOK, David Allen, b. 14 Aug. 1945, St Louis, Missouri, USA. Professor of Film and English Literature; Writer; Consultant. m. Diane Evelyn Holt, 28 Jan. 1967, College Park, Maryland, 1 son, 2 daughters. *Education:* BA, University of Maryland, 1967; PhD, University of Virginia, 1971. *Literary Appointments:* Assistant Professor, Purdue University, Indiana, 1971–73; Assistant Professor, 1973–76, Associate Professor, 1976–84, Professor, 1985, Emory University, Atlanta, Georgia. *Publications:* A History of Narrative Film, 1981; A Social History of Television. *Contributions to:* Victorian Poetry; Contemporary Literature; Comparative Literature; Modern Philosophy; Quarterly Review of Film Studies; Studies in Short Fiction; International Dictionary of Films and Filmmakers, 1984; Atlanta Magazine; Cinema Journal; International Encyclopedia of Communications, 1985. Numerous papers and public lectures. *Honours:* Elected to Maryland Gamma chapter, Phi Beta Kappa, University of Maryland, 1967; Fellow, NDEA, University of Virginia, 1968–70; Younger Humanist Fellow, National Endowment for the Humanities. 1973. *Memberships:* Modern Language Association; Society for Cinema Studies; Authors Guild of America. *Address:* Department of English, Emory University, Atlanta, GA 30322, USA.

COOK, Edgar Reginald (Eddie), b. 18 Apr. 1928, Billericay, Essex, England. Publisher; Journalist. m. Patricia Mary Beale, 26 Mar. 1955, Great Burstead, Essex, (deceased 12 Feb. 1977), 1 son, 1 daughter. *Education:* Dip P E; Qualifications in sports coaching and evening class teaching. *Literary Appointments:* Founding Editor, Coaching News; Current Editor-in-Chief, Jazz Journal International and Teeline. *Contributions to:* Coaching News; Car Mechanics; Motorcycle Mechanics; Cycling; Founding Publisher; Training; Memo; 2000; Office Skills; Jazz Journal International; Teeline; Taxi Globe. *Address:* c/o 35 Great Russell Street, London WC1B 3PP, England.

COOK, Gregory M, b. 3 Apr. 1942, Yarmouth, Nova Scotia, Canada. Writer. m. Miriam Langley, 14 June, 1961, Moncton, New Brunswick, 2 sons, 1 daughter. *Education:* BA, Acadia University, 1962, MA, 1967. *Appointments:* Chairman, Nova Scotia Writers' Council, 1975; Executive Director, Writers' Federation of Nova Scotia, 1978; Director, Evelyn Richardson Memorial Trust, 1979; Treasurer, Writers' Union of Canada, 1985; Director, PEN, Canada, 1985; Director, Writers' Development Trust, 1985. *Publications:* Ernest Buckler: Critical Views on Canadian Writers, 1972; Love from Backfield, 1980; Louve en Route, 1983; Love in Flight, 1985. *Contributions to:* Various journals and magazines. *Memberships:* The Writers' Union of Canada; The League of Canadian Poets: The Writers' Development

Trust. PEN CANADA, International. *Address:* RR1 Wolfville, Nova Scotia, Canada.

COOK, Judith Anne, b. 9 July 1933, Manchester, England. Journalist; Writer. m. Douglas Cook, 15 Sep. 1952, divorced 1974, 2 sons, 2 daughters. *Appointments:* Reporter, Guardian, 1962–64, 1968–70; Westward TV, 1968; B Post, 1972–74; Anglia TV, Parliamentary Reporting; Freelance Writing. *Publications:* Directors Theatre, 1972; The National Theatre, 1974; Women in Shakespeare, 1980; Shakespeare's Players, 1983; Apprentices of Freedom, 1979; Close to the Earth, 1984; The Waste Remains, 1984; The Price of Freedom, 1985; Who Killed Hilda Murrell?, 1985. *Contributor to:* Guardian; Sunday Times; Observer; New Statesman; New Society; Birmingham Post; Scotsman; Good Housekeeping; Cosmopolitan; She; etc. *Honours:* Margaret Rhondda Award, Society of Authors, 1981; PPA Runner Up, Campaigning Journalist of the Year, 1982. *Membership:* Society of Authors. *Literary Agent:* Tessa Sayle, 11 Jubilee Place, London SW3. *Address:* 3 West Terrace, Newlyn, Penzance, Cornwall, England.

COOK, Petronelle Marguerite Mary, b. 16 May 1925, Plymouth, Devon, England. Writer, Lecturer. m. Philip Remington Cook, 20 July 1949, Rome, Italy, divorced 1979, 2 sons, 1 daughter. *Education:* BA Honours, St Anne's College, Diploma in Archaeology and Anthropology with distinction, MA, University of Oxford. *Publications:* The Officer's Woman, 1972; The Villa on the Palatine, 1974; Marie, 1979; Marie, Voodoo Queen, 1981; Exit Actors, Dying, 1979; The Cape Cod Caper, 1980; Zadok's Treasure, 1980; Death of a Voodoo Doll, 1982; Lament for a Lady Laird, 1982; Death on the Dragon's Tongue, 1983; Affairs of State, 1983; Love Among The Allies, 1985; Desperate Measures, 1986; Short stories and articles. *Honours:* Prize Award, National Writers Club MSS Novel Contest, 1984. *Memberships:* Boston Authors Club; National Writers Club. *Literary Agent:* Collier Associates, New York. *Address:* 11 High School Road, Hyannis, MA 02601, USA.

COOKE, Brian, b. 3 Dec. 1937, Liverpool, England. Writer, m. Iris Hughes, 1960, Liverpool, 1 son, 1 daughter. *Literary Appointments:* Advisor/Consultant, Thames Television International. *Publications:* Writing Comedy for Television, 1984. *Contributions to:* Magazines and journals. *Honours:* Various television/writers guild awards. *Literary Agent:* Fraser and Dunlop. *Address:* Fraser and Dunlop, 91 Regent Street, London W1R 8RU, England.

COOLEY, Peter John, b. 19 Nov. 1940, Detroit, Michigan, USA. College Professor. m. Jacqueline Marks, 12 June 1965, Chicago, Illinois, 1 son, 2 daughters. *Education:* BA, Shimer College; MA, University of Chicago; PhD, University of Iowa. *Literary Appointments:* Poetry Editor, North American Review, 1970–; Professor of Creative Writing, Tulane University, 1975–. *Major Publications:* The Company of Strangers, 1975; The Room Where Summer Ends, 1979; Night-Seasons, 1983. *Contributor to:* Antaeus; Poetry; Atlantic Monthly; New Yorker; Harper's; Southern Review. *Honours:* Louisiana Division of the Arts Fellowship, 1981; Robert Frost Fellowship, Breadloaf Writers' Conference, 1982. *Memberships:* PEN; Poetry Society of America; Associated Writing Programs. *Address:* Department of English, Tulane University, New Orleans, LA 70118, USA.

COOMBS, David John, b. 8 Feb. 1937, Merton, Surrey, England. Magazine Editor. *Literary Appointment:* Editor, Antique Collector Magazine. *Publications:* Churchill: His Paintings, 1967; Sport and the Countryside in English Painting, 1978. *Contributions to:* The Economist; Good Housekeeping; Harpers & Queen. *Membership:* Society of Authors. *Address:* Meadow Barn, Priorsfield Road, Godalming, Surrey GU7 2RQ, England.

COOPER, Bryan, b. 6 Feb. 1932, Paris, France. Editor; Author. m. Judith Williams, 7 Apr. 1979, New York City, USA. 2 sons, 2 daughters (by previous marriage). *Appointments:* Editor, 1975–, Publisher, 1983–, Petroleum Economist. *Publications:* North Sea Oil – The Great Gamble, 1966; The Ironclads of Cambrai, 1967; Battle of the Torpedo Boats, 1970; The Buccaneers, 1970; PT Boats, 1970; Alaska – The Last Frontier, 1972; Tank Battles of World War I, 1973; Fighter, 1973; Bomber, 1974; Stones of Evil, (novel), 1974; The E-Boat Threat, 1976; The Wildcatters, (novel), 1976; The Adventure of North Sea Oil, 1982. *Contributor to:* The Times; Flying Review Magazine; Competition Press; many others; Scriptwriter, over 100 Radio and TV and Film Scripts. *Membership:* Writers Guild of Great Britain; Garrick Club; Press Club. *Address:* 74 Speed House, Barbican, London EC2, England.

COOPER, John Charles, b. 3 Apr. 1933, Charleston, South Carolina, USA. University Professor; Lutheran Pastor. m. Clelia Ann Johnston, 6 June 1954, Greer, South Carolina, USA, 2 sons, 2 daughters. *Education:* AB, University of South Carolina; MA, University of Chicago; PhD, University of Chicago; MDiv, Lutheran Seminary, Columbia, South Carolina; STM, Chicago Lutheran Seminary. *Publications:* The Roots of Radical Theology, 1967; Radical Christianity and Its Sources, 1968; The New Mentality, 1969; The Turn Right, 1970; A New Kind of Man, 1971; Religion in the Age of Aquarius, 1972; The Recovery of America, 1973; Religion After Forty, 1973; Finding a Simpler Life, 1974; Your Exciting Middle Years, 1975; Religious Pied Pipers, 1981; Not For a Million Dollars, 1980; The Joy of the Plain Life, 1982; Dealing with Destructive Cults, 1984, and others. *Contributions to:* Christian Century; Christianity Today; The Lutheran; Southern Humanities Review and numerous others. *Honours:* Phi Beta Kappa; Mensa; Thomas F Staley Foundation Distinguished Christian Scholar; Danforth Foundation Teacher Grant. *Address:* 718 Picnic Lane, Selinsgrove, PA 17870, USA.

COOPER, Lettice (Ulpha), b. 3 Sep. 1897, Lancashire, England. Author. *Education:* Lady Margaret Hall, Oxford. *Literary Appointment:* Associate Editor, Time & Tide, 1938. *Publications include:* The Ship of Truth, 1929; The New House, 1938; National Provincial, 1953; Fenny (Book Society selection), 1953; Three Lives, 1957; A Certain Compass, 1960; The Double Heart, 1962; Late in the Afternoon, 1971; Tea on Sunday, 1973; Snow and Roses, 1976; Desirable Residence, 1980; Unusual Behaviour, 1986; Juvenile Books include: The Young Florence Nightingale, 1960; Blackberry's Kitten, 1961; The Bear Who Was Too Big, 1963; The Twig of Cypress, 1965; The Fugitive King, 1965; The Life and Work of Charles Dickens, 1968; Gunpowder Treason and Plot, 1970; Other books: Yorkshire West Riding, 1950; George Eliot, 1951; Unusual Behaviour (novel) in progress. *Contributions to:* Times Literary Supplement; Observer; Spectator; Yorkshire Post and other newspapers and journals in England. *Honour:* OBE, 1980. *Memberships:* PEN, Vice-President, 1976; English Centre, President, 1977–79; Authors Society; Writers Guild. *Literary Agent:* A P Watt. *Address:* 95 Canfield Gardens, London, NW6 3DY, England.

COOPER, William Heaton, b. 6 Oct, 1903. Painter; Writer. m. Ophelia Gordon Bell, 25 May 1940, Grasmere, Cumbria, 2 sons, 2 daughters. *Publications:* The Hills of Lakeland, 1938, 3rd edition, 1984; The Tarms of Lakeland, 1960, 3rd edition, 1983; Lakeland Portraits, 1954, 3rd edition, 1986; The Lakes, 1966, 3rd edition, 1986; Mountain Painter, 1984, 85. *Contributions to:* Fell and Rock Climbing Club Journal; Lake Artists Society; Hon-member, Fell and Rock Climbing Club. Creswick Prize for Landscape, R A School. *Memberships:* Royal Institute of Painters in Watercolours; Lake Artists Society. *Address:* The Studio, Grasmere, Ambleside, Cumbria LA22 9SX, England.

COOPERMAN, Hasye, b. 2 Feb. 1909, New York City, USA. Author, Poetry & Criticism; College Teacher. m. N

B Minkoff, Oct. 1931, 2 sons. *Education:* BA, Hunter College; MA, PhD, Columbia University. *Literary Appointments:* Editorial Research, World Publishing Company, Ohio, 1937–43; Teacher, American & Comparative Literature, City College of New York, 1939–41; New School for Social Research, 1950–. *Publications include:* The Chase, poetry, 1932; Men Walk the Earth, poetry, 1953; The Making of a Woman, poetry, 1985. Criticism, The Aesthetics of Stéphane Mallarmé, revised edition 1971. *Contributions include:* Chapters in, Jewish Heritage Reader, The American Jew: A Reappraisal. 3 Radio Series on Yiddish Literature, 1979, 1980. Poetry in various anthologies & poetry magazines. *Honours:* National Poetry Ward, American Literary Association, 1957; Head of Literature Department, New School For Social Research, 1960–67. *Memberships:* Poetry Society of America; American Association of University Professors; International Platform Association. *Address:* 334 West 85th Street, New York, NY 10024, USA.

CORBALLIS, Michael Charles, b. 10 Sep. 1936, Marton, New Zealand. Professor of Psychology. m. Barbara Elizabeth Wheeler, 8 May 1962, Auckland, 2 sons. *Education:* BSc, MSc, BA, MA, PhD. *Literary Appointments:* Professor of Psychology, University of Auckland. *Major Publications:* The Psychology of Left & Right (with I L Beale), 1976; The Ambivalent Mind (with I L Beale), 1983; Human Laterality, 1983. *Contributor to:* Numerous professional journals, including Psychonomic Science, Nature, Perception & Psychophysics, Scientific American and many others. *Honours:* Fellow, New Zealand Psychological Society; Fellow, Royal Society of New Zealand; Fellow, American Association for the Advancement of Science; Fellow, American Psychological Association. *Address:* Department of Psychology, University of Auckland, Auckland, New Zealand.

CORBET, Philip Steven, b. 21 May 1929, Kuala Lumpur, Malaysia. Professor of Zoology. Separated, 1 daughter. *Education:* BSc, University of Reading, England; D Sc; PhD, University of Cambridge; ScD. *Publications:* Dragonflies, 1960; A Biology of Dragonflies, 1962; The Odonata of Canada and Alaska, Volume 3, 1975. *Contributions to:* about 200, to scientific journals on zoology, entomology, pest control and resource management. *Memberships:* Institute of Biology, London, Fellow; Entomological Society of Canada, President, Fellow; Society of Authors. London. *Address:* Department of Biological Sciences, The University, Dundee DD1 4HN, Scotland.

CORBETT, Edmund Victor, b. Birmingham, England. Librarian. *Education:* MA, FLA, University College, London, England. *Publications include:* Introduction to Public Librarianship, 1950, 2nd edition, 1952; Great True Mountain Stories, 1957; Great True Stories of the Sea, 1958; Waves of Battle, 1959; Public Library Finance, 1960; Librarianship, 1961; Great True Stories of Tragedy and Disaster, 1961; Public Library and its Control, 1962, 2nd edition, 1966; Introduction to Librarianship, 1963, 1966, 1970; By Car to the Continent, 1962, 2nd edition, 1969; Fundamentals of Library Organisation and Administration, 1978. *Contributions to:* Library Association Record; Journal of Librarianship; British Book News, etc. *Memberships:* Chairman, Publications Committee, 1967–72, Executive Committee 1973–74, President, 1975, Library Association. *Address:* 3 Grasmere Close, Merrow, Guildford, Surrey GU1 2TG, England.

CORCORAN, Barbara, b. 12 Apr. 1911, Hamilton, Massachusetts, USA. Writer. *Education:* BA, Wellesley College; MA, University of Montana. *Major Publications:* Sasha My Friend, 1968; A Dance to Still Music, 1973; The Clown, 1974; May I Cross Your Golden River?, 1974; Walk My Way, 1980; The Three Abigails, 1981; The Woman in Your Life, 1984. *Memberships:* Authors League of America; *Honours:* William Allen White Award, 1972; Junior Literary Guild, 1972, 1973, 1976; Childrens Book Council, Science Teachers of America, 1975, 1976; Pacific NW

Booksellers Award, 1975; National Endowment for the Arts Fellowship, 1978. *Literary Agent:* ICM. *Address:* PO Box 4394, Missoula, MT 59801, USA.

CORDER, George Edward, b. 14 Aug. 1904, California, USA. Human Behaviour Scientist, Writer, Educator, Expert Instructor. *Education:* BA cum laude, City College of New York, 1983; M Ed, University of California, Los Angeles, 1954; PhD Candidate, California University for Advanced Studies, 1986. *Publications:* Search Othello's Soul: A Sane Alternative to the Insanity of Psychology and Psychiatry, 1976; Your Brain-Image Power: How to Selfsex and Imagize Your Way to Super-Successful Living, 1983. *Membership:* Phi Beta Kappa. *Address:* Post Office Box 1723, Hollywood, CA 90078, USA.

CORLETT, William, b. 8 Oct. 1938, Darlington, England. Author; Playwright. *Education:* Diploma, Royal Academy of Dramatic Art. *Publications:* The Gate of Eden, 1974; The Land Beyond, 1975; Return to the Gate, 1975; The Dark Side of the Moon, 1976; The Question Series, six books on world religion, 1978–79; Bloxworth Blue, 1984. *Honours:* Pye Colour TV Award, Childrens TV Writer of 1978, 1981; TV Gold Award, IFT Festival of New York, 1980, 1983. *Memberships:* Writers Guild of Great Britain; Society of Authors. *Literary Agent:* Mark Lucas, Fraser & Dunlop Scripts Ltd. *Address:* c/o Fraser & Dunlop Scripts Ltd, 91 Regent Street, London W1, England.

CORMIER, Jean-Marc, b. 8 Feb. 1948, Quebec, Canada. Journalist. 2 sons, 2 daughters. *Literary Appointments:* Editor, Urgences, literary review, 1981, 1982; Chairman, Authors Group of East Quebec, 1982, 1983; Chairman, EDITEQ, Cooperative Editions of East Quebec, 1983; Vice-Chairman 1984–85, *Publications:* Poltergeists, 1972; On n'a pas Grand-Chose à Dire, 1980; Westernité, 1981; Poèmes d'Amour, 1982; La Symphonie Déconcertante, 1984. *Contributions to:* Le Jour, 1975; Nous, 1978; Urgences, 1981–84. *Honours:* Prize, Salon du Livre de Rimouski, 1981; Scholarships, Ministry of Cultural Affairs, Quebec, 1981, 1985. *Memberships:* Union of Quebec Writers; Authors Group of East Quebec. *Address:* CP 1525, Rimouski, Quebec, Canada G5L 8M4.

CORNWELL, Rupert Howard, b. 22 Feb. 1946, London, England. Journalist. m. Angela Doria, 1 Apr. 1972, 1 son. *Education:* Honours Degree, Modern Greek, Oxford University, 1967. *Publication:* God's Banker, 1983. *Contributor to:* Numerous Journals and Magazines including, The Listener; Economist; Times Literary Supplement; Banker; etc. *Address:* Konstantinstrasse 94, 5300 Bonn 2, Federal Republic of Germany.

COSTLEY, William Kirkwood, Jr, b. 21 May 1942, Salem, Massachusetts, USA. Writer, Journalist (print/broadcasting), Editor. m. Joan Helen Budyk, 6 June 1964, Brighton, Massachusetts, 1 son, 1 daughter; divorced 1985. *Education:* AB, Boston College, 1963; MFA, University of Boston, 1967. *Literary Appointments:* Associate Editor, IHS Review, Boston College, 1967–68; Junior College Instructor, Public Information Office; Newspaper Editor, 1968–73; Technical Editor, Writer, Course developer, 1974–; Host, Co-producer, Hyacinths & Biscuits, radio programme, WZLY-fm, Wellesley, 1981–84. *Major Publications:* Knosh I Cir, 1975; RAG(a)S, 1978; Anthologies include: The Movement towards a new America, 1971; 11 Young Poets, 1975; Blood of their Blood, 1980; Born Again Beef, 1980; Poetry of Motion, 1984. *Contributor to:* Ann Arbor Review; Antigonish Review; Arion's Dolphin; Arts in Society; Aspect; Black Rose; Bogg; Brown Sweater; Clear Creek; Clown War; Contraband; Cotyledon; Diana's Bi-Monthly; Hanging Loose; Hellcoal Annual(s); Out of Sight; Ploughshares; Poems of the People; Quabbin; Salt Lick; Sepia; The Small Pond; Stony Hills; The Smith; Washout Review; W End; Wormwood Review; Zahir; and others. *Honours:* Honorable mention, Spring Fling Poetry Competition,

Edinburgh, Scotland, 1985; National Poetry Competition, Greenwich, England, 1985. *Memberships:* Founder: Redbridge Collective, Lynn Voices Collaborative, Lynn Exiles Ltd; New England Writers for Survival; National Writers' Union, Boston (local secretary); Edinburgh Playwrights' Workshop, 1984. *Address:* c/o Arts End Books, PO Box 192, Waban, MA 02168, USA.

COTOLO, Frank Michael, b. 8 Dec. 1950, Brooklyn, New York, USA. Writer. *Education:* Bachelor of Fine Arts, New York Institute of Technology. *Literary Appointments:* Editor, Writer Co-publisher, Humorettes, 1976; Head Writer, Audio Stimulation, 1978; Editor-in-Chief, Fat Tuesday, 1981; Horse Racing Journalist, Gambling Times, 1982. *Contributor to:* Contents Under Pressure; Gambling Times; Fat Tuesday; Turf & Sports Digest; Recording Engineer & Producer; Paper Cinema; and others. *Address:* 853 N Citrus, Los Angeles, CA 90038, USA.

COURLANDER, Harold, b. 18 Sep. 1908, Indianapolis, USA. Author. *Education:* BA, University of Michigan, 1931; postgraduate work, Columbia University, 1939–50. *Publications include:* Haiti Singing, 1939; Kantchil's Lime Pit, 1960; The Hat Shaking Dance, 1957; The Drum and the Hoe, 1960; The King's Drum, 1962; Negro Folk Music USA, 1963; People of the Short Blue Corn, 1970; The Fourth World of the Hopis, 1971; Tales of Yoruba Gods and Heroes, 1973; A Treasury of African Folklore, 1975; A Treasury of Afro-American Folklore, 1976; The Crest and the Hide, 1982; The Heat of the Ngoni, 1982; Hopi Voices, 1982. Novels: The Caballero, 1940; The Big Old World of Richard Creeks, 1962; The African, 1967; The Son of the Leopard, 1974; The Mesa of Flowers, 1977; The Master of the Forge, 1985; Editor and annotatoor: Big Falling Snow, 1978. *Contributions to:* Musical Quarterly; Journal of Negro History. *Honours:* John Simon Guggenheim Fellowships, 1948, 1955; Various awards and academic grants in aid; University of Michigan Outstanding Achievement Award, 1984. *Address:* 5512 Brite Drive, Bethesda, MD 20014, USA.

COURTHION, Pierre-Barthelemy, b. 14 Jan. 1902, Geneva, Switzerland. Art Historian. *Education:* University of Geneva, Switzerland; Ecole des Beaux-Arts, Paris, France; Ecole du Louvre, Paris. *Publications include:* Vie d'Eugene Delacroix, 1927; Henri Matisse, 1934; Henri Rousseau le Douanier, 1944; Bonnard, Peintre du merveilleux, 1945; Utrillo, 1948; Peintres d'aujourd'hui, Raoul Dufy, 1951; Paris d'autrefois, 1957; Le Romantisme, 1961; Manet, 1962; Autour de l'impressionnisme, 1965; L'Ecole de Paris de Picasso a nos jours, 1968; Seurat, 1968; La Peinture flamande et hollandaise, 1984; Les Primitifs, naissance de la peinture europeanne, 1985. *Honour:* Silver Medal, Reconaissance francaise. *Memberships include:* Vice President, International Association of Art Critics. *Address:* 11 rue des Marronniers, Paris 16e, France.

COURTNEY, Nicholas Piers, b. 20 Dec. 1944, England. Author. m. Vanessa Hardwicke, London 1980. *Education:* ARICS, MRAC, Royal Agricultural College, Cirencester. *Publications:* Shopping & Cooking in Europe, 1980; The Tiger, Symbol of Freedom, 1981; Diana, Princess of Wales, 1982; Royal Children, 1982; Prince Andrew, 1983; Sporting Royals, 1983; Diana, Princess of Fashion, 1984; Queen Elizabeth, The Queen Mother, 1984; The Very Best of British, 1985; In Society The Brideshead Era, 1985. *Contributions to:* Times; Redbook. *Membership:* Hurlingham PEN Club. *Literary Agent:* Giles Gordon, Anthony Sheil Associates. *Address:* 9 Kempson Road, London SW6 4PX, England.

COURTNEY, Richard, b. 4 June 1927, England. Teacher; Writer. m. Maureen Rosemary Gale, 1 son, 1 daughter. *Education:* BA, Dip Ed, Leeds, England. *Publications:* Drama for Youth, 1964; Teaching Drama, 1965; The School Play, 1966; The Drama Studio, 1967; Teaching & The Arts, 1979; Learning in the Arts, with Paul Park, 1980; Play, Drama & Thought, 1968, 3rd edition, 1974; The Dramatic Curriculum, 1980; Drama in Therapy, 2 volumes with Gertrud Schattner, 1981; Re-Play: Studies of Human Drama in Education, 1982; Outline History of British Drama, 1982; Teacher Education in the Arts, co-author, 1985; Basic Books in Arts Education, co-author, 1985; Drama Education Canada, 1985; Plays: Lord of the Skies, 1985; Poetry: Beasts and Other People, 1985; Tales of a Travelling Man, 1985; The Turning of the World, 1985. *Contributor to:* Numerous professional journals and magazines including Journal of Aesthetics and Art Criticism; New Literary Theory; Connecticut Review; Proceedings, Research Conference; Contemporary Canadian Theatre, etc. *Honours:* Albera Achievement Award, 1973; Canadian Silver Jubilee Medal, 1977. *Address:* Ontario Institute for Studies in Education, 252 Bloor Street West, Toronto, Ontario M5S 1V6, Canada.

COURTNEY, Winifred Fisk, b. 29 Apr. 1918, Flushing, New York, USA. Editor/Writer. m. Denis A Courtney, 20 June 1942, Flushing, New York, 1 son, 1 daughter. *Education:* BA, English, Barnard College, 1941; MS, Elementary Education, State University of New York, New Paltz, New York, 1959. *Literary Appointments:* Freelance Copy Editor, 1941–42, 1959–62; Copy Editor – Special Books, 1962–66, Chief Copy Editor – Special Books, 1965–66, Readers Digest; Editor, Reader's Adviser R R Bowker Co, New York, 1966–71; Free-lance Writer, 1971–. *Publications:* Editor-Writer, Reader's Adviser 11th edition 1969–70; Young Charles Lamb, 1775–1802 1982; 3 entries in, British Literary Magazines Vol II, 1983. *Contributions to:* Many articles on Africa and UN in Friends Journal, Africa South etc, 1955–65; Recent articles in Charles Lamb Bulletin, London. *Memberships:* Authors Guild, New York; Charles Lamb Society, London; Keats-Shelley Association, New York. *Address:* 197 Cleveland Drive, Croton-on-Hudson, NY 10520, USA.

COURTWRIGHT, David Todd, b. 10 Apr. 1952, Kansas City, Missouri, USA. Professor of History. m. Shelby Marie Miller, 29 Dec. 1976, Houston, Texas, USA, 2 sons. *Education:* BA English, University of Kansas, 1974; PhD History, Rice University, 1979. *Literary Appointment:* Associate Professor and Chair of History, University of Hartford. *Major Publications:* The Architecture of John F Staub: Houston & the South, Austin and London (with others), 1979; Dark Paradise: Opiate Addiction in America before 1940, 1982. *Contributor to:* Civil War History; Journal of Drug Issues; Journal of Social History; Journal of Southern History; Journal of the Early Republic; Millbank Memorial Fund Quarterly; New Statesman; and others. *Honours:* Phi Beta Kappa, 1973; National Endowment for the Humanities Fellowship, 1981; Yale University Visiting Faculty Fellowship, 1983. *Memberships:* American Historical Association; Organisation of American Historians. *Address:* Department of History, University of Hartford, West Hartford, CT 06117, USA.

COUTINHO, Edilberto, b. 26 Sep. 1938, Paraiba, Brazil. Journalist. *Education:* PhD, Brazilian Literature, Universidade Federal do Rio de Janeiro; Law Degree, Universidade Federal de Pernambuco; World Press Institute, USA; Fellow, Writing, University of Iowa, USA. *Appointments:* Writer in Residence, University of Iowa, 1978–79; Visiting Professor, 15 Universities, USA, 1979–; Speeches in Paris, Madrid, Lisbon, Porto, 1984. *Publications:* Um negro vai à forra, 1977; Sangue na praça, 1979; Maracanã, adeus, 1980; A imaginação do real, 1983; O livro de Carlos, 1983; O jogo terminado, 1983. *Contributor to:* Literary Critics weekly in, O Globo, Rio de Janiero; Articles in various magazines including Revista do Brasil; Coloόuio; etc; short stories in Brazil, USA. *Honours:* Prêmio Casa de las Americas, Havana, Cuba, Maracanã, adeus, Academia Brasileira de Letras, 1980–81; Recipient various other honours and awards. *Memberships:* PEN; Academia Brasileira de Literatura. *Literary Agent:* Marie Ange Massom-Mosca, Paris, France. *Address:* Rua Antonio Parreiras, 94/303, Ipanema, CEP 22411 Rio de Janeiro – RJ, Brazil.

COVELL, Pauline, b. 8 June 1946, Liverpool, England. Journalist. m. Robert John Norris, Lytham, Lancashire, 1 son. *Education:* BSc Honours Geology, Sheffield University; Fellow, Institute of Packaging. *Literary Appointments:* Journalist, Composites; News Editor, European Plastics News; Assistant Editor – Editor, Packaging Review. *Contributions to:* Packaging Review; Financial Times. *Address:* Packaging Review, Business Press International, Quadrant House, The Quadrant, Sutton, Surrey, England.

COWAN, Brian Thomas, b. 26 Feb. 1944, Greymouth, New Zealand. Freelance Journalist. m. Kathleen Mary Hall, 27 Jan. 1967, Christchurch, 1 son, 2 daughters. *Education:* New Zealand Certificate of Civil Engineering. *Appointments:* Assistant Editor, Revs Motorcycle News, Sydney, Australia, 1976; Technical Editor, Modern Motor Magazine, Sydney, 1978; Editor, Two Wheels Magazine, Sydney, Australia, 1981. *Contributor to:* Freelance feature and technical stories in motorcycling and motoring magazines, Australia and United Kingdom, 1972–. *Address:* 94 Foremans Road, Christchurch 4, New Zealand.

COWAN, Evelyn, b. 18 Jan. 1924, Glasgow, Scotland. Journalist; Writer. *Publications:* Spring Remembered, 1975; Portrait of Alice, 1977. *Contributor to:* Glasgow Herald; BBC, Scotland, England & Overseas; Scottish Television; Sunday Post; Scots Magazine; Jewish Voice, England; Jewish Echo, Scotland; Paisley Gazette Group, 11 papers; Story included in, A Scottish Childhood Anthology, 1985. *Honours:* Short Story Silver Cup Award, Glasgow Literary Society, 1968; All-Scotland Writers Award, Short Story Competition, 1970. *Memberships:* Scottish Branch, PEN; Scottish Association of Writers; President, Glasgow Writers Club, 1979–81; National Union Journalists, Freelance Scottish Branch. *Address:* 12 Rostan Road, Glasgow G43 2XF, Scotland.

COWAN, Henry Jacob, b. 21 Aug. 1919. Professor Emeritus of Architectural Science. *Education:* BSc, MSc, Manchester University, England; PhD, DEng, Sheffield University; M.Arch, Sydney University, Australia. *Publications include:* The Design of Reinforced Concrete, 1963, 5th ed, 1986; An Historical Outline of Architectural Science, 1966, 2nd ed, 1977; Architectural Structures, 1971, 4th ed, 1980; Dictionary of Architectural Science, 1973, 2nd ed, 1985; The Master Builders, 1977, 2nd ed, 1985 (Russian translation, 1982, also Science and Buildings, 1982); Building Science Laboratory Manual, 1978; Solar Energy Applications in the Design of Buildings, 1980; Structural Systems, 1981; Environmental Systems, 1983; Predictive Methods for the Energy Conserving Design of Buildings, 1983; Energy Conservation in the Design of Multi-storey Buildings, 1984; Encyclopedia of Building Technology, 1986. *Contributor to:* Various journals. *Honours:* Recipient, Chapman Medal, Institution of Engineers Australia, 1956; Honorary Fellowship, Royal Australian Institute of Architects, 1980; Officer of the Order of Australia, 1984. *Memberships:* Fellow, Royal Society of Arts; Institution of Structural Engineers; FIE. *Address:* 93 Kings Road, Vaucluse, NSW 2030, Australia.

COWEN, Zelman (Sir), b. 7 Oct. 1919, Melbourne, Australia. Provost of Oriel College, Oxford. m. Anna Wittner, 7 June 1945, Melbourne, 3 sons, 1 daughter. *Education:* BA 1939, LLB, University of Melbourne, 1941; LLM 1942, BCL, MA, 1947, DCL, Oxford University, UK, 1968; Queen's Counsel of Queensland Bar, 1971. *Literary Appointments:* Chairman, British Press Council, 1983. *Publications include:* Australia and the United States: Some Legal Comparisons, 1954; Federal jurisdiction in Australia, 1959, (with Leslie Zines) 2nd Edition, 1978; The British Commonwealth of Nations in a Changing World, 1964; Sir Isaac Isaacs, 1967; The Private Man, 1969; Individual Liberty and the Law, 1975. *Contributor to:* Various journals. *Honours include:* Knight of the Order of Australia, 1977; Knight Grand Cross of the Order of St Michael and St George 1977; Knight Grand Cross, Royal Victorian Order, 1980. *Memberships include:* Foreign Honorary Member of the American Academy of Arts and Sciences, 1965; FRSA,

1971; Fellow, Academy of Social Sciences in Australia, 1971. *Address:* Provost's Lodgings, Oriel College, Oxford OX1 4EW, England.

COWLEY, Malcolm, b. 24 Aug. 1898, Belsano, Pennsylvania, USA. Writer. m. Muriel Maurer, 18 June 1932, 1 son. *Education:* AB, Harvard University, 1920; Hon DLitt, LHD, Franklin & Marshall, Colby, Warwick, New Haven; DLitt, Monmouth College, 1978. *Literary Appointments:* Literary Consultant, The Viking Press, 1948–; Literary Editor, The New Republic, 1930–40. *Publications include:* Blue Juniata (poems), 1929; Exile's Return, 1934, revised edition, 1951; Black Cargoes (with D P Mannix), 1962; Think Back on Us, 1967; Blue Juniata; Collected Poems, 1968; A Many-Windowed House, 1970; A Second Flowering, 1973; And I Worked at the Writer's Trade, 1978; The Dream of the Golden Mountains, 1980; The Flower and the Leaf, 1985. Numerous translations and edited books. *Contributions to:* Various magazines and newspapers, etc. *Honours Include:* Senior Fellowship, National Endowment for the Arts, 1968; Who's Who in America Achievement Award, 1984; Bobst Medal for Literary Criticism, 1984. *Memberships:* National Institute of Arts and Letters (President, 1956–59 and 1962–65); American Academy of Arts and Letters (Chancellor, 1967–77). *Address:* Church Road, Sherman, CT 06784, USA.

COX, Charles Brian, b. 1928, Grimsby, England. Professor of English. *Education:* MA, MLitt, Pembroke College, Cambridge. *Publications:* The Free Spirit, 1963; Modern Poetry, with A E Dyson, 1963; The Practical Criticism of Poetry, 1965; Dylan Thomas, 1967; The Black Papers on Education, with A E Dyson, 1971; The Twentieth Century Mind, 1972; Joseph Conrad: The Modern Imagination, 1974; Every Common Sight, 1981; Two-Headed Monster, 1985. *Contributor to:* Times Education Supplement; Critical Quarterly. *Address:* 20 Park Gates Drive, Cheadle Hulme, Cheshire, England.

COX, Molly (Marie-Therese Henriette), b. 18 Oct. 1925, Istanbul. TV Producer, BBC Childrens TV. m. Terence Cox, 28 June 1947, Kensington, London, England, 2 sons. *Publications:* Fabulous Animals, with David Attenborough, 1975; The Creation, 1977; The Family of Abraham, 1977; Moses and the Laws of God, 1978; The Kings of Israel, 1978; Breakthrough, with John Craven, 1981. *Contributor to:* Guest Contributor to TV World, 1985. *Address:* 4 Berwick Cottages, Marlow, Buckinghamshire, England.

COZAR SIEVERT, Rafael de, b. 10 Apr. 1951, Tetouan, Spanish Morocco. Professor, Spanish Literature, University of Seville, Spain. *Education:* Doctor of Spanish Philology. *Literary Appointments:* President, Andalusian Autonomous Section, Colegial Asociation of Spanish Writers; Professor of Spanish Literature. *Publications in Several Anthologues Include:* Nueva Poesia 1: Cadiz, 1976; Qadish: Muestra de la joven poesia gaditana, 1980; Antologia de la joven poesia andaluza; etc. *Honours:* Guernica Prize finalist with unpublished novel, Espumas de la memoria, 1979; Special Mention, Elysée Prize, manuscript novel, Jubilo final, 1981; Finalist, Ricardo Molina Prize, Cordoba; Finalist, Rafael Montesinos Prize, Seville. Manuscript book of poems published, 1980; various critical editions. *Address:* Imaginero Castillo Lastrucci 7-3, 41002 Sevilla, Spain.

CRAIG, Frederick Walter Scott, b. 10 Dec. 1929, Glasgow, Scotland. Journalist; Author; Publisher. *Publications:* British Parliamentary Election Statistics, 1968, 1971; British Parliamentary Election Results 1832–1983, 5 volumes, 1969–84; British General Election Manifestos, 1970, 1975; Boundaries of Parliamentary Constituencies 1885–1972, 1972; The Parliaments of England from 1715 to 1847, 1973; Greater London Votes: 1 The Greater London Council 1964–70, 1971; Minor Parties at British Parliamentary Elections 1885–1974, 1975; The Most Gracious Speeches to Parliament 1900–1974, 1975; British

Electoral Facts, 1976, 1980'; Britain Votes, 1977, 1980, 1984; Europe Votes, with T T Mackie, 1980, 1985. *Contributor to:* Joint Editor, Local Government Companion; BBC; ITN. *Address:* 18 Lincoln Green, Chichester, West Sussex PO19 4DN, England.

CRAIG, Malcolm McDearmid, b. 1 July 1937, South Shields, County Durham, England. Publisher/Writer. m. Jill Christine Hampson, 31 Jan. 1965, London, 1 son, 2 daughters. *Education:* BSc Econ (Home), Dip Cam; Sloan Fellow, London Graduate School of Business. *Literary Appointments:* Editor, Stockmarket Confidential; Editor, Finance Confidential; Editor. Craig's Investment Letter. *Publications:* The Sterling Money Markets, 1975; Successful Investment, 1977; Investing to Survive the 80's, 1979, 80; Invisible Britain, 1981; Making Money Out of Gold, 1982; Making Money Out of Shares, 1983; Successful Investment Strategy, 1984. *Contributions to:* All UK national and leading provincial press, specialist investment and financial publications; BBC Radio; BBC TV. *Literary Agent:* Dasha Shankman, Ed Victor Literary Agency. *Address:* 15 Dukes Ride, Gerrards Cross, Buckinghamshire, England.

CRAIG, Mary Francis, b. 23 Feb. 1927, Pratt, Kansas, USA. Writer. *Publications:* 23 children's books including: Runaway Home, 1965; Backwards for Luck, 1967; Pornada, 1970; Topcat of Tam, 1972; The Seven Stone, 1972; A Season of Silence, 1975; The Search for Grissi, 1985; The Josie Gambit, forthcoming, Spring, 1986; Adult publications include: Gillian's Chain, 1983, published in Finnish, Danish and Swedish, paperback USA, 1985; The Third Blonde, 1985; The Chicagoans, 1983–86; numerous other mystery and suspense publications for adult readers; Historical novels include: Williamsburg Saga, 1983; Lyon's Pride; Pirate's Landing. Books for teens and young adults include: The Silent Witness, 1983; My Roommate is Missing, 1983; Jessica, 1984; The Wrong Side of Love, 1985; Marilee, 1985. *Honours include:* Award candidates, NYTIMES; Best Books of the Year; Junior Literary Guild; Georgia Children's Award, 1982–83; Iowa Children's Choice, 1983–84 (Mister Wolf and Me); Candidate for Mark Twain, 1983–84 (Happles and Cinnamunger); Junior Literary Guild Selection and New York Public Library Childrens' Books, 1985 (The Search for Grissi). *Memberships:* Past National Vice President and current National Director, Mystery Writers of America, Inc; Authors' Guild and Authors' League of America; Crime Writers of Great Britain; Book League of Great Britain; Society of Midland Authors; Society of Childrens' Book Writers; Childrens' Reading Round Table. *Literary Agents:* Juvenile works: McIntosh and Otis; Adult publications: The Roslyn Targ Agency. *Address:* MFC Limited, 301 Lake Hinsdale Drive, 112 Clarendon Hills, IL 60514, USA.

CRAMPTON, Ellen Brooks, b. 20 Dec. 1946, Ohio, USA. Editor. m. John Crampton, 25 July 1970, Southend, Essex, England, 2 sons. *Education:* BA Honours, English, Wittenburg University/University of Leeds. *Literary Appointments:* Editor, George Rainbird Limited, 1969–73; Administrator, British Association of Picture Libraries and Agencies, 1977–81. Editor: The Pirbic Organisation, 1981–84; Ingersoll Engineers Incorporated, 1984–. *Publications:* The Asian Highway, with Jack Jackson, 1979. *Contributions to:* Educational and technical journals mainly as collaborating ghostwriter; over 50 indexes for books on wide ranging subjects. *Membership:* Society of Indexers. *Address:* 27 Orchard Way, Bubbenhall, Coventry CV8 3JQ, England.

CRANDALL, Norma Rand, b. New York, USA. Book Reviewer/Biographer/ Essayist/Editorial Consultant. m. Wilson McCarty (deceased). *Education:* Passy Lycee, Paris, France; Barnard College, New York. *Literary Appointments:* Editorial Consultant to Harcourt Brace, 1939 and also to other New York Publishers and individual writers. *Publication:* Emily Bronte: A Psychological Portrait, USA 1977, UK 1979. *Contributions to:* Reviews and essays in The New Republic; The New Leader; The North American Review; The New York Times; Trace; The English

Digest; The Humanist; The Chicago Review; America; The 19th Century; The New Review; The American Book Collector etc. Poetry in Town and Country Review, Boulder, Colorado, USA. *Honours:* Illustrated Lecture about the Brontes, Pace University, Pleasantville, New York; The Barnard College Club of New York; The Central Presbyterian Church, New York City etc. *Memberships:* The Poetry Society of America, New York; The Bronte Society of England. *Address:* 44 East 63rd Street, New York, NY 10021, USA.

CRANE, Richard Arthur, b. 4 Dec. 1944, York. England. Playwright. *Education:* BA (Hons), Jesus College, Cambridge, England, 1966; MA, 1970. *Literary Appointments:* Fellow in Theatre, University of Bradford, England, 1972–74; Board of Directors, Edinburgh Festival Fringe Society, UK, 1973 onwards; Resident Dramatist, National Theatre, England, 1974–75; Fellow in Creative Writing, University of Leicester, England, 1976; Literary Manager, Royal Court Theatre, England, 1978–79; Association Director, Brighton Theatre, England, 1980 onwards. *Publications:* Thunder – A Play of the Brontes, 1976; Gunslinger, 1979, Records: Mutiny!, 1983; Tahiti, 1983; Welcome, 1984; Mutiny! Cast Album, 1985, TV Plays: Rottingdean, 1980; The Possessed, 1985. Radio plays: Gogol, 1979; Decent Things, 1984. Stage plays: The Tenant, 1971; Crippen, 1971; Decent Things, 1972; Bleak Midwinter, 1972; The Blood Stream, 1972; David King of the Jews, 1973; Thunder, 1973; Secrets, 1973; The Quest, 1974; Mean Time, 1975; Venus and Superkid, 1975; Clownmaker, 1975; Bloody Neighbours, 1975; Gunslinger, 1976; Nero and the Golden House, 1976; Satan's Ball, 1977; Gogol, 1978; Vanity, 1980; Brothers Karamazov, 1981; The Possessed, with Yuri Lyubimov, 1985; Mutiny!, 1985. *Honours:* Literary Awards: Edinburgh Festival Fringe First Awards: Thunder, 1973; The Quest, 1974; Clownmaker, 1975; Satan's Ball, 1977; Vanity, 1980; Thames TV Bursary Awards: Thunder, 1974; Secrets, 1974; Arts Council Annual Writers Bursary, 1979. *Literary Agent:* Margaret Ramsay Ltd. *Address:* c/o Margaret Ramsay Ltd, 14A Goodwins Court, St Martins Lane, London WC2N 4LL, England.

CRANE, Sylvia E, b. 23 Feb 1918, New York City, USA. Freelance Journalist; Historian. BA, Brooklyn College, 1938; MA, Columbia University, 1941. *Pubications:* Thomas Jefferson: Philosopher of the Enlightenment, La Revue Libérale, Spring 1957, Paris; White Silence: Horatio Greenough, Hiram Powers, Thomas Crawford, American Sculptors in 19th Century Italy, 1972. *Contributions to:* Journal of Aesthetics and Art Criticism; Le Monde Diplomatique; Astrolabio. *Memberships:* Organisation of American Historians; American Historical Association; Trustee, Institute of Current World Affairs; Harvard Club. *Address:* 438 Wendover Drive, Princeton, NJ 08540, USA.

CRANE, Teresa Louise, b. 10 June 1938, Hornchurch, Essex, England. Writer. m. Anthony Charles Crane, 8 Oct. 1960, Hornchurch, 1 son, 1 daughter. *Education:* Hornchurch Grammar School. *Publications:* Spider's Web, 1980; Molly O'Dowd, 1982; A Fragile Peace, 1984; The Rose Stone, 1985. *Contributor to:* Short Story Writer, numerous magazines, England and Abroad, including 'Woman'. *Literary Agent:* Carol Smith.

CRANOR, Phoebe Anne, b. 22 Apr. 1923, Bayfield, Colorado, USA. Housewife; Lecturer; Writer. m. John A Cranor, 26 Oct. 1946, Phoenix, Arizona, 1 son, 3 daughters. *Education:* BA, Arizona State University. *Publications:* Why Did God Let Grandpa Die?, 1976; Why Doesn't God do Something?, 1978; How am I supposed to Love Myself, 1979; Is Anybody Listening When I Pray?, 1980. *Contributor to:* Childrens' Activities and Highlights for Children; Discovery; Family Circle; Farm Journal; 8 Leaflets, published by Dove Publications. *Honour:* Letter in Farm Journal, won Best Letter Award. *Address:* 3444 County Road 10, Gunnison, CO 81230, USA.

CRAWFORD, John Richard, b. 21 Aug. 1932, Karuizawa, Japan. Professor. m. Sylvia Jean Peresenyi,

27 May, 1956, Charlotte, North Carolina, USA, 2 sons, 2 daughters. *Education:* BA, History & Political Science, King College, Bristol, Tennessee, 1953; BD (Now MDiv), Union Theological Seminary, Richmond, Virginia, 1956; PhD, History, University of Aberdeen, Scotland. *Publications:* Only By Thumb, 1964; A Christian and His Money, 1967; Protestant Missions in the Congo, 1878–1969, 1973; Dieu et Votre Argent, 1974. *Contributions to:* Various journals & magazines. 90 articles, chiefly numismatic, theological, historical, anthropological; many concerning Congo region of Africa. *Address:* Black Mountain, NC 28711, USA.

CRAWFORD, John Sherman, b. 24 Jan. 1928, Sunnyside, Washington, USA. Nature Author; Photojournalist; Wildlife Researcher. *Education:* BA, University of Washington, Seattle, 1954. *Publications:* At Home with the High Ones, Comparative Observations of North American Mountain Sheep and the Rocky Mountain Goat, 1974; Wolves, Bears and Bighorns, Wilderness Observations and experiences of a Professional Outdoorsman, 1980: Contributor of Photographs of Northern Wildlife to Nature Books, North America and Europe. *Contributor to:* Outdoor Life; Field & Stream; Sunset; Alaska Magazine; True; National Geographic; The American Hunter; Alaska Geographic; National Wildlife; American Rifleman; Seattle Times; Seattle Post-Intelligencer; etc. *Honours:* Photographic Work represented, Exhibition of The Athapaskan Peoples: Strangers of the North, National Museum of Canada and Royal Scottish Museum, 1974; Alberta Achievement Award for Services to Canadian Red Cross, 1978; Merit Award Citation, for, Wolves, Bears and Bighorns, Western Books Exhibition, 1981. *Address:* c/o Alaska Northwest Publishing Company, 130 Second Avenue South, Edmonds, WA 98020, USA.

CRAWFORD POOLE, Shona, b. 17 June 1943, England. Journalist. m. Partington, 21 Oct. 1972, London. *Literary Appointments:* Cookery Correspondent, 1979–, Travel Editor, 1982–, The Times. *Publications:* The Christmas Cookbook, 1979; The Ice Cream Book, 1979; The Yoghurt Cookbook, 1980; The New Times Cook Book, 1983. *Contributions to:* Various magazines. *Literary Agent:* Toby Eady. *Address:* 134 Arlington Road, London NW1 7HP, England.

CRAWLEY, Charles William, b. 1 Apr. 1899, London, England. Fellow of Trinity Hall, Cambridge; University Lecturer in History (retired). m. Kathleen Elizabeth Leahy, 2 July 1930, Chichester, Sussex, 4 sons, 1 daughter. *Education:* MA, Trinity College, Cambridge; Fellow, Trinity Hall, Cambridge, 1924–66; Honorary Fellow, Trinity Hall, 1971–. *Publications:* The Question of Greek Independence 1821–1833, 1930; Chapter in A Short History of Greece, 1965; Editor, The New Cambridge Modern History, Volume 9 (3 chapters by Editor), 1965. *Contributions to:* Professional journals. *Membership:* Royal Historical Society (Fellow and one-time member of Council). *Address:* 1 Madingley Road, Cambridge CB3 0EE, England.

CRESSWELL, Jasmine Rosemary, b. 14 Jan. 1941, Wales. Writer. m. Malcolm Candlish, 15 Apr. 1963, Christ Church, London, England. 1 son, 3 daughters. *Education:* BA, Melbourne University; BA Honours, Macquarie University; MA, Case Western Reserve University. *Publications:* About 21 novels including: The Abducted Heiress, 1976; Tarrisbroke Hall, 1977; Caroline, 1979; Tender Triumph, 1981; Under Cover of Night, 1984; Traitor's Heir, 1984. *Memberships:* Vice President, Colorado Authors League; Romantic Novelists Association; Romance Writers of America; Authors Guild of America. *Literary Agent:* Curtis Brown, New York. *Address:* c/o Maureen Walters, 10 Astor Place, New York, NY 10003, USA.

CREWS, Frederick Campbell, b. 20 Feb. 1933, Philadelphia, Pennsylvania, USA. Professor of English; Writer. *Education:* AB, Yale University, 1955; PhD, Princeton University, 1958. *Publications:* The Tragedy of Manners, 1957; E M Forster: The Perils of Humanism, 1962; The Pooh Perplex, 1963; The Sins of the Fathers,

1966; The Patch Commission, 1968; The Random House Handbook, 1974, 4th edition 1984; Out of My System, 1975; Co-author, The Borzoi Handbook for Writers, 1985. Editor: Red Badge of Courage (Crane), 1967; Great Short Works on Nathaniel Hawthorne, 1967; Starting Over, 1970; The Random House Reader, 1981. *Honours:* Fulbright Lecturer, Turin, Italy, 1961–62; several fellowships including Guggenheim, 1970–71; Essay Prize, National Endowment for Arts, 1968; Dorothy T Burstein Lecturer, UCLA, 1984; Distinguished Teaching Award, University of California, Berkeley, 1985; Frederick Ives Carpenter Visiting Professor, University of Chicago, 1985. *Memberships:* MLA; National Council Teachers of English. *Address:* 636 Vincente Avenue, Berkeley, CA 94707, USA.

CRIBB, Julian Hillary James, b. 28 Dec. 1950, Halton, England. Newspaper Editor. m. Maureen Dorothy Feerry, 25 July 1979, Dimboola, Australia, 1 son, 1 daughter. *Education:* BA, Classics, Western Australia University. *Appointments:* Chief, Australian Agricultural News Bureau, ACT; News Editor, National Farmer Newspaper; Editor, Australian Country; Editor; Sunday Independant; Editor, National Farmer. *Publications:* The Forgotten Country, 1982; Australian Agricultural Year Book 1985, 1985; *Contributor to:* Sydney Morning Herald; Inside Australia; Dairy Foods, etc. *Honours:* 12 Press Awards including: UN Association Bronze Peace Citation, 1979; Best Contribution to Rural Journalism, Western Australia, 1979, 1980, 1981, 1982, 1983; Dalgety Award, 1983. *Membership:* National Rural Press Club, 1979–81; Vice President, 1980, 1981. *Address:* 18 Brinsmead St, Pearce, ACT 2607, Australia.

CRIBBIN, John, b. 26 July 1931, Melbourne, Australia. Writer. m. Jan Brand, 19 May 1962, Birmingham, England, 2 sons, 1 daughter. *Publications:* The Killing Times: The Coniston Massacre, 1984; The Making of ANZACS, 1983. *Contributor to:* Australian Broadcasting Corporation, 1970–82. *Honours:* Walkley National Award for Australian Journalism, 1978, 1981. *Membership:* Australian Writers Guild. *Address:* 22 Lindsay Avenue, Murrumbeena, Melbourne 3163, Australia.

CRIPPS, Joyce Beaudette, b. 13 June 1923, Brunswick, Melbourne, Australia, Poet; Photographer. m. Charles John Cripps, 2 Dec. 1944, 2 sons. *Publications:* Magpie Bridge, 1981; Actinia, 1983; Getting Published, 1983; Celebration, Editor, 1984; Poetry Day Australia, Editor, 1985; Tatters of Hessian, 1985; Papers: Leonardo Da Vinci's Ingenious Door to the Mind, 1982; Poetry and Time, 1984; Australian Editor Samvadana, 1983–84; Mainichi Newspaper, etc; Founder/Organiser, Poetry Day Australia Festival & Competitions, 1982–85; etc. *Contributor to:* Numerous journals & magazines including: Australian & International Magazines; Poetry; Mainichi Tokyo; Flowers of the Great South Land; Indo Australian Flowers; India; World Poetry Australia; Phrophetic Voices; Peace Poets International; World Poetry Korea; etc. *Honours:* Life Fellow, Academy of Poets, 1983; Premio Internazional La Gloire Dimploma D'Onore Leonardo Da Vinci, Rome, 1982; Master of Contemporary Poetry – Princess of Poetry, 1984; Commitato Internazionali D'Onore Centro Studi Scambi, 1985; Fellow, World Literary Academy, 1985; Australian Regent for California University of Advanced Studies International, 1985; Silver Medal, 1st 500 IBC, England, 1985. *Memberships Include:* Fellowship, Australian Writers; PEN; Australian Society of Authors; Society of Women Writers, Australia; Henry Lawson & Poetry Lovers; Melbourne Poetry Society; LFIAP; FWLA; etc. *Address:* 3 Mill St, Aspendale 3195, Victoria, Australia.

CROBAUGH, Emma Adelia Delozier Bleckner, b. 24 Jan. 1903, Harriman, Tennessee, USA. Writer. m. (1) Edward Bleckner, SR (dec.), 1 son, (2) Clyde Julian Crobaugh (dec.). *Publications:* Over 1000 poems published in national and international magazines; Poems translated and published in many foreign languages. *Honours include:* Honorary D Litt, World Academy of Arts and Culture with the World Congress of Poets, 1984; Honorary American-African Poet Laureate; Winner of numerous awards from poetry societies and in competitions; Diploma and Medal, Centre Studi E Scambi Internationali. *Memberships include:* National League of American Pen Women; Poetry Society of America; United Poets Laureate International; Composers, Authors, Artists of America; American Poets Fellowship Society; Avalon World Arts Academy; International Academy of Poets, London; American Poetry League; International Platform Association; Association for Poetry Therapy. *Address:* Seagate of Highland 821-C, 3300 S Ocean Boulevard, Highland Beach, FL 33431, USA.

CROCKETT, H Dale, b. 17 Feb. 1933, Reevesville, Illinois, USA. Clergyman – Ecumenical; Pastoral Therapist; Institutional Chaplain. m. Ruth A Bays, 5 June 1953, Marion, Illinois, 3 sons, 1 daughter. *Education:* BA, Union University; M Div, Southeastern Baptist Theological Seminary; D Min, San Francisco Theological Seminary. *Publications:* Focus on Watergate. An Examination of a Moral Dilemma in the Light of Civil Religion, 1982. *Contributions to:* Intercom; Christian Community; The Pastor's Journal; The Secret Place; The Upper Room; The Capital Baptist. *Address:* Union Church, Berea College Post Office, Berea, KY 40404, USA.

CROFT, Julian Charles Basset, b. 31 May 1941, Merewether, New South Wales, Australia. University Lecturer, divorced, 1 son. *Education:* BA, University of New South Wales; MA, University of Newcastle, New South Wales. *Literary Appointments:* Lecturer, English, Fourah Bay College, University of Sierra Leone; Lecturer, English, University of New England, Armidale, New South Wales, Australia. *Publications:* T H Jones, 1976; Breakfasts in Shanghai, poems, 1984; Their Solitary Way, novel, 1985. *Membership:* Foundation Executive, Association for the Study of Australian Literature, 1977–85. *Address:* Department of English, University of New England, Armidale, NSW 2351, Australia.

CRONER, Helga, b. 8 May 1914, Germany. Publisher; Editor. m. Ulrich Croner, 15 Aug. 1938, London, England, 2 daughters. *Education:* BA; MA. *Literary Appointments:* Editor-in-Chief, Stimulus Books. *Publications include:* Editor or co-editor: Stepping Stones to Further Jewish-Christian Relations; Issues in the Jewish-Christian Dialogue; Biblical Studies, Meeting Ground of Jews & Christians; Christian Mission – Jewish Mission; More Stepping Stones to Jewish-Christian Relations. *Contributions to:* Emuna; Freiburger Rundbrief. *Address:* New York, USA.

CROOKER, Barbara, b. 21 Nov. 1945, Cold Spring, New York USA. Writer. m. Richard McMaster Crooker, 26 July 1975, Corning, New York, 1 son, 3 daughters. *Education:* BA, Douglass College, Rutgers University; MS, Elmira College. *Literary Appointment:* Creative Writing Teacher, Cedar Crest College, 1982–. *Publications:* Writing Home, 1983; Moving Poems (forthcoming). *Contributions to:* McCalls; Family Circle; Organic Gardening; The Poetry Review; West Branch, Blue Unicorn; Poets On; Yarrow; The South Dakota Review; The Plains Poetry Journal; The John O'Hara Journal; Calyx; Riversedge; Bloodroot; Connections; The Plainswoman; Taxi; Telephone; Chomo-Uri; Circus Maximus; The Lyric; Phoebus; Creeping Bent; Sunrust; Moving Out; The Creative Woman, etc. *Honours:* Prize Winner, William Carlos Williams Poetry Center, 1978; Finalist, The John O'Hara Journal Poetry Contest, 1981; Honorable Mention, Blue Unicorn Poetry Contest, 1983; Honorable Mention, Westmoreland Arts Festival, 1983; Pennsylvania Council on the Arts Fellowship in Literature, 1985. *Membership:* Poetry Society of America. *Address:* 28 Woodsbluff Run, Fogelsville, PA 18051, USA.

CROSS, Gillian Clare, b. 24 Dec. 1945, London, England. Writer. m. Martin Francis Cross, 10 May 1967,

Oxford, 2 sons, 2 daughters. *Education:* BA (Hons), English Language and Literature, Somerville College, Oxford, 1969; D Phil, University of Sussex, 1973. *Publications:* The Runaway, 1979; The Iron Way, 1979; Revolt at Ratcliffe's Rags, 1980; Save Our School, 1981; A Whisper of Lace, 1981; The Demon Headmaster, 1982; The Dark Behind the Curtain, 1982; The Mintyglo Kid, 1983; Born of the Sun, 1983; On The Edge, 1984; The Prime Minister's Brain, 1985. *Contributions to:* The Times Literary Supplement (Reviewer); British Book News (Reviewer); Articles in, Children's Literature in Education, 1976, 79. *Honour:* Highly Commended for the Carnegie Medal 1982 for, The Dark Behind the Curtain. *Membership:* The Society of Authors. *Address:* 41 Essex Road, Gravesend, Kent DA11 0SL, England.

CROSSLEY-HOLLAND, Kevin John William, b. 7 Feb. 1941, Buckinghamshire, England. Writer. m. Gillian, 1 daughter; 2 sons by previous marriage. *Education:* Gregory Fellow, Poetry, University of Leeds, 1969–71; BA, Honours, Oxon. *Appointments:* Editorial Director, Victor Gollancz, Publishers, 1972–77; Arts Council Fellow, Writing, Winchester School of Art, 1983, 1984. *Publications:* The Rain-Giver, 1972; The Dream House, 1976; Time's Oriel, 1983; Waterslein, 1986, all poetry; The Norse Myths, 1981; Folk Tales of the British Islands, 1985; Editor, The Oxford Book of Travel Verse, 1986; Childrens Books: Regran Children, 1966; The Dead Moon, 1982; Brownie, 1982; Axe-Age, Wolf-Age, 1985; Translator, The Anglo-Saxon World, 1982. *Contributor to:* The Guardian; Sunday Times; Radio Times; Times Educational Supplement; etc. *Honour:* Arts Council Award for Best Book for Young Children, 1968. *Agent:* Deborah Rogers, London. *Address:* c/o Deborah Rogers, Literary Agency, 49 Blenheim Crescent, London W11, England.

CROUCH, Annette S, b. 22 Apr. 1957, Oakland, California, USA. Writer, Editor. Married, 1 son, 2 daughters. *Education:* Graduate, Writers Digest Fiction Course, 1983. *Literary Appointments:* President Founder, Wallowa County Writers, 1982–83, Enterprise, Oregon. *Major Publication:* More Damnations, 1985. *Contributor to:* Various fiction and poetry periodicals & anthologies. *Honours:* Honorable Mention, Special Poetry Contest, World of Poetry Press 1983. *Memberships:* National Writers Club; Science Fiction & Fantasy Workshop; Planetary Society; Horror-Occult Writers League; Small Press Writers & Artists Organisation; North Shore Womens Writers Association. *Address:* PO Box 5099, Lancaster, CA 93539, USA.

CROWE, Frederick Ernest, b. 5 July 1915, Canada. Professor of Theology. *Education:* BSc, University of New Brunswick, Canada, 1934; BA, Loyola College, University of Montreal, 1943; STD, Gregorian University, Rome, Italy, 1953. *Literary Appointments:* Professor, Regis College, Toronto, Canada, 1953–80, Emeritus, 1980–; Visiting Professor, Gregorian University, Rome, 1964, 1984. *Major Publications:* Spirit of Inquiry (editor), 1964; A Time of Change, 1967; Escatologia e missione terrena in Gesù di Nazareth, 1976; Theology of the Christian Word, 1978; The Lonergan Enterprise, 1980. *Contributor to:* Numerous Theological journals. *Honours:* Honorary D Litt, St Mary's University, Halifax, Nova Scotia, 1971; John Courtney Murray Award for Excellence in Theology, 1977; Honorary DD, Trinity College, Toronto, 1977; Honorary LLD, St Thomas University, Fredericton, 1982. *Memberships:* Canadian Theological Society, President 1974–75, Honorary Member, 1983–; Catholic Theological Society of America; American Catholic Philosophical Association; Jesuit Philosophical Association. *Address:* Regis College, 15 St Mary Street, Toronto M4Y 2R5, Canada.

CROZET, Charlotte, b. St Etienne, France. Novelist. m. Stefan Crozet, 1 son, 1 daughter. *Publications:* Les Petites Metamorphoses, 1957; le men piege, 1967; Les amours infantiles, 1967; Girltrap, 1968; Marianne ou les autres, 1972; Voie Privee, 1978; La Petite Fille a l'escarpolette, 1984. *Contributions to:* Diamanche a Navogne, short story in Le Mercure de France; Loin de Glasgow, short story in La Nouvelle Revue Francaise. *Memberships:* Societe des Gens de Lettre de France; Association des Amis du Nouveau Commerce. *Address:* Flat 7, 23 Compayne Gardens, London NW6 3DE, England.

CROZIER, Lorna Jean, b. 24 May 1948, Swift Current, Saskatchewan, Canada. Writer/Teacher. *Education:* BA, Hons, 1969, Professional A Teaching Certificate, 1970, University of Saskatchewan; MA, University of Alberta, 1980. *Literary Appointments:* Creative Writing Teacher, Saskatchewan Summer School of the Arts, 1975–82; Writer-in-Residence, Cypress Hills Community College, Swifts Current, Saskatchewan, Canada, 1980–81; Writer-in-Residence, Regina Rublic Library, Regina, Saskatchewan, Canada, 1984–85. *Publications:* Inside Is The Sky, 1976; Crows Black Joy; Humans and Other Beasts, 1980; No Longer Two People (with Patrick Lane Turnstone); The Weather, 1983; The Garden Going On Without Us, 1985. *Contributions to:* Ariel; Athanos; Event; Grain; Saturday Night; South Dakota Review; Prism International; The Fiddlehead; Canadian Forum; Prairie Fire; The Malahat Review; Moosehead Review; Boundary II; Fireweed; A Room of One's Own; Branching Out; Women and Words; Canadian Literature; Poetry Canada Review; Northern Journey; CVII; Waves; New Quarterly. *Honours:* University of Alberta Creative Writing Scholarship, 1978–79; Department of Culture and Youth Poetry Manuscript Award; Saskatchewan Writers' Guild Poetry Manuscript Award, 1983. *Memberships:* Saskatchewan Writers' Guild, Vice-President, President of Colony Committee; The League of Canadian Poets, Saskatchewan Representative, Chairman of Membership Committee. *Address:* 2265 Garnet Street, Regina, Saskatchewan, Canada S4T 3A1.

CRUICKSHANK, Charles Greig, b. 10 June 1914. Author. m. Maire Kissane, 1943, 3 sons. *Education:* Aberdeen University; Hertford College, Oxford; Edinburgh University; MA; DPhil; FR Hist S *Publications:* Elizabeth's Army, 1966; Army Royal, 1969; The English Occupation of Tournai, 1971; A Guide to the Sources of British Military History, co-author, 1971; The German Occupation of the Channel Islands, official history, 1975; Greece 1940–41, 1976; The V-Mann Papers, 1976; The Tang Murders, 1976; The Fourth Arm: psychological warfare 1938–45, 1977; The Ebony Version, 1978; The Deceivers, 1978; Deception in World War II, 1979; Kew for Murder, 1979; SOE in the Far East, official history, 1983; SOE in Scandinavia, official history, 1986; Scotch Murder, 1985. *Contributor to:* English Historical Review; Army Quarterly; History Today; Punch; War Monthly; History of Parliament; Dictionary of National Biography. *Address:* 15 McKay Road, Wimbledon Common, SW20 OHT, England.

CRUSSELL, Leah Ann, b. 22 Jan. 1960, Junction City, Kansas, USA. Editor. m. Donald Lee Crussell, 17 Dec. 1982, Manhattan, Kansas. *Education:* BS, Summa Cum Laude, Manhattan Christian College, 1982; Journalism and Mass Communications, Kansas State University, 1982. *Literary Appointments:* News and Information Officer, Manhattan Christian College, Manhattan, Kansas, 1978–80; Editor, Dimensions Magazine, Kansas State University, 1982; Editor, with special responsibility for Seek and Devotion magazines, Standard Publishing Company, Cincinnati, Ohio, 1982–85. *Publication:* A Man's Ministry, co-author, 1982. *Contributions to:* The Manhattan Mercury, 1981. *Honours:* Outstanding Young Woman of America, 1984; Delta Epsilon Chi, 1982; Fred M Parris Memorial Journalism Scholarship, 1982; National Dean's List, 1979, 80. *Memberships:* Past Chapter Treasurer, Women in Communications Incorporated. *Address:* 704 Mountain Road, Joppa, MD 21085, USA.

CUA, Antonio S, b. 23 July 1932, Manila, Philippines. Professor. m. Shoke-Hwee Khaw, 11 June 1956, Oakland, California, USA, 1 daughter. *Education:* BA, Far Eastern University, 1952; MA, 1954, PhD, 1958, University of California, Berkeley. *Publications:* Reason and Virtue: A Study in the Ethics of Richard Price, 1966; Dimensions of Moral Creativity: Paradigms, Principles & Ideals, 1978; The Unity of Knowledge and Action: A Study in Wang Yang-Ming's Moral Psychology, 1982; Ethical Argumentation: A Study in Hsun Tzu's Moral Epistemology, 1985. *Contributor to:* Ethics; American Philosophical Quarterly; International Philosophical Quarterly; Philosophy East and West; Philosophy and Phenomenological Research; Journal of Chinese Philosophy; Philosophical Inquiry; etc. *Honours:* Summer Faculty Fellow, State University of New York, 1966, 1967; Council on Philosophical Studies, 1967; Fellow, Woodrow Wilson Centre for International Scholars, 1982. *Memberships:* Society for Asian and Comparative Philosophy, President 1978–79; International Society for Chinese Philosophy, President, 1984–86; American Philosophical Association; Association for Asian Studies. *Address:* School of Philosophy, Catholic University of America, Washington, DC 20064, USA.

CULLEN, Lee Stowell, b. 31 July 1922, Massachusetts, USA. Senior Fiction Editor. *Contributions to:* over 200 fiction stories; photo-caption features and articles for Ranger Rick's Nature Magazine. *Address:* Ranger Rick Magazine, 8925 Leesburg Pike, Vienna, VA 22180, USA.

CUMMING, Patricia Arens, b. 7 Sep. 1932, New York City, New York, USA. Poet; Associate Professor of Humanities. *Education:* BA, Radcliffe College, Cambridge, Massachusetts, 1954; MA, Middlebury Graduate School of French in France, 1956. *Publications:* Afterwards, Poems, 1974; Letter from an Outlying Province, poems, 1976; Free Writing!, with Joseph Brown and others, 1977. *Contributions to:* Kayak; Shenandoah; Colorado Quarterly, and others. *Honours include:* Danforth Faculty Fellowship, 1975. *Memberships include:* Authors Guild; Poets, Playwrights, Editors, Essayists and Novelists. *Address:* Box 251, Adamsville, RI 02801, USA.

CUMMING, Peter, b. 23 Mar. 1951, Ontario, Canada. Writer; Teacher. m. (Mary) Shelleen Nelson, 14 Oct. 1970, 2 sons. *Education:* BA, Wilfrid Laurier University; Diploma, Education, McGill University, Montreal. *Appointments:* Resident Artist, Drama, Wilfrid Laurier University, 1972–73; Writer-in-Community, Truro, Nova Scotia, Autumn, 1983. *Publications:* Snowdreams, play, 1982; Ti-Jean, Children's play, 1983; A Horse Called Farmer, Children's book, 1984. *Contributor to:* Contributing Editor, Quill & Quire, 1982–84; various articles in journals and magazines. *Honours:* 1st Prizes, 1980, 1981, Writers' Federation of Nova Scotia Literary Competition; Winner, Canada-wide Playwriting Competition, Toronto Board of Education, 1981. *Memberships:* Writers' Federation of Nova Scotia (Executive); Dramatists' Co-op of Nova Scotia; Playwrights Union of Canada; Canadian Society of Children's Authors, Illustrators, and Performers. *Address:* General Delivery, Igloolik, Northwest Territories, Canada XOA 0L0.

CUMMING, William Patterson, b. 31 Oct. 1900, Nagoya, Japan. Professor; Author. *Education:* AB, Davidson College, USA, 1921; MA, 1922, PhD, 1925, Princeton University; DLitt, University of North Carolina at Chapel Hill, 1982. *Publications include:* Editor: The Revelations of St Birgitta, 1929; The Southeast in Early Maps, 1958; 2nd edition 1962; North Carolina in Early Maps, 1966; The Discovery of North America, (with R A Skelton, D B Quinn), 1971; The Exploration of North America (with S Hillier, D B Quinn, G Williams) 1974; British Maps of Colonial America 1974; The Fate of a Nation: The American Revolution through Contemporary Eyes, (with H Rankin), 1975. *Contributor to:* Various journals. *Honours include:* Lecturer and Fellow, Newberry Library, 1969, 1970. *Memberships include:* MLA; AAUP; Phi Beta Kappa. *Address:* 313 Woodland Street, Davidson, NC 28036, USA.

CUMMING-BRUCE, Nicholas, b. 22 June 1949, Zanzibar. Journalist. *Education:* BA, History, Exeter University; MSc, Politics, London School of Oriental & African Studies. *Contributor to:* The Guardian; The Economist; Euromoney. *Address:* 31 Moorhouse Road, London W2, England.

CUMMINGS, Richard, b. 23 Mar. 1938, New York, USA. Writer. m. Mary Hildreth Johnson, 3 Aug. 1965, New York, 2 sons. *Education:* AB, Princeton University; M Litt (Cantab); JD, Columbia University. *Literary Appointments:* Fellow, Princeton Inn College, Princeton; Writer-in-Residence, Southampton College; Fellow, New York Council for Humanities; Fellow, Albert & Bessie Warker Fund. *Publications:* Proposition 14, 1981; The Pied Piper, 1985. *Contributions to:* New York Times; Newsday; East Hampton Star; Empire State Report, etc. *Honours:* Buchanan Prize for Politics, Princeton, 1959; Kent Scholar, Columbia, 1962; Playwrights Unit Award, 1971. *Memberships:* American Society of Journalists and Authors; Overseas Press Club; Authors Guild. *Literary Agent:* Timothy Seldes, Russel and Volkening. *Address:* Box 349, Bridgehampton, NY 11932, USA.

CUMMINS, Walter (Merrill), b. 6 Feb. 1936, Long Branch, New Jersey, USA. Professor of English, Fairleigh Dickinson University. m. (1), 2 daughters, (2) Alison Cunningham, 14 Feb. 1981. *Education:* BA, Rutgers University; MA, MFA, PhD, University of Iowa. *Literary Appointments:* Associate Editor, 1979, Editor-in-Chief, 1982. The Literary Review. *Publications:* A Stranger to the Deed, novel, 1968; Into Temptation, novel, 1968; Witness, stories, 1975; Where we Live, stories, 1983. *Contributions to:* Stories: Florida Review; Kansas Quarterly; West Branch; Sou' Wester; Connecticut Quarterly; The Smith; St Andrew's Review; Wisconsin Review; Aspect; and others. *Honours:* Fiction Writing Fellowship for 1982–83 from New Jersey State Council on the Arts. *Address:* 98 Brandywyne Drive, Florham Park, NJ 07932, USA.

CUNHA CAMPOS, Maria Consuelo, b. 24 May 1947, Brazil. Writer/Teacher. *Education:* Master Brazilian Literature, PhD, Brazilian Literature, Pontifical Catholic University, Rio de Janeiro. *Literary Appointments:* 6th Brazilian Appointments of Criticism and Theory of Litterature, 1982; 4th National Appointment of Reading, Campinas SP, 1984; 17th Brazilian Appointments of Litterature and Language, 1985. *Publications:* About the Brazilian Short Story, essay, 1977; Mineiridade poetry, 1980. *Contributions to:* Nelida Pinon's, Republic of the Dreams (a study of the Galeguidade); Colonels and 'Jaguncos' in Autean Dourado's Fiction. *Honours:* Fernando Chinaglia's Prize for Essay, 1973; Brasilia's Prize for Essay, 1976; Fernando Chinaglia's Prize for short story book, 1982; Brasilia's Prize for Poetry, 1982. *Literary Agent:* Carmen Balcells – R Joao Lira. *Address:* 98, Conselheiro Lafayette 601, Rio de Janeiro, 22081 Brazil.

CUNLIFFE, Barrington Windsor, b. 10 Dec. 1939, Portsmouth, England. University Teacher. *Education:* BA, University of Cambridge, 1961; MA ibid 1963; PhD, 1966; D Litt, 1977. *Publications include:* Roman Bath Discovered, 1971; Fishbourne: A Roman Palace and its Garden, 1971; The Cradle of England, 1972; The Making of the English, 1973; Iron Age Communities in Britain, 1974; The Regni, 1974; Rome and the Barbarians, 1975; Hengistbury Head, 1978; Rome and Her Empire, 1978; The Celtic World, 1979; Julius Caesar: The Battle for Gaul, 1980, (2nd Ed 1986); Heywood Summers Wessex, 1985. *Contributions to:* Various journals etc. *Memberships:* FSA, 1964; Fellow, British Academy, 1979. *Literary Agent:* Curtis Brown (Acad) Ltd. *Address:* 31 Polstead Road, Oxford, England.

CUNLIFFE, Marcus Falkner, b. 5 July 1922, Rochdale, England. University Professor. *Education:* BA, MA, BLitt, Oriel College, Oxford University; Commonwealth Fellow, Yale University, USA. *Publications:* The Literature of the United States, 1954,

86; George Washington, Man and Monument, 1958, 82; Soldiers and Civilians: The Martial Spirit in America, 1968; American Presidents and the Presidency, 1972, 3rd editon, 1986; Chattel Slavery and Wage Slavery, 1979. *Contributions to:* Encounter; Guardian; Journal of American Studies; New Society; New Statesman; New York Review of Books; Washington Post. *Honours:* Honorary DLitt, New England College, 1979. *Memberships:* Society of American Historians; Fellow, Royal Historical Society. *Address:* George Washington University, 2110 G Street North West, Washington, DC 20052, USA.

CUNNINGHAM, Chet, b. 12 Dec. 1928, Shelby, Nebraska, USA. Freelance Writer, Novels, Screen Plays. m. Rose Marie Wilhoit, 18 Jan. 1953, Forest Grove, 2 sons, 1 daughter. *Education:* BA, Pacific University; BS, Columbia University. *Publications include:* New Mexico Sisters; Motor City Mayhem; Salt Lake Lady; Remember the Alamo; Inca Gold Hijack; Man in Two Camps; Arizona Gunfire; Gold Train; Blazing Blackout; Baja Bike; This Splendid Land; Rainbow Saga; Beloved Rebel; The Deadly Connection; The Power & The Prize; The Gold and the Glory; Bloody Boston; Dead Start Scramble; Northwest Contract; Bloody Gold; Sendai Purple; The Chicom Affair; Hijacking Manhattan; Blood on the Strip; Die of Gold; Fatal Friday; Demons of Highpoint House; Gold Wagon; Moscow at High Noon; Night of the Avengers; Killer's Range; Bushwhackers at The Circle K; etc. *Contributor to:* Hundreds of journals and magazines. *Membership:* San Diego Writers' Workshop. *Literary Agent:* Ashley Darlington Grayson. *Address:* 8431 Beaver Lake Drive, San Diego, CA 92119, USA.

CUNNINGHAM, Clifford Arnold Joseph, b. 31 Oct. 1955, Toronto, Canada. Astronomer. *Education:* BSc. University of Waterloo, Canada, 1976. *Major Publications:* Asteroids: The Next Frontier, 1986, Willmann-Bell Inc, Richmond, Virginia. *Contributor to:* The Minor Planet Bulletin; Journal of the Royal Astronomical Society of Canada, and others; Spaceflight; Geos; some 20 scientific papers and features in newspapers. *Honour:* Fellow, British Interplanetary Society, 1984. *Literary Agent:* Perry Remaklus, Willmann-Bell Inc. *Address:* 250 Frederick Street, Kitchener, Ontario, Canada, N2H 2N1.

CURL, James Stevens, b. 26 Mar. 1937, Belfast, Northern Ireland. Architect; Urbanist. m. Eileen Elizabeth Blackstock, 1 Jan. 1960, Belfast, 2 daughters. *Education:* PhD, London; Dipl Arch, Oxford; Dip T P, Oxford; RIBA; MRTPI; ARIAS; FSA; FSA Scot. *Publications:* European Cities and Society, 1970; The Victorian Celebration of Death, 1972; City of London Pubs, with T M Richards; Victorian Architecture: It's Practical Aspects, 1973; The Erosion of Oxford, 1977; English Architecture: An Illustrated Glossary, 1977; Mausolea in Ulster, 1978; Moneymore and Draperstown: The Architecture and Planning of the Estates of the Drapers' Company in Ulster, 1979; A Celebration of Death, 1980; Classical Churches in Ulster, 1980; The History, Architecture and Planning of the Fishmongers' Company in Ulster, 1981; The Egyptian Revival, 1982; The Life and Work of Henry Roberts 1803–1976 Architect, 1983; The Londonderry Plantation 1609–1914, 1986. *Contributor to:* Country Life; Journal of Royal Society of Arts; RIBA Journal; Journal of the RTPI; Progressive Architecture; Bauwelt; Oxford Mail; Journal of Garden History; etc. Awards: British Academy Research Awards, 1982, 1983; Research Grants, Society of Antiquaries of London, 1980, 1981. *Literary Agent:* A D Peters & Co. *Address:* c/o Bank of Scotland, PO Box 9, 110 Queen Street, Glasgow G1 3BY, Scotland.

CURNOW, Thomas Allen Monro, b. 17 June 1911, Timaru, New Zealand. Professor; Author. m. (1) Elizabeth J LeCren, Christchurch, 1936 (2) Jenifer Mary Tole, Auckland, 1965, 2 sons, 1 daughter. *Education:* BA, University of New Zealand, Canterbury & Auckland, 1933; St John's College of Theology, Auckland, 1931–33; LittD, University of Auckland, 1966. *Literary*

Appointments include: Reporter, Sub-editor, The Press, Christchurch, 1936–48; News Chronicle, London, England, 1949; Lecturer, Senior Lecturer in England, 1951–67; Associate Professor, University of Auckland, 1968–76. *Major publications:* Valley of Decision, 1933; Three Poems, 1935; Enemies, 1937; Not in Narrow Seas, 1939; Island & Time, 1941; Sailing or Drowning, 1943; Jack Without Magic, 1946; At Dead Low Water & Sonnets, 1949; Poems 1947–57, 1957; A Small Room with Large Windows, 1962; Trees, Effigies, Moving Objects, 1972; An Abominable Temper, 1973; Collected Poems, 1933–73, 1974; An Incorrigible Music, 1979; You will know when you get there, 1982; Selected Poems, 1982; The Loop in Lone Kauri Road, 1986; Plays: The Axe, The Overseas Expert, The Duke's Miracle (all in Four Plays), 1972; (editor) The Penguin Book of New Zealand Verse, 1960; A Book of New Zealand Verse, 1945. *Contributor to:* Penguin New Writing; Poetry Chicago; Times Literary Supplement; London Magazine; Encounter; PN Review; The Bulletin Literary Supplement (Sydney); The Age Monthly Review; Islands; Landfall. *Honours:* New Zealand Book Award for Poetry, 1957, 1972, 1974, 1979, 1982; Honorary Degree Litt D, University of Canterbury, 1975; Katherine Mansfield Memorial Fellowship, 1983. Various poetry readings & lectureships, USA & Canada. *Literary Agent:* Curtis Brown (Australia) Pty. *Address:* 62 Tohunga Crescent, Parnell, Auckland 1, New Zealand.

CURRAN, Colleen, b. 23 Aug. 1954, Montreal, Canada. Playwright. *Education:* BA, Hons, English, Loyola College, Concordia University, Montreal, 1976; Teaching Certificate, McGill College, Montreal, 1981. *Literary Appointment:* Playwright-in-Residence, Centaur Theatre, Montreal, 1984–85. *Publications:* Major Plays produced: El Clavadista, one act, Mayor's Council on the Arts, Burlington, Vermont, USA, 1982; Another Labor Day, one act, Montreal, 1983; Cake-Walk, comedy Blyth Festival, 1984; Nuclear Hollywood, performance piece-play, Playwrights' Workshop, Montreal, 1985; Moose County, comedy Blyth Festival, 1985. Maisonneuve, drama series for CBC Radio, 1984; Uluru, drama (play) for CBC Radio. *Contributor to:* Book Reviewer, The Gazette (Montreal) 1985–; Theatre writer, Montreal Review and Montreal Calendar; Writer, Loyola News, 1972–76. *Honours:* Honourable Mention for, Another Labor Day, Ottawa Little Theatre Playwrighting Competition, 1982; Dorothy White Playwrighting Award for, Amelia Earhart Was Not a Spy, Ottawa Little Theatre Playwrighting Competition, 1983; Best New Play, Another Labor Day, Quebec Drama Festival, 1984. *Membership:* Board Member, Playwrights Workshop, Montreal. *Address:* 148, Abbott Avenue, Montreal, Quebec, Canada H3Z 2J9.

CURRIE, Robert Duncan Mondy, b. 21 Sep. 1937, Lloydminster, Saskatchewan, Canada. High School English Teacher. m. Gwen Grieve 18 Aug. 1962, Moose Jaw, Saskatchewan, Canada, 1 son, 1 daughter. *Education:* BSP, 1961, BA, 1964, Honours English 1965, BEd 1966, University of Saskatchewan. *Literary Appointments:* Instructor in Creative Writing, Saskatchewan Summer School of the Arts, 1972–75. *Major Publications:* Sawdust & Dirt (poems), 1973; The Halls of Elsinore (poems), 1973; Moving Out (poems), 1975; Diving into Fire (poems), 1977; Yarrow (poems), 1980; Night Games (short stories), 1983. *Contributor to:* Canadian Forum; Fiddlehead; Nebula; Poetry Canada Review; Queen's Quarterly; Repository; and others. *Honours:* Ohio State Award for Radio Drama, 1977; 3rd Prize for Poetry, CBC national Literary Competition, 1980; Founders Award, Saskatchewan Writers Guild, 1984. *Memberships:* Saskatchewan Writers Guild, President 1973–74; League of Canadian Poets. *Address:* Moose Jaw, Saskatchewan, Canada.

CURRIE, Robert Frank, b. 26 Apr. 1918, London, England. Journalist. *Education:* National Certificate 1936, Higher National Certificate 1938, Engineering, City and Guilds. *Literary Appointments:* Assistant Editor, The TT Special, 1952–56; Midland Editor, The Motor Cycle, 1956–80; Editor, The Classic Motor Cycle, 1981–. *Publications:* The Art of Moto-Cross, 1960; Glory of the Manx TT, 1964; Motor Cycling in the 1930's, 1981; Great British Motor Cycles of the '50's, 1981; Great British Motor Cycles of the '60's, 1981; British Classics, The Final Years, 1984. *Contributions to:* Numerous including: Convoy; Exeter Echo; Worcester Evening News; Birmingham Mail; BBC Overseas Service; BRMB Radio; Radio West Midlands. *Address:* The Classic Motor Cycle, 18 Newtown Shopping Centre, Birmingham B19 2SB, England.

CURRY, Richard Orr, b. 26 Jan. 1931, White Sulphur, Springs, West Virginia, USA. Professor. *Education:* BA, 1952, MA, 1956, Marshall University; PhD, University of Pennsylvania, 1961. *Publications:* A House Divided, 1964; Conspiracy; Fear of Subversion in American History, 1972; Slavery in America, 1972; The Shaping of America, 1972; The Abolitionists, 1973; etc. *Contributor to:* Journal American History; American Historical Review; Civil War History; Journal of Negro History; Reviews in, American History; Mid America; Journal Southern History; Journal of the Early Republic; Canadian Review of American Studies. *Honours include:* National Endowment for Humanities, 1967; Award of Merit, 1971; Fulbright Lecturer, New Zealand, 1981. *Address:* Dept of History, University of Connecticut, Storrs, CT 06268, USA.

CURTIS, James Richard, b. 16 Nov. 1953, Los Angeles, California, USA. Writer. m. Debra R Reed, 4 June, 1978, Santa Ana, California. *Education:* AA, Fullerton College, 1974; BA, California State University, Fullerton, 1979. *Publications:* James Whale, 1982; Between Flops, 1982. *Contribution to:* American Film. *Literary Agent:* Davis S Hull, Peter Lampack Agency, New York. *Address:* 1051–C North Bradford Avenue, Placentia, CA 92670, USA.

CURTIS, John, b. 14 July 1937, Walton, Surrey, England. Management Consultant. m. Jane Margaret McCall-Smith, 15 Jan. 1966, Stradishall, Suffolk, 1 son, 1 daughter. *Education:* Qualified Chartered Accountant. *Literary Appointments:* Managing Editor, Career Accountant. *Publications:* Money Matters for Managers, 1975; Cost Effective Recruitment, 1976; Communicating for Results, 1979; IPM Guide to Cost Effective Recruitment, 1984; Bluffer's Guide to Management, 1985. *Contributions to:* Numerous publications on accounting, personel, medical, motoring and management. *Membership:* Society of Authors. *Address:* 31 Longmoore Street, London SW1V 1JQ, England.

CURTIS, Tony, b. 26 Dec. 1946, Carmarthen, Wales. College Teacher. *Education:* BA, University College, Swansea, 1968; MFA, Goddard College, Vermont, USA, 1980. *Publications:* Album, 1974; Preparations, 1980; The Art of Seamus Heaney, Editor; Letting Go, 1983; Dannie Abse, 1985; Wales the Imagined Nation, Editor, 1986; Selected Poems 1970–1986, 1986; Poems – Selected & New, 1986. *Contributor to:* The New Yorker; The Listener; Observer; Mississippi Valley Review; South Dakota Review; Kenyan Review; Stand; etc. *Honours:* Eric Gregory Award, 1972; Young Poets Prize, Welsh Arts Council, 1974; The Stroud Festival International Poetry Prize, 1980; Winner, National Poetry Competition, 1984; Short-listed for the 1985 Arvon/Observer Prize. *Memberships:* Chairman, Welsh Academy; Executive Member, Yr Academi Gymreig, 1976–. *Address:* Pentwyn, 55 Colcot Road, Barry CF6 8BQ, Wales.

CUSHMAN, Joseph David, b. 1 June 1925, Titusville, Florida, USA. Professor, History. m. Mary Susan Livingstone, 16 July 1955, Detroit, 2 sons. *Education:* BA, University of the South, 1949; MA, 1958;, PhD, 1962, Florida State University. *Publications:* A Goodly Heritage: The Episcopal Church in Florida, 1965; Through Some Eventful Years, by Susan Bradford Eppes, Editor, 1968; The Sound of Bells: The Episcopal Church in South Florida, 1976. *Contributor to:* Historical Magazine of the Protestant Episcopal Church; Florida Historical Quarterly;

Sewanee Review; etc. *Honours:* Writing Grants, Diocese of South Florida, 1965, Florida State University, 1966; Chairman, History, University of the South, 1978; Francis S Hoghteling Professor of American History, 1980; Trustee, University of the South, 1965–69, 1981–84. *Memberships:* Florida, Southern, American Historical Associations; Tallahassee Historical Society, President, 1964. *Address:* c/o History Dept, University of the South, Sewanee, TN 37375, USA.

CUTRUFELLI, Maria Rosa, b. 26 Jan. 1946, Messina, Italy. Journalist. *Education:* Degree, Literature, University Bologna. *Publications:* L'Invenzione Della Donna, 1974; Disoccupata Con Onore, 1975; Operaie Senza Fabbrica, 1977; Donna Perche Piangi? 1983; Economia E Politica Dei Sentimenti, 1980; Il Cliente-Inchiesta Sulla Prostitulione, 1981; Translated into French, German, Portuguese, English. *Contributor to:* Editorial Staff, Noi Donne; Contributor to various journals and newspapers. *Address:* Via Rendano 41, Rome, Italy.

CZAŁŁCZYNSKA, Barbara, b. 21 Apr. 1929, Lwow, Poland. Writer; Translator. *Education:* Jagiellonski University, Krakow.*Publications:* Pierwszy zakret, 1967; Proba zycia, 1969; Magdalena, 1974; Wielka cisza, 1967; Przesilenie wiosenne, 1980; Rozmowy z babka, 1982. Translations from French. *Address:* ul. Karłlowicza 5/5, 30-047 Krakow, Poland.

CZERMIŃSKA, Malgorzata, b. 22 Mar. 1940, Luboml, USSR. Literary Critic. *Education:* MSc, Polish Philology, University of Warsaw, 1962; Dr Human Science, High School of Education, Gdańsk, 1969. *Literary Appointments:* Lecturer, Assistant Professor, 1984, University of Gdańsk. *Major Publications:* Czas w powieściach Teodora Parnickiego, (Time in the novels of Teodor Parnicki), 1972; Teodor Parnicki, 1974. *Contributor to:* Nowa Kultura; Litery; Współczesność; Miesiecznik Literaski; Przeglad Hu manistyczny; Pamietnik Literacki. *Memberships:* Union of Polish Writers; Literary Society of Adam Mickiewicz; Editorial Board, PUNKT (Quarterly Review of Creative Groups in Gdańsk. *Honours:* Prize of Ministry of Science, High Schools & Technique, 1971; Prize of Miesiecznik Literacki, Warsaw, 1975. *Address:* 80-398 Gdańsk, ul. Obrońców Wybrzeze 6 A/90, Poland.

CZERNIAWSKI, Adam, b. 20 Dec. 1934, Warsaw, Poland. Philosophy Lecturer. m. Ann Daker, 27 July 1957, London, 1 son, 1 daughter. *Education:* BA English, 1955, BA, Philosophy, 1967, London; MA, Philosophy, Sussex, 1968; BPhil, Oxford, 1970. *Publications:* Liryka i druk (criticism), 1972; Akt (prose), 1975; Wybor Wierszy (selected poems 1953–78), 1982; Wiek Zloty (poems), 1982; Translator: Tadeusz Rozewicz, Conversation with the Prince and other poems, 1982; Leopold Staff, An Empty Room, 1983. *Contributor to:* Encounter, London, Kultura, Paris; Odra, Poland; Puls, London; Zeszyty Literackie, Paris; Oficyna Poetow, London; Polish Review, New York; Wiadomosci, London; Archipelag, Berlin. *Honours:* Woursell Foundation Literary Scholarship, Vienna, 1966–70; Koscielski Foundation Literary Prize, Geneva, 1971; L'Ordre du Merite Culturel, Polish Government, 1975; British Arts Council Translators Award, London, 1976; Hawthornden Castle Fellowship, 1985. *Address:* 6 Tylney Avenue, London SE19 1LN, England.

CZESTOCHOWSKI, Joseph Stephen, b. 6 Aug. 1950, New York, New York, USA. Executive Director, Museum of Art. m. Debra Nicholson, 19 Nov, 1972, Illinois, 1 son. *Education:* BA, University of Illinois, 1971; Diploma courses, Jageiellonian University, Cracow, Poland, 1971; MA, University of Illinois, 1973; Programme, National Endowment for the Arts on Art Museum Administration, 1972. *Publications:* Monographs: The Pioneers, 1977; Polish Posters, 1979; The Combined Works of Arthur B Davies, 1979; Prints by Childe Hassam, 1980; John S Curry and Grant Wood – A Portrait of Rural America, 1981; Great Drawings From 'The Masses'; The American Genre Tradition 1750–1915; A Catalogue Raisonne of the Graphics of Childe Hassam; Marvin D Cone, An American Tradition, 1985; various others. *Contributions to:* American Art Journal; American Art Review; The Tamarind Papers; numerous museum publications. *Honours:* Nancy Hanks Award, American Association of Museums, 1985. *Memberships:* American Association of Museums; Association of Art Museum Directors; International Council of Museums; College Art Association; American Council for the Arts; Affiliated State Art Agencies; Polish Institute of Arts and Sciences; Rotary International. *Address:* 2336 Grande Avenue South East, Cedar Rapids, IA 52403, USA.

D

DABBERDT, Walter F, b. 12 Oct. 1942, New York, USA. Research Scientist. m. Meredith Mueller, 26 Aug. 1967, 1 son, 1 daughter. *Education:* BS; MS; PhD. *Publications:* The Whole Air Weather Guide, 1975; Weather for Outdoorsmen, 1981; Atmospheric Dispersion of Hazardous/Toxic Materials from Transport Accidents, Editor, 1984. *Contributor to:* Journal of Climate and Applied Meteorology; Applied Optics; Journal Air Pollution Control Association. *Address:* 1176 Woodland Court, Boulder, CO 80303, USA.

DABYDEEN, Cyril, b. 15 Oct. 1945, Berbice, Guyana. Writer. *Education:* BA, First Class Hons. Lakehead University, 1973; MA, English, 1974, MPA, 1975, Queens University, Ontario. *Literary Appointment:* Unanimously elected Poet Laureate of Ottawa by City Hall, 1984–. *Publications include:* Distances, 1977; Goatsong, 1977; Heart's Frame, 1979; This Planet Earth, 1979; Still Close to the Island (fiction), 1980; Elephants Make Good Stepladders, 1983; The Wizard Swarni; To Monkey Jungle; Islands Lovelier Than a Vision, (Poetry), 1985. *Contributions to:* Breaking Silence; Asian American Poetry Anthology (winner of American Book Award, 1984). *Honours:* Okanagan Fiction Prize, 1982; Canada Council of the Arts Awards for Writing. *Membership:* League of Canadian Poets. *Address:* 23-2, Montcalm, Ottawa, Canada KIS 5K9.

DACE, Tish, b. 13 Sep. 1941, Washington, District of Columbia, USA. Theatre Critic; University Administrator. 2 sons. *Education:* BA, Sweet Briar College, Virginia, 1963; MA, 1967, PhD, 1971; Kansas State University. *Literary Appointments include:* Theatre Editor, Greenwich Village News, 1976–77. Theatre Critic: Soho Weekly News, 1977–82; Other Stages, 1978–82; Villager and Advocate, 1982–; Plays and Players, 1983–; Theatre Crafts, 1983–; New York Native, 1983–. Book Reviewer, Choice, 1984–. *Publications include:* LeRoi Jones (Imamu Amiri Baraka): A Checklist of Works by and About Him, 1971; The Theatre Student: Modern Theatre and Drama, 1973. *Contributions to:* Black American Writers: Bibliographical Essays, 1978; Great Writers of the English Language: Dramatists, 1979 and numerous other contributions to books. Articles featured in: New York Times; Kansas Quarterly; Shakespeare Newsletter; Soho Weekly News; Village Voice; American Theatre; Other Stages and numerous others. *Honours:* Judge: Tony Voter, 1978–; Joseph Maharam Foundation Awards, 1979–, Chair, 1985–. *Memberships include:* American Theatre Critics Association; American Society for Theatre Research; British Theatre Institute; New Drama Forum; Outer Critics Circle; Theatre Library Association; Modern Language Association of America; Phi Beta Kappa; Pi Epsilon Delta. *Address:* Dean, College of Arts and Sciences, Southeastern Massachusetts University, North Dartmouth, MA 02747, USA.

DACEY, (John) Philip, b. 5 Sep. 1939, St Louis, Missouri, USA. Teacher. m. Florence Pauline Chard, 25 May 1963, Grayslate, 2 sons, 1 daughter. *Education:* BA, St Louis University, 1961; MA, Stanford University, 1967; MFA, University of Iowa, 1970. *Appointments:* Professor, English, Southwest State University, Marshall, 1970–; Distinguished Poet-in-Residence, Wichita State University, Autumn 1985. *Publications:* How I Escaped From the Labyrinth and Other Poems, 1977; The Boy Under the Bed, 1981; Gerard Manley Hopkins Meets Walt Whitman in Heaven and Other Poems, 1982; The Man With Red Suspenders, 1986. *Contributor to:* American Poetry Review; Esquire; Poetry, Chicago; Paris Review; Partisan Review; New York Times; etc. *Honours:* 2 Puschart Prizes, 1977, 1982; National Endowment for the Arts Creative Writing Fellowships, 1975, 1980; Bush Foundation Fellowship, 1977. *Memberships:* Associated Writing Programmes; Poetry Society of America; PEN. *Address:* Box 346 Cottonwood, MN 56229, USA.

DACHY, Michel Roger Leona, b. 21 Jan. 1953, Bruxelles, Belgium, Industrial Draftsman. 1 son. *Education:* Diploma, 3 years architectural design, College. *Publication:* Perseverance, 1984. Contributor of Poems to: Vertet, Montreal; Arts et Lettres Francophones, Brussels; La revue litteraire de l'Alberta, Canada; L'Esperance, Brussels. *Memberships:* Arts et Lettres du Quebec; Arts et Lettres Francophones, Brussels, Belgium; Les 14 Salonniers Sonnettistes; Union des ecrivains Quebecois. *Honours:* 8 Prizes and 4 Honorary Mentions, Arts et Lettres du Quebec, 1982 and 1985; 3 Honorary Mentions, La cigale poetique (France), 1985. *Address:* 48 Rang Double, Napierville, Province of Quebec, Canada J0J 1L0.

DAGRIN, Bengt Gösta, b. 27 Apr. 1940, Örebro, Sweden, Author. *Education:* Commercial School. *Publications:* 35?! – Då Blir det fan inte lätt!, short stories, 1976; Hit! Men inte längre! (The Australian Aborigines of Today), 1978; Världen är skiti! leve Graffiti! (Swedish and World Graffiti from Yesterday and Today), 1980; Mellan Två Världar editor, short stories of New Zealand Maoris, 1982; Kakamoja, editor, graffiti and short poems 1700–1800, 1983; Klotter, 1982; Mera Klotter, 1983; Ännu Mera Klotter, 1984. *Contributions to:* Swedish Dagens Nyheter and various other Swedish newspapers and journals. *Honours:* Scholarships, Swedish Authors Fund, 1979, 1980, 1982 and 1983. *Memberships:* Swedish Union of Authors; Författarcentrum Öst och Riks. *Address:* Brages Väg 5, 6 trp, 145 69 Norsborg, Sweden.

DAIGNAULT, Claire, b. 5 Mar. 1950, Quebec, Canada. Writer. m. Gilles Thelland, 29 Dec. 1983, Longueuil, Canada. *Education:* BAC, Education. *Publications:* Le Cas Lembour, 1984; L'Amant De Dieu, 1979. *Memberships:* Union of Quebec Authors. *Address:* 155 de Jumonville, St Bruno, Quebec J3V 5C5, Canada.

DAIMS, Diva, b. 24 Aug. 1925, Albany, New York, USA. Professor of English. m. Leon Daims, 24 Apr. 1949, Albany, 3 sons. *Education:* PhD, Union Graduate School. *Appointments:* Instructor, English, 1965, Assistant Professor, Associate Professor, English, Women's Studies, 1975–, State University of New York, Albany. *Publications:* Novels in English by Women, 1891–1920, with Janet Grimes, 1981; Toward a Feminist Tradition in Novels by Women, 1891–1920, with Janet Grimes, 1982. *Contributor to:* A Criticism of their Own; Feminist Literary Criticism at the Turn of the Century, Turn of the Century Women. *Honours:* National Endowment for the Humanities Grant, The Feminist Tradition in Novels by Women; Co-Principal Investigator, 1977–78; NEH Grant for Project, 1978. *Memberships:* Modern Language Association; National Women Studies Association; National Council of Teachers of English. *Address:* Box 322 Oak Hill Rd, Esperance, NY 12066, USA.

DALBY, Richard Lawrence, b. 15 April, London, England. Bookseller, Writer, Researcher & Bibliographer. *Major Publications:* The Sorceress in Stained Glass, Stacey, 1971; The Best Ghost Stories of H Russell Wakefield (editor), J Murray, 1978; The Dervish of Windsor Castle: The Life of Arminius Vambery (with Lory Alder), Bachman & Turner, 1979; Bram Stoker: A Bibliography of First Editions, Dracula Press, 1983. *Contributor to:* Book & Magazine Collector; RSA Journal; Country Gentleman's Magazine; Times Educational Supplement. *Address:* 4 Westbourne Park, Scarborough, North Yorkshire, YO12 4AT, England.

DALE, Antony, b. 12 July 1912, Walton-on-the-Hill, Surrey, England. Civil Servant (retired). m. Yvonne Chevallier Macfie, 10 May 1941, Brighton, 1 daughter. *Education:* B Litt, Brighton College; MA, Oriel College, Oxford. *Publications:* Fashionable Brighton 1820–1860, 1946; The History of Architecture of Brighton, 1948; About Brighton, 1951; James Wyatt, 1953; Brighton Old and New, 1953; Brighton Town and Brighton People, 1976; The Wagners of Brighton, 1983.

Honours: FSA, 1951; OBE, 1973. *Membership:* Honorary Secretary, Regency Society of Brighton and Hove, 1945–. *Address:* 38 Prince Regent's Close, Brighton BN2 5JP, England.

DALE, Celia Marjorie, b. London, England. Novelist; Publishers' Adviser. *Publications:* The Least of These; To Hold the Mirror; The Dry Land; The Wooden O; Trial of Strength; A Spring of Love; Other People; A Helping Hand; Act of Love; A Dark Corner; The Innocent Party; Helping With Inquiries. *Contributor of:* Short stories to various volumes and to BBC Radio. *Memberships:* Crime Writers Association, Committee, 1981; Detection Club; PEN. *Literary Agents:* Curtis Brown Ltd, London; James Brown Associates, New York. *Address:* 44 Talbot Road, London N6, England.

DALE, Margaret Jessy, b. 27 Aug. 1911, Edinburgh, Scotland. Writer. m. Clunie Rutherford Dale, 3 Sep. 1938, Harrow on the Hill, 1 son, 2 daughters. *Education:* BA, Honours, Lady Margaret Hall, Oxford. *Appointment:* Assistant Editor, Shell Magazine, 1937–39. *Publications:* Seven Men of Wit, 1960; The Queens Music, 1961; The Powers of the Sapphire, 1962; Dr Boomer, 1964; Mouse Tails, 1967; Willow and Albert, 1968; Knights Beasts and Wonders, 1969; Emily, A Life of Emily Bronte, 1969; King Robert the Bruce, 1970; Billy Saturdays, 1972; The Fearsome Road, 1974; The Fearsome Island, 1975; The Fearsome Tide; The Far Castles, 1978; The Big Brown Teapot, 1979; The Mad Muddle, 1980; A Pocketful of Mice, 1982. *Contributor to:* BBC Schools Programmes; Times; Times Educational Supplement; Scottish Field; Scots Magazine; Scotlands Magazine. *Membership:* PEN. *Literary Agent:* John Johnson. *Address:* 26 Greys Hill, Henley, Oxon RG9 1SJ, England.

DALE, Peter John, b. 21 Aug. 1938, Addlestone, Surrey, England. Teacher. m. New Haw, 1 son, 1 daughter. *Education:* BA, Honours, Oxford. *Appointments:* Co-Editor, Agenda. *Publications:* Mortal Fire; One Another; Selected Poems of Villon; Narrow Straits, verse translated from French; Poems of Laforgue. *Contributor to:* Agenda; Listener; Times Literary Supplement; etc. *Honour:* Arts Council Bursary, 1970. *Address:* 5 Cranbourne Court, Albert Bridge Road, London SW11 4PE, England.

DALE, Robert Dennis, b. 23 Aug. 1940, Neosho, Missouri, USA. Professor. m. Carrie Lou Kondy. 25 Aug. 1962, Denver, 1 son, 1 daughter. *Education:* BA, Oklahoma Baptist University; BD, PhD, Southwestern Baptist Theological Seminary. *Publications:* Ten books in print including, Growing a Loving Church, 1974; To Dream Again, 1981; How to Encourage Others, co-author, 1983; Ministers as Leaders, 1984; Surviving Difficult Church Members, 1984. *Contributor to:* Over 100 articles in various religious journals including, Faith & Mission; Columnist, Mature Living. *Address:* 219 W Vernon Ave, Wake Forest, NC 27587, USA.

DALESKI, H M, b. 19 July 1926, Johannesburg, South Africa. Professor of English. *Education:* BA, BA Honours, MA, University of the Witwatersrand, Johannesburg; PhD, Hebrew University, Jerusalem, Israel. *Publications:* The Forked Flame: A Study of D H Lawrence, 1965; Dickens & The Art of Analogy, 1970; Joseph Conrad: The Way of Dispossession, 1977; The Divided Heroine: A Recurrent Pattern in Six English Novels, 1984; Unities: Studies in the English Novel, 1985. *Contributor to:* Nineteenth Century Fiction; Modern Fiction Studies; Critical Quarterly; Essays in Criticism. *Memberships:* President, The Dickens Society, 1985; Modern Language Association; D H Lawrence Society; International Association of University Professors of English; Joseph Conrad Society. *Address:* 7 Rashba St, Jerusalem, Israel.

D'ALFONSO, Antonio, b. 6 Aug. 1953, Montreal, Quebec, Canada. Writer/Editor/Publisher. *Education:* BA, Cinema, Loyola College; MSc, Semiology, Université de Montreal. *Publications:* La Chanson du Shaman à Sedna 1973; Queror 1979; Black Tongue

1983; Quêtes (with Fulvio Caccia) 1984; Dix Poetes anglophones du Quebec 1985; The Clarity of Voices, translation of Phillippe Haeck's poetry, 1985; The Other Shore, 1985. *Contributions to:* Vice Versa; Nos Livres; Poetry Canada Review. *Memberships:* League of Canadian Poets; Union des écrivains quebecois. *Address:* P O Box 633, Station N D G, Montreal, Quebec, Canada H4A 3R1.

DALLAS, Ruth, b. 29 Sep. 1919. Poet, Children's Author. *Publications include:* Country Road and Other Poems, 1953; The Turning Wheel, 1961; Day Book, Poems of a Year, 1966; Shadow Show, 1968; Walking on the Snow, 1976; Steps of the Sun, 1979; Children's books include: The Children in the Bush, 1969; A Dog Called Wig, 1970; The Wild Boy in the Bush, 1971; The Big Flood in the Bush, 1972; The House on the Cliffs, 1975; Shining Rivers, 1979; Holiday Time in the Bush, 1983. *Contributor to:* Landfall; Islands; Meanjin; Australian Quarterly. *Honours:* New Zealand Literary Fund Achievement Award, 1963; Robert Burns Fellowship, University of Otago, 1968; Shared Winner, Poetry section, New Zealand Book Awards, 1977; Buckland Literary Award, 1977; Honorary D Litt, University of Otago, 1978. *Membership:* PEN, New Zealand. *Address:* 448 Leith Street, Dunedin, New Zealand.

DALLIMORE, Arnold Arthur, b. 6 Sep. 1911, London, Ontario, Canada. Baptist Minister. m. May Bredin, 21 Aug. 1942, Toronto, Ontario, Canada. 1 son, 2 daughters. *Education:* Bachelor of Theology, Toronto Baptist Seminary; Doctor of Divinity, Northwest Baptist Theological College, Vancouver, British Columbia. *Publications:* Life of George Whitefield, two volumes; Life of Edward Irving, Forerunner of the Charismatic Movement; Only One Life: The Story of Dr Jack Scott; Spurgeon. *Contributions to:* The Man Who Loved His Critics' Christianity Today; John Cennick, The Evangelical Library Bulletin; Whitefield and Wesley in the West, Decision Magazine; Articles in, The Banner of Truth Magazine; Reformation Today; Reformation Canada; The Gospel Witness, Proceedings of The Wesley Historical Society. *Address:* 109 Hill Street, Cottam, Ontario, Canada NOR 1B0

DALLMAN, Elaine G, b. 8 Mar. 1934, Sacramento, California, USA. Founder & President, Women-in-Literature Inc & ARRA International Inc, 1977. m. Willard Ross, 18 Dec. 1954, San Francisco, USA, 1 son, 1 daughter. *Education:* BA, Stanford University; MA, San Francisco State University; PhD, Southern Illinois University, 1975. *Major Publications:* Editor-in-Chief, Woman Poet, series of Regional Poetry Anthologies: Woman Poet – The West, 1980; Woman Poet – The East, 1982; Woman Poet – The Midwest, 1985; Woman Poet – The South, forthcoming 1986; A Parallel Cut of Air (original poems), 1986. *Contributor to:* Numerous Literary Journals, including: Epoch; The Chowder Review. *Honours:* Over 120 awards in poetry contests 1974–85. *Memberships:* Poets & Writers, Inc; Authors Guild; Poetry Society of America; Executive Director, WILNA. *Address:* P O Box 60550, Reno, NV 89506, USA.

D'ALPUGET, Blanche, b. 3 Jan. 1944, Sydney, Australia. Writer. m. Anthony Ian Camden Pratt, 22 Nov. 1965, Sydney, 1 son. *Publications:* Mediator, A Biography of Sir Richard Kirby, 1977; Monkeys in the Dark, 1980; Turtle Beach, 1981; Robert J Hawke, A Biography, 1982; Winter in Jerusalem, 1986. *Honours:* PEN Sydney Centre Golden Jubilee Award for Literature, 1981; South Australian Government Award for Literature, 1982; Age, Novel of the Year, 1981; Braille Book of the Year, 1981, 1982; New South Wales Premier's Award for Literature, 1983. *Agent:* Robert Gottlieb, William Morris Agency, New York. *Address:* 6/8 Howitt Street, Kingston, ACT 2604, Australia.

DALRYMPLE, Byron William, b. 7 Aug. 1910, Michigan, USA. Freelance Writer; Journalist. m. Ellen F Christoffers, 30 Apr. 1949, Sarasota, Florida, 2 sons. *Education:* BA, University of Michigan. *Publications:*

Author of over 20 books including: Light Tackle Fishing, 1947; Doves and Dove Shooting, 1949; Fundamentals of Fishing and Hunting, 1959; Hunting Across North America, 1970; Modern Book of Black Bass, 1972; Complete Book of Deer Hunting, 1973; Game Animals of North America, 1978; Complete Guide to Game Fish, 1981. Contributions to: Field and Stream; Southern Outdoors, Special feature writer; Southwest Farm Press, Weekly Columnist; Sports Afield; Outdoor Life; Author over 3500 articles in range of outdoor and general magazines, 1940–. Honours: Award for film scripts and direction, Travel Film Festival, 1971, 75; Award for writing on Texas, Texas Tourist Development Award, 1973. Address: P O Box 709, Kerrville, TX 78029, USA.

DAMYANOV, Damyan, b. 18 Jan. 1935, Sliven, Bulgaria. Writer. Education: Bulgarian Philology, Sofia University. Publications: Poetry: If There Was No Fire, 1958; A Poem Of The Happiness, 1963; Love Above All, 1965; And The Summer Goes, 1968; I'm Knealing Before you, 1968; You Are Like a Teardrop, 1969. Contributor to: All main Bulgarian literary editons. Membership: Union of Bulgarian Writers. Address: bloc 22, boul. Lenin, Sofia, Bulgaria.

DANIEL, Errol Valentine, b. 17 Feb. 1946, Lindula, Sri Lanka. University Professor. Education: PhD, University of Chicago, 1979. Publications: Karma: An Anthropological Inquiry, co-editor with Charles F Keyes, 1983; South Asian Systems of Healing, co-editor with Judy F Pugh, 1984; Fluid Signs: Being a Person the Tamil Way, 1984. Contributions to: Medusa'a Hair: An Essay on Personal Symbols and Religious Experience in Culture, Medicine and Psychiatry. Address: Department of Anthropology, University of Washington, Seattle, WA 98103, USA.

DANIEL, Glenda Louise, 25 Apr. 1943, Mountain Home, Arkansas, USA. Writer. m. Jerry Sullivan, 4 Nov. 1974, Chicago, Illinois, 1 daughter. Education: BS, Arkansas State University; MJ candidate, University of Texas; Urban Journalism Fellowship, Northwestern University. Publications: Hiking Trails in the Midwest, with Jerry Sullivan, 1974, 80; Hiking Trails in the Southern Mountains, with Jerry Sullivan, 1975; Dune Country, 1977, 84; A Sierra Club Naturalists' Guide to the North Woods (of Minnesota, Wisconsin, Michigan), with Jerry Sullivan, 1981. Address: 4439 North Francisco, Chicago, IL 60625, USA.

DANIEL, Lorna MacLeod Lyons, b. 14 June 1953, Edmonton, AB, Canada. Communications. m. Patricia Lyons, 13 Jan. 1975, Lethbridge, AB (now divorced), 1 son, 1 daughter. Education: BA, Creative Writing, University of Lethbridge, 1975; Master of Communication Studies, University of Calgary (not yet completed). Publications: The Hunting Hand, 1973; Towards a New Compass, 1978; In the Flesh, 1982; Co-Editor, Ride Off Any Horizon, 1984. Contributions to: Over 30 periodicals including: Canadian Literature, Canadian Forum, Dandelion, Waves. Honours: Writing Grants from the Canada Council and Alberta Culture. Memberships: League of Canadian Poets, Alberta Representative, 1981–83; Writers Guild of Alberta, Vice-President, 1984–85. Address: 16 Openview Close, Red Deer, AB, T4P 1Z1, Canada.

DANIELS, Linda A (Paulin), b. 28 Nov. 1944, Tennessee, USA. Science Editor; Writer. Education: BFA, University of Chicago, 1969. Literary Appointments: Special Projects Editor 1982, Scientific Editor 1984, St Jude Children's Research Hospital. Publication Co-editor, Leukemia Research; Advances in Cell Biology & Treatment. Honours: PRISM Citations, PRISM Awards, 1980–85. Memberships: Council of Biology Editors; American Medical Writers Association; Society for Scholarly Publishing. Address: St Jude Children's Research Hospital, P O Box 318, Memphis, TN 38101, USA.

DANIELS, Marie-Therese, b. 27 June 1906. Librarian. Education: Licentiate Mathematics, University of Fribourg, Switzerland. Appointments:

Assistant History with Pierre de Zurich; Librarian, Provincial Library, University of Fribourg; General Advisor, City of Fribourg. Publications: Lampes et Minutes, Lights and Minutes, 1971; Passe-Ville, Passe-Maisons (Through Towns and Houses), 1975; a collabore au Florilege fribourgeouis de 1978 et 1979; Fribourg: Ses costumes regionaux, 1981. Memberships: Swiss Society of Writers; Cultural Romand Alliance; Past President, Fribourg Society of Writers. Address: Chemin des Grenadiers 5, CH–1700 Fribourg, Switzerland.

DANIELSSON, Bengt Emmerik, b. 1921, Krokek, Sweden. Explorer; Anthropologist; Swedish Consul, French Polynesia. Education: University of Uppsala, Sweden; University of Seattle, USA; PhD. Publications: Happy Island, 1952; Work and Life on Raroia, 1956; Love in the South Seas, 1956; Forgotten Islands of the South Seas, 1957; Terry in the South Seas, 1959; Terry in Australia, 1959; From Raft to Raft, 1961; What Happened on the Bounty, 1962; Gauguin in the South Seas, 1965; Decouverte and la Polynesia, 1972; Moruroa, mon Armour, 1974; La Memorial Polynesien, 6 volumes, 1975–81; Tahiti autrefois, 1982; Poisoned Reign, 1986. Television Script: Terry in the South Seas, 1963. Contributions to: Journal of Polynesian Society; Atoll Research Bulletin. Address: Papehue, Paea, Tahiti, French Polynesia.

DANINOS, Pierre Charles, b. 1913, Paris, France. Writer. Publications include: Les Carnets du Major Thompson. (Engl ed, Major Thompson Lives in France); Le Secret du Major Thompson (Engl ed, Major Thompson and I); Sonia, les autres et moi, (Engl ed, Life with Sonia); Les Carnets du Bon Dieu; Le Jacassid; Snobissimo; UnCertain Monsieur Blot; Ludovic Morateur, 1970; LePyjama, 1972; Les Touristocrates, 1974; Made in France, 1977; La Compostoin D'Histoire, 1979; La galerie des glaces, 1983; La France dans tous etats, 1985. Contributor to: Figaro; Punch; etc. Honours include: Prix Interaillie for Les Carnet du Bon Dieu; Prix Courteline for Somia, les autres et moi. Address: 81 rue de Grenelle, Paris 7, France.

DANN, Colin Michael, b. 10 Mar. 1943, Richmond, Surrey, England. Writer. m. Janet Elizabeth Stratton, 4 June 1977, Croydon, England. Major Publications: The Animals of Farthing Wood, 1979; In the Grip of Winter, 1981; Fox's Feud, 1982; The Fox Cub Bold, 1983; The Siege of White Deer Park, 1985. Honour: Arts Council National Book Award for Children's Literature, 1980. Membership: Society of Authors. Address: The Old Forge, Whatlington, East Sussex, England.

DAPUNT, Inge, b. 13 May 1943, Zams, Tirol, Austria. Writer. m. Edgar Morscher, 18 Aug. 1967, Innsbruck. Publications: Vom Schtadtle und vom Landle, 1964. Contributions to: Innsbruck, 1965, 67; Die Diagonale, 1968; Konfigurationen, 1969; Vorarlberg, 1969–72; Egoist, 1970; Bodensee Hefte, 1970, 77; Neue Wege, 1971; Podium, 1971, 75; Literatur und Kritik, 1972; Das Fenster, 1973; Neue Texte aus Vorarlberg, 1977, 83; Dialekt-Wienderentdeckung des Selbstverstandlichen, 1977; Machrichten aus dem Alemannischen, 1979; 'O Hoamatle! O Hoamatle?, 1985. Honours: Authors Prize of Rauris, 1973; Authors Prize of Vorarlberg, 1974. Membership: Grazer Autorenversammlung. Address: Kapellenweg 3, A– 5162 Obertrum am See, Austria.

DARBISHIRE, Peter Mark Dukinfield, b. 23 Oct. 1949, Norwich, England. Managing Editor. m. Julia Grace Overweel, 23 May 1980, Erin Mills, 2 sons. Education: Honours Degree, Mechanical Engineering, Leeds University, 1973. Contributor to: Agribook Magazine; Corn in Canada; Beans in Canada; Potatoes in Canada; Seed in Canada; Elevator Manager; Drainage Contractor; Farm Equipment Quarterly; Canadian Rental Service; Canadian Water Well; WFCD Communicator; Farm Light and Power; Soil and Water; The Soil; Fine Woodworking. Address: c/o AIS Communications Ltd, Box 1060, Exeter, Ontario, Canada N0M 1S0.

DARBY, John, b. 18 Nov. 1940, Belfast, Northern Ireland. University Professor. m. Marie McMahon, 13 Apr. 1966, Belfast, 2 sons. *Education:* BA 1960, H Dip Ed 1970, Queen's University, Belfast; D Phil, University of Ulster, 1985. *Publications:* Conflict in Northern Ireland, 1976; Violence and the Social Services in Northern Ireland (editor, with A Williamson), 1978; Dressed to Kill: Cartoonists and the Northern Ireland Conflict, 1983; Northern Ireland: Background to the Conflict, 1983. *Contributions to:* More than 30 articles. *Address:* University of Ulster, Coleraine, Northern Ireland.

DARBYSHIRE, Donald Edward, b. 27 Apr. 1934, Koondrook, Australia. Journalist. m. Danuta Agnieske Popkowski, 17 Nov. 1983, Hampton, 1 daughter, 4 sons by previous marriage. *Literary Appointments:* Numerous appointments as reporter, sub-editor or editor including: Reporter, Sub Editor, Sun News-Pictorial, The Herald, The Age. Reporter, ABC News; Writer, Sub-Editor, Stock and Land newspaper; Editor, SEC News, E Z Review; Principal Speechwriter to Honorable R J Hammer Premier of Victoria. *Publication:* Australia 2025, 1975. *Contributions to:* Flying; Aircraft; Circuit; Port of Melbourne Quarterly; This Australia; Business Review; Australasian Post; Rydges Journal; Business Bulletin; various Australian metropolitan daily newspapers. Various variety scripts for Australian Broadcasting Corporation. Talks for Radio Australia. *Address:* 3 Lewis Street, Mordialloc, Vic 3195, Australia.

DARE, Timothy Stephen, b. 17 Aug. 1940, Kiama, New South Wales, Australia. Author. m. Caroline Lamb, 18 Sep. 1971, South Yarra, Victoria, divorced 1980, 1 son. *Education:* Graded Journalist. *Publications:* Australians: Making a Great Nation, 1985. *Contributor to:* Various Magazines; Former Features Editor, The Australian, The Sydney Morning Herald; Numerous feature articles for Australian Newspapers, as well as columns and editorials. *Memberships:* Australian Society of Authors; Australian Journalists' Association. *Address:* 24 Colbourne Avenue, Glebe, NSW, 2037, Australia.

DARK, Harris Edward, b. 23 Nov. 1922, Springfield Missouri, USA. Writer, Author. m. Phyllis Betty Dolan, 29 Oct. 1949, Chicago, Illinois, USA, 1 son, 6 daughters. *Education:* BA English, BA Speech; 2 diplomas in electronics engineering; diploma in automotive engineering. *Major Publications:* The Wankel Rotary Engine 1974; Auto Engines of Tomorrow, 1975; The Greatest Ozarks Guidebook, 1978; Springfield of the Ozarks, 1981; Springfield, Missouri 40 Years of Growth & Progress, 1984. *Contributor to:* Numerous magazines of large circulation. *Honours:* Public Service Awards, National Safety Council, 1965, American Medical Association, 1966; Best Book, Missouri Writers Guild, 1975; Society of American Travel Writers Award, 1978. *Memberships:* Missouri Writers Guild, State President; Sigma Delta Chi; Society of Professional Journalists; Chicago Headline Club; Travel Journalists Guild; Chicago Press Club; Society of American Travel Writers; International Photography Society. *Address:* P O Box 1750, Bandera, TX 78003, USA.

DATHORNE, Oscar Ronald, b. 19 Nov. 1934, Guyana. Professor. m. Hilde Ostermaier, 11 Dec. 1959, Caxton Hall, 1 son, 1 daughter. *Education:* PhD, MBA, MPA. *Major Publications:* Dumplings in the Soup (novel), 1963; The Scholar Man (novel), 1964; Young Commonwealth Poetry '65 (edited African sections); Caribbean Narrative (editor), 2nd edition, 1972; Caribbean Verse; (editor), 2nd edition, 1972; *Contributions to:* Penguin Companion to Literature, 1968; African Poetry, 1968; African Prose (with W Feuser), 1969; The Black Mind: A History of African Literature, 1974; African Literature in the Twentieth Century, 1976; Kelly Poems, 1977; Dark Ancestor: Black Literature in the New World, 1981; Dele's Child, 1985. *Contributor to:* Journal of Commonwealth Literature; The London Magazine; Times Literary Supplement; Présence Africaine; Africa Quarterly; and others. *Honours:* Fellow, Royal Society of Arts; Fellow,

Royal Society of Economics: *Address:* 8901 Friedberg West, Lubeustrasse 2, Federal Republic of Germany.

DAUNT NETO, Ricardo Gumbleton, b. 17 July 1950, São Paulo, Brazil. Communication Advisor. *Education:* Business Administration, Fundacão Getúlio Vargas; Doctorate in Portuguese Literature, University of São Paulo. *Major Publications:* Juan, short stories, Livraria José Olympio Editora, Rio de Janeiro, 1975; Homem na Prateleira, short stories, Editora Ática, Sao Paulo 1979; 'Grito Empalhado', novel, Civilizaçao Brasileira, Rio de Janeiro, 1979; Manuário de Vidal, novel, RJ Codecri, 1981; Endereços Úteis, short stories, RJ, Codecri, 1984. *Contributor to:* Jornal do Brasil, O Globo, Folha de Sao Paulo (journals), Isto É, Encontros com a Civilização Brasileira (magazines) and others. *Honour:* Prêmio Remimgton, 1977. *Literary Agent:* Agência Literária Carmen Balcells. *Address:* Rua Visconde da Lus 88, apt. 84, CEP 04537, São Paulo, SP Brazil.

DAVEY, Thomas, b. 8 June 1930, Wigan, Lancashire, England. Writer. m. 19 June 1959, Toronto, Canada, 1 son, 1 daughter. *Education:* Courses at University of Toronto, University of Tasmania; Appointed Associate, Institute for Environmental Studies, University of Toronto, 1984. *Publications:* Recollections, an environmental history, 1985; All The Views Fit To Print, collection of scientific satires, 1985. *Contributions to:* Water and Pollution Control; Major Canadian Newspapers including Globe and Mail; Bridges. *Honours:* Winner Best Editorial Class A 1970, Award of Merit 1982, J H Neal Award, American Business Press, New York, USA; H Schlenz Medal, International Water Pollution Control Federation, Washington DC, USA, 1978; 4 awards, Canadian Business Press; Award, Canadian Science Writers Association; 12 Awards for Writing, Southam Business Communications Limited. *Memberships:* President 1978, Canadian Science Writers Association; Canadian Author's Association. *Address:* 37 Sandusky Cr Aurora, Ontario, L4G 3N3, Canada.

DAVI, Hans Leopold, b. 10 Jan. 1928. Bookseller. m. 3 children. *Publications:* Gedichte einer Jugen, 1952; Huellas en la Playa Spuren am Strand, 1956; Canciones de ninos Kinderlieder, 1959; Stein und Wolke, 1961; Aurmenta et nivel de los tios Es steigt der Wasserspiegel der Flusse, 1975; Distelund Distel-und Mistelworte, 1976; Der Herzmaler und andere Erzahlungen, 1982; Neue Distel-und Distelworte, 1984. *Contributor to:* Neue Zurcher Zeitung; Alzemte; Munich Humboldt; Revista de Occidente, Madrid; Peoples de Gen Armandans, Mallorca. *Honours:* Hons of Swiss Schiller Trust, 1959; Award of Appreciation by town of Lucerne, 1961. *Memberships:* Inner Swiss Authors Society; Society of Swiss Authors. *Address:* Hünenbergstr. 76, 6006 Lucerne, Switzerland.

DAVIAU, Diane-Monique, b. 18 April 1951, Montréal, Canada. Teacher. *Education:* MA, German Literature, University of Montr[a]eal, 1977. *Literary Appointments:* Teacher, German Literature, University of Montr[a]eal. *Major Publications:* Dessins à la plume, 1979; Histoires entre quatre murs, 1981. *Contributor to:* Liberté, Le Devoir, (reviews); X Y Z, (short stories). *Honour:* Finalist, 16th Grand Prix Littéraire de Montréal, 1980. *Membership:* Québec Writers' Union. *Address:* 2695 rue Goyer app 15, Montréal, Québec H3S 1H2, Canada.

DAVIAU, Donald George, b. 30 Sep. 1927, Medway, Massachusetts, USA. Professor of German and Austrian Literatures. *Education:* BA, Clark University, 1950; MA 1952, PhD, University of California, Berkeley, 1955. *Publications:* The Correspondence of Arthur Schnitzler and Racul Auernheimer together with Auernheimer's Unpublished Aphorisms, (with Jorun B Johns, co-author) Editor, 1972; Arthur Schnitzler, (transl), 1973; Ariadne auf Naxos of Hugo von Hofmannsthal and Richard Strauss, (with George Buelow), 1975; The Letters of Arthur Schnitzler to Hermann Bahr, 1978; Das Exilerlebis (co-editor with Ludwig M Fischer), 1982;

The Correspondence of Stefan Zweig with Raoul Auernheimer and Richard Beer-Hofmann, (Editor of volume; co-editor with Jorun B Johns), 1983; Der Mann von Obermorgen, Hermann Bahr, 1984; Stefan Zweig/Paul Zech: Briefe 1910–1942, 1984; Hermann Bahr, 1985; Exil: Wirking und Wertung, (co-edited with Ludwig M Fischer) 1985. *Contributor to:* Germanic Review; Monatshefte; German Quarterly; etc. *Honour:* Recipient, Ehrenkreuz fur Kunst und Wissenschaft, Austrian Government, 1977. *Memberships include:* MLA of America; Philology Association of the Pacific Coast; President, International Arthur Schnitzler Research Associate; President, American Council, Study of Austrian Literature. *Address:* Department of Literature and Languages, University of California, Riverside, CA 92521, USA.

DAVID, Joe, b. 9 July 1936, Chicago, Illinois, USA. Writer, Editor, Educator. *Education:* BA, Lake Forest College, Illinois, 1957; Northwestern University, Chicago, Evanston, Illinois, 1957–58; Graduate School of Journalism, University of Missouri, Columbia, Missouri, 1958–60; French Studies in France and Switzerland. *Appointments:* Editorial Board of Reading Improvement, 1973. *Major Publicatons:* The Fire Within, novel, 1981; Since You Asked, an investigation of Public Education, to be published 1986. *Contributor to:* Washington Star, Chicago Tribune, Los Angeles Herald-Examiner (newspapers); The Forum, College Student Journal, Education (journals); Family, American Atheist, Houston Home & Garden, Aldebaran, Executive Review (magazines); Travel articles in Jet Set and Space A (books). *Address:* P O Box 2, Alexandria, VA 22313, USA.

DAVIDKOV, Ivan, b. 9 Mar. 1926, Givovtzi, Bulgaria. Writer. *Education:* Slavonic Philology, Sofia University. *Literary Appointment:* An editor at The Bulgarian Writer, Publishing House. *Publications:* Poetry: Wings and Roots, 1964; Songs and Ballads, 1965; Thracian Mounds, 1968; Bridges of Clouds; A Lighting, 1970. Novel: The Winter Dreams of the Lyons, 1982. *Contributor to:* All main Bulgarian literary editions. *Honour:* A People's Worker of Culture, 1984. *Membership:* Union of Bulgarian Writers. *Address:* 128, Boulevard 9 September, Sofia, Bulgaria.

DAVIDSON, Caroline, b. 20 Jan. 1953, Washington, District of Columbia, USA. Writer. m. Clive Cookson, 7 Apr. 1978, 1 son. *Education:* BA, MA, King's College, Cambridge, England; Diploma, Journalism, University College, Cardiff. *Publications:* A Woman's Work is Never Done: A History of Housework in the British Isles, 1650–1950, 1982; The World of Mary Ellen Best, 1985. *Contributor to:* Petits Propos Culinaires; European Wine and Food; Homes & Gardens; Harpers' and Queen; Connoisseur; The Times; The Guardian; The Economist. *Membership:* Society of Authors. *Literary Agent:* Robert Ducas. *Address:* 5 Queen Anne's Gardens, London W4 1TU, England.

DAVIDSON, James Dale, b. 16 Apr. 1947, Washington, District of Columbia, USA. *Education:* M Litt, Oxon; MA and BA, University of Maryland. *Publications:* 'The Eccentric Guide to the United States', 1977, 1981; 'The Squeeze', 1980, 1981 ('Die Quetache'. 1982); 'Constitutional Economics' (Contributor), 1984; 'Beyond the Status Quo' (Contributor), 1985; 'Incentive-Based Reforms' (forthcoming). *Literary Agent:* Theron Raines. *Address:* 6200 Westchester Drive, #1614, College Park, MD 20740, USA.

DAVIDSON, Lionel, b. 31 Mar. 1922, Hull, England. *Publications:* The Night of Wenceslas, 1960; The Rose of Tibet, 1962; A Long Way to Shiloh, 1966; Making Good Again, 1968; Smith's Gazelle, 1971; The Sun Chemist, 1976; The Chelsea Murders, 1978; Under Plum Lake, 1980; various works for children. *Honours:* Authors Club Award, Most Promising First Novel of the Year & Crime Writers' Association Award, Best Thrill of Year, for, The Night of Wenceslas; Crime Writers' Association Awards for, A Long Way to Shiloh, & The

Chelsea Murders. *Agent:* Curtis Brown Ltd. *Address:* c/o 162 Regent Street, London W1R 5TA, England.

DAVIES, Frederick Herbert, b. 5 Aug. 1916, Birkenhead, England. Schoolmaster; Author; Translator. *Publications:* The Servant of Two Masters, 1961; The Liar, 1963; It Happened in Venice, 1965; The Italian Straw Hat, 1967; The Spelling Mistakes, 1967; The Fan, 1968; The Lucifer Stone (novel), 1965; Goldoni: Four Comedies, 1968; The Campiello, 1970; Three French Farces, 1973; Letters From My Windmill by Alphonse Daudet, 1976; The Gods Will Have Blood (Les Dieux on soif) by Anatole France, 1979; Death of a Hit-Man (novel), 1982; Show in Venice (novel), 1983. *Contributions to:* Literary journals. *Honour:* Fellow Commoner, Churchill College, Cambridge, 1969. *Memberships:* Society of Authors; Translators Association; Crime Writers Association. *Literary Agent:* Margaret Ramsay Ltd. *Address:* 5 Beaumaris Court, Charlesville, Oxton, Birkenhead, Merseyside, England.

DAVIES, Gill, b. 27 May 1945, Neath, Glamorgan, Wales. Publisher. *Education:* BSc, Sociology, London. *Appointment:* Editorial Director, Tavistock Publications Ltd. *Memberships:* Board Member, University, College and Professional Publishers Council, The Publishers Association. *Address:* 107 Bedford Court Mansions, Bedford Avenue, London WC1B 3AG, England.

DAVIES, John Christopher Hughes, b. 25 Dec. 1941, Sutton, England. Professor, Sociology, University of Reading. *Education:* BA, 1964, MA, 1969, Emmanuel College, Cambridge. *Appointments:* Radio Producer, BBC, 1967–69; Lecturer, University of Leeds, 1969–72; Lecturer, Senior Lecturer, Reader, 1972–84, Professor, Sociology, 1984–, University of Reading. *Publications:* Wrongful Imprisonment, Mistaken Convictions & Their Consequences, with Ruth Brandon, 1973; The Reactionary Jokebook, with Russell Lewis, 1973; Permissive Britain, Social Change in the Sixties & Seventies, 1975; Censorship & Obscenity, with R Dhavan, 1978; Welsh Jokes, 1978; Jokes Are About Peoples, forthcoming. *Contributor to:* British Journal of Sociology; American Journal of Sociology; Policy Review; Wall Street Journal; Irish Independant; Western Mail; Der Monat; Radio, TV Documentaries for BBC. *Membership:* President, Union Society Cambridge, 1964. *Literary Agent:* Laurence Pollinger. *Address:* Dept of Sociology, University of Reading, Whiteknights, Reading RG6 2AA, Berkshire, England.

DAVIES, Paul Charles William, b. 22 Apr. 1946, London, England. Professor of Physics. m. Susan Vivien Corti Woodcock, 27 July 1972, Epsom, Surrey, England, 1 son, 3 daughters. *Education:* BSc Physics, 1967; PhD, Theoretical Physics, 1970. *Literary Appointments:* Consultant, Nature, 1974; Consultant, The Economist, 1978. *Major Publications:* The Physics of Time Asymmetry, 1974; Space & Time in the Modern Universe, 1977; The Runaway Universe, 1978; The Forces of Nature, 1979; Other Worlds, The Search for Gravity Waves, 1980; The Edge of Infinity, 1981; The Accidental Universe, Quantum Fields in Curved Space, 1982 (Co-author with N D Birrell); God & the New Physics, 1983; Superforce, 1984; Quantum Mechanics, 1984. *Contributor to:* Numerous learned and scientific journals, including: Nature; New Scientist; The Sciences; The Economist; The Guardian; Science Digest. *Literary Agent:* Brockman Associates, New York, USA. *Address:* Department of Theoretical Physics, University of Newcastle-upon-Tyne, NE1 7RU, England.

DAVIES, Stevan Lawrence, b. 3 Sep. 1948, Hartford, Connecticut, USA. Associate Professor, Religious Studies. m. Sally Augusta Watkins, 27 Aug. 1973, Henderson, 1 son. *Education:* AB, Duke University, 1970; PhD, Temple University, 1978. *Publications:* The Revolt of the Widows – Social World of the Aprocryphal Acts, 1980; The Gospel of Thomas and Christian Wisdom, 1983. *Contributor to:* New Testament Studies; Biblical Archaeology; Semeia; Vigilia Christianae.

Address: College Misericordia, Department of Religion, Dallas, PA 18612, USA.

DAVIES-SHIEL, Michael, b. 5 June 1929, Rock Ferry, Birkenhead, England. School Master. m. Noreen Mary May, 29 Dec. 1956, Lancaster, 2 sons. *Education:* BSc, 1950, Educ Dip, 1951, Birmingham University. *Publications:* Industrial Archeology of the Lake Counties, with J D Marshall, 1969, 2nd edition 1975; Lake District at Work in Pictures, 1971; Wool is My Bread: History of Kendal's Wool Trade to 1575AD, 1975; Victorian & Edwardian Lake Counties, with J D Marshall, 1976; Watermills of Cumbria: How to Research Water Corn Mills, 1979. *Contributor to:* Transactions of Cumberland and Westmorland Archeological and Antiquarian Society; Bulletin of Historical Metallurgical Society; Isle of Thanet Geographical Association. *Honour:* Fellow, Royal Geographical Society. *Memberships:* Cumberland & Westmorland Archeological and Antiquarian Society; Historical Metallurgy Society; Cumbria Industrial History Society. *Address:* 12 St Mary's Park, Windermere, Cumbria LA23 1AY, England.

DAVIS, Dorothy Salisbury, b. 26 Apr. 1916, Chicago, Illinois, USA. Writer. *Education:* AB, Barat College, Lake Forest, Illinois. *Publications:* A Gentle Murderer, 1951; Men of No Property, 1956; The Evening of the Good Samaritan, 1961; Enemy and Brother, 1967; Where the Dark Streets Go, 1969; The Little Brothers, 1974; A Death in the Life, 1976; Scarlet Night, 1980; Lullaby of Murder, 1984; Tales for a Stormy Night, 1985. *Contributor to:* New Republic. *Honour:* Grand Master's Award, Mystery Writers of America, 1985. *Memberships:* President, Executive Vice President, Mystery Writers of America, Crime Writers Association, UK; Authors' Guild; Writers' Guild of America. *Literary Agent:* McIntosh and Otis. *Address:* Snedens Landing, Palisades, NY 10964, USA.

DAVIS, Flora Marion, b. 21 Dec. 1934, East Orange, New Jersey, USA. Author. m. Muhammad T Tayyabkhan, 1980, Princeton, 1 son, 1 daughter. *Education:* BA, McGill University. *Publications:* Inside Intuition – What We Know About Nonverbal Communication, 1971, 1972, 1973; Eloquent Animals, 1978; Living Alive!, 1981. *Contributor to:* 100 Articles in Woman's Day; Ladies Home Journal; Mademoiselle; Red Book; Glamour; Cosmopolitan; New York Times Magazine; Reader's Digest; etc. *Memberships:* ASJA, former Board Member; Authors Guild; National Writers Union. *Literary Agent:* Emilie Jacobson, Curtis Brown. *Address:* 62 Erdruan Avenue, Princeton, NJ 08540, USA.

DAVIS, Gary Alan, b. 28 July 1938, Salt Lake City, Utah, USA. Professor of Educational Psychology. m. Frances Clemmer (Davis), 19 Dec. 1961, Elko, Nevada, 3 daughters. *Education:* BA, University of Utah, 1962; MS, 1963; PhD, University of Wisconsin, 1965. *Publications:* Training Creative Thinking, 1971; Psychology of Problem Solving, 1973; Immagination Express, 1973; Psychology of Education, 1974; Stock Option Strategies, 1976; Creativity is Forever, 1983; Educational Psychology, 1983; Education of the Gifted and Talented, 1985. Contributor to various journals. *Honour:* Wilhelm, Wundt Award for organizing Creativity symposium, XXII International Congress of Psychology, Leipzig, 1980; Featured in Revue de Psychologie Applique, 1982. *Address:* Department of Educational Psychology, University of Wisconsin, Madison, WI 53706, USA.

DAVIS, James Madison, Jr, b. 10 Feb. 1951, Charlottesville, Virginia, USA. Writer; Professor. m. Simonne Evelyn Eck, 21 May 1977, Cumberland, Maryland, 2 sons. *Education:* BA, Anthropology, University of Maryland; MA, Writing Seminars, Johns Hopkins University; PhD, English, University of Southern Mississippi. *Publications:* Blackletter, 1986; Stanislaw Lem, 1986; Critical Essays on Edward Albee (co-Editor Philip C Kolin) (to be published 1986). *Contributions to:* Mississippi Review; Antietam Review;

From Mount San Angelo; article in, A 14th Century Analogue to Merchant of Venice in Shakespeare Quarterly, 1985, and many other publications. *Honours:* Third Prize, Virginia Highlands Festival Creative Writing Contest, 1981; Fellowship, Virginia Center for the Creative Arts, 1981; Fellowship, Hambidge Center for the Arts, 1982; Fellowship in Fiction, Pennsylvania Council of the Arts, 1984. *Memberships:* Poets and Writers Incorporated; Associated Writing Programs. *Address:* 9812 Stateline Road, North East, PA 16428, USA.

DAVIS, Louise, b. 1 Oct. 1950, Montreal, Canada. Writer. 1 daughter. *Education:* BA, University of Sherbrooke. *Appointments:* Literary Agent for a regional author association, Sherbroke, 1982–85; Literary Chronicle, Radio CIMO FM (Magog-Sherbrooke), 1984–85. *Publications:* La maternitude à bras ouverts, 1980; Le voile de la honte, 1983. *Contributor to:* Perspectives, Winter 1982, Montreal; Passages Autumn 1983 and Summer 1985; Soc et Foc, 1983, France. *Memberships:* Association des auteurs des Cantons de l'Est, President 1982–84; Salon du livre de l'Estrie, Board of Directors, 1982–83; Union des ecrivains quebecois, Montreal; Conseil de la culture de l'Estrie, President 1984–85. *Address:* 95 Bellevue app. 317 Sherbrooke, Quebec, Canada J1J 3Z2.

DAVIS, Michael Justin, b. 9 Feb. 1925, Oxted, Surrey, England. *Education:* BA, Pembroke College, Cambridge, 1949. *Publications:* William Blake a New Kind of Man, 1977; Supervisory Editor, The Kennet Shakespeare, 1964–74; Co-Editor, Words for Worship, 1969; Editor, More Words for Worship, 1980; (Poetry) The Way to the Tree of Life, 1983; To the Cross, 1984; Editor, Works By Alfred Williams: In A Wiltshire Village, 1981, Round About Middle Thames, 1982, Life in A Railway Factory, 1984; Editor, Edward Thomas's, A Literary Pilgrim, 1985. *Membership:* Alfred Williams Society. *Honour:* Recipient, Poetry Prize, Festival of St Cecilia, Bournemouth, 1976. *Literary Agent:* Curtis Brown Ltd. *Address:* Hyde Lodge, Hyde Lane, Marlborough, Wiltshire SN8 1JN, England.

DAVIS, Moshe, b. 12 June 1916, Brooklyn, NY, USA. Historian. *Education:* BA, Columbia University, NY, 1937; BJP, Teacher's Institute, 1937; MHL and Rabbinic Ordination, Jewish Theol, Seminary America, 1942; PhD, Hebrew University, Jerusalem, 1945. *Publications:* The Emergence of Conservative Judaism, 1963; American Jewish Community and World Jewry, 1970; Jewish Religious Life and Institutions, latest edition, 1971; (Editor) Yom Kippur Way – Israel and the Jewish People, 1974; With Eyes toward Zion, Volume I, 1977, Volume II, in press; (Project Director, General Editor), Guide to America-Holy Land Studies, Volume 4, 1880–84; Also Hebrew Publications. *Contributor to:* Various national and international scholarly journals. *Memberships include:* Study Circle of World Jewry; Home of Israel's Pres, (Chairman); Recipient, DHL, Hebrew Union College; Jewish Institute of Religion, 1974; Academic Chairman, International Center for University Teaching of Jewish Civilization. *Address:* Institute of Contemporary Jewry, Hebrew University of Jerusalem, Jerusalem, Israel.

DAVIS, Orville Kince, b. 26 July 1946, Many, Louisiana, USA. Journalist. *Education:* BA, magna cum laude, Journalism, Louisiana Technical University, 1969. *Literary Appointments:* Contributor, extensive biographical material. Outstanding Tennis Players of the Decade, 1972; Commissioned, series of articles on former great athletes, Louisiana Sportswriters Association, 1980; Research Committee, contributor, Louisiana Hall of Fame (published book). *Publication:* Grambling's Gridiron Glory, 1983. *Contributions to:* The Sporting News, USA Today (Louisiana correspondent); Over 300 articles in magazines and journals; Bylines in: Sports Illustrated; Grit; USA Today; Mainstream America; Louisiana Life; Football Digest; The Sporting News; Basketball Digest; Young Athlete; Holiday Inn Magazine; Basketball Times; Christian Single. *Honours:* 1st place, sportswriters feature story contest, Louisiana,

1969; Sweepstakes award winner, 1973, Best sports photo, Louisiana sportswriters contest, 1973; Best sports story, Louisiana, United Press International, 1978; Heisman Trophy certificate, Excellence as voter, 1981; 7th place, best article, National Writers Club contest, 1984. *Memberships:* Sigma Delta Chi; National Writers Club; Media Alliance; National Association of Sportswriters & Sportscasters; Football Writers Association of America; Basketball Writers of America; National Heisman Trophy Voting Committee. *Address:* PO Box 1427, Ruston, LA 71270, USA.

DAVIS, Owen, b. 27 Jan. 1939, Kuala Lumpur, Malaysia. Writer. m. Anne Philipsen, 2 Oct. 1982, London, England, 2 sons, 1 daughter. *Literary Appointments:* Editor, South West Review, 1979–81. *Publications:* Voice, 1973; Exile Within, 1975; Bruges, with Marcus Cumberlege, 1976; Reflective Arrangement, 1982; One Plus One, with Jeremy Hilton, 1985. Various others. *Contributions to:* Prism International, Canada; Poetry Australia; Parallel, Belgium; Voices, Israel; Grosseteste Review; Lettera, and others. *Honour:* Bursary, South West Arts (Writers), 1975. *Address:* 15 Argyle Road, Swanage, Dorset BH19 1HZ, England.

DAVIS, Peter Frank, b. 1 Feb. 1937, Los Angeles, California, USA. Writer. m. Karen Zehring, 10 June 1979, 3 sons, 1 daughter. *Education:* AB, Harvard College. *Publication:* Hometown, 1982. *Contributions to:* Esquire; The Nation. *Honours:* George Polk Award; 2 Awards, Writers Guild of America; Academy Award; Peabody Award; Award, Saturday Review of Literature. *Literary Agent:* Lynn Nesbit (ICM), 40 West 5th Street, New York, NY 10019. *Address:* 320 Central Park West, New York, NY 10025, USA.

DAVIS, Raecile Gwalthey, b. Louisville, USA. Teacher of Business Education. m. Fred Alvis Davis, 2 daughters. *Education:* Howard College; Samford University; Diploma, Wheeler Business College; BE, Alverspn-Draughn Business College; Speedwriting Institute, Teachers Certificate, New York. *Appointments:* Circulating Manager, Alabama Baptist Publications, 1950; First Director of Jr Clubs, Third Dis Ala Fed Women's Clubs Org. 1962; Historian Alabama Writers Conclave, 1975–80; Founder and first editor of, The Alalitcom, Litt. Anthology of Alabama Writers' Conclave, 1975; Historian, Alabama State Poetry Society, 1985. *Publications:* Giant Sages of the Pen, History of the Ala. Writers' Conclave, 1923–80; The Alalitcom, 1975, eleventh edition; I Remember Dad, memoirs, 1984. *Contributions:* Short stories, articles, poems in, Alalitcom; Poems on, Sampler; Progressive Farmer, Ideals etc; Four religious plays in, Alitcom. *Honours:* Morrison Silver Bowl Award, AFWC, 1974; Geneva Brush Silver Tray Award, AFWC, 1975; AWC Plaque for best essay in literary competiion, 1983; The Vatican Library, Rome, Diploma of Merit in Literature conferred by Universita Delle Arti of Italy; Inclusion of poems in Library of Congress; United Nations Peace Keeping Dept; Smithsonian Institute of Letters; AWC Plaque for best article, 1983; AWC Plaque for best play, 1983; AWC Plaque for best article written in seminar, etc. *Memberships:* President, Women's Club of Birmingham; President, Alabama State Poetry Society; President Alabama Writers' Conclave; President the Birmingham Quill Club; President, National League American Pen Women, Birmingham Branch, etc. *Address:* 5621 Sixth Avenue South, Birmingham AL 35212, USA.

DAVIS, (Walter) Burke, b. 24 July 1913, Durham, North Carolina, USA. Writer. m. Evangeline McLennan, 11 Aug. 1940, Augusta, 1 son, 1 daughter; Juliet Halliburton Burnett, 6 Feb. 1982, Queensboro. *Education:* AB, Journalism, University of North Carolina, 1937; Duke University, 2 years; Guildford College, 1 year. *Publications:* They Called Him Stonewall, 1954; Gray Fox: R E Lee of the Civil War, 1956; Jeb Stuart: The Last Cavalier, 1957; To Appomattox, 1959; Sherman's March, 1980; The Long Surrender, 1985. *Contributor to:* Harpers; Atlantic Monthly; New Republic; American Mercury. *Honours:*

Mayflower Cup, 1959; Fletcher Pratt Award, 1959; North Carolina Award, Literature, 1973. *Address:* Random House Inc, 201 East 50th, New York, NY 10022, USA.

DAVIS, William Sterling, b. 18 Apr. 1943, Pittston, Pennsylvania, USA. Professor, Systems Analysis. m. Catherine Ann Curcio, 2 July 1966, Easton, 1 son, 2 daughters. *Education:* BS, Industrial Engineering, Lafayette College; MA, Business Enterprise, SUNY, Binghamton. *Publications include:* Textbooks: Operating Systems: A Systematic View, 1977; Information Processing Systems, 1978; Business Data Processing, 1978; Cobol: An Introduction to Structured Logic and Modular Programme Design, 1979; The Information Age, 1979; Fortran 77: Getting Started, 1981; Basic: Getting Started, 1981; Computers and Business Information Processing, 1981; Information Processing Systems, 2nd edition 1981; Systems Analysis and Design: A Structured Approach, 1983; Computers and Business Information Processing, 2nd edition 1983; Tools and Techniques for Structured Systems Analysis and Design, 1983; True Basic Primer, 1985; Novel: The Neon Voyage: An Adventure in Computer Literacy, 1985; Fundamental Computer Concepts, 1986. *Address:* Department of Systems Analysis, Miami University, Oxford, OH 45056, USA.

DAVIS, William Virgil, b. 26 May 1940, Canton, Ohio, USA. Professor of English. m. Carol Ann Demske, 17 July 1971, Bristol, Connecticut, USA, 1 son. *Education:* M Div, Pittsburgh Theological Seminary, 1965; AB 1962, MA 1965, PhD 1967, Ohio University. *Literary Appointments:* Assistant Professor, University of Ohio, 1967–68; Assistant Professor, Central Connecticut State University, 1968–72; Assistant Professor, University of Illinois, Chicago, 1972–77; Associate Professor, Baylor University, 1977–79; Professor of English and Writer-in-Residence, Baylor University, 1979–. *Major Publications:* George Whitefield's Journals 1737–41, 1969; One Way to Reconstruct the Scene, 1980; The Dark Hours, 1984. *Contributor to:* Poetry; Hudson Review; Atlantic; Modern Poetry Studies; over 700 poems, 60 scholarly articles, also short stories, essays, reviews. *Honours:* Senior Fulbright Fellowship, University of Vienna, Austria, 1979–80; also University of Copenhagen, Denmark, 1984; Writer-in-Residence, University of Montana, 1983. *Memberships:* PEN; Academy of American Poets; Poetry Society of America; Poets & Writers; Texas Institute of Letters. *Address:* 2633 Lake Oaks Road, Waco, TX 76710, USA.

DAVISON, Peter Hubert, b. 27 June 1928, New York City, USA. Poet; Editor. m. (1) Jane Truslow Davison, 7 Mar. 1959, New York (deceased), 1 son, 1 daughter. (2) Joan Edelman Goody, 11 Aug 1984, Cambridge, Massachusetts. *Education:* AB, magna cum laude, Harvard College, 1949; Fulbright Scholar, St John's College, Cambridge, England, 1950. *Literary Appointments:* Assistant Editor, Harcourt Brace, 1950–51, 1953–55; Assistant to Director, Harvard University Press, 1955–56; Editor, Atlantic Monthly Press, 1956–63; Director, Atlantic Monthly Press, 1963–79; Poetry Editor, The Atlantic, 1972–; Senior Editor, Atlantic Monthly Press, 1979–85; Editor of, Peter Davison Books, Houghton Mifflin Co, 1985–. *Publications:* The Breaking of the Day and Other Poems, 1964; The City and the Island, 1966; Pretending to be Asleep, 1970; Half Remembered, A Personal History, 1973; Walking the Boundaries, 1974; A Voice in the Mountain, 1977; Barn Fever and Other Poems, 1980; Praying Wrong; New and Selected Poems 1957–84, 1984 USA, 1985 UK. *Contributions to:* The Atlantic; The New Yorker; Harper's; Encounter; Times Literary Supplement; New York Times Book Review; Washington Post Book World; The American Scholar; The New Criterion; Harvard Magazine; Hudson Review; Poetry (Chicago); New England Review/Breadloaf Quarterly; Country Journal; The New Republic and many others. *Honours:* Yale Series of Younger Poets Competition, 1963; Poetry Award, National Institute American Academy of Arts and Letters, 1972; James Michener Grant, Academy of

American Poets, 1980 and 1985. *Memberships:* National Translation Center 1964–67; Corporation of Yaddo, 1979–; Literature Panel, National Endowment for the Arts, 1979–82. *Address:* 70 River Street, Boston, MA 02108, USA.

DAWE, Gerald Chartres, b. 22 Apr. 1952, Belfast, North Ireland. Tutor in English. m. Dorothea Melvin, 28 Sep. 1979, Belfast, 1 son, 1 daughter. *Education:* BA Honours; Master of Arts, MA. *Literary Appointments:* Editor, Writing in the West Literary Supplement, Connacht Tribune, 1979–84. *Publications:* Sheltering Places, poems, 1978; The Younger Irish Poets, anthology, 1982; Across a Roaring Hill: The protestant Imagination in Modern Ireland, with Edna Longley, essays, 1985; The Lundys Letter, poems, 1985. *Contributions to:* Numerous publications. *Honours:* Major State Award for Research, 1974–77; Arts Council Bursary for Poetry, 1980; Macaulay Fellowship in Literature, 1984. *Memberships:* International Association of Anglo-Irish Literature and Language. *Address:* Glenrevagh, Corrandulla, County Galway, Republic of Ireland.

DAY, Beth, b. 25 May 1924, Fort Wayne, Indiana, USA. Freelance Writer. m. Carlos P Romulo, 1978, Manila (deceased 1985). *Education:* BA, University of Oklahoma, 1945; Honorary Doctor of Letters; Philippine Womens; University, Baguio Colleges Foundation. *Literary Appointment:* Teacher, Professional Writing, Adult School, Chappaqua, New York. *Publications:* Trade Books: Little Professor of Piney Woods, 1955; Grizzlies in Their Back Yard, 1956; Glacier Pilot, 1957; No Hiding Place, 1958; A Shirttail To Hang To, 1960; This Was Hollywood, 1959; Hey, I'm Alive, 1964; Passage Perilious, 1962; Special Agent, 1961; Sexual Life Between Blacks and Whites, 1972; I'm Done Crying, 1970; All My Children, 1971; Modern Motherhood, 1968; My Name is Dr Rantzau, 1970; The Philippines, Shattered Showcase of Democracy in Asia, 1974; The Manila Hotel, 1979; Juvenile Books: Will Rogers, 1952; Joshua Slocum, 1953; Talk Like a Cowboy, 1955; Eugene Rhodes, 1955; Lucille Mulhall, 1956; Grizzlies, 1971; Secret World of the Baby, 1968; Life on a Lost Continent, 1969; Speeches and Articles: Another Day (National Media), 1978; Persepective of a Diplomat's Wife, 1981; Aspects of Cultural Reporting (Foreign Service Institute), 1982. *Contributions to:* Magazines in USA, England, France, Germany, Italy and the Netherlands. *Honours:* Two Honorary Doctorates. *Memberships:* ASJA, formerly Society of Magazine Writers; Authors Guild; Authors League; Society of Women Geographers; Chaine des Rotisseurs; Les Disciples d'Auguste Escoffier. *Address:* 35 E 38th Street, New York, NY, USA.

DAY, Christopher Noel, b. 18 Nov. 1935, Harrow, England. Journalist. 1 son, 2 daughters. *Education:* GCE (Oxon). *Literary Appointments:* Editor, London Counties Newspapers; Foundation Editor, New Zealand Sunday News; Editor, Australian TV Times; Currently Freelance Writer of Sydney, Australia. *Publication:* Anzac 50th Anniversary of Gallipoli, 1965. *Contributions to:* National Times, TV Times, New Idea, Video Age, TV Guide, (USA); Woman's Day, Look & Listen, Australian TV: The First 25 Years, Broadcasting and TV, Sun-Herald. *Membership:* Australian Journalists Association. *Address:* 2 Margaret Street, Newtown, New South Wales 2042, Australia.

DAY, David Alan, b. 14 Oct. 1947, Victoria, British Columbia, Canada. Writer. Divorced, 1 daughter. *Education:* BA, University of Victoria. *Literary Appointment:* Writer-in-Residence, Aegean School of Arts, Greece. *Publications:* The Cowichan (poems), 1976; Many Voices: Canadian Indian Poetry (Anthology), Editor, 1977; The Burroughs Bestiary (fantasy), 1978; The Tolkien Bestiary (fantasy), 1979; The Scarlet Coat Serial (poems), 1981; The Doomsday Book of Animals (natural history), 1981; Castles (mythology), 1984; The Animals Within (poetry), 1984; The Emperor's Panda (novel), 1986; The Whale War (ecology), 1986; Gothic (poems), 1986. *Contributions*

to: Numerous publications (200-300). *Honours:* Canada Council Awards for Poetry, Fiction and Non-fiction, 1981, 83, 85; Canadian Broadcasting Corporation Prize for Poetry, 1982. *Memberships:* Writers Union of Canada; League of Canadian Poets. *Literary Agent:* Deborah Rogers Associates. *Address:* 23 Laurier Road, London, NW5, England.

DAY, Nancy Elizabeth (Raines), b. 15 Oct. 1951, Denver, Colorado, USA. Freelance Writer. m. Kenneth Gordon Day, 17 Aug. 1974, Greenwich, Connecticut, 1 son, 1 daughter. *Education:* BA, Journalism, University of Michigan, 1972; MA, Literary Journalism, Syracuse University, 1974. *Publications:* Tobacco: Facts for Decisions, 1978; Help Yourself to Health, 1980. *Contributions:* Russia in the USA, 1983; Bed & Breakfasts, 1982; Strawflowers, 1981; Fashions of the Past, 1980, etc, to Americana. *Honours:* National Merit Scholarship, 1969–72; College Honours Programme, University of Michigan; Mortar Board; Kappa Tau Alpha; Laubach Literary Assistantship; Award, Health Educators. *Memberships:* Authors Guild; Society of Childrens Book Writers; American Medical Writers Association; National Writers Club; Media Alliance; Women in Communications. *Address:* 598 Mariano Drive, Sonoma, CA 95476, USA.

DAY, Richard Somers, b. 14 June 1928, Chicago, Illinois, USA. Freelance Writer. m. Lois Patricia Beggs, 8 July 1950, Chicago, 2 sons, 1 daughter. *Publications include:* The New Concrete & Masonry Guide, 1966; MI Guide to Painting Your Home, 1967; The Practical Guide to Plumbing & Heating, 1968; The Practical Handbook of Concrete & Masonry, 1969; The Practical Handbook of Electrical Repair, 1969; Easy Things to Make with Concrete & Masonry, 1971; How to Service & Repair Your Own Car, 1973; The Home Owner Handbook of Plumbing & Heating, 1974; Patios & Decks, 1976; Plumb-It-Yourself the Easy Way with Genova, 1977; Automechanics, 1982; Automotive Engine Tuning, 1982; etc. *Contributions to:* Popular Science; Popular Mechanics; Homeowner; Family Handyman; Workbench; Home Mechanix. *Membership:* President & Director, National Association of Home & Workshop Writers. *Address:* Palomar Mountain, CA 92060, USA.

DAY-LEWIS, Sean Francis, b. 3 Aug. 1931, Cheltenham, England. Television and Radio Editor, Daily Telegraph. m. Anna Mott, 11 June 1960, Hampstead, England, 1 son, 1 daughter. *Publications:* Bulleid: Last Giant of Steam, 1964; C Day-Lewis: An English Literary Life, 1980. *Contributions to:* The Listener; Socialist Commentary; Radio Times; Broadcast; Drama; Plays versus Players. *Literary Agent:* Giles Gordon, Anthony Sheil Limited. *Address:* 38 Caithness Road, London W14 OJA, England.

DAYARATNAM, Pasala, b. 23 Nov. 1932, Rentachintala, India. Researcher; Teacher. m. Vijayalakshmi, 9 June 1959, 3 daughters. *Education:* BS, Madras; MS, PhD, Colorado, USA. *Literary Appointments:* Lecturer and Reader, Andhra University; Associate and Professor, ITT Kanpur. *Publications:* Prestressed Concrete Structures, 1970, 74, 78, 82; Analy. of Stat. Det. Structures, 1976; Analy. of Sta. Ind. Structures, 1976; Advanced Structural Analysis, 1978, 79, 82; Eng. Mechanics (Statics), 1979, 83; Structural Engineering Objective Questions, 1979, 82, 84; Design of RCC Structures, 1983, 84, 86. *Contributor to:* Journals of American Society Civil Engineers'; American Concrete Institue; International Association Bridge and Structural Engineering; IASS; Institute of Engineers, India; InternationalJournal of Building Science and Env; International Journal of Masonry; Indian Concrete Journal, (some 90 papers). *Honours:* TCM Scholarship, 1959; Aca. Exc. Citations, University of Colorado, 1982; Gold Medals from Institute of Engineers (India), 1976, 80. *Memberships:* Fellow, Institute of Engineers, India; Farmer Associate Member of ASCE. *Address:* Professor of Civil Engineering, ITT Kanpur 208 016 India.

DAYTON, Irene Catherine G, b. 6 Aug. 1922, Lake Ariel, Pennsylvania, USA. Poet & Novelist. m. Benjamin B Dayton, 16 Oct. 1943, North Chili, New York, 2 sons. *Education:* Roberts Wesleyan College, Associate Degree, 1942. *Literary Appointments:* Poet-in-Residence, Rochester, New York (State Arts Council), 1972–73; Poetry Consultant, Rochester, 1971–73; Instructor, Modern Poetry Writing & Creative Writing, Blue Ridge Technical College, Flat Rock, North Carolina, 1978–; Opportunity House, Hendersonville, North Carolina, 1982–. *Major Publications:* Poetry: In Oxbow of Time's River, 1978; Seven Times the Wind, 1977; The Panther's Eye, 1974; The Sixth Sense Quivers, 1970; Novels: Tale of the Vercors, 1984; The House of Zorayan, in progress. *Contributor to:* Literary Review; Malahat Review; Negative Capability; Poet Lore; and others. *Honours:* Finalist, Yale University Series of Younger Poets, 1958; 1st Prize Awards, Rochester Festival of Religious Arts 1959–60; Guiness Award, Cheltenham Festival of Literature, England, 1963; Distinguished Submissions Award, Shan andoah Valley Academy of Literature, 1979. *Memberships:* Rochester New York Poetry Society, Honorary Life Member, twice President; Poetry Society of America (Life Member); North Carolina Poetry Society; Founder Fellow, International Academy of Poets, Marquis Library Society, New York. *Address:* Pine Stone, 209 S Hillandale Drive, East Flat Rock, NC 28726, USA.

DE ARMAS, Frederick A, b. 9 Feb. 1945, Havana, Cuba, Professor. *Education:* BA, Stetson University, 1965; PhD, University of North Carolina, 1968, *Literary Appointments:* Editorial Advisory Board for 'Hispanofila, 1981–; for Bulletin of the Comediantes, 1981; Advisory Committee, PMLA, 1985–. *Major Publications:* The Four Interpolated Stories in the Roman Comique, 1971; Paul Scarron, 1972; The Invisible Mistress: Aspects of Feminism & Fantasy in the Golden Age, 1976; Co-editor, Critical Perspectives of Calderón de la Barca, 1981; The Return of Astraea: An Astral – Imperial Myth in Calderón, 1986. *Memberships:* Modern Language Association; American Association of Teachers of Spanish & Portuguese; Association International de Hispanistas; International Comparative Literature Association; Hispanic Society of America. *Honour:* Recipient, National Endowment for the Humanities Grant, 1979; National Endowment for the Humanities Fellowship for in-residence work, Newbury Library, 1985. *Address:* Department of Spanish & Portuguese, Louisiana State University, Baton Rouge, LA 70803, USA.

DE BLESER, Willy, b. 26 Feb. 1934, Boom, Belgium. Official. m. Hélène Van Dyck, 8 Dec. 1956, Boom, 2 sons, 2 daughters. *Publications:* Author, novels and short stories, De Adders, 1975; Het Verhaal van Teraja en Werjonjo, 1977; De Steniging, 1979; Het Koncert, 1981; Parijs-Tours, 1983. *Contributions to:* Various literary magazines. *Memberships:* Vereniging van Vlaamse Letterkundigen; Vereniging van Kempische Schrijvers; Vereniging van Vlaams Nationale Auteurs. *Address:* Sneeuwbesstraat 18, 2070 Antwerp, Belgium.

DE BOISSIERE, Ralph, b. 6 Oct. 1907, Trinidad, West Indies. Writer. m. Ivy Alcántara, 17 June 1935, Port-of-Spain, Trinidad, 2 daughters. *Publications:* Crown Jewel, 1952, 81 (translated into 8 languages); Rum and Coca-Cola, 1956, 84 (Translated into 6 langauges); No Saddle for Kangaroos, 1964. *Contributions to:* The Beacon, Trinidad; The Herald, Melbourne, Australia; Sun. *Membership:* Australian Society of Authors. *Literary Agent:* Dr R Sander, Bayreuth University. *Address:* 10 Vega Street, North Baldwyn, Victoria 3104, Australia.

DE CHAIR, Somerset, b. 22 Aug. 1911, Sunningdale, Berks, England. Writer. BA, Balliol College, Oxford. *Publications:* The Impending Storm, 1930; Divided Europe, 1932; Peter Public (Drama), 1932; Enter Napoleon, 1935; Red Tie in the Morning, 1936; The Golden Carpet, 1943; A Mind on the March, 1946; The Dome of the Rock, 1948; The Teetotalitarian State, 1949; The Story of a Lifetime, 1954; Bring Back the

Gods, 1962; Freinds, Romans, Concubines, 1971; The Star of the Wind, 1974; Legend of the Yellow River, 1979; (ed and transl) Napoleon's Memoirs, 1946; The First Crusade, Julius Caesar's Commentaries, 1951; The Millenium (Poems), 1949; Collected Verse, 1970; Buried Pleasure, 1985. *Address:* St Osyth Priory, Essex, England.

DE CLEMENTS, Barthe Faith, b. 8 Oct. 1920, Seattle, Washington, USA. Author. 2 sons, 2 daughters. *Education:* MEd, Educational Psychology, University of Washington, USA, 1970. *Major Publications:* Nothing's Fair in Fifth Grade, 1981; How Do You Lose Those Ninth Grade Blues?, 1983; Seventeen and In-between, 1984; Sixth Grade Can Really Kill, 1985; I Never Asked You to Understand Me, 1986. *Honours:* For Nothing's Fair in Fifth Grade, awards from 11 States, 1984–5. *Literary Agent:* William Reiss, John Hawkins & Associates Inc, New York. *Address:* 1511 Russell Road, Snohomish, WA 98290, USA.

DE CNODDER, Remi Frans Jozef, b. 23 Mar. 1919, Antwerp, Belgium. Art Critic. m. Marie-Thérèse van Lierop, Beveren, 24 Mar. 1979, 2 sons. *Literary Appointments:* Literary man; Art critic; Member, several committees and juries in Belgium & Italy. *Publications include:* Klein Boeket, 1941; Krans der Kleine Liederen, 1948; Weerspiegeling, 1979; Anti Pieta, 1980; Numerous translations. Young people's books: Een Pionier van de Luchtvaart; De Politieinspecteur, 1968; L'Inspecteur de Police, 1969. Art books: Oscar Verpoorten, 1951; Octave Landuyt, 1958; Rene de Coninck, 1965; Pol Mara, 1974; Ward Lernout, 1979; Piet Bekaert, 1982; Joz De Loose, 1984; etc. Aphorisms: Glossarium, 1982. Documentary films, television scripts, organiser for art exhibitions. *Contributions to:* Dailies and revues. *Honours include:* Silver Medal, City of Paris, 1961; Cavaliere nell' Ordine al Merito della Repubblica Italiana, 1962; Knight, Order of King Leopold II, Belgium, 1962; Gold Medal, City of Diano Marina, Italy, 1963; Gold Medal, City of Apricale, Italy, 1967; 2nd International Prize, Immagine per la Citta, Genova, Italy, 1972; Knight, Order of the Crown, Belgium, 1982; Officer, Order of Leopold II, Belgium, 1984. *Memberships:* Association Internationale des Critiques d'Art; VVL (Association of Flemish Authors). *Address:* House San Michele, Italiëlei 219 B.7, B–2000 Antwerpen, Belgium.

DE GROEN, Alma Margaret (Mathers), b. 5 Sep. 1941, Foxton, New Zealand. Playwright. *Publications:* Going Home & Other Plays, 1977; Vocations, 1983. *Contributions to:* Theatre Australia; Vogue (Australia). *Honour:* Australian Writers Guild Award, best TV adaptation, 1985. *Memberships:* Australian Writers Guild; Australian National Playwrights Conference. *Literary Agent:* Hilary Linstead. *Address:* c/o Hilary Linstead & Associates Pty Ltd, 223 Commonwealth Street, Surry Hills, NSW 2010, Australia.

DE HAMEL, Joan Littledale, b. 31 Mar. 1924, London, England. Writer; Former Teacher of French. m. Francis Alexander De Hamel, 24 Apr. 1948, London, 5 sons. *Education:* BA, 1944, MA, 1949, Lady Margaret Hall, Oxford University. *Publications:* X Marks the Spot, 1975; Take the Long Path, 1978; Hemi's Pet, 1985. *Contributions to:* Various journals and magazines; various radio and television scripts. *Honours:* Esther Glen Medal, New Zealand Library Association, 1979; A W Reed Memorial Award, 1985. *Membership:* Chairwoman, Dunedin Branch, PEN. *Literary Agents:* A P Watt, London, England; Ray Richards, Auckland, New Zealand. *Address:* 25 Howard Street, MacAndrew Bay, Dunedin, New Zealand.

DE JONG, Frank, b. 23 July 1930, The Hague, Netherlands. Journalist. m. 1956, 1 son. *Education:* Higher grade School, 5 years. *Publications:* Juliana & Bernhard in Indonesia, 1971, with H F van Loon. *Contributor to:* Daily Express, London; Sunday Tribune; Dublin; RTE Radio, Dublin; The Irish Press, Dublin; Dagens Nyheter, Stockholm. *Memberships:* Treasurer,

Acting Secretary, Foreign Press Association, Netherlands BPV, 1978–. *Address:* 23, Rijklof van Goensplein, NL 2024 An Haarlem, The Netherlands.

DE-LA-NOY, Michael, b. 3 Apr. 1934, Hessle, Writer. *Publications:* Elgar: The Man, 1983; The Journals of Denton Welch, Editor, 1984; Denton Welch: The Making of a Writer, 1984; The Honours System, 1985; Fragments of a Life Story: The Collected Short Works of Denton Welch, Editor, 1986. *Contributions to:* The Sunday Times; The Observer; The Illustrated London News; The Guardian; Books and Bookmen; New Society; The Musical Times; The Month; The Tablet; The Dublin Review. *Address:* c/o Penguin Books Limited, 536 King's Road, London SW10 OUH, England.

DE LA PESCA, Magda, b. 8 June 1946, Melbourne, Australia. Writer. *Education:* BA, Dip Ed, Monash University. *Literary Appointments:* Founding member, IMAGO Writers' Group, 1981; Grant for feature script, Australian Film Commission, 1982; Writer-in-Residence, Eltham High School, Victoria, 1983; Grant, Crafts Board, Australian Council, craft documentation, 1984. *Publications include:* Book, Raw Deal, 1975; Film & Television Dramas, Cop Shop, 1980, Home, 1981–82, Prisoner, 1983. *Contributions to:* Bulletin (Brussels); Bottom Line; Scientific Australian; Craft Victoria; Carringbush Writers; Juke; Nation Review; Herald; The Asian; The Age. *Memberships:* Australian Society of Authors; Australian Writers Guild; Fellowship of Australian Writers; Imago. *Address:* 159 Park Drive, Parkville, Victoria 3052, Australia.

DE LAET, Sigfried J L, b. 15 June 1914, Ghent, Belgium. Professor Emeritus, University of Ghent. *Publications include:* Aspects de la vie sociale et economique sous Auguste et Tibere, 1944; Portorium, 1949, 1975; Geschiedenis van Belgie, 1955, 5th edition, 1976; Archaeology & its Problems, 1957 (translated, French, Dutch, Danish, Italian, Swedish, Polish, Spanish); La prehistoire de l'Europe, 1967; La necropole gallo-romaine de Blicquy, 1972; Prehistorysche kulturen in het zuiden der Lage Landen, 1974, 2nd edition 1979; La Belgique d'avant les Romains, 1982; Dir., Volume I, UNESCO'S, A Scientific and Cultural History of Mankind, in preparation. *Contributor to:* Archaeological & historical journals, including, Helinium, Editor. *Honours:* FSA, Scotland, 1969, & London, 1972; Honorary Corresponding Member, Prehistory Society of Great Britain, 1968. *Memberships:* Honorary Member, Archaeological Associations in Denmark, Germany, Switzerland, Netherlands, Italy & France. *Address:* Soenenspark 45, 9820 St Denijs-Westrem, Ghent, Belgium.

DE LAUNAY, Jacques Forment, b. 28 Jan, 1924, Roubaix, France., Historian; Author. *Education:* JD. *Publications:* Secret Diplomacy of World War II, 1963; Major Controversies of Contemporary History, 1965; De Gaulle & His France, 1969; Great Decisions of World War II, 1973; La Grande Débâcle, 1944–45, 1985. *Membership:* VP European Press Association. *Address:* 211 Souverain BF4, B–1160 Brussels, Belgium.

DE MEJO, Oscar, b. 22 Aug. 1911, Trieste, Italy. Artist. m. Dorothy Graham, Dec 1967, Ciudad Juarez, Mexico. *Education:* Law Degree, University of Siena, Italy. 1935; Doctorate in political and social sciences, University of Padua, Italy, 1937. *Publications:* The Tiny Visitor, 1982; There's a Hand in the Sky, 1983; My America, 1983. *Contributions to:* From Trieste with Love, MD Magazine, 1985. Represented exclusively by the Nahan Galleries, New Orleans, Louisiana, USA. *Honour:* Award by The New York Times for one of ten best illustrated children's books of 1982. *Literary Agent:* Gloria Safier. *Address:* 322 West 57th Street, apt 10M, New York, NY 10019, USA.

DE PAGÈS, André Denis, b. 13 Jan. 1943, Grand-Combe, France. Writer, Historian. m. Johanne Doré, 22 June 1977, Montréal, Canada. *Education:* College

Alphonse Daudet, Nîmes, France. *Literary Appointments:* Lecturer, Salon International du Livre de Québec, 1985; Lecturer, Orandia Esoterical Program, Montréal, 1984. *Major Publications:* Nos ancêtres les Extraterrestres, 1979; Ile de Pâques – Miroir de Mu, 1984. *Membership:* Québec Writers' Union. *Literary Agent:* Jean Bergeron. *Address:* P.O. Box 596, Saint-Eustache, Québec, J7R 5W3, Canada.

DE PAUW, Wilfried Jan, b. 8 June 1927, Brussels, Belgium. Ambassador. *Education includes:* Masters and Educational degrees, Free University, Brussels, 1948; Studies, Universities of Amsterdam, Heidelberg and Pretoria; DLitt, Pretoria University, South Africa, 1954; Law studies; Honorary LLD, St Louis University, Philippines. *Publications:* Albert Verwey en Stefan George; Het talenvraagstuk in Belgisch-Kongo. *Honours:* War Palms, Red Cross of Belgium, 1940–45; Officer, Order of Leopold; Commander, Order of the Crown. *Address:* Koning Albertlaan 78, B–1080 Brussels, Belgium.

DE SCHUTTER, Willy Alfons Jan, b. 11 June 1906, Antwerp, Belgium. Journalist. m. Germaine Eug Liv Kenens, 3 Aug. 1929, 2 sons. *Education:* Diploma, Teacher, Antwerp, 1925. *Appointment:* Dramatic Critic, 1947–71. *Publications:* Play: Begin een nieuw Leven, 1950; Essay, 25 Years Youth Theatre of Antwerp, 1970; Portraits of Actors, 1979; etc. *Contributor to:* De Nieuwe Gazet. *Honours:* Knight Order Crown, 1950; Recipient, various Military Medals; Medal, Broken Pen, 1951; Knight Order Leopold, 1958; Officer Order Leopold II, 1968; Officer Order Crown, 1981; Literary Awards include: Four Flemish Provinces, 1952; International Home for Journalist, Hungary, 1967; Martini Award, 1968. *Address:* Smedenstraat 3, 2610 Antwerp, Wilrijk, Belgium.

DE WAAL, Ronald Burt, b. 23 Oct. 1932, Salt Lake City, Utah, USA. Librarian; Bibliographer. m. Gayle Lloyd, 7 Nov. 1963, Salt Lake City, 1 son. *Education:* BS, University of Utah, 1955; MA, University of Denver, 1958. *Publications:* The World Bibliography of Sherlock Holmes & Dr Watson, 1974; The International Sherlock Holmes, 1980; The Universal Sherlock Holmes, 1986. *Contributor to:* Baker Street Journal, New York; Sherlock Holmes Society Journal, London. *Honours:* Recipient, John H M Jenkins Award for best work of bibliography published in US, 1974, 1976; The Two Shilling Award,The Baker Street Irregulars, 1984. *Memberships:* Baker Street Irregulars; Colleagues of Lomax, Sub-Librarian (Pres); Sherlock Holmes Society of London. *Address:* 5020 Hogan Dr, Ft Collins, CO 80525, USA.

DE YOUNG, Mary Kay, b. 11 Aug. 1949, Chicago, Illinois, USA. College Professor. *Education:* BS, Grand Valley State College; MA, University of Chicago; DA, Western Colorado University. *Publications:* The Sexual Victimization of Children, 1982; Incest: An Annotated Bibliography, 1985. *Contributions to:* Child Welfare Journal; Victimology: The International Journal; Journal of Clinical Child Psychology; Human Organization; Journal of Humanics; Journal of Psychosocial Nursing. *Address:* 2226 Saginaw Road, SE, Grand Rapids, MI 49506, USA.

DEAGON, Ann, b. 19 Jan. 1930, Birmingham, Alabama, USA. Professor of Classical Studies. m. Donald D Deagon, 29 June, 1951, Birmingham, Alabama, 2 daughters. *Education:* AB, Birmingham-Southern College, 1950; MA, 1951, PhD, 1954, University of North Carolina, Chapel Hill. *Literary Appointments:* Editor, The Guildford Review, 1966–84; Director, Poetry Center Southeast, 1980–. *Publications:* Carbon 14 (poems), 1974; Poetics South (poems), 1974; There is No Balm in Birmingham (poems), 1978; Habitats (short stories), 1982; The Diver's Tomb (novel), 1985. *Contributions:* Poems and short stories included in some 100 magazines and anthologies, including: Georgia Review; New Letters; New York Quarterly; Ohio Review; Norton Introduction to Literature; Norton Introduction to Poetry, etc. *Honours:*

National Endowment for the Arts Literary Fellowship, 1981–82; Winthrop College Chapbook Award in Fiction, 1981; Watermark Press Breakthrough Award, 1983. *Memberships:* Poetry Society of America; Academy of American Poets; North Carolina Poetry Society (Past President); North Carolina Writers Conference (Past President); Greensboro Writers Club (Past President); Poetry Center Southeast (Director, 1980–). *Literary Agent:* Paula Diamond. *Address:* 802 Woodbrook Drive, Greensboro, NC 27410, USA.

DEAHL, James Edward, b. 5 Dec. 1945, Pittsburgh, USA. Writer and Editor. m. Gilda L Mekler, 23 May 1982, at Toronto, 1 daughter. *Education:* 2-year Apprenticeship under Master Poet, Milton Acorn. *Literary Appointments:* Currently employed by Maclean Hunter Publishers, Canada. *Major Publications:* Essay issued as chapbook, Real Poetry, 1981; In the lost Horn's Call, 1982; No Cold Ash, 1984; Blue Ridge, 1985. *Memberships:* League of Canadian Poets; Canadian Authors' Association; Canadian Poetry Association; Co-Founder & Director, LINK Poetry Workshop; Co-Founder & Director, Susan Chakraverty Institute; Canadian Society for Cultural Studies, York University. *Address:* Box 909, Adelaide St Station, Toronto, Ontario, Canada M5C 2K3.

DEAN, Nancy, b. 19 July 1930, New York City, New York, USA. Teacher of English. *Education:* BA, Honours, Vassar, 1952; MAT, Harvard, 1953; PhD, Medieval Literature, New York University, 1963. *Publications:* In the Mind of the Writer, 1973; Anna's Country, 1981. Co-Editor, In the Looking Glass, 1977. *Contributions to:* Hunter College Studies, 1967; Comparative Literature, 1967; Medium Aevum, 1975; The Gathering, in, Room of One's Own, volume 2, 1976; Requited Love, in, Ikon, Second series, 1985. Translation into German, Anna, novel. *Memberships:* Modern Language Association; Medieval Club of New York; Dramatists Guild. *Literary Agent:* Charlotte Sheedy. *Address:* Hunter College, 695 Park Avenue, New York City, NY 10021, USA.

DEANOVICH, Connie Marie, b. 8 Nov. 1960, East Chicago, Indiana, USA. Writer. m. David Michael Stevenson, 15 Oct. 1983, Chicago. *Education:* BA Writing/English, Columbia College, Chicago, 1983. *Literary Appointments:* Director of Publicity, Poetry Center, School of the Art Institute of Chicago, 1983; Editor, B-City magazine, poetry, 1983. *Contributions to:* Oink; Luna Tack; Another Chicago Magazine; Privates; Hairtrigger; Dial-a-poem: The Chicago Poetry Letter News; B-City. *Address:* 619 West Surf Street, Chicago, IL 60657, USA.

DEAR, Nick, b. 11 June 1955, Portsmouth, Hampshire, England. Playwright. *Education:* BA Honours, University of Essex. *Literary Appointments:* Script tutor, National Film and Television School, Beaconsfield, 1981; Playwright in Residence, University of Essex, 1985. *Publications:* Produced plays: The Perfect Alibi, 1980; Temptation, 1984, India and USA, 1984–85; Great Dreams from Heaven, 1984; The Bed, 1985. Filmed productions: Memo, 1980; The Monkey Parade, 1983; The Ranter, 1985. Radio and television productions: Matter Permitted, 1980; Pure Science, 1983; In The Ruins, 1984; Jonathan Wild, 1985. Currently working on a new play for the Royal Shakespeare Company. *Honours:* Radio Award, for Matter Permitted, Pye/Society of Authors, 1981. *Memberships:* Theatre Writers Guild; Writers Guild of Great Britain. *Literary Agent:* Joanna Marston, Rosica Colin Limited, London. *Address:* c/o Rosica Colin Limited, 1 Clareville Grove Mews, London SW7 5AH, England.

DeBAKEY, Michael Ellis, b. 7 Sep. 1908, Lake Charles, Louisiana, USA. Surgeon. *Education:* BS, 1930; MD, 1932; MS, 1935, Tulane University, School of Medicine, New Orleans, Louisiana. *Literary Appointments:* Editor, Journal of Vascular Surgery, 1984–. Author: Numerous Books. *Contributions to:* Numerous books, medical and scientific journals. *Honours include:* Distinguished Service Award, USA;

DSc, Hahnema Medical College and Hospital of Philadephia, 1973; American Surgical Association Distinguished Service Award, 1981; Presidential Medal of Freedom with Distinction, 1969. *Affiliation:* Chancellor, Baylor College of Medicine, 1979–. *Memberships:* Advisory Council, National Heart, Lung, Blood Institute, 1982–; Former Member, USSR Medical Academy, 1974; Honorary FRCS, England; Chairman, Albert Lasker Clinical Medicine Research Awards Jury, 1973; Stroke Council Fellow, American Heart Association, 1973; Trustee, China-America Relations Society, 1973; President, International Cardiovascular Society, 1959; President, Society of Vascular Surgery, 1954; President, Association of International Vascular Surgery, 1983; Member, American Surgical Association. *Address:* Baylor College of Medicine, One Baylor Plaza, Houston, TX 77030, USA.

DEBROEY, Marcel, b. 2 Apr. 1936, Buvingen. Master, Institute of Fine Arts, Hasselt, Belgium. m. Tress Vlaeminck, 7 Aug. 1973, Haasdonk, 1 son, 1 daughter. *Education:* Diploma, Institute of Fine Arts, Hasslet. *Literary Appointments:* Co-editor of literary magazines: De Tafelronde; Impuls; Vlaanderen. *Publications:* Poems: Kontrasten, 1959; Myriorama, 1962; Fazen, 1969; Suite, 1980. *Contributions to:* De Vlaamse Gids; Nieuw Vlaams Tydschrift; Dietse Warande Belfort; Muziek En Woord; De Tafelronde; Impuls; Vlaanderent; Deus Ex Machina; Phantomas; Kontrast. *Honours:* Literary Award of the Province of Limburg, 1960; The Hendrickvan Veldeke Award, 1961. *Membership:* The Flemish Literary Society. *Address:* Mgr Stillemansstraat 49, 2700 Sint Niklaas, Belgium.

DECAUNES, Luc, Writer; Educator; Theatre Animator; Composer; Collection Director. *Publications:* Haute-Provence, poems, 1976; La Poesie Parnassienne, 1977; Recreations, poems, 1978; Les Riches Heures de la Poesie Francaise, 1979; Chansons Pour Un Bichon, 1979; Les Etats-Generaux, poems, 1980; Les Riches Heures de la Chansons Francaise, 1981; Poesie au Grand Jour, Critique, 1982; Vie de Paul Eluard, 1982; Anthologie du Poeme en Prose, 1984. *Address:* 3 Square Beethoven, 93100 Montreuil, France.

DEDEYAN, Charles, b. 4 Apr. 1910, Smyrna, Turkey. Emeritus Professor, Comparative Literature, Sorbonne. *Education:* Lic Letters; Dip, Higher Studies of Classics; Certified Teacher of Classics; DLitt. *Publications include:* Montaigne Chez Bes Amis Anglo-Saxons, 1946; Stendhal Chroniquer, 1962; Victor Hugo et l'Allemagne, 1963, 1965; L'Italie dans l'oeuvre romanesque de Stendhal, 1963; Le Theme de Faust dans la Litterature europeinne 1954–67; Le Cosmopolitisme litteraire de Charles Du Bos, 1968, 1970; Racine et sa Phedre, 1968; Le Nouveau Mai de Siecle de Baudelaire a nos jours, 1968–72; Une guerre dans le mal des hommes, 1971; Chateaubriand et Rousseau, 1971; Le Cosmopolitisme europeen sous la Revolution et l'Empire, 1975; L'Arioste en France, 1975; Le Drame romantique en Europe, 1982; Le Roman Comipu de Scarron, 1983; Le Critique en Voyage, 1983. *Contributor to:* Magazines and journals. *Honours:* Legion d'Honneur; Commander, Palmes Academiques, 1979. *Memberships:* Numerous societies and academies. *Agent:* SEDES, Paris. *Address:* 27 rue de la Ferme, 92200 Neuilly, France.

DEEDES, Jeremy Wyndham, b. 24 Nov. 1943, York, England. Journalist. m. Anna Rosemary Gray, 2 May 1973, Hythe, Kent, 2 sons. *Education:* Eton College. *Literary Appointments:* Daily Sketch, 1966–69; Evening Standard, 1969–76; Deputy Editor, Daily Express, 1976–79; Managing Editor, The Standard, 1979–. *Address:* Hamilton House, Compton, Berkshire, England.

DEEMER, Bill, b. 4 Mar. 1945, USA. Poet. m. Toby Joy Murray, 4 Mar, 1966, San Francisco, California, USA. *Publications:* Poems, 1964; Diana, 1966; The King's Bounty, 1968; A Few For Lew, 1972; A Few For Lew & Other Poems, 1974; All Wet, 1975; This is Just to Say, 1981; Subjects, 1984. *Honour:* NEA Award, 1968.

Address: 92400 River Road, Junction City, OR 97448, USA.

DEER, Helen Glende, b. 8 April 1930, Indianapolis, USA. Poet; Director/Administrator (Education/Law/ Philanthropic). m. William H Deer, 4 Aug. 1978, Chicago, USA, 2 sons, 2 daughters. *Education:* BA, Butler University, Indianapolis; Graduate Creative Writing & International studies, University of Alabama. *Literary Appointments:* Editor, Wigwam, 1948–49; Associate Editor, Manuscripts, Butler University, 1949–51; Producer, Director, Writer, Internationally Speaking, 1966–72; Editor, Publisher, International Association of Educators for World Peace, Circulation Newsletter, 1979–81; Editor, Publisher, Peace Kaleidoscopes, 1981–83; Public Relations Director, Dr K F Luke Foundation, 1982–. *Major Publications:* Poetry included in various anthologies. *Contributor to:* Punjab Mail; This Womens' World; Peace Progress; Where on Earth? (television series, Alabama). *Honours:* Kiwanis Scholarship, Butler University, 1949; Medal for Journalism, Merit Scholar, Warren High School, Quill International 1949; Delta Tau Kappa, 1968; Bellevue American Spring Poetry Contest, winner 1972, 1973. *Memberships:* President, International Quill & Scroll, 1948–49; United Poets Laureate International; Women's Press Club; Huntsville Press Club (Founding Member). *Address:* Suite 206, 1350 East Sibley Boulevard, Dolton, IL 60419, USA.

DEFORD, Sara Whitcraft, b. 9 Nov. 1916, Youngstown, Ohio, USA. Professor. *Education:* BA, 1936, MA, 1938, Mount Holyoke College; PhD, Yale University, 1942. *Appointments:* College English Teacher, 1942–81. *Publications:* The Short Love Poems of John Donne, 1971; Forms of Verse, with Clarinda Lott, 1971; Lectures on Paradise Lost, I, II, 1970; The Pearl, 1966; The City of Love, 1958; Lectures on Modern American Poetry, 1957; The Return to Eden, 1940; Poetry Includes: Japanese Scroll Painting, 1969; Account in Gold, 1969; The Circle, 1969; High Wire Act, 1972; The Bridge, 1974; Plastic, 1974; Island Paradise, 1974; Magnolia, 1976; Lily of the Valley, 1976; etc. *Contributor to:* Numerous professional journals and magazines including, Poetry and Music; College Verse; Mount Holyoke Monthly; Poetry World; Westminster Magazine; Christian Science Monitor; Catholic World; Friends Journal; Arizona Quarterly; etc. *Honours:* Sigma Theta Chi Alumnae Poetry Prize, 1935; Albert Stanburrough Cook Prize, 1941; Eugene Saxton Memorial Fellowship, 1947; Fulbright Professor, Japan, 1954–55, 1961–62. *Membership:* Poetry Society of America. *Address:* 1961 So. Josephine #302, Denver, CO 80210, USA.

DEJASU, Lee, b. 18 Sep. 1940, New York City, USA. Artist; Visual Literatures; College Instructor. m. Francia Dejasu, 22 Sep. 1961, New York City, 1 son, 2 daughters. *Education:* Bachelor of Fine Arts, The Cooper Union, 1964; Master of Fine Arts, Rhode Island School of Design, 1970. *Visual Literature Exhibitions:* California Institute of Art; Virginia Commonwealth University; Centre de Arts y Communicacion, Buenos Aires, Argentina; Exhibition Hygiene, Paris, France; Galerie Kontact, Antwerp, Belgium; Kensington Arts Association, Toronto, Canada; Nova Scotia College of Art, Canada; NRA Gallery, Paris, France; and others. *Major Publication:* The Occurences of Duke Snider, 1980. *Contributor to:* New York Times; Boston Globe; Atlantic Monthly; and others. *Honour:* Rhode Island Council of the Arts Grant for Work in Visual Literature, 1979. *Address:* 16 Elton Street, Providence, RI 02906, USA.

DEJEVSKY, Nikolai James, b. 22 Sep. 1945, Hanau, Federal Republic of Germany. Publisher. m. Mary Peake, 13 Sep. 1975, Oxford, England. *Education:* BA, Cornell University, USA, 1968; MA, University of Pennsylvania, USA, 1971; D. Phil, Christ Church, University of Oxford, England, 1977. *Literary Appointments:* Assistant Editor, Clio Press Ltd, Oxford; 1977–80; Publishing Manager, Pergamon Press Ltd, Oxford, 1980–82; Publisher, Professional Publishing Ltd, London, 1982–84; Editorial

Director, Gower Publishing Ltd, Aldershot, 1984–85; Publisher, Longman Group Ltd, Harlow, 1985–. *Contributor to:* California Slavic Studies; Cambridge Encyclopaedia of Archaeology; Medieval Scandinavia; Solanus; Modern Encyclopaedia of Russian & Soviet History; Year's Work in Modern Language Studies. *Address:* c/o Longman Group Ltd, Longman House, Burnt Mill, Harlow, Essex, CM20 2JE, England.

DEKKER, Don, b. 24 Nov. 1944, Amsterdam. Author. *Education:* Rietveld Academy for Sculpture, Amsterdam. *Appointments:* Sculptur, 1966–68; Assistant Director, Director, Film Group One, Amsterdam, Paris, 1968–73; Director, Art Director, Copywriter, Maarten Toonder Studions, 1973–76; Sculptor, 1977–. *Publications:* Author, TV Drama Productions, TROS TV and NCRV TV; Scenario's, film, Border, My Sister the Negress; Stage Plays: At Lunchtime; Late in the Evening; The Plot; Total Freeze; The Renny Match Show; Cartoon Animations; Commercials, etc. *Address:* 2C Vander Helststraat 23/II, 1073 AG Amsterdam, The Netherlands.

deKOVEN, Don, b. 12 July 1928, New York City, USA. Medical Editor; Writer. m. Nancy Rees, 15 July 1967, Brooklyn, 2 sons. *Education:* AB, Harvard University, 1949. *Publications:* Surgical Infections, Selective Antibiotic Theraphy, co-editor, 1981. *Contributor to:* I–Am Magazine; Attenzione; North West Orient; 5000 stories on medicine and all sciences published; Chapters in several books (ghosted), etc. *Memberships:* Council of Biology Editors; Philosophy of Science Association. *Address:* 25 Circle Drive, Hastings/Hudson, NY 10706, USA.

DELAMAIDE, Darrell George, b. 25 Sep. 1949, Pittsburg, Kansas, USA. Journalist. *Education:* AB magna cum laude, St Louis University, St Louis, Missouri; Fulbright Scholarship, University of Munich, Federal Republic of Germany; MIA, Columbia University, New York, USA. *Literary Appointments:* Staff writer, Institutional Investor, monthly financial magazine. *Publications:* Debt Shock, 1984. *Literary Agent:* June Hall, London, England. *Address:* 10 Passage Turquetil, 75011 Paris, France.

DELANEY, Joseph David, b. 10 Oct. 1944, Grenada, Mississippi, USA. Journalist and Editor. *Education:* BS Political Science, Mississippi Valley State University; Master Studies, Atlanta University, Makato State College; Fellow, Certificate, Ford Foundation. *Literary Appointments:* Editor and Principal Journalist, Notes, legal publication. *Contributions to:* Newsweek; National Leader; Encore; American and Worldwise News; Black Enterprise; In These Times; Rural America. *Honours:* Writing Award, International Black Writers Conference, 1967 and 1968. *Memberships:* National Association of Black Journalists; International Black Writers Conference. *Address:* PO Box 103, Oxford, MS 38655, USA.

DELATUSH, Edith, b. 21 Nov. 1921, USA. Author. m. George A Delatush, 2 June 1943, Montclair, divorced 1983, 2 sons. *Education:* Registered Nurse. *Publications:* Beckoning Heart, 1981; West of the Moon, 1981; Midnight Wine, 1981; Dream Once More, 1982; Viscounts Witch, 1982; White Water Love, 1982; Delta River Magic, 1983; Rose Coloured Glass, 1983; No Other Love, 1983; Velvet is for Lovers, 1984; Color My Dreams, 1984; When Midnight Comes, 1985; Hand in Hand, 1985; Cape Cod Affair, 1986; Tonight You're Mine, 1986. *Agent:* The Robin Haigh Literary Agency, New York City, USA. *Address:* 200 Intracoastal Pl. #104, Tequesta, FL 33469, USA.

DELBANCO, Nicholas Franklin, b. 27 Aug. 1942, London, England. Writer. m. Elena Carter Greenhouse, 12 Sep. 1970, Pawlet, Vermont, 2 daughters. *Education:* BA History & Literature, Harvard College, 1963; MA English & Comparative Literature, Columbia University, 1966. *Literary Appointments:* Member, Language & Literature Division, Bennington College, 1966–; Director, Bennington Writing Workshops, 1977–;

Visiting Professor Iowa Writers Program, University of Iowa, 1979; Adjunct Professor, School of the Arts, Columbia University, 1979; Visiting Artist in Residence, Trinity College, 1980; Visiting Professor, Williams College, 1982; Professor of English, Skidmore College, 1984–85. *Major Publications:* The Martlet's Tale, 1966; Grasse 3/23/66, 1968; Consider Sappho Burning, 1969; News, 1870; In the Middle Distance, 1971; Fathering, 1973; Small Rain, 1975; Possession, 1977; Sherbrookes, 1978; Stillness, 1980; Group Portrait: Conrad, Crane, Ford, James & Wells, 1982; About my Table and Other Stories, 1983; The Beaux Arts Trio: A Portrait, 1985. *Contributor to:* Atlantic Monthly; Esquire; New York Times Book Review; The New Republic; and others. *Honours:* National Endowment for the Arts Creative Writing Fellowships, 1973, 1982; Guggenheim Fellowship, 1979; and others. *Memberships:* Authors League; Authors Guild; Signet Society; Phi Beta Kappa; New York State Writers Institute; PEN. *Literary Agent:* Brandt & Brandt, New York. *Address:* c/o Department of English, University of Michigan, 7601 Haven Hall, Ann Arbor, MI 48109, USA.

DELEU, Jozef Hugo Maria, b. 20 Apr. 1937, Roeselare, Belgium. Author, Publisher. m. Annemarie Deblaere, 22 Oct. 1960, Rekkem, Belgium, 2 sons, 1 daughter. *Literary Appointments:* Teacher, Moeskroen & Menen, 1960–70; Founder and Editor-in-Chief, Ons Erfdeel, 1957; Septentrion, 1972; De Franse Nederlanden, 1976; Co-Founder, Deputy Manager, Flemish-Netherlands Foundation Stichting One Erfdeel, 1970. *Major Publications:* Numerous works (in Dutch) including Poetry, Prose writing, anthologies, Essays, Cultural & Political writings, Children's literature. *Honours:* Numerous awards, including: Robert Schuman Silver Medal, Metz, 1973; Prix Descartes, Paris, 1980; 'sGravesande Price, The Hague, 1981. *Memberships:* Maatschappij van de Nederlandse Letteren, Leiden; Zuidnederlandse Maatschappij vour Taal-, Letterkunde en Geschiedenis, Brussels; Raad vour de Nederlandse Taal en Letteren, Nederlandse Taalunie, The Hague. *Literary Agent:* Stichting Ons Erfdeel. *Address:* Murissonstraat 220, 8530 Rekkem, Belgium.

DELEURAN, Aage, b. 11 Oct. 1925, Korslor, Denmark. Editor-in-Chief; Journalist. m. Birthe Braae, 1955. *Publications:* April 1940. Da krigen kom til Danmark, 1963. *Honours:* Commander, Order of Dannebrog; Officier, Legion d'Honneur. *Literary Agent:* Berlingske Forlag. *Address:* 1 Carl Johans Gade, 2100 Copenhagen ŁO, Denmark.

DELGADO, Ramon Louis, b. 16 Dec. 1937, Tampa, Florida, USA. College Professor. *Education:* BA, Stetson University, 1956; MA, Dallas Theater Center, 1960; MFA, Yale School of Drama, 1967; PhD, Southern Illinois University at Carbondale, 1976. *Literary Appointments:* New Plays Chairman, Dallas Theater Center, 1960; Fellow, Midwest Professional Playwrights Workshop, 1977; Playwright in Residence, INTAR, New York City, 1980; Editor, Best Short Plays series 1981–; Literary Consultant, Whole Theatre Company, 1981–83. *Publications:* Plays: Waiting for the Bus, in Ten Great One Act Plays, 1968; Once Below a Lighthouse, in Best Short Plays, 1972; Sparrows of the Field, 1973; The Knight-Mare's Nest, in A Pocketful of Wry, 1974; Omega's Ninth. 1975; A Little Holy Water, 1983. Books: Acting with Both Sides of Your Brain, 1985. *Contributions to:* Reviews and articles in Dramatics magazine; Cue; Journal of the Illinois Speech and Theatre Association; Florida Educational Journal; Players Magazine; The Statson Review. *Honours:* Theta Alpha Phi, First Prize for, Waiting for the Bus, 1959; University of Missouri, First Place, for The Knight-Mare's Nest, 1971; David Library American Freedom, Listen My Children, 1976; David Library American Freedom for, A Little Holy Water, 1977; Beverly Hills Theatre Guild 'STONES' Semifinalist, 1984. *Memberships:* The Dramatists' Guild; American Theatre Association. *Literary Agent:* Henry Dunmow, Curtis Brown Ltd, New York. *Address:* c/o Speech-Theatre

Department, Montclair State College, Upper Montclair, NJ 07043, USA.

DELIN, Bertil, b. 29 July 1922, Halmstad, Sweden. Editor-in-Chief. *Education:* HS of Commerce, 1974; HS of Forest Engineers, 1951; Graphic Institute, 1953; University of Stockholm, 1962–54. *Publications:* The Order of Charcoal Burners; Born in the Forest; The History of Swedish Workers' Protection. *Contributions to:* Working Environment. *Membership:* Swedish Publicists' Club. *Honour:* Scholarship of Publicists' Club. *Address:* Arbetsmiljo, Kungsholms Hamnplan 3, S–112 20 Stockholm, Sweden.

DELINS, Emils, b. 15 May 1921, Riga, Latvia. Journalist. m. Nina Sics, 18 Dec. 1948, Melbourne, Australia, 2 sons, 1 daughter. *Education:* Lycee Francais de Riga, 1940; University of Latvia, 1941–44; Technische Hochschule, Stuttgart, 1946. *Appointment:* Editor, Australian Latvian News, 1949–. *Publications:* 69 Hours, Essays on Latvian Life in three Continents, 1968; Executive Encounters, Travel notes on a Prime Ministerial Journey, 1980; Baltic States, 1980. Contributor to Australian Latvian News, Latvian journals and magazines in USA, Canada, England, West Germany and Sweden. *Memberships:* National Press Club, Canberra; Latvian Press Society, Boston, USA; Commonwealth Journalists' Association, London. *Honours:* Queen Elizabeth Silver Jubilee Medal, 1977; Honorary Consul for Latvia, 1982. *Address:* P O Box 23, Kew, Victoria 3101, Australia.

DELLING, Gerhard, b. 10 May 1905. University Professor Emeritus. *Education:* Studied theology, Erlangen, Berlin and Leipzig; Lic Theol, Leipzig, 1930; Inauguration, Greifswald, 1948, DTh, 1954. *Publications:* Der Gottesdienst im Neuen Testament, 1952; Die Zueignung des Heils in der Taufe, 1961; Die Taufe im Neuen Testament, 1963; Judische Lehre und Frommigkeit in den paralipomena Jeremiae, 1967; Bibliographie zur judisch-hellenistischen und intertestamentarischen Literatur 1900–1970, 1975; Studien zum Neuen Testament und zum hellenistischen Judentum, Gesammelte Aufsatze 1950–1968, 1970; Zeit und Endzeit, 1970; Der Kreuzestod Jesu in der urchristlichen Verkundigung, 1971; Wort Gottes und Verkundigung im Neuen Testament, 1971. *Contributions to:* Novum Testamentum; New Testament Studies; Zeitschrift fur die neutestamentliche Wissenschaft; Journal for the Study of Judaism; Theologische Literaturzeitung; Klio. *Membership:* Studiorum Novi Testamenti Societas. *Address:* Lafontainestrabe 14, DDR-402 Halle/Saale, Democratic Republic of Germany.

DELZELL, Charles Floyd, b. 6 Mar. 1920, Klamath Falls, Oregon, USA. Professor, History. m. Eugenia Robertson, 21 Mar. 1948, Eugene, 2 sons, 1 daughter. *Education:* BS, History, University of Oregon, 1941; MA, 1943, PhD, 1951, History, Stanford University; Istituto Italiano per gli Studi Storici, Naples, Italy, 1948–49. *Appointments:* Assistant Professor, History, University of Hawaii, 1949–50; Instructor, History, University of Oregon, 1950–51; Assistant to Professor, History, 1952–, Acting Director, Centre for European Studies, 1985–86, Vanderbilt University. *Publications:* The Meaning of Yalta, 1956, 3rd edition 1965; Mussolini's Enemies: The Italian Anti-Fascist Resistance, 1961, 1975; Italy in Modern Times, 1964, revised edition 1980; The Unification of Italy, 1859–1945, 1965; Mediterranean Fascism 1919–1945, 1970; The Future of History, 1977; Italy in the Twentieth Century, 1980. *Contributor to:* Numerous professional journals. *Honours:* Phi Beta Kappa, 1941; Phi Alpha Theta, 1948; Borden Award, Hoover Institution, Stanford University, 1960; George Louis Beer Prize, American Historical Association, 1961; Thomas Jefferson Award, Vanderbilt University, 1984. *Memberships:* American Historical Association, Council Member, numerous Committees; Southern Historical Association, Council Member, numerous committees; Society for Italian Historical Studies, President; American Committee for History of Second World War,

President; Phi Beta Kappa, Vanderbilt University Chapter, President. *Address:* 2303 Bernard Avenue, Nashville, TN 37212, USA.

DEMEDTS, Andre Maurits, b. 8 Aug. 1906. Former Regional Broadcasting Director. *Education:* Graduate, Commercial Sciences. *Appointments:* Farmer, 1921–37; High School Teacher, 1937–49; Director, Regional Broadcasting of W Flanders, 1949–71. *Publications:* Jamijnen, 1929; Geploegde Anarde, 1921; Vaarwel, 1940; Daarna, 1968; Verzamelde Gedichten, 1977; De Jaargetijden, 1979. *Contributor to:* De Standaard, Brussels; Dietsche Warande en Belfort, Antwerp; Tydskrif vir Letterkunde, Pretoria. *Memberships:* Koninklijke Academy voor Nederlandse Taalen Letterkunde of Belgium; Maatschappij der Nederlandse Lettermunde te Leiden, Netherlands; Comite flamand de France te Rijsel, Lille, France. *Address:* 77 Condédreef, 8500 Kortijk, Belgium.

DEMEDTS, Gabriëlle-Maria, b. 11 June 1909, St. Baafs-Vijve, West Flanders, Belgium. Former Bookseller. m. Lucien De Bosscher, 11 June 1957, Waregem. *Publications:* Poetry: Een Gevangene zingt, 1937; Een Twijg in den Wind, 1939; Morgen is alles uit, 1940; Verloren Thuis, 1946; De Doorgang, 1957; Levensberichten en Liederen, 1974; Klanken van Eeuwigheid in aardse Stem, 1974: Anthology in PEN series, Verzamelde Gedichten: De gulden Veder series. *Contributions to:* Dietsche Warande & Belfort; Hooger Leven; Nieuw Vlaanderen; Elckerlyc; Roeping; Europa; Vlaanderen; Astrid; Verzet om de Waarheid; Nieuwe Stemmen; Poëziekrant; Jong Deutschland (verses, essays, short stories). Founder, editor-in-chief, Handen. *Honour:* Knight, Order of Leopold II, 1954. *Memberships:* Union of Flemish Authors; Athena Club. *Address:* Residentie Marie-Josée B, Sint-Jansplein 14/26, 8500–Kortrijk, West-Vlaanderen, Belgium.

DEMETRAKOPOULOS, Stephanie, b. 18 Jan, 1937, Portland, Oregon, USA. University Professor. 1 son, 3 daughters. *Education:* BA, Portland State University, 1964; Reed College Graduate School, 1964–66; MA, 1968, PhD, 1971, University of Minnesota. *Appointments:* Teacher, Grant High School, Portland, 1964–66; Teaching Assistant, University of Minnesota, 1966–71; Assistant Professor, 1971–76, Associate Professor, 1977–82, Professor, 1983–, Western Michigan University. *Contributor to:* University Magazine; College English; The Explicator; Arizona English Bulletin; Milton Quartely; Mosaic; Comparative Drama; American Women Authors; Anima; Soundings; Canadian Literature; etc. *Honours:* Recipient, various honours and awards including Appointed, with Husband, Danforth Associate, 1980–86. *Memberships:* MLA; AAUP; NCTE; MMLA; Popular Culture Organisation; Chicago Jung Institute; Milton Society. *Address:* English Dept, Western Michigan University, Kalamazoo, MI 49001, USA.

DEMETRIUS, Lucia, b. 16 Sep. 1910, Bucharest, Rumania. Writer. m. 15 Sep. 1952, Constantin Cristel. *Education:* Bucharest University, 1931; Conservatory of Dramatic Art, 1931. *Publications include:* (novels) Youth, 1936; The World Begins With Me, 1968; Triptic, 3 volumes, 1980–84; (stories) Promises, 1964; At Five O'Clock Tea, 1970; Am An Earthling, 1973; The Coming to Miracle, 1974; The Happy Travel, 1979; Life I Love You, 1984; (plays) Three Generations, 1956; The Garden of God, 1966; The Cross Without a Well, 1972. *Contributor to:* poems, translations to various publications. *Honours:* State Prizes, 1950, 1952; Prize, Roumanian Writers Society, 1982. *Memberships:* Rumanian Writers Society; PEN. *Address:* Matei Millo Street, 12 Bucharest Section 1, code 70704, Rumania.

DEMPSEY, Hugh Aylmer, b. 7 Nov. 1929, Edgerton, Alberta, Canada. Historian. m. Pauline Sylvia Gladstone, 31 Aug. 1953, Edmonton, Alberta, Canada. 2 sons, 3 daughters. *Literary Appointments:* Editor, Alberta History 1958–; Northern and Canadian Editor, Montana Magazine of History, 1966–84; Editorial Advisory Board, Canadian Geographical Journal, 1966–83;

Editorial Advisory Committee, American West, 1978–83. *Publications:* Crowfoot, Chief of the Blackfeet, 1972; Charcoal's World, 1978; Red Crow, Warrior Chief, 1980; History in Their Blood, 1982; Big Bear, the End of Freedom, 1984. *Contributor to:* Alberta Through the Years, in Canadian Geographical Journal, 1955; Stone Medicine Wheels, in, Journal of the Washington Academy of Science, 1956; Religious Significance of Blackfoot Quillwork, in, Plains Anthropologist, 1963; Blackfoot Names for Animals indigenous to Alberta and Montana, Plains Indian Seminary Papers, and many others. *Honours:* Annual Award for Outstanding Contribution to Alberta History, 1963; Honorary Chieftainship, Blood Indian Tribe, 1967; Alberta Achievement Award, 1974 and 1975; Honorary Doctorate, University of Calgary; Alberta Non-Fiction Award, 1975; Order of Canada 1975; Bob Edwards Literary Award, 1982. *Address:* 95 Holmwood Avenue N W, Calgary, Alberta, Canada T2K 2G7.

DEMPSTER, Barry Edward, b. 17 Jan. 1952, Toronto, Canada. Writer. m. Karen Ruttan, 26 Sep. 1980, Toronto, Canada. *Publications:* Fables for Isolated Men, 1982; Globe Doubts, 1983; Real Places & Imaginary Men, 1984; David and the Daydreams, 1985. *Contributions to:* over 150 magazines. *Honour:* Governor General's Award Finalist for Poetry 1982. *Membership:* League of Canadian Poets. *Address:* 65 Woodrow Avenue, Toronto, Ontario M4C IG6, Canada.

DEMSKE, Richard John, b. 11 Feb. 1930, Buffalo, New York, USA. Writer. m. Arlene C Katz, 1 Jan. 1968, Brewster, New York, 4 sons, 2 daughters. *Education:* BA, Canisius College, Buffalo, New York. *Publications:* Author of approximately 45 books including: Handbook of Creative Crafts, 1966; Furniture Repair and Refinishing, 1973; Year-Round Outdoor Building Projects, 1979; The Home Repair Book, 1981; Professional Plumbing Series, 1985; Carpentry and Woodworking, 1985. *Contributor to:* Family Circle; Ladies' Home Journal; Newsday; Parade; Mechanix Illustrated; Family Handyman and other periodicals. *Memberships:* International Motor Press Association; Founding member, past President, Magazine Editors Association of New York; Past President, Member Board of Directors, National Association of Home and Workshop Writers. *Address:* 210 Longridge Court, Ventura, CA 93003, USA.

DENGLER, Sandy, b. 8 June 1939, Newark, Ohio, USA. Writer. m. William Frank Dengler, 11 Jan. 1963, Mesa, Arizona, 2 daughters. *Education:* BSc, Bowling Green State University, Ohio; MSc, Arizona State University. *Publications:* Yosemite's Marvellous Creatures, 1979; Getting into the Bible, 1979; Beats of the Field, 1979; Birds of the Air, 1979; Summer of the Wild Pig, 1979; Melon Hound, 1980; The Horse who Loved Picnics, 1980; Arizona Longhorn Adventure, 1980; Man and Beast Together, 1981; Rescue in the Desert, 1981; Mystery at McGeehan Ranch, 1982; Socorro Island Treasure, 1983; Chain Five Mystery, 1984; Summer Snow, 1984; Song of the Nereids, 1984; Fanny Crosby, Writer of 8000 Songs, 1985; Winterspring, 1985. *Address:* Tahoma Woods, Star Rte, Ashford WA 98304, USA.

DENHOLTZ, Elaine Grudin, b. New Jersey, USA. Writer. m. Melvin Denholtz, 2 sons, 1 daughter. *Education:* BA, Bucknell University; MAT, Seton Hall University. *Literary Appointments:* Adjunct Lecturer, Fairleigh Dickinson University, 1965–; Juror, New Jersey State Council of Arts Fellowships, 1982; Juror, Maryland State Arts Fellowships, 1984. *Publications:* Education, contributor, edited by Krajewski and Peltier, 1973; The Highchairs, 1975; How To Save Your Teeth and Your Money, 1977; The Dental Face Lift, 1981; Having It Both Ways, 1981 and 1983; Playing for High Stakes, 1986. *Contributions to:* Family Weekly; New Woman Magazine; The Dramatist Guild Quarterly; The Literary Review; NJEA Review; NEA Journal. *Honours include:* Playwriting Award, New Jersey State Council of Arts; Conkle Drama Prize; Dubuque Playwriting Award; Fenimore Drama Prize; Distinguished

Achievement Award for Excellence in Educational Journalism, Writers Guild of America. *Memberships:* Phi Beta Kappa; Writers Guild of America; The Dramatists Guild; Poets and Writers; The Authors Guild, National Academy of Television Arts and Sciences; American Federation of Television and Radio Artists. *Literary Agent:* Maria Carvainis Agency, New York. *Address:* 13 Birchwood Drive, Livingston, NJ 07039, USA.

DENNETT, Joann Taylor Temple, b. 24 Sep. 1938, Springfield, Illinois, USA. Science Writer. m. Roger Droppers Dennett 28 June 1969, Boulder, Colorado. *Education:* BSc Science Engineering, Northwestern University, 1961; MS, Journalism, Columbia University, 1962; PhD, Education, University of Colorado, 1985. *Contributor to:* Science Digest, Science 80-84, New Scientist, Science et Vie, Science & Mechanics; Denver Post, Empire, Miami Herald, Toronto Star, Boulder Camera; Feature articles for IBM Think, NOAA, European Community and others. *Honours:* Outstanding Young Women of America, 1969; Top Hand Award, Colorado Author's League, 1971; Numerous awards from Colorado Press Women, League of American Penwomen and Society for Technical Communication. *Memberships:* Society for Technical Communication; National League of American Penwomen; Colorado Press Women; National Press Women. *Literary Agent:* Joyce Flaherty. *Address:* 1206 Crestmoor Drive, Boulder, CO 80303, USA.

DENNEY, Diana Patience, b. 8 July 1910, Valetta, Malta. Teacher; Author. m. Antony Denney, 1939, divorced 1948, 1 son, 2 daughters. *Education:* BA, Honours, History, Girton College, Cambridge, England. 1931; Central School of Art, London 1932–34. *Appointments:* Art Teacher, 1930–34. *Publications:* The World at Work, 2 volumes 1939; The Story of the Beetle Who Lived Alone, 1941; Uncle Anty's Album, with Anthony Denney, 1942; The Golden Hen and Other Stories, 1942; The Little Red Engine Gets a Name, 1942; The Wild Cherry, 1943; Nursery Tales, 1944; The Story of the Little Red Engine, 1945; The Story of Louisa, 1945; The Little Red Engine Goes to Market (Goes to Town, Goes Travelling, and the Rocket, Goes Home, Goes to be Mended and the Taddlecombe Outing, Goes Carolling), 8 volumes 1946–71; Whoo Whoo, The Wind Blew, 1946; The Tooter and other Nursery Tales, 1951; The Enormous Apple Pie and Other Miss Pussy Tales, 1951; Ebenezer the Big Balloon, 1952; The Bridal Gown and Other Stories, 1952; The Bran Tub, 1954; William and the Lorry, 1956; Child of Air, 1957; The Dreadful Boy, 1959; The Merry-Go-Round, 1963; Old Perisher, 1963; Nothing to Do, 1966; I Love My Love with and A: Where is He?, 1972. *Membership:* Society of Authors. *Address:* Minster House, Shaw Hill, Melksham, Wiltshire, England.

DENNISON, George Harris, b. 10 Sep. 1925, Ashburn, Georgia, USA. Writer. m. Mabel H Chrystie, 1 son, 2 daughters. *Education:* BS, Columbia University, New York City, USA; BA, New School for Social Research, New York City; MA, New York University (incomplete). *Publications:* The Lives of Children, 1969; And Then a Harvest Feast, 1972; Oilers and Sweepers, 1979; Shawno, 1984; Luisa Domic, 1985. *Contributions:* Numerous reviews, essays, fiction in, New American Review; American Review; American Poetry Review; Commentary; New York Review of Books; Arts, magazine; New York Times Book Review, etc. *Honours:* Residence grants at Huntingdon Hartford Foundation, 1960; Yaddo, 1980, 1982; The Lives of Children was selected by the, New York Times, and the National Education Association as being among the ten best books of the year. *Memberships:* PEN. *Literary Agent:* Georges Borchardt. *Address:* Box 538, Temple, ME 04984, USA.

DENT, Harold Collett, b. 14 Nov. 1894, Scunthorpe, England. Writer. *Education:* BA, London University (External Student). *Publications:* The Education Act 1944, 1944; Education in Transition, 1944; Education in England & Wales, 1977; The Training of Teachers in England & Wales 1800–1975, 1977; 1870–1970

Century of Growth in English Education, 1970. *Contributor to:* Education; Times Educational Supplement. *Address:* Riccards Spring, Whatlington, Battle, East Sussex TN33 ONG, England.

DENT, Robert William, b. 8 Sept. 1917, Portland, Oregon, USA. Retired Professor of English. m. Ellen Margaret Quinlivan, 10 Aug. 1957, Gates Mill, Ohio, 2 sons, 3 daughters. *Education:* BA, 1940, MA, 1942, University of Oregon; PhD. University of Chicago, 1952. *Publications:* John Webster's Borrowing, 1960; Shakespeare's Proverbial Language: AN Index, 1981; Proverbial Language in English Drama Exclusive of Shakespeare 1495–1616: An Index, 1985. *Memberships:* Bibliographer, 1958–64, Shakespeare Society of America; World Shakespeare Society; Modern Language Association; Renaissance Society of America; Malone Society. *Address:* 15450 Deerhorn Road, Sherman Oaks, CA 91403, USA.

DEON, Michel, b. 4 Aug. 1919, Paris. Writer. m. Chantal Renaudeau D'er of Academie Francaise, 1978. *Publications:* Je ne Veux Jamais L'Oublier, 1950; La Corrida, 1952; Les Trompeuses Esperances, 1956; Tout L'Amour du Monde, 1957; Le Balon de Spetsai, 1961; Le Rendez Vous de Patmos, 1965; Les Poneys Sauvages, 1970; Un Taxi Mauve, 1974; Mes Arches de Noë, 1978; Un Dejeuner de Soleil, 1981; Je Vous Ecris d'Italie, 1984; Bagages pour Vancouver, 1985. *Contributor to:* Paris-Match; Figaro Magazine; House and Garden; L'Eventail; Decoration Internationale. *Honours:* Doctor Honoris Causa Universities of Ireland, Legion d'Honneur, Prix Interallie 1970; Prix du Roman de L'Academie Francaise, 1974. *Address:* Old Rectory, Tynagh, County Galway, Republic of Ireland.

DEPLAZES, Gion, b. 22 Mar. 1918, Surrein, Switzerland. Rector. *Education:* Teacher, Training Seminar, Chur; Universities Fribourg and Zurich. *Publications:* Geschichte der sprachlichen Lehrmittel, 1949; Marietta, 1951; Wir Sprechen Deutsch, 1955; Rugada, 1957; Il Cavrer da Vigliuz, 1957; La davosa untgida, 1958; Paun casa, 1960; Levzas petras, 1960; Passiuns, 1962; La bargia di tschess, 1964; Schibettas, 1965; Sentupadas, 1968; Sper via, 1970; La scappada, 1972; Purgina, 1976; Bittere Lippen, 1976; Marlengia, 1981; Ragischs 1982; Clavs, 1985. *Memberships:* Swiss PEN Club; Swiss Writers; Association; Society Retoumantscha, President 1964–; Union Scripturs Romontschs. *Address:* Buchenweg 2, 7000 Chur, Switzerland.

DEPPERT, Fritz, b. 24 Dec. 1932, Darmstadt, Federal Republic of Germany. Poet. m. Gabriella Döhner, 2 Feb. 1966, Darmstadt, 2 sons. *Education:* Studies, German Literature, History, Philosophy; Dr. Phil. *Literary Appointments:* Lecturer of the Literature März. *Publications:* Holzholeh, (Prose), 1970; Atemholen, (Poems), 1974; Wir, Jhr, Sie, (Poem), 1981; Atempause, (Poems), 1981; Zeit-Gedichte, (Poems), 1983. *Memberships:* Association of German Writers; Kogge. *Address:* Viktoriastr. 50a 61, Darmstadt, Federal Republic of Germany.

DEPREZ, Ada Vera, b. 12 Oct. 1928, Ostend, Belgium. University Professor, 1969–; Director, Cultural Documentation Centre, 1978–. *Education:* Dr Litt, 1964. *Publications include:* Numerous books & papers since 1960, on Dutch & Flemish literature, mainly 19th & 20th century. *Honours:* Joris Eeckhout Award of the Academy, 1962; Commander of the Leopoldsorde, 1971. *Memberships:* Past President, Royal Academy of Dutch Language & Literature, Gent; President 1982–85, Royal Southern Dutch Society for Language, Literature & History, Brussels; President 1983–, Contact Group 19th Century; Int. Verein für Germanistik (1963) and Ausschuss (1970–1985 for Dutch Literature. *Address:* Blandijnberg 2, B–9000 Gent, Belgium.

DERBY, Crispin John Alexander, b. 2 Jan. 1948, Rochford, Essex, England. Publisher and Director, BKT Publications; Editor, Local Government Chronicle. m. Pamela Anne Underwood, 4 Sep. 1971, Bentley,

Hampshire, 2 sons, 1 daughter. *Literary Appointments:* National Council for Training Journalists (Public Administration Board); Periodical Publishers Association (Editorial Committee). *Publications:* Vampire Bedside Companion, part author, 1974; Best Practice in Housing, part editor, 1981; Local Government for Journalists, editor, 1983. *Address:* BKT Publications, 11-12 Bury St, London EC3A 5AP. England.

DERICUM, Christa, b. 21 May 1932, Rheinberg/Niederrhein, Germany. Writer. 2 sons. *Education:* Studies of Sociology, History, History of Art, University of Heidelberg, Germany and University of Michigan, Ann Arbor, USA, PhD, 1961. *Appointments:* Editor, Suddeutscher Rundfunk, Stuttgart, 1961; Editor, Piper Verlag Munchen, 1962–63; First Editor, Radio Bremen, 1964–68. *Publications:* Burgund und seine Herzoge, 1966 and 1978; Belgien-Luxumborg, 1970; Holland, 1971; Fritz und Flori-Tagebuch einer Adoption, 1976 and 1980; Maximilian – Kaiser im Heiligen Romischen Reich Deutscher Nation, 1979; Florian Geyer und der Deutsche Vauernkrieg, 1980 and 1986; Editor, Alfred Weber, Haben vir Deutschen seit 1945 versagt, 1979. *Contributions include:* Many essays on history of democracy and anarchism in various publications; Die Zeit; Suddeutsche Zeitung; Basler Zeitung; Sankt Galler Tagblatt; Vorgange; Hessischer Bundfunk; Radio Bremen; Deutschlandfunk; Sender Freis Berlin. *Address:* Reingsen 10, 5840 Schwerte 4, Federal Republic of Germany.

DERRETT, John Duncan Martin, b. 30 Aug. 1922, London, England. University Professor Emeritus. *Education:* Doctor of Civil Law, Jesus College, University of Oxford; PhD, LLD, DD, School of Oriental & African Studies, London; Barrister. *Publications include:* Law in the New Testament, 1970; Critique of Modern Hindu Law, 1970; Jesus' Audience, 1973; Dharmasastra & Juridical Literature, 1973; Henry Swinburn 1551–1624–Civil Lawyer of York, 1973; Bharuchi's Commentary on the Manusmrti, 1975; Essays in Classical & Modern Hindu Law I – IV, 1976–78; The Death of Marriage Law, 1977; Studies in the New Testament I – IV, 1977–85; The Anastasis, 1982; The Making of Mark, 1985. *Contributor to:* Various learned journals in history, law & theology. *Memberships:* Gray's Inn; Royal Asiatic Society; Studiorum Novi Testamenti Societas. *Address:* Half Way House, Blockley, Gloucestershire, GL56 9EX, England.

DERRICOTTE, Toi, b. 12 Apr. 1941, Detroit, Michigan, USA. Poet; Teacher. m. Bruce Derricotte, 29 Dec. 1967, Detroit, Michigan, 1 son. *Education:* BA, Wayne State University, Special Education; MA, English Literature & Creative Writing, New York University. *Literary Appointments:* Poet-in-the-School, New Jersey State Council on the Arts, 1974–84; Master Teacher, Poet-in-the-School Program, New Jersey State Council on the Arts, 1984–. *Major Publications:* The Empress of the Death House, 1978; Natural Birth, 1983. *Contributor to:* The Iowa Review; Northwest Review; Pequod; Ironwood; Open Places; New York Quarterly; and others. Poetry in: An Introduction to Poetry, editor L Simpson, Home Girls: A Black Feminist Anthology; and others. *Honours:* Fellow, MacDowell Colony, 1982; New Jersey State Council on the Arts Poetry Fellow, 1983; National Endowment for the Arts Creative Writing Fellowship Grant, 1985. *Memberships:* PEN; Poetry Society of America; Academy of American Poets. *Address:* 237 Runnymead Road, Essex Fells, NJ 07021, USA.

DERRIMAN, James Parkyns, b. 19 Feb. 1922, London, England. Writer; Historical Researcher. m. Iris Ada Hogben, 17 Apr. 1948, Welwyn Garden City, Hertfordshire, 1 daughter. *Education:* Barrister, Lincolns Inn; Dip CAM, Diploma of Communications, Advertising and Marketing Educational Foundation. *Publications:* Pageantry of the Law, 1955; Discovering the Law, 1962; Public Relations in Business Management, 1964; Company-Investor Relations, 1969; The Bridge Builders, Editor with George Pulay, 1980. *Contributions to:* Daily, weekly and specialist publications of articles on Cornish local history. *Honours:* Fellow and Pat President, Institute of Public Relations; President's Medallist, Institute of Public Relations, 1978; Honorary Vice President, European Confederation of Public Relations. *Address:* 34 Mossville Gardens, Morden, Surrey SM4 4DG, England.

DERRY, Thomas Kingston, b. 1905, Glasgow, Scotland. Historian/Retired Schoolmaster. *Education:* MA, PhD, Queen's College, Oxford. *Publications:* The European World, W T L Jarman, 1950; The Campaign in Norway, 1952; The Making of Modern Britain, with T L Jarman, 1956; A Short History of Norway, 1957; A Short History of Technology, W T I Williams, 1960; The United Kingdom, 1962; Britain since 1750, 1965; Europe 1815–1914, and, Europe since 1914, with E J Knapton, USA 1965, UK 1966; Introducing Oslo, 1969; The Making of Britain, 2 volumes, with M G Blakeway, 1968, 1969; A History of Modern Norway 1914–1972, 1973; A History of St Edmund's Church, Oslo, 1976; A History of Scandinavia, 1979. *Honour:* OBE, 1976. *Address:* Nils Lauritssonsvei 27, Oslo 8, Norway.

DERUNGS, Ursicin Gion Gieli, b. 5 Jan. 1935, Villa, Italy. Teacher. m. Maria Cristina Bartolomei, 13 May 1976, Padua. *Education:* Doctor of Theology. *Publications:* Il saltar dils morts, 1983; Siemi de mesqstad, 1985. *Contributions to:* Igl Ischi; Litteratura. *Honour:* Drama Prize, LR, 1984. *Memberships:* Union of Romontsch Writers; Union of Swiss Writers; PEN Club. *Address:* Via Appiani 21, I–20121 Milano, Italy.

DES MARAIS, Louise Mercier, b. 28 Feb. 1923, Cambridge, Massachusetts, USA. Writer. m. Philip H Des Marais, 12 Aug. 1950, Washington DC, separated, 1 daughter. *Education:* BA, English, Emmanuel College, Boston, Massachusetts, USA. *Publications:* For Goodness Sake, 1966; Signs of Glory: Making Christian Choices, 1975. *Contributions to:* The Boston Herald; Catholic Action; The Sign; Action Now; Mission Digest; Information; Today; Our Sunday Visitor; Word; Marriage; Spiritual Life; Emmanuel Quarterly. *Memberships:* Washington Independent Writers; Washington Area Writers; Library of Human Resources. *Literary Agent:* Anita Diamant. *Address:* 1529, 44th Street NW, Washington, DC 20007, USA.

DEUTSCH, Helen, b. 21 March 1906, New York, USA. Writer. *Education:* BA, Barnard College, USA. *Literary Appointments:* Play-reader and General Executive, Provincetown Playhouse, New York, 1927–29; Free-lance writer in New York, 1929–42; Founder and Secretary, New York Drama Critics Circle, 1934–39; Assistant to Executive Director of New York Theatre Guild, 1937–38; Screenwriter, Metro-Goldwyn-Meyer, Hollywood, California, USA, 1942–56; Consultant on Motion Picture, Television and Broadway productions, 1956–. *Major Publication:* The Provincetown: A Story of the Theatre, Farrar & Rhinehart, 1931, reprinted Atheneum, 1972. *Screenplays include:* National Velvet; Lili; King Solomon's Mines; I'll Cry Tomorrow; Golden Earrings; The Seventh Cross; Kim; Plymouth Adventure; The Glass Slipper; The Unsinkable Molly Brown. *Contributor to:* (stories) Saturday Evening Post; McCall's; Ladies' Home Journal; Cosmopolitan; Redbook and others; (articles, some 200) New York Herald Tribune; New York Times; magazines and syndicated columns. *Honours:* Academy Award Nomination, Writers' Guild of America Screen Award for best musical, Cannes International Film Festival Award, Laurel Award, Golden Globe Award for best screenplay (all for Lili, 1953); Books and Authors' Award for I'll Cry Tomorrow (1954), Radio Daily Award (1956) and many others. *Memberships:* American Society of Composers, Authors and Publishers; Writers' Guild of America; Dramatists Guild; Academy of Notion Picture Arts and Sciences. *Address:* 1185 Park Avenue, New York, NY 10128, USA.

DEVANEY, John Francis, b. 15 Mar. 1926, New York City, USA. Writer. m. Barbara Masciocchi, 16 Apr. 1955, New York City, 2 sons. *Education:* BSc, New York University. *Publications:* The Killer Instinct, 1976;

Pictorial History of the World Series, 1977; Sports Stars of Yesteryear: Where Are They Now?, 1985. *Contributions to:* Saturday Evening Post; Redbook; Sport; Consumers Digest; Readers Digest. *Literary Agent:* Barbara Lowenstein, New York City. *Address:* PO Box 690, East Hampton, NY 11937, USA.

DEVITIS, Angelo A, b. 6 Nov. 1925, Akron, Ohio, USA. Teacher. *Education:* BA 1948, MA 1949, Western Reserve University; PhD, University of Wisconsin, 1954. *Appointment:* Professor, Purdue University, 1969-. *Publications include:* Roman Holiday: The Catholic Novels of Evelyn Waugh, 1955; Graham Greene, 1964, revised 1985-86; Anthony Burgess, 1972; J B Priestley, with A E Kalson, 1980. *Contributions to:* 20th Century Literature; College English; Contemporary Literature; etc. Reviews in, Saturday Review; Western Humanities Review; etc. *Address:* Department of English, Purdue University, W Lafayette, IN 47906, USA.

DEVLIN, Patrick, b. 25 Nov. 1905, Chislehurst, England. Lawyer. *Education:* BA, Christ's College, Cambridge, 1927; MA, 1960. *Publications:* Trial by Jury, 1956; The Criminal Prosecution in England, 1957; Samples of Lawmaking, 1962; The Enforcement of Morals, 1965; Too Proud to Fight: Woodrow Wilson's Neutrality, 1974; The Judge, 1979; Easing the Passing: The Trial of Dr John Bodkin Adams, 1985. *Honours:* Honorary LLD, Glasgow & Toronto, 1962, Cambridge, Leicester & Sussex, 1966, Durham 1968, Liverpool, 1970; Honorary DCL, Oxford, 1965. *Memberships:* Fellow, British Academy, 1963; Honorary Foreign Member, American Academy of Arts & Sciences. *Literary Agent:* Richard Scott Simon. *Address:* W Wick House, Pewsey, Wiltshire SN9 6JZ, England.

DEWEY, Priscilla Blackett, b. 16 Oct. 1924, Boston, Massachusetts, USA. Arts Educator; Administrator; Playwrite; Lyricist. m. Talbot Dewey, 21 Sep. 1946, Chestnut Hill, Massachusetts, 2 sons, 1 daughter. *Education:* School of the Museum of Fine Arts, Pine Manor College; MA, Theatre Arts, Goddard College. *Publications:* Book and Lyrics, Young Country, 1975; The Pied Piper, 1975; To Find a Rose, 1978; Multi Arts Summer Programmes: The Charles River Model, 1978; Rip's New Wrinkle, 1980; King Arthur's Knights and Days, 1980. *Contributor to:* One-Act Plays published in Plays Magazine; Poems, 'Arts & Leisure Section, Sunday New York Times; The Christian Science Monitor; The Boston Globe; The Bangkok World; Feature Stories and Articles, many newspapers in Boston area. *Honours:* Speaker, American Town Meeting for the Arts, Washington DC ACUCAA National Conference, New York; Catholic University, Washington DC; Womens' City Club, Boston; Alliance for Arts & Education, Boston; Antioch Institute of Open Education. *Memberships:* Dramatists Guild; Authors' League of America; Broadcast Music Inc. (Lyricist). *Address:* 307 Orchard Street, Millis, MA 02054, USA.

DEWHURST, Eileen Mary, b. 27 May 1929, Liverpool, England. Author. *Education:* BA (Hons), English Language and Literature, St. Anne's College, Oxford, 1951; MA, Oxon, 1958. *Publications:* Crime Novels: After the Ball, 1976; Curtain Fall, 1977, 82; Drink This, 1980; Trio in 3 Flats, 1981; Whoever I Am, 1982, 85; The House That Jack Built, 1983; There Was A Little Girl, 1985; Playing Safe, 1985. *Contributions to:* Various newspapers and magazines, 1964-68. *Memberships:* Crime Writers Association; Society of Authors. *Literary Agent:* Watson, Little Limited, London. *Address:* c/o Watson, Little Limited, 26 Charing Cross Road, London WC2H ODG, England.

DEXTER, Colin, b. 29 Sep. 1930, Stamford, Lincolnshire, England. Educational Administrator. *Education:* Christ's College, Cambridge; MA (Cantab); MA (Oxon). *Publications:* Last Bus to Woodstock, 1975; Last Seen Wearing, 1976; The Silent World of Nicholas Quinn, 1977; Service of All the Dead, 1979; The Dead of Jericho, 1981; The Riddle of the Third Mile, 1983. *Honours:* Recipient, Silver Dagger, Crime Writers'

Association, 1979 and 1980. *Memberships:* Crime Writers Association; Detection Club. *Address:* 456 Banbury Road, Oxford OX2 7RG, England.

DEY, Provash Ronjan, b. 1 Feb. 1933, Dacca, Bangladesh. Writer; Service. *Education:* BA, Sahitya Saraswati, Bidyaidhi. *Publications:* 14 works including: Arab Theke Araballi (Travelogue), 1964; Sonar Pakhi (Folk Tales), 1965; Galpa-Ar-Halla, (childrens stories), 1967; Kashmir-E-Kayekdin, (Travelogue), 1967; Childrens Literature of India, 1977; Children's Literature of Bengal, 1978; National Register of Writers for children, 1979; Japan-Dekhe-Elam, 1982. *Contributor to:* Corresponding Editor, Phaedrus, USA. *Memberships:* International Research Society for Children's Literature; All India Bengali Literature Conference; Author's Guild of India; Association of Writers & Illustrators for Children, India; Honorary Director, Academy for Documentation and Research on Children's Literaure; Chairman, Indian Chapter, International Rose O'Neill Club. *Honours:* Memento, National Seminar on Children's Literature, Punjab; Amtilá-Kamal Madel, 1984. *Address:* 4/2 Jadab Ghosh Road, Calcutta 700061, India.

DEZSERY, Endre Istvan, b. 27 Aug. 1920, Budapest, Hungary. Publisher. m. Maria Magdalene Ubelmesser, Aug. 1973, 2 sons, 3 daughters from previous marriage. *Education:* DPA, Budapest, 1942. *Literary Appointments include:* Assistant Editor, Vitezek Lapja, 1940-41; Managing Editor, Levente News Centre, 1942; Publisher, Dezsery Publications Private Limited, 1975-, Australia. *Publications:* Pirospottyos kisasszonyok, 1942; Bissatok a magyar ifjusagban, 1943; Visszatekintoes, 1975; English and Other Than English, Anthology in Community languages, 1979; Neighbours, Short stories, 1980; Katlaki, novel, 1980; The Amphibian, 1981. *Contributions to:* Hungarian Life; in Hungarian, weekly, Australia. *Honours:* 1st Class Levente Medal, 1943; Bronze Military Medal, 1944; Arpad Bronze, 1976, Gold, 1977, USA; St Laszlo Knight, 1982; Jubilee Corss of Knightly Order of Vites, 1984; Order of Australia Medal, 1985; New South Wales' Premier Award Committee, 1980. *Memberships:* Foundation Member and Vice President, Multilingual Authors Associaton of South Australia Incorporated; PEN, Sydney Centre; Writers Centre; Australian Book Publishers Association; Literary Division, Arpad Akademy, Cleveland, Ohio, USA; Federation of Free Hungarian Journalists, USA. *Address:* PO Box 1499, GPO Adelaide, SA 5001, Australia.

DI GIACOMO, James Joseph, b. 22 Nov. 1924, Brooklyn, New York, USA. Roman Catholic Priest; Teacher. *Education:* MA, Woodstock College, Maryland, 1952; Diplome de Lumen Vitae, International School of Religious Formation, Brussels, 1965. *Publications:* We Were Never Their Age, with Edward Wakin, 1972; Introduction to Bioethics, with Thomas Shannon, 1979; When Your Teenager Stops Going to Church, 1980; Understanding Teenagers, with Edward Wakin, 1983. *Contributions to:* Religion Teachers Journal; Witness; National Catholic Guidance Counselors Journal; Today's Catholic Teacher; NCEA Bulletin; US Catholic and Jubilee; The Catechist; Sign; Catholic Digest; Fordham; The Lamp; Catholic World; Conversations; National Catholic Reporter; New Catholic World; The Catholic Connection; America; The Living Light; Catholic Update; Marriage and Family Living; Modern Liturgy and various others. *Honours:* We Were Never Their Age, Selected by Catholic Book Club, 1972. *Address:* 106 West 56th Street, New York City, NY 10019, USA.

DI PRIMA, Diane, b. 6 Aug. 1934, New York City, USA, 2 sons, 3 daughters. Poet; Writer; Playwright. *Literary Appointments:* Contributing Editor, Kulchur magazine, NY, 1960-61; Co-editor with Leroi Jones, 1961-63, Editor, Floating Bear magazine, New York 1963-69; Associate with Yugen, Guerilla, SF Sunday Paper, Ralling Point; Publisher, Poets Press, New York 1964-69; Kidolon Editions, SF, 1974; Co-founder, New York Poets Theater, 1961-63; Core Faculty, NCOC, SF.

Publications: Dinners and Nightmares, 1961; New Handbook of Heaven, 1963; Earthsong, (poems), 1957–59; Hotel Albert, 1968; Revolutionary Letters, 1969; The Book of Hours, Loba, 1973; The Calculus of Variation, 1972; Poems for Freddie, 3 vols, 1972–78; Selected Poems, 1956–75. *Contributor to:* Numerous. *Honours:* National Institute Arts and Letters Grantee, 1965; National Endowment Arts Grantee, 1968, 1973; Coordinating Council of Little Magazines Grant, 1967, 1970. *Address:* Suite 103, PO Box 15068, San Francisco, CA 94115, USA.

DIBBEN, Margaret, b. 2 Apr. 1945, London, England. Journalist. *Publications:* The Guardian Money Guide, 1984. *Contributons to:* Guardian, Personal finance coverage. *Honour:* Insurance Journalist of the Year, 1983. *Address:* The Guardian, 119 Farringdon Street, London EC1R 3ER, England.

DICHLER, Gustav Carl, b. 15 May 1907, Vienna, Austria. Retired Professor; Author; Poet. *Education:* PhD, University of Vienna, 1930; Mag phil, ibid., 1972; Mag rernat, ibid, 1976. *Publications include:* English für der Kaufmann, 3 volumes (co-author), 5th edition 1972; English, Gate to the World, 2 volumes, 4th edition, 1973; Commercial Correspondence, 1966; 15 books poetry including: Das Waldviertel, 1975; Anekdoten aus meinem Leben, 1976; Der Apfel Evas, 1975; Narrenspiegel, 1976; Einfälle-Ausfälle, 1976; Poesie des Stichels, 1977; Masken, 1978; Harfenklang, 1978; Was mich geprägt, 1978; Geschürft, geschliffen, 1979; Die Nichtigkeit des Nichts, 1981; Im Zeichen des Stieres, 1981; Weisse Flügel, dunkle Schwingen, 1982; 3 x 13, 39 short stories, 1983; Der Arm, 30 short stories, 1985. *Contributions to:* Numerous journals. *Honour:* Title, Oberstudienrat, Federal President of Austria, 1960; Golden Doctor of Philosophy, work between 1930–80, 1980; Austrian Cross of Honour for Science and Art, 1982. *Memberships include:* President, Osterreichische Ex-libris Gesellschaft; President, Gesellschaft für zeitgenössische Graphik; Chairman, Osterreichischer Autorenverband; Austrian Textbook Writers Association. *Address:* Johann-Strauss Gasse 28, A–1040 Vienna XI, Austria.

DICKINSON, Harry Thomas, b. 9 Mar. 1939, Gateshead, County Durham, England. University Professor in History. *Education:* BA, Dip Ed, MA, PhD, Universities of Durham and Newcastle. *Publications:* The Correspondence of Sir James Clavering, editor, 1967; Bolingbroke, 1970; Walpole and the Whig Supremacy, 1973; Politics and Literature in the Eighteenth Century, editor, 1974; Liberty and Property, 1977; The Political Works of Thomas Spencer, editor, 1982; British Radicalism and the French Revolution, 1965; Caricatures and the Constitution 1760–1832, 1986. *Contributions to:* Various historical journals and reviews. *Honours include:* Earl Grey Fellow, University of Newcastle, 1964–66; Fulbright Travel Scholarship, 1973; Huntington Library Fellowship, 1973; Folger Shakespeare Library Fellowship, 1973; Winston Churchill Memorial Fellowship, 1980. *Membership:* Fellow Royal Historical Society. *Address:* 44 Viewforth Terrace, Edinburgh EH10 4LJ, Scotland.

DICKSON, Mora Agnes, b. 20 Apr. 1918, Glasgow, Scotland. Author. m. Alec G Dickson, 30 Aug. 1951, Moffat. *Education:* DA Edinburgh College of Art; Byam Shaw School of Drawing and Painting. *Publications:* New Nigerians, 1960; Baghdad And Beyond, 1961; A Season in Sarawak, 1962; A World Elsewhere, 1964; Israeli Interlude, 1966; Count Us In, 1967; School in The Round, 1969; Longhouse In Sarawak, 1971; Beloved Partner, 1974; The Inseparable Brief, 1976; A Chance To Serve, 1976; Asian Assignment, 1979; The Powerful Bond, 1980; The Aunts, 1981; Teacher Extraordinary, 1986; Nannie, 1986. *Honour:* Scottish Arts Council Book Award, 1975. *Address:* 19 Blenheim Road, London W4 1UB, England.

DICKSON, Niall Forbes Ross, b. 5 Nov. 1953, Glasgow, Scotland. Journalist. m. Elizabeth Selina, 20 Apr. 1979, Lisburn, 1 son, 1 daughter. *Education:* MA

Honours, Dip Ed, University of Edinburgh; Cert Ed, Moray House, College of Education. *Literary Appointments:* Head of Publishing, Age Concern England, 1979–81; Editor, Therapy Weekly, 1981–83; Editor, Nursing Times, 1983. *Publications:* Living in the '80's – What Prospects for the Elderly?, 1980; Age Concern at Work, 1981; Towards a Happy Retirement, (co-author), 1981. *Memberships:* National Union of Journalists; Medical Journalists Association. *Address:* Chestnut Cottage, Brasted, Kent TN16 1NT, England.

DIEHL, Digby Robert, b. 14 Nov. 1940, Boonton, New Jersey, USA. Writer; Editor. m. Kay Beyer, 6 June 1981, New Brunswick, New Jersey, 1 daughter. *Literary Appointments:* Editor: The Learning Center, Princeton, New Jersey, 1962–64; Coast Magazine, 1966–68; Show Magazine, 1968–69; Book editor, Los Angeles Times, 1969–78; Editor-in-Chief, Harry Abrams Inc, New York City, 1978–80; Book editor, Los Angeles Herald Examiner, 1980–. *Publications:* Supertalk: Extraordinary Conversations. 1974; Front Page, 1981. *Contributions to:* Numerous publications including, New York Magazine; Esquire; California Magazine; People; TV Guide; New York Times; Los Angeles Magazine; Family Weekly; Family Circle; etc. *Honour:* Irita Van Doren Award, 1977. *Memberships:* Vice President, National Bool Critics Circle; PEN International; American Society of Journalists & Authors; Phi Sigma Delta; Phi Beta Kappa. *Literary Agent:* George Diskant. *Address:* 788 South Lake Avenue, Pasadena, CA 91106, USA.

DIERENFIELD, Richard Bruce, b. 15 Oct. 1922, Aberdeen, SD, USA. Teacher; Author. *Education:* BA, MEd, Macalester College St Paul, Minnesota; EdD, University of Colorado, Boulder. *Publications:* Religion in American Public School, 1962; The High School Curriculum, (co-author), 1964; The Cinderella Subject: Religion In the County Secondary Schools of England, 1965; The Sociology of Religion (co-author), 1967; Learning to Teach, 1981. *Contributor to:* Religious Education; Journal of Teacher Education; Clearing House. *Address:* 1566 Cedar Road, St Paul, MI 55101, USA.

DIGGORY, Terence Elliott, b. 13 May 1951, Wallingford, Pennsylvania, USA. College Professor. m. Anne Parker, 5 June 1976, New Haven, Connecticut, 2 daughters. *Education:* BA, Yale University, 1973; D Phil, Oxford University, 1976. *Literary Appointments:* Instructor of English, 1975–76, Assistant Professor 1976–77, Yale University; Assistant Professor of English, 1977–84, Associate Professor 1984–, Skidmore College. *Contributions to:* Contributor to articles and reviews to journals and edited volumes including: Armoured Women, Naked Men: Dickinson, Whitman and Their Successors, in Shakespeare's Sisters; Feminist Essays on Women Poets edited by Sandra Gilbert and Susan Gubar, 1977. *Honours:* Summer Stipend, National Endowment for the Humanities, 1983; College Teachers Fellowship, National Endowment for the Humanities, 1984–85. *Membership:* Modern Language Association. *Address:* Department of English, Skidmore College, Saratoga Springs, NY 12866, USA.

DILKS, David Neville, b. 17 Mar. 1938, Coventry, England. Professor of History. m. Jill Medlicott, 15 Aug. 1963, Shrewsbury, 1 son. *Education:* BA, Hertford College and St Antony's College, Oxford University. *Publications:* Curzon in India, volume I 1969, Volume II 1970; The Diaries of Sir Alexander Cadogan, editor, 1971; The Conservatives, contributor, 1977; Retreat From Power, editor and contributor, 2 volumes, 1981; The Missing Dimension; Governments and Intelligence Communities in the Twentieth Century, edited with C Andrew, contributor 1984; Neville Chamberlain, Volume I; Pioneering and Reform, 1984. *Contributions to:* Time-Life History of the British Empire; Survey; Journal of Scandinavian History; BBC; etc. *Membership:* Royal Commonwealth Society. *Honour:* Visiting Fellow, All Souls' College, Oxford, 1973. *Literary Agent:* A D Peters Limited. *Address:* School of History, The University, Leeds, LS2 9JT, England.

DILL, William Joseph, b. 8 May 1935, Carmi, Illinois, USA. Editor. m. Marie Emilie Hubert, 14 Aug. 1965, Chicago, Illinois, USA, 2 sons, 2 daughters. *Education:* BSc, Southern Illinois University, Carbondale, Illinois. *Literary Appointments:* Editor, The Forum, Fargo, North Dakota, USA. *Contributor to:* Various newspapers. *Honours:* Pulitzer Prize Juror, 1985–86. *Address:* 105 19th Avenue North, Fargo, ND 58102, USA.

DILLARD, Annie, b. 30 Apr. 1945, Pittsburgh, Pennsylvania, USA. Writer. m. Gary Clevidence, 1 daughter. *Education:* BA, 1967, MA, 1968, Hollins College. *Appointments:* Contributing Editor, Harpers Magazine, 1974–; Adjunct Professor, Wesleyan University, 1980–. *Publications:* Pilgrim at Tinker Creek, 1974; Holy the Firm, 1978; Teaching a Stone to Talk, 1982; Living by Fiction, 1982; Encounter with Chinese Writers, 1984. *Contributor to:* Atlantic Monthly; Harpers Poetry; TriQuarterly; Sports Illustrated, Field; Esquire; etc. *Honours:* Phi Beta Kappa, 1966; Pulitzer Prize, 1974; Washington Governors Award, 1978; New York Press Club Award, 1975; NEA Grant, 1981; Guggenheim Foundation Grant, 1984–85. *Memberships:* Authors Guild; PEN; National Committee on US-China Relations; National Citizens for Public Libraries. *Literary Agent:* Blanche Gregory Inc, New York. *Address:* c/o Blanche Gregory Inc, 2 Tudor City Place, New York, NY 10017, USA.

DILLE, Denijs, b. 21 Feb. 1904, Aarschot, Belgium. Retired Head of Bela Bartok Archives, Budapest, Hungary. *Publications:* Béla Bartok, 1939, 3rd edition, 1974; Documenta Bartokiana I-IV, 1964–1970; Thematisches Verzeichnis der Jugenwerke Béla Bartok, 1974; Het Werk Van Béla Bartok, 1979; Genealogie Sommaire de la Famille Bartok, 1977. *Honours:* Golden Distinction, Ordre du Mérite pour le travail, Hungary, 1964–71; Officier de l'ordre de la Couronne, Belgium, 1974; Commandeur Dans L'ordre de Leopold II, Belgium, 1984; L'ordre du Drapeau de la Republique Populaire Hongroise, 1984. *Address:* Vöröshadsereg u 23, H 2000 Szentendre, Hungary.

DILLON, Lawrence Samuel, b. 10 Aprl 1910, Reading, Pennsylvania, USA. Professor. *Education:* BS, University of Pittsburg, 1933, MS, 1950, PhD, Texas A and M University, 1954. *Publications include:* Manual of the Common Beetles of Eastern North America, 1961, 2nd edition, 1970; The Science of Life, 1964; Principles of Animal Biology, 1965; Animal Variety, 1968, 3rd Edition, 1976; Evolution: Concepts and Consequences, 1973, 2nd Edition, 1978; The Genetic Mechanism and the Origins of Life, 1978; Ultrastructure, Macromolecules and Evolution, 1981; The Inconstant Gene, 1983. *Contributor to:* Various Scientific journals. *Honours include:* Phi Kappa Phi; Sigma Xi; Phi Sigma. *Memberships include:* Fellow, AAAS; American Institute of Biology Science; Fellow, Texas Academy of Science; American Society of Zoologists. *Address:* 1904 Cedarwood Drive, Bryan, TX 77801, USA.

DIMLER, G Richard, b. 21 Oct. 1931, Baltimore, Maryland, USA. Professor. *Education:* BA, MA, Fordham University; STL, STB, Woodstock College; MA, Middlebury College; PhD, University of California, Los Angeles. *Literary Appointment:* Editor-in-Chief, Thought Magazine, Fordham University, 1978–. *Publications:* Books include: Friedrich Spee's Trutznachtigall: Imagery and Function, 1973; Friedrich Spee's Trutznachtigall, 1983; Friedrich Spee's Von Langenfeld: Eine Beschreibende Bibliographie (awaiting publication). *Contributions to:* Professional publications and books; Translations; Book Reviews; Scholarly Papers and Addresses. *Honours:* NDEA Title IV, 1968; American Council of Learned Societies, 1974; National Endowment for Humanities, 1975. *Memberships:* Catholic Press Association; Modern Language Association of America; Society of Editors of Learned Journals; Society for Emblem Literature. *Address:* Fordham University, Loyola Hall 601, Bronx, NY 10458, USA.

DINESCU, Violeta, b. 13 July 1953, Bucharest, Romania, Composer. *Education:* Diploma for composition, piano, pedagogy, Conservatorium C Porumbescu, 1976; Special diploma for compositon, 1977. *Literary Appointments:* Co-author, Palestrina Melody, Editura muzicala 1978; Music and mathematics, Springer Verlag, 1985. *Publications:* Orchestral Compositions include: Memories, string orchestra; Anna Perenna, and Akrostichon, for orchestra; The Play, Children chorus and orchestra; Bewitch Me Into a Silver Bird, chorus and orchestra. Vocal compositions include: Flower Song; Song Remained in a Flute; Tamina; Country of Doina; Cat in Sentences; Sunset, chorus; The Play; Chamber Music includes: Echoes, 1-111; Satya, 1-V; Immagini; Improvisation; Dialogo; Arabesques; Alternances; Melismen; Three Miniatures; Aion; In Search of Mozart; Terra Lonhdana. *Contributions to:* Scinteia Tineretului; Romania Literara; Neuland. *Honours include:* George Enescu Stipend; Karl Klingler Stipend; Stipend and Union of Composers, Germany, Paul Hindemith, German Exchange Academy, Baden-Wurttemberg Foundation, 1983, City of Mannheim, 1984; Awards, Union of Composers of Rumania, 1975, 76, 80, National Council of Romania, 1982; 1st prize, International Music Competition, GB Viotti, Italy, 1983, International Competition for Composers, USA, 1983; Honorable mention, International League of Women Composers, USA, 1985; IAM Prize, Kassel, Germany, 1985; Valentin Becker Prize, Federal Republic of Germany, 1985; Terra Lonhdaa for chamber music, International Year of Music, World Music Days, Budapest, Hungary, 1985; various commissions. *Memberships:* Union of Composers of Rumania, Federal Republic of Germany, USA. *Address:* c/o von Knorr, Jahnstr 3, 6907 Nussloch-Heidelberg, Federal Republic of Germany.

DINTENFASS, Mark, b. 15 Nov. 1941, New York, NewYork, USA. Novelist. m. Phyllis Schulman, 10 June 1962, New York, 2 sons. *Education:* BA, 1963. MA, 1964, Columbia University; MFA, University of Iowa, 1968. *Literary Appointments:* Professor of English, Lawrence University, Appleton, Wisconsin. *Publications:* Make Yourself an Earthquake, 1969; The Case Against Org, 1970; Figure 8, 1974; Montgomery Street, 1978; Oldworld, New World, 1982. *Contributions to:* New York Times; Milwaukee Journal; Translantic; Wisconsin Academy Review. *Memberships:* Authors Guild; Poets, Playwrights, Editors, Essayists and Novelists. *Literary Agent:* Mitch Douglas, ICM. *Address:* Main Hall, Lawrence University, Appleton, WI 54911, USA.

DIONNE, René, b. 29 Jan. 1929, St Phillippe de Néri, Québec, Canada. University Professor. m. Gabrielle Poulin, 1970. *Education:* BA, Laval University; MA, University of Montreal; LPh, L'Immaculée Conception; Lic Letters, University of Montreal; D Litt, University of Sherbrooke. *Publications include:* Antoine Gérin-Lajoie, homme de lettres, 1978; La Patrie littéraire 1760–1895, 1978; Bibliographie de la littérature outaouaise et franco-ontarienne, 1978; Propos sur la littérature outaouaise et franco-ontarienne, 1978 (4 vols 1978–83); L-Âge de l-interrogation 1937–1952, 1980; Quatre Siècles d'identité canadienne, 1983; Le Quebecois et sa litterature, 1984. *Contributions to:* Lettres québécoises; Revue d'histoire littéraire du Québec et du Canada français, (Editor); Relations; Revue de l'Université d'Ottawa. *Honours:* Prize, Swiss Embassy, 1960; Literary Prize, La Presse, 1979; Champlain Literary Prize, 1980. *Memberships:* Union Québéçois writers; Associations of Canadian & Quebec Lits (Past President). *Address:* 1997 Avenue Quincy, Ottawa, Ontario, Canada K1J 6B4.

DIUGUID, Lewis Walter, b. 17 July 1955, St Louis, Missouri. Copy Editor; Automotive Editor; Assistant Minority Recruiting Co-ordinator. m. Valerie Gale Words, 25 Oct. 1977, Kansas City, 1 daughter. *Education:* Bachelor of Journalism, University of Missouri [md] Columbia School of Journalism, 1977; Graduate of the Editing Program for Minority Journalists Fellowship, 1984. *Contributions to:* Thousands of newspaper articles on various subjects published in Kansas City Times, 1977–; Article on Copy Editing for Capital Cities INK magazine, 1985 also published by Outlook publications of Institute of Journalism Education in California. *Honour:* Second Place, Investigative Reporting Award, Unity Awards in Media presented by the Journalism Department of Lincoln University, Jefferson City, Missouri, 1979. *Memberships:* Kansas City Association of Black Journalists; National Association of Black Journalists. *Address:* 3944 Charlotte Street, Kansas City, MO 64110, USA.

DIXON, Bernard, b. 17 July 1938, Darlington, England. Editor, Writer. *Education:* BSc, King's College, University of Durham; PhD, University of Newcastle upon Tyne. *Publications:* Journeys in Belief, 1968; What Is Science For? 1973; Invisible Allies, 1976; Magnificent Microbes, 1976; Beyond The Magic Bullet, 1978; Man and Medicine, 1986; Ideas of Science, 1985. *Contributions to:* New Scientist (editor); Spectator; World Medicine; British Medical Journal; Encyclopaedia Britannica; Biotechnology; New Society. *Honours:* Medical Journalists Association Award, 1978; Glaxo Travelling Fellowship for British Science Writers, 1980; Elected Fellow (in recognition of contributions to science writing), Institute of Biology. *Membership:* Chairman 1971–72, Association of British Science Writers. *Literary Agents:* Michael Sissons; A D Peters. *Address:* 81 Falmouth Road, Chelmsford, Essex, England.

DJAGAROV, Georghi, b. 14 July 1925, Sliven, Bulgaria. Writer. *Education:* The Moscow, Maxim Gorki, Literary Institution. *Literary Appointment:* Vice Chairman of The State Council of Bulgaria; Academician. *Publications:* Poetry: My Songs, 1954; Lyrics, 1956; In minutes of Silence, 1958; Drama: The Doors Are Closed, 1961; Tomorrow is a Day, Too, 1963; The Prosecutor, 1965; Essays: The Problems of Life – Problems of Literature. *Contributor to:* All main Bulgarian Literary editions. *Honours:* A Hero of Socialist Labour (twice); A People's Worker of Culture, 1971; Dimitrov Prize, 1976. *Membership:* Union of Bulgarian Writers, Chairman 1966–72. *Address:* 8 Boulevard Rouski, Sofia, Bulgaria.

DJERASSI, Carl, b. 29 Oct. 1923, Vienna, Austria. Professor of Chemistry. *Education:* AB summa cum laude, Kenyon College, 1942; PhD, University of Wisconsin, 1945. *Publications:* Optical Rotatory Dispersion, 1960; Steroid Reactions, editor, 1963; Interpretation of Mass Spectra of Organic Compounds, (with Herbert Budzikiewicz and Dudley Williams), 1964; Structure Elucidation of Natural Products by Mass Spectrometry, Volume 1, Alkaloids, (with Herbert Budzikiewicz and Dudley E Williams), 1964; Structure Elucidation of Natural Products by Mass Spectrometry, Volume 2, Steroids, Terpendoids, Sugars and Miscellaneous Classes, (with Herbert Budzikeiwicz and Dudley E Williams), 1964; Mass Spectrometry of Organic Compounds, (with Herbert Budzikiewicz and Dudley E Williams), 1967; The Politics of Contraception, 1980. *Contributions to:* Over 1000 articles in scientific journals; Poems in: Wallace Stevens Journal; Cumberland Review; Kenyon Review. *Honours:* Honorary doctorate from: Kenyon College, National University of Mexico, Federal University of Rio de Janeiro, Worcester Polytechnical Institute, Wayne State University, Columbia University, Uppsala Unversity, Coe College, University of Geneva, University of Ghent, University of Manitoba; National Medal of Science; Wolf Prize; Perkin Medals; American Chemical Society Award in Pure Chemistry; Award for Creative Inventing; *Memberships:* National Academy of Sciences; German Academy; Royal Swedish Academy; Royal Swedish Academy of Sciences; Brazilian Academy of Sciences; American Academy of Arts & Sciences; Mexican Academy Science Investigation; Bulgarian Academy Sciences; Phi Beta Kappa; Sigma Xi; Phi Lambda Upsilon. *Address:* Department of Chemistry, Stanford University, Stanford, CA 94305, USA.

DJUPALAEK, Kristjan fra, b. 16 July 1916, Djupilaekur, Iceland. Poet. *Education:* Eidar Public College, 1936–37; Akureyri College, 1937–38. *Major Publications:* (in Icelandic): 12 Collections of Poetry; selections of poems; tranlations of numerous books & plays for children & adults; (in English): The Song of the Stone (poetry), 1977; Akureyri & the Picturesque North (introductory text), 1977. *Contributor to:* Dagur. *Honours include:* Annual Artists' Grant, Icelandic State, 1948–; Writers Award, Icelandic Broadcasting Corporation, 1970; Artistic Award, Icelandic Ch, 1979. *Membership:* Icelandic Writers Association. *Literary Agent:* Icelandic Office, International Confederation of Societies of Authors & Composers. *Address:* Arnarsida 8a, 600 Akyureyri, Iceland.

DOBBS, Rosalyne Brown, b. 20 Aug. 1933, Little Rock, Arkansas, USA. Freelance Writer. m. John Allen Dobbs, 25 Aug. 1954, Little Rock, 1 daughter. *Education:* BA, English, Louisiana State University. *Contributor to:* American Rose Magazine; American Rose Annual; American Horticulturist; Garden; Organic Gardening; American Nurseryman; Southern Florist and Nurseryman; American Farmer; Progressive Farmer. *Memberships:* National Association of Science Writers. *Address:* 10934 Effringham Avenue, Baton Rouge, LA 70815, USA.

DOBRACZYNSKI Jan, b. 20 Apr. 1910, Warsaw, Poland. Writer. m. Danuta Kotowicz, 2 June 1935, 2 daughters. *Education:* High School of Commerce, Warsaw. *Publications include:* 67 books, translated into 19 languages including: Invaders, 1946; The Chosen of the Stars, 1948; The Key of Wisdom, 1951; The Letters of Nicodemus, 1952; The Desert, 1955; I Came To Separate, 1959; The Unvanquished Armada, 1960; Blue Helmets on the Dam, 1965; Captured, 1967; Poisoners, 1974; The Father's Shadow, 1977; Ann's Marriage, 1981; Anyone Who Puts You To Death, 1985. *Contributions to:* Slowo Powszechne. *Honours include:* Virluti, Militari; Commandeur Polonia Restituta Cross; Poland Popular Republic's Builder; Works Banner 1st Class; W Pietnak Prize, State's Literary Prize, Minister of Culture's Prize; Warsaw's Prize; Prato's Prize, Italy; Maksymilien Kolbe Prize, Federal Republic of Germany. *Memberships:* Polish Writers Association; Societé Européene de Culture; PEN Club. *Literary Agent:* Agencia Audorsche, 2 Hipokeene Street 2, Warsaw. *Address:* Hefmanska Street 42, 04305 Warsaw, Poland.

DOBSON, Sue (Susan Angela), b. 31 Jan. 1946, Maidstone, Kent, England. Magazine Editor. *Education:* Dip HE; BA, Hons. *Literary Appointment:* Editor, Woman and Home. *Publication:* The Wedding Day Book, 1981. *Contributor to:* Femina; Fair Lady; Wedding Day; Successful Slimming; Woman and Home. *Address:* Editor, Woman and Home, IPC Magazines, Kings Reach Tower, Stamford Street, London SE1 9LS.

DOCHERTY, John, b. 7 Jan. 1947, Bowden, Cheshire, England. Humorous Writer and Poet. *Education:* Fielden Park College, West Didsbury, Manchester; Poetry Workshop, Uniterity of Manchester. *Publications:* A Walk Around The City and Other Groans, 1969, special revised edition 1973; Words on Paper; A Run Around The Twilight Zones, 1977; From Bottoms To Tops and Back Again, 1977; Too Late Roles For Erogenous and Other Zones; Ballads of Fantasy and Reality, 1982. *Contributions to:* Sunday Times; Manchester Evening News; The Artful Reporter; Radio Manchester; Piccadilly Radio; South West Manchester Newsround; Daily Mail; What's On in Hulme; Dun and Bradstreet Report Magazine; The Times; The Susnday Telegraph; The Odd Fellow; Granada Television; North West Tonight; Stretford and Ormston Journal. *Honours include:* North West Arts Poetry Prize, 1978; Double Prize Winner, Tribute For St George's Day, Granada Television, 1978; North West Arts Letter Prize, 1980; Runners-up Prize, The Star Lovingest Bed Competition, 1984. *Memberships:* The Turner Society; Court School of Dancing, Subscriber, Manchester Academy of Fine Arts; Friend of Northwest

Arts; Friend of Manchester City Art Gallery; Authors North. *Address:* 43 Cornbrook Park Road, Old Trafford, Manchester M15 4EH, England.

DOCHNIAK, James M (Jeffrey Allan George), b. 22 July 1949, Greenbay, Wisconsin, USA. Poet. *Education:* BA, Experimental College, University of Minnesota. *Appointments:* Founding Board Member, The Loft, Minneapolis, 1974–76; Guest Editor, West End Magazine, New York, 1976–78; Regional Correspondent, Coordinating Council of Literary Magazines, New York, 1978–79; President, National Writers Union, Local 13, 1985. *Publications:* Friends, Pause and Look This Way, 1985; A Simple Exchange, 1986. *Contributor to:* Lake Street Review; Sing Heavenly Muse; Greenfield Review; One; North Stone Review; Northern Literary Quarterly; Maize; Moons & Lions Tales; Midwest; A Review; etc. *Honours:* Editorial Fellowships, Sez Magazine, Coordinating Council of Literary Magazines, 1977, Minnesota State Arts Board, 1980, National Endowment for the Arts, Washington DC, 1983. *Memberships:* Founding Member, Twin Cities Cultural Workers Association; President, National Writers Union. *Literary Agent:* Shadow Press, USA. *Address:* PO Box 8803, Minneapolis, MN 55408, USA.

DODD, Anne Wescott, b. 24 Apr. 1940, Bangor, Maine, USA. Freelance Writer. m. James H Dodd, 26 Feb. 1965, Maywood, California, 2 daughters. *Education:* BA, 1961, CAS; University of Maine, Orono, 1982; MA, California State University, Los Angeles, 1967. *Publications:* Write Now!, (Globe Book Company), 1973. *Contributor to:* English journal; Elementary English; Scholastic Teacher; NASSP Bulletin; Creative Teacher; Maine English Bulletin; NEATE Leaflet; Media and Methods; UMM Binnacle; Phi Delta Kappan; Yachting; Conn. English journal; Middle School journal; New England League of Middle Schools Journal; Ellsworth American; Maine Sunday Telegram; Brunswick Times Record; National Poetry Anthology. *Honour:* Phi Kappa Phi Member, 1983. *Memberships:* Society of Children's Book Writers; National Committee of National Council of Teachers of English; Secretary, Executive Board New England Association Teaccers of English; Vice President, Maine Council Teachers of English; Zonta Club; National Association Secondary School Prins.; Chair, Legis, Committee, Maine State Prins. Association. *Address:* 3095 Mere Point Road, Brunswick, ME 04011, USA.

DODD, Christopher John, b. 14 Feb. 1942, Bristol, England. Journalist. *Education:* BA Political Science, Nottingham University. *Publications:* Henley Royal Regatta, 1981; The Oxford and Cambridge Boat Race, 1983; Boating, 1983. *Contributions to:* Games of the 23rd Olympiad Commemorative Rock; The Guardian. *Literary Agents:* Malcolm Hamet, Headline Enterprises; Pamela Todd, A P Watt. *Address:* 73 Holmdene Avenue, Herne Hill, London SE24 9LD, England.

DODD, Wayne D, b. 23 Sep. 1930, Clarita, Oklahoma, USA. Professor, editor, writer. *Education:* BA 1955, MA 1957, University of Oklahoma; PhD, 1963. *Literary Appointment:* Editor, The Ohio Review, 1970–. *Publications:* A Time of Hunting, 1975; Made in America, 1975; We Will Wear White Roses, 1974; The Names You Gave It, 1980; The General Mule Poems, 1981; Sometimes Music Rises, 1986. *Contributions to:* American Review; Nation; Southern Review; Poetry North West; Georgia Review; Missouri Review; Shenandoah; Kayak; North West Review; Outerbridge; Black Warrior Review; Iowa Review; Lillabulero; Limberlost Review; etc. *Literary Agent:* James Brown Associates. *Address:* Route 3, Box 255, Athens, OH 45701, USA.

DODGE, Ellin, b. 7 Oct. 1932, New York City, New York, USA. Numerologist; Author. m. John C Young, divorced, 1 son, 1 daughter. *Publications:* The Vibes Books, a game of self analysis, with Carol Schuler, 1979; Help Yourself to Understand, 1980, 81; You Are Your First Name, 1983; Win The Lottery, 1985; You Are Your Birthday, 1986. *Memberships:* Authors Guild; American

Society of Journalists and Authors; National Writers Club. *Literary Agent:* Ellen Levine, New York. *Address:* 4216 West Missouri Avenue, Phoenix, AZ 85019, USA.

DOLING, Hilary, b. 14 Mar. 1957, London, England. Journalist. *Education:* BA, Honours, Sussex University. *Contributor to:* Sunday Express; The Accountant; Company; Cosmopolitan. *Address:* c/o Express Newspapers, Fleet Street, London, England.

DOLMETSCH, Christopher Lee, b. 22 Aug. 1950, Springfield, Missouri, USA. Professor. m. Nona Leigh Tapscott, Yorktown, Virginia, USA, 27 Aug. 1977. *Education:* BA German & European History, University of Pennsylvania, 1972; MA 1973, PhD 1979, German Language & Literature, University of Wisconsin at Madison. *Literary Appointments:* Professor of German, Marshall University, Huntingdon, West Virginia. *Major Publications:* The German Press of the Shenandoah Valley, (volume 4: Studies in German Literature, Linguistics & Culture), 1984. *Contributor to:* Moravian Music Journal; Journal of German-American Studies; Monatshefte; Report: Society of Germans in Md; and others. *Address:* Department of Modern Languages, Marshall University, Huntington, VA 25701, USA.

DOLSON, Franklin Robert, b. 22 Mar. 1933, New York City, USA. Sports Columnist; Sports Editor. *Education:* BSc Economics, Wharton School, University of Pennsylvania, USA; Beta Gamma Sigma (Honorary Fraternity). *Major Publications:* Always Young, World Publications, 1975; The Philadelphia Story, Icarus Press, 1981; Beating the Bushes, Icarus Press, 1982. *Contributor to:* Family Circle; Sports Illustrated, etc. *Honours:* Keystone Press Awards, 1967, 1968; National Sportscasters and Sportswriters Award, 1972, 1973, 1974, 1976. *Membership:* The Authors Guild. *Address:* Latches Lane Apts, Apt 404, Merion, PA 19066, USA.

DONAGUE, Francis J, b. 21 Nov. 1917, Chicago III, USA. Professor; Literary Critic. *Education:* BA, University of Nebraska, 1941; MA, University of Wisconsin, 1942; PhD, University of S California, 1965. *Publications:* Washington Irving; Su Mondo de Romance y Leyenda, 1958; Diez Figuras Ilustres de la Literatura Norteamericana, 1965; The Dramatic World of Tennessee Williams, 1964; Leandro F de Moratin: Dos Comedias, 1967; Alfonso Sastre: Dramaturgo y Preceptista, 1973. *Contributor to:* Books Abroad; Contemporary World Literature; Texas Quarterly; Michigan Quarterly; Saturday Review; etc. *Memberships include:* Corresponding Member, Academy Cubana de la Lengua. *Address:* California State University, Long Beach, CA 90840, USA.

DONCK, Carel, b. 11 Feb. 1946, Appingedam, Netherlands. Writer, translator. *Education:* Graduate, Gronningen University; 6 month course, Film Academy, Prague, Czechoslovakia. *Publications include:* Scenarios for short films; Splinters; Arthur and Eva; Bear or No Bear; Movies: My Nights with...; Debut, 1977; Series for television with Hugo Heinen; The Steamy Mirror, 1980; Weekend, 1982; Sanne, 1983; Translations and adaptations of operas into Dutch, with Hgo Heinen; The Impresario, Mozart's Der Schauspielddirektor; The Elixir of Love, Donizetti's L'élisir d'amore; The Poor Sailor, Milhaud/Cocteau's Le pauvre matelot. *Address:* Valeriusterras 3, 1075 BK Amsterdam, The Netherlands.

DONI, Rodolfo, b. 20 Mar. 1919, Pistoia, Italy. Writer. *Major Publications:* Sezione santo spirito, 1962; La Provocazione, 1967; I Numeri, 1969; Passaggio del fronte, 1971; Muro d'ombra, 1974; Giorno segreto, 1976; Se no, no, 1978; La Doppia vita, 1980; Il Senatore Mazzoni, 1981; Servo inutile, 1982; premio Vallombrora; Memoria per un figlio (diario), premio Selezione Estense; Legarne profondo, 1984; Meydugorge, 1985; TV scripts. *Contributor to:* La Nazione, Florence; Il Tempo, Rome; Avvenire, Milan; L'Osservatore Romano, Rome; principally reviews. *Honours include:* Selection Prize Campiello, Venice; Ceppo Prize, Pistoia; Palazzeschi Prize, Rome; Selection Prize, Naples, 1978; Castligoncello Prize,

Castiglioncello. *Literary Agent:* Editore Rusconi, Milan. *Address:* Spallanzani 2, Florence, Italy.

DONLEAVY, James Patrick, b. 26 Apr. 1926, Brooklyn, New York, USA. Author; Playwright. m. (1) Valerie Heron (div.) 1 son, 1 daughter. (2) Mary Wilson Price, 1 son, 1 daughter. *Education:* Trinity College, Dublin, Eire. *Publications include:* The Ginger Man, novel, 1955, adapted as play, 1959; Fairy Tales of New York, play, 1960; A Singular Man, novel, 1963, play 1964; Meet My Maker The Mad Molecule, short stories, 1964; The Beastly Beatitudes of Balthazar B, novel 1968, play 1981; The Onion Eaters, novel 1971; The Destinies of Darcy Dancer, Gentleman, novel, 1977; Schultz, novel, 1979; Leila: Further in the Destinies of Darcy Dancer, Gentleman, novel 1983; De Alfonce Tennis: The Superlative Game of Eccentric Champions. Its History, Accoutrements, Rules, Conduct & Regimen. A Legend, novel, 1984; J P Donleavy's Ireland: In All Her Sins and Some of Her Graces, biography, 1986; etc. *Contributions to:* Times, London; New York Times; Envoy; Punch; Guardian; Saturday Review; Playboy; Atlantic Monthly; New Yorker; Washington Post; Rolling Stone; Actuel; etc. *Honours:* Brandeis University Creative Arts Award, 1962; Evening Standard Drama Critic's Award, 1961; AAL Grantee, 1975. *Address:* Levington Park, Mullingar, Co Westmeath, Republic of Ireland.

DONNE, Michael Gerald, b. 6 Apr. 1928, London, England. Aerospace Correspondent, The Financial Times. m. Diana C Allsworth, 8 Sep. 1951, Coulsdon, Surrey. *Education:* Birkbeck College, University of London. *Publications:* Leader of the Skies, History of Rolls-Royce, 1981; Per Ardua ad Astra, History of the RAF and RFC, 1983. *Contributions to:* Aviation and technical magazines and journals world-wide over past 30 years, plus frequent radio and TV broadcasts in England and overseas. *Honour:* Honorary Companion, Royal Aeronautical Society. *Address:* Tresco, Blackheath, Guildford, Surrey, England.

DONNELLY, Augustine (Austin) Stanislaus, b. 1 June 1923, Port Douglas, Queensland, Australia. Investment Adviser/Writer. m. Sheila Bernadette O'Hagan, 15 Feb. 1947, Brisbane, 1 son, 2 daughters. *Education:* Bachelor Commerce, University of Queensland. *Literary Appointments:* Editor, Investing Today, 1970–83; Editor, Dynamic Investing Today, 1985–. *Publications:* Author of 31 books, most recently: Managing Cash Flow, 1979: Personal Money Management, 1979; Planning and Financing a Secure Retirement, 1980; Treasury Management, 1981; How to Generate and Control Cash Flow, 1982; Where to Park Your Cash, 1982; The three R's of Investing, 1985. *Contributions to:* Author of hundreds of articles on investing, finance, accounting, business communication and other subjects which have been published in Australia, USA, Canada, UK, Japan and New Zealand. *Honours:* Award for meritorious contribution to accounting literature for, Direct Costing by Australian Society of Accountants, 1958; Elected Fellow of The American Business Communication Association, 1980. *Address:* 31 King Arthur Terrace, Tennyson, Queensland, 4105, Australia.

DONOVAN, Hedley Williams, b. 24 May 1914. Brainerd, Minn, USA. Editor; formerly Senior Advisor to President of USA, 1979–80. *Education:* University of Minnesota; Hertford College, Oxford, England. *Publications:* Roosevelt to Reagan: A Reporter's Encounter with Nine Presidents, 1985. *Contributor to:* Reporter, Washington Post, 1937–42; Writer and Editor, 1945–53, Managing Editor, Fortune, 1953–59; Editing Director, Time Inc, 1959–64, Editor-in Chief, 1964–79, (ret'd). *Memberships:* Trustee, Asia Society; Aerospace Corporation; National Humanities Center; Member, Council on Foreign Relations; Fellow, American Academy of Arts and Sciences. *Address:* Harbor Road, Sands Point, NY 11050, USA.

DONTCHEV, Anton, b. 14 Sep. 1930, Bourgas, Bulgaria. Writer. *Education:* University Law Degree.

Publications: A Time To Split, 1964; The Leader of the Invisible Army; The Year 1191, 1967. *Contributor to:* All main Bulgarian literary editions. *Honour:* Dimitrov Prize, 1966. *Membership:* Union of Bulgarian Writers. *Address:* 23, Geo Milev Street, Sofia, Bulgaria.

DOOLEY, Brian J, b. 18 July 1954, Canadaqua, New York, USA. Writer. *Education:* BA English, McGill University, Montreal, Canada, 1976; Graduate courses in communications, University of Pennsylvania, USA. *Contributions to:* Today's Office; The Office; American Import/Export Bulletin; Printing Impressions; Graphic Arts Monthly; Computer Dealer; Datapro EDP Management Newsbrief; Datapro Management of: Microcomputers, Office Automation, Applications Software and Data Communications Newsbriefs. *Address:* 14 Northgate Village, Burlington, NJ 08016, USA.

DORFMAN, John R, b. 19 Apr. 1947, Chicago, Illinois, USA. Writer; Editor. m. Deborah Jane Levinson, 20 June 1971, New York, New York, 2 daughters. *Education:* BA, Princeton University, 1969; MFA, Columbia University, 1972. *Literary Appointments:* Reporter: New Brunswick Home News, New Jersey, 1970–72; Associated Press, 1972–73. Assistant Editor, Consumer Reports, 1973–74; Freelance Writer, 1974–81; Associate Editor, Forbes, 1982–84; Executive Editor, Consumer Reports, 1984–. *Publications:* Consumer Survival Kit, 1975; Well-Being, 1981' Stock Market Directory, 1982. *Contributions to:* Chicago; Consumer Reports; Forbes; Money; Parade; Playboy; Count Your Change, syndicated column. *Honours:* Family Investment Guide, Alternate selection, Book of the Month Club and Fortune Book Club, 1981. *Memberships:* American Society of Journalists and Authors; Authors Guild; American Society of Magazine Editors. *Literary Agent:* Dominick Abel. *Address:* 3547 Flanders Drive, Yorktown Heights, NY 10598, USA.

DORION, Hélène, b. 21 Apr. 1958, Québec, Canada. Writer. *Education:* BA (Philosophy), MA (Literature). *Major Publications:* L'Intervalle Prolongé Suiui De La Chute Requise, 1983; Hors Champ, 1985. *Contributor to:* Estuaire; Moebius; Possibles; Dérives; Le Sabord; Livre D'ici; Nuit Blanche; Dictionnaire des oeuvres littéraires du Québec; 'Québec Français; Livres et Auteurs québécois. *Membership:* Union des Ecrivains Québécois. *Address:* 990 Chemin Du Lac Connelly, St-Hippolyte, Québec, JOR IPO, Canada.

DOROSLOVAC, Milutin, b. 1923, Budapest, Hungary. Writer. *Education:* University of Vienna, Austria. *Publications:* (stories) On the Road, 1947; Death Leap, 1960; My Journeys to Vienna, 1974; (novels) Dead Men on Leave, 1952; Nothing but Memory, 1959; The White City, 1969; All My Brothers, 1979; The Last Sunday, 1982. *Honours:* Austrian State Prize, 1962; City of Vienna Prize, 1978; Anton Wildgans Prize, 1972. *Memberships:* Austrian PEN Centre, Vice President; Literary Performance Society, President. *Literary Agent:* Langen-Muller Verlag. *Address:* Pfeilgasse 32, A–1080 Vienna, Austria.

DOTSON, John L Jr, b. 5 Feb. 1937, Paterson, New Jersey, USA. Editor; Journalist. m. Peggy Elaine Burnett, 4 Apr. 1959, Montclair, 4 sons, 1 daughter. *Education:* BS, Temple University. *Contributor to:* Newark Evening News, 1959–64; Detroit Free Press, 1965; Newsweek Magazine, 1965–83; Philadelphia Inquirer, 1983–. *Honours:* Honorary PhD, 1982, Distinguished Alumnus, 1985, Temple University. *Address:* 400 N Broad St, Philadelphia, PA 19101, USA.

DOUBTFIRE, Dianne Joan, b. 18 Oct. 1918, Leeds, England. Novelist. *Education:* Diploma, Slade School of Fine Art; Art Teachers Diploma, University College, London. *Publications:* Lust for Innocence, 1960; Reason for Violence, 1961; Kick a Tin Can, 1964; The Flesh is Strong, 1966; Behind the Screen, 1969; Escape on Monday, 1970; This Jim, 1974; Girl in Cotton Wool, 1975; A Girl Called Rosemary, 1977; Sky Girl, 1978; The Craft of Novel-Writing, 1979; Girl in a Gondola,

1980; Sky Lovers, 1981; Teach Yourself Creative Writing, 1983; The Wrong Face, 1985. *Contributions to:* Books and Bookmen; Radio Times; Homes and Gardens; The Sun; Vogue; The Writer. *Memberships:* Writers Guild of Great Britain; PEN; Society of Authors. *Literary Agent:* Curtis Brown Limited. *Address:* April Cottage, Beech Hill, Headley Down, Hampshire GU35 8EQ, England.

DOUGALL, Donald Gillies, b. 22 Nov. 1920, Cheshire, England. Journalist. m. Oonagh Teresa Cassidi, 5 June 1954, Canterbury, 1 son, 2 daughters. *Publications:* Donald Dougall's TV Walkabout, 1975. *Contributions to:* Shooting Times and Country Magazine; The Field; Agricultural and rural journals; Countryside programme, Southern Television Ltd, 1968–81. *Membership:* Guild of Agricultural Journalists. *Address:* Stelling Minnis, near Canterbury, Kent, England.

DOUGALL, Robert Neill, b. 27 Nov. 1913, Croydon, Surrey, England. Writer, Broadcaster. m. Nancie Lockhart, London, 7 June 1947, 1 son. *Literary Appointments:* Newscaster, BBC, 1933–73. *Publications:* In and Out of the Box, 1973; Now For The Good News, 1976; A Celebration of Birds, 1978; British Birds, 1982. *Contributions to:* Newspapers and Magazines including: Sunday Telegraph Magazine; Spectator; Daily Mail; High Life. *Honour:* MBE, 1965. *Memberships:* Past President, Royal Society for the Protection of Birds; Garrick Club; Royal Society for Literature. *Literary Agent:* Curtis Brown, London. *Address:* c/o Curtis Brown Limited, 162-8 Regent Street, London W1R 5TA, England.

DOUGLAS, Carole Nelson, b. 5 Nov. 1944, Everett, Washington, USA. Journalist; Fiction Writer. m. Scott Douglas, 25 Nov. 1967, West St Paul, Minnesota, USA. *Education:* BA English, Speech & Drama, College of St Catherine, St Paul, Minnesota, 1966. *Major Publications:* Amberleigh, 1980; Fair Wind, Fiery Star, 1980; Six of Swords, In Her Prime, Her Own Person, 1982; The Best Man, Lady Rogue, 1983; Exiles of the Rynth, 1984; Azure Days, Quick-silver Nights, Probe (Science Fiction), 1985; The Exclusive, 1986. *Honours:* Porgie Award, 1982; Several Medallion Awards, 1982, 1983, 1984; Science Fiction Award, 1984. *Memberships:* Authors Guild; Romance Writers of America; Science Fiction Writers of America. *Literary Agent:* Frances Scwartz, New York.

DOUGLAS-HOME, Charles Cospatrick, b. 1 Sep. 1937. Editor. m. Jessica Violet Gwynne, 1966, 2 sons. *Literary Appointments:* Military Correspondent 1961, Political and Diplomatic Correspondent 1962, Daily Express; Defense Correspondent 1965, Features Editor 1970, Home Editor 1973, Foreign Editor 1978, Deputy Editor 1981, The Times. *Publications:* The Arabs and Israel, 1968; Britain's Reserve Forces, 1969; Rommel, 1973; Evelyn Baring: The Last Proconsul, 1978. *Address:* The Times, 200 Grays Inn Road, London WC1X 8EZ, England.

DOULIS, Thomas John, b. 31 Dec. 1931. Vandergrift, Pennsylvania, USA. Novelist; Professor of English. m. Nancy Barnes Ritter, 8 July 1962, Phaladelphia, Pennsylvania, 2 sons. *Education:* BA, English Literature, La Salle College, Philadelphia; MA, English/American Literature and Creative Writing, Stanford University. *Publications:* Path for our Valor, 1963; The Quarries of Sicily, 1969; George Theotokas, 1975; Disaster and Fiction, 1977; A Surge to the Sea, 1977, Landmarks of our Past, 1983. *Literary Agent:* Gunther Stuhlmann Becket, Massachusetts. *Address:* 2236 NE Regents Drive, Portland, OR 97212, USA.

DOWDEN, Kaviraj George, b. 15 Sep. 1932, Philadelphia, Pennsylvania, USA. Poet. *Education:* BA, Bucknell University, Lewisburg, Pennsylvania, 1957; MA, New York University, New York City, 1960. *Publications:* Flight from America, 1965; Birth Vision and Green Song, 1968; Renew Jerusalem, 1969; A Bibliography of Works by Allen Ginsberg, 1971; Earth

Incantations/Body Chants, 1976; A Message to Isis, 1977; From the Stone Through You and White Faces, 1978. *Contributions to:* Anthology of Little Magazine Poets; C'Mon Everybody: Poetry of the Dance; The Outsider; Win; Berkeley Barb; Second Aeon; Antigonish Review; Evergreen Review, etc. *Address:* Flat 7, 45 Upper Rock Gardens, Brighton, E Sussex BN2 1QF, England.

DOWLING, Basil Cairns, b. 29 Apr. 1910, Southbridge, New Zealand. Schoolmaster (Teaching English). m. Margaret Wilson, 11 June 1938, London, 1 son, 2 daughters. *Education:* MA, University of New Zealand; Diploma of Librarianship, New Zealand. *Literary Appointments:* South East Arts Literature Panel. *Publications:* A Day's Journey, 1941; Signs and Wonders, 1944; Canterbury and other Poems, 1949; Hatherley: Recollective Lyrics, 1968; A Little Gallery of Characters, 1971; Bedlam: A Mid-century Satire, 1972; The Unreturning Native, 1973; The Stream, 1979; Windfalls, 1983. *Contributions to:* Landfall, New Zealand; John O'London Weekly, England; Time and Tide; Times Literary Supplement; Outposts; South East Review. *Honour:* Jessie Mackay Memorial Award for Poetry, 1961. *Membership:* PEN. *Address:* 12 Mill Road, Rye, East Sussex, England.

DOWNES, Edward Olin Davenport, b. 12 Aug. 1911, Boston, Massachusetts, USA. Music Historian; Critic. m. Mildred Fowler Gignoux, New York City, 23 Oct. 1943. *Education:* Columbia College; Manhattan School of Music; University of Munich, West Germany; PhD, Harvard University, 1958. *Literary Appointments:* Assistant Music Critic, New York Post, 1936–38; Music Critic, Boston Evening Transcript, 1939–41; Programme Annotator, Boston Museum of Fine Arts, 1946–50; Assistant Music Critic, New York Times, 1955–58; Programme Annotator, New York Philharmonic, 1960–74. *Publications:* Verdi, the Man in his Letters, 1942; Adventures in Symphonic Music, 1943; Perspectives in Musicology, editor, 1972; New York Guide to the Symphony, 1976, revised as Guide to Symphonic Music, 1981. *Contributions include:* The Correspondence of Wagner & King Ludwig II, 2 articles, New York Times, 1937; Introduction to Wagner's Ring of the Nibelung, 1960; The Tast-Makers in, One Hundred Years of Music in America, 1961; Wozzeck in Art News Annual, 1962; American Music Criticism in Grove's Dictionary of Music in the United States, 1986. *Address:* 1 West 72nd Street, New York, NY 10023, USA.

DOWNEY, Charles Edward, b. 17 Nov. 1944, Memphis, Tennessee, USA. Journalist. m. Elsa Egemoes Snake-Jensen, 20 Jan. 1970. Copenhagen, 1 son. *Education:* BA, Journalism, California State University, Long Beach, 1972. *Appointments:* American Society of Journalists and Authors, 1975; GA Custer Native American Affairs Society, 1979; International Association of Business Communicators, 1980. *Publications:* Everyman's Prayer Book and Guide to Household Fiberglassing, 1978; Modern Daughters in Search of Selfhood and Awareness, 1982; Young Flesh's Burning, Yearning Hot Flush, 1983. Contributor to various Magazines and journals. *Honours:* L Fulton Memorial Award for Medical Writing, 1978; Anthony Hety Sportswriting Award, 1980; Norman-Mason Foundation Grant for Revealing Insights into Psychology, 1982; Thomas Meadow Waggner, new Fiction Writer Award, 1984. *Memberships:* ASJA. *Agent:* Thomas Jensen. *Address:* PO Box 271, Fawnskin, CA 92333, USA.

DOWNEY, James J, b. 19 Sep. 1920, Clinton County, Missouri, USA. Roman Catholic Priest. *Education:* BA, Economics, St Benedict's College, Atchison, Kansas; Theology, St Benedict's Abbey School of Theology, Atchison, Kansas; MA, Catholic Doctrine, St John's University, Jamaica, New York. *Appointments:* Editor: Raven Review, 1960–64; Religious Life, 1980 to present, English Edition Informationes SERIS Consecrated Life, 1980 to present. *Publication:* What the Church Teaches, Religious Life, 1985. *ADDRESS:*

Institute on Religious Life, 4200 North Austin Avenue, Chicago, IL 60634, USA.

DOWNIE, Mary Alice Dawe (nee Hunter), b. 12 Feb. 1934, Alton, Illinois, USA. Writer. m. John Downie, 27 June 1959, Toronto, 3 daughters. *Education:* BA (Hons), English Language and Literature, Trinity College, University of Toronto. *Literary Appointment:* Book Review Editor, Kingston Whig-Standard, 1973–78. *Publications include:* The Wind Has Wings; Poems from Canada, with Barbara Robertson, 1968; Sacked Sarah, 1974; Dragon on Parade, 1974; The Last Ship, 1980; A Proper Acadian, with George Rawlyk, 1982; Jenny Greenteeth, 1981; The Wicked Fairy-Wife, 1983; Alison's Ghosts, with Jon Downie, 1984; Stories and Cones, with Jillian Gilliland, 1984. Storiies: Four Short Stories, 1973; La Belle et la Ladde, 1978; Chapters from Honor Bound reprinted in Inside Outside and Measure Me Sky, 1979; Stories from The Witch of the North reprinted in Storytellers Rendezvous, 1980, Crossroads 1, 1979 and Out and About, 1981. *Contributions to:* The Hornbook Magazine; Pittsburgh Press; Kingston Whig-Standard; Ottawa Citizen; Globe and Mail; United Church Observer; OWL Magazine; Chickadee; Crackers. *Memberships:* Writers Union of Canada; CANSCAIP. *Address:* 190 Union Street, Kingston, Ontario, Canada K7L 2P6.

DOWNIE, Susanna Felder, b. 21 Nov. 1939, Philadelphia, Pennsylvania, USA. Journalist. *Education:* BA 1967, PhD studies, current, University of Pittsburgh. *Contributions:* Founding Editor, Allegheny Feminist, 1977, Pittsburgh Feminist Network News, 1981–; Numerous feminist periodicals, USA; Chapter, Communications at the Crossroads: The Gender Gap Connection, ed. Donna Allen & Ramona Rush, 1985. *Membership:* Womens Institute for Freedom of the Press. *Address:* 4312 Centre Avenue, Pittsburgh, PA 15213, USA.

DOWNING, Douglas Allan, b. 11 Oct. 1957, Seattle, Washington, USA. Assistant Professor of Economics. *Education:* BS, summa cum laude, 1979; M Phil, Yale University, 1982. *Publications:* Calculus the Easy Way, 1982; Encyclopedia of Computer Terms, 1983; Computer Programming in BASIC the Easy Way, 1983; Statistics the Easy Way (co-author with Jeff Clark), 1983; Algebra the Easy Way, 1983; Trigonometry the Easy Way, 1984; Computer Programming in Pascal the Easy Way (co-author with Mark Yoshimi), 1984; Business Statistics (co-author with Jeff Clark), 1985. *Membership:* Phi Beta Kappa. *Address:* 16760 Third Avenue NE, Seattle, WA 98155, USA.

DOWNING, Graham, b. 8 Oct. 1954, London, England. National Public Relations Officer. m. Veronica A M Samson, 20 May 1978, Wellingborough, 1 son, 1 daughter. *Education:* MA, St John's College, Oxford. *Literary Appointments:* Editor, Shooting and Conservation, 1983. *Contributions to:* Contributions on shooting to sporting and farming periodicals. *Address:* The Country Landowners Association, 16 Belgrave Square, London SW1X 8PQ, England.

DOWNS, Robert Conrad Smith, b. 23 Nov. 1937, Chicago, Illinois, USA. Professor. m. Barbara Lewry, 6 Sep. 1968, Ardmore Pennsylvania, USA, 2 daughters. *Education:* AB, Harvard College, 1960; MFA, University of Iowa, 1965. *Literary Appointments:* Hunter College, 1965–66; Colby-Sawyer, 1968–73; University of Arizona, 1973–80; Professor of English, Pennsylvania State University, 1980–. *Major Publications:* Novels: Going Gently, 1973; Peoples, 1974; Country Dying, 1976; White Mama, 1980; Living Together, 1983. *Honours:* Guggenheim Fellowship, 1979–80; Image Award, NAACP, 1979. *Literary Agent:* Don Congdon. *Address:* 764 West Hamilton Avenue, State College, PA, 16801, USA.

DOXAT, John, b. 28 June 1914, Isle of Wight, England. Author. *Publications:* Booth's Handbook of Cocktails & Mixed Drinks, 1966; Drinks & Drinking, 1971; The Book of Drinking, 1973; Stirred, Not Shaken, 1976; The Indispensable Drinks Book, 1981; Practical Cocktails, 1984; The Complete Drinker's Companion, 1985; The Living Thames, 1977; Israel, 1981; Shinwell Talking, 1984. *Contributor to:* Various articles to a variety of journals and magazines. *Memberships:* Society of Authors; Circle of Wine Writers. *Literary Agent:* John Pawsey. *Address:* 17 Grand Avenue, Camberley, Surrey GU15 3QJ, England.

DOYLE, Charles (Desmond), b. 18 Oct. 1928, Birmingham, England. Writer & Teacher. m. Doran Ross Smithells, 28 July 1959, 3 sons, 1 daughter. *Education:* MA, University of New Zealand; PhD, University of Auckland; Teaching Diploma, University of New Zealand. *Major Publications:* Earth Meditations, 1971; Stonedancer, 1976; James K Baxter, 1976; William Carlos Williams & The American Poem, 1982; A Steady Hand, 1983; The New Reality: The Politics of Restraint in British Columbia (co-editor), 1984. *Contributor to:* The Nation; Poetry (USA); Canadian Literature; Canadian Forum; Landfall (New Zealand); Meanjin; Quadrant (Australia); Akzente (Federal Republic of Germany); Tam Tam (Italy); and others. *Honours:* Macmillan Brown Prize, 1956; UNESCO International Artist's Fellowship, 1958–59; ACLS Fellowship, 1967–68. *Memberships:* Former Member, PEN International; Canadian Writers Union, Member, League of Canadian Poets (Executive Member 1979–81). *Address:* 759 Helvetia Crescent, Victoria, British Columbia, V8Y 1M1, Canada.

DRABEK, Jan, b. 5 May 1935, Prague, Czechoslovakia. Author. m. Joan M Sanders, 24 Oct. 1964, New York, USA, 2 daughters. *Education:* BA, English Literature, American University in Washington, DC, 1960; Graduate work at University of Mysore and University of British Columbia. *Publications:* Whatever Happened to Wenceslas? 1975; Report on the Death of Rosenkavalier, 1977; The Lister Legacy, 1980; The Statement, 1982; Blackboard Odyssey (non-fiction), 1973; Melvin the Weather Moose (Children's Book), 1976. *Contributions to:* The Reader's Digest; Crosscurrents, University of Michigan. *Memberships:* PEN International; Writers Union of Canada (former Member of National Council); Federation of British Columbia Writers (present Chairman). *Address:* 3330 West King Edward, Vancouver, Canada V65 1M3.

DRAGONWAGON, Crescent, b. 25 Nov. 1952, Manhattan, New York, USA. Freelance Writer. m. Ned Shank, 20 Oct. 1978, Eureka Springs, Arizona. *Publications:* The Year It Rained, 1985; The Dairy Hollow House Cookbook, 1986; Half a Moon and One Whole Star, 1986; Always, Always, 1984; Alligator Arrived with Apples: A Thanksgiving Potluck Alphabet, 1986. *Contributions to:* Ms Magazine; McCall's; Ladies Home Journal; Cosmopolitan. *Honours:* Wind Rose, Outstanding Science Trade Books for Children, 1976; To Take a Dare, American Library Association Best Book, 1982; Always, Always, Social Sciences Book of the Year, 1984; I Hate My Brother Harry, Childrens Choice Nominee, Georgia and Colorado, 1985. *Memberships:* American Society of Journalists and Authors; Authors Guild; Society of Childrens Book Writers; Women in Film. *Literary Agent:* Marilyn E Marlow, Curtis and Brown. *Address:* Dairy Hollow House, Route 4 Box 1, Eureka Springs, AR 72632, USA.

DRAKE, Walter Raymond, b. 2 Jan. 1913, Middlesborough, England. Retired Surveyor, HM Customs and Excise. m. Marjorie Cawthorne, 24 June 1944, Seaham, County Durham. *Education:* Inter-BA, London University; Associate, Institute of Linguistics; Fellow, British Esperanto Association; Doctor of Sacred Philosophy, World University, USA. *Publications:* Gods or Spacemen, 1964; Spacemen in the Ancient East, 1968; Gods and Spacemen in the Ancient Past, 1975; Gods and Spacemen in the Ancient West, 1974; Gods and Spacemen Throughout History, 1975; Gods and Spacemen in Greece and Rome, 1976; Gods and Spacemen in Ancient Israel, 1977; Messengers from the Stars, 1977; Titans Nell Antichita, 1982; Cosmic Continents, 1985. *Contributions to:* UFO Contract; Il

Giornale dei Misteri; Tamil News. *Honours:* Doctorate in Sacred Philosophy, World University, Tucson, Arizona, USA, 1983; Member, l'Academie Europeene des Sciences, des Arts et des Lettres, Paris, France, 1984. *Membership:* Society of Authors, England. *Address:* 2 Peareth Grove, Roker, Sunderland SR6 9NL, England.

DREW, Fraser Bragg Robert, b. 23 June 1913. University Teacher. *Education:* AB, University of Vermont, USA, 1933; AM, Duke University, 1935; PhD, University of Buffalo, 1952. *Literary Appointments include:* Instructor in English, 1945–47, Assistant Professor, 1947–52, Professor, 1952–73, Distinguished Teaching Professor, 1973–. SUNY, College at Buffalo. *Publications:* John Masefield's England: A Study of the National Themes in his Work, 1973. *Contributor to:* Ireland of Welcomes; The Housman Society Journal; Eire-Ireland; New Oxford Review; Western Humanities Review; In Britain; Philological Quarterly; Publ Bibliography Society of America; Modern Language Notes; Columbia University Library Columns; Yale University Library Gazette; Christian Science Monitor; Colby Library Quarterly; University Review; Canada Forum; Vermont History; CEA Critic; An Raiteas; Liber; Costerus; Trace; Library Journal; Fitzgerald-Hemingway Annual; American Book Collector; SUNY New Forum; Spirit; Mark Twain Journal. *Honours:* Distinguished Service Award, University of Vermont, 1968. *Memberships:* Academy of American Poets; Irish American Cultural Institute; American Committee for Irish Studies; Houseman Society; College of English Association; Friends of Thoor Ballylee; Robinson Jeffers Tor House Federation; IRA Allen Society. *Address:* Tralee House, 35 Danbury Lane, Kenmore, NY 14217, USA.

DREW, Philip, b. 28 Jan. 1943, Coff's Harbour, New South Wales, Australia. Architect. m. Julie Margaret Bisset, 28 June 1969, Scarborough, Ontario, Canada, 1 daughter. *Education:* B Arch, University of New South Wales, 1966; M Arch, The University of Sydney, 1979. *Literary Appointments:* Technical Editor, The Architectural Press, London, 1970–71; Visiting Professor, University of Idaho, USA. 1973–74; Lecturer University of Newcastle, New South Wales, New South Wales, 1974–76; Senior Lecturer, University of Newcastle, 1977–82; Visiting Associate Professor, Washington University, 1982–83. *Publications:* Third Generation: The Changing Meaning of Architecture, 1973; Frei Otto: Form and Structure, 1976; Tensile Architecture, 1979; Two Towers: Harry Seidler; Australia Square, MLC Tower, 1980; The Architecture of Arata Isozaki, 1982; Leaves of Iron: Glenn Murcutt, Pioneer of an Australian Architectural Form, 1985. *Contributions to:* Canadian Architect; Architectural Association Quarterly; Architecture Australia; Architecture and Urbanism; Space Design; Transition; AIA Journal; Vision; International Architect; Space and Society; Crit; The Architects Journal. *Memberships:* Australian Society of Authors; The Society of Architectural Historians, USA. *Literary Agent:* Victor Kline, Sydney. *Address:* 12 Turrug Street, Whitebridge, New South Wales 2290, Australia.

DROEGE, Thomas Arthur, b. 10 Apr. 1931, Seymour, Indiana, USA. Professor of Theology at Valparaiso University. m. Esther Elizabeth Kuehn, 29 Jan. 1956, Aberdeen, South Dakota, 3 daughters. BA, 1953, BD, 1956, Concordia Seminary, Missouri, MA, 1963, PhD, 1965, University of Chicago. *Publications:* Self-Realization and Faith: Beginning and Becoming in Relation to God, 1978; Theological Roots of Wholistic Health Care, 1979; Ministry to the Whole Person: Eight of Healing Ministry in Lutheran Congregation, 1982; Faith Passgaes and Patters, 1983. *Contributions to:* Concordia Theological Monthly; Journal of Religion and Health; Journal of Psychology and Christianity. *Honours:* Lilly Endowment Open Fellowship, 1982; O P Kretzmann Research Award, 1984. *Address:* Valparaiso University, Valparaiso, IN 46383, USA.

DRON, Tony, b. 29 Aug. 1946, London, England. Journalist. *Literary Appointment:* Editor, Thoroughbred & Classic Cars, Magazine. *Honour:* Sir William Lyons Award, 1968. *Membership:* Guild of Motoring Writers, Committee, 1983–84. *Address:* 57 Wales Avenue, Carshalton, Surrey, England.

DROTAR, David Lee, b. 20 Sep. 1952, Sidney, New York, USA. Writer. *Education:* BA, Magna cum laude, State University of New York, Oswego, New York, 1974. *Publications:* Pocket Calculators: How to Use and Enjoy Them. 1978; Microsurgery: Revolution in the Operating Room, 1982; Hiking: Pure and Simple, 1984. *Contributions to:* Boys' Life; Woman's World; New York Daily News; Houston Chronicle; Northeast Outdoors; Jack and Jill; Health Explorer; Children's Digest; Cobblestone; Humpty Dumpty; Ebony Journal; Children's Playmate; Trip and Tour; Highlights. *Honour:* One of the best 100 science and technical books of 1978 for, Pocket Calculators: How to Use and Enjoy Them, Library Journals. *Membership:* Society of Children's Book Writers. *Address:* PO Box 515, Clifton Park, NY 12065, USA.

DRUMMOND, Ian M, b. 4 June 1933, Vancouver, Canada. Professor of Economics. *Education:* BA Honours, University of British Columbia; MA, University of Toronto; PhD, Yale University, USA. *Major Publications:* The Canadian Economy, 1966, revised 1972; British Economic Policy & the Empire 1919–1939, 1972; Imperial Economic Policy, 1917–1939, 1974; Economics: Principles & Policies in an Open Economy, 1976; The Floating Pound & the Sterling Area 1931–39, 1981; Canada since 1945: Power, Politics & provincialism (with R S Bothwell & J English), 1981. *Contributor to:* Canadian Journal of Economics & Political Science, (Managing Editor, 1966–69); Canadian Forum, (Member of Editorial Board 1962–72); Journal of Economic History, (Member editorial Board 1977–). *Honour:* Fellow, Royal Society of Canada, 1981. *Address:* Department of Economics & Trinity College, University of Toronto, Toronto, Ontario, M5S 1H8, Canada.

DRUMWRIGHT, Charles McNeill, b. 18 Aug. 1930, Dallas, Texas, USA. Advertising executive. *Education:* BA, North Texas State University, Denton, 1952; MA, University of Texas, Austin, 1955. *Contributions to:* Decision Magazine; Poetry at the University of Texas, 1953; Avesta, North Texas State University; Decision Magazine, 1974. *Honours:* 1st Prize, Poetry writing, North Texas State University, 1952; Ralph Cheyney Memorial Award in Poetry, Southwest Writers Conference, 1956. *Memberships:* Poetry Society of Texas; Bryan-College Station Poetry Society. *Address:* 4639 McKinney, Apt P, Dallas , TX 75205, USA.

DRURY, Nevill, b. 1 Oct. 1947, England. Editor; Author; Publisher. m. Susan Pinchin 3 Jan. 1970 in Sydney, 1 son, 2 daughters. *Education:* MA Anthropology, Macquarie University, Sydney, Australia; Diploma in Education, Sydney Teachers' College. *Appointments:* Managing Editor, Harper & Row Australia, 1976–80; Managing Editor, Doubleday Australia, 1980–82; Editorial Director, The Craftsman's Press, 1982–; Managing Editor, Nature & Health magazine, 1983–. *Major Publications:* The Search for Abraxas (with S Skinner), Spearman, London, 1972; The Path of the Chameleon, Spearman, London, 1973; Don Juan, Mescalito and Modern Magic, Routledge & Kegan Paul, London & Boston, 1978; The Occult Sourcebook, (with G Tillett), Routledge & Kegan Paul, London & Boston, 1978; Inner Visions, Routledge & Kegan Paul, London & Boston, 1979; Other Temples, Other Gods (with G Tillett), Methuen Sydney, 1980; Hodder & Stoughton Sydney, 1982; The Healing Power, Muller, London, 1981; The Shaman and the Magician, Routledge & Kegan Paul, London & Boston, 1982; Vision-Quest, Prism Press, Dorchester, 1984; Dictionary of Mysticism and the Occult, Harper & Row, San Francisco, USA, 1985; Music for Inner Space, Prism Press, Dorchester, 1985; Inner Health, (editor), Harper & Row, Sydney, 1985; The Occult Experience, Collins, Sydney, 1985. *Contributor to:* Rolling Stone, Omega, Cosmos, Nature & Health, Healthy Living, Hi-Fi Review,

Nation Review. *Membership:* Society of Editors, 1980–83. *Literary Agent:* Early Works David Bolt; none at present. *Address:* 6a Ortona Road, Lindfield, NSW 2070, Australia.

DU MAURIER, (Dame) Daphne, b. 1907, London, England. Writer. *Publications include:* The Loving Spirit; I'll Never Be Young Again; Progress of Julius; Gerald; Jamaica Inn; Rebecca; Frenchman's Creek; Hungry Hill; The du Mauriers; The King's General; The Parasites; My Cousin Rachel; Mary Anne; The Apple Tree; The Scapegoat; The Breaking Point; The Glass Blowers; The Flight of The Falcon; Vanishing Cornwall; the House on the Strand; Not After Midnight; Rule Britannia; Golden Lads; The Winding Stair; (plays) Rebecca; The Years Between; September Tide; Castle Dor; Growing Pains: The Making of a Writer, 1977. *Membership:* FRLS. *Honour:* DBE. *Literary Agent:* Curtis Brown. *Address:* Kilmarth, Par, Cornwall, England.

DUBERMAN, Martin Bauml, b. 6 Aug. 1930, New York City, USA. Professor of History; Writer. *Education:* BA, Yale University, 1952; PhD, Harvard University, 1957. *Publications:* Charles Francis Adams, 1961; In White America, 1964; The Antislavery Vanguard, 1965; James Russell Lowell, 1966; The Uncompleted Past, 1970; The Memory Bank, 1970; Black Mountain, 1972; Male Armor, 1974; Visions of Kerouac, 1977. *Contributions to:* The New York Times; The New Republic; Partisan Review; Harpers; Atlantic Monthly; The New York Native; Christopher Street; Radical History Review; The Village Voice; Signs; Journal of Homosexuality; Show, etc. *Honours:* The Vernon Rice, Drama Desk Award, 1963–64; The Bancroft Prize, 1962; Finalist, The National Book Award, 1966; Special Award for 'contributions to literature' from The American Academy of Arts and Sciences, 1971. *Literary Agent:* Frances Goldin. *Address:* 475 West 22nd Street, New York, NY 10011, USA.

DUBERSTEIN, Helen Laura, b. 3 June 1926, New York City, USA. Writer. m. Victor Lipton, 10 Apr. 1949, New York City, 2 daughters. *Education:* City College of New York, 1947. *Appointments Include:* Co-Director, Four Corners Workshop, 1981; Creative Writing, PS97 Queens, 1981. *Publications:* Poetry: Arrived Safely; Changes; The Voyage Out; Succubs/Incubus; The Human Dimension; Fiction. *Contributor to:* Semiotext; Catalyst 87; New Letters for Now; Jewish Dialogue; Confrontation; Shantih; ingenue; Eidus: Erotica for Women; etc. *Honours include:* Interlochen Award for Best Play, 1979; Recipient, Various Grants, Awards, etc; Finalist, Semi-finalist, various short story competitions. *Memberships:* Dramatists Guild; Poetry Society of America. *Address:* 463 West Street 904D, New York, NY 10014, USA.

DUCKMAN, Baron Frederick, b. 20 May 1933, Leeds, England. University Professor; Head of Department. m. Helen Gertrud Ebbe Wegener, 30 Mar. 1959, Redcar, England, 2 sons, 1 daughter. *Education:* BA, MA, University of Manchester; Dip Ed; FRHistS, University of Leeds. *Literary Appointments:* Editor, Transport History, 1968–73. *Publications include:* The Yorkshire Ouse, 1967; The Transport Revolution 1750–1830, 1967; A History of the Scottish Coal Industry 1700–1815, 1970; The Inland Waterways of East Yorkshire 1700–1900, 1973; Great Pit Disasters: Britain 1700 to the Present Day, (with Helen Duckman), 1973; Steam Entertainment, (with John R Hume), 1974. *Contributor to:* Amateur Historian; Business History; Dalesman; History Today; Journal of Transport; Business History Review; Esso Magazine; History; Industrial Archaeology; Local Historian; Northern History; Scottish Historical Review; Transport History; Times Higher Education Supplement; etc. *Honour:* Fellow, Royal History Society, 1969. *Address:* c/o St David's University College, Lampeter, Dyfed, Wales.

DUCKWORTH, Renee, b. 8 Nov. 1928, Blackburn, Lancs, England. Student. *Education:* BA, Open University, 1979; BA, CNAA, 1983. *Contributor to:* Old Hillcrofters Magazine; Blackburn Times; Radio

Blackburn; Poems published in Galaxy of Verse, 1960; Calvacade of Poems, 1961; Poetical 60's, 1962. *Honours:* Dame Irene Vanbrugh Special Award, Verse Speaking, 1960; Gold Medal, L A M D A, Verse Speaking, 1965; 3rd Prize for Original Compositon, Nelson Festival, 1975; 3rd Prize for Original Composition, Burnley Festival, 1976; Silver Medal, Poetry Society, Watson School Dramatic Art, Clitheroe. *Address:* 916 Whalley New Road, Blackburn, Lancashire BB1 9BD, England.

DUCORNET, Erica, b. 19 Apr. 1943, Canton, New York, USA. Writer; Graphic Artist; Potter. *Education:* BA, Bard College, New York, 1962. *Publications include:* From the Star Chamber, 1974; Weird Sisters, 1976; Knife Notebook, 1977; The Illustrated Universe, 1979; The Butcher's Tales, 1980; The Stain, 1984; Entering Fire, 1986. Anthologies: Four Canadian Poets, 1977; Contemporary Surrealist Prose, volume 1, 1978; Magic Realism, 1980. *Contributions to:* Various journals including: Arsenal; Phases; Ellebore. *Literary Agent:* A M Heath and Company Limited. *Address:* Atelier de la Jaleterie, 49260 Le Puy Notre Dame, France.

DUERRSON, Werner, b. 12 Sep. 1932, Schwenningen/Neckar, German Republic. Writer. *Education:* Music Studies, Trossingen, 1953; German & French Literature Studies, Tubingen, Munich, 1957; PhD, 1962. *Publications:* Poetry, Prose, Essays, Dramas & Translations include: Dreizehn Gedichte, 1965; Schattengeschlecht, 1966; Flugballade, 1966; Drei Dichtungen, 1970; Mitgegangen mitgehangen, 1975; Werner Durrson liest Lyrik und Prosa, LP Record, 1978; Schubart; Feier-Eine deutsche Moritat, 1980; Schubert Drama, 1980; Zeit Gedichte, 1981; Stehend bewagt, Ein Poem, 1982; Der Luftkunstler, 13 short stories, 1983; Das Mattenhorner Schweigen, Gedichte, 1984; Feierabend, Gedichte, 1985; Translations of Authors including: Guillaume d'Aquitaine, Marguerite de Navarre, Mallarme, Rimbaud, yvan Goll, Rene Char, henri Michaux. *Contributor to:* Anthologies & broadcasting. *Honours include:* Recipient various honours and awards, most recent: German award for Short Stories, 1983; Bodensee Literary prize of Veberlingen, 1985. *Memberships include:* Association Internationale des Critiques litteraires, Paris; PEN; Association of German Writers. *Address:* Donau Schloss, D–7940 Neufra, Federal Republic of Germany.

DUFRESNE, Guy, b. 17 Apr. 1915, Montreal, Quebec, Canada. Apple Grower; Writer. m. Anne-Marie Lucier, 6 Nov. 1939, Maria, Quebec, 2 daughters. *Education:* BA, College Brebeuf, Montreal, 1935. *Literary Appointments:* Radio historical serial, Le Ciel Par-Dessus les Toits, 1947–55, Television serials, Cap-aux-Sorciers, 1955–58, Kanawio, 1960–61, Septieme-Nord, 1962–67, Les Forges de St Maurice, 1972–75, translation and adaptation of Of Mice and Men, 1973, Canadian Broadcasting Corporation. *Publications:* Plays: Docile, 1967; Les Traitants, 1968; Le Cri de l'Engoulevent, 1971. Extracts: Cap Aux-Sorcier, 1969; Ce Maudit Lardier, 1975. *Honours:* 1st prize of 1st Concours Radio-Canada for Le Contrebandier, 1946; Anik for Best Script for Johanne et ses Vieux, Canadian Broadcasting Corporation, 1976. *Memberships:* Societe des Auteurs, Recherchistes, Documentalistes et compositeurs; Union des Ecrivains du Quebec; Compositeurs et Auteurs Dramatiques Francaise. *Address:* 1 Chemin Abbott's Corner, Frelighsburg, Quebec, Canada J0J 1C0.

DUGMORE, Clifford William, b. 9 May 1909, Moseley, Birmingham, England. Clerk in Holy Orders, Deacon 1935, Priest 1936; University Professor. m. (1) Ruth Mabel Archbould Prangley, 23 Aug. 1938, Formby, Lancs, (dec. 1977), 1 daughter; (2) Kathleen Mary Whiteley, 17 Mar. 1979, Kings College, London Chapel. *Literary Appointments:* Senior Lecturer, Ecclesiastical History, 1946–58, Tutor, Faculty of Theology, University of Manchester, 1958; Professor, University of London, 1976–; Member, University Senate, 1964–71; Dean of Faculty of Theology, 1974–76. *Publications include:* Eucharistic Doctrine in

England from Hooker to Waterland, 1942; The Influence of the Synagogue Upon the Divine Office, 1944; Edited, The Interpretation of the Bible, 1944, 2nd edition 1946; The Mass and the English Reformers, 1958; Ecclesiastical History No Soft Option, 1959. Contributor to, Chambers's Encyclopaedia, 1950; Weltkirchenlixikon, 1960; Studia Patristica, 1961. *Contributions to:* Journal of Theological Studies; the Manchester Guardian; Studia Patristica. *Honours:* James New Rabbinical Hebrew Scholar, Oxford University, 1935; Norrisian prize, Cambridge University, 1940; Select Preacher 1956, Hulcan lecturer, Cambridge University, 1958–60. *Memberships:* Member, Advisory Board, Journal Ecclesiastical History, 1979–, Founder and Editor, 1950–78; British Member, Editorial Board, Novum Testamentum, 1956–76; Chairman, British Sous Commission of the Commission Internationale d'Histoire Ecclesiastique, 1952–62; President, Ecclesiastical History Society, 1963–64. *Address:* Thame Cottage, The Street, Puttenham, Guildford, Surrey GU3 1AT, England.

DUNAWAY, David King, b. 3 Oct. 1948, New York, USA. Biographer; Professor. *Education:* BA, Magna cum laude, University of Wisconsin, 1970; Diplôma. University of Aix en Provence; MAT, PhD University of California, Berkeley. *Publications:* How Can I Keep From Singing: Pete Seeger, 1981; Oral History: An Interdisciplinary Anthology, 1984; Huxley in Hollywood, in press. *Contributions to:* 48 articles, 1973–, The Nation; New York Times; Village Voice; Mother Jones; Country Music; Oral History Review; Journal of Integrated Education; New York Folklore; Folklore Forum; Ethno Musicology. *Honours:* Berkeley Folklore Prize, 1977; Regent's Fellow, Berkeley, 1977–79; ASCAP Deems Taylor Award; Excellence in a book on American Music and Culture, 1982; Fulbright Senior Lectureship, Kenya, 1984. *Memberships:* National Writers Union; Author's Guild. *Literary Agent:* Perry Knowlton, Curtis Brown. *Address:* Department of English, University of New Mexico, Albuquerque, NM 87131, USA.

DUNBAR, Charles Stewart, b. 14 Nov. 1900, Westminster, London, England. Transport Consultant; Technical Journalist. m. Emily May Bowler (deceased), 15 Oct. 1921, Soho, London, 1 son (deceased). *Literary Appointments:* Editor: Buses Illustrated, 1949–50; Passneger Transport, 1961–63. *Publications:* Goods Vehicle Operation, 1949, 53; Buses, Coaches and Lorries, 1960; Transport Oddities, 1962; Buses, Trolleys and Trams, 1967, 68; The Rise of Road Transport 1919–1939, 1981; various booklets and pamphlets. *Contributions to:* All British Transport journals; Pictorial Encyclopedia of Transport; Academic American Encyclopedia. *Honours:* Chartered Institute of Transport; British Electric Traction Award, 1956; Crow Medal, 1968. *Address:* 9 Christchurch Road, Malvern, Worcestershire WR14 3BH, England.

DUNCAN, Frances Mary (Sandy), b. 24 Jan. 1942, Vancouver, British Columbia, Canada. Writer. m. Norman James Duncan, 10 May 1963, Vancouver, 2 daughters. *Education:* BA, English and Psychology, 1962; MA, Clinical Psychology, 1963, University of British Columbia. *Publications:* Cariboo Runaway, 1976; Kap-Sung Ferris, 1977; The Toothpaste Genie, 1981; Dragon Hunt, 1981; Finding Home, 1982. *Contributions to:* Anthologies: New: West Coast, 1977; Common Ground, 1980; Canadian Short Fiction Anthology, Volume 2, 1982; Baker's Dozen, 1984; Vancouver Short Stories, 1985 and many other books and publications. *Honours:* Children's Book Centre Choice, 1979, 82; Greater Vancouver Library Federation Award, 1982, 83; Surrey Book of the Year, 1983. *Memberships:* The Writers Union of Canada, British Columbia-Yukon Representative, 1980–81; National Council, 1985–86; Federation of British Columbia Writers, Founding Chairman, 1980–82; PEN International Canadian Association of Children's Authors, Illustrators, Performers; West Coast Women and Words Society. *Literary Agent:* Nancy Colbert.

Address: c/o The Writers Union of Canada, 24 Ryerson Avenue, Toronto, Ontario M5T 2P3, Canada.

DUNETZ, Lora, b. New York, USA. Registered Occupational Therapist & Consultant. *Education:* MA, Education of Handicapped; Certificate, Occupational Therapy; Laval University, Canada; Dimplomé d'Etudes Francaises, Institut Ecole Pour Etrangers, Paris, France. *Appointments:* Occupational Therapist; French Teacher, High School, 4 years, Educable Retarded, 3 years; Designing & Direction Writing of Needlework for women's publications, several years. *Contributor to:* Numerous newspapers & anthologies: New York Sun; New York Times; New Poems by American Poets; Epos; Imagi; Discovery 5; Poet Lore; Educational Forum; Inferno; New Mexico Quarterly; Experiment; Instructor; Children's Friend; Furioso; Christian Century; Bluegrass Literary Review; Lyric; Ararat; Gazette; Distant Springs; Passaic Review; Coast; Anthology of American Magazine Verse, 1980–81, 1983–84; etc. *Honours:* Lyric Memorial Award, 1982. *Memberships:* Poetry Society of America; Chairman, Poetry Section, Baltimore Writers' Forum, Maryland, 3 years. *Address:* Box 113, Whiting, NJ 08759, USA.

DUNN, Stephen Elliott, b. 24 June 1939, Forest Hills, New York, USA. Poet; Teacher. m. 26 Sep. 1964, New York City, 2 daughters. *Education:* BA, History, Hofstra University, 1962; MA, Creative Writing, Syracuse University, 1970. *Literary Appointments:* Professor, Creative Writing, Stockton State College, New Jersey, 1974–; Visiting Professor of Poetry, Columbia University, 1984–86. *Publications:* Looking for Holes in the Ceiling, 1974; Full of Lust and Good Usage, 1976; A Circus of Needs, 1978; Work and Love, 1981; Not Dancing, 1984; Local Time, 1986. *Contributions to:* 'APR'; The Nation; The New Yorker; Poetry; Poetry Northwest; The Paris Review; Antacus, etc. *Honours:* The Theodore Roethke Prize, 1977; The Helen Bullis Prize, 1982; (both from, Poetry Northwest); Guggenheim Fellowship, 1984–85. *Address:* 445 Chestnut Neck Road, Port Republic, NJ 08241, USA.

DUNNAHOO, Terry, Author; Reviewer; Instructor; Consultant; Editor. *Literary Appointment:* Instructor, Creative Writing, University of California, Los Angeles, 1977–; Editor, Childrens books, West Coast Review of Books, 1979–. Consultant: Los Angeles Schools, 1975–; Asselin Television Productions (Childrens programming), 1976–. Reviewer: Los Angeles Herald-Examiner, 1979–85; West Coast Review of Books, 1978–. *Publications:* Nellie Bly; Annie Sullivan; Emily Dunning; Before the Supreme Court, Who Cares About Espie Sanchez?; This is Espie Sanchez; Who Needs Espie Sanchez?; Bridge to Tomorrow; The Last of April; Break Dancing; How to Write Children's Books. *Memberships:* Los Angeles Center, PEN International; Society of Childrens Books Writers; Southern Council of Literature for Children and Young People; Authors Guild of America; Women in Film. *Address:* 4061 Tropico Way, Los Angeles, CA 90065, USA.

DUNNAN, Nancy, b. 10 Jan. 1941, Fort Dodge, Iowa, USA. Writer. m. Jay J Pack, 1 Mar. 1981, New York, 2 step-children. *Education:* BS Library Science, Simmons College; MA American Studies, Western Reserve University. *Publications:* An Album of Roses, 1978; Financial Savvy for Singles, 1983; The $50 to $5,000 Investor, 1985; With a Little Bit of Luck, 1985; Dun and Bradstreet Guide to Investments, 1986. *Contributions to:* Savvy magazine; Self; Moneymaker; American Bar Association Journal; Fact magazine; Sylvia Porter's Personal Financial Magazine. *Honours:* Puckett Award for Academic Excellence, Western Reserve University, 1969. *Memberships:* American Association of Authors and Journalists. *Literary Agent:* Maria Carvainis. *Address:* 36 Gramercy Park, New York, NY 10003, USA.

DUPONT, Louis Jules Joseph, b. 14 Mar. 1924, Orp-Le-Grand. Teacher. m. Renée Deltenre, 6 July 1948, 1 son. *Education:* BA. *Appointments:* President, Midis De La Poésie, Brussels. *Publications:* Rever d'une eau si pure, 1960; La Nuit Veille, 1966; De L'Analyse

Grammaticale à L'Analyse Litteraire, 1969; Patience Connivence, 1972; Qui tait la vaste parole? 1976; Bêtes à Bon Dieu, 1982; Lumière sans visage, 1984. *Contributor to:* Marginales; Le Journal du Puc'tes; Le Soir; Revue Générale; Français 2000; Le Français dans le Monde. *Honours:* Chevalier, French Order Academic Palms, 1979; De Nayer Prize, Belgian Academy, 1985. *Memberships:* Association of Belgian Writers; Pen. *Address:* 15/3 Avenue De La Fulle Chanson, 1050 Brussels, Belgium.

DUPRÉ, Catherine, b. 26 June 1927, Oxford, England. Writer. m. Desmond Dupré (dec), 27 Jun 1949, Oxford, 3 sons, 2 daughters. *Literary Appointments:* Former member, Committee of English, PEN. *Publications:* Chicken Coop, 1967; Jelly Baby, 1968; Child of Julian Flynn, 1972; John Galsworthy: A Biography, 1976; Gentleman's Child. 1980. *Contributions to:* Reviews for: Daily Telegraph; Tablet; PEN. *Honour:* Runner-up, Yorkshire Post Book of the Year, 1967. *Membership:* PEN. *Literary Agent:* Deborah Rogers Ltd. *Address:* 94 Oxford Street, Woodstock, Oxford OX7 1TX, England.

DUQUIN, Lorene Hanley, b. 2 Oct. 1950, Buffalo, New York, USA. Freelance Writer of Magazine Articles and Books. m. Richard A Duquin Junior, 7 July 1973, Buffalo, New York, 2 sons, 2 daughters. *Education:* BA, Canisus College. *Publication:* Complete Guide to Starting a Food Buying Club, 1980. *Contributions to:* Family Circle; McCall's; Working Mother; Woman's Day; Seventeen; Modern Bride; Campaigns and Elections; American Baby; Mothers Today; Childbirth Educator; Facets; Kiwanis Magazine; Consumers Digest; Family Computing; Popular Computing; Lady's Circle; Home Life; Complete Woman, etc. *Honour:* Publicity Award, American Association of University Women, 1979. *Memberships:* Authors Guild; American Society of Journalists and Authors. *Literary Agent:* Anita Diamant. *Address:* 161 MacArthur Drive, Williamsville, NY 14221, USA.

DURACK (Dame) Mary, b. 20 Feb. 1913, Adelaide, South Australia. Writer. m. Horace Clive Miller, 1938 (Dec. 1980) 2 sons, 4 daughters (2 dec.) *Education:* Loreto Convent, Perth, Australia. *Publications include:* Kings in Grass Castles, 1959; To Ride a Fine Horse, 1963; An Australian Settler, 1964; A Pastoral Emigrant, 1964; The Rock and the Sand, 1969; To be Heirs Forever, 1976; Yagan of the Bibbulmun, 1976; Tjakamarra – Boy Between Two Worlds, 1977; The Way of the Whirlwind, 1979; Sons in the Saddle, 1983; Plays: The Ship of Dreams, 1968; Swan River Saga, 1972; Co-Author: Child Artists of the Australian Bush, 1952, (with Florence Rutter); The End of Dreaming, 1974, (with Ingrid Drysdale); The Land Beyond Time, 1984, (with Olsen, Serventy, Dutton, Bortignon); The Stockman, 1984, (with Mahood, Williams, Willey, Sawrey, Iddon-Ruhen); Libretto: for the Opera, Dalgeric, music by James Penberthy, 1966, replayed at Sydney Opera House, 1973; Numerous scripts for the Australian Broadcasting Commission. *Contributions to:* Australian Dictionary of Biog, Australian Broadcasting Commission; numerous newspapers and journals. *Honours:* OBE, 1966, DBE, 1978; Commonwealth Literary Grant, 1973 and 1977; Hon. D.Litt, University of Western Australia, 1978; Australian Research Grant, 1980 and 1984–85; Emeritus Fellowship, Literature Board of the Australia Council, 1983–84. *Memberships:* Honorary Life Member, Fellowship of Australian Writers; International PEN; Australian Society of Authors; National Trust; Royal Western Australian Historical Society; Australian Society of Women Writers; Stockman's Hall of Fame and Outback Heritage Centre. *Literary Agent:* Curtis Brown. *Address:* 12 Bellevue Avenue, Nedlands, WA 6009, Australia.

DURAIRAJ, Kaviarasu, b. 7 Oct. 1920, Periyakulam, Madurai. Writer. m. Kalaiselvi, 2 Feb. 1949, Pudukkotai, 3 sons, 3 daughters. *Education:* Vithvan in Tamil. *Literary Appointments:* Tamil Pandit at Madras, 1947; Tamil Pandit at Karaikudi, 1949. *Publications:* Mudiarasan Kavithaikal, 1954; Kaviappavai, 1959;

Kaviarangil Mudiarasan, 1960; Poonkodi, 1964; Veerakaviyam, 1970; Paadum Kuyil, 1983; Undrukol, 1983; Nenju Porokkuvillaiyae 1985. *Contributor to:* Murasoli; Tamilarasu. *Honours:* Mudiarasan Kavithaigal by Government of Tamilnadu, 1966; Honoured by Kundrakudi Adigalar for Nudiarasan Kavithaigal, Title Kaviarasu, 1966; Veerskaviam by Government of Tamilnadu, 1973; Honoured by Dravida Munatra Kazhagam and presented a Pruse, 1980; Tamil Laureate by Tamilega Pulavar Kuzhu, 1983. *Memberships:* Patron, Tamil Nadu Illakkia Ani; Patron, Anna Tamil Kazhegem, Karikudi. *Address:* Pavalar Mani A Palani, No. 48 Ambalakarar Street, Kattuthalai Vasal, Karaikudi 623 001, India.

DURANT, David Norton, b. 25 July 1925, Nottingham, England. Author. *Publications:* Bess of Hardwick, 1977; Arabella Stuart, 1978; Raleigh's Lost Colony, 1981. *Contributions to:* Today. *Membership:* Society of Authors. *Literary Agent:* Scott Ferris Associates. *Address:* The Old Hall, Bleasby, Nottingham NG14 7FU, England.

DURCAN, Paul, b. 16 Oct. 1944, Dublin, Republic of Ireland. Poet. *Education:* BA. *Publications:* Endsville, 1967; O Westport in the Light of Asia Minor, 1975; Teresa's Bar, 1976; Sam's Cross, 1978; Jesus, Break His Fall, 1980; Ark of the North, 1982; The Selected Paul Durcan, 1982, 85; Jumping the Train Tracks With Angela, 1983; The Berlin Wall Cafe, 1985. *Contributions to:* Irish Press; Irish Times; Hibernia; Magill; Cyphers; Honest Ulsterman; Gorey Detail; Cork Examiner; Aquarius. *Honours:* Patrick Kavanagh Poetry Award, 1974; Arts Council of Ireland Bursary for Creative Writing, 1976, 1980–81; Poetry Book Society Choice for the Berlin Wall Cafe, 1985. *Membership:* Aosdana. *Address:* 11 Lower Montenotte, Cork City, Republic of Ireland.

DUSKY, Lorraine Blanche, b. 13 June 1942, Detroit, Michigan, USA. Writer. m. Anthony Brandt, 20 Sep. 1981, Westhampton, New York, 1 daughter. *Education:* BA, Wayne State University, 1964. *Literary Appointments:* Theta Sigma Phi Scholar, 1964; Senior Editor, Town and Country, 1975–77; Adjunct Instructor, City College of New York, 1977. *Publications:* Total Vision, (with Richard Kavner), 1978; Birthmark, 1979; How to Eat Like a Thin Person, 1982. *Contributions to:* The New York Times Magazine; Newsweek; Savvy; McCalls; Ladies' Home Journal; Mademoiselle; Glamour; Cosmopolitan; Good Housekeeping; Harper's Bazaar; and others. *Honours:* New York State Award for Excellence in Medical Reporting, 1966; Public Service Award, American Optometric Association, 1975. *Memberships:* Author's Guild; Association of Journalists and Authors. *Literary Agent:* Alfred Lowman, Authors and Artists Group. *Address:* Box 968, Sag Harbor, NY 11963, USA.

DUSSINGER, John Andrew, b. 18 Nov. 1935, Reading, Pennsylvania, USA. College Teacher. m. Astrid Elisabeth Hammervig, 21 June 1959, Copenhagen, 2 daughters. *Education:* BA, English, Lehigh University, 1958; University of Copenhagen, 1958–59; MA, 1962, PhD, 1964, Princeton University. *Appointments:* Instructor, English, Rutgers University, 1962–65; Assistant Professor, 1965–68, Associate Professor, 1968–, University of Illinois; Lecturer, English, University of Aarhus, 1970–72; Visiting Professor, University of Southampton, England, 1979, University of Stockholm, 1982. *Publications:* The Discourse of the Mind in Eighteenth Century Fiction, 1974. *Contributor to:* Numerous articles in professional journals and magazines including Clarissa; Burlington Magazine; etc. *Honours:* Phi Beta Kappa, 1957; Fulbright Study Award to Denmark, 1958–59; Woodrow Wilson Fellowship to Princeton University, 1959–60; Fellowships at Princeton, 1960–63; Huntington Library Fellowship, 1970; Centre for Advanced Studies, University of Illinois, 1980. *Membership:* American Society for Eighteenth Century Studies. *Address:* 1612 Chevy Chase Drive, Champaign, IL 61821, USA.

DUTTON, Paul C, b. 29 Dec. 1943, Toronto, Ontario, Canada. Poet, Performer. *Publications:* Canada, phonograph album (with The Four Horsemen), 1973; Horse d'Oeuvres, (with The Four Horsemen), 1975; Live in the West, phonograph album, (with The Four Horsemen), 1977; The Book of Numbers, 1979; Right Hemisphere, Left Ear, 1979; The Prose Tattoo: Selected Performance Scores, (with The Four Horsemen), 1983; Spokesdlheards, (with Sandra Braman), 1983. *Contributions to:* Ganglia; a; The Kensington; Catalyst; Gryphon; Rune; Blew Ointment Tantrik Speshul; Missing Link; Light in Darkness; Earth and You; Kontakte; Wolly of Swot; Poetry Toronto; Canadian Forum; Writing; Curvd Haz; Rampike; Capitano Review. *Membership:* League of Canadian Poets. *Address:* 68 Kendal Avenue, Toronto, Ontario M5R 1L9, Canada.

DUVIVIER, Jean-Paul, b. 14 Aug. 1931, Flaudinne, Belgium. Town's Secretary. m. Bernadette Wagemans, 18 Mar. 1977, Chaudfontaine, 1 son, 2 daughters (from previous marriage). *Literary Appointments:* Adventure Writer; Poet. *Publications:* 11 books for adolescents (girls), 1962–63; 9 books for adolescents (young boys), 1962–69; 2 books of sea adventures for adults, 1975; 2 books of poetry, 1964; Book of child's souvenirs, 1979. *Honour:* A book about a Ship's Captain translated and shown in cinemas in Europe and on French Television (13 series), 1975. *Address:* Av Albert Ier, 17/2, Liege-Grivegnee, Belgium.

DYBA, Kenneth Walter, b. 9 May 1945, Nordegg, Alberta, Canada. Writer; Stage Director. *Education:* BA, Theatre/English, University of British Columbia. *Appointments:* Dramaturge, Theatre Calgary, Alberta, 1973; Dramaturge, Pleiades Theatre, Calgary Centennial Planetarium, 1974, 1975. *Publications:* Sister Roxy, 1973; Lucifer and Lucinda, 1977; The Long (and Glorious) Weekend of Raymond (and Bingo) Oblongh, 1983; The Sun Runner, stage play, 1983. *Contributor to:* Short stories, novel excerpts in Canadian Forum; Quarry; Grain; Matrix; Golden West; Cross-Canada Writers Quarterly; Descant; Rune; Origins; etc. *Honours:* Alberta Government Cultural Award, 1962; City of Calgary Award, 1964; University of British Columbia Bursary, 1964; Canada Council Award, 1980; Ontario Arts Council, 1983. *Membership:* Playwrights Union of Canada, Toronto. *Literary Agent:* Nancy Colbert, 303 Davenport Road, Toronto, Ontario, Canada M5R 1K5. *Address:* 120 Crescent Road, Toronto, Ontario, Canada M4W 1T5.

DYER, Charles, b. 2 July 1928, Shrewsbury, Shropshire, England. Playwright; Novelist. *Publications:* (novels) Rattle of a Simple Man, 1964; Charlie Always Told Harry Almost Everything, 1969; Staircase, 1969; Unter Der Treppe, 1970; La Crecelle, 1971; (plays) Wanted: One Body!, 1961; Time Murderers Place, 1962; Rattle of a Simple Man, 1963; Staircase, 1968; Mother Adam, 1972; Hot Godly Wind, 1973; A Loving Hallelujah, 1974; Dancers Circling, 1979; Lovers Dancing, 1981. *Contributions to:* Plays and Players; l'Avant Scene, Paris; Sipario, Rome; The Best Plays of New York, 1963, 1968; Best Plays in London, 1963. *Address:* Old Wob, Austenwood, Chalfont St Peter, Buckinghamshire SL9 85F, England.

DYER, Frederick C, Writer; Consultant. *Education:* BA, Holy Cross College, 1938; MBA, Dartmouth College, 1948. *Publications:* Author or co-author of 9 books for Prentice-Hall, Dow-Jones-Irwin, Stackpole and University of Miami, 3 replished in India, 2 in Latin America and 4 in Europe; 12 books for US Govrnment; over 70 pieces in over 30 periodicals. Contributing Editor, 4 journals. *Memberships include:* Army and Navy; Authors Guild; National Press Club; Cosmos Club; Washington Independent Writers. *Address:* 4509 Cumberland Avenue, Chevy Chase, MD 20815, USA.

DYER, James Frederick, b. 23 Feb. 1934, Luton, Bedfordshire, England. Archaeological Writer. *Education:* BA, MA Archaeology, University of Leicester, England; Diploma in Education, St John's College, York.

Literary Appointments: Editor, Bedfordshire Archaeological Journal, 1966–68, Bedfordshire Magazine, 1965–74, Shire Archaeology, 1974–. *Major Publications:* The Story of Luton, 1964; Discovering Archaeology in England & Wales, 1969; Discovering Archaeology in Denmark, 1972; Southern England: An Archaeological Guide, 1973; The Penguin Guide to Prehistoric England & Wales, 1981; Hillforts of England & Wales, 1981; Teaching Archaeology in Schools, 1983. *Contributor to:* The Illustrated London News; Antiquity; Bedfordshire Magazine. *Memberships:* Society of Authors. *Address:* 6 Rogate Road, Luton, Bedfordshire, England.

DYER, Roberta Coldren, b. 25 Aug. 1914, Dover, Delaware, USA. Counselor/Educator (Music). *Education:* American Conservatory of Music; North Park College, etc. *Appointments:* Teacher of Music (voice Theory); Investigator of religious cults; Counsellor, Educator in religion; Tutor in learning methods, music (piano), art and poetry; Lecturer; Writer. *Publications:* Sepher Yetzirah, 1940; Message from Gabriel, 1961. *Contributor to:* Various anthologies, journals and newspapers. *Honours include:* Recipient of several awards from Brownson Circle; Illinois Federation of Women's Clubs; Poets and Patrons; American Poetry League; Pennsylvania Poets Society etc. *Memberships:* Fellow, International Poetry Society; Workshop Director, Poets and Patrons; Poets Club of Chicago; Literary and Drama Chairman, Brownson Circle; Brownson Poets; Women's Literary Club of Chicago; Poetry Society (UK); Delta Omicron; American Poetry League; World Poetry Day; Pennsylvania Poetry Society; International Academy of Poets; American Poets Fellowship Society; National Writers Club; Theosophical Society in America; Poetry Society of America; Hospitalized Veterans' Writing Project; Paragraph Club; The Quill Pushers. *Address:* 1325 Manchester Road, Wheaton, IL 60187, USA.

DYKSTRA, Craig Richard, b. 31 May 1947, Detroit, Michigan, USA. Professor of Christian Education. m. Elizabeth Ann Hanson, 7 June 1969, Grosse Pointe, Michigan, 2 sons. *Education:* AB, Dinstinction, University of Michigan, 1969; MDiv 1973, PhD magna cum laude 1978, Princeton Theological Seminary, *Literary Appointments:* Instructor, Christian Education, 1976–77, Thomas W Synnott Professor 1984–, Princeton Theological Seminary; Assistant, Associate Professor, Louisville Presbyterian Theological Seminary, 1977–84. *Publications:* Vision & Character: A Christian Educator's Alternative to Kohlberg, 1981; Korean translation, ibid, 1984. *Contributions to:* Religious Education; Princeton Seminary Bulletin; Theology Today; Presbyterian Survey; New Ventures in Bible Study, 1981. *Honours include:* Phi Kappa Phi, 1968; Edward Howell Roberts Scholarship, 1972; William Tennent Scholarship, 1972; Fellowship. Practical Theology, 1973; Grawmeyer Award, instructional innovation, 1982; Outstanding Young Man of America, 1982. *Address:* Princeton Theological Seminary, CN 821, Princeton, NJ 08540, USA.

DYLAN, Bob, b. 24 May 1941, Duluth, Minnesota, USA. Singer; Composer. *Education:* University of Minnesota, 1960; Self-taught, guitar, piano, autoharp, harmonica. Honorary DMus, Princeton University, 1970. *Career includes:* Performer in numerous tours and concerts, 1960–; Devised and popularised folk-rock music, 1965–. Movies include: Don't Look Back; Pat Garrett and Billy the Kid; Renaldo and Clara. Numerous song compositions include: Blowin' in the Wind; A Hard Rain's A-Gonna Fall; Just Like a Woman; If Not For You; Simple Twist of Fate; Forever Young; Mozambique; Gotta Serve Somebody; numerous others. Recorded numerous albums including: The Freewheelin' Bob Dylan; Desire; Street Legal; Slow Train Coming. *Publications:* Tarantula, 1966, 71; Writings and Drawings of Bob Dylan, 1973; The Songs of Bob Dylan from 1966–1975, 1976; Lyrics 1962–85, 1985. *Address:* PO Box 870, Cooper Station, New York City, NY 10276, USA.

DYMOTT, Roderick, b. 14 Dec. 1945, Sussex, England. Publisher. m. Carol Atkinson, 7 Sep. 1968, Southwick, Sussex. 1 son, 1 daughter. *Literary Appointments:* Various senior publishing appointments. *Publications:* Fleet Air Arm, 1978; North Downs in Surrey, 1984; North Downs in Sussex, 1984; various childrens and local interest titles. *Contributions to:* Many professional publications. *Address:* 9 Clifton Close, Addlestone Moor, Weybridge, Surrey KT15 2EX, England.

DYSON, John Edward, b. 12 Mar. 1943, New Zealand. Journalist; Author. m. Kate Hedley, 27 Apr. 1967, Ledsham, 1 son, 3 daughters. *Publications:* The Prime Minister's Boat is Missing, 1974; The Pond Book, 1976; Motorcycling, 1977; Business in Great Waters, 1977; The Hot Arctic, 1979; The South Seas Dream, 1982; Blue Hurricane, 1983; China Race, 1984. *Contributor to:* Readers Digest Magazine; Observer Magazine; Weekend Telegraph; Sunday Times, etc. *Literary Agent:* Campbell Thomson & McLaughlin. *Address:* d'Antraigues, 27 The Terrace, Barnes, London SW13 0NR, England.

E

EASTMENT, Ian Raynor Handley, b. 26 Jan. 1948, London, England. Publisher; Scriptwriter. m. 5 Sep. 1970, Loughton, 1 son. *Literary Appointments:* Associate editor, Books and Issues, 1979–. *Publications:* Plays include: Tiptoe Through the Tulips, 1982; Bott and Ritter, 1985. *Address:* c/o Sage Publications Limited, 28 Banner Street, London EC1, England.

EASTON, Thomas Atwood, b. 17 July 1944, Bangor, Maine, USA. Writer. m. Elizabeth Susan Nelson, 13 June 1967, New York, 1 daughter. *Education:* BA, Biology, Colby College, 1966; PhD, Theoretical Biology, University of Chicago, 1971. *Appointment:* Book Columnist, Analog Science Fiction & Science Fact Magazine, 1979–. *Publications:* Bioscope, with Carl Rischer, 1979, 2nd edition 1984; How to Write a Readable Business Report, 1983; Working for Life: Careers in Biology, 1984; Careers in Science, 1984; Using Consultants: A Consumers Guide for Managers, with R Conant, 1985; Cutting Loose: Making the Transition from Employee to Entrepreneur, with R Conant, 1985. *Contributor to:* Numerous journals, magazines and newspapers. *Membership:* Science Fiction Writers of America, Grievance Committee, 1980–84. *Address:* Box 805, RFD 2, Belfast, ME 04915, USA.

EASTON, Thomas James, b. 5 Nov. 1919, Deceased. North Bondi, Australia. Journalist. m. Susan Priscilla Neven Read, Sydney, Australia, 23 Dec. 1965, 2 sons, 3 daughters. *Education:* Diploma, Public Administration, University of Sydney; Diploma; Magazine & Newspaper Advertising, Correspondence Schools. *Literary Appointments:* To write the history of Parramatta Rugby League Football Club (The Eels), 1978. *Publications:* Tennis Text Book (USSR), 1964; Tackling Rugby (Biography, Ken Thornett), 1966; History of The Eels (History, Parramatta Rugby League Club), 1978. *Contributions to:* Woman's Day (short stories); Sydney Morning Herald. *Honours & Literary Awards:* Best Story in Suburban Newspapers, 1981; 1st and 2nd places, RSL short story competition. *Membership:* Australian Journalist's Association. *Literary Agent:* Lansdowne Press & Cumberland Newspapers.

EATON, Lucy Ellen, b. 9 July 1905, Bridgeport, Connecticut, USA. Poet, Author. m. Howard Eldon Eaton, 11 Mar. 1931, Carlyle, Sask, 3 sons. *Publications:* Dear God, 1971; Mount up on Wings, 1971; Spring Up O Well, 1974; Acquiring Expertise with the Solomette, 1977; Love Drew a Circle, 1979; I Lift up my Eyes, 1979; Love Is, 1980; They Followed Their Star, 1981; Apples of Gold, 1981; Ordered Steps, 1983; Across Canada with a Cook Book, 1984. *Contributor to:* Castlegar News; Trail Times; Nelson Daily News; Regina Leader Post; United Poets Laureate; IBC; Masters of Modern Poetry (CSSI); Friendship; Full Moon Rising; Alta, Poetry Book; World Poetry; American Evangelist; Family Life Today; Bardic Echoes; Canadian Poets and Friends; Christian Life; The Christian; Family Life Today; Western People; Folklore; also to several anthologies and Historical Books. *Honours:* HLD, L'University Libre, Asia, 1978; Diploma D'Onore, Concorsa Letterario International, 1978; Poet Laureate with gold crown, United Poets Laureate Itern'l, 1977; Poet Laureate, CSSI, 1977; First Lady of the Year, Beta Sigma Phi International, 1981; over 30 Diplomas. *Memberships:* Saskatchewan Poetry Society; UAP. *Address:* 101 8th Avenue, Castlegar, BC Canada, V1N 1M7.

EATON, Trevor Michael William, b. 26 Mar. 1934, London, England. School Teacher. m. 29 Sep. 1958, Oxford, 2 sons, 2 daughters. *Education:* MA, New College, Oxford University. *Publications:* The Semantics of Literature, 1966; Theoretical Semics, 1972; Editor: Poetries: Their Media and Ends, 1974; Editor: Essays in Literary Semantics, 1978. *Contributions to:* Journal of Literary Semantics, Editor, 1972–; Linguistics; Style; Dutch Quarterly Review; Cahiers Roumains d'Etudés Littéraires; Times Higher Educational Supplement; Educational Studies. *Honours:* Schoolmaster Fellowships, Merton College, Oxford 1971 and Corpus Christi College, Cambridge, 1977. *Memberships:* Linguistics Association of Great Britain, Section Convenor, Linguistics and Literary Section, 1972–76; Poetics and Linguistics Association; International PEN. *Address:* Honeywood Cottage, 35 Seaton Avenue, Hythe. Kent CT21 5HH, England.

EBBETT, Frances Eva, b. 6 June 1925, Wellingborough, England. Author. *Publications:* as Eva Burfield: Yellow Kowhai, 1957; A Chair to Sit On, 1958; The Long Winter, 1964; Out of Yesterday, 1965; After Midnight, 1965; The White Prison, 1966; The New Mrs Rainier, 1967; The Last Day of Summer, 1968. As Eve Ebbett: Give Them Swing Bands, 1969; To the Garden Aline, 1970; In True Colonial Fashion, 1977; Victoria's Daughters: New Zealand Women of the Thirties, 1981; When the Boys Were Away: New Zealand Women in World War II, 1984. *Contributions to:* Magazines in New Zealand, Australia, UK and Scandinavia. *Literary Agent:* Kay Routledge and Associates. *Address:* PO Box 27, Waipawa, Hawkes Bay, New Zealand.

EBENER, Dietrich, b. 14 Feb. 1920, Berlin, Germany. University Teacher, Classical Philology. *Education:* Teachers' Examinations, Potsdam, 1948, 1949; State Examinations, Classics, History & Philosophy, Berlin, 1951; PhD, 1953; Habilitation, Halle, 1956; Professor, 1959. *Publications:* Euripides, Tragodien griechisch und deutsch, 6 volumes, 1971–79; Euripides Werke, 3 volumes, 1966, 1979; Homer Werke, 2 volumes, 1971, 1976, 1983; Theokrit Werke, 1973, 1983; Griechische Lyrik, 1976, 1980, 1985; Aischylos Werke, 1976; Lucanus, Burgerkreig, 1978, 1985; Novels: Landsknacht wider Willen, 1955; Kreuzweg Kalkutta, 1965; Nala und sein Sohn, 1977. *Address:* DDR 1505 Bergholtz-Rehbrücke, Alice-Bloch-Strasse 3, 3410 Democratic Republic of Germany.

EBNER-ALLINGER, Jeannie, b. 17 Nov. 1918, Sydney, New South Wales, Australia. Writer; Translator. *Education:* Academy of Fine Arts, Vienna, Austria, 4 years. *Publications include:* (poetry) Gedichte und Meditationen, Gesang an das Heute, 1952; Gedichte, 1965; Sag ich, 1978; (Novels) Z'sie Warten auf Antwort, 1954; Die Wildnis fruher Sommer, 1958; Figuren in Schwarz & Weiss, 1962; (short works) Der Konigstiger, 1959; Die Gotten reden nicht, 1961; Im Schatten der Gottin, 1963; Prosadichtungen, 1973; Protokoll aus einem Zwischenreich, 1975; Sag ich, 1978; Erfrorene Rosen, 1979; Drei Flotentone, 1981; Aktadn, 1983; Der Konigstiger, 1983; Das Bild der Beiden Schwestern (short works), 1983; Translation of 40 works from English. *Contributions to:* Literatur & Kritik, Salzburg (publisher and editor); numerous other journals and newspapers. *Honours:* Numerous prizes and medals. *Memberships include:* W Prikheimer Society (Board of Trustees); PEN (executive committee, Austrian Chapter). *Address:* Schlossgasse 3/8, 1050 Vienna, Austria.

EBY, Cecil, b. 1 Aug. 1927, Charles Town, West Vancouver, USA. Writer; Professor of American Culture; Professor of English, University of Michigan. *Publications:* The Old South Illustrated, 1959; Porte Crayon: The Life of David H Strother, 1960; A Virginia Yankee in the Civil War, 1961; The Siege of the Alcazar, 1965; Between the Bullet and the Lie, 1969; That Disgraceful Affair: The Black Hawk War, 1973. *Contributor to:* magazines and journals including American Literature; American Heritage; Der Spiegel; Book World; Washington Post; SW Review. *Honours:* Recipient, Rackham Awards, 1967, 69, 77, 79. *Memberships:* Mid-Continent American Studies Association; Michigan Academy. *Literary Agent:* Perry Knowlton, Curtis Brown. *Address:* Haven Hall, Department of English, University of Michigan, Ann Arbor, MI 49108, USA.

ECHOLS, Barbara Ellen, b. 29 Sep. 1934, Atlanta, Georgia, USA. 2 daughters. *Education:* MBA, Babcock Graduate School of Management, 1979. *Appointments:* Electroencephalography Technician, 1952–54, Chief, Electroencephalography Laboratory, 1954–67, Research Assistant, Medical Care and Hospitals, 1967–68, Assistant, Medical Care and Hospitals, 1968–69, Johns Hopkins University; Administrative Assistant, to President, Association of American Medical Colleges, 1969–71; Director, Grants and Contracts, Duke University Medical Centre, 1971–. *Publications:* The Commonsense Guide to Good Eating, co-author, 1978; Vegetarian Delights, 1981; Meatless Meals, 1983; Various book chapters. *Contributor to:* EEG & Clinical Neurophysiology; American Journal EEG Technicians'; Duke Alumni Newsletter; etc. *Honours:* Board of Examiners, American Board of Registration of Electroencephaolographic Technologists, 1964–66. *Memberships:* Member numerous professional organisations including: American Board of Registration of Electroencephalographic Technologists; American Society of Electroencephalographic Technicians, various offices; Association of American Medical Colleges, Health Benefits Committee, 1971; American Diabetes Association; etc. *Address:* Box 3001, Duke University Medical Centre, Durham, NC 27710, USA.

ECKARDT, Arthur Roy, b. 8 Aug. 1918, Brooklyn, New York, USA. Emeritus Professor. *Education:* BA, Brooklyn College, 1942; MDiv, Yale University, 1944; PhD, Columbia University, 1947. *Publications:* Christianity and the Children of Israel, 1948; The Surge of Piety in America, 1958; Elder and Younger Brothers, 1967, 1973; Encounter with Israel, (with Alice Eckardt), 1970; Your People, My People, 1974; Long Night's Journey into Day, (with Alice Eckardt), 1982. *Contributor to:* Various journals including, journal of the American Academy of Religion, Editor-in-Chief, 1961–69; The Christian Century; Commentary; Encounter, (Indianapolis); Evangelische Theologie, (Munich); Judaism. *Honours:* Phi Beta Kappa; Ford Fellow, Harvard University, 1955–56; Distinguished Alumnus Award, Brooklyn College, 1963; Lilly Fellow, University of Cambridge, UK, 1963–64; LHD, (hon) Hebrew Union College, 1969; Rockefeller Fellow, University of Tubingen, Germany; Hebrew University, Jerusalem, Israel, 1975–76; Jabotinsky Centennial Medal, 1980. *Address:* Beverly Hill Road, Box 619A, Coopersburg, PA 18036, USA.

EDBERG, Rolf Filip, b. 14 Mar. 1912, Lysvik, Sweden. Author. *Major Publications include:* On the Shred of a Cloud, 1957; At the Foot of the Tree, 1974; Letters to Columbus, 1973; House in Cosmos, 1975; Dream of Kilimanjaro, 1976; Shadows across the Savannah, 1977; Land of Glittering Waters, 1980; This is our Home, 1982; The Threats against our Home, 1982; Drops of Water, Drops of Life, 1982; ...and they always sailed, 1985. Several works on political & ecological questions in Scandinavian Languages. *Honours:* Socrates Prize, 1972; Gold Medal, Pro Mundo habitabili, Royal Swedish Academy of Sciences, 1974; Honorary PhD, 1974; Gold Medal, Swedish Anthropological & Geological Society, 1976; Dag Hammarskjöld Medal, 1978; King's Medal, 1981; Government's Medal, Illis quorum maruere labores, 1984; Let Live, Prize, 1985. *Memberships:* President, Swedish Press Club, 1951–53; Swedish Authors' Society; PEN; Royal Swedish Academy of Sciences. *Address:* Hagtornsgatan 3, 652 30 Karlstad, Sweden.

EDELMAN, Elaine, b. Indianapolis, MN, USA. Poet; Playwrite; Essayist. *Education:* BA, Sarah Lawrence College, NY, USA. *Literary Appointments include:* Reporter-Writer, CBS TV, NYC; Freelance Writer Producer, NBC TV, NET TV, NYC; Editor, American Heritage Book Company; Senior Editor, American Studies Professional and Reference Book Division, McGraw-Hill Books; Senior Editor, Harper and Row Publishing Company, Children's Books. *Publications:* Noeva: Three Women Poets, 1975; Boom-de-Boom, 1980; I Love My Baby Sister (Most of the Time), 1985. *Contributor to:* numerous magazines and anthologies including Young North American Poets; I Hear My Sister Saying (T Y Crowell); American Poetry Review; New American and Canadian Poets; Perspective; New; The SD Review; Prairie Schooner; Vanity Fair; Esquire; McCall's; Confrontation. *Honours include:* American Film Festival Prizes, 1963, 1965; Barcourt Brace Jovanovich Poetry Fellowship, University of Colorado Writers Conference, 1970; Dramatists Guild Grant, 1973; Fellow, Virginia Center for Creative Arts, 1983. *Memberships:* The New Dramatists Incorporated, (Fellow, Executive Board, 1973–74); The Writers Guild; PEN America. *Address:* New York NY, USA.

EDEN, Robert, b. 25 July 1942, Washington, District of Columbia, USA. Professor of Political Philosophy and Political Science, m. Anne Shotz, 18 June 1970, Newton, Massachusetts, USA, 1 son, 1 daughter. *Education:* BA, University of California, Berkeley, 1966; PhD, Government Department, Harvard University, 1974. *Publications:* Political Leadership and Nihilism: A Study of Weber and Nietzsche, 1984. *Contributions to:* The Review of Politics, Political Theory; Nietzsche-Studien. *Honours:* Nominated for Kayden Award for Best Book in Humanities published in 1984. *Address:* Department of Political Science, Dalhousie University, Halifax, Nova Scotia, B3H 4H6, Canada.

EDFELT, Bo Johannes, b. 21 Dec. 1904, Kyrkefalla, Skaraborgs Ian, Sweden. Author; Poet. *Education:* Fil mag, Uppsala University, 1930; Fil Lic, Stockholms Hogskola, 1952; Fil dr, hc, Stockholm University, 1960. *Publications include:* (poetry) Hogmassa, 1934; I denna natt, 1936; Vintern ar lang, 1939; Elden och Klyftan, 1943; Braddjupt eko, 1947; Hemliga slagfalt, 1952; Under Saturnus, 1956; Insyn, 1962; Adernat, 1968; Brev fran edn atelje, 1976; various essays, translations of lyric poetry. *Contributor to:* Dagens Nyheter; Svenska Dagbladec; Bonniers Litterara Magasin, etc. *Honours include:* Svenska Akademiens Bellmanspris, 1954, 1971; Kellgrinpris, 1983; Boklotteriets stora pris, 1962; Henrik Steffens-Preis, Germany, 1967; Goethe-Medaille, 1984. *Address:* Bergviksvägen 38, 150 24 Rönninge, Sweden.

EDLIN, John Bruce, b. 21 Aug. 1945, Invercargill, NZ. News Agency, Correspondent. *Contributor to:* The Associated Press; Newsweek; London Sunday Express; Yorkshire Post; The Australian; Toronto Star. *Memberships:* Quill Club, Harare; City Club, Harare. *Address:* c/o Associated Press, Box 785, Harare, Zimbabwe.

EDMOND, Lauris Dorothy, b. 2 Apr. 1924, Dannevirke, New Zealand. Writer; Part-time University Lecturer. m. Trevor Edmond, 16 May 1945, Tauranga, New Zealand, 1 son, 5 daughters. *Education:* MA (1st Class), English, Victoria University, Wellington; Speech Therapy Diploma; Teacher's Certificate. *Literary Appointments:* Tutor, Poetry School, Victoria University, Wellington, 1983; Tutor, Summer School, Wanganui College of Advanced Education, 1984; Writer-in-Residence, Deakin University, Melbourne, 1985. *Publications:* (Poems), In Middle Air, 1975; The Pear Tree, 1977; Wellington Letter, 1980; Salt from the North, 1980; Catching It, 1983; Selected Poems, 1984; Selected Letters of A R D Fairburn, Editor, 1981; High Country Weather, (novel), 1984. *Contributor to:* (in New Zealand), Listener; Landfall; Islands; P N Review, (UK); Meanjin; Westerly; Mattoid; Poetry Australia; Critical articles in, Affairs, (New Zealand); Reviews in New Zealand, Listener. *Honours:* Best First Book, New Zealand PEN Award, 1975; Katherine Mansfield Memorial Fellowship, 1981; Commonwealth Poetry Prize, 1985. *Membership:* PEN, Past President, New Zealand Center. *Address:* 22 Grass Street, Oriental Bay, Wellington, New Zealand.

EDMONDS, Vernon H, b. 18 Dec. 1927, Clinton, Oklahoma, USA. College Professor. *Education:* BA, Oklahoma State University, 1954; MS, Purdue University, 1955; PhD, University of Missouri, 1962. *Publications:* Human Behavior, Volume 2, 1967; Social Behavior, 1964; Social Behavior, 2nd Edition, 1967.

Contributor to: Journal of Marriage & Family; Social Forces. *Memberships:* American Sociological Association; National Council on Family Relations (Associate Editor, JMF); Southern Sociological Association. *Address:* College of William & Mary, Williamsburg, VA 23185, USA.

EDSON, J T, b. 17 Feb. 1928, Worksop, Nottinghamshire, England. Author. Div, 2 sons, 1 daughter. *Publications include:* Trail Boss, 1961; Ole Devil Hardin series; Civil War series; Floating Outfit series; Waco series; Calamity Jane series; Waxahachie Smith series; Alvin Dustine 'Cap' Fog series; Rockabye County series; Bunduki series. Over 120 titles. *Contributions to:* Victor boys paper Boys World in early career. *Honours & Literary Awards:* 2nd Prize, Brown Watson Literary Competition (Western Section), 1960; Approx. 20,000,000 Copies of books sold worldwide. *Membership:* Western Writers of America. *Literary Agent:* Joanna Marston, Rosica Colin Ltd, 1 Clareville Grove News, London SW7, England. *Address:* P O Box 13, Melton Mowbray, Leicestershire, England.

EDWARDS, George Charles III, b. 3 Jan. 1947, Rochester, New York, USA. Professor of Political Science. m. Carmella Pierce, 22 May 1981, Waco, Texas, 1 son. *Education:* BA, Stetson University, 1969; MA, 1970, PhD, 1973, University of Wisconsin. *Publications:* Perspectives on Public Policy Making, 1975; The Policy Predicament, 1978; Presidential Influence in Congress, 1980; Implementing Public Policy, 1980; The Public Presidency, 1983; Studying the Presidency, 1983; Public Policy Implementation, 1984; Presidential Leadership, 1985; The Presidency and Public Policy Making, 1985. *Contributions to:* Numerous publications including: American Political Science Review; American Journal of Political Science; Journal of Politics; American Politics Quarterly; Policy Studies Journal; Presidential Studies Quarterly; Public Opinion; essays in many books. *Address:* Department of Political Science, Texas A&M University, College Station, TX 77843, USA.

EDWARDS, Gillian Mary, b. 7 Oct. 1918, Soham, England. Secretary. *Education:* BA, University of Reading, England. *Publications:* Sun of My Life, 1951; The Road to Hell, 1967; Uncumber and Panaloon, 1968; I am Leo, 1969; Hogmanay and Tiffany, 1970; Tower of Lions, 1971; Hobgoblin and Sweet Puck, 1974; Accidental Visitor, 1974; Fatal Grace, 1978. *Address:* 19 Primary Court, Chesterton, Cambridge CB4 1NB, England.

EDWARDS, Michael, b. 29 Apr. 1938, Barnes, Surrey, England. University Teacher. m. Danielle Bourdin, 7 July 1964, Paris, 1 son, 1 daughter. *Education:* BA 1960, MA, 1964, PhD. 1965. Christ's College, Cambridge. *Publications:* Poetry: To Kindle the Starling, 1972; Where, 1975; The Balad of Mobb Conroy, 1977; The Magic Unquiet Body, 1985. Radio Play: Commonplace, 1971. Criticism: La Tragédie racinienne, 1972; Towards a Christian Poetics, 1984. *Contributions to:* Poems, translations and articles in Adam; Agenda; Critical Quarterly; Delta; London Magazine; PN Review; Prospice; Samphire; Action poétique (France); Nuova Rivista Europea (Italy). Joint Editor of Prospice, 1972–82. *Address:* 30 Alma Street, Wivenhoe, Essex CO7 9DL, England.

EDWARDS, Philip Walter, b. 7 Feb. 1923, Barrow-in-Furness, Lancashire, England. University Professor of English Literature. *Education:* BA, MA, PhD, University of Birmingham. *Publications include:* Kyd, The Spanish Tragedy, Editor, 1959; Shakespeare & The Confines of Art, 1968; Pericles Prince of Tyre, Editor, 1976; Massinger, Plays & Poems, Editor, 1976; Threshold of a Nation, 1979; Hamlet, Prince of Denmark, Editor, 1985; Shakespeare: A Writer's Progress, 1986. *Contributor to:* Shakespeare Survey; Proceedings of the British Academy. *Address:* 12 South Bank, Oxton, Birkenhead, Merseyside, L43 5UP, England.

EDWARDS, Robert John, b. 26 Oct. 1925. Non-Executive Deputy Chairman, Mirror Group Newspapers, London, England. m. (1) Laura Ellwood (1952–72), 2 sons, 2 daughters; (2) Brigid O'Neil Forsyth Segrave, 27 July 1977. *Literary Appointments:* Editor, Tribune, 1951–54; Deputy Editor, Sunday Express, 1957–59; Managing Editor, Daily Express, 1959–61; Editor, Daily Express, 1961– 1963–65; Editor, Evening Citizen, Glasgow, 1962–63; Editor, Sunday People, 1966–72; Editor, Sunday Mirror, 1972–84; Deputy Chairman and Senior Group Editor, Mirror Group Newspapers, 1985–; Director, Mirror Group Newspapers, 1976–; *Address:* Mirror Group Newspapers, 33 Holborn Circus, London, EC1P 1DQ, England.

EDWARDS, Ronald George, b. 10 Oct. 1930, Geelong, Australia. Writer. m. Anne Edwards, 1 son, 1 daughter. *Education:* Diploma of Art. *Appointment:* Editor, Australian Folklore Society Journal. *Publications include:* The Overlander Songbook, 1958, 1969, 1971; Index of Australian Folksong 1857–1970, 1971; Australian Folksongs, 1972; Australian Traditional Bush Crafts, 1975; The Big Book of Australian Folksong, 1976; The Australian Yarn 1977–78; Skills of the Australian Bushman, 1979; Yarns and Ballads, 1981; Making a Stock Saddle, 1981; Mud Brick & Earth Building, with Lin Wei-hao, 1983; Bush Leatherwork, 1985. *Honours:* Australian Folk Trust Fellowship, 1985. *Address:* Box 274 Kuranda, Queensland 4872, Australia.

EELLS, George, b. 20 Jan 1922, Winslow, Illinois, USA. Writer. *Education:* Northwestern University; Columbia University; American Theater Wing. *Literary Appointments:* Entertainment Editor, Parade magazine, 1945; Entertainment Editor, Look Magazine, 1946–60; Editor, Theatre Arts Magazine, 1962; Editor, Signature Magazine, 1963–67. *Publications:* Cole Porter: The Life That Late He Led, 1967; Hedda and Louella, a duel biography, 1972 (re-issued in paperback as, Malice in Wonderland, 1985); Ginger, Loretta and Irene WHO?, 1976; Merman, with Ethel Merman, 1978; High Times, Hard Times, with Anita O'Day, 1981; Mae West, a biography, with Stanley Musgrove, 1982; Robert Mitchum, a biography, 1984. *Honours:* ASCAP Biographical Award, 1967; The Life That Late He Led, chosen one of 20 outstanding non-fiction books, New York Times, 1967; High Times, Hard Times, chosen New York Times Notable Books of the Year, 1981. *Memberships:* Authors Guild Inc; Writers Guild of America, West. *Literary Agent:* Gloria Safier Inc. New York. *Address:* c/o Gloria Safier Inc. 244 East 52nd, New York, NY 10022, USA.

EGAN, Desmond, b. Athlone, Co Westmeath, Republic of Ireland. Teacher. *Education:* MA. *Publications:* Midland, 1972; Leaves, 1974, Siegel, 1976; Woodcutter, 1978; Athlone?, 1980; Seeing Double, 1983; Snapdragon, 1983; Collected Poems, (USA) 1983, (Europe) 1984; A soup for My Father, (USA) 1986; Collected Prose,(USA) 1986. *Contributor to:* Editor, Era Literary Review; Co-Editor, Choice (Contemporary Irish Verse); Feathers and Bones (Modern Irish Poetry USA Anthology); The Wearing of the Black; Lines Review; The Review of Irish Literature (USA); Poetry Wales; Aquarius; Times Literary Supplement; Irish Times. *Honours:* Winner, National Poetry Foundation of USA Award, 1983. *Literary Agent:* Goldsmith Press Limited. *Address:* Martinstown Road, The Curragh, Co Kildare, Republic of Ireland.

EGAN, Harvey Daniel, b. 6 Nov. 1937, Connecticut, USA. Jesuit Priest; Theology Professor. *Education:* BS, Electrical Engineering, 1959; MA, Philosophy, Boston College, 1965; MA, Theology, Woodstock College, 1969; ThD, University of Muenster, Germany, 1973. *Publications:* The Spiritual Exercises and the Ignatian Mystical Horizon, 1967; What Are They Saying About Mysticism? 1982; Christian Mysticism: The Future of Tradition, 1984. *Contributions to:* Theological Studies; Word and Spirit; Studies in Formative Spirituality; Canadian Journal of Religion; Horizons; National Catholic Reporter; Thought; America; Homiletic and

Pastoral Review; Listening. *Honour:* Merit Scholarship from the State Government of Nordrhein-Westfalen, Germany, 1969–73. *Memberships:* The Catholic Theological Society of America; The College Theology Society; American Academy of Religion. *Address:* St. Mary's Hall, Boston College, Chestnut Hill, MA 02167, USA.

EGAN, Pamela Grace, b. 28 Nov. 1933, Bolton, Lancashire, England. Author; Editor. m. William Egan, 12 Dec. 1959, Oxford, 1 son, 1 daughter. *Education:* MA (Oxon). *Literary Appointments:* Journalistic work on Church of England Newspaper, Good Housekeeping; Mind Alive; Publications Officer, General Synod Board of Education, 1968–. *Publications:* Author, Editor, Compiler of many religious education books for those working with children, including Rainbow Series (1972–) and Benjamin Series (1975–). *Contributions to:* Together, Magazine of Board of Education, 1968–. *Address:* Tower House, Wells, Somerset BA5 2UN, England.

EHLE, John Marsden, b. 13 Dec. 1925, Asheville, North Carolina, USA. Author. m. Rosemary Harris, Oct. 1967, 1 daughter. *Education:* AB, MA, University of North Carolina. *Publications:* Novels: Move Over, Mountain, 1957; Kinstree Island, 1959; Land Breakers, 1964; Journey of August King, 1971; Winter People, 1982; Last One Home, 1983. *Honours include:* Walter Raleigh Award, 1961, 1964, 1970, 1975; North Carolina Award for Literature; Lillian Smith Award, 1981; Thomas Wolfe Prize, 1983; Distinguished Alumni Award, University of North Carolina, Chapel Hill, 1984; Wetherford Award, 1985. *Memberships;* Authors Guild; Century Club, New York City. *Literary Agent:* Candada Donadio, 231 West 22nd Street, New York, NY 10011. *Address:* 125 Westview Road NW, Winston-Salem, NC 27104, USA.

EHRHART, William Daniel, b. 30 Sep. 1948, Roaring Spring, Pennsylvania, USA. Writer. m. Anne Senter Gulick, 27 June 1981. *Education:* BA, English Literature, Swarthmore College, 1973; MA, Creative Writing, University of Illinois, 1978. *Publications:* Vietnam: Perkasie, 1983; To Those Who Have Gone Home Tired: New & Selected Poems, 1984; The Outer Banks and Other Poems, 1984; Those Who Were There (contributing Editor), 1984. *Contributions to:* The Virgina Quarterly Review; TriQuarterly; New Letters; The Chronicle of Higher Education; Humanistic Judaism; The Greenfield Review; The Connecticut Poetry Review; Voices Israel; Svetova Literature; and others. *Honours:* Academy of American Poets Collegiate Prize, 1972; Circle Center Poetry Prize, 1978; Mary Roberts Rinehart Foundation Grant, 1980; Pennsylvania Counsil on the Arts Fellow, 1981. *Memberships:* Poets and Writers Incorporated; Poetry Society of America; Society of Professional Journalists. *Address:* Philadelphia, PA, USA.

EICHER, David John, b. 7 Aug. 1961, Oxford, Ohio, USA. Editor. *Education:* Miami University, 1979–81. *Literary Appointments:* Editor, Deep Sky, Magazine; Assistant Editor, Astronomy. *Major Publication:* Deep Sky Observing with Small Telescopes, 1986. *Contributor to:* Sky & Telescope; Star & Sky; Odyssey; Telescope Making. *Honour:* Carles Messier Award from Astronomical League, 1978. *Address:* 625 East St Paul Avenue, Milwaukee, WI 53202, USA.

EICHLER, Margrit, b. 28 Sep. 1942, Berlin, Federal Republic of Germany. Professor of Sociology. 1 son. *Education:* MA Sociology, 1968; PhD Sociology, 1972. *Publications include:* Martin's Father, children's book, 1977; The Double Standard: A Feminist Critique of Feminist Social Science, 1980; Women in Futures Research, 1981; Canadian Families Today: Recent Changes and their Policy Consequences, 1983. *Contributions to:* Numerous publications including: Journal for the Scientific Study of Religion; Women in Canada; Atlantis; Women's Studies International Quarterly; Canadian Journal of Sociology; Perspectives on Women in the 1980's. *Address:* Department of Sociology, OISE, 252 Bloor Street West, Toronto, Ontario, Canada M5S IV6.

EICHLER, Richard W, b. 8 Aug. 1921, Liebenau, Bohemia. Writer, Professor. *Education:* Studies in Vienna. *Publications:* Koehner-Kuenstler Scharlatane, 1960, 7th edition, 1978; Kuenstler und Werke, 1962, 3rd edition, 1968; Der gesteuerte Kunstverfall, 1965, 3rd edition, 1985; Die taetowierte Muse, 1965; Viel Gunst fur schlechte Kunst, 2nd edition, 1969; Verhexte Muttersprache, 1974; Die Wiederkehr des Schoenen, 1984, 2nd edition, 1985. *Honours:* Schiller Prize, Munich, Germany, 1969; Adalbert-Stifter Medal, 1982. *Memberships:* Sudeten-German Academy of Sciences and Arts; Praesidium; German Arts Foundation of Commerce. *Address:* Steinkirchner Strasse 15, D 8000 Munich 71, Federal Republic of Germany.

EIGEN, Michael Edward, b. 11 Jan. 1936, Passaic, New Jersey, USA. Psychoanalyst; Psychologist. m. Betty Gitelman, 28 Dec. 1980, New York City, 2 sons. *Education:* BA, University of Pennsylvania, 1957; PhD, New School for Social Research, 1974. *Publications:* Evil: Self and Culture, (co-editor), 1984; The Psychotic Self and Its Treatment, 1986. *Contributor to:* Professional journals including: International Journal of Psycho-Analysis; American Journal of Psychoanalysis; Psychoanalytic Review; Journal of the American Academy of Psychoanalysis; Journal of Humanistic Psychology; Psychocultural Review, etc; Chapters in books; Book reviews. *Membership:* Phi Beta Kappa. *Address:* 225 Central Park West, New York, NY 10024, USA.

EISELE, Robert H, b. 9 June, 1948. Writer; Professor. *Education:* BA, MFA, UCLA, USA, 1971. *Appointments:* Playwrighting Fellow and Actor, American Conservatory Theatre, 1975–76; Associate Professor, Theatre Arts, Rio Hondo College, California, 1976–. *Publications:* Plays: Animals are Passing from our Lives; A Dark Night of the Soul; A Garden in Los Angeles; Goats; The Green Room; Film: Breach of Contract, 1982; TV: Murder of Einstein, aired on PBS, 1981; Ordinary Hero (episode of, Cagney and Lacey) aired on CBS, October 1985. *Honours include:* Samuel Goldwyn Writing Awards, 1973; Oscar Hammerstein Playwriting Fellowship, 1973–74; Donald Davis Dramatic Writing Awards, 1974; American Conservatory Theatre Playwriting Fellowship, 1975–76; 1st Prize, Theatre Arts Corporation playwriting contest, 1979. *Memberships:* Writers' Guild of America; Western Dramatists Guild and Authors' League of America; Actors' EQUITY Association; PEN International; Eugene O'Neill Memorial Theatre Centre. *Address:* 404 N Sweetzer Avenue, Los Angeles, CA 90048, USA.

EISENBERG, Phyllis, b. 26 June 1924, Chicago, Illinois, USA. Writer. m. Emanuel M Eisenberg, 2 Sep. 1945, Los Angeles, 1 son. *Literary Appointments:* California Professional Writers' Workshop, University of California at Los Angeles, 1978; Los Angeles Valley College Writers' Conference, Van Nuys, California, 1978. *Major Publications:* A Mitzvah is Something Special, 1978; Don't tell me a Ghost Story, in Impressions (anthology), 1982; This is a Picnic, in Stories for Free Children (anthology), 1982. *Contributor to:* Ms Magazine; The Progressive; Instructor; Cricket Magazine; Woman's World; Moment Magazine; Playgirl; View Magazine; The Rotarian; Pen Magazine; World Over; Backpacker; Wall Street Journal; People & Places; Together Magazine; Los Angeles Times; Sign; School Magazine (Sydney, Australia); Baltimore Jewish Times; Christian Science Monitor; WOW (American Baptist Board of Education). *Honours:* Honorable mention, Unitarian Universalist Play-writing Competition. 1974; Entry in World Book Encyclopaedia, 1979; Don't Tell me a Ghost Story, exhibited at international children's & Youth Exhibition, Munich, Federal Republic of Germany, 1983. *Memberships:* Society of Childrens' Book Writers; Authors Guild of America; PEN. *Address:* 5703 Ventura Canyon Avenue, Van Nuys, CA 91401, USA.

EISENHAUER, Gale Ann, b. 3 Oct. 1955, Newcastle, Wyoming, USA. Editor; Information Director, Wyoming Rural Electric Association. m. Patrick Maurice Eisenhauer, 7 July 1979, Casper, Wyoming, 1 son, 1 daughter. *Education:* Design, Massey Junior College, Atlanta, Georgia; Editing and Production, Casper College, Wyoming. *Contributions to:* Wyoming Rural Electric News; Wyoming Wool Grower. *Memberships:* Wyoming Press Association; Wyoming Federation of Press Women; National Federation of Press Women; Wyoming Heritage Society; Casper Business Women. *Address:* P O Box 3805, Casper, WY 82602, USA.

EISENSTEIN, James, b. 3 Feb. 1940, St Louis, USA. University Professor, m. Virginia B Woodcock, 6 Sep. 1963, Garden City, New York, USA, 2 sons, 1 daughter. *Education:* BA, Oberlin College, 1962; PhD, Yale University, 1968. *Publications:* Politics and the Legal Process. 1973; Counsel for the United States: US Attorneys in the Political and Legal Systems, 1977; Felony Justice: An Organizational Analysis of Criminal Courts, with Herbert Jacob, 1977. *Contributions to:* Political Science Quarterly; American Political Science Review. *Address:* Department of Political Science, Pennsylvania State University, University Park, PA 16802, USA.

EKERWALD, Carl-Göran, b. 30 Dec. 1923, Östersund, Sweden. Writer. *Education:* MA. *Literary Appointments:* Serving on Committee awarding the Norrland Prize; Serving on Committee awarding the Nordcouncil Prize. *Publications:* The Wolfe's Castle, 1963; The Lotus Eaters, 1966; Polish Sugar from Norway, 1967; The Ascension of Bertrand Russell, 1974; Diogenes' Lantern, 1983. *Contributions to:* Dagens Nyheter since 1978. *Honours:* The Norrland Prize, 1967; The Olof Hogberg Prize, 1969; The Peterson-Berger Prize, 1973; The Irma and Einer Forseth Prize, 1984. *Memberships:* Swedish Writers Union; Swedish Union of Playwriters; Swedish PEN Club. *Address:* Box 3617, 831 93 Östersund, Sweden.

EKNER, Reidar, b. 25 July 1929. Writer. *Education:* PhD, Stockholm University, 1962. *Literary Appointments:* Docent, Stockholm University, Sweden, 1962–; Member, Sveriges Forfatterforbund. *Publications:* Etnografika, 1960; Skiljaktigheter, 1963; Andhämtning, 1969; Efter flera tusen rad, 1974; Varje meddelande, 1974; Den svenske toalettsabotoren, 1975; Halvvägs mot mörkret, 1979; Mellan polerna, 1982; Stenarna i skrinct, 1984; Poetry translations: Helgon & Hetsporrar, 1960; Sigbjorn Obstfelderr Här är så underligt, 1975; Gary Snyder: Tingens ådring, 1975; Gary Snyder: Sköldpaddsön, 1976; Denise Levertov: Känna det okända, 1977. *Contributor to:* Ord och Bild; Lyrikvannen; Bonniers Litterara Magasin; Horisont etc. *Honour:* Swedish Academy Literary Award, 1982. *Address:* Alsike 719, S–741 00 Knivsta, Sweden.

EKSTROM, Margareta, b. 23 Apr. 1930, Stockholm, Sweden. Author. *Education:* BA, Stockholm University, 1956. *Publications include:* Evenings in St Petersburg, 1960; Breakfast Time 1961; The Attack, 1962; The Girls, 1963; Domestic Scenes, 1964; The Birth Book, 1965; Berling Island, 1965; When They Rode About, 1969; Words to Johanna, 1973; Relations To Foreign Powers, 1972; On the Nature of Stora Skuggan, a nature diary, 1979; Words in Freedom, diary, 1982; Death's Midwives, Collection of Stories, USA; Numerous stories, novels and poems; various books for children; various translations from African Poetry. *Contributor to:* Literary Critic Expressen; Dagens Nyheter; Swedish Radio; Columnist, Skona Hem; Film Critic, Morgonbladet, 1956–58. *Honours:* Recipient, Bonnier Prize, 1967; Doblough Prize, 1975. *Memberships include:* Board Member, Swedish Writers Association, 1964–69; Vice Chairman. Swedish PEN; Board Member, Swedish Institution, 1979–83. *Address:* Stora Skuggan, 115 42 Stockholm, Sweden.

EL MALLAKH, Ragaei William, b. 5 Mar. 1935, Tanta, Egypt. Professor of Economic/Editor/Director, International Research Center for Energy and Economic Development. m. Dorothea Hendry, 26 Aug. 1962, Boise, Idaho, 2 daughters. *Education:* BA, Faculty of Commerce, Univerity of Cairo, 1947; MA, School of Law, University of Cairo, 1949; MA, Economics, 1951, PhD, Economics, 1955, Rutgers University. *Literary Appointments:* Board of Editors, American Journal of Arabic Studies, 1972–; Board of Editors, Middle East Journal, 1977–84; Board of editors, International Journal of Middle East Studies, 1977–84; Editor, Journal of energy and Development, 1975–. *Publications:* Economic Development and Regional co-operation: Kuwait, 1968; Capital Investment in the Middle East, 1977; The Middle East in the Coming Decade, 1978; Kuwait: Tade and Investment, 1979; Qater: Development of an Oil Economy, 1979; The Economic Development of the United Arab Emirates, 1981; The Absorptive Capacity of Kuwait, 1981; Saudi Arabia: Energy, Development Planning and Industrialization, 1982; OPEC: Twenty Years and Beyond, 1982; Saudi Arabia: Rush to Development, 1982; Petroleum and Economic Development: The Cases of Mexico and Norway, 1984; Mexico's Energy Resources, 1985; Qater: Energy and Development, 1985. *Contributions to:* Articles and reviews on economic development, Middle East economics and energy economics in Journal of Economic Literature; Land Economics: OPEC Review; Current History; Rivista Internationale di Scienze Economiche e Commerciali; International Journal of Middle East Studies; Investigacion Economia; The Wharton Magazine; Energy Policy; Middle East Journal; The World Today; Kyklos. *Honour:* 1984 Award for research and writing, from the Kuwait Foundation for the Advancement of Sciences. *Address:* 216 Economics Building, Box 263, University of Colorado, Boulder, CO 80309–0236, USA.

ELAGIN, Ivan, (real name Matveiev), b. 1 Dec. 1918. Poet; Translator. Education: PhD, New York University, USA, 1970. *Appointments include:* Currently, Professor, Russian Literature, University of Pittsburgh. *Publications:* (In Russian), Journey From There, 1953; Gleaming in the Night, 1963; The Slanted Flight, 1967; Dragon on the Roof, 1973; Under the Constellation of the Axe, 1976; In the Hall of the Universe, 1982; Translator into Russian, John Brown's Body, by S V Benet, 1979; 3 Collections of early works. *Contributor to:* New Review; America; Dailogue-USA; Kontinent; Grani; Novoye Russkoye Slovo; La Pensse Russe. *Address:* 1715 Murdoch St, Pittsburgh, PA 15217, USA.

ELBOGEN, Paul b. 11 Nov. 1894, Vienna, Austria, Writer. *Education:* BA, University of Vienna. *Publications:* Numerous Books including: Letters of Famous Men to their Mothers, 1929; Abandoned Women, 1933, 2nd Edition 1962; Life as an Adventure, 1938; Genius in the Making, documents of the youth of geniusses, 1963; Humour since Homer, the one and only collection of antique jokes, 1964; (novels) Hunt after Life, 1961; Transl. Dutch, English and Spanish, The Jealous Mistress, 1953; The Dark Star, 1960; A Dark Cloud Cometh In, 1983. *Contributor to:* All major newspapers and magazines in Germany, Austria and Switzerland; Editor, Magazine Moderne Welt, Vienna; Long biog. in, German Exile Literature, since 1933 by Professor J Petzer, 1976. *Address:* 218 21 Avenue, San Francisco, CA 94121, USA.

ELBORN, Geoffrey Sheridan, b. 27 Feb. 1950, Edinburgh, Scotland. Writer. *Education:* BA (Hons), English and Music. *Publications:* Poems, 1971; Edith Sitwell, A Life, 1981; Princess Alexandra, 1982; John Piper, 1983; Hand and Eye (anthology of poems), 1977. *Contributions to:* Books and Bookmen; Literary Review; The Times; The Scotsman; Book and Magazine; Woman and Home; The Frog Journal. *Membership:* Society of Authors. *Literary Agent:* Richard Scott Simon, London. *Address:* Ochilview Airth, Falkirk, Stirlingshire, Scotland.

ELDER, Gary, b. 16 Apr. 1939, Poet; Editor. *Publications:* Arnulfsaga, 1970; Making Touch, 1971; Grosser Fagott Fugit, 1973; A Vulgar Elegance, 1974;

Eyes on the Land, 1980; Hold Fire, 1985. *Contributions to:* Amphicrosia; Assembling; Dust; Hyperion; Open Places; Pig Iron; SHY; Greece; The Smith; Snowy Egret; The Vagabond; West Coast Poetry Review; Wood Ibis; Wormwood Review; various others. *Address:* 95 Carson Court, Shelter Cove, Whitehorn, CA 95489, USA.

ELDJÁRN, Thorarinn, b. 22 Aug. 1949, Reykjavik, Iceland. Writer. m. Unnur Olafsdottir, 26 Aug. 1972, Reykjavik, 4 sons. *Education:* Fil. Kand., University of Lund, Sweden. *Publications:* Kvaedi, 1974, 4th edition, 1979; Disneyrimur, 1978; Erindi, 1979; Ofsogum sagt, 1981; Kyrr kjor, 1983; Ydd, 1984; Margsaga, 1985; O muna hif, 1986. *Memberships:* Writers Union of Iceland, Member of Board, 1985; Icelandic PEN Centre. *Address:* Asvallagata 12, 101 Reykjavik, Iceland.

ELDRED-GRIGG, Stevan Treleaven, b. 5 Oct. 1952, Greymouth, New Zealand. Writer. m. Lauree Arlene Hunter, 13 Nov. 1976, Christchurch, New Zealand, 2 sons. *Education:* MA, Honours, University of Canterbury, 1975; PhD, Australian National University, 1978. *Literary Appointment:* Judge, New Zealand Book Awards, 1984. *Publications:* A Southern Gentry, 1980; A New History of Canterbury, 1982; Pleasures of the flesh: Sexuality and Drugs in colonial New Zealand, 1984. *Contributor to:* Short Stories in: Islands; Landfall; New Zealand Listener; Historical Essays in: New Zealand Journal of History; Journal of the Royal Australian Historical Society, *Honour:* A V Reed Memorial Book Award, 1984. *Memberships:* PEN, New Zealand Centre, Canterbury Provincial Committee. *Address:* 377 River Road, Christchurch, New Zealand.

ELDRIDGE, Colin Clifford, b. 16 May 1942, Walthamstow, England. University Lecturer. m. Ruth Margaret Evans, 3 Aug. 1970, Lampeter, 1 daughter. *Education:* BA, Honours, 1963, PhD 1966, Nottingham University. *Publications:* England's Mission: The Imperial Idea in the Age of Gladstone & Disraeli, 1868–1880, 1973; Victorian Imperialism, 1978; British Imperialism in the 19th Century, editor, 1984. *Contributions:* Articles & book reviews in various learned journals. *Honour:* Fellow, Royal Historical Society, 1980. *Address:* Tanerdy, Ciliau Aeron, Lampeter, Dyfed SA48 8DL, Wales.

ELEKTOROWICZ, Leszek, b. 29 May 1924, Lwow, Poland. Writer. m. Maria Kruszynska, 4 Dec. 1948, Krakow, 1 daughter. *Education:* MA, Jagiellonian University. *Literary Appointments:* Editorial Board, literary weekly, Zycie Literackie, Krakow, 1957–72; Literary Manager, Theatre, Krakow, 1972–77; Freelance Writer, 1977–80; Editorial Board, literary monthly, Pismo Krakow, 1980–83. *Publications:* Poetry: Swiat niestworzony, 1957; Kontury, 1962; Przedmowy do ciszy, 1968; Cale klamstwo swiata, 1983. Fiction: Rejterada, 1963; Przechadzki Sylena, 1971; Gwiazdy drwiace, 1974; Przeklety teatr, 1977; w lochu Ferrary, 1980. Essays: Zwierciadlo w okruchach, 1966; Z Londynu do Teksasu, 1970; Motywy zachodnie, 1973. Translations from English: R Frost, D H Lawrence, F B Shelley, W H Auden, etc. *Contributions to:* All major literary magazines in Poland. Some of his works translated and published in French, English, German, Czech, anthologies and magazines. *Honour:* Golden Cross of Merit, 1975. *Memberships:* Polish Writers Association, 1958–83, Vice-President Krakow section, 1975–83, Main Board, 1980–83; PEN Club; ZAIKS, Society of Authors. *Literary Agent:* Agencja Autorska, Warsaw. *Address:* Mazowiecka 8 m 4, 30-036 Krakow, Poland.

ELGARRESTA RAMIREZ DE HARO, Jose, b. 18 May 1945, Madrid Spain. Economist. *Education:* Graduate of Law, University of Madrid; Graduate of Business Administration, ICADE. *Publications:* Monologos (poetry) editor Libros Dante, 1977; Grito y Piedra (poetry) editor Sala, 1979; El Suplantador de Personalidades y Otros Cuentos (short stories) editor participation, 1979; Raices en la Niebla (poestry) editor C Carballo, 1980; Parpado y Hierba (poetry) editor Anthropos, 1982; El Pais de Ninguna Parte, editor

Origenes, (short stories) 1984; Estudio Del IGTE y los Impuestos Especiales por Actividades Economicas (Laws) editor Civitas, 1984. *Memberships;* Collegiate Association of Spanish Writers; European Academy of Arts, Sciences and Letters. *Address:* Fernandez de la Hoz 76, Madrid 28003, Spain.

ELIACH, Yaffa, b. 31 May 1935, Vilna, Poland. Professor of History & Literature. m. David Israel Eliach, 12 Aug. 1953, 1 son, 1 daughter. *Education:* Teachers Diploma, 1954; BA, 1967; MA, 1969; PhD, History, 1973. *History Appointments:* Professor of History & Literature, Brooklyn College, 1969–; Founder, Director, Center for Holocaust Studies, Documentation and Research, 1974–. *Publications:* The Fisherman's Wife/Eishet Ha-Dayag, (poetry), 1965; The Last Jew, with Uri Assaf, (play), 1977; Editor with Brana Gurewitsch, The Liberators: Eyewitness accounts of the Liberation of Concentration Camps, 1981; Hasidic Tales of the Holocaust, 1982. *Contributor to:* Many magazines in USA and Israel. *Honours:* Christopher Award for Literature, 1983; Jewish Women's Leadership Award, Brookly, 1983; The Last Jew, selected by the Commission to the Arts to commemorate the Holocaust on Heroes & Martyrs Day in Israel, 1975; Myrtle Wreath Award for Humanitarian Activities, 1979; Woodrow Wilson Dissertation Award, 1971. *Memberships:* Historical Societies; Various national and international committees; Appearances American television and radio. *Literary Agent:* Russell & Volkening Inc, 50 West 29 Street, New York City, USA. *Address:* City University of New York, Brooklyn College, Brooklyn, NY 11210, USA.

ELIAS, STEPHEN ROGER, b. 7 June 1941, Los Angeles, California, USA. Editors; Writer. m. Catherine Jermany, 22 May 1983, Las Vegas, Nevada, 1 son, 2 daughters. *Education:* AB, University of California, Berkeley, 1963; JD, University of California, Hastings College of Law, 1969. *Publications:* Legal Research: How to Find and Understand the Law, 1982; Dictionary of Intellectual Property Law, 1985. *Contributions;* Articles to Nolo News, a quarterly self-help law journal; Copy Protection for Software, A+, a national magazine for Apple Computer Users. *Address:* c/o NO1o Press, 950 Parker Street, Berkeley, CA 94710, USA.

ELISA, Victoria Ireland Elisa-Grey, b. 21 June 1958, Georgia, USA. Newsletter Writer-Editor. *Education:* Suffolk University; Magna cum laude Communication/Political Science, Spelman College. *Literary Appointments:* Editor, Academic Textbooks, Winthrop Publishers, Cambridge, 1976–78; Editor, Software Metrics, Design News, EDN Magazine/Cahners Publishers, 1979; Writing Consultant, Ogilvy and Mather, New York; Writer, Martin Luther King Jr Centre, 1981–82; Editor, Lay-out Director, The Amplifier, 1982–84; Editor, Writer, The Prime Times, 1984–. *Publications:* Major television scripts: Behind the Changing Scene; If Toes Could See, 1979; Rhetorical Criticism, 1981; Sweet Auburn Avenue, 1984; Community Calendar, 1984–; I Remember DeKalb, 1983. *Contributions to:* EDN Magazine, DeKalb News Sun; The Amplifier; The Prime Times. *Honours Include:* 2nd place, New England Poetry Competition, 1979; 2nd place, New England Prose Competition, 1979; Communications Service Award, 1983; Community Calendar Scriptwriter, National Association of Black Journalists, 1984. *Memberships:* Publication in Services Guild; DeKalb Council for Arts/Village Writers Group; Secretary 1984, Video Writers for Visual Arts. *Address:* Dyno Pub, PO Box 519, Marietta Street, Atlanta, GA 30302, USA.

ELISHA, Ron, b. 19 Dec. 1951, Jerusalem. Playwright. m. Bertha Rubin, 6 Dec. 1981, Melbourne, Australia, 1 son. *Education:* Bachelor of Medicine; Bachelor of Surgery. *Publications:* Dramatic Works for the Stage: In Duty Bound, 1979; Einstein, 1981; Two, 1983; Pax Americana, 1984. *Honours:* Australian Writers Guild Award for Einstein; Best Stage Play, 1982; Australian Writers Guild Major Award for Best Script in any category, 1982; Australian Writers Guild Award for Two,

Best Stage Play, 1984. *Memberships:* Australian Writers Guild. *Address:* 4 Bruce Court, Elsternwick, Victoria 3185, Australia.

ELIZAGARAY, Alga Marina, b. 17 Sep. 1937, Cuba. Children's Literature Writer. *Literary Appointments:* Research Advisor on Children's Literature, National Library Jose Marti, Havana, Cuba, 1967–77; Specialist in Literature for Children, Literature Department, Ministry of Culture, Cuba; Advisor to Editorial Gente Nueva, Jose Marti. *Major Publications include:* Cuentos Lunares, 1974; El Poder de la literatura para ninos y jovenes (essays), 1979; La iniciación del niño en la literatura, 1979; La literatura de la Revolución Cubana para niños y jovenes, 1979; Por el Mar de las Antilias (Anthology of Cuban Poetry), 1983; Fábulas cubanas, 1985. *Contributor to:* Zlaty Maj (Czechoslovakia); Phaedrus (USA); Dotskaya Literatur (USSR). *Memberships:* International Association of Literature for Children in Spanish; International Research Society for Children's Literature; President, Cuban Section, International Board on Books for Children. *Address:* Apartado 4061, Havana, 4, Cuba.

ELKHADEM, Saad Eldin Amin, b. 12 May 1932, Cairo, Egypt. Professor; Editor; Author. m. Madiha, 16 Aug. 1962, 1 daughter. *Education:* PhD, University of Graz, Austria, 1961. *Appointments:* President, International Fiction Association; Editor, International Fiction Review, 1974–; Editor, Authoritative Studies in World Literature, 1984–. *Publications:* Author, 7 Plays, 1965; Collection of Short Stories, 1967; 4 Novels, 1971, 1975, 1979, 1985, in Arabic; 7 scholarly books in German & English, 1969, 1970, 1973, 1976, 1978, 1981, 1985; 4 books translated from German into Arabic, 1966, 1967, 1969, 1971; Editor, 16 scholarly books. *Contributor to:* Al Ahram, Cairo; Bina al-Watan, Cairo; International Fiction Review, Canada; Canadian Review of Comparative Literature; Sabah al-Khayr, Cairo; Manuskript, Austria. *Membership:* International Fiction Association, President. *Address:* 96 Meadow Green Ct, Fredericton, NB, Canada E3B 5LB.

ELKINS, Thomas Henry, b. 3 Aug. 1926, London, England. Retired University Teacher. m. Dorothy Elkins, 1 son, 1 daughter. *Education:* BA, London University, 1950. *Publications:* Germany, 1960, revised edition, 1968, New York, 1968; The Urban Explosion, 1973; Translation of Ph Pincheinel's La France, with Dorothy Elkins. *Contributions to:* Numerous publications. *Address:* 2 Watergate Lane, Lewes, East Sussex BN7 1UG, England.

ELLERBECK, Rosemary (Anne L'Estrange), b. Cape Town, South Africa, Novelist. *Publications:* (As Nicola Thorne) Where the Rivers Meet, 1982; (As Katherine Yorke) A Woman's Place, 1983; The Pair Bond, 1984; (As Nicola Thorne) Affairs of Love, 1983; Never Such Innocence; The Enchantress Saga, 1985; Yesterday's Promises, 1986; (As Anne L'Estrange) Return to Wuthering Heights, 1976. *Membership:* PEN. *Literary Agent:* Richard Scott Simon Ltd. *Address:* 96 Townshend Court, Mackennal Street, London NW8 6LD, England.

ELLIOT, Alistair, b. 13 Oct. 1932, Liverpool, England. Poet; Verse-Translator. *Education:* MA Christ Church Oxford University, 1955. *Publications:* (poems): Contentions, 1977; Talking Back, 1982; On the Appian Way, 1984; (translations): Euripides' Alcestia, 1965; Aristophanes' Peace, 1965; Verlaine's Femmes/Hombres, 1979; Heine's The Lazarus Poems, 1979; Sophocles' The Oedipus Plays, 1986; Editor, Virgil's Georgics with Dryden's translation (parallel text with notes), 1981. *Contributions to:* Ten English Poets, Editor Michael Schmidt, 1979; The Greek Anthology, Editor Peter Jay, 1973; The Picador Book of Erotic Verse, Editor Alan Bold, 1978; magazines, journals and newspapers; BBC radio and TV. *Honours:* Arts Council of Great Britain Award, 1979 Ingram Merrill Foundation Award, 1983; Djerassi Foundation Fellow, 1984; Judge, EEC Verse Translation Competition, 1979.

Address: 27 Hawthorn Road, Newcastle-upon-Tyne, NE3 4DE, England.

ELLIOTT, Janice, b. 14 Oct. 1931, Derby, England. Novelist. *Education:* BA, St Anne's College, Oxford. *Publications:* Cave With Echoes, 1962; The Somnambulists, 1964; The Godmother, 1966; The Buttercup Chain, 1967; The Singing Head, 1968; Angels Falling, 1969; The Kindling, 1970; A State of Peace, 1971; Private Life, 1972; Heaven on Earth, 1975; A Loving Eye, 1977; The Honey Tree, 1978; Summer People, 1979; Secret Places, 1981; The Country of Her Dreams, 1982; Magic, 1983; The Italian Lesson, 1985; (children's books) The Birthday Unicorn, 1970; Alexander in the Land of Mog, 1973; The Incompetent Dragon, 1982. *Contributions to:* Numerous magazines and newspapers; collections of short stories; Reviewer, Sunday Telegraph, 1969–. *Honour:* Southern Arts Award for Literature (for novel Secret Places), 1981. *Memberships:* PEN; Society of Authors. *Literary Agent:* Richard Scott Simon. *Address:* c/o Hodder and Stoughton, 47 Bedford Square, London WC1B 3DP, England.

ELLIOTT, John Huxtable, b. 23 June 1930, Reading, Berkshire, England. Historian. *Education:* MA, 1955, PhD, 1955, Trinity College, Cambridge University. *Publications:* The Revolt of the Catalans, 1962; Imperial Spain 1469–1716, 1963; Europe Divided 1559–1598, 1968; The Old World and the New 1492–1650, 1970; A Palace for a King, with Jonathan Brown, 1980; Richelieu and Olivares, 1984; The Count-Dukes of Olivares, 1986. *Contributions to:* New York Review of Books. *Memberships:* Corresponding Fellow: Royal Academy of History, Madrid, Spain; Royal Academy of Letters, Seville, Fellow, American Academy of Arts and Sciences; FBA, 1972. *Address:* Institute for Advanced Study, Princeton, NJ 08540, USA.

ELLIOTT, Lawrence, b. 18 Jan. 1924, New York City, USA. Writer. m. Gisèle Suzanne Kayser, 19 July 1969, Paris, France, 1 son. *Education:* BSS, City College of New York, 1950. *Literary Appointments:* Associate Editor, Coronet Magazine, 1948–54; Freelance; Staff Writer, Reader's Digest, 1961–70; Roving Editor, Reader's Digest, 1970–. *Publications:* A Little Girl's Gift, 1963; George Washington Carver, 1966; On the Edge of Nowhere (with James Huntington), 1966; Journey to Washington (with Senator Daniel Inouye), 1967; The Legacy of Tom Dooley, 1969; I Will Be Called John (Biography of Pope John XXIII), 1973; The Long Hunter: A Life of Daniel Boone, 1976; Little Flower: The Life and Times of Fiorello La Guardia, 1983. *Contributions to:* Reader's Digest (over 150 articles) and similar number in other magazines and newspapers. *Honours:* Freedoms Foundation Medal, 1950; Alaska Press Club Award, Best Book 1966, On The Edge of Nowhere; German Jugenbuchpreis for biography of George Washington Carver, 1970. *Memberships:* Overseas Press Club of America; Anglo-American Press Club, Paris; Authors Guild. *Literary Agent:* Ronald P Sokol. *Address:* c/o Reader's Digest, 54 rue de Varenne, 75007, Paris, France.

ELLIS, Ella Thorp, b. 14 July 1928, Los Angeles, California, USA. *Education:* BA, University of California, Los Angeles, 1966; MA, San Francisco State University, 1975. *Publications:* Roam the Wild Country, 1967; Riptide, 1969; Celebrate the Morning, 1972; Where the Road Ends, 1974; Hallelujah, 1976; Hugo and the Princess Nena, 1983. Paperback editions: Roam the Wild Country, 1970; Riptide, 1971; Sleepwalker's Moon, 1980. *Honours:* Honor Book, for Roam the Wild Country, American Library Association; Celebrate the Morning, Junior Literary Guild Selection; Represented USA, Buenos Aires Book Fair, 1985. *Memberships:* Sierra Club; World Affairs Council of California; California Writers Club; American Civil Liberties Union; Audubon Society. *Literary Agent:* Julie Fallowfield, McIntosh and Otis. *Address:* 1438 Grizzly Peak Boulevard, Berkeley, CA 94708, USA.

ELLIS, Peter Berresford, b. 10 Mar. 1943, Coventry, England. Author. m. Dorothea P Cheesmur, Sep. 1966. *Appointments:* Chairman, Scrif Celt '85; Chairman, Scrif-Celt '86. *Publications include:* Over 40 books including, A History of the Irish Working Class, 1972; The Cornish Language and its Literature, 1974; A Voice from the Infinite, 1978; The Liberty Tree, 1981; The Last Adventurer, 1984; Celtic Inheritance, 1985; (as Peter Tremayne), The Lan-Kern Trilogy, 1980, 1983, 1983; Raven of Estiny, 1984; Angelus, 1985; (as Peter MacAlan), The Judas Battalion, 1983; Airship, 1984; The Confession, 1985, etc; Works translated into 10 languages. *Contributor to:* Numerous articles and short stories to professional journals. *Agent:* A M Heath & Co Ltd, London. *Address:* c/o A M Heath & Co Ltd, 40-42 William IV Street, London WC2N 4DD, England.

ELLIS, Royston, b. 10 Feb. 1941, Pinner, Middlesex, England. Author. *Appointments:* Assistant Editor, Jersey News & Features Agency, 1961–62; Associate Editor, The Canary Islands Sun, 1963–66; Editor, The Educator, Dominica, 1975; Managing Editor, Wordsman Ltd, Guernsey, 1976–84. *Publications:* Jiving to Gyp, 1959; Rave, Driftin' with Cliff, 1960; A Seaman's Suitcase, The Big Beat Scene, The Shadows By Themselves, 1961; The Mattress Flowers, Rebel, 1962;Myself for Fame, 1964; The Flesh Merchants, 1966; The Rush At the End, The Cherry Boy, 1967; The Bondmaster, 1977; Blood of the Bondmaster, 1978; Bondmaster Breed, 1979; Fleur, 1979; Bondmaster Fury, 1982; Bondmaster's Revenge, 1983; Bondmaster Buck, Master of Black River, 1984; Black River Affair, Black River Breed, Bloodheart, 1985; Bloodheart Royal, Bloodheart Feud, 1986. *Contributor to:* Institute of Small Business Guide to Import/Export; Generation X, 1965; Business Traveller (Asia/Pacific), 1983–. *Honours:* Croix de Valeur, Redonda, 1961; Dominica National Day Poetry Prizes, 1969, 1973. *Memberships:* Life Fellow, Royal Commonwealth Society; Institute of Journalists. *Agent:* Leslie Gardner Literary Agency Ltd, London. *Address:* PO Box 110, Roseau, Dominica, West Indies.

ELLISON, Eugenia Irene Adams, b. 28 Nov. 1916, Cadiz, Texas, USA. Teacher of English. m. James T Ellison, San Francisco, California, 21 Sep. 1942, 1 daughter. *Education:* BA, Tex A & I University, Kingsville; MA, University of Texas, Austin; Work completed for PhD, University of Texas, except dissertation. *Literary Appointments:* Teacher, Creative Writing. *Publications:* Teacher, Teacher, Don't Whip Me, 1955; Exiled Heart: The Ballad of Sam Houston, 1965; The Innocent Child in Dickens & Other Writers, 1982. *Contributions to:* The Grade Teacher Magazine; National Education Association Journal; The Texas Outlook; Our Navy; The Delta Kappa Gamma Journal; 1960 Yearbook, Poetry Society of Texas. *Honours & Literary Awards:* 1st Prize, poem, Night, Border Poets, Kingsville, Texas, 1933; 1st Prize, collection of lyrics, Fine Arts Colony, Corpus Christi, Texas, 1957; 1st Prize, poem, Defenders of the Alamo, Poetry Society of Texas, 1960; Several 1st prizes, Southwest Writers Conference, Corpus Christi. *Memberships:* Former member, Poetry Society of Texas; Fine Arts Colony, Corpus Christi. *Address:* 408 E. 10th Street, Bishop, TX 78343, USA.

ELLISON, Joan Audrey Anderson, b. 1928, Workington, Cumberland, England. Microbiologist; Assistant Lecturer; Food Consultant. *Education:* BSc, Queen Elizabeth College, London. *Publications:* The Great Scandinavian Cook Book (translator and editor), 1966; The Findus Book of Fish Cookery, 1968; Time-Life Foods of the World Series, 1969–70; The World Atlas of Food (contributing author), 1974; Vegetable Cook Book (with Clay Jones), 1978; Editor and Publisher, Norman Tucker, Musician, 1978; Contributing Author, Encyclopaedia of Herbs and Herbalism, 1979; Traditional British Cookery, 1980. *Memberships:* Society of Chemical Industry; Fellow, Institute of Food Science and Technology; Fellow, Linneon Society; Fellow, Institute of Home Economics; Nutrition Society; Guild of Food Writers; Institute of Journalists. *Address:* 74 Doneraile Street, London SW6 6EP, England.

ELLMANN, Richard, b. 15 Mar. 1918, Highland Park, Michigan, USA. University Professor. *Education:* BA; MA; PhD; Yale University; LittB, Trinity College, Dublin, Ireland; MA, Oxford; LittD (Hon), National University of Ireland; Several Hon. Doctorates. *Publications include:* Yeats: The Man and the Masks, 1948; The Identity of Yeats, 1954; James Joyce, 1959; Eminent Domain, 1968; Ulysses on the Liffay, 1972; Golden Codgers, 1974; The Consciousness of Joyce, 1977; Four Dubliners: Wilde, Yeats, Joyce and Beckett, 1986. *Honours:* National Book Award, 1959; Duff Cooper Prize, 1982; James Tait Black Prize, 1982. *Address:* 39 St Giles, Oxford OX1 3LW, England.

ELMAN, Richard, b. 23 Apr. 1939, New York City, USA. Writer. m. Alice Cooke, 9 Apr. 1979, Long Island, New York, 2 dughters. *Education:* BA, Syracuse University, 1955; MA, Stanford University, 1957. *Literary Appointments:* Professor, Creative Writing, columbia University, 1968–76; Professor, Creative Writing, Bennington College, 1966–68; Professor, Creative Writing, University of Pennsylvania, 1981–83. *Publications include:* A Coat for the Tsar, 1959; The Poorhouse State, 1966; The 28th Day of Elul, 1967; Freda and Slurl and the Kids, 1971; An Education in Blood, 1970; Cocktails at Somoza's; 1980. *Contributions to:* The Nation; New York Times Book Review; New Republic; Paris Review; Geo; atlantic; New Statesman; Commonweal; Oui; Trans-Atlantic Review; etc; Book reviewer, Nat Public Radio, 1979–84. *Honour:* Fellow, National Endowment for the Arts, 1974; Fellow, CAPS (New York), 1975. *Memberships:* PEN; Authors Guild; NBCC. *Literary Agent:* Roberta Pryor, New York City. *Address:* Box 216, Stony Brook, NY 11790, USA.

ELMSLIE, Kenward, b. 27 Apr. 1929, New York City, USA. Poet. *Education:* BA, Harvard College, 1950. *Publications:* Motor Disturbance, 1971; The Seagull, 1974; The Orchid Stories, 1975; Tropicalism, 1975; Washington Square, 1976; Moving Right Along, 1980; Bimbo Dirt, 1982. *Contributions to:* Poetry: The Paris Review; The Oxford Literary Review; The Partisan Review; Sun & Moon; Oink!; Mississippi Review; Barney; Kulchur; Art and Literature; Locus Solus; Penguin Modern Poets 24; Folder; Parnassus; Big Sky; Nomad; Poetry (Chigaco); Adventures in Poetry; Yale Literary Magazine. *Honour:* Frank O'Hara Poetry Award, 1971. *Memberships:* ASCAP; Dramatists Guild; Authors League, *Literary Agent:* Mitch Douglas, c/o ICM, 40W 57th Street, New York, NY 10018, USA. *Address:* Poets Corner, Calais, VT 05648, USA.

ELRICK, George Seefurth, b. 7 Oct. 1921, Evanston, Illinois, USA. Writer; Editor; Publisher. m. Marilyn Jean Wharton, 11 Jan. 1947, Chicago, 2 sons. *Education:* BS, Northwestern University, 1943. *Publications include:* Exciting Africa, 1965; Exotic Asia, 1965; Australia and Oceania, 1965; North America, 1966; The Bubble Gum Kid, 1967; Adventure in Alaska, 1967; Night of Terror, 1968; The Shabby Sheik, 1968; The Cheetah Caper, 1969; The Yellow Moth, 1970; Mission Possible: The Zenolta Leak Story, 1970; The Joyce Murff Story, 1971; The Emmett Stovel Story, 1972; The Dog Who Could Talk Business, 1972; Lassie and the Sasquatch, 1975; Spiderman Zaps Mr Zodiac, 1976; The Collected Works of Buck Rogers in the 25th Century, with Robert Dille, 1977; The Science Fiction Handbook, 1978; You Can Negotiate Anything, with Herb Cohen, 1980; Hearts and Dollars: How to Beat the High Cost of Falling In and Out of Love, co-author, 1983; A History of the Solomon Islands, 1946. *Contributions to:* Editorial Director, Abstract Publishing, Illinois; Field correspondent, Stars and Stripes, World War II; Former Editor, Holiday Inn Magazine and United Airlines Maxinliner Magazine. *Honours:* Included in Contemporary Authors. *Memberships:* Dickens Fellowship; Cakes and Ale Booksellers Club; Science Fiction Research Association; Past Editorial Board member, Classic Press Incorporated. *Literary Agent:* Carol DeChant. *Address:* 2136 Fir Street. Glenview, IL 60025, USA.

ELSBERG, John William, b. 4 Aug. 1945, New York City, New York, USA. History Book Editor. m. 1 son. *Education:* MA, Cantab. *Literary Appointments:* Editor and Publisher, Bogg magazine, UK and USA; Fellow, Virginia Center for the Creative Arts; The writer's Center, Glen Echo, Maryland. *Publications:* Home-Style Cooking on Third Avenue, 1982. *Contributions to:* Over 100 publications including: Orbis, UK; Outposts, UK; Tribune, UK; Poetry Now; Gargoyle; Porch; Real Poetry, Australia; Pierian Spring, Canada. *Membership:* Poetry Society of America. *Address:* 422 N Cleveland, Arlington, VA 22201, USA.

ELSEN, Albert Edward, b. 11 Oct. 1927, New York City, USA. Teacher. Scholar. *Education:* AB, 1949, MA, 1951, PhD, 1955, Columbia University, New York, USA. *Publications include:* Rodin's Gates of Hell, 1960; Purposes of Art, 1962, 3rd edition, 1972; Rodin, 1962; Auguste Rodin: Readings on His Life and Work, 1965; The Partial Figure in Modern Sculpture, Rodin to 1969; Seymour Lipton, 1972; The Sculpture of Henri Matisse, 1973; Paul Jenkins, 1973; Origins of Modern Sculpture, Pioneers and Premises, 1974; Modern European Sculpture, 1918–45, 1979; In Rodin's Studio, 1980; Rodin Rediscovered (editor), 1981; The Gates of Hell by Auguste Rodin, 1985; Rodin's Thinker and the Dilemma of Modern Public Sculpture, 1985. *Contributions to:* Art News; Art International, etc. *Honours include:* Senior Fellow, National Endowment Humanities, 1976; Distinguished Teaching Award, Stanford University, 1978–89. *Memberships:* The College Art Association of America Director 1966–70, Secretary 1970–72; Vice President 1972–74, President, 1974–present. *Address:* 10 Peter Coutts Circle, Stanford, CA 94305, USA.

ELSOM, John Edward, b. 31 Oct. 1934, Leigh-on-Sea, England. Author; Journalist. m. Sally Ann Mays, 3 Dec. 1955, Surrey, England, 2 sons. *Education:* BA (Hons), Cambridge, England. *Literary Appointments:* Senior Fellow, Gresham College, London, 1985–6. *Publications:* Theatre Outside London, 1971; Erotic Theatre, 1973; Post-War British Theatre, 1976 rev. 1979; The History of the National Theatre, 1978; Post-War British Theatre Criticism, 1980. *Contributions to:* Various newspapers, journals, etc. as theatre critic and general correspondent. *Memberships:* Chairman, British Section International Association of Theatre Critics: Vice President, IATC. *Literary Agent:* John McLaughlin, Campbell Thomson and McLaughlin. *Address:* 'Stella Maris', Anglesea Road, Kingston-upon-Thames, Surrey, KT1 2EW, England.

ELSTOB, Peter, b. 22 Dec. 1915, London, England. Author. *Education:* University of Michigan, USA. *Major Publications:* Warriors for the Working Day, 1960; The Armed Rehearsal, 1964; Hitler's Last Offensive (military history), 1971; Scoundrel, 1986. *Former Contributor to:* Numerous magazines & journals. *Memberships:* Savage Club; Society of Authors; Authors' Guild, New York, USA; Vice-President, International PEN; Garrick Club. *Address:* Burley Lawn House, Burley Lawn, Hampshire BH24 4AR, England.

ELY, Janina Meigs, b. 20 July 1944, Oakland, California, USA. Editor; Writer. *Education:* BA English, University of California, Davis, 1967; Non degree training programme in biomedical editing/publishing/writing, University of Texas M D Anderson Hospital and Tumor Institute, Houston, 1968–70. *Literary Appointments:* Programmer, TV Guide magazine, Washington DC, 1964: Assistant Editor, Publications Department, University of Texas M D Anderson Hospital and Tumor Institute, Houston, 1968–70; Editor II, Publications Department, UCLA Latin American Center, 1971–72; Technical Editor, NW Regional Educational Laboratory, Portland, 1973–76; Science Editor, Oregon Regional Primate Research Center, Beaverton, 1976–. *Contributions to:* The Cal Aggie; M D Anderson Hospital and Tumor Institute Hospital Newsletter; Editorial Consultant, Primate News, 1976–. *Memberships:* Council of Biology Editors; American Medical Writers Association; Senior member,

Scoeity for Technical Communication. *Address:* Post Office Box 1072, Beaverton, OR 97075, USA.

EMANUEL, James Andrew, b. 15 June 1921, Alliance, Nebraska, USA. University Professor (retired). m. Mattie Etha Johnson, 1 Oct. 1950, Chicago, Illinois, divorced 1974, 1 son, (deceased). *Education:* BA, Howard University, Washington DC, 1946–50; MA, Northwestern University, Evanston, Illinois, 1950–53; PhD, Columbia University, New York City, 1953–62. *Literary Appointments:* Instructor 1957–62, Assistant Professor, 1962–70, Associate Professor, 1970–72, Professor of English, 1972–84, City College of the City University of New York; Fulbright Professor of American Literature, University of Grenoble, France, 1968–69, University of Warsaw, Poland, 1975–76; Visiting Professor of American Literature, University of Toulouse, France, 1971–73, 1979–81. *Major publications:* Langston Hughes, 1967; Dark Symphony: Negro Literature in America, 1968; Black Man Abroad: The Toulouse Poems, 1978; A Chisel in the Dark: Poems Selected & New, 1980; A Poet's Mind, 1983; The Broken Bowl (New & Uncollected Poems), 1983. *Contributor to:* American Speech, Books Abroad, Black World, Negro Digest, Black Expression, The Black Aesthetic, Modern Black Poets,Dictionary of American Negro Biography, and many others. *Honours:* John Hay Whitney Foundation Opportunity Fellowship, 1952–54; Eugene F Saxton Memorial Trust Fellowship, 1964–65; Flame Magazine Award for sonnet, 1958; Black American Literature Forum Award for poems, 1980. *Address:* c/o Department of English, City College of CUNY, Coinvent Avenue at 138th Street, New York, NY 10031, USA.

EMANUEL, Lynn Collins, b. 14 Mar. 1949, New York, USA. Associate Professor of English. m. Jeffrey Hugh Schwartz, 4 Oct. 1975, Pittsburgh. *Education:* BA, Bennington College, 1972; MA, City College of New York, 1975; MFA, The University of Iowa, 1983. *Literary Appointments:* Associate Professor, Department of English, University of Pittsburgh. *Publications:* Hotel Fiesta, 1984. *Contributions to:* Magazines and Journals including: The American Poetry Review; The Georgia Review; The Morrow Anthology of Younger American Poets; Poetry. *Honours include:* The John Atherton Scholarship in Poetry, Bread Loaf Writers' Conference, Middlebury College, Vermont, 1980; Flora Strosse Memorial Award, University of Nebraska at Lincoln, 1980; Pennsylvania Council on the Arts Fellowship, 1981; National Endowment for the Arts Fellowship, 1984; The Great Lakes Associated Colleges Award for Poetry, 1985. *Memberships:* The Academy of American Poets; The Poetry Society of America. *Address:* 4017 Windsor Street, Pittsburgh, PA 15217, USA.

EMERY, John Cameron, b. 19 Feb. 1947, Cairns, Australia. Writer. m. Audrey Joan Rau, 18 July 1969, Canberra, 1 son, 1 daughter. *Education:* BA, Library Studies, SAIT. *Appointments:* Chairman, Writers Week, Adelaide Festival of Arts, 1984. *Publications:* Summer Ends Now, 1980; The Sky People, 1984. *Contributor to:* Numerous magazines and journals, Australia, UK, USA, Kiev. *Honours:* National Short Story of the Year, Australia, 1974; Awgie Award, Best Childrens TV Adaptation, 1984. *Memberships:* Australian Society of Authors; Executive Committee, Australian Writers Guild, 1979–84. *Address:* 59 Sparks Terrace, Rostrevor, South Australia 5073, Australia.

EMILSSON, Tryggvi, b. 20 Oct. 1902, Akureyri, Iceland. Worker. m. Steinunn Gudrún Jónsdóttir, 28 June 1925, 2 daughters. *Publications:* Poetry; Rimud ljod, rhymed poetry, 1967; Ljodmaeli, 1971. *Memoirs:* Fataekt folk (poor people), 3rd edition 1980; Barattan um braudid (The struggle for bread), 3rd edition 1980; Fyrir sunnan (In the south), 2nd edition 1980. Translated, German, Novel & short stories, Kona sjomannsins (The fisherman's wife), 1981. *Contributions to:* Various Icelandic magazines, anticles & essays. *Honours:* Dagsbrun Literary Award & Medal of Honour, Trade Unions, 1977; Designated, Literary Award, Nordic Council, 1977, 1978. *Membership:*

Writers Union of Iceland. *Literary Agent:* Mal og menning, Laugavegi 181 101 Reykjavik, Iceland. *Address:* Safamyri 56, 108 Reykjavik, Iceland.

EMMET, Dorothy Mary, b. 29 Sep. 1904, London, England. University Professor (retired). *Education:* BA, Lady Margaret Hall, Oxford, 1927; AM, Radclife College, Cambridge, Massachusetts, USA. *Appointment:* Editor, Theoria to Theory, 1966–81. *Publications:* Whitehead's Philosophy of Organism, 1932; The Nature of Metaphysical Thinking, 1946; Function, Purpose and Power, 1957; Roles, Rules and Relatives, 1965; The Moral Prism, 1979; The Effectiveness of Causes, 1984. *Contributions to:* Mind; Philosophy; Proceedings of Aristotelian Society, etc. *Honours:* Hon D Litt, Glasgow, 1974, Leicester, 1976. *Address:* 11 Millington Road, Cambridge, England.

EMMOTT, William John, b. 6 Aug. 1956, London, England. Journalist. m. Charlotte Andrea Crowther, 17 Apr. 1982, Brussels, Belgium.*Education:* BA, Honours, Oxford University; PPE. *Literary Appointments:* Staff Writer, The Economist, 1980–; Variously Brussels, Economics, Tokyo Corespondent, ibid. *Publication:* The Pocket Economist, with Rupert Pennant-Rea, 1983. *Address:* The Economist, Nikkei Building 8F, 1-9-5 Otemachi, Chiyoda-ku, Tokyo 100, Japan.

EMRY, Douglas Kriss, b. 19 Sep. 1938, Topeka, Kansas, USA. Publisher; Writer. m. Juanita Pearl Blackwood (div.), 1 son, 1 daughter. *Education:* Studies, Economics & Accounting, San Diego State College. *Publications include:* Collection, short stories & poetry, 1984; Writer, West magazine, West Books, California. *Contributions also to:* San Diego Business Journal. *Memberships:* President, Linda Vista Branch, Friends of the Library; San Diego Writers & Editors Guild. *Address:* P O Box 16097, San Diego, CA 92116, USA.

EMSLEY, Clive, b. 4 Aug. 1944, London, England. Historian. m. Jennifer Elizabeth Noble, 28 Mar. 1970, Brighouse, Yorkshire, 1 son, 1 daughter. *Education:* BA Honours, York University, 1966; MLitt, Cambridge University, 1970. *Literary Appointments:* General Editor, Themes in Comparative History, Macmillan, 1979–. *Publications:* British Society and the French Wars 1793–1815, 1979; Policing and its Context: 1750–1870, 1983. *Contributions to:* English Historical Review; History Today; History; Social History. *Honour:* Fellow, Royal Historical Society, 1982. *Address:* Faculty of Arts, The Open University, Walton Hall, Milton Keynes MK7 6AA, England.

ENCKELL, Martin Olof Toussaint, b. 8 Jan. 1954, Helsinki, Finland. Poet. *Publications:* Kristalltårar, 1974; Ingen & Den Knottriga Damen, with Johan Donner, 1978; Sortie, 1979; Pravda-Love, 1983. *Contributor to:* Fågel Fenix; Otid; BLA. *Membership:* Finlands Svenska Författareförening. *Address:* Eino Leinonkatu 2 B 30, 00250 Helsinki, Finland.

ENGEL, Howard, b. 2 Apr. 1931, Toronto, Canada. Writer. m. (1) Marian Passmore, 27 Jan. 1962, London, England (2) Janet Evelyn Hamilton, 9 Jun. 1978, Kleinberg, Ontario, Canada, 1 son, 1 daughter. *Education:* BA 1954, Secondary School Teaching Certificate, 1955, McMaster University, Hamilton, Ontario, Canada. *Major publications:* The Suicide Murders, 1980; The Ransom Game, 1981; Murder on Location, 1982; Murder Sees the Light, 1984. *Contributor to:* Tamarack Review; Queen's Quarterly; Books in Canada; Toronto Globe & Mail; Toronto Star. *Membership:* Founding Member, Crime Writers of Canada (currently Membership Chairman). *Literary Agent:* Beverley Slopen, Toronto, Canada. *Address:* 281 Major Street, Toronto, Ontario, M5S 2L5, Canada.

ENGELHARDT, M Veronice (Sister), b. 29 Mar. 1912, Syracuse, New York, USA. Educator; Psychologist. *Education:* BS Education; MA Psychology; MA Education; PhD Higher Education, Educational Psychology and Psychology; Postgraduate work in Reading, Administration and Psychology. *Publications:* Science series for Catholic elementary grades: Learning About God's World; Creatures in God's World; Learning More About God's World; Songs About God's World songbook, (co-author); Community's Jubilee Books, (author and editor), 1978, 1979 and 1980. *Contributions to:* Community's Newsletter (and editor). *Memberships:* National League of American Pen Women. *Honours include:* Notable American Award, 1976–77. *Address:* St Anthony Convent and Motherhouse, Syracuse, NY 13208, USA.

ENGELMANN,, Ruth Marie (née Gould), b. 6 Nov. 1919, Hurley, Wisconsin, USA. Fiction Writer. m. Hugo Engelmann, 24 Oct. 1941, Madison, Wisconsin, USA. 1 son. *Education:* BA, 1943, MA, 1944, University of Wisconsin. *Literary Appointments:* Instructor in English, Michigan State University 1945–47; Instructor in English, University of Wisconsin, 1949–51; Editorial Work & Private Tutoring in English, 1951–64; Instructor in Creative Writing, Adult Education Program, University of Wisconsin, 1965–67; Editorial Work, 1968–. *Major Publication:* Leaf House, 1982, also published in Finnish as, Lehtimaja. *Contributor to:* Partisan Review; Readings & Reviews; Literary Half-Yearly; DePaul Literary Magazine; Saturday Review. *Address:* 421 West Hillcrest Drive, DeKalb, IL 60115, USA.

ENGH, Jeri, b. 28 Apr. 1938, Ossining, New York, USA. Writer. m. Rohn Engh, 23 Jan. 1960, Tepoztlan, Mexico, 2 sons. *Education:* BA, Mount Holyoke College, 1959. *Literary Appointments:* Editor, Apple River Journal, 1975; Editorial Director, Photoletter, 1980, Photosource International 1982–. *Publications:* Co-author, A Very Simple Garden Book, 1977, Sell & Resell Your Photos, 1980. *Contributions to:* Saturday Review; Reader's Digest; Redbrook; Parents Magazine; Christian Science Monitor; Kiwanis Magazine; Chicago Tribune; Ford Times; Today's Health; Woman's Day; Parade Mademoiselle. *Honours:* Freedom Foundation Award, 1963; Bolex Film Script Award, 1964; Centennial Award, Mount Holyoke College. 1974. *Memberships:* Current, American Society of Journalists & Authors; Formerly, Society of American Travel Writers. *Address:* Pine Lake Farm, Osceola, WI 54020, USA.

ENGLISH, John Wesley, b. 5 Oct. 1940, Kansas, USA. Professor of Journalism, Freelance Writer. *Education:* ABJ, University of Tulsa, 1962; MSJ Graduate School of Journalism, Columbia University, 1966; PhD, Union Graduate School, 1977. *Literary Appointments include:* Copy Editor and arts critic, Wisconsin State Journal, 1968–69; Professor, University of Georgia, School of Journalism, 1970–; Editor and Publisher, Contemporary Art/Southeast, Atlanta, Georgia, 1979–80. *Publications:* Criticising The Critics, 1979; Georgia Legal Services Program: The First Decade, 1981; Foto Berita Malaysia, 1983; When Men Were Boys, 1985; Chapters in 4 books; Feature films: The Secret of Nikola Tesla, 1980; Pertama, 1982. *Contributions to:* Contemporary Art/Southeast; IPI Report, London; United Press International; Atlanta; Atlanta Weekly; American Film; New York Times; The Quill; Village Voice; Gazette, Amsterdam. *Honour:* Silver Gavel Award, Georgia Bar Association, 1981. *Memberships:* American Society of Journalists and Authors; Society of Professional Journalists, SDX. *Address:* 565 Prince Avenue, Athens, GA 30601, USA.

ENRIGHT, Dennis Joseph, b. 11 Mar 1920, Leamington Spa, England. Writer. m. Madeleine Harders, 3 Nov. 1949, Alexandria Egypt, 1 daughter. *Education:* BA, MA, Cambridge University; D Litt, Alexandria, Egypt. *Literary Appointments:* Co-editor, Encounter 1970–72; Director, Chatto and Windus/The Hogarth Press, Publishers, 1973–82. *Publications:* Memoirs of a Mendicant Professor 1969; Shakespeare and the Students 1970; Collected Poems 1981; A Mania for Sentences 1983; Editor: The Oxford Book of Death 1983; Instant Chronicles 1985. *Contributor to:* The Listener; The Observer; Times Literary Supplement; New York Review of Books etc. *Honours:* Queen's Gold

Medal for Poetry, 1981; Doctor of Letters (honoris
cansa) University of Warwick, 1982, D Univ. University
of Surrey, 1985. *Membership:* Fellow, Royal Society of
Literature. *Literary Agent:* Watson, Little Ltd. *Address:*
35A Viewfield Road, London SW18 5JD, England.

ENSLER, Eve, b. 25 May 1953, New York City, USA.
Writer; Playwright; Poet; Peace Activist. m. Richard
McDermott, 15 Sep. 1979, 1 stepson. *Education:* BA,
Middlebury College. *Appointment:* Editor, Central Park
Magazine. *Publications:* Plays Produced: When I Call
My Voices, 1979; Rendezvous, 1983. *Contributor to:*
Over 25 magazines including Chicago Review; Win
Magazine; The Third Wind; Peace or Perish: A Crisis
Anthology. *Honour:* Art of Peace, Poetry, 1984.
Address: 16 West 16th Street 14 SN, New York, NY
10011, USA.

ENSOR, Alick Charles Davidson, b. 27 Nov. 1906,
Sheerness, England. Retired Solicitor and Member of
Parliament; Author; Farmer; Journalist. *Education:*
Westminster School; Law Society School of Law.
Publications: Thirty Acres and A Cow, 1954; I Was a
Public Prosecutor, 1958; Verdict Afterwards, 1960;
With Lord Roberts through the Khyber Pass, 1966.
Contributions to: All national daily newspapers, many
provincial newspapers and many magazines. Films
include: The Trials of Oscar Wilde; The Pot Carriers;
Death in the Sky Above. *Honours:* Member of
Parliament, 1964–70; Member, Estimates Committee,
1964–69; Chairman, Committee on Catering in the
House of Commons, 1969–70; Chairman, Private Bills
Committee, 1965–69. *Address:* 107 l'Etoile d'Or, 66701
Argeles sur Mer, France.

ENYEART, James Lyle, b. 13 Jan. 1943, Auburn,
Washington, USA. Administrator. m. Roxanne Malone,
7 Sep. 1964, Topeka, 3 daughters. *Education:* BFA,
Kansas City Art Institute, 1965; MFA, University of
Kansas, 1972. *Publications:* Francis Bruguiere, 1977;
Heinecken, Editor, 1980; Jerry Uelsmann: Twenty-five
Years, 1982; Edward Weston's California Landscapes,
1984; Judy Dater: Twenty Years, 1986. *Contributor to:*
The History of Photography; American Photographer;
Exposure; Journal of the Royal Photographic Society of
Great Britain; Book Review, Steichen, The Master
Printer, for, The History of Photography, 1979.*Honours:*
Fellowship, Organisation of American States, 1966–67;
National Humanities Faculty, 1971–72, 1976–77;
Honorary Research Fellow, University of Exeter,
England, 1974; National Endowment for the Arts
Grants, 1973, 1974, 1975. *Address:* c/o Centre for
Creative Photography, 843E University Blvd, Tucson,
AR 85719, USA.

EPPARD, Philip B(lair), b. 13 Jan. 1945,
Cumberland, Maryland, USA. Archivist. *Education:* AB,
Lafayette College, 1967; MA, Andover Newton
Theological Scool, 1973; PhD, Brown University, 1979;
MS, Simmons College, 1984. *Appointments:* Curatorial
Associate in Manuscripts, Andover-Harvard Theological
Library, Harvard Divinity School, 1979–81; Archivist,
Joel Dean Papers, Baker Library, Harvard Business
School, 1981–83; Survey Archivist,Harvard College
Library, 1984–. *Publications include:* Introduction,
Views of Christian Nurture, Horace Bushnell, 1975; Co-
author, Guide to the Atlantic Monthly Contributors Club,
1983. *Contributions to:* American Women Writers:
Bibliographical Essays, 1983; Critical Essays on Sarah
Orne Jewett, 1984; First printings of American Authors,
1977–79. Henry Adams and Diaries of John Hay, in
Books at Brown, 1982–83; John O'Hara in the New
Masses, in John O'hara Journal, 1982–83; Mark Twain
dissects an overrated book, in, American Literature,
1977. Others in: Recources for American Literary Study;
Papers of the Bibliographical Society of America;
American Literary Realism; etc. *Memberships:*
Bibliographical Society of America; Phi Beta Kappa.
Address: 136 Irving Street, Cambridge, MA 02138,
USA.

EPSTEIN, Ellen Robinson, b. 2 Sep. 1947,
Washington, DC, USA. Writer; Historian. m. David
Epstein, 15 Aug. 1971, Washington, 3 sons, 2
daughters. *Education:* BA, Connecticut College, USA,
1969. *Publications:* Record and Remember: Tracing
Your Roots Through Oral History, 1978; The Bar/Bat
Mitzvah Planbook, 1982. *Contributions:* Records of the
Columbia Historical Society, The East and West Wings
of the White House, Washington DC, 1971–72.
Address: 7507 Wyndale Road, Chevy Chase, MD
20815, USA.

ERDRICH, Louise, b. 7 June 1954, Little Falls,
Minnesota, USA. Novelist. m. Michael Dorris, 10 Oct.
1981, Cornish, New Hampshire, 2 sons, 3 daughters.
Education: BA, Dartmouth College, New Hampshire,
1976; MA, Johns Hopkins University, 1979.
Publications: Jacklight (poems), 1984; Love Medicine
(novel), 1984; The Best Queen (novel), 1986.
Contributions to: Atlantic Monthly; The Paris Review;
Ms; Antaeus; Mother Jones; North American Review;
Formations; Kenyon Review; Georgia Review; Chicago;
Mississippi Valley Review; Woman; Redbook; New
America. *Honours:* Nelson Algren Award, 1981; NEA
Fellowship, 1983; National Book Critics Circle for
Fiction, 1984; Sue Kaufman Prize for First Fiction,
American Academy, 1984; American Book Award,
1984; Scully Prize, 1984; Great Lakes College Prize,
1984; Los Angeles Times Award for Fiction,
1985.*Memberships:* Board Member, PEN; Authors
Guild. *Literary Agent:* Michael Dorris. *Address:* c/o
Michael Dorris, PO Box 70, Cornish Flat, NH 03746,
USA.

ERICHSEN Eli Store, b. 23 Jan. 1894, Mosjoen,
Norway. Housewife. *Publications:* Eventyr og historier
for barn, 1942; Istrollene, 1947; Ole Jakobs tur til
Finnmark, 1948; Ole Jakob oppdager Island, 1950;
Eventyret om Sildine, 1956; Signe I del, 1965; Signes
nye verden 2 del, 1967; Signe og Signore 3 del, 1970;
Tine, Tom og Trine, 1969; Oldemors Visebok, 1976.
Contributor to: Fairytales to Magazines: articles to
newspapers. *Honours:* Recipient, 2 prizes from
Department of Education for children's books, 1965 and
1970. *Memberships:* Ungdomslitteraturens Forfatterlag.
Address: Majorstuveien 25 b, Oslo 3, Norway.

ERICSSON, Ronald James, b. 17 July 1935, Belle
Fourche, South Dakota, USA. President, Commercial
Biotechnology Firm. m. Jean Marie Hodge, 19 Aug.
1956, 1 son, 1 daughter. *Education:* BS, Colorado State
University, 1953–57; MS 1961, PhD 1964, University
of Kentucky; Postdoctoral Fellow, University of
Wisconsin, 1963–64. *Publications:* Getting Pregnant in
the 1980's: New Advances in Infertility Treatment and
Sex Presolection, (with Robert Glass), 1982; 7 patents
as inventor or co-inventor; 66 publications in medical-
biological journals and textbooks. *Memberships:*
American Association for the Advancement of Science;
American Association of Tissue Banks; American
Society of Andrology; Association for the Study of
Animal Behaviour; Endocrine Society; Society for the
Advancement of Contraception; Society for Exper-
imental Biology and Medicine; Society for the Study of
Fertility; Society for the Study of Reproduction.
Address: Gametrics Limited, Colony Route, Alzada, MT
59311, USA.

ERKELIUS, Per Agne, b. 1 July 1935, Hofors,
Sweden. Writer. m. Kerstin M Lundberg, 22 Apr. 1975,
Sigtuna, Sweden. 1 son, 3 daughters. *Publications:*
Staderna vid havet, 1961; Cirkeln, 1963; Processen mot
Egil, 1966; Amatorerna, 1970; Hemma i Sverige, 1972;
Final for otrogna, 1974; Fotografen, 1976; Drommen
om Johannes, 1978; Resan till Kristin, 1980; Min svager
och jag, 1983; Minnet av Nanny, 1985 (novels).
Contributions to: Dagens Nyheter. *Membership:* PEN,
Board Member. *Address:* Mardstigen 8, S–171 71
Solna, Sweden.

ERNE, Nino, b. 31 Oct. 1921, Berlin, German Republic.
Writer. *Education:* University studies in philosophy,
languages, literature, art; PhD. *Publications:* Der
sinnende Bettler, 1947; Kunst der Novelle, 1956;
Junger Mann in der Stadtbahn, 1959; Monolog des

Foschkönigs, 1966; Murmelpoeme, 1967; Italien süss und sauer, 1975; Nachruf auf Othello, 1976; Kellerkneipe und Elfenbeinturm, 1979; Fahrgäste, 1981; Rom – ein Tag, eine Nacht, 1982; Vorschlag zur Güte, 1984. *Contributor to:* TV; ZDF. *Honours:* Die Zukunft Novel Prize; Arts Prize for Literature, Rhineland-Palatinate, 1979. *Memberships:* PEN Club; German Writers' Association; ETA Hoffmann Society; German Journalists' Association. *Address:* Ebersheimer Weg 37, 6500 Mainz, Federal Republic of Germany.

ERNST, Eldon G, b. 27 Jan. 1939, Seattle, Washington, USA. Professor. m. Jay S, 12 June 1959, Seattle, 4 sons, 1 daughter. *Education:* BA Linfield College; BD, Colgate Rochester Divinity School; MA; PhD, Yale University. *Literary Appointments:* Editor, Foundations, 1975–77; Editor, GTU Library Bulletin, 1983–. *Publications:* Moment of Truth for Protestant America: In Ten Church Campaigns following World War I, 1974; Without Help or Hindrance: Religious Identity in American Culture, 1977. *Contributor to:* Ethics and Policy, 1983; Articles in, Foundations; Church History; Journal of Presbyterian History; Action/Reaction; GTU Library Bulletin; Chapters in, Understanding The New Religions, Editors: J Needleman and G Baker, 1978; In The Great Tradition, Editors: J Ben and P Dekar, 1982; A Guide to The History of California, Editors: D Nunis and G Lothrop, 1986; Encyclopedia of Religion in America, Editors: C Lippy and P Williams, 1986. *Honourt:* Howd Sociology Prize, Linfield College, 1961. *Memberships:* American Academy of Religion, President, Western Region; American Society of Church History. *Address:* 1855 San Antonio Avenue, Berkeley, CA, USA.

ERON, Carol Lehman, b. 11 Jan. 1945, Pennsylvania, USA. Writer. m. Lawrence Eron, 2 Jan. 1967, 1 son, 2 daughters. *Education:* BA, Douglass College, 1966. *Publication:* The Virus That Ate Cannibals, 1981. *Contributions to:* The Washington Post; International Herald-Tribune; Boston Globe; New York Post; The Phoenix; Public Health Reports. *Membership:* Washington Independent Writers. *Literary Agent:* Theron Raines,New York. *Address:* Hamilton Spring Court, Bethesda, MD 20817, USA.

ESCARPIT, Robert, b. 24 Apr. 1918, Saint-Macaire, France. Professor (retired). m. Denise Dupont, 22 Aug. 1942, Bordeaux, France, 1 son, 2 daughters. *Education:* Alumnus of the Ecole Normale Supérieure, 1938; Graduate Teacher of English Certificate, 1942; Doctorate of Letters, 1952. *Major Publications:* Rudyard Kipling, 1955; Lord Byron, 1957; Sociologie de la Littérature, 1958; Peinture fraîche, 1960; L'humour, 1960; Hemingway, 1963; Le Littératron, 1964; La Révolution du Livre, 1965; Lettre ouverte à Dieu, 1968; Les Contes de Saint Glinglin, 1973; Appelez-moi Thérèse, 1976; Théorie générale de l'information et de la Communication, 1976; Les reportages de Rouletabosse, 1978; Le jeune homme et la nuit, 1979; Les voyages d'Hazembat, Marin de Gascogne, 1984; Le Prisonnier de Trafalgar, 1985. *Contributor to:* Le Monde (daily columnist), 1949–80; Sud-Ouest-Dimanche (weekly columnist). *Honours:* Edouard Herriot Prize, 1958 Grand Prix for Humour, 1960; Literary Grand Prix, City of Bordeaux, 1967; International Prize for Peace, 1967; International Maritime Prize, 1984; Aigue Marine Prize, 1985; Honorary Doctorate, Universities of Brussels (Belgium) and Loughborough (England). *Membership:* Society of Men of Letters, Paris, France. *Address:* 7 Avenue des Chasseurs, 33600 Pessac, France.

ESHRAW, Ra, b. 1926. Metaphysical Writer and Painter. *Education:* Academie de la Grande Chaumiere, Paris, France, 1954–56; Ecole des Beaux Arts, Paris, 1955–56; Academie Ranson, Paris, 1956. *Publications:* Vox Humana, 1967; Homo Cosmicus, 1970; Ad Astra, 1973; Intergalactic Revelation, 1975; The Bermuda Triangle (A Teleportation Chamber of the Gods), 1975; Planet in the Sun, 1977; Souvenir of Atlantis, 1979; The Creators, 1980; Timetraveller, 1981; The Jupiter Effect, 1983; Universal Love, 1984; The Surveyors, 1985.

Honour: Statue of Victory Award, World Culture Prize for 1985; Centro Stodi E Ricerthe Delle Nazioni, Accademia Italia, Italy, 1985. *Membership:* Centro Studi e Ricerche Delle Nazioni, Italy. *Address:* Hägur, Eksta, 62020 Klintehamn, Sweden.

ESKENAZY SABBADINI, Sarita, b. 1 Jan. 1927, Madrid, Spain. Writer. m. Bruno Sabbadini, 21 Jan. 1946, Milan, Italy, 1 son, 1 daughter. *Education:* Classical Studies, Milan. *Publications:* Le Courage du Bonheur, 1984; El Coraje de la Dicha. *Membership:* Societe Gens de Lettres, Paris. *Literary Agent:* Milan; Barcelona. *Address:* Rue des Vergers 9, 3965 Chiffus; Switzerland.

ESKOW, Dennis M, b. 8 Sep. 1946, Weehawken, New Jersey, USA. Writer, Editor. m. 22 Oct. 1967, at Bradley Beach, New Jersey, 1 son, 3 daughters. *Literary Appointments:* Freelance music critic and entertainment writer, 1969–73; Poet, New Creation Anthology, 1974 and 1976; Science Writer, AP Broadcasting, 1974–76; Playwright, Raft Theatre, New York, 1980; Science Editor, Popular Mechanics magazine, 1981–. *Honours:* Fellow American Political Science Association, 1971; Transition Award for Best Science Story, 1975. *Membership:* National Association of Science Writers. *Address:* 224 W 57th Street, New York, NY 10019, USA.

ESLER, Anthony James, b. 20 Feb. 1934, West Mystic, Connecticut, USA. Novelist; Historian. m. Carol Eaton Clemeau, 17 June 1961, Glen Ellyn, Illinois, 2 sons. *Education:* BA, University of Arizona, Tucson, 1956; MA, 1958, PhD, 1961, Duke University. *Publications:* The Aspiring Mind of the Elizabethan Younger Generation, 1966; Bombs, Beards, and Barricades, 1971; The Youth Revolution, 1974; Castlemayne, 1974; Hellbane, 1975; Lord Libertine, 1976; Forbidden City, 1977; The Freebooters, 1979; Babylon, 1980; Bastion, 1980; Generations in History, 1982; The Generation Gap, 1984; The Human Venture, 1985; (in press). *Contributions:* Articles and reviews to scholarly journals. *Membership:* Authors Guild. *Literary Agent:* Scott Meredith Literary Agency. *Address:* 1523 Jamestown Road, Williamsburg, VA 23185, USA.

ESPAILLAT, Rhina Polonia, b. 20 Jan. 1932, Dominican Republic. Former High School Teacher of English. m. Alfred Moskowitz, 28 June 1952, 3 sons. *Education:* BA, Hunter College; MSE, Queen's College. *Major Publications:* Poems included in following Anthologies: Riverside Poetry, 1953; Hymns for Children & Grown-ups, 1953; The Golden Year, 1960; The Muse Anthology, 1962; Parthenon Anthology, Black Washed & Ghost Bright, 1981; Modern Lyrics Anthology, 1982; Lyrical Treasures Classic & Modern, 1983; Chester H Jones Poetry Competition Winners Anthology, 1984. *Contributor to:* Ladies Home Journal; Woman; Home Chat; Poetry Chap Book; The Lyric; Encore; Voices International; Commonweal; Poet Lore; The Poetry Review; Blue Unicorn; North American Mentor Magazine; Plains Poetry Journal; Moonlight Review; High Points; Manhattan Poetry Review. *Honours:* Various commendations for poetry. *Memberships:* Poetry Society of America; The Shelley Society; Women Poets of New York. *Address:* 72-04 162nd Street, Flushing, NY 11365, USA.

ESPINO, Federico Junior, b. 10 Apr. 1939, Pasig, Rizal, Philippines. Journalist. *Education:* Bachelor of Literature, Journalism, Faculty of Philosophy and Letters, University of Santo Tomas, 1959. *Literary Appointment:* Poet of the Year, Institute of National Language, Metro Manila, Philippines, 1967. *Publications:* Lightning Road: Pararrayos, Bilingual Edition, 1980; Rhapsody on Thames of Brecht, Racto and Others (poems and plays), 1983; Lady Macbeth: A Black Symphony in Three Movements, 1983. *Contributions to:* Hemisphere, Australia; International Portland Review, Portland, USA (poems). *Honours:* First Prize in Tagalog Poetry, Palanca Award, 1967; First Prize in English Poetry, Palanca Award, 1969; Premin de Poesia Ramon de Basterra, Bilbao, Spain, 1977.

Memberships: Catholic Writers Guild, President, 1959; University of Santo Tomas, Espana, Metro Manila. *Address:* 178 M H del Pilar, Palatiw Kaliwa, Pasig, Metro Manila, Philippines.

ESPOSITO, Joseph L, b. 2 Nov. 1941, New Haven, Connecticut, USA. Philosophy Professor. m. (1) Nancy Giller Esposito, June 1967, (2) Maddalena Florillo, 12 Dec. 1977. 1 son. *Education:* BS Chemistry, Fairfield University, 1960; MA Philosophy 1967, PhD Philosophy 1970, New York University; JD Law, University of Arizona, 1986. *Publications:* Schelling's Idealism and Philosophy of Nature, 1977; Evolutionary Metaphysics, 1980; The Transcendence of History, 1984; The Obsolete Self: Philosophical Dimensions of Aging, 1986. *Contributions to:* Numerous articles to scholarly publications in philosophy. *Honour:* Academic Achievement Founders Day Award, New York University, 1970. *Memberships:* American Philosophical Association; Hegel Society; Charles S Peirce Society; Society for the Advancement of American Philosophy. *Address:* 1817 E Tenth Street, Tucson, AZ 85719, USA.

ESPY, Richard, b. 4 Sept. 1952, Denver, Colorado, USA. Writer. m. Monica Friedman, 8 July, 1978. *Education:* BA Social Sciences, University of the Pacific; Master of International Studies, Claremont Graduate School. *Major Publications:* The Politics of the Olympic Games, 1979; Epilogue to the former, 1981. *Address:* 324 N Francisca apt 3, Redondo Beach, CA 90277, USA.

ESSEN-HOLMQVIST, von Barbro Elsa, b. 30 Sep. 1915, Jakobstad, Finland, Dispenser and Pharmacist. m. Lars Robert Holmqvist, 9 Apr. 1950, 2 sons 1 daughter. *Education:* Graduated in Pharmacy, University of Helsinki, 1938. *Publications:* poems in anthologies: (Svenska Österbottens Litteraturför) 1972, 1978, 1982 (Författarnas Fredsanth) Poems: I jordiska labyrinter 1974, Så fjärrsynt ler mitt hjärta, 1975 (Författarnas Andelslag), Stum stiger frågan (Maskrosorna) 1976, Två strängar på min luta-Kaksi on viulussa kieltä (Horisont) 1979 (in Swedish and Finnish); Långa Livs Längtan I (own publication) 1981; Långa Livs Längtan II (own publication) 1982. *Contributor to:* Horisont; Kuriren; Wasabladet. *Memberships:* Finlands Svenska Författareförening r.f.; Finlands Publicistföround r.f.; Kirjailijakeskus-Författarcentrum; Pand-Konstnärer för fred; Svenska Österbottens Littleför. Nylands. Mitt. för. *Literary Agent:* Författarnas andelslag r.f. Jeppo. *Address:* Aleksis Kiventie 4, 01900 Nurmijärvi, Finland.

ETCHELLS, Andrew (Jeffrey), b. 17 May 1954, Woodley, England, Editor, 'Running Magazine'. m. Isabel Walker, 25 May 1985. *Education:* BA, Oxon (PPE), 1976. *Publications:* The Marathon Book (with N Wilson and B Tulloh), 1982; The AAA Runner's Guide (contributor), 1983. *Contributions to:* Running Magazine; Fleet Street Newspapers, colour supplements; Radio and TV Shows; Trade Journals. *Memberships:* Association Internationale de la Preise Sportive; Sports Writers Association (UK); British Athletics Writers Association, Committee Member, 1983–. *Literary Agent:* John Pawsey. *Address:* Flat 1, 2-4 College Cross, London N1 1PP, England.

ETKIND, Efim, b. 26 Feb. 1918, Leningrad, USSR. Professor of Literature. m. Zvorykina Catherine, 20 Jan. 1940, Leningrad, 2 daughters. *Education:* Cand. Degree, University Leningrad, 1936–41; PhD, 1965; State Doctorate in Letters & Hymanesiences, Sorbonne, France, 1975. *Publications include:* Poetry & Translation, 1963; Bertolt Brecht, 1970; The Russian Poets as Translators, 1973; Notes of a Non-Conspirator, 1978; The Matter of Verse, 1978; Un art en crise X-Essai d'une poetique de la traduction poetique, 1982; Russian Poetry of the XX Century, (in German), 1984. *Honours:* Prize, Academic Francaise for Translation, 1982. *Memberships:* Corres, Bavarian Academy of Fine Arts, Academy of Science & Literature, Mainz, Academy of Language & Literature, Darmstadt; PEN Centre,

Federal German Republic. *Address:* 31 Jardins Boieldieu, 92800 Puteaux, France.

ETTO, Jorma Heikki, b. 13 Oct. 1931, Rovaniemi, Finland. Author. m Eila Viio, 8 July 1952, Rovaniemi, 1 son, 2 daughters. *Education:* BA. *Publications:* Elämä on, poems, 1955; Rakkauden oppi, short stories, 1957, Väärää rahaa, novel, 1959; Merkkitulia, novel, 1961; Joulupukin päiväkirja, novel, 1963; Ajastaikaa, poems, 1964; oksat ja omenat, television play, 1969; Kirjailijat rakastavat toisiaan, novel, 1972; Häkki, drama, 1974; Valtias, drama, 1975; Läskikapina, drama, 1980; Kalenterinlehtiä, poems, 1982; Suomalainen, poems, 1985. *Honours:* Cultural Prize for Northern Scandinavia, 1968; State Prize for Playwrights, 1968; State Prize for Information, 1975. *Memberships:* Writers' Union of Finland; Playwrights' Union of Finland; Union for Translators of Finland. *Address:* Ahkiomaantie 18-20 C 29, 96300 Rovaniemi, Finland.

EVANS, David Stanley, b. 28 Jan. 1916, Cardiff, Wales. Jack S Josey Centennial; Professor of Astronomy, University of Texas at Austin, USA. *Education:* BA 1937, MA and PhD 1941, ScD 1971, Cambridge University, England. *Publications:* Frontiers of Astronomy, 1946; Teach Yourself Astronomy, several editions, 1952–75; Observation in Modern Astronomy, 1968; Herschel at the Cape, editor, 1969; The Shadow of the Telescope, editor, 1970; External Galaxies and Quasi Stellar Objects, editor, 1972; Photometry, Kinematics and Dynamics of Galaxies, editor, 1979; Proceedings of the Eleventh Texas Symposium on Relativistic Astrophysics,editor, 1984. *Contributions to:* Professional journals including: The Observatory Magazine (editor); Discovery (Science advisory editor 1942–44; Sky and Telescope; Royal Astronomical Society; Astronomical Journal; Astrophysical Journal. *Honours include:* Visiting Professorships of Science include: Austin (USA); Cape Town (Republic of South Africa), Geneva (Switzerland), Victoria (Canada), Tromsło (Norway; McIntryre Award, Astronomical Society of Southern Africa. *Memberships include:* American Astronomical Society; Past President, Commission 30, International Astronomical Union; Honorary Member, Astronomical Society of Southern Africa; Fellow, Royal Astronomical Society; Fellow, Institute of Physics. *Address:* 6001 Mountainclimb Drive, Austin, TX 78731, USA.

EVANS DAVIES, Gloria, b. 17 Apr. 1932, Maesteg, South Wales, Poet. *Publications:* Words for Blodwen, 1962; Her Name Like The Hours, 1974. *Contributions to:* The Times Literary Supplement; New York Times; Spectator; Listener; BBC Radio and TV; Harlech TV; The Oxford Book of Welsh Verse in English; The Oxford Companion to the Literature of Wales; Arts Council Anthologies; T R Anthology; Quartet Books Anthology; Feminist Review; Spare Rib; Writing Women; Poetry Wales; Radical Wales; Planet; Anglo-Welsh Review. *Honours:* Grants from Gulbenkian Foundation and Royal Literary Fund, London and to write third book of poems. *Address:* 25C High Street Superior, Brecon LD3 7LA, Powys, South Wales.

EVANS, George Ewart, 1 Apr. 1909, Abercynon, Glamorganshire, Wales. Writer. m. Florence Knappett, 23 Apr. 1938, Cambridge, 1 son, 3 daughters. *Education:* Doctor of the University, University of Essex, 1982; Honorary D. Litt, University of Keele, 1983; BA, University of Wales. *Publications include:* Ask the Fellows Who Cut The Hay, 1956; The Horse in the Furrow, 1960; The Pattern Under the Plough, 1966; The Farm and the Village, 1969; Where Beards Wag All, 1970; The Leaping Hare (co-author), 1972; Acky, 1973; The Days That We Have Seen, 1975; Let Dogs Delight, 1975; From Mouths of Men, 1976; Horse Power and Magic, 1979; The Strength of the Hills (autobiography, Volume 1), 1983; (Volume II in process). *Contributions to:* Various journals and magazines. *Membership:* Executive, Oral History Society. *Address:* 19 The Street, Brooke, Norwich NR15 1JW, England.

EVELYN, John Michael, b. 2 June 1916, Worthing, Sussex, England. Retired Lawyer; Writer. *Education:* MA, Oxford University; Barrister-at-Law. *Publications include:* 40 crime novels, 1954–86. *Honour:* CB, 1976. *Memberships:* Detection Club; Chairman, Crime Writers Association, 1964–65. *Literary Agent:* A M Heath & Company Ltd. *Address:* c/o A M Heath & Company Ltd, 40/42 William IV Street, London WC2N 4DD, England.

EVERETT, Joann Marie, b. 26 Nov. 1950, Philadelphia, Pennsylvania, USA. Author. m. Dale Wayne Everett, 12 Aug. 1972, 1 son. Education: BS, Education-English, Kutztown University, Pennsylvania; MS, Education, Temple University. *Literary Appointments:* Honorary Doctorate in Literature from World University, 1980; Director, Bensalem Association of Women Writers, 1983. *Publications:* Wandering Song (poetry), 1980; Whispered Beginnings (poetry), 1984; A Christmas Memory (non-fiction), Unpublished 1985. *Contributions:* Over 500 poems in many literary journals; Short story, Alien Christmas in Icicle Carnical; Aliens on Ghosts, in, The Book of the Living Dead; Greeting Cards, Maine Line Card Co, 1985. *Honours:* First Prize, PMA Memorial Contest. 1978; Honorable Mention in Gusto Contest 1980; Honorary Doctorate in Literature from World University, 1980; First Prize, Nashville Newsletter Contest, 1981; First Prize, Joan Rossi Award in Poetry, 1981; 1st Prize, Submit!, 1985; 2nd Prize, Poets at work, 1985. *Memberships:* International Women's Writing Guild; World Poetry Society; Bensalem Association of Women Writers. *Address:* Box 236, Croydon, PA 19020–0940, USA.

EVERSON, Ronald Gilmour, b. 18 Nov. 1903, Oshawa, Ontario, Canada. Poet. m. Lorna Austin, 15 Apr. 1931, Toronto, Ontario. *Education:* BA, University of Toronto; Law Degree, Upper Canada Law School, Toronto. *Publications:* Three Dozen Poems, 1957; A Lattice for Momos, 1958; Wrestle With an Angel, 1962; The Dark Is Not So Dark, 1966; Incident at Cote des Neiges, 1966; Baby Head, 1967; Selected Poems, 1970; Indian Summer, 1976; Carnival, 1978; Everson at Eighty, 1983. *Contributions to:* Poetry; Chicago; Atlantic Monthly. *Membership:* League of Canadian Poets. *Address:* 4855 Ch. Cote St-Luc (608), Montreal, Quebec, Canada H3W 2H5.

EWALD, William Bragg, Junior, b. 8 Dec. 1925, Chicago, Illinois. Writer; Public Affairs Analyst. m. Mary Cecilia Thedieck, 6 Dec. 1947, Suffolk, Virginia, 3 sons. *Education:* AB, Washington University, 1946; MA, 1947, PhD, 1951, Harvard University. *Publications:* The Masks of Jonathan Swift, 1954; The Newsmen of Queen Anne, 1956; Eisenhower The President: Crucial Days 1951–60, 1981; Who Killed Joe McCarthy?, 1984. *Contributions to:* New York Times; Greenwich Time. *Honour:* Eisenhower Exchange Fellowship, 1959–60. *Membership:* Phi Beta Kappa. *Literary Agent:* Knox Burger Assiciates,New York City. *Address:* Dewart Road, Greenwich, CT 06830, USA.

EWART Gavin Buchanan, b. 4 Feb. 1916, London, England. Poet (Freelance Writer). m. Margaret Adelaide

Bennett, 24 Mar. 1956, London, 1 son, 1 daughter. *Education:* BA, Classics and English 1937, MA, Classics and English, 1942, Cambridge University. *Literary Appointments:* Literary Editor, The Granta; Chairman, The Poetry Society. *Publications:* Poems and Songs, 1939; Londoners, 1964; The Collected Ewart 1933–80, 1980; The New Ewart, Poems 1980–82; 1982; The Young Pobble's Guide to his Toes, 1985. *Contributions to:* New Verse; The Listener; Times Literary Supplement; Ambit; London Magazine; Encounter; New Statesman; The New Yorker; Grand Street (USA). *Honours:* Cholmondeley Award, 1971; Fellow of Royal Society of Literature, 1984. *Membership:* The Poetry Society (Chairman). *Address:* 57 Kenilworth Court, Lower Richmond Road, London SW15 1EN, England.

EWELL, Barbara Claire, b. 10 Mar. 1947, Baton Rouge, Louisiana, USA. Teacher. m. Jerry L Speir, New Orleans, 20 May 1979. *Education:* BA (sumna cum laude), University of Dallas, Texas, USA, 1969; PhD, University of Notre Dame, 1974. *Appointments:* Visiting Assistant Professor, Tulane University, USA, 1975–79; Assistant Professor, University of Mississippi, USA, 1975–79; Associate Professor, Loyola University, 1984–present. *Publication:* Kate Chopin, 1986. *Contributions to:* So. Lit Journal, (John Barth), 1973; Essays on Michael Drayton to: SP, 1976; JEGP, 1983; MLQ, 1983; Centennial Review (Margaret Atwood), 1981; and others. *Honours:* Woodrow Wilson Dissertation Fellowship, 1972–73; Monticello College Foundation Fellowship for Women, Newberry Library, Chicago, 1982–83; American Council of Learned Societies, Grant in Aid, 1983. *Memberships:* MLA; Renaissance Society of America; South Central MLA Women's Caucus, Chair, 1980; Southeastern Women's Studies Association, President, 1985–86. *Address:* Box 14 City College, Loyola University, New Orleans, LA 70118, USA.

EWELSON SOARES PINTO, b. 9 Mar. 1926, Itaperuna, Brazil. Judge, Sao Paulo Criminal Court. *Education:* Graduate in Social & Juridical Sciences (Law Degree). *Major Publications:* A Crônica do Valente Parintins (novel), 1976; O Rei dos Paus (novel) 2nd edition, 1980. *Honours:* Honorable mention for fiction in State Government contests. *Literary Agent:* Carmen Balcells, Rio de Janeiro. *Address:* Rua São Vivente de Paula 395, apto 141, 01229 São Paulo SP, Brazil.

EWING, David Walkley, b. 19 May 1923, Grand Rapids, USA. Editor. m. Elizabeth Bennett, 11 Sep. 1948, Hingham, 1 son, 3 daughters. *Education:* JD, Harvard Law School, 1949. *Publications:* Long Range Planning for Management, 1958; The Managerial Mind, 1964; The Human Side of Planning, 1968; Writing for Results, 1974; Do It My Way Or You're Fired!, 1985. *Contributor to:* Numerous articles, Harvard Business Review; Psychology Today; Harper's; Saturday Review; The New York Times; The Walls Street Journal; etc. *Membership:* Monday Club, Winchester, Massachusetts. *Literary Agent:* Julian Bach. *Address:* Harvard Business Review, Boston, MA 02163, USA.

F

FABRY, Joseph Benedikt, b. 6 Nov. 1909, Vienna, Austria. Writer; Translator. *Education:* Dr Jur, University of Vienna, 1933. *Publications:* Wer Zuletzt Lacht, (Appleton-Century-Crofts), 1952; Lacht Am Besten, (Appleton-Century-Crofts), 1957; The Pursuit of Meaning, (Beacon Press), 1968; Editor, Logotherapy in Action, (J Aronson), 1979; Swing Shift, (Strawberry Hill), 1982; (transls.) Three Comedies, (Frederick Ungar), 1970; Haas-Bert Brecht, (Frederick Ungar), 1970; Heine – Poems (Random House), 1973; Brecht – Schweyk in the Second World War, (Random House), 1975; Kraus – Last Days of Mankind, (Carcanet), 1984; Lukas – Meaningful Living, (Grove Press), 1986. *Contributor to:* Various journals. *Memberships include:* California Writers Club. *Address:* 315 Carmel Avenue, El Cerrito, CA 94530, USA.

FAERBER, Meir Marcell, b. 29 Apr. 1908, Ostrava. Journalist. m. Sara Ilana Tutelman, 31 Jan. 1941, Tel Aviv, Israel, 2 sons. *Education:* Commercial Academy, Brno, Czechoslovakia. *Literary Appointments:* Chairman, Association of German Writing Authors in Israel, 1975–. *Publications:* Auf der Flucht erschossen, Drama, 1933; Residenz Schuschan, 1944; Marchen und Sagen aus Israel, 1960; Die Israel fuhren, 1971; Ringende Seelen, 1974; Worte, Poems, lyrics, 1980; Brennende Eifersucht, stories, 1983; Drei mal drei Glieder einer Kette, novel, 1985. *Contributions to:* Die Stimme, Tel Aviv; Aufbau, USA; Allgemeine judische Wochenzeitung, Germany; Das neue Israel, Switzerland; Illustrierte Neue Welt, Austria; Nieuw Israelietisch Weekblad, Netherlands. *Honours:* Golden Award of Honour, Republic of Austria, 1971; Jacob Landau Award, Bne-Brith Lodge, Theodor Hezzel, 1980; Studiosis Humanitatis Medal, Litterary Union, Federal Republic of Germany, 1981; Order of Merit Cross 1st class, Federal Republic of Germany, 1983. *Memberships:* Chairman, Association of German writing Authors in Israel; Executive, Organisation of Authors Association in Israel; National Federation of Israeli Journalists; PEN Club Centre of Israel; International Autorenkreis Plesse, Federal Republic of Germany; Executive, Federal Association of German Authors Organisations, Berlin. *Address:* 56 Yitzhak Sadeh St, 67065 Tel Aviv, Israel.

FAIERS, Christopher Fordham, b. 28 June 1948, Hamilton, Ontario, Canada. Library Assistant. *Education:* AA, Miami-Dade Community College. *Literary Appointments:* Founder, Unfinished Monument Press and Main Street Library Poetry Series. *Publications include:* Collections: Cricket Formations, 1969; Dominion Day in Jail, 1978; Unacknowledged Legislator, 1981; White Rasta in Wintertime, 1982; Island Women, 1983; The Unfinished Anthology, editor, volume 1, 1984; 5 Minutes Ago They Dropped the Bomb, 1984. *Contributions to:* Anthologies and textbooks including: Poems for Sale in the Street, 1979; The Canadian Haiku Anthology, 1979; Modern English Haiku, 1981; The Toronto Collection, 1984; Other Channels, 1984; Anti-war Poems, 1984; Various works forthcoming. Other contributions include: Alchemist; Alive; Canadian Book Review Annual, 1983; Grain; Haiku Highlights; Origins; Poetry Toronto; Waitaka Press Broadsheet; Waves; Writers Quarterly. Various readings and broadcasts. *Memberships:* Haiku Society of Canada; Canadian Poetry Association, Founding Member; Publisher, Unfinished Monument Press. *Address:* c/o Unfinished Monument Press, Box 67 Station H, Toronto, Ontario, Canada M4C 5H7.

FAINLIGHT, Ruth Esther, b. 2 May 1931. USA. Writer. *Literary Appointment:* Poet-in-Residence, Vanderbilt University, Tennessee, Spring 1985. *Publications:* Cages, 1966; To See The Matter Clearly, 1968; All Citizens Are Soldiers, 1969; Daylife and Nightlife, 1971; The Region's Violence, 1973; Another Full Moon, 1976; Sibyls and Others, 1980; Fifteen to Infinity, 1983; Climates, 1983. *Contributions to:* TLS; Poetry; London Review of Books; Hudson Review; Grand Street; English; Critical Quarterly. *Membership:* PEN; London and National Poetry Secretariats. *Address:* 14 Ladbroke Terrace, London, W11 3PG, England.

FAIRBAIRN, Garry Lawrence, b. 5 June 1947, Arcola, Saskatchewan, Canada. Journalist. m. Lorna Bratvold, 9 Dec. 1977. Alexandria, Virginia, USA, 1 son, 1 daughter. *Education:* MA, Carleton University, Ottawa, Canada, 1969. *Publications:* From Prairie Roots: The Remarkable Story of Saskatchewan Wheat Pool, 1984; Will the Bounty End?: The Uncertain Future of Canada's Food Supply, 1984. *Contributions to:* Numerous newspapers and Newsmagazines, 1969–. *Address:* 604 McPherson Avenue, Saskatoon, Saskatchewan, Canada S7N 0X6.

FAIRBURN, Eleanor M, b. 23 Feb. 1928, Republic of Ireland. Author; Writer. m. Brian Fairburn, 1 daughter. *Literary Appointments:* Past Member of Literary Panel for Northern Arts; Tutor in Practical Writing, University of Leeds Adult Education Centre. *Publications:* (historical novels): The Green Popinjays, 1962, 68; The White Seahorse, 1964, 1970, 1985; Lady Mary, 1982; The Golden Hive, 1966; Crowned Ermine, 1968; (thrillers): A Silence with Voices, 1971; The Rose in Spring, 1971, 1972 and 1973; White Rose, Dark Summer, 1972, 1973; The Semper Inheritance, 1972–75, 1986; To Die a Little, 1972, 1973, 1979 and 1986; The Sleeping Salamander, 1973, 1981, 1986; The Rose At Harvest End, 1975, 1976; Winter's Rose, 1976; (light romantic fiction): House of the Chestnut Trees, 1977; Cousin Caroline, 1981, 1986; The Haunting of Abbotsgarth, 1980, 1982; Frenchman's Harvest, 1982, 1986; Ascent of Lilacs, 1982. *Contributions to:* Brief biography of Nurse Edith Cavell for This England, autumn, 1985. *Memberships:* Middlesbrough Writers Group. *Address:* 199 Oxford Road, Linthorpe, Middlesbrough, Cleveland TS5 5EG, England.

FAIRFAX, John, b. 9 Nov. 1930, London, England. Poet. *Publications:* (poems): This I Say, 1968; The 5th Horseman of the Apocalypse, 1969; Adrift on the Star Brow of Taliesin, 1975; Bone Harvest Done, 1980; Wild Children, 1985. *Contributions to:* Times Literary Supplement; The Times; Poetry Review; Two Cities; Stand; Partisan Review; Look; Poetry Editor, Resurgence. *Membership:* Co-Founder, Arvon Foundation (Creative Writing Centers). *Literary Agent:* A D Peters. *Address:* The Thatched Cottage, Eling, Hermitage, Newbury, Berkshire RG16 9XR, England.

FAIRWEATHER, Leslie Stephen, b. 7 Mar. 1929, London, England. Managing Director, m. Anne Williamson, 26 Oct. 1963, London, England, 3 sons, 2 daughters. *Education:* Department of Architecture, Brighton Polytechnic; Member of the Royal Institute of British Architects. *Literary Appointments:* Technical Editor, 1967–73; Editor, 1973–84, The Architects' Journal; Managing Director, The Architectural Press Limited, 1984–. *Publications:* A Metric Handbook, 1968; Prison Architecture, 1975. *Contributions to:* The Architects' Journal, 1960–; British Journal of Criminology! Apr. 1961; Oct. 1961. *Honour:* RIBA Ashpitel Prize, Distinction in Thesis, 1957. *Address:* The Architectural Press Limited, 9 Queen Anne's Gate, London SW1H 9BY, England.

FALESSI, Alessandro, b. 3 Oct. 1945, Castellina, Siena, Italy. Professor, Cultural Anthropology. *Education:* Doctorate, Sociology, Universita Di Firenze, Gonzaga University, 1968; MA, Folklore, 1973, PhD, 1975, University of California, Berkeley, USA. *Publications:* La Terra in Piazza, 1975; Proverbi Toscani, 1979; La Santa Dell'Oca, 1980; Per Forza E Per Amore, 1980; Folklore by the Fireside, 1980; Palio, 1982; Italian Folklore: An Annotated Bibliography, 1985. *Contributor to:* 100 articles in professional journals. *Honours:* Chicago Folklore Prize, 1976. *Memberships:* Life Member, American Anthropological Association, American Folklore Society. *Address:* 340 Royce Hall, University of California, Los Angeles, CA 90024, USA.

FALK, Lee Harrison, b. St Louis, Missouri, USA. Writer. *Education:* BA, University of Illinois. *Major Publications:* Creator of Mandrake the Magician, The Phantom (international syndicated comic strips); Playwright: Festival at Salzburg; The Katatonics; Happy Dollar; The Passionate Congressman; Eris; Home at Six; Long after Gath; The Big Story (with A Cranston); and others. Author, 6 Phantom Novels 1972–75. *Memberships:* President, Provincetown Academy of Living Art, Massachusetts, 1970–76; President, Truro Center of the Arts, Massachusetts, 1979–81. *Honours:* Salon Internationale dei Comics, Lucca, Italy, 1971; Adamson Award, Stockholm, Sweden, 1978; Lifetime Achievement Award, Lucca, Italy, 1984; City of Rome Award, Italy, 1984. *Address:* PO Box Z, South Pamet Road, Truro, MA 02666, USA.

FALK, Peter Hastings, b. 27 Oct. 1950, New Haven, Connecticut, USA. Fine Arts researcher; Publisher. m. Margaret Lake, at Chicago, Illinois, 28 May 1977, 2 daughters. *Education:* AB, Brown University; MA, Rhode Island School of Design. *Publications:* The Photographic Art Market, 1981; Who Was Who In American Art, 1985. *Contributions to:* Numerous monographs on American artists, for museum journals. *Address:* 883 Boston Post Road, Suite 150, Madison, CT 06443, USA.

FALKUS, Hugh, b. 15 May 1917, Surrey, England. Writer. *Publications:* Sea Trout Fishing, 1st edition, 1962, 2nd edition, 1975; The Stolen Years, 1963, 79; Signals for Survival, 1970; Falkus & Bullers Freshwater Fishing, 1975; Nature Detective, 1978; Sydney Cove to Duntroon, 1982; Master of Cape Horn, 1982; Salmon Fishing, 1984. *Address:* Watcarrick Cottage, Eskdalemuir, Dumfriesshire, Scotland.

FALLOWS, Carolyn Lois, b. 10 Dec. 1949, Melbourne, Australia. Editor. m. Ralph Martin Fallows, 19 Aug. 1972, St Ives, New South Wales, Australia, 2 sons, 1 daughter. *Education:* BA, Macquarie University; Associate of the Library Association of Australia. *Literary Appointments:* Founding Editor, Parents & Children Magazine (Australia); Founding Editor, My Baby: All about Your Child's First Year of Life from A–Z; Editor, Slimming, Health & Nutrition Magazine and attendant publications, now ceased. *Address:* 23 Willoughby Road, Crows Nest, 2065, Australia.

FANCUTT, Walter, b. 22 Feb. 1911, Blackburn, Lancashire, England. Baptist Minister. m. Amy Florence Muriel Hawkins, 28 Dec. 1933, Ash Vale, England. *Education:* Blackburn College of Technology; All Nations Bible College; Central School of Art, London. *Literary Appointments:* Editorial Secretary, 1967–70, Editorial Consultant, 1970–75, The Leprosy Mission; General Secretary, Southern Baptist Association, 1971–76. *Major Publications:* The Royal Review; 1942; The Kingsgate Pocket Poets, (8 volumes) 1943–46; Then Came Jesus, 1944; From Vision to Advance, 1950; The Story of Whitchurch Baptist Church, 1952; In This I Will be Confident, 1957; Beyond the Bitter Sea, 1958; Escaped as a Bird, 1962; Present to Heal, 1964; The Mission to Lepers: 90 Years of Leprosy Service, 1964; Daily Remembrance, 1966; The Imprisoned Splendour, 1970; With Strange Surprise, 1974; The Southern Baptist Association & Its Church, 1974; The Luminous Cloud, 1980; His Excellent Greatness; East Dene: Ventnor Local History Society, 1982. *Memberships:* Baptist Union Council, 1948–76; Chairman, Baptist Mission Committee, 1972–77; President, Southern Baptists Associaton, 1950–51. *Honours:* Poetry Prize, School of Religious Journalism, 1942; UNFAO Medal, 1984. *Address:* 4B St Boniface Gardens, Ventnor, IOW, PO38 1NN, England.

FANTHORPE, Ursula Askham, b. 22 July 1929, Lee Green, England. Hospital Clerk; Poet. *Education:* BA, MA (Oxon). *Literary Appointment:* Arts Council Fellow, St Martin's College, Lancaster. *Publications:* Side Effects, 1978; Standing to, 1982; Voices Off, 1984; The Crystal Zoo (with John Cotten and L J Anderson), 1985. *Contributions to:* (Poems): TLS; Encounter;

Outposts; Firebird; Bananas; South West Review; Quarto; Tribune; Country Life; Use of English; Poetry Review; Poetry Book Society Supplement; Writing Women; Spectator, BBC, etc. *Honour:* Travelling Bursary from Royal Society of Authors, 1984. *Memberships:* Poetry Society; PEN. *Address:* Culverhay House, Wotton-under-Edge, Gloucestershire GL12 7LS, England.

FARHI, Musa Moris, b. 5 July 1935, Ankara, Turkey. Writer. m. Nina Ruth Sievers, 2 July 1978, London, England, 1 step-daughter. *Education:* BA, Humanities, American College, Istanbul; Diploma, Royal Academy of Dramatic Art, London. *Publications:* The Pleasure of Your Death, 1972; The Last of Days, 1983; Included in Anthology, Voices Within the Ark, The Modern Jewish Poets, 1980; From The Ashes of Thebes, play, Mercury Theatre, 1969. *Contributor to:* Modern Poetry in Translation. *Memberships:* Society of Authors; Writers Guild of Great Britain; PEN; Authors Guild of America. *Literary Agent:* A D Peters & Co Ltd. *Address:* 24 Heathgate, London NW11 7AN, England.

FARINA, John, b. 17 Apr. 1950, Hartford, Connecticut, USA. Writer; Editor. m. Paula Diesel, 27 Oct. 1979, Newington, Connecticut, USA. 1 son, 2 daughters. *Education:* BA, 1972, Vassar College; MDiv, 1974, Yale Divinity School; PhD, 1979, Columbia University. *Literary Appointments:* Associate Editor, Paulist Press, Mahwah, New Jersey, 1980; Editor-in-Chief, Classics of Western Spiritually series, Paulist Press, 1983; General Editor, Sources of American Spirituality series, Paulist Press, 1985. *Publications:* An American Experience of God: The Spirituality of Isaac Hecker, (New York: Paulist Press), 1981; Hecker Studies: Essays on the Thought of Isaac Hecker, (Ed. New York: Paulist Press), 1983. *Contributions to:* Catholic Historical Review; US Catholic Historian; The Journal of Formative Spirituality; Spirituality Today; The New Catholic World; Paulist '83. *Honour:* Phi Beta Kappa. *Memberships:* American Catholic Historical Association; United States Catholic Historical Association; American Academy of Religion; Society of Documentary Editors. *Address:* Paulist Press, 997 Macarthur Boulevard, Mahwah, NJ 07430, USA.

FARQUHAR, Betty Murphy, b. 17 June 1924, Germany. Artist. *Education:* Administrative Assistant's Diploma, German Business School; Secretary's Diploma, USBusiness College; Mexican American Cultural Exchange Institute; San Antonio Art Institute. *Literary Appointment:* Appointed Poet Laureate by Dr Stella Woodall, 1979. *Contributions to:* Publications including: Poet, India; Adventures in Poetry (anthology); Anthology of Texas Poems, 1975; Shadows of the Elusive Dream, 1975; Tracings of the Valiant Soul, 1978; Magic of the Muse, 1978; Great Contemporary Poems, 1978; Lyrical Voices, 1979; Quiet Thoughts, 1979; Visions of the Enchanted Spirit, 1979; Mirrors of the Wishful Dreamer, 1980; Today's Best Poems, 1980; Best Poems of the Western World, 1980; The Album of International Poets, India, 1981; Images of the Mystic Truth, 1981; Premier Poets Anthologies, 1982 and 1984; Life and Love, 1984. *Honours include:* Prize for Patriotic Poetry, 1978; Winner, Poems of Wisdom Contest, 1978; Winner, Poetry Contest, New World Unlimited, 1978; CSSI Poet Laureate Award, 1981; Diploma of Honour and International Great Prize- The Glory, Rome, 1982; Diploma d'Honore – Palme d'Oro Accademiche, Rome, 1982; Golden Poet Award, 1985. *Memberships include:* United Poets Laureate International; Stella Woodall Poetry Society; World Poetry Society; The Academy of American Poets. *Address:* PO Box 127, Marion, TX 78124, USA.

FARR, Diana, b. Surrey, England. Author. *Publications:* 31 Books include: I Wanted a Pony, 1946; The Boy and the Donkey, 1958; The Secret Dog, 1959; Bindi Must Go, 1962; Ponies in the Valley, 1976; Ponies on the Trail, 1978; Gilbert Cannan: A Georgian Prodigy, 1978; Ponies in Peril, 1979; Cassidy in Danger, 1979; Five at 10, 1985; over 21 other books many in foreign editions. *Contributions to:* Daily Telegraph; Pony; Bookseller; The Author; Good Housekeeping; and others. *Memberships:* Children's Writers Group, Founder member; Poets, Playwrights, Editors, Essayists and Novelists; PEN; Society of Authors. *Literary Agent:* Jerome Epstein. *Address:* 12 Blandford Road, Chiswick, London W4 1DU, England.

FARRANT, Trevor, b. South Australia. Writer. m. 1965, Adelaide, 2 sons. *Education:* BA, Honours, University of Adelaide, 1966. *Publications:* Winter Grass, 1969; The Pirate Movie, 1982; HooRoo Saves the Whale, 1985; The Laugh-in Scripts, 1972; The Best of Norman Gunston, 1976. *Contributor to:* Founding Contributor, Matilda, 1985. *Honours:* Australian Film & TV Arts & Sciences Awards, 1977, 1978, 1980; Australian Writers Guild Award, 1981. *Memberships:* Writers Guild of America; West Australian Writers Guild. *Literary Agent:* Philip Gerlach, Woolloomooloo, New South Wales. *Address:* 46 Monmouth Road, South Australia 5041, Australia.

FARRELL, Bernard, b. 21 July 1939, Sandycove, County Dublin, Republic of Ireland. Playwright. *Education:* Monkstown Park College. *Publications:* Goodbye Smiler, It's Been Nice, 1975; I Do Not Like Thee, Doctor Fell, 1979 (performed in Abbey Theatre, Dublin); Legs Eleven, 1979; Canaries, 1980 (performed in Abbey Theatre, Dublin); All in Favour Said No! (performed Abbey Theatre, 1981); Petty Sessions (Abbey Theatre), 1982; Don Juan (Abbey Theatre), 1982; Then Moses Met Marconi (Project Theatre), 1983; All the Way Back (Abbey Theatre), 1985; One-Two-Three-O'Leary (Adapted Grips Play), 1985. Various BBC-RTE Radio Plays. *Contributions to:* Beacon, Assistant Editor, 1974–76; Sunday Times; Reality; Triangle; Irish Times; Dublin Evening Press; Radio Telefis Eireann; Anthology of Modern Fiction, 1983. *Honour:* Rooney Prize for Irish Literature Award, 1980. *Memberships:* Lantern Theatre Workshop; Irish PEN; Society of Irish Playwrights. *Literary Agent:* Joanna Marston, Rosica Colin Limited, London. *Address:* 5 St Peters Terrace, Sandycove, County Dublin, Republic of Ireland.

FARSON, Daniel Negley, b. 1927, London, England. Writer; Journalist; Television Interviewer. *Education:* USA and England; attended Pembroke College, Cambridge, under GI Bill of Rights. *Appointments include:* Parliamentary and Lobby Correspondent for the Central Press; Staff Photographer, Picture Post, magazine; TV interviewer and presenter, programmes including, Farson's Guide to the British; Farson in Australia; Time Gentlemen, Please!. Full time writer since 1964. *Publications include:* Transplant, 1971; Jack the Ripper, 1972; Out of Step (autobiography), 1973; The Man Who Wrote Dracula, (biography of great-uncle, Bram Stoker), 1975; Window on the Sea, 1978; Hamlyn Books of: Horror; Ghosts; Monsters; Clifton House Mystery (for children), 1980; Curse, 1980; The Biography of Henry Williamson, 1982; A Traveller in Turkey, 1985; Swansdowne, 1986. *Contributions to:* The Mail on Sunday; Susnday Telegraph Magazine; Daily Telegraph; Spectator, etc. *Honour:* Recipient of nomination as Best Interviewer by British TV Critics, 1959. *Literary Agent:* Irene Josephy. *Address:* 129, Irsha Street, Appledore, North Devon, England.

FASEL, Ida, b. 9 May 1909, Portland, Maine, USA. Professor of English. m. Oskar A Fasel, 24 Dec. 1945, New York, USA. *Education:* BA, MA, University of Boston; PhD, University of Denver. *Major Publications:* On the Meanings of Cleave, 1979; Thanking the Flowers, 1981; West of Whitecaps, 1982; All of Us, Dancers, 1984; Amphora Full of Light, 1985. *Contributor to:* Various publications, of scholarly papers, poetry, translations, articles & reviews. *Memberships:* Poetry Society of America; Poetry Society of Texas; National League of American Pen-women; Milton Society of America; Friends of Milton's Cottage. *Address:* 165 Ivy Street, Denver, CO 80220, USA.

FAUST, Irvin, b. 11 June 1924, New York City, New York, USA. Author, Educator. m. Jean D Satterthwaite, 29 Aug. 1959, New York City. *Education:* BS, City College of New York; MA, EdD, Columbia University. *Publications:* Roar Lion Roar and other stories, 1965; The Steagle, novel, 1966; The File on Stanley Patton Buchta, novel, 1970; Willy Remembers, 1971; Foreign Devils, 1973; A Star in the Family, novel, 1975; Newsreel, novel, 1980; The Year of the Hot Rock and other stories, 1985. *Contributions to:* Sewanee Review; Paris Review; Atlantic monthly; Esquire; New Black Mask Quarterly; Sunday Times; New Republic. *Honours:* Listed in Best Books of the Year, New York Times Book Review, 1965, 1971, 1980; Inclusion in, O'Henry Prize Stories, 1983 and 1986. *Membership:* American PEN. *Literary Agent:* Gloria Loomis Agency. *Address:* c/o Watkins-Loomis Agency, 150 E 35th Street, New York, NY 10016, USA.

FAUST, Naomi F, Salisbury, North Carolina, USA. Educator; Author; Poet. *Education:* AB, Bennett College, Greensboro, North Carolina; MA, University of Michigan, Ann Arbor; PhD, New York University. *Literary Appointments:* Teacher of English; Professor of English; Professor of English Education. *Publications:* Speaking in Verse (book, poems), 1974; Discipline & the Classroom Teacher, 1977; All Beautiful Things (book, poems), 1983. *Contributions to:* Poet; Poetry Prevue; South & West Inc, literary quarterly; Cyco-Flame; Poems by Blacks; Written Word; National Poetry Anthology; Afro-American Paper; Biennial Anthology of Premier Poets; The New York Amsterdam News; Parnassus Literary Journal; Gusto (A literary Poetry Journal); Bitterroot, quarterly poetry magazine; Nature Anthology. *Honours & Literary Awards:* Alpha Epsilon; Alpha Kappa Mu; Prize & Certificate, Cooper Hill Writers Conference; Certificate, Poems by Blacks, 1970; Honoured by Long Island Branch, National Association of University Women. *Memberships:* American Association of University Professors; World Poetry Society; National Council of Teachers of English; New York Poetry Forum; Womens National Book Association. *Literary Agent:* Alex Jackson. *Address:* 112-01 175th Street, Jamaica, NY 11433, USA.

FAUVET, Jacques, b. 9 June 1914, Paris, France. Ex-Director, Le Monde Newspapers; Chairman, French Commission on Data Protection. *Education:* LLB, Faculty of Law, Paris. *Publications:* The Cockpit of France; La France Dechiree, 1957; La IVe Republique, 1959; Histoire du Parti Communiste Francais, 1977. *Contributions to:* Le Monde. *Honours:* Legion d'Honneur. *Address:* 5 Rue Louis Boilly, 75016 Paris, France.

FAYE, Jean-Pierre, b. 19 July, 1925, Paris, France. Writer. *Education:* Sorbonne University, Paris. *Publications include:* (novels) entre les Rues, 1958; La Cassure, 1961; Battement, 1962; Analogues, 1964; Les Troyens, 1970; Inferno, 1975; L'Ovale, 1975; poems: Fleuve Renverse, 1959; Couleurs Pliees, 1965; Essays: Le Recit Hungue, 1967; Langages Totalitaires, Theorie du recit, 1972; La Critique de Langage et son Economie, 1973; Migrations des Recits sur le Peuple Juif, 1974; Verres, 1977; Syeeda, 1980 (poems). *Memberships:* Editor, Change, 1968; Founder, Centre for the Analysis and Sociology of Languages. *Honour:* Prix Renaudot (L'ecluse), 1964. *Address:* Founder of the European Philosophical University, 1 Rue Descartes, Paris 5, France.

FEAVER, George Arthur, b. 12 May 1937. Professor of Political Science. *Education:* BA Honours, University of British Columbia, 1959; PhD, London University, England, 1962. *Publications:* From Status to Contract: A Biography of Sir Henry Maine, 1969; Lives, Liberties and the Public Good, 1986. Editor: Our Partnership, by Beatrice Webb, 1975. *Contributions to:* The New Left: Six Critical Studies, edited by maurice Cranston, 1970; Encounter; Lugano Review; Journal of Politics; Studies in Comparative Communism. *Honours:* Leave Fellowships, Canada Council, 1970–71, 1974–75, 1980–81; Fellow, American Council of Learned

Societies, 1974–75. *Memberships:* Society of Authors; Travellers Club, London, England. *Address:* Department of Political Science, University of British Columbia, Vancouver, British Columbia, Canada V6T 1W5.

FECK, Luke, b. 15 Aug. 1935, Cincinnati, Ohio, USA. Journalist. m. Gail Schutte, 12 Aug. 1962, Cincinnati, 1 son, 2 daughters. *Education:* BA, English, University of Cincinnati. *Publication:* Yesterday's Cincinnati, 1976. *Memberships:* Literary Club, Cincinnati; Kit Kat Club, Columbus. *Address:* 34 S Third Street, Columbus, OH 43216, USA.

FEDCHAK, Gregg, b. 17 Dec. 1956. Waverley, New York, USA. Writer. m. M Elaine Robinson, 11 Aug. 1979, Canton, New York. *Education:* BA, St Lawrence University, 1979; Graduate Studies, Catholic University of America, 1980; Korean Language Certification, National Crypotologic School, Department of Defence, USA. *Literary Appointments:* Correspondent, Park Newspapers of St Lawrence Incorporated, Ogdensburg, New York. *Contributions to:* Park Newspapers, Weekly Columnist of 'Letters Home' column; Earthwise; The Country Poet; Hieroglyphics. *Memberships:* National Writers Club; Writers Association of State of New York. *Address:* 414 West Thomas Street, Rome, NY 13440, USA.

FEDDER, Norman Joseph, b. 26 Jan. 1934, b. New York City, NY, USA. Professor of Theatre. m. Deborah Pincus, 24 Nov. 1955, NYC, 1 son, 1 daughter. *Education:* BA, Brooklyn College, 1955; MA, Columbia University, 1956; PhD, NY University, 1962. *Publications:* The Influence of D H Lawrence on Tennessee Williams, 1966; Tennessee Williams: 13 Essays, (Co-Author), 1980; Plays- We Can Make Our Lives Sublime, 1970; The Betrayal, 1978; The Buck Stops Here, 1983. *Contributor to:* Godspiel Dramatics Magazine, 1978, 1981; The Kansas Quarterly, Beyond Absurdity and Sociopolitics: The Religious Theatre Movement in the Seventies, 1980; Modern Liturgy, Unstiffening Those Stiffnecked People, 1985. *Honours:* Winner, Sacramento State College National Playwriting Competition, 1970; Travelling Fellowship to Israel, American Jewish Committee, 1975; Grant to Develop Jewish Heritage Theatre, National Foundation for Jewish Culture, 1978. *Memberships:* Chairperson, Religion and Theatre Program, American Theatre Association, 1975–80; Dramatists Guild. *Literary Agent:* Mitch Douglas, ICM, New York, NY. *Address:* 1903 Crescent Drive, Manhattan, KS 66502, USA.

FEELEY, Malcolm M, b. 28 Nov. 1942, New Hampshire, USA. Professor of Law. m. Margo Peller, 8 June 1969, 1 son, 1 daughter. *Education:* BA, Austin College, 1964; MA, PhD, University of Minnesota. *Publications:* Affirmative School Integration, 1968; Impact of Supreme Court Decisions, 1973; The Process is the Punishment, 1979; The Policy Dilemma, 1980; Court Reform on Trial, 1983; American Constitutional Law, 1985. *Contributions to:* Law and Society Review; Ethics; Polity; USA Today. *Honours:* Silver Gavel Award, American Bar Association, 1980; Gavel Certificate of Merit, American Bar Association, 1984. *Memberships:* Law and Society Association; American Political Science Association. *Address:* School of Law, University of California, Berkeley, CA 94720, USA.

FEELY, Terence John, b. 20 July 1928, Liverpool, England. Playwright; Novelist. m. Elizabeth Adams, York. *Education:* BA 1st University of Liverpool. *Literary Appointments:* Head of Story: Thames Television; Paramount Films; Warner Brothers. *Publications:* Arthur of the Britons, 1973; Rich Little Poor Girl, 1981; Number 10, 1982; Lime Light, 1984. *Honours:* Best Television Series, Screen Writers Guild, 1973; Best Theatre Play, Elek, 1974; Henry James Circle, Boston, 1975. *Literary Agent:* DRM. *Address:* c/o DRM, 28 Charing Cross Road, London, England.

FEENEY, Christopher John, b. 20 Mar. 1955, Meriden, Warwickshire, England. Editor. m. Ann Cook, 1 Sep. 1984, Bromsgrove. *Education:* University of Bristol, 1977. *Appointments:* Books Editor, British Psychological Society, Leicester, 1984–. *Publications:* Guide and Index to the Archives of Harper and Brothers, 1980; Studying the West Midlands, 1983. *Membership:* Society of Indexers. *Address:* The British Psychological Society, St Andrews House, Princess Road East, Leicester LE1 7DR, England.

FEHER, Klára, b. 21 May 1923, Ujpest, Hungary. Writer, Playwright. *Major Publications include:* (novels): The Sea, 1956; translated into German, Russian & Georgian; Don't Sleep Tonight, 1960; Marcosis, 1969; Four Days in Paradise, 1976; (comedies) We are no Angels, 1958; We are the Bespectacled one, 1975; (science fiction) Earthquake Island, 1958; Oxygenia, 1972; (short stories) We are No Devils, 1968; What's the Elephant Made of, 1973; (childrens' books), Dreams of a Teenager, 1966; Gilly the Fish, 1974; (travel books with L Nemes) Japan, 1965; Canada, 1968; Aústralia, 1970; Turkey, 1971. *Contributor to:* Various magazines: Hungarian Radio and TV. *Honours:* Jozsef Attila Literary Prize, 1950. *Memberships:* Hungarian Writers' Association; PEN. *Literary Agent:* Artisjus. *Address:* Munkas u 3/B, 1074 Budapest, Hungary.

FEHR, Karl, b. 8 Aug. 1910, Berg am Irchel, Switzerland. Professor. m. Marg. Stettbacher, 19 Nov. 1938, 1 son, 2 daughters. *Education:* PhD, Universities of Zurich & Paris, 1935; Titular Professor, 1959. *Publications:* Jeremias Gotthelfs Schwarze Spinne als Christliches Mythos, 1942; Besinnung auf Gotthelf, 1946; Jeremias Gotthelf, 1954; Das Bild des Menschen b J Gotthelf, 1954; Der Zweite Bildungsweg, 1962; Der Realismus in der schweizerischen Literatur, 1965; J Gotthell, 1967, 2nd edition 1985; J V Kopp, 1968; C F Meyer, 1971, 2nd edition 1980; G Keller, Aufschlüsse und Deutungen, 1972; J V Kopp, Aphorismen, Editor, 1972; Meta Heusser, Hauschronik, 1980; Abseits in grechischen Meer, 1985; J Gotthelf Studien, 1986; Heinrich Leuthold: Die Schonbeit die ich fr[u]auh geliebt, 1985. *Contributor to:* Neue Zürcher Zeitung; Zürichsee Zeitung. *Honours:* Literary Prize, Canton of Zurich, 1954, 1965, 1972, 1985; Gold Medal, E Alker Stiftung, 1980; Literary Prize, SBG, 1982. *Membership:* Academic Society of Swiss Germanists. *Address:* Kanzlerstr. 24, 8500 Frauenfeld, Switzerland.

FEHRENBACH, T R, b. 12 Jan. 1925, San Benito, Texas, USA. Author. *Education:* BA, Princeton University. *Publications:* Author of 18 books including: This Kind of War, 1963; Gnomes of Zurich, 1966; This Kind of Peace, 1966; FDR's Undeclared War, 1967; Lone Star, 1968; Greatness to Spare, 1968; Fire and Blood, 1973; Comanches, 1974. *Contributions to:* Various magazines, journals and newspapers including: Satevepost; Argosy; Esquire; Banker's; American Legion; New Republic; Atlantic; This Week; Analog; Sunday Times, England; Zurich Woche. *Honours include:* Freedom Foundation, 1965; Evelyn Oppenheimer, 1968; St Marys University, 1969; Texas House of Representatives, 1969, 73; Texas State Legislature, 1977. *Memberships:* Authors Guild; Science Fiction Writers of America. *Literary Agent:* Richard Curtis Associates. *Address:* PO Box 6698, San Antonio, TX 78209, USA.

FEIBLEMAN, Peter, b. 1 Aug. 1930, New York, USA. Writer. *Education:* Student, Drama, Carnegie Institute of Technology; Columbia University. *Publications:* A Place Without Twilight, 1958; The Daughters of Necessity, 1959; Tiger Tiger Burning Bright, (Play), 1963; Strangers and Graves, (4 Novellas), 1966; The Columbus Tree, 1973; Charlie Boy, 1980; Eating Together – Recollections and Recipes, (with Lillian Hellman), 1984. *Contributor to:* Travel and Leisure; Food and Wine Magazine; Time/Life Books – Foods of the World; Atlantic Monthly; Holiday; many others. *Honours:* Guggenheim Fellowship Award to Creative Writing, 1958; Gold Pen Award, 1983. *Membership:* PEN. *Literary Agent:* Robert Lantz. *Address:* 8263 Hollywood Blvd, Los Angeles, CA 90069, USA.

FEIN, Helen, b. 17 Sep. 1934, New York City, USA. Sociologist. m. Richard J. Fein, 10 Sep. 1955, New York City, 2 daughters. *Education:* BA 1955, MA 1958, Brooklyn College; PhD; Sociology, Columbia University, 1971. *Publications include:* Imperial Crime & Punishment: The Jallianwala Bagh Massacre & British Judgement 1919–1920, 1977; Accounting for Genocide: National Responses & Jewish Victimization During the Holocaust, 2nd edition 1984; Towards Understanding, Intervention and Prevention of Genocide, 1984. *Contributions to:* Midstream; Society; Worldviews; Contemporary Sociology; International Human Rights: Contemporary Issues, ed. Jack L Nelson & Vera Green, 1980; Genocide & Human Rights, ed. Jack N Porter, 1982; Encountering the Holocaust, ed. Byron Sherwin, 1979; etc. Various book reviews, review essays. *Honour:* Sorokin Award, American Sociological Association, 1979. *Address:* 33 Elting Avenue, New Paltz, NY 12561, USA.

FEIN, Leonard, b. 1 July 1934, New York, USA. Writer. 3 daughters. *Education:* BA, MA, University of Chicago; PhD, Political Science, Michigan State University. *Literary Appointment:* Editor-in-Chief, Moment Magazine, 1973–. *Publications:* Politics in Israel, 1967; The Ecology of the Public Schools, 1971. *Contributions to:* Moment; New Republic; Saturday Review; etc. *Literary Agent:* Pam Bernstein, William Morris. *Address:* 462 Boylston Street, Boston, MA 02116, USA.

FEINBERG, Nathan, b. 6 June 1895, Kovno, Russia. Professor emeritus, International Law, Hebrew University of Jerusalem. *Education:* Dr Jur Utr, University Zurich; Graduate Institute of International Studies, Geneva. *Publications include:* La juridication de la Cour Permanente de Justice Internationale dans le Systeme des Mandats, 1930; La Petition en Droit International, 1933; L'Admission de nouveaux membres a la Societe des Nations et a l'Organisation des Nations Unies, 1952; The Jewish Struggle Against Hitler in the League of Nations (The Bernheim Petition), 1957, in Hebrew; Palestine under the Mandate and the State of Israel – Problems in International Law, 1963, in Hebrew; The Jewish League of Nations Societies, 1967, in Hebrew; Studies in International Law, with special reference to the Arab-Israeli Conflict, 1979; Essays on Jewish Issues of our Time, 1980, in Hebrew; Reminiscences, 1985, in Hebrew; Co-Editor, The Jewish Yearbook of International Law, 1949; Editor, Studies in Public International Law in Memory of Sir Hersch Lauterpacht, 1961, in Hebrew. *Memberships:* Perm. Court Arbitration; Institute of International Law; Board of Governors, Hebrew University. *Address:* 6 Ben Labrat Street, Jerusalem 92307, Israel.

FEINBERG, Renee, b. 10 Apr. 1940, New York City, USA. Librarian. *Education:* BA, University of Chicago, 1961; MA, Columbia University, Teachers College, 1966; MLS, Columbia University, School of Library Service, 1969. *Publications:* Women, Education and Employment: A bibliography of periodical citations, 1970–80; SHARE Directory of Feminist Librarians, 1975; Shoe String, 1982. *Contributor to:* Finding Homes for Children, Reference Services Review 12(1):43-48; The Jewish Caucus and the Jewish Question, ALA Yearbook 1976; What Price Professionalism?, Library Journal, 2.15.71:242-47. *Address:* Brooklyn College Library, Brooklyn, NY 11210, USA.

FEINSTEIN, Lloyd Leonard, b. 28 August, 1941, Jersey City, New Jersey, USA. Career Marketing. m. Joan Gritz, 3 July 1965, Short Hills, New Jersey, USA, 2 sons. *Education:* BA, Kean College of New Jersey; MA, Rutgers University. *Major Publications:* It's Your Money, parts 1 & 2, 1973; Career Changing: The Worry-Free Guide, 1983. *Contributor to:* Innumerable periodicals. *Honour:* Woodrow Wilson National Fellowship (honorable mention), 1964. *Literary Agent:* Barbara Grant. *Address:* 60 Colonial Way, New Providence, NJ 07974, USA.

FEIR, Dorothy Jean, b. 29 Jan. 1929, St Louis, Missouri, USA. University Professor. *Education:* BS, University of Michigan, Ann Arbor; MS, University of Wyoming, Laramie; PhD, University of Wisconsin, Madison. *Appointment:* Editor, Environmental Entomology, 1977–84. *Contributor to:* 50 research articles published in Nature; Annals of the Entomological Society of America; Journal of Insect Physiology; Insect Biochemistry; Experientia; Comparative Biochemistry and Physiology, etc. *Memberships:* Council of Biology Editors. *Address:* Biology Dept, St Louis University, St Louis, MO 63103, USA.

FEJES, Endre, b. 15 Sep. 1923, Budapest, Hungary. Writer. m. Eva Balàzs, 10 Sep. 1952. *Publications:* The Liar, 1958 and 1973; Generation of Rust, 1962, play 1963, 15th edition in Hungary and 30th in other languages 1985; Merry Fellows, short stories 1966; Mocorgo, play 1966; Good Evening Summer, Good Evening Love, 1969, 3rd edition 1973, television play 1973; Vono Ignác, 1969, play 1969 and 1984; The Marriage of Margit Cserepes, play 1972 and 1985; About Love on a Crazy Night, 1975; Whoever Would Think of it, pamphlet 1979; The Boy Whose Had a Face, 1982. *Contributions to:* Theatre; Magyar Hirlap; Magyar Ifjùsàg. *Honour:* Short Film Prize, Öberhausen, 1960; SZOT Literature Prize, 1962; Attila Jòzsef Literature Prize, 1968; Kossuth Literature Prize, 1975; Fòv, Tanace Mürèazeti dij, 1979; Szocialista Magyarorszàgèri, 1983. *Memberships:* Feszek Artists' Club; Hungarian PEN. *Address:* Normafa ut 15/b, 1121 Budapest, Hungary.

FELDMAN, Ruth (Wasby), b. 21 May 1911. Poet, translator. m. Moses O Feldman (deceased). *Education:* BA, Wellesley College, 1931; Workshops, Boston University, Radcliffe Institute. *Publications include:* Books: The Ambition of Ghosts, Poetry 1979, and, Poesie di Ruth Feldman, Poetry 1981. Co-editor and Translator: Collected Poems of Lucio Piccolo, translator, 1973; Selected Poems of Andrea Zanzotto, 1975; Shema, 1976; Italian Poetry Today, 1979; The Dawn is Always New, 1980; The Hands of the South, 1980; The Dry Air of the Fire, 1981; Moments of Reprieve, sole translator, 1986. Anthologies: The New York Times Book ofVerse; Anthology of Magazine Verse; Voices Within The Ark; Peter Kaplan's Book; Sotheby's Poetry Competition Prize Anthology; Poesia Bele Metamorfosi; Poetry Society of America Diamond Anthology; Penguin Book of Women Poets; Barnstone Book of Women Poets; Gates To The New City; In The Pink. *Contributions to:* Numerous literary magazines and reviews; Poetry translated into Italian in Italian magazines. *Honours include:* Devil's Advocate Award, 1972; Monthly Awards and One Annual Award, Poetry Society of America; Co-winner, John Florio, 1976; Circe-Sabaudia, 1983. *Memberships:* Poetry Society of America; New England Poetry Club; American Literary Translators Association. *Address:* 221 Mount Auburn Street, Cambridge MA 02138, USA.

FELSENTHAL, Carol, b. 25 Apr. 1949, Chicago, Illinois, USA. Writer. m. Steven Felsenthal, 14 June 1970, Chicago, 2 daughters. *Education:* BA, University of Illinois – Urbana; MA, Boston College. *Publications:* The Sweetheart of the Silent Majority, 1981; A Cry for Help, 1983. *Contributions to:* Contributor of numerous articles to a variety of national and local magazines. *Membership:* Authors' Guild. *Literary Agent:* Philippa Brophy, The Sterling Lord Agency. *Address:* 2920 N Commonwealth Apt 9A, Chicago, IL 60657, USA.

FELSTEIN, Ivor Leslie, b. 14 May 1933, Scotland. Physician; Psychotherapist. m. Juliet Miller, 25 Feb. 1958, Glasgow, 1 son, 1 daughter. *Education:* MB, CH B, University of Glasgow, 1956; Member, Institute of Psychosexual Medicine, London. *Publications:* Later Life, 1969; Change of Face & Figure, 1971; Living to Be A Hundred, 1974; Sexual Pollution, 1974; Medical Shorthand Typist, with Mitson & Barnard, 1973; Looking at Retirement, 1975; Sex in Later Life, 1980. *Contributor to:* Consulting Editor, British Journal of Sexual Medicine; Columnist: Medical News Tribune, Rostrum, Spectrum, MIMS Magazine, Doctor Weekly,

Therapy Weekly; Articles in, Parents; Geriatric Medicine; Mirror News Group; Update Publications; Marshall Cavendish Publications. *Membership:* Society of Authors, London. *Address:* 11 Chorley New Road, Bolton, Lancashire, England.

FENBY, Eric William, b. 22 Apr. 1906, Scarborough, York, England. Musician. *Publications:* Delius as I Knew Him, 1936, revised edition 1966; Delius (Great Composer Series), 1971. *Contributions to:* Books and Bookmen. *Honours:* OBE; Honorary RAM; Award winning script for A Song of Summer (TV documentary film); Honorary Doctorate, Music, Jacksonville; Honorary Doctorate Litt, Bradford; Honorary Doctorate Litt, Warwick, all 1978. *Memberships:* President, Delius Society of Great Britain; Royal Academy of Music; Honorary Member, the Royal Philharmonic Society; Honorary Fellow, Royal College of Music, 1985; The Society of Authors. *Address:* 35 Brookfield, Highgate West Hill, London N6, England.

FENG, Zong Pu, b. 26 July 1928, Beijing, Peoples Republic of China. Research Fellow, Research Institute of Foreign Literature, Chinese Academy of Social Sciences. m. Cai Zhong De, 17 Sep. 1969, Beijing, 1 daughter. *Education:* BA, Qiunghua University. *Publications:* The Red Beans, 1957; Melody in Dreams, 1978; Who Am I?, 1979; Lu Lu, 1980; The Everlasting Rock, 1980; Selection of Zong Pu's Stories and Prose, 1981; Fairy Tales from A Wind Cottage, 1984; Bear Palm (selection of stories), 1985; Heads in the Marsh, 1985; A Shadowless Pine, 1985; Stars' Tears, 1985. A Sketch on West Lake (prose), 1962 became a text in The Chinese Textbook for all the Senior High Schools in China, 1985. *Honours:* Winner of The National Best Short Stories Award for, Melody in Dreams, 1978; Winner of the National Best Novelette Award for, The Everlasting Rock, 1980. *Memberships:* Chinese Writers Association; PEN; Council of Chinese Writers Association, 1984–. *Address:* Research Institute of Foreign Literature, Chinese Academy of Social Sciences.

FERGUSON, Evelyn Cook, b. 22 Feb. 1910, Council Bluffs, Iowa, USA. Editor; Author; Teacher. m. (1) John H Nevin, Colville, Washington; (2) Dr William B Ferguson, Philadelphia, Pennsylvania. *Education:* Washington State University; New York University. *Publications:* Books for Young People: The Lost Children of Shoshones; The Sign of the Anchor; Underground Escape; Captive of the Delawares; The River Spirit and the Mountain Demons; The Extraordinary Adventures of Chee Chee McNerney; Grandma Tilbury (short story) used for several years by Office of Audio Education, Empire State FM Educational Network. Books published in Germany, Austria, Norway, Holland, England, New Zealand and Australia. *Contributions to:* Jack and Jill; Boy's Life. *Honours:* Underground Escape chosen for James Weldon Johnson Memorial Collection, Countee Cullen Branch of New York City Library; Member of College Honorary in the 1930s, Euradelphian Literary Honorary. *Address:* 432 N Avenida Felicidad, Tucson, AZ 85705, USA.

FERGUSON, John, b. 2 Mar. 1921, Manchester, England. Former University and College Professor and Administrator. (Retired). *Education:* MA, Cambridge University; BD, London University. *Publications include:* Religions of the Roman Empire, 1970; A Companion to Greek Tragedy, 1972; The Place of Suffering, 1972; The Heritage of Hellenism, 1973; Illustrated Encyclopaedia of Mysticism and Mystery Religions, 1976; War and Peace in the World's Religions, 1977; (co-author) Political and Social Life in the Great Age of Athens, 1978; Juvenal: The Satires, 1979; Jesus in the Tide of Time, 1980; Disarmament: The Unanswerable Case, 1982; Catullus, 1985, numerous other books and plays. *Contributions to:* Reconciliation Quarterly (Joint Editor). *Honours:* Fellow, International Institute of Arts & Letters; Fellow, Royal Society of Arts; Knight, Mark Twain Society. *Memberships include:* Various international, religious, educational and classical associations. *Address:* 102

Oakfield Road, Selly Park, Birmingham B29 7ED, England.

FERGUSON, Peter Roderick Innes, b. 30 Dec. 1933, Bromley, Kent, England. Writer; Lecturer. *Education:* BA, Balliol College, Oxford, 1958; PhD, University of London, 1978. *Publications include:* Autumn for Heroes, 1959; Monster Clough, 1962; A Week Before Winter (in the Year of the Great Reaping), 1971; A Week by the Sea, 1976; It Never Snows in England, 1979. *Contributions to:* Best Sports Stories, 1966; Truth; Listen; Departure; Daily Telegraph Magazine, etc. *Address:* 74 W Riding, Bricket Wood, St Albans, Hertfordshire AL2 3QQ, England.

FERGUSSON, Adam, b. 10 July 1932, Haddington, England. Special Adviser on European Affairs, Foreign and Commonwealth Office, 1985–; Member, European Parliament, 1979–84. *Education:* BA, Trinity College, Cambridge, 1955. *Publications:* Roman Go Home, 1969; The Lost Embassy, 1972; The Sack of Bath, 1973; When Money Dies, 1975. *Contributor to:* Times; Glasgow Herald; Scotsman; Sunday Times; Sunday Telegraph; Daily Telegraph; Spectator; Illustrated London News; etc. *Agent:* Curtis Brown Ltd. *Address:* 15 Warwick Gardens, London W14, England.

FERNANDEZ, Gladys Vivian Craven, b. 3 Mar. 1939, Scranton, Pennsylvania, USA. Professor. m. Richard R Fernandez, 10 June 1961, Garden City, New York, 3 sons. *Education:* BA, Wellesley College; MAT, Harvard Graduate School of Education; MA, University of Pennsylvania; Ed D, Temple University. *Publications:* Parents Organizing To Improve Schools, 1976, 2nd edition 1985; The Child Advocacy Handbook, 1981. *Contributions to:* The Urban Review; Philadelphia Inquirer; Bulletin of the National Association of Secondary School Principals; Eye on Education; PAR Analysis. *Honours:* Wellesley College Scholar, 1960 and 1961; Merit Award for Teaching and Service, Temple University, 1978, 1979, 1982 and 1983. *Address:* 3400 Baring Street, Philadelphia, PA 19104, USA.

FERNANDEZ DE LA REGUERA UGARTE, Ricardo, b. 27 Apr. 1914, Barcenillas, Spain. Writer. *Education:* Degree; Philosophy and Letters. *Publications:* Cuando voy a morir, 1951; Cuerpo a tierra, 1954; Perdimos el Paraiso, 1955; Bienaventurados los que aman, 1956; Vagabundos provisionales, 1959; Espionaje, 1963; Episodios nacionales contemporaneos, (11 volumes), 1963–79; works translated into many languages. *Contributions to:* Literary Reviews etc, Spain, Germany, USA and France. *Honours:* Novel Prize, Ciudad de Barcelona, 1950; International Novel Prize, Club Espana, Mexico, 1954; Novel Prize, Concha Espina, 1955; Two Literary Awards. Juan March Foundation, 1962–63. *Address:* Rda Gral Mitre 144, Barcelona–6, Spain.

FERNEYHOUGH, Frank, b. 2 June 1911, Bucknall, Stoke-on-Trent, Staffordshire, England. Professional Writer. *Publications:* Railways, 1948; Booking and Parcels Office Clerical Work, 1949; Railways-A Picture History, 1970; Choosing a Job on the Railways, 1973; Steam Trains Down the Line, 1975; The History of Railways in Britain, 1975; Liverpool and Manchester Railway, 1830–1980, 1980; Steam Up!, (autobiography), volume I, 1983, volume II, 1986. *Contributions to:* Chambers Journal; Housewife; Psychology; Daily Mirror; Dean's Annuals; English Digest; Musical Times; Lecturer on writing for the Press, St Albans College of Further Education. *Memberships:* FRSA; Authors' Society; London Press Club; Institute of Directors. *Address:* 25 Rose Walk, St Albans, Hertfordshire, England.

FERNEYHOUGH, Roger Edmund, b. 28 Aug. 1941, Nothampton, England. Publisher. *Education:* MA Pembroke College, Oxford. *Literary Appointments:* Assistant Editor, B T Batsford and Company, 1965–66; Editor, Weidenfeld Publishers Limited, 1966–69; Editorial Director, Wayland Publishers Limited, 1969–79; Publisher, Macdonald and Evans Limited, 1983–85;

Editorial Director, Northcote House Publishers Limited (Plymouth), 1985–. *Publications:* English Life in the 18th Century, 1970, English Life in the 17th Century, 1970; English Life in the 19th Century, 1971; English Life in Tudor Times, 1972; English Life in Chaucer's Day, 1972; Witchcraft, 1972; England Expects, 1972; Nelson's Navy, 1972; Battle of the Spanish Armada, 1973; Men in the Air, 1973; Voyages of Captain Cook, 1973; The Industrial Revolution, 1978. *Contributions to:* Times; Times Educational Supplement; Economist; New Society; Journal of the Royal Society of Arts; Mind Alive; The School Librarian. *Address:* Northcote House, Ugborough, Devon, England.

FERREIRA, Alfonso Antonio, b. 4 Sep. 1934, Mount Vernon, New York, USA. Priest, Psychotherapist. *Education:* MA, Psychology; MA, Divinity; PhD Candidate. *Contributor to:* Topic Magazine (of the Order of Friars Minor). *Honour:* Silver Award for Dissertation, 1969, Immaculate Conception College of Philisophy. *Membership:* President and Director, The Listening Place. *Address:* Topic Magazine, Provincial Spiritual Assistant, 38 Michigan Avenue, Lynn, MA 01902, USA.

FERRETT, Mabel, b. 30 Apr. 1917, Leeds, England. Teacher. m. Harold Ferrett, 7 Aug. 1947, Ossett, Yorkshire, England, 1 son. *Education:* Teacher's Certificate, Ripon Training College, Yorkshire, England. *Literary Appointments:* Teacher, Leeds, Yorkshire; Freelance Writer; Adjudicator, Wharfedale Music Festival Poetry Competition 1984 and 1985; Editor, Pennine Platform, 1973–76; Editor, Fighting Cock Press Productions, 1973–85; Part Editor, Ipso Facto, 1975; Editor, Orbis, 1978–80. *Publications:* Lynx-Eyed Strangers, 1956; The Angry Men, novel 1965; The Tall Tower, 1970; The Years of the Right Hand, 1975; The Brontes in the Spen Valley, topography 1978; Poetry Tape, Poems by Ian Emberson and Mabel Ferrett, 1983; A Question of Menhirs, 1984; Humber Bridge, selected poems 1986. *Contributions to:* BBC; Radio Leeds Educational Services (poems); Yorkshire Post; Outposts; John O'London's Weekly; Orbis; The Woman Journalist; Pennine Platform; New Hope International; Yorkshire Ridings Magazine; Chamber's Journal; John Bull; The Dalesman etc. *Honours include:* Kirklees Festival 1975; Phoenix Competition 1975; 1st Prize, Julian Cairns Poetry Competition 1976; Yorks Arts Association Bursaries 1976 and 1984. *Memberships:* Society of Women Writers and Journalists; Halifax Authors' Circle; Pennine Poets; Kirklees Poetry Society; Life President, Spen Valley Historical Society. *Address:* 2 Vernon Road, Heckmondwike, West Yorkshire WF16 9LU, England.

FERRISS, Lucy, b. 14 Jan. 1954, St Louis, Missouri, USA. Novelist. m. Mark P Couzens, 19 May 1984, New York. *Education:* BA, Pomona College; MA, San Francisco State University. *Appointment:* Writer-in-Residence, Phillips Exeter Academy. *Publications:* One Step Closer, Anthology, 1976; Philip's Girl, 1985; The Gated River, 1986. *Contributor to:* Pequod; Transfer; Marilyn; Seven Stars; Northern New England Review; San Francisco Chronicle Magazine. *Honours:* Alliance Francaise Deuxieme Prix, 1970; Dole Prize, 1975; Women's Commission Writing Prize, 1975; Redbook Short Fiction Finalist, 1979; Bennett Fellowship, 1979; Yaddo Fellowship, 1983, 1986. *Literary Agent:* Carole Abel. *Address:* Bard College, Annandale on Hudson, NY 12504, USA.

FERTIG, Nelle, b. 1 Oct. 1919. Teacher. *Education:* AB, Whittier College, USA, 1940; MA, California State University, Los Angeles, 1965. m. Norman R Fertig. *Literary Appointments:* Elementary School Teacher; Part-time Faculty, California State University, Los Angeles; Adult Education Teacher of Poetry. *Publication:* The Brittle Distance, 1974. *Contributor to:* Poet Lore; S & W; Descant; California State Poetry Quarterly; A Fine Frenzy, 2nd edition; Cardinal; Imprints; Legend; Poet, India; Poetry Parade; Quoin; Voices International California English Journal; Modern Haiku; Haiku West; Janus South; Dragonfly; Encore,

etc. *Honours include:* Golden Pegasus, 1972; Roadrunner-Up Trophy, 1979. *Memberships:* California State Poetry Society, Founder and Past President, Southern California Chapter; Poetry Society of Texas, Past Contest Chairman; California Federation of Chaparral Poets. *Address:* 743 Puma Canyon Lane, Glendora, CA 91740, USA.

FICHTER, George S, b. 17 Sep. 1922, Hamilton, Ohio, USA. Editor; Writer; Publisher. m. Nadine K Warner, 1945, 1 son, 2 daughters. *Education:* BA, Miami University, Ohio; MSc, Entomology, North Carolina State College, 1948; Graduate work in Sociology and Anthropology, University of North Carolina. *Literary Appointments:* Vice-President and Editor-in-Chief, Fisherman Press Incorporated, 1950–55; Freelance Writer and Editor including production of a natural history encyclopedia and editing Florida Outdoors, 1957–63; Editor, Golden Guides, Western Publishing Company, 1963–67; Director, Golden Guides, 1967–68; Freelance Writer and Editor; Senior Editor-Consultant, Western Publishing Company; Bi-weekly newspaper Column, Science World; Writer-in-Residence, Stetson University, 1968–. *Publications:* Fishing, 1954; Good Fishing (co-author), 1959; Reptiles and How They Live, 1960; Flying Animals, 1961; Snakes, 1963; Fishes, 1963; Insects, 1964; Reptiles, 1965; Fishing (co-author), 1965; Insect Pests, 1966; Rocks, 1966; Bicycle Racing (co-author) 1978; The Future Sea, 1978; Fishing the Four Seasons, 1978; Iraq, 1978; Pet Amphibians and Reptiles, 1978; Working Dogs, 1978; Florida: A Visual Geography, 1979; Racquetball, 1979; Snakes of the World, 1979; Space Shuttle, 1981; Karts and Karting, 1982; Comets and Meteors, 1982 and many others. *Contributions to:* Magazines, books, encyclopedias etc. Editor of many books and encyclopedias. *Address:* PO Box 3280, DeLand, FL 32720, USA.

FICOWSKI, Jerzy, b. 4 Sep. 1924, Warsaw, Poland. Writer, poet, novelist, essayist, translator. m. Elzbieta Bussold, 21 Nov. 1968, 3 daughters. *Education:* Studies Philosophy and Sociology, University of Warsaw, 1946–50. *Publications include:* Poetry: Leaden Soldiers, 1948; My Sides of the World, 1957; Bird Beyond Bird, 1968; Selected Poems, 1970; Note Smuggled Through, 1979; Reading of Ashes, 1979; Fiction: Waiting for the Dog's Sleep, 1970, 1973 and 1986; Essays: Regions of Great Heresy, essays on the life and work of Bruno Schulz, 1967 and 1975; Gypsies on Polish Roads, history and folklore, 1965 and 1986; Translations from Yiddish, Spanish, Roumanian and Romany including: Raisins With Almonds, anthology of Jewish Folk Songs, 1964 nd 1986; F Garcia Lorcas–Selected Poems, 1958, 1968 and 1975; As Editor: Bruno Schulz–Book of Letters, 1975. *Contributor to:* Journals of the Gypsy Lore Society, England, 1949–63; Zapis, 1978–81. *Memberships:* Zwiazek Literatow Polskich (1978–1983); Member of the Board, Polish PEN Centre, 1972–. *Honours:* Polish PEN Club Award, 1977; Alfred Jurzykowski Foundation, USA, Award, 1983. *Address:* Plac Inwalidow 4/6/8, 01-553 Warsaw, m 41 Poland.

FIEDLER, Lesle A, b. 8 Mar. 1917. Professor of English. m. Sally Anderson Fiedler, 8 children. *Education:* BA, NY University, 1938; MA 1939; PhD, University of Wisconsin, 1941; Postdoctoral study Harvard University, 1944–47. *Literary Appointments:* Montana State University, 1941–63, Chairman of Department, 1954–56; Professor of English, SUNY, Buffalo, 1964–; Associate Fellow, Calhoun College, Yale University; Visiting Professor, various overseas and American Universities. *Publications:* (books) Waiting for the End, 1964; Back to China, 1965; The Continuing Debate (with Jacob Winocur), 1964; Love and Death in the American Novel (revised new edition), 1966; The Last Jew in America, 1966; The Return of the Vanishing American, 1968; Nude Croquet and Other Stories, 1969; Being Busted, 1970; The Collected Essays of Leslie Fiedler, 1971; The Stranger in Shakespeare, 1972; The Inadvertent Epic, 1979; Olaf Staledon, 1982; Freaks, 1982. *Contributor to:* Numerous critical and review articles as well as poetry and short fiction to periodicals in many countries. *Honours:* Furioso Poetry Prize; Prize story reprinted in the Martha Foley College; Prize awarded by the National Institue of Arts and Letters, 1957. *Memberships:* AAUP; MLA; English Institute; PEN Club; Dante Society of America. *Address:* 154 Morris Avenue, Buffalo, NY 14214, USA.

FIELD, Ian Harcourt, b. 10 Aug. 1930, Melbourne, Australia. Real Estate Agent. m. Janet Ford, 7 Dec. 1957, Melbourne, 2 sons, 1 daughter. *Publications:* The Engineers Thumb, 1953; The Touch of Saint Valery, 1955; A Career in Steel, Great Expectations, Air Hostess, 1956; When Shall I Awake?, 1962; Lights Behind the Curtain, 1968; One Sided Triangle, 1968; The Poet Gordon, The Lady with the Red Boots, The Hill, 1977; Odyssey of an Outback, 1978; The Tuesday Game, 1981; Two Slices of Cake, 1983; Simon Has a Godson, (Theatrical Play), Stand in for Freddie, (Feature Film), Go For It, (Feature Film), Remission, (TV Mini-series). *Membership:* Australian Writers Guild. *Address:* Princefield, 23 King Street, East Ivanhoe, Victoria 3079, Australia.

FIELD, Mark (George), b. 17 June 1923, Lausanne, Switzerland. Educator in Sociology. *Education:* AB, Harvard College, USA, 1948; AM, 1950, PhD, 1955, Harvard University. *Publications:* Doctor and Patient in Soviet Russia, 1957; Social Approaches to Mental Patient Care, (with MS Schwartz, C G Schwartz, et al), 1964; Soviet Socialized Medicine, 1967; Evaluating Health Program Impact: The US-Yugoslav Cooperative Research Effort, (with R E Berry et el). 1974; The Social Consequences of Modernization in Communist Societies (Editor), 1976. *Contributor to:* numerous journals including: American Journal of Sociology; New England Journal of Medicine; Social Problems; Journal of Health and Human Behavior; Soviet Survey, etc. *Memberships include:* International Sociological Association; Research Committee on the Sociology of Medicine (Chairman); American Sociological Association; Societe Europeenne de Culture (Member, Executive Council); Club International de Cooperation (Honorary President for US), Former Chairman, Research Committee, Sociology of Medicine, International Sociological Association. *Address:* 40 Peacock Farm Road, Lexington, MA 02173, USA.

FIENNES, Ranulph Twisleton-Wykeham, (Sir) b. 7 Mar. 1944, Windsor, Berkshire, England. Writer; Traveller; Speaker. *Publications:* Talent for Trouble, 1970; Ice Fall in Norway, 1972; The Headless Valley, 1973; Where Soldiers Fear to Tread, 1975; Hell on Ice, 1979; To The Ends of the Earth, 1983; Bothie, The Polar Dog, 1984. *Contributions to:* Geological Magazine; Observer. *Memberships:* FRGB; Vintner's Company. *Literary Agent:* John Farquarson Limited. *Address:* Robins, Church Lane, Lodsworth, Sussex, England.

FIGES, Eva, b. 15 Apr. 1932, Berlin, Germany. Writer. 1 son, 1 daughter. *Education:* BA (Hons), London University. *Literary Appointments:* C Day Lewis Fellowship, University College, 1973–74; Fellowship (Arts Council), Brunel University, 1977–79. *Publications:* Novels: Equinox, 1966; Winter Journey, 1967; Konek Landing, 1969; B, 1972; Days, 1974; Nelly's Version, 1977; Waking, 1981; Light, 1983; Non-Fiction: Patriarchal Attitudes: Women in Society, 1970; Tragedy and Social Evolution, 1976; Little Eden, 1978; Sex and Subterfuge: Women Writers to 1850, 1982. *Honour:* Guardian Fiction Prize, 1967. *Membership:* Writers Guild, Executive Council. *Literary Agent:* Deborah Rogers Limited. *Address:* 24 Fitzjohns Avenue, London NW3 5NB, England.

FILBY, P William, b. 10 Dec. 1911, Cambridge, England. Appraiser of Literary Properties; Director, Maryland Historical Society, USA, (retired); Consultant, Gale Research Company, Detroit. *Education:* Cambridge University & Foreign Office Courses. *Publications:* Calligraphy & Handwriting in America, 1963; Two Thousand Years of Calligraphy, 1965; American & British Genealogy & Heraldry, 1970, 2nd edition 1975; Star Spangled Books, 1972; Passenger &

Immigration Lists Index, 7 volumes, 1981–; Bibliography of American County Histories, 1985; Philadelphia Maturalizations, 1983; Bibliography of Passenger Lists, 2 volumes, 1981, 1984; American & British Genealogy & Heraldry, 3rd edition, 1981, supplement, 1986. *Honours:* Fellow, Society of Genealogists, London; National Genealogical Society, Washington DC. *Memberships:* New York Typophiles; Baltimore Bibliophiles; Wynkyn de Worde Society. *Address:* 8944 Madison St, Savage, MD 20763, USA.

FILION, Pierre, b. 27 June 1951, Montréal, Québec, Canada. Editor. m. Lucie Désaulniers, 5 Aug. 1978. Montréal, 1 son, 1 daughter. *Education:* PhD, Lettres, University of Montréal, 1984. *Publications:* Le Personnage, 1972; La Brunante, 1973; Impromptu pour deux virus, Théâtre, 1973; Sainte Bénite de sainte bénite de mémére, 1975; Jure craché, 1981; Le chat de Greene street, 1984; Axes intérieurs poems, 1982; La Lady, 1985. *Contributions to:* Le Devoir; Livres d'ici; Études francaises. *Memberships:* CAPAC, UNEQ. *Address:* 560 Champagneur, Outremont, Montréal, Québec, Canada H2V 3P5.

FILIP, Raymond John, b. 1 Aug. 1950, Lübeck, Federal Republic of Germany. Writer, Musician. *Education:* BA McGill University, 1973; Diploma in Education, McGill University, 1975. *Literary Appointments:* Contributing Editor, Books in Canada, Columnist, Poetry Canada Review. *Major Publications:* Poetry: Jaws in a Fish-Bowl, 1976; Somebody Told Me I Look Like Everyman, 1978; Hope's Half-Life, 1983; Flakes (Short stories), forthcoming. *Contributor to:* Numerous periodicals, including: Canadian Forum; Poetry Australia; Canadian Author & Bookman; Canada Writers' Quarterly; Poetry Canada Reveiw. *Membership:* League of Canadian Poets, Quebec Representative on Executive Committee. *Address:* 254 6th Avenue, Verdun, Quebec, H4G 3A1, Canada.

FILKIN, David Shenstone, b. 22 Nov. 1942, Birmingham, England. BBC TV Executive. m. Angela Elizabeth Callam, 31 Aug. 1968, Richmond on Thames, 3 sons. *Education:* BA, honours, Politics, Philosophy, Economics, University College, Oxford. *Publications:* Tomorrow's World Today, 1984. *Contributor to:* The Listener; other trade journals. *Literary Agent:* Jonathan Clowes. *Address:* 29 Bloomfield Road, Kingston upon Thames, Surrey KT1 2SF, England.

FINALE, Frank, b. 10 Mar. 1942. Teacher. *Education:* BS, Education, Ohio State University, 1964; MA, Human Development, Fairleigh Dickinson University, 1976. *Literary Appointments:* Teacher, Poetry Workshops, 1984, 1985. *Contributions to:* Georgia Review; Kansas Quarterly; Poet Lore; Cedar Rock; Poetry Now; Descent; New Laurel Review; Poem; Blue Unicorn; The New Renaissance; Long Pond Review; Negative Capability; De Kalb Literary Arts Journal; Plains Poetry Journal; The Mendocino Review; The Long Story; The Smith; The Princeton Packet; Tempest; Wind Literary Journal; Visions; The Small Pond; Hiram Poetry Review; Phantasm; Anthology of Magazine Verse & Yearbook of American Poetry 1985 (ed. Alan F Pater); Dear Winter (ed. Marie Harris) 1984; Blood to Remember: American Poets on the Holocaust (ed. Charles Fishman), forthcoming. Plus many more. *Honours include:* Writers Digest Poetry Contest, 1966, Honourable Mention; Winner, Cardinal Poetry Quarterly, Best Poem of 1968 Series; Writers Digest Poetry Contest 1976, 1979, 1980; North American Mentor Certificates of Merit for Poetry, 1977, 1978. *Memberships:* Founding member, Ocean County Poets Collective; Founding Editor, Without Halos, annual magazine of poetry & art. Secretary, OCPC. *Address:* 921 Riverside Drive, Pine Beach, NJ 08741, USA.

FINCKE, Gary William, b. 7 July 1945, Pittsburgh, Pennsylvania, USA. Writing Program Director, Susquehanna University. m. Elizabeth Locker, 17 Aug. 1968, 2 sons, 1 daughter. *Education:* BA, Thiel College, 1967; MA, Miami University, 1969; PhD, Kent State University, 1974. *Publications:* Poetry: Breath, 1984;

The Coat in the Heart, 1985; The Days of Uncertain Health, 1986. *Contributions to:* Poetry; Cimarron Review; Poetry Northwest; The Literary Review; The Paris Review; Ontario Review; Southwest Review; Chariton Review; Beloit Poetry Journal; Florida Review; Pequod; Memphis State Review; Southern Poetry Review, etc. *Honours:* Poetry Fellowship, Pennsylvania Arts Council 1982 and 1985; Purchase Prize, Pen Syndicated Fiction Project, 1984; Gamut Fiction Prize, 1984; Footwork Poetry Prize, 1984; Poetry Fellowship, Pennsylvania Arts Council, 1985. *Membership:* Poets and Writers. *Address:* 3 Melody Lane, Selinsgrove, PA 17870, USA.

FINDLEY, Timothy Irving Frederick, b. 30 Oct. 1930, Toronto, Canada. Writer. *Literary Appointments:* Playwright-in-residence, National Arts Centre, Ottawa, Canada, 1974–75; Writer-in residence, University of Toronto, 1970–80, Trent University, Peterborough, Canada, 1984, University of Winnipeg, Canada, 1985. *Major Publications:* The Last of the Crazy People, 1967; The Butterfly Plague, 1969; Can You See Me Yet?, play, 1977; The Wars, 1977; Famous Last Words, 1981; Dinner Along the Amazon, collected short fiction, 1984; Not Wanted On The Voyage, 1984. *Honours & Literary Awards:* Armstrong Award, radio, 1971; ACTRA Award, TV documentary, Canada, 1975; Toronto Book Award, 1977; Governor General's Award, fiction, 1977; Anik Award, TV, Canada, 1980; Honorary DLitt, Trent University, 1982; Author of the Year, Periodical Distributors of Canada 1983, Canadian Booksellers Association 1984; Honorary DLitt, University of Guelph, Canada, 1984; Novel of the Year, Canadian Authors Association, 1985. *Memberships:* Association of Canadian Television & Radio Artists (ACTRA); Writers Union of Canada (Chairman 1977–78); PEN International. *Literary Agent:* Colbert Agency, Toronto, Canada. *Address:* c/o The Colbert Agency, 303 Davenport Road, Toronto, Ontario, Canada M5R 1K5.

FINE, Carla, b. 29 May 1946, New York City. Writer. m. Harry Reiss, 3 Sep. 1968. *Education:* MSc, Columbia University Graduate School of Journalism; BA, New York University. *Publications:* Barron's Guide to Foreign Medical Schools: Selecting Them, Surviving Them and Successfully Practising in the United States, 1979; Married to Medicine: An Intimate Portrait of Doctors' Wives, 1981. *Contributor to:* Cosmopolitan, US, France, Italy, Germany and South America; Omni; Woman's Day. *Membership:* Author's Guild. *Literary Agent:* Dominick Abel. *Address:* 477 West 22nd Street, New York, NY 10011, USA.

FINE, Gary Alan, b. 11 May 1950, New York City, USA. Professor of Sociology. m. Susan Baker Hirsig, 9 June 1972, Jacksonville, Florida, 2 sons. *Education:* BA, University of Pennsylvania, 1972; PhD, Harvard University, 1976. *Literary Appointments:* Assistant Professor, University of Minnesota, 1976–80; Associate Professor, 1980–85; Professor, 1985–. *Publications:* Rumor and Gossip: The Social Psychology of Hearsay (with Ralph Rosnow), 1976; Shared Fantasy: Role-Playing Game as Social Words, 1983; Talking Sociology, 1985. *Contributions to:* American Journal of Sociology; American Sociological Review; Journal of American Folklore. *Memberships:* Phi Beta Kappa; The Loft, Minneapolis–St Paul; American Folklore Society; American Sociological Association. *Address:* Department of Sociology, University of Minnesota, Minneapolis, MN 55455, USA.

FINEGAN, Jack, b. 11 July 1908, Des Moines, Iowa, USA. Professor. *Education:* BA, MA, BD, MTh Lic Theol, LLD, LittD. *Publications include:* Light from the Ancient Past, (Princeton University Press); The Archeology of World Religions, (Princeton University Press); The Archeology of the New Testament, (Princeton University Press), 1969; The Orbits of Life, (Bethany Press); Wanderer Upon Earth, (Harper); Encountering New Testament Manuscripts, 1974/75; Archeological History of the Ancient Middle East, 1979; In the Beginning, (Harper); Jesus, History and You, (John Knox Press); The Christian Church, (Cathedral

Publishers). *Contributions:* Various encyclopaedias and journals. *Memberships include:* Phi Beta Kappa. *Address:* 1116 Cragmont Avenue, Berkeley, CA 94708, USA.

FINK, Louis Charles, b. 15 Sep. 1910, St Louis, Missouri, USA. Editor. m. Vera Baxter. 3 May 1947, Rutherford, 1 son. *Education:* Bankers School of Public Relations, Syracuse University. *Appointments:* Adveritising Director, Hanover Bank, New York; Advertising Manager, Trust Company of Georgia, Atlanta; Editor, Holy Name Newsletter, Rocky Mount. *Publications:* Hallowed Be Thy Name, 1984. *Contributor to:* Over 700 articles in Boys' Life; Liguorian; Burroughs Clearing House; Decor; Our Sunday Visitor; etc. *Honours:* Silver Beaver, Boy Scouts of America, Ver elli Medal, Holy Name Society. *Address:* L-6 Tau Valley, Rocky Mount, NC 27801, USA.

FINLEY, Michael Craig, b. 7 Apr. 1950, Flint, Michigan, USA. Editor. m. Rachel M Frazin, 25 July 1980, Minneapolis, USA, 1 daughter. *Education:* BA, 1972, University of Minnesota. *Publications:* The Movie Under the Blindfold, 1978; Home Trees, 1978; Water Hills, 1984. *Contributions to:* Paris Review; Rolling Stone. *Honour:* Pushcart Prize, 1984. *Memberships:* Wisconsin Arts Board Evaluations Panel, (literature); Poets & Writers Inc. *Address:* 2320 E Bradford Avenue 2, Milwaukee, WI 53211, USA.

FINN, Mary Beavers, b. 14 Apr. 1907. Teacher. *Education:* Life Teaching Certificate, NYS, USA; New York State Teachers College, USA, 1927. *Appointments Include:* Tutor, Grade School, Children, Summers, WWII; Collector, School Taxes, Cornwall-on-Hudson School District, 1943–49. *Contributor to:* North American Mentor Magazine; Cyclo-Flame; Lyrical Parnassus Magazine; Ames Daily Tribune; Des Moines Register; Max Barker Anthologies; The Club Woman; Numerous Year Books; Creative Writing Brochures. *Memberships include:* Secretary Treasurer, 1937–40, Cornwall Writers Club, New York; Area Representative, Board Member, 1967–, 2nd Vice President, 1967–71, Nominating Committee, 9 years, Iowa Poetry Association; Editor, The North American Mentor Magazine, 2 years; Avalon Poets; National League of American Pen Women, Des Moines Branch Treasurer 1980–; National League of American Pen Women Inc, Iowa State Organiser; Academy of American Poets; etc. *Honours:* Award 1973, 1978, 1979, North American Mentor Magazine; numerous similar honours. *Address:* 805 Top-O-Hollow Road, Ames, IA 50010, USA.

FIRKINS, Peter Charles, b. 19 July 1926, Penang, Straits Settlement. Company Director. m. Audrey Adele Field, 24 Mar. 1950, Sydney, Australia, 3 daughters. *Publications:* Strike and Return, 1963; The Australian in Nine Wars, 1971; Of Nautilus and Eagles, 1975; From Hell to Eternity, 1979; The Golden Eagles, 1981. *Membership:* Australian Society of Authors. *Literary Agent:* Watson, Little and Company, London, England. *Address:* 22 Sudbury Way, City Beach, WA 6015, Australia.

FISCH, Harold, b. 25 Mar. 1923, Birmingham, England. University teacher, literary critic. m. Frances Joyce Roston, 26 Aug. 1947, London, England, 4 sons, 1 daughter. *Education:* BA English 1st class honours, University of Sheffield, 1946; BLitt, University of Oxford, 1948. *Literary Appointments:* Lecturers in England Language and Literature, University of Leeds, 1947; Associate Professor of English 1957, Full Professor 1964, Bar-Ilan University, Israel. *Publications:* The Dual Image, 1959, revised edition 1971; Jerusalem and Albion, 1964; Hamlet and the Word, 1971; S Y Agnon, 1975; The Zionist Revolution, 1978; A Remembered Future, 1984. *Contributions to:* Commentary; Yale Review; Midstream; Shakespeare Survey; New Leader; Mozyayim; Molad; Keshet; Haaretz. *Memberships:* Israel Writers' Association; International Association of University of Professors of English. *Address:* 4 Shmaryahu Levin Street, Jerusalem 96664, Israel.

FISHBANE, Michael A, b. 18 Feb. 1943, Cambridge, Massachusetts, USA. Professor of Jewish Religious History and Social Ethics. m. Mona DeKoven, 27 July 1969, 2 sons. *Education:* MA 1967, PhD 1971, Brandeis University. *Publications:* Texts and Responses, co-editor, 1975; Text and Texture – Close Readings of Selected Biblical Texts, 1979; Biblical Interpretation in Ancient Israel, 1985; Harper's Bible Dictionary, co-editor, 1985; Judaism, forthcoming. *Contributions to:* Interalia; Journal of Biblical Literature; Journal of American Oriental Society; Vetus Testamentum; Catholic Judaism; Hebrew Union College Annual; Tarbiz; Annals of the Swedish Theological Institute; Journal of Jewish Studies; Encyclopaedia Judaica; Encyclopaedia Biblica (Hebrew); Abingdon Dictionary of Living Religions; MacMillan Encyclopaedia of Religion. *Honours:* Stipend, National Endowment for the Humanities, 1977; Grants, Memorial Foundation for Jewish Culture, 1977 and 1984–85; Grant, John Simon Guggenheim Memorial Foundation, 1984–85. *Memberships:* Editorial Board 1980–85, Executive Board 1982–, President New England Region 1984–85, Society of Biblical Literature; Executive Board 1972–75 and 1983–86, Association for Jewish Studies; American Oriental Society; Catholic Biblical Society; Colloquium for Biblical Research. *Address:* Department of Near Eastern and Judaic Studies, Brandeis University, Waltham, MA 02254, USA.

FISHER, Benjamin Franklin IV, b. 21 July 1940, Orwigsburg, Pennsylvania, USA. University Professor of English. *Education:* BA, Ursinus College, 1962; MA, 1963, PhD, 1969, Duke University. *Literary Appointments:* Instructor, 1967–69, Assistant Professor, 1969–73, University of Pennsylvania; Assistant Professor, 1973–75, Associate Professor, 1975–79, Director, General Studies, 1976–79, Hahnemann University; Associate Professor, 1979–84, Professor, 1984–, University of Mississippi. *Publications:* Poe at Work: Seven Textual Studies, Editor, 1978; The Very Spirit of Cordiality: The Literary Uses of Alcohol and Alcoholism in the Tales of Edgar Allan Poe, 1978. *Contributions to:* American Literature; Texas Studies in Literature and Language; Victorian Poetry; University of Mississippi Studies in English. *Honours:* Departmental Honours in English, Ursinus College, 1962; Graduate Student Summer Research Grant, Duke University, 1967; Editorial Intern, Cooperative Humanities Programme, Duke University and University of North Carolina, 1966–67. *Memberships:* Past Vice President and President, Poe Studies Association; Life, Chairman of Annual Lecture Series, Edgar Allan Poe Society; Life, Bibliographer, USA Evaluator of Manuscripts, Houseman Society; Life Member, Nathaniel Hawthorne Society; Life Member, Dickens Society. *Address:* Box 816, University, MS 38677, USA.

FISHER, Eugene Joseph, b. 10 Sep. 1943, Grosse Pointe, Michigan, USA. Ecumenist-Catholic/Jewish Relations. m. Catherine Ambrosiano, 31 Dec. 1970. *Education:* BA magna cum laude, Sacred Heart College, Detroit, 1965; MA, Catholic Theology, University of Detroit, 1967; MA Hebrew Studies 1970, PhD Hebrew Culture and Education 1976, New York University. *Literary Appointments:* Ecumenical Events Editor, Journal of Ecumenical Studies, 1983–. *Publications include:* Faith Without Prejudice: Rebuilding Christian Attitudes Toward Judaism, 1977; Homework for Christians Preparing For Christian-Jewish Dialogue, 1982; Liturgical Foundations of Social Policy in the Catholic and Jewish Traditions, (co-editor with Rabbi Daniel Polish), 1983; Seminary Education and Catholic-Jewish Relations, 1983; From Death to Hope: Liturgical Reflections on the Holocaust, (with Rabbi Leon Klenicki), 1983. *Contributions to:* Over 100 articles in major religious journals. *Honours include:* Edith Stein Guild Award, 1983. *Memberships include:* Society of Biblical Literature; Catholic Biblical Association; Executive Council, National Association of Professors of Hebrew, 1978–; Biblical Archaeology Society; Service Internationale de Documentation Judeo-Chretienne; American Academy of Religion; National Conference of Christians and Jews. *Address:* 11296 Spyglass Cove Lane, Reston, VA 22091, USA.

FISHER, Leonard Everett, b. 24 June 1924, New York City, USA. Painter; Illustrator; Author; Visiting Professor, Arts; Dean Emeritus. m. Margery Meskin, 21 Dec. 1952, Rockville Centre, 1 son, 2 daughters. *Education:* BFA, 1949, MFA, 1950, Yale University School of Fine Arts. *Appointments:* Delegate-At-Large, White House Conference on Library & Information Services, 1979. *Publications:* The Death of Evening Star, 1972; The Art Experience, 1973; Across the Sea from Galway, 1975; Alphabet Art, 1978; A Russian Farewell, 1980; The Seven Days of Creation, 1981; Storm at the Jetty, 1981; Number Art, 1982; Symbol Art, 1985; The Statue of Liberty, 1985; Masterpieces of American Painting, 1985; The Great Wall of China, 1986; The Colonial Americans, 19 volumes, 1964–1977; Nineteenth Century America, 7 volumes, 1978–1983. *Honours:* Pulitzer Prize, Painting, 1950; Premio Grafico Fiera Di Bologna, Italy, 1968; Medallion of the University of Southern Mississippi, Children's Literature, 1979; Christopher Medal, 1980; National Jewish Book Award, Children's Literature, 1981; Various Citations, 1959–; etc. *Membership:* Authors Guild. *Agent:* John Hawkins & Associates. *Address:* 7 Twin Bridge Acres Road, Westport, CT 06880, USA.

FISHER, Neal Floyd, b. 4 Apr. 1936, Washington, Indiana, USA. Minister; Seminary President. m. Ila Alexander, 18 Aug. 1957, Marion, Indiana, 1 son, 1 daughter. *Education:* BA, DePauw University; MDiv, School of Theology, PhD, Graduate School, Boston University. *Publications:* The Parables of Jesus: Glimpses of the New Age, 1979; Context for Discovery, 1981. *Honours:* Honorary LHD, De Pauw University, Greencastle, Indiana, 1983; Distinguished Alumnus Award, Boston University School of Theology, 1985. *Address:* 2426 Lincolnwood Drive, Evanston, IL 60201, USA.

FISHLOCK, David Jocelyn, b. 9 Aug, 1932, Bath, England. Journalist. m. Mary Millicent Cosgrove, 19 Dec. 1959, Hampstead, 1 son. *Education:* Bristol College of Technology (now Bath University); Hon D Litt, Salford University, 1982. *Literary Appointments:* Associate Editor, Metalworking Production, 1959–62; Technology Editor, New Scientist, 1962–67; Science Editor, Financial Times, 1967–. *Publications:* The New Materials, 1967; A Guide to the Laser (Editor), 1967; Man Modified, 1969; The Business of Science; The Business of Biotechnology, 1982. *Contributions to:* The Energy Daily, Washington, DC (London Correspondent); Nuclear Europe, (Columnist). *Honours:* Queen's Silver Jubilee Medal, 1977; Glako Travelling Fellowship, 1978; Worthington Pump Award, 1982; Chemical Writer of the Year Award, 1982; OBE, 1983. *Membership:* Association of British Science Writers. *Literary Agent:* Campbell, Thomson, McLaughlin. *Address:* Traveller's Joy, Copse Lane, Jordans, Buckinghamshire HP9 2TA, England.

FISHMAN, Katharine Davis, b. 13 June 1937, Paterson, New Jersey, USA. Writer. m. Joseph Louis Fishman, 19 July 1959, New York City, 2 daughters. *Education:* BA, Cornell University, 1958. *Literary Appointment:* Assistant Editor, Mademoiselle Magazine, 1960–64. *Publication:* The Computer Establishment, 2nd edition 1982. *Contributions to:* New York magazine; Atlantic; New York Times magazine; New York Times Book Review; etc. *Memberships:* Authors Guild; American Society of Journalists & Authors; Womens Ink. *Literary Agent:* Curtis Brown Ltd, USA. *Address:* 316 West 79th Street, New York, NY 10024, USA.

FISHOF, David, b. 18 June 1956, New York City, USA. Theatrical and Sport Entertainer. m. Monica Belmont, 20 Feb. 1977, New York, 1 son, 1 daughter. *Education:* BS. *Publication:* Putting It On The Line, 1984. *Literary Agent:* Mel Berger, c/o William Morris Agency. *Address:* 1775 Broadway, New York, NY 10019, USA.

FITTS, Henry King, b. 21 Dec. 1914, Boston, Massachusetts, USA. Teacher of High School, English. m. Brenda Skene, 23 June 1937, Winchester, Massachusetts, 1 son, 1 daughter. *Education:* BS, Harvard College; MA, Columbia Teacher's College. *Publications:* I Begged for Bread in Russia, (with Paul Bergman), 1976; Winnowings from the Granite State, 1982. *Contributions to:* Open Road for Boys; Yachting; Rudder; Popular Mechanics; Mechanics Illustrated; and others. *Address:* RFD 180 Trow Hill Road, Sunapee, NH 03782, USA.

FITZGERALD, Arlene Janiece, b. 22 Feb. 1927, Orleans, Nebraska, USA. Author; Writer. m. Ralph Lester Fitzgerald, 1944, Medford, Oregon, 1 son, 2 daughters. *Education:* Art, Literature and Psychology, Southern Oregon State College. *Publications:* As Monica Heath: Falconlough, 1966; Hawkshadow, As Arlene J Fitzgerald: Everything You Always Wanted to Know About Sorcery; Numbers for Lovers; Windfire. *Contributions to:* Numerous publications of factual articles and short fiction. *Literary Agent:* Jane Rotrosen Agency. *Address:* c/o Jane Rotrosen Agency, 226 East 32nd Street, New York City, NY 10016, USA.

FITZGERALD, Jeanne Tashian, b. 18 Apr. 1942, Chicago, Illinois, USA. Medical Editor; Writer. *Education:* BA, Chicago State University; MA, University of Chicago. *Appointments:* Associate Managing Editor, Annals of Vascular Surgery, 1985–. *Major Publications:* Every Woman's Pharmacy: A Guide to Safe Drug Use (co-author with W R Rayburn & F Zuspan), 1983. *Contributor to:* Annals of Thoracic Surgery; Journal of Family Practice; Emergency Medicine; Michigan Academician; Ann Arbor Observer; Chronicle. *Honour:* Fellow, American Medical Writers Association. *Memberships:* American Medical Writers Association, Michigan Chapter President 1985–86. *Address:* 821 Hewett Drive, Ann Arbor, MI 48103, USA.

FITZGERALD, Penelope Mary, b. 17 Dec. 1916. Writer. m. 15 Aug. 1942, 1 son, 2 daughters. *Education:* BA, Oxford. *Publications:* Edward Burne Jones (biography), 1975; The Golden Child, 1976; The Bookshop, 1977; The Knox Brothers, 1977; Offshore (fiction), 1979; Human Voices (fiction), 1980; At Freddie's (fiction), 1981; Charlotte Mew and Her Friends (biography), 1984. *Contribution to:* William Morris: The Novel on Blue Paper (Dickens Studies Annual, 1982). *Honours:* Booker McConnell Prize for Fiction, 1979; Rose Mary Crawshaw Award, 1985. *Address:* c/o William Collins, 8 Grafton Street, London W1, England.

FITZHENRY, Robert Irvine, b. 10 Apr. 1918, New York City, USA. Book Publisher. m. Hilda A Anderson, 22 Jan. 1949, Slingerlands, New York, 3 daughters. *Education:* BA, University of Michigan. *Publications:* Fitzhenry and Whiteside Book of Quotations, 1981; Barnes and Noble Book of Quotations, 1983; David and Charles Book of Quotations, 1985. *Address:* Box 508 – 62 Mill Street, Uxbridge, Ontario LOC ITO, Canada.

FITZMYER, Joseph Augustine, b. 4 Nov. 1920, Philadelphia, Pennsylvania, USA. Priest; Professor. *Education:* AB, 1943, AM, 1945, Loyola University; STL, Facultes St Albert de Louvain, Belgium, 1952; PhD, Johns Hopkins University, USA, 1956; SSL, Pontificio Istituto Biblico, Rome, Italy, 1957. *Appointments:* Instructor, Gonzaga High School, Washington DC, 1945–48; Assistant Professor, New Testament, Woodstock College, 1958; Associate Professor, 1959, Professor, 1964–69, Woodstock College; Professor, University of Chicago, 1969–71, Fordham University, 1971–74, Weston School of Theology, 1974–76, Catholic University of America, 1976–. *Publications:* The Genesis Apocryphon of Qumran Cave 1, 1966; The Aramaic Inscriptions of Sefire, 1967; Co-Editor, The Jerome Biblical Commentary, 1968; Essays on the Semitic Background of the New Testament, 1971; Co-Author, A Manual of Palestinian Aramaic Texts, 1978; The Gospel According to Luke, 1981–85. *Contributor to:* Catholic Biblical

Quarterly; Journal of Biblical Literature: Theological Studies; New Testament Studies; Biblica; etc; Editor, Journal of Biblical Literature, 1971–76, Catholic Biblical Quarterly, 1980–84. *Honours:* LHD, University of Scranton, 1979; Litt D, College of Holy Cross, Worcester, 1979; LHD, Fairfield University, 1981; Teol H Dr, Lunds Universitet, Sweden, 1981; Burkitt Medal for Biblical Studies, British Academy, 1984. *Memberships:* Studiorum Novi Testamenti Societas, Editorial Board 1983–86; Society of Biblical Literature, President 1978–79; Catholic Biblical Association, President, 1969–70. *Address:* Jesuit Community, Georgetown University, 37th + 0 Sts, NW, Washington DC 20057, USA.

FITZPATRICK, Kevin, b. 3 Oct. 1949, St Paul, Minnesota, USA. *Education:* BA, University of Minnesota, 1971; MEd, College of St Thomas, 1977. *Literary Appointment:* Editor, Lake Street Review, 1977–. *Contributions to:* Poet's Voices '84; Milkwood Chronicle; Santuary Si!; Visions, and others. *Honour:* Joseph O'Brien Creative Writing Award, 1967. *Membership:* Board Member, Minnesota Literature Newsletter. *Address:* Box 7188, Powderhorn Station, Minneapolis, MN 55407, USA.

FITZSIMMONS, Thomas, b. 21 Oct. 1926. Professor of English. *Education:* Fresno State College, USA, 1947; Sorbonne & Institute de Scie. Pol. France, 1949–50; BA, English Literature, Stanford University, 1951; MA, English & Comparative Literature, Columbia University, 1952. *Appointments:* Cons, History Section, Office of Secretary of Defence, 1952; Foreign Affairs Writer & Editor, New Republic Magazine; Assistant Professor, American University, 1955–59; Research Chairman, 1955–56, Director, Research, 1956–58, Director & Editor, HRAF Press, 1953–59, HRAF, Yale University; Assistant Professor, 1959–60, Associate Professor, 1961–66, Professor, 1966–, Oakland University; Visiting Professor, Tokyo University of Education, Keio University, Japan Women's University, Tokyo, Japan, 1973–75; Director, Asian Artists in Res., Editor, Asian Poetry in Translation, 1979; Publisher, Katydid Books. *Publications include:* USSR, 1960; Downingside, 1969; This Time, This Place, 1969; Zenjoints, 1970; Morningdew, 1970; Meditation Seeds, 1971; Japanese Poetry Now, 1971; Mooning, 1971; Playseeds, 1973; Some Other American Poets, (videotape), 1974; The Great Hawaiin Conquest, 1979; Rocking Mirror Daybreak, 1982; Japan Personally, 1986 (in Japanese). *Contributor to:* Numerous journals and magazines. *Honours:* Recipient, various honours including: National Endowment for the Arts Award in Poetry, 1967, 1982. *Memberships:* Various professional associations. *Address:* Dept of English, Oakland University, Rochester, MI 78063, USA.

FJÄLLSTEDT, Linnea, b. 4 Sep. 1926, Vilhelmina, Sweden. Author; Painter. *Education:* Self Taught. *Publications:* Hungerpesten, 1975; Ödeslotten, 1977; Befrielsen, 1979; Missgärningen, 1984; Poas Söner, 1986; En Gång I Lappland, 1985; Unpublished, Wilderness Drama, (with Bert L Gilleroth). *Contributor to:* Husmodern; Allers; Kvällsposten; Hemmets Journal; Svenska Journalen; Svenska Turistföreningens Årsbok, 1980; most National Newspapers; Radio and TV Programmes; working on TV series for Children. *Honours:* Scholarships: Landstingets Kulturstipendium, 1976; Norrlandsförbundets Kulturstipendium, 1976; Landsbygdens Kulturstipendium; ABF Kulturstipendium; Vilhelmina Kommuns Kulturstipendium. *Memberships:* Writers Association, Sweden; KACV, Cultural Working Centre, ibid. *Address:* Rönnäs 5026, 912 00 Vilhelmina, Sweden.

FLEET, Judith Van Wyck, b. 4 Apr. 1937. Port Washington, New York, USA. Clinical Research. m. Anthony J Zagarella, 2 June 1962, deceased, 1 daughter. *Education:* BA, Biology, Florida State University. *Contributor to:* Numerous articles in professional journals, and papers presented including: Clinical Pharmacological Therapy; Drug Metabolism and Disposition; Journal Pharmaceutical Science; Life

Sciences; European Journal of Clinical Pharmacology; Progressive Neuropsychopharmacology Biological Psychiatry; etc. *Memberships:* American Medical Writers Association; Drug Information Association; Society for Clinical Trials; American Society of Clinical Phamacology and Therapeutics; New York Academy of Sciences. *Address:* Medical Division, Burroughs Wellcome Co, Research Triangle Park, NC 27709, USA.

FLEETWOOD, Frances, b. 24 May 1902, London, England. Writer. *Education:* Sorbonne University, Paris, France. *Publications:* U Nobile, With the Italia to the North Pole, translator, 1930; Conquest, The Story of a Theatre Family, 1953; My Polar Flights, translator, 1961; Historical monographs on Rimini and Casertavecchia, in Italian and English, 1968 and 1973; Concordia, 1971; Concordia Errant, 1973; Beloved Upstart, (with V Schuyler), 1974; Translator of 2 novels by Dekobra; Flashback (Romance of Casertantica, Yesterday and Today), 1980; Collaboration with M Tabanelli: Castles, Fortresses and Towers of the Malatesti, 1963; Women of the Malatesti, 1984; Romagna, 1984. *Contributions to:* Times Educational Supplement; La Pie. *Honours:* Honourable mention, Gradara International Prize Competition, 1973; Silver Medal, Friends of Gradara. *Address:* Via del Golfo 4, 04028 Scauri (Latina), Italy.

FLEGG, Henry Graham, b. 10 June 1924, London, England. University Teacher. m. 7 Oct. 1950, Woodeaton, 1 son, 4 daughters, 1 deceased. *Education:* MA, St Andrews; DCAE, Cranfield; CEng; FIMA; MIEE; MRAeS; FRMetS. *Appointment:* Reader, History of Mathematics, The Open University. Editor, Journal of the Anglican and Eastern Churches Association. *Publications:* Boolean Algebra and its Application, 1964; Boolean Algebra, 1972; An Introduction to Calculus & Algebra, I-III, 1972; Basic Mathematical Structures, I-II, with N Gowar, 1973–74; From Geometry to Topology, 1975; Number: Its History & Meaning, 1983–84; Nicolas Chuquet: Renaissance Mathematician, with C Hay & B Moss, 1984. *Contributor to:* Control; Journal RAF Technical College; Bulletin IMA; International Journal Mathematical Education Science Technology; Editor, Studies in Maths; New Scientist; Journal French Society Historical Mathematics; etc. *Literary Agent:* Messrs A D Peters & Co. *Address:* 20 Clapham Road, Bedford MK41 7PP, England.

FLETCHER, Barbara Rainbow, b. 15 Oct. 1935, San Francisco, California, USA. Freelance Author. m. Donald D Fletcher, 28 May 1977, Seattle, Washington, 2 sons, 1 daughter. *Education:* AA, Seattle, Washington, USA. *Literary Appointments:* Braille Edition of publication, 1984. *Publication:* Don't Blame the Stork, 1981. *Membership:* American Name Society. *Address:* 18916 68th Avenue NE #E101, Bothell, WA 98011, USA.

FLETCHER, David Richard, b. 21 May 1939, Leicester, England. Journalist. m. Joy, 1 son, 1 daughter. *Education:* BA (Hons), Leeds University. *Literary Appointments:* Lancashire Evening Telegraph, 1960–63; Birmingham Post, 1963–66; The Daily Telegraph, 1966–. Correspondent, Health Services, 1979–. *Address:* 135 Fleet Street, London EC4, England.

FLETCHER, Ian, b. 22 Aug. 1920, London, England. University Professor. m. Loraine McQueen, 14 Aug. 1965, Woodford Bridge, 2 daughters. *Education:* Goldsmith's College, London University; PhD, University of Reading. *Literary Appointments:* Editorial Board: Nine, 1949–51; Colonnade, 1952; Assistant Lecturer, 1956–58, Lecturer, 1958–66, Reader in English Literature, 1966–78, Professor, 1978–82, University of Reading; Selector Poetry Book Society, 1961–63; Professor, Arizona State University, USA, 1982. *Publications:* Orisons, Poems, 1947; Springtime, anthology, with G S Fraser, 1953; The Lover's Martyrdom, 1957; Motets, poems, 1962; Romantic Mythologies, editor, 1965; The Milesian Intrusion, translation, 1968; Meredith Now, Editor, 1972; Lauds, poems, 1978; Decadence and the 1890s, Editor, 1979;

Poems in Continuities, 1980; An Octagon for Peter Russell, 1982. *Contributions to:* Poetry Review; Encounter; London Magazine; Times Literary Supplement; Southern Quarterly; Victorian Studies; Victorian Poetry, and others. *Address:* 8 Warwick Road, Reading, Berkshire, England.

FLETT, Ethel Snelson, b. 24 July 1912, Christchurch, New Zealand. Novelist. m. Rev William Nugent Flett, 18 May 1940, Christchurch, 1 son, 1 daughter. *Publications:* Author of 51 published works including: New Zealand Inheritance, 1957; The Essie Sommers Story, 1974. *Contributions to:* Australian Woman's Mirror; New Zealand Mirror; New Zealand Home Journal; New Zealand Womens Weekly; New Zealand Dairy Exporter; Womans Weekly, UK, serials; Columnist, Timaru Herald; Good Housekeeping, UK; Scots Magazine; numerous newspapers. *Address:* Jesmond Cottage, 32a Tom Parker Avenue, Napier, New Zealand.

FLiTNER, Andreas, b. 28 Sep. 1922, Jena, Federal Republic of Germany. Professor, Education, University of Tubingen. m. Sonia Christ, 14 Aug. 1950, Basel. *Education:* Dr Phil, MA, Basel, 1951; Habil, 1954. *Publications:* Erasmus im Urteil seiner Nachwelt, 1952; Polit.Erziehung, 1957; Soziologische Jugendforschung, 1963; Brennpunkte gegenw. Padagogik, 1969; Spielen-Lernen, 1972; Missratener Fortschritt, 1977; Konrad...Uber Erziehung and Nicht; Erziehung, 1982–85; Lernen mit Kopf und Hand, 1983; Editor: Wilhelm v. Humboldt, Werke in 5 Banden, 1960–81; Erziehung in Wissenschaft u. Praxis, 30 volumes, 1967–; Zeitschrift f.Padagogik, 1962–. *Contributor to:* Numerous professional journals. *Address:* Im Rotbad 43, D7400 Tübingen, Federal Republic of Germany.

FLOURNOY, Sheryl Diane Hines, b. 12 Nov. 1951, Mishawaka, Indiana, USA. Author. m. Keith Hays Flournoy, 7 Mar. 1970, Marshall, Texas, 2 daughters. *Education:* Creative Writing, University of Houston, Texas. *Publications:* Historical Novels: Flames of Passion, 1982; Destiny's Embrace, 1984; Reckless Desire, 1985; Duskfire, 1987. Contemporary Novels: Make No Promises, 1982; Share Your Tomorrows, 1983. *Literary Agent:* Denis Marcil Literary Agency. *Address:* 3325 West Paradise Lane, Phoenix, AZ 85023, USA.

FLOWER, Raymond Charles, b. 2 July 1921, Bexhill, Sussex. Author; Social Historian. *Publications Include:* Napoleon to Nasser: The Story of Modern Egypt, 1972; Lloyd's of London, An Illustrated History (with M Wynn Jones), 1974, 1981; Motor Sports, 1974; The Story of Skiing & Other Winter Sports, 1976, 1977; Chianti: The Land, The People & The Wine, 1978, 1979; Chianti: Storia e Cultura, 1981; A Hundred Years of Motoring: An RAC History of the Car (with M Wynn Jones), 1981; The Palace, A Profile of St Moritz, 1982; Raffles: The Story of Singapore, 1984; Year of the Tiger, 1985. Editor, In Search of the Holy Land, 1979. In Progress, The Old Ship: A Prospect of Brighton, 1986. *Honours Include:* Numerous motor-racing trophies; Nominated Gonfaloniere della Lega del Chianti, 1978. *Address:* Torre di Grignano, Castellina in Chianti, Siena, Italy.

FLURY, Alfred, b. 16 Apr. 1934, Wangen, Switzerland. Chaplain; Composer; Lyricist; Singer. *Education:* Theology; Philosophy; Music. *Contributions to:* Various newspapers on education and drugs problems. *Memberships:* Pen Club; Swiss Authors Association. *Address:* c/o Kaplan Flury, Dorfstrasse 243, CH–4612 Wangen, Switzerland.

FOGARTY, Robert Stephen, b. 30 Aug. 1938, Brooklyn, New York, USA. Editor, Professor of History. *Education:* BA, Fordham College, 1960; MA, University of Denver, 1962; PhD, University of Denver, 1968. *Literary Appointments:* Editor, The Antioch Review, 1977–. *Major Publications:* Letters from a Self-made Merchant to his Son (editor), 1971; American Utopianism (editor), 1974; American Utopian Adventure (editor), 1975; Dictionary of American & Communal History, 1980 ; The Righteous Remnant: The

House of David, 1981. *Contributor to:* Prospects: Annual Studies in American Culture; Missouri Review; American Studies International; Journal of American Studies; Labor History; New England Quarterly. *Honour:* Fellow, National Endowment for the Humanities, 1983. *Memberships:* Bibliographical Committee, American Studies Association; Historic Communal Societies Organisation; Organisation of American Historians. *Address:* Antioch Review, PO Box 148, Yellow Springs, Oh 45387, USA.

FOGDALL, Alberta Frances Brooks, b. 1 Sep. 1912, Clay Centre, Kansas, USA. Educator; Homemaker; Writer. m. Dr Vergil S Fogdall, 27 Dec. 1934, Ottowa, Kansas, 2 sons, 1 daughter. *Education:* BA, Ottawa University, 1933; MAT, Lewis & Clark College, Portland, Oregon. *Publications:* A Golden Anniversary: A Brief History of the Lake Grove Presbyterian Church, 1974–75; Royal Family of the Columbia: Dr John McLoughlin and His Family, 1978, 2nd edition 1982; Father of the Pacific Northwest: Dr John McLoughlin, 1984 for youth. *Contributor to:* Clark County Historical Journal; The Columbian; The Oregonian; The Review; The Enterprise Courier. *Honours:* Recipient of various honours and awards including: Tied for Top Place, in WWA Non-fiction, 1983; Western Writers of America; 2nd edition, Royal Family of the Columbia placed 1st, votes of national newspapers; Scholarships to French Language Institute, sponsored by National Defense Education Association, New York State. *Memberships:* Washington County Historical Society; Fort Vancouver Historical Society; Oregon Historical Society; Clackamas County Historical Society. *Address:* 2943 S.W. Lake View Blvd, Lake Oswego, OR 97034, USA.

FONTAINE, André Lucien Georges, b. 30 Mar. 1921, Paris, France. Journalist. *Education:* Lic es Lettres, Diplôme d'etudes Superieures, Law and Economics, Paris University. *Literary Appointment:* Editor, Le Monde. *Publications include:* Histoire de la Guerre Froide, 2 volumes, 1965 and 1966 (English translation: The History of the Cold War, 2 volumes, 1966 and 1967); La Guerre Civile Froide, 1969; Le Dernier Quart de Siécle, 1976 and 1981; La France au Bois Dormant, 1978; Un Seul Lit Pour Deux Rêves, 1981; Sortir de l'hexagonie, (with Pierre Li), 1984. *Contributions to:* BBC; New York Times; Foreign Affairs; Affari; Ester; etc. *Honour:* Atlas International editor, 1976. *Address:* 5 rue des Italiens, 75427 Paris, Cedex 09, France.

FONTANA, Thomas, Michael, b. 12 Sep. 1951, Buffalo, New York, USA. Writer. m. Sagan Lewis, 18 Dec. 1982, Santa Monica, California. *Education:* BA Speech & Theatre Arts, State University College at Buffalo, New York. *Literary Appointments:* Playwright-in-Residence, The Writer's Theatre, 1976–; Playwright-in-Residence, Williamstown Theatre Festival, 1978–81. *Major Publications:* Currently Producer/Writer of TV series, St Elsewhere. *Honours:* Various TV writing awards, including Emmy Award 1983–84. *Memberships:* Dramatists' Guild; Authors League of America; Writers Guild of America; Board of Directors, American Writers Theatre Foundation, 1975–. *Address:* 304 East 52nd Street, 3rd Floor, New York, NY 10022, USA.

FONTANET, Jean-Claude, b. 16 Feb. 1925, Geneva, Switzerland. Writer. m. Paule van Hollebeke, 5 May 1949, Geneva, 1 son. *Education:* Collège Calvin, Geneva. *Publications:* La Mascogne ou le péché mignon du collégien, 1962; La Montagne, 1970; Mater dolorosa, 1977; Les Panneaux, 1978; Printemps de beauté, 1983. *Honours:* Schiller Prize, 1976; Alps-Jura Prize, 1976; Short Story Prize, Town of Le Mans, 1978. *Memberships:* Swiss Society of Writers; Association of French-Speaking Writers. *Address:* 32 route de l'Hospice, 1247 Anieres/Geneva, Switzerland.

FONTIER, Jaak, b. 27 July 1927, Bruges, Belgium. Author, Art Critic, Retired teacher. m. Christiane Brynooghe, 26 Dec. 1953, Furnes, 1 son, 2 daughters. *Education:* Teacher of Germanic Languages, Training College, Ghent, 1946–48. **Publications:** Swimberghe,

Monograph, 1970; Zen, maan en sterren, essay, 1975; In de zon van zen, essay, 1977; Friedrich Hölderlin. Wat blijft stichten de dichters. Duits-Nederlandse bloemlezing, traduction of 48 poems, 1981; Luc Peire, monograph, 1984. *Contributions to:* Nieuw Vlaams Tijdschrift; De Vlaamse Gids; Het 5de Wiel; Yang; Ons Erfdeel; Kreatief. *Honour:* Award Essay Province West-Flanders, 1969. *Memberships:* Vereniging Westvlaamse Schrijvers; Vereniging Vlaamse Letterkundigen; Association Internationale des Critiques d'Art. *Address:* Sint-Ewoudsstraat 34, B 8200 Brugge, Belgium.

FOON, Dennis Todd, b. 18 Nov. 1951, Detroit, Michigan, USA. Playwright; Director. m. Jane Howard Baker, divorced, 1 daughter. *Education:* BA, University of Michigan, USA, 1973; MFA, University of British Columbia, Canada, 1975. *Publications:* The Windigo, 1979; Raftbaby, 1979; Heracles, 1979; New Canadian Kid, 1982; Trummi Kaput, 1983; Hunchback of Notre Dame, 1983; Am I The Only One, 1985. *Contributions to:* Canadian Theatre Review; Contemporary Canadian Theatre; New World Visions. *Honours:* Avery Hopwood Award, University of Michigan, 1972; Writers Digest Award, 1975; Literary Prize, Canadian Broadcasting Corporation, 1985. *Membership:* Playwrights Union of Canada. *Literary Agent:* Great North Artists, Toronto. *Address:* 1-2975 Oak Street, Vancouver, British Columbia, Canada V6H 2K7.

FOOTE, Thomas Howard, b. 1 Feb. 1950, La Jolla, California, USA. Editor, Profiles Magazine. *Education:* BS, 1968, MA, 1978, MA 1979, PhD 1985, Stanford University. *Literary Appointments:* Lecturer in Educational Research Methods, Lecturer in Business Statistics and Operations Research College of Education, San Diego State University; Co-Director, Social Equity Center, funded by Ford Foundation; Editorial Consultant to PWS Publishers Division of Wadsworth Inc, Richard D Irwin Inc, and others. *Publications:* Ethnic Groups and Public Education in California, 1978; Intuitive Themes of Operations Research and Practical Applications for Managers, 1983; Intuitive Themes of Statistics and Practical Applications for Managers, 1983; Student Disinterest in School and the Microeconomics of Reversing it, 1985. *Contributions to:* Reader; Profiles. *Honours:* Ford Foundation Fellowship for graduate study in Educational Policy Analysis at Stanford University; Associated Business Students' Appreciation Award for Outstanding Professor; Professor of the Month. *Address:* 5661 Lake Park Way, #10, La Mesa, CA 92041, USA.

FOQUÉ, Richard K V, b. 21 Nov. 1943, Willebroek, Belgium. Professor of Architecture, Antwerp; Partner, F.A.A.D. Architects-Engineers-Planning Consultants, Antwerp. m. Bie Wellens, 15 Apr. 1972, Wilrijk, 2 sons, 1 daughter. *Education:* Burg.Ir.Architect, University of Leuven, Belgium; MSc, Design Technology, University of Manchester, UK. *Literary Appointments:* Member, International Editorial Board of Design Studies. *Publications:* Alleen Kringen, poetry, 1967; De Dieren Komen, poetry, 1969; De Mekanische Priester, poetry, 1971; Drie millivolt van oneindig, poetry, 1972; Ontwerpsystemen, 1975; Wonen met de wereld, 1978. *Contributions to:* Poetry in Heibel, Yang. Article in design studies: DMG-Journal; AA-Quarterly; Neuf; Bouw; A-Plus; Intermediair; Streven; Wetenscharp en Samenleving; Elsevier-Techno. *Membership:* V.V.L. (Society of Flemish Authors). *Address:* Hortside, Bruinstraat 14, B–2418 Lille, Belgium.

FORD, Brian J(ohn), b. 13 May 1939, Chippenham, Wiltshire, England. Scientist; Broadcaster; Lecturer. *Education:* University of Wales. *Publications include:* German Secret Weapons: Blueprint for Mars, 1969; Allied Secret Weapons: War of Science, 1970, editions in Portuguese, French, Italian, Japanese, Spanish and Dutch; Microbiology and Food, 1970; Nonscience...Or How to Rule the World, 1971; The Earth Watchers, 1973; Optical Microscope Manual; Past and Present Uses and Techniques, USA, Australia and UK edition, 1973; Revealing Lens: Mankind and the Microscope,

1973; Microbe Power: Tomorrow's Revolution, 1976, USA, 1977, Japan, 1979; Patterns of Sex: The Mating Urge and Our Sexual Future, 1979, USA, 1980; The Cult of the Expert, 1982, 83, Germany, 1985; 101 Questions About Science, 1983; 101 More Questions..., 1984; Compute: How, Why, Do I Have To?, 1985; Sexually Transmitted Diseases and their Mimics (in Sex and Your Health), 1985; Single Lens: The Story of the Simple Microscope, UK and USA, 1985; The Food Book, 1986. *Contributions to:* Journals and British Broadcasting Corporation. *Memberships include:* Savage Club; British Broadcasting Corporation Glub; Architecture Club. *Address:* Mill Park House, 57 Westville Road, Cardiff, Wales.

FORD, Herbert Paul, b. 27 Aug. 1927, San Benito, Texas, USA. Vice-President for Development and College Relations, Pacific Union College, Angwin, California. m. Anita Cavagnaro, 7 Sep. 1952, 3 daughters. *Education:* BA, Pacific Union College, 1954; MA, California State University, Northridge, 1975. *Publications include:* Wind High, Sand Deep, 1965; Flee The Captor, 1966; No Guns On Their Shoulders, 1968; Crimson Coats and Kimonos, 1968; Affair of the Heart, 1969; Rudo the Reckless Russian, 1970; For The Love of China, 1971; Pitcairn, 1971; The Miscellany of Pitcairn's Island, 1980. *Contributor to:* Time; Newsweek; Saturday Evening Post, various religious journals. *Memberships include:* Association for Education in Journalism; President, Christian Writers Club, Napa Valley, California; Kappa Tau Alpha. *Address:* 531 Sunset Drive, Angwin, CA 94508, USA.

FORD, Jesse Hill, b. 28 Dec. 1928, Troy Alabama, USA. Writer. m. Lillian P Chandler, 15 Nov. 1975, Nashville, Tennessee, USA. 2 sons, 2 daughters. *Education:* BA, Vanderbilt University; MA, University of Florida; Fulbright Scholar, University of Oslo, Norway; Post-graduate Studies Center for Advanced Study, Middletown, Connecticut, USA. *Major Publications:* Mountains of Gilead, 1961; The Liberation of Lord Byron Jones, 1965; The Feast of St Barnabas, 1967; The Raider, 1975 (novels); Fishes, Birds & Sons of Men (short stories), 1968; The Conversion of Buster Drumwright (play), 1963; Mister Potter & His Bank (biography), 1978. *Contributor to:* Atlantic Monthly; Cosmopolitan; Esquire; Paris Review; Playboy. *Honour:* Edgar Allen Poe award (from Mystery Writers of America), 1976. *Literary Agent:* Harold Ober Associates, New York City, USA. *Address:* P O Box 43, Bellevue, TN 37221, USA.

FORD, Lee Ellen, b. 16 June 1917, Auburn, Indiana, USA. Attorney-at-Law; Writer. *Education:* BS, Wittenberg College, Ohio, 1947; MS, University Minnesota, 1949; PhD, Iowa State Campus, Ames, 1952; JD, Notre Dame University, Indiana, 1972. *Publications:* Editor and compiler and author of some 1,000 publications in Women's Legal Handbook Series. Over 100 scientific research publications; numerous books on dogs, collies in particular, including: Novice Obedience, 1957; The White Collie, 1957; Illustrated History of Collies; Elementary Genetic Lessons, 2 vols; Showing and Judging Collies, 1955. Contributor to many magazines and other publications including: Cytology, Cytologia, Women's Law Journal and American Kennel Club Gazette. *Address:* 824 E Seventh Street, Auburn, IN 46706, USA.

FORD, Philip John, b. 28 Mar. 1949, Ilford, Essex, England. University Lecturer. m. Lenore Joyce Muskett, 17 July 1982, Cambridge. *Education:* BA, 1971, MA, 1975, PhD, 1977, King's College, University of Cambridge; M.és Llettres, Bordeaux III, France, 1977. *Literary Appointments:* Lecturer in French, University of Cambridge. *Major Publications:* George Buchanan, Prince of Poets, 1982; Alexandre Hardy, Panthée: édition critique, 1986. *Contributor to:* Bibliothèque d'Humanisme et Renaissance, French Studies, Seventeenth Century French studies. *Address:* Clare College, Cambridge CB2 1TL, England.

FORD, Sarah Litsey, b. 23 June 1901, Kentucky, USA. Writer; Teacher. m. (1) Frank Wilson Nye, (2) William Walace Ford. *Literary Appointments:* Instructor: Mary Baldwin School, Virginia; Atherton High School, Kentucky; Famous Writers School, Connecticut. Conducted numerous independent writing workshops. *Publications:* Poetry: Legend, 1936; For the Lonely, 1937; The Oldest April, 1957; Toward Mystery, 1974. Novels: There Was a Lady, 1945; The Intimate Illusion, 1955; A Path to the Water, 1962. *Contributions:* Numerous Magazines, journals and reviews including: Saturday Evening Post; New York Times; New York Herald Tribune; Contemporary Verse; Poetry; Poetry World; Poetry Digest. *Honours include:* 1st Prizes: Poetry World, 1935; Poetry Society of America, 1940; New York Women Poets, 1958, 59, 74; New York Women Poets, 1976, 83; Memorial Prize, 1983, Quarterly Prize, 1983, 85, The Lyric. *Memberships:* PEN International; Vice President, Connecticut Branch, American Pen Women; President, New York Women Poets; Poetry Society of America. *Literary Agent:* Julian Bach Junior. *Address:* 248 Newtown Turnpike, West Redding, CT 06896, USA.

FORESTER, Bruce, b. 25 May 1939, New York, USA. Physician; Psychiatrist. m. Erica Simms, at New York, 21 Dec. 1962, 2 sons, 1 daughter. *Education:* BA, Dartmouth College, Hanover, New Hampshire, 1961; MD, Columbia University College of Physicians & Surgeons, 1965. *Publications:* In Strict Confidence, Ashley Books, 1982; Signs & Omens, Dodd/Mead, 1984. *Contributions to:* Seventeen; Red Book; Yours Miss; House & Garden; Cosmopolitan; American Journal of Psychiatry. *Membership:* Mystery Writers of America. *Address:* 145 East 74th Street, New York, NY 10021, USA.

FORFREEDOM, Ann, b. 3 Jan. 1947, Wolfratshausen, Federal Republic of Germany. Feminist Activist & Writer. *Education:* BA, University of California at Los Angeles, USA; Postgraduate Study, California State University at Sacramento, California, USA. *Literary Appointments:* Editor & Publisher of, The Wise Woman; Editor, Goddess Rising Movement. *Major Publications:* Editor & Publisher, Women Out of History: A Herstory Anthology, 1972; Co-editor & Publisher, Book of the Goddess, 1980. *Contributor to:* Ms Magazine; Circle Network News; Beltane Papers; and others. *Address:* 2441 Cordova Street, Oakland, CA 94602, USA.

FORGUE, Janis Marie Pinson, b. 21 May 1948, Chicago, Illinois, USA. Writer, Editor. m. Les Richard Forgue, 16 Mar. 1968, Chicago. *Education:* BA with honours writing and journalism, Columbia College, Chicago. *Literary Appointments:* Writer, The Neighbourhood Institute, Chicago, 1981; Editorial Assistant, Department of Obstetrics and Gynaecology, Mount Sinai Hospital, Chicago, 1981–82; Writer/Reporter, Thomas Reports, Chicago, 1982; Writer/Researcher, Authors' Research, Chicago, 1982–85; Managing Editor/Co-publisher, My Father's House Magazine, Maywood, Illinois, 1983–; Assistant Managing Editor, General Dentistry – Journal of the Academy of General Dentistry, Chicago, 1985–. *Contributions to:* My Father's House; General Dentistry. *Membership:* American Medical Writers Association. *Address:* PO Box 346, Maywood, IL 60153, USA.

FORISHA-KOVACH, Barbara Ellen, b. 28 Dec. 1941, Ann Arbor, Michigan, USA. Dean/Professor/Consultant. m. Randy Louis Kovach, 3 May 1981, Ann Arbor, Michigan, 1 son, 2 daughters. *Education:* BA, 1963, MA 1964, Stanford University; PhD University of Maryland, 1973. *Publications:* Sex Roles and Personal Awareness, 1978; Outsiders on the Inside, 1981; Power and Love, 1982; Experience of Adolescence, 1983; Organizational Sync, 1983; The Flexible Organisation, 1984. *Contributor to:* Journal of Mental Imagery; Perceptual and Motor Skill; Small Group Behavior; Journal of Humanistic Psychology; Journal of Developmental Psychology. *Address:* 38 Evans Drive, Cranbury, NJ 08512, USA.

FORMAN, Joan, b. Louth, Lincs, England. Author. *Publications:* (plays) The Turning Tide; End of a Dream; Freedom of the House; Westward to Canaan; (other publications), Princess in the Tower, 1973; Haunted East Anglia, 1974; The Mask of Time (Macdonald), 1978; The Haunted South (Hale), 1978. *Contributor to:* Various journals; UK and Canadian TV, Radio and Lectr. *Memberships:* Society of Authors; Educational Writers' Group; League of Dramatists. *Address:* 89 Newton Street, Newton St Faiths, Norwich, NR10 3AD, England.

FORMAN, Max L, b. 6 Mar. 1909, Albany, New York, USA. Retired Clergyman. m. (1) Diana Slavin, 4 July 1933 (deceased), New York City; (2) Sade S Fischbein, 6 July 1971, Queens, New York, 1 son, 2 daughters (one deceased). *Education:* BA, University of Pennsylvania, 1930; Rabbi, 1934, MHL, 1948, DD, 1966, Jewish Theological Seminary of America. *Publications:* Capsules of Wisdom, 1948; Ideas That Work, 1952; World's Greatest Quotations, 1970; Rx for Living, 1983. *Contributions to:* Poetry: Junto (literary magazine); Professional articles: Fellowship; Jewish Times of Philadelphia; Post and Opinion; Torch; Rabb. Assembly Yearbook; Post-Times of Palm Beach. *Memberships:* Zelosophic Society; Philomathean Society. *Address:* 2860 South Ocean Boulevard, Palm Beach, FL 33480, USA.

FORRESTER, Martyn John, b. 27 Sep. 1952, Guernsey, Channel Islands, England. Writer. m. Evie Hume. 5 Jan. 1980, London, 1 daughter. *Education:* BA (Hons) Social Administration, University of Exeter, England. *Major Publication:* Breaking Wind, 1984. *Literary Agent:* Mark Lucas, Fraser & Dunlop. *Address:* c/o Fraser & Dunlop Scripts Limited, 91 Regent Street, London W1, England.

FORRESTER, Victoria Wadsworth, b. 28 Mar. 1940, Pasadena, California, USA. Story-teller/Poet/Librarian/Illustrator of children's books. m. Alan Harry Forrester, 14 June 1960, Carmel California, 1 son. *Education:* BA, English Literature, 1960; MLS, Library Science, 1962; MA, Art, 1970, University of California at Los Angeles. *Publications:* Bears and Theirs, 1982; Oddward, 1982; The Touch Said Hello, 1982; The Magnificent Moo, 1983; Words to Keep Against the Night, 1983; The Candlemaker and other Tales, 1984; A Latch Against the Wind, 1985. *Address:* One Owlswood Drive, Larkspur, CA 94939, USA.

FORSBERG, (Charles) Gerald, b. 18 June 1912, Vancouver, British Columbia, Canada. Writer; Former Naval Officer and Civil Servant. m. Joyce Whewell Hogarth, 16 Apr. 1952, Morecambe, England, 1 son, 1 daughter. *Publications:* Long Distance Swimming, 1957; First Strokes in Swimming, 1961; Modern Long Distance Swimming, 1963; Salvage from the Sea, 1977; Practical Pocket Book for Seamen, 1980. *Contributions to:* Nautical Magazine; Swimming Times; Blackwoods; Bassey's Annual; several encyclopedias and maritime and professional journals. *Honours include:* OBE, 1955; Marathon Swimming Hall of Fame, USA, 1965; Davids-Wheeler Award, for services to swimming, USA, 1971. *Memberships:* President, Channel Swimming Association, 1963–; Freeman, City of London; Fellow, Nautical Institute; Liveryman, Honourable Company of Master Mariners; Younger Brother, Trinity House. *Address:* c/o Barclays Bank, 13 Marine Road West, Morecambe LA3 1BX, England.

FORSBLOM, Harry Hjalmar, b. 2 Nov. 1943, Jyväskylä, Finland. Literary Critic; Writer. m. Anne Elisabeth Nordgren, 25 Mar. 1970, Helsinki, 2 sons. *Education:* BA, University of Helsinki, Finland. *Literary Appointments:* Literary critic, Helsingin Sanomat (newspaper), 1969–1985; Free Writer, Critic, Translator, 1985–. *Publications:* in Finnish: Jees, maailman dialektiikka, poems, 1973; Toivakan kirkon kattomaalaus, poems, 1975; Tomumajayllatys, poems, 1978; Aurinkolinna, novel, 1980; Kun legendasta tulee tosi, novel, 1984. *Honours:* Honorary Fellow in Writing, University of Iowa, USA, 1984. *Memberships:* Suomen Kirjailijaliitto (Finnish Writers Association). *Literary Agent:* Werner Soderstrom Oy, Helsinki. *Address:* Kauppakartanonkatu 26 G 86, 00930 Helsinki, Finland.

FORSTER, Robert, b. 1926, New York City, USA. Professor of Modern European History, Johns Hopkins University. *Education:* BA, Swarthmore College, Pennsylvania, 1949; MA, Harvard University, 1951; PhD, Johns Hopkins University, 1956; University of Toulouse, France, 1953–55. *Publications:* The Nobility of Toulouse in the 18th Century, 1960; 1970; The House of Saulx Tavanes: Versailles & Burgundy, 1700–1830, 1971; Merchants, Landlords, Magistrates: The Depont Family in 18th Century France, 1980. *Contributor to:* Professional Journals, including, American Historical Review; Journal of Economic History; Past and Present; Annales-ESC. *Honours:* John Simon Guggenheim Fellow, Paris, 1969–70; Fellow, Institute for Advanced Study, Princeton, 1975–76; Fellow, Centre for Advanced Study in Behavioural Sciences, Stanord, California, 1979–80; National Humanities Foundation Fellow, Paris, 1983–84. *Memberships include:* Several professional organisations: American Historical Association; Society for French Historical Studies (President, 1974). *Address:* 208 Oakdale Road, Baltimore, MD 21210, USA.

FOSTER, David Manning, b. 15 May 1944, Sydney, Australia. Writer. m. (1) Robin Bowers, (2) Gerda Hageraats, 2 sons, 4 daughters. *Education:* BSc, Syndey; PhD, Australian National University. *Literary Appointments:* Senior Fellow, Australian Literature Board, 1973–85. *Publications:* Novels: The Pure Land, 1974; Moonlite, 1981; Plumbum, 1983; Dog Rock, 1985; Christian Rosy Cross, 1986. *Honours:* The 'Age' Award, 1974; National Book Council Award, 1981. *Memberships:* Australian Society of Authors. *Literary Agent:* Rosemary Creswell, Glebe, New South Wales. *Address:* Bundanoon, NSW 2578, Australia.

FOSTER, Janet, b. 18 Nov. 1935, Stockton-on-Tees, England. Writer; TV Production Assistant. m. David Edward Foster, 2 May 1975, Hatfield. *Education:* ALAM, Honours. *Publications:* The Trouble at Aquitaine; Fatality at Bath & Wells, 1986. *Literary Agent:* Mark Lucas, Fraser & Dunlop. *Address:* c/o Fraser and Dunlop Scripts Ltd, 91 Regent Street, London W1 8RU, England.

FOSTER, John Philip, b. 19 Mar. 1958, Pembury, Sussex, England. Journalist. m. Marian Ann Sellers, 5 Apr. 1980, Holy Cross, Uckfield. *Education:* BA (Honours) London. *Appointments:* Trainee Reporter, Features Writer, Farming Press Group; Feature Writer, 1982, Deputy Editor, 1984–, Pig Farming. *Contributor to:* Pig Farming; Dairy Farmer; Arable Farming. *Address:* 20 Hamilton Road, Ipswich, Suffolk IP3 9AL, England.

FOSTER, Linda Nemec, b. 29 May 1950, Garfield Heights, Ohio, USA. Poet, Teacher of Creative Writing. m. Anthony Jesse Foster, 26 Oct. 1974, Maple Heights, Ohio, USA, 1 son, 1 daughter. *Education:* BA, Aquinas College, Grand Rapids, Michigan; MFA Creative Writing, Goddard College, Plainfield, Vermont. *Literary Appointments:* Board member, Cranbrook Writers Guild, Birmingham, Michigan; Creative Writers in Schools Programme, Michigan Council for the Arts, Detroit; Board Member, Mecosta County Council for the Humanities, Big Rapids, Michigan. *Publications:* A History of the Body, chapbook of prose poems. 1986. *Contributions to:* Poetry Now; Nimrod; Tendril; Invisible City; Chowder Review; Midwest Poetry Review; Another Chicago Magazine; Croton Review; The Alchemist; University of Windsor Review, Canada; Escarpments; Sierra Madre Review; Room; and others. *Honours:* Poetry manuscript nominated for Anne Sexton Prize, 1979; 2 poems nominated for Pushcart Prize, 1982; Poetry Grant, Michigan Council for the Arts, 1983–84; Prizewinner, Croton Review poetry competition, 1985. *Memberships:* Detroit Women Writers; Poetry Society of America; Academy of

American Poets. *Address:* 427 W Pere Marquette, Big Rapids, MI 49307, USA.

FOSTER, Paul, b. 15 Oct. 1931, Pennsgrove, New Jersey, USA. Writer. *Education:* BA, Rutgers University; LLB, New York University Law School. *Publications:* 25 books of plays including: Tom Paine, 1971; The Madonna in the Orchard, 1971; Elizabeth I, 1972; The Off-Off-Broadway Book: Satyricon, 1972; Elizabeth I, The Madonna in the Orchard, 1974; The Best American Plays of the Modern Theater: Tom Paine, 1975; Marcus Brutus and Silver Queen Saloon, 1976; Tom Paine, Silver Queen Saloon, Elizabeth I, 1978; A Kiss Is Just a Kiss, 1984; Films: Smile, 1980; The Cop & The Anthem, 1982; When You're Smiling, 1983; Cinderella, 1984; Home Port, 1984. Plays: Mellon & The National Art Gallery, 1980, New Works: Three Mystery Comedies, The Dark & Mr Stone, 1985. *Contribution to:* New Stages. *Honours:* Rockefeller Foundation Fellowship, 1967; J S Guggenheim Fellowship, 1974; British Arts Council Award, 1973; Theater Heute Award, 1977. *Memberships:* Dramatists Guild; Society of Composers and Dramatic Authors, France; The Players Club, New York City, *Address:* 242 E 5 Street, New York, NY 10003, USA.

FOTHERGILL, (Arthur) Brian, b. 3 Apr. 1921, Lytham St Annes, Lancashire, England. Author. *Education:* King's College, London. *Publications:* The Cardinal King, 1958; Nicholas Wiseman, 1963; Mrs Jordan, Portrait of an Actress, 1965; Sir William Hamilton, Envoy Extraordinary, 1969; The Mitred Earl, 1974; Backford of Fonthill, 1979; The Strawberry Hill Set, 1983. *Contributions to:* Corvo 1860-1960 (New Quests for Corvo); Encyclopaedia Britannica; Times Literary Supplement. *Honours:* Heinemann Award, 1969 and 1980; Silver Pen Prize, 1970. *Memberships:* FSA; FRSL; PEN Club. *Address:* 7 Union Square, London N1 7DH, England.

FOUGERE, Jean, b. 5 May 1914, St Amand, Cher, France. Writer. *Publications include:* (Novels) La Pouponniere, 1948; La Cour des Miracles, 1955; La Vie de Chateau, 1958; Les Petits Messieurs, 1963; Nos Tantes d'Avallon, 1968; Destinee City, 1983; (Short Stories) Un Cadeau Utile, 1953; La Belle Femme, 1971; (Essays) Voulez-vous Voyager Avec Moi?, 1957; Les Nouveaux Bovides, 1966; Lettre Ouverte a un Satyre, 1969; Les Passengers, 1975. *Contributor to:* Le Figaro; les Nouvelles Litteraires. *Memberships:* Former Vice President, Society of Men of Letters. *Honours:* Grand Prix de la Nouvelle, Academy Francaise, 1972; Chevalier Legion d'Honneur. *Address:* 22 Quai de Bethune, 75004 Paris, France.

FOULKES, Albert Peter, b. 17 Oct. 1936, Rotherham, England. University Professor. *Education:* BA, Sheffield University, England; MA, McMaster University; PhD, Tulane University. *Publications:* The Reluctant Pessimist: A Study of Frank Kafka, 1967; The Search for Literary Meaning, 1975; The Uses of Criticism, 1976; Literature and Propaganda, 1983. *Contributions to:* Comp Lit; Seminar; Journal of Literary Semantics; Germanic Review; German Quarterly, etc. *Honours:* Alexander von Humboldt Research Fellow, 1972-74; Visiting Professor of Comp Lit, University of Mainz, 1976. *Address:* Panty-y-Cosyn House, Shirenewton, Gwent, Wales.

FOUTCHEDJIEV, Diko, b. 16 July 1928, Gramatikovo, Bulgaria. Writer. *Education:* Law Degree, Sofia University. *Literary Appointment:* Director of The National Theatre, Ivan Vazov. *Publications:* Prose: The Sky above Veleka, 1963; A Furious Journey, 1970; The River, 1974; The Green Grass of the Desert, 1978; The World in our Hearts, 1978. *Contributor to:* All main Bulgarian literary editions. *Honours:* Dimitrov Prize, 1980; People's Worker of Culture, 1985. *Membership:* Union of Bulgarian Writers. *Address:* 120 A, Rakovski Street, Sofia, Bulgaria.

FOWKE, Edith Margaret, b. 30 Apr. 1913, Lumsden, Saskatchewan, Canada. Folklorist. m. Franklin G Fowke,

1 Oct. 1938, Saskatoon. *Education:* BA, MA, University of Saskatchewan. *Literary Appointments:* Editor, The Western Teacher; Associate Editor, Magazine Digest; Professor of English, York University. *Publications include:* Sally Go Round the Sun, 1969; Lumbering Songs from the Northern Woods, 1970; The Penguin Book of Canadian Folk Songs, 1973; Folklore of Canada, 1976; Ring Around the Moon, 1977; Folklores of French Canada, 1979; A Bibliography of Canadian Folklore in English (with Carole Henderson Carpenter), 1981; Riot of Riddles, 1982; Singing Our History, revised edition of Canada's Story in Song, 1984; Explorations in Canadian Folklore (with Carole H Carpenter), 1985. *Contributions to:* Western Folklore; Midwest Folklore; Canadian Literature; The Literary History of Canada; Journal of American Folklore; Ethnomusicology; The Canada Music Book; Canadian Folk Music Journal; The Oxford Companion to Canadian Literature, etc. *Honours:* Honorary LL.D, Brock University, 1974; Honorary D.Litt, Trent University, 1975, York University, 1982; Vicky Metcalf Award, 1985. *Memberships:* Fellow, American Folklore Society; Member of the Order of Canada; Fellow, Royal Society of Canada. *Address:* 5 Notley Place, Toronto, Ontario M4B 2M7, Canada.

FOWLER, Marian Elizabeth. b. 15 Oct. 1929, Newmarket, Ontario, Canada. Writer. m. Dr Rodney Singleton Fowler, 19 Sep. 1953, Toronto, divorced 1977, 1 son, 1 daughter. *Education:* BA Honours in English 1951, MA (English) 1965, PhD (English) 1970, University of Toronto. *Publications:* The Embroidered Tent, Five Gentlewomen in Early Canada, 1982; Redney: A Life of Sara Jeannette Duncan, 1983; Below the Peacock Fan: First Ladies of the Raj, pending 1986. *Contributions to:* English Studies in Canada; University of Toronto Quarterly; Dalhousie Review; Ontario History; Dictionary of Canadian Biography; Oxford Companion to Canadian Literature; New Canadian Encyclopaedia. *Honours:* Governor-General's Gold Medal in English, 1951; Canadian Biography Award, 1979. *Memberships:* International PEN; Writers' Union of Canada. *Address:* Kilmara, RR2, Lisle, Ontario, Canada.

FOWLER, Richard Alan, b. 2 Dec. 1948, San Jose, California, USA. College Professor. m. Jerilyn Rowell, 24 Aug. 1968, Pekin, Illinois, 1 son, 1 daughter. *Education:* MA, University of Wisconsin, EdS, University of Georgia; EdD, Highland University; Clinical Psychology License, State of Texas, University of Texas. *Publications:* The Christian Confronts His Culture, 1983; Christian Activism in Secular America, 1986; Illusion or Delusion?, 1986. *Contributions to:* NIAI Journal; Coach and Athlete; Christian Life; Good News Broadcaster; Moody Monthly; Discipleship Magazine; Computer Instructor. *Address:* 1312 Lawndale, Longview, TX 75604, USA.

FOWLER, William Morgan Jr, b. 25 July 1944, Clearwater, Florida, USA. Professor; Editor. m. Marilyn Louise Noble, 11 Aug. 1968, Wakefield, Massachusetts, 1 son, 1 daughter. *Education:* BA, Northeastern University; MA, PhD, University of Notre Dame. *Appointments:* Assistant Professor 1971, Professor of History 1980-, Northeastern University; Managing Editor, New England Quarterly, 1981-. *Publications:* Rebels Under Sail: The American Navy in the Revolution, 1976; The American Revolution: Changing Perspectives, editor with Wallace Coyle, 1979; The Baron of Beacon Hill: A Biography of John Hancock, 1980; Jack Tars & Commodores: The American Navy 1783-1815, 1984. *Contributions to:* American Neptune; Pennsylvania Magazine of History & Biography; Proceedings, US Naval Institute; Collections, Essex Institute; Mariners Mirror; Rhode Island History; Various newspapers. *Honours:* Fellow, Pilgrim Society; Member, Colonial Society of Massachusetts. *Memberships:* Trustee, New England Historic Genealogical Society; Trustee, Pilgrim Society; Trustee, USS Constitution, Museum Foundation; Trustee, Old South Association. *Address:* Department of

History, Northeastern University, Boston, MA 02115, USA.

FOX, Daniel Michael, b. 20 Aug. 1938, New York, USA. Public Official; Historian. *Education:* AB, 1959, AM, 1961; PhD, 1964, Harvard University. *Appointments:* Assistant Professor, History, Public Administration, Harvard University, 1967; Associate Professor, Professor, Humanities in Medicine, State University of New York, Stony Brook, 1971–; Director, New York State Center for Assessing Health Services, 1985–. *Publications:* Engines of Culture, 1963; The Discovery of Abundance, 1967; Economists and Health Care, 1979; Health Policies, Health Politics: The Experience of Britain and America, 1986. *Contributor to:* Bulletin of the History of Medicine; Journal of Social History; Milbank Memorial Quarterly/Health and Society, etc. *Honours:* Albert J Beveridge Prize, American Historical Association, 1967. *Memberships:* Chair, Association for Faculty in the Medical Humanities, 1982–84; American Association for the History of Medicine, Council, 1984–87. *Address:* Health Sciences Centre 4L–215, State University of New York, Stony Brook, NY 11794, USA.

FOX, Frank Wayne, b. 7 Oct. 1940, Salt Lake City, Utah, USA. Professor of History. m. Elaine Tabbs, 9 Sep. 1969, Salt Lake City, 2 sons. *Education:* BA, 1966; MA, 1969, University of Utah; PhD, 1973, Stanford University. *Literary Appointments:* Special Consulting Editor, BYU Centennial History, 1975–76; Consultant with Prentice-Hall on development of American History Texts; Consultant for BYU Press. *Publications:* include: The Eden World of William Bartram, Phi Alpha Theta Journal, 1967; Washington, DuBois, and the Problem of Negro, Two-ness, Markham Review, 1975; The Genesis of American Technology, American Studies, 1976; Madison Avenue Goes to War: The Strange Military Career of American Advertising, 1941–45, Charles E Merrill Monographs, 1974; J Reuben Clark: The Public Years, BYU Press, 1980; American Heritage: An Interdisciplinary Approach, Morton, 1982; The Founding Fathers, Ensign, 1976; Jim Stewart: A Face in the Crowd, Utah Holiday, 1978. *Contributions to:* Various journals. *Honours:* Graduated cum laude; Henry D Newell, Ford Foundation Fellowships, Stanford University; Phi Alpha Theta Teacher of the Year, 1975; Phi Kappa Phi; Association for Mormon Letters prize for best general publication of 1980; BYU Professor of the Month, February 1983; BYU Professor of the Year, 1983; Karl G Maeser Distinguished Teaching Award, September 1984. *Memberships:* Phi Alpha Theta, Chapter President, 1968; Organization of American Historians; American Studies Association; Society for Early American History and Culture. *Address:* Department of History 322 KMH, Brigham Young University, Provo, UT 84604, USA.

FOX, Gail Talmadge, b. 5 Feb. 1942, Willimantic, Connecticut, USA. Poet. m. Michael Allen Fox, 11 June 1963, Ithaca, New York, 2 sons. *Education:* BA, Cornell University, 1964; Pontifical Institute of Mediaeval Studies, 1964–65. *Literary Appointments:* Editor, Quarry Magazine, 1975–78. *Publications:* Dangerous Season, 1969; God's Odd Look, 1976; In Search of Living Things, 1980; Houses of God, 1983. *Contributions to:* Numerous Publications. *Honours:* 11 Canada Council Grants, 1975–85; 13 Ontario Arts Council Grants, 1977–85. *Memberships:* League of Canadian Poets; past member, Flat Earth Society. *Address:* Oberon Press, 401 A Inn of the Provinces, Ottawa, Canada.

FOX, Robert Richard, b. 2 Feb. 1943, Brooklyn, New York, USA. Writer in Residence. m. Susan H Goldstein, 27 Aug. 1967, Queens, New York, 1 son, 1 daughter. *Education:* BA, Brooklyn College, New York, 1967; MA, Ohio University, 1970. *Literary Appointments:* Writer in Residence, Rider College, Lawrenceville, New Jersey, 1971–72, Ohio Arts Council, Columbus, Ohio, 1977–. *Publications:* Destiny News, short stories, 1977. Featured in Anthologies: Short Stories from the Literary Magazines, 1970; Three Stances of Modern Fiction,

1971; Currents: Concerns and Composition, 1972; Literature: An Anthology, 1975; Literature: Fiction, 1976; Challenge of Conflict, 1976; From the Hudson to the World, 1978; A Reader of New American Fiction, 1980. *Contributions to:* Salmagundi; Trace; The North American Review; December; Prism International; The Colorado State Review, Pulpsmith; The Memphis State Review; Mundus Artium. *Honours:* Ohioana Citation, Martha Kinney Cooper Foundation, 1982. *Membership:* Associated Writing Programs. *Address:* Route 4, Pomeroy, OH 45769, USA.

FOX HUTCHINSON, Juliet Mary, b. 13 Jan. 1911, London, England. Writer of Verse. m. Alan Hutchinson, 6 Sep. 1934, London. *Publications:* The Harbour, 1962; The Third Day, 1963; A Rainbow of Paths; Remembering Vernon: A Memoir of the Late Lord Barnby. *Contributor to:* Country Life; Field; House & Gardens; The Lady, Yorkshire Post; Scotsman; Glasgow Herald; New York Times; Herald Tribune; Christian Science Monitor. *Address:* Kyloe Old Vicarage, Berwick on Tweed, Northumberland TD15 2PG, England.

FOXALL, Raymond, b. 26 Mar. 1916, Iriam, Lancashire, England. Author/Journalist. *Education:* Manchester College of Commerce. *Publications:* Here Lies the Shadow, 1957; Songs for a Prince, 1959; The Devil's Smile, 1960; The Wicked Lord, 1962; John McCormack, 1963; The Devil's Spawn, 1965; Squire Errant, 1968; The Little Ferret, 1968; Brandy for the Parson, 1970; The Dark Forest, 1972; The Silver Goblet, 1974; Society of the Dispossessed, 1976; The Amorous Rogue, 1977; The Noble Pirate, 1978; The Last Jacobite, 1979; The Amateur Commandos, 1981; The Guinea-Pigs, 1982. *Contributor to:* Scottish and Universal Newspapers. *Memberships:* Society of Authors; National Union of Journalists. *Literary Agent:* David Bolt Associates. *Address:* The Old Crossings House, Balgowan by Tibbermore, Perthshire PH1 1QW, Scotland.

FOXWORTH, Thomas G, b. 11 Nov. 1939, Rahway, New Jersey, USA. Air Line Pilot. m. (2) Jennifer Oliver, 9 Feb. 1979, 2 daughters by 1st marriage. *Education:* BSc, Aeronautical Engineering, Princeton University, 1959. *Publications:* The Speed Seekers, 1975; Passengers, with Michael Laurence, 1983. *Contributor to:* Numerous professional journals including, Newsweek; USA Today; Air & Space; trade and technical society journals. *Honours:* Flight Safety Foundation Annual Publications Awards, 1969, 1971; Aviation/Space Writers Association Strebig Award, 1976. *Memberships:* Authors Guild; Aviation/Space Writers Association; Washington Independent Writers. *Literary Agent:* Fraser & Dunlop Scripts, London, England. *Address:* 5449 Rutherford Drive, Woodbridge, VA 22193, USA.

FRAILE, Medardo, b. 21 Mar. 1925, Madrid, Spain. Professor in Spanish. *Education:* DPh, DLitt, University of Madrid, 1968. *Publications:* Cuentos con Algun Amor, 1954; A La Luz Cambian las Cosas, 1959; Cuentos de Verdad, 1964; Descubridor de Nada y Otros Cuentos, 1970; Con Los Dias Contados, 1972; Hacia una Generacion Sin Critica, 1972; La Penultima Inglaterra, 1973; Poesia y Teatro Espanoles Contemporaneos, 1974; Ejemplario, 1979. *Contributions to:* Cuadernos de Agora, Sub-Editor, Drama Critic, 1957–64; Abside; Revista de Occidente, Caravelle; Clavileno; Cuadernos Hispano-Americanos; numerous other publications. *Honours include:* Critics Book of the Year, 1965; Hucha de Oro Prize, 1971; Research Grant, Carnegie Trust for Universities of Scotland, 1975. *Memberships:* General Society of Spanish Authors; Working Community of Book Writers, Spain; Association of University Teachers; College of Doctors of Philosophy and Letters, Officer; Membre Correspondant de L'Académie Européenne des Sciences, des Arts et des Lettres, Paris. *Address:* 24 Etive Crescent, Bishopbriggs, Glasgow G64 1ES, Scotland.

FRANCA, Jose-Augusto, b. 18 Nov. 1922, Tomar, Portugal. Art Historian; University Professor; Editor.

Education: D'es Lettres, Paris University; DHist, University of Paris. *Publications include:* Natureza Mona, 1949; Azasel, 1955; Despidida Breve, 1956; Une Ville des Lumieres: La Lisbonne de Pombal, 1965; A Arte em Portugal no seculo XIX, 2 volumes 1967; A Arte em Portugal no seculo XX, 1975. *Contributor to:* Coloquio/Artes, Editor; etc. *Honours:* Recipient, Knight Order of Arts et Lettres, Order Nat. du Merite, France; Commander, Order of Rio Branco, Brazil. *Memberships include:* International Committee, Art History, Chairman, Portugal; National Academy of Fine Arts, Vice President, 1975, President, 1976–80; Academy of Sciences; Portuguese Academy of History; International Association of Art Critics, Vice President, 1971–73, President, 1984–; European Academy of Sciences; etc. *Address:* 75116 Paris, France.

FRANCE, Thelma Edith Minnie, b. Wellington, New Zealand. Nurse; Author. *Education:* BA, Vic, University of Wellington, 1972. *Publications:* The Glitter not the Gold, 1974; Talisman for a Bride, 1976; Legacy of Thorns, 1977; An Orchid for Belinda, 1977; Decision for Nurse Lewis, 1978; Dr Herbert's Dilemma, 1979; A Doctor's Marriage, 1980; Doctor on Safari, 1982. *Contributor to:* New Zealand Women's Weekly; Evening Post; Nelson Mail; Southland News; H B Herald Tribune; Radio New Zealand; Australian Religious Magazines. *Memberships:* PEN; New Zealand Women Writers & Journalists; Federation of University Women; New Zealand Romantic Novelists Association; Past President, Secretary, Treasurer & Committee Member, New Zealand Women Writers' Society. *Agent:* Laurence Pollinger Ltd. *Address:* 68 Mairangi Road, Wadestown, Wellington 1, New Zealand.

FRANCIS, Clare, b. 17 Apr. 1946, Surrey, England. Writer. 1 son. *Education:* Economics Degree, University College, London. *Publications:* Come Hell or High Water, 1977; Come Wind or Weather, 1978; The Commanding Sea, 1981; Night Sky, 1983; Red Crystal, 1985. *Honours:* MBE; Honorary Fellow, University College, London. *Membership:* Society of Authors. *Literary Agent:* John Johnson, London. *Address:* c/o William Heinemann, 10 Upper Grosvenor Street, London W1, England.

FRANCK, Frederick, b. 12 Apr. 1909, Maastricht, Netherlands. Painter; Author. m. Caske Maria Berndes, 1960, 1 son. *Education:* LDS, RCS, Edinburgh, Scotland; DMD, University of Pittsburgh, USA; DFA, Pittsburgh. *Publications:* Open Wide, Please, 1957; Days with Albert Schweitzer, 1959; My Friend in Africa, 1960; African Sketchbook, 1961; My Eye is Love, 1963; Outsider in the Vatican, 1965; I Love Life, 1967; Exploding Church, 1968; Simenon's Paris, 1970; Pilgrimage to Nowhere, 1973; The Zen of Seeing, 1973; The Book of Angelus Silesius, 1976; Zen and Zen Classics, 1977; Everyone: The Timeless Myth of Everyman Reborn, 1978; The Awakened Eye, 1979; The Buddha Eye, 1981; The Supreme Koran; 1982; Echoes from a Bottomless Well, 1985; several textbooks; Cons. Ed. Parabola, Quarterly. *Contributions:* Numerous magazines and papers including, Parabola, quarterly; Eastern Buddhist; etc. *Honours:* Drawings and Paintings in Museum of Modern Art, Whitney, USA, and in Tokyo National Museum, etc. *Memberships:* Hon Dir Artists Equity Association; NY PEN; Fellow, Int. Inst. for Arts and Letters; Fellow, Society for Arts, Religious and Contemporary Culture. *Literary Agent:* Joan Daves. *Address:* 96 Covered Bridge Road, Ontwyck, Pacem in Terris, Warwick, NY 10990, USA.

FRANK, Joseph Nathaniel, b. 6 Oct. 1918, New York, New York, USA. Professor of Comparative Literature. m. Marguerite J Straus, 11 May 1953, 2 daughters. *Education:* Studied, New York University, 1937–38, University of Wisconsin, 1941–42, University of Paris, 1950–51; PhD, University of Chicago, 1960. *Literary Appointments include:* Editor, Bureau of National Affairs, Washington, 1942–50; Lecturer, Department of English, Princeton University; Associate Professor, Rutgers University, 1961–66; Professor of Comparative Literature, Director of Christian Causs

Seminars, Princeton University, 1966–. *Publications:* The Widening Gyre, Crisis and Mastery in Modern Literature, 1963; F M Dostoevsky: The Seeds of Revolt, 1821–1849, 1976; F M Dostoevsky: The Years of Ordeal, 1850–1859, 1983. Editor, A Primer of Ignorance, 1967. *Contributions to:* The Southern Review; The Sewanee Review; The Hudson Review; The Partisan Review; Art News; Critique; The Chicago Review; The Minnesota Review; The Russian Review; Le Contract Social; Commentary; Encounter; New York Review, and others. Contributions to various books, numerous book reviews and translations. *Honours include:* Fulbright Scholar, 1950–51; Rockefeller Fellow, 1952–53, 53-54; Guggenheim Fellow, 1956–57, 1975–76; Award, National Institute of Arts and Letters, 1958; Fellow, American Academy of Arts and Sciences, 1969. Research Grants: American Council of Learned Societies, 1964–65, 1967–68, 1970–71; Rockefeller Foundation, 1979–80, 1983–84. *Address:* Department of Comparative Literature, 326 East Pyne, Princeton University, Princeton, NJ 08544, USA.

FRANKEL, Sandor, b. 16 Nov. 1943, NYC, USA. Attorney; Author. *Education:* BA, NY University, 1964; LLB, Harvard Law School, 1967. *Publications:* Beyond a Reasonable Doubt, 1971; The Aleph Solution, 1978; How to Defend Yourself Against the IRS, 1985. *Honour:* Recipient, Edgar Allen Poe Prize for, Beyond a Reasonable Doubt, 1971. *Address:* 225 Broadway, NY 10007, USA.

FRANKLIN, Ursula, b. 3 July 1929, Germany. Professor of French. *Education:* BA, 1964, MA, 1966, PhD, 1971, Michigan State University, USA. *Publications:* An Anatomy of Poesis: The Prose Poems of Stephane Mallarine, 1976; The Rhetoric of Valery's Prose Aubudes, 1979; The Broken Angel: Myth and Method in Valery, 1984. *Contributions to:* Various scholarly journals in USA, France, Australia, Canada and Germany. *Honours:* Fellowships: American Council of Learned Societies, 1978–79; John Simon Guggenheim Foundation, 1982–83. *Memberships:* International and American Comparative Literature Associations; Modern Language Association; Societe Paul Valéry. *Address:* 3331 Campus View Apartments, 10255 42nd Street, Allendale, MI 49401, USA.

FRANZÉN, Nils-Olof, b. 23 Aug. 1916, Oxel[u]osund, Sweden. Broadcaster; Programme Director. m. Birgit Levihn (dec), 31 Aug. 1940, Stockholm, 1 son, 2 daughters. *Education:* BA, Stockholm University, 1941; Doctor Honoris Causa, Stockholm University, 1984. *Literary Appointments:* Biographies of Rossini, 1951; Zola, 1958; Moliere, 1960; Christina Nilsson, 1976; Mozart, 1978; Jenny Lind, 1982; Hjalmar Branting, 1985; Thesis, Zola et La Joie de vivre, 1958; Series of Detective Stories for Children, Agaton Sax, 1953–78. *Literary Agent:* Bonniers, Stockholm. *Address:* Sandelsgatan 40, 115 33 Stockholm, Sweden.

FRASER, Anthea Mary, b. Blundellsands, Lancashire, England. Author. *Publications include:* Laura Possessed, 1974; Home Through the Dark, 1974; Whistler's Lane, 1975; Breath of Brimstone, 1977; Presence of Mind, 1979; Time of Trial, 1979; Island-in-Waiting, 1979; The Stone, 1980; Summer in France, 1981; Second Time Around, 1982; A Shroud for Delilah, 1984; A Necessary End, 1985; Pretty Maids All in a Row, 1986. *Contributor to:* Homes & Gardens; Woman's Own; New Idea, Australia; Fair Lady; Femina, South Africa; Cosmopolitan; Woman's Weekly; Woman's Realm. *Memberships:* Society of Women Writers & Journalists; Crime Writers' Association. *Agent:* Laurence Pollinger Ltd. *Address:* c/o Laurence Pollinger Ltd, 18 Maddox Street, London W1R OEU, England.

FRASER, Douglas Jamieson, b. 12 Jan. 1910. Retired. *Education:* George Heriot School, Edinburgh, Scotland. *Appointments:* Insurance Clerk, Standard Life Assurance Company, Edinburgh, 1927–71. *Publications:* Landscape of Delight, 1967; Rhymes O' Auld Reekie, 1973; Where the Dark Branches Part, 1977. *Contributor to:* Scots Magazine; Lines Review; Lallans;

Burns Chronicle. *Honours:* Scotsman Burns Bi-Centenary Competition Prize, 1959; International Who's Who in Poetry Competition Prize, 1974; Queen's Silver Jubilee Medal, 1977. *Memberships:* Scottish PEN; Vice Chairman, Honorary Treasurer, Scottish Associaton for the Speaking of Verse; Honorary Secretary, Edinburgh Poetry Club; Scots Language Society. *Address:* 2 Keith Terrace, Edinburgh EH4 3NJ, Scotland.

FRASER, John Anderson, b. 5 June 1944, Montreal, Canada. Writer. m. Elizabeth Scott MacCallum, 8 Mar. 1975, Toronto, 2 daughters. *Education:* BA Honours, Memorial University of Newfoundland, 1969; MA, University of East Anglia, Norwich, Norfolk, England, 1970. *Literary Appointments:* Music and Dance Critic, Toronto Telegram, 1970–72; Dance Critic and Feature Writer 1972–74, Theatre Critic 1974–77, Peking Correspondent 1977–79, National Affairs Columnist 1979–82, Toronto Globe and Mail; National Editor, Globe and Mail, 1982–84; European Bureau Chief in London, Globe and Mail, 1984–. *Publications:* Kain and Augustyn: The Story of Two Canadian Dancers, 1977; The Chinese: Portrait of a People, 1980; China Hands, contributor, 1984. *Contributions to:* Saturday Night; New York Times; Washington Post; Christian Science Monitor; The Times of London; The New Republic, USA. *Honours:* National Newspaper Awards for criticism, 1974 and 1976; National Newspaper Award for Spot reporting, 1978; The Chinese, chosen as main selection, Book of the Month Club, January 1981. *Memberships:* Canadian Writers Association; Toronto Arts and Letters Club; Wig and Pen Club, London, England; Foreign Press Association, London. *Literary Agent:* Nancy Colbert, Colbert and Associates, Toronto, Canada. *Address:* 167 Temple Chambers, The Globe and Mail, Temple Avenue, London EC4Y OEA, England.

FRASER, Peter, b. 28 Apr. 1928, Inverness, Scotland. Writer. m. 2 sons, 3 daughters. *Education:* BA (Cantab), 1952; PhD, London, 1957. *Publications:* The Intelligence of the Secretaries of State and their Monopoly of Licensed News 1660–1688, 1956; Joseph Chamberlain's Radicalism and Empire 1868–1914, 1966; Lord Esher: A Political Biography, 1973. *Contributions to:* English Historical Review; Historical Journal; History; Journal of Modern History; Canadian Journal of History, etc. *Honour:* Prince Consort Prize, Cambridge University. 1954. *Membership:* Fellow, Royal Historical Society. *Address:* 1596 Vernon Street, Halifax, Nova Scotia B3H 3M7, Canada.

FRASER, Ronald Angus, b. 9 Dec. 1930, Hamburg, Germany. Writer. 1 son, 1 daughter. *Publications:* Work, 1968; Work 2, 1969; In Hiding, 1972; The Pueblo, 1973; Blood of Spain, 1979; In Search of a Past, 1984. *Contributor to:* New Left Review. *Literary Agent:* Tessa Sayle, 11 Jubilee Place, London SW3. *Address:* 16 Evangelist Road, London NW5 1UB, England.

FRAWLEY, William John, b. 17 Sep. 1953, Newark, New Jersey, USA. Professor. m. Maria Hinkle-Frawley, 6 Sep. 1985, Wilmington, Delaware, USA. *Education:* BA English, Glassboro State College, 1975; MA Linguistics, Louisiana State University, 1977; PhD Linguistics, Northwestern University, 1979. *Major Publications:* Instead of Music, 1980; Linguistics & Literacy, 1982; Translation, 1984; Text & Epistemology, 1986. *Contributorto:* Text (Conjunctive Cohesion in 4 English Genres), 1983; Applied Linguistics (Second Language Discourse), 1985; Studies in Second Language Acquisition (Speaking & Self-Order, 1984. *Honour:* Fulbright Professor, University of Kraków, Poland, 1985–86. *Address:* 24 Centre Street, 2N, Newark, DE 19711, USA.

FRAYN, Michael, b. 1933, London, England. Author; Journalist. *Education:* BA, Emmanuel College, Cambridge University. *Publications:* (Novels): The Tin Men, 1966; The Russian Interpreter, 1967; Towards the End of the Morning, 1969; A Very Private Life, 1968; Sweet Dreams, 1973; (philosophy): Constructions, 1974; (plays): The Two of Us, 1970; Alphabetical Order and Donkeys' Years, 1977; Clouds, 1977; Make and Break, 1980; Noises Off, 1982; Benefactors, 1984; (translations) Chekhov: The Cherry Orchard, 1978; Tolstoy: The Fruits of Enlightenment, 1979; Chekhov: Three Sisters, 1983; Chekhov, Wild Honey, 1984; (stage productions include): Make and Break, Lyric, Hammersmith, 1980, Haymarket, 1980; Noises Off, Lyric, Hammersmith, 1982, Savoy, 1982, Brooks Atkinson, New York, 1983; Three Sisters (Chekhov translation), Royal Exchange, Manchester, 1985; Benefactors, Vandeville 1984; Brooks Atkinson, New York, 1985; TV (Plays, series and documentaries include): Making Faces (6 plays for Eleanor Bron), 1975 BBC; Jerusalem, 1984 BBC. *Honours:* Somerset Maugham Award, 1966; Hawthorndon Prize, 1967; National Press Award, 1970; Evening Standard Drama Award, 1975. *Memberships:* FRSL. *Literary Agent:* Elaine Greene Limited. *Address:* c/o Elaine Greene Limited, 31 Newington Green, London N16 9PU, England.

FRAZIER, Anitra, b. 13 Aug. 1936, Philadelphia, Pennsylvania, USA. Feline Groomer-Nutritionist. *Education:* BS, Music Education, Lebanon Valley College, 1958. *Publications:* The Natural Cat, 1982; It's A Cat's Life, 1985. *Contributor to:* Vegetarian Times; Whole Life Times; Cat Fancy; British Family Circle. *Literary Agent:* Robert Gotlieb, William Morris Agency. *Address:* 5D 309 W 99th St, New York, NY 10025, USA.

FREBURGER, William Joseph, b. 6 Oct. 1940, Baltimore, Maryland, USA. Editor. Author. m. Mary Elizabeth Algeo, 23 Feb. 1979, Missouri, 1 son. *Education:* BA, 1962; St Mary's Seminary, Baltimore, Maryland; STL, 1966, Gregorian University, Rome, Italy. *Literary Appointments:* Editor, Celebration: A Creative Worship Service, 1978–; Editor, Eucharistic Minister, 1984–; Editor, The Caring Community, 1985–. *Publications:* Repent and Believe, 1972; This Is The Word Of The Lord, 1974; Eucharistic Prayers for Children, 1976; The Forgiving Christ, 1977; Liturgy: Work of the People, 1984; Birthday Blessings, 1985. *Contributions to:* numerous theological journals including, National Catholic Reporter. *Address:* 11211 Monticello Avenue, Silverspring MD 20902, USA.

FREEBORN, Richard H, b. 19 Oct. 1926, Cardiff, Wales. University Professor. m. Anne Davis, 14 Feb. 1954, Moscow, 1 son, 3 daughters. *Education:* MA, PhD, Brasenose College, Oxford University. *Literary Appointments:* Professor of Russian Literature, University of London, England. *Publications:* Turgenev, The Novelist's Novelist: A Study, 1960; A Short History of Modern Russia, 1966; Two Ways of Life, 1962; The Emigration of Sergey Ivanovich, 1963; Turgenev: Sketches from a Hunter's Album, 1967; Turgenev, Home of the Gentry, 1970; The Rise of the Rusian Novel, 1973; Turgenev: Rudin, 1975; Russian Roulette, 1979; The Russian Revolutionary Novel, 1982, paperback 1985; Love and Death, Six Stories by Ivan Turgenev, 1983. *Contributions to:* Times Literary Supplement; Times Higher Education Supplement; The London Review of Books; Slavonic and East European Review; ATR Journal; Oxford Slavonic Papers; Modern Languages Review; Journal of European Studies, and others. *Honours:* Honorary DLitt, University of London, England, 1984. *Memberships:* Crime Writers Association. *Literary Agent:* Rosalind Battersby. *Address:* School of Slavonic and East European Studies, University of London, London, England.

FREEDLAND, Michael, b. 18 Dec. 1934, London, England. Author; Journalist; Broadcaster. m. Sara Hockerman, 3 July 1960, London, 1 son, 2 daughters. *Publications:* Al Jolson, 1972 (republished as, Jolie – The Story of Al Jolson, 1985); Irving Berlin, 1974 (republished as, Salute to Irving Berlin, 1986); James Cagney, 1975; Fred Astaire, 1976; 1984; Sophie, 1977; The Two Lives of Errol Flynn, 1979; Jerome Kern, 1978; Gregory Peck, 1980; Maurice Chevalier, 1981; Peter O'Toole, 1982; The Warner Brothers, 1983; So Let's Hear The Applause, 1983; Katharine Hepburn, 1984; Dino, The Dean Martin Story, 1984; Jack Lemmon, 1985; The Secret Life of Danny Kaye, 1985; Shirley

Maclaine, 1986. *Contributor to:* The Times, London; Jewish Chronicle, London; TV Times, London; National Enquirer, USA. *Address:* 35 Hartfield Avenue, Elstree, Herts. UD6 3JB, England.

FREEDMAN, Lloys-Nancy Mars, b. 4 July 1920, Evanston, Illinois, USA. Author. m. Benedict Freedman, 29 June 1941, Evanston, Illinois, USA, 1 son, 2 daughters. *Publications include:* Novels with Benedict Freedman: Mrs Mike, 1949; This and No More, 1951; The Spark and the Exodus, 1954; Lootville, 1957; Tresa, 1959; The Apprentice Bastard, 1966. Novels: Cyclone of Silence, 1969; Joshua Son of None, 1973; The Immortals, 1976; Prima Donna, 1981; Sappho. *Contributions to:* The Atlantic Monthly; Readers Digest; King Features Syndication; Little Brown Handbook. *Honours:* Selection, The Literary Guild, 1949; Selection, The Literary Guild, 1973; Collection of Memorabilia, Boston University, 1968; Selection of The Book of the Month, 1981. *Literary Agent:* Scott Meredith. *Address:* 5837 Latigo Bluffs, Malibu, CA 90265, USA.

FREEDMAN, Nancy (Mars), b. 4 July 1920, Chicago, Illinois, USA. Author; Novelist. m. Benedict Freedman, 29 June 1941, Evanston, Illinois, 1 son, 2 daughters. *Education:* University of Southern California. *Publications:* (novels): (co-author Benedict Freedman): Mrs Mike, 1949; This And No More, 1952; The Spark and the Exodus, 1954; Lockville, 1957; Tresa, 1959; The Apprentice Bastard, 1966; (author): Cyclone Silence, 1969; Joshua Son Of None, 1973; The Immortals, 1976; Prima Donna, 1981; Sappho (in press). (Books translated into 27 languages). *Contributions to:* The Atlantic Monthly; King Features Syndicate; Reader's Digest. *Honours:* Mrs Mike, feature film, 1947; Bavarian Festival in honour, 1958; A Collection of Memorabilia at Boston University Mugar Library; Main selection Literary Guild; Alternate selection Literary Guild; Alternate selection Book of Month Club; Main Boekenclub Success, The Netherlands. *Literary Agent:* Scott Meredith. *Address:* 5837 Latigo Bluffs, Malibu, CA 90265, USA.

FREELING, Nicolas, b. 3 Mar. 1927, London, England. Fiction Writer. m. Cornelia Termes, 4 sons, 1 daughter. *Publications include:* 30 books, 1961–. Titles include: Love in Amsterdam, 1961; Because of the Cats, 1962; Gun Before Butter, 1962; Valparaiso, 1963; Double Barrel, 1963; Criminal Conversation, 1964; King of the Rainy Country, 1965; Dresden Green, 1966; Strike Out Where Not Applicable, 1967; This is the Castle, 1968; Tsing-Boum, 1969; Kitchen Book, 1970; Over the High Side, 1971; Cook Book, 1971; A Long Silence, 1972; Dressing of Diamond, 1974; What Are the Bugles Blowing For?, 1975; Lake Isle, 1976; Gadget, 1977; The Night Lords, 1978; The Widow, 1979; Castang's City, 1980; One Damn Thing After Another, 1981; Wolfnight, 1982; Back of the North Wind, 1983; No Part in Your Death, 1984; A City Solitary, 1985; Cold Iron, 1986. *Contributions to:* Various journals. *Honours:* Approximately six, 1963–. *Literary Agent:* Curtis Brown, London/New York. *Address:* Grandfontaine, 67130 Schirmeck, France.

FREELY, Maureen, b. 28 July 1952, Neptune, New Jersey, USA. Writer. m. Paul Spike, 26 Mar. 1976, London, England, 1 son, 1 daughter. *Education:* AB, magna cum laude, Harvard College, 1974. *Publications:* Mother's Helper, 1979; The Life of the Party, 1985. *Literary Agent:* Helen Brann. *Address:* c/o The Helen Brann Agency, 157 West 57th Street, New York, NY 10019, USA.

FREEMAN, David Edgar, b. 7 Jan. 1945, Toronto, Canada. Writer. *Education:* BA, Political Sciences, McMaster University. *Publications:* Battering Ram, 1974; Creeps, Canadian Plays Series, 1972; The Penguin Book of Modern Canadian Drama; The Burns Mantle Yearbook; The Best Plays of 1973-74, 1971; Flytrap, 1976; You're Gonna Be Alright Jamie-Boy, 1974. *Contributor to:* Maclean's Magazine; Star Weekly; The Silhouette; Stage Voices, 1978. *Honours:* Chalmers Awards for best Canadian Play of 1971-72

Season; New York Drama Desk Award for Outstanding New Playwright, 1973; One of 6 First Prizes, Edinburgh Fringe Festival, 1979; Three Los Angeles Critics Circle Awards, 1983. *Literary Agent:* John C Goodwin, Canada; Ellen Neuwald, New York. *Address:* c/o John C Goodwin, 4235 Avenue de l'Esplanada, Montreal H2W 1T1, Quebec, Canada.

FREEMAN, Gillian, b. London, England. Writer. *Education:* BA, Reading University. *Publications:* The Liberty Man, 1955; Fall of Innocence, 1957; Jack Would be a Gentleman, 1959; The Leather Boys, 1962; The Campaign, 1963; The Leader, 1964; The Alabaster Egg, 1970; The Marriage Machine, 1975; Nazi Lady, 1978; An Easter Egg Hunt, 1981; Love Child (under Elaine Jackson), 1984; (non-fiction) The Story of Albert Einstein, 1959; The Undergrowth of Literature, 1968; The Schoolgirl Ethic; The Life and Work of Angela Brazil, 1976; Films: The Leather Boys; That Cold Day in the Park; I Want What I Want. *Contributions to:* The Times; Sunday Times; Spectator; New Statesman; Listener; London Magazine; The Guardian. *Literary Agent:* Richard Scott Simon. *Address:* c/o Richard Scott Simon, 32 College Cross, London N1, England.

FREEMAN, Lucy, b. New York City, USA. Author. Divorced. *Education:* BA, Bennington College. *Appointments:* Reporter, New York Times, 1942-53. *Publications:* 54 books including: Fight Against Fears, 1951; Betrayal, 1976; Freud and Women, 1980. *Contributor to:* Cosmopolitan; New York Times Magazine; McCall's. *Memberships:* President, Mystery Writers of America; PEN; National Association of Science Writers; American Society of Journalists and Authors. *Address:* 210 Central Park South, New York, NY 10019, USA.

FREEMAN-GRENVILLE, Greville Stewart Parker, b. 29 June 1918, Hook Norton, Oxfordshire, England. Historian. *Education:* BA, 1939, BLitt, 1940, MA, 1942, DPhil, 1957, Worcester College, Oxford. *Publications include:* The East African Coast; Select Documents, 1962, 2nd edition, 1976; Muslim and Christian Calenders, 1963, 2nd edition, 1977; Chronology of World History, 1976; The Queen's Lineage, 1977; The Mombasa Rising Against the Portuguese, 1631, 1980. *Contributions to:* Various encyclopaedias and professional journals. *Honours:* Recipient of Overseas Travel Awards, British Academy, 1976, 1979, 1982; Knight of the Holy Sepulchre, 1982; Papal Gross Pro Exclesia et Pontifice, 1984. *Memberships:* FSA; Fellow Royal Asiatic Society; Royal Numismatic Society; Royal Commonwealth Society. *Address:* North View House, Sheriff Hutton, York, England.

FREEMANTLE, Michael Harold, b. 27 Sept. 1942, Southampton, Hampshire, England. Writer, Editor. m. Mary Therese McHale, 4 May 1968, Harrow, Middlesex, 1 son, 3 daughters. *Education:* BSc, PhD, MRSC, C Chem. *Literary Appointments:* Part-time Consultant Editor to UNESCO Division of Scientific Research and Higher Education, 1975-85; Editor: Chemistry International. *Major Publications:* Chemist in Industry: Management & Economics, 1975; Slim for Life, 1980; Essential Science: Chemistry (with J Tidy), 1983; Chemistry Quizzes & Puzzles (with G Curtis), 1985. *Contributor to:* Journal of the Chemical Society; Pure & Applied Chemistry; New Scientist; and others. *Membership:* Society of Authors. *Address:* 11 Plover Close, Kempshott, Basingstoke, Hampshire, RG22 5PQ, England.

FREIBERG, Stanley Kenneth, b. 26 Aug. 1923, Merrill, Wisconsin, USA. Teacher, Writer. m. Marjorie Ellen Speckhand, 29 June 1947, Clintonville, Wisconsin, 1 son, 1 daughter. *Education:* BA 1948, MA 1949, PhD 1957, University of Wisconsin, Madison. *Literary Appointments include:* Assistant Professor 1963-64; Associate Professor of English Literature 1965-66, University of Nevada, Reno; Professor of English Literature, University of Calgary, Alberta, Canada, 1966-79; Writer, Teacher of writing and drama at University of Ottawa and of literature at University of

Victoria and University of Calgary, 1979–. *Publications:* The Baskets of Baghdad: Poems of the Middle East, 1968; Plumes of the Serpent: Poems of Mexico, 1973; The Caplin-Crowded Seas: Poems of Newfoundland, 1975; Nightmare Tales (Short Stories of Nova Scotia), 1980. *Contributions to:* Dalhousie Review; Queen's Quarterly; Ariel. *Honours:* Canada Arts Council Grant, 1980. *Address:* 1523 York Place, Victoria, British Columbia, V8R 5XI, Canada.

FREIRE-MAIA, Newton,b. 29 June 1918, Boa Esperanca, MG. Professor. m. (1) Flavia Leite Naves, 26 Sep. 1948 (deceased 1972), Boa Esperanca, MG, 2 sons, 2 daughters (2) Eleidi A Chautard, 1974. *Education:* DDS, 1945; ScD, Natural Sciences, 1960. *Publications:* Genetica Medica, 1966; Populacoes Brasileiras, 1967; Problems of Human Biology, 1970; Radiogenetica Humana, 1972; Brasil: Laboratorio Racial, 1973, 7th editon, 1985; Genetica de Populacoes Humanas, 1984; Topicos de Genetica Humana, 1976; Ectodermal Dysplasias: A Clinical and Genetic Study, 1984, etc. *Contributions to:* American Journal of Human Genetics; American Journal of Medical Genetics; Journal of Medical Genetics, Human Heredity; Human Biology; Social Biology, and several other professional publications. Articles and Papers mainly on human population genetics and medical genetcis. *Honours:* Brazilian National Prize of Genetics and many others. *Membeerships:* Editorial Board of Scientific Journals; Full Member, Brazilian Academy of Sciences; Brazilian Society of Genetics; Brazilian Society for the Progress of Sciences; Brazilian Society of History of Science. *Address:* Department of Genetics, UFPR, Caixa Postal 19.071, 81504 Curitiba, PR Brazil.

FRENCH, Dorothy Kayser, b. 11 Feb. 1926, Milwaukee, Wisconsin, USA. Writer. *Education:* BA Journalism, University of Wisconsin. *Publications:* Mystery of the Old Oil Well, 1963; Swim to Victory, 1969; A Try at Tumbling, 1970; Pioneer Saddle Mystery, 1975; I Don't Belong Here, 1980; Out of the Rough, 1981. *Contributions to:* Teen; Oklahoma Today Dodge Adventurer; Humpty Dumpty; Hi Call; Dallas Times Herald; Milwaukee Journal; Modern Baby; Modern Romances; True Story, and others. Former Womens Editor, Wisconsin State Journal, Former Social Editor, Shorewood Herald, and Bartlesville Record. Staff Member, Tampa Book Fair, Florida, 1974, 76, 77. *Honours:* Listing in Sequoyah List of Recommended Books for Oklahoma Schools and Libraries, 1964, 65. *Memberships:* Women In Communications; Mortar Board; Kappa Delta. *Address:* 2136 South East Starlight Court, Bartlesville, OK 74006, USA.

FRENCH, Raymond James, b. 23 Dec. 1939, St Helens, Lancashire, England. Schoolmaster; Television Commentator. m. Helen French, 1 June 1963, St Helens, 1 son, 1 daughter. *Education:* BA Honours, Leeds University; Certificate of Education. *Publications:* My Kind of Rugby, 1979; Running Rugby, 1980; Coaching Rugby League, 1982; The Rugby League Lions, 1985. *Contributions to:* Rugby Leaguer; Open Rugby. *Literary Agent:* Malcolm Hamer. *Address:* 50 Kiln Lane, St Helens, Lancashire, England.

FRENKEL, Karen A, b. 7 Sept. 1955, New York City, USA. Features Writer. *Education:* BA, Philisophy of Science, Hampshire College, 1978; MS, Science Communication, Boston University, 1982. *Publications:* Robots: Machines in Man's Image, with Isaac Asimov, 1985. *Contributions:* Science & technology articles for: Forbes; Technology Review; Medical World News; Communications of the ACM. *Memberships:* Society of Professional Journalists; Sigma Delta Chi. *Address:* 240 W 98th Street, Apt 14A, New York, NY 10025, USA.

FRENKIEL, Zygmunt (Freddie), b. Czestochowa, Poland. (British Subject). Journalist; Writer. m. Eunice Barbara Hutching, 1947, 1 son, 1 daughter. *Education:* CEng, FIMechE University of Caén, France; FILing; Dipl Colonial Institute, University of Nancy, France. *Publications:* Paryz, 1939; Speak English, 1946; English Letters for Poles, 1946; Polish Technician in British Industry, 1947; Be A Gentleman, 1947; The Easy Way to Speak Polish, 1948; New English-Polish Secretary, 1959. *Contributions to:* BBC, 1948; Encyclopaedia Britannica, 1969; Lift, Elevator and Ropeway Engineering, 1974 (editor); Wire Machinery Guide, 1981 (Editor); Wire Industry, 1981 (asst editor); Kempe's Engineering Year Book, 1985; various professional journals. *Honours:* Officer d'Academie, 1938; International Literary Prize of French Tourism, 1939; Officer de l'I l'Instrn Publ France, 1953. *Memberships:* Institute of Journalists (Member); Society of Authors; Translations Association; and others. *Address:* 11 Rotherfield Road, Carshalton, Surrey, SM5 3DN, England.

FREUNDLICH, Eisabeth, b. 21 July 1906, Vienna, Austria. Writer. *Education:* PhD, University of Vienna; MA, Columbia University, New York, USA. *Publications:* Invasion Day, 1948; Der Eherne Reiter, 1961; Die Ermordung einer Stadt namens Stanislau, 1986; Finstere Zeifen, 1986; Der Seelenvogel, 1986. Translations of plays and novels by various authors including: Sean O'Casey; Joseph Conrad; P V Carroll. *Contributions to:* Various German language magazines including: Frankfurter Hefte. Various broadcasting stations including: Austrian Radio; Radio Bremen. Contributor to, O'Casey Studies, New York, USA. *Honours:* Prize of Achievement, Theodor Korner Foundation, 1970; Grant, Austrian Ministry of Science and Research, 1978. *Memberships:* Austrian Section, Poets, Playwrights, Editors, Essayists and Novelists Club. *Address:* Florianig 55/18, A–1080 Vienna, Austria.

FRIAR, Kimon, b. 18 Nov. 1911, Imrale, Turkey. Author. *Education:* BA, University of Wisconsin, USA, 1934; MA, University of Michigan, 1939; State University of Iowa; Yale Graduate School of Drama. *Publications include:* The Nativity, A Poem for Dance, 1974; The Spiritual Odyssey of Nikos Kasantakis: A Talk, 1979. Translations: Numerous of works by Nikos Kazantzakis, Takis Sinopoulos, Yannis Ritsos and others. Editor: The Poetry Center Presents, 1947; The Greeks, A Celebration of the Greek People through Poetry and Photography, 1984. Has produced numerous translations with introductions and notes from Greek to English, and into Greek. *Contributions to:* Numerous translations of works in anthologies. *Honours:* Award and Diploma, Athens Academy, 1976; Honorary Citizen, Iraklion, Crete, 1976; Greek World Award, 1978; Ford Foundation Grant; Imgram-Merrill Foundation Grant; National Foundation for the Arts Grant; Insugurator of newly formed Kazantzakis Chair, San Francisco State University, 1986. *Memberships:* American Greek Studies Association. *Address:* Kallidromiou 10, Athens 706, Greece.

FRIED, Philip Henry, b. 8 Jan. 1945, Editor. m. Lynn Saville, 5 Oct. 1985, New York City. *Education:* BA, Antioch College, USA, 1966; MFA, University of Iowa Writer's Workshop, 1968; PhD, English, State University of New York, Stony Brok, 1978. *Literary Appointments include:* Editor: Mitchell, Titus and Company Certified Public Accountants, 1979; Hold, Rinehart and Winston Publishers, New York City, 1984–. Administrative Assistant, Gloria Stern Literary Agency, 1978–79. *Contributions to:* Partisan Review; Paris Review; Massachusetts Review; Chicago Review; Beloit Poetry Journal; Poetry Northwest; North American Review; Antioch Review; Falcon; The Little Mag; New Voices; Egg; Bits; Soundings. Founder and Editor, The Manhattan Review, poetry journal. *Honour:* Grant, Coordinating Council ofLiterary Magazines, 1984. *Memberships:* Poetry Society of America; Writers Union; Poets and Writers Incorporated; Coordinating Council of Literary Magazines. *Address:* 304 Third Avenue, 4A, New York City, NY 10010, USA.

FRIEDERICHS-FITZWATER, Marlene Marie von, b. 14 July 1939, Beatrice, Nebraska, USA. University Professor. m. Robert B Desaeger, 18 June 1983, Montreal, Quebec, Canada, 4 sons (previous marriages). *Education:* BS, Communication, Westminster College, Utah; MA, Communication, University of

Nebraska, Omaha; PhD Communication, University of Utah, Salt Lake City. *Literary Appointments:* General Assignment Reporter, Los Angeles Times, 1957–60; Publicist and Script Writer, Walt Disney Studios, California, 1960–63; Copywriter and Newsletter Editor, Ross Jurney Advertising, Salt Lake City, 1963–65; Freelance Writer and Editor, 1965–71; Information Specialist for Model Cities, Salt Lake City, 1971–74; Managing Editor, Utah Magazine, and Utah Life Magazine; President, First Edition Publishing Company, Salt Lake City, 1974–76; Information Specialist and Writer, Nebraska ETV Network, 1976–77; Director, Public Relations, College of St Mary, 1977–79; Public Relations Specialist, Editor, Archbishop, Bergan Mercy Hospital, Omaha, 1979–81; Teaching Fellow, Communication, University of Utah, 1981–83; Currently, Assistant Professor, Department of Communication Studies, California State University, 1985–. *Publications:* Over 200 articles; Contributing Editor, Biographical Dictionary of America Journalism (in process); Mass Media Content, Political Opinion and Social Change (in process). *Honours:* Numerous Honours and Awards including; Award for Excellence, Photography: Human Interest, International Association of Business Communications, 1982. *Memberships:* Member professional organizations. *Address:* 5230 Greenberry Drive, Sacramento, CA 95841, USA.

FRIEDMAN, Alan Howard, b. 4 Jan. 1928, New York City, USA. Writer. m. (1), Lenore Ann Helman, 1 Aug. 1950, New York City, (div.) 1 son. (2). Kate Miller Gilbert, 30 Oct. 1977, New York City. *Education:* BA (Magnacum laude), Harvard College, 1949; MA, Columbia University, 1950; PhD, University of California, Berkeley, 1964. *Publications:* The Turn of the Novel, (1966; Hermaphrodeity: The Autobiography of a Poet, (novel. National Book Award nominee), 1972. *Contributor to:* (Stories): Hudson Review; Mademoiselle; Contact; Partisan Review; New American Review; Paris Review; Fiction International; Kansas Quarterly, 1985; Formations; articles, chapters and reviews: The Stream of Conscience, Hudson Review, Winter 1964–65; The Other Lawrence, Partisan Review, No. 2 1970; The Novel, The Twentieth Century Mind, Edited by C B Cox and A E Dyson, 1972; Reviews in New York Times Book Review. *Honours:* D H Lawrence Fellowship, 1974; National Endowment in the Arts Award, 1975. *Membership:* PEN Club, Phi Beta Kappa. *Literary Agent:* Lynn Nesbit, New York City. *Address:* Program for Writers, English Department, University of Illinois at Chicago, Chicago, IL 60680, USA.

FRIEDMAN, Jacob Horace, b. 11 Mar. 1916, Cape Town, South Africa. Priest. *Education:* Medical Studies, CT University, 1933–38; Various Hospitals; Student, Catholic Institute, Lyon, France, 1953–54; Priestly Ordination, Metropolitan Cathedral, Avignon, 1953. *Publications include:* The Redemption of Israel, 1947; In Praise of Night (poems), 1969; La Terre Sainte, 1982; Jerusalem Sonnets (poems), 1982; Monte Carmelo, 1983; The Spirituality of a Hebrew-Catholic; Poems from Mount Carmel, 1985; Numerous translations. *Contributor to:* Groote Schuur; Contrast; Voices, Israel; Chapters in Books: A New Book of South African Verse in English; Monte Carmelo; The Orders and Churches of Crusader Acre. *Honours:* Best Speaker Prize from Cape Zionist Youth Movement, 1931; Several Scholarships; General Service Medal; Africa Medal; Certificate from Association of Israeli Guides for services rendered to visitors and pilgrims to Stela Maris, 1966; Olive Schreiner Debut Prize for volume of original poems, In Praise of Night, by S A Academy of Arts and Science, 1971; Jerusalem Medal, Department of Tourism of State of Israel, 1979; Diploma of Merit, University of Arts, Parma, Italy, 1981; Plaque by Winfield Oratorio Society, Kansas City, USA for services rendered, 1984. *Memberships:* Foundation Member, International Academy of Poets, 1976; Life Member, World Literary Academy. *Address:* 'Stella Maris' Monastery, POB 9047, 31090 Haifa, Israel.

FRIEDMAN, Kathi Vallone, b. 26 Sep. 1943, Rochester, New York, USA. Sociologist. *Education:* BA,

Cornell University, Ithaca, New York, 1965; MA, 1970; PhD, 1979, University of North Carolina. *Publications:* Legitimation of Social Rights and the Western Welfare State: A Weberian Perspective, 1981; Beyond the Welfare State: Institution Building for the 21st Century. *Contributions to:* Introduction to Sociology, 1977. *Honours:* Guldin Award in Journalism for article in Cornell Countryman Magazine, 1962; National Defense Education Act Fellowship, 1968–70. *Address:* PO Box 1251, Washington, DC 20013, USA.

FRIEDMAN, Rosemary, b. 5 Feb. 1929, London, England. Writer. *Education:* University College, London University. *Publications:* No White Coat, 1957; Love On My List, 1959; We All Fall Down, 1960; Patients of a Saint, 1961; The Fraternity, 1963; The Commonplace Day, 1964; The General Practice, 1967; Practice Makes Perfect, 1969; Aristide, 1966; The Life Situation, 1977; The Long Hot Summer, 1980; Proofs of Affection, 1982; A Loving Mistress, 1983; Rose of Jericho, 1984; A Second Wife, 1986. *Contributions to:* The Times Literary Supplement; Financial Times; The Times. *Membership:* PEN. *Address:* 2 St Katharine's Precinct, Regent's Park, London NW1 4HH, England.

FRIEDMANN, John, b. 16 Apr. 1926, Vienna, Austria. Professor. *Education:* MA, PhD 1955, University of Chicago, USA. *Major Publications:* The Spatial Structure of Economic Developments in the Tennessee Valley, 1955; Regional Development & Planning (with W Alcaso), 1964; Venezuela: From Doctrine to Dialogue, 1965; Regional Development Policy: A Case Study of Venezuela, 1966; Urbanization, Planning & National Development, 1973; Retracking America: A Theory of Transactive Planing, 1973, reissued 1981; Regional Policy (with W Alonso), 1975; The Urban Transition (with R Wulff), 1975; The Good Society, 1979; Territory & Function (with C Weaver), 1979. *Contributor to:* Numnerous journals. *Honours include:* Honorary Doctorate, Universidad Católica de Chile, 1969. *Address:* Urban Planning Programme, School of Architecture & Urban Planning, University of California at Los Angeles, 405 Hilgard Avenue, Los Angeles, CA 90024, USA.

FRIEDRICH, Eduard Georg Jr, b. 21 Oct. 1937, Chicago, Illinois, USA. University Professor. 2 daughters. *Education:* HAB, Xavier University, 1959; MD, The Johns Hopkins University School of Medicine, 1963; LLD (Honoris Causa), Xavier University 1982. *Literary Appointments:* Special Editorial Consultant, Obstetrics and Gynecology, 1975–; Editorial Board, Sexually Transmitted Disease, 1977; Editorial Consultant, American Journal of Ob-Gyn, 1979–; Guest Editor, Clinical Obstetrics and Gynecology, 1981 and 1985; Editorial Board, The Journal of Reproductive Medicine, 1981–; Editorial Advisory Board, The Journal of Family Practice, 1983–. *Publications:* Vulvar Disease 1976, 2nd edition 1983; Poems 1983. *Contributions to:* American Journal of Obstetrics and Gynecology; Clinical Obstetrics and Gynecology; Obstetrics and Gynecology; Journal of Reproductive Medicine; New England Journal of Medicine; Linacre Quarterly; Contemporary Obstetrics and Gynecology; Journal of the Florida Medical Association; International Journal of Gynecology and Obstetrics; American Family Physician. *Honours:* AMA Physician's Recognition Award, 1974; Senior Class Award for Teaching Excellence, Medical College of Wisconsin, 1974; ACOG Film Award for Outstanding Motion Picture of the Year, 1979; Outstanding Residency Program Director, District IV ACOG, 1983. *Memberships:* American Medical Writers Association; Florida State Poets Association. *Address:* Box J-294, JHMHC, Gainesville, FL 32610, USA.

FRIEDRICH, Gustav, William, b. 2 Mar. 1941, Hastings, Nebraska, USA. Professor of Communication. m. Erena Rae Bakeberg, 4 Aug. 1962, Hopkins, Minnesota, 1 son. *Education:* AA, Concordian College, 1961; BA, summa cum laude, University of Minnesota, 1964; MA, University of Kansas, 1967; PhD, (Hons), University of Kansas, 1968. *Literary Appointments:* University of Kansas, 1964–68; Purdue University,

1968–77; University of Nebraska, 1977–81; University of Oklahoma, 1982–. *Publications:* Teaching Speech Communication in the Secondary School, 1973; Public Communication, 1975; Growing Together...Classroom Communication, 1976; Education in the 80's: Speech Communication, 1981; Public Communication, 1983. *Contributions to:* Speech Monographs; Speech Teacher; Journal of Communication; Journal of Personality and Social Psychology; Journal of Applied Social Psychology; International Journal of Instructional Media, etc. *Honours:* SCA Golden Anniversary Monograph Award, 1974; CSSA Service Award, 1978; Outstanding Young Man of America, 1973; CSSA Outstanding Young Teacher Award, 1970. *Memberships:* CSSA, President and Executive Secretary; SCA, Administrative Committee; ICA, Board of Directors. *Address:* Department of Communication, 331 Kaufman Hall, University of Oklahoma, Norman, OK 73019, USA.

FRIEDRICH, Heinz, b. 14 Feb. 1922, Rossdorf, Kreis Darmstadt, Federal German Republic. Publisher of, Deutscher Taschenbuch Verlag. *Publications:* Im Narrenschiff des Zeitgeistes, 1972; Kulturkatastrophe, 1979; Kulturverfall und Umweltkrise, 1982. *Contributor to:* Newspapers: Die Welt; Rheinischer Merkur; Suddeutsche Zeitung; Die Presse; Broadcasting Corporations Bayerischer Rundfunk; Osterreichischer Rundfunk. *Memberships:* German-Swiss PEN Ctr, Zurich, Switzerland; President of the Bavarian Academy of Fine Arts, Munich, Germany. *Address:* Deutscher Taschenbuch Verlag, Friedrichstrasse la, D–8000 Munich 40, Federal Republic of Germany.

FRIEL, Brian, b. 9 Jan. 1929, Ireland. Writer. m. Anne Morrison, 28 Jan, 1954, Derry City, 1 son, 4 daughters. *Publications:* The Saucer of Larks; The Gold in the Sea; Plays: The Enemy Within; Philadelphia, Here I Come!; The Loves of Cass McGuire; Lovers; The Freedom of the City; Living Quarters; Aristocrats; Volunteers; Faith Healer; Translations; The Communication Cord; Translation: Three Sisters. *Contributor to:* New Yorker. *Honours:* D Litt, National University of Ireland, 1982; McAuley Fellowship, 1964; Harvey Award, 1980. *Memberships:* Irish Academy of Letters; Aosdana. *Literary Agent:* Curtis Brown, London. *Address:* Drumaweir House, Greencastle, County Donegal, Ireland.

FRIESEN, Patrick Frank, b. 5 July 1945, Canada. Media Specialist. m. Carol Anne, 9 May 1970, Winnipeg, 1 son, 1 daughter. *Education:* BA, Honours. *Publications:* The Lands I am, 1976; Bluebottle, 1978; The Shunning, 1980; Unearthly Horses, 1984. *Contributor to:* Various magazines and journals. *Honours:* 2 Arts Council Grants. *Memberships:* Manitoba Writers' Guild, President, 1981–83; The League of Canadian Poets, Manitoba Representative on Executive, 1980–. *Address:* Winnipeg, Manitoba, Canada.

FRISBIE, Louise Kelley, b. 18 Oct. 1913, Jacksonville, Florida, USA. Journalist. *Education:* BS, Florida Southern College. *Publications:* Here's How, Notes on News Writing, 1957; Peace River Pioneers, 1974; Yesterday's Polk County, 1976; Florida's Fabled Inns, 1980. *Honours:* Citation for Contribution to History, Florida Senate, 1976; Outstanding Service to Humanity, Florida Southern College, 1977. *Memberships:* Editor Executive Committee, Polk County Historical Association; Tampa Historical Society; Florida Historical Society; Historical Association of Southern Florida; Orange County Historical Society; Historical Association of Palm Beach County. *Address:* PO Box 120, Bartow, FL 33830, USA.

FRISÉ, Adolf, b. 29 May 1910, Euskirchen, Federal Republic of Germany. Writer. m. Maria von Loesch, 25 May 1957, Bad Homburg. *Education:* PhD, studies of German Literature, Philosophy and History of Art, 1932. *Literary Appointments:* Freelance writer and critc, 1932–40; Editor politics and culture, Hamburg, 1946–50; Editor culture, Hessischer Rundfunk Frankfurt an

Main, 1956–75.*Publications:* Reise-Journal, travel diaries, 1967–-68; Plädoyer für Robert Musil. Hiaweise und Essays 1931–1980, 1980; Collected Works of Robert Musil, (editor), 3 volumes, 1952–57; Robert Musil's Tagebucher 1699–1942, (editor), 2 volumes, 1978; Robert Musil's Briefe 1901–1942, (editor), 2 volumes, 1981. *Contributions to:* Neue Rundschau; Die Tat; Nerkur; Die Zeit; Frankfurter Allgemeine Zeitung; Neue Zurcher Zeitung. *Honours:* Honorary Professor, nominated by the President of Austria, 1974; Honorary President, International Robert Musil Society, 1979; Decorated Bundesverdienstkreuz 1st class, 1981; Dr Phil honoris causa, University Klagenfurt/Autriche, 1982. *Memberships:* PEN; Deutsche Schillergesellschasft; International Robert Musil-Gesellschaft. *Address:* Am Zollstock 24, D6380 Bad Homburg vdH, Federal Republic of Germany.

FRITH, David Edward John, b. 16 Mar. 1937, London, England. Writer (Cricket). m. Oriel Christina Debbie, 11 May 1957, Ipswich, Queensland, Australia, 2 sons, 1 daughter. *Education:* Matriculation from Canterbury High School, Sydney, New South Wales. *Literary Appointments:* Editor, The Cricketer, 1972–78; Editor, Wisden Cricket Monthly, 1979–. *Publications:* Biographies of A E Stoddart, 1970; Archie Jackson, 1974; Jeff Thomson, 1979; England and Australia tour accounts, 1977 (with Greg Chappell) and 1979; The Fast Men, 1975; The Slow Men, 1984; Editor, Cricket Gallery, 1974; England and Australia: A Pictorial History, 1977; The Golden Age of Cricket, 1978; Cricket's Golden Summer (with Gerry Wright), 1985. *Contributions to:* Wisden Cricket Monthly; The Cricketer; The Journal of the Cricket Society; Sportsworld (India); Cricketer (Australia); South African Cricketer. *Honours:* Cricket Society Jubilee Literary Award, 1970; Cricket Writer of the Year, Wombwell Cricket Lovers Society, Yorkshire, 1984. *Membership:* Cricket Writers Club, Committee Member. *Address:* 6 Beech Lane, Guildford, Surrey, England.

FRITZ, Walter Helmut, b. 26 Aug. 1929. Writer. *Education:* Literature & Philosophy, University of Heidelberg. *Publications:* Achtsam sein, 1956; Veranderte Jahre, 1963; Umwege, 1964; Zwischenbemerkungen, 1965; Abweichung, 1965; Die Zuverlassigkeit der Unruhe, 1966; Bemerkungen zu einer Gegend, 1969; Dies Verwechslung, 1970; Aus der Nahe, 1972; Die Beschaffenbeit solcher Tage, 1972; Bevor uns Horan und Sehen Vergeht, 1975; Schwierige Uberfahrt, 1976; Auch jetzi und morgan, 1979; Gesammelte Gedichte, 1979; Wunschtraum Alptraum, 1981; Werkzenge der Freiheit, 1983; Cornelias Trau und andere Aufzeichnungen, 1985. *Contributor to:* Neue Rundschau; Neue Deutsche Hefte; Frankfurter Hefte; Jahresring Ensemble; Universitas; Tages-speigel, and others. *Honours:* Lierature Prize of the City of Karlsruhe, 1960; Prize, Bavarian Academy of Fine Arts, 1962; Heine-Taler, Lyrik Prize, 1966; Prize, Culture Circle, Federation of German Industry, 1971. *Memberships:* German Academy for Speech & Poetry; Academy for Science & Literature, mainz; Bavarian Academy of Fine Arts, Munich; PEN; Union of German Writers. *Address:* Kolbergerstr 2a, 75 Karlsruhe 1, Federal Republic of Germany.

FROMER, Margot Joan, b. 30 Aug. 1939, New York City, USA, Writer. *Education:* BS, Boston University, 1961; MA 1964, MEd 1967, Columbia University, New York; Doctoral Program, Georgetown University, Washington DC, 1980–81. *Literary Appointments:* Assistant Professor, Rutgers University, New Jersey, 1974–78; Assistant Professor, University of Delaware, 1978–80; Feature Writer, Emergency Department News, New York City, 1981–82; Adjunct Professor (part-time), American University, Washington DC, 1983; Consultant; Resource Applications, Baltimore, Maryland, 1982–84; Contributing Editor, The Washington Blade, 1983. *Major Publications:* Community Health Care & The Nursing Process, 1979; Ethical Issues in Health Care, 1981; Ethical Issues in Sexuality & Reproduction, 1983; How to Quit Smoking in 30 Days...Without Cracking Up, (with F G Conn),

1982. Instructors Guide, for use with, Fundamentals of Nursing, (Kozier & Erb). *Contributor to:* Washington Post; New York Times; Baltimore Sun; Psychology Today; The New Physician; Nursing Law & Ethics; and others. *Honours:* National Endowment for the Humanities grant, 1979. *Memberships:* American Civil Liberties Union; American Medical Writers Association; American Society of Law & Medicine; Institute for Society, Ethics & Life Sciences; Authors Guild; Washington Independent Writers; Women & Health Roundtable. *Literary Agent:* John Farquharson Ltd, New York & London. *Address:* 1606 Noyes Drive, Silver Spring, MD 20910, USA.

FROMMER, Harvey, b. 10 Oct. 1937, Brooklyn, New York, USA. Professor; Author. m. Myrna Katz, 23 Jan. 1960, Brooklyn, New York, 2 sons, 1 daughter. *Education:* BS, Journalism; MA, English; PhD, Communications, New York University. *Literary Appointments:* Professor of Writing and Speech, New York City Technical College, City University of New York, 1970–; Reviewer for; Yankees Magazine, Library Journal, Choice, Kliatt Paperback Book Guide. *Publications:* A Baseball Century, 1976; A Sailing Primer, 1978; The Martial Arts Book, 1978; Sports Lingo, 1979, 83; Sports Roots, 1979; The Great American Soccer Book, 1980; New York City Baseball 1947–57, 1980, 85; The Sports Date Book, 1981; Basketball My Way, Nancy Lieberman, 1982; Rickey and Robinson, 1982; Baseball's Greatest Rivalry, 1982, 84; Sports Genes, 1982; Baseball's Greatest Records, 1983; Jackie Robinson, 1984; National Baseball Hall of Fame, 1985; Baseball's Greatest Managers, 1985; The Autobiography of Red Holzman, 1986; City Tech: The first Forty Years, 1986; Olympic Controversies, 1987. *Contributions to:* Golf Digest; Yankees Magazine; The New York Times; Queens Magazine; United Features; Staten Island Magazine; New Brooklyn; New York Daily News; Newsday Long Island Magazine; St Louis Post-Dispatch; The Los Angeles Times; New York University Alumni News. *Honours:* Official guest of Mexican Government to tour nation to write about Mexican Sports, Summer 1983; Salute to Scholars Award, City University of New York, 1984; As result of nationwide search chosen to be Editor and Chief Author of Games of the XXIIIrd Olympiad Los Angeles 1984 Commemorative Book. *Literary Agent:* Arthur Pine, New York City. *Address:* 791 Oakleigh Road, North Woodmere, NY 11581, USA.

FROMMER, Myrna, b. 29 Mar. 1940, New York City, USA. Teacher of Rhetoric. m. Harvey Frommer, 23 Jan. 1960, New York City, 2 sons, 1 daughter. *Education:* BS, New York University; PhD Candidate, New York University. *Appointments:* Editor, Games of the XXIIIrd Olympiad, Los Angeles 1984 Commemorative Book. *Publications:* Sporting Green, 1982; The Sports Date Book, 1981; Basketball My Way – Nancy Leiberman, 1982, all with Harvey Frommer. *Contributor to:* Numerous professional journals, newspapers and magazines. *Address:* 791 Oakleigh Road, N Laadmere, NY 11581, USA.

FRØOYDARLUND, Jan-Anker, b. 6 May 1911, Skien, Norway. Author; Poetry Translator. *Education:* BA, Bennett College, England, 1931; Authorised Translator, SPU, Amsterdam, The Netherlands, 1948; Graduate Poetry Translator, Laureate, World Academy of Languages and Literature, 1975; Doctor of Letters, University of Danzig, American Faculty, USA, 1976; PhD, Honours, Theological Faculty, Bodkin Institute, USA, 1981. *Appointments include:* Journalist, 1932–35; Lecturer, English & French Literature, Junior Colleege of Ulefoss; Principal and Lecturer, Froydarlund Institute of Languages and Literature, 1940; Folk University, 1960–75; Literary Critic, 1975–80; Editorial Board, World Poetry, 2 Europe, 1982. *Publications include:* Fanga av min tid, 1966; Kjaerleik den einaste rosa, 1966; Den Kortaste dagen, selections from Dr Negalha's Poetry, 1977; Curriculum Vitae, 1978; Loynleg Liv, 1979; Horisonten og Regnbogen, including Poetry of Ondra Lysohorsky, 1980. *Contributor to:* Numerous professional journals,

including, Poet; Madras; Laurel Leaves; Dagbladet; etc. *Honours:* Award, Distinguished Achievement, Translation of the Nobel Prize Poet Juan Ramón Jiménez, Madrid, Spain, 1967; Poet Laureate for distinguished achievement, World Academy of Arts and Culture, 1981, numerous academic grants etc. *Memberships include:* Norwegian Writers Centre; International PEN Club, Oslo; Founder Fellow, Honorary Secretary, Societas Polyglotta Universalis, Amsterdam; Felow, International Academy of Poets; etc. *Literary Agent:* Dreyers Forlag, Oslo; Solum Forlag, Oslo. *Address:* Tamburgata 3, 3700 Skien, Norway.

FRUCHTER, Rena Harriet, b. 26 Apr. 1947, Philadelphia, Pennsylvania, USA. Music Critic; Columnist. m. Brian F Dallow, 4 Aug. 1968, Philadelphia, Pennsylvania, 1 son, 3 daughters. *Education:* BA, Brandeis University; Associate, Royal College of Music, London, England; Licentiate, Trinity College, London; Certificate, Fontainebleau, France. *Literary Appointments:* Boston Herald-Traveler, 1965–68; Music Critic, New Brunswick Home News, 1970–85. *Contributor to:* Boston Herald-Traveler; Boston After Dark; New Haven Register; Chamber Music Magazine; New York Times; New Jersey Weekly; Los Angeles Herald-Examiner. *Honours:* Stein Creative Arts Award; Mayoral Citations, Philadelphia, Pennsylvania and Plainfield, New Jersey. *Address:* Martine Avenue, Plainfield, NJ 07060, USA.

FRUMKES, Lewis Burke, b. 10 May 1939, New York City, USA. Writer. 2 children. *Publications:* How To Raise Your IQ By Eating Gifted Children, 1983; The Mensa Think-Smart Book, 1986. *Contributions to:* Harpers; Punch; The New York Times; Travel and Leisure; Town and Country, etc. *Honours:* Pick of Punch, 1982, 83 and 1985. *Memberships:* American Society of Journalists and Authors; Poets and Writers; Authors Guild. *Literary Agent:* Dorothy Pittman. *Address:* 1 Gracie Terrace, New York, NY 10028, USA.

FRYER, Alan David Thompson, b. 13 May 1949, Liverpool, England. Computer Language Specialist. m. Margaret Ann Helsby, 15 Mar, 1975, Egham, Surrey, 2 daughters. *Education:* BSc, 1972, MSc, Computer Science, London University. *Publications:* Micro Computers for Business and Home, 1982; Cobol on Microcomputers, 1984. *Contributor to:* DP Magazine, 1984. *Membership:* Society of Authors. *Address:* 20 Terncliff, Covingham, Swindon, Wiltshire SN3 5BB, England.

FUCCILLO, Domenic Anthony, b. 1 Jan. 1930, New York, USA. Managing Editor. m. Mary Patricia Halloran, 11 July 1953, Alton, Illinois, 2 sons, 2 daughters. *Education:* AB, BJ, University of Missouri, Columbia, Missouri. *Literary Appointments:* Desk Editor, The Prescott Evening Courier, The Arizona Republic, 1957–61; Editor, Biology Division, Oak Ridge National Laboratory, Tennessee, Associate Editor, Isotopes and Radiation Technology, 1961–66; Director, Scientific and Technical Information, US Health Research Program, 1966–73; Managing Editor: Agronomy Journal, Crop Science, and Journal of Agronomic Education, 1973–. *Publications:* Information Work With Unpublished Reports, (with A H Holloway and others), 1976; Many reports and papers. *Contributions to:* AIBS Bulletin; Oak Ridge National Laboratory Memo; NIH Program Notes; Journal of Agronomic Education; CBE Views. *Honours:* Harold Swanberg Medical Writing Scholarship, 1955; Lecturer, University of Wisconsin, Madison, 1972; Editor in residence, Colorado State University, Fort Collins, 1981. *Memberships:* Chairman of Journal Economics Committee, Council of Biology Editors; Society for Technical Communication; Sigma Delta Chi. *Address:* American Society of Agronomy, 677 South Segoe Road, Madison, WI 53711, USA.

FUENTES, Martha Frances Ayers, b. 21 Dec. 1923, Ashland, Alabama, USA. Author. m. Manuel Solomon Fuentes, 11 Apr. 1943. *Education:* BA English, University of South Florida, Tampa, 1969. *Publications:* Two Characters in Search of Agreement, one act play,

1970; The Rebel, television drama; Faith for Today; Mama Don't Make Me Go To College, My Head Hurts, 1969. *Contributions to:* Japanophile; National and regional magazines. *Memberships Include:* Literary Representative 1983, Florida Women in the Arts; Authors Guild; Authors League of America; Dramatists Guild; Society of Children's Book Writers; Southeastern Writers Association; American Association of University Women. *Honours:* Ione Lester Creative Writing Award, University of Southern Florida, 1965; George Sergel Drama Award, University of Chicago, 1969. *Hobbies:* Gourmet cooking; Animal Rights and Protection; Theatre; Swimming; Gardening; Travel; Bird Watching. *Address:* 102 Third Street, Belleair Beach, FL 33535, USA.

FUKUDA, Haruko, b. 21 July 1946, Tokyo, Japan, Member of the Stock Exchange. m. J I Dunnett, 28 Sep. 1973, London. *Education:* BA, Honours, 1968, MA, 1971, Cambridge University, England. *Publications:* Britain in Europe: Impact of the Third World, 1973; Japan and World Trade: Years Ahead, 1974. *Contributions to:* Numerous professional journals and magazines. *Address:* Creems, Wissington, Nayland, Nr Colchester, Essex, England.

FUKUTAKE, Tadashi, b. 12 Feb. 1917, Okayama, Japan. Professor Emeritus, University of Tokyo, Director of the Social Development Research Institute. *Education:* BA, Tokyo Imperial University, Japan, 1940; PhD, University of Tokyo, 1962. *Publications:* Man and Society in Japan, 1962; Asian Rural Society, China, India, Japan, 1967; Japanese Rural Society, 1967; Japanese Society Today, 1974; Rural Society in Japan, 1980; The Japanese Social Structure: Its' Evolution in the Modern Century, 1983; Collected Works (in Japanese), Vol 3 1975–86. *Honours:* Manichi Publications Prize, 1963. *Memberships:* International Sociological Association; Japan Sociological Association. *Address:* 6-31-20-Daita, Setagaya-Ku, Tokyo, Japan.

FULTON, Robin, b. 6 May 1937, Arran, Scotland. Writer. *Education:* MA (Hons), Edinburgh, 1959; PhD, Edinburgh, 1972; Litt D. *Literary Appointment:* Editor, literary quarterly Lines Review, 1967–76. *Publications:* (poetry): Instances, 1967; Inventories, 1969; The Spaces Between the Stones, 1971; The Man With the Surbahar, 1971; Tree-Lines, 1974; Music and Flight, 1975; Between Flights, 1976; Places to Stay In, 1978; Following a Mirror, 1980; Selected Poems 1963–78, 1980; Fields of Focus, 1982; (Criticism): Contemporary Scottish Poetry: Individuals and Contexts, 1974; (editorial): Trio: New Poets from Edinburgh, 1971; Iain Crichton Smith: Selected Poems 1955–80, 1982; Robert Garioch: The Complete Poetical Works, with notes, 1983; Robert Garioch: A Garioch Miscellany, Selected Prose and Letters, 1986; (translations): An Italian Quarter, 1966; Blok's Twelve, 1968; Five Swedish Poets, 1972; Lars Gustafason, Selected Poems, 1972; Gunnar Harding, They Killed Sitting Bull and Other Poems, 1973; Tomas Tranströmer, Citoyens, 1974; Tomas Tranströmer, Selected Poems, 1974, expanded 1975; Werner Aspenström 37 Poems, 1976; Tomas Tranströmer, Baltics, 1980; Johannes Edfelt, Family Tree, 1981; Werner Asperström, The Blue Whale and Other Prose Pieces, 1981; Kjell Espmark, Béla Bartok against The Third Reich and Other Poems, 1985; Olav Hauge, Don't Give Me the Whole Truth and Other Poems, 1985. *Contributions to:* Numerous publications including magazines, periodicals. *Honours:* Gregory Award, 1967; Writers Fellowship, Edinburgh University, 1969; Scottish Arts Council Writers Bursary, 1972; Arthur Lundevist Award for translations from Swedish, 1977; Swedish Academy Award for translations from Swedish, 1978. *Address:* Postboks 467, N 4001 Stavanger, Norway.

FURNELL, Michael, b. 3 Mar. 1924, London, England. Journalist. m. Barbara Grace Noble, 23 June 1956, London, 1 daughter. *Literary Appointments:* Editor, Homefinder Magazine, 1955–84; Editor, Homes Overseas magazine, 1965–; Editor, New Homes News,

1978–. *Publications:* Buying A House or Flat, 1955; Buying Overseas Property, 1983. *Contributions to:* Property Correspondent, Sunday Telegraph; Financial Times; Daily Mail; Surrey County magazine; Telegraph magazine; The Peak, Hong Kong. *Address:* 10 East Road, London N1 6AU, England.

FURNESS, Edna Lucinda, b. Wausa, Nebraska, USA. Professor Emeritus; Translator; Author. *Education:* BA, MA, PhD, University of Colorado. *Literary Appointments:* Poet Lore, Member of the Advisory Board, 1962–72; Book Reviewer, Johnson Boulder Company, 1985. *Literary Appointments:* Diagnostic and Instructional Procedures in the Language Arts, (Co-Author); New Dimensions in the Teaching of English, (Co-Author): Spelling for the Millions, (revisions), 1977; Furness Test of Aural Comprehension in Spanish, 1947. *Contributor to:* Various magazines and journals, such as, American Mercury; Arizona Quarterly; American School Board Journal; Clearing House; College English; Delta Kappa Gamma Bulletin; Education; Educational Administration and Supervision; Educational Forum; Education Digest; Elementary English; English Journal History of Education Quarterly; Journal of Educational Psychology. *Honours include:* Fellowship, University of Colorado, 1939–41, 1950–51; Trustee Fellowship, Smith College, 1941–42; Rockefeller Fellowship, Inter-American Studies, University of Denver, 1944; Faculty Research Grant, University of Wyoming, 1957. *Memberships include:* Delta Kappa Gamma; Gamma Phi Beta; Kappa Delta Pi; Phi Sigma Iota; Pi Delta Phi; Pi Lambda Theta; National Council of Teachers of English. *Address:* 725 South Alton Way, Denver, CO 80231, USA.

FURNIVAL, Christine Mary Twiston, b. 21 Jan. 1931, London, England. Teacher; Writer. m. Robert Graham Furnival, 6 June 1957, London (div. 1983), 3 daughters. *Education:* Honours degree, English Literature, Cambridge University, 1953; Diploma, Italian Language & Literature, Florence, Italy, 1954. *Literary Appointments:* Teacher, Creative Writing, Borough of Hounslow Adult Education Department, Greater London. *Publications include:* 4 pamphlets, poetry, 1968–78; Several radio plays; Full-length stage play, The Starving of Sarah, produced 1980. *Contributions to:* Anthologies: New Stories 2; Dismays & Rainbows, 1979; Pieces of Eight, 1982. Journals: New Stateman; Poetry Wales; Workshop; Anglo-Welsh Review; Meridian; etc. *Honour:* MA, 1983. *Memberships:* Theatre Writers Union; Writers Guild; PEN. *Address:* 4 Sion Row, Riverside, Twickenham, Middlesex TW1 3DR, England.

FURSDON, Francis William Edward, b. 10 May 1925, London, England, Regular British Army (Major-General), retired; Defence Correspondent, The Daily Telegraph. m. Joan Rosemary Worssam, 25 Mar. 1950, Seal Chart, 1 son, 1 daughter. *Education:* MLitt, Aberdeen; DLitt, Leiden; FBIM. *Literary Appointment:* Defence Correspondent, The Daily Telegraph, 1980–. *Publications:* Grains of Sand, 1971; There Are No Frontiers, 1973; The European Defence Community: A History, 1980. *Contributions to:* numerous journals over the past 30 years. *Honours:* MBE for Gallantry, 1956; CB, 1980; KS:J, 1980. *Address:* c/o National Westminster Bank Limited, 1 St James's Square, London, SW1, England.

FURTADO, Celso, b. 26 July 1920, Pombal, Brazil. Professor of Economics. *Education:* BA, University of Brazil: MA, University of Cambridge, UK; Dr, University of Paris, France. *Publications include:* (all books originally in Portuguese, some translations in English and French). Diagnosis of the Brazilian Crisis, (University of Columbia Press), 1965; Economic Development of Latin America, (Cambridge University Press), 1970; Obstacles to Development in Latin America, (Doubleday), 1970; Analyse du Modèle Brésilien, 1974; Le Mythe du Développment Economique, 1976; Publisher, Anthropos. *Address:* Rua Anita Garibaldi, 38/401 Rio de Janeiro, Brazil.

FURTWANGLER, Virginia W, b. 16 Dec. 1932, Hartford, Connecticut, USA. Fiction writer. m. Albert J Furtwangler, 17 Aug. 1968, Ithaca, New York, 2 sons. *Education:* BA cum laude, College of New Rochelle, 1954; MA, Catholic University of America, 1959; PhD, Cornell University, 1970. *Literary Appointments:* College of New Rochelle, 1963–66; Indiana University Northwest, 1970–71; Université de Moncton, 1971–72; Mount Allison University Extension, New Brunswick, Canada, 1971–76; Visiting Fiction Writer, College of Idaho, 1980; Visiting Professor of English, Linfield College, 1980–81; Visiting Fiction Writer, University of Idaho, 1982, 1986. *Publications include:* At Peace, short fiction, 1978; The Back Room, short fiction, 1979; Earthen Vessels, short fiction, 1984. *Contributions to:* Western Humanities Review; Canadian Fiction Magazine; The Ontario Review; The Fiddlehead; The University of Windsor Review; Snapdragon; The Long Story. *Honours:* Canada Council Short Term Grant, 1977; National Endowment for the Arts Fellowship, 1978; At Peace, selected for Best American Short Stories, 1977; Canada Council B Grant, 1980–81; CC Short Term Grant, 1982; Artist Award, New Brunswick Department of Culture, 1982. *Memberships:* International Women's Writing Guild; The Canada Writers Union. *Literary Agent:* Barbara Kouts, c/o Philip G Spitzer, New York, USA. *Address:* PO 1450, Sackville, New Brunswick, EOA 3CO, Canada.

FYSON, Anthony John Cedric, b. 8 Feb. 1943, England. Editor. m. Hilary Anne Suffern, 1 Mar. 1980, Harrogate, England, 1 son, 1 daughter. *Education:* BA, MA, Geography, Oxford University. *Literary Appointments:* Co-Editor, Bulletin of Environmental Education, 1971–80; Editor/Press Officer, Royal Town Planning Institute, 1983–. *Publications:* Streetwork (with Colin Ward) 1973; Change the Street, 1976. *Contributor to:* Town and Country Planning; The Planner of articles mainly on education and town planning. *Address:* 124 Brampton Road, St Albans, Herts AL1 4PY, England.

FYSON, Jenny Grace, b. 3 Oct. 1904, Bromley, Kent, England. Writer. m. Christopher Fyson, 8 Mar. 1940, Hale, Hampshire, 1 son (adopted). *Publications:* Saul and David, I and II, Religious Interludes for Schools Radio, 1952; The Three Brothers of Ur, 1964; The Journey of the Eldest Son, 1965; Friend Fire and the Dark Wings, 1983; Father Pierre (a true story told as a myth. MSS retained for use by the Religious Drama Society of Great Britain). *Contributions to:* Edward Blisheu's; Miscellany 5. *Honours:* Finalist, Carnegie Medal, 1964 and 1965. *Membership:* Society of Authors. *Address:* c/o Children's Department, Oxford University Press, Walton Street, Oxford, England.

G

GABBARD, Gregory N, b. 4 Oct. 1941, Fort Smith, Arkansas, USA. Teacher. *Education:* BS, MIT; MA, PhD, University of Texas. *Publications:* Runes from an Infant Edda, 1980; Tiger Webs, 1982. *Contributor:* Numerous poems, stories, essays and cartoons, various newspapers and magazines. *Honour:* John Masefield Award, Poetry Society of America, 1978. *Address:* Box 781, New Boston, TX 75570, USA.

GABBARD, Lucina Paquet, b. 16 Jan. 1922, New Orleans, USA. Professor, English, Drama. m. Earnest Glendon Gabbard, 29 Jan. 1942, Baton Rouge, 2 sons. *Education:* BA, Louisiana State University, 1942; MA, University of Iowa, 1947; PhD, University of Illinois, 1974. *Publications:* The Dream Structure of Pinter's Plays, 1976; The Stoppard Plays, 1982. *Contributor to:* Modern Drama; Twentieth Century Literature; Journal of Evolutionary Psychology. *Honours:* Eastern Illinois University's, Distinguished Faculty Award, 1981, Merit Award for Teaching, 1978, 1979, 1980, 1981; National Endowment for the Humanities' Summer Fellowship, 1980. *Memberships:* Modern Language Association; Midwest Modern Language Association; National Council of Teacher's of English. *Address:* 4 Orchard Drive, Charleston, IL 61920, USA.

GABRIEL, Juri Evald, b. 27 July 1940, Tallinn, Estonia. Writer; Photographer; Lecturer; Literary Agent. m. Margaret Lynette Hemmant, 26 Aug. 1962, Pyrford, England. *Education:* MA, Jesus College, Oxford, England. *Appointments:* Lecturer in Creative Writing, Morley College, 1979–; MA Course in Creative Writing, Antioch University, 1984–. *Publications:* Victoriana, 1969; Thinking About Television, 1973; Guide to European Campgrounds, 1974, 1975, 1976, 1977, 1978; RAC Guide to British and Continental Camping and Caravaning Sites, 1981; Unqualified Success, 1984, revised edition 1986. Contributor to: Times Educational Supplement. *Memberships:* Member of Writers' Guild of Great Britain, since 1977, on Executive Council, 1982–85; Writers' Guild of Great Britain representative on British Copyright Council, since 1978 Current Vice Chairman of Copyright Licensing Agency. *Literary Agent:* Curtis Brown. *Address:* 35 Camberwell Grove, London SE5 8JA, England.

GACH, Michael Reed, b. 19 Aug. 1952, Los Angeles, USA. Acupressure Training & Programme Development. *Education:* BA, Immaculate Heart College, 1975. *Publications:* Acu-Yoga: Self Help Techniques, 1981; The Bum Back Book, 1983; The Lazy Way to Greater Energy, 1983. *Contributor to:* Glamour; Prevention; Redbook. *Memberships:* Founder, Acupressure Institute. *Literary Agent:* Joyce Cole, Berkeley. *Address:* Acupressure Institute, 1533 Shattuck Avenue, Berkeley, CA 94709, USA.

GADDIS ROSE, Marilyn, b. 2 Apr. 1930, Fayette, Missouri, USA. University Professor. m. Stephen David Rose, 16 Nov. 1968, Binghamton, 1 son. *Education:* PhD, University of Missouri, 1958. *Publications:* Translator, Axel, by Villiers de l'Isle-Adam, 1970; Julian Green, Gallic-American Novelist, 1971; Jack B Yeats, Painter & Poet, 1972; Katharyn Tynan, 1975; Editor, Contributor, Translation Spectrum, 1981; Translator, Eve of the Future Eden, by Villiers & l'Isle-Adam, 1981; etc. *Contributor to:* Essays in London Magazine; Translation Review; French Review; etc. *Honours:* Fellowship, Australian National University Humanities Research Centre, 1977. *Memberships:* PEN American Centre; American Literary Translators Association, Secretary 1981–83; American Translators Association, Man Ed of Series, 1985–. *Address:* Translation Research and Instruction Programme, University Centre at Binghamton, Binghamton, NY 13901, USA.

GAGE, Joy P, b. 7 June 1930, Anthonies Mill, Missouri, USA. Author; Writer. m. Kenneth G Gage, 5 June 1952, Douglas, Arizona, 3 daughters. *Education:* Diploma in Christian Education, Biola College. *Publications:* When Parents Cry, 1980; Broken Boundaries/Broken Lives, 1982; Restoring Fellowship, Judgement and Church Discipline, 1984 (co-authored with husband, Kenneth Gage); But You Don't Know Harry; Lord, Can We Talk This Over? 1980. *Contributions to:* Success Magazine; The Pastor's Manual; The CB; The Christian Writer; The Christian Single and numerous others. *Honour:* Writer of the Year, Mt Hermon Writers Conference, 1980. *Memberships:* American Association of State and Local History; National Trust for Historic Preservation. *Address:* 99 Yosemite Road, San Rafael, CA 94903, USA.

GAGE, Mary, b. 6 May 1940, Stanmore, Middlesex, England. Writer; Playwright. m. Ulick Gage, 12 Dec. 1964, London, 1 son, 1 daughter. *Education:* MA, History, Girton College, Cambridge, 1967; Graduate Trainee with, The Times, London. *Publications:* Overlanders Handbook, 1976; The New Life, 1977; Praise The Egg, 1980; My Name Is Pablo Picasso, 1984. *Contributions to:* The National Times; The Sydney Morning Herald; The West Australian; etc. *Honours:* First Prize Western Australia's 150th Anniversary Playwrighting Competition with, The Price of Pearls, 1979; Angus Robertson Fellowship for, Praise The Egg, 1980. *Membership:* Australian Writers Guild. *Literary Agent:* Tim Curnow, Curtis Brown, Paddington, New South Wales. *Address:* Unit 1/52-54 Stanley Street, East Sydney, NSW 2010, Australia.

GAGNON, Cécile, b. 7 Jan. 1936, Quebec, Canada. Writer; Illustrator. m. Michel Bergeron, 31 Aug. 1963, 1 son, 1 daughter. *Education:* BA, Laval University; Boston University School of Fine and Applied Arts; Ecole Normale Supérieurs des Arts Décoratifs, Paris. *Literary Appointments:* Chief Editor, Passe-Partout magazine for Children, Director, Brindille Collection, Héritage Publishers, 1980; Director, Coulicou magazine for children, 1983; Chief of children's publications, Pierre Tisseyre Publishers, Montreal, 1982–. *Publications include:* La Pêche a l'horizon, 1959; Martine-auroiseux, 1964; Le Voyage d'un cerf-volant, 1972; Plumeneige, 1976; L'Epouvantail et le champignon, 1978; Le Parapluie Rouge, 1979; Lucienne, 1980; Alfred Dans le Métro, 1980; Johanne du Québec, 1982; Une Grosse Pierre, 1983; Opération Marmotte, 1985; Illustrator of several books. *Contributions to:* Yakari; Eclats de Lire; Jeunes Années; Hibou; Coulicou. *Honours:* Prize, Grand Jury des Lettres, Montreal, 1962; Award of Merit, International Leipzig Fair, 1964; Province of Québec Literary Prize, 1970; Association Canadian Teachers of French, 1980. *Memberships:* Union des Ecrivains Quebecois; IBBY-Canada; President, Communication-Jeunesse, Montreal. *Address:* 12 avenue de la Brunante, Montreal, Quebec, H3T IR4, Canada.

GAIDA-GAIDAMAVICIUS, Pranas, b. 26 Jan. 1914, Lithuania. Priest, Editor. *Education:* Doctor of Theology. *Literary Appointments:* Editor of Gimtoji [uv]salis (Lithuanian monthly, Belgium), 1947–50; Editor, Tevi[uv]skès [uv]ziburiai (Lights of Homeland) Lithuanian weekly, Canada), 1961–. *Major Publications:* Homeless Man, 1951; Giant, Hero, Saint, 1954; The Great Unrest, 1961; The Undying Mortal, 1981; (all published in Lithuanian language); Lithuanians in Canada, 1967. *Contributor to:* Naujoji Romuva; Aidai; Draugas; Tevi[uv]skès [uv]ziburiai; Ateitis; Zidinys. *Honours:* For Journalism; For the Book The Undying Mortal, 1983. *Memberships:* Lithuanian Catholic Academy of Sciences; Institute of Lithuanian Studies. *Address:* 2185 Stavebank Road, Mississauga, Ontario, L5C 1T3, Canada.

GALAND, René, b. 27 Jan. 1923, Brittany, France. Professor of French. m. France Texier, 23 Dec. 1955, Paris, 1 son, 1 daughter. *Education:* Licence es Lettres, University of Rennes, 1944; PhD, Yale University, 1952. *Publications:* L'Ame Celtique de Renan, 1959; Baudelaire: Poetiques et Poesie, 1959; Saint-John Perse, 1972; Levr ar Blanedenn, 1981; Klemmgan Breizh, 1985. Co-Author: Baudelaire as a Love Poet and

Other Essays, 1969; Homosexualities and French Literature, 1979; The Binding of Proteus, 1980. *Contributions to:* Philadelphia; Yale French Studies; The French Review; The Romanic Review; Sumposium; Dada/Surrealism; World Literature Today; Al Liamm; Keltica; Skrid; Bro Neves; The American Legion of Honor Magazine; Bulletin Baudelairien; Barr-Heol and others. *Honours:* Chevalier, Ordre des Palmes Academiques, 1971; Xavier de Langlais Prize in Breton Literature, 1979. *Membership:* Kevredigezh ar Skrivagnerien. *Address:* 8 Leighton Road, Wellesley, MA 02181, USA.

GALE, Robert Lee, b. 27 Dec. 1919, Des Moines, Iowa, USA. Educator; Author. *Education:* BA, Dartmouth College, 1942; MA, 1947; PhD, 1952, Columbia University. *Publications:* Thomas Crawford, American Sculptor, 1964; The Caught Image! Figurative Language in Henry James, 1964; Plots & Characters in the Fiction of Henry James, 1965, ...in Nathaniel Hawthorne, 1968; ...in Herman Melville, 1970: ...in Edgar Allan Poe, 1970; ...in Mark Twain, 1973; Simplified Approach to Emerson & Transcendentalism, 1966; Richard Henry Dana, Jr, 1969; Francis Parkman, 1973; John Hay, 1978; Luke Short, 1981; Will Henry, 1984; Louis L'Amour, 1985. *Contributions to:* American Literature; 19th Century Fiction; Modern Fiction Studies, etc. *Memberships:* Phi Beta Kappa; MLA; Western Writers of America, Inc. *Address:* 131 Techview Terrace, Pittsburgh, PA 15213, USA.

GALL, Sally Moore, b. 28 July 1941, New York City, USA. Author. m. William Einar Gall, 8 Dec. 1967, New York City. *Education:* BA, Harvard, Radcliffe, 1963; MA, 1971, PhD, 1976, New York University. *Literary Appointments:* Poetry Editor, Free Inquiry, 1981–84; Editor, Eidos, The International Prosody Bulletin, 1984–. *Publications:* The Modern Poetic Sequence: The Genius of Modern Poetry (co-author), 1983; Ramon Guthrie's Maximum Security Ward: An American Classic, 1984; Editor, Maximum Security Ward and Other Poems by Ramon Guthrie, 1984. *Contributions to:* Modern Poetry Studies; American Poetry Review; American Literature; The Nation; The Massachusetts Review, etc. (articles, reviews, reference works, poems; Reference works such as DLB; Contemporary Poets; Funk and Wagnalls New Encyclopedia, etc. *Honour:* Explicator Literary Foundation Award (joint recipient with M L Rosenthal) for The Modern Poetic Sequence, 1984. *Memberships:* Conference of Editors of Learned Journals; National Poetry Foundation; Modern Language Association. *Address:* 29 Bayard Lane, Suffern, NY 10901, USA.

GALLAGHER, Katherine, b. 7 Sep. 1935, Maldon, Australia. Teacher; Poet. m. Bernard Londeix, 8 Apr. 1978, Boulogne, France. 1 son. *Education:* BA, Melbourne University, 1962; Diploma of Education, Melbourne University, 1963. *Publications:* (Poetry): The Eye's Circle, 1974; Tributaries of the Love-Song, 1978; Passengers to the City, 1985. *Contributions to:* (In Australia): Luna; The Age; Overland; Meanjin; Nation Review; Quadrant; Mattoid; Words and Visions; The Bulletin Literary Supplement; Contempa; Poetry Australia; Ear in a Wheatfield; The Bendigo Advertiser; The Secondary Teacher; The Great Auk; Fitzrot; New Poetry; The Canberra Times; Magic Sam; The Realist; (In England): New Poetry; She; London Poetry Times; Pink Peace; Wild Words; Ludd's Mill; Acumen; Basa; Bark; Poetry Review; Writing Women; Lancaster Festival Anthology; Tribune; The Honest Ulsterman; Brecht Times; Poems in Kunapipi, Denmark; Waves, Canada; stories in, Inprint; Tabloid Story, Australia. *Honours:* First Prize (equal with Finola Moorhead), Melbourne Sun-Pictorial Short Story Festival, 1975; First Prize, Brisbane Festival Poetry Award, 1981. *Memberships:* Poetry Society, London; Victorian Branch, Fellowship of Writers, Melbourne; PEN, Victorian Branch. *Address:* 49 Myddleton Road, Wood Green, London N22 4LZ, England.

GALLAGHER, Rachel Mary, b. 31 July 1941, New York City, New York, USA. Assistant to Director, Film Department, New York City Museum of Modern Art.

Education: BA English, Roanoke College, Salem, Virginia, 1959. *Literary Appointments:* Editor-in-chief, Peter Max Magazine, 1969; Open Forum Letters Editor, Forum Magazine, 1976–79. *Publications:* The New York In/Out Quiz Book, (with Daphne Davis), 1966; Letting Down My Hair, (with Lori Davis), 1973; Games in the Street, 1976. *Contributions to:* Esquire; Cue; New York; New York Times Travel Section; Self; Rags; Hanson Music Books; National Forum; Esquire's Good Grooming Guide. *Membership:* American Society of Journalists and Authors; National Writers Union.

GALLAHUE, David L, b. 15 Feb. 1943, USA. Professor of Physical Education. m. Elnora Bredenberg, 20 Aug. 1964, 1 son, 1 daughter. *Education:* BS, Indiana University, 1964; MS, Purdue University, 1967; Ed D, Temple University, 1971. *Literary Appointments:* Teaching Assistant, Purdue University, 1966–67; Teaching Fellow, Temple University, 1967–70; Assistant Professor 1970–75, Associate Professor 1975–82, Assistant Chairman, Department of Physical Education, 1982–83, Professor of Physical Education, 1983–, Indiana University, Assistant Dean for Research & Development, School of Health, Physical Education & Recreation, 1978–. *Major Publications include:* Motor Development & Movement Experiences for Young Children, 1975; (with others), A Conceptual Approach to Moving & Learning, 1976; Understanding Motor Development in Children, 1982; Developmental Physical Education for Today's Children, 1987. *Contributor to:* Various journals (25 articles). *Memberships:* American Alliance for Health, Physical Education, Recreation & Dance: National Association for Sport & Physical Education; Motor Development Academy of NASPE; Phi Epsilon Kappa; Phi Delta Kappa; North American Society for Psychology of Sport & Physical Activity; American Association for Leisure & Recreation; International Playground Association. *Address:* Blackberry Ridge Farm, 8010 North State Road 37, Bloomington, IN 47401, USA.

GALLE, Janet Ruth Schmidt, b. 25 Sep. 1942, Fort Wayne, Indiana, USA. Educator. m. A W Galle Jr, 16 Mar. 1963, Fort Wayne, Indiana, 2 sons, 1 daughter. *Education:* BA, Miami University, Oxford, Ohio; MSc, University of Maine. *Contributor to:* Story Friends, 1979, Lutheran Women, 1981, Family Life Today, 1981; Editor, Merrymeeting Audubon Society, Maine, Newsletter, 1979–82; Columnist, (Country Ways), for Bath-Brunswick, Times Record, newspaper, 1981–, regular contributor to Times Record on special assignments; Contributing Editor, Maine Science Teachers Association Newsletter, 1986–. *Address:* RFD 1 Millay Road Box 222A Apple Creek Farm, Bowdoinham, ME 04008, USA.

GALLOWAY, Priscilla, b. 22 July 1930, Montreal, Canada. m. Bev Galloway, 17 Sep. 1949, Ottawa, deceased 25 Oct. 1985, 2 sons, 1 daughter. *Education:* BA, First Class Honours, Queen's University; MA, PhD, University of Toronto. *Publications:* Good Times, Bad Times, Mummy and Me, 1980; What's wrong with high school English?...It's Sexist, unCanadian, outdated, 1980; Timely and Timeless: Contemporary Prose, 1983; Timely and Timeless: a Teacher's Guide, 1984; When you were Little and I was Big, 1984; Jennifer Has Two Daddies, 1985. *Contributions to:* Short stories, Poetry, Articles and Book Reviews in many journals including, Waves; Chatelaine; Atlantis; Orbit; Contemporary Voices; Indirections; Journal of Reading; The Human; Canadian Book Review Annual; English Quarterly. *Honours:* Teacher of the Year, Ontario Council of Teachers of English, 1976; Marty Memorial Scholarship, Queen's University, 1976; Touring Author for Canadian Children's Book Festival week, Nov. 1982. *Memberships:* The Writers' Union of Canada, (Chair, Curriculum Committee, 1983–84); Canadian Society of Children's Authors, Illustrators and Performers; PEN International. *Address:* 209K, 2911 Bayview Ave, North York, Ontario, Canada M2K 1E8.

GALT, Tom, b. 29 July 1908, Michigan, USA. Poet. m. Florella, 12 Dec. 1929, Boston. *Education:* BA, Harvard,

1932. *Publications:* Volcano, 1946; How the UN Works, 1947, 3rd edition 1965; Peter Zenger, 1951; Native Place, 1983; The World Has A Familiar Face, 1981; The Little Treasury, translated from Japanese, 1982. *Contributor to:* Virgil; Revue d'Historia du Theatre, Paris; VIIeme Siede, Paris; 52 Poetry magazines in USA. *Memberships:* Poetry Society of America; New England Poetry Club; Authors League of America. *Address:* Box 417, Wellfleet, MA 02667, USA.

GAMBINO, Diane R, b. New York City, USA. Sportswriter. *Education:* BA, English Literature, 1974, 1st Female Sportswriter for College Newspaper, Queens College, City University of New York. *Appointments:* One of 1st Women Sportswriters to cover professional Baseball, 1973–; Initiated Project to Revise Baseball's All Star Game; 1st Female Sportswriter to attend Baseball Chapel with Major League Teams, various Stadiums, 1979. *Contributor to:* Diamond Report, Contributing Writer, 1976–79; Sports Facts Weekly, 1974; Queens Tribune, Sports Staff, 1973–75; Sports Editor, Queens Magazine, 1979–81. *Honours:* Recognised by Optimists Club, New York Chapter, Optimistic Work in Sports Journalism, 1974. *Memberships:* Editorial Freelancers Association; National Baseball Congress, National Association of Baseball Writers. *Address:* 150-23 24th Road, Whitestone, NY 11357, USA.

GAMESTER, Brandon Richard, b. 27 May 1951, Wolverhampton, England. Journalist. m. Helen Drummond Morrison, 25 Oct. 1978, 1 daughter. *Education:* BSc (Hons). *Literary Appointments:* Features Editor, Electrical Review; Speech Writer, Department of Industry; Editor, Computer Weekly; Editor, Micro Business. *Contributions to:* The Guardian; The Times; New Scientist; Trade journals. *Address:* 64-66 Central Buildings, 24 Southwark Street, London SE1, England.

GANDLEY, Kenneth Royce, b. 11 Dec. 1920, Croydon, England. Writer. *Publications:* No Paradise, 1960; The Long Corridor, 1961; The Night Seekers, 1962; The Angry Island, 1963; The Day the Wind Dropped, 1964; Bones in the Sand, 1967; A Peck of Salt, 1968; A Single to Hong Kong, 1969; The Woodcutter Operation, 1975; Assination Day, 1975; Bustillo, 1976; (Book Club Choices), The XYY Man, 1970; The Concrete Boot, 1971; The Miniatures Frame, 1972; Spider Under-ground, 1973; Trapspider, 1974; Man on a Short Leash, 1975; The Satan Touch, 1978; Third Arm, 1980; 10,000 Days, 1981; Channel Assault, 1982; The Stalin Account, 1983; The Crypto Man, 1984; The Mosley Receipt, 1985; The XYY Man, Concrete Boot, and Miniatures Frame, were all adapted for Television and Bulman, a character in this series, was used in three series of Strangers and subsequently another series called Bulman. *Address:* c/o David Higham Associates, 5-8 Lower St John Street, Golden Square, London, W1R 4HA, England.

GANDOLFI, Simon, b. 11 Feb. 1933, London, England. 2 sons. *Publications:* Even with the Shutters Closed, 1970; The One Hundred Kild Club, 1978; France Security, 1983; The Reluctant Stud, 1984. *Literary Agent:* Christopher Little. *Address:* 269-271 Sandycombe Road, Kew Gardens, Richmond, Surrey, England.

GANN, Lewis Henry, b. 28 Jan. 1924, Mainz, Germany. Historian. m. Rita Nissler, 30 Sep. 1950 (deceased), 1 son. *Education:* MA; MLitt; DPhil (Oxon). *Literary Appointments:* Historian, Rhodes-Livingstone Institute (now Institute for Social Research, University of Zambia), 1950–52; Assistant Lecturer, University of Manchester, England, 1952–54; Archivist and Editor, National Archives of Rhodesia and Nyasaland, 1954–63; Associate, then Senior Fellow, Hoover Institution Stanford University, 1964–. *Publications:* The Birth of a Plural Society: The Development of Northern Rhodesia under the British South Africa Company 1894-1914, 1958, 61; White Settlers in Tropical Africa (with Peter Duigan), 1962,

63; A History of Northern Rhodesia: Early Days to 1953, 1964, 69; A History of Southern Rhodesia: Early Days to 1934, 1965, 69; Central Africa: The Former British States, 1971; Several books with Peter Duigan including: The Rulers of Belgian Africa 1884-1914, 1979; Why South Africa Will Survive, 1980, 81; The United States and Africa: A History, 1984, 86; The Hispanic Americans (in preparation). *Contributor to:* Numerous scholarly journals. *Honours:* Domus Scholar, Balliol College. Oxford; Grants from Earhart Foundation, Helm Foundation, National Endowment for the Humanities, Historische Kommission zu Berlin, etc; Fellow of Royal Historical Society. *Address:* Hoover Institution, Stanford University, Stanford, CA 94305, USA.

GANNON, Robert Haines, b. 1 Mar. 1931, White Plains, New York, USA. Writer; Teacher. *Appointment:* Associate Professor, Penn State, 1974–. *Publications:* The Complete Book of Archery, 1962; Time is Short and the Water Rises, 1968; What's Under a Rock?, 1972; Great Survival Adventures, 1973; Why Your Home May Endanger Your Health, 1980; Half Mile Up Without an Engine, 1982. *Contributions to:* Reader's Digest; Popular Mechanics; Look; Saturday Evening Post; TV Guide and many others (approximately 200); Contributing Editor, Popular Science, 1969–. *Honour:* Lincoln Award for Outstanding Aviation Writing, 1982. *Memberships:* American Society of Authors and Journalists; National Science Writers. *Literary Agent:* Theron Raines. *Address:* English Department, Burrowes Building, The Pennsylvania State University, University Park, PA 16802, USA.

GARAY, Ronald Gene, b. 13 Apr. 1947, Gary, West Virginia, USA. College Professor of Journalism. m. Mary Sue Sanders, 20 Dec. 1970, Texarkana, Texas. *Education:* BFA, 1969, MFA, 1970, Texas Christian University; PhD, Ohio University, 1980. *Publications:* Congressional Television: A Legislative History, 1984. *Contributions to:* Communications Yearbook VII, 1983; Journal of Broadcasting; Journalism Quarterly; Quarterly Journal of Speech. *Address:* Manship School of Journalism, Louisiana State University, Baton Rouge, LA 70803, USA.

GARCITORAL, Alicio, b. 6 Oct. 1902, Gijón, Spain. Author; Politican in Exile, 1936–. *Education:* Merchant Marine Studies; Courses in Economics, University of Madrid. *Publications:* Tercer Frente, 1939, 2nd Edition, 1954; Interpretación de Espana, 1945; El Amor Divino, 1946; Meditaciones Religiosas, 1949; Diccionario del Hombre, 1949; Primera Categoría, 1950; The Fifth Door and Manifests of Integral Democracy; La Edad Democrática, 1965; La Espana de los Reyes Catolicos, 1950; various other works. *Contributions to:* La Prensa; La Nacion; El Mundo; several papers and magazines in Spain, Buenos Aires and USA. *Address;* 37 Richie Road, Quincy, MA 02169, USA.

GARD, Joyce, b. 1911, London, England. Author. *Education:* BA, Lady Margaret Hall, Oxford University. *Publications:* Woorroo, 1961; The Dragon of the Hill, 1963; Talargain the Seal's Whelp, 1964; Smudge of the Fells, 1965; The Snow Firing, 1967; The Mermaid's Daughter, 1969; Handysides Shall Not Fall, 1975; The Hagwaste Donkeys, 1976; Translation of Jules Verne's Journey to the Centre of the Earth, 1961. *Contributions to:* Miscellany Five. Translations from French of works on contemporary art. *Memberships:* Royal Archaeological Institute; Society of Authors. *Address:* 1 Eliza Cottages, Charing, Ashford, Kent, England.

GARDINIER, David Pierre Elmer, b. 13 Oct. 1932, Syracuse, New York, USA. University Professor. m. Josefina Sevilla y Zialcita, 2 July 1966, Manila, Philippines, 1 son, 2 daughters. *Education:* AB, SUNY-Albany, 1953; MA, 1954, PhD, 1960, Yale University; University of Paris. *Literary Appointments:* University of Delaware, 1959–60; Bowling Green State University, 1960–65; Ohio University 1965–66; Marquette University 1966–. *Publications:* Cameroon: UN Challenge to French Policy, 1963; Historical Dictionary of Gabon, 1981. *Contributions to:* Dozen articles and chapters of history of western education in Cameroon and states of ex-French Equatorial Africa; historiographical chapters on French colonial rule and decolonization. *Honours:* Fulbright Scholarship to University of Paris, 1958–59; Hoover Institution Fellowship, 1977; Fulbright Scholar at Ministry of Co-operation, Paris, 1979. *Memberships:* French Colonial Historical Society, President 1978–80, Vice-President 1976–78. American Historical Association, Africana bibliographer 1964–. *Address:* 21845 Gareth Lane, Brookfield, WI 53005, USA.

GARDNER-THORPE, Christopher, b. 22 Aug. 1941, Cosham, Hampshire, England. Consultant Neurologist. *Education:* MB BS, 1964, MRCP 1968, MD, 1974, FRCP, 1985, St Thomas' Hospital, University of London. *Contributor to:* Neurology; Medical Journal of Australia; Quarterly Journal of Medicine; Journal of Neurology, Neurosurgery and Psychiatry; Clinica Chimica Acta; Acta Neurologica Scandinavica; Postgraduate Medical Journal; Journal of the Neurological Sciences; Modern Medicine; South African Medical Journal; many other professional journals. *Memberships include:* Association of British Neurologists; Founder Member, Treasurer, South West of England Neurosciences Associaton; British Epilepsy Association, Medical Advisory Committee; International League Against Epilepsy; Royal Society of Medicine; Harveian Society; South West Physicians Club; International Society of Internal Medicine. *Address:* The Coach House, 1A College Road, Exeter EX1 1TE, Devon, England.

GARDONYI, Zoltan, b. 25 Apr. 1906, Budapest, Hungary. Composer; Musicologist. m. Ilona Wallrabenstein, 26 Dec. 1942, Budapest, 1 son, 1 daughter. *Education:* Academy Music, Budapest; DMus, University of Berlin, 1931. *Publications:* Die ungarischen Stileigentumlichkeiten in den musikalischen Werken F Liszts, 1931; Liszt Ferenc magyar stilusa – Le Style Hongro de F Liszt, 1936; Elemzo formatan, 1963, 2nd edition 1979; J S Bach ellenpontmuveszetenek alapjai, 1967; J S Bach kanon – es fugaszerkeszto muveszete, 1972. *Contributor to:* Encyclopedia's and Musical Journals on Hungarian Music in Hungary, Germany, France, England; Contributing Editor, New Liszt Ed, Volumes 1-4, 1970–73. *Honour:* Recipient, Francis Joseph Music Prize, Budapest, 1931. *Membership:* Foundation & Honorary Member, Hungarian Feren Liszt Society. *Address:* Roonstrasse 40, D–4902 Bad Salzuflen, Federal Republic of Germany.

GARFINKEL, Patricia Gail, b. 15 Feb. 1938, New York City, USA. Writer. 2 sons. *Education:* BA, New York University. *Publications:* Ram's Horn, 1980, (poems), Window Press, Washington, DC. *Contributions to:* numerous publications and anthologies, including, Hollin's Critic; Seattle Review; Cedar Book; Washington Magazine; Black Box; City Lights Anthology, 1976; Anthology of Magazine Verse/Yearbook of American Poetry, 1980; Poet Upstairs Anthology; Miller Cabin Anthology, 1984; Montpelier Culture Arts Center Anthology, 1984; Snow Summits in the Sun Anthology, 1985. *Honour:* Poetry in Public Places Award for New York State, 1977. *Memberships:* Poets and Writers Inc; Writers' Center, Glen Echo, Maryland; Academy of American Poets. *Address:* 2031 Approach Lane, Reston, VA 22091, USA.

GARLICK, Raymond, b. 21 Sep. 1926, London, England, Anglo-Welsh Poet. *Education:* BA, University of Wales. *Literary Appointment:* Foundation Editor, Dock Leaves, now called The Anglo-Welsh Review, 1949–60. *Publications:* A Sense of Europe: Collected Poems, 1954–68; A Sense of Time: Poems and Antipoems 1969–72; Incense: Poems 1972–85; An Introduction to Anglo-Welsh Literature, 1972; Anglo-Welsh Poetry 1480–1980 (with Roland Mathias), 1984; The Hymn to the Virgin, 1985. *Contributions to:* Numerous magazines, etc. *Honours:* Welsh Arts Council

Poetry Award, 1969, 73, 77. *Memberships:* Welsh Academy; Fellow of Royal Society of Arts. *Address:* 30 Glannant House, College Road, Carmarthen SA31 3EF, Wales.

GARNER, Alan, b. 17 Oct. 1934, Congleton, Cheshire, England. Author. m. (1) Ann Cook, 1 June 1956, (2) Griselda Greaves, 14 Jan. 1972, 2 sons, 3 daughters. *Education:* Magdalen College, Oxford. *Publications include:* The Weirdstone of Brisingamen, 1960; The Moon of Gomrath, 1963; Elidor, 1965; Holly From the Bongs, 1966; The Old Man of Mow, 1967; The Owl Service, 1967; The Hamish Hamilton Book of Goblins, 1969; Red Shift, 1973; The Breadhorse, with A Trowski, 1975; The Guizer, 1975; The Green Mist, (dance drama) 1970; (Libretti) The Bellybag 1971; Potter Thompson, 1972; Holly from the Bongs, 1974; Rascally Tag, 1979; The Fine Anger, 1979; The Stone Book, 1976; Tom Fobble's Day, 1977; Granny Reardun, 1977; The Aimer Gate, 1978; Fairy Tales, 1979; The Lad of the Gad, 1980; Book of British Fairy Tales, 1984; A Bag of Moonshine, 1986. Plays: Lamaload, 1978; Lurga Lom, 1980; To Kill a King, 1980; Sally Water, 1982; The Keeper, 1983. Films: Red Shift, 1978, with J Mackenzie; Places and Things, 1978; Images, 1981. *Contributor to:* Times Literary Supplement; Library Association Carnegie Medal, 1967; Guardian Award, 1968; First Prize, Chicago International Film Festival, 1981, for Images. *Literary Agent:* David Higham Associates Ltd. *Address:* Blackden, Holmes Chapel, Crewe CW4 8BY, Cheshire.

GARNER, Patrick C, b. 17 Mar. 1948, Bradenton, Florida, USA. Playwright; Novelist; Poet. m. Deborah L Knight, 29 Dec. 1972, 2 sons. *Education:* BVA, Georgia State University, 1971. *Publication:* A Series of Days of Change, 1972. *Contributor to:* Hiram Poetry Review; Local Storms; Northwoods Press; Salt River Anthology; Southern Poetry Review; Old Red Kimono; Biterroot; Cumberland Review; Four Elements; Green River Review; Rhode Island Review; Sierra Madre Review; Northeast Journal; Lodestar. *Honours:* 2nd Prize, Actor's Contemporary Ensemble, Charlotte, 1983; Finalist, National Reportory Theatre Foundation, California, 1984. *Address:* 8-12th Street, Providence, RI 02906, USA.

GARNER, Stuart, b. 14 July 1944, Wisbech, England. Newspaper Editor. m. Gillian, 16 Apr. 1977, North Shields. *Education:* Joint Honours Degree, History and Economics, Bristol University, 1966. *Literary Appointments:* Editor, Cambridge Evening News, 1982; Editor-in-Chief, Eastern Counties Newspapers, 1984; Director, 1985. *Address:* c/o Eastern Counties Newspapers, Prospect House, Rouen Road, Norwich, NR1 1RE, England.

GARNETT, Eve C R, b. Upper Wick, Worcestershire, England. Author; Illustrator. *Education:* Scholarship, Royal Academy Schools (School of Painting). *Publications:* With Illustrations: The Family From One End Street, 1937; Is It Well With the Child, with Foreward by Walter de la Mare, 1938; In and Out and Roundabout: Stories of a Little Town, 1948; A Book of the Seasons: An Anthology, 1952; Further Adventures of the Family from One End Street, 1956; Holiday at the Dew Drop Inn, 1962. To Greenlands Icy Mountains: The Story of Hans Egede, Explorer, Coloniser, Missionary, with Foreward by Professor N E Bloch-Hoell, University of Oslo, Norway, 1968; Lost and Found, 4 stories, 1974; Illustrations to Penguin R L Stevensons's A Child's Garden of Verses, 1948; First Affections; Some Autobiographical Chapters of Early Childhood, 1982. *Contributions to:* Various journals. *Honour:* Carnegie Gold Medal, 1938. *Memberships:* PEN; Society of Authors. *Address:* c/o Lloyd's Bank Limited, 29-31 Grosvenor Gardens, London SW1W 0BU, England.

GARRETT, Edward Cortez, b. 25 Sep. 1948, Quezon City, Republic of the Philippines. Security Officer. *Education:* AA, Journalism, Marketing, Pima Community College, Arizona; BA Literature, Social Sciences, De le Salle College, Manila; MA, Speech Communication,

English, University of Arizona. *Contributions to:* Thirdwind; Negative Capability; Nightsun; Undinal Songs; Men of War; New Kauri; Prickly Pears Poetry Quarterly; Inago Newsletter; Inago Anthology; Sunday Times Magazine (Philippines); Horizon; Horizons Quarterly. *Honours:* First Place Award from American Academy of Poets for Dawn, 1976; Fellowship to National Summer Creative Writing Workshop at Silliman University, Philippines; Many other school related awards; Awards for debate, oratory, interpretative reading, dramatics; Honoured by readings on TV, Radio and at many literary cafes; Art work, Graphics, have been included in Prickly Pears, Horizons and New Kauri; Oneman painting exhibition in 1971. *Memberships:* Prickly Pears Poetry Society, Tucson (Vice-President, 1979; President, 1980); Northwest Neighborhood Center, Tucson (Coordinator, 1984–85); Bethesda Players and Eccles Street Performers (Co-Founder and Director of Performances, 1979–80). *Address:* 455 South Irving Avenue, Apartment 101, Tucson, AZ 85711, USA.

GARRETT, Leslie, b. 5 July 1932, Philadelphia, Pennsylvania, USA. Writer. m. Linda Kerby, 18 Mar. 1973, Maryville, 1 son, 1 daughter. *Publication:* The Beasts, 1966. *Contributor to:* New World Writing; Evergreen Review; Confrontation; Four Quarters; Karamu; American Courier; Nugget; Climax 2. *Honours:* Maxwell E Perkins Commemorative Novel Award, for The Beasts, 1966. *Literary Agent:* Ellen Levine Literary Agency Inc. *Address:* 1409 Clinch Avenue, Knoxville, TN 37916, USA.

GARRETT, Richard, b. 15 Jan. 1920, London, England. Author; Journalist. m. Margaret Anne Selves, 20 Aug. 1945, Chelsea, 2 sons, 1 daughter. *Publications:* 42 books including: Fast and Furious, 1968; The Motor Racing Story, 1969; Cross Channel, 1972; General Gordon, 1974; General Wolfe, 1975; Robert Clive, 1976; Scharnhorst and Gneisenau, 1978; Mrs Simpson, 1979; The Raiders, 1980; POW, 1981; Royal Travel, 1982; The Story of Britain, 1983; Atlantic Disaster, 1986; 16 childrens books, etc. *Contributor to:* County Magazine. *Membership:* Society of Authors. *Agent:* Watson Little Limited. *Address:* The White Cottage, 27A Broadwater Down, Tunbridge Wells, Kent TN2 5NL, England.

GARRETT, Thomas Kenneth, b. 21 Oct. 1919, Brentford, Middlesex, England. Author, Journalist, Engineer. m. Dorothea Johanna Elisabeth Haellmigk, 16 Aug. 1972, Hemel Hempstead, Hertfordshire. *Education:* C Eng, Fellow, Institute of Mechanical Engineers, MRAeS. *Literary Appointments:* Editorial Staff, 1951, Editor, 1958–72, Automobile Engineer; Freelance writer, 1972–. *Major Publications:* The Motor Vehicle, 10th edition, 1983; Q & A Automobile Fuel Systems, 1985. *Contributor to:* Numerous magazines, including: Automotive Engineer; Design Engineering; Truck Australia; International Law Enforcement; and others. *Memberships:* Society of Authors. Guild of Motoring Writers. *Literary Agent:* Max Press Ltd. (Japan). *Address:* 51 Crossfell Road, Leverstock Green, Hemel Hempstead, Hertfordshire, HP3 8RQ, England.

GARRISON, Joseph Marion, Jr, b. 25 July 1934, Columbia, Missouri, USA. College Teacher. m. Ann Dexter Herron, 27 Aug. 1980, Laurinburg, North Carolina, 1 son, 1 daughter. *Education:* AB, Davidson College, 1956; MA, 1957, PhD, 1960, Duke University. *Literary Appointments:* Instructor of English, College of William and Mary; Associate Professor of English, St Andrews Presbyterian College; Associate Professor of English, Mary Baldwin College; Professor of English, Mary Baldwin College; Professor of English and Chairman, Mary Baldwin College. *Contributions To:* (Poems): Poetry Northwest; Southern Poetry Review; Kansas Quarterly; Poetry Row; Southwest Review, etc. Articles published in magazines such as College English; American Quarterly; Studies in Short Fiction, etc. Major essay on Robert Frost in Centennial Essays on Robert Frost, 1972. *Honours:* Louise McNeill Pease Prize for Poetry, 1973; Finalist for Phillipe Award, 1974.

Membership: Poets and Writers. *Address:* 265 Thornrose Avenue, Staunton, VA 24401, USA.

GARRONE, Gabriel Marie (His Excellency, Cardinal), b. 21 Oct. 1901, Aix-le-Bains, Savoie, France. Ecclesiastic. *Education:* PhD, Institute of Notre-Dame de la Villette; University of Grenoble; Pontifica Universitas Gregoriana, Rome, Italy. *Publications:* La Porte des Ecritures; Panorama du Credo; Ce que croyait Therese de Lisueux; La Religieuse Signe de Dieu dans le Monde; Ce que croyait Pasal; Le Gout de pain; La foi au fil des jours; Le credo lu dans l'historie; Ce que croyait Jeanne Jugan. *Honours:* Grand Cross, Legion of Honour, France; Croux de Guerre. *Address:* Largo del Colonnato 3, 00193, Rome, Italy.

GARTNER, Chloe Maria, b. 21 Mar. 1916, Troy, Kansas, USA. Writer. m. Peter Godfrey Trimble, 22 Jan. 1942, San Francisco, California, (divorced 1957), 1 daughter. *Education:* University of California; Mesa College, Grand Junction, Colorado; College Marin, Kentfield, California. *Publications:* The Infidels, 1960; Drums of Khartoum, 1967, 2nd edition, 1968; German translation, Die Trommein von Khartoum, 1970; Die Longe Sommer, 1970; Woman From The Glen, 1973; Mistress of the Highlands, 1976; Anne Bonney, 1977; The Image and the Dream, 1980, UK, 1986; Still Falls the Rain, 1983, UK, 1985; Greenleaf (in production). *Contributions to:* Cosmopolitan; Good Housekeeping, etc. *Memberships include:* Authors' Guild. *Honours include:* Silver Medal, Commonwealth Club of California for, The Infidels, 1960. *Literary Agents:* John Hawkins & Associates, New York City; Murray Pollinger, London. *Address:* John Hawkins & Associates, Suite 1600, 71 West 23 Street, New York, NY 10010, USA.

GASCAR, Pierre, b. 13 Mar. Paris, France. Writer. *Education:* BA. *Publications:* Les Meubles, 1949; Les Betes, 1953; Les Temps des Morts, 1953; Les Femmes, 1955; Chine Ouverte, 1956; La Graine, 1956; Soleils, 1960; Le Meilliur de la Vie, 1964; Les Charmes, 1965; Les Chimeres, 1969; L'Arche, 1971; Quartier Latin, 1972; Le Presage, 1972; L'Homme et L'Animal, 1974; Le bal des Ardents, 1978; Un Jardin de Cure, 1979; L'Ombre de Robespierre, 1979; Les Secrets de Maitre Bernard, 1980; Le Regne Vegetal, 1981; Buffon, 1983; Le Fortin, 1983; Le Diable a Paris, 1985. *Contributor to:* La Nouvelle Revue. *Honours:* Critics' Prize, 1953; Goncourt Prize, 1953; Grand Prix Literature de L'Academie Francaise, 1969. *Address:* 13 bd du Montparnasse, 75006, Paris, France.

GASCOYNE, David Emery, b. 10 Oct. 1916, Harrow, Middlesex, England. Writer; Poet; Critic. m. Judy Lewis Tyler, 17 May 1975, Newport, Isle of Wight, 2 step-sons, 2 step daughters. *Publications:* A Short Survey of Surrealism, 1935; Holderlin's Madness, 1938; Poems, 1937–42, 1943; A Vagrant & Other poems, 1951; Night Thoughts, 1956; Collected Poems, 1965; Journal, 1936–37, Paris Journal, 1937–39, 1978, 1980; Journal de Paris et d'ailleurs 1936–42, 1984. (translated by Christine Jordis). *Contributions to:* New English Weekly; New Verse; Times Literary Supplement; Partisan Review; Malahat Review; Botteghe Oscure; Nouvelle Revue Francaise; Nuova Revista Europea; Poesie 84; Ambit; The Tablet, etc. *Honours:* Atlantic Award, 1946, 47; Premio Biella Poesis Europea, 1982. *Memberships:* Fellow, Royal Society of Literature; Honorary Member of Committee of Belgian Biennales Internationales de Poesis. *Literary Agent:* Alan Clodd, Enitharmon Press, London. *Address:* 48 Oxford Street, Northwood, Cowes, Isle of Wight PO31 8PT, England.

GASKELL, Jane, b. 7 July 1941, Grange-over-Sands, Lancashire, England. Writer. 1 daughter. *Literary Appointment:* USA Correspondent, Daily Mail, 1974–76. *Publications include:* Strange Evil, 1957; King's Daughter, 1958; Attic Summer, 1960; The Serpent, 1961; Atlan, 1962; The Shiny Narrow Grin, 1963; The Fabulous Heroine, 1963; The City, 1964; All Neat in Black Stockings, 1965; A Sweet Sweet Summer, 1971; Summer Coming, 1973; Some Summer Lands, 1979. *Contributions:* Astrological column, Observer, 1977–

79. *Honour:* Somerset Maugham Award, 1971. *Literary Agent:* Fraser & Dunlop. *Address:* c/o Fraser & Dunlop, 91 Regent Street, London W1, England.

GASKELL (John) Philip (Wellesley), b. 1926, London, England. Bibliographer; College Fellow. *Education:* MA, PhD, Litt D, University of Cambridge, England. *Publications:* William Mason, 1951; John Baskerville, 1959; Caught! 1960; The Foulis Press, 1964; Morvern Transformed, 1968; A New Introduction to Bibliography, 1972; From Writer to Reader, 1978; Trinity College Library, 1980. *Contributions to:* The Lib; Transactions of Cambridge Bibliographical Society; Studies on Bibliography; The Times Literary Supplement. *Membership:* Bibligraphical Society. *Address:* Trinity College, Cambridge CB2 1TQ, England.

GASKIN, Catherine Majella, b. 2 Apr. 1929, Dundalk, Co Louth, Ireland. Novelist. m. Sol Cornberg, 1 Dec. 1955. *Publications:* This Other Eden, 1946; With Every Year, 1947; Dust in Sunlight, 1950; All Else is Folly, 1951; Daughter of the House, 1952; Sara Dane, 1955; Blake's Reach, 1958; Corporation Wife, 1960; I Know My Love, 1962; The Tilsit Inheritance, 1963; The File on Devlin, 1965; Edge of Glass, 1967; Fiona, 1970; A Falcon for a Queen, 1972; The Property of a Gentleman, 1974; The Lynmara Legacy, (completely rewritten and enlarged version of, This Other Eden), 1975; The Summer of the Spanish Woman, 1977; Family Affairs, 1980; Promises, 1982; The Ambassador's Women, 1985. *Memberships:* Society of Authors; Authors Guild of America. *Address:* White Rigg, East Ballaterson, Maughold, Isle of Man.

GASTON, Georg M A, b. 22 Oct. 1938, Kiev, Ukranie. English Professor. m. Karen Carmean, 2 Aug. 1968, Denton, Texas, USA. *Education:* BA, Texas A & M University; MA, PhD, Auburn University. *Publications:* Karel Reisz, 1980; Jack Clayton, 1981; The Pursuit of Salvation: A Critical Guide to the Novels of Graham Greene, 1984. *Contributions:* The Function of Tom Sawyer, in Huckleberry Finn, Mississippi Quarterly, 1974; The Structure of Salvation, in The Quiet America, Renascence, 1979; The Uses of Music, in Who'll Stop the Rain, Kentucky Folklore, 1979; Russell Baker's Political Satire, Studies in Contemporary Satire, 1980; The French Lieutenant's Woman, Novel and Film, Film Quarterly, 1981; Comic Celebration, John Fowles' Mantissa, Washington Book Review, 1982. *Honours:* Allan Edgar Fellow, 1963; NEH Grant, 1978. *Memberships:* Phi Kappa Phi; Modern Language Association. *Address:* 405 Stadium Drive, Boone, NC 28607, USA.

GATER, Dilys, b. 17 Apr. 1944, Wrexham, Wales. Author. m. (1) Dennis Owen, 27 Sep. 1963, Wrexham (divorced 1969), 1 daughter; (2) Philip Gater, 21 May 1977, Stoke-on-Trent. *Literary Appointment:* Theatre Critic, 8 years. *Publications:* Over 40 books and plays including: Sophy, 1974; Leo Possessed, 1975; The Witch-Girl, 1979; Emily, 1980; Jenni, 1982; A Man of Honour, 1983; Sing No Sad Songs, 1983; Lallie, 1983. *Contributions to:* Over 30 magazines and journals including syndicated work world-wide. Articles, short stories, poems. *Address:* 31 Carlton Road, Shelton, Stoke-on-Trent, Staffordshire, England.

GATES, Henry Louis Jr. b. 16 Sep. 1950, West Virginia, USA. University Professor. m. Sharon Adams, 1 Sep. 1979, Paterson, New Jersey, 2 daughters. *Education:* BA, Yale University, 1972; MA, 1974, PhD, 1979, University of Cambridge. *Literary Appointments:* Assistant Professor of English, 1979–84, Associate Professor of English, 1984–85, Yale University; Professor of English, Cornell University, 1985–. *Publications:* Editor: Black is the Color of the Cosmos, 1982; Our Nig, 1983; Black Literature and Literary Theory, 1984; The Slave's Narrative, 1985 (with Charles T Davis); etc. *Contributions to:* Essays, Review Essays and Book Reviews in numerous journals and magazines including: New York Times Book Review; Journal of Negro History; Saturday Review, The Times Literary Supplement; The American Book Review; The Yale

Review; Race Today; Time Out; The Spectator; Black Enterprise; Antioch Review; Harper's Magazine; Transition. *Honours:* Phi Beta Kappa, 1972; Summa Cum Laude, 1973; Mellon Fellow, 1973–85; MacArthur Prize Fellow, 1981–86. *Membership:* President, Afro-American Academy. *Literary Agent:* Carl Brandt. *Address:* 503 Triphammer Road, Ithaca, NY, USA.

GATTEY, Charles Neilson, b. 1921, London, England. Author; Playwright; Lecturer. *Education:* London University. *Publications include:* (3 Act Plays) The White Falcon; The Colour of Anger; True Love – or the Bloomer; (1 Act Plays) Queen of a Thousand Dresses; Farewell Pots & Pans; Mrs Adams & Eve; Mrs Griggs Loses Her Bed; Fair Cops; (Biographies) The Bloomer Girls, 1967; Gaugin's Astonishing Grandmother, 1970; A Bird of Curious Plumage, 1971; The Incredible Mrs Van de Elst, 1972; (Historical Novel) The King Who Could Not Stay the Tide, 1971; Occult: They Saw Tomorrow, 1976; Music – Queen's of Song, 1979; The Elephant That Swallowed a Nightingale, 1981; Peacocks on the Podium, 1982; Great Dining Disasters, 1984; Fois Gras and Trumpets, 1984. *Membership:* President, Society of Civil Service Authors. *Address:* The White House, 15 St Lawrence Drive, Pinner, Middlesex HA5 2RL, England.

GAUDIOSE, Dorothy M, b. 27 Nov. 1917, Crabtree, Pennsylvania, USA. Teacher. *Education:* BS Education, Lock Haven State College, Pennsylvania, 1940; MEd, Pennsylvania State University, State College, 1961; French Language & Culture, Sorbonne University, Paris. *Major Publications:* Prophet of the People, (a biography of Padre Pio), 1974; Mary's House (a biography of Mary M Pyle, disciple of Padre Pio), in progress. *Contributor to:* Voice of Padre Pio; La Casa; San Giovanni Rotondo, Italy; News Reporter, Collegian, Altoona Cathedral Register, Lock Haven Express. *Honour:* Consultant for documentary film on life of Padre Pio. *Memberships:* NEA; Local President, Pennsylvania State Education Association; Catholic Daughters of America; Red Cross Association. *Address:* 344 West Water Street Apt B, PO Box 685, Lock Haven, PA 17745, USA.

GAUDREAULT LABRECQUE, Madeleine, b. 25 Apr. 1931, Le Malbaie, Quebec, Canada. Writer. m. Victor Labrecque, 3 Sep. 1955, La Malbaie, Quebec, Canada, 1 son, 1 daughter. *Education:* Masters degree in Creative Writing; Licence in Literature and Journalism. *Appointments:* Lecturer to adults and children at libraries and schools, 1979 to present; Following 'Salon du Livre de Quebec' invited with other writers to discuss literary matters on Radio Quebec, 1983–1985; Teacher of Creative Writing, Laval University, Quebec, Fall 1984. *Publications:* Michel Labre collection of adventure novels for teenagers: Vol à bord du Concordia, 1968; Alerte ce soir à 22 heures; Gueule-de-loup, 1985. Books for teenagers and children: Le mystère du grenier, 1982; 'Le merle odieux', 1983. Contributor to magazines and journals. *Memberships:* Quebec Writers Federation; Union of Writers for the Youth; Quebec Professional Journalists Federation. *Honours:* Radio-Canada Society, 1946; French-Canadian Poets Society, 1963. *Address:* 4887 Saint Felix, C P 1081, Cap Rouge, Quebec, Canada G1Y 3E4.

GAUGER, Wilhelm Peter Joachim, b. 13 July 1932, Wuppertal, Germany. Professor of English Literature. m. Christel Kaiser, 19 Dec. 1964, Möchmühl, 1 son, 1 daughter. *Education:* Secondary School Teachers Diplomas, 1959, 62; PhD, 1965; Habilitation, 1971. *Publications:* Geschlechter, Liebe und Ehe in Londoner Zeitschriften um 1700, 1962; Wandlungsmotive in Rudyard Kiplings Prosawerk, 1975; Y Paranormale Welt, Wirklichkeit und Literatur, 1980. *Contributions to:* Numerous periodicals on literature, parapsychology and art. *Address:* Schopenhauerstr 7, D–1000 Berlin 38, Federal Republic of Germany.

GAUHAR, Altaf, b. Mar. 1923, Pakistan, Editor-in-Chief, South Magazine; Secretary-General, Third World Foundation, 1 son, 2 daughters. *Education:* MA, English, Government College, Lahore. *Literary Appointments:*

Editor-in-Chief, Herald Group of Newspapers, Pakistan; Editor, Dawn Newspaper (concurrent); Secretary-General, Third World Foundation (publishes Third World Quarterly); Co-Editor, Guardian Third World Review; Editor-in-Chief, South Magazine. *Publications:* Challenge of Islam, 1974; Islamic Concept of Economic Order, 1977; Editor, Talking About Development, 1983; Editor, The Rich and the Poor, 1983; Editor, Third World Strategy, 1983. *Contributions to:* South Magazine (Editorials); Third World Quarterly (Editorials). *Honour:* British Press Award, 1978. *Membership:* Vice-President, Federation of International Languages and Literature. *Address:* 13th Floor, New Zealand House, Haymarket, London SW1, England.

GAULDIE, William Sinclair, b. 29 Dec. 1918, Dundee, Scotland. Architect. m. Enid Elizabeth MacNeilage, 4 Dec. 1949, St Andrews, 1 son, 2 daughters. *Education:* School of Architecture, Dundee College of Art; ARIBA, 1943; FRIBA, 1954. *Appointments:* Member, Editorial Board, Prospect, 1954–60, British Journal of Aesthetics, 1968–75. *Publications:* Looking at Scottish Buildings, 1947; Fortesquieu, with Harold Scott, 1953; Architecture, 1969; Architects and Architecture on Tayside, with Bruce Walker, 1984. *Contributor to:* Numerous articles to, The Illustrated Carpenter & Builder; The Architects Journal; The Architectural Review; Prospect; Modulus; British Journal of Aesthetics, 1950–. *Honours:* President, Royal Incorporation of Architects in Scotland, 1963–65; Commander, Order of the British Empire, 1970. *Address:* 2 Osborne Place, Dundee DD2 1BD, Scotland.

GAUTHIER, Bertrand, b. 3 Mar. 1945, Montreal, Canada. Publisher. *Education:* BA, MA, McGill University. *Publications:* Hou Ilva, 1976; Hébertluée, 1981; Les Amantures, 1982; Zunik, 1985. *Honours:* Quebec-Wallonie-Bruxelles Prize, 1985; Prize, Conseil des Arts du Canada, 1981. *Membership:* Quebec Writers Union. *Address:* 458 Blvd St Joseph E, No 4, Montreal, Quebec, Canada H2J 1J7.

GAVIN, Catherine, b. Aberdeen, Scotland. Author. *Education:* MA, PhD, University of Aberdeen; Sorbonne, Paris, France. *Literary Appointments:* War Correspondent, Kemsley Newspapers and Daily Express. *Publications:* Madeline, 1959; The Cactus and The Crown, 1962; The Fortress, 1964; The Moon into Blood, 1966; The Devil in Harbour, 1968; The House of War, 1970; Give me the Daggers, 1972; The Snow Mountain, 1973; Traitors' Gate, 1976; None Dare Call It Treason, 1978; How Sleep the Brave, 1980; The Sunset Dream, 1983; A Light Woman, 1986. *Honour:* Recipient of University Medal of Honour, Helsinki, 1970. *Literary Agent:* Scott Ferris Associates. *Address:* 120 California Street, San Francisco, CA 94111, USA.

GAY, Michel, b. 5 Aug. 1949, Montreal, Quebec, Canada. Writer. m. Michele Deraiche, 1 Feb. 1972, Montreal, 1 son, 1 daughter. *Education:* Specialised Baccalaureat in cultural information, University of Quebec, 1971. *Literary Appointments:* Secretary General, Union des ecrivains quebecois; Federation internationale des ecrivains de langue fracaise; Director, La Nouvelle Barre du jour, 1977. *Publications:* L'Implicite/Le Filigrane, 1978; Oxygene/Recit, 1978; Metal Mental, 1981; Plaque tournante, 1981; Eclaboussures, 1982; Ecrivains, intellectuels, 1984; Ecrire la nuit, 1985. *Contributions to:* La Barre du jour; La Nouvelle Barre du jour; Coincidences; Ellipse; Estuaire; Action poetique; Levres urbaines; Odradek; Docks; Montreal Now; and others. *Memberships:* Union des écrivains québécois. *Address:* 119 rue Westhill, Saint-Bruno, Quebec, Canada J3V 1N7.

GAY, Pamela, b. 1 Dec. 1947, Dayton, Ohio, USA. Author/Poet/Translator/Critic and Historian of Performing Arts. *Education:* AA, The American College of Paris; BA, MA Professional Equivalency, The University of California, Berkeley. *Literary Appointment:* Editorial Board, Dance Scope, 1978–82. *Publication:* In Search of Bejart, contracted by Marcel Dekker Inc, New

York City, 1978–80. *Contributions to:* Essays, interviews and reviews in The Dial; The New York Times; Dance Magazine; Les Saisons de la Dance (Paris); The Christian Science Monitor; The Dancing Times (London) particularly, Portrait of Kyra Nijinsky, Dance Magazine, 1974; Legacy of the Minstrel Show, Dance Scope, 1978; Conversation with Leonide Massine, Dance Scope, 1979; France and the Dancing Kings, The Dancing Times, 1985. International Correspondent, Les Saisons de la Danse. *Honours:* Member, Breadloaf Writers Conference, 1970; Visiting Scholar, University of Calgary, 1980. *Membership:* Newsletter Editor, American Medical Writers Association, 1983–85. *Literary Agent:* Linda Allen, 1929 Divisidero Street, San Francisco, California. *Address:* PO Box 53108, Washington, DC 20009, USA.

GAYRE of GAYRE and NIGG, Robert, Ethnologist. *Education:* MA, University of Edinburgh; Exeter College, Oxford; DPolSc, Palermo, DPhil, Messina; DSc, University of Naples. *Publicatons include:* Teuton and Slav on the Polish Frontier, 1944; Wassaill In Mazers of Mead, 1948; Gayre's Books, 4 volumes, 1948–49; The Nature of Arms, 1961; A Case for Monarchy, 1962; Roll of Scottish Arms, Part 1 (3 volumes), 1964, 69, 75; Armorial Who is Who, 1960–62, 1963–65, 1966–69, 1970–75, 1976–79; Ethnological Elements of Africa, 1966; Zimbabwe, 1972; The Knightly Twilight, 1972; More Ethnological Elements of Africa, 1973; Miscellaneous Essays on Ethnology (2 volumes), 1943–72, 1973; The Lost Clan, 1974; British and Continental Heraldry, 1975; Minard Castle, 1979. *Contributions to:* Encyclopaedia Britannica; English Encyclopaedia, etc. *Honour:* Bronze Medal, Institute of Genealogy, Rome. *Membership:* National Academy of Science. *Address:* Lezayre Mount, Ramsey, Isle of Man, England.

GEDDES, Paul, b. 1922, England. Writer. 2 daughters. *Publications:* The High Game, 1968; A November Wind, 1970; The Ottawa Allegation, 1973; Hangman, 1977; A State of Corruption, 1985. *Literary Agent:* Tessa Sayle, 11 Jubilee Place, London SW3, England.

GEE, Maurice Gough, b. 22 Aug. 1931, Whakatane, New Zealand. Writer. m. Margaretha Garden, 1 son, 2 daughters. *Education:* MA, Auckland University, 1954. *Appointments:* Robert Burns Fellow, University of Otago, 1964. *Publications:* The Big Season, 1962; In My Fathers Den, 1972; Games of Choice, 1976; Plumb, 1978; Meg, 1981; Sole Survivor, 1983; 3 novels for children including, Under the Mountain, 1979; The Halfmen of O, 1982. *Honours:* New Zealand Literary Fund Scholarship, 1962, 1976; New Zealand Fiction Award, 1976, 1979, 1982; James Tait Black Memorial Prize, 1979; New Zealand Book of the Year Award, 1979. *Memberships:* PEN; New Zealand Writers Guild. *Literary Agent:* Richards Literary Agency, Auckland 9, New Zealand. *Address:* 125 Cleveland Terrace, Nelson, New Zealand.

GEGGUS, David Patrick, b. 19 Nov. 1949, Romford, Essex, England. University Professor. *Education:* BA, Oxford University, 1971; MA, distinction, London University, 1972; PhD, York University, 1979. *Literary Appointments:* Junior Research Fellow, Wolfson College, Oxford University, 1976–80; Hartley Research Fellow, Southampton University, 1980–82; Assistant Professor, 1983–85, Associate Professor, 1985–, University of Florida, Gainesville, Florida, USA; Associate Book Editor, Hispanic American Historical Review, 1985–. *Publications:* Slavery, War and Revolution: The British Occupation of Saint Dominique, 1982; Slave Resistance Studies and the Saint Dominique Slave Revolt, 1983. *Contributions to:* Slavery and British Society, 1982; English Historical Review; Medical History; The Historical Journal; Caribbean Studies; various others. *Honours:* French Government Scholarship, 1974; Leverhulme Overseas Award, 1975; British Academy Thank-Offering to Britain Fellowship, 1980; Roger Brew Memorial Prize, Cambridge University Press, 1980; Fellowship, Royal Historical Society, 1982; Guggenheim Foundation

Fellowship, 1984. *Address:* History Department, University of Florida, Gainesville, FL 32611, USA.

GEIJERSTAM, Carl-Erik af, b. 11 Feb. 1914, Skovde, Sweden. Teacher. *Education:* Fil lic, University of Uppsala, 1944. *Publications:* Vaktare vid spannet, 1936; Bortom ordens skyar, 1941; Bindemedel, 1950; Det personliga experimentet, stud i Vilhelm Ekelunds aforismer, 1963; Uppenbar hemlighet, 1967; Genomfard, 1972; Varseblivet, 1975; Ur fromma intet, 1976; Den brutna fortroliningen, 1979; Oppenheter, 1981; Fardsatt, 1983; Strimmor av Vanlighet, 1985. *Contributor to:* Artes; Bonniers Litterare Magasin; Forfattarforlagets tidskrift; Horisont; Lyrikvannen; Nya Argus; Ord och Bild; Var Losen. *Honour:* Uppsala Landstings Kulturpris, 1973. *Memberships:* Swedish Authors Union; PEN. *Address:* Gropgrand 2A, 75235, Sweden.

GEISSLER, Christian, b. 25 Dec. 1928, Hamburg, Germany. Writer; Documentary Film Maker. *Publications:* Anfrage, (novel), 1960; Schlachtvieh, (TV play), 1963; Kalte Zeiten, (novel), 1965; Ende der Anfrage, (stories and plays), 1967; Das Brot met der Feile, (novel), 1973; Wird Zeit. das vir leben, (novel), 1976; Im Vorfeld einer Schussverletzung, (poems), 1980; Speil auf augeheuer, (poems), 1983. *Contributor to:* Werkhefte Katholischer Laien; Kurbiskern; Konkret; blatter fur Deutsche und internationale Politik; Film; Plamen, (Prague, Czechoslovakia); Neutralitat, (Basle, Switzerland); Ramparts, (USA). *Honours include:* Premio Speciale della Rivista, Milanese, Questro e Altro, 1964. *Memberships:* PEN, West Germany; German Authors Society (VS). *Address:* Aaltuikerei 180, D 2955 Dollart, Federal Republic of Germany.

GELB, Norman, b. 9 Nov. 1929, New York City, USA. Author. *Education:* BA, Brooklyn College. *Publications:* Enemy in the Shadows, 1976; The Irresistible Impulse, 1979; The British, 1982; Less Than Glory, 1984. *Contributor to:* The New Leader; New York Times; San Francisco Chronicle. *Membership:* Society of Authors. *Address:* c/o Foreign Press Association, 11 Carlton Gardens Terrace, London SW1, England.

GELFAND, Lawrence E, b. 20 June, 1926, Cleveland, Ohio, USA. Historian. m. Miriam J Ifland, 14 June 1953, Seattle, 2 sons, 1 daughter. *Education:* BA, MA, Western Reserve University, Cleveland; PhD, University of Washington, Seattle. *Appointments:* Assistant Professor, University of Hawaii, 1956–58; Acting Assistant Professor, University of Washington, 1958–59; Assistant Professor, University of Wyoming, 1959–62; Assistant Professor, to Professor, University of Iowa, 1962–. *Publications:* The Inquiry: American Preparations for Peace 1917–1919. 1963; Editor, A Diplomat Looks Back (Memoirs of Lewis Einstein, 1968); Herbert Hoover: The Great War and Its Aftermath. Editor, 1979. *Memberships:* American Historical Association; Organization of American Historians, Co-Chairman, Membership Committee, 1982–85; Society for Historians of American Foreign Relations, President, 1982. *Address:* Dept of History, University of Iowa, Iowa City, IA 52242, USA.

GELLER, Uri, b. 20 Dec. 1946, Tel Aviv, Israel. Author; Lecturer. m. Hanna Strang, 1 son, 1 daughter. *Publications:* Uri Geller, Praeger Publishers 1975, Warner Paperback 1976; Geller Papers, Houghton and Mifflin, 1976; Pampini World Authors Ltd, 1980. *Contributions to:* Columns in psychic phenomenon to magazines and newspapers throughout the world. *Literary Agent:* Andrew Mann International Ltd, London. *Address:* c/o Andrew Mann International Ltd, 1 Old Compton Street, London W1, England.

GELLERT, Gyorgy, b. 17 Oct. 1922, Budapest, Hungary. Literary Translator. *Education:* DEcons. *Publications include:* Translations from Russian of works by Tolstoy, Gorky, Leskov, Korolenko, Saltikov, Goncharov, Bunin, Leonov, Fedin, Nekrasov, Panteleiev, Aksionov and others. Translations from French: La Joie de Vivre, by Emil Zola; Catherine de

Russie, by Z Oldenbourg: Books by Teilhard de Chardin and nunmerous other French writers. Translations from German: Novels by modern German writers. The Life of the Poet, Biography of Pushkin by A Gessen, translated from Russian; A Guide Book of Budapest for Russian Readers. Various forewords to translation volumes. *Contributions to:* Numerous literary journals. *Honours include:* Diploma Moscow, Soviet Writers Association, 1967, 69, 71. *Memberships include:* Hungarian Writers Association; PEN. *Address:* XI Somloi ut 50/A, 1118 Budapest, Hungary.

GEMS, Jonathan Malcolm Frederick, b. 7 Jan. 1952, London, England. Playwright. *Publications:* Naked Robots, 1982. Plays: The Tax Exile, Bush Theatre, 1979; Naked Robots, Royal Shakespeare Company, 1981; The Pakanormalist, Greenwich Theatre, 1983; Susan's Breasts, Royal Court Theatre, 1985. *Honour:* George Devine Award, 1980. *Membership:* Theatre Writers Union. *Literary Agent:* Judy Daish. *Address:* c/o Judy Daish Associates, 83 Eastbourne Mews, London W2 6LQ, England.

GENET, Jean, b. 19 Dec. 1907, Paris, France. Playwright. *Publications include:* Le Condamne a Mort, 1942; Notre-Dame-des-Fleurs, 1944; Chants Secrets, 1945; Miracle de la Rose, 1946; Les Bonnes, 1947; Pompes Funebres, 1947; Querelle de Brest, 1947; Haute Surveillance, 1949; Le Journal du Voleur, 1949. Plays: Le Balcon, 1956; Les Negres, 1958; Les Parvents, 1961. Poems: La Galerie; Le Parade; Un Chant d'Armour; LePecheur di Susquet. *Address:* c/o Rosica Colin, 1 Clareville Grove Mews, London SW7 5AM, England.

GENSER, Cynthia Kraman, b. 3 June 1950. Writer. *Education:* BA, University of Massachusetts, USA. 1972; MFA Programme, Columbia University. *Publications:* Taking on the Local Colour, 1977; Club 82, 1979; New York Poems, anthology, 1980. *Contributions to:* Paris Review; Antaeus. *Memberships:* Poets and Writers Incorporated. *Address:* 16 Charles Street, New York City, NY 10014, USA.

GERMAN, Donald Robert, b. 11 Feb. 1931, Philadelphia, Pennsylvania, USA. Author. m. Joan Alice Wolfe, 4 Sep. 1954, Philadelphia, 1 son. *Education:* BS, Temple University, Pennsylvania, 1955; MA, 1984, PhD Candidate, Columbia Pacific University. *Publications:* The Banker's Complete Guide to Advertising, 1966; The Bank Employee's Security Handbook, 1972; Money and Banks, 1979; Mattie's Money Tree, 1984; The Banker as Financial Adviser, 1986; Co-author Joan W German: Passkeys, 1967; Dividends, 1969; The Bank Teller's Handbook, 1970; Successful Job Hunting for Executives, 1974; Bank Employee's Marketing Handbook, 1975; Tested Techniques in Bank Marketing, Volume 1, 1977; Tested Techniques in Bank Marketing, Volume 2, 1979; Make Your Own Convenience Foods, 1979; The Bank Teller's Handbook (new edition), 1981; How to Find a Job When Jobs Are Hard to Find, 1981; The Bank Employee's Security Handbook (new edition), 1982; Checklists for Profitability, 1983; The Only Money Book for the Middle Class, 1983; Money A to Z: A Consumer's Guide to the Language of Personal Finance, 1984; Ninety Days to Financial Fitness, 1986. *Contributions to:* ABA Journal; Bankers Magazine; Brides; Compass; Consumer Life; Consumers Digest; Cosmopolitan; Dynamic Years; Easy Living; Family Weekly; Friendly Exchange; Magazine Age; Money Maker; RABW Journal; National Enquirer; Tables; Woman's Day; Chapters in: Investment Guide, 1980–85; The Complete Guide to Writing Nonfiction, 1984. Author-Editor: Bank Tellor's Report, 1968–; Branch Banker's Report, 1969–; Contributing Editor: Bank Marketing Report, 1967–. *Memberships:* American Society of Journalists and Authors Inc. (Director-at-large 1979–81); Authors Guild; Boston Authors Club. *Address:* West Mountain Road, Cheshire, MA 01225, USA.

GERMAN, Joan Alice (Wolfe), b. 9 Feb. 1933, Philadelphia, Pennsylvania, USA. Author. m. Donald R

German, 4 Sep. 1954, Philadelphia, 1 son. *Education:* Temple University, Philadelphia, 1951–54. *Publications:* Passkeys, 1967; Dividends, 1969; The Bank Teller's Handbook, 1970; Successful Job Hunting for Executives, 1974; Bank Employee's Marketing Handbook, 1975; Tested Techniques in Bank Marketing, Volume 1, 1977; Tested Techniques in Bank Marketing, Volume 2, 1979; Make Your Own Convenience Foods, 1979; The Money Book, 1981; The Bank Teller's Handbook, new edition, 1981; How To Find a Job When Jobs Are Hard to Find, 1981; The Bank Employee's Security Handbook, new edition, 1982; Checklist for Profitability, 1983; The Only Money Book for the Middle Class, 1983; Money A to Z: A Consumer's Guide to the Language of Personal Finance, 1984; Forthcoming Books: What Am I?; Guess What?; Co-author with Donald R German of all books except, The Money Book, 1981. To be published in 1986: Ninety Days to Financial Fitness. *Contributions to:* Bankers Magazine; Brides; Compass; Cosmopolitan; Dynamic Years; Easy Living; NABW Journal; National Enquirer; Tables; Woman's Day; Author/Editor: Bank Teller's Report, 1968–; Branch Banker's Report, 1969–. *Memberships:* American Society of Journalists and Authors Incorporated, Chairperson, Berkshire Hills Chapter, 1983–85; Authors Guild; National League of American Pen Woman, President, Berkshire Branch, 1974–76; Massachusetts State President, 1976–78. *Address:* West Mountain Road, Cheshire, MA 01225, USA.

GEROV, Alexander, b. 15 May 1919, Sofia. Writer. m. Tamara Gerova, 24 July 1949. *Education:* University Law Degree. *Publications:* Poetry: We, People; Our Power; The Best Thing; Political Poetry; Particles of Dust; Ingections; Prose: Science Fiction Stories. *Contributor to:* All main Bulgarian literary editions. *Honours:* People's Worker of Culture, 1979; Dimitrov Prize, 1980. *Membership:* Union of Bulgarian Writers. *Address:* 50, T Petrov Street, Sofia, Bulgaria.

GERRISH, Brian Albert, b. 14 Aug. 1931, London, England. University Professor. *Education:* BA, Queens College, Cambridge, England, 1952; Exit Certificate, Westminster College, Cambridge, 1955; MA, ibid. 1956, STM, Union Theol Sem, New York, USA, 1956; PhD, Columbia University, USA, 1958. *Appointments:* Editor, Journal of Religion, 1972–85; John Nueven Professor, Divinity School, University of Chicago, Illinois, USA. *Publications:* Grace and Reason; A Study in the Theology of Luther, 1962; Tradition in the Modern World; Reformed Theology in the Nineteenth Century, 1978; The Old Protestantism and the New: Essays on the Reformation Heritage, 1982; A Prince of the Church: Schleiermacher and the Beginnings of Modern Theology, 1984; Editor: The Faith of Christendom, A Source Book of Creeds and Confessions, 1963; Reformers in Profile, 1967; Reformatio Perennis: Essays on Calvin and the Reformation in Honor of Ford Lewis Battles, 1981. *Contributor to:* Various professional journals. *Honours:* Guggenheim Fellowship, 1970; National Endowment for the Humanities Fellowship, 1980; DD, Honoris Causa, University of St Andrews, Scotland, 1984. *Address:* 301 Swift Hall, University of Chicago, 1025 East 58th Street, Chicago, IL 60637 USA.

GERSHATOR, David, b. 2 Dec. 1937, Mount Carmel, USA. Lecturer/Writer. m. Phillis, 19 Oct. 1963, Oakland, California, 1 son 1 daughter. *Education:* BA, C U N Y, 1959; MA, Columbia University, 1960; PhD, New York University, 1967. *Literary Appointment:* Fiction Lecturer, Rotterdam World Cruise, 1980. *Publications:* Play Mas, West Indian Poems, Downtown Poets, 1981; The Selected Letters of Federico Garcia Lorca Editor and Translator, 1983. *Contributions to:* Confrontation; Revista Review; Interamericana; Snakeroots; Stroker; Montemora; Passages; Jewish Currents; Antaeus etc. Associated Editor, Home Planet News, New York. *Honours:* NER, National Endowment for the Humanities, 1971; CAPS grant, New York State Creative Artist Public Service, 1978. *Membership:*

Poetry Society of America. *Address:* P O Box 3353, St Thomas, VI 00801, USA.

GESSERT, Kate Rogers, b. 25 Jan. 1948, Santa Barbara, California, USA. Writer, Gardener; Peace Activist. m. George Gessert, 16 Apr. 1974, Briarcliff Manor, New York, 1 son, 1 daughter. *Education:* BA English, Wellesley College, Wellesley, Massachusetts, 1969; MS Education, Bank Street College of Education, New York, 1975; Graduate Student in Horticulture, Oregon State University, 1975–78. *Major publications:* The Beautiful Food Garden, 1983. *Contributor to:* American Horticulturalist; Mother Earth News; Gardens for All News; Pacific Northwest; American Community Gardening Association Journal; Organic Gardening. *Honours:* 1st place award for garden book for general readership, Garden Writers of America Association, 1983. *Memberships:* Garden Writers of America Association; Lane Literary Guild; Families for Survival. *Address:* 1230 West Broadway, Eugene, OR 97402, USA.

GETHING, Michael John, b. 13 May 1949, Bridlington, Yorks, England. Editor. *Literary Appointments:* Managing Editor, Whitton Press, Defence series of magazines, 1979–. *Publications:* Modern Fighters, Part 2 (Phoebus Publishing Company), 1980/81; Nato Air Power ingl 1980's, (Arms and Armour Press), 1982; Warsaw Pact Air Power in 1980's, (A and AP), 1982; F-15 Eagle, (Salamander), 1983; Military Helicopters, (A and AP), 1983; Harrier, (A and AP), 1983; RAF Air Power Today, with L Peacock, (1 and AP), 1984; Nato Air Power Today, (A and AP), 1986. *Contributor to:* Various magazines including: Miltronics (Ed Cons); Aerospace (Asst Ed, 1973–76); Air Cadet News (Aviation and Modelling Corres, 1975–83); Defence Helicopter World; Combat Weapons. *Memberships:* (Assoc) Royal Aeronautical Society; Institute of Journalists; Aviation and Space Writers Association; Royal United Services Institite; Air Britain. *Address:* Havelet Cottagè, 23 Grasmere Road, Cove, Farnborough, Hants GU14 OLE, England.

GEYER, Georgie Anne, b. 2 Apr. 1935, Chicago, Illinois, USA. Syndicated Columnist. *Education:* BS, Medill School of Journalism, Northwestern University, 1956; Fulbright Scholarship, University of Vienna, Australia, 1956–57. *Literary Appointments:* General Assignment Report, Chicago Daily News, 1960–64; Foreign Correspondent, Chicago Daily News, 1964–75; Syndicated Columnist, Los Angeles Times Syndicate, 1975–80; Syndicated Columnist, Universaly Press Syndicate and The Washington Star, 1980–81; Syndicated Columnist, Universal Press Syndicate, 1981–. *Publications:* The New Latins 1970; The New 100 Years' War, 1972; The Young Russians, 1976; Buying the Night Flight, 1983. *Contributor to:* Three-times-a-week column on domestic, foreign and women's affairs in more than 100 newspapers in US including The Chicago Sun-Times; The Philadelphia Inquirer; The Seattle Times; The Providence Journal; The Miami News and The Washington Times. Regular contributor to such magazines as The Saturday Review; The Atlantic; The New Republic; The Progressive; The Nation; Ladies Home Journal; Encyclopedia Britannica; People; Signature; Notre Dame Magazine and many others. *Honours:* Chicago Newspaper Guild Prize for best human interest story, 1962; Overseas Press Club Latin America Award 1967; the National Council of Jewish Women's Hannah Solomon Award for public service, 1971; The Maria Moors Cabot Award, Columbia University. 1971; Who's Who in America Women Award for outstanding woman journalist in USA, 1971; Picked by Newsweek Magazine as one of four outstanding women journalists in USA; Illinois State Merit Award 1975; Nortwestern University Merit Award, 1968; Northwestern Alumnae Award, 1981; Distinguished Fellow, Mortar Board National Senior Honor Society, American University, 1982. Honorary Doctor of Letters, Lake Forest College, Lake Forest, Illinois, 1980. *Memberships:* International Institute for Strategic Studies, London; Women in Communications; Sigma Delta Chi; Midland Authors; Mortar Board, the

Women's Institute for Freedom of the Press; National Press Club. *Address:* The Plaza, 800 25th Street, NW, Washington, DC 20037, USA.

GHANEM, Shihab Muhammad Abduh, b. 16 Oct. 1940, Aden. Engineer. m. Jihad Ali Luqman, 11 Aug. 1968, 2 sons, 1 daughter. *Education:* BSc, Mechanical & Electrical Engineering, Aberdeen University, 1964; PG Dip (WRD) 1st Division, 1970, ME (WRD) 1st Division, 1975, Roorkee University. *Literary Appointments:* Editor, Aden College Magazine, 1957–60; Founder members, committee member (1983–), Almuntada, Arabic cultural magazine published in Dubai, United Arab Emirate. *Publications:* Bayn Shat wa Akher (Arabic verse). 1982; Tanwiat (Arabic verse, co-author), 1982; Basamat Ala al-Rimal (Arabic verse), 1983; Shawath fi al-Atma (Arabic verse), in press; Tafaraqat Aydi Sabaa (Arabic Verse), under publication. *Contributions to:* Over 100 poems, 10 literary articles in Arabic, various magazines and journals. *Honours & Literary Awards:* Education Department Arabic Essay Prize, Aden, 1958; British Council English Essay Prize, Aden, 1960; UAE Arabic Poetry Prize, Sharjah, 1984. *Address:* PO Box 10949, Dubai, United Arab Emirate.

GHEERAERT, John, b. 19 July 1939, Ostend, Belgium, Teacher. m. Dina Clybouw, 5 Aug 1966, Bredene, Belgium, 2 sons, 1 daughter. *Education:* Licentiate Germanic Philology. *Publications:* Paardjes uit Polen (Little Horses from Poland) 1981; De Non (The Nun) 1983; Trekuogels (Birds of Passage) 1984. *Contributor to:* Short stories in the literary magazine, Dietsche Warande en Belfort. *Honours:* The Ary Sleeks Award, Royal Academy, 1978–80; The Literary Award of the Osstendse Compagnie, 1983; The Daan Inghebram Award, 1985; other Awards for short stories. *Literary Agent:* De Vries-Brouwers, Antwerp, Belgium. *Address:* Duinhelmlaan 7, Bredene 8401, Belgium.

GHEZZI, Bertil William, b. 12 July 1941, Pittsburgh, Pennsylvania, USA. Editor. m. Mary Lou Cuddyre, 20 June 1964, Pittsburgh, 4 sons, 3 daughters. *Education:* BA Classics magna cum laude, Duquesne University; PhD History, University of Notre Dame. *Literary Appointments:* Editorial Director, Servant Publications, 1974–85; Editor, New Covenant, 1974–85; Editor, Pastoral Renewal, 1976–81; Editorial Director, Charisma, 1985–; Editorial Director, Ministries, 1985–; Editorial Director, Strang Communications Company, 1985–. *Publications:* Build With The Lord, 1976; The Angry Christian, 1980; Getting Free, 1982; Facing Your Feelings, 1983. *Contributions to:* Our Sunday Visitor; National Catholic Register; Christian Life; HIS; Eternity; Charisma; New Covenant; Pastoral Renewal. *Honours:* Graduated magna cum laude; Awarded First Year Fellowship, University of Notre Dame, 1963–64. *Address:* 2417 Tioga Trail, Winter Park, FL 32789, USA.

GHIGNA, Charles, b. 25 Aug. 1946, Poet-in-Residence. m. Debra Holmes. *Literary Appointments:* Poet-in-Residence, Alaska School of Fine Arts. *Contributor to:* Numerous magazines and journals including, Harper's; The Village Voice; Southern Poetry Review; The Saturday Evening Post; Good Housekeeping; Playboy; Rolling Stone; (children's magazines) Humpty Dumpty; Child Life; Children's Digest; Highlights for Children. *Honours:* Fellowships from, John F Kennedy Center for the Performing Arts; Rockefeller Brothers Fund; Mary Roberts Rinehart Foundation; NEA. *Address:* 204 W Linwood Drive, Homewood, AL 35209, USA.

GHNASSIA, Maurice Jean-Henri, b. 23 July 1920, Paris, France; Writer; Communications Consultant; Lecturer; Film Writer; Director; Producer. m. Dr Jill Dix, 18 Dec. 1980. *Literary Appointments:* Internship, New York Herald Tribune, Paris Edition, 1937–40; Associate Managing Editor, Grolier Incorporated, 1959– (Publishers of La Science pour tous, 8 volume encyclopedia in French); United Nations Representative for Grolier Incorporated, 1972. *Publications:* Foule aux Dames, 1952; Un Dimanche pour Pleurer, 1954; Arena: A Novel of Spartasus and Crassus, 1969; Charlie

Brown, 8 volume series in French. Film, Writer, Director and Producer, A Profession Integrates. *Contributions to:* Quarte et Trois; France Dimasnche; Le Temps de Paris; L'Aurore; France Observateur; Europe no 1; Renascita; Le Monde, 1948–; La Tribune de Geneve, Switzerland; Die Welt, Germany; Frankfurter Allgemeine; Grolier's Year Books, and various others. *Honours:* Best Short Story, Jazz, 1949; Book of the Month Club, 1969. *Memberships:* Societe des Gens de Lettres de France; Society of Authors and Composers; Authors Guild; Foreign Press Association; United Nations Correspondents Association. *Address:* PO Box 611, New Hartford, CT 06057, USA.

GIANNINI, David, b. 19 Mar. 1948, New York, New York, USA. Poet; Writer. *Appointments:* Co-Editor/Co-Founder, Genesis; Grasp Magazine, 1968–72; Adjunct Professor of English, Williams College, Massachusetts, USA, 1980; Poet in Residence, Mark Hopkins School, Massachussetts, 1979–80. *Publications:* Opens, 1971; Stories, 1974; Fourfield, 1976; Close Packet, 1978; 3, 1978; Stem, 1981. *Contributor to:* New Directions, annuals, Nos. 23, 26 and 40; Longhouse Journal; Quarterly Review of Literature; Chelsea Review. *Honour:* Osa and Lee Mays Award, 1971. *Address:* Wendling Farm, Williamstown, MA 01267, USA.

GIBBONS, Reginald, b. 7 Jan. 1947, Houston, Texas, USA. Poet; Editor. *Education:* AB, Princeton, 1969; MA, 1971, PhD, 1974, Stanford. *Publications:* Roofs Voices Roads, 1979; The Ruined Motel, 1981; Saints, 1986; 5 other books. *Contributor to:* The New Republic; The Nation; The Yale Review; New York Times Book Review; Critical Inquiry; Hudson Review; Southern Review, etc. *Honours:* Guggenheim Fellowship in Poetry, 1984; National Endowment for the Arts Fellowship in Poetry, 1984–85. *Memberships:* Associated Writing Programmes, Vice President, 1985–86; PEN American Centre; Poetry Society of America; Texas Institute of Letters, etc. *Address:* c/o TriQuarterly, 1735, Benson Avenue, Evanston, IL 60201, USA.

GIBSON, Evan Keith, b. 4 July 1909, Everett, Washington, USA. University Professor. m. Mary Eleanor Burns, 7 Oct. 1932, Arlington, Washington, 1 son, 3 daughters. *Education:* AB, Seattle Pacific College, 1933; MA, 1935, PhD, 1947, University of Washington. *Publications:* C S Lewis, Spinner of Tales, a Guide to his Fiction, 1980; Heinrich Hoffmann: Der Struwwel Peter Polyglott (English version) 1984. *Contributions to:* Alastor: A Reinterpretation PMLA, 1947; Conception is a Blessing PMLA, 1949; Literary Trends after Hiroshima, The Elensis of Chi Omega, 1949; A number of other articles, stories and poems. *Address:* 14318 – 68th Avenue NW, Gig Harbor, WA 98335, USA.

GIBSON, Graeme Cameron, b. 9 Aug. 1934, London, Ontario, Canada. Writer. married, 2 sons, 1 daughter. *Education:* BA, English and Philosophy, University of Western Ontario. *Appointments:* Writer-in-Residence, University of Waterloo, Waterloo, Ontario, Canada, 1982–83; Writer in Residence, University of Ottawa, Ontario, Canada, 1985. *Publications:* Five Legs, (novel), 1969; Communion, (novel), 1971; 11 Canaan Novelists, (intereviews), 1973; Perpetual Motion, (novel), 1982. *Honours:* First Recipient Canada-Scotland writers' exchange; several senior Canada Council grants and awards. *Memberships:* Writer's Union of Canada, Chairman, 1974–75; Book and Periodical Development Council, Chairman, 1976; Writers' Development Trust, Chairman, 1978, Vice-Chairman, 1985. *Literary Agent:* Charlotte Sheedy Agency. *Address:* 105 Admiral Road, Toronto, Ontario, Canada M5R 2L7.

GIBSON, Margaret, b. 17 Feb. 1944, Philadelphia, Pennsylvania, USA. Poet. m. David McKain, 27 Dec. 1975, Friend's Meeting. *Education:* BA, English, Hollins College; MA, English, University of Virginia. *Publications:* Signs, 1979; Long Walks in the Afternoon, 1982; Memories of the Future, forthcoming. *Contributor to:* Georgia Review; New England Review; Crazy

Horse; Parnassus; Michigan Quarterly Review. *Honours:* Phi Beta Kappa, 1965; Woodrow Willson Fellowship, 1966–77; Lamont Selection Academy of American Poets, 1982; National Endowment for the Arts Grant, 1985. *Address:* RFD # 1 Watson Road, Preston, CT 06360, USA.

GIBSON, Morgan, b. 6 June 1929, Cleveland, Ohio, USA. Author; Professor of English. m. (1) Barbara Brown, 1950, divorced 1972, 2 daughters; (2) Keiko Matsui, 14 Sep. 1978, Kobe, Japan. *Education:* BA, Oberlin College, 1950; MA, 1952, PhD, 1959, University of Iowa; Studied Philosophy, Paul Goodman, Masao Abe, Buddhist Seminars, Myoshinji Temple, Kyoto, 1976–78. *Publications:* (Poetry) Our Bedroom's Underground, 1962; Mayors of Marble, 1966; Stones Glow Like Lovers' Eyes, 1970; Dark Summer, 1977; Wakeup, 1978; Speaking of Light, 1979; Kokoro: Heart Mind, with Keiko Matsui Gibson, 1980; (Poetic Fiction) The Great Brook Book, 1981; Tantric Poetry of Kukai (Kobo Daishi) Japan's Buddhist Saint, 1982; Revolutionary Rexroth: Poet of East-West Wisdom, 1986; Among Buddhas in Japan: Autobiographical Essays, 1986; Poetry Editor: Arts in Society, 1965–72; Editor, Anthology, The Arts of Activism, 1972. *Contributor to:* Numerous professional journals and magazines. *Honours:* Recipient, Poetry and Fiction Awards, Oberlin College, University of Wisconsin-Milwaukee. *Memberships:* PEN; Academy of American Poets; Poetry Society of America; Associated Writing Programs; Buddhist Publications Society, Sri Lanka; World Fellowship of Buddhists, Bangkok; Buddhist Peace Fellowship. *Address:* Chukyo University, Nagoya, Japan.

GIBSON, Robert Donald Davidson, b. 21 Aug. 1927, Hackney, London, England. University Professor. m. Sheila Elaine Goldsworthy, 21 Dec. 1953. Walthamstow, 3 sons. *Education:* BA, Honours, French, King's College, London, 1948; PhD, Cambridge, 1953. *Publications:* The Quest of Alain-Fournier, 1953; Modern French Poets on Poetry, 1961; Editor, A-Frontier: Le Grand meaulnes, 1968; The Land Without a Name, 1975. *Contributor to:* Times Literary Supplement; French Studies; Modern Language Review; Times Higher Educational Supplement; Czhiers proustiens. *Address:* 7 Sunnymead, Tyler Hill, Canterbury, Kent, England.

GIBSON, Sue, b. 16 Sep. 1948, Madras, India. Publisher/Writer. *Literary Appointment:* Former NUJ; Member of British Equestrian Writers Association. *Publications:* Rusty's Foal, 1981 2nd edition 1982, serialised in PNY magazine 1981; The Story of Rusty, serialised in PONY magazine 1983; Glorious Uncertainty: The Autobiography of Jenny Pitman, 1984; The Family Outdoor Book, (Ed Edwards) Pony Section, 1984. *Contributions to:* Sporting Chronicle; Light Horse later called Horse and Rider; Pony Magazine; She Magazine; Daily Mail; Editor Horse and Rider magazine, 1982–83. *Address:* Barn Cottage, 4 Church Lane, Ditchling, East Sussex, England.

GIGGAL, Kenneth, b. 19 Mar. 1927, Dewsbury, Yorks, England. *Publications include:* The Manchester Thing, 1970; The Huddersfield Job, 1971; The London Assignment, 1972; The Dunfermline Affair, 1973; The Bradford Business, 1974; The Amsterdam Diversion, 1974; The Leeds Fiasco, 1975; The Edinburgh Exercise, 1975; The Ampurias Exchange, 1976; The Aberdeen Conundrum, 1977; The Congleton Lark, 1979; The Hamburg Switch, 1980; A Bad April, 1980; The Menwith Tangle, 1982; The Darlington Jaunt, 1983; The Luxembourg Run, 1985; Doom Indigo, 1986; Scripts and films for TV. *Contributor to:* Many magazines, national and international. *Memberships:* The Savage Club; The Arms and Armour Society; The Writers Guild of Great Britain; The Crime Writer's Association. *Address:* The Old Granary, Bishop Monkton, Near Harrogate, N Yorks, England.

GILBERT, James Robie, b. 15 May 1948, Rochester, New York, USA. Editor: Journalist. m. Nancy Wood, 8

Sep. 1979, Truro, Massachusetts, 1 son, 1 daughter. *Education:* BA, Sociology, Occidental College. *Appointments:* Editor, Seven Seas Press, Newport, Rhode Island; Associate Editor, Cruising World, Newport; Managing Editor, Caribbean Business; The Advocate, Provincetown. *Publications:* Editor, 30 books, 1981–85. *Contributor to:* Numerous professional journals. *Honours:* Award, Investigative Reporting, Overseas Press Club of Puerto Rico, 1980. *Address:* 16 Galley Street, James Town, RI 02835, USA.

GILBERT, John Raphael, b. 1926, London, England. Freelance Author; Editor; Translator. *Education:* Columbia University, New York, USA; University of London, England; BA. *Publications:* Modern World Book of Animals, 1948; Cats, Cats, Cats, 1961; Famous Jewish Lives, 1970; Myths of Ancient Rome, 1970; Charting the Vast Pacific, 1971; Pirates and Buccaneers, 1971; Highwaymen and Outlaws, 1971; National Costumes of the World, 1972; Pirates and Buccaneers, 1975; Miracles of Nature, 19754; Knights of the Crusades, 1978; Prehistoric Man, 1979; Translations: World of Wildlife, 1971–74; Leonardo da Vinci, 1977; La Scala, 1979. *Address:* 28 Lyndale Avenue, London NW2, England.

GILBERT, Martin, b. 25 Oct. 1936, London, England. Historian; Official Biographer of Sir Winston Churchil, 1968–. *Education:* BA, MA, Oxford University; Magdalen, St Antony's & Merton (Fellow 1962–), Colleges, Oxford. *Publications include:* The Appeasers, with Richard Gott, 1963; The European Powers 1900–1945, 1966 Historical Atlases on recent history, British and American History & many aspects of Jewish history; Winston S Churchill, volume III 1914–1916, 1971 (2 pt companion volume 1973), volume iv, 1917–1922, 1975 (3 part companion volume 1977), volume v, 1922–1939, 1976 (3 part companion volume 1979–80), volume vi, 1939–41, 1983, volume vii, 1941–45, 1986; Exile & Return, The Emergence of Jewish Statehood, 1978; Children's Illustrated Bible Atlas, 1979; Auschwitz & The Allies, 1980; Churchill's Wilderness Years, 1981; The Holocaust Atlas, 1984; Jerusalem, Rebirth of a City, 1985; several publications translated into other languages. *Contrubutor to:* The Guardian; Sunday Times; Observer; TV Times; Jerusalem Post; New York Review of Books. *Membership:* FRSL. *Agent:* A P Watt. *Address:* Merton College, Oxford University, Oxford, England.

GILCHRIST, Martyn Wright, b. 1 Feb. 1941, Leeds, Yorkshire, England. Indexer. m. Sandra Eldridge, at Newport, Isle of Wight, 8 May 1965, 3 daughters. *Education:* Registered Indexer. *Publications:* Compiler of indexes from 1984. *Contributions to:* The Indexer. *Membership:* Society of Indexers. *Address:* 22 Fernhill Road, New Milton, Hampshire BH25 5JZ, England.

GILL, Anton, b. 22 Oct. 1948, Essex, England. Writer. m. Nicola Browne, 6 Nov. 1982, London. *Education:* MA, Cambridge University. *Literary Appointments:* Drama Officer, Arts Council of Great Britain, 1976–78. *Publications:* Martin Allen Is Missing, 1984; Mad About the Boy, 1984; How to be Oxbridge, 1985. *Contributions to:* Plays and Players; Time Out. *Membership:* Theatre committee, Writers Guild of Great Britain. *Literary Agent:* Mark Lucas. *Address:* c/o Fraser and Dunlop Scripts Limited, 91 Regent Street, London W1, England.

GILL, Stephen, b. 25 June 1932, Sialkot. Writer; Book publisher; Editor. m. Sarala, 1 son, 2 daughters. *Education:* MA, English literature. *Literary Appointments:* Past President, Cornwall branch, Canadian Authors Association; Editor, Writers Lifeline, currently. *Publications include:* Political Convictions of G B Shaw; Six Symbolist Plays of Yeats (literary criticism); Life's Vagaries, stories; English Grammar for Beginners; Why, novel; Immigrant, novel; Sketches of India, essays; Moans and Waves, poems; Simon and the Snow King, children's story; The Blessings of a Bird, children's story; Scientific Romances of H G Wells (literary criticism); Reflections and Wounds (Poems); Discovery of

Bangladesh (History); The Loyalist City, (Novel). Editor and Co-editor of anthologies: Green Snow; Poets of the Capital; Tales from Canada for Children Everywhere; Anti-War Poems; Seaway Valley Poets; Anti-war Poems, volume 2. *Contributions to:* Journal of Modern Literature; Books in Canada; Calcutta Review; The Literary Half-Yearly; Canadian World Federalist; The Ottawa Journal; Quill and Quire; Christian Monitor, India; The Canadian India Times; and others. *Memberships:* Educational Press Association of America; Canadian Society of Childrens Authors, Illustrators and Performers. *Address:* PO Box 32, Cornwall, Ontario, Canada K6H 5R9.

GILL Elaine Goldman, b. 28 Apr. 1924, Boston, Massachusetts. Publisher. m. John Gill, 26 Jan. 1954, New York, 2 sons. *Education:* BA, University of California, Berkeley; MA, New York University; PhD studies, Columbia University. *Publications:* Mountain Moving Day, Poems By Women, 1973; An Herbal Sampler, 1984. *Address:* PO Box 640, Trumansburg, NY 14886, USA.

GILLAM, Anthony John, b. 20 Jan. 1943, Derby, England. Publisher. m. Mary, 1 Apr. 1967, Chesterfield, 1 son, 2 daughters. *Education:* College of Education, Clifton, Nottingham, 1963–66; Dip Ed. *Publications:* Starting Chess (originally, Play Chess), 1978; Simple Chess Tactics, 1978; Simple Checkmates, 1978. *Address:* 12 Burton Avenue, Carlton, Nottingham NG4 1PT, England.

GILLE, Hans-Werner, b. 18 May 1928, Glogau, Germany. *Education:* PhD, Munich University. *Publications:* Katholiken gegen Rom, Catholics Versus Rome, 1969; Play Bluff, novel, 1971; Politik Staat und Nation in der Dritten Welt, Policy, State and Nation in the Third World, 3rd edition, 1974; Das Antliz Chinas, The Face of China, 1976; Nation heute, The Idea of Nation Today, 4th Edition, 1977; Sibirien, Siberia, 1978; Australien, Ein Kontinent in Aufbruch, Australia, A Continent on the Point of Emerging, 1981; Drei Fragen zu Deutschland (Anthologie), Three Questions on Germany, 1985. *Contributions to:* German Broadcasting of features, dramas and essays. *Membership:* International Press Club, Munich. *Address:* Fafnerstrasse 32, D–8000 Munich 19, Federal Republic of Germany.

GILLES, Anthony Eugene, b. 8 Oct. 1945, Owensboro, Kentucky, USA. Writer. m. Andrea Brennan, 21 Nov. 1981, Sunny Hills, Florida. *Education:* BA, Magna cum laude, University of Tennessee, 1967; MA, Rutgers University, 1969; JD, University of Tennessee, 1973; various studies, St Joseph's Abbey, 1976–77, St Charles College, 1978–79. *Publications:* The People of the Book: The Story Behind the Old Testament, 1983; The People of the Way: The Story Behind the New Testament, 1984; Fundamentalism: What Every Catholic Needs to Know, 1984; The People of the Creed: The Story Behind the Early Church, 1985; Living Words: A Simple Study of Key New Testament Concepts for People Who Don't Know a Word of Greek, 1985; the People of the Faith: The Story Behind the Church of the Middle Ages, 1986; The People of Anguish: The Story Behind the Reformation, 1986; The People of Hope: The Story Behind the Modern Church, 1987. Series of taped talks for St Anthony Messenger Press, 1984, 85. *Contributions to:* Romance Paroles; The Teilhard Review; America; God's Word Today; St Anthony Messenger; Bread; The Good News Visitor; Spirituality Today; Stamp World; Sunday Publication; Today's Parish; US Catholic; In Spirit and In Truth, column, St Anthony Messenger, 1985–. *Honour:* 3rd Place, Contest, Catholic Press Association, 1981. *Address:* 3484 Wellington Road, Pensacola, FL 32504, USA.

GILLET, Philippe, b. 13 July 1923, France. Engineer. *Education:* Ecole Polytechnique, Paris. *Publications:* La Meilleure Part, novel, 1954; La Machine a Faire des Dieux, novel, 1956; Dialogues a une Voix, 1967; Romantismes, 1976. *Honours:* Jean Cocteau Poetry Prize, 1967. *Memberships:* Society of Men of Letters, Paris; Society General Jean Cocteau, Prize Jury; Leader, Artistic Chapter, Montmarte. *Address:* 64 Rue de Longchamp, 92 200 Neuilly, Fance.

GILLILAND, Hap Cleburne, b. 26 Aug 1918, Willard, Colorado, USA. University Professor. m. Erma Rodreick, 21 Apr 1946, Denver, Colorado, 1 son, 2 daughters. *Education:* EdD, University of Northern Colorado; MA, BA, Western State College of Colorado. *Literary Appointments:* Editor, Montana Journal of Reading, 1964–70; Editorial Boards of: Journal of Reading 1971–72, The Reading Teacher, 1972–76, Reading Horizons 1975–77; Editor, Indian Culture Series (102 books) Council for Indian Education, 1969–. *Publications:* Corrective and Remedial Reading, 1973; Chant of the Red Man, 1976; Indian Children's Books 1976, Materials for Remedial Reading and Their Use, 1965, revised editions 1966, 1967, 1972, 1976; A Practical Guide to Remedial Reading, 1974, 1978; 10 children's books. *Contributions to:* Humor in the Classroom, The Reading Teacher; Who has the Best Methods for Beginning Reading, Reading Horizons; Reading for the Child with Learning Disabilities, journal, Reading Association of Ireland; Teaching Reading to the Culturally Different Child, Reading Process and Success, New Zealand; The New View of Native Americans in Children's Books, The Reading Teacher. *Honours:* 1,000 Merit Award for Research and Creative Endeavor, Committee on Evaluation, Eastern Montana College, 1977; Bronze Plaque, In Recognition of Outstanding Contributions to Child's Rights and Education, Billings Committee, International Year of the Child, 1978; Outstanding Alumnus Award, Western State College of Colorado, 1979. *Memberships:* Rocky Mountain Reading Specialists Association; Council for International Co-operation in Reading Research; International Reading Association. *Address:* Eastern Montana College, Montana University System, Billings, MT 59101, USA.

GINDIN, James, b. 23 May 1926, Newark, New Jersey, USA. Professor. *Education:* BA, Yale University, 1949; MA 1950, PhD 1954 Cornell University. *Literary Appointments:* Professor of English. *Major Publications include:* Postwar British Fiction: New Accents and Attitudes, 1962; Norton Critical Edition of Thomas Hardy's The Return of the Native (editor), 1969; Harvest of a Quiet Eye: The Novel of Compassion, 1971; The English Climate: An Excursion into a Biography of John Galsworthy, 1979; John Galsworthy's Life & Art: An Alien's Fortress. 1986. *Contributor to:* Various academic journals. *Honours include:* Harvest of Quiet Eye, and alternative selection, Reader's Subscription Book Club, 1971. *Address:* 1615 Shadford Road, Ann Arbour, MI 48104, USA.

GINIGER, Kenneth Seeman, b. 18 Feb. 1919, New York City, USA. Publisher. *Education:* University of Virginia; New York Law School. *Publications:* The Compact Treasury of Inspiration, 1955; America, America, America, 1957; A Treasury of Golden Memories, 1958; What is Protestantism, 1965; A Little Treasury of Hope, 1968; A Little Treasury of Comfort, 1968; A Little Treasury of Healing, 1968; A Little Treasury of Christmas, 1968; The Sayings of Jesus, 1968; Heroes for our Times, 1969; The Family Advent Book, 1979. *Contributor to:* Variety; True; Publishers Weekly; American Weekly; New York Post; Chicago Daily News; Chicago Sun Times. *Honour:* Recipient, French Legion of Honour. *Memberships include:* PEN American Centre; Overseas Press Club of America; National Press Club, Washington; Authors Club, London. *Address:* K S Giniger Company Inc, 1133 Broadway, New York, NY 10010, USA.

GINSBURG, Mirra, b. Bobruisk, USSR. Translator; Editor; Author. *Education:* Various schools in various countries. *Literary Appointments:* Member, Translation Juries: NBA, 1974, ABA, 1982, PEN, 1984. *Publications include:* (Editor and Translator), The Fatal Egg and Other Soviet Satire, 1965, 68; The Dragon, 15 Stories by Yevgeny Zamyatin, 1966, 68, 72, 75, 76; A

Soviet Heretic: Essays of Zamyatin, 1970, 75; The Last Door to Aiya, 1968 (German, 1970); The Ultimate Threshold, 1970, 76 (Portuguese 1971), The Air of Mars, 1976 (3 anthologies of Soviet Science Fiction); Translations of works by Bulgakov, Zemyatin, Dostoyevsky and Platonov; (children's books and folk tales, Edited, Adapted, Translated) The Master of the Winds, Folk Tales from Siberia, 1970; Three Rolls and One Doughnut, Fables from Russia, 1970, 73 (Afrikaans 1976); How Wilka Went to Sea, 1975; The Twelve Clever Brothers and Other Fools, Folk Tales from Russia, 1979; Picture Books, translated, adapted and written, published in several countries. (14 books published in England, 14 in Japan (in Japanese) and others in Sweden, Denmark, France, Spain, Germany, Austria, etc.). *Honours:* Lewis Carroll Shelf Award, 1972; Guggenheim Fellowship, 1975–76; Honor List of the Austrian National Award for Books for Children. *Memberships:* PEN American Centre; The Dramatists Guild; American Association of Literary Translators. *Address:* 150 W 96th Street, New York, NY 10025, USA.

GINSBURG, Philip Eliot, b. 4 Apr. 1940, New York, New York, USA. Writer. m. Elizabeth Holsinger, 14 July 1964, Scarsdale, New York, divorced 1983, 2 sons. *Education:* BA, Cornell University; MS Journalism Columbia University Graduate School of Journalism PhD, Brown University. *Publications:* Higher Education and Political Development in the People's Republic of China, 1976; New Hampshire Political Almanac, 1980; Poisoned Blood, 1986. *Contributions to:* New Republic; Fine Woodworking; Camp Kenwod Camper. *Literary Agent:* Elizabeth Knappman. *Address:* RFD 1, Lee, NH 03857, USA.

GINTER, Maria, b. 23 Nov. 1922, Poland. Painter; Writer. m. (1) 19 Mar. 1943, (2) 26 Aug. 1946, (3) 23 Apr. 1964, 1 son. *Education:* BA, French; MA, Art. *Publications:* Life in Both Hands, 1964; Ali Baba and his 40 Adventures, 1974; Poems of Visual Linages, 1975; Galopem Na Przelaj, 1983. *Contributor to:* Amerika; Literature; Kierunkt; Scene; Mowia Wieki; Guardian; Nowa Kultura; Polish Daily News. *Address:* 555 Jericho Tpk Jericho, Long Island, NY 11753, USA.

GIOSEFFI, Daniela Dorothy, b. 12 Feb. 1941, Orange, New Jersey, USA. Writer/Poet/Novelist. Divorced, 1 daughter. *Education:* BA, English and Speech, Montclair State College, Montclair, New Jersey, USA, 1963; MFA, Speech and Drama, The Catholic University of America, Washington DC, 1965. *Literary Appointments:* Poet/Consultant, The New York State Poets-in-the-Schools Inc Program of the National Endowment on the Arts for fifteen years. *Publications:* The Great American Belly, 5 editions, 1977–80; Eggs in the Lake, 1979; Earth Dancing: Mother Nature's Oldest Rite, 1980; Various plays produced in New York City; Fiction and poetry published in many anthologies. *Contributor to:* Poetry, fiction and criticism in the magazine; The Paris Review; The Nation; Antaeus; Fiction International; Modern Poetry Studies; Choice; Chelsea; New Letters; The Library Journal; The New York Times; New American Review; Forbes; East/West journal; Ambit (England); Quadrant (Australia) The Pearl (Denmark) The London Daily Mail; American Review of Books; The Psycho-cultural Review etc. *Honours:* Award/Grant from the Creative Artists Public Service Program of The New York State Council on the Arts, in poetry and fiction, 1972 and 1977; Fellowship/residency at the Edna St Vincent Millay Colony for the Arts, 1982. *Memberships:* PEN American Center; The Poetry Society of America; The Academy of American Poets; The Writers' Guild; Executive Member and Board Member, The Writers' and Publishers' Alliance for Nuclear Disarmament. *Address:* GPO Box 197, Brooklyn Heights, New York City, NY 11202–0197, USA.

GIOSEFFI, Dorothy, b. 12 Feb. 1941, Orange, New Jersey, USA. Writer; Poet; Novelist. Reviewer. divorced. 1 daughter. *Education:* BA, Montclair State College, New Jersey, 1963; MFA, CUA, Washington, DC, 1965.

Publications: The Great American Belly Dance, Novel, 1977–79; Eggs in the Lake, Poetry, 1979; Earth Dancing: Mother Nature's Oldest Rite, non fiction, 1980. *Contributions to:* Anthologies: Contemporaries, 1972l; Rising Tides, 1973; 20th Century American Women Poets; We Become New, 1976; Seasons of Women, 1980; Options for Reading and Writing, 1985; An Introduction to Literature: Structure and Meaning, 1984. Journals including: The Journal of the Poetry Society of America; Antaeus; The Nation; Chelsea; Quadrant, Australia; Ms Magazine; USA; Contact 11. *Honours:* Grant in Poetry and Multi-Media, CAPS, New York State Council of the Arts, 1971, 77; Judge of Award, Poetry Society of America, 1981. *Memberships:* Executive Member, Writers and Publishers Alliance for Nuclear Disarmament; Poetry Society of American; PEN International. *Address:* PO Box 197, Brooklyn, NY 11202, USA.

GIRAUDIER, Antonio, Poet, Painter, Musician. *Publications:* 55 books, in English, Spanish and French; 17 musical salutes and remembrances for American and foreign composers; 34 songs composed. *Honours include:* Laureate Marguerite d'Or, France, 1960; Gold Laurel Cup and Silver Star Laurel Cup, 1978 and 1979; Golden Crown Arts and Letters, Manila, 1978; Diploma Speaker, IBC, Cambridge, England, 1979; Diploma Universal Intelligence Data Bank, Albert Einstein Academy Foundation, USA; Grand Prize of the Nations, Italy, 1983; Diploma, Lincoln Institute, Washington DC, 1985; Academician of Italy with Gold Medal. *Address:* 215 East 68th Street, New York, NY 10021, USA.

GIROUD, Francoise, b. 21 Sept. 1916, Geneva, Switzerland. Journalist. *Education:* Baccalaureat. *Publications:* Si je mens... 1971, USA, 1974; La Comedie du Pouvoir, 1977; Ce que je crois... 1978; Une femme honorable Marie Curie, 1981 (USA 1985); Le Bon Plaisir, 1983. *Contributions to:* New York Times Magazine; Le Monde, France; Corriera della Serra, Italy; Le nouvel Observateur, France. *Honours:* Honorary DHL, University of Michigan, Ann Arbor, Michigan, USA; Marie Curie prix de Litterature de l'Academie de Florence, Italy, 1984. *Literary Agent:* Max Becker, New York, USA. *Address:* 41 Boulevard de Latour Mauborg, 75007 Paris, France.

GIROUX, Joye S, b. 31 May 1930. Teacher. *Education:* BA, Ctrl. Michigan University, 1952; University of Michigan; Michigan State University; Wayne State University; Ctrl. Michigan University. *Appointments include:* Teacher, South Lake Schools, St Clair Shores, 1954–56, 1962–66; Teacher, Rapids Public Schools, 1969–. *Publications:* A Grain of Sand, No More, 1976; Where Lies the Dream, 1976; Four Women...Getting On With It, with others, 1977; The Whispering of Leaves, 1978; Draw Me a Morning or Two, 1978; Dust I Cannot Hold, 1978; Whispers Lost in Thunder, 1980; Survivor, 1981; And Who's To Pay Your Passage, 1984. *Contributor to:* Various anthologies including: Poetry of Our Time; Notable American Poets; The Lark and the Dawn; Journal of Contemporary Poets; Forty Salutes to Michigan Poets; American Poetry Fellowship Society Bi-Centennial Anthology; Convergence 1980; Golden Song, 1985, 1985; Ezra Ound Memorial Anthology, 1985; Access to Literature (a college literature text) 1981. Poetry in various journals including: Bardic Echoes; Peninsula Poets; Driftwood E; Gusto; Woods Runner; Adventures in Poetry; American Poet; Jeans's Journal; Wayside Quarterly; Wayside Poetry Forum; Kansas Quarterly. *Memberships:* President 1980–84, Poetry Society of Michigan. *Address:* 825 Cherry Avenue, Big Rapids, MI 49307, USA.

GITTINS, Rob, b. 18 Apr. 1956, Manchester, England. Writer. m. Mary Deere, 8 Mar. 1985, 1 son, 1 daughter. *Education:* BA, English, Economics; MA, English Literature; M Phil, Modern Drama. *Publications:* Rock and Roll to Paradise, 1982; Dylan Thomas: The Last Days, 1986; Dylan Thomas' Wales, 1987. *Literary Agent:* Jill Foster. *Address:* 19 Glynderi, Carmarthen, Dyfed, Wales.

GIZZI, Michael Anthony, b. 13 Feb. 1949, New York, USA. Writer. m. Barbara Tarleton Astlett, 28 Aug. 1971, Chester, Connecticut, divorced 1979, 1 daughter. *Education:* BA, MFA, Brown University. *Literary Appointments:* Union College, New York, 1984. *Publications:* Bird As, 1976; Avis, 1979; Species of Intoxication, 1983. *Contributions to:* Diana's Work-In-Progress; Action Poetique, Paris; Berkshire Sampler. *Honours:* Academy of American Poets, 1974 and 1978; Kim Ann Arstark Award, 1976. *Memberships:* Directory of American Poets; International Who's Who in Poetry; The Sphinx. *Address:* Box 1029, Stockbridge, MA 01262, USA.

GJESSING, Ketil, b. 18 Feb. 1934. Evaluator of Manuscipts. *Education:* Mag art and Cand Philos, Oslo University. *Literary Appointments:* Teacher, Atlantic College, St Donat's Castle, Llantwit Major, Glamorgan, South Wales; Programme Selector, Norwegian Broadcasting Corporation. *Publications:* Collections of Poetry: Kransen om et møote, 1962; Frostjern, 1968; Private steiner bl a, 1970; Utegaende Post, 1975; Snøoen som faller i Fjor, 1977; Bjelle, malm, 1979; Vinger, røotter, 1982; Som pila synger i flukten, 1985. Represented in Anthologies: Ti unge Studentlyrikk, 1958; Nye navn i norsk kunst, 1962; I grenselandet, 1969; Lahahure blomster blomstre, 1974. *Contributions to:* Dagbladet; Aftenposten; Vinduet; Filologen, England. *Honour:* Gyldendals legat, 1983. *Address:* Betzy Kjelsbergs V 15, Oslo 4, Norway.

GLADSTONE, Arthur M, b. 22 Sep. 1921, New York, USA. Writer. m. Helen Worth, Andover, New Jersey, 1980. *Education:* BA, Chemistry, MS, Chemistry, New York University. *Publications:* The Honourable Miss Clarendon, 1975; The Poor Relation, 1978; My Lord Rakehell, 1977; Bow Street Gentleman, 1977; Bow Street Brangle, 1977; The Young Lady from Alton-St Pancras, 1977' Miss Letty, 1977; That Savage Yenkee Squire! 1978; Lord Dedringham's Divorce, 1978; The Honorable Miss Clarendon, 1978; The Courtship of Colonel Crowne, 1978; The Awakening of Lord Dalby, 1979; Dilema in Duet, 1980; Byway To Love, 1980; Meg Miller, 1981; Lord Orlando's Protegee, 1981; The Plight of Pamela Pollworth, 1982; Dilema in Duet, 1982; Byway to Love, 1982; A Keeper for Lord Linford, 1982, and many others. *Memberships:* Authorised League; Virginia Writers Club; Entomological Society of America. *Literary Agent:* Collier Associates. *Address:* 1701 Owensville Road, Charlottesville, VA 22901, USA.

GLANVILLE, Brian Lester, b. 24 Sep. 1931. Author; Journalist. *Publications:* Along the Arno, 1956; The Bankrupts, 1958; A Bad Streak (stories), 1961; Diamond, 1962; The Rise of Gerry Logan, 1963; The Director's Wife (stories) 1963; A Second Home, 1965; The King of Hackney Marshes (stories), 1965; A Roman Marriage, 1966; The Artist Type, 1967; The Olympian, 1969; A Cry of Crickets, 1970; The Financiers, 1972; The Thing He Loves (stories), 1973; The Comic, 1974; The Dying of the Light, 1976; Never Look Back, 1980; Kissing America, 1985; Love is not Love (stories), 1985. *Contributor to:* The Sunday Times. *Literary Agent:* John Farquharson Limited. *Address:* Sunday Times, London, WC1, England.

GLASER, Michael Schmidt, b. 20 Mar. 1943, Chicago, Illinois, USA. Professor of Literature and Creative Writing. m. Kathleen Webbert, 8 May, 1976, The Ocean, USA, 3 sons, 2 daughters. *Education:* BA, Denison University, 1965; MA, Kent State University, 1966, PhD, 1971. *Appointments:* Assistant Professor, St Mary's College of Maryland, USA, 1970, Associate Professor, 1976, Professor, 1983. *Publication:* Marmalade, 1976. *Contributions:* Cottonwood Review; Christian Science Monitor; Christian Century; Poets on Poems; Eleven; Samasad; Milkwood Chronicle; Colorado North Review, etc. *Honour:* Honourable Mention, Chester Jones Prize. *Membership:* AWP, Writer's Centre. *Address:* PO Box 1, St Mary's City, MD 20686, USA.

GLASGOW, Eric, b. 10 June 1924, Leeds, Yorkshire, England. Historical Researcher. *Education:* MA, St Johns College, Cambridge University, 1948; PhD, Manchester University, 1951; Lundie Reader, St Deiniol's Library, Hawarden, 1970-. *Appointments:* School Teacher, 1954-74 (retired); Tutor, Modern British History, North West Region, Open University, 1975-78; Adjunct Consultant, Modern British History, Kensington University College, Cambridge, California, USA, 1980-; Tutor, History, National Extension College, Cambridge, England, 1984-. *Contributions to:* Spring Anthology, 1971-73; Treasury of Modern Poets, 1973; History; Contemporary Review; Postal History International; Greek Gazette; Postal Historty Bulletin; Salzburg Studies in English Literature; Reader's Encyclopedia of English Literature; Victorian Institute Journal, University oif East Carolina, USA, 1985-. *Honours:* Melville Cup, National Philatelic Society, London. 1951-52. *Address:* Flat 37, Clairville, 21 Lulworth Road, Birkdale, Southport, Merseyside PR8 2BG, England.

GLASSER, Selma L, b. New York. Freelance Writer. Widow, 1 son, 1 daughter. *Publications:* Analogy Anthology, 1973-; The Complete Guide to Prize Contests, Sweepstakes & How to Win Them, 1980; Prize Winning Recipes, 1984. *Contributions to:* Numerous journals, including, The Writer; Prizewinner; Golden Chances; Reader's Digest. *Memberships:* Brooklyn Writers' Club; California Writers' Club. *Literary Agent:* Allan Lang. *Address:* 10240 Camarillo Street, Suite #210 Toluca Lake, CA 91602, USA.

GLASSMAN, Ronald M, b. 6 Jan. 1937, Brooklyn, New York, USA. Professor of Sociology. m. Urania Glassman, 10 Jan. 1972, New York City, USA, 2 sons. *Education:* BA, Queen's College, New York City; MA, Ohio State University; PhD, New School for Social Research, New York City. *Major Publications:* The Political History of Latin America, 1969; (edited with A J Vidich) Conflict & Control: The Challenge to Legitimacy of Modern Governments, 1979; (edited with V Muruar) The Political Sociology of Max Weber, 1983; (edited with R J Antonio) A Max Weber Dialogue, 1984. Democracy and Despotism in Primitive Society, 1985; (edited with W Swatus), Charisma & Social Structure, 1985; The New Middle Class & Democracy, 1986; Bureaucracy Against Democracy & Socialism, 1986. *Contributor to:* Social Research; Conflict & Control. *Honour:* Ford Foundation Grant, Venezuela, 1965. *Memberships:* American Sociological Association, President, Section on History of Sociology; Convenor, Max Weber Colloquium. *Address:* 372 Central Park West apt 4c, New York, NY 10025, USA.

GLÜCK, Robert, b. 2 Feb. 1947, Cleveland, Ohio, USA. Writer, Teacher. *Education:* BA, University of California at Berkeley; MA, San Francisco State University. *Literary Appointments:* Writer-in Residence, Small Press Traffic Literary Resource Centre in San Francisco, Funded by National Endowment for the Arts 1977-79, California Arts Council 1979-85; Assistant Director of Poetry Centre, San Francisco, State University, 1985-. *Major Publications:* Andy, 1973; Family Poems, 1979; La Fontaine (with B Boose), 1982; Elements of a Coffee Service, 1982; Jack the Modernist, 1985. *Contributor to:* Numerous Journals & Literary Magazines, including: Poetics Journal; Ironwood; The Advocate; New Directions Anthology; Writing/Talks Anthology; and others. *Honours:* Browning Prize 1972; Academy of American Poets Award, 1973. *Membership:* National Writers Union. *Address:* 16 Clipper Street, San Francisco, CA 94114, USA.

GLEASNER, Diana Cottle, b. 26 Apr. 1936, New Brunswick, New Jersey, USA. Writer. m. G William Gleasner, 12 July 1958, Highland Park, New Jersey, 1 son, 1 daughter. *Education:* BA, Ohio Wesleyan University; MA, State University of New York, Buffalo. *Publications:* Hawaiian Gardens, 1978; Kauai Traveler's Guide, 1978; Oahu Traveler's Guide, 1978; Big Island Traveler's Guide, 1978; Maui Traveler's Guide, 1978; Breakthrough: Women in Writing, 1980; Illustrated

Dictionary of Surfing, Swimming and Diving, 1980; Sea Islands of the South, 1980; Rock Climbing, 1980; Inventions That Changed Our Lives: Dynamite, 1982; Charlotte: A Touch of Gold, 1983; Breakthrough: Women in Science, 1983; Inventions that Changed Our Lives: The Movies, 1983; Windsurfing, 1985. *Contributions to:* Over 1000 articles in publications including: Good Housekeeping; Field and Stream; Travel/Holiday; New Woman; Boating; Argosy; Better Homes and Gardens; Jack and Jill; Exploring; American Airlines Inflight Magazine. *Memberships:* American Society of Journalists and Authors; Society of American Travel Writers; Outdoor Writers Association of America; Women in Communications. *Address:* 132 Holly Court, Denver, NC 28037, USA.

GLENN, Edmund S, b. 12 Apr. 1915, Poland. University Professor. m. Marjorie Rugg, 10 Jan. 1946, Washington, District of Columbia, USA, 2 sons, 2 daughters. *Education:* PhD equivalent, based on research. *Literary Appointments:* Professor emeritus, Council for International Understanding, University of Delaware. *Publications:* Man and Mankind, Conflicts and Communication Between Cultures, 1981. *Contributions to:* ETC; Journal of Communication; Semiotica; Communication and Cognition; Language; Word, and others. *Honours:* Saxton Memorial Fellowship, 1946; Social Science Faculty Fellowship, 1960; Brookings Federal Executive Fellowship, 1967. *Address:* 8 The Horseshoe, Newark, DE 19711, USA.

GLOAG, Julian, b. 2 July 1930, London, England. Novelist. 1 son, 1 daughter. *Education:* Exhibition, BA 1953, MA 1959, Magdalene College, Cambridge. *Publications:* Our Mother's House, 1963; A Sentence of Life, 1966; Maundy, 1969; A Woman of Character, 1973; Sleeping Dogs Lie, 1980; Lost and Found, 1981; Blood For Blood, 1985. *Memberships:* Fellow, Royal Society of Literature; Authors Guild. *Literary Agent:* Georges Borchardt Inc, New York, USA; Richard Scott Simon Limited, London; Michelle Lapautre, Paris. *Address:* c/o Richard Scott Simon Limited, 32 College Cross, London N1 1PR, England.

GLOVER, Judith Mary, b. 31 Mar. 1943, Penn, Staffordshire, England. Author. *Major Publications:* The Place-names of Sussex, 1975; The Place-names of Kent, 1976; Drink Your Own Garden, 1979; The Stallion Man, 1982; Sisters & Brothers, 1984; To Everything a Season, 1986. *Literary Agent:* Leslie Gardner. *Address:* Mount Sion, Tunbridge Wells, Kent, TN1 1TN, England.

GLÜCK, Louise Elisabeth, b. 22 Apr. 1943, New York, USA. Writer. m. John Dranow, 1 Jan. 1977, Cabot, Vermont, USA, 1 son. *Literary Appointments:* Visiting Lecturer, Goddard College, University of North Carolina, University of Virginia; Visiting Professor, University of Iowa; Elliston Professor, University of Cincinnati; Visiting Professor, Columbia University; Holloway Lecturer, University of California at Berkeley; Visiting Professor, University of California at Davis; Also University of California at Irvine; Scott Professor, Williams College; Faculty & Board Member, MFA Program, Warren Wilson College. *Major Publications:* Firstborn, 1968; The House on Marshland, 1975; Descending Figure, 1980; The Triumph of Achilles, 1985. *Honours:* Rockefeller Foundation Grant, 1968–69; National Endowment for the Arts Fellowship, 1969–70, 1979–80; Eunice Tietjena Prize, Poetry Magazine, 1971; Guggenheim Foundation Fellowship, 1975–76; American Academy & Institute of Arts & Letters, Award in Literature, 1981. *Address:* Creamery Road, Plainfield, VT 05667, USA.

GLYN, Anthony, b. 13 Mar. 1922, London, England. Author. *Publications:* Romanza, 1953; The Jungle of Eden, 1954; Elinor Glyn, a biography, 1955; The Ram in the Thicket, 1957; I Can Take it All, 1959; Kick Turn, 1963; The Terminal, 1965; The Seine, 1966; The Dragon Variation, 1969; The British Portrait of a People, 1970; The Companion Guide to Paris, 1985; work translated into French, Spanish, Dutch, Japanese, Finnish, Swedish, Italian. *Contributor to:* Times;

Spectator; Listener; Musical Times; Truth; Saturday Book. *Honours:* Book Society Choice, 1955, 1959; Dollar Book Club Choice, 1958; TV Play Prize, ITV, 1960. *Agent:* A M Heath & Co. *Address:* 13 rue le Regrattier, Paris 75004, France.

GLYN JONES, Kenneth, b. 13 Nov. 1915, New Tredegar, Wales. Air Navigator m. Brenda Margaret Thomas, 8 June 1969, Bracknell, Berkshire, England. *Education:* Royal Air Force Staff Navigation School, 1944; Civil Aviation Flight Navigator's Licence, 1946. *Publications:* 2 Science Survey broadcasts on BBC, 1950; Messier's Nebulae and Star Clusters, 1968; The Search for the Nebulae, 1975; The Webb Society Deep Sky Observer's Handbook, (editor), 5 volumes 1979–82. *Contributions to:* British Astronomical Association Journal; Journal for the History of Astronomy; The Aeroplane, 1950; Editor, The Webb Society Quarterly Journal. *Membership:* President, The Webb Society, 1967–. *Address:* Wild Rose, Church Road, Winkfield, Windsor, Berkshire SL4 4SF, England.

GOBAR, Ash, b. 7 Apr. 1930, Poti, Georgia, USSR. Author, Professor of Philosophy. *Education:* AB, College of Wooster, 1952; PhD, University of Wisconsin, 1959; Fellow, University of Geneva, Switzerland, 1960. *Major Publications:* Philosophic Foundations of Genetic/Gestalt Psychology, 1968; Integral Philosophy, Kosmos Island (forthcoming); A Lamp in the Forest, 1982; Modern Concepts in Philosophy (forthcoming). *Contributor to:* (essays) Proceedings of the American Philosophical Society; Philosophy Today; Studies in Soviet Thought; Philosophical Studies; Philosophical Inquiry; Dialectics; Critica. *Memberships:* American Philosophical Association; History of Science Society; World Congress of Philosophy. *Honours:* Recipient of several awards. *Literary Agent:* Anita Gobar. *Address:* Route 1, Lawrenceburg, KY 40342, USA.

GODDARD, Hazel Idella Firth, b. 12 Dec. 1911, Jordan Ferry, Novia Scotia, Canada. School Teacher; Secretary; Nurse/Aid. m. Roland Bernard Goddard, 8 July 1930, Shelburne, Nova Scotia, 1 son. *Education:* Business School, Canada. *Publications:* Prisms in Print, 1966; Hazel Bough, 1972; Chestnuts and Autumn Leaves, 1980; Scattered Stars, 1984. *Contributor to:* Canadian Poets and Friends; Amber; Marsh and Maple; Harbour Lights; Prophetic Voices; Our World's Best Beloved Poems; The Poet; Parnassus; Quickenings; Poet's Study Club; Haiku Column in Mainichi Daily News, Tokyo, Japan. *Honours:* 6 Honourable Mentions in World of Poetry and Golden Poet Award; Honourable Mention, Kentucky State Contest, 1985; First Prize and Golden Poet Award; Honorable Mention, Kentucky State Contest, 1985; First Prize Haiku and Second Prize Sonnet in International Poetry Contest, Canadian Authors Association, Alberta, 1985. *Memberships:* Canadian Authors Association; Scotian Pen Guild, President, Editor; Poet's Study Club, Terre Haute, Indiana, USA. *Address:* 404 40 Rose Street, Dartmouth, Nova Scotia, Canada B3A 2T6.

GODDEN, Geoffrey Arthur, b. 2 Feb. 1929, Worthing, West Sussex, England. Antique Dealer in Porcelain. m. Jean Magness, 29 Aug. 1964, Worthing, 1 son. *Publications:* Encyclopedia of British Pottery and Porcelain Marks, 1964; English China, 1984; Author of some further 25 titles relating mainly to British pottery and porcelain. *Contributions:* Most antique collecting magazines and learned journals. *Address:* 19a Crescent Road, Worthing, West Sussex, England.

GODEL, Vahe, b. 16 Aug. 1931, Geneva, Switzerland. 2 sons, 2 daughters. Teacher of French. *Education:* Arts Degree, University of Geneva, Switzerland. *Publications include:* Signes particuliers, 1969; Cendres Drulantes, 1970; L'oeil etant la fenetre de l'ame, 1972; Coupes sombres, 1974; Lac(i)s, 1974; Poussieres, 1977; Voies d'eau, 1977; Du meme desert a la meme nuit, 1978; Obscures besognes, 1979; Papiers d'armenie, 1979; Qui Parle? que voyez-vous?, 1982; Faits et gestes, 1983; L'heure d'or, 1985; Les frontieres naturelles, 1986. *Contributor to:* Cahiers du Sud; Europe; Esprit;

Courrier due Ctr. Int. d'Etudes poetiques; POESIE, L'VII: Encres Vives; Entailles; Gradiva; Journal des Poetes; Journal de Geneve; Revue de Belles-Lettres: Ecriture; VWA Reperes; Construire; POESIE I; Armenia; etc. *Honour:* Prix Schiller, 1982. *Memberships:* Olten Group SCAM (Paris); Correspondent, International Center of Poetic Studies (Brussels). *Address:* 25 ave. des Cavaliers, 1224 Chene-Bougeries/Geneva, Switzerland.

GODFREY, Laurie Ann (Rohde), b. 27 Aug. 1945, New York City, USA. Biological Anthropologist – University Professor. m. Paul Joseph Godfrey, 15 June 1968, Brookline, Massachusetts, 1 son, 1 daughter. *Education:* BA Biology/Geology, Tufts University, 1967; MA 1969, PhD 1977, Anthropology, Harvard University. *Publications:* Scientists Confront Creationism (edited with WW Norton), 1983; What Darwin Began, editor, 1985. *Contributions to:* Natural History; The Skeptical Inquirer; Journal of Human Evolution; American Journal of Physical Anthropology; Current Anthropology; American Anthropologist. *Honours:* Honorary Fellow, American Association of University Women, 1983–84; Mary Ingraham Bunting Science Scholar, 1983–85; University of Massachusetts' Presidential Writers' Award, 1985. *Address:* Department of Anthropology, Machmer Hall, University of Massachusetts at Amherst, Amherst, MA 01003, USA.

GODFREY, Peter, b. 8 Sep. 1918, Vereeniging, Republic of South Africa. Author. m. Nina Cowan, Johannesburg, 2 sons. *Education:* BA, Witwatersrand University; Literature and Psychology, University of South Africa. *Publications include:* Death Under The Table, 1954; Four O'Clock Noon, play, 1959; Various radio, television and screen plays: Over 2000 short stories; Anthologies: The Queen's Awards – 5th Series; South African Saturday Book; 4th Mystery Bedside Book; Creasey Mystery Bedside Books, 1972, 1974 and 1976; Worse Verse; John Creasey Crime Collection, 6 editions 1978 to 1984; I Witness, 1978; Best Detective Stories of the Year, 1978 and 1979; Ellery Queen's Scenes of the Crime, 1979; Year's Best Mystery and Suspense Stories, 1983; Ellery Queen's Memorable Characters, 1984; The Deadly Arts, 1985. *Honours:* Ellery Queen Short Story Awards, 1948, 1949 and 1953. *Memberships:* Several professional organisations. *Address:* 62 Richmond Hill Court, Richmond, Surrey TW10 6BE, England.

GODMAN, Arthur, b. 10 Oct. 1916, Hereford, England. Author. *Education:* BSc Honours, Chemistry, University College, University of London; Diploma in Education, Institute of Education, London University. *Publications:* Health Science for the Tropics, 1962; Chemistry a New Certificate Approach, 1969; Additional Mathematics, 1971; Physical Science, 1972; Human and Social Biology, 1973; Longman Dictionary of Scientific Usage, 1979; Longman Illustrated Science Dictionary, 1981; Longman Illustrated Dictionary of Chemistry, 1982; Colour-Coded Guide to Microcomputers, 1983; Thesaurus of Computer Science, 1984. *Contributions to:* Hong Kong Council for Educational Research; Overseas Education. *Honour:* Honorary Research Fellow, Department of South East Asian Studies, Eliot College, University of Kent. *Memberships:* Royal Chemical Society; Royal Asiatic Society (Fellow); Society of Authors. *Address:* Sondes House, Patrixbourne, Canterbury, Kent CT4 5DD, England.

GOEBEL-SCHILLING, Gerhard, b. 20 July 1932, Berlin, Germany. Professor of Romance Philology. *Education:* Dr Phil, Romance & English Philology, Berlin, 1965; Venia Legendi, Romance Philology & Comparative Literature, 1970. m. Silke Schilling, 23 Sep. 1981. *Major Publications:* Poeta Faber: Erdictete Architektur in der italienischen, spanischen und französischen Literatur der Renaissance und des Barock, 1971. *Contributor to:* Asthetick und Kommunikation; Alternative; GRM; Lendermains; Lettres Nouvelles; Romanische Forschungen;

Romanistisches Jahrbuch. *Address:* J W von Goethe Universität, Romanisches Seminar, Gräfatraße 76, D–6000 Frankfurt/Main, Federal Republic of Germany.

GOEDICKE, Patricia, b. 21 June 1931, Boston, Massachusetts, USA. Poet. m. Leonard Wallace Robinson, 3 June 1971, San Miguel Allende, Mexico. *Education:* BA, Middlebury College, 1953; MA, Ohio University, 1965. *Literary Appointments:* Editorial Secretary, Harcourt, Brace and World Inc, 1953–54; Editorial Assistant, T U Crowell Co 1955–56; Lecturer in English, Ohio University, 1963–68; Lecturer in English, Hunter College, 1969–71; Associate Professor, Creative Writing, Institute Allende, 1972–79; Visiting Writer-in-Residence, Kalamazoo College, 1977; Guest Faculty, Writing Program, Sarah Lawrence College, 1980; Visiting Poet-in-Residence, 1981–82, 1982–83, Associate Professor, Creative Writing, 1983–, University of Montana. *Publications:* Between Oceans, 1968; For the Four Corners, 1976; The Trail that Turns on Itself, 1978; The Dog that was Barking Yesterday, 1980; Crossing the Same River, 1980; The King of Childhood, 1984; The Wind of Our Going, 1985. *Contributions to:* New Yorker; Hudson Review; Poetry; The Nation; The American Poetry Review; Ploughshares; Paris Review; The New Republic; Agai Review; New England Review; Dowa Review; Canyon Review; New Letters; Missouri Review; Virginia Quarterly Review; Poetry Northwest; Tar River Review; North American Review; etc. *Honours:* COLM Prize, 1976; NEA Creative Writing Fellowship, 1976; William Carbon Williams Prize, New Letters, 1977; Pushcart Prize II Anthology, 1977–78. *Memberships:* PEN; Poetry Society of America; AWP; Academy of American Poetry. *Address:* 310 McLeod, Missoula, MT 59801, USA.

GOELDLIN, Michel, b. 3 Aug. 1934, Lausanne, Switzerland. Novelist. m. Yucki, 1 son, 1 daughter. *Publications:* Les Sentiers Obliques, 1972; Le Vent Meurt à Midi, 1976; Juliette Crucifieé, 1977, Radio; A l'Ouest de Lake Placid, 1979; Les Desemparés, 1982; Les Moissons du Désert, 1984; 60 Photos romanesques, with Yucki, 1985; L'Espace d'un Homme, part 1, 1986. *Memberships:* Société Suisse des Ecrivains; Pro Litteris. *Literary Agent:* P & P Fritz, Zurich, Switzerland. *Address:* c/o Editions de l'Aire, POB, CH–1000 Lausanne 21, Switzerland.

GOKAK, Vinayak, b. 10 Aug. 1909. Teacher; Educator. *Education:* MA, Bombay University, India, 1931; MA, Oxford University, 1938, DLitt, h c, Karnatak University, India, 1967. *Appointments include:* Principle Professor, English, Karnataka, Maharashtra, Gujaratg and Andhra Colleges, 1931–58; Director, Central Institute of English, 1959–66; Director, Indian Institute of Advanced Study, Simla, 1970–71; Vice Chancellor, Bangalore University, 1966–69; Vice Chancellor, Shri Sathya Sai Institute of Higher Learning, 1981–85. *Publications:* The Song of Life, 1948; In Life's Temple, 1965; Toleridge's Aesthetics, 1975; An Integral View of Poetry, 1975; Kashmir and the Blind Man, 1977; The Concept of Indian Writing, 1979; 20 Collections of Poems. *Contributor to:* Mother India; Verse Today; Commonwealth Journal; Literature Today. *Honours include:* Academie of India Award for Dyara-Prithui, 1961; Padma Sri, President of India, 1961; Various other literary awards. *Memberships include:* Chairman, Jnanprith Selection Board for Highest Indian Literary Award, 1978–81; Vice Chairman, National Akademi of Letters, India, 1978–82, Chairman, 1981. *Address:* Lake Raburn Road, Box 7, Lakemont, GA 30552, USA.

GOLD, Geoffrey Maurice, b. 5 Aug. 1950, London, England. Book & Magazine Publisher. m. Louise Naomi, 28 Jan. 1973, Adelaide, Australia, 2 sons. *Publications:* China Through Australian Eyes, 1974; Eureka-Rebellion Beneath the Southern Cross, 1977; Home Video in Australia, 1982. *Contributor to:* Nation Review; Video & Cinema; Video Business; Music Business; Fiji Video Today; A-Z Music; Score Magazine; Video & Communications; The Australian. *Address:* 9 Paran Place, Glen Iris, Victoria 3146, Australia.

GOLD, Jordan Jay, b. 31 Mar. 1957, Chicago, Illinois, USA. Writer. m. Fara Lynée Miller, Dallas, Texas, 15 Sep. 1984. *Education:* BSc, Technical Careers, ASc, Electronics Technology, Southern Illinois University, 1980. *Literary Appointments:* Contributing editor, Audio-Video. International, 1980–84; Computer Merchandising 1982–85; Senior editor Microsystems, Computer Decisions, current. *Publication:* The Word Perfect Workbook, Wordware Publishing & Prentice-Hall, 1984. *Contributions to:* Audio Digest; Consumer Electronics Monthly; PC Consumer; Personal Computing; Soft Side; Vegetarian Times, Video Retailing. *Memberships:* National Writers Club (professional); Computer Press Association; Past member, Society of Technical Communication. *Address:* 4409 Amherst Lane, Grand Prairie, TX 75052, USA.

GOLDBERG, Barry, b. 27 Dec. 1942, New York City, USA. Writer. m. Linda, 2 Feb. 1978, Congers, New York, USA, 2 daughters. *Education:* Diploma in Journalism, Defence Information School, 1966; BA, History, City College of New York, 1969. *Appointment:* Editor, Journal, Jack Anderson Scholarship Fund. *Contributions:* Numerous reports on convention seminars and articles in the Journal of the New York State School Boards Association; Why the Budget Goes Up Though Enrollment Goes Down, in School Budgeting: Problems and Solutions, 1982 (award-winning article). *Honours include:* Distinguished Achievement Award, EDPRESS, 1980, 1981, 1984; awards for Overall Graphics and Design, Budget Report, EDPRESS, 1980, 1982, 1983, 1984, 1985; Award of Honour, special purpose community newsletter, A Fact Sheet, NYSPRA,, 1984; Award of Merit, internal publication, Chalk Talk, NYSPRA, 1984; Award of Honour, special purpose publication, East Ramapo Update, NYSPRA, 1985; Award of Merit, community newsletter, East Ramapo Report, NSPRA, 1985. *Memberships:* National School Public Relations Association, 1978–; New York School Public Relations Association, 1978–, (president 1981–82, editor, NYSPRA News, 1981–83; Rockland School Public Relations Association (founder, 1980, president, 1980–82); Educational Press of America, 1978–; New York State Parents-Teachers Association, honorary life member for distinguished volunteer service, 1983. *Address:* 139 Massachussetts Avenue, Congers, NY 10920, USA.

GOLDENTHAL, Jolene Bleich, b. Boston, Massachusetts, USA. Playwright, Art Critic. m. Carol Goldenthal, 2 sons. *Education:* AB, Smith College; MA, Trinity College, Hartford, Connecticut. *Literary Appointments:* Art Critic, West Hertford News, 1966–70; Art Critic Hartford Courant, 1970–80. *Major Publications:* Prize Winning Plays: A Stranger in a Strange Land, 1977; The Station, 1978; Mequasset By The Sea, 1983; Gallery, 1984; Rachel's Gifts, 1984. *Contributor to:* Antiques World; Sunday Magazine; Trinity Reporter; National Antiques Review; and others. *Honours:* Various competitive awards for drama scripts. *Memberships:* Dramatists' Guild; New England Theatre Conference; Stage Source; Women in Communications, Inc. *Address:* 132 Jefferson Street, Hartford, CT 06106, USA.

GOLDKORN, Isaac, b. 1 Oct. 1911, Szydlowiec, Poland. Writer (Essays, Literary Criticism, Epigrams, Parables). m. Irene, Toronto, 29 Mar. 1969, 1 son. *Education:* Hebrew Religious Schools. *Literary Appointments:* Reporter, Unzer Express, Warsaw, 1939; Staff writer, Bafreiung, Munich, 1947–50; Editor, Unzer Heint, Munich 1951, Widerstand, Montreal 1957–59, Israelite Press, Winnipeg 1960–64; News editor, Keneder Adler, Montreal, 1965; Staff writer, Jewish Daily Forward, New York, 1967–77. *Major Publications:* Nokturns, 1938; Literarishe Siluetn, 1949; Lieder, 1950; Epigramatish, 1954; Fun Weltkval, 1963; Lodzher Portretn, 1963; Zingers un Zoggers, 1971; Heimishe un Fremde, 1973; Mesholim, 1975; Farkishefter Yarid, 1976; Yellow Letters – Green Memories, 1978; Kurtz un Sharf, 1981; Letzter Shnit, 1984. Various anthologies, English & Yiddish. *Contributions to:* Os Neier Folksblat,

Lodz; Bafreiung, Neivelt, Unzer Weg, Shriftn, Munich; Zein, Oifsnei, Freie Arbeter Stimme, Zukunft, Unzer Tsait, New York; Unzer Weg, Mexico; Keneder Adler, Montrealer Heftn, Widerstand, Montreal; Writer's Lifeline, Kornwall, Ontario; Jewish Standard, Toronto; Yiddishe Post, Melbourne; Dorem Afrike, Johannes-burg; Cross-Canada Writers' Quarterly; and others. *Honour:* Jacob Glatstein Award, Congress for Jewish Culture, New York 1976. *Memberships:* Jewish Writers Union, Munich, 1948–50 (Secretary); Yiddish PEN Club, New York; International Academy of Poets, Cambridge, UK. *Address:* 3300 Don Mills Road, No. 1401, Willowdale, Ontario, Canada M2J 4X7.

GOLDMAN, Bernard, b. 30 May 1922, Toronto, Canada. Professor of Art History. m. 1 Aug. 1943, Colorado, 1 son, 1 daughter. *Education:* PhD. Ex-Director, Wayne State University Press; Editor, Bulletin of the Asia Institute. *Publications:* The Sacred Portal, 1966; Reading and Writing in the Arts, 1972, 78. *Contributions to:* American Journal of Archaeology; Berytus; Journal of Aesthetics and Art Criticism; Journal of Near Eastern Studies; Jahrbuch fuer ethnographische und praehistorische Kunst; East and West; Natural History; Ars Orientalis; Iranica Antique, Studia Iranica; The Etruscans; Catholic Encyclopaedia; Encyclopaedia Judaica. *Membership:* Phi Beta Kappa. *Address:* 6239 Eastmoor, Birmingham, MI 48202, USA.

GOLDMAN, Bo, b. 10 Sep. 1932, New York City, USA. Screenwriter. m. Mab Ashforth, 2 Jan. 1954, New York City, 2 sons, 4 daughters. *Education:* Diploma, Phillips Exeter Academy; AB, Princeton University. *Publications:* Co-Author: Screenplay, One Flew Over the Cuckoo's Nest, 1975; The Rose, 1979; Author: Melvin and Howard, 1980; Shoot the Moon, 1981. *Honours:* Academy Awards, Best Screenplay based on material from another medium, 1976, Best Original Screenplay, 1981; New York Film Critics Awards, Best Screenplay. *Membership:* Academy of Motion Picture Arts and Sciences. *Literary Agent:* International Creative Management. *Address:* c/o James Wiatt, ICM, 8899 Beverly Blvd, Los Angeles, CA 90048, USA.

GOLDMAN, Howard Hirsch, b. 20 Mar. 1949, Detroit, Michigan, USA. Psychiatrist. m. Debra Ann Josefchak, 31 July 1976, Cambridge, Massachusetts, 1 son, 1 daughter. *Education:* BA, Brandeis University, 1970; MD, Harvard Medical School, 1974; MPH, Harvard School of Public Health, 1974; PhD, Brandeis University, Heller School, 1978. *Appointments:* Research Psychiatrist, National Institute of Mental Health, 1978–80; Assistant Professor, of Psychiatry, University of California, San Francisco, 1980–83; Associate Professor of Psychiatry, University of California, San Francisco, 1983–85; Assistant Director, National Institute of Mental Health, 1983–85; Associate Professor of Psychiatry, University of Maryland, Baltimore, 1985–; Director of Mental Health Policy Studies. *Publications:* Enduring Assylum (with J P Morrissey, L V Klerman, etal), 1980; The Chronically Mentally Ill (with R C Tessler), 1982; Editor, Review of General Pshychiatry, 1984. *Contributions:* 50 articles, editorials, book chapters on epidemiology and mental health services research to professional publications. *Address:* 10600 Trotters Trail, Potomac, MD 20854, USA.

GOLDMAN, James A, b. 30 June 1927, Chicago, USA. Playwright; Screenwriter; Novelist; Lyricist. m. (1) 1962, divorced 1972, (2) 1975. *Education:* PhB, 1947, MA, 1950, University of Chicago; Post-graduate, Columbia University, New York, 1950–52; US Army, 1952–54. *Publications:* (Plays) They Might Be Giants, 1961; Blood, Sweat and Stanley Poole, 1961, with William Goldman; The Lion in Winter, 1966; (Musicals) A Family Affair, with William Goldman, music by John Kander, 1962; Follies, music by Stephen Sondheim, 1972; (Novels) Waldorf, 1965; The Man from Greek and Roman, 1974; Myself as Witness, 1980; (Screenplays) The Lion in Winter, 1968; They Might Be Giants, 1970; Nicholas and Alexandra, 1971; Robin and Marian, 1976; White Nights, with Eric Hughes, 1985;

(TV) Evening Primrose, 1967; Oliver Twist, 1982; Anna Karenina, 1985. *Contributor to:* Food & Wine Magazine; Penthouse; Harpers Bazaar; Dramatics; Chicago Tribune Book World; Atlantic Monthly. *Honours:* Motion Pictures Academy of Arts & Sciences (Oscar), 1968; American Screenwriters Award, 1968; British Screenwriters Award, 1969, All for the Lion in Winter; Drama Critics Awards, Best Musical, Follies, 1972; Tony Award, Best Musical, Follies, 1972; WGA Nomination, Best Teleplay, CBS, Oliver Twist, 1983. *Memberships include:* Dramatist Guild, Council Member, 1966–; Author's League of America, Council Member, 1966–; French Academy of Playwrights; National Academy of Recording Artists; PEN; Explorer's Club, Fellow; etc. *Address:* C/o Sam Cohn, International Creative Management, 40 West 37th Street 18th Floor, New York, NY 10019, USA.

GOLDSCHMIDT, Hermann Levin, b. 11 Apr. 1914, Berlin, Germany. Author. m. Mary Bollag, 6 Apr. 1962, Zürich, Switzerland. *Education:* PhD Professor, h c. *Publications include:* Der Geist der Erziehung bei Jeremias Gotthelf, 1939; Der Nihilismus im Licht einer kritischen Philosophie, 1941; Philosophie als Dialogik, 1948; Das Vermächtnis des deutschen Judentums, 1957, 3rd expanded edition, 1965; Dialogik, Philosophie auf dem Boden der Neuzeit, 1964; Abschied von Martin Buber, 1966; Filosofia come Dialogica, 1970; Freiheit fur den Widerspruch, 1976; Pestalozzis unvollendete Revolution, 1977; Haltet euch an Worte: Betrachtungen zur Sprache, 1977; Selbstentfaltung und Selbstanalyse, 1980; Jüdisches Ja zur Zukunft der Welt. Eine Schweizerische Dokumentation eigener Mitwirkung seit 1938, 1981; Weg und Weisung des Alten Lehrers, 1982, 2nd edition, 1985; *Contributions to:* Numerous articles in field of philosophy and religous history. *Honours:* Erster Leo Baeck Preis des Zentralrats der Juden in Deutschland, 1957. *Membership:* Schweizerischer Schriftsteller-Verband. *Address:* Balgriststrasse 9, CH–8008 Zürich, Switzerland.

GOLDSTEIN, Laurence Alan, b. 5 Jan. 1943, Los Angeles, California, USA. Professor of English. m. Nancy Copeland, 28 Apr. 1968, Providence, Rhode Island, 2 sons. *Education:* BA, University of California, 1965; PhD, Brown University, 1970. *Literary Appointments:* University of Michigan, 1970–; Editor, Michigan Quarterly Review, 1977–. *Publications:* Ruins and Empire: The Evolution of a Theme in Augustan and Romantic Literature, 1977; Altamira, 1978; The Flying Machine and Modern Literature, 1985. *Contributions to:* Essays: ELH; JEGP; Iowa Review; Centennial Review; Parnassus; Prospects. Fiction: Sewanee Review; Iowa Review. Poetry: Poetry; Ploughshares; Ontario Review; Southern Review; MSS. *Address:* Department of English, University of Michigan, Ann Arbor, MI 48109, USA.

GOLDSWORTHY, Graeme, b. 7 Sep. 1934, Sydney, New South Wales, Australia. Minister of Religion. m. Miriam Heideman, 19 Dec. 1964, Sydney, 2 sons, 2 daughters. *Education:* BA, Sydney; ThL, Australian College of Theology; BD, London; MA, Cambridge; ThM, PhD, Union Theological Seminary, Virginia, USA. *Publications:* Gospel and Kingdom, 1981; The Gospel in Revelation, 1984 (Published as, The Lamb and the Lion, USA, 1984). *Contributions to:* Present Truth; Verdict; Journal of Christian Education. *Address:* 47 Ferol Street, Coorparoo, Qld 4151, Australia.

GOLIN, Milton b. 2 Apr. 1921, Oak Park, Illinois, USA. Editor; Writer. m. Carol Brierly, 12 Dec. 1975, Northbrook, Illinois, 2 sons, 1 daughter. *Education:* Wright City College; Roosevelt College, Chicago. *Literary Appointments:* Assistant Editor, Radio and TV, City News Bureau of Chicago; Assistant Editor, Journal of American Medical Association; Editor, Medicolegal Digest; Editor, Publisher: Medicine at Work; Ob-Syn News; Pediatric News; Diagnosis News; Adolescent Medicine; Medical Group News; Computers and Medicine; Surgery Update. *Publication:* Business Side of Medical Practice, 1958. *Contributions to:* Readers

Digest; Saturday Evening Post; Today's Health; Journal of American Medical Association; Mechanix Illustrated; Mademoiselle; Changing Times; Best Articles and Stories; Catholic Digest; American Medical News; Prism, etc; Over 200 articles in national periodicals. *Honour:* Editor and Publisher, America's First regional broadcast news service, 1955. *Memberships:* Sigma Delta Chi; National Association of Science Writers; American Society of Journalists and Authors (Chairman, Washington, DC Chapter); American Medical Writers Association. *Address:* 168 Indian Tree Drive, Highland Park, IL 60035, USA.

GOMBRICH, Sir Ernst (Hans Josef), b. 30 Mar. 1909, Vienna, Austria. Professor. *Education:* PhD, University of Vienna, Fellow of the British Academy, 1960; Fellow, Society of Arts, 1961. *Major Publications include:* The Story of Art, 1950, 12th edition 1972; Art & Illusion, 1960; Aby Warburg (biography), 1970; The Sense of Order, 1979; Das Österreichische Ehrenzeilen für Wissenschaft und Kunst, 1975. *Contributor to:* Learned journals. *Honours include:* CBE, 1966; Knight, 1972; Pour le Mérite, 1977; W H Smith Literary Award, 1964; Erasmus Prize, 1975; numerous honorary doctorates. *Memberships include:* Trustee, British Museum, 1974–79; Member, Standing Committee on Museums & Galleries, 1976–83; Foreign Honorary Member, American Academy of Arts & Sciences, 1964. *Address:* 19 Briardale Gardens, London NW3, England.

GOMERY, John Douglas, b. 5 Apr. 1945, New York City, USA. University Professor. m. Marilyn L Moon, 13 Jan. 1973. *Education:* BS, Economics, cum laude, Lehigh University, Bethlehem, Pennsylvania, USA, 1967; MA, Economics, 1970, PhD, Communication Arts, 1975, University of Wisconsin, USA. *Literary Appointments:* Assistant Professor, Milwaukee, 1974–80, Visiting Professor, Communication Arts, Madison, 1977, University of Wisconsin; Visiting Professor, Radio Televison Film, School of Speech, Northwestern University, 1981; Associate Professor, Mass Communication, University of Wisconsin, Milwaukee, 1980–81; Visiting Professor, Mass Communication, Theatre Arts, University of Iowa, 1982; Associate Professor, Communication Arts and Theatre, University of Maryland, 1981–. *Publications:* The Hollywood Studio System, 1986; Film History: Theory and Practice, with Robert C Allen, 1985; High Sierra: Screenplay and Analysis, 1979. *Contributor to:* Numerous articles to professional journals including Journal of Film and Video; Popular Culture and Media Studies; Marquee; Screen; Film Actors and Actresses: An Encyclopedia; Quarterly Review of Film Studies; etc; Associate Editor, Journal of the University Film and Video Association, 1983–; Associate Editor, Cinema Journal, 1983–; Editorial Board, IRIS (Paris), 1982–; Contributing Editor, Film Studies Annual, 1977–80; Reviewer, numerous manuscripts for various journals, university and trade presses. *Honours:* Phi Beta Kappa; Beta Gamma Sigma; Phi Kappa Phi; Recipient, various Research Fellowships; Bernhart C Korn Grant, Milwaukee County Historical Society, 1981. *Memberships:* Dissertation Award Committee, Society for Cinema Studies; Nominations Committee, Officers of the Society for Cinema Studies; Organizer, Theatrical Historical Society Annual Convention, Milwaukee, 1981; etc. *Address:* Department of Communication Arts, Tawes Hall, University of Maryland, College Park, MD 20742, USA.

GOMEZ-SICRE, José, b. 6 July 1916, Matanzas, Cuba. Art Historian; Art Critic. Divorced. *Education:* University of Havana, Cuba; Licenciado en Derecho Diplomatico y Consular; Doctor en Ciencias Sociales, Politicas y Economicas. *Appointments:* Lecturer, Latin American Countries, Spain, Japan, Italy, etc; Chief, Visual Arts, Organization of American States, Washington DC, 1946–81; Director, Museum of Modern Art of Latin America, 1976–83. *Publications:* Carreño, 1943; Cuban Painting of Today, 1944; Spanish Drawings, 1951; Leonardo Nierman, 1968; Jose Luis Cuevas, 1983. *Contributor to:* Norte; Americas; Vanidades; Hombre de Mundo; Articles in professional journals and magazines in Latin America, Spain, Paris. *Honours:* One in Madrid, 1953; Knight of Republic of Colombia, 1983. *Address:* 1756 Lanier Place NW, Washington, DC 20009, USA.

GONSALVES, Norman A, b. 15 Nov. 1934, Honolulu, Hawaii. Vice President, Pacific Intelligence Inc. Widower, 2 sons, 1 daughter. *Education:* Security Management, Southern States University, USA; Administration of Justice, Long Beach College; Hawaiian-Polynesian Research & Documentation. *Literary Appointments:* Lecturer, recognised authority on ancient Hawaiian culture; Director, 12-year study of Ancient Hawaii, to document endangered knowledge. *Contributions to:* Voice of Hawaii; Hawaiian Studies, Polynesian Research Foundation Journal; The Factfinder; Hilo Tribune Herald; The Two Fifty; Hui O Lehualena; Various group study manuals. *Address:* 5600 Orangethorpe No.310, La Palma, CA 90623, USA.

GOOCH, Steve, b. 22 22 July 1945, Walton-on-Thames, Surrey, England. Playwright. *Education:* BA, Hons, Trinity College, Cambridge University. *Literary Appointments:* Resident Playwright, Open Space Theatre, London, 1973, Half Moon Theatre, London, 1974, Greenwich Theatre, London, 1975, Solent People's Theatre, Southampton, 1982, Theatre Venture at the Tom Allen Centre, London. 1983–4. *Publications:* Female Transport, 1974; The Motor Show, 1975; Will Wat, If Not What Will? 1975; The Women Pirates, 1978; Landmark 1982; Fast One, 1982; All Together Now 1984. Translations: Big Wolf (Harald Mueller) 1972; Poems and Ballads (Wolf Biermann) 1977; Wallraff, the Undesirable Journalist, 1978; The Mother (Brecht) 1978; Gambit 39/40 (Fassbinder, Kroetz and Harald Mueller) 1982. *Contributor to:* Plays and Players (Assistant Editor 1973); Theatre Quarterly; Platform; Drama. *Memberships:* Negotiating Committee, Theatre Writers Union; Theatre Writing Committee, Arts Council of Great Britain, 1984–86. *Honours:* Harper-Wood Scholarship, 1967; Arts Council Award, 1973; Thames TV Award, 1974. *Literary Agent:* Margaret Ramsay Ltd.

GOODE, John, b. 15 Oct. 1927, London, England. Writer – Photographer. *Publications:* More than 20 published books include: Freshwater Tortoises of Australia and New Guinea, 1967; World Guide to Cooking With Fruit and Vegetables, 1974; Rape of the Fly, 1977; The Original Australian and New Zealand CookBook, (with Carol Willson), 1979. *Contributions to:* Sydney Morning Herald; Sun Herald; Australian Financial Review; Cosmopolitan; Good Housekeeping; Geo; Epicurean and others, on travel and food, co-author with Carol Willson. *Honours:* Fellow, Royal Geographical Society, London. *Memberships:* Former Management Committee member, Australian Society of Authors; Former Vice-president, Victorian Fellowship of Australian Writers. *Address:* P O Box 191, Glebe, NSW 2037, Australia.

GOODERSON, David Richard, b. 24 Feb. 1941, Lahore, Pakistan. Actor; Writer. m. Deirdre Margaret Jane Bath, 18 May 1968, Grayswood, Surrey, England, 3 daughters. *Education:* Law and English MA (Cantab), 1963; Certificate of Education, Cambridge, 1984. *Publications:* The Castaway (one-man show), toured in England, 1974–81; Upstream Theatre Club, London, 1978; TV adaptation, BBC-TV, 1975; The Killing of Mr Toad (play), Salisbury Playhouse, 1982; Kings Head Theatre Club, London, 1983; Radio adaptation, BBC Radio 4, 1984. *Membership:* Writers Guild, 1982. *Literary Agent:* Michael Imison (Michael Imison Playwrights Limited) *Address:* 167 Elborough Street, London, SW18 5DS, England.

GOODFELLOW, William S(cott), b. 2 Dec. 1941, Los Angeles, California, USA. Music Critic. m. Susan Stücklen, 23 July 1974, Logan, Utah. *Education:* BA, Stanford University, 1967; MA, University of Chicago, 1968; Doctoral Candidate, University of Chicago. *Literary Appointments:* Chicago Sun-Times, 1968–74; Deseret News, 1977–; Part-time Faculty, Brigham Young University, 1985–. *Contributions to:* Chicago

Sun-Times; Deseret News; High Fidelity/Musical America; Shakespeare Quarterly; Milton quarterly plus occasional syndication or individual publications in other newspapers. *Memberships:* Music Critics Association; Modern Language Association. *Address:* Deseret News, 30 E 100 South, Salt Lake City, UT 84111, USA.

GOODHEART, Barbara Jean, b. 13 July 1934, Chicago, USA. Author. m. Clyde R Goodheart, 26 Dec. 1953, Chicago, Illinois, 1 son, 2 daughters. *Education:* BA, Northwestern University, Evanston, Illinois, USA. *Publication:* A Year on the Desert (1969). *Contributor to:* Better Homes and Gardens; Companion; Discovery; Family Weekly; Holiday Inn Magazine; Lady's Circle; Today's Health; Trailer Travel; Westways; various medical publication; numerous books. *Honours:* Special audiovisual award, Greater Chicago Area Chapter, American Medical Writers Association, 1981; Honorable Mention, the Morris Fishbein Award for Distinguished Achievement in Medical Writing, 1984. *Memberships:* American Society of Journalists and Authors; Chairperson, Midwest Chapter, 1973–75 and 1982–83; National Press Club; American Medical Writers Association; Society of Professional Journalists/Sigma Delta Chi. *Literary Agent:* Anita Diamant. *Address:* 15 Sheffield Court, Lincolnshire, IL 60015, USA.

GOODMAN, Edward J, b. 19 Nov. 1916, Dubuque, Iowa, USA. Teacher. m. Jeanne Finch, 22 Sep. 1945, Chicago, Illinois, 2 sons, 2 daughters. *Education:* AB, Loras College, Dubuque; MA, PhD, Columbia University. *Literary Appointments include:* Professor, Professor Emeritus, Xavier University, Cincinnati, Ohio, 1950–82; Visiting Professor, Catholic University, Washington 1963, University of Illinois 1965–66. *Publications:* The Explorers of South America, 1972; The Exploration of South America: An Annotated Bibliography, 1983. *Contributions:* Articles, book reviews in, American Historical Review; Hispanic American Historical Review; Terrae Incognitae; Review of Politics; Thought. Articles in, Encyclopedia Americana, New Catholic Encyclopedia. *Memberships:* Hakluyt Society; Council member 1980–81, Society for the History of Discoveries. *Address:* 5578 Buring Court SW, Fort Myers, FL 33907, USA.

GOODMAN, Geoffrey George, b. 2 July 1921, Stockport, England. Journalist. m. Margit Freudenbergova, 9 Jan. 1947, London, 1 son, 1 daughter. *Education:* BSc Economics, London School of Economics. *Publications:* Europe After UNRRA, 1949; The General Strike, 1951; The Awkward Warrior – Life and Times of Frank Cousins, 1978; The Miners Strike, 1985. *Contributions to:* New Statesman; BBC television and radio; Weekend World television programme; LBC Radio; Canadian and Australian Broadcasting Corporations. *Honours:* MA, Honorary, Oxon, 1974. *Address:* c/o Daily Mirror, Holborn Circus, London EC1, England.

GOODMAN, Melissa, b. 14 July 1952, Malden, Massachusetts, USA. Medical Writer; Editor. *Education:* BA, University of Massachusetts; MS, Boston University. *Literary Appointments:* Editor, Respiratory News. *Contributions to:* Medical Tribune; Medical World News; Various other publications for professional and lay audiences. *Memberships:* Past Treasurer, Past Meeting Reporter, New England Chapter, American Medical Writers Association. *Address:* 189 Sackett Street, #3, Brooklyn, NY 11231, USA.

GOODMAN, Michael Barry, b. 10 July 1949, Dallas, Texas, USA. University Professor; Writer; Consultant. m. Karen Edna Cook, 4 June 1977, Rocky Point, New York, 2 sons. *Education:* BA, University of Texas, 1971; MA 1972, PhD 1979, State University of New York, Stony Brook. *Appointments include:* Assistant Professor, SUNY, Stony Brook, 1979–81; Assistant Professor, Northeastern University, 1982–. *Publications:* William S Burroughs: An Annotated Bibliography, 1975; Contemporary Literary Censorship, 1981; Write to the

Point: Effective Communication in the Workplace, 1984. *Contributions:* George Munro, Norman L Munro, US Book Company in Publishers for Mass Entertainment in 19th Century America, ed. Stern, 1980; The Customs Censorship of William Burroughs, Naked Lunch, in Critique, 1980; etc. Articles, reviews, to American Book Review. *Honours:* Resident Faculty Member, National Humanities Faculty; Excellence in teaching, 1984. *Memberships:* Modern Language Association; Authors Guild; Authors League; National Council of Teachers of English; Society for Technical Communication; American Business Communication Association. *Address:* 470 2nd Avenue, 18B, New York, NY 10016, USA.

GOODWIN, Geoffrey Lawrence, b. 14 June 1916, London, England. University Professor. m. Janet Audrey Sewell, 6 Jan. 1951, Dorking, Surrey, 1 son, 2 daughters. *Education:* BSc, London School of Economics, 1945. *Literary Appointments:* Lecturer, 1948–62, Professor, 1962–78, Emeritus Professor, 1978–, International Relations, University of London. *Publications:* Britain and the United Nations, 1958; Research on International Organisation, 1968; Die Politik Gorssbritanniens in den Vereinten Nationen, 1974. Editor: University Teaching of International Relations, 1951; New Dimensions of World Politics, 1975; A New International Commodity Regime, 1979; Ethics and Nuclear Defences, 1982. *Contributions to:* Numerous professional publications including: The Listener; The Times; The Observer; International Affairs; World Today; International Organization; Millenium; Review of International Studies; Political Quarterly. *Honours:* Fellow, Royal Society of Arts; Honorary President, British International Studies Association, 1977–82. *Membership:* Council Member, Royal Institute of International Affairs, 1968–71, 1974–77. *Address:* Webbs Farm, Church Lane, Headley, Epsom, Surrey KT18 6L2, England.

GOODWIN, H Eugene, b. 19 Dec. 1922, Council Bluffs, Iowa. University Professor. m. Frances Prudhon, 3 July 1943, Columbus, Ohio, 2 sons, 2 daughters. *Education:* BA, Journalism and Political Science, 1946, MA, Journalism, 1947, University of Iowa. *Literary Appointments:* Reporter, Columnist and Editor for Baltimore Sun, Associated Press and Washington Star, 1947–57; Teacher of Journalism, The Pennsylvania State University, 1957–. *Publications:* Grouping for Ethics in Journalism, 1983. *Contributions to:* The Ethics of Compassion, in The Quill magazine, 1983, reprinted in Impact of Mass Media, 1985. *Honour:* Frank Luther Mott-Kappa Tau Alpha Award for best researched book about journalism published in 1983. *Address:* 119 Bathgate Drive, State College, PA 16801, USA.

GOODY, John Rankine, b. 27 July 1919. Professor Emeritus of Social Anthropology, University of Cambridge. *Education:* BA; Diploma Anthropol; BLitt; PhD; ScD; FBA, St John's College, Cambridge and Balliol College, Oxford. *Publications:* The Social Organisation for the LoWiili, 1956 The Development Cycle in Domestic Groups, (Ed), 1958; Death, Property and the Ancestors, 1962; Succession to High Office, (Ed), 1966; Salaga: The Struggle for Power, (W J A Braimah), 1967; Literacy in Traditional Societies, (Ed), 1968; Comparative Studies in Kinship, 1969; Technology, Tradition and the State in Africa, 1971; The Myth of the Bagre, 1972; Bridewealth and Dowry, (W S J Tambiah), 1973; The Character of Kinship, (Ed), 1973; Production and Reproduction, 1977; The Domestication of the Savage Mind, 1977; Cooking, Cuisine and Class, 1982; The Development of the Family amd Marriage in Europe, 1983. *Contributor to:* Professional Journals. *Address:* St Johns College, Cambridge, England.

GOODYER, Paula Ann, b. 16 Jan. 1947, Nottingham, England. Journalist. m. Rick Stevens, 26 Mar. 1977, Sydney, Australia, 1 daughter. *Education:* Associate, Institute of Linguists, (French). *Contributor to:* Cleo; Family Circle; New Woman, USA. *Honour:* Walkley Award for Journalism, Best Magazine Story, 1977.

Address: 11 Prince Edward Road, Seaforth 2092, Australia.

GOOLD-ADAMS, Richard John Moreton, b. 24 Jan. 1916, Brisbane, Australia. Economist; Company Director. *Education:* MA, New College, Oxford, England. *Publications:* South Africa Today & Tomorrow, 1936; Middle East Journey, 1947; The Time of Power: a Reappraisal of John Foster Dulles, 1962; The Return of the Great Britain, 1976. *Contributions to:* The Economist, (Assistant Editor, 1950's); Sunday Times; radio and TV. *Honour:* CBE, 1974. *Address:* 11 Richmond Road, Bath BA1 5TU, England.

GOONERATNE, Malini Yasmine Dias Bendaranaike, b. 22 Dec. 1935, Colombo, Sri Lanka. Associate Professor English Lieterature, m. Dr Brendon W M Gooneratne, 31 Dec. 1962, Colombo, 1 son, 1 daughter. *Education:* BA (Hons), University of Ceylon, 1959; PhD, Cambridge University, England, 1962; D Litt, Macquerie University, Australia, 1981. *Literary Appointments:* University of Ceylon, 1959–71; Macquarie University, 1972–. *Publications:* English Literature in Ceylon 1815–1878, 1968; Jane Austen, 1970; Word, Bird, Motif: 53 Poems, 1971; The Lizards, Cry and other Peoms, 1972; Alexander Pope, 1976; Editor, Stories from Sri Lanka, 1979; Editor, Poems from India, Sri Lanka, Malaysia and Singapore, 1979; Diverse Inheritance: A Personal Perspective on Commonwealth Literature, 1980; 6000 Ft. Death Divet Poems, 1981; Silence, Exile and Cunning: The Fiction of R F Jhabvala, 1983; Relative Merits: The Banderanaika Family of Sri Lanka, 1986. *Contributor to:* Literary publications, magazines, journals, etc. *Honours:* Senkadagala Memorial Prize for Poetry, 1953; Pettah Library Prize, 1955; Leigh Smith Memorial Prize, 1958; Government of Ceylon University Scholarship in Arts, 1958; Sir Bartle Frere Exhibition, Cambridge University, 1968; Lawn Foundation Research Grant, University of London, 1968; Ida Woolley International Research Fellowship, 1968; Macquerie University Research Grant, 1984–, etc. *Address:* School of English and Linguistics, Macquarie University, North Ryde, New South Wales 2113, Australia.

GOOR, Nancy Miller, b. 27 Mar. 1944, Washington, DC, USA. Writer. m. Ronald Goor, 12 Mar. 1967, 2 sons. *Education:* BA, University of Pennsylvania; MFA, Boston University. *Publications:* Shadows: Here, There and Everywhere, 1981; In the Driver's Seat, 1982; Signs, 1983; All Kinds of Feet, 1984. *Honours:* American Library Association Notable Book (Shadows), 1981; Library of Congress Children's Book of the Year (Shadows), 1981; School Library Journal Best Book of the Year (Driver's Seat), 1982; Library of Congress Children's Book of the Year (Driver's Seat), 1982; Notable Children's Trade Book for the Language Arts (Signs), 1983; Outstanding Science trade books for children (All Kinds of Feet and Shadows), 1984. *Membership:* Children's Book Guild of Washington, DC, Treasurer. *Address:* 9301 Cedarcrest Drive, Bethesda, MD 20814, USA.

GOOR, Ronald Stephen, b. 31 May 1940, Washington DC, USA. Health Scientist. m. Nancy Ruth Miller, 2 sons. *Education:* BA, Swarthmore College, 1962; PhD, Biochemistry, 1967, MPH, 1976, Harvard University. *Publicatioans:* Backyard Insects, with Millicent Selsam, 1981; With Nancy Goor; Shadows: Here, There and Everywhere, 1981; In the Driver's Seat, 1982; Signs, 1983; All Kinds of Feet, 1984; Pompeii: A Roman Ghost Town, 1986; Eater's Choice, 1986. *Contributor to:* Country Road, Attenzione, 1983. *Honours:* American Library Association Notable Book, 1981, Outstanding Science Trade Book for Children, National Science Teachers' Association and Children's Book Council, One of the Best Books of the Year, Library of Congress, 1981, for, Shadows : Here, There and Everywhere; In the Driver's Seat, chosen Junior Literary Selection, Best Book by School Library Journal, one of 15 best books of the year, New York Times, 1982; Recipient of numerous other awards for books.

Membership: Children's Book Guild. *Address:* 9301 Cedarcrest Drive, Bethesda, MD 20814, USA.

GOPEN, George David, b. 24 Sep. 1945, Cambridge, Massachusetts, USA. English Professor. m. Gillian Einstein, 3 Aug. 1980, Newton, Massachusetts. *Education:* BA English, Brandeis University, Waltham, Massachusetts, 1967; JD, Harvard Law School, Cambridge, 1972; PhD English and American Language and Literature, Harvard Graduate School of Arts and Sciences, 1975. *Literary Appointments:* Visiting Assistant Professor of English, University of Utah, 1975–78; Assistant Professor of English and Director of Writing Programmes, Loyola University of Chicago, 1978–85; Lecturer, Harvard Law School, 1983–; Assistant Professor of English and Director of Writing Programmes, Duke University, Durham, North Carolina, 1985–. *Publications:* Writing From a Legal Perspective, 1981; The Moral Fables of Robert Henryson, 1986. *Contributions to:* Journals including: Journal of Legal Education; College English; Harvard Law School Bulletin; Studies in Philology. *Memberships:* Phi Beta Kappa; Modern Language Association; Philological Association of the Pacific Coast; National Council of Teachers of English; South Atlantic Modern Language Association. *Address:* 613 Swift Avenue, Durham, NC 27706, USA.

GORDON, Angela, b. 27 Mar. 1957, Scotland. Diary Editor, The Times. *Literary Appointment:* Diary Editor, The Times. *Honours:* Scotland's Young Journalist of the Year, 1980. *Address:* 'The Times', 200 Gray's Inn Road, London, WC1, England.

GORDON, Bonnie Heather, b. 18 Oct. 1952, Philadelphia, Pennsylvania, USA. Editor; Writer. m. Edward Kaplan, 2 Apr. 1978, 1 son. *Education:* BA, English, Temple University. *Publication:* Thus May Be Figured in Numberless Ways, 1985. *Contributions:* of stories to, Zone; Sarcophagus; Tracks; Assembling; Adz; Alph Null; Sapiens. *Address:* 3704 Hyde Park Avenue, Cincinnati, OH 45209, USA.

GORDON, Giles Alexander Esme, b. 23 May 1940, Edinburgh, Scotland. Lecturer; Literary Agent; Writer; Theatre Critic. m. Margaret Gordon, 2 sons, 1 daughter. *Education:* Edinburgh Academy. *Appointments:* Adveritising Manager, Secker & Warburg; editor, Hutchinson & Co, & Penguin Books; Editorial Director, Victor Gollancz Ltd; Member, Literary Panel, Arts Council of Great Britain; Chairman, Society of Young Publishers; Lecturer, Creative Writing, Tufts University, Massachusetts, USA. *Publications:* Two & Two Make One, 1966; Two Elegies, 1968; Pictures from an Exhibition, 1970; The Umbrella Man, 1971; Twelve Poems for Callum, 1972; About a Marriage, 1972; Girl with Red Hair, 1974; Farewell Fond Dreams, 1975; Beyond the Words, editor, 1975; 100 Scenes from Married Life, 1976; Members of the Jury, Editor with Dulan Barber, 1976; Prevailing Spirits, 1976; A Book of Contemporary Enemies, 1977; Nightmares, Editor, 1977; The Illusionist, 1978; Ambrose's Vision, 1980. *Contributor to:* Theatre Critic, Spectator, 1983–84; Deputy Theatre Critic, Punch, 1985–; Reviewer of Plays, Observer, Plays & Players, Editor, Drama Magazine, 1982–84; Theatre Critic, The House Magazine, 1985–; Articles in various journals, magazines & newspapers including, the Times, Bookseller, etc. *Membership:* Society of Authors. *Address:* 9 St Ann's Garden's London NW5, England.

GORDON, John Fraser, b. 1916, London, England. Company Director. *Education:* City of London College. *Publications include:* The Staffordshire Bull Terrier Owner's Encyclopaedia, 1967; All About the Boxer, 1970; All About the Cocker Spaniel, 1971; The Beagle Guide, 1968; The Miniature Schnauzer Guide, 1968; The Staffordshire Bull Terrier, 1970; The Bull Terrier, 1973; The Bulldog, 1973; The Dandie Dinmont Terrier, 1973; The Pug, 1973; The Borzoi, 1974; The Irish Wolfhound, 1974; Some Rare & Unusual Breeds, 1975; Dogs, 1976; The German Shepherd Dog, 1978; Schnauzers, 1979; Map of World's Dogs, 1978; The Alaskan Malamute, 1979; All About the Staffordshire Bull Terrier, 1984. *Contributor to:* Dog World. *Memberships:* Wig & Pen; Society of Authors. *Honours:* Freeman, City of London; Cruft's & International Judge of Dogs. *Address:* Suite 79, London Wool Exchange, Corporation London House, Brushfield Street, London E1 6EP, England.

GORDON, Lawrence A, b. 15 Apr. 1943. Ernst & Whinney Alumni Professor of Accounting, The University of Maryland College of Business and Management, USA. m. Hedy, 2 children. *Education:* BSc, 1966, MBA, 1967; State University of New York at Albany; PhD, Management Accounting, Economic Theory, Renaselaer Polytechnic Instiute, 1973. *Literary Appointments:* Co-Editor, Journal of Accounting and Public Policy, 1982–; Editorial Board Member, The Accounting Review, 1981–83; Management International Review, 1982–; Contemporary Accounting Research, 1984–; Ad Hoc Reviewer, Journal of Financial and Quantitative Analysis: Accounting Organizations and Society; The Accounting Review; Journal of Business and Economic Statistics. *Publications:* Improving Capital Budgeting: A Decision Support System Approach, (with G Pinches), 1984; The Pricing Decision, (with R Cooper, H Falk and D Miller) 1980; Accounting and Corporate Social Responsibility, 1978; Normative Models in Managerial Decision Making (with D Miller, H Mintzberg), 1975. *Contributor to:* The Accounting Review; The Journal of Accounting and Public Policy; Accounting, Organisations and Society; Public Budgeting and Finance; Journal of Financial and Quantitative Analysis; Policy Studies Journal, etc. *Honours:* Research Grants; Outstanding Teacher Award, University of Maryland, 1984; Outstanding Faculty Award, Alumni Association, University of Maryland College of Business and Management, 1983. *Memberships:* American Accounting Associaton; American Economic Association; Institute for Decision Sciences; Association of Government Accountants, etc. *Address:* College of Business and Management, University of Maryland, College Park, MD 20742, USA.

GORDON, Maclaren, b. 21 Jan. 1916, Melbourne, Australia. Journalist. m. Claire Perry, 8 Feb. 1940, Melbourne, 1 son, 1 daughter. *Education:* Arts & Commerce, University of Melbourne. *Appointments:* Writer, sub-editor, features editor, editor; Australian Army Journal, Salt; Melbourne, Age; Melbourne, Argus; Sydney, Daily Telegraph; Food Store News; Editor, Overseas Trading, Australian Department of Trade. Writer, editor, publisher, Food Store News, national supermarket management journal, 15 years. *Contributions:* Verse in anthology, Poets of Australia. *Address:* 2 Chambers Street, South Yarra, Victoria 3141, Australia.

GÖRGEY, Gábor, b. 22 Nov. 1929, Budapest, Hungary. Author. *Education:* University of Linguistics, Budapest. *Publications:* Smoke and Light, lyric poetry, 1956; Meridian, lyric poetry, 1963; One Pistol for Five, 5 plays, 1969; I'm Fine Thanks, lyric poetry, 1970; Ararat Small, 2 comedy plays, 1971; Hunter's Fortune, lyric translation, 1974; Sharks in the Garden, 3 plays, 1976; Hallway of Air, Lyric poetry, 1977. *Contributions to:* Publications including: Columnist, Magyar Nemzet, 1959–; Modern International Drama, USA; American Review; Confrontation, USA; Les lettres Nouvelles, France. *Honour:* Robert Graves Prize, 1976. *Memberships:* Society of Hungarian Authors; PEN. *Literary Agent:* Artisjus. *Address:* Szalonka ut 16, Budapest 1025, Hungary.

GOSHGARIAN, Gary, b. 20 Aug. 1942, Hartford, Connecticut, USA. Professor of English. m. Kathleen Krueger, 26 Aug. 1978, 2 sons. *Education:* BS, Physics; MA, English; PhD, English. *Literary Appointment:* Professor of English, Northeastern University, 1969– *Publications include:* Exploring Language, 4th edition 1986; Atlantis Fire, novel, 1980; The Contemporary Reader, 1984. *Contributions to:* Boston Globe; Northeastern Edition; Bedford Reader; Today's

Education; Sportscape. *Membership:* PEN (Poets, Essayists, Novelists). *Literary Agent:* Esther Newberg, International Creative Management. *Address:* Department of English, Northeastern University, Boston, MA 02115, USA.

GOTHE, Jurgen R, b. 4 Apr. 1944, Barwalde, Germany. Writer (journalist, columnist, broadcaster). *Contributor to:* International Music Guide (UK & USA); Fanfare Magazine (USA); CBC Radio Network; various journals concerned with entertainment, travel and leisure. Member, Music Critics Association of America, Recipient National Magazine Awards, Canada, for Humor, 1978. *Address:* Quincy Gothe Inc, 300-845 Cambie St, Vancouver, BC Canada V6B 4Z9.

GOTLIEB, Phyllis, b. 25 May 1926, Toronto, Canada. Writer. *Education:* BA, MA, University of Toronto. *Publications:* Poetry: Within the Zodiac, 1964; Ordinary Moving, 1969; Doctor Umlaut's Earthly Kingdom, 1974; The Works, 1978; Novels: Sunburst, 1964; Why Should I Have All the Grief? 1969; O Master Caliban, 1976; A Judgement of Dragons, 1980; Emperor, Swords, Pentacles, 1982; The Kingdom of the Cats, 1985; Collection: Son of the Morning and Other Stories, 1983. *Contributor to:* Various magazines and journals including Tamarack Review; Queen's Quarterly; Amazing Science Fiction; Fantastic Science Fiction; If Science Fiction; Galaxy Science Fiction. *Membership:* Science Fiction Writers of America. *Literary Agent:* Virginia Kidd. *Address:* 29 Ridgevale Drive, Toronto, Canada M6A 1K9.

GOTTFRIED, Robert Steven, b. 13 Jan. 1949, Philadelphia, USA. University Professor. m. Jane Rudes, 10 Nov. 1970, Ann Arbor, Michigan, 1 son, 1 daughter. *Education:* BA, Penn State University, 1970; MA, 1971, PhD, 1975, University of Michigan. *Literary Appointments:* University of Michigan, 1974–75; Rutgers University, 1975–. *Publications:* Epidemic Disease in Fifteenth Century England, 1978; Bury St Edmunds and the Urban Crisis, 1290–1539, 1982; The Black Death, 1983. *Contributions to:* American Historical Review; Speculum; Journal of Modern History; Journal of Economic History; Journal of British Studies; Albion; Journal of Interdisciplinary History; Historian; Bulletin of the History of Medicine; and others. *Honours:* Danforth Fellow, 1971; Fulbright Fellow, 1972–73; NEH Fellow, 1977; ACLS Fellow, 1982–83; Member, Institute for Advanced Study, 1983. *Memberships:* Economic History Association; Economic History Society; Conference on British Studies; Past and Present Society; Medieval Academy of America; and others. *Literary Agent:* Georges Bourcherdt, New York. *Address:* Department of History, Rutgers University, New Brunswick, NJ 08903, USA.

GOTTLIEB, Moshe Raphael, b. 15 Feb. 1931, Dusseldorf, Germany. University Lecturer. m. Ziporah Atarah Levinstein, 25 Nov. 1964, New York City, USA, 3 sons, 1 daughter. *Education:* Hebrew Teachers Institute, Yeshiva University, 1951; BA, Brooklyn College, 1952; MHL Rabbi, Jewish Theological Seminary, New York City, 1956; MA, Near Eastern and Judaic Studies, Brandeis University, 1961; PhD, Brandeis University. *Literary Appointments:* Instructor, Modern and American Jewish History, Queens College, New York; Instructor, Modern Jewish History, New School for Social Research; Lecturer, American Jewish History, Tel-Aviv University; Visiting Senior Lecturer, Haifa University; Chairman, Judaic Studies, SUNY; Senior Researcher, Holocaust, Bar-Ilan University. *Publications:* American Anti-Nazi Resistance 1933–41, 1982; The American Struggle Against Hitler Germany: An Episodic History, 1986; The Anti-Nazi Boycott Movement in the American Jewish Community, 1933–41 (doctoral thesis), 1967. *Contributions to:* American Jewish Historical Quarterly; Jewish Social Studies; Encyclopedia Judaica, etc. *Honours include:* Prize in Modern Hebrew Literature, Rabbinical School, JTS, 1953–54; Fellowship, Brandeis University, Waltham, 1960–61. *Memberships:* Hebrew Teachers Union, New

York City; Member, Rabbinical Assembly, New York City. *Address:* 34 Bar-Ilan Street, Ra-anana, Israel.

GOULD, Roberta, b. 16 July 1938, Brooklyn, New York, USA. *Education:* MA, University of California at Berkeley. *Major Publications:* Dream Yourself Flying, 1979; Writing Air, Written Water, 1982; Punch Drunk & Other Poems, 1985; Only Rock, 1985. *Contributor to:* New York Times; Catholic Worker; Poetry Now; Response; Blue Unicorn; Pax; Village Voice; Confrontation; and others. *Memberships:* Poetry Society of America; PEN Club; New York Poets Cooperative. *Address:* 315 East 18th Street, New York, NY 10003, USA.

GOULET, Denis A, b. 27 May 1931, Fall River, Massachusetts, USA. Professor. *Education:* BA 1954, MA 1956, St Paul's College, Washington DC; MA, IRFED, Paris, France, 1960; PhD, University of Sao Paulo, Brazil, 1963. *Literary Appointments:* O'Neill Professor in Education for Justice, University of Notre Dame, Indiana, USA. *Major Publications include:* The Myth of Aid (with M Hudson), 1971; The Cruel Choice: A New Concept in the Theory of Development, 1971; A New Moral Order: Development Ethics & Liberation Theology, 1974; The Uncertain Promise: Value Conflicts in Technology Transfer, 1977; Survival with Integrity: Sarvodaya at the Crossroads, 1981; Mexico: Development Strategies for the Future, 1983. *Contributor to:* Numerous journals. *Honour:* Chevalier, Ordre National du Cedre, Republic of Lebanon, 1960. *Address:* 432 Decio Faculty Building, Box 1068, Notre Dame, IN 46556, USA.

GOWIN, Dixie Bob, b. 11 Dec. 1925, West Palm Beach, Florida, USA. University Professor. Divorced, 2 sons, 1 daughter. *Education:* BA, University of Texas, 1948; MA, Stanford University, 1952; PhD, Yale University, 1956. *Literary Appointments:* Board of Editors, Studies in Philosophy and Education, 1961–72; Chairman, John Dewey Society Lecture Commission, 1980–. *Publications:* Appraising Educational Research with J Millman, 1974; Educating 1981; Boundaries, a book of poems, 1981; Learning How to Learn, with Joseph D Novak, 1984. *Contributions to:* Some 60 professional journals since 1956. *Honours:* Postdoctoral Fellowship, Yale University, 1958; One of twelve recipients of national competition for a year's stipend from US Office of Education, 1967–68. *Address:* Roberts Hall, Cornell University, Ithaca, NY 14853, USA.

GRAB, André b. 26 July, 1952, Zürich, Switzerland. Bookseller. *Major Publications:* Er, 1981, Normal, 1983 (both short stories). *Contributor to:* Der Rabe; Volksrecht (regular columnist). *Honours:* 1st prize in short story competition, Zürich, 1979; Awards of the City of Zürich, 1981, 1983. *Membership:* Swiss Writers' Union, Zürich. *Literary Agent:* Ms Marianne Fabrin, Zürich. *Address:* P O Box 2133, CH–8028, Zürich, Switzerland.

GRABOWSKA-STEFFEN, Alicja Wanda, b. 24 July 1936, Warsaw, Poland. Poet; Playwright; Teacher. m. Jan Steffen, 9 Dec. 1978, 1 son. *Education:* MA, Warsaw University. *Publications:* Z Kregu, 1968; Adam-Eva, 1975; Drzewo od Wewnatrz, 1975; Kolysanka, Verses for children, 1981; Anthology of the Polish Erotic Poetry written by Women, 1982; Rana Ziemi, 1983; Oto Ja Kobieta, 1984. *Contributions to:* Numerous publications including: Poezja; Kultura; Literatura. *Honour:* Golden Cross of Merit for didactic work. *Memberships:* Societe Europene de Culture; Society of Authors, Zaiks; Polish Writers Union. *Literary Agent:* Agrncja Autorska (Authors Agency). *Address:* Orłowicza 6 m 30, 00–414 Warsaw, Poland.

GRACE, John Patrick, b. 6 Sep. 1942, Chicago, Illinois, USA. Professor of Romance Languages. m. (1) Joan Spitzer, 17 July 1965, Glenview, Illinois, 3 sons, 1 daughter, 2) Jennifer Mock, 29 Sep. 1979, Chapel Hill, North Carolina, 1 daughter. *Education:* BA, Loyola University, Chicago, Illinois, 1964; MS, Columbia

University, 1965; MA, 1980, PhD, pending, University of North Carolina. *Literary Appointments:* Various freelance appointments; Writer, Editor, Foreign Corespondent, Associated Press, Chicago, New York and Rome, 1965–72; Reporter, Columnist, Greensboro Record, 1973–75; Consultant, Institute for Southern Studies, 1977–78; Teaching Assistant, Department of Romance Languages, University of North Carolina, 1977–. *Publications:* Jerusalem Lives!, 1976; Greensboro: A Pictorial History, 1977; Hearing His Voice, 1979. *Contributions to:* Associate Press; Time; Newsweek; The Atlantic Monthly; IBM Think Magazine; America; Washington Post; Boston Globe; Christian Science Monotor. *Honours:* 1st, Feature writing, North Carolina Press Association, 1974; Landmark Newspaper Group award for sustained excellence in reporting, 1975; Honorable Mention, American Academy of Family Physicians, 1975. *Address:* Ecole de Commerce, 74 allées de Morlaas, 64000 Pau, France.

GRACE, Sherrill Elizabeth, b. 18 Aug 1944, Ormstown, Quebec, Canada. University Professor. m. John R Grace, 20 Dec. 1964, Sudbury, Ontario, Canada, 1 son, 1 daughter. *Education:* BA, 1965; MA, 1970; PhD, 1974. *Publications:* Violent Duality: A Study of Margaret Atwood, 1980; The Voyage That Never Ends: Malcolm Lowry's Fiction, 1982; Margaret Atwood: Language, Text and System, co-edited with L Weir, 1983. *Contributor to:* Numerous articles on modern literature in scholarly journals such as, Modern Fiction Studies, Canadian Literature, Mosaic and Journal of Modern Literature. *Honours:* Canadian Council Doctoral Fellow, 1971–74; Canadian Federation for the Humanities Publishing Grant, 1982; Social Sciences and Humanities Research Council of Canada, International Travel Grants 1984, 1985. DAAD Research Grant in Germany, 1985. *Memberships:* Modern Language Association; Association of Canadian University Teachers of English; Executive Member, Canadian Association of American Studies, 1983–87; Association of Canadian Studies; Canadian Comparative Literature Association. *Address:* Department of English, The University of British Columbia, Vancouver BC, Canada V6T 1W5.

GRAFF, Henry Franklin, b. 11 Aug. 1921, New York City, USA. University Professor of History; Historian; Author. *Education:* BSS, City College of New York, 1941; MA 1942, PhD 1949, Columbia University. *Publications:* Bluejackets with Perry in Japan, 1952; The Modern Researcher (with J Barzun), 4th ed. 1985; The Adventure of the American People (with J Krout), 3rd ed. 1973; The Grand Experiment (Vol. 1, The Call of Freedom, Vol. 2, The Promise of Democracy) (with P Bohannan), 1978; The Free & The Brave, revised ed. 1980; This Great Nation, 1983; America: The Glorious Republic, 1985. Ed: American Imperialism & The Philippine Insurrection, 1969; The Tuesday Cabinet: Deliberation & Decision on Peace & War Under Lyndon B Johnson, 1970. *Contributions to:* New York Times Book Review; New York Times Magazine; etc. *Memberships:* PEN; Authors Guild. *Address:* 47 Andrea Lane, Scarsdale, NY 10583, USA.

GRAGASIN, Jose Valliente, b. 28 Feb. 1900, Gerona, Tarlac, Philippines. Retired Educator; Economist; Author; Poet. m. Socorro C Patricio, 5 Oct. 1930, Echague, 4 sons, 4 daughters. *Education:* AB, 1922, BCS, 1923, Kansas City University, USA; BD, Garrett Theological Seminary, 1926; PhD, Graduate Seminar of Social Science, Chicago Law School, 1927; Hon DH, Kansas City University, 1928. *Appointments include:* Educational Consultant, United Bretheren Mission Schools, concurrently English Editor, NAIMBAG A DAMAG, 1928–33; Education Consultant, Osias Colleges, Director-Founder, Gerona Instiute, 1933–35; Agrarian Problems Researcher, President Manuel L Quezon, 1936–37; Economist-Adviser, Agriculture, Philippine Commonwealth, 1938–47; Economist, Philippine Farmers Federation, 1948; Professor, Lecturer, Graduate Schools of: National University, 1949–56, National Defence College,

Philippines, 1957–59, Feati University, 1949–56, etc; Acting Dean, Graduate School, Jose Rizal College, 1956; Vice President, Academic Affairs, Dean, Graduate School, Northeastern College, 1972–74; Professor, Lecturer, University of the East, 1947–67. *Publications include:* 13 College Texts: Methodology of Research, 1949; Comparative Education, 1953; Philippine Economic Problems and Their Solutions, 1964; etc; Poetry: The Attributes to the Greatness of the American People, 1980; What Makes the Filipinos A Great People, 1984; etc. *Contributor to:* Numerous books of Poetry. *Honours:* Inductee, Personalities of America Hall of Fame, 1984; Golden Poetry, World of Poetry, 1985; Recipient of numerous honours and other awards. *Memberships:* Fellow Vice Chancellor, International Academy of Poets for South East Asia; Fellow, World Literary Academy; Associate Member, Academy of American Poets, Poetry Society of America; United States Capitol Historical Society; American Economic Association; American Statistical Society; Asia Research Foundation; International Academy of Leadership; Epsilon Tau Chi; Phi Beta Kappa. *Address:* 104 South Collins Avenue, Baltimore, MD 21229, USA.

GRAHAM, Ian, b. 9 Sep. 1953, Belfast, Northern Ireland. Author. *Education:* BSc, Applied Physics, The City University, London, 1975; Postgraduate Diploma Journalism, The City University, London, 1978. *Publications:* Computer and Video Games, 1982; The Inside Story: Computer, 1983; Information Revolution (with Lynn Myring), 1983; The Personal Computer Handbook (with Helen Varley), 1983; Step-By-Step Programming for the BBC Micro (Books 1 and 2), Acorn Electron (Books 1 and 2), Sinclair Spectrum (Books 1 and 2), Sinclair Spectrum + (Books 1 and 2), 1984. *Contributions:* on Video, Computers, Spaceflight to: Marketing Week, What MSX?; Which Video?; Next...; Space Voyager; Science Now; Popular Hi-Fi; Computer Games and System Retailer; The Optician, etc. *Literary Agent:* Barbara Levy, Carol Smith Agency. *Address:* c/o Carol Smith Literary Agency, 25 Hornton Court, Kensington High Street, London W8 7RT, England.

GRAHAM, Neile, b. 8 Oct. 1958, Winnipeg, Manitoba, Canada. Poet. m. James Gurley, 20 June 1983. *Education:* BA, University of Victoria, Canada, 1980; MFA, University of Montana, USA, 1984. *Publication:* Seven Robins, Penumbra Press, Ontario, 1983. *Contributions to:* Fiddlehead (3 poems), 1981; Malahat Review (3 poems), 1982; Canadian Literature (4 poems), 1983; Anthology of Magazine Verse & Yearbook of American Poetry (1 poem), 1984; Various Canadian & American periodicals (25 poems). *Memberships:* Associated Writing programs. *Address:* 733 Walnut Street, Missoula, MT 59801, USA.

GRAHAM, Teresa A, b. 4 Aug. 1964, Albany, New York, USA. Newspaper Editorial Clerk. *Education:* AAS, Hudson Valley Community College, Troy, New York; BS Russell Sage College, Troy, New York. *Contributor to:* The Hudsonian; Gleanings; Tiers Magazine; etc, and various other periodicals; Essay: Reflections of a Suicide, 1980 was taught as part of a private secondary school religion course, 1981, Contemporary Moral Problems. *Honour:* Lorica Chapter, National Honour Society, 1982. *Membership:* Hudson Valley Literary Club. *Address:* 314 Chiswell Road, Schenectady, NY 12304, USA.

GRAHAM, W(illiam) Fred, b. 31 Oct. 1930, Columbus, Ohio, USA. Professor of Religious Studies, m. Jean Garrett, 12 Aug. 1953, Braddville, Iowa, 4 daughters. *Education:* BA, Tarkio College, Missouri, 1952; MDiv, Pittsburgh Theological Seminary, 1955; ThM, Louisville Presbyterian Seminary, 1958; PhD, University of Iowa, 1965. *Publications:* The Constructive Revolutionary: John Calvin's Socio-Economic Impact, 1971,81; Picking Up the Pieces, 1978. *Contributions to:* The Christian Century; Christianity Today; The Reformed Journal; Church History; The Journal of the American Historical Association; Christian Scholars Review, and others. *Memberships:* American Society of Church History;

American Academy of Religion; 16th Century Studies Society; Calvin Studies Society; Phi Kappa Phi. *Address:* Department of Religious Studies, Michigan State University, East Lansing, MI 48824, USA.

GRAHAM-YOOLL, Andrew Michael, b. 5 Jan. 1944, Buenos Aires, Argentina. Journalist; Writer. m. Micaela Isabel Meyer. 17 Jan. 1966, San Isidro, Argentina, 1 son, 2 daughters. *Publications:* Time of Tragedy, 1966–71; Time of Violence – Argentina 1972–73, 1974; Lancelot Holland, Journey to the River Plate in 1807, 1976; Arthur Koestler, From Infinity to Zero, 1978; Censorship in the World (Anthology), 1980; Venezuela's Independence as Seen by The Times, 1980; Rosas as Seen by the British 1829–1852, 1980; The Press in Argentina 1973–78, 1979; Portrait of an Exile, 1981; The Forgotten Colony, 1981; Small Wars You May Have Missed, 1983; (Poetry) Spanglish Spoken, 1972; Day to Day, 1973. *Contributor to:* Political Columnist, News Editor, Buenos Aires Herald 1966–76; Foreign Correspondent, Daily Telegraph, 1970–77; Foreign Desk, Sub Editor, Correspondent, The Guardian, 1977–84; Editor, South Magazine, 1984–; Freelance, San Francisco Chronicle, USA, 1967–70; *Contributor to:* Miami Herald; Baltimore Sun; Kansas City Star; New York Times; Newsweek; Cambio 16; many other professional journals, magazines and newspapers. *Memberships:* International PEN, Press Officer, 1979–; Writers' Guild of Great Britain, Executive Council, 1983;. *Address:* 10 Rotherwick Road, London NW11 7DA, England.

GRAMS WEHDEKING, Alma Luise, b. Bremen, Federal Repulic of Germany. Librarian. *Education:* Bookselling Certificate, Leipzig; Library practice, State Library, Hamburg, 2 years; Diploma of Librarianship, Berlin. *Publications:* Das Haus an der Weide, Geschichte einer Bremer Familie, 1962, 63; Worpswede um die Jahrhundertwende, Ein Ruckblick, 1978; Caroline von Humbolt und ilive Zeit. 1980. *Memberships:* Lyceum Club, Munich; International Federation of Business and Professional Women, Munich; Society for Overseas Studies Munich; German English Society. Munich; Friends of the Evangelical Academy, Munich. *Address:* Münchnerstrasse 11, 8036 Breitbrunn am Ammersee, Federal Republic of Germany.

GRANATSTEIN, Jack Lawrence, b. 21 May 1939, Toronto, Ontario, Canada. Historian. m. Elaine Hitchcock, 29 Nov. 1961, Toronto, 1 sons, (deceased) 1 daughter. *Education:* BA, RMC, Canada; MA, University of Toronto; PhD, Duke University. *literary Appointments:* Professor of History, York University, 1966–. *Publications:* The Politics of Survival, 1967; Canada's War, 1975; Broken Promises, 1977; A Man of Influence, 1981; TheOttawa Men, 1982; Canada 1957–67, 1986. *Contributions to:* Saturday Night; Maclean's; Canadian Forum; Canadian Historical Review; International Journal, and others. *Honours:* Killam Research Fellow, 1982–84; Fellow, Royal Society Canada, 1982. *Literary Agent:* The Colbert Agency, Toronto. *Address:* 53 Marlborough Avenue, Toronto, Ontario, Canada M5R 1X5.

GRANLID, Hans Olov, b. 22 Dec, 1926, Sundsvall, Sweden. Writer, m. Gundula Braun, 20 Aug. 1985, Höganäs, 2 sons, 1 daughter by previous marriages. *Education:* Doctor of Philosophy, 1957. *Publications:* Nertrappning, 1969; Mottagning, 1970; Rackarsång, Själasörjaren, 1978; Varma fiskar, 1981; Sicksakeldar, 1982; Stekta sparvar, 1984. *Honours:* The great novel prize of, Litteraturframjandet, (a Board for the advancement of literature) for, Mottagning, 1971; The prize of the Association, The Nine (co-recipient with Tomas Transcromer), 1979; The great prize of, Litteraturframjandet, (known as the Little Nobel Prize), 1984. *Membership:* PEN, Sweden. *Address:* Säterbacken 6, 142 00 Trångsund, Sweden.

GRANT, Bruce Alexander, b. 4 Apr. 1925, Perth, Australia. Author/Government Adviser. m. Joan Constance Pennell, 20 Oct. 1963, Singapore, 2 sons. *Education:* BA, Diploma of Journalism, Melbourne

University; Niemann Fellow, Harvard University. *Literary Appointments:* Adviser on Arts to Government of Victoria 1982; Chairman, Premier's Literary Awards Committee, 1984. *Publications:* Indonesia 1964; The Crisis of Loyalty, 1972; Arthur and Eric, 1978; The Boat People, 1979; Cherry Bloom, 1980; Gods and Politicians, 1982; The Australian Dilemma, 1983. *Contributor to:* The New Yorker; Esquire; Mademoiselle; Playboy; Cleo; Meanjin; Quadrant; Overland; Bulletin; Foreign Affairs (US); International Affairs; Pacific Community; Australian Outlook. *Literary Agent:* Curtis Brown. *Address:* 11/63 Domain Street, South Yarra 3141, Australia.

GRANT, Claude DeWitt, b. 20 Dec. 1944, New York City, New York, USA. Writer. m. Ginger B Waters, 7 Aug. 1982, New York City, 1 son. *Education:* BA, Hunter College, New York City; MA, Mercy College, Dobbs Ferry, New York. *Literary Appointments:* Guest Lecturer, Bronx Community College, York College, Fordham University. *Publications:* Fables From The Far Side; Images in a Shaded Light, poetry; Keeping Time, poetry. *Contributions to:* Essence Magazine; Players Magazine; Soul Magazine; Amsterdam News; Critical Perspectives of 3rd World America. *Memberships:* Association for Education in Journalism and Mass Communication; College Media Advisors; Poets and Writers Inc; Community College Journalism Association. *Address:* 1783 Bussing Avenue, Bronx, NY 10466, USA.

GRANT, Frederic Delano Junior, b. 16 July 1954, Boston, Massachusetts, USA. Attorney. *Education:* BA with high honours, Bates College, Lewiston, Maine, 1976; JD cum laude, Boston College Law School, Newton, Massachusetts, 1983. *Contributions to:* American Bar Association Journal, 1982; Boston Bar Journal, 1981, 79, 77 and others. *Address:* McCabe/Gordon PC, One Post Office Square, Boston, MA 02109, USA.

GRANT, Gwendoline Ellen, b. 5 May 1940, Worksop, Notts, England. Writer. m. Ian Grant, 13 July 1964, Worksop, 2 sons. *Education:* BA (Open); Diploma (Adult) Education. *Literary Appointments:* Creative Writing Tutor, Worksop Technical College, 1976–83; Writer-in-Residence, Museum of Childhood, Sudbury, Derbyshire, 1983; Writer Attached, Earl's Barton Junior School, Northampton, 1985. *Publications:* Private – Keep Out, 1978; Knock and Wait, 1979; Enemies Are Dangerous, 1980; The Lily Pickle Band Book, 1982; One Way Only 1983. *Contributions to:* Woman and Home; Sunday Telegraph; Woman Writer and Journalist; Meridian; Orbis; Poetry Nottingham, etc. *Memberships:* Writers' Guild of Great Britain; Theatre Writers' Union. *Literary Agent:* David Higham Associates Ltd. *Address:* 95 Watson Road, Worksop, Nottinghamshire, England.

GRANT, Michael, b. 21 Nov. 1914, London, England. Writer; Former University Professor & Vice-Chancellor. m. Rut Anne Sophie Beskow, 2 Aug. 1944, Istanbul, Turkey, 2 sons. *Education:* BA, MA, LITT.D, Trinity College, Cambridge; *Publications include:* From Imperium to Auctoritas, 1946; Roman Imperial Money, 1954; The World of Rome, 1960; Myths of the Greeks & Romans, 1962; The Civilizations of Europe, 1965; The Climax of Rome, 1968; The Ancient Mediterranean, 1969; Julius Caesar, 1969; The Ancient Historians, 1970; The Roman Forum, 1970; Herod the Great, 1971; The Jews in the Roman World, 1973; Cleopatra, 1972; The Fall of the Roman Empire, 1976; The Dawn of the Middle Ages, 1981; From Alexander to Cleopatra, 1982; History of Ancient Israel, 1984; The Roman Emperors: 31BC – AD476, 1985. *Contributions to:* Various journals. *Honours:* OBE, 1946; CBE, 1958; Honorary Litt.D. Dublin, 1961; Honorary LLD, Belfast, 1967; Gold Medal for Education, Sudan, 1977; Premio del Mediterraneo, Mazara del Valio, 1983. *Memberships:* President, Medallist, Honorary Fellow, Royal Numismatic Society; Huntingdon Medalist, American Numismatic Society; President, Virgil Society; President, Classical Association. *Address:* Le Pitturacce, Gattaiola, 55050 Lucca, Italy.

GRANT, Nigel Duncan Cameron, b. 8 June 1932, Glasgow, Scotland. University Professor. m. Valerie Keeling Evans, 16 July 1957, 1 son, 1 daughter. *Education:* MA Honours English Literature & Language, University of Glasgow, 1954; Teacher Training Certificate (Secondary), Jordanhill College, 1955; Dip Ed, 1954, M Ed, 1957, PhD, 1969, University of Glasgow. *Literary Appointments:* Editor, 1973–77, Editorial Board, 1977–, Comparative Education. *Major Publications:* Soviet Education, 1964, 1968, 1972, 1979, translated into German, Italian, Dutch & Thai; Society, Schools & Progress in Eastern Europe, 1969; Education & Nation-building in the Third World, (edited with J Lowe & T D Williams), 1971; A Mythology of British Education, (with R E Bell), 1973; Scottish Universities: The Case for Devolution, (with a Main), 1975; Patterns of Education in the British Isles, (with R E Bell), 1977; The Crisis of Scottish Education, 1982. *Contributor to:* Numerous periodicals, including: Comparative Education, School & Society, Journal of Education, Times Educational Supplement, Times Higher Education Supplement, The Scotsman, Glasgow Herald, Edinburgh International Review, Scottish Educational Review, and others. *Address:* Department of Education, The University, Glasgow G12 8QQ, Scotland.

GRANT, Verne, b. 17 Oct. 1917, San Francisco, California, USA. University Professor. *Education:* AB, 1940, PhD, Botany and Genetics, 1949, University of California, Berkeley. *Publications:* Natural History in the Phlox Family, 1959; The Origin of Adaptations, 1963, paperback edition 1971; The Architecture of the Germplasm, 1964; Flower Polination in the Phlox Family, 1965 and, Hummingbirds and their Flowers, 1968 (both with Karen Grant); Plant Speciation, 1st edition 1971, 2nd edition 1981, German translation 1976, Russian translation 1984; Genetics of Flowering Plants, 1975, paperback editon 1978; Organismic Evolution, 1977, Russian translation 1980; The Evolutionary Process, 1985. *Contributions to:* Contributor of numerous papers to professional journals, encyclopaedias. *Honours include:* Phi Beta Kappa Award in Science, 1964; Member of National Academy of Sciences, 1968; Certificate of Merit, Botanical Society of America, 1971; Fellow, American Academy of Arts and Sciences, 1975. *Memberships include:* American Society of Naturalists; Genetics Society of America; Society for the Study of Evolution (past President); Botanical Society of America; Several editorial boards. *Address:* 2811 Fresco Drive, Austin, TX 78731, USA.

GRANT, Wynford Paul, b. 11 Jan. 1947, Greenwich, England. University Lecturer. m. Margaret Elliott, 20 July 1978, 3 daughters. *Education:* 1st Class Honours, Politics, University of Leicester, 1968; MSc, Politics, University of Strathclyde, 1969; PhD, University of Exeter, 1973. *Appointment:* Associate Editor, Political Studies, 1982–. *Publications:* The Confederation of British Industry, with David Marsh, 1977; Independent Local Politics in England and Wales, 1977; The Political Economy of Industrial Policy, 1982; The Politics of Economic Policymaking, with Shiv Nath, 1984; Editor, The Political Economy of Corporation, 1985. *Contributor to:* Political Studies; Journal of Public Policy; West European Politics; Journal of Common Market Studies; British Journal of Political Science; Parliamentary Affairs; Public Money; Government and Opposition; Political Quarterly; Policy and Politics; Public Administration; New Society. *Address:* Dept of Politics, University of Warwick, Coventry CV4 7AL, England.

GRASSWILL, Helen, b. 5 Aug. 1952, Perth, Australia. Writer; Producer; Editor. m. Bruno Jean Grasswill, 7 Aug. 1976, Sydney. *Publications:* Australia, A Timeless Grandeur, 1981. *Contributions to:* Numerous publications. *Honours:* Best Produced Book Award, ABPA and Galley Club of Australia, 1982; Publishers Gold Award, 1982. *Memberships:* Australian Society of Authors; Australian Journalists Association. *Address:* 30 Dibbs Street, Alexandria, Sydney, NSW 2015, Australia.

GRAU, Shirley Ann, b. 8 July 1930, New Orleans, Writer. m. James Feibleman, 4 Aug. 1955, New York City, 2 sons, 2 daughters. *Education:* BA, Tulane University, New Orleans. *Publications:* The Black Prince, 1955; The Hard Blue Sky, 1958; The House on Coleseum Street, 1961; The Keepers of the House, 1964; The Condor Passes, 1971; The Wind Shifting West, 1973; Evidence of Love, 1977; Nine Women, 1985. *Contributor to:* New Yorker; Saturday Evening Post; etc. *Honour:* Pulitzer Prize for Fiction, 1965. *Literary Agent:* Brandt and Brandt, New York City. *Address:* 1314 First N B C Building, New Orleans, LA 70112, USA.

GRAVAGNUOLO, Benedetto, b. 10 Nov. 1949, Naples, Italy. Architect. *Education:* Degree in Architecture, University of Naples, 1973. *Literary Appointments:* Lecture on occasion of exhibition, Design by circumstance, Columbia University, New York City, New York, USA, 1981; Lecture on occasion of International congress on Adolf Loos, Sorbonne, Paris, France, 1983. *Publications:* Design by circumstance, with Alessandro Mendini, 1981; Adolf Loos, Theory and Works, 1982, English translation, 1982; Gli studi Nizzoli, editor, 1983. *Contributions to:* Casabella; Controspazio; Domus; Laica Journal; Modo; Skyline; 9A. *Address:* Via dei Mille no 1, Napoli, Italy.

GRAVES, Roy Neil, II, b. 2 Feb. 1939, Medina, Tennessee, USA. College Teacher. m. Sue Lain Hunt, 5 June 1965, Trenton, Tennessee, 1 son, 2 daughters. (divorced 1982). *Education:* Union University, Jackson, Tennessee, 1957–59; B.Arts, Princeton University, 1961; M.Arts, Duke University, 1964; D.Arts, University of Mississippi, 1977. *Literary Appointments:* Teaching Assistant, Duke University, 1964; Assistant Professor of English; University of Virginia, Lynchburg, 1965–67; Associate Professor of English, Central Virginia Community College, Lynchburg, 1967–69; Assistant, Associate, Professor of English, University of Tennessee, Martin, 1969–. *Publications:* Medina and Other Poems, 1976; John Massey Un-hyd, 1977; Shakespeare's Lost Sonnets, 1979. *Contributions to:* Appalachian Journal; The Goddard Journal; Mississippi Review; Vanderbilt Poetry Review; etc. (over 50 poems). Articles on Fortinbras (Upstart Crow, 1963); Richard Wright (Phylon); D H Lawrence (Tenn. Phil. Bull, 1943); and several reviews. *Honours include:* NIEA Fellow, Duke University, 1961–64; NEH Grant Stipend, 1975; Carnegie Fellow, Mississippi, 1976–77; First Place for Poetry, Annual Contest of, The Miscellany, 1976. *Memberships:* Tennessee Philological Association; Mississippi and Arkansas Philological Associations; Early English Text Society; Poetry Society of Tennessee; Southern Appalachian Writers' Cooperative. *Address:* Route 2, Box 473, McClain Road, Martin, TN 38237, USA.

GRAY, Clayton, b. Montreal, Canada. Writer; Historian. *Education:* Archives Diploma, McGill University, 1963. *Appointments:* Lecturer, History of Canadian Literature, Concordia University, Montreal, 1960–70. *Publications:* The Montreal Story, 1949; Conspiracy in Canada, 1959; Le Vieux Montreal, 1964. *Contributions to:* The Montrealer, Magazine; National and International Services, Educational Script Services, Drama Department, Canadian Broadcasting Corporation. *Honours:* Numerous grants. *Memberships include:* Lake Saint Louis Historical Society; Fellow, Royal Commonwealth Society; Historian, MacDodnald-Stewart Foundation; Secretary, Canadian Centre, International PEN; National Library Club. *Address:* 1495 Ste Croix, Montreal, Quebec, Canada H4L 3Z5.

GRAY, Denis John Pereira, b. 2 Oct. 1935, Exeter, England. Medical Practitioner. m. Jill Margaret Pereira Hoyte, 28 Apr. 1962, 1 son, 3 daughters. *Education:* BA, Cambridge, England 1957, MB BChir. 1960, MA, 1962, MRCGP 1967, FRCGP 1973. *Literary Appointments:* Editor, Journal of the Royal College of General Practitioners, 1972–80; Hon Editor, Royal College of General Practitioners publications 1981–. *Publications:* Running a Practice, (joint author) 1978, 3rd edition

1985; Training for General Practice, 1982; The Medical Annual, 1983/84/85. *Contributions to:* Numerous medical journals including the, British Medical Journal, Journal of the Royal College of General Practitioners, Practitioner, etc. *Honours:* George Abercrombie Award of Royal College of General Practitioners for Literature, 1978; OBE, 1981. *Address:* 9 Marlborough Road, Exeter, Devon, EX2 4TJ, England.

GRAY, Edwyn, b. 17 July 1927, London, England. Author. *Publications:* (non-fiction) A Damned Un-English Weapon, 1971; The Killing Time, 1972; The Devil's Device, 1975; Few Survived, 1986; (fiction) No Survivors, 1974; Action Atlantic!, 1975; The Tokyo Torpedo, 1975; The Last Command, 1976; Fighting Submarine, 1977; Devil Flotilla, 1978; Diving Stations, 1980; Crash Dive, 1981. *Contributor to:* Popular Magazines in UK, USA and Australia, 1952–. *Memberships:* Society of Authors; Authors' Guild Incorporated; Authors' League of America, nomination as Choice of the Month, American Military Book Club, (The Killing Time). *Literary Agent:* Nat Sobel Associates (US); Jacintha Alexander (UK). *Address:* 8 Sycamore Close, Attleborough, Norfolk, England.

GRAY, Harold James, b. 17 Oct. 1907, London. Retired Civil Servant; Former Director, Confederation of British Industry. m. Katherine Starling, 18 Oct. 1928, Snaresbrook, 1 daughter. *Education:* BSc Honours, MSc, LLB, London; MPA, Harvard; C Phys; MInstP; FRSA. *Publications include:* Electricity in Service of Man, 1949; Economic Survey of Australia, 1955; Dictionary of Physics, 1958; New Dictionary of Physics, 1975; Booklets on small firms, industrial relations, etc. *Honours:* CMG, 1956; Commonwealth Fund Fellowship, 1949–50. *Address:* 27 Byron Road, Penenden Heath, Maidstone, Kent ME14 2HA, England.

GRAY, Marianne Claire, b. 21 Sep. 1947, Cape Town, Republic of South Africa. Journalist; Author. *Education:* Diploma, Foreign Institute, University of Aix-Marseilles; 1st year BA, University of South Africa; EFL Teaching Diploma, International House, London; Secretarial/Business Diploma, Cambridgeshire Technical College. *Literary Appointments:* Reporter, The Star, Johannesburg, 1969; Reporter and showbiz writer, The Cape Times, 1972; Reporter, Sunday Express, Cape Town, 1974; Editor, Athens News, 1974; Sub-editor Buckinghamshire Advertiser, 1978; Freelance, 1978–. *Publications:* Indians and Palefaces, 1978; The Other 'Arf, 1980; Working From Home, 1982; Thoughts About Architecture, (editor), 1982. *Contributions to:* Publications in South Africa, Australia and United Kingdom including: Cosmopolitan; Honey; Woman's Journal; Company; Working Woman; Annabel; What Investment; Photoplay; She; Screen International; Woman and Home; Over 21; Sunday Times Colour Supplement; Observer Colour Supplement; Sunday Mirror; Daily Mail; Cachet; The Face; Ideal Home, etc. *Literary Agent:* Julian Friedman. *Address:* 32 Eburne Road, London N7 6AU, England.

GRAYSON, Cecil, b. 5 Feb. 1920, Batley, Yorks, England. University Professor. *Education:* MA, St Edmund Hall, Oxford. *Publications:* Early Italian Texts, (with Professor C Dionisotti); Opuscoli Inediti L B Alberti; Alberti and The Tempio Malatestiano; Vincenzo Calmeta; Prose e Lettee edite e inedite; L B Alberti, Opere volgari, 3 volumes; Life of Savonarola (transl); Life of Machiavelli (transl); Cinque saggi su Dante; L B Alberti, On Painting and on Sculpture. *Contributor to:* Bibliofilia; Burlington Magazine; English Miscellany; Italian Studies; Letter e Italiane; Lingua Nostra; Rinascimento; Years Work in Modern Languages. *Honours:* Premio International Galileo Galilei, 1974; Commendatore dell'Ordine al Merito della Repubblica Italiana, 1975; Serena Medal for Italian Studies, British Academy, 1976. *Memberships:* Fellow, British Academy; Former Member, Accademia Nazionale dei Lincei; Accademia della Crusca; Accademia dell'Arcadia. *Address:* 11 Norham Road, Oxford, England.

GREEN, Andrew Malcolm, b. 28 July 1927, London, England. Freelance Tutor and Journalist. m. Norah Bridget Cawthorne Styles, 3 Feb. 1979, Hastings, 1 stepson. *Education:* MPh, London University. *Literary Appointments:* Group Editor, Trade and Technical Press, 1963–65; Editorial Director, Thomson Organisation, 1965–71; Managing Director, Malcolm Publications, 1971–74. *Publications:* Our Haunted Kingdom, 1972; Ghost Hunting: A Practical Guide, 1972; Ghosts of the South East, 1976; Phantom Ladies, 1977; Haunted Houses, 1979; The Ghostly Army, 1980; Ghosts of Today, 1980. *Contributions to:* Prediction; Social Work Today; Police Journal; She; Fate; Theta; Daily Mirror; Weekend; Nursing Times; Woman's Journal; Doctor; Southern Life; British Book News, book reviewer. *Honours:* Award, American Parapsychological Research Fellowship; Gold Medallion Award for Design Unit at Exposition de Bruxelles, 1960. *Memberships:* Society of Authors; Fellow, Institute of Scientific and Technical Communicators and Royal Society of Arts. *Literary Agent:* Sheila Watson, London. *Address:* Scribes, Church Cottage, Mountfield, Robertsbridge, Sussex TN32 5JS, England.

GREEN, Clifford, b. 6 Dec. 1934, Melbourne, Victoria, Australia. Author; Scriptwriter. m. Judith Irene Painter, 16 May 1959, Melbourne, 1 son, 3 daughters. *Education:* Trained Primary Teachers Certificate, Toorak Teachers College. *Publications:* Marion, 1974; The Incredible Steam-Driven Adventures of Riverboat Bill, 1975; Picnic at Hanging Rock, film, 1975; Break of Day, 1976; The Sun is Up, 1978; Four Scripts, 1978; Burn the Butterflies, 1979; Lawson's Mates, 1980; The Further Adventures of Riverboat Bill, 1981; Art of Dale Marsh, 1981; Plays for Kids, 1981; Cop Out!, 1983; Evergreen, 1984; Riverboat Bill Steams Again, 1985. *Honours:* Australian Writers Guild Awards, 1973, 74, 76, 78, 79; Television Society of Australia Awards, 1974, 78, 80; Variety Club of Australia Ward, 1978. *Memberships:* Australian Society of Authors; Past Vice President, Australian Writers Guild and Melbourne Writers Theatre. *Address:* 23 Webb Street, Warrandyte Victoria 3113, Australia.

GREEN, Geoffrey Frederic, b. 22 Aug. 1947, Bradford, England. Publishing Director, T & T. Clark Ltd, Edinburgh. m. Ellen Clare Hughes, at New Orleans, 25 Nov. 1974, 1 son, 1 daughter. *Education:* MA 1970, PhD 1975, University of Edinburgh. *Literary Appointments:* Editor, New Edinburgh Review, 1974; Project Editor, Reader's Digest Books, 1982–84. *Publications:* (As Executive Editor) You & Your Rights in Scotland, 1984; The Family Guide to the Bible, 1984. *Address:* 35 Dick Place, Edinburgh EH9 2JA, Scotland.

GREEN, Harvey, b. 15 Sep. 1946, Buffalo, New York, USA. Historian; Museum Deputy Director. m. Susan R Williams, 21 June 1980, Rochester, New York. *Education:* BA, Rochester University; MA, PhD, Rutgers University. *Publications:* The Light of the Home: An Intimate View of the Lives of Women in Victorian America, 1983; Fit for America: Health, Fitness, Sport and American Society 1830–1940, 1986. *Contributions to:* Victorian Furniture, 1983; Points of View, 1978; American Quarterly, and various others. *Address:* Strong Museum, 1 Manhattan Square, Rochester, NY 14607, USA.

GREEN, Janet, b. 30 Oct. 1939, Burnley, Lancashire, England. Religious Education Teacher. m. John Green, 8 Aug. 1964, Blackpool, divorced 1983. *Education:* BA, Theology, Durham University; Diploma, Education, Oxford University. *Appointments:* Consultant, Scriptwriter, Scene, BBC Schools' TV, 1977–; Scriptwriter, Radio Bristol, 1984–. *Publications:* The Six, 1976; Getting By Turning Points, 1977; The Jesus Puzzle, 1978; Love at a Bus Stop, 1979; Homemade Prayers, 1982; Harlequinade, 1982; God's Rules OK, 1983; Best Bible Bits, 1984. *Contributor to:* Together, numerous other magazines. *Membership:* West Country Writers. *Address:* 25 Yeomeades, Long Ashton, Bristol BS18 9BE, England.

GREEN, Jim, b. 6 July 1941, High River, Alberta, Canada. Writer. m. Jeneva Boyden, 10 June 1967, Alberta, 1 son, 1 daughter. *Education:* BSc, Journalism. *Publications:* North Book, 1975; Beyond Here, 1983; Album, Flint & Steel, 1984. *Contributor to:* Numerous professional journals and magazines. *Honours:* Canadian Author's Award, 1976; Province of Alberta Award of Excellence for Poetry, 1976. *Memberships:* League of Canadian Poets; Writers Guild of Alberta. *Address:* Box 508, Fort Smith, NWT, XOE OPO, Canada.

GREEN, Joseph Lee, b. 14 Jan. 1931, Compass Lake, Florida, USA. Public Affairs Writer, NASA, John F Kennedy Space Centre. *Education:* AA, Brevard Community College, 1967. *Publications:* The Loofers of Refuge, 1965; An Affair with Genius, 1969; Gold the Man, 1971; Conscience Interplanetary, 1972; Star Probe, 1976; The Horde, 1976; Some 65 stories and articles, in British & American Magazines. *Honours:* Guest of Honour, Professional Writer, Deep South Science Fiction Convention, 1973, and Vulcon B, 1981, New Orleans, USA. *Memberships:* American Association for the Advancement of Science; Science Fiction Writers of America; World Future Society. *Agent:* E J Cornell Literary Agency. *Address:* 1390 Holly Ave, Merrit Island, FL 32952, USA.

GREEN, Michael Frederick, b. 2 Jan. 1927, Leicester, England. Author. *Education:* BA, Open University. *Publications:* Stage Noises & Effects, 1958; The Art of Coarse Rugby, 1960; The Art of Coarse Sailing, 1962; Don't Print My Name Upside Down, 1963; Even Coarser Rugby, 1963; The Art of Coarse Acting, 1964; The Michael Green Book of Coarse Sport, 1965; The Art of Coarse Golf, 1967; A Roof Over My Head The Art of Coarse Moving, 1969; Michael Green's Rugby Alphabet, 1971; The Arts of Coarse Drinking, 1973; Squire Haggard's Journal, 1975; The Arts of Coarse Cruising, 1976; Four Plays for Coarse Actors, 1978; Even Coarser Sport, 1979; The Art of Coarse Sex, 1981; The Coarse Acting Show Two, 1981; Tonight Josephine, 1981; Don't Swing From the Balcony Romeo, 1983; The Third Great Coarse Acting Show, 1985; The Art of Coarse Office Life, 1985. *Contributor to:* Observer; Times; Sunday Times; Daily Telegraph; Punch; BBC. *Memberships:* National Union of Journalists; Society of Authors. *Address:* 78 Sandall Road, London W5 1JB, England.

GREEN, Rose Basile, b. 19 Dec. 1914, New Rochelle, New York, USA. Poet; Critics Educator. m. Raymond S Green, at Torrington, Connecticut, 1 son, 1 daughter. *Education:* BA, College of New Rochelle, 1935; MA, Columbia University. 1941; PhD, University of Pennsylvania, 1963. *Literary Appointments include:* Professor of English, University of Tampa, Florida; Chairman of Department of English, Cabrini College, 1958–74; Chairman, Advisory Council of Ethnic American Studies, Washington DC, 1982–; Board Editor, National Italian-American Newsletter. *Publications include:* The Cabrinian Philosophy of Education, 1967; The Violet & the Flame, poetry, 1968; Lauding the American Dream, poetry, 1971; To Reason Why, poetry, 1971; The Italian-American Novel, criticism, 1974; Primo Vino, poetry, 1974; 76 for Philadelphia, poetry, 1975; Woman, The Second Coming, poems, 1977; Century-Four, poetry, 1982; Songs of Ourselves, poetry, 1982; The Pennsylvania People, poetry, 1984; The Life of St Frances Cabrini, Translation, 1984. *Contributions to:* A-Zimuth, Cabrini College Faculty Journal (editor & contributor); Kappa Gamma Pi News; American Ethnics Studies; National Italian-American Foundation Newsletter; and others. *Honours:* Cavalier, Republic of Italy, 1975; Distinguished Daughter of Pennsylvania, 1978; National Amita Award for Literature, 1976; Bicentennial Award for Poetry, Daughters of the American Revolution, 1976; Citation, City of Philadelphia, Poetry, 1977. *Memberships include:* Philadelphia Art Alliance (Director, Literary Committee); Free Library of Philadelphia (Director & Trustee); American Academy of Political & Social Science; Academy of American Poets; National Council

of Teachers of English. *Address:* 308 Manor Road, Philadelphia, PA 19128, USA.

GREEN, Samuel Leonard, b. 2 Dec. 1948, Sedro Woolley, Washington, USA. m. Sally Green, 18 Dec. 1971, Seattle, Washington, 1 son. *Education:* BA, English Philosophy, Western Washington State College; MA, English, Creative Writing, Western Washington University. *Literary Appointments:* Poet-in-Residence, Poetry in the Schools Program, Washington State, 1978, 79, 80, 83, 85; Poet-in-Residence, King County Arts Commission, Seattle, Washington; Visiting Professor, Southern Utah State College, 1986; Editor, Jawbone Press, 1977–83. *Publications:* Gillnets, 1978; Wind, 1980; Hands Learning to Work, 1984. *Contributions to:* Poet and Critic; Poetry Northwest; Poetry Now; Southern Poetry Review; Four Quarters; Blackwater Review; Cut Bank; Willow Springs Magazine, etc. *Address:* Waldron Island, WA 98297, USA.

GREEN, William M, b. 3 Nov. 1936, New York City, USA. Writer. m. Lindsay Waggener, New York, 1 son. *Education:* Bachelor of Fine Arts, University of Texas, Austin, Texas. *Publications:* Spencer's Bag, published in Britain as, The Plutonium Heist, 1971; Avery's Fortune, 1972; The Salisbury Manuscript, 1973; See How They Run, 1975; The Man Who Called Himself Devlin, 1978; The Romanov Connection, 1984. *Memberships:* Mystery Writers of America; Authors League. *Literary Agent:* Jo Stewart. *Address:* 303 West 66th Street, New York, NY 10023, USA.

GREENBERG, Alvin David, b. 10 May 1932. Author; Teacher. *Education:* BA, MA, University of Cincinnati, USA; PhD, University of Washington. *Literary Appointments:* University of Kentucky, 1963–65; Professor of English, Macalester College, St Paul, Minnesota. *Publications:* The Metaphysical Giraffe, 1968; Going Nowhere, 1971; House of the Would-Be Gardener, 1972; Dark Lands, 1973; Metaform, 1975; The Invention of the West, 1976; In Direction, 1978; The Discovery of America and Other Tales, 1980; And Yet, 1981; Delta Q, 1983; The Man in the Cardboard Mask, 1985. *Contributions to:* American Review; Antioch Review; Ploughshares; Poetry North West; American Poetry Review; Mississippi Review. *Honours:* Bush Foundation Artist Fellowships, 1976, 80; National Endowment for the Arts Fellowship, 1972; Short Fiction Award, Associated Writng Programmes, 1982. *Address:* Department of English, Macalester College, St Paul, MN 55105, USA.

GREENBIE, Barrie Barstow, b. 29 Mar. 1920, New York, New York, USA. Professor, Landscape Architecture and Regional Planning. m. Vlasta Koran, 20 July 1965, 3 daughters by previous marriage. *Education:* BS, University of Miami; MS, PhD, University of Wisconsin; studied, Corcoran School of Art and Art Students League. *Literary Appointment:* Editorial Board, Land Use Policy. *Publications:* Design for Diversity, 1976; Design for Communality and Privacy, Co-editor, 1978; Spaces: Dimensions of the Human Landscape, 1981. *Contributions to:* Journal of the American Institue of Planners; Man-Environment Systems; Traffic Quarterly; Landscape Design, UK; Landscape Research, UK. *Address:* 15 Cortland Drive, Amherst, MA 01002, USA.

GREENBLAT, Cathy Stein, b. 11 Mar. 1940, New York City, USA. Professor of Sociology, Rutgers University. 1 son, 1 daughter. *Education:* AB, Vassar College, 1961; MA, Teachers College, Columbia University, 1964; PhD, Columbia University, 1968. *Publications include:* The Marriage Game: Understanding Marital Decision-Making (with P J Stein and N F Washburne), 1973, revised, 1977; Blood Money (with J H Gagnon), 1976; Life Design (with J H Gagnon), 1977; Getting Married (with T Cottle), 1980; Principles and Practices of Gaming, Simulations (with R Duke), 1981; Introduction to Sociology, 1981. *Contributor to:* (Editor), Simulation and Games; Simulation-Gaming News; Teaching Sociology; Health Education Monographs; American Sociology; Youth and Society; Victimology; Journal of Marriage and the Family; Sociological Perspectives; Signs; Society. *Memberships:* American Sociological Association, Executive Board Member, 1973–78; President, 1973–74; International Simulation and Gaming Association. *Address:* 34 Bayard Lane, Princeton, NJ 08540, USA.

GREENE, Freda Hannah, b. 29 Mar. 1929, London, England. Freelance Writer, Journalist. m. 12 April 1953, New York, 1 daughter. *Education:* Regent Street Polytechnic, London, England, RSA French; University of Southern California at Los Angeles. *Literary Appointments:* Consultant Writer, National Center on Deafness, California State University, Northridge, USA; Contributing editor, California Good Life; International Correspondent: Giftware News (US), Tableware International (UK). *Major Publications:* How to Get a Job in Los Angeles, 1985; *Contributing Writer:* California (Los Angeles edition); Contributing Writer, Book of Lists, 1977 #01. *Contributor to:* Scanorama Europe (Magazine of the EEC, Washington DC); Travel & Leisure; Deaf American; The Financial Weekly (London); Los Angeles Times; German American Trade News; Collector Editions; Automobile International; Australian Giftguide. *Honours:* Writers' Digest, 1975, 1977; Foreign Press Award, 1982. *Memberships:* American Society of Journalists & Authors (Events Chair); PEN International; Womens' National Book Association; Book Publicists of Southern California. *Literary Agent:* Elaine Berman. *Address:* 6624 Newcastle Avenue, Reseda, CA 91335, USA.

GREENE, James, b. 20 Jan. 1938, Berlin, Germany. Writer. *Education:* BA, French and Russian, Oxford University, England, 1961. *Publications:* Osip Mandelstam, 1977, 1980; Dead Man's Fall, 1980; I Have Come to You to Greet You, (translation of poems of Olav H Hauge), 1982; Don't Give Me the Whole Truth, (with Robin Fulton and Siv Hennum), 1985; Surprise of Being, (with Clara Mafra), 1986; Author of BBC Radio 3 programmes on, Mandelstam, FET, Valery, and Grimm's The Goldern Bird. *Contributor to:* Comparative Criticism; Encounter; Lines Review; London Magazine; London Review of Books; New Review; New Statesman; Poetry Durham; Poetry and Audience; Poetry Nation Review; Poetry Review; Verse; International Journal of Psycho-Analysis; Contemporary Psycho-Analysis; Isis; Views; New Society; Harvest; Energy and Character. *Honours:* 1st Prize in Comparative Literature Associations annual translation competition for poems by Fernando Pessoa, 1985. *Address:* 45 Shirlock Road, London NW3, England.

GREENE, Oscar Herbert, b. 28 May 1918, New York City, USA. Retired Manager, General Electric; Author; Lecturer; Media Scout. m. Ruby Frierson, 29 Sep. 1942, St Louis, Missouri, 1 son. *Education:* Diploma Certifcate, Hampton Institute (now Hampton University), 1941. *Literary Appointments:* Book Review Staff, Boston Globe, 1965–75; Trustee, Medford Public Library, Massachusetts, 1968–75; New England Media Scout, Guideposts Magazine, 1984–; Contributing Writer, Guideposts, Book Division, 1984–. *Publications:* The Episcopal Diocese of Massachusetts 1784–1984 (contributor); Daily Guideposts, 1980, 81, 86 (contributor). *Contributor to:* Guideposts; Highlights for Children; Power for Living; Purpose; The Boston Globe; The Gem; Guideposts Femily Christmas Books; The Christian Writer; The Lookout; Sunday Digest. *Honour:* Winner, Guideposts National Writing Competition, 1977. *Address:* 121 Sharon Street, West Medford, MA 02155, USA.

GREENE, Robert Everett, b. 14 February 1936, Portland, Maine, USA. Reporter; Writer; Editor. m. Helky Jaatinen, 9 Nov. 1971, Rockville, Maryland, USA. *Education:* University of Kansas. *Publications:* Century of Champions; World of Tennis, 1983, 84, 85. *Contributor to:* New York Magazine and various tennis publications. *Memberships:* United States Tennis Writers Association (President); Lawn Tennis Writers (British); Football Reporters of Canada. *Honour:* Co-

writer of the Year, Women's Tennis Association, 1985. *Address:* 150 Joralemon Street, Apt. 46, Brooklyn, NY 11201, USA.

GREENE, (Sir) Hugh (Carleton), b. 15 Nov. 1910, Berkhamstead, England. Publisher; Former Broadcasting Official. *Education:* Merton College, Oxford. *Publications:* The Spy's Bedside Book, 1957; The Third Floor Front, 1969; The Rivals of Sherlock Holmes (editor) 1970; More Rivals of Sherlock Holmes, (editor) 1971; The Future of Broadcasting, in Britain, 1972; The Crooked Counties (editor) 1973; The American Rivals of Sherlock Holmes (editor) 1976. *Honours:* Honorary DCL, University of East Aglia, 1969; Dr hc, Open University and York University, 1973. *Address:* Earls Hall, Cockfield, Bury St Edmunds, Suffolk, England.

GREENE, Victor Robert, b. 15 Nov. 1933, Newark, New Jersey, USA. Historian. *Education:* BA, Harvard University, 1955; MA, University of Rochester, New York, 1960; PhD, University of Pennsylvania, 1963. *Publications:* The Slavic Community on Strike, 1968; For God and Country: Rise of Polish and Lithuanian Ethnic Consciousness in America 1860–1910, 1975. *Contributions to:* Church History; The Polish Review; American Historical Review; Journal of American History; *Honours:* Grants: National Endowment for the Humanities, 1965, 76. *Membership:* President and Executive Board Member, Immigration History Society. *Address:* Department of History, University of Wisconsin, Milwaukee, WI 53201, USA.

GREENHILL, Basil Jack, b. 26 Feb. 1920, Weston-Super-Mare, Somerset, England. Chairman, SS Great Britain Project; Company Director. m. Ann Giffard, 2 June 1961, Fyfield, 2 sons. *Education:* BA, PhD, Bristol University. *Publications:* The Merchant Schooners, 2 volumes 1968; Boats & Boatmen of Pakistan, 1972; A Victorian Maritime Album, 1974; A Quayside Camera, 1975; Archaeology of Boats, with Ann Giffard, 1976; Westcountrymen in Prince Edward's Ise, 1967; Travelling by Sea in the 19th Century, 1972; Victorian & Edwardian Sailing Ships, 1976; Westcountry Coasting Ketches, with W J Slade, 1974; The Coastal Trade: Sailing Craft of British Waters 900-1900, with L Willis, 1975; Victorian & Edwardian Steamships, with A Giffard, 1978; The Life and Death of the Merchant Sailing Ship, 1980; Schooners, 1980; The British Seafarer, 1980; Seafaring under Sail, 1981; Karlsson, 1982; Grain Race, 1986; The Woodshipbuilders, 1986. *Contributor to:* Numerous professional journals. *Honours:* Award of Merit, American Association for State & Local History, 1968; Commander, Order of St Michael & St George; Companion, Order of the Bath, 1981; Knight Commander, Order of White Rose of Finland. *Address:* West Boethevic Farm, St Dominic, Saltash, Cornwall PL12 6SZ, England.

GREENMAN, Robert Stephen, b. 11 Dec. 1939, Brooklyn, New York, USA. High School English Teacher. m. Carol Nina Sokolov, 28 May, 1960, Cambridge, Massachusetts, USA, 3 daughters. *Education:* BS, Emerson College, Boston, USA. *Publications:* The Rap Book, 1979; The New York Times Captive Vocabulary, 1980; Words in Action, 1983. *Contributor to:* The Adviser's Companion (a series of articles about the principles and problems of advising secondary school student newspapers. Appearing in the journal of the Columbia Scholastic Press Association, Columbia University, New York, 1985 to 1986. *Honour:* Gold Key, Columbia Scholastic Press Association, 1984. *Address:* 4272 Bedford Avenue, Brooklyn, NY 11229, USA.

GREER, Germaine, b. 29 Jan. 1939. Writer, Broadcaster. Divorced. *Education:* BA Honours, University of Melbourne, Australia, 1959; MA Honours, Sydney University, 1963; PhD, Cambridge, England, 1968. *Literary Appointments:* Senior tutor in English, 1963–64; Lecturer in English, University of Warwick, 1968–73; Visiting Professor, University of Tulsa, USA, 1979; Director, Tulsa Centre for the Study of Women's Literature, 1980–82. *Publications:* The Female Eunuch,

1968; Foreword, Autobiography of Anna Kollontai, 1970; Introduction, Goblin Market, 1971; The Revolting Garden, 1971; The Obstacle Race, 1979; Sex and Destiny, 1982; Women and Power in Cuba, in, Women: A World Report, 1985; Shakespeare, 1986; Collected Essays, in press; An Anthology of Seventeenth Century Women's Verse, (co-editor), 1987. *Contributions to:* Publications including: Columnist, The Sunday Times, 1971–73; Esquire; Harper's; Playboy; The Listener; The Spectator. *Honour:* Journalist of the Year, Playboy. *Address:* c/o Gillon Aitken Limited, 29 Fernshaw Road, London SW10 OTG, England.

GREET, Brian Aubrey, b. 12 June 1922, Bristol, England. Methodist Minister. m. Jill Margaret Edwards, 3 July 1954, Birmingham, 1 son, 1 daughter. *Education:* BA, Birmingham University; BD, Manchester University; STM, Drew University, Madison, New Jersey, USA. *Publications:* To Communion with Confidence, 1970; What Makes a Minister?; Contributor to Symposia: In Church; Preachers Handbook Number II. *Contributor to:* Epworth Review; Methodist Recorder; Expository Times. *Honours:* 1st Prize, Manuscript Competition, 1969. *Address:* 37 Sutton Passeys Crescent, Wollaton Park, Nottingham NG8 1BX, England.

GREET, Kenneth Gerald, b. 17 Nov. 1918, Bristol, England. Writer. m. Mary Edbrooke, 26 July 1947, Bristol, 1 son, 2 daughters. *Education:* Hamdsworth College, Birmingham; DD, Ohio, USA. *Publications:* Large Petitions, 1958; The Mutual Society, 1962; Man and Wife Together, 1962; The Debate About Drink, 1969; The Sunday Question, 1970; The Art of Moral Judgement, 1970; When the Spirit Moves, 1975; A Lion from a Thicket, 1978; What Shall I Cry? 1986. *Contributions to:* Methodist Recorder; Epworth Review; Tablet; Guardian; Times and others. *Address:* 89 Broadmark Land, Rustington, Sussex BM16 2JA, England.

GREGOR-DELLIN, Martin, b. 3 June 1926, Naumburg, Germany. Writer. *Publications include:* Jakob Haferglanz, 1956, 2nd edition, 1963; Der Mann mit der StOpphuhr, 1959; Der Nullpunki, 1959; Der Kandelaber, 1962; Moglichkeiten einer Fahrt, 1964; Einer, 1964; Markwerben, 1967; Aufbruch ins Ungewisse, 1968; Unsichere Zeiten, 1969; Ferdinand wird totgereder, 1971; Wagner-Chronik, 1976; Das Gastehaus, 1972; Richard Wagner – die Revolution als Oper, 1973; Fohn, 1974; Deutsche Erzahlungen aus drei Jahrzehnten (anthology), 1975; Das Riesenrad, 1976; Im Zeitalter Kafkas, 1979; Richard Wagner, Sein Leben, sein Werk, sein Jahrhundert, 1980; Schlabrudorf oder Die Republik, 1982; Heinrich SchuTz, SeiN liben, sein Werk, sein Zief, 1984; Was ist Grope? Sieben Deutsche und ein deutsohes Problem, 1985. *Honours:* Munich Literary Prize; Critics Prize, Die Goldene Feder; SterEo Radio Play Prize; Federal Cross of Merit, 1st Class. *Memberships:* German Academy for Language and Literature; Bavarian Academy of Fine Arts; Association of German Writers; PEN Center, Federal German Repubic, General Secretary. *Address:* Kochelseestrasse 57, D–8038 Gröbenzell bei München, Federal German Republic.

GREGORIOS, Paulos Mar, b. 9 Aug. 1922, Tripunithura, Kerala, India. Bishop; Educator; Writer; Editor. President, World Council of Churches. *Education includes:* BA, Goshen College, Indiana, USA, 1952; MDiv, Princeton Theological Seminary, 1954; STM, Yale University, 1960; D Th, Serampore University, India, 1975. *Literary Appointments:* Journalist, India, 1937–42; Teacher, Secondary Schools, Ethiopia, 1947–50; Honorary Lecturer, Union Christian College, 1954–56, University College of Addis Ababa, 1956–59. Various others. *Publications:* The Joy of Freedom, 1967; The Gospel of the Kingdom, 1968; The Freedom of Man, 1972; Be Still and Know, 1974; Freedom and Authority, 1974; The Quest for Certainty, 1975; The Human Presence, 1978, Indian Edition, 1980; Truth Without Tradition? 1978; Science for Sane Societies, 1980;

Cosmic Man, 1980; The Indian Orthodox Church, 1982. *Contributions to:* Hundreds of journals. Editor and Contributor: Koptisches Christentum, 1973; Die Syrischen Kirchen in Indien, 1974; Burning Issues, 1977; Science and Our Future, 1978; Does Chalcedon Divide or Unite? 1981. *Honours include:* Certificate of Merit for Distinguished Service and Inspired Leadership of World Church, Dictionary of International Biography, Cambridge, England; Order of St Vladimir, USSR; Order of St Sergius, USSR; Order of St Mary Magdalene, Poland; Honorary D Th, Leningrad Theological Academy, USSR, Lutheran Theological Academy, Budapest, Hungary and Jan Hus Faculty, Prague. *Memberships include:* Comparative Education Society in Europe. *Address:* Delhi Orthodox Centre, 2 Institutional Area, Tughlakabad, New Delhi 110062, India.

GREGORY, Timothy Edmund, b. 1 Apr. 1943, Flint, Michigan, USA. Professor. 4 daughters. *Education:* AB, University of Michigan, 1963; AM, 1965; PhD, 1971; American School of Classical Studies, Athens, 1967–68. *Literary Appointments:* Pennsylvania State University, 1969–72; Ohio State University, 1972–; American School of Classical Studies, 1979–81. *Publications:* Editor with Anthony J Podlecki, Panathenaia, 1978; Violence and Popular Involvement in the Religious Controversies of the Fifth Century A D, 1979; Nauplion, 1980. *Contributions to:* Greek, Roman and Byzantine Studies; Byzantion; Hesperia; Byzantine Studies/Etudes Byzantines; and others. *Memberships:* American Philological Association; Archaeological Institute of America; US National Committee on Byzantine Studies; Association of Ancient Historians; Modern Greek Studies Association. *Address:* Department of History, Ohio State University, Columbus, OH 43210, USA.

GRENDLER, Paul Frederick, b. 24 May 1936, Armstrong, Iowa, USA. Historian; Professor of History. *Education:* BA, Oberlin College, 1959; MA, 1961; PhD, 1964, University of Wisconsin. *Publications:* Critis of the Italian World, 1530–1560, 1969; The Roman Inquisition and the Venetian Press 1540–1605, 1977, Italian translation, 1983; Culture and Censorship in Late Renaissance Italy and France, 1981. *Contributions to:* Various professional journals. *Honours include:* Marraro Prize, American Catholic Historical Association, 1978; Various fellowships and grants. *Memberships:* Renaissance Society of America; American Historical Association; Society for Italian Historical Studies; Past President, American Catholic Historical Association. *Address:* Department of History, University of Toronto, Toronto, Ontario, Canada M5S 1A1.

GRESS, Esther, Editor. *Literary Appointments:* Editor, Encyclopedia Vor Tids Konversations Leksikon Supplement, 1948; Mentor, 1949; Dansk Rim-Ordbog, 1950; Newspaper Berlingske Tidende, 1950–; Publications of Det Berlingske Officin A/S including Radiolytteren, Landet, Det Danske Magasin and Berlingske Aftenavis; Radio, film and theatre columnist; Picture Editor. *Publications:* Skal, 1974; Liv, 1977; Ville-vejenivejen 1979; Det Sker – måske, 1982; Det gik, 1983; Raise, with English poems, 1984; Og Se, 1984; Noget, 1985; Let Us, with poems in 10 languages, 1985. *Contributions to:* Anthologies, papers and magazines including: Lyrikarbogen, 1974 and 1977; Citatbogen, 1977 and 1979; Spejlinger, 1977; Digte 80, 1980; Lyriksafe, 1980; Frederiksborg Amts Avis; Berlingske Tidende; Barlingske Aftenavis; Politiken; Kristelight Dagblad; Svenska Dagbladet; Jul i Nordsjoelland; Nuancer; English poems in magazines in United Kingdom, USA, Italy, Switzerland, Austria, Korea and India. *Honours include:* Awards in USA and Italy; Academy Consul for Denmark, Accademia d'Europa, Naples, 1982; Guest of Honour, New York Poetry Forum, 1983; Grand Dame in Knight of Malta, 1984; Doctor of Literature, 1984. *Memberships include:* World Poetry Society Intercontinental; United Poets Laureate International; Danish Authors Association; Accademia Internazionale di Lettere; Arti Virgiglio-Mantegna; Accademia Internazionale Leonardo da Vinci; New York

Poetry Forum. Inc; National Federation of States Poetry Societies Inc; Danish Press Historic Association. *Address:* Ny Strandvej 27, 3050 Humlebaek, Denmark.

GREY, Beryl Elizabeth, b. 11 June 1927, London, England. Former Prima Ballerina; Producer, London Classical Ballets. m. Sven Gustav Svenson, 15 July 1950, 1 son. *Publications:* Red Curtain Up, 1959; Through the Bamboo Curtain, 1965; My Favourite Ballet Stories, 1981; Biography, Beryl Grey, by David Gillard, 1979. *Contributions to:* Numerous Publications. *Honours:* Companion, Order of the British Empire (CBE), 1973; Honorary DLitt, London City University, 1974; Honorary DMus, Leicester University, 1971. *Literary Agent:* Higham Associates. *Address:* Fernhill, Priory Road, Forest Row, E Sussex, England.

GREY, Ian, b. 5 May 1918, Wellington, New Zealand. Author, Editor. *Education:* LL B, University of Sydney, Australia. *Major Publications:* Peter the Great, 1960; Catherine the Great, 1961; Ivan the Terrible, 1964; The First Fifty Years: Soviet Russia 1917–67; The Romanovs: Rise & Fall of the Dynasty, 1970; A History of Russia, 1970; Boris Godunov, 1973; Stalin: Man of History, 1979; Parliamentarians, The History of the Commonwealth Parliamentary Association 1911–1985, 1986. *Literary Agent:* John Farquharson Ltd. *Address:* 10 Alwyn Avenue, Chiswick, London W4, England.

GRIFFIN, Johy Eleanor Fogleman Phelps, b. 21 Nov. 1905, Pollock, Louisiana, USA. Teacher. m. (1) Iley O Fogleman, 26 Dec. 1928 (dec. 1934), 2 sons, 1 daughter. (2) Earl J Phelps (dec. 1965), *Education:* BA, Northwestern State University, 1940; Postgraduate work, University of Virginia, George Washington University etc; Diploma, Writers School, Richmond, Virginia, 1982; Writers Conferences. *Literary Appointments:* Teacher; Lecturer; Annual Literary Programme for NE American Mothers on Great Authors & Poets; Manuscripts for Meditation Booklet, on assigned scripture, in press. *Contributions to:* Louisiana Teachers Journal (article). Poems in: American Poet; Writers Exchange; American Haiku; Swordsman Review; Sea to Sea in Song; Mature Living; Home Life; Monroe News Star; Springfield Daily News; Louisiana Lyric; Haiku Highlights. Mature Living, articles, essays, profiles; Pre-School Leadership Journal, articles, poems. *Honours include:* Delta Kappa Gamma Award, Biography; Two 1st Place Awards, Poetry, Louisiana Federation of Womens Clubs; 1st Place, Essay, American Mothers, New York, 1979; 1st Place, Louisiana State, short story, 1980, 1981; Story & Poem, Louisiana Writers Conference, 1984; Short Story, National, 1984, etc. *Memberships include:* Louisiana State Poetry Society (President, Northeast Branch, 1968–70); National League of American Pen Women; De Nova Federation Club; American Mothers (Literary Chairman, 1984–86). *Address:* Joy Eleanor Phelps, Royal North Apts. 1–1603 Erin Avenue, Monroe, LA 71201, USA.

GRIFFIN, Russell Morgan, b. 29 Apr. 1943, Stamford, Connecticut, USA. Professor of English. m. Sheila Vaznelis, 25 Aug. 1965, New Britain, Connecticut, 1 son, 1 daughter. *Education:* BA, Trinity College, Connecticut, 1965; MA, Case Western Reserve University, 1969; PhD, Case Western Reserve University, 1970. *Publications:* Makeshift God, 1979; Century's End, 1981; The Blind Man and the Elephant, 1982; The Timesavers, 1985. *Contributions to:* Extrapolation; Redbook; Omni, Best of Omni; Analog; Fantasy and Science Fiction. *Honour:* NDEA Fellow, 1967–70. *Membership:* Science Fiction Writers of America. *Literary Agent:* Jet Literary Associates. *Address:* 102 Old Field Lane, Milford, CT 06460, USA.

GRIFFITHS, Bryn, b. Swansea, Wales. Writer. *Literary Appointments:* Editor, Welsh Voices; Writer-in-Residence, West Australia College, 1983; Writer-in-Residence, Australian Merchant Navy, 1985. *Publications:* The Mask of Pity, 1966; The Stones Remember, 1967; Welsh Voices (Editor), 1967; Scars, 1969; The Survivors, 1971; Starboard Green, 1971;

Beast Hoods, 1972; The Dark Convoys, 1973; Love Poems, 1981. *Contributions to:* Poetry Wales; Poetry Review; Blackfriars Magazine; Western Mail; Transatlantic Review; Tribune; Critical Quarterly; Sunday Times; The Australian; Meanjin Review; The Listener, *Literary Agent:* Jill Campbell, Mckay, London. *Address:* 65 Gwili Terrace, Mayhill, Swansea, Wales.

GRIFFITHS, (Edith) Grace (Chalmers), b. 9 Feb. 1921, Devon, England. Librarian. m. Gordon Griffiths, 14 Oct. 1948, Newton Abbot, Devon, England. *Major Publications:* History of Teignmouth, 1965; Mattie, 1967; Silver Blue, 1971; Abandoned, 1973; Days of my Freedom, 1978; Book of Dawlish, 1984. *Address:* 3 Winterbourne Road, Teignmouth, Devon, TQ14 8JT, England.

GRIFFITHS, Helen, b. 8 May 1939, London, England. Writer. *Publications:* Horse in the Clouds, 1957; Wild and Free, 1958; Moonlight, 1959; Africano, 1960; The Wild Heart, 1962; The Greyhound, 1963; The Wild Horse of Santander, 1965, (Highly Commended by Carnegie Comm, 1966): The Dark Swallows, 1965; Leon, 1966; Stallion of the Sands, 1967; Moshie Cat, 1968; Patch, 1969; Federico, 1970; Russian Blue, 1973; Just a Dog, 1974; Witch Fear, 1975 (Silver Pencil Award, Netherlands, for Best Children's Book of the Year, 1978); Pablo, 1976; The Kershaw Dogs, 1978; The Last Summer, 1979; Blackface Stallion, 1980; Dancing Horses, 1981; Hari's Pigeon, 1982; Rafa's Dog, 1983; The Dog at the Window, 1984. *Address:* 42 New Bridge Road, Bath, Avon BA1 3JZ, England.

GRIFFITHS, Linda Pauline, b. 7 Oct. 1956, Montreal, Canada. Writer, Actor. *Education:* CEGEP Diploma, Dawson College; Teaching Certificate, McGill Teachers' College. *Publications:* Maggie & Pierre, 1980; O D On Paradise, 1985. *Honours:* Dora Mavor Moore Award, 1980, 1984. *Membership:* Playwright's Union of Canada. *Literary Agent:* Ralph Zimmerman. *Address:* c/o Ralph Zimmerman, Great North Artists, 345 Adelaide Street West, Suite 500, Toronto, Ontario M5U IR5, Canada.

GRIFFITHS ORMHAUG, Ella, b. 22 Mar. 1926, Oslo, Norway. Author; Copywriter; Radio Reporter; Journalist; Columnist; Translator. *Education:* Oslo University; Conservatory of Music, Oslo; Mass Media Studies, American University, The Salzburg Seminar in American Studies, Salzburg, Austria; Certificate of Proficiency, English, University of Cambridge; Film/Video Seminar, Norwegian Film Industries. *Publications:* Some 25 adult books including the police procedurals: The Water Widow; Unknown Partner; Murder on Page 3; Five to Twelve; 12 Children's and Youth Novels including: Pia, Kim and Tiny, 1979; Tiny and Bombastus, the Cat, 1981; Tiny and Pepper, the Tortoise, 1983; Fiddle-Diddle Grasshopper and other Fairytales, 1984; Thursday, January 32, (science fiction), 1985; Short Stories in The John Creasey Crime Collections, 1980, 1983, 1984, 1986; Several of her works are published in Sweden, Denmark, Finland, United Kingdom, USA, and Unknown Partner in USSR, 1986–87. *Memberships:* Norwegian Authors Association, Norway; Association of Authors of Children's Books and Youth Novels; Norwegian Authors Centre; Crime Writers' Association, England, PEN. *Honours include:* United States Information Agency (Washington) Award for Meritorious Service, 1962; Department of State AID-USIA (Washington) Outstanding Services Award, 1977; etc. *Literary Agents:* Ulla Lohren (Nordic Countries); Laurence Pollinger Limited, London, (the rest of the World). *Address:* Kirkeveien 99A, 1344 Haslum, Norway.

GRIGG, John Edward Poynder, b. 15 Apr. 1924, London, England. Author; Journalist. *Education:* MA New College, Oxford. *Publications:* Two Anglican Essays, 1958; The Young Lloyd George, 1973; Lloyd George: The People's Champion, 1978; 1943: The Victory that Never Was, 1980; Nancy Astor, Portrait of a Pioneer, 1980; Lloyd George: from Peace to War, 1985. *Contributor to:* The Guardian; Listener; many newspapers & periodicals. *Honours:* Recipient, Whitebread Prize for Best Biography of Year, 1978; Wolfson Award, 1985. *Address:* 32 Dartmouth Row, London SE10 8AW, England.

GRIGORESCU, Ioan, b. 20 Oct. 1930, Ploiesti, Romania. Writer. m. Maria, 9 Nov. 1950, 1 son. *Education:* Diploma, Gorki Literary Institute, Moscow, USSR, 1955; Diploma, Institute of Journalism, Strasbourg, France, 1960. *Literary Appointments:* Paustowski, 1950–55; Sadoveanu, 1956; Ehrenbourg, 1956; Arghezi, 1958; Neruda, 1959; Mauriac, 1960; Toffler, 1971; Jouvenel, 1973; Boisdeffrs, 1976; Kessler, 1984, etc. *Publications:* Cinema Madagascar, 1956; The Obsession, 1959; The Struggle Against Sleep, 1969; Inflammable Phoenix, 1971; The World Spectacle, 1973; The Dirty Paradise, 1974; I Swear! 1974; The American Dilemma, 1982; Fifth Cardinal Point, 1984; 18 Art Films Scenarios; 100 short TV Films. *Contributor to:* Contemporenul, (former Editor); Cinema, (former Editor); other literary publications; radio and TV. *Honours:* Prize Italia, 1968; Prize of Association of Filmakers, 1971; Prize, Writers Union, 1971, 83. *Memberships:* Filmakers Association (Vice-President, 19781–85); Writers Union Bucharest, 1957–85; Society of Authors, Paris, 1969. *Literary Agents:* SACD, Paris; Fondul Literer, Bucharest. *Address:* Bvld. Primaverii 32, Cod Postal 71297, Bucharest, Romania.

GRIGSON, Jane, b. 13 Mar. 1928. Gloucester, England. Cookery Writer. *Education:* BA Honours, Newnham College, University of Cambridge, 1946–49. *Major Publications:* Charcuterie & French Pork Cookery, 1967; Good Things, 1971; Fish Cookery, 1973; English Food, 1974, revised 1979; The Mushroom Feast, 1975; Jane Grigson's Vegetable Book, 1978; Food with the Famous, 1979; Jane Grigson's Fruit Book, 1982; Observer Guide to European Cookery, 1983; Observer Guide to British Cookery, 1984. *Contributor to:* Observer Magazine; A la Carte. *Honour:* John Florio Prize for Italian Translation (with Fr K Foster) of Beccaria's Of Crimes & Punishments, 1966. *Literary Agent:* Jacqueline Korn, David Higham Associates. *Address:* Broad Town Farmhouse, Broad Town, Swindon, Wiltshire, England.

GRIM, William Edward, b. 29 Aug. 1955, Columbus, Ohio, USA. Professor. m. Deborah Binkley, 26 May 1979, Coshocton, Ohio, USA. *Education:* BM Music, Ohio Wesleyan University, 1977; MM Music Performance, University of Akron, 1979; PhD, Musicology, Kent State University, 1985. *Literary Appointments:* Review Editor, The Flute Journal, 1982–83; Poetry Editor, 1983–84, Executive Editor, 1984–, The St Andrews Review. *Major Publicatons:* Max Reger A Bio-Bibliography, 1987. *Contributor to:* St Andrews Review; Cairn; The Clarinet; The Flute Journal; The National Association of College Wind & Percussion Instructors Journal; The Student Scholar. *Honours:* Independent Research Fellowship, Ohio Wesleyan University, 1977; Faculty Research Grants, St Andrews Presbyterian College, 1982–85. *Memberships:* North Carolina Writers; Association; Association of Affiliated Writing Programs. *Address:* 2119 Thomas Avenue, Apt. C, Alamosa, CO 81101, USA.

GRIMES, Naomi, b. 20 Oct. 1950. Writer, Photojournalist, Lecturer. *Education:* BA, Livingston College – Rutgers University, 1974. *Appointments:* Proof Reader, Board of Education Community Publishing, KWELI; Talent coordinator, Blackfrica Promotions; Instructor, creative writing and applied socio-linguistics, Livingston College and Rutgers University Graduate School of Education; Literary Consultant, Hunter College; Radio producer, The Kids Show, WBAI FM, New York, Literary Consultant, Cultural Council Foundation CETA Arts project. *Publications:* Poems By, 1970; Something on My Mind, 1978; Growin, juvenile novel, 1977; *Contributions to:* Newspaspers and magazines including: Today's Christian Woman; Sunday Woman; Journal of Black Poetry; Obsidian; Greenfield Review; Essence; Drum; Voice; Black Forum. *Honours:* Various. *Memberships*

include: Poets and Writers Incorporated; Authors Guild Incorporated. *Address:* The Dial Press, E P Dutton, 2 Park Avenue, New York, NY 10016, USA.

GRIMSHAW, James Albert, b. 10 Dec. 1940, Kingsville, Texas, USA. Educator. m. Glenda Darlene Hargett, 10 June 1961, Lubbock, Texas, USA. 1 son, 1 daughter. *Education:* BA 1962, MA 1968, Texas Technological University; PhD, Louisiana State University, 1972. *Publications:* Cleanth Brooks at the USAF Academy, 1980; The Flannery O'Connor Companion, 1981; Robert Penn Warren: A Descriptive Bibliography, 1982; Robert Penn Warren's, Brother to Dragons: A Discussion, 1983. *Contributions to:* Shakespeare Quarterly; The Southern Review; Southern Literary Journal; Kentucky Review; South Central Review; Explicator; Resources for American Literary Study; Papers of the Bibliographical Society of America; Notes on Modern American Literature; College English. *Honours:* Flannery O'Connor Visiting Professor of English, Georgia College, 1977; Visiting Fellow in Bibliography, Beinecke Rare Book and Manuscript Library, Yale University, 1979–80. *Memberships:* Texas Folklore Society; Chairman 1983–84, South Central Association of Departments of English; Modern Language Association of America; Society for the Study of Southern Literature. *Address:* Rt 2 Box 40T, Greenville, TX 75401, USA.

GRIMSHAW, Peter John, b. 13 May 1940, London, England. Journalist; Broadcaster. m. Margaret Sabey, 12 Dec. 1964, Huntingdon, 1 son, 1 daughter. *Education:* HND, Agriculture; CDA, Agriculture, Chelmsford. *Appointments:* Former Staff Journalist, major farm and agricultural journals; Currently, free-lance journalist. *Contributor to:* Local radio on rural and agriculture matters. *Honour:* Fisons Award for Agricultural Radio. *Memberships:* Council Member, Vice Chairman, UK Guild of Agricultural Journalists. *Address:* The Rockery, Bath Road, Devizes, Wiltshire SN10 1PL, England.

GROENE, Janet. Writer – Photographer. (Partner, Gordon Groene). *Publications:* The Galley Book, 1977; How To Live Aboard A Boat, 1983; Cooking On The Go, 1984; Living Aboard Your Recreational Vehicle, 1986. *Contributions to:* Numerous publications. *Memberships:* American Society of Journalists and Authors. *Literary Agent:* Ray Lincoln. *Address:* c/o Hearst Marine Books, 105 Madison Avenue, New York, NY 10016, USA.

GRÖHLER, Harald O, b. 13 Oct. 1938, Bad Warmbrunn, Federal Republic of Germany. Freelance Writer. *Education:* Studies Psychology, Gottingen, Kiel and Cologne Universities. *Literary Appointments:* Freelance Writer, 1960s-; Literary Critic, Freelance for numerous West German radio stations and newspapers including Frankfurter Allgem and Zeitung; Manager and Moderator, Published authors discussions, Cologne and others, 1971; Founder, Group-Intermedia (Artistic group), 1970; Managing podium-discussions, jury member, Literary Prize Competition, Cologne at the Cathedral, 1980. *Publications:* Stories with Children and Without, progressive prose, 1981; Red, novel, 1984; Editor, Into the own net, by Gerhard Uhlenbruck, 1977; Co-Editor, Cologne, Anthology, 1980. *Contributions to:* Over 40 anthologies and numerous journals including: Suddeutsche Zeitung; Frankfurter Allgem Zeitung; Akzente; Neue Deutsche Hefte; Dokumente; Dimensions, USA; Znaky, Poland; Lieraturmagazin; Jahresring; Die Horen; Jahrburch fur Lyrik. Translations into Turkish and Arabic. *Honours:* Working Scholarship, Ministry of Education, 1973, 81; Scholarship AtelierhausWorpsede, 1974; Promotion Prize, City of Cologne, 1975; Honorary Member, Literature Society, Cologne, 1974–; Visiting Professor, University of Texas, USA, 1976, University of New Mexico, 1976; Manager, Literary Arrangement, Ankara, Turkey, 1980. *Memberships include:* Managing Committee, Literarian Society, Cologne, 1976–84; Association of German Writers; General Society of

Philosophy on Germany. *Address:* Siebengebirgsallee 17, D–5000 Cologne 41, Federal Republic of Germany.

GRONEWOLD, Sue, b. 18 Apr. 1947, Peoria, Illinois, USA. Writer; Consultant. m. Peter Winn, 22 May 1976, Princeton, New Jersey, USA, 1 son. *Education:* BA, History and French, 1969, MA, European History and Education, 1973, University of Wisconsin; MA, Chinese History, 1980, M Phil, Chinese History, 1983, Columbia University. *Literary Appointments:* Lecturer on Asia, American Museum of Natural History, Education Department, 1980–84; Visiting Lecturer, Department of History, Smith College, 1984–85; New York Council for Humanities Program Office, 1985–. *Publication:* Beautiful Merchandise: Prostitutes in China 1860–1936, 1982. *Contributor to:* Yankee Doodle Comes to China, in natural History, 1984; Chinese Women: A Revolution of Their Own? in, Trends in History, 1985; Numerous articles and reviews in, Focus on Asian Studies. *Memberships:* Association for Asian Studies; Committee on Teaching About Asia; Association of American Museums. *Address:* 315 West 106th Street Apt. 10C, New York, NY 10025, USA.

GROSS, Ludwik, b. 11 Sep. 1904, Crakow, Poland. Physician; Researcher in Cancer and Leukemia. *Education:* MD, Lagellon University, Crakow, Poland, 1929. *Publications:* Oncogenic Viruses, UK and USA. 1961, 3rd edition, 1983; Ludzkosc W Walce o Zdrowie, 3 editions; Siewcy Chorob i Smierci, 2 editions. *Contributions to:* Various professional journals and numerous articles. *Honours include:* United Prize, World Health Organisation, New York, USA, 1962; Founders Award for Cancer And Ummunology, New York City, 1975; Prix Griffuel for Cancer Research, Paris, France, 1978. *Memberships include:* National Academy of Sciences, USA; Board of Directors (Past), American Association for Cancer Research. *Address:* Cancer Research Unit, Veterans Administration Unit, 130 West Kingsbridge Road, Bronx, NY 10468, USA.

GROSS, Natan, b. 16 Nov. 1919, Cracow, Poland. Film Director; Journalist; Poet; Translator. *Education:* Law and Art Studies, 1939; Polish Film Institute, 1945–46. *Publications:* Wybor Wspolczesnej Poezji Hebrajskiej (Selection of New Hebrew Poetry), 1947; Puesni o Izraelu (Songs of Israel), 1948; Ca nam zostalo z tych lat (What Remaines of Us from Those Years), 1971; Ha'shoa be'shira ha'ivrit (Holocaust in Hebrew Poetry), (Co-ed anthology), 1974; Wiersze buntu i zaglady (Songs of Holocaust and Rebellion), 1975; Okruszyny mlodosci (Crumbs of Youth), 1976; Yeladim be'geto (Children in the Ghetto) (with Sarah Nishmith), 1978; Palukst: The Rediscovered Artist, 1982; Hommage to Janusz Korczak (in Hebrew), anthology of poems, awaiting publication; Al Gesher Tsar (On a Narrow Bridge), awaiting publication; Na Waskiej Kladce (One Narrow Bridge), awaiting publication; The History of Israeli Film (in Hebrew), scheduled for 1985. *Contributions to:* various publications including, Slowo Mlodych, youth monthly (Editor, 1946–49) Poland; Al Hamishmar Daily (Film Critic, 1962–); Leksikon ha'omanuyoth (Arts Lexicon), Israel Film (Editor, 1975), etc. *Honours:* Numerous Israeli and International Film Festival Awards; Ben-Dor Prize, Davar newspaper, 1960. *Memberships:* Film Critics Section, Association Israeli Journalists; Film and TV Directors Guild, Israel. *Address:* 14 Herzog Street, Givataim, Israel 53686.

GROSSER, Alfred, b. 1 Feb. 1925, Frankfurt, Germany. Professor, Political Science. *Education:* Universities of Aix en Provence & Paris; Agrege de L'University; Doct es Letrtres. *Publications include:* La Politique Exterieure e la V Republique, 1965; English translation 1967; Au Nom de Quoi Fondemonts d'une Morale Politique, 1969; L'Allmagne de Notre Temps, 1970, Englsh translation 1971; L'Explication Politique, 1972; Gegen den Strom, 1975; La Politique en France, co-auther, 1975; La Passion de Comprendre, 1977; Les Occidentaux, 1978; English translation, 1982; Le Sel de la Terre, 1981; Versuchte Beeinflussung, 1981; Affaires exterieures, 1984; L'Allamagne en Occident, 1985. *Contributor to:* Le Monde, Political Column; various

international political publications; German TV. *Honours:* Prix Broquette-Gonin, Academy Francaise, 1965; 1 Peace Prize, German Publishers, 1975. *Memberships:* PEN, France & Germany. *Address:* 8 Rue Dupleix, 75015 Paris, France.

GROSSINGER, Tania, b. 17 Feb. 1937, Evanston, Illinois, USA. Writer; Public Relations Consultant. *Education:* BA, Brandeis University, 1956. *Publications:* The Book of Gadgets, 1974; Growing Up At Grossinger's, 1975; The Great Gadget Catalogue, 1977; Weekend, with Andrew Neiderman, 1980. *Contributor to:* Good Housekeeping; Working Woman; New York Times Travel Section. *Membership:* American Society of Journalists & Authors, Executive Council, 1984. *Literary Agent:* Anita Diamant, New York City. *Address:* 1 Christopher Street, New York City, NY 10014, USA.

GROSSMAN, Ron, b. 18 Nov. 1934, Chicago, Illinois, USA. Journalist; Educator. m. Tina Timberlin, 19 Feb. 1972, Chicago, 1 son, 5 daughters. *Education:* PhD, University of Chicago. *Literary Appointment:* Columnist (Chicago Bookshelf), for the Chicago Tribune's Bookworld, 1981–. *Publications:* Italians in America, 1965; Guide to Chicago Neighbourhoods, 1981. *Contributions to:* Chicago Tribune; Philadelphia Inquirer; Washington Post; San Francisco Chronicle; Los Angeles Times; Cosmopolitan; Present Tense; Inland Architect; Chicago Magazine. *Memberships:* American Society of Journalists and Authors; National Book Critics Circle. *Address:* 554 Roscoe, Chicago, IL 60657, USA.

GROSSMAN, Samuel, b. 6 Dec. 1897. Philadelphia, Pennsylvania, USA. Author; Publisher. *Education:* CCNY; American Business Institute; Mechanical Institute of New York, New York School of Industrial Art. *Publications:* Regent World Album. 1946; Capitol US Stamp Album, 1959; Philatelic World Gazetteer, 1960; Postage Stamp Identifier & Guide, 1961; Transworld Stamp Album, 1965; US Plate Block Album, new editions to 1975; Stamp Collectors Handbook, 15 editions to 1978. *Address:* 15 East 17th St, New York, NY 10003, USA.

GROSSRIEDER, Hans, b. 30 Sep. 1912, Düdingen, Fribourg, Switzerland. Professor. m. Alice Seewer, 22 July 1942, Fribourg, 1 daughter. *Education:* College St Michael; Maturité, University of Fribourg; Dr Phil. *Literary Appointment:* Writer, translator from French and English. *Publications:* Coll. Drei Schweizer Kunstwerke in Fryburg, 1943; Lexikon der Waltliteratur, 1960–61; Freiburg (essay), 1946; Der Stern im Schnee, 1953; Das Kollegium Sankt Michael, 1980. *Contributions to:* Schweizer Rundschau; Einsiedelun-Zurich; Wort und Wahrheit, Vienna. *Membership:* Schweizer Schriftstellerverband. *Address:* 2 Rte Ste-Agnes, 1700 Fribourg, Switzerland.

GROULT, Benoite, b. 31 Jan. 1920, Paris, France. Writer. m. (1) Georges de Caunes, 1946, (2) Paul Guimart, 1951, 3 daughters. *Education:* Latin-Greek Philology Licence. *Publications:* Le Journal à 4 mains, 1960; Le Feminin Pluriel 1965; La Part des Choses, 1972; Ainsi Soit-elle 1975; Adaptation de Claudine en Ménage, for TV, 1978; Les Trois Quarts du Temps novel, 1982. *Contributor to:* Elle; Marie-Claire; F Mag (co-founder and editor). *Membership:* Jury for Femina Prize. *Honour:* Prize of Academy of Britanny for, La Part des Choses, 1973. *Address:* 54 rue de Bourgogne, Paris 75007, France.

GROVER, John Charles, b. 25 Nov. 1920, Sydney, Australia. Consultant; Engineer/Earth Scientist; Writer; Speaker. m. Caroline Sandon, 1 son, 2 daughters. *Education:* BE (Min & Met); MSc; FRGS; FIMM; FGS; FIEAust; MAuslMM. *Appointments:* D & W Murray Ltd, 1935–39; Royal Australian Engineers, 1939–45; Founded, Geological Survey, Solomon Islands, 1950–67; Director, Geological Surveys; Chairman Mining Board with British Solomon Islands Protectorate Government; Corresponding Member, Seismological Subcommittee, British National Committee for Geodesy and Geophysics; Director, Geological Surveys, Chairman, Minerals Development Committee, Government of Fiji, 1967–69; General Manager, Kathleen Investments Ltd, Sydney, 1969–70; UNDP Project Manager in Ethiopia, 1975–77; Co-Ordinator, Special Projects, Peko-Wallsend Ltd, Sydney, 1977–82. *Publications:* 5 Official Volumes on Earth Sciences related to the Solomon Islands, 1950–67; Numerous scientific papers; The Struggle for Power, 1980; Struggle for Cargo, 1983. *Honours:* Galathea Medal, from King of Denmark, 1956; United National Fellowship, 1957; Officer, Order of the British Empire, 1963; Royal Society and Nuffield Grant, 1967. *Address:* 66 Castle Circuit, Seaforth, NSW 2092, Australia.

GROVES, Donald George, b. Syracuse, New York, USA. Scientist. m. Barbara Lee Matticks, 18 Mar. 1949. *Education:* BSc, MSc, Syracuse University. Diplomas, Various US Navy and industrial companies technical courses. *Publications:* A Glossary of Ocean Science and Underseas Terms; The Ocean World Encyclopedia, 1980. *Contributions to:* Over 250 published articles in various magazines and international journals. *Honours:* Various awards – latest Honorable Mention for Best Article, The Officer Review Magazine, 1984. *Memberships:* Washington (DC) Writers; Hudsons Directory of Writers. *Address:* National Academy of Sciences, 2101 Constitution Avenue NW, Washington, DC 20418, USA.

GRUBER, Karl J, b. 3 May 1909, Innsbruck, Austria. Politician. *Education:* Universities of Innsbruck and Vienna, Austria; Dr Jur. *Publications:* Die Politik der Mitte, 1943; Voraussetzungen der Vollbeschaftigung, 1946; Zusammenhang zwischen Grosse, Kosten und Rentabilitat industrieller Betriebe, 1948; Zwischen Befreiung und Freiheit, 1953; Ein Politisches Leben. *Honours:* Honorary LLD, University of Southern California, USA. *Memberships:* Former Vice President, OEEG; Past Special Adviser, International Atomic Energy Agency; Austrian People's Party. *Address:* Rennweg 6A, A–1030 Vienna, Austria.

GRUMMER, Arnold Edward, b. 19 Aug. 1923, Spencer, Iowa, USA. Lecturer/Writer. m. Mabel Emmel, 11 Aug 1948, Denver, Iowa, 2 sons, 1 daughter. *Education:* BA, Iowa State Teachers College; MA, State University of Iowa. *Literary Appointment:* Editor of General Publications, The Institute of Paper Chemistry. *Publication:* Paper By Kids, 1980. *Contributions to:* The Development of Test Tube Trees, Paper Magazine, London; Paper, series of three articles in the Correspondent; Paper and other Writing Materials, Collier's Encyclopedia; Paper, Scribner's Dictionary of American History. *Membership:* Wisconsin Regional Writers. *Address:* 63 Bellaire Court, Appleton, WI 54911, USA.

GRUNBAUM, Adolf, b. 15 May 1923, Cologne, Germany. Educator. m. Thelma Braverman, 26 June 1949, Bethlehem, Pennsylvania, USA, 2 son, 1 daughter. *Education:* BA, Wesleyan University (Mathematics and Philosophy) 1943; MS, Yale University (Physics) 1948; PhD, Yale University (Philosophy) 1951. *Academic Appointments:* Andrew Mellon Professor of Philosophy, Research Professor of Psychiatry, Chairman, Center for Philosophy of Science, University of Pittsburgh. *Publications:* Philosophical Problems of Space and Time, 1963, Russian translation 1969, 2nd enlarged edition, 1973; Modern Science and Zeno's Paradoxes, 1967, British Education, 1968; Geometry and Chronometry in Philosophical Perspectove, 1968; The Foundations of Psychoanalysis: A Philosophical Critique, 1984. *Contributor to:* Over 130 articles to scientific journals including: British Journal for the Philosophy of Science; Erkenntis; Journal of Philosophy; American Philosophical Quarterly; Psychoanalysis and Contemporary Thought; Psychological Medicine; Free Inquiry; The Behavioural and Brain Sciences. *Honours:* President, Philosophy of Sciences Association, 1965–70; President, American Philosophical Association, Eastern Division, 1982–83; Gifford Lectures, University of St Andrews, Scotland,

1985; Werner Heisenberg Lecture, Bavarian Academy of Science, Munich, Federal Republic of Germany, 1985; Senior US Scientist Award, Alexander von Humboldt Foundation, Federal Republic of Germany, 1985. *Memberships:* Fellow, American Association for the Advancement of Science; American Academy of Arts and Sciences; Laureate, Academy of Humanism. *Address:* 2510 Cathedral of Learning, University of Pittsburgh, Pittsburgh, PA 15260, USA.

GRUNDY, Joan, b. 17 Aug. 1920, Ulverston, England. University Teacher. *Education:* Graduated First Class Honours in English, Bedford College, University of London, 1943; MA with Distinction, Bedford College, 1947. *Literary Appointments:* Assistant Lecturer, English, University of Edinburgh 1947–50; Lecturer in English, University of Liverpool, 1950–65; Reader in English Literature, Royal Holloway College, University of London, 1965–79; Professor of English Literature, Royal Holloway College, 1979–80; Professor Emeritus of English Literature, London University, 1980–. *Publications:* Editor: The Poems of Henry Constable, 1960; The Spenserian Poets, 1969; Hardy and the Sister Arts, 1979. *Contributions to:* Modern Language Review; Review of English Studies; Essays in Criticism; Encyclopaedia Britannica; Britannica Book of the Year; Powys Review; Shakespeare Survey; Macmillan Hardy Annual (articles and reviews, 1950–). *Membership:* Thomas Hardy Society. *Address:* Rose Cottage, Lamb Park, Rosside, Ulverston, Cumbria LA12 7NR, England.

GUADAGNA, Ingeborg, b. 23 Mar. 1914, Heidenheim-Brenz, Federal German Republic. Writer; Housewife. *Education:* Universities of Tubingen, Munich, Perugia. *Publications:* (Novels): Die sizilianischen Schwestern, 1946; Die Ehe der Vanna Licusu, 1950; (Proceed to Judgement, 1953); Das Landhaus bein Florenz, 1952; Die Fahrt zur Insel, 1953; 4 travel books: Auf Korsika, 1963, 72, 76, 81; Sardinien, 1967, 84; Sizilien, 1973, 81; ØO Toskane und Umbrien, 1975, 80; Novel in press; Der Besuch, 1976; I cugini Buonaparte e Altre visite, 1985. *Contributor to:* Merian; Nuova Sadegna; Cassella-Riedel-Archiv. *Honours include:* Mundela Prize, Cagliari, 1973, 77; Romena Prize, 1980; Premio Citta di Fuecchio, 1983, 85. *Memberships:* Italian Federation Artists, Professionals and Business Women (FIDAPA-IFBPW) in Writers' Group, Florence. *Address:* Via del Renaio 13, 50061 Girone-Fiesole, Florence, Italy.

GUAY, Georgette Marie Jeanne, b. 18 Oct. 1952, Windsor, Ontario, Canada. Writer. m. Jim Biros, 7 May 1972, Windsor, 1 daughter. *Education:* BA, English & Drama, University of Windsor; BEd, University of Toronto. *Literary Appointments:* Playwright-in-Residence, Theatre on the Move, Frog Print Theatre. *Publications:* The Bling Said Hello, You'll Never Be The Same, 1979; Kid's Plays, anthology, 1980; Sense & Feeling, anthology, 1982. *Honours:* Chalmer's Award, honourable mention (1st), 1982; Dora Mavor Moore Award, best children's play, 1983. *Membership:* Playwrights Union of Canada. *Address:* c/o Playwrights Union of Canada, 8 York Street, 6th Floor, Toronto, Ontario, Canada M5J 1R2.

GUDAUSKAS, George, b. 4 June 1940, Brooklyn, New York, USA. Journalist. m. Linda Anne Hales, 13 May 1982, Southwest Harbor, Maine, USA, 1 son, 1 daughter, from previous marriage. *Education:* Quinnipiac College, 1963–64; University of Connecticut, 1965–66; University of Hartford, 1972–73; Fellowship programme, University of Massachusetts, 1968–70; Non-fiction writing course, Famous Writers School, Connecticut, 1966–68. *Literary Appointments:* Editor, Reporter, Torrington Register, 1966–67; Assistant State Editor and Urban Affairs reporter, Waterbury Republican and American, 1967–69; Washington Correspondent, Capitol Correspondent and Columnist and Day Editor, United Press International, 1969–75; Reporter, Rocky Mountain News, 1976–77; Washington Corespondent, States News Service, 1979–80; Supervising Editor, Journal Inquirer, 1980–82; Assistant National Editor, The Washington Times, 1982–

; Associate Editor, Elle International, 1984. *Contributions to:* Publications including Torrington Register; Waterbury Republican and American; Rocky Mountain News; Journal Inquirer; Washington Times; Elle International; The New York Times; International Herald Tribune. *Memberships:* Association de la Presse Anglo-Americaine de Paris; Sigma Delta Chi, USA; International Foreign Corespondents Association, London. *Address:* 6 rue Vineuse, 75116 Paris, France.

GUENTHER, Charles John, b. 29 Apr. 1920, St Louis, Missouri, USA. Teacher; Poet; Translator. m. Esther Laura Klund, 11 Apr. 1942, St Louis, 1 son, 2 daughters. *Education:* AA, Harris Teachers College, 1940; BA, MA, Webster University, St Louis, 1973–74; Completed Doctoral Course Work, St Louis University, 1979; LHD, Southern Illinois University, Edwardsville, 1979. *Appointments:* Creative Writing Instuctor, People's Art Centre, St Louis, 1953–56; Director, McKendree Writers' Conference, 1969–72; Instructor, various US Writers' Conferences, 1955–; Adjunct Professor, various colleges and Universities, 1976–84. *Publications:* Modern Italian Poets, 1961; Phrase/Paraphrase, 1970; Paul Valery in English, 1970; Voices in the Dark, 1974; High Sundowns, translation of J R Jimenex, 1974; Jules Laforgue: Selected Poems, 1984; Co-Translator, Alain Bosquet, Selected Poems, 1963. *Contributor to:* 300 magazines and anthologies worldwide including: Poetry; The Nation; Quarterly Review of Literature; Literary Review; etc. *Honours:* Decorated Commander, Order of Merit, Italian Republic, 1973; James Joyce Award, 1974; Witter Bynner Poetry Translation Grant, Poetry Society of America, 1979; Missouri Library Association Literary Award, 1974; St Louis Arts & Humanities Fellowship, 1981. *Memberships:* Poetry Society of America, Midwest Regional Vice-President, 1977–; Missouri Writers' Guild, President, 1973–74; St Louis Writers' Guild, President, 1959, 1976–77; St Louis Poetry Centre, President 1974–76, Member, Board of Chancellors, past Chairman. *Address:* 2935 Russell Blvd, St Louis, MO 63104, USA.

GUERIN, Daniel, b. 19 May 1904, Paris, France. Writer. *Publications:* Numerous including: La Lutte de Classes sous la Premiere Republique, 1946, 68; Shakespeare et Gide en correctionnaelle? 1959; Le Grain sous la Niege, 1961; L'Anarchisme, 1965; Pour un Marxisme, Libertaire, 1969; Front Populaire revolution manquee, 1970; Ni Dieu ne Maitre, 1971; Autobiographie de jeunesse, 1971; Rosa Luxembura, 1971; Sur le Fascisme, I and II, 1975; Bourgeois et bras nus, 1973; De l'Oncle Tom aux Penthizes, 1973; Ci-git la Colonialisme, 1930–1972, 1974; L'Armen en France, 1974; La Revolution Francaise et Nous, 1976; Le Feu du Sang, 1977; Prouhon oui et non, 1978; Son Testament, 1979; Quand l'Algerie s'insurgeait, 1979; Homosexualite et Revolution, 1984; A le Rechezche d'un communisme Libertaire, 1984. *Contributions to:* Various journals. *Memberships:* Various academic organisations. *Address:* 5 Square de Port-Royal, 75013 Paris, France.

GUERNSEY, Bruce Hubbard, b. 10 Mar. 1944, Boston, Massachusetts, USA. Professor of English, Eastern Illinois University. m. Janet Louise Fallon, 7 June 1969, Clifton, New Jersey, 1 son, 1 daughter. *Education:* BA, Colgate University, 1966; MA, University of Virginia, 1967; MA, The Johns Hopkins University, 1971; PhD, University of New Hampshire, 1978. *Literary Appointments:* Teaching Fellow in Poetry, The Johns Hopkins University, 1970–71; Poet-in-Residence, Virginia Wesleyan College, 1971–75; Scholar in Poetry, Bread Loaf Writers Conference, 1972; Editor, Karamu, 1978–82. *Publications:* Lost Wealth, 1975; January Thaw, 1982. *Contributions to:* (Poetry); The Atlantic; Poetry; The Nation; New Letters; Harvard Magazine; College English; Yankee; Country Journal; Poetry Now; Ascent; Shenandoah; Quarterly West; Ironwood; Tendril, etc. *Honours:* Scholarship in Poetry, Bread Loaf Writers Conference, 1972; Illinois Arts Council Literary Fellowships, 1983, 84, 85; National Endowment of the Arts Creative Writing Fellowship, 1984. *Membership:*

PEN International. *Address:* RR 4, Box 123, Charleston, IL 61920, USA.

GUEST, Barbara, b. 6 Sept. 1920, USA. Writer. m. Prof. Trumbull Higgins, 1954, 1 son, 1 daughter. *Education:* BA, University of California at Berkeley, USA. *Major Publications:* Poems: The Location of Things, 1960; Poems, 1963; The Blue Stairs, 1968; Moscow Mansions, 1973; The Countess from Minneapolis, 1976; Seeking Air (fiction), 1978; Herself Defined: H D, The Poet & Her World (biography), 1984; Poems: Turler Losses, 1979; Quilts, 1980; Biography, 1980. *Contributor to:* Partisan Review; Paris Review; and others. *Honours:* National Endowment for the Arts, 1980; Longview Award, 1960. *Memberships:* PEN; Poetry Society of America. *Address:* 37 Pleasant Lane, Southampton, NY 11968, USA.

GUEST, Lynn Doremus, b. 6 Oct. 1939, Missouri, USA. Writer. m. Harry Guest, 28 Dec, 1963, Delaware, USA, 1 son, 1 daughter. *Education:* BA, Sarah Lawrence College, Edinburgh University. *Publications:* Post-War Japanese Poetry, 1972; (novels) Children of Hachiman, 1980; Yedo, 1985. *Honour:* Georgette Heyer Historical Novel Prize for Children of Hachiman, 1980. *Address:* 1 Alexandra Terrace, Exeter, Devon EX4 6SY, England.

GUINNESS, Bryan Walter (Lord Moyne), b. 27 Oct. 1905. Poet; Novelist; Playwright. *Education:* MA, Modern Languages, Oxford University, England; Fellow, Royal Society Literature. *Publications include:* 23 Poems, 1931; Singing Out of Tune, 1933; Landscape with Figures, 1934; Under the Eyelid, 1935; Johnny and Jemima, 1936; A Week by the Sea, 1936; Lady Crushwells Companion, 1938; The Children in the Desert, 1947; Reflexions, 1947; The Animals Breakfast, 1950; Story of a Nutcraker, 1953; Collected Poems, 1956; A Fugue of Cinderellas, 1956; Catriona & the Grasshopper, 1957; Priscilla & the Prawn, 1960; Leo & Rosabelle, 1961; The Giant's Eye, 1964; The Rose in the Tree, 1964; The Engagement, 1969; The Clock, 1973; Diary Not Kept, 1975; Hellenic Flirtation, 1978; Potpouri from the Thirties, 1982; etc. *Contributor to:* London Mercury; Harpers Bazaar; Sunday Times; Country Life; Irish Times; Poetry Review; Listener; Ariel. *Address:* Knockmaroon House, Castleknock, Co Dublin, Eire.

GUISEWITE, Cathy Lee, b. 5 Sep. 1950, Dayton, Ohio, USA. Syndicated Cartoonist. *Education:* BA, University of Michigan, 1972. *Publications:* The Cathy Chronicles, 1978; What Do You Mean, I Still Don't Have Equal Rights??!, 1980; What's a Nice Single Girl Doing with a Double Bed!, 1981; I Think I'm Having a Relationship with a Blueberry Pie!, 1981; It Must Be Love, My Face is Breaking Out, 1982; Another Saturday Night of Wild and Reckless Abandon, 1982; Cathy's Valentine's Day Survival Book, How to Live Through another February 14th, 1982; How to Get Rich, Fall in Love, Lose Weight and Solve all Your Problems by Saying No, 1983; Eat Your Way to a Better Relationship, 1983; A Mouthful of Breath Mints and No One to Kiss, 1985; Climb Every Mountain, Bounce Every Check, 1983; Men Should Come with Instruction Booklets, 1984; Wake me up When I'm a size 5, 1985. *Contributions to:* Glamour Magazine, monthly comic strip. *Honours:* Honorary LHD, Rhode Island College, 1979; Eastern Michigan University, 1980; Poetry/Literature Award, Matrix Midland, 1984; Distinguished Women Award, Northwood Institute, 1984. *Memberships:* National Cartoonists Society. *Literary Agent:* Universal Press Syndicate. *Address:* c/o Universal Press Syndicate, 4400 Johnson Drive, Fairway, KS 66205, USA.

GULA, Richard Michael, b. 11 Apr. 1947, Sharpsville, Pennsylvania, USA. Roman Catholic Priest. *Education:* STM 1973, STL 1981, St Mary's Seminary and University, Baltimore, Maryland; PhD, St Michael's College, Toronto, Canada. *Publications:* What Are They Saying About Moral Norms?, 1982; To Walk Together Again: The Sacrament of Reconciliation, 1984. *Contributions to:* The Priest; American Ecclesiastical

Review; Eglise et Theologie Bulletin de Saint Sulpice; Pastoral Life; The Living Light; Christian Initiation Resources; New Catholic World; Spirituality Today. *Address:* St Patrick's Seminary, 320 Middlefield Road, Menlo Park, CA 94025, USA.

GULLANS, Charles Bennett, b. 5 May 1929, Minneapolis, Minnesota, USA. Professor of English and Creative Writing. *Education:* BA, cum laude, 1948; MA, 1951, Minnesota; PhD, Stanford University, 1956. *Literary Appointments:* Publisher of The Symposium Press (established 1978) and others include Edgar Bowers, Turner Cassity, J V Cunningham, John Espey, Janet Lewis and Timothy Steele. *Publications:* Translator with Franz Schneider, Last Letters from Stalingrad, 1962; Arrivals and Departure, 1962; Editor, The English and Latin Poems of Sir Robert Ayton, 1963; A Checklist of Trade Bindings Designed by Margaret Armstrong, 1968; A Bibliography of the published works of J V Cunningham, 1973; Imperfect Correspondences, 1978; Many Houses, 1981; A Diatribe to Dr Steele, 1982; Under Red Skies, 1983; The Bright Universe, 1983; Local Winds, 1985. *Contributions to:* Hudson Review; Southern Review. *Honours:* Fellow of Institute of Creative Arts, University of California, 1965–66; Fulbright Fellow, 1953–55. *Membership:* Vice-President, Scottish Text Society. *Address:* Department of English, University of California Los Angeles, 405 Hilgard Avenue, Los Angeles, CA 90024, USA.

GUNARATNE, Victor Thomas Herat, b. 1912, Madampe, Sri Lanka. Regional Director Emeritus, South East Asia Region, World Health Organisation. *Education:* Qualified, Medical College, Colombo, Sri Lanka, 1935; Diploma in Tropical Medicine and Hygiene, 1947, Diploma of Public Health, University of London, England; MRCP, Edinburgh, Scotland, 1950. *Publications include:* Selected Addresses, 1972; Challenges and Responses – Health in South East Asia Region, 1977; Voyage Towards Health, 1980. Scientific Publications include: A History of Medicine and Public Health in Sri Lanka; The Child, The Environment and the Future; The Intense Wavelengths of Noise; The Age of Maturity; An Effort of Will; Bringing Down Drug Costs, the Sri Lanka Example. *Contributions to:* Various professional journals including: Indian Journal of Cancer; Journal of Diabetic Association of India; World Health. Various daily newspapers. *Honours include:* Fellow, Royal College of Physicians, Scotland; 1st Fellow, Sri Lanka Public Health Association. Honorary Fellow, 1st Non-Indian, Indian Academy of Medical Sciences, 1975; 1st Honorary Fellow, Ceylon College of Physicians, 1976. Honorary Degrees: DPH, Mahidol University, Thailand, 1977; DSc, University of Sri Lanka, 1978; MD, State Medical Institute of Mongolia, 1978; DSc, Bernaras Hinud University, 1980; World Health Organisation, Regional Director Emeritus, 1980. *Address:* 4 Rosmead Place, Colombo 7, Sri Lanka.

GUNN, James Ewin, b. 1923, Kansas City, Missouri, USA. Professor, English & Journalism, University of Kansas; Writer (mainly science fiction). m. Jane Frances Anderson, 6 Feb. 1947, Lawrence, 2 sons. *Education:* BS, 1947, MA, 1951, University of Kansas. *Publications include:* This Fortress World, 1955, 1957. 1979; Star Bridge, with J Williamson, 1955, 1956, 1961, 1977; The Immortals, 1962, 1968, 1979 (also TV play & series); Man & the Future, Editor, 1968; The Witching Hour, 1970; Breaking Point, 1972, 1973; The Listeners, 1972, 1974; Nebula Award Stories Ten, 1975, 1976; Alternate Worlds, The Illustrated History of Science Fiction, 1975, 1976; The Magicians, 1976, 1980; Kampus, 1977; The Road to Science Fiction from Gilgamesh to Wells, 1977; From Wells to Heinlein, 1979; From Heinlein to Here, 1979; The Dreamers, 1981; Isaac Asimov: The Foundations of Science Fiction, 1982; The Road to Science Fiction – From Here to Forever, 1982; Crisis, 1986. *Contributor to:* More than 80 published stories; many articles. *Honours:* Science Fiction Research Association, President, 1978–80; Science Fiction Achievement Award for Non-Fiction, for Isaac Asimov: The Foundations of Science Fiction, 1983; etc. *Agent:*

Richard Curtis; Maggie Noach. *Address:* 2215 Orchard Lane, Lawrence, KS 66044, USA.

GUNN, Thomson William, b. 29 Aug. 1929, Gravesend, England. Freelance Writer. *Education:* BA, 1953, MA, 1958, Cambridge University, Trinity College; Stanford University, California, USA, 1954–55, 1956–58. *Publications:* Fighting Terms, 1954; The Sense of Movement, 1957; My Said Captains, 1961; Positives, with Ander Gunn, 1966; Touch, 1967; Moly, 1971; Jack Straw's Castle, 1976; Selected Poems, 1979; The Passages of Joy, 1982; The Occasions of Poetry, 1982. *Honours:* Levinson Prize, 1955; Maugham Award, 1959; Arts Council of Great Britain Award, 1959; National Institute of Arts & Letters Grant, 1964; Rockefeller Award, 1965; Guggenheim Fellowship, 1971. *Address:* 1216 Cole St, San Francisco, CA 94117, USA.

GUNNELL, Bryn, b. 24 Oct. 1932, Esher, Surrey, England. University Lecturer. *Education:* BA, MA, London; Diploma in Translation, University of Paris. *Publications:* Calabrian Summer, 1964; The Cashew Nut Girl & Other Stories, 1974; Delhi Edition 1975. *Contributor to:* London Magazine; Contemporary Review; Stand; Cornhill Magazine; Good Housekeeping. *Address:* 66 Rue De La Fontaine, Bagneaux 92, France.

GUNNLAUGSDOTTIR, Alfrun, b. 18 Mar. 1938, Reykjavik, Iceland. University Lecturer in Comparative Literature. m. 1 son. *Education:* License in Philosophy and Letters, 1965, Doctor of Philosophy and Letters, 1970, University of Barcelona, Spain. *Publications:* Tristan en el Norte, non-fiction, 1978; Af manna Voldum, short stories, 1982; Thel, novel, 1984. *Contributions to:* Um Parcevals sogu; Stofnun Arna Magnussonar. *Honours:* Literary Award, Dagbladid and Visir Newspaper, 1984. *Membership:* Writers Union of Iceland. *Address:* Skerjabraut 9, IS–170 Seltjarnarnesi, Iceland.

GUNTER, Addison Yancey (Pete) III, b. 20 Oct. 1936, Hammond, Indiana, USA. University Professor. *Education:* BA Magna cum laude. University of Texas, 1958, University of Cambridge, England, 1960; PhD, Yale University, 1963. *Publications:* Bergson and the Evolution of Physics, 1969; The Big Thicket: A Challenge for Conservation, 1972; International Bergson Bibliography, 1974; Process Philosophy: Basic Writing, with J R Sibley, 1978; Memoirs of W R Strong, with Robert Calvert, 1982; Creative Evolution, by Henri Bergson, Editor, 1983; River in Dry Grass, novel, 1984; Present Tense, Future Perfect?: A Symposium on Widening Choices for the Visual Environmental Resource, with Bobette Higgins, 1984; Whats is Living and What is Dead in the Philosophy of Hegel, by Benedetto Croce, re-edition with new introduction, 1985. *Contributions to:* Main Currents in Modern Thought; National Wildlife and others, *Honours include:* Authors Citation, Texas Council of Teachers of English. 1972; Writers Roundup Prize, Theta Sigma Phi, 1972; Dallas Public Library Literary Map of Texas, 1976; Faculty Excellence Award, North Texas Area Phi Beta Kappa, 1984. *Memberships include:* Texas Institute of Letters; Western Division, American Philosophy Society. *Address:* Department of Philosophy, North Texas State University, Denton, TX 76203, USA.

GUNTER, Gordon, b. 18 Aug. 1909, Goldonna, Louisiana, USA. Marine Zoologist. *Education:* BA, Louisiana State Normal College, 1929; MA, 1931, PhD, 1945, University of Texas. *Contributor to:* 350 articles, science and professional journals and popular articles, reviews; Editor, Publications of Institute of Marine Science, 1950–55; Associate Editor, Bulletin of Marine Science, Gulf and Caribbean, 1961–64; Editor, Gulf Reach Reports, Gulf Coast Research Laboratory, 1961–74; Consultant Editor, 1975; Papers handed over to The University of Wyoming Library, Laramie, 1984. *Address:* Rt.6, Box 22B, Ocean Springs, MS 39564, USA.

GURA, Philip Francis, b. 14 June 1950, Ware, Massachusetts, USA. Professor of English. m. Leslie Ann Cobig, 4 Aug. 1979, Cherry Hills, Colorado, 1 son. *Education:* BA, (magna cum laude), 1972; PhD, 1977, Harvard University. *Publications:* The Wisdom of Words: Language, Theology and Literature in the American Renaissance, 1981; Critical Essays on American Transcendentalism, (co-edited with Joel Myerson), 1982; A Glimpse of Sion's Glory: Puritan Radioalism in New England, 1620–1660, 1984. *Contributions to:* American Literature; New England Quarterly; Virginia Quarterly; William and Mary Quarterly; Early American Literature; Yale Review; Sewanee Review; ESQ; A Journal of the American Renaissance; New England Historical and Genealogical Regier, Journal of Presbyterian History, etc. *Honours:* Norman Foerster Prize in American Literature, Awarded by Modern Language Association, 1977; Fellow, Charles Warren Center for Studies in History, Harvard University, 1980–81; Fellow, Institute of Early American History and Culture, Williamsburg, Virginia, 1985–86. *Address:* Department of English, University of Colorado, Boulder, CO 80309, USA.

GURAVICH, Daniel, b. 22 Feb. 1918, Winnipeg, Canada. Photojournalist. m. Betty Ruth Kraus, June 1942, Ottawa, 1 son, 2 daughters. *Education:* BSc, University of Manitoba, 1939; MSc, 1948, PhD, 1949, University of Wisconsin. *Publications:* The Grand Banks, 1968; The Man and the River, 1969; Northwest Passage, 1970; Gulf of Mexico, 1972; Inside Passage, 1975; Mormon Trek West, 1978; Yesterdays Wings, 1982; Lords of the Arctic, 1982; Return of the Brown Pelican, 1983; Field Guide to Southern Fungi, 1984. *Contributions to:* Smithsonian; Natural History; Science Digest; Sports Afield; Exxon USA; Town and Country; Science 80; Signature; PMW World Friends; Ranger Rick; Life; Newsweek; Time; Popular Photography; and others. *Honours:* Award of Merit, Art Directors Club of Metropolitan Washington, 1968; Publication Award, Geographic Society of Chicago, 1970; Golden Eagle for Exxon Film, in the Path of History, 1970; Certificate of Merit, Society of Publication Designers, 1973; Gold Quill, International Association of Business Communicators, 1975; Honor Book, Mouisiana Library Association, 1984; Annual Award for Outstanding Achievement, Mississippi Academy of Science. *Memberships:* American Society of Journalists and Authors; Society of American Travel Writers; Travel Journalists Guild. *Address:* 407 Rebecca Drive, Greenville, MS 38701, USA.

GURLEY BROWN, Helen, b. 18 Feb. 1922, Green Forest, Arkansas, USA. Editor in Chief. m. David Brown, 25 Sep. 1959. *Education:* Texas State College for Women, 1941; Woodbury College, 1942. *Publications:* Sex and the Single Girl, 1962; Sex and the Office, 1965; The Outrageous Opinions of Helen Gurley Brown, 1967; Helen Gurley Brown's Single Girl Cookbook, 1969; Sex and the New Single Girl, 1970; Having It All, 1982. *Contributor to:* Editor-in-Chief, Cosmopolitan Magazine. *Honours:* Francis Holmes Achievement Award for Outstanding Work in Advertising, 1956–59; Distinguished Achievement Award, University of Southern California, School of Journalism, 1971; American Newspaperwomens Association Annual Award, 1972; American Society Journalism School Administrators, 1972; Distinguished Achievement Award in Journalism, Hon. Alumnus, Stanford University, 1977; New York Women in Communications Inc, annual Matrix Ward in Magazine Category, 1985; The establishment of the Helen Gurley Brown Research Professorship, North Western University's Medill School of Journalism. *Memberships:* Authors League of America; American Society Magazine Editors. *Literary Agent:* Irving Lazar. *Address:* 224 West 57th Street, New York, NY 10019, USA.

GURNEY, Lawrence Stuart, b. 17 Feb. 1921, Geologist; Illustrator; Draftsman. *Education:* BA, University of Southern California, 1943; Postgraduate work in Geology and English Literature. *Appointments:* Aerospace Draftsman and Illustrator, US Geological

Survey; Retired from J Paul Getty Museum. *Contributions to:* American Weave; Coastlines; Curled Wire Chronicle; Epos; Fiddlehead; Kaleidograph; Rocky Mountain Herald; New York Herlad-Tribune; Starlanes; Talaria; Trace; Poetry Pub; The Golden Year Anthology; Diamond Anthology of The Poetry Society of America. *Memberships:* Poetry Society of America; Poetry Society of Southern California. *Address:* 945 14th Street, Apr. E, Santa Moniea, CA 90403, USA.

GÜRT, Elisabeth, b. 18 May 1917, Vienna, Austria. Freelance Writer. *Education:* Examination as School Teacher; Studies of languages. *Publications:* Author of over 40 novels, childrens books and short stories including: Eine Frau für drei Tage, 1942; Es gehört dir nichts, 1947; Bis dass der Tod euch scheidet, 1953, 79; Ein Stern namens Julia, 1955; Kein Mann für alle Tage, 1961, 75; Verzaubert von Tuju, 1980; Vierzig Jahre und ein Sommer, 1981; Denkst du noch an Korfu?, 1982; Hinter weissen Türen, 1984. Young Peoples Novels: Vor uns das Leben; Wolken im Sommer; Du bist kein Kind mehr, Gundula, 1982; Erwachsen wirst du über Nacht, 1984. Short Stories: Wunsche sind wie Sommerwolken; Flammen im Schnee; Die Stunde zwischen acht und neun; Immer werde ich dich lieben. *Contributions In:* Many weekly magazines, Germany, Austria, Switzerland and Canada, various works translated in to English. *Honours:* Silver Honorary Award of Merit, Republic of Austria, 1981. *Memberships:* Austrian Writers Association; Der Ereis; Austrian Womens Club; Association of Female Writers and Artists; Landtmannkreis. *Address:* Schaumburger Gasse 16, A–1040 Vienna, Austria.

GUSSOW, Mel, b. 19 Dec. 1933, New York City, New York, USA. Drama Critic. m. Ann Beebe, 12 Aug. 1963, New York City, 1 son. *Education:* BA, Middlebury College, Vermont, 1955; MS, Columbia University Graduate School of Journalism, New York, 1956. *Publications:* Don't Say Yes Until I Finish Talking: A Biography of Darryl F Zanuck, 1971, 80. *Contributions to:* The New Yorker; The New York Times Magazine; New York; Esquire; Horizon; Holiday; McCall's; and various others. *Honours:* George Jean Nathan Award for Dramatic Criticism, 1977–78; Guggenheim Fellowship, 1979. *Address:* The New York Times, 229 West 43rd Street, New York City, NY 10036, USA.

GUSTAFSON, Ralph Barker, b. 16 Aug. 1909, Line Ridge, Quebec, Canada. *Education:* BA, Bishops University, 1929, MA, 1930; BA, 1933, MA, 1963, Oxford University; DLitt, Mt Allison, 1973I DCL, Bishops University, 1977. *Publications:* Author, many books & poems including: The Golden Chalice, 1935; Lyrics Unromantic, 1942; Rocky Mountain Poems, 1960; Sift in an Hourglass, 1966; Ixion's Wheel, 1969; Selected Poems, 1972; Fire on Stone, 1974; Corners in Glass, 1977; Soviet Poems, 1978; Sequences, 1979; The Moment is All, Selected Poems 1944–83, 1983; Solidarnosc: Prelude, 1983; Impromptus, 1984; Directives of Autumn, 1984; Twelve Landscapes, 1985; etc; Editor, various anthologies including Anthology of Canadian Poetry, 1952; Canadian Accent, 1944; Penguin Book of Canadian Verse, 1958; etc. *Memberships:* Founding Member, League of Canadian Poets; Keble College Association, Oxford. *Honours:* Recipient, numerous honours and awards including: Queen's Silver Jubilee Medal, 1978; Poetry Delegate to UK, 1972, to USSR, 1976, Washington DC, 1977, Italy, 1981. *Address:* North Hatley, Quebec J0B 2C0, Canada.

GUSTAFSSON, Lars Erik Einar, b. 17 May 1936, Vasteras, Sweden. Writer. m. D Alexandra Chasnoff, 6 Nov. 1982, Austin, Texas, USA. *Education:* D Phil, Uppsala, 1978. *Literary Appointments:* Associate Editor, Albert Bonniers Publishing House, Bonniers Litterara Magasin, 1960–65; Reader and Adviser to Fiction Department of Bonniers Publishing House; Adjunct Professor, University of Texas, USA. *Publications include:* (novels): Herr Gustafsson Sjalv, 1971; Yllet, 1973; Familjefesten, 1975; Sigismund (in English with John Weinstock), 1985; (poetry): Warm Rooms and

Cold, translated by Yvonne L Sandstroem, 1975; Ballongfararne, 1962; Varma rum och Kalla, 1972; Varldens tystnad fore Bach, 1982; Faglarna, 1984; (prose fiction); Vagvila, 1957; scholarly works and translations. *Contributions to:* Svenska Dagbladet, Stockholm; Les Lettres Internationales, Paris; Der Spiegel, Hamburg. *Honours include:* Henrik Steffen Preis, Hamburg, 1985. *Membership:* PEN. *Literary Agent:* Carl Hanser, Munich. *Address:* PO Box 8047, Austin, TX 78712, USA.

GUTIERREZ, Donald Kenneth, b. 10 Mar. 1932, Alameda, California, USA. College English Professor, Scholar, Writer. m. Marlene Cecilia Zander, May 1957, 2 sons. *Education:* BA English 1956, MLS 1958, Berkeley, MA 1966, PhD 1969, Los Angeles, University of California. *Literary Appointments:* Assistant Professor of English, University of Notre Dame, 1968–75; Professor of English, Western New Mexico University, 1984–. *Publications:* Lapsing Out: Embodiments of Death and Rebirth in the Last Works of D H Lawrence, 1980; The Maze in the Mind and the World : Labyrinths in Modern Literature, 1985. *Contributions to:* 52 articles mainly on literary scholarship or criticism in magazines and journals. *Honours:* Honourable mention and 2nd place, new Mexico Humanities Council Prize Essay Award, 1984. *Membership:* Rio Grande Writers Association. *Address:* Department of English, Western New Mexico University, Silver City, NM 88061, USA.

GUTTON, Andre, b. 8 Jan. 1904, Fonteay sous Bois, Seine, France. Architect. *Education:* Government Certificate of Architecture; Diploma in Urbanism, Institute of Urbanism, University of Paris; Award, Institute of France. *Publications include:* La Charte de l'Urbanisme, 1941; Conversations sur l'Architecture; L'edifice dans le Cite, 1952; La Maison de l'Homme, 1954; Les Edifices Religieux et Culturels, 1956; Les Ecoles et Universites, 1959; L'Urbanisme au service de l'Homme, 1962; De la Nuit a l'Aurore, 1985. *Contributions to:* Urbanisme; Vie Urbaine; Monuments Historiques. *Honours:* Officer, Legion of Honour, France, 1958; Officer, Arts and Letters, 1962, Officer, Academy, 1949, Legion of Honour; Officer, Various foreign orders. *Memberships include:* Academy of Architecture, France; Royal Academy, Belgium; Honorary Fellow, American Institute of Architects. *Address:* 3 Avenue Vavin, 75006 Paris, France.

GUTZIN, Harold H., b. 15 Sep. 1938, Toronto, Ontario, Canada. Pharmacologist; Poet; Novelist. m. Lorie Gutzin, Toronto, Canada, Mar. 1983, 1 son, 1 daughter. *Education:* BSc, MSc, DSc. *Publications:* Currently working on a collection of poetry and two novels. *Contributions to:* Numerous anthologies in North America (poetry). *Membership:* Associate member, League of Canadian Poets. *Literary Agent:* Mrs Reva Gutzin. *Address:* 1 Codsell Avenue, Downsview, Ontario, Canada M3H 3V6.

GUY, David McCutcheon, b. 19 Aug. 1948, Pittsburgh, Pennsylvania, USA. Author. m. Elizabeth Ramsey Heard, 20 June 1970, Sewickley, Pennsylvania, 1 son. *Education:* BA, Duke University, North Carolina. *Publications:* Football Dreams, 1980; The Man Who Loved Dirty Books, 1983; Second Brother, 1985. *Contributions to:* The Sun, Chapel Hill, North Carolina; The Washington Post; Philadelphia Inquirer; Chicago Tribune; USA Today. *Honours:* Voted one of Best Books for Young Adults, with Football Dreams, American Library Association, 1980. *Membership:* National Book Critics Circle. *Literary Agent:* Virginia Barber Literary Agency. *Address:* 2117 Wilson Street, Durham, NC 27705, USA.

GUYER, Paul David, b. 13 Jan 1948, New York City. University Professor. m. Pamela Susan Paola Foa, 21 May 1978, Pittsburgh, Pennsylvania, 1 daughter. *Education:* AB, Harvard College, 1969; PhD, Harvard University, 1974. *Literary Appointments:* Assistant Professor of Philosophy, University of Pittsburgh, 1973–78; Associate Professor of Philosophy, University of Illinois, Chicago, 1978–83; Professor of Philosophy,

University of Pennsylvania, 1983–. *Publications:* Kant and the Claims of Taste, 1979; Essays in Kant's Aesthetics, co-edited with Ted Cohen, 1982. *Contributions to:* Kant's Tactics in the Transcendental Deduction in Philosophical Topics, 1981; Kant's Distinction Between the Beautiful and Sublime in Review of Metaphysics, 1982; Antonomy and Integrity in Kant's Aesthetics, Monist, 1983; Kant's Intentions in the Refutation of Idealism, Philosophical Review, 1983 etc.*Honour:* Matchette Prize of the American Philosophical Association, 1982. *Memberships:* American Philosophical Association; American Society of Aesthetics. *Address:* Department of Philosophy, 305 Logan Hall CN, University of Pennsylvania, Philadelphia, PA 19104, USA.

GWYNN, Eireen Meiriona, b. 1 Dec. 1916, Liverpool, England. Science Journalist; Broadcaster; Retired Tutor-Organiser for WEA. m. Harri Gwynn, 1 Jan. 1942, Bangor, Wales, 1 son. *Education:* BSc (Hons. Physics), 1937, PhD, 1940. *Publications:* I'r Lleuad a Thu Hwnt, 1964, (Science: To the Moon and Beyond); Priodi, 1966, (Marriage), editor; Dau Lygad Du, 1979, (short stories and essays); Caethiwed, 1981 (novel); Cwsg ni Ddaw, 1982, (essays); Hon, 1985 (novel): Bwyta i Fyw (pending, 1986), Eating to Live – on nutirition). *Contributions to:* Y Gwyddonydd, (The Scientist – University of Wales publication); Y Cymro; Y Faner. *Honours:* 1st Prize, BBC Wales Drama Competition, 1970; Honorary Member of the Gorsedd of Bards, Wales, 1985. *Address:* Tyddyn Rhuddallt, Llanrug, Caernarfon, Gwynedd, Wales.

GWYNN, Harri, b. 14 Feb. 1913, London, England, Dec. 24 Apr. 1985. Broadcaster; Formerly Civil Servant and Farmer. *Education:* BA(Hons), DipEd, MA. *Publications:* Barddoniaeth Harri Gwynn, 1955; Y Fuwch a'i Chynffon, 1957; Yng. Nghoedwigoedd y Ser, 1975. *Contributions to:* Y Llenor; Taliesin; Barn; Traethodydd, etc. Various Elsteddfondic Crowns; Member Gorsedd of Bards, 1982. *Membership:* Yr Academi Gymreig. *Address:* Tyddyn rhuddallt, Llanrug, Caernarfon, Gwynedd, Wales.

GYGER, Alison Isabel, b. 17 June 1933, Newcastle, Australia. Journalist. m. David Gyger, 4 Mar. 1967, Newcastle, 2 sons, 1 daughter. *Education:* BA, Sydney; Litt B, PhD, University of New England. *Contributor to:* Medium Aevum, 1966, 1969, 1971; 24 Hours, 1981–85; Opera Australia, 1978–85. *Address:* 6 Mitchell Street, Greenwich, NSW 2065, Australia.

GYGER, David Elliott, b. 7 Aug. 1931, East Sebago, Maine, USA. Editor/Manager, Opera Australia (monthly newspaper). m. Alison Jones, Newcastle, NSW, 4 Mar. 1967, 2 sons, 1 daughter. *Education:* BA, Amherst College, Massachusetts, USA, 1952. *Literary Appointments:* Reporter/photographer, Wooster (Ohio) Daily Record, USA, 1954–55; Reporter, Sydney Daily Telegraph, Australia, 1956–57; Editor/Manager, Riverina Express, Wagga Wagga, New South Wales, Australia, 1958–63; Sub-Editor, The Australian, Canberra/Sydney, 1964–75; Freelance Arts Journalist, 1976–77; Editor/Manager, Opera Australia, Sydney, 1978–. *Contributions to:* Sydney music critic, The Australian (national newspaper), 1971–75; Opera critic, Theatre Australia (monthly magazine), 1978–80; Music critic, feature writer, 24 Hours (monthly magazine), 1974–84; Classical record critic, music critic, The Bulletin (weekly magazine), 1975–76; Australian critic. Opera Canada, 1975–; Performance & record critic, Opera Australia, 1978–. *Address:* 6 Mitchell Street, Greenwich, New South Wales 2065, Australia.

GYLLENSTEN, Lars Johan Wictor, b. 12 Nov. 1921, Stockholm, Sweden. Former Professor of Histology; Author. *Education:* MD. *Publications include:* Camera obscura (poetry with T Greitz), 1946; Moderna myter (miscellany), 1949; Barnabok (novel), 1952; Senilia (novel), 1956; Sokratesdod, (novel) 1960; Desperados (short stories), 1962; Juvenilia, (novel), 1965; Palatset i parken (novel), 1970; Ur min offentiga sektor, (essays), 1971; Grottan i oknen (novel), 1973; I skuggan av Don

Juan (novel), 1975; Ballangesminnen (novel), 1978; Skuggans aferkowst (novel), 1985. *Honours include:* Lilla Nobelpriset, 1972. *Memberships:* Swedish Adacemy; Royal Swedish Academy of Sciences; Nobel Committee for Literature. *Address:* Karlavagen 121, 115 26 Stockholm, Sweden.

GYSI, Charles L III, b. 21 Dec. 1957, Philadelphia, USA. Journalist. m. Janet Lynn Lammers, 5 Oct. 1985, Burlington. *Education:* BA, Journalism, Temple University, Philadelphia. *Publications:* Scanner Master Greater Philadelphia/South Jersey Guide, 1983, 2nd edition 1985. *Contributor to:* Contributing Editor, Popular Communications. *Address:* P O Box 144, Rosemont, NJ 08556, USA.

H

HAAGE, Peter, b. 28 July 1940, Dresden, Germany. Author. *Publications:* Editor: Wozu das Theater Essays Satiren, Humoresken von Egon Friedell, 1965; Der Partylowe der nur Bucher frass, Egon Friedell und sein Kreis, biography, 1971; Ludwig Thoma, Mit Nagelstiefeln durchs Kaiserreich, biography, 1975; Wilhelm-Busch, Ein weises Leben, biography, 1960. *Address:* Klein Flottbeker Weg 14, D–2000 Hamburg 52, Federal Republic of Germany.

HAAKANA, Anna-Lisa, b. 30 Jan. 1937, Rovaniemi, Finland. Author. m. Veikko Olavi Haakana, 27 Feb. 1963, 1 son, 1 daughter. *Education:* Literature studies, University of Tempere. *Publications include:* 3 children's books, 1978–84; 3 books for young people, Ykï All Alone, 1980; Top Girl, 1981; A Flower, Nevertheless, 1983. *Honours:* National Award for Literature, 1981; Anni Swan Medal, 1982; H C Andersen's Certificate of Honour, 1982; Church's Award for Literature, 1982. *Memberships:* Trustee, 1984–, Finnish Provincial Writers; Trustee, 1983–, Northern Writers; Finnish Society of Authors; Association of Finnish Writers for Children & Youth. *Literary Agent:* Werner Söderström Oy. *Address:* 99600 Sodankylä, Finland.

HABGOOD, John Stapylton (Archibishop of York), b. 23 June 1927, England. m. Rosalie Mary Ann Boston, 7 June 1961, Neston, 2 sons, 2 daughters. *Education:* MA, PhD, King's College, Cambridge; Cuddesdon College, Oxford. *Publications:* Religion and Science, 1964; A Working Faith: Essays and Addresses on Science, Medicine and Ethics, 1980; Church and Nation in a Secular Age, 1983; Contributor to many symposia including, Soundings (Ed A Vidler), 1962. *Contributor to:* Numerous essays, and reviews in, Journal of Physiology, Nature, New Scientist, Theology, Expository Times, Frontier, Journal of Theological Studies, Crucible, Times Supplements, etc. *Honours:* Honorary DD, Durham, 1975, Cambridge 1984; Honorary Fellow, King's College, Cambridge, 1985. *Address:* Bishopthorpe, York, YO2 1QE, England.

HACKETT, Cecil Arthur, b. 19 Jan. 1908, Birmingham, England. Emeritus Professor of French; Literary Critic. *Education:* MA, Emmanuel College, Cambridge University; Doctoral Degree, University of Paris, France. *Publications:* Le Lyrisme de Rimbaud, 1938; Rimbaud l'Enfant, 1948; Anthology of Modern French Poetry from Baudelaire to the Present Day, 1952, 4th edition 1978; Rimbaud, 1957; Autour de Rimbaud, 1967; New French Poetry an Anthology, 1973; Rimbaud: A Critical Introduction, 1981; Rimbaud: Poesies, 1986. *Contributor to:* Numerous academic journals in England, France, USA & Canada. *Honours:* Recipient, Chevalier de la Legion d'Honneur. *Memberships:* Society for French Studies, Advisory Board. *Address:* Shawford Close, Shawford, Winchester, Hants, England.

HACKETT, Vernell, b. 31 Jan. 1949, Waco, Texas, USA. Entertainment journalist. *Education:* BS, Sam Houston State University. *Contributions to:* Country News; American Songwriter; Comptons Yearbook; Satelite TV Week; Country Rhythms; Grit; Camping Journal. *Honours:* Journalist of the Year, National Entertainment Journalists Association, 1982. Member National Entertainment Journalists Association, Past President, currently Parliamentarian, Member, Nashville Songwriters Association International. *Address:* 1719 West End No. 511, Nashville, TN 37203, USA.

HADDAD, Yvonne Yazbeck, b. 23 Mar. 1935, Syria. Professor. m. Wadi Z Haddad, 2 Nov. 1958, Jerusalem, 1 son, 1 daughter. *Education:* BA, Beirut College for Women, Lebanon, 1958; MRE, Boston University, 1966; MA History, University of Wisconsin, 1971; PhD, Islamic Studies, Hartford Seminary, 1979. *Literary Appointments:* Editor, The Muslim World, Hartford,

1980–; Associate Professor 1980–85, Professor 1985–, of Islamic Studies, Hartford Seminary, Hartford, Connecticut. *Major Publications:* The Islamic Understanding of Death & Resurrection (with J L Smith), 1981; Contemporary Islam & the Challenge of History, 1982; The Islamic Impact (with B Haines & E Findly), 1984; The Muslim Experience in North America, 1986; Women, Religion & Social Change, 1985. *Contributor to:* Muslim World; Middle East Journal; The Link; Journal of the American Oriental Society; Journal of the American Academy of Religion; and others. *Honours:* Various scholarships and grants, including: National Endowment for the Humanities, 1983–85; Fulbright Senior Research Fellowship, 1985. *Memberships:* American Academy of Religion; Middle East Studies Association; American Oriental Society. *Address:* 77 Sherman Street, Hartford, CT 06105, USA.

HADENHAM, Judith Sara, b. 23 Oct. 1953, England. Editor. m. Warren William Hadenham, 21 Aug. 1983, Sydney, Australia. *Appointment:* Editor in Chief, Portfolio Magazine, 1983–. *Contributor to:* Fashion Editor, Dolly; Creator, Mode Magazine; Editor, Bystander Magazine; Editor in Chief, Portfolio Magazine. *Address:* 3/51 Wolseley Road, Point Piper, Sydney, Australia.

HADLEIGH, Boze, b. 15 May 1954, Syria. Author; Journalist; Actor. m. 5 Oct. 1975, San Jose, California, USA. *Education:* BA, Spanish Literature, University of California, Santa Barbara, USA; MS Journalism, San Jose State University. *Publications:* Chairman Meow; Midnight Madonna; The Films of Jane Fonda, 1981. *Contributions to:* Magazines and papers in USA and Japan. *Address:* 810 Polhemus 63, San Mateo, CA 94402, USA.

HADLEY, Charles David, Junior, b. 5 June 1942, Springfield, Massachusetts, USA. Associate Professor of Political Science, divorced, 1 son. *Education:* BA, University of Massachusetts, Amherst, 1964; MA, 1967; PhD, University of Connecticut, 1971. *Publications:* Political Parties and Political Issues: Patterns in Differentiation Since the New Deal (Monograph with Everett C Ladd, Jr), 1973; Transformations of the American Party System: Political Coalitions from the New Deal to the 1970s (with Everett C Ladd, Jr), 1975, 2nd editon, 1978. *Contributions to:* The Public Interest; The Public Opinion Quarterly; Dictionary of American History, 1976; American Politics Quarterly; The Journal of Politics; Southeastern Political Review; State Government; Party Politics in the South, 1980; Political Ideas and Institution, 1983; The Journal of Political Science; The Journal of Social and Political Attitudes; The 1984 Presidential Election in the South, 1985. *Honour:* Younger Humanist Fellowship, National Endowment for the Humanities, May–Dec 1973. *Memberships:* American Political Science Association; Southern Political Science Association, Executive Council, 1978–81; Corresponding Secretary, 1984–85; Committee for Party Renewal, Executive Committee, 1984–87. *Address:* Department of Political Science, University of New Orleans, New Orleans, LA 70148, USA.

HAENEN, Paul, Journalist; Writer. *Literary Appointment:* As Margaret Dolman on Dolman Show every Friday on Radio Stad Amsterdam. LP on show came out in Oct. 1981. Author of satirical texts spoken during the show. *Publications:* Commissioned by Toneelgroep Theater in Arnhem to write plays for their school program and three plays are: U Kunt Beter Van School Gaan Meneer (You Had Better Leave School, Sir); Ik Mag Nooit lets (I Am Not Allowed to do Anything); De Boodschappenjongen (The Errand Boy). *Address:* Valeriusstraat 276/11, 1075 GN Amsterdam, The Netherlands.

HAEVEN, Paul b. 13 June 1893, Hasselt, Belgium. Retired. m. (1) Bertha Dejoncker, 1917, dec. 1944, 2 sons, 1 son dec. 1944, (2) Julienne Hoolans, 1954. *Publications:* Ecce Homo, collected poems, 1967; De Witte Dood, 1956; Honger Naar Macht, 1971;

Avondlandse Haikoes, 1975; Kosmos en Ziel, 1979. *Contributions to:* Oostland; Kruispunt; 't Kofschip; Spectraal. *Memberships:* Association of Flemish Authors; Association of Limburg Writers. *Address:* Oude Pastoriestraat 21, 1080 Brussels, Belgium.

HAFEN, Brent Que, b. 17 July 1940, Salt Lake City, Utah, USA. Professor of Health Sciences. m. Sylvia Ann Jacobson, 23 July 1959, Manti, 5 sons, 2 daughters. *Education:* BS, 1958, MS, 1962, University of Utah; PhD, Southern Illinois University, 1969. *Appointment:* Professor, Health Sciences, Brigham Young University. *Publications:* Numerous books including: Utah and Federal Drug Laws, 1970; Crisis Intervention for Prehospital Personnel, 1979; Surviving Health Emergencies & Disasters, 1979; First Aid for Health Emergencies, 2nd edition 1980; Food, Nutrition and Weight Control, 1981; Alcohol and Alcoholism, 2nd edition, 1983; Medicines and Drugs, 3rd edition, 1985; (Chapter Author), Counseling: A Guide to Helping Others, Volume II, 1985; Co-Author, Emotional Survival, 1983; Medical Self-Care and Assessment, 1983; An A-Z of Alternative Medicine, 1984; Psychological Emergencies and Crisis Intervention, 1985; etc. Editor, many books including Addictive Behavior: Alcohol Abuse, 1985; Nutrition & Health: New Concepts & Issues, 1985; etc. *Contributor to:* Numerous professional journals and magazines including, Nursing; Nursing Life; Health and Longevity Report; New Woman; Health Education; AMCAP Journal; etc. *Memberships:* American Association of Trauma Specialists; National Association of Emergency Medical Technicians; American Public Health Association. *Address:* Department of Health Sciences, 229 A Richards Bldg, Brigham Young University, Provo, UT 84602, USA.

HAFTMANN, Werner, b. 28 Apr. 1912, Glowno, Federal Republic of Germany. Art Historian. *Education:* PhD. *Publications:* Das Italienische Saulenmonument, 1939, latest edition, 1974; Paul Klee, Wege blidnerschen Denkens, 1950, latest edition, 1976; Malerei im 20 Jahrhundert, 2 volumes, 1954, latest edition, 1976; Emil Nolde, 1958, 75; Skizzenbuch zur Kultur der Gegenwart, 1960; E W Nay, 1960; Guttuso, 1971; Marc Chagall, 1972; Hans Uhlmann, Leben und Werk, 1975; Willi Baumeister Gilgamesch, 1976; Klaus Fubmann, 1976; Der Bildhauer Ludwig Kasper, 1978; Der Mensch und sine Bilder, 1980; Horst Antes 25 votive, 1984. *Honours:* Lessing Prize, 1962; Goethe Plaque, 1964; Reuter Plaque, 1974; Federal German Cross of Merit, 1st class, 1973. *Memberships:* Academy of Arts, Berlin; Poets, Playwrights, Essaysists, Editors and Novelists Club. *Address:* Bernockerweg 22, 8184 Gmund a Tegernsee, Federal Republic of Germany.

HAGEN, Siegfried Gerhard Werner, b. 17 Oct. 1925, Bad Charlottenbrunn, Schlesien, Germany. Editor, DuMont Buchverlag, Cologne. *Education:* School leaving examination; Study of German and Classical Philology. *Publications:* Fritz Usinger, (monograph), 1973; Henry Benrath. Der Dichter und sein Werk, (monograph), 1978; Chimärische Geschichten, 1979; Entwurf zu einam Menschenbild, 1980; Weil Form nur fasst. Hommage à Beauclair, 1985; Einige Gedichte, 1985; Gingo biloba. Gedichte, in preparation. Editor, Fritz Usinger Werke, 1984; Biographies of poets of the twentieth century; Poetry; Essays. *Contributor to:* Castrum Peregrini, Amsterdam; Neue Deutsche Hefts, Berlin. *Honour:* Ehrenschild, of the town of Friedberg/Hessen. *Memberships:* Deutsche Schillergesellschaft, Marbach a.N; Humboldt-Gesellschaft für Wissenschaft, Kunst und Bildung; Freier Deutscher Autorenverband, Bonn. *Address:* Türnicher Str. 3, D–5000 Köln 51, Federal German Republic.

HAGERTY, William John, b. 23 Apr. 1939, Ilford, Essex, England. Journalist. m. Lynda Ann, 5 June 1965, Edgware, Middlesex, 1 son, 1 daughter. *Publications:* Flash Bang Wallop (with Kent Gavin), 1978. *Contributions To:* Mirror Group Newspapers; Cosmopolitan; Company; Radio Times; TV Times. *Literary Agent:* Abner Stein, 10 Roland Gardens,

London SW7, *Address:* Mirror Group Newspapers, Holborn Circus, London EC1, England.

HÄGG, Tomas, b. 16 Nov. 1938, Uppsala, Sweden. Professor of Classical Philology, University of Bergen, Norway. m. Birgitta Nilsson, 23 June 1975, Uppsala, 1 daughter. *Literary Appointments:* Lecturer in Greek, University of Uppsala, 1972–77; Professor, Classical Philology, University of Bergen, 1977–. *Publications:* Narrative Technique in Ancient Greek Romances, 1971; Photios als Vermittler antiker Literatur, 1975; The Novel in Antiquity, 1983, Swedish Edition, 1980. *Contributions to:* Professional journals on Greek and Byzantine language and literature. *Literary Agent:* Carmina, Uppsala. *Address:* Department of Classics, Sydnespl. 9, N–5000 Bergen, Norway.

HAGGERTY, Joan, b. 26 Apr. 1940, Vancouver, British Columbia, Canada. Writer. 2 sons, 1 daughter. *Education:* BA, English and Theatre, University of British Columbia, 1962. *Appointment:* Instructor, Department of Creative Writing, University of British Columbia, 1979–83. *Publications:* Please Miss, Can I Play God? 1965; Daughters of the Moon, 1971. *Contributions to:* MS Magazine; CBC; BBC Radio; Books in Canada, Toronto; Room of One's Own, Vancouver; The Capilano Review, Vancouver; McCall's Magazine; B C Monthly, Vancouver. *Honours:* Four Canada Council Grants for Writing. *Membership:* Writers Union of Canada, B.C. Co-ordinator, 1983. *Address:* 168 West 19th Avenue, Vancouver, British Columbia, Canada V5Y 2B4.

HAGLUND, Elaine Jean, b. 1 Apr. 1937, Los Angeles, California, USA. Professor. *Education:* BA, University of California at Los Angeles, 1958; MA 1970, PhD 1972, Michigan State University. *Major Publications:* Resource Guide for Mainstreaming, 1980; On This Day, 1983. *Contributor to:* Peabody Journal of Education; Journal of Developing Areas; Curriculum Inquiry; International Journal of Intercultural Relations; International Education; School Psychology International. *Honour:* Fulbright Hays Fellow, 1978–80. *Membership:* Friends of the Library, University of California at Irvine. *Address:* California State University, Department of Educational Psychology, Long Beach, CA 90840, USA.

HAIGH, Jack, b. 21 Feb. 1910, West Hartlepool, England. Journalism. m. Josephine Agnes Mary McLoughlin, 7 July 1949, London. *Appointments:* Script Writer, The Rascals, official soldiers' concert party for Palestine, 1939–41; Staff, The Racing Calendar, 1956–68; Sports Sub Editor, The Daily Sketch, 1968–71; The Daily Mirror, 1971–72; The Daily Mail, 1972–84; Proprietor, Greenfriar Press. *Publications:* Theory of Genius, 1972; Constellation of Genius, 1982; Phillimore: The Postcard Art of R P Phillimore, 1985. *Contributions to:* 30 Children's Radio plays broadcasts from Jerusalem, 1941–44; Special Feature Programme introduced by Prince Peter of Greece & Denmark, 1944; 116 Radio Programmes broadcast, Forces Broadcasting Service, 1945–47. *Memberships:* Honorary Secretary, Freelance Specialist Panel, Institute of Journalists, 1951–53, 1964–72; Society of Indexers, 1958–. *Address:* 28 Manville Road, London SW17 8JN, England.

HAIKARA, Kalevi Ilmari, b. 8 Sep. 1938, Oulu, Finland. Author; Critic. m. Helly Kiviholma-Haikara, 29 Dec. 1965, 2 sons. *Education:* MA, Helsinki University. *Literary Appointments:* Otava Publishing House, 1969. *Publications:* Se oli se kultamaa, (That Was the Eldorado, Otava) 1969; Isanmaan vasen laita, (Left Side of the Fatherland, Otava), 1975; Kuka surmasi sananvapauden, (Who Killed the Freedom of Speech?, Otava), 1984; Aseita vastustajien kasiin, (Weapons for the Adversaries, play), 1984; Leikki kaukana, (Far From Joke), Radio Play, 1978. *Contributions to:* Parnasso; Suomen Kuvalehti; Ydin, (Finland); Kentering, (Netherlands); Nordisk Tidskrift, (Sweden). *Memberships:* Finnish PEN, (Secretary 1970–74; Vice-President, 1975–78; Board Member, 1981–); Finnish Playwrights' Union. (Board Member, 1978–, Vice-

President, 1980–). *Address:* Kontulankaari 2nA, 00940 Helsinki, Finland.

HAINES, Pamela Mary, b. 4 Nov. 1929, Harrogate, Yorkshire, England. Writer. m. Dr Anthony Haines, 24 June 1955, 2 sons, 3 daughters. *Education:* MA, English Literature, Cambridge University, 1952. *Publications include:* Tea at Gunter's, 1974; A Kind of War, 1976; Men on White Horses, 1978; The Kissing Gate, 1981; The Diamond Waterfall, 1984. *Honours:* Spectator New Writing Prize, 1971; Yorkshire Arts Young Writers Award, 1974. *Memberships:* Authors Society; Committee 1980–84, English branch, PEN. *Literary Agent:* Pat Kavanagh, A D Peters, 10 Buckingham Street, London WC2. *Address:* 57 Middle Lane, London N8 8PE, England.

HAIR, Nellie Eileen Donovan, b. 22 Nov. 1913, Wellington, New Zealand. Writer; Journalist. *Education:* Marsden Collegiate College; Gilby's Business College, Wellington. *Publications:* Short stories: Children's stories & serials; poems, etc. *Contributions to:* (Staff Writer) The Dominion; Hawke's Bay Herald-Tribune; New Zealand Women's Weekly; Weekly News, (Auckland); New Zealand Information Service, (Sr Press Office); Overseas Information Service, Tourist and Publicity Department; Colombo Plan, WHO & other New Zealand Government Aid Programmes; New Zealand Herald; Evening Post; South East Asian and African newspapers; Australian magazines; (plays) radio. *Memberships:* Professional and Literary organisations, including New Zealand Women's Writers Society, (Founder 1932, Past President, Secretary and Treasurer; active VP, Life Member); Society of Women Writers and Journalists; London Society of Women Writers; Australian Journalists' Union, New Zealand; Women's Press Club, London. *Address:* 65 Ravenwood Drive, Milford, Auckland 9, New Zealand.

HAIRSTON, William, b. 1 Apr. 1928, Goldsboro, North Carolina, USA. Writer; Consultant; Public Administrator. *Education:* New York University; Columbia University, New York City; BSc, Political Science. *Publicatioans:* Book Novel: The World of Carlos, 1968. Productions. Plays: Walk in Darkness; Black Antingone; Ira Aldridge; Creator and Editor, Newspaper, DC Pipeline for Washington, DC Government; Motion Picture and TV Shows for US Information Agency, Washington, DC; Apollo 11; Man on the Moon; Media Hora; Yosemite National Park; Jules Verne vs Real Flight to the Moon; Festival of Heritage, etc. *Honours:* Grant, Ford Foundation, 1965; Fellowship, National Endowment for the Arts, 1967. *Memberships:* Dramatists Guild; Authors League. *Address:* 9909 Conestoga Way, Potomac, MD 20854, USA.

HAITOV, Nikolai, b. 15 Sep. 1919, Yavorovo, Bulgaria. Writer. *Education:* Faculty of Arboriculture, Sofia University. *Literary Appointment:* Chief Editor of the, Rodopi, magazine. *Publications:* Wild Stories,short stories, 1967; Captain Petko voivoda, biography,1974; The Thorny Rose, essays, 1975; A Look in the Most Cherished, 1977; Selected Works, 1979. *Contributor to:* All main Bulgarian literary editions. *Honours:* People's Worker of Culture, 1976; Dimitrov Prize, 1979. *Membership:* Union of Bulgasrian Writers. *Address:* 15 Latinka Street, Sofia, Bulgaria.

HAKKARAINEN, Olli, b. 10 Oct. 1971, Tampere, Finland. Journalist. m. (2) Leena Salminen, 12 June 1976, Anjala, 2 sons, 3 daughters. *Education:* Helsinki University, 1963–72. *Publications:* 20 books including: Pienet Tytot Keinuva Kesaillassa, poems, 1979; Huppunmies eijalkia Jata, 1980; Kahden Miljonnan Markan Unelma, novel, 1981; Kuutamokeikka, 1984. *Contributions to:* Helsingin Sanomal. *Membership:* Finnish Writers Guild. *Literary Agent:* Arvi A Karisto Limited. *Address:* Pohjoiskaari 6A2, 00200 Helsinki 20, Finland.

HALBAN, Peter Francis, b. 1 June 1946, New York City, USA. Publisher. m. Martine Mizrahi 20 Feb. 1985,

London, 1 son. *Education:* BA, cum laude, History, Princeton University, 1969. *Literary Appointments:* Sales and Rights, Weidenfeld Publishers, 1971–73; Literary Agent, Peter Janson-Smith, 1973–74; Own Literary Agency, Jerusalem, 1978–82; Partner and Publisher, Domino Publishers, Jerusalem, 1982–; Own Publishing List, London, 1986–. *Honours:* Prize, Italian, Princeton University, 1968. *Memberships:* Book Publishers Association, Israel; Board of Directors, Jerusalem International Book Fair; Princeton Club of New York (affiliated). *Address:* 10 Montagu Square, London W1H 1RB, England.

HALDAR, Gopal, b. 11 Feb. 1902, Vidgamom, Dacca, India (now Bangladesh). Author, Journalist. *Education:* BA, MA, BL, University of Calcutta. *Major Publications:* 12 works of fiction, 1 collection of short stories, 6 works on cultural history, 6 on history of language & literature, 6 collections of belles lettres, 6 books of essays & criticisms, 2 critical editions, 4 books of grammar & compositions, 3 scholarly works, including, Ekada, translated as, One Day, Vidya Sagar – A New Assessment. *Contributor to:* Hindustan Standard; Parichay; numerous standard literary, research & foreign journals. *Honours:* National Fellowship in Literature & the Arts, 1976; Sharat Chandra Award, 1977; Tagore Award for Literature, 1980; Rabindra Puraskar Award, 1980; Sarojini Medal for best researches, University of Calcutta; Vidya Sagar Lectures, D L Roy Lectures, Khudiyam Lectures, Universities of Bombay & Calcutta. *Memberships include:* Executive, Asiatic Society; Pavlov Institute; Sahitya Parishad, Calcutta. *Address:* C I T Buildings, B1 H Flat No 19, Christopher Road, Calcutta, 700014, India.

HALE, Judson Drake, b. 16 Mar. 1933, Boston, Massachusetts, USA. Editor of, Yankee Magazine and The Old Farmers Almanac. m. Sally Huberlie, 6 Sep. 1958, Rochester, New York, 3 sons. *Education:* AB, Dartmouth College; Doctor of Journalism (Honorary), New England College. *Publications:* Inside New England, 1982, Paperback, 1986; The Best of Yankee Magazine (Editor), 1985; Other anthologies published by Yankee Publishing Incorporated. *Contributions to:* Yankee Magazine; Old Farmers Almanac; American Heritage. *Address:* Vallex Road, P O Box 251, Dublin, NH 03444, USA.

HALE, Kathleen, b. 24 May 1898, Broughton, Lancashire, England. Author, Artist. *Education:* Art Department Scholar, University of Reading. *Major Publications:* Orlando the Marmalade Cat, series; Manda the Jersey Calf; Henrietta the Faithful Hen; Henrietta's Magic Egg. *Contributor to:* Home & Garden; Child Education; Orlando Ballet; Festival of Britain; and other publications. *Memberships:* Chelsea Arts Club; Society of Authors; International Artists. *Honour:* OBE, 1976. *Address:* Tod House, Forest Hill, Oxford, England.

HALE, Robert William, b. 21 Apr. 1937, Denver, Colorado, USA. Professor, History of Spirituality. *Education:* BA, Pomona College, 1959; STB, Ponticium Athenaeum Anselmianum, Rome, Italy, 1964; MA, St John's University, 1968; PhD, Fordham University, 1972. *Appointments:* Professor Adiunctus, Pontificium Athenaeum Anselmianum, Rome, 1972–79; Visitng Professor, Theology, Holy Family College, California, 1980–; Visiting Associati Professor, Spirituality, Jesuit School of Theology, Berkely, 1980–. *Publications:* Christ and the Universe: Teilhard de Chardin and the Cosmos, 1973; Canterbury and Rome: Sister Churches, 1982. *Contributor to:* Various professional journals including, Vita Monastica; total of 80 articles. *Memberships:* American Academy of Religion; Pacific Coast Theological Society; Collaborator, Vita Monastica; President's Council, Religious Sciences in Italy. *Address:* Incarnation Priory, 1601 Oxford St, Berkeley, CA 94709, USA.

HALL, Alan Wilburn, b. 2 Apr. 1928, Enfield, Middlesex, England. Publisher. m. Betty Rosina Wesley, 24 July 1959, Ealing, 1 son, 1 daughter. *Education:* Art Teachers Diploma; National Diploma in Design.

Publications: The Avro Anson, 1969; RAF Fighters of World War 2, 1975; American Fighters of World War 2, 1976; Aircraft Conversions, 1979. *Contributions to:* Founder-Editor, Airfix Magazine; Editor, Royal Aircraft Establishment News; Publisher–Editor, Aviation News, Scale Aircraft Modelling; RAF News; Air Pictoria; L'Album du Fanaticue; Air Cadet News. *Address:* 226 High Street, Berkhamsted, Hertfordshire HP4 1AD, England.

HALL, Alfred Rupert, b. 26 July 1920, Stoke-on-Trent, England. Professor. *Education:* MA 1944, PhD 1950, Litt D, 1974, Christ's College, University of Cambridge, England. *Major Publications:* Ballistics in the 17th Century, 1952; The Scientific Revolution, 1954; A History of Technology (co-editor), 1953–58; From Galileo to Newton, 1962; The Cambridge Philosophical Society: A History, 1969; Philosophers at War, 1980; (co-author) Correspondence of Henry Oldenburg, 1965–80; Brief History of Science, 1964; Correspondence of Isaac Newton volumes 5-7, 1975–78; Short History of the Imperial College, 1982; The Revolution in Science 1500–1750, 1983. *Memberships:* Fellow, British Academy, Past President, International Academy of the Historty of Science; Past President, British Society of the History of Science. *Honours:* Silver Medal, Royal Society of Arts, 1974; Sarton Medal (JTLY), 1981. *Address:* 14 Ball Lane, Tackley, Oxford, England.

HALL, David Robert, b. 22 Jan. 1943, Manchester, England. Publisher. m. Patricia Kay, 1 May 1971, 2 sons, (divorced). *Publications:* Complete Coarse Fisherman, 1980; The Match Fisherman, 1982. *Contributions to:* Coarse Fisherman Magazine; Fisherman Magazine; Water. *Address:* 49 High Street, Daventry, Northants, England.

HALL, Durell, Jr b. 29 Sep. 1954, Canton, Ohio, USA. Photojournalist, 1 daughter. *Education:* BFA, Ohio University. *Contributions to:* Akron Beacon Journal; Louisville Courier Journal; Washington Post; New York Times; Ebony. *Honours:* Ohio New Photographic Illustration, 1978; Akron Media Award, 1979; Picture of the Year Contest, National Press Photographic Association, 1981; Frederick Douglass Award, National Association of Black Journalists, 1981. *Address:* 5125 Quial Court, No 8, Louisville, KY 40213, USA.

HALL, Elsie Irene, b. 3 Nov. 1914, Eveleth, Minnesota, USA. Housewife. m. John E Hall, 14 May 1936, Duluth, Minnesota, 2 sons. *Contributions to:* Of Theel Sing; The 1971 Shore Poetry Anthology; The Lyric; And So It Is; Reflections of the Inward Silence; Shadows of the Elusive Dream; North Country Cadence; Poetry of Our Times; Heartsong and Northstar Gold, League of Minnesota Poets Anthology, 1984. *Honours:* Life Member, 1981, Editor Emeritus, 1984, Numerous awards, Poetry Seminars, 1970–84, League of Minnesota Poets. *Memberships:* Secretary of Manuscripts, Arrowhead Poetry Society; League of Minnesota Poets; Academy of American Poets; National Association of State Poetry Societies. *Address:* Star Route Box 66, Brimson, MN 55602, USA.

HALL, Ernest (George), b. 18 May 1921, Tidworth, Hampshire, England. Author; Journalist. m. Heather Ina Gilbert, 27 Apr. 1946, Ilford, 2 sons. *Education:* Qualified Environmental Health Officer; Fellow, Royal Society of Health; Further Education Teachers Certificate, City & Guilds of London Institute. *Publications:* Home Plumbing; Beginner's Guide to Domestic Plumbing; Teach Yourself; Plumbing; Questions & Answers on Home Plumbing; David & Charles Manual of Home Plumbing. *Contributions to:* Do-It-Yourself, magazine; Various camping & caravanning magazines; Feature Writer, columnist, local press. *Membership:* Society of Authors. *Literary Agent:* Donald Copeman. *Address:* 88 Dudley Road, Clacton-on-Sea, Essex CO15 3DJ, England.

HALL, Gerald L, b. 27 Oct. 1936. College Professor. m. Mary Lise, 11 May 1984, Saginaw, Michigan.

Education: BA, 1961, MA, 1963, ABD, 1967, Michigan State University. *Literary Appointments:* Instructor, 1967, Assistant Professor, 1969, Associate Professor, 1974–, Delta College, University Center, Michigan; Advisory Board for Literature, Michigan Council for the Arts, 1984–86. *Publications:* Pick-A-Duck, 1973; Poemontage, 1974; Poems for the Bicentennial, Michigan, Co-Editor, 1976; Dad, 1977; Concrete Poetry, Co-author, 1977; 1,365 Ways and Days to Love, 1979; Key West Love Poems, Co-author, 1979; Eclipse, 1979; US '79, Poetry-by-the-Sea, Publisher, 1979; Loving Foreward and Backward, 1980; 13 Dreams of ESQ, Co-author, 1981; For Our Eyes Only, Co-author, 1981; What Is, What Might Have Been, What Might Be, 1982; Michigan Writers, Editor, 1984. *Contributions to:* Red Cedar Review; Backfire; New Poets Review; Main Street; Cranberries; Poetry of Love; Peninsula Poets; Review; Exhibit. *Memberships:* College English Association; Past Michigan Vice President, Past Michigan President, Member, Executive Board, National Memberships Committee; Poetry Society of Michigan; Nationl Society of Literature and the Arts; Michigan Academy of Sciences; Arts and Letters; Modern Language Association; National Council of Teachers of English. *Address:* English Division, Delta College, University Center, MI 48710, USA.

HALL, James B(yron), b. 21 July 1918, USA. Writer, Professor. m. Elizabeth Cushman, 14 Feb. 1946, 1 son, 4 daughters. *Education:* BA, MA, PhD 1953. *Literary Appointments:* Cornell University, 1952–54; University of Oregon, 1955–65; University of California at Irvine, 1966–69; Provost University of California at Santa Cruz, 1969–75; Professor 1975–84. Emeritus 1984. *Major Publications:* Not by Door, 1954; Us He Devours, 1964; The Hunt Within, 1973; The Short Hall, 1981. *Contributor to:* Esquire; Atlantic; New Letters; Omni; Sewanee; and others. *Honours:* Several awards for writing. *Membership:* National Writers Union, Past President, local Chapter. *Address:* 31 Hollins Drive, Santa Cruz, CA 95060, USA.

HALL, J(ohn) C(live), b. 12 Sep. 1920. *Education:* Leighton Park, Reading; Oriel College, University of Oxford. *Major Publications:* Selected Poems (with Keith Douglas & Norman Nicholson), 1943; The Summer Dance (poems), 1951; The Burning Hare (poems), 1966; A House of Voices (poems), 1973; Selected and New Poems 1939–84, 1985; Edwin Muir (critical pamphlet), 1956. *Address:* 198 Blythe Road, London W14 OHH, England.

HALL, N John, b. 1 Jan. 1933, Orange, New Jersey, USA. Professor of English. m. Marianne E Gsell, 13 Oct. 1968, New York City, New York, 1 son. *Education:* PhD, New York University, 1970. *Literary Appointments:* Distinguished Professor of English, Bronx Community College and Graduate Center, City University of New York, 1983–. *Publications:* Salmagundi: Byron, Allegra and the Trollope Family, 1975; Trollope and His Illustrators, 1980. Editor: Anthony Trollope's The New Zealander, 1972; The Trollope Critics, 1982; The Letters of Anthony Trollope, 2 volumes, 1983; Beerbohn's Illustrated Zuleika Dobson, 1985. *Contributions to:* 19th Century Fiction; Princeton University Library Chronicle. *Honours:* Fellowships: National Endowment for the Humanities, 1974; Guggenheim Foundation, 1977, 84; American Council of Learned Societies, 1980. *Memberships:* Past Board of Directors, City University of New York Academy of Humanities and Sciences; Executive Director, Maximillian Society 11. *Address:* 44 West 10th Street, New York City, NY 10011, USA.

HALL, Peter Geoffrey, b. 19 Mar. 1932, London, England. University Professor. *Education:* BA 1953, MA 1957, St Catharine's College, University of Cambridge, 1959. *Publications include:* The World Cities, 1966; Theory and Practice of Regional Planning, 1970; Urban and Regional Planning, 3rd edition, 1974; The Containment of Urban England (co-author), 1973; Planning and Urban Growth: An Anglo-American Comparison (with Marion Clawson), 1973; Europe 2000 (co-author), 1977; Growth Centres in the

European Urban System, 1980; Great Planning Disasters, 1980. *Contributor to:* New Society. *Honour:* Recipient, Gill Memorial Prize, RGS, 1968. *Literary Agent:* A D Peters and Co. *Address:* Department of Geography, University of Reading, Whiteknights, Reading, Berkshire RG6 2AB, England.

HALL, Rand, b. 17 July 1945, New Jersey, USA. Writer; Dental Laboratory Owner & Operator. 1 son, 1 daughter. *Education:* Hofstra University, New York; New York Agricultural & Technical Institute, Farmingdale. *Editor & Publisher of:* Womonwrites Anthology '84; Southern Exposure Womonwrites, 1985. *Contributions:* Poetry, essays in: Sinister Wisdom; Feminary; Common Lives/Lesbian Lives; Oblisk periodicals; Books, Voices in the Night, McNaron & Morgan; The Alternative Papers. *Memberships:* Feminist Writers Guild; Womonwrites – Southeastern Lesbian Writers Conference, registrar, 1981–. *Address:* 7134 5th Avenue N, St Petersburg, FL 33710, USA.

HALL, Rodney, b. 18 Nov. 1935, Solihull, England. Writer. m. Bet MacPhail, Brisbane, 3 daughters. *Education:* BA, Queensland University. *Appointments:* Poetry Editor, The Australian, 1967–78; Creative Arts Fellow, Australian National University, 1968–69. *Publications:* (Poetry) Penniless Till Doomsday, 1962; Selected Poems, 1975; Black Ragatelles, 1978; (Novels) The Ship on the Coin, 1972; A Place Among People, 1975, 2nd edition 1984; Just Relations, 1982, 4th edition 1985. *Contributor to:* Hundreds of poems and several short stories in, Australian Literary Magazines, Newspapers, Journals; Book Reviews, The Australian; Sydney Morning Herald; The Bulletin. *Honours:* Grace Leven Prize for Poetry, 1973; Australia Council, Senior Fellowships, 1973, 1976, 1983, 1985; Miles Franklin Award, for Novel, 1982. *Literary Agent:* Elaine Markson, New York. *Address:* PO Box 7, Bermagui South, NSW 2547, Australia.

HALL, Roger Dennis, b. 13 May 1945, Regina, Canada. Professor of History. m. Sandra Martin, 21 Oct. 1971, Cambridge, England, 1 son, 1 daughter. *Education:* BA Honours, University of Victoria, British Columbia, 1967; MA, University of Sussex, England, 1968; PhD, Cambridge University, 1974. *Literary Appointments:* Editor, Ontario History, 1981–85; Co-editor, Canadian Review of American Studies, 1985–. *Publications:* With Sandra Martin: Rupert Brooke in Canada, 1978; Where Were You? Memorable Events of the 20th Century, 1981. With Gordon Dodds: A Picture History of Ontario, 1978; Canada: A History, 1981; The World of William Notman; The Rising Country: The Correspondence of Elizabeth Hale of Quebec with her brother Lord Amherst, Governor-General of India, forthcoming. *Contributions to:* Canadian Historical Review; Canadian Journal of History; Dalhousie Review; Canadian Forum; Ontario History; Saturday Night Magazine; Books in Canada; Quill and Quire; Toronto Globe and Mail; Toronto Star and others. *Honours:* Doctoral Fellowships, Canada Council, 1972–74; Research Grants, Social Science and Humanities Research Council, 1979–82. *Literary Agent:* John Duff. *Address:* Department of History, University of Western Ontario, London, Ontario, Canada N6A 5C2.

HALLER, John S Jr, b. 22 July 1940, Pittsburgh, Pennsylvania, USA. Professor of History. *Education:* AB, Georgetown University, Washington DC; MA, John Carroll University, Cleveland, Ohio; PhD, University of Maryland. *Major Publications:* Outcasts from Evolution: Scientific Attitudes of Racial Inferiority 1899–1900, 1971, 1974; The Physician & Sexuality in Victorian America, 1974, 1977; American Medicinein Transition, 1840–1910, 1981. *Contributor to:* Professional journals, including: Journal of the History of Medicine, Bulletin of the History of Medicine, New York State Journal of Medicine, Journal of Medicine, American Anthropology, medical History. *Memberships:* American Association for the History of Medicine; American Institute for the History of Pharmacy; Organisation of American Historians; Association for the History of Anthropology. *Honours:* Anisfield-Wolf prize in Race

Relations for book, Outcasts, 1971. *Address:* 4788 Dogwood Avenue, Seal Beach, CA 90740, USA.

HALLERAN, Dorothy Eleanor Wilder, b. 7 Mar. 1919, Lynn, Massachusetts, USA, Administrative Assistant, Public Relations, Employment Security, State Government, Retired 1977. m. Frank David Halleran, 2 Jan. 1975, Lynn, Massachusetts. *Education:* BLS, English, Boston University, 1975. *Contributor to:* (Poetry): North Shore Magazine; Earthwise; The Villager; Alura; Encore; The Pen Woman, magazine of National League of American Pen Women; Anthologies include: Anthology of The Massachusetts State Poetry Society; North Shore Poets Forum; Maine Poets and Their Poems; The Art of Poetry: A Treasury of Contemporary Verse? *Honours:* First, second and third prizes for poetry sponsored by Lynn Sunday Post, Poetry Society of New Hampshire, Massachusetts State Poetry Society, North Shore Poets Forum and the North Shore Branch of national league of American Pen Women. *Memberships:* North Shore Poets Forum, Treasurer 7 terms; President, 2 terms; Poetry Society of New Hampshire; Poetry Fellowship of Maine; Massachusetts State Poetry Society, Board member, 2 terms; North Shore Branch, NLAPW, Secretary. *Address:* 30 Chestnut Street, Peabody, MA 01960, USA.

HALLETT, Hugh Victory Dudley, b. 16 Jan. 1919, Poole, Dorset, England. Senior Police Officer. *Publications:* International Bibliography of the Police, 2 editions; IPA Travel Scholarship Papers, 6 editions, 1968–75; Survey of the Present and Past Police Forces of England and Wales, 1975. *Contributions to:* Police World, (Editor-in-Chief); Police Journal; Police World Ed. Bd. Abstracts on Police Science, (Editor); Police Chief; Criminal Law Review, etc. *Honour:* Queens Police Medal, 1983. *Memberships:* Association of Industrial Editors; Institute of Personnel Managers; Association of Conference Organizers; Henry Fielding Society. *Address:* Sparrow Hatch, 20 Sportsfield, Maidstone, Kent ME14 5LR, England.

HALLGARTEN, Siegfried Solomon 'Fritz', b. 6 June 1902, Winkel (Rhg) Germany. Lawyer. m. Friedel Liselotte Liebaraum, 28 Oct. 1930, 2 sons. *Education:* Dr of Law, Heidelberg University, University Frankfurt and Maine, Germany. *Publications include:* Rhineland-Wineland, 1951 (Elek), Paperback, 1967: The Great Wines of Germany (with Andre Simon), 1963; Alsace and its Winegardens; Alsace, its Winegardens, Cellars and Cuisine, 1978; Guide to the Vineyards, Estates and Wines of Germany, 1974; German Wines, (Faber and Faber), 1976, 1981 (Publivin London); (Contributor) Wines and Spirits of the World, 1972; Wines of the World, (editor, Andre Simon), 1972; Wines and Wine Gardens of Austria (with wife), 1979; Der Konflikt zwischen geographischer Herkunftsbereichnung und Warenzeichen, 1985; Wine Scandal, 1986 (Weidenfeld and Nicholson). *Contributor to:* Harper's Wine and Spirit Gazette; Wines and Spritis; Wine World; Deutsche Weinfach zeitung; House and Garden; Magazine of Wine Club of America German Legal Papers, ZLR, EWR, GROR. *Memberships:* German Lawyers' Association, West Germany. *Address:* 20 Bracknell Gardens, London NW3 7ED, England.

HALLIDAY, David G, b. 2 Apr. 1948, Toronto, Canada. Computer Typesetter. m. Anne-Marie Von Vosselen, 16 Nov. 1979, Hamme, Belgium, 1 son. *Education:* BA, MA, Philosophy, University of Windsor, Canada. *Publications:* Crowd Noises, 1975; Murder, 1979; The Black Bird, 1983; Making Movies, 1983. *Contributor to:* over 10 magazines throughout the USA and Canada including, Antigonish Review; New Quarterly; Canadian Fiction Magazine; Quarry; New Writer's News; Matrix; Waves; Mosshead Review; Grain. *Membership:* Writer's Union of Canada. *Address:* 36 Botfield Ave, Islington, Ontario, Canada.

HALLIDAY, William R(oss), b. 9 May 1926, Emory University, Georgia, USA. Thoracic Surgeon, Medical Administrator; Speleologist. *Education:* BA, Swarthmore College, PA, 1946; MD, George

Washington University, Washington DC, 1948. *Publications:* Adventure is Underground, 1959; pirate Russian ed, 1963; Caves of California, 1962; Caves of Washington, 1963; Depths of the Earth, 1966; revised edition, 1976; American Caves and Caving, 1974, revised edition 1982. *Contributor to:* Science; Pacific Discovery; Pacific Search; Desert; National Parks Magazine; Various Technical and outdoors magazines. *Honours include:* Desert Magazine Award, 1960; Governer's Award, 1968. *Memberships:* Past President, Seattle Free Lances; Past Trustee, Pacific NW Writers Conference. *Address:* 1117 36th Avenue East, Seattle, WA 98112, USA.

HALLOREN, Christopher Lewis, b. 17 July 1947, DeKalb, Illinois, USA. Technical Writer. m. 29 Nov. 1979, Toronto, 2 sons, 1 daughter. *Education:* BA, University of Illinois. *Publications:* Tangled Passage, 1974; Westroy Hotel, 1978. *Contributor to:* Mayday magazine; Scene Changes; Toronto Theatre Review. *Honours:* Ontario Arts Council Grant, 1977; Canada Council explorations Award, 1977; Write Your Own Ticket Runner Up, 1979. *Memberships:* Guild of Canadian Playwrights; Playwrights Union of Canada. *Address:* 7 George St S, Toronto, Ontario M5A 4B1, Canada.

HALLY, Simon, b. 27 Sep. 1949, London, England. Magazine Editor. m. Linda Irvin, 23 June 1984, Toronto, Ontario, Canada. *Education:* BSc, University of Toronto. *Literary Appointments:* Editor, Canadian Driver/Owner, 1977, Canadian Jeweller, 1979; Editor, Publisher, Canadian Jeweller, 1983–. *Contributions to:* Numerous journals. *Honours:* Kenneth R Wilson Memorial Awards, 1977–79, 1981–84. *Address:* 192 Macpherson Avenue, Toronto, Ontario, Canada M5R 1W8.

HALPRIN, Lawrence, b. 1 July 1916, New York City, USA. Landscape Architect; Planner. m. Anna, 19 Sep. 1941, Chicago, Illinois, 2 daughters. *Education:* BS, Cornell University, 1939; MS, University of Wisconsin, 1941; BLA, Harvard School of Design, 19421. *Publications:* Freeways, 1966; New York, New York, 1968; RSVP Cycles, 1970; Cities, 1972; Notebooks of Lawrence Halprin, 1959–71, 1972; Take Part, 1972; Taking Part: A Workshop Approach to Collective Creativity, (with Jim Burns), 1974; City Spirit (with Roundhouse), 1976; Process Architecture, Lawrence Halprin (with Proc. Arch.), 1978; Sketchbooks of Lawrence Halprin, (with Proc. Arch.), 1981. *Contributor to:* Progressive Architecture; Process Architecture; AIA Journal; Landscape Architecture; Landscape; RIBA Journal; Architecture/West; Ridge Review. *Honours:* Gold Medal for Distinguished Achievement in Allied Professions, American Institute of Architects; Fellow, American Society of Landscape Architects; Honorary Fellow, American Institute of Interior Design; Thomas Jefferson Gold Medal Award in Architecture; Leaders of Tomorrow, Time Magazine; Design Award of Excellence, Smithsonian Institution; Award of Excellence, San Francisco Arts Commission; Collaborative Medal of Honor, Architecture League of New York; Numerous Awards of Excellence from AIA, ASLA, P/A, HUD, etc. *Membership:* The Academy of Arts and Sciences, National Endowment for the Arts. *Address:* 444 Brannan Street, San Francisco, CA 94107, USA.

HALSALL, Eric, b. 18 Mar. 1920, Burnley, Lancashire, England. Retired Estate Manager; Author. m. Rita Greenwood, 12 Dec. 1941, Burnley. *Publications:* Hill Dog, 1961; Meg of Lonktop, 1967; Sheepdogs, My Faithful Friends, 1980; Sheepdog Trials, 1982; Gael, Sheepdog of the Hills, 1985; Sheepdogs, My Faithful Friends, revised, 1985. *Contributions to:* Farmers Guardian; Burnley Express; most farming and country magazines. *Honours:* Television Commentator, One Man and His Dog, 10 annual series, British Broadcasting Corporation television; various radio and television programmes. *Memberships:* Guild of Agricultural Journalists; Press Officer, Ribblesdale Farmers Club; Director, International Sheep Dog Society; Secretary, Derbyshijre Gritstone Sheep Breeders Society;

President, Burnley Branch, Guide Dogs for the Blind Association. *Address:* 528 Red Lees Road, Cliviger, near Burnley, Lancashire, England.

HAMALAINEN, Helvi Helena, b. 16 June 1907, Hamina, Finland. Author. *Publications include:* Katuojan vetta, 1935; translated into French, Norwegian & Swedish; Saadyllinen murhenaytelma, 1939; Ketunkivi, 1948; Tuhopolttaja, 1949; Karkuri, 1961, translated into Russian & Tsekki, 1961; Suden kunnia, 1962; Valitut runot (selected poems), 1973. *Honours:* Pro Finlandia Medal, 1961; Aleksis Kivi Prize, 1958; Kordelin Prize of Merit, 1962; Prize, Foundation of Finnish Culture, 1971; State Prizes, 1936, 1943. *Membership:* of Honour, Finnish Authors' Society, 1973. *Address:* Ukonvaaja 2 B 27, Tapiola 02130, Espoo 13, Finland.

HAMBURGER, Anne Ellen, b. 10 Sep. 1928, Redhill, England. m. Michael Hamburger, 28 July 1957, London, 1 son, 2 daughters. *Education:* Trained at Central School of Speech and Drama, London, England. *Literary Appointments:* Worked with Poets in Schools projects since 1973; also worked for the Anvon Foundation Writng Courses. *Publications:* Walking Without Moving; The Lair; Footsteps in Snow; The Curving Shore; Songs a Thracion Taught Me; Songs of Almut. *Contributor to:* Akzente; Agenda; New Statesman; The Observer; The Scotsman; The Literary Review; Rialto; Boston University Journal; Kayak; Arc; Aquarius; Kurbiskern; and other publications. *Memberships:* Member of the Poetry Society of Great Britain; committee member, 1976–79. *Address:* Marsh Acres, Middleton, Saxmundham, Suffolk IP17 3NH, England.

HAMBURGER, Jean, b. 15 July 1909, Paris, France. Professor of Medicine. *Education:* MD, PhD, Faculty of Medicine, Sorbonne, Paris. *Publications:* Nephrologie, 1979; Nefrologia, 1967; Nephrology, 1979; La Transplantation Renale, 1970; Renal Transplantation, 1971; Structure and Function of the Kidney, 1971; La Puissance et la Fragilite, 1972, translated into 7 languages; Discovering the Individual, 1978; Demain, Les Austres, 1979; Le Journal d'Harvey, 1983; La Raison et la Passion, 1984. *Honour:* Grand Officer, Legion d'Honneur, France. *Memberships:* Vice President, Foundation for French Medical Research; Institute of France, Academy of Sciences, 1974; National Academy of Medicine; Former President, International Society of Transplantation; International Society of Nephrology; Fellow, Royal College of Physicians, London, Edinburgh and Canada. *Address:* 38 rue Mazarine, Paris 6e, France.

HAMBURGER, Käte, b. 21 Sep. 1896, Hamburg, Federal Republic of Germany. Emeritus University Professor. *Education:* Doctor magna cum laude, 1922; Dr h c, University of Siegen, 1980. *Publications:* Thomas Mann und die Romantik, 1932; Thomas Manns Roman, Joseph und seine Br[em]uder, 1945, 2nd edition as, Der Humor bei Thomas Mann, 1965; Tolstoi, 1950, 2nd edition 1963; Die Logik der Dichtung, 1957, 3rd edition 1977; Von Sophokles zu Sartre, 1962, 5th edition 1974; Philosophie der Dichter, 1966; Rilke, 1976; Wahrheit und ästhetische Wahrheit, 1979; Das Mitleid, 1985. *Contributions to:* Numerous German journals. *Memberships:* German Schiller Society; Goes the Society; Thomas Mann Society; Heine Society; Honorary member, MLA, USA; PEN. *Honour:* Grand Cross of Merit, Federal Republic of Germany, 1966. *Address:* Hegelstrasse 51 (1009), 7000 Stüttgart, Federal Republic of Germany.

HAMBURGER, Philip, b. 2 July 1914, Wheeling, West Virginia, USA. Writer. *Education:* BA, Johns Hopkins University, 1935; MS, Graduate School of Journalism, Columbia University, 1938. *Publications:* The Oblong Blur & Other Odysseys, 1949; JP Marquand, Esquire, 1952; Mayor Watching & Other Pleasures, 1958; Our Man Stanley, 1963; An American Notebook, 1965. *Contributor to:* New Yorker Magazine, Staff Writer, 1939–; The Century Association, New York; The Coffee House, New York. *Memberships:* Member, Authors Guild; PEN, American Central; Board of Directors, Authors League Fund; National Press Club, Washington DC. *Address:* The New Yorker, 25 W 43rd St, New York, NY 10036, USA.

HAMEL DOBKIN, Kathleen L, b. 18 May 1945, Wisconsin, USA. Writer. *Education:* BA, Humanities, Liberal Arts, University of Wisconsin, Madison. *Publications:* The Red Room, 1981; The Queen of Hearts, 1982; The White Rabbit, 1983; A Valentine for Betsy, 1984; Desire and Dream, 1984; All-Nighter, 1985. *Honour:* Residency, The Helene Wurlitzer Foundation of New Mexico, Taos, New Mexico. *Literary Agent:* Barbara Lowenstein Associates, New York City. *Address:* New York State, USA.

HAMELL, Patrick Joseph (Right Reverend Monsignor), b. 11 Dec. 1910, Cloughjordan, County Tipperary, Republic of Ireland. Vicar General of Killaloe Diocese; Parish Priest of Birr, County Offaly, Republic of Ireland; University Professor of Theology. *Education:* BA, 1931, MA, 1940, Maynooth College, National University of Ireland; DD, Maynooth Pontifical University, 1937. *Publications:* Patrology: An Introduction; Index to Irish Ecclesiastical Records, 1864–1964; Maynooth Students and Ordinations Index, Volume 1, 1795–1895, Volume 11, 1895–1984; Jacques Paul Migne; The Resurrection of the Just; The Church in Africa in St Cyprian's Writings; Membership of the Mystical Body, Editor, Irish Ecclesiastical Record, 1948–64. *Contributions to:* Various theological journals. *Membership:* Co-Founder and 1st Chairman, Irish Theological Association. *Address:* St Brendan's Birr, Offaly, Republic of Ireland.

HAMEY, John Anthony, b. 17 Feb. 1956, Hitchin, Hertfordshire, England. Barrister. *Education:* BA (Cantab), 1977; Called to Bar of England and Wales by Inner Temple, 1979; MA (Cantab), 1981. *Publication:* The Roman Engineers, 1981, reprinted 1983, American edition, 1982. *Contribution to:* Scottish Home & Country, 1977. *Address:* 29 Trinity Court, Gray's Inn Road, London WC1X 8JX, England.

HAMILTON, Morse, b. 16 Aug. 1943, Detroit, Michigan, USA. Teacher. m. Sharon Saros, 20 Aug. 1966, Detroit, 3 daughters. *Education:* BA, University of Michigan, 1967; MA, 1968, PhD, 1974, Columbia University. *Publications:* Children's Books: My Name is Emily, 1979; Big Sisters Are Bad Witches, 1980; Who's Afraid of the Dark?, 1983; How Do You Do, Mr Birdsteps?, 1983. *Honours:* Hopwood Award, 1967; Woodrow Wilson Dissertation Fellow, 1971; George Bennett Memorial Fellow, 1973. *Literary Agent:* Emilie Jacobson, Curtis Brown Ltd. *Address:* 49 Cottage St, Watertown, MA 02172, USA.

HAMILTON, Richard Frederick, b. 18 Jan. 1930, Kenmore, New York, USA. Professor of Sociology. m. Irene Maria Elisabeth Wagner, 12 Aug. 1957, Heidelberg, Germany, 2 sons. *Education:* AB, University of Chicago, 1950; MA, 1953, PhD, 1963, Columbia University. *Appointments:* Instructor, Skidmore College, 1957–59; Instructor, Harpur College, 1959–64; Assistant Professor, Princeton University, 1964–66; Associate Professor to Professor, University of Wisconsin, 1966–70; Professor, McGill University, Montreal, Canada, 1970–. *Publications:* Affluence and the French Worker, 1967; Class and Politics in the United States, 1972; Restraining Myths, 1975; Who Voted for Hitler?, 1982; The State of the Masses, (with James D Wright), 1985. *Contributor to:* Various journals and magazines. *Address:* 473 Argyle Ave, Westmount, Quebec H3Y 3B3, Canada.

HAMLEY, Ernest Basil, b. 30 June 1926, London, England. Fisheries Adviser. m. 6 June 1953, 2 daughters. *Education:* College of Engineering and Navigation; Kennington College of Commerce and Law; Diploma in English; FIIM; FBIM; MIFM; MRSH; MRIPHH. *Literary Appointments:* Editorial duties, Assistant Secretary, Education and Examinations department, Royal Society of Health, London, 1948–64; Senior Administration Officer, Union of Educational Institutions, Birmingham, 1964–65, NDLB, London, 1965–68; Secretary General, Fisheries Organization Society and Editor, FOS Year book and Directory, annually, 1968–80. *Publications:* Various technical studies and recent reports including: Fish Production and Cooperative Marketing Projects in the Khartoum, White Nile, Blue Nile and Wadi Halfa Regions of the Sudan, 1979; Development of Fish Production and Marketing in Indonesia, with P R Walters, 1983; 10-Element Fisheries Cooperatives Management Training Package, 1983–85. *Contributions to:* Numerous fishing technical and trade publications including: World Fishing; La Peché Maritime; Fishing News International; Fishing News; Fish Trades Gazette. Reviewer of technical books for UN Food and Agriculture Organisation, ILO and FN Books Limited. Author of Visual Aids in First Aid, series for St John Review, 1973. *Honours:* Commander, Order of St John of Jerusalem, 1973; Honorary Life member, St John Ambulance Association. *Memberships Include:* Society of Authors; Technical Writers' Group; Folklore Society; Nautical Research Society; FIBA. *Address:* c/o Foreign and Commonwealth Office (Jakarta), King Charles Street, London SW1A 2AH, England.

HAMLIN, Griffith Askew, b. 24 Feb. 1919, Richmond, Virginia, USA. College Professor (retired). m. Margaret Geneva Cook, 1 June 1943, Cedar Grove, North Carolina, 2 sons. *Education:* BA, Atlantic Christian College; M Rel Ed, Lexington Theological Seminary; BD, Duke University; MS in Education, Southern Illinois University; ThD, Iliff School of Theology; Honorary DD, William Woods College, 1982. *Publications:* The Old Testament: Its Content and Intent, 1959; In Faith and History: The Story of William Woods College, 1965; Montecello: The Biography of a College, 1976; William Woods College, 1965; The Cutlip Years, 1960–1980, 1981; Frontier Discipleship, 1983; A Community and Its Schools, 1984. *Address:* 201 Lynn Avenue, Fulton, MO 65251, USA.

HAMMEL, Eric M, b. 29 June 1946, Salem, Massachusetts, USA. Writer. m. Barbara Sidman, 7 Aug. 1966, Philadelphia, Pennsylvania, 1 son, 1 daughter. *Education:* BS, Journalism, Temple University, Pennsylvania. *Publications:* 76 Hours: The Invasion of Tarawa, 1979 & 1985; Chosin: Heroic Ordeal of the Korean War, 1981; The Root: The Marines in Beirut, September 1982–February 1984, 1985; ACE!: A Marine Night Fighter Pilot in World War II, 1985. *Contributions to:* Marine Corps Gazette; Leatherneck; Sea Power; World War II Magazine; The Elite; The Hook, and other military professional magazines. *Honour:* Award of Merit for the Root, Marine Corps Combat Correspondents Association, 1985. *Literary Agent:* Clyde Taylor, Curtis Brown Ltd. *Address:* 1149 Grand Teton Drive, Pacifica, CA 94044, USA.

HAMMER, David Lindley, b. 6 June 1929, Newton, Iowa, USA. Barrister. m. Audrey Lowe, 20 June 1953, Grinnell, Iowa, 1 son, 2 daughters. *Education:* BA, Grinnell College; J D, University of Iowa. *Publications:* The Game is Afoot; A Travel Guide to the England of Sherlock Holmes; Poems From The Ledge. *Contributor to:* Baker Street Journal; Baker Street Miscellanea; Sherlock Holmes Journal. *Agent:* Ann Elmo Agency. *Address:* 720 Laurel Park Road, Dubuque, IA 52001, USA.

HAMMER, Emanuel Frederick, b. 15 Aug. 1926, Brooklyn, New York, USA. Psychoanalyst, Clinical Psychologist. *Education:* Brooklyn College, Columbia University, New York, 1945–46; BA, Syracuse University, New York, 1946; PhD, New York University, 1951; Certified Psychoanalyst, National Psychologic Association for Psychoanalysis, 1965. *Publications include:* The Clinical Application of Projective Drawings, 1958; Use of Interpretation in Treatment; Technique and Art, 1958; Anti-achievement; Perspectives on School Drop-Outs, 1972; Creativity, Talent and Personality, 1984. *Contributions to:* Various professional journals. *Memberships include:* President 1964–65, New York Society of Clinical Psychologists.

Address: 381 West End Avenue, New York, NY 10024, USA.

HAMMER, Lillian, Poet and Writer in 2 languages. m. Jack Hammer. *Education:* Numerous University courses, History, Far Eastern Arts, Humanities, Philosophy; Psychology, Science, Language in today's world, etc. *Publications:* Waves of Fire, 1972; The Seeker, 1977. *Contributor to:* International Belle Lettres News; Courier; Press Angus; IAP Fellows Magazine; Poet International Monthly; Pancontinental Premier Poets; Eastern Sun; Laurel Leaves; Pancontinental Premier Poets; World Poetry Society. *Honours:* Numerous honours and awards including Cultural Doctorate, World University, 1979; Awarded States of Victory Personality of the Year Award, 1984; World Culture Prize, Centro Studi a Recerche della nazioni, Italy. *Memberships:* Honorary Member for Philippines, United Poets Laureate International; National Member, Smithsonian Association; World Poetry Society Intercontinental; International Belles Lettres Society (Life Member); American Society Writers; Founder Fellow, IAUP, UK; Acad. International Leonardo da Vinci; Association CSESI Culturale, Italy; Centro Studi e Scambi Int, (Past Vice-President); Poetry Society Hall of Fame; Historical Preservations of America Incorporated. *Address:* 15 Elmwood Street, Albany, NY 12203, USA.

HAMMICK, Charles Cyril Willmott, b. 24 Oct. 1927, England. Bookseller; Publisher. 2 sons, 3 daughters. *Education:* ACIS. *Memberships:* Society of Bookmen; National Book League Executive Committee, 1977–83. *Address:* Hammick's Bookshops Limited, Albany Park, Frimley, Surrey, England.

HAMMOND, Ian Raymond, b. 11 Dec. 1943, Adelaide, South Australia. Freelance Journalist. m. Marrilyn Joy Townley, 26 June 1971, Adelaide, 1 daughter. *Appointments include:* South Australian Correspondent, Truck & Bus Transportation; South Australian Editorial Representative: Aviation News; Australian Hospital; Graphix; Hospitality & Convention News; Pacific Computer Weekly; Travel Week; Engineers Australia; Australian Editor, International Rail Journal; South Australian Correspondent: Transport and Distribution Letter; Australian Correspondent: World Mining Equipment; World Construction. *Address:* 467 Grenfell Road, Banksia Park, South Australia 5091.

HAMMOND, Karla M, b. 26 Apr. 1949, Middleton, CT, USA. Freelance Writer. *Education:* BA, Goucher College; MA, Trinity College. *Literary Appointments:* Contributing Book Reviewer, Connecticut Fireside Press, 1976–77; Contributing Editor, Puckerbrush Press, 1978–79; Poetry Interviewer, Benington Review, 1978–80; Contributing Editor, Thunder City Press, 1979–84; Special Book Review Contributor, Paintbrush, 1979–84. *Publications:* (Chapbook) No Name For Season, 1986. *Contributor to:* around 150 literary magazines in USA, Canada, UK, Australia, Italy, Japan and Greece; magazines including Ann Arbor Review; Anthology of Magazine Verse and Yearbook American Poetry; Colorado Northern Review; Concerning Poetry; Counterpoint (UK); Dice (Canada); Eurika II (Sweden); First Encounter (Canada); Heart and Helix (Australia); etc. *Honours:* Chase Going Woodhouse Poetry Award, 1st Prize, 1976 and finalist, 1977; Bucknell University Festival Poet, 1977 and 1978; nominated for Pushcart prize, Absinthe Magazine, 1979. *Address:* RR No 7, 12 West Drive, East Hampton, CT 06424, USA.

HAMMOND, Peter, b. 13 July 1942. Materials Distributor. m. Alice Hammond. *Publications:* Two in Staffordshire, with Graham Metcalfe (artist), 1979. *Contributions to:* New Poetry; New Age; Outposts; Arvon Foundation, publications; Staffs Conservation Society; Charter, and others. *Honour:* Poetry Prize, North Walsall School, 1956. *Memberships:* Rugeley Literary Society; Co-Founder, Cannock Poetry Group. *Address:* 14 Ascot Drive, Cannock, Staffordshire WS11 1PD, England.

HAMMOND INNES, Ralph, CBE, b. 15 July 1913. Author. m. Dorothy Mary Lang, 1937. *Literary Appointments:* Staff, Financial News, 1934–40. *Publications include:* 27 novels, 2 travel books, 1 history, etc. Titles include: Wreckers Must Breathe, 1940; The Trojan Horse, 1940; Attack Alarm, 1941; Dead & Alive, 1946; The Lonely Skier, 1947; The Killer Mine, 1947; Maddon's Rock, 1948; The Blue Ice, 1948; The White South, 1949; The Angry Mountain, 1950; Air Bridge, 1951; Campbell's Kingdom, 1952; The Strange Land, 1954; The Mary Deare, 1956; The Land God Gave to Cain, 1958; Harvest of Journeys, 1959; The Doomed Oasis, 1960; Atlantic Fury, 1962; Scandinavia, 1963; The Strode Venturer, 1965; Sea & Islands, 1967; The Conquistadors, 1969; Levkas Man, 1971; Golden Soak, 1973; North Star, 1974; The Big Footprints, 1977; The Last Voyage (Cook), 1978; Solomon's Seal, 1980; The Black Tide, 1982; High Stand, Adaptations for films, television, various titles; Book Club Choices. *Contributions to:* Numerous journals & magazines. *Honours:* CBE, 1978; DLitt, 1985. *Memberships:* Various Writing, Sailing, Forestry committees, Society of Authors. *Literary Agent:* Curtis Brown. *Address:* Ayres End, Kersey, Suffolk IP7 6EB.

HAMPL, Patricia, b. 12 Mar. 1946, St Paul, Minnesota, USA. Writer. *Education:* BA, University of Minnesota, 1968; MFA, University of Iowa, 1970. *Literary Appointments:* Visiting Assistant Professor, English Department, University of Minnesota, 1978–79, 81. *Publications:* Woman Before an Aquarium, 1978; A Romantic Education, 1981; Resort and Other Poems, 1983. Writer of Libretto for choral work, In a Winter Garden, 1983. *Contributions to:* the New Yorker; Paris Review; Antaeus; Iowa Review; Ironwood; American Poetry Review. *Honours:* Fellowship: National Endowment for the Arts, 1976; Bush Foundation, 1979; Houghton Mifflin (Literary), 1981. *Address:* 286 Laurel Avenue, St Paul, MN 55102, USA.

HANANI, Joseph, b. 6 Dec. 1908. Supervisor of Schools, Lecturer. *Education:* Hebrew Teachers College; University of London. *Literary Appointments:* Director of Schools; Supervisor of Schools; Lecturer. *Major Publications:* (novels) Bintiv Hayisourim; Be'ol Hakiboush; Bait Malbin Bapardess; Mazal; Hamehalel Mi me'ah Shearim; Rega Shel Haine; (short stories) Me'arat Haplaim; Kad Haress; Shlosha Haveriru Vehaver; Shnei Limonim Velimon; Saudol Yatza Ladereh; Rashim Prouim; Gam Havered Rakad; Hagom Ha'aroch Shel Erau; Hamitria Ha'adouma; Ehad Neged Joulam; Yesh Li Yedid. *Contributor to:* Various Hebrew journals. *Honours:* London Prize for Youth & Childrens Literature, 1969; Honorary Citizen of Petah Tikva, 1978. *Address:* 18 Hedva Rashish Avenue, Petah-Tikva 49505, Israel.

HANBURY-TENISON, Airling Robin, b. 7 May 1936, London, England. Farmer; Association Chairman. m. (1) Marika Hopkinson, 20 Jan. 1959, London, 1 son, 1 daughter, (2) Louella Edwards, 14 Nov. 1983, London, 1 son. *Education:* MA, Magdalen College, Oxford. *Publications:* The Rough and the Smooth, 1969; A Question of Survival, 1973; A Pattern of Peoples, 1975; Mulu: The Rain Forest, 1980; Aborigines of the Amazon Rain Forest: The Yarowami, 1982; Worlds Apart, 1984, Autobiography; White Horses over France, 1985. *Contributor to:* The Times; Spectator; Blackwood's Magazine; Geographical Magazine; Ecologist; Traveller. *Honours:* OBE, Gold Medal, Royal Geographical Society, 1979; Krug Award of Excellence, 1980; Special Mention, Thomas Cook Travel Book Award, 1984. *Memberships:* President, Survival International; Member, Council Royal Geographical Society; Society of Authors. *Literary Agent:* A D Peters and Company. *Address:* Maidenwell, Cardinham, Bodmin, Cornwall, England.

HANCOCK, Beryl Lynette, b. 5 Jan. 1938, East Fremantle, West Australia. Writer, photographer, lecturer and teacher. *Education:* MA (Comm), Simon Fraser University, Canada; B Ed Simon Fraser University, Canada; LRAM, England; LTCL, England;

LSDA, Australia. *Publications:* There's a Seal in My Sleeping Bag; The Mighty McxKenzie; There's a Raccoon in my Parka; Love Affair with a Cougar; An Ape came out of my Hatbox; Vanderhoof – A History; Tell Me Grandmother. *Contributor to:* Canadian Geographic; BC Outdoors; North West Explorer;Skyword; Globe and Mail; Nature Canada; Up Here; Motor Boat and Sailing; Australian Women's Weekly; Outdoor Canada. *Literary Awards:* Pacific Northwest Booksellers' Award (1972); Francis Kortright Conservation Award for Excellence in Outdoor Writing (1978); American Express Travel Writing Award (1981 and 1983). *Member of:* The Writers' Union of Canada. *Address:* 2457 Baker View Road, Mill Bay, British Columbia, Canada VOR ZPO.

HANCOCK, Geoffrey White, b. 14 Apr. 1946, New Westminster, Canada. Writer, literary journalist. m. Gay Allison, 6 Aug. 1983, Toronto, 1 daughter. *Education:* BFA 1973, MFA 1975, University of British Columbia. *Literary Appointments:* Editor in chief, Canadian Fiction magazine, 1975; Consulting editor, Canadian Author and Bookman, 1978; Fiction editor, Cross-Canada Writers Quarterly, 1980; Literary Consultant, CBC Radio, 1980. *Publications:* Magic Realism, 1980; Illusion: fables, fantasies and metafictions, 1983; Metavisions, 1983; Shoes and Shit: Stories for Pedestrians, 1984; Visible Stories and Invisible Fictions from Quebec, 1986; Published in Canada, 1985; Moving Off the Map: From Story to Fiction, 1985. *Contributions to:* Toronto Star; Writer's Quarterly; Canadian Author and Bookman; Books in Canada; Canadian Forum. *Honour:* Fiona Mee Award for Literary Journalism, 1979. *Memberships:* Periodical Writers of Canada; Director, Canadian Periodical Publishers Association. *Address:* c/o Canadian Fiction Magazine, Box number 946 Station F, Toronto, Ontario M4Y 2N9, Canada.

HANDY, Mary Nixeon Civille, b. 5 Mar. 1909, Ocean Park, California, USA. Teacher; Poet; Speaker. m. 14 Feb. 1932, 3 sons, 1 daughter. *Education:* BE, University of California, Los Angeles, 1930; ME, Central University of Washington, Ellensburg, 1958; Advanced work, University of Washington, 1972. *Literary Appointments:* English, Wenatchee Valley College, Wenatchee Washington; Journalism, Director Poetry Workshop, Dean of Women. *Publications:* (Poetry): Do Not Disturb The Dance: Enter It, 1973; Earth House, 1978. *Contributions to:* Texas Revue; New England Journal; St Andrews Review; Creative Women; Wind; Cincinnati Review; Pegasus; Wellspring; Poetry Now; Blackwater Review; Buffalo Spree; Stone Country; Kalliops; Charlton Review; Spoon River Quarterly; En Passant; Ally; Puget Soundings; Old Hickory Review; Snapdragon; Fragments; Colorado N Review; Blue Unicorn; New York Quarterly; Sawtooth; Higginson Journal, etc. *Honours:* Grant Alpha Sigma for poetry at University of Washington, 1972; Grant for workshops in libraries, Seattle, 1979; Nixeon Civille Handy Poetry Prize at University of Puget Sound, Tacoma, Washington. *Memberships:* Poetry Society of America; Washington Poets Association (Board Member); National League of American Pen Women (Secretary; Correspondence Secretary). *Address:* 19240 Tenth N E, Seattle, WA 98155, USA.

HANEY, Siobhan Mary, b. 8 Sep. 1961, London, England. Technology Editor. *Education:* BSc, Hons, Economics, Queen Mary College, London. *Literary Appointment:* Technology Editor, The Banker. *Contributions to:* Articles on Technology in Banks and other Financial Institutions for, The Banker; The Financial Times; The Investor's Chronicle; Datamation. *Address:* The Banker, 102-108, Clerkenwell Road, London EC1M 5SA, England.

HANF, James Alphonso, b. 3 Feb. 1923. Naval Architect Technician. m. Ruth Golda Eyler, 1 daughter. *Education:* Graduate, Centralia Junior College, Washington, 1943. *Literary Appointments:* Poetry editor, Coffee Break magazine, 1977–82; Lecturer, new Americana version of Haiku, 1977 (originator);

Lecturer, Haiku & Siamese poetry, to professional and civic groups. *Contributions to:* New York Culture Review; Forum; Mercury Magazine; ABIRA Digest; History of International Literature; Washington Verse; Adventurers in Poetry; World Poetry Day; Journal of Contemporary Poets; Best Poets of the 20th Century; Dragonfly; Modern Haiku; Leatherneck; Quintessence; Hoosier Challenge; Japan Forum; New World Unlimited; Inky Trails; Vices International; Publications of The World Poetry Society; numerous other books, magazines, anthologies, newspapers. *Honours:* Poet Laureate Award, Outstanding Poet of the Year, Inky Trails, 1978; Award, Dragonfly; Numerous other poetry awards. Diploma di Merito, Universita Delle Arti, Italy; Distinguished Service Award, American Biographical Institute, 1981; Honorary Member, Stella Woodall Poetry Society, 1981; Honorary DLitt, World University, 1981; Nomination, Poet Laureate, Washington State, 1981. *Memberships Include:* World Poets Resource Centre; California Federation of Chaparral Poets; Ina Coolbrith Circle; Literarische Union of West Germany; New York Poetry Forum; Illinois State Poetry Society; World & National Poetry Day Committees; Western World Haiku Society of Oregon; International Poetry Society of India. *Address:* P O Box 374, Bremerton, Washington 98310, USA.

HANKLA, (Bonnie) Susan, b. 22 Sep. 1951, Roanoke, Virginia, USA. Writer; Teacher; Poet-in-the-Schools. m. Jack Glover, 22 Apr. 1981, Roanoke. *Education:* BA, Hollins College; MA, Creative Writing, Brown University. *Literary Appointments:* Fellow, Virginia Center for the Creative Arts, Sweet Briar, Virginia, 1985. *Publications:* I Am Running Home, 1979; Mistral for Daddy and Van Gogh, 1976. Co-Editor, Sermons in Paint, 1985. *Contributions to:* Artemis; Boys and Girls Grow Up; The Burning Deck Anthology; Film Journal; Gargoyle; Hollins Critic; Intro 5; Laurel Review; New Virginia Review; Open Places; Poetry Northwest; Richmond Arts Magazine; Richmond Quasrterly Review; Southern Poetry Review. Fiction: Commonwealth; Michigan Quarterly Review; Artemis; New Virginia Review; American Signatures. *Honours:* Nancy Thorpe Memorial Prize for Poetry, Hollins College, 1973; Finalist, Virginia Prize for Fiction, 1985. Founder and Coordinator, 1708 East Main Poetry and Fiction Series. *Membership:* Chair, Wednesday Night Circle. *Address:* 1109 West Avenue, Richmond, VA 23220, USA.

HANLEY, Boniface Francis, b. 21 Sep. 1924, Brooklyn, New York, USA. Roman Catholic Priest. *Education:* BA Philosophy, St Bonaventure University; MS Theology, Holy Name College, Washington DC; MS Business, Columbia University, New York. *Publications:* Love at Work, 1962; Ten Christians, 1979; No Strangers to Love, 1983; No Greater Love, 1981. *Contributions to:* Biographical profiles to, The Athonian; Articles in religious magazines. *Honours:* 1st prize 12 years and older, Catholic Press Association of USA and Canada, 1984. *Address:* St Joseph's Friary, 454 Germanstown Road, West Milford, NJ 07480, USA.

HANLEY, Clifford, b. 28 Oct. 1922, Glasgow, Scotland. Writer. m. Anna Clark, 10 Jan. 1948, Glasgow, 1 son, 2 daughters. *Appointments:* Professor, Creative Writing, York University, Toronto, Canada, 1979–80. *Publications:* Dancing in the Streets, 1958; The Taste of Too Much, 1960; Nothing but the Best, 1964; A Skinful of Scotch, 1965; The Redhaired Bitch, 1969; The Unspeakable Scot, 1977; The Scots, 1980; Another Street Another Dance, 1983. *Contributor to:* Numerous professional journals and magazines. *Memberships:* International PEN, Scottish President, 1970–72; Scottish Chairman 1963–70; Glasgow Philosophy and Literary Society, President, 1965. *Literary Agent:* Curtis Brown, London; J de S Associates, Connecticut, USA. *Address:* 36 Munro Road, Glasgow G13 1SF, Scotland.

HANNAH, Betty (Elizabeth Weir), b. 22 Jan. 1918, New Jersey, USA. Writer. m. Charles Robert Hoffman, 6 June 1942, Essex Fells, 2 sons, 1 daughter. *Education:* BA, Smith College. *Publications:* My Husband, Author

Murray, with Kathryn Murray, 1959; Queen of the Golden Age, 1956; Contributor to Notable American Women, 1971; What to do When There's Nothing to Do, 1968–. Contributor to: Columnist, Can This Marriage Be Saved, Ladies Home Journal, 14 years; Articles on American Family Life and Celebrities in, Ladies Home Journal; McCalls; Readers' Digest; Saturday Evening Post, Cosmopolitan. Honours: Benjamin Franklin Award, University of Illinois, 1956; Smith College Mosaic of 150 Outstanding Alumnae, 1972; Exceptional Achievement Award, Council for Advancement and Support of Education, 1976. Membership: American Society of Journalists and Authors. Address: 2237 Marin Avenue, Berkeley, CA 94707, USA.

HANNAU, Hans Walter, b. 5 Aug. 1904, Vienna, Austria. Author. Education: JD, University of Vienna. Publications: USA in Full Color (Merriam), 1972; Caribbean Island, 1970; The Behama Islands, 1969; Bermuda in Full Color, 1971; In the Coral Reefs of the Caribbean, 1974. Honours: Gold Cross of Honour, Austria; Title of Professor, Austria; Officers Cross of Merit, Order of Merit, Federal Republic of Germany. Address: 20 Island Avenue, Apt 1208, Miami Beach, FL 33139, USA.

HÄNNINEN, Anne Anita, b. 7 Feb. 1958, Konnevesi, Finland. Poet. Publications: Poems: The Tin of the Night Melts into the Morning, 1978; Sunset Stairway, 1980; Temple of Fire, 1982. Membership: Finnish Authors Union. Address: Vapaudenkatu 67 A 22, 40100 Jyväskylä 10, Finland.

HANSEN, Leonard J, b. 4 Aug. 1932, San Francisco, California, USA. Writer; Editor. m. Marcia Ann Rasmussen, 18 Mar. 1966, Seattle, Washington, 2 sons. Education: BA, San Francisco State College, 1956; Postgraduate work, San Francisco College, 1956–57. Publications: Two books accepted for publication but publication date not yet set. Contributor to: Senior World, newsmonthlies; Senior News Service, nationally; Senior Edition; Denver and other mature market newspapers, magazines and journals. Memberships: National Writers Club; San Diego Press Club. Honours: Communicator of the Year, San Diego Press Club, 1982; Best Investigative Reporting Awards, San Diego Press Club, Sigma Delta Chi and others. Address: 2612 Bayside Walk, San Diego, CA 92109, USA.

HANSON, Jim, b. 6 May 1953. Education: BA, 1976, MBA, 1982, University of Chicago. Literary Appointments: Editor, In The Light, 1975–80. Publications: Three Numbers, (with S Levine), 1976; Reasons for the Sky, 1979. Contributor to: The Denver Post; Mag City; 432 Review; Out There. Memberships: Poets and Writers; Co-chairman, University of Chicago Poetry Speakers Series, 1975–78; Co-ordinator, Still Light Reading Series, 1984. Address: 2114 Glenn Lane, Glenn Heights, TX 75115, USA.

HANSON, Kenneth O, b. 24 Feb. 1922. Professor of Literature. Education: BA University of Idaho, Pocatelo and Moscow, Idaho, 1942; Graduate, Chinese Languages and English Literature, 1946–54. Literary Appointment: Professor of Literature, Reed College, Portland, Oregon, 1954–. Publications: 8 Poems (folio), 1958; The Distance Anywhere, 1966; Saromikos and Other Poems, 1970; The Uncorrected World, 1970; Growing Old Alive, (translation from Chinese of Han Yu), 1978; Portraits, Friends, Artists, (folio, with prints by LaVerne Krause), 1979; Lighting the Night Sky, (poems), 1983. Contributions to: Accent; Botteghe Oscure; The New Yorker; The Nation; Poetry Northwest; Northwest Review; Transatlantic Review; Iowa Review; Sewannee Review; Kayak; Massachusetts Review; Accent Anthology. 1954; Oregon Signatures, 1960; Five Poets of the Pacific Northwest, 1964; Contemporary American Poets, 1969; Modern Poetry of Western America, 1975. Honours: Fulbright Fellowship, 1962; Bollingen Translation Grant, 1962; Theodore Roethke Award, Poetry Northwest, 1964–65; Lamont Award, Academy

of American Poets, 1966; Rockefeller Grant, 1966–67; Helen Bullis Award, 1970; Asia Society Translation Commemoration, 1970; Amy Lowell Poetry Travelling Scholarship, 1973; National Endowment for the Arts Grant, 1976 and 1982. Address: Department of English, Reed College, Portland, OR 97202, USA.

HANTON, E Michael, b. Gary, Indiana, USA. Public & Personnel Relations Consultant. Education: AB, Indiana University, 1951, MA 1955; Graduate, US Air Force Air War College, 1968. Publications include: The New Nurse, 1973. Contributions: Reporter, Muncie Evening Press, Indiana, 1952; Gary Post-Tribune, 1952–53. Memberships include: American Medical Writers Association; Association for Education in Journalism & Mass Communication. Address: POB 803, Plattsburgh, NY 12901, USA.

HARAHAP, Marwali, b. 4 Mar. 1932, Pematang Siantar, Indonesia. Dermato-Venereologist. m. Dalina, 23 Nov. 1961, Bandung, 4 sons, 1 daughter. Education: MD, University of Indonesia, 1960; Doctor, University of North Sumatra, 1968; Postgraduate: University of California, 1964–66, Tokyo Womens Medical College 1977. Publications: Skin Surgery, Warren Green, St Louis, 1985; Principles of Dermatologic Plastic Surgery, S P Scientific Medical Books, New York, in press; Penyakit Menular Seksual, Gramedia, Jakarta, 1984. Contributions to: International Journal of Dermatology; Journal of Dermatologic Surgery & Oncology; Environmental & Occupational Dermatitis, Copenhagen; Modern Medicine of Asia, Hongkong; Excerpta Medica, Amsterdam/Oxford; Medical Progress, Sydney; International Journal of Leprosy; Journal of Perinatal Medicine; Indian Journal of Medical Education; numerous other scientific papers and books. Address: 55 Jalan Ir Juanda, Medan, Indonesia.

HARALDSDOTTIR, Ingibjörg, b. 21 Oct. 1942, Reykjavik, Iceland. Translator; Poet. m. Eirikur Gudjonsson, 2 Apr. 1981, Reykjavik, 1 son, 1 daughter. Education: Diploma as feature film director, MA, All Union State Institute of Cinematography, Moscow, USSR. Publications: Poetry: Thangad vil eg fljuga, 1974; Ordspur daganna, 1983. Translations: Mikhail Bulgakov: Master and Margarita, 1981; Fyodor Dostoyevsky's, Crime and Punishment, 1984 and, The Idiot, 1986. Contributions to: Timarit Mals og menningar; Translations of poetry, short stories from Spanish in numerous magazines. Memberships: Writers Union of Iceland. Address: Baronsstig 63, 101 Reykjavik, Iceland.

HARDIN, Linda Anne (Garr), b. 29 Jan. 1954, Newnan, Georgia, USA. Music Educator. m. James Neal Hardin, Jr. 15 Nov. 1983, Columbia, South Carolina. Education: BMus, Georgia State University, Atlanta, 1976; M.Mus.Ed, University of South Carolina; Trumpet Performance Certificate, 1978. Literary Appointment: Editor, International Trumpet Guild Journal, (quarterly), 1978–. Publications: A Trumpeter's Guide to Orchestral Excerpts, 1977, 2nd revised edition, 1986; A Horn Player's Guiide to Orchestral Excerpts, 1978. Contributor to: The Instrumentalist; Hand Booster. Honour: AMOCO Outstanding Graduate Teacher Award, University of South Carolina, 1978. Address: 132 Norse Way, Columbia, SC 29223, USA.

HARDY, David Andrews, b. 10 Apr. 1936, Birmingham, England. Space/Science Artist; Writer. Education: Birmingham College of Art. Publications: New Challenge of the Stars, (with Patrick Moore), 1972, 1977; The Solar System, 1975; Rockets and Satellites, 1976; Air and Weather, 1977; Light and Sight, 1977; Energy and the Future, 1979; Galactic Tours, (with Bob Shaw), 1981; Atlas of the Solar System, 1982, 1986. Contributor to: Leonardo; Canvas; Arts Review; Various professional journals. Honours: Nominated for Hugo Award, World Science Fiction Convention, 1979. Memberships include: Fellow, Royal Astronomical Society; Fellow, British Interplanetary Society; Licentiate, Royal Photographic Society.

Address: 99 Southam Road, Hall Green, Birmingham B28 OAB, England.

HARE, William Francis, b. 7 Feb. 1944, Leicester, England. University Professor. m. Niki Liasi, 27 Aug. 1966, London, England, 3 sons. *Education:* BA, London, 1965; MA, Leicester, 1968; PhD, Toronto, 1971. *Publications:* Open-mindedness and Education, 1979; Controversies in teaching, 1985; In Defence of Open-Mindedness, 1985. *Contributor to:* 50 articles to various journals including, Oxford Review of Education; Metaphilosophy; Journal of Applied Philosophy. *Honours:* Canada Council Leave Fellowship, 1976; SSHRC of Canada Leave Fellowship, 1981. *Address:* Dept of Education, Dalhousie University, Halifax, Nova Scotia, Canada B3H 3J5.

HARE DUKE, Michael Geoffrey, b. 28 Nov. 1925, Calcutta, India. Bishop in the Scottish Episcopal Church. m. Grace Lydia (Baa) Dodd, 6 July 1950, Ickford, Oxfordshire, 1 son, 3 daughters. *Education:* MA, Oxford University. *Publications:* Understanding The Adolescent, 1969; Break of Glory, 1970; Freud, 1972; Good News, 1977; Stories, Signs and Sacraments, 1982. *Address:* Bishop's House, Fairmount Road, Perth, PH2 7AP, Scotland.

HAREWOOD, George Henry Hubert (The Right Honorable the Earl of), b. 7 Feb. 1923, London, England. Governor, British Broadcasting Corporation; President, British Board of Film Classification; Artistic Director, Adelaide Festival. m. (1) Maria Donata Stein, 1949, London, (2) Patricia Elizabeth Tuckwell, 1967, USA, 4 sons. *Education:* MA, Kings College, Cambridge University. Kobbe's Complete Opera Book, Editor and Reviser; Benjamin Britten: A Symposium; The Tongs and the Bones, autobiography, 1981. *Contributions to:* Opera on Record; Daily Mail; New Statesman; Opera, Editor, 1950–53. *Honours:* Honorary LLD: University of Leeds; University of Aberdeen, Scotland; Honorary DMus, University of Hull; Honorary DLitt, University of Bradford; Honorary Member, Royal Academy of Music. *Address:* Harewood House, Leeds LS17 9LG, England.

HARFIELD, Alan, b. 12 Dec. 1926, Gosport, Hampshire, England. Deputy Director, Royal Signals Museum. m. June Bowler, 6 June 1966, Salisbury, 1 daughter. *Publications:* A History of the Village of Chilmark, 1961; The Royal Brunei Malay Regiment, English and Malay, 1977; Headdress and Badges of the Royal Signals, 1982; British and Indian Armies in the East Indies 1685–1935, 1984; Blandford and the Military, 1984; Life and Times of a Victorian Officer, 1985. Specialist books written for UK based charity, British Association of Cemeteries in South Asia: Fort Canning Cemetery Singapore, 1981; Christian Cemeteries and Memorials in Malacca, 1984; Bencoolen, Sumatra – The Christian Cemetery, 1985. *Contributions to:* Crown Imperial; Hamilton's Medal Journal 'Despatch'; The Military Chest, 13 articles and continuing series, A Corner of Some Foreign Field, stories relating to military graves in foreign countries; Military Historical Society; Orders and Medal Research Society; Society for Army Historical Research. *Honours:* Military, British Empire Medal, 1953; Most Blessed Order of the Setia Negara Brunei, 3rd class for writing the History of the Royal Brunei Malay Regiment, 1977. *Memberships:* Royal Historical Society, Fellow; Honorary Editor, Military Historical Society; Society for Army Historical Research; Malaysian Branch, Royal Asiatic Society; Company of Military Historians of USA. *Address:* Little Beechwood, Childe Okeford, Dorset DT11 8EH, England.

HARJO, Joy, b. 9 May 1951, Tulsa, Oklahoma, USA. Poet. 1 son, 1 daughter. *Education:* BA, Creative Writing, University of New Mexico, 1976; MFA, Creative Writing, University of Iowa, 1978; Anthropology Film Center, 1982. *Appointments:* Policy Panel, National Endowment for the Arts, Literature, 1979–81; Assistant Professor, English, University of Colorado, Boulder, 1985. *Publications:* The Last Song, 1975; What Moon Drove Me to This, 1980; She Had Some Horses, 1983. *Contributor to:* Massachusetts Review; Beloit Poetry Journal; River Styx; Conditions; etc. *Honours:* Academy of American Poetry Award, University of New Mexico, 1st Place, 1976; Writers Forum, University of Colorado, 1st Place, Poetry, 1977; National Endowment for the Arts Creative Writing Fellowship, 1978; Santa Fe Festival for the Arts, 1st Place, Poetry, 1980; etc. *Memberships:* International PEN; Poets & Writers. *Address:* Dept of English, University of Colorado, Boulder, CO 80209, USA.

HARKAVY, Robert E, b. 19 Nov. 1936, New York, New York, USA. Professor of Political Science. m. Jane T Frew, 9 July 1963, Kensington, California, 1 son. *Education:* BA, Cornell University, 1958; MA, University of California, 1964; PhD, Yale University, 1973; Studied, Basel University, Switzerland and Harvard Business School, USA. *Publications:* The Arms Trade and International Systems, 1975; Great Power Competition for Overseas Bases: The Geopolitics of Access Diplomacy, 1982. Co-Editor: Arms Transfers in the Modern World: Problems and Prospects, 1979; American Security Policy and Policy Making: The Dilemmas of Using and Controlling Military Force, 1980; Security Policies of Developing States: Implications for Regional and Global Security, 1981; The Lessons of Recent Wars in The Third World, 2 volumes. *Contributions to:* Michigan Academician, Policy Studies Journal; Journal of International Affairs; International Organization; The Jerusalem Journal of International Affairs; Works contributed to numerous professional books and reprinted as book chapters. Various book reviews and monographs. Papers presented at national and international conferences. Numerous lectures and invited lectures. *Honours include:* New York State and Cornell State Scholarships; Phi Beta Kappa; Fellowships and Graduate Assistantships, Berkeley and Yale; Alexander Von Humboldt Fellowship, Institute of Political Science, Christian-Albrechtes University, Kiel, Federal Republic of Germany, 1983, 84; Fulbright Research Grant, Stockholm, Sweden, 1985. *Memberships:* American Political Science Association; International Studies Association; Institute of Strategic Studies, International; various others. *Address:* 450 Sierra Lane, State College, PA 16803, USA.

HARLAN, Elizabeth, b. 11 Nov. 1945, New York City, USA. Writer. m. Leonard Harlan, 27 Aug. 1969, New York City, 2 sons. *Education:* BA, Barnard College, 1967; M Phil, Yale Graduate School, 1970. *Publications:* Footfalls, novel, 1982; Watershed, 1986. *Contributions to:* New York Times; Harpers. *Literary Agent:* Rosalie Siegel. *Address:* Windmill Farm, Cranbury, NJ 08512, USA.

HARLOW, Neal, b. 11 June 1908, Columbus, Indiana, USA. Former Librarian; Dean. m. Marian Gardner, 12 Sep. 1936, Los Angeles, California, 2 daughters. *Education:* EdB; MA. *Publications:* The Maps of San Francisco Bay, 1951; Maps and Surveys of the Pueblo Lands of Los Angeles, 1976; California Conquered, 1982. *Contributions to:* Numerous magazines and journals, etc. *Honour:* LHD (Doctor of Humanities), Moravian College, Pennsylvania. *Address:* PO Box 26101, Los Angeles, CA 90026, USA.

HARMAN, Jeanne Perkins, Writer. m. Harry Elliott Harman III, St Thomas. *Education:* Smith College, USA. *Publications:* Love Junk, Travel Book of the Month Club, Literary Guild Clubs Selection; Fielding's Guide to the Caribbean to the Bahamas, 1969–78; Hilton Hotel Report; Harman's Official Guide to Cruise Ships, St Semons, Sea Isle, The Virgins, Magic Islands. *Contributions to:* New York Times; Business Week; McGraw-Hill World News' Services; Syndicated Princeton Features; Times-Mirror News Syndicate, Cox Newspapers; Knight-Ridder Newspapers; Life Writer, Correspondent, Time Incorporated. *Memberships:* Society of American Travel Writers; Overseas Press Club; American Society of Journalists and Authors; International Platform Association. *Literary Agent:*

Robert Roestacher, New York City. *Address:* 3105 Country Club Drive, Valdosta, GA 31602, USA.

HARMSEN, Frieda, b. 8 July 1931, Amsterdam, Netherlands. Art Historian. m. Jacob van Proosdij, 27 Nov. 1970, Pretoria. *Education:* BA, Fine Arts, BA Honours, Witwatersrand; MA-SA, Landscape in Painting and Literature, Witsrand; Tvl. Higher Education Diploma; Ac.Dip, Courtauld Institute, University of London. *Appointments:* Lecturer, Senior Lecturer, University of South Africa, 1964–80; Editor, De Arte, 1967–80. *Publications:* Editor, Art and Articles in Honour of Heather Martienssen, 1973; The Women of Boonefoi: the Story of the Everard Group, 1980; Looking at South African Art: A Guide to the Study and Appreciation of Art, 1985. *Contributor to:* Numerous Articles in: Lantern; SA Panorama; De Arte; Quarterly Bulletin of SA National Gallery; Dictionary of SA Biographies. *Memberships:* SA Association of Art Historians, elected Assistant Editor of Envisaged Academic Journal. *Address:* 266 Aries Street, Waterkloof Ridge, 0181 Pretoria, South Africa.

HARNER, James Lowell, b. 24 Mar. 1946, Washington, Indiana, USA. Professor of English. m. Darinda Jane Wilson, 26 Aug. 1967, Washington, Indiana, 1 daughter. *Education:* BS magna cum laude, Indiana State University, 1968; MA 1970, PhD 1972, University of Illinois. *Literary Appointments:* Assistant Editor, Seventeenth-Century News, 1972–82; Head, Festshchriften section, MLA International Bibliography; Advisory Editor, Medieval and Renaissance Literature, G K Hall Reference Guides in Literature Series. *Publications:* English Renaissance Prose Fiction, 1500–1660: An Annotated Bibliography of Criticism, 1978; Samuel Daniel and Michael Drayton: A Reference Guide, 1980; On Compiling an Annotated Bibliography, 1985; English Renaissance Prose Fiction, 1500–1660; An Annotated Bibliography of Criticism, 1976–1983, 1985. *Contributions to:* Papers of the Bibliographical Society of America; Book Collector; Library; Notes and Queries; Moreana; Explicator. *Memberships:* The Bibliographical Society, London; Bibliographical Society of America; Renaissance Society of America. *Address:* Department of English, Bowling Green State University, Bowling Green, OH 43403, USA.

HARPER, Kenneth, b. 4 Sep. 1942, California, USA. Diesel Mechanic. m. Olivia, 16 June 1962, Everson, Washington, 1 son, 1 daughter. *Education:* AA Liberal Arts. *Publications:* Casey's Cavalier, with Olivia Harper. *Memberships:* Romance Writers of America. *Literary Agent:* Denise Marcil Literary Agency. *Address:* 293 Casper Place, San Ramon, CA 94583, USA.

HARPER, Olivia, b. 9 Aug. 1942, Texas, USA. Author. m. Kenneth, 16 June 1962, Everson, Washington, 1 son, 1 daughter. *Education:* AA, Business Certificate of Accounting. *Publications:* As JoAnna Brandon: The Devil's Playground; Sing to Me of Love; Love, Bid me Welcome; Just a Kiss Away; Lingering Laughter; The World in His Arms; Suspicion and Desire. From This Day Forward, as Jolene Adams; Casey's Cavalier, with Kenneth Harper. *Memberships:* Romance Writers of America; National League of American Pen Women. *Literary Agent:* Denise Marcil Literary Agency. *Address:* 293 Casper Place, San Ramon, CA 94583, USA.

HARPER, Stephen, b. 15 Sep. 1924, Newport, Monmouthshire, England. Journalist. *Publications:* (novels) A Necessary End, (Collins), 1975; Mirror Image, (Doubleday, NY), 1976; Live Till Tomorrow, (Collins), 1977; Miracle of Deliverance, (Sidgwick and Jackson), 1985; (non-fiction), Last Sunset, (Collins), 1978. *Address:* Green Dene Lodge, Green Dene, East Horsley, Surrey, England.

HARR, Lorraine Ellis, b. 31 Oct. Illinois, USA. Writer, Poet, Housewife. m. Carl Frederick Harr, 18 Aug. 1958, Stevenson, Oregon, USA, 2 sons, 1 deceased. *Literary Appointments:* Editor, Dragonfly (Haiku quarterly) for 13 years; Founder of Western World Haiku Society. *Major Publications:* Cats, Crows, Frogs & Scarecrows,

(Haiku); The Red Barn (Haiku); Tombo; Snowflakes in the Wind (Haiku); Ripe Papaya & Orange Slices (poems); Selected Senryu of Leh; Poems for Peter K; Poems for Sarah J (childrens poems); Anthology of Western World Haiku Society Award Winners, 1974–75, 1976–77, 1978, 1979, 1980, 1981; China Sojourn (Haibun); A Flight of Herons (Haiku); Sundowners (Haiku). *Contributor to:* Dragonfly; Writers Digest; American Haiku; Oregon Journal; Denver Post; Modern Haiku; Haiku West; and others. *Honours:* Various awards for Haiku. *Memberships:* Western World Haiku Society; North Carolina Haiku Society; Cape Cod Haiku Society; American Haiku Society; and others. *Address:* 4102 NE 130th Place, Portland, OR 97230, USA.

HARRIET, Sydney Harvey, b. 2 May 1944, Pawtucket, Rhode Island. University Professor. *Education:* BA, Hons, Michigan State University; MA, San Francisco State College; PhD, University of Oregon; MSW, Fresho State University. *Literary Appointment:* Editor, Potpourri Literary Magazine, 1978–. *Contributor to:* Zeitgeist; Coven; Arx; University of Oregon Supplement; Confrontation; Minataur, MMPI; Music Guide; KUPR Folio. *Address:* Potpourri Literary Magazine, Fresho City College, 1101 University Avenue, Fresho, CA 93741, USA.

HARRIMAN, Ann Lyall, b. 23 July 1932, Concord, California, USA. Professor. m. Malcolm A White, 3 Jan. 1984, The Sea Ranch, California, 4 sons from previous marriage. *Education:* BS, University of California, Berkeley; MBA, California State University, Sacramento; MPA, DPA, University of Southern California. *Literary Appointments:* Professor of Human Resource Management, California State University, Sacramento. *Major Publications:* Women/Men/Management, 1985; The Work-Leisure Trade-off: Reduced Worktime for Managers & Professionals, 1982. *Contributor to:* National Forum; Journal of College Placement; Review of Public Personnel Administration. *Address:* School of Business & Public Administration, California State University, Sacramento, CA 95819, USA.

HARRINGTON, Paul, b. 21 Apr. 1938, Maidstone, Kent, England. Journalist. *Literary Appointments:* Editor; Australian Auto Action; Fabulous 500; Motor Manual; Best Buys; Car Life and Style, Hong Kong; Caravan Life; Turbo Australia. *Contributions to:* Car and Driver; Motor; Motoring News; Autosport; 4X4 Australia; Motor Manual; Caravan World; Let's Travel; Asia Magazine, Motoring column. *Membership:* Australian Society of Travel Writers. *Address:* c/o Newspress Pty Ltd, 603-611 Little Lonsdale Street, Melbourne 3000, Australia.

HARRIS, Aurand, b. 4 July 1915, Jamesport, Missouri, USA. Playwright; Teacher. *Education:* AB, University of Kansas City; MA, Northwestern University; special studies, Columbia University. *Publications include:* (Plays, Juvenile), Simple Simon, 1953; The Plain Princess, 1955; Circus in the Wind, 1960; The Brave Litle Tailor, 1961; Androcies & the Lion, 1961; Rags to Riches, 1966; Punch & Judy, 1968; Just So Stories, 1970; Steal Away Home, 1972; Peck's Bad Boy, 1974; A Toby Show, 1978; The Arkansaw Bear, 1980; Treasure Island, 1983; The Magician's Nephew, 1984; The Flying Prince, 1985; (Anthologies), Six Plays for Children by Aurand Harris, 1977. *Contributor to:* Other books & anthologies. *Honours:* John Golden Award, Columbia University, 1945; Anderson Award, Stanford University, 1948; Marburg Prize, Johns Hopkins University, 1956; Chorpenning Cup, American Theatre Association, 1967; Creative Writing Fellowship, National Endowment for the Arts, 1976; Ohio State Theatre Alliance Award, 1984; A Fellow, American Theatre Association, 1985. *Memberships:* American & Children's Theatre Associations; Advisory Board, Institute for Advanced Studies in Theatre Arts. *Address:* C/o Anchorage Press, Box 8067, New Orleans, LA 70182, USA.

HARRIS, Christie Lucy, b. 21 Nov. 1907, Newark, New Jersey, USA. Author. m. 13 Feb. 1932, Hall Prairie, 3 sons, 2 daughters. *Education:* Teacher's Certificate, British Columbia. *Publications:* Cariboo Trail; Once upon a Totem; You Have to Draw the Line Somewhere; West with the White Chiefs; Raven's Cry; Confessions of a Toe-hanger; Forbidden Frontier; Let X be Excitement; (with Moira Johnston) Figleafing Through History: The Dynamics of Dress...; Secret in the Stlalakum Wild; (with Tom Harris) Mule Lib; Once More upon a Totem; Sky Man on the Totem Pole?; Mouse Woman and the Vanished Princesses; Mouse Woman and the Mischief Makers; Mystery at the Edge of Two Worlds; Mouse Woman and the Muddleheads; The Trouble with Princesses; The Trouble with Adventurers. *Literary Awards:* Book of the Year for Children medal (Canadian Association of Children's Librarians); Pacific Northwest Booksellers' Award; Vicky Metcalf Award for Body of Work for Young People (Canadian Authors Association); BC Library Commission Award; The Order of Canada; Canada Council Children's Literature Prize. *Membership:* The Writers' Union of Canada. *Agent:* McIntosh and Otis. *Address:* 1604–2045 Nelson Street, Vancouver, British Columbia, V6G 1N8, Canada.

HARRIS, David Kenneth, b. 11 Nov. 1919, South Wales. Journalist. *Literary Appointments:* Associate Editor, The Observer Limited. *Publications:* Travelling Tongues, 1947; Attlee, (Biography), 1982. *Contributions to:* Washington Correspondent, The Observer, 1950–53; Column, Pendennis, The Observer, 1956–; Interviews for The Observer; Contributions to Horizon Magazine (US); New York Times Magazine. *Memberships:* Society of Writers and Authors. *Address:* 45 Molyneux Street, London W1H 5HW, England.

HARRIS, Ian Richard, b. 26 July 1949, Bexleyheath, Kent, England. Journalist. *Education:* Diploma of Higher Education, Modern History; BA Honours, Warwick University; PhD candidate. *Publications:* Bikers–The Making of a Modern Day Outlaw, 1985. *Contributions to:* Back Street Heroes, monthly column; Easy Riders, overseas correspondent. *Literary Agent:* Rosica Colin Limited. *Address:* 22 Freta Road, Bexleyheath, Kent, England.

HARRIS, Jana N, b. 21 Sep. 1947. Writer. m. Mark Allen Bothwell. *Education:* BS, University of Oregon, 1969; MA, San Francisco State University, San Francisco, California, 1972. *Literary Appointments:* Poet-in-Residence, Alameda County Neighborhood Arts; Instructor, California Poetry in Schools; Instructor, Creative Writing, Modesto Junior College, Modesto, California; Instructor. Creative Writing, New York University Department of Liberal Studies, New York City, 1950, Director, Writers in Performance, Manhattan Theatre Club, New York, 1981. *Publications:* This House that Rocks with Every Truck on the Road, 1976; Pin Money, 1977; The Clackamas, 1980; Who's That Pushy Bitch, 1981; Running Scared, 1981; Manhatten as a Second Language, 1982. *Contributions to:* US Congressional Record; New Letters; Berkeley Monthly; Berkeley Poetry Review; Sunbury; Black Maria; Napa College Catalog; East Bay Review Performing Arts; San Francisco Bay Guardian; Room; Beatitudes, and others. *Honours:* Berkeley Civic Arts Commemoration Grant, 1974. *Memberships:* Poets and Writers Incorporated. Poets and Wirters, New Jersey; Feminist Writers Guild; Associated Writing Programs; Women's Salon, New York City. *Address:* PO Box 352, La Conner, WA 98257, USA.

HARRIS, Jennifer Rosemary, b. 18 Nov. 1939, London, England. Journalist. *Education:* BA, Open University; Press Fellow, Wolfson College, Cambridge, 1983. *Literary Appointments:* Editor, West London Observer, 1978–83; Editor, Post Magazine and Insurance Monitor, Reinsurance, 1984–. *Address:* 58 Fleet Street, London, EC4Y 1JU, England.

HARRIS, John, b. 18 Oct. 1916, Rotherham, Yorkshire, England. Author. *Publications:* Over 70 books including: The Sea Shall Not Have Them, 1953; Covenant with Death, 1961; Light Cavalry Action, 1967; Ride Out the Storm, 1975; The Gallant Six Hundred, 1973. *Memberships:* Author's Society. *Agent:* Curtis Brown Ltd. *Address:* Merston Cottage, Jerusalem Bottom, W Wittering, Sussex, England.

HARRIS, John, b. 1931, London, England. Historian. *Publications include:* English Decorative Ironwork, 1960; Regency Furniture Designs, 1961; Lincolnshire (co-author), 1964; Italian Architectural Drawings, 1966; Illustrated Glossary of Architecture (co-author), 1966; Georgian Country Houses, 1968; Buckingham Palace (co-author), 1968; The Country Seat (co-author), 1970; Sir William Chambers, 1970; A Catalogue of British Drawings for Architecture, Decoration, Sculpture and Landscape Gardening in American Collections, 1970; The King's Arcadia, 1973; Catalogue of Drawings Inigo Jones, 1972; Catalogue of Drawings Colin Campbell, 1973; Headfort House and Robert Adam, 1973; The Destruction of the Country House (co-author), 1974; A Garden Alphabet, 1979; The Garden, Book of the Garden Exhibition, (ED.), 1979; The Artist and the Country House, 1979; A Country House Index, new edition, 1979; The Palladians, 1981; Design of the English House, 1985. *Contributor to:* Architecture Review; Country Life; Burlington Magazine; Apollo; Connoisseur; Journal Society Architectural Historians, etc. *Honours:* FRIBA; OBE, 1986. *Memberships:* FSA; FRSA. *Address:* 16 Limerston Street, London SW10, England.

HARRIS, Louise, b. Pawtuxet, Rhode Island, USA. Former Recitalist of Organ & Piano; Researcher. *Education:* BA, Brown University, 1926. *Publications Include:* Comprehensive Bibliography of C A Stephens, 1965; None But the Best, 1966; A Chuckle & a Laugh, 1967; The Star of the Youth's Companion, 1969; The Flag Over the Schoolhouse, 1971; C A Stephens Looks at Norway, 1970; Charles Adams Tales, 1972; Little Big Heart, (compiled from C A Stephens' stories), 1974; Under the Sea in the Salvadore, 1969; Our Great American Story-Teller, 1978. *Contributor to:* Intercontinental Biography Magazine; Dime Novel Round-up; East Providence Post & Seekonk Star. *Honours:* Recipient, Diplomas, Certificates, Plaques & medals. *Memberships:* Life Member, American Biographical Institute Research Asociation; Institute for Community Service. *Address:* 395 Angele Street, Apt 111, Providence, RI 02906, USA.

HARRIS, Marie, b. 7 Nov. 1943, New York City, USA. Writer. *Education:* BA, Goddard College, 1971. *Publications:* Raw Honey, 1975; Interstate, 1981; Dear Winter, Editor, 1984. *Contributor to:* Parnassus; Poetry Now; Country Journal; 13th Moon; Choomia; American Book Review. *Honours:* National Endowment for the Arts Fellowship, 1976; N H Commission on the Arts Fellowship, 1982. *Membership:* Poetry Society of America. *Address:* Scruton Pond Rd, RFD #2, Barrington, NH 03825, USA.

HARRIS, Robert Stone, b. 10 Mar. 1925, Carlow, Republic of Ireland. Journalist. *Literary Appointments:* Advertisement Manager, West London & Middlesex Newspapers Ltd, 1960–72; General Manager, London & Westminster Newspapers Ltd, 1972–78, Managing Director, 1978–. *Membership:* Fellow of the Institute of Directors. *Address:* Newspaper House, Winslow Road, London, W6, England.

HARRIS, Robert van Dassanowsky, b. 28 Jan 1956, New York, USA. Playwright, Poet, Essayist. *Education:* Graduate, American Academy of Dramatic Arts; BA, Political Science & German Literature, University of California, Los Angeles. *Literary Appointments:* Board of Advisors, Committee Art for Olympia, New York, 1984–. *Major Publications:* Telegrams from the Metropole (poems), forthcoming: Numerous play productions and readings. *Contributor to:* Poetry/LA; California Quarterly; Modern Poetry Studies; Osiris; Crosscurrents; LA Weekly; Piedmont Review; Gryphon; Dreamworks; Allin (UK) Europa, Gypsy, Papyrus (Federal Republic of Germany); Printed

Matter (Japan) Poet India; Poetry Australia; and others. *Honours:* Karolyi Memorial Foundation Residency Award, France, 1982; Beverly Hills Theatre Guild Playwriting Award; and others. *Memberships:* Dramatists Guild, New York; Authors League, New York; Poets & Writers, New York; German-American Congress; Paneuropa Union (Germany & Austria); Heinrich von Kleist Gesellschaft (Germany). *Address:* 4346 Matilija Avenue 27, Sherman Oaks, CA 91423, USA.

HARRIS, Ronald Walter, b. 19 Aug. 1916, Bradford-on-Avon, England. Historian. *Education:* MA, Bristol University. *Literary Appointments:* Editor, Blandford History Series; Editor, Gollancz Men and Ideas Series; etc. *Publications:* England in the 18th Century, 1963; Political Ideas, 1963; Science Mind and Method, 1960; Absolution and Enlightenment, 1964; Introduction to the 20th Century, 1966; Reason and Nature, 1968; Romanticism and the Social Order, 1969; Clarendon and the English Revolution, 1983. *Address:* 14 Barton Road, Canterbury, Kent, England.

HARRIS, Stacy, Minneapolis, Minnesota, USA. Writer. *Education:* BA, University of Maryland, 1973. *Literary Appointments:* Columnist and Staff Writer, Countryside, Minneapolis, Minnesota, 1972–76; Contributing author, Researcher, Country Music Stars and the Supernatural, Dell Publishing Incorporated, 1978–79; Contributing editor, Inside Country Music, Nashville, Tennessee, 1981–83; Nashville entertainment writer, Newsweek, Washington, 1983–; Nashville editor, Spotlight on Country, New York, 1984–. *Publications:* Comedians of Country Music, 1978; The Carter Family, 1978. *Contributions to:* Country Song Roundup, 1976–; Nashville; Country Rhythms; Horoscope; Country Music; Music City News; Performance; Country News; People on Parade; American Songwriter; Amusement Business; Country Style; Satellite Business; The Nashville Gazette; Country Music Scene; The Music City Loafer; Beauty Dealer Press; Writer of press releases for Country music associations and other publications, biographies for various recording companies; Book reviewer, Nashville Banner. *Memberships:* Charter member and Past President , National Entertainment Journalists Association (Past newsletter editor, historian and official photographer), Treasurer, 1985–. *Address:* The Windsor Tower, 4215 Harding Road, #107, Nashville, TN 37205–2028, USA.

HARRIS, Theodore Wilson, b. 24 Mar. 1921, New Amsterdam, British Guiana. *Appointments include:* Visiting Professor, Yale University, 1979, University of Texas at Austin, 1980, 81, 82; Regents Lecturer, University of California, 1983. *Publications:* The Guyana Quartet, (includes, Palace of the Peacock, 1960; The Far Journey of Oudin, 1961; The Whole Armour, 1962; The Secret Ladder, 1963); The Eye of the Scarecrow, 1965; Tumatumari, 1968; Ascent to Omai, 1970; The Sleepers of Roraima, 1970; Black Marsden, 1972; Companions of the Day and Night, 1975; The Tree of the Sun, 1978; Da Silva da Silva's Cultivated Wilderness, 1977; Eternity to Season, 1978; The Angel at the Gate, 1982; Carnival, 1985. *Honours:* Commonwealth Fellow, University of Leeds, England, 1971; Guggenheim Fellow, USA, 1973; Henfield Writing Fellow, University of East Anglia, 1974. *Address:* c/o Faber and Faber Limited, 3 Queen Square, London WC1 3AU, England.

HARRISON, Claire Ellen, b. 12 Feb. 1946, Brooklyn, New York, USA. Writer. m. John Edward Harrison, 11 Apr. 1965, Binghamton, New York, 2 sons. *Education:* BA, Carleton University, Ottawa, Ontario, Canada. *Publications:* Silhouette Romances: Mistaken Identity, 1981; Summer Magic 1982; Flight of Fancy, 1983. Mills and Boon (Harlequin) Romances: Prophecy of Desire, 1983; Dance While You Can, 1984; Leading Man, 1984; Once A Lover, 1984; An Independent Woman, 1984; Dragon's Point, 1984; One Last Dance, 1984; Diplomatic Affair, 1985; Arctic Rose, 1985; Wildflower, 1985. *Contributions to:* Poetry (1978–1980): Makara;

Quarry; Arc; Room of One's Own; Canadian Literature; The Ear's Chamber. Short Fiction: The Leopard, Ladies' Home Journal, 1984. *Memberships:* Co-founder and Past President, Washington Romance Writers; Co-founder and Newsletter Editor, Ottawa Independent Writers; Charter Member, Romance Writers of America. *Literary Agent:* Steven Axelrod, New York. *Address:* 136 Brighton Avenue, Ottawa, Ontario, Canada K1S OT4.

HARRISON, Elizabeth Fancourt, b. 12 Jan. 1921, Watford, Hertfordshire, England. Author. *Publications include:* Coffee at Dobree's, 1965; The Physicians, 1966; The Ravelston Affair, 1967; Corridors of Healing, 1968; Emergency Call, 1970; Accident Call, 1971; Ambulance Call, 1972; Surgeon's Call, 1973; On Call 1974; Hospital Call, 1975; Dangerous Call, 1976; To Mend a Heart, 1977; Young Dr Goddard, 1978; A Doctor Called Caroline, 1979; A Surgeon Called Amanda, 1982; A Surgeon's Life, 1983; Marrying a Doctor, 1984; Surgeon's Affair, 1985; paperback editions UK & USA. *Honours:* Runner-Up, 1970, & Short listed, 1971, 1972, 1973, Major Award, Romantic Novelists Association. *Memberships:* Editor, Overseas Secretary, Chest & Heart Association, 1947–72; Society of Authors; Romantic Novelists Association, Honorary Secretary, 1972–77, Chairman 1977–79. *Literary Agent:* Mary Irvine. *Address:* 71 Wingfield Road, Kingston-on-Thames, Surrey KT2 5LR, England.

HARRISON, George, b. 14 Feb. 1936, Pennsylvania, USA. Nature Journalist. m. Kit Harrison, 15 Oct. 1975, West Bend, Wisconsin, 1 son, 1 daughter. *Education:* BA Journalism, Pennsylvania State University, USA. *Literary Appointments:* Associate Editor, Virginia Wildlife, 1959–61; Editor, Pennsylvania Game News, 1961–65; Managing Editor, National/International Wildlife, 1965–74; Field Editor, 1974–; Nature Editor, Sports Afield, 1977–. *Major Publications:* Roger Tory Peterson's Dozen Birding Hot Spots, 1976; America's Great Outdoors, 1976; Treasury of Wildlife (Encyclopaedia Britannica co-author), 1979; The Backyard Birdwatcher, 1979; America's Favorite Backyard Birds (co-author with K Harrison), 1983; America's Favorite Backyard Wildlife (co-author with K Harrison), 1985. *Contributor to:* Audubon; Better Homes & Gardens; Natural History; Living Bird Quarterly; Ranger Rick's Nature Magazine; National/International Wildlife. *Honour:* Jade of Chiefs Award (Outdoor Writers Association of America), 1981. *Memberships:* Board of Directors, 1978–81, President, 1985–86, Outdoor Writers' Association of America; Wisconsin Outdoor Communicators Association. *Address:* Willowmere, Hubertus, WI 53033, USA.

HARRISON, Royden John, b. 3 Mar. 1927, London, England. University Teacher. *Education:* BA, 1951, MA, 1955, PhD, 1955, Oxford University. *Publications:* Before the Socialists, 1965; The English Defence of the Commune, 1971; British Labour and Politics, in Japanese, 1975; Warwick Guide to British Labour Periodicals, 1977; Independent Collier, 1978. *Contributions to:* International Review of Social History; Economics Journal; Political Quasrterly; Times Literary Supplement, and various others. Co-Founder and Co-Editor, Bulletin of Society for Study of Labour History, 1960–. Guest, Japanese Society for the Promotion of Science, 1976. *Literary Agent:* Hilary Rubenstein. *Address:* Centre for the Study of Social History, University of Warwick, Coventry, Warwickshire CV4 7AL, England.

HARRISON, Sarah, b. 7 Aug. 1946, Devon, England. Writer. m. Jeremy Richard Douglas Harrison, 7 June 1969, Littleham, Devon, 1 son, 2 daughters. *Education:* English Hons, London University. *Publications:* In Granny's Garden, 1980; The Flowers of the Field, 1980; A Flower That's Free, 1984; Hot Breath, 1985. *Contributions to:* Woman's Realm; Woman's Own; She; Sunday Express Magazine; Spare Rib; articles and short stories. *Honour:* Runner-up, Best Romantic Novel for Flowers of the Field, R.N.A., 1981. *Literary Agent:* Carol Smith. *Address:* Holmcrest, 17 Station Road, Steeple Morden, Royston, Hertfordshire, England.

HARRISON, (Sir) Richard (John), b. 8 Oct. 1920, Dulwich, England. Professor. *Education:* Cambridge University; St Bartholomew's Hospital Medical College; MRCS; LRCP; MA; MD; DSc; FRS. *Publications include:* Man the Peculiar Animal, 1958; Marine Mammals, 1965; Behaviour and PHysiology of Pinnidpeda, 1968; Anatomical Terms, 3rd edition, 1969; Functional Anatomy of Marine Mammals, volume 1, 1972, volume II, 1974, volume III, 1977; Handbook of Marine Mammals, volumes I-III, 1981–85; Research on Dolphins, 1986. *Contributor to:* various professional journals; Encyclopaedia Britannica. *Honour:* Knight Bachelor, 1984. *Memberships:* Anatomical Society of Great Britain and Ireland, Secretary, 1956–64, President, 1978–79; Garrick Club; American Association of Anatomists, Honorary Member; International Federation of Associations of Anatomists, President, 1985–. *Address:* Downing College, Cambridge CB 1DQ, England.

HARRISON, Tony, b. 30 Apr. 1937, Leeds, Yorkshire, England. Poet. *Literary Appointments:* Northern Arts Fellow in Poetry; UNESCO Fellow in Poetry; Resident Dramatist, National Theatre of Great Britain. *Publications:* Poetry: Earthworks, 1964; Newcastle is Peru, 1969; The Loiners, 1970; Palladas, 1975, 1984; from, The School of Eloquence, 1978; Continuous 1981; A Kumquat for John Keats, 1981; US Martial, 1981; Selected Poems, 1984; Dramatic Verse 1973–85, 1985; V, 1985; The Fire-Gap, 1985. Theatre: Aikin Mata, 1966; The Misanthrope, 1973; Phaedra Britannica, 1975; Bow Down, 1977; The Passion, 1977; The Bartered Bride, 1978; The Oresteia, 1981; The Mysteries, 1985. *Contributions to:* Stand; New Statesman; Observer; Times Literary Supplement; PN Review; Encounter; London Review of Books. *Honours:* Geoffrey Faber Memorial Prize 1972; Cholmondeley Award for Poetry; European Poetry Translation Prize, 1983. *Membership:* Fellow of Royal Society of Literature. *Literary Agent:* Kenneth Ewing, Fraser and Dunlop (Scripts) Ltd, London. *Address:* c/o Fraser and Dunlop (Scripts) Ltd, 91 Regent Street, London W1R 8RU, England.

HARRISON MATTHEWS, Leonard, b. 1901. Biologist; Author. *Education:* MA, ScD, King's College, Cambridge. *Publications include:* Wandering Albatross; Sea Elephant; British Mammals; Beasts of the Field; Animals in Colour; The Senses of Animals, (co-author); The Whale; The Life of Mammals, (2 volumes); Editor, Waterton's Wanderings in South America; Introduction to Derwin's Origin of Species; Man and Wildlife; Penguin, (with foreword by HRH The Duke of Edinburgh); The Natural History of the Whale; The Seals and the Scientists. *Contributor to:* numerous radio and TV broadcasts; Times Literary and Educational Supplements; Nature; New Science; Endeavour; Listener; Observer; Geographic Magazine; Countryman; Field; Sunday Times; Country Fair; Punch. *Membership:* Fellow, Royal Society. *Address:* The Old Rectory, Stansfield, Via Sudbury, Suffolk, England.

HARROD, Nicholas, b. 7 May 1952, Glasgow, Scotland. Playwright. m. Judi Massey, 7 Aug. 1976, Kirkintilloch, Scotland, 1 son, 1 daughter. *Education:* BA English Literature, San Carlos State University, California, USA. *Literary Appointments:* Writer-in-Residence, Waystrode College, Kent, England, 1983–84. *Major Publications:* Plays: The Crew, 1982; Events in the Dressing-Room, 1982; Pull-up for Car Girls, 1983; Final Draft, 1984; The Wind Up, 1985. *Contributor to:* Autocar; Truck Drivers Gazette; Theatre; and others, including Scottish Television. *Honour:* Cottelsoe Award, Best Short Play for 1982 (The Crew). *Literary Agent:* Michael Whitehall of Leading Artists. *Address:* 60 St James's Street, London, SW1, England.

HARROLD, William Eugene, b. 24 June 1936, Winston-Salem, North Carolina, USA. University Professor. *Education:* BA, Wake Forest University, 1959; MA 1961, PhD, 1967, University of North Carolina. *Literary Appointments:* Instructor to Professor of English, University of Wisconsin, Milwaukee, 1965–

85. *Major Publications:* The Variance & the Unity: A Study of the Complementary Poems of Robert Browning, 1973; Beyond the Dream (poems), 1972. *Contributor to:* Paris Review; Antioch Review; Midwest Quarterly; Modern Language Review; California Quarterly; Poetry Now; Wormwood; Sparrow Magazine; Florida Quarterly; South Carolina Review; Image; Blue Unicorn; Rapport; Poet Lore; and others. *Honours:* Winner, North Carolina Poetry Council Award, 1973, International Poetry Award, 1978; and others. *Memberships:* Modern Language Association; Browning Institute; Tennyson Society; Browning Society; MMLA; MHRA. *Address:* 1982 North Prospect 2A, Milwaukee, WI 53202, USA.

HARSHAM, Philip, b. 2 Jan. 1924, Carter, Kentucky, USA. Writer, primarily magazine articles. m. Diane Dorothy Hart, 16 Apr. 1960, Louisville, Kentucky, 2 sons. *Education:* BA, English, Tulane University; Diploma, Advanced International Reporting, Columbia University. *Literary Appointments:* Louisville, Courier-Journal; New York Times; Medical Economics; Currently Southeast Editor, Medical Economics, & Contributing Editor, Florida Tend, Georgie Trend. *Publication:* The Beginning Investor, 1984. *Contributions:* Regular articles on money management, Medical Economics, Florida Trend, Georgia Trend; Freelance, wide range of subjects, numerous national publications. *Honours:* Reid Foundation Fellow, study of Africa, 1955; Consultant, Rockefeller Foundation, needs of African press, 1961; Ford Foundation Fellow, international reporting, 1963. *Address:* 2057 Kansas Avenue NE, St Petersburg, FL 33703, USA.

HART, Edward Warrener, b. 25 Dec. 1924, Strensall, Yorkshire, England. Agricultural Journalist and Author. m, 1 son, 1 daughter. *Education:* Certificate in Agriculture, Askham Bryan College of Agriculture. *Literary Appointments:* Agricultural Correspondent, Northern Echo, 1966–; Currently Agricultural Editor. *Publications:* Over 20 books on farming and the countryside including: The Sheep Dog: Its Work and Training (with Tim Longton), 1976; The Golden Guinea Book of Heavy Horses Past and Present, 1976. *Contributions to:* Horse and Hound and many other country journals. *Address:* Vince Moor East, Dalton-on-Tees, Darlington DL2 2PN, England.

HART, Francis Dudley, b. 4 Oct. 1909, Glossop, England. Consulting Physician. m. Mary Josephine Tully, 18 Dec. 1944, 1 son, 2 daughters. *Education:* MD Edinburgh; FRCP, London. *Publications:* Editor, French's Index of Differential Diagnosis, 10th edition, 1973, 11th edition, 1979; Editor, Drug Treatment of the Rheumatic Diseases, 1st Edition, 1978, 2nd Edition 1972; Overcoming Arthritis, 1981; Practical Problems in Rheumatology, 1983. *Contributions to:* Numerous publications on medical subjects, most recent: William Harvey and His Gout, Annals of the Rheumatic Diseases, 1984; Drug Induced Arthritis and Arthralgia, Drugs, 1984; Non-Steriodal Anti-inflammatory Drugs, (with E C Huskisson), Drugs, 1984. *Address:* 24 Harmont House, 20 Harley Street, London W1N 1AN, England.

HART, Jeffrey Allen, b. 29 Dec. 1947, New Kensington, Pennsylvania, USA. University Professor. m. Joan Goldhammer, 9 June 1968, Portland, Oregon, USA. *Education:* BA, Swarthmore College; PhD, University of California, Berkeley. *Publications:* The Anglo-Icelandic Cod War of 1972–73, 1976; The United States and the World Community, 1982; The New International Economic Order, 1983; Interdependence in the Post Multilateral Era, 1985. *Contributions to:* World Politics; International Organization; Journal of Conflict. *Honours:* Lewis Lehrman Visiting Fellow, 1980; Paul Henri Spaak Fellow, 1982–83. *Membership:* Phi Beta Kappa. *Address:* Department of Political Science, Indiana University, Bloomington, IN 47405, USA.

HART, Joseph Patrick, b. 1 May 1945, New York, USA. Playwright. m. Victoria Jane Pacey, 18 Sep. 1969,

New York City, 2 sons, 2 daughters. *Education:* BA, Fordham University; MA, New York University. *Literary Appointments:* Resident Playwright: Aspen Playwrights' Conference; Philadelphia Festival; Theater-In The-Works; Rutgers Theater Arts. *Publications:* (All Plays) Sosnata for Mott Street; Ghost Dance; Wigleaf; Window and Wall; Lot's Wife; Simon of Cyrene; Triple Play. *Honours:* Aspen Playwrights Award; University of Massachusetts Playwriting Award. *Membership:* Dramatists' Guild. *Literary Agent:* William Craver, c/o Helen Merrill. *Address:* 155 No 6th Avenue, Highland Park, NJ 08904, USA.

HART, Ron, b. 26 Sep. 1929, London, England. Playwright; Insurance Company Director. m. Carmel Levine, 5 Jan. 1964, London, 3 sons. *Publications:* Lunch Girls, 1983; Book Depository Blues, Play, 1985; A Fortunate Man, filmscript, 1974. *Contributions to:* various publications with short stories and articles. *Honours:* Oxford Experimental Drama Award, 1974; Verity Bargate Award, 1983; South London Arts Award, 1983. *Membership:* Writers Guild. *Literary Agent:* Rosica Colin Limited. *Address:* Heathcote, Totteridge Green, London N20, England.

HART, Sandra Lynn (Housby), b. 24 Mar. 1948, Aurora, Illinois, USA. Writer. m. William M Hart, 16 Dec. 1967, Denver, Colorado, 1 son, 2 daughters. *Publications:* The Snows of Craggmoor, 1978; Angel, 1982; Hurricane Sweep, 1984; Kiss of Gold, 1985; Sweet Whispers; 1986; Over 125 short stories. *Memberships:* Romance Writers of America; Authors Guild; Vice President Central Illinois Branch, League of American Pen Women, 1984–86; Illinois State Vice President, National League of American Pen Women, 1986–88. *Address:* RR13 Box 345, Bloomington, IL 61701, USA.

HART (Dame) Judith Constance Mary, b. Lancashire, England. Member of Parliament. *Education:* BA, Honours, London School of Economics, 1945. *Publication:* Aid and Liberation, 1973. *Contributor to:* Various publications including reviews. *Honour:* OBE, 1979. *Address:* House of Commons, London SW1, England.

HART-SMITH, William, b. 23 Nov. 1911, Tonbridge Wells, Kent, England. Poet. *Publications:* Columbus Goes West, 1943; Harvest, 1944; The Unceasing Ground, 1946; Christopher Columbus, 1948; On The Level, 1950; Poems in Doggerel, 1955; Poems of Discovery, 1959; The Talking Clothes, 1966; Minipoems, 1974; Let Me Learn The Steps, 1977. *Contributions to:* Various journals, Australia, New Zealand, UK, USA. *Honours:* Grace Leven Poetry Prize, 1964; Crouch Memorial Gold Medal, 1959. *Memberships:* Editor, Poetry Society of Australia, 1964–66; Jindyworobak Club, New South Wales. *Literary Agent:* Angus & Robertson. *Address:* 16A Hamilton Place, Glenfield, Auckland, New Zealand.

HARTCUP, Adeline, b. 26 Apr. 1918, Isle of Wight, England. Writer. m. John Hartcup, 11 Feb. 1950, 2 sons. *Education:* MA, Oxon, Classics and English Literature. *Appointments:* Editorial Staff, Times Educational Supplement; Honorary Press Officer, Kent Voluntary Service Council. *Publications:* Angelica, 1954; Morning Faces, 1963; Below Stairs in the Great Country Houses, 1980; Children of the Great Country Houses, 1982; Love and Marriage in the Great Country Houses, 1984. *Contributor to:* Times Educational Supplement; Harpers; Queen; Times Higher Educational Supplement; etc. *Address:* Swanton Court, Sevington, Ashford, Kent TN24 OLL, England.

HARTLEY, Dorothy Rosaman, b. 4 Oct. 1893, Skipton-in-Craven, England. Writer, Historian, Artist. *Major Publications:* Life and Work of the People of England (6 volumes), 1925; Medieval Costume and Life, 1931; Thomas Tusser, 1931; Here's England, 1934; Countryman's England, 1935; Made in England, 1939; Holiday in Ireland, 1938; Food in England, 1954; Water in England, 1964; The Land of England, 1979.

Contributor to: Daily Sketch; Countryman Magazine; The Manchester Guardian; Life & Letters Today; Country Quest; and others. *Honour:* Civil List Pension awarded for work. *Membership:* Society of Authors. *Address:* Fron House, Froncysyllte, Nr Llangollen, North Wales.

HARTLEY, Jean Ayres, b. 21 Dec. 1914, California, USA. Writer. m. William Hartley, 24 July 1942, Stanford University, 1 son, 1 daughter. *Education:* AB, Stanford University. *Contributor to:* Over 300 articles published in numerous magazines and newspapers including, Family Weekly; Points; Off Duty; Modern Maturity; Rotarian; Bon Appetit; Chevron USA; These Times; NRTA Journal; Christian Science Monitor; etc. *Memberships:* International Platform Association; American Society of Journalists and Authors; National Writers Club; California Writers Club, Secretary; International Travel Writers. *Address:* 5020 Winding Way, Sacramento, CA 95841, USA.

HARTLEY, Keith, b. 14 July 1940. Economist; Director of IRISS. m. Winifred Keally, 12 Apr. 1966, Easington, England, 1 son, 2 daughter. *Education:* BSc (Economics Class 1); PhD. *Publications:* Co-author, Export Performance and Pressure of Demand, 1970; Problems of Economic Policy, 1977; Co-author, Micro-Economic Policy, 1981; NATO Arms Co-operation, 1983. *Contributions to:* Applied Economics; Economic Journal; Journal of Industrial Economics; International Journal of Industrial Organisation; Social Science Information. *Honours:* Visiting Associate Professor, University of Illinois, 1974; NATO Research Fellowship, 1977; Visiting Professor, University of Kernagan, Malaysia, 1984. *Membership:* Royal Economic Society. *Address:* Institute for Research in Social Sciences, University of York, York YO1 5DD, England.

HARTMAN, Evert, b. 12 July 1937, Avereest, Netherlands. Teacher of Geography. m. Tjitske D Medema, 11 June 1963, Kampen, 2 sons. *Education:* University Geography Degree. *Publications:* Signalen in de nacht, 1973; Machinist op dood spoon, 1975; De Laatste Stuw, 1977;)Oorlog zonder vrienden, (War Without Friends), 1979; Vechten voor Overmorgen, 1980; Het onzichtbare licht, 1982; Gegyzeld, 1984. *Honours:* European Juvenile Award for Contemporary Literature. *Membership:* Vereniging van Letterkundigen (Union of Authors). *Address:* Eddingtonlaan 4, 7904 EE Hoogeveen, The Netherlands.

HARTMAN, George E, b. 20 Oct. 1926, Newton, Kansas, USA. University Professor; Attorney. *Education:* BS, University of Kansas, 1950; MBA, Indiana University, 1951; PhD, University of Illinois, 1958; JD, University of Cincinnati, 1964. *Publications include:* Export Trade Workshop Handbook, 1968. *Contributions to:* Handbook of Modern Marketing, ed. Victor Buell, 1970, revised edition 1984; Environment 1984, ed. Henry Baker, 1975; Managerial Finance, 1981, revised edition 1984; Journal of Marketing; Marketing News; Enterprise Magazine. *Memberships:* Various professional organisations. *Address:* College of Business Administration, University of Cincinnati, OH 45221, USA.

HARTSTON, William Roland, b. 12 Aug. 1947, London, England. Writer; Industrial Psychologist. m. Elizabeth Bannerman, 26 Aug. 1978, Cambridge. *Education:* MA, Mathematics, Jesus College, Cambridge University, 1972. *Publications:* The Benoni, 1969; How to Cheat at Chess, 1976; Soft Pawn, 1980; The Penguin Book of Chess Openings, 1981; The Ultimate Irrelevant Encyclopedia, with Jill Dawson, 1984; Teach Yourself Chess, 1985; Kings of Chess, 1985. Co-Author, The King's Indian Defence, 1969, 73; Korchnoi-Karpov, 1974. *Contributions to:* British Chess Magazine; Chess; The Mail on Sunday, Chess columnist. *Literary Agent:* Jonathan Clowes, London. *Address:* 14 Willow Walk, Cambridge CB1 1LA, England.

HARVEY, Ian Douglas, b. 25 Jan. 1914, Ft Wellington, Madras, India. Public Relations Consultant; Freelance Journalist. m. Clare Mayhew, Nov. 1949, London, 2 daughters. *Education:* Fettes College, Edinburgh; BA (Hons); MA, Oxford University; Staff College, Camberley; Paddington College (Governor). *Publications:* Talk of Propaganda, 1947; The Technique of Persuasion, 1951; Arms and Tomorrow, 1954; To Fall Like Lucifer, 1971. *Contributions to:* Police Quarterly; Spectator; New Statesman; Daily Telegraph; Guardian; Gay News; Scotland. *Honours:* Territorial Decoration; Former Member of Parliament for Harrow East; Junior Minister, Foreign Office. *Literary Agent:* John Farquharson Limited, London. *Address:* 62D St Michael's Street, London W2 1QR, England.

HARVEY, John Robert, b. 25 June 1942, Bishops Stortford, Hertfordshire, England. University Lecturer, Cambridge English Faculty. m. Julietta Chloe Papadopoulou, 1 Sep. 1968, Thessalonika, Greece, 1 daughter. *Education:* BA, Honours Class I in English 1964, MA 1967, PhD 1969, University of Cambridge. *Literary Appointments:* Editor, Cambridge Quarterly, 1978–. *Publications:* Victorian Novelists and Their Illustrators, 1970; The Plate Shop novel, 1979; Coup d'Etat novel, 1985. *Contributions to:* London Review of Books; Sunday Times; Listener; Encounter; Cambridge Quarterly; Essays in Criticism; Delta; Cambridge Review; Times Higher Education Supplement. *Honours:* David Higham Prize , 1979. *Literary Agent:* Curtis Brown. *Address:* c/o English Faculty, 9 West Road, Cambridge, England.

HARVEY, Paul Dean Adshead, b. 7 May 1930, London, England. University Professor, Retired, Medieval History. m. Yvonne Crossman, 6 July 1968, Hockley, Essex. *Education:* BA, 1953, MA, 1960, D Phil, 1960, Oxford University. *Literary Appointments:* Assistant Archivist, Warwick County Record Office, 1954–56; Assistant Keeper, Department of Manuscripts, British Museum, 1957–66; Lecturer, Department of History, Southampton University, 1966–78; Professor of Medieval History, 1978–85 and Professor Emeritus 1985, Durham University; General Editor, Southampton Records Series, 1966–78, Portsmouth Record Series, 1969–. *Publications:* Printed Maps of Warwickshire 1576–1900, with H Thorpe, 1959; A Medieval Oxfordshire Village: Cuxham 1240–1400, 1965; Memorial Records of Cuxham c. 1200–1359, 1976; The History of Topographical Maps, 1980; Manorial Records, 1984. Editor: The Peasant Land Market in Medieval England, 1984; Local Maps and Plans from Medieval England, 1986. *Contributions to:* Victoria History of Oxfordshire, volume 10, 1972; Agricultural History Review; British Museum Quarterly; Economic History Review; Past and Present. *Memberships:* Fellow: Royal Historical Society, 1981; Society of Antiquaries, 1963. Vice President, Surtees Society, 1978. *Address:* Lyndhurst, Farnley Hey Road, Durham DH1 4EA, England.

HARWOOD, Alan, b. 20 Mar. 1935, Tarrytown, New York, USA. Anthropologist. 1 son, 1 daughter. *Education:* AB, Harvard College; MA, University of Michigan; PhD, Columbia University. *Appointment:* International Board of Consulting Editors, Culture, Medicine and Psychiatry. *Publications:* Witchcraft Sorcery and Social Categories among the Safa, 1970; Rx: Spiritist As Needed: A Study of a Puerto Rican, Community Mental Health Resource, 1977; Ethnicity and Medical Care, Editor, 1981. The Hot-Cold Theory of Disease: Implications for Treatment of Puerto Rican Patients (article), Journal of the American Medical Association. *Honours:* Phi Beta Kappa; Wellcome Medal, Royal Anthropological Institute of Great Britain & Ireland. *Address:* Dept of Anthropology, University of Massachusetts, Boston, MA 02125, USA.

HARWOOD, Alice Mary, b. 7 July 1909, West Bromwich, England. Authoress. *Education:* BA, University of London. *Publications:* Caedmon: A Lyrical Drama, 1937; The Star of the Greys, 1939; She Had to be Queen, 1948; Merchant of the Ruby, 1951; The

Strangeling, 1954; At Heart a King, 1957; No Smoke Without Fire USA, 1964; The Living Phantom, 1973; The Clandestine Queen, 1979; The Uncrowned Queen, 1983. *Contributor to:* Magazines and journals including: The Fortnightly; Sunday Telegraph; Radio Times; Country Life; Good Housekeeping; The Lady; Birmingham Post; etc. *Honours:* Bodley Head Prize, 1944; Honorary Member, Mark Twain Society, USA. *Memberships:* Society of Authors; PEN; Shakespeare Club, Stratford on Avon. *Address:* Green Hedges, Oversley, Alcester, Warwickshire B49 5AQ, England.

HASENHÜTTL, Gotthold, b. 2 Dec. 1933, Graz, Austria. Professor. *Education:* Ordination as priest, 1959; ThD, 1962, PhD, 1971. *Major Publications:* Der Glaubensvollzug: Eine Begegnung mit Rudolf Bultmann aus katholischen Glaubensverständnis, 1963; Charisma, Ordnungsprinzip der Kirche, 1969; Füreinander Dasein: Brennpunkte moderner Glaubensproblematik, 1971; Gott ohne Gott: Ein Dialog mit J P Sartre, 1972; Herrschaftsfreie Kirche: Sozio-theologische Grundlegung, 1974; Kritische Dogmatik, 1979; Einführung in die Gotteslehre, 1980; Freiheit in Fesseln: Die Chance der Befreiungstheologie. Ein Erfahrungsbericht, 1985. *Address:* Philippinenstrasze 23, D–6600 Saarbrücken, Federal Republic of Germany.

HASHMI, (Auranzgeb) Alamgir, b. 15 Nov. 1951, Lahore, Pakistan, Lecturer; Writer. m. Beatrice, 15 Dec. 1978. Winterthur, Switzerland, 1 son. *Education:* MA; D Litt. *Literary Appointments:* Assistant Editor, The Ravi, 1970–71; Faculty Adviser, Folio, 1973–74; Editor and Broadcaster, English Magazine, 1973–74; Foreign Editor, Explorations, 1978–; Member, Editorial Board, Poetry Europe, 1982; Correspondent, The Journal of Commonwealth Literature, 1979–; Editor, Helix, 1978–83; Editorial Adviser, Kunapipi, 1981–; Editorial Adviser to several other publications. *Publications:* The Oath and Amen, 1976; Pakistani Literature, 1978; America is a Punjabi Word, 1979; My Second in Kentucky, 1981; This Time in Lahore, 1983; Commonwealth Literature, 1983; Neither This Time/Nor That Place, 1984; The Worlds of Muslim Imagination, 1985. *Contributions to:* The Pakistan Times; Viewpoint; Journal of South Asian Literature; World Literature Written in English; CRNLE Reviews Journal; Poetry Australia; Westerly; Poetry Review; James Joyce Broadsheet; D H Lawrence Review; Ariel; Wascana Review; Asiaweek; Chandrabhaga; Landfall; DeKalb Literary Arts Journal; Washington Review, etc. *Honours:* Poetry Prize, All-Pakistan Creative Writing Contest, 1972; University of Panjab Certificate of Merit, 1973; Academic Roll of Honour, Government College, Lahore, 1972; The Pakistan Academy of Letters, Patras Bukhari Award (National Literature Prize), 1985. *Memberships:* Several professional organizations. *Address:* c/o Mr J Stork, Hohenkrahenstrasse 5, CH–8200 Schaffhausen, Switzerland.

HASKELL, Francis James Herbert, b. 7 Apr. 1928, London, England. Professor of History of Art. m. 10 Aug. 1965, Leningrad. *Education:* MA, King's College, Cambridge University, 1951. *Publications:* Patrons and Painters: A Study of the Relations between Art and Society in the Age of the Baroque, 1963, 80, Italian editions, 1966, 85, Spanish edition, 1984; Rediscoveries in Art, 1976, 80, Italian edition, 1982; L'Arte e il linguaggio della politica, 1977; Taste and the Antique, 1981, 1982, Italian edition, 1985, with Nicholas Penny. *Contributions to:* Burlington Magazine; Journal of Warbury and Courtauld Institutes; New York Review of Books, and others. *Honours:* Fellow, British Academy, 1971; Foreign Honorary Member, American Academy of Arts and Sciences, 1979–; Corresponding Member, Accademia Portaniana, Naples, Italy, 1982–. *Address:* Department of History of Art, 35 Beaumont Street, Oxford OX1 2PG, England.

HASSAN, Ihab, b. 17 Oct. 1925, Cairo, Egypt. Professor; Literary Critic. *Education:* BSc, University of Cairo, 1946; MS, University of Pennsylvania, USA, 1948; MA, 1950, PhD, 1953. *Publications include:* Radical Innocence; Studies in the Contemporary

American Novel, 1961; The Literature of Silence: Henry Miller & Samuel Beckett, 1967; The Dismemberment of Orpheus Toward a Postmodern Literature, 1971, 1982; Paracriticisms: Seven Speculations of the TImes, 1975; The Right Promethean Fire: Imagination, Science & Cultural Change, 1980; Editor, Liberations, 1971; Co-Editor with Sally Hassan, Innovation/Renovation, 1983. *Contributor to:* Various journals. *Honours:* Recipient, various academic honours. *Memberships include:* MLA; American Comparative Literature Association; PEN. *Address:* 2137 N Terrace Ave, Milwaukee, WI 53202, USA.

HASTINGS, Max Macdonald, b. 28 Dec. 1945, London, England. Writer. m. Patricia Mary Edmondson, 27 May 1972, Hallaton, 2 sons, 1 daughter. *Education:* Exhibitioner, University College, Oxford. *Appointments:* Researcher, BBC TV, 1963–64; Reporter, London Evening Standard, 1965–67, 1968–70; Fellow, US World Press Institute, 1967–68; Reporter BBC TV, 24 Hours, 1970–73; Freelance Author, Broadcaster, Journalist, 1973–; Editor, Evening Standard Londoner's Diary, 1976–77; Columnist, Daily Express, 1981–83; Columnist, Sunday Times, 1985–. *Publications:* America 1968: The Fire This Time, 1968; Ulster 1969: The Struggle for Civil Rights in Northern Ireland, 1970; Montrose: The King's Champion, 1977; Yoni: Hero of Entebbe, 1979; Bomber Command, 1979; Contributor, Battle of Britain, 1980; Das Reich, 1981; Battle for the Falklands, with Simon Jenkins, 1983; Overlord, 1984; Victory in Europe, 1985; The Oxford Book of Military Anecdotes, Editor, 1985. *Contributor to:* The Standard; The Spectator; The Field. *Honours:* Somerset Maugham Prize, 1979; Yorkshire Post Book of the Year, 1983 & 1984; Cited, British Press Awards, 1973, 1980; Journalist of the Year, 1982; Granada TV Reporter of the Year, 1982. *Literary Agent:* A D Peters. *Address:* Guilsborough Lodge, Northamptonshire, England.

HAUGEN, Paal-Helge, b. 26 Apr. 1945, Valle, Norway. Author. *Education:* Studied medicine, film and theatre, Norway and USA. *Publications:* Poetry: På botnen av ein møork sommar, 1967; Sangbok, 1969; Det synlege menneske, 1975; Fram i lyset, tydeleg, 1978; Steingjerde, 1979; Spor, Selected and new poems, 1981; I dette huset, 1984; Det overvintrå Lyset, 1985; Anne, novel, 1968; Herr Tidemann reiser, 1980, Childrens book. Inga anna tid, ingen annan stad, stage play, 1986. *Contributions to:* Various professional journals; Plays for radio, television and stage. *Honours include:* Literary Prize, Norwegian Cultural Council, 1968; The English edition of Steingierde (Stone Fences, University of Missouri Press), translated by Roger Greenwald and William Mishler, awarded, The American Translators Association's Richard Wilbur Prize, 1986. *Memberships:* Vice Chairman, Board of Literary Advisers, Society of Norwegian Writers; Society of Norwegian Playwrights; Society of Norwegian Translators; Chairman, Norwegian State Council of Film Producers. *Literary Agent:* Det Norske Samlaget. *Address:* Skrefjellv 5, 4645 Nodeland, Norway.

HAULE, James Mark, b. 26 Nov. 1945, Detroit, Michigan, USA. Professor of English. m. Margaret Ann Cyzeska, 29 Nov. 1968, 2 daughters. *Education:* BA, 1968; MA, 1970; PhD, 1974, Wayne State University. *Literary Appointments:* NDEA Title IV Fellow, Department of English, 1971–74; Instructor to Assistant Professor of English, 1974–75; Wayne State University, Detroit; Faculty Coordinator, 1975–76, Detroit College of Business; Associate Professor of English and Associate Dean, 1976–78, Detroit College of Business; Associate Professor of English and Assistant Dean, 1978–80; School of Humanities, Pan American University, Edinburg, Texas; Associate Professor of English, Director, Humanities Community Services, General Editor, Living Author Series, Pan American University, 1980–84; Professor of English and General Editor, Living Author Series, 1985, Pan American University. *Publications:* A Concordance to, The Waves, by Virginia Woolf, (with PH Smith, Jr), Oxford Microform Publications Ltd 1981; A Concordance to, Between the Acts, by Virginia Woolf, (with PH Smith

Jr), 1985; A Concordance to, To The Lighthouse, by Virginia Wolf, (with PH Smith, Jr), 1983; A Concordance to, The Years, by Virginia Woolf, (With PH Smith, Jr), 1984; A Concordance to, Mrs Dalloway, by Virginia Woolf, (with PH Smith, Jr), 1984; A Concordance to, Orlando, by Virginia Woolf, (with PH Smith, Jr), 1985. *Contributions to:* Literature & Psychology; Studies in American Humor; Twentieth Century Literature; Virginia Woolf Miscellany; Critique: Studies in Modern Fiction, and others. Detroit College of Business Grant, 1977–78; Faculty Research Council Grant, Pan American University, 1979–80; and 1980–81; and 1981–82; and 1982–83; Social Sciences and Humanities Research Council of Canada Grant, 1982–83, 1983–84 and 1984–85. *Memberships:* Modern Language Association and others. *Address:* Department of English, Pan American University, Edinburg, TX 78539, USA.

HAUSERMANN, Gertrud, b. 7 Aug. 1921, Gebenstorf, Switzerland. Writer. m. Hans Walter Hausermann, Egliswil, Switzerland, 21 Jan. 1967. *Major Publications:* Irene, 1947; Perdita, 1948; Anne und Ruth, 1949; Die Fischermädchen, 1950; Marianne, 1952; Franziska und Renato, 1954; Heimat am Fluß, 1953; Die silberne Kette, 1956; Die Geschichte mit Leonie, 1958; Simone, 1960; Simone in der Bretagne, 1962. *Honours:* Swiss Children's Books Award (Heimat am Fluß), 1954; Hans Christian Anderson Award, Diploma of Merit (Die silberne Ketter), 1958. *Membership:* Swiss Writers' Union, Zürich. *Address:* Reußdörflistraße 12, CH-5412 Reuß-Gebenstorf, Switzerland.

HAUSMAN, Gerald Andrews, b. 13 Oct. 1945, Baltimore, Maryland, USA. Teacher. m. Loretta Ruth Wright, 17 June 1968, La Cueva, New Mexico, 2 daughters. *Education:* BA, English Literature, New Mexico Highlands University. *Literary Appointments:* Editor, Bookstore Press, Lenox, Massachusetts, 1970–77; Literary Arts Consultant, Southern Berkshire Community Arts Council, Great Barrington, Massachusetts, 1975–76; Editor-in-Chief, New Mexico Craft Magazine, Santa Fe, 1977–79; Managing Editor, Sunstone Press, Santa Fe, 1979–83. *Publications:* Eight Poems (with D Kherdian), 1968; New Marlboro Stage, 1969, Second Edition, 1971; Circle Meadow, 1971; Night Herding Song, 1980; No Witness, 1980; Runners, 1984; Meditations With Animals, 1986. *Contributions to:* (articles and poems); Bloomsbury Review; Small Press; Crab Creek Review; Willow Springs Review; Studia Mystica; New Mexico Wildlife; The Christian Science Monitor; Waterways; Oyez Review; The Amicus Journal; The Greenfield Review; Ararat; Longhouse; Southwestern Review; Arizona Quarterly; Country Journal; From Seedbed to Harvest. *Honours:* Poetry Award, Union College, New Jersey, 1965; Children's Protective Services Award, Boston, Massachusetts, 1973; Gerald Hausman Scholarship Fund, Santa Fe, 1985. *Memberships:* Board of Directors, Sunstone Press, 1979–84; Poets in the Schools, Massachusetts, 1972–76. *Address:* PO Box 517, Tesuque, NM 87574, USA.

HAVEL, J E, b. 16 June 1928, Le Havre, France. Professor. *Education:* Lic. en Droit, Paris, 1950; Diploma, Institute of Political Studies, University of Paris, 1952; DLit, University of Paris, 1956. *Publications include:* La Condicion de la femme, 1961; Les etats scandinaves et l'integration europeenne, 1970; La Finlande et la Suede, 1978; Habitat et logement, 5th edition, 1985. *Contributor to:* Various professional journals. *Honours:* Disting. by French Academy of Moral and Political Sciences, 1961; Prize, Carnegie Endowment for International Peace, European Centre, 1958; Canadian Centennial Medal, 1967. *Address:* 175 Boland Avenue, Sudbury, Ontario, P3E 1YI, Canada.

HAVENS, Murray Clark, b. 21 Aug. 1932, Council Grove, Kansas, USA. Political Scientist; Educator. m. Agnes Marie Scharpf, 5 July 1958, New York, USA. (deceased 1969), 1 son, 1 daughter. *Education:* BA, University of Alabama, 1953; MA, Johns Hopkins

University, 1954; PhD, ibid. 1958. *Appointments:* Book Review Editor, The Journal of Politics, 1972–83. *Publications:* City Versus Farm? 1957; The Challenges to Democracy, 1965; The Politics of Assassination, 1970; Assassination and Terrorism, 1975; Texas Politics Today, 1984. *Contributions to:* Journal of Politics; Presidential Studies Quarterly; Issues and Ideas in America; New Republican. *Address:* 7408 Topeka Avenue, Lubbock, Texas 79424, USA.

HAVIGHURST, Alfred Freeman, b. 30 Sep. 1904, Mount Pleasant, USA. Educator. *Education:* BA, Ohio Wesleyan University, 1925; MA, University of Chicago, 1928; PhD, Harvard University, 1936. *Publications:* Twentieth Century Britain, 1962, 2nd edition, 1966; Radical Journalist: H W Massingham 1860–1924, 1974; (bibliography handbook) Modern England 1901–70, 1976; The Pirenne Thesis; Analysis, Criticism and Revision, 3rd edition, 1976; Britain in Transition: The Twentieth Century, 1979; 4th edition, 1985. *Contributor to:* American Historical Review; Journal of Modern History; Annals of American Academy of Political and Social Science; Journal of British Studies; Law Quarterly Review; Encyclopedia Britannica. *Memberships:* Member, American Historical Association and Fellow, Royal Historical Society. *Address:* 11 Blake Field, Amherest, MA 01002, USA.

HAVRAN, Martin Joseph William, b. 12 Nov. 1929, Windsor, Ontario, Canada. Professor of History. m. Clara Lily, 30 Aug. 1958, Windsor, 1 son, 1 daughter. *Education:* PhD, University of Detroit, 1951; MA, Wayne State University, 1953; PhD, Case Western University, 1957. *Publications:* Readings in English History, (co-editor), 1967; England: Prehistory to the Present, (co-author, 1968; The Catholics in Caroline England, 1962; Caroline Courtier: The Life of Lord Cottington, 1973. *Contributor to:* Numerous journals and essayist; Latest forthcoming essay: The Counter-Reformation in the Britsh Isles, in Catholicism in Early Modern Europe, Editor, John O'Malley, 1986. *Honour:* Fellow, Royal Historical Society, 1973. *Memberships:* American Catholic Historical Association, President, 1982; North American Conference on British Studies, President, 1979–81; American Historical Association; The Historical Association. *Address:* Corcoran Department of History, Randall Hall, University of Virginia, Charlottesville, VA 22903, USA.

HAWKEN, Marjorie Monica Walker, b. 10 Aug. 1918, Orange, New South Wales, Australia. Journalist. m. Russell Hawken, 14 June 1945, Sydney, New South Wales, Australia, 2 sons, 1 daughter. *Education:* Macquarie Secretarial School, Sydney, Australia. *Literary Appointments:* Editor, Mia-Mia, national Christian Family magazine, 1972–76; Sydney Editor, Church Scene, national Anglican weekly newspaper, 1976–79. *Publications:* An Open Door, daily readings, 1974. *Contributions to:* Southern Cross, Sydney Anglican News Magazine, 1979–82; Mia-Mia; Church Scene. *Honours:* Vietnamese Childen article recieved Highly Commended Certificate 1975, The Rich Wine of Marriage article received Commended Certificate 1976, Australian Religious Press Association; Award Certificate for article, Do Australian Aborigines Need Another Wilberforce? *Address:* 31 Milson Road, Cremorne Point, Sydney, NSW 2090, Australia.

HAWKES, John Clendennin Talbot Burne, b. 17 Aug. 1925, Stamford, Connecticut, USA. University Teacher; Writer. m. Sophie Tazewell, 5 Sep. 1947, Fort Peck, Montana, 3 sons, 1 daughter. *Education:* AB, Harvard University, 1949. *Publications include:* The Cannibal, 1949; The Lime Twig, 1961; Second Skin, 1964; The Blood Oranges, 1971; Travesty, 1976; The Passion Artist, 1979; Virginie, 1982; Adventures in the Alaskan Skin Trade, 1985; Short Stories include: Humors of Blood & Skin; A John Hawkes Reader, 1984; Plays include: The Innocent Party, 1966; The Wax Museum, 1966. *Honours include:* Recipient, Award in Literature, American Academy and Institute of Arts and Letters, 1962; Guggenheim Fellowship, 1962; Ford Fellowship for Drama, 1964; Rockefeller Fellowship,

1968; Le Prix du Meilleur Livre Etranger, Paris, 1973. *Memberships:* American Academy and Institute of Arts and Letters; American Academy of Arts and Sciences; International Authors and Writers. *Literary Agent:* Lynn Nesbit, New York City, USA. *Address:* 18 Everett Avenue, Providence, RI 02906, USA.

HAWKESWORTH, John, b. 1920, London, England. Film and Television Producer and Writer. *Education:* BA, Oxford University. *Publications:* Film and Television Scripts: Tiger Bay; The Conan Doyle Series; The Million Pound Bank Note, Adaptation; The Elusive Pompernel; The Goldrobbers; Upstairs, Downstairs, television series 1-5. Novels: Upstairs: Secrets of An Edwardian Household, 1972; Upstairs, Downstairs in My Lady's Chamber, 1973; The Duchess of Duke Street, 2 television series; Danger UXB. Creator and Scriptwriter (Television): The Flame Trees of Thika; The Tales of Beatrix Potter; By The Sword Divided, 2 series; Oscar, The Adventures of Sherlock Holmes, Presented and adapted. *Literary Agent:* Douglas Rae Management and Deborah Rogers Limited. *Address:* Flat 2, 24 Cottesmore Gardens, London W8, England.

HAWKINS, Harriett Bloker, b. 29 Apr. 1934, Memphis, Tennessee, USA. Shakespeare Critic. m. Eric Buckley, 15 Mar. 1978, Charlotte, North Carolina. *Education:* BA, Tulane University; MA, PhD, Washington University; MA, Oxford University. *Literary Appointments:* Instructor in English, Swarthmore College; Assistant, Associate and Professor of English, Vassar College; Senior Research Fellow, Linacre College, Oxford. *Publications:* Likenesses of Truth in Elizabethan and Restoration Drama; Poetic Freedom and Poetic Truth; Chaucer, Shakespeare, Marlow, Milton; The Devil's Party: Critical Counter-Interpretations of Shakespearean Drama. *Contributions to:* Shakespeare Studies; Modern Philology; Studies in English Literature; Reviewer for Shakespeare Survey, Review of English Studies and Essays in Criticism. *Honours:* Gugenheim Fellowship, 1975–76; Rose Mary Crayshaw Prize, British Academy, 1977. *Memberships:* International Shakespeare Association; Modern Language Association. *Address:* 43 Sandfield Road, Headington, Oxford OX3 7RN, England.

HAWLEY, Donald Frederick, (Sir), b. 22 May 1921, Essex, England. Chairman, Ewbank Preece Ltd; Retired Ambassador. m. Ruth Morwenna Graham Howes, 16 June 1964, Charmouth, 1 son, 3 daughters. *Education:* MA, New College, University of Oxford, England; Member of the English Bar (Inner Temple). *Major Publications:* Courtesies in the Trucial States, 1965; The Trucial States, Oman and its Renaissance, 1977; Courtesies in the Gulf Area, 1978; Manners and Correct Form in the Middle East, 1983. *Contributor to:* Journal of the Royal Society for Asian Affairs. *Honours:* Knight Commander of the Order of St Michael and St George; Member of the Order of the British Empire. *Address:* Little Cheverell House, Nr Devizes, Wiltshire, SN 10 4JS, England.

HAYASHI, Tetsumaro, b. 22 Mar. 1929, Sakaide City, Japan. University Professor. m. Akiko Sakuratani, 14 Apr. 1960, 1 son. *Education:* BA, Okayama University, Japan; MA, University of Florida, Gainesville, USA; MALS, PhD, Kent State University, Ohio, USA. *Literary Appointments:* Editor, Steinbeck Quarterly, 1968–; Editor, Steinbeck Monograph Series, 1970–. Author/Editor of 27 books including: The Poetry of Robert Greene, 1977; A Study Guide to Steinbeck: A Handbook to His Major Works, Editor; Translated into Japanese, 1978; Steinbeck and Hemingway: Dissertation Abstracts and Research Opportunities, Editor, 1980; William Faulkner: Research Opportunities and Dissertation Abstracts, Editor, 1982; Eugene O'Neill: Research Opportunities and Dissertation Abstracts, Editor, 1983; Steinbeck's Travel Literature, Editor, 1984; James Joyce: Reserach Opportunities and Dissertation Abstracts, Editor, 1985; 11 Monographs; 6 Pamphlets; Reviews: *Contributor to:* Professional journals, etc, short stories, papers, articles. *Memberships:* Modern Language Association of

America; Steinbeck Society of America, Director, 1966–77; President, 1977–81; International John Steinbeck Society, President, 1981–85, 1985–90. *Address:* c/o English Department, Ball State University, Muncie, IN 47306, USA.

HAYES, Paul Martin, b. 12 Feb. 1942, London, England. Fellow, Keble College; University Lecturer in Modern History; Former Junior Proctor. m. Ursel Kiehne, 3 Feb. 1981, Oxford, 1 son. *Education includes:* MA, 1967, PhD, 1969, Nuffield College, Oxford. *Publications:* Quisling, 1971; Fascism, 1973; The Nineteenth Century 1814–1880–, 1975 and, The Twentieth Century 180-1939, 1978 (books for Modern British Foreign Policy Series). Publisher, A and C Black. *Contributions to:* New Statesman; History Today; English History Review; Times Literary Supplement, and others. *Honour:* Larsen Prize, 1966. *Memberships:* Fellow, Royal History Society. *Address:* Keble College, Oxford OX1 3PG, England.

HAYES, Steven Charles, b. 12 Aug. 1948, Philadelphia, Pennsylvania, USA. Clinical Psychologist; Researcher; Educator; Practitioner. m. Angela Fe Butcher, 8 June 1972, San Diego, California (divorced), 1 daughter. *Education:* BA, Psychology (cum laude), Loyola University of Los Angeles, 1970; Psychology, California State University, San Diego, 1971–72; MA, Clinical Psychology, 1974; PhD, Clinical Psychology, 1977, West Virginia University, Morgantown. *Literary Appointments:* Editor, The Student Recorder, 1974–75; Guest Associate Editor, 1983 and Editorial Consultant, 1979–82 Behavioral Assessment; Associate Editor, Journal of Applied Behavior Analysis; Member of Board of Editors, several professional publications including: Journal of Consulting and Clinical Psychology, 1979–. *Publications include:* Books in Press: Co-editor, Conceptual Foundations of Behavioral Assessment; Co-author. The Scientist-Practitioner. *Contributions to:* Numerous professional journals, etc. *Memberships:* AAAS; Sigma Xi; American Psychological Association, Division 12, Fellow, Division 25; Association for Behavior Analysis. *Address:* Department of Psychology, University of North Carolina et Greensboro, Greensboro, NC 27412, USA.

HAYNES, Brian, b. 2 Apr. 1939, Shrewsbury, England. Television/Journalist. *Education:* Associate, Royal College of Art. *Publications:* Spyship (with Tom Keene), 1980; Sky Shroud (with Tom Keene), 1981; Posers Guide (with Sue Read), 1985. *Contributions to:* Sunday Times Magazine; Observer Magazine. *Literary Agent:* Julian Freidmann, Blake/Friedmann. *Address:* 106 Hurlingham Road, London SW6, England.

HAYNES, David Michael, b. 8 Nov. 1940, Subiaco, Western Australia, Australia. Chartered Secretary. *Education:* ACIS. *Literary Appointments:* Founding Director, J H Haynes and Company; Finance director and Company Secretary, Haynes Publishing Group PLC. *Address:* Haynes Publishing Group PLC, Sparkford, near Yeovil, Somerset BA22 7JJ, England.

HAYS, Howard H, b. 2 June 1917, Chicago, Illinois, USA. Editor & Publisher. m. Helen Cunningham, 27 May 1947, Riverside, California, USA, 2 sons. *Education:* BA, Stanford University, 1939; LLB, Harvard University, 1942. *Contributor to:* Bulletin of the American Society of Newspaper Editors; Riverside Press-Enterprise. *Address:* Press-Enterprise Company, 3512–14th Street, Riverside, CA 92501, USA.

HAYTER, Alethea, b. 1911, Cairo, Egypt. Former British Council Representative and Cultural Attache. *Education:* MA, University of Oxford. *Publications:* Mrs Browning: A Poet's Work and Its Setting, 1962; A Sultry Month: Scenes of London Literary Life in 1846, 1965; Elizabeth Barrett Browning, 1965; Opium and the Romantic Imagination, 1968; Horatio's Version, 1972; A Voyage in Vain, 1973; Fitzgerald to His Friends: Selected Letters of Edward Fitzgerald, 1979. *Contributor to:* Sunday Times; Times Saturday Review; Times Literary Supplement; New Statesman; History

Today; Arield. *Honours:* W H Heinemann Prize, RSL for, Mrs Browning: A Poet's Work and Its Setting; Rose Mary Crawhay Prize, British Academy for, Opium and the Romantic Imagination; OBE. *Memberships:* FRSL; Society of Authors, Committee of Management, 1975–79. *Address:* 22 Aldebert Terrace, London SW8 1BJ, England.

HAYTHORNTHWAITE, Philip John, b. 22 April 1951, Colne, Lancashire, England. Company Director; Author. *Publications:* Uniforms of the Napoleonic Wars, 1973, latest edition, 1985; Uniforms of Waterloo, 1975, latest edition, 1983; Uniforms of the American Civil War, 1975, latest edition, 1985; World Uniforms and Battles 1815–50-, 1976; Uniforms of the Retreat from Moscow, 1976, latest edition, 1977; Uniforms of the Peninsular War, 1978; Weapons and Equipment of the Napoleonic Wars, 1979; Uniforms of the French Revolutionary Wars, 1981; Uniforms of 1812, 1982; Napoleon's Line Infantry, 1983; Napoleon's Light Infantry, 1983; The English Civil War: An Illustrated Military History, 1983, latest edition, 1985; Napoleon's Guard Infantry: Part I, 1984; Napoleon's Guard Infantry: Part II, 1985; Civil War Soldiers, 1985; The Alamo and War of Texan Independence, forthcoming 1986; Austrian Troops of the Napoleonic Wars: Infantry, forthcoming, 1986; Austrian Troops of the Napoleonic Wars: Cavalry, Forthcoming, 1986; The Boer War, forthcoming, 1986. *Contributions to:* numerous historical, antiquarian, military history publications in UK and USA including journal of Society for Army Historical Research. *Address:* Park Hill, Parrock Road, Barrowford, Nelson, Lancashire BB9 6QP, England.

HAZEN, Robert M, b. 1 Nov. 1948, New York, USA. Research Scientist. m. Margaret Hindle, 9 Aug. 1969, Ridgewood, New Jersey, 1 son, 1 daughter. *Education:* BS, SM, MIT, 1971; PhD, Harvard University, 1975. *Literary Appointments:* Associate Editor, American Mineralogist; Associate Editor, Geophysical Research Letters; Editorial Consultant, George Allen and Unwin. *Publications:* American Geological Literature, 1979; The Poetry of Geology, 1982; Comparative Crystal Chemistry, 1982; Wealth Inexhaustible, 1985. *Contributions to:* More than 90 articles in periodicals such as Science; Nature; Scientific American; American Scientist; Physical Review. *Honour:* Mineralogical Society of America Award, 1982. *Address:* Carnegie Institution of Washington, Geophysical Laboratory, 2801 Upton Street NW, Washington, DC 20008, USA.

HAZLEHURST, Cameron, b. 12 Oct. 1941, Harrogate, England. Historian. *Education:* BA, Honours, University of Melbourne, Australia, 1963; DPhil, University of Oxford, England, 1969. *Publications:* Politicans at War, July 1914 to May 1915, 1971; Menzies Observed, 1979. *Contributor to:* Various publications including: The Times; The Sunday Times; Times Higher Educational Supplement, (Contributing Editor, to 1972); The Observer (Historical Correspondent 1970–71); New Statesman; History; English Historical Review; Paladin History of England, (Advisory Editor); Series Research Consultant, BBC TV, British Empire Series, 1968–72, ABC TV Mastermind, 1977–82, Close Up, 1983. *Memberships:* FRSL; FRHist S; FRSA. *Literary Agents:* Hilary Rubinstein; A P Watt & Son. *Address:* 8 Hunter St, Yarraluma, ACT 2600, Australia.

HAZLITT, Henry, b. 28 Nov. 1894, USA. Editor & Author. m. Frances S Kanes. *Education:* City College of New York, USA. *Literary Appointments include:* Wall Street Journal, 1913–16; Financial Staff, New York Evening Post, 1916–18; Financial Editor, New York Evening Mail, 1921–23; Editorial Writer, New York Herald, 1923–24, The Sun, 1924–25; Literary Editor, The Sun, 1925–29; The Nation 1930–33; Editor, American Mercury, 1933–34; Editorial Staff, New York Times, 1934–46; Business Tides for Newsweek, 1946–66; Co-founder & Co-editor (with J Chamberlain), The Freeman, 1950–52; Editor in Chief, 1953–; Columnist, Los Angeles Times Syndicate, 1966–69. *Major Publications include:* Thinking as a Science, 1916,

1969; The Anatomy of Criticism, 1933; A New Constitution Now, 1942, 1974; Economics in One Lesson, 1946, 1979; Time Will Run Back, 1951, 1966; The Failure of the New Economics: An Analysis of the Keynesian Fallacies, 1959, 1984; The Foundations of Morality, 1964, 1972; Man vs The Welfare State, 1969; The Conquest of Poverty, 1973; The Inflation Crisis & How to Resolve it, 1978; From Bretton Woods to World Inflation, 1984. *Honours:* Honorary Degrees: D Litt; Grove City College, Pennsylvania, 1958; LL D, Bethany College, West Virginia, 1961; ScD, Universidad Francisco Marroquin (Guatemala), 1976. *Address:* Bethel-Springvale Inn, 500 Albany Post Road, Croton-on-Hudson, NY 10520, USA.

HEAD, Bessie Amelia, b. 6 July 1937, Pietermaritzburg, Republic of South Africa. m. 1 Sep. 1961, Cape Town, divorced. 1 son. *Education:* Primary Teaching Certificate. *Publications:* When Rain Clouds Gather, novel, 1966; Maru, novel, 1970; A Question of Power, novel, 1973; The Collector of Treasures, short stories, 1977; Serowe! Village of the Rain Wind, social life, 1983; A Bewitched Crossroad, novel, 1984. *Literary Agent:* John Johnson, Clerkenwell House, 45/47 Clerkenwell Green, London EC1R OHT, England. *Address:* PO Box 15, Serowe, Botswana.

HEAL, Jeanne, b. 25 May 1917, Cambridge, England. Journalist; Author; Graphologist; Printer. *Education:* Beneden School; Ecole du Louvre, Paris, France; Architectural Association School, London; MSc. *Publications:* Jeanne Heal's Book of Careers for Girls, 1955; A Thousand and One Australians, 1959; New Zealand Journey, 1963; You and Your Handwriting, 1973. *Contributor to:* Picture Post; Sunday Empire News; Sunday Graphic; Sydney Morning Herald, Australia; various United Kingdom National Newspapers and Magazines. *Address:* Grey Walls, Aldeburgh, Suffolk, England.

HEALE, Jeremy Peter Wingfield, b. 28 June 1937, Burnham-on-Sea, England. Schoolmaster; Author. *Education:* MA Brasenose College, Oxford University, 1963; Higher Diploma in Education, with Distinction, University of Cape Town, Republic of South Africa, 1980. *Literary Appointments:* Managing Director, Fenrose Limited (Specialist publishers), 1973–75; General Publications Planner, Maskew Miller Limited, 1982. *Publications:* The Teacher's Relief Book, 1973; Far Fierce Hour, 1974; School Quad, 1974; They Made This Land, 1981; Southern African Booklist, 1983; Young Africa Booklist, 1985. *Contributions to:* Book Reviews: Sunday Times, Johannesburg; Fair Lady, Cape Town; Frontline Books, Johannesburg; Bookchat, Book Group newsletter, Somerset West. *Memberships:* Individual Member, International Board on Books for Young People; Founder, Editor, Jay Heale's Childrens Book Group, 1976–; International Poets, Playwrights, Editors, Essayists and Novelists. *Address:* Somerset House School, Somerset West, 7130, Republic of South Africa.

HEATER, Derek Benjamin, b. 31 Nov. 1931, Sydenham, England. Writer. m. (1) Joyce Dean, 1956, 1 son, 1 daughter. (2) Gwyneth Owen, 1982. *Education:* BA (Hons), History, Postgraduate Certificate in Education, University of London, England. *Publications:* Political Ideas in the Modern World, 1960, 4th edition, 1971; Order and Rebellion; A History of Europe in the 18th Century, 1964; The Cold War, 1965, 2nd edition, 1970; Editor, The Teaching of Politics, 1969; World Affairs, (with Gwyneth Owen), 1972, 3rd edition 1978; Contemporary Political Ideas, 1974, 1978; Britain and the Outside World, 1976; Essays on Political Education, (with Bernard Crick), 1977; Peace and War since 1945, 1979, 2nd edition 1980; Essays on Contemporary Studies, 1979; World Studies: Education for International Understanding in Britain, 1980; Political Education in Flux, (co-Editor with Judith A Gillespie), 1981; Our World This Century, 1982, 2nd editon, 1986; Human Rights Education in Schools, 1984; Peace Through Education: the Contribution of CEWC, 1984; Our World Today, 1985. *Membership:* Fellow, Royal Society of Arts. *Address:* 3 The Rotyngs, Rottingdean, Brighton BN2 7DX, England.

HEATH, Beth LaPointe, b. 1 June 1906, Boston, Massachusetts. Writer. m. Corey A Heath. *Appointments:* Nurse; Demonstrator of Make-up; Handwriting Analysis; Reading poetry to children in public schools, Hudson. *Publications:* Time of Singing, 1966; Pixie Places, 1979; Anthologies; Golden Quill, 1962, 1966, 1968, 1969, 1970, 1971; Sea to Sea in Song, 1966, 1967, 1969, 1971, 1972, 1975; Jewels on a Willow Tree, 1966; Melodies from a Jade Harp, 1968; Windsong II, 1978. *Contributor to:* Expanding Horizons; Author-Poet; New England Review; Midwest Chaparral; Maj Haiju; Modern Haiku; Haiku World; The Green World; American Poets; Jeans Journal; Poems of America. *Honours:* Recipient, numerous literary honours and awards. *Memberships:* Massachusetts State Poetry Society; National Federation of State Poetry Societies. *Address:* 29 Tower St, Hudson, MA 01749, USA.

HEATH, Edward (Richard George) (Right Honorable), b. 1916, Broadstairs, Kent, England. Member of Parliament, Bexley, Sidcup; Former Prime Minister, UK and Leader of the Conservative Party. *Education:* Balliol College, Oxford University. *Publications include:* One Nation: A Tory Approach to Social Problems, co-author, 1950; Old New Horizons, 1970; Sailing – A Course of My Life, 1975; Music – A Joy for Life, 1976; Travels – People and Places in My Life, 1977; Carols – The Joy of Christmas, 1977. *Honours include:* MBE, Honorary Degrees: Oxford; Bradford; Westminster College, Salt Lake City, Utah, USA; Paris-Sorbonne, France; Honorary Kent University DCL, England, 1985. Visiting Chubb Fellow, Yale University and Montgomery Fellow, Dartmouth College, USA; Lecturer several universities; Guest conductor, various orchestras; Numerous yachting trophies. *Memberships include:* Past Chairman, Gala Concert Conductor, London Symphony Orchestra Trust; President and Past Tour Conductor, European Economic Community Youth Orchestra; Independent Commission on International Development Issues. *Address:* c/o House of Commons, Westminster, London SW1, England.

HEATH, Richard John, b. 29 Oct. 1934, Western Australia. Freelance Writer; Public Relations Writer. m. Eva Heath, 1 Aug. 1962, Melbourne, 1 son. *Education:* Study, Management, Melbourne (4 years of 6-year course). *Literary Appointments:* Editor, Shell Times, 1964, Imagineer, 1966; Chief of Editorial Staff, Peter Isaacson Publications Australia, 1970; Editor, Insurance Broker, 1983. *Contributions to:* Asia Pacific Travel; The Convention; Rydge's; Marketing World; In-Marketing; Insurance Broker; The Age; Sun News-Pictorial; Quorum; Open House; Various other Australian periodicals, ad-hoc basis. *Honours:* Best In-House-Produced Marketing Magazine (Imagineer), 1968, 1969; Best Business Newspaper, International Travel, 1970. *Address:* 2 Jocelyn Court, Doncaster East, Victoria 3109, Australia.

HEATHCOTT, Mary, b. 30 Sep. 1914, Manchester, England. Journalist. m. E A Keegan, 10 Sep. 1938, London, 1 son, 1 daughter. *Literary Appointments:* London Evening News; Singapore Free Press; MOI; Time and Tide; John Herling's Labor Letter, Washington, USA. *Publications:* If Today Be Sweet; Island of the Heart; Love Be Wary; The Day of Return; Her Part of the House; Hide my Heart; Thief of My Heart; Never Doubt Me; Shadow of a Star; Change my Heart; Take-Over; Girl in a Mask; The Divided House; The Long Journey Home; I Have Three Sons; That Summer; Surety for a Stranger; The Pimpernel Project; The Silver Girl; April Promise; Grandma Tyson's Legacy; Villa of Flowers. *Address:* Cockenskell, Blawith, Ulverston, Cumbria, England.

HEATON, Eric William, b. 15 Oct. 1920, Bradford, England. Clergyman; College Dean. *Education:* MA, Christ's College, Cambridge. *Publications:* His Servants the Prophets, 1949, revised as, The Old Testament

Prophets, 1958, further revision, 1977; Everyday Life in Old Testament Times, 1956; The Book of Daniel, 1956; Commentary on the Sunday Lessons, 1959; The Hebrew Kingdoms, 1968; Solomon's New Men, 1974. *Contributor to:* Journal of Theology Studies. *Honours:* Honorary Felow, St John's College, Oxford, 1979; Honorary Fellow, Christ's College, Cambridge, 1983. *Address:* The Deanery, Christ Church, Oxford OX1 1DP, England.

HEBALD, Carol, b. 6 July 1934, New York City, USA. Writer. *Education:* BA, 1969, City College of the City University of New York; MFA, 1971, University of Iowa. *Literary Appointments:* Instructor of Creative Writing for Theatre Artists, New York University, 1975–76; Visiting Lecturer in Creative Writing, University of Wisconsin at Madison, 1976–77; Associate Professor of Creative Writing, University of Kansas, 1977–84; Visiting Professor, Creative Writing, Warsaw University, 1981–82. *Contributions to:* Dekalb Literary Arts Journal; Free Inquiry; Our World's Best Lived Poems; Our World's Greatest Poems; Ararat; Parthenon Poetry Anthology; Cottonwood Review, and numerous others. *Honours:* Graduated Phi Beta Kapa, Magna Cum Laude; William Bradley Otis Fellowship; Elias Lieberman Poetry Award; Ralph Weinberg Poetry Award; Theodore Goodman Short Story Award; Teaching and Writing Fellowship at University of Iowa; Utica College Creative Writing Grant, 1974, 1975; Residences at MacDowell and Millay Colonies; Creative Writing Grant, University of Kansas Research Fund, 1978; Residences at Virginia Center for the Creative Arts, 1981, 1983, 1984; Finalist in one-act play contest for, Last Evening at Pitzer's; Residence at Edward Albee Foundation, 1984. *Memberships:* Poetry Society of America; Phi Beta Kappa. *Literary Agent:* Jeanne Drewsen. *Address:* c/o West 5E, 132 West 28th Street, New York, NY 10001, USA.

HECKLER, Jonellen Beth, b. 28 Oct. 1943, Pittsburgh, Pennsylvania, USA. Novelist. m. Louis Roy Heckler, 17 Aug. 1968, Pittsburgh, 1 son. *Education:* BA, English Literature, University of Pittsburgh, 1965. *Publication:* Safekeeping, 1983; A Fragile Peace, 1986. *Contributor to:* 8 poems, 9 short stories, Ladies Home Journal, USA, 1975–83; 15 songs, lyricist, published, 1979–84. *Membership:* Authors Guild. *Literary Agent:* Elizabeth Trupin, Jet Literary Associates, New York. *Address:* 5562 Pernod Drive SW, Fort Myers, FL 33907, USA.

HEDDEN, Jay W, b. 13 Oct. 1920, Dalton, Illinois, USA. Editor. m. Honey G Mais, 7 Aug. 1942, Portland, Maine, 1 daughter. *Publications:* How to Build Mediterranean Furniture; Successful Living Rooms; Successful Baths; Modern Plumbing for Old and New Houses; How to Solarize Your Home; Heating, Cooling and Ventilation; The Dremel Guide to Compact Power Tools. *Contributions to:* Popular Mechanics, Assistant editor, 1953–59; Workbench, Editor, 1959–. *Address:* 3911 West 100 Terrace, Leawood, KS 66207, USA.

HEDIN, Mary Ann, b. 3 Aug. 1929, Minneapolis, Minnesota, USA. Writer; Professor, English. m. Roger Willard Hedin, 3 sons, 1 daughter. *Education:* BS, University of Minnesota; MA, University of California, San Francisco. *Appointments:* Fellow, Yaddo, 1974; Writer in Residence, Robinson Jeffers Tor House Foundation, 1984–85. *Publications:* Fly Away Home, 1980; Direction, 1983. *Contributor to:* McCalls; Red Book; Southwest Review; South Dakota Review; Descant; O Henry Prize Short Stories; Best American Short Stories; Poems in, Shenandoah; South; Perspective; World Order. *Honours:* John H McGinnis Memorial Award, 1979; Iowa School of Letters Award for Short Fiction, 1979. *Memberships:* Authors Guild; PEN; American Poetry Society. *Address:* 182 Oak Avenue, San Anselmo, CA 94960, USA.

HEDLEY, (Gladys) Olwen, b. 28 Apr. 1912, London, England. Author. *Publications:* Round and About Windsor and District, (Oxley and Son), 1948; Windsor Castle, (Robert Hale), 1967, 2nd edition, 1972; Royal Palaces, (Robert Hale), 1972; Queen Charlotte, (John Murray), 1975; The Queen's Silver Jubilee, (Pitkin Pictorials), 1977; A Child's Guide to Windsor Castle, 1979; The Royal Foundation of Saint Katharine, 1984; Editor, The Court Journals of Fanny Burney, 1786–1791, 1986. *Contributor to:* Times: History Today; Annual Report of Society of Friends of St George's and the Descendants of the Knights of the Garter; Berkshire Archaeology journal; 1st Windsor Literary Arts Festival, 1977. *Memberships:* Fellow, The Royal Society of Literature, 1975. *Literary Agent:* John Johnson. *Address:* 15 Denny Crescent, London SE11 4UY, England.

HEDLEY, Leslie Woolf, b. 23 Mar. 1921, Newark, New Jersey, USA. Writer; Editor; Publisher; Consultant. m. Koky Olson, 28 Nov. 1946, Los Angeles. *Education:* PhD. *Publications include:* The Edge of Insanity, poems, 1948; Selected Poems, 1953; Zero Hour, poems, 1957; Motions & Notions, aphorisms, 1961; Abraxas & Other Poems, 1961; On My Way to the Cemetery, poems, 1981; The Day Japan Bombed Pearl Harbor & Other Stories, 1984; Confessions, aphorisms, 1984; XYZ & Other Stories, 1985. *Contributions to:* Numerous periodicals including New York Times; Times Literary Supplement, UK; Minority ofO ne; San Francisco Examiner; Kansas Quarterly; Meanjin; Malahat Review; Colorado Quarterly; San Jose Studies; Southwest Review; etc. *Address:* c/o Exile Press, P O Box 1768, Novato, CA 94948, USA.

HEDMAN, Kaj William, b. 9 July 1953, Gamlakarleby, Finland. Writer, Free-lance Journalist. *Education:* Studied History, Swedish Correspondence Institute in Finland and University of Helsinki. *Major Pubications:* Morgonen har vaknat, 1977; En verklig dröm, 1980 (poems). *Contributor to:* Österbottningen, 1981–, Horisont, 1983– (Freelance literary critic); Kyrkpressen, 1984–; Hufvudstadbladet; and others. *Honours:* Swedish Culture Foundation in Finland Scholarship; Scholarship, Cultural Commission of Vasa Country, Finland. *Membership:* Swedish Writers Association in Finland, 1980–. *Literary Agent:* Publisher Holger Schildts förlag. *Address:* Rosundsvägen 14, SF–67700 Karleby, Finland.

HEFFER, Eric Samuel, b. 12 Jan. 1922, Hertford, England. Member of Parliament. *Publication:* The Class Struggle in Parliament, 1972. *Contributions to:* New Society; New Statesman; Tribune; New Left Review; New Politics; Politics Quarterly; Spectator; The Times; Guardian; Liverpool Daily Post; Sunday Times; Sunday Observer; and others. *Address:* House of Commons, London SW1A OAA, England.

HEFFERNAN, Thomas Carroll, b. 19 Aug. 1939, Hyannis, Massachusetts, USA. University Lecturer, English, Philosophy. m. Nancy Elizabeth Iler, 15 July 1972, Vineyard Haven, divorced 1977. *Education:* MA, English Literature, University of Manchester, 1963; BA, English, Boston College, 1961. *Appointments:* Poet in Residence, 3 Colleges, North Carolina Dept, of Community Colleges, 1977–81; Poet in the Schools, North Carolina Dept of Public Instruction, 1973–77. *Publications:* Mobiles, 1973; A Poem is a Smile You Can Hear, Editor, 1976; A Narrative of Jeremy Bentham, 1978; The Liam Poems, 1981; City Renewing Itself, 1983. *Contributor to:* Numerous journals, magazines and newspapers. *Honours:* Dillard Award, 1973, 1975; Literary Fellowship, National Endowment for the Arts, 1977; Crucible Award, Poetry, 1977, 1979; Gordon Barber Memorial Award, Poetry Society of America, 1979. *Memberships:* Poetry Society of America; MLA; Poetry Society of North Carolina; Poetry Centre South, Board Member; Greensboro Writers Club, Past President. *Address:* University of Maryland, Asian Division, Box 100, APO San Francisco, CA 96328, USA.

HEFFRON, Dorris M, b. 18 Oct. 1944, Canada. Novelist. m. D L Gauer, 29 Oct. 1980, Toronto, 1 son, 3 daughters. *Education:* Honours BA; MA. *Literary Appointments:* Tutor and Lecturer, Oxford University External Studies, England, 1970–80; Tutor, The Open

University, 1972–78. *Publications:* A Nice Fire and Some Moonpennies, 1971; Crusty Crossed, 1976; Rain and I, 1982. *Contributions to:* Queen's Quarterly. *Honour:* Canada Council Arts Grant, 1974. *Memberships:* Authors Society; Ontario Representative, Writer's Union of Canada; Executive Committee, PEN Canada. *Literary Agent:* Sheila Watson, Watson Little Limited. *Address:* 202 Riverside Drive, Toronto, Ontario, Canada M6S 4A9.

HEGELER, Sten, b. 28 Apr. 1923, Copenhagen, Denmark. Psychoanalyst and Psychologist. *Education:* Candidate for Psychology, University of Copenhagen, 1953. *Major Publications include:* Peter & Caroline; Fem sma matroser; Jorn pa Kostskole; Lise; i pension; Choosing Toys for Children; What Everybody Should Know About AIDS; On Selenium; (co-author with I Hegeler) An ABZ of Love; Ask Inge & Sten; World's Best Slimming Diet; On Being Lonesome; XYZ of Love; Living is Loving. *Contributor to:* Politiken; Aktuelt; Info; Editor, Taenk (Danish Consumer Magazine). *Memberships include:* Danish Psychological Association; Danish Journalist Association; Danish Authors Association. *Honour:* Recipient (with wife) PH-Fund 1970. *Address:* Frederiksberg Alle 25, DK-1820 Copenhagen V, Denmark.

HEIKKINEN, Helge Birger, b. 20 Dec. 1910, Helsinki, Finland. Ship's Captain; Author. m. Margit Viola Svensson, 2 May 1941, Rauma, 3 sons, 1 daughter. *Education:* National Nautical College, Rauma; Journalism, College, Oslo, Norway, University of Helsinki. *Appointments:* Captain, Sailing Vessels, Steamers, Motor Vessels and Naval Vessels, 20 years; Assistant Instructor of Limnologie, University of Helsinki, 5 years; Author, 1950–. *Publications Include:* Sailing Round Cape Horn, 1947; Navigation 1958; 1981; On Dangerous Waters, 1960; The Unknown Sailor, 1975; Finnish Deep Sea Fishing, 1981; etc. *Contributor to:* Approximately 1000 articles in professional journals and magazines. *Honours:* Suomalaisen Kiriallisuudden edistamisvarojen valtuuskunta 1971; Par le Merit, France, 1980; World War II decorations. *Memberships:* World Ship Society, London; Finnish Society of Authors; many other organisations. *Literary Agent:* WSOY. *Address:* EkändaVägen 31, 02730 Esbo 73, Finland.

HEIL, Ruth, b. 25 Jan. 1947, Rohrbach, Germany. Former Registered Medical Nurse; Writer; Lecturer; Counsellor. m. Hans-Joachim Heil, 5 Jan. 1967, Mannheim, 4 sons, 6 daughters. *Education:* Diploma, Registered Medical Nurse; Qualified, Marriage Counselling, Family Life Mission. *Publications:* Du in mir; My Child Within; Das seltsame Gasthaus; Un restaurant pas comme les autres; Was schwach ist vor der Welt, with her father Ludwig Katzenmaier. *Contributor to:* Editor, German, English and French Newsletters, Family Life Mission. *Honour:* Recipient, Prize, Contest of Christian Poets. *Literary Agent:* Editions Trobisch, West Germany. *Address:* Ortsstrasse 1, 6781 Fischbach/Dahn, Federal Republic of Germany.

HEILMAN, Robert Bechtold, b. 18 July 1906, Philadelphia, Pennsylvania, USA. University Professor; Critic. m. Ruth Delavan Champlin, 31 July 1935, Cortland, 2 sons. *Education:* AB, Lafayette College, 1927; AM, Ohio State University, 1930; AM, 1931, PhD, 1935, Harvard University. *Appointments include:* Instructor, English, Ohio University, 1928–30; University of Maine, 1931–33, 1934–35; Instructor, 1935–36, Assistant Professor, 1936–42, Associate Professor, 1942–46, Professor, 1946–48, English, Louisiana State University; Professor, English, University of Washington, 1948–75. *Publications:* America in English Fiction 1760–1800, 1937; This Great Stage : King Lear, 1948; Magic in the Web: Othello, 1956; Tragedy and Melodrama, 1968; The Iceman, the Arsonist, and the Troubled Agent, 1973; The Charliad, (light verse), 1973; The Ghost on the Ramparts and Other Essays in the Humanities, 1974; Editor, 2 Shakespeare Plays, 1964, 1966; Editor, Collection of Essays on shakespeare, 1984. *Contributor to:* Editorial

Board Member: Sewanee Review; Studies in the Novel; Poetry Northwest; Shakespeare Studies; Critical Quarterly; Contributed essays and reviews to various professional journals. *Honours:* Arizona Quarterly Essay Prize, 1956; Longwood Essay Prize, 1962; Explicator Prize, 1957; Christian Gauss Prize, 1978; Guggenheim Fellowships, 1964–72; Honorary Degrees, various Universities. *Memberships:* Philological Association of the Pacific Coast, President, 1959; Modern Language Association of America, Executive Council, 1966–70; Shakespeare Society of America, Trustee, 1977–80; Jane Austen Society of America; International Shakespeare Association. *Address:* 4554 45th Ave NE, Seattle, WA 98105, USA.

HEINEMANN, Katherine, b. 13 Aug. 1918, St Louis, Missouri, USA. Writer. m. (1) Morton D May, 30 Dec. 1937, St Louis, Missouri, (2) Sol Heinemann, MD, 8 July 1950, St Louis, Missouri. 2 sons, 1 daughter. *Education:* Bachelors 1950, Masters 1956, Washington University, St Louis, Missouri. *Publications:* Brandings, 1968; Some Inhuman Familiars, 1983. *Contributions to:* New York Times; University Review; Prairie Schooner; Southwest Review. *Honours:* Arts and Sciences Faculty Award, Washington University, 1950. *Membership:* PEN American Center. *Address:* 4252 Ridge Crest Drive, El Paso, TX 79902, USA.

HEINEN, Hugo, b. 7 Mar. 1944, Utrecht, The Netherlands. Dramaturge, writer. *Education:* Dutch and Theater Scholarship. *Plays:* A Dog's Life; Lermontov; The Marriage; The Blurred Mirror; Weekend; Dubbel Spy; The Little Titans; Pickpockets; Sanne; The Gideons Bunch; The Execution. *Musicals:* Adapted, The Club, and, Rocky Horror Show. Film: That Must be Possible. *Translations:* Numerous stage and television plays, musicals and operas. *Literary Awards:* Silver Dove for the Best Drama Production, Monte Carlo. *Membership:* Board of the VVL (Union for Literature). *Address:* Valeriusterras 3, 1075 Bk Amsterdam, The Netherlands.

HEINRICH, Bernd, b. 19 Apr. 1940, Germany. Professor of Zoology. m. Margaret Heinrich, 1 son, 1 daughter. *Education:* BA, 1964, MS, 1966, University of Maine, USA; PhD, Zoology, University of California, Los Angeles, 1970. *Appointments:* Teacher, Research Assistant, University of California, Los Angeles, 1966–70; Assistant Professor, 1971–75, Associate Professor, 1975–78, Professor, 1978–80, Entomology, University of California, Berkeley; Professor, Zoology, University of Vermont, 1980–. *Publications:* Bumblebee Economics, 1979; Biology, co-author, 1979; Insect Thermoregulation, 1981; In a Patch of Fireweed, 1984. *Contributor to:* Numerous scientific journals. *Honours:* Guggenheim Fellow, 1976–77; Fellow, AAAS, 1978; Winship Award, 1984. *Address:* Dept of Zoology, University of Vermont, Burlington, VT 05405, USA.

HEISSERER, Andrew Jackson, b. 2 June 1935, St Louis, Missouri, USA. Professor of Ancient History. m. Margaret Lloyd, 29 May 1964, 1 son. *Education:* BS, History, 1958; MA, History, 1962, St Louis University; PhD, Classics and History, University of Cincinnati, 1971. *Literary Appointments:* Dubourg High School, St Louis, Missouri, 1960–62; Instructor, Texas Woman's University, Denton, Texas, 1962–64; Part-time Instructor, Xavier University, Cincinnati, Ohio, 1967–70; Assistant Professor of Ancient History, 1970–79, Associate Professor of Ancient History, 1979–, University of Oklahoma; Curator of Classical Art & Archaeology, Stovall Museum, University of Oklahoma 1981–. *Publications:* Alexander the Great and the Greeks: The Epigraphic Evidence, 1980; Editor and Contribution, A Catalogue of the Classical Antiquities in the Stovall Museum, University of Oklahoma (forthcoming). *Contributions to:* Classical Texts and Their Traditions, 1984; The Monetary Pact Between Mytilene and Phokaia, 1984; Gerion 4, 1986; Historia; Hesperia; Zeitschrift fur Papyrologie und Epigraphik, 1981; La Parola del Passato, 1981. *Honours:* Outstanding Senior Award, St Louis University Senior Year, 1958; AMOCO Teaching Award, University of Oklahoma 1977; Associates' Distinguished Lecturer at

University of Oklahoma, 1984–85; Various Researcxh Grants. *Memberships:* Classical Association of England; American Association of Ancient Historians; American Philological Association; American Classical League; Classical Association of the Middle West and South (USA). *Address:* Department of History, 455 W Lindsey, Room 406, University of Oklahoma, Norman, OK 73019, USA.

HEITZMANN, William Ray, b. 12 Feb. 1948, Hoboken, New Jersey, USA. Professor; Mens Basketball Coach. *Education:* BS, Villanova University; MAT, University of Chicago; PhD, University of Delaware; Student, Northwestern University, California State University. Professor, Villanova University, Pennsylvania. *Publications include:* Minicourses, 1977; Opportunities in Marine and Maritime Careers, 1979; Using the Newspaper in the Classroom, 1979; Opportunities in Sports and Athletics, 1980, 85; Political Cartoons, 1980; Educational Games and Simulations, 2nd edition, 1984; Opportunities in Sports Medicine, 1984. *Contributions to:* Consulting Editor, Social Studies; Contributing Editor, Sea History, and Beachcomber. *Honour:* Outstanding Service Award, National Council for the Social Studies, 1980. *Memberships:* Past President, Pennsylvania Council for the Social Studies. *Address:* 132 Sycamore Road, Havertown, PA 19083, USA.

HELBO, André, b. 25 Sep. 1947, Brussels, Belgium. Professor. *Education:* Dr of Philos and Letters. *Publications include:* Michel Butor vers une littérature do signe, 1975; Sémiologie de la représentation, 1975; L'enjeu du discours, lecture de Sartre, 1978; Publr: Complexe-P U F; Le champ sémiologique. Perspectives internationales (Complexe) 1979; Sémiologie des Messages Sociaux (Edilig), 1983; Les mots et les gestes. Essai sur le théâtre (Pulille), 1983; Editor: Journal Degrés. *Contributions to:* Co-editor, Zeitschrift für Semiotik; Cahiers roumains d'études litéraires etc. *Memberships include:* President, Association Internationale de recherche et de sémiologie dans le domaine du spectacle; PEN. *Address:* Pl.C. Meunier 2, 1180 Brussels, Belgium.

HELIN, Hannu Aukusti, b. 23 Apr. 1944, Kuopio, Finland. m. Anja Tuominen, 29 Oct. 1984, Helsinki. *Education:* Degree, Theoretical Philosophy. *Publications:* Poetry: Tarisen maailman Ryljessa, 1978; Niin paljon heikkoa voimaa, 1979; Tanaan on houmenna eilen, 1981; Ruusun varjossa, 1984; Novel, Sanna Sannaseih, 1980. *Honour:* Literary Award, J H Erkko, 1978. *Membership:* Finnish Society of Authors. *Address:* Helsinginkatu 23 A 15, 00510 Helsinki, Finland.

HELKA, Leena Kyllikki, b. 29 Dec. 1924, Rauma, Finland. Teacher; Writer. 1 son. *Education:* MA, University of Helsinki, 1951. *Publications:* In Swedish: 4 Books of Poetry, 1960–65; In Finnish: Books for Children and Teenagers, Children's Encyclopedia, short stories, 1951–78; A Novel: The Seven Words of Edith, 1982. *Honour:* Nortamo Prize, Finland, 1978. *Address:* Valtakatu 30 A 53, 28100 Pori, Finland.

HELLBERG, Hans-Eric, b. 11 May 1927, Borlänge, Sweden. Writer. *Publications:* Jan får en vän, 1958; Morfars Maria, 1969; Martins Maria, 1970; Jag är Maria Jag, 1971; Alskade Maria, 1974; Kram, 1973; Puss, 1975; Love Love Love, 1977; Jag är Maria, film, 1979; Busungen, 1979; Pojken som hade tur, 1983; Osynlig närvaro, 1984; Det är jag som är Gry, 1984; Flickan som dog, 1986 with Ulf Nilsson and Hans Erik Engqvist. *Honours:* Nils Holgersson Plaketten, 1971; Certificate of Honour for Bogserbaten, 1971; Astrid-Lindgrenpriset, 1975; Diploma, Swedish Academy of Detection, 1976. *Address:* Vasagatan 12 a, 781 00 Borlange, Sweden.

HELLE, Steven James, b. 9 Nov. 1954, Manchester, Iowa, USA. Associate Professor. m. Susan Lynn Hanes, 12 Aug. 1978, Mason City, Iowa. *Education:* BS 1976, MA 1979, JD 1979, University of Iowa. *Contributions*

to: Duke Law Journal I; DePaul Law Review; Journalism Quarterly. *Address:* 119 Gregory Hall, 810 S Wright Street, University of Illinois, Urbana, IL 61801, USA.

HELLER, Michael David, b. 11 May 1937, Poet; Writer. m. 1 child. *Education:* BS, Engineering, Rennselaer Polytechnic Institute; Philosophy courses, New York University. *Literary Appointments:* Chief Technical Writer, Norelco, 1963–65; Freelance writer, 1965–67; Instructor, New York University, 1967–. *Publications:* Accidental Center, 1972; Two Poems, 1970; Figures of Speaking, 1977; Knowledge, 1979; Convictions Net of Branches, Criticism, 1985. *Contributions to:* The Paris Review; The Nation; Chelsea; Sumac; Caterpillar; Extensions; Equal Time; The Park; The Young American Writers, 1967; Inside Outer Space, 1970; Open Poetry, 1973; Caterpillar Anthology, 1971; The New York Times Sunday Book Review. *Honours:* Coffey Poetry Prize, New School for Social Research, 1964; New York State CAPS Fellow in Poetry. *Memberships:* PEN; Poets and Writers. *Address:* PO Box 981, Stuyvesant Station, New York City, NY 10009, USA.

HELLER, Walter Wolfgang, b. 27 Sep. 1915, Buffalo, New York, USA. Regent's Professor of Economics, University of Minnesota. *Publications:* New Dimensions of Political Economy, 1966; Monetary versus Fiscal Policy, (co-author), 1969; Economic Growth and Environmental Quality: Collision or Co-Existence? 1973; The Economy: Old Myths and New Realities, 1976. *Contributions to:* American Economic Review; Wall Street Journal; Board of Economists; Time; Economics in the Public Service. *Honours:* LLD, Oberlin, 1964; Riponu, 1968, University of Wisconsin, 1969, Long Island University, 1968; LHD, Loyola University, 1970, Roosevelt University, 1976, Coe College, 1967; DLitt, Kenyon, 1965. *Address:* 2203 Folwell Street, St Paul, MN 55108, USA.

HELLERSTEIN, Kathryn Ann, b. 27 July 1952, Cleveland, Ohio, USA. Translator; Scholar; Critic; Assistant Professor. *Education:* PhD in English and American Literature, Stanford University, USA; MA in English and Poetry Writing, Stanford University, USA; BA in English, Brandeis University, USA. *Literary Appointments:* Assistant Professor of English, Wellesley College, Wellesley, Massachusetts, USA, 1982–86. *Publications:* Moyshe-Leyb's In New York: A Modern Yiddish Verse Narrative; In New York: A Selection (edited, translated and introduced by Kathryn Hellerstein); Translations of Yiddish poems in, American Yiddish Poetry; Women Poets in Yiddish; Yiddish Voices in American English. *Contributor to:* Kenyon Review; Partisan Review; Present Tense; Grove; Imagine; Midstream; Poetry; Networks; I That am Ever Stranger; Jewish Book Annual; Religion and Literature. *Literary Awards:* National Endowment for the Arts Literature Program Fellowship for Translators Grant, 1986; National Endowment for the Humanities Travel to Collections Grant, Summer 1985; Memorial Foundation for Jewish Culture Grant, 1982–83; Edith Mirrielees Fellowship in Creative Writing, Stanford University, 1974–75. *Memberships:* American Literary Translators Association; YIVO Institute for Jewish Research. *Address:* Department of English, Wellesley College, Wellesley, MA 02181, USA.

HELLWIG, Claes Peter, b. 1 Jan. 1951, Stockholm, Sweden. Dramaturg; Dramatic writer. m. Hilda Hellwig, 8 June 1976. *Education:* University of Stockholm; Dramaturg Diploma, Dramatiska Institutet. *Literary Appointments:* Svenska Riksteatern; Teater Aurora; Teacher in Dramaturgi, Dramatiska Institutet. *Publications:* Och mörkret täcker jorden, (And the Darkness covers the Earth); Den Osinliga Trädgården (The Invisible Garden); Våta Drömmar (Wet Dreams); Tivoli (Carnival). *Contributor to:* Nya Teatertidningen (New Theater Journal). *Literary Awards:* Swedish Arts Council, 1980, 1982, 1984; Andrew Sandrew Foundation, 1984; Goetheinstitut, 1984; Swedish Dramatic Writers Foundation, 1985. *Agent:* Folmer

Hansen Sthlm. *Address:* Västmannag. 53 113, 25, Stockholm, Sweden.

HELM, Peter James, b. 16 June 1916, Waterfoot, England. Teacher; Author. *Education:* MA, Cambridge University. *Publications:* Dead Men's Fingers, 1960; History of Europe, 1450–1660, 1961; Death Has a Thousand Entrances, 1963; Alfred the Great, 1963; Modern British History, 1813–1964, 1963; The Man With No Bones, 1966; Jeffreys, 1966; England Under the Yorkists and Tudors, 1471–1603, 1968; Exploring Prehistoric England, 1971; Exploring Roman Britain, 1975; Exploring Saxon and Norman England, 1976; Exploring Tudor England, 1981; The Brainpicker, 1981. *Contributor to:* Ambit: Archaeol, Journal; Time and Tide. *Address:* The Croft, Bradford-on-Tone, Taunton, Somerset TA4 1HW, England.

HELM-PIRGO, Marian, b. 25 Mar. 1897, Lwow, Poland. Architect. *Education:* Technical University of Lwow, 1918–20; Degree in Architecture, Technical University of Warsaw, 1925; Warsaw School of Fine Arts, 1926–28. *Publications:* (in English): Virgin Mary, Queen of Poland (historical essay), 1957, 2nd Edition, 1966; Royal Dragoons (historical novel), 1976; (in Polish, titles translated): Cartography and Military Use of the Terrain, 1928; The Legend of the Helm, 1931; The Grotto of Stradcz, 1932; For Raising the Standard of Architecture and Building Crafts, 1936; In Fetters and Fight, 1946; The Beginnings of Military Cartography in Restored Poland 1918–20, 1971. *Contributions to:* Journals in Poland, USA and Canada. *Honours:* First Prize, for architecture and planning, Association of Polish Town Planners, 1929 and Golden Cross of Merit, Government of Republic of Poland, 1939; Chivalric Cross, (for science and art), 1973 and Officers Cross, 1979, Polonia Restituta, Polish Government in Exile. *Memberships include:* Polish Institute of Arts and Sciences in America, Lit. and Art Section. *Address:* c/o Polish Institute of Arts and Sciences in America, 59 East 66th Street, New York, NY 10021, USA.

HELMINEN, Jussi, b. 7 Oct. 1947, Turku, Finland. Dramatist; Theatre Director. m. Tellervo Helminen, 25 Sep. 1973, 3 sons. *Education:* Finnish Theatre Academy. *Publications:* (Plays) The Drugstory, 1972; Hello World, 1973; The Numskulls, 1977; Yellowcloth, 1985, etc; (TV Plays) Mother Gets Married, 1973; Bigboy and the Boot, 1975; Hands, 1975; Mother's Difficult Age, 1983; Reflection, 1984; Smiley, 1984, etc. *Honours:* Finnish State drama Award, 1971, 1972; TV (Eurovision) Prix Jeunesse in Munich, 1974; TV (Intervision) Prix Donau, Bratislava, 1975; Tampere Theatre Summer Award, 1972, 1973. *Membership:* Finnish Dramatists Union. *Literary Agent:* Finnish Dramatists Union. *Address:* Oulu City Theatre, 90100 Oulu, Finland.

HELMLINGER, Trudy, b. 2 Jan. 1942, Seattle, Washington, USA. Psychotherapist. *Education:* BA 1967, Master's Social Work 1969, California State University, Sacramento; PhD Psychology, Professional School of Psychology, San Francisco, 1985. *Publications:* After You've Said Goodbye, 1977, revised edition 1982; Adoptions Archives Registry, 1985. *Contributions to:* New Woman; Working Woman. *Memberships:* American Society of Journalists and Authors; Author's League of North California; National Association of Social Workers; World Federation of Mental Health; Academy of Certified Social Workers. *Honours:* National Association of Social Workers Scholarships, 1967 and 1968. *Literary Agent:* Multimedia Product Development Inc. *Address:* 2740 Fulton Avenue 113, Sacramento, CA 95821, USA.

HELMREICH, William B, b. 25 Aug. 1943, Zurich, Switzerland. Professor. m. Helaine, 28 June 1970, New York City, 3 sons. *Education:* BA, Yershiva University; MA, PhD, Washington University, St Louis. *Literary Appointments:* Chairman, Department of Sociology, City College of New York, CUNY Graduate Centre. *Publications:* The Black Crusaders, 1973; Wake Up, Wake Up, To Do The Work of The Creator, 1976; Afro-Americans and Africa, 1976; The World of The Yeshiva,

1982; The Things They Say Behind Your Back, 1982. *Contribution to:* New York Times, 1981. *Honours:* Woodrow Wilson Fellowship, 1971; Outstanding Young Man of America, 1977, 1982. *Address:* Department of Sociology, City College of New York, 138th Street & Convent Avenue, New York, NY 10031, USA.

HELMS, Sandra Ann, b. 27 Apr. 1945, San Antonio, Texas, USA. Medical Editor. m. (1) Harvey Michael Fleming, 1 Jan. 1964, San Antonio, Texas, Div. 1972, 1 son, (2) William Radford Helms, 22 Mar. 1980, San Antonio, 1 stepson, 1 stepdaughter. *Literary Appointments:* Medical Editor, Department of Medicine, Managing Editor, BAMC Progress Notes, Brooke Army Medical Center, Fort Sam Houston, Texas, 1975–79 and 1983–. *Publications:* Managing Editor, House Staff Guide-BAMC Progress Notes, annually 1975–79. *Honours:* Many sustained superior performance awards and outstanding performance appraisals, Brooke Army Medical Center, Fort Sam Houston. *Memberships:* Council of Biology Editors Inc; American Medical Writers Association; American Association for Medical Transcription. *Address:* Route 1, Box 252, Hampshire, TN 38461–9998, USA.

HELYAR, Jane Penelope Josephine, b. 12 Feb. 1933, London, England. Writer. m. (1) T R Poole, 1956, (2) V J H Helyar, 1975, 1 son, 5 daughters. *Major Publications:* A Dream in the House, 1961; Moon Eyes, 1965; The Lilywhite Boys, 1968; Catch as Catch Can, 1969; Yokeham, 1970; Billy Buck, 1972; Touch & Go, 1976; When Fishes Flew, 1978; The Open Grave, The Forbidden Room, (remedial readers), 1979; Hannah Chance, 1980; Diamond Jack, 1983; The Country Dairy Companion (to accompany Central TV series), 1983; Three for Luck, 1985; Collection of animal stories, due 1986. Televisions scripts: The Harbourer, 1975; The Sabbatical, The Breakdown, Miss Constantine (all 1981); Ring a Ring a Rosie, With Love, Belinda, The Wit to Woo (all 1983); in West Country Stories series; Fox, Buzzard, Dartmoor Pony, (all 1984) in Three in the Wild series. *Literary Agent:* A P Watt Limited, London. *Address:* Poundisford Lodge, Poundisford, Taunton, Somerset TA3 7AE, England.

HEMLOW, Joyce, b. 30 July 1906, Liscomb, Nova Scotia, Canada. Writer. *Education:* BA 1941, MA 1942, Queen's University; AM 1944, PhD 1948, Harvard University, USA; Professor Emeritus, McGill University, Montreal, Canada, 1975. *Publications include:* the History of Fanny Burney, 1958; A Catalogue of the Burney Family Corespondence 1749–1878, 1971; The Journals and Letters of Fanny Burney (Madame d'Arblay) 1791–1840, 12 volumes (with associated editors), 1972–84. *Honours include:* James Tait Black Memorial Prize, 1958; Medal for Academic Non-Fiction, 1958; British Academy Award, The Rose Mary Crawhay Prize, 1960; FRSC, 1960. *Memberships include:* Johnsonians; New York International Association of University Teachers of English; Conference of British Studies; Phi Beta Kappa. *Address:* Liscomb, Guysboro County, Nova Scotia, Canada.

HEMMING, John Henry, b. 5 Jan. 1935, Vancouver, Canada. Publisher. m. Sukie Babington-Smith, 19 Jan. 1935, London, England, 1 son, 1 daughter. *Education:* BA; MA; DLitt; Oxford University. *Publications:* The Conquest of the Incas, 1970; Tribes of the Amazon Basin in Brazil, (co-author), 1972; Red Gold: The Conquest of the Brazilian Indiana, 1978; The Search for El Dorado, 1978; Machu Picchu, 1980; Monument of the Incas, 1982; Change in the Amazon Basin, 2 volumes, (Editor), 1985; Amazon Frontier, (in press). *Contributor to:* Numerous magazines and journals including: The Times; Times Literary Supplement; Times Educational Supplement; Sunday Times; Observer; Geographical Journal; Vogue. *Honours:* Pitman Prize, 1970; Christopher Award, New York, 1971. *Address:* 178-202 Great Portland Street, London W1N 6NH, England.

HEMMINKI, Heikki Veli Matti, b. 7 June 1931, Kauhava, Finland. Writer. m. 7 Apr. 1958, Maiju, 1 son, 1

daughter. *Education:* Bachelor of Humanistic Arts. *Publications include:* Along The Roadside, collection of poems, 1964; Songs of Development, collection of poems, 1966; Flood, play, 1968; People From Raamattusaari, play, 1970; Piiskawedding, play, 1974; Gold and Honour, play, 1972; Spaceplay, children's play, 1974; Two Patrons, documentary television play, 1978; The Olympic Games in Arts, 1981; A Computer Fiancee, play, 1982; Laugh at Plain, novel, 1985. *Contributions to:* Radio and magazines including: Vaasa; Kurikka. *Honours:* A cultural prize awarded by Seinäjoki town, 1973; An artistic prize awarded by Vassa administrative district, 1976; The State Prize, play. *Memberships:* Finnish Association of Writers; Finnish Association of Playwriters. *Literary Agent:* The Finnish Association of Writers. *Address:* Pajupolku 2 as 1, 61300 Kurikka, Finland.

HEMPHILL, Penny, b. 18 Oct. 1955, Sydney, Australia. Writer. *Literary Appointments:* Cadet Journalist, Manly Daily Newspaper, 1974; Editor, Where Magazine, 1978; Assistant Editor, Shree Media, 1979; Freelance Journalist, Writer, 1979–85. Currently self-employed writing comedy for theatre, film, stand-up, newspapers and magazines. *Contributions to:* Home Journal; Pol; Woman's Day; People; Matilda; Readers Digest; Family Circle; Better Homes & Gardens; Cleo; Cosmopolitan; Nature and Health; Simply Living; Good Housekeeping. *Memberships:* Australian Writers Guild; Australian Journalists Association; Fellowship of Australian Writers; The Society of Women Writers (Australia). *Address:* 36 Gloucester Street, West Pymble 2073, Sydney, New South Wales, Australia.

HENDERSON, Bruce Bradley, b. 18 Dec. 1946, Oakland, California, USA. Author. m. Cynthia Newcomb, 1 son, 2 daughters. *Education:* AA, Chabot College. *Literary Appointments:* Senior Lecturer, School of Journalism, University of Southern California. *Publications:* Empire of Deceit, 1985; The Black Cats, 1980; Ghetto Cops, 1974. *Contributions to:* Reader's Digest; Esquire; Playboy; California; Family Weekly and others. *Memberships:* American Society of Journalists and Authors; Authors Guild; Investigative Reporters and Editors. *Literary Agent:* Michael Hamilburg. *Address:* c/o Mitchell J Hamilburg Agency, 292 South La Cienega, Suite 212, Beverly Hills, CA 90211, USA.

HENDERSON, Lawrence (Larry) Austin, b. 21 July 1915, Portland, Oregon, USA. Sign Painter; Freelance Cartoonist. *Publications:* Bitter Harvest (fiction set in Eastern Oregon during the great depression years of 1930's), 1975. *Contributor to:* Rural Economic Development Article Series, Lovelock Review-Miner Newspaper Weekly; Lovelock Nevada 89419. *Honours:* President, Pershine County Chamber of Commerce, 2 concurrent terms. *Membership:* Western Writers of America. *Address:* 250 8th Street, PO Box 1031, Lovelock, NV 89419, USA.

HENDERSON, Michael Douglas, b. 15 Mar. 1932, London, England. Voluntary Religious Worker. m. Erica M Hallowes, 16 Apr. 1966, Guildford, England, 1 daughter. *Literary Appointments:* Editor, New World News, 1963–1968, 1971–1978; Moderator, World Press In Review, KOAPTV 1979–1981; Commentator, KBOO Radio, Portland, 1982–; Columnist. Lake Oswego Review, 1984–; Union Jack, 1985–; Center Island Pennysaver, 1985–; Commentator, KOAP Radio, Portland, 1985. *Publications:* From India With Hope, 1972; Experiment With Untruth – India Under Emergency, 1977; A Different Accent, 1985. *Memberships:* Institute of Journalists; Willamette Writers, President 1982; Oregon Association of Christian Writers. *Address:* 10605 SW Terwilliger Boulevard, Portland, OR 97219, USA.

HENDERSON, Patricia Jean, b. 26 June 1955, Montreal, Canada. Stage Manager; Writer. *Education:* BA, Theatre, Queens University, Ontario; Graduate, Production Course, National Theatre School, Montreal. *Publication:* Beyond the End of Your Nose, 1984. *Honours:* Non-equity productions of: Adaptations of

Sword in the Stone, Showcase Series, Toronto, 1983; Arthur-The Once and Future King, 1985. *Membership:* Playwrights Canada. *Address:* #809-145 St George St, Toronto, Ontario M5R 2M1, Canada.

HENDON, Donald W, b. USA. University Professor of Marketing; Author. *Education:* MBA, University of California, Berkeley; PhD, BBA, University of Texas, Austin. *Appointments:* Professor of Marketing, Arkansas State University; President, Business Consultants International; Adviser to firms in USA and worldwide, including manufacturers, retailers, wholesalers, market research firms, advertising agencies, media, trade associations, lobbyists, educational institutions, hospitals, chambers of commerce, government agencies, land developers, etc. *Publications:* Author of 257 separate works, including a book, Battling for Profits, 4 monographs and 3 forthcoming full length books. 37 journal articles (22 academic, 15 business and other non-academic), 26 articles in Proceedings, 4 case studies, 3 original articles in textbooks, 136 miscellaneous and privately-circulated works and 15 training manuals and has presented 28 papers at meetings. *Contributions to:* 20 American journals including: Marketing Times; Journal of Applied Psychology, Business Horizons; 5 journals in the UK, Singapore, Hong Kong, Mexico and Peru and 5 in Australia. *Memberships include:* 23 professional associations such as Academy of International Business, Academy of Management, Mensa, Sales and Marketing Executives International. *Address:* Arkansas State University, Department of Marketing and Management, College of Business, P O Box 59, State University, AK 72467, USA.

HENDRY, Joy McLaggan, b. 3 Feb. 1953, Perth, Scotland. Writer. *Education:* MA (Hons), Mental Philosophy, University of Edinburgh; DipEd, Moray House College of Education and University of Edinburgh. *Literary Appointments:* Joint Editor, with Walter Perrie, of Chapman, 1972–; Sole Editor, 1976. *Publications:* Scots: The Way Forward, 1981; Editor; Wendy Wood: Poems and Pictures, 1985; Critical Essays on Sorley MacLean, Edited with Raymond J Ross, 1985. *Contributions to:* Scotia Review; Chapman; The Scotsman; The Glasgow Herald; The Scots Magazine. *Address:* 35 East Claremont Street, Edinburgh EH7 4HT, Scotland.

HENLEY, Gail Olsheski, b. 6 Dec. 1952, Barry's Bay, Ontario, Canada. Author. *Education:* BA, McGill University, 1972; Diploma, Jagiellonian University, Cracow, Poland. 1973; MA, University of Toronto, Canada, 1974; Diploma, CSI, Canadian Securities Institute, Toronto, Canada, 1981. *Publication:* Where the Cherries End Up, (novel), (McClelland & Stewart/Little, Brown), 1978, (Bantam-Seal), 1980. *Contributions to:* Cinema Canada, in the form of regular leading feature articles. *Memberships:* Alliance of Canadian Cinema. Television & Radio Artists; British Actor's Equity Association; Academy of Canadian Cinema; McGill Glub. *Agent:* McClelland & Stewart. *Address:* 25 Hollinger Road, Toronto, Canada.

HENNESSEE, Judith Adler, b. 4 Mar. 1932, New York, New York, USA. Journalist. *Education:* BA, Barnard College. *Contributions to:* Contributing Editor: Manhattan Inc; The New York Times; Columbia Journalism review; Vanity Fair; Esquire; Mademoiselle; Redbook; MS; The Dial; The Village Voice; Publishers Weekly; New Times; Viva; The Washingtonian; and others. *Honour:* Compton Journalism Award, 1982. *Memberships:* American Society of Journalists and Authors, Society of Professional Journalists; Authors Guild; Women's Ink. *Literary Agent:* Ellen Levine. *Address:* 3 East 85th Street, New York, NY 10028, USA.

HENNESSEY, A Patricia Jaysane, b. 9 Sep. 1946, New York City. Professor of English. m. Richard E Hennessey, 20 Mar 1971, Hartford, Connecticut, 2 sons. *Education:* BA, Philosophy, 1969, MA, English, 1972, University of Hartford, Connecticut; Université Laval, Québec, Canada, studying for PhD. *Literary*

Appointment: Fiction Editos, The Long Story, 1983–. *Contributor to:* 100 articles for The Encyclopedic Dictionary of Religion. *Address:* Hill Road, West Bath, ME 01830, USA.

HENRARD, Roger Jean Albert, b. 13 Aug. 1921, Ans, Liège, Belgium. Professor. *Education:* Doctor in Germanic Philology. *Publications:* Grammaire du Néerlandais, 1960; Thèmes et exercices appropriés à la grammaire du Néerlandais, 1961; Menno ter Braak in het licht van Fr Nietzsche, 1963; Menno ter Braak, 1967; Wijsheidsgestalten in dichterwoord, 1977. *Contributions to:* Dietsche Warande en Belfort; Spiegel der Letteren; Ons Erfdeel; Septentrion; Etudes Germaniques; De Nieuwe Taalgids; Levende Talen; Forum der Letteren; De Vlaamse Gids. *Honour:* J Eeckhoutprijs, 1965. *Memberships:* Nederlandse Maatschappij voor Taal – en Letterkunde; Zuidnederlandse Maatschappij voor Taal – en Letterkunde en Geschiedenis; Het Spinozahuis. *Address:* 9 rue Dehin, 4000 Liège, Belgium.

HENRY, Marguerite, b. Milwaukee, Wisconsin, USA. Author. *Publications include:* Eight Pictured Geographies, Mexico, Canada, Alaska, Brazil, Argentina, Chile, West Indies and Panama, 1941; A Boy and A Dog, 1944; King of the Wind, 1948; Black Gold, 1957; Album of Dogs, 1970; San Domingo, The Medicine Hat Stallion, 1972; The Little Fellow, revised, 1975; Our First Pony, 1984. Films include: Misty of Chincoteague; Justin Morgan Has a Horse; Brighty of the Grand Canyon. Many publications in foreign editions, in Braille and as recordings for the blind. *Honours include:* John Newberry Award, 1948; William Allen White Award, 1956; Clara Ingram Judson Award, Society of Midland Authors, 1961; Western Heritage Award, 1970; Society of Midland Authors Award, 1973. *Address:* Rancho, Santa Fe, CA 92067, USA.

HENRY, Peter (born Hans Peter Zuntz), b. 21 Apr. 1926, Marburg, Germany. Professor, Slavonic Languages and Literatures. m. Brenda Grace Lewis, 3 Aug. 1951, Newport, divorced 1969, 1 son, 3 daughters. *Education:* MA, German & Russian, St John's College, Oxford University, 1950; DipEd, Leeds University, 1951. *Appointment:* Editor, Scottish Slavonic Review, 1983–. *Publications:* Editions of Russian Literary Works: Pushkin, The Gypsies; Chekhov, The Seagull; Bunin, Selected Stories; Paustovsky, Selected Stories (Introduction, Notes, Vocabulary), all 1962–67; Author, Modern Russian Prose Composition, 2 volumes, 1963, 1964; Manual of Modern Russian Usage, 1963; Anthology of Soviet Satire, 2 volumes, 1972, 1974; A Hamlet of his Time – Vsevolod Garshin: The Man, His Works, and His Milieu, 1983; GAZETA. Clippings from the Soviet Press (with K Young), 1983. *Contributor to:* Slavonic and East European Review; Critical Survey; Modern Language Review; Essays in Poetics; Journal of Russian Studies; Britain-USSR; Scottish Slavonic Review; to The Monster in the Mirror: Studies in 19th Century Realism, 1978; etc. Translations: short stories by Paustovsky, Sholokhov and Tendryakov in Winter's Tales, 7, 1961; Stand: Quarterly for the Arts, 1966, 1967; by Tyuntyunnik in Soviet Literature, Moscow, 1973; by Garshin in, The Penguin Book of Russian Short Stories, 1981; etc. *Memberships:* British Universities Association of Slavists; Scottish Publishers Association; etc. *Address:* Dept of Slavonic Languages and Literatures, Hetherington Building, University of Glasgow, Glasgow G12 8QQ, Scotland.

HENSCHEL, Elizabeth Georgie, b. London, England. Author of Equestrian books; Stud Owner. *Publications:* Thomas, A Pony, 1960; Careers With Horses, 1966; Kingfisher Guide to Horses and Ponies, 1979; Illustrated Guide to Horses and Ponies, 1980; Basic Riding Explained, 1981; Horses and Ponies, 1984. *Contributions to:* Encyclopedia of Horse, 1977; Country Life Book of Horses, 1978; Riding Magazine, 1969–; Horse and Hound; Horse and Driving, 1962–; Horse and Pony; Scottish Farmer. *Memberships:* Society of Authors; British Equestrian Writers Association.

Address: Ballintean, Kincraig, Kingussie, Inverness-shire PH21 1NX, Scotland.

HERALD, George William, b. 3 Jan. 1911, Berlin, Germany. Author; Foreign Correspondent. m. Martha A Dubois, 23 Mar. 1948, Paris, France, 1 son, 1 daughter. *Education:* Columbia University, New York City, USA; LLD, cum laude, University of Basle. *Literary Appointments:* International News Service Diplomatic Correspondent, London, Paris, 1945–46; Berlin Bureau Chief, 1946–47; Vienna Bureau Chief, 1947–49; Special Writer, United Features, New York City, 1949–52, European Editor, United Nations World, 1952–54; Paris Bureau Chief, Vision Inc, New York, 1954–. *Publications:* My Favourite Assassin, 1943; Off the Record, 1952; The Double Dealers, 1958; My Life as an Empress, (with Soraya Esfandiary), 1962; The Big Wheel, 1963; Art and Money, 1977. *Contributor to:* Readers Digest; Harper's Magazine; McCall's; Maclean's; over 200 articles to magazines in 10 countries. *Honour:* Honorary Member, International Arts Council. *Memberships:* Authors League of America; International Press Institute; Overseas Press Club of America. *Literary Agent:* B Klausner, New York, USA. *Address:* c/o Vision Inc, Vision Building, 13 East 75th Street, New York, NY 10022, USA.

HERBERT, (Dennis) Nicholas, Lord Hemingford, b. 25 July 1934, Watford, England. Journalist. m. Jennifer Mary Toresen Bailey 8 Nov. 1958, Harrogate, 1 son, 3 daughters. *Education:* MA Cambridge University. *Appointments:* Sports Desk, Reuters, 1956–57; Diplomatic Desk, Reuters, 1957–60; Washington Bureau, Reuters, 1960–61; Assistant Washington Correspondent, 1961–65, Middle East Correspondent, 1966–68, Deputy Features Editor, 1968–70, The Times; Editor, Cambridge Evening News, 1970–74; Editorial Director, Westminster Press, 1974–. *Publications:* Jews and Arabs in Conflict, 1969; Press Freedom: The Lifeblood of Democracy, Editor, 1974. *Memberships:* Guild of British Newspaper Editors, President, 1980–81; Media Society, President, 1982–84; British Executive, International Press Institute; Association of British Editors, Secretary, 1985–; East Anglian RegionalCommittee, National Trust, 1984–. *Address:* The Old Rectory, Hemingford Abbots, Huntingdon, Cambridgeshire PE18 9AH, England.

HERBERT, (Edward) Ivor (Montgomery), b. 20 Aug. 1925, Johannesburg, South Africa. Author; Journalist; Playwright; Scriptwriter; Partner, Equus Productions (video). *Education:* MA, Trinity College, Cambridge. *Publications include:* Eastern Windows, novel, 1953; Point-to-Point, 1964; Arkle, 1966; The Queen Mother's Horses, 1967; The Winter Kings, 1968; The Way to the Top, 1969; Night of the Blue Demands, play, 1971; Over Our Dead Bodies, novel, 1972; The Diamond Diggers, history, South African diamond industry, 1972; Winter's Tale, 1973; Red Rum, 1974; Come Riding, 1975; L'Equitation, 1975; The Filly, 1978; Vincent O'Brien's Great Horses, 1984. *Films include:* The Great St Trinian's Train Robbery, 1966; Numerous documentaries. *Contributions to:* Mail on Sunday (travel writer, racing editor); Horse & Hound. *Memberships:* Writers Guild; Society of Authors; National Union of Journalists; Guards Club. *Agent:* David Higham Associates. *Address:* The Old Rectory, Bradenham, Nr High Wycombe, Buckinghamshire, England.

HERBERT, Peter Desmond, b. 1 May 1952, Australia. Writer for Television and Film. *Education:* Diploma of Electrical Engineering, Crippsland Institute of Advanced Education; BA Honours, University of Melbourne. *Memberships:* Victoria Branch, Australian Writers Guild. *Address:* 33 Kay Street, Carlton, Victoria 3053, Australia.

HERMAN, Ira, b. 13 June 1948, Huntington, West Virginia, USA. Novelist; Publisher. m. Claire Marie Nudd, 9 May 1981. *Education:* BA, University of California, Los Angeles. *Appointments:* Co-ordinator, Mountain State Press, 1979–82; WVA Writer in Residence,

National Endowment for the Arts, 1983; Publisher, Aegina Press, University Editions, 1984–85. *Publications:* Dark Horses Leaping into Flame, poetry, 1978; The Two Tzaddiks, Del Rey Books, 1981. *Contributor to:* Numerous magazines in USA, and abroad. *Honour:* Winner, Writers of the Future Contest, Science Fiction, 1985. *Membership:* Science Fiction Writers of America. *Address:* 4937 Humphrey Road, Huntington, WV 25704, USA.

HERMAN, Roger E, b. 11 Dec. 1943, San Francisco, California, USA. Management Consultant; Trainer. m. Sandra J Herman, 2 May 1974, Stow, Ohio, 3 sons, 1 daughter. *Education:* BA, Hiram College; MA, Ohio State University. *Publications:* Disaster Planning for Local Government, 1982; Emergency Operations Plan, 1983. *Contributions:* Over 100 published, various periodicals. *Memberships:* Director, Annual Writers Conference, University of Akron, Ohio; National Speakers Association; American Society for Training and Development. *Address:* c/o Herman Associates, 19 North Main Street, Rittman, OH 44270, USA.

HERMAN, Rosalind Susan, b. 17 Jan. 1954, London, England. Journalist. *Education:* MA, Cambridge University, 1978; MSc, London University, 1982. *Literary Appointments:* Science Policy Editor, New Scientist, 1982–. *Publication:* The European Scientific Community, 1986. *Contributions to:* New Scientist; Science and Government Report, USA; La Recherche; Scienza due Mille. *Membership:* Vice Chairman, 1985–86, Association of British Science Writers. *Literary Agent:* Murray Pollinger. *Address:* c/o New Scientist, Commonwealth House, 1-19 New Oxford Street, London WC1 1NG, England.

HERR, Ethel Louise, b. 17 Nov. 1936, Tacoma, Washington, USA. Freelance Author; Teacher. m. Walter Ellsworth Herr, 28 Mar. 1958, Turlock, California, 1 son, 2 daughters. *Education:* Multnomah School of the Bible, 1954–56; Modesto Junior College, 1956–57. *Publications:* Chosen Women of the Bible, 1976; Growing Up is a Family Affair, 1978; Schools: How Parents Can Make a Difference, 1981; Chosen Families of the Bible, 1981; Bible Study for Busy Women, 1982; An Introduction to Christian Writing, 1983. *Contributions to:* Eternity; Moody Monthly; Decision; Family Life Today; Sunday Digest; Purpose; Church Herald; Christian Leader; Success; Alive Now; Scope; Young Musician; The Evangel; Looking Ahead; Teens Today; Young Calvinist; The Evangelical Beacon; Vital Christianity; The Edge; Baptist Leader; The Mennonite; Gospel Carrier; Pentecostal Evangel. *Honour:* Pacesetter Award, Mount Hermon Christian Writers Conference, 1982. *Memberships:* Co Founder and Leader, Santa Clara Valley Christian Writers, 1970–; Director, Literature Ministries Prayer Fellowship, 1984–; Institute for Historical Study, 1984–. *Address:* 731 Lakefair Drive, Sunnyvale, CA 94089, USA.

HERRGARD, Elin, b. 18 Aug. 1907, Malax, Finland. Writer. m. Ernst Ragnar Herrgard, May 1928 (deceased), 2 sons, 2 daughters. *Major Publications:* Slattbygd, 1963; Fackelblomst, 1965; Amerikabrevet, 1973; Lovjerskan, 1976; Renfana, 1982. *Memberships:* Svenska Österbottens Litteraturforening (of honour); Finlands Svenska Forfattareforening. *Address:* 7 Kolmilevägen, SF–65230 Vasa 23, Finland.

HERRING, Reuben, b. 14 July 1922, Tifton, Georgia, USA. Journalist. m. Dorothy L McCorvey, 2 Dec. 1942, Athens, Georgia, USA, 5 sons, 1 daughter. *Education:* ABJ, University of Georgia. *Publications:* Two Shall Be One, 1964; Men Are Like That, 1967; Building a Better Marriage, 1975; Baptist Almanac and Repository of Indispensable Knowledge, 1976; Your Family Worship Guide Book, 1978; Fire in the Canebrake, 1980; Becoming Friends with Your Children, (with Dorothy Herring), 1984. *Contributions to:* Numerous theological journals, including Home Life, Brotherhood Journal, The Deacon, Church Administration. *Honours:* Southern Baptist Historical Commission Award, 1976; Baptist Sunday School Board Career Professional, 1983.

Address: 127 Ninth Avenue North, Nashville, TN 37234, USA.

HERRMANN, Dorothy, b. 27 July 1941, Brooklyn, New York, USA. Writer. m. Lance David Silverman, 26 Dec. 1976, New York. *Education:* BA, English, Middlebury College, Vermont, 1963. *Publication:* With Malice Toward All: The Quips, Lives & Loves of Some Celebrated 20th Century American Wits, 1982. *Contributor to:* Ms; Cosmopolitan; Smithsonian; Ladies Home Journal. *Membership:* Authors Guild. *Literary Agent:* Owen Lester, William Morris Agency. *Address:* c/o William Morris Agency, 1350 Avenue of the Americas, New York, NY 10019, USA.

HERSH, Burton David, b. 18 Sep. 1933, Chicago, Illinois, USA. Freelance writer. m. Ellen Eiseman, 3 Aug. 1957, Augusta, Georgia, 1 son, 1 daughter. *Education:* BA, magna cum laude, Harvard College, 1955; Fulbright Scholar, 1955–56. *Literary Appointments:* Fellow, Bread Loaf Writers Conference, 1964; Martin Memorial Lecturer, The Blake School, 1973. *Publications:* The Ski People, 1968; The Education of Edward Kennedy, 1972; The Mellon Family, 1978. *Contributor to:* Many major US magazines including, Holiday; Esquire; Washingtonian; etc. *Honours:* History & Literature Prize, Harvard College, 1954; Bowdoin Prize 1955, Senior Phi Beta Kappa 1955, Harvard; Book Club Final Selection, 1972; Book-of-the-Month Club Selection, 1978. *Memberships:* Authors Guild; American Society of Journalists & Authors. *Literary Agent:* Ned Leavitt, William Morris Agency Inc. *Address:* Box 204, Bradford, NH 03221, USA.

HERSHEY, Jonathan, b. 14 Apr. 1956, Bon Secour, Alabama, USA. University Professor. *Education:* BA in English; MFA in Creative Writing. *Literary Appointments:* Teaching-Writing Fellowship, University of Alabama, 1982; Former Fiction Editor, Black Warrior Review; Editor, Old Red Kimono. *Contributions to:* Fiction; Beloit Fiction Journal; Indiana Review; Black Warrior Review; Intro. Poetry; Vanderbilt Review. *Honours:* Nominated for Pushcart Prize, 1982; Finalist, Indiana Review Fiction Award, 1984. *Memberships:* Board Member, Rome Area Council for the Arts; Associated Writing Programs. *Address:* P O Box 5785, Rome, GA 30162, USA.

HERZBERG, Gerhard, b. 25 Dec. 1904, Hamburg, Germany. Physicist. *Education:* Dipl Ing, 1927; Dr Ing, 1928, Darmstadt Institute of Technology; University of Gottingen, 1928–29; Bristol University, England, 1929–30. *Publications include:* Molecular Structure, I, Spectra of Diatomic Molecules, 1939; 2nd edition, 1950; IL Infrared and Raman Spectra of Polyatamic Molecules, 1945; III Electronic Spectra and Electronic Structure of Polyatomic Molecules, 1966; IV Constants of Diatomic Molecules, (with K P Huber), 1979; works translated into various languages. *Contributor to:* Scientific journals. *Honours include:* Nobel Prize in Chemistry, 1971. *Membership:* Honorary Member Mark Twain Society. *Address:* Hersberg Institute of Astrophysics, National Research Council of Canada; Ottawa, Ontario K1A OR6, Canada.

HESKETH, Phoebe, b. 29 Jan. 1909, Editor; Writer. *Education:* Cheltenham Ladies College. *Literary Appointments:* Editor, Woman's Page, Bolton Evening News; Lecturer, Woman's College, Bolton; Leader, Creative Writing Group, Bolton School. *Publications:* Lean Forward, Spring, 1948; No Time for Cowards, 1952; Out of the Dark, 1954; Between Wheels and Stars, 1956; The Buttercup Children, 1958; Prayer for Sun, 1966; Song of Sunlight, 1974; Preparing to Leave, 1977; The Eighth Day, Selected poems, 1980; (prose) My Aunt Edith, 1966; Rivington, the Story of a Village, 1972; What Can the Matter Be? 1985; A Ring of Leaves, (poems) 1985; Over the Brook, 1986. *Contributor to:* Sunday Times; Observer; Listener; New Statesman; Times Literary Supplement; Punch; Countryman; Country Life; etc. *Honours:* Greenwood Prize, Poetry Society, 1947, 1966; FRSL, 1971. *Memberships:* Royal College of Literature; Poetry

Society; Lancashire Authors' Association. *Address:* 10 The Green, Heath Charnock, Near Chorley, Lancashire PR6 9JH, England.

HESSIE, Bettie Jean, b. 28 July 1938, Olney, Maryland, USA. Editor; Writer. *Education:* BSc, Distributed Science, American University, 1978. *Publication:* Assistant Editor, Anti-Epileptic Drugs, 2nd editon 1982. *Contributions:* As Co-author: Cleveland Clinical Quarterly; Federal Proceedings. As sole author: Washington Star; Washington Post. *Memberships:* Council of Biology Editors; American Medical Writers Association; Washington Society for the History of Medicine; Phi Kappa Phi. *Address:* 10500 Rockville Pike No. 1114, Rockville, MD 20852, USA.

HESTER, Martin L, b. 16 Aug. 1947, Greensboro, North Carolina, USA. Poet; Novelist; Editor. Divorced, 1 daughter. *Education:* University of North Carolina, Greensboro; University of North Carolina, Chapel Hill (special student of poet Charles Edward Eaton). *Literary Appointment:* Senior Editor, Tudor Publishers Incorporated. *Publications:* Penny Progressions, 1973; Looking at You, 1984; Meryl Streep: A Critical Biography (co-author) (forthcoming). *Contributions to:* American Scholar; Confrontation; Minnesota Review; Mississippi Review; Denver Quarterly; International Poetry Review; Chariton Review; Kudos (UK); Bogg (USA & UK); Arte Quincenal (Venezuela); etc. *Honours:* St Andrews Prize for Poetry, 1976; Kansas Quarterly/Kansas Arts Council Prize for Fiction, 1985; Various Editor's choice awards, nominations, etc. *Memberships:* Associated Writing Programs; Society of Children's Book Authors; Poets & Writers Incorporated Directory of American Poets and Fiction Writers. *Address:* 3007 Taliaferro Road, Greensboro, NC 27408, USA.

HESTERMAN, Vicki Lynn, b. 16 Mar. 1951, Napoleon, Ohio, USA. Writer, Photographer, Teacher. *Education:* BA, English & Biology, Secondary Teachers' Certificate, Adrian College, Michigan; MA, College Student Personnel & Journalism, Bowling Green State University, Bowling Green, Ohio, USA; PhD Graduate Studies in Mass Communications, Ohio University, Athens, Ohio, 1985–. *Literary Appointments:* Magazine Writing Instructor, Bowling Green State University, 1983–85; Advisor & Feature Writer, Literary Magazine, Miscellany, 1984–85. *Major Publications:* Angels in Faded Jeans (photographer), 1979; Walking Home (co-author), 1982. *Contributor to:* Good Housekeeping; Toledo Blade Magazine; Genetics; Toledo Alive Magazine; News Photographer Magazine. *Honour:* Outstanding Young Woman of America, 1984. *Memberships:* Lambda Iota Tau, Secretary 1970–73; Northwest Ohio Writers Forum, 1984–85; Association of Educators, Journalism and Mass Communications; Society of Professional Journalists. *Address:* P O Box 333, Stevenson Street, Napoleon, OH 43545, USA.

HETHERINGTON, Hector Alastair, b. 31 Oct. 1919, Llanishen, Glamorgan, Wales. Journalist. m. Miranda Oliver, 27 June 1957, Manchester, England, 2 sons, 2 daughters. *Education:* MA Honours, Oxford University. *Literary Appointments:* Staff Member, Glasgow Herald, Scotland, 1946–50; Foreign Editor, Manchester Guardian, 1953; Editor, The Guardian, 1958–75; Controller, British Broadcasting Corporation Scotland, 1975–78; Research Professor in Media Studies, University of Stirling, Scotland, 1982–. *Publications:* The Guardian Years, 1981; News, newspapers and Televison, 1985. *Contributions to:* The Listener; New Statesman; Spectator; British Broadcasting Corporation. *Honours:* Journalist of the Year, National Press Awards, 1971. *Address:* 38 Chalton Road, Bridge of Allan, Stirling FK9 4EF, Scotland.

HEUTERMAN, Thomas H, b. 13 Aug. 1934, Yakima, Washington, USA. Department Chair, Journalism Professor. m. Gretchen Ann Dow, 22 June 1957, Burlington, 2 sons. *Education:* BA, 1956, PhD, 1973, Washington State University; MA, University of Washington, 1961. *Publications:* Movable Type :

Biography of Legh Freeman, 1979. *Contributor to:* Assessing the Press on Wheels : Individualism in Frontier Journalism, Journalism Quarterly, 1976; Racism in Frontier Journalism: A Case Study, Journal of the West, 1980. *Honours:* Distinguished Reporting Award, American Political Science Association, 1960; Distinguished Campus Adviser Award, Society of Professional Journalists, 1980. *Memberships:* Society of Professional Journalists; Association for Education in Journalism and Mass Communication; Past President, American Society of Journalism School Administrators. *Address:* NW 500 Polaris St, Pullman, WA 99163, USA.

HEUZEL, John Lal, b. 23 Sep. 1945, Ostend, Belgium. Translator. m. Marie-Thérèse van Dycke, 24 Dec. 1968, Assebzoek. *Education:* Secretarial & Modern Language Studies, 1964. *Contributor to:* De Brugse Gazette; Volksopuoeding; Yang; Kruispunt; Publisher, Kruispunt, 1981–; Editor, Kruispunt No. 85: James Joyce. *Memberships:* Association of Flemish Writers; Vice President, Jan Vercammen Foundation, Brugge. *Address:* Boeveriestraat 8, B–8000 Brugge, Belgium.

HEWAT, Alan Vaill, b. 4 Aug. 1940, Massachusetts, USA. Writer. m. Emily J Joselson, 2 July 1983, North Calais, Vermont, USA. *Education:* AB, Dartmouth College. *Major Publication:* Lady's Time, 1985. *Contributor to:* Esquire Magazine; Iowa Review; Ascent; Massachusetts Review. *Honours:* Artists Fellowship, Massachusetts Council on the Arts & Humanities, 1978; Vermont Council on the Arts Fellowship in Literature, 1984. *Literary Agent:* Thomas S Hart, Literary Enterprises. *Address;* RD 2, Brandon, VT 05733, USA.

HEYDEN, Haye van der, b. 20 Feb. 1957. Actor; Singer; Writer; Director. *Education:* Gymnasium A, 1976; Dutch Literature, State University, Utrecht, The Netherlands. *Publications:* Three Girls, Three Boys; For Queen and Country; And Provo is their Name. *Performed in:* The Film Van Ome Willem; Nelson Revue. *Television and Radio Appearances:* Martine Bijl; Mies Bouwman; Ivo Niehe; Alfred Biolex. *Directed:* Adèle's Choice; Frisse Jongens; And Provo is their Name. *Literary Awards:* Visser Neerlandia Award, 1980; Ministry of Culture stipendium. *Address:* 3e Helmersstraat 72/US, 1054 BL Amsterdam, The Netherlands.

HEYM, Stefan, b. 10 Apr. 1913, Chemnitz, Germany. Author. *Education:* University of Berlin; MA, University of Chicago, Illinois, USA, 1935. *Literary Appointments:* Editor, Deutsches Volksecho, New York, USA, 1937–39. *Publications include:* Fiction: Hostages, 1942, 43, republished as Glasenapp Case, 1962; Of Smiling Peace, 1944, 46; The Crusaders, 1948; Goldsborough, 1953, 61; Die Kannibalen und andere Erzahlungen, 1953; The Lenzpapers; Die Papiere des Andreas Lenz, 1963–69; The King David Report (Der Konig-David-Bericht), 1972; The Queen Against Defoe, 1975; Märchen Für Kludge Kinder, 1975; Die richtige Einstellung und andere Erzahlungen, 1976; Five Days in June, 1977; Collin, 1979; Ahasver, 1981; Schwarsenberg, 1984. Non-fiction: Nasis in USA: An Expose of Hitler's Aims and Agents in the USA, 1938; Im Kopt sauber: Schriften zum Tage, 1954; Wege und Umwege: Streitbare Schfiten aus funf Jahrzehnten, 1980; Auskunft 1-2: Neue Prose aus der DDR, Editor, 1974–78; King Leopold's Soliloquy, by Mark Twain, translated, 1961. Tom Sawyers grosses Abenteuer, play, 1952. Numerous of his works have been translated into English and re-issued. *Honours:* Henrich Mann Prize, 1953; National Prize, Democratic Republic of Germany. *Address:* Rabindranath-Tagore-Strasse 9, 118 Berlin-Grunau, Democratic Republic of Germany.

HEYNEN, James A, b. 14 July 1940, USA. Writer. m. Carol Bangs, 1 Aug. 1973, Eugene, 1 son, 1 daughter. *Education:* BA, Calvin College; MA, University of Iowa; MFA, University of Oregon. *Appointments:* Writer-in-Residence, University of Alaska, 1974; Distinguished Writer in Residence, University of Idaho, 1981. *Publications:* The Man Who Kept Cigars in his Cap,

1979; A Suitable Church, 1981; You Know What is Right, 1985. *Contributor to:* Numerous professional journals including, Redbook; North American Review; Poetry Northwest; Prairie Schooner; Georgia Review. *Honours:* National Endowment for the Arts Fellowship, 1975; US-UK Bicentennial Exchange Fellowship, 1977–78. *Address:* 624 Lincoln Street, Port Townsend, WA 98368, USA.

HEYUM, Monica. Literary Agent. *Literary Appointments:* Literary agent, representing authors worldwide, and USA-UK and French agents and publishers in Scandinavia, Holland and France. *Address:* Box 3300, Vendelso, S–136 03 Handen, Sweden.

HEYWORTH, Peter, b. 3 June 1921, New York, USA. Music Critic. *Education:* Charterhouse and Balliol College, Oxford, BA Honours. *Literary Appointments:* Music Critic, The Observer, 1955–. *Publications:* Otto Klempererer: His Life and Times, Volume I 1885–1933. *Address:* 32 Bryanston Square, London W1, England.

HIBBEN, Frank Cummings, b. 5 Dec. 1910, Lakewood, Ohio, USA. Professor; Author. *Education:* AB, Princeton University, 1933; MS, University of New Mexico, 1936; PhD, Anthropology, Harvard University, 1940. *Appointments:* Teaching Assistant to Professor, Anthropology, University of New Mexico, 1933–; Director, Maxwell Museum, 1961–67; Director, Albuquerque Zoo, 1977–, publications: The Lost Americans, 1946; Hunting American Lions, 1948; Hunting American Bears, 1950; Treasure in the Dust, 1951; Prehistoric Man in Europe, 1958; Digging Up America, 1960; Hunting in Africa, 1962; Kiva Art of the Anasazi, 1975. *Contributor to:* Reader's Digest; Field and Stream; Outdoor Life; Denver Post; Empire; many sporting magazines; Technical reports in professional journals. *Honours:* Legion of Merit; Phi Beta Kappa; Phi Kappa Phi; Fellow, Explorers Club. *Memberships:* Ecological Society; Ethnological Society; Society for American Archaeology; American Anthropological Association; American Society for the Advancement of Science; Texas Archaeological & Palaeological Society. *Address:* Dept of Anthropology, University of New Mexico, Albuquerque, NM 87131, USA.

HIBBERT, Christopher, b. 5 Mar. 1924, Enderby, Leicestershire, England. Author. m. Susan Piggford, 12 Aug. 1948, Harrogate, 2 sons, 1 daughter. *Education:* MA, Oriel College, Oxford University; FRSL; FRGS. *Publications:* The Destruction of Lord Raglan, 1961; Corunna, 1961; Benito Mussolini, 1962; The Battle of Arnheim, 1962; The Roots of Evil, 1963; The Court at Windsor, 1964; Agincourt, 1964; Garibaldi and His Enemies, 1965; The Making of Charles Dickens, 1967; Charles I, 1968; The Grand Tour, 1969; London: Biography of a City, 1969; The Search for King Arthur, 1970; The Dragon Wakes: China and the West, 1973–1911, 1970; The Personal History of Samuel Johnson, 1971; George IV, Prince of Wales, 1972; George IV, Regent and King, 1812–1830, 1973; The Rise and Fall of the House of Medici, 1974; Edward VII: A Portrait, 1976; The Great Mutiny: India 1857, 1978; Disraeli and His World, 1978; The French Revolution, 1981; Editor, Greville's England, 1981; Africa Explored: Europeans in the Dark Continent 1769–1889, 1982; Edited with Ben Weinreb, The London Encyclopedia, 1983; Queen Victoria in Her Letters and Journals, 1984; Rome: Biography of a City, 1985. *Honour:* Heinemann Award for Literature, 1962. *Memberships:* Fellow, Royal Society of Literature; President, Johnson Society, 1980. *Literary Agent:* David Higham Associates. *Address:* The Old Post Office, Storor, Henley-on-Thames, Oxfordshire, England.

HIBBS, John Alfred Blyth, b. 5 May 1925, Birmingham, England. Lecturer. *Education:* BComm, University of Birmingham; MSc, Economics, University of London; PhD, Birmingham University. *Publications:* Transport for Passengers, 1963, 71; The History of British Bus Services, 1968; Transport Studies: An Introduction, 1970; The Omnibus, 1971; How to Run the Buses, 1972; The Bus and Coach Industry, 1975;

Transport Without Politics [el]?, 1982; Bus and Coach Management, 1985; Regulation-An International Study of Bus and Coach Licensing, 1985; The Country Bus, 1986. Poetry written under pen name: Being a Patient, 1965; New Found Land, 1963. *Contributions to:* Journal of Transport Economics and Policy; Journal of Transport History; Transportation Research Record, USA; Transport Reviews. *Honours:* BET Road Passenger Transport Award, Chartered Institute of Transport, 1981. *Membershiops:* PEN English Centre. *Address:* 134 Wood End Road, Birmingham B24 8BN, England.

HICKEY, Raymond, b. 21 Apr. 1936, Dublin, Eire, Catholic Missionary Priest. *Education:* DD, Faculty of Theology, Gregorian University, Home, Italy, 1977. *Publications:* Africa: The Case for an Auxiliary Priesthood, 1980, USA, 1982; A History of the Catholic Church in Northern Nigeria, 1981; Christianity in Borno State and Northern Gongola, 1985. Editor: Modern Missionary Documents and Africa, 1982. *Contributions to:* Clergy Review; Doctrine and Life; Religious Life Review; AFER, Kenya; African Affairs; International Journal of African Historical Studies; Nigrizia. *Address:* St Patrick's Cathedral, PO Box 58 Maiduguri, Nigeria.

HICKS, Alice Louise, b. 24 Nov. 1914. Writer. *Education:* DePauw University, Indiana, USA, 1932–34; Spring Hill College, Alabama, 1975–77. *Appointments include:* Teacher, Pascagoula, Mississippi, 1961–68; St Mary's School, Christiansted, St Croix, US Virgin Islands, 1979–; St Joseph's High School, St Croix, 1981–82. *Major Publications:* I Sing My Amazement, 1968; Lyrics from Cor Meum, 1969. *Contributor to:* Voices International; Negative Capability; Yearbook of Texas Poetry Society; The Sampler; Jean's Journal; Various anthologies. *Honours:* Winner, Western World Haiku Society Competition, 1977, 1979; Dragonfly Award, 1980; Beaudoin Gemstone Awards, 1976, 1977, 1978, 1980; Featured Writer, Voices International, 1983. *Memberships:* Founding Member, Kenwigs Club, Auburn, Indiana; Life Member, Poetry Society of Texas; Founder, Writers Unlimited of Pascagoula, Mississippi, 1968–79; Alabama Conclave of Writers; Alabama State Poetry Society. *Address:* P O Box 278, Unit F–40, Christiansted, St Croix, US Virgin Islands, 00820.

HIEBERT, D(avid) Edmond, b. 21 July 1910, Corn, OK, USA. Seminary Professor; Author. *Education:* AB, John Fletcher College, 1935; ThM, 1939, ThD, 1942, Southern Baptist Theology Seminary. *Publications:* Introduction to the Pauline Epistles, 1954, 11th edition, 1976; revised edition, 1977; Introduction to the Non-Pauline Epistles, 1962, 8th edition, 1976; The Thessalonian Epistles, 1971; Personalities Around Paul, 1973; Mark: Portrait of the Servant, 1974; Introduction to the New Testament; The Non-Pauline Epistles and Revelation, 1977; The Pistle of James: Tests of a Living Faith, 1979; First Peter, An Expositional Commentary, 1984. *Contributor to:* religious journals. *Memberships:* Evangelical Theological Society. *Address:* 4864 East Townsend, Fresno, CA 93727.

HIGDON, Hal, b. 17 June 1931, Chicago, Illinois, USA. Freelance Writer. m. Rose Musacchio, 12 Apr. 1958, Chicago, 2 sons, 1 daughter. *Education:* BA, Carleton College, 1953. *Publications:* The Union vs Dr Mudd, 1964; Heroes of the Olympics, 1965; Pro Football, USA, 1968; The Horse That Played Center Field, 1969; The Business Healers, 1969; On the Run from Dogs and People, 1971; Thirty Days in May, 1971; Champions of the Tennis Courts, 1971; The Electronic Olympics, 1971; Finding the Groove, 1973; Find the Key Man, 1974; The Last Series, 1974; The Crime of the Century, 1975; Six Seconds to Glory, 1975; Showdown at Daytona, 1976; Summer of Triumph, 1977; Fitness After Forty, 1977; Beginner's Running Guide, 1978; Hitting, Pitching and Fielding, 1978; Runner's Cookbook, 1979; Johnny rutherford, Indy Champion, 1980; The Marathoners, 1980; The Team that Played in the Space Bowl, 1981. Ghosted: Together: A Casebook of Joint Practices in Primary Care (Editor, Elaine Katz,

1977; 400 Novels: The Future of School Health in America (by Godfrey E Cronin and William M Young), 1979; Introduction to Sport Studies (by Harold VanderZwaeg and Thomas J Sheehan), 1978; The Complete Diet Guide, 1978. Queen of the Demo Derby (awaiting publication); Falconara (in progress). *Contributions to:* Reader's Digest; Sports Illustrated National Geographic; Playboy; People Weekly, etc. *Memberships:* American Society of Journalists and Authors; Writer's Guild. *Literary Agent:* Edward J Acton. *Address:* 2815 Lake Shore Drive, Michigan City, IN 46360, USA.

HIGGINS, Lionel George, b. 26 May 1891, Bedford, England. Medical Profession. m. 16 July 1925, 3 sons, 1 daughter. *Education:* MA; MD Cantab; FRCS, England; FRCOG. *Publications:* Field Guide to Butterflies of Britain and Europe (with N D Riley), 1970; Butterflies of Britain and Europe, 1983. *Contributions to:* Transcripts Entomological Society, London. *Honours:* Raffles Award, Zoological Society of London, 1972; H H Bloomer Award, Linnean Society of London, 1982. *Address:* Focklesbrook Farm, Chobham, Woking, Surrey, England.

HIGH, Graham John, b. 3 Apr. 1948, Painter; Sculptor; Author. *Education:* BA, Leeds University, 1973. *Publications:* Ravens of Unresting Thought, 1975; Attempts to Love, 1977. *Contributions to:* Workshop New Poetry; Incept; Overspill; Little Word Machine; Pick; Sandwiches; Radix; Promontary; Envoi; Poetry One Assegai; Headland; Orbis; Poetry Society Bulletin. *Honours:* 1st Poetry Society Premium Competition, 1973; 1st, Students in Hall Competiton, Leeds University, 1970. *Memberships:* Co-Organiser, Rummage; Leeds Poetry Society; Questors Theatre, Ealing, London. *Address:* 13 Witham Road, Isleworth, Middlesex TW7 4AJ, England.

HIGH, Katherine M Adams, b. 16 Oct. 1952, Pittsburgh, Pennsylvania, USA. Broadcast Journalist. m. Donald J High, 1 son. *Education:* Malone College, Canton, Ohio, 1970–72; Kent State University, Kent, Ohio, 1972–74. *Literary Appointments:* Copywriter, WJKW-TV, Storer Broadcasting, Cleveland, 1974–75; Production Assistant 1975–76, Reporter 1976–, noon news anchor 1976–82, 6 to 11 o'clock anchor WJBK-TV, Storer Broadcasting Company, Detroit, 1983–. *Memberships:* American Federation Television and Radio Artists. *Address:* 2 Storer Place, Southfield, MI 48037, USA.

HIGHAM, Robin David Stewart, b. 20 June 1925, London, England. Professor of History. m. Barbara Jane Davies, 5 Aug. 1950, Scranton, Pennsylvania, 3 daughters. *Education:* AB cum laude, Harvard, 1950; MA Claremont Graduate School, 1953; PhD Harvard University, 1957. *Literary Appointments:* Editor, Military Affairs; Editor, Aerospace Historian; Editor, Journal of the West; President, Sunflower University Press. *Publications:* Britain's Imperial Air Routes, 1960; The British Rigid Airship, 1961, 1982; Armed Forces in Peacetime, 1963; The Military Intellectuals in Britain, 1966; Air Power: A Concise History, 1973, 1984; The Diary of a Disaster, 1986. *Contributor to:* The American Neptune; Balkan Studies; Business History Review; Airpower Historian; Military Affairs; Naval War College Review; and numerous other publications. *Literary Awards:* Aviation and Space Writers' Award, 1973; History Book Club selection, 1973. *Memberships:* Publications Committee, Conference of British Studies; Editorial Advisory Board, Technology and Culture. *Agent:* Bruce Hunter of David Higham; Claire Smith of Harold Ober. *Address:* 2961 Nevada Street, Manhattan, KS, 66502, USA.

HIGSON, Philip John Willoughby, b. 21 Feb. 1933, Newcastle under Lyne, Staffordshire, England. Author; Lecturer. *Education:* BA, 1956, MA, 1959, PhD, 1971, Liverpool University; Post Graduate Certificate of Education, University of Keele, 1972. *Literary Appointments:* Lecturer, Senior Lecturer, Chester College of Higher Education, 1972–; Chairman,

President, Chester Poets, 1974–. *Publications:* Poetry: Poems of Protest and Pilgrimage, 1966; To Make Love's Harbour, 1966; The Riposte and Other Poems, 1971; Sonnets to My Goddess, 1983; Maurice Rollinat: Les Nevroses, A Selected English Version, 1986. The Bizarre Barons of Rivington, Historical, 1965. Baudelaire: Flowers of Evil and Other Authenticated Poems, Editor and Translator with E E Ashe, 1975. *Contributions to:* Making Love, Picador Anthology containing translations of poems by D'Annunzio, 1978; Ciritical Quarterly; International Rhyme Revival Anthology; Onadelebrum Poetry Magazine; Chester Poets, Anthologies 1-12; Collegian. Historical features contributed to: Antiqueries Journal; Northern History; Genealogists Magazine; Coat of Arms; Complete Peerage; Antiquarian Society, Lancashire and Cheshire; Historical Society, Lancashire and Cheshire. *Honour:* Competition Awards, Poetry, Chester Festival, 1981–83. *Memberships:* Society of Authors; Fellow, Society of Antiquaries; Fellow, Royal Society of Arts. *Address:* Senior Common Room, Chester College of Higher Education, Cheyney Road, Chester CH1 4BJ, England.

HILD, Nancy Blanchette, b. 21 Nov. 1942, Hartford, Connecticut, USA. Writer. m. Robert Alexander Hild, 27 May 1972, Falls Church, Virginia, 1 daughter. *Education:* BS, University of Maryland, 1965; MS, University of Tennessee, 1984. *Literary Appointments:* Reporter, United Press International, Washington, District of Columbia, 1964; Columnist, Ankara Daily News, Ankara, Turkey, 1966; US Information Agency International Press Service, 1968; Faculty, University of Tennessee College of Communications, 1978; Editor, Networker, University of Tennessee Commission for Women, 1982. *Contributions to:* The Bent Magazine; Topic Magazine, Africa; Journalism Educator, USA; Al Arabi Magazine, Kuwait; Span Magazine, Iran; Marzhaye Now Magazine; Del Yagui Tribune, Mexico; al-Majal Magazine, Lebanon; Panorama Magazine, Pakistan; Hindusthan Standard, India. *Honours:* One Show Merit Award, Art Directors Club and Copy Club of New York, 1974; Photography Award for exhibit on Community Life, Tennessee Agricultural and Industrial Fair, 1976. *Memberships:* Past Chapter President, Women in Communications Incorporated; Past Chapter Vice President, International Association of Business Communicators; Kapa Tau Alpha. *Address:* 2623 Joneva Road, Knoxville, TN 37932, USA.

HILL, Gladwyn, b. 16 June 1914. Writer. m. Elisita Stuntz, 19 Aug. 1942, New York, USA, 1 son, 1 daughter. *Education:* BSc, Harvard University, Cambridge, Massachusetts, USA. *Major Publications:* Dancing Bear: An Inside Look at California Politics, 1968; Madman in a Lifeboat: Issues of the Environmental Crisis, 1972. *Contributor to:* New York Times; California Magazine; California Journal; World's Fair; Los Angeles Times. *Honour:* Thomas L Stokes International Award for Environmental reporting, 1972. *Memberships:* Authors Guild. *Address:* 6207 Mulholland Highway, Los Angeles, CA 90068, USA.

HILL, Hamlin, b. 7 Nov. 1931, Houston, Texas, USA. Professor. *Education:* BA University of Houston, 1953; MA, University of Texas, 1954; PhD, University of Chicago, 1959. *Publications:* The Art of Huckleberry Finn, (with W Blair), 1962, revised edition 1969; Mark Twain and Elisha Bliss, 1964; Mark Twain's Letters to His Publishers, 1867–1894, 1967; Mark Twain: God's Fool, 1973; America's Humour from Poor Richard to Doonesbury, (with W Blair), 1978. *Contributions to:* American Literature; American Literature Realism; American Literature Scholarship; Studies in American Humor, and others. *Honours include:* Grants-in-Aid, American Council of Learned Societies, 1963, 1965 and 1967; Guggenheim Fellow, 1971–72. *Membership:* Modern Language Association. *Address:* Department of English, University of New Mexico, Albuquerque, NX 87131, USA.

HILL, Niki, b. 19 June 1938, Belfast, Northern Ireland. Journalist. m. Ian Julian Hill, Belfast, Northern Ireland, 2 daughters. *Education:* BSc Economics, Queen's

University, Belfast. *Literary Appointments:* Freelance Journalist working in radio and television, newspapers and magazines, 1977; Feature Writer, Belfast Telegraph, 1977; Present Woman's Editor, Belfast News Letter. *Publications:* Culinary Tales, 1974. *Contributions to:* The Grocer; Catering Review; Woman's Own; London Daily Telegraph; Belfast Telegraph; Belfast News Letter; and others. *Honours:* Glenfiddich Awards, 1973 and 1974; Argos Award, 1977. *Address:* 19 Windsor Road, Belfast BT9 6FR, Northern Ireland.

HILL, Robert White, b. 17 Jan. 1941, Anniston, Alabama, USA. University Professor. m. Jane Bowers, 16 Aug. 1980, Mountain Rest, South Carolina, 2 sons, 1 daughter. *Education:* AB, 1963, MA, 1964, University of North Carolina; PhD, University of Illinois, 1972. *Literary Appointment:* Co-editor, South Carolina Review, 1973–. *Publications:* Billy Goat, 1978; James Dickey with R J Calhoun, 1983. *Contributions to:* Southern Poetry Review; Southern Review; Shanandoah; Hopkins Quarterly; REAL. *Honours:* Tricentennial South Carolina Poetry Fellow, 1968; Anna Rena Blake, 1972; McKinley Peace Prize (2nd place) 1980; Davidson Miscellany Fiction (2nd place) 1982; Greenville, South Carolina, Arts Festival, 1984. *Memberships:* Modern Language Association; South Atlantic MLA; Philological Association of the Carolinas; Emrys Foundation. *Address:* 105 Lark Circle, Clemson, SC 29631, USA.

HILLERT, Margaret, b. 22 Jan. 1920. Teacher. *Education:* RN, University of Michigan School of Nursing, USA; AB, Wayne University College of Education. *Appointments include:* Registered Nurse, 3 years; Primary Teacher, 34 years. *Publications:* Farther Than Far, 1969; I Like to Live in the City, 1970; Who Comes to Your House, 1973; Come Play With Me, 1975; The Sleepytime Book, 1975; What Is It?, 1978; I'm Special...So Are You!, 1979; Action Verse for the Primary Classroom, 1980; Doing Things, 1980; Let's Take a Break, 1981; Rabbits and Rainbows, 1985; 55 juvenile books, 12 in, Dear Dragon Series; various translations into Swedish, Danish, German, Portuguese. *Contributor to:* Numerous literary magazines & journals; numerous anthologies. *Honours include:* Various 1st Prizes; TV Interview, Channel 7, WXYZ Detroit, 1979. *Memberships:* Detroit Women Writers; Poetry Society of Michigan; International League of Children's Poets; Society of Children's Book Writers; Emily Dickinson Society. *Address:* 31262 Huntley Square, E Birmingham, MI 48009, USA.

HILLGRUBER, Andreas Fritz, b. 18 Jan. 1925, Angerburg, Federal Republic of Germany. University Professor, m. Karin Zierau, 11 Jan. 1960, 2 sons, 1 daughter. *Education:* PhD, 1954; Habilitation, 1965. *Publications:* Hitler, König Carol und Marysthall Antonescu, 1954, 2nd edition 1965; Hitler's Strasstegie-Politik und Kriegführung 1940–41, 1965, 2nd edition 1982; Deutschlands Rolle in der Vorgeschichte der beiden Weltkriege, 1967, 2nd edition 1979; Grossmachtpolitik und Militarismus im 20 Jahrhundert, 1974; Bismarcks Aussenpolitik, 1972, 2nd edition 1981; Deutsche Grossmacht und Weltpolitik im 19 und 20 Jahrhundert, 1977, 2nd edition 1979; Europa in der Weltpolitik der Wachkriegszeit (1945–1963), 1979, 2nd edition 1981; Der Zweite Weltkrieg 1939–1945– Kriegsziele und Strategie der großen Mächte, 1982, 4th edition 1985; Die Last der Nation, 1984. *Contributions to:* Militärgeschichtliche Studies; Militärgeschichtliche Mitteilungen; Kölner Historische Abhandlungen; Historische Zeitschrift. *Memberships:* Historische Kommission bet der Bayerischen; Akademie der Wissenschaften; Rheinisch-Westfälische Akademie der Wissenschaften. *Address:* Gyrofstraße 21, D–5000 Köln 41, Federal Republic of Germany.

HILLIARD, Noel Harvey, b. 6 Feb. 1929, Napier, NZ. Journalist, Author. m. Kiriwai Mete, 8 Sep. 1954, Wellington, NZ. 2 sons, 2 daughters. *Education:* Victoria University of Wellington; Teachers Certificate, Wellington Teachers' College, 1955. *Literary Appointments:* New Zealand Literary Fund Scholarship in Letters, 1962, 1975; Robert Burns Fellowship in Literature, Otago University, Dunedin, New Zealand, 1971–72. *Publications:* Maori Girl, 1960; (9th Edition 1983); A Piece of Land, 1963; Power of Joy, 1965; A Night at Green River, 1969, 1975; We Live By a Lake, 1972; Maori Woman, 1974; Send Somebody Nice, 1976; Wellington, City Alive, 1976; Selected Stories, 1977; The Glory and the Dream, 1978. *Honour:* Hubert Church Memorial Award, 1961. *Memberships:* New Zealand Journalists' Union; PEN (New Zealand Centre); New Zealand Educational Institute. *Address:* 28 Richard Street, Titahi Bay, Wellington, NZ.

HILLIARD, Robert L, b. 25 June 1925, New York, New York, USA. Educator; Author. 1 son, 1 daughter. *Education:* BA; MA; MFA; PhD. *Publications:* Blue Rock Land, 1956; Writing for Television and Radio, 1962, 4th edition, 1984; Understanding Television, 1964; Radio Broadcasting, 1967, 3rd edition, 1985; Television and the Teacher, 1976; Television Broadcasting, 1978; Television and Adult Education, 1985. *Contributions to:* Communication, education and general journals, about 40 articles in the field. *Address:* 38 Essex Street, Cambridge, MA 02139, USA.

HILLIER, Jack Ronald, b. 1912, London, England. Wood Engraver; Book Illustrator; Art Critic; Writer; Art Historian. *Publications include:* Japanese Masters of the Colour-Print, 1954; Hokusai, 1955; Utamaro, 1961; Hokusai Drawings, 1966; The Japanese Print, A New Approach, 1960; Landscape Prints of Old Japan, 1960; Japanese Drawings, 1965; The Harari Collection of Japanese Paintings and Drawings, 1970; Japanese Paintings and Prints in the Collection of Mr and Mrs Richard P Gale, 1970p The Uninhibited Brush: Japanese Art in the Shijo Style, 1974; Japanese Prints and Drawings from the Vever Collection, 1976; Japanese Drawings of the 18th and 19th Centuries, 1980; The Art of Hokusai in Book Illustration, 1950; Japanese Prints, 300 Years of Albums and Books, (with Lawrence Smith), 1980. *Contributor to:* Connoisseur. *Address:* 27 White Post Hill, Redhill, Surrey RH1 6DA, England.

HILLS, Ida, b. Casper, USA. Writer. m. Wesley Hills, 29 May 1943, Albuquerque, 1 son, 2 daughters. *Education:* BA, University of Wyoming. *Publications:* A Love to Remember, 1980; Shalom, My Love, 1981; Heartbreaker Mine, 1983. *Contributor to:* Santa Cruz (CA) Sentinel; Western Treasures; Single Life; Flower & Garden. *Membership:* Romance Writers of America. *Agent:* Ann Elmo. *Address:* 3920 Porter Gulch, Aptos, CA 95003, USA.

HILTON, Margot Pamela, b. 18 Aug. 1947, London, England. Arts Administrator; Writer. m. Graeme Binndell, 3 Oct. 1979, Melbourne, Australia, 1 son, 1 daughter. *Education:* BA, English, Honours, 1971, MA, Drama & Theatre Arts, 1972, Leeds University, England. *Appointments:* Drama Adviser, Victorian Ministry for the Arts, 1974–79; Storyliner & Scriptwriter with Grundy Organisation, 1980; Australian National Playwrights Conference, 1981; Executive Officer, Australian Society of Authors, 1981–84; Playwright in Residence, Australian National Playwrights Conference, 1983; Executive Secretary, Victorian Premier's Literary Awards, 1984–88; Promotions Manager, August Robertson Publishers, 1985–. *Publications:* (Performed Plays) Potiphar's Wife; Marmalade File, 1983; Sanealing Pips, 1983. *Contributor to:* Theatre Australia; Playboy; The New Review; Australian Author; The Bulletin; Architecture Australia. *Memberships:* Australian Writers Guild; Victorian Writers Theatre; Fellowship of Australian Writers. *Agent:* Curtis Brown. *Address:* 84 Surrey Street, Potts Point, NSW 2011, Australia.

HIMROD, Brenda Lee, b. 10 Apr. 1945, Danville, Virginia, USA. Author. m. Robert Himrod, 31 Dec. 1974, California. *Education:* AA. *Publications:* As Brenda Trent: Rising Star, 1981; Winter Dreams, 1981; A Stranger's Wife, 1981; Run From Heartache, 1982; Stormy Affair, 1982; Runaway Wife, 1982; Steal Love

Away, 1983; Hunter's Moon, 1983; Without Regrets, 1984; Bewitched By Love, 1986. As Megan Trent: Bitter Vines, 1982; Hold Love Tightly, 1983; Tenderness at Twilight, 1983; Tomorrow Will Come, 1984; Live Together as Strangers, 1984; Twice the Loving, 1985; The Trouble with Magic, 1985; Gypsy Renegade, 1986. *Contributions to:* Personal Romances; Intimate Story; True Love; Modern Love; True Life Secrets. *Memberships:* Romance Writers of America. *Literary Agent:* Teal and Watt Literary Agency. *Address:* 329 Wilson Road, Danville, VA 24541, USA.

HINCE, Michael Anthony, b. 29 June 1947, Melbourne, Australia. Writer, Broadcaster. *Education:* BA, La Trobe University, Melbourne, Australia. *Literary Appointments:* Former editor, 'Epicurean magazine; Production editor, Australian Journal of Optometry; Editor, Australian Wine and Spirit Brewing Review; Editor, Victorian Farmers and Graziers Association Newsletter. *Publication:* The Great Weekend Escape Book, 1986. *Contributions to:* The Age Newspaper; Epicurean magazine; Signature; ABC radio 3LO and 3AR; This Australia magazine; Australian Gourmet magazine; Age Good Food Guide; Australian. *Memberships:* Graduate Union, University of Melbourne; Wine Press Club of Victoria; Wine and Food Society of Victoria; Society of Business Communicators. *Address:* 342 Rathdowne Street, Carlton North, Victoria 3054, Australia.

HINCHLIFFE, Bruce Daniel, b. 21 July 1935, Rockhampton, Queensland, Australia. Journalism. m. Jocelyn Margaret Prouten, Toowoomba, 2 sons. *Appointments:* Chief of Staff, Toowoomba Chronicle; Sub-Editor, Hong Kong Star, The Courier Mail, Brisbane; Editor, The Chronicle, Toowoomba. *Publications:* Editor: They Meant Business – An Illustrated History of Eight Toowoomba Enterprises, 1984. *Honours:* Recipient Commonwealth Press Union Scholarship to study at Thomson Foundation Journalism Course, Cardiff, Wales. *Address:* 5 Range Street, Toowoomba, Queensland, Australia.

HINDMARCH, Gladys Maria, b. 1 Jan. 1940, Ladysmith, British Columbia, Canada. Writer, College Instructor. 1 son, 1 daughter. *Education:* BA and MA, University of British Columbia. *Publications:* The Peter Stories; A Birth Account. *Contributor to:* The Capilano Review; Writing; Periodics. *Memberships:* Writers' Union of Canada. *Address:* 1750 Parker Street, Vancouver, BC, V5L 2K8, Canada.

HINRICHSEN, Donald David, b. 22 Apr. 1946, Savanna, Illinois, USA. Journalist, Editor. *Education:* BA, American University, Washington DC, USA. *Literary Appointments:* Associate Editor, 1978–81, Editor in chief, 1981–85 AMBIO, Stockholm, Sweden; Science and Technology Editor, Sweden Now, 1978–85, Stockholm Sweden; Editor in chief, World Resources Report, World Resources, Washington DC, 1985–. *Publications:* The Future Works editor, Swedish Institute, Stockholm, 1980; Nuclear War: The Aftermath, Co-editor, 1983. *Contributions to:* Sweden Now, Stockholm; New Scientist, London; International Wildlife; Scientific American; Biotechnology, New York; Compass News Features, Luxembourg; Christian Science Monitor, Boston; Scanorama, Stockholm. *Memberships:* Association of Scientific Journalists, Sweden; Foreign Press Association of Sweden; Foreign Press Association of Denmark; European Association of Science Writers. *Address:* World Resources Institute, 1735 New York Avenue NW, Washington, DC 20006, USA.

HINSON, Edward Glenn, b. 27 July 1931, St Louis, Missouri, USA. Professor of Church History. m. Martha Anne Burks, 1 Sep. 1956, Affton, Missouri, 1 son, 1 daughter. *Education:* BA, Washington University, St Louis; BD, ThD, The Southern Baptist Theological Seminary; D.Phil, Oxford University. *Literary Appointments:* Editor, Review and Expositor; Editor, Baptist Peacemaker; Consulting Editor, Weavings. *Publications:* The Church; Design for Survival;

Glossolalie; Seekers, after Mature Faith; I and II Timothy, Titus, in, Broadman Bible Commentary; A Serious Call to a Contemplative Lifestyle; Saul Liberty; Jesus Christ; The Integrity of the Church; Doubleday Devotional Classis; The Reaffirmation of Prayer; The Early Church Fathers; A History of Baptists in Arkansas; The Evangelization of the Roman Empire; Are Southern Baptiste Evangelicals? *Contributor to:* Revie de Qumran; Church History; Review and Expositor; Christian Century; Sojourners; Baptist Peacemaker; Religion in Life; Search; Perspectives in Religious Studies; Baptist History and Heritage; Foundations; Journal of Ecumenical Studies; The Deacon; Ecumenical Trends; Biblical Illustrator; Seeds; One in Christ; Liturgy; Worship; Canadian Churchman; NICM Journal. numerous Baptist periodicals. *Memberships:* Fellow, American Association of Theological Schools; Fellow, Association of Theological Schools in the USA and Canada. *Address:* Box 1856, Southern Baptist Theological Seminary, 2825 Lexington Road, Louisville, KY 40280, USA.

HINTIKKA, Kaarlo Jaakko Juhani, b. 12 Jan. 1929, Helsingen pitäjä, Finland. Philosopher. m. Merrill Bristow Provence, 11 Feb. 1978. *Education:* Cand Phil, Lic. Phil 1952, DPh 1956, University of Helsinki. *Literary Appointments:* Editor in Chief, Synthese, 1965–76. *Publications include:* Models for Modalities, 1969; Logic, Language-Games and Information, 1973; Knowledge and the Unknown, 1974; Induzione accettazione, informazione, 1974; The Intentions of Intentionality, 1975; Aristotle on Modality and Determinism, 1977; The Game of Language, (with J Kulas), 1983; Anaphora and Definite Descriptions, (with J Kulas), 1985; Investigating Wittgenstein, (with M Hintikka), 1986. *Contributions to:* over 250 professional journals including: Synthese; Several philosophical journals in English. *Honours include:* Guggenheim Fellow, Centre of Advance Study in Behavioral Sciences, 1970–71; Wihuri International Prize, 1976; Honorary Doctorate, University of Liege, Belgium 1984. *Memberships include:* President 1975–76, Pacific Division, American Philosophical Association; Member and official of various academic organisations. *Address:* Department of Philosophy, Florida State University, Tallahassee, FL 32306, USA.

HITCHCOCK, Henry-Russell, b. 3 June 1903, Boston, MA, USA. Archtectural Historian. *Education:* AB 1924, MA, Harvard, 1927; LHD, University of Pennsylvania, 1976; DHL, Wesleyan University, 1979. *Publications:* Modern Architecture, 1929, 1971; The International Style, 1932; 1966; Architecture of H H Richardson, 1936, 1961, 1966; In the Nature of Materials, Buildings of Frank Lloyd Wright, 1942, 1974; American Architectural Books, 1946, 1962; Early Victorian Architecture in Britain, 1954, 1974; Architecture, 19th and 20th Centuries, 1958, 1963, 1969, 1971; The Brothers Zimmermann, 1968; Rococo Architecture in Southern Germany, 1968; German Renaissance Architecture, 1981. *Honours include:* Honorary DFA, NY University, 1969; Honorary DLitt, University of Glasgow, 1973; Benjamin Franklin Medal, Royal Society of Arts, 1979. *Address:* 152 East 62nd Street, New York, NY 10021, USA.

HJARTARSON, Snorri, b. 22 Apr. 1906, Iceland. Librarian. *Education:* Studied painting, Copenhagen, Denmark, 1931, Academy of Fine Arts, Oslo, Norway, 1932–33. *Literary Appointments:* Librarian, 1939–43, Chief Librarian, 1943–66, Reykjavik City Library. *Publications:* Hljot flyver Ravnen, novel, 1934. Poetry: Kvaedi, 1944; A Gnitaheioi, 1952; Lauf og stjornur, 1966; Haustrokkrid yfir mer, 1979. *Contributions to:* Timarit Mals og menningar; Helgafell; Thjodviljinn, and various others. *Honours:* State Honorary Stipend Award, 1976–; Nordic Council Literary Prize, 1981; Honorary Member, Writers Union of Iceland. *Memberships:* Writers Union of Iceland; Past President, Federation of Icelandic Artists. *Address:* Eiriksgata 27, Reykjavik, Iceland.

HOAGLAND, Edward, b. 21 Dec. 1932, New York City, New York, USA. Writer. m. Marion Magid, 28 Mar. 1968, 1 daughter. *Education:* BA, Harvard University, 1955. *Literary Appointments:* Instructor, University of Iowa, University of Columbia, Rugtgers University, Sarah Lawrence University, City College of New York and New School for Social Research. *Publications:* Cat Man, 1956; The Circle Home, 1960; The Peacock's Tail, 1965; Notes from the Century Before, 1969; The Courage of Turtles, 1971; Walking the Dead Diamond River, 1973; Red Wolves and Black Bears, 1976; African Calliope, 1979; The Edward Hoagland Reader, 1979; The Tugman's Passage, 1982. *Contributions to:* Numerous publications. *Honours:* Guggenheim Award, twice; Prix de Rome and others. *Memberships:* American Academy and Institute of Arts and Letters. *Literary Agent:* Robert Lescher. *Address:* 463 West Street, New York, NY 10014, USA.

HOBERMAN, Gerald, b. 2 Jan. 1943, Cape Town, Republic of South Africa. Company Executive Director. m. Hazel Suchet, 17 Dec. 1970, 2 sons, 1 daughter. *Education:* Studied with Ted Harrison, Studio Briggs, London, England, 1968–70. *Literary Appointments:* Mounted exhibition, Oriental Portfolio, 1967; Managing director, Phototecnic Laboratories, Cape Town, South Africa, 1970–71, Phototecnic Laboratories Limited, London, England, 1971–73. *Publications:* The Art of Coins and Their Photograph, 1981; Boer War Tribute Medals, photographic illustrator, 1982; Coins of South Africa, Photographic illustrator, 1983; Publishing History of the Art of Coins and Their Photography, 1985; Oriental Portfolio, 1985; Time Life Planet Earth Series/Noble Metals, 1984, photographic illustrator. *Contributions to:* Connoisseur; Hasselblad Magazine; Canadian Collector; Norwegian Numismatic Journal; auction catalogue for Spink and Son, London, England. *Memberships:* Fellow, Royal Numismatic Society, President, South African Numasmatic Society; Royal Photographic Society; American Numismatic Society; American Numismatic Association; Classical Association of South Africa; Historical Society of Cape Town; Botanical Society of South Africa. *Address:* 2 Avenue Bordeaux, Constantia, 7800, Republic of South Africa.

HOBSON, Anthony Robert Alwyn, b. 5 Sep. 1921, Rhyl, North Wales. Bibliographical Historian. *Education:* MA, Oxford University (New College). *Publications:* French and Italian Collectors and their Bindings, 1953; Great Libraries, 1970; Apollo and Pegasus, 1975. *Contributions to:* Times Literary Supplement; The Library, Transactions of the Bibliographical Society; La Bibliofilia, and others. *Honours:* Cavaliere Ufficiale, Al Merito della Republica Italiana, 1979. *Memberships:* Past President, Bibliographical Society; Honorary President, Edinburgh Bibliographical Society, Scotland; President, Past Vice President, Association Internationale de Bibliophilie. *Address:* The Glebe House, Whitsbury, Fordingbridge, Hampshire, England.

HOCH, Edward D, b. 22 Feb. 1930, Rochester, NY, USA. Author. *Education:* University of Rochester. *Publications:* The Shattered Raven, 1969; The Transvection Machine, 1971; The Fellowship of the Hand, 1973; The Frankenstein Factory, 1975; Best Detective Stories of the Year (editor), 1976–81; The Thefts of Nick Velvet, 1978; Year's Best Mystery and Suspense Stories, (editor), 1982–86; The Quest of Simon Ark, 1984; Leopold's Way, 1985. *Contributor to:* Ellery Queen's Mystery Magazine; Alfred Hitchcock's Mystery Magazine; etc. *Honours:* Recipient, Edgar Award, Mystery Writers of America, 1968. *Memberships include:* Board of Directors, Mystery Writers of AMerica; Crime Writers Association. *Address:* 2941 Lake Avenue, Rochester, NY 14612, USA.

HOCHWALDER, Fritz, b. 28 May 1911, Vienna, Austria. Playwright. *Publications:* (plays) Esther, 1940; Das heilige Experiment, 1942; Hotel du Commerce, 1944; Der Fluchtling, 1945; Donadieu, 1953; die Herberge, 1956; Fer Unschuldige, 1958; Donnerstag, 1959; I003, 1963; Der Himbeerpflucker, 1964; Der Befehl, 1968; Lazaretti, 1974; Dis Prinsessin von Chimay, 1981; Der verschwundene Mond, 1982; Die Burgschaft, 1984. *Honours:* Literary prize, City of Vienna, 1955; Grillparzer Prize, Austrian Academy of Science, 1956; Anton Wildgans Prize, 1963; Austrian State Prize for Literature, 1966; Ehrenkreux fur Wissenschaft and Kunst, 1971; Ehrenring der Stadt Wien, 1972. *Address:* Am. Oeschbrig 27, 8053 Zurich, Switzerland.

HODDER-WILLIAMS, Mark, b. 24 Mar. 1939, Bickley, Kent, England. Book Publishing Executive. m. Janette Elspeth Cochran, 14 Oct. 1961, 3 sons, 1 daughter. *Education:* MA, Politics, Philosophy and Economics (Oxon). *Literary Appointments:* Chairman, Publishers Association Distribution Committee, 1978–80; Member, Publishers Association Management Advisory Panel, 1982–. *Contributions to:* The Bookseller; Publishing News. *Address:* Hodder & Stoughton Limited, Mill Road, Dunton Green, Sevenoaks, Kent TN13 2YA, England.

HODGE, Jane Aiken, b. 4 Dec. 1917, Boston, MA, USA. Author. *Education:* BA, Somerville College, Oxford, England; AM, Harvard University, USA. *Publications include:* The Adventurers, 1965; Watch the Wall, My Darling, 1966; Here Comes a Candle, 1967; The Winding Stair, 1968; Marry in Haste, 1969; Greek Wedding, 1970; Savannah Purchase, 1971; The Double Life of Jane Austen, 1972; Strangers in Company, 1973; Shadow of a Lady, 1974; One Way to Venice, 1975; Rebel Heiress 1975; Runaway Bride, 1976; Judas Flowering, 1976; Red Sky at Night, 1977; Last Act, 1979; Wide is the Water, 1981; The Lost Garden, 1982; The Private World of Georgette Heyer, 1984; Secret Island, 1985. *Memberships:* Society of Authors; Authors' League of America. *Literary Agent:* David Higham Associates Limited. *Address:* 23 Eastport Lane, Lewes, Sussex BN7 1TL, England.

HODGELL, Patricia Christine, b. 16 Mar. 1951, Des Moines, Iowa, USA. Writer. *Education:* BA, (Comparative Literature), 1973, Eckerd College; MA, 1976; ABD, (English), 1981, University of Minnesota. *Publications:* God Stalk, 1982; Dark of the Moon, 1985. *Contributions to:* Riverside Quarterly; Berkley Showcase; Clarion SF; Elsewhere III; Imaginary Lands. *Membership:* Science Fiction Writers of America. *Literary Agent:* Adele Leone Agency. *Address:* 1237 Liberty Street, Oshkosh, WI 54901, USA.

HODGES, C(yril) Walter, b. 18 Mar. 1909. Freelance Writer; Book Illustrator; Theatrical Historian and Designer. *Education:* Goldsmiths' College School of Art, London, England. *Publications:* Columbus Sails, 1939; The Flying House, 1947; Shakespeare and the Players, 1948; The Globe Restored, 1953, 1968; The Namesake, 1964; Shakespeare's Theatre, 1964; The Norman Conquest, 1966; Magna Carta, 1966; The Marsh King, 1967; The Spanish Armada, 1967; The Overland Launch, 1969; The English Civil War, 1972; Shakespeare's Second Globe, 1973; Playhouse Tales, 1974; The Emperor's Elephant, 1975. *Contributor to:* Shakespeare Survey; Illustrator; advertising; magazines, especially Radio Times; Children's books; designer; stage productions; exhibitions murals; art Director, Encyclopedia Britannica Films; Illustrations of original staging, for The New Cambridge Shakespeare, 1984–, 36 volumes altogether. *Honours:* Kate Greenaway Medal, illustration, 1965; Honours List, Hans Christian Anderson International Award, 1966; DLitt, (Hon causa), University of Sussex, 1979. *Literary Agent:* Laura Cecil. *Address:* 36 Southover, High Street, Lewes, East Susex, England.

HODGES, Harold Mellor, b. 9 Apr. 1922, Beverly Hills, USA. Professor; Author. *Education:* AB, Stanford University, 1944; MA 1952, PhD, University of Southern California 1953. *Publications include:* Cosnflict and Consensus, Readings Toward a Sociological Prospective, Exploring Sociology, 1976; On Becoming Fully Human: Search for Self, Topdogs, Underdogs and Middle Americans; Social Inequality in a Post Peninsular People: Social Class in a Metropolitan

Complex, 1964, 2nd editon, 1976; The New Humanists; Synergy as Metaphor; Hodge/Podge: Random but Related Quotations, 1984; Hodge/Podge II, 1985; The Day After Tomorrow, 1985, 1986. *Contributor to:* Numerous book reviews. *Honours include:* Distinguished Visiting Professor,Yale University, 1969–70. *memberships:* American Sociology Association. Centre for Creative Arts and Sciences (Chairman of Board). *Address:* 19875 Park Drive, Saratoga, CA 95070, USA.

HODGSON, Marion Foster Stegeman, b. 16 Dec. 1921. Writer. m. Edward McCullough Hodgson, 1 June 1944, Fort Worth, Texas, 2 sons, 1 daughter. *Education:* BA Journalism, University of Georgia; Women Airforce Service Pilot, US Air Force. *Publications:* College Kids Cookbook, 1967; The Bride's Survival Kit, 1970; What's Your Beef?, 1973; One-Armed Cooking, for new mothers and others, 1979; Where Thunder Hides, 1979. *Contributions to:* McCall's; Good Housekeeping; Texas Metro; Guideposts. *Membership:* Authors Guild. *Literary Agent:* Curtis Brown Limited. *Address:* 624 North Bailey, Fort Worth, TX 76107, USA.

HODGSON, Neville, b. 13 Feb. 1929, Birmingham, England. BBC Radio Actor; Drama Lecturer. *Education:* LRAM; LGSM. *Appointments:* National Poetry Secretariat, 1978; BBC Radio Actor, 1955–65; Lecturer, College of Further Education, Shropshire. *Publications:* They Watch the President, play, 1967; 20 poems. *Contributor to:* Contemporary Review; Poetry Review; York Anthology; Australian Telegraph; Australian Argus; many others. *Honours:* 3 Bursaries, Yorkshire Arts: 1978, 1979, 1983. *Memberships:* York Poetry Society; Pennine Platform; Bradford Quarterly; Founder, Boulton Poetry Society. *Address:* 35 Wensleydale Rise, Shipley, Bakdon, West Yorkshire BD17 1GA, England.

HODSON, Henry Vincent, b. 12 May 1906, London, England. Newspaper and periodical Editor. m. Margaret Elizabeth Honey, 28 Mar. 1933, Brisbane, Queensland, Australia, 4 sons. *Education:* MA, Balliol College, Oxford University; Fellow, All Saints College, Oxford, 1928–35. *Literary Appointments:* Editor, the Round Table, 1933–39; Assistant Editor, 1945–50, Editor, 1950–61, The Sunday Times; Editor, The Annual Register, 1973–. *Publications:* Economics of a Changing World, 1933; Slump and Recovery 1929–34, 1938; Twentieth Century Empire, 1948; The Great Divide: Britain–India–Pakistan, 1969, 85; The Diseconomics of Growth, 1942. *Contributions to:* The Times; The Sunday Times; Illustrated London News; Encounter, and others. *Membership:* Society of Authors. *Address:* 23 Cadogan Lane, London SW1X 9DP, England.

HOEY, Joanne Nobes, b. 8 Dec. 1936, Rochester, New York, USA. Poet, Speaker. m. Charles Hoey, 25 Aug. 1956, Auburn, New York, USA, 3 sons, 3 daughters. *Education:* BA Communications; Diploma in Secretarial Science. *Publications:* Listen To My Touch, 1981; May I Touch You Now, 1983. *Contributions to:* Asphodel; Jersey Woman; Dragonfly; Avant. *Honours:* Ester Bovard Creative Writing Award, Glassboro State College, 1981. *Memberships:* Secretary, New Jersey Forum For the Arts. *Address:* 33 East Centennial Drive, Medford, NJ 08055, USA.

HOFF, Kay, b. 15 Aug. 1924, Neustadt, Holstein, Germany. Writer. *Education:* Dr Phil, University of Kiel, 1945–49. *Major Publications:* Poems: Zeitzeichen, 1962; Netzwerk, 1969; Bestandsaufnahme, 1977; Gegen den Stundenschlag, 1982; Radio-plays: Alarm, 1963; Die Chance, 1964; Spiegelgespräch, 1968; Ein Schiff bauen, 1970; Hörte ich recht?, (8 radio plays, printed 1980); Novels: Bödelstedt, 1966; Ein ehrlicher Mensch, 1967; Drei, 1970; Wir reisen nach Jerusalem, 1976; Janus, 1984. *Memberships:* PEN Chapter, Federal Republic of Germany. *Honours:* Poetry Prize, Competition for Young Authors from Schleswig-Holstein, 1952; 2nd Prize, Radio Play Competition, Süddeutscher Rundfunk, 1957; Achievement award, Nordehein-Westfalen, 1960; Ernst-Reuter Prize, 1965;

Georg Mackenses Prize, 1968. *Address:* Stresemannstraße 30, D–2400 Lübeck, Federal Republic of Germany.

HOFFMAN, William M, b. 12 Apr. 1939, New York City, USA. Writer. *Education:* BA, cum laude, City College of New York, 1960. *Literary Appointments:* Assistant Editor, Associate Editor, Drama Editor, Hill and Wang, 1961–68. Playwriting Consultant, CAPS Program of the New York State Council on the Arts, 1975–77; Playwriting Consultant, Massachusetts Arts and Humanities Foundation, 1978; Playwright-in-Residence, American Conservatory Theatre, San Francisco, 1978; Playwright-in-Residence, La Mama Theatre, New York City, 1978–79; Visiting Professor in Playwriting, Hofstra University 1980–. *Publications:* Plays: Thank You, Miss Victoria, in New American Plays, 1970; Saturday Night At the Movies, in The Off-Off-broadway Book, 1973; X's, in More Pays From Off-Off-Broadway, 1973; A Quick Nut Bread to Make Your Mouth Water, in Spontaneous Combustion, 1973; The Last Days of Stephen Foster, in Dramatics Magazine, 1978; Connbury, in Gay Plays, 1979; From Fool to Hanged Man, in Scenarics, 1980, ASIS, 1985. Anthologies: Gay Plays: The First Collection, 1979; New American Plays, Vols 2,3,4, 1968,1970,1971. Poetry and Lyrics: The Cloisters, song cycle included in 31 New American Poets, 1970 and Fine Frenzy, 1972; Wedding Song, 1979. *Contributions to:* Vogue, Village Voice, New York Nativ. Author of motion picture, television and radio scripts. *Honours:* Phi Beta Kappa; MacDowell Fellowship, 1971; Gugenheim Fellowship, 1974–75; National Endowment for the Arts, Librettist's Grant, 1975–76; National Endowment for the Arts, Creative Writing Fellowship, 1976–77; Metropolitan Opera, Commission for libretto for 100th Anniversary Opera, Final Figaro, 1980–; New York Foundation for the Arts Fellowship, 1985; Nominated for Tony Award for Best Play, ASIs, 1985; Dramadesk Award and Obie Award for, ASIs, 1985. *Memberships:* Dramatists Guild; Writer's Guild; ASCAP; PEN; Circle Repertory Theatre's. *Address:* c/o Luis San Jurjo, International Creative Management, 40 West 57th Street, New York, NY 10019, USA.

HOFFMANN, Ann Marie, b. 6 May 1930, Abingdon, Berkshire, England. Author; Author's Researcher; Indexer. *Literary Appointments:* Establishment of Authors' Research Services, 1966. *Publications:* The Dutch: How They Live and Work, 1971, 2nd edition 1973; Research: A Handbook for Writers and Journalists, 1975, 2nd edition 1979, 3rd edition 1986; Bocking Deanery, 1976; Lives of the Tudor Age, 1977; Majorca, 1978. *Contributions to:* Various professional journals. *Memberships:* Society of Authors; PEN (English Centre); Society of Women Writers & Journalists; Society of Indexers; Society of Genealogists; Society of Sussex Authors. *Address:* 104 Russell Court, Woburn Place, London WC1H 0LP, England.

HOFFMANN, Hilmar, b. 25 Aug. 1925, Bremen. City Councillor for Cultural Affairs. m. Brunhild Huelsmann, 1960, 1 son, 1 daughter. *Appointments:* Lecturer, Universities in Bochum, Frankfurt, Marburg; Guest Professor, University Tel Aviv; Professor, State Academy for Music & Theatre, Frankfurt. *Publications:* Erwachsenenbildung, 1962; Der tschechoslowakische Film, 1964; Fernsehdokumentation Castros Cuba, 1969; Tauben – reisende Boten, 1965; Theorie der Filmmontage, 1969; Perspektiven der Kulturpolitik, 1974; Kultur fur alle, 1979; Das Taubenbuch, 1981; Kultur-Zerstorung, 1983; Kultur Fuer Morgen, 1985. *Contributor to:* Several books on film and cultural policy; Lexica; etc. *Honours:* Ring of Honour, City of Oberhausen, 1970; Deutsches Filmband in Gold, 1976; Chevalier de L'Ordre Des Arts et Des Lettres, France; Goethe-Plakette Land Hessen. *Membership:* Deutscher Schriftsteller-Verband. *Agent:* S Fischer-Verlag, Frankfurt. *Address:* Buchrainstr. 94, 6 Frankfurt/Main 70, Federal Republic of Germany.

HOFFMANN, John Henry, b. 30 July 1928, Milwaukee, Wisconsin, USA. Dentist. m. Gloria Betty Lange, 14 Apr. 1950, at Milwaukee, Wisconsin, USA, 2 sons. *Education:* DMD, University of Oregon; DDPH, University of Toronto; FICD, Fellow, International College of Dentists; Certification, Dental Administration, State of Illinois; Certification, Dental Editor, Ohio State School of Journalism. *Publications:* Psycological Aspects of Dental Decay, 1968; Mandatory Flouridation in Illinois, 1970; Dental Sociology, 1972; Inside Dentistry, 1984. *Contributions to:* Over 200 articles or programs for newspapers, magazines, radio and television. *Honours:* United States Public Health Service, 1970; American Dental Association, 1983 and 1984; Philippine Dental Association, 1985. *Memberships:* American Association of Dental Editors; Guam Press Club; American Medical Writers Association; American Poetry Association. *Address:* Drawer 8170, Tamuning, Guam 96911, USA.

HOFFMANN, Stanley, b. 27 Nov. 1928, Vienna, Austria. Douglas Dillon Professor of the Civilisation of France, Harvard University. *Education:* MA, Harvard University, USA; Diploma of Political Science, Paris, France; LLD, University of Paris. *Publications:* In Search of France, Co-Author, 1963; The State of War, 1965; Gulliver's Troubles, 1968; Decline or Renewal?: France Since the 30s, 1974; Primacy or World Order, 1978; Duties Beyond Borders, 1981; Dead Ends, 1983; Living with Nuclear Weapons, Co-Author, 1983. *Contributions to:* Daedalus; Foreign Affairs; Foreign Policy; New York Review of Books; Esprit. *Address:* 91 Washington Avenue, Cambridge, MA 02140, USA.

HOGG, Ian Vernon, b. 29 Oct. 1926, Durham, England. Writer. m. Anna Trebinska, 10 Mar. 1962, Birmingham, 2 sons, 1 daughter. *Literary Appointments:* Editor, Jane's Military Review, 1982–; Editor, Jane's Infantry Weapons, 1983–. *Publications:* The Guns 1939–45, 1970; Artillery, 1973; Coast Defences of England and Wales, 1974; Military Small Arms of the 20th Century, 1973–; Fortress, 1975; Pistols of the World, 1978; Armour in Conflict, 1980; History of Fortification, 1981; Patton: A Biography, 1982; Encyclopedia of Ammunition, 1985. *Contributions to:* Defence; National Defense, USA; Armada, Switzerland; Defence Today, Italy; Nato's Fifteen Nations, Belgium; Defense Afrique, France; International Combat Arms, USA; Jane's Defence Review; Jane's Defence Weekly. *Membership:* Institute of Journalists. *Literary Agent:* Watson, Little Limited, 26 Charing Cross Road, London. *Address:* 15 Packers Hill, Upton-upon-Severn, Worcestershire WR8 OSG, England.

HOGGARD, James Martin, b. 21 June 1941, Wichita Falls, Texas, USA. Professor of English. m. Lynn Taylor, 23 May 1976, 1 son, 1 daughter. *Education:* BA, Southern Methodist University; MA, University of Kansas. *Literary Appointments:* Newspaper Reporter; University Professor of English, currently. *Publications:* Eyesigns, 1977; Trotter Ross, 1981; The Shaper Poems, 1983; Elevator Man, 1983; Two Gulls, One Hawk, 1983. *Contributions to:* Beyond Baroque; Blackbird Circle; Descant; Alembic; Cedar Rock; Mississippi Review; Poet and Critic; Poet; Poet Lore; Southern Poetry Review; South West Review; The Smith; Karamu Latin American Literary Review; Ohio Review; Mundus Artium; Texas Observer. *Honours:* David Russell Poetry Award, 1963; Fine Arts Festival Award, Midwest University, 1968; Hart Crane and Alice Crance Williams Memorial Award, 1969. *Memberships:* Texas Institute of Letters; Texas Association of Creative Writing Teachers. *Address:* 2414 Leighton Circle North, Wichita Falls, TX 76309, USA.

HOHENBERG, John, b. 17 Feb. 1906, New York City, USA. Journalist. m. (1). Dorothy Lannuier, 1928–77,(2). Joann Fogarty, 9 Mar. 1979, Nashville, Tennessee, 1 son, 1 daughter. *Education:* BLitt, Columbia University, 1927; PhD (hon causa) Wilkes College, 1978. *Literary Appointments:* Professor of Journalism, Columbia University, 1950–76; Meeman Professor, University of Tennessee, 1976–77; 78-81;

Gannett Professional in Residence, University of Kansas, 1977–78; Gannett Professor, University of Florida, 1981–82; Visiting Professor, University of Miami, 1982–83; Newhouse Professor, Syracuse Univerity, 1983–85; Distinguished Research Fellow, Gannett Center for Media Studies, Columbia, 1985–. *Publications:* The Pulitzer Prize Story, 1959; The Professional Journalist (now in 5th edition) 1960; Foreign Correspondence 1964; The New Front Page, 1965; Between Two Worlds 1968; The News Media 1968; Free Press/Free People 1971; New Era in the Pacific, 1972; A Crisis for the American Press, 1978; The Pulitzer Prizes, a history 1974; The Pulitzer Prize Story II 1980. *Honours Include:* Administrator, The Pulitzer Prizes, 1954–76; Pulitzer Prize Special Award for services to American journalism, 1976; Grantee for various studies by Knight, Ford and Gannett Foundations. Council on Foreign Relations appointee for Asian/ American Relations Study; Gold Key Award from Columbia Scholastic Press Association, Distinguished National Teaching Award, Society of Professional Journalists; Three Prizes for Distinguished Research, Society of Professional Journalists; Elected to Journalism Hall of Fame, Deadline Club, New York City. *Address:* 6212 Pleasant Ridge Road, Knoxville, TN 37952, USA.

HOHOL, Roman Stepan, b. 17 Apr. 1956, England. Editor. m. Erena Makowecky, 9 Aug. 1980, Toronto, 1 son, 1 daughter. *Education:* Bachelor of Journalism, Carleton University, Ottawa, Ontario; Bachelor of Arts, University of Toronto, Ontario. *Literary Appointment:* Editor, Pulp & Paper Journal, Toronto, Ontario, 1982. *Address:* 777 Bay Street, Toronto, Ontario M5W 1A7, Canada.

HOLBORN, Gerd, b. 9 May 1921, Berlin. Journalist. m. Wendy Cynthia Harington-Ray, 2 Nov. 1944, died 1981, 1 daughter. *Education:* BA Journalism and European History cum laude, Syracuse University, New York, USA. *Literary Appointments:* Reuters; Reader's Digest; Fin Times, 1963–67; AP Down-Jones Business News, 1967–. *Contributions to:* Everybody's; Geographical Magazine; TV Times; Wall Street Journal; Investors' Review. *Address:* Bromley, Kent, England.

HOLBROOK, Cyril Raymond, b. 26 July 1935, Cambridgeshire, England. Journalist; Editor. m. Anne Ward, 11 July 1959, Wisbech, Cambridgeshire, 1 son. *Literary Appointments:* Western Daily Press, Bristol, 1958; Eastern Evening News, Norwich, 1959; Evening Telegraph, Peterborough, 1971; Angling Times, Peterborough, 1972; Editor, Tackle and Guns, 1976–. *Contributor to:* Articles and photographs in many angling publications. *Honours:* 4 awards within East Midland Allied Press Group, 3 years to 1973. *Address:* The Shrubbery, Chatteris, Cambridgeshire PE16 6JE, England.

HOLBROOK, David Kenneth, b. 9 Jan. 1923, Norwich, England. Author. *Education:* MA, Downing College, Cambridge University. *Literary Appointments:* Fellow and Director of English Studies, Downing College, Cambridge University; Hooker Distinguished Visiting Professor, MacMaster University, Hamilton, Ontario, Canada, 1984. *Publications:* Children's Games, 1957; Imaginings, 1961; English for Maturity, 1961; Iron Honey Gold, 1961; People and Diamonds, 1962; Against the Cruel Frost, 1963; Lights in the Sky Country, 1963; Thieves and Angels, 1963; English for the Rejected, 1964; The Secret Places, 1964; Visions of Life, 1964; The Quest for Love, 1965; Flesh Wounds, 1966; I've Got to Use Words, 1966; Object Relations, 1967; The Exploring Word, 1967; Children's Writing, 1967; The Cambridge Hymnal and, The Apple Tree (with Elizabeth Poston) 1967 and 1976; Plucking the Rushes, 1968; Old World, New World, 1969; Human Hope and the Death Instinct, 1971; English in Australia Now, 1972; Sex and Dehumanisation, 1972; The Masks of Hate, 1972; Dylan Thomas: The Code of Night, 1972; The Pseudo-revolution, 1972; (Editor) The Case Against Pornography, 1972; The Honey of Man (with Christine MacKenzie), 1972 and 1975; Moments in

Italy, 1976; Sylvia Plath: Poetry and Existence, 1976; Education, Nihilism and Survival, 1977; Lost Bearings in English Poetry, 1977; Chance of a Lifetime, 1978; A Play of Passion, 1978; Selected Poems, 1980; English for Meaning, 1980; Education and Philosophical Anthropology, 1986; Evolutionary Theory and the Humanities, 1986. *Contributor to:* Encounter; Critical Quarterly; Universities Quarterly; 20th Century; and numerous other newspapers and journals. *Literary Awards:* Keats Memorial Prize, 1973; Prize, International Who's Who in Poetry, 1974; Arts Council Grant, 1975 and 1979. *Agent:* Bolt & Watson. *Address:* Demore Lodge, Brunswick Gardens, Cambridge, England.

HOLDEN, James Milnes, b. 2 Sep. 1918, Preston, Lancashire, England. Professor of Business Law. *Education:* LLB 1948, PhD 1950, LLD 1973, University of London; Barrister, Lincoln's Inn, London, 1948. *Publications:* History of Negotiable Instruments in English Law, 1955; Chalmer's Marine Insurance Act 1906 (co-editor), 5th edition 1956; The Law and Practice of Banking, volume 1, Banker and Customer, 4th edition 1986, and volume 2, Securities for Bankers' Advances, 7th edition 1986; Jones and Holden's Studies in Practical Banking, 6th edition 1971. *Contributions to:* Law Quarterly Review; Modern Law Review; Journal of the Institute of Bankers; Bankers' magazine; and other professional journals. *Honours:* Hirst Essay Prize, University College, London, 1948; Institute Prize, Institue of Bankers, 1970. *Address:* University of Stirling, Stirling FK9 4LA, Scotland.

HOLDER, Nancy L, b. 29 Aug. 1953, Palo Alto, California, USA. Writer. m. Wayne Holder, 27 Dec. 1980, La Mesa, California, USA. *Education:* BA,summa cum laude, University of California, San Diego. *Publications:* Teach Me to Love, 1982; Boundless Love, 1983; Shades of Moonlight, 1984; His Fair Lady, 1985; Stories in Shadows 8, 1985; Stories in Shadows 9, 1986; Once in Love with Amy, 1986. *Honours:* Best Rapture Romance 1984 and 1985; San Diego Writers and Editors Guild Award for Best Horror Fiction, 1985. *Memberships:* Romance Writers of America; Horror Writers of America. *Literary Agent:* Joseph Elder Agency.*Address:* 11365 Lake Rim Road, San Diego, CA 92131, USA.

HOLFORD, Ingrid, b. 10 Jan. 1920, Kingston on Thames, England. m. Garth Holford, 14 July 1948, Surbiton, 1 son, 1 daughter. *Education:* BSc (Econ). *Publications:* Interpreting the Weather, 1973; British Weather Disasters, 1976; Guinness Book of Weather Facts & Feats, 1978, 1982; Yachtsman's Weather Guide, 1979; Looking at Weather, 1985. *Contributor to:* Yachting Journals; Amateur Gardening; BBC Radio; etc. *Memberships:* Society of Authors; Royal Meteorological Society. *Address:* 5 Oberfield Road, Brockenhurst, Hampshire SO4 7QF, England.

HOLIERHOEK, Kees, b. 14 Oct. 1941, Delft, The Netherlands. Writer. *Education:* Dutch Language and Literature, University of Leiden. *Publications:* Cocks in the Convent Garden; Mark and the Soldiers; Fingers of Power; Cycling in the Dark; Nightwatch. *Television Plays:* Unfinished Past; The Shadow of the Water; and numerous others. *Film Scenarios:* Turkish Earth, Dutch Soil; Soldier of Orange (co-scenarist). *Address:* Reviusdreef 2, 2353 BE Leiderdorp, The Netherlands.

HOLL, Hristi Diane, b. 8 Dec. 1951, Iowa, USA. Writer, Teacher. m. Randy Holl, 17 June 1973, Beaman, Iowa, 1 son, 3 daughters. *Education:* BA in Elementary Education. *Publications:* Just Like a Real Family, 1983; Mystery by Mail, 1983; Footprints up my Back, 1984; The Rose Beyond the Wall, 1985; First Things First, 1986; Cast a Single Shadow, 1986; Perfect or Not, Here I Come, 1986. *Contributor to:* Jack & Jill; Touch; Family Life Today; Your Life and Health; and numerous other magazines. *Literary Awards:* Nominated for the 1986 Mark Twain Award; Nominated for the 1986 Iowa Children's Choice Award; Nominated for the 1986 Sequoya Children's Book Award (Oklahoma); Junior

Literary Guild selection, 1984. *Memberships:* Authors Guild; Society of Children's Book Writers. *Address:* Route 2, Box 26, Conrad, IA 50621, USA.

HOLLAHAN, Eugene, b. 27 Feb. 1933, Memphis, Tennessee, USA. Poet; Professor. m. Carol Honeycutt, 6 Apr. 1963, Raleigh, North Carolina, USA, 2 sons. *Education:* BA, MA, PhD, University of North Carolina, USA. *Literary Appointments:* Poetry Reviewer, Atlanta Journal-Constitution; National Book Critics Circle; American Institute for Writing Research, Inc; Advisory Board, Saul Bellow Journal; Advisory Board, Journal of Evolutionary Psychology. *Publications:* Stone Mountain Escape (poems), 1976; Philosophical Dimensions of Saul Bellow's Fiction, 1984. *Contributions to:* Contributor to various journals including, PMLA; Studies in Philology; Studies in the Novel; Modern Fiction Studies; Georgia Review. *Honours:* Bain-Swiggett Poetry Prize, University of Tennessee, USA, 1961. *Memberships:* Charter member, Nathaniel Hawthorne Society; Charter member, Saul Bellow Society; National Book Critics Circle. *Address:* Georgia State University, Atlanta, GA 30303, USA.

HOLLAND, Elizabeth Anne, b. 11 Jan. 1928, Farnborough, Hampshire, England. Lecturer; Research Worker. *Education:* BSc Economics, London; MA, Edinburgh University, Scotland. *Publications:* A Separate Person, 1962; The House in the North, 1963; The House by the Sea, 1965; The Adding-Up, 1968; New Maps of Tolkein Land, with Robert Giddings, 1981. *Contributions to:* The New Tolkein Newsletter, Co-Editor; The Scotsman; Winter's Tales. *Honours:* Isbister Scholarship, University of Manchester, 1943. *Address:* 16 Prior Park Buildings, Bath, Avon BA2 4NP, England.

HOLLAND, Isabelle Christian, b. 16 June 1920, Basel, Switzerland. Writer. *Education:* Liverpool University, England, 2 years; BA, Tulane University, New Orleans, Louisiana, USA. *Publications include:* Childrens Books: Amanda's Choice, 1970; The Mystery of Castle Rinaldi, 1972; The Man Without A Face, 1972; Heads You Win, Tails I Lose, 1973; Of Love and Death and Other Journeys, 1975; Alan And The Animal Kingdom, 1977; Hitchhike, 1977; Dinah and the Green Fat Kingdom, 1978; Now Is Not Too Late, 1980; Summer of My First Love, 1981; A Horse Named Peaceable, 1982; Abbie's God Book, 1982; Perdita, 1983; God, Mrs Muskrat and Aunt Dot, 1983; After The First Love, 1983; The Empty House, 1983; Kevin's Hat, 1984; The Island, 1984; The Empty House, 1985. Adult books: Cecily, 1967; Kilgaren, 1974; Trelawny, 1974; Moncrieff, 1975; Darcourt, 1976; Grenelle, 1976; The DeMaury Papers, 1977; Darcourt, 1977; Grenelle, 1978; The DeMaury Papers, 1978; Tower Abbey, 1978; The Marchington Inheritance, 1979; Counterpoint, 1980; The Lost Madonna, 1981; A Death at St Anselms, 1984; Cecily, 1985. *Memberships Include:* Author's Guild; PEN. *Literary Agent:* JCA Literary Agency. *Address:* 1199 Park Avenue, New York, NY 10028, USA.

HOLLANDER, John, b. 28 Oct. 1929, New York City, USA. University Professor, Poet. m. (1) 15 June 1952, Cleveland, Ohio, (2) Anne Loesser, 15 Dec. 1982, New Haven, Connecticut, 2 daughters. *Education:* BA, Columbia University; MA, Columbia University; PhD Indiana University; Litt D (Hon), Marietta College. *Publications:* A Crackling of Thorns, 1958; The Untuning of the Sky, 1961; Movie-Going and Other Poems, 1962; Visions from the Ramble, 1965; Types of Shape, 1968; Images of Voice, 1970; The Night Mirror, 1971; The Head of the Bed, 1974; Tales Told of the Fathers, 1975; Vision and Resonance, 1975; Reflections on Espionage, 1976; Spectral Emanations, 1978; In Place, 1978; Blue Wine, 1979; The Figure of Echo, 1981; Rhyme's Reason, 1981; Looking Ahead, 1982; Powers of Thirteen, 1983; Dal Vere (with Saul Steinberg), 1983. *Edited:* The Wind and the Rain (with Harold Bloom), 1961; Poems of Ben Jonson, 1961; Jiggery-Pokery (with Anthony Hecht), 1966; Poems of our Moment, 1968; Modern Poetry: Essays in Criticism, 1968; American Short Stories Since 1945, 1968; The

Oxford Anthology of English Literature (with Frank Kermode, Harold Bloom, J B Trapp, Martin Price, Lionel Trilling), 1973; I A Richards: Essays in his Honor (with R A Brower and Helen Vendler), 1973; Literature as Experience (with David Bromwich and Irving Howe), 1979. *Literary Awards:* Yale Younger Poets, 1958; Poetry Chapter Book Award, 1962; National Institute of Arts and Letters Grant, 1963; Levinson Prize, 1976; Mina P Shaughnessy Award, 1983; Bollinger Prize, 1983. *Memberships:* Chancellor, Academy of American Poets; Member, American Academy, Institute of Arts and Letters; Fellow, American Academy of Arts and Sciences. *Address:* c/o English Department, Yale University, New Haven, CT 06520, USA.

HOLLANDS, Roy Derrick, b. 20 July 1924, Canterbury, Kent, England. Author. m. Sarah Hollands, 14 Apr. 1945, Pembroke Dock, 1 daughter. *Education:* BSc, 1951, Teachers Certificate, 1953, Southampton University; Advanced Certificate in Education, Sheffield University, 1967; MA, Exeter University, 1969; MEd, University of Newcastle, 1980. *Literary Appointments:* Adviser to 10 major publishers, England; Editor, 8 major mathematics schemes; Freelance writer. *Publications:* Author or co-author over 150 books including: Mathematics for General Education, 1975; Headway Mathematics, 1977; Puzzle Mathematics, books 1 and 2, 1977; Primary Mathematics for Nigeria, 1979–82; Dictionary of Mathematics, 1980; Foundations of Arithmetic, 1980; Ginn Primary Mathematics, 1982–84; Sum It Up, 1983; Success with Numbers, 1983; Development of Mathematics Skills, 1983; Primary Mathematics for Lesotho, 1985; Let's Solve Problems, 1985. *Contributions to:* Over 350 articles published in mathematics journals and numerous reviews. *Honours:* Fellow, College of Preceptors, 1984. *Memberships:* Deputy Chairman, Educational Writers Committee, Society of Authors; MENSA. *Address:* 2 Furse Feld, Aldwick Felds, Bognor Regis, West Sussex PO21 2RE, England.

HOLLES, Robert, b. 11 Oct. 1926. Author and Playwright. m. Philippa Elmer, 12 July, 1952, 2 sons, 1 daughter. *Appointments:* Former Member, Broadcasting Commission, Society of Authors; Artist in Residence, Central State University of Oklahoma, USA, 1981–82. *Publications:* Now Thrive the Armourers, 1952; The Bribe Scorners, 1956; Captain Cat, 1960; The Siege of Battersea, 1962; Religion and Davey Peach, 1964; The Nature of the Beast, 1965; Spawn, 1978; I'll Walk Beside You, 1979; Sunblight, 1981; The Guide to Real Village Cricket, 1983; The Guide to Real Subversive Soldiering, 1985; screenplay: Guns at Batasi, 1965; some 30 plays in TV series such as, Armchair Theatre; Play for Today, etc. *Contributor to:* Various magazines and journals. *Literary Agent:* David Higham Associates. *Address:* Ware House, Stebbing, Essex, England.

HOLLIDAY, David, b. 20 Aug. 1941, Isleworth, England. m. Ruth Brick, 29 Feb. 1960, Hounslow, England, 1 son. *Education:* Member of the Association of Accounting Technicians. *Appointment:* Johnt Editor, Deuce; Central Editor, Envoi; Editor, Scrip. *Publications:* Pictures from an Exhibition, 1959 (with Patrick Snelling). Pepper to Taste, (as Alfred Cunning), 1960; Compositions of Place, 1961; A Dusty Answer, 1973; Jerusalem, 1982. *Contributor to:* Cornhill; Envoi; Here Now; Limbo; Littack; Manifold; New Christian; Orbis; Outposts; Two Tone; etc. *Honour:* Fellow, International Poetry Society, 1976. *Memberships:* Chairman, Wensley Poetry Group; Secretary, Nottingham Poetry Society. *Address:* 67 Hady Crescent, Chesterfield, Derbyshire S41 OEB, England.

HOLLIDAY, Joyce, b. 13 July 1932, Sheffield, England. Playwright. *Education:* BA (Hons), Sheffield University, England. *Literary Appointments:* Resident Playwright, Pentabus Theatre Company, 1976; Chairwoman, West Midlands Arts Drama Panel, 1977–82. Plays produced: Adaptations of Arnold Bennett novels, Victoria Theatre, Stoke, UK: Clayhanger, 1967; Anna of the Five Towns, 1969; The Old Wives Tale, 1971; The Card, 1973; Riceyman Steps, 1982. Also

Anna of the Five Towns produced for BBC Radio, 1969, and ATV, 1969. Other productions include: Getaway, 1976; Cottage in the Country, 1976; The Woman's Story, 1979; Domestic Front, 1980; Celebration: Arnold Bennett, 1981; Tall Tales of Finn Mac Cool, 1983; adaptation of Patience and Sarah, 1983; Suit of Lights, 1984; Anywhere to Anywhere, 1985; What Did You Do In The War Mum?, 1985; Can We Afford The Doctor?, 1985. Numerous short documentary programmes for theatre and radio. Numerous Contributions to magazines. *Address:* 19 The Greenway, May Bank, Newcastle, Staffordshire, ST5 ORY, England.

HOLLIMAN, Mary Constance, née Bloom, b. 28 Jan. 1930, Bethlehem, Pennsylvania. Editor, Writer. m. Rhodes Burns Holliman, 17 Dec. 1950, Birmingham, Alabama, USA, 2 sons; dissolved 1980. *Education:* BA, Howard College, Birmingham, Alabama, 1951; MA, University of Miami, Florida, 1953. *Literary Appointments:* Editor, Howard College Crimson, 1950–51; Reporter, Tooele Daily News, Tooele, Utah, 1953–55; Managing Editor, Journal of the Mineralogical Society of America, 1972–75; Communicator, Sea Grant at Virginia Tech, 1975–79; Director for Information & Awareness, National Sea Grant College Program, 1979–81; University Research Editor, Virginia Tech, Blacksburg, VA, 1981–; President, Pocahontas Press Inc (Publishers), 1984–. *Major Publications:* Index to volumes 51-60, The American Mineralogist 1966–75, edited 1976; Environmental Impact in Antarctica, editor, 1978; Endangered & Threatened Plants & Animals of Virginia, editor, 1980; Seafood Processing Pest Management, editor, 1983; A Teacher's Story: An Autobiography editor, 1985; Sea Grant Biennial Report 1977–79 (author & editor), 1980. *Contributor to:* Various publications on experimental agriculture and marine science; Weekly seafood column taken by various newspapers. *Honours:* Numerous awards for editing. *Memberships:* Western District Director, Virginia Press Women; National Federation of Press Women; American Association of University Women; Society for Scholarly Publishing; Council of Biology Editors. *Address:* 2805 Wellesley Court, Blacksburg, VA 24060, USA.

HOLLINGWORTH, Clare, b. Leicester, England. Foreign Correspondent; War Correspondent; Defence Corespondent; Writer. m. Geoffrey E Hoare, 14 Apr. 1951, Kensington, deceased. *Education:* Scholar, School of Slavonic Studies, London University; Balkan History Diploma, 1937; University of Zagreb, Yugoslavia, 1938; Research Fellow, Centre of Asian Studies, University of Hong Kong. *Appointments:* Daily Telegraph Correspondent, German Polish Board, reported outbreak of World War II; War Correspondent, Middle East, Persia, North Africa, Italy, Greece, France; Guardian Correspondent, Paris, Algeria, during war against France; Covered Troubles in Aden, War in Vietnam, 2 Wars between Pakistan and India; Defence Correspondent, Guardian, 1962–65, Daily Telegraph, 1976–80; etc. *Publications:* Three Weeks War in Poland, 1940; There's a German Just Behind Me, 1942; The Arabs and the West Methuen, 1952; Mao and the Men Against Him, 1985. *Contributor to:* Numerous articles in various journals, magazines and newspapers. *Honours:* Corespondent of the Year, 1962; OBE, 1982. *Address:* 19 Dorset Square, London NW1, England.

HOLLOWAY, Glenna Rose, b. 7 Feb. 1928, Nashville, Tennessee, USA. Silversmith; Enamelist. m. Robert Wesley Holloway. *Contributions to:* Western Humanities Review; Georgia Review; Poet Lore; Christian Science Monitor; Modern Maturity; Manhattan Review; Orbis; Voices International; Poetry International; Northwest Magazine; The Lyric; Connecticut River Review; Pennsylvania Prize Poems; Pegasus; Sandcutters; The Pen Woman; Lincoln Log; Writers Digest; Modern Lyrics; Kansas City Star; American Collector; Lapidary Journal. Various anthologies. *Honours include:* Dellbrook-Shenendoah, 1979. Firsts: National Federation of State Poetry Societies, 1978–84; World Order of Narrative Poetry, 1980–83; Sterling Pegasus Grand Prize, 1982, 83;

Georgia State Poetry Society, 1982; Poetry Society of Virginia; Beach Poets, 1984; Poetry Society of West Virginia; Bright Horizons; Poetry Society of California; Chapparral Poets; Texas Poetry Society; National League of American Penwomen. Numerous other firsts and seconds. *Memberships:* National League of American Penwomen; Poetry Societies of America, Illinois; National Federation of State Poetry Societies; Poets Club of Chicago; Poetry Chairman, Chicago Branch, NLAPW. *Address:* 913 East Bailey Road, Naperville, IL 60565, USA.

HOLLOWAY, John, b. 1 Aug. 1920, Croydon, Surrey, England. University Professor (retired). *Education:* MA, D Phil, Oxford University; D Litt, Aberdeen University; Litt D, Cambridge University. *Literary Appointments:* Fellow, All Souls College, Oxford, 1946–60; Lecturer in English, Aberdeen University, 1949–54; Lecturer in English, Cambridge University, 1954–; Byron Professor, Athens, Greece, 1961–63; Reader in Modern English, 1966–72, Professor of Modern English, 1972–82, Cambridge University, Retired 1982. *Publications:* Prose: Language and Intelligence, 1951; The Victorian Sage, 1953; The Story of the Night (Shakespeare's Tragedies), 1961; The Proud Knowledge (English Poetry 1610–1910) 1977; Narrative and Structure, 1979; The Slumber of Apollo, 1983. Verse: The Minute, 1956; The Fugue, 1960; The Landfallers, 1962; Wood and Windfall, 1965; New Poems, 1970; Planet of Winds, 1977. *Contributor to:* Many contributions to, British and overseas literary and academic journals and BBC and New Zealand Radio Literary talks. *Honours:* The Minute, and Wood and Windfall, choices of the Poetry Book Society, London. *Memberships:* Literature Panel, Eastern Arts Association; Royal Society of Literature, Fellow 1957–1975. *Address:* Queen's College, Cambridge, England.

HOLLOWAY, Marcella M, CSJ, b. 1 Dec. 1913, St Louis, Missouri, USA. Teacher. *Education:* MA, Columbia University, Columbia, Missouri; PhD, Catholic University, Washington DC; Sabbatical, University of Oxford, 1970. *Literary Appointments:* Secretary, National League of American Penwomen, 1980–85; Secretary, T S Eliot Society, St Louis, 1980–85; President, St Louis Writers Guild, 1983–84. *Major Publications:* The Prosodic Theory of G M Hopkins, 2nd edition, 1963; Should You Become a Sister?, 1978, Plays: The Last of the Leprechauns, 1957; The Little Juggler, 1963; A Christmas Carol, 1975. *Contributor to:* Downside Review; Catholic World; Sign; The Critic; Studies in Philosophy; Catholic Digest; and others. *Memberships:* Senior Scholar, International Hopkins Society; National League of American Penwomen; Modern Language Association of America. *Address:* Fontbonne College, St Louis, MO 63105, USA.

HOŁUJ, Tadeusz, b. 23 Nov. 1916, Krakow, Poland. Writer. m. Leokadia Stefania Kałuska, 10 Nov. 1950, Krakow, 1 son. *Education:* Polish Language Department, Jagiellonian University, Krakow, 1936–39. Prisoner in Nazi concentration camps, 1942–45; Secretary General, International Auschwitz Committee, 1957–67. *Publications:* Author over 20 books of poetry, novels, short stories and dramas including; Dziewczyho płyniemy naprzod, 1936; Wiersze z obozu, 1946; Probaognia, 1946; Krolestwo bez ziemi, 1954–56; Koniec naszego swiata, 1958; Wiersze, 1960; Drzewo rodzi owoc, 1963; Roza i płłonacy las, 1971; Osoba, 1974. *Contributions to:* Zycie Literackie; Polityka; Kultura; Zdanie; various daily newspapers and other publications; Editor-in-Chief, Echo Krakowa, 1946–47. *Honours:* City of Krakow Award, 1946, 58; Ministry of National Defense Award, 1961; Minister of Art and Culture Award, 1962–75; National Award in Literature, 1966; Central Council of Trade Unions Award, 1972–74. *Memberships:* Polish Writers Union (Past National Board member, President, Crakow Branch, 1983–85); Polish Pen Club. *Address:* ul Emaus 14a 30-201 Krakow, Poland.

HOLM, Ingvar Hans, b. 25 Oct. 1923, Vik, Rörum, Kristianstads län, Sweden. Professor, Chairman. m.

Gunnel Skantz, 9 May 1954, deceased 1983, 1 son, 1 daughter. *Education:* BA 1945, Fil.lic, 1950, PhD 1958, University of Lund, Sweden. *Literary Appointments:* Assistant Professor of History of Literature, University of Lund, Head of Department of Drama, Theatre & Film, 1966; Director, Institute of Research into Dramatic Arts, 1968; Visiting Professor, University of Cologne, Federal Republic of Germany, 1969; Professor, University of Copenhagen, Denmark, 1970–71; Visiting Professor, University of Minnesota, USA, University of California USA, 1972 & 1981; Professor of History of Literature, Chairman of Department of Drama, Film & Theatre Research, University of Lund. *Major Publications:* Ola Hansson, Romanticism of the Eighties, 1957; La Littérature suèdoise, (co-author), 1957; Harry Martinson: Myths, Paintings, Motives, 1960; From Baudelaire to World War I, 1964; Drama on Stage, Forms & Functions of Drama, 1969; Theatre, Polemics, Theories, Manifestos, 1970; Strindberg et l'expressionisme, (in L'Expressionisme dans le théâtre, edited E Bablet), 1971; Swedish Film & Art in Senegal, 1973; Novels turned into Films, 1975; Holstebro, Studies of Culture Policy in a Danish Town, (co-author), 1976 (Swedish), 1977 (Danish), 1985 (English). Industrialism on Stage, 1979, German edition 1985; Anthology of Children's Theatre i-iii, 1980; Miranda-Under Sail through the Culture of the Baltic, 1980 (novel); Theatre 1-3, 1982; Willy Weberg, 1982; The Witch Sycorax– Song of North Sea (novel), 1984; My Book of Osterlen, 1986; The Dramaturgy of Political Events, 1987. *Honours:* Various Scholarships; King Oscar II Prize, University of Lund, 1962; Schück Prize, Swedish Academy, 1964. *Memberships:* Society of Art & Science, Lund; Royal Society of Arts, Lund; International Federation for Theatre Research (Executive Committee), 1970; Executive Committee, International Association of Theatre Critics, 1975–; Head of Swedish Drama Critics Association, 1975–80; Head, Harry Martinsson Society, 1984–. *Address:* Vik, Vikarevägen 25, S–272 00 Simrishann, Sweden.

HOLM, Peter Rowde, b. 5 Apr. 1931, Oslo, Norway. Writer. m. 28 Sep. 1954, 1 son, 1 daughter. *Education:* Grad St Gallen; Certificate of Proficiency in English, Cambridge, England, 1955. *Publications:* 20 books of poetry; Literary reviews, articles on arms control; 2 books on East-West tension and the arms race; 1 anthology, translated into 12 languages. *Contributor to:* Numerous Norwegian, Swedish and Danish journals and periodicals; many articles on international security problems. *Honours:* Sarpsborg Literary Prize, 1957; Mads Wiel Nygaards prize, 1962; Dagbladets Poetry Prize, 1964; Norwegian Cultural Council Prize, 1966; Literary Critics Prize, 1966; Riksmals Prize, 1977. *Memberships:* Norwegian Union of Authors; de Niderton; The Johnson Society. *Literary Agent:* Aschehoug, Oslo. *Address:* Ostre Holmensvingen 4, 0387 Oslo 3, Norway.

HOLMBERG, Theodore, b. 16 July 1931, Richmond, New York, USA. Newspaperman. m. Carol Kenyon Caffrey, (div), 21 Nov. 1962, 2 sons, 1 daughter. *Education:* BA, Brooklyn College; MS, Columbia University. *Literary Appointments:* Journalism Teacher, Providence College. *Contributions to:* Editor & Publisher; daily newspapers. *Honours:* New England Newspaper Award, best column, 1976, 1978. *Membership:* New England Society of Newspaper Editors. *Address:* The Moorings, East Greenwich, RI 02818, USA.

HOLMERIN, Funny Eva-Annette, b. 6 Feb. 1952, Stockholm, Sweden. Actress. divorced, 1 son, 1 daughter. *Education:* Institution of Dramatic Art, Stockholm, 1973. *Publications:* Plays: Drugs, 1969; The Fountain, 1976; A New Jazz Review, 1978; The Diamond, 1985; A Dream of Living, translation of work by Robert Muller, 1985. Poetic Dramatic Productions: The Fountain, 1975; One Seasons Fall, 1977; The Stone of Fortune, 1978. *Contributions to:* Various live and radio performances, 1969–. *Memberships:* Sveriges Dramatikerförbund. *Literary Agent:* Addi Grini. *Address:*

c/o Addi Grini, Rosenhill, Djurgården, 115 25 Stockholm, Sweden.

HOLMES, Clyde, b. 20 Oct. 1940, Friern Barnet, England. Painter. m. Gudrun Jakob, 10 Oct. 1971, Hampstead Town Hall, London, 1 son, 1 daughter. *Education:* Hornsey College of Art, London, England; ibid. St Martin's School of Art. *Publications:* Cwyn Hesgin, 1977; Standing Stone, 1978; Westering, 1981. *Contributor to:* Welsh Review; Country Life; Aquarius; Gall; Honest Ulsterman; London Magazine; New Poetry; Outposts; Poetry Review; Poetry Wales; Samphire; Counterpoint; Poetry Nottingham; Vision On; Anthologies: Here in North Wales; Speak to the Hills. *Honours:* Poems read on HTV Cymru's close down sequence; 2nd place, Edmund Blunden prize, 1979; Commendation, Welsh Arts Council New Poet's Competition, 1978; Cert. Dist. 1977; finalist, Stroud Festival, 1977; 1978 shortlisted and included, Vision on, Michael Johnston Mem. Prize, 1977, 79; New poetry Prize, 1976; Dip. Winner, Scottish Open Poetry Comp. 1976, 77, 78; Finalist, Arnold Vincent Bowen Competition, 1976. *Memberships:* International Poetry Society. *Address:* Cwym Hesgin, Bala, Gwynned, North Wales.

HOLMES, John Wendell, b. 17 June 1910, London, Ontario, Canada. Professor. *Education:* BA, University of Western Ontario, 1932; MA, University of Toronto, 1933; University of London, 1938–40. *Publications:* The Better Part of Valour: Essays on Canadian Diplomacy, 1970; Canada: A Middle-Aged Power, 1976; The Shaping of Peace: Canada and the Search for World Order, 1943–57. Volume 1, 1979, Volume 2, 1982; Life with Uncle: the Canadian-American Relationship, 1982. *Contributor to:* International Journal; Foreign Policy; Orbis; International Organization; Foreign Affairs; the Round Table; Politique Etrangère; Atlantic Community Quarterly; The World Today; Pacific Affairs; Pacific Community; International Perspectives; Survival; Etudes Internationales, etc; Chapters in numerous books. *Honours:* Officer, Order of Canada, 1969; LLD, University of Western Ontario, 1973, University of New Brunswick, 1975, University of Waterloo, 1976, York University, 1981, St Lawrence University and Carleton University, 1983, DCL, Acadia University, 1977; DLitt, University of Windsor, 1980; Fellow, Royal Society of Canada, 1977. *Address:* Canadian Institute of International Affairs, 15 King's College Circle, Toronto, Canada M5S 2V9.

HOLMES, Marjorie, b. 22 Sep. 1910, Storm Lake, Iowa, USA. Freelance Writer; Columnist; Teacher. m. (1) Lynn Burton Mighell, 1932, deceased, 1 son, 2 daughters, (2) Dr George P Schmieler, 1981. *Education:* Buena Vista College, 1927–29; BA, 1931. *Appointments include:* Author, Weekly Column, Love and Laughter, Washington DC Star, 1959–73. *Publications:* World by the Tail, 1943; Ten O'Clock Scholar, 1947; Saturday Night, 1959; Cherry Blossom Princess, 1960; Follow Your Dream, 1961; Senior Trip, 1962; Love is a Hopscotch Thing, 1963; Love and Laughter, 1967; I've Got to Talk to Somebody God, 1969; Writing the Creative Article, 1969; Who Am I, God?, 1971; To Treasure Our Days, 1971; Two from Galilee, 1972; Nobody Else Will Listen, 1973; You and I and Yesterday, 1973; As Tall as My Heart, 1974; How Can I Find You God?, 1975; Beauty in your Own back Yard, 1976; Hold Me Up a Little Longer, Lord, 1977; Lord Let Me Love, 1978; God and Vitamins, 1980; To Help You Through the Hurting, 1983; Three from Galilee (Young Man from Nazareth), 1985; Author, Filmscript for, The General Comes Homes, and film adaptation of book, Two from Galilee. *Contributor:* Short stories, articles and poetry to magazines and journals. *Honours:* Recipient, numerous honours and awards including: Award for Literature, American Association for SOcial Psychiatry, 1964; Honor Iowans Award, Buena Vista College, 1966; D.Litt., Buena Vista College, 1976; Freedom Foundation of Valley Forge Award, 1977; Distinguished Service Award, Buena Vista College, 1978. *Memberships:* Member, numerous professional organisations including: Children's Book Guild;

American Newspaper Women's Club; Washington National Press Club; etc. *Address:* 637 E McMurray Rd, McMurray, PA 15317, USA.

HOLMQVIST, Nils (Oskar Anders), b. 18 Nov. 1925, Abo, Finland. Literary Translator; Lecturer; Advertising Copywriter; Musician. *Education:* University courses, languages, social sciences, musical theory; private musical study (opera), Italy; Examination for Authorised Translators, Finland, 1969. *Publications:* Translations into Swedish: Allardt-Littunen: Sociologi, 1975; Uusitalo: Samhällsplaneringens mål och medel, 1976; Hyrynen-Hautamäki: Människans bildbarhet och utbildnings-politiken, 1977; Hetzler: I behov av vård?, 1978; Szasz: Psykiatrins slavar, 1979; Nojonen: Freuds fatala förkylning, 1974; etc. *Contributions to:* Newspapers, trade & professional publications including: Taucher-Skruven (editorial secretary). *Honours include:* Several Inter-Scandinavian scholarships, 1972–. *Memberships:* Literary Translators Section, Swedish Authors Association; Finnish Marketing Association; Finnish Copywriters Guild. *Address:* Sjötullsgatan 25A9, 00170 Helsingfors 17, Finland.

HOLMSTEN, Aldona, b. 2 Mar. 1932, Karcevishkiu, Lithuania. Writer; Painter. *Publications include:* Lyric Poetry: Nachtstrassen, 1962; Grasdeuter, 1963; Blaue Straucher, 1967; Liebedichtexte, 1968; Worterotik, 1971; Frankierter Morgenhimmel, 1975; Puppenruhe, 1977; Eine Welle, eine Muschel oder Venus personlich, 1979, includes 3 books with own illustrations. *Contributions to:* Over 40 anthologies. *Membership:* Association of German Writers. *Address:* Elssholzstrasse 19, 1000 Berlin 30, Federal Republic of Germany.

HOLMSTEN, Georg, b. 4 Aug. 1913, Riga, Livonia, USSR. Writer. *Education:* Studies of Literature and History, 1933–39. *Publications:* Berliner Miniaturen, 1946; Der Bruckenkopf, 1948, 2nd edition, 1971; Lucrezi Borgia, historical novel, 1951, 79; Rembrandt, biographical novel, 1952, 77; Ludwig XIV, Historical novel, 1952. Author of 6 other biographical novels including: Friedrich II von Preussen, 1969; Voltaire, 1971; Rousseau, 1972. Die Berlin-chronik, 1984; Buntesrertienstkreutz i Klause, 1981. *Memberships:* Association of German Writers. *Address:* Ellssholzstrasse 19, D–1000 Berlin 30, Federal Republic of Germany.

HOLOIEN, Martin Olaf, b. 13 Nov. 1928, Wolf Point, Montana, USA. College Professor. m. Edith I Kobbervig, 14 Aug. 1948, Moorhead, Minnesota, USA, 2 sons. *Education:* BS Mathematics, Moorhead State University, 1951; MS Mathematics, North Dakota State University, 1959; PhD Mathematics Education, University of Minnesota, Minneapolis, 1970. *Publications:* Computers and Their Societal Impact, 1977; Problem Solving and Structured Programming with Fortran 77, 1983; Problem Solving and Structured Programming with Pascal, 1985. *Address:* Department of Computer Science, University of California Santa Barbara (UCSB), Santa Barbara, CA 93106, USA.

HOLOWAY, Nigel Robert, b. 16 Nov. 1953, London, England. Journalist. *Education:* BA. *Literary Appointment:* South-east Asia correspondent, The Economist newspaper. *Contributions to:* The Economist. *Address:* International Building, #05-01B, 360 Orchard Road, Singapore 0923.

HOLT, Gary Arthur, b. 23 June 1950, Fort Worth, Texas, USA. Drug-Health Educator. m. Linda Kay Edde, 30 June 1984, 1 daughter. *Education:* Associate in Biology, Eastern Oklahoma State, 1970; MEd, Central State University, 1980; BS Zoology 1974, BS Pharmacy 1977, Studying for PhD Social Pharmacy 1987, Oklahoma University. *Contributions to:* Over 40 in magazines, journals and newspapers. *Memberships:* American Medical Writers Association; Correspondent, National Center for Health Education. *Address:* Department of Pharmacy Practice, College of Pharmacy,

Oklahoma University Health Sciences Center, Oklahoma City, OK 73190, USA.

HOLT, Pat Mayo, b. 5 Sep. 1920, Gatesville, Texas, USA. Foreign Affairs Consultant. m. LaVerne Bryson, 18 June 1941, Bastrop, Texas, 2 sons. *Education:* BA, BJ, University of Texas, 1940; MS Journalism, Columbia University, New York, 1941. *Major Publications:* Colombia Today – And Tomorrow, 1964; US Policy in Foreign Affairs, 1971; The War Powers Resolution: The Role of Congress in US Armed Intervention, 1978; Invitation to Struggle: Congress, The President & Foreign Policy (with C V Crabb Jnr) 2nd edition, 1984. *Contributor to:* Various periodicals & journals. *Address:* 7510 Exeter Road, Bethesda, MD 20814, USA.

HOLT, Rochelle Lynn, b. 17 Mar. 1946. Writer. *Education:* BA English, University of Illinois, 1964; MFA English, University of Iowa Writer's Workshop, 1970; PhD English and Psychology, Columbia Pacific University, 1980. *Literary Appointments include:* Editor, Valhalla literary magazine, 1970–80; Co-owner and operator, Letterpress Ragnarok Press, 1970–78; Consulting Editor, Merging Media offset editions, 1978–86; NEA Writer in residence, Miles College, Birmingham, Alabama, 1978; Union College, Cranford 1983, Kean College, Elizabeth, 1985, New Jersey. *Publications include:* Poetry volumes: From One Bird, 1978; Train in the Rain, 1982; Timelapse, 1983; The Blue Guitar, 1984; Extended Family, 1985; Drama includes: Walking Into The Dawn: A Celebration, 1975; One Day In Life Of Woman, Radio Station Boston, 1984; Non-fiction includes: Timesharing: Consumer's Guide, 1982; Fiction, children's literature, translations. *Contributions to:* Various magazines including: Writer's Digest; Calyx; Telewoman; Thirteen; Nassau. *Honours include:* NEA Poets in Schools, Virginia, 1977; Dodge Foundation Grant, 1981; New Jersey Humanities Council Grant, 1985. *Memberships:* Poetry Society of America; International Women Writer's Guild: Academy of American Poets; Feminist Writer's Guild; Association of Writers; Poets and Writers; Associated Writers Programmes.

HOLTON, Felicia Antonelli, b. 28 Nov. 1921, Flushing, New York, USA. Magazine Editor; Author, divorced, 1 daughter. *Education:* BA, University of Chicago, 1950. *Publications:* Koster: Americans in Search of Their Prehistoric Past, with Stuart Struever, 1979; Compukids: A Parent's Guide to Computers and Learning, 1965. *Contributions to:* New York Times; Encyclopedia Science Britannica Yearbook, 1979. *Membership:* American Society of Journalists and Authors. *Literary Agent:* Virginia Barber Literary Agency. *Address:* 525 Grove Street, Evanston, IL 60201, USA.

HOLTZ, Barry W, b. 26 Mar. 1947, Boston, Massachusetts, USA. Educator. *Education:* BA, Tufts University, 1968; PhD, English & American Literature, Brandeis University, 1973. *Appointments:* Chairman, English, Akiba Academy, Philadelphia, 1974–77; Chairman, Publications, 1976–80, Co Director, 1980–, Melton Research Center, New York. *Publications:* Your Word is Fire, 1977; Back to the Sources, 1984. *Contributor to:* Present Tense; Midstream; Response; Teachers College Record; Religious Education; Melton Journal; Jerusalem Post Magazine; English Journal. *Address:* 711 West End Avenue, New York, NY 10025, USA.

HOLUB, Robert Charles, b. 22 Aug. 1949, New Jersey, USA. Professor. m. Renate Wiesner, 25 Nov. 1975, Madison, Wisconsin, 1 son. *Education:* BA, University of Pennsylvania; MA, PhD, University of Wisconsin-Madison. *Literary Appointments:* University of California, Berkeley, 1979–. *Publications:* Heinrich Heine's Reception of German Grecophilia: The Function and Application of the Hellenic Tradition in the First Half of the 19th Century, 1981; Reception Theory: A Critical Introduction, 1984. Co-Editor: Heinrich Heine: Poetry and Prose, 1982; Heinrich Heine: Critical Essays, 1984. *Contributions to:* New German Critique; Comparative Literature Studies; Heine-Jarhrbuch; Germano-Slavica;

German Quarterly; Monatshefte; Enclitic; Deutsche Vierteljahrsschrift; Modern Language Notes; Colloquia Germanica; Southern Review. Book contributions include: Collier's Encyclopedia, 81, 82, 83; Stereotyp und Vorurteil in der Literatur, 1978; Karl Marx und Friedrich Neitzsche: Acht Beitrage, 1978; The Dialogical and the Dialectical Neveu de Rameau, 1983. Numerous book reviews in, German Quarterly; Monatshefte, and others. *Honour:* Humboldt Fellow, 1983–85. *Memberships:* Heinrich Heine Society; American Association of Teachers of German. *Address:* Department of German, University of California, Berkeley, CA 94720, USA.

HOME OF THE HIRSEL, DOUGLAS-HOME, Alexander Frederick, (Baron of Coldstream), b. 1903. Former Prime Minister and First Lord of the Treasury. *Education:* Oxford University. *Publications:* The Way The Wind Blows, autobiography, 1976; Border Reflections, 1979. *Memberships:* Member of Parliament (Conservative); South Lanark 1931–45; Lanark Division 1950–51; Kinross and West Perthshire 1963–74. *Honours:* Knight; Life Peer Created 1974, (Former 14th Earl of Home, renounced Peerage on becoming Prime Minister, 1963). *Address:* The Hirsel, Coldstream, Berwickshire and Castlemains Douglas, Lanarkshire, Scotland.

HOMER, Arthur Thomas, b. 19 May 1951, Ellington, Missouri, USA. Poet; Professor. *Education:* BA, English, Portland State University, 1977; MFA, Creative Writing, University of Montana, 1979. *Appointments:* Editor, Portland Review, 1974–77; Teaching Assistant, University of Montana, 1977–79; Editor, CutBank & SmokeRoot Press, 1977–79; Poet in Residence, Montana Arts Council, 1979–81; Instructor Colleges & Universities, 1981–83; Assistant Professor & Chair, UNO Writer's Workshop, 1983–; Editor, The Nebraska Review, 1984–. *Publications:* What We Did After the Rain, 1984; Tattoos, 1985. *Contributor to:* Antaeus; Chariton Review; College English; Midwest Quarterly; Missouri Review; New Jersey Poetry Journal; Poetry Review; etc. *Honours:* Co-ordinating Council of Literary Magazines Editor's Award; Grants from National Endowment for the Arts; Oregon Arts Commission; Nebraska Arts Council. *Memberships:* Associated Writing Programmes; Programme Director's Council; Poetry Society of America. *Address:* Writer's Workshop, Arts & Sciences Hall 215, University of Nebraska, Omaha, NE 68182, USA.

HOMOLA, Samuel, b. 10 June 1929, Dothan, Alabama, USA. Chiropractor. *Education:* Dr Chiropractic. *Publications:* Bonesetting, Chiropractic & Cultism, 1963; Backache: Home treatment & Prevention, 1968; Muscle Training for Athletes, 1968; A Chiropractor's Treasury of Health Secrets, 1970; Secrets of Naturally Youthful Health & Vitality, 1971; Doctor Homola's Life Extender Health Guide, 1975; Doctor Homola's Fat Disintergrator Diet, 1977; Peter Lupus' Guide to Radient Health & Beauty, with Peter Lupus, 1978; Peter Lupus' Celebrity Body Book, with Peter Lupus, 1980. *Contributor to:* Numerous articles to Magazines. *Address:* 1307 E 2nd Ct, Panama City, FL 32401, USA.

HONDERICH, Ted, b. 30 Jan. 1933, Baden, Ontario, Canada. University Professor. *Education:* BA, University of Toronto; PhD, University College, London, England. *Publications:* Punishment, The Supposed Justifications, 1969, 1971, 1976; Essays on Freedom of Action, Editor, 1973; Three Essays on Political Violence, 1976; Social Ends and Political Means, Editor, 1976; Philosophy As It Is, with M Burnyeat, 1979; Violence for Equality: Inquiries in Political Philosophy, 1980; Philosophy Through Its Past, Editor, 1984; Morality and Objectivity, Editor, 1985. *Memberships:* Aristotelian Society; Mind Association; Beefsteak Lunch Club. *Address:* Dept of Philosophy, University College London, Gower St, London WC1, England.

HONEYCOMBE, Gordon, b. 27 Sep. 1936, Karachi, Pakistan. Writer. *Education:* BA, University College, Oxford, England. *Publications:* Neither the Sea Nor the

Sand, 1969; Dragon Under the Hill, 1972; Adam's Tale, 1974; Red Watch, 1976; The Edge of Heaven, 1981; Nagasaki, 1945, 1981; Royal Wedding, 1981; The Year of the Princess, 1982; The Murders of the Black Museum, 1982; Selfridges, 1984; TV plays: The Golden Vision, 1968; Time and Again, 1974; The Thirteenth Day of Christmas; 1985. Stage Plays: The Redemption, 1965; Lancelot and Guinivere, 1980; Radio dramatisations: Paradise Lost, 1974; A King Shall Have a Kingdom, 1977; screenplay: Neither the Sea nor the Sand. *Literary Agent:* A D Peters and Co Ltd. *Address:* c/o A D Peters & Company Limited, 10 Buckingham Street, London WC2N 6BU, England.

HONHART, Frederick Lewis, b. 29 Oct. 1943, San Diego, California, USA. Archivist. m. Barbara Ann Baker, 27 Aug. 1966, Hanover, Indiana, 2 Sons. *Education:* BA, Wayne State University, 1966; MA 1968; PhD 1972, Case-Western Reserve University. *Publications:* Guide to Manuscript Collections and Institutional Records in Ohio, (Assistant Editor), 1974; Guide to the Michigan State University Archives and Historial Collections (Editor), 1976. *Contributions to:* Journal of Forest History; College and Research Libraries; Acronyms; Journal of American History Newsletter. *Address:* University Archives and Historical Collections, Michigan State University, East Lansing, MI 48824-1048, USA.

HONIG, Edwin, b. 3 Sep. 1919. University Professor. *Education:* BA, 1942, MA, 1947, University of Wisconsin, USA. *Literary Appointments include:* Harvard University, 1949–57; Professor, Brown University, Providence, Rhode Island, 1957–. *Publications:* The Moral Circhs, 1955; The Gazebos, 41 poems, 1959; The Gazebos, 41 Poems and The Widow, play, 1961; Survivals; Spring Journal Poems, 1968; Four Springs, 1972; At Sixes, 1974; Shake a Spear With Me, John Berryman, 1975; The Afinities of Orpheus, 1976; Selected Poems 1955–76, 1979; The Poet's other Voice: On Translation, criticism, 1985; Fernando Pessoa's Keeper of Sheep, Translation, 1986; Fernando Pessoa's Selected Poems, Co-translator, 1986; Gifts of Light, Poetry, 1983; Interrupted Praise: Poems 1955–1976; Foibles and Fables of an Abstract Man, 1979; Ends of the World and Other Plays, 1983. *Contributions to:* New York Times; Nation; New Republic; New Mexico Quarterly; Kenyon Review; Virginia Quarterly Review; Michigan Quarterly; Poetry. *Honours include:* Guggenheim Fellowship, 1948, 62; Amy Lowell Travelling Scholarship in Poetry, 1968; Grant for translation, 1975, 1977–80, NEH; Grant in Creative Writing, 1977, Grant to write libretoo, 1981, National Education Association; 1st Prize in Translation, Poetry Society of America; national Prize in Translation, Columbia University Translation Center, 1985. *Memberships:* PEN; Past Executive Board Member, Poetry Society of America; Dante Society of America. *Address:* English Department, Box 1852, Brown University, Providence, RI 02912, USA.

HOOD, Christopher, b. 7 May 1943, Lancashire, England. Writer. m. twice, 4 children. *Major publications:* The Mullenthorpe Thing, 1971; The Other Side of the Mountain, 1979; Contact with Maldonia (with Jasper Hood), 1982; Banana Cat, 1985. *Contributor to:* Touch & Go; Swansea Evening Post. *Honour:* Shortlisted for National Book Award for Fiction, 1980 (The Other Side of the Mountain). *Memberships:* Co-Founder, The Napolean Club, 1978; Society of Authors; Theatre Writers' Union; Crime Writers' Association. *Literary Agent:* Jacintha Alexander. *Address:* c/o Jacintha Alexander, 47 Emperor's Gate, London, SW7, England.

HOOD, Hugh, b. 30 Apr. 1928, Toronto, Canada. Novelist; Short Story Writer; Essayist. m. Ruth Noreen Mallory, 22 Apr. 1957, Toronto, 2 sons, 2 daughters. *Education:* BA, 1950, MA, 1952, PhD, 1955, University of Toronto. *Publications:* Flying a Red Kite, stories, 1962; White Figure, White Ground, novel, 1964; The New Age/Le nouveau siecle, 12 volume Roman-fleuvy; 6 story collections, 10 novels, 4 non-fiction volumes and

hundreds of stories and articles. *Contributions to:* Numerous publications. *Honours:* Numerous. *Address:* 4242 Hampton Avenue, Montréal, Quebec, Canada H4A 2K9.

HOOGLAND, Claes Abraham, b. 11 Jan. 1916, Gothenburg, Sweden. Drama critic; Radio producer. m. Signe Claesson, 2 Feb. 1946, Stockholm, 3 sons. *Education:* University of Stockholm; Sorbonne. *Literary Appointments:* Editor, Literary Review '40-TAL', 1944–46; Literary Assistant, Municipal Theatre, Gothenburg, 1947–49; Literary Assistant, Royal Dramatic Theatre, Stockholm, 1949–52; Producer and Drama Critic, Swedish Radio, 1952–81. *Publications:* Translation: Milne När vi var mycket små, 1941; Maneten, 1949; Amorina (adaptation), 1951; Den briljante Anouilh, 1952; Scenens Ungdom, 1954; Den satiriske Holberg, 1963; Diktaren och tiden, 1965; Bilder ur Svensk Teaterhistoria, 1970; translations and adaptations of numerous plays. *Contributor to:* AO-TAL8; Stockholm-Tidningen; Ord och Bild; Entre; numerous radio programmes. *Literary Awards:* French legate, 1946; Publicistklubbens stip., 1967; Swedish Academy legate, 1985. *Memberships:* Göteborgs författarsällskap, Vice-President, 1949; Svenska Dramatikerförbundet, Vice-President, 1958–62; Svenska Teaterkritikers Förening, President, 1971–75; AICT, International Association of Theatre Critics, Member of Board, 1972–75; Almquistsällskapet, 1980. *Literary Agent:* Svenska Dramatikerförbundet. *Address:* Valhallavägen 104, 114 41 Stockholm, Sweden.

HOOGVELD, Jos, b. 20 Mar. 1948, The Hague, The Netherlands. Writer; Actor; Illustrator; Designer. *Publications:* 1002 Figures, 1982; series of illustrated cards, 1983. *Contributor to:* Ariadne. *Address:* Wibautstraat 36/III, 1091 GM Amsterdam, The Netherlands.

HOOK, Sidney, b. 20 Dec. 1902, New York City, USA. Professor of Philosophy; Senior Research Fellow, Hoover Institution of War, Revolution and Peace. *Education:* BS, City College New York, 1923; MA, 1926; PhD, 1927; Columbia University; LHD; LLD, 1960. *Publications include:* Education for Modern Man, 2nd edition, 1963; Heresy, Yes-Conspiracy, No, 1953; Political Power and Personal Freedom, 1959; The Quest for Being, 1961; The Paradoxes of Freedom, 1962; The Place of Religion in a Free Society, 1968; Academic Freedom and Academic Anarchy, 1970; Education and the Taming of Power, 1973; Fragmatism and the Tragic Senses of Life, 1974; Revolution, Reform and Social Justice, 1975; Philosophy and Public Policy, 1980; Marxism and Beyond, 1983; Editor, several books including: American Philosophers at Work; The Current Philosophic Scene, 1956. *Contributor to:* Philosophical Journals. *Honours include:* Guggenheim Fellow, 1928–29, 1961–62; Fellow; American Academy Arts and Sciences; American Academy of Education; Jefferson Lecturer awarded by the National Endowment for the Humanities, 1984; Presidential Medal of Freedom, 1985. *Address:* Hoover Institution, Stanford, CA 94305, USA.

HOOKER, Morna Dorothy, b. 19 May 1931, Surrey, England. Professor. m. W David Stacey, 30 Mar. 1978, Bristol. *Education:* BA 1953, MA 1956, University of Bristol; University of Manchester, 1957–59, PhD 1967; MA, University of Oxford, 1970, MA, University of Cambridge,1976. *Literary Appointments:* Editor, Journal of Theological Studies, Oxford University Press, 1985–. *Major Publications:* Jesus & the Servant, 1959; The Son of Man in Mark, 1967; Pauline Pieces (A Preface to Paul), 1979; Studying the New Testament, 1979; The Message of Mark, 1983; What about the New Testament, (joint editor), 1975; Paul & Paulinism, (joint editor), 1982. *Contributor to:* Journal of Theological Studies; new Testament Studies; Epworth Review; Expository Times; Theology. *Honours:* Fellow, King's College, University of London, 1979; Honorary Fellow, Linacre College, Oxford, 1980. *Address:* the Divinity School, St John's Street, Cambridge, CB2 1TW, England.

HOOKER, (Peter) Jeremy, b. 23 Mar. 1941, Warsash. Writer; Former University Lecturer. Divorced, 1 son, 1 daughter. *Education:* BA, 1963, MA, 1965, Southampton University, England. *Appointments:* Lecturer, English, University College of Wales, 1965–84; Arts Council Creative Writing Fellow, Winchester School of Art, 1981–83; Writer-in-Residence, Kibbutz Gezer, Israel, 1985. *Publications:* John Cowper Powys, 1973; Solicoquies of a Chalk Giant, 1974; David Jones: An Exploratory Study, 1975; Solent Shore, 1978; Englishman's Road, 1980; A View from the Source, 1982; Poetry of Place, 1982; Itchen Water, 1982. *Contributor to:* Essays, Reviews, etc; Poetry in, Anglo Welsh Review; Agenda; Poetry Nation Review; Poetry Wales; Stand; etc. *Honours:* Eric Gregory Award for Poetry, 1969; Welsh Arts Council Literary Prize, 1974; Welsh Arts Council Representative, Conference, Sligo, 1984. *Memberships:* Powys Society; Richard Jefferies Society; Former Committee Member, Welsh Arts Council Literature Committee. *Address:* Korreweg 80, 9715 Ag Groningen, The Netherlands.

HOOPER, John, b. 17 July 1950, Westminster, London, England. Journalist. m. The Honourable Lucinda Evans, 19 July 1980. *Education:* Exhibitioner, BA honours, St Catherine's College, Cambridge. *Literary Appointments:* Energy and Trade Correspondent, The Guardian newspaper. *Publication:* The Spaniards – A Portrait of the New Spain, 1986. *Literary Agent:* Anthony Sheil. *Address:* 1 Bevan Street, London N1, England.

HOOVER, Helen Mary, b. 5 Apr. 1935, Stark County, Ohio, USA. Writer. *Publications:* Children of Morrow, 1973; The Lion's Cub, 1974; Treasures of Morrow, 1976; The Delikon, 1977; The Rains of Eridan, 1977; The Lost Star, 1979; Return to Earth, 1980; This Time of Darkness, 1980; Another Heaven, Another Earth, 1981; The Bell Tree, 1982; The Shepherd Moon, 1984. *Contributions to:* Language Arts; Top of the News, Journal of American Library Association. *Honours:* Best book list, for Another Heaven, Another Earth, American Library Association, 1981; Ohioana Award, for Another Heaven, Another Earth, 1982; Award for Outstanding Contribution to Children's Literature, Central Missouri State University, 1984. *Membership:* Authors Guild. *Address:* c/o Viking Penguin Children's Books, 40 West 23rd Street, New York City, NY 10010, USA.

HOOVER, Herbert Theodore, b. 3 Sep. 1930, Minnesota, USA. Professor of History. m. 25 June 1958, Minnesota, 1 son, 1 daughter. *Education:* BA, 1960, MA, 1961, History, New Mexico State University; PhD, History, University of Oklahoma, 1966. *Literary Appointments:* Professor of History, University of South Dakota, 1968–; Director, Indian Center, Newberry Library, Chicago, 1981–83; Research Fellowship, National Endowment for the Humanities, 1978–81. *Publications:* To Be An Indian, 1971; The Chitimacha People, 1975; Practice of Oral History, 1975; The Sioux, 1979; Bibliography of the Sioux, 1980. *Contributions to:* The Past Before Us, 1979; Historians and the American West, 1983; Western Historical Quarterly, 1976; South Dakota History, 1983; Last Years of Sitting Bull, 1984, etc. *Honours:* Research Award, National Endowment for the Humanities, 1978–81; Newberry Library Fellowship, 1977; Western America Achievement Award, Augustana College, 1984. *Memberships:* Western Historical Association (5 offices); Organization of American Historians (2 offices); Board of Editors, Western Historical Quarterly; International Councillor, Phi Alpha Theta. *Address:* Department of History, University of South Dakota, Vermillion, SD 57069, USA.

HOOYKAAS, Reijer, b. 1 Aug. 1906, Schoonhoven, Netherlands. University Professor. *Education:* DSc, Urecht University. *Publications include:* The Principle of Uniformity in Geology, Biology and Theology, 1959, 1963, 1976; Physik und Mechanik in historischer Hinsicht, 1963; Introducao a Historia deas Ciencias, 1965; Nature and History, 1966; Catastrophism in Geology, 1970; History of Science, from Babel to Bohr, 1971; Religion and the Rise of Modern Science, 1972,

1973; Humanism and the Portuguese Discoveries, 1979. *Contributor to:* International historical and scientific journals. *Honours include:* Knight, Order of Nederlandse Leeuw. *Memberships include:* Royal Netherlands Academy of Sciences and Letters. *Address:* Krullelaan 35, Zeist, Netherlands.

HOPE, Ronald, b. 4 Apr. 1921, London, England. Director, The Marine Society. *Education:* MA, PhD, Oxford University. *Publications:* Spare Time at Sea, 1954, 74; Economic Geography, 1956, 5th edition, 1969; Dick Small in the Half-Deck, novel, 1958; Ships, 1958; The Shoregoer's Guide to World Ports, 1963; Introduction to the Merchant Navy, 1965, 4th edition, 1973; Retirement from the Sea, 1967; In Cabined Ships at Sea, 1969; The Merchant Navy, 1980. Editor: The Harrap Book of Sea Verse, 1960; Seamen and the Sea, 1965; Voices from the Sea, 1977; John Masefield: The Sea Poems, 1978; Twenty Singing Seamen, 1979; The Seamens World, 1982; Sea Pie, 1984. *Contributions to:* Fairplay; Natucial Review. *Address:* The Marine Society, 202 Lambeth Road, London SE1 7JW, England.

HOPE MASON, John, b. 17 Sep. 1943, England. Writer. *Education:* Scholar in History, 1st Class Degree Anglo-Saxon Tripos, Cambridge University. *Literary Appointments:* Thames Television Playwright in Residence, Queens Theatre, Hornchurch, 1975–76; Leverhulme Trust Fund Research Award, 1981–83; Arts Council of Great Britain Writers Bursary, 1983–85. *Publications:* The Indispensable Rousseau, 1979; The Irresistable Diderot, 1982. *Contributions to:* Literary Review; Modern Language Review; PN Review; Times Educational Supplement; Times Literary Supplement; Times Higher Education Supplement. *Address:* 1 Wendover Court, Chiltern Street, London W1, England.

HOPKINS, Leon John, b. 30 Oct. 1944, England. Journalist. m. Joanne, 28 Oct. 1967, Southgate, 2 sons. *Education:* Chartered Accountant; Certified Accountant; FCA; FCCA. *Literary Appointments:* Editor: Accountancy Age, Accountants Weekly, Certified Accountant, Audit Report, World Accounting Report. *Publications:* The Hundredth Year, 1980; The Audit Report, 1984; World Accounting Survey, 1984. *Address:* Chapter Three Publications Limited, 8A Hythe Street, Dartford, Kent DA1 1BX, England.

HORAN, Michael, b. 17 Jan. 1943, Washington DC, USA. College Professor; Psychiatric Social Worker. *Education:* BA, Psychology and Sociology, 1973, Master of Social Work, 1975, Indiana University. *Publications:* Index to Parachuting 1900–1975, 1979; Parachuting Folklore, The Evolution of Free, 1980; Index to Parachuting 1976–80, 1982. *Contributions to:* Over 50 articles pertaining to Parachuting for all the major magazines in the United States and Canada. *Address:* President, Parachuting Resources, MC PO Box 1291, Dayton, OH 45402, USA.

HORECKY Paul Louis, b. 8 Sep. 1913, Trutnov, Czechoslovakia. Writer; Librarian. m. Emily M Ivey, 12 Dec. 1949, 1 son. *Education:* Sorbonne, University of Paris, France, 1934; Doctor of Law & Political Science, University of Prague, Czechoslovakia, 1936; MA, Harvard University USA, 1951. *Appointments:* Law Practice, Prague, 1936–37; Trial Attorney (US) Nuremberg, 1947–49; Researcher, Russian Research Centre, Harvard University, 1949–51; Assistant Chief, East European Specialist, Library of Congress, Washington DC, 1951–72; Chief, Slavic & Central European Division, 1972–77; Senior Research Fellow, Institute for Sino-Soviet Studies, George Washington University, Washington DC, 1978–79; Visiting Professor, Slavic Research Centre, Hokkaido University, Japan, 1979–80; Guest Lecturer, Institute of World Politics, Chinese Academy of Social Sciences, 1980. *Major Publications:* Trials of War Criminals before the Nuremberg Military Tribunals, Vols. X & XI (co-editor), 1950–51; Various bibliographical volumes of Library of Congress, 1959–76. *Contributor to:* Encyclopaedia Americana; Several Library of Congress bibliographical monographs. *Memberships:* American Political Science

Association; American Association for the Advancement of Slavis Studies; American Library Association; Cosmos Club, Harvard Club, Washington DC. *Address:* 2207 Paul Spring Road, Alexandria, VA, 22307, USA.

HORIC, Alain, b. 3 Jan. 1929, Bosnia, Croatia. Publisher. m. Jacqueline Rivard, 6 Dec. 1952, Montreal, Canada, 3 sons, 1 daughter. *Education:* MA, University of Montreal, Quebec, Canada, 1957. *Literary Appointments:* Publisher, Editions de l'Hexagone, Editions Les Herbes Rouges, Editions Parti Pris. *Publications:* Poetry: L'aube assassinee, 1957; Nemir duse, 1959; Blessure au flanc du ciel, 1962; Cela commenca par un reve et ce fut la Creation, 1969; Les coqs egorges, 1972. *Contributions to:* Many magazines and newspapers, represented in numerous Quebec poetry anthologies. *Memberships:* Writers Union of Quebec; Croatian Academy of America. *Address:* 3425 avenue Laval, Montreal, Quebec, Canada H2X 3C7.

HORIUCHI, Toshimi, b. 5 Sep. 1931, Japan. Instructor in English. m. Yoskiko Takayama, 25 Mar. 1958. *Education:* BA, Tohokugakuin College, 1956; Studies in Poetry and Creative Writing, St John's University, Minnesota, USA, 1981–82 and 1984–85. *Publications:* Drops of Rainbow (poems), in English, 1979; Minnesota Songs (poems), in English, 1982. *Contributions to:* Poetry Nippon, The Poetry Society of Japan; Laurel Leaves, United Poets Laureate International; Mainichi Daily News, Tokyo. *Honour:* For Drops of Rainbow. *Memberships:* Core member, The Poetry Society of Japan; Advisory Council, The Poetry Reading Circle of Tokyo; The Christian Literature Society of Japan. *Address:* 2-10-12-105 Satsukigaoka, Chiba-chi 281, Japan.

HORN, Sabine, b. 10 Apr. 1918, Konigsberg, East Prussia. *Education:* Private study. *Literary Appointments:* Writer, Radio Station, NDR, Norddeutscher Rundfunk. *Publications:* Aus der Stille; Geliebter Tag-Geliebts Nacht; Klingendes Mosaik; Ein Leben im Rollstuhl, autobiography; Fensterglas, lyrics; Eck woll met di plachandern, lyrics in East Prussian dialect. *Honours:* Awarded Literary Youth Prize, 1935. *Memberships:* Interessengemeinschaft Deutschsprachiger Autoren. *Address:* Wuelfelerstrasse 60A, Haus Roderbruch, D–3000 Hannover 72, Federal Republic of Germany.

HORNBAKER, Alice J, b. 2 Mar. 1927, Cincinnati, Ohio, USA. Journalist; Author; TV News Broadcaster. Divorced, 2 sons, 1 daughter. *Education:* BA, English, Journalism, San Jose State University. *Publication:* Preventive Care: Easy Exercise Against Aging, 1974. *Contributor to:* Poeple; Modern Maturity, New York Times Sunday Magazine; Nature Journal; Cincinnati Magazine; The Sunday Enquirer Magazine. *Honours:* Bronze Award, American Chiropractic Association, 2 years; National Health Journalism Award, 1976, 1977; Numerous, 1st, 2nd Awards for Feature Writing, columns, critical book reviews, etc, 1977–85. *Memberships:* President, Blue Ribbon Society, Ohio State University; Vice President, ONWA Ohio, Newspaper Women's Association; Treasurer, Society of Professional Journalists. *Address:* 617 Vine St, Cincinnati, OH 45201, USA.

HORNE, Alistair Allan, b. 9 Nov. 1925, London, England. Author; Farmer. *Education:* MA, Jesus College, Cambridge, England. *Publications:* Back Into Power, 1956; Return to Power, 1956; The Land is Bright, 1958; Canada and the Canadians, 1961; The Price and the Commune, 1870–71, 1965; To Lose a Battle: France 1940, 1969; Death of a Generation, 1970; The Terrible Year, 1971; Small Earthquake in Chile, 1972; A Savage War of Peace: Algeria, 1964–62, 1978; Napoleon, Master of Europe 1805–1907, 1979; French Army and Politics, 1870–1970, 1985. *Contributor to:* Spectator; Evening Standard; Esquire. *Honours include:* Hawthornden Prize, 1963; Wolfson Prize, 1978; Enid Prize for Literature, 1985. *Memberships include:* Comm of Mgmt; Royal Lit Fund;

FRSL. *Address:* c/o Macmillans, 4 Little Essex Street, London WC2, England.

HORNE, Donald Richmond, b. 26 Dec. 1921, Sydney, Australia. Author; Professor. m. Myfanwy Gollan, 22 Mar. 1960, Sydney, 1 son, 1 daughter. *Literary Appointments:* Editor, The Observer, 1958–61; Editor, The Bulletin, 1961–62, 1967–72; Co-editor, The Quadrant, 1963–66; Contributing Editor, Newsweek International, 1973–77; Professor of Political Science, University of New South Wales; Chairman, Australia Council, 1985–. *Major Publications:* The Lucky Country, 1964; The Permit, 1965; The Education of Young Donald, 1967; Southern Exposure (with D Beal), 1967; God is an Englishman, 1969; The Next Australia, 1970; But what of there are no Pelicans?, 1971; The Australian People, 1972; The Story of the Australian People, expanded version, 1985; Death of the Lucky Countruy, 1976; Money Made us, 1976; His Excellency's Pleasure, 1977; Right Way, Don't go Back, 1978; In Search of Billy Hughes, 1979; Time of Hope, Australia, 1966–72, 1980; Winner Take All, 1981; The Great Museum, 1985; Confessions of a New Boy, 1985; (editor) Change the Rules (with S Encel & E Thompson). *Contributor to:* Various books and papers on Australia. *Honours:* Oficer, Order of Australia, 1982. *Memberships:* Council, Australian Society of Authors, 1982–85, President, 1984–85; Chairman, Copyright Agency Ltd, 1983–85; New South Wales Cultural Affairs Advisory Council, 1976–80. *Address:* 53 Grosvenor Street, Woolahra 2025, Australia.

HORNE, Ralph Albert, b. 10 Mar 1929, Haverhill, Massachusetts, USA. Scientist. *Education:* SB, MIT, 1950; MS, University of Vermont, 1952; MA, Boston University, 1953; PhD, Columbia University, 1955; JD, Suffolk University, 1979. *Publications:* Marine Chemistry, 1969; Water and Aqueous Solutions, 1971; The Chemistry of Our Environment, 1978. *Contributions to:* Over 100 articles in scientific and scholarly periodicals. *Address:* RFD 3, Raymond, NH 03077, USA.

HORNSTEIN, Patricia, b. 10 July 1928. Poet; Freelance Writer. *Education:* BA, University of Connecticut. *Literary Appointments include:* Advertisement Sales, Fairfield News; Women's Editor, Westport Town Crier; Horse and Dog Columnist, Bridgeport Post; Freelance Writer specializing in gardening and nature. *Publications:* (poetry for children) The Apple Vendor's Fair, 1963; 8 a.m. Shadows, 1965; Catch Me a Wind, 1968; more than 200 anthologies and textbooks. *Memberships:* Authors Leage and Authors Guild. *Address:* 90 Norton Road, Easton, CT 06612, USA.

HOROVITZ, Israel, b. 31 Mar. 1939. Playwright; Poet. *Education:* Diploma, RADA, London, England; MA, CUNY, USA. *Appointments:* Founding Playwright, Eugene O'Neil Memorial Theatre Foundation; Director, Playwrights' Laboratory, Actors' Studio. Artistic Director/Producer of The Gloucester Stage Company, Gloucester, Massachusetts, USA, 1979–. *Publications:* Plays: The Wakefield Plays, including trilogy, Alfred the Great, Our Father's Falling, Alfred Dies; Quanna-Powitt Quartet, Hopscotch, The 75th, Stage Directions, Spared; The Indian Wants the Bronx; Line; Its Called Sugar Plumb; Morning; Dr Hero; Primary English Class; Shooting Gallery; Rats; The Reason We Rat; Mackerel; Sunday Runners in the Rain; The Good Parts; Today I Am A Fountain Pen; A Rosen by any Other Name; The Chopin Playoffs; The Widow's Blind Date; Park Your Car in Harvard Yard; Henry Lumper; North Shore Fish; Firebird Champiion, and others; All these plays produced professionally; Adaptation of Dickens' A Christmas Carol – Scrooge and Marley; Films: Strawberry Statement, Author! Author!; TV Film: Play foir Germs (for VD blues); Bartleby the Scrivener; Playcycle for Canadian TV: Groiwing up Jewish in Sault Ste Marie; Novel: Cappella, Novella: Nobody Loves Me. *Honours:* 2 Obies for Best Plays off Broadway; Emmy for TV Plays; Prix du Jury, Cannes Film Festival; French Critics Prize; Drama Desk Award; Vernonn Rice Award;

Boston Critics Prize; French Critics Prize, etc. *Address:* c/o Margaret Ramsey Limited, Goodwin's Court, St Martins Lane, London WC2, England.

HOROVITZ, Michael William, b. 4 Apr. 1945, Frankfurt, Germany. Writer. m. 12 June 1964, 1 son. *Education:* BA and MA (Hons), English Language and Literature, Oxford University. *Literary Appointments:* Founder-Editor, New Departures: Originator, Poetry Olympics. *Publications:* Children of Albion, 1969; The Wolverhampton Wanderer, 1971; Growing Up: Selected Poems and Pictures, 1951–79, 1979; Midsummer Morning Jog Log, 1986. *Contributor to:* Spectator; Vogue; Books and Bookmen; numerous other publications. *Literary Awards:* Arts Council Translator's Award, 1964; Arts Council Writer's Award, 1978. *Address:* Piedmont, Bisley, Gloucestershire GL6 7BU, England.

HORST, Eberhard, b. 1 Feb. 1924, Düsseldorf, Federal Republic of Germany. Writer. m. Eva Maskopf, 28 Feb. 1955, Munich, 1 son. *Education:* Studied Philosophy, Theology, Literature and Theatre, Universities of Bonn and Munich; PhD, 1956. *Publications:* Sizilien, 1964–85; Venedig, 1967–86; 15 mal Spanien, 1975; Friedrich der Staufer, biography, 1975–85; Was ist anders in Spanien?' 1975; Sudliches Licht, prose, 1978; Caesar, biography, 1980–82; Geh ein Wort weiter, literary essays, 1983; Konstantin der Grobe, biography, 1984–85. *Contributions to:* Various journals and radio and television plays. *Honours:* Literary Prize, Foundation for Advancement of Writing, 1975. *Memberships:* PEN Center, Federal Republic of Germany; Co-Founder, Union of German Writers; Past President, Union of German Writers, Bavaria; Board of Directors, Society for Fulfillment of Expression. *Address:* Weiherweg 41, D–8038 Gröbenzell, Federal Republic of Germany.

HORTON, Louise Charlotte Walthall, b. 23 June 1916, Texas, USA. Writer. m. Professor Claude Wendell Horton, 23 Nov. 1938, Houston, Texas, USA, 1 son, 1 daughter. *Education:* BA, Rice University. *Publications:* Samuel Bell Maxey: A Biography, 1974; In the Hills of the Pennyroyal, 1973; Houston. A Novel, 1981. *Contributions to:* Texana; Southwestern Historical Quarterly; The Texas Review; Southwestern Magazine; Kentucky Poetry Review; Bluegrass Literary Review; Columbia Road Review. *Honours:* Honourable mention for portion of novel, Charlotte Collingtree, Southwest Writers Conference, 1978; 1st Prize for poem at San Antonio Writers Conference. *Membership:* National League of American PEN Woman. *Address:* 7804 Rutgers Ave, Austin, TX 78757, USA.

HORTON, Susan R, b. 16 Nov. 1941, Defiance, Ohio, USA. University Professor. m. 5 May 1964, 1 son. *Education:* BA, Defiance College; MA, PhD, Brandeis University. *Literary Appointment:* Professor of English, University of Massachusetts, 1972–. *Major Publications:* Interpreting Interpreting, 1979; The Reader in the Dickens World, 1981; Thinking Through Writing, 1982. *Contributor to:* Genre; Comparative Literature; Modern Fiction Studies; Victorian Studies; Modern Language Association. *Memberships:* Dickens Society; Trustee, Current Secretary & Treasurer; Modern Language Association; College English Association; English Institute. *Address:* Department of English, University of Massachusetts, Boston, MA 02125, USA.

HORVATH, Tibor, b. 28 July 1927, Banhida, Hungary. Professor of Systematic Theology. *Education:* MA, LPhil, College Philosophique, St Albert, Louvain, Belgium; STL, Facutad Teologica, Granada, Spain; STD, Universita Gregoriana, Rome, Italy. *Literary Appointments:* General Editor, Encyclopaedia of Ultimate Reality and Meaning, 1970–; General Editor, journal Ultimate Reality and Meaning, 1978–. *Publications:* Caritas est in ratione. Die Lehre des hl. Thomas Über die Einheit der intellektiven und affektiven Begnadung des Menschen, 1966; Encyclopedia of Human Ideas on Ultimate Reality and Meaning, A Plan and List of Topics for a New Encyclopedia, 1970; Faith Under Scrutiny, 1975; A Kinyilatkoztatas Toclogiaja. A Kinyilatkoztatas

Kiritkaja, 1975; The Sacrificial Interpretation of Jesus' Achievement in the New Testament. *Contributions to:* Journals including: Revue de l'Universite d'Ottawa; Science et Esprit; Novum Testamentum; Heythrop Journal; Rassegna di Teologia; Journal of Ecumenical Studies; Current Anthropology. *Membership:* President, International Society for the of Ultimate Reality and Meaning, 1985–. *Address:* Regis College, 15 St Mary Street, Toronto, Ontario M4Y 2R5, Canada.

HOSKEN, Fran(ziska) Porges, b. 12 July 1919, Vienna, Austria. Journalist. m. James C Hosken, 14 Feb. 1947 (divorced 1961) 2 sons, 1 daughter. *Education:* BA, Smith College, 1940; Master of Architecture, Harvard Graduate School of Design, 1944; Postgraduate work in City Planning, MIT, 1963–66. *Literary Appointments:* Development of multi-media urban teaching programs and teaching experiments with Urban Field Service (Harvard) and Urban Projects Laboratory (MIT) 1970–71; Associate Professor of Urban Studies, University Without Walls, Boston, 1971–74; Lecturer on the Status of Women and Women's Rights at universities, women's groups, international development organisations all over Europe and USA; Consultant to UN HABITAT (Conference on Human Settlements) Preparatory Planning Group 1975; to World Bank on Integration of Women in Sites and Services Programs, 1975; to World Health Organisation/EMRO Alexandria (Temporary Adviser) and member of Secretariat of Seminar on Traditional Practices Affecting the Health of Women and Children 1979, Khartoum Sudan International Journalist – specialist in Urban Affairs, Housing and Development. Publisher and Editor, Win News (Women's International Network News). Development, publication and worldwide distribution by Win News of Childbirth Picture Book Program, 1980–. *Publications:* The Childbirth Picture Book, 1981; The Childbirth Picture Book Flip Chart, The Universal Childbirth Picture Book, 1982; The Childbirth Picture Book Color Slide Program 1982; Female Sexual Mutilations; The Facts and Proposals for Action – An Action Guide, 1980; The Hosken Report; Genital/Sexual Mutilation of Females, 1979; International Directory of Women's Development Organizations 1977; The Kathmandu Valley Towns, 1974; The Functions of Cities, 1972; The Language of Cities, 1968, 1971. *Contributor to:* Christian Science Monitor; Boston Herald; Boston Globe; St Louis Post-Dispatch; Progressive Architecture; Design and Environment; Society of International Development Journal; Development Digest; Architecture Canada; Arts and Architecture; Women Speaking; Women and Health; Women's Agenda and many more. *Memberships:* National Association for Female Executives etc. *Address:* 187 Grant Street, Lexington, MA 02173, USA.

HOSKING, Eric, b. 1909, London, England. Writer. *Publications:* Co-Author of numerous books including: Intimate Sketches from Bird Life, 1940; The Art of Bird Photography, 1944; Birds of the Day, 1944; Birds of the Night, 1945; Birds in Action, 1949; Bird Photography as a Hobby, 1961; Birds Fighting, 1955; Nesting Birds, Eggs and Fledglings, 1967; An Eye for a Bird, autobiography with Frank Lane, 1970; Wildlife Photography, 1973; Minesmere, 1977; Birds of Britain, 1978; Eric Hosking's Birds, 1979; Eric Hosking's Owls, 1982; Antarctic Wildlife, 1982; Eric Hosking's Waders, 1983; Eric Hosking's Seabirds, 1983; Eric Hosking's Wildfowl, 1985; Just a Lark, 1984. Photographic illustrator of numerous natural history books. *Contributions to:* Country Life; Field; British Birds; Birds; Wildlife; Shooting Times. *Honours:* FRPS; FIIP; FZS; OBE. *Memberships:* Vice President, Royal Society for the Protection of Birds; President, Nature Photographic Society. Vice President: British Naturalists Association; Zoological Photographic Club. *Address:* 20 Crouch Hall Road, London N8 8HX, England.

HOSPITAL, Janette Turner, b. 12 Nov. 1942, Melbourne, Australia. Author. m. Clifford G Hospital, 5 Feb. 1965, Brisbane, 1 son, 1 daughter. *Education:* BA, University of Queensland, 1965; MA, Queens

University, Canada, 1973. *Literary Appointments:* Librarian, Harvard University, USA, 1971–74; Lecturer, Writers Workshop, University of Calgary, Canada, 1983, 84. *Publications:* Novels: The Ivory Swing, 1982, 83, 84; The Tiger in the Tiger Pit, 1983, 84, 85; Borderline, 1985. *Contributions to:* Numerous literary magazines in USA, Canada and Uk and Australia including: Atlantic Monthly; North American Review; Mademoiselle; Saturday Night; Canadian Fiction Magazine; Encounter. *Honours:* Atlantic First, citation for short story, Atlantic Monthly, 1978; Seal Award for The Ivory Swing, Canada, 1982; 1st Prize, Magazine Fiction, Canada, 1982. *Memberships:* Poets, Playwrights, Editors, Essayists and Novelists International; American Authors Guild; Writers Union of Canada. *Literary Agent:* Blanche C Gregory, USA; Murray Pollinger. *Address:* c/o Blanche C Gregory, 2 Tudor City Place, New York, NY 10017, USA.

HOUGHTON, Barbara Coan, b. 11 Aug. 1932, Philadelphia, PA, USA. Homemaker. m David D Houghton, 22 June 1963, Solebury, PA, 2 sons, 1 daughter. *Education:* BS, University of Pennsylvania; MA, University of Washington. *Publications:* City of the Second Lake, A History of McFarland, Wisconsin, 1976; By Special Request, 1985. *Contributor to:* Christian Science Monitor; Primipara; Voices International; Country Poet; Poetry Out of Wisconsin; Ezra Pound in Memorian; Wisonsin Poets' Calendar; Stoughton Courier Hub; Friends Journal; Wisconsin School News. *Memberships:* Wisonsin Fellowship of Poets; Wisconsin Regional Writers' Association. *Address:* 2447 Highway AB, McFarland, WI 53558, USA.

HOULDIN, Michael Christopher, b. 12 Oct. 1953, Philadelphia, Pennsylvania, USA. Managing Editor, Columnist. *Education:* English, Villanova University, 1971–73; BA Journalism, St Bonaventure University, 1973–75. *Literary Appointments:* Sportswriter 1977, General Assignment Reporter 1979, Columnist-General Commentary 1980, News Editor 1984, Managing Editor 1984, The Catholic Standard and Times. *Contributions to:* The Catholic Standard and Times; The Philadelphia Inquirer; The Philadelphia Bulletin; The Camden Courier Post; National Catholic News Service; Religious News Service and National Christian Council. *Honours:* Best Regular Column, Catholic Press Association, 1980; General Excellence in Newspapering, Catholic Press Association, 1984. *Memberships:* Catholic Press Association; Philadelphia Writers Organization; Philadelphia Sportswriters Association; Philadelphia Writers Conference; Metropolitan Christian Council of Philadelphia. *Address:* The Catholic Standard and Times, 222 N 17th Street, Philadelphia, PA 19103, USA.

HOWARD, Anthony Michell, b. 12 Feb. 1934, London, England. Journalist. *Education:* BA, Christ Church, Oxford, 1955; Called to the Bar, Inner Temple, 1956. *Publications:* The Baldwin Age, contributor, 1960; The Age of Austerity, contributor, 1960; The Making of the Prime Minister, with Richard West, 1965; Richard Crossman: Selections from the Diaries of a Cabinet Minister, Editor, 1979. *Contributor to:* Editor, New Statesman, 1972–78; Editor, Listener, 1979–81; Deputy Editor, The Obserever, 1981–; New York Times Book Review; New Republic; etc. *Agent:* A D Peters. *Address:* 17 Addison Avenue, London W11, England.

HOWARD, Edward Davenport, b. 23 Dec. 1945, Cleveland, Ohio, USA. Journalist. *Education:* Columbia University and The University of Sydney; BA, Sydney. *Contributions to:* The Australian; The National Times (Sydney); Sydney Morning Herald; Theatre Australia, etc. *Membership:* St Anthony Hall, New York City, USA. *Address:* Flat 1, 87 Francis Street, Bondi, NSW, 2026, Australia.

HOWARD, Helen Addison, b. 4 Aug. 1904, Missoula, Montana, USA. Historian. m. Ben Overland, 24 April 1946, Hollywood, California. *Education:* BA, University of Montana, 1927; MA, University of Southern California, 1933. *Literary Appointments:* Editorial Advisory Board, Journal of the West, Scholarly Historical Quarterly, Kansas State University, Manhattan, Kansas, 1978. *Publications:* War Chief Joseph, 1941–78; Northwest Trail Blazers, 1963; Saga of Chief Joseph, 1965–75; Hiawatha: Co-Founder of an Indian United Nations, 1971; Literary Translators and Interpreters of Indian Songs, 1973; An Introduction to Pre-Missionary Indian Religion, 1974, (in journal of the West); A Survey of American Indian Music: A Critique of 5 vols. from the Densmore Collection, 1974; American Indian Poetry, 1979–85, an ethnohistory, Literary critique; American Frontier Tales, 1982. *Contributor to:* The Puzzle of Baptiste Charbonneau, Frontier Times Magazine, 1970; The Men Who Saved the Buffalo, 1975; Editor, American Indian Poetry, 1979; Unique History of Fort Tejon, Journal of the West, 1979; Dictionary of Indian Tribes of the Americas, 1980; Numerous articles in specialist horse magazines. *Honours:* Recipient, several academy honours. *Memberships:* California Writers Guild, 1973–78; PEN International, Los Angeles Center, 1979–81. *Address:* 410 South Lamer Street, Burbank, CA 91506, USA.

HOWARD, Marghanita, b. 24 Oct. 1915, London, England. Writer. m. John Howard, 1938, Paris, France, 1 son, 1 daughter. *Education:* Somerville College, Oxford; MA, Oxon. *Literary Appointments:* Annan Committee of Inquiry into Future of Broadcasting, 1974–77; Arts Council, 1979–, Vice-Chairman, Drama Adv. Panel, 1980–; Chairman, 1980; Chairman, Literature Adv. Panel, 1980–, Vice-Chairman, 1982; Honorary Fellow, Manchester Polytechnic, 1971; F D Maurice Memorial Lectures, 1974. *Publications:* Love on the Supertax (novel), 1944; The Patchwork Book (anthology), 1946; To Bed With Grand Music, 1946; Editor, Stories of Adventure, 1974; Editor, Victorian Tales, 1948; Tory Heaven (novel), 1948; Little Boy Lost (novel), 1949; Mrs Ewing, Mrs Molesworth, Mrs Hodgson Burnett (criticism), 1950; The Village (novel), 1952; The Victorian Chaise-Longue (novel), 1953; The Offshore Island (play), 1959; Ectasy: A Study of Some Secular and Religious Experiences, 1961; Domestic Life in Edwardian England, 1964; Co-Editor, A Chaplet for Charlotte Yonge, 1965; Jane Austen and Her World, 1969; George Eliot and Her World, 1973; Kipling's English History, 1974; Everyday Ecstasy, 1980; Ferry The Jerusalem Cat (children's novel), 1983; Reviews, Radio and TV programmes. *Contributions to:* Numerous publications. *Literary Agent:* David Higham Associates. *Address:* c/o 5-8 Lower John Street, Golden Square, London W1, England.

HOWARD, Patricia, b. 18 Oct. 1937, Warwickshire, England. Musician/Lecturer in Music, The Open University. *Education:* Lady Margaret Hall, Oxford; University of Surrey, BA Hons (Music), MA, PhD. *Publications:* Gluck and the Birth of Modern Opera, 1963; The Operas of Benjamin Britten: An Introduction, 1969; Haydn in London, 1980; Mozart's Marriage of Figaro, 1980; C W von Gluck; Orfeo, 1981; Beethoven's Eroica Symphony, 1984; Haydn's String Quartet, 1984; Benjamin Britten: The Turn of the Screw, 1985. *Contributions to:* Musical Times; Music and Letters; The Consort; The Listener. *Honours:* Susette Taylor Travelling Fellowship, 1971; Leverhulme Research Award, 1976. *Address:* Stepping Stones, Gomshall, Surrey, England.

HOWARD, Philip N C, b. 2 Nov. 1933, London, England. Journalist. *Education:* King's Scholar, Eton College; MA, Trinity College, Oxford University. *Publications:* The Royal Palaces, 1970; London's River, 1975; The British Monarchy, 1977; New Words for Old, 1977; Weasel Words, 1978; Words Fail Me, 1980; A Word in Your Ear, 1983; The State of the Language, English Observed, 1984; We Thundered Out, 200 Years of the Times 1785–1985, 1985. *Contributor to:* Literary Editor, The Times, 1978–; Punch; New Society; Verbatim; Illustrated London News; Homes & Gardens; BBC Radio & TV. *Honours:* Recipient, IPC Press Award for descriptive writing, 1970. *Memberships:* National Union of Journalists; Liveryman, Wheelwrights' Company. *Address:* Flat 1, 47 Ladbroke Grove, London W11 3AR, England.

HOWARD, Roger, b. 19 June 1938, Warwick, England. Theatre Writer, Poet, Lecturer. *Education:* MA Litt Drama. *Literary Appointments:* Founder and Director, Theatre Underground; Lecturer in Literature, University of Essex. *Publications:* New Short Plays, 1968; Slaughter Night and Other Plays, 1971; A Break in Berun, 1979; Mao Tse Tung and the Chinese People, 1977; Contemporary Chinese Theatre, 1978; The Siege, 1981; Partisans, 1983. *Contributions to:* Transatlantic Review; Stand; Bananas; Times Literary Supplement; Double Space; New Society; Times Education Supplement; Minnesota Review; Theatre Quarterly; Play and Players; Theatre Research International. *Membership:* Theatre Writers Union. *Address:* c/o Theatre Underground, Department of Literature, University of Essex, Wivenhoe Park, Colchester, Essex, CO4 3SQ, England.

HOWARD, Theresa Lizbeth, b. 25 Apr. 1957, London, England. Literary Agent. *Education:* BA, Honours, Performing Arts. *Plays produced:* Jo's Story, Street Theatre, London, 1979; The Rev Luke's Useful Show, devised with Mountebank Theatre Company, performed Oxford 1980; Stone Fist, Soho Poly, 1981; Grock, Liverpool 1984. *Memberships:* Theatre Writers Union; Women in Entertainment; Script Reading Panel, Womens Playhouse Trust. *Literary Agent:* Genista McIntosh. *Address:* c/o Genista McIntosh, Marmont Management Ltd, 308 Regent Street, London W1, England.

HOWARTH, Stephen William Russell, b. 19 Apr. 1953, Farnborough, Kent, England. Writer. m. Marianne Stella Vanek, 3 July 1981, Tunbridge Wells, Kent. *Education:* Certificate of Education, Oxford University; TEFL (IH). *Publications:* The Koh-i-Noor Diamond: The History and the Legend, 1980; The Knights Templar, 1982; Morning Glory: A History of the Imperial Japanese Navy, 1983 (published in USA as, The Fighting Ships of the Rising Sun). *Contributions to:* The Geographical Magazine; the Daily Express. *Memberships:* Fellow of the Royal Geographical Society; Associate Member of the US Naval Institute; Sub-lieutenant, Royal Naval Reserve. *Literary Agent:* Curtis Brown Spokesmen, London. *Address:* c/o Curtis Brown Spokesmen, 162-168 Regent Street, London W1R 5TA, England.

HOWE, James, b. 2 Aug. 1946, Oneida, New York, USA. Writer. m. Betsy Imershein, 5 Apr. 1981, New York, New York, USA. *Education:* BFA, Boston University, 1968; MA, Hunter College, 1977. *Publications:* Bunnicula, 1979; Teddy Bear's Scrapbook, 1980; The Hospital Book, 1981; Holiday Inn, 1982; A Night Without Stars, 1983; The Celery Stalks at Midnight, 1983; Morgan's Zoo, 1984; The Day The Teacher Went Bananas, 1984; What Eric Knew, 1985; Stage Fright, 1986; When You Go to Kindergarten, 1986. *Contributions to:* Writing for the Hidden Child in The Horn Book Magazine, 1985. *Honours:* Golden Sower Award, 1981; South Carolina Childrens Book Award, 1981; Dorothy Canfield Fisher Award, 1981; Iowa Childrens Choice Award, 1982; Sequoya Childrens Book Award, 1982; Young Readers Choice Award, 1982; Land of Enchantment Childrens Book Award, 1982; Nene Award, 1983; Sunshine State Young Readers Award, 1984; Boston Globe-Horn Book Honor Award, 1981; American Book Award Nominee, 1982; Tennessee Children's Choice Award, 1984. *Memberships:* Authors Guild; Mystery Writers of America; Poets, Playwrights, Editors, Essayists and Novelists. *Literary Agent:* Amy Berkower, New York, USA. *Address:* Writers House, 21 West 26 Street, New York, NY 10010, USA.

HOWE, Stephen Douglas, b. 28 Feb. 1948, Brentwood, Essex, England. Journalist. m. Susan Jane Apps, 24 Apr. 1971, Blindley Heath, Surrey, 1 son, 1 daughter. *Education:* College Diploma in Agriculture; National Diploma in Agriculture; College Diploma in Farm Management; Seale Hayne Agricultural College, Devon. *Literary Appointments:* Technical Editor, Power Farming Magazine, 1978; Editor, Power Farming, 1982.

Contributions to: Power Farming; Farmers Weekly; The Scotsman; Agribooks, Canada; BBC Radio, Farming Today (regular contributor). *Honours:* Perkins Award, 1973; Fisons Award, 1973; Perkins Award, 1975; Fisons Award, 1978; John Deere Award, 1980. *Membership:* Guild of Agricultural Journalists, Council Member. *Address:* Springfield Cottage, Byers Lane, South Godstone, Surrey, England.

HOWE ELKINS, Valmai Jennifer, b. 4 Nov. 1947, Australia. Writer; Lecturer. m. David Elkins, 9 May 1970, Peacham, Vermont, USA, 1 step-son, 1 daughter. *Education:* MFA, Physiotherapy. *Publications:* The Rights of the Pregnant Parent, 1976; The Birth Report, 1983. *Contributor to:* Canadian Doctor Magazine; Canadian Physiotherapy Association; Doctors Review; Bennington Review. *Address:* 707 Grosvenor Avenue, Westmount, Quebec, Canada H3Y 2T3.

HOWELL, Freda, b. 18 Jan. 1912. Retired Bank Clerk. *Publications:* The Wind in the Corn, 1968; Stone Angels, 1980. *Contributor to:* Anthologies: Stroud Festival Poems, 1967; Lambda Anthology, column VII, 1969; Ipso Facto; Masques of Love; Sugar and Spice; Rhyme Revival, 1982; Orbis; Candelabrum; Contemporary Comunications; Ipse; Envoi. *Honours:* Premium Prize, Poetry Society, 1971-72; Arnold Vincent Bowen Award, 1972; 3rd Prize, Canterbury Literary Award Poetry Competition, 1977; Interview and reading of poems, Radio Medway, 1978. *Address:* 63 St John's Road, Swalecliffe, Whitstable, Kent CT5 2RJ, England.

HOWELLS, William Herbert Roscoe, b. 27 Oct. 1919, Saundersfoot. Writer. m. (1) Lucie Winifred Taylor, 28 June 1943, Birmingham (deceased Feb. 1979) (2) Margaret Olive James, 1 Oct. 1979, Amroth, 1 son. *Publications:* Cliffs of Freedom, 1961; Farming in Wales, 1965; The Sounds Between, 1968; Across the Sounds, 1972; What Price Abortion?, 1973; Total Community, 1975; Old Saundersfoot, 1977; Herons Mill, 1979; Tenby Old and New, 1981; Caldey, 1984. *Contributions to:* Various publications. *Memberships:* Guild of Agricultural Journalists; Institute of Journalists. *Literary Agent:* Rosemary Bromley, Hampshire. *Address:* Glan-y-Môr Amroth, Narberth, Pembrokeshire SA67 8NG, Wales.

HOWER Edward, b. 10 Jan. 1941, New York, USA. Writer. *Education:* BA, Cornell University; Dip Ed, Makerere University, Uganda; MA, University of California, Los Angeles. *Publications:* The New Life Hotel (novel); Wolf Tickets (novel); Kikuyu Woman (short fiction). *Contributions to:* Atlantic Monthly; Transatlantic Review; Epoch; East Africa Journal; Transition (Ghana). *Honour:* National Endowment for the Arts Award. *Membership:* PEN. *Literary Agent:* Liz Darhansoff. *Address:* 1409 Hanshaw Road, Ithaca, NY 14850, USA.

HOWES, Barbara, b. 1 May 1914, New York City, USA. Poet, Anthologist. m. William Jay Smith, 1 Oct. 1947, Mountainville, New York, USA, 2 sons. *Education:* BA, Bennington College, 1937. *Literary Appointments:* Editor, Chimera, literary quarterly, 1943-47. *Major Publications:* Poetry: The Undersea Farmer, 1948; In the Cold Country, 1954; Light & Dark, 1959; Looking up at Leaves, 1966; The Blue Garden, 1972; A Private Signal: Poems New & Selected, 1977; Moving, 1983; Short Stories. The Road Commissioner & other Stories, (with block prints by Gregory Smith), 1983. Anthologies: 23 Modern Stories, 1963; From the Green Antilles: Writings of the Caribbean, 1966; The Sea-Green Horse, (with Gregory Smith), 1970; The Eye of the Heart, Stories from Latin America, 1973. *Contributor to:* The New Yorker; Antaeus; Southern Review; Virginia Quarterly Review; Atlantic; and others. *Honours:* Guggenheim Fellowship, 1955. *Membership:* PEN Club. *Literary Agent:* Tim Schaffner, New York. *Address:* Brook House, North Pownal, VT 05260, USA.

HOWLAND, Carol, b. 19 June 1953, Troy, New York, USA. Medical Writer, Scientific Editor. *Education:* BA

English, Indiana University of Pennsylvania; Postgraduate study, Literacy Communications, Syracuse University; Certification in Biomedical Communications. *Literary Appointments:* Assistant Editor, Environmental Periodicals Bibliography, 1977; Editor, Literacy Advance, 1978–79; Scientific Editor, Current Concepts in Rehabilitation Medicine, 1982–; Research Instructor, Department of Physical Medicine, Baylor College of Medicine. *Major Publications:* Editor: Psychophysiological Aspects of Sleep, 1980; Late Effects of Poliomyelitis, 1985; Medical Rehabilitation, 1985. *Contributor to:* Consultant; Medical Aspects of Human Secuality; Psychiatric Annals; American Journal of Psychiatry; Sleep; Heart & Lung; Archives of Phsyical Medicine & Rehabilitation; Annals of the Academy of Medicine, Singapore; Archives of Surgery; Cardiovascular Research Bulletin; Southern Medical Journal. *Memberships:* American Medical Writers Association, President-elect, Southwest Chapter; Chairperson, AMWA Southwest Conference, 1985, Board of Directors, Southwest Chapter; Council of Biology Editors; Society for Technical Communication; Society for Scholarly Publishing; National Association for Literary Advance. *Address:* 7321 Staffordshire apt 4, Houston, TX 77030, USA.

HOWSON, Frank Michael, b. 10 Mar. 1952, Melbourne, Australia. Writer (Film & Theatre) Lyricist. m. Lynn Murphy Howson. *Major Publications:* Plays: Magical Frank, 1976; The Boy who dared to Dream, 1978; Squizzy, 1978; Aladdin, 1981; Sinbad–The Last Adventure, 1982; Films: Backstage, Something great; Heaven Tonight; Hunting. *Contribution to:* Tagg; A–Z; (short stories & interviews). *Membership:* Australian Writers Guild. *Literary Agent:* Boulevard Organisation, Melbourne, Australia. *Address:* 22 Nelson Street, Balaclava, 3183 Victoria, Australia.

HOYLAND, Michael David, b. 1 Apr. 1925. Senior Art Lecturer. m. Marette N Hoyland. *Appointments:* Whitford Hall School, Bromsgrove, 1951–57; Art, Patchway Secondary School, Bristol, 1957–63; Senior Art Lecturer, Kestevn College of Education, 1963–. *Publications:* Art for Children, 1970; Variations, 1975; Love Affair with War, 1981; The Bright Way In, 1984. *Contributions to:* The Listener; The New Statesman; The Scotsman; Tribune; Numerous anthologies of the Arts Council. *Memberships:* PEN; Fellow, Society for Art Education. *Address:* Foxfoot House, South Luffenham, Near Oakham, Rutland, Leicestershire LE1 8NP, England.

HOZESKI, Bruce William, b. 28 Feb. 1941, Grand Rapids, Michigan, USA. University Professor. m. Kathleen Antoinette Tuma, 9 Sep. 1967, Grand Rapids, 1 daughter. *Education:* BA, Aquinas College, Grand Rapids, 1964; MA 1966, PhD 1969, Michigan State University. *Literary Appointments:* Editor, Nuntia, newsletter, Medieval Association of the Midwest, 1982–85; Editor, Ball State University Forum, 1983–; Editor, Newsletter, International Society of Hildegard von Bingen Studies, 1984–. *Publications:* First English Critical Edition/Translation, Hildegard von Bingen's Scivias, 1985. *Contributions to:* Mystics Quarterly; Annuale Mediaevale; etc. *Memberships:* Treasurer 1981–, Lambda Iota Tau; Founder & President, International Society of Hildegard von Bingen Studies, 1984–; etc. *Address:* Department of English, Ball State University, Muncie, IN 47306, USA.

HRDY, Sarah Blaffer, b. 11 July 1946, USA. University Professor. m. Daniel B Hrdy, 2 children. *Education:* BA summa cum laude, Radcliffe College, 1969; PhD, Harvard University, 1975. *Publications:* The Blackman of Zinacantan: A Central American Legend, 1972; The Langurs of Abu: Female and Male Strategies of Reproduction, 1977, 80; The Woman that Never Evolved, 1981, Japanese editon, 1982, 5th printing 1984, French edition, 1984; Infanticide: Comparative and Evolutionary Perspectives, co-editor, 1984. *Contributions to:* Folia Primatologica; Advances in the Study of Behavior, 1976; Science; American Scientist; Natural History; Recent Advances in Primatology,

1978; Quarterly Review of Biology; Harvard Magazine; Other Ways of Growing Old, 1981; International Journal of Primatology; Social Behavior of Female Vertebrates, 1983; Perspectives in Primate Biology, 1983; Encyclopedia of Mammals, 1984; various other books and journal contributions. *Honour:* Phi Beta Kappa; Numerous public addresses by invitation; Various International symposium invitations; Consulting Editor, American Journal of Primatology and Primates; Editorial Board, Cultural Anthropology. *Address:* Department of Anthropology, Young Hall, University of California, Davis, CA 95616, USA.

HUANT, Ernest Albin Camille, b. 29 Oct. 1909, Vouziers, Ardennes, France. Doctor; Writer; Philosopher; Sociologist. *Education:* Faculty of Medicine, Paris. *Publications include:* L'Unite Romaine de l'An 1000: Othon III, 1971; Non a l'Avortement, 1972; La Nouvelle face de Meduse, 1974; Cybernetique des 3/Economie, Environnement, Ecologie, 1975; Temperalite, Survie, Analyse Psycho-Cybernetique, 1975; Les etranges courses du Colonel d'Hourdoff, 1986. *Honours include:* Chevalier, Legion d'Honneur; Carnegie Foundation Medal, USA; Prix rechercho Scient. Acad. de Medecine, 1965; Prix Littre des Eorir Med. Prix Audiffred de l'Acad des Sciences Morales et Polit. 1968. *Memberships include:* Society d'Economie Politique, Paris, 1958–; President, Founder, Centre International Humanae Vitae, 1968. *Address:* 9 Ave Niel, Paris 17e, France.

HUBBARD, L Ron, b. 13 Mar. 1911, Deceased. Tilden, Nebraska, USA. Writer, explorer, philosopher, humanitarian. m. Mary Sue Whipp, 1 son, 2 daughters. *Education:* George Washington University, 1932; Princeton School of Government, 1945. *Publications include:* Over 240 novels and short stories, 1934–50; Non-fiction writing include: Dianetics: The Modern Science of Mental Health, 1950; Science of Survival, 1951; The Fundamentals of Thought, 1956; Scientology: A New Slant on Life, 1966; Self-Analysis, 1968; Dianetics Today, 1975; Battlefield Earth – A Saga of the Year 3000, 1982; The Invaders Plan – Volume I, 10 volume Mission Earth series, 1985. *Contributions to:* Various publications. *Honours include:* Community Service awards internationally; Over 75 awards for musical creations; International Social Reform Award, 1976; Ingrams West Award, 1977; National Life Acievement Award, Illinois, Society of Psychic Research, 1978; International Professional Association Award, 1978; Numerous honorary citizenships and keys to cities in USA; Special Achievement Award, Academy of Science Fiction, Fantasy and Horror Films, 1984. *Memberships include:* Authors League of America; Writers Guild of Great Britain; American Society of Composers, Authors and Publishers. *Address:* Saint Hill Manor, East Grinstead, Sussex RH19 4JY, England.

HUBER-ABRAHAMOWICZ, Elfriede, b. 19 Dec. 1922, Vienna, Austria. Writer. m. Gerhard Huber, 7 Sep. 1948, Basel, 2 daughters. *Education:* PhD. *Publications:* Das Problem der Kunst bei Platon, 1954; Verhaengnis. Gedichte, 1957; Der unendliche Weg. Prosa und Gedichte, 1964; Seiltanz und Waage. Gedichte, 1974; Parallel, Roman, 1979; Spiegelspannung. Sonette, 1981; Muttergestirn. Gedichte, 1984. *Contributions to:* Neue Zuercher Zeitung; Badener Tagblatt. *Honours:* Preis des Basler Literaturkredits, 1960; C F Meyer-Preis, 1965. *Memberships:* Schweizerischer Schriftsteller-Verband; Internationale Assoziation von Philosophinnen. *Address:* Berghaldenstrasse 36 c, CH–8053 Zuerich, Switzerland.

HUBLER, David Elliot, b. 3 Sep. 1941, New York City, USA. Writer. m. Rebecca Summer 4 Sep. 1966, Plainview, New York, 2 sons. *Education:* BA, New York University, 1963; MA, University of New Hampshire, 1965. *Literary Appointments:* Secondary School English Teacher, 1965–66; Instructor in Writing, Northern Virginia Community College, 1983. *Major Publications:* You Gotta Believe !, 1983; The Politicians' Health, Diet & Sex Guide, 1984. *Contributor to:* Washington Post; McCall's; Washington Times; and others. *Membership:* Washington Independent Writers. *Literary Agent:* Alyss Dorese. *Address:* 4109 Breezewood Lane, Annandale, VA 22003, USA.

HUDGINS, Patricia Jo, b. 1 Apr. 1943, North Carolina, USA. Executive Secretary, Romance Writers of America. m. William W Hudgins, 8 Apr. 1966, 1 son, 1 daughter. *Education:* BFA, Art Education, Mississippi University for Women, 1965; University of Mississippi, 1961–62; Creighton University, 1971–72. *Literary Appointments:* Editor, Capitol Ideas; Staff Writer, Report (Romance Writers of America); Editor, Romance Writers Report, 1982–84; Assistant Editor, The State of Art, newspaper; Editor, Enrich, magazine. *Publications:* Media on the Move, 1980; numerous poetry anthologies. *Contributor to:* Enrich; Media Library Services Journal; Reader's Digest; Christian Single Magazine; Romance Writers Report; State of Art. *Literary Awards:* Oklahoma Poetry Society, 1st, 2nd and Special Award, 1974; Romance Writers of America, Honorable Mention, 1982; Oklahoma Federated Writer, 1st place, 1983, 3rd, 1984, Honorable Mention, 1985; Texas Press Women, 2nd Prize, 1984, 2nd Prize, 1985, Honorable Mention, 1985; Byliners, Honorable Mention, 1984, Honorable Mention, 1985. *Memberships:* National Federation of Press Women; Texas Press Women; Romance Writers of America; Oklahoma Writers Federation. *Address:* 6911 Fawn River Drive, Spring, TX 77379, USA.

HUDSON, Christopher, b. 29 Sep. 1946, England. Writer. m. Kirsty McLeod, 10 Mar. 1978, 1 son. *Education:* Scholar, Jesus College, Cambridge. *Literary Appointments:* Editor, Faber & Faber, 1968; Literary Editor, The Spectator, 1971, The Standard, 1981. *Publications:* Overlord, 1975; The FinalAct, 1980; Insider Out, 1982; The Killing Fields, 1984. *Literary Agent:* Toby Eady. *Address:* 64 Westbourne Park Road, London W2, England.

HUDSON, Derek (Rommel), b. 20 July 1911, London, England. Author/Journalist. *Education:* MA, Oxford University. *Publications include:* Thomas Barnes of The Times, 1943, 2nd edition 1973; Lewis Carroll, 1954, 2nd edition 1976; Arthur Rackham: His Life and Work, 1960, 2nd edition 1974; Writing Between the Lines, 1965; Holland House in Kensington, 1967; Kensington Palace, 1968; Minby: Man of Two Worlds, 1972 paperback edition 1974; For Love of Painting, Sir Gerald Kelly, 1975. Editorial staff, The Times 1939–49; Literary Editor, Spectator, 1949–53, Oxford University Press 1955–75; anthologies and 2 collections of essays. *Contributor to:* Times Literary Supplement; Cornhill National Review etc. *Membership:* FRSL, 1955. *Address:* 33 Beacon Hill Court, Hindhead, Surrey GU26 6PU, England.

HUDSON, Robert Vernon, b. 29 Aug. 1934, Indianapolis, Indiana, USA. Writer, Educator. 2 sons. *Education:* BS, Indiana University, 1954; MS, University of Oregon, 1966; PhD, University of Minnesota, 1970. *Publications:* The Writing Game: A Biography of Will Irwin, 1982. *Contributions to:* Books including: Newsletters to Newspapers;: Eighteenth-Century Journalism; Academic American Encyclopedia; Dictionary of Literary Biography; Biographical Dictionary of Internationalists; Biographical Dictionary of American Journalism; Magazines and journals including: Journalism Quarterly; Journalism History; Grassroots Editor; Writer's Digest; Ensign; Lakeland Boating; Together; Journalism Educator. *Memberships:* The Society of Professional Journalists; Kappa Tau Alpha; Association for Education in Journalism and Mass Communication. *Address:* School of Journalism, Michigan State University, East Lansing, MI 48824, USA.

HUDSON, Thomas Cyril, b. 25 Aug. 1910. Retired Estimator and Planning Engineer. *Publications:* Kairos, 1960. *Contributions to:* Boys' Own Paper; Humour Variety; Southern Evening Echo; Hampshire Poets; Isle of Wight Poets, Nos. 1 and 2; The Islander; Country Life; This England; Island Images (anthology). *Honours:* First Prize, Isle of Wight Writers' Circle, 1971–72; Margery Hume Cup, Isle of Wight Musical Festival, 1972, 73, 79, 82, 84, 85; WG & SF Tillyard Cup, Isle of Wight Writers' Circle, 1974; Runner-up, Southern Evening Echo, Poetry Competition (over 2000 entires); 1 of 6 Runners-up, Chichester Festival Theatre Competition; First Prize in Competition, Isle of Wight Council for the Arts. *Address:* Wyvern, Newport Road, Cowes, Isle of Wight PO31 8PE, England.

HUFF, Robert, b. 3 Apr. 1924, Evanston, Illinois, USA. Professor of English; Poet. Single, 1 son, 2 daughters. *Education:* AB, English Literature (with distinction), 1949, AM, Humanities, 1952, Wayne State University. *Literary Appointments:* Instructor of Composition: University of Oregon, Fresno State College, Oregon State University; Poet-in-Residence, University of Delaware, 1960–64; Associate Professor, Modern Poetry, Humanities, etc. Western Washington State College, 1964–66; Writer-in-Residence, University of Arkansas, 1966–67; Professor, Modern Poetry, Humanities, Introductory Literature and The Writing of Poetry, Western Washington University, 1967–. *Publications:* Colonel Johnson's Ride, 1959; The Course, 1966; The Ventriloquist, 1977; Shore Guide to Flocking Names, 1985; Numerous poems recorded. Books in progress: Taking Her Sides on Immortality; Beginning in Winter. *Contributions to:* Numerous magazines, journals and newspapers, also anthologies. *Honours include:* Robert Huff Manuscript Collections at University of Kentucky, Wayne State University and Carnegie Library, Syracuse University; Student Fellowship, School of Letters, Indiana University, 1957; Writing Scholarship, Bread Loaf Writers Conference, 1961; Writing Fellowship, The MacDowell Colony, 1963; several other honours and awards. *Memberships include:* Northwest Poetry Circuit (Member, Selection Committee). *Address:* Department of English, Western Washington University, Bellingham, WA 98225, USA.

HUGGETT, Frank Edward, b. 25 Mar. 1924, London, England. Writer. *Education:* BA, Wadham College, Oxford, England. *Publucations:* Life Below Stairs, 1977; Victorian England as seen by Punch, 1978; Goodnight Sweetheart, 1979; Carriages at Eight, 1979; Cartoonists at War, 1981; The Dutch Connection, 1982; Teachers, 1986. *Address:* Flat 6, 40 Shepherd Hill, London N6, England.

HUGHES, Graham, b. 17 Apr. 1926, London, England. Editor, Arts Review Magazine. m. 7 Sep. 1951, St Giles in the Fields, London, 1 son, 3 daughters. *Education:* MA, History & Law, Trinity College, Cambridge. *Publications:* Modern Jewelry, 1963; Modern Silver, 1967; Jewelry, 1966; Art of Jewelry, 1972; Gems & Jewelry, 1976; Barns of Rural Britain, 1985. *Contributor to:* Many articles on Art History, special emphasis on modern design and crafts; many catalogues. *Honours:* Liveryman, Goldsmiths' Hall; Honorary Brother, Art Workers' Guild; Gold Medal, Royal Society of Arts; Fellow, Society of Antiquaries. *Address:* 16 St James' Gardens, London W11, England.

HUGHES, Monica, b. 3 Nov. 1925, Liverpool, England. Novelist. m. Glen Hughes, 22 Apr. 1957, Ottawa, 2 sons, 2 daughters. *Appointments:* Writer-in-Residence, University of Alberta, 1984–85. *Publications:* Crisis on Conshelf Ten, 1975; Earth Dark, 1977; The Tomorow City, 1978; Beyond the Dark River, 1979; The Keeper of the Isis Light, 1980; The Guardian of Isis, 1981; The Isis Pedlar, 1982; Ring Rise, Ring-Set, 1982; Hunter in the Dark, 1982; Space Trap, 1983; Devil on my Back, 1984; Sandwriter, 1985. *Honours:* Vicky Metcalf Award, 1981; Alberta Culture Juvenile Novel Award, 1981; Canada Council Prize for Children's Literature, 1981, 1982; IBBY Certificate of Honour, 1982; Runner Up, The Guardian Award, 1983. *Memberships:* Writers Union of Canada; Alberta Writers' Guild; Canadian Society of Children's Authors, Illustrators & Performers. *Literary Agent:* Nancy Colbert, Toronto. *Address:* 13816 – 110A Avenue, Edmonton, Alberta T5M 2M9, Canada.

HUGHES, Retha Ellen Glidewell, b. 24 Oct. 1959, North Carolina, USA. Documentation Specialist; Technical Writer. m. Earl Kevin Hughes, Cape Carteret, N Carolina, 20 June 1981. *Education:* BA, English & Secondary Education, University of North Carolina, Chapel Hill, 1981; MA candidate, Technical Writing & Editing, George Mason University, Virginia. *Major Publications:* Computer Software Documentation, 1984–85: Decision Master User's Manual; CHEETAH User's Manual; ProCalc User's Manual. CAMM (Computer-Aided Manufacturing Management) Operator's Manuals: TCS Interface; Allen-Bradley Interface; Series Six Interface; Analogic Interface; Kastle Interface; Modicon Interface. *Contributions to:* Medical Advances for Divers, Naval Medical Research Institute, 1984. *Honours:* Dean's Honour List, 1977–81; Whitaker Academic Scholarship, 1979–81. *Memberships:* American Medical Writers Association; Council for Biology Editors; Society for Technical Communications. *Address:* 623 Center Street, No. 204, Herndon, VA 22070, USA.

HUGHES, Spike (Patrick Cairns), b. 1908, London, England. Writer. *Publications:* Cinderella (Opera for TV), 1938; Opening Bars; Second Movement; The Art of Coarse Cricket; The Art of Coarse Bridge; The Art of Coarse Cookery; The Art of Coarse Entertaining; The Art of Coarse Language; Great Opera Houses; Out of Season; Famous Verdi Operas; Famous Mozart Operas; Famous Puccini Operas; The Toscanini Legacy; Glyndebourne; How to Survive Abroad; Editor, The International Encyclopaedia of Opera, 1974. *Contributor to:* Observer; Times; Daily Express; Musical Times; Opera; etc. *Agent:* Richard Scott Simon Ltd. *Address:* Broyle Gate Farmhouse, Ringmer, Sussex, England.

HUIE, William Bradford, b. 13 Nov. 1910, Hartselle, Alabama, USA. Author. m. (1) Ruth Puckett (deceased), 27 Oct. 1934, Hartselle, (2) Martha Hunt Robertson, 16 July 1977, Huntsville, Alabama. *Education:* BA, University of Alabama, 1930 . *Publications:* Mud on the Stars; The Fight for Air Power; Can Do! The Story of the Seabees; From Omaha to Okinawa; The Revolt of Mamie Stover; The Case Against the Admirals; The Americanisation of Emily; The Execution of Private Slovik; The Hero of Iwo Jima; The Crime of Ruby McCollum; Wolf Whistle; He Slew the Dreamer; The Hiroshima Pilot; Three Lives For Mississippi; In the Hours of Night; The Klansman; A New Life to Live; It's Me, O Lord. *Contributions to:* Numerous magazines including: American Mercury; Reader's Digest; Colliers; Saturday Evening Post; Cavelier; True; Ebony; Look; Life; Esquire. *Membership:* Phi Beta Kappa. *Literary Agent:* Ned Brown, Beverley Hills, California. *Address:* PO Box 1567, Scottsboro, AL 35768, USA.

HUMBLE, William Frank, b. 22 Dec. 1942, Surrey, England. Writer. 1 son, 1 daughter. *Education:* BA Honours, Drama and Theatre Arts, Birmingham University. *Literary Appointments:* Script Editor, BBC Television, 1973–76. *Publications Include:* A Tale of Arthur, 1967; Many scripts performed include: On Giant's Shoulders (TV), 1979 Fly Away Home (stage play), 1983; Talk To Me (TV), 1984; Poppyland (TV), 1985. *Memberships:* Writers Guild; Theatre Writers Union. *Literary Agent:* Norman North, A D Peters Limited. *Address:* c/o A D Peters Limited, 10 Buckingham Street, London WC2N 6BU, England.

HUMPHREY, Belinda, b. 3 Oct. 1938, Kettering, England. University Lecturer. *Education:* MA, B Litt, St Hugh's College, Oxford, England, 1958–64. *Publications:* Essays on John Cowper Powys, 1972; Recollections of the Powys Brothers, 1980 (Peter Owen); John Dyer 1699–1957, 1980 (UWP). *Contributions:* The Powys Review (Editor), 1977–; Anglo-Welsh Review; Poetry Wales; Peake Review; Durham University Journal; Trivium; Blake Studies. *Memberships:* English Language Section Yr Academi Gymreig; Comm. Powys Society and various other literary societies. *Address:* Department of English, St David's University College, Lampeter, Dyfed, Wales.

HUMPHREY, Jennifer Margaret, b. 1 May 1946, London, England. Writer; Researcher; Journalist; Consultant. m. Isadore William Deiches, 30 Apr. 1981, London. *Education:* Institute of Linguists; Drama examination, with merit, Guildhall School of Music and Drama. *Literary Appointments:* Journalist: Hornchurch Echo; Retail Chemist; Brentwood Argus, Freelance Writer and English Teacher, Malaga, Spain; Writer, Researcher, Essex Countryside and East Coast Digest; Journalist and Researcher, Homes Overseas and Homefinder. *Publications:* The Hundreds of Essex, 1972; Too Soon Our Past? – East Anglian Tales, 1973; A Guide to Living Abroad, 1980; Pyramids, co-author, 1983. *Contributions to:* Homes Overseas; Homefinder; Essex Countryside; East Coast Digest; Retail Chemist; Hornchurch Echo; Brentwood Argus. *Honours:* Winner, Writers Cup, All-Age Section, Harold Wood Eisteddford, Essex, 1954, 55, 56. *Address:* 14 Railway Square, Brentwood, Essex CM14 4LN, England.

HUMPHRY, Derek John, b. 29 Apr. 1930, Bath, Somerset, England. Writer. *Literary Appointments:* Writer on staff, Sunday Times, London, 1967–78; Writer on staff, Los Angeles Times, 1978–80. *Publications:* Because They're Black, 1971; Police Power and Black People, 1972; Passports and Politics, 1974; False Messiah, 1977; The Cricket Conspiracy, 1976; Jean's Way, 1978; Let Me Die Before I Wake, 1982; The Right to Die: Understanding Euthanasia, 1986. *Honours:* Martin Luther King Memorial Prize for Because They're Black, 1971. *Literary Agent:* Robert Ducas, New York City. *Address:* PO Box 66218, Los Angeles, CA 90066, USA.

HUMPHRYS, Leslie George, b. 22 Feb. 1921, England. Headmaster (retired). m. Jeanette Lilian Graver, 29 June 1978, North Walsham, England. 3 sons, 1 daughter from first marriage, first wife deceased. *Education:* Qualified Teachers Diploma, Camden College. *Publications:* Time to Live, 1959; Wonders of Life, books 1–4, 1959–61; Weather in Britain, 1963; Your Body At Work, 1963; Men Learn to Fly, 1966; Life is Exciting, 1966; Science is Exciting, books 1–3, 1967–69; Fruit and Fruit Growing, 1969; Drinks, 1970; Men Travel in Space, 1971; Glass and Glassmaking, 1971; Motion and Power, 1974; Tools, 1975; Machines, 1976. *Contributions to:* Punch; Illustrated London News; Contemporary Review; House and Garden; The Lady; varied Gardening and Women's magazines. *Membership:* Society of Authors. *Address:* 27 Litester Close, North Walsham, Norfolk NR28 9JA, England.

HUNGRY-WOLF, Adolf, b. 16 Feb. 1944. Writer. m. Beverly Little-Bear, 3 sons, 1 daughter. Raising family in the wilderness of Canadian Rockies. *Publications:* The Good Medicine Book, 1973; The Blood People, 1976; Rails in the Canadian Rockies, 1979; Der Rabe weiss, Wod die sonne Wohnt, 1983; Shadows of the Buffalo, with Beverly Hungry-Wolf, 1983. *Honours:* Prize of the Reading Rats, German Students Federation, 1983. *Literary Agent:* Peter Fritz. *Address:* Box 844, Skookumchuck, British Columbia, Canada VOB 2EO.

HUNT, Annice Elizabeth, b. 30 Mar. 1934, Palmetto, Florida, USA. Editor. *Education:* BA Social Studies, Education, English; Graduate Work, Library Sciences. *Major Publications:* Squirrels in Your Tree, Planting Hedges to Attract Songbirds, 1976; Why Plant Trees?, Bird Tales, Becky Squirrel, 1977; Feeding Hungry Birds, 1979; Audubon Wardens, 1980. *Contributor to:* Calli's Tales' (as editor). *Address:* P O Box 1224, Palmetto, FL 3356, USA.

HUNT, Joyce, b. 31 Oct. 1927, New York City, USA. Writer. m. Irwin Hunt, 25 June 1950, New York City, 2 sons. *Education:* BA, Brooklyn College; MA, Hunter College. *Publications:* Co-author with Irwin Hunt, Watching Orangutans, 1983; Co-author with Millicent Selsam series of science books for children: A First Look at: Leaves, 1972; Fish, 1972; Mammals, 1973; Birds, 1973; Insects, 1974; Frogs and Toads, 1976; Animals Without Backbones, 1976; Flowers, 1977; Snakes, Lizards and other Reptiles, 1977; Animals with

Backbones, 1978; The World of Plants, 1978; Monkeys and Apes, 1979; Sharks, 1979; Whales, 1980; Cats, 1981; Dogs, 1981; Horses, 1981; Dinosaurs, 1982; Spiders, 1983; Seashells, 1983; Rocks, 1984; Bird Nests, 1984; Kangaroos, Koalas and Other Animals With Pouches, 1985. *Honours:* Outstanding Science Books for Children Award, 1977 for A First Look at Animals Without Backbones and A First Look at Sharks, 1979. *Address:* 131 Riverside Drive, New York, NY 10024, USA.

HUNT, Linda (Christenses), b. 3 Sep. 1940, Spokane, Washington, USA. College English Faculty, Freelance Writer. m. James Barton Hunt, 21 Feb. 1969, Seattle, Washington, USA, 1 son, 2 daughters. *Education:* BA, History/English, University of Washington; Master of Arts in Teaching, Whitworth College. *Major Publications:* Loaves & Fishes, 1980; Celebrate the Seasons, 1980; Christina's World, 1985. *Contributor to:* Psychology Today; Reader's Digest; Family Circle; Christian Science Monitor; Woman's Day; Guideposts; and others. *Literary Agent:* Lois Curley (for Christina's World only). *Address:* N9115 Mountain View Lane, Spokane, WA 99218, USA.

HUNT, Peter Leonard, b. 2 Sep. 1945, Rugby, England. Lecturer in English Literature and Language. m. Sarah Wilkinson, 24 Oct. 1981, Yalding, Kent, 2 daughters. *Education:* BA, University College of Wales, Aberystwyth; MA, PhD, University of Wales. *Publications:* Children's Literature Research in Britain, 1977; Further Approaches to Research in Children's Literature, 1981; The Maps of Time, 1982; A Step Off The Path, 1985. *Contributions to:* Times Literary Supplement; Studies in the Literary Imagination; Children's Literature (Yale); Signal; Children's Literature in Education; The Advocate; Journal of Technical Writing, USA; Social Work Today. *Address:* Department of English, University of Wales (UWIST), Cardiff, Wales.

HUNT, Tony, b. 21 Mar. 1944, Bebington, England. Reader in French. *Education:* MA, B Litt, Worcester College, Oxford University. *Contributions to:* Numerous professional and literary journals including: Romania; Zeitschrift für Romanische Philologie; Modern Language Review; French Studies; Romanische Forschungen; Studi Francesi; Journal of European Studies; Durham University Journal; Forum for Modern Language Studies; Studia Celtica; Mediaeval Scandinavia; Zeitschrift für centische Philologie; Medium Aevum Trivium; Neophilologus; Studies in Philology; Orbis Letterarum; Mediaeval Studies. *Memberships include:* International Arthurian Society; Bibliographer British branch, International Courtly Literature Society; International Society for the History of Rhetoric; Anglo-Norman Text Society; Société Rencesvals. *Address:* Department of French, University of St Andrews, Fife, Scotland.

HUNT, V Daniel, Principal Investigator, Technology Research Corporation. *Education:* BS Electronic Engineering, 1961, MBA Management, 1965, University of Maryland, USA. *Major Publications:* Energy Dictionary; Windpower; The Synfuels Handbook; Handbook of Energy Technology; Handbook of Conservation & Solar Energy; Solar Energy Dictionary; Energy Issues in Health Care; Gasohol Handbook; Industrial Robots Handbook; Smart Robots, 1984. *Address:* Technology Research Corporation, Springfield Professional Park, 8328–A Traford Lane, Springfield, VA 22152, USA.

HUNTER, Alan James Herbert, b. 25 June 1922, Hoveton St John, Norwich, England. Author. m. Adelaide Cubitt, 14 Feb. 1944, Norwich, England, 1 daughter. *Education:* Electrical School, RAF Henlow, England. *Publications:* The Norwich Poems, 1945; 34 crime novels, including, Gently Does It, 1955; Gently in the Sun, 1959; Gently Go Man, 1961; Gently Continental, 1967; Gently With the Innocents, 1970; Gently With Love, 1975; Gently to a Sleep, 1978; The Honfleur Decision, 1980; Gabrielle's Way, 1981; Fields

of Heather, 1981; Gently Between Tides, 1982; Amorous Leander, 1983; The Unhung Man, 1984; Once a Prostitute, 1984; The Chelsea Ghost, 1985. *Honour:* Literary Critic, Eastern Daily Press. *Memberships:* Society of Authors; Crime Writers' Association. *Address:* 3 St Lawrence Avenue, Brundall, Norwich, NR13 5QH, England.

HUNTER, Brian, b. 14 May 1932, London, England. Librarian. *Education:* BA, Dip Lib, University of London. *Literary Appointments:* Slavonic Librarian, London School of Economics, 1960–. *Publications:* Soviet-Yugoslav Relations 1948–72: A Bibliography, 1976; Official Publications of the Soviet Union & Eastern Europe, 1945–1980 (co-author), 1982. *Contributions to:* Librarianship journals; Books (NBL); Statesman's Year Book; LSE Magazine. *Membership:* Society of Indexers. *Address:* BLPES, London School of Economics, 10 Portugal Street, London WC2A 2HD, England.

HUNTER, Norman George Lorimer, b. 23 Nov. 1899, London, England. Author. *Publications include:* Incredible Adventures of Professor Branestawm, 1933, 14th edition, 1974; Professor Branestawm's Treasure Hunt, 1934, 6th edition, 1974; Puffin Book of Magic, 1968, 7th edition, as, Norman Hunter's Book of Magic, 1974; The Home Made Dragoon, 1971, 3rd Edition, 1974; Professor Branestawm up the Pole, 1972; Professor Branestawm's Dictionary, 1973, 2nd edition, 1974; The Frantic Phantom, 1973; Wizards Are a Nuisance, 1973; Professor Branestawm's Great Revolution, 1974; Professor Branestawm's Compendium, 1975; Dust-up at the Royal Disco, 1975; Professor Branestawm's Do-It-Yourself Handbook, 1976; Count Bakwerdz on the Carpet, 1979; Professor Branestawm's Perilous Pudding, 1979. *Contributor to:* Various newspapers and magazines in UK and USA. *Memberships include:* Savage Club; Society of Authors; Children's Writers' Circle; Association Inner Magic Circle. *Literary Agent:* Bodley Head. *Address:* 23 St Olave's Close, Staines, Middx, TW18 2LH, England.

HUNTER BLAIR, Pauline. Author. *Education:* BA (Hons) Somerville College, Oxford. m. Peter Hunter Blair, Feb. 1969. *Publications:* The Pekinese Princess, 1948; The White Elephant, 1952; Five Dolls in a House; Smith's Hoard, 1955; The Boy with the Erpingham Hood, 1956; Sandy the Sailor, 1956; Bel the Giant, 1956; James the Policeman; Torolv the Fatherless, 1959; The Robin Hooders, 1960; Keep the Pot Boiling, 1961; The Twelve and the Genii, 1962; The Return of the Twelves, 1963; Silver Bells and Cockle Shells, 1962; Merlin's Magic, 1963; Crowds of Creatures, 1964; The Two Faces of Silenns, 1972. *Contributor to:* Times Daily Press; Times Literary Supplement. *Literary Awards:* Carnegie Medal, 1962; Lewis Carroll Shelf Award, 1963; Deutsche Jungenbuch Preis, 1968. *Memberships:* Society of Authors; National Book League. *Agent:* Curtis Brown Ltd. *Address:* Church Farm House, Bottisham, Cambridge CB5 9BA, England.

HUNTING, Constance, b. 15 Oct. 1925, Providence, Rhode Island, USA. Poet; Editor; Publisher; Professor. m. Robert Hunting, 28 Aug. 1948, Providence, 1 son, 1 daughter. *Education:* BA, Brown University, Providence, 1947. *Appointments:* Poet in Schools, 1979; Poet in Library, 1985; Lecturer, University of Maine, Orono, 1978–. *Publications:* After the Stravinsky Concert, 1969; Nightwalk, 1981; Dream Cities, 1982; Collected Poems, 1969–82; A Day at the Shore, 1983; Looking Glass Days, 1985; etc. *Contributor to:* Numerous articles in professional journals and magazines including Puckerbrush Review. *Honours:* Sesquitennial Indiana Poet 1961. *Memberships:* Founding Member, Virginia Woolf Society. *Address:* 76 Main Street, Orono, ME 04473, USA.

HUREAU, Jean Emile Pierre, b. 2 Feb. 1915, Paris, France. Journalist; Holiday Travel Writer; Editor. *Publications:* La Tunisie aujourd 'hui; Le Maroc aujourd 'hui; L'Algerie aujourd 'hui; L'Iran aujourd 'hui; L'Espagne aujourd 'hui; La Corse aujourd 'hui; La

Provence et la Cote d'Azur aujourd 'hui; La Bretagne aujourd 'hui; L'Egypte aujourd 'hui; La Syrie aujourd 'hui; La Sicile aujourd'hui; Le Portugal aujourd 'hui; La Hollande aujourd 'hui; L'Auvergne et le Massif Central aujourd 'hui; La Normandie; Jerusalem; L'ile de la Reunion aujourd 'hui; L'Italie (Nouvelles Fronteires); Thal der Louire. General Editor, Les Guides Aujourd'hui, series. *Contributions to:* Clartes, encyclopedia; Jeune Afrique. *Honours include:* Premier Periodistas Extranjeros, Madrid, Spain, 1966; International Tourism Prize, 1967. *Memberships include:* International Federation of Travel Journalists and Writers (Executive committee). *Address:* 2 residence du Parc, F–91300 Massey, France.

HURREN, Bernard John, b. 1907, London, England. Author; Freelance Journalist; former Press Executive. *Publications include:* Eastern Med, 1943; No Specific Gravity and Second Dog, 1944–46; Fellowship of the Air; Official History of the Royal Aero Club, 1951; ABC of Atomic Energy, 1956; The Awful Motorist, 1965; Airports of the World Guide, 1970; Waterloo, as a Wargame, 1975; Insomniac's Dictionary, 1980. *Contributions to:* Illustrated Guide to Britain, 1971; New Book of the Road, 1974; Reader's Digest, Consultant and contributor; Treasures of Britain; French Aviation Magazine, English editor and various antional newspapers. *Membership:* Society of Authors. *Literary Agent:* Donald Copeman. *Address:* 1/43 Wilbury Road, Hove, Sussex, England.

HUSER, Laverne (Verne) C, b. 2 Mar. 1931, Texas, USA. Mediator, Environmental Disputes. m. Jean Hurlbert, 3 May 1961, Carmel, California (div. 1969), 1 son, 1 daughter. *Education:* BS, University of Texas; MEd, Hardin-Simmons University. *Literary Appointments:* High School English Teacher, 1958–72; Literary Editor, River Runner, 1985–. *Publications include:* Snake River Guide, 1972; River Running, 1975; Canyon Country Paddles, 1978; River Camping, 1981; River Reflections, 1984. *Contributions to:* Adventure Travel; American Forests; Audubon; Backpacker; Canoe; Dynamic Years; High Country News; Mariah; National Parks Magazine; Outdoor Life; Passages; River World; Small World; Sports Illustrated; Alaskafest; Western's World; Wildlife News; Living Wilderness; Teton Magazine; etc. *Memberships:* Outdoor Ethics Committee, Nominating Committee, Outdoor Writers Association. *Address:* 23020 SE 6th Place, Redmond, WA 98053, USA.

HUSSEY, Elizabeth, b. 23 Apr. 1929, London, England. Journalist. *Literary Appointments:* Editor, Ski Survey Magazine. *Publication:* Worlds Greatest Ski Holiday, 1982. *Address:* 118 Eaton Square, London SW1W 9AF, England.

HUTCHIN, Kenneth Charles, b. 8 Dec. 1908, Mitcham, Surrey, England. General Medical Practitioner, Medical Consultant, Daily Telegraph, London. *Education:* MB, ChB, MD, University of Glasgow. *Publications:* Your Diet & Your Health, 1959; Heart Disease & High Blood Pressure, 1960; Allergy, 1961; Coughs Colds & Bronchitis, 1961; Slipped Discs, 1962; The Change of Life, 1963; Diabetes, 1964; How Not to Kill Your Husband, 1962; How Not to Kill Your Wife, 1965; How Not to Kill Your Children, 1968; How Not to Kill Yourself, 1973; several translations of, How Not to Kill Series: Your Health, 1962, A Young Man's Guide to Health, 1964; The Health of the Businessman, 1966; Health & Sex, 1969; Family Health & First Aid, 1964. *Contributor to:* Several magazines & encyclopaedias. *Memberships:* Several professional organisations. *Honours:* Recipient, Military Honours. *Address:* Wold Cottage, Broad Campden, Chipping Campden, Gloucestershire, England.

HUTCHINSON, (David) Robert, b. 2 Oct. 1948, Perivale, Middlesex, England. Journalist; m. Broadcaster Marie Richardson, 15 Apr. 1972, Cheam, Surrey, England. *Education:* Proficiency Test, National Council Training of Journalists. *Literary Appointments:* Defence Correspondent, Press Association, 1977–83; News Editor 1983–84, Deputy Editor in Chief, Jane's Defence Wekly. *Contributions to:* International Defense Review; The Diplomatist; Royal United Services Institute Journal. *Honours:* NATO Defence Writers' Prize, 1978. *Address:* PO Box 30, 13 High Street, Horley, Surrey, England.

HUTCHINSON, (Sir) Joseph Burtt, b. 21 Mar. 1902, Burton Latimer, England. Professor of Agriculture. *Education:* ScD, St John's College, Cambridge. *Publications:* The Genetics of Gossypium, 1956; Genetics and the Improvement of Tropical Crops, 1958; Application of Genetics to Cotton Improvement, 1959; Farming and Food Supply, 1972; Editor: Essays on Crop Plant Evolution, 1965; Population and Food Supply, 1969; Evolutionary Studies in World Crops, 1974. *Honours include:* Royal Medal, Royal Society, 1967. *Memberships include:* Fellow, St John's College, Cambridge; Linnean Society; British Association for Advancement of Science, President, 1965–66; FRS. *Address:* Huntingfield, Huntingdon Road, Cambridge CB3 OLH, England.

HUTCHISON, David, b. 24 Sep. 1944, West Kilbride, Scotland. Lecturer, Communication Studies. m. Pauleen Frew, 28 June 1967, Stevenson, 2 daughters. *Education:* MA 1966, MLitt 1975, University of Glasgow. *Publications:* The Modern Scottish Theatre, 1977; Headlines: The Media in Scotland, editor, 1978; Plays: The Plan for Greenhills, 1977; Deadline, 1980. *Contributor to:* Glasgow Herald; Scotsman; Scottish Theatre News; etc. *Address:* Department of Humanities, Glasgow College of Technology, Cowcaddens Road, Glasgow G4 OBA, Scotland.

HUTSCHNECKER, Arnold A, b. 13 May 1898, Austria. Psycho-Analytic Physician; Writer. *Education:* MD, University of Berlin, Germany; Postgraduate, University Hospital, Berlin. *Publications:* The Will to Live, 1951; Cornerstone; Love & Hate in Human Nature, 1955; The Will to Happiness; The Drive for Power, 1974; The Psychodynamics of Hope; Hope The Dynamics of Self-Fulfilment, 1981. *Contributor to:* (Editorials) to various publications including: Look Magazine; New York Times; Vogue Magazine; Archives of Foundation of Thanetol. *Memberships:* The Royal Society of Hith, England, Past President; American Association of Psychoanalytic Physicians; AMM; New York Academy of Science; Academy Psychosomatic Medicine; etc; Authors Guild of America; Authors League Foundation; Mark Twain Society, Honorary Member; Past President, American Association Psychoanalytic Physicians. *Agent:* Bill Adler Brooks. *Address:* 1230 Avenue of the Americas, New York, NY 10020, USA.

HUTTERLI, Kurt, b. 18 Aug. 1944, Bern, Switzerland. Writer. m. Marianne Büchler, 7 July 1966, Bern, 1 son, 1 daughter. *Education:* Secondary School Teacher Diploma, University of Bern. *Publications:* Various Poems, novels, short stories, theatre and radio plays, 1962–. *Contributions to:* Various magazines and journals. *Honours:* Gedichtpreis de Stadt Bern, 1971; Buchpreis de Stadt Bern, 1972, 78; Jugendtheaterpreis SADS, 1976; Welti-preis fur das Drama, 1982. *Memberships:* PEN Swiss Centre; Schweizer Autoren Gruupe Olten; Managing Committee, Berner Schrifteller-Verein. *Address:* Luisenstrasse 30, CH–3005 Bern, Switzerland.

HUUSKONEN, Taisto Kalevi, b. 14 Nov. 1925, Tampere, Finland. Author. m. Enni Etelainen, Tampere, 1 June 1975. *Literary Appointments:* Permanent Assistant, Soviet-Karelia paper, 1954–76; Editor, Red Flag paper. *Major Publications:* (5 books published in USSR, 1963–74); Children of Finland, 1979; Steel Storm, 1980; War Mates, 1982; Enni's Story, 1984. *Honours:* Scholarship, Cordelin Foundation, 1982; Scholarship, WSOY, 1984. *Memberships:* The Finnish Society of Authors; The Pirtkalain Writers. *Literary Agent:* Werner Söderström (WSOY). *Address:* Hopunhovi, 38460 Mouhijärvi, Finland.

HUXLEY, Anthony Julian, b. 2 Dec. 1920, Oxford, England. Writer; Editor; Photographer. *Education:* MA, Cambridge University, England. *Publications:* Standard Encyclopaedia of the World's Mountains, Oceans and Islands, Rivers and Lakes (Editor), 1962. 1968; Flowers of the Mediterranean (with O O Polunin), 1965; Mountain Flowers, 1967; House Plants, Cacti and Succulents, 1972; Plant and Planet, 1974; The Financial Times Book of Garden Design, (Editor), 1975; Flowers of Greece and the Aegean (with W Taylor), 1977; An Illustrated History of Gardening, 1978; Success with House Plants (Gen Ed), 1979; Penguin Encyclopaedia of Gardening, 1981; Wild Orchids of Britain and Europe (with P & J Davies), 1983; The Macmillan World Guide to House Plants (Editor), 1983; Green Inheritance, 1985. *Contributor to:* Country Life; The Garden; House and Garden (US). *Honour:* Award of the Victorian Medal of Honour from the Royal Horticultural Society. *Memberships:* Horticultural Club (London); President; Royal Horticultural Society (Council, various Committees). *Literary Agent:* Margaret Hanbury. *Address:* 50 Villiers Avenue, Surbiton, Surrey, England.

HUXLEY, George Leonard, b. 23 Sep. 1932, Leicester, England. Scholar. *Education:* MA, Magdalen College, Oxford University, 1951–55; Fellow, All Souls College, 1955–61; Honorary DLitt, Dublin, Republic of Ireland. *Publications:* Early Sparta, 1962; The Early Ionians, 1966; Greek Epic Poetry from Eumelos to Panyassis, 1969; Pindar's Vision of the Past, 1975; On Aristotle and Greek Society, 1979. Editor, Kythera, with J N Coldstream, 1972. *Contributions to:* Times Literary Supplement; Greek and Byzantine periodicals. *Honours:* Cromer Greek Prize, British Academy, 1963. *Memberships:* Royal Irish Academy. *Address:* Forge Cottage, Church Enstone, Oxfordshire OX7 4NN, England.

HUYLER, Jean Wiley, b. 30 Mar. 1935, Seattle, Washington, USA. Communications Management Consultant; Author-Writer; Editor; Photojournalist. Widowed, 1 son, 1 daughter. *Education includes:* Business Administration, University of Washington, 1953–55; BA, Marylhurst College, 1978; MA, Pacific Lutheran University, 1979. *Literary Appointments:* Various newspaper and magazine editorships, 1963–75; Editor, books for education system managers, Washington School Directors Association, 1977–81; Designer and Editor, For The Record (A History of Tacoma Public Schools), Tacoma SchoolDistrict, 1985–. *Publications:* Demystifying the Media, 1980, 81; Crisis Communications, 1983; Campaign Savvy – School Support, 2nd edition, 1981; Communications is a People Process, 1981; How to Get Competent Communications Help, 1983. *Contributions to:* Press Woman; C:JET (Communications: Journalism Education Today); Publishers Auxiliary; American Banker; The Lion; Kiwanis; Lottery Players Magazine. *Honours:* Over 100 awards for assorted writings including: Superior Performance, 1964, Torchbearer, 1984, Washington Press Association; Excellence in Educational Communications, National Association of State Education Department Information Officers, 1978; National Federation of Press Women Awards. *Memberships include:* Past President and various other offices, National Federation of Press Women. *Literary Agent:* B J Simon. *Address:* 922 North Pearl A–27, Tacoma, WA 98406, USA.

HYAMS, Jay, b. 13 Sep. 1949, New York City, USA. Writer. *Education:* BA, Harpur College, State University of New York, Binghampton. *Publications:* The Life and Times of the Western Movie, 1983; War Movies, 1984; Poisons, 1986; The Complete Book of American Trivia (with co-author Kathy Smith), 1983; The Best Book of Trivia (under pseudonym Veneto Schei with co-author

Jack Griffin), 1985. *Address:* 421 East 64 Street, New York, NY 10021, USA.

HYMAN, (Robert) Anthony, b. 5 Apr. 1928, London, England. Historian of Science. m. Laura Alice Boyd, 14 Jan. 1961, St Marylebone, 2 sons, 1 daughter. *Education:* MA, Trinity College. *Appointment:* Alistair Horne Fellow, St Antony's College, Oxford, 1977–78. *Publications:* The Computer in Design, 1973; Computing: A Dictionary of Terms, Concepts and Ideas, 1976; The Coming of the Chip, 1980; Charles Babbage: Pioneer of the Computer, 1982. *Contributor to:* Times Literary Supplement; Nature; Proceedings of the Physical Society; Annals of the History of Computing; Biographical Companion to Modern Thought, etc. *Honours:* Leverhulme Award, 1978–79; Arts Council, 1984–85. *Memberships:* Society of Authors; Authors Lending & Copyright Society. *Address:* 38A Downshire Hill, London NW3 1NU, England.

HYMES, Dell Hathaway, b. 7 June 1927, Portland, Oregon, USA. Anthropologist; Linguist. *Education:* BA, Reed Colege, 1950; MA, 1953, PhD, 1955, Indiana University. *Publications:* Language in Culture and Society, 1964; Pidginization and Creolization of Languages, 1971; Reinventing Anthropology, 1972; Foundations in Sociolinguistics, 1974; Studies in the History of Linguistics, 1975; Language in Education, 1980; In Vain I Tried to Tell You: Studies in Native American Ethnopeotics, 1981; Essays in the History of Linguistic Anthropology, 1983; Vers la competence de communication, 1984. *Contributions to:* The Nation. *Honours include:* Phi Beta Kappa, 1950; Guggenheim Fellow, 1969; Senior Fellow, National Endowment for the Humanities, 1972–73; Fellow, American Academy of Arts and Sciences. *Address:* Graduate School of Edcuation, University of Pennsylvania, Phildelphia, PA 19174, USA.

HYVÄRINEN, Rakel Johanna, b. 23 Jan. 1923, Pyhäjärvi, Finland. Author. m. Antti, 31 May 1953, Haukivuori, 1 son, 1 daughter. *Publications:* Nauta, 1978; Kiikaritahtain, 1980; Punainen tytto, 1981; Viiden marken kesa, 1982; Kaivo, 1983; Isan varjo, 1984; Sputnik, 1985. *Contributions to:* Kansanvakuutus. *Honours:* Second Prize for novel with an animal theme, Nauta 1978; First Prize in writing contest of the child's year, Kiikaritahtain, 1980; Literary Award of Finnish Government, Punaimen tytto, 1981. *Membership:* Finnish Society of Authors. *Literary Agent:* Tammi and Wsoy. *Address:* Kanneljärventie 12, SF–02130 Espoo, Finland.

HYYPIA, Jorma, b. 13 Aug. 1918, Gardner, Massachusetts, USA. Writer; Editor. m. Bethea Jeanne MacMullin, 17 June 1944, 1 son. *Education:* BS, University of Rhode Island, 1940; MS, Middlebury College, Vermont, 1942; Cornell University, 1942–44. *Literary Appointments:* Markets Editor, Chemical Week, 1955–60; Reports Editor, Chemical Week, 1960–62; Contributing Editor: Science and Mechanics, Camping Journal, Income Opportunities, Elementary Electronics, and others. *Publications:* The Complete Tiffen Filter Manual, 1981; Science and Mechanics Handyman Encyclopedia, 1975 (379 pages text, 277 photos, 115 drawings); New photography book and photography invention in production at this time. *Contributions:* of many hundreds of feature articles and columns on general science, electronics, computers, CB radio, Hi-Fi audio, camping, business opportunities, home construction and repair, photograph, workshop practices, environment and ecology, architecture. *Honour:* Jesse H Neal Editorial Achievement Award, 1961. *Memberships:* Phi Kappa Phi, American Chemical Society. *Address:* 90 Bowman Drive North, Greenwich, CT 06831, USA.

I

IBARRURI, Dolores, b. 9 Dec. 1895, Gallarta, Spain. Publicist. m. Julian Ruiz, 15 Feb. 1916, Gallarta, 1 son, 5 daughters. *Publications:* El Unico Camino, 1960; En La Lucha, 1968; Memorias de Pasionaria, 1984; Memorias de Dolores Ibarruri – La Lucha y La Vida. 1985. *Contributions to:* Numerous publications. *Honour:* Doctor honoris causa. History, University of Lomonoscov, Moscow, USSR. *Address:* Santisima Trinidad 5, Madrid 28010, Spain.

IDDON, Josephine, b. 14 Jan. 1926, Free Lance Writer. m. Edwin Iddon. *Publications:* Reflections; Red Rose; The Record. *Contributions to:* Lancashire Life; The Sun; Just Sithabogd; Chey'p at Price; Clattering Clogs; Woven in Lancashire, 1983; Lancashire Authors Anthology, Verse and Prose, 1984. 2 Taped contributions to, Lancashire Miscellany. *Honours:* E M Rose Bowl, Preston Poets, 1972; 3rd Prize, Dialect Verse, Lancashire Authors Association; Pomfret Poets Society; Angus Butterworth Trophy, Lancashire Authors Association, 1980. *Memberships:* Lancashire Authors Association; Leyland Writers. *Address:* Ash Villa, Gill Lane, Walmer Bridge, Longton, Neat Preston, Lancashire PR4 5GN, England.

IDSTRÖM, (Ilse) Annika, b. 12 Nov. 1947, Helsinki, Finland. Author. *Education:* Diploma, Film and photography, Art School. *Publications:* Sinitaivas, Blue Sky, 1980; Isani rakkaani, My Father, My Love, 1981; Valjeni Sebastian, By Brother Sebastian, 1985. *Contributions to:* Grand Street, USA. 1985. *Honours:* Award for 1st novel, 1981; Kalevi Jantti prize. *Memberships:* Finnish Union for Writers; Pen Club. *Address:* Prinsessantie 4 H 79, 00820 Helsinki 82, Finland.

IEWIN Theodore, b. 17 Sep. 1907, USA. Writer. m. Helen Ross, 12 Apr. 1964, New York, 2 sons, 1 daughter. *Education:* BS, New York University. *Publications:* Collusion, 1932; Strange Passage, 1935; Practical Birth Control, 1937; Instant Shrink, 1971; Understanding and Overcoming Depression, 1973; Stop, Thief!, 1978. *Contributions to:* The New York Times; Reader's Digest; Parade; many others. *Membership:* President, American Society of Journalists and Authors. *Address:* 250 East 73rd Street, New York, NY 10021, USA.

IGNATOW, David, b. 7 Feb. 1914, Brooklyn, New York, USA. Poet; Teacher. m. Rose Graubart. *Education:* Academic degree, New Utrecht HS, Brooklyn, New York, 1932. *Literary Appointments:* President Emeritus, Poetry Society of America; Visiting Professor, New York University, 1985. *Publications:* Poems, 1948; The Gentle Weight Lifter, 1955; Say Pardon, 1962; Figures of the Human, 1964; Rescue the Dead, 1968; Earth Hard, 1968; Poems: 1935–69, 1970; Selected Poems, 1975; Facing the Tree, 1975; Tread the Dark, 1978; New and Collected Poems, 1970–85, 1986; Chaptbooks: The Animal in the Bush, 1978; Sunlight: A Sequence for My Daughter, 1979; Conversations, 1980; Whisper to the Earth, 1981. Prose: The Notebooks of David Ingnatow, 1973; Open Between Us, 1980. *Contributions to:* Various journals and magazines. *Honours include:* National Institute of Arts and Letters, 1964; Guggenheim Fellowship, 1965 and 1973, Shelley Memorial Prize, 1965; Rockefeller Foundation Fellowship, 1968; Wallace Stevens Fellowship, 1977; Bollinger Prize, 1977. *Memberships:* PEN; Poetry Society of America. *Address:* PO Box 1458, East Hampton, NY 11937, USA.

ILES, Robert LeRoy, b. 26 Sep. 1934, Logan, Ohio, USA. Writer. m. Phyllis Jean Hutchinson, 17 Dec. 1955, Waterville, Ohio, 2 sons, 2 daughters. *Education:* BA, English Literature, 1956, MA, English Literature, 1960, Bowling Green State University, Ohio. *Literary Appointment:* Medical Editor, Marion Laboratories, Kansas City, Missouri, 1973. *Contributions:* Of articles

to, British Journal of Venereal Disease; Clinical Medicine; Eye, Ear, Nose and Throat Monthly; Journal of Clinical Gastoenterology; Focus; Clinical Research Practices and Drug Regulatory Affairs, etc. *Literary Agent:* Joyce Flaherty, St Louis, Missouri. *Address:* 601 Drury Lane, Olathe, KS 66061, USA.

ILMER, Walter, b. 4 Mar. 1926, Cologne, Germany. Senior Civil Servant. *Publications:* Das Netz, 1958; Totentanz in Mersley Hall, 1958; Schatten ungreifbarer Machte, 1956; Morders Letzte Zuflucht, 1952; Der Geist der Vendetta, 1954; Schrecken um Hillsboro, 1950; Der Schattenreiter, 1951; 29 other novels. *Contributor to:* Jahrbuch der Karl-May-Gesellschaft; Mitteilungen der Karl-May-Gesellschaft, etc. *Membership:* Karl-May-Gesellschaft. *Address:* Letterhausstrasse 4, 5300 Bonn 1, Federal Republic of Germany.

INCE, Martin Jeffrey, b. 29 Apr. 1952, Birkenhead, England. Journalist. m. Victoria Claire Hutchings, 20 Jan. 1979, London. *Education:* BSc Geology and Chemistry, University of Newcastle upon Tyne, 1973. *Literary Appointments:* Deputy Editor, Freight Management, IPC, 1976–77; Resources Editor, Technology Editor, Features Editor, Engineering Today, 1977–82; Associate Editor, Technology and New Technology, 1982–85; Features Editor, The Engineer, 1985. *Publications:* Space, 1981; Energy Policy, 1983; Sizewell Inquiry Evidence on UK Power Industry, 1983; Sizewell Report, 1984; Space Wars, 1986; Politics of British Science, 1986. *Contributions to:* The Economist; New Statesman; The Times; New Scientist; and others. *Membership:* National Union of Journalists. *Address:* 17 Brenda Road, London SW17 7DD, England.

ING, Dean Charles, b. 17 June 1931, Austin, Texas, USA. Novelist. m. Gina Baker, 21 Aug. 1959, Lake Tahoe, 4 daughters. *Education:* BA, Fresno State College, 1956; MA, San Jose State University, 1970; PhD; University of Oregon, 1974. *Literary Appointments:* Assistant Professor, Media writing, Unnamed Midwest University. *Publications:* Soft Targets, 1979; Anasazi, 1980; Systemio Shock, 1981; Pulling Through, 1983; Single Combat, 1983; Mutual Assured Survival, with Jerry Pournelle, 1984; The Future of Flight, with Leik Myrabo, 1985; Wild Country, 1985. *Contributions to:* American Society of Engineering Educators; Bulletin of Missouri English Teachers'; Analog; Destinies; Far Frontiers; Omni; Road and Truck; Survive; Survival Tomorrow and others. *Honours:* 1st Prize, Holt-Rinehart-Winston Award for scholarly paper, 1969. *Membership:* Science Fiction Writers of America. *Literary Agent:* Joe Elder. *Address:* c/o Tor Books, 8 West 36th Street, New York City, NY 10018, USA.

INGALLS, Jeremy, b. 2 Apr. 1911. Poet; Retired University Professor; Translator. *Education:* Tufts University, BA, MA, LittD; University of Chicago. *Literary Appointments:* Assistant Professor of English Literature, Western College, 1941–43; Professor, Head of Department of English and American Literature, Director of Asian Studies, Rockford College, 1950s; Rockefeller Foundation Lecturer, American Poetry; Ford Foundation Fellowship, Asian Studies; Fulbright Professor of American Literature; Japan, 1957, 58. *Publications:* The Metaphysical Sword, 1941; Tahl, 1945; The Galilean Way, 1953; The Woman from the Island, 1958; These Islands Also, 1959; Nakagawa's Tenno Yugao, 1975; The Malice of Empire, 1970; This Stubborn Quantum, 1983; Summer Liturgy, 1985. *Contributions to:* Poetry Now, Michigan Quarterly Review; Christianity and Crisis; Religion in Life; The Classical Journal; Yearbook of General and Comparative Literature; Literature East and West; East-West Review; Poetry, New Republic; Saturday Review; Accent; American Mercury; American Prefaces; Atlantic Monthly; Beloit Poetry Journal; Chicago Review; Common Sense; Maryland Quarterly, etc. *Honours:* Guggenheim Fellowship, Poetry, 1943; American Academy of Arts and Letters Grant, 1944; Shelley Memorial Award, 1950; Lola Ridge Memorial

Awards, 1951, 52; Honorary LHD, Rockford College, 1960; University of Arizona Poetry Center Lectureship, 1964; Epic Poet Laureate, UPLI, 1965; Steinman Foundation. *Memberships:* Life Member, Poetry Society of America and several other professional organisations. *Address:* 6269 East Rosewood, Tucson, AZ 85711, USA.

INGBER, Dina Adele, b. 18 May 1948, USA. Freelance Writer. *Education:* BA Anthropology, Brooklyn College; MA Journalism, Pennsylvania State University. *Literary Appointments:* Contributing Editor, Science Digest Magazine; Contributing Editor, Success Magazine. *Contributions to:* America's Health; Cosmopolitan; Family Circle; Harper's Bazaar; Magazine Age; McCall's; Christian Science Monitor; Success; Science Digest; US; Celebrity. *Honour:* Front Page Award, Newswomen's Club of New York, 1981. *Memberships:* Kappa Tau Alpha; American Society of Journalists and Authors. *Address:* 333 East 66 Street, New York City, NY 10021, USA.

INGHAM, Jennie, b. 7 May 1944, Nottingham, England. Educational Researcher. Single Parent, 1 son, 1 daughter. *Education:* Research Fellow. *Appointments:* General Editor, Kingfisher Books. *Publications:* The Tiger and the Woodpecker; Reading Materials for Minority Groups Project Pack; The Naughty Mouse; The Golden Apples. *Membership:* Society of Authors. *Literary Agent:* Andrew Best, Curtis Brown. *Address:* 22 Newbury Road, Highams Park, London E4, England.

INGLIS, Brian, b. 31 July 1916, Dublin, Ireland. Journalist. m. Ruth Langdon (divorced), 1 son, 1 daughter. *Education:* BA (Oxon); PhD, Dublin. *Publications:* The Story of Ireland, 1956; Revolution in Medicine, 1958; Fringe Medicine, 1964; Abdication, 1966; Poverty and the Industrial Revolution, 1971; Roger Casement, 1973; The Forbidden Game, 1975; Natural and Supernatural, 1977; Natural Medicine, 1978; The Alternative Health Guide (with Ruth West), 1953; Science and Parascience, 1984; The Paranormal: An Encyclopedia of Psychic Phenomena, 1985. *Contributions to:* The Lancet; World Medicine; The Guardian; The Times; The Spectator; Punch; Encounter; Vogue. *Membership:* Fellow, Royal Society of Literature. *Literary Agent:* Curtis Brown, *Address:* Garden Flat, 23 Lambolle Road, London, NW3, England.

INGLOT, Mieczyslaw Stefan, b. 11 Jan. 1931, Lvov, Poland. Polish Literary Historian; University Professor. m. 29 June 1957, 1 son, 1 daughter. *Education:* PhD, Jagellonian University. *Literary Appointment:* Member of Editorial Board, Ze Skarbca Kultury. *Publications:* Polskie czasopisma literackie ziem litewskoruskich w latach, 1832–1851, 1966; Mysl historyczna w Kordianie, 1973; Komedie Aleksandra Fredry. Literatura i teatr, 1978; Norwid.Z dziejow recepcji tworczosci, 1983. *Contributions to:* Biblioteka Narodowa; Nasza Biblioteka (Editor); Pamietnik Literacki; Prace Literackie; Polonistyka; Studia Norvidiana. *Memberships:* Governing Body, Adam Mickiewicz Literary Society; Governing Body, M Konopnicka Society. *Address:* ul. Czarnieckiego 38 m.4, 53–651 Wroclaw, Poland.

INGOLFSSON, Viktor Arnar, b. 12 Apr. 1955, Akureyri, Iceland. Editor. *Education:* BS in Civil Engineering. *Literary Appointments:* Editor, Newsletter of Public Roads Administration, Iceland. *Publications:* Daudasok, 1978; Heitur Snjor, 1982. *Memberships:* Writers Union of Iceland. *Address:* Alfheimar 70, 104 Reykjavik, Iceland.

INGRAM-BROWN, Leslie, b. 24 May 1947, Glasgow, Scotland. Printing; Publishing; Trade Bookbinding. m. Susanna Lockhart MacDonald, 5 Feb. 1979, Glasgow. *Education:* Shawlands Academy; Hutchesons' Boys' Grammar School. *Literary Appointments:* Assistant Editor, Nautical Magazine, 1975–80; Editor, Nautical Magazine, 1980–. *Address:* 4/10 Darnley Street, Glasgow G41 2SD, Scotland.

INKSTER, Ian Edward, b. 4 Aug. 1949, Warrington, England. Academic. m. Anne Lorraine Rich, 15 Aug. 1970, Epping, 1 son, 1 daughter. *Education:* BA, Honours, University of East Anglia; PhD, Economic History, University of Sheffield, 1977. *Publications:* Japan as a Development Model, 1980; Metropolis and Province; with Jack Morrell, 1983; The Steam Intellect Societies, 1985. *Contributions to:* Annals of Science; Journal of European Economic History; East Asia; The Developing Economies; British Journal for the History of Science; Oxford Review of Education; Paedogogica Historica; Development and Change; Social Studies of Science. *Membership:* Fellow, Royal Historical Society. *Address:* Department of Economic History, University of New South Wales, PO Box 1, Kensington, NSW 2033, Australia.

INMAN, Will, formerly McGirt, William Archibald Junior, b. 4 May 1923, Habilitation Technician. *Education:* Duke University, 1943. *Literary Appointments:* Library Assistant, 1956–67; Instructor, American University, 1967–71; Instructor, Montgomery College, Maryland, 1969–73; Habilitation Technician for Mentally Disabled. *Publications include:* The Wakers in the Tongue, 1977; Voice of the Beach Oracle, 1977; A Way Through for the Damned, 1983; A Trek of Waking, 1985. Anthologies include: Southwest; A Geography of Poets; The Face of Poetry; Focus 101; Editor, Kauri, 1964–71; New Kauri, 1980–84. *Contributions to:* Pembroke Magazine; The Spirit that Moves Us; The Mickle Street Review. *Address:* 2551 W Mossman Road, Tucson, AZ 85746, USA.

INNES, Brian, b. 4 May 1928, Croydon, Surrey, England. Publisher; Writer; Designer. m. (1) Felicity Anne McNair Wilson, 5 Oct. 1956, Chelsea, diss. 1964, (2) Eunice Mary Lynch (Smith), 2 Apr. 1971, Hampstead, diss. 1984, 3 sons. *Education:* BSc, Kings College, London; Chelsea College of Art; Central School of Arts and Crafts; London College of Printing; MIOP; MSIAD. *Literary Appointments:* Assistant editor, Chemical Age, 1953–55; Associate editor, The British Printer, 1955–60; Art director, Hamlyn Group, 1960–62; Director, Animated Graphic and Publicity, 1964–65; Proprietor, Immediate Books, 1966–70, FOT Library, 1970–; Creative director, 1970–, currently Deputy Chairman, Orbis Publishing Limited, 1970–. *Publications:* Book of Pirates, 1966; Book of Spies, 1967; Book of Revolutions, 1967; Book of Outlaws, 1968; Flight, 1970; Saga of the Railways, 1972; Horoscopes, 1976; Tarot, 1977; Alchemy, 1976; Book of Change, 1979; The Red Baron Lives!, 1981; The Red Red Baron, 1983; The Havana Cigar, 1983; editor, Rococo to Romanticism, 1977. *Contributions to:* Encyclopedia Britannica; Man, Myth and Magic; British Printer; editor, Fact of Print series; History of English Speaking Peoples; American Destiny; All About Science; On Four Wheels; The Unexplained; History of Rock and others. *Memberships:* Arts Club, London; Society of Authors; National Union of Journalists; Society of Industrial Artists and Designers; Institute of Printing. *Address:* 23 Islington Green, London N1, England.

INNES, Christopher David, b. 6 Oct. 1941, Liverpool, England. Professor. m. Eva Maria Felsöeornagy, 12 June 1971, Edgbaston, 1 son. *Education:* BA, English Language & Literature, B Phil, Comparative Literature, D Phil, German Literature, Oxford Univerity. *Appointments:* Contributing Editor, Modern Drama, Toronto, Canada, 1979–; General Editor, Directors in Perspective Series, Cambridge University Press, 1980–; General Editor, Canadian Dramatist Series, 1983–; Editorial Board, Cambridge Guide to World Drama, Cambridge University Press, 1984–. *Publications:* Erwin Piscator's Political Theatre; Modern German Drama: A Study in Form; Holy Theatre: Ritual & The Avant Garde; Edward Gordon Craig. *Contributor to:* English Studies in Canada; Drama Review; Modern British Dramatists: New Perspectives; Canadian Drama; etc. *Honour:* Fellow, Royal Society of Arts, 1983. *Memberships:* Canadian Association for Irish Studies, Treasurer. *Address:* Dept of English, York University, 4700 Keele St, Toronto, Ontario, Canada.

INSALL, Donald W, b. 7 Feb. 1926, Clifton, Bristol, England. Architect; Planner; Conservationist. *Education:* ARIBA, now FRIBA, Royal W of England Academy, School of Architects; Post Graduate Royal Academy School of Architecture, London; S P Dip. (Hons.) AMTPI, now FRTPI; School of Planning and Research for Reg. Dev. *Publications:* The Care of Old Buildings Today, (Archtl. Press); Chester: A Study in Conservation, (HMSO), 1969; Historic Buildings: Action to Maintain the Expertise for their Care and Repair, (Coun. of Europe). *Contributor to:* Tech Press; Ency. Britannica. *Honours include:* 4 European Architectural Heritage Year Awards and Medal; The Queen's Silver Jubilee Medal, 1977; OBE, 1981; Academician, Royal West of England Academy, 1983. *Memberships include:* FRSA; FSA; Commissioner, Historic Buildings and Monuments Commission for England. *Address:* 19 West Eaton Place, London SW1X 8LT, England.

INSINGEL, Mark, b. 3 May 1935, Lier, Belgium. Author. *Education:* Koninklijk Vlaams Muziekconservatorium, Antwerp, 1955–58; MA. *Publications:* Author of some 17 books, novels, poetry, essays and radio plays including: Relections, 1971; A Course of Time, 1977; When a Lady Shakes Hands with a Gentleman, 1982; My Territory, 1985. *Contributions to:* Main literary magazines in the Netherlands and Dutch speaking areas of Belgium. *Honours:* Biennal Prize, De Vlaamse Gids, 1970; Visser-Neerlandiaprijs for radio plays, 1974; Arthur Merghelynckprijs, Academy of Dutch Language and Literature, Ghent, 1974–75; Dirk Martensprijs, 1978. *Memberships:* Flemish Center, PEN Club; Maatschappij der Nederlandse Letterkunde; Flemish Writers Association. *Address:* Zwanenlaan 1, B–2610 Antwerpen-Wilrijk, Belgium.

INVERARITY, Robert Bruce, b. 5 July 1909, Seattle, Washington, USA. Museologist; Anthropologist; Artist. *Education:* BA, University of Washington; MFA, PhD, Fremont University. *Publications include:* Block Printing and Stenciling, 1930; The Rainbow Book: Batik Making, 1930; Playable Puppet Plays, 1933; Manual of Puppetry, 1933; Masks and Marionettes of the North West Coast Indians, 1940; Twelve Photographs by R B Inverarity, 1940; Northwest Coast Indian Art, 1946; Art of the North West Coast Indians, 1950; Winslow Homer in the Adirondacks, Editor and Compiler, 1959; Visual File Coding Index, 1960; Accessioning and Cataloguing, 1965; The Use of Computers in Anthropology, Co-author, 1965; Early Chinese Art and Its Possible Influence in the Pacific Basin, co-author, 1972; Early Marine Navigation, 1976; Philadelphia, Port of History 1609–1837, Editor, 1976. *Contributions to:* Various journals. *Memberships include:* American Association of Museology, 1966–76; Phi Beta Kappa. *Address:* 2610 Torrey Pines Road, C22, La Jolla, CA 92037, USA.

IOANNOU, Susan, b. 4 Oct. 1944, Toronto, Canada. Writer; Editor. m. Lazaros Ioannou, 28 Aug. 1967, Toronto, 1 son, 1 daughter. *Education:* BA, Honours, English Language & Literature, 1966, MA, English Literature, 1967, University of Toronto. *Appointments:* Managing Editor, Coiffure du Canada, 1979–80; Associate Editor, Cross-Canada Writers Quarterly, 1980–; Poetry Editor, Arts Scarborough Newsletter, 1980–85; Managing Editor, Columbine Editions, 1981–; Poetry Instructor, Toronto Board of Education, 1982–; Director, Wordwrights Canada, 1985–. *Publications:* Spare Words, 1984; Motherpoems, 1985; The Crafted Poem, 1985. *Contributions include:* Magazines: Alberta Poetry Yearbook, Alchemist; First Encounter; Nebula; Northward Journal; Poetry Toronto; Waves; West Coast Review; etc. Anthologies: Here is a Poem; Modern Lyrics Anthology; Parthenon Poetry Anthology; Nelson Canada Flip Flops; Toronto Collection; Womansong; Other Channels. Columns: Poetry, Arts Scarborough Newsletter, 1980–85; Cross-Canada Writers Quarterly, 1980–. *Honours:* Norma Epstein Foundation Award, poetry, University of Toronto, 1965; Honorary Member, Cross-Canada Writers' Workshop, 1980–; Award, Book Cellar Mother's Day, poem, 1982. *Memberships:*

Canadian Poetry Association; Freelance Editors Association of Canada; League of Canadian Poets (associate); Media Club of Canada. *Address:* 36 Elvaston Drive, Toronto, Ontario, Canada M4A 1N3.

IODICE, Ruth Genevieve, b. 16 Aug. 1925, Crystal Lake, Illinois, USA. Editor; Writer; Teacher. *Education:* BA, Ind. State University; Graduate Work, Universities of Chicago & California. *Publications:* Editor, The Singing East Bay & Beyond – Fifty Years of the Poets' Dinner (Anthology), 1976; Editor, Little Voices from the Hilltop I & II (Children's Anthologies), 1976 & 1979. *Contributor to:* Numerous magazines, journals, etc., including, California State Poetry Quarterly, Editor in Chief, 1976–77; Founding Editor, Blue Unicorn; Poet Lore; Cedar Rock; The Woods-Runner; Attention Please; Haiku (Toronto); Modern Haiku; Haiku W; Haiku Highlights; Red Bluff Daily News; Founder, Trinity Gallery. *Honours:* Numerous prizes and awards including: 2nd Prize, Emma Brimm Memorial Award, NFSPS, 1977; 2nd Prize, La State Poetry Society Award, 1976; several 1st Prizes, California Federation of Chaparral Poets Contests. *Memberships:* Poetry Society of America; National Federation State Poetry Societies California Federation Chaparral Poets; Ina Coolbirth Circle (Literary & California Historical). *Address:* 22 Avon Road, Kensington, CA 94707, USA.

IORIO, James, b. 7 Apr. 1921. School Principal. *Education:* MA, University of Chicago, USA. 1948; MEd, DePaul University, 1956. *Appointments:* Public School Teacher, 1948–56, Vice-Principal, 1961–. *Publications:* The Fifth Season, 1974; Silence Interrupted, 1976; Ring of Fire, 1978; Journeys, 1983. *Contributions to:* University of Chicago Magazine; Encore; Notable American Poets; Chicago Harlem-Foster Times; Poetry Today; Voices International; View; MTI. Ars Poetica (Northeastern University, Illinois); National Federation of State Poetry Societies Anthology of Prize Poems, 1976; The Republic. *Memberships:* Illinois State Poetry Society; National Federation of State Poetry Societies. *Address:* 2018 Habberton Avenue, Park Ridge, IL 60068, USA.

IRWIN, Patricia Kathleen, b. 23 Nov. 1916, Dorset, England. Writer. m. W Arthur Irwin, 16 Dec. 1950, Ottawa, Canada. *Publications:* Poetry: As Ten as Twenty, 1946; The Metal and the Flower, 1954; Cry Ararat! Poems New and Selected, 1967; P K Page: Poems Selected and New, 1974; Evening Dance of the Grey Flies, 1981; The Glass Air, 1985. Fiction: The Sun and the Moon, 1944; The Sun and the Moon and other fictions, 1973; Editor, To Say the Least, 1979. *Contributions to:* Malahat Review; Queens Quarterly; Alphabet; ariel; Artscanada; Canadian Forum; Canadian Literature; Canadian Poetry Magazine; Contemporary Verse, CVII; Encounter; First Statement; Here and Now; Northern Review; The Observer; Poetry; Preview; Saturday Night; Tamarack Review; Ellipse and others. *Honours:* Bertram Warr Award, 1940; Oscar Blumenthal Award, 1944; Governor General's Award, 1954; Officer, Order of Canada, 1977; National Magazines Award, 1985; D Litt, University of Victoria, 1985. *Memberships:* League of Canadian Poets. *Address:* 3260 Exeter Road, Victoria, British Columbia, Canada V8R 6H6.

ISAACS, Ann Fabe, b. 2 July 1920, Cincinnati, Ohio, USA. Educator; Author; Artist; Composer; Elected Official. m. S Ted Isaacs, 7 June 1939, Cincinnati, 2 daughters. *Education:* BA, University of Cincinnati, 1944; MEd, Xavier University, 1952; PhD, National Science Foundation, 1977. *Appointments:* Editor, The Gifted Child Quarterly, 1956–79; Editor, Publisher, The Creative Child and Adult Quarterly, 1976–. *Publications:* Acrostic on Giftedness for Home & School, 1964; Crossroads of Talent, Editor, 1965; The Creative Cat, 1972; How to Teach Ourselves to Be Good to One Another, 1975; Commonsense Creativity, 1982; How to Be Personally Creative, 1986. *Contributor to:* More than 400 articles in journals including, The School Administrator; The Reading Teacher; etc. *Honours:* Educational Press Award for Excellence, 1967. *Address:* 8080 Spring Valley Dr, Cincinnati, OH 45236, USA.

ISAACS, Florence, b. 2 July 1937, New York City, USA. Non-Fiction Writer. m. Harvey A Isaacs, 1 Sep 1962, New York City. *Education:* BBA, Baruch College. *Contributor to:* Good Housekeeping; Parade; Family Circle; Readers Digest; Dynamic Years; Mademoiselle. *Memberships:* American Society of Journalists and Authors; Women in Communications. *Address:* 175 W 13 St, New York, NY 10011, USA.

ISAEV, Mladen, b. 20 June 1907, Balyuvitza, Bulgaria. Writer. m. Lyudmila Antonova, 31 Oct. 1952, 3 daughters. *Publications:* 20 books of poetry including Fires, 1932; Victims, 1934; The Fire; Youth; Star of Peace; Love; The Green Tree; Generosity; A Vault of Heaven; There's No Rest For Your; The Fury; A Poem About September; The Man Meets The Sun. Memoirs, The Memorable; About 15 books for children. *Contributor to:* All main Bulgarian literary editions. *Honours:* Four awards from the Union of Bulgarian Writers; People's Worker of Culture, 1970; A Hero of People's Republic of Bulgaria; Dimitrov Prize, 1971; The Big Award of Sofia, 1978. *Memberships:* Union of Bulgarian Writers, Secretary 1944–47, 1956–58, Vice President 1962–66, 1984. Union of Bulgarian Translators, Member of Governing Body. *Address:* 145 Rakovski Street, Sofia, Bulgaria.

ISRAEL, Charles Edward, b. 15 Nov. 1920, Evansville, Indiana, USA. Writer. m. Gloria Varley, 23 Sep. 1979. *Education:* BA, University of Cincinnati, 1942; BHL, Bachelor of Hebrew Letters, Hebrew Union College, 1943. *Publications:* How Many Angels, 1956; The True North (with T C Fairley), 1956; The Mark, 1958; Rizpah, 1961; Who Was Then The Gentleman? 1963; Shadows on a Wall, 1965; Five Ships West, 1965; The Hostages, 1966. *Contributions to:* Features on wines and spirits to magazines including: Toronto Life; Wine Tidings; Toronto Calendar. *Honours:* City of Genoa Award, Prix Italia, 1964; Best Scenario, Prague Film Festival, 1965. *Memberships:* Academy of Television Arts and Sciences; Academy of Canadian Cinema; Writers Union of Canada; Periodical Writers Association of Canada; Writers Guild of America West; Alliance of Canadian Cinema, Television and Radio Artists. *Literary Agent:* Harvey Unna, London; Roslyn Targ, New York; Triad Artists, Los Angeles. *Address:* 113 Howland Avenue, Toronto, M5R 3B4, Canada.

ISRAEL, Martin Spencer, b. 30 Apr. 1927, Johannesburg, South Africa. Pathologist; Clerk in Holy Orders. *Education:* MB; MRCP; FRC.Path. *Publications:* General Pathology, (with J B Walter), 1963, 5th Edition, 1979; Summons to Life, 1974; Precarious Living, 1976; Smouldering Fire, 1978; The Pain that Heals, 1981; Living Alone, 1982; The Spirit of Counsel, 1983; Healing as Sacrament, 1984. *Contributor to:* Various medical publications and theological journals. *Literary Agent:* Edward England, 12 Highlands Close, Crowborough, East Sussex. *Address:* Flat 2, 26 Tregunter Road, London SW10 9LS, England.

ITKONEN, Jukka Olavi, b. 7 Oct. 1951, Varkaus, Finland. Author. m. Inga Lindroos, 25 Sep. 1981, Varkaus, 1 son. *Publications:* Käsipuoli Amor, 1974; Isänmaata kynnen alla, 1974; Vallaton kuningas, 1975; Kultainen Omena, 1983. *Contributor to:* Raketti. *Memberships:* The Finnish Dramatists' Society. *Address:* Halmekatu 3 B 22, 78300 Varkaus 30, Finland.

ITZIN, Catherine Lenore, b. 29 May 1944, Iowa, USA. Author. m. 1 son, 1 daughter. *Education:* BA, University of Iowa, 1967; MPhil, University of London, England, 1970. *Literary Appointments:* Founder, Editor, Theatre Quarterly, 1970–77; Drama Critic, Tribune, 1972–81; Script Editor and Producer, British Broadcasting Corporation Radio drama, 1973–75; Drama Editor, Pluto Press, 1978–80; Editor, Explorations in Feminism, 1982–. *Publications:* Stages in the Revolution, 1980, 82; Splitting Up, 1980; Tax Law and Childcare, 1980; 20th Century Polish Theatre, 1980; New Theatre Voices of the Seventies, 1981; British Alternative Theatre Directory, 1979–85; Directory of Playwrights, Directors and Designers,

1985; How to Choose a School, 1985. *Contributions to:* Guardian; Time Out; Tribune; Plays and Players; Red Letters; Gambit; Gulliver; Marxism Today; Womens Studies' International Forum, Times Educational Supplement. *Honours:* Plays: Ever After, Tricycle Theatre, 1982; Let's Murder the Moonshine, British Broadcasting Corporation Radio 3, 1984. *Memberships:* British Society of Gerontology; British Sociological Association; Support and Housing Assistance for People with Disabilities (SHAD). *Literary Agent:* Deborah Rogers, London. *Address:* c/o Deborah Rogers, Literary Agent, 49 Blenheim Crescent, London W11 2EF, England.

IVANNIKOFF, Lydia, b. 22 Feb. 1909. Teacher. *Education:* University of Belgrade, Yugoslavia. *Appointments:* High School Teacher, Belgrade 1834–44; Secretary, UNRRA camp, 1945–49; Clerk, 1949–60; Technical Assistant, New York Public Library, USA. 1960–78 (Retired). *Publications:* Lesboe solntze (Forest Sun), 1954; V puti (On the Way), 1959; Prozrachnyi sled (Translucent trace), 1964; Vremya razluk (Time of Partings), 1971; Stikhi, poems, 1980. *Contributions to:* Various Russian language journals, USA, Canada, France and Germany. *Address:* 203 West 98th Street, Apt 1D, New York City, NY 10025, USA.

IVES, Richard, b. 8 Feb. 1951, Aberdeen, South Dakota, USA. Writer. *Education:* BA, Eastern Washington University; MFA, University of Montana. *Literary Appointments:* Editor and Publisher: Owl Creek Press, 1979–; The Montana Review, 1979–. Associate Editor, Crosscurrents, 1984–. *Publications:* Notes from the Water Journals, 1980; Rain in the Forest, Light in the Trees, 1983; The Other Image, 1984; From Timberline to Tidepool, 1985; Time Enough for the World, 1985. *Contributions to:* Virginia Quarterly Review; Iowa Review; Quarterly West; Poetry Northwest; Northwest Review; Malahat Review; Denver Quarterly; Seneca Review; The Nation; Numerous others. *Address:* 1620 North 45th Street, 205, Seattle, WA 98103, USA.

IVIE, Robert Lynn, b. 29 July 1945, Medford, Oregon, USA. Professor. m. Nancy Lee Haagensen, 11 Dec. 1965, San Leandro, California, 1 son, 1 daughter. *Education:* BA, California State University, Hayward, 1967; MA 1968, PhD 1972, Washington State University. *Literary Appointments:* Editor, Western Journal of Speech Comunication, 1984–87; Associate Editor, Quarterly Journal of Speech, 1986–89; Professor of Communications, Washington State University. *Major Publication:* Congress Declares War: Rhetoric, Leadership & Partnership in the Early Republic, 1983. *Contributor to:* Various periodicals, including: Communication Monographs, Social Science History, Central States Speech Journal Souther Speech Communication Journal, and others. *Memberships:* Speech Communication Association; Western Speech Communication Association (2nd Vice-President); International Society for the History of Rhetoric; Rhetoric Society of America. *Address:* Department of Communications, Washington State University, Pullman, WA 99164-2520, USA.

IYENGAR, Bellur Khishnamachar Sundararaja, b. 14 Dec. 1918, Bellur, India. Yoga Teacher. m. Ramamani, 13 July 1943, 6 children. *Publications:* Light on Yoga; Body The Shrine Yoga; The Light, 1978; Light on Pranayama, 1981; Art of Yoga, 1985. *Contributor to:* Yoga & Health; Yoga Journal; Yoga To-day; Bharatiya Vidhya Bhavan; etc. *Address:* Ramamani Iyengar Memorial Yoga Institute, 1107/B–1, Shivajinagar, Pune 411–016, India.

IZBAN, Samuel, b. 26 Sep. 1905, Warsaw, Poland. Author; Journalist; Book Critic. *Education:* Hebrew University, Jerusalem, Israel. *Publications:* Queen Jezebel; Rahab of Jericho; Heroes of the Desert; The Belated Heirs; The City of Wrath; New York Tales; After the Storm; A Whale in Jaffa; A Dream in the Desert; Stories of Jerusalem; Within Hundred Gates. *Contributions to:* Hebrew press in Israel; Yiddish press, USA; Magazines, periodicals, USA, Israel, South Africa,

Australia, Europe and Latin America. *Honours:* Haint Literature Prize, 1932; Zukunft Prize, 1944; Kessel Prize, 1950; Yiddische Zeitung, Tel Aviv, Israel, 1972; Annual Literary Prize, World Jewish Culture Congress, New York, USA, 1980; Annual Itzik Manger Literary Prize, Israel, 1984. *Memberships:* World Organisation of Hebrew Writers; I L Peretz Writers Union; International PEN. *Address:* 2475 East 22nd Street, Brooklyn, NY 11235, USA.

J

JACHIMOWSKI, Henryk, b. 16 Apr. 1938, Roznica, Poland. Editor. m. 1 son. *Education:* Master of Polish Philology, Higher School of Pedagogics, Cracow. *Publications:* I'm going on the River's Bottom, 1965; Salamanders, 1966; Flaw, 1969; Sun Songs, 1970; Returning Mythes, 1975; Fog, 1976; Paralysis, 1984; Dramas, 1985. *Literary Awards:* Red Rose Award, 1963; Joseph Czechowicz Laurel, 1966; Stanislaw Pigtak Literary Award, 1970; Stanislaw Staszic Award, 1975. *Memberships:* Polish Writers Union, 1968–83. *Address:* Interpress, Bagatela 12, 00-585 Warszawa, Poland.

JACKOWSKA, Nicki, b. 6 Aug. 1942, Brighton, England. Writer; Actress. m. Andrzej Jackowski, 1 May 1970, Penzance, 1 daughter. *Literary Appointments:* Reg. Coordinator, New Activities Committee, Arts Council of Great Britain, 1969–70; Freelance Writer and Performer, 1968–74; Tudor, Arvon Foundation, Devon and Yorks, 1977–; Tutor, Center for Continuing Edcuation, University of Sussex, 1979–; Numerous poetry readings in UK and BBC Radio. *Publications:* (Poetry): Song for the Beginning of it, 1972; Nightride, 1973; Today's Flower is White, 1973; House of Effigies, 1973; The Bride Month, 1973; The King Rises, 1973; The Flower Waker, 1974; The Words That Manda Spoke, 1974; Night of the Bird; Wife, 1975; The Bone Palaces, 1977; The House That Manda Built, 1981; Incubus, 1981; Earthwalks, 1982; Letters to Superman, 1984; Gates to the City, 1985; (Fiction): Doctor Marbles and Marianne, 1982; The Road to Orc, 1985. *Contributor to:* Various professional journals and magazines;s; Anthologies: Bread and Roses, 1983; Purple and Green, 1985; Editor and Introduction, Voices from Arts for Labour, 1985; Angels of Fire, 1986. *Honours:* Winner, Stroud Festival Poetry Competition, 1972; Grant, Society of Authors, 1973; Continental Bursary, S E Arts, 1978; Arts Council Writers Fellowship, 1984–85; Prize Winner, Stand, Magazine International Short Story Competition, 1985. *Membership:* Poetry Society. *Literary Agent:* Bill Hamilton at A M Heath, London. *Address:* 40 Hanover Terrace, Brighton BN2 2SN, England.

JACKSON, John Graeme, b. 28 Mar. 1953, Dundee, Scotland. Journalist. m. Amanda Lucy Relph, 1 Sep. 1982, Woking, Surrey. *Education:* BSc Honours Physiology, University of St Andrews, 1976; Diploma in Dietetics, The Queen's College, Glasgow, 1979. *Literary Appointments:* Assistant Editor, International Journal of Refrigeration, 1979–80; Assistant Editor, Geriatric Medicine, 1980–81; Editor, Medical Digest, 1981–84; Managing Editor, Maclean Hunter Medical Division, 1984; Editor, Medical Digest and Geriatric Medicine, 1984; Editor, Kitchens 1985–; Freelance Editor, Diabetes Bulletin. *Memberships:* Medical Journalists Association. *Address:* 75 Meadway Drive, Horsell, Woking, Surrey, England.

JACKSON, Richard Eugene, b. 25 Feb. 1941, Helena, Arkansas, USA. Professor of Drama. Divorced, 1 son. *Education:* BS, Memphis State University, 1963; MA, Kent State University, 1964, PhD, Southern Illinois University, 1971. *Publications:* Little Red Riding Wolf, 1973; Popeye the Sailor, book and lyrics, 1984; Boogie Man Rock, book and lyrics, 1984. Over 30 additional plays. *Contributions to:* Children's Theatre is a Seed, in San Francisco State University's Theatron, 1970 and Children's Theatre Review, 1970; The Theatre Scene, South Alabama; Toward 2000, 1978. *Honours:* Winner of Atlanta Junior League Children's Theatre Contest, 1966 with, Ferdinand and the Dirty Knight; Winner of Pioneer Drama Service Contest, 1981 with, Snowhite and the Space Gwarfs; Winner of several other playwriting competitions. *Membership:* Dramatists Guild. *Address:* 1901 Oakleaf Court, Mobile, AL 36609, USA.

JACKSON, Robert Louis, b. 10 Nov. 1923, New York, USA. Professor of Russian Literature. m. Elizabeth Mann Gillette, 28 July 1951, 2 daughters. *Education:* BA, Cornell University, 1944; MA 1949, Certificate of Russian Institute 1949, Columbia University; PhD, University of California, Berkeley. *Literary Appointments:* Instructor 1954, Assistant Professor 1958, Professor of Russian Literature 1967, Yale University. *Publications:* Dostoevsky's Underground Man in Russian Literature, 1958; Dostoevsky's Quest For Form: A Study of His Philosophy of Art, 1966; Chekhov collection of critical essays, editor, 1967; Crime and Punishment collected critical essays, editor, 1974; The Art of Dostoevsky, 1981; Dostoevsky collected critical essays, editor, 1984. *Contributions to:* Numerous articles in publications including: The Yale Review; Yale French Studies; Comparative Literature; Slavic Review; Slavic and East European Journal; Scando-Slavica; Slavica Hierosolymitana; Russian Literature; Ricerche Slavistiche; The Sewanee Review; Dostoevsky Studies. *Honours:* Fellow, American Council of Learned Societies, 1950, 1951; Yale Morse Fellowship, 1961–62; Guggenheim Fellow, 1967–68; National Endowment for the Humanities Fellowship, 1974. *Memberships:* Phi Beta Kappa; President 1971–77, North American Dostoevsky Society; President 1977–83, International Dostoevsky Society; President, International Chekhov Society, 1977–; President, Vyacheslav Ivanov Convivium, 1981–; AAASS; AATSEEL. *Address:* Box 3, Hall of Graduate Studies, Yale University, New Haven, CT 06520, USA.

JACKSON, William Godfrey Fothergill (General Sir), b. 28 Aug. 1917, Blackpool, Lancashire, England. Regular Army Officer. *Education:* Royal Military Academy, Woolwich; MA, King's College, Cambridge University. *Publications:* Attack in the West, 1953; Seven Roads to Moscow, 1957; Battle for Italy, 1967; Battle for Rome, 1959; Alexander of Tunis, 1971; Battle of Northern Africa, 1975; Overlord, 1976; Official historian, Cabinet Office, London, Editor of Volume VI Parts 1-3, Mediterranean and Middle East Campaigns and other publications. *Contributions to:* Royal United Services Journal; Royal Engineers Journal. *Honours include:* Gold Medals for Prize Essays, Royal United Service Institution, 1950, 65; MC and Bar, 1940–44; OBE, 1957; KCB, 1970; GBE, 1975; Knight of Justice of St John, 1978. *Memberships:* Fellow, British Institute of Management; Various military organisations. *Address:* c/o Williams and Glyns Bank, Whitehall, London SW1, England.

JACOBS, Louis, b. 17 July 1920, Manchester, England. Rabbi. *Education:* BA, PhD, University College, London University. *Publications:* We Have Reason to Believe, 1957; Studies in Talmudic Logic and Methodology, 1962; Principles of the Jewish Faith, 1964; Faith, 1966; A Jewish Theology, 1974; The Chain of Tradition, 5 vols, 1967–77. *Contributor to:* Jewish Chronicle: Journal of Jewish Studies; Journal of Semitic Studies; Hebrew Union College Annual. *Honours:* Jerusalem Prize (Aaron Zeitlin), 1959; Jewish Chronicle Award, 1975. *Memberships include:* Society of Old Testament Study; British Conference of Jewish Studies. *Addresss:* 27 Clifton Hill, St John's Wood, London NW8 OQE, England.

JACOBSEN, Claus, b. 7 Oct. 1940, Copenhagen, Denmark. Television Producer; Author; Teacher. *Education:* School of Journalism. *Literary Appointments:* Head of Information, Nordic Council Stockholm. *Publications:* Baukauli – en nordindisk landsby, (Baukauli – a Village in North India), 1976; TV-avisen – medie og virkelighed, (TV News – Medium and Reality), 1978, 1979; Danmark – kursen er sat, (Denmark – the Course is Decided), 1979, 1980; Bordtennis, (Table Tennis), 1973, 1977, 1980; TV in the 1980's, 1981; From Old Paintings to TV-satellites. *Contributor to:* Table Tennis Magazine of Denmark; Sailing Magazines; Various newspapers. *Memberships:* Danish Federation of Journalists; Danish Authors Association. *Address:* Ternevej 5 B, 8240 Risskov, Denmark.

JACOBSON, Beverly, b. 17 Apr. 1927, New York City, USA. Writer. m. Dr Julius H Jacobson II, 26 June

1949, Mahopac, New York, 2 sons, 3 daughters. *Education:* BA, Mount Holyoke College. *Publications:* Young Programs for Older Workers, 1980; Money in Your Attic: How to Turn Your Furniture, Antiques, Silver & Collectibles into Cash, 1985. *Contributions to:* Ladies Home Journal; Good Housekeeping; McCalls; Parade; National Forum; Public Affairs Committee pamphlets; Medica; Seventeen; etc. *Memberships:* Delegate, Executive board member (Westchester), National Writers Union; Programme chair, Writers Referral Service Committee, American Society of Journalists & Authors. *Literary Agent:* Nancy Love. *Address:* 125 Brite Avenue, Scarsdale, NY 10583, USA.

JACOBSON, Dan, b. 7 Mar. 1929. Johannesburg, South Africa. Writer. m. Margaret Pye, 3 sons, 1 daughter. *Education:* BA, University of the Witwatersrand, Johannesburg, South Africa. *Literary Appointments:* Fellow in Creative Writing, Stanford University, California, 1956; Professor, Syracuse University, New York, 1965–66; Fellow, State University of New York, Buffalo NY, 1972; Fellow Royal Society of Literature, 1974; Lecturer, 1975–80, Reader in English 1980–, University College, London; Fellow, Humanities Research Centre, Australian National University, 1981. *Publications:* The Trap 1955; A Dance in the Sun 1956; The Price of Diamonds 1957; The Evidence of Love 1960; The Beginners 1965; The Rape of Tamar 1970; The Wonder-Worker 1973; The Confessions of Josef Baisz 1979; The Story of the Stories 1982; Time and Time Again 1985. *Contributions to:* New Yorker; Commentary; Grand Street; London Magazine; London Review of Books; The Guardian etc. *Honours:* John Llewelyn Rhys Memorial Award, 1958; W Somerset Maughan Award, 1964; H H Wingate Award, 1979. *Literary Agent:* A M Heath and Co Ltd, London. *Address:* c/o A M Heath and Co Ltd, 40-42 King William IV Street, London WC2, England.

JAEGER, Gerard A, b. 1 Dec. 1952, Fribourg, Switzerland. Writer; Historian; Stage Producer. m. Angelica Pitteri, 21 May 1977, Fribourg, 1 son, 1 daughter. *Education:* Doctor of Letters, University of Fribourg. *Publications:* L'Age de Bronze, 1978; Le Grand Largue, 1981; Anthologie Critique de la Poésie Fribourgeoise (1426–1973), 1982; Les Aventuriers de la Mer, Bibliographie Thématique (XVIe-XXe Siècle), 1983; Les Femmes d'Abordage, Chronique des Aventurières de la Mer, 1984; Approche Critique et Bibliographique des Frères Rosny, 1985. *Contributor to:* Reviews, poetry anthologies, 1972–85. *Membership:* Swiss Society of Writers. *Address:* 71 Boulevard du Montfleury, Cannes, France.

JAEGGI, Urs, b. 23 June 1931, Solothurn, Switzerland. Professor of Sociology. *Education:* Universities of Bern & Berlin; Dr rer pol, University of Bern, 1959. *Major Publications include:* Kapital und Arbeit in der Bundesrepublik, 1973; Sozialstruktur, und politische Systeme, 1976; Brandeis, (novel), 1978; Grundrisse, 1981; Versuch über den Verrat, 1984. *Contributor to:* Various journals. *Memberships include:* West German PEN; Schweizerische Schriftsteller-Verband. *Honours include:* Literary Prize, City of Bern, 1963; Theodor-Heuß Professorship, New School for Social Research, New York, USA, 1970–71. *Address:* Fritschestraße 66, D–1000 Berlin 10, Federal Republic of Germany.

JAFAREY, Ada, b. 22 Aug. 1924, Badayun, Uttar Pradesh, India. Creative Writer, Poetry. m. Nurul Hasan Jafarey, 29 Jan. 1947, Lucknow, 2 sons, 1 daughter. *Literary Appointments:* Member Judges Panel, Pakistan Writers Guild, 1975; Editors Panel, Qaumi Zaban, Monthly magazine, 1983. *Publications:* In Search of Symphony, 1950; Universe of Pain, 1967; Gazelles of Course You Know, 1974; Symphony of Verses is a Veil, 1982. *Contributions to:* Rooman; Adabi Duniya; Adabi Latif; Shahkar; Funoon; Auraq; Nugoosh; Asloob; Naya Daur; Qaumi Zaban. *Honours:* Adamjee Award for Literature; Best Poetry Book, Pakistan Writers Guild, 1967; Tamghai Imtiaz, conferred by Government of Pakistan for contribution to enrichment of Urdu

language, 1980. *Memberships:* Pakistan Writers Guild; Executive Committee, Sind Zone, Pakistan Writers Guild; Governing Body, Pakistan National Language Authority; Haiku Advisory Committee, Japanese Embassy Organization. *Address:* 43/8/B Block 6, Pechs, Karachi 29, Pakistan.

JAFFE, Aniela, b. 1903, Berlin, Germany. Analytical Psychologist. *Education:* Universities of Hamburg & Zurich, Switzerland. *Publications:* Editor, Memories, Dreams, Reflections of C G Jung; Co-Editor, C J Jung's Collected Letters; Apparitions & Precognition, 1963; The Myth of Meaning, 1970; From the Life & Work of C G Jung, 1971 (all originally published in German). *Contributor to:* Several, Eranos Jahbulcher; Acad. Journals. *Memberships:* Swiss Society for Practical Psychology; Swiss Parapsychological Society; Zurich Society of Arts. *Address:* Hochstr. 73, 8044 Zurich, Switzerland.

JAFFE, Harold, b. 8 July 1940, New York, USA. Writer. m. Maggie Aronoff, 25 Aug. 1979, Sag Harbor. *Education:* BA, Grinnell College, 1960: Ma, New York University, 1961; PhD, Honours, Ibid, 1968. *Literary Appointments:* Co-Director, Fiction Collective, 1980–83; Editor, Fiction International, 1983–. *Publications:* Mole's Pity, novel, 1979; Mourning Crazy Horse, stories, 1982; Dos Indios, novel, 1983; Beasts, short fiction, 1986. *Contributions to:* Chicago Review; New Directions Annual; Boundary 2; Minnesota Review; O Ars; Fiction; Fiction International; American Made; etc. *Honours:* Fulbright Fellowship, American Literature, to India, 1971–72; Grant, National Endowment for the Arts, 1983. *Memberships:* PEN; Poets & Writers; Fiction Collective. *Literary Agent:* Gunther Stuhlmann. *Address:* 3551 Granada Avenue, San Diego, CA 92104, USA.

JAFFE, Jacob Harry, b. 18 June 1918, Newport, Rhode Island, USA. Professor of Journalism. m. Anne Papernik, 25 Dec. 1949, New York, 1 son. *Education:* Litt.B, Rutgers University; MA, Columbia University. *Literary Appointments:* Editor-in-Chief, Journalism Educator, 1966–68; Editorial Advisory Board, Journalism Quarterly, 1972–. *Publications include:* Career Opportunities in Journalism, 1960; 100 Books for New Journalists, 1963; History of World Journalism, Basic English Guide, in progress. *Contributions to:* Saturday Review of Literature; The Progressive; Journalism Educator. *Honours include:* Philosophian, Rutgers University English Department; Honour Society, 1940; Kappa Tau Alpha, 1940; Plaque & Citation, contributions to journalism, numerous newspapers, press associations; Elected Professor Emeritus of Journalism, Long Island University, 1980. Currently Professor at Rutgers University. *Memberships include:* American Society of Journalism School Adminstrators (President 1964–65); Secretary, Kappa Tau Alpha 1967–68; Society of Professional Journalists. *Address:* 321 Stevens Avenue, Jersey City, NJ 07305, USA.

JAGER, Hugo de, b. 26 Feb. 1931, Bandung, formerly Dutch East Indies. Retired Professor of Sociology. *Education:* BA, MA, PhD, State University of Utrecht, Netherlands. *Publications:* Grondbeginselen der Sociologie, with Dr A L Mok, 1964, 8th edition, 1983, German and Italian translations; Cultuuroverdracht en Concertbezoek, 1967; Mensbeelden en Maatschappymodellen, 1975. *Contributions to:* Mens en Maatschappij; Sociologia Neerlandica; Music and Man; International Review of the Aesthetics and Sociology of Music. *Literary Agent:* H E Stenfert Kroese BV. *Address:* Lv Suchtelen v.d. Haere 41, 1045 AR Bussum, Netherlands.

JAKOBSDÓTTIR, Svava, b. 4 Oct. 1930, Neskaupstadur, Iceland. Author; Former Member of Parliament. m. J[sc]on Hnefill Aoalsteinsson, 11 June 1955, Reykjavik, 1 son. *Education:* BA, Smith College, Massachusetts, USA; Somerville College, Oxford University, England; University of Uppsla, Sweden. *Publications:* Tolf konur, short stories, 1965; Veizla undir grjotvegg, short stories, 1967; Legjandinn, novel,

1969; Sogur, 2nd edition of 3 previous books, 1979; Gefio hvort ooru, short stories, 1982; Oskubuska i austri og vestri, Translation of fairy tales, 1982. Plays: Hvad er i blyholkmum?, 1970; Fridsael verold, 1974; Aeskuvinir, 1976; I takt vid timana, 1980; Lokaaefing, 1983. *Honours:* Literary prize, Icelandic Writers Fund, 1968; Literary prize, Icelandic State Radio Literary Fund, 1984. *Memberships:* Union of Icelandic Writers; Icelandic Pen Club. *Address:* Einarsnes 32, 101 Reykjavik, Iceland.

JAMES, David Geraint, b. 2 Jan. 1922, Treherbert, Wales. Dean, Consultant Physician, Royal Northern Hospital. m. Professor Dame Sheila Sherlock, 2 daughters. *Education:* Jesus College, Cambridge, 1939; Middlesex Hospital Medical School, University of London, 1941–44. *Publications:* Diagnosis and Treatment of Infections, 1957; Sarcoidosis, 1970; Circulation of the Blood, 1978; A Colour Atlas of Respiratory Diseases, 1984; Sarcoidosis and Other Granulomatous Disorders, 1985. *Honours:* Comyns Berkeley Fellow, Middlesex Hospital Medical School, 1950–51; Research Fellow, Columbia University, New York City; Ethel Reilly Scholarship, 1955, Leverhulme Scholar, 1955–57, Middlesex Hospital Medical School; 1st Prize, Scientific Exhibition, British Medical Association Congress, Newcastle Upon Tyne, 1957; Chesterfield Medallist, Institute of Dermatology, University of London, 1957; 1st Prize, Barraquer Institute of Opthalmology, Barcelona, 1958; Honorary LLD, University of Wales, 1982; Carlo Forlaninin Gold Medal, Italian Thoracic Society, 1983; White-Robed Member of the Gorsedd, 1984. *Address:* 149 Harley Street, London W1 1HG, England.

JAMES, Kathleen Ann Lapp, b. 10 May 1950, Milwaukee, Wisconsin, Editor. m. Randall James, 3 Sep. 1977, 1 son., *Education:* BA; MS. *Literary Appointments:* Executive Editor, American Health Consultants, Publishers of 15 Health Care Newsletters. *Honours:* Newsletter Association of America, Best Investigative Reporting, 1982. *Address:* 451 Valley Creek Road, Mableton, GA 30059, USA.

JANDL, Ernst, b. 1 Aug. 1925, Vienna, Austria. Writer. *Education:* Teaching Certificate, 1949; PhD, 1950, University of Vienna. *Publications:* Andere Augen, 1956; Laut und Luise, 1966 3rd edition 1976; Sprochblasen, 1968, 2nd editon 1979; Der kunstliche Baum, 1970; Funt Mann Menschen, with Friederike Mayröcker, 1971; Dingfest, 1973; Fur alle, 1974; Serienfuss, 1974; Die schone Kunst des Schreibens, 1976; Die Bearbeitung der Mutze, 1978; Aus der Fremde, 1980; Der gelbe Hund, 1980; Selbstporträt des Schachspielers als trinkende Uhr, 1983; Das Öffnen und Schliessen des Mundes, 1985; Collected Works in 3 volumes, 1985. *Contributor to:* Various literary journals. *Honours:* Radio-play prize for, War-Blinded Men, with Friederike Mayröcker, 1968; Georg Traki Prize for Poetry, 1974; City of Vienna Prize, 1976; Austrian State Prize, 1978; Mulheim Prize for Dramatists, 1980; Manuscript Prize of the County of Styria, 1982; Anton-Wildgans Prize of the Austrian Industry, 1982; Great Austrian State Prize, 1984; Georg Buchner Prize, 1984. *Memberships:* Academy of Arts, West Berlin; Forum Stadtpark, Graz; President, Graz Association of Authors; German Academy of Language and Literature, Darmstadt; Vice President, Austrian Arts Senate. *Address:* Box 227, A–1041 Vienna, Austria.

JANES, Percy Maxwell, b. 12 Mar 1922, St John's, Newfoundland, Canada. Writer. Divorced. *Education:* BA, University of Toronto, 1948. *Appointments:* Editorial Reader, Harry Cuff Publications, St John's. *Publications:* House of Hate, 1970; Eastmall, 1981; Requiem for a Faith, 1983; No Cage for Conquerors, 1984; Poetry: Light and Dark, 1982; Short Stories: Newfoundlanders, 1982. *Contributor to:* Numerous Magazines and Journals. *Honours:* Lydia Campbell Award for Writing, St John's, 1984. *Membership:* Honorary Member, Newfoundland Writers' Guild, St John's. *Address:* Box 77, St Thomas, C B, Newfoundland A0A 2E0, Canada.

JANIW, Wolodymyr, b. 21 Nov. 1908. Professor; University Rector; Psychologist; Sociologist. *Education:* Licence, Psychology, University of Lwiw, Ukraine, 1927–34; PhD, Friedrich-Wilhelss University, Berlin, 1944; Dr Phil. habil, Ukrainian Free University, Munich, Federal Republic of Germany, 1949. *Appointments include:* Lecturer, 1946–49, Assistant Professor, 1949–55, Associate Professor, 1956–63, Professor, 1963–; Rector, 1968–, Ukrainian Free University, Munich. *Major Publications:* 4 Anthologies of Poetry; Studies and Materials on Modern Ukrainian History (in Ukrainian), volume 1 1970, volume 2 1983. *Honours include:* 1st Literary Prize for anthology The Life, 1978; Bayrische Staatsmedaille für soziale Verdienste, 1980. *Memberships include:* Science Secretary, 1952–68 & Vice-President, 1968–, Shevchenko Science Society; Professional Association of German Psychologists; German Society of Psychology; Free International Academy of Sciences & Letters, Paris, France. *Address:* 29 Rue des Bauves, F–95200 Sarcelles, France.

JANKO, Richard Charles Murray, b. 30 May 1955, England. Classicist. m. Michele Hannoosh, 26 May 1984, Wakefield, USA. *Education:* BA, Classics, 1976, MA, PhD, 1980, Trinity College, Cambridge University. *Appointments:* Temporary Lecturer, Greek, University of St Andrews, 1978–79; Research fellow, Trinity College, Cambridge, 1978–82; Assistant Professor, Classics, Columbia University, USA, 1982–; Associate Professor, 1985–. *Publications:* Homer Hesiod and the Hymns: Diachronic Development in Epic Diction; 1982; Aristotle on Comedy: Towards a Reconstruction of Poetics II, 1984; The Iliad: A Commentary, Volume IV Books 13-16, forthcoming; Aristotle: Poetics and related texts, forthcoming. *Contributor to:* Numerous Articles on Ancient Greek Language and Literature. *Honours:* Prize Fellowship, Trinity College, 1978. *Memberships:* American Philological Society; Cambridge Philological Society. *Address:* Dept of Classics, 617 Hamilton Hall, Columbia University, New York, NY 10027, USA.

JANKUHN, Herbert, b. 8 Aug. 1905, Angerburg, Prussia. Full Professor. *Education:* Universities of Konigsberg, Jena, Berlin; PhD, Berlin, 1931; Habilitation, University of Kiel, 1935. *Publications:* Various in field of archaeology, early history and economics including: Die Ausgrabungen in Haithabu, 1937, 6th edition, 1976; Die Befestigungen der Wikingerzeit zwischen Schlei und Treene, 1938; Geschichte der Landwirteschaft von Neolithikum bis zur Wolkerwanderungszeit, 1967; Einfuhrung in die Siedlungsarchaologie, 1975. *Contributions to:* Prehistorische Zeitschrift. *Honour:* Grand Cross of Merit, Lower Saxony OM. *Memberships:* Academy of Sciences, Gottingen; Science Academy of Stockholm, Sweden; Austrian Academy of Sciences; Anthropology Society, Austria; Fryske Akademy, Leeuwarden; Society of Sciences, Lund, Sweden. *Address:* Ewaldstrasse 103, D–3400 Göttingen, Federal Republic of Germany.

JANOWITZ, Phyllis, b. 3 Mar. 1940, New York City, USA. Poet. Divorced, 1 son, 1 daughter. *Education:* BA, Queens College; MFA, University of Massachusetts, Amherst, 1970. *Literary Appointments:* Hodder Fellow in Poetry, Princeton University, 1979–80; Assistant Professor in English and Poet in Residence, Cornell University, 1980–. *Publications:* Rites of Strangers, 1978; Visiting Rites, 1982. *Contributions to:* Poems in The New Yorker; Atlantic; The Nation; The New Republic; Paris Review; Ploughshares; Radcliffe Quarterly; Prairie Schooner; Esquire; Andover Review; Harvard Magazine Backbone; The Literary Review; The Mid-Atlantic Review; Anthology of Magazine Verse; Mississippi Review; Moving Out; Beyond Baroque; DeKalb Literary Review; Bellingham Review; Concerning Poetry etc. *Honours:* Fellow, Bunting Institute, 1973; Stroud International Poetry Festival Award, 1978; National Endowment of the Arts Award, 1974–75; Alfred Hodder Fellow in Humanities, Princeton University, 1979–80; Emily Dickinson Award, Poetry Society of America, 1983. *Memberships:* PEN; Poetry Society of America; Association Writing

Program; MacDowell Colony. *Address:* One Lodge Way, Ithaca, NY 14850, USA.

JANSEN, Godfrey Henry, b. 2 Dec. 1919, Akyab (Sittwe), Burma. Foreign Correspondent. m. Michael Elin Fancher, 31 Oct. 1967, Beirut, Lebanon, 1 daughter. *Education:* BA, Christian College, Madras, India; MA, University of Madras. *Literary Appointments:* Foreign Correspondent, The Statesman, New Delhi and Calcutta, 1960–70; Middle East Correspondent, The Economist, London, 1970–. *Publications:* Afro-Asia and Non-Alignment, 1966; Why Robert Kennedy Was Killed, 1970; Zionism, Israel and Asian Nationalism, 1971; Militant Islam, 1979; The Battle of Beirut (with Michael Jansen), 1982. *Contributions to:* The Statesman; The Economist; The Los Angeles Times; Middle East International, London. *Literary Agent:* Jacqueline Korn, David Higham, London. *Address:* 5 John Metaxas Street, Ayois Dhometios, Nicosia, Cyprus.

JANSSONIUS, Mart, b. 1 Oct. 1907, Godlinze, The Netherlands. Former Secretary at a Multinational. *Literary Appointments:* Chosen Member of Maatschappij der Nederlandse Letteren. *Publications:* Mijn Man Gaat uit (My Man Steps Out), 1959; Agnes Sorel-Koningin van de Linkerhand (Agnes Sorel-Queen of the Left Hand), 1966; Maria van Bourondie-Bruid van Europa (Mary of Burgundy-Bride of Europe), 1978; Isabella van Portugal-Moeder van Karel de Stoute (Isabella of Portugal-Mother of Charles the Bold), 1985. *Contributions to:* Avenue, Amsterdam; DAFkrant, Eindhoven; Elsevier's Weekblad, Amsterdam; Nieuwsblad van het Noorden, Gronongen; Nieuwe Rotterdamse Courant; NRC-Handelsblad Rotterdam; De Vecature, Zutphen; Die Kunst und das schone Heim, Munchen; Radioprograms, Hilversum. *Memberships:* Maatschappij der Nederlandse Letteren, Leiden; Vereniging van Letterkundigen, Amsterdam. *Address:* Kroonlaan 44, 1217 AX Hilversum, The Netherlands.

JAPIASSU, Hilton Ferreira, b. 26 Mar. 1934, Carolina, MA, Brazil. Professor. *Education:* Licence in Philosophy; Philosophy Doctor. *Publications:* Interdisciplinarity and Knowledge Pathology, 1976; To Read Bachelard, 1976; Introduction to Psychology's Epistemology, 1978; The Myth of Scientific Neutrality, 1980; Birth and Death of Human Sciences, 1981; The Modern Scientific Revolution, 1985. *Contributions to:* Cuadernos de Filosofia Latinoamericana; Revista de Cultura Vozes; Reflexão. *Membership:* Brazilian Society for the Progress in Science. *Literary Agent:* Carmen Balcells, C Postal 33.113 Rio de Janeiro. *Address:* Rue Marquês de S Vicente 225, Filosofia, 22453 Rio de Janeiro, Brazil.

JARRETT, Dennis Evan, b. 17 Jan. 1949, England. Author, Editor. *Education:* Dip AD; BA Honours. *Literary Appointments:* Staff Writer, Computer Digest; Editor, Computer Management; Managing Editor, Which Computer; Managing Editor, Practical Computing; Managing Editor, Commodore User; Managing Editor, 16 BIT Computing. *Publications:* Good Computing Book, 1980; The IBM PC Book, The Electronic Office, Getting the Most from the Vic-20, The Commodore 64, The Victor/Sirius Book, all 1984. *Contributions to:* Numerous professional publications. *Address:* Paradox Group, The Metropolitan, Enfield Road, London N1 5AZ, England.

JÄRV, Harry Johannes, b. 27 Mar. 1921, Korsholm, Finland. Deputy National Librarian, Director, Library Department, Swedish National Library. m. Barbro Lundin, 27 Dec. 1947, Kiruna, Sweden. *Education:* Helsinki University, 1944–45; PhLic, Uppsala University, 1954. *Publications:* Kritik av den nya kritiken, 1953; Klassisk horisont, 1960; Die Kafka-Literatur, 1961; Varaktigare än koppar, 1962; Introduktion till Kafka, 1962; Illuminated Manuscripts, 1963; D H Lawrences Studier, 1964; Strindbergsfejden, 2 volumes, 1968; Den seriöse konstnären, 1969; Läsarmekanismer, 1971; Mallarmë, 1972; Frihet, jämlikhet, konstnärskap, 1974; Ezra Pounds Litteräca essäer, 1975; Victor Svanbergs skrifter, 1976; Tycke och smak, 1978; Konst är kvalitet, 1979; Den 'goda tvåan, 1981; Enfald eller mångfald, 1982; Den svenska boken 500 år, 1983; Vinghästen, 1984. *Contributor to:* Arbetaren; Joint Editor, 1954–71, Horisont Magazine; Editor, 1978–81, Parnasso Magazine; Radix Magazine; Editor, Fenix Magazine, 1983–. *Honours include:* Literary Awards, Swedish Academy 1969, 1980; PhD h.c., Uppsala University, 1973; Elsa Thulin Award, 1976; Tegnér Award, 1977; Läkerol Award, 1981; Blytypen, 1983. *Memberships include:* Royal Society for Publishers of MSS; Finnish Society of Letters; Board, Strindberg Society; Board, Early Swedish Text Society; Royal Swedish Academy of Letters; Honorary Member, Swedish East Bothnia Writers' Association; Swedish Writers' Union; Swedish PEN Club. *Address:* Fyrverkarbacken 32, S–112 60 Stockholm, Sweden.

JARVIS, Martin, b. 4 Aug. 1941, Cheltenham, Gloucestershire, England. Actor; Writer. m. (2) Rosalind Ayres, 23 Nov. 1974; 2 sons (from previous marriage). *Education:* Diploma, Royal Academy of Dramatic Art, 1962. *Appointments:* Numerous acting roles on stage, film & television productions. *Major Publications:* (play) Bright Boy, 1977; (short stories) Name out of a Hat, 1967; Alphonse, 1972; Late Burst, 1976; adapted 20, Just William, stories of Richmal Crompton for BBC Radio, 1972–76; adapted, Goodbye Mr Chips, by James Hilton for BBC Radio & Television, 1973. *Honours:* Vanburgh Award, Silver Medal, Royal Academy of Dramatic Art, 1968; National Theatre Player, 1982–84. *Membership:* Council Member, National Youth Theatre. *Literary Agent:* Michael Whitehall Ltd. *Address:* 82 Eaton Terrace, London, SW1, England.

JASPERT, Werner Pincus, b. 21 Mar. 1926, Frankfurt, Germany. Journalist. *Publications:* Encyclopaedia of Type Faces, 1986; State of the Art, 1984. *Contributor to:* Numerous magazines, journals and newspapers. *Agent:* McLean Hunter, USA; ITP International, The Netherlands. *Address:* 93a Belsize Lane, London NW3 5AY, England.

JAY, Peter, b. 7 Feb. 1937, England. Writer; Broadcaster. 1 son, 2 daughters. *Education:* 1st class degree PPE. *Literary Appointments:* Economics Editor, The Times, 1967–69; Associate Editor, Times Business News, 1969–77; Editor, Banking World, 1983–. *Publications:* The Budget, 1972; The Crisis for Western Political Economy and Other Essays, 1984. *Contributions to:* Foreign Affairs-America and the World, 1979; and others. *Honours:* Harold Wincott Financial and Economic Journalist of the Year, 1973; Wincott Memorial Lecturer, 1975; Fellow of the Royal Society of Arts, 1975. *Literary Agent:* Curtis Brown. *Address:* 39 Castlebar Road, London W5, England.

JEBB, Robert Dudley, b. 1 Feb. 1944, Connecticut, USA. Writer; Publisher. m. Jeanne Elliott, 23 Dec. 1973, New Mexico. *Education:* MS Journalism, 1972, University of Utah; BA International Relations, 1966, University of the Pacific. *Publication:* Mirages My Father Left Me, 1973. *Contribution to:* Publishers Weekly. *Address:* P O Box 136, Kittery Point, ME 03905, USA.

JEFFARES, Alexander Norman, b. 11 Aug. 1920, Dublin, Republic of Ireland. Professor. *Education:* MA, PhD, University of Dublin; MA, DPhil, Oxford University. W B Yeats: Man and Poet, 1949; 1962; A Commentary on the Collected Poems of Yeats, 1968; A Commentary on the Collected Plays of Yeats, (with A S Knowland), 1972; Restoration Drama, 1974; A History of Anglo Irish Literature, 1982; A New Commentary on the Poems of Yeats, 1984; The Poems of Yeats: A New Selection, 1984; (Editor) A Review of ENglish Literature; Ariel: A Review of International English Literature; Several Literary Series. *Contributor to:* Numerous Professional journals. *Honours:* Honorary Fellow, Trinity College, Dublin; Fellow, Australian Academy of the Humanities; Honorary Doct, l'Universite, Lille, France. *Memberships:* FRSL; FRSE; FRSA; Life President, International Associate for the

Study of Anglo-Irish Literature; Life Fellow, Associate for C'with. Lit. and Lang. Studies; Chairman, National Book League (Scotland); Member Executive Committee, NBL, London. *Address:* Department of English Studies, University of Stirling, Stirling, FK9 4LA, Scotland.

JEFFERSON, Alan, b. 20 Mar. 1921, Ashtead, Surrey, England. Author. Formerly stage-manager/director, musical administrator. *Education:* Rydal Schl, Colwyn Bay, 1935–37; Old Vic Theatre Schl. (Prod), 1947–48. *Publications:* The Operas of Richard Strauss in Great Britain, 1910–63, 1963; The Lieder of Richard Strauss, 1971 1910–63, 1963; Delius (Master Musicians), 1972; Richard Strauss (The Music Masters); 1975; Sir Thomas Beecham: A Centenary Biography, 1979; The Complete Gilbert and Sullivan Opera Guide, 1984; Der Rosenkavalier (Cambridge Opera Guides), 1986. *Memberships:* Administrator, London Symphony Orchestra, 1967–68; Professor, Vocal Interpretation, Guildhall Schl of Music, London, 1967–74; Orchestral manager, BBC, 1968–73; Editor, The Monthly Guide to Recorded Music, 1980–82. *Agent:* David Higham Associates. *Address:* c/o David Higham Associates, 5-8 Lower John Street, Golden Square, London, W1R 4HA, England.

JEFFREY, Lloyd Nicholas, b. 26 Nov. 1918, Temple, Oklahoma, USA. University Professor. *Education:* BA, 1939, MA, 1947, PhD, 1951, University of Texas. *Literary Appointments:* Associate Editor, Studies in the Novel (journal). *Major Publications:* Thomas Hood, 1972; Fears Related to Death & Suicide, (co-author), 1974; Shelley's Knowledge & Use of Natural History, 1976. *Contributor to:* Various Professional & literary journals, including: Coll Engl Bulletin of Bibliography; Western Folklore; Southwest Review; Keats-Shelley Journal; Psychoanalytic Review; Classical Journal. *Memberships:* Texas Association of College Teachers (President, North Texas Chapter); Modern Language Association (Section Chairman); American Classical League; S Ctrl Coll Engl Association; Phi Beta Kappa. *Honours:* University Doctoral Fellowship, 1939; Outstanding Educators of America, 1973, 1974, 1975; Numerous University Research Grants. *Address:* 625 Linwood Drive, Denton, TX 76201, USA.

JELLICOE, Marguerite Ruth, b. 2 Dec. 1913, Southampton, England. Retired Third World Community Development Officer. *Education:* MA African Studies, Makerere University, Uganda, 1969; Academic postgraduate diploma in Social Studies in Tropical Territories, London School of Economics, England, 1958. *Publications:* The Long Path, 1978. *Contributions to:* East Africa Journal; Transition, Africa, a Swedish school book, 1981. *Memberships:* Society of Authors, London. *Address:* Tremithousa, Old Church Road, Bothernhampton, Bridport, Dorset, DT6 4BP, England.

JENCKS, Harlan Wardell, b. 4 Aug. 1941, Ellensburg, Washington, USA. Professor. *Education:* BA 1963, MA 1971, PhD 1978, in Political Science, University of Washington; Diploma, 1980, US Army Command & General Staff College. *Literary Appointments:* Professor of National Security Affairs, Naval Postgraduate School, California. *Major Publications:* From Muskets to Missiles: Politics & Professionalism in the Chinese Army 1945–81, 1982; Contributing Editor (with F Gilbert Chan): Chinese Communist Politics: Selected Studies, 1982. *Contributor to:* Current History; China Quarterly; Chinese Defence Policy. *Address:* Department of National Security Affairs code 56JE, Naval Postgraduate School, Monterey, CA 93943, USA.

JENKINS, Mike Geraint, b. 16 Jan. 1953, Aberystwyth, Wales. Teacher. m. Marie Greagsby, 30 Oct. 1976, Belfast, Northern Ireland, 1 son, 1 daughter. *Education:* BA English, Post-graduate Certificate in Education. *Literary Appointments:* Member of Executive Committee, The Welsh Academy. *Major Publications:* The Common Land, 1981; Empire of Smoke, 1983; The Valleys (co-editor) with John Davies), 1984.

Contributor to: Encounter; New Statesman; Poetry Review; Anglo-Welsh Review; Poetry Wales; 2 plus 2; Poetry London/ Apple Magazine; Planet; The Honest Waterman; and others. *Honour:* Eric Gregory Award (Society of Authors), 1979; Welsh Arts Council Young Writers Prize, 1984. *Memberships:* Executive Committee, The Welsh Academy; Welsh Union of Writers. *Address:* 26 Andrews Close, Merthyr Tydfyl, CF48 1SS, Wales.

JENKINS, Simon David, b. 10 June 1943, Birmingham, England. Journalist. m. Gayle Hunnicutt, 1978. *Education:* St John's College, Oxford University. *Literary Appointments:* Member, Board of London Regional Transport, 1984; Historic Buildings Commission, 1985; Museum of London, 1985. *Publications:* City at Risk, 1971; Landlords to London, 1974; Outer London, 1981; Hampstead, 1982; Battle for the Falklands, 1983; With Respect, Ambassador, 1985. *Contributor to:* News Editor, Times Educational Supplement, 1966; Features Editor, London Evening Standard, 1970; Insight Editor, Sunday Times, 1974; Editor, London Evening Standard, 1976; Political Editor, Economist, 1979; Encounter; Politics Quarterly. *Memberships:* Board, British Rail; Municipal Journal Limited. *Literary Agent:* A D Peters. *Address:* 174 Regents Park Road, London NW1, England.

JENKINSON, Keith Anthony, b. 16 May 1938, Rawdon, England. Author/Publisher. m. Maureen Swain, 24 Sep. 1972, Rawdon, 2 sons. *Literary Appointments:* Editor, Historic Commerical, 1972–; Managing Editor, Bus Fayre, 1978–. *Publications:* Preserved Buses, 1976, 2nd revised edition, 1978; Preserved Lorries, 1977; History of West Yorkshire Road Car Co Ltd, 1977; Ledgard Way, 1981; Preserving Commercial Vehicles, 1982; Preserved Military Vehicles, 1983; H V Burlingham of Blackpool, 1983; York City Buses, 1984; Focus on Bristol Lodekka, 1984; National Express – Together We Have Gone Places, 1985. *Contributions to:* Buses Magazine; Historic Commerical; Bus Fayre. *Address:* 42 Coniston Avenue, Queensbury, Bradford, West Yorkshire BD13 2JD, England.

JENNINGS, C Robert, b. 12 Sep. 1929, Eufaula, Alabama, USA. Freelance Writer. m. Mary Alice Robertson, 10 Sep. 1954, Cincinnati, Ohio, 2 daughters. *Education:* BA, English & American Civilisation, Princeton University. *Play:* Confessions of a Nightingale, co-author, based on interviews with Tennessee Williams. *Contributions to:* New York Times; Time Magazine; New York Magazine; Esquire; Saturday Evening Post; Horizon; Playboy; Chatelaine; Cosmopolitan; Ladies Home Journal; Town & Country. *Honour:* Best Articles of the Year, Crown, 1967. *Membership:* Writers Guild. *Literary Agent:* Roberta Pryor, ICM. *Address:* 122 Hart Avenue, Santa Monica, CA 90405, USA.

JENNINGS, Kate, b. 30 May 1946, Brooklyn, New York, USA. Poet. m. Michael Channer McPeak, 9 Aug. 1969, New York City, 2 sons, 1 daughter. *Education:* Hon Degree in English, Marymount College, Tarrytown, New York, *Publications:* Second Sight, 1976; 30th Year to Heaven, 1980. *Contributions to:* American Scholar; Atlantic Monthly; Carleton Miscellany; Carolina Quarterly; Hudson Review; London Magazine; New Republic; North American Review; Poetry; Prairie Schooner; Redbook; Shenandoah; Southern Humanities Review; Southern Poetry Review; Virginia Quarterly. *Honours:* Grand Prize, Writer's Digest Creative Writing Contest, 1974; Visit at Yaddo, 1976; Borestone Mountain Poetry Awards, 1976; Anthology of Magazine Verse and Yearbook of American Poetry, 1980, 81, 84; Sotheby's International Poetry Competition, 1982. *Address:* 34 Chemin Francois Lehmann, 1218 Grand Saconnex, Geneva, Switzerland.

JENNINGS, Paul, b. 20 June 1918, Leamington Spa, England. Journalist. m. Celia Blom, 9 Feb. 1952, London, 3 sons, 3 daughters. *Publications:* Oddly Enough, 1951; Even Oddlier, 1952; Oddly Bodlikins,

1953; Next to Olliness, 1955; Gladly Oddly, 1957; Oodles of Oddlies, 1963; I Was Joking of Course, 1968; The Living Village, 1968; Just a Few Lines, 1969; It's an Odd Thing, But, 1971; I Must Have Imagined It, 1977; Companion to Britain, 1981; A Feast of Days, 1982; Golden Oddlies, 1983; The Book of Nonsense, Editor, 1977; And Now for Something Exactly The Same (novel); for children, The Great Jelly of London, 1967; The Train to Yesterday, 1974. *Contributor to:* The Observer (humour columnist, 1949–66); Punch (regular contributor); Telegraph Magazine; Sunday Times. *Honours:* Recipient, Silver Medal, Royal Society of Arts, 1969. *Memberships:* FRSL; FRSA. *Address:* 25 High Street, Orford, Woodbridge, Suffolk, England.

JENOFF, Marvyne, b. 10 Mar 1942, Winnipeg, Canada. Teacher. *Education:* BA, University of Manitoba, Canada, 1964; Teacher Training. *Literary Appointments:* Fiction Editor: Waves Magazine, Toronto; Editor, New Poet's Handbook, League of Canadian Poets, 1984 and 1985; Judging Committee, Gerald Lampert Memorial Award, League of Canadian Poets, 1984 and 1985. *Publications:* No Lingering Peace (Poetry) 1972; Hollandsong (Poetry) 1975; Editor: New Poet's Handbook 1984 and 1985; The Orphan and the Stranger (Poetry) 1985; The Singular Sister (short fiction), 1986. *Contributions to:* (Reviews) Canadian Forum and Books in Canada; (Poem) Germination etc. *Honour:* Chancellor's Prize for Poetry, University of Manitoba, 1962. *Membership:* League of Canadian Poets. *Address:* c/o League of Canadian Poets.

JEROME, Judson Blair, b. 8 Feb. 1927, Tulsa, Oklahoma, USA. Poet. *Education:* MA, University of Chicago, 1950; PhD, Ohio State University, 1955. *Publications include:* Light in the West (poetry), 1962; The Poet and the Poem (essays), 1963, 3rd edition 1979; The Fell of Dark (novel), 1966; Plays for an Imaginary Theatre (verse plays and autobiographical essays) 1970; I Never Saw... (poetry), 1974; Families of Eden: Communes and the New Anarchism (social criticism), 1974; Thirty Years of Poetry, 1949–79 (collected poems), 1979; Partita in Nothing Flat (poems), 1983; On Being a Poet... (essays); 1986 Poet's Market: How and Where to Publish Your Poetry (markets), 1985. *Contributions to:* Numerous journals. *Honours include:* Amy Lowell Travelling Poetry Fellowship, 1960–61; William Carlos Williams Award for short fiction, 1963. *Address:* 917 Xenia Avenue, Yellow Springs, OH 45387, USA.

JERSILD, Per Christian, b. 14 Mar. 1935, Katrineholm, Sweden. Writer. m. Ulla J, 1960, 2 sons. *Education:* MD. *Publications:* The Animal Doctor, 1975; After the Flood, 1986; also 20 books published in Sweden. *Literary Awards:* Swedish Grand Novel Prize, 1981; Swedish Academy Award, 1982. *Memberships:* Swedish Pen Board. *Address:* Rosensdalsv. 20, 5-19454 Uppl. Vasby, Sweden.

JESIONOWSKI, Jerzy, b. 7 Nov. 1919, Ponikiew Duza. Writer. *Publications:* Niewygodny czlowiek, 1965; Dwadziescia batow, 1966; Nieosadzony, 1968; Z drugiej strony Nieba, 1969; Przygoda w czasie, 1970; Powret pozegnanych, 1971; Przed drugim brzegiem, 1974; Drugi brzeg, 1977; Surmak, 1977; Przystanek w biegu, 1981; Dobrze urodzony, 1982; Nad urwiskiem, 1982; Poszukiwany Albert Peryt, 1983; Rzeka czasu, 1984; Egzylia, 1985. *Literary Awards:* Polish State Priez, 1976. *Memberships:* Member of Management, Association of Polish Writers. *Address:* Solec 115-42, 00-382 Warszawa, Poland.

JETT, Stephen Clinton, b. 1938, Cleveland, Ohio, USA. University Professor. m. 1 son. *Education:* AB, Princeton University, 1960; University of Arizona; PhD, Johns Hopkins University, 1964. *Publications:* Tourism in the Navajo Country; Resources and Planning, 1967; Navajo Wildlands: as long as the rivers shall run, 1967; Man Across the Sea: Problems of Pre-Columbian Contracts, (contributing author), 1971; The House of Three Turkeys, 1977; Ancient Native Americans

(contributing author), 1978; Navajo Architecture: Forms, History and Distributions (co-author), 1981; Navajo Religion and Culture: Seleted Studies (contributing author), 1982; Ancient North Americans (contributing author), 1983; Ancient South Americans (contributing author), 1983. *Contributions to:* Numerous publications including: American Antiquity; Annals of the Association of American Geographers; Encyclopedia Britannica; Economic Botany. *Honours:* Navajo Wildlands, named one of 50 Books of the Year, American Institute of Graphic Arts, 1967, and one of 20 Merit Books of the Year, American Institute of Graphic Arts, 1967, and one of 20 Merit Book Awards, World Publishers Association, 1969; Navajo Architecture, named one of the Outstanding Academic Books and Non-Print Materials of 1981, by Choice, The Journal of College and Research Libraries, American Library Association, 1981. *Membership:* Fellow, Explorers Club. *Address:* Department of Geography, University of California, Davis, CA 95616, USA.

JILER, John Hayes, b. 4 Apr. 1946, New York City, New York, USA. Actor. Writer. *Education:* BA, University of Hartford. *Publications:* Wild Berry Moon, 1982. *Contributor to:* Village Voice. *Literary Awards:* Los Angeles Dramalogue Short Play Award, 1982; San Francisco Dramathon Winner, 1982. *Address:* 93 Nassau Street, No. 915, New York, NY 10038, USA.

JIMENEZ DE CISNEROS Y BAUDIN, Consuelo, b. 24 May 1956, Alicante, Spain. Teacher, Spanish Language and Literature. *Education:* Lic. Philosophy & Letters; Certificate, Teacher of Spanish Language & Literature, 1979. *Publications:* Poetry: El Canto Alucinado, 1975; A Lo Largo del Camino, 1975; Con Las Manos Alzadas, 1978; Diez Canciones para la Escuela, 1983. *Contributor to:* Arbol de Fuego; Item (magazine of University of Alicante); Molinos. *Honours:* Several Literary Prizes. *Memberships:* Sagrada Familia College for Teaching, Alicante; Liceo Español de París; Aula de INBAD (Institute Nacional de Educación a Distancia) de Eindhoven (NL). *Address:* Pintor Velázques 16, 4° izd, Alicante, Spain.

JIRGENS, Karl Edward, b. 5 Sep. 1952, Toronto, Canada. Writer. *Education:* BA, University of Toronto; OCA, Ontario College of Art; MA, PhD, York University, Toronto, Canada. *Literary Appointments:* Editor-in-Chief, Rampike Magazine, 1979–; Managing Editor, Open Letter Magazine, 1980–81; English Instructor, York University, Toronto, 1982–. *Major Publication:* Strappado, 1984. *Contributor to:* Only Paper Today; Impulse; Writing; Open Letter; Books in Canada; Canadian Literature Magazine; Rampike Magazine; and others. *Honours:* Ontario Arts Council Award for Writing, 1978, 1982. *Memberships:* Freelance Editors Association of Canada; Writers Union of Canada; League of Canadian Poets; Canadian Periodical Publishers Association. *Literary Agent:* Lucinda Vardey, Toronto, Canada. *Address:* 95 Rivercrest Road, Toronto, Ontario, M6S 4H7, Canada.

JOANS, Barbara, b. 28 Feb. 1935, New York, USA. Anthropologist; Writer. m. Kenneth Harmon, 2 sons. *Education:* BA Philosophy, Brooklyn College, 1958–61; MA Sociology-Anthropology, New York University, 1961–65; PhD Anthropology, City University of New York Graduate Centre, 1968–75. *Publications:* Identity: Female, 1975; The Women's Workshop, 1979; How The Youth View the Youth Entitlement Demonstration, 1961; Sex Roles, 1982. *Contributions to:* Medical Menopause, 1976; Health in the Middle Years, 1977; University Under Siege, 1978; Encyclopedia of Indians of the Americas, 1979; Criminal Justice Ethics; National Women's Anthropology Newsletter; Practicing Anthropology; Lilith: A Feminist Quarterly; Sacramento Anthropological Society Journal. *Honours Include:* Charles Kriser Foundation Fellowship, 1962–63; Research Associate, Anthropology Board, UCSC, California, 1982–85. *Memberships:* Academy of Criminal Justice Sciences; American Anthropological Association; Society of Anthropology and Humanism; National Women's Studies Association; Women and

Anthropology Association; Association of Political and Legal Anthropologists; Institute for Criminal Justice Ethics; Institute for the Cross-Cultural Study of Crime and Justice; Society for Applied Anthropology. *Address:* Department of Anthropology, San Jose State University, San Jose, CA 95192, USA.

JOENPELTO, Eeva Elisabet, b. 17 June 1921, Sammatti, Finland. Writer. m. Jarl Hellemann, 5 Jan. 1945, separated 1975, 1 son. *Publications:* Johannes, 1953; Neito kulkee vettan paella, 1955; Betas kaikista ovista, 1974; Kuin kekale kadessa, 1976; Sataa suolaista vetta, 1978; Eteisiin ja Kynniksille, 1980; Elaman rouva, rouve Glad, 1982 (29 novels). *Honours:* State Prize, 1951, 55, 61, 69, 74, 83; Phil. doctor honoris cause, 1982. *Memberships:* Writers Society of Finland; PEN. *Address:* 09220 Sammatti, Myllykylä, Finland.

JOENPOLVI, Martti Kalewi, b. 19 Apr. 1936, Käkisalmi, Finland. Author. *Publications:* 14 short stories and novels. *Honours:* Literary Prize, State of Finland, 1974, 1981; Literary Prize, City of Tampere, 1960, 1962, 1972, 1976, 1978, 1981, 1983, 1985. *Memberships:* Suomen Kirjailijaliitto r y; Finnish PEN Club. *Address:* K J Gummerus Oy, PL 479, 00101 Helsinki, Finland.

JOHANNESSEN, Matthias, b. 3 Jan. 1930, Reykjavik, Iceland. m. Johanna Kristveig Ingolfsdottir, 2 sons. *Education:* MA, University of Iceland, 1955. *Literary Appointments:* Past Chairman, Union of Icelandic Authors; Society of Icelandic Writers; Journalist 1951–59, Chief Editor, Morgunbladid, 1959; Chairman, Council of Icelandic Writers, 1976. *Publications:* 30 to 40 books, twelve being of poetry, the most notable being, Njala islenskem skaldskap, 1958; Borgin hló, 1958; Hólmgönguljoo, 1960; Jörd úr aegi, 1961; Vor ur vetri, 1963; I dag skein sól, höf. raedir vio Pál Isófsson, 1964; Mörg eru dags augu, 1972; Visur um vötn, 1972; Biographies, Kjarvalsker, 1974; Gunnlagur Scheving, 1974; Dagur ei meir, (poetry), 1975; Morgunn i Mai, (poetry), 1978; Tveggia bakha Vedur, Poetry 1981; Djafur Thors, Biography 1952; Several books translated into Danish, Swedish and English, poems into other languages. *Contributor to:* Numerous articles, poems and short stories, periodicals; plays presented on radio, television and National theatre. *Memberships:* Celebration Committee, 1966; Board Member, Menntamalarad Islands (Cultural Council of Iceland, 1972; Chairman, Committee 1100 Years of Settlement, Iceland, 1974; Member, Literacy Council Alemna bokafelagid. *Literary Agent:* AB Almenua Dokafelagid, Rykjavik. *Address:* Reynimel 25A, 107 Reykjavik, Iceland.

JOHANSEN, Bruce Elliott, b. 30 Jan. 1950, San Diego, California, USA. Author; Professor; Newspaper Reporter; Social Activist. *Education:* BA, University of Washington, 1972; MA, University of Minnesota, Minneapolis, 1975; PhD, University of Washington, Seattle, 1979. *Literary Appointments:* Seattle Times, 1970–76; Assistant Professor, University of Nebraska at Omaha, 1982–. *Publications:* Wasi' chu: The Continuing Indian Wars (New York: Monthly Review, 1979; Spanish; Fondo de Culture y Economics, Mexico City) (with Roberto F Maestas); The Forgotten Founders: Benjamin Franklin, the Iroquois and the Nationale for American Revolution, 1982; El Pueblo: The Gallegos Family's American Journey 1503–80 (Monthly Review) (with Roberto F Maestas), 1983; This New Man, the American: Ideas, Experience, Imagination (in press). *Contributions to:* History Today (London); Washington Post; Seattle Times; The Nation; The Progressive; Los Angeles Times; International Herald-Tribune; Newsday; Denver Post, etc. *Honours:* Sigma Delta Chi, First Place, Public Affairs Reporting for Seattle Times, 1974; University of Nebraska Research Fellowship, 1983; Carey McWilliams Fellowship (La Vuz, Seattle), 1985. *Address:* Department of Communication, University of Nebraska at Omaha, Omaha, NE 68182, USA.

JOHANSON, Donald Carl, b. 28 June 1943, Chicago, Illinois, USA. Paleoanthropologist. Divorced.

Education: BA, University of Illinois, 1966; MA, 1970, PhD, 1974, University of Chicago; DSc, (Hon), John Carro University, 1979. *Publications:* Lucy: The Beginning of Humankind, 1981; Book Review: The Fossils Hominids and an Introduction of their Context, 1980; Dating of South Africa Hominids Sites, 1982; The Human Career, The Humanist, 1983. *Contributor to:* Science Year – The World Book Science Annual; National Geographic Magazine. *Honours:* American Book Award, 1982; Distinguished Service Award, American Humanist Association, 1983; Golden Plate American Academy of Achievement, 1976; Professional Achievement Award, 1980; Outstanding Achievement Award, 1979; Golden Mercury International Award, 1982. *Literary Agent:* Donald Cutler, Sterling Lord Agency, New York City, USA. *Address:* Institute of Human Origins, 2453 Bridge Road, Berkeley, CA 94709, USA.

JOHANSSON-BACKE, Karl Erik, b. 24 Nov. 1914, Stockholm, Sweden. Teacher (retired 1963); Author. m. Kerstin Gunhild Bergquist, 21 Nov. 1943, 1 son, 3 daughters. *Education:* Degree, High School Teacher. *Publications:* A Pole in the River, 1950; Daybreak (novel), 1954; Lust and Flame (poetry), 1981; The Mountain of Temptation (novel), 1983; The Ghost Aviator (documentary), 1985; author of 21 books and 12 plays. *Honours:* Many literary awards from 1961–85. *Memberships:* The Swedish Authors Federation; The Swedish Playwrights Federation. *Literary Agents:* Folmer Hansen (plays); Bonniers Norsbits, Stockholm; CEWE, Bjasta (books). *Address:* Kopmangstan 56, 83133 Östersund, Sweden.

JOHN, Donas, b. 25 Nov. 1937, USA. Writer. *Education:* AA, Los Angeles Technical College, California, USA. *Contributions to:* Peace is Our Profession, anthology, 1981; TAMJ anthology; Vega; Tradewinds; Connecticut Fireside and Review of Books; West Coast Writer's Conspiracy; Lyrical Voices; An international Poetry Anthology; Writing; Electrum; Lean-Frog; Valballa; Princeton Spectrum Greyledge Review; North Country Anvil; Poetry of the Year; Cyclo-Flame; Notable Poets; Grass Roots Forum; The Archer; Best in Poetry; Poet Lore; Anthology of World Poets; Cathartic; Chaparral Poet; Stonecloud-Pacific Perceptions; Western Poetry; Poetry Venture; Voices International; Encore; Yearbook of Modern Poetry; others. *Honours include:* Guest Poet, Santa Monica City College Creative Writing Classes. *Membership:* Feminist Writers Guild. *Address:* 10110 Regent Street, Palms, CA 90034, USA.

JOHN, M P, b. 29 Sep. 1911, Kerala, India. Editor, New Times Observer. *Publications:* Eternal Christ; Inner Space Voyages, Poems; Evolving Reality; In His Own Image Man Created God; Earth's Flowers, poems; Cosmic Culture for Peace and Progress; The City Down Below, poems. *Honours:* President: Pondicherry Cultural Academy; World Union, Pondicherry Branch; Pondicherry Environmental Society. *Address:* New Times Observer, Pondicherry, India.

JOHN, Ursula Moran, 19 Apr. 1911, Petersfield, Hampshire, England. Writer of Children's books. m. Conrad Southey John, 28 Sep. 1935, North Stoneham, England, 4 sons. *Education:* private; Winchester Art College. *Major Publications:* Some 70 titles since 1931, including: Jean-Pierre (A & C Block); Adventures of the little Wooden Horse; Gobbolino the Witch's Cat; Further adventures of Gobbolino & the little Wooden Horse; The Nine Lives of Island Mackenzie; The Noble Hawks; Bogwoppit; Jeffy the Burglar's Cat; The Good Little Christmas Tree; The Cruise of the Happy-Go-Gay; Bellabelinda & the No-Good Angel; The Moonball. *Contributions to:* Cricket USA; Puffin Post; The EGG; Storyteller 1, 2, Christmas Numbers; Australian Magazines. *Memberships:* West of England Writers' Guild. *Literary Agent:* Curtis Brown. *Address:* Court Farm House, Beckford, Nr Tewkesbury, Gloucestershire, England.

JOHNSON, Anthony Leonard, b. 4 May 1939, London. University Professor; Editor; Writer. m. Rosanna Autera, 14 Sep. 1968, London, 1 son. *Education:* Wellington College, 1952–57; Oxford University, 1957–62; British Council Research Scholar, 1963–64. *Appointments:* Lecturer in English, Siena University, 1964–66; Faculty of Languages, 1966–67, Associate Professor in English Language, Faculty of Economics and Commerce, 1967–84, Pisa University; Lecturer in English Language, Scuola Normale Superiore, Pisa, 1970–81; Faculty of Education, 1974–81, Professor of English Language and Literature, Faculty of Education, 1981–83, Florence University; Professor of English Language and Literature, Faculty of Letters and Philosophy, Pisa University, 1983–; Correspondent, TES, 1969–72; Correspondent, TLS, 1972–76; Review Editor, Poetics Today, Tel Aviv, 1981–. *Publications:* Poetry: The Arc of the Sun, 1974; Marigolds, Stilts, Solitudes: Selected Poems, 1956–84, 1984. Literary Criticism: Sign and Structure in the Poetry of T S Eliot, 1976; Readings of Anthony and Cleopatra and King Lear, Pisa 1979; W B Yeats: The Tower Pisa, 1985. *Contributor to:* Poems in Littack; Expression One; New Headland; Pick; Orbis; Tomorrow; Oxford; The Village Review; Chapman; Acumen; L'Immaginazione; Lecce; Hellas, Florence. Papers in ELH (English Literary History); Poetics Today; Anglistica, Naples; Linguistica E Lettratura, Pisa; Analysis: Quanerni di Anglistica, Pisa. *Memberships:* Italian Association for English Studies, 1977–, Member of Executive Council, 1981–86. Editor of Association's Journal, Analysis: Quanderni di Anglistiuca, 1982–86. *Address:* Le Gondole, Via Zamenhof, 14–57, I–56100 Pisa, Italy.

JOHNSON, Edwin Clark (Toby), b. 4 Aug. 1945, San Antonio, Texas, USA. Psychotherapist. *Education:* BA, University of St Louis, Missouri, 1968; MA, Philosophy & Religion, CIIS, 1976; PhD, Integral Counselling & Psychotherapy, California Institute of Integral Studies, 1978. *Major Publications:* The Myth of the Great Secret: A Search for Spiritual Meaning in the Face of Emptiness, 1982; In Search of God in the Sexual Underworld: A Mystical Journey, 1983. *Contributor to:* Psychological Perspectives; The Advocate; New York Native; Philadelphia Gay News; Blueboy Magazine; Firsthand Magazine; and others. *Honours:* 2 citations, Atlantic Monthly Writing Centest, 1965; Phi Beta Kappa, Alpha Sigma Nu, 1968. *Literary Agent:* John Brockman, New York City. *Address:* 915 E Elmira, San Antonio, TX 78212, USA.

JOHNSON, Elizabeth Scott (Serson), b. 11 Sep. 1921, Ottawa, Canada. Editor. m. (1) Harry G Johnson, 26 May 1948, Cambridge, Massachusetts, USA (2) John A Simpson, 23 Aug. 1980, Chicago, Illinois, 1 son, 1 daughter. *Education:* BA, University of Toronto; MS, Columbia University. *Literary Appointments:* Member, Keynes Memorial Committee, Royal Economic Society, 1953–73; Editor, University of Chicago Press, 1978–83; Consulting Editor, Basil Blackwell, 1984–. *Publications:* Editor, The Collected Writings of John Maynard Keynes, Volumes XV and XVI, 1971, XVII, 1977, XVIII, 1978, The Shadow of Keynes (with Harry G Johnson), 1978. *Contributions:* of articles to various professional journals. *Address:* 1119 East 53rd Street, Chicago, IL 60615, USA.

JOHNSON, James Ralph, b. 20 May 1922, Fort Payne, Alabama, USA. Artist; Author. *Education:* BS, Howard College, Birmingham, Alabama, 1943. *Publications include:* Anyone Can Live Off the Land, 1961; Anyone Can Backpack in Comfort, 1965; Advanced Camping Techniques, 1967; Pepper, 1967; Blackie, The Gorilla, 1968; Ringtail, 1968; Moses' Band of Chimpanzees, 1969; Animal Paradise, 1969; Everglades Advanture, 1970; Southern Swamps of America, 1970; Photography for Young People, 1971; Zoos of Today, 1971; Animals and Their food, 1972. *Honour:* Junior Literary Guild Selection, 1971. *Memberships include:* Western Writers of America; Outdoors Writers of America. *Address:* Box 5295, Santa Fe, NM 87501, USA.

JOHNSON, James Richard, b. 28 June 1947, England. Journalist. m. Pauline Dawn Wheatley, 11 Sep. 1971, Leigh-on-Sea, 2 sons. *Literary Appointments:* Technical Reporter, Technical Editor, Deputy Editor, Motor Boat and Yachting Magazine; Editor, Yachting World magazine, 1981. *Contributions to:* Marine and marine technical journals, 1970–. *Address:* 42 Chapmans Walk, Leigh-on-Sea, Essex, England.

JOHNSON, Jennifer Hilary, b. 2 Nov. 1945, Bristol, England. Writer of Poetry. 1 son. *Publications:* (poems) Going Home, 1980; Becoming and Other Poems, 1983. *Contributions to:* Poems in Circle in the Square Poetry Anthology, 1982; Arvon Foundation Poetry Competition, 1980, anthology; South West Review; A Celebration. *Honours:* Awards from South West Arts for Poetry Collection, 1978, 1979, 1982, 1983. *Memberships:* The Poetry Society; The Circle in the Square. *Address:* Flat 1, Style House, 7 Raddenstile Lane, Exmouth, Devon EX8 2JH, England.

JOHNSON, (John) Stephen, b. 3 June 1947, Mansfield, Notinghamshire, England. Inspector, Ancient Monuments, English Heritage. m. Margaret Stephens, 26 July 1975, Norwich, 1 son, 1 daughter. *Education:* BA, MA, DPhil, Oxford University. *Publications:* The Roman Forts of the Saxon Shore, 1976; Later Roman Britain, 1979; Late Roman Fortifications, 1983. *Contributor to:* Numerous Archaelogical Journals. *Address:* English Heritage, Fortress House, 23 Savile Row, London W1X 2HE, England.

JOHNSON, Louis (Albert), b. 27 Sep. 1924, Wellington, New Zealand. Writer; Teacher. m. Cecilia Margery Ware Wilson, 15 Dec. 1970, Melbourne, 1 son, 1 daughter. *Education:* New Zealand Teacher's Certificate, 1951. *Literary Appointments:* Editor, Junior School Publications, Department of Education, Wellington, 1963–69; OIC Bureau of Literature Papua New Guinea, 1969; Writers; Representative, New Zealand Literary Fund Advisory Committee, 1982–. *Publications:* Editor, New Zealand Poetry Yearbook (Annual) 1951–64; New Worlds for Old, 1956; Bread and a Pension, 1964; Land Like a Lizard, 1970; Fires and Patterns, 1975; Coming and Going, 1981; Winter Apples, 1984. *Contributor to:* Poetry London; Poetry, Chicago; Poetry Australia; The Austrlian Landfall; Islands; Meanjin; Coastlines; Epoch; Yorkshire Post; Critical Quarterly; Ariel; Sydney Bulletin; Compass; Melbourne Age; Outposts; Angry Penguins; Artisan; Nimrod, etc. *Honours:* New Zealand Book Award (poetry) for Fires and Patterns, 1975; Writers Fellowship, Victoria University of Wellington, 1980. *Memberships:* PEN (New Zealand) Centre, 1950–, Secretary 5 years; Fellowship of Australian Writers, 1970–79. *Address:* 4 Te Motu Road, Pukerva Bay, New Zealand.

JOHNSON, Michael Ross, b. 23 Nov. 1938, Delphi, Indiana, USA. Journalist. m. Jacqueline Zimbardo, 28 May 1966, Brie-comte-Robert, France, 3 daughters. *Education:* BA, San Jose State College, California; Certificate, Columbia University, New York. *Literary Appointments:* Paris Bureau Chief, McGraw-Hill World News, 1971–76; Director, McGraw-Hill World News, New York, 1976–82; Editor-in-Chief, International Management, 1982–. *Address:* 45, Abbey Gardens, London NW8 2AS, England.

JOHNSON, Owen Verne, b. 22 Feb. 1946, Madison, Wisconsin, USA. Journalism Teacher; Historian. m. Marta Kucerova, 17 July 1969, Zelezny Brod, Czechoslovakia, 2 daughters. *Education:* BA, Washington State University, 1968; MA, 1970, PhD, 1978, History, University of Michigan. *Appointments:* Sports Editor, General News Reporter, Pullman (Wash) Herald, 1961–67; Reporter, KWSU Radio/TV, Pullman, 1965–74; Producer, Editor, Reporter, WUOM, Ann Arbour, 1969–77; Instructor, Russian and European Studies, History, 1970–79, Administrative Assistant, Russian & European Studies, 1978–79, University of Michigan; Assistant Professor, School of Journalism, S Illinois University, 1979–80; Assistant Professor, School of Journalism, Indiana University, 1980–. *Publications:* Slovakia 1918–1838: Education and the Making of a Nation, 1985. *Contributor to:* 14 Scholarly articles, essays, in numerous journals including, East European Social History; East Central Europe; Slavic and European Education Review; Bohemia etc; Editor, Clio Among the Media, 1983–84; Editor, Czech Marks, 1982–84. *Honours:* Sigma Delta Chi Excellence in Journalism Award, State of Washington, 1966; Many Grants and Fellowships; etc. *Memberships:* American Historical Association; American Association for the Advancement of Slavic Studies; Association for Education in Journalism and Mass Communication, many offices; Czechoslovak History Conference; Immigration History Society; International Association for Mass Communication Research; etc. *Address:* School of Journalism, Indiana University, Bloomington, IN 47405, USA.

JOHNSON, Stella Gertrude, b. 23 May 1910. Civil Servant. m. Harold Leland Johnson. *Education:* Sacramento City College, University of California, Berkeley, California, USA. *Appointments:* Ed: Instrimentation Techn; Tax Cons; Editor, Poetry magazines. *Publications:* Dressing for the Part, 1976; Notes for the First Orchestra, 1977; Slice of Time/Bone in My Throat, 1978; Three Panels for December, 1979; numerous anthologies. *Contributor to:* Blue Unicorn; Attention Please; In a Nutshell; Ninbus Basin 3; Impulse Press; Voices Int. *Honours:* Over 60 Awards, various poetry competitions, including 2 1st awards, 1979. *Memberships:* Poetry Society; American League of American Penwomen; Ina Coolbirth Cir; Poetry Organisation of Women. *Address:* 708 Inglewood Drive, Broderick, CA 95605, USA.

JOHNSON, Stowers, b. Brentwood, Essex. Headmaster (retired). *Education:* BA, College of St Mark, Chelsea; Queen Mary College School of Slavonic Studies, University of London. *Literary Appointments:* Principal, Dagenham Literary Institute, 1936–39; Headmaster, Aveley School, 1939–68; Editor, Anglo-Soviet Journal, 1966–68. *Major Publications:* Branches Green & Branches Black, 1944; London Saga, 1946; The Mundane Tree, 1947; Mountains and No Mules, 1949; Sonnets, They Say, 1949; When Fountains Fall, 1961; Prose, before and after Puck, 1953; Gay Bulgaria, 1964; Yugoslav Summer, 1967; Turkish Panorama, 1969; Collector's Luck, 1968; The Two Faces of Russia, 1969; Agents Extraordinary, 1975; Headmastering Man, 1986. *Contributor to:* Various journals. *Memberships:* Past Treasurer, Poetry Society; International PEN; Fellow, Royal Society of Arts; Fellow, PEN. *Address:* Corbiere, 45 Rayleigh Road, Hutton, Brentwood, Essex, England.

JOHNSON, William Weber, b. 18 Dec. 1909, Mattoon Illinois, USA. Writer. *Education:* BA, DePauw University, 1932; MA, University of Illinois, 1933. *Publications:* Sam Houston, 1953; Kelly Blue, 1960 revised edition 1979; Birth of Texas, 1960; Captain Cortés Conquers Mexico, 1960; Mexico 1962; Andean Republics 1965; Forty-Niners 1968; Heroic Mexico, 1968; Baja California, 1971; Story of Sea Otters, 1974; Cortés, 1975. *Contributor to:* Newspapers and magazines including: Saturday Evening Post; Holiday; New York Times Book Review; Los Angeles Times Book Review; Smithsonian. *Honours:* Guggenheim Fellowship 1959; Commonwealth Gold Medal for non-fiction, 1969. *Address:* 4285 Maryland, San Diego, CA 92103, USA.

JOHNSTON, George Benson, b. 7 Oct. 1913, Hamilton, Ontario, Canada. Retired University Professor, m. Jeanne McRae, 3 July 1944, White Lake, 3 sons, 3 daughters. *Education:* BA, MA, Toronto. *Publications:* The Cruising Auk, 1959; The Saga of Gisli, 1963; Home Free, 1966; Happy Enough, 1972; The Faroe Islanders Saga, 1974; The Greenlanders Saga, 1975; Taking a Grip, 1978; Rocky Shores, 1981; Auk Redivivus, 1981; Wind Over Romsdal, 1982; Ask Again, 1985; Pastor Bodvar's Letter, 1985. *Contributor to:* New Yorker; University of Toronto Quarterly; Atlantic;

Harpers; Spectator; London Mercury; Canadian Literature; Malahat Review; etc. *Honours:* LL D Honoris causa, Queen's University, 1972; D Litt, Honoris causa, Carleton University, 1978; Canada Council Senior Arts Fellowship, 1973. *Membership:* Viking Society for Northern Research. *Address:* RR1 Athelstan, Quebec J0S 1A0, Canada.

JOHNSTON, (Sir) Charles Hepburn, b. 11 Mar. 1912, London, England. Retired Diplomat. *Education:* Winchester School; Balliol College, University of Oxford, England, 1930–34. *Major Publications:* The View from Steamer Point, 1964; Mo & Other Orignals, 1971; The Brink of Jordan, 1972; Estuary in Scotland & Other poems, 1974; Pushkin's Eugene Onegin (translation), 1977; Selected Poems, 1985. *Address:* 32 Kingston House South, London SW7, England.

JOHNSTONE, Iain Gilmour, b. 8 Apr. 1943, England. Film Critic. m. Maureen Hammond, 1957, 2 daughters. *Education:* LL B Honours; Distinction, Solicitor's finals. *Literary Appointments:* Film Critic, The Sunday Times. *Publications:* The Arnhem Report, 1977; The Man With No Name, 1980; Dustin Hoffman, 1984. *Address:* 16 Tournay Road, London SW6, England.

JOHNSTONE, Robert. b. 30 Oct. 1951, Belfast, Ireland. Author. *Education:* BA, English, New University of Ulster, 1973. *Appointments:* Editorial Committee, Fortnightly Magazine; Co-Editor, Honest Ulsterman Magazine. *Publications:* Our Lives Are Swiss, 1976; Trio Poetry 1, with Will Colhoun & David Park, 1980; Images of Belfast, 1983; Breakfast in a Bright Room, 1983; All Shy Wildness, Editor, 1985. *Contributor to:* Caret; Connacht Tribune; Fortnight; Gown; Honest Ulsterman; Aquarius; North New Poetry; Oxford Poetry; Poetry Review; Paris-Atlantic; Trimestrial Poetry Review; Northern Lights; Sunday Independent; Ulster Architect; etc. *Honour:* Walter Allen Prize, 1973. *Membership:* English Society, Queen's University, Belfast. *Address:* 7 Lower Crescent, Belfast BT7 1NR, Northern Ireland.

JOKINEN, Ulla Kaarina Vellamo, b. 26 Nov. 1921, Viipuri, Finland. University Professor. m. Olavi 28 June 1944, Tampere, 2 sons, 2 daughters. *Education:* PhD, University of Helsinki. *Publications:* Doctoral thesis: Les relatifs en moyen francais. Formes et fonctions. Annales Academiae Scientiarum Fennicae, Dissertationes Humanarum Litterarum 14, Helsinki 1978; Reviews in the Neuphilologische Mitteilungen, Helsinki, 1962, 1984, 1985; 60 Literary translations mainly from French and Italian. *Contributions to:* Verlaine; Lyric Poet; Suomalainen Suomi, Helsinki, 1967; Numerous articles and reviews in Aamulehti, Tampere, Finland. *Honours:* Coppet Literary Award 1959, 1967. *Memberships:* Finnish Society of Authors; Finnish Society of Playwrights; Federation of Finnish Translators and Interpreters. *Literary Agent:* Finnish Society of Playwrights. *Address:* Uudenmaankatu 31 A 4, 00120 Helsinki, Finland.

JOKOSTRA, Peter, b. 5 May 1912. Literary Critic; Novelist. *Education:* Degrees, Universities of Frankfurt, Munich and Berlin, Germany. *Literary Appointments include:* Publisher's Reader; Press Officer; Publicity Officer. *Publications:* An der besonnten Mauer, 1958; Magische Strasse, 1960; Hinab zu den Sternen, 1961; Die gewendete Haut, 1967; Feuerzonen, 1976. *Contributions to:* Die Welt; Rheinische Post; Munchner Merkur; Akzente; Merkur; Westermanns Monatshefte Eckart; Sinn Und From; Neue Deutsche Literatur; La Voix des Poetes. *Honours:* Poetry Prize, Ministry of Culture, Democratic Republic of Germany, 1958; Andreas Gryphius Prize, 1965; Rheinland Pfaiz Maj Art Prize, 1979. *Address:* In der Stehle 38, 5461 Kasbach, Federal Republic of Germany.

JOLLIFFE, Lee Baldwin, b. 25 Aug. 1953, Fredericksburg, Virginia, USA. Writer. *Education:* BA, Lindenwood College, St Charles, 1974; MA, Ohio State University, Columbus, 1978; PhD Candidate, Ohio University, Athens, Ohio. *Appointments:* Newspaper Columnist, North Side Herald, Columbus, 1982, The

Booster, Columbus, 1983–84; Restaurant Reviewer, Ohio Magazine, Columbus, 1982–84; Contributing Editor, Living Single Magazine, Columbus, 1983–84; Research Writer, Battelle Memorial Institute, 1984–85; Lecturer, Ohio State University, 1982–84; Teaching Associate, Ohio University, Athens, 1984–85. *Contributor to:* More than 120 articles in professional magazines, books, journals in USA; Science writing published in magazines, in US, Canada, Japan. *Honour:* Feature Writing Award, University of Missouri, Columbia, 1974. *Memberships:* American Society of Journalists and Authors; Kappa Tau Alpha; Sigma Delta Chi. *Address:* 458 Vermont Place, Columbus, OH 43201, USA.

JONAS, Ann, b. 15 July 1919, Joplin, Missouri, USA. Poet. m. Walter H Jonas, 30 Mar. 1944, Louisville, Kentucky, USA, 1 daughter. *Education:* Graduate, Goodman Theatre, Chicago, Illinois. *Contributions to:* Several anthologies including: Dark Unsleeping Land, 1960; The Diamond Anthology, 1971; Ipso Facto, 1975; Dan River Anthology, 1985; Lawrence of Nottingham: A Poetry Anthology for D H Lawrence, 1985; Literary journals including: Adena; Approacher; The Poetry Review; Haiku Journals including: American Haiku; Haiku (Canada); Haiku West. *Honours:* Yaddo Fellowship, 1968; Cecil Hemly Memorial Award, Poetry Society of America, 1972; Henry Rago Award, The New York Poetry Forum, 1972; Edwin Markham Poetry Prize, Eugene V Debs Foundation, co-winner, 1977; Eleanor B North Award, International Poetry Society, England, finalist, 1975; Caddo Writing Center Award, 1985. *Membership:* Poetry Society of America. *Address:* 2425 Ashwood Drive, Louisville, KY 40205, USA.

JONASSON, Jonas, b. 3 May 1931, Reykjavik, Iceland. Broadcaster. m. Sigrun Sigurdardottir, 14 Mar. 1964, Reykjavik, 3 daughters. *Publications:* Bru milli heima, (Bridge Between Worlds), 1972; Polli, (Story of Me and the Boys), 1973; Glerhusid, (Glasshouse; Play), 1978; Einbjorn Hansson, (Dear Me), 1981; Kvoldgestir, (Evening Guests), 1983. *Contributions to:* Numerous weekly and daily papers as columnist. *Honour:* Reykjavik City Council Award, Best Book for Young People, 1974. *Membership:* Writer's Union of Iceland. *Literary Agent:* Vaka-Helgafell. *Address:* PO Box 525, 602 Akureyri, Iceland.

JONES, Christopher Dennis, b. 13 Dec. 1949, New York, New York, USA. Playwright. m. Gwendoline Shirley Rose, 18 Aug. 1979, London. *Education:* BA English Literature, University of Pittsburgh. *Literary Appointments:* Resident Playwright, Carnaby Street Theatre, London, England, 1975–76; Resident Playwright, New Hope Theatre Company, London, 1977–78. *Publications:* Plays: Passing Strangers, 1976; Nasty Corners, 1977; New Signals, 1978; In Flight Reunion, 1979; Sterile Landscape, 1982; Ralph Bird's River Race, 1985; Dying Hairless With A Rash, 1985. *Contributions to:* Arts Review. *Membership:* Writer's Guild of Great Britain. *Literary Agent:* Fraser and Dunlop, 91 Regents Street, London W1R 8RU. *Address:* c/o Richard Wakeley, Fraser and Dunlop, 91 Regent Street, London W1R 8RU, England.

JONES, David Gareth, b. 28 Aug. 1940, Cardiff, Wales. University Professor. m. Beryl Watson, 30 July 1966, Newcastle-upon-Tyne, 2 sons, 2 daughters. *Education:* BSc, University College, London, 1961; MBBS, University College Hospital Medical School, London, 1965; DSc, University of Western Australia, 1976. *Major Publications:* Teilhard De Chardin, 1965; Synapses & Synaptosomes, 1975; Genetic Engineering, 1978; Our Fragile Brains, 1981; Neurons & Synapses, 1981; Brave New People, 1984; Current Topics in Research on Synapses Volumes 1 & 2 (editor), 1984. *Contributor to:* Numerous Scientific & Christian magazines. *Address:* Department of Anatomy, University of Otago, P O Box 913, Dunedin, New Zealand.

JONES, Glyn, b. 28 Feb. 1905. School Teacher, Retired, *Education:* St Paul's College, Cheltenham,

England. *Publications:* Short Stories: The Blue Bed, 1937; The Water Music, 1944; Selected Short stories, 1971; Welsh Heirs, 1977. Verse: Poems, 1939; The Dream of Jake Hopkins, 1954; Selected Poems, 1975; The Beach of Falesa, verse libretto, 1974. Novels: The Valley, The City, The Village, 1956, 80; The Learning Lark, 1960; The Island of Apples, 1965. Essays: The Dragon Has Two Tongues, 1968; Profiles, with J Rowlands, 1980. Translations of Welsh Poetry into English: When the Rosebush Brings Forth Apples, 1980; Honeydew on the Wormwood, 1984. *Contributions to:* The Adelph; Life and Letters Today; Guardian; Times; Anglo-Welsh Review; Poetry, Chicago, USA; Poetry, Hong Kong; Fine Madness, USA; Lingus; Helix, Australia. *Honours:* Major Prize, Welsh Arts Council, 1972; DLitt, University of Wales, 1974. *Memberships:* 1st Chairman, English Language Section, Yr Academi Gymreig. *Address;* 158 Manor Way, Whitchurch, Cardiff, South Glamorgan, Wales.

JONES, Gwyn Owain, b. 29 Mar. 1917, Cardiff, Wales. Director, National Museum of Wales, 1968–77, Author. *Education:* MA, DSc, Jesus College, University of Oxford; PhD, University of Sheffield. *Major Publications:* Atoms & the Universe, 1956, 3rd edition, 1973; Glass, 1956, 2nd edition, 1971; (novels) The Catalyst, 1960; Personal File, 1962; Now, 1965; The Conjuring Show, 1981. *Contributor to:* Anglo-Welsh Review; Planet; formerly to various professional & physical journals. *Honours:* CBE, 1978. *Memberships:* English Language Section, Yr. Academi Gymreig (Chairman 1978–81). *Address:* Ivy Cottage, Hudnall's Loop, St Briavel's Common, Nr Lydney, Gloucestershire, GL15 6SG, England.

JONES, Heather Windsor, b. 18 July 1955, Shrewsbury, Shropshire, England. Journalist. *Education:* HND Agriculture, Harper Adams Agricultural College. *Literary Appointments:* Agricultural Correspondent, Shropshire Weekly Newspapers, 1982–. *Contributions to:* The Farmer; Farmers' Guardian; Farmers Weekly. *Membership:* Guild of Agricultural Journalists. *Address:* 127 Wenlock Road, Shrewsbury, Shropshire, England.

JONES, Jay Jeffrey, b. 18 Feb. 1946, Albuquerque, New Mexico, USA. TV Commercials Writer/Director. m. Frances Bruce, 21 Dec. 1979, Prestwich, 1 son. *Appointments:* Joint Editor, Word Works Magazine, 1974–76; Editor, New Yorkshire Writing, 1976–78. *Publications:* Plays Produced: The Lizard King, 1981; Rivers of Blood, commission by Foco Novo, New York, 1982, London, 1983. *Contributor to:* Transatlantic Review; Agenda; Science Fiction Monthly; The Savoy Book; International Times; etc. *Membership:* Directors' Guild of Great Britain. *Address:* 13/15 Northgate, Heptonstall, Hebden Bridge, West Yorkshire HX7 7ND, England.

JONES, John, b. 1924, Burma. College Fellow. *Education:* MA, University of Oxford, England. *Publications:* The Egotistical Sublime: A History of Wordsworth's Imagination, 1954; On Aristole and Greek Tragedy, 1962; John Keats Dream of Truth, 1969; The Same God, 1971; Editor, The Study of Good Letters, by H W Garrod, 1963; Dostoevsky, 1983. *Contributor to:* Blackfriars; Observer; Times Literary Supplement; Sunday Telegraph; New Statesman; Spectator; Proceedings of the British Academy. *Address:* c/o Merton College, Oxford, England.

JONES, John Griffin, b. 18 Oct. 1955, Jackson, Mississippi, USA. Attorney. m. Mary Arrington, 27 June 1981, Prentiss, Mississippi, 1 son. *Education:* BA, JD, University of Mississippi. *Publications:* Mississippi Writers Talking, volume 1, 1982, volume 11, 1983. *Contributions to:* Journal of Mississippi History, book reviewer. *Address:* 1833 Laurel, Jackson, MS 39202, USA.

JONES, John Llewelyn, b. 14 June 1916, Llangunllo, Wales. Journalist. m. Dorothy Beryl Goodwin Hawkins, 13 Sep. 1952, Bristol, 1 son, 1 daughter. *Education:*

University of Wales; Jesus College, Oxford. *Publications:* Crafts from the Countryside 1975; Schoolin's Log, 1980. *Contributions to:* Country Life; Farmers Weekly; Country Quest and regional countryside monthlies. *Address:* 46 Edward Road, Clevedon, Avon, BS21 7DT, England.

JONES, Madison Percy, b. 1925, Nashville, Tennessee, USA. Writer; Professor of English. *Education:* MA, Vanderbilt University; University of Florida. *Literary Appointment:* University Writer-in-Residence, Professor of English, Auburn University, Alabama. *Publications:* The Innocent Forest of the Night; Dog Days; Best American Short Stories; A Cry of Absence, 1971; Passage Through Gehenna, 1978; A Buried Land, 1963; An Exile, 1967; Seasons of the Strangler, 1982. *Contributor to:* Sewanee Review. *Memberships:* South Atlantic MLA. *Literary Agent:* McIntosh, McKee and Dodds Incorporated. *Address:* 800 Kuderna Acres, Auburn, AL 36830, USA.

JONES, (Morgan) Glyn, b. 28 Feb. 1905, Merthyr Tydfil, Glamorgan, Wales. Teacher of English. m. Phyllis Doreen, 1935, Cardiff. *Education:* St Pauls College, Cheltenham, England. *Publications:* The Blue Bed, 1937; Poems, 1939; The Water Music. 1944; The Dream of Jake Hopkins, 1954; The Saga of Llywarch The Old (with T J Morgan), 1955; The Valley, The City, The Village, 1956, 80; The Learning Lark, 1960; The Island of Apples, 1965; The Dragon Has Two Tongues, 1968; Selected Short Stories, 1971; The Beach of Falesa, 1974; Selected Poems, 1975; Welsh Heirs, 1977; Profiles (with J Rowlands), 1981. *Contributor to:* New Verse; Poetry London; Poetry Chicago; Poetry Wales; The Adelphie; The Guardian; Planet; The Times; Life and Letters Today; Wales; The Welsh Review; Dock Leaves; Madog. *Honours:* Welsh Arts Council Literature Prize, 1969; D Litt, University of Wales, 1974. *Membership:* The Welsh Academy, former Chairman and Vice-President. *Literary Agent:* Laurente Pollinger, London. *Address:* 158 Manor Way, Whitchurch, Cardiff, Glamorgan, Wales.

JONES, R Ben, b. 29 Jan. 1933, Bakewell, Derbyshire. England. Schoolmaster. *Education:* MA, B Litt, Oxford University. *Publications:* French Revolution, 1968; Approaches to the New History (Editor), 1970; The Hanoverians, 1972; The Victorians, 1974; Napolean, Man and Myth, 1978; Social and Economic History, 2nd edition, 1979; The Making of Contemporary Europe, 1980, The Challenge of Greatness: A Political, social and economic history, 1986. *Contributor to:* History; Teaching History; Contemporary Europe. *Address:* Yew Court, 93 Stockton Lane, York, England.

JONES, Rhiannon Davies, b. 4 Nov. 1921, Llanbedr, Meirionnydd, Wales. Teacher Training College Lecturer. *Education:* MA, University College of North Wales, Bangor. *Publications:* Fy Hen Lyfr Cownt, 1961; Lleian Llan Llŷr, 1965; Llys Aberffraw, 1977; Eryr Pengwern, 1981; Dyddiadur Mari Gwyn, 1985. *Contributions to:* Seren Gomer; Cyfansoddiadau yr Eisteddfod Genedlaethol; Barn. Adjudicator at major literature competitions, National Eisteddfod of Wales, 1967–68, 70, 74, 1977–80, 1982–84. *Honours:* Awards for Novels, 1952, 56, Short stories, 1954, Prose Medals, 1960, 64, National Eisteddfod; Crown Award for Novel, Anglesey County Eisteddfod; Welsh Arts Council Awards, 1966, 78, 82. *Address:* Glynor, Llanfair, Harlech, Gwynedd, Wales.

JONES, Richard Andrew, b. 8 Aug, 1953, London, England. Poet; Editor; Teacher. *Education:* BA 1975, MA 1976, University of Virginia, USA. *Literary Appointments:* Editor, Poetry East, 1979–; Scandinavian Review 1982–83; Lecturer in English, University of Virginia, 1982–. *Publications:* Windows & Walls, Poems, 1982; Editor, Of Solitude & Silence: Writings on Robert Bly, 1982; Editor, Poetry & Politics, 1984; Innocent Things, poems, 1985; The Lake, poems, 1986; Country of Air, poems, 1986. *Contributions:* Poems, short stories essays in: Agni Review; New Letters; American Book Review; Crazyhorse; Quarry West; etc. *Honours:*

Swedish Writers Union Award, 1982; CCLM Editors Award, 1985. *Membership:* National Book Critics Circle. *Address:* Department of English, Wilson Hall, University of Virginia, Charlottesville, VA 22903, USA.

JONES, Richard Preston, b. 25 July 1942, New York City, USA. Associate Professor of English, Pacific Lutheran University. Divorced, 1 son, 2 daughters. *Education:* AB, Harvard University, 1964; MA, University of Massachusetts, Amherst, 1969; MFA, Poetry, University of Massachusetts, 1969. *Literary Appointments:* Visiting Artist, Artist-in-the-Schools Program, 1970–76; Port Townsend Writers Conference, 1974, 75. *Publications:* Waiting For Spring, 1978; The Rest Is Silence, 1984. *Contributions to:* Harvard Review; Seattle Review; Portland Review; Capilano Review; Art Reach; West Coast Poetry Review; Paintbrush; Seattle Times. *Honours:* William Stafford Award, 1979; Regency Award, 1984. *Membership:* Pacific Northwest Renaissance Conference, President, 1982–83, Secretary/Treasurer, 1980–82. *Address:* Box 44471, Tacoma, WA 98444, USA.

JONES, Robert (Bob) Reynolds, b. 19 Oct. 1911, Montgomery, Alabama, USA. Educator. *Education:* BA, Bob Jones College, 1931; MA, University of Pittsburgh, 1932; LittD, Asbury College, 1935; LKHD, John Brown University, 1941; LLD, Houghton College, 1943; DD, Northwestern Schools, 1950; STD, Mid-Western Bible College, 1974; LittD, Chung-ang University, Seoul, Korea, 1972. *Publications:* All Fullness Dwells, 1942; As the Small Rain, 1945; Showers Upon the Grass, 1951; Ancient Truths for Modern Days, 1963; Prologue: A Drama of Jon Hus, 1968, with B Jones Senior and B Jones III; Heritage of Faith, 1973; Old Testament Sermons, 4 volums, 1973; Rhyme and Reason, 1982; Daniel of Babylon, 1984; Cornbread and Caviar, 1985. *Contributions to:* Various professional journals and religious magazines, Editor, Faith for the Family; Syndicated column, A Look at the Book, in about 300 newspapers, magazines throughout the world. *Honours:* Selected as Best Religious Film Actor of the Year, National Evangelical Film Foundation, 1964; Congress of Freedom Liberty Award, 1978; Silver Good Citizenship Medal, Birmingham Chapter, Sons of the American Revolution, 1984. *Address:* Bob Jones University, Greenville, SC 29614, USA.

JONES, Rodney W, b. 16 July 1943, India. Educator; Policy Analyst. m. Dawn Elaine, 4 Sep. 1965, Williamsport, USA, 2 sons. *Education:* BA, Juniata College, 1964; MA, 1965, PhD, 1970, Columbia University. *Appointments:* International Affairs Fellow, Council on Foreign Relations, 1977–78; Associate Professor, Political Science, Columbia University, 1978–80; Senior Fellow, Director, Nuclear Policy Studies, Centre for Strategic and International Studies, Georgetown University, 1980–. *Publications:* Urban Politics in India; Area, Power and Policy in a Penetrated System, 1974; Nuclear Proliferation: Islam, the Bomb, and South Asia, 1981; Small Nuclear Forces, 1984; Modern Weapons and Third World Powers, co-author, 1984; Smal Nuclear Forces and US Security Policy: Threats and Potential Conflicts in the Middle East and South Asia, 1984; The Nuclear Suppliers and Nonproliferation: Dilemmas and Policy Choices, 1985. *Contributor to:* Numerous professional journals including, Washington Quarterly; Society; Arms Control Today; Pacific Affairs; Journal of Asian Studies; etc. *Honours:* Richard M Simpson Memorial Scholarship, Juniata College, 1961–64; Juniata Honour Society, 1963; Baccalaureate Degree, Magna cum Laude, 1964; Danforth Graduate Fellow, 1964–69; International Fellows Program, Columbia University 1965–66; Dissertation Awarded, Distinction, nominated for Ausley prize, Columbia University, 1970; American Institute of Indian Studies Senior Fellow, 1974–75s; Book, Urban Politics in India, received Imprimatur, Center for South and Southeast Asia Studies, University of California, & nominated for Wattamull Prize, 1976. *Memberships:* International Institute of Strategic Studies; Association for Asian Studies; Society for

Values in Higher Education. *Address:* CSIS, 1800 K St, N W, Washington DC 20006, USA.

JONES, Sally Roberts, b. 30 Nov. 1935, London, England. Librarian/Housewife. m. Alwyn Bowen Jones, 2 June 1969, Carmarthen, 3 sons. *Education:* BA, Hons, History, Diploma in Archive Administration, University of Wales; Associate of the Library Association (ALA) North Western Polytechnic, London. *Publications:* Romford in the Nineteenth Century, 1969; Turning Away (poems) 1969; The Forgotten Country (poems) 1977; Elen and the Goblin, 1977; Allen Raine (Writers of Wales Series) 1979; Relative Values (poems) 1985. *Contributions to:* Numerous contributions to Poetry Wales; Anglo-Welsh Review; Tribune; Planet; Essex Journal. Numerous articles on local history and bibliographies. Editor of, Dragon's Tale, (magazine of children's literature in Wales). *Honour:* Welsh Arts Council Award, 1969–70. *Membership:* Vr Academi Gymreig. *Address:* 3 Crown Street, Port Talbot, West Glamorgan SA13 1BG, Wales.

JONES, Trevor, b. 5 Sep. 1936, Manchester, England. University Lecturer. m. Marion Jenkinson, 12 Aug. 1974, 1 daughter. *Education:* BA 1st Class Geography and History 1959, MA 1972, Cambridge University. *Publications:* Ghana's First Republic, 1977; A Final Note (?) On Trebitsch-Lincoln, 1985. *Contributions to:* Review articles; Times Literary Supplement; Journal Political Economy, Accra, Ghana. *Honours:* Figgis Memorial Prize, Cambridge, 1958; Fulbright Travel Award, 1960–62. *Literary Agent:* Curtis Brown, London. *Address:* c/o Department of History, University of Keele, Staffordshire, ST5 5BG, England.

JONG, Erica, b. 26 Mar. 1942, New York City, USA. Writer. *Education:* BA, Barnard College, 1963; MA, Columbia University, 1965. *Publications:* Fruits & Vegetables, 1971; Half-Lives, 1973; Fear of Flying, 1973; Loveroot, 1975; How to Save Your Own Life, 1977; At the Edge of the Body, 1979; Here Comes and Other Poems, 1975; Fanny: Being the True History of the Adventures of Fanny Hackabout-Jones, 1980; Ordinary Miracles, 1983; Megan's Book of Divorce, 1984; Parachutes and Kisses, 1984. *Contributor to:* New York Times Book Review; Los Angeles Times; New Republican; New York Magazine; New Yorker; Ms; Vogue; News Day. *Honours:* Bess Hokin Prize, 1971; Alice Faye di Castagnola, 1972; National Endowments for the Arts Grant, 1973; Premio International Sigmund Freud, 1979. *Memberships:* Poets & Writers; Author's Guild; PEN; Poetry Society of America; Phi Beta Kappa. *Address:* Morton L Janklow Associates Inc, 598 Madison Avenue, New York, NY 10022, USA.

JONSDOTTIR, Thora, b. 17 Jan. 1925, Iceland. Housewife. m. Pall Flygenring, 20 Aug. 1949, Bessastadir, 1 son, 2 daughters. *Education:* Degree from Teachers' University of Iceland. *Publications:* 4 Books of Poems: 1973, 1975, 1978, 1983. *Membership:* Writers' Association of Iceland. *Address:* Njörvasund 13, 104 Reykjavik, Iceland.

JONSSON, Jon Dan, b. 10 Mar. 1915, Iceland. Former Treasurer of the State. m. Halîdora Eliasdottir, 18 Dec. 1943, Reykjavik, 1 son, 3 daughters. *Education:* Commercial School. *Appointment:* Writers Salary, State of Iceland, annually, last 12-15 years. *Publications:* A Blast in the Night, 1956, Tides, 1958; Two Tales of Captives, 1960; Barefooted Words, 1967; The Happenings at Mountain Farm, 1973; Last Night at Sea, 1977; The Stargazers, 1980; Sabotage, 1981; Bondage, 1982. *Contributor to:* Numerous magazines and journals. *Honours:* 3rd Prize, 1951, 1st Prize 1953, Short Stories, Samvinnan Magazine; 1st Prize, Short Story, Helgafell Magazine, 1953. *Membership:* Writers Union of Iceland, with Revisory Post. *Address:* Storageroi 13, 108 Reykjavik, Iceland.

JONSSON, Kristjan Johann, b. 10 May 1949, Iceland. Writer. m. Dagny Kristjansdottir, 6 Nov. 1970, Reyjavik, 2 sons. *Education:* BA, Icelandic language and literature and General literature history. *Appointments:*

Teacher of Icelandic Literature, University of Oslo, Norway, 1983. *Publications:* Haustio er rautt, novel, 1981. Translations from Danish: Haltu kjafti og vertu saet, short stories by Vita Andersen, 1981; Fotboltaengillinn, novel by Hans-Jorgen Nielsen, 1983. *Contributions to:* Pdooviljinn, Literature critic, 1976–79; contributor of short stories and poems in various Icelandic literature magazines. *Honours:* Annual Contributions from Writers Salary Fund, Iceland, 1981–. *Memberships:* Rithofundasamband Islands Mal og menning, Iceland. *Literary Agent:* Mal og menning. *Address:* Osterasbakken 81 A, 1345 Osteras, Norway.

JOOSSE, Barbara M, b. 18 Feb. 1949, Grafton, Wisconsin, USA. Writer; Mother. m. Peter C Joosse, 30 Aug. 1969, Grafton, 1 son, 2 daughters. *Education:* BA, University of Wisconsin. *Publications:* Picture Books: The Thinking Place, 1982; Spiders in the Fruit Cellar, 1983; Fourth of July, 1985. *Contributions to:* Milwaukee Magazine, Columnist; Instructor; Cricket; School Magazine, New South Wales. *Honours:* 1st Place, Picture Book, Coucil for Wisconsin Writers (for The Thinking Place), 1982. *Memberships:* Society of Childrens Book Writers; Council for Wisconsin Writers. *Literary Agent:* Andrea Brown. *Address:* 2953 Little Moraine Drive, Hartford, WI 53027, USA.

JORDAN, Barbara Leslie, b. 30 Sep. 1915, New York City, USA. Poet. m. John I Yellott, MBE CSJ, 2 June 1951, New York, 2 sons, 1 stepson, 1 stepdaughter. *Education:* Special poetry workshop, Columbia University, New York, 1933–34; Workshops, of various poets. *Publications:* Web of Days, 1949; Comfort the Dreamer, 1955; Silver Song, selected poems, 1980. *Contributions to:* Various works including: The Golden Year, 1960; Diamond Anthology, 1971; New York Times; New York Herald Tribune; Denver Post; Paris Herald Tribune; Christian Science Monitor; Poetry Chapbook; Voices; Sharing; Point West; Taleria; The Arizona Republic. *Honours:* 3 Critics Award, New York Women Poets, 1953; Poem used in National Contest – Modern Dance, 1985. *Memberships:* Treasurer, John Yellott Engineering Association Inc. 1958–; Past Literary Chairman, Past Historian, Poetry Chairman, Valley of the Sun Chapter, National Society of Arts and Letters; Poetry Society of America; New York Women Poets; Chapter 100; Cum laude Society, Orme School, 1973; Phoenix Branch, The English-Speaking Union. *Address:* 901 West El Caminito Drive, Phoenix, AZ 85021, USA.

JORDAN, William Johnston, b. 9 Sep. 1924, Ireland. Veterinary Surgeon. m. Brenda R Foster, 2 Feb. 1950, Wallasey, 2 sons, 1 daughter. *Education:* MVSc; BSc; MRCVS; CBiol; MIBiol; FZS. *Publications:* Last Great Wild Beast Show, 1978; Care of the Wild, 1982; A-Z of Pet Care, 1985. *Contributions to:* Various journals and encyclopaedias including: Veterinary Record; British Encyclopedia; British Airways Magazine; Contemporary Review; Country Life; Veterinary Journal; BBC Wildlife Magazine. *Literary Agent:* Donald Copeman. *Address:* Ashfolds, Rusper, Horsham, Sussex RH12 4QX, England.

JOSEFOWITZ, Natasha, b. 31 Oct. 1926, Paris, France. Professor; Author; Lecturer; Syndicated Columnist. m. Sam Josefowitz, 15 Apr. 1949, Beverley Hills, USA, 1 son, 1 daughter. *Education:* BA, Soupps College, Claremont, USA; MSW, Columbia University, New York; Doctoraus, Lausanne University, Switzerland. *Publications:* Paths to Power, 1980; Is this where I was Going?, 1983; You're the Boss!, 1985. *Contributor to:* Harvard Business Review; Personnel Administrator; Psychology Today; Ms; L A Times. *Honours:* Recipient, Award for Contribution to Education, California Women in Government. *Memberships:* National Society of Arts & Letters; Authors Guild Inc. *Literary Agent:* Margaret McBride. *Address:* 2235 Calle Guaymas, La Jolla, CA 92037, USA.

JOSEPH, James, b. 12 May 1924, Terre Haute, Indiana, USA. Writer; Photographer; Editor. m. Marjorie Waterman, 1950 (divorced), 1 son, 1 daughter.

Education: BA, Stanford University, California; Scholarship course, Medill School of Journalism, Northwestern University. *Literary Appointments:* Self-syndicated column, Western Round-Up; Founder, Owner, Writer's World (seminars); Founder, President, World Reach (world-wide marketing communications), Founder, Executive Editor, Robomation Report, and others. *Publications:* 20 books, magazine articles including: How to Start a Successful Small Business, 1956; Income Opportunities, 1956; Poolside Living, 1962; Better Water Skiing for Boys, 1963; You Fly It, 1965; I Lived Inside the Campus Revolution (with William Divale), 1970; Here is Your Hobby: Snowmobiling, 1972; The Complete Out-of-Doors: Job, Business and Profession Guide, 1974; Chilton's Diesel Guide, 1980; The Car-Keeper's Guide, 1982; Float Free, 1986; Car Cures: Car-Trouble Symptons, Causes and Cures, 1986; Interstate Highway Quick-Stops. *Contributions to:* more than 500 magazines and journals worldwide, in some 30 nations and 25 languages. *Honours include:* Melville Jacoby Award, Stanford University, 1949. *Memberships:* American Society of Journalists and Authors; Authors Guild; Newsletter Association of America; Society of Photographers in Communications. *Literary Agents:* Arthur Pine & Associates; D Michael Tomkins, Agent, Attorney. *Address:* PO Box 24678, Los Angeles, CA 90024, USA.

JOSEPH, Jenny, b. 7 May 1932, Birmingham, England. Writer; Lecturer. *Education:* BA, Hons, Oxford University. *Publications:* The Unlooked-For Season; 1960; Rose in the Afternoon, 1974; The Thinking Heart, 1978; Beyond Descartes, 1983; Persephone, 1985; 6 children's books, 1960s. *Honours:* Gregory Award, 1961; Cholmondeley Award, 1975; Arts CNCL, 1978. *Memberships:* National Poetry Society, former Council Member; Festival of Spoken Poetry, former Committee Member. *Literary Agent:* John Johnson. *Address:* c/o John Johnson, 45-47 Clerkenwell Green, London EC1R OHT, England.

JOSEPH, Joan Judith, b. 13 July 1937, Israel. Author. Divorced, 1 son. *Education:* BA, (Hons) History, MA, History, McGill University Montreal, Canada, 1959; Centre Universitaire Mediterranee, Nice, France Institut de l'Universite d'Aix Marseille, 1963–64; Certificate, Spoken French, L'Alliance Francaise, Paris, 1964; Equivalent of MA, University of Paris, 1964; Graduate School of History, University of Miami, 1965; 13th Century Medieval Latin Palegraphy, Wellcome Historical Institute and British Public Record Office, 1970; Intensive Latin Reading, City University of New York Graduate Center, 1985. *Literary Appointments:* With Grolier Publishing Company, 1959–61, 1965; French Translator, US Department of Commerce, 1966–68; Historical Summaries, Aurora Toys, 1971. *Publications include:* Robert Levy's Magic Book, 1976; For love of Liz, 1976; Love's Frantic Flight, 1980; In Joy and In Sorrow, 1982; A World for the Taking, 1983; Now Is the Hour, 1985. *Contributions to:* Reader's Digest Books; McGraw-Hill Encyclopedia of World Drama, 1973; Time-Life, Encyclopedia of Gardening, Lawn Covers, Volume 3; Travelage East. Travelage Southeast, 1983, 84, 85. *Honours include:* The Dropsie University Center for Manuscript Research and the Lucius N Littauer Foundation, Grant for Studies in Medieval Anglo-Jewry, 1971; Teaching Fellowship, University of Miami and Columbia University. *Address:* 10 West 66th Street, New York, NY 10023, USA.

JOSEPH, Terri Brint, b. 15 Sep. 1940, Oklahoma City, Oklahoma, USA. Writer; Teacher. m. Roger Joseph, 28 May 1963, Santa Monica, California. *Education:* BA, cum laude, University of California, Los Angeles; MA, English Literature, PhD, English Literature, University of California, Irvine. *Literary Appointments:* Leader, Poetry Workshops for Poetry in Schools, 1977; Visiting Lecturer, English, University of California, Los Angeles, 1981–82; Assistant Professor, English, Director of Creative Writing and Criticism, Chapman College, 1982–. *Publication:* Ezra Pound's Epic Variations, 1985. *Contributor to:* Poetry: Numerous publications in variety

of journals including North American Mentor; The Archer; Manifest; New Women; Articles in Signs; Real; Paideuma. *Honours:* 272 Old Topanga Canyon Road, chosen for inclusion in Poetry of the Year: Best in Poetry, 1973; Honour and Merit Awards for Poetry, North American Mentor, 1974–76; Chapman Research Fellowship, 1983–85. *Memberships:* Member, delegate assembly, Modern Language Association, 1981–84; Poetry Society of America; modern Poetry Asssociation; Semiotic Society of America, Programme Committee, 1983–85. *Address:* Department of English and Comparative Literature, Chapman College, Orange, CA 92666, USA.

JOSEPHS, Ray, b. 1 Jan. 1912, Philadelphia, Pennsylvania, USA. Chairman, International Public Relations Company Ltd (New York). m. Juanita Wegner, 22 Feb. 1941. *Education:* University of Pennsylvania, Philadelphia, Pennsylvania, USA. *Publications include:* Argentine Diary, 1944; Spies and Saboteurs in Argentina, 1943; Latin America, Continent in Crisis, 1948; Those Perplexing Argentines (with James Bruce), 1952; How To Make Money From Your Ideas, 1954; How To Gain An Extra Hour Every Day, 1955; Memoirs of a Live Wire, (with David Kemp), 1956; Streamlining Your Executive Workload, 1958; Our Housing Jungle and Your Pocketbook, (with Oscar Steiner), 1960; The Magic Power of Putting Yourself Over With People, (with Stanley Arnold), 1962; Contributor to several other books. *Contributions to:* Magazines and newspapers including; Washington Post; Christian Science Monitor; Time Magazine; Reader's Digest; Charm; Saturday Review of Literature. *Memberships:* Charter accredited, Public Relations Society of America; Brandeis University Development Council; Writers Guild of America; Society of Magazine Writers. *Address:* 860 United Nations Plaza, New York, NY 10017, USA.

JOY, David Anthony Welton, b. 14 June 1932, Ilkley, Yorkshire, England. Publisher. m. Judith Margaret Agar, 29 Mar. 1967, York, 2 sons, 1 daughter. *Literary Appointments:* General Reporter, Yorkshire Post, 1962–65; Editorial Assistant, 1965–70, Books editor, 1970–, Dalesman Publishing Company. *Publications include:* Main Line Over Shap, 1967; Cumbrian Coast Railway, 1968; Railways in the North, 1970; Traction Engines in the North, 1970; Steamtown, 1972; Railways of the Lake Counties, 1973; Regional History of the Railways of Great Britain: South and West Yorkshire, 1975, 84; Railways in Lancashire, 1975; Railways in Yorkshire: Teh West Riding, 1976; Steam of the North Yorks Moors, 1978; Steam on the Settle and Carlisle, 1981; Yorkshire Dales Railway, 1983; Settle-Carlisle in Colour, 1983; Regional History of the Railways of Great Britain: The Lake Countries, 1983; Portrait of the Settle-Carlisle, 1984. Co-Authorships include: Settle-Carlisle Railway, 1966; George Hudson of York, 1971; North Yorkshire Moors Railway, 1977; Yorkshire Railways, 1979. *Contributions to:* The Dalesman Magazine. *Address:* Hole Bottom, Hebden, Skipton, North Yorkshire BD23 5DL, England.

JOY, Thomas Alfred, b. 30 Dec. 1904, Oxford, England. Bookseller. *Education:* Bedford House, Oxford. *Publications:* The Right Way to Run a Library Business, 1949; Bookselling, 1953; The Truth About Bookselling, 1964; The Bookselling Business, 1974; Mostly Joy (autobiography), 1971. *Contributor to:* The Bookseller. *Honours include:* Lieutenant, Royal Vic Order, 1979; Queen's Silver Jubilee Medal, 1977; FRSA, 1967; First Curators Prize, Bodleian Library, Oxford, 1920. *Memberships:* Honorary Life Member, Society of Bookmen; Book Trade Benevolent Society, President, 1974–; Booksellers Association of Great Britain, President, 1957–58; Chairman Education Board, 1954, Honorary Treasurer, 1951–55; Employers Representative, Bookselling and Stationery Trades Wages Council, 1946–, Chairman, 1957; FRSA. *Address:* Velden, 13 Cole Gardens, Twickenham, Middlesex, England.

JUDELL, Brandon, b. 22 Jan. 1951, Bronx, New York, USA. Writer; Editor. *Education:* BA, City College, New York; Parsons H B Studio; Herbert H Lehman College; The New School. *Appointments:* Head, Writers' Caucaus, 1984; Vice President, Gay and Lesbian Press Association, 1985. *Publications:* Anthologized in Lavender Culture, 1979. *Contributor to:* The Other Side of Christopher St, Village Voice, 1981; They're Just Wilde About Werner, Village Voice, 1979; Kiss My Ash, New York Daily News Sunday Magazine, 1984; Regular Contributor to, Daily News; Village Voice; Advocate; Entertainment New York; High Society; Diverson. *Memberships:* Authors Guild; Gay and Lesbian Press Association; National Writers Union. *Literary Agent:* Jed Mattes, ICM. *Address:* 5 West 91 Street, New York City, NY 10024, USA.

JUERGENS, George Ivar, b. 20 Mar. 1932, Brooklyn, New York. Professor. *Education:* BA, Columbia College; BA, MA, Oriel College, Oxford University, England; PhD, Columbia University. *Major Publications:* Joseph Pulitzer & The New York World, 1966; News From the White House, 1981. *Literary Agent:* Gerald McCauley. *Address:* 2111 Meadowbluff Court, Bloomington, IN 47401, USA.

JUNOR, John (Sir), b. 15 Jan. 1919, Glasgow, Scotland. Journalist. m. Pamela Mary Welsh, 21 Apr. 1942, Newcastle-on-Tyne, 1 son, 1 daughter. *Education:* MA honours English, Glasgow University. *Publication:* The Best of J J, 1982. *Contributions to:* Sunday Express. *Honours:* Honorary LLD, New Brunswick, 1973; Knight, 1980. *Address:* Sunday Express, Fleet Street, London EC4, England.

JUNQUERA-HUERGO Y TORRES, Felipe Neri, b. 9 Jan. 1928, Gijón, Spain. Technical Administrator, Spanish Treasury. *Education:* Business studies. *Publications:* Las Presencias (Nueva voz en la carne), 1960; Otras Tierras, 1961; Antologia de Urgencia, 1962; Diario Poetico 1942-1954 (Breve antologia), 1980; Veinte Sonetos para el Ajedrez, 1985; Numerous unpublished works of poetry. *Contributions to:* Rumbos; Poesia Española; Cuadernos de Agora; Anthology of Asturian Poets; Gran Enciclopedia Asturiana. *Address:* Calle Armando Ojanguren 10, 33002 Oviedo, Spain.

JURGENSEN, Manfred, b. 26 Mar. 1940, Flensburg, Federal Republic of Germany. Professor of German, Personal Chair. m. Uschi Fischer, 1986. *Education:* BA, Honours, 1964, MA, 1966, Melbourne University, Australia; PhD, Zurich University, Switzerland, 1968. *Literary Appointments:* Editor: Outrider, Journal of Multicultural Literature; Queensland Studies in German Literature. Co-Editor, Seminar; Director, Phoenix Publications. *Publications:* Poetry: Stations, 1968; Places, 1969; Signs and Voices, 1973; A Kind of Dying, 1977; A Winter's Journey, 1979; South Africa Transit, 1979; State Security, 1979; The Skin Trade, 1983; Waiting for Cancer, 1985. Novels: Conscientious Objection, 1979; Break-Out, 1979; Experimental Man, 1982; A Difficult Love, 1985; The Age of Man, 1986. Criticism: Symbol as Idea, 1968; Max Frisch: The Dramatic Works, 1968; Max Frisch: The Novels, 1972; German Literary Theory, 1973; On Gunter Grass, 1974; The Fictional I, 1979; Narrative Forms of the Fictional I, 1980; Thomas Bernhard, 1980; Bachmann: The New Language, 1981; Contemporary German Women Writers, 1982; Women as Authors, 1982; Literature and Pornography, 1985; Keith Leopold: Selected Writings, 1985; Karin Struck: An Introduction, 1985. Critical Anthologies: Grass, 1973; Boll, 1975; Frisch, 1977; Handke, 1979; Bernhard, 1981; Wolf, 1984; Ethnic Australia, 1981-84. *Contributions to:* Numerous professional journal, various poetry magazines and journals; Reviewer of German literature books in International publications. *Memberships:* Australian Fellowship of Writers; Australian Society of Authors; International PEN; Deutscher Schriftstellerverband; Humbolt Fellowship; AULLA. *Literary Agent:* Hans Erpf. *Address:* c/o Department of German, University of Queensland, St Lucia, Brisbane 4067, Australia.

JUSTICE, Donald, b. 12 Aug. 1925, Miami, Florida, USA. Professor of Literature. m. Jean Ross, 22 Aug. 1947, Norwood, North Carolina, 1 son. *Education:* AB, University of Miami; AM, University of North Carolina; PhD, University of Iowa. *Literary Appointments:* Professor, University of Iowa; Professor, Syracuse University; Visiting Professor, University of California, Irving; Visiting Professor, Princeton University; Visiting Professor, University of Virginia; Professor, University of Florida. *Publications:* The Summer Anniversaries, 1960; Night Light, 1967; Departures, 1973; Selected Poems, 1979; Platonic Scripts, 1984. *Contributions to:* Antaeus; The New Criterion; The New Yorker. *Honours:* Lamont Prize for a first book, 1959; Guggenheim Fellowship, 1976; Pulitzer Prize in poetry, 1980; Harriet Monroe Award, 1984. *Address:* English Department, University of Florida, Gainesville, FL 32611, USA.

K

KACHEL, Zeev Zew Wolf, b. 8 Apr. 1912, Brest Lotowsk, USSR. Safety Engineer; Electro-Mechanical Engineer. m. Judith Jolanta Joseph, 12 Mar. 1952, 1 son, 1 daughter. *Education:* Diploma of Engineer in Electro-Mechanics; Technical Institute of Normandy of the University of Caen, France, 1930–34. *Publications:* Ethiopie, poem in Yiddish, 1937; Scharim Baperets, (Dams in Storm or Steming the Flood), in Hebrew, prose, 1957; Can We Still Love, in Hebrew, poems, 1961; Which Day is Today, poems in Hebrew, 1977. Horizons, Literary journal appearing only once in Yiddish, 1938. *Contributions to:* Davar; Ha'Arets; Ba Hagshama; Ma'ariv, Ediot Acronot; Bticut Bo'awoda; Bticut; Eitanim; Hacablan, Whabone; Laisha; Handasa w'adricalut; Poet International, and others. Numerous translations. Since retirement has become prolific painter. *Honours:* 2nd Prize for best reporting, Neie Presse, Paris, France, 1936–37. Work has received much critical acclaim. *Memberships:* Societe de Auteurs, Compositeurs et Editeurs de Musiq ue en Israel; World Poetry Society Intercontinental; Israel Union of Editors of Periodicals. *Address:* Yocheved St no 13, Haifa 34674, Israel.

KAECH, René Edgar, b. 19 Apr. 1909, Paris, France (Swiss Citizen). Doctor of Medicine; Physician; Writer. m. Colette Vonnez, 29 Apr. 1944, Lausanne, 2 sons. *Education:* MD, Lausanne, Switzerland, 1938; FMH, Psch, 1939. *Publications:* Le Poete-Gueux, 1941; L'Epopee interieure, 1944; Heros de roman, 1948; Discors pour un mort, 1959; Cecile au miroir, 1960; Veuves et Veufs, 1966; Blason de la Diletta, 1976; Erwartungen, 1979; Mythes at entimythes, 1980. *Contributor to:* Various journals. *Honours:* Gold Medal, Arts-Sciences-Lettres, Paris, 1964; Gold Medal, Columbus Association, Trieste, 1964; Silver Medal, Giuliani Lit. Prizes, Milan, 1956; Chevalier de l'Ordre des Arts et des Lettres, Paris, 1976; Ehrenmitglied Freier Deutscher Autorenverband, 1978. *Memberships include:* Swiss Writers Association, President 1972–74; PEN Club, Basle, President, 1964–68; Swiss Association of Writing Physicians, Founding Member, 1956, Hon President, 1965–; Works Union of Writing Doctors, President, 1973–79, Hon President, 1980. *Address:* Benkenstrasse 7, CH 4054, Basle, Switzerland.

KAGAN, Diane Janet, b. 25 Nov. 1940, Maplewood, New Jersey, USA. Actress; Playwright; Poet; Writer. *Education:* BA, Florida State University; Graduate, Martha Green School of Contemporary Dance, New York City, New York, Stella Adler Theatre Studio; Eugene O'Neill Playwrights Conference. *Publications:* Who Won Second Place at Omaha?, 1975. Plays: Luminosity Without Radiance; The Corridor; Marvelous Gray; Phoebus; The Final Voyage of Aphrodite. *Honours:* Nominated for Harvard Fellowship, 1984; Participant, 1982, Semi-finalist, 1984, Eugene O'Neill Playwrights Conference. *Memberships:* Dramatists Guild; Executive Committee, Admissions Committee, The New Dramatists; The Women's Project, American Place Theatre. *Literary Agent:* Audrey Wood, Luis Sanjurjo, ICM. *Address:* c/o Sanjurjo, ICM, West 57th Street, New York, NY 10019, USA.

KAIGHIN, Sheila M, b. 21 Nov. 1942, Toronto, Canada. Editorial Director. m. Ronald F Kaighin, 26 Aug. 1961, Barrie, Ontario, 1 son, 1 daughter. *Education:* Diplomas in Interior design and Early childhood education. *Literary Appointments:* Director, Outdoor Writers of Canada, 6 years. *Contributions to:* Outdoor Canada Magazine, Editor, 12 years; Editorial director, Ontario and British Columbia sections, Outdoor Canada; Boating Business. *Honours:* F H Kortright Outdoor Writing Awards, 1973–75; Greg Clark Outdoor Editorial Awards, 1977, 81. *Memberships:* Outdoor Writers of Canada, Director; Outdoor Writers of America. *Address:* 22 Glenorchy Road, Don Mills, Ontario, Canada M3C 2P9.

KAILA, Tiina Elisabet, b. 16 Aug. 1951, Helsinki, Finland. Author. m. Kai Kalervo Kaila, 29 Dec. 1971, Helsinki, 2 sons. *Publications:* Poems: Keskustelu hamarassa, 1974; Talven talossa, 1978; Kala on meren kuva, 1984. Faiory tale novels: Auringonlaskun torni, 1976; Simon matkat Peilikaupunkiin, 1978. *Honours:* National Literature Prize, Auringonlaskun torni, 1977. *Membership:* Finnish Society of Authors. *Address:* Simeonintie 4, 00730 Helsinki, Finland.

KAINZ, Howard Paul Junior, b. 9 June 1933, Inglewood, California, USA. Professor. m. Cathryn Louise Drozdik, 28 Feb. 1970, Chicago, Illinois, 1 son, 2 daughters. *Education:* BA, Loyola University, 1958; MA, St Louis University, 1964; PhD, Duquesne University, 1968. *Publications:* Hegel's Philosophy of Right, with Marx's Commentary, 1974; Hegel's Phenomenology, part 1, 1976, part 2, 1983; Ethica Dialectica, A Study of Ethical Oppositions, 1979; The Philosophy of Man, 1980; Democracy East and West, 1984; Philosophical Perspectives on Peace, 1986. *Contributions:* American Philosophical Quarterly; Idealistic Studies; Hegel-Studies; The Modern Schoolman; The Journal of Thought; The New Scholasticism; The New Orleans Review, and others. *Honours:* Best Persuasive Essay, Catholic Press Association, 1971; Fellow, National Endowment for the Humanities, 1977–78; Fulbright Fellow, Germany, 1981–82. *Address:* Department of Philosophy, Marquette University, Milwaukee, WI 53233, USA.

KAIPAINEN, Aune Helina, b. 14 Mar. 1933, Mudlaa, Finland. Author. m. Osmo Kaipainen, 27 Dec. 1955, Kiuruvesi (deceased 15 May 1985), 3 sons. *Education:* Candidate in Philosophy (MA). *Publications:* Arkkiemkeli Oulussa (The Angel in Oulussa), 1967; Magdaleena ja Maailman Upsbt (Magdalene and the World's Children), 1969; Naistentanssit (Woman's Dances), 1975; Poimisin Heliat Hiekat (I Would Pick Up Perle-Like Sands), 1983. *Contributions to:* numerous publications. *Honours:* National Prize, 1966, 69; Prize Finlandia 1968. *Memberships:* Society of Finish Drama Authors, President, 1979; Literary Society of Finland, Vice-President, 1975–76; Central Society of Theater Organizations of Finland, President, 1977–79. *Literary Agent:* WSOY. *Address:* Sinebrychoffinkatu 11 B 17, 00120 Helsinki 12, Finland.

KAISER, Dave, b. 20 Nov. 1943, Pennsylvania, USA. Writer; Editor. *Appointments:* Director, Associated Business Writers of America, Business Press Editors Association. *Publications:* Outdoor Recreation Areas, 1978; Outdoor Structures, 1980; Complete Guide to Writing Non-Fiction, 1984; Tips for Writers, 2nd edition, 1984; Freelance Business Writing, 1984; Swimming Pool Weekly/Age Data and Reference Annual, 1969, 11th editon 1979; Swimming Pools, A Guide to their Design and Operation, 1969, 3rd editon 1977. *Contributor to:* Arab News; Newsday; Air Conditioning, Heating and Refrigeration News; Around Mercy, Mercy Medicine; Baths Service; Florida Golf News; Florida Golfer; Florida Government; Greyhound Racing Record; Saudi Business; Saudi Report; Tennis USA; etc. *Memberships:* American Society of Journalists and Authors; Florida Freelance Writers Association; National Writers Club; Associated Business Writers of America; Investigative Reporters & Editors Association. *Address:* 4211 NW 10 Terrace, Fort Lauderdale, FL 33309, USA.

KAJIMA, Shozo, 12 Jan. 1923, Tokyo, Japan. Teacher; Writer; Translator. m. Toshiko, 1953, Yokohama, 2 sons. *Education:* MA, Waseda University, Tokyo. *Publications:* Editor, Translator, Post War Japanese Poetry, 1972; (Essays): At Faulkner's Town, 1984; (Poems): Bansei, 1985. *Membership:* Japan Poets Association. *Literary Agent:* UNI Agency, Kanda, Tokyo. *Address:* 8 Uchikoshi, Naka-ku, Yokohama, Japan 231.

KALAMARAS, Vasso, b. Athens, Greece, Lecturer, Modern Greek Language; Writer. m. Leon Kalamaras, 2 sons. *Education:* Associateship in Fine Arts, Western

Australia Institute of Technology, Perth, Australia. *Publications include:* Poetry: Stalagmites, 1960; A Bilingual Volume of Poetry, 1977; Landscape and Soul, 1980. Short Stories: Pikres, 1976; Other Earth, 1977; Bitterness, 1983. Other works: Alla Homata, Estia Athens; Etchings by Leon Kalamaras; Designs and Sculptures by Leon Kalamaras; Impression of Journey, 1978; The Hammer of the Sculptor, in Greek, 1979; The Breadtrap, play, 1982; Holiday Stin Ellada, one-act play, 1983. *Contributions to:* Numerous reviews, seminars, television interviews, literary journals and anthologies. *Honours include:* Tsakalos Literary Prize, Athens, Greece, 1978; Grant, Literary Board, 1976, Special Purpose Grant, 1977, Australian Council; Represented in various anthologies; Plays produced in English by Patch Theatre, Perth. *Memberships:* PEN International; National Society for Greek Writers; Australian Society of Authors; Fellowship of Australian Writers; Australian Society of Authors; Fellowship of Australian Writers; Poets Union; World Poetry Intercontinental. *Address:* 71 Selby Street, Daglish, WA 6008, Australia.

KALCHEV, Kamen, b. 31 July 1914, Kereka, Bulgaria. Writer. m. Maria Stolarova. *Education:* Finance, Free University, Sofia. *Publications:* A Son of the Working Class, 1949; The Alives Remember, 1950; The Weavers Family, 1956; Two Ones In The New Town, 1964; At The Source of Life, 1964; Sofia Tales, 1967; A Burning Summer, 1973; Selected Works, 1974. *Contributor to:* All main Bulgarian editions. *Honours:* Dimitrov Prize, 1950; A People's Worker Of Culture, 1972; A Hero of Socialist Labour 1974 and 1984. *Membership:* Vice President, Union of Bulgarian Writers. *Address:* 11 Lyuben Karavelov, Sofia, Bulgaria.

KALECHOFSKY, Roberta, b. 11 May 1931, New York, New York, USA. Writer; Publisher. m. Robert Kalechofsky, & June 1953, Brooklyn, New York, 2 sons. *Education:* BA, Brooklyn College, 1952; MA, 1956, PhD, 1970, New York University. *Publications:* George Orwell, 1973; Stephen's Passion, 1975; Orestes in Progres, 1976; La Hoya, 1977; Solomon's Wisdom, 1978. *Contributions to:* Western Humanities Review; Confrontation; Works; Ball State University Forum; Pulpsmith. *Honours:* Best American Short Stories inclusion, 1972; Honorable Mention, Best American Short Stories, 1976, 77; Grant for pubishing, 1977, for Litrary writing, 1982, for publishing, 1984, National Endowment for the Arts. *Address:* 255 Humphrey Street, Marblehead, MA 01945, USA.

KALIN, Robert, b. 11 Dec. 1921, Everett, Massachusetts, USA. Professor of Mathematics Education. m. Madelyn Pildish, 17 Aug. 1962, Dover, Delaware, USA, 2 sons, 2 daughters. *Education:* BA, University of Chicago, 1947; MA, Harvard University, 1948; PhD, Florida State University, 1961. *Major Publications:* (Co-author) Holt School Mathematics, Grades k-8, 1974, revised 1978; Analytical Geometry, 1973; Elementary Mathematics, Patterns & Structures Grades k-8, 1966, revised 1968; Modern Mathematics for the Elementary School Teacher, 1966; Holt Mathematics, Grades k-8, 1981, revised 1985. *Contributor to:* Dimensions in Mathematics; The Mathematics Teacher; The Arithmetic Teacher. *Memberships include:* Mathematical Association of America. *Address:* 1120 Cherokee Drive, Tallahassee, FL 32301, USA.

KALLIR, Jane Katherine, b. 30 July 1954, New York, USA. Gallery Director. m. Gary Cosimini, 25 Jan. 1985, New York. *Education:* BA, Brown University. *Publications:* Gustav Klimt/Egon Schiele, 1980; Austria's Expressionism, 1981; The Folk Art Tradition: Naive Painting in Europe and the United States, 1981; Grandma Moses, The Artist Behind the Myth, 1982; Arnold Schoenberg's Vienna, 1985. *Contributions to:* Southwest Art; The Clarion; Bulletin of the Center for Austrian Studies, University of Minnesota. *Honour:* Award, Art Libraries Society, 1981. *Address:* c/o Galerie St Etienne, 24 West 57th Street, New York, NY 10019, USA.

KAMEN, Betty, b. 23 June 1925, New York City, USA. Writer; Lecturer. m. Si Kamen, 29 Dec. 1946, Brooklyn, New York, 2 sons, 1 daughter. *Literary Appointments:* Feature Columnist for: Let's Live Magazine; Health Freedom News; Health Business News; Pacific Sun Newspaper. *Publications:* Total Nutrition During Pregnancy, 1981; Kids Are What They Eat, 1983; In Pursuit of Youth, 1984; Osteoporosis: What It Is, How to Prevent It, How to Stop It, 1984; The Breastfeeding Bible, 1986. *Contributor:* Of over 200 articles in Health and Nutrition Journals. *Honours:* Total Nutrition During Pregnancy, accepted in permanent library of World Health organisation, 1984; Kids Are What They Eat, voted among 10 best by MS Magazine; 1984. *Literary Agent:* Evan Marshall, Sterling Lord Agency. *Address:* Box 689, Larkspur, CA 94939, USA.

KAMENETZ, Herman L (Leo), b. 1 Sep. 1907, Kaunas, Lithuania. Physician. m. Georgette Barbaix, 13 Feb. 1947, Paris, France. *Education:* German Abitur, Berlin; French Baccalaureat, MSc, MD, University of Paris, France. *Appointments:* Editorial Assistant, Physical Library, New Haven, Connecticut, 1958–63; Associate Editor, Physical Medicine Library for: Medical Hydrology, 1963, Medical Climatology, 1964, Therapeutic Heat and Cold, 1965, Orthotics Etcetra, 1966, Rehabilitation and Medicine, 1968, Arthritus and Physical Medicine, 1969. *Publications:* Physiatric Dictionary, 1965; The Wheelchair Book, 1969; Dictionnaire de Medecine Physique, de Reeducation et Readaptation Fonctionnelles, with Georgette Kamenetz, 1972; English-French and French-English Dictionary of Physical Medicine and Rehabilitation, with Georgette Kamenetz, 1972; Dictionary of Rehabilitation Medicine, 1983. Chapters in medical books; articles in medical magazines and journals. *Honours:* Doctoral Thesis Tres Honorable, Paris, 1952; Editorial Committee, Scandinavian-English Rehabilitation Terminology, Copenhagen, 1968. *Memberships:* American Medical Writers Association. *Address:* The Chatham, Apt 824, 4501 Arlington Boulevard, Arlington, VA 22203, USA.

KAMENETZ, Rodger, b. 20 Jan. 1950, Baltimore, Maryland. USA. Poet. m. Moira Crone, 15 Oct. 1979, Baltimore, 1 daughter. *Education:* BA, Yale College; MA, Johns Hopkins University; MA, Stanford University. *Literary Appointments:* Director, Creative Writing Program, Louisiana State University. *Publications:* The Missing Jew, 1979; Nympholepsy, 1985; Terra Infirma, 1986. *Contributions to:* Antioch Review; Southern Review; Shenandoah; Mississippi Review; Grand Street. *Address:* 3175 Hundred Oaks Avenue, Baton Rouge, LA 70808, USA.

KAMER, Rienk Hendrikus, b. 12 Apr. 1943, Rotterdam, Netherlands. Author; Financial Adviser. m. Gyde Knebusch, 20 Apr. 1964, Enschede, 2 sons. *Education:* Journalism and law. *Publications:* Roeland and Dany Visiting the Petroleum Sheiks, Dutch and German, 1974; All About Money, Dutch, 1976; Condemned Without Judgement, Dutch, 1984; The Tyranny of Money, Dutch, 1985. *Contributions to:* Various publications including: Der Spiegel, Germany; Capital, Germany. *Memberships:* Vlaams Verbond van Letterkundigen, Belgium. *Literary Agent:* Omega Books b v, Amsterdam. *Address:* P O Box 882, 2501 CW The Hague, The Netherlands.

KAMINSKY, Alice R, b. New York City, USA. Teacher. *Education:* BA, 1946, MA, 1947, PhD, 1952, New York University. *Publications:* George Henry Lewes Literary Criticism, Editor, 1964; George Henry Lewes as Literary Critic, 1968; Logic: A Philosophic Introduction, 1974; Chaucer's Troilus and Cresyde and the Critics, 1980; The Victim's Song, 1985. *Contributor to:* PMLA; Bibliography of Philosophy; Nineteenth Century French Studies. *Honours:* Tuition Scholarship, 1946; 2 Research Foundation Fellowships, State University of New York, 1965, 69; Doctoral Fellowship, New York University, 1949–52. *Membership:* MLA. *Address:* SUNY-Cortland, Cortland, NY 13045, USA.

KAMM, Phyllis S, b. 12 July 1918, Philadelphia, Pennsylvania, USA. Freelance journalist. m. Herbert Kamm, 6 Dec. 1936, Highlands, New Jersey, 3 sons. *Publications:* Co-author, About Mourning: Support & Guidance for the Bereaved, 1984. *Contributions to:* United Feature Syndicate; Womens News Service; Newspaper Enterprise of America; The Cleveland (Ohio) Press; Cleveland Magazine. Variety of feature subjects, book reviews, travel, problems of ageing, education, etc. *Literary Agent:* Joan Fulton, Harold Matson Company, New York, NY. *Address:* 1155–B Ash Street, Arroys Grande, CA 93420, USA.

KAMPF, Louis, b. 12 May 1929, Vienna, Austria. Professor of Literature. *Education:* BA, Long Island University, USA, 1951; Graduate School, University of Iowa, 1954–58; Society of Fellows, Harvard University, 1958–61. *Publications:* On Modernism, 1967; The Politics of Literature, 1972. *Contributions to:* Harper's; The National Coll Eng; The Humanist; Change; PMLA, etc. *Membership:* MLA, President, 1971. *Honour:* Old Dominion Fellowship, 1964. *Address:* 14N418, MIT, Cambridge, MA 02139, USA.

KANE, Peter Evans, b. 27 Feb. 1932, Beverly Hills, California, USA. College Professor. m. Marguerite Coniff, 30 May 1982, St Croix, 1 son, 3 daughters by previous marriage. *Education:* BA, 1954, MA, 1960, University of California; PhD, Purdue University, 1967. *Literary Appointments:* Reviewer, Choice, 1965–; Book Review Editor, Today's Speech, 1971–72. Associate Editor: Communication Quarterly, 1977–78; Free Speech Yearbook, 1973–78, 1982–. *Publications:* Speech Communication in a Democratic Society, 1974, 77, 79; Free Speech Yearbook, Editor, 1979, 80, 81; Murder, Courts and the Press, 1986. *Contributions to:* Choice; Free Speech Yearbook; 1983 Philosophic Exchange. *Memberships:* Sustaining Life Member, Eastern Communication Association; Sustaining Member, Speech Communication Association. *Address:* 138 Erie Street, Brockport, NY 14420, USA.

KANE, Thomas Anthony, b. 27 June 1945, Philadelphia, Pennsylvania, USA. University Professor. *Education:* MA, Notre Dame University; STL, Catholic University of America; PhD, Ohio State University. *Literary Appointment:* Editor, The Paulist. *Publication:* Introducing Dance in Christian Worship (with Ronald Gagne and Rovert VerEcke), 1984. *Contributions to:* The Sacred Play of Children, Edited by Diane Apostolos Cappadona, 1982; Life Gifts (column), Nov. 1980; The Year of the Spirit, 1980; Celebrating 1980: A Ministry Day Book, Planner, 1980; Celebrating, 1979; Liturgy, Sep-Oct, 1979; Jan-Feb, 1979. *Address:* Weston School of Theology, 3 Phillips Place, Cambridge, MA 02138, USA.

KANERVA, Erkki Olavi, 14 Oct. 1936, Tampere, Finland. Editor. m. 1 Feb. 1958, 1 son, 1 daughter. *Major Publications:* 16 Causerie books called Yrjö (George), 1969–84. Contributor to: Various publications – several thousand stories. *Membership:* Finnish Writers Society. *Address:* Takahuhdintie 31, 33530 Tampere 53, Finland.

KANETZKE, Howard William, b. 25 Feb. 1932, Racine, Wisconsin, USA. m. Lucetta Caroline Bloedow, 15 Sep. 1956, Oconomowoc, Wisconsin, 1 son, 1 daughter. *Education:* BA, History, University of Wisconsin. *Appointments:* Editor, juvenile publications, State Historical Society, Wisconsin, 1965–. *Publications:* Grade A Level, ibid: Airplanes, Trains, Automobiles, (History). *Contributions:* Editor, The 30th Star, 1959–65, Badger History, 1965–, State Historical Society publications for school students. *Address:* 5726 Elder Place, Madison, WI 53705, USA.

KANTONEN, Taito Almar, b. 24 Apr. 1900, Karstula, Finland. Educator. *Education:* BA, University of Minnesota, USA. 1924; MA Harvard University, 1926; STB, 1928, PhD, 1931, Boston University. *Publications:* The Message of the Church to the World Today, 1941; Resurgence of the Gospel, 1948; Risti ja Tahtilippu, Finnish, 1950; Theology of Evangelism, 1954; The Christian Hope, 1954; Theology for Christian Stewardship, 1956; Life After Death, 1962; Man in the Eyes of God, 1972; Christian Faith Today, 1974; Good News for all Seasons, 1975; To Live is Christ, 1977. *Contributions to:* Various philosophy and religious journals including: religion in Life, Editorial Board; Philosophy Review; Church History; Theology Today; Encyclopedia of Religion. *Honours:* Book of the Month, Religious Book Club, 1948; Knight, Order of the White Rose, Finland, 1954; Honorary Doctorates, Augustana College, University of Helsinki and Ohio Wesleyan University. *Memberships:* Various professional organisations including: American Philosophical Association; Past Chairman, Division of Theology Studies, Lutheran Council in USA. *Address:* 816 Snowhill Boulevard, Springfield, OH 45504, USA.

KANTZER, Kenneth Sealer, b. 29 Mar. 1917, Detroit, Michigan, USA. Minister; Educator. m. Ruth Forbes, 21 Sep. 1939, Ashland, Ohio, 1 son, 1 daughter. *Education:* BA, Ashland College, 1938; MA, Ohio State University, 1939; BD, STM, Faith Theological Seminary; PhD, Harvard University, 1950; Post graduate, Goettingen, Germany, 1954, Basel, Switzerland, 1955. *Publications:* Editor: Evangelical Roots, 1978; Perspectives in Evangelical Theology, 1979. Editor in Chief, Christianity Today, 1978–82. *Contributions to:* Religions in a Changing World; The Evangelicals; Inspiration and Interpretation; The Word for this Century; Jesus of Nazareth, Saviour and Lord; Journal of Evangelical Theology Society, Book Editor; His Magazine, Contributing Editor; Christianity Today, Editorial Adviser and Dean of Research Institute, 1984–. *Honours:* Honorary Degrees: DD, Ashland Theological Seminary, 1981; DD, Gordon College, 1979; DHUm, John Brown University, 1981. Hopkins Scholar, Harvard University, 1944–46; Teacher of the Year, Wheaton College, 1962. *Memberships:* President 1983–84, Chancellor 1984– Trinity College, Deerfield, Illinois; Past Secretary, IFACS Educational Foundation; Board of Directors, Heritage Christian School, Lincolnshire, Illinois, 1984–; American Theological Society; President, Evangelical Theology Society; Evangelical Philosphy Society. *Address:* 1752 Spruce Avenue, Highland Park, IL 60035, USA.

KAPLAN, Lois, b. 6 Feb. 1932. Freelance Writer; Composer; Sculptor; Recreation Consultant; Lecturer, Fine Arts & Humanities. *Education:* BMus, DePaul University, 1958; MSc, University of Wisconsin, 1963; MArts, Jacksonville State University, 1978; Postgraduate Studies, Florida State University, 1981; Graduate, Cmd & General Staff College, Ft Leavenworth, Kansas, 1981; Sculpture, Arrowment School of Arts & Crafts, University of Tennissee. *Appointments include:* Fellow, International Academy of Poets (Cambridge); Fellow, Centro Studi E Scambi Internazionali Accademia Leonardo Da Vinci, (Rome); Fellow, World Literature Academy; Chairman Steering & Finance Committees & Programme Executor for the Alabama Council of the Arts and Humanities; Freelance Writer; Teacher; Choir Director; Professional Trombonist & Private Music Instrument Teacher. *Publications:* Music compositions with Lyrics; Pallas Athens March & Son, 1973; Salute to the Citizen Soldier, 1980; This Indeed We'll Defend, 1981. *Contributor to:* Annual Anthology of College Poetry; Poetry Magazine; The DePaulia; Cardinal Magazine; New Yorker Magazine; Chicago Daily News; Chicago Today; Chicago Tribune. *Address:* 616 Lenwood Dr, Anniston, AL 36206, USA.

KAPLAN, Nathan O(ram), b. 25 June 1917, New York, USA. Professor of Chemistry. *Education:* University of California, Los Angeles; University of California Berkeley; PhD. *Literary Appointments:* Co-Chairman, Editorial Committee, Analytical Biochemistry; Co-Editor-in-Chief, Methods of Enzymology, 63 volumes. *Publications:* Author and co-author of almost 438 articles in various journals. *Honours Include:* Eli Lilly Award in Biochemistry, 1953; Guggenheim Fellowship, 1964–65; American Association for Clinical Chemistry Award, 1976; Honorary DSC Degree, Brandeis University, 1982; Fogarty Scholar-in-Residence (NIH), 1982. *Memberships:* National Academy of Sciences;

AAAS; American Society of Biochemistry; American Society of Bacteriologists; American Academy of Arts and Sciences; Sigma Xi. *Address:* University of California, San Diego, La Jolla, CA 92093, USA.

KAPLAN, Norman M, b. 2 Jan. 1931, Dallas, Texas, USA. Professor of Internal Medicine (Medical Teaching). m. Audrey Richman, 27 Nov. 1975, Dallas, Texas, 2 sons, 4 daughters. *Education:* BS Pharmacy, University of Texas, 1947–50; MD, University of Texas Southwestern Medical School, Dallas, 1950–54; Rotating Internship, Parkland Memorial Hospital, Dallas, 1954–55; Residency in Internal Medicine, Parkland, 1955–58. *Literary Appointments:* Instructor, 1961–62, Assistant Professor, 1962–68, Associate Professor, 1968–70, Professor of Internal Medicine, University of Texas Southwestern Medical School, Dallas, 1970–75; Deputy Vice-President for Research Programs, American Heart Association, Dallas, 1975–76; Professor of Internal Medicine, Dallas, 1977–. *Major Publications:* Clinical Hypertension, 3rd edition, 1982; Prevent Your Heart Attack, 1983; Prevention of Coronary Heart Disease, 1984. *Contributor to:* Journal of Clinical Endocrinology & Metabolism; Seminars on Nephrology; American Heart Journal; American Journal of Nephrology; Journal of Hypertension; American Journal of Cardiology. *Honours:* National Institute of Health Preventative Cardiology Academic Award, 1979–84. *Memberships include:* American Federation for Clinical Research; Endocrine Society; Fellow, American College, of Physicians; American Public Health Association; American College of Preventative Medicine. *Address:* 5323 Harry Hines, Dallas, TX 75235, USA.

KARAKORPI, Liisa Helena, b. 23 Feb. 1943, Helsinki, Finland. Teacher of Native Language. *Education:* MA. *Publications:* Children's Books: Omenaiset Pajut, 1971; Salaisten Lintujen Linnunrata, 1973; Jannitysmaa, 1980; Outi Ja Kultamuna, 1983; Noiden Kummitytto, 1985. *Memberships:* Suomen Kirjailijaliitto (The Society of Finland's Authors); Sudmen Nuorisokirjaillijat (Organization for Authors of Youth Literature). *Honours:* The Award of the City of Turku, 1971; The Awards of Kustannusosakeyhtio Otava, 1982, 1983. *Address:* Tyysterniementie 5 B 12, 53900 Lappeenranta, Finland.

KARAMFILOV, Efrem, b. 27 Nov. 1911, Kyustendil, Bulgaria. Writer. m. Lada Galina. *Education:* Law Degree, Sofia University. *Literary Appointments:* Director, The Literary Institution of the Bulgarian Academy of Science. *Publications:* Essays: Shadows of the Past, 1960; Heroes and Characters, in three volumes, 1962–67; George Dimitrov at the Leipzig Court, 1972; The Most Bulgarian Time, 1976. *Contributor to:* All main Bulgarian literary editions. *Honours:* Dimitrov Prize, 1972; A People's Worker of Culture, 1974. *Memberships:* Union of Bulgarian Writers. *Address:* bloc 98 B, complex Mladost, Sofia, Bulgaria.

KARASLAVOV, Slav Chr, b. 26 Mar 1932, Debar, Bulgaria. Writer. m. Anetta Tzvetanova Karaslovova, 30 Dec. 1959, 2 sons. *Education:* History Degree. *Publications:* Poetry, Privately With My Son, 1966; After A Time, 1966; Poems, 1973; Novel, The Despot Slav, 1970; The Decay of Ivanko; The Brothers from Soloun, novel; I've walked So Many Paths, 1976. *Membership:* Secretary, Vice President, Union of Bulgarian Writers. *Address:* bloc 315, Nezabravka Street, Sofia, Bulgaria.

KARKHANIS, Sharad, b. 8 Mar. 1935, Khopili, India. Librarian/Professor of Library Science. *Education:* Diploma in Library Science, Bombay Library Association, Bombay, India, 1956; BA, Economics, University of Bombay, India, 1958; MLS, Library Science, Rutgers: The State University, 1962; MA, Political Science, Brooklyn College of City University of New York, 1967; PhD, Political Science, New York University, 1978. *Literary Appointments:* Library Trainee, United States Information Library, Bombay,

1955–58; Library Trainee, Layton Public Library, England, 1958–59; Librarian, Montclair Public Library, Montclair, New Jersey, 1959–60; Librarian, East Orange Public Library, East Orange, New Jersey, 1960–63; Librarian, Brooklyn College of CUNY, Brooklyn, New York, 1963–64; Professor Library Department and Political Science Department, 1964–. *Publications:* Indian Politics and the Role of the Press, 1981. *Contributions to:* Numerous book reviews to American Reference Books Annual; Acquisition of Asian Material of North American and European Libraries, in Library Acquisition: Theory and Practice, 1984; Contributor to numerous professional journals. *Honours:* Certificate of Appreciation, Distinguished Service, Library Association of the City University of New York, 1972; Tarakanath Das Award, New York University, 1977. *Memberships:* Past president, Asian/Pacific American Librarians Association; Past president, Library Association of the City University of New York; American Library Association; Asian Society. *Address:* Kingsborough Community College Library, Oriental Boulevard, Brooklyn, NY 11235, USA.

KARLSSON, Dick Viking, b. 16 Aug. 1952, Pargas, Finland, Laboratory Engineer. m. Anneli Alice Asunta, 11 Mar. 1976, Helsinki, 1 son, 1 daughter. *Education:* MSc (Civil Engineering). *Publications:* Mellan Infrarott Och Ultraviolett (poetry), 1980; Forenklad Bild Av Tystnaden (poetry), 1982. *Membership:* Finlands Svenska Forfattareforening. *Literary Agent:* Söderströms. *Address:* Malmnäs Strandväg 1, 21600 Pargas, Finland.

KARLSSON, Throstur Julius, b. 1 Nov. 1948, Reykjavik, Iceland. Author. m. 6 Feb. 1976, 2 sons, 2 daughters. *Literary Appointment:* Poet and Adventure Writer. *Publications:* Floskuskeytio, 1971; Leitin ao Nattulfinum, 1973; Gullskipio tynda, 1975; Sagan af Villa Villiketti, 1976; Aokomuhundurinn, 1976; Strutsunginn, 1976; Illfyglio, 1976; Leppaluoi fer a Kreik, 1976; Konungur Loftsins; Silkinattfotin, 1978; Ognvaldurinn, 1978; Gamlarskvold i sv, 1979; Litli apakotturinn, 1980; Praelar soldansins, 1978; Uglan (poems), 1980; Fralandsvidar, 1981; Eltingaleikurinn mikli, 1982. *Membership:* The Writers Association of Icelend. *Address:* Selvogsgata 1, Hafnarfjörour, Iceland.

KARNOW, Stanley, b. 4 Feb. 1925, New York City, New York, USA. Writer. m. Annette Kline, 21 Apr. 1959, Gibraltar, 2 sons, 1 daughter. *Education:* BA, Harvard University, USA; Sorbonne, France; Ecole des Sciences Politques; Nieman Fellow, Fellow of Kennedy School of Government and East Asia Research Center, Harvard University. *Publications:* Southeast Asia, 1963, 65; Mao and China: From Revolution to Revolution, 1972; Vietnam: A History, 1983. *Contributions to:* New York Times; GEO; Atlantic; Foreign Affairs; Foreign Policy; Esqire; Saturday Review; Le Point; Le Matin; Paris; Encounter. Weekly column in 40 newspapers including: Washington Star; Baltimore Sun; Boston Globe; Nashville Tennessean; Miami Herald. *Honours:* Overseas Press Club, 1967, 68, 83; Dupoont, Polk and Emmy Awards, 1984. *Memberships:* White House Correspondents Association; Foreign Correspondents Club, Hong Kong. *Literary Agent:* Ronald Goldfarb, Washington. *Address:* 10850 Springknoll Drive, Potomac, MD 20854, USA.

KARP, David, b. 5 May 1922, New York City, USA. m. Lillian Klass, 25 Dec, 1944, Neosho, 2 sons. *Education:* BSc, Social Sciences, City College of the City of New York. *Publications:* Platoon, 1953; One, 1954; The Day of the Monkey, 1955; All Honorable Men, 1956; Leave Me Alone, 1957; Enter, Sleeping, 1960; The Last Believers, 1964; Vice President in Charge of Revolution, with M D Lincoln, 1960. *Contributor to:* Short Stories in, Esquire; The American Magazine; Saturday Evening Post; Collier's; Park East; Argosy; Articles, Book Reviews in, The Nation; New York Times; Book Review; Saturday Review; Los Angeles Times; New York Herald Tribune; Journal of the National Academy of Television Arts & Sciences. *Honours:* Ohio State University First Award for TV Drama, 1948, 1958; Guggenheim Fellow,

1956; Look Magazine Award for TV Drama, 1958; Mystery Writers of America 'Edgar' for Best TV Drama, 1959; American Bar Association Silver Gavel Award for TV Drama, 1963; Emmy Award for TV Drama, 1965. *Memberships:* Writers Guild of America, Council Member, 1963–66, Board of Directors, 1968–74, President, TV Radio Branch, 1969–71, Trustee, Penions Plan, 1969–, various other offices; PEN; Dramatists Guild. *Literary Agent:* Frank Cooper, Los Angeles, California, USA. *Address:* The Cooper Agency, 10100 Santa Monica Boulevard, Los Angeles, CA 90067, USA.

KARSEN, Sonja Petra, b. 11 Apr. 1919, Berlin, Germany (US Citizen 1945–). Professor of Spanish. *Education:* BA, Carleton College, USA, 1939; MA, Bryn Mawr College, 1941; PhD, Columbia University, 1950. *Publications include:* Guillermo Valencia, 1951; Eduational Development in Costa Rica with UNESCO's Technical Assistance, 1951–54, 1954; Jaime Torres Bodet: A Poet in a Changing World, 1963; Selected Poems of Jaime Torres Bodet, 1964; Versos y prosas de Jaime Torres Bodet, 1966; Jaime Torres Bodet, 1971; Editor, Language Association Bulletin, 1980–82; numerous articles, reviews and translations; numerous papers read to colleges and conferences, etc. *Contributor to:* World Literature Today; Hispania; Symposim; Americas; Texas Quarerly, etc. *Honours include:* Chevalier dans l'ordre des Plamas Académiques, Paris France, 1963; numerous grants and fellowships; Fulbright Lecturer, Freie Unversität Berlin, 1968; National Distinguished Leadership Award, New York State Association of Foreign Languages Language Techers, 1979; Alumni Achievement Award, Carleton College, 1982; Member, Ateuco Doctor Jaime Torres Bodet, Mexico, 1984; Spanish Heritage Award, 1981. *Memberships include:* Phi Sigma Iota; Delagate Assembly, MLA, 1976–78; numerous committees. *Address:* Department of Foreign Languages and Literatures, Skidmore College, Saratoga Springs, NY 12866, USA.

KARSIKAS, Leevi Kustavi, b. 5 June 1933, Haapavesi, Finland. Author. m. Anna Maria Jaakola, 4 Nov. 1960, Nurmijärvi, 1 son, 1 daughter. *Publications:* Hukkuva erämaa, 1969; Riekko Jäniksenjalka, 1975; Meri veti henkeä, 1977; Lintuvuonna, 1980, Karhunpiilo, 1981; Hiljainen erämaa, 1982; Tuntureita ja outamaita, 1983; Seitatunturut, 1984; Unelma suurlohesta, 1985. *Contributions to:* Kaleva; Kalajokilaasko; Ase and Erä. *Honours:* Awards of State, 1982, 1983, 1984 and 1985; Award of Arvi A Karisto Foundation, 1982; Award of the Finnish Society of Authors, 1984. *Memberships:* Society of Authors. *Literary Agent:* Publisher, Arvi A Karisto Ltd. *Address:* Oulaistenkatu 24 B 22, 86300 Oulainen, Finland.

KASNER, Nancy Anne, b. 6 Nov. 1948, Minneapolis, Minnesota, USA. Editor. *Education:* BA Cum laude, College of Liberal Arts, University of Minnesota; graduate credits, University of Minnesota; graduate credits, University of Minnesota. *Literary Appointments:* Manuscript editor, American Journal of Ophthalmology, Chicago, Illinois, 1978–80; Free-lance manuscript editor, Archives of Physical Medicine and Rehabilitation, Chicago, 1981–; Publications editor, College of American Pathologists, Skokie, 1983–. *Membership:* American Medical Writers Association. *Address:* 644 East ShaBonne Trail, Mount Prospect, IL 60056, USA.

KASSELL, Paula, b. 5 Dec. 1917, New York City, New York, USA. Editor, Writer. m. Gerson Friedman, 16 Aug. 1941, New York City, 1 son, 1 daughter. *Education:* BA, Barnard College, Columbia University, 1939. *Literary Appointments:* Editor, New Directions for Women, 1971. *Contributions to:* Hundreds of articles and editorial in New Directions for Women. *Memberships:* Author's Guild; Women's National Book Association; Feminist Writers' Guild. *Address:* P O Box 27, Dover, NJ 07801, USA.

KATSARAKIS, Joan, b. 23 Oct. 1922, South Wales. Writer. m. George Katsarakis, 17 Apr. 1963, Chicago, 1 daughter. *Education:* BS, Elementary Education; MS,

English, Northwestern University. *Literary Appointments:* Special Features Editor, Lancaster Newspapers Inc, Pennsylvania, 1951–58; Childrens Editor, religious publishing house, 1959–62. *Publication:* They Triumphed Over Their Handicaps, 1981. *Contributions to:* Various school journals including, Pennsylvania School Journal, Indiana Teacher, Young American Teacher, North Dakota Teacher, etc, 1940's. *Honours:* National Dorothy Dowe Award, coverage of home furnishings news, 1950's; 1st prize, fiction contest, Iota Sigma Epsilon, Northwestern University. *Memberships:* Society of Childrens Book Writers; League of Vermont Writers. *Address:* 10 Briar Lane, Essex Junction, VT 05452, USA.

KATZ, Pierre, b. 8 Jan. 1941, Cluj, Romania. Librarian. *Education:* Licencie es Sciences Politiques; Diplome superieur de bibliothecaires. *Publications:* Tours, Poetry, 1970; Angoisses, Poetry, 1977; L'Inferno Quotidien, Novel, 1979; La Ligne du Destin, 1984. *Contributions to:* Service de Presse Suisse. *Memberships:* PEN; Groupe d'Olten; Association Vaudoise des Ecrivains (Membership committee member). *Address:* 6 Primerose, 1007 Lausanne, Switzerland.

KATZMAN, Martin Theodore, b. 15 July 1941, Boston, Massachusetts, USA. Economics Professor. m. Arlene Cohen, 31 July 1966, Teaneck, New Jersey, 1 son 2 daughters. *Education:* AB summa cum laude, Harvard College, 1963; PhD, Yale University, 1966. *Publications:* Political Economy of Urban Schools, 1971; Cities and Frontiers in Brazil, 1977; Solar and Wind Energy, 1984; Chemical Catastrophes, 1985. *Contributions to:* Academic and popular journals on public finance, urban development, renewable energy and education. *Honours:* Woodrow Wilson Graduate Fellow, 1964; NSF Graduate Fellow, 1965–67; Guggenheim Fellow, 1980. *Memberships:* Phi Beta Kappa; American Association for the Advancement of Science; American Economic Association. *Address:* University of Texas at Dallas, Box 688, Richardson, TX 75080, USA.

KAUFMAN, Martin, b. 6 Dec. 1940, Boston, Massachusetts, USA. Professor of History. m. Henrietta Flax, 22 Dec. 1968, Milton, Massachusetts, USA, 2 sons (1 deceased), 1 daughter. *Education:* BA, 1962, Boston University; MA, 1963, University of Pittsburgh; PhD, 1969, Tulane University. *Literary Appointments:* Editorial Director, Historical Journal of Massachusetts, 1972–. *Publications:* Homeopathy in America, 1971; American Medical Education, 1976; The University of Vermont College of Medicine, 1979; Dictionary of American Medical Biography, 1984. *Contributions to:* American History Illustrated; Yankee Magazine, and others. *Address:* 666 Western Avenue, Westfield, MA 01085, USA.

KAUFMAN, Shirley, b. 5 June, 1923, Seattle, Washington, USA. Poet. m. H M Daleski, 3 daughters by previous marriage. *Education:* BA, University of California at Los Angeles, 1944; MA State University of California at San Francisco, 1967. *Appointments:* Visiting Lecturer, University of Massachusetts, 1974; Visiting Professor, Department of English, University of Washington, 1977; Poet in Residence, Oberlin, 1979; Teaching Association, Hebrew University, 1980; Visiting Professor, 1983–84. *Publications:* The Floor Keeps Turning, 1980; Gold Country, 1974; A Canopy on the Desert (translation from the Hebrew of the poems of Israeli poet Abba Kovner), 1973; The Light of Lost Suns (translations from the Hebrews of the poems of Amir Gilboa), 1979; From One Life to Another, 1979; Claims, 1984; My Little Sister and Selected Poems 1945–1985, (translation from the Hebrew of Israeli poet Abba Kovner), 1986. *Contributions to:* American Poetry Review; The Atlantic Monthly; Choice; European Judaism; Field; Harper's; The Iowa Review; Kayak; Massachussetts Review; The Nation; The New Yorker; Poetry North West; The Southern Review. *Memberships:* Poetry Association of America. *Honours:* 1st Prize, San Francisco State College Academy of American Poets, 1964; US Award of the International

Poetry Forum, 1969; Association of American University Professional Award for the International Council for the Arts Selection in Poetry, 1970; NEA Fellowship, 1979. *Address:* 7 Rashba Street, Jerusalem, Israel.

KAURAKA, Kauraka, b. 5 Sep. 1951, Rarotonga, Cook Islands, South Pacific. Education Officer. *Education:* BA, Sociology & Education, University of the South Pacific; Teaching Certificate, New Zealand, 1973. *Major Publications:* Tales of Manihiki (folktales); 1982; Legends from the Atolls (folktales), 1983; Return to Havaiki (poetry), 1985. *Contributor to:* Mana (Literary journal, Fiji); Taunga '84 (Rarotonga). *Memberships:* Taunga Creative Writers Society, Rarotonga, 1984; PEN Auckland Branch, New Zealand, 1985; Polynesian Society, Auckland, 1985. *Address:* PO Box 503, Rarotonga, Cook Islands, South Pacific.

KAURANEN, Anja Kyllikki, b. 23 May 1954, Helsinki, Finland. Writer. *Education:* Ba, University of Helsinki, 1977. *Publications:* Sonja O kävi täällä, 1981, Tushka, 1983; Kiltasuu, 1985. *Honour:* J H Erkko Award for the best novel of the year, 1982. *Memberships:* The Finnish Writer's Association; The Stormy Group, group of young Finnish writers. *Literary Agent:* Publishing Company; WSOY. *Address:* RJP 17, 04370 Rusutjärvi, Finland.

KAVANAGH, (P)atrick (J)oseph, b. 6 Jan. 1931, Sussex, England. Writer. 2 daughters. *Education:* MA, Oxford University. *Publications:* Novels: A Son and Dance; A Happy Man; People and Weather. Books for Children: Scarf Jack; Rebel for Good. Poems: One and One, 1960; On the Way to the Depot, 1967; About Time, 1970; Edward Thomas in Heaven, 1974; Life Before Death, 1979; Selected Poems, 1982. Editor: Collected Poems of Ivor Gurney, Boxford Book of Short Poems; Collected Poems of G K Chesterton. *Contributor to:* The Guardian; New Statesman; New Yorker; Encounter; London Magazine. Columnist for The Spectator, 1983–. *Honours:* Richard McCleary Prize, 1966; Guardian Fiction Prize, 1968. *Literary Agent:* A D Peters, London. *Address:* A D Peters, 10 Buckingham Street, London WC2N 6BU, England.

KAWALEC, Julian, b. 11 Oct. 1916, Wrzawy, Poland, Writer. m. Irene Wierzbanowska, 2 June 1948, Cracow, 1 daughter. *Education:* Graduate, Jagellonian University, Cracow. *Publications:* Paths Among Streets, 1957; Scars, 1960; Bound to the Land, 1962; Overthrown Elms, 1963; In The Sun, 1963; The Dancing Hawk, 1964; Black Light, 1965; Wedding March, 1966; Appeal, 1968; Searching for Home, 1968; Praise of Hands, 1969; To Cross the River, 1973; Grey Aureole, 1974; Great Feast, 1974; To Steal the Brother, 1982. *Contributor to:* Literary Life, Cracow; Literary Monthly, Warsaw. *Honours:* Prize Plish Editors, 1962; Prize of Minister of Culture and Art, 1967, 85; Prize of State, 1975. *Memberships:* Polish Pen Club; Polish Writers Association; Society European Culture. *Address:* 39 Zaleskiego, 31-525 Krakow, Poland.

KAY, Mara, b. Europe. Retired. *Publications:* In Place of Katia, 1964; The Burning Candle, 1966; Masha, 1969; The Youngest Lady in Waiting, 1971; The Circling Star, 1973; The Storm Warning, hard cover, 1976; Lolo, 1981; One Small Clue, 1982. *Memberships:* PEN, London, England; Marquis Library Society. *Address:* 2 Lent Avenue, Hempstead, NY 11550, USA.

KAY, Stephen Douglas, b. 29 Jan. 1949, Christchurch, New Zealand. Journalist. m. Margaret Victoria Michael, 21 Aug. 1981, London, England, 1 son, 1 daughter. *Education:* MA Honours; Diploma of Journalism with distinction, Canterbury University, New Zealand. *Literary Appointments:* Christchurch Press, New Zealand, 1970–71; Hawke's Bay Herald-Tribune, 1972–76; Farmers Weekly, London, England, 1979–. *Contributions to:* New Zealand Travel Magazines, 1976–79, Variety of agricultural publications in UK and worldwide, 1979–. *Honours:* Travel Scholarship, Food From Britain, 1984. *Membership:* Guild of Agricultural

Journalists. *Address:* 26 Thorpebank Road, London W12 0PQ, England.

KAYE, Geraldine, b. 14 Jan. 1925, Watford, England. Writer. *Education:* BSc, University of London. *Publications:* The Pony Raffle, 1966; The Blue Rabbit, 1967; Kassim and the Sea Monkey, 1967; Tawno, Gypsy Boy, 1968; Koto and the Lagoon, 1968; Nowhere to Stop, 1972; Runaway Boy, 1972; Kassim Goes Fishing, 1972; Kofi and the Eagle, 1973; Marie Alone, 1973; Joanna All Alone, 1974; Billy-Boy, 1976; A Different Sort of Christmas, 1976; Children of the Turnpike, 1976; Penny Black, 1976; Joey's Room, 1979; King of the Knockdown Gingers, 1979; The Day After Yesterday, 1981; Frangipani Summer, 1982; The Blue Dragon, 1982; The Donkey Strike, 1984; Comfort Herself, 1984; The Biggest Bonfire in the World, 1985; The Call of the Wild Wood, 1986. *Honours:* Winner, The Other Award, for a book Comfort Herself, 1985. *Memberships:* PEN; Society of Authors; West Country Writers; Association; National Book League. *Address:* 39 High Kingsdown, Bristol BS2 8EW, England.

KAYE, Marvin Nathan, b. 10 Mar. 1938, Philadelphia, Pennsylvania, USA. Writer. m. Saralee Bransdorf, 4 Aug. 1963, Wilkes-Barre, Pennsylvania, 1 daughter. *Education:* BA, MA, Pennsylvania State University; Graduate study, University of Denver, Colorado. *Literary Appointments:* Senior Editor, Harcourt Brace Jovanovich; Adjunct Assistant Professor of Creative Writing, New York University. *Publications:* The Histrionic Holmes, 1971; A Lively Game of Death, 1972; A Toy is Born, The Stein and Day Handbook of Magic, 1973; The Grand Ole Opry Murders, The Handbook of Mental Magic, 1974; Bullets for Macbeth, Fiends and Creatures (Editor), 1975; Brother Theodore's Chamber of Horrors (Editor), 1975; Catalog of Magic, My Son the Druggist, The Laurel and Hardy Murders, 1977; The Masters of Solitude, 1978; The Incredible Umbrella, My Brother the Druggist, 1979; Ghosts (Editor), 1981; The Amorous Umbrella, The Possession of Immanuel Wolf, 1981; Wintermind (with Parke Godwin), 1982; The Soap Opera Slaughters, 1982; A Cold Blue Light (with Parke Godwin), 1983; Masterpieces of Terror and the Supernatural (Editor), 1985. *Contributions to:* (essays) Amazing; Fantastic; Galileleo, Family Digest, etc. Columnist, Science Fiction Chronicle. *Honours include:* First runner-up, best novel, British Fantasy Awards, 1978. *Memberships:* Several professional organizations. *Literary Agents:* Mel Berger, William Morris Inc. (books); Mitch Douglas, ICM (plays, films, TV). *Address:* c/o William Morris Inc, 1350 Avenue of the Americas, New York, NY 10019, USA.

KEALY, Sean Patrick, b. 29 Mar. 1937, Thurles, Republic of Ireland. Professor of Scripture. *Education:* BA, MA Ancient Classics, University College, Dublin; BD, STW, Gregorian University, Rome, Italy; BSS, LSS, Biblical Institute, Rome. *Publications:* The Early Church and Africa, 1975; The Changing Bible, 1977; Who is Jesus of Nazareth ?, 1977; Jesus the Teacher, 1978; That You May Believe, 1978; Luke's Gospel Today, 1979; Mark's Gospel, 1982; Soundings in Irish Spirituality, 1983; Towards Biblical Spirituality, 1985. *Contributions to:* Doctrine and Life; Furrow; Tablet; Catholic Biblical Quarterly. *Memberships:* Chairman, Kenyan Association for Liturgical Music; Committee, Irish Biblical Association; Catholic Biblical Association in USA. *Address:* House of Theology, Holy Ghost Missionary College, Kimmage Manor, Dublin 12, Republic of Ireland.

KEARNS, Lionel John, b. 16 Feb. 1937, Nelson, British Columbia, Canada. Writer; Educator. m. Geraldine Sinclair, 31 Dec. 19 , 3 sons, 1 daughter. *Education:* BA 1961, MA, University of British Columbia, 1964. *Literary Appointments:* Associate Professor, Simon Fraser University, English Department, 1966. *Publications:* Songs of Circumstance, 1963; Listen George, 1965; Pointing, 1967; By the Light of the Silvery McLune: Media Parables, Poems, Signs, Gestures and other assaults on the Interface, 1969; The Brith of God, (with Gordon Payne), cine-poem, 1973;

About Time, 1974; Negotiating a New Canadian Constitution, (with Gordon Payne) cine-poem, 1974; Practicing up to be Human, 1978; Ignoring the Bomb: New and Selected Poems, 1982; Convergences, 1984; Critical Studies: George Bowering, Metaphysic in Time: The Poetry of Lionel Kearns, A Way With Words, 1983. *Contributions to:* Numerous. *Address:* 1616 Charles Street, Vancouver, B C, Canada, V5L 2T3.

KEATING, Donald Robert, b. 9 Dec. 1925, Silver Creek, Manitoba, Canada. m. Gloria Maytot Bower, 5 Sep. 1952, Killarney, Manitoba, 2 sons, 2 daughters. *Education:* BA; BD; MES. *Publications:* The Power to Make It Happen, 1975; The Future of Neighbourhood Organizing, in Participatory Democracy in Action, 1979. *Contributions to:* Winnipeg Tribune, various series of articles; Renewal Magazine; Chicago City Magazine; Looking Back at Community Organizing. *Address:* 283 Booth Avenue, Toronto, Ontario, Canada M4M 2M7.

KEATING, L(ouis) Clark, b. 20 Aug. 1907, Philadelphia, Pennsylvania, USA. Author; Professor. *Education:* BA, Colgate University, 1928; MA, 1930, PhD, 1934, Harvard University. *Publications:* Numerous including: Audubon, The Kentucky Years, general, 1976; Andre Maurois, scholarly, 1969; Etienne Pasquier, 1972. Textbooks: Conversational French, with H V Besso, 1944; A Short Review of French Grammar, with C A Choquette, 1948; Impressions d'Amerique, with K Huvos, 1970; Selections de Moliere, Voltaire, Hugo, with M Moraud, 1972. Translations including: An Introduction to American Literature, 1971; An Introduction to English Literature, 1974 both by J L Borges and translated with R O Evans; Life in Rosu. *Honours:* Palmes academiques, Officer, France; QBK. *Memberships include:* American Association of University Professors; American Association of Teachers of French; Modern Language Association. *Address:* 608 Raintree Road, Lexington, KY 40502, USA.

KEATING, Reginald James Thomas (Rex), b. 14 Feb. 1910, London, England. Writer; Broadcaster; Mass Media Consultant. *Publications:* Nubian Twilight, 1962; Nubian Rescue, 1975; Grass Roots Radio, 1978; UNESCO in Africa, 1983; Booklets: Man and the Biosphere: After Ten Years, 1982; Microbes in the Service of Man, 1983. *Contributor to:* Open University; UNESCO Courier; UNESCO Features; Encyclopedia Britannica; BBC and other broadcasting organizations. *Memberships:* Royal Institute of Internaitonal Affairs; Egypt Exploration Society. *Literary Agents:* Harvey Unna & Stephen Durbridge Limited. *Address:* Orcemont, 78120 Rambouillet, France.

KECSKESI, Tibor, b. 21 Dec. 1920. Journalist; Newspaper Editor. m. Dr Maria Kecskesi, 3 children. *Education:* Military Academy, Budapest, Hungary. *Appointments:* Editor in Chief, Hungarian Paper, Nemzetor. *Publications:* 4 volumes of poetry; Editor, 2 int anthologies and 1 Hungarian anthology. *Contributor to:* Numerous major newspapers, journals, reviews and anthologies in various languages. *Honours:* Various poetry prizes; Hon Citizens, 4 cities. *Address:* Postfach 70, 8 Munich 34, German Federal Republic.

KEE, Robert, b. 5 Oct. 1919, Calcutta, India. Author; Broadcaster. *Education:* MA, Magdalen College, Oxford University. *Publications:* A Crowd is not Company, 1948; The Impossible Shore, 1949; A Sign of the Times, 1954; Broadstrop in Season, 1959; Refugee World, 1961; The Green Flag, 1972; Ireland: A History, 1980; The World We Left Behind, 1984; The World We Fought For, 1985. *Contributor to:* New Statesman; Times Literary Supplement; Spectator (Literary Editor, 1957–58); Observer, Sunday Times; NY Review of Books. *Honours:* Atlantic Award for Literature, 1946; Richard Dimbleby British Academy of Film and TV Arts Award, 1976; Jacobs Award (Dublin), 1981. *Memberships:* Society of Authors; ACTT, Equity. *Literary Agent:* Anthony Sheil Associates. *Address:* c/o Anthony Sheil Associates, 43 Doughty Street, London, WC1N 2LF, England.

KEEBLE, John Robert, b. 24 Nov. 1944, Winnipeg, Manitoba, Canada. Writer; Professor. m. Claire Sheldon, 3 Sep. 1964, National City, California, USA. 3 sons. *Education:* BA, (Magna Cum Laude), University of Redlands; MFA, University of Iowa. *Publications:* Crab Canon, 1971; Mine, 1974, Yellowfish, 1980. *Contributions to:* Confluence; Works In Progress; American Review; Traces; Willow Springs; Northwest Review. *Honour:* John Simon Guggenheim Memorial Foundation Fellowship, 1982–83. *Membership:* PEN, American Center. *Literary Agent:* Georges Borchardt. *Address:* RR 2, Box 142-7, Medical Lake, WA 99022, USA.

KEEGAN, William James, b. 3 July 1938, London, England. Journalist. m. Tessa Ashton, 7 Feb. 1967 London, (divorced 1982), 2 sons, 2 daughters. *Education:* BA Honours, Cantab. *Literary Appointments:* Economics Editor 1977–, Associate Editor 1983–, The Observer. *Publications:* Consulting Father Wintergreen, novel, 1974; A Real Killing, novel, 1976; Who Runs The Economy?, 1979; Mrs Thatcher's Economic Experiment, 1984; Britain Without Oil, 1985. *Contributions to:* The Tablet. *Literary Agent:* Anne McDirmid, Curtis Brown. *Address:* c/o Garrick Club, London WC2, England.

KEIDEL, Eudene Evelyn, b. 9 Feb. 1921, Flanagan, Illinois, USA. Missionary Nurse. m. Levi O Keidel, 24 Sep. 1948, Flanagan, Illinois, 2 sons, 2 daughters. *Education:* Diploma, 1944, Fort Wayne Bible Institute; RN, 1948, Mennonite Hospital School of Nursing; Certificate Lere Degree, Alliance Francaise, Paris, France; BS in Missions, 1975, Fort Wayne Bible College, Fort Wayne, Indiana, USA. *Publications:* African Fables, Book I, 1977; African Fables, Book II, 1981, (several editions, translated into 3 European languages). *Contributions to:* Missions Today; The Mennonite; Pastor's Manual, (Baptist Publication); Congo Missionary Messenger. *Honour:* Medaille du Merite Civique, Government of Republic of Zaire, 1972. *Membership:* Christian Writers' Club, Abbotsford, BC. *Address:* Box 1170, Sumas, WA 98295, USA.

KEIRSTEAD, Phillip Owen, b. 1 May 1938, Waterville, Maine, USA. Professor of Journalism. m. Sonia-Kay Piekos, 20 Apr. 1963, Lowell, Massachusetts. *Education:* BS, Radio & Television, Summa cum laude, Boston University, 1960; MA, Journalism, University of Iowa, 1966. *Publications:* Journalists' Notebook of Live Radio-TV News, 1976; Modern Public Affairs Programming, 1979; All-News Radio, 1980; The Complete Guide to Newsroom Computers, 2nd edition 1984. *Contributions:* News Technology Editor, 1981–. Television/Broadcast Communications; Quill; Broadcast Management/Engineering; National Law Journal; Feedback; RTNDA Communicator; Video Age International; Radio/Active; etc. Book reviewer: Journalism Quarterly; Journal of Broadcasting. *Honours:* Award, American Medical Association, 1975; Silver Gavel Award, American Bar Association, 1976; Ohio State Award 1976; Alumni Award, College of Communication, Boston University, 1983. *Address:* 6252 Bradfordville Road, Tallahassee, FL 32308, USA.

KEISER, Beatrice, b. 8 Jan. 1931, Philadelphia, Pennsylvania, USA. Homemaker. *Education:* University of Pennsylvania. *Publication:* All Our Hearts Are Trumps, 1976. *Contributions to:* Family Circle. *Membership:* National League of American Penwomen. *Address:* 257 Sandpiper Drive, Palm Beach, FL 33480, USA.

KEITH-LUCAS, Bryan, b. 1 Aug. 1912, Cambridge, England. Retired Professor. m. Mary Ross Hardwicke, 24 Oct. 1946, London, 1 son, 2 daughters. *Education:* MA, Pembroke College, Cambridge; MA, Nuffield College, Oxford; D Litt. Professor of Government, University of Kent. *Publications:* The English Local Government Franchise, 1952; History of Local Government in the 20th Century (with P G Richards) 1978; The Unreformed Local Government System,

1980; The Hansard Society: the first 40 years, 1984. *Contributions to:* Numerous contributions to learned journals. *Honours:* D Litt, University of Kent, 1980; CBE, 1983. *Address:* 7 Church Street, Wye, Ashford, Kent TN25 5BN, England.

KELL, Richard Alexander, b. 1 Nov. 1927, Youghal, County Cork, Republic of Ireland. Lecturer. *Education:* BA, H Dip Education, Trinity College, Dublin, 1946–52. *Publications:* Poems: Control Tower, 1962; Differences, 1969; Humours, 1978; Heartwood, 1978; The Broken Circle, 1981. *Contributions to:* Listener; London Magazine; New Statesman; Stand; Observer; Irish Times; Irish Press; Irish Writing; Poetry Ireland; Bell; etc. *Honour:* Poetry Book Society, recommendation, 1962. *Membership:* Composers Guild of Great Britain. *Address:* 18 Rectory Grove, Gosforth, Newcastle upon Tyne, NE3 1AL, England.

KELLER, Mark, b. 21 Feb. 1907, Austria. Editor. m. Sarah Vivienne Hirsh, 30 Dec. 1930, New York, USA, 1 daughter. *Education:* Private. *Literary Appointments:* Managing Editor, Editor, Quarterly Journal of Studies on Alcohol, Yale University, 1941–61; Editor, Journal of Studies on Alcohol, Rutgers University, 1962–77; Emeritus Professor of Documentation, Rutgers University, 1977–; Editor, Data (Johnson Institute), 1984–. *Major Publications:* (with J R Seeley), The Alcohol Language, 1958; (with V Efron & E M Jellinek), CAAAL Manual, 1965; (editor), International Bibliography of Studies on Alcohol, volume 1 1966, volume 2 1968, volume 3 1980; (with V Efron & M M McCormick), A Dictionary of Words about Alcohol, 1982. *Contributor to:* British Journal of Addiction; Medical Tribune; Cancer Research. *Honours:* Hammond Award for Distinguished Medical Journalism, American Medical Writers Association, 1976; Jellinek Memorial Award, 1977. *Memberships:* American Medical Writers Association; Council of Biology Editors. *Address:* Centre of Alcohol Studies, Rutgers University, New Brunswick, NJ 08903, USA.

KELLEY, Win (David), b. 6 Nov. 1923, Pryor, Oklahoma, USA. Emeritus Professor. *Education:* BA, Pacific University, Oregon, 1950; MEd, University of Oregon, 1954; EdD, University of Southern California, 1962. *Publications:* Waiilatpu (The Place of Rye Grass), 1952; The Art of Public Address, 1963; Teaching in the Community Junior College, with Leslie Wilbur, 1970; Breaking the Barriers in Public Speaking, 1978. *Contributions to:* Talent Review, 1947–48; Coos Bay Times, 1954–56; Community Junior College Research Quarterly, 1977–81; Speech Teacher; Improving University and College Teaching Community College Journal etc. *Honours include:* 2nd National Play Contest, Portland Civic Theatre, Waiilatpu, 1953; George Washington Honorary Medal, Freedoms Foundation, Valley Forge, Pennsylvania, 1973. *Memberships include:* Honorary Member, Mark Twain Society; AAUP; Speech Communications Association; American Forensics Association; National Education Association; Faculty Association of Californian Community Colleges; Dramatists Guild; Authors League of America. *Address:* 1913E Foothill Boulevard, Glendora, CA 91740, USA.

KELLMAN, Steven G, b. 15 Nov. 1947, Brooklyn, New York, USA. Critic; Professor. *Education:* BA, State University of New York, 1967; MA, 1969, PhD, 1972, University of California, Berkeley. *Appointments:* Editor in chief, Occident, 1969–70; Assistant Professor, Bemidji State University, Minnesota, 1972–73; Lecturer, Tel-Aviv University, 1973–75; Visiting Lecturer, University of California, Irvine, 1975–76; Fulbright Senior Lecturer, USSR, 1980; Visiting Associate Professor, University of California, Berkeley, 1982; Assistant Professor, 1976–80, Associate Professor, 1980–85, Professor, 1985–, University of Texas, San Antonio; Literary Scene Editor, USA Today, magazine. *Publications:* The Self-Begetting Novel, 1980; Editor, Approaches to Teaching Camus's The Plague, 1985; Loving Reading : Erotics of the Text, 1985. *Contributor to:* San Antonio Light; Village Voice;

The Nation; The Georgia Review; Moment; Newsweek; Modern Fiction Studies; Midstream; Novel; New Republic; Comparative Literature; etc. *Honours:* Fulbright Senior Lectureship, American Literature, USSR, 1980; Danforth Teaching Associate, 1981–86; ACLS Travel Grant, 1984; Finalist, NBCC Citation for Excellence in Reviewing, 1984. *Memberships:* PEN American Centre; National Book Critics Circle; Modern Language Association; Popular Culture Association; South Central Modern Language Association. *Address:* 302 Fawn Drive, San Antonio, TX 78231, USA.

KELLMAN, Tony, b. 24 Apr. 1958, Barbados, West Indies. Journalist; Public Relations Practitioner. m. Pamela Emptage, 19 Dec. 1981, Barbados, 1 daughter. *Education:* Diploma, London School of Journalism, England; BA, English, History, University of THe West Indies. *Appointments:* Participated, as Poet, Third International Book Fair of Radical and Third World Books, London, 1984. *Publication:* In Depths of Burning Light, poetry, 1982. *Contributor to:* Articles, Art and Literary Reviews; Poems and Short Stories in, New Voices; Kyk-Over-Al; Bajan Magazine; Poems in, North American Mentor Magazine; Wascana Review, Canada; etc. *Honours:* 2 Awards, Creative Writing, Barbados National Independence Festival of Creative Arts, 1973; 2 Awards, Ecellence, NIFCA, 1974; 2 Special Awards, Excellence, NIFCA, 1975; 2nd Award, North American Mentor Magazine"s International Poetry Contest, 1984; Award of Merit, North American Mentor Magazine, 1985. *Address:* First Avenue, Birds River, Deacons Road, St Michael, Barbados, West Indies.

KELLY, James Plunkett, b. 21 May 1920, Dublin, Ireland. Author. m. Valerie Koblitz, 4 Sep. 1945, Dublin, 3 sons, 1 daughter. *Appointments:* Assistant Head, Drama, Radio Eireann, 1955; Head, Features, Telefis Eireann, 1969. *Publications:* Short Stories: The Trusting and the Maimed, 1955; Novels: Strumpet City, 1969; Farewell Companions, 1977; Essays; The Gems She Wore, 1972. *Contributor to:* The Bell; Irish Writing; Writing Today; etc. *Honour:* Yorkshire Post Literary Award, 1969–70. *Memberships:* Society of Irish Playwrights; Irish Academy of Letters, President; Aosdana (Toscaire). *Literary Agent:* A D Peters, London. *Address:* Coolakeagh, Old Long Hill, Kilmacanogue, Co Wicklow, Republic of Ireland.

KELLY, Richard, b. 16 Mar. 1937, New York City, New York, USA. Professor of English. m. Barbara Hunter, 17 June 1961. *Education:* BA, City College of New York, 1959; MA 1960, PhD 1965, Duke University. *Literary Appointments:* Professor of English, University of Tennessee, 1965–. *Major Publications:* The Best of Mr Punch: The Humorous Writing of Douglas Jerrold, (editor), 1970; Douglas Jerrold, 1972; Lewis Carroll, 1978; The Andy Griffith Show, 1981; George du Maurier, 1982; Grahame Greene, 1984. *Contributor to:* Studies in English Literature; Studies in Browning; other essays and chapters. *Honour:* Phi Beta Kappa. *Membership:* Lewis Carroll Society of North America. *Address:* Department of English, University of Tennessee, Knoxville, TN 37916, USA.

KELLY, Tim, b. 2 Oct. 1937, Saugus, Massachusetts, USA. Playwright. *Education:* BA, MA, Emerson College, Boston, Yale University. *Literary Appointments:* Fellow, American Broadcasting Company. *Major Publications:* Some 160 Plays, unnumerable Western Novels. *Contributor to:* Point West; Arizona Highways; For Men Only; Mystery Magazine; and others. *Honours:* Winner of several major writing awards. *Memberships:* Writers Guild of America West; Authors' League; Dramatists Guild of America. *Literary Agent:* Samuel French, New York City. *Address:* 8730 Lookout Mountain Avenue, Hollywood, CA 90046, USA.

KELTON, Elmer Stephen, b. 29 April 1926, Andrews County, Texas, USA. Novelist. Livestock Journalist. m. Anna Lipp, 3 July 1947, Midland, Texas, USA, 2 sons, 1 daughter. *Education:* BA Journalism, University of Texas, 1948. *Publications:* The Day the Cowboys Quit, 1971; The Time It Never Rained, 1973; The Good Old

Boys, 1978; The Wolf and the Buffalo, 1980; Stand Proud, 1984. *Contributions to:* Numerous agricultural publications. *Honours:* Four Spur Awards from Western Writers of America. *Memberships:* Western Writers of America; Texas Institute of Letters, 1983–; Texas Folklore Society, 1984–. *Literary Agent:* John Payne. *Address:* 2460 Oxford, San Angelo, TX 76904, USA.

KEMELMAN, Harry, b. 24 Nov. 1908, Boston, Massachusetts, USA. Writer. m. Anne Kessin, 29 Mar. 1936, Boston, USA, 1 son, 2 daughters. *Education:* AB, Boston University, 1930; MA, Harvard Graduate School, Cambridge, Massachusetts, 1931. *Major Publications:* Friday, the Rabbi Slept Late, 1963; Saturday the Rabbi Went Hungry; The Nine-Mile Walk; Sunday, the Rabbi Stayed Home; Commonsense in Education; Monday, the Rabbi Took Off; Tuesday, the Rabbi Saw Red; Wednesday, the Rabbi Got West; Thursday, the Rabbi Walked Out; Conversations with Rabbi Small; Someday, the Rabbi Will Leave. *Contributor to:* The Bookman. *Honours:* Edgar Award, Mystery Writers Association, 1964; Faith & Freedom Award for Fiction, Religious Heritage of America, 1967. *Memberships:* Authors' Guild. *Literary Agent:* Scott Meredith. *Address:* P O Box 674, Marblehead, MA 01945, USA.

KEMMIS BETTY, Peter Arthur John, b. 11 Aug. 1936, London, England. Book Publisher. m. Sarah Margaret Mason, 1 April 1971, Broadway, Gloucestershire, England, 1 son, 2 daughters. *Education:* MA, Cantab. *Literary Appointments:* Managing Director, B T Batsford Limited. *Address:* B T Batsford Limited, 4 Fitzhardinge Street, London W1H OAH, England.

KEMP, Martin John, b. 5 Mar. 1942, Windsor, Berkshire, England. University Professor. m. Jill Lightfoot, 27 Aug. 1966, Windsor, 1 son, 1 daughter. *Eduation:* MA, University of Cambridge, 1963; Academic diploma in the history of art, University of London, 1965. *Publication:* Leonardo da Vinci, The Marvellous Works of Nature and Man, 1981. *Contributions to:* Journals including; Art Journal; Art Bulletin; Burlington magazine; Bibliotheque; de Humanisme et Renaissance; The Guardian; Journal of the Warburg and Courtauld Institutes; Medical History; Sunday Times; Visitor. *Honour:* Mitchell Prize for the Best First Book on Art History, 1981. *Literary Agent:* Caroline Dawnay, A D Peters and Company. *Address:* 45 Pittenweem Road, Anstruther, Fife, Scotland.

KEMP, Peter, b. 11 Feb. 1904, Eastcote, Middlesex, England. Naval Officer (invalided from Navy 1928); Historian. m. (1) Joyce, 1930 (deceased), 1 son (deceased), 2 daughters; (2) Eleanor Rothwell, 1950. *Literary Appointments:* Assistant Editor; Sporting and Dramatic; Editorial Staff, The Times; Editor, Royal United Services Journal; Head, Naval Historical Branch, M O D. *Publications:* Nine Vanguards, 1951; Victory at Sea, 1959; Brethren of the Coast (with C Lloyd), 1960; History of Royal Navy, 1969; The British Sailor, 1970; A History of Ships, 1978; Editor: Fisher's First Sea Lord Papers, 2 volumes, 1960, 64; Oxford Companion to Ships and The Sea, 1976; Encyclopaedia of Ships and Seafaring, 1980. *Honours:* OBE, 1963. *Memberships:* Fellow, Royal Historical Society; Navy Records Society. Editorial Adviser, Board of Military Affairs (US). *Literary Agent:* Campbell Thomson & McLaughlin Limited. *Address:* 53 Market Hill, Maldon, Essex CM9 7QA, England.

KEMPTER, Lothar, b. 1 May 1900, Zürich, Switzerland. Teacher; Author. m. Anna Bänninger, 17 Oct. 1929, 1 son, 2 daughters. *Education:* Universities of Zürich and Berlin; Dr Phil, German, History, History of Art, University of Zürich, 1929. *Appointment:* Teacher, Winterthur Canton School. *Publications:* Hölderlin und die Mythologie, 1929; Hölderlin in Hauptwil, 1946; Das Musikkollegium Winterthur, 1959; Aphorismen, 1973; Schleppe und Flügel, poems, 1974; Hans Brühlmann.Leben-Werk-Welt, 1985. *Contributor to:* Winterthurer Jahrbuch; Neue Zurcher Zeitung; Der Landbote, Winterthur. *Honours:* Honorary Awards, City of Winterthur, 1959, Canton of Zürich, 1972; Honorary Member, Hölderlin Society, Tübingen; Arts Prize, Carl Heinrich Ernst Foundation, Winterthur, 1974. *Memberships:* Theatre Commission, Winterthur, 1950–70; Literature Commission, Canton of Zürich, 1954–70; Swiss Writers' Union; Literary Association, Winterthur; Curatorium of Martin Bodmer Foundation. *Address:* Weinbergstr. 97, CH 8408 Winterthur, Switzerland.

KEMPTON, Karl, b. 1 July 1943, Chicago, Illinois, USA. Poet. m. Ruth Ann, 21 June 1983. *Education:* BS, Economics, University of Utah, Salt Lake City. *Publications:* Lost Alfabet Found, 1979; Rune, 1980; Rune 2: 26 Voices, 1980; Black Strokes White Spaces, 1984; Ko, with Loris Essary, 1984; The Light We Are, 1985; Alignment, 1985. *Contributions to:* (poems): Atticus Review; The Gamut; Graphis; Inkblot; Invisible City; Irno; Interstate; Konglomerati; Lightworks; NRG; O.ARS; Scree; Score; Shishi; West Coast Poetry Review. *Honour:* Co-winner of The Gamut Concrete Poetry Contest. *Address:* PO Box 7036, Halycon, CA 93420–7036, USA.

KENDALL, Carol, b. 13 Sep. 1917, Bucyrus, Ohio, USA. Writer. *Education:* AB, Ohio University, Athens, Ohio. *Publications include:* (juvenile) The Other Side of the Tunnel, 1957; The Gammage Cup, 1959; also 2nd publisher, title The Minnipins: The Big Splash, 1960; The Whisper of Glocken, 1965; also 2nd publisher; Sweet and Sour, Tales from China, retold by C Kendall and Yaowen Li, 1979; also 2nd publisher; The Firelings, 1981, Bodley Hed, London; Atheneum US, 1982; Haunting Tales from Japan, 1985. *Honours include:* Ohioana Award, 1960 and Finalist Newberry Award, 1960 for the Gammage Cup; Parents; Choice Award for The Fireling, 1982; Aslan Award, Mythopoeic Society, The Firelings, 1983. *Address:* 928 Holiday Drive, Lawrence, KS 66044, USA.

KENDALL, Elizabeth Ann Fenella, b. 6 Jan. 1939, Gerrards Cross, England. Archaeologist. *Education:* Dip Ad Ctrl School of Art and Design, London, 1966; MA, University of California, Los Angeles, 1970; Phd, Institute of Archaeology, London University, England, 1974. *Literary Appointments:* Director, Cusichaca Archaeological Project, 1977–. *Publications:* Everyday Life of the Incas, 1973; editor, Current Archaeological Projects in the Central Andes, 1984; Author, Aspects of Inca Architecture. Description, Function, Chronology, 1985. *Contributor to:* Various professional journals in Peru, 1969–; Germany, 1974, 76; Early Stages in the Cusichaca Archaeological Project, Bulletin No 16, Institute of Archaeology, London University, 1978; Middle Stages of the Cusichaca Archaeological Project, Bulletin No 20, 1983; Archaeological Investigation of the Late Intermediate Period and the Late Horizon Period at Cusichaca, Peru, BAR 210, Oxford, 1984. *Honours:* Winston Churchill Memorial Trust Fellowship, 1968; Parry Award, Department of Education and Science, 1971–73; Order of Merit awarded by Peruvian Government for work on Archaeology in Peru, 1980; Leverhulme Research Grant, 1978. *Membership:* Institute of Andean Studies. *Address:* Springfields, 62 High Street, Belbroughton, Worcestershire, England.

KENDALL, M Sue, b. 19 July 1951, Virginia, USA. Americanist, Art Historian. m. Philip Charles Kendall, 24 Aug. 1974, Virginia, 2 sons. *Education:* BS, Old Dominion University, magna cum laude; MA, PhD, University of Minnesota. *Publications:* Rethinking Regionalism: John Stewart Curry and the Kansas Mural Controversy, in the series, New Directions in American Art, 1986. *Contributor to:* Gold's Fool and God's Country: The Coronado Craze of 1940–41, in Prospects, The Annual Journal of American Cultural Studies, vol. II, 1986; John Stewart Curry's Kansas Pastoral; The Modern American Family on the Middle Border, in Joseph S Crestochowski; John Stewart Curry and Grant Wood: A Portrait of Rural America, 1981. *Memberships:* American Studies Association; College Art Association. *Address:* 238 Meeting House Lane, Merion Station, PA 19066, USA.

KENDRICK, Walter, b. 23 Apr. 1947, Providence, Rhode Island, USA. Associate Professor. *Education:* BA, Wesleyan University, 1968; PhD, Yale University, 1975. *Appointments:* Associate Professor, English, Fordham University. *Publications:* The Novel-Machine: The Theory and Fiction of Anthony Trollope, 1980; The Treasury of English Poetry, Editor with Mark Caldwell, 1984. *Contributor to:* More than 100 essays and reviews in New York Times Book Review; Village Voice; London Review of Books; The Nation; Academic literary journals. *Honours:* National Endowment for the Humanities Fellowship, 1980. *Membership:* National Book Critics Circle. *Literary Agent:* Robert Cornfield Literary Agency. *Address:* 300 W 12th Street, New York, NY 10014, USA.

KENNEDY, David Michael, b. 22 July 1941, Seattle, Washington, USA. Educator. *Education:* BA, Stanford University, USA, 1963; MA, Yale University, 1964; PhD, ibid, 1968. *Publications:* Birth Control in America: The Career of Margaret Sanger, 1970; The American Pageant (with Thomas A Bailey), 1987; Over Here: The First World War and American Society, 1980. *Contributor to:* American Historical Review; Journal of American History; Reviews in: American History; Nation; New York Times; Atlantic Monthly; The New Republic. *Honours include:* John Gilmary Shea Prize, 1970; Bancroft Prize, 1971. *Memberships:* American Historical Association; Organisation of American Historians; Society of American Historians; American Studies Association. *Address:* History Department, Stanford University, Stanford, CA 94305, USA.

KENNEDY, Joseph, b. 26 Jan. 1923, Bolton Lancashire. England. Lecturer. *Education:* BA, MA, University of London. *Publications:* A History of Malaya, 1962, 2nd edition, 1970; Asian Nationalism, in the Twentieth Century, 1968, (Urdu edition 1970); Madeley: A History of a Staffordshire Parish, 1970; Biddulph: A Local History, 1980; Newcastle-under-Lyme: A Town Portrait, 1984; British Civilians & the Japanese War in Malaya & Singapore 1941-45, 1986. *Contributor to:* Handbuch der Orientalistik; Local History Journals of Hampshire & Staffordshire, including Proceedings of the Hants Field Club. *Memberships:* Historical Association; Fellow, Royal Historical Society. *Address:* 14 Poolfield Avenue, Newcastle-under-Lyme, Staffordshire ST5 2NL, England.

KENNEDY, Joseph Charles, b. 21 Aug. 1929, Dover, New Jersey, USA. Writer. m. Dorothy Mintzlaff, 25 Jan. 1962, Ann Arbor, 4 sons, 1 daughter. *Education:* BS, Seton Hall University, 1950; MA, Columbia University, 1951; Certificat Litteraire, University of Paris, 1956. *Appointments:* Poetry Editor, Paris Review, 1961-64; Co-Editor, Counter/Measures, 1971-74. *Publications:* Nude Descending a Staircase, 1961; Growing into Love, 1969; Breaking and Entering, 1971; Emky Dickinson in Southern California, 1974; One Winter Knight in August, 1975; The Phantom Ice Cream Man, 1979; Knock at a Star: A Child's Introduction to Poetry, with Dorothy M Kennedy, 1982; The Owlstone Crown, 1983; Literature, 3rd edition, 1983; The Forgetful Wishing Well, 1985; Cross Ties: Selected Poems, 1985; An Introduction to Poetry, 6th edition 1986; Brats, 1986. *Contributor to:* Numerous journals & magazines. *Honours include:* Lamont Award, Academy of American Poets, 1961; Shelley Memorial Award, 1970; Guggenheim Fellow, 1973-74; Bruern Fellow, American Civilisation, University of Leeds, 1974-75; Los Angeles Times Book Award for Poetry, 1985. *Memberships:* PEN; Authors Guild; Children's Literature Association. *Agent:* Curtis Brown Ltd, New York, USA. *Address:* 4 Fern Way, Bedford, MA 01730, USA.

KENNEDY, Michael, b. 19 Feb. 1926, Manchester, England. Journalist. m. Eslyn Durdle, 16 May 1947, Altrincham. *Literary Appointments:* Staff music critic 1950-, Northern Editor 1960-, The Daily Telegraph. *Publications:* The Halle Tradition, 1960; The Works of Ralph Vaughan Williams, 1964; Portrait of Elgar, 1968; Barbirolli, 1971; Mahler, 1974; Strauss, 1976; Britten,

1980; Oxford Dictionary of Music, 1985. *Contributions to:* Musical Times; The Listener; Music and Letters; Gramophone. *Honours:* FRNCM, 1981; OBE, 1981. *Address:* The Daily Telegraph, Manchester, England.

KENNEDY, Robert, b. 18 May 1938, England. Writer/Photo Journalist. *Education:* British Government's National Diploma in Art, Norwich College of Art; Art Teacher's Diploma. *Literary Appointments:* Editor, Musclemag International (Canada), Foreign Correspondent, Bodypower, (England). *Publications:* Shape-Up, 1972; Start Bodybuilding, 1975; Bodybuilding for Women, 1975; Hardcore Bodybuilding, 1981; Beef It!, 1982; Unleashing the Wild Physique, 1984; Pumping Up!, with Ben Weider, 1985; Reps!, 1985. *Contributions to:* Numerous articles to magazines on Art, Angling, Physical Culture, Sport and Fitness. *Honours:* WBBG Publisher of the Year, New York City, 1975; IFBB Award of Merit, Montreal, 1985. *Address:* 2 Melanie Drive, Bramalea, Ontario, Canada L6T 4K8.

KENNELLY, Brendan, b. 17 Apr. 1936. Professor of Modern Literature. *Education:* BA (Hons), English and French, Trinity College, Dublin Ireland, 1961; MA Ibid, 1963; Study for PhD, Leeds University, England. *Appointments:* Junior Lecturer, Lecturer, Associate Professor, Trinity College, Dublin, 1963-; Chairman, English Department, ibid, 1973-76; Visiting Professor, English (Cronell Prof Lit), Swarthmore College, Pennsylvania, USA, 1971-72. *Publications include:* Good Souls to Survive, 1967; Dream of a Black Fox, 1968; Selected Poems, 1969; American edition, 1971; Drinking Cup, 1970; Bread, 1971; Love Cry, 1972; Salvation, The Stranger, 1972; Voices, 1973; Shelley in Dublin, 1974; Kind of Trust, 1975; New and Selected Poems, 1976; Island Man, 1977; Visitor, 1978; Small Light, 1979; The Boats are Home, 1980; The House that Jack Didn't Build, 1982; Cromwell, 1984; Moloney up and At It, 1984; Selected Poems, 1985; Editor, Penguin Book of Irish Verse, 1970, 1974, 1976, 2nd enlarged edition, 1981. *Contributions to:* International magazines, *Honours:* AE Memorial Prize, 1967. *Memberships:* Fellow, Trinity College, Dublin, 1967. *Address:* Department of English, Arts Building, Trinity College, Dublin 2, Republic of Ireland.

KENNET, Elizabeth (Lady), b. London, England. Writer. 1 son, 5 daughters. *Education:* Somerville College, Oxford; BA (Hons), Modern Greats, Philosophy, Politics and Economics; Ma, Oxford. *Publications:* Old London Churches (with Wayland Young), 1956; Time Is As Time Does (poetry), 1958; A Farewell to Arms control, 1972; Quiet Enjoyment: Arms Control and Police Forces for the Ocean (with Ritchie Calder), 1972; Sea Use Planning, Fabian Society, 1975. *Contributions to:* Leading journals in the UK, USA, France, Canada and Italy. *Address:* 100 Bayswater Road, London W2 3HJ, England.

KENNET, Wayland Hilton Young (Lord), b. 2 Aug. 1923. Author; Politician. *Education:* Trinity College, Cambridge; Harvard University, USA. *Publications:* As Wayland Young: The Italian Left, 1949; The Dead Weight, 1952; Now or Never, 1953; Old London Churches, with Elizabeth Young, 1956; The Montesi Scandal, 1957; Still Alive Tomorrow, 1958; Strategy for Survival, 1959; The Profumo Affair, 1963; Eros Denied, 1965; Thirty Four Articles, 1965; Existing Mechanisms of Arms Control, Editor, 1965. As Wayland Kennet: Preservation, 1972; The Future of Europe, 1976; The Rebirth of Britain, editor, 1982. *Honours:* FRIBA, 1970. *Address:* 100 Bayswater Road, London W2, England.

KENNY, Anthony James Patrick, b. 16 Mar. 1931, Liverpool, England. Master of Balliol College, Oxford. *Education:* Gregorian University, Rome, Italy; DPhil, St Benet's Hall, Oxford. *Publications:* Action Emotion and Will, 1963; Descartes, 1968; The Five Ways, 1969; Wittgenstein, 1973; The Anatomy of the Soul, 1974; Will, Freedom and Power, 1975; The Aristotelian Ethics, 1978; Freewill and Responsibility, 1978; Aristotle's Theory of the Will, 1979; The God of the Philosophers,

1979; Aquinas, 1980; The Computation of Style, 1982; Faith and Reason, 1983; Thomas More, 1983; The Legacy of Wittgenstein, 1984; A Path From Rome, 1985; The Logic of Deterrence, 1985; The Ivory Tower, 1985; Wyclif, 1985; Wyclif's De Universalibus, 1985; Rationalism, Empiricism and Idealism, 1986; Wyclif in His Times, 1986; The Way from the New Ireland Forum, 1986. *Honour:* FBA. *Address:* Balliol College, Oxford, England.

KENRICK, Douglas Moore, b. 3 Sep. 1912, Waihi, New Zealand. Creator and Organiser of International Business. *Edcuation:* PhD; Master Commerce; Diploma in Banking; Chartered Accountant. *Publications:* The Theory of Price Control and Its Practice in Hong Kong, 1946/47, 1954; The Book of Sumo, 1969; Death in a Tokyo Family, 1979; A Century of Western Studies of Japan, 1980. *Contributions to:* Monumenta Nipponica; Contemporary Japan; Japan Illustrated; Far Eastern Economics Review; Asahi Evening News. *Membership:* Tokyo Poetry Circle. *Address:* Kowa Daisan Building, 11-45 I-chome Akasaka, Minato-ku, Tokyo 107, Japan.

KENRICK, Vivienne Mary, b. 23 Apr. 1920, London, England. Writer. *Publications:* Tokyo Days, 1956; Side Winds in Kinuta, 1963; Horses in Japan, 1964; Taste the Dust, 1968; Portrait of Japan, 1974; Too Far East Too Long, with Miranda Kenrick, 1977; They Dared to Do It, 1980; Light Traveller in India, 1985. *Contributor to:* The Japan Times, Columnist 1963; Far East Traveler, Contributor, 1970–; Fodor's guide Japan, Area Editor, 1971–84; Numerous magazines published in English in Japan. *Address:* 5-6-28 Higashi Gotanda, Shinagawa-ku, Tokyo 141, Japan.

KENT, Homer Austin Junior, b. 13 Aug. 1926, Washington, District of Columbia, USA. President, Grace Theological Seminary and College; Professor of Greek and New Testament. *Education:* BA, Bob Jones University, 1947; BD, 1950, ThM, 1952, ThD, 1956, Grace Theological Seminary. *Publications:* The Pastoral Epistles, 1958; Ephesians, The Glory of the Church, 1971; Jerusalem to Rome, 1972; The Epistle to the Hebrews, 1972; Light in the Darkness: Studies in the Gospel of John, 1974; The Freedom of God's Sons: Studies in Galatians, 1976; Treasures of Wisdom: Studies in 2 Corinthians, 1982. *Contributions to:* Several theological publications including: The Wycliffe Bible Commentary; Baker's Dictionary of Theology; Bibliotheca Sacra; The Expositor's Bible Commentary; Evangelical Dictionary of Theology. Journals including: Grace Theological Journal. *Address:* 305 6th Street, Winona Lake, IN 46590, USA.

KENTON, Leslie, b. 24 June 1941, Los Angeles, USA. Writer; Broadcaster; Journalist, 3 sons, 1 daughter. *Education:* Philosophy, Stanford University. *Literary Appointment:* Health and Beauty Editor, Harpers and Queen Magazine. *Publications:* The Joy of Beauty, 1983; Raw Energy, 1984; Ultra Health, 1984; Raw Energy Recipes, 1985; Ageless Ageing, 1985; The 10 Day Plan, 1985. *Contributor to:* Harpers and Queen; Vogue; Mademoiselle; Ms; Cosmopolitan; Brides; Woman's Day etc. *Honour:* PPA Award for Technical Writer of the Year 1984; McCarrison Lecture, Royal Faculty of Medicine, 1984. *Literary Agent:* A D Peters and Co Ltd, 10 Buckingham Street, London WC2. *Address:* 72 Broadwick Street, London W1, England.

KENYON, Karen Beth, b. 4 Sep. 1938, Oklahoma City, Oklahoma, USA. Writer. m. Richard Bertram Kenyon, 14 Feb. 1963, Albuquerque, New Mexico, 1 son. *Education:* BA, English. *Publications:* Many Faces, 1971; Sunshower, 1981. *Contributions to:* Newsweek; Redbook; Ladies' Home Journal. *Honours:* Creativity Award, San Diego Institute for Creativity for, Many Faces, 1974; Certificate of Merit (Poetry), Atlantic Monthly, 1975. *Membership:* PEN, L A Center. *Literary Agent:* Jane Jordan Browne. *Address:* PO Box 12604, La Jolla, CA 92037-0660, USA.

KERCKHOFF, Alan C, b. 14 Mar. 1924, Lakewood, Ohio, USA. Professor of Sociology. m. Sylvia Stansbury,

11 June 1949, Toledo, Ohio, 1 son, 1 daughter. *Education:* Kent State University, 1942–43; AB, Oberlin College, 1946–49; MA, PhD, University of Wisconsin, Madison, 1949–53. *Literary appointments:* Advisory Editor, Social Forces, 1969–71; Associate Editor, American Sociological Review, 1976–78; Editor, Research in Sociology of Education and Socialization: An Annual Compilation of Research, JAI Press, 1978–: Editor, Sociology of Education, 1978–81; Advisory Editor, Sociological Quarterly, 1982–84. *Publications:* The June Bug: A Study of Hysterical Contagion, (with Kurt W Back), 1968; Socialization and Social Class, 1972; Ambition and Attainment: A Study of Your Samples of American Boys, 1974; Research in Sociology of Education and Socialisation, editor, 5 volumes, 1980–85. *Contributions to:* Sociological journals. *Honours:* Senior Postdoctoral Fellow, Stanford University 1964–65, University of London 1971–72, National Science Foundation. *Address:* Department of Sociology, Duke University, Durham, NC 27706, USA.

KERN, Edith, b. 7 Feb. 1912, Dusseldorf, Germany. University Professor, Writer, Early Education in Europe. *Education:* BA, Bridgewater College, Bridgewater, Virginia, USA; MA, PhD 1946, The Johns Hopkins University, Baltimore, Maryland, USA. *Literary Appointments:* Assistant Professor, Romance Language, University of Kansas, USA, 1947–52; Associate Professor, St Johns University, 1952–65; Professor Romance Language and Literatures, Graduate School, University of Washington, 1965–72; D Silbert Professor Humanities, Smith College, 1972–77; John Cranford Adams Professor Literature, Hofstra University, 1977–80; Faculty, New School for Social Research, 1980–. *Publications:* The Influence of Heinsuis and Vossius Upon French Dramatic Theory, 1949; Jean-Paul Sartre (20th Century Views), editor, 1962; Existential Thought and Fictional Technique: Kierkegaard, Sartre, Beckett, 1970; The Absolute Comic (A Study of Farcical Laughter), 1980. *Contributions to Books:* Publications including: Samuel Beckett, 1959; Disciplines, 1959; Disciplines of Criticism, 1968; The Hero in Literature, 1970; Boccaccio, 1974; Moliere and the Commonwealth of Letters, 1975; Literary Theory and Criticism, 1984. Articles in Publications: PMLA; Romantic Review; Journal of Modern Literature; Comparative Literature. *Honours include:* Guggenheim Fellow, 1976; Rockefeller Foundation Fellow, 1982. *Memberships include:* Vice President, 1965–66, President, 1977, Modern Language Association America; Executive Board, 1973–75, Comparative Literature Association; Executive Board, Philological Association Pacific Coast; International Comparative Literature Association. *Address:* 1025 Fifth Avenue, apt 5-F-s, New York, NY 10028, USA.

KERN-FOXWORTH, Marilyn, b. 3 Apr. 1954, Kosciusko, Mississippi, USA. University Professor. m. Gregory Lamar Foxworth, 7 Mar. 1982, 1 son. *Education:* BS, Jackson State University, 1974; MS, Mass Communication, Florida State University, 1976; PhD, Mass Communication, University of Wisconsin, 1980. *Literary Appointments:* Public Relations Assistant; Communications Specialist; Coordinator of Advertising; College Relations Representative; AM Traffic Manager, Production Manager; Columnist and Staff Reporter, Mid-West Observer, Madison, Wisconsin, 1979–80; Assistant Professor, University of Tennessee-Knoxville, School of Journalism, 1980–. *Publications:* Minority Affairs Program in Pharmacy: A Guide to Your Career in Pharmacy, 1980; All Minority Grads: Opportunity is Knocking, 1982; Career Guide for Minority Journalism Students, 1983 and several other booklets. Film: Minority Enrollment, WHA-TV, Madison, 1980. *Contributions to:* Nashville Banner and numerous presentation. *Honours:* Recognition of Excellence Award, Volunteer Chapter PRSA, 1985; Unity Awards in Media, Second place for Reporting of Education, 1984; Various other grants and awards. *Memberships include:* Black Media Association; National Federation of Executive Women; Public Relations Society of America; National Council of Negro Women; Association for Education in Journalism (various offices); Alpha Kappa Alpha; Association of Black Communicators, Founder and Adviser; Public Relations Student Society of America, Adviser, 1983–. *Address:* 729 W Meadecrest Drive, Knoxville, TN 37923, USA.

KERNAGHAN, Eileen Shirley, b. 6 Jan. 1939, Enderby, British Columbia, Canada. Writer. m. Patrick Walter Kernaghan, 22 Aug. 1959, Enderby, 2 sons, 1 daughter. *Education:* Elementary Teaching Certificate, University of British Columbia. *Publications:* The Upper Left-Hand Corner: A Writer's Guide for the Northwest, co-author, 1975, revised, 1984; Journey to Aprilioth, 1980; Songs from the Drowned Lands, 1983. *Contributions to:* Galaxy, USA; Room of One's Own, Canada; Womanspace, USA; The Window of Dreams; Canada; Northern Journey; Branching Out; Canadian Review; Origins; Nimbus; Tesseracts and others. *Honours:* Silver Porgy Award for original paperback (Journey to Aprilioth), West Coast Review for Books 1981; Canadian Science Fiction and Fantasy Award (for songs from the Drowned Lands), 1985. *Memberships:* Writers Union of Canada; Federation of British Columbian Writers; Secretary, Treasurer, Newsletter editor, Burnaby Writers Society. *Literary Agent:* Virginia Kidd Literary Agency. *Address:* c/o Burnaby Arts Council, 6450 Gilpin Street, Burnaby, British Columbia, Canada V5G 2J3.

KERNOHAN, Robert Deans, b. 9 Jan. 1931, Glasgow, Scotland. Journalist. m. Margaret Bannerman, 17 Sep. 1956, Glasgow, 4 sons. *Education:* MA; Glasgow University; Balliol College, Oxford. *Literary Appointments:* Assistant Editor 1965–66, London Editor 1966–67, The Glasgow Herald; Editor, Life and Work, Edinburgh, 1972–. *Publications:* Scotland's Life and Work, 1979; William Barclay: The Plain Uncommon Man, 1980; Thoughts through the Year, 1985; Our Church, 1985. *Contributions to:* Numerous publications including: Contemporary Review; The Scotsman; Listener; Radio Times. *Address:* 121 George Street, Edinburgh, EH2 4YN, Scotland.

KERSHAW, Harvey, b. 20 Jan. 1908. Retired Paper Stockkeeper. m. Mary Alice Ridehaigh, 14 Aug. 1937, Rochdale. *Appointments:* Edwun Waugh Dialect Society, President 1964–, Life Member 1978. *Publications:* Lancashire Sings Again, 1958; Lancashire Sings Again – First Encore, 1963; Local History Books: Over My Shoulder, 1976; Beyond the Boubda ries, 1979; Growing Up, 1980; Lancashire's Industrial Legacies, 1974; Lancashire Metal, 1984; Among My Souvenirs, 1984; From the Fylde to the Pennine Range, 1985; The Day Before Yesterday, 1985. *Contributor to:* Rochdale Observer; Lancashire Life; Lancashire Magazine; Pennine Magazine; Manchester Literary Society Journal; Lancashire Authors Quarterly Record; etc. *Honours:* President's Cup Award, for outstanding work in LAA, Dialect and Local History, 1975; MBE. *Memberships:* Lancashire Authors Association; Honorary Member, Manchester Dialect Society. *Address:* 11 Holmes Street, Rochdale OL12 6AQ, Greater Manchester, England.

KERTZER, David Israel, b. 20 Feb. 1948, New York City, USA. Social Anthropologist; Professor. m. Susan Dana, 24 May 1970, Augusta, 1 son, 1 daughter. *Education:* BA, Brown University, 1969; PhD, Brandeis University, 1974. *Publications:* Comrades and Christians, 1980; Urban Life in Mediterranean Europe, with Michael Kenny, 1983; Family Life in Central Italy, 1984; Age and Anthopological Theory, with Jennie Keith, 1984. *Contributor to:* American Journal of Sociology; American Ethnologist; Journal for the Scientific Study of Religion; Journal of Family History; Demography; Social Science History; Historical Methods; etc. *Honours:* Phi Beta Kapp, 1969; Fellow, Center for Advanced Study in the Behavioral Sciences, Stanford, 1982–83; Marraro Prize for 'Family Life in Central Italy, 1984. *Address:* Department of Sociology & Anthropology, Bowdoin College, Brunswick, ME 04011, USA.

KESSELMAN-TURKEL, Judi, b. 3 Jan. 1934, New York City, USA. Author, Journalist. 2 sons. *Education:* BA, English and Education, Brooklyn College. *Publications:* Stopping Out: A Guide to Leaving College and Getting Back In, 1975; Co-author with Franklynn Peterson: The Do-It-Yourself Custom Van Book, 1977; Eat Anything Exercise Diet (third author Dr Frank Konishi), 1979; Handbook of Snowmobile Maintenance and Repair, 1979; Good Writing (textbook), 1980; Test Taking Strategies, 1981; Study Smarts, 1981; Homeowner's Book of Lists, 1981; How To Improve Damn Near Everything Around Your Home, 1981; Author's Handbook, 1982; The Grammar Crammer, 1982; Research Shortcuts, 1982; Note-Taking Made Easy, 1982; The Magazine Writer's Handbook, 1983; Getting It Down: A Guide to Writing Paper, 1983; Spelling Simplified, 1983; The Vocabulary Builder, 1983; For Children: Vans, 1979; I Can Use Tools, 1981. *Contributions to:* Magazines including: Playgirl; Modern Maturity Magazine; New Dawn Magazine; Seventeen; McCall's; Be Alive Magazine; Popular Science; Science Digest; Money Magazine; Women's Day; Co-author syndicated newspaper column, The Business Computer, 1983–. *Honours:* Jesse H Neal Award of American Business Press Association, 1977; Citation for Excellence in Consumer Journalism from National Press Club, 1984. *Memberships:* American Society of Journalists and Authors; Council for Wisconsin Writers, Authors guild. *Address:* P/K Associates Incorporated, 4348 West Beltline Highway, Madison, WI 53711, USA.

KESSLER, Jascha. *Education:* BA, 1950, New York University; MA, 1951, PhD, 1955, University of Michigan. *Literary Appointments:* University of Michigan, 1951–54; New York University, 1954–55; Hunter College, New York City, 1955–56; Hamilton College, New York, 1957–61; UCLA, 1961–. *Publications:* Include (in translation), The Magician's Garden, with Charlotte Rogers), from Hungarian, 1982; Bride of Acacias: The Selected Poems of Forugh Farrokhzad, (with Amin Banani), from Persian, 1983; Opium and Other Stories, (with Charlotte Rogers), from Hungarian, 1983; Rose of Mother-Of-Pearl: A Fairytale, (with G Olujic), from Serbo-Croatian, 1984; Time As Seen from Above and Other Poems, (with Alexander Shurbanov), from Bulgarian, 1984; Under Gemini: The Selected Poems of Miklos Radnoti, from Hungarian, 1985. Editor, American Poems: A Contemporary Collection, 1972; An Egyptian Bondage and Other Stories, 1967; Whatever Love Declares, Poetry, 1969; After The Armies Have Passed, Poem, 1970; In Memory of the Future, Poetry, 1976; Bearing Gifts: Two Mythologems, 1979; Lee Mullican, 1980; Death Comes for the Behaviorist, A Novella & 3 Long Stories, 1983; Transmigrations: 18 Mythologems, 1985; Courtly Love; 28 Stories, 1985; Medusa: The Selected Poetry of Nicolai Kantchev, (with Alexander Shurbanov) from Bulgarian 1985; The Face of Crection, 26 Hungarian Poet, (with Julie Kode, Maria Körösy) 1986. *Contributions to:* Lecture Program for 11 Western States. *Honours:* Include Fellow, Rockefeller Foundation, Italy, 1978; Hungarian PEN Club Memorial Medal, 1979; Artisjus Award, Budapest, 1980; IREX Fellow, International Research & Exchanges Scholarship Board, 1983–84; *Memberships:* Include California Arts Council; Executive Vice-President, PEN, Los Angeles, 1983–84. *Address:* Department of English, UCLA, 405 Hilgard Avenue, Los Angeles, CA 90024, USA.

KESSLER, Kaye Warren, b. 20 Dec. 1923, Toledo, Ohio, USA. Sportswriter; Columnist. m. Rosemary Maxine Reeder, 3 Apr. 1948, at Worthington, Ohio, 1 son, 1 daughter. *Education:* BSc, Journalism, Ohio State University, 1951. *Publications:* The Golf Club, 1982. *Contributor to:* Sports Illustrated, 1955– Golf World; Golf Digest; Golf Magazine; PGA Magazine; Football Yearbooks; Professional football publications; NCAA Guides; national Golf Tournament programmes and publications; NCAA Basketball Tournament publications; Rose & Orange Bowl Publications. *Honours:* Many Golf Writer of the Year Honours; College Baseball

Writing Contest; Ohio UPI Firsts in columns and news 1977, 1979, 1981, 1982, 1983, 1984; Ohio Sportswriter of the Year, 1984. *Address:* 52 Wilson Drive, Worthington, OH 43085, USA.

KESTEMAN, Emile, b. 6 July 1922, Brussels, Belgium. Professor. m. Madeleine Fonteyn, 6 Aug. 1949, Louvain, 2 sons, 3 daughters. *Education:* Licencié en Philologie Romane; Agrégé. *Publications:* Tentations, 1955; Holmead, 1973; L'Ere de l'Errance, 1974; Je suis descendu pour to voir danser, 1977; Ton Corps Végétal, 1978. *Contributions to:* Les, Elytres du Hammeton; Revue M. La Derneère Heure; Le Spantole; Marginales. *Memberships:* Association des Ecrivans Belges; PEN International; Grenier Jane Tony. *Address:* 112 Rue Colonel Bourg, Bte 23, 1040 Brussels, Belgium.

KETCHUM, William Clarence, b. 29 Mar. 1931, Columbia, Missouri, USA. Author. m. Erica Stoller, New York, 2 sons, 2 daughters. *Education:* BA, Union College; JD, Columbia University Law School. *Publications:* American Basketry and Woodenware, 1974; A Treasury of American Bottles, 1975; Hooked Rugs, 1976; A Catalogue of American Antiques, 1977; A Catalogue of American Collectables, 1979; Collecting Amerian Craft Antiques, 1980; Auction, 1980; Western Memorabilia, 1980; Toys and Games, 1981; Furniture volume II, 1981; The Catalog of World Antiques, 1981; Boxes, 1982; American Furniture, 1982; Pottery and Procelain, 1983; American Folk Art of the 20th Century, 1983; Collecting Toys for Fun and Profit, 1985. *Contributions to:* Publications including: Contributing Editor, Antique Monthly; Better Homes and Gardens; Country Home; Early American Life. *Honour:* Ambassador of Honor Award, English Speaking Union, 1983. *Memberships:* Commission of the Arts, New York Bar Association; New York Historical Society. *Address:* 241 Grace Church Street, Rye, NY 10580, USA.

KEULS, Yvonne, b. Indonesia. Writer. m. with children. *Education:* Teacher Training. *Publications:* The Mother of David S, 1970's; Book portraying the plight of young female drug addicts who often find themselves forced to work as prostitutes in order to pay for their heroin shots; Short Plays: Little Mice; Rainsnakes; Full-length Plays: Every Tom, Dick and Harry; Mother of David S; TV adaptations: The Copper Garden; Mother of David S. *Address:* Beeklaan 492, 2562 Bm Den Hagg, The Netherlands.

KEY-ABERL, Sandro Gustav, b. 6 May 1922, Radebeul Bei Dresden, Sweden. Writer. m. (1) Lodron Larson, 27 Oct. 1959 (deceased) (2) Berit Roos, 18 Oct. 1985. *Education:* Fil Kand, Stockholm, 1953. *Publications:* Poetry: Skramdas Lekar, 1950; Bittersok, 1954; Levit en Stor Sak, 1963; Pa Jin Hojd, 1972; Till de Sorjande, 19875; Prose: Salolik, 1964; Bildade Mauniskor, 1964; Deloda Manniskorna, 1976; Fridhem, Shaland, Sverke, 1982; Drama: O, Scenprator, 1965; Harhga Tidson Randas, 1968; Hederslasterna, 1981; Works of Pedagogics: Poetisklek, 1962; Ordelk Diktlek, 1985. *Contributor to:* Various newspapers and magazines. *Honours:* Svenska Halbladets Literary Prize, 1952; ABFS Literary Prize, 1957; Kunlastipendium, 1959; FIBS Lyrik Prize, 1962; Ferlin Prize, 1972; Carl Emil Lund Prize, 1972; Bellman Prize, 1973; Liiteratur Framhanders Stora Pris, 1976; Dubloua Priset, 1983. *Memberships:* Penklubben, 1966–; Sverkes Forfattarforbund, Director, 1965–71; Witeraturframjandet, Director, 1965–; Ferlinsalskapet, Chairman, 1974–85, etc. *Address:* Telnerlunden 10, 11359 Stockholm, Sweden.

KEYS, Kerry Shawn, b. 25 June 1946, Harrisburg, Pennsylvania, USA. Poet. *Education:* BA, English Literature, University of Pennsylvania; MA, English Literature, Indiana University, Bloomington. *Publications:* Swallowtails Gather These Stones, (poems), 1973; Jade Water (poems), 1974; Loose Leaves Fall (poems), 1977; Quingumbo, Nova Poesia Norte-Americana, Brazil (anthology), 1980; A Knife All Blade, João Cabral de Melo Neto (translation), 1980; Seams (poems), 1985; A Gathering of Smoke (prose-poem), India, 1985. *Contributions to:* The Nation; Kayak; Michigan Quarterly Review; Denver Quarterly; Milkweed Chronicle; Chandrabhaga; Prairie Schooner; Prism International, etc. *Honours:* Fellowship in Literature, Pennsylvania Council on the Arts, 1983; Fulbright Senior Research Grant, 1983, 84, Bahia, Brazil; Associate Fellow in English, Dickinson College, 1981–85. *Membership:* Poets and Writers, New York. *Address:* OAK-OMOLU, Box 530 RD 1, Landisburg, PA, 17040, USA.

KEYSER, Samuel Jay, b. 7 July 1935, Philadelphia, Pennsylvania, USA. Associate Provost and Professor of Linguistics. m. Margaret Joan Horridge, 18 Mar. 1959, Oxford, England. 1 son, 2 daughters. *Education:* BA, George Washington University, 1956; BA, Oxford University, 1958; MA, Yale University, 1960; MA, Oxford University, 1962; D Phil, Yale University, 1962. *Publications:* English Stress: Its Form, Its Growth and Its Role in Verse, with Morris Halle, 1971; Beginning English Grammar, with Paul Postal, 1973; Recent Studies in European Transformational Grammar, Editor, 1979; CV Phonology: A Generative Theory of the Syllable, with G N Clements, 1983; Rule Generalisation and Optionality in Language Change, with Wayne O'Neil, 1985. *Contributions to:* 35 articles, reviews and notes in professional journals in the field of linguistics, English Literature. *Honours:* University Trustee Scholarship, George Washington University, 1952–56; Fulbright Scholarship, Merton College, Oxford University, 1956–58; University Fellowship, Yale University, 1958–61; Senior Fulbright Fellowship University College, London 1971–72. *Address:* Office of the Provost, 3-234 MIT 77 Massachusetts Avenue, Cambridge, MA 02139, USA.

KHATCHADOURIAN, Haig, b. 22 July 1925, Jerusalem. Palestine, Professor of Philosophy. m. Arpineé Yaghlian, 10 Sep. 1950, Jerusalem, 2 sons, 1 daughter. *Education:* BA, MA, American University of Beirut, Lebanon; PhD, Duke University, USA. *Publications:* The Coherence Theory of Truth: A Critical Evaluation, 1961; (poetry) Traffic of Time (with others), 1963; A Critical Study in Method, 1967; The Concept of Art, 1971; Shadows of Time (poetry), 1983; Music, Film & Art, 1985. *Contributor to:* Numerous professional & literary journals. *Memberships include:* National Society for Literature & The Arts, USA; Various Philosophical Societies. *Honours include:* Phi Beta Kappa, 1966; 2nd Prize, World Essay Contest, International Humanist & Ethical Union, Netherlands, 1959; 1st Prize, poetry contest, 1962; Prize, essay contest, 1964, Ararat, New York, USA; Distinguished Visiting Professor, University of Mexico, 1978–769; Liberal Arts Fellow, Philisophy & Law, Harvard Law School, 1982–83; Phi Kappa Phi, 1985. *Address:* Department of Philosophy, University of Milwaukee, WI 53201, USA.

KHOSLA, Gopal Das, b. 15 Dec. 1901, Lahore, India. High Court Judge, Writer. m. Shakuntla Singh, 15 May 1928, Lahore, 3 sons, 1 daughter. *Education:* BA, University of Cambridge, England, Barrister-at-Law, Lincoln's Inn, London. *Literary Appointments:* President, Authors' Guild of India, 1974. *Major Publications:* Stern Reckoning, 1940; Himalayan Circuit, 1956; Price of a Wife, 1962; Murder of the Mahatma, Horoscope Cannot Lie, 1963; Grim Fairy Tales, 1967; The Last Mughal, 1965; A Way of Loving, A Taste of India, 1969; Memories & Opinions, 1973; Indira Gandhi, 1974; Last Days of Netaji, 1974; Pornography & Censorship, 1976; Of Mountains & Men, Never the Twain, 1983; Memory's Gay Chariot, 1985. *Contributor to:* Illustrated Weekly of India; Caravan; Thought; Statesman; Times of India; Hindustani Times; Indian Express; and others. *Honours:* 1st Prize Short Stories in English, Illustrated Weekly 1950, Hindustani Times 1952. *Memberships:* Authors' Guild of India. *Address:* C-9 Maharani Bagh, New Delhi 110065, India.

KHOURI, Fred John, b. 15 Aug. 1916, Cranford, New Jersey, USA. College Professor. *Education:* BA, 1938; MA, 1939; PhD, 1953; Columbia University. *Literary*

Appointment: Associate Editor, Journal of South Asian and Middle Eastern Studies. *Literary Appointments:* Associate Editor, Journal of South Asian and Middle Eastern Studies. *Publications:* The Arab States and the UN (monograph), 1954; The Arab-Israeli Dilemmma, 1968, 2nd edition, 1976, 3rd edition 1985; (contributing author); To Make War or to Make Peace, 1969; The Politics of International Crises, 1970; People and Politics in the Middle East, 1975; Dictionary of American History, 1976; Lebanon in Crisis, 1979; UN Reform and Reconstruction, 1980; The Middle East in the 1980s: Problems and Prospects, 1983. *Contributor to:* Various journals. *Honour:* Order of the Cedars, Lebanon, 1969. *Memberships include:* Fellow, Middle East Studies Association; Middle East Institute. *Address:* 1209 W Wynnewood Road, Apr 310, Wynnewood, PA 19096, USA.

KICKNOSWAY, Faye, b. 16 Dec. 1936, Detroit, Michigan USA. Poet; Illustrator. 1 son, 1 daughter. *Education:* BA, Wayne State University. 1967; MA, San Francisco State College, 1969. *Publications:* O, You Can Walk On the Sky? Good, (Capra Press), 1972; A Man Is a Hook. Trouble, (Capra Press) 1974; Asparagus, Asparagus, Ah Sweet Asparagus, (Toothpaste Press), 1981; She Wears Him Fancy In Her Night Braid, (Toothpaste Press), 1983; Who Shall Know Them?, (Viking Penguin), 1985. *Contributions to:* New Letters; TriQuarterly; Ironwood; and others; (poems). *Honours:* Woodrow Wilson Fellowship, 1967; Academy of American Poets, 1969; Michigan Foundation for the Arts Award, 1980; Michigan Artist Grant, 1981; Artist Achievement Award, 1983; Michigan Artist Grant, 1985; NEA, 1985. *Memberships:* Poetry Society of America; Associated Writing Program. *Address:* c/o Stacy Schiff, Viking Penguin Inc, 40 West 23 Street, New York, NY 10010, USA.

KIDD, Virginia, b. 2 June 1921, Germantown, Pennsylvania, USA. Literary Agent; Writer; Editor; Publisher. *Publications:* (Co-Editor with Roger Elwood) Saving Worlds, 1973, reprinted as, The Wounded Planet, 1974; Editor, The Best of Judith Merril, 1976; Assistant Editor with Ursula K Le Guin, Nebula Award Stories Eleven, 1976; Editor, Millennial Women, 1978, 1979; Co-Editor with Ursula K Le Guin, Interfaces, 1980, Edges. *Contributor to:* Several magazines & anthologies. *Memberships include:* Science Fiction Writers of America; Authors League. *Address:* 538 E Hartford St, Milford, PA 18337, USA.

KIHLMAN, Christopher Alfred, b. 14 June 1930, Helsinki, Finland. Author. m. Selinda Enckell, 5 Jan. 1956, Helsinki, 1 son, 1 daughter. *Publications:* Se upp Salige!, 1960; Den bla modern, 1963; Manniskan som skalv, 1971; Dyre prins, Sweet Prince, 1983; Alla mina soner, All My Sons, 1984. *Memberships:* International PEN. *Literary Agent:* Peter Owen, London. *Address:* Sveinsgatan 27 B, 02730 Esbo 73, Finland.

KIKKAWA, Jun'chi, b. 7 Feb. 1922, Tojo, Horishima, Japan. Assistant Professor. English, Kyoto University of Foreign Studies. m. Atsumi Tokimoto, 27 Oct. 1958, Kobe, 1 daughter. *Education:* Special Student, English Literature Department, Doshicha University, Kyoto, 1950. *Literary Appointments:* Reporter, Mainichi Daily News 1970–76; Part-time Lecturer, 1977, Full-time Lecturer, 1980, Assistant Professor, 1985, Kyoto University of Foreign Studies. *Publications:* Blue-eyed Bonze, novel in English, 1976; Guide Book for English Newspaper, Japansese & English, 1978; Current English: Feature Stories, Interviews & Other Stroes, in English, 1981; The Gist of English Composition, textbook, 1981; A Bridge for Peace, collection of essays, short stories and poems, 1986. *Contributor to:* Michi; Kenkyu Ronso; Sell, Kufs Organ. *Memberships:* English Literary Society of Doshisha University; Poetry Society of Japan, Advisory Committee; Japan Forum, Tokyo. *Address:* 5-23 2–chome, Kunokidai, Tondabayashi City, Osaka, Japan 584.

KILBY, Howard Lee, b. 28 Dec. 1943. Broadcaster; Poet; Writer. *Education:* AA, Miami Dade Community

College, 1974; BA, University of Hawaii, Manoa, Honolulu, 1979. *Literary Appointments:* Newspaper Reporter, Radio Announcer, 1974; Production Technicial, Hawaii TV, 1975; Radio Announcer, 1979–80. *Publications:* Poems by Round Table Poets of Arkansas, 1978, 1979, 1980, 1981; Poets of Arkansas, 1981. *Contributor to:* Honolulu Advertiser; Sentinel Records; Hot Springs News; Arkansas Gazette; The Avatar. *Memberships:* National Federation of State Poetry Societies; Vice President, Hot Springs Chapter, Poets Round Table of Arkansas; Vice President, Tri-Arts Chapter, Arkansas Authors, Composers & Artists Society, 1980–91; Hawaii Writers Club. *Honours:* Arkansas Traveler Award, 1979; National Poetry Day Award, 1979. *Address:* 218 Pullman Avenue, Hot Springs, AR 71901, USA.

KILCHENMANN, Ruth J, b. 1 Jan. 1917, Langnau, Switzerland. Professor of German and Comparative Literature. *Education:* Certified Secondary School Teacher, University of Bern, 1940; PhD, University of Southern California, Los Angeles, USA, 1956. *Publications:* Die Kurzgeschichte, Formen und Entwicklung, 1967; 5th edition, 1978; Panorama, Ausdrucksformen moderner Autoren, 1967; Bilder aus Deutschlands Gegenwart und Vergangenheit, 1967; Rezept fur die bosen Weiber, 1970; Schlaue Kisten machen Geschichten (for IBM), 1977. *Contributions to:* German Quarterly, USA; Kansas Foreign Language Quarterly; Der Bund, Switzerland; Die Brucke, Germany; Comparative Literature, USA; The Minnesota Language Bulletin; Encyclopedia of World Literature in 20th Century, USA. *Honours:* Several honours, USA. *Memberships:* Modern Language Association (holder of various offices); American Association of Teachers of German. *Address:* Haus Vasudeva, CH–1531 Gletterens, Switzerland.

KILMINSTER, Clive William, b. 3 Jan. Epping, Essex, England. Professor of Mathematics. *Education:* BSc 1944, MSc 1948, PhD 1950, Queen Mary College, University of London. *Major Publications include:* Hamiltonian Dynamics, 1964; The Environment in Modern Physics, 1965; Men of Physics: Sir Arthur Eddington, 1966; Language, Logic & Mathematics, 1967; Lagrangian Dynamics, 1970; Special Theory of Relativity, 1970; The Nature of the Universe, 1972; General Theory of Relativity, 1973; Philosophers in Context: Russell, 1984. *Contributor to:* Times Higher Education Supplement. *Membership:* Fellow, Institute of Mathematics & its Applications. *Address;* 11 Vanburgh Hill, Blackheath, London SE3 7UE, England.

KILPI, Eeva Karin, b. 18 Feb. 1928, Hiitola, Finland. Author. m. Mikko Kustaa Kilpi, 1949 (div 1966), 3 sons. *Education:* Cand phil, Helsinki University, 1953. *Publications include:* Novels: Elämä edestakaisin, 1964; Tamara, 1972; Häätanhu, 1973; Elämän evallona, 1983. Short story collections: Rakkauden ja kuolemen pöytä, 1967; Kesä ja keski-ikäinen nainen, 1970; Hyvän yön tarinoita, 1971; Se mitä ei koskaan sanota, 1979. Poetry collections: Laulu rakkaudesta, 1972; Terveisin, 1976; Ennen kuolemaa, 1982. Collection of essays: Ihmisen ääni, 1976. *Honours:* National Book Prizes, 1968, 1974, 1984. *Memberships:* Chairman, Finnish PEN, 1970–75; Society of Finnish Authors. *Literary Agent:* Werner Söderström Oy. *Address:* c/o Werner Söderström Publishers, Bulevardi 12, 00120 Helsinki, Finland.

KILPI, Irja Marjatta, b. 19 Apr. 1940, Helsinki, Finland. Author. m. Mikko, 1966, 1 son. *Education:* MA. *Publications:* Lasisormus, 1967; Ruusu ja ritari, 1971; Aurora ja rakkaus, 1974; Ala kutsu kukkaseksi, 1976; Kuin vasilintu Lahdella, 1977; Koti-isa, 1979; Halkeilevat kehykset, 1980. *Contributions to:* Various magazines (short stories). *Honours:* Awards of: Wihuri Foundation, 1974; Kordelin Foundation, 1981. *Membership:* Finnish Authors Society. *Address:* Marjatta Kilpi, Snellmaninkatu 25 B 28, 00170 Helsinki, Finland.

KILROY, Thomas, b. 23 Sep. 1934, Callan, Republic of Ireland, Professor of Modern English; Playwright;

Novelist. m. Patricia Cobey, 1963, 3 sons, (2) Julia Lowell Carlson, 1981. *Education:* BA, 1956, MA 1959, National University of Ireland. *Publications:* The Death and Resurrection of Mr Roche, play, 1968; The Big Chapel, 1971; Talbot's Box, play, 1977; The Seagull, an adaptation of Chekhov's play, 1981. *Contributions to:* Literature and Changing Ireland, 1981; The Gentle Master, 1985; Sagetrieb, 1984; The Genius and Irish Prose, 1985. *Honours:* Nominated for Booker prize, 1971; Gucrovian Fiction prize, 1971; American–Irish Foundation Literary Award, 1974. *Memberships:* Fellow, Royal Society of Literature; Academy of Irish Letters. *Literary Agent:* Margaret Ramsay, 14a Goodrian Court, St Martin's Lane, London, England. *Address:* English Department, UCG, Galway, Republic of Ireland.

KIM, Hyun Kap, b. 17 Nov. 1934, South Korea. Associate Professor of Communication. m. Maria Hija Lee, 26 Mar. 1968, Seoul, Korea, 2 sons, 1 daughter. *Education:* LL.B, Seoul National University; MA, Southern Illinois University, USA; PhD, Journalism, Southern Illinois University. *Appointment:* Associate Professor of Communication, University of Wisconsin, Stevens Point, USA. *Contributions:* A Review of College-Level Texts for the Introductory Mass Communication Course, Journal of Wisconsin Communication Association; Fall 1978; Editorial Assertions on Panmunjom Crisis; Content Analysis of US and South Korean Newspapers;. Journal of Korean Society of Mass Communication and Journalism, Winter 1982 and six other articles. *Membership:* Korean Journalists Association, Vice-President, 1967–68. *Honours:* Fulbright Grant, 1970–71; University of Wisconsin Stevens Point Research Grant, 1978. *Address:* 721 Mary Ann Avenue, Stevens Point, WI 54481, USA.

KIM, Jennifer Gi-won, b. 22 Apr. 1964, Monterey, California, USA. Editor; Writer; Dancer. *Education:* BA Candidate, University of California, Los Angeles. *Literary Appointments:* Dance and Theatre Critic, Daily Bruin, Associate Editor-in-Chief, Daily Bruin Review, Editor-in-Chief, Westwind (Journal of the Arts), University of California, Los Angeles. *Contributions:* Daily Bruin; Westwind. *Honour:* Grant, College of Honors (for continued publication of Westwind), University of California, Los Angeles, 1984–. *Address:* 1409 Thayer Avenue, Los Angeles, CA 90024, USA.

KIM, Soon Jin, b. 24 Oct. 1927, Korea. Professor. m. Aie Kyung Yoon, 14 Oct. 1960, Seoul, Korea, 4 daughters. *Education:* AS, Kagoshima College, Japan 1945; BA, Spanish, Korea University of Foreign Studies, 1960; MA Journalism, University of Missouri, USA, 1970; MA History, San Carlos University, Guatemala, 1972; PhD, Humanities, American Studies, University of Maryland, USA, 1982. *Literary Appointments:* Reporter-Writer, The Korean Republic, 1958–61; Latin Correspondent, The Korea Daily News (Chosun Ilbo), 1961–68; Writer-Editor, The Columbia Missourian, USA, 1968–70; Founding Foreign Editor, La Nación Guatemala, 1970; Founder, Editor & Advisor, Towsonian (College Newspaper), 1980; Writer-contributor, News-Post News Service, Frederick, Maryland, USA, 1985–. *Major Publication:* EPE: Spain's World News Agency, 1986. *Contributor to:* Journalist (USA); The Democratic Journalist (Czechoslovakia), 1985; IAMCR, (Prague, Czechoslovakia), 1984. *Address:* 3717 Springdell Avenue, Randallstown, Baltimore, MD 21133, USA.

KIMES, Beverly Rae, b. 17 Aug. 1939, Aurora, Illinois, USA. Writer; Editor. m. James H Cox, 6 July 1984, Eagle River, Wisconsin. *Education:* BS, Journalism, University of Illinois; MA, Journalism, Pennsylvania State University. *Publications:* The Classic Tradition of the Lincoln Motor Car, 1968; Oldsmobile: The First Seventy-Five Years, 1972 (with Richard M Langworth); The Cars that Henry Ford Built, 1978; Editor: Great Cars and Grand Marques, 1976; Editor: Packard: A History of the Motor Car and the Company, 1979; Editor: Automobile Quarterly's Handbook of Automotive Hobbies, 1981; My Two Lives: Race Car to

Restaurateur (with Rene Dreyfus), 1983; Chevrolet: A History from 1911 (with Robert C Ackerson), 1984; Standard Catalog of American Cars: 1805–1942, 1985. *Contributions to:* Automobile Quarterly; The Classic Car; Automobiles Classiques; Wheels; Car and Driver; Road and Track. *Honours:* Cugnot Award, Society of Automotive Historians, 1978, 79, 84; McKean Trophy, Antique Automobile Club of America, 1984; Moto Award, First Annual Automotive Journalism Conference, 1984. *Membership:* Society of Automotive Historians. *Address:* 215 East 80th Street, New York, NY 10021, USA.

KIMMINS, Sybil Jean, b. 23 Nov. 1923, Homemaker. m. William Phillip Kimmins. *Publications:* The Musings of a Mountain Maid, 1969; 72; More Musings, 1980. *Contributions to:* The North Australia Monthly; North Queensland Register; Endeavour; Phoenix Australia; People; Expression Australia; Catholic Leader; Queensland Methodist Times; Poets of Australia, volumes 1, 2 and 3; various other contributions. *Memberships include:* Secretary and President, Womens Committee, Sub-Normal Children's Welfare Association; Treasurer and Secretary, Womens Guild of Methodist Church; Sunshine Coast Literary Society; Queensland Writers Workshop; Newspaper reporter, North Queensland Naturalists Club. *Honours include:* 1st prize, 1950, 2nd prize, 1951, 4CA Radio Competition; Commended, Phoenix Australia competition 3, 1976; Quarterly Award for Best Poems, Sunshine Coast Literary Society, 1979; 4th Prize, Ernestine Hill Memorial Competition, 1976; 2nd Prize, North Queensland Eisteddfod, 1981. *Address:* 231 Lyons Street, Westcourt, Cairns, North Queensland 4870, Australia.

KINDING, (Sven) Thomas, b. 12 Oct. 1939, Örgryte-Goteborg, Sweden. Literary Advisor, Theatre (to Gothenburg Municipal Theatre). *Education:* BA, Royal University of Uppsala. *Publications:* Etthundrafemtio terminer, 1966; Kantat vid invigningen av ett paradhus, 1967; Faidra, Swedish translation of Racine's drama (in Litteratur genom tiderna 3), 1974; TV and radio dramas for Swedish Broadcasting Company (several with L E Larsson and H Sandblad); translations into Swedish of operas and dramas (from English, German, French, Italian) performed at major Swedish theatres. *Honours:* State Grant, 1977; Royal Society (Sweden) Pro Patria Silver Medal for Civic Merits, 1978; Chevalier, Royal Belgian Order of Leopold II, 1984; State Grant, 1985. *Membership:* Sällskapet Gnistan, Göteborg. *Literary Agent:* Opinicus AB. *Address:* Göteborgs Stadsteater, PO Box 5094, 402 22 Gothenburg, Sweden.

KINDT, Guido J F, b. 13 July 1934, Roeselare, Belgium. Journalist. m. Paule Breesch, 19 Sep. 1959, Laken. *Education:* Press-house, Brussels; University of Brussels; Licensed Private Pilot, Cessna Pilot Centre, Brussels. *Contributions to:* De Standaard; Het Nieuwsblad; De Gentenaar. *Memberships:* Association of Professional Scientific Journalists; Aviation Press Club. *Address:* G Delathouwerstraat 7/B 1, 1090 Brussels, Belgium.

KING, David John, b. 31 Jan. 1955, Melbourne, Australia. Freelance Writer. *Education:* Diploma of Arts/Humanities, Gordon Institute of Technology, Geelong, 1975. *Literary Appointments include:* Freelance scriptwriter/editor/story consultant, Australian Broadcasting Commission Education Department, Victoria and Queensland, 1980–84; Freelance Scriptwriter/Storyliner, ABC Television Drama Department, 1982–83; Freelance Scriptwriter, Australian Children's Television Foundation, 1983–84; Freelance Scriptwriter, independent producers 1980–85; Freelance travel journalist, Geelong Advertiser, Bellarine Echo, 1980–84; Freelance scriptwriter, ATV Channel 10, Melbourne, Victoria. *Credits:* Series of short, historical radio documentaries broadcast throughout throught South-East, West Asia, the Pacific and Europe by Radio by Radio Australia; Contributed to ABC Education Department radio programmes Story Work, What If...?, Listen and Read; Television drama/documentary, What Killed Cobb and Co? for Queensland ABC Education Department, Episodes 10, 18, 27, 28 of award-winning young people's television series 'Home' for ABC TV Drama Department; episodes 1 to 5 of science fiction television series for young people 'The Parallax Factor' for Australian Children's Television Foundation; Erotic rock 'N' roll comedy video release feature film 'Coming of Age' (with Brian Jones); Developed treatments of original mystery thriller feature film 'Entangled' for David Hannay Production, Sydney and Satori Entertainment Corporation, New York; Developed series of short, original documentaries for Deafness Foundation Telethon '85. *Contributor to:* Geelong Advertiser, Bellaraine Scho of over 30 travel articles. *Honour:* Young Australian National Short Story Award for 'Aeons After', 1971. *Memberships:* Victorian Fellowship of Australian Writers; Australian Writers Guild. *Address:* C/–9 Robertson Street, East Geelong, 3219 Victoria, Australia.

KING, Deborah Jane Munro, b. 21 Nov. 1950, Dorset, England. Author; Artist; Part-time Art Lecturer. *Education:* First Class Honours Diploma in Illustation, Hornsey School of Art, 1972. *Literary Appointments:* Lecturer, Drawing, Middlesex Polytechnic, London; Lecturer, Drawing, Bournemouth & Poole College of Art & Design. *Publications:* Rook, 1980; Sirius and Saba, 1981; Puffin, 1984; Swan, 1985. *Contributions to:* Reader's Digest; MacDonald Educational; BBC Publications: Mitchell Beazley; Ladybird Books; Hodder-Stoughton; Weidenfield and Nicholson. One-man Exhibition at Portal Gallery, London, 1980. *Address:* 3 Harmony Terrace, Studland, Dorset, England.

KING, Francis Henry, b. 4 Mar. 1923, Adelboden, Switzerland. Author. *Education:* MA, University of Oxford, England. *Publications:* To the Dark Tower, 1946; The Dividing Stream, 1951; The Widow, 1957; The Man on the Rock, 1957; The Custom House, 1961; The Last of the Pleasure Gardens, 1965; A Domestic Animal, 1969; Flights, 1973; A Game of Patience, 1974; The Needle; Danny Hill, 1977; The Action, 1978; E M Foster and His World, 1978; Indirect Method, 1980; Act of Darkness, 1983; Voices in an Empty Room, 1984; One is a Wanderer, 1985. *Contributions to:* Sunday Telegraph; Spectator. *Honours:* Somerset Maugham Prize, 1952; Katherine Mansfield Short Story Prize, 1964; Yorkshire Post Prize, 1984. *Memberships:* Fellow, Royal Society of Literature; President, Poets, Playwrights, Editors, Essayists and Novelists; Society of Authors; President, International PEN; Society for Psychical Research. *Literary Agent:* A M Heath and Company Limited. *Address:* 19 Gordon Place, London W8 4JE, England.

KING-HELE, Desmond George, b. 3 Nov. 1927, Seaford, England. Scientist. *Education:* BA, 1948; MA, 1952; Trinity College, Cambridge. *Publications:* Shelley: His Thought and Work, 1960, 2nd edition, 1971; Satellites and Scientific Research, 1960, 2nd edition, 1962; Erasmus Darwin, 1963; Theory of Satellite Orbits in an Atmosphere, 1964; Observing Earth Satellites, 1966; Essential Writings of Erasmus Darwin, 1968; The End of the Twentieth Century, 1970; Poems and Trixies, 1972; Doctor of Revolution, 1977; The Letters of Erasmus Darwin (Editor), 1981; The RAE Table of Earth Satellites 1957–82 (Editor), 1983; Animal Spirits, 1983; Erasmus Darwin and the Romantic Poets, 1986. *Contributor to:* Numerous scholarly journals. *Honours:* FRS and several awards. *Memberships:* Member of Fellow of Science Organizations. *Address:* 3 Tor Road, Farnham, Surrey, England.

KING-SMITH, Ronald Gordon, b. 27 Mar. 1922, Bitton, Gloucestershire, England. Children's Author. m. Myrle England, 6 Feb. 1943, Bitton, 1 son, 2 daughters. *Education:* B.Ed, Bristol University. *Publications:* The Fox Busters, 1978; Daggie Dogfoot, 1980; The Mouse Butcher, 1981; Magnus Powermouse, 1982; The Queen's Nose, 1983; The Sheep-Pig, 1984; Harry's Mad, 1984; Saddlebottom, 1985. *Honour:* The Guardian Award for Children's Fiction (The Sheep-Pig), 1984. *Literary Agent:* Pamela Todd, A P Watt, London.

Address: Diamond's Cottage, Queen Charlton, Keynsham, Avon, England.

KINNELL, Galway, b. 1 Feb. 1927. Poet-in-Residence. *Education:* BA, Princeton University, New Jersey, USA, 1948; MA, University of Rochester, New York, 1949; Fulbright Fellow, Paris, France, 1955–56. *Publications:* What a Kingdom It Was, 1960; Flower Herding on Mount Monadnock, 1964; Poems of Night, 1968; Body Rags, 1968; Black Light, 1965; The Book of Nightmares, 1971; Mortal Acts, Mortal Words, 1980; Selected Poems, 1982; The Past, 1985. Translations: The Poems of Francois Villon, 1963, 78; On the Motion and Immobility of Douve, 1968. *Contributions to:* Anthologies: New Poets by American Poets, 1953; Pocket Book of Modern Verse, 1954; New Poets of England and America, 1962; Poets Choice, 1962; Modern Poets, 1963; Poems of Doubt and Belief, 1964; A Controversy of Poets, 1965; Poems on Poetry, 1965. Journals including: Poetry; Nations; Sixties, and others. *Honours:* Guggenheim Fellowship,1961–62; Longview Foundation Award, 1962; National Institute of Arts and Letters Grant, 1961; Rockefeller Foundation Grant, 1967–68; Brandeis University Creative Arts Award, 1969; Amy Lowell Travelling Scholarship, 1969–70; American Book Award, 1982; Pulitzer Prize, 1982. *Address:* Sheffield, VT 05866, USA.

KINNUNEN, Eino, b. 11 Jan. 1930, Nilsiä, Finland. Author. m. Maire Hartikainen, 5 Dec. 1954, Nilsiä, 1 son, 1 daughter. *Publications:* Tie paattyy, 1960; Satssessa asuu ikava, 1963; Elaman avaimet 1-11, 1964–66; Matalapaine, 1969; Suomalainen hamara, 1970; Varpusen polska, 1972; Lapsuuden muisto, 1974; Mirjami, 1979. Translated, Varpisen polska into Russian, 1976. *Contributions to:* Magazine Pellervo, stories. *Memberships:* Suomen Kirjailijaliitto; Pohjois-Savon kirjallinen yhdistys Vestaja r y. *Literary Agent:* Kirjayhtyma Oy. *Address:* Majalahti, 73300 Nilsiä, Finland.

KINSELLA, William Patrick, b. 25 May 1935, Edmonton, Alberta, Canada. Author. m. Ann Knight, 30 Dec. 1978, Iowa City, USA, 2 daughters. *Education:* BA, University of Victoria, 1974; MFA, University of Iowa, USA, 1978. *Publications:* Dance Me Outside, 1977; Scars, 1978; Shoeless Joe Jackson Comes to Iowa, 1980; Born Indian, 1981; Shoeless Joe, 1982; The Balad of the Public Trustee, 1982; The Moccasin Telegraph, 1983; The Thrill of the Grass, 1984; The Alligator Report, 1985; The Iowa Baseball Confederacy, 1986; The Fencepost Chronicles, 1986. *Contributor to:* 200 articles in professional journals & magazines, USA & Canada. *Honours:* Houghton Mifflin Literary Fellowship, 1982; Books in Canada First Novel Award, 1983; Canadian Author's Association Prize for Fiction, 1983; Writers' Guild of Alberta Award for Fiction, 1983, 1984. *Membership:* President, The Enoch Emery Society. *Agent:* Colbert Agency, Ontario, Canada. *Address:* Box 400, White Rock, BC V4B 5G3, Canada.

KIRCHNER, William James, b. 9 July 1955, Tucson, Arizona, USA. Professional Philatelist. m. Carla Saba, 15 May 1974, Tucson, 2 sons. *Education:* University of Arizona. *Contributor to:* Linn's Stamp News; The Practical Investor; Stamp Auction News. *Honours:* Silver Award, Philatelic Literature, Cardinal Spellman Philatelic Museum, 1985. *Membership:* Society of Philaticians. *Address:* P O Box 12865, Tucson, AZ 85732, USA.

KIRK, Russell, b. 19 Oct. 1918, Mecosta, Michigan, USA. Writer; Editor. *Education:* BA, Michigan State University, USA; MA, Duke University; D Litt, St Andrews University. *Publications include:* John Randolph of Roanoke, 1951; The Conservative Mind, 1953; St Andrews, 1954; A Program for Conservatives, 1954; Academic Freedom, 1955; Beyond the Dreams of Avarice, 1956l The American Cause, 1957; The Surly Sullen Bell, 1962; Confessions of a Bohemian Tory, 1963; The Intemperate Professor, 1965; A Creature of the Twilight, 1966; Edmund Burke, 1967; Enemies of the Permanent Things, 1969; Eliot and His Age, 1971;

The Roots of American Order, 1974; The Princess of All Lands, 1979; Decadence and Renewal on the Higher Learning, 1979; Lord of the Hollow Dark, 1979; Portable Conservative Reader, 1982; Watchers at the Straig Gate, 1984; Reclaiming a Patrimony, 1983. *Contributor to:* Numerous magazines and journals including, The University Bookman Quarterly (Editor, 1961–) Modern Age Quarterly (past Editor). *Honours:* Ann Radcliffe Award, 1964; Christopher Award, 1973; Ingersoll Prize 1984. *Membership:* President, Marguerite Ever Wilbur Foundation for literature, 1979. *Agent:* Kirby McCauley. *Address:* Piety Hill, Mecosta, MI 49332, USA.

KIRKALDY, John Francis, b. 14 May 1908, Eastbourne, Sussex, England. Emeritus Professor of Geology, Queen Mary College, London. *Education:* BSc, 1939, MSc, 1932, DSc, 1946, King's College, London. *Publications:* General Principles of Geology, 1954; Rocks and Minerals in Colour, 1963; Fossils in Colour, 1967; Geological Time, 1971; Outline of Historical Geology (with A K Wells), 1938; Field Geology in Colour (with D E B Bates), 1976. *Contributor to:* Quarterly Journal Geological Society; Proceedings of Geologists Association; Geological Magazine; Weather, etc. *Honours include:* Fellow, King's College and Queen Mary College, London. *Membership:* Society of Authors. *Address:* Stone House, Byfield Road, Chipping Warden, Banbury, Oxon OX17 1LE, England.

KIRP, David L, b. 15 Apr. 1944, New York City, USA. Professor; Journalist. *Education:* BA, Amherst College, 1965; LLB, Harvard University, 1968. *Publications:* Doing Good By Doing Little, 1974; Just Schools, 1981; Gender Justice, 1985. *Contributions to:* T E S; New Republic; Wall Street Journal; Commentary; Public Interest; Nation; Christian Science Monitor; Harvard Educational Review; Stanford Law Review; Policy Analysis, and others. *Address:* 1058 Greenwich, San Francisco, CA 97133, USA.

KIRSTILÄ, Pentti Olavi, b. 26 May 1948, Turku, Finland. Author. *Education:* MA, Social Sciences. *Publications:* Farewell to the Dearest, 1977; Farewell Without Tears, 1978; Farewell to the President, 1979; Farewell to the Glass Horse, 1981; Do Not Offend the Gods, 1982; A Shot in the Vein, 1982; A Blow Across the Face, 1983; Munthe, 1984; Farewell in Bright Yellow, 1985. *Contributor to:* Several Newspapers and magazines. *Membership:* Union of Finnish Writers. *Address:* Topeliuksenkatu 29 B 33 00250 Helsinki, Finland.

KISHON, Ephraim, b. 23 Aug. 1924, Budapest, Hungary. Writer, Film Producer and Director, Theatre Play Writer and Director. m. 3 children. *Education:* History of Art, Budapest University. *Publications include:* About 30 books, satires, novels and plays on Hebrew including: Marriage Licence, play; Sallah, film comedy, 1965; The Policeman, film comedy, 1972; Look Back Mrs Lot, book; Noah's Ark, Tourist Class, book; Unfair to Goliath, book; Blow Softly in Jericho; The Seaside Whale, book; Wise Guy, Solomon, book; No Oil Moses, book; Sorry We Won, book; Woe to the Victors, book. *Contributions to:* Daily satirical column, Maariv, Israel, 1952–. *Honours include:* Nordau Prize for Literature, Israel, 1953; Sokolov Prize for Outstanding Journalistic Achievements, 1958; 3 Israeli Kinor David Prizes, 1964 amd 1971; 3 Hollywood Golden Globe Awards, Hollywood Foreign Press Association, USA. 1965 and 1972; Israeli Hertzl Prize for Literature, 1970; Oscar Nomination, The Academy of Motion Picture Arts and Sciences, 1972; Das Goldene DTV-Taschenbuch, 1976; Der Till Eulenspiegel Preis, Hamburg, Federal Republic of Germany, 1980; The Shalom Aleichen Prize, Tel Aviv, Israel, 1984; Die Goldene Kamera for Outstanding TV films, 1984, Berlin, Federal Republic of Germany, 1985. *Address:* 48 Hamitnadev Street, Afeka 69 690, Israel.

KISNER, James Martin, b. 26 Mar. 1947, Evansville, Indiana, USA. Advertising Copywriter. m. Carole

Kleckner, 24 Jan. 1969, 1 son, 1 daughter. *Education:* MA, 1973, BA, 1970, Indiana University. *Publications:* (Fiction) Nero's Vice, 1981; Slice of Life, 1982; (Anthology) Cold Sweat, 1985. *Contributor to:* Former Editor, Cinema Review. *Memberships:* Poets & Writers Inc; Author's Guild. *Literary Agent:* Mary Williamson, Midwest Literary Agency. *Address:* c/o Midwest Literary Agency, 3660 Alsace Dr, Indianapolis, IN 46260, USA.

KITCHER, Philip Stuart, b. 20 Feb. 1947, London, England. Professor of Philosophy, University of Minnesota, USA. m. Patricia Williams, 21 Aug. 1971, New Haven, Connecticut, 2 sons. *Education:* BA (Cantab); PhD, Princeton University. *Publications:* Abusing Science: The Case Against Creationism, 1982; The Nature of Mathematical Knowledge, 1983; Vaulting Ambition: Sociobiology and the Quest for Human Nature, 1985. *Contributions to:* Philosophical Review; Philosophy of Science; British Journal for the Philosophy of Science; Journal of Philosophy; Nous; Philosophical Studies; Philosophical Quarterly; Isis; Studies in the History and Philosophy of Science; Journal of Philosophical Logic; Australasian Journal of Philosophy; Philosophical Topics; Journal of College Science Teaching; Reviews in: Nature; Science; New York Times, etc. *Address:* Minnesota Center for the Philosophy of Science, 315 Ford Hall, 224 Church Street S E, Minneapolis, MN 55455, USA.

KITCHIN, Laurence, b. 21 July, 1913, Bradford, England. *Education:* BA, King's College, London University, 1934. *Publications:* Len Hutton, 1953; Three on Trial (Byron, Bowdler, Machiavelli), 1959; Mid-Century Drama, 1960, 62; Drama in the Sixties, 1966. *Contributions to:* Times; Observer; Encounter; London Magazine; New Hungarian Quarterly; Shakespeare Survey; Times Literary Supplement. *Memberships:* The Athenaeum. *Address:* c/o National Westminster Bank, 1 St James's Square, London, England.

KITSON, Vivian Ian, b. 20 Dec. 1944, Perth, Western Australia. Journalist. m. Tamara Lensky, 15 Jan. 1971, Sydney, 1 son. *Education:* BA, University of Western Australia. *Literary Appointments:* Executive member, Western Australia branch, Fellowship of Australian Writers, 1967–68. *Publication:* Life, Death and some Words About Them, 1978. *Contributions to:* Over 50 poems in Australian literary journals including: Meanjin; Quadrant; Overland; Poetry Australia; New Poetry; Westerly. *Honours:* Highly commended for 1st collection of verse, Anne Elder Poetry Award, 1978. *Memberships:* Australian Society of Authors; associate, Australian Writers Guild. *Address:* 102 Cavendish Street, Stanmore, NSW 2048, Australia.

KIVISTÖ Pentti Eino Johannes, b. 11 Aug. 1922, Lappee, Finland. Author. *Education:* Central Art School, Finland. *Publications:* Loulakuvat, 1952; Vedenharmaat Urut, 1956; Urho, 1958; Naamiot, 1965. *Contributions to:* Numerous publications. *Honours:* Literary Prize, Finnish Society of Authors, 1957; Lauritsale Medal, 1970; Golden Mark, Society of Young Spirit Award, 1969. *Memberships:* Finnish Society of Authors; Union of Finnish Critics. *Literary Agent:* WSOY, Karisto. *Address:* Lauritsalantie 73, 53300 Lappeenranta, Finland.

KIYOTA, Minoru, b. 12 Oct. 1923, Seattle, Washington, USA. Professor of Buddhist Studies. m. Noriko Motoyoshi, 6 Mar. 1951, at Japan, 2 sons. *Education:* BA, University of California at Berkeley, USA; MA, PhD, Tokyo University, Japan. *Literary Appointments:* Assistant Professor 1962, Professor 1978, University of Wisconsin-Madison. *Publications:* Shingon Buddhism: Theory and Practice, 1978; Mahayana Buddhist Meditation: Theory and Practice, editor, 1978; Gedatsukai: Its Theory and Practice, 1982; Tantric Concept of Bodhicitta: A Buddhist Experiential Philosophy, 1982. *Memberships:* International Association of Buddhist Studies. *Address:* 2422 Chamberlain Avenue, Madison, WI 53705, USA.

KJAER, Niels, b. 27 Apr. 1949, Aarhus, Denmark. Minister. m. Elisabeth ØOllgaard, 10 Aug. 1973, Vorde, 2 daughters. *Education:* Candidatus Theologiae, Minister of Divinity equivalent, Aarhus University, 1975. *Literary Appointments:* Literary critic, Høojskolebladet, 1978-. *Publications:* Papir, poems, 1977; Lyøo Logbog, poems, 1978; ØO-liv, essays, 1982; Den grøonne Kristus, essays, 1983; John Greenleaf Whittierog Den evige Godhed, biography, 1983; Editor and translator, Emily Dickinson's Elysium and Hesperidernes sommer, 1984, 85. *Contributions to:* Høojskolebladet; Lyrik; Nuancer; Church and Life, USA; Dickinson Studies, USA. *Memberships:* Danish Authors Association; Emily Dickinson Society; Søoren Kierkegaard Society; Grundtvig Society. *Address:* Lyøo Bygade 6, Lyøo, 5600 Faaborg, Denmark.

KLAASSEN, Walter, b. 27 May 1926, Laird, Saskatchewan, Canada. University Professor. m. Ruth Dorean Strange, 7 June 1952, Weyburn, Saskatchewan, 3 sons, 3 daughters. *Education:* BA, McMaster University, Hamilton, Ontario, 1954; BD, McMaster Divinity School, 1957; D Phil, University of Oxford, England, 1960. *Major Publications:* Anabaptism: Neither Catholic nor Protestant, 1973; Michael Gaismair: Revolutionary & Reformer, 1978; The Writings of Pilgram Marpeck (with William Klaassen), 1978; Anabaptism in Outline: Selected Primary Sources, 1981. *Contributor to:* The Baptist Quarterly, London; The Mennonite Quarterly Review; Church History; Peace Research Reviews, 1962-. *Address:* Site 12A C23 R R 7, Vernon, British Columbia, V1T 723, Canada.

KLAHR, Myra, b. 16 Apr. 1933, New York, USA. Poet; Arts Administrator. m. 1 son, 3 daughters. *Education:* BA, 1954, MA, 1960, Queens College. *Literary Appointments:* Poet, Teacher, 1971; Founder, Executive Director, New York State Poets in the Schools, 1973-. *Publication:* The Waiting Room, 1972. *Contributions to:* Hanging Loose; Sesheta; Small Pond; Unicorn; The Teacher. *Honours:* Phi Beta Kappa. 1952; Dylan Thomas Poetry Award, 1970. *Memberships:* Directory of American Poets; Board Member, New York State Alliance for Arts Education. *Address:* 57 Old Farm Road, Pleasantville, NY 10570, USA.

KLAPPERT, Peter, b. 14 Nov. 1942, Rockville Center, New York, USA. Poet; Educator. *Education:* BA, Cornell University, 1964; MA, 1967, MFA 1968, University of Iowa. *Literary Appointments:* Instructor, Rollins College, 1968–71; Briggs-Copeland Lecturer, Harvard University, 1971–74; Visiting Lecturer, New College, Florida, 1972; Writer-in-Residence, College of William and Mary, 1976–77; Assistant Professor, 1977–78; Assistant Professor, George Mason University, 1978–81; Director of The Graduate Writing Program, 1979–80, 1985–; Associate Professor, 1981–. *Publications:* Lugging Vegetables to Nantucket, 1971; Circular Stairs, Distress in the Mirrors, 1975; Non Sequitur O' Connor, 1977; The Idiot Princess of the Last Dynasty, 1984; 52 Pick-Up; Scenes from The Conspiracy, A Documentary, 1984; Internal Foreigner (audio cassette), 1984. *Contributions to:* Antaeus; The Atlantic Monthly; Harper's; American Poetry Review; Agni Review; Ploughshares; Missouri Review, Paris Review; Parnassus; Poetry in Review, etc. *Honours:* Yales Series of Younger Poets, 1971; MEA Fellowships in Creative Writing, 1973, 79; Lucille Medwick Award of Poetry Society of America, 1977; Ingram Merrill Foundation Grant in Creative Writing, 1983; Resident Fellowships at Yaddo, The MacDowell Colony, The Virginia Center for the Creative Arts, The Millay Colony, La Fondation Maroly. *Memberships:* Academy of American Poets; Associated Writing Programs; PEN; Poetry Society of America; Washington Independent Writers; National Writers Union. *Literary Agent:* Sandra Hardy, Wald-Hardy Associates, New York City. *Address:* Graduate Writing Program, Department of English, George Mason University, Fairfax, VA 22030, USA.

KLARE, Hugh John, b. 22 June 1916, Berndorf, Austria. Criminologist, Penologist. *Publications:* Anatomy of Prison, 1960, 1962 and USA in 1980; Changing Concepts of Crime and its Treatment, 1966; Frontiers of Criminology, (co-author), 1966; People in Prison, 1973. *Contributions to:* Various Newspapers and journals including: JP; Encyclopedia Britannica; International Yearbook. *Membership:* Authors Club. *Honour:* Commander of the British Empire, 1967. *Address:* 28 Pittville Court, Albert Road, Cheltenham, Gloucestershire GL52 3TA, England.

KLEHR, Harvey Elliott, b. 25 Dec. 1945, Newark, New Jersey, USA. Professor of Political Science. m. Elizabeth Jordan Turner, July 1970, Chapel Hill, North Carolina, 3 sons. *Education:* BA, Franklin and Marshall College, 1967; PhD, University of North Carolina, Chapel Hill, 1971. *Publications:* Communist Cadre, 1978; The Heyday of American Communism: The Depression Decade, 1984. *Contributions to:* Encounter, 1982; New York Review of Books, 1982. *Literary Agent:* Maggie Curran. *Address:* Department of Political Science, Emory University, Atlanta, GA 30322, USA.

KLEMETTINEN, Yrjö Johannes, b. 14 Feb. 1920, Oulu, Finland. Author. m. Salme Stenius, 17 Feb. 1945, Oulu, 2 sons, 1 daughter. *Education:* Chief of Printing Office. *Publications:* Drama: Pohjoisesta tuulee, 1974; Ihmisen hinta, 1976; Ohi taivaan ja meren, 1977; Verenpunainen ruusu, 1977; Perhonen, 1978; Leikkipulsto, 1981; Soraniityt, 1981; Viattomat leikit, 1982; Eilisen varjot, 1982; Pieni Prinsessa ja uljas Gladiaattori, 1984; Rikasta elamaa, 1984; Ei yolla paista aurinki, 1985; Elisan unet, 1985; Ihmisia valimaastossa, 1985. *Contributions to:* About 200 short stories published. *Membership:* Finnish Dramatists Society. *Literary Agent:* Finnish Dramatists Society. *Address:* Kaislatie 11 L 43, 90160, Oulu, Finland.

KLEVIN, Jill Ross, b. 7 Sep. 1935, New York, USA. Writer. m. Bruce M Klevin, 7 Apr. 1960, New York, 1 son, 1 daughter. *Education:* BS Writing, Columbia University, New York. *Major Publications:* The Summer of the Sky-Blue Bikini, 1979; That's my Girl, 1980; The Best of Friends, 1981; Far From Home, 1982; The Turtle Street Trading Company, 1982; Turtles Together Forever, 1982; Miss Perfect, 1983. *Memberships:* PEN; Society of Children's Book Writers. *Literary Agent:* Writers' House Inc. *Address:* 5252 Winnetka Avenue, Woodland Hills, CA 91364, USA.

KLINGER, Eric, b. 23 May 1933, Vienna, Austria. Professor of Psychology. *Education:* BA, Harvard University, USA, 1954; PhD, University of Chicago, 1960. *Publications:* Structure and Functions of Fantasy, 1971; Meaning and Void: Inner Experience and the Incentives in People's Lives, 1977; Imagery, Volume 2, 1981. *Contributions to:* Psychology Review; Psychology Bulletin; Journal of Personality and Social Psychology. *Honours:* Horace T Morse Amoco Award, 1972; Fulbright Research Grant to Germany, 1975–76. *Memberships:* Past President, American Association for the Study of Mental Imagery; Fellow, American Psychology Association; Sigma Xi; Psychonomic Society; American Association of University Professors. *Address:* University of Minnesota. Division of Social Sciences, Morris, MN 56267, USA.

KLINGER, Mary, b. 20 Nov. 1953. Registration Assistant at Boston College, USA. *Education:* BA, English Sociology, Boston College, USA, 1976. *Appointments:* Editorial Assistant, Porter Sargent Publishers; Freelance Writer. *Contributions to:* Christian Science Monitor. *Honours:* Hon Mention, Scholastic Magazine, 1967; National Poetry Press, 1968/69/71; Hon Mention, Nancy Thorp Memorial Contest, Hollins College, 1970; Cardinal Cushing Award, Boston College, 1976; 4 awards for editorial, literary magazines, Empire State Press Association, 1971. *Address:* 281 Antlers Drive, Rochester, NY 14618, USA.

KLINKOWITZ, Jerome, b. 24 Dec. 1943, Milwaukee, Wisconsin, USA. Author. m. (1) Elaine Ptaszynaki, 29 Jan. 1966, Milwaukee, Wisconsin; (2) Julie Huffman, 27 May 1978, Cedar Falls, Iowa, 1 son, 1 daughter.

Education: BA, 1966, MA, 1967, Marquette University; PhD, University of Wisconsin, 1970. *Literary Appointments:* University Fellow, University of Wisconsin, 1968–69; Assistant Professor, English, Northern Illinois University, 1969–70; Associate Professor, English, University of Northern Iowa, 1972–75; Professor of English, University of Northern Iowa, 1975–; University Distinguished Scholar, University of Northern Iowa, 1985–. *Publications:* Literary Disruptions, 1975; The Life of Fiction, 1977; The American 1960s, 1980; The Practice of Fiction in America, 1980; Kurt Vonnegut, 1982; The Self-Apparent Word, 1984; Literary Subversions, 1985; The New American Novel of Manners, 1986. *Contributions:* Over 250 essays in Partisan Review, The New Republic, The Nation, American Literature, etc. Short stories in The North American Review, The Chicago Tribune, The San Francisco Chronicle. *Honours:* National Endowment for the Arts/PEN Syndicated Fiction Prizes, 1984, 85. *Memberships:* Modern Language Association of America; PEN American Center. *Address:* 1904 Clay Street, Cedar Falls, IA 50613, USA.

KLOEPFER, Marguerite Fonnesback, b. 13 Nov. 1916, Logan, Utah, USA. Writer. *Education:* BS, Utah State University, 1937. *Publications:* Non-Fiction: Singles Survival, 1979. Novels: Bentley, 1979; But Where Is Love?, 1980; The Heart and the Scarab, 1981. *Contributions to:* Seventeen; Woman's Day; Nineteen From Seventeen, anthology, 1952; Widening Views, textbook, 1958. *Address:* 306 East Hawthorne Street, Ontario, CA 91764, USA.

KLOPFENSTEIN, Freddy, b. 25 June 1934, Bex, Switzerland. Journalist; Director of La Vie Protestante, m. Valérie Martinoglio, 13 Sep. 1958, 1 son, 1 daughter. *Publications:* Le Soleil est nouveau tous les jours, 1977; Humanitude, 1980; Le Décor de l'envers, 1981; Méditation teintée d'humour noir, 1983; 'Ministre porté disparu, 1985. *Memberships:* President 1980–81, Geneva Society of Writers; Swiss Society of Writers; Geneva National Institute. *Address:* 26 chemin François-Lehmann, CH–1218 Le Grand-Saconnex, Genèva, Switzerland.

KNAPP, Ronald Gary, b. 15 Aug. 1940, Pittsburgh, Pennsylvania, USA. College Professor. m. May Tse, 15 Sep. 1968, 2 sons, 1 daughter. *Education:* BA, Stetson University, Florida, 1962; PhD, University of Pittsburgh, 1968. *Publications:* Co-editor: Chinese Walled Cities, 1979; Editor: and contributor: China's Island Frontier: Studies in the Historical Geography of Taiwan, 1980. *Contributions to:* Journal of Geography; Annals; Association of American Geographers; The China Geographer; Annals; Association of American Geographers; The China Geographer; Comparative Frontier Studies; American Philosophical Society Proceedings; The China Quarterly; Pacific Historical Review; Orientations; Journal of Cultural Geography. Also, China Perceived, Perceiving China, In A Preface to East Asia; Geographical and Historical Approaches to Foreign Area Studies, edited by Clifton W Pannell, 1983. *Honours:* Woodrow Wilson Fellowship, 1962–63; American Council of Learned Societies, Mellon Foundation Fellow, 1978; National Endowment for the Humanities Fellowship, 1984; Grants from American Philosophical Society, State University of New York, Association of American Geographers. *Memberships:* Association for Asian Studies; Association of American Geographers. *Address:* 5 Van Kleeck Avenue, New Paltz, NY 12561, USA.

KNAUS, William A, b. 13 Aug. 1946, Pittsburgh, Pennsylvania, USA. Physician. *Education:* Widener College, 1968; MD, West Virginia University, 1972. *Major Publications:* Inside Russian Medicine, 1981. *Contributor to:* New York Times Magazine; New York Times; Washington Post; American Medical Association News. *Honour:* Recipient, Annual Scientific Writing Award, American Medical Writers Association, 1978, 1979. *Membership:* American Medical Writers Association. *Literary Agent:* John Schaffner. *Address:* 5320 37th Street, North Arlington, VA 22207, USA.

KNEBEL, Fletcher, b. 1 Oct. 1911, Dayton, Ohio, USA. m. Constance Wood, 28 Apr. 1985, Hawaii, USA. *Education:* Miami University, Ohio, USA, 1934. *Literary Appointments include:* Washington Correspondent, Cleveland Plain Dealer, 1937–50; Look Magazine, Des Moines Register, Minneapolis Tribune, 1950–64; Syndicated column, Potomac Fever, 1951–64. *Publications:* No High Ground, 1960; Seven Days in May, 1962; Convention, 1964; Night of Camp David, (with Charles W Bailey II), 1965; The Zinzin Road, 1966; Vanished, 1968; Trespass, 1969; Dark Horse, 1972; The Bottom Line, 1974; Dave Sulkin Cares, 1978; Crossing in Berlin, 1981; Poker Game, 1983. *Address:* 1119 Kaumoku Street, Honolulu, HI 96825, USA.

KNECHT, Robert Jean, b. 20 Sep. 1926, London, England. Professor of French History, University of Birmingham, England. m. Sonia Mary Fitzpatrick Hodge (deceased), London. *Education:* BA, 1948, Diploma in Education, 1949, MA, 1953, University of London; D Litt, 1984, University of Birmingham. *Publications:* The Voyage of Sir Nicholas Carewe, 1959; Francis I and Absolute Monarchy, 1969; The Fronde, 1975; Wealth and Power in Tudor England, 1978; Francis I, 1982; French Renaissance Monarchy: Francis I and II, 1984. *Contributions to:* The Courts of Europe, edited by A G Dickens, 1977; Times Literary Supplement; English History Review; History; European Studies Review; Encyclopedia Britannica. *Memberships:* Societe de l'Histoire de France; Fellow, Royal Historical Society. *Address:* 22 Warwick New Road, Leamington Spa, Warwickshire CV32 5JG, England.

KNEIPP, Marianne Hagar, b. 14 Feb. 1948, Davenport, Iowa, USA. Medical Writer. 1 daughter. *Education:* BA, University of Iowa. *Literary Appointments:* Editorial Associate, St Luke's Episcopal Hospital, 1976–80; Medical Writer, Texas Heart Institute, 1980–; Editorial Consultant, Texas Heart Institute Journal, 1976–. *Publications:* Editor: Techniques in Cardiac Surgery, by Denton A Cooley MD, 1984; Reflections & Observations: Essays of Denton A Cooley MD, 1985; Surgical Treatment of Airtic Aneurysms, by Denton A Cooley MD, 1985. Editor, Writer, numerous scientific manuscripts, essays, speeches, for Texas Heart Institute Staff. *Honours:* Academic Commendation, University of Iowa, 1970; Core Curriculum Certification, English/Writing, American Medical Writers Association, 1985. *Memberships:* American Medical Writers Association; Membership Chairman, Southwest Chapter, ibid; Council of Biology Editors; Women in Communications. *Address:* Texas Heart Institute; P O Box 20345, Houston, TX 77225, USA.

KNIBB, Shirley Marion, b. 24 Apr. 1948, Potters Bar, England. Technician (Biology); Author. m. Colin W J Knibb, 15 Sep. 1969, Potters Bar, 1 son, 2 daughters. *Education:* Certificate in Journalism. Specialised training in Microscopical techniques. *Publications:* Smaller Pets, 1981; Rattus Norvegicus, 1983. *Contributions to:* Country Quest; Natural History. *Memberships:* Authors Society; Technical Authors Society. *Address:* 49 Nodes Drive, Marymead, Stevenage, Hertfordshire, England.

KNIGHT, Arthur Winfield, b. 29 Dec. 1937, San Francisco, California, USA. Writer, University Professor. m. Kathleen (Kit) Duell, 25 Aug. 1976. Cumberland, Maryland, USA, 1 daughter. *Education:* BA English, 1960, MA Creative Writing, 1962, San Francisco State University. *Major Publications:* A Marriage of Poets (with Kit Knight), 1984; Golden Land, 1985. *Contributor to:* The Spoon River Quarterly; Wormwood Review, Mississippi Arts & Letters Review; Poetry Now; Bogg; The Greenfield Review; Truly Fine Review; Review of Contemporary Fiction; Puerto Del Sol; Gypsy. *Address:* P O Box 439, California, PA 15419, USA.

KNIGHT, Frida Frances Emma (Nee Stewart), b. 11 Nov. 1910, Cambridge, England. m. Professor B C J G Knight, 28 Dec. 1943, Cambridge, England, 2 sons, 2 daughters. *Education:* Hich's Konservatorium, Frankfurt a-M, Germany; Association of the Royal College of Music, London, England. *Publications:* Dawn Escape, 1943; The Strange Case of Thomas Walker, 1956; University Rebel - Life of William Frend, 1971; Beethoven and the Age of Revolution, 1973; The French Resistance, 1975; Cambridge Music, 1979; Translations from the French to works by Sadoreann (1953) and Caragiale (1956). *Contributions to:* BBC Music Magazine and Women's Hour; ITV programmes on French Resistance; 1984; New Statesman; Daily Telegraph; Morning Star; New Hungarian Quarterly; Cambridge Review. *Address:* 28 Park Parade, Cambridge CB5 8AL, England.

KNIGHT, Kathleen (Kit) Duell, b. 21 Sep. 1952, N Kingston, Rhode Island, USA. Writer; Publisher; Editor. m. Arthur Winfield Knight, 25 Aug. 1976, Cumberland, Maryland, 1 daughter. *Education:* BA, Communications, California University of Pennsylvania, 1975. *Publications:* The Best Road (co-editor with Arthur Knight), 1984; A Marriage of Poets (co-author with Arthur Knight), 1984. *Contributions:* Poetry and Prose to: The Spoon River Quarterly; Home Planet News; Poetry Now; Ludd's Mill; Waterways; Random Weirdness; Second Coming and numerous other publications. *Honour:* Coordinating Council of Literary Magazines, for co-editing the unspeakable visions of the individual, 1982. *Address:* PO Box 439, California, PA 15419, USA.

KNIGHTS, Lionel Charles, b. 15 May 1906, Grantham, England. University Teacher. *Education:* BA, MA, PhD, Selwyn College and Christs College, Cambridge University. *Publications:* Drama and Society in the Age of Jonson, 1937; Exploration: Essays in Criticism, 1946; Some Shakespearean Themes, 1959; An Approach to Hamlet, 1960; Further Exploration, 1965; Public Voices: Literature and Politics, 1971; Explorations 3, 1976; Metaphor and Symbol, Co-Editor with Basil Cottle, 1960. *Contributions to:* Scrutiny; The Criterion; Southern Review; Sewanee Review; New York Review of Books, and others. *Honours:* Honorary Doctorates: University of Bordeaux, France, 1964; University of York, England, 1969; Literature, University of Manchester 1974; Sheffield University, 1978; Warwick University, 1979; Bristol University, 1984. Honorary Foreign Member, American Academy of Artsand Sciences, 1980. *Memberships:* Association of University Teachers; Royal Commonwealth Society. *Address:* 57 Jesus Lane, Cambridge CB5 8BS, England.

KNOEBEL, Joseph Alfred, b. 19 Sep. 1933, Rochester, New York, USA. Clergyman, Editor. *Education:* BA, 1957, St Mary's Seminary, Techny; MA, 1964, Catholics University of America, Washinton DC. *Literary Appointments:* Editor, Divine Word Missionaries, 1983. *Contributions to:* Numerous theological and professional journals. *Address:* 1835 Waukegan Road, Techny, IL 60082, USA.

KNORR, Dandi Daley, b. 24 Mar. 1949, Kansas City, Missouri, USA. Writer. m. 19 May 1973, Hamilton, Missouri, 2 daughters. *Education:* BA, University of Missouri. *Literary Appointments:* Freelance Reviewer, Prentice Hall. *Publications:* The Blessing is in the Doing, 1983; A Spiritual Handbook for Women, 1984; When the Answer is No, 1985; Remembering..., 1985. *Contributions to:* Moody Monthly; Worldwide Challenge; Eternity; Faith at Work; various minor Christian publications. *Address:* 2118 Sharman Avenue, Evanston, IL 60201, USA.

KNOWLES, Dorothy, b. 28 Mar. 1906, Johannesburg, Republic of South Africa. University Lecturer (Retired). m. John Stephenson Spink, 27 July 1940, Liverpool. *Education:* BA, 1928; Diploma in Education, 1929, MA, 1931, Leeds University, England; Licenciate, Royal Academy of Music, 1926; Dr ès Lettres, Sorbonne, France, 1934. *Publications include:* La Reaction idealiste au Theatre depius, 1934; The Censor, The Drama and Film 1900-1934, 1934; French Drama of the Inter-War Years 1918-1939, 1968; Forces in

Modern French Drama, Co-Author, 1972; The Wild Duck Flies Against the Wind, Armand Gatti's Theatrical Activities, 1986. *Contributions to:* French Studies; Modern Language Review and others. *Honours:* Medal, French Academy, 1935; Officer of the Academy, 1947. *Address:* 48 Woodside Park Road, London N12 8RS, England.

KNOWLTON, Edgar Colby,b. 14 Sep. 1921, Delaware, Ohio, USA. Professor. *Education:* AB, magna cum laude, 1941, AM, Harvard, 1942; PhD, Stanford University, 1959. *Publications:* The Conquest of Malacca, (translation, Sa de Meneses). *Education:* AB, magna cum laude, 1941, AM, Harvard, 1942; PhD, Stanford University, 1959. *Publications:* The Conquest of Malacca, (translation, Sa de Meneses). *Education:* AB, magna cum laude, 1941, AM, Harvard, 1942; PhD, Stanford University, 1959. *Publications:* The Conquest of Malacca, (translation, Sa de Meneses); 1971; V Blasco Ibanez, (co-author with A Grove Day), 1972; Esteban Echeverria, 1986. *Contributor to:* Articles and reviews in: World Literature Today; Romance Philology; Romance Notes; Hispania; Hispanic Review; Studies in Short Fiction: Revista portuguesa de filologia: Notes and Queries; American Speech: The Explicator; Gavea-Brown; Tamil Culture; Chinese Culture; The Linguist; The Hawaiian; Journal of History; Boletim Eclesial, (Diocese de Macau), etc. *Honour:* Translation Prize, 1973. *Address:* 1026 Kalo Place, Apt 403, Honolulu, HI 96828, USA.

KNOX, Ray, b. 23 Sep. 1926, Wellington, New Zealand. Editor. m. Heather Douglas, 23 Feb. 1955, Christchurch, 3 daughters. *Education:* Victoria University, Wellington. *Literary Appointments include:* Feature Writer, 1956, Chief Reporter 1964, New Zealand Listener; Editor-in-Chief, New Zealand's Heritage, 1971; Editor-in-Chief, New Zealand Today, 1973; Editor-in-Chief, New Zealand's Nature Heritage, 1974. *Publications:* Editor, Collins Nature Heritage, series; A Thousand Mountains Shining, 1984. *Contributions to:* New Zealand Listener; Here and Now; New Zealand Nature Review; New Zealand Mirror; Radio documentaries, talks and criticism to New Zealand Broadcasting Corporation; television documentaries on New Zealand novelists. *Honour:* Toured Great Britain as a guest of the Commonwealth Relations Office, 1965. *Membership:* PEN. *Address:* 1 Bayview Road, Paremata, New Zealand.

KNOX, Robert Buick, b. 10 Oct. 1918, Banbridge, Down, Northern Ireland. Retired Professor of Ecclesiastical History, Cambridge College, Cambridge University, England. *Education:* MA, BD, Presbyterian College, Belfast, Northern Ireland; BA, PhD, London University, England. *Publications:* James Ussher, Archbishop of Armagh, 1967; Voices from the Past: History of the English Conference of the Presbyterian Church of Wales, 1969; Wales and Y Goleuad 1869-1879, 1969. *Contributions to:* A History of Christian Doctrine, 1979; Studies in Church History; Scottish Journal of Theology; Expisitory Times; Records of Scottish Church History Society. *Honours:* DD, Presbyterian Theological Faculty of Ireland, 1980. *Membership:* Ecclesiastical History Society. *Address:* 26 Killicomaine Drive, Portadown, County Armagh, Northern Ireland.

KNOX-JOHNSTON, Robin, b. 17 Mar. 1939, Putney, London, England. Master Mariner; Company Director; Author. *Publications:* A World of My Own, 1969; Robin Round the World, 1969; Sailing, 1976; Last But Not Least, 1978; Twilight of Sail, 1978. *Contributions to:* True, USA; Yachting World; Yachting Monthly; Rudder; Woman's Own, and others. *Honours:* CBE, 1969. *Memberships:* Fellow, Royal Geographical Society. *Address:* 26 Sefton Street, Putney, London SW15, England.

KNUUTTILA, Rauha Katri, b. 1 Nov. 1924, Ilmajoki, Finland, Playwright. m. Väinö Johannes, 9 Feb. 1944, Nurmo, 3 sons. *Publications:* Poems in anthologies, 1972, 77, 79; Radio play, A Piece of Everyday Life (Ote arjesta), 1972; Play, The Village of Peltokulma Must Not Die (Ei tapeta Peltakulmaa), 1979; Play, Farms Wanting in Mistresses (Emannattomat farmit), 1981; Play, Home Rapids (Kotikoski), 1984. *Contributor to:* Various magazines and newspapers and radio programs of short stories, articles, etc. *Honours:* First Class Medal with Golden Cross given by the Order of the White Rose of Finland, 1982; Award from Society for Support of Finnish Scenic Art, 1980, 85. *Memberships:* Society of Finnish Playwrights; Association of Ostrobothnian Writers; Association of Finnish Provincial Writers. *Address:* Sepäntie 7, 60800 Ilmajoki, Finland.

KOBRE, Sidney, b. 7 Sep. 1907, Winston-Salem, North Carolina, USA. Journalist; Editor; Teacher. m. Reva Hoppenstein, 4 Mar. 1939, Baltimore, 1 son, 1 daughter. *Education:* BA, Johns Hopkins University; Pulitzer School of Journalism, Columbia University; MA, PhD, Columbia University. *Literary Appointments:* Freelance Journalist, Baltimore Sunday Sun; Reporter, Star-Eagle, Newark, New Jersey; Reporter/Editorial Writer, Newark New Jersey Ledger; Assistant Editor, Home News, Baltimore; Managing Editor, Guide Publications, Baltimore; Columnist, Tallahassee Florida Post; Reporter, York Gazette and Daily, Pennsylvania. *Publications:* Backgrounding the News, 1939; Development of Colonial Newspaper, 1944, 1960; News Behind the Headlines, 1955; Psychology and the News, 1955; Journalism History Guidebook, 1955; Press and Ccopntemporary Affairs, 1957, 1969; Behind Shocking Crime Headlines, 1957; Foundations of American Journalism, 1958; Modern American Journalism, 1959; Yelow Press and Gilded Age Journalism, 1964; Development of American Journalism, 1969; Reporting News in Depth, 1982; Successful Public Relations for Colleges and Universities, 1974. *Contributions to:* Social Sciences and the Newspaper, Journalism Quarterly, 1938; First American Newspaper, A Product of Environment, Journalism Quarterly; Sociological Approach to Research in Newspaper History, Journalism Quarterly, 1945; The Zangara Case, Journalism Quarterly, 1936; Celia Cooney Case, Journalism Quarterly, 1937. *Memberships:* Association for Education in Journalism (Co-Founder, History Division); American Journalism Historians Association (Co-Founder, Member of Board of Directors). *Address:* 8215 Scotts Level Road, Baltimore, MD 21208, USA.

KOCH, Claude Francis, b. 28 Nov. 1918, Philadelphia, Pennsylvania, USA. Professor of English. m. Mary P Kane, 7 Sep. 1941, 5 sons, 1 daughter. *Education:* BS, La Salle University; MA, University of Florida. *Publications:* Island Interlude, 1951; Light in Silence, 1958; The Kite in the Sea, 1964; A Casual Company, 1965. *Contributions to:* Sewanee Review; Southern Review; Antioch Review; Kansas Quarterly; Four Quarters; Northwest Review; Ave Maria; Delta Review. *Honours:* Dodd, Mead Intercollegiate Literary Fellowship, 1949; Sewanee Review Fellowship in Fiction, 1957; La Salle College Centenary Award, 1965; Rockefeller Foundation Fellowship in Fiction, 1966; Lindback Award for Distinguished Teaching, 1968. *Address:* 128 West Highland Avenue, Philadelphia, PA 19118, USA.

KOCH, Joanne Barbara, b. 28 Mar. 1941, Chicago, Illinois, USA. Author; Playwright. m. Lewis Z Koch, 30 May 1964, Chicago, 1 son, 2 daughters. *Education:* BA, Hons, Cornell University; MA (Woodrow Wilson Fellowship), Columbia University. *Literary Appointments:* Guest Lecturer: Loyola University, DePaul University; Writer-in-Residence, Lake Forest College. *Publications:* The Marriage Savers (with Lewis Koch), 1976; Contributor: Readings in Psychology Today, 1978; Children: Development through Adolescence, 1983; Marriage and the Family, 1983; Child Development: Topical Approach, 1985; Plays: Haymarket: Footnote to a Bombing; Teeth; XX-XY; Grant 5742; Danceland (musical with Julie Shannon); Teleplays: Today I Am a Person; The Price of Daffodils. *Contributions to:* Parade; Psychology Today; Newsday; McCall's; Washingtonian; etc; Communicated Columnist, Newspaper Enterprise Association. *Honours:* Woodrow Wilson Fellow; First Place Media Award, Family Service Association; Harris Media Award, American Psychoanalytic Association; Grants from Illinois Arts Council for Playwriting. *Memberships*

include: Phi Beta Kappa; Phi Kappa Phi; Society of Midland Authors, President, 1978–80; Chairperson, Drama Award, Society of Midland Authors, 1980–84; Dramatists Guild; Women in Theater; Women in Film; American Association of Authors and Journalists. *Literary Agent:* Timoth Seldes, Russell & Volkening, New York City. *Address:* 343 Dodge Avenue, Evanston, IL 60202, USA.

KOCH, Kurt E, b. 16 Nov. 1913, Berghausen, Germany. Lutheran Minister; Lecturer. m. Bärbel Meyer, Aglasterhausen, 21 Mar. 1974, 2 daughters. *Education:* Dr of Theology, University of Tübingen, Germany; Professor of Theology, Christian University, Manzini, Swaziland. *Literary Appointments:* Writer & Lecturer, 1949–; Founder, Bible & Literature Mission, over 120 countries. *Major Publications:* Seelsorge und Okkultismus, 1952–85, 26 editions, Antwerp, 1984. Okkultes ABC, 1982–84, 2 editions: Total of more than 70 books with 76 foreign translations. *Contributions to:* Over 100 publications incl. Baker's Dictionary; Contemporary Authors. Also 19 books translated into English; 9 into French; 3 Spanish; Japanese, Korean, Chinese, Taiwanese; Burmese; Afrikaans; Telegu; Pidgin English; Most European Languages. *Honours:* Doctorate, Tübingen University; Honorary US Degrees Book Prizes; Between Christ & Satan, US evangelical prize; Occultism, Antwerp, 1984; Occult ABC, Luxembourg 1985. *Address:* D–6955 Aglasterhausen, Federal Republic of Germany.

KOCH, Thilo, b. 20 Sep. 1920, Canena, Federal Republic of Germany. Writer. m. Susanne Gaertner, 22 May 1944, Berlin, 1 son, 1 daughter. *Publications:* Stille und Klang, poems, 1947; Die Opfer, novel, 1948; Gottfried Benn, 1956; Washington Diary, 1965; Interview Mit Südamerika, 1966; Die Goldenen Zwanziger Jahre, 1968; Briefe Aus Krähwinkel, 1966; Begegnungen, 1970; Reporter-Report, 1972; Deutschland War Teilbar, 1972; Berlin 1st Wunderbar, 1985; 150 television documetaries. *Contributions to:* Chief Editor, Aral Journal; Special Correspondent, German Television, Hamburg; Columnist for a German newspaper chain. *Honour:* Bundesverdienstkreuz 1 Klasse. *Membership:* Honorary International Treasurer, PEN Club. *Address:* D 7201 Hausen ob Verena, Württemberg, Federal Republic of Germany.

KOEHLER, Isabel Winifred, b. 5 Feb. 1903, Boston, Massachusetts, USA. Poet; Artist; Writer; Illustrator. m. F Mills Koehler, 16 April 1925, Boston, Mass, 1 son, 1 daughter. *Appointments include:* New England Women's Press Association; Massachusetts State Poetry Society. *Publications:* Bouquets of Poems, 1974; Versified Variety, 1978. *Contributor to:* Bay State Echo; Houston Post; Boston Post; Boston Herald Traveler; Boston Herald America; Boston Daily Globe; Melrose Free Press; Everett Leader, Herald and Gazette; Albo d'Oro; Masters of Modern Poetry; Quarderni de Poesia; Digest, American Biographical Research Instiute; Poetical Rainbow; Fort Lewis College Magazine; Massachusetts State Poetry Society Anthologies, 1981, 1982, 1983, 1984. *Honours:* Recipient of numerous honours including, Poet Laureate Award, 1980; Bouquets of Poems, Library and Archives, North Carolina, 1983; Diploma d'onore, 1982; Rome Diploma of Recognition, Rome 1983; Diploma of Honor, 1984; Star of Contemporary Poetry, 1984; Princess of Poetry, 1985; Masters of Modern Poetry, Rome, Gold Medal, 1983–84; Silver Medal, 1984; Gold Medal, Leonardo Da Vinci Accademie, Rome, 1982. *Memberships:* New England Woman's Press Association; Massachusetts State Poetry Society; American Biographical Institute Research Association; Member, National Board of Advisors, 1983–85. *Address:* 30 Fremont Avenue, Everett, MA 02149, USA.

KOEHN-VAN ZWIENEN, Ilse Charlotte, b. 6 Aug. 1929, Berlin, Germany. Graphic Designer/Writer. *Education:* Illustration, Graphic Design & Fashion Graphics, Art Academy, Berlin. *Publications:* Mischling, Second Degree, 1977; Tilla, 1981, (Greenwillow Books div. of William Morrow & Co). *Honours:* Nominee,

National Book Awards, 1978; Boston Globe-Horn Book Award, best non-fiction, 1978; Jane Addams Peace Association Inc Honorary Award, 1978; Lewis Carroll Shelf Award, 1978. *Memberships:* Authors Guild; Graphic Artists Guild. *Literary Agent:* Janet Loranger. *Address:* 50 Sound Beach Avenue, Old Greenwich, CT 06870, USA.

KOENIGSBERGER, Helmut George, b. 24 Oct. 1918, Berlin, Germany. Professor Emeritus of History, King's College, London, England. *Education:* BA, MA, PhD, Cambridge University. *Literary Appointment:* Fellow of Institute of Advanced Historical Studies, Munich, Germany, 1984–85. *Publications:* The Practice of Empire, 1951, 69; Europe in the Sixteenth Century (with G L Mosse), 1968; Estates and Revolutions, 1971; The Habsburgs and Europe, 1516–1660, 1971; Politicians and Vitruosi, 1986; Medieval Europe 400-1500, 1986; Early Modern Europe 1500–1789, 1986; Editor: Republics and Republicanism in Early Modern Europe 1500–1789, 1986; Editor: Republics and Republicanism in Early Modern Europe. *Contributor to:* Professional journals including: English Historical Review; Journal of Modern History; European Studies Review. *Honour:* J S Guggenheim Fellowship, 1970–71. *Memberships include:* Fellow, Royal Historical Society; Associate, Real Academia de Madrid, Spain; International Commission for the History of Republic and Parliamentary Institutions, Secretary-General, 1955–75, Vice-President, 1975–80, Pr, 1980; President, International Commission for the History of Representative and Parliamentary Institutions, 1980–85; Vice-President, Royal Historical Society, 1982–85. *Address:* 41A Lancaster Grove, London NW3 4HB, England.

KOFALK, Harriet, b. 12 Oct. 1937, New Jersey, USA. Writer/Historical Researcher. Divorced, 1 son, 1 daughter. *Education:* BA, University of New Mexico, 1959. *Publications:* Apple Encore, 1977; Tamotzu in Haiku, 1977. *Contributions to:* The Christian Science Monitor; New Mexico Magazine; New Mexico Architecture; Harper's Weekly; Sew Business; Bird Watcher's Digest. *Honours:* Second Honorable Mention, Kansas Poetry Contest, 1982; Honorable Mention, San Diego Historical Society Annual Institute, 1984 and 1985. *Membership:* Rio Grande Writers' Workshop. *Address:* 2128 Stonyvale, Tujunga, CA 91042, USA.

KOFOED, Rud, b. 25 Apr. 1945, Holeby, Denmark. Journalist. *Education:* School of Journalism, Aarhus University. *Publications:* Kritiske Tekster, 1972; Gurotro og Jesus Revolution, 1974; The Book About Abba, 1977; Rock-Arbogen, 1978. *Contributions to:* Ekstra Bladet, Copenhagen. *Membership:* Dansk Journalistforbund. *Address:* Piledammen, Bolbrovej 63, 2960 Rungsted Kyst, Denmark.

KOGAWA, Joy Nozomi, b. 6 June 1935, Canada. Writer. *Literary Appointment:* Writer-in-Residence, University of Ottawa, 1978. *Publications:* A Choice of Dreams, 1974; Jericho Road, 1978; Obasan, 1981; David Godine (US), 1982, Futami Shobo (Japan), 1983, Penguin (Canada), 1983, Penguin (UK), 1984. *Honours:* First Novel Award, Books in Canada, 1981; Book of the Year, Canadian Authors, 1982; Notable Book, American Library Association, 1982; American Book Award, Before Columbus Foundation, 1983; Paper back Award, Canadian Periodical Distributor, 1983. *Memberships:* PEN International; League of Canadian Poets; Writers Union of Canada. *Address:* 447 Montrose Avenue, Toronto M6G 3H2, Ontario, Canada.

KOHFELDT, Mary Lou, b. 5 Feb. 1939, Fort Worth, Texas, USA. Writer; Investor. m. Dr Philip John Stevenson, 11 May 1968, Durham, North Carolina, 1 son, 1 daughter. *Education:* BA, Stanford University, 1960; MA, Duke University, 1965; PhD, University of North Carolina, 1977. *Publications:* Lady Gregory: The Woman Behind the Irish Renaissance, 1985. *Literary Agent:* Rosalie Siegel. *Address:* 42 Cleveland Lane, Princeton, NJ 08540, USA.

KOHLER, Foy D, b. 15 Feb. 1908, Oakwood, Ohio, USA. Diplomatist. *Education:* Toledo and Ohio State Universities; BA. *Publications:* Understanding the Russians – A Citizen's Primer, 1970; Science and Technology as an Instrument of Soviet Policy, Co-Author, 1972; Convergence of Communism and Capitalism, 1973; Soviet Strategy for the 70s: From Cold War to Peaceful Coexistence, 1973; The Role of Nuclear Forces in Current Soviet Strategy, 1974; The Soviet Union – Yesterday, Today, Tomorrow, 1975; Custine's Eternal Russia, 1976; Salt II: How Not to Negotiate with the Russians, 1979. *Contributions to:* Innumerable professional publications. *Honours:* Honorary DHum, Ohio State University; Honorary LLD, University of Toledo, Ohio. *Address:* 215 Golf Club Circle, Tequesta, FL 33469, USA.

KOISTINEN, Vuokko, b. 14 July 1931, Ruokoiahti, Finland. Author. m. Paavo, 24 June 1953 (divorced, 1976), 1 son, 2 daughters. *Literary Appointments:* Kirjayhtyma. *Publications:* Poikkiviivat, 1969; Vihreat tomaatit, 1970; Yksityisalue, 1971; Tassa maisemasse, 1973; Saahan aurinko olla, 1974; Rakkaampi Kivi rakkaampi Kukka, 1981. *Membership:* Suomen Kirjailijaliitto. *Address:* Livisniemenaukio 2 E 55, 02260 Espoo, Finland.

KOIVISTOINEN, Eino Hannes, b. 10 May 1907, Kuopio, Finland. Author. m. Salme Mirjam Soininen, 30 Aug. 1936, 2 sons, 1 daughter. *Education:* Navigation Institute, Master 1938; Navy Reserve Officers' School, 1st Lieutenant, 1941. *Major Publications:* The Sea Protest of SS Orpheus, 1964; An Angel Without Wings (novel), 1962; The Blue Sea and other stores, 1967; Swelling Sails, 1970; The Old Tramp, 1973; Tahiti, 1977; Telegram to God, (short stories), 1979; Gustav Erikson, King of Sailing Ships, 1981; Cargo of Coal to Chile (short stories), 1982; The Voice of Sea and Wind (poems & translations from Polynesian and Indian poems), 1985. *Contributor to:* Various Travel weekly magazines and journals in Finland. *Honours:* Winner Television play-writing contest, 1960; State Prize of Literature for The Old Tramp (novel), 1974; Art Prize of Literature, Kymenlaasko County, 1979; Knight of the White Rose (Finland), 1969; Cross of Liberty IV Class with Swords & several War Medals. *Memberships:* Authors League of Finland; Dramatists' League of Finland; Society of Cape Horners. *Literary Agent:* Werner Söderström Osakeyhtiö, Helsinki, Finland. *Address:* Kalliolankatu 3 B 52, 48100 Kotka 10, Finland.

KOLATCH, Alfred Jacob, b. 2 Jan. 1916, Seattle, Washington, USA. Publisher. m. Thelma Rubin, 16 June 1940, New York City, 2 sons. *Education:* BA, Yeshiva University, 1937; MHL and Rabbinical Degree, Jewish Theological Seminary, 1941. *Publications:* These Are the Names, 1948; Who's Who in the Talmud, 1964; The Name Dictionary, 1967; Names for Pets, 1971; Dictionary of First Names, 1980; Jewish Book of Why 1981; Complete Dictionary of English and Hebrew First Names, 1984; Second Jewish Book of Why, 1985. *Address:* 72-08 Juno Street, Forest Hills, NY 11375, USA.

KOLOZSVARI GRANDPIERRE, Emil, b. 15 Jan. 1907. Kolozsvár, Hungary. Writer. *Education:* DPhil. *Publications include:* A rosta, 1932; A nagy ember, 1935; Alvarjarok, 1938; Tegnap, 1942; Szabadság, 1945; Lofo es kora, 1946; Lelkifinomasgok, 1948; Mergelen, 1950; A csodarfurulya, 1954; A torokfejes kopja, 1955; A buvos kaptafa, 1957; Legendak nyomaban, 1959; Parbeszed a sorsall, 1962; A burok, 1964; Drama felvalrol, 1966; Szelleoi galeri, 1968; Utosolo hullam, 1072; Harmazcseppek, 1974; Beklyok es Baratok, 1979; Arnyak az alagutban, 1981; Egy házasság elotottenete, 1982; Eretnek essezék, 1983. *Contributor to:* Kotars; Uj Iras; Jelenkor (former editor); Magyarok. *Honours:* Baumgarten Literary Prizes, 1938, 1942 and 1975; Jozsef Attila Literary Prizes, 1964, 1973; Kossuth Prize, 1980. *Memberships:* PEN. *Address:* 11 Berkenyeutca 19, 1025 Budapest, Hungary.

KOMISAR, Lucy, b. 8 Apr. 1942, New York, USA. Journalist. *Education:* BA History, Queens College, City University of New York, 1964. *Literary Appointments:* Editor, Mississippi Free Press, 1962–63; Associate Editor, The Hatworker, 1966; Reporter, The Bergen Record, 1978–80; Radio and television reporter, freelance writer, 1968–78, 1981. *Publications:* The New Feminism, 1971; Down and Out in the USA; A History of Public Welfare, 1973. *Contributions to:* Numerous magazines and journals including: Miami Herald; Toronto Star; San Diego Union; The New Leader; The Record; The Progressive; Newsday; Worldview; Washington Post; San Francisco Chronicle; Pacific News Service; Sacramento Bee; The Economist Development Report, London; Marie Claire, Paris; New York Times. *Honours include:* 3 times Fellow, Macdowell Writers Colony, Peterborough, New Hampshire, 1970's; John J McCloy Fellowship, American Council on Germany, 1979; Grant, Ploughshares Fund, 1983 and 1985. *Membership:* Executive Board, Pen American Center, 1976–. *Address:* 100 West 12 Street, New York, NY 10011, USA.

KONICK, Marcus, b. 27 Oct. 1914, Philadelphia, Pennsylvania, USA. College Administrator. *Education:* BS, Education, Temple University, 1936; MA, 1937; PhD, 1953; University of Pennsylvania. *Publications include:* History of American Literature, in Study of Literature, 1959; Plays for Modern Youth, (Editor and Author), 1961; Tales in Verse, (Co-Editor), 1963; Six Complete World Plays, (Editor), 1963; Edward Fitzgerald's Rubaiyat of Omar Khayyam, (Editor), 1967; some 100 plays for stage, radio and TV. *Contributor to:* Magazines and journals including: Plays Magazine; Educational Screen and Audiovisual Guide; 18th Century Studies. *Honours:* Awards and Medals from Pennsylvania Department of Public Instruction, 1964; Pennsylvania Learning Resources Association, 1966; Marie Curie Sklodowska University, Poland, 1977; Ministry of Education, Taiwai, 1978. *Memberships:* Pennsylvania Council of Teachers of English, President, 1957–58; National Council of Teachers of English, Chairman, Member of various committees; Member, Joint Committee on Liaison with American Educational Theatre Association and Speech Association of America; Phi Delta Kappa; Pennsylvania Federation of Music Clubs; Lock Haven Rotary Club. *Address:* 1214 Hillview Street, Lock Haven, PA 17745, USA.

KONIECZNY, Stanley J Jr, b. 14 Apr. 1955, East St Louis, Illinois, USA. Associate Editor, Catholic weekly newspaper. *Education:* BA, Summa cum laude, St Mary's University, San Antonio, Texas. *Contributions to:* Liguorian; Grit; Family; Minkus Stamp & Coin Journal; Linn's Stamp News; Delta Epsilon Sigma Bulletin; PolAmerica; Today's Parish; Our Lady's Digest; Polish Heritage; Journal of the St Clair Country Historical Society; Momentum. *Honours:* 2nd place, Texas, Catholic Daughters of America Essay Contest, 1974; Citation, news & features coverage of the handicapped, Victim Missionaries, 1983; Silver Bronze Medal, American Philatelic Society Writers Unit, 1984. *Memberships:* Catholic Press Association: Society of Philaticians. *Address:* 201 Clearview, Belleville, IL 62223, USA.

KÖNIG, Josef Walter, b. 16 Feb. 1923, Hotzenplotz, Czechoslovakia. Teacher, writer. *Education:* University of Prague, Czechoslovakia; University of Munich, Federal Republic of Germany. *Publications:* Das Schrifttum des Ostsudentenlandes, 1964; Ihr Wort wirkt weiter, 1966; Viktor-Heeger-Bibliographie, 1966; Donauwörth im Spiegel der Literatur, 1968; Strassenrandbemerkungen, 1972; Donauwörth, 1974; Erkrandstück mit Sonderstempel, 1975; Heimat im Widerschein, 1978; Schwarzes Kreuz auf weissem Grund, 1981; Vorderösterreich, 1982; Viktor Heeger – Leben und Werk, 1985. *Contributions to:* Altvater-Jahrbuch. *Honours:* Christophorus Prize, 1969; AWMM Prize, 1984. *Memberships:* Free German Authors Association; International Group of Writers in Regensburg; Lions Club. *Address:* Johann Wiedemann

Strasse 2, D 8850 Donauwörth, Federal Republic of Germany.

KONING, Hans, b. 12 July 1924, Amsterdam, Netherlands. Writer. m. Kathleen Scanlon, 1 son, 3 daughters, USA. *Education:* Universities of Amsterdam, Zurich and Paris-Sorbonne. *Publications:* The Affair, 1958; A Walk With Love and Death, 1960; The Revolutionary, 1967; Death of a Schoolboy, 1974; A New Yorker in Egypt, 1976; The Kleber Flight, 1981; America Made Me, 1983; DeWitt's War, 1983; Acts of Faith, 1986. *Contributions to:* The New Yorker; Nation; Atlantic Monthly; and others. *Honours:* NEA Award, 1978; Connecticut Arts Award, 1980. *Literary Agent:* Lantz Office, New York City. *Address:* c/o The Lantz Office, 888 Seventh Avenue, New York, NY 10106, USA.

KONSTANTINOV, Georghi, b. 20 Dec. 1943, Pleven, Bulgaria. Writer. *Education:* Bulgarian Philosophy. Sofia University. *Literary Appointment:* Editor-in-Chief of literary magazine Plamak. *Publications:* Poetry: One Smile Is A Capital To Me, 1967; Love Me On Sunday, 1970; A Personal Time, 1974; A Dove With Burning Wings, 1976; Illiterate Heart, 1984. *Contributor to:* All main Bulgarian literary editions. *Honour:* An Honoured Worker of Culture, 1985. *Membership:* Union of Bulgarian Writers. *Address:* 33 A, Nezabravka Street, Sofia, Bulgaria.

KONVITZ, Milton Ridras, b. 12 Mar. 1908, Safad, Israel. Professor. *Education:* BS, MA, JrD, New York University, USA; PhD, Cornell University, USA. *Publications include:* The Constitution & Civil Rights, 1947; Civil Rights in Immigration, 1953; Fundamental Liberties of a Free People, 1957; Expanding Liberties, 1966; Religious Liberty & Conscience, 1968. *Contributor to:* American Scholar; Commentary; New Leader; Law Reviews; etc; Editorial Board, various magazines. *Honours include:* Various honorary degrees & distinguished awards from National Universities, 1954–75; numerous fellowships including Gugenheim, 1953, Ford Foundation, 1952, National Endowment for the Humanities, 1975. *Address:* 16 The Byway, Ithaca, NY 14850, USA.

KOONTS, J(ones) Calvin, b. 19 Sep. 1924. Educator. m. 1 son, 1 daughter. *Education:* AB 1945, Litt D 1969, Catawba College, Salisbury, North Carolina; MA 1949, PhD 1958, George Peabody College, Nashville, Tennessee; Postdoctoral Study, Harvard University, 1960; Postdoctoral Study, Smithsonian/Oxford Seminar, Oxford University, England, 1965. *Publications:* I'm Living in a Dream, song 1947; Straws in the Wind, book of collected verse, 1968; Under the Umbrella, book of poetry; Editor, Green Leaves in January, 1972; A Slice of the Sun, 1976; Poems represented in National Poetry Anthology, 1957, 1959, 1960 and 1962; editor, Inklings, 1983. *Honours:* Algernon Sydney Sullivan Award, 1951; Holds Governor's appointment as Commissioner of Piedmont Technical Education Centre, Greenwood, South Carolina; Winner, William Gilmore Simms Poetry Prize in South Caroline, 1973; University of California at Los Angeles Research Scholar, 1977. *Memberships include:* NEA; Fellow, Academy of American Poets. *Address:* PO Box 163, Erskine College, Due West, SC 29639, USA.

KOPLEWICZ, Rebecca, b. 2 Jan. 1910, Warsaw, Poland. Poet, Essayist, Novelist. m. Koplewicz Israel, 6 Feb. 1932, Paris, 1 daughter. *Publications:* La Rosee du Silence, 1951; A New Life, 1959; Stars on My Window, 1961; Colours and Sounds, 1967; Intimate with Books I, 1973; Symphony in the Wind, 1978; Intimate with Books II, 1983. *Contributions to:* International publications. *Honour:* Diploma of Journalists and Writers Association, 1984. *Membership:* Yiddish PEN CLub. *Address:* 10 Rue Claude Nicolas Ledoux 92350, Le Plessis-Robinson, France.

KOR, Billa Dickson Buma, b. 19 May 1948, Bali-Gham, Cameroon. Publisher; Bookseller. m. Claudia Fokam, 9 June 1984, 1 son. *Education:* Diploma in

Education, Ibadan, Nigeria. *Publications:* Searchlight, poems, 1975; In Defence of the Cross, 1973. *Contributions to:* Fako Magazine; New Delhi CBT; Tokyo ACCU Newsletter, Japan; Prague IBBY Journal. *Honours:* Award for poem, African Africanism, 1970, for short story, Frightened Mamas and Dogs, 1975, British Broadcasting Corporation. *Memberships:* In charge of publishing matters, Association of Cameroon Poets and Writers; Promoter and International Representative, Cameroon section, International Board on Books for Young People. *Address:* B P 727, Yaounde, Cameroon.

KORAN, Dennis Howard, b. 21 May 1947. Publisher; Writer. *Education:* University of California, Berkeley, 1964–69; University of Leeds, England, 1966–67; Loyola Law School, 1982–84. *Literary Appointments:* Founder and Co-Editor, Cloud Marauder Press, Berkeley, California, 1967–71; Founder and Editor, Panjandrum Press, San Francisco, 1971–. *Publications:* Vacancies, 1975. *Contributions to:* Amphora; Abraxas; Cloud Marauder; Kasaba; Fuse; Panjandrum; San Francisco Phoenix; Skywriting; Sonoma County Stump; Aldebaran Review; Electrum; Beatitude; Lyrical Voices, 1979; Poetry Now Magazine; Urthkid; Peace and Pieces, 1973; The San Francisco Bark; Berkeley Anthology, 1977. *Honours:* Honorable Mention, University of Leeds Poetry Contest, England, 1966. *Memberships:* Committee of Small Magazines and Press; Coordinating Council of Literary Magazines; Poets and Writers Incorporated. *Address:* 11321 Iowa Avenue, Suite 1, Los Angeles, CA 90025, USA.

KOREN, Henry Joseph, b. 30 Dec. 1912, Roermond, Netherlands. Professor, Philosophy. *Education:* STB, 1937, STL, 1939, Gregorian University, Rome, Italy; STD, Catholic University of America, Washington DC, USA, 1942. *Publications include:* Introduction to Philosophy of Nature, 1960; Knaves of Knights, 1962; Research in Philosophy, 1966; Marx & The Authentic Man, 1968; Introduction to Existential Phenomenology, co-author, 1969; Religion & Atheism, co-author, 1971; To the Ends of the Earth, 1982; The Serpent and the Dove, 1985; Publisher, Duquesne. *Contributor to:* Editor, Duquesne Studies, 1953–; General Editor, Spiritana Monumenta Historica, 1965–71. *Memberships:* Metaphysical Society of America. *Address:* Box 2328 St Leo, FL 33574, USA.

KORIYAMA, Naoshi, b. 3 Nov. 1926, Professor of English. *Education:* University of New Mexico, USA, 1950–51; BA, State University of New York, Albany, USA, 1954. *Literary Appointments include:* Instructor, Assistant Professor, English, Obirin Junior College, Tokyo, Japan, 1956–61; Faculty Member, 1961–, Professor, English, 1967–, Tokyo University. *Publications:* Coral Reefs, 1957; Plum Tree in Japan & Other Poems, 1959; Songs from Sagamihara, 1967; By the Lakeshore & Other Poems, 1977; Time and Space and Other Poems, 1985. *Contributor to:* Poetry Nippon. *Membership:* Poetry Society of Japan. *Address:* 2-15-9 Yaei, Sagamihara-shi, Kanagawa-ken, 229, Japan.

KORMAN, Gordon, b. 23 Oct. 1963, Montreal, Quebec. Writer. *Education:* BFA, New York University, USA, 1985. *Publications:* This Can't Be Happening, At MacDonald Hall, 1978; Go Jump in the Pool, 1980; Beware the Fish, 1980; Who Is Bugs Potter?, 1981; I Want To Go Home, 1981; Our Man Weston, 1982; The War With Mr Wizzle, 1983; Bugs Potter Live at Nickaninny, 1984; No Coins Please, 1984; Don't Care High, 1985; Son of Interflux, 1986. *Honours:* Air Canada Award, Canadian Authors Association, 1981; Ontario Youth Medal, 1985. *Memberships:* Canadian Authors Association; Writers Union of Canada; Canadian Society of Childrens Authors, Illustrators and Performers. *Literary Agent:* Curtis Brown, New York, USA. *Address:* 20 Dersingham Crescent, Thornhill, Ontario, Canada L3T 4E7.

KORN, Charles Paul, b. 31 July 1939, Philadelphia, Pennsylvania, USA. University Professor. m. Anne Storer, 26 Aug. 1963, Los Angeles. *Education:* BA 1961, MA 1965, PhD (with Distinction) 1969,

University of California, Los Angeles. *Publications:* Cromwell and the New Model Foreign Policy, 1975; West Ham United: The Making of a Football Club, 1986. Contributor to various journals and reviews. *Honour:* Fellow of Royal Historical Society, 1976. *Address:* Department of History, University of Missouri–St Louis, St Louis, MO 63121, USA.

KORNFELD, Robert Jonathan, b. 3 Mar. 1919, Massachusetts, USA. Playwright. m. Celia Seiferth, 23 Aug. 1945, New York City, 1 son. *Education:* AB, Harvard University; Graduate Studies, Havard, Columbia, Tulane, New York Universities. *Publications:* Great Southern Mansions, 1977. *Contributor to:* Many travel articles to New York Times. Many theatrical works produced in America, France, Mexico, etc. *Honours:* 2 1st Prizes, National Theatre Contests; Winner, Broadway Drama Guild Competition, 1979. *Memberships:* Trustee, Bronx Society of Science & Letters; Authors League; Dramatists Guild; Board Member, Riverdale Contemporary Theatre; Bronx Arts Ensemble. *Literary Agent:* Curtis Brown Ltd. *Address:* 5286 Sycamore Avenue, Riverdale on Hudson, New York, NY 10471, USA.

KOROLKO, Miroskaw, b. 25 Jan. 1935, Pruzana, Poland. Polish Literary and Cultural Historian. m. Kazimierz Kinga, 18 Oct. 1975. *Education:* Catholic University, Lubelski, University Warsaw. *Publication:* Jana Kochanowskiego zywot i sprawy, 1985. *Address:* ul. Szolc-Rogozinskiego 8 m. 8, 02-777 Warsaw, Poland.

KORP, Maureen Elizabeth, b. 18 May 1945, New Jersey, USA. Consultant in Public Administration. 1 daughter. *Education:* BA, Douglass College, 1966; MA, Rutgers University, 1976; Certificate in Public Administration, University of Buffalo, 1979. *Publications:* Editor, several book length technical manuscripts in education, health and public affairs. *Contributions to:* Canadian and American small literary magazine press, 1962–68, 1983–, including: Anthologies; Hornbook; Mosaic; Mississippi Magazine; Canadian Forum; Quarry; Queens Quarterly; Matrix; Arc; Cross-Canada Literary Quarterly. *Honours:* Scholarships, Breadloaf Writers Conference, Middlebury College, 1965, 68. *Address:* 693–B King Edward Avenue, Ottawa, Ontario, Canada.

KOSSOFF, David, b. 24 Nov. 1919 (Russian parentage). Actor; Designer; Illustrator. *Publications:* Bible Stories retold by David Kossoff, 1968; The Book of Witnesses, 1971; The Three Donkeys, 1972; The Voices of Kasada, 1973; You Have a Moment Lord? 1975; The Little Book of Sylvanus, 1975; A Small Town is a World, 1979; Sweet Nutcracker; Own Bible Storytelling programmes (writer & teller) on radio & TV; Appeared, many plays & films & on radio & TV; since 1972, one-man performances: As According to Kossoff, & A Funny Kind of Evening. *Honours:* British Academy Award, 1956; Elected Member, Society Industrial Artists, 1958; FRSA, 1969. *Address:* 45 Roe Green Close, Hatfield, Hertfordshire, England.

KOSTER, Simon, b. 13 June 1900, Rotterdam, Netherlands. Author, Editor. *Education:* School for Continued Education, Rotterdam. *Literary Appointments:* Editor-in-Chief, daily newspaper, Haarlems Dagblad, 1956–65; Dutch theatrical magazine, Het Mesker (The Mask), Spel en Dans (Play & Dance); and several other art magazines. *Major Publications:* De Razende Saxofoon, 1931; Als ik Greta Garbo was, 1934 (english Edition, Leading Ladies, 1936); Storm in't Paradijs, 1937; The Snowball, 1943; (books on theatre & cinema history); German Film Art, 1931; Van Schavot tot Schouwburg, 1970; De Bouwmeesters, 1973; Fabrication & Truth about Sarah Bernhardt, 1974; Komedie in Gelderland, 1979; (Film scenarios): Das Lied einer Nacht, 1932; Dood Water (Dead Water), 1933; Malle Gevallen (Funny Happenings), 1934; Lentelied (Spring Song), 1936; Buiten de Grenzen (Outside the Borders), 1942; Sky Over Holland, 1967; (stage-plays): Madame La Mode, 1925; Camelia, 1926;

Nul Uur Nul, 1928; Bob und Bobby (Juvenile), 1931. *Contributor to:* (Drama & cinema critic). Numerous magazines and newspapers, including: Neue Zürcher Zeitung, Switzerland (on Dutch Theatre). *Memberships include:* PEN (Honorary Secretary, National Chapter, 1966–71, Honorary Member, 1980); Foreign Press Association of New York (Life Member, President, 1946–48); Honorary Member, Netherlands Society of Editors-in-Chief, President 1959–65; Society for Netherlands Literature. *Honours:* Knight, Royal Netherlands Order or Orange-Nassua, 1953. *Address:* Beekhuizense weg 15, 6881 AB Velp, Netherlands.

KOTARBA, Joseph Anthony, b. 11 Apr. 1947, Chicago, Illinois, USA. Associate Professor of Sociology. m. Polly Lodema Peterson, 16 Aug. 1975, Weston, Missouri, 1 son, 1 daughter. *Education:* BA Sociology, Illinois State University, 1969; MA, Arizona State University, 1975; PhD, University of California, San Diego, 1980. *Literary Appointments:* Review Editor, Journal of Symbolic Interaction, 1982–; Advisory Editor, Journal of Youth and Society, 1982–. *Publications:* Introduction to the Sociologies of Everyday Life, 1980; Chronic Pain: Its Social Dimensions, 1983; The Existential Self in Society, 1984. *Contributions to:* Journal of Urban Life: Social Science and Medicine; Journal of Health and Social Behavior. *Honour:* Teaching Excellence Award, University of Houston, College of Social Science, 1982–83. *Address:* 3812 Oberlin, Houston, TX 77005, USA.

KOTLER, Philip, b. 27 May 1931, Chicago, Illinois, USA. University Professor. *Education:* MS, Economics, University of Chicago, 1953; PhD, Economics, Massachusetts Institute of Technology, 1956; Postgraduate work in Sociology, University of Chicago; Maths, Harvard University. *Publications:* Marketing Management: Analysis, Planning and Control, 1967, 71, 76, 80, 84; Creating Social Change, 1972; Marketing for Non-Profit Organisations, 1975, 82; Principles of Marketing, 1980, 83, 86; The New Competition, 1985; Marketing Professional Services, 1985; Strategic Marketing for educational Institutions, 1985. *Contributor to:* Professional journals including: Harvard Business Review; Journal of Marketing, *Honours:* Graham and Dodd Award, 1962; McLaren Advt Research Award, 1964; Media/Scope Merit Award, 1964; McKinsey Award, 1965; Alpha Kappa Psi Award, 1978; Stewart Henderson Britt Award, 1983; Distinguished Marketing Educator Award, 1985. *Address:* 624 Central Street, Evanston, IL 60201, USA.

KOUNS, Alan Terry, b. 31 Dec. 1941, Long Beach, California, USA. Medical Writer; Journalist. *Education:* MA Communications, University of Pennsylvania, 1967. *Literary Appointments:* Writer-producer in radio and television; Writer and consultant in educational multimedia; Public relations writer, University of Southern California, 1965; Health Sciences writer, 1970–72; Correspondent, U S Information Agency, 1975–81 and 1982–; Fund raising consultant in educational film, One World Foundation, 1978; Lecturer in Communication Arts, California State Polytechnic University, Pomona, 1981; Writer-publicist, City of Hope National Medical Center, 1981–82. *Contributions to:* Third World Development (chapter) 1985; Periodicals including: Africa; Dialysis and Transplantation; Dreamworks; Emergency Medical Services; Los Angeles Times; The Progressive. *Honours:* Ford Motor Company Scholarship in Journalism, 1958; University of Pennsylvania Communications Scholarship, 1966. *Memberships:* American Medical Writers Association; Greater Los Angeles Press Club. National Association of Science Writers. *Address:* 9936 Ramona Street, Apartment 21, Bellflower, CA 90706, USA.

KOVARIK, William Joseph, b. 22 Oct. 1951, Belvoir, Virginia, USA. Journalist. Science Writer. m. Linda L Burton, 20 May, 1979. Copper Hill, Virginia, 1 son. *Education:* BS Journalism, Virginia Commonwealth University, 1974; MA Communications, University of South Carolina, 1984. *Literary Appointments:* Researcher, Jack Anderson, 1977; Editor, Latin American Energy Report, 1978–80; Editor, Appropriate Technology Times, 1980–81; Assistant Instructor, University of South Carolina, 1981; Reporter, Charleston SC News and Courier, 1982–84; Instructor, Virginia Polytechnic Institute, 1985–. *Publications:* Fuel Alcohol: Energy, Environment and a Hungry World, 1981; The Forbidden Fuel: Power Alcohol in the 20th Century, 1982. *Contributions to:* Renewable Energy News; Solar Age; New York Times; Time Magazine; Sciphers; Genetic Engineering News; Solar Energy Intelligence Report; Floyd Ag News. *Honours:* Sabre Fund for Investigative Journalism, 1978. *Memberships:* Sigma Delta Chi; Kappa Tau Alpha. *Literary Agent:* Raines and Raines, New York. *Address:* Rt 1 Box 232, Check, VA 24072, USA.

KOWIT, Steve, b. 30 June 1938, New York City, New York, USA. Poet. m. Mary Petrangelo, 11 Aug. 1967, Seattle, Washington, USA. *Education:* MA, San Francisco State College, California. *Literary Appointments:* Professor of Writing, San Diego State University; Professor of Literature, San Diego City College; Faculty Member, Napa Valley Poetry Conference. *Publications:* Incitement to Nixonicide and Praise for the Chilean Revolution, Translation of Neruda, 1978; Cutting Our Losses, 1981; Heart in Utter Confusion, 1982; Lurid Confessions, 1983; Passionate Journey, 1984. *Contributions to:* New York Times; Beloit Poetry Journal; Vagabond; Wormwood Review; American Book Review; New York Quarterly; Abraxas; Maelstrom; Little Caesar; Sierra Madre Review; Friction; Beatitude. *Honours:* Joseph P Slomovitch Memorial Award, 1980; National Endowment for the Arts Fellowship, 1985. *Address:* 1868 Ebers Street, San Diego, CA 92107, USA.

KRAEMER, Kenneth Leo, b. 29 Oct. 1936, Plain, Wisconsin, USA. University Professor. m. Norine Florence Bindl, 13 July 1959, Plain, 1 son, 1 daughter. *Education:* B Arch, Notre Dame, 1959; MSC, RP, 1962, MPA, PhD, 1967, University of Southern California. *Publications:* Computers in Local Government, 1979, 1978; Policy Analysis in Local Government, 1973; Technological Innovation in American Local Government, 1979; The Management of Information Systems, 1980; Computers and Politics, 1982; Public Management: Public and Private Perspectives, 1983; Modeling as Negotiating, 1985; The Dynamics of Computing, 1985; People and Computers, in press; Computer Models in Federal Policy Making, in press. *Contributor to:* Communications of the ACM; Public Administration Review; Telecommunications Policy; Systems, Objectives, Solutions; American Review of Public Administration; Public Administrators Quarterly; International Review of Public Administration; etc. *Address:* 3811 E Fernwood Ave, Orange, CA 92669, USA.

KRAFT, Eric, b. 29 Oct. 1944, Bay Shore, New York, USA. Writer. m. Madeline M Canning, 9 Feb. 1963, Babylon, New York, 2 sons. *Education:* AB, Harvard College, 1965; MAT, Harvard Graduate School of Education, 1966. *Publications:* My Mother Takes a Tumble, 1982; Do Clams Bite?, 1982; Life on the Bolotomy, 1983; The Static of the Spheres, 1983; The Fox and the Clam, 1983; The Girl with the White Fur Muff, 1984; Take the Long Way Home, 1984. *Literary Agent:* Nat Sobel Associates, New York. *Address:* Newburyport, Massachusetts, USA.

KRAFT, Herbert, b. 5 June 1938, Walsum, Federal Republic of Germany. Professor of German and Head of Department. *Education:* Universities of Tubingen and Newcastle-upon-Tyne, UK, D Phil, 1962, D Phil habil, 1970. *Publications:* Schillers Kabale und Liebe, 1963; J H Merck, Briefe, 1968; Poesie der Idee, Die tragische Dichtung Friedrich Hebbels, 1971; Schillers Werke, Nationalausgabe, Bd. 11 (Demetrius), 1971; Kunst und Wirklichkeit im Expressionismus, 1972; Kafta, Wirklichkeit und Perspektive, 1972; Die Geschichtlichkeit literarischer Texte, 1973; Das Schicksalsdrama, 1974; Andreas Streichers Schiller-Biographie, 1974; Das literarische Werk von Walter

Jens, 1975; Um Schiller betrogen, 1978; Schillers Werke, Nationalausgabe, Bd 12 (Dramatische Fragmente), 1982; Mondheimal, Kafka, 1983. *Address:* Els-Brandstrom-Str 9, D–4416 Everswinkel, Federal Republic of Germany.

KRAMARAE, Cheris, b. 10 Mar, 1938, South Dakota. USA. Professor. m. Dale Kramer 21 Dec. 1961, 2 daughters. *Education:* BS, South Dakota State University, 1959; MS, Ohio University, 1963: PhD, University of Illinois at Urbana/Champaign, 1975. *Publications:* The Voices and Words of Women and Men, editor, 1980; Women and Men Speaking; Frameworks for Analysis, 1981; Language, Gender and Society, co-editor, 1983; Language and Power, co-editor, 1984; For Alma Mater: Feminist Scholarship in Theory and Practice, co-editor, 1985; A Feminist Dictionary: In Our Own Words, co-editor, 1985. *Contributions to:* Anthropological Linguistics; Language and Speech; Psychology Today; Signs: Journal of Women in Culture and Society; Women's Studies International Quarterly; Communication Quarterly. *Address:* Department of Speech Communication, University of Illinois, Urbana, IL 61801, USA.

KRAMER, Aaron, b. 13 Dec. 1921, Brooklyn, New York, USA. Professor of English; Poet. m. Katherine Kolodny, 10 Mar. 1942, Washington, DC, 2 daughters. *Education:* BA, 1941, MA, 1951, Brooklyn College; PhD, New York University, 1966. *Publications:* The Glass Mountain; The Poetry and Prose of Heinrich Heine, 1948; Rolle the Forbidden Drums! 1954; The Tune of the Calliope, 1958; Rumshinsky's Hat, 1964; Rulke: Visions of Christ, 1967; The Prophetic Tradition in American Poetry, 1968; Melville's Poetry, 1972; On Freedom's Side, 1972; On the Way to Palermo, 1973; Carousel Parkway, 1980; The Burning Bush: Poems and Other Writings, 1940–1980, 1983. *Contributor to:* Numerous magazines and journals including, West Hills Review, Co-editor, 1978–85; American Annals of the Deaf; Massachusetts Review; Midstream; Modern Poetry Review; New York Times; Village Voice; Kenyon Review; Missouri Review; New England Review; Writers Forum. *Honours:* Numerous honours and awards including: ASCAP Awards, 1971–74, 1976–79, 1981–86; All Nations Poetry Contests, 1975–79; Fellowship Memorial Foundation for Jewish Culture, 1978–79; Eugene O'Neill Theatre Center Award, 1983; Abraham Jenofsky Yiddish Culture Award, 1983. *Memberships:* PEN; Internaional Academy of Poets; NE MLA; Assocaition for Poetry Therapy (Executive Board, 1969–); ASCAP; Edna St Vincent Millay Society; Dramatists Guild; Walt Whitman Birthplace Association, Board of Trustees, 1982–85. *Literary Agent:* August Lenniger Agency. *Address:* English Department, Dowling College, Oakdale, NY 10769, USA.

KRAMER, John Eichholtz Jr, b. 19 May 1935, Philadelphia, Pennsylvania, USA. Professor, Sociology, State University of New York. m. Joan Andrews, 10 Apr. 1958, Easton, Connecticut, 1 son, 1 daughter. *Education:* AB, Dartmouth College, 1956; MA, George Washington University, 1961; MA, 1963, PhD, 1965, Yale University. *Publications:* North American Suburbs, 1972; Strategy and Conflict in Metropolitan Housing, with Ken Young, 1978; The American College Novel, 1981; College Mystery Novels, with John Kramer III, 1983. *Contributor to:* Numerous articles in sociology and higher education journals. *Address:* Dept of Sociology, State University of New York, Brockport, NY 14420, USA.

KRAMER-BADONI, Rudolf, b. 22 Dec. 1913, Rüdesheim, Federal Republic of Germany. Freelance Writer. *Education:* PhD. *Publications:* 8 novels including: Jacobs Jahr, 1943, 78; Bewegliche Ziele, 1962, French translation as, Les realities mouvantes; Gleichung mit einer Unbekannten, 1977. Polish works including: Anarchismus, 1970; Die niedliche revolution, 1973. Religious works include: Revolution in der Kirche-Lefebvre und Rom, 1980. Galileo Galilei, biography, 1983. Zwischen allen Stuhlen, autobiography, 1985. *Contributions to:* Die Welt, Bonn.

Honour: Konrad Adenauer Literature Prize, 1979. *Memberships:* Past German Secretary, PEN Club; PEN Club, Switzerland. *Address:* Brunnen Strasse 6, D–6200 Wiesbaden, Federal Republic of Germany.

KRANTZ, Kermit Edward, b. 4 June 1923, Oakpark, Illinois, USA. Physician (Gynecologist and Obstetrician). m. Doris Cole, 7 Sep. 1946, 1 son, 2 daughters. *Education:* BS, Northwestern University, Evanston-Chicago, 1945; BM, 1947, MS, Anatomy, 1947, MD, 1948, Northwestern University School of Medicine. *Literary Appointment:* Member, International Editorial Review Board, King Faisal Specialist Hospital Medical Journal, Riyadh, Saudi Arabia, 1981–85. *Publications:* The Adolescent Experience: A Counseling Guide to Social and Sexual Behavior (with J P Semmens), 1970. *Contributions to:* Books, Textbooks and professional journals including: American Journal of Obstetrics and Gynecology; Annals of New York Academy of Science; American Medical Association Journal of Dis Child; Ob/Gyn Digest; British Journal of Sexual Medicine; Journal of Reproductive Medicine; Bulletin of the American College of Surgeons. *Honours include:* Numerous Awards and Honours including: Distinguished Service Award, American College of Obstetricians and Gynecologists, 1982; Edward Crown Memorial Lecturer, Columbus Hospital, Chicago, Illinois, 1983; William Heaty Byford Award, Northwestern University Medical School Alumnus in Obstetrics and Gynecology, Chicago, 1984. *Memberships:* Member of numerous professional organizations. *Address:* The University of Kansas Medical Center, Rainbow Boulevard at 39th Street, Kansas City, KS 66103, USA.

KRANZBERG, Melvin, b. 22 Nov. 1917, St Louis, Missouri, USA. College Professor. *Education:* BA, Amherst College; MA, PhD, Harvard University. *Publications:* The Siege of Paris: 1870–71, 1951; A Turning Point? 1959; By the Sweat of Thy Brow: Work in the Western World, with Joseph Gies, 1975, 76, Italian translation; Ethics in an Age of Pervasive Technology, Editor, 1980. Co-Editor: Technology in Western Civilization, 2 volumes, 1967, Japanese and Spanish translations; Technology and Culture: An Anthology, 1972, 75 and Arabic translation; Technological Innovation: A Critical Review of Current Knowledge, 1978; Energy and the Way We Live, 1979; Bridge to the Future: A Centennial Celebration of the Brooklyn Bridge, 1984. Advisory Editor: Science, Technology and Human Values; Knowledge. *Honours include:* Leonardo da Vinci Medal, Society for History of Technology, 1967; Jabotinsky Centennial Medal, State of Israel, 1980; Roe Medal, American Society of Mechanical Engineers, 1980; President, Society for History of Technology, 1983–84; Honorary Foreign Member, Czechoslovak History of Science and Technology Society, Czech Academy of Sciences, 1985. *Memberships include:* Founder, Editor of Journal, Society for the History of Technology; Past National President, Sigma Xi; Committee Chairman, American Association for the Advancement of Science. *Address:* Department of Social Science, Georgia Institute of Technology, Atlanta, GA 30332, USA.

KRATCOSKI, Peter Charles, b. 25 Nov. 1936, Mildred, Pennsylvania, USA. Professor. m. Lucille Dunn, 1 June, 1960, Dushore, Pennsylvania, 1 son, 1 daughter. *Education:* BA Sociology, King's College, 1961; MA Sociology, University of Notre Dame, 1962; PhD Sociology, Pennsylvania State University, 1969. *Literary Appointments:* Associate Editor, Sociological Analysis, 1973–77; Article Reviewer, Sociological Quarterly, 1980–81; Article Reviewer, Justice Quarterly, 1984–; Assistant Editor, Journal of Crime & Justice, 1984–; Life in America Editor for, USA Today, 1980–; Chairperson, Department of Criminal Justice Studies; Professor of Criminal Justice Studies and Sociology, Kent State University. *Major Publications:* Correctional Counselling & Treatment, 1981; Criminal Justice in America: Process & Issues, 2nd edition, 1984; Juvenile Delinquency, 2nd edition 1986. *Contributor to:* Various criminal justice & sociological journals. *Address:* 113

Bowman Hall, Kent State University, Kent, OH 44242, USA.

KRAUS, Wolfgang, b. 13 Jan. 1924, Vienna, Austria. Writer. *Education:* PhD, University of Vienna, 1948. *Publications:* Der funfte Stand, 1966; Die stillen Revolutionare, 1970; Kulturund Macht, 1975; Die verratene Aubetung, 1978; Die Wiederkehr des Einzelnen, 1980; Nihilismus heute, 1983; Die Spuren des Paradieses, uber Ideale, 1985. *Contributor to:* Zsolnay Publing, Vienna, Editor, 1949–56; Europa Verlag, Editor, 1971–75; Neue Zurcher Zeitung; Die Presse, Vienna; Stuttgarter Zeitung. *Honours:* Anton Wildgans Prize, Austrian Ind, Vienna, 1979; Osterr. Staatspreis fur Kulturpublizistik, 1983. *Memberships:* PEN, Board Member. *Address:* Berggasse 6, 1090 Vienna, Austria.

KRAUT, Benny, b. 24 Dec. 1947, Munich, Federal Republic of Germany. Professor of Judaica. m. Penina Lea Besdin, 21 Nov. 1972, Queens, New York, USA, 1 son, 2 daughters. *Education:* BA, Yeshiva University; MA, PhD, Brandeis University. *Publications:* From Reform Judaism to Ethical Culture: The Religious Evolution of Felix Adler, 1979; Jews and the Founding of the Republic, (co-editor with J D Sarma), 1985. *Contributions to:* Association for Jewish Studies Review; Judaism; Modern Judaism; Journal of Ecumenical Studies. *Honours:* Orentlicher Prize for Excellence in Philosophy. 1966; Doctoral Fellow, Canada Council, 1970–72; Fellow, Memorial Foundation, 1972–75; Jacob's Fellow, 1979, Loewenstein-Wiener Fellow 1980; American Jewish Archives. *Memberships:* Association for Jewish Studies; World Union of Jewish Studies; Organization of American Historians; Ohio Academy of History. *Address:* Judaic Studies Program, Loc. 169, University of Cincinnati, OH 45221, USA.

KREITER-KURYLO, Carolyn, b. 20 Dec. 1946, Farmville, Virginia, USA. Language Arts Resource Teacher. *Education:* BA, Mary Washington College, 1969; MEd 1973, MA 1979, George Mason University; D Arts in Education, George Mason University, 1983. *Literary Appointments:* Teacher Consultant of Writing, Fairfax Country Public Schools & George Mason University, 1978–; Poet/Artist-in-Residence, 1983–. *Major Publications:* Instructional Guide (co-author) (for television), 1983. *Contributor to:* Poet Lore; Mid-American Review; Wind Literary Journal; Antioch Review; Spree; Negative Capability; Anthology of Magazine Verse & Yearbook of American Poetry 1984; and others. *Honours:* Various awards for poetry, including: Annual Phoebe Awards 1980, 1981; 1st Place awards, poetry, Alexandria Pen-women nationwide competition 1981, Spree Contest 1984–85. *Memberships:* Writers Center, Bethesda, Maryland; Writers Club, George Mason University (Vice-President). *Address:* 5966 Annaberg Place, Burke, VA 22015, USA.

KREJČÍ, Jaroslav, b. 13 Feb. 1916, Polesovice, Czechoslovakia. Professor Emeritus. m. Anna Cerna, 11 May 1940, Prague. *Education:* Dr jur, Charles University, Prague. *Publications:* Income Distribution (in Czech), 1947; Social Change and Stratification in Postwar Czechoslovakia, 1972; Social Structure in Divided Germany, 1976; Sozialdemokratie und Systemwandel, (Ed), 1978; Political and Ethnic Nations in Europe, (with V Velimsky), 1980; National Income and Outlay in Czechoslovakia, Poland and Yugoslavia, 1982; Great Revolutions Compared, the Search for a Theory, 1983. *Contributor to:* Soviet Studies; Revue d'etudes comparatives est cuest; Yearbook of E European Econs, History of European Ideas; Religion. *Memberships:* British Sociology Association; National Association for Soviet and E European Studies University Associate for Contemporary European Studies; International Society for Comparative Study of Civilizations; Czechoslovakian Society of Arts and Sciences in America; Council for European Studies (US). *Address:* Lonsdale College, University of Lancaster, England.

KREMEN, Bennett, b. 12 Aug. 1936, Chicago, Illinois, USA. Author. m. Jeanette Arnone, 7 Apr. 1973, New York City, 1 son. *Education:* BA, Antioch College; MA, New School of Social Research. *Publications:* Date Line: America, 1974. *Contributions to:* New York Times; Holiday Mag; Village Voice; The Nation; Dissent; The American Journal of Psychoanalysis and numerous others. *Honours:* Breadloaf Writers Conference, 1973. *Membership:* Authors Guild Incorporated. *Address:* 151 East 26th Street, New York City, NY 10010, USA.

KRESH, Paul, b. 3 Dec. 1919, New York, New York, USA. Writer and Publicist. m. Florence Werner, 1 Apr. 1940 (divorced 1943). *Education:* BA, College of the City of New York, 1939; Fellow, MacDowell Colony and Virginia Centre for the Creative Arts. *Literary Appointments include:* Vice President 1975, Governor 1975–79, National Academy of Recording Arts and Sciences; Commissioner, White House Record Library Commission, 1979–; Supervisor of courses and lectures in creative writing, Elgin Community College, Elgin, Illinois, 1983 and 1985. *Publications include:* Tales Out Of Congress (with Senator Stenhen M Young), 1966; The Power of the Unknown Citizen, 1969; Isaac Bashevis Singer – The Magician of West 86th, 1979; Isaac Bashevis Singer, The Story of a Storyteller, 1984. *Contributions to:* Stereo Review; American Record Guide; Saturday Review; Playboy; Pageant; Lithopinion; Performing Arts; High Fidelity; New York Times. *Honours include:* Several Ohio State Awards, 1941–68; Golden Eagle Award, Council of International Theatrical Events, 1965; Faith and Freedom Award, Religious Heritage Foundation, 1968; Grammy Award Nominations, National Academy of Recording Arts and Sciences; Emmy Award for Outstanding Individual Craft, 1980; Film Awards from International Film and Television Festivals. *Memberships:* PEN American Center: American Society of Journalists and Authors; American Academy of TV Arts and Sciences; NARAS. *Literary Agent:* Theron Raines. *Address:* One David Lane, Yonkers, NY 10701, USA.

KRIEGER, Murray, b. 27 Nov. 1923, Newark, New Jersey, USA. Professor & Literary Critic. m. Joan Alice Stone, 15 June 1947, New Jersey, USA, 1 son, 1 daughter. *Education:* MA, University of Chicago, 1948; PhD, Ohio State University, 1952. *Literary Appointments:* Assistant, Associate Professor of English, University of Minnesota, 1952–58; Professor of English, University of Illinois, 1958–63; Carpenter Professor of Literary Criticism, University of Iowa, 1963–66; Professor of English, University of California, Irvine, 1966–, Los Angeles, 1973–; University Professor, University of California, 1973–. *Major Publications:* The New Apologists for Poetry, 1956; The Tragic Vision, 1960; A Window to Criticism: Shakespeare's Sonnets and Modern Poetics, 1964; The Play and Place of Criticism, 1967; the Classic Vision, 1971; Theory of Criticism, 1976; Poetic Presence & Illusion, 1979; Arts on the Level: The Fall of the Elite Object, 1981. *Contributor to:* Many literary and scholarly journals. *Honours:* Guggenheim Fellowships, 1956–57, 1961–62; Fellowship, American Council of Learned Societies, 1966–67; Humanities Fellowship, Rockefeller Foundation, 1978; Elected Fellow, American Academy of Arts & Sciences, 1983. *Memberships:* Modern Language Association of America; English Institute (Chairman, 1982–83); International Association of University Professors of English; Academy of Literary Studies (elected 1974). *Address:* Department of English & Comparative Literature, University of California, Irvine, CA 92717, USA.

KRIGE, Mattheus Uys, b. 4 Feb. 1910, South Africa. Author. m. Lydia Lindeque, 1937, Cape Town, 1 son, 1 daughter. *Education:* BA, University Stellenbosch; Honorary Doctorates: Universities of Rhodes, Natal and Stellenbosch. *Appointments:* Founder Editor, Vandag, Johannesburg; War Correspondent, Egypt, Abyssinia, World War II. *Publications:* Kentering, 1935; The Wit Muur, 3 plays, 1940; Die Gove Kring, 1956; The Sniper and Other One Act Plays, 1962; Elvard & die Surealisme, 1962; The Two Lamps, 1964; Vooraand, 1964;

Versamelde Gedigte, 1985; etc. *Contributor to:* Numerous professional journals including, Harpers Magazine; Readers Digest; Nederlandse Post; etc. *Honours:* Twice Winner, Hertzog Prize; Academy Prize; Carnegie Scholarship, 1959; French Government Bursary, 1952. *Literary Agent:* Dalro, Johannesburg. *Address:* PO Box 25, Onrust River 7201, Cape, South Africa.

KRISPÉ, Randel, b. 9 Dec. 1955, Ho-Ho-Kus, New Jersey, USA. Editor. m. Trudy Kramden, 14 Feb. 1980, Bayonne, 2 sons, 2 daughters. *Education:* MBS, Technical Editing; PhD, World Literature. *Literary Appointments:* Assistant Professor, Apex Tech; Associate Editor, Harlequin Romance. *Publications:* Saturday Night Curiosity, 1979; Understanding Office Machines, 1980; The Grapevine is Listening, 1984. *Contributions to:* Harlequin Romance series; Journal of Forensic Medicine; Journal of Electroshock Theraphy; Journal of Electro-Therapy Mechanics; Mechanics; Popular Office Design; Highlights; Swank. *Honours:* New Jersey Scholastic Science Awards, 1983; Herlequin Novelette of the Month Award, 1984. *Memberships:* Harlequin Romance Novel Society; Society of Technical Editors.

KRISTJANSDOTTIR, Filippia S, b. 3 Oct. 1905, Eyjafjardarsysla, Iceland. Author; Housewife; Nurse; Christian work. m. (1) Valdimar Jonsson, 1931, 2 sons, 1 daughter, (2) Einar Eriksson, 1972. *Education:* Literary courses, Denmark, Norway. *Publications:* 11 books for children and young people, 5 full length novels, 4 books of short stories, 3 biographies, 7 books of poetry; Numerous contributions to radio including plays, travel stories, lectures, poetry, short and continual stories; Translated books into Icelandic. *Contributions to:* Newspapers, magazines and radio. *Honours:* Honorary Awards, State of Iceland; Working Grants for literary work, Government of Iceland; Literary Awards, Memorial and Educational Fund for Women and Danish-Icelandic Writers Foundation. *Memberships:* Icelandic Authors Association: Women's Missionary Society. *Address:* Baldursgata 3, 101 Reykjavik, Iceland.

KROETSCH, Robert Paul, b. 26 June 1927, Canada. Writer. *Education:* University of Alberta, 1948; MA, Middlesbury College, Vermont, USA, 1956; PhD, University of Iowa, 1961. *Literary Appointments:* Professor: State University of New York, Binghamton, New York, USA, 1961–78; University of Manitoba, Canada, 1987–. *Publications:* Novels: The Words of My Roaring, 1966; The Studhorse Man, 1969; Badlands, 1975; What the Crow Said, 1978; Alibi, 1983. Poetry: Field Notes, 1981; Advice to My Friends, 1985. *Honours:* Governor General's Award for Fiction, 1969. *Literary Agent:* Ed Carson, General Publishing Company Limited, Ontario. *Address:* Department of English, University of Manitoba, Winnipeg, Canada R3T 2N2.

KRUEGER, Treila, b. 2 Jan. 1954, USA. Researcher; Writer; Consultant. *Education:* Masters, University of Texas; Postgraduate, University of California; Graduate, Stanford University Publishing Procedure Programme. *Publications:* Preventive Medicine Services for Children in Colombia: A Strategy for Delivery, 1979; All Clear: An Everyday Guide to Total Skin Care, 1984. *Contributions to:* Public Health, and Others. *Memberships:* American Medical Writers Association; Society for Nutrition Education; American Association of University Women; American Association for the Advancement of Health Education. *Address:* PO Box 60966, Sacramento, CA 95860, USA.

KRUGMAN, Dean Mark, b. 15 Mar. 1948, Chicago, Illinois, USA. University Professor. m. Vicki K Phillips, 12 Aug. 1976, 2 daughters. *Education:* BS, Southern Illinois University; MS, PhD, University of Illinois. *Contributions to:* Journal of Advertising Research; Journal of Advertising; Journalism Quarterly; European Reasearch; Journal of Broadcasting and Electronic Media; Journal of the Academy of Marketing Sciences; Journal of Macro-Marketing. *Address:* School of Journalism and Mass Communication, University of Georgia, Athens, GA 30602, USA.

KRUMINS, Anita Ilze, b. 15 Nov. 1946, Flensburg, Germany. Educator. Writer. m. George Swede, 23 July 1975, Toronto, 2 sons. *Education:* BA summa cum laude 1973, MA 1974, York University, Canada. *Literary Appointments:* Children's Rock Review Editor, Writer's Quarterly, 1984–. *Publications:* Quillby, The Porcupine Who Lost His Quills, 1980; Who's Going to Clean Up The Mess, 1981; Mr Wurtzel and the Hallowe'en Bunny, 1982; Who's Going To Clean Up The Mess, revised edition, 1985. *Contributions to:* Waves; Writer's Quarterly; Tall Tales. *Honours:* York Scholarship, 1973; Canada Council Doctoral Fellowship, 1974. *Memberships:* Canadian Society of Children's Authors, Illustrators and Performers; The Writer's Union of Canada; American Business Communication Association; Association of Teachers of Technical Writing. *Address:* 70 London Street, Toronto, Ontario M6G IN3, Canada.

KRUPP, Edwin Charles, b. 18 Nov. 1944, Chicago, Illinois, USA. Astronomer, Director of Public Observatory. m. 31 December, 1968, Claremont, California, 1 son. *Education:* BA Physics/Astronomy, Pomona College, 1966; MA 1968, PhD 1972, Astronomy, University of California, Los Angeles. *Literary Appointment:* Editor-in-Chief, Griffith Observatory, monthly magazine. *Publications:* In Search of Ancient Astronomies, 1978; Echoes of the Ancient Skies, 1983; Archaeoastronomy and the Roots of Science, 1984; The Comet and You, 1985. *Contributions to:* New Scientist; Griffith Observer; Sky and Telescope; The Sciences; American Antiquity; Southern California Quarterly; Physics Today; Archaeoastronomy. *Honours:* American Institute of Physics – United States Steel Foundation Award for best science writing, 1978; American Institute of Physics Award, 1985. *Literary Agent:* Jane Jordan Browne, Chicago. *Address:* Griffith Observatory, 2800 East Observatory Road, Los Angeles, CA 90027, USA.

KUBLY, Herbert Oswald, b. New Glarus, Wisconsin, USA. Novelist; Author; Retired Educator. Divorced, 1 son. *Education:* BA, University of Wisconsin. *Literary Appointment:* Professor Emeritus of English, University of Wisconsin – Parkside, Kenosha. *Publications:* American in Italy, 1955; Easter in Sicily, 1956; Varieties of Love (Short Stories), 1958; Italy, 1961; The Whistling Zone (novel), 1963; Switzerland, 1964; At Large (essays), 1964; Gods and Heroes, 1969; The Duchess of Glover (novel), 1975; The Native's Return, 1981; The Parkside Stories, 1985. Plays: Men to the Sea, National Theater, New York; The Cocoon, Playhouse Theater, London; The Virus, University of Wisconsin Parkside Theater; Perpetual Care, University of Wisconsin Parkside Theater. *Contributions to:* Esquire; Atlantic; Saturday Review and other magazines; Editor, Time Magazine and Writer for Life and Holiday magazines; Currently Gourmet and Travel Writer for Wisconsin Magazine of Sunday Milwaukee Journal. *Honours:* Rockefeller Grants, 1947, 48; Fulbright Research Grant, Italy, 1950; National Book Award, 1956; First Award, Wisconsin Council for Writers, 1970, 76; Citations for Distinguished Service in Letters by Wisconsin State Legislature and Wisconsin Academy of Science, Arts and Letters, 1982. *Memberships:* Authors League of America; Dramatists Guild of America (National Secretary, 1947–49); Council of Wisconsin Writers; Wisconsin Academy of Science, Arts and Letters; Poetry Society of America. *Literary Agent:* Harold Ober Associates, New York City. *Address:* W4970 Kubly Road, New Glarus, WI 53574, USA.

KUDELKA, Jan, b. 25 Jan. 1952, Canada. Playwright. m. Barry Eldridge, 12 Nov. 1981, Toronto, 1 son, 1 daughter. *Publication:* Circus Gothic. *Membership:* Regional representative, Playwrights Union of Canada. *Address:* 41 Cowan Avenue, Toronto, Ontario, Canada M6K 2N1.

KUDIAN, Mischa, b. Alexandria, Egypt. Writer. *Education:* Victoria College, Alexandria, Egypt; University of London, England. *Publications:* Three Apples Fell From Heaven, 1969; The Saga of Sassoun, 1970; Soviet Armenian Poetry, 1974; Candy Floss, 1980; Flutterby, 1983; This Day and Age, 1983; Tenpence a Laugh, 1983; More Apples Fell From Heaven, 1983; Witricks Galore!, 1984. Translations: Scenes from an Armenian Childhood, 1962; The Bard of Loree, 1970; Tell Me, Bella, 1972; The Muse of Sheerak, 1975; Selected Works: Avetik Issahakian, 1976; Lamentations of Narek, 1977; Honorable Beggars, 1978; Retreat Without Song, 1982; Komitas, The Shepherd of Songs, 1983; The Tailor's Visitors, 1984; Jonathan Son of Jeremiah, 1985. *Contributions to:* Various journals and magazines. *Memberships:* Society of Authors; Translators Association. *Address:* c/o Barclays Bank Limited, 15 Langham Place, London W1, England.

KUDRLE, Robert Thomas, b. 23 Aug. 1942, Sioux City, Iowa, USA. Professor, Public Affairs. m. Venetia Hilary Mary Thomas, 24 July 1970, Oxford, England, 2 sons. *Education:* AB, 1964, PhD, 1974, Harvard University; M Phil, Economics, University of Oxford, England, 1967. *Publications:* Agricultural Tractors: A World Industry Study, 1975; Reducing the Cost of Dental Care, co-editor, 1983; The Industrial Future of the Pacific Basin, co-editor, 1984. *Contributor to:* Canadian Journal of Economics; Policy Analysis; Public Finance; International Studies Quarterly; International Organization; World Politics, etc. *Honours:* Rhodes Scholarship, 1964; Nuffield College Studentship, 1966; Graduate Research Assistantship, Harvard Centre for International Affairs, 1969; Co-Editor, International Studies Quarterly, 1980-84. *Address:* 4155 Garfield Ave S, Minneapolis, MN 55409, USA.

KÜHNELT, Wilhelm A, b. 28 July 1905, Linz, Oberösterreich, Austria. University Professor. m. Getraud Kitzler, 20 July 1942, Vienna, 1 son, 1 daughter. *Education:* PhD, University of Vienna, 1927. *Publications:* Bodenbiologie, 1950; Soil Biology, 1961 and 1976; Gundriss der Okologie, 1965 and 1971; Ecologie Générale, 1969. *Contributions to:* Various scholarly journals. *Honours:* Corresponding member 1955, full member 1959, Osterreichische Akademie der Wissen-schaften; Honorary member: Naturwissenschaftlicher Verein für Kärten; Abeitsgemeinschaft österreichischer Wissenschafter für Umweltschutz. *Address:* Goldschlagstrasse 120, Vienna XV, Austria.

KUHNER, Herbert, b. 29 Mar. 1935, Vienna, Austria. Writer; Translator. *Education:* BA, Columbia University, USA. *Publications:* Nixe, 1968; Vier Einakter, 1973; Broadsides & Pratfalls, 1976; The Assembly-Line Prince; Translations include: Borders/Grenzen, poetry by Peter Paul Wiplinger, 1977; Infanticide/Kindsmord, drama by Peter Turrini, 1978; Carinthian Slovenian Poetry, with Feliks J Bister, 1984; Austrian Poetry Today, with M Holton, 1985. *Contributor to:* Dimension; Translation; Confrontation; Mundus Artium; Portland Review; Webster Review; American Pen; Christian Science Monitor; Stand; Modern Poetry in Translation; Malahat Review; Prism International; Poetry Australia; Skylark; etc. *Honours:* Golden Pen for Translation, Struge Poetry Evenings Festival, Yugoslavia; Complete Works and papers collected by Boston University Libraries. *Memberships:* PEN; Poetry Society of America. *Literary Agent:* Andrew Hewson, London. *Address:* Gentzgasse 14/4, A-1180 Vienna, Austria.

KUHNS, Dennis R, b. 28 Jan. 1947, Maugansville, Maryland, USA. Clergyman, Mennonite Church. m. Joyce Eberly, 1 Aug. 1970, 2 daughters. *Education:* BA, Psychology, 1971, M Div, 1983, Eastern Mennonite Seminary. *Publications:* Women in the Church, 1978; Frauen in der Gemeinde, 1980. *Contributor to:* Gospel Herald; Seminarian. *Address:* 2450 Biglerville Road, Gettysburg, PA 17325, USA.

KULSKI, Wladyslaw Wszebor, b. 27 July 1903, Warsaw, Poland. Former Polish Diplomat; American University Professor. m. Antonina Reutt, 28 Oct. 1938. *Education:* MA, Warsaw University, School of Law, 1925; JD, Paris University Law School, 1927. *Appointments:* Polish Diplomatic Service, 1928-45; Public Lecturer, USA, 1946-47; Lecturer, Political Science, University of Alabama, 1947-48; Professor, Political Science, University of Alabama, 1948-51, Syracuse University 1951-64, Duke University 1964-73. *Publications:* Le Probleme de la Securite Internationale, 1927; Contemporary Europe, in Polish, 1939; Editor, Polish White Book, 1940; Thus Spake Germany, 1941; Germany from Defeat to Conquest: 1913-33, 1945; The Soviet Regime: Communism in Practice, 1954, 4th edition 1964; Peaceful Co-existence: An Analysis of Soviet Foreign Policy, 1960; International Politics in a Revolutionary Age, 1964, 2nd edition 1968; De Gaulle and the World: The Foreign Policy of the Fifth French Republic, 1966; The Soviet Union in World Affairs (1964-72), 1973; Germany and Poland, 1976. *Contributor to:* Numerous professional journals including, Journal of Central European Affairs; Contemporary Review; American Journal of International Law; Russian Review; High School Journal; Problems of Communism; Europa Archiv; etc. *Honours:* Fulbright Research Award and John Simon Guggenheim Memorial Foundation Research Fellowship, 1961-62; 2nd Guggenheim Research Fellowship, 1970. *Memberships:* American Society of International Law; American Political Science Association; American Association for Slavic Studies; American Association of University Professors; Southern Conference on Slavic Studies, President 1963-70. *Address:* 1624 Marion Avenue, Durham, NC 27705, USA.

KUMAR, Krishna, b. 14 Mar. 1940, Meerut, India. Professor; Researcher. m. Dr Parizad Tahbazzadeh, 18 May 1977, Delhi, 2 daughters. *Education:* MA, Economics and Sociology; PhD, Sociology. *Publications:* The Social and Cultural Impact of Transnational Enterprises, 1979; Ethics and Politics of International Collaborative Research: From Praxis to Practice, co-author. Editor: Transnational Enterprises: Their Impact on Third World Societies and Cultures, 1960; Bonds Without Bondage: Explorations in Transnational Cultural Interactions, 1979; Democracy and Nonviolence: A Study of Their Relationships, 1968. Co-Editor: Racial Conflict, Discrimination and Power: Historical and Comparative Studies, 1976; Multinationals from Developing Countries, 1981. *Contributions to:* Various publications including: Journal of Political and Military Sociology; .International Studies Quarterly; International Journal of Business Studies; Euro-Asia Business Review; Indian Journal of Extension Education; American Sociological Review; International Journal of Comparative Sociology; Southeast Asian Journal of Social Science; Social Welfare; Indian Journal of Social Defense. *Address:* 261 Congressional Lane Apt T-19, Rockville, MD 20852, USA.

KUMAR, Satish, b. 27 May 1933, Moga, India. University Professor. m. Manjari, 7 May 1963, Dehradun, 2 daughters. *Education:* MA, Political Science, Delhi University; PhD, Indian School of International Studies, Delhi University. *Literary Appointments:* Assistant Professor in South Asian Studies, Indian School of International Studies, Jawaharlal Nehru University, New Delhi, 1961-67; Senior Research Officer (Pakistan) Ministry of External Affairs, New Delhi, 1967-72; Associate Professor in Diplomacy, 1972-83, Professor of Diplomacy, 1983-, School of International Studies, Jawaharlal Nehru University, New Delhi. *Publications:* Rana Polity in Nepal, 1967; The New Pakistan, 1978; CIA and the Third World, 1981; Bangladesh Documents, two volumes 1971, 1972; Documents on India's Foreign Policy, three volumes 1975, 1976, 1977; Yearbook on India's Foreign Policy, 1982-83, 1985. *Contributions to:* About 40 research articles in Indian and foreign journals. *Honours:* Senior Fulbright Fellowship at School of Advanced International Studies, John

Hopkins University, Washington DC, Jan–Sep 1978; Ford Foundation Fellowship at University of California, Berkeley, Oct–Dec 1978. *Memberships:* Authors Guild of India, New Delhi; Institute of Defence Studies and Analyses, New Delhi; Indian Council of World Affairs, New Delhi; India International Centre, New Delhi. *Literary Agent:* Third World Book Review, London. *Address:* 60 Dakshinapuram, New Campus, Jawaharlal Nehru University, New Delhi 110067, India.

KUMIN, Maxine Winokur, b. 6 June 1925, Philadelphia, Pennsylvania, USA. Writer. m. Victor M Kumin, 29 June 1946, Philadelphia, 1 son, 2 daughters. *Education:* AB 1946, AM 1948, Radcliffe College. *Literary Appointments include:* Brandeis University 1975; Hurst Professor of Literature, Washington University 1977, Woodrow Wilson Visiting Fellow, 1979; Consultant in Poetry, Library of Congress, 1981–82; Poet-in-Residence, Bucknell University, 1983; Master Artist, Atlantic Center for the Arts, Florida, 1984. *Publications include:* Poetry: Halfway, 1961; The Privilege, 1965; Up Country, 1972; Our Ground Time Here Will Be Brief, 1982; Closing the Ring, 1984; The Long Approach, 1985. Novels: Through Dooms of Love, 1965, The Passions of Uxport, 1968; The Abduction, 1971; The Designated Heir, 1974. Also short stories, essays, children's books. *Contributions to:* Numerous magazines & journals. *Honours include:* Various honorary degrees: Eunice Tietjens Memorial Prize, Poetry Magazine, 1972; Politzer Prize in Poetry, 1973; 1st Prize, Borestone Mountain, 1976; Recognition Award, Radcliffe College Alumnae, 1978; Award, American Academy & Institute, Arts & Letters, 1980; Arts America Tour, US Information Agency, 1983; Academy of American Poets Fellowship, 1985; Fellowships, scholarships. *Memberships:* Poetry Society of America; PEN. *Literary Agent:* Emilie Jacobson, Curtis Brown Ltd. *Address:* c/o Curtis Brown Ltd, 10 Astor Place, New York, NY 10003, USA.

KUNCEWICZ, Maria Sophia, b. 30 Oct. 1897, Samara, Russia. Novelist; Essayist. m. Ferzy Karol Kuncewicz, 13 May 1921, Warsaw, Poland, 1 son. *Education:* Certificat d'etudes françaises, Universities of Nancy, Krakow and Warsaw. *Appointments include:* Columnist, Bluszcz Kobieta Wspotczesna, Gazeta Polska, Warsaw; Collaborator, Nowa Polska, London; Professor, Polish Literature, University of Chicago, USA, 1962–70. *Publications include:* Two Moons, 1933; The Stranger, 1936; Tristan, 1967; The Keys, 1948; The Forester, 1961; etc. *Contributor to:* Numerous journals including Now, London; Bonniers Magazine, Stockholm; The Nation, New York; Herald Tribune, New York; East European Review, USA. *Honours:* Gold Laurel, Polish Academy of Letters, 1938; Gold Cross of Merit, 1939; Literary Prize, City of Warsaw, 1939; The Kosciuyzro Foundation Medal of Recognition, 1971; National Grand Prix, 1974; Sociètè Europèenne de culture Medal, 1983; etc. *Memberships:* International PEN; Polish English & American Centres; Founder, International PEN for writers in exile; Pre War Polish Writers' Union, now dissolved. *Address:* Old Kennels, Flint Hill, VA 22627, USA.

KUNDERA, Milan, b. 1 Apr. 1929, Prague, Czechoslovakia. Writer. *Education:* Institute of Cinematography, Prague. *Publications:* The Joke, 1965; Laughable Loves, 1968; Life is Elsewhere, 1969; The Farewell Party, 1971; The Book of Laughter and Forgetting, 1979; The Unbearable Lightness of Being, 1984. *Honours:* Jerusalem Prize, 1985. *Literary Agent:* Francois Prdel, Paris. *Address:* Ecole des Hautes Etudes, 54 blo Raspail, Paris 6, France.

KUNERT, Gunter, b. 6 Mar. 1929, Berlin. Author. m. Marianna Todten, 1 Apr. 1952. *Publications include:* Abtotungverfahren, 1980; Verspatete Monologe, 1981; Diesseits Des Erinnerns, 1982; Die Letzten Indianer Europas, 1983; Mein Lesebuch, 1983; Stilleben, 1983; Auf Der Suche Nach Der Wirklichen Freiheit, 1983; Leben Und Schreiben, 1983; Zuruck Ins Paradies, 1984; Kain Und Abels Bruderlichkeit, 1984. *Contributions to:* numerous publications. *Honours:*

Heinrich-Man-Price, 1962; Johannes-R-Becher-Price, 1973; Poet of the Town in Bergen Engheim, 1983; Heinrich-Heine-Price, 1985. *Memberships:* Academy of Art, (Berlin West); Academy of Poetry and Protection of Language, (Darmstadt); PEN Club, Germany. *Address:* Schulstrasse 7, D–2216 Kaisborstel, Federal Republic of Germany.

KUNZ, Günter, b. 30 Nov. 1921, Berlin, Germany. Journalist. *Publications:* Problem Fortschritt, 1975; Friede durch Zusammenarbeit, (Co-Author), 1980; Die ökologische Wende (Editor and Co-Author), 1983. *Contributor to:* Z I P (Publisher until 1975); PRISMA TV Science Report (Editor); Problem Fortschritt – TV Environmental Report (Author). *Memberships:* Technisch-Literarische Gesellschaft; Luftfart-Presse Club e.v. *Honours:* Recipient, Glaxo International Prize for Science Journalists, 1977. *Address:* Schoenaich-Carolath-Str, 10, D–2000 Hamburg 52, Federal Republic of Germany.

KUNZE, Reiner Alexander, b. 16 Aug. 1933, Oelsnitz, Germany. Writer. *Education:* Studies of philosophy & journalism, literary history, art history, music history, University of Leipzig, 1951–55; Master's degree, ibid. *Publications include:* Poetry, prose, translations, films. Sensible Wage, 1969; Der Löwe Leopold, 1970; Zimmerlautstärke, 1972; Brief mit blauem Siegel, 1973; Die wunderbaren Jahre, 1976; Film script, Die wunderbaren Jahre, 1979; Auf eigene Hoffnung, 1981; Eine stadtbekannte Geschichte, 1982; In Deutschland zuhaus, 1984; Gespräch mit der Amse, 1984. *Honours:* Translation Prize, Czech Writers Association, 1968; German Young People's Book Prize, 1970; Mölle Literary Prize, Sweden, 1973; Literary Prize, Bavarian Academy of Fine Arts, 1973; Georg Trakl Prize, Austria, 1977; Andreas Gryphus Prize, 1977; Georg Büchner Prize, 1977; Geschwister Scholl Prize, 1981; Eichendorff Literature Prize, 1984; Bundesverdienstkruez 1st Class, 1984. *Memberships:* Bavarian Academy of Fine Arts; Academy of Arts, Berlin; German Academy for Language & Literature, Darmstadt; PEN Club. *Address:* Am Sonnenhang 19, D–8391 Obernzell I–Erlau, Federal Republic of Germany.

KUO, Alex, b. 19 Jan. 1939, Boston, Massachusetts, USA. Writer; Teacher. *Education:* BA, Knox College, 1961; MFA, University of Iowa, 1963. *Literary Appointments:* Co-Editor, Statements, 1961–63; Consulting Editor, Wisconsin Review, 1965–69; Literary Editor, Journal of Ethnic Studies, 1973–85. *Publications:* The Window Tree, 1971; New Letters from Hiroshima and Other Poems, 1974; Changing the River, 1985. *Contributions of poems and stories to:* Journal of Ethnic Studies; The Malahat Review; The Literary Review; New Letters; Boundary 2; The Minnesota Review; Cincinnati Poetry Review; Wisconsin Review; Tin Can Journal; Snapdragon; Bulletin of Concerned Asian Scholars; Greenfield Review; Bartleby's Review; Ironwood; Poetry Nortwest; Shenandoah; Northwest Review; Cheshire; Motive; Arts in Society; Beloit Poetry Journal; New Mexico Quarterly; Trace; Unicorn; Statements; Sciamachy; Forum; Discourse; American Weave; Descant; Castalia. *Honours:* Davenport Drama Award, 1960; Greig Post Poetry Award, 1961. *Literary Agent:* Spike Mulligan. *Address:* P O Box 8824, Moscow, ID 83843, USA.

KUPER, Leo, b. 24 Nov. 1908, Johannesburg, Republic of South Africa. *Education:* BA, LLB, University of Witwatersrand, Johannesburg, 1931; MA, University of North Carolina, Chapel Hill, USA, 1948; PhD, University of Birmingham, England, 1952. *Publications:* Passive Resistance in South Africa, 1955; An African Bourgeoisie, 1965; Pluralism in Africa, Co-Editor, 1969; Race, Class and Power, 1974; The Pity of It All, 1977; Genocide, 1982; The Prevention of Genocide, 1985. *Honours:* Herskowits Award, 1966; Spivak Fellowship Award, American Sociological Association, 1978. *Address:* 1282 Warner Avenue, Los Angeles, CA 90024, USA.

KURIKKA, Pirkko Marjatta, b. 9 June 1949, Urjala, Sweden. Dramatist. *Education:* The Theatre Academy, 1970–74. *Literary Appointments:* Teacher of Dramaturgy, Theatre Academy, 1975–78. *Publications:* Heinaaikaan (At hay-making time), 1974; Kullervo, 1975; Sarjetty viulu (The Wrecked Violin), 1979; Kevaan Musta valo (The Black Light of Spring), 1982; Pimean poika (Son of Darkness) 1982; Kerikansan kronikat (The Chronicles of the Kerikabsa Folk), 1984; Uppotukki (The Sunken Log), 1984. *Honour:* The National Award for TV-Film Script, 1985. *Membership:* The Finnish Dramatists Union. *Literary Agent:* The Finnish Dramatists' Union. *Address:* The Finnish Dramatists' Union, Vironkatu 12B, 00170 Helsinki, Sweden.

KURZWEIL, Edith, b. Vienna, Austria. Professor of Sociology; Editor. Widowed, 2 sons, 1 daughter. *Education:* BA, Queens College, City University of New York, 1967; MA, 1969, PhD, 1973, Graduate faculty, New School for Social Research, New York. *Literary Appointments:* Corresponding editor, Theory and Society, 1977–; Contributing editor, 1977–79, Executive editor, 1978–, Partisan Review; Associate editor, Current Perspectives in Social Theory, 1984–. *Publications:* The Age of Structuralism, 1980; Italian Entrepreneurs, 1983; Co-editor, Writers and Politics, 1983, Literature and Psychoanalysis, 1983, Cultural Analysis, 1984. *Contributions to:* Essays and book reviews: Partisan Review; Commentary; Contemporary Sociology; Theory and Society; Worldview; American Journal of Religion; American Journal of Sociology and others. *Honours:* Rockefeller Humanities Fellowship, 1982–83; Resident Scholar, Bellagio, 1977; Rutgers University Travel Grant, 1979–83; Research, Sigmund Freud Institutes, Vienna and Frankfurt; Maison des Sciences de l'Homme, Paris, France, 1982–83; CES, Harvard, 1982–83; Visiting professor, University of Frankfurst, 1984. *Memberships:* American Sociological Association (Chair, Theory section, 1982–83); International Sociological Association; Tocqueville Society; Cosmep; Groves Conference; Eastern Sociological Society; Poets, Playwrights, Editors, Essayists and Novelists. *Address:* 1 Lincoln Plaza, New York, NY 10023, USA.

KUSCHE, Lothar, b. 2 May 1929, Berlin, Germany. Author. *Publications:* Satirical novels and essays including: Das bombastische Windei, 1958; Nanu, wer schiesst denn da?, 1960; Uberall ist Zwergenland, 1960; Quer durch England in anderthelb Stunden, 1961; Kase und Locher, 1963; Kein Woodka fur den Staetsanwalt, 1967; Wie man einen Haushalt aushalt, 1969; Patientenfibel, 1971; Kusches Drucksachen, 1974; Kellner Willi serviert, 1978; Knoten im Taschentuch, 1980; Donald Duck sishe unter Greta Garbo, 1981; Laute im Hinterkopf, 1983; Der Mann auf dem Kleiderschrank, 1985; Nasen, die man nicht vergisst, 1986. *Contributor to:* Die Weltbuhne; Eulenspiegel, Berlin. *Honours:* Heinrich Heine Prize, 1960; Heinrich Greif Prize, 1973; National Prize DDR, 1984. *Memberships:* International PEN Democratic German Republic Center; Writers Association of Democratic German Republic; Association of Journalists of Democratic German Republic. *Address:* Woelckpromenade 5, DDR–1120 Berlin, Democratic German Republic.

KUSHLAN, James A, b. 10 Nov. 1947, Ohio, USA. Professor of Biological Sciences. *Education:* PhD, University of Miami, Florida, 1975. *Literary Appointments:* Editorial Board, Colonial Waterbirds, scientific journal, 1981–85; Editor, Florida Field Naturalist, 1981–86; Editorial Board, Wetlands, 1982; Editor, Colonial Waterbirds, 1985–. *Publications:* The Herons Handbook, 1984. *Contributions to:* Over 100 top scientific and technical journals. *Membership:* Council of Biological Editors, 1981–. *Address:* Department of Biological Sciences, East Texas State University, Commerce, TX 75428, USA.

KUSHNER, Rose, b. 22 June 1929, Baltimore, Maryland, USA. Medical Writer. m. Harvey D Kusner, 14 Jan. 1951, Baltimore, 2 sons, 1 daughter. *Education:* Pre-Med Studies, McCoy College, 1946–47, Baltimore Junior College, 1950–51, Montgomery College, 1963–65; Experimental Psychology, 1965–68, BS, Journalism, 1972, University of Maryland. *Appointments:* Free-lance Science Writer, 1965–; President, Executive Director, Breast Cancer Advisory Centre, Kensington, Maryland, 1975. *Publications:* Breast Cancer: A Personal History & Investigative Report, 1975; Why Me: What Every Woman Should Know About Breast Cancer to Save Her Life, 1977; Alternatives: New Developments in the War on Breast Cancer, 1984–85. *Contributor to:* Health Annual; CA: A Cancer Journal for Clinicians; etc. *Honours:* Summa Cum Laude, University of Maryland, 1972; National Media Award (Newspapers), American Phsychological Association, 1974; Distinguished Medical Writing Award, American Medical Writers Association; National Cancer Advisory Board. *Memberships include:* New York Academy of Sciences; Association of Community Cancer Centres; American Society of Clinical Oncology; Federation of American Scientists; National Press Club. *Address:* 9607 Kingston Road, Kensington, MD 20895, USA.

KUWABARA, Takeo, b. 10 May 1904, Turuga, Japan. Writer. m. Tazu Tanaka, 8 May 1933, 1 son, 3 daughters. *Education:* Bungakusi, Faculty of Letters, Kyoto University. *Publications:* (In Japanese) Reality and Fiction, 1943; Introduction to Literature, 1950; Essays on French Literature, 1967; Selected Works, 10 volumes, 1980–81; Interdisciplinary Researches: J-J Rousseau, 1951; Encyclopedie, 1954; French Revolution, 1959; Comparative Studies on Bourgeois Revolutions, 1964; Nakae Chomin, 1966; Theories of Literature, 1967; Studies on Rouseau, 1970; In English: Japan and Western Civilization, 1983. *Contributor to:* Various professional journals and magazines. *Honours:* Asahi Prize, 1975; Chevalier de la Legion D'Honneur, 1975; Man of Cultural Merit, 1979. *Memberships:* Honorary member, Japan Pen Club, former Vice President; Honorary Member, Japanese Society of French Literature; Academy of Arts (Japanese). *Address:* 421 Tonodan Yabunosita, Kamikyo-ku, Kyoto 602, Japan.

KWAN, William Chao-Yu, b. 7 Aug. 1916, Shanhaikuan, Peoples Republic of China. Advertising/Commercial Artist. m. Emily Wei-Tan Wang, 24 Feb. 1939, Tientsin, China, 1 son, 1 daughter, 1 adopted daughter. *Education:* St Francis Xavier's College, Shanghai, China; Diploma in Advertising, ICS, Scranton, Pennsylvania, USA; Diploma in Creative and Article Writing, Palmer Institute of Authorship, Hollywood, California, USA. *Literary Appointments:* Associate Editor, The Advertiser, Tientsin, Peoples Republic of China; Advertising Copywriter/Layout man, China Press, Shanghai; Editor, HAEC Newsletter, In-house publication of Hong Kong Aircraft Engineering Company Limited, Hong Kong, 1958–61; Editorial Adviser, HAEC Welfare Society Magazine, Hong Kong, 1968–74. *Publications:* English Precis, 1978–79; English Composition, 1978–79. *Contributions to:* China Mail, Hong Kong; The Asia Magazine, Hong Kong; Fate Magazine, USA; Beyond Magazine, USA; Successful Beekeeping Magazine, USA; Elite Magazine, USA; American Poetry Anthology, USA. *Memberships:* Past Associate Member, Society of Authors, London, England; Past Member, Hong Kong Journalists Association. *Literary Agent:* Anita Diamant Literary Agent, New York, New York, USA. *Address:* Tappan Oaks, 12 Carol Lane, Tappan, NY 10983, USA.

KWEIT, Robert William, b. 2 July 1946, New York City, USA. Professor of Political Science. m. Mary Elizabeth Grisez, 16 Nov. 1976, Charlottesville, Virginia. *Education:* AB, Syracuse University, 1967; MA 1968, PhD 1974, University of Pennsylvania. *Publications:* Concepts & Methods for Political Analysis, co-author, 1981; Implementing Citizen Participation in a Bureaucratic Society: A Contingency Approach, co-author, 1981. *Contributions:* Permeability of Political Parties: Continuity & Change among Delegates to State

Party Conventions, in, The Life of the Parties: Activists in Presidential Politics, eds. Abramowitz et al, in press. Politics of Policy Analysis: The Role of Citizen Participation in Analytical Decision-Making, co-author, in Policy Studies Review, 1984; Bureaucratic Decision-Making: Impediments to Citizen Participation, co-author, in Polity, 1980. *Honour:* Pi Sigma Alpha, 1982. *Address:* 3823 Fairview Place, Grand Forks, ND 58201, USA.

KYTÖHONKA, Arto Olavi, b. 27 Jan. 1944, Pori, Finland. Writer. m. Riitta Helena Alanen, 7 Apr. 1978, 3 daughters. *Appointments:* Editor, Parnasso, 1978; Artist of State, Hame, Finland, 1983–. *Publications:* Ollakseni kaihoisa, 1970; Illilla jatan oven valmiiksi auki, 1974; Toinen teos, 1982; Satunais Run, 1983; Satunaiz Run, 1984. *Contributor to:* Ilta-Sanomat; several other magazines and journals. *Memberships:* Suomen kirjailijaliittoo; Finnish Union of Writers; PEn Finland. *Address:* Casa Bianca, SF–16100 Uusikylae, Finland.

L

LA BARRE, Weston, b. 13 Dec. 1911, Uniontown, Pennsylvania, USA. Anthropologist. *Education:* BA, Princeton University, 1933; PhD, Yale University, 1937. *Publications:* The Peyote Cult, 1938; The Aymara Indians of the Lake Titicaca Plateau, Bolivia, 1948; The Human Animal, 1954; Materia Medica of the Aymara, 1960; They Shall Take up Serpents: Psychology of the Southern Snakehandling Cult, 1962; The Ghost Dance: Origins of Religion, 1970; Muellos: A Stone Age Superstition About Sexuality, 1985. Editor-in-Chief: Landmarks in Anthropology. *Contributions to:* American Anthropology; Current Anthropology; Psychology; Journal of American Folklore; Science. *Honours:* Sterling Fellow of Yale, 1937; Guggenheim Fellow, 1946; Rockefeller Fellow, Villa Serbelloni, Lake Como, Italy, 1981; Geza Roheim Memorial Award, 1958. *Memberships:* Phi Beta Kappa; Sigma Xi. *Address:* 172 Carol Woods, Chapel Hill, NC 27514, USA.

LA CAPRA, Dominick, b. 13 July 1939, New York City, USA. Historian; Critic. Divorced, 1 daughter. *Education:* BA, Cornell University, 1961; PhD, Harvard University, 1970. *Literary Appointment:* Goldwin Smith Professor of European Intellectual History, Cornell University. *Publications:* Emile Durkheim: Sociologist and Philosopher, 1972; A Preface to Sartre, 1978; Madame Bovary, on Trial, 1982; Co-editor: Modern European Intellectual History, 1982; Rethinking Intellectual History, 1983; History and Criticism, 1985. *Contributions to:* Diacritics; MLN; History and Theory; Representations; The French Review; Boundary 2; Telos. *Honours:* Phi Beta Kappa, 1960; Phi Kappa Phi, 1961; Senior Fellowship from National Endowment for the Humanities, 1976; Senior Fellowship from The Society for the Humanities at Cornell, 1979. *Memberships:* International Association for Philosophy and Literature; American Historical Association; Society for Existential and Phenomenological Philosophy. *Address:* c/o History Department, McGraw Hall, Cornell University, Ithaca, NY 14853, USA.

LA FOLLETTE, Marcel Evelyn Chotkowski, b. 4 July 1944, Little Rock, Arkansas, USA. Professor; Policy Analyst. *Eduation:* BS, Little Rock University, Arkansas, 1967; MS, Boston University, 1968; PhD, Indiana University, 1979. *Literary Appointments:* Editor, Science, Technology and Human Values, 1978–; Assistant Professor, Writing Program, 1985–, Massachusetts Institute of Technology, Cambridge, Massachusetts. *Publications:* Editor: Law and Science, 1979; Quality in Science, 1981; Creationism, Science, and the Law, 1982. *Contributions to:* Daedalus; Environment; The Sciences; Science, Technology and Human Values. *Address:* c/o Science, Technology and Human Values, Editorial Offices E51-207, Massachusetts Institute of Technology, Cambridge, MA 02139, USA.

LA FOREST, Gerard V, b. 1 Apr. 1926, Grand Falls, New Brunswick, Canada. Judge, Supreme Court of Canada. m. D Marie Warner, 27 Dec. 1952, St John, New Brunswick, 5 daughters. *Education:* 2 years Arts, St Francis Xavier University, 1944–46; BCL, University of New Brunswick, 1949; BA Jurisprudence 1951, MA 1956, Oxford University, England; LL M 1965, JSD 1966, Yale University, USA. *Publications:* Disallowance and Reservation of Provincial Legislation, 1955, 2nd edition 1965; Extradition to and From Canada, 1961, 2nd edition, 1977; The Allocation of Taxing Power Under the Canadian Constitution, 1967, 2nd edition 1981; Natural Resources and Public Property Under the Canadian Constitution, 1969; Le Territoire Quebecois (co-author), 1970; Water Law in Canada – The Atlantic Provinces, (co-author), 1973. *Contributions to:* Numerous periodical journals. *Honours:* Rhodes Scholar, 1949–51; Yale Graduate Fellow, 1964–65; Queen's Counsel, New Brunswick, 1968; Fellow, Royal Society of Canada, 1975; Fellow, World Academy of Art and Science, 1975; LL D, University of Basel,

Switzerland, 1981; DU, University of Ottawa, 1985; DCL, University of New Brunswick, 1985. *Address:* 170 Minto Place, Rockcliffe Park, Ottawa, Ontario, Canada.

LA TOUSCHE D'AVRIGNY de, (Baronne) Francoise Anne, b. 19 Mar. 1907, Vern d'Anjou, France. m. Jean, Baron de la Tousche d'Avrigny, 14 Oct. 1937, 2 sons, 1 daughter. *Publications:* Nocturnes, 1967, Les Mots Historiques, Lettres anciennes et modernes, forthcoming. *Contributor to:* La Legion Violette; Academy of French Thought; Savoir, Angers. *Honours:* Prize, Belgian Association for Modern Poetry in Wallonia, 1970, 1975; Prize, Academy of French Thought, 1970, 1980. *Memberships:* La Legion Violette, Paris; Friends of Alfred de Vigny, Paris; Academy of French Thought, Niort. *Address:* 22 rue Kliber, 49000 Angers, France.

LAABS, Joochen, b. 3 July 1937, Dresden, Democratic Republic of Germany. Author. 3 daughters. *Education:* Diplom-Ingenieur, Hochschule für Verkehrswesen, Dresden. *Publications:* Eine Straßenbahn für Nofretete (poems), 1970; Das Grashaus oder Die Aufteilung von 35000 Frauen auf zwei Mann (novel), 1971; Die andere Hälfte der Welt (stories), 1974; Himmel sträflicher Leichtsinn (poems), 1978; Der Ausbruch (novel), 1979; Jeder Mensch will König sein (stories), 1983. *Contributions to:* Neue Deutsche Literatur; Sinn und Form; Litfass; L'80; Neue Literatur; Connaissance de la RDA, Literarni mesicnik; Plamaki; Revue svetovej literatury; Union; Uj Tükör. *Honours:* Förderungspreis des Mitteldeutschen Verlages Halle, 1971; Erich-Weinert-Medaille, Kunstpreis der FDJ, 1972; Martin-Andersen-Nexö-Preis der Stadt Dresden, 1973. *Memberships:* Schriftstellerverband der DDR (Authors Associations of DDR); PEN – Zentrum der DDR (PEN – centre of DDH). *Address:* Husstr, 126, 1199 Berlin, Democratic Republic of Germany.

L'ABATE, Luciano, b. 19 Sep. 1928, Brindisi, Italy. Psychologist. m. Bess Lukas, 30 Aug. 1958, Chicago, Illinois, USA, 1 son, 1 daughter. *Education:* BA, Tabor College, Kansas, USA; MA, Wichita University; PhD, Duke University. *Publications:* Principles of Clinical Psychology, 1964; Teaching Exceptional Children, (with L Curtis), 1975; Understanding and Helping the Individual in the Family, 1976; How To Avoid Divorce: Help for Troubled Marriages, (with Bess L'Abate), 1977; Enrichment Skills Training for Family Life, (with Gary Rupp), 1980; Approaches to Family Therapy, (with J C Hansen), 1982; Enrichment: Structured Approached with Couples, Families and Groups, 1977; Paradoxical Psychotherapy: Theory and Practice with Individuals, Couples and Families, (with G Weeks), 1982; Values, Ethics, Legalities and the Family Therapist, editor, 1983; Family Psychology: Theory, Therapy and Training, 1983; Handbook of Marital Interventions, (with Sherry McHenry), 1983; A Dictionary of Family Therapy Terms, (with R Sauber and G Weeks), 1985; Handbook of Social Skills Training and Research, (edited with M Milan), 1985; Handbook of Family Psychology, editor, 1985; Systematic Family Therapy, 1986. *Contributions to:* Over 180 papers, chapters and reviews in professional journals. *Honour:* Alumni Distinguished Professor Arts and Sciences, Georgia State University, 1983. *Memberships:* Diplomate and Examiner, American Board of Examiners in Professional Psychology; Fellow, Approved Supervisor, American Association of Marriage and Family Therapists; Fellow, American Psychological and American Orthopsychiatric Association; Charter Member, American Family Therapy Association. *Address:* Department of Psychology, Georgia State University, Atlanta, GA 30303, USA.

LABOVITCH, Carey Elizabeth, b. 20 Apr. 1960, London, England. Magazine Publisher & Editor. *Education:* BA Honours, French, St Hilda's College, Oxford University. *Literary Appointments:* Founder publisher, Blitz, magazine; Founder publisher, Managing editor, The Beat magazine, 1984; Founder publisher, The Magazine Distribution Book, 1st edition 1985.

INTERNATIONAL AUTHORS AND WRITERS WHO'S WHO 351

Judge, Publisher Magazine, publishing awards, 1985. *Contributions to:* Blitz; The Beat; Fashion Year Book, 1984; Media Week. *Honours:* Guardian/NUS Student Media Award, 1981; The 1984 Magazine Publishing Entrepreneur of the Year Award; highly commended, 1984; The BBC Enterprise Award for Small Businesses, 1985. *Address:* 1 Lower James Street, London W1R 3PN, England.

LABRIE, Roger P, b. 5 Feb. 1952, Manchester, New Hampshire, USA. Research Associate in Defence and Foreign Policy. *Education:* BA, Saint Anselm College, Manchester, New Hampshire; MSFS, Georgetown University, School of Foreign Service, Washington DC; M Phil, Columbia University, New York. *Literary Appointment:* Acting Managing Editor, AEI Foreign Policy and Defense Review, a quarterly journal published by the American Enterprise Institute. *Publications:* Nuclear Strategy and National Security, co-edited with Robert J Pranger, 1977; SALT Handbook: Key Documents and Issues, 1972–1979, editor, 1979; US Arms Sales Policy: Background and Issues, co-author, 1982. *Contributions to:* The FY 1982–1986 Defense Program: Issues and Trends (co-author) in AEI Foreign Policy and Defense Review, 1981; The Press Rewrites SALT II Columbia Journalism Review (co-author) 1983; Editor and author of introduction to Dealing with the Soviet Union, AEI Foreign Policy and Defense Review, 1985. *Honour:* Recipient of a Hubert H Humphrey Research Fellowship from the US Arms Control and Disarmament Agency, 1982–83. *Address:* American Enterprise Institute for Public Policy Research, 1150 Seventeenth Street NW, Washington, DC 20036, USA.

LACEY, Robert, b. 3 Jan. 1944, Guildford, Surrey, England. Author. m. Alexandra Jane Lacey, 2 sons, 1 daughter. *Education:* MA, Selwyn College, Cambridge. *Publications:* Robert, Earl of Essex, 1971; Sir Walter Raleigh, 1974; Majesty, 1977; The Kingdom, 1981; Princess, 1982; Aristocrats, 1983. *Contributions to:* New York Times; Sunday Times, UK; Books & Bookmen; Life. *Memberships:* Society of Authors; Writer Guild of Great Britain; Writers Guild of America. *Literary Agent:* Curtis Brown. *Address:* c/o Curtis Brown, 163 Regent Street, London W1, England.

LACOSTE, Beatrice Paule Emilie Andrée Marie, b. 27 Nov. 1947, Washington DC, USA. Journalist. *Education:* Degree, English and American Literature, Sorbonne, Paris, France; History and Geography of the USSR, National School of Oriental Languages, Paris. *Literary Appointments:* Assistant, American Literature & Civilization, Sorbonne, Fulbright Foundation Project, 1973–75; Freelance Journalist, Travel Writer, until 1983; Researcher, Dan Rather, American TV Programme 60 Minutes; Frequent Contributor to BBC World Service Programmes; Currently, Journalist, BBC Radio. *Publications:* Contributing Writer, Energy Coverage – Media Panic, 1983. *Contributor:* L'Express; Radio France International Radio; Canadian News; Continent; Renewable Energy News; Africa Events. *Membership:* Association of Anglo American Press, Paris. *Address:* Flat 6 Avis Court, 50 Ladbroke Grove, London W11 2PA, England.

LACY, Creighton Boutelle, b. 31 May 1919, Kuling, China. Seminary Professor. m. Frances McGuire Thompson, 20 June 1944, Greensboro, USA, 1 daughter. *Education:* AB, Summa cum laude Political Science, Swarthmore College, 1941; BD, magna cum laude, Missions, 1944, PhD, Christian Ethics, 1953, Yale University. *Publications:* Is China A Democracy?, 1943; The Conscience of India, 1965; Frank Mason North, 1967; Indian Insights, 1972; The Word-Carrying Giant, 1977; Coming Home – To China, 1978; Editor, Christianity Amid Rising Men and Nations, 1965. *Contributor to:* Christian Century; International Bulletin of Missionary Research; New World Outlook; Pacific Affairs; American Review; Asia and the Americas. *Honours:* Phi Beta Kappa, 1941; Phi Tau Phi, 1947; Kent Fellowship, Yale, 1944; Day Felowship, Yale, 1944; Fulbright Research Grant for India, 1966.

Memberships: Association of Professors of Missions, Chairman, 1964–66; American Society of Missology. *Address:* Divinity School of Duke University, Durham, NC 27706, USA.

LADELL, John Lindsay, b. 30 Sep. 1924, Bangkok, Siam (Thailand). Freelance Writer; Author. m. Monica Southey, 8 Oct. 1955, Ottawa, Canada, 1 son, 1 daughter. *Education:* BScF, Toronto, 1951; DPhil, Oxon, 1961. *Publication:* Inheritance: Ontavio's Century Farms, Past and Present (with Monica Ladell), 1979. *Contributor to:* The Loyal Canadians; Quest, Dr George Douglas: History's Forgotten Hero in Medical Post, April 1982; In Praise of Other Roses (with Monica Ladell) in Ontario Living, July 1985, etc. *Honour:* Ontario Bicentennial Award of Merit, 1984. *Memberships:* Writers' Union of Canada; Periodical Writers Association of Canada. *Address:* 1176 Tecumseh Park Drive, Mississauga, Ontario, Canada L5H 2W1.

LADELL, Norah Monica, b. 16 Mar. 1925, South Africa. Freelance Writer; Author. m. John Ladell, 8 Oct. 1955, Ottawa, Canada, 1 son, 1 daughter. *Education:* BA, Natal, 1944; Dip Lib, Cape Town, 1946. *Publication:* Inheritance: Ontavio's Century Farms; Past and Present, (with John Ladell), 1979. *Contributor:* of articles on agricultural and medical history, antiques, architecture, travel, rural life and living. *Honour:* Ontario Bicentennial Award of Merit, 1984. *Memberships:* Freelance Editors Association of Canada; Periodical Writers Association of Canada, Treasurer, Toronto Chapter, 1985–86. *Address:* 1176 Tecumseh Park Drive, Mississauga, Ontario, Canada L5H 2W1.

LADWIG, Zita, b. 4 Mar. 1919, Rothau, Graslitz, Czechoslovakia. Freelance Writer; Retired Secretary. m. Johannes Stefan Ladwig, 26 Sep. 1942. *Education:* Commercial Studies; Industrial Further Education School. *Publications:* Mascha-Ein Frauenschicksal, 1973; Walderdbeeren, 1978; Märchenschloss des Markus Frey, 1979; Gedichtla u Gschichtla in der Mutterschprauch, 1979; Waldkraiburg neue Heimat nach der Vertreibung, 1980; Moishe und Rachele, 1981; Blumen am Wege, 1982; Im Strom der Zeit, 1983; Humor und Witz in Reimen, 1984; Ein Kleines Glück, 1985. *Contributor to:* 800 single titles in journals, 1969– ; songs, yearbooks and anthologies. *Honours:* Federal Honorary Needle of Egerlander Gmoin, 1980; Federal Honorary Award, Egerlander Gmoin, 1985; Poetry Distinction, Professor Karlheinz Urban Written Competition. *Memberships:* Working Circle of Egerland Culturally Creative; Authors Association, Littera, Munich; Dialect Group, Weiss-Blaustrumpf, Munich; Bavarian Authors' Association. *Address:* Böhmerwaldstr. 3, D–8264 Waldkraiburg, Federal Republic of Germany.

LAEL, Richard Lee, b. 16 Sep. 1946, Hickory, North Carolina, USA. College Professor. *Education:* MA, PhD, University of North Carolina, Chapel Hill. *Publications:* The Yamashita Precedent: War Crimes and Command Responsibility, 1982; Versailles and After: An Annotated Bibliography of American Foreign Relations, 1919–1933, (co-author), 1983. *Contributions to:* Diplomatic History; Mid-America; Business History Review. *Honours:* Winner of the Missouri Conference on History Distinguished Book Award for, The Yamashita Precedent. *Memberships:* Society for Historians of American Foreign Relations: Organisation of American Historians; American Historical Association. *Address:* Department of History, Westminster College, Fulton, MO 65251, USA.

LAFEBER, Walter Frederick, b. 30 Aug. 1933, Indiana, USA. Professor of History and US Foreign Policy. m. Sandra Jane Gould, 11 Sep. 1955, Mt Carmel, Illinois, 1 son, 1 daughter. *Education:* BA, Hanover College, Indiana, 1955; MA, Stanford University, 1956; PhD, University of Wisconsin, 1959. *Publications:* The New Empire: An Interpretation of American Expansion, 1865–1898, 1963; America, Russia, and the Cold War, 1966, 5th edition 1985; The Creation of the American

Empire, (co-author), 1973 and 1979; The American Century, (co-author), 1975, 3rd edition 1986; Inevitable Revolutions: The U S In Central America, 1983. *Contributions to:* Atlantic Monthly; New York Times; Washington Post Book Week; Political Science Quarterly; American Historical Review; Journal of American History; Diplomatic History; Foreign Service Journal. *Honours:* Beveridge Prize, American Historical Associaton, 1963; Clark Teaching Award, 1966. *Memberships:* American Historical Association; Organization of American Historians; Society of Historians of American Foreign Policy. *Literary Agent:* Gerard McCauley, Katonah, New York and New York City. *Address:* History-McGraw Hall, Cornell University, Ithaca, NY 14853, USA.

LAFFAN, Kevin Barry, b. 24 May 1922, Reading, Berkshire, England. Dramatist; Scriptwriter. *Productions:* Stage Plays: It's a 2'6'' Above the Ground World, 1970; Zoo Zoo Widdershins Zoo, 1971; The Super Annuatroman, 1972; Wandering Jew, 1978; Neber So Good, 1979; There are Humans at the Bottom of My Garden, 1977. Television Plays: Lucky for Some; Best Legs in the Business; Decision to Burn; Fly on the Wall; You Can Only Buy Once. Television Series: Kate; Justice; Beryl's Lot; Emmerdale Farm. *Honours:* ATV Award, 1960; Dublin Theatre Festival Award, 1968; NSU and Sunday Times Best Play Award, 1969. *Literary Agent:* Actac Limited. *Address:* 16 Cadogan Lane, London SW1, England.

LAFFIN, John, b. 21 Sep. 1922, Sydney, Australia. Military & Political Historian; Novelist; Poet; Lecturer; Journalist; Broadcaster. m. Hazelle Gloria Stonham, 6 Oct. 1943, Sydney, Australia, 1 son, 2 daughters. *Education:* MA; DLitt. *Publications:* Over 100 books including: Digger – Story of the Australian Soldier, 1959; Jackboot, 1965; Links of Leadership, 1966; The Hunger to Come, 1966, 1971; New Geography, 1967, 1968–69, 1970–71; Anatomy of Captivity, 1968; Surgeons in the Field, 1970; Devil's Goad, 1970; Letters From the Front, 1914–18, 1973; French Foreign Legion 1974; The Arab Mind, 1974; Americans in Battle, 1975; The Israeli Mind, 1979; The Dagger of Islam, 1979; Damn the Dardanelles! – The Story of Gallipoli, 1980; Fight for the Falklands!, 1982; The PLO Connections, 1982; The Arabs as Master Slavers, 1982; The Australian Army At War 1899–1975, 1982; The Israeli Army in the Middle East Wars 1948–73, 1982; The Arab Armies of the Middle East Wars 1948–75, 1982; The Man the Nazis Couldn't Catch, 1984; Know the Middle East, 1985; Stories from the Western Front 1914–18, 1985; Dictionary of Battles, Campaigns & Wars, 1985; A Passion of Poetry, 1985; The War of Despiration: Lebanon 1982–85, 1985; Battlefield Archaeology, 1986; A Kind of Immorality, 1986; Dictionary of Battles, 1986. *Contributor to:* Daily Telegraph; International Herald Tribune; BBC; many other professional journals. *Memberships:* Society of Authors; Poetry Society. *Address:* Oxford House, Church Street, Knighton, Powys, Wales.

LAFKY, Sue Ann, b. 28 Sep. 1953, Portland, Oregon, USA. Journalist; Educator. *Education:* BS, Journalism, University of Oregon, 1975; MA, Journalism, 1985, Studies for PhD, Mass Communications, current, Indiana University. *Literary Appointments:* Editor/Reporter, Sandy Cor Post, 1976–78; Reporter, Gresham Outlook, Oregon, 1978–79; Correspondent, Oregonian, 1979–80; Reporter/Wire Service Editor, Bloomington Herald-Telephone, 1980–. *Contributions:* Co-Founder, Contributor, Feminist Teacher; Newspaper Research Journal. *Address:* 7121/2 E Cottage Grove, Bloomington, IN 47401, USA.

LaHOOD, Marvin J, b. 21 Mar. 1933, Auburn, New York, USA. College Professor. m. Marjorie Braun, 27 Aug. 1959, Dunkirk, New York, 2 sons, 1 daughter. *Education:* BS, Boston College, 1954; MA 1958, PhD 1962, English University of Notre Dame. *Literary Appointments:* Instructor 1960–61, Associate Professor 1962–64, Niagara University; Professor and Dean, Salem State College, 1972–75; Professor and Dean,

D'Youville College, 1975–78; Associate Professor 1964–67, Professor 1967–71 and 1978–, State University of New York, Buffalo. *Publications:* Latvian Literature, consulting editor, 1964; Tender is the Night : Essays in Criticism, editor, 1969; Conrad Richter's America, 1974; State University College at Buffalo; 1946–1972, 1980. *Contributions to:* Journals including: Philological Quarterly; University Review; The English Record; English Journal; Mark Twain Journal; Revue des Langues Vivantes; World Literature Today; American Literary Criticism. *Honours:* Faculty Research Fellowships 1967 and 1968, Chancellors Award for Excellence in Teaching 1985, State University of New York; Massachusetts Council on the Arts and Humanities Panel on Writing, 1973–75. *Address:* 93 Parkhaven Drive, Amherst, NY 14226, USA.

LAHR, John Henry, b. 12 July 1941, Los Angeles, USA. Author. m. Anthea Mander, 12 Aug. 1965, London, England, 1 son. *Education:* BA, Yale University; MA, Worcester College, Oxford University, England. *Appointments:* Drama Critic, Manhattan East, 1966–68; Drama Critic, Free Press, 1968–70, Village Voice, 1970–75; Contributing Editor, Evergreen Review, 1969–72, Harper's, 1976–81; Drama Critic, New Society, 1978–. *Publications:* Notes on a Cowardly Lion, 1969; Acting Out of America, 1972; The Autograph Hound, 1973; Hot to Trot, 1974; Prick Up Your Ears, 1978; Coward: The Playwright, 1982; Automatic Vaudeville, 1984. *Honours:* Yale Writing Prize, 1963; George Jean Nathan Award for Dramatic Criticism, 1969; Gay New Literary Prize, 1979; ASCAP Deems Taylor Award, 1980, 1982. *Literary Agent:* Richard Simon, UK; Georges Borchardt USA. *Address:* 11 a, Chalcot Gdns, Englands Lane, London NW3, England.

LAHTINEN, Anni, b. 2 Feb. 1914, Kuhmalahti, Finland. Writer. *Publications:* Ystavani Elviira, Mustalaistytto, 1973; Hiiret, 1974; Kakstoista Meren Rannalla, 1976; Jattilaisen Tasku, 1980; Voi Elaman J Kevat, 1981; Sinappia, Olkaa Hyva, 1982; Tuku Tuku Lampaitani, 1983; Tunturikurmitsa Kutsuu, 1984; Kyynelia Joulupuurossa, 1985. *Contributions to:* various publications and broadcasting. *Honours:* Country Award for Literature, 1980; Finnish State Prize for Literature, 1981; City Prize, 1981; Publishing Company's Prize, 1983. *Memberships:* Finnish Writers' Society: Finnish Provincial Writers' Society; Finnish Dramatists' Society; Local Literary Society. *Address:* Yrjönkatu 3 – 5 A 7, 33100 Tampere, Finland.

LAING, Ronald David, b. 7 Oct. 1927. Psychologist. *Education:* MB, ChB, Glasgow University, Scotland; Diploma of Psychological Medicine. *Publications:* The Divided Self, 1960, 1962, 1971; The Self and Others, 1961, 1969, 1971; (jointly) Reason and Violence (with introduction by J P Sartre) 1964, 1971; (jointly) Sanity, Madness and the Family 1965; The Politics of Experience and the Bird of Paradise, 1967, 1971, 1972; Knots 1970, 1971; The Politics of the Family 1971; The Facts of Life, 1976; Do You Love Me, 1977; Conversations with Adam and Natasha, 1977; Conversations with Children, 1978; Sonnets, 1979; The Voice of Experience, 1982; Wisdom, Madness and Folly, 1985. *Address:* 2 Eton Road, London NW3, England.

LAIR, Helen Humphrey, b. 3 Jan. 1918, Indiana, USA. Art Teacher (retired), Artist, Poet, Newspaper Columnist. m. 2 July 1966, 1 son, 2 daughters. (1 deceased.) *Education:* John Herron Art School, Anderson College, University of Wisconsin; Gloucester School of Art; Brown County School of Art (with Curry Boehm). *Major Publications:* Lair of the Four Winds; Earth Pilgrim. *Contributor to:* Hibiscus Press; Poetry Review; Today's Best Poetry; Contemporary Poetry of Today; Pharnassus Press; Footprints in the Sand; Mincie Star; and others. *Honours Include:* DLitt; Farnell Award, New York; Richard Miller Award, New York; International Clover Award; Dr Stella Woodall Poetry Award; Golden Poetry Award, National Federation of Poetry, 1980; Hibiscus Press Short Story Award; Campbell Historial Award. *Memberships: include:*

Founder, Henry County Art Guild; Founder, Mid-Ctrl Indiana Poetry Contest; Indiana State Federation of Poetry; National Federation of Poetry; World Poetry Society Intercontinental; Chaparral Poets; Academy of American Poets; International Poets of Achievement; President, Raintree Writers. *Address:* 1202 Mourer Street, New Castle, IN 47362, USA.

LAIRD, Robbin Frederick, b. 6 Oct. 1946, Los Angeles, California, USA. International Affairs. m. Nancy Croft, 16 June 1970, New York, USA. *Education:* PhD, Columbia University, 1974. *Publications:* The Politics of Economic Modernization in the Soviet Union (with Erik Hoffmann), 1982; The Scientific–Technological Revolution and Soviet Foreign Policy, (with Erik Hoffmann), 1982; The Soviet Polity in the Modern Era, (with Erik Hoffmann), 1984; The Soviet Union and Strategic Arms, (with Dale Herspring), 1984; Technocratic Socialism: The Soviet Union in the Advanced Industrial Era, (with Erik Hoffmann), 1985; France, the Soviet Union and the Nuclear Weapons Issue, 1985, French Edition 1986; Soviet Foreign Policy in a Changing World, (with Erik Hoffmann), 1986. *Contributions include:* Chapters in books and articles. *Honours:* National Science Foundation Award, 1979–81. *Memberships:* Institut Francais des Relations Internationales, Paris; International Institute for Strategic Studies, London; Royal Institute of International Affairs, London. *Address:* Box 627, Arlington, VA 22216, USA.

LAKEMAN, Enid, b. 1903, Hadlow, Kent, England. Editorial Consultant. *Education:* BSc, London University. Director & Secretary, Electoral Reform Society 1945–79; Editorial Consultant 1979–. *Publications:* When Labour Fails; Report on Malaya; Voting in Democracies, with James D Lambert; How Democracies Vote, Power to Elect. *Contributions to:* Contemporary Review; Parliamentary Affairs; National Review; Liberal News; etc. *Memberships:* National Book League; Liberal Party; Royal Institute of International Affairs; Politics Association; Liberal International; European Movement; United Nations Association, International Political Studies Association; Amnesty International; Consumers' Association. *Address:* 37 Culverden Avenue, Tunbridge Wells, Kent, TN4 9RE, England.

LAKRITZ, Esther (née Himmelman), b. 11 Apr. 1928, Milwaukee, Wisconsin, USA. Freelance Writer. m. Leo W Lakritz, 26 Dec. 1951, Milwaukee, Wisconsin, 2 sons, 1 daughter. *Education:* BS Secondary Education, University of Wisconsin Milwaukee, 1949; MLS, University of Wisconsin, Madison, 1976. *Major Publication:* Randy Visits the Doctor, 1962. *Contributor to:* California State Patrolman; Family Health; On Computing; Sea Classics; Real West; Wisconsin Weekend; Woman's World; Alive & Well; Life & Health; Physicians Management; Medical Economics; Medical Secretaries; The Professional Medical Assistant; and others. *Address:* 2661 East Collingswood, Beloit, WI 53511, USA.

LAL, P, b. 28 Aug. 1928, Kapurthala, India. Professor of English Literature. m. Shyamasree Devi, 31 Jan, 1955, Calcutta, 1 son, 1 daughter. *Education:* MA English Literature, Calcutta University, 1952. *Literary Appointments:* Professor of English 1952–67, currently Honorary Professor, St Xavier's College, Calcutta; Visiting Professor, Hofstra University, University of Illinois, Albion College, Ohio University, Berea College, Western Maryland College, 1962–82. *Publications:* Great Sanskrit Plays, 1964; The Bhagavad Gita, 1965; The Dhammapada, 1967; The Man of Dharma and the Rasa of Silence, 1974; The Collected Poems of P Lal, 1977; The Mahabharata of Vyasa, 1980; The Ramayana of Valmiki, 1981; A Premchand Dozen (with Nandini Nopany), 1983. *Contributions to:* The Atlantic Monthly; Poetry, Chicago; The Nation; Thought; Quest; Quadrant; The Illustrated Weekly of India; Visva-Bharati Quarterly; Journal of Indian Writing in English; The Miscellany; The Literary Criterion; and others. *Honours:* Jawaharlal Nehru Fellowship, 1969–70; Padma Shri,

Government of India, 1970; D Litt, Western Maryland College, 1977. *Membership:* Secretary, Writer's Workshop, Calcutta, 1958–. *Address:* 162/92 Lake Gardens, Calcutta 700 045, India.

LAM, Andrzej, b. 26 Dec. 1929, Grudziadz, Poland. Professor. m. 17 Sep. 1960, Donata. *Education:* PhD; Habilitation; Professor. *Literary Appointments:* Professor, Warsaw University, 1979–; Professor, Mainz University, 1982–83; Editor-in-Chief, Semi-monthly Wspolłczesnosc, 1962–66; Editor, Miesiecznik Literacki, 1966–; Editor-in-Chief, Rocznik Literacki, 1980–; *Publications:* Wyobraznia ujarzmiona (Guided Imagination), 1967; Polska awangarda poetycka (The Vanguard of Polish Poets), 1969; Pamietnik Krytyczny (Critical Diary) 1970; Z teorii i praktyki awangardyzmu (From Theory and Practice of the Vanguard), 1976; Mainzer Vorlesungen (Munchen), 1983; The Anthology of Polish Poetry since 1939, 1972; The Polish Poets 1918–1978 (An Anthology), 1980. *Honour:* The Cavalier Cross of Polonia Restituta Order, 1974. *Memberships:* Polish Writers Association; International Association of Literary Critics. *Address:* ul. Brandta 5, 01-472 Warsaw, Poland.

LAMAR, Howard Roberts, b. 18 Nov. 1923, Tuskegee, Alabama, USA. Professor of History; Academic Administrator. m. Doris Shirley White, 3 Sep. 1959, Amherst, Massachusetts, 2 daughters. *Education:* BA, 1944, Emory University; MA, 1945; PhD, 1951, Yale University; Doctor of Humane Letters, 1975, Emory University. *Literary Appointments:* Dean, Yale College, 1979–85. *Publications:* Dakota Territory, 1861–1889: A Study of Frontier Politics, 1956; The Far Southwest, 1846–1912, 1966; Reader's Encyclopedia of the American West, 1977; The Frontier in History: North America and Southern Africa Compared, 1981. *Contributions to:* Western Historical Quarterly; Reviewer for, American Historical Review; Journal of American History; History Book Club, Monthly Magazine. *Honours:* Eggleston Prize, Yale University, 1951; Southwestern Library Association, 1968. *Memberships:* President, American Historical Association, 1971–72; Organization of American Historican Historians: American Antiquarian Society; Western History Association; Elizabethan Club; Yale University. *Address:* Department of History, Yale University, New Haven, CT 06520, USA.

LAMAR, Quinton Curtis, b. 2 Apr. 1942, Mississippi, USA. Professor, History & Latin; Editor. m. Dana Ruth Townes, 22 Dec. 1963, McComb, Mississippi, 1 son, 2 daughters. *Education:* BA cum laude, European History, Millsaps College; MA, US Social & Cultural History, University of North Carolina; PhD, Latin History, Louisiana State University. *Literary Appointment:* Editor, Delta Scene, Delta State University, 1976–. *Publications include:* A History of Rosedale, Mississippi, 1876–1976, 1976. *Contributions to:* Hispanic American Historical Review; The Americas; Quarterly Review of Inter-American Cultural History; Phi Kappa Phi Journal; Journal of Bolivar County Historical Society; Mississippi Libraries; South Eastern Latin Americanist; Quarterly Review, South Eastern Council of Latin American Studies; 50 Plus Magazine; Delta Scene. *Honours:* College Public Relations Association of Mississippi Award, 1977–78, 1978–79; 1981–82, 1983–84. *Address:* Department of History, P O Box 3162, Delta State University, Cleveland, MS 38733, USA.

LAMB, Elizabeth Searle, b. 22 Jan. 1917, Topeka, Kansas, USA. Writer/Editor. m. F Bruce Lamb, 11 Dec. 1941, Port of Spain, Trinidad, 1 daughter. *Education:* BA, 1939, Bachelor of Music, 1940, University of Kansas. *Literary Appointment:* Editor, Frogpond, Haiku Quarterly, 1984–. *Publications:* Pelican Tree and Other Panama Adventures, co-author, 1953; Today and Every Day, 1970; Inside Me, Outside Me, 1974; In this Blaze of Sun, 1975; Picasso's, Bust of Sylvette, 1977; 39 Blossoms, 1982; Casting Into a Cloud: Southwest Haiku, 1985. *Contributions to:* Americas; Etude; Family Circle; Christian Science Monitor; East West Journal; Studia Mystica; Lookout; The Mennonite; Daily Word;

Purpose; Ideals; Augsburg Christmas Annual; The World of English (Belding), etc; Juvenile journals: Jack and Jill; The Children's Friend; Highlights for Children; Wee Wisdom. Poetry journals: Frogpond; Cicada; Haiku; Tweed; Outch; Poets On; Blue Unicorn; Modern Haiku; Bonsai. *Honours:* Ruth Mason Rice Awards, 1966, 1967, 1972, 1975 and 1977; Graham Peace Award 1965 and 1969; Ruben Dario Memorial Award (2nd place, from CAS) 1972; National League of American Pen Women Awards, 1964, 1968, 1976 and 1978; Henderson Awards, 1978 and 1981; Dellbrook Poetry Award, 1979; Yuki Taikai 1981; Mainichi Daily News (Tokyo) Award 1984 (Haiku). *Memberships:* Past president and vice-president, Haiku Society of America; Past Vice-President, New York Women Poets; National League of American Pen Women; Poetry Society of America; Rio Grande Writers Association. *Literary Agent:* Mrs Bertha Klausner, 71 Park Avenue, New York, NY 10016, USA. *Address:* 970 Acequia Madre, Santa Fe, NM 87501, USA.

LAMB, F(rank) Bruce, b. 27 July 1913, Cotopaxi, Colorado, USA. Forester; Writer. m. Elizabeth Searle, 11 Dec. 1941, Port of Spain, 1 daughter. *Education:* BS, 1940, MF, 1941, PhD, 1954, University of Michigan. *Appointment:* Editor, Caribbean Forester, 1958–60. *Publications:* Bosques de Guatemala, co-author, 1952; Mahogany of Tropical America, 1966; Wizard of the Upper Amazon, 1971; Rio Tigre and Beyond: Jungle Medicine of Manuel Cordova, 1985. *Contributor to:* Americas; Caribbean Forester; American Forests; Papers of Sixth World Forestry Congress, 1966; Journal of Forestry; Natural History; Economic Botany; Viva. *Honours:* Diploma of Honour, Ministry of Agriculture, Guatemala, 1955. *Membership:* Rio Grande Writers Association. *Literary Agent:* International Literary Agency, New York. *Address:* 970 Acequia Madre, Sante Fe, NM 87501, USA.

LAMBELET, Foula, b. 15 June 1925, Thessaloniki, Greece. Bacteriologist/Doctor of Medicine. m. Albert Paul Lambelet, 10 Sep. 1950, Zurich. *Education:* Graduated, Medical School, University of Thessaloniki; Medical Doctor, University of Zurich. *Publications:* Zitite prassini gata (Search for a Green Cat); I Defteri valiza (The Second Luggage); Zoni agnotitas (Chastity Belt); Planaria; Christofis (Christopher); Ispaniko pandochio (A Spanish Inn). *Contributions to:* Nea Poria; Tetramina; Tomes Smyrna; Diavazo; Ipirotiki Estia. *Memberships:* Literary Societies of Thessaloniki, Greece, Switzerland and Zurich. *Address:* Rebbergstrasse 49, 8102 Oberengstringen, Switzerland.

LAMBERT, David Wesley, b. 10 Nov. 1948, Fullerton, California, USA. Editor, 1 son, 3 daughters. *Education:* AB, Creative Writing, California State University, 1971; MFA, Fiction Writing, University of Montana, 1974. *Literary Appointments:* Managing Editor, Young Ambassador, Nebraska, 1982–85; Editor of Youth Books, Zondervan Publishing House, Grand Rapids, Michigan, 1985–. *Contributions include:* Poems, fiction, essays, articles in religious, outdoors, literary magazines, 1970–. *Address:* 2097 60th SE, Kentwood, MI 49508, USA.

LAMBERTON, Donald McLean, b. 29 July, 1927, Casino, New South Wales, Australia. University Professor. m. Clare Margaret McSullea, 20 Nov. 1965, Sydney, 1 son, 1 daughter. *Education:* BEc, University of Sydney, 1949; D Phil, Oxford University, England, 1963. *Publications:* The Theory of Profit, 1965; Science, Technology and the Australian Economy, 1970; Economics of Information and Knowledge (editor), 1971; The Information Revolution, (editor), 1974; Communication Economics and Development (joint editor), 1982; Economic Effects of the Australian Patent System (co-author), 1982; The Trouble With Technology (co-editor), 1983. *Contributions to:* Economic Journal; Economic Record; Journal of Business; Quarterly Journal of Economics; Technology and Culture; Australian Journal of Politics and History; International Social Science Journal; Media Information Australia; Search; The Information Society. *Honours:*

Australian Services Canteens Postgraduate Overseas Scholarship, 1957; Australian-American Educational Foundation Travel Grant, 1966; Rockefeller Foundation Bellagio Center Residency, 1985. *Memberships:* Chairman of Scientific Committee for Economics, Pacific Science Association; Royal Economic Society; Economic Society of Austrlia; American Economic Society. *Address:* 10 Clarina Sreet, Chapel Hill, Queensland 4069, Australia.

LAMBOT, Isobel Mary, b. 21 July 1926, Birmingham, England. Novelist. m. Marice Edouard Lambot, (dec), 19 Dec. 1959. Smethwick, England. *Education:* BA, Liverpool University, Teaching Certificate, Birmingham University. *Literary Appointments:* Tutor in Creative Writing, Lichfield Evening Institute, 1973–80. *Publications:* 16 detective stories, latest Rooney's Gold, 1984; 4 historical novels, latest Runaway Lady, 1980. *Contributor to:* Women's journals. *Memberships:* Crime Writers' Association: Society of Authors; Writers' Guild of Great Britain. *Literary Agent:* Mary Irvine. *Address:* Ty Twt, Montfort Fields, Kington, Herefordshire HR5 3AT, England.

LAMIRANDE, Emilien, b. 22 May 1926, St Georges De Windsor, Quebec, Canada. Professor. m. Claire Guillemette, 3 Apr. 1971, Ottawa. *Education:* MPh, LPh, LTh, University of O'Hara; STM, Union Theological Theology, New York; DTh, Leopold Franzens Universitat, Innsbruck. *Appointments:* Professor, Theology, University of Ottawa, 1954–65, Professor, Chairman, Religous Studies, 1971–; Professor, Theology, 1965–71, Dean, 1967–69, University of Saint Paul, Ottawa. *Publications:* Un siecle et demi d'etudes sur l'ecolesiologie de saint Augustin, 1962; L'Eglise celeste selon saint Augustin, 1963; Etudes sur l'ecclesiologie de saint Augustin, 1969; La situation ecclesiologique des Donatistes d'apres saint Augustin, 1972; Church, State and Toleration: An Intriguing Change of Mind in Augustine, 1975; Paulin de Milan et la 'vita Ambrosli,' 1983. *Contributor to:* Numerous professional journals. *Memberships:* Fellow, Royal Society of Canada; Canadian Society of Patristic Studies, Honorary President; Societe Canadienne de theologie, former Vice-President. *Address:* Dept of Religious Studies, University of Ottawa, Ottawa, Canada K1N 6N5.

LAMONT-BROWN, Raymond, b. 20 Sep. 1939, Horsforth, Yorkshire, England. Author/Broadcaster. m. (1) Jean Elizabeth Adamson (died 1979); (2) Dr Elizabeth Moira MacGregor, Sep. 1985. *Education:* MA; AMIET; FRGS; MJS; FSA(Scot); MRAS. *Literary Appointment:* Managing Editor, Writers' Monthly, 1984–. *Publications:* Most recently: Growing Up with the Highland Clans, 1978; Scottish Epitaphs, 1977, 1979; Lothian and Southeast Borders: Walks for Motorist, 1980, 1981; Phantoms of the Theatre, 1978; My Fun Book of Scotland, 1980; East Anglian Epitaphs, 1980; Victorian and Edwardian Fife from Old Photographs (with Peter Adamson), 1980; The Victorian and Edwardian Borderland from Rare Photographs (with Peter Adamson), 1981; Victorian and Edwardian Dundee and Broughty Ferry from Rare Photographs (with Peter Adamson), 1981; Mary, Queen of Scots, 1982; Mysteries and Legends, 1982; Fife: Portrait of a Country from Rare Photographs, 1910–1950 (with Peter Adamson), 1982; Drives around Edinburgh, 1983; Drives around Glasgow, 1983; Mothers-in-law, 1983; A Visitor's Guide to St Andrews, 1984; A Book of British Eccentrics, 1984; St Andrews: City of Change (with Peter Adamson), 1984. *Contributor to:* Over 250 magazines and newspapers. *Membership:* Society of Authors in Scotland, Secretary 1983–. *Address:* Crawford House, 132 North Street, St Andrews, Fife KY16 9AF, Scotland.

LAMOTTE, Angela (Alice-Clemence), b. 6 June 1908, Ghent, Belgium. Writer. *Education:* Studies of Humanities. *Publications:* L'estrange destin de Fumu Za: roman pour la jeunesse, 1964; Les Contes de Ma Barza, 1965; Sous les Jacarandas, 1967; De Roses et d'Epines, 1972; La Grande Aventure, 1974; Medaillons,

1977; Un peu d'eeame au oreuf de la main, poems, 1982. *Contributions to:* Presence; Altair. *Honours include:* Silver Medal, Academy of Lutece, Paris, 1978; Golden Medal, Academy of Lutece, Paris, 1980. *Memberships include:* Poets, Playwrights, Editors, Essayists and Novelists Club International; Association of Belgian Writers; Writers Action Group. *Address:* 324 Avenue Brugmann, Boite 30, 1180 Brussels, Belgium.

LANCASTER-BROWN, Peter, b. 13 Apr. 1927, Leeds, England. m. Johanne Nyreröd, 17 Aug. 1953, Tönsberg, Norway, 1 son (deceased). *Education:* BSc. *Publications:* Twelve Came Back, 1957; Call Of The Outback, 1970; What Star Is That?, 1971; Coast of Coral and Pearl, 1972; Astronomy in Colour, 1972; The Seas and Oceans in Colour, 1973; Comets, Meteorites and Men, 1973; Star and Planet Spotting, 1974; Planet Earth in Colour, 1976; Megaliths, Myths and Men, 1976; Megaliths and Masterminds, 1979; Fjord of Silent Men, 1983; Astronomy, 1984; Halley and His Comet, 1985; The Story of Halley's Comet, 1985; The Comet Man: Memoirs of Edmond Halley, 1986. *Contributions to:* Numerous magazines and journals. *Address:* 10A St Peter's Road, Aldeburgh, Suffolk, England.

LANCE, Jeanne Louise, b. 21 May 1945, New Jersey, USA. Poet. m. Peter John Holland, 18 Nov. 1975, Oakland, California. *Education:* AB, Bryn Mawr College, 1967; MA, University of Toronto, 1971. *Publications:* Mass Psychosis, prose, 1983; Water Burial, prose, 1985. *Contributions to:* Ear Magazine; Telephone; Laurel Review. *Honour:* Fellow, Squaw Valley Community of Writers, 1974. *Membership:* Poets and Writers Incorporated, New York City. *Address:* 25 Carlin Street, Norwalk, CT 06851, USA.

LANCZKOWSKI, Cl, b. 24 Jan. 1958, Wabern, Federal Republic of Germany. Author. *Education:* Studium der Theologie und der Klassischen Philologie. *Literary Appointments:* Verbandslektor des FDA, 1985. *Publications:* Denkturm, 1982/1983 Eliade: Geschichte der rel. Ideen; Frankfurt 2000 – Paradise Regained, 1984. *Contributions to:* Rhein-Neckar-. Zeitung; HLS; Vis-a-Vis; Co-editor; Tabula Rasa, Philodendron, NAOS; Fränkische Nachrichten; Aargauer Anzeiger; VlaB; Katalog der Mainzer Mini-Pressen Messe; Bayernkurier; Auto Motor und Sport, and others. *Honours:* Scheffel Preis, 1978; Filmpreis der Stadt Frankfurt am Main, 1983. *Membership:* Freier Deutscher Autorenverband, FDA. *Address:* Liebermannstrasse 45, D–6900 Heidelberg 1, Federal Republic of Germany.

LANDAU, Edwin Maria, b. 20 Sep. 1904, Coblenz, Rhine. Private Scholar. m. Heidi Schneebeli, 6 July 1946, Zurich, 2 sons. *Education:* PhD. *Appointments:* Secretary, to Director of Deutsche Verlagsanstalt, Stuttgart; Founder, Director, Verlag Die Runde, Berlin; Director, Collected Works of Paul Claudel, in German Translation; Director, Collected Works of Reinhold Schneider, Insel Verlag. *Publications:* Claudel in Friedrichs Dramatiker des Welttheaters; Paul Claudel on German Speaking Theatres; Translations of Malègue, Claudel, Mallarmé, Supervielle, Cocteau, Belloc, Hersey, Voltaire, Corneille, Racine, Moliere. *Contributor to:* Claudel Studies, USA; Dokumente (Cologne); Bulletin de la Societe Paul Claudel; Bonner Generalanzeiger; Wiesbadener Kurier; Deutsche Tagespost Wurzburg. *Honours:* Officer, Order of Arts and Letters, France, 1979; Translation Prize, German Academy for Language & Literature, Darmstadt, 1977; Cultural Prize, Coblenz, 1983. *Memberships:* Society Paul Claudel, Paris, Belgium & USA; President, Swiss Association of Friends of Paul Claudel; President, Reinhold Schneider Society, Freiburg i.Br.; PEN for German Writers Abroad; Association of Foreign Press Members in Switzerland. *Address:* Beustweg 7, CH 8032, Zurich, Switzerland.

LANDER, Ernest McPherson, Jr, b. 16 Dec. 1915, Calhoun Falls, South Carolina, USA. Professor. m. Sarah Ray Shirley, 1 Sep. 1947, Clemson, South Carolina, 2 daughters. *Education:* AB, Wofford College, 1937; MA, 1939, PhD, 1950, University of North Carolina, Chapel Hill. *Literary Appointments:* Alumni Professor of History, Clemson University, 1975–. *Major Publications:* History of South Carolina, 1865–1960, 1960; A Rebel Came Home: Civil War Diary of Floride Clemson (co-editor), 1961; South Carolina: The Palmetto State, 1969; The Textile Industry in Antebellum, South Carolina, 1970; Reluctant Imperialists: Calhoun, The South Carolinians and the Mexican War, 1980; The Calhoun Family and Thomas Green Clemson: Decline of a Southern Patriarchy, 1983. *Contributor to:* Journal of American History; Mississippi Valley Historical Review; Journal of Southern History; North Carolina Historical Review; South Carolina Historical Magazine; and others. *Honours:* Phi Beta Kappa, 1961. *Memberships:* South Carolina Historical Association (President, 1960); Southern Historical Association (Board of Editors, Executive Council); South Carolina Historical Society. *Address:* 217 Riggs Drive, Clemson, SC 29631, USA.

LANDER, Harold, b. 17 Aug. 1923, Chester-le-Street, County Durham, England. Writer; Story Editor. m. Lorna Morwood, 31 Mar. 1964, Lincoln, 3 daughters. *Appointments:* Head, Writing, 1974–78, 1985–. Australian Film & Television School. *Publicaitons:* TV Adaptations, Hal Porter's Stage Play, Eden House, 1970, D'Arcy Niland's Novel, Dead Men Running, 1970; TV Film , Flashpoint, 1971; Documentary Film, What is Psychology?, 1974; Radio Play, Down the Snakes, 1978. *Contributor to:* The Observer; The Australian; The Sydney Morning Herald; The Australian Author; National Review; New Theatre Magazine. *Honours:* Australian Writers Guild, Awgie Awards, 1974, 1978. *Memberships:* Australian Writers Guild; Australian Society of Authors. *Address:* 13 Borambil Place, Longueville, NSW 2066, Australia.

LANDERT, Walter, b. 3 Jan. 1929, Zurich, Switzerland. Merchant. *Education:* Higher School of Commerce, Neuchatel; Merchant apprentice w. dip; Dip, Swiss Mercantile School, London; Student Trainee, Westminster Bank, London. *Publications:* Manager auf Zeit (novel), 1968; Selbstbefragung (poems), 1969; Entwurf Schweiz (literary essay), 1970; Koitzsch (novel), 1971; Traum einer besseren Welt (short stories and poems), 1980; UnKraut inhelvetischen Kulturgartchen (literary essay), 1981; Meine Frau baut einen Bahnhof (short stories), 1981; Klemms Memorabilien–ein Vorspiel (novel), 1986; s Huus us Pilatusholz (monodrama), first performance, 1985. *Contributor of* short stories to various newspapers. *Honours:* Artemis Jubilee Prize, 1969; Poetry Prize, Literary Union, Saabrucken, 1977. *Memberships:* Swiss Authors; Olten Group. *Address:* Lendikonerstrasse 54, CH–8484 Weisslingen/ZH, Switzerland.

LANDGRAF, Wolfgang, b. 5 Dec. 1948, Langenchursdorf, Germany. Author. m. 13 June 1973, 1 son. *Education:* Scientist of Literature. *Publications:* Like Birds in a Cage: A Legend from the Children's Crusade, 1977; Martin Luther, Reformer and Rebel (biography), 1981; The Sign of Glory, 1984: Saw the Dawn: Life and Death of Emperor Henry IV; Stories, Features and Scenarios. *Contributor:* Dragonships on the Rhein and contributions to Children's and Youth's Literature. *Membership:* Writers League of GDR. *Address:* Greifenhagener Str. 39, 1071 Berlin, Democratic Republic of Germany.

LANDMAN, David, b. 24 Oct. 1917, Philadelphia, Pennsylvania, USA. Editor; Writer. m. (1) Joan Klein, 1 Sep. 1946, (dec.) (2) Hedy Macklin, 30 Dec. 1964, New York, 1 son, 1 daughter. *Education:* AB, Magna cum laude, Brown University, 1939; AM, Columbia University, 1963. *Literary Appointments:* Associate Editor 1939–40, Secretary & Chief Executive 1950–60, Universal Jewish Encyclopedia; Director of Information, Harvard Business School, Boston, 1969–73; Editor, Special Projects &, Medical Center Alumni News, University of Illinois, 1979–83; Director, Conference Publications Associates, 1983–. *Publications include:* Look at America: Central Northeast, 1948; Where to Ski, with Joan Landman, 1949; America Faces the Nuclear Age, co-editor, 1961; Population: Theory & Policy, co-editor, 1982; Occupational Therapy Over Forty Years, editor, in press. *Contributions to:* New Republic; Nation's Business; Collier's Redbook; Cosmopolitan; Coronet; Pageant; True; Argosy; etc. Also: Techniques, Journal of American College Public Relations Association; Prose by Professionals, 1961. *Honours:* Bronze Star, US Army, 1945; Fellowship to Indonesia, Ford Foundation, 1955–56. *Membership:* Midwest Chairman 1983–84, American Society of Journalists & Authors. *Address:* 40 East Cedar, Suite 20-C, Chicago, IL 60611, USA.

LANE, Frank Walter, B. 15 Aug. 1908, London, England. m. Barbara Katherine Mace, 27 Sep. 1952, at Horsham, Sussex, England, 1 son, 2 daughters. *Publications:* Nature Parade; 1939; The Elements Rage, 1945; Animal Wonderland, 1948; Kingdom of the Octopus, 1957; An Eye For A Bird, (with Éric Hosking), 1970; Zoo Animals, 1977; The Violent Earth, 1986. *Contributions to:* Various magazines and journals in Europe and USA. *Memberships:* Vice President, Society of Civil Service Authors; Life Fellow, Zoological Society of London. *Address:* 17 Azalea Walk, Pinner, Middlesex HA5 2EJ, England.

LANE, M Travis (Millicent Elizabeth Travis), b. 23 Sep. 1934, USA. Writer. m. Lauriat Lane Jr, 26 Aug. 1957, 1 son, 1 daughter. *Education:* MA, PhD, Cornell University, USA. *Literary Appointments:* Assistantships at Cornell University and University of New Brunswick; Honorary Research Associate, Unviersity of New Brunswick. *Publications:* Five Poets: Cornell, 1960; An Inch Or So Of Garden, 1969; Poems 1968–72, 1973; Homecomings, 1977; Divinations and Shorter Poems, 1973–78, 1980. *Contributions to:* Canadian Literature; Dalhousie Review; Ariel; Essays on Canadian Writing; University of Toronto Quarterly, Fiddlehead Magazine, Contemporary Canadian Verse and Alternatives to Narrative (poems, reviews and essays on Canadian and Commonwealth writers). *Honour:* Pat Lowther Prize from League of Canadian Poets, 1980. *Address:* 807 Windsor Street, Fredericton, New Brunswick, Canada E3B 4G7.

LANE, Richard, b. 9 Feb. 1926, Florida, USA. Research Scholar. *Education:* BA, University of Hawaii, 1948; MA, 1949, PhD, 1958, Columbia University; Graduate, Universites of Tokyo, Japan and Kyoto, London, England; Tokyo National Museum. *Publications include:* Saikaku: Novelist of the Japanese Renaissance, 1957; Six Masterpieces of the Ukiyo-e, 1958; Masters of the Japanese Print: Their World and Their Work, 1962; Shunga Books of the Ukiyo-e School: Moronobu, Series, 1, 1973 to Series V, 1979; Images from the Floating World, 1978; The Erotic Theme in Japanese Painting and Prints, 1979; Hiroshige's Kameara, 1985; The Provinces of Japan, 1986; Hokusai, 1986; Studies in Edo Literature, 1986. *Contributions to:* Contributor and translator of several books and stories. Contributor to: Inside Japan; Journal of Royal Asiatic Society; Atlantic; Monuments Nipponica; Japan Quarterly; Ukiyo-e and others. *Honours:* Recipient of several academic awards. *Address:* Yamashina Koyama, Gobo-No-Uchi 57, Kyoto, Japan 607.

LANE, Ronald James, b. 11 Aug. 1931, Horsham, Victoria, Australia. Education. m. Jean Deborah King, 2 Jan. 1954, Geelong, 2 daughters. *Education:* BA, BEd, Melbourne; MEd, Canberra College of Advanced Education. *Publications:* Beginning Precis Writing, 1962; Language and Ideas, Book 1 1963, Book 2, 1964, Book 3, 1965; Language and Opinions, 1967. *Contributor to:* various professional journals. *Address:* Dickson College, Phillip Avenue, Dickson, Canberra, Australia.

LANG, Fredrik Vilhelm, b. 9 Mar. 1947, Narpes, Finland. Writer. m. Sunniva Elisabeth Drake, 29 June 1975, 2 sons. *Education:* MA (Abo Akademi), 1976; Licentiate of Philosophy, Helsinki University, 1983. *Publications:* Ockupationen (The Occupation), 1978; Nar Thales Myntade Uttryck (As Thales Coined Expressions), 1982; Sabotaget (The Sabotage), 1983; Sommaren Med Sue (Summer With Sue), 1984. *Honour:* Government Literature Prize, 1985. *Address:* Rulludden, SF–02260 Esbo, Finland.

LANG-DILLENBURGER, Elmy, b. 13 Aug. 1921, Pirmasens, Federal Republic of Germany. Writer. *Education:* Interpreter's Diploma. *Publications:* (Poetry) Mitternachtsspritzer, 1970; Das Wort, 1980; (Novels) Fruhstuck auf franzosisch, 1971; Der Rabenwald, 1985; (Radio Plays) Die Verfolgung, 1974; Dani und Heseki reisen zur Erde, 1975; Der Flacon, 1981; Spate Gaste am Heiligen Abend, 1982; (Play) Der Fall Chardon; (English-German Poetry) Pingpong Penguin, 1978, 1980; (Story) Die Bodenguckkinder, 1977; (Short Stories & Poetry) Blick ins Paradies, 1980; (Limericks), 1984. *Contributor to:* Book Anthologies: Neue Texte Rhld-Pfalz Jg, 1975, 1976, 1977; Local Authors Present Themselves, Berlin at the Hour Zero, 1980; numerous articles and short stories in professional journals and magazines. *Honours:* Accademia Italia, Universita delle Arti, Diploma di Merito, Salsomaggiore; Final Prize, 20th Grand Prix International de Peinture de la Cote d'Azur. *Memberships:* Union of German Writers; Europaische Autorenvereiningung Die Kogge; Literarischer Verein der Pfalz; Carl Zuckmayer Association. *Address:* Postbox 2120, 6780 Pirmasens, Federal Republic of Germany.

LANGDON, Robert Adrian, b. 3 Sep. 1924, Adelaide, Australia. Historian. *Education:* Adelaide Technical High School. *Major Publications:* Tahiti: Island of Love, 5th edition, 1979; The Lost Caravel, 1975; The Language of Easter Island, (with D Tryon), 1983. *Contributor to:* Pacific Islands Monthly; Pacific Islands Yearbook; Journal of Pacific History; World Book Yearbook. *Honours:* Research Fellow, Research School of Pacific Studies, Australian National University, Canberra, 1977–79; Caballero de la Orden de Isabela la Católica, Spain, 1980. *Memberships:* Société des Etudes Océaniennes, Tahiti; Polynesian Society, Auckland, New Zeland; Hakluyt Society, London, England; Société des Océanistes, Paris, France. *Address:* 15 Darambal Street, Aranda, ACT 2614, Australia.

LANGE, Victor, b. 13 July 1908, Leipzig, Germany. Professor. m. Frances Olrich Lange, 23 Feb. 1945, 1 son, 1 daughter. *Education:* MA, Toronto; PhD, Leipzig. *Literary Appointments:* Lecturer in German, University of Toronto; Professor of German Literature, Cornell University; Professor of German and Comparative Literature, Princeton University. *Publications:* Die Lyrik und ihr Publikum; Modern German Literature; Contemporary German Literature; New Perspectives in German Literary Criticism; The Classical Age of German Literature. *Contributions to:* Saturday Review of Literature; Yale Review; Atlantic Monthly; PMLA; Die Zeit; Comparative Literature. *Honours:* Goethe Medal in Gold; Gundolf – Prize of German Academy; Commander's Cross, German Federal Republic; Chancellor's Citation, University of California. *Memberships:* President: American Society for 18th Century Studies; International Association of Germanists; Goethe Society of North America; Friends of Wolfenbuebel Library. *Address:* 343 Jefferson Road, Princeton, NY 08540, USA.

LANGER, Rudolf, b. 6 Nov. 1923, Neisse, Germany. Writer. m. 31 Oct. 1942, Breslau/Silesia, 3 sons, 2 daughters. *Publications:* First publication of, Die Muhle, newspaper, 1945; Ortswechsel, 1973; Uberholvorgang, poetry, 1976; Gleich morgen, 1978; Wounded No Doubt, 1979. *Honours:* Arts Prize, City of Ingolstadt, 1975; Andreas Gryphius Prize, 1977; Neisse Cultural Prize, 1984. *Memberships:* Reading for, Gruppe 47, in Jugenheim 1948; Kogge; Esslingen Artists Guild; Eichendorff Society. *Address:* Heppstr 1, 8070 Ingolstadt, Federal Republic of Germany.

LANGEVIN, Michael Peter, b. 30 Dec. 1952, Lawrence, Massachusetts, USA. Publisher. *Education:* Associate degree, Northern Essex College; Bachelors degree, University of Massachusetts; Masters degree,

University of California at Berkeley. *Literary Appointments:* Editor, Open Door, 1975; Editor, Parnassus, 1976; Editor, Critical Review, 1977; Publisher, Poor Farm Stories, 1978–81; Publisher, Shoot in the Dark literary review, 1980; Publisher/Managing Editor, Magical Blend magazine, 1982–85. *Publications:* The Porcelain Underground, 1984; Living Magically at the End of the 20th Century, 1985. *Contributions to:* Magical Blend; Poor Farm Stories; Shoot in the Dark. *Literary Agent:* Michael Epstein and Company, 3005 20th Street, San Francisco, CA 94110, USA. *Address:* PO Box 11303, San Francisco, CA 94101, USA.

LANGFORD, David, b. 10 Apr. 1953, Newport, Gwent, South Wales. Weapons Physicist, Author, Editor, Consultant. m. Hazel Langford, 12 June 1976. *Education:* BA Honours Physics 1974, MA 1978, Brasenose College, Oxford. *Literary Appointments:* Contributing editor, White Dwarf magazine, 1983–; General Editor, Starlight SF News pages, Prestel; editor, Ansible. *Publications Include:* War on 2080: The Future of Military Technology, non fiction, 1979; An Account of a Meeting with Denizens of Another World, 1871, 1979; The Leaky Establishment, 1984; Accretion in Andromeda 2, 1977; The Final Days short story in Destinies 3:1, 1981; Cube Root short story in Interzone 11, 1985. *Contributions to:* Numerous books, anthologies and magazines including: University Desk Encyclopaedia, 1977; Ad Astra magazine; What Micro? magazine; New Scientist; SF Chronicle. *Honours include:* Winner with Nicholls and Stableford of Special European SF Award, 1984; Winner of SF Achievement (Hugo) Award, 1985. *Memberships:* Council member, British SF Association; Society of Authors; SF Foundation UK. *Literary Agent:* Hilary Rubinstein of A P Watt Ltd, 26/28 Bedford Road, London WC1R 4HL, England. *Address:* 94 London Road, Reading, Berkshire RG1 5AU, England.

LANGFORD, Gerald, b. 20 Oct. 1911, Montgomery, Alabama, USA. Professor of English. m. Anne Crenshaw Phelps, 17 Dec. 1938, Cloverport, Kentucky, 2 daughters. *Education:* BA 1933, MA 1934, PhD 1940, University of Virginia. *Literary Appointments:* Associate Professor of English, Winthrop College, 1940–43; Assistant Professor of English 1946–50, Associate Professor 1950–62, Professor 1962–83, Professor Emeritus 1983–, University of Texas at Austin. *Publications:* Alias O Henry, A Biography of William Sidney Porter, 1957; The Richard Harding Davis Years, 1961; The Murder of Stanford White, 1962; Ingenue Among The Lions, editor, 1965; Faulkner's Revision of, Absalom, Absalom!, editor, 1971; Faulkner's Revision of, Sanctuary, editor, 1972; Destination, novel, 1981. *Membership:* Texas Institute of Letters. *Address:* English Department, University of Texas at Austin, Austin, TX 78712, USA.

LANGLAND, Elizabeth Jean, b. 11 Aug. 1948, Iowa City, Iowa, USA. Associate Professor of English. m. Jerald D Jahn, 20 May 1978, 1 son, 1 daughter. *Education:* BA, Summa cum laude, Barnard College, 1970; MA, Honours, 1971, PhD, Honours, 1975, University of Chicago. *Appointments:* Assistant Professor, English, Vanderbilt University, 1975–82; Associate Professor/Chair, English Department, Converse College, 1982–85; Associate Professor, English, University of Florida, 1985–. *Publications:* A Feminist Perspective in the Academy, co-editor, 1983; The Voyage In: Fictions of Female Development, co-editor, 1983; Society in the Novel, 1984. *Contributions to:* Women's Studies International Forum, 1983; Critical Inquiry, 1982. *Honours:* Phi Beta Kappa, 1970; Woodrow Wilson Fellowship, 1970; Ford Foundation Fellowship, 1970–74; NEH Summer Seminar Award, University of California, Berkeley, 1983. *Memberships:* Modern Language Association; South Atlantic Modern Language Association; National Womens Studies Association; National Council of Teachers of English. *Address:* Department of English, University of Florida, Gainesville, FL 32601, USA.

LANGSLET, Lars Roar, b. 5 Mar. 1936, Nesbyen, Norway. Minister of Cultural and Scientific Affairs, Norway; Assistant Professor. *Education:* MA, 1962. *Publications:* Heritage & Perspective, 1962; Young Karl Marx & the Alienation of Man, 1963; Conservatism, 1965; The Church in Dialogue, 1968; Unity & Diversity, 1969; Seen from the Side Line, 1974; Freedom & Order, 1974; etc. *Memberships:* Norwegian Authors Union; Norwegian Academy for Language & Literature, Secretary, 1973–. *Address:* Stortinget, Oslo 1, Norway.

LANGTON, Jane, b.30 Dec. 1922, Boston, Massachusetts, USA. Writer. m. William Langton, 10 June 1943, 3 sons. *Education:* Wellesley College, 1940–42; BS Astronomy 1944, MA History of Art 1945, University of Michigan; MA History of Art, Radcliffe College, 1948. *Publications:* The Diamond in the Window, children's book, 1962; The Transcendental Murder, 1964; Dark Nantucket Noon, 1975; The Memorial Hall Murder, 1978; The Fledgling, children's book, 1980; Natural Enemy, 1982; Emily Dickinson is Dead, 1984; The Fragile Flag, children's book, 1984. *Honours:* Nominee in children's book category, Edgar Allen Poe Award, Mystery Writers of America, 1963; Newbery Honor Book – The Fledgling, 1981; Nero Wolfe Award 1984, Edgar nomination 1985 for, Emily Dickinson is Dead. *Memberships:* Authors Guild; Mystery Writers of America. *Literary Agent:* McIntosh and Otis, 475 Fifth Avenue, New York, NY 10017, USA. *Address:* 9 Baker Farm Road, Lincoln, MA 01773, USA.

LANGWORTH, Richard Michael, b. 7 July 1941, Rye, New York, USA. Writer; Publisher. m. Barbara Dunbar Francis, 5 Feb. 1966, Staten Island, New York, 1 son. *Education:* BA, History, Wagner College, 1963. *Publications:* Publisher: The Packard Cormorant, magazine, Packard Club, 1975–; The Hot One: Chevrolet 1955–57, Pat Chappell, 1977; Finest Hour, magazine, International Churchill Society, 1981–; The Studebaker Century, Asa Hall & Richard Langworth, 1982; Chevy U-8s, Terry Boyle 1986. Author. Books include: Consumer Guide Classic Car Series, 1977–; Personal Luxury: The Thunderbird Story, 1980; Books on Packard, Studebaker, Triumph, Hudson, Chrysler, Oldsmobile; Encyclopedia of American Cars 1940–70, 1980; Complete Book of Collectable Cars 1940–80, with Graham Robson, 1982. *Contributions to:* American Way; Car Collector; National Review; Special Interest Autos. Associate Editor, 1970–74; Host, vintage car tours, UK, 1977–86; Churchill's England, 1983, 1985. *Honours:* McKean Award, Antique Auto Club of America, 1975; Cugnot Award, Society of Automotive Historians, 1975, 1979. *Memberships:* Guild of Motoring Writers; Board Chairman, International Churchill Society, 1982–86. *UK Representative:* Graham Robson, Girt House, Dorset, England. *Address:* Dragonwyck Publishing Inc, Burrage Road, Contoocook, NH 03229, USA.

LANHAM, Richard A, b. 26 Apr. 1936, Washington DC, USA. Professor of English. m. Carol Dana, 7 Sep. 1957. *Education:* BA, 1956, MA 1960, PhD, 1963, Yale University. *Appointments:* Instructor, 1962–64, Assistant Professor, 1964–65, English, Dartmouth College; Assistant Professor, 1965–69, Associate Professor, 1969–72, Professor, 1972–, English, Vice Chairman, Composition, English Dept, 1980–, University of California, Los Angeles. *Publications:* Sydney's Old Arcadia, 1965; A Handlist of Rhetorical Terms, 1968; Tristram Shandy: The Games of Pleasure, 1973; Style: An Anti-textbook, 1974; The Motives of Eloquence: Literary Rhetoric in the Renaissance, 1983; Revising Business Prose, 1981; Analyzing Prose, 1983; Literacy and the Survivor of Humanism, 1983. *Contributor to:* Victorian Newsletter; English Record; Pacific Coast Philology; English STudies; Studies in Short Fiction; Modern Language Quarterly; Southern Review; Experiment and Innovation; English Literary Renaissance; Virginia Quarterly Review; Bulletin; many other professional journals. *Honours:* Summer Research Fellowship, University of California Institute for the Humanities, 1966; Sabbatical Supplementation Grant, University of California Institute for the Humanities,

1967, 1972, 1980; Senior Fellowship, National Endowment for the Humanities, 1973–74. *Memberships:* Executive Committee, Section for Renaissance Literature excluding Shakespeare, Modern Language Association of America. *Address:* 371 Kinsey Hall, University of California, Los Angeles, CA 90024, USA.

LANOUETTE, William J, b. 14 Sep. 1940, New Haven, Connecticut, USA. Writer; Editor. m. Joanne M Sheldon, 12 Apr. 1969, St Paul, Minnesota, 2 daughters. *Education:* BA, Fordham College, New York City, New York, 1963; MSc 1966, PHD 1973, London School of Economics. *Literary Appointments:* Researcher, Reporter, Newsweek, 1961–64; Staff Writer, The National Observer, 1969–70, 72-77; Staff Correspondent, 1977–82, Contributing Editor, 1982–83, National Journal, Washington; Communications Director, 1983–85, Senior Associate 1985, World Resources Institute, Washington. Currently. Working on biography of Leo Szilard. *Contributions to:* Arms Control Today; The Atlantic Monthly; The Bulletin of the Atomic Scientists; Commonweal; The Economist; Environment; The Far Eastern Economic Review; New York; Parliamentary Affairs; The Wilson Quarterly. *Honours:* Forum Award, for significant print media contributions to public understanding of atomic energy, 1974. *Memberships:* Washington Independent Writers. *Literary Agent:* F Joseph Spieler, New York. *Address:* 326 Fifth Street South East, Washington, DC 20003, USA.

LANSBURGH, Werner, b. 29 June 1912, Berlin, Germany. Writer. m. Elisabeth Almquist, 12 Aug. 1944, Uppsala, Sweden, 1 son, 1 daughter. *Education:* LLD, University of Basel, Switzerland. *Publications:* Blod och Bläck, in Swedish, 1944; Dear Doosie, Eine Liebesgeschichte in Briefen, 1977; Wiedersehen mit Doosie, 1980; Strandgut Europa, 1982, translated as Driftwood, 1985. *Contributions to:* Various leading German magazines. *Honour:* Alexander Zinn Prize, City of Hamburg. *Memberships:* PEN Centre of German-Speaking Writers Abroad, London. *Address:* Colonnaden 25, D–2 Hamburg 36, Federal Republic of Germany.

LANSBURY, Angela, b. 16 Mar. 1946, London, England. Freelance Journalist. m. Trevor Sharot, 11 Apr. 1977, 1 son. *Education:* BA, Honours, University College, London; Teacher of English, Institute of Education; Trained Journalist, National Union of Journalists. *Literary Appointments include:* Personal Assistance, Copywriter, Sub-Editor; Freelance Journalist; Travel Writer; Photographer. *Publications:* Enquire Within Upon Travel and Holidays, 1976; See Britain at Work, 1977; The A to Z of Shopping by Post, 1978; Etequette for Every Occasion, 1985. *Contributions to:* Numerous magazines including: Parents; Under-5; Brides; Wedding and Home; American in Britain; Resident Abroad, TV and radio broadcasting. *Membership:* Institute of Journalists. *Address:* 6 Hillview Road, Hatch End, Pinner, Middx, HA5 4PA, England.

LANT, Jeffrey Ladd, b. 16 Feb. 1947, Maywood, Illinois, USA. *Education:* BA, University of California, Santa Barbara, 1969; Certificate, Advanced Graduate Studies, Higher Education Administration, Northeastern University, 1975; MA, 1970, PhD, 1975, Harvard University. *Publications:* Insubstantial Pageant: Ceremony and Confusion at Queen Victoria's Court, 1979; Development Today: A Guide for Nonprofit Organizations, 1980, 2nd edition 1983; The Consultant's Kit: Establishing and Operating Your Successful Business, 1981, 2nd edition, 1984; Editor: Our Harvard: Reflections on College Life by Twentytwo Distinguished Graduates, 1982; The Unabashed Self-Promoter's Guide: What Every Man, Woman, Child and Organization in America Needs to Know about Getting Ahead by Exploiting the Media, 1983; Money Talks: The Complete Guide to Creating a Profitable Workshop or Seminar on any Field, 1985. *Contributor to:* Over 400 articles in professional journals. *Address:* 50 Follen St, Suite 507, Cambridge, MA 02138, USA.

LANTZ, Frances Lin, b. 27 Aug. 1952, Trenton, New Jersey, USA. Writer of novels for young adults. m. John M Landsberg, 30 Apr. 1984, Brookline, Massachusetts. *Education:* BA Music, Dickinson College, Carlisle, Pennsylvania; MLS, Simmons College, Boston, Massachusetts. *Publications:* Good Rockin' Tonight, 1982; 4 caprice romances for Berkley Books, 1983–85; Can't Stop Us Now; Making It On Our Own, 1986; Woodstock Magic, 1986. *Contributions to:* Book reviewer, Paperback Book Guide; Former record reviewer, Rockingchair. *Membership:* PEN. *Literary Agent:* Merrilee Heifetz, Writer's House, New York. *Address:* c/o Writers House, 21 West 26th Street, New York, NY 10010, USA.

LAPIDUS, Jacqueline, b. 6 Sep. 1941, New York City, USA. Poet, Editor. *Education:* BA, Swarthmore College, Pennsylvania, 1962. Ready to Survive, 1975; Starting Over, 1977; (with Tee Corinne), Yantras of Womanlove, 1982; Ultimate Conspiracy, 1985. *Contributor to:* Amazon Quarterly; Calyx; Conditions; Sinister Wisdom (magazines), Amazon Poetry; I Hear My Sisters Saying; Lesbian Poetry; The Lesbian Reader; New Lesbian Writing (anthologies), and others. *Address:* PO Box 963, Provincetown, MA 02657, USA.

LAPONCE, Jean A, b. 4 Nov. 1925, Decize, France, Professor. m. (2) Iza Fiszhaut, 4 Oct. 1972, 2 sons, 2 daughters. *Educatons:* Diploma, Institut d'Etudes Politiques, France, 1947; PhD, University of California, Los Angeles, USA, 1966. *Publications:* Protection of Minorities, 1961; Government of France under the Fifth Republic, 1970; Left and Right, 1981, Langue et Territoire, 1984. *Contributions to:* Western Political Quarterly; Canadian Journal of Political Science; Political Studies; Revue Francaise de science politique; American Political Science Review; Comparative Political Studies; Comparitive Politics; British Journal of Political Science Review; Politics and the Life Sciences; Journal of Commonwealth and Comparative Politics. *Honours:* Harry Guggenheim Fellow, 1973–74; Fellow, Royal Society of Canada, *Address:* Department of Political Science, University of British Columbia, C472 – 1866 Main Mall Vancouver, British Columbia, Canada V6T 1W5.

LAPP, Rudolph Mathew, b. 19 Aug. 1915, Chicago, Illinois, USA. Professor of History. m. Patricia Teeling, 23 Jan. 1943. *Education:* BA, Roosevelt University, Chicago; MA, PhD, University of California, Berkeley. *Publications:* Archy Lee: A California Fugitive Slave Case, 1969; Blacks in Gold Rush California, 1977; Afro-Americans in California, revised edition, 1985. *Contributions to:* Journal of Negro History; California Historical Society Quarterly. *Honours:* American Philosophical Society Grant, 1966; Fellowship, National Endowment for the Humanities, 1972–73. *Address:* College of San Mateo, 1700 Hillsdale Boulevard, San Mateo, CA 94402, USA.

LAQUEUR, Walter, b. 26 May 1921, Breslau, Germany. History Teacher, Author. m. Barbara Koch, 29 May 1941, 2 daughters. *Education:* Graduate, Johannesgymnasium, Breslau, 1938; Student, Hebrew University, Jerusalem, 1938–39. *Literary Appointments:* Newspaper Correspondent, Free-lance author, 1944–55; Founder, editor, Survey, London, England 1955–67, Washington Papers 1972–; Co-editor, founder, Journal of Contemporary History, 1966–; Founder, Co-editor, Washington Quarterly of Strategic and International Studies, 1977–. *Publications include:* Communism and Nationalism in the Middle East, 1956; The Soviet Union and the Middle East, 1959; Young Germany, 1962; Russia and Germany, 1966; The Fate of the Revolution, 1967; The Road to War, 1967; Road to Jerusalem, 1969; The Struggle for the Middle East, 1969; Europe since Hitler, 1970; Out of the Ruins of Europe, 1971; A History of Zionism, 1972; Confrontation: The Middle East and World Politics, 1974; Weimar, 1975; Geurrilla, 1976; Terrorism, 1977; A Continent Astray, 1979; The Missing Years, 1980; Political Psychology of Appeasement, 1980; Farewell to Europe, 1981; The Terrible Secret, 1981; America, Europe and the Soviet

Union, 1983. *Honour:* First Distinguished Writer's Award, Center of Strategic and International Studies, 1969. *Address:* Center of Strategic and International Studies, 1800 K Street North West, Washington, DC 20006, USA.

LARDAS, Konstantinos, b. 3 Aug. 1927. Professor of English and Comparative Literature. *Education:* BA, University of Pittsburgh, Pennsylvania; MA, Columbia University, 1951; PhD, University of Michigan, 1966. *Literary Appointments:* Teaching Fellow, 1961, Pre-Doctoral Instructor 1964, University of Michigan; Assistant Professor, 1966, Associate Professor, 1970, Professor of English, 1976–, City College of New York. *Publications:* And In Him, Too, In Us, Selected and introduced by A Warren, Generation, University of Michigan, 1964. *Contributions to:* Numerous magazines and journals including: America; Antioch Review; Ararat; Atlantic Monthly; Chicago Review; College English; Fulbright Review; Harvard Advocate; Harper's Bazaar; Literary Review; Michigan Quarterly Review; Modern Poetry; Nea Estia, Greece; New York Times; North America; Mentor; Poetry East West; Prairie Schooner; Southern Review; Spectrum; Yale Literary Review. *Honours include:* Brain-Swiggett Poetry Award, University of Michigan, 1962; Borestone Mountains Poetry Awards, Palo Alto, California, 1962, 63; Pulitzer Prize Nomination, 1964. *Memberships:* Modern Greek Language Association; Academy of American Poets. *Address:* 68 Wakefield Avenue, Yonkers, NY 10704, USA.

LARN, Richard James, b. 1 Sep. 1930, Norwich, England. Writer/Diver. m. Bridget Teresa McBride, 1 Nov. 1980, St Austell, Cornwall, 2 daughters. *Literary Appointments:* Editor, Newsletter, Nautical Archaeology Society. *Publications:* Cornish Shipwrecks – 2 The South Coast 1969; Cornish Shipwrecks – The Isles of Scilly, 1971; Devon Shipwrecks 1974; Goodwin Sands Shipwrecks 1976; Shipwrecks of Great Britain and Ireland 1979; Commercial Diving Manual 1984. *Contributor to:* Diver Magazine (UK); Tauchen Magazine (Germany); Diver Magazine (New Zealand). *Honour:* Fellow of Mark Twain Society (USA) 1971. *Address:* 50 Sea Road, Carlyon Bay, St Austell, Cornwall PL25 3SG, England.

LAROCHE, Maximilien, b. 5 Apr. 1937, Cap-Haitien, Haiti. Professor of Literature. m. Louise Goyer, 12 Sep. 1964, Montreal, 1 son, 1 daughter. *Education:* Licence en Droit, Universite d'Haiti, 1958; Licence es-Lettres 1962, MA Litt esp 1962, Université de Montréal, Canada; Doctorat Litt Comp, Université Toulouise, France, 1971. *Literary Appointments:* Professor, Université Laval, 1979; Editor, Livres et Auteurs Québécois, 1980–83. *Publications:* Le Miracle et la Métamorphose, 1971; L'Image Comme Écho, 1978; La Littérature Haitienne, 1981. *Contributions to:* Casa De Las Americas; Oitenta; Anthropologie et Societes. *Honours:* Member Jury Casa de las Americas Prize, 1979; Invited Writer, Rencontre Québécoise Internationale des Écrivans, 1980–83. *Memberships:* International Commmittee of Creole Studies; Comité international des études créoles; Circulo de estudos francofonos, Brazil; Union of Quebec Authors: Union des écrivains Quebecois. *Address:* 1100 av Ploermel, Sillery, Quebec G1S 3R9, Canada.

LAROUCHE, Jean-Claude, b. 15 June 1944, Roberval, Quebec, Canada. Book Publisher. m. Anne-Marie Tremblay, 10 Sep. 1967, 1 son, 2 daughters. *Education:* BA, Physical Education & Recreation. *Major Publicaitons:* Alexis le Trotteur, 1971; Alexis le Trotteur: Athlète ou Centaure?, 1977; La Grande Aventure, 1980; Rapport Officiel des Vème Jeux d'Hiver du Canada, 1983. *Memberships:* Quebec Writers Union; Society of Canadian Authors. *Address:* 867 Rang no 8, St Nazaire, Quebec, GOW 2V0, Cananda.

LARRICK, Nancy, b. 28 Dec. 1910, Winchester, Virginia, USA. Writer; Lecturer. m. Alexander L Crosby, 15 Feb. 1958 (dec 1980), Winchester. *Education:* AB, Goucher College; MA, Columbia University; EdD, New

York University. *Literary Appointments:* Editor, Young America Readers, children's magazines, 1946–52; Associate Editor, Children's Books, Random House, 1952–59. *Publications include:* Printing & Promotion Handbook, with Daniel Melcher, 1949; A Parent's Guide to Children's Reading, 5th edition, 1982; A Teacher's Guide to Children's Books, 1960; A Parent's Guide to Children's Reading Begins At Home, 1980. Editor, 15 poetry anthologies for young readers including: One City Streets, 1968; Piping Down the Valleys Wild, 1968; I Heard a Scream in the Street, 1972; Room for Me & a Mountain Lion, 1974; Bring Me All of Your Dreams, 1980; When the Dark Comes Dancing, 1983. *Contributions to:* Numerous periodicals including: New York Times Educational Supplement; Christian Science Monitor; Saturday Review; Publisher Weekly; School Library Journal; Reading Teacher; Learning. *Honours:* Edison Foundation Award, 1958; International Reading Association Citation of Merit, 1977; Drexel University Citation, contributions to children's literature, 1977; Indiana University Citation, 1982; Helen Keating Ott Award, 1984. *Literary Agent:* Joan Daves, 59 E 54th Street, New York, NY 10022, USA. *Address:* 330 W Cecil Street, Winchester, Virginia 22601, USA.

LARROWE, Charles P, b. 1 May 1916, Portland, Oregon, USA. Professor of Economics. *Education:* BA, University of Washington, Seattle, 1946; MA, Economics, ibid, 1948; PhD, Economics, Yale University, 1952. *Publications:* Shape-up and Hiring Hall, 1955; Harry Bridges, 1972. *Contributor to:* New Times, NYC; Nation, USA; California Law Review. *Honour:* Reserve Index-A, FBI, USA, 1969. *Address:* Department of Economics, Michigan State University, East Lansing, MI 48824, USA.

LARSEN, Egon, b. 13 July, 1904, Writer. m. Ursula Lippmann, 3 July 1940, London. *Publications:* Men Who Changed the World (scientists, inventors) 1952; An American in Europe: Count Rumford (biography) 1953; Men Who Fought for Freedom (biography) 1958; A History of Invention, 1961; The Deceivers, 1966; Lasers, 1968; Strange Sects and Cults, 1971; Weimar Eyewitness (Germany 1918–33), 1977; A Flame in Barbed Wire (Amnesty International), 1978; Wit as a Weapon (The Political Joke in History), 1980. *Contributions to:* Radio; Television – thousands since 1945. *Honour:* Diesel Medal (silver) 1963. *Memberships:* Fellow, English Centre PEN; Society of Authors. *Literary Agent:* Doris von Bendemann, 8b Oakhill Avenue, London NW3. *Address:* 34 Dartmouth Road, London NW2 4EX, England.

LARSEN, Gaylord, b. 4 Jan. 1932, Canova, South Dakota, USA. College Teacher. m. Muriel Geiger, 28 July 1956, Los Angeles, USA, 3 sons, 1 daughter. *Education:* BA, Sioux Falls College, 1953; MA Theatre Arts, University of California at Los Angeles, 1959. *Major Publications:* The Kilbourne Connection, 1980; Trouble Crossing The Pyrenees, 1983. *Honours:* Cornerstone Magazine Best Christian Fiction Award, 1983. *Memberships:* Writers' Guild of America West. *Address:* 1200 Seafarer Street, Ventura, CA 93001, USA.

LARSEN, Torben B, b. 12 Jan. 1944, Copenhagen, Denmark. *Education:* MSc, Economics; DSc, Natural Sciences, University of Copenhagen. *Publications:* India's Fight against the Population Explosion, 1970; The Population Explosion, 1970; Butterflies of Lebanon, 1974; Butterflies of Oamn, 1980; Butterflies of Saudi Arabia and its Neighbours, 1985. *Contributor to:* Numerous professional journals. *Honour:* Said Akl Award, Lebanon, 1973. *Address:* c/o 29C Snoghoj Alle, DK 2770, Kastrup, Denmark.

LARSON, Arthur, b. 4 July 1910, Sioux Falls, South Dakota, USA. Legal Writer. m. 31 July 1935, Sioux Falls, South Dakota, 1 son, 1 daughter. *Education:* AB, Augustana College, South Dakota, 1931; University of South Dakota Law School, 1931–32; BA, Jurisprudence, 1935, MA, Jurisprudence, 1938,

Bachelor of Civil Laws, 1957, Doctor of Civil Law, 1957, Oxford (Rhodes Scholar). *Publications:* The Law of Workmen's Compensation (10 volumes with two annual Supplements and Revisions); The Law of Employment Discrimincation (with Lex K Larson) (4 volumes with two annual Revisions and Supplement); Workmen's Compensation for Industrial Injury and Death (2 volumes with Annual Supplement and Revision) Eisenhower: The President Nobody Knew, 1968; A Republican Looks at His Party, 1956; When Nations Disagree, 1961; Ten other books on law and public affairs. *Contributions to:* Encyclopedias: Colliers; United Nations: Americana Annual, 1967–70; International Law; Britannica, Great Ideas Today, 1965, Progress-Sharing: West, Guide to American Law, 1982, Affirmative Action. Contributions to 24 other books, also 135 articles in law reviews and national periodicals. *Honours:* Honorary Fellow, Pembroke College, Oxford, England; World Peace Award, American Freedom Association; Henderson Memorial Prize, Harvard University; Fulbright Advance Research Award; Horovitz Award, American Trial Lawyers Association; Seven honorary doctor's degrees. *Address:* Duke University Law School, Durham, NC 27706, USA.

LARSON, Charles Lester, b. 23 Oct. 1922, Portland, Oregon, USA. Author, Television writer and producer. m. Alice Mae Dovey, 25 Aug. 1966, Las Vegas, Nevada, 1 stepson. *Publications:* The Chinese Game, 1969; Someone's Death, 1973; Matthew's Hand, 1974; Muir's Blood, 1976; The Portland Murders, 1983. *Contributions to:* Freelance magazine writer, 1941–51. *Honours:* Special Award for Someone's Death, Mystery Writers of America, 1974. *Memberships:* Writers Guild of America, West; Mystery Writers of America; Author's League. *Literary Agent:* JCA Literary Agency. *Address:* 2422 SW Broadway Drive, Portland, OR 97201, USA.

LARSSON, Zenia, b. 2 Apr. 1922, Lodz, Poland. Authoress; Sculptoress. *Education:* Matriculation examinations, Lodz, Poland, 1941; Swedish Academy of Arts, Stockholm, 1947–52. *Publications:* Skuggorna Vid Träbron, 1960; Lång Ar Gryningen, 1961; Livet Till Mötes, 1962; Ater Till Babel, 1964; Mejan, 1966; Fotfäste, 1968; Morfars Kopparslantar, 1970; Brev Från En Ny Verklighet, 1972; Vägen Hem, 1975; Stadens Fyrhantiga hyjärta, 1980; Mellan Gårdagen och Nuet, 1985; Radio Play, Vem Saknar Johnathan?, for Swedish Radio, 1979. *Honours:* Several grants. *Memberships:* Association of Swedish Authors; Swedish Association of Artists. *Agent:* AB Raben & Sjögren, Bokforlag. *Address:* Box 45022, 104 30 Stockholm, Sweden.

LASDUN, Susan Virginia, b. 23 Apr. 1929, London, England. Author; Artist. m. Denys Lasdun, 26 Apr. 1954, London, 2 sons, 1 daughter. *Publications:* Victorians at Home, 1981; Making Victorians, 1983. *Contributions to:* Country Life; Saturday Book; Architectural Review; RIBA Journal; Harpers & Queen. *Literary Agent:* Andrew Hewson of John Johnstone. *Address:* 51 Rowan Road, London W6 7DT, England.

LASKER, David Raymond, b. 21 Apr. 1950, New York City, New York, USA. Writer; Musician, Double-bassist. *Education:* BS, 1972, MMus, 1974, Yale University; studies, Juilliard School of Music, New York, 2 years. *Publications:* The Boy Who Loved Music, 1979. *Contributions to:* Ontario Living; Western Living; Toronto Life; City and Country Home; Atlanta Weekly; Arts Manitoba; Music and Fitness; Muscle Magazine International; Ovation; Bravo and others. *Honours:* Notable book, for Boy Who Loved Music, American Library Association, 1980. *Memberships:* Fees Committee, Periodical Writers Association of Canada. *Address:* 533 Logan Avenue, Toronto, Ontario, Canada M4K 383.

LASKOWSKI, Jacek Andrzej, b. 4 June 1946, Edinburgh, Scotland. Writer, Translator. m. Anne G Howieson, 8 July 1978. *Education:* Pembroke College, Cambridge; Mag Fil., Jagiellonian University, Krakow; University of St Andrews. *Literary Appointments:* Literary Manager, Haymarket Theatre, Leicester.

Publications: Plays and production dates: Silver Lining, 1977; Dreams To Damnation, 1978; Pawn Takes Pawn, 1979; The Secret Agent, 1983; Translations: Clouds of Unknowing (Konwicki et al), 1981; On Foot (Mrozek), 1983; A Summer's Day (Mrozek), 1985; Translations from English: Lunar Caustic (Lowry), 1971; The Ginger Man (Donleavy), 1973; Translation from Polish: The Book of Lech Walesa, 1982. *Contributions to:* Tygodnik Powszechny; Literatura; Literatura na Swiecie; Poets and Painters Press; Television Today; London Review of Books. *Honours:* Fellow, International Writing Program, Iowa, 1973; Best Script Awards, NSDF, 1977; Arts Council Bursaries, 1978 and 1981. *Memberships:* Secretary 1982, Negotiating Team, Theatre Writer's Union; Broadcasting Committee, Deputy Chairman 1983–84, Society of Authors; International Pen. *Literary Agent:* Drama: Penny Tackaberry; Other: Tessa Sayle. *Address:* c/o Tessa Sayle Literary and Dramatic Agents, 11 Jubilee Place, London SW3 3TE, England.

LASKY, Jesse Louis Jnr, b. 19 Sep. 1910, New York City, USA. Writer. m. Barbara Hayden, 13 Feb. 1960, 1 stepson, 1 stepdaughter. *Literary Appointments:* Former Vice President, Screen Branch, Writers Guild of America; Writers Guild of Great Britain; Company of Military Historians. *Publications:* 3 volumes of Poetry; 5 novels including, The Offer (with Pat Silver); Whatever Happened to Hollywood? Non-fiction, (with Pat Silver); Love Scene; Men of Mystery. *Contributor to:* Cosmopolitan; Writers Guild of America Book on TV and Screen Writing; Writers Guild of Great Britain publication Lookout; Spanish Home; Sunday Times Book Review; etc; Poetry Reviews: Los Angeles Times; La Prensa, Argentina. *Honours:* Poetry Awards; Short Story Award for one of ten best published in Cosmopolitan, Christopher Award; American University Woman's Award for most original play for verse play Ghost Town (with Pat Silver), etc. *Literary Agent:* Andrew Mann, London; Lantz Office, New York. *Address:* c/o Andrew Mann Ltd, 1 Old Compton Street, London W1.

LASKY, Melvin Jonah, b. 15 Jan. 1920, New York City, USA, Editor; m. Brigitte Newiger, 1947, divorced, 1 son, 1 daughter. *Education:* BSS, City College of New York; MA, University of Michigan; Columbia University. *Appointments:* Literary Editor, The New Leader, New York, 1942–43; US Combat Historian in France and Germany, 1944–45; Captain, US Army, 1946; Foreign Correspondent, 1946–48; Editor, Publisher, Der Monat, Berlin, 1945–58, 1978–; Co-Editor, Encounter Magazine, London, 1958–; Editorial Director, Library Press, New York, 1970–; Publisher, Alcove Press, London, 1972–; Regular TV Broadcaster, Cologne, Zurich, Vienna, 1955–. *Publications:* Reisemotizen and Tagebucher, 1958; Africa for Beginners, 1962; Utopia and Revolution, 1976. *Contributor to:* America and Europe, 1951; New Paths in American History, 1965; Sprache und Politik, 1969; Festchrift for Raymond Aron, 1971; Editor The Hungarian Revolution, 1957. *Address:* c/o Encounter, 59 St Martins Lane, London WC2N 4JS, England.

LASKY, Victor, b. 7 Jan. 1918, Liberty, New York, USA. Author; Commentator; Lecturer. m. Patricia Pratt, 6 Sep. 1952, New York City. *Education:* BA, Brooklyn College, 1940; Honorary Doctor of Letters, Ashland College, 1983. *Publications:* Seeds of Treason, (with Ralph de Toledano) 1950; J F K: The Man and The Myth, 1963; The Ugly Russian, 1965; Robert F Kennedy: The Myth and The Man, 1968; Say, Didn't You Used to be George Murphy? (with George Murphy), 1970; It Didn't Start with Watergate, 1977; Jimmy Carter: The Man and the Myth, 1979; Never Complain, Never Explain: The Story of Henry Ford II, 1981. *Honour:* Accuracy in Media Award: Best Book of the Year, 1978. *Memberships:* Overseas Press Club; National Press Club; Authors Guild. *Literary Agent:* Mrs Lucianne Goldberg, 255 West 84th Street, New York, NY 10024, USA. *Address:* 3133 Connecticut Avenue NW, Washington, DC 20008, USA.

LASSAM, Robert Errington, b. 19 Mar. 1914, Harrow, Middlesex, England. Museum Curator. m. Margaret Perry, 26 Apr. 1944, Harrow, 2 daughters. *Education:* Higher Diploma, Institute of Chemistry; Honorary Fellow, Royal Photographic Society, Society of Industrial Artists; Fellow, Royal Society of Arts. *Literary Appointments:* Curator, Fox-Talbot Museum, Lacock, Wiltshire. *Major Publications:* Fox-Talbot – Photographer. *Contributor to:* Amateur Photographer; British Journal of Photography; History of Photography. *Honours:* President's Medal, Institute of Professional Photographers, 1980; Salverte Medal, French Photographic Society, 1983; Corresponding Member, German Photographic Society, 1978. *Address:* 7 Forester Road, Bath, Avon BS2 6GF, England.

LAST, Joan Mary, b. 12 Jan. 1908. Professor of Piano; Composer; Writer; Teacher; Lecturer. *Education:* LRAM; ARCM. *Publications:* The Young Pianist, UK 1954, Japan 1972, Finland 1985; Interpretation in Piano Study, UK 1961, Japan 1972; Freedom in Piano Technique, 1980. *Contributions to:* Music Teacher; EPTA Journal; Clavier, USA; Keys, USA. *Honour:* Honorary RAM, 1975. *Address:* 11 St Mary's Close, Littlehampton, West Sussex, BN17 5PZ, England.

LATIMER, Dan Raymond, b. 15 July 1944, San Angelo, Texas, USA. University Professor. m. Renate Schmidt, 2 May 1970, Detroit, Michigan, USA, 1 daughter. *Education:* BA English, University of Texas, Austin, 1964–66; MA 1966–68, PhD 1969–72, Comparative Literature, University of Michigan, Ann Arbour. *Literary Appointments:* Assistant Professor 1972–78, Associate Professor 1978–, Auburn University; Co-editor, Southern Humanities Review, Auburn University. *Publications:* The Elagiac Mode inMilton and Rilke: Reflections of Death, 1977; Essays, papers, translations, book reviews. *Contributions to:* Modern Language Notes; Literature and Psychology; New Orleans Review; Southern Humanities Review; New Left Review; Michigan Quarterly; The Literary Review; Contemporary Literature in Translation; Philosophy and Literature; Rackham Literary Studies; Modern Austrian Litrature. *Honours include:* Exchange Scholarship, Universität Erlangen-Nürnberg; Rackham Fellowship; Fellowships; National Endowment for the Humanities for Summer Seminars, 1978, 1981, 1985; Institute for the Marxist Interpretation of Culture, 1983; Consultant for Travel Division 1985, National Endowment for the Humanities; The Humanities Fund Award for Instructional Innovation, Auburn University, 1982. *Address:* Co-editor, Southern Humanities Review, Auburn University, 9088 Haley Center, Auburn University, AL 36849, USA.

LATTA, Richard John, b. 16 Oct. 1946, East Chicago, Indiana, USA. Freelance Writer, Puzzle Creator. m. Mary Tripodi, 24 Aug. 1968, 4 daughters. *Education:* BS Biology, Illinois Benedictine College. *Major Publications:* Concrete Poems, 1974; Rain (poems), 1972; Games for Travel, 1976; Series of 10 Educational books, 1978–; Series of 12 Maze books, 1983–; Wordfind books, 1984–. *Contributor to:* Chicago Review; Carolina Quarterly; Reader's Digest; Family Circle; National Geographic World Magazine; Instructor; Early Years; Teacher; Learning; and many others. *Address:* 126 N Indian Bound Road, Plainfield, IL 60544, USA.

LATTA, William Charlton Jr, b. 24 Sep. 1929, E Liverpool, Ohio, USA. University Professor. m. Nancy Carolyn Carnahan, 22 July 1952, Manhattan, Kansas, 2 sons, 2 daughters. *Education:* BA, Sterling College, Kansas, 1952; Diploma, Russian Language Specialist, US Army Language School, 1963; MA, Kansas State University, Manhattan, 1960; PhD, University of Nebraska, Lincoln, 1965. *Appointments:* Editorial Assistant, University of Nebraska Curriculum Development Centre, 1963–65; Fiction Editor, Wascana Review, 1965–67; Member, Editorial Board, Prairie Forum, 1981–84; Guest Editor, Special Alberta Issue – Contemporary Verse Two, 1983. *Publications:* Summer's Bright Blood, 1976; Drifting into Grey, 1977; Included in: Draft: An Anthology of Prairie Poetry,

1983; Ride Off Any Horizon, 1983; Dancing Visions, 1985. *Contributor to:* Canadian Forum; Queen's Quarterly; Prairie Schooner; Prism International; Kansas Quarterly; Wascana Review; Camrose Review; Repository; Canada Goose; Criticism and Reviews in numerous journals. *Honours:* Winner, Prairie Schooner Fiction Award, 1961; John H Vreeland Award, University of Nebraska, 1963; Co-Winner, Saskatchewan Arts Board Poetry Competition, 1966; Inclusion in, Best Poems of 1966, Borestone Mountain Poetry Awards, 1967. *Memberships:* League of Canadian Poets; Writers' Guild of Alberta, Member-at-Large, Executive Committee, 1979–80, 1983–84, Judge, Annual Poetry Prize, 1983, 1985. *Address:* 408 14th Street So, Lethbridge, Alberta T1J 2X7, Canada.

LATZ, Dorothy L, b. 8 Dec. 1930. New York City, USA. College Professor; Writer. *Education:* BA, College, New Rochelle, New York; MA, Fordham University, New York, 1962; Fordham MA, University of Edinburgh, Scotland; Doctor, University of Paris, Sorbonne, 1969; Licence, University of Grenoble, 1971; Doctorate, Sciences Religieuses, Faculty de Theologie Catholique de University SH de Strasbourg. *Appointments:* English Instructor, Seton Hall University, New Jersey, 1964–66; Assistant Professor of English, Marywood College, Pennsylvania, 1969–70; Associate Professor, Humanities Division and Department Chairperson, St Thomas Aquinas College, New York, 1975–78; Faculty, English, St Peters Collge, Nassau Community College, New York, 1979; Associate Professor, English, Hofstra University, New York, 1985. *Publications:* First Chapter, Le Theatre Au Moyen Age, 1981; Chapter, Mary Ward, 17th Century Women Writers. *Contributor to:* Christianity and Literature; Mystics Quarterly; Responsibilita. *Honours:* Various Scholarships. *Memberships:* American Modern Language Association; Renaissance Seminars, Columbia University; Alliance Francaise; 16th Century Studies Conference; Poetry Society of America. *Address:* PO Box 265, New Rochelle, NY 10802, USA.

LAUBIN, Gladys Winifred, b. Paterson, New Jersey, USA. Writer; Photographer; Helps husband with concerts and lecturers; Indian Dancer. m. Reginald K Laubin. *Education:* Norwich Free Academy; Norwich Art School. *Publications:* Co-author, The Indian Tipi, 1957, 2nd Edition, 1979; Indian Dance of North America, 1977, 79; American Indian Archery, 1980. *Contributor to:* Encyclopaedia Britannica. *Honours:* Adopted into Sitting Bull Family,Hunkkapa Sioux, 1934; Capegio Dance Award, 1972 (highest award in dance world for contribution to ethnic dance); Peace Pipe Award, Indian Lore Association, 1976. *Address:* PO Box 4, Grand Teton National Park, Moose, WY 83012, USA.

LAUBIN, Reginald Karl, b. Detroit, Michigan, USA. Performer of American Indian Dances; Lecturer. m. Gladys W Tortoiseshell. *Education:* Hartford Art School; Norwich Art School. *Publications:* The Indian Tipi, 1957, 2nd edition 1979; Indian Dances of North America, 1977, 79; American Indian Archery, 1980 (all books co-authored with Gladys W Laubin). *Contributions to:* Adventure; Boy's Life; Scouting; Encyclopaedia Britannica. *Honours:* Adopted by Sioux Tribe, 1984; Guggenheim Fellowship, 1957; Capezio Dance Award, 1972 (highest award in dance world for contribution to ethnic dance); Peace Pipe Award, 1976 (American Indian Lore Association). *Address:* PO Box 4, Grand Teton National Park, Moose, WY 83012, USA.

LAUDER, Phyllis Anna Lynn, b. 16 June 1898, London, England. Housewife; Writer. m. Dr H V Lauder, 3 Oct. 1925, Paddington, London, England, 1 son, 1 daughter. *Education:* Oxford and Cambridge Higher Certificate. *Literary Appointment:* Columnist for The Siamese News Quarterly, Colorado, USA. *Publications:* Siamese Cats, 1950, 53; New Siamese Cats, 1953; The Siamese Cat, 1971; Siamese Cats, 1963; The Batsford Book of the Siamese Cat, 1974; The Rex Cat, 1974; The Siamese Cat 1978; The British, European and North American Shorthair Cat, 1981. *Contributions to:* Journal of Cat Genetics, Sacramento, California; Cats Magazine,

USA; Cat-Lovers Bedside Book. *Address:* Mulberry Cottage, Exlade Street, Near Woodcote, Reading, England.

LAUDON, Hasso, b. 23 Jan. 1932, Berlin, Germany. Writer. m. 1955, 1 son, 1 daughter. *Publications:* The Labyrinth (novel), 1964; Adrian (novel), 1970; The Eternal Heretic (novel, Life of Dostoevsky), 1983; Legend from the Sea (novel), 1984. *Membership:* Writers Union German Democratic Republic. *Address:* Murtzaner Ring 31, 1140 Berlin, Democratic Republic of Germany.

LAUFMAN, Harold, b. 6 Jan. 1912, Milwaukee, Wisconsin, USA. Surgical Consultant, Emeritus Professor of Surgery. m. (1) Marilyn Joselit (dec.), 1 Sep. 1940, 2 daughters, (2) June Friend Moses, 10 Apr. 1980. *Education:* BS 1932, MD Rush Medical College 1937, University of Chicago; MS Surgery 1946, PhD Surgery 1948, Northwestern University Medical School. *Literary Appointments:* Editor, Chicago Medicine, 1959–63; Consulting Editor, Modern Medicine, 1965–69; Editorial boards, Health Devices, 1969–; Acting Editor in Chief, Modern Medicine, 1970; Editorial Board, Medical Research Engineering, 1970–75; Editorial Board, Emergency Medicine, 1971–79; Editor in Chief, Diagnostica, 1972–76; Associate Editor, Medical Instrumentation, 1976–83; Editorial Boards, Infection Control, 1979–. *Publications:* Surgical Exposures of the Extremities, (with S W Banks), 1953; Hematologic Problems in Surgery, (with R B Erichson), 1970; Hospital Special Care Facilities, 1981; Silvergirl's in Surgery: The Veins, 1985. *Contributions to:* Author or co-author of 265 articles and book chapters in medical and scientific literature. *Honours:* Prize Essayist, Chicago Surgical Society, 1947; Harold Swanberg Award, American Writers Association, 1973. *Memberships:* President, American Medical Writers Association, 1968–69. *Address:* 31 East 72 Street, New York, NY 10021, USA.

LAURIE, Rona, b. 16 Sep. 1926, Derby, England. Professor of Drama. *Education:* BA Honours English; Licentiate, Royal Academy of Music; Licentiate, Guildhall School of Music. *Publications:* 8th Anthology, (co-editor) 1964; Speaking Together Books I and II, (co-editor), 1964; A Hundred Speeches From The Theatre, 1966; Scenes and Ideas, 1967; 11th, 1969; 13th, 1973; Festivals and Adjudication, 1975; Children's Plays From Beatrix Potter, 1980; 17th, 1981; Auditioning, 1985. *Contributions to:* Speaking Shakespeare Today; On Stage, Australia; Numerous on theatre and on acting technique. *Honours:* Fellow, Guildhall School of Music and Drama, 1967; Exponent Poetry Lovers Fellowship, 1968. *Address:* 2 New Quebec Street, London W1H 2DD, England.

LAVELL, Stephen Michael, b. 23 Feb. 1956, London, England. Writer. *Education:* BA, University College, London, UK; Sorbonne, Paris. *Publications:* Almost Hampstead, 1976; Olympic Games, 1977; Had I Been Alone, 1978; Absolutely Free, 1980; Star Turns, 1984; Family Business, 1985. *Contributor to:* Arts Review; Artline; Campaign; Company. Literary Awards: Winner, International Student Playscript Competition, 1978 (finalist, 1977; semi-finalist, 1976). *Address:* 29B Gloucester Avenue, London NW1, England.

LAVELLE, Sheila, b. 12 July 1939, Gateshead, England. Writer. m. Derek James Lavelle, 13 Sep. 1958, Newcastle, 2 sons. *Education:* Certificate of Education (Primary), 1968. *Publications:* Children's Books: Ursula Bear, 1977; Everybody Said No, 1978; Oliver Ostrich, 1978; Too Many Husbands, 1978; Ursula Dancing, 1979; My Best Friend, 1979; Ursula Exploring, 1980; Ursual Flying, 1981; The Fiend Next Door, 1982; Myrtle Turtle, 1981; Mr Ginger's Potato, 1981; Ursula Flying, 1984; The Big Stink, 1984; Trouble With the Fiend, 1984; Ursula Riding, 1985; The Disappearing Granny (to be published 1985); Harry's Aunt (to be published 1985); Various short stories. *Honours:* Silver Pencil Award, Amsterdam, 1979. *Address:* 47 Chalklands, Bourne End, Buckinghamshire SL8 5TH, England.

LAVER, Michael John, b. 3 Aug. 1949, London, England. University Professor. m. Brid Goretti O'Connor, 28 July 1976, Liverpool, 1 son, 1 daughter. *Education:* BA, MA, University of Essex; PhD, Liverpool. *Publications:* Playing Politics, 1979; The Politics of Private Desires, 1981; The Crime Game, 1982; Invitation to Politics, 1983. *Contributor to:* Wide range of magazines & journals. *Address:* Dept of Politics & Sociology, University College, Galway, Republic of Ireland.

LAVIN, John Halley, b. 27 Oct. 1932, Queens, New York, USA. Writer; Editor. m. Bernadette Manning, 2 Mar. 1957, 2 sons, 2 daughters. *Education:* BA, Queens College, New York; Certificate, Health Administrators Development Conference, Cornell University. *Publications:* Hospital Administrator's Guide to Purchasing, 1981; Stroke: From Crisis to Victory, 1985. *Contributions to:* Good Housekeeping; Dial; Self; Us; Medical Economics; Modern Naturity; Redbook; etc. *Honours:* Jesse H Neal Award, 1975; Jesse H. Neal Certificate of Merit, 1975; Outstanding Journalist Award, American Academy of Family Physicians, 1981. *Memberships:* American Society of Journalists & Authors; Society of Professional Journalists; Sigma Delta Chi. *Literary Agent:* Jean V Naggar, New York. *Address:* 44 Greenbrier Street, Marco Island, FL 33937, USA.

LAVIOLETTE, Gontran, b. 7 Apr. 1911, Clarence, Ontario, Canada. Editor. *Education:* Matriculation, University of Ottawa; LPh, Bth, Oblate, Catholic Seminary, Saskatchewan. *Literary Appointments:* Editor: Sunday Herald, Winnipeg, 1957–69; The Canadian League, Winnipeg, 1969–79. *Publications:* Indian Record, 1938; Sioux Indians in Canada, 1944; The Canadian Dakota Indians, 1985. *Contributions to:* Anthropologica, Ottawa University; Dictionary of Canadian Biography. *Memberships:* Societe Historique du Manitoba, 1981; Manitoba Historical Society, 1982. *Address:* 503-480 Aulneau Street, Winnipeg, Manitoba, Canada R2H 2V2.

LAVIOLETTE, Gontran, b. 7 Apr. 1911, Clarence, Ontario, Canada. Editor. *Education:* Matriculation, University of Ottawa; LPh, Bth, Oblate, Catholic Seminary, Saskatchewan. *Literary Appointments:* Editor: Sunday Herald, Winnipeg, 1957–69; The Canadian League, Winnipeg, 1969–79. *Publications:* Indian Record, 1938; Sioux Indians in Canada, 1944; The Canadian Dakota Indians, 1985. *Contributions to:* Anthropoligica, Ottawa University; Dictionary of Canadian Biography. *Memberships:* Societe Historique du Manitoba, 1981; Manitoba Historical Society, 1982. *Address:* 503-480 Aulneau Street, Winnipeg, Manitoba, Canada R2H 2V2.

LAWDEN, Derek Frank, b. 15 Sep. 1919, Birmingham, England. University Professor. m. Dorothy Mary Smith, 13 June 1940, Birmingham, 3 sons. *Education:* MA, ScD, St Catherine's College, Cambridge, 1937–39 and 1946–47. *Publications:* Mathematics of Engineering Systems, 1954; A Course in Applied Mathematics volumes I and II, 1960; Optimal Trajectories for Space Navigation, 1963; Mathematical Principles of Quantum Mechanics, 1967; Analytical Mechanics, 1972; Electromagnetism, 1973; Analytical Methods of Optimization, 1975; Introduction to Tensor Calculus, Relativity and Cosmology, 1982. *Contributions to:* Research papers on control theory, rocket flight and psychophysics. *Honours:* Fellow, Royal Society of New Zealand, 1962; Hector Medal, Royal Society of New Zealand, 1964; Mechanics and Control of Flight Award, American Institute of Aeronautics and Astronautics, 1967. *Address:* 36 Mackenzie Road, Birmingham, B11 4EL, England.

LAWRENCE, D Baloti, b. 3 June 1951, Washington, District of Columbia, USA. *Education:* BA Media Communications; MA Psychology; Doctoral candidate, administration. *Publications:* Massageworks, 1983; Massage Techniques, 1985. *Contributions to:* Cosmopolitan magazine; Massage Journal; Studio

Photography; Essence; Futurific; Health and Diet Times. *Membership:* New York Academy. *Literary Agent:* Michael B Kent. *Address:* 1990 Broadway, 1206, New York, NY 10023, USA.

LAWRENCE, Dana Jeffrey, 5 Apr. 1953, Detroit, Michigan, USA. Chiropractic Physician. m. Randee Lipson, 21 June 1976, Detroit, Michigan, 2 sons. *Education:* BA, Biology, Michigan State University, 1975; BS, Human Biology, 1978, DC, 1979, National College of Chiropractic, 1979. *Literary Appointments:* Assistant to Director, Editorial Review and Publication, National College of Chiropractic, 1983; Associate Editor, Journal of Manipulative and Physiological Therapeutics, 1984. *Publications:* Co-Editor, States Manual of Spinal, Pelvic and Extravertebral Technique, in preparation. *Contributor to:* Pes Planus: A Review of Etiology, Diagnosis and Chiropractic Treatment, Journal Manipulative Physiological Therapy, 1983; A Radiographic Method of Determining Short Leg Mensuration, Journal American Chiropractic Association, 1984; Other articles in Climbing, etc. *Honours:* A Radiographic Method of Determining Short Leg Mensuration, presented, 1st Advances in Conservative Health Science Research Symposium; Paper Presented at 2nd Annual ACHSR Symposium; Recipient many other honours and awards. *Memberships:* American Medical Writers Association; Council of Biology Editors. *Address:* National College of Chiropractic, 200 E Roosevelt Road, Lombard, IL 60148, USA.

LAWRENCE, John Shelton, b. 30 Mar. 1938, Amarillo, Texas, USA. Professor of Philosophy. m. Nancy Cummings, 10 June 1961, San Anselmo, 1 son, 1 daughter. *Education:* BA, Stanford University, 1960; PhD, University of Texas, Austin, 1964. *Publications:* The American Monomyth, with Robert Jewett, 1977; Fair Use & Free Inquiry, with Bernard Timberg, 1980; The Electronic Scholar, 1984. *Contributor to:* Numerous professional Journals. *Address:* Philosophy Dept, Morningside College, Sioux City, IA 51106-1751, USA.

LAWRENCE, William Henry (Fr Neal, OSB), b. 22 Jan. 1908. Catholic Priest, Benedictine Order; University Professor. *Education:* AB, English Literature, Harvard College, 1929; US Naval Military Government School, Columbia University, USA, 1944; MA, Public Law and Government, Columbia University, 1947; St John's Seminary, Minnesota, 1954–60; Ordained Priest, 1960; Franciscan Language School, Japan, 1960–62; Oxford University, England, Commonwealth in Asia, 1965. *Appointments include:* University Professor, Ethics, International Relations, English Language, Commonwealth of Nations, St John's University, Minnesota, USA, 1954–60; University of Tokyo, Japan, 1962–68; International College, Sophia University, 1963–80; Shirayuri Women's College, Japan, 1966–84; Keio & Seikei Unviersities, 1968–83; Catholic Priest, St Anselm's Benedictine Priory, Japan, 1960–. *Publications:* Soul's Inner Sparkle, Moments of Waka Sensations, 1978, 2nd edition, 1980; Rushing Amid Tears, Tanka Poems in English, 1983. *Contributor to:* Poetry Nippon; Verbeia 3; Dragonfly; Ocarina's Anthology of International Poetry; Laurel Leaves; Anthology, 5th World Congress of Poets, USA. *Memberships include:* Advisory Committee, Poetry Society of Japan; Poetry Reading Circle of Tokyo; Tokyo English Literary Society; MPA, USA; United Poets Laureate International, Philippines. *Address:* St Anslem's Benedictine Priory, 6-22 Kamiosaki 4–chome, Shinagawa-ku, Tokyo 141, Japan.

LAZARUS, Arnold Leslie, b. 20 Feb. 1914, Revere, Massachusetts, USA. Freelance Writer. m. Keo Smith Felker, 24 July 1938, Santa Barbara, 2 sons, 2 daughters. *Education:* BA, University of Michigan; MA, PhD, University of California, Los Angeles. *Appointments:* Technical Director, Ford Hall Forum Little Theatre, Boston, Santa Monica Little Theatre; Teacher, Latin, English, Santa Barbara Public Schools; Associate Professor, English, University of Texas, Austin; Professor, English & American Literature, Purdue University. *Publications:* Co-Editor, Harbrace

Adventures in Literature, series, 1956–70; Entertainments & Valedictions, 1970; The Grosset Modern English, 1970; Editor, The Indiana Experience, 1976; Beyond Graustark: George Barr McCutcheon, 1981; The NCTE Glossary of Literature & Composition, 1983; Editor, The Best of George Ade, 1985. *Contributor to:* various professional journals, magazines and newspapers. *Honours:* Phi Beta Kappa, 1935; Purdue University School of Humanities Best Teacher Award, 1974; Kemper McComb, 1976. *Memberships:* Poetry Society of America; Screenwriters Guild of Santa Barbara. *Literary Agent:* Andrea Brown, New York City. *Address:* 945 Ward Drive #69, Santa Barbara, CA 93111, USA.

LAZARUS, John (Sidney), b. 24 Dec. 1947, Montreal, Canada. Playwright. Divorced, 2 daughters. *Education:* McGill University, 1965–66; Graduate, National Theatre School of Canada, 1969. *Literary Appointments:* Playwright-in-Residence, Arts Club Theatre, Vancouver, 1984. *Publications:* Plays: Dreaming and Duelling, 1980; Schoolyard Games, 1981. Productions: Babel Rap, 1972; Dreaming and Duelling, 1980; The Late Blumer, 1984; Village of Idiots, 1985. Childrens Plays: Schoolyard Games, 1981; Not So Dumb, 1984. *Contributions to:* The Vancouver Province, Theatre Critic, 1974; Interface; Canadian Theatre Review; Quarry; Canadian Broadcasting Corporation, Radio theatre critic, 1978–83, numerous radio and television plays, 1970–. *Honours:* 1st Prize, Playwriting Contest, Performing Arts Magazine, 1972; 2nd Prize, Playwriting contest, Clifford E Lee, 1974; Chalmers Award, 1980. *Memberships:* Playwrights Union of Canada; Past member, Guild of Canadian Playwrights, Playwrights Canada. *Literary Agent:* Mark Bolton, The New Play Centre. *Address:* 228 West 16th Avenue, Vancouver, British Columbia, Canada V5Y 1Y9.

LAZARUS, Pat, b. 1 Oct. 1935, Bridgeton, New Jersey, USA. Writer. m. Joseph Lazarus, 25 Feb. 1961, Oakland, California. *Education:* Temple University, Philadelphia, Pennyslvania. *Publication:* Keep Your Pet Healthy the Natural Way, 1983. *Contributions to:* Let's LIVE; Newsart; Backstage; Total Health magazine; Associate Editor: Alcoholism Update; Dialogues in Pediatric Urology; Occupational Health. *Memberships:* National Association of Science Writers; Editorial Freelancers' Association. *Literary Agent:* Denise Marcil, New York City. *Address:* 338 Devoe Street, Brooklyn, NY 11211, USA.

LAZER, William, b. 4 July 1924, Estevan, Saskatchewan, Canada. Professor, Marketing. m. Joyce Meriam Trepel, 1 son, 1 daughter. *Education:* B Com, University of Manitoba, 1949; MBA, University of Chicago, 1950; PhD, Ohio State University, 1956; Post-Doctoral Work, Ford Foundation Fellow, Harvard University, 1959–60. *Appointment:* Library Committee, 1969–72, Graduate Council 1974–77, Academic Senate 1975–78, Presidential Search and Selection Committee 1978–79, Advisory Committee Wharton Fine Arts Center 1979–81, Michigan State University. *Publications:* Basic Bibliography on Industrial Marketing, 1958; Mathematical Models and Methods in Marketing, 1961; Managerial Marketing: Perspectives and Viewpoints, 1958, 3rd edition, 1967, Japanese Translation, 1969, Indian. Marketing Management: A Systems Perspective, 1971; Marketing Management: A Systems Perspective, Instructors Manual, 1971; Managerial Marketing: Policies, Strategies and Decision, 1973; Social Marketing: Perspectives and Viewpoints, 1973; Marketing Management: Policies, Strategies and Decision, 1973; Marketing Management: Foundation and Practices, 1983, Instructors Manual 1983. Translation into Chinese 1984. *Contributor to:* Enterprise; Drugstore Merchandising; Business Quarterly; Western Buyers' Market; Australian Accountant; Business Topics; Journal of Marketing; Public Opinion Quarterly; Business Horizons, Journals of Advertising Research. *Honours:* Mu Kappa Tau; Visiting Scholar, National Science Foundation, 1972; Marketing Educator of the Year, Sales & Marketing Executives International, 1972;

Honorary Advisor, Japan Marketing Association, 1973; Distinguished Faculty Award, Michigan State University, 1974; Alpha Iota Delta, 1974; Phi Kappa Phi 1974; Alpha Mu Alpha, 1977; Beta Gamma Sigma, Distinguished Scholar, 1980. *Memberships include:* President, Vice President, Executive Committee, American Marketing Association, 1973–74; Board Chairman, Bio-Gas Detectors, 1979–; Screening Committee, Fulbright Commission, 1982–; Academic Senate; Various Government Committees including: Official Delegate, White House Conferences on: Industrial World of the 1990's, Inflation, Trade Negotiations, 1974. *Address:* PO Box 539, Boca Raton, FL 33429, USA.

LAZEROWITZ, Morris, b. 22 Oct. 1907, Lodz, Poland. Educator & Writer. m. Alice Ambrose, 15 June 1938, Northampton, Massachusetts, USA. *Education:* AB, 1933, PhD, 1936, University of Michigan; Post-doctoral research, University of Cambridge, England, Harvard University, 1937–38. *Appointments:* Faculty Member, Smith College, 1938–73; Sophia & Austin Smith Professor of Philosophy, 1964–73; Fulbright Professor, Bedford College, University of London, England, 1951–52; Distinguished Visiting Professor of Philosophy, University of Delaware, 1975; Visiting Professor, Hampshire College, 1977, 1979, 1981; Cowling Professor of Philosphy, Carleton College, 1979. *Major Publications:* The Structure of Metaphysics, 1955; Studies in Metaphilosophy, 1964; Philosophy & Illusion, 1968; The Language of Philosophy, 1977. Co-author (with A Ambrose): Fundamentals of Symbolic Logic, Rev.ed. 1962; Logic: The Theory of Formal Inference, Rev.ed. 1972; Philosophical Theories, 1976; Essays in the Unknown Wittgenstein, 1984; Necessity & Language, 1983; Co-editor (with A Ambrose), G E Moore: Essays in Retrospect, 1970; Ludwig Wittgenstein: Philosophy & Language, 1972; (with W E Kennick), Metaphysics: Readings and Reappraisals, 1966; (with C Hanley) Psychoanalysis & Philosophy, 1970. *Contributor to:* Learned Journals in USA, Poland, Japan, Mexico, Puerto Rico, Britain. *Honours:* Phi Kappa Phi, 1933; Alfred H Lloyd post-doctoral Fellowship, 1936–37; Katherine Asher Engel Lecture, Smith College, 1983. *Memberships:* American Philosophical Association; American Association of University Professors. *Address:* 126 Vernon Street, Northampton, MA 01060, USA.

le CLERE, René b. 5 June 1940, Oise, France. Society Secretary General; Terminologist. *Education:* National Technical College, Beauvais, France; Diploma, Psycho-Pedagogy, University of Québec, Canada; courses in various universities in Canada, USA and Colombia. *Publications:* Jean-Francois Battellier (1744–1812) feudiste du marquis de Gaudechart, 1974; Henry Aux Cousteaux de Conty: Lettres d'interêt généalogique (1887–1975), 1976. *Contributions to:* Le Devoir; La Presse; SEM; Actualités; The Augustan Magazine; The Heraldry in Canada; Bulletin de la Societe des ecrivains canadiens; Mémoires de la Société généalogique canadienne-française and others. *Honours:* Air Canada Literary Prize, 1977 and 1984; Fellow, Augustan Society 1978; Member of Honour, Society of French-Speaking Canadian Writers, 1985; Personally dubbed Chevalier by HMSH the Prince of Lippe, Germany, 1977; French-Alliance-Canada Cultural Prize, 1984; Grand Prize for Literature, City of Montreal 1980; Society for Studies and Lectures, 1983. *Memberships:* Secretary General, Society of French-Speaking Canadian Writers; Executive, Francophone PEN International Canadian Centre; Executive Federation of the French Alliances; Executive, Château Ramezay; Executive, Augustan Society. *Address:* PO Box 329 Victoria Station, Montréal-Westmount, Québec, Canada H3Z 2V8.

LE GUIN, Ursula, b. 21 Oct. 1929, Berkeley, USA. Writer. m. 22 Dec. 1953, Paris, 1 son, 2 daughters. *Education:* AB, Radcliffe College, 1951; AM, Columbia University, 1952. *Appointments:* Resident, or Visiting Lectureship at: Mercer University, University of Idaho, University of Washington, Portland State University,

Pacific University, Reading University, England, Indiana University, University of California, etc. *Publications:* Rocannon's World, 1966; 2 Planet of Exile, 1966; City of Illusions, 1966; The Left Hand of Darkness, 1969; A Wizard of Earthsea, 1968; The Lathe of Heaven, 1971; The Tombs of Atuan, 1970; The Farthest Shore, 1974; Poems: Wild Angels, 1974; Hard Words, 1981; Short Stories: The Wind's Twelve Quarters, 1975; Orsinian Tales, 1976; The Compass Rose, 1982; Essays: The Language of the Night; Screenplay: King Dog, 1985; The Word for World is Forest, 1976; Very Far Away from Anywhere Else, 1976; Malafrena, 1979; The Beginning Place, 1981; The Eye of the Heron, 1983; Always Coming Home, 1985. *Contributor to:* Numerous professional journals and magazines. *Honours:* Boston Globe Hornbrook Award, 1968; Nebula Award, 1969, 1974, 1975; Hugo Award, 1969, 1972; 1973, 1974; Newbery Honour Medal, 1972; National Book Award, 1972. *Memberships:* PEN; SFRA: Authors League. *Agent:* Virginia Kidd, Pennsylvania, USA.

LE MAY, Godfrey Hugh Lancelot, b. 7 Sep. 1920, Johannesburg, Republic of South Africa. Fellow and Tutor, Worcester College, Oxford. m. Penelope Mary Tugman, 15 Nov. 1963, Johannesburg, Republic of South Africa, 2 sons. *Education:* BA (Rhodes); MA (Oxon). *Publications:* British Government 1914–1963, 1955 2nd edition 1964; British Supremacy in South Africa 1899–1907, 1965; Black and White in South Africa, 1971; The Victorian Constitution, 1979. *Contributions to:* South African Law Journal; The Economist; History Today; History of the Twentieth Century. *Honours:* Milner Memorial Prize, 1941; Gladstone Memorial Prize, 1951; CNA Literary Award, 1965. *Address:* Worcester College, Oxford OX1 2HB, England.

LE QUESNE, Suzanne Elizabeth, b. 6 Mar. 1953, Jersey, Channel Islands. Editor; Journalist. m. Stephen Vibert Le Feuvre, 25 Apr. 1981, Grouville, 1 daughter. *England:* BSc Honours: Microbiology; Proficiency test in Journalism. *Literary Appointments:* Editor, Information Retrieval Limited, London, England; Reporter, Jersey Evening Post, Jersey, Channel Islands; Freelance reporter, British Broadcasting Corporation Radio, Jersey; Editor, The Jersey at Home; Publications editor, States of Jersey/States Greffe, Jersey. *Contributions to:* Fruit Trades Journal; Flower Trades Journal; Grower. *Membership:* Associate member, Guild of Agricultural Journalists. *Address:* 4 Old Lawn La Grande Route de la Côte, Pontac, St Clement, Jersey, Channel Islands.

LEAK, Gordon, b. 18 June 1936, Bramham, Yorkshire, England. Journalist. m. 17 Aug. 1957, Lewisham, 1 son, 2 daughters. *Literary Appointments:* Parliamentary Correspondent, Glasgow Herald; Parliamentary Correspondent, Yorkshire Post; Political Correspondent, Thomson Regional Newspapers; Political Editor, News of the World; Industrial Editor, Sunday Express. *Address:* 121 Fleet Street, London EC4, England.

LEALE, B C, b. 1 Sep. 1930, Ashford, Middlesex, England. Bookseller; Poet. *Publications:* Under a Glass Sky, 1975; Preludes, 1977; Leviathan and other poems, 1984; The Colours of Ancient Dreams, 1984. *Contributor to:* Magazines and journals including: Ambit; Encounter; The Fiction Magazine; Kayak; The Listener; The Literary Review; London Review of Books; Montana Gothic; The Observer; Pacific Quarterly; Poetry Review; A Review of English Literature; Second Aeon; the Spectator; Stand; The Times Literary Supplement; Tribune. Anthologies: Best of the Poetry Year 6 (Robson Books); A Group Anthology (Oxford University Press); New Poems 1963 and 1977–78 (PEN/Hutchinson); New Poetry 1,2,4,6,7 and 9 (Arts Council/Hutchinson); New Writing and Writers 16 and 18 (John Calder). *Membership:* Poetry Society. *Address:* Flat E10, Peabody Estate, Wild Street, London WC2B 4AH, England.

LEAN, Geoffrey, b. 21 Apr. 1947, London, England. Journalist; Author. m. Judith Eveline Wolfe, 24 June

1972, Cork, Eire, 1 son. *Education:* BA, Oxford University. *Literary Appointments:* Graduate Trainee, 1969, Feature Writer, 1973, Environment Correspondent, 1973, Yorkshire Post; Reporter, 1977, Environment Correspondent, 1979, The Observer. *Publications:* Rich World, Poor World, 1978. *Contributor to:* Numerous contributions to international and specialist journals; Consultancies to Food and Agriculture Organisation, 1981; United Nations Environment Programme, 1982–; Edited, State of the Environment Report, UNEP, 1983, 1984; Environment: A Dialogue Among Nations, UNEP, 1985; Radiation: Doses, Effects, Risks, UNEP, 1985. *Honours:* Runner up, Young Journalist of the Year, British National Press Awards, 1972; Yorkshire Council for Social Service Press Award, 1972; Glaxo Travelling Fellowship, 1973. *Literary Agent:* Caradoc King, AP Watt and Son. *Address:* The Observer, 8 St Andrew's Hill, London EC4V 5JA; 56 Middleton Road, London E8 4BS, England.

LEAPMAN, Michael Henry, b. 24 Apr. 1938, London, England. Writer; Journalist. m. Olga Mason at London 15 July 1965, 1 son. *Literary Appointments:* Journalist; The Times, 1969–81. *Publications:* One Man and His Plot, 1976; Yankee Doodles, 1982; Companion Guide to New York, 1983; Barefaced Cheek, 1983; Treachery, 1984. *Contributions to:* Numerous magazines and journals. *Honours:* Campaigning Journalist of the Year. British Press Award, 1968; Thomas Cook Travel Book Award, Best Guide Book of 1983. *Memberships:* Society of Authors; National Union of Journalists. *Literary Agent:* Felicity Bryan, Curtis Brown. *Address:* 13 Aldebert Terrace, London SW8 1BH, England.

LEASOR, (Thomas) James, b. 20 Dec. 1923, Erith, Kent, England. Author; Member of Lloyds. m. Joan Margaret Bevan, 1 Dec. 1951, London, 3 sons. *Education:* BA, MA Honours, Oriel College, Oxford. *Literary Appointments:* Feature Writer, Foreign Correspondent, Daily Express, London; Editorial Advisor, Newnes & Pearsons (later IPC); Director, Elm Tree Books Ltd. *Publications include:* The One That Got Away, with K Burt, 1956; Follow the Drum, 1972; Passport series, adventure novels, featuring Dr Jason Love, 1964–79; Boarding Party, 1980; Who Killed Sir Harry Oakes, 1983; etc. *Contributions to:* Readers Digest; Argosy; Sunday Express; Sunday Times. Also USA. *Memberships:* Society of Authors; Crime Writers Association. *Literary Agent:* Michael Shaw of Curtis Brown, 192-168 Regent Street, London, UK. *Address:* Swallowcliffe Manor, Salisbury, Wiltshire, England.

LEBEL, Robert, b. 5 Jan. 1901, Paris, France. Art Expert, French Courts of Justice; President, French Chamber of Art Experts. *Education:* Sorbonne; Dip Ecole du Louvre. *Publications:* Leonardo de Vinci, 1952; Marcel Duchamp, 1959; Gericault, 1960; La Double Vue, 1964; L'Envers de la Peinture, 1964; L'Oiseau Caramel, 1969; Traite des Passions, 1972; La Saint-Charlemagne. *Contributor to:* Preuves; L'oeil; Art and Artists, etc. *Honour:* Prix du Fantastique, 1965. *Address:* 16 Boulevard Raspail, Paris 75007, France.

LECLERC, Ivor, b. Dordrecht, South Africa. m. Joan Pirie, 6 Sep. 1975, Cambridge, USA, 1 son, 1 daughter. *Education:* BA, University of South Africa, 1942; MA, University of Capetown, 1946; PhD, University of London, England, 1949. *Publications:* Whitehead's Metaphysics, 1958; Nature of Physical Existence, 1972; Philosophy of Nature, 1986; Editor: The Relevance of Whitehead, 1961; The Philosophy of Leibniz and the Modern World, 1973. *Contributor to:* The Ontology of Descartes, Review of Metaphysics; Metaphysics and the Theory of Society, Philosophoha Miasl; God and the Problem of Being, Religious Studies; Metaphysics of the Good, Review of Metaphysics. *Address:* Box 799, Camden, ME 04843, USA.

LEDDY, Mary Jo, b. 1 Feb. 1946, Toronto, Canada. Journalist. *Education:* BA, BEd, MA, PhD (philosophy). *Literary Appointments:* Founding member, 1977–, Editor, 1977–79, Co-Editor, 1981–85, Catholic New

Times; Columnist Toronto Star, 1978–; Commentator, CBC TV, 1985–. *Contributions to:* Catholic New Times: Toronto Star; Prairie Messenger; Catalyst; Mandate; Presbyterian Record; National Catholic Reporter. *Honours:* Canadian Council Doctoral Fellowship, 1972; Canadian University President's Award: One of the Outstanding Young Women of 1978; Canadian Church Press Award, Best Editorial, Best Feature, 1978, 1979; Award from Catholic Press Association of North American for 'Best National Newspaper'. *Memberships:* Catholic Church Press; Canadian Catholic Church Press. *Address:* 489 Brunswick Avenue, Toronto, Ontario M5R 2Z6, Canada.

LEDER, Lawrence H, b. 23 Feb. 1927, New York, USA. Professor of History. m. Bernice E Kadish, 16 Mar, 1968, New York City, 1 son, 2 daughters. *Education:* AB cum laude, Long Island University, 1949; AM 1950, PhD 1960, New York University. *Publications:* Robert Livingston, 1654–1728, and the Politics of Colonial New York, 1961; The Glorious Revolution in America; Documents on the Colonial Crisis of 1689, 1964 and 1972; Liberty and Authority: Early American Political Ideology, 1689–1763, 1968 and 1976; America, 1603–1789: Prelude to a Nation, 1972 and 1978; Dimensions of Change: Problems and Issues of American Colonial History, 1972. *Contributions to:* New York Historical Society Quarterly; New York History; Business History Review; The William and Mary Quarterly; Mississippi Valley Historical Review; New York Public Library Bulletin; Huntington Library Quarterly. *Honours include:* Penfield Fellowship in History, New York University, 1955; James C Healey Medal, New York University Graduate School, 1961; Distinguished Faculty Citation, Louisiana State University Alumni Association, 1964; Distinguished Alumni Citation, Long Island University Association, 1975. *Address:* Lehigh University, Bethlehem, PA 18015, USA.

LEDERER, Paul Joseph, 2 July 1944, San Diego, California, USA. Author. 2 sons. *Education:* San Diego State University. *Publications:* The Sun Flower's Issue, 1978; A History of the Early Theater, 1979; Tecumseh, 1982; Manitou's Daughters, 1982; Shawnee Dawn, 1982; Cheyenee Dreams, 1985. *Honours:* Porgie Award, West Coast Review of Books, 1982. *Literary Agent:* Richard Curtis, 164 E Street, New York. *Address:* Box 107, Pine Valley, CA 92062, USA.

LEE, Alfred McClung, b. 23 Aug. 1906, Oakmont, Pennsylvania, USA. Social Scientist. m. 15 Sep. 1927, Pittsburgh, 2 sons. *Education:* MA, 1931, BA, 1927, University of Pittsburgh; PhD, Yale University, 1933. *Publications:* The Daily Newspaper in America, 1937, 3rd edition 1973; The Fine Art of Propaganda, co-author, 1939, 3rd edition 1979; Race Riot, co-author, 1943, 2nd edition 1968; Principles of Sociology, Editor, Co-author, 1946, 3rd edition 1969; Social Problems in America, co-author, 1949, 2nd edition 1955; Readings in Sociology; Editor, Co-Author, 1951; How to Understand Propaganda, 1952; Public Opinion and Propaganda, co-editor, co-author, 1954; Fraternities Without Brotherhood, 1955; La Sociologia delle Communicazioni, UNESCO Italian Lectures, 1960; Marriage and the Family, co-author, 1961; 2nd edition 1967; Che Cose'e' la Propaganda, Fulbright Lectures, 1961; Multivalent Man, 1966, 2nd edition 1970; Toward Humanist Sociology, 1973; Sociology for Whom?, 1978; 2nd edition 1986; Human Rights in the Northern Ireland Conflict, 1980; Terrorism in Northern Ireland, 1983. *Contributor to:* Numerous professional journals. *Honours:* KT Friend Fellow, 1931–33, Sterling Postdoctoral Fellow, 1933–34, Yale University; Award of Honour, Corriere della Sera Nespapers, Milan, Italy, 1967; Merit Award, Eastern Sociological Society, 1974; Lee & Lee Founders Award, Society for the Study of Social Problems, 1981; Distinguished Career Award, Clinical Sociological Association, 1984; Recipient, various other honours and awards. *Memberships include:* American Sociological Association, Council member, 1953–54, 1955–57, 1961–64, President 1975–76; Michigan Sociological Society, President, 1946–47; Eastern Sociological Society, President,

1954–55; International Sociological Association, USA Representative on Council, 1965–70; Society of Professional Journalists (National Research Award 1937, Certificate of Appreciation 1984); Sigma Xi; etc. *Address:* 17 Holden Lane, Madison, NJ 07940, USA.

LEE, Audrey M, b. USA. Writer. *Publications:* "The Clarion People", 1968; The Workers, 1969. *Contributor to:* Playgirl; Essence; Black World; Negro Digest; Anthologies: What We Must See; Hartford Courant Newspaper; etc. *Memberships:* Authors Guild; Poets & Writers. *Address:* P O Box 16622, Philadelphia, PA 19139, USA.

LEE, Dennis Beynon, 31 Aug. 1939, Toronto, Canada. Writer. m. (1) Donna Youngblut, 1962, Toronto (divorced) 1 son, 2 daughters, (2) Susan Perly, 1985. *Education:* BA, English, 1962, MA, English, 1965, University of Toronto. *Literary Appointments:* Writer-in-residence, Trent University, Ontario, 1975; Writer-in-residence, University of Toronto, 1978–79; Holder of Scottish-Canadian exchange fellowship in Edinburgh, 1980–81. *Publications:* Kingdom of Absence (poetry) 1967; Civil Elegies (poetry) 1968; Civil Elgies and Other Poems (expanded version) 1968; Wiggle to the Laundromat (children's poetry) 1970; Alligator Pie (children's poetry) 1974; Nicholas Knock and Other People (children's poetry) 1974; Garbage Delight (children's Poetry) 1977; Savage Fields: An Essay in Literature and Criticism (non-fiction, literary theory) 1977; The Gods (poetry) 1979; The Ordinary Bath (children's tale) 1979; Jelly Belly (children's poetry) 1983; Lizzy's Lion (children's poetry) 1984; Editor: The New Canadian Poets; 1970–1985 (anthology) 1985; Writer of song lyrics, children's TV series 'Fraggle Rock'. *Contributor to:* Numerous magazines and journals. *Honours:* Governor General's Award for Poetry, 1972; Canadian Association of Children's Librarians' Medal for Best Children's Book, 1974 and 1977; Philips Literary Prize, 1984. *Membership:* Writers' Union of Canada; PEN Canada. *Literary Agent:* Murray and Gina Pollinger, London (for children's writing).

LEE, Donald Lewis, b. 29 Nov. 1931, Blaydon/Tyne, England. University Professor. m. Shirley Hepple. 24 Aug. 1959, Gateshead/Tyne, 2 sons, 1 daughter. *Education:* BSc, King's College, University of Durham, 1956; PhD, Christ's College, University of Cambridge, 1959. *Literary Appointments:* Editorial Board, Parasitology. *Publications:* The Physiology of Nematodes, 1965; Symbiosis, (with D H Jennings), 1975; Physiology of Nematodes (with H J Atkinson), 2nd edition, 1976. *Contributions to:* Over 80 contributions to scientific journals including: Parasitology; International Journal of Parasitology; Experimental Parasitology; Journal of Zoology; Tissue and Cell. *Honours:* Scientific Medal, Zoological Society of London, 1971. *Membership:* Leeds Philosophical and Literary Society. *Address:* 970 Scott Hall Road, Leeds LS17 6HH, England.

LEE, Hun, b. 17 Sep. 1917, Biologist. *Education:* National Cultural University, China, 1942; BA 1949; MA 1951, University of Texas, Austin, USA; University of California, Berkeley, 1951–52; Studied poetry with Chinese poets Shih-fan Pu and Lin-Sheng Liu. *Contributions to:* China Poetry Studies; Min-tsu Evening News; Cultural Daily; San Francisco Chinese Times; Tien-Sheng Weekly; World-wide Manchingyee Poetry Association publications. *Memberships:* Co-chairman 1975–78, World-wide Manchingyee Poetry Association; Fellow, Institute of Poetry Studies. *Address:* 1223 16th Avenue, San Francisco, CA 94122, USA.

LEE, Joyce Isabel, b. 19 June 1913, Murtoa, Australia. Pharmacist; Lecturer. m. Norman Edward, 18 Dec. 1937, 2 sons. *Education:* Methodist Ladies' College; Registered Pharmacist, Victorian College of Pharmacy, Melbourne. *Literary Appointments:* Lecturer/Tutor (Poetry Writing) Victoria College of Advanced Education, Toorak Campus, 1981–. *Publications:* Sisters Poets 1, 1979, reprinted 1979 and 1980; Abruptly from

the Flatlands, 1984 reprinted 1984. *Contributions to:* Meanjin; Poetry Australia; The Age; The Bulletin; Luna; Compass; Contempa; New Europe; Premier Poets and various anthologies. *Honours:* Literature Board Grants 1977 and 1982; Maryborough Golden Wattle Festival, 1st Prize for Poetry; Grenfull Henry Lawson Prize for Verse, 1978; Poetry Prize, Communicating Arts Centre, 1981; MacGregor Prize for Poetry 1982. *Memberships:* Committee Member, International PEN Melbourne; Fellowship of Australian Writers; Poets Union; Society of Women Writers (Australia). Treasurer Parish Press Co-op Ltd. *Address:* 5 Morrison Street, Hawthorn, Victoria 3122, Australia.

LEE, Kuei-shien, b. 19 June 1937, Taipei, Taiwan, Republic of China. Patent Agent; Chemical Engineer; Corporation President. m. Huei-uei Wang, 1965, 1 son, 1 daughter. *Education:* Chemical Engineering, Taipei Institute of Technology, 1958; German Literature, European Language Center of Educational Ministry, 1964. *Literary Appointments:* Director, Li Poetry Society; Publisher, Inventors Journal; Examiner, Wu Tzu-lieu New Poetry Award. *Publications:* Essays include: Journey to Europe, 1971; Profile of the Souls, 1972; Essays on German Literature, 1973; On International Patent Practices, 1975; Critical Essays on Chinese Translation of English Poetry, 1976; Poetry includes: Pagoda and Other Poems, 1963; The Loquat, 1964; Poems on Nankang, 1966; Naked Roses, 1976; Collected poems, 1985; Anthologies include: Anthology of German Poems, 1970; Anthology of Black Orpheus, 1974; Translations include: The Trial by Franz Kafka, 1969; Cat and Mouse by Gunter Grass, 1970; Rainer Maria Rilke by H E Holthusen, 1969. *Contributions to:* Numerous magazines and journals including: Taiwan Literature; Modern Poetry; Epoch Poetry Quarterly. *Honours include:* Outstanding Poet Award, 1967; Wu Tzu-lieu New Poetry Award, 1975; Chung Hsing Literary Medal for Poetry, 1978. *Memberships include:* Supervisor, Chinese New Poetry Association; founder Fellow, International Academy of Poets; Rilke-Gesellschaft. *Address:* Room 705, Asia Enterprise Center, No 600 Minchuan East Road, Taipei, Taiwan, Republic of China.

LEE, Lance, b. 25 Aug. 1942, New York, New York, USA. Writer; Poet; Playwright. m. Jeanne Barbara Hutchings, 30 Aug. 1962, Laconia, New Hampshire, 2 daughters. *Education:* Boston University; BA, Brandeis University, 1964; MFA, Yale School of Drama, 1967. *Literary Appointments include:* Lecturer, Speech, Bridgeport University, 1967–68; Instructor, Creative writing, Southern Connecticut State College, 1968; Assistant Professor, Playwriting, Senior Lecturer, 1968–71, University of Southern California; Lecturer, Playwriting, University of California, 1971–73; Lecturer, Screenwriting, California State University, 1981–. *Publications:* Plays: Fox, Hound and Huntress, 1973; Time's Up, 1979; Productions: Time's Up; Gambits; Fox Hound and Huntress; Rasputin. *Contributions to:* Numerous including: Glass Onion; The Journal; Voices International; Poem; Lake Superior Review; Midwest Poetry Review; Cottonwood Review; San Fernando Poetry Journal; Poetry Project One; Whiskey Island Quarterly; Riverside Quarterly; Literary Quarterly; Coast Magazines; Chicago Review; Los Angeles Times; Pulpsmith (the Smith); Poetry Northwest; Poetry/LA; Hiram Poetry Review. *Honours:* Fellowships: National Endowment for the Arts, 1976; Theatre Development Fund, 1976; Rockefeller Foundation, 1971; University of Southern California Research and Publication Grants, 1970–71; Arts of the Theatre Foundation, 1967; Squaw Valley Community of Writers, 1982; Port Townsend (Centrum), 1985; Theron Bamberger Award in Playwriting, Brandeis University, 1964; Wells Scholar in Poetry, 1983. *Memberships:* Dramatists Guild; Authors League; American Academy of Poets; Poetry Society of America. *Address:* 1127 Galloway Street, Pacific Palisades, CA 90272, USA.

LEE, William David, b. 13 Aug. 1944, Matador, Texas, USA. Professor of English. m. Jan Miller Lee, 13 Aug. 1971, Moss Ledge, Wasatch Forest, 1 son, 1 daughter.

Education: BA, 1967, Colorado State University; MA, 1970, Idaho State University; PhD, 1973, University of Utah. *Literary Appointments:* Professor of English, Southern Utah State College, Cedar City, Utah, 1971–. *Publications:* The Porcine Legacy, 1978; Driving amd Drinking, 1979, 1982; Shadow Weaver, 1984; The Porcine Canticles, 1984. *Contributions to:* Midwest Quarterly; Willow Springs Magazine; Kayak; Chowder Review; Pebble; Oregon Horseman; 7 Poets. *Honours:* Finalist, honorable mention, Elliston Award, 1978. First Place, serious poetry, 25th Utah Original Writing Contest. *Memberships:* Utah Arts Council; Utah Artist in Education; AWP; Poetry Society of America. *Address:* Box 62, Paragonah, UT 84760, USA.

LEE, William Rowland, b. Uxbridge, Middlesex, England. m. Zdena Pausarova, 9 July 1948, Prague, 2 daughters. *Education:* Teacher's Diploma, University of London, 1934; Certificates in English, Phonetics and French Phonetics, 1934, 35; PhD, Charles University, Prague, 1950; MA, Linguistics, University of London, 1954. *Literary Appointments:* Lecturer, Department of English, Charles University, Prague, 1946–51; Lecturer, English as a Foreign Language, University of London Institute of Education, 1952–57, 1959–62; Language Teaching Adviser, British Council, London, 1958, 59; Freelance Textbook Writer, Examiner and Lecturer, 1963–; Editor: English Language Teaching Journal, 1961–81; World Language English, 1982–84. *Publications:* English Intonation: A New Approach, 1958; Teach Yourself Czech (with Z. Lee), 1959; An English Intonation Reader, 1960; Spelling Irregularity and Reading Progress, 1960, 1972; Time for a Song (with M Dodderidge, 1963; Simple Audio-Visual Aids to Foreign Language Teaching (with H Coppen, 1964, 68; Language Teaching Games and Contests, 1979–82, The Dolphin English Course, 1970, 1973; A Study Dictionary of Social English, 1984. *Contributions to:* Magazines and professional publications. *Honours:* Honorary Fellow, Trinity College London, 1972; OBE, 1979. *Memberships:* Founder and Chairman (1967–84), The International Association of Teachers of English as a Foreign Language and other professional organizations. *Literary Agent:* Passim Ltd. *Address:* 16 Alexandra Gardens, Hounslow, Middlesex TW3 4HU, England.

LEECE, William John, b. 21 Dec. 1951, Wrexham, England. Journalist. *Education:* St Catherine's College, Oxford. *Literary Appointments:* Journalist, 1972–; Music and Opera Reviewer, 1975–, Business Writer, 1980–, Liverpool Daily Post and Echo. *Contributor to:* Occasional contributor to specialist magazines. *Address:* Liverpool Daily Post and Echo, PO Box 48, Old Hall Street, Liverpool L69 3EB, England.

LEECH, Geoffrey Neil, b. 16 Jan. 1936, Gloucester, England. University Professor. m. Frances Anne Berman, 29 July 1961, Watford, 1 son, 1 daughter. *Education:* BA, English Language and Literature, 1959, MA, 1963, PhD, 1968, University College, London. *Publications:* English in Advertising, 1966; A Linguistic Guide to English Poetry, 1969; Towards a Samantic Description of English, 1969; Meaning and the English Verb, 1971; A Grammar of Contemporary English (with R Quirk, 5 Greenbaum and J Svartvik), 1972; Samantics, 1974, 2nd edition 1981; A Communicative Grammar of English (with J Svertvik), 1975; Explorations in Samantics and Pragmatics, 1980; Style in Fiction (with Michael H Short), 1981; English Grammar for Today (with R Hoogenread and M Deucher), 1982; Principles of Pragmatics, 1983; A Comprehensive Grammar of the English Language (with R Quirk, 5 Greenbaum and J Svartvik), 1985. *Contributions to:* A Review of English Literature; Lingua; New Society; Linguistics; Dutch Quarterly Review of Anglo-American Letters; TL5; Prose Studies; The Rising Generation; Transactions of the Philological Society. *Address:* 12 Clougha Avenue, Lancaster LA1 3JG, England.

LEEDS, Barry Howard, b. 6 Dec. 1940, New York, USA. Professor of English. m. Robin Leigh Flowers, 20 Apr. 1968, New York, 2 daughters. *Education:* BA, 1962, MA, 1963, Columbia University; PhD, Ohio University, 1967. *Literary Appointments:* Lecturer in English, City University of New York, 1963–64; Instructor in English, University of Texas at El Paso, 1964–65; Teaching Fellow in English, Ohio University (Athens), 1965–67; Assistant Professor of English, 1968–71, Associate Professor of English, 1971–76, Professor of English, 1976–, Central Connecticut State University. *Publications:* The Structured Vision of Norman Mailer, 1969; Ken Kesey, 1981. *Contributions to:* Various magazines, journals and anthologies, articles and reviews, including; Saturday Review, Modern Fiction Studies, Journal of Modern Literature, Columbia Review, Contemporary Literary Critism. *Honours:* Central Connecticut State University Distinguished Service Award, 1982; Visiting Faculty Fellowship at Yale University, 1984–85. *Address:* 133 Jerome Avenue, Burlington, CT 06013, USA.

LEEDS, Morton Harold, b. 15 May, 1921, New York, USA. Writer; Management Consultant. m. Ingrid Rheinstrom, 25 June 1948, New York, 3 daughters. *Education:* BSSc, City College of New York, 1944; MA, 1948, PhD, 1950, Graduate Faculty, New School for Sociel Research, New York. *Publications:* Ageing in Indiana, 1959; The Aged, the Social Worker and the Community, 1961; Geriatric Institutional Management, with H Shore, 1964; Washington Colloquium on Science and Society, 2nd series 1967; Jackstones, poetry, 1970; Outgrowing Self-Deception, 1975, The Paranormal and the Normal, 1979, with Gardner Murphy. *Contributor to:* About 90 articles, book chapters, reviews, monographs, 50 additional poems; etc. *Address:* 6219 Lone Oak Drive, Bethesda, MD 20817, USA.

LEERBURGER, Benedict, A, b. 2 Jan. 1932, New York, USA. Writer. m. Julie Loeb, 22 June, 1958, White Plains, New York, 2 daughters. *Education:* BA, Colby College. *Literary Appointments:* Assistant Editor, Product Engineering, 1956–61; Science Editor, Grolier Inc, 1961–63; Managing Editor, Book Division, Look, Magazine, 1963–68; Director of Micropublications, Greenwood Press, 1968–69; Vice-President & Editorial Director, National Micropublishing Corporation, 1969–71; Director of Publications, MCA Division, New York Times, 1971–73, KTO Press 1973–76; Editor-in-Chief, Webster Division, McGraw-Hill Book Co, 1976–79; Freelance Writer & Editorial Consultant, 1979–. *Publications:* Josiah Willard Gibbs: American Theoretical Physicist, 1967; Marketing the Library, 1983; Flight, 1985; Automobiles, 1985; The Complete Consumer's Guide to the Latest Telephones, 1985. *Contributor to:* Look; Popular Science; Science Digest; Science News; Venture; Think; Guide to New England; Upcountry; Product Engineering; Scanorama; Orion Nature Review; Book of Popular Science; Book of Knowledge; Encyclopaedia Britannica, and others. *Memberships:* National Association of Science Writers (Life Member); American Society of Journalists & Authors; Explorers Club. *Literary Agent:* John Wright. *Address:* 338 Heathcote Road, Scarsdale, NY 10583, USA.

LEESON, Robert Arthur, b. 31 Mar. 1928, Barnton, Cheshire, England. Writer. m. Gunvor Hagen, 25 May 1954, Oslo, 1 son, 1 daughter. *Education:* English (Hons) Degree, London University (external). *Publications:* For Children: Third Class Genie, 1975; The White Horse, 1977; Silver's Revenge, 1978; It's My Life, 1980; Grange Hill Goes Wild, 1980; Candy For King, 1983; For Adults: Strike: A Live History, 1887–1971; 1973; Travelling Brothers: The Six Centuries; Journey from Craft Fellowship to Trade Unionism, 1979; Reading and Righting: The Past Present and Future of Fiction for the Young, 1985. *Contributions to:* all major journals concerned with children's literature; Literary and Children's Editor of the 'Morning Star', 25 years to 1984. *Honour:* Eleanor Farjeon Award for Services to Children's Literature, 1984. *Memberships:* Writers Guild of Great Britain, Chair, Books Committee, 1984–85; International Board on Books for Young

People, British Section, Treasurer, 1978–. *Address:* 18 McKenzie Road, Broxbourne, Hertfordshire, England.

LEFF, Gordon, b. 9 May 1926, London, England. University Professor. 1 son. *Education:* BA 1st Class Honours Historical Trinos 1950–51, PhD 1954. Litt D 1968; Cambridge. *Publications:* Bradwardine and the Pelagians, 1957; Medieval Thought, 1958; Gregory of Rimini, 1961; The Tyranny of Concepts, 1961 and 1969; Richard Fitzralph, 1964; Heresy on the Later Middle Ages, 2 volumes, 1967; Paris and Oxford Universities, 1968; History and Social Theory, 1969; William of Oakham, 1975; The Dissolution of the Medieval Outlook, 1976. *Address:* The Sycamores, 12 The Village, Strensall, York YO3 5XS, England.

LEFORT, Suzanne-Jules, b. 18 July 1951, Montréal, P Québec, Canada. Writer. *Education:* Secondaire V = 12° Sciences Lettres. *Publications:* Sortie Exit Salida, 1973. *Contributions to:* La Libidienne in La Nouvelle Barre Du Jour, 1979; La Pyramide De Cristal in XYZ, 1985. *Memberships:* L'Union des Écrivains Quebécois, 1978; Société des Auteurs, Recherchistes, Documentalistes et Compositeurs, 1982. *Address:* 12051 Boul St Germain, Montréal, P Québec H4J 2A4, Canada.

LEGAGNEUR, Serge, b. 10 Jan. 1937, Jérémie, Haiti. Professor, Writer, Poet. *Literary Appointments:* Professor of French Literature; Reader and Re-writer in publishing Houses. *Major Publications:* Zextes Interdits; Textes en Croix; Le Crabe; Inaltérable. *Contributor to:* Semences; Rond-Point; Conjunction; Lettres et écritures; Passe-Partout; Estuaire; Nouvelle Optique; Possibles; Mot pout Mot; Nouvelliste; Panorama; Haiti-Littéraire; Le Matin. *Memberships:* Founder, Haiti-Littéraire; Qu[ec]ebec Writers Union; Attended various international Writers' conferences. *Address:* 3320 Boulevard Gouin E, app 101, Montréal, Québec, H1H 5P3, Canada.

LEGAT, Michael Ronald, b. 24 Mar. 1923, London, England. Author. m. Irene Rosetta Clark, 20 Aug. 1949, Norbury, London, 2 sons. *Literary Appointments:* Editorial Director, Transworld Publishers Limited, 1956–73, Cassell Limited, 1973–78. *Publications:* Dear Author... 1972; Mario's Vineyard, 1980; The Silver Fountain, 1982; An Author's Guide to Publishing, 1983; Putting on a Play, 1984; The Shapiro Diamond, 1984; The Silk Maker, 1985. *Memberships:* Society of Authors; Society of Sussex Authors; Chairman, Haywards Heath Literary Society; President, Weald of Sussex Authors. *Literary Agent:* Campbell Thomson and McLaughlin Limited. *Address:* Brevic, Lewes Road, Horsted Keynes, Haywards Heath, West Sussex RH17 7DP, England.

LEGERE, Werner, b. 28 May 1912, Hohenstein-Ernstthal, Germany. Author; Former Clerk. m. Ruth Corsa, 10 Oct. 1942, Hohenstein-Er, 2 sons. *Publications:* Ich War in Timbuktu, 1955; Unter Korsaren Verschollen, 1955; Die Verschworung von rio Cayado, 1956; Schwester Florence, 1956; Der Ruf Von Castiglione, 1960; Stern Aus Jakos, 1963; Die Stiere von Assur, 1969; Der Geforchtete Gaismai, 1976; In Allen Meinen Taten, 1982; *Honours:* First Prize Group Adventure Books for Children and Young People for, Ich War in Timbuktu, from Board of Literature of the GDR, 1953; Art Prize of the County Karl-Marx-Stadt, 1961; Artur-Becker Medal in Silver of Free German Youth Organization, 1962; Johannes R Becher Medal in Silver of the Kulturbund (Cultural Association) of the GDR, 1982; Culture Prize of the County Karl-Marx-Stadt, 1982. *Membership:* Schriftstellerverband der DDR (Authors organization of GDR). *Address:* Lutherstrasse 1, GDR-9270 Hohenstein-Ernstthal, Democratic Republic of Germany.

LEGGATT, Alexander, Maxwell, b. 18 Aug. 1940, Trafalgar Township, Ontario, Canada. Professor of English. m. Margaret Ann Thomas, 31 Mar. 1964, Wolverton, Warwickshire, 4 daughters. *Education:* BA, University of Toronto, 1962; MA 1963, PhD 1965, University of Birmingham. *Literary Appointments:* Associate Editor, Modern Drama, 1972–75; Editorial Board, English Studies in Canada, 1984–. *Publications:* Citizens Comedy in the Age of Shakespeare, 1973; Shakespeare's Comedy of Love, 1974; Ben Jonson: His Vision and His Art, 1981. *Contributions to:* Articles and reviews in publications including: Book Forum; Canadian Drama; CRNLE Reviews Journal; English Studies in Canada; Journal of English and Germanic Philology; Modern Drama; Modern Language Notes; Modern Language Quarterly; Modern Language Review; Mosaic; Queen's Quarterly; Renaissance and Reformation; Shakespeare Quarterly; Shakespeare Studies; Southern Review, Adelaide; Studies in English Literature. *Honours:* Guggenheim Fellowship, 1985–86. *Memberships:* Association of Canadian University Teachers of English; International Association of University Professor of English; Shakespeare Association of America. *Address:* University College, University of Toronto, Toronto M5S 1A1, Canada.

LEGLER, Philip, b. 7 Mar. 1928, Dayton, Ohio, USA. Professor; Poet. m. Martha Jane Prater, 26 Aug. 1950, Dayton, 1 son, 2 daughters. *Education:* A Change of View, 1964; The Intruder, 1972. *Contributor to:* Poetry; Poetry Northwest; Prairie Schooner; New York Times; Paris Review; Antioch Review; Quarterly Review of Literature; etc. *Memberships:* Poetry Society of America; Michigan Council for the Arts Poetry in the Schools Project. *Address:* 128 E Magnetic, Marquette, MI 49855, USA.

LEHMANN, Johannes Asirvadam Arno, b. 7 Sep. 1929, Madras, India. Editor, Radio Stuttgart, Germany. m. 19 May 1956, Geneva, 2 daughters. *Publications:* Jesus Report, in nine languages, 1970; Die Hethiter: Volk der Tausend Gotter, 1974; Die Kreuzfahrer: Abenteurer Gottes, 1976; Die Staufer, 1978; Buddha: Leben, Lehre Wirkung, 1980; Moses: Der Mann aus Agypten, 1983; Das Geheimnis des Rabbi J, 1985. *Contributor to:* Various publications including, Merian. *Membership:* Deutscher Schriftstellerverband (Association of German Writers). *Address:* Degerlocher Strasse 8, 7000 Stuttgart, Federal Republic of Germany.

LEHMANN, Jürgen, b. 26 Dec. 1934, Grossdubrau, Democratic Republic of Germany. Editor. m. Eva Hollmann, 8 Aug. 1956, Görlitz, 1 son, 1 daughter. *Education:* Diploma, Germanistics, University. *Publications:* Begegnung mit einem Zauberer, short stories, 1976; (Novels) Strandgesellschaft, 1980; Hochzeitsbilder, 1983. *Contributor to:* Literary Journals. *Honours:* Förderungspreis des Mitteldeutschen Verlages, 1977; Kunstpreis der Stadt Leipzig, 1982. *Memberships:* Society of Authors and Writers of the Democratic Republic of Germany, Board Member, Leipzig District. *Address:* Pösnaer Strasse 17, 7027 Leipzig, Democratic Republic of Germany.

LEHMANN, Marlies, b. 11 Oct. 1931, Hamelin, Germany. Writer. m. Hans-Joachim Lehmann, 10 June 1955, 3 sons, 1 daughter. *Publication:* Im Schatten des Obelisken, 1982. *Contributions to:* Hamburger Abendblatt; Frankfurter Rundschau; Schleswig-Holstein-Monatshafte; Hoerzu and TV Hoeren und Sehen; Tina; Husumer Nachrichten and others. *Honours:* Hamburg Literary Prize for short prose, 1981. *Memberships:* Hamburg Authors Association; Writers in Schleswig-Holstein, Kiel. *Literary Agent:* Doernersche Verlagsgesellschaft Reinbek. *Address:* Carstensstr 9, D-2250 Husum, Federal Republic of Germany.

LEHMBERG, Stanford Eugene, b. 23 Sep. 1931, McPherson, Kansas, USA. Historian. m. Phyllis Barton, 23 July 1962, Austin, Texas. 1 son. *Education:* BA, 1953, MA, 1954, University of Kansas; PhD, Cambridge University, 1956. *Publications:* Sir Thomas Elyot, Tudor Humanist, 1960; Sir Walter Mildmay and Tudor Government, 1966; The Reformation Parliament, 1529–36, 1970; The Later Parliaments of Henry VIII, 1536–47, 1977. *Contributions to:* English Historical Review; Historical Journal; Studies in the Renaissance; Archiv fur Reformationsgeschichte; The Historian. *Honour:*

Guggenheim Fellowships, 1965–66, 1985–86. *Memberships:* President, Midwest Conference on British Studies, 1982–84; Council, American Historical Association, 1975–78. *Address:* Department of History, University of Minnesota, Minneapolis, MN 55455, USA.

LEIBRANDT, Thomas J, b. 3 May 1948, Philadelphia, Pennsylvania, USA. Editor; Writer. m. Linda Jeanne Lynott, 7 Oct. 1972, Abington, 1 son. *Education:* BA, LaSalle University, 1970; MA, Temple University, 1974. *Literary Appointments include:* Senior Editor, 1979–80, Editorial Manager, 1980–81, Nurse's Reference Library, Springhouse Corporation; Associate Editor, Nursing 82 and 83; Acquisitions Editor, Reference Book Division, Springhouse Corporation, 1983–84; Rewrite Editor, Catalyst Group, 1982–84; Editor, Educational Coordinator, Department of Surgery, Abington Memorial Hospital, 1984–. Numerous other editorial positions. *Contributions to:* Surgical Endoscopy; The Philadelphia Inquirer; The Sunday Bulletin; Inquirer; Chicago Tribune; Indianapolis Star; Cleveland Plain Dealer; The Poet; Creative Review; Poetry Scope; Alura; Poetry Quarterly. Participant in various seminars and conferences. *Honours:* Jesse H Neal Award for editorial excellence, American Business Press, 1983. *Memberships:* American Medical Writers Association; McKenna Society; Military History Society of Ireland. *Address:* 1104 Wheatsheaf Lane, Abington, PA 19001, USA.

LEIST, Otmar, b. 16 Jan. 1921, Breman, Federal Republic of Germany. Writer. *Publications:* Poetry: Helm ab zum Denken, 1975; In halber Helle, 1976; Jahre des Feuerteufels, 1976; Mobilmachung, 1977; Im Goldenen Westen, 1978; Menschenwerk, 1979; Die Stadt fur uns, 1981; Springende Punkte, 1984. *Contributions to:* die horen; Zivilcourage. *Memberships:* Association of German Writers; Literary Working Group of the Working World. *Address:* Löningstr. 35, 2800 Bremen 7, Federal Republic of Germany.

LELCHUK, Alan, b. 15 Sep. 1938, Brooklyn, New York, USA. Novelist m. Barbara Kreiger, 5 Oct. 1980, Hanover, 1 son. *Education:* BA, Brooklyn College, 1960; University of London, 1962–63; MA, PhD, 1965, Stanford University. *Appointments:* Writer-in-Residence, Brandeis University, 1966–81; Visiting Writer, Amherst College, 1982–84; Associate Editor, Modern Occasions, 1970–72. *Publications:* American Mischief, 1973; Miriam at Thirty-Four, 1974; Shrinking, 1978; Miriam in her Forties, 1985. *Contributor to:* Short Stories: New American Review; The Atlantic; Transatlantic Review; Modern Occasions; Work in Progress; Articles: Sewanee Review; Possent; Partisan Review; New York Times Book Review. *Honours:* Guggenheim Fellow, 1976–77; Guest Resident, MishKenot Sha'Ananim, Jerusalem, 1976–77. *Membership:* PEN. *Literary Agent:* Georges Borchardt Inc, New York City. *Address:* RFD 2, Canaan, NH 03741, USA.

LeMASTER, J R, b. 29 Mar. 1934, Pike County, Ohio, USA. Professor of English. m. Wanda May Ohnesorge, 22 May 1966, Defiance, Ohio, 1 son, 2 daughters. *Education:* BS, Defiance College, Ohio, 1959; MA, 1962, PhD, 1970, Bowling Green State University, Ohio. *Literary Appointments:* Editor, Texas Writers Newsletter, 1979–80; Founder and Director, Defiance College Poetry Day, 1970–77; Founder and Director, Baylor University Poetry Festival, 1979–. *Publications:* The Heart is a Gypsy, 1967; Children of Adam, 1971; Weeds and Wildflowers, 1975; Jessa Stuart: A Reference Guide, 1979; Jessa Stuart: Kentucky's Chronicler-Poet, 1980; First Person, Second, 1983; Editor: Poets of the Midwest, 1966; Jesse Stuart: The World of Jesse Stuart: Selected Poems, 1975; Jesse Stuart: Essays on His Work (with Mary W Clarke), 1977; Jesse Stuart: Selected Criticism, 1978; John Clarke Jordan: Making Sense of Grammar, 1980. *Contributor to:* Numerous magazines and journals. *Honours:* South and West Incorporated Publishers Award, 1970; Ohio Poet of the Year, 1976; Dean of the College Award for Academic Excellence, 1977. *Memberships:* Modern

Language Association; Southwest Modern Language Association; Texas Association of Creative Writing Teachers, etc. *Address:* 201 Harrington Avenue, Waco, TX 76706, USA.

LEMERT, James Bolton, b. 5 Nov. 1935, Sangerfield, New York, USA. University Professor. m. Rosalie Bassett, 23 Mar. 1972, Mill City, Oregon. *Education:* BA 1957, MJ 1959, University of California; PhD, Michigan State University, 1964; Post Doctoral work, University of Michigan, 1980. *Literary Appointments:* Sports Stringer, Oakland Tribune, 1954–56, Editor, Daily California, 1957; Education and Features Writer, Chico Enterprise-Record, 1957; Publications Writer, Institute for Transportation and Traffic Engineering, University of California, Richmond Research Station, 1957–58; Feature Writer, Chico Enterprise-Record, 1958–60. *Publications:* Does Mass Communication Change Opinion After All?, 1981, Spanish edition, 1983; Criticising the Media: Empirical Approaches. *Contributions to:* Editor and Publisher, columnist, 1966–67; Journalism Quarterly; Communications Research; Journal of Communication; Journal of Broadcasting; Public Opinion Quarterly; Political Communication Review. Obituary and analysis of pollster George Gallup in, The American Annual, 1985. *Honours include:* 6 Undergraduate Scholarships, University of California; Professional Chapter Award, San Francisco Bay Area, Society of Professional Journalists, 1956; Phi Beta Kappa, 1957; Fellow, National Science Foundation, 1963–64. *Address:* School of Journalism, University of Oregon, Eugene, OR 97403, USA.

LEMING, Ronald Lee, b. 9 Nov. 1950, Hercules, California, USA. Fiction Writer; Editor. *Education:* Black Belt Holder in several martial arts; BS, Abnormal Psychology. *Publications:* Damnations, 1984; More Damnations, 1986. *Contributor to:* Modern Haiku; The Horror Show; Eldritch Tales; Etchings and Odysseys; Approaching Critical Mass; Space Grits; The Arkham Companion; The Australian Horror and Fantasy Magazine; Timewarp; Mayfair; Upon a Star; Labyrinth; Potboiler; Grue Magazines; Haunts; Outlaw Biker; Twisted; Writer's Lifeline; SF&FW; Svavengee's Newletter; Fangoria; Weirdbook; Weirdbook Sampler. *Honour:* Short Story, Fox Goes Fission, nominated for a World Fantasy Award, 1968. *Memberships:* Science Fiction and Fantasy Workshop; Small Press Writers and Artists Organisation; Horror and Occult Writer's League; Science Fiction Writers of America. *Literary Agent:* Jean Teresa Sumner. *Address:* PO Box 5099, Lancaster, CA 93539, USA.

LEMKE, Alexander-Gotthilf, b. 28 Aug. 1908, Stettin. Writer and Linguist. m. Amalie-Gisea, 29 Aug. 1958. *Education:* University of Hamburg. *Publications:* Die dreizehn südchilenischan Lieder, 1932; Heiters Peil-Ergebnisse, 1941; Weltbild nach Augenmass, 1942; Schnappachüsse, 1943. *Address:* Max-Brauer-Allee 36, D–2000 Hamburg 50, Federal Republic of Germany.

LEMKE, Johannes, b. 6 Apr. 1921, Polchow, Cammin, Pomerania. Retired. m. Charlotte Lemke, 15 Apr. 1944, Germany, 2 sons, 1 daughter. *Education:* Agricultural College; Courses in Journalism, Literary Authorship. *Literary Appointments:* Started Journalism with the, Norddeutsche Zeitung. *Publications:* Bauerngeneral Blex, 1981; Kurz vor der grossen Reise, 1982; Der endlose Weg, 1983. *Contributor to:* Pommersche Zeitung; Camminer Heimatgrusse. *Membership:* Journalistic Working Group. *Address:* Mönichhusen 25, D–4970 Bad Oeynhausen 2, Federal Republic of Germany.

LEMON, George Edward, b. 23 June 1907, Youngstown, Ohio, USA. Former Bookkeeper; Steelworker; Army Officer. *Education:* 1 year, Ohio State University. *Publications:* Birdbrain Brainbeau's Bible, weekly publication. *Contributions to:* Numerous local & national creative contests; Advertisements, mail order publications. *Membership:* National Contesters Association. *Address:* 286 Lora Avenue, Youngstown, Ohio 44504, USA.

LEMON, Lee Thomas, b. 9 Jan. 1931, Kansas City, Kansas, USA. Professor. m. Maria Mullinaux, 5 May 1972, Lincoln, Nebraska, 3 sons, 3 daughters. *Education:* BA, St Louis University; MA, Southern Illinois University; PhD, University of Illinois. *Publications:* Partial Critics, 1975; Russian Formalist Criticism, 1965; Glossary for the Study of English, 1971; Portraits of the Artist in Contemporary Fiction, 1985. *Address:* 849 South 40th Street, Lincoln, NE 68510, USA.

LEMOS, Ramon Marcelino, b. 7 July 1927, Mobile, Alabama, USA. Professor of Philosophy. m. Mamia Lou McCrory, 26 Dec. 1951, Forest Home, Alabama, 4 sons. *Education:* BA, University of Alabama, 1951; MA, 1953, PhD, 1955, Duke University; Postdoctoral Student, University of London, 1955–56. *Publications:* Experience, Mind and Value: Philosophical Essays, 1969; Rousseau's Political Philosophy: An Exposition and Interpretation, 1977; Hobbes and Locke: Power and Consent, 1978; Rights, Goods and Democracy, 1986. *Contributions:* Conceptual and Conventional Necessity, Studium Generale, 1969; Emotion, Feeling and Behavior, Critica, 1970; Locke's Theory of Property, Interpretation, 1975; A Moral Argument for Democracy, Social Theory and Practice, 1976; A Defense of Retributivism, The Southern Journal of Philosophy, 1977 and others. *Address:* Department of Philosophy, University of Miami, Coral Gables, FL 33124, USA.

LEMP, Liselotte (Annemarie), b. 4 Apr. 1916, Oppeln, Germany. Writer. *Education:* 2 years study with Dr Frank Thiess. *Publications:* Stage plays: Die Augen, 1946; Das dunkle Jahr, 1947; Die Lilith, 1981; Zwei Maenner oder Verwirrung einer jungen Frau, 1982; Several radio plays, 1944–47; Poems in anthologies; Junges Berlin, 1948; Hamburger Anthologie, 1965; Lyrische Texte, 1982; Hinter den Traenen ein Laecheln, 1984; Lyrik Heute, 1984; ...und das kleine bisschen Hoffnung, 1985. *Contributions to:* Berliner Hefte für geistiges Leben: Verse, 1946; Perikles in Hellbrunn, 1947; Eine Flucht, 1948; Gedichte, 1949; Ettlinger Hefte: AD 1945: Im Gefängnis, 1979; Erinnerungen an Frank Thiess, 1979; Contributor to various other magazines and journals. *Honours:* Grant for travel, Vereinigung Deutscher Schriftstellerverbände e. V (Hamburg) and Foreign Office, Bonn, 1958. *Memberships include:* Freier Deutscher Autorenverband, Munich and Hamburg. *Address:* Alexander-Zinn-Strasse 6, D–2000 Hamburg 52, Federal Republic of Germany.

LEMPP, Karl Ferdinand, b. 14 Oct. 1913, Schwäbisch Gmünd, Federal Republic of Germany. Writer. m. (1) Lena Fliedner, 1937, Omaruru, Namibia, (2) Ingrid Becker, 1958, Luderitz, Namibia. 3 sons, 2 daughters. *Education:* Primary School Teacher, Namibia, 1932–36. *Literary Appointments:* Editor, Allgemeine Zeitung, Namibia, 1950–60; Editor, S W A Farmer, S W A Bulletin, Der Kreis, Namibia, 1957–64; Publisher, S W A Farmer, Der Kreis. *Publications:* Windhoek, 1964; Unsere Verantwortung, by H A Fagan, Afrikaans/German translation; Quacksalber, by James Harvey Young, English/German translation; Quintessenz, poems, 1973; Homer's Odyssee, in new German prose, 1985. *Contributions to:* Numerous publications in English, German and Afrikaans. *Memberships:* Literateam, German; Littera, Munich; Lübecker Autorenkreis, German. *Address:* Bahnhofstrasse 2, D 2081 Prisdorf, Federal Republic of Germany.

L'ENGLE, Madeleine, b. 29 Nov. 1918, New York, USA. Writer. m. 26 Jan. 1946, 1 son, 2 daughters. *Education:* AB, Honours, Smith College; D Humane Letters, Honorary, Gordon College; D Letters, Honorary, Miami University, Ohio; D Litt, Honorary, Wheaton College. *Appointments:* Writer in Residence, several US Universities; Writer in Residence, Cathedral St John the Divine, New York, 1965–. *Publications:* The Small Rain, 1945; Ilsa, 1946; And Both Were Young, 1949; Camilla, 1952; A Winter's Love, 1957; Meet the Austins, 1961; A Wrinkle in Time, 1962; The Moon by Night, 1963; The Arm of the Starfish, 1964; The Love Letters, 1965; The Journey with Jonah, 1966; The Yound Unicorns, 1967; Lines Scribbled on an Envelope, 1968; The Other Side of the Sun, 1969; A Circle of Quiet, 1970; A Wind in the Door, 1971; The Summer of the Great Grandmother, 1974; Dragons in the Waters, 1975; The Irrational Season, 1976; A Swiftly Titling Planet, 1977; A Ring of Endless Light, 1978; Walking on Water, 1980; The Sphinx at Dawn, 1981 A Severed Wasp, 1982; And It was Good, 1983; A House Like a Lotus, 1984. *Contributor to:* Numerous magazines and journals. *Honours:* Recipient numerous honours and awards including Smith College Medal, 1980; Sophie Award, 1984; Regina Medal, 1984; etc. *Memberships:* President, Authors Guild of America; Council Member, Authors League of America; Board of Directors, Authors League Fund. PEN. *Literary Agent:* Robert Lescher. *Address:* c/o Farrar Straus Giroux, 19 Union Square West, New York, NY 1003, USA.

LENHART, Gary, b. 15 Oct. 1947. Associate Director, Teachers and Writers Collaborative. m. Louise Hamlin. *Education:* BA, Sienna College, 1969; MA, University of Wisconsin, 1973; Graduate Study, Department of Comparative Literature, Rutgers University, 1973–74. *Publications:* Drunkard's Dream, 1978; Bulb in Socket, 1980; One at at Time, 1983. *Contributions to:* The World; In the Light; Saturday Morning; Poetry Project Newsletter; Dodgems; Lumen Avenue; A Little Light; American Book Review; Sagetrieb; Exquisite Corpse; Red Weather; Mag City Co-Editor. *Address:* 248 West 105th Street, Apt 6D, New York City, NY 10025, USA.

LENTNER, Howard H, b. 8 Sep. 1931, USA. College Professor. Divorced, 1 son, 2 daughters, 1 deceased. *Education:* BS, Miami University, 1958; MA, 1959, PhD, 1964, Syracuse University. *Publications:* Chapter in, International Crises, 1972; Foreign Policy Analysis : A Comparative and Conceptual Approach, 1974. *Contributor to:* Western Political Quarterly; Journal of Politics; Social Education; Toronto Daily Star; Freedom at Issue; World Politics; Orbis; International Perspectives; Comparative Politics. *Address:* 19 Abeel Street, 6H, Yonkers, NY 10705, USA.

LEONARD, Constance, b. 27 Apr. 1923, Pennsylvania, USA. Mystery Writer. m. John D Leonard, 21 June 1949, Caxton Hall, London, (divorced 1969), 1 daughter. *Education:* BA, Wellesley College. *Publications:* The Other Martha, 1972; Steps To Nowhere, 1974; Hostage in Illyria, 1976; Shadow Of a Ghost, 1978; The Marina Mystery, 1981; Stowaway, 1983; Aground, 1984; Strange Waters, 1985. *Contributions to:* Redbrook; Woman Grazia. *Memberships:* The Authors Guild; The Authors League of America. *Address:* Francestown, NH, USA.

LEONARD, Elmore, b. 11 Oct. 1925, New Orleans, Louisiana, USA. Novelist. m. Joan Shepard, 15 Sep. 1979, Birmingham, Michigan, USA. 3 sons, 2 daughters. *Education:* Bachelor's degree University of Detroit, 1950. *Publications include:* 21 novels including: Hombre, 1961; City Primeval, 1980; Split Images, 1981; Cat Chaser, 1982; Stick, 1983; Labrava, 1983; Glitz, 1985. *Honours:* Edgar Allen Poe Award for, Labrava, Mystery Writers of America, 1984; Michigan Foundation for the Arts award for literature, 1985. *Memberships:* Writers Guild of America Inc. West; Pen American; The Authors Guild; Western Writers of America; Mystery Writers of America. *Literary Agent:* H N Swanson. *Address:* c/o H N Swanson Literary Agent, 8523 Sunset, Los Angeles, CA 90069, USA.

LEONARD, George Burr, b. 9 Aug. 1923, Macon, Georgia, USA. Author. Lecturer. m. Annie Styron, 14 Feb. 1981, Mill Valley, California, 4 daughters. *Education:* BA, University of North Carolina, 1946; LHD, Lewis and Clarke, 1972. *Literary Appointments:* Senior Editor, Look Magazine, 1953–70; Contributing Editor, Esquire, 1984–. *Publications:* Shoulder the Sky, 1959; Education and Ecstacy, 1968; The Man and Woman Thing, 1970; The Transformation, 1972; The Ultimate Athlete, 1975; The Silent Pulse, 1978; The End of Sex, 1983. *Contributions to:* Numerous articles, including: Look; Esquire; Harper's; Atlantic; New York; Saturday Review; Reader's Digest. *Honours:* 7 National School Bell Awards, 1956–65; Education Writers Association Award, 1956, 1957, 1958; Certificate of Recognition, National Conference of Christians and Jews, 1967; Presidential Citation, American Alliance for Health and Physical Education, 1976. *Memberships:* Authors Guild; Authors League. *Literary Agent:* Sterling Lord, 660 Madison Avenue, New York, NY 10021. *Address:* Box 609, Mill Valley, CA 94942, USA.

LEONARD, Tom, b. 22 Aug. 1944, Glasgow. Freelance Writer/Poet. m. Sonya O'Brien, 24 Dec. 1971, Edinburgh, 2 sons. *Education:* MA, Scottish Literature and English Literature, Glasgow University. 1976. *Publications:* Poems, 1973; Intimate Voices: Writing 1965–1983, 1984; Satires and Profanites, 1984. *Contributor to:* Poetry Information of, The Locust Tree in Flower and Why it had Difficulty Flowering in Britain (essay on W C Williams) Winter 1976/77; Edinburgh, Review of Mater Tenebrarum (essay on James Thomson 1834–82) 1985. *Honours:* Scottish Arts Council Awards 1978, 1984; Joint Winner, Scottish Book of the Year Award, Saltire Society, 1984. *Membership:* Scottish Society of Playwrights. *Address:* 56 Eldon Street, Glasgow G3 6NJ, Scotland.

LEONHARD, Wolfgang, b. 16 Apr. 1921, Vienna, Austria. Author, Professor of History. m. Elke Schmid, 10 Oct. 1974, 1 son. *Education:* English Department, Moscow State Pedagogical Institute, USSR, 1940–41; School of the Communist International, USSR, 1942–43; St Antony's College, University of Oxford, England, 1956–58; Senior Research Fellow, Russian Institute, Columbia University, New York, USA, 1963–64. *Literary Appointments:* Professor of History and International Communism, Yale University, USA, 1966–. *Major Publications include:* Child of the Revolution, 1955; The Kremlin Since Stalin, 1959; Soviet Ideology Today, 1962; Kruschev, the Rise & Fall of a Soviet Leader, 1965; Three Faces of Marxism, 1970; Soviet Union: Future Prospects, 1975; Euro-Communism – A Challenge to East & West, 1978; all available in various translations. *Contributor to:* International Affairs; Problems of Communism; Foreign Affairs; Osteuropa; Schweizer Rundschau; Aus Politik und Zeitgeschichte; Der Monat; Samtiden (Oslo). *Honour:* DeVane Medal. *Membership:* PEN Club. *Address:* Kirchstraße 24, D–5562 Manderscheid/Eifel, Federal Republic of Germany.

LEONHARDT, Roland, b. 23 Jan. 1957, Gössnitz, Thuringia. *Education:* Commercial School; Evening School; Self-taught studies; University Giessen. *Appointments:* Aphorisums, Jenseits der Welt des Bosen, 1980; Leben, weil Gott uns Liebt, 1982; Segenswunsche zum Geburtstag, 1985; Herr, dein Licht lass mich schauen, 1985. *Publications:* Neue Sicht unseres Weltbildes (der Immanente Positivismus), with Professor Jonas-Lichtenwallner, 1979; Und jeder Tag ist ein Geschenk, 1984; Book Reviews in the association journal, I gd A-aktuell. *Honours:* Literary Scholarship, City of Bad Harzburg in association with the Free German Authors Association, 1982. *Memberships:* Free German Authors Association; Christian Authors Group; Group for Interests of German-speaking Authors; Association Authors in Kassel, Circle of Friends; Founder, Giessen Literary Circle. *Address:* Leipzigerstr. 15, 6336 Albshausen/Solms bei Wetzlar, Federal Republic of Germany.

LEONHARDT, Siegmund, b. 12 May 1939, Leipzig, Germany. Painter; Etcher; Illustrator; Teacher of Arts. m. Christel Rothley, 28 Sep. 1962, 2 sons. *Education:* Kunstakademie Dusseldorf; Johannes-Gutenberg Universitat Mainz; Philipps Universitat, Marburg. Academic Distinction, Studiendirektor. *Publications:* Russel in Komikland, 1972; Glucksucher in Venedig, 1973; Leben und Traum mit Schellenfusz, 1975; Schimpferd und Nilpanse, 1975; Barlamms Verwandlung, 1976; Der Prozess um des Esels Schatten, 1978. *Honours:* Bronze and Silver Medals for picture

books, International Book Exhibition, IBA, Leipzig, Germany, 1979. *Address:* Sandstr 18, 6101 Bickenbach, Federal Republic of Germany.

LEPORE, Dominick James, b. 1 July 1911, Enfield, Connecticut, USA. Retired Educator; Writer; Poet. m. Agatha Maggio, 15 Jan. 1949, Enfield, 1 daughter. *Education:* AB, College of the Holy Cross, 1933; MA, University of Connecticut, 1959; Graduate Work, Georgetown University, University of Hartford. *Appointments:* Public Relations Representative, National Council of Teachers of English, Committee on the Reading and Study of Poetry; Assistant Chairman, Pre-Conv Group, Effective English. *Publications:* The Praise and the Praised, 1955; Within His Walls, 1968. *Contributor to:* Arizona Quarterly; Blue Unicorn; Denver Quarterly; Cedar Rock; English Journal; Prairie Schooner; etc. *Honours:* DHL, Honoria Causa, L'Universite Libre (Asia) 1970; Diploma di Benemerenga, Centra Studi e Scambi 1972; Diploma, di Signalizione, Centro di Cultura, Taranto, 1975–81; Culta di Cagliari, Special Poetry Prize, 1977. *Memberships:* Poetry Society of America; New England Poetry Club. *Address:* 4 Mitchell Drive, Enfield, CT, 06082, USA.

LERMAN, Rhoda, b. 18 Jan. 1936, New York City, New York, USA. Novelist. m. Robert Lerman, 16 Aug. 1957, Los Angeles, California, 1 son, 2 daughters. *Education:* BA. *Literary Appointments:* Writer in Residence, University of Colorado, 1982–84; National Endowment for the Humanities Distinguished Professor in Humanities, Hartwick, 1984–; Visiting Professor, Creative Writing, Syracuse University, 1985. *Publications:* Call Me Ishtar, 1973; Girl That He Marries, 1967; Eleanor, A Novel, 1979; Book of the Night, 1984 and others. *Literary Agent:* Owen Lester, William Morris Agency. *Address:* Shore Acres, Cazernova, NY 13035, USA.

LERNER, Arthur, b. 10 Jan. 1915, Chicago, Illinois, USA. Author. m. Matilda T Fisher, 24 Nov. 1955, Los Angeles. *Education:* AB, Central YMCA College, Chicago, 1942; AM, Northwestern University, Evanston, 1946; PhD, 1953, MEd, 1960, MS, 1961, MA, 1964, PhD, 1968, University of Southern California, Los Angeles. *Publications:* Rhymed and Unrhymed, 1965; Follow-up, 1967; Psychoanalytically Oriented Criticism of Three American Poets: Poe, Whitman, and Aiken, 1970; Starting Points, 1971; Editor, Poetry in the Therapeutic Experience, 1978; Words for All Seasons, 1983. *Contributor to:* Los Angeles Mirror-News; Los Angeles Times; Chicago Sun-Times; Poet and Critic; APA Monitor; Voices; AHP Perspective; The Arts in Psychotherapy; ETC; The Clearing House. *Honours:* Literary Acheivement Book Award; International Poets Shrine, 1971. *Memberships:* PEN, Los Angeles Centre, Vice President, 1973; Poetry Society of America; Authors Guild. *Literary Agent:* Bertha Klausner, International Literary Agency, New York. *Address:* 520 South Burnside Avenue, Apt. 11C, Los Angeles, CA 90036, USA.

LERNER, Laurence David, b. 12 Dec. 1925, Cape Town, South Africa. Poet/University Professor. m. Natalie Hope Winch, 15 June 1948, Cambridge, 4 sons. *Education:* BA, 1944, MA, 1945, University of Cape Town; BA, Pembroke College, Cambridge, 1949. *Publications:* Poetry: Domestic Interior, 1959; The Directions of Memory, 1964; Selves, 1969; A.R.T.H.U.R. 1974; The Man I Killed, 1980; A.R.T.H.U.R. & M.A.R.T.H.A., 1980; Selected Poems, 1984; Chapter and Verse, 1984. Fiction: The Englishmen, 1959; A Free Man, 1968; My Grandfather's Grandfather, 1985. Criticism: The Truest Poetry, 1960; The Truthtellers, 1967; The Uses of Nostalgia, 1972; An Introduction to English Poetry, 1975; Love and Marriage, 1979; The Literary Imagination, 1982. *Contributor to:* Poems: TLS; New Statesman; Encounter; London Magazine; Observer; Sunday Times; Critical Quarterly; Jewish Quarterly etc. Frequent contributor of reviews, articles, stories etc to Encounter; also various academic journals e.g. Essays in Criticism. *Honours:* Various poetry prizes; South-East Arts

Literature Prize for 'Love and Marriage', 1979; Fellow of the Royal Society of Literature, 1984. *Literary Agent:* Jennifer Kavanagh. *Address:* 50 Compton Avenue, Brighton, Sussex BN1 3PS, England.

LERNER, Max, b. 20 Dec. 1902, Minsk, Russia. Professor; Writer; Columnist, Lecturer. m. (1) Anita Marburg, 20 July 1928, (2) Edna Albers, 16 Aug. 1941. 3 sons, 2 daughters. *Education:* AB 1923, Law student 1923–24, Yale University, USA; AM, Washington University, 1925; PhD, Robert Brookings Graduate School of Economics and Government, 1927. *Literary Appointments:* Assistant Editor, Managing Editor, Encyclopedia of Social Sciences, New York City, 1927–32; Editor, The Nation, 1936–38; Editorial Director, PM, 1943–48; Colmnist, New York Star, 1948–49; Syndicated Columnist, New York Post, 1949–. *Publications:* Ideas Are Weapons, 1939; Ideas For The Ice Age, 1941; It Is Later Than You Think, 1928 and 1943; The Mind and Faith of Justice Holmes, 1943; Public Journal, 1945; The Third Battle For France, 1945; The World of the Great Powers, 1947; The Portable Veblen, 1948; Actions and Passions, 1949; America As A Civilisation, 1957; The Unfinished Country, 1959; The Essential Works of John Stuart Mill, 1961; The Age of Overkill, 1962; Education and A Radical Humanism, 1962; Tocqueville and American Civilization, 1966; Values in Education, 1976; Ted and the Kennedy Legend, 1980. *Contributions to:* Magazines including: The New Republic; Quest; Foreign Affairs; McCalls; Encounter. *Honours include:* Albion College; Wilberforce University; New School for Social Research; Williams College; Brandeis University. *Address:* New York Post, 210 South Street, New York, NY 1002, USA.

LERNER, Robert Earl, b. 8 Feb. 1940, New York, USA. Historian. m. Erdmut Krumnack, 25 Oct. 1963, Princeton, 2 daughters. *Education:* BA, University of Chicago, 1960; MA, 1962, PhD, 1964, Princeton University. *Publications:* The Age of Adversity, 1968; The Heresy of the Free Spirit in the Later Middle Ages, 1972; One Thousand Years, co-author, 1974; The Powers of Prophecy, 1983; Western Civilizations, co-author, 10th edition 1984. *Contributor to:* Numerous articles and reviews in professional journals, *Honours:* Fulbright Fellow, 1967; National Endowment for Humanities Fellow, 1972; American Council of Learned Societies Fellow, 1979; Guggenheim Foundation Fellow, 1983; American Academy in Rome Fellow, 1983. *Address:* Dept of History, Nothwestern University, Evanston, IL 60201, USA.

LESLIE, John Andrew, b. 2 Aug. 1940, Calcutta, India. Philosopher. m. Gillian Margaret Alliston, 8 Aug. 1964, Southampton, England, 1 son, 1 daughter. *Education:* BA, Philosophy and Psychology, Oxford, 1962; MA, Oxford, 1967; M Litt, Literae Hymaniores, Oxford, 1970. *Literary Appointments:* Lecturer in Philosophy, 1968, Professor of Philosophy 1982, University of Guelph. *Publication:* Value and Existence, 1979. *Contributions to:* Articles in American Philosophical Quarterly; Philosophy; Mind and other philosophical journals; Also chapters in philosophical books. *Honour:* Leave Fellowship, Social Sciences and Humanities Research Council of Canada, 1980–81. *Membership:* Canadian Philosophical Association, Secretary 1983–84. *Address:* Department of Philosophy, University of Guelph, Guelph, Ontario, Canada.

LESLY, Philip, b. 29 May 1918, Chicago, Illinois, USA. Management Counsel, Mass Communications & Public Relations. m. (1) Ruth Edwards, 17 Oct. 1940, divorced 1971, (2) Virginia Barnes, 11 May 1984, 1 son. *Education:* BS, magna cum laude, Northwestern University, 1940. *Publications:* Public Relations: Principles & Procedures, co-author, 1945; Public Relations in Action, Editor, 1947; Everything and the Kitchen Sink, 1955; Public Relations Handbook, 1950, 3rd edition 1967, Author, Editor; Lesly's Public Relations Handbook, Author, Editor, 1971, 3rd edition 1983; The People Factor, 1974; Selections from

Managing the Human Climate, 1979; How We Discommunicate, 1979; Overcoming Opposition, 1984. *Contributor to:* Wall Street Journal; Industry Week; Management Review; Management Digest; Northliner; Commerce; Public Opinion Quarterly; Public Relations Journal; International Public Relations Association Review; etc. *Honours:* Silver Anvil Award of Merit, Public Relations Society of America, 1946, 1963, 1966; Named, Leading Active Public Relations Practitioner, Poll by PR Reporter, 1978; Gold Anvil, 1979. *Address:* 155 Harbor Drive, Chicago, Il 60601, USA.

LESSER, Wendy, b. 20 Mar. 1952, California, USA. Writer, Editor. m. Richard Rizzo, 18 Jan. 1985, San Francisco, USA, 1 son. *Education:* BA, Harvard University, USA, 1973; MA English, University of Cambridge, England, 1975; PhD English, University of California, Berkeley, 1982. *Literary Appointments:* Founding editor, The Threepenny Review, 1979–; Visiting Writer, Northwestern University, USA, 1984; Visiting Lecturer in American Literature, University College, Santa Cruz, 1984. *Contributor to:* The Hudson Review; Southwest Review; ELH; New York Times (Book reviews). *Honours:* James Essay Prize, (King's College, Cambridge), 1974; NEH Fellowship for Independent Research, 1983; Residency at Rockefeller Foundation's Bellagio Center, 1984. *Literary Agent:* Tim Seldes (Russell & Volkening), New York. *Address:* PO Box 9131, Berkeley, CA 94709, USA.

LESSING, Charlotte, b. London, England. Magazine Editor. m. 25 May 1948, London, 3 daughters. *Education:* Diploma English Literature. *Literary Appointments:* Editorial Assistant, Lilliput Magazine, 1945–50; Deputy Editor 1964–74, Editor 1974–. Good Housekeeping magazine; Editor-in-Chief, Good Housekeeping's Country Living. *Contributions to:* Punch; Lilliput; Good Housekeeping; Various women's magazines. *Address:* National Magazine House, 72 Broadwick Street, London W1, England.

LESTER, Andrew D, b. 8 Aug. 1939, Coral Gables, Florida, USA. Professor of Psychology of Religion. m. Judith A Laesser, 8 Sep. 1960, 1 son, 1 daughter. *Education:* BA, Mississippi College, 1961; BD, 1964, PhD, 1968, Southern Baptist Theological Seminary; Clinical training, Louisville General Hospital, Childrens Hospital, General State Hospital, Personal Counseling Service, 1964–67. *Publications:* Sex is More Than a Word, 1973; It Hurts So Bad, Lord!, 1976; Coping with your Anger: A Christian Guide, 1983; Pastoral Care for Children in Crisis, 1985. Co-Author, Understanding Aging Parents, 1980, Co-Editor: Pastoral Care in Crucial Human Situations, 1969; Spiritual Dimensions for Pastoral Care, 1985. *Contributions to:* The Baptist Student; Church Administration; Home Missions; Review and Expositor. *Honours:* Chaplain Supervisor affiliation, Association of Clinical Pastoral Education; Diplomate, American Association of Pastoral Counsellors; Fellow, College of Chaplains, American Protestant Hospital Association. *Membership:* Clinical Member, American Association of Marriage and Family Therapists. *Address:* Southern Baptist Theological Seminary, Box 1918, Louisville, KY 40280, USA.

LESTER, David, b. 1 June 1942, London, England. Professor. m. dissolved, 1 son. *Education:* BA, 1964, MA, 1968, University of Cambridge, England; MA, 1966, PhD, 1968, Brandeis University, USA. *Literary Appointments:* Assistant Professor, Wellesley College, 1967–69; Director of Research & Evaluation, Suicide Prevention & Crisis Service, Buffalo, New York, 1969–71; Professor of Psychology, Richard Stockton State College, 1971–; Coordinator & Founder, Psychology Program, 1971–74, Coordinator, Criminal Justice Program, 1977–78, Richard Stockton State College. *Major Publications include:* Suicide (with G Lester), 1971; Comparative Psychology, 1973; Unusual Sexual Behavior, 1975; Psychotherapy for Offenders, 1981; (editor) The Elderly Victim of Crime, 1981; (with M E Murrell) Introduction to Juvenile Delinquency, 1981; The Structure of the Mind, 1982; Why People Kill Themselves, 2nd edition 1983. *Contributor to:*

Numerous scholarly periodicals, newspapers and magazines. *Address:* Psychology Program, Richard Stockton State College, Pomona, NJ 08240, USA.

LESTER, Paul Alfred, b. 11 June 1949, Birmingham, England. Writer; Lecturer. *Education:* lst Class honours in English Literature and Economic History, Manchester University; PhD Thesis, Birmingham University. *Publications:* A Funny Brand of Freedom, 1975; Songs and Wrongs, 1980; Changing Chennels, Illustrated by Les Roadhouse, 1980; Mirror on Megalopolis, illustrated by Les Roadhouse, 1981; Minding the Animals, 1982; The Great Sea-Serpent Controversy, 1984; Animal Morals, 1985. *Contributions to:* Poetry: Bogg; Brecht Times; Contac; Grok; Radix; Hope; Krax; Kudos; Ostrich; Pink Hippo; Poetry One; Sydelines; Tincan; Scrip; Sepia; Streetpoems; Voices. *Address:* Flat 4, 34 Summerfield Crescent, Edgbaston, Birmingham B16 OER, England.

LEUTENEGGER, Gertrud, b. 4 Dec. 1948, Schwyz, Switzerland. Writer. *Education:* Regisseurin. *Publications:* Vorabend, 1975; Ninive, 1977; Lebewohl, Gute Reise, 1980; Gouverneur, 1981; Wie in Salomons Garten, 1981; Kommins Schiff, 1983; Das verlorene Monument, 1985; Kontinent, 1985. *Contributions to:* Manuskripte, Graz; Tages Anzeiger Magazin, Zurich; Frankfurter Allgemeine Zeitung, Frankfurt. *Honours:* Kritikerpreis des Ingeborg Bachmann Preises, 1978; Meersburger Drostepreis, 1979. *Membership:* Gruppe Olten Schweiz. *Address:* Casa Bacciarini, CH-6831 Cabbio, Switzerland.

LEVE, Charles Steven, b. 30 Oct. 1948, Chicago, Illinois, USA. Writer; Editor; Expert, Racquetball. m. Barbara Lynn Turcot, 10 July 1977, Northfield, 2 sons. *Education:* BA, University of Miami, Florida, 1970. *Publications:* Inside Racquetball, 1972; Winning Racquetball, 1976. *Contributor to:* Over 1000 articles on Racquetball, 1970–; Inaugural Editor, Racquetball Magazine, 1972, National Racquetball Magazine, 1973; Editor, National Racquetball Magazine, 1973–79, 1981–; Contributor, Racquetball, Encyclopedia Britannica, annually, 1980–. *Address:* 1701 Silver Pine Drive, Northbrook, IL 60062, USA.

LEVENDOSKY, Charles (Leonard), b. 4 July, 1936. Journalist; Poet. *Education:* BS, 1958, University of Oklahoma, USA, BA, 1960; Graduate studies, Universities of Hawaii and Oklahoma, 1961; MA, New York University, 1963. *Appointments:* HS Teacher, US Virgin Islands, 1963–65; Tutot, Kyoto University, Japan, 1965–66; HS Tutor, New York, USA, 1966–67; Instructor of English, New York University, 1967–70; Poet in Residence, New York, New Jersey and Ga. 1971–72 and Wyoming Council on the Arts, 1972; Editor for annual arts edition for the Casper Star-Tribune; Columnist for the Casper Star-Tribune, Wyoming, USA. *Publications:* Perimeters, 1970; Small Town America, 1974; Words and Fonts, 1975; Aspects of the Vertical, 1978; Distances, 1980; Wyoming Fragments, 1981; Nocturnes, 1982; Hands, 1986. *Contributions to:* Numerous magazines and journals including: El Corno Emplumado; New York Quarterly; Thoreau Journal Quarterly; American Poetry Review; Poetry Now; Writers Forum; Northwest Review; Sun Dog; Sulphur River; Negative Capability; Posts on; Blue Light Review; Dacotah Territory; etc. *Honours:* National Endowment for the Arts Fellowship–Grant as Librettist for composer Wendell Logan; Small Town America, silver medal at Internationale Buchkunst-Austellung in Leipzig for book design, 1977; Wyoming Governor's Award for the Arts, 1983; Wyoming Writers' Arizola Magnenat Award, 1984. *Memberships:* PEN: Wyoming Writers; Poetry Progs. of Wyoming (Founder and Director, 1973–78). *Address:* Poetry Progs. of Wyoming, PO Box 3033, Casper, WY 82606, USA.

LEVI, Helen Isabel, b. 30 Oct. 1929, Winnipeg, Canada. Teacher. m. David Trilling Levi, (deceased), 2 Feb. 1951, 1 son, 1 daughter. *Education:* BA; Certificate of Education, University of Manitoba; BEd Brandon University. *Publications:* A Small Informal Dance, 1977;

Tangle Your Web and Dosey-Do, 1978; Honour Your Partner, 1979. *Membership:* Writers' Union of Canada. *Address:* 108 Christie Street, Glenboro, Manitoba, Canada ROK OXO.

LEVI, Leo, b. 15 Jan. 1926, Mannheim, Federal Republic of Germany. Physicist. m. Miriam Wechsler, 17 Feb. 1957, New York, USA, 3 sons. *Education:* BEE, City College of New York; M Sc, PhD, Polytechnic Institute, Brooklyn, New York; Professor, Dean, Jerusalem College of Technology. *Publications:* Vista From Mt Moria, 1959; Jewish Chrononomy, 1967; Applied Optics, volume 1 1968, volume 2 1980; Handbook of Tables of Functions for Applied Optics, 1974; Tractate Shevi'ith of Jerusalem Talmud with New Commentary, (with A Carmell), Hebrew, 1979; Torah and Science, Their Interplay In the World Scheme, 1983. *Contributions to:* Journals of science, technology and Jewish thought including; Journal of Optical Society of America, HaMa'ayan; No'am. *Honours:* Federal Award for Torah and Science. Abramowitz-Zeitlin prize for Jewish Literature. *Address:* Jerusalem College of Technology, 21 HaVaa'ad Haleumi, Jerusalem 91, 160, Israel.

LEVI, Primo, b. 31 July 1919, Turin, Italy. Writer. m. Lucia Morpurgo, 8 Sep. 1947, Turin, 1 son, 1 daughter. *Education:* Laurea Degree, Chemistry, 1941. *Publications:* Sequesto e un Uomo, 1947, as If This is a Man, UK, 1949; Le Tregua, 1962, as, The Truce, UK, 1965; Il Sistema Periodico, 1975, as The Periodic Table, UK, 1985; Se Non Ora, Quando?, 1982, as If Not Now, When?, UK, 1986. *Contributions to:* La Stampa, of over 100 articles. *Honours:* Premio Campiello, 1962, 82; Premio Strega, 1979; Premio Viareggio, 1982. *Literary Agent:* Ali v Manzomi. *Address:* Corso re Umberto 75, 10128 Torino, Italy.

LEVIN, Betty, b. 10 Sep. 1927, New York, USA. Writer; Teacher; Sheep Farmer. m. Alvin Levin, 3 Aug. 1947, 3 daughters. *Education:* BA, University of Rochester; MA, Radcliffe College; AMT, Graduate School of Education, Harvard University. *Literary Appointments:* Fellow in Creative Writing, Bunting Institute, 1968–70; Adjunct Professor, Simmons College Center for the Study of Childrens Literature. *Publications:* The Sword of Culann, 1973; A Griffon's Nest, 1974; The Forespoken, 1976; Landfall, 1979; The Keeping Room, 1981; A Binding Spell, 1984; Put on My Crown, 1985; The Ice Bear, 1986. *Contributions to:* The Horn Book Magazine; The Christian Science Monitor; The Boston Herald; Children's Literature in Education. *Honours:* Parents' Choice for Put on My Crown, Literary Remarkable, CSM Best Books, 1985. *Literary Agent:* D Markinko, McIntosh and Otis Incorporated. *Address:* Old Winter Street, Lincoln, MA 01773, USA.

LEVIN, Richard Louis, b. 31 Aug. 1922, Buffalo, New York, USA. University Professor. m. Muriel Renee Abrams, 22 June 1952, New York City, 2 sons. *Education:* BA, 1943, MA, 1947, PhD 1957, University of Chicago. *Literary Appointments:* Instructor in English, 1949–53, Assistant Professor, 1953–57, University of Chicago; Professor, State University of New York at Stony Brook, 1957. *Publications:* Tragedy: Plays, Theory and Criticism, 1960 revised edition 1965; The Question of Socrates, 1961; Thomas Middleton's Michaelmas Term (editor) 1967; The Multiple Plot in England Renaissance Drama, 1971; New Readings vs Old Plays: Recent Trends in the Reinterpretation of English Renaissance Drama, 1979. *Contributions to:* Modern Philology; Modern Language Review; Modern Language Quarterly; Essays in Criticism; Skakespeare Survey; Shakespeare Quarterly; Medieval and renaissance Drama; Mosaic, PMLA; Philological Quarterly; Review of English Studes; ELH; Studies in English Literature; Huntington Library Quarterly; Literature and Psychology; Studes in Philology; Clio; College English. *Honours:* American Council of Learned Societies Fellow, 1963–64; Explicator Award, 1971; National Endowment for Humanities Senior Fellow, 1974; Guggenheim Foundation Fellow, 1978–79; Fulbrighr Lecturer 1984–85. *Memberships:* Modern

Language Association; Shakespeare Association of America; Advisory Council Member, Shakespeare Globe Center; Internaitonal Shakespeare Association; Joseph Crabtree Foundation; Malone Society; Marlowe Society of America. *Address:* English Department, State University of New York, Stony Brook, NY 11794, USA.

LEVINE, Faye Iris, b. 18 Jan. 1944, Connecticut, USA. Writer. *Education:* AB, cum laude, Radcliffe College, 1965; Ed M, Harvard University, 1970. *Appointments:* Teacher, Shirley Industrial School for Boys, 1970; Adjunct Instructor, Freshman Composition, Polytechnic Institute of New York, 1982; Faculty, Special Subjects, The New School, 1982. *Publications:* The Strange World of the Hare Krishnas, 1974; The Culture Barons: An Analysis of Power and Money in the Arts, 1976; Solomon & Sheba, novel, 1980; Splendor & Misery, A Novel of Harvard, 1983. *Contributor to:* Nations War Under the Spell of Kashmir, Newsweek, 1965; Life, Love and the Movies in India, Atlantic, 1966; The End of the Maharajaha, Atlantic, 1967; The New Calcutta, Atlantic, 1967; Articles in, New York Times Book Review; Jewish Daily Forward; Rolling Stone; Harper's; Ms; Physician's World; Penthouse; etc. *Honours:* Dana Reed Prize, best writing in a Harvard Undergraduate Publication, Honorable Mention for, The Three Flavors of Radcliffe, 1963; Fulbright Fellowship, 1965–66. *Memberships:* PEN; Authors' Guild; National Press Club. *Address:* 20 E 9th St, New York, NY 10003, USA.

LEVINE, Israel, E, b. 30 Aug. 1923, New York, USA. Editor & Publicist. m. Joy Elaine Michael, 23 June 1946, Monroe, Louisiana, USA, 1 son, 1 daughter. *Education:* Bachelor of Social Science, City College of New York. *Major Publications:* The Discoverer of Insulin: Dr Frederick G Banting, 1959; Conqueror of Smallpox: Dr Edward Jenner, 1960; Behind the Silken Curtain: The Story of Townsend Harris, 1961; Inventive Wizard: George Westinghouse, 1962; Champion of World Peace: Dag Hammerskjold, 1962; Miracle Man of Printing: Ottmar Mergenthaler, 1963; Electronics Pioneer: Lee DeForest, 1964;Young Man in the Whihte House: John Fitzgerald Kennedy, 1964; Oliver Cromwell, 1966; Spokesman for the Free World: Adlai Stevenson, 1967; Lenin: the Man Who Made a Revolution, 1969;The Many Faces of Slavery, 1975. *Contributor to:* Many National magazines & professional journals. *Honour:* 125th Anniversary Award, City College of New York, 1972. *Memberships:* Authors Guild; Authors League of America; Society of Silurians; New York Press Club. *Address:* 140-41 69 Road, Flushing, NY 11367, USA.

LEVINE, Stuart, b. 25 May 1932, New York City, USA. College Professor, Editor. m. Susan Fleming Matthews, 6 June 1963, 2 sons, 1 daughter. *Education:* AB, Harvard University, 1954; MA 1956, PhD 1958, Brown University. *Literary Appointments:* Editor, American Studies, 1959–. *Major Publications:* Materials for Technical Writing, 1963; The American Indian Today (with N C Lurie), 2nd edition 1970; Charles Caffin: The Story of American Painting (editor), 1972; Edgar Poe: Seer and Craftsman, 1972; The Short Fiction of Edgar Allan Poe (with Susan Levine), 1976. *Contributor to:* American Quarterly; American Studies; Canadian Review of American Studies; Comparative Literature; Colorado Quarterly; Midwest Quarterly; Forum; Harvard English Studies; and others. *Honours:* Phi Beta Kappa, 1954; Anisfield-Wolf Award in Race Relations, 1968; Citation, National Conference of Christians & Jews, 1969; Exxon Intra-University Professorship 1982–83; Gabriel PrizeJury, 1983–85; Chairman of Jury, 1985; 5 Fulbright Awards. *Memberships:* American Studies Association; Chairman, prize Committees; chairman, Major Speakers Committee, 1967 National Convention, Executive Board, Mid-America Branch, 1960–, American Studies Association. *Address:* 1846 Barker, Lawrence, KS 66044, USA.

LEVINSON, Harry, b. 16 Jan. 1922, Port Jervis, New York, USA. Clinical Psychologist; Management Consultant. m. Roberta Freiman, 11 Jan. 1946, divorced 1972, 2 sons, 2 daughters. *Education:* BS, 1943, MS, 1947, Psychology, Emporia (Kansas) State University; PhD, Clinical Psychology, University of Kansas, 1952. *Appointments:* Editorial Board, Consultation, 1981–; Editorial Advisory Board, Administration in Mental Health, 1977–; Administrative Science Quarterly, 1972–76; etc. *Publications:* Men, Management and Mental Health, 1962; Organizational Diagnosis, 1972; Executive Stress, 1970; The Great Jackass Fallacy, 1973; Psychological Man, 1976; Emotional Health in the World of Work, 1964, revised 1980; The Exceptional Executive, 1968, revised as, Executive, 1981; CEO: Corporate Leadership in Action, 1984. *Contributor to:* Numerous Professional Journals & magazines. *Honours:* Massachusetts Psychological Association's Career Award, 1985; 1st Award of Psychologists in Management, 1985; Perry L Rohrer Consulting Psychology Practice award, 1984; many other honours and awards. *Address:* The Levinson Institute, PO Box 95, Cambridge, MA 02138, USA.

LEVINSON, Henry Samuel, b. 2 Nov. 1948, Cincinnati, Ohio, USA. Professor of Religious Studies. m. Catherine Ellen Kaplan, 30 Aug. 1969, Denver, Colorado, 2 daughters. *Education:* BA, Humanities, 1970; MA, Religion, 1974, PhD, Religion, 1976, Princeton University. *Literary Appointments:* Assistant Professor, Stamford University, 1975–82; Assistant Professor, University of North Carolina – Greensboro, 1982–. *Publications:* Science, Metaphysics and the Chance of Salvation: An Interpretation of the Thought of William James, 1978; The Religious Investigations of William James, 1981. *Contributions to:* William James and the Federal Republican Principle, Publius, 1978; Traditional Religion, Modernity and Unthinkable Thoughts, Journal of Religion, 1981; Religious Criticism, Journal of Religion, 1984; Santayana's Contribution to American Religious Philosophy, Journal of the American Academy of Religion, 1984. *Honours:* Danforth Fellowship, 1970–75; Mellon Faculty Fellowship, Harvard University, 1982–83; MEH Fellowship for Independent Study and Research, 1985–86. *Memberships:* American Academy of Religion; C S Peirce Society. *Address:* 5151 North Church Street Extension, Greensboro, NC 27405, USA.

LEVISON, Alfred, b. 30 Dec. 1924, Southampton, England. Writer. m. (1) Eva Dropkin, 1 Oct. 1945, Chicago, Illinois, USA. (deceased 1978); (2) Claudie Calvez, 26 Oct. 1979, Sag Harbor, 2 sons, 1 daughter. *Education:* BA, MA, Brooklyn College & University of Wisconsin, 1940–44. *Literary Appointments:* Playwright-in-residence, Office for Advanced Drama Research, University of Wisconsin, 1968; Post-in-residence, Mamaroneck Senior High School, New York, 1982. *Major Publications:* Socrates Wounded in New American Plays (Hill & Wang, New York, 1965); Travelogs (poetry), Signford Press, London, 1981; Shipping Out and Millwork, volumes 1 & 2 of a series of 10 novels Fishtales, Signford Press/Oracle Press, Louisiana, USA, 1984. *Literary Agent:* Joanna Marston, Rosica Colin Ltd, London, England. *Address:* Henry Street, Sag Harbour, NY 11963, USA.

LEVITSKY, Serge L, b. 23 Sep. 1926. Professor of Law. m. Alice Marie Boulin, 30 June 1956, 2 sons, 2 daughters. *Education:* LL B 1947, Licencié en Droit 1948, LL D 1951, Sorbonne, Paris, France. *Literary Appointments:* Editor in Chief, Deadline Data on World Affairs, 1957–60. *Publications:* Copyright, Defamation, and Privacy in Soviet Civil Law, 1979; KAMAZ: The Billion Dollar Beginning, 1974; The American Bibliography of Slavic and East European Studies, Co-editor, 1957–60; International Contracts, co-editor, 1981. *Contributions to:* Numerous publications including: Encyclopedia of Soviet Law; Journal of Media Law and Practice; Review of Socialist Law; Tijdschrift voor Rechtsgeschiedenis; Auteursrecht; Gewerblicher Rechtsschutz in Ost und West; Sonderstudie; The Trademark Reporter; Revue Internationale du Droit d'Auteur; Etudes Slaves et Est-Européennes; Bulletin of the Copyright Society of the USA. *Honours:* Research and writing grant, Netherlands Organization for the Advancement of Scientific

Research and University of Leyden, 1978–79; Visiting Scholar grant, Max-Planck Gesellschaft, 1980. *Address:* 620 Barrymore Lane, Mamaroneck, NY 10543, USA.

LEVITT, Morton P, b. 22 Dec. 1936, Brooklyn, New York, USA. University Professor. m. Annette Shandler, 7 Sep. 1963, Philadelphia. *Education:* AB, Dickinson College, 1958; MA, Columbia University, 1960; PhD, Pennsylvania State University, 1965. *Literary Appointments:* Instructor in English, Pennsylvania State University, 1960–62; Assistant Professor, Associate Professor then Professor of English, Temple University, 1962–; Fulbright Professor, Zagreb University, Yugoslavia, 1974–75; Visiting Professor, University of Granada, Spain, 1983, Concordia University, Montreal, Canada. 1983. *Publications:* Bloomsday: An Interpretation of James Joyce's Ulysses, 1972; The Cretan Glance: The World and Art of Nikos Kazantzakis, 1980; Modernist survivors: The Contemporary Novel in England, France, The United States and Latin America, forthcoming 1986. *Contributions to:* Many articles on contemporary fiction in England, France, the US, Latin America and Greece in various collections and in such journals as Modern Fiction Studies; James Joyce Quarterly; The Kenyon Review; Critique; Mosaic; Comparative Literature Studies; Journal of Modern Literature, translated into Greek, Italian, Spanish and Serbo-Croatian. *Memberships:* James Joyce Foundation; Modern Greek Studies Association; Modern Language Association. *Address:* Department of English, Temple University, Philadelphia, PA 19122, USA.

LEVY, Alan, b. 10 Feb. 1932, New York City, USA. Author, Foreign Correspondent, Dramatist. m. Valerie Wladaver, 7 Aug. 1965, New York City, USA, 2 daughters. *Education:* AB, Brown University, Rhode Island, USA; 1952; MS Columbia Graduate School of Journalism, New York, 1953. *Publications include:* Operation Elvis, 1960; Kind-Hearted Tiger, 1964; The Culture Vultures, 1968; God Bless You Real Good, My Crusade With Billy Graham, 1969; Rowboat to Prague, 1972; Good Men Still Live, 1974; The Bluebird of Happiness, 1976; Forever, Sophia, 1979; Biographies of Ezra Pound, W H Auden and Vladimir Nabokov, 1983–84; Adapter of Play The World of Ruth Draper, 1982; Text author for symphonic requiem Just an Accident? with music by René Starr, 1983. *Contributions to:* Newspapers, magazines and anthologies including: New York Times; International Herald Tribune; Harpers; Horizon. *Honours:* New Republic Young Writers Award, Washington DC, 1958; Bernard De Voto Fellowship in Prose, Middlebury College, Vermont, 1963; Pacific Area Travel Association Excellence Award, 1978; Government of Malto Bronze Plume for Travel Writing, 1985. *Memberships include:* PEN; Overseas Press Club, America; American Society of Journalists and Authors; Authors Guild; Dramatists Guild; Vienna Foreign Press Association; Trustee, Thomas Nast Foundation, Landau, Federal Republic of Germany. *Literary Agent:* June Hall, 19 College Cross, London, England. *Address:* Bennogasse 8 Apt 7, A 1080 Vienne, Austria.

LEVY, Jonathan Frederick, b. 20 Feb. 1935, New York City, USA. Teacher; Writer. m. Geraldine Carro (deceased), 24 Nov. 1968, 1 daughter. *Education:* MA, PhD. *Literary Appointments:* Playwright-in-Residence, Manhattan Theatre Club, New York, 1973–78; National Endowment for the Arts, (Chairman, Theatre for Youth Panel, 1979–81, Policy Panel, 1980–81); Literary Advisor, Manhattan Theatre Club, 1982–. *Publications:* Turandot, 1967; The Play of Innocence and Change, 1967; The Marvellous Adventures of Tyl, 1971; Boswel's Journal, 1972; Marco Polo, 1977; Charlie the Chicken, 1982. *Contributions to:* The New York Times; The Village Voice, etc. of light verse, book and play reviews. *Honour:* Charlotte Chorpennig Award in Best Short Plays of 1983. *Memberships:* The Dramatists Guild; ASCAP; Playwrights for Children's Theatre (President, 1971–75). *Literary Agent:* Susan Schulman. *Address:* 1165 Fifth Avenue, New York, NY 10029, USA.

LEVY, Paul, 26 Feb. 1941, Lexington, Kentucky, USA. Journalist; Author; Food and Wine Editor. m. Penelope Marcus, 24 June 1977, London, England, 2 daughters. *Education:* BA, MA, University of Chicago; Postgraduate studies, University College, London, England, Nuffield College, Oxford; PhD, Harvard University, USA. *Literary Appointments:* Trustee, Co-Literary Executor (with Michael Holroyd) of the Strachey Trust; Journalist, Author, Food and Wine Editor, The Observer. *Publications:* Lytton Strachey: The Really Interesting Question, 1972; Moore: GE Moore and the Cambridge Apostles, 1979; The Shorter Strachey, (with Michael Holroyd), 1980; The Official Foodie Handbook, (with Ann Barr), 1984. *Contributor to:* The Observer; Harpers & Queen; A la Carte; The Wall Street Journal; Homes and Gardens; Connoisseur; Paris en Cuisine; The New York Times; Literary Review; Books and Bookmen; Times Literary Supplement. *Memberships:* FRSL; Society of Authors. *Literary Agent:* Ed Victor Ltd. *Address:* The Observer, 8 St Andrew's Hill, London EC4V 5JA, England.

LEVY, William, b. 10 Jan. 1939, New York, USA. Author; Correspondent. m. 1 daughter. *Education:* BA, University of Maryland; Post-Graduate studies, Temple University; Printing, Ealing College of Art, London, England. *Publications:* The Virgin Sperm Dancer, 1972; Wet Dreams, 1973; Certain Radiospeeches of Ezra Pound, 1975; Natural Jew Boy, 1981; Voicings and Transmissions, 1983; Blood, 1985. *Contributions to:* Co-Founder, Chief Editor: Insect Trust Gazette; International Times; Suck; The Fanatic; Radio Art and Atom Club. European Correspondent, High Times, USA. Amsterdam Correspondent, Exquisite Corpse, Louisiana. *Address:* Postbus 2080, 1000 CB Amsterdam, The Netherlands.

LEWANDOWSKI, Herbert, b. 23 Mar. 1896, Kassel, Germany. Writer. m. 5 June 1924, Utrecht, Netherlands, 1 son, 1 daughter. *Education:* PhD, Bonn, 1923. *Publications:* Genius and Eros, 2 volumes, German, 1947, 49, Spanish 1947, Japanese, 1984; Paintings of Gauguin with introduction in English, French and German, 1947; Flight from Civilization, German, 1948, Italian, 1955, English in preparation; First Oeuvre: Catalogue of Paul Gauguin, 1951; Gauguin: The Truth, English, 1961, Spanish 1969, German, 1973. *Contributor to:* German, Dutch and Swiss press of many handreds of articles, 1916–85. *Memberships:* Swiss PEN Club; Association of German Language;s Writers in Switzerland. *Address:* 69 rue de la Servette, CH[nd1202, Geneva, Switzerland.

LEWIN, Hugh Francis, b. 3 Dec. 1939, Lydenburg, Republic of South Africa. Media Trainer. m. Patricia Davidson, 19 June 1972, 2 daughters. *Education:* BA, English, History; BA Honours English; Higher Diploma in Library Science. *Publications:* Bandiet – Seven years in a South African prison, 1974; Jafta: Jafta – My mother; Jafta – my father; Jafta – the wedding, 1981; Jafta – the Journey, 1983; Jafta – the town, 1983; An Elephant Came to Swim, 1985. *Contributions to:* Poets to the People, poems. *Address:* P O Box HG236, Highlands, Harare, Zimbabwe.

LEWIN, Leonard C, b. 2 Oct. 1916, New York, USA. Writer. 1 son, 1 daughter. *Education:* BA, Harvard University. *Publications:* A Treasury of American Political Humor, 1964; Report from Iron Mountain, 1967; Triage, 1972. *Contributor to:* Numerous professional journals, magazines, newspapers. *Memberships:* Various professional organisations. *Literary Agent:* Wallace & Sheil. *Address:* 6 Long Hill Farm, Guilford, CT 06437, USA.

LEWIN, Michael Zinn, b. 21 July 1942, Springfield, Massachusetts, USA. Writer. m. Marianne Grewe, 11 Aug. 1965, New York, 1 son. *Education:* AB, Harvard College. *Publications:* How To Beat College Tests, 1969; Ask The Right Question, 1971; The Way We Die Now, 1973; The Enemies Within, 1974; The Next Man, 1976; Night Cover, 1976; The Silent Salesman, 1978; Outside In, 1980; Missing Woman, 1981; Hard Line,

1982; Out of Season (UK Title, Out of Time), 1984. *Contributions to:* Penthouse; A Hitchcock; Crime Wave; Winter's Crimes 16; The Eyes Have It. *Honours:* Edgar nomination for Best First Novel, 1971; Prizewinner, International Crime Congress Competition, Stockholm, 1981; Edgar Nomination for Best Short Story, 1984. *Memberships:* Authors Guild; Mystery Writers of America: Crime Writers Association: Private Eye Writers Association: Playwrights Company. *Literary Agent:* Giles Gordon, Anthony Sheil Associates, UK; Lois Wallace, Wallace and Sheil, USA. *Address:* 5 Welshmill Road, Frome, Somerset BA11 2LA, England.

LEWIS, Cherie Sue, b. 6 Feb. 1951, Cleveland, Ohio, USA. Professor; Author. *Education:* BA, History, University of Michigan, 1973; MS, Journalism, Boston University, 1975; PhD, Mass Communication, University of Minnesota, 1985. *Literary Appointments:* Lecturer, Universities of Minnesota (1976–78), Southern California (1978–80), California, Los Angeles (1980–83), Southern California (1985–86). *Publications:* Citizen Activism & Television, in press. *Contributions to:* Various newspapers including 'Sun Press', Cleveland, Ohio. *Honour:* Moeller Award, journalism research, Association for Education of Journalism, 1976. *Literary Agent:* Michael Larsen, San Francisco. *Address:* 3104 4th Street, Suite 106, Santa Monica, CA 90405, USA.

LEWIS, Ernest Michael Roy, b. 6 Nov. 1913, England. Retired Journalist/Writer. m. Cristine Tew, 1939, 2 daughters. *Education:* BA, Oxford University. *Literary Appointments:* The Statist, 1936–39; The Economist 1952–61; The Times 1961–81. *Publications:* The English Middle Classes (with A Maude), 1949; Professional People (with A Maude), 1953; The Boss: Life and Times of the British Business Man (with R Stewart), 1958; Evolution Man, 1959; The British in Africa, 1971; Enoch Powell, a Political Biography, 1979. *Contributor to:* Various magazines and journals. *Literary Agent:* David Higham Associates. *Address:* 26 Sydney Road, Richmond, Surrey TW9 1UB, England.

LEWIS, Flora, b. Los Angeles, USA. Journalist. m. Sydney Gruson, 17 Aug. 1945 (div), 1 son, 2 daughters. *Eduation:* BA, University of California, Los Angeles, 1941; MS, Columbia University, 1942. *Literary Appointments include:* Freelance or contract for, Observer, Economist, Financial Times, France-Soir, Time Magazine, New York Times Magazine, London, Warsaw, Berlin, The Hague, Mexico City, Tel Aviv, 1946–54, Prague, Warsaw 1956–58; Editor, McGraw Hill, New York City, 1955; Bureau Chief, Washington Post, Bonn, London, New York, 1958–66; Syndicated Columnist, Newsday, Paris, New York, 1967–72; Bureau Chief, New York Times, Paris, 1972–76; European correspondent 1976–80; Foreign Affairs Columnist, New York Times, 1980–. *Publications include:* Case History of Hope, 1958; Red Pawn, 1964; One of our H-Bombs is Missing, 1967. *Contributions to:* Anthologies, books, magazines; New York Times; New Yorker; Atlantic Monthly; Foreign Affairs Quarterly; etc. *Honours Include:* Awards: Best interpretation, foreign affairs, 1956; Best reporting foreign affairs, 1960, Overseas Press Club; Columbia Journalism School 50th Anniversary Honor Award, 1963; Phi Beta Kappa; Aspen Instututes Award, Journalistic excellence, 1977; Award, Distinguished Diplomatic Reporting, Georgetown University School for Foreign Affairs, 1978; French Legion of Honour, 1981; Various honorary doctorates; UCLA Alumnae Awards of Excellence, 1984. *Address:* c/o New York Times, 229 West 43rd Street, New York City, USA.

LEWIS, Greg, b. 3 Sep. 1945, USA. Asociate Professor of Photojournalism. m. Mary Ann Knudsen, 1 son, 1 daughter. *Education:* Bachelors Degree, Masters Degree, California State University, Northridge. *Publications:* Wedding Photography for Today, 1980; Photographing Your Family, 1981. *Contributions to:* Numerous professional periodicals. *Address:* Journalism Department, California State University Fresno, Fresno, CA 93740, USA.

LEWIS, Hywel David, b. 21 May 1910, Llandudno, North Wales. Emeritus Professor of Philosophy. m. (1) Megan Elias Jones, 17 Aug. 1943, Bangor, North Wales (deceased 1962). (2) Kate Alice Megan Prichard, 17 July 1965, London. *Education:* BA, Philosophy 1st Class & MA (Distinction), Bangor University College; BLitt, Jesus College, Oxford University. *Literary Appointments:* Editor: Muirhead Library of Philosophy, 1948–78; Religious Studies (CUP), 1965–82. *Publications include:* Our Experience of God, 1959; Freedom & History, 1962; The Elusive Mind, 1969; The Self & Immortality, 1973; Persons & Life After Death; The Elusive Self, 1982; Jesus in the Faith of Christiana, 1981; Freedom & Alienation, 1985. In Welsh: Diogelu Diwylliant, 1945; Gwybod am Dduw, 1952; Pwy yw Iesu Grist?, 1979; Numerous other books including, Morals & Revelation, 1951. *Contributions to:* Mind; Aristotelian Society Proceedings; Philosophy; Philosophical Quarterly; Hibbert Journal; Idealism; Review of Metaphysics; Archives de Philosophie; etc. In Welsh: Y Llenor; Y Traethodydd; Efrydiau Athronyddol; Y Faner; Y Goleuad. *Honour:* Honorary DD, St Andrews University, 1964; Honorary DLitte, Emory University, Georgia, USA, 1977; Energeia Medal EL Ateneo Filosofico de Mexico, 1980; Honorary Vice President, Federation Internationale des Sociétés de Philosophe, 1984–. *Memberships:* President 1949, Mind; President 1962, Aristotelian Society; Chairman of Council 1965–, Royal Institute of Philosophy; Chairman 1964–66, Society for the Study of Theology; President 1975–82, International Society for Metaphysics. *Address:* Normandy Park, Normandy, Nr Guildford, Surrey, England.

LEWIS, Jacqueline Rose (Guccione), b. 11 Aug. 1934, New Jersey, USA. Editor. 2 sons, 2 daughters. *Education:* BA, Sociology, University of Evansville; MA, Sociology, University of Connecticut. Editor, Co-founder, Publisher, Espionage Magazine, 1st issue 11 Oct. 1984. *Contributions to:* Various periodicals; short stories, advice for women. *Address:* Teaneck, New Jersey, USA.

LEWIS, Lesley (Lawrence), b. 8 Mar, 1909, Brentwood, Essex, England. Writer. m. David James Lewis, 12 July 1944, Bentley, Brentwood, Essex. *Education:* BA, 1935, MA, 1938, History of Art, London University, Courtauld Institute; Barrister-at-law, Called Lincoln's Inn, 1956. *Publications:* Connoisseurs and Secret Agents in Eighteenth Century Rome, 1961; The Private Life of a Country House, 1980. *Contributions to:* Warburg Institute Journal, 1938; Stuart and Revett: Their Literary and Architectural Careers (by Lesley Lawrence); Apollo, Philip von Stasch, 1967; Burlington Magazine, 1964; Elizabeth, Countess of Home and Her House in Portman Square; The Jamaican Historical Review, 1972; Hird's Annals of Bedale, North Yorkshire County Record Office, 1975; English Commemorative Sculpture in Jamaica, etc. *Memberships:* Fellow, Society of Antiquaries of London, Vice-President, 1980–84; Royal Archaeological Institute, Vice-President; Society of Authors. *Literary Agent:* Anne Harrel. *Address:* 38 Whitelands House, Cheltenham Terrace, London SW3 4QY, England.

LEWIS, Marjorie Schwartz, b. 3 May 1929, New York City, USA. Librarian. m. Philip Lewis, 12 Sep. 1954, Woodmere, Long Island, New York, 2 sons, 2 daughters. *Education:* BA, Russell Sage College, Troy, New York, 1949; MLS, Rutgers, The State University, New Brunswick, New Jersey, 1970. *Publications:* The Boy Who Would Be A Hero, 1982; Ernie and the Mile Long Muffler, 1982; Wrongway Applebaum, 1984. *Contributions to:* Articles and book reviews in School Library Journal. Charlie's Garden, a story for free children, in MS Magazine, 1984. *Honour:* Beta Phi Mu. *Address:* 13 Hubbard Drive, White Plains, NY 10605, USA.

LEWIS, Norman, b. 30 Dec. 1912, New York, USA. Author; College Professor. m. Mary Goldstein, 28 July 1934, New York, 2 daughters. *Education:* BA, City College of New York, 1937; MA, Columbia University,

1941. *Publications:* Vocabulary and Spelling, Books I, II, 1941; Journeys through Wordland, Books I-IV, 1942; Power with Words, 1943; The Lewis English Refresher and Vocabulary Builder, 1945; How to Speak Better English, 1948; The Rapid Vocabulary Builder, 1951, 2nd edition 1980; How to Get More Out of Your Reading, 1951; Twenty Days to Better Spelling, 1953; Better English, 1956; Dictionary of Correct Spelling, 1962; Correct Spelling Made Easy, 1963; Dictionary of Modern Pronunciation, 1963; New Guide to Word Power, 1963; How to Become a Better Reader, 1964; The New Power with Words, 1964; The Modern Thesaurus of Synonyms, 1965; Thirty Days to a More Powereful Vocabulary, co-author, 1970; RSVP – Reading, Spelling, Vocabulary, pronunciation, Books I, II, III, 1972; See, Say and Write, Books I, II, 1973; Instant Spelling Power for College Students, 1976; RSVP for College English Power, Book I, 1977, Book II, 1978; How to Read Better and Faster, 4th edition 1978; The New Roget's Thesaurus in Dictionary Form, 1978; Word Power Made Easy, 1978; Instant Word Power, 1981, 2nd edition 1982; RSVP, Books I-III, 1982–83, IV, 1984, Books A,B, 1985; 30 Days to Better English, 1985. *Contributor to:* Numerous Professional journals including: College English; English Journal; etc. *Address:* c/o Rio Hondo College, Whittier, CA 90608, USA.

LEWIS, Patricia Ann, b. 7 Apr. 1933, Cincinnati, Ohio, USA. Writer; Educational Consultant; Astrologer. *Education:* BA, University of Miami; Graduate Studies of Econometrics, Hofstra University, New York. Literary Appointments: Senior Editor, The Professional Poet. *Publications:* Songs of these Who Love, 1981; Butterfly Love, 1981; Off Other Realms, 1982; How To Write Prize Winning Poems, 1984; Astros, Difinitive Astrology for the novice, 1985. *Contributions to:* Regular columnist, The Professional Poet; Guest colmnist, The Editor's Desk. *Honours:* Poetry awards from: Edward A Fallot Competition; The Connecticut Writer; Carlisle Poets Workshop; Ursus Press; World of Poetry; The Professional Poet; American Poetry Association. *Memberships:* International Women's Writers Guild; The Women Writer's Alliance; Connecticut Writer's League; Poetry Society of Georgia; California State Poetry Society; Poetry Society of Texas; Poetry Society of Oklahoma; National Council for Geocosmic Research; AFA; NAS. *Literary Agent:* Mrs Betty Wright, Rainbow Books, PO Box 1069, Moore Haven, FL 33471, USA. *Address:* 1800 Wildcat Trail SW, Stuart, FL 33497, USA.

LEWIS, Robert William, b. 15 Dec. 1930, Elrama, Pennsylvania, USA. Professor; Editor. *Education:* BA, English, University of Pittsburgh, 1952; MA, English, Columbia University, New York, 1958; PhD, English, University of Illinois, Urbana, 1963. *Literary Appointments:* University of Nebraska, Lincoln, 1955–58; University of Illinois, Urbana, 1958–63; University of Texas, Austin, 1963–69; University of Catania, Italy, 1967–68; University of North Dakota, 1969–; Ain Shams University, Cairo, Egypt, 1975–76; American University in Cairo, Egypt, 1975; editor, North Dakota Quarterly, 1982–. *Publications:* Hemingway on Love, 1965; Contributions to 'Seven Contemporary Authors', 1966, Editor, Thomas B Whitbread; Literature in Critical Perspectives, 1968, editor Walter K Gordon; Hemingway's African Stories, 1969, editor John M Howell; Hemigway: In Our Time, 1974, Editors Jackson J Benson and Richard Astro; The Short Stories of Ernest Hemingway, 1975, Editor Jackson J Benson; Ernest Hemingway: The Writer in Context, 1984, editor James Nagel. *Contributions to:* The Humanist; North Country. *Honours include:* Outstanding Educator of American 1975 and several other honours. *Memberships:* Modern Language Association; Executive Committee, Conference on College Composition and Communication, 1970–73; Executive Committee, The Hemingway Society, 1980–83; Editorial Board, The Hemingway Review, 1980–; Iota Tau Alpha. *Address:* Department of English, University of North Dakota, P O Box 8237, Grand Forks, ND 58202, USA.

LEWIS, Theodore Gyle, b. 2 Dec. 1941, Lebanon, Oregon, USA. Computer Scientist. m. Molly Humphrey, 28 Sep. 1984; 1 son, 1 daughter by previous marriage. *Education:* BA Mathematics, Oregon State University, 1966; MS 1970, PhD 1971, Computer Science, Washington State University. *Literary Appointments:* Assistant Professor, Computer Science, University of Missouro, 1971–73; Associate Professor, Computer Science, University of Southwest Lousiana, 1973–76; Associate Professor, Computer Science, Oregon State University, 1976–; Various editorial responsibilities in computer publishing. *Major Publications include:* How to profit from your Personal Computer, 1978; Applying Data Structures (with M Z Smith), 1982; Using the Osborne – 1 Computer, Using the IBM Personal Computer, 1982; Database Management made Easy, (with G Barnes & J Wilson), 1983; and others. *Contributions to:* Numerous scientific journals and proceedings on computer science. *Honours:* Various Research grants awarded. *Memberships include:* Association for Computing Machinery; IEEE Computer Society. *Address:* Department of Computer Science, Oregon State University, Corvallis, OR 97331, USA.

LEWIS, William Arthur, b. 23 Jan. 1915, St Lucia, British West Indies. Professor of Economics. m. 3 May 1947, Grenada, 2 daughters. *Education:* The Theory of Economic Growth, 1955; Development Planning, 1967; Growth and Fluctuations, 1870–1913, 1978; Racial Conflict and Economic Development, 1985. *Contributor to:* Numerous economic journals. *Honours:* Nobel Prize, Economics, 1979. *Membership:* Corresponding Fellow, British Academy. *Address:* c/o Woodrow Wilson School, Princeton, NJ 08544, USA.

LEWIS-SMITH, Anne Elizabeth, b. 16 Apr. 1925, London, England. Writer; Poet. m. Peter Lewis-Smith, 17 May 1944, Postishead, 1 son, 2 daughters. *Literary Appointments:* Editor, 1st WRNS magazine; Editor, Aerostat, 1952–57; Editor, West Wales Naturalist Trust Bulletin, 1980–83; Editor, British Association Friend of Museums Broadsheet and Yearbook, 1983–; Editor, Envoi, 1984–; Publisher, Envoi Poets, 1985–. *Publications:* Seventh Bridge, 1963; The Beginning, 1964; Flesh and Flowers, 1967; Dandelion Flavour, 1970; Dinas Head, 1979; Places and Passions, 1986. *Contributions to:* Over 40 magazines in UK and abroad. *Honours:* Medal dUhonour studi e scanbi International, 1970; Tissandier Award, 1978; Debbie Warley Award, 1981. *Memberships;* Fellow, PEN; Council member, BAFM. *Addres:* Pen Ffordd, Newport, Dyfed SA42 0QT, Wales.

LEY, Alice Chetwynd, B. 12 Oct. 1913, Halifax, Yorkshire, England. Novelist. m. Kenneth James Ley, 3 Feb. 1945, 2 sons. *Education:* Diploma in Sociology, Gilchrist Award, London University, 1962. *Literary Appointments:* Tutor in Creative Writing, Harrow College of Further Education, 1963–83. *Publications:* Jewelled Snuff Box 1959; Georgian Rake 1960; Guinea Stamp 1961; Master of Liversedge 1966; Clandestine Betrothal 1967; Toast of the Town 1968; Letters for a Spy 1970; Season at Brighton 1971; Tenant of Chesdene Manor 1974; Beau O The Blue Stocking 1975; At Dark of the Moon 1977; An Advantageous Marriage 1977; Regency Scandal 1979; Conformable Wife (USA only) 1981; Intrepid Miss Haydon (USA only) 1983; A Reputation Dies 1984. *Honour:* USA Paperback Books Awards (Classic Regency) 1985. *Memberships:* Romantic Novelists' Association, Chairman 1971–73, Public Relations Officer, 1975–85; Society of Women Writers and Journalists; Jane Austen Society; Crime Writers' Association. *Literary Agent:* Curtis Brown. *Address:* 42 Cannonbury Avenue, Pinner, Middlesex HA5 1TS, England.

LI, Fang Kuei, b. 20 Aug. 1902, Canton. University Professor/Researcher. m. Hsu Ying, 21 Aug. 1932, Peking, 1 son, 2 daughters. *Education:* AB, University of Michigan, 1926; MA, 1927, PhD, 1928, University of Chicago. *Literary Appointments:* Fellow of the Institute of History and Philology, Academia Sinica, Peking, 1929; Visiting Professor, Chinese Studies, Yale

University, 1937-39; Professor, Chinese Linguistics, University of Washington, 1948-68; Professor, Linguistics, University of Hawaii, 1949-73. *Publications:* Mattole, an Athabaskan Language, 1931; Chipewyan Texts, co-author R Scallon, 1976; A Handbook of Comparative Tai, 1977. *Contributor to:* Bulletin of the Institute of History and Philology, Academia Sinica; International Journal of American Linguistics; T'oung Pao; Language etc. *Honours:* Doctor of Letters (honoris causa) University of Michigan, 1972; LLD (honorary) Chinese University of Hong Kong, 1976; Professor Emeritus, University of Washington and University of Hawaii. *Address:* 3326 Oahu Avenue, Honolulu, HI 76822, USA.

LI, Yao-wen (Kwang), b. 7 May 1924, Canton, China. Writer. m. Chu-tsing Li, 18 June 1948, New York, 1 son, 1 daughter. *Education:* BA, Ginling College, Nanking, China, 1947; MA, University of Iowa, USA, 1951. *Literary Appointments:* Teaching Assistant, Botany, Ginling College, Nanking, China, Spring 1947; Research Assistant, Department of Obstetrics and Gynecology and Department of Surgery, University of Iowa, Iowa City, 1951-59; Free lance writer since 1975. *Publications:* Sweet and Sour, with Carol Kendall, 1978; 1979; Three Folktales with Daisy Kouzel and Gloria Skurzynski, 1981. *Contributor to:* Asia Magazine New York, 1980; Crickets, Boston, 1980, 1985; Houghton Mifflin Reading Program, Boston, 1981; Orientations, Hong Kong, 1983; Crosscurrents, Westlake Village, California, 1984; New Mexico Humanities Review, Socorro, New Mexico. *Honour:* Books of the Year, Child Study Associaton, USA for, Sweet and Sour, 1980. *Address:* 1108 Avalon Road, Lawrence, KS 66044, USA.

LIBERMAN, Serge, b. 14 Nov. 1942, Russia. Medical Practitioner; Author. m. Eva Matzner, 19 Jan. 1969, Melbourne, Australia, 1 son, 2 daughters. *Education:* Bachelor of Surgery; Bachelor of Medicine; MB BS, Melbourne, Australia. *Literary Appointments:* Editor, Melbourne Chronicle, 1977-84. Associate Editor, Outride, 1984-. *Publications:* Story collections: On Firmer Shores, 1981; A Universe of Clowns, 1983. A Bibliography of Australasian Judaica, 1985. *Contributions to:* Melbourne Chronicle; Overland; Outrider; Scopp; Nepean Review; Kivun; Australia-Israel Review; Inprint; Access; Jewish Quaterly, England; Anthologies: Joseph's Coat 1985; Jewish Down Under - Australia and New Zealand, 1984. Australia and New Zealand Jewish Year Book. 1985; Classic Australian Short Stories, 1965. *Honours:* Alan Marshall Awards, 1980, 81, 85; New South Wales Premier's Literary Award, 1984. *Memberships:* Vice President, PEN International, Melbourne Centre; Australian Society of Authors; Fellowship of Australian Writers, Victorian branch. *Address:* 16 Ward Avenue, North Caulfield,. Victoria 3161, Australia.

LIBMAN, Carol, b. 9 June 1928, Montreal, Canada. Writer. m. Sydney Libman, 16 Sep. 1948, Montreal, 1 son, 2 daughters. *Publications:* Follow the Leader (play) included in an anthology entitled 'Dialogue & Dialectic', 1972; (play) Wintersong, 1982. *Contributions to:* numerous professional publications. *Honours:* 1st Prize, Ottawa Little Theatre, 1956; Finalist, Clifford E Lee Awards, 1975; Semi Finalist, Fireweed Competition, 1980. *Memberships:* Life Member, Playwrights; Workshop (Montreal) Inc; Playwrights Union of Canada; Dramatist Guild (US). *Literary Agent:* Larry Hoffman. *Address:* 300 Antibes Drive, Apt 2102 Willowdale, Ontario, Canada M2R 3N8.

LICHNIAK, Zygmunt, b. 28 Apr. 1925, Wilczyn, Poland. Editor; Author. m. Zofia Czartoryska, 18 Apr. 1954, Warsaw. *Education:* Polish Philology, University of Warsaw. *Literary Appointments:* Literary Editor, Dzis i Jutro (Today and Tomorrow), weekly; Literary Editor, Instytut Wydewniczy PAX; Chief Editor, Zycie i mysl (Life and Thought), monthly; Deputy Chief Editor, Instytut Wydewniczy PAX; Chief Editor, Kierunki, weekly. *Publications:* Obrachunki ze wspitires noscie, 1955; Mowy i nemowy, 1969; 2 mojego ivieriwiezzo,

1972; W duchu diologu, 1984; Zanim powstenie penorume, 1983; Kupa lat, 1985. *Contributor to:* Zis; Yutro; Stowo Powszechne Zycie i Mysl; Tu; Teraz; Kierunki. *Honours:* Wlodzinnerz Dietizak Literary Awards, 1949, 58, 72; Kerol Irzykowski Film Critic Award, 1973; Literary Fund Award, 1984; First Degree Award of Minister of Culture and Arts. *Memberships include:* ZLP (Polish Writers Association); SEC; SDPRL (Journalists Association of Polish People's Republic); International Critic Association; Kreg (Literary Club, President). *Address:* ul Oolyrice f in 2, 02-606 Warsaw, Poland.

LICHT, (Edgar) Wolfgang, b. 1 Nov. 1928, Leipzig, Germany. Physician. *Education:* Government examination in Medicine, Graduate, MD. University of Leipzig. *Publications:* Bilanz mit VierunddreiBig oder Die Ehe der Claudia M, 1978; Die Haut, in 'Die Tarnkappe', 1978; Vision, in Das erste Haus am Platz, 1982. *Address:* Zum Viertelsberg 5, DDR 7232 bad Lausick, Democratic Republic of Germany.

LICHTBLAU, Myron Ivor, b. 10 Oct. 1925, New York City, USA. University Professor. m. Bernice Glanz, 23 June 1956, New York City, 2 sons (1 deceased) 1 daughter. *Education:* BA, The City College of New York, 1947; MA, Universidad Nacional de Mexico, 1948; PhD, Columbia University, 1957. *Literary Appointments:* Executive Secretary, Revista Iberoamericana, 1959-63; Book Review Editor, Symposium, 1967-; Book Review Editor, Hispania, 1974-83; Member, Editorial Board, Critica Hispanica. *Publications:* The Nineteenth Century Argenitine Novel, 1959; A College edition of, Las Dos Vidas del Pobre Napoleon, 1963; El arte estilistico de Eduardo Mallea, 1967; Manuel Galvez, 1972; A Practical Reference Guide to Reading Spanish, 1978; Annotated edition of, Manuel Pacho, 1980; Translation and edition of, A History of an Argentine Passion, 1983; Editor, Mallea Ante la Critica, 1985. *Contributions to:* Poetic Expression in Roa Bastos, Hijo de hombre; Le ironico y lo Picaresco en Hijo de Ladron; El Papel del Narrador, en La herencia de M Arcangel; Recent Spanish American Fiction: Trial and Success; The Short Stories of Manuel Galves; Theme and Content; Towards a Stylistic Appreciation of One Hundred Years of Solitude. *Honours:* Honorary Diploma from School of Humanities of La Universidad de Nuevo Leon (Mexico), 1964. *Memberships:* Modern Language Association of America; The American Association of Teachers of Spanish and Portuguese; Revista Iberoamericana. *Address:* Department of Foreign Languages and Literature, Syracuse University, Syracuse, NY 13210, USA.

LICHTENBERG, Philip, b. 1 Oct. 1926, Schenectady, New York, USA. Psychologist, Professor. m. Elsa Russell, 15 June 1949, New York, 4 sons. *Education:* BS 1948, MA 1950, PhD 1952, Psychology, Western Reserve University. *Publications:* Motivation for Child Psychiatry Treatment, (with Robert Kohrman and Helen MacGregor), 1960; Psychoanalysis: Radical and Conservative, 1969; Cognitive and Mental Development in the First Five Years of Life, (with Dolores G Norton), 1970; Lectures in Psychoanalysis for Social Workers. *Contributions to:* AMA Archives of Neurology and Psychiatry; Journal of Abnormal and Social psychology; Journal of Sociology and Social Welfare; and others. *Membership:* Phi Beta Kappa. *Address:* 25 Lowry's Lane, Rosemont, PA 19010, USA.

LICHTENFELD, Herbert, b. 16 June 1927, Leipzig, Germany. Author. m. Winnie 24 Aug. 1957, Bühl, 1 daughter. *Education:* Akademy of Music. *Publications:* Diestunde Des Lowen, 1979; Nachtaufnahme, 1981; Topliche Beziehungen, 1984. *Contributor to:* Horzu; Tunkuhr; Bild und Funk, etc. *Honours:* Adolf Grimme Preis, 1971; Preis der Akademie fur Sprache und Dichtung, Darmstadt, 1978. *Address:* Wandsbeker Schützenhof 18, 2000 Hamburg 70, Federal Republic of Germany.

LICHTY, Lynn, b. 5 Aug. 1935, Antwerp, Ohio, USA. Writer; Personal Manager. *Literary Appointment:*

Contributing Editor, Sick Magazine, New York City, New York, 3 years. *Contributions to:* Good Old Days; World of Yesterday; Lackawanna Independent; Flintstone's Comic Strips; Sick Magazine; Reader's Digest; Playboy's Party Joke Book; Earl Wilson Column, Author and Journalist; Playboy; Humor Exchange Newsletter and Gag Recap; Modern People,; Ring Wrestling; Yesterday's Magazine; Orben's Current Comedy; Arizona Republic; TV Digest; Under Western Skies; American Billiard Review. Local Radio and WWJ-TV, Detroit. *Honours:* World's Champion Gagwriter, 1966; Finished highly in World Champion Gagwriter Contest, 1968; Member, All American Team of Comedy Writers, 1970; Contest Winner, Cracked Magazine and Bowling Green Radio Station. *Address:* RR2 Box 130A, Antwerp, OH 45813, USA.

LICKONA, Thomas Edward, b. 4 Apr. 1943, Poughkeepsie, New York, USA. Professor. m. Judith Barker, 10 Sep. 1966, Albany, New York, USA, 2 sons. *Education:* BA, MA (English); PhD Psychology. *Literary Appointments:* In Psychology & Education: State University of New York at Cortland, 1970–78; Harvard University, 1978–79; Boston University, 1979–80; Professor, State University of New York at Cortland, 1980–. *Major Publications:* Moral Development & Behaviour: Theory, Research & Social Issues, 1976; Raising Good Children: Helping Your Child through the Stages of Moral Development, 1983; and numerous chapters on moral development & moral education in the family and in school. *Contributor to:* Various popular magazines & scholarly journals in field of moral development & education. *Honours:* Faculty Exchange Scholar, 1984–87, State University of New York Awards Committee. *Memberships:* Association for Moral Education (Past President); North American Society of Adlerian Psychology. *Literary Agent:* Robin Straus. *Address:* Department of Education, State University of New York at Cortland, Cortland, NY 13045, USA.

LIDSTONE, John Barrie Joseph, b. 21 July 1929, Salisbury, England. Marketing Consultant; Author. m. Primrose Vivien Russell, 30 Mar. 1957, 1 daughter. *Education:* Fellow, British Institute of Management; Institute of Management Consultants; Member, Institute of Personnel Management; Fellow, Institute of Marketing. *Publications:* Training Salesmen on the Job, 1975, 85; Recruiting and Selecting Successful Salesmen, 1976, re-issued as 'How to Recruit and Select Successful Salesmen', 1983; Negotiating Profitable Sales, 1977; Motivating Your Sales Force, 1978; Making Effective Presentation, 1985; The Sales Presentation, co-author, 1985. *Contributions to:* The Times; Financial Times; Observer; Daily Telegraph; Director; Management To-Day; Marketing Week; Chief Executive; International Management; Executive Times, USA; Personnel Magazine; Marketing Handbook, 1981; Managing Marketing and Sales Training, 1984; The Sales Management Handbook, 1985. *Honours:* Two books filmed by Rank and Video Arts; Award for Creative Excellence for film of book 'Training Salesmen on the Job', USA. 1981; Freeman, City of London, 1978; Voted Top Speaker on Marketing in Europe, 1974. *Memberships:* British Academy of Film and Television Arts. *Address:* 17 Ulster Terrace, Regents Park, London NW1 4PJ, England.

LIDZ, Theodor, b. 1 Apr. 1910, New York City, USA. Psychiatrist. m. Ruth Wilmanns, MD, 23 Nov. 1939, 3 sons. *Education:* AB, MD, Columbia University. *Publications:* The Family and Human Adaptation, 1963; Schizophrenia and the Family, co-author, 1965; The Person, 1968, revised edition 1976; The Origin and Treatment of Schizophrenic Disorders, 1973; Training Tomorrow's Psychiatrist, (M Edelson, co-editor), 1970; Hamlet's Enemy, 1974. *Contributor to:* More than 160 articles in scientific journals. *Honours:* MA, Honorary, Yale University, 1951; Frieda Fromm-Reichmann Award, 1961; Salmon Lecturer Medal, 1967; William C. Menninger Award, 1972; Van Giesen Award, 1973; Stanley R Dean Award, 1973; Laughlin Award, 1982; American Family Therapy Association Award, 1985. *Address:* 25 Park Street, New Haven, CT 06519, USA.

LIEBER, Robert James, b. 29 Sep. 1941, Chicago, Illinois, USA. Professor of Government. m. Nancy Lee Isaksen, 20 June 1963, Madison, Wisconsin. 2 sons. *Education:* BA High Honours, University of Wisconsin, 1963; PhD, Harvard University, 1968. *Publications include:* British Politics and European Unity, 1970; Theory and World Politics, 1972; Oil and the Middle East War; Europe in the Energy Crisis, 1976; Eagle Entangled: US Foreign Policy in a Changing World, (co-editor, co-author), 1979; The Oil Decade, 1983; Eagle Defiant, (co-editor, co-author), 1983. *Contributions to:* Journals including: International Affairs; American Political Science Review; International Security; Foreign Policy; Politique Etrtangere; Washington Quarterly; Washington Post; New York Times; Harpers. *Honours:* Graduate Prize Fellowship, Harvard University, 1964; Guggenheim Fellow, 1972; Council on Foreign Relations International Affairs Fellow, 1972; Rockefeller Foundation International Relations Fellowship, 1978; Woodrow Wilson International Center for Scholars Fellow, 1980. *Membership:* Phi Beta Kappa. *Address:* Department of Government, Georgetown University, Washington, DC 20057, USA.

LIEBERMAN, Herbert, b. 22 Sep. 1933, New Rochelle, New York, USA. Editor; Novelist. m. Judith Barsky, 9 June 1963, Port Washington, 1 daughter. *Education:* AB, City College of New York, 1955; AM, Columbia University, 1957. *Publications:* Matty and the Moron and Madonna, 1965; The Adventures of Dolphin Green, 1967; Crawlspace, 1970; The Eighth Square, 1972; Brilliant Kids, 1974; City of the Dead, 1978; The Climate of Hell, 1980; Nightcall from a Distant Time Zone, 1982; Nightbloom, 1984. *Honours:* Charles Sergel Drama Award, University of Chicago, 1964; Guggenheim Fellowship, Playwriting, 1966; Grand Prix du Litterature, Policier, France, 1978. *Literary Agent:* Georges Borchardt. *Address:* c/o Georges Borchardt, 136 East 57th Street, New York, NY 10022, USA.

LIEBERMAN, Jethro Koller, b. 23 Oct. 1943, Washington, District of Columbia, USA. Writer. m. Susan E Vucker, divorced, 1 son, 1 daughter. *Education:* BA, Yale University, 1964; JD, Harvard Law School, 1967. *Literary Appointment:* Legal Affairs Editor, Business Week, 1973–82. *Publications:* The Tyranny of the Experts, 1970; How the Government Breaks the Law, 1972; Milestones! 200 Years of American Law, 1976; Crisis at the Bar, 1978; Free Speech, Free Press and the Law, 1980; The Litigious Society, 1981; Business Law and the Legal Environment, 1985; Author of 10 other books. *Contributions to:* Philosophy and Public Affairs, and various others. *Honours:* Phi Beta Kappa Bicentennial Fellowship, 1972; National Council for the Social Studies, Notable Book of the Year, 1981; Silver Gavel Award, American Bar Association, 1982. *Literary Agent:* Georges Borchardt New York. *Address:* c/o Georges Borchardt, 136 East 57th Street, New York, NY 10022, USA.

LIEBERMAN, Laurence, b. 16 Feb. 1935, Detroit, Michigan, USA. Professor of English. m. Bernice Braun, 17 June 1956, 1 son, 2 daughters. *Education:* BA English 1956, MA English 1958, University of Michigan. *Literary Appointments:* Poetry Editor, University of Illinois Press, 1971–. *Publications:* Unassigned Frequencies: American Poetry in Review, 1977; Poetry: The Unblinding, 1968; The Osprey Suicides, 1973; God's Measurements, 1980; Eros at the World Kite Pageant, 1983; The Mural of Wakeful Sleep, 1985. *Contributions to:* The New Yorker; The Atlantic; Harper's; American Poetry Review; Paris Review; Poetry; Sewanee Review; Partisan Review; Kenyon Review; Hudson Review; The Nation; New Republic. *Honours:* National Endowment for the Arts Award, Poetry, 1968; Illinois Arts Council Grant, 1982. *Membership:* Poetry Society of America. *Address:* 1304 Eliot Drive, Urbana, IL 61801, USA.

LIEBERMAN, Shari, b. 24 June 1958, New York, USA. Nutritionist. m. Darwin Buschman, 4 Apr. 1982, New York City. *Education:* MA Clinical Nutrition, New York University; Registered Dietician. *Publication:* How

To Design Your Own Vitamin-Mineral Program, 1986. *Contributions to:* Nutrition Health Review; Tennis Around Town; Women's World; MS Magazine; Mademoiselle; Coping with Chemotherapy; Television and radio appearances and lectures. *Literary Agent:* Susan Protter, New York. *Address:* 60 East 8th Street, New York, NY 10003, USA.

LIEBMANN, Irina, b. 23 July 1943, Moscow, USSR. Writer; Scripter; Reporter. 2 daughters. *Education:* MA, Sinology and Arts, Leipzig University. *Publications:* Berliner Mietschaus (Berlin Apartment House), 1983; Neune Berichte uber Ronald, der seine Grossmutter begraben wollte (Nine Reports on Ronald, Who Wanted to Bury His Grannie), radio-play reprinted in Dialog 1981, Berlin; Henschelverlag; Sie mussen jetzt gehen, Frau Muhsam (You'd Better Go Now, Frau Muhsam), radio play reprinted in Dialog, Berlin. Henschelverlag. *Contributor to:* Wochenpost; Temperamente, Berlin, 1975–80. *Honours:* 2nd Prize, Radio Drama Competition, 1979; Radio-drama Award for the GDR (Preis der Horer), 1980; 1st Prize of radio-drama competition, 1981; Award for the benefit of Young Writers, 1984. *Membership:* Schriftstellerverband der DDR (Writers Union of the GDR). *Literary Agent:* Mitteldeutscher Verlag Halle/Saale. *Address:* Wolfshagener Str, DDR–1100 Berlin, Democratic Republic of Germany.

LIEHR, Heinz Fritz Siegfried, b. 24 Jan. 1917, Berlin, Germany. Medical Secretary, Scientific Cooperator. *Literary Appointments:* Scientific Cooperator to Institut für Konstitutionsbiologie und menschliche Verhaltensforschung, Hamburg, 1955–67, Kronburg/Taunus, 1967–84; Freelance author in fiction; Translator. *Major Publications:* Unten ohne (short stories), 1976; Gen – Italien (novel), 1977; Work on drawings in, Ägäische Legende (R de Saint-Privat), 1971; Author's Assistant for, Sex im Volksmund (E Bornemann), 1971; Jungenfreundschaften, Volume 2 (novel), 1984; Männerliebe (short stories in anthology), 1985. *Contributor to:* HIM-Applaus; DON-Magazine; ADONIS-Magazine (editorial assistant). *Honour:* Scholarship from State of Hesse, 1983. *Membership:* Freier Deutscher Autoren-Verband. *Literary Agent:* Karl-Ludwig Leonhardt, Hamburg, Federal Republic of Germany. *Address:* 314 Via Pasitea, I–84017 Positano, Prov. Salerno, Italy.

LIETZ, Walter, b. 27 July 1914, Elbing, West Prussia. Retired Police Officer. *Literary Appointments:* Readings in various German towns and Luxembourg, on a Russian cruise ship MS Dnjpr and MS Europa (German). *Publications:* Des Kohlerkindes Weihnachtsabend, 1952; Licht und Schatten, 1959; Manchmal, 1966; Kaleidoskop, 1967; Pfoten und Krallen, 1968; Dazwishen die Lust und die Pein, 1976; Mach dir nicht das Leben schwer, 1982; Manchmal solltest du verweilen, 1983; Unkraut verdirbt nicht, wächst stets raus, 1985. *Contributions to:* DAS Boot, Stadthefte; Deutsche Lebensret-lungs-Gesellschaft; Streife; General-Anzeiger; Neue Ruhr Zei-lung; Ruhrwacht; Elbinger Hefte; Silhoutte; Pegasus-Hyde Park' Kultur Korrespondenz; Schuim; VDI-Zeiting and others. *Honours:* Honoury Rose, Authors Competition, the Herne Meeting, 1957, 60; Lyric Prize, Working Association for Advertising Market and Opinion Research, Switzerland, 1985. *Memberships:* Association of German Writers; North Rhineland-Westphalian Artists Guild. *Address:* Beckerstr 23, 4200 Oberhausen 1, Federal Republic of Germany.

LIFSHIN, Lyn, b. 12 July 1949, Burlington, Vermont, USA. Poet; Editor. *Education:* BA, Syracuse University; MA, University of Vermont. *Publications:* 60 Books including: Black Apples; Upstate Madonna; Offered by Owner; Leaving South; Plymouth Women; Kiss The Skin Off; Madonna Who Shifts For Herself; Naked Charm. *Contributions to:* Chelsea; American Poetry Review; MS; Rolling Stone; Poetry Now; Chicago Review; Mississippi Review; Carolina Quarterly and most poetry magazines. *Honours:* Harcourt Brace Scholarship to Boulder; Boulder Manuscript Award;

Hart Crane Memorial Award; New York CAPS Grant; Fellowship to Yaddo, MacDowell, Millay, Bread Loaf, Jack Kerouac Award. *Literary Agent:* Charlotte Raymond. *Address:* 2142 Appletree Lane, Niskagona, NY 12309, USA.

LIGI, b. 11 Dec. 1946, Ravenswood, USA. m. Frieda Jean Rogers, 3 Aug. 1970, Pickens, South Carolina, USA. *Publications:* Stinking and Full of Eels, 1975; Some Accident Between the Grass and My Feet, 1976; News and Rejected Poems, 1980; The Cambridge Years, 1981; Killing the Magistrate, 1983; The Landlady's Lampwhite Hands, 1985. *Contributions to:* Abbey; Outlaw; Abraxos; Greenfield Review; New York Quarterly; Soho Arts Weekly; Northern Pleasure; Poetry Motel; The Archer; Nausea, and numerous others. *Address:* PO Box 40710, Portland, OR 97240, USA.

LIMA, Robert F, Jr, b. 7 Nov. 1935, Havana, Cuba. Professor. m. Sally Ann Murphy, 27 June 1964, Upper Darby, Pennsylvania, USA, 2 sons, 2 daughters. *Education:* BA English/Philosophy, 1957, MA Theatre & Drama, 1961, Villanova University, Pennsylvania; PhD Romance Literatures, New York University, 1968. *Literary Appointments:* Lecturer in Romance Languages & Literatures, Hunter College, City University of New York, 1962–65; Assistant Professor, 1965–69, Associate Professor, 1969–73, Professor of Spanish & Comparative Literatures, Pennsylvania State University, 1973–; Visiting Professor, Pontificia Universidad Catolica del Peru, 1976–77. *Major Publications:* The Readers Encyclopaedia of American Literature, 1962; The Theatre of Garcia Lorca, 1963; Borges the Labyrinth Maker, translation of work by A M Barrenechea, 1965; Valle-Inclan: Autobiography, Aesthetics, Aphorisms, translation, 1966; An Annotated Bibliography of Ramon del Valle-Inclan, 1972; Ramon del Valle-Inclan, 1972; Dos Ensayos Sobre Teatro Espanol de los Veinte (with D Doughterty), 1984; Fathoms, Poetry 1981; The Olde Ground; 1985. *Contributor to:* Hispania; Latin American Literary Review; Modern Fiction Studies; Studies in American Fiction; Romance Notes; Washington Post; Chicago Tribune; Christian Science Monitor; Library Journal; Saturday Review; Literary Review; Mundus Artium; and many others. *Honours:* CINTAS Foundation Fellow in Poetry 1971–72; Phi Sigma Iota (Honorary Fellow), 1977; Senior Fulbright-Hays Fellow, 1976–77; Fellow, Pennsylvania Humanities Council, 1981–83; Phi Kappa Phi (Honorary Fellow), 1984. *Memberships:* International PEN – American Center; Poetry Society of America; Pennsylvania Humanities Council. *Address:* 485 Orlando Avenue, State College, PA 16803, USA.

LIMBACHER, James Louis, b. 30 Nov. 1926, St Mary's, Ohio, USA. Film Historian; Teacher; Author. *Education:* BA, MA, Bowling Green University; MS Education, Indiana University; MS Library Sciences, Wayne State University. *Major Publications:* Using Films, 1967; Four Aspects of the Film, 1969; A Reference Guide to Audiovisual Information, 1973; Film Music: From Violins to Video, 1974; Haven't I seen you somewhere before?, 1979; Keeping Score, 1980; Feature Films in 8mm, 16mm and videotape, 1985; Television series: Shadows on the Wall, 1974; The Screening Room, 1978; Talking Pictures, 1984; Script Writer: Our Modern Art – The Movies, 1972. *Contributor to:* Film Journals; Monthly column in, Previews. *Honours:* Gold Medal for script of, The Man Called Edison, Atlanta Film Festival; Michigan Librarian of the Year, 1974. *Address:* Morley Manor Apt. 1201, 21800 Morley Avenue, Dearborn, MI 48124, USA.

LIMBURG, James Wallace, b. 2 Mar. 1935, Minnesota, USA. Professor of Old Testament. m. Martha Ylvisaker, 3 Aug. 1957, Decorah, Iowa, USA, 3 sons, 1 daughter. *Education:* BA, Luther College; BD, Luther Theological Seminary; PhD, Union Theological Seminary, Virginia. *Major Publications:* The Prophets and the the Powerless, 1977; Old Stories for a New Time, 1983. *Contributions to:* Journal of Biblical Literature; Catholic Bible Quarterly; Interpretation; Word & World. *Honours:* Distinguished Service Award, Luther College. *Membership:* Society of Biblical

Literature. *Address:* Luther Northwestern Theological Seminary, 2481 Como Avenue, St Paul, MN 55108, USA.

LIMET, Elizabeth, b. 15 Apr. 1915, Namur, Belgium. Writer, Author, Painter, Musician. m. R Borremans, 1 Feb. 1933, Veuve, Belgium. 2 sons, 2 daughters. *Education:* Belgian Academy of Music. *Literary Appointments:* Various responsibilities for poetry on Canadian television and radio. *Major Publications:* La Voix de mes Pensées; Le Phare des Amants; Gel de Feu; Rosétendre- J'aime L'éspace. *Honour:* Citation au Congrès des éducateurs du Québec, 1975. *Memberships:* French Literary Society; Québec Writers Union. *Address:* C.P. 905 – Succ. H, Montréal, Québec, H3G 2M9, Canada.

LIN, Jain I, b. 18 Mar. 1938, Taiwan, Republic of China. Pathologist. m. Elizabeth Lin, 24 June 1968, Ping Tung, 2 daughters. *Education:* MD, Kaohsiung Medical College, Kaohsiung, Taiwan. *Publications:* Death of a Kaiser, the story of Frederick III's illness, 1985. *Contributions to:* The New England Journal of Medicine; Laboratory Medicine; Taiwan Medical Journal. *Memberships:* American Medical Writers Association: *Literary Agent:* Landfall Press Inc, Dayton, Ohio, USA. *Address:* 100 Terrace Villa Dr, Centerville, OH 45459, USA.

LINCOLN, Bruce Kenneth, b. 5 Mar. 1948, Philadelphia. University Professor. m. Louis Gibson Hassett, 17 Apr. 1971, Baltimore, 2 daughters. *Education:* BA (with High Honours) Haverford College, 1970; PhD (with Distinction) University of Chicago, 1976; *Publications:* Priests, Warriors and Cattle: A Study in the Ecology of Religions, 1981; Emerging from the Chrysalis: Studies in Rituals of Women's Initiation, 1981; Religion, Rebellion, Revolution, editor 1985. *Contributions to:* Articles in Comparative Studies in Society and History; History of Religions; Journal of Indo-European Studies and other scholarly journals. *Honours:* American Council of Learned Societies Award for Best New Book in History of Religions for 'Priests, Warriors and Cattle', 1981; John Simon Guggenheim Memorial Fellowship 1983–84. *Address:* Humanities Program, 314 Ford Hall, University of Minnesota, Minneapolis, MN 55455, USA.

LINDBERG, Richard C, B. 14 June 1953, Chicago, Illinois, USA. Writer; Scriptwriter. m. Denise Kay Janda, 1 July 1978, Chicago, Illinois. *Education:* BA, MA candidate, History, Northeastern Illinois University. *Publications:* Stuck on the Sox, 1978; Who's On Third: The Chicago White Sox Story, 1983; The Chicago White Sox, 1984; Chicago Ragtime: Another Look at Chicago 1880–1920, 1985. *Contributions to:* Chicago Tribune magazine, 1980; Chicago History Magazine, 1981. *Memberhips:* Phi Alpha Theta. *Address:* 10069 Linda Lane, Des Plaines, IL 60016, USA.

LINDE, Nancy, b. 21 Dec. 1949. Teacher. m. Stephan Khinov. *Education:* BA, Philos. 1971, MFA, 1972, CCNY, USA. *Appointments include:* Adjunct Lecturer, College of Staten Island, CUNY: Adjunct Lecturer, Rutgers University; Adjunct Lecturer, Rochester Institute of Technology; Adjunct Lecturer, Community College of the Finger Lakes, Staten Island; ZC Community College, CUNY; Adjunct Lecturer, Bronx Community College, CUNY; Adjunct Lecturer, The College of New Rochelle. *Memberships:* Poets and Writers; Fellow, Poetry Centre, College of Staten Island. *Contributor to:* Buckle; Parachute; Earth's Daughters; Symposium; Sojourner; 13th Moon; Endymion; Anduril; Balaam's Ass; Promethean. *Honours:* Poetry Prize, City College, 1970. *Address:* 366 Woodstock Avenue, Staten Island, NY 10301, USA.

LINDE, Shirley Motter, b. 22 Mar. 1929, Cincinnati, USA. Author; publishing executive. m. Douglas W Londe, 1954, (divorced 1967), 2 sons. *Education:* BS, 1951, University of Cincinnati; MS, 1973, University of Michigan. *Publications:* The Big Ditch-Story of the Suez Canal, 1962; Science and the Public, 1962; Response of the Nervous System to Ionizing Radiation, 1962; Medical Science in the News, 1965; Heart Attacks That Aren't, 1966; Airline Stewardess Handbook, 1968; Modern Woman's Medical Dictionary, 1968; Cosmetic Surgery – What It Can Do For You, 1971; Emergency Family First Aid Guide, 1971; Sickle Cell – a Complete Guide to Prevention and Treatment, (with Arthur Michels), 1972; Orthotherapy, (With Howard G Rapaport), 1971; The Complete Allergy Guide, 1970; The Sleep Book, (with Frank Finnerty, Jr,) High Blood Pressure, 1975; Now That You've Had Your Baby, (with Gideon Panter), 1976; Dr Atkins' Superenergy Diet, 1977; Shirley Linde's Whole Health Catalogue, 1977; The Whole Health Catalogue, 1980; The Joy of Sleep, 1981; How to Beat a Bad Back, 1981; Lifegain, (with Dr Robert Allen), 1981; 201 Medical Tests You Can Do At Home, 1983; US Directory to Wholistic Medicine and Alternate Health Care, 1984. *Contributions to:* Numerous publications. *Honour:* Outstanding Service Award, 1972, American Medical Writers' Association. *Memberships:* Include National Association of Scientific Writers; American Medical Writers' Association; AAAS; Authors' League. *Address:* 152 First Avenue N, Tierra Verde, FL 33715, USA.

LINDEBERG, Per Sten Karl, b. 18 May 1938, Stockholm, Sweden. Writer; Journalist. *Education:* Fil kand, University of Stockholm. *Literary Appointment:* Drama Series (each a 4-part play) for the Swedish Broadcasting Corporation: Vedergallningen, 1974; Ansiktet i skuggan, 1976 (The plays have also been broadcast in West Germany, Switzerland, Italy, Norway, Finland and Czechoslovakia). *Publication:* Blylarmet, 1983. *Contributor:* Short stories and articles to Swedish daily and periodic press since mid-sixties; Programmes for Swedish Broadcasting Corporation. *Honour:* Fellowship from Swedish Authors Fund, 1984. *Memberships:* Member, Swedish Union of Playwriters. *Address:* Hantverkargatan 81, 112 38 Stockholm, Sweden.

LINDEMAN, Jack, b. 31 Dec. 1924, Philadelphia, Pennsylvania, USA. Teacher. *Education:* BS, West Chester University, 1949; Universities of Pennsylvania, 1949, Mississippi, 1949–50, Villanova, 1973. *Appointments:* Editor, Whetstone, 1955–61; Poetry Editor, Time Capsule, 1981–. *Publications:* Twenty-One Poems, 1963; The Conflict of Convictions, 1968. *Contributor to:* Beloit Poetry Journal; Christian Science Monitor; Colorado Quarterly; Harper's; Literary Review; The Nation; New World Writing; New York Times; Perspective; Poetry; Southern Poetry Review; Southwest Review; Anthologies: Best Poems of 1966; Where is Vietnam?; The Writing on the Wall; From Paragraph to Essay; etc. *Membership:* Walt Whitman Society. *Address:* 133 S Franklin St, Fleetwood, PA 19522, USA.

LINDENBERG, Vladimir Tchelistcheff, b. 16 May 1902, Moscow, Russia. Physician; Psychiatrist; Neurologist. *Education:* Universities of Bonn, Heidelberg, Vienna until 1925; Medical Diploma, 1928. *Publications include:* Schicksalsgefahrte sein, 1964; Richter Staatsanwaite, Rechtsbrecher, 1965; Das Yoga Bilderbuch, 1967; Gottes Boten unter uns, 1968; Bobik begegnet der Welt, 1969; Bobik in der Fremde, 1970; Jenseits der Funfzig, 1971; Uber die Schwelle, 1973; Wolodja. Portrait einer jungen Arztes, 1974; Von Mensch zu Mensch, 1973; Geheimnisvolle Krafte um uns, 1974; Reise nach Innen, 1976; Tag um Tag ist guter Tag, 1976; Stufen und Riten der Einweihung, 1978; Mit Freunde leben, 1979. *Honours include:* Literary Prize of the VDK; Fed. Cross of Merit, 1978. *Membership:* German Authors Association. *Address:* Beyschlagstrasse 13A, D–1000 Berlin 27, Federal Republic of Germany.

LINDHOLM, Gösta Olof Ferdinand, b. 30 Apr. 1921, Ekenäs, Finland. Teacher of Psychology; Rector. m. Katri-Helena Nelimarkka, 27 Sep. 1949, Helsinki, (deceased 1983), 3 daughters. *Education:* PhD, 1967. *Publications:* Plays: Flower Blooming for Sun, 1959; Admission Test, 1961; Background, 1962; Good

Morning Life, 1976. Radio plays: The Latest Craze, 1950; Two People in the Night, 1954; Beauty Balsam, 1960; Admission Test, 1966; Three Monks, Theme of Leo Tolstoy, 1982. Radio Play Trilogy, The Slave of God, I; The Green Staff, 1984; The Brotherhood of Ants, 1984; Astapovo, 1984; Free dramatizations of Decameron by Boccaccio, Confession of a Beauty, tale III, 2nd day 1985, St. Julian, Patron Saint of Travellers, tale II, 2nd day, 1986, Saint Ciappelletto, tale I, 1st day 1986. *Membership:* Finnish Dramatists Society. *Address:* Parivaljakonkuja 4 A 13, 00410 Helsinki, Finland.

LINDOW, Rainer, b. 23 Apr. 1942, Berlin, Germany. Author, m. Berlin, 2 sons, 1 daughter. *Education:* Diploma (Director of Film). *Publications:* Under the Hat in the Sun on the New Book Nichel (Novel), 1979; Stories, 1973, 77, 78; Pieces for radio, television and theater; Feature films and documentary films. *Honour:* Silver Laurel, Television of German Democratic Republic. *Memberships:* Union of Writers of German Democratic Republic. *Address:* Leunistrasse 1, 1500 Potsdam, Democratic Republic of Germany.

LINDSAY, John Maurice, b. 21 July 1918, Glasgow, Scotland. Former Director; Consultant. m. Aileen Joyce Gordon, 3 Aug. 1946, Glasgow, 1 son, 3 daughters. *Education:* Royal Scottish Academy of Music, 1936–39. *Literary Appointments:* Editor, Scottish Review. *Publications:* Poetry Includes: The Advancing Day, 1940; Perhaps Tomorrow, 1941; No Crown for Laughter; Selected Poems, 1947; At the Wood's Edge, 1950; The Exiles Heart, 1957; This Business of Living, 1969; Comings and Goings, 1971; Selected Poems 1942–1972, 1973; Walking Without and Overcoat, 1972–77; French Mosquitoes Woman, 1986. Prose includes: A Pocket Guide to Scottish Culture, 1947; The Scottish Renaissance, 1949; Robert Burns, The Man, His Work, The Legend, 3rd edition, 1980; The Burns Encyclopedia, 1959, 3rd edition, 1980; Killochan Castle, 1960; Portrait of Glasgow, 1972; 1981; History of Scottish Literature, 1977; Lowland Scottish Villages, 1980; Thank You for Having Me: A Personal memoir, 1983; Castles of Scotland: A Constable Guide, 1986. Editor of numerous works including: Scotland: An Anthology, 1974; As I Remember, 1979; Scottish Comic Verse, 1425–1980, 1980. *Honours:* Rockefeller Atlantic Award, 1946; Commander of British Empire, 1979; Honorary DLitt, Glasgow University, Scotland, 1982; Honorary Fellow, Royal Institute of Architects, Scotland, 1985. *Memberships:* Council members, Association of Scottish Literary Studies. *Address:* 7 Milton Hill, Milton, Dumbarton, Scotland.

LINDSAY, Kenneth C, b. 23 Dec. 1919, Milwaukee, Wisconsin, USA. Art Historian. m. Christine Charstrom, 18 Oct. 1947, Madison, Wisconsin, 1 son, 1 daughter. *Education:* MA, PhD, University of Wisconsin. *Literary Appointment:* Professor of Art History, SUNY at Binghamton. *Publications:* The Harpur Index of Masters Theses in Art Written in American Institutions of Higher Learning, 1956; The Works of John Vanderlyn, 1970; Angelo Ippollto, 1975; Kandinsky: Complete Writings on Art (co-editor), 1982 (2 volumes). *Contributions to:* Journal of Aesthetics and Art Criticism; Art News; Prints; Computers and Their Potential Application on Museums, 1962; The Burlington Magazine. *Honours:* Fulbright Award, 1949–50; Hilla Rebay Kandinsky Award, 1953. *Address:* Box 24 RD 7, Binghamton, NY 13903, USA.

LINDSAY, Rae, b. Garfield, New Jersey, USA. Writer. m. Alexander M Lindsay, deceased, 2 sons, 1 daughter. *Education:* BA, Wellesley College. *Literary Appointments:* Center for Research on Women, co-sponsored by Wellesley College and Federation of Organisations for Professional Women, 1976; Jew Jersey State Council on the Arts, for Alone and Surviving, 1976. *Publications:* The Pursuit of Youth, 1976; Alone and Surviving, 1977; The Left-Handed Book, 1980; How to Look as Young as Feel, 1980; George Michael's Secrets for Beautiful Hair, 1981; How to be a Perfect Bitch, 1983. *Contributions to:* Associated Press Newsfeatures,

syndicated columnist, 1978–84; Woman's World Magazine, contributing editor, curently; Family Weekly; The Woman's Home Companion; Cosmopolitan; Eve; Single Magazine; Runners World; Travel world; Sunday Woman; National Enquirer. *Memberships:* National Press Club; Authors Guild; Authors League; National Association of Journalists and Authors. *Literary Agent:* R & R Writers/Agents Incorporated. *Address:* 364 Mauro Road, Englewood Cliffs, NJ 07632, USA.

LINE, Maurice Bernard, b. 21 June 1928, Bedford, England. Librarian. m. Joyce Gilchrist, 12 Apr. 1954, Paisley, 1 son, 1 daughter. *Education:* BA, Oxford, 1950; MA, Oxford, 1954; Fellow of the Library Association; Fellow of the Institute of Information Scientists; Fellow of the British Institute of Management. *Literary Appointments:* Library Trainee, Bodleian Library, Oxford, 1950–51; Library Assistant, University of Glasgow, 1951–53; Sub-Librarian, University of Southampton, 1954–65; Deputy Librarian, University of Newcastle-upon-Tyne, 1965–68; Librarian, University of Bath, 1968–71; Librarian, National Central Library, 1971–73; Director-General, British Library Lending Division, 1974–. *Publications:* Library Surveys, 1967, revised 1982; National Libraries, 1979; Universal Availability of Publications, 1983. *Contributions to:* 200 Articles mostly on professional topics. *Honour:* Honorary D Litt, Heriot-Watt University, Edinburgh. *Address:* 10 Blackthorn Lane, Burn Bridge, Harrogate, North Yorkshire HG3 1NZ, England.

LINGARD, Joan Amelia, b. Edinburgh, Scotland. Author. 3 daughters. *Publications:* Liam's Daughter, 1963; The Prevailing Wind, 1964; The Tide Comes In, 1966; The Headmaster, 1967; A Sort of Freedom, 1968; The Lord on Our Side, 1970; The Second Flowering of Emily Mountjoy, 1979; Greenyards, 1981; Sisters by Rite, 1984; Children's books: The Twelfth Day of July, 1970; Frying As Usual, 1971; Across the Barricades, 1972; Into Exile, 1973; The Clearance, 1974; A Proper Place, 1975; The Resettling, 1975; Hostages To Fortune, 1976; The Pilgrimage, 1976; The Reunion, 1977; Frying As Usual, 1977; The Gooseberry, 1978; The File on Fraulein Berg, 1980; Strangers In The House, 1981; The Winter Visitor, 1983. *Honour:* Scottish Arts Council Bursary, 1967–68. *Memberships:* Chairman, Society of Authors in Scotland; Scottish Pen; Director, Edinburgh Book Festival; Chairman, Meet the Author Committee, Edinburgh; Council member 1980–84, Literary Committee 1980–84, SAC. *Literary Agent:* David Higham Associates Ltd. *Address:* c/o David Higham Assoc Ltd, 5-8 Lower John Street, Golden Square, London W1R 4HA, England.

LINGENFELIER, Richard Emery, b. 5 Apr. 1934, New Mexico, USA. Physicist. m. Naomi Brefka, 27 Dec. 1957, 1 daughter. *Education:* AB, University of California, Los Angeles, 1956. *Publications:* Songs of the Gold Rush, 1964; Presses of the Pacific Islands, 1967; Songs of the American West, 1968; The Hardrock Miners, 1974; Steamboats on the Colorado, 1978; Gamma Ray Transients, 1982; The Newspapers of Nevada, 1984; Lying on the Eastern Slope, 1984; Death Valley & The Amargosa, 1986. *Contributions to:* Over 100 articles in Nature; Astrophysical Journal; Physical Review; Science; Philosophical Transactions of the Royal Society of London; Space Science Reviews; Reviews of Geophysics; Annual Reviews of Nuclear and Particle Science. *Honours:* Fulbright Research Scholar, India, 1968–69. *Memberships:* Fellow, American Physical Society; International Astronomical Union; American Astronomical Society. *Address:* Center for Astrophysics and Space Sciences, C-011, University of California, San Diego, La Jolla, CA 92093, USA.

LINTERMANS, Gloria, b. 11 May 1947, Brooklyn, New York, USA. Fashion and Beauty columnist. m. Eric Lintermans, 15 June 1968 (div. 1981) 2 sons. *Literary Appointments:* Columnist, Looking Great, Inter-Continental Press Syndicate, Glendale, California, 1978–82; Universal Press Syndicate, Fairway, Kansas, 1982–; International Columnist, Editor's Press, New York City, 1980–; Author, Capistrano Press, Long

Beach, California, 1980. *Publications:* The Professional Babysitter's Guide; Internationally syndicated column, Looking Great; Looking Great newsletter. *Memberships:* Society of Professional Journalists; Fashion Group International; Women in Communications; American Federation of Television and Radio Artists. *Hobbies:* Gardening; Chinese History; Ballet. *Address:* PO Box 675, Van Nuys, CA 91408-0675, USA.

LIPMAN, David, b. 13 Feb. 1931, Springfield, Missouri, USA. Newspaper Editor. m. Marilyn Lee Vittert, 18 Dec. 1961, 1 son, 1 daughter. *Education:* BJ, University of Missouri, Columbia, 1953. *Appointments:* Sports Editor, Post-Tribune, Jefferson City, 1953; General Assignment Reporter, Springfield, Daily News, 1953–54; Reporter, Copy Editor, Springfield, Leader & Press, 1956–57; Reporter and Copy Editor, Kansas City Star, 1957–60; Sports Reporter, St Louis Post-Dispatch, 1960–66; Assistant Sports Editor, 1966–68, News Editor, 1968–71, Assistant Managing Editor, 1971–78, Managing Editor, 1979–, Vice President, Director, 1981–, Pulitzer Productions Inc. *Publications:* Maybe I'll Pitch Forever, 1962; Mr Baseball, The Story of Branch Rickey, 1966; Ken Boyer, 1967; Joe Namath, 1968; The Speed King, The Story of Boby Hayes, co-author, 1971; Bob Gibson Pitching Ace, 1975; Jim Hart, Underrated Quarterback, 1977. *Memberships:* Sigma Delta Chi; Mid-American Press Institute, Board of Directors, 1973–, Chairman, 1975–77; Mid-America Newspaper Conference, Board of Directors, 1973–75; Football Writers Association of America, Board of Directors, 1968; American Society of Newspaper Editions, 1979–; University of Missouri School of Journalism National Alunmi Association, National Chaman, 1980–83. *Address:* St Louis Post Dispatch, 900 North Tucker Blvd, St Louis, MO 63101, USA.

LIPMAN, Matthew, b. 24 Aug. 1923, Vineland, New Jersey, USA. Professor of Philosophy. m. Theresa Smith, 26 Dec. 1974. *Education:* BS, 1948, PhD, 1954, Columbia University. *Publications:* What Happens in Art, 1967; Discovering Philosophy, 1969; Contemporary Aesthetics, 1973; Harry Stettlemeier's Discovery, 1974; Lisa, 1976; Mark, 1980; Pixie, 1981; Kip and Gus, 1982. *Contributions to:* Psychiatry, 1956; Journal of Philosophy; New York Times. *Honours:* Fulbright Scholar, Sorbonne, 1950–51; Matchette Prize in Aesthetics, 1956; Rockefeller Foundation Research Grant, 1978–81; Schumann Foundation Grant, 1982–85. *Literary Agent:* Susan Schulman. *Address:* Institute for the Advancement of Philosophy for Children, Montclair State College, Upper Montclair, NJ 07043, USA.

LIPMAN, Vivian David, b. 27 Feb. 1921, London, England. Editor; Author; Retired Governmental Officer. m. Sonia Lynette Sersuve, 21 June 1964, 1 son. *Education:* BA, MA, PhD, Oxford University. *Literary Appointments:* Editor, Littman Library of Jewish Civilisation; Coordinator, Britain, America-Holyland Project. *Publications:* English Local Government Areas, 1949; A Social History of the Jews in Britain, 1954; A Century of Social Service, 1959; Jews of Medieval Norwich, 1964; The Century of Moses Montefoire, editor with S L Lipman, 1985. *Contributions to:* Public Administration; Jewish Journal of Sociology; Transactions of Jewish Historical Society and others. *Honours:* CVO, 1977. *Memberships:* Fellow, Royal Historical Society and Society of Antiquaries. *Address:* 9 Rotherwick Road, London NW11 7DG, England.

LIPP, Frederick John, b. 23 July 1916, Toledo, Ohio, USA. Writer; Journalist. m. Marian Ruth Bechstein, 7 Sep. 1946, Toledo. *Education:* PhB, University of Toledo, 1939; MA, University of Iowa, 1941. *Publications include:* Rulers of Darkness, novel, 1966; Some Lose Their Way, young adult novel, 1980; Radio & Televison plays, 1941–60. *Contributions to:* American Writing 1943; Various literary magazines, 1940–45; The Explorer, journal, Cleveland Museum of Natural History, 1982–85. *Honours:* 1st Prize, novel, Friends of American Writers, 1967; Literary Award, Cleveland Arts Prize, 1968. *Literary Agent:* McIntosh & Otis Inc., 475

5th Avenue, New York. *Address:* 3223 Rocky River Drive No. 20; Cleveland, OH 44111, USA.

LIPPMANN, Alfred Lothar. b. 25 Oct. 1917, Frankenberg, Germany. Writer. m. Liselotte Rossberg, 2 Sep. 1950, Frankenberg, Germany, 2 daughters. *Education:* Abitur, Technical University for Mechanical Engineering and Physics, Germany. *Appointments:* Literary critic and essayist. *Publications:* Ausserhalb der Zeit, 1967; Augen der Zeit, 1979; Auskunft über unsere Zeit, 1981; Auf den Strassen der Zeit, 1982; Aus dem Happtbuch meiner Zeit (pending). *Contributor to:* Actuell, journal; Frankenband, and others. *Memberships:* Regensburger Schriftstellergruppe International; Interessengemeinschaft deutschsprachiger Autoren; Kreis der Freunde um Peter Coryllis. *Address:* Lothar Lippmann, Postfach 3012, D 8500 Nurnberg, Federal Republic of Germany.

LIPSKA, Ewa Aleksandra, b. 8 Oct. 1945, Krakow, Poland. Writer. m. 24 July 1982. *Education:* Krakow Academy of Fine Arts. *Major Publications:* Poems, 1967; Second Collection of Poems, 1970; Third Collection of Poems, 1972; Fourth Collection of Poems, 1974; Fifth Collection of Poems, 1978; Selected Poems, 1979; Living Death (novel), 1979. *Contributor to:* Various literary journals and anthologies. *Honours:* Koscielski Prize, Switzerland, 1973; General Poetry Polish Prize, Kodz, 1972; Andrew Bursa Poetry Prize, Krakow, 1972; Robert Graves Prize, PEN Club. *Address:* 200 East Ohio Street, Chicago, IL 11606, USA.

LIPSON, Leslie Michael, b. 14 Nov. 1912, London, England. University Professor of Political Science. m. Helen M Fruchtman, 2 Oct. 1980, Oakland, California, USA, 1 son by previous marriage. *Education:* BA, 1935, MA, 1945, Oxford University; PhD, Chicago, Illinois, USA, 1938. *Publications:* The American Governor, 1939, 68; The Politics of Equality, 1948; The Great Issues of Politics, 1954, 7th edition, 1985; The Democratic Civilization, 1964; Values and Humanity, with Elizabeth M Drews, 1971. *Contributions to:* American Political Science Review; Political Quarterly; Public Administration; Public Administration Review; Journal of Politics; Revue Francaise de Science Politque; Political Studies; Encyclopedia Britannica; Dictionary of the Social Sciences, and others. *Honour:* Berkeley Citation, University of California, 1980. *Address:* 25 Stoddard Way, Berkeley, CA 94708, USA.

LIPTON, Leonard, b. 18 May 1940, New York City, USA. Inventor. Divorced, 1 daughter. *Education:* AB, Cornell University, 1962. *Appointments:* Researcher, Time Inc, 1963; Editor, Popular Photography Magazine, 1965. *Publications:* Independent Filmmaking, 1972; Super 8 Book, 1976; Foundations of the Stereoscopic Cinema, 1982. *Contributor to:* Film Reviewer, Berkeley Barb, 1965–69; Regular Contributor, Popular Photography, 1966–80; Articles in: American Cinematographer; SMPTE Journal; SPIE Proceedings; SID Proceedings. *Membership:* American Society of Composers, Authors and Publishers. *Address:* 236 Water St, Pt Richmond, CA 94801, USA.

LIPTZIN, Sol, b. 27 July 1901, Satanov, USSR. Educator. *Education:* BA, CCNY, 1921; AM, Columbia, 1922; PhD, Columbia, 1924. *Publications:* Shelley in Germany, 1924; Arthur Schnitzier, 1932; Germany's Stepchildren, 1944; Generation of Decision, 1958; The Jew in American Literature, 1966; History of Yiddish Literature, 1972; Biblical Themes in World Literature, 1985. *Contributor to:* Encyclopedia Americana; Columbia Dictionary of Modern European Literature. *Membership:* President, Jewish Book Council of America. *Address:* 21 Washington St, Jerusalem, Israel.

LISH, Gordon, b. 11 Feb. 1934, Hewlett, New York, USA. Writer; Teacher; Editor. m. Barbara Works, 30 May 1968, Carmel, 1 son, 3 children by previous marriage. *Appointment:* Teacher, Yale, Columbia, New York Universities. *Publications:* English Grammar; A Man's Work; Why Work; Secret Life of Our Times; New Sounds in American Fiction; All Our Secrets Are the

Same; (Novels) Dear Mr Capote; Peru; (Short Stories) What I Know So Far; (Ghostwritten Book) Coming Out of the Ice, by Victor Herman, 1977. *Honours:* 2 Awards, Columbia Graduate School of Journalism. *Literary Agent:* Georges Borchardt. *Address:* c/o Alfred A Knopf, Inc, 201 East 50, New York, NY 10022, USA.

LISSENS, René Felix, b. 27 Mar. 1912, Louvain, Belgium. Emeritus Professor. m. Berthe van den Begin, 29 June 1938, Kessel-Lo, 1 son, 1 daughter. *Education:* PhD, University of Louvain, 1933; Postgraduate studies, University of Hamburg, Rostock, Berlin and Paris. *Literary Appointments:* Founder and Director, Center for Studies of Guido Gezelle, Antwerp, 1966–81; Co-Editor, Vormen, 1937–40; Founder and Editor in Chief, De Periscoop, 1950–59; Co-Editor, Dietsche Warande den Belfort, 1960–, Gezelliana, 1970–. *Publications:* Het Impressionisme in de Vlaamsche letterkunde, 1934; Brieven van A Rodenbach, 1942; Rien que l'homme, 1944; De Vlaamse letterkunde van 1780 tot heden, 1967, 4th edition; Gezellebriefwisseling I, 1970; Letter en geest, 1982; Contributions to various English, Dutch, American, French, Italian encyclopedias and reference books. *Honours:* Commander, Order of Leopold II, 1962; Commander, Order of Leopold, 1966; Grand Officer, Order of the Crown, 1974; Grand Officer, Order of Leopold, 1981; Beernaert Prize, Royal Flemish Academy, 1952–53; Prize, Flemish Provinces, 1955. *Memberships:* Ex-President, Royal Flemish Academy of Language and Letters; South Netherlands Society of Language, Literature and History; Dutch Society of Literature; Commission for National Biographical Dictionary; Consultant, Commission of Archives and Museum of Flemish Cultural Life; Guido Gezelle Society; Accademia Internationale de Leonardo da Vinci, Italy; Society of Flemish Men of Letters; Flemish Pen Club; Past President, Scriptores Christiani. *Address:* Gebladertelaan 2A, 1180 Brussels, Belgium.

LIST, Anneliese, b. 6 Jan. 1922, Heroldsberg, Federal Republic of Germany, Soubrette. *Education:* State examination and permission as dancer. *Publications include:* Der Baum, 1974; Die Arbeit war umsonst 1974; Wunder gibt es immer wieder, 1974; Was ich nie im Leben verges sen Kann, 1975; Mein Weiter Weg vom Kreig bis heute, 1975; Erst heute versteche ich warum meine Mutter mich verlieB, 1975; Wie ich mein erstes Geld verdiente, 1977; Der erste Tanz, 1977; Das Hexlein, 1977; Fröhliche Weihnacht überall, 1985; Das Lebkuchenherz, 1985; Das Glück hinter den Bergen, 1978. *Honours:* 2nd prize, for best story, Wahre Geschichten Magazine, 1975. *Address:* Fünfbronn 26, 8545 Spalt, Federal Republic of Germany.

LISTER, Raymond (George), b. 28 Mar. 1919. Cambridge, England. Author; m. Pamela Helen Brutnell, 7 June 1947, Cambridge, 1 son, 1 daughter. *Education:* MA, Cantab; Fellow, Wolfson College, Cambridge; Syndic., Fitzwilliam Museum, Cambridge. *Publications:* Decorative Wrought Ironwork in Great Britain, 1957; Edward Calvert, 1962; William Blake, 1968; Samuel Palmer and His Etchings, 1969; British Romantic Art, 1973; Samuel Palmer: A Biography, 1974; Editor, The Letters Of Samuel Palmer, 1974; Prints & Printmaking, 1984; The Paintings of Samuel, 1985. *Contributions to:* various professional journals. *Literary Agent:* Stephen Aske. *Address:* Windmill House, Linton, Cambridge CB1 6NS, England.

LITSEY, Sarah, b. 23 June 1901, Springfield, Kentucky, USA. Writer; Conductor of Writers Workshops. m. (1) E W Nye, 17 June 1933, 1 son; (2) W W Ford, 1 Dec. 1979. *Education:* Sargent School for Physical Education. *Literary Appointments:* Famous Writers School, Westport, Connecticut, 1961–; Independent classes, 1950–. *Publications:* Poetry: Legend, 1936; For The Lonely, 1937; The Oldest April, 1957; Toward Mystery, 1974; Novels: There Was a Lady, 1945; The Intimate Illusion, 1955; A Path to the Water, 1962. *Contributions to:* Numerous magazines, journals and reviews including: Saturday Evening Post; Colliers; Cosmopolitan; Good Housekeeping; Scribners; The Writer; New York Times; New York

Herald-Tribune; Poetry: Magazine of Verse; christian Science Monitor; McCall's Ladies Home Journal; American; Poetry World; Poetry Digest. *Honours include:* First Prize, New York Women Poets, 1974, 83, 84; Memorial Prize, Dec. 1984; Third Prize, Brooklyn Poetry Circle, 1984. *Memberships:* President, New York Women Poets; American PEN; Poetry Society of America. *Literary Agent:* Julian Bach Junior. *Address:* 248 Newtown Turnpike, W Redding, CT 06896, USA.

LITTLE, Flora Jean, b. 2 Jan, 1932, Taiwan, SE Asia. Writer. *Education:* BA, University of Toronto, Canada. *Appointments:* Lecturer, Children's Literature University of Guelph, Canada, 1979–83. *Publications:* Mine for Keeps, 1962; Look Through My Window, 1970; From Anna, 1972; Listen for the Singing, 1977; Mama's Going to Buy You a Mockingbird, 1984; Lost and Found, 1985. *Honours:* Little-Brown Canadian Children's Book Award, 1961; Vicky Metcalf Award, 1974; Canada Council Children's Book Award, 1977; Canadian Library Association Award, 1985; Ruth Schwartz Children's Book Award, 1985. *Address:* 198 Glasgow Street North, Guelph, Ontario, Canada N1H 4X2.

LITTLE, Geraldine Clinton, b. 20 Sep. 1925, Portstewart, Ireland. Poet; Teacher. m. Robert K Little, 26 Sep. 1953, Philadelphia, Pennsylvania, USA, 3 sons. *Education:* Master's Degree in English. *Literary Appointments:* Past President of The Haiku Society of America; Vice-President of The Poetry Society of America. *Publications:* Contrast in Keenings: Ireland, 1982; Hakugai, Poem from a Concentration Camp, 1983; Endless Waves, 1984. *Contributions to:* Published in over 60 literary journals including: Poetry Northwest; Poetry Now; California Quarterly, Northwest Review; Shenandoah; 13th Moon; Blue Unicorn; Poet Lore; The Literary Review; Christian Science Monitor. *Honours:* 5 major awards from The Poetry Society of AMerica, 1977–1982; The Grand Prize of The National Federation of State Poetry Societies, Inc., 1979; The Daniel Varoujan Award from The New England Poetry Club, 1982. *Memberships:* The Poetry Society of America, Vice President; The Haiku Society of America, President; Authors' Guild. *Address:* 519 Jacksonville Road, Mount Holly, NJ 08060, USA.

LITTLE, Larry Douglas, b. 13 Apr. 1948. Bookseller. *Education:* BA, Creative Writing, Purdue University, West Lafayette, Indiana. *Contributor to:* Sunshine Review; Poet's Pulse; Sunshine; Eternity; Orphic Lute. *Membership:* South and West Incorporated. *Address:* 1024 25th Street, Bedford, IN 47421, USA.

LITTLE, Stuart W, b. 19 Dec. 1921, Hartford, Connecticut, USA. Writer, Editor, Book Catalogue Company President. m. Anastazia Lillie Marie Raben-Levetzau, 25 Sep. 1945, London, 1 son, 2 daughters. *Education:* BA, Yale University. *Literary Appointments:* Editor, Authors Guild Bulletin, 1968–81. *Publications:* The Playamakers, (with Arthur Cantor), 1970; Off Broadway, 1972; Enter Joseph Papp, 1974; After The Fact, 1975. *Contributions to:* New York Times arts and leisure section; Playbill; Saturday Review; New York Magazine. *Membership:* The Authors Guild. *Literary Agent:* Melanie Jackson. *Address:* 131 Prince Street, New York, NY 10012, USA.

LITVEN, Walter, b. 5 July 1934, Poland. Editor; Writer. m. Joanne P Moisuk, 5 Sep. 1965, Edmonton, Alberta, Canada. *Education:* BA (Hons), University of British Columbia, Vancouver; Graduate Studies, University of Michigan, Ann Arbor, USA. *Literary Appointment:* Editor, Chronic Diseases in Canada, 1 Jan. 1980. *Publications:* Various articles on United Nations Youth in Canada; Observations and Comparisons of Field Work Operations of Five Study Areas in the WHO/ICS-MCU Study, 1969; Alberta Health Care Study: Health Care Utilization Patterns of Albertans 1968 and 1970. Final Report, 1972; Health Care: An International Study (co-author), 1976; Prevalence of Chronic Respiratory Disease and possible Determinants in the Cities of Ottawa and Sudbury, Ontario (co-author), 1975;

Chronic Diseases in Canada (Editor); Recent Trends in Lung Cancer Mortality (co-author), 1980; Decline in Eschemic Heart Disease Mortality (co-author), 1980; Recent Respiratory Disease Mortality Trends in Canada (co-author), 1980; Respiratory Disease Statistics in Canada: A Survey Summary (co-author), 1984. *Memberships:* Founding President, Canada Chapter, American Medical Writers Association; Council of Biology Editors; Secretary, Epidemiology and Disease Control Division Canadian Public Health Association; Member Standards Committee, Canadian Lung Association; Information Services Institute. *Address:* 7 Castelbeau, Aylmer, Quebec, Canada J9J 1C9.

LITVIN, Martin Jay, b. 31 Mar. 1928, Galesburg, Illinois, USA. Author; Lecturer. *Education:* BA, University of Southern California, 1949; Law school, University of Iowa, 1953–54. *Publications:* Sergeant Allen and Private Renick, 1971; Voices of the Prairie Land, 2 volumes, 1972; Black Angel, 1973; Hiram Revels in Illinois, 1974; Chase the Prairie Wind, 1975; The Young Mary, 1976; The Journey, 1981; A Rocking Horse Family, 1982; A Daring Young Man, 1983; Black Earth, 1984. *Contributions to:* Galesberg Post, and Knoxville Journal, weekly columnist as New York correspondent, 1954–72. *Memberships:* Associate member, Dramatist Guild. *Address:* Rural Route 2, Box 15, Wataga, IL 61488, USA.

LIU, Wu-Chi, b. 27 July 1907, Wu-Chiang, China. Educator; University Professor. m. Helen Gaw, 20 Apr. 1932, 1 daughter. *Education:* BA, Lawrence University; PhD, Yale University, USA. *Appointments:* Visiting Professor, Chinese Literature, Yale University 1951–53; Professor, Chinese Comparative Literature, Indiana University, 1961–76. Senior Editor, Associate Director, Research, Human Relations Area Files, Yale University; Consultant, Chinese Literature & Philosophy, Funks & Wagnalls New Encyclopedia; Consultant, Chinese Literature, Encyclopedia of World Literature in the 20th Century; Chairman, Editorial Committee, Tsing Hua Journal of Chinese Studies. *Publications:* A Short History of Confucion Philosophy, 1955; Confucius, His Life and Time, 1955; An Introduction to Chinese Literature, 1966; Su Man-shu (World Authors Series), 1972; Sunflower Splendor – Three Thousand Years of Chinese Poetry, Co-editor, 1975. *Contributor to:* Biographical Dictionary of Republican China; Dictionary of Oriental Literatures; Encyclopedia of World Biography; Encyclopedia of World Literature; Encyclopedia of Philosophy. *Honours:* Senior Fellowship, National Foundation on the Arts and Humanities, 1967–68. *Address:* 2140 Santa Cruz Ave, #E305, Menlo Park, CA 94025, USA.

LIVELY, Penelope Margaret, b. 17 Mar. 1933, Cairo, Egypt. Writer. m. Jack Lively, 27 June 1957, London, 1 son, 1 daughter. *Education:* Honours degree Modern History, St Anne's College, Oxford. *Publications include:* Fiction: Judgement Day, 1980; Nothing Missing But The Samovar and other stories, 1978; Corruption and other stories, 1984; According to Mark, 1984; Non-Fiction: The Presence of the Past: An Introduction to landscape history, 1976; Children's books: The Ghost of Thomas Kempe, 1973; A Stitch in Time, 1975; The Voyage of Qubb, 1976; Uninvited Ghosts and other stories, 1984. *Contributions to:* Short stories and reviews in publications including: Encounter; Quarto; The Literary Review; Good Housekeeping; Vogue; Cosmopolitan; Options; Over 21; Women's Own; Sunday Telegraph; Books and Bookmen; Times Educational Supplement. *Honours:* Arts Council National Book Award; Southern Arts Literature Prize; Twice shortlisted for the Booker Prize; Carnegie Medal; Whitbread Award. *Memberships:* Society of Authors; English Branch of Pen; Fellow, Royal Society of Literature. *Literary Agent:* Murray Pollinger, 4 Garrick Street, London WC2E 9BH, England. *Address:* Duck End, Great Rollright, Chipping Norton, Oxfordshire OX7 5SB, England.

LIVERSIDGE, (Henry) Douglas, b. 12 Mar. 1913, Swinton, Yorkshire, England. Journalist/Author. m.

Cosmina Pistola, 25 Sep 1954, Holborn, London, 1 daughter. *Publications include:* White Horizon 1951; The Last Continent 1958; The Third Front 1960; The Whale Killers 1963; Saint Francis of Assisi 1968; Peter the Great 1968; Lenin 1969; Joseph Stalin 1969; Saint Ignatius of Loyola 1970; The White World 1972; Queen Elizabeth II 1974; Prince Charles 1975; Prince Phillip 1976; Queen Elizabeth the Queen Mother 1977; The Mountbattens 1978. *Contributor to:* Numerous journals and newspapers. *Address:* 56 Love Lane, Pinner, Middlesex HA5 3EX, England.

LIVINGSTON, Elizabeth Jane, b. 15 Sep. 1952, Niagara Falls, USA. Former Elementary School Librarian; Homemaker. m. William Robert Livingston, 27 Dec. 1980, 1 son, 1 daughter. *Education:* BA, Wheaton College; MS, University of Illinois, 1975. *Publications:* The Hideout, 1983; Zach & the Scary Phone Calls, 1984. *Contributor to:* Dare to Be Different, Evangelizing Today's Child, 1981; An Everything's Going Wrong Day, Evangelizing Today's Child, 1981. *Address:* 10 Geyer Road, Elma, NY 14059, USA.

LIVINGSTON, Myra Cohn, b. 17 Aug. 1926, Omaha, Nebraska, USA. Poet. m. Richard Roland Livingston, 14 Apr. 1952, 2 sons, 1 daughter. *Education:* BA, Sarah Lawrence College, 1948. *Literary Appointments:* Poet-in-Residence, Beverly Hills Unified School District; Senior Lecturer, UCLA Extension. *Publications:* 40 books beginning with, Whispers, 1958 and including: Monkey Puzzle and Other Poems, 1984; The Child as Poet: Myth or Reality?, 1984; Celebrations, 1985; Worlds I Know, 1985; A Learical Lexicon, 1985. *Contributions to:* More than 60 articles in The Horn Book; Childhood Education; Wilson Library Journal; The Advocate; The Writer and others. *Honours:* Texas Institute of Letters, 1961 and 1980; National Council of Teachers of English Excellence in Poetry Award, 1980, and others. *Memberships:* Author's Guild; PEN International; Reading is Fundamental (advisory board); Poetry Therapy Institute (advisory board); Society of Children's Book Writers. *Literary Agent:* McIntosh and Otis. *Address:* 9308 Readcrest Drive, Beverly Hills, CA 90210, USA.

LIVINGSTONE, Douglas (James), b. 5 Jan 1932, Kuala Lumpur, Malaysia. Microbiologist. *Education:* Dip. Bact. *Publications:* Sjambok and Other Poems from Africa, 1964; Eyes Closed Against the Sun, 1970; A Rosary of Bone, 1975, enlarged edition 1983; The Anvil's Undertone, 1978; Selected Poems, 1984. *Contributions to:* The London Magazine. *Honours:* Guinness Prize, 1965; Cholmondeley Award, 1970; Olive Schreiner Prize, 1975; English Association Prize, 1978; CNA Literary Prize, 1984. *Address:* PO Box 17001, Congella 4013, South Africa.

LLYWELYN-WILLIAMS, Alun, b. 27 Aug. 1913. Broadcaster; Adult Educator; Poet; Critic. *Education:* MA, University of Wales, Cardiff. *Literary Appointments:* BBC, Cardiff and London, 1935–40, Bangor, 1946–48; Director, Extra-mural Studies, University College of North Wales, Bangor, 1948–79, now Professor Emeritus. *Publications:* Cerddi, 1944; Pont y Caniedydd, 1956; Y Golau yn y Gwyll, 1979. *Contributor to:* (Y Llenor); Y Traethodydd; Taliesin; Y Faner; Oxford Book of Welsh Verse; (in transl) Oxford Book of Welsh Verse in English; Penguin Book of Welsh Verse; Poetry of Wales, 1930–1970; Presenting Welsh Poetry; Twentieth Century Welsh Poems, (Joseph P Clancy), 1982; International Poetry Review; Vol. V, No. 1. *Honours:* Recipient, WElsh Arts Council Main Award, 1980; Honorary DLitt, 1983. *Memberships:* Welsh Committee, Arts Council of GB, 1958–67; North Wales Arts Assn., 1967–; (Chmn, 1977–81); Yr Academi Gymreig, 1959–; (Chmn, 1979–82). *Address:* Cwm Bychan, 11 Ffordd Ffiddoedd, Bangor, Gwynedd, Wales.

LOBRON, Barbara L, b. 19 Mar. 1944, Philadelphia, Pennsylvania, USA. Editor; Writer. *Education:* BA, Speech and Dramatic Arts, Temple University, Pennsylvania; Majored in English, Dean's List,

Pennsylvania State University, University Park, 1962–63. *Publication:* Chapter on Photography, Grolier's Popular Book of Science. *Contributions to:* US Camera Annual, 1976; Popular Photography; Lens Magazine; Camera 35; Camera Arts; Photograph. *Honour:* Winner First Prize for external newsletter, International Association of Business Communicators, District 1, 1977. *Membership:* Authors Guild. *Address:* 85 Hicks Street, Apt 7, Brooklyn Heights, NY 11201, USA.

LOBSENZ, Amelia, b. Greensboro, North Carolina, USA. Public Relations Executive. m. Harry Abrahams, 1 son, 1 daughter. *Education:* BA, Agnes Scott College. *Publications:* Kay Everett Calls, 1951; Kay Everett Works, 1952. *Contributions to:* Readers Digest; McCalls; Parents; Coronet; Parade; Nations Business; Family Circle; Pageant; Womans Day; Good Housekeeping; Ladies Home Journal; Family Weekly; etc. *Honours include:* Best article, insurance magazine writers; 5 President's Awards, Public Relations Society of America; President International, Public Relations Association, 1986. *Memberships:* American Society of Journalists & Authors; National Association of Science Writers; American Medical Writers Association. *Address:* Lobsenz-Stevens Inc, 460 Park Avenue South, New York, NY 10016, USA.

LOBSENZ, Norman Mitchell, b. 16 May 1919, New York, USA. Book & Magazine Writer. m. Dorothea Harding 23 May 1929, New York, USA, 3 sons. *Education:* BS, New York University, MS, Graduate School of Journalism, Columbia University. *Literary Appointments:* New York City Newspapers 1940–43; News Editor, British Information Service, 1943–44; Editor Quick Magazine (New York), 1950–54; Editorial Director, Hillman Periodicals (New York), 1954–55. *Major Publications:* How to Stay Married, 1968; No-fault Marriage, 1976; Styles of Loving, 1980; Nobody's Perfect, 1981; Equal Time, 1983. *Contributor to:* Readers Digest; McCall's Ladies' Home Journal; Good Housekeeping; Woman's Day; Parade; Family Weekly; Success; Self; Redbook; New York Times Magazine; Playboy; and others. *Honours:* 1st Prize, Medical Journalism, American Academy of Family Physicians, 1978; Science Writing Award, American Dental Association, 1966. *Memberships:* Honorary Member, American Association of Marital & Family Therapists; American Society of Journalists & Authors (President, 1965); Overseas Press Club. *Address:* 2216 Westridge Road, Los Angeles, CA 90049, USA.

LOCHHEAD, Douglas Grant, b. 25 Mar. 1922, Guelph, Ontario, Canada. Professor of Canadian Studies, Director of Centre for Canadian Studies. m. Jean St Clair Beckwith, 17 Sep. 1949, Ottawa, Ontario, 2 daughters. *Education:* BA 1943, BLS 1951, McGill University; MA, Toronto, 1947. *Literary Appointments:* Professor of English, York University, Toronto, 1960–63; Professor of English, University of Toronto, 1965–75. *Publications:* Poetry: The Heart is Fire, 1959; It Is All Around, 1960; Poet Talking, 1964; A and B and C, 1969; Millwood Road Poems, 1970; Prayers in a Field, 1974; The Full Furnace: Collected Poems, 1975; High Marsh Road, 1980; Battle Sequence, 1980; A and E, 1980; The Panic Field, 1984; Dykelands, 1985. *Contributions to:* Numerous publications. *Honours:* Golden Dog Award, 1974; Fellow, Royal Society of Canada, 1976. *Memberships:* Vice-Chairman, 1967–71, League of Canadian Poets. *Address:* P O Box 1108, Sackville, New Brunswick, EOA 3CO, Canada.

LOCK, Stephen Penford, b. 8 Apr. 1919, Romford, Essex, England. Editor, British Medical Journal. m. Shirley Gillian Walker, 19 Feb. 1955, Chelsea Old Church, 1 son, 1 daughter. *Education:* MA; MB; FRCP. *Literary Appointments:* Junior Assistant Editor, The Lancet, 1959; Assistant Editor 1964–69, Senior Assistant Editor 1969–74, Deputy Editor 1974–75, Editor 1975–, British Medical Journal. *Publications:* An Introduction to Clinical Pathology, 1965; Better Medical Writing, (co-author), 1970; The Medical Risks of Life, (co-author), 1975; Thorne's Better Medical Writing, 2nd edition 1977; Adverse Drug Reactions,

(editor), 1977; Remembering Henry, (editor), 1977. *Contributions to:* British, American, Swiss and Finnish journals. *Honours:* Donders Medal, Ned Tidsch Gneesk, 1981; International Medical, Finnish Medical Society Duodecim, 1981; Officer, 1st Class, White Rose of Finland, 1982. *Memberships:* Medical Group, Society of Authors; Council of Biology Editors USA; President, European Association of Life Science Editors, 1982–. *Address:* 115 Dulwich Village, London SE21 7BJ, England.

LOCKE, Elsie Violet, b. 17 Aug. 1912, New Zealand. Writer. m. John Gibson Locke, 7 Nov. 1941, Christchurch, 2 sons, 2 daughters. *Education:* BA, University of Auckland. *Publications:* (Juveniles), The Runaway Settlers, 1965; The End of the Harbour, 1968; The Boy with the Snowgrass Hair, (with co-author Ken Dawson) 1976; Moko's Hideout, 1976; Explorer Zach, 1978; The Gaoler, 1978; The Kauri and the Willow, 1984; Journey Under Warning, 1984; A Canoe in the Mist, 1984; (Adult), Student at the Gates, 1981. *Contributor to:* Numerous contributions to New Zealand School Journal and other New Zealand periodicals for adults and children. *Honour:* Katherine Mansfield Award for non-fiction, 1959. *Memberships:* PEN, New Zealand; New Zealand Children's Literature Association. *Address:* 392 Oxford Tce, Christchurch 1, New Zealand.

LOCKE, Hubert G, b. 30 Apr. 1934, Detroit, Michigan, USA. Educator. m. Linda K Christian, Seattle, Washington, 2 daughters. *Education:* BA, Wayne State University; BD, University of Chicago; AM, University of Michigan. *Literary Appointments:* Associate Editor, Holocaust and Genocide. *Publications:* The Detroit Riot of 1967, 1969; The Care and Feeding of White Liberals, 1970; The German Church Struggle and the Holocaust, (with F H Littell), 1974; The Church Confronts The Nazis, 1984; The Prison Letters of Martin Niemoller, 1985. *Contributions to:* New York Times Book Review; Social Development Issues; Journal of Urban Law. *Address:* Graduate School of Public Affairs DP 30, University of Washington, Seattle, WA 98195, USA.

LOCKHART, Kim Lawrence, b. 4 Sep. 1948, Toronto, Canada. Writer. m. Renée Bonard, 29 Sep. 1978, Toronto, Canada, 1 son. *Education:* Honours Degree in Business Administration, University of Western Ontario, 1972. *Appointments:* Feature Writer and Editor, Globe and Mail, Newspaper, 1977–83; Senior Writer, Global Television, 1983–84; Editor, Canadian Lawyer, Magazine, 1984–present. *Publications:* Revenge on the G Spot, 1982. *Contributor to:* Numerous Legal, Business and Travel Publications. *Memberships:* Consultant to Port Stanley Summer Theatre, Ghost Lake Films. *Literary Agent:* Jacky Schaefer. *Address:* 60 Pavane Linkway, PH 4, Don Mills, Ontario, Canada M3C 1A1.

LOCKHART, Saul, b. 31 Oct. 1940, Pittsburgh, Pennsylvania, USA. Writer; Editor. m. Alison Ann Kemp, 15 Aug. 1971, Hong Kong, 1 son, 1 daughter. *Education:* BA, Washington and Jefferson College, Washington, Pennyslvania, USA. *Literary Appointments:* Associate Editor, Off Duty Publications, 1971–75; Hong Kong Editor, Insight Guide to Hong Kong, 1980–81; Deputy Editor, Cathay Pacific Airways Publications, 1980–82; Area Editor, Fodor's Guide to Hong Kong and Macau; Publications Editor, Hong Kong Trade Developments Council, 1982–. *Publications:* Hong Kong Good Food Guide, 1970; A Diver's Guide to Asian Waters, 1978; Manila By Night, 1981; Complete Guide to the Philippines, 1981; Insight Guide to Hong Kong, 1981; Business Visitors' Guide to Hong Kong, 1984; Fodor's Guide to Hong Kong and Macau, 1984. *Contributions to:* Geo, German edition; Orientations; Far Eastern Economic Review; Asian Wall Street Journal; International Herald Tribune; Asiaweek; Asia Magazine; San Francisco Chronicle; Melbourne Herald; Vancouver Sun; Clipper; Travel and Leisure; Signature; and numerous hotel and airline magazines. *Honours:* Best Story, Hotel Magazine Category, Pacific Travel Association Annual Contest, 1984. *Memberships:*

American Society of Journalists and Authors; American Society of magazine Photographers; Past Officer, Foreign Correspondents Club of Hong Kong; Hong Kong Journalists Association. *Address:* c/o Foreign Correspondents Club, 2 Lower Albert Road, Hong Kong.

LODGE, David John, b. 28 Jan 1935. Professor of Modern English Literature. m. Mary Frances Jacob, 1959, 2 sons 1 daughter. *Education:* BA, Hons, MA, London University; PhD, Birmingham University. *Appointments:* British Council, London, 1959–60; Assistant Lecturer in English, 1960–62, Lecturer 1963–71, Senior Lecturer, 1971–73, Reader in English 1973–76, Professor of Modern English Literature 1976–, University of Birmingham; Harkness Commonwealth Fellow 1964–65; Visiting Associate Professor, University of California, Berkeley, 1969; Henfield Writing Fellow, University of East Anglia, 1977. *Publications:* Novels: The Picturegoers, 1960; Ginger, You're Barmy, 1962; The British Museum is Falling Down, 1965; Out of the Shelter, 1970 revised edition 1985; Changing Places, 1975; How Far Can You Go?, 1980; Small World, 1984; Criticism: Language of Fiction, 1966; The Novelist at the Crossroads, 1971; The Modes of Modern Writing, 1977; Working with Structuralism, 1981. *Honours:* Yorkshire Post Fiction Prize, 1975; Hawthornden Prize 1976; FRSL 1976; Whitbread Book of the Year Award for, How Far Can You Go?, 1980. *Address:* Department of English, University of Birmingham, Birmingham B15 2TT, England.

LOEBNER-FELSKI, Erika, b. 3 Mar. 1922, Rathenow. Writer. m. 9 Nov. 1959, Munich. *Education:* Teacher Training College. *Publications:* Klawa, das Mädchen aus Charkow; Puderdose, Lippenstift und Weltgeschichte; Und morgen wieder einen Tag jünger. *Contributions:* Articles, numerous magazines & journals. *Membership:* Berlin Authors Association. *Address:* D–8262 Altoetting, Federal Republic of Germany.

LOEPER, John Joseph, b. 9 July 1929, Ashland, Pennsylvania, USA. Educator; Artist; Author. m. Jane Knawa Loeper, 13 June 1959, Notley. *Education:* BS; MA; PhD. *Publications:* Men of Ideas, 1969; Going to School in 1776, 1974; The Flying Machine, 1976; The Shop on High Street, 1977; Mr Marley's Main Street Confectionery, 1978; The Golden Dragon, 1979; By Hook & Ladder, 1980; Galloping Gertrude, 1980; Away We Go!, 1981; Going to School in 1872, 1983. *Contributor to:* Gourmet; Coronet; The Instructor; Pennsylvania School Board Journal. *Honours:* American Educator's Medal, 1965; Hands Across the Sea, English Speaking Union, 1982. *Address:* New Hope, PA, USA.

LOETHER, Herman John, b. 27 Feb. 1930, Pittsburgh, Pennsylvania, USA. Professor, Sociology. m. Carolyn Louise Jackson, 15 June 1957, Seattle, 1 son. *Education:* BA, California State University, Los Angeles, 1951; MA, 1953, PhD, 1955, University of Washington, Seattle. *Appointments:* Consulting Editor, Research Methods, Allyn and Bacon Inc, Boston, 1976–82; Consulting Editor, Special Edition, Western Sociological Review, 1982. *Publications:* Problems of Aging, 1967, 2nd edition 1975; Descriptive and Inferential Statistics, co-author, 1976, 2nd edition, 1980. *Contributed to:* Organizational Context and the Professorial Role, Varieties of Work, 1982. *Address:* Dept of Sociology, California State University, Dominguez Hills, Carson, CA 90747, USA.

LOETSCHER, Hugo, b. 22 Dec. 1929, Zürich, Switzerland. Writer; Journalist. *Education:* Studies in Political Science, Sociology, Economic History, Literature at University of Zurich and Sorbonne. *Literary Appointments:* Literary Editor, Du, 1958–62; Literary Editor and Member of Editorial Board, Die Weltwoche, 1964–69; Writer-in-Residence, University of Southern California, Los Angeles, USA, 1979–80; Lecturer, University of Fribourg, 1981; First Holder of Pro Helvetia Swiss Lectureship, City University of New York, 1981–82. *Publications:* Abwässer: Ein Gutachten

(Sewage: An Expert Opinion) (novel), 1963; Die Kranzflechterin (The Wreath Weaver) (novel), 1964; Noah; Roman einer Konjunktur (Noah: Novel about an Economic Boom), 1967; Der Immune (The Man with Immunity) (novel), 1969; Zehn Jahre Fidel Castro: Bericht und Analyse (Ten Years of Fidel Castro: Report and Analysis), 1970; Wunderwelt: Eine brasilianische Begegnung (Miracle World: A Brazilian Encounter), 1979; How Many Languages Does Man Need?, Lectureship CUNY New York, 1982; Herbst in der Grossen Orange (Fall in the Big Orange) (novel), 1983. *Contributions to:* Magazines, journals etc. also radio and television broadcasts in Switzerland and Federal Republic of Germany. *Honours include:* Mozart Prize Goethe Stiftung, 1983; Prize der Schweizerischen Schiller Stiftung, 1985. *Memberships:* Schweizerischer Schriftstellerverban 1973; PEN Club Schweiz; Deutsche Akademis fur Sprache ujnd Dichtung, Darmstadt. *Address:* Storchengasse 6, CH–8000, Zürich, Switzerland.

LOEWEN, Walter, b. 18 Mar. 1927, Friedensfeld, Germany. Editor & Publisher. m. Brigitte Mossler, 29 Nov. 1952, 1 son, 1 daughter. *Education:* MA, University of Leipzig; Dr Phil, University of Jena, German Democratic Republic. *Major Publications:* (novels): Der Richter, 1977; Jenny Marx, 1978; Spiel mit dem Schicksal, 1982; Und die Elbe schweigt, 1985; (tragedies): Die deutsche Tragödie – Trilogie mit Bernhard von Weimar, Marx in Köln, Stauffenberg, 1978; Dmitri Samoswanex, 1980; (comedies): 13 deutsche Komödien, 1978; Goethes letzte Liebe, 1981; (social-critical writings): Die Solidargesellschaft, 1972; Der dritte Weg zur gerechten Gesellschaft, 1980. *Address:* Kampstraße 91D, D–3000 Hannover 61, Federal Republic of Germany.

LOEWIG, Roger, b. 5 Sep. 1930, Striegau, Federal Republic of Germany. Painter; Drawer; Writer. *Publications:* Poems: Und verliebt in mein land, 1972; Ewig rauchende Kaltezeit, 1979; Bis ein Stuck Himmel die Brust trägt, 1982. Poems and drawings: Odysseus Heimwehgesange, 1975; Sei ein Himmel gnadig, 1977; Zeichnungen und Terte in der Hamburger Kunstnalle, 1978; Ein Vogel bin ich ohne Flugel, 1979. Documentation: Licht und Schatten, 1979. Prose: Eine Hinterlassenschaft, 1981. *Contributions to:* Various anthologies include: Jahrbuch fur Lyrik, 1979, 80, 81; Die Halfte der Stadt, 1982. Anuario de letras modernas, 1983; Berliner Malerpoeten, 1973–. *Address:* Wilhelmsruher Damm 120, D–1000 Berlin 26, Federal Republic of Germany.

LOFTUS, Elizabeth, b. 16 Oct. 1944, Los Angeles, California, USA. Professor of Psychology. m. Geoffrey R Loftus, 30 June 1968. *Education:* BA, 1966, University of California, Los Angeles; MA, 1967; PhD, 1970, Stanford. *Publications:* Eyewitness Testimony, 1979; Memory, 1980; Mind at Play (with G Loftus), 1983; Eyewitness Testimony: Psychological Perspectives, (with G Wells), 1984; Psychology, (with C Wortman). *Contributions to:* Various professional journals. *Honour:* National Media Award, Distinguished Contribution, 1980. *Address:* Psychology Department, University of Washington, Seattle, WA 98195, USA.

LOGUE, Christopher John, b. 23 Nov. 1926, Portsmouth, England. Writer. *Publications include:* Ode to the Dodo, poems, 1953–78, 1981; War Music, 1981. *Contributions to:* Private Eye; Times; etc. *Literary Agent:* Diana Baring at Curtis Brown. *Address:* 18 Denbigh Close, London W11 2QH, England.

LOHMANN, Harald, b. 31 Jan. 1926, Hamburg, Germany. Lawyer. *Education:* Doctor and Magister juris, University of Innsbruck. *Publications:* Ausklarieren – Geschichten vom Mittelmeer, 1980; Zu Ehren der Malariamucke, 1985. *Contributions to:* Diners Club Magazine, Vienna; Motor Review; Yacht Review; Eternit Magazin. *Address:* Borromäustrabe 13, A–5020 Salzburg, Austria.

LOMBARDO, Gian S, b. 24 Sep. 1953, Hartford, Connecticut, USA. Poet. *Education:* BA, Comparative Literature, Trinity College, Hartford; MA, Creative Writing, Boston University. *Publication:* Between Islands, 1984. *Contributions to:* Poems, prose poems, verse translations in, Boston Literary Review; Big Time Review; Brown Review; Another Small Magazine; Trinity Review. Biographical essays in, The Annual Obituary, 1981. *Address:* 25 Quimby Street, Watertown, MA 02172, USA.

LONDON, Herbert I, b. 6 Mar. 1939, New York, USA. Dean of New York University, Senior Fellow of Hudson Institute. m. Vicki Pops London, 27 Nov. 1976, 2 daughters. *Education:* BA, Columbia College, 1960; MA, Columbia University, 1961; PhD, New York University, 1966; Post-doctoral study, Australian National University, 1966–67. *Literary Appointments:* Managing Editor, Gallatin Review; Contributing Editor, Defense Science. *Publications:* Non-White Immigration and The White Australia Policy, 1970; Fitting In: Crosswise At Generation Gap, 1974; The Overheated Decade, 1976; The Seventies: Counterfeit Decade, 1979; Myths That Rule America, 1981; Why Are They Lying To Our Children, 1984; Closing The Circle: A Cultural History of the Rock Revolution, 1984. *Contributions to:* New York Magazine; Orbis; Defense Science; New York Times; Washington Post; Wall Street Journal; Dictionary of American Biographies; Journal of Higher Education; Los Angeles Times; Saturday Review; National Review; Freedom at Issue; Human Events. *Honours:* Founder Day Award, 1966; Fulbright Award, 1966–67; Honorary Doctorate, University of Aix. *Literary Agent:* Jan Flatt. *Address:* 715 Broadway, New York, NY 10003, USA.

LONDRÉ, Felicia Hardison, b. 1 Apr. 1941, Fort Lewis, Washington, USA. Professor of Theatre, University of Missouri-Kansas City. m. Venne-Richard Londré, 196 Dec. 1967, Madison, Wisconsin, 1 son, 1 daughter. *Education:* BA, French, University of Montana, 1962I Fulbright Study Grant, Universite de Caen, France, 1962–63; MA, Romance Languages, University of Washington, 1964; PhD, Theatre, University of Wisconsin, Madison, 1969. *Literary Appointments:* Committee of Consultants, American Women Writers, F Ungar Publishing Company; Advisory Board, Bookmark Press, 1981–; Editorial Board, Theatre History Studies, 1981–; Elected Daughter of Mark Twain Society, 1981; University of Missouri Press Committee, 1982–84; Book Review Editor, Theatre Journal, 1984–87; Advisory Editor, Nineteenth Century Theatre Research, 1984–; Editorial Board: Studies om American Drama, 1945–80, 1984–; Tennessee Williams Review, 1985–. *Publications:* Tennessee Williams 1979, Paperback Edition 1983; Tom Stoppard, 1981; Federico Carcia Lorca, 1984; 18 entries in, American Women Writers, 4 volumes, 1979–82; Associate Editor, Notable International Shakespeare production: Postwar Years, 1986. *Contributions to:* Magazines and journals. *Honours:* Consul General's Award in French, University of Montana, 1961–62; Second Prize, John Gassner Memorial Playwright Award Competition for, Miss Millay Was Right, 1982. *Memberships:* Several professional organizations. *Address:* Department of Theatre, University of Missouri-Kansas City, 5100 Rockhill Road, Kansas City, MO 64110, USA.

LONG, Anthony Arthur, b. 17 Aug. 1937, Manchester, England. University Professor. m. (1) Janice Galloway, (2) Mary Kay Flavell, 1 son, 1 daughter. *Education:* BA, Honours, Classics, University College, London, 1960; PhD, University of London, 1964. *Appointments:* Editor, The Bulletin, University College, London, 1970–72; Co-Editor, The Classical Quarterly, 1975–80; Professor, Classics, University of California, USA. *Publications:* Language and Thought in Sophocles, 1968; Problems in Stiocism, 1971; Hellenistic Philosophy, 1974; The Hellenistic Philosophers, 2 volumes with D N Sedley, 1986–87. *Contributor to:* Times Literary Supplement; Classical Review; Journal of Hellenic Studies; Philosophical Quarterly; Phronesis, etc. *Honour:* Cromer Greek Prize,

British Academy, 1968. *Address:* Department of Classics, University of California, Berkeley, CA 94720, USA.

LONG, Edward Gerald Hanslip, b. 16 Sep. 1941, Bury St Edmunds, Suffolk, England. Agricultural Journalist/Broadcaster. m. Moya Gibson, 4 Sep. 1965, Caversham, 1 son, 1 daughter. *Education:* NDA; MRAC. *Contributions to:* Farming journals throughout Europe and the USA. *Honours:* Norsk Hydro Travel Scholarship, 1984. *Address:* The Old School House, Hundon, Sudbury, Suffolk CO10 8ED, England.

LONG, Virginia Love, b. 21 Aug. 1941, Roxboro, North Carolina, USA. Poet. 2 sons, 1 fosterson. *Education:* Catawba College, Salisbury, North Carolina, 1958–61. *Publications:* After the Ifaluk and Other Poems, 1974; The Gallows Lord, 1978; Letters of Human Nature (with Rochelle Holt), 1985; Upstream: A Celebration of Kenneth Clyde Wagstaff, 1985; Shared Journey: A Journal of Two Sister Souls (with Rochelle Holt), 1986. *Contributions to:* Pembroke; El Nahuatzen; Crucible; Hyperion; The Sun; Southern Exposure; International Poetry Review; Amorotica; New Kauri; Poema Convidado; Windhover, Leaves of Greens; Miscellany; Bay Leaves; Tar Heel; The Unrealist; Pan-Erotic Review; Writer's Choice; Black Sun New Moon; Crossroads; Southern Accent; Illuminations. *Honours:* First Place: Greensboro Writers Poetry Contest, 1964; James Larkin Pearson Free Verse Contest, North Carolina Poetry Council, 1975; Sunbonnet Literary Contest, 1976; North Carolina Press Award Recipient, 1969, 73. *Memberships:* Poetry Council of North Carolina, Secretary, 1977, 78, 79; North Carolina Poetry Society, Membership Chairman, 1980–81; Feminist Writers Guild; The Byron Society, American Chapter; Triangle Area Women Poets. *Address:* Rte 2 Box 54, Hurdle Mills, NC 27541, USA.

LONGCHAMPS, Renaud, b. 5 Nov. 1952, St Ephren, Quebec, Canada. Poet. m. Charlotte Poulin, 29 July 1973, Notre Dame de la Providence, 1 son, 2 daughters. *Education:* Diploma d'etudes collegiales, 1973; Francois-Xavier Garneau College. *Publications:* Poems: Paroles d'ici, l'Homme Imminent, 1973; Anticorps, Charpente charnelle, Sur l'aire du Lire, 1974; Ditactique, 1975; Main armee, Terres rares, 1976; Comme d'hasard ouvrables, 1977; L'Etat de matiere, 1978; Le desir de la production, 1981; Miguasha, 1983; Anomalies, 1985; Le detail de l'apocalypse, 1985. Novels: Après le deluge, 1981; L'Escarfe, 1984. *Contributions to:* La Nouvelle Barre du Jour; Estuaire; Hobo Quebec; Cross Country; Possibles; Les Herbes Rouges; Action poetique; France; Jungle; Sud; L'Ivraie; Identites, Belgium. *Honours:* Arts Grants: Canada Council, 1974, 75, 76, 82; Ministers des Affaires Culturelles, Quebec, 1975, 77, 78, 81, 83, 84, 85. *Memberships:* Quebec Writers Union. *Literary Agent:* Charlotte Poulin. *Address:* 24 boulevard Chartier, Saint-Ephrem, Beauce, Québec, Canada G0M 1R0.

LONGFORD, Elizabeth, b. 30 Aug. 1906, London, England. Writer. m. Hon. Frank Pakenham (now Earl of Longford), 3 Nov. 1931, London, 4 sons, 4 daughters (1 dec.). *Education:* MA, Oxford University. *Literary Appointments:* Advisory Board, British Library; Vice President, London Library. *Publications include:* Jameson's Raid, 2nd edition 1982; Victoria R.I., 1964; Wellington: Years of the Sword, 1969; Wellington: Pillar of State, 1972; Pilgrimage of Passion, 1979; Churchill, 1974; Eminent Victorian Women, 1981; Elizabeth R, 1983. *Contributions to:* Literary Review; Books & Bookmen; Majesty; Washington Post. *Honours:* James Tait Black Memorial Prize, 1964; Yorkshire Post Book of the Year, 1972; Honorary DLItt, Sussex University; CBE. *Memberships:* Fellow, Honorary Life President, Royal Society of Literature; PEN International: Society of Women Writers & Journalists; London Writers Circle. *Literary Agent:* Curtis Brown. *Address:* 18 Chesil Court, Chelsea Manor Street, London SW3 5QP, England.

LONGMATE, Norman Richard, b. 15 Dec. 1925, Newbury, Berkshire, England. Author. m. Elizabeth Jean Taylor, 8 Aug. 1953, Kew, 1 daughter. *Education:* BA,

Modern History, Oxford, 1950; MA, 1953. *Publications include:* King Cholera, 1966; The Waterdrinkers, 1968; How We Lived Then, 1971; If Britain Had Fallen, 1972; The Workhouse, 1974; The Real Dad's Army, 1974; The G.I.'s, 1975; Air Raid, 1976; When We Won The War, 1977; The Hungry Mills, 1978; The Doodlebugs, 1981; The Bombers, 1983; The Breadsnatchers, 1984; Hitler's Rockets, 1985; etc. Editor: The Home Front, 1981; Writing for the BBC, various editions 1966–83. *Contributions to:* The Listener; Radio Times; New Society; The Standard. *Membership:* Broadcasting Committee, Society of Authors. *Address:* c/o Century Hutchinson Ltd, 62-65 Chandos Place, London WC2N 4NW, England.

LONGRIGG, Roger Erskine, b. 1 May 1929, Edinburgh, Scotland. Writer. m. Jane Chichester, 20 July 1957, Winchester, 3 daughters. *Education:* BA Honours, Magdelen College, Oxford University. *Publications:* A High Pitched Buzz, 1956; Switchboard, 1957; Wrong Number, 1959; Daughters of Mulberry, 1961; The Paper Boats, 1963; Love Among the Bottles, 1967; The Sun on the Water, 1969; The Desperate Criminals, 1971; The Jevinton System, 1973; History of Horse Racing, 1972; Their Pleasing Sport. 1975; History of Fox Hunting, 1975; The Babe in the Wood, 1976; The English Squire and His Sport, 1977; Bad Bet, 1982. *Contributions to:* Times; Times Literary Supplement; Sunday Times; Sunday Telegraph; Weekend Telegraph; Spectator; Punch; Illustrated London News; Cosmopolitan; Horse and Hound. *Memberships:* Society of Authors; Crime Writers' Association; Mystery Writers of America. *Literary Agent:* Curtis Brown. *Address:* Orchard House, Crookham, Hampshire, England.

LONGSTREET, Stephen, b. 1907, USA. Novelist. *Education:* Attended Rutgers University, Harvard University, New York School of Fine and Applied Art; Studied Art in London, Paris & Rome. *Publications include:* Decade 1929–1939, 1940; The Golden Touch, 1941; The Gay Sisters, 1942; The Last Man Comes Home, 1942; The Land I Live, 1943; Stallion Road, 1945; The Beach House, 1952; The Real Jazz, Old and New, 1956; The Promoters, 1957; The Burning Man, 1958; Never Look Back: The Autobiography of a Jockey, co-author, 1958; Eagles Where I Walk, 1961; The Flesh Peddlers, 1962; The Figure in Art, 1963; The Golden Runaways, 1964; The Young Men of Paris, 1967; Senator Silverthorn, 1968; She Walks in Beauty, 1970; The Pedlock Inheritance, 1972; The Divorce, 1974; etc; Numerous screenplays including, The Jolson Story, 1946; Duel in the Sun, 1946; The Greatest Show on Earth, 1952; Stars and Stripes Forever, 1962; Houdini, 1953; Untamed Youth, 1957; The Helen Morgan Story, co-author, 1957; Born Reckless, 1959; Wild Harvest, 1961; Rider on a Dead Horse, 1963; etc.*Honours include:* Photoplay Gold Medal, for the Jolsen Story; Nominee for Academy Award, Greatest Show on Earth; etc. *memberships include:* Member, Board of Directors, Graphic Society of Los Angeles County Museum of Art; Trustee, Los Angeles Art Association, President 1970–82. *Address:* 1133 Miradero Road, Beverly Hills, CA 90210, USA.

LONGSWORTH, Polly Ormsby, b. 21 Oct. 1933, Buffalo, New York, USA. Writer. m. Charles R Longworth, 30 June 1956, Troy, New York, 4 daughters. *Education:* BA, Smith College, Massachusetts. *Publications:* Exploring Caves, 1958; Emily Dickinson: Her Letter to the World, 1965; I, Charlotte Forten Black and Free, 1970; Austin and Mabel: The Amherst Affair and Love Letters of Austin Dickinson and Mabel Loomis Todd, 1984. *Membership:* Authors Guild. *Address:* Coke-Garret House, Williamsburg, VA 23185, USA.

LOPATIN, Judy, b. 5 Oct. 1954, Detroit, Michigan, USA. Fiction Writer. *Education:* AB, University of Michigan, 1976; MFA, Columbia University, 1979. *Publications:* Modern Romances, collection of short fiction, 1986. *Contributions to:* Mississippi Review; Benzene; Zone; Diana's Almanac. *Honours:* Phi Beta Kappa, 1975; Graduate Fellowship, Columbia University School of the Arts, 1978. *Literary Agent:*

Alison M Bond, 171 West 79th Street, New York, NY 10024. *Address:* 601 West 110th Street, (Penthouse), New York, NY 10025, USA.

LOPES, Henri, b. 12 Sep. 1937, Kinshasa, Zaire. Educationalist. m. Nirva Pasbeau, 13 May 1961, Paris, 1 son, 3 daughters. *Education:* Licence D'Histoire et Geographie; Diplome D'Etudes Superieures D'Histoire, Faculte des Letters et Sciences Humaines de Paris, Sorbonne. *Appointments:* Minister of National Education, 1968–71, Foreign Affairs, 1971–73; Member, Political Bureau, Congolese Labour Party, 1973; Prime Minister, & Minister of Planning, 1973–75, Finance 1977–80; UN Assistant Director General for Programme Support, 1982–. *Publications:* Tribaliques, short stories; La Nouvelle Romance, Novel; Learning to Be, co-author; Sanstam-tam, Novel, 1977; Le Pleurer Rire, novel, 1982; Author of National Anthem. *Honours:* Commander du Merite, Congolais, etc; Prix litteraire de l'Afrique noire, 1972; Prix SIMBA de litterature, 1978; Prix de litterature du President (Congo). *Address:* Assistant Director General for Culture and Communication, UNESCO, 7 Place de Fontenoy, F75700 Paris, France.

LOPEZ, Barry Holstun, b. 6 Jan. 1945, Port Chester, New York, USA. Writer. m. Sandra Jean Landers, 10 June 1967, Medford, New Jersey. *Education:* BA, University of Notre Dame, 1966; MA, 1968. *Publications:* Desert Notes, 1976; Giving Birth to Thunder, 1978; Of Wolves and Men, 1978; River Notes, 1979; Winter Count, 1981. *Contributions to:* Searching for Ancestors, Outside, Apr. 1983; Renegotiating the Contracts, Parabola, Spring 1983; Story at Anaktuvuk Pass, Harper's, Dec. 1984. *Honours:* John Burroughs Medal for Distinguished Natural History Writing, 1979; Distinguished Recognition Award in Fiction, Friends of American Writer, 1982. *Memberships:* PEN, American Center; Aamerican Center; Authors Guild. *Address:* Finn Rock, OR 97488, USA.

LORANT, Stefan, b. 22 Feb, 1901, Budapest, Hungary. Writer. *Education:* Academy of Economics, Budapest, 1919; MA, Harvard University, 1960; Honorary Doctor Degree, Know College, Galesberg, Illinois, 1958; Syracuse University, Syracuse, New York. *Publications:* I Was Hitler's Prisoner, 1935; Lincoln, His Life in Photographs, 1941; The New World, 1946; 1965; FDR, A Pictorial Biography, 1950; The Presidency, 1951; Lincoln, A Picture Story of His Life, 1952, 1957, 1969; The Life of Abraham Lincoln, 1954; The Life and Times of Theodore Roosevelt, 1959; Pittsburgh, the Story of an American City, 1964, 1975, 1980; The Glorius Burden, 1969, 1976; Sieg Heil!, 1974. *Contributor to:* Look; Saturday Evening Post; New York Times Magazine; etc. *Honours:* Recipient of over 12 honours and awards. *Memberships:* Authors Guild; PEN Club. *Address:* Farview, Lenox, MA 01240, USA.

LORD, Doreen Mildred Douglas, b. 25 Sep. 1904, Southsea, England. Writer/Reporter. *Publications:* Spirit of Wearde Hall, 1927; Horned Priests, 1928; Magic Arrow; 1934; Christopher Stories, 1935; Joan at Seascale, 1936; Lynette at Carisgate, 1937; Yellow Flower, 1935; Kiwi Jane, 1962; To Win Their Crown, 1962; Children at Court of Saint Peter, 1963; Cypress Box, 1963; Going to God (translation from French), 1964. *Contributor to:* Numerous journals and magazines of poems, articles and plays; Numerous translations from French and German; Writer of words for three cantatas. *Honour:* De Grummond Collection, Hattiesberg, Mississippi, 1964. *Membership:* Society of Women Writers and Journalists. *Address:* Home of Comfort, 17 Victoria Grove, Southsea PO5 1NF, Hampshire, England.

LORD, Graham John, b. 16 Feb. 1943, Mutare, Zimbabwe. Journalist. m. Jane Carruthers, 12 Sep. 1962, Littleport, Cambridgeshire, England, 2 daughters. *Education:* BA Honours, Cambridge University, 1965. *Literary Appointments:* Literary editor, Sunday Express, London, 1969–. *Publications:* Novels: Marshmallow

Pie, 1970; A Roof Under Your Feet, 1973; The Spider and the Fly, 1974; God and All His Angels, 1976; The Nostradamus Horoscope, 1981; Time Out of Mind, 1986. *Literary Agent:* A M Heath, London. *Address:* Sunday Express, Fleet Street, London EC4, England.

LORD, Walter, b. 8 Oct. 1917, Baltimore, Maryland, USA. Author. *Education:* BA, Princeton University, 1939; LLB, Yale University Law School, 1946. *Publications include:* The Fremantle Diary, 1954; A Night to Remember, 1955; Day of Infamy, 1957; The Good Years, 1960; A Time to Stand, 1961; Peary to the Pole, 1963; The Past That Would Not Die, 1965; Incredible Victory, 1967; The Dawn's Light, 1972; Lonely Vigil, 1977; Illustrated edition, Night to Remember, 1976; The Miracle of Dunkirk, 1982. *Contributions to:* Life; Reader's Digest; American Heritage; etc. *Honours:* Summerfield Roberts Award, Texas history, 1961; Colonial Dames Award, colonial history, 1972; Andres White Medal, Public service, Loyola College, Maryland, 1984. *Memberships:* Council 1972–83, Authors Guild; Council 1975–80, Authors League; President 1981–83, Society of American Historians; ASCAP. *Literary Agent:* Sterling Lord. *Address:* 116 E 68th Street, New York, NY 10021, USA.

LORENT, Hans-Peter de, b. 2 Mar. 1949, Neumünster. Teacher. 3 daughters. *Education:* Studied, Education, Psychology. *Publications:* Die Hexenjagd, 1980; Diskrete Karriere, 1984; Schule unterm Hakenkreuz, 1985. *Contributor to:* several journals. *Memberships:* Verband Deutsches Schriftsteller. *Address:* Bernadottestr. 38, 2000 Hamburg 50, Federal Republic of Germany.

LORENZEN, Coral E, b. 2 Apr. 1925, Hillsdale, Wisconsin, USA. Writer, Editor. m. Leslie J Lorenzen, 29 Sep. 1943, Austin, Minnesota, 1 son, 1 daughter. *Literary Appointments:* Editor, The APRO Bulletin, 1952–. *Publications:* The Great Flying Saucer Hoax, 1962; Flying Saucers – The Startling Evidence of the Invasion from Outer Space, 1966; Flying Saucer Occupants, 1967; UFOs over the Americas, 1968; UFO Occupants, 1969; UFOs, The Whole Story, 1969; Shadow of the Unknown, 1970; Abducted, 1977. *Contributions to:* Fate; The APRO Bulletin. *Address:* 3597 W Grape Road, Tucson, AZ 85741, USA.

LORTS, Jack E, b. 4 Sep. 1940, Wichita, Kansas, USA. Teacher; Writer; Poet. m. Cecilia Ann Kennedy, 9 Nov. 1960, Artesia, California, USA. 3 daughters. *Education:* BA, 1962, California State University; MEd, 1978, University of Oregon. *Literary Appointments:* Teacher, Middle School English, Los Angeles County, 1962–68, 1969–74; Teacher, Secondary School English/Drama, Myrtle Creek, Oregon, 1968–69, 1974–; Teacher, Umpqua Community College, Roseburg, Oregon, 1975–, (part-time). *Contributions to:* English Journal; Arizona Quarterly; Kansas Quarterly; Vis-a-Vis; Oregon English; Nomad; Ninth Circle; all poems. *Honours:* Coe Fellowship in American Studies, 1968, 1969; National Endowment for the Humanities, Fellowship for Secondary Teachers, 1984. *Membership:* National Council for Teachers of English. *Address:* PO Box 279, 991 Mason Street, Myrtle Creek, OR 97457, USA.

LOSCHIAVO, Linda Ann, b. 24 Oct. 1947, New York City, USA. Freelance Writer; Non Fiction Author. m. Sergei Brozski, P E (legally separated), 3 Sep. 1977, New York City. *Education:* BA, 1971, MA, 1976, Hunter College, New York City; PhD Candidate, New York University, New York City. *Appointments:* E P Dutton Book Company, 1968; MacFadden Bartell Publishers, 1969; Universal Publishing Co, 1970; Reese Publishing Co, 1971; American Journal of Nursing Publishers, 1975. *Publications:* Contributor to various magazines. *Honours:* Marquis Award, 1964; Writer's Digest Writing Competition (won 1978 and 1980); Mensa journalis Award, 1978; Mensa Owl Award and other journalism awards, 1979. *Memberships:* Sigma Tau Delta; American Society of Journalists and Authors; American Mensa Ltd. (Editor 1978–1979, Board Member 1979–

1980). *Address:* 24 Fifth Avenue, New York, NY 10011, USA.

LOTTMAN, Herbert R, b. 16 Aug. 1927, New York City, USA. Writer. *Major Publications:* Albert Camus, 1979; The Left Bank: Writers, Artists & Politics; From the Popular Front to the Cold War, 1982; Pétain: Hero or Traitor?, 1985. *Contributor to:* Publishers Weekly (International Correspondent); New York Times; Washington Post Book World; Harper's; Saturday Review; and others. *Address:* B P 214, 75264 Paris Cédex 06, France.

LOUIS, Arthur Murray, b. 21 Jan. 1938, Toledo, Ohio, USA. Journalist. m. Ann Debra Dransfield, 6 Aug. 1984, Virginia City, Nevada, 2 sons (by previous marriage). *Education:* AB, Columbia College, 1959; MA, Columbia University Graduate School of Journalism, 1960. *Literary Appointments:* Writer, Philadelphia Inquirer, 1960–64; Writer/Editor, McGraw-Hill, 1964–66; Writer, Fortune Magazine, 1966–. *Major Publications:* The Tycoons, 1981. *Contributor to:* Fortune; Columbia University Forum; The Nation; Saturday Review; New York; Harper's; Psychology Today. *Honour:* Deadline Award, Sigma Delta Chi, New York Chapter, 1978. *Literary Agent:* Meredith Bernstein, New York City. *Address:* 333 East 79th Street, New York, NY 10017, USA.

LOVESEY, Peter, b. 10 Sep. 1936, Whitton, Middlesex, England. Writer. m. Jacqueline Ruth Lewis, 30 May 1959, Whitton, Middlesex, 1 son, 1 daughter. *Education:* BA, Honours, English, University of Reading, 1958. *Publications:* The Kings of Distance, non-fiction, sports, 1968; Wobble to Death, crime fiction, 1970; The Detective Wore Silk Drawers, 1971; Abracadaver, 1972; Mad Hatter's Holiday, 1973; Invitation to a Dynamite Party, 1974; A Case of Spirits, 1975; Swing, Swing Together, 1976; Goldengirl, as Peter Lear, 1977; Waxwork, 1978; Official Centenary History of the Amateur Athletic Association, 1979; Spider Girl, as Peter Lear, 1980; The False Inspector Dew, 1982; Keystone, 1983; Butchers; short stories, 1985. *Honours:* MacMillan/Panther 1st Crime Novel Award, 1970; Crime Writers Association Silver Dagger, 1978, Gold Dagger 1982; Grand Prix de Littérature Policière, 1985. *Memberships:* Crime Writers Association; Detection Club; Writers Guild. *Literary Agent:* John Farquharson Ltd. *Address:* c/o John Farquharson Ltd, 162-168 Regent Street, London W1R 5TB, England.

LOW, Alfred David, b. 28 Feb. 1913, Vienna, Austria. Professor of History (retired). m. Rose Seelenfreund, 30 June 1938, Vienna, 2 daughters. *Education:* PhD, University of Vienna, 1936; Retraining Project, Haverford College, 1940–41; Columbia University, 1953–54; A M In Rel, 1956; Certificate of Russian Institute, 1957. *Publications:* Lenin on the Question of Nationality, 1958; The Soviet Hungariian Republic and the Paris Peace Conference, 1963; The Anschluss Movement, 1918–1919, and the Paris Peace Cnference, 1974; The Sino-Soviet Dispute. An Analysis of the Polemics, 1976; Jews in the Eyes of the Germans. From the Enlightenment to Imperial Germany, 1979. The Anschluss Movement 1918–1938: Background and Aftermath. An Annotated Bibliography in German and Austrian Nationalism, 1964; The Anschluss Movement, 1931–1938, and the Great Powers, 1985. *Contributions to:* American History Review; Social Studies; The Russian Review; Journal of Central European Affairs; jahrbücher fosteurop. Gesch.; Austrian History Yearbook; East Central Europe; Canadian Journal of History; Canadian Review of Studies in Nationalism; Journal of Modern History; Jahrbuch d. Deutsch. Gesch. (Tel-Aviv). *Honours:* Prize, 1975, First Prize, 1977, First Prize, 1980, The Council for Wisconsin Writers; Board of Editors; Canadian Review of Studies in Nationalism, 1980–; Scholarship at Columbia University Ford Fellow, 1953–54; American Philosophical Society, Marquette University, Research Grants. *Address:* 1840–184th Street, Bellevue, WA 98008, USA.

LOW, Ann Marie, b. 1 May 1912, Kensal, ND, USA. Teacher. m. Seth H Low, 21 Aug. 1937, Kenmare ND, 1 son, 1 daughter. *Education:* BA, English. *Publications:* Dust Bowl Diary, 1984. *Honours:* Dust Bowl Diary, featured by the History Book Club; Also selected by Board of Editors of the National Library Journal, Best Books, 1984. *Address:* 210 Last Wagon Drive, Sedona, AZ 86336, USA.

LOWBURY, Edward Joseph Lister, b. 6 Dec. 1913, London, England. Writer. m. Alison Young, 6 June, 1954, London, 3 daughters. *Education:* MA, DM, University College, Oxford, England; FRCP; FRCS; FRC.Path. *Appointments:* Formerly Member of Literature Panel, West Midlands Arts, England, 1976–79; President Smethwick Society of Arts, 1980. *Publications include:* Time for Sale, 1961; Daylight Astronomy, 1968; Thomas Campion, Poet, Composer, Physician, (with T Salter and A Young), 1970; The Night Watchman, 1974; Selected Poems, 1978; Masada – Byzantium – Celle: Apocryphal Letters, 1985; The Poetical Works of Andrew Young, (co-editor), 1985. Numerous contributions to magazines and journals. *Honours:* John Keats Memorial Lecturer, 1973; FRSL, 1974; Hon DSC, Aston, 1977; OBE 1979; Hon LLD, Birmingham, 1980. *Memberships:* Fellow of Royal Society of Literature and Member of Poetry Society. *Address:* 79 Vernon Road, Birmingham B16 9SQ, England.

LOWE, Jonathan F, b. 29 Sep. 1953, Minneapolis, Minnesota, USA. Journalist. *Education:* Degree in Business Management. *Literary Appointments:* Editor, The Struggling Writer', 1982–83. *Contributions to:* Poem; Phoebe; Modern Keyboard Review; Dekalb Arts Journal; Sunshine; Buffalo Spree; Wind; Rampike; Seek; Gray's Sporting Journal; Medical Blend. *Honours:* 3rd prize, International Writer's Digest Competition in fiction, 1982; 1st prize in poetry, Roger C Peace Competition, 1982; Best in Science Fiction, Roger C Peace Competition, 1984. *Memberships:* Poets and Writers NYC; Furman Theater Guild. *Literary Agent:* Criterion Agency, BX 16315 Greenville, South Carolina. *Address:* Box 16315, Greenville, SC 29606, USA.

LOWNDES, Ginny, b. 21 Mar. 1945, Mitchell, Queensland, Australia. Writer; Script Editor. 2 daughters. *Education:* Graduate, Writing, Film & TV, Australian Film & TV School 1980. *Appointments:* Lecturer, media & Children's TV, Sydney High Shool, 1981; Challenge of Kids TV, 1985. *Publications:* Stories of Her Life, 1981; The Collection, 1983, 1984. *Contributor to:* Billy Blue; Woman's Day; Playboy; The Nation Review, etc; Radio Broadcasts; Extensive TV writing & script editing credits. *Honours:* The Billy Blue/John Clemenger Short Story Award, 1982. *Memberships:* Australian Writers Guild; Australian Society of Women Writers; Australian Society of Authors; Australian Screenwriters Guild; Australian Film Institite. *Address:* P O Box 904, Darlinghurst 2010, Sydney, Australia.

LOWRY, Robert James, b. 28 Mar. 1919, Cincinnati, Ohio, USA. Writer. 3 sons. *Publications include:* Casualty, 1946; Find Me In Fire, 1948; The Wolf That Fed Us, 1949; The Big Cage, 1949; The Violent Wedding, 1953; Happy New Year, Kamerades!, 1954; What's Left of April, 1956; New York Call Girl, 1959; The Prince of Pride Starring, 1959; Party of Dreamers, 1962. *Address:* 3747 Hutton Street, Cincinnati, OH 45226, USA.

LOYDELL, Rupert Michael, b. 7 July, 1960, London, England. Writer; Publisher; Artist. m. Susan Patricia Callaghan, 3 Sep. 1982, Tring, Hertfordshire, England. *Education:* Art Foundation Course, Richmond College of Further Education, England; BA(Hons), Creative Arts, Crewe and Alsager College of Further Education. *Publications:* Songs From the Silence, 1980; Madness and Other Voyages, 1981; Lonely City, 1982; Dark Angel, 1983; Missing Persons, 1984; On the Coast, 1985; Shadows and Forefiles, 1985, *Contributor to:* Editor, Stride magazine and publications series;

Anthologies: Richmond Poetry, 1980 and 1981; Richmond College Makers Dozen; 100 Contemporary Christian Poets; Pomander; Concrete and Cupid; magazines: Folio; Frames; Acumen; Straig; The New Writer; Only Prose; Label; Snake; Tears in the Fence; Poems by Strangers, Fisheye, etc. *Honours:* 1st Prize, Richmond Borough Poetry Competition, 2978. *Address:* 80 Lord Street, Crewe, Cheshire CW2 7DL, England.

LUBINGER, Eva, b. 3 Feb. 1930, Steyr, Austria. Writer. m. Dr Walter Myss, 7 Oct. 1952, 2 sons. *Appointment:* Wort und Welt, Innsbruck, Austria. *Publications:* Paradies mit Kleinen Fehlein, 1976; Gespenster in Sir Edward's Haus, 1978; Pflücke den Wind, (lyric) 1982; Verlieb Dich nicht in Mark Aurell, 1985; Zeig mir Lamorna, 1985. *Contributions to:* Präsent, weekly newspaper. Honours; Literature Prize for Lyrics, Innsbruck, 1963; Literature Prize for Drama, Innsbruck, 1969. *Membership:* PEN, Austria. *Literary Agent:* Wort und Welt, Innsbruck. *Address:* Lindenbühelweg 16, 6020 Innsbruck, Austria.

LUCAS, Christopher John, b. 21 Feb. 1940, Indianapolis, USA. University Professor/Administrator. 1 son. *Education:* BA, Psychology, Syracuse University, 1962; MAT, Education and English, Northwestern University, 1964; PhD, Philosophy and Education, The Ohio State University, 1967. *Literary Appointments:* Research Assistant, Psychology Department, Syracuse University, 1961–62; Secondary English Teacher, Chicago, 1963–64; Teaching Associate, Ohio State University, 1964–67; Co-Director, International Summer Courses, University of Salzburg, Australia, 1966–71; Professor of Education, 1967–, Director, Center for International Programs and Studies, 1984–, University of Missouri. *Publications:* What is Philosophy of Education! 1969; Our Western Educational Heritage, 1972; Challenge and Choice of Contemporary Education, 1976; Yesterday's China, 1982; School, Society and Scribal Culture in Ancient Mesopotamia, 1982; Schooling and the Social Order: Foundations of Eduction, 1984. *Contributor to:* Author of 63 pubished journal articles, 3 monographs, 25 newspaper articles, 8 book chapters and 24 book reviews. *Honours:* Phi Beta Kappa, 1962; Phi Kappa Phi, 1975; Kappa Delta Pi; Delta Tau Kappa; Phi Delta Kappa; Lorberg Memorial Award. *Memberships:* President, American Educaitonal Studies Association; National Fellow, Philosophy of Education Society; American Education Research Association; John Dewey Society; Comparative and International Education Society; International Council on Education for Teaching; Association for Supervision and Curriculum Development; President, Society of Professors of Education; Executive Secretary, Co-ordinating Council for Learned Societies in Education. *Address:* Hill Hall, College of Education, University of Missouri – Columbia, Columbia, MO 65211, USA.

LUCAS, Henry C Junior, b. USA. Professor, Graduate School of Business, New York University. *Education:* BS Magna Cum Laude, Yale University, 1966; MS, 1968, PhD, 1970, Sloan School of Mangement, Massachusetts Institute of Technology. *Literary Appointments:* Associate editor, Information and Management. Performance Evaluation Review, 1972–73; Industrial Management, Sloan Management Review, Reviewer, Computing Reviews; Editorial Board, Sloan Management Review; Chairman, IFIP Working Group, 1975–80. *Publications:* Computer Based Information Systems in Organizations, 1973; The Information Systems Environment, Senior Editor, 1980; Casebook for Management Information Systems, 2nd edition, 1981; The Analysis, Design and Implementation of Information Systems, 3rd edition, 1985; Information Systems Concepts for Management, 3rd edition, 1986. Introduction to Computers and Information Systems, 1986. *Contributions to:* Various monographs; Computing Surveys; Data Base; Sloan Management Review; Special Libraries; Management Informatics; Computer Journal; Decision Sciences; Management Science; Journal of Marketing Research; The Accounting Review; Various other journals and numerous conference proceedings. *Honour:* Award for

Excellence in Teaching, Schools of Business, 1982. *Memberships:* Association for Computing Machinery; Institute of Management Sciences; Tau Beta Pi; Phi Beta Kappa. *Address:* 18 Portland Road, Summit, NJ 07901, USA.

LUCAS, Martin Charles John, b. 4 Feb. 1944, England. Television Producer and Director. m. Hilary, 22 July 1963, Coventry, 1 son, 2 daughters. *Education:* BSc, Honours in Psychology. *Publications:* All In The Mind, 1984; The Human Race, with T Dixon, 1982. *Contributions to:* Time Out; The Guardian. *Address:* Harrow, London, England.

LUCIA, Ellis Joel, b. 6 June 1922, Watsonville, California, USA. Author; Freelance Writer. m. Elsie Eleanor Kemmling, 6 Nov. 1965, North Plains Oregon. *Education:* BA; History, Literature, Political Science, Pacific University, 1944; Honorary Doctor of Letters, Pacific University, 1965. *Publications:* The Saga of Ben Holladay, 1959; Klondike Kate, 1962; Tough Men, Tough Country, 1963; The Big Blow, 1963; Don't Call It Or-E-Gawn, 1964; Head Rig, 1965; Wild Water, 1965; Sea Wall, 1966; This Land Around Us, 1969; Mr Football: Amos Alonzo Stagg, 1970; Editor, The Gunfighters, 1971; (with Mike Hanley) Owyhee Trails, 1974; The Big Woods, 1975; Cornerstone, 1975; Magic Valley, 1976; Editor, Oregon's Golden Years, 1976; Seattle's Sisters of Providence, 1978; Tillamook Burn Country, 1983. *Contributor to:* Over 1,000 magazine, newspaper, journal and anthologie articles including, New York Times; The Nation; King Features, etc. *Honours:* Best Western, The Wrangler, Western Heritage, 1974; Trophy, Citation, Founder-Public Relations Director, All Northwest Barber Shop Ballad Contest and Gay 90's Festival, 1953. *Memberships:* Authors Guild of America; Western Writers of America; Oregon Freelance Club, President, twice, 1950's. *Address:* P O Box 17507, Portland, OR 97217, USA.

LUDEL, Jacqueline, b. 17 Mar. 1945, Boston, Massachusetts, USA. Teacher. *Education:* BA, Queens College, Flushing, New York, 1966; PhD, Indiana University, Bloomington, Indiana, 1971. *Publications:* Introduction to Sensory Process, 1978, also issued in an Italian edition, I Processi Sensoriali, 1981; Margaret Mead (an Impact Biography), 1983. *Contributions to:* Papers and reviews in Greensboro News and Record; Co-evolution Quarterly; Contemporary Psychology; Spectrum; Journal of the Florida Academy of Science; Teaching of Psychology etc. Prose and poetry in Guildford Review and Womansprouts. *Honours:* Listed as a Notable Children's Trade Book in the Field of Social Studies by National Council for the Social Studies in Social Education – Margaret Mead, 1984; Guildford College Board of Visitors Excellence in Teaching Award, 1979–80; Danforth Associate 1979–85; National Science Foundation Graduate Fellow, 1966–71; Phi Beta Kappa; Beta Beta Beta (Sigma Phi Chapter) Charter Member; National Biology Honor Society; Jacksonville University Honor Society; Psi Chi; National Psychology Honor Society; Sigma Delta Epsilon; National Honor Society of Women in Science; Woodworth Award in Psychology; Queens College. *Address:* Departments of Biology and Psychology, Guilford College, Gueensboro, NC 27410, USA.

LUDLOW, Howard Thomas, b. 7 Sep. 1921, New York. University Professor. m. Catherine Evelyn Packard, 28 June 1952, New York, 2 sons, 1 daughter. *Education:* BS, Economics, Fordham College, 1947; MA, Economics, 1949, PhD, Economics, 1955, Fordham University. *Publications:* Business Management, 1965; Labour Economics, 1966. *Contributions to:* Jack and Jill and Justice, Mid-Atlantic Journal of Business, 1962; The Fourth Argument, Labour Law Journal, 1964; Big Mediator is Watching You, America, 1964; Formal Education and Mediator Acceptability, Labour Law Journal, 1966; The Role of Trade Unions in Poland, Political Science Quarterly, 1975; Polish Trade Unions, Mercurio, 1976 and also book reviews. *Address:* Seton Hall University, South Orange, NJ 07079, USA.

LUECKE, Janemarie, b. 24 Apr. 1924, Okeene, Oklahoma, USA. Teacher. *Education:* BA, Benedictine Heights College, 1948; MA, Marquette University, 1956; PhD, Notre Dame University, 1964. *Literary Appointments:* Teacher of English and Journalism, High School, 11 Years; Director of Public Relations Programme; Dean and Assistant Professor of English, Benedictine Heights College, 5 years; Professor of English, Oklahoma State University, 1966–. *Publications:* Books: A Prosody Manual, 1971; Measuring Old English Rhythm, 1978; The Rape of the Sabine Women, poems, 1978; Wild Bird Eggs, poems, 1984. *Contributions to:* 50 poems in 30 journals and anthologies; 17 articles in scholarly journals and anthologies; 16 articles in trade and general journals and magazines. *Memberships:* Benedictine Order of Catholic Sisters; Fellow, International Poetry Society, Modern Poetry Society, Academy of American Poets, Medieval Academy of America, Modern Language Association. *Address:* Department of English, Oklahoma State University, Stillwater, OK 74078, USA.

LUESMA CASTAN, Miguel, b. 2 Feb. 1929, Zaragoza, Spain. Writer; Bank Employee. *Publications include:* Solo Circunferencia, 1965; Poemas en voz baja, 1966; Riglos, 1967; Las Trilogias, 1968; Sembrando en el viento, 1971, 2 editions; En el Lento Morir del Planeta, 1972, 2 editions; Antologia, 1973; Aragon, sinfonia incompleta, 1976, 3 editions; Acordes para andar por un planeta vivo, 1979; Editor, of cycles of South American Poetry and Youth Poetry; Concierto No 9 para solo de flauta y orquesta, 1979; En los infernos y en algun que otro paraiso, 1982. *Contributor to:* Various Spanish and North and South American Publications. *Honours:* Numerous prizes including: San Jorge Prize, 1970; City of Barcelona Prize for Poetry in Spanish, 1976. *Memberships:* Peña Nike; Peña Ramón J Sender, Vice President; for some years, Coordinator, Poetry Session of the Fernando el Católica Institute; International Biographical Association: Asociación Colegial de Escritores de España. *Address:* Camino de las Torres 101–7°A, Zaragoza 50007, Spain.

LUH, Bor Shiun, b. 13 Jan. 1916, Shanghai, China. Food Science & Technology. m. Bai Tsain Liu Luh, 23 Nov. 1940, 1 daughter. *Education:* BS, Chiao Tung University, Shanghai, 1938; MS, Food Science, PhD, Agricultural chemistry, University of California, Berkeley, USA. *Literary Appointments:* Food Technologist, University of California, 1952–. *Publications include:* Baby Food, 1971; Commercial Vegetable Processing (with J G Woodroof), 1975; Rice Production and Utilization, 1980; Commercial Fruit Processing, (with J G Woodroof) 1975; etc. *Contributor to:* Philip E Nelson and D K Tressler (Editors), Fruit and Vegetable Juice Processing Technology, 3rd edition 1980 (Chapters 8, 9, 10); Journal of Food Science; Food Technology; Confructa; Journal of Science Food & Agriculture, England; Plant Physiology; California Agriculture; many other professional journals. *Honours:* Tippet Award, Chiao Tung University, 1983; Consultant to FAO, United Nations; Consultant, United Nations Industrial and Development Organization, Vienna, Austria, 1968, 1972, 1980, 1981–82; Achievement Award, Chinese American Food Society. *Memberships include:* American Chemical Society; American Oil Chemists Society; American Association of Cerial Chemists; American Association for the Advancement of Science; Institute of Food Technologists; American Association Horticultural Society; Chinese American Food Society; North American Phytochemical Society; Sigma Xi; Phi Tao Sigma. *Literary Agent:* The Avi Publishing Co Inc Westpoint, Connecticut. *Address:* Department of Food Science and Technology, University of California, Cruess Hall, Davis, CA 95616, USA.

LUHR, William George, b. 31 Mar. 1946, Brooklyn, New York, USA. Associate Professor of English and Film, St Peter's College, Jersey City, New Jersey. m. Judith Challop, 16 Aug. 1981, Roslyn, New York. *Education:* BA, English, Fordham University, 1967; MA, English, New York University, 1969; PhD, English and

American Literature, New York University, 1978. *Publications:* Authorship and Narrative in the Cinema (with Peter Lehman), 1977; Blake Edwards (with Peter Lehman), 1981; Raymond Chandler and Film, 1982; Currently writing Blake Edwards, Volume 2. *Contributions:* of articles to professional publications including Wide Angle, Journal of the Media Educators Association, Michigan Academician, etc; Book Reviews and Book Chapters. *Memberships:* The Modern Language Association; The College English Association; The Society for Cinema Studies. *Address:* 180 West Poplar Street, Floral Park, NY 11001, USA.

LUKAS, Josef, b. 23 Jan. 1899, Frankstadt, Bern, Switzerland. Journalist; Editor. m. Hanni Dora Stotzer, 21 May 1938, Bern, 1 daughter. *Education:* College of Fine Arts, Berlin; Fichtehochschule, Leipzig; Journalism Seminar, University of Zurich; University Bern. *Publications:* Zur Geschichte des Streiks, 1926; Vom Fichtenholz zum Modestrumpf, 1929; Weberkampfe vor 100 Jahren, 1928; Bei clen happländern auf Besuch, 1981; Geschichte der Textilarbeiter in der Schweiz, 1933; Spinnstubengeschichten, 1935; Goethe und die textile Arbeit, 1932; Der Maschinensturm von Uster, 1932; Pioniere der Freiheit, 1943; Peter Bratschi and seine Heimat, 1946; Das Spinnen und Weben in Sprichwort & Redensart, 1976; Die goldene Spindel, 1978; Der silberne Faden, 1980; Die blaue Blume, 1981; Von der Volkskunst des Klöppelns, 1982; Das ehrbare Handwerk, 1985. *Contributor to:* Numerous newspapers, journals and yearbooks. *Memberships:* Association of Swiss Journalists; International Association of the Specialist Press; General Writers' Association, Berlin; Society for Preservation of European People's Fairytale Heritage; Working Friends of Art; Political Economy Society. *Address:* Weiherstrasse 11, CH 3073 Gümligen– Bern, Switzerland.

LUKASIEWICZ, Jacek, b. 21 June 1934, Lwow, Poland. Writer. m. Teresa Mercik, 2 June 1934. 2 sons. *Education:* M.Philol; Dr Humane Sciences, 1972; Habilitation, 1980; University Wroclaw. *Publications:* (Poems): Mine and Yours, (Moje i Twoje), 1959; Winters Plays (Zabawy Zimowe), 1968; The Valley (Dolina), 1972; Journeys (Padroze), 1976, Album, 1983; (Essays): Nag-man and Heroes, 1963; Zagloba in Hell, 1965; Laur and Body, 1971; Mitings in the Time, with Mieczyskaw Jastrun, 1982. *Contributions to:* Wiez; Odra; Tworczosc. *Membership:* Polish PEN Club. *Address:* ul. Popowiska 92 m. 6, 54-238 Wroclaw, Poland.

LUMPKIN, Angela, b. 17 May 1950, Helena, Arkansas, USA. University Professor. *Education:* BSE, University of Arkansas, 1971; MA, 1972; PhD, 1974, Ohio State University. *Publications:* Women's Tennis, A Historical Documentary of the Players and Their Game, 1981; History and Principles of Physical Education, 1981, 83; A Guide to the Literature of Tennis, 1985; Physical Education: A Contemporary Introduction, 1985. Co-Author: Racquetball Everyone, 1984. Co-Editor: Sport in American Education: History and Perspective, 1979. *Contributions to:* Biographical Dictionary of Americana Sport; Sports Encyclopedia North American; The North Carolina Journal; Journal of Physical Education and Recreation; Quest; Journal of Popular Culture; Coach; Womens Athletics; Scholastic Coach. Book chapters: Sport in American Education: History and Perspective; Her Story in Sport: A Historical Anthology of Women in Sport. *Honours:* Mabel Lee Award, American Alliance of Health, Physical Education, Recreation and Dance, 1984; North Carolina Delegate, National Women's Leadership Conference on Fitness, 1984; University Scholarship for Programme for Technical Managers, 1985. *Address:* 205 Woollen Gym, University of North Carolina, Chapel Hill, NC 27514, USA.

LUNAN, Duncan Alasdair, b. 24 Oct. 1945, Edinburgh. Author. m. Linda Joyce Donnelly, 16 Apr. 1975, Hamilton, Div. July 1984. *Education:* MA, Hons, English and Philosophy, Glasgow University, 1968;

Diploma in Education, Glasgow University, 1984. *Publications:* Man and the Stars, 1974; New Worlds for Old, 1979; Man and the Planets, 1983. Contributor to eight other books including, Extraterrestrial Encounter, by Chris Boyce, 1979; The Science Fictional Solar System ed. Asimov, Greenberg and Waugh, 1980. *Contributor to:* Glasgow University Magazine; Galaxy; If; Anolog; Spaceflight; Pursuit; Journal of the Society of Electronic and Radio Technicians; Griffith Observer; Astronomy Quarterly; Journal of the British Interplanetary Society; second Look etc. *Honour:* Fellow of the British Interplanetary Society, 1984. *Memberships:* President, Association Research into Astronautics, 1966–72, 1978–86; Chairman, Glasgow Science Fiction Circle, 1971–76; Science Fiction Writers of America, 1974–. *Literary Agent:* The Adele Leone Agency, Scarsdale, New York, USA. *Address:* c/o Campbell, 16 Oakfield Avenue, Hillhead, Glasgow G12, Scotland.

LUND, Jøorgen-Richard, b. 7 Aug. 1923, Copenhagen, Denmark. Editor, Film Adviser, Script Writer. m. 26 Dec. 1950, 1 son, 1 daughter. *Education:* Film studies, Denmark, England, Germany, Italy. *Publications:* Naval Home Guard, 1952–1977; Thoughts For The Future, 1983. *Contributions to:* Home Guard; Civil Servant; Defence Civil Servant; SMK Contact (Royal Danish Navy); The Wing (Royal Danish Air Force); The Outlook (Royal Navy Veterans). *Honour:* Recipient, Chief of Army Dip., 1975. *Memberships:* Danish Press Association; Delegate to Danish Press Association Congress, 1985. *Address:* Ruskaer 17, 2610 Roedovre, Denmark.

LUND, Reinhard, b. 8 Mar. 1933, Copenhagen, Denmark. Professor, Organizational Sociology. m. Karen-Johanne Halkjaer Kristensen, 11 Aug. 1962, Copenhagen, 1 son, 1 daughter. *Education:* Cand. Polit., University of Copenhagen, 1959; Dr Merc., Copenhagen School of Economics, 1979. *Publications:* Employees' Influence on Management's Decisions, 1972; Centralization and Bureaucratization, 1979; International Handbook of Industrial Relations, (with A A Blum), 1981; International Handbook of Trade Unions (German), with S Mielke, 1983. *Contributor to:* Organisation Studies. *Membership:* International Industrial Relations Association, Council Member. *Address:* Institute of Production, Aalborg University Centre, DK–9220 Aalborg, Denmark.

LUNDBERG, Ulla-Lena, b. 14 July 1947, Kökar, Aland, Finland. Writer. *Education:* MA, Abo Akademi, Finland, 1985. *Publications:* Utgangspunkt, poetry, 1962; Novels, 1966 and 1968; Gaijin, travel book, 1970; Volume of radio-plays, 1974; Kökar, documentary work, 1976; Tre Afrikanska herättelser, short stories, 1977; Öar i Afrikas inre, documentary work, 1981; Kungens Anna, novel, 1982; Ingens Anna, novel, 1984; Franciskus i Kökar, ethnological thesis, 1985. *Honours:* Finnish State Award, 1971 and 1982. *Memberships:* Society of Swedish Authors in Finland; Finnish Pen Club. *Address:* Radmansgatan 4 B 37, SF 06100 Borga, Finland.

LUNDHOLM, Anja, b. 28 Apr. 1928, Düsseldorf, Federal Republic of Germany. Writer. *Publications:* Halb Und Halb, 1966; Via Tasso, 1969; Morgenfrauen, 1970; Bluff, 1971; Ein Ehrenhafter Bürger, 1972; Zerreissprobe, 1974; Nesthocker, 1977; Mit Ausblick Zum See, 1979; Jene Tage in Rom, 1981; Geordnete Verhältnisse, 1983; Narziss Postlagernd, 1985; Short stories; Translations. *Honours:* Literary Award, Ministry of Foreign Affairs, Bonn, 1970; Literary Promotion Award, Sweden, 1975; Yearly allotment 'to express our gratefulness for your cultural contribution to this country', President of the Federal State of Germany, 1981. *Address:* Ostendstrasse 1, 6000 Frankfurt/Main, Federal Republic of Germany.

LUNT, James Doiran, b. 13 Nov. 1917, Liverpool, England. Writer/Former Army Officer. m. Muriel Byrt, 19 Oct 1940, Mandalay, Burma, 1 son, 1 daughter. *Education:* MA Hon, Oxford University; FRGS; FR Hist

S; Emeritus Fellow, Wadham College, Oxford University. *Publications:* Charge to Glory, 1960; Scarlet Lancer, 1964; The Barren Rocks of Aden, 1966; Bokhara Burnes, 1969; Editor: From Sepoy to Subedar, 1970; The Duke of Wellington's Regiment, 1971; The 16th/5th The Queen's Royal Lancers, 1973; John Burgoyne of Saratoga, 1975; Imperial Sunset, 1981; Glubb Pasha, 1984. *Contributions to:* Blackwoods Magazine; most British Army journals; The Times; She; Country Life; The Field etc. *Honours:* OBE 1959; CBE 1964; Order of Independence (Jordan) 1955; Order of South Arabia 1965. *Memberships:* Chairman of Council, Society for Army Historical Research; Council Member, Army Records Society. *Literary Agent:* Bruce Hunter, David Higham Associates Ltd. *Address:* Hilltop House, Little Milton, Oxfordshire, England.

LURIE, Alison, b. Sep. 1926, Chicago, Illinois, USA. Writer. div. 3 sons. *Education:* BA magna cum laude, Radcliffe College, 1947. *Literary Appointments:* Professor of English, Cornell University, New York, 1975–. *Publications:* Love and Friendship, 1962; The Nowhere City, 1965; Imaginary Friends, 1967; Real People, 1969; The War Between the Tates, 1974; Only Children, 1979; The Language of Clothes, 1981; Foreign Affairs, 1984. *Contributions to:* Harpers; Horizon; House and Garden; Ms; The New Republic; New York Review of Books; New York Times Book Review; The Observer; Times Literary Supplement; Vanity Fair, and others. *Honours:* Guggenheim Foundation Grant, 1966; Rockefeller Foundation Grant, 1968; New York State Grant, 1972; American Academy of Arts Award in Literatire, 1978; Pulitzer Prize in Fiction, 1985. *Memberships:* Poets, Playwrights, Editors, Essayists and Novelists; Authors Guild. *Literary Agent:* A P Watt, London, England. *Address:* English Department, Cornell University, Ithaca, NY 14853, USA.

LUST, Peter, b. 15 Jan. 1911, Nuernberg, Federal Republic of Germany, Journalist, Author. m. Evelyn Heymannsohn, 23 June 1953, Montreal, 2 sons, 1 daughter. *Education:* Master's Degree, History, University of Geneva, Switzerland. *Publications:* Two Germanies, Mirror of an Age, 1966; The Last Seal Pup, 1967; Cuba, Time Bomb at our Door, 1969; Break Up Canada, 1970. *Contributions to:* Various publications including, Der Spiegel; Stern; Montreal Star. *Honour:* Best Non-Fiction Award by Province of Quebec, 1967. *Address:* 13 Thompson Point, Beaconsfield, Quebec, Canada.

LÜTH, Paul, b. 20 June 1921, Perleberg. Doctor; University Teacher; Medical Journalist. 2 sons, 2 daughters. *Education:* Universities Rostock, & Mainz; Dr Med; Professor, Medical Sociology, Mainz and University General College, Kassel. *Publications:* Niederlassung und Praxis, 1969; Ansichten einer Kunftigen Medizin, 1970; Kritische Medizin, 1977; Das Medikamentenbuck; Das Krankheitenbuch; Tagebuch eines Landarztes, 1985; Der Mensch ist kein Zufall, 1983; Medizin in unserer Gessellschaft, 1986; Das Ende der Medizin – Die Entdeckung der Neuer Gesundheit, 1986. *Contributor to:* Medical Tribune, Column, Wie ich es sehe. *Honours:* 1st Prize, Ana Aslan Foundation for Gerontology, 1983; Literary Prize, Federal Chamber of Doctors, 1984; Medizin im Wort, Publicity Prize, Medical & Scientific Journalists, 1985. *Address:* Arzt 1, Aligemeinmedizin, Nentaroder Str. 6, 3589 Knüllweid, Federal Republic of Germany.

LUTTMANN, Gail Jane, b. 29 Feb. 1944, Denver, Colorado, USA. Writer. *Education:* BS, University of Arizona. *Publications:* Co-author, Chickens in Your Backyard, 1976; Ducks & Geese in Your Backyard, 1978. *Contributions to:* Animal News; AP&WS Magazine; Backyard Poultry; Cloverdale Reveille; 1979 CORD/NDA Proceedings; Farmstead; Feather Fancier; Focus on Dance; Fox River Patriot; Herb Quarterly; Poultry Press; Rodale's New Shelter; Tennessee Conservationist. *Address:* RR 2, Box 341, Gainesboro, TN 38562, USA.

LUTTWAK, Edward Nicolae, b. 4 Nov. 1942, Arad, Romania. Military Consultant. *Education:* BSc Honours, London School of Economics, London, England, 1964; PhD, Johns Hopkins University, USA, 1975. *Publications:* Coup d'Etat, 1968; Dictionary of Modern War, 1971; The Israeli Army, (with Dan Horowitz), 1975; The Grand Strategy of the Roman Empire, 1975; The Political Uses of Sea Power, 1976; Strategy and Politics, 1979; The Grand Strategy of the Soviet Union, 1983; The Pentagon and the Art of War, 1985. *Contributions to:* Commentary; Times Literary Supplement, London; American Historical Review; Survival. *Address:* c/o CSIS, 1800 K St NW, Washington, DC 20006, USA.

LUTYENS, Mary, b. 31 July 1908, London. Author. m. 1 Anthony Sewell, 18 Feb. 1930, 1 daughter, divorced, 1945, 2 Joseph Gluckstein Links, 22 June 1945. *Publications include:* Perchance to Dream, 1935; Cleo, 1973; Julie and the Narrow Valley, 1944; Lady Lytton's Court Diary, 1961; Miller's and the Ruskins, 1967; Krishnamurti: the years of awakening, 1977; The Lyttons in India, 1979; Edwin Lutyens, 1980; Krishnamurti: the years of fulfilment, 1982; numerous serials. *Contributor to:* The Cornhill; The Times Literary Supplement; The Spectator; The Walpole Society Journal; Apollo; Woman and Home; Woman's Weekly; Woman's Realm. *Honour:* Fellow, Royal Society of Literature, 1967. *Literary Agent:* Curtis Brown. *Address:* 8 Elizabeth Close, Randolph Avenue, London W9 1BN, England.

LUTZ, John Thomas, b. 11 Sep. 1939, Dallas, Texas, USA. Writer. m. Barbara Jean Bradley, 15 Mar. 1958, 1 son, 2 daughters. *Education:* Meramac Community College. *Publications:* The Truth of the Matter, 1971; Buyer Beware, 1976; Bonegrinder, 1977; Lazarus Man, 1979, 80; Jericho Man, 1980, 81; The Shadow Man, 1981, 82; Exiled, with Steven Greene, 1982; The Eye, with Bill Pronzini, 1984; Nightlines, 1985; The Right to Sing the Blues, 1986. *Contributions to:* Ellery Queens Mystery Magazine; Hitchcock's Mystery Magazine; Mike Shayne Mystery Magazine; Executioner; Charlie Chan Mystery Magazine; Cavalier; Espionage. Works featured in numerous foreign publications, textbooks and anthologies. Several adaptation for radio mystery dramas. *Honours:* Scroll, Mystery Writers of America, 1981; Shamus Award, 1982, Shamus nominee, 1983, Private Eye Writers of America; Peer Award nominee, 1985. *Memberships:* Board of Directors: Private Eye Writers of America; Midwest chapter, Mystery Writers of America. *Literary Agent:* Dominick Abel, New York. *Address:* 880 Providence Avenue, Webster Groves, MO 63119, USA.

LUTZKER, Edythe, b. 25 June 1904, Berlin, Germany. Historian; Writer; Researcher. m. Philip Lutzker (d. 1981), 14 June 1924, Bronx, New York, 3 sons. *Education:* BA, City College of New York, 1954; MA Columbia University, 1959. *Publications:* Medical Education for Women in Great Britain, 1959; Women Gain a Place in Medicine, 1969; Edith Pechey-Phipson MD, The Story of England's & India'a Foremost Pioneering Woman Doctor, 1973; Haffkine, A Historical Appreciation, 1974. *Contributions include:* Numerous Radio & Television Interviews from New York, India, Israel, UK. Lectures & Addresses, Papers published at many scientific meetings including International Congress for the History of Medicine Proceedings, Canada, 1976. *Honours include:* Fellow, Royal Society of Medicine, 1973; Member, Jewish Academy of Arts & Sciences, 1974; Numerous grants including National Library of Medicine, US Department of Health, Education & Welfare. *Memberships include:* American Association for the History of Medicine; American Historical Association. American Society for Microbiology; Apothecaries Hall, London, UK; Fawcett Society, UK; History of Science Society; Institute for Research in History; Society for the Social History of Medicine; Waldemar M. Haffkine International Memorial Committee. *Address:* 201 West 89th Street, New York, NY 10024, USA.

LYALL, Gavin Tudor, b. 9 May 1932, Birmingham, England. Author. m. Katherine Whitehorn, 4 Jan. 1985, Marlborough, 2 sons. *Education:* BA (Hons), English Literature, Cambridge University, 1956. *Publication:* The Wrong Side of the Sky, 1961; Six similar thrillers; The Secret Servant, 1980; The Conduct of Major Maxim, 1982; The Crocus List, 1985. *Contributions to:* The Observer; Punch; Sunday Telegraph, etc. Reviews, articles and travel writing. *Honours:* CWA Silver Dagger Awards, 1964, 65. *Memberships:* Crime Writers Association, Chairman, 1966–67; Detection Club; Society of Authors. *Literary Agent:* A D Peters & Company. *Address:* 14 Provost Road, London NW3 4ST, England.

LYDOLPH, Paul Edward, b. 4 Jan. 1924, Iowa, USA. University Professor. m. Mary J Klahn, 17 Dec. 1966, Milwaukee, Wisconsin, USA, 5 sons. *Education:* University of Iowa, 1941–43, 1948–50, BS 1948; University of Wisconsin, 1943, 1950–52, MS 1951, PhD 1956; Harvard University, 1944–45; MIT 1945; UCLA 1956; Berkeley 1956–57. *Publications:* Geography of the USSR, 1964, 1970, 1977; Climates of the Soviet Union, 1977; Geography of the USSR: Topical Analysis, 1979; Weather and Climate, 1985; The climate of the Earth, 1985. *Contributor to:* Articles in professional journals on the geography and climate of the USSR and other parts of the world. *Honour:* Ford Foundation Fellow 1956–57. *Address:* Box 323 Rt 2, Elkhart Lake, WI 53020, USA.

LYKIARD, Alexis Constantine, b. 2 Jan. 1940, Athens, Greece. Writer. m. Erica Bowden, 1984, 1 son. *Education:* BA, 1st Class Honours, Cantab, 1962; MA Cantab, 1966. *Appointments:* C Day Lewis/GLAA Creative Writing Fellowship, Sutton Central Library, 1977; Arts Council of Great Britain Fellow, Creative Writing, Loughborough College of Art, 1982–83; Devon Libraries' Writer in Residence, Tavistock Library, 1983–85. *Pubications:* Novels: The Summer Ghosts, 1964; Zones, 1966; Sleeping Partner, 1967; Strange Alphabet, 1970; Instrument of Pleasure, 1974; Last Throes, 1976; The Drive North, 1977; Scrubbers, 1983; Poetry: Lobsters, 1961; Journey of the Alchemist, 1963; Paros Poems, 1967; Robe of Skin, 1969; Eight Lovesongs, 1972; Greek Images, 1972; Lifelines, 1973; Milesian Fables, 1976; A Modern Tower Reading, 1976; Out of Exile, 1985; Cat Kin, 1985; 16 books of translations; Editor, numerous books including New Stories 2, 1977; Memoirs of Dolly Morton, 1984, etc. *Contributor to:* Numerous Magazines, Journals and Anthologies in United Kingdom and abroad. *Honours:* Arts Council of Great Britain Awards, 1973, 1978. *Memberships:* Literature Panel, ACGB, 1974–76; Literature Panel, South West Arts, 1977–84, Chairman, 1981–84; Writers; Guild; ACTT. *Address:* c/o W H Allen & Co PLC, 44 Hill Street, London W1X 8LB, England.

LYLES, Donald, b. 11 Apr. 1946, Palestine, Texas, USA. Freelance Writer; Magazine Columnist; Job Resume Writer; Manuscript Typist; Editor; Lecturer. m. Juanita Collins, separated, 2 sons. *Education:* BS, California State University, 1980; Certificate, Artillery and Missile School, US Army. *Literary Appointments:* Founder, Fellow and Chancellor, American Academy of Authors. *Publications:* The ABCs of Classified Advertising, 1986; Everybody's Job Hunting and Job Promotion Guidebook, 1987; Memories of Interviews with Millionaires, Musicians and Movie Stars, 1987; The Billionaire's and Multimillionaire's Quotebook, 1987. *Contributions:* Columnist: Bronze Thrills Magazine, 1972–83; Frontier News, 1974–76; Lyric Writer Magazine, 1983; The Houston Informer and Texas Freeman, 1974; The National Afro-American, 1973. Freelance articles contributed to: Black Stars, Help Magazine and others. *Honour:* Certificate of Honour, American Poets Fellowship Society, 1973. *Memberships:* Founding President, American Academy of Authors. *Address:* PO Box 3689, Los Angeles, CA 90078, USA.

LYNDS, Dennis, b. 15 Jan. 1924, St Louis, Missouri, USA. Writer. m. (1) Doris Flood, 1949 (divorced 1956);

(2) Sheila McErlean, 1961, 2 daughters (divorced 1985); (3) Gayle Hallenbeck Stone, 1986. *Appointments include:* Assistant Editor, Chemical Week, New York, 1951–52; Editorial Director, American Institute of Management, New York, 1952–54; Associate Editor, then Managing Editor, Chemical Engineering Progress, 1955–61; Editor part-time, Chemical Equipment, and Laboratory Equipment, New York, 1962–66; Instructor, Santa Barbara City College Adult Education Division, Santa Barbara, California, 1966–68; Self-employed writer since 1961. *Publications include:* Combat Soldier, 1962; Uptown Downtown, 1963; Why Girls Ride Sidesaddle (short stories) 1980; The Slasher 1980, paperback 1981; Freak, 1983, 1984; Touch of Death, 1981; Deadly Innocents, 1986. *Contributor to:* Numerous short stories in journals and anthologies. *Honours:* Mystery Writers of America Edgar Allan Poe Award, 1968; Mystery Writers of America, Special,Award 1969; Arbeitsgemeinschaft Kriminalliteratur Special Commendation for entire body of work, 1981; Private Eye Writers of America, Shamus Nominee, 1984; President, Private Eye Writers of America, 1985; Guest of Honor, 8th Festival du Roman et du Film Policiers, Reims, France, 1986. *Literary Agent:* Harold Ober Associates, 40 East 49th Street, New York, NY 10017, USA. *Address:* 234 S Voluntario, Apt F, Santa Barbara, CA 93103, USA.

LYNN, Jonathan Adam, b. 1943, England. Writer Director. *Literary Appointments:* Artistic Director, Cambridge Theatre Co, 1976–81. *Publications:* (with George Leyton) Doctor in Charge; Doctor at Sea; Doctor on the Go (television series), 1971–74; (with George Layton) My Name is Harry Worth (television series) 1973; Pig of the Month (play), 1974; (with Barry Levinson) The Internecine Project (screenplay), 1974; (with George Layton) My Brother's Keeper (2 television series), 1975, 76; A Proper Man (novel), 1976; (with Antony Jay) Yes Minister (television series), 1980, 81, (book form), 2 vols, 1980, 81, (book form), 2 vols, 1981, 82. *Address:* c/o Dr Uan van Loewen Limited, 21 Kingly Street, London W1R 5LB, England.

LYNN, Mary Elizabeth, b. 17 Mar. 1939, Enid, Oklahoma, USA. Writer. m. Ted Lynn, 6 Nov. 1966, Miami, Florida, USA, 2 sons, 2 daughters. *Education:* Associate of Arts; Licensed Private Pilot; Radiologic Technologist; Real Estate Broker. *Publications:* Autumn Harvest, 1982; Snow Spirit, 1983; Sonatina, 1983; Summerson, 1983; Out of Bounds, 1984; Danielle's Doll, 1984; Sea of Dreams, 1984; Sugarfire, 1985; Anna's Child, 1985; Knock Anytime, 1986. *Memberships:* Romance Writers of America; New Mexico Romance Writers (President 1984–85); Southwest Writers Workshop (Adviser 1985–86). *Literary Agent:* Anita Diamant. *Address:* 2804 Vermont NE, Albuquerque, NM 87110, USA.

LYONS, David Barry, b. 6 Feb. 1935, New York City. University Professor. m. Sandra Yetta Nemiroff, 18 Dec 1955, New York City, 2 sons, 1 daughter. *Education:* Cooper Union of Engineering; BA, Brooklyn College, City University of New York, 1960; PhD + MA, Harvard University, 1963; Oxford University. *Literary Appointments:* Editor, 1968–70, 1973–75, Managing Editor, 1978–81, The Philosophical Review. *Publications:* Forms and Limits of Utilatarianism, 1965; In the Interest of the Governed: A Study in Bentham's Philosphy of Utility and Law, 1973; Rights, edited with an introduction, 1979; Ethics and the Rule of Law, 1984. *Contributor to:* Times Literary Supplement; Philosophical Studies; American Philosophical Quarterly; Journal of Philosophy; Philosophy Review; Nous; Cornell Law Review; Philosophy; Journal of Value Inquiry; Ethics; Social Theory and Practice; Yale Law Journal; Canadian Journal of Philosophy; Virginia Law Review; Midwest Studies in Philosophy, etc. *Honours:* Guggenheim Foundation Fellowship, 1970–71; Society for the Humanities Fellowship, 1972–73; Clark Distinguished Teaching Award, 1976; Distinguished Alumnus Award, Brooklyn College, 1980; National Endowment for the Humanities Fellowships, 1977–78,

1984–85. *Address:* 309 Mitchell Street, Ithaca, NY 14850, USA.

LYONS, Garry Fairfax, b. 5 July 1956, Kingston-upon-Thames, England. Writer. *Education:* BA, English Literature, University of York, 1978; MA, Drama & Theatre Arts, University of Leeds, 1982. *Literary Appointments:* Playwright in Residence, Major Road Theatre Company, 1983; Fellow in Theatre, University of Bradford, 1984–. *Major Productions:* Echoes from the Valley, 1983; Mohicans, 1984; St Vitus' Boogie, 1985; Urban Jungle, 1985. *Memberships:* Theatre Writers' Union (Secretary, West Yorkshire branch, 1983–). *Literary Agent:* Michael Imison, London. *Address:* c/o Michael Imison, 28 Almeida Street, London N1 4TD, England.

LYONS, Grant Maxwell, b. 19 Aug. 1941, Butler, Pensylvania, USA. Writer, Teacher. m. Bonnie Carol Kaplan, 1 Sep. 1965, Austin, Texas, 1 daughter. *Education:* BA, Tulane University; MA, University of New Orleans; MLS, University of Texas at Austin. *Publications:* Tales The People Tell in Mexico, for children, 1973; Andy Jackson and the Battles for New Orleans, for children, 1976; 4.4.4., 1977; The Creek Indians, for children, 1978; Mustangs, Six-Shooters, and Barbed Wire, for children, 1981; Pacific Coast Indians of North America, for children, 1983. *Contributions to:* Redbook; Cimarron Review; New Orleans Review; Seattle Review; Confrontation; Northwest Review; Other magazines. *Address:* 2923 Woodcrest, San Antonio, TX 78209, USA.

LYONS, Jerry L, b. 2 Apr. 1939, St. Louis, USA. Engineer. *Education:* BSME, MSME and PhD, Engineering Management, Southwest University; Diploma in Mechanical Engineering, Oklahoma Institute of Technology; Certified and Registered Profl. Engineer. *Publications include:* The Lyons' Encyclopedia of Valves, (Van Nostrand Reinhold Publ), 1975; Home Study Series Course on Actuators & Accessories (Instrument Soc of Am), 1977; The Designers Handbook of Pressure Sensing Devices (Van Nostrand Reinhold Publ), 1980; Special Process Applications (Instrument Soc of Am), 1980; The Valve Designer's Handbook, (Van Nostrand Reinhold Publ), 1981; America's Greatest Challenge, 1986; Co-Authored 3 other books. *Contributions to:* Articles, numerous magazines and papers. *Honour:* Award of Merit for Publishing, St Louis Engineers Club. *Memberships:* Writer Digest Club; International Platform Association. *Address:* 7535 Harlan Walk, St Louis, MO 63123, USA.

LYONS, Thomas Tolman, b. 21 June 1934, Stoneham, Massachusetts, USA. Teacher. m. Eleanor F Conconey, 31 Aug. 1958, Reading, Massachusetts, 3 sons, 1 daughter. *Education:* MAT, BA, Harvard. *Appointments:* Teaching appointments: Mount Hermon School, 1958–63; Coe Fellow, Stanford University, 1963; Philips Academy, Andover, 1963–68; Visiting Fellow, Dartmouth College, 1968–69; Phillips Academy 1969–; Instructor on Independence Teaching Foundation. *Publications:* Presidential Power in the Era of the New Deal, 1963; Realism and Idealism in Wilson's Peace Program, 1965; Reconstruction and the Race Problem, 1968; Black Leadership in American History, 1971; The Supreme Court and Individual Rights in Contemporary Society, 1975; The Expansion of the Federal Union, 1978; After Hiroshima: America Since 1955, 1979 revised edition 1985; The President: Preacher, Teacher, Salesman, 1985. *Contributor to:* Independent School Bulletin; Andover Review. *Honours:* Distinguished Secondary School Teaching

Award, Harvard University, 1966; Kidger Award, 1985. *Memberships:* American Historical Association; Organization of American Historians; National Council for the Social Studies; New England History Teachers Association. *Address:* 38 Phillips Street, Andover, MA 01810, USA.

LYONS, W T, b. 10 Aug. 1919, Griffin, Georgia, USA. Metaphysician; Poet; Technical Writer; Management Analyst. *Education:* BA 1949; MA 1952, Howard University, University of Pennsylvania; MScB 1981, MScM 1982, MScD 1983 (Metaphysical Science), University of Metaphysics, Los Angeles, DD 1984, ThD 1984, University College Seminary, Los Angeles, California. *Major Publications:* Soul in Solitude (poetry), Exposition Press, 1970; The Odyssey of Godwin Gipson & Other Poems (poetry of black experience), Carlton Press, 1974; The Heartbeat of Soul, Exposition Press, 1975. Technical Publications: Handbook for Staffing Criteria Development for Activities Ashore, OPNAV Publications, 1967; The Analysis of Staffing Criteria Evaluation Reports, ibid, 1969. Metaphysical publications: Psychic-Mystical Aspects of Metaphysics (Masters thesis), 1982; Metaphysics & The New World of the Mind (Doctoral thesis), 1983. *Address:* 4208 East Capitol Street NE, No. 204, Washington DC 20019, USA.

LYROT, Alain Hervede, b. 19 Aug. 1926, Paris, France. Journalist. m. Mary-Elizabeth Allen, 21 Dec. 1961, Paris, 2 sons. *Literary Appointments:* New York Herald Tribune, USA; International Herald Tribune, Paris; Continent, Paris; French Information Ministry; Editor in Chief, Selection of Reader's Digest; Executive Editor, International, Readers Digest. *Contributor to:* New York Herald Tribune; International Herald Tribune; The Statesman. *Honours:* Knight Legion of Honour, France; Knight National Order of Merit, France; Commander of Merit, Luxembourg. *Membership:* Anglo-American Press Association, Paris. *Address:* 23 Rue Du Cherche-Midi, 75006, Paris, France.

LYTLE, Andrew Nelson, b. 26 Dec. 1902, Murfreesboro, Tennessee, USA. Novelist. m. Edna Langdon Barker, 20 June 1938, 3 daughters. *Education:* Sewanee Military Academy; Vanderbilt University, 1921–25; George Pierce Baker's School of Drama at Yale, 1927 and 1928. *Literary Appointments:* Managing Editor, Sewanee Review, 1942–43; Editor, Sewanee Review, 1961–73; Lecturer in Creative Writing, University of Florida 1948–61; Leader of Humanities Division International Seminar, Harvard, 1954; Teacher, Vanderbilt University, Nashville, 1974; Teacher, University of Kentucky, Lexington, 1976. *Publications:* Bedford Forrest and His Critter Company 1931; The Long Night, 1936; At the Moon's Inn, 1941; Alchemy, 1942; A Name for Evil, 1947; The Velvet Horn, 1957; A Novel, Novella and Four Stories, 1958; A Hero with the Private Parts, literary criticism, 1966; A Wake for the Living, a family chronicle, 1975. *Contribtor to:* Kenyon Review; Sewanee Review; The American Review; Virginia Quarterly; Southern Review; Hound and Horn, Daedalus. *Honours:* Honorary degrees (Doctor of Letters) Kenyon College, 1965; University of Florida, 1970; University of the South, 1973; Hillsdale College, 1985. Guggenheim Fellowship, 1940–41, 1941–42, 1960–61; Kenyon Review Fellow for Fiction, 1956; National Foundation Arts and Humanities Award 1966–67; First Class, Lyndhurst Foundation, 1985; Phi Beta Kappa etc. *Memberships:* Little Magazines of America; Southern Academy of Letters, Arts and Sciences; Council of Little Magazines. *Address:* Monteagle Sunday School Assembly, Monteagle, TN 37356, USA.

M

MABEY, Richard Thomas, b. 20 Feb. 1941, Berkhamsted, England. Writer. *Education:* BA, Hons, 1964, MA, 1971, St Catherine's College, Oxford. *Literary Appointment:* Senior Editor, Penguin Books, 1966–73. *Publications:* Editor: Class, 1967; The Pop Process, 1969; Food for Free, 1972; The Unofficial Countryside, 1973; The Common Ground, 1980; The Flowering of Britain, 1980; Oak and Company, 1983; In a Green Shade, 1983; Editor: Second Nature, 1984; The Frampton Flora, 1985; Gilbert White: A Biography, 1986. *Contributor to:* The Times; Sunday Times; Observer; Sunday Telegraph; Radio Times; New Society; Nature; New Scientist; Good Housekeeping; In Britain; Harpers; Arts Express; Illustrated London News; Times Educational Supplement; The Countryman. *Honours:* Times Educational Supplement Information Book of the Year, 1977; New York Academy of Science Junior Science Book of the Year, 1984; Leverhulme Trust Research Award, 1983–84. *Literary Agent:* Richard Scott Simon, London. *Address:* c/o Richard Scott Simon, 32 College Cross, London N1 1PR, England.

MAC, Maggie, b. 1940, London, England. *Education:* Certificate in English language and literature, Oxford University; Certificates, Royal Society of Arts, London. *Literary Appointments:* Worked in newspapers, television, commercials and films; Teacher of English. *Publications:* Two novels in progress about South Africa and opals; Television script on the Fire Brigade. *Contributions to:* Modern Poets, 1978; Welwyn Garden City Times, 1969; Readers Digest. *Memberships:* Past President, Sydney Fellowship of Writers, Australia; Australian Women Authors; Melbourne Professional Writers' Service; Justice of the Peace; Sydney Masonic Club; Australian Actors Equity. *Address:* 14/31 Churchill Crescent, Concord, NSW 2131, Australia.

McADOO, Henry Robert, b. 10 Jan. 1916, Cork, Ireland. Retired Archbishop of Dublin. m. Lesley Weir, 1 Feb. 1940, Dublin, 1 son, 2 daughters. *Education:* PhD, DD, Trinity College, Dublin; STD, honoris causa, Seabury-Western College, USA. *Publications:* No New Church, 1946; The Structure of Caroline Moral Theology, 1949; John Bramhall and Anglicanism, 1964; The Spirit of Anglicanism, 1965; Where Do Anglicans Stand?, 1970; Modern Eucharistic Agreement, 1973; Marriage & The Community – The Inter Church Marriage, 1974; Being an Anglican, 1977; The Identity of the Church of Ireland, 1980; Rome and the Anglicans, 1982; The Unity of Anglicanism: Catholic and Reformed, 1983. *Contributor to:* Theology; The Furrow; New Divinity; Doctrine & Life. *Honours:* Scholar of Trinity College, Dublin, 1936; 1st Class Moderatorship Gold Medalist, 1938; Bedel, White, Kyle Downes Prizeman. *Address:* 2 The Paddocks, Dalkey, Co Dublin, Republic of Ireland.

McALEAVEY, David Willard, b. 27 Mar. 1946. University Professor. *Education:* BA Summa cum laude, 1968, MFA, 1972, PhD, 1974, Cornell University, USA. *Literary Appointments:* Instructor, English, 1974–75, Assistant Professor, 1975–80, Associate Professor, 1980–, George Washington University. *Publications:* Sterling 403, 1971; The Forty Days, 1975; Shrine, Shelter, Cave, 1980; Holding Obsidian, 1985. *Contributions to:* Poetry; Poetry Now; The Little Magazine; Ascent; Denver Quarterly; Chicago Review; Hollow Spring Poetry; Seneca Review. *Honours:* Corson-Morrison Poetry Prize, 1968; Afred M Kreymborg Award, Poetry Society of America, 1983. *Memberships:* Board of Directors, Poetry Committee of Washington Area, District of Columbia; Modern Language Association; PEN; AWP. *Address:* Associate Dean for Student Services, Columbia College of Arts and Sciences, Washington, DC 20052, USA.

McARTHUR, Harvey King, b. 9 May 1912, Billingsville, Missouri, USA. Professor of New Testament, Ordained Minister. m. Elizabeth R Dimock, 21 Oct. 1941, Scranton, Pennsylvania, 2 sons, 1 daughter. *Education:* B Ph; STM; PhD. *Publications:* New Testament Sidelights, 1960; Understanding The Sermon on the Mount, 1960; The Quest Through The Centuries, 1966; In Search of the Historical Jesus, 1969. *Contributions to:* Journals including: New Testament Studies; The Expository Times: Novum Testamentum; Interpretation; Catholic Biblical Quarterly. *Memberships:* Society of Biblical Literature; Studiorum Novi Testamenti Societas; Catholic Biblical Association of America. *Address:* Box 128, Wilmington, VT 05363, USA.

McAULEY, James J, b. 8 Jan. 1936, Dublin, Republic of Ireland. Author, Poet. m. Deirdre O'Sullivan, 17 Feb. 1982, Spokane, Washington, USA; 5 sons by 2 previous marriages. *Education:* BA, University College, Dublin, 1962; MFA, University of Arkansas, 1971. *Literary Appointments:* Journalist, editor, art & book critic in Dublin for the Electricity Supply Board, 1954–66; Lecturer in Art, Queen's University, Belfast, Northern Ireland, Municipal Gallery of Modern Art, 1965–66; Graduate Teaching Assistant, Department of English, University of Arkansas, 1966–68; Assistant Professor of English, Director of Creative Writing Programme, Lycoming College, Pennsylvania, 1968–70; Assistant Professor of English, Eastern Washington State University, 1970–77; Professor of English, Eastern Washington State University, 1970–77; Professor of English, Eastern Washington University, 1977–, Director of Creative Writing Programme, 1971–74, 1977–79, 1981–83. *Major Publications:* Poems: Observations, 1960; A New Address, 1965; Draft Balance Sheet, 1970; After the Blizzard, 1975; Recital, 1982; (Satire): The Revolution, 1966; Verse & Prose in various anthologies. *Contributor to:* The Kilkenny Magazine; Hibernia!; The Irish Press; The Irish Times; Poetry Ireland; Radio Telefis Eireann. *Honours:* Various awards in USA & Ireland for poetry. *Address:* 1011 West 25th Avenue, Spokane, WA 99203, USA.

McCABE, John (Charles III), b. 14 Nov. 1920, Detroit, Michigan, USA. Writer. m. Vija Valda Zarina, 19 Oct. 1962, New York City, 2 sons, 1 daughter. *Education:* PhB, English, University of Detroit, 1947; MFA, Theatre, Fordham University, 1948; PhD, English Literature, Shakespeare Institute, University of Birmingham, UK, 1954. *Literary Appointment:* Author-in-residence, Lake Superior State College, Michigan, 1970–. *Publications include:* Mr Laurel & Mr Hardy, 1961 (et seq); George M Cohan: The Man Who Owned Broadway, 1973; The Comedy World of Stan Laurel, 1975; Laurel & Hardy, 1975; Proclaiming the Word, with G B Harrison, 1977; Charlie Chaplin, 1979. Chief consultant, James Cagney's autobiography, Cagney By Cagney, 1976. *Contributions to:* Anniversary issue, Variety (annually); Book reviews, theatre, film, Detroit News, 1972–. *Address:* Box 363, Mackinac Island, MI 49757, USA.

McCAFFERY, Margo, b. 29 Sep. 1938, Corsicana, Texas, USA. Nursing Consultant in Pain. Divorced, 1 daughter. *Education:* BS, Baylor University, 1959; MS, Nursing, Vanderbilt University, 1961. *Appointments:* Various Nursing Positions including: Workshop Leader, Lecturer, Consultant, Nursing Care of Patients with Pain, 1970–. *Publications:* Nursing Practice Theories Related to Cognition, Bodily Pain, and Man-Environment Interactions, 1968; Nursing Management of the Patient with Pain, 1972; Behavioral Responses to Sensory Deprivation and Cognitive Disorders, 1978; Dealing with Pain: A Handbook for Persons with Cancer and Their Families, co-author, 1980; Pain: A Nursing Approach to Assessment and Analysis, 1983; Nursing the Patient in Pain, 1983. *Contributor to:* Numerous journals and magazines. *Honours:* Recipient, numerous honours and awards including: Sigma Theta Tau; Alpha Chi. *Address:* 1458 Berkeley St Apt 1, Santa Monica, CA 90404, USA.

McCAFFREY, Anne, b. 1 Apr. 1926, Cambridge, Massachusetts, USA. Science Fiction Novelist. divorced, 2 sons, 1 daughter. *Education:* Cum laude Slavonic languages and literatures, Radcliffe College, Cambridge, Massachusetts. *Publications:* Restoree, 1967; Dragonridgers of Pern, trilogy; The Ship Who Sang, 1970; Mark of Merlin, 1971; To Ride Pegasus, 1973; Dinosaur Planet, 1978; Crystal Singer, 1982; Moreta, Dragonlady of Pern, 1983; Dinosaur Planet Survivors, 1984; Stitch in Snow, 1984; Killashandra, 1985; The Lucy, 1985; Nerilka's Story, 1986; Dragonsong, Dragonsinger, and Dragondrums, constitute Harper Hall Trilogy. *Contributions to:* Short stories and novellas contributed to numerous publications including: Science Fiction; F&SF Mag; Galaxy; Analog; Crime Prevention in the 30th Century; The Disappearing Future; The Many Worlds of SF; Get Off the Unicorn, short story collection. *Honours:* Hugo World SF Award, 1968; Nebula SFWA Award, 1969; E Doc Smith Lensman Award, 1975; Ditmar Award, Australia, 1979; Eurcon SF Award, 1979; Gandalf Award, 1979; Balrog Awards, 1980. *Memberships:* Past Secretary and Treasurer, SFWA; Authors Guild; Poets, Playwrights, Editors, Essayists and Novelists, Dublin. *Literary Agent:* Virginia Kidd Agency, Pennsylvania, USA. *Address:* Dragonhold, Kilquade, Greystones, County Wicklow, Ireland.

McCALL, Grant Edwin, b. 22 Aug. 1943, USA. Anthropologist. m. Julia Jane West, 12 Mar. 1971, Wandsworth, England. 3 sons. *Education:* AA, Orange Coast College, Costa Mesa, California, 1965; BA, University of California, Berkeley, 1966; MA, San Francisco State College, 1968; Diploma of Social Anthropology, 1970, Bachelor of Letters, 1971, University of Oxford; D Phil, Australian National University, 1977. *Literary Appointments include:* Research Assistant, Canadian National Museum, Pitt-Rivers and Horniman Museums, 1971; Part-time Tutor, Department of Anthropology and Prehistory, School of General Studies, The Australian National University, 1974; Lecturer, School of Sociology, The University of New South Wales, 1979–82; Reader in and Head of Sociology, The University of the South Pacific, 1981; Associate Professor; School of Sociology, The University of New South Wales, 1983–. *Publications:* Basque-Americans and a Sequential Theory of Migration and Adaptation, 1973; Edited with Alexander F Mamak, Paradise Postponed: Research for Development in the Pacific 1978; Rapanui: Tradition and Survival on Easter Island, 1980; Dharma Dynamic, 1982; Anthropology in Australia: Essays to Honour 50 Years of Mankind, 1982; Edited with I H Burnley and S Encel, Immigration and Ethnicity in the 1980s, 1985. *Contributions to:* Viltis; Boletin del Instituto-Americano de Estudios Vascos; Journal of Popular Culture; Journal of Anthropological Society of Oxford; Current Anthropology; Journal of Pacific History; Journal of the Polynesian Society; Third World Quarterly etc. Book reviews in Oceania; Mankind; Man; Journal of Pacific Studies etc. *Honours:* Stanley M Tashira Memorial Scholarship, University of California, Berkeley, 1965–66; Fellow, Royal Anthropological Institute (London) 1976–; Fellow, American Anthropological Association (Washington) 1976–; Honorary Research Fellowship, Department of Anthropology, University College, London, 1979; Australian Research Grants Scheme funding for South Pacific Islanders in Australia project, with Alex Mamak, 1979; Australian Research Grants Scheme funding for Rapanui (Easter Island) Development, 1984–. *Memberships include:* Association of Social Anthropologists of the Commonwealth, 1980–. *Address:* School of Sociology, The University of New South Wales, PO Box 1, Kensington, New South Wales 2033, Australia.

McCALL, James Robertson, b. 3 Jan. 1948, Moffat, Dumfriesshire, Scotland. Publisher. m. Janette Anderson Barr, Prestwick, 22 Aug. 1970, 1 son, 1 daughter. *Education:* MA, Honours, English Literature & Philosophy, Glasgow University. *Literary Appointments:* President, Glasgow University Literary Society, 1969; Editor, Humanities, Blackie & Son; Chairman, Scottish Young Publishers' Society, 1977; Director, Blackie Publishing Group, 1980; Consultant Editor, Macmillan Publishers, 1985. *Contributionsto:* Various educational journals, 1974–85; Fiction reviewer, Glasgow Herald, 1984–. *Honour:* Buchanan Prize, Glasgow University, 1970. *Membership:* Board, Educational Publishers Council, 1980–84. *Address:* 26 Middlemuir Road, Lenzie, Glasgow, Scotland.

McCALL-NEWMAN, Christina, b. 29 Jan. 1935, Toronto, Canada. Writer; Editor. m. (1) Peter C Newman, 22 Oct. 1959, 1 daughter. (2) Stephen Clarkson, 1 Sep. 1978, 2 daughters. *Education:* BA, University of Toronto.*Literary Appointments:* Editorial Assistant 1957–59, Associate Editor 1971–75, Maclean's magazine; Assistant Editor, Chatelaine magazine, 1959–66; Ottawa Editor, 1967–70, Executive Editor 1977–, Saturday Night magazine; National Correspondent, Globe and Mail, 1975–77. *Publications:* The Man From Oxbow, 1967; Grits: A Portrait of the Liberal Party, 1982; Les Rouges: un portrait du intime parti Liberal, 1983. *Contributions to:* Several hundred articles mainly on Canadian politics in a Maclean's Saturday Night. *Honours include:* President's Medal for Best Magazine Article, 1970; Southam Fellowship, University of Toronto, 1977; National Magazine Award Gold Medal, 1980; Canadian Authors Association Prize, 1982. *Membership:* Writers Union. *Address:* Saturday Night, 70 Bond Street, Toronto, Canada.

McCALLUM, Phyllis, b. 5 Apr. 1911, Pacific Grove, California, USA. Playwright. m. Dr George Alexander McCalum, 20 Dec. 1936, Salinas, 1 son, 1 daughter. *Education:* BA, English, Stanford University. *Literary Appointment:* Advisory Board, Pioneer Drama Service, Denver, Colorado. *Publications:* The Pale Pink Dragon, 1966; The Uniform Unicorn, 1967; The Tough and Tender Troll, 1967; The Grateful Griffin, 1968; The Vanilla Viking, 1969; Hansel and Gretel and the Golden Petticoat, 1973; Crumple Rumpelstiltskin, 1974; Jack and the Beanstalk, 1976; The Dignified Donkey of New Almaden, (written for US Bicentennial 1976 and musical version for San Jose Bicentennial, 1977); The Swiss Family Robinson 1978, musical version 1976; The Twelve Dancing Princesses, 1978; Christmas with Little Women, 1980. *Contributor to:* Eleusis; Pen Women; Lutheran; Vista; Instructor; Days; Discovery. *Honours:* First Prize, Seattle Junior Programs 1958 for, The Pale Pink Dragon; First Prize, Kansas City Community Children's Theatre Inc. for, Kangalou, and Second Prize 1967 for, The Tough and Tender Troll, Second Prize, Pioneer Drama Service 1967 for, The Tough and Tender Troll; First Prizes, National League of American Pen Women, 1974, 1976, 1978 and 1979. *Memberships:* President, Santa Clara County branch, National League of American Pen Women, 1972–74; President, San Jose Junior Theatre Advisory Board, 1976–79; National Letters Board, National League of American Pen Women, 1974–76.*Literary Agent:* Helen McGrath and Associates, 1406 Idaho Court, Concord, CA 94521, USA. *Address:* 1187 Clark Way, San Jose, CA 95125, USA.

McCANN, Jean, Medical Journalist. *Education:* BA, Northwestern University; Regents College. *Literary Appointments:* Currently: National News Editor, Oncology Times and Emergency Department News, New York; International Correspondent, Physicians Radio Network; President, Medical News Inc. *Contributions to:* Numerous magazines and periodicals in USA, Canada and Europe. *Memberships:* Section Chairman, American Medical Writers Association; International Science Writers Association; National Association of Science Writers; Society of Professional Journalists; Overseas Press Club. *Address:* P O Box 18600, Cleveland, OH 44118, USA.

McCARTHY, Gary W, b. 23 Jan. 1943, California, USA. Western and Historical Novelist. m. Virginia Kurzwel, 14 June 1969, 1 son, 3 daughters. *Education:* BS Agriculture, California State University, Pomona; MS Economics, University of Nevada, Reno. *Publications:* The Derby Man, (9 books), 1976–80; Winds of

Gold, 1980; Legend of the Lone Ranger, 1981; Silver Winds, 1983; Wind River, 1984; Powder River, 1985. *Literary Agent:* Joseph Elder Agency. *Address:* 1005 Brown Avenue, Ojai, CA 93023, USA.

McCARTHY, Martha May, b. 9 July 1945, Louisville, Kentucky, USA. Professor. m. George Dennis Kuh, 1 son, 1 daughter. *Education:* BA, 1966, MA, 1969, University of Kentucky; Specialist in Education, Educational Administration, University of Florida, 1974; PhD, Educational Administration, University of Florida, 1975. *Literary Appointments:* Finance Law Co-Editor, Journal of Education Finance, 1977–; Law Editor, Journal of Educational Equity and Leadership, 1981–; Editorial Board: Education Law Reporter, 1982–; Issues in Education, 1982–; National Forum on Educational Administration and Supervision, 1983–; Educational Administration Quarterly, 1985; Legal Columnist for Indiana Elementary Principal, 1979–; Educational Horizons, 1984–. *Publications:* Law and the Indiana Educator, (Co-author), 1979; Public School Law: Teachers' and Students' Rights, (Co-author), 1981; What Legally Constitutes an Adequate Public Education?, (Co-author), 1982; A Delicate Balance: Church, State and the Schools, 1983; Educators and the Law, (Co-Editor), 1983. *Contributions of:* More than 100 articles to professional journals, etc. including, Phi Delta Kappan; Educational Administration Quarterly; Journal of Education Finance; Harvard Educational Review; Education Law Reporter; Technical Reports and Book Reviews. *Honours:* Recipient of several awards, scholarships, grants, honours. *Memberships include:* Phi Delta Kappa; American Educational Research Association; Pi Lambda Theta; American Education Finance Association, etc. *Address:* School of Education 241, Indiana University, Bloomington, IN 47405, USA.

McCARTHY, Mary, b. 21 June 1912, Seattle, Washington, USA. Author. m. (1) Harold Johnsrud, 21 June 1933, divorced 1936; (2) Edmund Wilson, Feb. 1938, divorced 1946, 1 son; (3) Bowden Broadwater, 6 Dec. 1946, divorced 1961; (4) James Raymond West, 15 Apr. 1961. *Education:* AB, Vassar College, 1933. *Literary Appointments:* Editor, Covici Friede, 1936–37; Editor, Partisan Review, 1937–38; Drama critic, 1937–48; Instructor in Literature, Bard College, 1945–46; Instructor of English, Sarah Lawrence College, 1948; Northcliffe Lecturer, University College, London, 1980. *Publications:* The Company She Keeps, 1942; The Oasis, 1949; Cast A Cold Eye, 1950; The Groves of Academe, 1952; A Charmed Life, 1955; Sights and Spectacles, 1956; Venice Observed, 1956; Memories of a Catgolic Girlhood, 1957; The Stones of Florence, 1959; On The Contrary, 1961; The Group, 1963; Mary McCarthy's Theatre Chronicles, 1963; Vietnam, 1967; Hanoi, 1968; The Writing on the Wall, 1970; Birds of America, 1971; Medina, 1972; The Seventeenth Degree, 1974; The Mask of State, 1974; Cannibals and Missionaries, 1979; Ideas and the Novel, 1980; The Hounds of Summer and other Stories, 1981; La Traviata, adaptation, 1983; Occasional Prose, 1985. *Contributions to:* Numerous magazines. *Honours include:* Horizon Prize, 1949; Doctor of Letters, Syracuse University, 1973; Doctor of Letters, University of Hull, 1974; Doctor of Literature, Bard College, 1976; Doctor of Laws, Aberdeen University,1977; Doctor of Literature, University of Maine, 1982; National Medal for Literature, 1984; Edward MacDowell Medal, 1984; Friends of Rochester Library Award, 1985. *Memberships include:* Phi Beta Kappa; National Institute of Arts and Letters. *Literary Agent:* A M Heath, London. *Address:* 141 rue de Rennes, Paris 75006, France.

McCARTNEY, Dorothy Eleanor Wilson, b. 12 June, 1914, Stroudsburg, Pennsylvania, USA. Housewife; Poet. m. John R McCartney, 23 Jan. 1943, Ithaca, New York, 1 son, 1 daughter. *Education:* AB, Pennsylvania State University, USA, 1934; MA, English Literature and Music, Cornell University, USA, 1943. *Appointments:* Teacher, High School and Elementary Schools; Music Librarian, Cornell University, USA; Assistant Librarian, Francis Harvey Green Library, W Chester State College,

Pennsylvania, USA; Pianist, Gilbert and Sullivan productions; Music Arranger, Accompanist, revised silent movies; Private Secretary to Consultant husband, 1976–81, 1976–84. *Publication:* Lemmus Lemmus and Other poems, 1973. *Contributor to:* Anthologies; First State Writers, 1951; NC Poetry Award Winning Poems, 1966/68/69/72; Bay Leaves, (NC Poetry Council), 1975; American Poetry League Bulletin, 1968; Badge of Promise, 1968; The American Poet, 1968; From Sea to Sea in Songs; Festival Poets, 1969; Friendship Trail, 1970; The Sandcutters, 1971; Red Horse Hill; Moon Age Poets; Yearbook of Modern Poetry; Lyrics of Love NFSPS, Prize Poems, 1969/72; Haiku Drops from the Great Dipper; Oriole; Poetry Society Prize Poems, 1968/69/71/73; Sixty Eight Poets; Prairie Poet Anthology, 1970; Selected Poems, Florida State Poetry Society, 1968; A Patrick Cavanaugh (anthology); Golden Eagle (anthology); Ipso Facto, 1975; Poetry Society Award Winning Poems, 1966/68/69/72/76/77/79; Bayleaves, etc. *Honours include:* 24 first prizes; 21 second prizes; 20 third prizes; 54 honorable mentions. Pennsylvania Poetry Society Prize Poems 1968/69/71/73/74/75/80; Pennsylvania Writers Collection, 1984/85/856; National Federation of State Poetry Societies Prize Poems 1969/70/72. *Memberships:* Poets and Writers Inc. *Address:* PO Box 29, Westtown, PA 19395, USA.

McCARTNEY, Lucinda Lee, b. 1 June 1933, Chicago, USA. Journalist. m. (1) Robert Blenker, 26 Aug. 1961, Oshkosh, (2) R G McCartney, 8 May 1972, Cincinnati, 3 sons. *Education:* University of Wisconsin, 1956; University of Cincinnati, Ohio State University, GRI, 1980. *Publication:* Contributing Editor, Investors Guide. *Contributor to:* Sylvia Porter's Personal Finance Magazine; Money Maker; Physicians Guide to Money Management; London Travel Letter; Living/Working Abroad; Family Motor Coaching; Look Magazine; Oshkosh Northwestern. *Honours:* Criminal Justice Institute 1st Award for Excellence, Newsletter of Cincinnati, 1976, 1977. *Memberships:* American Society Journalists & Authors; Authors Guild/League of America; Florida Freelance Writers Association; National Writers Club; Manatee Writers Guild. *Address:* PO Box 1027, Palmetto, FL 33561, USA.

McCARTY, Clifford, b. 13 June 1929, Los Angeles, California, USA. Bookseller. m. Maxine Reich, 21 July 1955, Beverly Hills, 1 son, 2 daughters. *Education:* BA, California State University, Los Angeles, 1952. *Publications:* Film Composers in America: A Checklist of Their Work, 1953; Bogey: The Films of Humphrey Bogart, 1965; The Films of Errol Flynn, co-author, 1969; The Films of Frank Sinatra, with Gene Ringgold, 1971; Published Screenplays, A Checklist, 1971. *Contributor to:* Armchair Detective; Down Beat; Film and TV Music; Film Careers; Films in Review; The Gissing Newsletter; Notes; Screen Facts. *Address:* PO Box 89, Topanga, CA 90290, USA.

McCASLIN, Nellie, b. 20 Aug. 1914, Cleveland, Ohio, USA. Writer. *Education:* BA, English, MA, Theatre, Case Western Reserve University; PhD, Dramatic Art, New York University; Certificate, Ouspenskaya Studio. *Publications:* Legends in Action, 1945; More Legends in Action, 1950; Pioneers in Petticoats, 1961; Tall Tales and Tall Men, 1956; The Little Snow Girl, 1963; The Rabbit Who Wanted Red Wings, 1963; Creative Drama in the Classroom, 1968, 4th edition 1984; Theatre for Children in the United States: A History, 1971; Children and Drama, 1975, 2nd edition, 1981; Act Now!, 1975; Puppet Fun, 1977; Theatre for Young Audiences, 1978; Shows on a Shoestring, 1979. *Contributor to:* Numerous Articles, Book Reviews; Chapters in: Drama in Therapy, Volume 1, 1981; Children's Theatre and Creative Dramatics: Principles and Practices, 1961; Resources for Early Childhood, 1983; Introductions to: Dress the Show, 1976; Audience Participation, 1981; Understanding Your Child's Entertainemnt, 1977; The Peddler's Dream, 1963. *Honours:* Distinguished Scholar Award, New York University, 1957; Jennie Hedden Award, Children's Theatre Association, 1967; Fellow, American Theatre Association, 1977; Newton D. Baker

Award, Western Reserve Alumni Association, 1983. *Memberships:* Children's Theatre Association of America, Past President; American Theatre Association. *Address:* 40 E 10 St, New York, NY 10003, USA.

McCAULEY, Martin, b. 18 Oct. 1934, Omagh. Senior Lecturer. m. Marta Kring, 26 Aug. 1966, Siegen, Federal Republic of Germany, 1 son. *Education:* BA, PhD, University of London: Diplome d'etudes de civilisation francaise, Sorbonne, University of Paris, France; Professional Associate, Royal Institution of Chartered Surveyors. *Publications:* Leadership and Succession in the Soviet Union, Eastern Europe and China, editor, 1985; The Russian Revolution and the Soviet State 1917–1921, 1975; Khrushchev and the Development of Soviet Agriculture, 1976; The Soviet Union since 1917, 1981; Stalin and Stalinism, 1983; The Origins of the Cold War, 1983; The Soviet Union Since Brezhnev, 1984. *Contributions to:* Soviet Jewish Affairs, 1984; Contemporary Review, 1984, 85. *Address:* School of Slavonic and East European Studies, University of London, Senate House, Malet Street, London WC1E 7HU, England.

McCLATCHY, Joseph Donald, b. 12 Aug. 1945, Bryn Mawr, Pennsylvania, USA. Poet; Critic; Teacher. *Education:* AB, summa cum laude, 1967, Georgetown University; PhD, 1974, Yale University. *Literary Appointments:* Assistant Professor, English Department, Yale University, 1974–81; Lecturer, Creative Writing Program, Princeton University, 1981–; Contributing Editor, American Poetry Review; Poetry Editor, The Yale Review. *Publications:* Anne Sexton: The Artist and Her Critics, (Editor), 1978; Scenes from Another Life, 1981; (London 1983); Stars Principal, 1986; Inventing Artists, 1986. *Contributions to:* Numerous journals and poetry publications. *Honours:* Phi Beta Kappa, 1966; Woodrow Wilson Fellowship, 1967; Ingram Merrill Foundation Grant, 1979; Connecticut Commission on the Arts Grant, 1981; Witter Bynner Prize, American Academy & Institute of Arts & Letters, 1984. *Address:* Creative Writing Program, Princeton University, 185 Nassau Street, Princeton, NJ 08544, USA.

McCLELLAND, Charles Edgar, b. 29 July 1940, San Antonio, Texas, USA. Professor of History. Divorced, 1 daughter. *Education:* BA, Princeton University, 1962; MA, 1963, PhD, 1967, Yale University. *Publications:* The German Historian and England, 1971; Postwar German Culture, with S P Scher, 1974, 80; State, Society and University in German 1700–1914, 1980. *Address:* Department of History, University of New Mexico, Albuquerque, NM 87131, USA.

McCLOY-DRESSER, Helen Worrell Clarkson, b. 8 June 1904, New York City, USA. Writer. m. 13 Oct. 1948, Islip, New York, 1 daughter. *Literary Appointments:* Paris Correspondent, International Studio, 1930–31; London Fine Arts Letter, Sunday Edition New York Times, 1930–31; Book Reviewer, Westport Crier & affiliated newspapers, 1950's. *Publications include:* Dance of Death; The Deadly Truth; Cue for Murder; The Goblin Market; The One That Got Away; Thro' A Glass, Darkly; Unfinished Crime; Two-Thirds of a Ghost; The Last Day; The Singing Diamonds; Mr Splitfoot; A Change of Heart; Minotaur Country; The Imposter; Burn This; etc. *Contributions to:* Various journals. *Honours:* Edgar Allan Poe Award, mystery criticism, Mystery Writers of America, 1953; Nero Wolfe Award, Wolfe Pack, 1980. *Memberships:* Treasurer 1947, President 1953, Mystery Writers of America; Crime Writers Association, UK; Overseas Press Club, New York. *Literary Agent:* Gerald Pollinger, 18 Maddox Street, Mayfair, London W1R OEU, UK. *Address:* Dodd, Mead & Company, 79 Madison Avenue, New York, NY 10016, USA.

McCLUNG, Robert Marshall, b. 10 Sep. 1916, Butler, Pennsylvania, USA. Writer & Illustrator. m. Gale Stubbs, 23 July 1949, Cleveland, Ohio, USA, 2 sons. *Education:* AB, Princeton University, 1939; MS, Cornell University, 1948. *Literary Appointments:* Editor, National Geographic Magazine, Washington DC, 1958–62.

Major Publications: Wings in the Woods, 1948; Sphinx, 1949; Major, 1956; All About Animals & Their Young, 1958; Shag, 1960; Lost Wild America, 1969; Mice, Moose & Men, 1973; Lost Wild Worlds, 1976; Hunted Mammals of the Sea, 1978; America's Endangered Birds, 1979; The Amazing Egg, 1980; Vanishing Wildlife of Latin America, 1980; Last of the Bengal Tigers, 1982; Gorilla, 1984; The True Adventures of Grizzly Adams, 1985; 42 other children's books. *Contributor to:* Various magazines. *Honours:* Numerous Awards, especially Outstanding Science Trade Books for Children 7 times 1972–84. *Literary Agent:* Janet D Chenery. *Address:* 91 Sunset Avenue, Amherst, MA 01002, USA.

McCLUNG, William Alexander, b. 22 Jan 1944, Norfolk, Virginia, USA. University Professor. *Education:* BA, 1966, Williams College, Williamstown, Massachusetts; AM, 1967, PhD, 1972, Harvard University. *Literary Appointments:* Assistant Professor of English Literature, 1971–76, Associate Professor, 1976–84, Professor, 1984–, Mississippi State University; Visiting Associate Professor, Connecticut College, 1980; Visiting Fellow, Huntington Library, 1985; Visiting Scholar in English, University of California, 1985. *Publications:* The Country House in English Renaissance Poetry, 1977; The Architecture of Paradise: Survivals of Eden and Jerusalem, 1983. *Contributions to:* Articles on literature and architecture in Journal of the Society of Architectural Historians; Journal of Architectural Education; Milton Quarterly; Notes and Queries; VIA: Publications of the Graduate School of Fine Arts, University of Pennsylvania; The Explicator. *Honours:* Dexter Fellowship, Harvard University for travel in England, 1970; Visiting Fellow, The Huntington Library, San Marino, California, 1985. *Memberships:* Phi Beta Kappa; Phi Kappa Phi; Milton Society of America; Modern Language Association; Mississippi Institute of Arts and Letters. *Address:* Department of English, Mississippi State University, MS 39762, USA.

McCLURE, Charles Robert, b. 24 May 1949, Syracuse, New York, USA. Librarian; Information Science. m. Victoria A Jones, 29 Dec. 1970, Oklahoma City, 1 daughter. *Education:* BA, Spanish, MA, History, Oklahoma State University, Stillwater; MLS, Library Science, University of Oklahoma, Norman; PhD, Information Studies, Rutgers University, New Brunswick, New Jersey. *Literary Appointments:* Assistant Editor, Government Publications Review, 1980–83; Associate Editor, Government Information Quarterly, 1983–. *Publications:* Information for Academic Library Decision Making, 1980; Strategies for Library Administration, editor, 1982; Planning for Library Services, editor, 1982; Improving the quality of Reference Services, with Peter Hernon, 1983; Public Access to Government Information, with Peter Hernon, 1984; Research for Decision Making, with Robert Swisher, 1984; Descriptive Analysis for the US Depository Library Program, with Peter Hernon, 1985. *Contributions to:* Management Information for Library Decision Making, in Advances in Librarianship edited by W Simarton, 1984; An Assessment of the GPO Biennial Survey in Government Information Quarterly, 1985. Total of 65 articles/chapters written between 1976–85. *Honours:* Best Research Paper of the Year Award, Association for Library and Information Science Education, 1982; Visiting Scholar, Syracuse University, 1983; Distinguished Lectureship, University of Oklahoma, 1984. *Memberships:* Board of Director, Association for Library and Information Science Education, 1983–85; American Library Association; American Society for Information Science. *Address:* School of Library and Information Studies, University of Oklahoma, Norman, OK 73019, USA.

McCLURE, Gillian Mary, b. 29 Oct. 1948, Bradford, England. Author; Illustrator. m. Ian Patrick McClure, 26 Sep., 1970, Steyning, 3 sons. *Education:* Combined Honours, 2nd Class, French, English, History of Art. *Publications:* The Emperor's Singing Bird, 1974; Prickly Pig, 1976; Fly Home McDoo, 1979; What's the Time Rory Wolf, 1982. Illustrations for Tog the Ribber, 1985.

Membership: Society of Authors. *Literary Agent:* Curtis Brown. *Address:* Hamilton Kerr Institute, Mill Lane, Whittlesford, Cambridgeshire, England.

McCLURE, Michael Thomas, b. 20 Oct. 1932, Marysville, Kansas, USA. Poet; Playwright. m. Joanna Keera, 1 daughter. *Education:* BA, San Francisco State College, 1955. *Literary Appointments:* Professor of English and Humanities, California College of Arts and Crafts, Oakland, California; Editorial Board, Evergreen Review and New York Review; Honorary Associate Fellow, Pierson College, Yale. *Publications include:* Nine volumes of poetry; Two novels; Essays published in one volume; 2 volumes of essays; Numerous volumes of plays, 1956–85. *Contributions to:* Life; Atlantic; The Nation; Poetry; Vanity Fair; Semine; Paris Review; Rolling Stone; Clear Creek; Planet Drum; Evergreen Review; Co-Evolution Quarterly. *Honour:* Guggenheim Award; Magic Theatre Alfred Jarry Award; National Education Association Grants; California Arts Council Awards. *Membership:* Sons of Anacreon. *Literary Agent:* (For Drama) Helen Merrill, New York City. *Address:* 264 Downey Street, San Francisco CA 94117, USA.

McCLURE, Ruth Koonz, b. 13 Oct. 1916, Santa Ana, California, USA. (Retired) Editor; Writer. m. Walter McClure Junior, 10 Apr. 1954, Kingston, New York. *Education:* AB, summa cum laude, Vassar College, New York; MA, MPhil, PhD with distinction, Columbia University, New York. *Literary Appointment:* Associate Editor, Yale Editon of Horace Walpole's Correspondence, 1975–81. *Publications:* Coram's Children: The London Foundling Hospital in the Eighteenth Century, 1981; Editor: Eleanor Roosevelt, An Eager Spirit: The Letters of Dorothy Dow 1933–45, 1984. *Contributions to:* Review of English Studies; Studies in Eighteenth Century Culture; American Historical Review. *Honour:* Coram's Children awarded honorable mention and special commendation by Louis Gottschalk Prize Committee of American Society for Eighteenth Century Studies. *Memberships:* Phi Beta Kappa; Conference on British Studies; American Historical Association; Organization of American Historians. *Address:* 24 Sycamore Drive, Hyde Park, NY 12538, USA.

McCOMB, Gordon, b. 12 May 1957, Barstow, California, USA. Writer, non-fiction. m. Jennifer L. Carper, 20 Nov. 1976, Oceanside, California, 1 daughter. *Education:* 2 years' college; Self-taught. *Publications:* Lotus 1-2-3 etc, 1984; Macintosh User's Guide, 1984; Macintosh Graphics, 1985; Presentation Graphics on your Personal Computer, 1985. *Contributions to:* Numerous magazines including: Popular Science; Omni; High Technology; Computers & Electronics; Video; Macworld; etc. *Memberships:* Authors Guild; Computer Press Association. *Address:* 2127 Penasquitas, Aptos, CA 95008, USA.

McCONNELL, William Tate, b. 29 Apr. 1941, San Antonio, Texas, USA. Missionary; Editor; Administrator; Teacher. m. Lu Beth McLeran, 13 June 1964, Denver, Colorado, 2 sons, 2 daughters. *Education:* BA Honours, University of Colorado, 1963; BD summa, Denver Theological Seminary, 1966; DMin, Luther Rice Theological Seminary, Jacksonville, Florida, 1982. *Literary Appointments:* ABU Editora, 1975–85; Adjunct Professor, Creative Writing and Journalism, Faculdade Batista, Sao Paulo, Brazil, 1985–. *Publications:* The Gift of Time, 1983; Tive Fome, Editor, 1983. *Contributions to:* His Magazine; FES Review; Fides et Historia; Comunidad. *Honours:* Christian Scholars Book Grant, Evangelical Literature Trust, 1983. *Literary Agent:* Intervarsity Press. *Address:* ABU Editora, Caixa Postal 30.505, 01.051 São Paulo SP, Brazil.

McCORMACK, Kenneth Anthony, b. 11 Feb. 1945, Birmingham, England. Writer. m. Lydia Catherine Andrews, 2 Apr. 1966, St Chads Church, 2 sons, 1 daughter. *Publication:* Broken Promise. *Literary Agents:* The Penman Literary Service. *Address:* 6 Nuthurst, Sutton Coldfield, West Midlands B75 7EZ, England.

McCORMICK, (George) Donald (King), b. 9 Dec. 1911, Rhyl, Wales. Author. m. (3) Eileen Chellinor James, 1963, London, 1 son. *Publications include:* The Talkative Muse, 1934; The Wicked City, 1956; Blood on the Sea, 1962; The Unseen Killer, 1964; The Red Barn Mystery, 1967; One Man's Wars, 1972; The Master Book of Spies, 1973; Islands of England and Wales, 1974; Taken for a Ride, 1976; Who's Who in Spy Fiction, 1977; Approaching, 1984; Love in Code, 1980; Books published under Richard Deacon: The Private Life of Mr Gladstone, 1965; Madoc and The Discovery of America, 1966; John Dee, 1968; A History of the British Secret Service, 1969, A History of the Russian Secret Service, 1972; A History of the Chinese Secret Service, 1974; Matthew Hopkins: Witchmaster-General, 1976; The Book of Fate: Its Origin and Uses, 1976; The Silent War, 1978; The British Connection, 1979; Spy: Six Stories of Modern Espionage, 1979; Escape, 1980; A History of the Japanese Secret Service, 1982; With My Little Eye: Memoirs of a Spy-Hunter, 1982; Zita: A Do-It-Yourself Romance, 1983; "C": A Biography of Sir Maurice Oldfield, Head of M1 6, 1985. *Address:* 8 Barry Court, 36 Southend Road, Beckenham, Kent BR0 2AD, England.

McCORMICK, John Owen, b. 20 Sep. 1918, Thief River Falls, Minnesota, USA. Professor of Comparative Literature. m. Mairi MacInnes, 4 Feb. 1954, London, 3 sons, 1 daughter. *Education:* BA, 1941, MA, 1947, University of Minnesota; PhD, Harvard University, 1951. *Publications:* Catastrophe and Imagination, 1957; Versions of Censorship, (with Mairi MacInnes), 1962; The Complete Aficionado, 1967; The Middle Distance: A Comparative History of American Imaginative Literature, 1919–1932, 1971; Fiction as Knowledge; The Modern Post-Romantic Novel, 1975; George Santayana: A Biography, 1986. *Contributions to:* Numerous magazines and journals. *Honours:* Guggenheim Fellow, 1964–65; Longview Award for Non-Fiction, 1960; Guggenheim Fellow, 1980–81; Senior Fellow National Endowment for the Humanities, 1983–84. *Literary Agent:* ICM (International Creative Management), New York. *Address:* 158 Terhune Road, Princeton, NJ 08540, USA.

McCORMICK, Richard Arthur, b. 3 Oct. 1922, Toledo, Ohio, USA. Professor. *Education:* AB, 1945; MA, 1950, Loyola University, Chicago; STD, 1957, Gregorian University, Rome. *Publications:* Ambiguity in Moral Choice, 1973; Doing Evil to Achieve Good, 1978; How Brave a New World? 1981; Notes on Moral Theology, 1965, 1980, 1981; Health and Medicine in the Catholic Tradition, 1984. *Contributions to:* numerous national and professional publications. *Honours:* Honorary PhD, 1975, University of Scranton; Honorary PhD, 1976, Wheeling College; Honorary PhD, 1982, Jesuit School of Theology, California; Honorary PhD, 1985, Siena College. *Membership:* Catholic Theological Society of America. *Address:* Georgetown University, USA.

McCORMICK, Scott, Junior, b. 6 Apr. 1929, Evanston, Illinois, USA. College Professor (Religion). *Appointments:* Professor of Religion, Hastings College, Nebraska, 1970–; Minister, Tyler Memorial Presbyterian Church, Radford, Virginia, 1958–65; Associate Professor of Religion, Washington and Jefferson College, Pennsylvania, 1965–70; Consultant, World Council of Churches, 1967–71 and National Council of Churches, 1970–72. *Publication:* The Lord's Supper, 1966. *Address:* 1120 Pleasant Street, Hastings, NE 68901, USA.

McCOY, Barbara Anne, b. 25 May 1936, Erwin, North Carolina, USA. Poet & Editor. m. R F McCoy, 23 Dec. 1970, Williamsburg, Virginia, USA. *Education:* BA, Creative Writing, 1966, MA, English, 1968, University of North Carolina, Chapel Hill, North Carolina, USA. *Appointments include:* English Teacher, John Graham High School, Warrenton, North Carolina, 1966–67; English Teacher, Louisburg College, 1968–70; Teacher, Henderson Institute Junior High School, Henderson NC, 1970–71; Teacher, Vaiden Whitley High School,

Wendell NC, 1971–72. *Major publications:* A Christmas Death: Mini-Chapbook of Haiku, 1979. *Contributor to:* The Anthology of Western World Haiku Society Award Winners 1980 & 1981; Na Pua old Puke, ekolu 1981–83; Haiku Journal Members, Anthology 1983 & 1984; The Outside of a Haiku (Rebecca Rust), 1984; Award-Winning Poems 1980–84 (North Carolina Poetry Society); Poets of the Vineyard Anthology 1984. *Contributor to:* Channels; Jean's Journal; Reflect; The Yellow Butterfly; Prophetic Voices; Parnassus; Manna; Amelia; Piedmont Literary Review; Dragonfly; Haiku Journal; Modern Haiku; Frogpond; Virtual Image; Wind Chimes; The Red Pagoda; Outch. *Honours:* Numerous awards for Poetry and Haiku. *Memberships include:* Western World Haiku Society; North Carolina Poetry Society; Haiku Society of America Inc; Yuki Teikei Haiku Society of USA & Canada; Piedmont Literary Society; P.O.E.T.S.; North Carolina Haiku Society; Christian Writers League of America; Poetry Council of North Carolina Inc. *Address:* 861 Wimbleton Drive, Raleigh, NC 27609, USA.

McCRACKEN, Melinda Jane, b. 1 June 1940, Winnipeg, Manitoba, Canada. Writer. 1 daughter. *Education:* BA (English), University of Manitoba, Canada, 1961. *Publications:* Memories Are Made of This, 1975; Her Own Woman, 1975 (with others); Winnipeg 8: The Ice Cold Hothouse, 1983 (with others). *Contributions to:* Quill and Quire; Maclean's 1972; The Globe and Mail. *Memberships:* The Writers' Union of Canada; Manitoba Writers' Guild. *Address:* 336 Balfour Avenue, Winnipeg, Manitoba R3L 1N8, Canada.

McCRANK, Lawrence J, b. 17 Apr. 1945, Fargo, North Dakota, USA. Librarian/Archivist/Historian. m. Ruth Diane Madson, 23 Dec. 1967, Moorhead, Minnesota, 2 daughters. *Education:* BA, History, Moorhead St University, Minnesota, 1967; MA, History, University of Kansas, 1970; PhD, History, University of Virginia, 1974; MLS, University of Oregon, 1976. *Publications:* Introduction to Basic Information Sources in American History, 1978; Introduction to Basic Information Sources in the Humanities, 1978; Education for Rare Book Librarianship: Trends and Problems, 1980; Automating the Archives: Current Trends and Future Problems, 1981; Mt Angel Abbey: A Centennial History of the Benedictine Community and its Library, 1882–1982, 1983; The Rare Book and Manuscript Collections of Mt Angel Abbey Library: A Catalog and Index, 1983. *Contributions:* 37 articles, 16 reviews, 3 bibliographies on subjects of monastic history, medieval and early modern Iberian history, historical bibliography, manuscripts and rare books, library, archival and information science and administration. *Honours:* Essays in History Award, University of Virginia, 1971; American Library Association first prize essay award for article co-authored with Ruth D McCrank, 1977; Maryland Association for Higher Education Certificate of Merit, 1981. *Memberships:* American Historical Association; American Library Association; Society of American Archivists etc. *Address:* 326 Navajo Drive, Arrowhead, Montgomery, AL 36117, USA.

McCROHAN, Donna Marie, b. 20 Sep. 1947, New York, USA. Author. m. 1969, div. *Education:* BA, Barnard College, New York; MA, Columbia University, New York. *Publications:* The Honeymooners' Companion: The Kramdens and the Nortons Revisited, 1978; The Love Trial, 1982; Bedside Book of Celebrity Gossip, (Celebrity Research Group), 1984. *Contributions to:* Video Review Magazine; Humour News; Cosmopolitan, short story, Foolsrush Inn. *Memberships:* Authors' Guild. *Literary Agent:* Denise Marcil. *Address:* c/o Denise Marcil Literary Agency, 316 West 82 Street, New York, NY 10024, USA.

McCULLOUGH, Constance Mary, b. 15 Jan. 1912, Indianapolis, Indiana, USA. Professor of Education (Language Arts & Reading). *Education:* AB, Vassar College, 1932; MS, Butler University, 1933; PhD, University of Minnesota, 1938; advanced study, University of California at Berkeley, Teachers College, Columbia University, New York. *Major Publications* include: Basal readers for Ginn & Company, 27 years; Problems in the Improvement of Reading, (co-author); The Improvement of Reading, (co-author); Teaching Elementary Reading, (co-author); Preparation of Textbooks in the Mother Tongue, (published by International Reading Association in India for all countries), 1965; Consultant & Author in India, Nepal & Japan. *Contributor to:* The Reading Teacher. *Memberships include:* International Reading Association (President, 1974–75). *Honours include:* Citation in Reading, International Reading Association, 1969; Fellow, American Biographical Institute, 1979. *Address:* 1925 Cactus Court apt 4, Walnut Creek, CA 94595, USA.

McCUTCHAN, Philip Donald, b. 13 Oct. 1920, Cambridge, England. Author. m. Elizabeth May Ryan, 30 June 1951, 1 son, 1 daughter. *Publications include:* Nearly 100 novels, 1957–, including series featuring Commander Shaw; Detective Chief Superintendent Simon Shard; Lieutenant St Vincent Halfhyre, RN; Donald Cameron, RNVR; Commodore John Mason Kemp, RNR. As Duncan MacNeil, series featuring Captain James Ogilvie of the 114th Highlanders; Fighting, Indian NW Frontier, 1890's. Non-fiction: Tall Ships; The Golden Age of Sail, 1976; Great Yachts, 1979. *Membership:* Chairman, 1965–66, Crime Writers Association. *Address:* Myrtle Cottage, 107 Portland Road, Worthing, West Sussex BN11 1QA, England.

MACDERMOTT, Mercia, b. 7 Apr. 1927, Plymouth, England. University Lecturer. m. James MacDermott, 31 Dec. 1948, London, divorced, 1 daughter. *Education:* MA, Russian,s St Annes College, Oxford University; Academic diploma, Bulgarian Regional Studies, School of Slavic Studies, London; Doctor of Historical Sciences, Sofia University. *Publications:* A History of Bulgaria 1393–1885, 1962; The Apostle of Freedom, Biography of Vasil Levsky, 1967; Freedom of Death, Biography of Gotse Delchev, 1978. *Honours:* 1st Class, Order of Cyril and Methodius, Bulgarian Government, 1963, 70; Order of the Rose, Bulgarian Government, 1977; Paisi Hilendersky Prize, Sofia University and Bulgarian Academy of Sciences, 1979. *Address:* Boulevard 9 IX, 12-18 Apt 54, Sofia, Bulgaria 1612.

MACDONALD, David Whyte, b. 30 Sep. 1951, Oxford, England. Biologist. m. Jennifer Mary Wells, 2 Aug. 1976, Oxford, 1 son. *Education:* BA, Zoology; MA, Oxford University; DPhil. *Publications:* Vulpina – Story of A Fox, 1976; Rabies and Wildlife – A Zoologists Perspective, 1980; Expedition to Borneo, 1982; The Encyclopaedia of Mammals, Volume 1, 1984, Volume 2, 1984; Mammalian Social Odours, 1985. *Contributions to:* Numerous scientific and natural history magazines including: Wildlife; New Scientist; Geo; Naturopa. *Honours:* Winston churchill Award, 1976; T H Huxley Award for contributions to zoology, Zoological Society of London, 1978. *Membership:* Society of Authors. *Address:* Department of Zoology, University of Oxford, Oxford OX1 3PS, England.

MACDONALD, Dennis Ronald, b. 1 July 1946, Chicago, Illinois, USA. Associate Professor of New Testament and Christian Origins. m. Diane Louise Prosser, 9 June 1973, Chicago, 1 son, 1 daughter. *Education:* Princeton Theological Seminary, 1969–70; Trinity Evangelical Divinity School, 1970–72; MDiv, McCormick Theological Seminary, 1974; PhD, Harvard University, 1978. *Publications:* Rediscovering Paul, 1980; The Legend and the Apostle: The Battle for Paul in Story and Canon, 1983. *Contributions to:* The Iliff Review; Harvard Theological Review; Which Way Women?; Reformed Journal; Post American; Seminary Papers, Society of Biblical Literature. Book Reviews: Journal of Biblical Literature; Mennonite Quarterly Review. *Honours:* BA cum laude; 1st alternate for St Andrews Society Fellowship, 1968–69; Clarence G Campbell Fellowship, Harvard University, 1975–76; Doctoral Examination and Disseration Passed with distinction. *Address:* The Iliff School of Theology, 2201 South University Boulevard, Denver, CO 80210, USA.

McDONALD, Eva Rose, b. 30 Mar 1909, London. Author. *Publications:* 38 books published including: Lazare the Leopard 1959; The Runaway Countess 1966; The White Petticoat 1971; The Lady from Yorktown 1972; Roman Conqueror 1975; Dearest Ba 1976; The Road to Glencoe 1977; Norman Knight 1977; Queen Victoria's Prince 1978; Candlemas Courtship 1978; Napoleon's Captain 1979; John Ruskin's Wife 1979; Chateau of Nightingales 1979; House of Secrets 1980. *Memberships:* The Society of Authors; National Book League; Authors' Lending and Copyright Society. *Address:* Wyldwynds, 105 Bathurst Walk, Iver, Buckinghamshire SL0 9EF, England.

MACDONALD, John M, b. 11 Sep. 1920, Dunedin, New Zealand. Physician. m. Lucy, 13 Dec. 1952, Chicago, Illinois, USA, 2 sons, 1 daughter. *Education:* University of Otago Medical School, 1940–45, MB, University of New Zealand, MD with distinction, University of Otago, University of London, 1948–49, Diploma in Psychological Medicine, University of Edinburgh, Postgraduate Training in Internal Merdicine, 1949–50. *Publications:* The Murderer and His Victim, 1961; Homicidal Threats, 1968; Indecent Exposure, 1973; Armed Robbery: Offenders and Their Victims, 1975; Psychiatry and the Criminal 3rd editon 1976; Bombers and Firesetters, 1977; Rape: Offenders and Their Victims, 3rd printing 1979; Burglary and Theft, 1980; Criminal Investigation of Drug Offenses, with J Kennedy, 1983. *Address:* 4200 East Ninth Avenue, Denver, CO 80262, USA.

McDONALD, Roger, b. 23 June 1941, Young, New South Wales, Australia. Writer. m. 1967, 3 daughters. *Education:* Arts, Sydney University. *Publications:* Poems: Citizens of Mist, 1968; Airship, 1975; Novels: 1913, 1979; Slipstream, 1982. *Honours:* Winner, Age Book of the Year, 1979; South Australian Government Literary Award, 1980; Australia-Canada Prize, 1982. *Address:* c/o University of Queensland Press, PO Box 42, St Lucia, Queensland, 4067, Australia.

MacDONALD, Ruby D, b. 27 June 1930, California, Ontario, Canada. Author/Writer. m. Thomas Wayne MacDonald, 5 Apr. 1975, San Francisco, California, USA, 2 sons, 3 daughters. *Education:* BS candidate. *Publications:* Ruby MacDonald's Forty Plus and Feeling Fabulour Book, 1982. *Contributions to:* Virtue; Scripture Press; Moody Monthly; Catholic Digest; Aglow; Nor'westing; Woman; Grit; Shriners; Forty Plus Newsletter; Speakers and Writers Ink Newsletter. *Honours:* Writer of the Year, Warner Christian Writers Conference Inspirational, Warner Pacific College, 1983; Angel Award, for excellence for religion in media, 1983. *Memberships:* Authors Guild; Authors League of America; Oregon Association of Ghristian Writers; Pacific Northwest Writers; Willamette Writers; President, Speakers and Writers, Ink. *Literary Agent:* Sherry Robb, Andrews-Robb. *Address:* 6209 Riverside Drive, Vancouver, WA 98661, USA.

McDONALD, Walter R (Robert), b. 18 July 1934, Lubbock, Texas, USA. Professor of English. m. Carol Ham, 28 Aug. 1959, Amarillo, 2 sons, 1 daughter. *Education:* BA, 1956, MA, 1957, Texas Technological College; PhD, University of Iowa, 1966. *Appointments:* Instructor, Assistant Professor, Associate Professor, US Air Force Academy, 1960–62, 1965–71; Lecturer, University of Colorado, 1967–69; Associate Professor, Professor, Texas Tech. University, 1971–73, 1975–. *Publications:* (Poetry) Caliban in Blue, 1976; One Thing Leads to Another, 1978; Anything, Anything, 1980; Working Against Time, 1981; Burning the Fence, 1981. *Contributor to:* Numerous journals and magazines including Poetry; American Poetry Review; Poetry Northwest; Poet Lore; New York Quarterly; College English; etc. *Honours:* Voertman Poetry Award, Texas Institute of Letters, 1977; Best Short Story Award, Texas Institute of Letters, 1977; National Endowment for the Arts Creative Writing Fellowship, 1984. *Memberships:* Texas Association of Creative Writing Teachers, President, 1974–76; PEN; Poetry Society of America; Associated Writing Programmes. *Address:* Department of English, Texas Tech University, Lubbock, TX 79409, USA.

McDONALD, William Andrew, b. 26 Apr. 1913, Warkworth, Ontario, Canada. University Professor (retired). m. 28 June 1941, Bethlehem, Pennsylvania, USA, 1 daughter. *Education:* BA, 1935, MA, 1936, University of Toronto; PhD, The Johns Hopkins University, Baltimore, 1940. *Publications:* The Political Meeting Places of the Greeks, 1943; The Place Names of South-West Greece, with D J Georgacas, 1965; Progress into the Past: The Rediscovery of Mycenaean Civilization, 1967; The Minnesota Messenia Expedition: Reconstructing a Bronze Age Regional Environment, co-editor with George R Rapp Jr. 1972; Excavations at Nichoria in South-West Greece: The Dark Age and Byzantine Occupation, editor with W D E Coulson and John Hosser, 1983. *Contributions to:* Archaeological and Philological Journals such as American Journal of Archaeology; Hesparia; Journal of Field Archaeology. *Honours:* Gold Medal Award of Archaeological Institute of America, 1981; Contributions to Aegean Archaeology (in honour of W A McDonald) 1983. *Address:* Department of Classical Studies, 310 Folwell Hall, University of Minnesota, Minneapolis, MN 55455, USA.

MacDOUGALL, Mary Katherine, b. Mount Auburn, Illinois, USA. Ministry; Writing; Teaching. m. (1) Wayne Fox, Bowling Green, deceased. (2) Harold Alexander MacDougall, 4 sons, 1 daughter. *Education:* BA, University of Michigan. *Publications:* Black Jupiter, 1960; What Treasure Mapping Can Do For You, 1968; Prosperity Now, 1969; Healing Now, 1970; Making Love Happen, 1970; Happiness Now; Dear Friend, I Love You, 1980; *Contributor to:* Numerous articles in professional journals & magazines. *Honours:* Recipient, various honours & awards. *Address:* 2511 Hartford Road, Austin, TX 78703, USA.

McDOWELL, Frederick P N, b. 29 May 1915, Philadelphia, Pennsylvania, USA. Professor of English. m. Margaret Louise Blaine, 29 May 1953, Pittsburg, Kansas, 2 sons, 3 daughters. *Education:* BS, University of Pennsylvania, 1937; MA 1936 and 1947, PhD 1949, English, Harvard University. *Literary Appointments:* Instructor in English, Washington and Jefferson College, 1937–38; Instructor in English, University of Delaware, 1939–41; Instructor 1949–51, Assistant Professor 1951–58, Associate Professor 1958–63, Professor 1963–65, Emeritus Professor 1985, University of Iowa. *Publications:* Ellen Glasgow and the Ironic Art of Fiction, 1960; Elizabeth Madox Roberts, 1963; Caroline Gordon, 1966; E M Forster, 1969, revised 1982; E M Forster: An Annotated Bibliography of Writings About Him, 1977. *Contributions to:* Magazines and journals including: PMLA; Modern Drama; Drama Survey; English Literature in Transition; Philological Quarterly; Contemporary Literature; Modern Fiction Studies; Shaw Reviewed; Conradiana. *Honours:* Senior Fellow, National Endowment for the Humanities, 1973–74; Fulbright Lecturer, Université Paul-Valéry, Montpellier, France. *Memberships:* President 1975, Ellen Glasgow Society; Modern Language Association of America; Shaw Society, New York; Joseph Conrad Society; D H Lawrence Society; Virginia Woolf Society. *Address:* 1118E Court Street, Iowa City, IA 52240, USA.

McDOWELL, Michael McEachern, b. 6 Jan. 1950, Enterprise, Alabama, USA. Writer. *Education:* BA, Harvard College, 1972; PhD, Brandeis University, 1978. *Major publications:* The Amulet, 1979; Cold Moon Over Babylon, Gilded Needles, 1980; The Elementals, 1981; Katie, 1982; Blackwater, 1983; Toplin, 1985. Jack & Susan in 1953, 1985; (under Pseudonym Aldyne with Dennis Schuetz) Vermilion, 1980; Cobalt, 1982; Slate, 1984; (under Pseudonym Axel Young with Dennis Schuetz): Blood Rubies, 1982; Wicked Stepmother, 1963. *Literary Agent:* The Otte Company, Belmont, Massachusetts. *Address:* 117 Mystic Street, Medford, MA 02155, USA.

MACE, Vera Chapman, b. 24 Jan. 1902, Leeds, Yorkshire, England. Marriage and Family Life Educator. m. David Robert Mace, 26 July 1933, London, 2 daughters. *Education:* Board of Education Diploma, Bingley Teachers College, England; MA, Drew University, USA; DHL (Hon), Alma College, Michigan; DSS (Hon), Brigham Young University, Utah. *Publications:* Marriage: East and West (with David Mace), 1960; The Soviet Family (with David Mace), 1963; Sex, Love and Marriage in the Carribean (with David Mace), 1965; Sex, Marriage and the Family in the Pacific (with David Mace), 1969; We Can Have Better Marriages: If We Realy Want Them (with David Mace), 1974; Christian Freedom for Women (contributions to symposium, edited by Harry Hollis), 1975; Men, Woman and God (with David Mace); Marriage Enrichment in the Church (with David Mace); Toward Better Marriages (with David Mace), 1976; How to Have a Happy Marriage (with David Mace), 1977; What's Happening to Clergy Marriages? (with David Mace); In the Presence of God: Readings for Christian Marriage (with David Mace), 1985; Letters to a Retired Couple: Marriage in the Later Years (with David Mace), 1985; Translations of books and articles in Afrikaans, French, Italian, Swedish and Urdu. *Honours include:* Distinguished Service to Families Award from National Council on Family Relations, 1975; First Annual Award, The National Symposium on Family Strength and numerous other honours and awards. *Memberships include:* National Marriage Guidance Council of Great Britain; World Council of Churches; Founder with husband, the Associaton of Couples for Marriage Enrichment. *Address:* C21 Highland Farm, Black Mountain, NC 28711, USA.

McEACHERN, Dona Morrison, b. 1 May 1948. Artist; Writer. m. Marion Kelley McEachern. *Education:* BA, La Grange College, USA; Breadloaf Writers Conference; Special Studies with R Constantine, Atlanta, Georgia, USA. *Publications:* Of Northern Lights, Chapbook of poetry, 1977; Cover and all book illustrations for Lawyers Title Cookbook, Atlanta Branch, 1983; Cover and all book illustrations for Driftwood Garden Club, 1985. *Contributor to:* Albany Herald; The Scroll Quarterly, The La Grange College; NAFAC-NATO Base Paper, Keflavik, Iceland; The Washout Review, New York. *Honour:* Second Place Poetry Award, NATO Base Paper, Keflavik, Iceland, 1973. *Memberships:* The Academy of American Poets, New York; Daughters of the American Revolution, Atlanta Chapter; The Clan Morrison Society, Scotland; The Platform Society; Chatotuckee Valley Art Association. *Address:* 198 Jackson Street, Newnan, GA 30263, USA.

McELROY, Ilse Editha, b. 27 Jan. 1904, Seguin, Texas, USA. Retired Medical Secretary and Ward Administrator. m. James Lafayette McElroy (deceased), 24 Dec. 1935, Boerne, Texas. *Education:* Certificate, Lutheran College, Seguin. *Publications:* Poems, 1976; To the Hills, 1981; Vapors, 1982; Children & Animals and Animal Children, Illustrations by Marguerite Lindner, 1985. *Contributions to:* Anthology of Texas Poems; Those Comforting Hills; World Poetry Anthologies; Comfort News; Seguin Enterprise; The Torch. *Honours include:* 8 Awards, World Poetry Association; Golden Poet of 1985; Fellow, World Literary Academy; Honorary mention, World Poetry; Patron and Honorary Life Member, National Day Poetry Association and World Day Poetry Association. *Memberships:* San Antonio Poetry Association; Stella Woodall Poetry Association; Comfort Art Guild; Community Library. *Address:* POB 363, Comfort, TX 1983, USA.

MACER-STORY, Eugenia, b. 20 Jan. 1945, Minneapolis, Minnesota, USA. Poet; Playwright; Essayist on the supernatural. 1 son. *Education:* BS, Northwestern University, 1965; MFA, Columbia University, 1968. *Publications:* Congratulations: The UFO Reality, 1978; Angels of Time, 1982. *Contributions to:* Triquarterly Literary Review; Manhattan Poetry Review; Pursuit Magazine; Articles, poems and plays also in other specialized magazines. *Honours:* Schubert Fellowship, Columbia University, 1968; Paper included in convention proceedings of the American Association for the Advancement of Science, 1985. *Memberships:* Dramatists Guild; American Association for the Advancement of Science. *Literary Agent:* c/o Magick Mirror Communications. *Address:* Box 854, Woodstock, NY 12498, USA.

MACESICH, George, b. 27 May 1927, Cleveland, Ohio, USA. Director, Centre for Yugoslav-American Studies, Research, Exchanges; Teacher; Author. m. Susanna S Macesich, 20 Feb. 1955, 1 son, 2 daughters. *Education:* AA, 1951, BA, 1953, MA, 1954, Economics, George Washington University; PhD, Economics, University of Chicago, 1958. *Appointments:* Institute for International Education, National Screening Committee, 1984–87; Director, Senior Faculty Member, Institute in Yugoslavia, 1969–; National Advisory Council, University of Montenegro, Yugoslavia, 1972–76; etc. *Publications:* 21 books, most recent include: Monetarism: Theory and Policy, 1983; Money and Finance in Yugoslavia: A Comparative Analysis, co-author, 1983; Politics of Monetarism: Its Historical and Institutional Development, 1984; World Crises and Developing Countries, 1984; World Banking and Finance: Cooperation Versus Conflict, 1984; Banking and the Third World Debt: In Search of Solutions, 1985; Economic Nationalism and Stability, 1985. *Contributor to:* Numerous professional journals and magazines; Editorial Consultant, Journal of Money, Credit and Banking, 1977–; Editorial Board, Southern Economic Journal, 1972–76; Editorial Consultant, Journal of Political Economy, 1968–81; Editorial Board, Foreign Trade and Cycles, 1970–78; Founding Editor, Proceedings and Reports, formerly known as, FSU Slavic Papers, 1967–; etc. *Honours:* Order of the Yugoslav Star with Gold Wreath, 1983. *Memberships:* Numerous professional organisations. *Address:* Centre for Yugoslav-American Studies, Research & Exchanges, Florida State University, 930 West Park Avenue, Tallahassee, FL 32306, USA.

McEVOY, Marjorie, b. York City, England. Novelist. m. William Noel McEvoy, Cramlington, Northumberland, 1 son, 1 daughter. *Publications:* Doctors in Conflict, 1962; The Grenfell Legacy, 1967; Dusky Cactus, 1969; Echoes from the Past, 1978; Calabrian Summer, 1980; Sleeping Tiger, 1982; Star of Randevi, 1984; Temple Bells, 1985. *Contributions to:* The Caravan; Modern Caravan; various newspapers and magazines. *Membership:* RNA. *Address:* 54 Miriam Avenue, Chesterfield, Derbyshire, England.

MACEWEN, Gwendolyn Margaret, b. 1 Sep. 1941, Toronto, Canada. Writer. *Appointments:* Writer in Residence, University of Western Ontario, 1984–85. *Publications:* Julian the Magician, 1963; King of Egypt, King of Dreams, 1971; Short Stories: Noman, 1971; Noman's Land, 1985; Travel: Mermaids and Ikons, A Greek Summer, 1978; Juvenile: The Chocolate Moose, 1979; The Honey Drum, 1983; Theatre: The Trojan Women; Radio Plays: Terror and Frebus, 1965; Tesla, 1966; The World of Neshiah, 1967; The Last Night of James Pike, 1976; Poetry includes: Magic Animals, 1975; Earthlight, 1982; LP Recordings and Tapes include: Gwendolyn Macewen; Canadian Poets 1, 1966; 20 Pen Secrets, 1972; Canadian Poets on Tape. *Contributor to:* Numerous Canadian literary magazines. *Honours:* Governor General's Award, 1969; A J M Smith Poetry Award, for Armies of the Moon, 1973; CBC Literary Competition V, Short Story, 1983; Gold, Silver Prizes, Du Maurier Awards for Poetry, 1983; etc.*Memberships:* Writers Union of Canada; League of Canadian Poets; Playwrights Canada; PEN. *Literary Agent:* Virginia Kidd, USA. *Address:* C/o Writers Union of Canada, 24 Ryerson Avenue, Toronto, Ontario M5T 2P3, Canada.

McFADDEN, Roy, b. 14 Nov. 1921, Belfast, Northern Ireland. Writer. m. Margaret Ferguson, 10 June, 1952, Belfast, Northern Ireland, 3 sons, 2 daughters. *Publications:* Swords and Ploughshares, 1943; Flowers for a Lady, 1945; The Heart's Townland, 1947; Elegy For the Dead of the Princess Victoria, 1953; The Garryowen, 1971; Verifications, 1977; A Watching Brief, 1979; The

Selected, Roy McFadden, 1983; Letters to the Hinterland, 1986. *Address:* 13 Shrewsbury Gardens, Belfast 9, Northern Ireland.

McFALL, Catherine Gardner, b. 10 July 1952, Jacksonville, Florida, USA. Poet; Critic; Teacher. m. Peter Forbes Olberg, 21 Oct. 1978. *Education:* BA, magna cum laude, Wheaton College, Massachusetts, 1974; MA, Johns Hopkins University, 1975. *Literary Appointments:* Director, Poetry Society of America, 1981–83; Instructor, Expository Writing Program, 1983–, Assistant Director, Poetics Institute, 1984–, New York University. *Publication:* For children: Jonathan's Cloud, 1986. *Contributor to:* Poems in The New Yorker; Shenandoah; Georgia Review; The New York Times; Ploughshares; Agni Review; Seattle Review; Tendril; Poetry Miscellany; Crazyhorse etc. Reviews in Newsday; the Washington Post; Ms. Magazine; Dallas Times-Herald; Florida Times Union etc. *Honours:* Fellowships to the MacDowell Colony, 1980 and Yaddo 1981 and 1984; National Arts Club Scholarship in Poetry, The Bread Loaf Writers' Conference, 1983. *Memberships:* Poets and Writers Inc; the Poetry Society of America; Associated Writing Programs; Modern Languages Association. *Literary Agent:* Edite Kroll, 31E 31st Street, New York, NY 10016, USA. *Address:* 48 East 13th Street Apt. 9–A, New York, NY 10003, USA.

McFARLAND, Dalton Edward, b. 23 Sep. 1919, USA. Freelance Writer, Business & Social Subjects. m. Jean A Brown, 17 Mar. 1972, Phoenix, Arizona, 1 son. 3 sons by previous marriage. *Education:* BS, Western Michigan University 1943; MBA, University of Chicago, 1947; PhD, Cornell University, 1952. *Literary Appointments:* Associate Editor/Editor, Journal of the Academy of Management, 1957–64; Editorial Boards, Academy of Management Journal, Journal of Business Research, Journal of Management, Journal of Behavioural Economics, 1972–85. *Publications include:* Management: Principle & Practices, 5th edition, 1979; Action Strategies for Managerial Achievement, 1977; Managerial Innovation & Change in the Metropolitan Hospital, 1979; Management & Society, 1982; The Managerial Imperative: The Coming Age of Macromanagement, 1986. *Contributions to:* Scholarly & Trade Journals; Editor, conference proceedings; Chapters, anthologies; Case materials; Numerous book reviews. *Honour:* Frederick W Conner Prize in History of Ideas, 1984. *Address:* 2720 Highland Court South, Birmingham, AL 35205, USA.

McFARLAND, Ronald E, b. 22 Sep. 1942, Bellaire, Ohio, USA. Professor of English. m. Elsie Watson, 29 Jan. 1966, Trenton, Florida, 1 son, 2 daughters. *Education:* AA, Brevard Junior College; BA, MA, Florida State University; PhD, University of Illinois. *Literary Appointments:* Instructor, San Houston State College, 1965–67; Assistant Professor to Professor, University of Idaho, 1970–; Writer-In-Residence, Idaho State (2 Year Governor's Appointment), 1984–85. *Publications:* American Controversy, 1968; Poems, Certain Women, 1977; Anthology, Eight Idaho Poets, 1979; Poems, Composting at Forty, 1984. *Contributions to:* English Miscellaney, Teratology in Late Renaissance Popular Literature; Modern Poetry Studies, The Contemporary Villanelle; Italian Quarterly, Thematic Variations on the Myth of Dedalus and Icarus; Northwest Magazine, Father's Day, story. *Memberships:* Editor, Slackwater Review, 1978–84; Editor, Snapdragon, 1977–. *Address:* 857 East 8th Street, Moscow, ID 83843, USA.

McFARLANE, Roy Livingstone Clare, b. 20 July 1925, Kingston, Jamaica, West Indies; Retired Teacher. m. Ruby Jane Palmer, 26 Feb. 1950, Washington, District of Columbia, USA, 2 sons, 2 daughters. *Education:* BA, London, England, 1947; MA, Howard University, USA, 1950, *Publications:* Selected Poems 1943–1952; Hunting the Bright Stream, Poems 1954–60; Poems in Three Phases 1947–76; Suddenly the Lignum Vitae Poems 1976–78; Buttercups in a Drytime, Poems 1978–81. *Honours:* Founder Fellow, International Academy of Poets, 1976; Diploma of

Merit, University of Art, Italy, 1982. *Address:* 4 Lemon Close, Kingston 8, Jamaica, West Indies.

McGAHEE, Welbourne Dawson, b. 21 Dec. 1925, Tampa, Florida, USA. Inventor; Author; Patentee; President, Founder and Chairman of the Board, Loop-A-Line, Inc. m. Barbara Warren, 2 May 1943, Reno, Nevada, 7 sons, 6 daughters. *Education:* Graduate, US Air Force Dental Laboratory, 1947; Advanced Chrome Cobalt, 1960; Non-Commissioned Officers Academy, 1962. *Publications:* Riche$, Your$ for Thinking, book I, 1974, book II, 1984. *Contributions to:* US Air Force Dental Laboratory Technical Manual. *Membership:* Dame Sybil Leek's Poetry Club, Melbourne, Florida. *Literary Agent:* Sharon D Kirk. *Address:* 1896 Coolidge, Melbourne, FL 32935, USA.

McGARVEY, Robert, b. 13 Dec. 1948, Elizabeth, New Jersey, USA. Writer. m. Elise Caitlin, July 1975. *Education:* AB Philosophy summa cum laude, Rutgers College, Rutgers University. *Publications:* Leisure Alternatives Catalog, (contributor), 1980; Terror in Turin, Battle in Botswana, King of Kingston, 1981–82; Sex Lives of Famous People, (contributor), 1982; The Complete Spy, (with Elise Caitlin), 1983. *Contributions to:* Various Magazines, including: Playboy; Boys' Life; Los Angeles; Success. *Membership:* Authors Guild. *Address:* 327 N Orlando, Los Angeles, CA 92714, USA.

McGEE, Robert William, b. 12 Apr. 1947, Erie, Pennsylvania, USA. University Professor. m. Margaret Fealko, 27 June 1970, Warren, Ohio, USA, 2 daughters. *Education:* BA, Gannon University; MST, DePaul University; JD, Cleveland State University; CPA, CMA, CIA, CBA, CCA, CSP. *Publications:* Author or co-author of 14 books published by Prentice Hall, Harcourt Brace, Dow Jones – Irwin and National Association of Accountants. *Contributor to:* More than 70 articles in US and UK journals including Computer Law Journal; Western New England Law Review; Cooley Law Review; Hamline Law Review; Management Accounting; World Accounting Report; ABA Banking Journal; Taxation for Accountants; Taxation for Lawyers; Taxes; Practical Accountant; Controller's Quarterly; Monthly Digest of Tax Articles; CPA Digest. *Honours:* Faculty Merit Award for excellence in teaching, research and service, Seton Hall University, 1983; Golden Loophole Award for excellence in tax planning, CPA Digest, 1984. *Address:* 236 Johnson Avenue, Dumont, NJ 07628, USA.

McGILL, Angus, Journalist. *Publications:* Yea Yea Yea, novel; Clive; Clive in Love; I Augusta; Augusta The Great; Live Wires. *Honours:* IPC Award, Descriptive Writer of the Year, 1968. *Literary Agent:* Andrew Hewsen. *Address:* The London Standard, Fleet Street, London EC4, England.

McGILLIARD, Lon Dee, b. 9 Aug. 1921, Manhattan, Kansas, USA. Professor of Dairy Science. m. Nancy D, 31 Aug. 1975, East Lansing, Michigan, 3 sons, 4 daughters. *Education:* BS, Oklahoma A&M College, 1942; MS, Michigan State College, 1947; PhD, Iowa State College, 1952. *Literary Appointments:* Editorial Board, 1965, Associate Editor, 1970, Editor in Chief, 1973, Journal of Dairy Science. *Publications:* Nutritional and Economic Aspects of Feed Utilization by Dairy Cows, 1959, Editor; Animal Agriculture – Research to Meet Human Needs in the 21st Century, Editor, 1980. *Contributions to:* Journal of Dairy Science; Theoretical Applied Genet; North Central Region Research Publication. *Membership:* Council of Biology Editors. *Address:* Animal Science, Michigan State University, East Lansing, MI 48824, USA.

McGINNIS, Terry Jack, b. 5 Sep. 1950, Omaha, Nebraska, USA. Freelace Writer. m. Andriette K Cowan, Las Vegas, Nevada, 16 Apr. 1982, 1 daughter. *Education:* BA, Fine Arts. *Literary Appointments:* Staff Artist 1971, Director & Copywriter 1972, Grand Island Daily Independent; Advertising Manager, Universal Publishing, 1975; Editor, Ad-Art Advertising, 1976; President, Writer's Ink, 1984. *Publications:* Industrial

Adhesives Facts Booklet, Feb. 1985; Fastener Facts Book, Feb. 1985. *Contributions to:* Sargents Magazine (poetry); McFadden's Womens Group (True Romance), five poems; American Poetry Anthology, 1982; American Poetry Association, Hearts on Fire Edition; T.V. Guide. *Honours & Literary Awards:* Best Small Ad Campaign, Nebraska Newspaper Association 1974; Best Ad, Sylvania Corporation, 1974; Best Colour Promotion 1975, Best Copy for Institutional Ad, 1975, Nebraska Newspaper Association & National Print Media Association; Most Original Idea, National Newspaper Association 1975. *Membership:* National Writers Club. *Address:* Suite 193, 5078 South 108th, Omaha, NE 68137, USA.

McGRADY, Patrick Michael Jr, b. 17 July 1932, Shelton, Washington, USA. Author; Journalist; Consultant; Director, CANHELP, a cancer patient information service. m. (1) Elizabeth Rosenbaum, 4 Apr. 1964, Larchmont, NY, 1 son, (2) Colleen Yvonne Bennett, 7 Jan. 1967, Northport, NY, 1 son, 1 daughter. *Education:* BA, Political Science (International Relations), Yale University 1954; Certificat d'études, Institut d'études politiques de Paris. *Literary Appointments:* Chairman, Professional Rights Committee, American Society Journalists and Authors (ASJA), 1974–1984; President, ASJA, 1973–76; Medical Advisory Board, American Medical Writers Association, Northwest Chapter, 1984–. *Publications:* TV Critics in a Free Society, 1959; The Youth Doctors, 1968; The Love Doctors, 1972; The Pritikin Program for Diet & Exercise (with Nathan Pritikin), 1979. *Contributions to:* Reader's Digest, Vogue, True, Family Circle, Ladies Home Journal, Esquire, Woman's Day, Coronet, Status, Newsday Magazine, Atlanta Weekly, Townsend Medical Letter. *Honour:* The Youth Doctors, one of 100 best books of the year by Book World, 1968. *Membership:* The Elizabethan Club, Yale University. *Literary Agent:* Julian Bach, New York City. *Address:* 221 West 82nd Street, New York, NY 10024, USA.

McGRATH, John, b. 1 June 1935, Birkenhead, England. Writer. m. 23 Mar. 1962, 2 sons, 1 daughter. *Education:* BA, Dip Ed, St John's College, Oxford. *Literary Appointment:* Judith E Wilson Visiting Fellow, Cambridge. *Publications:* Events While Guarding the Bofors Gun, 1966; Random Happenings in the Hebrides, 1972; Bakke's Night of Fame, 1973; The Cheviot, The Stag and The Black Oil, 1974; 2nd Edition 1981; The Game's A Bogey, 1974; Fish in the Sea, 1977; Little Red Hen, 1977; Yobbo Nowt, 1978; Joe's Drum, 1979; Blood Red Roses and Swings and Roundabouts, 1981; A Good Night Out, 1981. *Literary Agent:* Margaret Ramsey Limited. *Address:* c/o Freeway Films, 7 Royal Terrace, Edinburgh, Scotland.

MacGREGOR, David Roy, b. 26 Aug. 1925, London, England. Author. m. Patricia Margaret Aline Purcell-Gilpin, 26 Oct. 1962, London. *Education:* BA, 1948, MA, 1950, Trinity College, Cambridge University; Hammersmith School of Building, 1954–55; Associate, Royal Institute of British Architects, 1957. *Publications:* The Tea Clippers, 1952, revised edition 1983; The China Bird, 1961; Fast Sailing Ships 1775–1875, 1973; Clipper Ships, 1977; Merchant Sailing Ships, 1775–1815, 1980; Merchant Sailing Ships, 1815–1850, 1984; Merchant Sailing Ships, 1850–1875, 1984. *Contributions to:* Mariner's Mirror; Journal of Nautical Archaeology. *Memberships:* Fellow, Royal Historical Society, 1957; FSA, 1975; Council Member, Society of Nautical Research, 1959–63, 1965–69, 1974–77, 1980–85; Ship's Committee, Maritime Trust, 1974. *Honour:* Gold Medal from Daily Express for Best Book of the Sea in 1973 for Fast Sailing Ships. *Address:* 99 Lonsdale Road, London SW13 9DA, England.

MacGREGOR, Geddes, b. 13 Nov. 1909, Glasgow, Scotland. University Professor, Emeritus. m. Elizabeth Sutherland McAllister, 14 Aug. 1941, Edinburgh. 1 son, 1 daughter. *Education:* D ès L, Sorbonne, Paris; DPhil, DD, BD, Oxford; BD, LLB, Edinburgh. *Publications:* Aesthetic Experience in Religion, 1947; Christian Doubt, 1951; Les Frontières de la morale et de la Religion, 1952; From a Christian Ghetto: Letters of Ghostly Wit, Written AD 2453, 1954; The Tichborne Impostor, 1957; The Vatican Revolution, 1957; The Thundering Scot, 1957; Corpus Christi: The Doctrine of the Church in the Reforme Tradition, 1959; The Bible in the Making, 1959; Introduction to Religious Philosophy, 1959; The Coming Reformation, 1960; The Hemlock and the Cross, 1963; God Beyond Doubt, 1966; The Sense of Absence, 1967; A Literary History of the Bible, 1970; So Help Me God: A Calendar of Quick Prayers for Half-Skeptics, 1970; Philosophical Issues in Religious Thought, 1973; The Rhythm of God, 1974; He Who Lets Us Be, 1975; Reincarnation in Christianity, 1978; Gnosos, 1978; Scotland Forever Home, 1980 and 1985; The Nicene Creed, 1981; The Gospels as a Mandala of Wisdom, 1982; Reincarnation as a Christian Hope, 1982; The Christening of Karma, 1984; Immortality and Human Destiny, (Editor) 1986; Apostles Extraordinary, 1986. *Contributions to:* Encyclopedias Scholarly journals and other periodicals. *Honours:* Fellow of the Royal Society of Literature, 1948; California Literature Award, Gold Medal nonfiction category, 1964; LHD (Hebrew Union, h c) 1978; Phi Kappa Phi Distinguished Award, 1982. *Memberships:* Senior Research Fellow, International Society for Philosophical Enquiry; Mensa; Speculative Society, Edinburgh; Dialectic Society of Edinburgh, past President and honorary life member. *Address:* 876 Victoria Avenue, Los Angeles, CA 90005-3751, USA.

McGREW, Janice Olive Waggener, b. Humboldt, Nebraska, USA. Speech Pathologist; Poet; Public Speaker. *Education:* AB; MA; Graduate Study, University of Colorado School of Medicine, University of Northern Colorado, University of Denver. *Contributor to:* Colorado Newspapers (also consultant on grammar); occasionally to National Organisation Magazines; formerly Staff Assistant, Special correspondence, Dwight D Eisenhower Presidential Campaign, 1952. *Honours:* State Poetry Society Awards, 1978–79; Arapahoe County Fair, 1984; Elbert County Fair, 1984. *Memberships:* Poetry Societies of Colorado, Arizona and Kentucky Nebraska, Kentucky and Colorado Historical Societies, (Life Member); Colorado Secretary, National Society US Daughters 1812, & National Society Dames of the Court of Honour; Elder Captain (Chap.) Sons & Daughters of the Pilgrims & Peace Pipe, NSDAR; Denver Press Council; Civic Commissioner, Kiowa Planning Commission. *Address:* Box #71, Kiowa, CO 80117, USA.

McGURN, Barrett, b. 6 Aug. 1914, New York City, USA. Journalist. m. Janice Ann McLaughlin, 19 June 1962, Rome, Italy, 5 sons, 1 daughter. *Education:* AB, Fordham University, 1935; Honorary DLitt, 1958. *Literary Appointments:* Reporter, New York Herald Tribune, 1936–66: Bureau Chief, Rome, Paris, Moscow, 1946–62; South Pacific War Corespondent, Washington Bureau Chief, YANK, Army Weekly 1943–45; Press Attaché, US Embassy, Rome, Italy, 1966–68; Press Counsellor, US Embassy, Vietnam, 1968–69; Press Spokesman, US Supreme Court 1973–82. *Major publications:* Decade in Europe, 1958; A Reporter Looks at The Vatican, 1962; A Reporter Looks at American Catholicism, 1967; The Best from YANK, 1945 (co-author); YANK – the GI Story of the War, 1946; Combat, 1950; I Can Tell It Now, 1964; How I Got That Story, 1967; Heroes for Our Times, 1968; Newsbreak, 1975; Saints for all Seasons, 1978. *Contributor to:* Reader's Digest; Catholic Digest; America; Commonweal; Encore; This Week; Mademoiselle; Colliers; Sign; Family Weekly; Popular Science. *Honours:* Various awards for Foreign Correspondents. *Memberships:* Stampa Estera (Foreign Press in Italy), Vice-President, 1951–52, President 1961–62; Anglo-American Press Club, Paris, Governor, 1955; Overseas Press Club of America, President, 1963–65; Correspondents at Supreme Allied Headquarters in Paris, Treasurer, 1955. *Literary Agent:* Curtis Brown Ltd, New York, USA. *Address:* 5229 Duvall Drive, Westmoreland Hills, MD 20816, USA.

MACHADO, Ana Maria Martins, b. 24 Dec. 1941, Rio de Janeiro, Brazil. Journalist. 2 sons, 1 daughter. *Education:* Graduate, Romance Languages; Master in Spanish Literature, Federal University of Rio de Janeiro; Postgraduate, Linguistics, Ecole Pratique des Hautes Studes, Paris, France. *Literary Appointments include:* Professor of Brazilian Literature & Literary Theory, University of Rio de Janeiro, 1969–; Member, Hans Christian Anderson Jury, 1978–80; International Women Writers Conference, Ottawa, 1979, Prague 1980, Cambridge 1982, Nicosia 1984; International Board on Books for Youth Congresses; Casa de las Americas Jury, 1982–. *Publications include:* Recado do Nome, 1976; Historia Meio ao Contrario, 1978; Raul da Ferrugem Azul, 1979; Bem do seu Tamanho, 1979; Do outro lado tem segredos, 1980; De Olho nas Penas, 1981; Bisa Bia Bisa Bel, 1982; Alice e Ulisses, 1983; Passarinho me contou, 1984. *Contributions to:* Elle magazine, France; Journal do Brazil; Isto E; Parapara, Venezuela, Bookbird, Austria. *Honours include:* Joan de Barro Award, 1978; International Women Writers Conference, Ottawa, 1979; IBBY Congresses, Prague 1980, Cambridge 1982, Nicosia 1984; Best Book of the Year FNLIJ Award, 1979, 1981, 1982; Jabuti Award; Fernando Chinaglia Award; Casade las Americas Award, 1980; Crefisul Award, 1981; Art Critics Association of S. Paulo Award, 1982; S. Paulo Biennial Award, 1984. *Memberships:* Former Board Member, Rio de Janeiro Union of Writers; Vice President, International Board on Books for Youth. *Literary Agent:* Carmen Balcells; Copyright Brasileira. *Address:* Rua Marques de S. Vicente 52/367, 22451 Gavea, Rio de Janeiro, Brazil.

MacINNIS, Austin Joseph Michael, b. 15 Mar. 1931, Virginia, Minnesota, USA. Professor. m. Virginia A Reese, 21 Mar. 1957, Fargo, North Dakota, 3 daughters. *Education:* AS; BS; MS; PhD; PDS. *Literary Appointments:* Editorial Board, 1970–73, Committee for Selection of Reviews, 1970–73, Experimental Parasitology; Editorial Board, 1977–78, Editor, 1979–83, Journal of Parasitology; Co-Editor, Elsevier Monographs: Human Parasitic Disease, 1982–; Consultant, Journal of Parasitology, 1984–. *Publications:* Experiments and Techniques in Parasitology, 1970. *Contributions to:* Various professional journals and publications of about 75 scientific manuscripts, reviews and book reviews. *Honours:* Special Citation, for services as editor, American Society of Parasitology, 1983. *Membership:* Council of Biology Editors. *Literary Agent:* Eleanor B Harder, Los Angeles, California. *Address:* Department of Biology, University of California, Los Angeles, CA 90024, USA.

MacINNIS, Frank, b. 25 Jan. 1914, P.E.I., Canada. Medicine. m. Adele Margaret Irving, 2 Dec. 1946, Sydney, Nova Scotia, Canada, deceased 1971, 3 sons, 1 daughter. *Education:* MD, CM, Queens University, Kingston, Ontario, Canada; Fellow, Royal College Physicians, Canada; Fellow, American College of Physicians. *Contributor to:* Numismatic Columnist, Coin World, 1967–79; Geriatric Medicine Columnist, Canadian and US Newspapers including Gannett News Service to its client newspapers, 1981–. *Memberships:* American Medical Writers Association; British Institute of Journalists. *Literary Agent:* HFM Literary Enterprises, Box 307. *Address:* PO Box 307, Edmonton, Alberta, Canada T5J 2J7.

McINTOSH, George, b. 28 May 1930, Clayton-Le-Moors, England. Journalist. m. Mary Margaret McIntosh, 19 June 1954, Accrington, 2 sons, 1 daughter. *Literary Appointments:* Reporter: Accrington Observer and Times; Northern Daily Telegraph; News Chronicle; Northern News Editor, Deputy Northern Editor, Northern Editor, News of the World. *Address:* Middle Barn, Lowgill, Wray, Lancaster, England.

McINTOSH, Michael Scott, b. 7 Dec. 1945, Ottumwa, Iowa, USA. Editor; Writer. m. Dana Mallinson Clemens, 27 Mar. 1975, St Joseph, Missouri. *Education:* BA, Iowa Wesleyan College, 1968; MA, University of Iowa, 1970; Studies, University of California, Los Angeles, Princeton University. *Publications:* The Best Shotguns Ever Made in America, 1981; Practical Shotgunning, 1986. Editor: John Madson: Out Home, 1979; Classics of American Sporting Fiction, 1984. *Contributions to:* Over 100 published magazine articles. Assistant Editor, Missouri Conservationist; Firearms Columnist, Sporting Classics. *Membership:* Outdoor Writers Association of America. *Address:* Route 2 Oakdale, Jefferson City, MO 65101, USA.

McINTOSH, Robert Patrick, b. 24 Sep. 1920, Milwaukee, Wisconsin, USA. Professor. m. Joan A Wright, 24 May 1947, Milwaukee, 1 son, 1 daughter. *Education:* BS, Lawrence College, Wisconsin, 1942; MS, 1948, PhD, 1950, University of Wisconsin. *Literary Appointments:* Editorial Board, Ecology, 1961–64; Associate Editor, Ecological Monographs, 1969–72; Editor, American Midland Naturalist, 1970–; Consultant, History of Ecology Reprint Collection, Arno Press, 1976. *Publications:* Phytosociology, 1978; The Background of Ecology: Concept and Theory, 1986. *Contributions to:* Ecology Since 1900 – Issues and Ideas in America, 1976; Synthese 48, 1980; E L Greene The Man – Landmarks in the History of Botany, 1983. *Address:* Department of Biology, University of Notre Dame, Notre Dame, IN 46556, USA.

McINTYRE, W(illiam) David, b. 4 Sep. 1932, Hucknall, Nottinghamshire, England. Historian. University Professor. m. Marion Jean Hillyard, 14 Dec. 1957, 4 sons, 1 daughter. *Education:* BA, Peterhouse, Cambridge, 1955; MA, University of Washington, Seattle, 1956; PhD, University of London, 1959. *Literary Appointments:* New Zealand Government Historical Advisory Committee, 1967–73; Advisory Board, Historical Abstracts. *Publications:* Colonies Into Commonwealth, 1966; The Imperial Frontier in the Tropics, 1967; Neutralism, non-alignment and New Zealand, 1969; Britain, New Zealand and the Security of South East Asia, 1969; Britain and the Commonwealth Since 1907, 1970; Speeches and Documents on New Zealand History (with W J Gardner), 1971; The Commonwealth of Nations 1869–1971, 1977; The Rise and Fall of the Singapore Naval Base, 1979; The Journal of Henry Sewell, 2 volumes, 1980; Provincial Perspectives (with L Richardson), 1980. *Contributions to:* Articles in journals including: Historical Journal; Journal of Pacific History; Historical Studies Australia and New Zealand. *Honour:* J B Wilson Prose for New Zealand History, 1982. *Memberships:* Chairman 1967, Canterbury Historical Association; New Zealand Historical Association. *Address:* 54a Bryndwr Road, Christchurch 5, New Zealand.

MACK, Carol K, b. 20 Nov. 1941, New York City. Playwright. m. Peter R Mack, 1 son, 2 daughters. *Education:* BA, Mount Holyoke College; Columbia Teachers College. *Publications:* The Chameleon Variant with Dr Ehrenfeld, 1980; Territorial Rites (play) included in Women's Project Anthology II, Performing Arts Journal, 1984; Halftime at Halcyon Days (play) Best Short Plays, Chilton, 1985. *Contributions to:* Moment Magazine. *Honours:* Stanley Drama Award, 1976; University of Jacksonville One Act Play Award, 1982; John Gassner Memorial Award, 1982; Finalist, Susan Smith Blackburn Prize, 1983; Beverly Hills Theatre Guild Playwright Award, 1985; Finalist, Sergel Award, 1985. *Membership:* Dramatists' Guild; League of Professional Theatre Women, New York. *Literary Agent:* Joan Scott, Writers & Artists Agency. *Address:* 115 Central Park West, New York, NY 10023, USA.

MACKAY, Allan Marshall, b. 25 Mar. 1940, New South Wales, Australia. Writer. m. Lesley, Wollongong, New South Wales, 17 Dec. 1971, 1 daughter. *Education:* BA, BLitt, Diploma of Education. *Major Publications:* Imagine – Ten Plays for Young Actors, 1976; Life Pieces – Ten Australian Plays, 1979; Life Pieces 2 – Ten More Australian Plays, 1982; A Wind in Heaven – and other plays, 1985. *Honour:* Winner, Goethe Institute National Playwriting Competition, 1980. *Membership:* Australian Writers' Guild. *Address:* R M B 217, Rose Valley Road, Gerringong, NSW 2534, Australia.

MACKAY, Claire Lorraine, b. 21 Dec. 1930, Toronto, Ontario, Canada. Writer. m. Jackson F Mackay, 12 Sep. 1952, Toronto, Ontario, Canada, 3 sons. *Education:* BA, Political Science, University of Toronto, 1952; Post-graduate studies, Social Work, University of British Columbia, 1968–69; Certificate in Rehabilitation Coun-selling, University of Manitoba, 1971. *Appointments:* Writer-in-Residence, Metropolitan Toronto Library, 1987. *Publications:* Mini-Bike Hero, 1974, 78, 84; Mini-Bike Racer, 1976, 79, 84; Mini-Bike Rescue, 1982; Exit Barney McGee, 1979; One Proud Summer, 1981; The Minerva Program, 1984. Articles, columns, short stories, verse and book reviews in newspapers and magazines. *Memberships:* Canadian Society of Children's Authors, Illustrators and Performers (various offices); Writers Union of Canada; Writers Copyright Agency of Canada Trust; Canadian Authors Associ-ation; Children's Book Centre; Writers Development Trust, etc. *Honours include:* Ruth Schwartz Foundation Award for Best Children's Book, 1982; Vicky Metcalf Award for Body of Work for Children, 1983. *Address:* 6 Frank Crescent, Toronto, Ontario, Canada M6G 3K5.

McKEAN, John Maule Laurie, b. 7 Nov. 1943, Glasgow, Scotland. Architectural Critic; Designer; Illus-trator; Teacher. m. Marion Adler, 4 July 1985, 1 son, 1 daughter. *Education:* B Architecture Honours, Strathclyde University; MA Architectural Theory and History, Essex University, England; Registered Archi-tect. *Literary Appointments:* News and Features Editor, The Architects Journal, 1972–75; United Kingdom Correspondent, Architecture, Paris, France 1975–77, Architektur und Wettbewerbe, Stuttgart, Federal Re-public of Germany 1980–. *Publications:* Essex: Ten Years of a New University, 1972; Architecture of the Western World, (co-author), 1980; Masterpieces of Architectural Drawing, (ghosted), 1982; Architecture: Style, Structure and Design, (co-author), 1984. *Contributions to:* Studio International; Files of the Architectural Association; Architectural Association Quarterly; Spazio e Società; Building Design; Architects Journal; Parametro; Architectural Design. *Member-ships:* Associate, Sri Lanka Association of Architects; Associate, Royal Incorporation of Architects in Scot-land. *Address:* 34 Dukes Avenue, London N10 2PU, England.

MACKEDANZ, Hubert, b. 9 Apr. 1920, Köln am Rhein, Federal Republic of Germany. Male nurse. m. Hannelore Horst, 3 Aug. 1944, Groß Gerau, 1 son, 2 daughters. *Publications include:* Der Flursegler, novel, 1978; Zuletzt nach Manching, notes on a former soldier, 1980; Prüfstand Erde, a philosophical contemplation about human beings, 1982; Lisbeth, narrative, 1984. *Contributions to:* Darmstädter Tagblatt; Darmstädter Echo. *Membership:* Verband Deutscher Schriftsteller (German Association of Authors). *Address:* Bismarckstrasse 17 a, 6100 Darmstadt, Federal Repub-lic of Germany.

McKEE, Louis, b. 31 July 1951, Philadelphia, Pennsyl-vania, USA. Poet; Teacher. m. Christine Caruso, 19 Aug. 1978. *Education:* BA, LaSalle University, 1974; MFA, Columbia University, 1976. *Literary Appointments:* Editor: Carousal Quarterly Review, 1974–76; Mickle Street Review, 1982–84; Painted Bride Quarterly, 1984–; Axe Factory Review, 1984–. *Publications:* Schuylkill County, 1982; The True Speed of Things, 1984; Roses, 1985; Safe Water, 1985. *Contributions to:* (Poetry): American Poetry Review; Poetry Now; Liter-ary Review; Abraxas; Laurel Review; Tar River Review; Event; Mississippi Mud; Centennial Review; Four Quarters, etc. Reviews and Criticisms: Small Press Review; Contact II; Greenfield Review; Gargoyle Sec-ond Coming; Menu, etc. *Memberships:* Poets and Writers Incorporated; PEN. *Address:* PO Box 11186, Philadelphia, PA 19136, USA.

McKENNA, Marian Cecilia, b. 3 July 1926, Scarsdale, New York, USA. College Professor. *Educa-tion:* BS, Teachers College, Columbia University, 1949; MA, 1950, PhD, 1953, Columbia University. *Publica-tions:* Borah, 1960; Pictorial History of Catholicism,

1961; Myra Hess: A Portrait, 1976; The Litchfield Law School: A History, 1986. *Contributor to:* Book Reviews, Canadian Journal of History; Articles, Ethnic Studies Review; Icelandic-Canadian. *Honours:* Erb Fellow, 1953; Danforth Fellow, 1963–66; Canada Council Awards, 1967, 1976, 1969, 1978; American Philosophical Society Award. *Membership:* Writers Guild. *Address:* Dept of History, University of Calgary, 2500 University Drive NW, Calgary, Alberta, Canada T2N 1N4.

MacKENZIE, Andrew Carr, b. 30 May 1911, Oamaru, New Zealand. Journalist; Author. m. Kaarina Sisko Sihvonen, 1 Mar. 1952, London, England, 1 son, 2 daughters. *Education:* Victoria University College, Wellington, New Zealand, 1930–33. *Literary Appoint-ments:* Editorial Staff, Evening Post, Wellington, New Zealand, 1928–38; Kemsley (Later Thomson), Newspapers, London, England, 1946–63; United Newspapers, London, 1963–76 (retired). *Publications:* The Unexplained, 1966; Frontiers of the Unknown, 1968; Apparitions and Ghosts, 1971; A Gallery of Ghosts, editor, 1972; Riddle of the Future, 1974; Dracula Country, 1977; Hauntings and Apparitions, 1982; Romanian Journey, 1983; A Concise History of Romania, editor, 1985. *Contributions to:* Journal of the Society for Psychical Research, reviewer. *Literary Agent:* A M Heath and Company, 40-42 William IV Street, London WC2, England. *Address:* 18 Castlebar Park, London W5 1BX, England.

MacKENZIE, David, b. 10 June 1927, Rochester, New York, USA. Professor of History. m. Patricia Williams, 8 Aug. 1953, Weymouth, Massachusetts, 3 sons. *Education:* AB, University of Rochester, 1951; MA, Certificate of Russian Institute, 1953, PhD, 1962, Columbia University. *Literary Appointments:* Princeton University, 1959–61; Wells College (Aurora, New York) 1961–68; University of North Carolina at Greensboro, 1969–. *Publications:* The Serbs and Russian Pan-Slavism, 1875–1878, 1967; The Lion of Tashkent; The Career of General M G Cherniaev, 1974; A History of Russia and the Soviet Union, 1977, 1982; Ilija Garasanin: The Balken Bismarck, 1985; A History of the Soviet Union, 1986. *Contributions to:* The Journal of Modern History; Slavic Review; Canadian Slavic Studies; Russian Review; International History Review; East European Quarterly. *Honours:* Phi Beta Kappa, 1950; Fellowships from Ford Foundation, ACLS, Inter-University Committee on Travel Grants, American Philosophical Society. *Address:* 1000 Fairmont St, Greensboro, NC 27401, USA.

MACKENZIE, Debora Olivia, b. 1 July 1954, Toronto, Canada. Journalist; Science Writer. *Education:* BSc Honours, Dalhousie University, Halifax; MS, Purdue University, Indiana, USA. *Literary Appointment:* European Editor, New Scientist magazine. *Contributions to:* New Scientist; Various European and North Ameri-can newspapers and magazines. *Memberships:* Associ-ation of British Science Writers; Schweizer Klub der Wissenschafts Journalista. *Address:* c/o New Scientist, 1-19 Oxford Street, London WC1A 1NG, England.

MACKENZIE, Helen Joan, b. 23 Nov. 1925, Ottawa, Ontario, Canada. Writer. m. Charles Grant Mackenzie, 23 May 1949, Kingston, Ontario (dec. 1965), 2 sons, 1 daughter. *Education:* Journalism, Carleton University, Ottawa; BA, Queen's University, Kingston. *Publica-tions:* Through the Glass, Darkly, poetry, 1963; A Dream of Lilies, poetry, 1965; Canada in Bed; Entrance to The Greenhouse, poetry, 1968; It Was Warm and Sunny When We Set Out, poetry, 1970; In The Brown Cottage on Lougborough Lake, poetry, 1970; Kingston: Cele-brate This City, literary history, 1976; Living Together, poetry, 1976; I Come From the Valley, literary history, 1976; Canadian Colonial Cooking, 1976; A Reminder of Familiar Faces, poetry, 1978; This Series has Been Discontinued, poetry, 1980; Some Of The Stories I Told You Were True, oral history, 1981; Giants of Canada's Ottawa Valley, biography, 1981; Look! The Land Is Growing Giants, children's literature, French and English editions, 1983; Laughing All the Way Home, oral history, 1984; Legacies, Legends and Lies, oral history, 1985. *Honours include:* Centennial Prize for Poetry, 1968; 11 out of 13 Canadian Film Awards for screenplay, The Best Damn Fiddler From Calabogie to Kaladar, 1973. *Literary Agent:* Bella Pomey, Toronto. *Address:* Hartington, Ontario, KOH 1WO, Canada.

MACKENZIE, Jean Kathleen, b. 22 Mar. 1928, Traynor, Saskatchewan, Canada. Writer. m. Edward Duncan MacKenzie, 5 July 1952, 2 sons. *Publications:* Storm Island, 1968; River of Stars, 1971. *Contributions to:* Canadian and overseas magazines of travel, religious and general interest articles.*Honour:* First Prize, Canadian Centennial Literary Competition, Juvenile Books, for Storm Island, 1967. *Membership:* Canadian Authors Association. *Address:* 3815 Merriman Drive, Victoria, British Columbia, Canada V8P 2SB.

McKENZIE, Lillian Crawford, b. 15 June 1905. m. E Norton McKenzie. *Education:* Wesleyan College, Macon, Georgia; Graduate, Huntington College, Alabama; Art Students League, New York City; AB; Diploma of Art. *Publications:* Dear Family, 1966. *Contributions to:* Poems to magazines and anthologies including: Ideals; Listen; Link; World Anthology on Peace. *Honour:* State Prize for poem Grandaughter, sponsored by Pen Women. *Memberships:* Vivian Laramore Poetry Club; Florida Poets Association; Vice-President, Board, Miami branch, National League of American Pen Women. *Address:* 3120 Brickell Avenue, Miami, FL 33129, USA.

MacKENZIE, Norman Hugh, b. 8 Mar. 1915, Salisbury, Rhodesia. Professor of English. m. Rita Hofmann, 14 Aug. 1948, Melbourne, Australia, 1 son, 1 daughter. *Education:* BA 1934, MA 1935, University Education Diploma 1936, Rhodes University, South Africa; PhD, University of London, England, 1940. *Literary Appointments:* Lecturer in English, Rhodes University, 1937; Lecturer in English, University of Hong Kong, 1940–41; Lecturer in English, University of Melbourne, Australia, 1946–48; Senior Lecturer, University of Natal, South Africa, 1949–55; Professor of English, 5 years Dean of Faculty of Arts, University College of Rhodesia, 1955–65; Professor, Lawrentian University, Ontario, Canada, 1965–66; Professor 1966–80, Emeritus Professor 1980–, Queen's University, Ontario. *Publications:* The Poems of Gerard Manley Hopkins (Edited with W H Gardner), 1967; Hopkins, 1968; Poems by Hopkins (Editor), 1974; A Readers Guide to Gerard Manley Hopkins, 1981. *Contributions to:* Articles and chapters in books in publications including: The Outlook for English in Central Africa: English Proficiency Testing in the British Commonwealth; Sir Thomas Herbert of Tintern; The Place of English in African Education; The Tests Yeats Canon and Recent Scholarship; Forensic Document Techniques Applied to Literary Manuscripts. *Honours:* Union Scholar, 1939–40; Killam Fellow, 1979–81; Fellow, Royal Society of Canada. *Memberships include:* President 1972–75, International Hopkins Society; Executive 1972–74, Canadian Association for Irish Studies; Life member, Modern Language Association of America; Life member, Yeats Association. *Address:* 416 Windward Place, Kingston, Ontario K7M 4E4, Canada.

MACKENZIE, R Alec, b. 29 Jan. 1923, Genoa, Illinois, USA. Lecturer/Author. m. Gay Rowena Wood, 16 Aug. 1953, 1 son, 1 daughter. *Education:* BS Degree from US Military Academy at West Point; Juris Doctorate from University of Iowa Law School; Graduate Studies in Management and Education at the University of Chicago and Columbia University. *Publications:* Managing Your Time, 1967; The Time Trap, 1972; New Time Management Methods for You and Your Staff, 1975; About Time! A Woman's Guide to Time Management, 1981. *Contributions to:* Management Review Magazine; Harvard Business Review; Personnel Magazine; US News and World Report; Business Quarterly; Influential Business; Life Association News; Registered Representative. *Address:* Alec Mackenzie and Associates, PO Box 130-88 Salem Street, Greenwich, NY 12834, USA.

McKEOWN, Lorraine Laredo, b. New York City, USA. Writer. m. 9 July 1964, New York City, 3 daughters. *Literary Appointments:* Columnist, Mobile Home Journal; Colomnist, Camping Journal. *Contributions to:* Mobile Home Journal; Camping Journal; Popular Mechanics; Popular Science; Mechanix Illustrated; Motor Boating. *Membership:* Free Lance Associates. *Address:* 52 Monell Place, Beacon, NY 12508, USA.

McKEOWN, William Taylor, b. 4 July 1921, Fort Collins, Colorado, USA. Journalist. m. Lorraine Laredo, 9 July 1964, New York City, 3 daughters. *Education:* BA, Bowdoin College; Pilot Officer, USAF Fighter School; Columbia University; University of Vermont. *Literary Appointments:* Editor: Fawcett Books; Popular Boating; Popular Mechanics; Outdoor Life. *Publications:* Outboard Boating Handbook, 1955; Boating in America, 1962. *Contributions to:* Yachting; Boating; Saturday Evening Post; Argosy; True; Esquire; Popular Mechanics; Popular Science; Outdor Life; Woman's Day. *Honours:* Ole Evinrude Award, 1981; NMMA Directors Award, 1984. *Membership:* Overseas Press Club. *Address:* Outdor Life, 380 Madison Avenue, New York, NY 10017, USA.

McKERNAN, Llewellyn Teresa, b. 12 July 1941, Hampton, Arkansas, USA. Poet; English Instructor. m. John Joseph McKernan, 3 Aug. 1967, El Dorado, Arkansas, 1 daughter. *Education:* BA cum laude, English, Hendrix College, 1963; MA, English, University of Arkansas, 1966; MA, Creative Writing, Brown University, 1976. *Publications include:* Copper Beech Anthology of Translations, 1975; Short & Simple Annals: Poems About Appalachisa, 2nd edition 1983. *Contributions to:* Nimrod; West Virginia Hillbilly; Aspen Anthology; Cat Fancy; Laurel Review; Kenyon Review; Kentucky Monthly; Columbus Dispatch; North Carolina Arts Journal; Mountain Life & Work; Crescent Review; Poet & Critic; Artemis; Agni Review; Inlet; Pilgrim Review; etc.*Honours include:*Grant, American Association of University Women, 1978–79; Fellowship, West Virginia Arts & Humanities Commission, 1981; Grant, West Virginia Humanities Foundation, 1982; Grant, Poet & Writers Inc., 1984; 3rd Prize, Chester H. Jones National Poetry Competition, 1982. *Address:* 1012 Chesapeake Court, Huntingdon, WV 25701, USA.

MACKERRAS, Colin Patrick, b. 26 Aug. 1939, Sydney, Australia. Professor. m. Alyce Barbara Brazier, 29 June 1963, 2 sons, 3 daughters. *Education:* BA, University of Melbourne, 1961; BA, Honours, 1962, PhD, 1970, Australian National University; MLitt, University of Cambridge. *Appointments:* English Teacher, Peking Foreign Languages Institute, 1964–66; Research Scholar, 1966–69, Research Fellow, 1969–73, Far Eastern History, Australian National University; Foundation Professor, 1974–, Dean, 1979–85, School of Modern Asian Studies, Griffith University. *Publications:* China Observed 1964–67, with Neale Hunter, 1967; The Uighur Empire According to the T'ang Dynastic Histories, A Study in Sino-Uighur Relations 744-840, 1972; The Rise of the Peking Opera, 1770–1870, Social Aspects of the Theatre in Manchu China, 1972; Amateur Theatre in China 1949–66, 1973; Essays on the Sources for Chinese History, co-editor, 1973; The Chinese Theatre in Modern Times from 1840 to Present Day, 1975; China: The Impact of Revolution, Editor, 1976; The Performing Arts in Contemporary China, 1981; Modern China: A Chronology, 1982; Chinese Theatre from Its Origins to the Present Day, Editor, 1983; From Fear to Friendship, Australia's Policies Towards the People's Republic of China, 1966–82, Co-author; Marxism in Asia, 1985, co-editor. *Contributor to:* Numerous professional journals. *Honours:* International Visitor, Department of State, 1977; Gold Citation, media Peace Prize, United Nations Association of Australia, 1981. *Membership:* Australian Studies Association of Australia, Councillor, 1978–81. *Address:* School of Modern Asian Studies, Griffith University, Nathan, Queensland 4111, Australia.

MACKERRAS, Malcolm Hugh, b. 26 Aug. 1939, Turramurra, Australia. University Lecturer. *Education:* BEconomics. *Publications:* The 1968 Federal Redistribution, 1969; Australian General Elections, 1972; New South Wales Elections, 1973; Elections, 1975, 1975; Elections, 1980, 1980; Victorian Elections, 1980. *Contributions to:* The Bulletin. *Literary Agent:* Curtis Brown. *Address:* 35 Creswell Street, Campbell, ACT 2601, Australia.

McKERROW, Gordon, b. 14 Nov. 1952, Birkenhead, Merseyside, England, Writer, Film Maker. m. Susan Musty. *Education:* BA Film PCL. *Publications:* Plays include: Any Other Business, 1977; Support Your Local Tattooist, 1978; The Infamous Mr Georgie, 1978; Fictions, 1980; We will Know Them, 1981; Bran Underground, 1984; Almost Time For School, 1984; Who Was Algy Geddes?, 1985; A Courtly Dance, 1985. *Literary Agent:* Tessa Sayle. *Address:* Flat 1, 8 Thornton Hill, Wimbledon, London SW19 4HS, England.

McKEY, Eleanor Frances, b. 14 March, 1913, Fall River, Massachussetts, USA. Teacher; Administrator. m. Gordon Wells McKey, 19 Apr. 1941, Sutton, Massachussetts, USA. *Education:* AB, Boston University, USA, 1934, MA, 1940. *Appointments:* Advisor, Chanticleer, Weston High School, USA, 1940–47; Editor of, Reed, Anthology of Poetry Fellowship of Maine, USA, 1951; Advisor, Swampscott High School, Yearbook, 1965–69. *Publications:* Cross Currents, 1978. *Contributor to:* English Journal; English Leaflet; Boston Herald; Boston Post; Driftwood East; Hamilton Historical Society Bulletin. *Honours:* Latin Poetry Prize, 1931; Pan-Hellenic Prize, 1931; Hon. Mention American Pen Womens' Contest, 1980; Maine Writers' Conference, 1983 and 1985; Numerous prizes Poetry Fellowship of Maine. *Memberships:* Poetry Fellowship of Maine; League of American Pen Women; American Association of University Women. *Address:* 296 Essex Street, South Hamilton, MA 01982, USA.

MACKIE, B(ernard) Allan, b. 16 Oct. 1925, Canada. Teacher, Builder. m. Ida Mary Luxton, 3 June 1953, Victoria, British Columbia, Canada, 1 son, 1 daughter. *Education:* Teaching Certificate, University of British Columbia; Graduate, British Columbia Forest Service Ranger School. *Publications:* Building With Logs, 7 editions, 1st edition 1971; Notches of All Kind, A Book of Timber Joinery, 1977; Log House Plans, 1977; Picture Book of Log Homes, 1982; Log Span Tables, 1979. *Contributions to:* Log House magazine; ForesTalk magazine. *Address:* RR1, Pender Island, British Columbia, VON 2MO, Canada.

MACKIE, Philip, b. 26 Nov. 1918, Broughton, Lancashire, England. Author. m. Cynthia Louise Curtis Clarke, 24 Jan. 1948,4 daughters. *Education:* BA (Hons), University College, London, 1939. *Literary Appointment:* Drama Staff Scriptwriter, BBC Television, 1945–55. *Publications:* Hurrah! The Flag, 1957; All The Way Up, 1970; Napoleon and Love, 1974; The Organization, 1974; The Cleopatras, 1983; Plays: The Whole Truth, 1956; Open House, 1957; The Key of the Door, 1959; The Big Killing, 1962; The Chairmen, 1976. *Honours:* Writers Guild of Great Britain Awards for The Caesars, 1968 and The Organization, 1972; Broadcasting Press Guild Award, 1975; Prix Italia,1976; Emmy Award for The Naked Civil Servant, 1976.*Memberships:* Writers Guild of Great Britain, Ex-Executive Councillor; PEN Club; Society of Authors and League of Dramatists.*Literary Agent:* Judy Daish. *Address:* LowerHouse, Kelmscott, Lechlade, Gloucestershire GL7 3HG, England.

MacKILLOP, James John, b. 31 May 1939, Pontiac, Michigan, USA. Professor of English; Author; Journalist. m. Patricia Joan Kahan, 29 Aug. 1964, 1 son, 1 daughter. *Education:* AB 1962, MA, 1968, English Literature, Wayne State University; PhD English Literature, Syracuse University, 1975; Visiting Fellow in Celtic Languages, Harvard University, 1975–76. *Literary Appointments:* Instructor of English, Michigan Technological University, 1963–66; Professor of English, Onondaga Community College, 1967–; Lecturer in English, part-time, State University of New York, Utica-Rome, 1974; Lecturer in Cinema, State University of New York, Cortland, 1978–84. *Publications:* Conflict in Ireland, (editors E Sullivan and H Wilson), 1976; The Irish Peasant 1800–1916, (editors D Casey and R Rhodes), 1977; Speaking of Words, (with D W Cross), 1978, 3rd edition 1985; The Copy Book, (with T Friedmann), 1980; Fionn mar Cumhaill, 1985. *Contributions to:* Eire-Ireland; Antigonish Review; International Fiction Review; Syracuse University Magazine; World Book Encyclopaedia; American Short Stories on Film. *Honour:* National Endowment for the Humanities Fellowship for Independent Study, 1983–84. *Memberships:* Modern Language Association; National Council of Teachers of English; American Committee for Irish Studies; Canadian Association for Irish Studies. *Address:* 108 Limestone Lane, Syracuse, NY 13219, USA.

MacKINLAY, Leila Antoinette Sterling, b. 5 Sep. 1910, London, England. Novelist. *Education:* Diploma, English Literature, London University, 1950. *Literary Appointments:* Dancing Times, 1930s; Amateur Stage, 1946–; Writing and English Literature, London County Council and Greater London Council, to 1965; Teacher of Ordinary Level English Literature. *Publications:* Little Mountebank, 1930; No Room for Loneliness, 1965; numerous other books published, 3 before the age of 21 years. *Contributions to:* Romantic Novelists Association News, Editor. *Honours:* Presidents Prize, Romantic Novelists Association, 1965; Adjudicator, Waterford Festival of Light Opera, 3 years. *Memberships:* Life Member, Society of Authors and NBL; Romantic Novelists Association; Society of Literature.*Address:* 4P Portman Mansions, Chiltern Street, London W1M 1LF, England.

McKINLEY, Hugh, b. 18 Feb. 1924, Oxford, England. m. Deborah Waterfield, 15 Sep. 1979. *Literary Appointments:* Literary Editor, Athens Daily Post, 1966–77; European Editor, Poet India, 1967–; Editorial panel, Bitterroot (USA), 1980–. *Publications include:* Poetry: Starmusic, 1976; Transformation of Faust, 1977; Poet in Transit, 1979; Exulting for the Light, 1983. *Contributions to:* Publications worldwide including London Magazine; Orbis; Weyfarers; Pennine Platform; Candelabra; Poetry Wales; Poet's Voice (UK); Hibernia; Kilkenny Magazine; Dublin Magazine (Ireland); Malahat Review (Canada); Bitterroot, The Smith, Poetry International; (USA); Laurel Leaves (Philippines); Poet India; Skylark, (India); etc. *Honours:* LittLD, International Academy of Leadership & President Marcos Medal, Phillippines, 1967; Honorary DLitt, Free University of Asia, Karachi, India, 1973; Directorate, Academia Pax Mundi, Israel, 1978. *Memberships:* Vice Chairman, Suffolk Poetry Society, UK; International PEN, Irish Centre. *Address:* Roseholme, Curlew Green, Kelsale, Suffolk, England.

MacKINNON, Sue, b. 14 July 1942, Hamilton, Victoria, Australia. Managing Editor. *Education:* BA, University of Melbourne, Victoria, Australia. *Literary Appointments:* Editor 1984–, Managing Editor 1985–, This Australia. *Publications:* Life on the Australian Goldfields, 1978; Waterfront, 1984. *Memberships:* Australian Fellowship of Writers. *Address:* Greenhouse Publications P/L, 385 Bridge Road, Richmond, Victoria 3121, Australia.

MACKSEY, Kenneth John, b. 1 July 1923, Epsom, England. Historian; Author. m. Catherine Angela Joan Little, 22 June 1946, Leckhampton, 1 son, 1 daughter. *Education:* British Army Staff College, PSC. *Literary Appointment:* Deputy Editor, Purnell's History of the Second World War and First World War, 1968–70. *Publications:* To The Green Fields Beyond, 1965; The Shadow of Vimy Ridge, 1965; Armoured Crusader; the Biography of Major-General Sir Percy Hobart, 1967; Afrika Korps, 1968; Panzer Division, 1968; Crucible of Power, 1969; Tank, 1970; Tank Force, 1970; Beda Fomm, 1971; Tank Warfare, 1971; Vimy Ridge, 1972; Guinness Book of Tank Facts and Feats, 1972; The

Guinness History of Land Warfare, 1973; Battle, 1974; The Partisans of Europe, 1975; The Guinness History of Sea Warfare, 1975; Guderian, Panzer General, 1975; The Guinness Guide to Feminine Achievements, 1975; The Guinness History of Air Warfare, 1976; The Guinness Book of 1952, 1977; The Guinness Book of 1953, 1978; The Guinness Book of 1954, 1978; Kesselring: The Making of the Luftwaffe, 1978; Rommel: Battles and Campaigns, 1979; The Tanks volume 3, 1979; Invasion, 1980; The Tank Pioneers, 1981; A History of the Royal Armoured Corps, 1914–75, 1983; Commando Strike, 1985; First Clash, 1985. *Contributions to:* Magazines etc. *Honours:* Knight Clowes Military Essay, 1956, 58. *Literary Agent:* Sheila Watson, Watson, Little Limited. *Address:* Whatley Mill, Beaminster, Dorset DT8 3EN, England.

McLANE, Nancy Baxter, b. 3 Oct. 1950, Grand Rapids, Michigan, USA. Medical Writer; Editor. m. Edward Timothy McLane, 23 May 1982, Pluckemin, New Jersey. *Education:* BA, Journalism, American University, Washington DC, 1972. *Appointments:* Editor, Water Pollution Control Federation, Washington DC, 1972–73; Assistant Director, Publications, American Speech and Hearing Association, Washington DC, 1973–77; Editor, Biomedia Inc, Princeton, 1977–79; Editor, Am Best Co, Oldwick, 1979–81; Managing Editor, Continuing Professional Education Centre, Princeton, 1981–82; Editor, Biomedical Information Corp, New York, 1982–83; President, McLane Media Inc, Summit and Greenwich, New Jersey, 1983–. *Contributor to:* Major medical newsletters and journals. *Memberships:* American Medical Writers Association; Women in Communications. *Address:* McLane Media Inc, 47 Woodland Ave, Summit, NJ 07901, USA.

McLAREN, Colin Andrew, b. 14 Dec. 1940, Middlesex, England. Manuscript Librarian. m. Jan Foale, 25 Mar. 1964, 1 son, 1 daughter. *Education:* BA, MPhil, DipArch Admin, University of London. *Publications:* Rattus Rex, 1978; Crows in a Winter Landscape, 1979; Mother of the Free, 1980; A Twister over the Thames, 1981; The Warriors Under the Stone, 1983. *Memberships:* Society of Authors; Crime Writers' Association. *Literary Agent:* A P Watt Ltd *Address:* c/o The Library, University of Aberdeen, Aberdeen, Scotland.

McLAREN, Peter Lawrence, b. 2 Aug. 1948, Toronto, Canada. Professor of Education. m. Jennifer Carter, 14 Feb. 1976, Toronto, 1 son, 1 daughter. *Education:* BA; BEd; MEd; PhD. *Literary Appointment:* Advisory Panel, Orbit. *Publications:* Cries from the Corridor; The New Surburban Ghettos, 1980; Schooling as a Ritual Performance; Towards a Political Economy of Educational Symbols and Gestures, 1986. *Contributions to:* Journal of Education, University of Boston; Educational Studies; Semiotic Inquiry; Etc: A Review of General Semantics. *Honour:* Editor's Choice, Books in Canada, 1980. *Literary Agent:* Bella Pomer. *Address:* 116 North Bishop Avenue, Oxford, OH 45056, USA.

McLAUGHLIN, William DeWitt, b. 26 Aug. 1918, Youngstown, Ohio, USA. Retired Educator. *Education:* BA, Western Reserve University, Ohio, 1948; MS, University of Wisconsin, Madison, 1950. *Publications:* Poetry: Ourselves at One Remove, 1972; At Rest in the Midwest, 1982. *Contributor to:* Ariel; Concerning Poetry; The English Record; Counter/Measures; Beloit Poetry Journal; Cape Rock Journal; College English; Colorado Quarterly; Cottonwood; Epoch; Epos; The Davidson Miscellany; Folio; Kansas Quarterly; The Little Magazine; The Malahat Review; Midwest Quarterly; New American Review; Poetry Cleveland; Poetry Northwest; Poetry Venture; Queen's Quarterly; Satire Newsletter; The Small Pond; Southern Humanities Review; Southern Poetry Review; Goodard Journal; Hollins Critic; Pembroke Magazine; Poetry Now; Sou'Wester; Ball State Forum; Cape Rock; Chowder Review; Colorado State Review; Denver Quarterly; Hampden-Sydney Poetry Review; Kansas Quarterly; Laurel Review; Louisville Review; Prairie Schooner; West Branch; Wooster Review. *Honours:* $6,000 Grant from The Ohio Arts Council for writing in poetry, 1983.

Address: 20865 Chagrin Boulevard #1, Cleveland, OH 44122, USA.

MACLEAN, Charles Peter Bruce, b. 23 Aug. 1951, Glasgow, Scotland. Writer. *Education:* MA, St Andrews University; LL.B, Dundee University; WS, Edinburgh University. *Literary Appointment:* Managing Director, Maclean Dubois Limited, Copywriters of Literary Agents, 1977. *Publication:* The Fringe of Gold, 1985. *Memberships:* Society of Authors; Scottish Arts Club; Creative Forum. *Address:* 3 Rutland Square, Edinburgh, Scotland.

McLEAN, Cheryl Raye, b. 30 Apr. 1957, Oregon, USA. Writer; Editor. m. Clint Brown, 16 June 1984, Portland, Oregon. *Education:* BA, Oregon State University, 1979; MA, University of Oregon, 1985. *Literary Appointments:* Managing Editor for Literature, Calyx (Journal of Art and Literature by Women), Gorvallis, Oregon. *Contributions to:* Sunset; Ceramics Monthly; Aura; Prism. *Honours:* Graduate Teaching Fellow, 1984–85, Best Thesis Award, 1985, University of Oregon; Kappa Tau Alpha. *Memberships:* Kappa Tau Alpha; Vice President and Board of Directors, Calyx. *Address:* 33058 Southeast Peoria Road, Corvallis, OR 97333, USA.

McLEAN, Eric Donald, b. 25 Sep. 1919, Montreal, Canada. Music Critic. *Education:* Mus Bac, McGill University. *Publications:* The Living Past of Montreal, 1964 and 1976; The Early Furniture of French Canada, translation of French original by Jean Palardy, 1963. *Contributions to:* Antiques Magazine; Maclean's Chateleine; Chimo; The World of Music; and others. *Honours:* Canadian Music Council Award, 1973; OC, Officer of Order of Canada, 1975. *Memberships:* International PEN; Royal Society; President 1964, Music Critics' Association of America; Vice President, Jacques-Viger Commission, 1985. *Address:* 440 Rue du Bon-Secours, Montreal H2Y 3C4, Canada.

McLEAN, Sammy, b. 29 Sep. 1929, USA. University Professor; Literary Translator. *Education:* PhD, Germanic Languages and Literatures, University of Michigan, 1963. *Literary Appointments:* Dartmouth College; University of Maryland Overseas Program; University of Washington. *Publication:* The Bankelsang and the Work of Bertolt Brecht, 1972. *Contributions to:* Poems and translations of poetry and prose from German in literary magazines in USA and Canada; Scholarly articles on Brecht, Kafka, G Hauptmann, etc. in academic journals in USA. *Memberships:* American Literary Translators Association; International Brecht Society. *Address:* Comparative Literature and Germanics DH–30, University of Washington, Seattle, WA 98195, USA.

McLEISH, Kenneth, b. 10 Oct. 1940, Glasgow, Scotland. Author; Broadcaster. m. Valerie, 30 May 1967, Sherburn, 2 sons. *Education:* MA; BMus. *Publications:* Books for Adults include: The Theatre of Aristophanes, 1980; The List of Books, with F Raphael, 1981; Children of the Gods, complete Greek myths, 1983; Penguin Companion to the Arts in the 20th Century, 1985; Shakespeare's Characters A–Z, 1985; Longman Music Guide, with V McLeish, 1986. Books for Children include: Oxford First Companion to Music, with V McLeish, 1983; British myths and folk-tales, 1986. *Contributions to:* Reviewer, The Literary Review, Country Life and others. *Literary Agent:* Hilary Rubinstein, A P Watt. *Address:* c/o A P Watt Limited, 26/28 Bedford Row, London WC1R 4HL, England.

McLELLAN, David Stanley, b. 24 Dec. 1924, New York City, USA. Professor of International Relations. m. Ann Handforth, 1 son, 3 daughters. *Education:* BA 1949, MA 1951, PhD 1954, Yale University; Licence es Science Politique, University of Geneva, Switzerland, 1949. *Publications:* The Cold War Transition, 1965; Dean Acheson: The State Department Years, 1976; Among Friends: The Personal Letters of Dean Acheson, 1980; The Theory and Practice of International Relations, (co-editor with W C Olson), 6th edition, 1982; Cyrus Vance, 1985. *Contributions to:* Scholarly articles to journals including: Political Science Quarterly; International Studies Quarterly; Yale Review; Worldview. *Honours:* David Lloyd Prize, Truman Library, 1976–78; Woodrow Wilson Fellow, 1983. *Address:* Department of Political Science, Miami University, Oxford, OH 45056, USA.

McLENDON-HOUSTON, Gloria Sue, b. 24 Nov. 1940, Marion, North Carolina, USA. Educator; Writer. divorced, 2 adopted daughters. *Education:* BS, Appalachian State University, Boone, North Carolina, 1963; MEd, 1983, PhD, 1986, University of South Florida. *Literary Appointments:* Professor, Childrens Literature, 1985–, English Education, 1984–, University of South Florida, Tampa, Florida. *Publications:* My Brother Joey Died, 1982; Be Still Prepared..., 1984; My Great Aunt Arizona, 1987; The Perfect Balsam Christmas Tree, 1987. *Contributions to:* Eric Data Base; Instructor; AB Bookman's Weekly; Sunday Woman; Childrens House; Florida Truck News; Music Educators Journal; Journal of Death Education; Thanatos; Tampa Tribune, review columnist. *Honours:* Nomination for My Brother Joey Died, various awards. *Memberships:* Vernician Literary Society, Appalachian State University. *Literary Agent:* Louise des Jardins. *Address:* 801 Hunter Court, Brandon, FL 33511, USA.

MacLEOD, Doug, b. 13 Oct. 1959, Melbourne, Australia. Scriptwriter. *Education:* Diploma of Arts, Victorian College of Arts. *Literary Appointments:* Contributing Editor, Puffinalia Magazine, 1981. *Publications:* (Children's titles), Tales of Tuttle, 1980; Knees, 1982; In the Garden of Badthings, 1982;The Fed Up Family Album, 1984; Frank Boulderbuster, 1985. *Contributions to:* Puffinalia; Melbourne Age. *Memberships:* Australian Writers' Guild; Fellowship of Australian Writers. *Address:* c/o Penguin Books Australia Limited, P O Box 257, Ringwood, Victoria 3134, Australia.

MACLEOD, Ellen Jane, b. Glasgow, Scotland. Author. m. Donald M MacLeod, 15 Dec. 1953, Callander, Scotland. *Education:* American High School; Washington State University, USA. *Publications:* 14 Youth books, 1956–71; Orchids for a Rose, 1963; Stranger in the Glen, 1969; The Broken Melody, 1970; The Kelpie Ledge, 1972; Isle of Shadows, 1974. *Contributions to:* 8 Serials; various magazines; 2 radio plays for BBC. *Memberships:* Society of Authors; Radiowriters Association. *Address:* 12 Montgomery Place, Buchlyvie, Stirlingshire, FK8 3NF, Scotland.

MacLEOD, Jean Sutherland, b. 20 Jan. 1908, Glasgow, Scotland. Novelist. m. Lionel Walton, 1 Jan. 1935, Newcastle, 1 son. *Publications include:* The Wild MacRaes (as Catherine Airlie); Sugar Island, 1964; The Wolf of Heimra, 1965; The Moonflower, 1967; The Joshua Tree, 1968; Moment of Decision, 1970; The White Cockade (historical romance); The Dark Fortune (historical); Time Suspended, 1973; The Restless Years; Search For Yesterday, 1981; Moreton's Kingdom, 1982; A Distant Paradise, 1983; Beyond the Reef, 1984; etc. *Contributor to:* Woman & Home; Woman's Own; Woman's Weekly. *Honours:* Recipient, Historical Award, Romantic Novelists; Association, 1962. *Memberships:* Romantic Novelists Association; St Andrew Society, York. *Literary Agent:* Mills & Boon Ltd, London. *Address:* Rose Garth, Thornton-Le-Beans, Northallerton, North Yorkshire, England.

McMAHON, Joseph H, b. 21 Oct. 1930, New York City. University Professor; Literary Critic. *Education:* AB, Manhattan College, 1952; MA, 1959, PhD, 1960, Stanford University. *Literary Appointments:* Instructor, Assistant Professor, Associate Professor, Yale University, 1960–68; Associate Professor, Professor, Wesleyan University, 1968–82; Hollis Professor of French, Wesleyan University, 1982–. *Publications:* The Imagination of Jean Genet, 1963; Humans Being: The World of Jean-Paul Sartre, 1971; In Progress, Haunting Heros, Sexuality, Death and the Heroic Order. *Contributions to:* Yale French Studies, Editor 1963–67; The French Review, Assistant Editor 1977–; Marxist Fictions: The Novels of John Berger; Contemporary

Literature, XXIII, 2, 1982; Michel Tournier's Books for Children, 1985. *Honours:* Fulbright Fellowship 1952; Morse Fellowship 1967; Guggenheim Fellowship 1972. *Memberships:* American Association of Teachers of French; The Authors' Guild. *Literary Agent:* Curtis Brown Ltd. *Address:* 35 Phedon Parkway, Middletown, CT 06457, USA.

McMANUS, Kay, b. 4 July 1922, Nottingham, England. Writer. m. James Alexander McManus (deceased), 17 May 1947, Streatham, London, 1 son, 1 daughter. *Publications:* Raven, 1966; Listen and I'll Talk, 1968. *Contributions to:* Radio and TV plays for BBC, Granada TV etc. 1953–85. *Memberships:* Writers' Guild of Great Britain; International PEN (English Centre). *Address:* Farm Cottage, Bow Brickhill, Buckinghamshire MK17 9JT, England.

McMASTER, Beth Brown, b. 15 Apr. 1935, Peterborough, Ontario, Canada. m. Stuart McMaster, 24 Aug. 1956, Ottawa, 2 sons, 1 daughter. *Publications:* Stick With Molasses, 1973; Which Witch is Which?, 1974; Put On The Spot, 1975; When Everybody Cares, 1975; Christmas Cards, 1981; Happy Holly, 1981. *Honours:* Nova Scotia Drama League Award, 1972; Touring Players Foundation Award, 1973; Ontario Multicultural Theatre Award, 1976; City of Peterborough Cultural Achievement Award, 1981. *Memberships:* Chairman 1977, Eastern Ontario Drama League; Festival Chairman 1980, Theatre Ontario; President 1975, Peterborough Theatre Guild. *Literary Agent:* Simon and Pierre Publishing, Toronto. *Address:* RR#2, Peterborough, Ontario K9J 6X3, Canada.

MacMASTER, Eve Ruth Bowers, b. 24 Sep. 1942, Baltimore, Maryland, USA. Writer. m. Richard Kerwin MacMaster, 3 Feb. 1968, Camp Hill, Pennsylvania, 2 sons, 1 daughter. *Education:* BA, Pennsylvania State University; MA, George Washington University. *Publications:* God's Family, 1981; God Rescues His People, 1982; God Gives the Land, 1983; God's Chosen King, 1983; God's Wisdom and Power, 1984; God's Justice, 1984; God Comforts His People, 1985. *Contributions to:* Christian Living; Highlights for Children; Gospel Herald; Purpose; Report on women in Church and Society; Adult Bible Study Guide; Parables of the Kingdom Study Guide; Voice Magazine. *Address:* 105 West College Street, Bridgewater, VA 22812, USA.

McMASTER, Juliet Sylvia, b. 2 Aug. 1937, Kisumu, Kenya. Professor of English. m. Roland McMaster, 10 May 1968, Edmonton, Canada, 1 son, 1 daughter. *Education:* BA, MA, Oxford University, 1959; MA 1962, PhD 1965, University of Alberta, Canada. *Literary Appointments:* Assistant Professor 1965–70, Associate Professor 1970–76, Professor 1976–, University of Alberta. *Publications:* Thackeray: The Major Novels, 1971; Jane Austen's Achievement (editor), 1976; Trollop's Palliser Novels, 1978; Jane Austen on Love, 1978; The Novel from Sterne to James, (with R D McMaster),1981; Dickens The Designer, in press. *Contributions to:* Journals including: Nineteenth-Century Fiction; Studies in English Literature; English Studies in Canada; Modern Language Quarterly. *Honours:* Guggenheim Fellow, 1976–77; Fellow, Royal Society of Canada, 1981; *Membership:* President 1976–78, Association of Canadian University Teachers of English. *Address:* Department of English, University of Alberta, Edmonton, Alberta T6G, Canada.

McMILLAN, James, b. 30 Oct 1925, Glasgow, Scotland. Journalist. m. Doreen Smith, 7 Apr 1953, Glasgow, 3 sons, 1 daughter. *Education:* MA, Hons, Economics, Glasgow University. *Literary Appointments:* Deputy Editor, Evening Citizen, Glasgow; Political Adviser, Express Newspapers, London. *Publications:* The Glass Lie 1965; The American Take-over 1967; The Honours Game 1968; Anatomy of Scotland 1969; The British Genius (with Peter Grosvenor) 1973; The Way We Were (Trilogy) 1978–80; Five Men at Nuremberg 1985. *Contributor to:* Various British and US trade journals. *Literary Agent:* Peter Knight, 20 Crescent

Grove, London SW4 7AH. *Address:* Thurlestone Fairmile Park Road, Cobham, Surrey, England.

McMORROW, Thomas Evers, b. 17 Nov. 1920, New York. Journalist; Writer. m. Joan Lowell, 28 Aug. 1947, New York, 1 son 2 daughters. *Education:* Yale, 1938–39. *Literary Appointments:* Writer, Producer and Director of Hall of Fame official films The Legendary Greats and Baseball's Golden Moments. *Publications:* Plays: The Celebrity, 1984; The Sawdust Murders and Other Crimes of 1885. *Contributions to:* Short stories for Saturday Evening Post in 1950's and 60's, e.g. The Most Valuable Louse in the League, The Psychological Halfback, etc. Fantasy Science Fiction; Alfred Hitchcock's Mystery Magazine; Amazing Stories. Articles for Argosy; TV Guide; True; Smart Living etc. Articles, critiques, reviews and columns for newspapers including New York Daily News and magazines. Theatre Editor and Critic for The City, 1982. *Memberships:* Member of Executive Committee (Past President) The Drama Desk, The Association of New York Theatre critics, writers and editors; American Theatre Critics Association. *Address:* 245 E 40th Street, New York, NY 10016, USA.

McMURTRY, R Gerald, b. 17 Feb. 1906, Elizabethtown, Kentucky, USA. Library and Museum Director, (retired). m. Florence Louise Koberly, 22 Dec. 1932, Fort Wayne, Indiana, 1 son, 4 daughters. *Education:* AB, Centre College, Danville, Kentucky, 1929; LittD, 1953, LLD Indiana Wesleyan College, 1946; DHL, Lincoln College, Lincoln, Illinois, 1962. *Literary Appointments:* Librarian/Member of Research Staff, Lincoln National Life Foundation, 1931–35; Director, Department of Lincolniana, Assistant Professor of American History, Administrative Secretary, Lincoln Memorial University, Harrogate, Tennessee, 1937–56; Director, Lincoln National Life Foundation, 1956–; Lecturer, International Educational Exchange Service, State Department, 1959. *Publications include:* The Kentucky Lincolns on Mill Creek; Ben Hardin Helm, Rebel, Brother-in-Law of Abraham Lincoln with a Biographical sketch of his Wife and an account of the Todd Family in Kentucky; Lincoln's Other Mary (with Olive Carruthers); Lincoln's Favorite Poets (with David J Harkness); My Lifelong Pursuit of Lincoln. *Contributions to:* Historical Journals; Parade Magazine; Antiques Magazine. Editor of: Lincoln Herald; Lincoln Lore. *Memberships:* Historical Societies and Civil WasRound Tables. *Address:* 910 West Rudisill Boulevard, Fort Wayne, IN 46807, USA.

McNAIR SCOTT, Ronald Guthrie, b. 29 May 1906, Bromley, Kent, England. m. Hon Mary Cecilia Berry, Longcross, Surrey, 2 sons, 3 daughters. *Education:* BA, University of Oxford, England, 1927. *Literary Appointments:* Book Reviewer, The Sunday Times, The English Review, 1931–35. *Major Publications:* Misogyny Over the Weekend, 1931; Dead Mr Nixon, 1931; Robert the Bruce, 1982. *Contributor to:* The English Review; London Mercury; Life & Letters. *Membership:* Fellow, Royal Society of Literature. *Address:* Huish House, Old Basing, Basingstoke, Hants, England.

McNAMARA, Eugene Joseph, b. 18 Mar. 1930, Oak Park, Illinois, USA. Professor, Editor, Poet, Writer. m. Margaret Lindstrom, 19 July 1952, Chicago, Illinois, USA, 4 sons, 1 daughter. *Education:* BA, MA, DePaul University; PhD, Northwestern University, 1964. *Literary Appointments:* Editor, Mainline, 1967–72; Editor, University of Windsor Review, 1965–; Editor, Sesame Press, 1973–80. Professor of English, University of Windsor. *Major Publications:* (Poems:) For the Mean Time, 1965; Outerings, 1970; Dillinger Poems, 1970; Love Scenes, 1971; Passages, 1972; Screens, 1977; Forcing the Field, 1980; Call it a Day, 1984; (short stories): Salt, 1977; Search for Sarah Grace, 1978; Spectral Evidence, 1985. *Contributor to:* Queens Quarterly; Saturday Night; Chicago; Quarry; Denver Quarterly; and others (several hundred poems). *Address:* 166 Randolph Place, Windsor, Ontario, N9B 2T3, Canada.

McNAMEE, Maurice Basil, b. 5 June 1909, Montello, Wisconsin, USA. Professor; Priest. *Education:* AB, 1933, MA, 1934, St L, 1941, PhD, 1945, St Louis University. *Literary Appointments:* Instructor in English, Creighton University High School, 1936–37; English Faculty, St Louis University, 1944; Chairman, English Department, 1956–71; Full Professor of English, 1960; Director of Honors Program, 1950–61; Full Professor of Art History, 1966; Professor Emeritus of English and Art History, 1970; Director, Cupples House and Gallery, 1971; Lecturer in Art in Foreign Workshops five summers. *Publications:* English Literature: Reading for Understanding, 1950; Literary Tynes and Thames, 1960; Honor and the Epic Hero, 1960; Essays in Exposition, 1950; Essays by the Masters, 1956. *Contributions to:* Magazines and journals. *Honours:* The Nancy Ring Outstanding Faculty Award, 1975; The Fleur de Lis Medal, St Louis University's highest award for outstanding services to the University, 1981; Research Grants: Faculty Grant for Study in England, St Louis University, 1955; Ford Foundation Grant, 1965; Fulbright Research Fellowship in Belgium, 1966; Several Research Grants in the Humanities. *Memberships:* Phi Beta Kappa; Modern Language Association; Renaissance Society of American Medieval Academy; College Arts Association; Midwest Society of Art Historians; National Council of Teachers of English. *Address:* Jesuit Hall, 3601 Lindall Boulevard, St Louis, MO 63108, USA.

McNAY, Michael, b. 7 Mar. 1935, Rawalpindi. Journalist. m. (1) Marian Milne, 24 Aug. 1957, Edinburgh, 1 son, 1 daughter; (2) Susan Pilkington, 26 Jan. 1974, 1 daughter. *Publication:* East Malling: Portrait of a Kentish Village, 1978; *Contributions to:* Design; Illustrated London News; The Guardian. *Address:* c/o The Guardian, 119 Farringdon Road, London EC18 3ER, England.

MACNEACAIL, Aonghas, b. 7 June 1942, Uig, Isle of Skye, Scotland. Writer. m. Gerda Stevenson, 21 June 1980, West Linton, Peeblesshire. *Publications:* Poetry Quintet, 1976; Imaginary Wounds, 1980; Sireadh Bradain Sicir/Seeking Wise Salmon, 1983; An Cathadh Mor/The Great Snowbattle, 1984; An Seachnadh/The Avoiding, 1985. *Contributions to:* Gairm, Gaelic: Cencrastus; Words; Acuarius; Cracked Locking Glass; Chapman; Lines Review; Scottish Review; Edinburgh Review; Scotlsman; West Highland Free Press; Akros; Poetry Australia; Pembroke magazine, USA; International Poetry Review, USA; Tijdschrift Voor Poezie, Belgium; Honest Ulsterman, Ireland. *Honours:* Grampian Television Gaelic Poetry Award; Diamond Jubilee Award, Scottish Association for the Speaking of Verse, 1985. *Memberships:* Council member 1974–77, The Poetry Society, London, 1973–77; Council member 1984–, Scottish Poetry Library Association. *Address:* 13 Murieston Crescent, Edinburgh EH11 2LJ, Scotland.

McNEAL, Robert Hatch, b. 8 Feb. 1930, Newark, New Jersey, USA. Professor of History. m. Jacqueline P Frost, 25 Oct. 1952, 3 sons, 1 daughter. *Education:* BA, Yale University; MA, PhD, Columbia University. *Publications:* The Bolshevik Tradition, 1963; Bride of the Revolution. Krupskaya and Lenin, 1972; Tsarand Cossack, 1855–1914, 1985. *Address:* Department of History, University of Massachusetts, Amherst, MA 01003,USA.

MACNEIL, Ian Roderick, b. 20 June 1929, New York City, New York, USA. Law Professor. m. Nancy Carol Wilson, 29 Mar. 1952, Ottawa, Canada, 3 sons (1 deceased), 1 daughter. *Education:* BA, University of Vermont, 1950; LL B, Harvard University, 1955. *Publications:* Bankruptcy Law in East Africa, 1966; Formation of Contracts: Common Core Legal Systems (co-author), 1969; Contracts: Instruments of Social Co-operation – East Africa, 1968; Contracts: Exchange Transactions and Relations 2nd edition, 1978; The New Social Contract – An Inquiry Into Modern Contractual Relations, 1980. *Contributions to:* Southern California Law Review: Nw U L Review; Ethics.*Honours:* Emil Brown Preventive Law Award, 1971; Guggenheim

Fellow, 1978–79; Rosenthal Lecturer, 1979; Honourable mention. Order of Coif Triennial Book Award, 1979–81. *Memberships:* Phi Beta Kappa. *Address:* 3500 N Lake Shore Drive, Chicago, IL 60657, USA.

MACNEIL, Robert Breckenridge Ware, b. 19 Jan. 1931, Montreal, Canada. Broadcast Journalist. m. Donna Powell, 20 Oct. 1984, New York City, USA, 2 sons, 2 daughters from previous marriage. *Education:* BA, Carleton University, Canada, 1955. *Publications:* The People Machine, 1968; The Right Place at the Right Time, 1982; The Story of English (co-author), 1986. *Contributions to:* Harpers; New York Times Magazine; TV Guide; Readers Digest; The Listener; The Nation; New York Times Book Review; Show; Travel and Leisure; Washingtonian; Television Quarterly. *Honours:* Numerous honorary degrees. *Literary Agent:* Bill Adler. *Address:* MacNeil/Lehrer News Hour, 356 West 58th Street, New York, NY 10019, USA.

McNEILL, Anthony, b. 17 Dec. 1941, St Andrew, Jamaica, West Indies. Poet. m. Olive Samuel, 29 Aug. 1970, New York City, 1 son. *Education:* MA, Writing Seminars, Johns Hopkins University, 1971; MA, English, University of Massachusetts, 1976. *Literary Appointments:* Teaching Fellow, Johns Hopkins University, 1970–71; USIS Fellow, International Writing Programme, University of Iowa, 1985. *Publications:* Hello Ungod, 1971; Reel from The Life-Movie, 1975; Credences at The Altar of Cloud, 1979. *Contributions to:* Arts Review; Bim; Bête Noire; Caliban; Canto; Casa de las Americas; Contraband; Cultural Worker; Drum; Focus; Jamaica Journal; Now; Nimrod; Okike; Partisan Review; Poetry Now; Pendulum; Greenfield Review; Iowa Review; Massachusetts Review; Trinidad & Tobago Review, etc. *Honours:* 1st Prize & Silver Medal, Jamaica Festival Literary Competition (poetry), 1966, 1971; Silver Musgrave Medal for Poetry, 1972. *Address:* c/o L Wint, Linstead PO, Jamaica, West Indies.

McNEILL, William Hardy, b. 31 Oct. 1917, Vancouver, British Columbia, Canada. University Professor. m. Elizabeth St John Dukinfield Darbishire, 6 Sep. 1946, Colebrook, Connecticut, USA, 2 sons, 2 daughters. *Education:* PhD, Cornell University, 1947. *Publications:* Author of twenty-two books including: Greek Dilemma: War and Aftermath, 1947; America, Britain and Russia: Co-operation and Conflict 1941–46, 1954; The Rise of the West: A History of the Human Community, 1964; Venice: The Hinge of Europe, 1974; Plagues and Peoples, 1976; The Pursuit of Power, Technology, Armed Force and Society since 1000 AD, 1982. *Contributor to:* Numerous magazines and journals. *Honour:* National Book Award, 1964. *Literary Agent:* Gerald Macauley, Katonah, New York. *Address:* P O Box 45, Colebrook, CT 06021, USA.

McNERNEY, Joan, b. 13 July 1945, New York City, USA. Typographer; Graphic Artist. *Education:* BA, English Literature (externally through Board of Regents), State University of New York, Albany; University of Mexico School for Foreign Students, San Antonio. *Literary Appointments:* Radio Programs (readings, discussions, performances), KPFT Pacific, WBAI Pacific, Houston, Texas; WTBS Massachusetts Institute of Technology, Boston. *Publications:* (Poetry) Crossing the River Rubicon, 1975; Crazy Flowers, 1984; Noah's Daughters, 1984. *Contributions to:* (Poetry) Skydog; Oregon; Studio; Texas; Touchstone; Copula; Washington; Art Scenes; Texas; Look Quick; Passaic Review; High Coo; Texas Artists, Writers, Thinkers in Exile; Modern Haiku; Frologue, etc. *Address:* 1042 Colgate Avenue, Bronx, NY 10472, USA.

McPHAIL, Thomas Lawrence, b. 13 Apr. 1942, Hamilton, Ontario, Canada. Professor of Communications. m. Brenda Mary Downey, 17 Aug. 1985, Ottawa, 3 daughters. *Education:* BA Economics, McMaster University, 1965; MA Communications, State University of New York at Buffalo, 1967; PhD Communications, Purdue University, 1971. *Publications:* Electronic Colonialism; The Future of International Broadcasting and Communication, 1981; Communications in the '80's; Major Issues (with S Hamilton), 1984; Telecom 2000: Canada's Telecommunications Future(with B McPhail), 1985. *Contributions to:* Associate Editor, Canadian Journal of Communications; Contributing Editor, Communication Monographs; Associate Editor, Journal for Advances in Telematics. *Honours:* David A Rose Award, Purdue University, 1969. *Membership:* Banff School of Fine Arts.*Address:* Communications Studies Programme, The University of Calgary, 2500 University Drive NW, Calgary, Alberta T2N 1N4, Canada.

MacPHEE, Rosalind Roberts, b. 29 Jan. 1946, Summerland, British Columbia, Canada. Writer; Ambulance Attendant. m. Peter Leslie MacPhee, 27 June 1970, 2 daughters. *Education:* Diplomas and certificates in Industrial Relations and Advanced Interviewing and Counselling; BFA to be completed, University of British Columbia, Canada. *Publications:* (Poetry): Scarecrow, (Fiddlehead Poetry Books), 1979; Maggie, (Coach House Press), (Fourth Printing), 1979; What Place Is This?, (Coach House Press), 1983; O Lord Won't You Buy Me a Mercedes Benz, (in Progress); Far Countries of the Heart, (In Progress); A Village Like Ours, (In Progress); (radio play): Down North to the Palace Grand. *Honours:* Canada Council Arts Awards 1975, 1977, 1979, 1980, 1981, 1983; numerous literary and magazine awards. *Memberships:* League of Canadian Poets, (Chair of Membership Committee, 1983–85); Family Court and Youth Justice Committees, (annual appointment 1983–); Howe Sound Search & Rescue, (Deputy Leader 1983–). *Address:* PO Box 74, Lions Bay, BC VON 2EO, Canada.

McPHERSON, James Allen, b. 16 Sep. 1943, Savannah, Georgia, USA. Writer; Teacher. 1 daughter. *Education:* BA, Morriss Brown College, Atlanta, Georgia, 1965; LLB, Harvard Law School, Cambridge, Massachusetts, 1968; MFA, University of Iowa, 1971. *Literary Appointments:* University of California at Santa Cruz, 1969–70; Morgan State University, Baltimore, Maryland, 1974–75; University of Virginia, Charlottesville, Virginia, 1976–81; University of Iowa, Iowa City,Iowa, 1981–. *Publications:* Hue and Cry, 1969; Railroad, 1976; Elbow Room, 1977. *Contributions to:* Atlantic Monthly (Contributing Editor); Atlantic; Esquire; New York Times Magazine; New York Times Book Review: Reader's Digest; Chicago Tribune; Playboy; Ploughshares; Iowa Reviews. *Honours:* Atlantic First Award, 1968; Atlantic Grant, 1969; Award in Literature, National Academy of Arts and Letters, 1970; Guggenheim Fellowship, 1973; Pulitzer Prize,1978; McArthur Award, 1981. *Membership:* Authors League. *Literary Agent:* Carl Brandt. *Address:* c/o Carl Brandt, 1501 Broadway, New York, NY 10036, USA.

McPHERSON, James Munro, b. 11 Oct. 1936, Valley City, North Dakota, USA. Professor. m. 28 Dec. 1957, St Peter, Minnesota, 1 daughter. *Education:* BA, Gustavus Adolphus Coleige, 1958; PhD, Johns Hopkins University, 1962. *Appointments:* Instructor, 1962–65; Assistant Professor, 1965–66, Associate Professor, 1966–72, Professor, 1972–82, History, Edwards Professor of American History, 1982–, Princeton University. *Publications:* The Struggle for Equality: Abolitionists and the Negro in the Civil War and Reconstruction,1964; The Negro's Civil War, 1965; The Abolitionist Legacy: From Reconstruction to the NAACF, 1975; Ordeal by Fire: The Civil War and Reconstruction, 1982. *Contributor to:* American Historical Review; Journal of American History; Journal of Southern History; Journal of Social History; Journal of Negro History; Civil War History; etc; Reviews,New York Times Book Review; PeopleMagazine; etc. *Honours:* Anisfield-Wolf Award in Rave Relations for book Struggle for Equality, 1965. *Memberships:* American Historical Association, Programme Committee, 1979–80; Organization of American Historians; Southern Historical Association, Programme Committee, 1967–68. *Address:* 15 Randall Road, Princeton, NJ 08540, USA.

MACPHERSON, Jean Jay, b. 13 June 1931, London, England. *Education:* BA, Carleton University, Ottawa, 1951; MA, PhD, University of Toronto, 1955, 1964. *Publications:* The Boatman, 1957; Four Ages of Man, 1962; Welcoming Disaster, 1975; Poems Twice Told, 1981; The Spirit of Solitude, 1982. *Honour:* Governor-General's Poetry Award, 1957. *Membership:* Association, Canadian University Teachers of English; Canadian Society for Eighteenth-Century Studies; League of Canadian Poets. *Address:* Northrop Frye Hall 315, Victoria College, University of Toronto, Canada M5S 1K7.

McPHERSON, Sandra, b. 2 Aug. 1943, San Jose, California, USA. Writer; Teacher. m. Henry Carlile, 24 July 1966, Seattle, Washington, 1 daughter, (Divorced 4 Nov. 1985). *Education:* BA, English, San Jose State, 1965. *Publications:* Elegies for the Hot Season, 1970, 1982; Radiation, 1973; The Year of Our Birth, 1978; Sensing, 1980; Patron Happiness, 1983; Pheasant Flower, 1985; Responsibility For Blue, 1985; Floralia, 1985. *Contribution to:* (Poetry): American Poetry Review; Field; Grand Street; The Yale Review; The New Republic; and many other publications. *Honours:* Ingram Merrill Foundation Grant, 1972, 84; National Endowment for the Arts Grant, 1974, 80, 85; Guggenheim Foundation Fellowship, 1976; National Book Award Nominee, 1979; Oregon Arts Commission Fellowship, 1984. *Address:* c/o English Department, University of California, Davis, CA 95616, USA.

McQUOWN, Judith Hershkowitz, b. 8 Apr. 1941, New York City, USA. Author. m. Harrison Roth, 1985. *Education:* AB, Hunter College, 1963; New York Institute of Finance. *Publications:* Inc. Yourself: How To Profit By Setting Up Your Own Corporation, 1977, 4th edition 1984; Tax Shelters That Work For Everyone, 1979; The Fashion Survival Manual, 1981; Playing The Takeover Market, 1982; How To Profit After You Inc. Yourself, 1985; Start With $5,000, 1966. *Contributions to:* Boardroom Reports; Bottom Line/Personal; Privileged Information; Fact/Money Management; Financial World; Medica; Pan Am Clipper; Physician's Financial News; Physician's Guide to Money Management. *Membership:* American Society of Journalists and Authors. *Literary Agent:* Ms Robin Rue, Anita Diamant Agency, 310 Madison Avenue, New York, NY 10017. *Address:* 333 East 80th Street, New York, NY 10021, USA.

McRAE, Hamish Malcolm Donald, b. 20 Oct. 1943, Devon, England. Journalist. m. Frances Cairncross, 10 Sep. 1971, London, 2 daughters. *Education:* BA (Hons), Trinity College, Dublin. *Literary Appointments:* Assistant Editor, 1969, Deputy Editor, 1971, The Banker; Editor, Euromoney, 1972; Financial Editor, The Guardian, 1975. *Publications:* Capital City-London as a Financial Centre, with Frances Cairncross, 1973 and 1984; The Second Great Crash, with Frances Cairncross, 1975. *Contributions to:* Various magazines and journals. *Honours:* Harold Wincott Award – Young Financial Journalist of the Year, 1971, Financial Journalist of the Year, 1979. *Address:* c/o The Guardian, 119 Farringdon Road, London EC1, England.

MACSHANE, Frank Sutherland, b. 19 Oct. 1927, Pittsburgh, Pennsylvania, USA. Writer. m. Virginia Lynn Fry, 23 July 1959, Cincinnati, Ohio, USA, 1 son. *Education:* AB, Harvard University, USA; MA, Yale University, USA; DPhil, Oxford University, England. *Publications:* Many Golden Ages, 1962; The Life and Work of Ford Madox Ford, 1965; The Life of Raymond Chandler, 1976; The Life of John O'Hara, 1981; Into Eternity, The Life of James Jones, American Writer, 1985. *Contributions to:* New York Times; New York Times Book Review; The New Republic; The London Magazine; Sunday Times, (London); Magazine Littéraire, (Paris); Art News; New American Review; and others. *Honours:* Fulbright Awards, 1959, 1962, 1978; Guggenheim Fellowship, 1974. *Memberships:* PEN American Centre; Authors Guild; Poets and Writers; The Translation Centre. *Literary Agents:* Aaron M Priest New York, Abner Stein, London. *Address:*

Columbia University, 404 Dodge, New York, NY 10027, USA.

McSHANE, Mark, b. 28 Nov. 1929, Sydney, Australia. Writer. m. Rosemary Armstrong, 15 Oct. 1963, Palma, Majorca, Spain, 2 sons, 1 daughter. *Publications:* Over 40 novels. *Literary Agent:* Collier Associates, 875 Fifth Avenue, New York, USA. *Address:* Can Tumi, La Cabaneta, Majorca, Spain.

MACSWEEN, Roderick Joseph, b. 8 May 1915, Nova Scotia, Canada. Clergyman. *Education:* BA. *Appointments:* Editor, The Antigonish Review. *Publications:* The Forgotton World, (poems), 1971; Double Shadow, (poems), 1973; The Secret City, (poems), 1977; The Burnt Forest, 1975; Furiously Wrinkled, 1976; Called from Darkness, (poems). *Contributions to:* The Antigonish Review. *Address:* St Francis Xavier University, Box 23, Antigonish, Nova Scotia, Canada B26-1C0.

MACVEAN, Jean Elizabeth, b. Bradford, Yorkshire, England. Writer. m. James Bernard Wright, 11 Oct. 1952, 1 son, 1 daughter. *Publications:* Ideas of Love, 1956, The Intermediaries, 1965. *Contributions to:* numerous publications. *Membership:* PEN. *Address:* 21 Peel Street, London W8 7PA, England.

McWHIRTER, George, b. 26 Sep. 1939, Belfast, County Antrim, Northern Ireland. Writer; Translator; University Professor. m. Angela Mairead Cold, 26 Dec. 1963, Belfast, 1 son, 1 daughter. *Education:* BA Honours, Diploma in Education, Queen's University Belfast; MA, University of British Columbia, Canada. *Literary Appointments:* Co-editor in chief 1977, Advisory Editor 1978–, 'Prism' international magazine; Head, Department of Creative Writing, University of British Columbia, Canada, 1982–. *Publications:* Catalan Poems 1971; Bodyworks, 1974; Queen of the Sea, 1976; Twenty-Five, 1978; God's Eye, 1981; Coming To Grips With Lucy, 1982; The Island Man, 1980, Fire Before Dark, 1983; Paula Lake, 1984. *Contributions to:* Poetry Australia; The Irish Universities Review; The Malahat Review; The London Magazine; Saturday Night; The Meanjin Quarterly; Helix; The Honest Ulsterman; Quarry; The Canadian Forum; Prism International; The Beloit Poetry Journal; Epoch; Poetry Review Canada; CBC's Anthology; Books in Canada; Interface; Canadian Literature; The Fiddlehead; Event; Ariel. *Honours:* Macmillan Prize for Poetry, 1969; Commonwealth Poetry Prize, shared with Chinua Achebe, 1972. *Memberships:* League of Canadian Poets; B C Writer's Federation; Writer's Union of Canada. *Address:* 4637 West 13th Avenue, Vancouver B C, V6R 2V6, Canada.

McWHIRTER, Norris Dewar, b. 12 Aug. 1925, London, England. Author; Broadcaster; Publisher. m. Carole Eckert, 28 Dec. 1957, Totteridge, England, 1 son, 1 daughter. *Education:* BA, Economics and Int. Relations, MA, Contract Law, Trinity College, Oxford, England. *Appointments:* Athletics Correspondent, Star, London, Observer, London; Editor, Athletes' World. *Publications:* Get to Your Marks, 1950; Guinness Book of Records, 218 editions published in 26 languages, 1955–86; Guinness Book of Answers, 5 editions, 1967–86; Ross–Story of Stored Life. *Contributions to:* Encyclopaedia Britannica; Yen books; Life magazine; Daily Telegraph. *Honour:* CBE, 1980. *Address:* 33 London Road, Enfield, Middlesex, England.

McWILLIAMS, Margaret, b. 26 May 1929, Osage, Iowa, USA. Professor of Food and Nutrition. 1 son, 1 daughter. *Education:* BS, MS, Iowa State University; PhD, Oregon State University. *Publications:* Food Fundamentals,1966, 4th edition 1985; Nutrition For The Growing Years, 1967, 4th edition 1986; Understanding Food, (with L Kotschevar), 1969; Living Nutrition, (with F Stare), 1973,4th edition 1984; Food for You, (with L Davis), 2nd edition 1976; Illustrated Guide to Food Preparation, 4th edition 1982; Modern Food Preservation, (with H Paine), 1977; Fundamentals of Meal Management, 1978; Experimental Foods Laboratory Manual, 2nd edition 1981; Nutrition for Good Health, (with F Stare), 2nd edition 1982; World of Nutrition, (with H Heller), 1984. *Contributions to:* Journals of American Diatetic Association: Journal of Food Sciences; World Book Encyclopaedia; Arete Encyclopaedia; Salvate Encyclopaedia. *Honours:* Centennial Alumni Award 1971, Professional Achievement Award 1977, Iowa State University; Outstanding Professor 1975, Meritorious Service Award 1985, California State University. *Address:* P O Box 720, Redondo Beach, CA 90277, USA.

MACWORTH, Cecily de Chobannes la Palice, b. Llantillio Pertholey, Gwent, Wales. Writer. m. Marquis de Chobannes la Palice, 1956, London, 1 daughter (by first husband). *Publications:* I Came Out of France, 1942; Francois Villon, A Study, 1947; A Mirror for French Poetry, 1942; The Mouth of the Sword, 1949; Springs Green Shadow (novel), 1953; Guillaume Apollinaire and the Cubist Life, 1961; English Interludes, 1974; Memoirs programmed for 1987. *Contributions to:* Horizon; Life and Letters Today; Poetry Quarterly; Cornhill; Twentieth Century; Cultures for all Peoples (UNESCO); Critique; Les Lettres Mouvelles and several other French publications. *Honour:* Darmstadt Award, 1965. *Memberships:* PEN (French); Association Internationale des Critiques Littersires; Society of Authors (GB). *Address:* 6 Rue des Coutures St Gervais, Paris 75003, France.

MADDEN, David, b. 25 July 1933, Knoxville, Tennessee, USA. Writer. m. 6 Sep. 1956, Knoxville, 1 son. *Education:* BS, University of Tennessee; MA, San Francisco State College; Yale Drama School. *Literary Appointment:* Assistant Editor, Kenyon Review. *Publications:* Cassandia Singing, 1969; Bijou, 1974; The Suicide's Wife, 1977; The New Orleans of Possibilities, stories, 1982. *Contributions to:* Various literary and mass circulation magazines of stories, poems and essays. *Honours:* Fiction Selection, National Council on the Arts, 1971; Rockefeller Grant in Fiction, 1979. *Memberships:* Board, Associated Writing Programmes; Poets, Playwrights, Editors, Essayists and Novelists; Authors Guild. *Literary Agent:* Georges Borchardt. *Address:* 614 Park Boulevard, Baton Rouge, LA 70806, USA.

MADGE, Tim Justin, b. 13 Apr. 1947, England. Writer. m. Nicola Jane Hylton, 28 May 1982, Beaconsfield, 1 son. *Education:* BSc Social Sciences, Politics and International Relations; PhD Political Sociology. *Publications:* Beyond The BBC, 1986; Future of Communication, forthcoming. *Contributions to:* Magazines and journals including: Guardian; Observer; Economist; New Society; New Scientist; Times Higher Education Supplement. *Address:* 3 Barnsbury Terrace, London N1 1JH, England.

MADGETT, Naomi Long, b. 6 July 1923, Norfolk, Virginia, USA. Professor of English. *Education:* BA, Virginia State College, 1945; MEd, English, Wayne State University; PhD, International Institute for Advanced Studies, 1980. m. Leonard P Andrews Sr. *Appointments:* Staff Writer, The Michigan Chronicle; Service Representaive, Michigan Bell Telephone Co; Teacher of English, Northwestern High School, Detroit, Michigan; Lecturer in English, University of Michigan, Ann Arbor; Associate Professor, Professor of English, now Emeritus Professor, Eastern Michigan University; Editor, Lotus Press, 1974–. *Publications include:* Songs to a Phantom Nightingale, 1941; One and the Many, 1956; Star By Star, 1965, 1970; A Student's Guide to Creative Writing, 1980; Pink Ladies in the Afternoon, 1972; Exits and Entrances, 1978; Phantom Nightingale: Juvenilia, 1981. *Contributor to:* Numerous anthologies and journals including: Beyond the Blues, 1962; Afro-Amerikaanse Poezie, 1964; Ik Ben De Nieuwe Negar, 1965; Kaleidoscope, 1967; Ten, 1968; Black Voices, 1968; Black Poetry, 1969; Michigan Signatures, 1969; Black America, Yesterday and Today, 1969; The Harlem Renaissance and Beyond, 1969; Poems to Enjoy, 1970; Soulscript, 1970; Britain America, 1970; The Black Poets, 1971; New Black Voices, 1972; Modern and Contemporary Afro-American Poetry, 1972; Afro-

American Writing, 1972; The Poetry of Black America, 1973; Within You, Without You, 1973; Love Has Many Faces, 1973; American Negro Poetry (revised editon) 1974; The Touch of a Poet, 1975; One Little Room, an Everywhere 1975; The Freelance; Poet; English Journal; Poetry Broadsides; Ebony; Phylon; Nigro Digest; Michigan Challenge; Freedom Ways; Poetry Digest; American Pen; Journal of Black Poetry; Negro History Bulletin; Poetry Newsletter; Blue River Poetry Magazine; Missouri School Journal; Detroit News; Michigan Chronicle; The Nor'wester; Virginia Statesman etc. *Honours:* Poetry Award, National Writers' Club, 1955; Robert Hayden Runagate Award, 1985; Wayne State University Arts Achievement Award (Literature) 1985. *Membership:* Detroit Women Writers. *Address:* 16886 Inverness Ave, Detroit, MI 48221, USA.

MADSEN, Christian, b. 19 Oct. 1927, Uglerup, Holbaek, Denmark. Journalist. *Education:* Agriculture and Journalism. *Contributions to:* Sjaellands Tidende; Slagelse. *Address:* Nansensgade 14, 4200 Slagelse, Denmark.

MADSEN, Truman Grant, b. 13 Dec. 1926, Salt Lake City, Utah, USA. Professor of Philosophy; Author. m. G Ann Nicholls, 16 June 1953, Salt Lake City, 1 son, 2 daughters. *Education:* BS/MS, University of Utah, 1951; MA, 1957, PhD, 1960, Harvard University. *Publications:* Eternal Man, 1966; Four Essays on Love, 1969; Christ and the Inner Life, 1970; The Highest In Us, 1978; Defender of the Faith, 1980. *Contributions to:* Ensign; New Era; BYU Studies. Editor, Religious Studies Center Monograph Series, 3 volumes. *Honours:* F C S Schiller Philosophical Essay Prize, 1952, Mudd Fellowship in Philosophy, 1952–53, University of Southern California; Honors Professor of the Year, 1968, Karl G Maeser Distinguished Teacher, 1967, Mormon History Association Award, 1969, Outstanding Educator Award, 1972, Brigham Young University, Utah; Chairman, Public Programmes Committee, National Endowment for the Humanities, 1973–79; Kennedy International Center Research Fellow, 1985. *Memberships:* Society of Biblical Literature; American Philosophical Association; American Academy of Religion. *Address:* 165 Joseph Smith Building, Brigham Young University, Provo, UT 84602, USA.

MAEMPA, John T, b. 13 Oct. 1950, Cascade, Idaho, USA. Editor of elementary Sunday School curriculum. m. Janice L Figart, 29 Aug. 1970, Garden City, Idaho, 1 son, 1 daughter. *Education:* BA Religion, Northwest Nazarene College; MA Biblical Studies, Assemblies of God Theological Seminary. *Publications:* Foundations for Faith, 1980. *Contributions to:* Pentecostal Evangel; Advance magazine; Sunday School Counselor. *Address:* 914 E Powell, Springfield, MO 65807, USA.

MAGEE, Wes, b. 20 July 1939, Greenock, Scotland. Headteacher; Writer; Broadcaster. m. Janet Elizabeth Parkhouse, 10 August 1967. Plymouth, 1 son, 1 daughter. *Education:* Teaching Certificate, 1967; Advanced Certificate in Education, 1972. *Publications:* Poetry: Urban Gorilla, 1972; No Man's Land, 1978; A Dark Age, 1982; Other: Oliver the Daring Birdman, 1978; The Real Spirit of Christmas, 1979; All the Day Through, 1982; Dragon's Smoke, 1985; A Shooting Star, 1985. *Contributions to:* Journals and publications including poetry and reviews. *Honours:* New Poets Award, 1972; Poetry Book Society Recommendation, 1978. *Membership:* Poetry Society of Great Britain. *Address:* Sunnybank, Low Street, Sancton, Near York, England.

MAGGAL, Moshe Morris, b. 16 March 1908, Hungary. Rabbi, Author, Lecturer, Journalist. m. Rachel Delia Diamond, 8 July 1951, New York, USA, 3 daughters. *Education:* BA, National Rabbinical Seminary, Budapest, Hungary, 1933; Rabbinical Degree, 1934; Postgraduate, University of Zurich, Switzerland, 1935; Hebrew University, Jerusalem, Israel, 1936. *Literary Appointments:* Editor, Iton Meyuhad, Israel, 1940–47; Associate Editor, Heritage Newspaper, Los Angeles, USA, 1958–68; Publisher and Editor, The Voice of Judaism, 1960; Founder and President, National Jewish Information Service, 1960-. *Publications:* Acres of Happiness, 1968; The Secret of Israel's Victories – Past, Present, and Future, 1982. *Contributions to:* numerous newspapers, magazines and periodicals. *Memberships:* Southern Pacific Region of the Zionist Organization of America; Greater Los Angeles Press Club; Town Hall of California; World Affairs Council; International Visitors Programme; United States Congressional Advisory Board. *Address:* 5174 West 8th Street, Los Angeles, CA 90036, USA.

MAGGS, Colin Gordon, b. 1 June 1932, Bath, England. Deputy Headmaster. *Education:* BA. *Publications:* Including Railways to Exmouth, 1980; Taunton to Barnstaple Line, 1980; Hail Centres: Bristol, 1981; Railways of the Cotswolds, 1981; The Bath to Weymouth Line, 1982; Rail Centres, Swindon, 1983; The Camerton Branch, 1985; The Honeybourne Line, 1985; Rail Centres: Exeter, 1985. *Contributions to:* Various publications. *Address:* 8 Old Newbridge Hill, Bath BA1 3LN, Avon, England.

MAGNER, James Jr, b. 16 Mar. 1928, New York City. University Professor. m. Mary Ann Dick (deceased), 13 July 1957, Cleveland, 3 sons, 1 daughter. *Education:* BA, Duquesne University, 1957; MA, 1961, PhD, 1966, University of Pittsburgh. *Publications:* Toiler of the Sea, 1965; Although There Is The Night, 1968; Gethsemane, 1969; John Crowe Ransome: Critical Principles and Preoccupations, 1971; The Dark is Closest to the Noon, 1973; The Women of the Golden Horn, 1976; To Whom You Shall Go, 1978; Till No Light Leaps, The Selected Poems, 1981; Rose of My Flowering Night, 1985. *Contributions to:* The Mickle Street Review; College English; The Christian Century; Hiram Poetry Review; Illinois Quarterly; The Carroll Quarterly; Fine Arts; Free Lance; American Bard; The Back Door; The Jam Today; Blue River Poetry Magazine; Podium; Poet; Spherje; Spirit; Tangent; Bitterroot; The Cleveland Plain Dealer; The Mediterranean Review; The New England Review; The American Weave; Review '74; Review '75 and other journals. *Honours:* George E Granel Memorial Fellowship, 1968 and 1981; Ohio Poet of the Year 1981; Hart Crane Memorial Award 1984; Special Commendation, Ohio House of Representatives for Poetic Achievement. *Address:* English Department, John Carroll University, Cleveland, OH 44118, USA.

MAGNUSSON, Geirlaugur, b. 25 Aug. 1944, Iceland. Teacher. 1 daughter. *Education:* Studies, Slavic Languages, Warsaw, Poland, 1968-70; Literature Studies, University of Provence, France, 1975-80. *Publications:* Annadhooteda, 1974; Beneath the Axe, 1980; On No Occasion, 1981; Little Bits from the Solitaire, 1983; Impletamps, 1985. *Contributor to:* Various literary journals. *Membership:* Icelandic Writers Union. *Address:* Vidigrund 14, 550 Sandailesoluce, Iceland.

MAGNUSSON, Sigurdur A, b. 31 Mar. 1928, Reykjavik, Iceland. Writer. Twice married, twice divorced, 2 sons, 2 daughters. *Education:* University of Iceland; BA, New School for Social Research, New York, 1955. *Appointments:* Literary and Drama Critic, Morgunbladid, 1956-67; Editor in Chief, Samvinnan, 1967-74; Member, International Writing Programe, University of Iowa, 1976, 1977; Member, West Berlin International Artists' Programme, 1979-80; Member, 11 man 1986 Jury, Neustadt International Prize for Literature, Oklahoma. *Publications:* (Poems): Scribbled in Sand, 1958; The Sea & The Rock, 1961; This is Your Life, 1974; In the Light of Next Day, 1978; (Essays): The Emperor's New Clothes, 1959; Sown to the Wind, 1967; In the Limelight, 1982; (Novels): Night Visitors, 1961; Under a Dead Star, 1979; The Meshes of Tomorrow, 1981; Jacob Wrestling, 1983; The Tree of Knowledge, 1985; (short stories): Trivialities, 1965; (play): Visiting, 1962; Travel Books on Greece and India, 1953, 1962; (In Greek), Death of Balder and Other Poems, 1960; (In English), Norther Sphinx – Iceland and the Icelanders from the Settlement to the Present, 1977, 2nd edition 1984; Iceland Country and People, 1978; The Iceland Horse, 1978; The Postwar Poetry of Iceland, 1982; Icelandic Writing Today, 1982; Iceland Crucible – A Modern Artistic Renaissance, 1985. *Contributor to:* Numerous professional journals & magazines. *Honours:* Golden Cross of Phoenix, Greece, 1955; Cultural Council's Prize for Best Play, 1961; Cultural Prize for Best Novel, 1980. *Memberships:* Society of Icelandic Drama Critics, Chairman, 1963-71; Writers Union of Iceland, Chairman, 1971-78. *Address:* Háaleitisbraut 22, 108 Reykjavik, Iceland.

MAGORIAN, James, b. 24 Apr. 1942, Palisade, Nebraska, USA. Writer. *Education:* BS, University of Nebraska, 1965; MS, Illinois State University, 1969; Oxford University, England, 1971; Harvard University, USA, 1973. *Publications:* Almost Noon, 1969; Ambushes and Apologies, 1970; The Garden of Epicurus, 1971; The Last Reel of the Late Movie, 1972; Distances, 1972; The Red, White and Blue Bus, 1975; Bosnia and Herregovina, 1976; Alphabetical Order, 1976; The Ghost of Hamlet's Father, 1977; Safe Passage, 1977; Phases of the Moon, 1978; The Edge of the Forest, 1980; Travel Expenses, 1984; Keeper of Fire, 1984; Weighing The Sun's Light, 1985. *Contributions to:* Abbey; American Mosaic; Ararat; Bardic Echoes; Bits; Bitterroot Journal; The Eye; The Green Fuse; etc. *Address:* 1225 N 46th Street, Lincoln, NE 68503, USA.

MAGOWAN, Robin, b. 4 Sep. 1936, San Francisco, USA. Writer. m. Carol Marcoux, 21 Mar. 1979, 3 sons, 1 daughter. *Education:* BA 1958, Harvard; MA 1961, Columbia; PhD 1964, Yale. *Literary Appointments:* Assistant Professor, University of Washington, 1962-65; Assistant Professor, University of California at Berkeley, 1965-70. *Publications:* Voyages, 1967; Tour de France: the 75th Anniversary Race, 1979; Burning the Knife, 1985. *Memberships:* PEN; Royal Society of Authors. *Literary Agent:* Leslie Gardner. *Address:* 20 Brook Green, London W6, England.

MAHANTI, Prabhat Kumar, b. 5 Nov. 1947, Jharbagda, India. Teacher: Researcher. m. Malina Sinhababu, 27 Jan. 1974, 2 sons. *Education:* BSc, 1968; MSc, IIT Kharagpur, 1971; PhD, IIT, Bombay 1976. *Appointments:* Visiting Professor; IIT Bombay, India, Basrah University, Iraq, Ilorin University, Nigeria, Saskatchewan University, South American University. *Publications:* Book to be published shortly by Pergamon Press, London, England, 11 Scientific and Research papers published in national and international journals of repute. *Memberships:* Life Member, Indian Math. Society; Reviewer for Math Reviews and Xentrablat Fur Mathematik in USA & Germany; American Math. Society. *Honours:* National Scholarship, Government of India, 1969; CSIR, India, 1974; Euratom, Italy, 1975; NSERC, Canada, 1980; Commonwealth Foundation Fellowship, 1983; CNPQ, Brazil, 1985. *Address:* P O Jharbagda District, Purulia, West Bengal, India.

MAHAPATRA, Jayanta, b. 22 Oct. 1928, Cuttack, India. Writer. m. Jyotsna Das, 16 Jan. 1951, 1 son. *Education:* MSc, Physics, Patna University, 1949. *Appointments:* Editor, South & West, 1973; Poetry Editor, Graybook, 1972-73; Editor, Chandrabhaga, 1979; Poetry Editor, The Telegraph Sunday Magazine. *Publications include:* (Poetry) Close the Sky, Ten by Ten, 1971; A Rain of Rites, 1976; The False Start, 1980; Relationship, 1980; Life Signs, 1983; Burden of Waves & Fruit, 1986 etc. *Contributor to:* Boundary 2; Critical Quarterly; Chicago Review; Helix; Hudson Review; Dalhousie Review; Kenyon Review; Kunapipi; Malahat Review; Meanjin Quarterly; New York Quarterly; Poetry, Chicago; Sewanee Review; Queen's Quarterly; Quadrant; Times Literary Supplement; etc. *Honours:* 2nd Prize, International Who's Who of Poetry, London, 1970; Jacob Glatstein Memorial Award, Poetry Chicago, 1975; National Academy of Letters Award, New Delhi, 1981. *Address:* Tinkonia Bagicha, Cuttack 753 001, India.

MAHER, The Reverend Trafford P, b. 17 Apr 1914, Nebraska, USA. Jesuit Priest; University Professor (retired). *Education:* Creighton University 1931-52;

AB, 1935, AM, 1938, Saint Louis University, Saint Louis, Missouri; Ordained Priest 1946; University of Minnesota 1948; PhD, Catholic University of America, Washington, DC, 1952. *Appointments:* Director of Department of Education, 1954–68, Founder and Director, Human Relations Center for Training and Research, 1954–82, St Louis University; First Governor appointed Chairman of First Missouri State Commission on Human Rights, 1957–63; Appointed by President John F Kennedy, Chairman of Advisory Committee to The United States Commission on Civil Rights, 1964; Elected member of St Louis University Board of Trustees and its Executive Committee, 1964–67; President, Missouri Association of Social Welfare 1970–71; Extensive teaching experience in both schools and universities; Conducted Workshops in Human Relations in many countries; Designer and presenter of radio and television programmes in Human Relations. *Publications:* Books: Lest We Build on Sand; Self-A Measureless Sea; Urban Renewal and Social Renovation; Religious Education for a Lunar Age; Editor: Socio-Psychological Concepts and Skills; Editor: Reading Skills and Literature For The Culturally Deprived; Editor: Action Research on the Culturally Deprived; Chapters in: Vows But No Walls, and, The High School of the Future. Contributor of numerous articles on subjects such as Religious Education, Human Relations, Civil Rights etc. *Honours include:* St Louis University Board of Trustees for distinguished service as Board Member; Member, Board of Trustees of Medical Schools of Eastern Virginia; Saint Louis Board of Education for distinguished public service to public schools, etc. *Memberships:* Board Member, American Social Health Association; Board Member, The Saint Louis United Nations Chapter; Board Member, Saint Louis Mental Health Association; President, Missouri Association of Social Welfare; Board Member, Saint Louis Social Health Association, etc. *Address:* Jesuit Hall, 3601 Lindell Boulevard, St Louis, MO 63108, USA.

MÄHLQVIST, K(arl) Stefan, b. 7 Aug. 1943, Nyköping, Sweden. University Teacher. m. Karin Johannisson, 26 July 1967, Paris, France, 2 sons. *Education:* PhD, Literature, University of Uppsala. *Publications:* Inte farligt pappa, Krokodilerna klrar jag, (I'll Take Care of the Crocodiles), 1978; Kom im i min natt, Kom in i min dröm (Come Into My Night, Come Into my Dream), 1981; Drakberget (Dragon's Mountain), 1981; Apan i arken (The Ape in the Ark), 1982; Er hårt paket (A Hard Parcel), 1983; Biggles i Sverige (Biggles in Sweden), 1983; Nattens svarta flagga (Black Flag of Night), 1985. *Contributions to:* Dogens Nyheter, Critic; Swedish television, book promoter. *Honours:* Honour Prize Provinzia di Trento, for Dragons Mountain, 1982. *Memberships:* Board Member, Swedish Union of Authors; Swedish PEN. *Literary Agent:* Raben and Sjogren bokfum]orlag AB. *Address:* Bredmansgatan 4A, S–75224 Uppsala, Sweden.

MAHY, Margaret May, b. 21 Mar. 1936. Writer. 2 daughters. *Education:* BA, University of New Zealand; Diploma, New Zealand Library Association. *Literary Appointments:* Writer-in-Residence, Canterbury University, 1984; Writer-in-Residence, Western Australian College of Advanced Education, 1985. *Publications include:* A Lion in the Meadow, 1969; The First Margaret Mahy Story Book, 1972; The Man Whose Mother Was a Pirate, 1972; The Witch in the Cherry Tree, 1974; The Boy Who Was Followed Home, 1977; Nonstop Nonsense, 1977; Raging Robotsand Unruly Uncles, 1981; The Chewing Gum Rescue and Other Stories, 1982; The Haunting, 1982; The Pirates Mixed Up Voyage, 1983; The Birthday Burglar and a Very Wicked Headmistress, 1984; The Changeover, Jan, 1984. *Honours:* Esther Glenn Medal, 1970, 1972–73, 1984; Carnegie Medal, 1982, 84; Een Zilveren Griffel, 1978. *Address:* No. 1 R.D., Lyttelton, New Zealand.

MAI, Gottfried Erhard Willy, b. 11 May 1940, Finsterwalde, Federal Republic of Germany. Theologian. m. Gunhild Flemming, 1 Sep. 1962, Schönenberg, 2 sons, 2 daughters. *Education:* Navigation Certificate, Nautical School, Bremen; Study of Theology and History at Universities of Bonn, Gottingen, Hamburg and Copenhagen; Dr Theol; Dr Phil. *Literary Appointment:* Freelance writer. *Publications include:* The Protestant Church and the German Emigration to North America (1815–1914), 1972; Die niederdentsche Reformbewegung, 1979; The German Federal Armed Forces 1815–1864, 1977/1982; Geschichte der stadt Finsterwalde, 1979; Der Uberfall des Tigers, 1982; Chronicle of the 4th Minesweeper-Squadron Wilhelmshaven, 1985; Buddha, 1985. *Contributor to:* Hospitium ecclesiae (Society for History) Bremen; Annual Books of Hermannsburg Mission Society; Annual Books of Gustav-Adolf-Werk, Kassel; Readers Digest of World Mission, Erlangen; Annual Book of Lower-Saxonian Church-History, Blomberg; German Soldier-Annual Book, Bonn, etc. *Honour:* International Book Prize for History of AWMM, 1983. *Address:* Harlinger Weg 2, D–2948 Grafschaft, Federal Republic of Germany.

MAIER, Paul Luther, b. 31 May 1930, St Louis, Missouri, USA. University Professor. m. Joan M. Ludtke, 17 June 1967, Kalamazoo, Michigan, 4 daughters. *Education:* Harvard College, 1948–50; BD, Concordia Seminary, St Louis, Missouri, 1955; MA, Harvard University, 1954; PhD, University of Basel, 1957. *Literary Appointments:* Editorial Board, Christian Herald Family Bookshelf; Resource Scholar, Christianity Today Institute. *Publications:* Caspar Schwenckfeld on the Person and Work of Christ, 1959; A Man Spoke, A World Listened – The Story of Walter A Maier, 1963; Pontius Pilate, 1968; First Christmas, 1971; First Easter, 1973; First Christians – Pentecost and the Spread of Christianity, 1976; The Flames of Rome, 1981; Editor: The Best of Walter A Maier, 1980; Associate Editor: Josephus – The Jewish War, 1982. *Contributions to:* Over 200 articles in Faculty Contributions, Western Michigan University, Kalamazoo. *Honours:* Harvard Detur Award, 1950; Fulbright Scholarship, 1955; Alumni Award for Teaching Excellence, Western Michigan University, 1974; Outstanding Educator of America, 1974; Distinguished Faculty Scholar Ward, Western Michigan University, 1981; Professor of the Year Award, Council for Advancement and Support of Education, 1984; Academy Citation for 1985, Michigan Academy of Science, Arts and Letters. *Address:* Department of History, Western Michigan University, Kalamazoo, MI 49008, USA.

MAILLOUX, Steven John, b. 23 Mar. 1950, La Jolla, California, USA. Associate Professor of English. m. Mary Ann Young, 3 Aug. 1975, Northridge, California, 1 son, 1 daughter. *Education:* BA, Loyola University, 1972; MA, 1974, PhD, 1977, University of Southern California. *Literary Appointments:* Assistant Professor of English, Temple University 1977–79; Assistant Professor of English, 1979–81, Associate Professor of English, 1982–, University of Miami. *Publications:* Interpretive Conventions: The Reader in the Study of American Fiction, 1982. *Contributions to:* Style; Studies in the Literary Imagination; MLN; New Literary History; Critical Inquiry. *Honours:* National Endowment for the Humanities Fellowship, 1979–80; Orovitz Summer Award in Arts and Humanities, University of Miami, 1981, 1984; Fellowship to the School of Criticism and Theory, Northwestern University, 1982; National Endowment for the Humanities Summer Fellowship, 1983; Fellowship to the Stanford Humanities Center, 1985–86. *Address:* Department of English, University of Miami, Coral Gables, FL 33124, USA.

MAINPRIZE, Donald Charles, b. 28 Aug. 1930, Coleman, Michigan, USA. Teacher, Writer. m. Doris Olive Humphrey, 27 July 1952, Houghton Lake, Michigan, USA, 2 sons, 2 daughters. *Education:* Pastor's Diploma, Grand Rapids School of the Bible & Music; BA Professional Writing, University of Oklahoma; MA English, Central Michigan University. *Major Publications:* Christian Heroes of Today, How to Enjoy the Christian Life, 1966; Enjoy the Christian Life, 1971; Good Morning, Lord: Meditations for Teachers, 1974; Happy Anniversary (with Doris Mainprize), 1975; ABCs for Educators, 1976, 1985; Stars, Stars, Stars (poems),

Stonesville USA, 1977. *Contributor to:* English Journal; Language Arts; Today's Catholic Teacher; Kansas English Bulletin; Missouri English Bulletin; Pentecostal Evangel; and others. *Honours:* Two 1st prizes, Poetry Society of Michigan, 1972. *Address:* P O Box 117, Houghton Lake Heights, MI 48630, USA.

MAIR, Victor Henry, b. 25 Mar 1943, Canton, Ohio, USA. University Professor. m. 15 Dec. 1970, 1 son. *Education:* BA, Hon, Dartmouth College; BA, Hon, M Phil, University of London; MA, PhD, Harvard University. *Literary Appointments:* Editor and Founder, Tang/New China; Editor and Founder, Jinri Medguo/America Today. *Publications:* Tun-huang Popular Narratives, 1983; Experimental Essays on Chuang-tau, 1983. *Contributions to:* Harvard Journal of Asiatic Studies; T'oung Pao; Journal of the American Oriental Society; Chinese Literature: Essays, Articles, Reviews, etc. *Address:* Oriental Studies, University of Pennsylvania CU, Philadelphia, PA 19104, USA.

MAIRINGER, Hans Dieter, b. 12 Apr. 1943, Linz, Donau, Austria. Teacher. m. Wels, 16 July 1974. *Education:* Masters Degree, Doctorate, Economic & Social Sciences. *Appointments:* Dialect Texts; Standard Speech Satirical Texts; Standard Speech Satirical Poetry; Dramatic Texts; Dialect Translations. *Publications:* Waunn ih so schau, 1976; Herrgott-Meditationen in der Umgangssprache, 1979; Es is a Gfrett, 1979; Demnächet in diesem Theater, 1980; So wie bei Sonnenuhren..., 1980; Wehrgraben, 1981; Onkel Ferdinand, 1982; In Bethlehem im Stall, 1982; Langschläfer Leben länger, 1985. *Contributor to:* rampe, (Weu ma so fad is); Resident Writer, Standard Speech Satires, O O Nachrichten; Resident Article Writer, Muhlviertler Kulturzeitschrift. *Honours:* Public Jury Prize, Literary Competition of Upper Austrian Chamber of Workers, Linz, 1976; Dr Ernst Koref Prize, Short Prose, Linz, 1979; Dialect Prose Prize, Stelzhamerbund, Linz, 1982. *Memberships:* Meeting Club, Linz; International Dialect Institute, Vienna; Hublviertel Artists' Guild; Steizhamerbund, Linz. *Address:* Gusen 253, A-4222 St Georgen, Austria.

MAJOR, Clarence, b. 31 Dec. 1936, Atlanta, Georgia, USA. Novelist. m. Pamela Jane Ritter. *Education:* BS, State University of New York, Albany; PhD, Union Graduate School. *Appointments:* Professor, English & Literature, University of Colorado, Boulder, 1977–. *Publications include:* The Cotton Club, 1972; The Syncopated Cakewalk, 1974; The Dark & Felling, 1974; Reflex & Bone Structure, 1975; Emergency Exit NY : Fiction Collective – Geo Braziller, 1979. My Amputation, 1986; Inside Diameter : The France Poems, 1985. *Contributions to:* American Book Review; numerous other professional journals, magazines and newspapers. *Honours:* Recipient, various grants and awards; Fulbright, 1981–82. *Memberships include:* South West Region Executive Board, Poetry Society of America, 1978–; Fulbright, 1981–82. *Address:* Dept of English, University of Colorado, Boulder, CO 80309, USA.

MALCOLM, Derek Elliston Michael, b. 12 May 1932, London, England. Film Critic. *Education:* BA, History, Merton College, Oxford. *Literary Appointments:* Film Critic, The Guardian, 1971–; Film Critic, Cosmopolitan, 1972–; Director, London International Film Festival, 1984–86. *Publication:* Robert Mitchum, 1984. *Contributions to:* Articles in Sight and Sound (UK); New Republic (USA); New Society (UK). Regular broadcaster for BBC. *Honour:* Critic of the Year Award, International Publishing Company, 1972. *Memberships:* President, Critics Circle UK, 1980; Chairman, Film Section, Critics Circle UK, 1979–82; Chairman, UK Branch of International Critics Association, 1982–. *Literary Agent:* Ann McDermid, Curtis Brown and Co. *Address:* 28 Avenue Road, Highgate, London N6, England.

MALCOMSON, Anthony Peter William, b. 12 Mar. 1945, Belfast. Archivist. *Education:* MA, Cantab, 1966; PhD, Queen's University, Belfast, 1970. *Appointment:* Deputy Director, Public Record Office, Northern Ireland.

Publications: John Foster: The Politics of the Anglo-Irish Ascendancy, 1978; The Pursuit of the Heiress: Aristocratic Marriage in Ireland, 1750–1820, 1982; Absenteeism in 18th Century Ireland, Irish Economic and Social History, volume 1, 1974, and numerous articles and introductions on Irish political history, c 1750–1820. *Address:* Public Record Office of Northern Ireland, 66 Balmoral Avenue, Belfast BT9 6NY, Northern Ireland.

MALEK, James S, b. 11 Aug. 1941, Hampton, Nebraska, USA. Professor of English. *Education:* BA, Earlham College, 1963; MA, 1966, PhD, 1968, University of Chicago. *Publications:* The Arts Compared: An Aspect of 18th Century British Aesthetics, 1974; The Plays of John Home, Editor, 1980. *Contributions to:* Modern Philology; Neuphilologische Mitteilungen; Journal of Aesthetics and Art Criticism; English Language Notes; The New Rambler; Studies in Scottish Literature; Texas Studies in Literature and Language and various others. *Honours:* Woodrow Wilson Fellowship, 1963–64; Fellowships, National Endowment for the Humanities, 1971–72, 1983–84; BA, MA, PhD, with Honours. *Address:* Department of English, DePaul University, 2323 North Seminary, Chicago, IL 60614, USA.

MALERBA, Luigi, b. 11 Nov. 1927, Berceto, Italy. Author; Scriptwriter. m. Anna Lapenna, 1962, 2 sons. *Education:* Liceo Classico Romagnosi di Parma; Faculty of Law, University of Parma. *Literary Appointments:* Editor, 1960–65, Discoteca. *Publications:* La scoperta dell' alfabeto, 1963; Il Serpente, 1966; Salto mortale, 1968; Storie dell'Anno Mille, with Tonino Guerra, 1969–71; Il Protagonista, 1973; Le rose imperiali, 1974; Mozziconi, 1975; Storiette, 1977; Le parole abbandonate, 1977; Pinocchio con gli stivali, 1977; Il pataffio, 1978; C'era und volta la citta di Luni, 1978; La storia e la gloria, 1979; Dopo il prescecane, 1979; Le galline pensierose, 1980; diario di un sognatore, 1981; Storiette Tascabili, 1984; Cima chima, 1985. *Honours include:* Premio Selezione Campiello, for Il Serpente, 1966; Golden Nymph Award, International Television Festival, Monte Carlo, France; Premio Sila, 1969; Prix Medicis, France, 1970. *Address:* Via Tor Millina 31, Rome, Italy.

MALIN, Howard Gerald, b. 2 Dec. 1941, Providence, Rhode Island, USA. Podiatrist; Journalist; Lecturer. *Education:* AB, Biology, University of Rhode Island, 1964; Certificate, Cytotechnology, Our Lady of Fatima Hospital, Institue of Pathology, North Providence, 1965; Certificate d'Etudes, Universite de Poiters, France, 1965; Stage Hospitalier en Cytologie, Universite de Tours, France, 1967; MA, Brigham Young University, 1969; BSc, 1969, MPM, 1972, California College of Podiatric Medicine, San Francisco; Certificate, Podiatric Medicine and Surgery, New York College of Podiatric Medicine, 1974; Certificate, Instructor, Advanced Cardiac Life Support, American Heart Association, & David Grant USAF Medical Centre, 1978; MSc, Pepperdine University, 1978. *Literary Appointments:* Editorial Board, Archives of Podiatric Medicine and Surgery, 1978–81, David Grant USAF Medical Centre (MAC), Travis AFB, 1979–80; Editorial Consultant, Classical Medicine, Current Podiatry, 1984–. *Publications:* An English Translation of Marc-Antoine Muret's Play entitled Julius Caesar, 1969. *Contributor to:* Archives of Podiatric Medicine and Foot Surgery; Sports Medicine; etc. *Honours:* Certificate of Volunteer Service, Miriam Hospital, Providence, 1960; Certificate of Achievement, Region 4, Foreign Language Fair, Brigham Young University, 1968; Veterans Administration Service Award, West Virginia, 1983; Recipient numerous other honours and awards. *Memberships include:* American Chemical Society; American Association for the Advancement of Science; Mediaeval Academy of America; American College of Foot Orthopedics; Association of Military Surgeons of the United States: Phi Delta Kappa. *Address:* Chief, Podiatric Section, c/o Veterans Administration Medical Centre, Martinsburg, WV 25401, USA.

MALIN, Irving, b. 18 Mar. 1934, New York City, USA. University Professor. *Education:* BA, Queens College, 1955; PhD, Stanford University, 1958. *Literary Appointments:* Reviewer for Review of Contemporary Fiction, Hollins Critic; Advisory Editor of Saul Bellow Journal, Twentieth Century Literature, Studies in American Jewish Literature. *Publications include:* William Faulkner: An Interpretation, 1957; New American Gothic, 1962; Jews and Americans, 1965; Saul Bellow's Fiction, 1969; Nathanael West's Novels, 1972; Isaac Bashevis Singer, 1972; Editor; Psychoanalysis and American Fiction, 1965; Saul Bellow and the Critics, 1967; Trumann Capote's In Cold Blood: A Critical Handbook, 1968; Critical Views of Isaac Bashevia, Singer, 1969; Contemporary American-Jewish Literature: Critical Essays, 1973; Co-editor, Breakthrough: A Treasury of Contemporary American-Jewish Literature, 1964; William Styron's Confessions of Nat Turner: A Critical Handbook, 1970; The Achievement of William Styron, 1975; Editor: Conrad Aiken's Prose, 1982. *Contributions to:* Journals including: New Republic; Commonweal; Nation; Virginia Quarterly Review; London Magazine; Kenyon Review. *Honours:* Fellow, Yaddo, 1963; Fellow, National Foundation for Jewish Culture, 1963; Fellow, Huntington Lib. 1978. *Memberships:* PEN; MLA; Authors Guild; Society for the Study of Southern Literature; Phi Beta Kappa; American Studies Association; Poetry Society of America; International Association of University Professors of English; National Book Critics Circle. *Address:* 96-13 68th Avenue, Forest Hills, NY 11375, USA.

MALKIEL, Yakov, b. 22 July 1914, Kiev, Russia. University Professor; Scholar, Widower. *Education:* PhD, Friedrich Wilhelms (Humboldt) University, Berlin, Germany, 1938. *Publications include:* Essays on Linguistic Themes, 1968; From Particular to General Linguistics, 1984. *Contributions to:* Numerous publications including: Times Literary Supplement; Modern Language Review; Medium Aevum; French Studies; Bulletin of Hispanic Studies; etc. *Honours:* Honorary Doctorates: LHD, University of Chicago, 1969; LLD, University of Illinois, 1976; LLD, Université de Paris, France, & Freie Universität, Berlin, Germany, 1983. *Membership:* Modern Language Association. *Address:* 1 Arlington Lane, Berkeley, CA 94707, USA.

MALLET, Marilu Marie Louise, b. 2 Dec. 1945, Santiago, Chile. Writer and Film Director. *Education:* OCIC, School of Films, Santiago, Chile, 1968; Architecture Degree, University of Chile, Santiago, Chile, 1969; MA, University of Montreal, Canada, 1985. *Publications:* Les Compagnons de l'Horlorge Pointeuse, 1981; Voyage to the Extreme, 1985. *Contributions to:* Liberte; Chatelaine; Moeubius; Format Cinema; Possibles; (magazines). *Memberships:* Quebec Union's Writers. *Address:* Montreal, Quebec, Canada.

MALLIK, Umesh Charan, b. 1 March 1916, Havaribagh-Biher, India. Film Producer, Script Writer. *Education:* BA. *Publications:* Treason and Trumpets; The Beggar Empress, (with Terence Young); When the Elephants Stampede, (with Janet Bennett); Kubla Khan; Beethoven – The God and Man, (with Michael Powell); Dabi and Detective, (with Provash Hallik). *Contributions to:* numerous publications. *Honours:* Subol Chand Dey Memorial Award; Gokul Chandra Sil Award. *Membership:* Formerly Writers Guild. *Address:* Royal Overseas League, St James's Street, London SW1A 1LE, England.

MALLIN, Jay, b. 1927, USA. Journalist. *Literary Appointments:* Stringer Correspondent, Time Magazine, New York City, 1956–; Editor, The Met, 1974–; Stringer Corespondent in Cuba during 1950's; City Editor, Havana Herald, Cuba, 1951–53; Correspondent, Miami News, Florida, 1957–63; Research Scientist, Center for Advanced International Studies, University of Miami, Florida, 1967–69; Correspondent, Copley News Service, 1972–74. *Publications:* Fortress Cuba, 1965; Caribbean Crisis, 1965; Terror in Vietnam, 1966; Che Guevera on Revolution, 1969; Strategy for Conquest, 1970; Terror and Urban Guerrillas, 1971; Marc: American Soldiers of Fortune, 1978. *Address:* 406 Savons Avenue, Coral Gable, FL 33146, USA.

MALLINSON, Vernon, b. 16 Feb. 1910, Barnsley, England, University Professor of Comparative Education; *Education:* BA, Honours School of French, 1931, Diploma in Education 1932, MA Honours, School of French 1936, University of Leeds, UK. *Major Publications:* Tendances Nouvelles dans la littérature anglaise contemporaine, Brussels, 1947; Teaching a Modern Language, London 1953; None Can Be Called Deformed, London, 1956, reissued Arno Press, New York, 1980; Introduction to the Study of Comparative Education, London 1957, 4th edition rewritten & revised, 1975; Power & Politics in Belgian Education, London, 1963; Modern Belgian Literature 1830–1960, London, 1966; Belgium, London 1969; The Western European Idea in Education, Oxford, 1980. *Contributions to:* Times Literary Supplement; Times Educational Supplement; Modern Languages; Journal of Education; British Journal of Educational Studies; Revue Générale (Belgium); Comparative Education; Compare; Comparative Education Review (USA). *Honours:* Officier de l'Ordre de Léopold II, Belgium, 1947; Officier de l'Ordre de Léopold, Belgium, 1972; Honorary Degree, Doctor of Civil Laws, University of Kent at Canterbury, 1985. *Memberships:* Past Chairman, Modern Languages Association; Founding member, Comparative Education Society, Europe, past President, British section. *Address:* 23 Palmerston Court, Walmer, Deal, Kent CT14 7JU, England.

MALLIS, Jacqueline Montgomery, b. 1 Nov. 1922, Corning, New York, USA. Publishing. m. Milton M Mallis, 22 Dec. 1950, Tucson, Arizona, 2 sons. *Education:* BA English; MA Education; PhD Gifted Child Education. *Literary Appointments:* Freelance writer, Science Research Associates Inc, Chicago; Senior Editor, Educational Developmental Laboratories Inc, division of McGraw-Hill Book Company, New York; Materials Developer for Education Service Center, Region XIII, Austin, Texas. *Publications:* Reaching for the Stars (a 10-book series): A Minicourse for Education of Gifted Students, (senior author), 1979; Ideas for Teaching Gifted Students, 8 books, (compiler, editor), 1980; Diamonds in the Dust: Discover and Develop Your Child's Gifts, 1982; Pathways to Poetry: Mosaics, 1984. *Contributions to:* the English Journal; Clearing House. *Honour:* BA cum laude, 1945. *Membership:* Phi Delta Kappa. *Address:* Austin, Texas, USA.

MALMSTROM, Vincent Herschel, b. 6 Mar. 1926, Evanston, Illinois, USA. University Professor. m. Ruth Marie Midtskog, 2 daughters. *Education:* AB, Geography, 1947, MA, Geography, 1948, PhD, Geography, 1954, University of Michigan; Advanced graduate work, University of Oslo, 1950–52, University of Texas 1949–50. *Literary Appointments:* Geographer, Army Map Service, Washington DC, 1942; Instructor, Michigan Technological University, 1953–54; Assistant Professor, Bucknell University, lewisburg, Pennsylvania, 1953–56; Instructor, Midlebury College, Middlebury, Vermont, 1956–57; Assistant Professor, University of Minnesota, 1957–58; Assistant Professor, 1958–64, Acting Chairman 1953–60, Associate Professor, 1965–70, Professor 1971–75, Chairman 1974–85, Department of Geography, Middlebury College, Middlebury, Vermont; Professor and Chairman, Department of Geography, Dartmouth College, Hanover, New Hampshire, 1975–. *Publicatiaons:* Life in Europe: Norway with Ruth M Malmstrom, 1955; Life in Europe: Sweden, with Ruth M Malmstrom, 1956; Life in Europe: The Britsh Isles, with Ruth M Malmstrom, 1957; A Regional Geography of Iceland, 1958; Norden: Crossroads of Destiny, 1965; Geography of Europe: A REgional Analysis, 1971; Place: A Computer Manual in Introductory Geography, 1975 etc. *Contributor to:* Scientific articles and book reviews in numerous journals including American-Scandinavian Review; Geographical Review; The Professional Geographer; Journal of Geography; The Vermont Geographer; Journal of the History of Stronomy etc. Author of chapters in many scientific books and presenter of scientific papers to numerous geographical associations. *Honours include:* Second Prize, Association of American Geographers Participation Awards, Stockholm, Sweden, 1960; Awarded travel grant, American Council of Learned Societies to attend XXIII International Geographical Congress, Moscow, USSR, 1976, Awarded Fellowship, Swedish Institute, Stockholm, Sweden, 1979. *Address:* Department of Geography, Dartmouth College, Hanover, New Hampshire 03755, USA.

MALOUF, George Joseph David, b. 20 Mar. 1934, Brisbane, Australia. Writer. *Education:* BA, English, Honours, University of Queensland. *Publications:* Bicycle & Other Poems, 1970; Neighbours in a Thicket, 1974; Johanno, 1975; An Imaginary Life, 1978; Selected Poems, 1981; First Things Last, 1981; Child's Play, 1982; Fly Away Peter, 1982; Harland's Half Acre, 1984; Antipodes, 1985. *Honours:* Gold Medal, Australian Literature Society, 1975, 1983; Grace Leven Prize for Poetry, 1975; James Cook University Award, 1975; NSW Premier's Prize for Fiction, 1981; Age Australian Book of the Year, 1982. *Membership:* Australian Society of Authors. *Literary Agent:* Curtis Brown Pty Ltd, London, Sydney, New York. *Address:* c/o Curtis Brown, P O Box 19, NSW 2021, Australia.

MALPASS, Eric Lawson, b. 14 Nov. 1910, Derby, England. Author. m. Muriel Barnett, Derby, 3 Oct. 1936, 1 son. *Publications:* Beefy Jones, 1957; Mornings at Seven, 1965; At the Height of the Moon, 1967; Fortinbras Has Escaped, 1970; Oh My Darling Daughter, 1970; Sweet Will, 1973; The Cleopatra Boy, 1974; A House of Women, 1975; The Wind Brings Up The Rain, 1978; Summer Awakening, 1978; The Long, Long Dances, 1978; Liebe Blüht Zu Allen Zeiten, 1981; Und Doch Singt die Amsel, 1983; Lampenschein und Sternenlicht, 1985. *Honours:* Palma d'Oro, Italy; Goldene Leinwand, Germany. *Membership:* Society of Authors. *Literary Agent:* Campbell Thomson & McLaughlin Ltd. *Address:* 216 Breedon Street, Long Eaton, Nottingham, England.

MALTMAN, Kim Rendal, b. 23 Aug. 1950, Medicine Hat, Alberta, Canada. Physicist; Poet. *Education:* BSc, 1970, BSc, 1972, MSc, 1973, University of Calgary; PhD, University of Toronto, 1983. *Publications:* The Country of the Mapmakers, 1977; The Sickness of Hats, 1982; Branch Lines, 1982; Softened Violence, 1985; The Transparence of November/Snow, with Rob Borson, 1985. *Contributions to:* Malahat Review; Canadian Literature; Tamarack Review; Prism International; Grain; Dandelion; Quarry; and others. *Honour:* 1st Prize, CBC Literary Competition, Poetry Division, 1984. *Address:* 244 Alvarado Road, Berkeley, CA 94705, USA.

MANAF, Mohammed Zaini (Sir), b. 24 Feb. 1941, Muar, Malaysia. Management Consultant. *Education:* Technical/Polytechnic Colleges, United Kingdom; City of London College; London School of Economics, University of London; State University of New York, USA; Kesington University; PhD, MSc; numerous professional qualifications in engineering & management. *Publications:* Professional Organisations in Malaysia, 1979; The Malaysian Universities, 1980. *Contributor to:* Journal of Royal Aeronautical Society; Journal of the Institute of Traffic Administration (UK); Journal of the Institution of Sales Engineers (UK); etc. *Memberships include:* Institute of Management Consultants, Malaysia (President); Institute of Road Transport Engineers, United Kingdom (Chairman, Malaysia Branch); Association of Business Executives, United Kingdom (Representative in Malaysia); Institute of Engineers, (UK); Representative, Malaysia, Oxford Society; Member, Malaysian Council of LSE Society. *Honours:* Honorary D.Sc, Aeronautical, Pepperdine University; Honorary D. Litt, Clayton University; Honorary LL.D, Pacific Western University; DBA, Pacific Western University; Honorary Admiral, State of Alabama Navy, Created Knight Commander of Merit, Souvreign Order of Saint John of Jerusalem, 1985.

Address: Hampstead Lodge, PO Box 1052 J Semangat, 46860 Petaling Jaya, Malaysia.

MANBY, Frederic, b. 2 Apr. 1946, Skipton-in-Craven, England. Journalist. m. Hilary, 29 Nov. 1974, Skipton, 1 son, 1 daughter. *Education:* NCTJ Diploma, Sheffield. *Literary Appointments:* Craven Herald and Pioneer, Skipton; Yorkshire Post, Leeds, 1969–. *Contributions to:* Craven Herald and Pioneer; Yorkshire Post. *Memberships:* Institute of Journalists. *Address:* c/o The Yorkshire Post, Wellington Street, Leeds 1, Yorkshire, England.

MANCHESTER, William, b. 1 Apr. 192, Attleboro, Massachusetts, USA. Writer. m. 27 Mar. 1948, Ruxton, 1 son, 2 daughters. *Education:* AB, University of Massachusetts, AM, University of Missouri, 1947; LHD, University of Massachusetts, University of New Haven. *Appointments:* Guggenheim Fellow, 1959–60; Fellow Centre for Advanced Studies, 1959–60; Fellow, Wesleyan University East College, 1968–; Member, Wesleyan University Faculty, 1968–; Writer in Residence, 1975–; Adjunct Professor, History, 1979–; Official Historian, Kennedy Assassination, 1963–67. *Publications include:* Disturber of the Peace, 1951; The City of Anger, 1953; Shadow of the Monsoon, 1956; Beard the Lion, 1958; A Rockefeller Family Portrait, 1959; The Long Gainer, 1962; Portrait of a President, 1962; The Death of a President, 1967; The Arms of Krupp, 1968; The Glory & the Dream 1932–72, 1974; Controversy & Other Essays in Journalism, 1976; American Ceasar, 1978; Good-bye Darkmen, 1980; The Last Lion: Winston Spencer Churchill 1874–1932, Volume 1 Visions of Glory, 1983; One Brief Shining Moment: Remembering Kennedy, 1983. *Honours include:* Hammarskjold International Prize, Literature, 1966–67; Overseas Press Club for Best Book on Foreign Affairs, 1969; New York Public Library Literary Lion, 1983; Frederick S. Troy Award, 1980; Abraham Lincoln Literary Award, 1985; Distinguished Public Service Award of the Connecticut Bar Association, 1985, etc. *Memberships:* PEN: Author's Guild; Society of American Historians; etc. *Address:* Alin Library, Wesleyan University, Middletown, CT 06457, USA.

MANDEL, Ernest, b. 5 Apr. 1923, Frankfurt, Germany. Professor, Free University of Brussels. m. Anna Sprimont. *Education:* Licence, Ecole Pratique des Hautes Etudes, Sorbonne, Paris, France; Dr Phil, Free University of Berlin, Germany. *Publications include:* Marxist Economic Theory, 1962; The Formation of the Economic Thought of Karl Marx, 1967; Europe vs. America, 1969; Late Capitalism, 1972; Revolutionary Marxism Today, 1979; Trotsky: A Study in the Dynamics of his Thought, 1979; The Long Waves of Capitalist Development, 1980; Delightful Murder, 1984; Dix Ans de Crise, 1985. *Honours:* Alfred Marshall Lectures, Cambridge University, UK, 1978. *Address:* 127 rue Jos.Impens, 1030 Brussels, Belgium.

MANFRED, Frederick Feikema, b. 6 Jan. 1912, Doon, Iowa, USA. Writer, divorced, 1 son, 2 daughters. *Education:* BA, Calvin College; Honorary Litt D, Augustana College; Honorary DHL, Morningside College and Buena Vista College. *Literary Appointments:* Writer-in-Residence: Macalester College, St Paul, Minnesota, 1949–51; University of South Dakota, 1968–82; Chair for Regional Heritage, Augustana College, Sioux Falls, Dakota, 1984. *Publications:* Author of 25 books including: This Is the Year, 1947; Lord Grizzly, 1954; Conquering Horse, 1959; Wanderlust, Trilogy, 1962; King of Spades, 1966; Milk of Wolves, 1976; The Manly-Hearted Woman, 1976; Green Earth, 1977; Sons of Adam, 1980. *Contributions to:* New Republic; Esquire; Minnesota History. *Honours:* Grant in Aid, American Academy of Arts and Letters, 1945; Honorary Life Membership, Western Literature Association, 1967; Iowa's Most Distinguished Contribution to Literature, 1980. *Memberships:* Authors League; Society of Midland Writers; The Players. *Address:* Roundwind HR3, Luverne, MN 56156, USA.

MANHEIM, Jarol Bruce, b. 17 Apr. 1946, Cleveland, Ohio, USA. Political Science Educator. m. Amy Lowen, 6 Sep. 1969, Needham, 1 daughter. *Education:* BA, Rice University, 1968; MA, 1969, PhD, 1971, Northwestern University. *Appointments:* Associate Editor, Journal of Politics, 1978–79; Advisory Editor, Political Science, Longman Inc, 1979–; Literature Review Editor, 1980–82, Editorial Board, 1980–83, Policy Studies Journal. *Publications:* Annual Editions Readings in American Government, Editor, 1974, 1975, 1976; The Politics Within: A Primer in Political Attitudes and Behavior, 1975, 1982; Deja Vu: American Political Problems in Historical Perspective, 1976; Empirical Political Analysis, with R C Rich, 1981, 1986; American Politics Yearbook, 1982; Datamap: Index of Published Tables of Statistical Data, with A Ondrasik, 1983 & after, (serial). *Contributor to:* Numerous professional journals. *Honours:* Datamap designated an, Outstanding Reference Source of 1984, by American Library Association. *Address:* 709 Circle Drive, NW, Blacksburg, VA 24060, USA.

MANHEIM, Werner, b. 17 Feb. 1915, Poland. Pianist-Musicologist; Professor of Modern Foreign Languages. m. Eliane Housiaux, 18 Aug. 1951, Chicago. *Education:* Bachelor of Education, University of Berlin, Germany; Bachelor of Music, Master of Music, Cincinnati Conservatory of Music; Doctor of Fine Arts, Chicago Musical College. *Publications:* Monograph Martin Buber, 1974; Sonette von der Vergänglichkeit, 1975; Klänge der Nacht, 1977; Im Abendrot versunken, 1983; A Spark of Music, 1983; Wenn das Morgenrot aufbluht, 1985; Many translations and contributions in anthologies. *Contributor to:* Encounter; Poet; Poesie und Prosa; Lyrikmappe; Ocarina; Machrichten aus den Staaten; UNIO; World Poetry, Gauke Jahrbuch: Anthology on World Brotherhood and Peace, etc. *Honours:* Medal studiosis humanitatis, Poetenmunze zum Halben Bogen; Certificate of Merit, Adolf-Bartels-Gedächtais Ehrung. *Memberships:* International Circle of Authors; Please International; Board of German Senryu Center Regensburg Autorenkreis; International Contributing Editor, Ocarina. *Address:* 2906 Hazelwood Avenue, Fort Wayne, IN 46805, USA.

MANLOVE, Colin Nicholas, b. 4 May 1942, Falkirk, Scotland. University Teacher. m. Evelyn Mary Schuftan, 2 Sep. 1967, Richmond-upon-Thames, England, 2 sons. *Education:* MA Honours 1st class; B Litt (Oxon). *Literary Appointments:* Lecturer 1967–84, Reader 1984–, English Literature, University of Edinburgh, Scotland. *Publications:* Modern Fantasy: Five Studies, 1975; Literature and Reality 1600–1800, 1978; The Gap in Shakespeare: The Motif of Division From Richard II to The Tempest, 1981; The Impulse of Fantasy Literature, 1983; Science Fiction: Ten Explorations, 1986. *Contributions to:* Books: The Dictionary of National Biography, 1961–1970, 1981; New Perspectives on Melville, F Pullin, editor, 1978; Nineteenth Century Scottish Fiction, I Campbell, editor, 1979; The Aesthetics of Fantasy Literature and Art, R Schlobin, editor, 1982; Articles in: Studies in Scottish Literature; Essays in Criticism; Mosaic; Studies in English Literature 1500–1900; Journal of Narrative Technique; Mervyn Peake Review; Essays and Studies; Dickens Studies Annual; Durham University Journal; Extrapolation; Kansas Quarterly. *Address:* Department of English Literature, University of Edinburgh, David Hume Tower, George Square, Edinburgh EH8 9JX, Scotland.

MANN, Emily, b. 12 Apr. 1952, Boston, Massachussetts, USA. Playwright; Director (Theatre). m. Gerry Bamman, 12 Aug. 1981, 1 son. *Education:* BA, Harvard-Radcliffe, 1974; MFA, Theater Arts, (Bush Fellow), University of Minnesota, 1976. *Publications:* Still Life (play), anthologized in New Plays USA, also in Coming to Terms, American Plays of the Vietnam War, 1985; Execution of Justice (play) in New Plays USA, 1986. *Contributor to:* American Theater Magazine. *Honours:* OBIE Award (Off-Broadway), Best Play, Still Life, 1981; Fringe First (Edinburgh), Best Play, Still Life, 1984; Co-winner, Great American Play Contest for, Execution, 1983; Guggenheim Fellowship, 1983; NEA

Fellow, 1985; McKnight Fellow, 1985; Rosamond Gilder Award, 1983. *Memberships:* Phi Beta Kappa. *Literary Agent:* George Lane, William Morris Agency Incorporated, New York. *Address:* c/o George Lane, William Morris Agency Incorporated, 1350 Avenue of the Americas, New York, NY 10019, USA.

MANN, Francis Anthony, b. 10 June 1914, Bolton, England. Foreign Correspondent; Journalist; Author. m. Traute Eichwede, 8 Oct. 1937, Berchtesgaden, Germany, 2 daughters. *Education:* BA (Hons), Oxford. *Literary Appointments:* London Staff, Daily Telegraph, 1937. Thereafter Vienna, Berlin; Chief Berlin Correspondent at outbreak of WWII, 1939; Copenhagen; Interned on German invasion of Denmark, 1940; Correspondent, Germany, 1945–; Nuremberg Tribunal; Berlin, Dusseldorf, Bonn; Chief Correspondent for Mediterranean and Middle East, Rome, 1952; Chief European Corespondent, Sunday Telegraph, 1961; Chief Paris Corespondent, Daily Telegraph, 1965–73; Special Correspondent in numerous European and African countries and USA; Retired from Daily Telegraph, 1973. *Publicatons:* Where God Laughed: The Suden Today, 1954; Well Informed Circles, 1961; Zelazny: Portrait Sculpture 1917–70,1970; Tiara (novel), 1973; Comeback: Germany 1945–52, 1980. *Contributions to:* Daily Telegraph; Sunday Telegraph; Sunday Telegraph Magazine; Politiken, Copenhagen and publications in USA, Canada, Italy, Germany, etc. Articles mainly on Foreign affairs. *Honours:* Humboldt Medallist of Germany Academy, Munich; Rustichello de Pisa Prize for International Journalism, Italy. *Membership:* Ex-President, Anglo-American Press Association, Paris. *Literary Agent:* Clarke Conway Gordon, London. *Address:* 58018 Porto Ercole, Prov. Grosseto, Italy.

MANN, Jessica, b. London, England. Writer. m. Charles Thomas, 2 sons, 2 daughters. *Education:* MA, Cambridge University; LLB, Leicester University. *Publications include:* Fiction: A Charitable End, 1971; Mrs Knox's Profession, 1972; The Only Security (USA, Troublecross), 1973; The Sticking Place, 1974; The Eighth Deadly Sin, 1976; The Sting of Death, 1978; Funeral Sites, 1981; No Man's Island, 1983; Grave Goods, 1984. (Also published, USA). Non-fiction: Deadlier Than the Male: An Investigation into Feminine Crime Writing, UK 1981, USA 1982. *Contributions to:* Times Literary Supplement; Observer; Western Morning News; British Book News. Numerous programmes, BBC Radio, BBC & ITV Television. *Address:* Lambessow, St Clement, Cornwall TR1 1TB, England.

MANN, Ralph Emerson, b. 3 June 1943, Freeport, Texas, USA. College History Teacher. m. Nancy Dawson, 30 Aug. 1969, Palo Alto, California, USA, 1 son, 1 daughter. *Education:* BA, Duke University, 1965; AM, Stanford University, 1966; PhD, Stanford University, 1970. *Literary Appointments:* University of California, San Diego; University of Colorado, Boulder. *Major Publication:* After the Gold Rush: Family, Work and Ethnicity in Two Californian Mining Camps, 1982. *Contributor to:* Pacific Historical Review; American Studies; Southern California Quarterly. *Honour:* Phi Beta Kappa, 1965. *Memberships:* Organisation of American Historians; Virginia Historical Society. *Address:* Department of History, Campus Box 234, University of Colorado, Boulder, CO 80309, USA.

MANNE, Henry Girard, b. 10 May 1928, New Orleans, Louisiana, USA. Educator. m. Bobbette L Manne, 19 Aug. 1968, Arlington, Virginia, 1 son, 1 daughter. *Education:* BA, Vanderbilt University, 1950; JD, University of Chicago, 1952; LL M 1963, JSD 1966, Yale University. *Literary Appointments:* Associate Editor, University of Chicago Law Review, 1950–52; Board of Editors, Heritage Foundation, Policy Review, 1977–; Board of Editors, International Review of Law and Economics, 1983–; Economics columnist, Atlanta Journal and Constitution, 1984–. *Publications:* Insider Trading and the Stock Market, 1966; Supplementary Cases and Material For Business Associations II, (editor), 1967; Economic Policy and the Regulation of

Corporate Securities, (editor), 1969; The Modern Corporation and Social Responsibility, (with H C Wallich), 1972; Wall Street in Transition, (with E Solomon), 1974; The Economics of Legal Relationships, (editor), 1975; Gold, Money and the Law, (editor with R L Miller), 1975; Auto Safety Regulation: The Cure or the Problem?, (editor with R L Miller), 1976; Corporate Governance: Past and Future, (editor), 1982. *Contributions to:* Numerous journals and law reviews. *Honours:* Order of the Coif; Award for Excellence, Freedom's Foundation at Valley Forge, 1979. *Membership:* Phi Beta Kappa. *Address:* Emory University, Law and Economics Center, School of Law, Atlanta, GA 30322, USA.

MANNERS, David X, b. 23 Feb. 1912, Zanesville, Ohio, USA. Public Relations Counsel. m. Ruth Ann Bauer, 22 Feb. 1945, New York City, 4 sons. *Education:* BA, University of Cincinnati, 1933. *Literary Appointments:* Editor; Popular Publications, Incorporated, New York City; Editor, Standard Magazine, New York City; Editorial Director, Universal Publishing Company New York City; Editor, Hearst Magazine, New York City; President, David X Manners Company Incorporated. *Publications:* Original story, motion picture, Humphrey Bogart in Conflict, 1943; Novels: Memory of a Scream, 1946; Dead to the World, 1947; Non-fiction: Isn't It a Crime, 1947; Handyman's Handbook, 1958; Complete Book of Home Workshops, 1969; The Great Tool Emporium, 1980 and eight other books. *Contributions to:* Reader's Digest; Science Digest; House Beautiful; Popular Science. *Honours:* Silver Platter Award, Water Quality Association, 1979; Superior Achievement in Press Relations, 1982. *Membership:* The Authors Guild. *Address:* 237 East Rocks Road, Norwalk, CT 06851, USA.

MANNES, Totte Irmeli, b. 15 Mar. 1933, Kajaani, Finland. Painter; Writer. m. Eero Mannes, 26 June 1964, Copenhagen, Denmark, 2 sons. *Publications:* Tummien Laulujen Maa, Documents on Colombia, 1967; Paakallotanssi Meksikossa, Documents on Mexico, 1968; Taiteilijaihminen, stories of 22 Spanish artists, 1974; Ars Gratia Artis, Process of Artistic Creation, 1982. All books self-illustrated. *Contributions to:* Dozens of illustrations and drawings by author from places in which she has lived, Helsinki, Hong Kong, Bogota, Madrid. *Membership:* Circulo de Bellas Artes, Madrid, Spain. *Address:* Moreto 10, 28014 Madrid, Spain.

MANNING, Ambrose Nuel, b. 18 May 1922, Bailey, North Carolina, USA. Professor of English. m. Mary Ella Dailey, 30 June 1948, Deposit, 4 daughters. *Education:* AB, Atlantic Christian College, 1943; MA, University of North Carolina, Chapel Hill, 1947; Ed S, George Peabody College, 1955. *Appointments:* Oak Ridge Military Academy, 1947–48; East Tennessee State University, Johnson City, 1948–83; Professor Emeritus, 1983–. *Publications:* Collection of Folklore by Undergraduate Students of East Tennessee State University, 1966; Folklore: Folksongs, 1967; Folklore: Folksongs, II, 1969; Voices from the Hills: Selected Readings of Southern Appalachian Literature, with Dr R Higgs, 1975. *Contributor to:* Numerous professional journals including: Tennessee Folklore Society Bulletin; Appalachian Journal; Chapters in two books. *Honours:* Distinguished Faculty Award, 1975; Laurel Leaves Award, Appalachian Consortium for outstanding contributions to Appalachian Culture, 1982. *Memberships:* Tennessee Folklore Society, president; Folklore Section, South Atlantic Modern Language Association, Chairman and Secretary; Chairman, Board, Appalachian Consortium. *Address:* 1607 Seward Drive, Johnson City, TN 37601, USA.

MANNING, Paul, b. 22 Nov. 1912, Pasadena, California, USA. Author; Journalist; Commentator CBS News London. m. Louise Margaret Windels, 22 Mar. 1947, Brooklyn, New York, 4 sons. *Education:* Alumnus, Occidental College, Los Angeles. *Publications:* Mr England, Biography of Winston Churchill, 1941; Martin Bormann, Nazi in Exile, 1981; Hirohito, the War Years, 1986; Churchill, The War Years, 1986. *Contributions to:*

Saturday Evening Post; The New York Times; Reader's Digest; Formerly Chief European Correspondent, Scripps-Howard Newspaper Group and Newspaper Enterprise Association. *Honours:* 2 Pulitzer Prize nominations; Special citations, Secretary of War Robert Patterson and Secretary of Navy James Forrestal, for outstanding and conspicuous service as an accredited war correspondent serving with the armed forces overseas; Nomination for Congressional medal, 1947. *Literary Agent:* Ira Blue Esq, PO Box 759, Norwalk, CT. *Address:* PO Box 3129, Jersey City, NJ 07302, USA.

MANNING, Rosemary Joy, b. 9 Dec 1911, England. Writer. *Education:* BA, Hons, Classics, London University, 1933. *Publications include:* Look, Stranger 1960; The Chinese Garden 1962, republished 1984; Man on a Tower 1965; A Time and a Time 1971, to be republished 1985/86; Open the Door 1983. *Membership:* Writers' Guild. *Literary Agent:* Curtis Brown. *Address:* 20 Lyndhurst Gardens, London NW3 5NR, England.

MANSELL, Chris, b. 1 Mar. 1953, Sydney, Australia. Poet. *Education:* BEc, Sydney University; Dip Ed, Sydney Teachers College. *Appointments:* Secretary, Poets Union, Sydney, 1978, Treasurer, 1983–85; Editor, Compass, 1978–; Member, Copyright Council, 1980–84; Writer in Residence, WAIT, 1985. *Publications:* Delta, 1978; Head, Heart & Stone, 1982. *Contributor to:* Aspect; Bulletin; Brave New World; Compass; Image Fling; New Poetry; Poetry Australia; Open Door; Southern Review; etc. *Address:* P O Box 51, Burwood 2134, NSW, Australia.

MANSERGH, (Philip) Nicholas (Seton), b. 1910, Tipperary, Republic of Ireland. Master of St John's College, Cambridge, 1969–79. *Education:* Dublin, Republic of Ireland; Pembroke College, University of Oxford; DPhil, 1936; D Litt (Oxon), 1960; Litt D (Cantab), 1970; Fellow of the British Academy, 1973. *Literary Appointments:* Editor-in-Chief, India Office Records on the Transfer of Power, 1967–72. *Major Publications include:* The Irish Free State: Its Government & Politics, 1934; Britain & Ireland, 1942, 2nd editon 1946; Surver of British Commonwealth Affairs: Volume 1 1931–39, 1952, Volume 2 1939–52, 1958; Documents & Speeches on Commonwealth Affairs 1931–62 (3 volumes), 1953–63; The Multiracial Commonwealth, 1955; South Africa 1906–61, 1962; The Irish Question 1840–1921, 1965, 3rd edition 1975; The Commonwealth Experience, 1969, 2nd edition 1982. *Memberships include:* Editorial Board, Annual Register, 1947–73; Advisory Council on Public Records, 1966–. *Honours include:* OBE, 1945. *Address:* The Lodge, Little Shelford, Cambridge, England.

MANSFIELD, Charles, b. 10 Nov. 1955, Ashbourne, England. Writer; Freelance Journalist. *Education:* Matlock College of Education, 1975–77; Dublin Communications Centre, School of Journalism, 1983. *Literary Appointments:* Staff writer, Computing, 1983; Freelance Series Editor, New Technology Publishers, 1984; Editor, Start Magazine of Literature and the Arts, 1984–. *Publication:* Review of Computer Systems, 1985. *Contributions to:* Non-fiction: Computing; Dec User; Dec Professional (USA); Middle East Computing; Computer Weekly; Tractor Trader; Far Eastern Agriculture; Which Computer?; Short Stories: Start Magazine; Published Short Stories: First Piece, Man and Boy, The Translator, Real Times, 1985. *Honours:* Iris Harvey Scholarship, Swanwick Writers; School for Short Story; Elected to membership without examination, Institute of Scientific and Technical Communicators. *Memberships:* Executive, Society of Authors in London; PEN International; Association British Science Writers; Institute of Journalists; Guild of Agricultural Journalists. *Address:* Editor, Start Magazine of Literature and the Arts, Queen's Chambers, King Street, Nottingham, England.

MANSFIELD, Jayne Diana, b. 22 June 1962, Ashbourne, England. Writer. *Education:* BA (Hons), English and Psychology, Salford University, England,

1983. *Appointments:* Theatre Correspondent for, Start, Magazine of Literature and the Arts, Nottingham, England, 1984. *Publications:* (Co-author) Systems Design, 1985. *Contributions to:* Start; Tractor Trader; Businessman. *Address:* The Waterings Farm, Blore, Ashbourne, Derbyshire, England.

MANUS, Willard, b. 28 Sep. 1930, New York City. Writer. m. Mavis Ross, 9 Oct. 1960, New York City, 1 son, 1 daughter. *Education:* BA, Adelphi College, Garden City, New York. *Publications:* The Fixers, 1957; Mott the Hoople, 1967; The Fighting Men, 1982. *Contributions to:* Sight and Sound, New York Times; Washington Post; Chicago Tribune; Newsday; The Observer (UK); Blackwood's Argosy; The Nation; New Letters; Venture; Financial Post (Canada); Canadian Geographic; Holiday and many others. *Memberships:* Writers Guild of America, West; Los Angeles. Film Critics Association; American Theatre Critics Association. *Literary Agent:* Carole Abel, New York City. *Address:* 248 Lasky Drive, Beverly Hills, CA 90212, USA.

MANWELL, Reginald D(ickinson), b. 24 Dec. 1897, Hartford, Pennsylvania, USA. University Professor. m. Elizabeth Skelding Moore, 6 Aug. 1930, Williamsburg, Massachusetts, USA, 2 sons. *Education:* AB, AM, Amherst College; ScD, Johns Hopkins University. *Publications:* The Church Across the Street, 1946; Practical Malariology (with Russell, West and MacDonald), 1947; Introduction to Protozoology, 1961. *Contributor to:* Some 200 articles mostly in scientific journals. *Honours:* Honorary ScD, Syracuse University, 1963; President, Rocky Mountain Biological Laboratory, Crest Butts, Colorado, 1963–64. *Memberships:* Society of Protozoology; American Society of Parasitologists; American Society of Tropical Medicine and Hygiene; Society of Zoologists; American Microscopical Society; American Society of Naturalists; Marine Biological Laboratory; Sigma Xi. *Address:* 909 4th Street, Liverpool, New York, 13210, USA.

MAPLE, Eric William, b. 22 Jan. 1915, London, England. Author; Broadcaster; Lecturer. m. Dora, 22 Dec. 1951, London. *Publications:* The Dark World of Witches, 1962; The Realm of Ghosts, 1964; The Domain of Devils, 1966; Magic Medicine and Quackery, 1968; Superstition and the Superstitious, 1971; Witchcraft: Man's Quest for Supernatural Power, 1973; Supernatural England, 1977; The Secret Lore of Plants and Flowers, 1980; Old Wives' Tales, 1981. *Contributions to:* Reader's Digest Books, In Britain, British Tourist Authority; Adviser, Man, Myth and Magic. *Address:* 52 Buckingham Road, Wanstead, London E11 2EB, England.

MAPLE, Gordon Extra, b. 6 Aug. 1932, Jersey, Channel Islands. Writer. m. Mabel Atkinson-Frayn, 29 Jan. 1953, Bristol, England, 1 son, 1 daughter. *Publications:* Plays: Limeade, 1963; Dog, 1967; Here's a Funny Thing, 1964; Elephant, 1968; Tortoise, 1974; Singo, 1975; Napoleon Has Feet, 1977; Pink Circle, 1984; Chateau Scholoss, 1985; Popeye, Theatr Hafren, 1985. *Honours:* Evening Standard Awards, 1964, 73; Oscar Nomination for, The Crack, 1964. *Memberships:* BPM, Oxford Yec; Fellow, Royal Society of Letters. *Literary Agents:* Fraser and Dunlop Limited (Scripts). *Address:* The Rectory, Hopesay, Shropshire, England.

MAPP, Alf Johnson, Junior, b. 17 Feb. 1925, Portsmouth, Virginia, USA. Author; Historian; Educator. m. (1) Hartley Lockhart, 3 Mar. 1953, Charlotte, North Carolina, 1 son; (2) Ramona Hartley Hamby, 1 Aug. 1971, Williamsburg, Virginia. *Education:* AB summa cum laude, College of William and Mary, 1961. *Appointments:* Editorial Writer, Portsmouth Star, 1945–46; Associate Editor, 1946–48; Editorial Chief, 1948–54; News Editor, Editorial Writer, Norfolk Virginian-Pilot, 1954–58; Freelance Writer, 1958 to present; Lecturer, Old Dominion University, 1961–62; Instructor, 1962–67; Assistant Professor, 1967–73; Associate Professor, 1973–79; Professor, 1979–81; Eminent Professor (endowed rank), 1981–; Non-fiction Editor, New

Virginia Review, 1982–83. *Publications:* The Virginia Experiment, 1957, 2nd Edition 1974; Frock Coats and Epaulets, 1963, 71, 85; America Creates Its Own Literature, 1965; Just One Man, 1968; The Golden Dragon: Alfred the Great and His Times, 1974, 75, 80; Thomas Jefferson: A Strange Case of Mistaken Identity, 1986; Co-author, Chesapeake Bay in the American Revolution, 1981. Author of Television and Film Scripts. Contributor to magazines and journals. *Memberships:* Virginia Authors Club; Authors Guild; Phi Kappa Phi. *Honours include:* Bicentennial Medal of the US, 1976; Medal Comité Francais, Republic of France, 1976; Cultural Laureate, Commonwealth of Virginia, 1981. *Address:* Willow Oaks, 2901 Tanbark Lane, Portsmouth, VA 23703, USA.

MAR, Elias, b. 22 July 1924, Reykjavik, Iceland. Writer. *Education:* Teachers Seminary; Studied Literature, London, England and Copenhagen, Denmark. *Publications:* Vogguvisa, novel, 1950, (German Publication) 1958; Soleyjarsaga I-II, novel, 1954–59; Speglun, poems, 1977; New Collection of Short Stories 1949–84, 1985. *Contributions to:* Timarit Mals og menningar; Thjodviljinn; Helgafell; Konkret, Germany; Nya Pressen, Finland. *Honours:* Numerous awards for Literary contributions, Iceland State. *Membership:* Past Secretary and other offices, Icelandic Writers Association. *Literary Agent:* Helgafell, Reykjavik. *Address:* Bjargi, Sundlaugav, 37, 105 Reykjavik, Iceland.

MARANGELL, Virginia Johnson, b. 8 July 1924, New Haven, Connecticut, USA. Writer. *Education:* Diploma, Stone College; Certificate, Newspaper Institute of America. *Publications:* Gianna Mia, 1969. *Contributions to:* War Cry; Vista; Home Life; Lutheran Women; Lutheran Standard; Evangelical; Alive; Standard; Lookout; Miraculacous Medal; Live; Young Judaean. *Address:* 165 Farifield Street, c/o PO Box 1132, New Haven, CT 06505, USA.

MARCEAU, Felicien, b. 16 Sep. 1913, Cortenberg, Belgium. Author; Playwright. *Education:* Law Faculty, Louvain University. *Publications:* Plays: L'Oeuf, 1956; La Bonne Soupe, 1958; La Preuve par Quatre, 1964; Madame Princess, 1965; Le Babour, 1968; L'Homme en Question, 1973; A Nous de Jouer, 1979; Novels: Bergère Légère, 1953; Les Elans du Couer, 1955; Creezi, 1969; Le Corps de mon Ennemi, 1975; Appelez-moi Mademoiselle, 1984; La Carriole du Père Juniet, 1985; Essays: Casanova ou l'Anti Don Juan, 1949; Balsac et son Monde, 1955; Le Roman en Liberté, 1977; Memoirs, Les Annés Courtes, 1968. *Honours:* Priz Pelman du Théatre, 1954; Prix Interallie, 1955; Prix Goncourt, 1969; Grand Prix Prince Pierre de Monaco, 1974; Grand Prix du Théatre, 1975. *Memberships:* Academie Francaise, 1975. *Address:* c/o Eds. Gallimard, 5 Rue Sebastien-Bottin, Paris 75007, France.

MARCH, Katherine Burmann, b. 16 Mar. 1910, Torzsa, Hungary (arrived in USA in 1914). Housewife; Poet; Writer. m. Hugo March, 9 July 1949, Murrysville, Pennsylvania, USA, 2 sons (1 deceased). *Literary Appointment:* Correspondent, Mt Holly Herald. *Contributor to:* Grit; Fellowship in Prayer; Jean's Journal; Burlington County Times; New Jersey Poetry Society; Anthologies; Amber; Harbor Lights; Mount Holly Herald; The Messenger; Hoosier Challenger; Quintessence; Bardic Echoes; Dragonfly; Hob-Nob Annual; Four Seasons Poetry Club Magazine; Quickenings; Elmside Echoes; Encore! *Honours:* Brightners Trophy; Life Member, International Belles Lettres Society; Award for a poem from Walt Whitman Poetry Center, Camden, New Jersey. *Memberships:* American Legion Auxiliary; Adventures in Poetry, Chairman, Advisory Board; Poet Laureate, Stella Woodall Poetry Society; United Poet Laureate International, Life Member; Inky Trails; The Academy of American Poets; Friend of Amherst College; National League of American Pen Women; Centro Studi e Scambi International; The Poetry Society of America. *Address:* Acacia-Lumberton Manor, Building 4, Apt. 0, Lumberton, NJ 08048, USA.

MARCHAK, Maureen Patricia, b. 22 June 1936, Lethbridge, Alberta, Canada. Professor of Sociology. m. William Marchak, 31 Dec. 1956, Vancouver, 2 sons. *Education:* BA, 1958; PhD, 1970, University of British Columbia, Vancouver. *Literary Appointments:* Assistant Professor, 1973–75, Associate Professor, 1975–80, Professor, 1980–, University of British Columbia. *Publications:* Ideological Perspectives on Canada, 1975, 2nd Edition 1981; In Whose Interests, on Multinational Corporations in a Canadian Context, 1979; Green Gold: The Forest Industry in British Columbia, 1983. *Contributions to:* Numerous professional journals of sociology, political economy, and popular publications. *Honours:* Research Grants awarded by Social Science and Humanities Research Council of Canada, to study Forest Industry, 1977–78; and Fisheries Industry, 1981–84, (Director of Team Project). *Memberships:* International Sociological Association; Canadian Political Science Association; Network Foundation for Educational Publishing, (founding Member); President, 1979, Canadian Sociology and Anthropology Association; Member, Advisory Board, Association for Canadian Studies; Member, Editorial Boards of Studies in Political Economy; Current Sociology; Pacific Group, Canadian Centre for Policy Alternatives, etc. *Address:* Department of Anthropology and Sociology, University of British Columbia, 6303 Marine Drive, Vancouver, BC V6T 2B2, Canada.

MARCUM, Virginia Shires, b. 21 Aug. 1944, Tennessee, USA. Editor. m. Dudley R Marcum, 12 Apr. 1968 (now div.), 1 son. *Education:* BA, Divisional Humanities, Michigan State University; MA, History & Philosophy of Science, Indiana University. *Literary Appointments:* Houghton & Mifflin Company, Boston, 1966–67; Office of Agricultural Publications, University of Illinois, Urbana, Champaign, 1968–78; American Association for Clinical Chemistry, 1978–. *Honours:* National Merit Scholar, 1962–66; NDEA Title IV Fellowship, 1967–69. *Memberships:* Council of Biology Editors: Society for Scholarly Publishing. *Address:* 1101 Cypress Circle, Winston-Salem, NC 27106, USA.

MARE, William Harold, b. 23 July 1918, Portland, Oregon, USA. Professor of New Testament. m. Clara Elizabeth Potter, 23 Mar. 1945, Wilmington, Delaware, 1 son, 4 daughters. *Education:* BA 1941, MA 1946, Wheaton College, Wheaton, Illinois; BD, Faith Theological Seminary, Wilmington, Delaware, 1945; PhD, University of Pennsylvania, Philadelphia, 1961. *Publications:* I Corinthians, Expositor's Bible Commentary, volume 10, 1976; Mastering New Testament Greek, 1979; The Archaeology of the Jerusalem Area, 1986. *Contributions to:* Westminster Theological Journal; Festschrift; Near East Archaeological Society Bulletin; New International Version Study Bible. *Memberships:* Wheaton College Scholastic Honor Society; Society of Biblical Literature; American Schools of Oriental Research; President, Near East Archaeological Society, 1971–; President 1977–79, Classical Club of St Louis, Missouri; President St Louis Society 1979–80, Archaeological Institute of America. *Address:* Covenant Theological Seminary, 10330 Conway Road, St Louis, MO 63141, USA.

MAREK, Jaroslav, b. 13 Sep. 1940, Prague. Author; Lecturer. *Education:* Master's Degree, Charles University, Prague; University of Bern. *Literary Appointments:* Prose, scripts for films, translations, etc. *Publications:* Plujici andele, letici ryby (Floating Angels, Flying Fishes), short stories, 1974; Osal aneb splynuti (The Monkey or Melting), novel, 1977; Ptaci (Birds), short stories, 1981; Wohltatigkeitsbasar (The Charity Bazaar), short stories, 1981; Co-author: Hunderennen (Dog Race) (with B Safarik, screen play and film, 1983 (Switzerland), Book, 1585 (Canada); Zelene Vino (Green Wine), novel, 1985. *Contributions to:* Neue Zurcher Zeitung, Zurich; Tages Anzeiger, Zurich. *Honours:* Egon Hostovsky's Memory Award, New York, 1975; Literarische Auszeichnung der Stadt Zurich, 1983. *Memberships:* Union of Swiss Writers; PEN Club. *Address:* Buchholzstr 155, 8053 Zürich, Switzerland.

MARGALITH, Pinhas Z, b. 9 July 1926, Vienna, Austria. Microbiologist. m. Ruth Hanaor, 19 Aug. 1954, 1 son, 2 daughters. *Education:* PhD, Hebrew University, Jerusalem, Israel. *Publications:* Flavor Microbiology, 1981. *Contributions to:* Scientific journals. *Address:* 10a Litanis Str, Haifa 34337, Israel.

MARGOLIS, Diane Rothbard, b. 11 Sep. 1933, Newark, New Jersey, USA. Professor of Sociology. m. Richard J Margolis, 3 Apr. 1955, St Paul, Minnesota, 2 sons. *Education:* Cornell University, 1951–54; BA, University of Bridgeport, 1969; MA, 1973, PhD, 1976, New York University. *Publications:* The Managers: Corporate Life in America, 1979. *Contributions to:* Social Problems; Women in Local Politics; Social Problems; Impact, Process and Solution, 1984; Change; Women on Campus; Colliers Year Book; Politics and Society, 1985; Working paper for Wellesley Center for Research on Women, 1984; Paper for Center for the American Woman and Politics, 1981. Reviews: SWS Network; Contemporary Sociology. *Honours include:* University Fellow, New York University, 1972–83; Florence Eagleton Grant, Rutgers University, 1974–75; Bonus Award, University of Connecticut, 1979; National Science Foundation Travel Grant, 1980; Educational Foundation Fellowship, American Association of University Women, 1980; Bunting Fellowship, Radcliffe College, 1980–81; Yale Visiting Faculty Programme, 1982–83; Research Foundation Grant, University of Connecticut, 1983–84, 76; Member, Mellon Seminar on Curriculum, 1984–86, Member, Mellon Seminar, 1983–, Wellesely College; Visiting Scholar, Harvard University, 1983–85. *Address:* University of Connecticut, Scofieldtown Road, Stamford, CT 06903, USA.

MARIANI, Paul (Louis), b. 29 Feb. 1940, New York City, USA. Writer; Teacher. m. Eileen Spinosa, 24 Aug. 1963, New York City, 3 sons. *Education:* BA, 1962, Manhattan College; MA, 1964, Colgate University; Graduate Center, City University of New York, 1968. *Literary Appointments:* John Jay College, 1967–68; Professor of English, University of Massachusetts, Amherst, Massachusetts, 1968–. *Publications:* A Commentary on the Complete Poems of Gerard Manley Hopkins, 1970; William Carlos Williams: A New World Naked, 1981; Timing Devices, 1979; Crossing Cocytus, 1982; A Usable Past: Essays on Modern and Contemporary Poetry, 1984; Prime Mover, 1985. *Contributions to:* TriQuarterly; Tendril; Parnassus; The Massachusetts Review; Contemporary Literature; Hudson Review; Field; Sagetrieb; Boundary 2; New England Review/Bread Loaf Quarterly. *Honours:* National Endowment for the Humanities Fellowship, 1972–73 and 1981–2; National Endowment for the Arts, 1983–84; Guggenheim Fellowship, 1986; Nomination for American Book Award for WcW: A New World Naked. *Memberships:* Modern Languages Association; Poetry Society of America; Associated Writers' Program. *Literary Agent:* John Brokman Associates. *Address:* 24 Main Street, Montague, MA 01351, USA.

MARINO, Carolyn Fitch, b. 17 Apr. 1942, Mebane, North Carolina, USA. Writer; Editor. m. John J. Marino, 23 Nov. 1968, Brulington, North Carolina, 2 daughters. *Education:* BA, History, University of North Carolina; MA, History, George Washington University; Participant in Writers Program, Columbia University. *Literary Appointments:* Reporter: The Reston Times, The Washington Post; Associate Editor, Energy Digest; Editor, Troll Associates (Book Publishers). *Publications:* Yesterday's Bride, 1982; Children's Books to be published in 1986; My Sister Bean; The Magic Wishbone; Gabby Gus; Lions' Lunch. *Contributions to:* Capital Shopper Magazine (Contributing Editor). *Address:* 190 Glen Road, Woodcliff Lake, NJ 07675, USA.

MARITZ, Magdalena Petronella, b. 15 Sep. 1922, Bethal, Transvaal, Republic of South Africa. Housewife. m. D J J Maritz, 28 June 1947, Johannesburg, 1 son. *Education:* Diploma, Medical and Surgical Nursing; Diploma, Midwifery. *Publications include:* 59 publications including: Die Wit Kleed, 1956, 2nd edition 1970; Koraalkop se dogters, 1957; Ryp Graan, 1958, 2nd edition 1959; Velde Vol Vygies, 1958, 2nd edition 1979; Die Helder Vlam, 1960; Suster Nelia, 1967; Blou Vuur, 1971; Carlien Al Vlug Jy, 1972; Vlam in die Namib, 1973, 4th edition 1978; Stemme uit die Fundudzi, 1975; Angsvlug uit Anglola, 1978; Beloftes van Môre (novel and film). *Contributions to:* Various publications. *Honour:* Publishers Award for Youth Book, 1957. *Memberships include:* South African Author's Association. *Address:* 103 Flamingo, c/o Walker and Cellier Street, Mucklenuek, 0002 Pretoria, Republic of South Africa.

MARK, Paul J, b. 11 Oct. 1931, Sur, Grisons, Switzerland. Trustee; Writer. *Education:* Federal Diploma of Accountancy. *Publications:* Randsteine, 1968; Amethyst, 1977; Obsidian, 1981; Ofenrauch, 1983; Flugsand, 1984; Editor, Lysohorsky; Co-Editor, The Pasternak Family. *Contributions to:* Various Literary magazines. *Memberships:* L F International Academy of Poets; Schweiz Schriftsteller-Verein. *Address:* Bucholzstr 119, CH–8053, Zurich, Switzerland.

MARK Jan, b. 22 June 1943, Welwyn, England. Freelance Writer. m. Neil Mark, 1 Mar. 1969, Gravesend, 1 son, 1 daughter. *Education:* National Diploma in Design, Canterbury College of Art, 1965. *Literary Appointment:* Writer Fellow in Children's Literature, Oxford Polytechnic, 1982–84. *Publications:* Thunder and Lightnings, 1976; The Ennead, 1978; Divide and Rule, 1979; Nothing To Be Afraid of, 1980; Aquarius, 1982; Feet and Other Stories, 1973; Handles 1983. *Contributor to:* Various magazines and journals. *Honours:* Penguin/Guardian Award, 1975; Library Association Carnegie Medal 1976; Bank/Observer Award for Teenage Fiction 1982; Angel Award for Fiction 1983; Library Association Carnegie Medal 1983. *Membership:* Society of Authors. *Literary Agent:* Murray Pollinger, 4 Garrick Street, London WC2E 9BH. *Address:* 10 Sydney Street, Ingham, Norfolk NR12 9TQ, England.

MARKANDAYA, Kamala, Writer. m. 1 child. *Publications:* Nectar in a Sieve, 1955; Some Inner Fury, 1956; A Silence of Desire, 1961; Possession, 1964; A Handfull of Rice, 1968; The Coffer Dams, 1969; The Nowhereman, 1973; Two Virgins, 1974; The Golden Honeycomb, 1977; Pleasure City, 1982. *Address:* c/o Barclays Bank, 25 Soho Square, London W1, England.

MARKEL, Geraldine, b. 1 Apr. 1939, Brooklyn, New York, USA. Educational Psychologist. m. 5 July 1958, New York, 2 sons, 1 daughter. *Education:* BA, 1959, MA, 1964, PhD, 1975, University of Michigan; EdS, George Washington University, 1968. *Publications:* The ABC's of the SAT: A Parents Guide to College Entrance Examinations, co-author, 1983; Parents are to be Seen and Heard: Assertiveness in Educational Planning for Handicapped Children, co-author, 1979. *Contributions to:* Personnel Development Series; Teacher Education and Special Education; Career Development for Exceptional Individuals; Academic Therapy. Numerous presentations and workshops. *Literary Agent:* Jane Gelfman, John Farquharson Limited. *Address:* Department of Educational Resources, B322 School of Dentistry, University of Michigan, Ann Arbor, MI 48109, USA.

MARKERT, Joy, b. 8 May 1942, Tuttlingen. Author. *Literary Appointments:* Films: Harlis, 1973; Der Letzte Schrei, 1975; Belcanto, 1977; Das Andere Lacheln, 1978 (with Robert Van Ackeren); Ich Fuhle Was, Was du Nicht Fuhlst, 1982; Theatre: Asyl, 1984; Erich's Tag, 1985; Radio: 30 Radio Plays since 1976. *Publications:* Asyl, 1985; Malta, 1986. *Contributions to:* German, Austrian Radio Stations, and various literary publications. *Honours:* German Film Prize, 1972; 1977, 1980 German Film Awards; 1982, 1984 Berlin Literary Awards. *Membership:* VS German Authors; BAF Berlin Film Makers. *Address:* Bredowstrasse 33, D–1000 Berlin, Federal Republic of Germany.

MARKO, Katherine Dolores, b. 26 Nov. 1913, Allentown, Pennsylvania, USA. Writer. m. Alex Marko,

20 Oct. 1945, Allentown, 2 sons, 1 daughter. *Publications:* Juvenile books: The Sod Turners, 1970; God, When Will I Ever Belong?, 1979; Whales, Giants of the Sea, 1980; How The Wind Blows, 1981; God, Why Did Dad Lose His Job?, 1982; Away To Fundy Bay, 1985. *Contributions to:* Children's Encyclopedia Britannica; Jack and Jill; Highlights for Children; Children's Playmate; Straight; Alive; The Friend; On The Line; Childlife; Christian Science Monitor; Young Catholic Messenger; Wow. *Honours:* Prizes for short stories, 1967; Child Study Association List, 1970; Honorable mention for manuscript at conference, 1973. *Memberships:* Children's Reading Round Table, Chicago; Society of Children's Book Writers, Los Angeles; Off Campus Writer's Workshop, Winnetka. *Address:* 471 Franklin Boulevard, Elgin, IL 60120, USA.

MARKS, John David, b. 21 Feb. 1943, Orange, New Jersey, USA. Executive Director, Search for Common Ground. Divorced, 1 son. *Education:* AB, Cornell University. *Publications:* The CIA and the Cult of Intelligence, (co-author), 1974; The Search for the Manchurian Candidate, 1979. *Contributions to:* New York Times; Washington Post; Rolling Stone; Washington Monthly; Columbia Journalism Review; Saturday Review; Ramparts; Playboy; Los Angeles Times. *Honour:* Best Investigative Book of 1979 Award from Investigative Reporters and Editors Inc, 1980. *Address:* 1851 Mintwood Place, NW, Washington, DC 20009, USA.

MARLATT, Daphne Shirley, b. 11 July 1942, Melbourne, Australia. Writer; Editor. m. G Alan Marlatt, 24 Aug. 1963, Vancouver, 1 son (Dissolved 1972). *Education:* BA English & Creative Writing, University of British Columbia, 1964; MA Comparative Literature, Indiana University, 1968. *Literary Appointments:* English Instructor, Capilano Community College, 1973–76; Various Summer Schools, 1980, 1982. *Major Publications:* Vancouver Poems, 1972; Steveston, 1974, 1984; Zocalo, 1977; What Matters, 1980; Selected Writing: Net Work, 1980; How Hug a Stone, 1983; Touch to my Tongue, 1984. *Contributor to:* Is; Capilano Review; Canadian Forum; B C Monthly; Open Letter; Island; Writing; Periodics; Tessera; HOW(ever); Origin; Co-editor for several of these. *Honours:* McMillan Award; Brissenden Award; Canada Council Arts Grants. *Memberships:* Writers' Union of Canada; West Coast Women & Words. *Address:* c/o Talonbooks, 201-1019 East Cordova Street, Vancouver, British Columbia, V6A 1M8, Canada.

MARLOW, Joyce Mary, b. 27 Dec. 1929, Manchester, England. Writer. m. Patrick Connor, July 1955, Manchester, 2 sons. *Publications:* The Peterloo Massacre, 1969; The Tolpuddle Martyrs, 1971, (paperback reprint 1985); The Uncrowned Queen of Ireland, 1975; Captain Boycott and the Irish, 1973; Life and Times of George I, 1973; Mr and Mrs Gladstone, 1977; Kessie, 1985. *Memberships:* Director, Authors' Lending & Copywright Society; Director, Copywright Licensing Agency; PLR Advisory Committee. *Address:* 109 St Albans Road, Sandridge, St Albans AL4 9LH, Hertfordshire, England.

MARLOWE, Stephen, b. 7 Aug. 1928, Brooklyn, New York, USA. Novelist. m. Ann Humbert, 28 Nov. 1964, New York, 2 daughters. *Education:* AB, College of William and Mary, 1950. *Literary Appointments:* Writer in Residence, College of William and Mary, 1980–81, inaugurated programme, 1974–75. *Publications:* Colossus, 1972; The Man with No Shadow, 1974; Translation, 1976; The Valkyrie Encounter, 1978; 1956, 1982; The Memoirs of Christopher Columbus, pending 1986. *Memberships:* New York Vice President, Mystery Writers of America. *Literary Agent:* Campbell Thomson and McLaughlin. *Address:* El Sol, Punta de la Mona, La Herradura (GR), Spain.

MARMO, Frank C, b. 9 Jan. 1930, Rome, Italy. International Journalist; Editor; Publisher. *Education:* BS, Newark State College, USA, 1952; MA, Seton Hall

University; PhD, Fordham University. *Literary Appointments Include:* Journalist and editor for many publications; Former President, South Florida Publishing Company; Teaching appointments at universites including: Fairleigh Dickinson University, Rutgers University, New York University, University of Mexico, University of Western Ontario, University of Toronto. *Contributions to:* Publications including: Italian Tribune News; Newark Evening News; Newark Stater; Newark Sunday Call; Oklahoma City Journal; Florida on Patrol Magazine; Halifax Reporter; Ottawa Journal; New York Herald Tribune; North Florida Times Journal. *Honours:* Eloy Alfaro Grand Cross, Republic of Panama, 1968. *Address:* Box 1735 North Beach Street, Daytona Beach, FL 32015, USA.

MAROWITZ, Charles, b. 26 Jan. 1934, New York City, USA. Writer. m. Jane Elizabeth Allsop, 14 Dec. 1982, Los Angeles. *Literary Appointment:* Senior Editor, Matzoh Ball Gazette. *Publications:* The Method as Means, 1961; The Marowitz Hamlet, 1966; The Shrew, 1972; Artaud at Rodez, 1975; Confessions of a Counterfeit Critic, 1976; Marowitz Shakespeare, 1980; Act of Being, 1980; Sex Wars, 1983; Sherlock's Last Case, 1984; Prosperous Staff, 1986; Potboilers, Play Collection 1986. *Contributions to:* New York Times; The Guardian; Sun Times; Plays and Players; Encore; New Statesman; Spectator; Village Voice. *Honours:* Order of the Purple Sash, Denmark, 1965; Whitbread Award for Drama, 1967; 1st prize, Louis B Mayer Award, 1984. *Membership:* Dramatists Guild. *Literary Agent:* Gary Salt, c/o Paul Kohner Agency, California. *Address:* 3058 Sequit Drive, Malibu, CA 90265, USA.

MARQUEZ RODRIGUEZ, Alexis, b. 12 Apr. 1931, Venezuela. Professor Universitario, Periodista, Abogado. m. 15 Aug. 1953, 2 sons. *Publications:* Doctrina y proceso de la educacion en Venezuela, 1964; Aquellos mundos tersos–Analisis de la poesia de Alberto Arvelo Torrealba, 1966; La obra narrativa de Alejo Carpentier, 1970; La Comunicacion Impresa–Teoria y practica del lenguaje periodistico, 1976; Lo barroco y lo real maravilloso en la obra de Alejo Carpentier, 1982. *Contributor to:* Colaboraciones publicadas en diario, El Nacional (Caracas); Uno mas uno (Mexico); El dia (Mexico); El Pais (Madrid); magazines Casa de las Americas (La Habana); Plural (Mexico); Lamigal (Caracas). *Honours:* Premio Municipal de Literatura (Caracas), 1975, 1982; Premio Municipal de Literatura, Manuel Diaz Rodriguez (Petare-Venezuela), 1983; Premio Nacional de Periodismo (Venezuela), 1974. *Memberships:* Asociacion de Escritores de Venezuela. *Address:* Apartado postal No 100, Caracas 1010, Venezuela.

MARR, William W, b. 3 Sep. 1936, China. Engineer. m. Jane J Liu, 22 Sep. 1962, Milwaukee, Wisconsin, USA, 2 sons. *Education:* MS, Marquette University, 1963; PhD, University of Wisconsin, 1969. *Literary Appointments:* Editing Adviser, Li Poetry Magazine, 1985; Editor, Modern Poetry in Taiwan, published in Hong Kong, 1986. *Publications:* In the Windy City, 1975; Selected Poems, 1983; White Horse, 1984; Selected Poems of Fei Ma, 1985. *Contributions to:* Li Poetry Magazine; The Epoch Poetry Quarterly; Literary Taiwan; Taiwan Literature; Unitas, Literary magazine; Hong Kong Literature Monthly; Haizia; The Taiwan Poetry Quarterly. *Honours:* Wu Cho Liu Poetry Award, 1982; Li Poetry Translation Award, 1982; Li Poetry Award, 1984. *Memberships:* Li Poetry Society; Society of Taiwan Literature Studies. *Address:* 737 Ridgeview Street, Downers Grove, IL 60516 USA.

MARRIS, Peter Horsey, b. 6 July 1927, London, England. University Professor. *Education:* BA, Cambridge University, 1951. *Publications:* Widows and Their Families, 1958; Family and Social Change in an African City, 1962; The Experience of Higher Education, 1964; Dilemmas of Social Reform, 1967, 2nd edition, 1973, with Martin Rein; African Businessmen, with Anthony Somerset, 1971; Loss and Change, 1974; Community Planning and Conceptions of Change, 1982. *Contributions to:* New Society; Social Policy;

International Journal of Urban and Regional Research; Times Higher Education Supplement; various others. *Honours:* John Simon Guggenheim Fellowship, 1983; German Marshall Fund Fellowship, 1984. *Address:* School of Architectural and Urban Planning, University of California, Los Angeles, CA 90024, USA.

MARSCH, Lucy-Leone, b. 13 Oct. 1912, Alexandria, Minnesota, USA. Writer. *Publications include:* A Thousand Rainbows; Collection of Early Verse; White Wine; Grapes of Thorns; Out of the Darkness; Way of Escape; The Wine Cup; Harps Upon the Willows; I Am the Vine. *Contributor to:* Grit; Ideals; The Farmer; The Moccasin; The American Bard; Anthologies; International Anthology on World Brotherhood & Peace, 1979; Young's Yearbook of Modern Poetry, 1971; Pied Piper Press Anthology; Outstanding Contemporary Poetry, 1972; American Poets' Best, 1962; Poets' Haven Anthologies, 1962, 1965, 1970; etc. *Memberships:* Academy of American Poets; League of Minnesota Poets; Charter Member, Midwest Federation of Chaparral Poets; Honorary Member, Poets' Haven. *Honour:* Golden Poet Award, World of Poetry, 1985. *Address:* Rte 6, Box 93, Jesse Glen Farm, Alexandria, MN 56308, USA.

MARSH, John, b. 5 Oct. 1904, Brighton, Sussex, England. Theologian/University Professor. m. Gladys Walker, 3 Sep. 1934, Cockermouth, Cumbria, England. 2 sons, 1 daughter. *Education:* MA, Hons, Edinburgh University, 1928; Ordination Course, Mansfield College, Oxford, 1928–31; Post Graduate Study, Marburg University, 1931–32; MA, D Phil, Oxford University, 1946; Hon DD, Edinburgh University, 1955. *Publications:* The Living God, 1942; The Fulness of Time, 1952; A Year with the Bible, 1957; Amos and Micah, 1959; St John's Gospel, 1968. Contributed to: Congregationalism Today 1943; A Book of Congregational Worship, 1948; Intercommunion, editor, 1952; Ways of Worship, 1957; Biblical Authority, 1951; Essays of Karl Barth, 1957; Jesus in His Lifetime, 1981; Translations: Bullmann, The History of the Synoptic Tradition, 1963; Straffer, Theology of the New Testament, 1952. *Honour:* CBE, 1964. *Address:* Dale House, High Corton, Cockermouth, Cumbria CA13 9UQ, England.

MARSH, Norman Stayner, b. 26 July 1913, Bath, Avon, England. Barrister. m. Christiane Christinnecke, 8 July 1939, London, 2 sons, 2 daughters. *Education:* MA, BCL, Oxford University; Barrister, Queen's Counsel. *Literary Appointments:* Editor, Journal of the International Commission of Jurists, 1957–58; General editor, 1960–65, Member of Editorial Board, 1965–, International and Comparative Law Quarterly. *Publications:* The Rule of Law in a Free Society, 1960; Interpretation in a National and International Context, 1973; Access to Government-Held Information: A Comparative Study, editor and co-author, forthcoming. *Contributions to:* International Law Quarterly; International and Comparative Law Quarterly; American Journal of Comparative Law; Rabel's Zeitschrift. *Honours:* CBE, 1977; QC, 1967. *Membership:* Executive Committee, Authors Club. *Address:* 13 North Side, Clapham Common, London SW4, England.

MARSH, Susan R, b. 23 Jan. 1914, Jersey Shore, Pennsylvania, USA. Professional Musician; Free Lance Writer. m. Thompson G Marsh, 2 June 1935, Westport, Connecticut, 4 daughters. *Education:* BA, Smith College; Graduate work, University of Denver. *Publications:* All About Maps and Mapmaking, 1963; Teaching About Maps, 6 volumes, 1965. *Contributions to:* New York Times, over 70 articles and 20 photographs; Glamour; Denver Post; American Institute of Architects Journal; Journal of Geography; String Teachers Journal; Nordic World. *Address:* 199 Ash Street, Denver, CO 80220, USA.

MARSHALL, Elizabeth Margaret, b. 24 Aug 1926, Scotland. Writer. m. Reverend John D Marshall, 31 Dec. 1946, Fortrose, 2 sons, 1 daughter. *Education:* Certificate in Social Science, Edinburgh University. *Publications:* The Black Isle: A Portrait of the Past 1972; Lent

Term, 1973; The Seer of Kintail, 1974; Hannah Hereafter, 1976; The Eye of God 1977; The Weeping Tree,
1980; Ravens and Black Rain: The Story of Highland
Second Sight 1985; Edited and introduced: The
Prophecies of the Brahan Seer by Alexander Mackenzie,
1977. *Contributor to:* Scottish papers and magazines
e.g. The Scots Magazine. *Honours:* Constable Trophy –
Scottish Association of Writers for Lent Term 1972;
Scottish Arts Council Book Award for Hannah Hereafter
1976. *Memberships:* Glasgow Writers Club (former Vice
President); Scottish PEN. *Literary Agent:* Murray
Pollinger, 4 Garrick Street, London. *Address:* 17 Mac-
kenzie Terrace, Rosemarkie, Ross-shire IV10 8UH,
Scotland.

MARSHALL, Evelyn, b. 2 Dec. 1897, Pershore,
Worcestershire, England. Author; Broadcaster. m.
Lieutenant Gerald Eric Marshall, 26 June 1917,
Halesowen, 1 son (deceased 1944), 1 daughter. *Literary
Appointments:* Serial and Ghost writer, Amalgamated
Press (now IPC), 1922–1939; Broadcaster, World War
II, Kitchen Front and Overseas Services; Script writer,
Childrens Hour, British Broadcasting Corporation radio,
1946–56. *Publications include:* Shore House Mystery,
1931; Murder Next Door, 1933; Death Visits the Circus,
1947; Death Among the Stars, 1954; On the Trail of the
Albatross, 1950, childrens book; Valley of Silent Sound,
for children 1962; Sand Against the Wind, 1973; The
Family at Castle Trevissa, 1979; Sawdust and Dreams,
1980; Mistress of Tanglewood, 1981; Unbidden Dream,
1981; The Rekindled Flame, 1982; This Foolish Love,
1982; The Divided Heart, 1983; Quest for Love, 1984;
Destiny at Castle Rock, 1985; Pride of Vallou, forthcoming. Numerous books translated into Danish, German
and Dutch. *Contributions to:* Very numerous over the
years most recently serials for Woman's Story Magazine.
Memberships: Society of Authors; Radio Writers Association. *Literary Agent:* Rupert Crew of King's Mews,
London. *Address:* Bewdley, Worcestershire, England.

MARSHALL, Jack, b. 25 Feb. 1937, Brooklyn, New
York, USA. Writer. *Literary Appointments include:* Guest
Lecturer, Modern and Contemporary Poetry, University
of Iowa Writers Workshop; Teacher, Modern Fiction and
Poetry, US International University, San Diego; Teacher,
Poetry Writing, San Francisco State University. *Publica-
tions:* The Darkest Continent, 1967; Bearings, 1970;
Surviving in America, 1971; Floats, long poem, 1972;
Bits of Thirst, 1976; Arriving on the Playing Fields of
Paradise, 1984; Arabian Nights, poems, 1986; Messiah
of Izmir, play. *Contributions to:* Anthologies: Of Poetry
and Power, 1964; Young American Poets, 1968;
Journals: New Yorker; Hudson Review; Harper's;
Kayak; Big Moon. *Honours:* Discovery Award, Young
Mens Christian Association, New York City, New York,
1966; Bay Area Book Reviewers Award for Poetry, for
Arriving on the Playing Fields of Paradise, 1984.
Address: 1056 Treat Avenue, San Francisco, CA 94110,
USA.

MARSHALL, Margaret Wiley, b. 17 Apr. 1908,
Portland, Oregon, USA. Professor of English (Emerita).
Education: BA, Reed College, Portland, Oregon, USA,
1929; MA, 1931; PhD, Harvard-Radcliff, Cambridge,
Massachusetts, 1940. *Publications:* The Subtle Knot:
Creative Scepticism in 17th Century England, 1952;
Creative Sceptics, 1966. *Contributions to:* Hibbert
Journal; Journal of History of Ideas; West Humanities
Review; Journal of Higher Education. Various others.
Honours: Scholarship, Oregon section, American Asso-
ciation of University Women, 1937–38; Fulbright
Scholar, India, 1957–59. *Memberships:* English Renais-
sance Society; Modern Language Association. *Address:*
Fyfield Lodge, Fyfield Road, Oxford OX2 6QE, England.

MARSHALL, Mel, b. 8 Oct. 1911, San Antonio, Texas,
USA. Writer. m. Aldine Thompson, Santa Fe. *Publications:* Author, 72 books. *Contributor to:* 250 magazine
articles. *Membership:* President, Western Writers of
America, 1976–77. *Literary Agent:* Richard Curtis
Associates. *Address:* 1100 Rosemont, Amarillo, TX
79106, USA.

MARSHALL, Muriel Joyce, b. Nara Visa, New
Mexico, USA. Writer; Editor. m. Walter Raymond
Marshall, 1 son, 2 daughters. *Education:* University of
Colorado; University of Denver. *Publications:* Lovely
Rebel; Uncompahgre. *Contributor to:* Woman's Day;
Colliers; Readers Digest; University of New Mexico
Quarterly; University of Texas Quarterly. *Address:* Box
139, Delta, CO 81416, USA.

MARSHALL, Rosalind Kay, b. Dysart, Scotland.
Curator. *Education:* MA, Dip.Ed, PhD, FRSL, FSA Scot,
Edinburgh University, Scotland. *Literary Appointments:*
Associate Editor of The Review of Scottish Culture,
1983–. *Publications:* The Days of Duchess Anne, 1973;
Mary of Guise, 1977; Virgins and Viragos: A History of
Women in Scotland, 1983. *Contributions to:* various
publications on social history. *Honours:* Hume Brown
Senior Prize for PhD Thesis, also Jeremiah Dalziel Prize,
1970; Scottish Arts Council New Writing Award, 1973;
Fellow of the Royal Society of Literature, 1974.
Membership: PEN International, 1980–85. *Address:*
Scottish National Portrait Gallery, Edinburgh, Scotland.

MARSHALL, Tom, b. 9 Apr. 1938, Niagara Falls,
Ontario, Canada. University Professor. *Education:* BA
History 1961, MA English 1965, Queen's University.
Literary Appointments: Editor, Quarry, 1965–66 and
1968–70; Editor, Quarry Press, 1965–76; Poetry Editor,
Canadian Forum, 1973–78. *Publications:* The Psychic
Mariner: A Reading of the Poems of D H Lawrence,
1970; Rosemary Goal, fiction, 1978; Harsh and Lovely
Land: The Major Canadian Poets and the Making of a
CanadianTradition, 1979: The Elements poetry, 1980;
Glass Houses, fiction, 1985. *Contributions to:* Quarry;
Queen's Quarterly; Canadian Forum; Canadian
Literature: Tamarack Review. *Memberships:* League of
Canadian Poets; Chairman of membership committee
1984–85, Writer's Union of Canada. *Address:*
Department of English, Queen's University, Kingston,
Ontario K7L 3N6, Canada.

MARSMAN, Hendrik Jan, b. 14 Jan. 1937. *Publica-
tions include:* 20 novels; Plays; Sterf de Moord; In
Verwachting; Deuren; Nachtrich. *Address:*
Valeriusstraat 104, 1075 GC Amsterdam, Netherlands.

MARSZALEK, John Francis, b. 5 July 1939, Buffalo,
New York, USA. University Professor. m. Jeanne Ann
Kozmer, 16 Oct. 1965, Niles, Michigan, 3 sons.
Education: AB, Canisius College, 1961; AM, PhD,
University of Notre Dame, 1964, 1968. *Appointments:*
Instructor, history, Canisius College, 1967–68; Assistant
Professor, Associate Professor, Gannon University,
1968–73; Associate Professor, Professor, Mississippi
State University, 1973–. *Publications:* Court Martial: A
Black Man in America, 1972; Black Businessman in
White Mississippi, 1977; Diary of Miss Emma Holmes
1861–1866; Black Physician: Bringing Hope in Missis-
sippi, 1985. *Contributor to:* American Heritage; Civil
War Times Illustrated; Georgia Historical Quarterly;
Military Law Review; Negro History Bulletin; etc.
Honours: National Endowment for the Humanities
Grants, 1969, 1984; American Council of Learned
Societies Grant, 1973–74. *Membership:* Organization of
American Historians; Southern Historical Association;
Mississippi Historical Society, Board of Directors.
Address: Department of History, Mississippi State
University, MS 39762, USA.

MARTH, Elmer H, b. 11 Sep. 1927, Jackson, Wisconsin, USA. University Professor. m. Phyllis E Menge, 10
Aug. 1957, Madison, Wisconsin. *Education:* BS, Bacte-
riology, 1950, MS, Bacteriology, 1952, PhD, Bacteri-
ology, 1954, University of Wisconsin – Madison.
Literary Appointments: Editor, Journal of Milk and Food
Technology, 1967–77; Editor, Journal of Food
Protection, 1977–. *Publications:* Low-Temperature
Preservation of Foods and Living Matter, co-author,
1973; Staphylococci and Their Significance in Foods,
co-author, 1976; Editor: Standard Methods For the
Examination of Dairy Products, 14th edition, 1978;
Microbial Survival in the Envrionment: Bacteria and
Rickettsiae Important in Human and Animal Health co-

author, 1984. *Contributions to:* Over 400 scientific research and review papers that have appeared in 35 different scientific journals. *Honours:* Fellow, World Health Organization, 1975; Pfizer Award for Research (American Dairy Science Association), 1975; Educator Award for Research (International Association of Milk and Food Sanitarians), 1977; Nordica Award for Research (American Cultured Dairy Products Institute) 1979; Dairy Research Foundation Award (American Dairy Science Association), 1980; Fellow, Institute of Food Technologists, 1983; Heritorious Service Award (American Public Health Association), 1983; Citation Award for Research (International Association of Milk and Food Sanitarians), 1984. *Membership:* Council of Biology Editors. *Address:* Department of Food Science, University of Wisconsin – Madison, Madison, WI 53706, USA.

MARTIN, Adrian Wolfgang, b. 29 Apr. 1929, St Gallen, Switzerland. Writer and Painter. m. Regina Brunnschweiler, 12 Mar. 1971, Hauptwil Switzerland, 1 son, 1 daughter. *Education:* University of Bern. *Literary Appointment:* As independent writer. *Major Publications:* Apollinische Sonette, 1950; Phoenix (poems), 1955; Requiem für den verlorenen Sohn (novel), 1962; Janus von Neapel (novel), 1966; Gedichte 1957–66 (poems), 1967; Salina (novel), 1977. *Honours:* Cultural Awards, Bern 1953, St Gallen 1962, 1978; Premio Sicillia (Italy), 1980. *Memberships:* Writers Union, Bern; PEN-Club Liechtenstein; Accademia Tiburina Ros (Italy); Universita Popolare Sanfilippese Sicilia. *Address:* Kaufhaus, CH–9213 Hauptwil, Switzerland.

MARTIN, David Alfred, b. 30 June 1929. Writer. m. Bernice, 30 June 1962, Chiswick, London, 3 sons, 1 daughter. *Education:* BSc, 1959; PhD, 1964. *Literary Appointments:* Varied Guest Lectureships at Universities of Birmingham, Durham, Manchester, Exeter, Liverpool and Nottingham. *Publications:* Pacifism, 1965; A Sociology of English Religion, 1967; The Religious and the Secular, 1969; A General Theory of Secularisation, 1978; Dilemmas of Contemporary Religion, 1978; The Breaking of the Image, 1980. *Contributor to:* The Times Higher Education Supplement; The Times Literary Supplement; The Times Education Supplement. *Honour:* President, Conference Internationale de Sociologie des Religions, 1975–83. *Address:* 174, St John's Road, Woking, Surrey, England.

MARTIN, David Victor, b. India. Journalist. m. Mary Katherine Purves, 29 June 1963, Sidcup, 1 son, 1 daughter. *Education:* BSc, Bristol University. *Literary Appointments:* Assistant Editor, British Chemical Engineering: Deputy Editor, Process Engineering; Editor, Tunnels and Tunnelling. *Contributions to:* Technical Journals. *Address:* 30 Faraday Avenue, Sidcup, Kent DA14 4JF, England.

MARTIN, Ernest Walter, b. 31 May 1914, Devon, England. Author. m. Elisabeth Editha Mallandaine, 24 Apr. 1943, Croydon, England. *Education:* Shebbear College, Seale-Hayne College and others. *Major Publications:* In Search of Faith, 1944; A Wanderer in the West Country, 1950; Dartmoor, 1958; The Secret People, 1954; Where London Ends, 1958; The Tyranny of the Majority, 1961; The Book of the Village, 1962; The Book of the Country Town, 1962; The Shearers and the Shorn, 1965; Country Life in England, 1966; Comparative Development in Social Welfare, 1978. *Contributor to:* The Observer; The Listener; Town & Country Planning; History Today; The Times Literary Supplement; Country Life; The Tablet; Journal of Social Policy; Sociological Review; and others. *Honours:* Leverhulme Research Fellowship, 1965–67; Civil List Pension awarded for services to literature and Social History, 1972; Honorary Research Fellow, University of Exeter, England, 1974–83. *Membership:* Fellow, Royal Historical Society. *Address:* Editha Cottage, Black Torrington, Beaworthy, Devon, EX21 5QF, England.

MARTIN, Geoffrey Haward, b. 27 Sep. 1928, Colchester, England. Archivist (Keeper of Public Records). m. 12 Sep. 1953, Oxford, 3 sons, 1 daughter. *Education:* MA, 1950, MA, 1954, Merton College, Oxford; DPhil, 1955; University of Manchester, 1951–52. *Publications:* The Town: A Visual History of Britain, 1961; The Royal Charters of Grantham 1463–1688, 1963; A Bibliography of British and Irish Municipal History, 1 General Works, with S C McIntyre, 1972; The Ipswich Recognizance Rolls, 1294–1327: A Calendar, 1974. *Contributor to:* Archives; Journal of Society of Archivists; Journal of Transport History; English Historical Review. *Honour:* Besterman Medal, Library Association, 1972. *Memberships:* Fellow, Royal Historical Society, Vice President 1985–; FSA. *Address:* Public Record Office, Chancery Lane, London WC2A 1LR, England.

MARTIN, George Thomas Junior, b. 17 Nov. 1931, Norfolk, USA. Freelance Writer; Major USAF (Retired). m. Catherine Jean Myers, 24 Oct. 1977, Jacox, West Virginia, 1 son, 1 daughter. *Education:* BA; MS; PhD, Public Administration; Greenbrier Military School; University of New Mexico; Ohio State University; West Virginia University; West Virginia State College; International University; Armed Forces Technical Training (Communications); DEKTOR Counterintelligence. *Contributor to:* Aviation and communications trade journals; various technical and religious newsletters, contract commercial publications; Editor, The Discriminator. *Memberhips:* MENSA, Editor, Mensanear, Local Secretary, West Virginia; Intertel, Associate Editor, Integra. *Address:* 301A Rosemont Avenue, 2 Charleston, WV 25303, USA.

MARTIN, George Whitney, b. 25 Jan. 1926, New York City. *Education:* BA 1948, Harvard College; LLB 1953, University of Virginia Law School. *Publications:* The Opera Companion: A Guide for the Casual Operagoer, New York, 1961, London, 1962, 3rd Edition US 1982; The Battle of the Frogs and the Mice: An Homeric Fable, 1962; Verdi, His Music, Life and Times, New York, 1965, London 1965, 3rd Edition US 1983; The Red Shirt and the Cross of Savoy: The Story of Italy's Risorgimento, 1748–1871, New York 1969, London 1970; Causes and Conflicts, the Centennial History of the Association of the Bar of the City of New York, 1870–1970, 1970; Madam Secretary, Frances Perkins, 1976; The Companion to Twentieth Century Opera, New York 1979, London 1980, 2nd Edition US 1984; The Damrosch Dynasty, America's First Family of Music, 1983. *Contributions to:* Various musical publications. *Address:* 333 East 68th Street, New York City, NY 10021, USA.

MARTIN, Gerald, b. 28 Sep. 1916, St Leonard, Canada. Chemist; Writer. m. Claire Daoust, 28 Oct. 1961, 1 daughter from 1st marriage. *Education:* BL; BSc, PhD, Chemistry. *Appointments:* Chemist; Writer. *Publications:* Genealogie ascendante et descendante de Omer Daoust, 1983; Ou Va Le Monde?, 1980; Martin, Qui Es-Tu, 1981; Editor, La Societe Genealogique Des Martin. *Contributor to:* The Gloucester Northern Light; La Presqu'Ile; L'Echo; L'Etoile; Le Brayon; La Sentinelle. *Honours:* Percy W Foy Award for book, Martin, Qui Es-Tu?, Societe Genealogique Canadienne-Francaise, 1981; Chevalier de l'Ordre de la Republique, Edmundston. *Membership:* La Societe Genealogique des Martin, President. *Address:* 70 des Ormeaux, Ville Ile Perrot, Quebec J7V 7T3, Canada.

MARTIN, Graham Dunstan, b. 21 Oct. 1932, Leeds, England. University Lecturer. m. Anne M Crombie, 14 June, 1969, Edinburgh, Scotland, 2 sons. *Education:* BA, Oxford, 1954; BLitt, Oxford, 1965; Graduate Certificate of Education, Manchester, 1955. *Publications:* Language, Truth and Poetry, 1975; Giftwish, 1980; Catchfire, 1981; The Architecture of Experience, 1981; The Soul Master, 1984; Time-Slip, 1986. *Contributions to:* Lines; London Magazine; Modern Language Review; French Studios; Forum; British Journal of Aesthetics; Philosophy; Poetics Today. *Membership:* Society of Authors. *Address:* French Department, University of Edinburgh, 4 Buccleuch Place, Edinburgh EH8 9LW, Scotland.

MARTIN, Gunther Heinrich Maximilian, b. 12 Dec. 1928, Rodaun, Austria. Writer; Translator. *Education:* Diploma, Special School of Photography, Vienna, 1951. *Literary Appointments:* Journalist, Press Officer, Phillips Austria, 1959–61; Freelance in press and radio, 1961–. *Publications:* Das Silberne Vlies; Schnapsbrevier; Zu Gast in Wien; Das ist Osterreichs Militarmusik; Wien, Gestichter einer Stadt; Als, Victorianer in Wien; Numerous books translations English-German. *Contributions to:* Austrian, German and Swiss newspapers, magazines and anthologies; various adaptations and editorships. *Honours:* Medal of Merit for Conservation of Cultural Monuments, Republic of Austria, 1975; Title of Professor, Federal President conferred, 1984; Golden Cross of Merit, Lower Austria Region, 1985. *Membership:* British Council, Vienna. *Address:* Altmannsdorfer Strasse 164/12//17, A–1232 Vienna, Austria.

MARTIN, Jean-Georges, b. 3 Mar. 1902, Morges, Switzerland. Newspaper Journalist; Writer. m. Adrienne Rod, 20 Feb. 1932, 2 sons, 1 daughter. *Education:* Licence degree in Arts, University of Lausanne, Switzerland. *Literary Appointments:* Freelance Journalist; Editor in Chief, Pour Tous, 1945–53, l'Illustre, 1953–59. *Publications:* Contes du Leman, 1932; Histoire du Sport Suisse, 1945; La Roue, poems, 1975; Nu, poems, 1976; Les Uns Pas Comme Les Autres, poems, 1980; Le bal des Jours Perdus, poems, 1985. *Contributions to:* L'Illustration, Paris, France, 1928–39; Gazette de Lausanne; Tribune de Geneve; Neue Zurcher Zeitung; L'Illustre. *Honours:* Honorary Member: Paderewski Society; Polono-Swiss Society, Lausanne. *Memberships:* Vaud Society of Writers; Society of Swiss Writers, Greco-Swiss Friendship. *Address:* 56 Chemin de la Rosière, 1012 Lausanne, Switzerland.

MARTIN, Joseph Hirsch, b. 12 Aug. 1953, Norwalk, Connecticut, USA. Writer. *Education:* Comparative Literature, University of Bergen, Norway, 1978; BA, American Literature, George Washington University, Washington DC, USA; MFA, Creative Writing, University of British Columbia, Canada. *Appointments:* Drama and Translations Editor, PRISM International, Vancouver, Canada, 1983–85; Dramaturg, Open Theatre Company, Vancouver, 1983–85. *Publications:* (Plays): Unconditional Surrender; Platform or The Behemoth; The Dust Conspiracy; Passion Play; The Dealers of San Juan. *Contributions to:* PRISM International; Woordloom; Antigonish Review; San Fernando Poetry Journal; Greenfield Review; Vancouver Sun; Radical America; West Coast Review; GW Forum. *Honours:* Washington DC Consortium Poetry Prize, 1978; Alice Goddard Prize in American Literature, 1979; University Graduate Fellowships for work in Comparative Literature, UBC, 1981–85; Grant Redford Memorial Prize in Playwriting, 1981; American Scandanavian Foundation Fellowship for work in Comparative Drama, 1985–86; Source Theatre Literary Prize, Washington DC, 1985. *Memberships:* Playwrights Union of Canada; The New Play Centre. *Literary Agent:* Joy Westendarp, International Copyright Bureau. *Address:* 2060 Trafalgar Street, Vancouver BC, V6K 3S6, Canada.

MARTIN, Marjorie, b. 18 July 1942, Brooklyn, New York, USA. Freelance writer. *Education:* 2-year Certificate, Newspaper Institute of America; 2-year Certificate, Christian Writers Institute. *Literary Appointments:* Poetry Editor, Coney Island Times, Williamsburg News, Town & Country Newspaper, 1960–80. *Publications:* A Friend Asked Me, 1963; The Span of Dreams, 1970. *Contributions to:* Numerous periodicals including Globe; Coney Island Times; Williamsburg News; The Village; The Post; Daily News; Modern Maturity; Empire State Beacon; Christian Women; Grit; The Entertainer. *Honour:* New York State Freedom Award, 1982. *Memberships:* Vice President, Brooklyn Poetry Club, 1975; Composers, Authors & Artists Association; New York Poetry Forum; Christian Writers Club. *Address:* P O Box 1035, F D R Sta, New York City, NY 10150, USA.

MARTIN, Philip (John Talbot), b. 28 Mar. 1931, Melbourne, Australia. Poet; Teacher; Translator; Critic; Radio Programmer. *Education:* BA, University of Melbourne. *Appointments:* Tutor, English, University of Melbourne, 1960–62; Lecturer, English, Australian National University, 1963; Lecturer, Senior Lecturer, English, Monash University, 1964–; Visiting Lecturer, University of Amsterdam, 1967; Visiting Professor, University of Venice, 1976, Carleton College, Northfield, Minnesota, 1983. *Publications:* Voice Unaccompanied, 1970; A Bone Flute, 1974; From Sweden, 1979; A Flag for the Wind, 1982; Lars Gustafsson: Selected Poems, translation, 1982; Shakespeare's Sonnets: Self, Love and Art, criticism, 1972. *Contributor to:* Times Literary Supplement; Stand; The Age; The Australian; Helix; Meanjin; New Hungarian Quarterly; Carleton Miscellany; Poetry (Chicago); Quadrant; Scripsi; Southerly; also to numerous anthologies, from Australian Poetry 1957 to Poet's Choice (1972–78) and Da Slessor a Dransfield (English/Italian, 1977); poems also broadcast by BBC and Australian Radio. *Memberships:* Amnesty International; PEN, Melbourne Centre; Poets' Union of Australia, Melbourne Branch; Fellowship of Australian Writers; Association for Study of Australian Literature. *Address:* c/o English Department, Monash University, Clayton, Victoria 3168, Australia.

MARTIN, Robert Allen, b. 25 June 1930, Toledo, Ohio, USA. Teacher, Writer. Editor. Married, 2 sons, 2 daughters. *Education:* BA, University of Toledo, 1958; BA 1959, PhD 1965, University of Michigan. *Publications:* Editor: The Theater Essays of Arthur Miller, 1978; Arthur Miller: New Perspectives, 1981; The Writer's Craft, 1982. *Contributions to:* Michigan Quarterly Review; Theatre Journal; Studies in American Fiction: Mid America; Modern Drama; American Notes and Queries; CEA Critic; Journal of Popular Culture; Michigan Academician; Philosophy and Literature; The Centennial Review; Notes on Contemporary Literature; College Literature; Others. *Honours include:* Several Academic Fellowships, 1958–81; Woodrow Wilson Fellowship, 1964; Thomas Clarkson Trueblood Fellowship, 1958; Editorial Consultant for several presses and journals, 1975–. *Memberships:* Phi Kappa Phi; Modern Language Association; Michigan College English Association: Society for the Study of Midwestern Literature; American Literature section, Modern Language Association; The Hemingway Society. *Literary Agent:* International Creative Management, New York, New York. *Address:* Department of Humanities, University of Michigan, Ann Arbor, MI 48109, USA.

MARTIN, Robert Bernard, b. 11 Sep. 1918, La Harpe, Illinois, USA. Writer. *Education:* AB, University of Iowa; AM, Harvard University; B Litt, Oxford University. *Literary Appointments:* Professor of English, 1951–75, Emeritus Professor, 1975–, Princeton University; Citizens Professor of English, University of Hawaii, 1981–82, 1984–. *Publications:* The Dust of Combat: A Life of Charles Kingsley, 1959; Enter Humour: Four Early Victorian Scandals, 1962; Victorian Poetry, Ten Major Poets, 1964; The Accents of Persuasion: Charlotte Bronte's Novels, 1968; The Triumph of Wit: A Study of Victorian Comic Theory, 1974; Tennyson: The Unquiet Heart, 1980; With Friends Possessed: A Life of Edward Fitz Gerald 1985; also four pseudonymous novels. *Contributor to:* Numerous magazines and journals. *Honours:* Fellow, American Council of Learned Societies, 1966–67; Fellow, Guggenheim Foundation, 1971–72, 1983–84; Senior Fellow, National Endowment for the Humanities, 1976–77; Fellow, Rockefeller Research Center, Bellagic, 1979; Duff Cooper Award for Biography, 1981; James Tait Black Prize for Biography, 1981; Royal Society of Literature's W H Heinemann Award, 1981; Christian Gauss Award for Literary Scholarship and Criticism, 1981. *Membership:* Fellow, Royal Society of Literature. *Literary Agent:* Curtis Brown, London. *Address:* 8 Walton Street, Oxford OX1 2HG, England.

MARTIN, Roderick, b. 18 Oct. 1940, Lancaster, England. University Professor. *Education:* BA, Balliol College, Oxford University; Studied, University of Pennsylvania, Philadelphia, USA; MA, PhD, Nuffield College, Oxford University, England. *Publications:* Communism and the British Trade Unions 1924–33, 1969; Redundancy and Paternalist Capitalism, with R H Fryer, 1973; The Sociology of Power, 1977; New Technology and Industrial Relations in Fleet Street, 1981; Working Women in Recession, with J Wallace, 1984; Ballots and Trade Union Democracy, with R Undy, 1984. *Contributions to:* Various learned journals. *Address:* Department of Social and Economic Studies, Imperial College of Science and Technology, 53 Princes Gate, Exhibition Road, London SW7 2PG, England.

MARTIN, William, b. 31 Jan. 1933, England. m. 13 June 1975, Haringay, London, 1 daughter. *Education:* London School of Economics; Trent Park College of Education. *Literary Appointments:* Northern Arts Playwright Fellowship, 1975–78; Writer in Residence, Sunderland Polytechnic, 1978; Playwriting Bursary, East Midlands Arts, 1979–80. *Publications:* Exploration Drama, with G Vallin, 1968; Dramawork, with G Vallins, 1972; Drama, 1975; Vacuees, 1983. *Contributions to:* Theatre Quarterly, 1972, 80. *Literary Agent:* Margaret Ramsay, London. *Address:* 6 Elm Terrace, Elm Grove Lane, Steyning, West Sussex BN4 3RB, England.

MARTINEAU, Francis Edward, b. 15 Jan. 1921, Attleboro, Massachusetts, USA. Editor; Publisher; Former Assistant Director of Public Affairs, USAF Reserve, Pentagon, Washington, District of Columbia (retired Colonel). *Education:* RCAF and USAF Pilot and Instructor Schools; Graduate, Air University, USAF; Industrial College of Armed Forces, Department of Defence; Studied, Brown University, Universities of California and Rhode Island; Accredited, Public Relations Society of America, 1970; Certified, American Society of Association Executives, 1972. *Contributions to:* Various publications including: Editor and Publisher of, Association Trends Weekly Newspaper, 1973–; Past Executive Director; Aircraft Owners & Pilots Association; Air Safety Foundation; American League of Lobbyists; Armed Forces Writers League; National Association of Government Communicators; Past Director of Public Relations, Airline Pilots Association. *Address:* 7204 Clarendon Road, Bethesda, MD 20814, USA.

MARTINES, Lauro, b. 22 Nov. 1927, Chicago, Illinois, USA. University Professor. *Education:* BA, 1950, PhD, 1960, Harvard University, USA. *Literary Appointments:* Visiting Professor of History, Warburg Institute, University of London, England, 1985. *Major Publications:* The Social World of the Florentine Humanists, 1963; Lawyers & Statecraft in Renaissance Florence, 1968; Not in God's Image; Women in History from the Greeks to the Victorians (with Julia O'Faolain), 1973; Violence & Civil Disorder in Italian Cities 1200–1500 (editor), 1971; Power & Imagination: City States in Renaissance Italy, 1970; Society & History in English Renaissance Verse, 1985. *Contributor to:* American Historical Review; Renaissance Quarterly; Speculum; The Washington Post; The American Scholar; The Times Literary Supplement. *Memberships:* Medieval Academy of America (Fellow); American Historical Association; Member of Board, Renaissance Society of America. *Honour:* Citation from Society for Italian Historical Studies in America 1963 for Social World of the Florentine Humanists. *Address:* 15 Glenloch Road, London NW3, England.

MARTY, Sid, b. 20 June 1944, South Shields, England. Writer. m. Myrna Jamison, 28 Sep. 1968, Calgary, Canada, 2 sons. *Education:* BA, Honours, English, Sir George William University, Montreal, 1970. *Appointment:* Poet in Residence, Banff School of Fine Arts, 1981. *Publications:* Poetry: Headwaters, 1973; Nobody Danced with Miss Rodeo, 1981; Non-fiction: Men for the Mountains, 1978: A Grand and Fabulous Notion, Centennial History, National Parks of Canada, 1984. *Honours:* Alberta Government Award, Best non-fiction, 1976; Canadian Author's Association Award, best non-fiction, 1976. *Membership:* Writer's Union of Canada. *Address:* c/o Box 22, Lundbreck, Alberta T0K 1H0, Canada.

MARTZ, Georg, b. 10 Feb. 1923, Lodz, Poland. Professor of Fachhochschule Rheinland-Pfalz. Author. m. Margarethe Martz, 25 Oct. 1958, Graz, Austria. *Education:* Dipl-Ing, Technical University of Graz. *Publications:* Siedlungswasserbau, (3 volumes), from 1970; Einführung in den Ökologischen Umweltschutz, 1975; Fabeln und Florabeln, (poems), 1979; Am Donnerstag jeder Woche, (stories), 1983. *Contributions to:* Lexikothek; Kosmos. *Memberships:* Künstlergilde, Esslingen (Artists Guild, Esslingen); Verband Deutscher Schriftsteller (German Association of Authors); Autorengruppe, Mainz (Author's Group, Mainz). *Address:* D–6500 Mainz 1, Heiligkreuzweg 65, Federal Republic of Germany.

MARTZ, Margarethe, b. 11 Nov. 1925, Lukac/Virovitica. Yugoslavia. m. Georg Martz, 25 Oct. 1958, Graz, Austria. *Education:* PhD, University of Graz. *Publications:* Poems: Was den Tag trägt, 1976; Stockwerke nach innen, 1979; Vom Hochhaus Zum Monddach, 1983; Schnecken Geduld, 1983. *Contributions to:* Mainz; Südostdeutsche Vierteljahresblätter; Kulturpolitische Korrespondenz. *Memberships:* Künstlergilde Esslingen (Authors Guild, Esslingen); Verband Deutscher Schriftsteller (German Association of Authors); Autorengruppe Mainz (Authors Group, Mainz). *Address:* D–6500 Mainz 1, Heiligkreuzweg 85, Federal Republic of Germany.

MARUYAMA, Masao, b. 22 Mar. 1914, Osaka, Japan. Historian. m. Yukari Koyama, 24 Mar. 1944, Tokyo, 1 son. *Education:* Graduate, Law, Imperial University of Tokyo. *Literary Appointments:* Professor, Political Theory, University of Tokyo, 1940–70. *Publications:* Thought and Behaviour in Modern Japanese Politics, 1963; Studies in the Intellectual History of Tokugawa, 1974. *Honours:* Honorary Degree, Law, Harvard University, USA, 1973; Honorary Degree, Letters, Princeton University, 1973. *Memberships:* Japan Academy, 1978; Elected, Correspondent Fellow, Royal Historical Society, 1981; Elected, Foreign Correspondent, British Academy, 1982; Elected, Honorary Member, American Historical Association, 1984. *Address:* 2-44-5 Higashicho, Kichijoji, Musashino–shi, Tokyo, Japan.

MARVIN, Blanche, b. 17 Jan. 1925, New York City, New York, USA. Writer, Actress, Agent. m. Mark Marvin, 31 Oct. 1950, Paris, 1 son, 1 daughter. *Education:* BA, Antioch. *Literary Appointments:* Liaison Officer, Writer's Guild; Secretary, Agents Associate, Personal Managers Association: Artistic Director, Cricket Theatre, 1958–68. *Publications include:* Scarface and Blue Water; Series of children's plays and fairy tales in anthologies. *Contributions to:* Articles, stories and poems in publications including: Woman's Own; Dance magazine. *Honours:* Nomination for the Tony Award, 1961; Community Fiver Award, 1963; Cue Magazine Valentine, 1963; Hall of Fame, 1965. *Memberships:* Writers' Guild of Great Britain; Theatre Writers' Union; Dramatist Guild; Personal Manager Association; Association of Independent Producers. *Literary Agent:* Blanche Marvin. *Address:* 21A St John's Wood High Street, London NW8 7NG, England.

MARX, Anne, b. Bleincherode am Harz, Germany. Poet; Author; Lecturer; Critic; Translator; Editor. *Education:* Medical Schools, Heidelberg, Berlin; Various colleges, USA. *Literary Appointments include:* Iona College; Wagner College, Fairleigh Dickinson University; PSA Poetry Workshops; Arkansas Writers Conference; Jakarta Arts Centre, Indonesia; Conventions, National Federation of State Poetry Societies, 1974, 81, 82, 86; Penn State University. *Publications include:* Ein Buchlein: German Lyrics; Into the Wind of Waking, 1960; The Second Voice: A Collection of Poems, 1963; By Grace of Pain, 1966; By Way of People, 1970; A Time to Mend, 1973; Hear of Israel and

Other Poems, 1975; 40 Love Poems for 40 Years, 1977; Face Lifts for All Seasons, 1980: Forty-five Love Poems for 45 Years, 1982; Holocaust: Hurts to Healings, 1984; A Further Semester, 1984. *Contributions to:* Numerous USA and other journals; Co-Editor, Pegasus in the Seventies, The World's Love Poetry. Anthologies include: The Enjoyment of Literature; Talking Book for the Blind; A Conversation with Anne Marx with selections from her works; The Golden Year; The Diamond Year; Fro Grand-dad, A Gift of Love; The Destruction of the Jewish Community of Worms; Eve's Eden; Eve's Legacy; American Women Discuss Their Craft. *Honours include:* Greenwood Prize, 1966; Fellowships, Poetry Society of America; American Weave Publication Award, 1960; V H Parsons Award, 1977; Biennial Book Award, National League of American Pen Women, 1967; Publications Award, The Crossroads Press, 1984. *Memberhsips:* Past Executive Board and Vice President, Poetry Society of America; Past National Poetry Editor, Pen Woman; National Vice President, National League of American Pen Women. *Address:* 315 The Colony, Hartsdale, NY 10530, USA.

MARX, Gary T, b. 10 Jan. 1938, California, USA. Professor of Sociology. m. 18 Aug. 1962, Tucson, 2 sons. *Education:* BA, UCLA, Los Angeles, 1960; MA, 1962, PhD, 1967, University of California, Berkeley. *Appointments:* Lecturer, University of California, Berkeley, 1966–67; Assistant Professor, Harvard University, 1967–73; Associate Professor, Professor, Massachusetts Institute of Technology, 1973–. *Publications:* Protest and Prejudice, 1967; Confrontation: Psychology and Problems of Today, co-editor, 1970; Racial Conflict: Tension and Change in American Society, Editor, 1971; Inquiries in Sociology, Co-author, 1972; Muckraking Sociology: Research as Social Criticism, Editor, 1972; Society Today, 4th Edition 1982; Sociology: Classic and Popular Approaches, co-editor, 1980; etc. *Contributor to:* Berkeley Journal of Sociology; Phylon; Journal of Social Issues; Annals of the American Academy of Political and Social Science; American Behavioral Scientist; Sociologie du Travail; Crime and Justice Systems Annuals; Journal of Urban Life and Culture; Victimology; Theory and Society; etc. *Honours:* Recipient numerous Grants and Awards. *Address:* Department of Urban Studies and Planning, Massachusetts Institute of Technology, 77 Massachusetts Avenue, Cambridge, MA 02139, USA.

MARZECKI, Longin Walter (Wladyslaw), b. 4 Jan. 1918, Albany, New York, USA. Journalist; Illustrator; Retired US Army Officer. *Education:* BS Military-Science. *Publications:* Peas In A Nutshell, 1965; Lights On Arthur Kill, 1968; East and Willow, 1974; A Trilogy and a History in preparation. *Contributions to:* Sunday New York Times; Sunday NB Home News; GAN Press; Independent Leader; News Tribune; National Fisherman; Polish-American World; Rola Boza (God's Field). *Memberships:* Past member, New York and New Jersey Press Associations; Professional Artists' League of New York. *Address:* Box 202, Avenel, NJ 07001, USA.

MASCALL, Eric Lionel, b. 12 Dec. 1905, Sydenham, Kent, England. Anglican Priest; Theological Professor. *Education:* BSc, 1st Class Mathematics, University of London, 1927; BA 1st Class Mathematics, University of Cambridge, 1928; DD University of Cambridge, 1958; DD University of Oxford, 1948; Honarary DD, St Andrew's 1967. *Literary Appointments:* Sub-Warden, Lincoln Theological College, 1937–45; Student, Christ Church, Oxford, 1946–62; Professor of Historical Theology, King's College, University of London, 1962–73; Bampton Lecturer, Oxford, 1946; Bampton Lecturer, Columbia University, New York, 1958; Gifford Lecturer, Edinburgh, 1970–71; FBA, 1974–. *Publications:* He Who Is, 1943, 1966; Christ, the Christian and the Church, 1946; Christian Theology and Natural Science, 1956; Corpus Christi, 1953; Words and Images, 1957; The Secularization of Christianity, 1956; The Openess of Being, 1971; Theology and the Gospel of Christ, 1977, 1984; Whatever Happened to the Human Mind?, 1980. *Contributions to:* Theological journals and others.

Honour: Fellow of the British Academy, 1974–. *Address:* 30 Bourne Street, London SW1W 8JJ, England.

MASON, Haydn Trevor, b. 12 Jan. 1929, Saundersfoot, Dyfed, Wales. University Professor. m. (1) 1 son, 2 daughters. (2) Adrienne Mary Redshaw, 14 Sep. 1982, Bristol. *Education:* BA, Wales. 1949; AM, Middlebury, 1951; D Phil, Oxford, 1960. *Publications:* Pierre Bayle and Voltaire, 1963; Marivaux: Les Fausses Confidences (Editor), 1964: Leibniz/Arnauld Correspondence (Editor and translator), 1967: Voltaire: Zadig and other tales, 1971; Voltaire, 1975; Voltaire: A Biography, 1981; French Writers and their Society 1715–1800, 1982; Vita di Voltaire, 1984; Cyrano de Bergerac: L'Autre Monde, 1984; Voltaire and His World (co-editor), 1985; Studies on Voltaire and the Eighteenth Century (Editor) 66 volumes 1977–. *Contributions to:* Journals including: Times Literary Supplement; Studies on Voltaire: French Studies; Modern Language Review; Journal of European Studies; Forum, (Austin, Texas); Studi Filosofici. *Honours:* Special commendation, American Society for Eighteenth Century Studies, 1982. *Memberships:* President 1984–86. British Association for Eighteenth Century Studies; President 1982–84, Society for French Studies; President 1981–82, Association of University Professors of French. *Address:* French Department, University of Bristol, 19 Woodland Road, Bristol, BS8 1TE, England.

MASON, Stanley, b. 16 Apr. 1917, Blairmore, Alberta, Canada. Editor, Translator. m. Cloris, Ielmini, 29 July 1944, Zurich, 1 daughter. *Education:* MA. English Literature. Oriel College, Oxford. *Literary Appointments:* Literary Editor, Graphis magazine, 1963–83; Editor, Elements, Dow Chemical Europe house organ, 1969–75. *Publications:* Modern English Structures (with Ronald Ridout), 4 volumes, 1968–72; A Necklace of Words, poetry, 1975; A Reef of Hours, poetry, 1983. *Contributions to:* UK: Adelphi; Poetry Review; Envoi; Orbis; Doors; Pennine Platform; others; Canada: Canadian Forum; Dalhousie Review. *Honours include:* 2 poems in Best Poems of 1964, Borestone Mountain Poetry Awards, 1965; 3 diplomas, Scottish National Open Poetry Competitions, including 1984 and 1985. *Address:* Im Zelgli 5, 8307 Effretikon, Switzerland.

MASON, Theodore Charles, b. 27 July 1921, Berkeley, California, USA. Writer. m. (1) Betty Jane Baker, 25 Mar. 1945, Carson City, Nevada, 1 daughter. (2) Rita Jeannette Bolduc, 28 Apr. 1978, North San Juan, California. *Education:* Graduated in English, University of Southern California, Los Angeles, 1949. *Literary Appointments:* Proof Reader, Los Angeles Times, 1950–51; Reporter, Arizona Republic, Phoenix, 1951–52; Reporter, Editor, Columnist, Arizona Free Press, 1952–53; Copywriter, 1953, TV Director, 1954, Advertising Counselors of Arizona, Phoenix; Copy Chief and Radio-TV Director, Louis Landau Advertising Agency, Sacramento, California, 1954–58; Copy Chief 1958–66, Vice President-Creative Director, 1966–69, Ramsey Advertising Agency, Los Angeles; Self-employed freelance writer and author, 1969–. *Publications:* Applied Engineered Cementing, 1969; Applied Engineered Stimulation, 1970; Contributor to, Air Raid: Pearl Harbor! Recollections of a Day of Infamy, edited by Paul Stillwell, 1981; Battleship Sailor, 1982; South Pacific Sailor, 1986. *Contributor to:* A number of business and professional publications including, American School and University; Architectural Forum; Engineering News Record; Marine Engineering Log; The Military Engineer and the Proceedings of the United States Naval Institute. *Honours:* Battleship Sailor, was selected by Professor Craig L Symonds as one of the Notable Naval Books of 1982; Military Medals and Decorations; American Defense with, Fleet, Clasp; American Campaign; Asiatic-Pacific Campaign, with Silver and Bronze Stars; World War II Victory; Good Conduct; Philippine Liberation Medal; Phillipine Republic Presidential Unit Citation. *Membership:* Founder of, Works in Progress, a local writers' group, 1982. *Address:* 38253 Via Del Largo, Murrieta Hot Springs, CA 92362, USA.

MASOTTI, Louis Henry, b. 16 May 1934, New York, USA. Professor, Consultant, Author. m. (2) Rosemary Scanlon, 14 June 1985, New York City; 1 son, 3 daughters. *Education:* AB Princeton University, 1956; MA 1961, PhD 1964, Northwestern University. *Major Publications Include:* (editor) The Suburban Seventies, 1975; (Co-editor with R L Lineberry) The New Urban Politics, 1976; (co-editor with J. Walton) The City in Comparative Perspective, 1976; (co-editor with S Gove) After Dace: Chicago Politics in Transition, 1982; Downtown Development: Chicago 1979–84. *Contributor to:* Numerous professional journals etc; chapters in books; numerous articles, book reviews & reports. *Memberships include:* Policy Studies Organisation; Urban Land Institute; National Council on Urban Economic Development. *Honours:* Various Awards. *Address:* Kellogg Graduate School of Management, Northwestern University, Evanston, IL 60201, USA.

MASSIALAS, Byron G, b. 1 Nov. 1929, Greece. Professor of Education. m. 2 sons. *Education:* BA, cum laude, Butler University, 1957; MA, 1958, PhD, 1961, Indiana University. *Appointments:* Instructor, Social Studies, University High School, Indiana University, USA, 1959–61; Assistant Professor, University of Chicago, 1961–65; Associate Professor, Education, University of Michigan, 1963–70; Professor, Education, Florida State University, 1970–. *Contributor to:* Numerous articles in professional journals including: Encyclopedia of Education; School Review; Educational Leadership; Comparative Education Review; Social Education; International Encyclopedia of Education; World Education Encyclopedia; etc. *Memberships:* American Educational Research Association; Modern Greek Studies Association; National Council for Social Studies; Comparative and International Education Society; Middle East Institute; Asian Regional Population Education Association; National Association for Bilingual Education; Society for Population Educators. *Address:* 2402 Killarney Way, Tallahassee, FL 32308, USA.

MASSON, David Irvine, b. 1915, Edinburgh, Scotland. Retired University Rare Books Librarian. m. Olive Newton, 1 daughter. *Education:* BA (Oxon); MA (Oxon). *Publications:* The Caltraps of Time, 1968, translation: An den Grenzen der Zeit, 1984. *Contributions to:* Modern Language Review; ELH; Journal of Aesthetics; British Journal of Aesthetics; Encyclopedia of Poetry and Poetics; Neophilologus; Proceedings of the Leeds Philosophical and Literary Society; Science Fiction: New Worlds; Science fiction anthologies in USA and in translation; Reviews and articles: Foundation. *Memberships:* Modern Humanities Research Association. *Address:* 38 Whinfield, Adel, Leeds, LS16 7AE, England.

MASTERS, Roger D, b. 8 June 1933, Boston, Massachusetts, USA. University Professor. m. Susanne R Putnam, 25 Aug. 1984, South Woodstock, Vermont, 2 sons, 1 daughter. *Education:* AB, Harvard University, 1955; MA 1958, PhD 1961, University of Chicago. *Publications:* Rousseau's First and Second Discourses, translation, 1964; The Nation is Burdened, 1967; Political Philosophy of Rousseau, 1968; Rousseau's Social Contract with Geneva MS and Political Economy, editor, 1978. *Contributions to:* American Political Science Review; World Politics; Quarterly Review of Biology; Le Monde; Le Figaro; La Recherche; Washington Post; New York Times; Numerous scholarly journals. *Honours:* Guggenheim Fellowship, 1967. *Memberships:* American Association for the Advancement of Science; International Political Science Association; Association for Politics and the Life Sciences. *Address:* c/o Department of Government, Dartmouth College, Hanover, NH 03755, USA.

MASTERTON, Graham, b. 16 Jan. 1946, Edinburgh, Scotland. Author. m. Wiescka Walach, 11 Nov. 1975, Guildford, Surrey. England, 3 sons. *Publications:* The Manitou, 1975; Charnel House, 1976; Rich, 1977; Railroad, 1980; Solitaire, 1983; Maiden Voyage, 1984; Tengu, 1984; Lady of Fortune, 1985; Corroboree, 1985.

Contributions to: The Writer, article on technique, 1985. *Honours:* Special Award, Mystery Writers of America, 1977; Silver Medal, West Coast Review of Books, 1984. *Membership:* Authors Guild. *Literary Agent:* Wiescka Masterton, *Address:* c/o Sphere Books, 30-32 Grays Inn Road, London WC1X 8JL, England.

MASTERTON, Murray Strachan, b. 12 July 1929, Christchurch, New Zealand. University Lecturer. m. Moya Wendy, 2 Nov. 1953, Oslo, 2 daughters. *Education:* BA (Hons) Newcastle, New South Wales, Australia, 1967; MS (J) Ohio, USA, 1977. *Publications:* Great Ugly River, 1965; ...but you'll never be bored: the Five W's of Australian Journalism, 1983; And Now the News in Detail, (with R Patching), 1985. *Contributions to:* Australian Journalism Review. *Address:* Journalism/Humanities, Deakin University, Victoria 3127, Australia.

MATERNA, Thomas Walter, b. 24 Oct. 1944, Passaic, New Jersey, USA. Medicine. m. Jorunn Aronsen, 18 Aug. 1973, Bethesda, Maryland, 1 son, 1 daughter. *Education:* AB, Holy Cross College; MD, State University of New York. *Contributor to:* Medical Writer, Commission for the Blind, State of New Jersey; Staff Writer, Health and Science, WRNU Radio, Newark, New Jersey. *Membership:* American Medical Writers Association. *Address:* 654 E Jersey St, Elizabeth, NJ 07206, USA.

MATEV, Pavel, b. 6 Dec. 1924, Orizovo, Bulgaria. Writer, *Education:* Slavonic Philology, Sofia University. *Literary Appointments:* Chairman, The Committee for Culture, 1966–75; Chairman, The Committee for Bulgarians Abroad. *Publications:* Poetry: Clear Days, 1953; With The Belief of the People, 1959; The Seagulls Rest on the Waves, 1965; Unpolluted Worlds, 1969; Stores Silences, 1973; A Severe Summer, 1974; Sudden Pauses, 1976. *Contributor to:* All main Bulgarian editions. *Honours:* Dimitrov Prize; A People's Worker of Culture, 1971; A Hero of Socialist Labour, 1980. *Membership:* Union of Bulgarian Writers, Secretary 1958–62. *Address:* 21 Boulevard P Evtimi, Sofia, Bulgaria.

MATHESON, John Ross (Colonel The Honourable), b. 14 Nov. 1917, Arundel, Quebec, Canada. Judge. m. Edith May Bickley, 4 Aug. 1945, Kingston, Ontario, 4 sons, 2 daughters. *Education:* BA Honours, Queen's University; MA, Mount Allison University; Barrister-at-Law, Osgoode Hall; LL M, University of Western Ontario. *Publications:* Canada's Flag: A Search For a Country, 1980; Sinews of the Heart, collection of poetry, 1982. *Contributions to:* Encyclopaedia Canadiana; The Canadian Encyclopaedia; My Canada; Genealogical and heraldic publications. *Honours:* Queens Counsel, 1967; Knight of Justice Most Venerable Order of St John, 1974; Knight Commander of Merit Order of St Lazarus, 1975; Canadian Forces Decoration, 1975; Honorary 33° Scottish Rite of Freemasonry, 1977; Distinguished Service Award 1977, Montreal Medal 1980, LL D Honoris Causa 1984, Queen's University; Elected fellow: Royal Economic Society, Society of Antiquaries of Scotland, Heraldry Society of Canada. *Address:* Rideau Ferry, Ontario K0G1W0, Canada

MATHEWS, Walter Michael, b. 13 Nov. 1942, Philadelphia, USA. University Professor and Administrator. m. Mary Florence Richardson, 13 June 1964, Philadelphia, 1 son, 1 daughter. *Education:* BA, La Salle College, 1964; M Ed, Temple University, 1967; PhD, University of Wisconsin – Madison, 1971. *Literary Appointments:* Associate Editor, Mid-South Educational Researcher, 1972–74; Associate Editor, AEDS Journal Association for Educational Data Systems, 1977 -; Consulting Editor, Research in Rural Education, 1982–; Facilitating Editor American Educational Research Association, 1984–. *Publications:* Editor, Monster or Messiah?: The Computer's Impact on Society, 1980; Editor, Mississippi 1990, 1981; Rural Education in Encyclopedia of Educational Research edited by Harold E Mitzel, 5th edition 1982, etc.

Contributions to: Articles in Journal of Educational Data Processing, NCME Measurement News; Journal of Educational Measurement; Educational Researcher; Journal of Educational Technology Systems; Journal of Drug Education; Journal of Ceylon Association for the Mentally Retarded; Phi Delta Kappan; Public Personnel Management; Australian Journal of Mental Retardation; Journal of Cross-Cultural Psychology; Compact; Research in Rural Education; etc. Ten book reviews in AEDS Journal; AEDS Monitor and Educational Forum. *Address:* 27 Midway Avenue, Locust Valley, Long Island, NY 11560, USA.

MATHIAS, Paul Stuart, b. 27 Sep. 1940, Beckenham, Kent, England. Teacher; Lecturer; Writer; Editor; Consultant. *Education:* BA Honours in History, Wales, 1964; Certificate in Education, with distinction, Cambridge, 1965; MA Music Education, London University, 1983. *Publications:* Conceived and Edited, Blandford Social Studies Series, 1971–74; Teacher's Handbook for Social Studies, 1973; Some People Are Different, 1975; Groups and Communities, 1974, revised international edition 1984; Multiple Choice Questions for CXC Social Studies, 1984; Man In His Environment, editor, 3 books in the Sierra Leone National Programme in Social Studies, 1985. *Contributions to:* Social Studies Education, 1981. *Honour:* Fellow, Royal Society of Arts, 1979. *Address:* Blencathra, Paynesfield Road, Tatsfield, Westerham, Kent TN16 2BG, England.

MATHIAS, Peter, b. 10 Jan. 1928, Somerset, England. Professor of Economic History. m. Elisabeth Ann Blackmore, 5 Apr. 1958, Bath Abbey, 2 sons, 1 daughter. *Education:* BA 1951, MA 1954, Jesus College, Cambridge; D Litt, Oxford University, 1985. *Literary Appointments:*; FBA, 1977; Honorary Treasurer, British Academy, 1979. *Publications:* The Brewing Industry in England 1700–1830, 1959; English Trade Tokens, 1961; Retailing Revolution, 1967; The First Industrial Nation, 1969 and 1983; The Transformation of England, 1979. *Contributions to:* Various historical learned journals in UK and USA. *Honour:* CBE, 1984. *Memberships:* President 1974–78, Honorary President 1978–, International Economic History Association; President, Business Archives Council, 1984–; Honorary Treasurer, Economic History Society, 1967–; FRHS, 1972; Advisory Board of the Research Council. *Address:* All Souls College, Oxford, England.

MATHIAS, Roland Glyn, b. 4 Sep. 1915, Talybont-on-Usk, Breconshire, Wales. Schoolmaster. m. Mary (Molly) Hawes, 4 Apr. 1944, Chipping Norton, Oxfordshire, England, 1 son, 2 daughters. *Education:* BA, Modern History, 1936, BLitt (by thesis) 1939, MA, 1944, Jesus College, University of Oxford, England; Doctor of Humane Letters (honoris causa), Georgetown University, Washington, USA, 1985. *Literary Appointments:* Editor, The Anglo-Welsh Review, 1961–76; Member, Welsh Arts Council, 1970–79; Chairman, Literature Committee, Welsh Arts Council, 1976–79; Visiting Professor, University of Alabama at Birmingham, 1971; Extra-Mural Lecturer, University College, Cardiff, 1970–77. *Major Publications:* Break in Harvest, (poems), 1946; The Roses of Tretower, (poems), 1952; The Eleven Men of Eppynt, (short stories), 1956; The Flooded Valley, (poems), 1960; Whitsun Riot, (historical research),1963; Absalom in the Tree, (poems), 1971; Vernon Watkins, (literary criticism), 1974; Snipe's Castle, (poems), 1979; John Cowper Powys as Poet, (literary criticism), 1979; Burning Brambles, (selected poems), 1983; A Ride Through the Wood, (critical essays), 1985. *Contributor to:* Very many periodicals and literary journals. *Honours:* Welsh Arts Council Prizes for Poetry, 1972, 1980; Honorary Doctorate, Georgetown University (USA) for services to literature of Wales. *Memberships:* The Welsh Academy of Writers, Chairman 1975–78; The Powys Society; The David Jones Society. *Address:* Deffrobani, 5 Maescelyn, Brecon, Powys, LD3 7NL, Wales.

MATHIESEN, Thomas James, b. 30 Apr. 1947, Roslyn Heights, New York, USA. Musicologist. m. Penelope Jay Price, 11 Sep. 1971, Brea, California, USA. *Education:* B Mus Willamette University, 1968; M Mus, 1970, Doctor of Musical Arts, 1971, University of Southern California. *Literary Appointments:* General Editor, Greek & Latin Music Theory, 1982–. *Major Publications:* A Bibliography of Sources for the Study of Ancient Greek Music, 1974; A Style Guide for Text Criticism, Translation and the Preparation of Camera-ready Typescript, 1982; Aristides Quintilianus on Music in Three Books: Translation, with Introduction, Commentary & Annotations, 1983. *Contributor to:* Music Theory Spectrum 7; Journal of Musicology 3; Acta Musicologica. *Honours:* Grant-in-Aid, American Council of Learned Societies, 1977; Senior Fellowship, National Endowment for the Humanities, 1985–86. *Address:* Rt 2, Box 172, Hobble Creek Canyon, Springville, UT 84663, USA.

MATHIS-EDDY, Darlene, b. 19 Mar. 1937, Elkhart, Indiana, USA. Professor of English; Poet. m. Spencer Livingston Eddy, 23 May 1964, Boonton, deceased 1971. *Education:* BA, Goshen College, 1959; MA, 1961, PhD, 1967, English, Rutgers University. *Appointments:* Instructor, Lecturer, Douglass College, Rutgers University, 1962–66; Assistant Professor, 1967–71; Associate Professor, 1971–75, Professor, 1973–, Ball State University. *Publications:* The Worlds of King Lear, 1968; Leaf Threads, Wind Thymes, 1985; Weathering, 1986; The Green Sea and the Azur'd Valt: Essays in Shakespearean Studies, 1986. *Contributor to:* Numerous articles, reviews to American Literature; English Language Notes; Forum; The Steinbeck Quarterly; etc; Poetry in Calyx; Barnwood; Green River Review; Pebble; etc. *Honours:* Woodrow Wilson National Fellow, 1959–62; Rutgers University Graduate Honours Fellow, 1964–65; Poetry Editor, Forum, 1985–; etc. *Memberships include:* Modern Language Association; National Council of Teachers of English; Shakespeare Association; College English Association. *Address:* Department of English, RB 248, Ball State University, Muncie, IN 47303, USA.

MATON, Jean, b. 4 June 1926. Writer; Librarian. *Education:* Instn. Saint Antoine de padoue; Eccle nat Profl, Chalon sur Saone. *Literary Appointments:* Librarian, Orleans, 1956–; Founder, Secretary General Grands Prix de l'Humour noir, 1954. *Publications:* Vers trop verts, 1947; Morceaux choisis, suivis des Poems a Re, 1948; Un Sermon a Parisvaque, 1948; Fiasco, 1953; Commerce, 1955; Amour Noir, 1955; L'Oiel fondant, 1957: Aux Mauvaises Langues, 1960: Spectacle gratuit, 1961; 13 poems express, 1961: Le Pain Complet, 1965; Chants du haut de ma Tour, 1967; Pour une date un seul amour, 1970; Elements pour un poeme, 1972; Les Quat'Saisons, 1975; La Lune mange le violet, 1981; X F humoriste noir blanc de visage, 1984. *Contributor to:* Various literary journals. *Honours include:* Poet Laureate, Society, Men of Letters, 1962; Commander of Order of St Constantin, Knight of National Merit, France; Officer, Order of Clou, 1964; Officer of Order of Arts and Letters, 1984; Knight of Order of Arts and Letters, 1979; Laureat du Prix Thyde Monnier, 1981; du Prix des Ecrivains de France, 1984; du Prix Aram Sayabalian de la Societe des Gens de Lettres, 1984. *Memberships:* Secretary General Cep Burgone, 19460; Jury, International Prize of Golden Rose; Academy of Morvan; Academy of Treize; Founder, Literary Prize of Morvan and Poetry Prize Gustave Gasser, 1965; Honorary Committee, Marie Noel Prize; PEN; Associate Society Men of Letters; Committee, Union of Writers. *Address:* 3 Blvd, de Quebec, 45000 Orleans, France.

MATSUMOTO, Shigeharu, b. 2 Oct. 1899, Osaka, Japan. Chairman, Board of Directors, International House of Japan Incorporated. *Education:* LLB, University of Tokyo, 1923; Yale University, USA and Universities of Wisconsin, Geneva (Switzerland) and Vienna (Austria), 1924–27. *Publications include:* Shanghaijidai (My Shanghai Days), 1975; Kindai Nihon no Gaiko (Modern Japanese Diplomacy), Co-Author, 1962; Genten Amerika Shi (A Documentary History of American People), Co-Editor, 6 volumes, 1950–58; Kabayama Aisuke O (Recollections of Aisuke Kabayama), Editor, 1955; Editor of Several books of lectures, various translations. *Honours include:* Various Honours Degrees; 1st Class Order, Sacred Treasure, 1969; Named Person of Cultural Merit, Ministry of Education, Japan, 1976; Japan Foundation Award, 1976. *Memberships include:* Past President, Japan Association for American Studies; Council Member, Institute of Asian Economic Affairs; Director, English Language Education Council. *Address:* c/o International House of Japan Incorporated, 11-16 Roppongi 5-chome, Minato-ku, Tokyo 106, Japan.

MATSUNAGA, Alicia Orloff, b. 25 May 1937, Livermore Valley, California, USA. Buddhist Theologian. *Education:* AB, University of California, Davis, 1958; MA, University of Redlands, 1960; PhD, Claremont Graduate School, 1964. *Publications:* Buddhist Philosophy of Assimilation, 1969; Buddhist Concept of Hell, co-author, 1971; Foundation of Japanese Buddhism: The Aristocratic Age, co-author, 1974; Foundation of Japanese Buddhism: The Mass Movement, co-author, 1976. *Contributor to:* Monumenta Nipponica. *Honours:* Recipient, Cultural Award, Nippon Hoso Kyokai (Japanese National Broadcasting Co), 1970. *Memberships:* Sapporo Director, Buddhist Books Invernational. *Address:* Eikyoji Institute of Buddhist Studies, Tadoshi, Fukagawa, Hokkaido, Japan 074-01.

MATTAR, Denis de Brong, b. 27 July 1946, São Paulo, Brazil. Advertiser. m. Talitha Camargo Silva Mattar, 2 July 1971, São Paulo, 2 sons. *Education:* Movie Director, Higher School of Cinema; Law Faculty, University of São Paulo. *Literary Appointments:* Escritor Brasileiro, 1980; Semana do Escritor Brasileiro, 1981. *Publications:* A Caminho do Sotao, novel, 1978. *Contributions to:* Movie reviews, A Gazeta, 1970; Short stories, Editora Abril, 1971. *Memberships:* Brazilian Writers Union. *Literary Agent:* Estela dos Santos Abreu. *Address:* Alameda Ministro Rocha Azevedo 384-11° andar, 01410 São Paulo, Brazil.

MATTHEW, Christopher Charles Forest, b. 8 May 1939, London, England. Writer; Broadcaster. m. Wendy Mallinson, 19 October 1979, 2 sons, 1 daughter. *Education:* BA (Hons) Oxford. *Literary Appointments:* Editor, Times Travel Guide, 1975-76. *Publications:* A Different World; Stories of Great Hotels, 1976; Diary of a Somebody, 1978; Loosely Engaged, 1980; The Long Haired Boy, 1980; The Crisp Report, 1981; Annotated Three Men in a Boat, (with Benny Green), 1982; The Junket Man, 1983; How to Survive Missile Age, 1983. *Contributions to:* Punch, Vogue, The Observer, Highlife, World of Interiors. *Honour:* Arts Council Award, 1977. *Literary Agent:* Deborah Rogers Limited. *Address:* c/o Deborah Rogers Limited, 49 Blenheim Crescent, London W11 2EF, England.

MATTHEWS, John Harold, b. 22 July 1925, Columbus, Ohio, USA. Writer; Professor of English. m. Barbara Reese, 16 Sep. 1947, Granville, Ohio, 1 son, 2 daughters. *Education:* BA, MA, Ohio State University. *Publications:* Hanger Stout, Awakel, novel, 1967; The Charisma Campaigns, novel, 1971; Dubious Persuassions, stories, 1982; Sassafras, novel, 1983; Crazy Women, stories, 1985. *Contributions to:* Kenyon Review; Malahat Review; Yale Review; etc.*Honours include:* Oihioana Fiction Award, 1964; Guggenheim Fellowship, 1974–75; Sherwood Anderson Prize, 1985. *Address:* 24 Briarwood Drive, Athens, OH 45701, USA.

MATTHEWS, John Herbert, b. 11 Sep. 1930, Swansea, Glamorgan. University Professor. m. Jeanne Brooks, 23 July, 1955, Swansea, 1 son, 2 daughters. *Education:* BA, English and French, 1949, BA (Hons) French, 1951, University of Wales; D de I'U, University of Montpellier, 1955; D Litt, University of Wales, 1977. *Literary Appointment:* Editor, Symposium, a quarterly journal in modern literatures, 1965–. *Publications:* Author of 24 books, 17 on surrealism, including Les deux Zola, 1957; An Introduction to Surrealism, 1965. *Address:* R R #3, Box 275, Tully, NY 13159, USA.

MATTHEWS, Patricia Anne, b. 1 July 1927, San Fernando, California, USA. Author. m. (1) Marvin Owen Brisco, 1946 (divorced, 1961), 2 sons; (2) Clayton Hartly Matthews, 1971. *Education:* Pasadena Junior College; California State University at Los Angeles. *Literary Appointments:* Freelance writer of short stories, poetry and novels. *Publications include:* Love's Daring Dream, 1978; Love's Pagan Heart, 1978; Love's Magic Moment, 1979; Love's Golden Destiny, 1979; Love's Raging Tide, 1980; Love's Sweet Agony, 1980; Love's Bold Journey, 1980; Tides of Love, 1981; Embers of Dawn, 1982; Flames of Glory, 1983; Dancer of Dreams, 1984; Gambler in Love, 1985; Tame the Restless Heart, 1986; Love's Many Faces (poetry), 1979; The Night Visitor (occult), 1979; Juveniles: Merry's Treasure, 1969; The Carnival Mystery, 1974; The Campus Mystery, 1977; Raging Rapide, 1978; Too Much in Love, 1979. *Contributions to:* Alfred Hitchcok's Mystery Anthology; Microcosmic Tales, Asimov; Escapade Annual; Ellery Queen Anthology; The Oregonion; The American Bard; Ladies' Home Journal; Cosmopolitan; Ellery Queen's Mystery Magazine, etc. *Honours:* Porgie Award, West Coast Review of Books, Silver Medal for The Night Visitor, 1979; Silver Medal for Empire, 1983; Bronze Medal for Flames of Glory, 1984; Romantic Times Team Writng Award, with Clayton Matthews, 1983. *Memberships include:* Mystery Writers of America; PEN, etc. *Literary Agent:* Jay Garon, New York City. *Address:* P O Box 277, Bonsall, CA 92003, USA.

MATTHEWS, Peter John, b. 6 Jan. 1945, Fareham, Hampshire, England. Freelance Author and Broadcaster. m. Diana Randall, 1975, London, 2 sons. *Literary Appointments:* Editorial Director, Guinness Superlatives, 1981–84; Sports Editor, Guinness Book of Records, 1982–. *Publications:* Guinness Book of Athletic Facts and Feats, 1982; International Athletics Annual, 1985. *Contributions to:* Athletics publications. *Address:* 6 Broadfields, Goffs Oak, Waltham Cross, Hertfordshire EN7 5JU, England.

MATTHEWS, Robert Andrew James, b. 23 Sep. 1959, Carshalton, England. Journalist. *Education:* BA, Honours, Physics, University of Oxford, 1981. *Appointments:* Associate Editor, Technology Week, 1981–82; Technology Reporter, 1982–84, Technology Editor, 1984–, Building. *Publications:* Consultant Editor, Physics Today, 1984. *Contributor to:* Sunday Times; New Scientist; The Economist; Science Now; Designing; Public Service & Local Government; Popular Astronomy; etc. *Honours:* Periodical Publishers Association, Campaigning Features of the Year, 1984. *Memberships:* Association of British Science Writers; Fellow, Royal Astronomical Society; Associate Member, Institute of Physics. *Address:* 42 Ashdown Way, London SW17 7TH, England.

MATTHEWS, Thomas Stanley, b. 16 Jan. 1901, Cincinnati, Ohio, USA. Journalist. m. (1) Juliana Stevens Cuyler, 16 May 1925, Dec. 1949; (2) Martha Gellhorn, 1954; (3) Pamela Peniakoff, 1964. 4 sons. *Education:* BA, Princeton University, USA, 1922; MA, New College, Oxford, England. *Publications:* To The Gallows I Must Go, 1931; The Sugar Pill, 1957; Name and Address, 1960; O My America, 1962; The Worst Unsaid, verse, 1962; Great Tom, 1974; Jacks or Better, 1977; Angels Unawares, 1985. *Contributions to:* Many varied contributions to magazines and journals. *Honours:* Doctor of Humane Letters, Kenyon College, 1952; Doctor of Letters, Rollins College, 1953. *Literary Agent:* Deborah Owen, 78 Narrow Street, London E14 8BP, England. *Address:* Cavendish Hall, Cavendish, Suffolk, England.

MATTHEWS, William P, b. 11 Nov. 1942, Cincinnati, Ohio, USA. Poet; College Teacher. m. Marie Murray Harris, 4 May 1963, Rye, New York, divorced 1973, 2 sons. *Education:* BA, Yale University, 1965; MA, University of North Carolina at Chapel Hill, 1966. *Literary Appointment:* Distinguished Writer-in-Residence, City College of the City University of New York. *Publications:* Ruining the New Road, 1970; Sleek for the Long Flight, 1972; Sticks and Stones, 1975; Rising and Falling, 1979; Flood, 1982; A Happy Childhood, 1984. *Contributions to:* American Poetry Review;

Antaeus; Atlantic Monthly; Field; Georgia Review; Kayak; The Nation; The New Republic; The New Yorker; Ohio Review; Paris Review; Poetry etc. *Honours:* Fellowship, National Endowment for the Arts, 1974, 1984; Fellowship, Guggenheim Foundation, 1980–81; Fellowship, Ingram Merrill Foundation, 1984. *Memberships:* Associated Writing Programs, President 1979–80; PEN; Poetry Society of America, President 1985–87. *Address:* 523W 121 Street, New York City, NY 10027, USA.

MATTHIAS, Klaus, b. 1 June 1929, Lübeck, Federal Republic of Germany. Studiendirektor, Institut für Literaturwissenschaft Universität Kiel. m. Gabriele Delbrück, 1960, 4 daughters. *Education:* University studies of German Literature, musicology, history of arts and history; State diploma for secondary school teaching; Phil doctor, University of Kiel. *Publications:* Die Musik bei Thomas Mana und Hermann Hesse, 1956; Studien zum Werk thomas Manus, 1967; Thomas Mann und Skandinavien, 1969; Heinrich Mann 1871/1971. Bestandsaufnahme und Untersuchung, 1973. *Contributions to:* Lübeckische Blätter 1950–71, 1982; Literatur in Wissenschaft und Unterricht II, 1970, 75; Hamburger Bibliographien Band 9, 1970, Literaturlexikon 20 Jahrhundert, 1971; Die deutsche Exilliteratur 1933–45, 1973; Jahrbuch des Freien Deutschen Hochstifts 1973, 75; Modern Language Notes, Vol. 90, 1975; Die Großen der Weltgeschichte VII, 1976; Nordelbingen, 46, 1977; Die Welt der Bücher 1972–74, 1981–83; Die Musik in Geschichte und Gegenwart 16, 1979; Formen realistische Erzählkunst. Festschrift für Ch Jolles (Nottingham H B) 1979; Hermann Sudermann. Werk und Wirkung, 1980; 800 Jahre Musik in Lübeck, 1982; II Oeswagen 16 Ein Lübeckisches Jahrbuch, 1954–56, 1969, 1984. *Memberships:* Founder and President 1965–74 of Thomas-Mann-Gesellschaft Lübeck; Founder and Director of Thomas-Mann-Archiv Lübeck 1985; Freies Deutsches Hochstift. *Address:* 2409 Scharbeutz/Ostsee, Konsulweg 5, Federal Republic of Germany.

MATTHIASDOTTIR, Magnea Johanna, b. 13 Jan. 1953, Reykjavik, Iceland. Writer. *Publications:* Kopar, (poems), 1976; Haegara Paelt en Kylt, 1978; Goturaesiskandidatar, 1979; Saetir Strakar, 1981. *Contributions include:* Numerous poems and short stories to magazines and journals. *Membership:* The Writers' Union of Iceland. *Address:* Reykjavikurvegur 29, 101 Reykjavik, Iceland.

MATTHIES, Frank-Wolf, b. 4 Oct. 1951, Berlin, Germany. Author. m. Petra Neumann, 26 May 1977, Berlin, 2 sons, 2 daughters. *Major Publications:* Morgen, 1979; Unbewohnter Raum mit Möbeln, 1980; Für Patricia im Winter, 1981; Exil, 1983; Tagebuch Fortunes, 1985; Die Stadt, 1985. *Contributor to:* Sinn und Form; Schreibheft; Litfass; Dimension; and others. *Honour:* Villa Massimo Stipendium, Rome, Italy, 1983. *Literary Agent:* Petra Matthies, Berlin. *Address:* Rowohlt-Verlag GmbH, Postfach 1349, D–2057 Reinbek, Federal Republic of Germany.

MATTINGLEY, Christobel Rosemary, b. 26 Oct. 1931, Adelaide, South Australia, Australia. Writer. m. Cecil D Mattingley, 17 Dec. 1953, Melbourne, 2 sons, 1 daughter. *Education:* BA 1st class honours, 1951; Certificate in Proficiency in Librarianship, 1952; Registration Certificate and Associate, Library Association of Australia, 1971. *Literary Appointments include:* Librarian: Department of Immigration, Canberra, 1953; Prince Alfred College, Adelaide, 1956–57; St Peters Girls School, Adelaide, 1966–70; Reader Services, Murray Park CAE, 1973–74. Editor, Researcher, Aboriginal History Volume for South Australia, 1983–; Public Lending Right Committee member, 1984–. *Publications include:* Windmill at Magpie Creek, 1971; Tiger's Milk, 1974; New Patches for Old, 1977, 80; The Jetty, 1978, 82; Rummage, 1981, 82; Brave with Ben, 1982; The Magic Saddle, 1983, 84; Duck Boy, 1983; Southerly Buster, 1983; The Angel with a Mouth Organ, 1984; Ghost Sitter, 1984; The Miracle Tree, 1985; Survival in Our Own Land: Aboriginal Experience in South Australia

1836–1985, 1986. *Contributions to:* Numerous professional journals, magazines and publications. Commissioned script writer for South Australian Film Corporation, 1978–79. *Honours:* Fellowship, Australian Council Literature Board, 1975, 83; International Youth Library Scholarship, Munich, Federal Republic of Germany, 1976–77; Writers Award, National Parks and Wildlife Services of New South Wales, 1983. *Memberships include:* Australian Society of Authors; Childrens Book Council; Co-Founder, Community Aid Abroad. *Literary Agent:* A P Watt Limited, England. *Address:* 18 Allendale Grove, Stonyfell, SA 5066, Australia.

MATTSSON, Leni Johanna, b. 25 Nov. 1955, Turku, Finland. Writer. *Major publications:* Isoja Ja Pieniä, 1979; Varhain Läntivät Linnut, 1981; Kylmän Sodan Lapset, 1984. *Contributor to:* Kultuurivihkot; Uusi Nainen on a freelance basis, and others. *Membership:* Finnish Literary Society. *Address:* Poclalankatu 9A11, 20100 Turku 10, Finland.

MATUSZEWSKI, Reinhard, b. 30 July 1951, Ricklinghausen, Westfalen, Germany. Writer. *Education:* Diploma, Secondary Technical School. *Publication:* Aus dem Krankenhaus, 1977. *Contributions of:* Short Stories and Poems in Kaktus and Klinke; Poem in City Magazine; Short story about journey to France in Stadtblatt. *Address:* Hammer Strasse 37, 44 Münster, Federal Republic of Germany.

MAUGHAM, (Lord) Robin, b. 17 May 1916, London, England. Writer. *Education:* BA, Trinity Hall, Cambridge University. *Publications include:* Come to Dust, 1945; Nomad, 1947; Approach to Palestine, 1947; North African Notebook, 1947; The Servant, 1948; Behind the Mirror, 1955; The Man with Two Shadows, 1958; The Slaves of Timbuktu, 1961; November Reef, 1962; The Green Shade, 1968; Somerset & All The Maughams, 1966; The Second Window, 1968; The Wrong People, 1970; Escape from the Shadows, 1972; The Last Encounter, 1972; The Barrier, 1973; The Black Tent & Other Stories, 1974; The Sign, 1974; Search for Nirvana, 1975; Knock on Teak, 1975; Conversations with Willie, 1978; The Dividing Line, 1979. *Member:* Garrick Club. *Agent:* Eric Glass Ltd. *Address:* c/o Eric Glass Ltd, 28 Berkeley Square, London W1, England.

MAUMELA, Titus Ntsieni, b. 25 Dec. 1924, Sibasa. Teacher. m. Rose Mawila, 27 June 1949, Sibasa, 2 sons, 1 daughter. *Education:* BA, University of South Africa. *Publications:* Elewani, novelette, 1954; Mafangambiti, novelette, 1956; Tshililo, drama, 1957; Vhavenda Vho-Matshivha, novel, 1958; Vhuhosi Vhu Tou Bebelwa, novel, 1962; Zwa Mulovha Zwi A Fhelsa, novel, 1963; Zwiitavhathu, short stories, 1965; Masle Wa Vho-Mathavha, novel, 1967; Musandiwa Da Khotei, novel, 1967; Dzingano pa Daithai, folktales, 1968; Thikho ya Luvenda, language manual series, 1970; Matakadzambilu, short stories, 1970; Luvenda, language manual series, 1975 and 1976; Ndi Vho-Muthukhuthukhu, novel, 1977; Vho-Rammbebo, novel, 1981. *Contributions to:* Muvenda. *Honours:* SABC Venda short story competition, 1966; Bantu Education novel writing competition, 1966; Die Suid Afrikaanse Akademie vir Vetenskan en Kuns, 1967; Bantu Education short stories competition, 1971. *Address:* P O Box 2, Vhufuli, Venda, Southern Africa.

MAUNULA, Allan Arthur, b. 24 Sep. 1924, Arthyde, Minnesota, USA. Property Manager. divorced, 2 sons, 2 daughters. *Education:* AA, Grossmont College; BA, San Diego State University; Cultural Doctorate in the Philosophy of Literature, World University. *Contributions to:* 175 poems published in various works including: The Moccasin; The Farmer; Argus; Yearbook of Modern Poetry; Quality Poetry; Poet; Epos; Book Anthology; Bardic Echoes; Midwest Chaparral; Poetry View; Dawn Anthology; Hearts Secrets; The Sandcutters; Rhyme Time for the Very Young: A Vision of Verse. *Honours:* Recipient of numerous literary honours and awards including: Jewel Award, Robert Frost Chapter, Chaparral Poets, 1978; 1st Prize, Pennsylvania Poetry Society, 1979; Grand Prize, Poets of the

Vineyard, 1980. *Memberships:* President: San Diego Torrey Pines Poets; Tierra del Sol Writers Club. 2nd Vice President, Showcase Writers Club; World Poetry Society; San Diego Poets; League of Minnesota Poets; Arizona and California States Poetry Societies; Award Director, Midwest Federation of Chaparral Poets. *Address:* 8835 La Mesa Boulevard, Apt L, La Mesa, CA 92041, USA.

MAURER, Joseph, b. 10 Apr. 1914, Bolzano-Bozen, Italy. Professor of Philosophy; Poet; Scriptor; Translator. m. Maria Luise Zagler, 2 Oct. 1971, 3 daughters. *Education:* PhD, University of Florence, 1938. *Publications:* Italienische Lyrik aus 7 Jahrhunderten von Dante bis Quasimodo, 1978; Italienische Lyrik aus acht Jahrhunderten von Frenz von Assiisi bis Pasolini, 1985; Giovanni Segantini Maler der Alepn, 1982; Commemoration of Spinoza, 1982; Witches and Devils in Alpine Folklore, 1979; Aphorism and Epigramms, 1985. *Contributions to:* Alto Adige; Dolomiten; Schlern; Arunda; Adige-Panorama; Il quadrifoglio; Nuova Rivista Europa; Duomo-Citta-Territorio; speaker in Radio Bolzano. *Honours:* Accademia degli Agiati in Rovereto, Trento; Accademia del Buonconsiglio Trento; Accademia del Bronzi di Riace in Catanzaro; Internationale Burckhardt-Akademie in St Gallen and Rome; Spinozahius in Amsterdam; Accademmia d'Europe in Viterbe. *Memberships:* Sudtiroler Kunsterbund; Turmbund Inssbruck; Holderilu Gesellschaft; Stefan Zweig Gesellschaft; Robert Musil Gesellschaft. *Literary Agent:* Manfrini Editor, Calliano, Trento, Italy. *Address:* Manfrini Editor, Arti Grefiche ed Editoria, I–38060 Calliano, Trento, Italy.

MAUSER, Patricia Rhoads, b. 14 Jan. 1943, Sacramento, California, USA. Author. divorced, 1 son, 1 daughter. *Education:* Washington State University; University of Oregon. *Publications:* How I Found Myself at the Fair, 1980; A Bundle of Sticks, 1982; Rip-Off, 1985. *Contributions to:* Various small publications. *Honour:* Washington State Governor's Award, 1983; Dorothy Canfield Fisher Award, 1984. *Literary Agent:* Amy Berkower, Writers House Incorporated, New York. *Address:* 5111 26th Street North East, Puyallup, WA 98372, USA.

MAXFIELD-MILLER, Elizabeth, b. 20 July 1910, Philadelphia, Pennsylvania, USA. Retired Teacher; Researcher. *Education:* BA, Swarthmore College; MA, 1936, PhD. 1938, Radcliffe-Harvard. *Publications include:* Cent ans de recherches sur Moliere sur sa famille et sur les comediens de sa troupe, Co-Author, 1963; Romansh Poems and Short Stories, Translations, 1971. *Contributions to:* Various learned periodicals; author of articles on Concord Authors. *Honours include:* Chavalier des Palmes Academiques, 1966. *Address:* 159 Elsinore Street, Concord, MA 01742, USA.

MAXWELL, Patricia Anne, b. 9 Mar. 1942, Louisiana, USA. Author. m. Jerry R Maxwell, 1 Aug. 1957, Quitman, Louisiana, 2 sons, 2 daughters. *Literary Appointments:* Writer-in-Residence, University of Northeastern Louisiana. *Publications:* Love's Wild Desire, 1977; Tender Betrayal, 1979; The Storm and the Splender, 1979; Golden Fancy, 1980; Embrace and Conquer, 1981; Royal Seduction, 1983; Surrender in Moonlight, 1984; Midnigt Waltz, 1985; Fierce Eden, 1985; Royal Passion, 1986. *Honours:* Historical Romance Author of the Year, 1985. *Literary Agent:* Donald MacCampbell, Inc. *Address:* Route 1, Box 133, Quitman, LA 71268, USA.

MAY, Gita, b. 16 Sep. 1929, Brussels, Belgium. Professor of French Literature. m. Irving May, 21 Dec. 1947, Waco, Texas, USA. *Education:* BA, Hunter College, 1953. *Literary Appointments:* Lecturer of French, Hunter College, 1953–56; Lecturer of French, 1953–56; Instructor of French, 1956–58; Assistant and Associate Professor of French, 1958–68; Professor, 1968–83; Professor and Chair of Department of French and Romance Philology, Columbia University, 1983–. *Publications:* Diderot et Baudelaire, Critiques d'Art, 1957; Diderot Studies III (co-editor), 1961; De Jean-

Jacques Rousseau a Madame Roland; Essai sur la sensibilite preromentique et revolutionnaire, 1964; Madame Roland and the Age of Revolution (Winner of Columbia University's Van Amringa Distinguished Book Award), 1971; Standhal and the Age of Napoleon, 1978; Critical Edition of Diderot's Essais sur la peinture for the Edition des Oeuvres completes de Diderot, Vol. XIV, 1984. *Contributions to:* professional journals, etc. of essays, reviews and review articles. *Honours:* Numerous honours and awards including: Guggenheim Fellowship, 1964; Fulbright Research Grant, 1965; Chevalier dans l'Urdre des Palmes Academiques by Government of France, 1968, promoted to Officier, 1981; National Endowment for the Humanities Senior Fellowship, 1971; Faculty Award for Distinguished Teaching, Columbia University, 1980. *Memberships:* Member, Executive Council, Modern Language Association of America, 1980–83; President, American Society for Eighteenth Century Studies, 1985–86. Member and Officer of professional organizations. *Address:* 404 West 116th Street, New York, NY 10027, USA.

MAY, John Richard, b. 16 Sep. 1931, New Orleans, Louisiana, USA. Professor and Chairman of English. m. Janet Peroyes, 22 May 1973, New Orleans, 2 sons, 2 daughters. *Education:* BBA, Loyola University, 1951; MA, Spring Hall College, 1957; STL, St Louis University, 1965; PhD, Emory University, 1971. *Publications include:* The Pruning Word; The Parables of Flannery O'Connor, 1976; Film Odyssey: The Art of Film as Search for Meaning (with E Ferlita), 1976; The Parables of Lina Wertmuller (with E Ferlita), 1977; Toward a New Earth: Apocalypse in the American Novel, 1972; Religion in Film, Edited with Michael Bird, 1982. *Contributor to:* numerous magazines and journals. *Memberships include:* Modern Language Association; American Academy of Religion; College Theological Society; Alpha Sigma Nu; Honorary Member, Loyola University APO-LS1. Serv. Org., 1975. *Address:* Department of English, Louisiana State University, Baton Rouge, LA 70803, USA.

MAY, Robin Stephen, b. 26 Dec. 1929, Deal, Kent, England. Author. m. (1) Joan Clarke (dec) 7 June 1958. (2) Maureen Filipkiewicz, 4 Dec. 1976; 2 sons, 1 daughter. *Publications:* Operamania, 1966; Theatremania, 1967; Who Was Shakespeare?, 1974; The Gold Rushes, 1978; Cowboy: The Man and the Myth, (with Joseph G Rosa), 1980; History of the American West, 1984, etc. *Contributions to:* Look & Learn 1965–80, and other educational publications. *Membership:* Society of Authors. *Literary Agent:* Rupert Crew Limited. *Address:* 5 Ridgway Place, London SW19 4EW, England.

MAYCHICK, Diana, b. 23 Feb. 1955, New York, USA. Journalist. m. L Avon Borgo, 23 Sept. 1982, New York, USA. *Education:* BA Cum Laude, Vassar College, 1977; MA (with Distinction), John Hopkins University, 1979. *Publication:* Meryl Streep: The Reluctant Superstar, 1984. *Contributions to:* Various publications. *Honours:* Callan Wolde Writer's Prize; W K Rose Fellowship. *Literary Agent:* Scott Meredith. *Address:* 15 Washington Place, New York, NY 10003, USA.

MAYCOCK, Robert Frederick, b. 21 Feb. 1948, Potters Bar, England. Editor; Journalist. *Education:* BA History and Philosophy of Science, Trinity College, Cambridge, 1966–69; Postgraduate study of musical analysis, University of Leeds, 1974–75. *Literary Appointments:* Staff Journalist, Nature, 1969; Editor, Macmillan Press, 1971; Assistant Editor 1976, Editor 1977, Classical Music Weekly (Classical Music from 1978). *Contributions to:* Sunday Times; Observer; Daily Telegraph; British Music Yearbook; Music and Musicians; Records and Recording. *Membership:* Founder member 1983, Arts Correspondents Group. *Address:* 73 Cromwell Avenue, London N6 5HS, England.

MAYER, Gerda Kamilla, b. 9 June 1927, Karlsbad, Germany. Poet. m. Adolf Mayer, 3 Sep. 1949. *Education:* BA. *Publications:* Treble Poets 2, (with Elon & Halpern); The Knockabout Show, 1978; Monkey on the

Analyst's Couch, 1980; The Candy-Floss Tree, (with Norman Nicholson & Frank Flynn), 1984. *Contributions to:* Encounter; Argo; Writing Women; Poetry Durham; Ambit; She; Arc; Anthologies: Poems for Fun; Sweet & Sour; New Poetry; The Funny Songbook; Poems for 9 Year Olds and Under; Poems for 10 Year Olds and Over. *Honour:* Poetry Book Society recommendation for, Monkey on the Analyst's Couch. *Memberships:* PEN; Poetry Society. *Address:* 12 Margaret Avenue, Chingford, London E4 7NP, England.

MAYER, Hannelore, b. 23 Jan. 1929, Donawitz, Austria. Writer. m. (2) Viktor Mayer, 28 Apr. 1962, 1 son. *Education:* PhD, Physics, University of Graz, Styria, Austria. *Publications:* Novels: Die Hohlen Noahs, 1961; Ein fremder Garten, 1964, 70; Zuflucht hinter der Zeit (As Fenster um Sommer), 1967, 77; Vorhof der Wirklichleit, 1972; Das magische Tagebuch, 1981. Various short stories, poetry and books for young people. *Contributions to:* Neue Deutsche Hefte; Literatur und Kritik; Dimension, USA and others. *Honours:* National Advancement Award, 1957; Peter Rosegger Prize, Styrian Regional Government, 1966; Austrian Children's Book Prize, 1977; Amade Prize, Monaco, 1978; various other awards. *Memberships:* Austrian PEN Club; Austrian Writers Union; Styrian Writers Union; Podium. *Address:* Schwarzspanier-strasse 15/11/8, A-1090 Vienna, Austria.

MAYER, Henri André Van Huysen, b. 19 Dec. 1946, New Haven, Connecticut, USA. Historian; Higher Education Administrator. 1 son, 1 daughter. *Education:* BA, Harvard University; MA, CPhil, University of California, Berkeley. *Publications:* King's Chapel (Boston), 1976; The Crocodile Man, 1982. *Contributor to:* The Atlantic Monthly; Daedalus; etc. *Literary Agent:* The Otte Company, Belmont. *Address:* Board of Regents of Higher Education, 1 Ashburton Place, Boston, MA 02108, USA.

MAYHAR, Ardath (Frances), b. 20 Feb. 1930, Timpson, Texas, USA. Writer; Teacher. m. Joe E Mayhar, 7 June 1958, Nacogdoches, Texas, 2 sons. *Publications:* How The Gods Move in Kyrannon, 1979; Seekers at Shar-Nuhn, 1980; Soul-Singer of Tyrnos, 1981; Warlock's Gift, 1982; Golden Dream: A Fuzzy Odyssey, 1982; Runes of the Lyre, 1982; Khi to Freedom, 1983; Lords of the Triple Moons, 1983; Exile on Vlahil, 1984; The Absolutely Perfect Horse, 1983; The World Ends in Hickory Hollow, 1985; The Saga of Grittel Sundotha, 1985; Medicine Walk, 1985; Carrots and Miggle, 1986; Makra Choria, 1987. *Contributions to:* (stories): The Twilight Zone Magazine; Isaac Asimov's Science Fiction Magazine; Espionage Magazine; Mike Shayne's Mystery Magazine, and many small and literary magazines; Narrative poetry to: Fantasy Book; Pulpsmith; Tempest. *Honour:* Balrog Award, Best Poet, 1985. *Memberships:* Science Fiction Writers of America; Western Writers of America. *Literary Agent:* Ray Puechner. *Address:* Route 1, Box 146, Chireno, TX 75937, USA.

MAYHEW, Christopher Paget (Lord), b. 12 June 1915, London, England. Member of House of Lords. m. Cicely Elizabeth Ludlam, 12 Aug. 1949. *Education:* MA, Christ College, Oxford University. *Publications:* Men Seeking God, 1955; Britain's Role Tomorrow, 1967; Party Game, 1969; Publish It Not..., 1975. *Contributions to:* Numerous publications. *Address:* 39 Wood Road, Wimbledon, London SW20, England.

MAYHEW, David Raymond, b. 18 May 1937, Putnam, Connecticut, USA. College Professor. *Education:* BA, 1958, Amherst College; PhD, 1964, Harvard University. *Literary Appointments:* Instructor, 1963–64; Assistant Professor, 1964–67, University of Massachusetts; Assistant Professor, 1968–72; Associate Professor, 1972–77; Professor, 1977–82; Alfred Cowles Professor of Government, 1982–. Yale University, Department of Political Science. *Publications:* Party Loyalty Among Congressmen, 1966; Congress: The Electoral Connection, 1974; Placing Parties in American Politics, 1986. *Contributions to:* Political journals. *Honours:* Phi Beta Kappa, 1958; Woodrow Wilson Fellowship, 1958–59; American Political Science Association Congressional Fellowship, 1967–68; co-winner, Washington Monthly Annual Political Book Award, 1974; Guggenheim Fellowship, 1978–79; Hoover National Fellowship, 1978–79. *Memberships:* Chairman, Nominating Committee, American Political Science Association, 1976–78; Fellow, American Academy of Arts and Sciences, 1984–. *Address:* Department of Political Science, Yale University, New Haven, CT 06520, USA.

MAYMAN, Janice, b. 15 Aug. 1945, Perth, Western Australia, Australia. Journalist. *Education:* BA, Politics and Economics. *Contributions to:* London Economist; London Sunday Times and National Times of Australia; Perth correspondent, The Age, specialising in the diamond industry and racial issues. *Honours:* Winner, Golden W G Walkley Award for best piece reporting, print, radio or TV for series of articles on John Pat; Walkley Award for best newspaper report, Death, 1984, also published in The Age, 1984. *Address:* 66 Clifton Road, Hollywood, Western Australia, Australia.

MAYNARD, Nancy Kathleen Brazier, b. 25 June 1910, Maidenhead, Berkshire, England. Author. m. Geoffrey Mansfield Maynard, 17 Sep. 1939, Maidenhead, 1 daughter. *Publications:* This Is My Street, 1962; Weep Not, My Wanton, 1964; The Bawdy Wind, 1965; Flesh and Blood, 1967; All Sauce for the Gander, 1968; The Wayward Flesh, 1969; Almost An Affair, 1969; A Fig for Virtue, 1970; Strumpet Voluntary, 1970; Rings for Her Fingers, 1971; When the Devil Drives, 1972; Leaf in the Wind, 1973; A Crumb for Every Sparrow, 1974; Red Roses Dying, 1974; If You Can't Catch, Don't Throw, 1976; A Grief Agoi, 1976; Losers Weepers, 1977; Table 21, 1978; Not Quite Summer, 1980; The Last Dawn, 1981; One for the Stairs, 1982; Too Near The Sun, 1983; Springtime of Tears, 1984; The Distance and the Dark, 1984; Silence and Tears, 1985; Big Girls Don't Cry, 1985. *Address:* Morven House, 5 Keble Road, Maidenhead, Berkshire SL6 6BB, England.

MAYNE, William, b. 16 Mar. 1928, Hull, England. Writer of Children's Fiction. *Publications include:* Follow the Footprints, 1953; A Swarm in May, 1955; The Blue Boat, 1957; A Grass Rope, 1957; (Carnegie Medal, Brit Lib Assn); The Long Night, 1957; The Gobbling Billy, (with R D Caesar, as Dynely James), 1959; The Fishing Party, 1960; The Changeling, 1961; The Twelve Dancers, 1962; Water Boatman, 1964; (Ed., with E Farjeon), The Hamish Hamilton Book of Kings, (in US as A Cavalcade of Kings), 1964; The Hamish Hamilton Book of Queens, (in US as A Cavalcade of Queens), 1965; Fig in the Middle, 1965; The Big Egg, 1967; (compiler), The Hamish Hamilton Book of Heroes (in US as William Mayne's Book of Heroes), 1967; The Hamish Hamilton Book of Giants, (in US as William Mayne's Book of Giants), 1968; Royal Harry, 1971; Game of Dark, 1971; The Incline, 1972; Skiffy, 1972; Robin's Real Engine, 1972; The Jersey Shore, 1973; A Fear and a Day, 1976; Party Pants, 1977; Max's Dream, 1977; It, 1977; While the Bells Ring, 1979; Salt River Times, 1980; The Mouse and the Egg, 1980; The Patchwork Cat, 1981; Skiffy and the Twin Planets, 1982; A Small Pudding for Wee Gowrie, 1982; All the King's Men, 1982; Winter Quarters, 1982; The Red Book of Hob Stories; The Green Book of Hob Stories, The Yellow Book of Hob Stories, The Blue Book of Hob Stories, 1984; Drift, 1984. *Literary Agent:* David Higham Associates. *Address:* c/o David Higham Assocs, 3-5 Lower John Street, London W1R 4HA, England.

MAYO, Margaret Mary, b. 10 May 1935, London, England. Teacher. m. Peter Mayo, 26 July 1958, 2 sons, 1 daughter. Welling. *Education:* B Sc, University of Southampton; Postgraduate Certificate in Education. *Publications:* The Book of Magical Horses, 1976; The Book of Magical Birds, 1977; The Book of Magical Cats, 1978; Saints, Birds and Beasts, 1980; The Italian Fairy Book, 1981; Fairy Tales From France, 1983. *Address:* 85 Peacock Lane, Brighton, Sussex BN1 6WA, England.

MAYO, Patricia Elton, b. 7 Sep. 1915, Australia. Sociologist; Author. m. Dunstan Curtis, 22 May 1950, London, England. *Education:* Studies, History, Economics, Cambridge University, England. *Publications:* The Making of a Criminal, 1969; The Roots of Identity, 1974. Author: Probation and Aftercare in Europe, Stationery Office, 1963 (European Commission on Crime Problems); The State of the Union of Europe, Co-author, 1979. *Honours:* Chevalier, L'Ordre des Palmes Academiques, France, 1960. *Membership:* Welsh Union of Writers. *Literary Agent:* M Hanbury, 27 Walcot Square, London SE11. *Address:* Bryn Awel House, Montgomery, Powys SY15 6PU, Wales.

MAYRÖCKER, Friederike, b. 20 Dec. 1924, Vienna, Austria. Writer and Poetess. *Publications include:* More than 40 books of Poetry, Childrens' books, Prose, Radio Plays, most recent being: Reise durch die Nacht, 1984; Das Herzzerreiszende der Dinge, 1985. *Contributions include:* Numerous articles in literary journals and magazines since 1966. *Honours:* Hörspielpreis der Kriegsblinden, 1968; Osterrichischer Wurdigungspeiz, 1975; Preis der Stadt Wien, 1976; George-Trankl-Preis, 1977; Roswitha-von-Gandersheim-Preis, 1982; Anton-Wildgans-Preis, 1982; Grosser Osterreichischer Staatspreis, 1982; Literaturpreis des Südwestfunk, 1985. *Memberships:* Österreichischer Kunstsenat Wien; Akademie der Künste Berlin-West; Internationales Künstlergremium; Grazer Autorenversammlung; Deutsche Akademie für Sprache und Dichtung Darmstadt. *Address:* Sentagasse 16/40, A–1050 Vienna, Austria.

MAZLISH, Bruce, b. 15 Sep. 1923, New York City, USA. Historian; Writer. *Education:* BA, Columbia College, 1944; MA, 1946, PhD, 1955, Columbia University. *Publications include:* The Western Intellectual Tradition: From Leonardo to Hegel with J Bronowski, 1960; In Search of Nixon: A psychohistorical study, 1972; Kissinger: The European Mind in American Policy, 1972; The Revolutionary Asceti, 1976. *Contributor to:* Various journals and magazines. *Honours:* Fellow, American Academy of Arts and Sciences, 1967; Clement Staff Essay Award, 1968. *Address:* 11 Lowell Street, Cambridge, MA 02138, USA.

MAZUR, Gail Lewis Beckwith, b. Cambridge, Massachusetts, USA. Writer. m. Michael Mazur, 28 Dec. 1958, Belmont, Massachusetts, USA, 1 son, 1 daughter. *Education:* BA, Smith College; MA, Lesley College. *Publications:* Nightfire, 1978; The Pose of Happiness, 1985. *Contributions to:* Contributor to various journals including, The New Republic; The Hudson Review; The Boston Review; The Boston Globe. *Honours:* National Endowment for The Arts Award, 1978; Poetry Society of America Prize, 1980. *Memberships:* PEN; PEN New England, Executive Committee; Poetry Society of America. *Address:* 5 Walnut Avenue, Cambridge, MA 02140, USA.

MAZZAROLO, Evo Andrea, b. 1 May 1953. Storeman Stock Controller. *Appointments:* Sub-Manager, Supermarket; Forklift Truck Driver. *Contributions to:* North American Mentor. *Address:* 15 Aveland Avenue, Trinity Gardens, SA 5068, Australia.

MBITA, Hashim Iddi, b. 2 Nov. 1933, Tabora, Tanzania. Army Officer. *Education:* E African School of Coops, Kabete, Kenya; American Press Institute, Columbia University, New York, USA; Mons. Off, Cadet School, Aldershot, England. *Memberships:* Publicity Secretary, Tanganyika African National Union, 1967–78; National Executive Secretary, 1970–71; Executive Secretary, OAU Liberation Committee, 1972–. *Address:* OAU Liberation Committee, PO Box 1767, Dar es Salaam, Tanzania.

MBITI, John Samuel, b. 30 Nov. 1931, Kitui, Kenya. Clergyman, Professor. m. Verena Siegenthaler, 15 May 1967, Bern, Switzerland, 1 son, 3 daughters. *Education:* BA (London), Makerere University, Kampala, Uganda; AB, ThB, Barrington College, Rhode Island, USA; PhD, Cambridge, England. *Publications include:* Akamba Stories, 1966; African Religions and Philosophy, 1969;

Poems of Nature and Faith, 1969; Concepts of God in Africa, 1970; New Testament Eschatology in an African Background, 1971; The Crisis of Mission in Africa, 1971; Love and Marriage in Africa, 1973; The Voice of Nine Bible Trees, 1973; Introduction to African Religion, 1974; The Prayers of African Religion, 1975; Confessing Christ in Different Cultures (editor), 1977; Indigenous Theology and the Universal Church (editor), 1979; Christian and Jewish Dialogue on Man (editor), 1980; Evangelische Kirchenlexikon (co-editor) 5 volumes, 1985–89; Bible and Theology in African Christianity, 1986. *Contributions to:* Worldview; Presence; Africa Theology Journal; International Review of Mission; and others. *Honour:* Honorary LHD, Barrington College, Rhode Island, USA, 1973. *Membership:* Studiorum Novi Testamenti Society. *Address:* Einschlagweg 11, CH 3400 Burgdorf, Switzerland.

MEACHER, Michael Hugh, b. 4 Nov. 1939, Hemel Hempstead, Hertfordshire, England. Member of Parliament. m. Molly Christine Reid, 11 Apr. 1962, Little Goddesden, Herts, 2 sons, 2 daughters. *Education:* Greats, Philosophy and History, Class 1, New College, Oxford, 1962; Diploma in Social Administration, London School of Economics, 1963. *Publications:* Taken For A Ride: Residential Homes For The Elderly Mentally Infirm: A Study of Separatism in Social Policy, 1972; Socialism With A Human Face, 1982. *Contributions to:* Several hundred articles in newspapers and journals, 1970–. *Memberships:* Shadow Cabinet, 1983–; Chief Opposition Spokesman, Health and Social Security, 1983–; Labour Party National Executive Committee, 1983–. *Literary Agent:* Andrew Best. *Address:* 45 Cholmeley Park, London N6, England.

MEADE, Richard Oron, b. 21 July 1946, Clinton, Iowa, USA. Editor. Divorced, 1 daughter. *Education:* BA, Earlham College, 1968; MA, Clark University, 1974. *Publications:* Swimming The Channel, 1981. *Contributions to:* Poetry in magazines. *Honours:* Worcester Poetry Festival Winner, 1972. *Memberships:* Poets and Writers Inc; Illinois Writers Inc. *Address:* 4142 Rose Avenue, Western Springs, IL 60558, USA.

MEADOW, Charles T, b. 16 Dec. 1929, Paterson, New Jersey, USA. Professor. m. (1) Harriet Reiss, 9 Sep. 1956, New York. (2) Mary Louise Shipskey, 24 June 1977, Baltimore, 1 son, 3 daughters. *Education:* BA Mathematics, University of Rochester, 1951; MS Mathematics, Rutgers University, 1954. *Literary Appointments:* Editor, Journal of the American Society for Information Science, 1977–84; Editor, Canadian Journal of Information Science, 1985–. *Publications:* The Analysis of Information Systems, 1967; Man-Machine Communication, 1970; The Story of Computers, 1970; Sounds and Signals: How We Communicate, 1975; Applied Date Management, 1976; Basics of Online Searching (with Pauline A Cochrane), 1981; Telecommunications for Management (with Albert S Tedesco), 1985. *Contributions to:* Bulletin of the American Society for Information Science; Journal of the American Society for Information Science; Online; Online Review; Information Services and Use; Special Libraries. *Honours:* Honorable mention, Children's Science Book Awards, New York Academy of Science, 1975; Visiting Professor, University of Sheffield, 1980–81; Research Grantee of: National Science Foundation, US Department of Energy, Online Computer Library Center Inc. *Memberships:* Association for Computing Machinery; American Society for Information Science; Fellow, Institute of Information Scientists; Canadian Association for Information Science; Sigma Xi. *Address:* Faculty of Library and Information Science, University of Toronto, 140 St George Street, Toronto, Ontario, M5S 1A1, Canada.

MEANS, Gordon Paul, b. 9 May 1927, Spokane, Washington, USA. University Professor. m. Ingunn Norderval, 12 June 1956, Eugene, Oregon, USA, 2 sons, 2 daughters. *Education:* University of Oregon, 1946–47; Grinnell College, 1947–48; BA, Political Science, Reed College, 1950; MA, Political Science, 1952, PhD,

Political Science, 1960, University of Washington. *Literary Appointments:* Assistant Professor. Willamette University, 1958–60; Assistant Professor, Gustavus Adolphus College, 1960–65; Assistant Professor, University of Iowa, 1965–66; Associate Professor, Willamette University, 1958–60; Assistant Professor, Gustavus Adolphus College, 1960–65; Assistant Professor, University of Iowa, 1965–66; Associate Professor, University of Washington, 1966–67; Associate Professor, 1967–73; Professor, 1973–, McMaster University, Hamilton, Ontario, Canada. *Publications:* Malaysian Politics 1970, 2nd revised edition 1976; Editor: Development and Underdevelopment in Southeast Asia 1977; Editor: The Past in Southeast Asia's Present 1978. *Contributions to:* The Role of Islam in the Political Development of Malaysia Comparative Politics, 1969; Public Policy Toward Religion in Malaysia Pacific Affairs, 1978, Energy Resource Development and Management in Malaysia Contemporary Southeast Asia, 1983. Other articles in Pacific Affairs; Asian Survey; Comparative Politics; Canadian Journal of Political Science etc. *Honours include:* Ford Foundation Fellowship, 1954–55; Smith-Mundt visiting Professor, University of Malaya, 1962–63; Ford Foundation Fellowship, 1974–75; Canada Council Leave Fellowship, 1974–75; Max Bell Foundation ASEAN Research Fellowship, 1984. *Memberships:* Canadian Council for Southeast Asian Studies; Canadian Society for Asian Studies; Malaysian Branch Royal Asiatic Society; Association for Asian Studies; Canadian Political Science Association. *Address:* 1271 King Street West, Hamilton, Ontario, Canada L8S 1M5.

MEBS, Gudrun, b. 8 Jan. 1944, Bad Mergentheim, Federal Republic of Germany. Author. *Education:* Diploma of Frankfurt State Academy of Acting. *Publications:* Birgit, eine Geschichte von Sterben, 1982; Sonntagskind, 1983; Oma, schreit des Frieder, 1984; Meistens Gert's Mir Gut Mit Dir, 1985; Und Wieder schreit des Frieder: Oma! 1985. *Contributions to:* Numerous magazines and journals. *Honours:* Scholarship of the German, Litteraturfonds; German Children's Book Prize, 1984; German Children's Book Prize, 1983 Honour List; La Vache Qui Lit, Zurich 1984; Janus Horczak Prize Medaille, 1985. *Address:* Schleissheimer Str 64, 8000 Munchen 40, Federal Republic of Germany.

MECH, L David, b. 18 Jan. 1937, Auburn, New York, USA. Wildlife Research Biologist. m. Betty Ann Smith, 30 Aug. 1958 (divorced July 1985), 3 sons, 1 daughter. *Education:* BS Conservation, Cornell University, Ithaca, New York, 1958; PhD Wildlife Ecology, Purdue University, Lafayette, Indiana, 1962. *Publications:* Wolves of Isle Royale, 1966; The Wolf: Ecology and Behavior of an Endangered Species, 1970, paperback reprint 1981; Handbook of Animal Radio-Tracking, 1983. *Contributions to:* About 200 scientific, semi-technical, and popular articles on wolves, deer, raccoons, ecology, predation, radio-tracking and conservation. *Honours:* Special Achievement Award for wolf reserach in Minnesota, United States Fish and Wildlife Service, 1970; Terrestrial Wildlife Publication Award for, The Wolf, The Wildlife Society, 1972; Civil Servant of the Year, Region III, United States Fish and Wildlife Service, 1973; Best Wildlife Book for, The Wolf, Symposium on Threatened and Endangered Wildlife, Washington, District of Columbia, 1974; Distinguished Service in Science Education and Science Research, Minnesota Academy of Sciences, 1981; Special Achievement Award for publication record 1975–80, United States Fish and Wildlife Service, 1981; Gulf Oil Professional Conservationist Award, 1984. *Address:* 2400 West Larpenteur #6, St. Paul, MN 55113, USA.

MEDLICOTT, William Norton, b. 11 May 1900, Wandsworth, England. Professor of History. m. Dr Dorothy Kathleen Coveney (dec), 18 July 1936. *Education:* MA (Distinction), 1926; DLit(Modern History), 1952, University College and Institute of Historical Research, London. *Literary Appointments:* Official Historian to Ministry of Economic Warfare, London, 1942–58; Editor, Longman's Series A History of England, 1946–; Senior Editor, Documents on British Foreign Policy 1919–39, 1965–. *Publicatons include:* The Congress of Berlin and After, 1938, 1976; British Foreign Policy since Versailles, 1940, 1968; The Economic Blockade, volume I 1952, volume II 1959; Bismarck, Gladstone, and the Concert of Europe, 1956; Bismarck and Modern Germany, 1965; Contemporary England, 1967, 1976; The Lion's Tail, (with D K Coveney), 1971; Bismarck and Europe, 1971. *Contributions to:* numerous Reviews and Journals. *Honours:* Honorary DLitt, 1970, Wales; Honorary LittD 1975, Leeds; Honorary DLitt 1984, Buckingham; CBE, 1982. *Memberships:* Governing body, Historical Association, 1930–; Royal Historical Society, 1953–56; Royal Institute of International Affairs, 1955–70; The Annual Register, 1947–70. *Address:* 172 Watchfield Court, Sutton Court Road, London W4 4NE, England.

MEDVEDEV, Roy Aleksandrovich, b. 14 Nov. 1925, Tbilisi, USSR. Historian; Sociologist. m. Galina A Gaidina, 1956, 1 son. *Education:* Leningrad State University PhD. *Literary Appointments:* Editor, Academy of Pedagogical Sciences, USSR; Deputy to Editor-in-Chief, Publishing House of Pedagogical Literature, Moscow, 1957–59; Freelance Author, 1972–. *Publications:* Vocational Education in Secondary Schools, 1960; Faut-il rehabiliter Staline?, 1969; A Question of Madness, with Zhores Medvedev, 1971; Let History Judge, 1972; On Socialist Democracy, 1975; Qui a ecrit le Don Paisible?, 1975; La Revolution d'octobre etait-elle ineluctablee, 1975; Solschenizyn und die Sowjetische Linke, 1976; Khrushchev – The Years in Power, with Z Medvedev, 1976; Political Essays, 1976; Problems in the Literary Biography of Mikhail Sholokhov, 1977; Samizdat Register, 1978; Philip Mironov and the Russian Civil War, with S Starikov, 1978; The October Revolution, 1979; On Stalin and Stalinism, 1979; On Soviet Dissent, 1980; Nokolai Bukharin – The Last Years, 1980; Leninism and Western Socialism, 1981; An End to Silence, 1982; Krushchev, 1983; All Stalin's Men, 1983; China and the Superpowers, 1986; Author of over 150 professional and general articles. *Address:* c/o Z A Medvedev, National Institute for Medical Research, The Ridgeway, Mill Hill, London NW7 1AA, England.

MEDVEDEV, Zhores Alexandrovich, b. 14 Nov. 1925, Thilisi, USSR. Research Scientist; Biochemist. m. Margarita Nikolaevna Busina, 21 Oct. 1951. Moscow, 2 sons. *Education:* BSc, K A Timiriasev Agricultural Academy, Moscow, 1950; PhD, Research Institute of Plant Physiology, Academy of Sciences of the USSR, 1951. *Publications:* Protein Biosynthesis, 1963; The Rise and Fall of T D Lysenko, 1969; The Medvedev Papers, 1971; One Day in the Life of Ivan Denisovich, 1973; Khrushchev : The Years in Power, with Roy Medvedev, 1976; Soviet Science, 1978; Nuclear Disaster in the Urals, 1979; Andropov, 1983. *Contributor to:* Over 200 articles in scientific and political journals. *Honours:* Book Award, Moscow Naturalist Society, 1965. *Memberships include:* New York Academy of Sciences; American Gerontological Society; Biochemical Society, England; Genetic Society. *Address:* National Institute for Medical Research, Mill Hill, London NW7 1AA, England.

MEEK, Forrest B (Burns), b. 11 June 1928, Tustin, Michigan, USA. Educator; Writer. m. Jean Grimes, 24 June 1953, Lansing, Michigan, 2 sons, 2 daughters. *Education:* AA, Spring Arbor College; BA, Michigan State University; MA, Central Michigan University. *Literary Appointments:* Historian, Clare County Bicentennial Committee, 1974; Historian, White Pine Historical Society, 1979. *Publications:* Michigan's Timber Battle Ground, 1976; Michigan's Heartland 1900–1918, 1979; White Pine, due to be published 1987. *Contributor to:* The Fortune Forest, Timberman's Journal, 1981; A Close Look at P.L.480, Asia, 1962. *Honour:* Outstanding Historian, Michigan Bicentennial Series. *Membership:* Executive Secretary, White Pine historical Society. *Literary Agent:* Edgewood Press, Clare, Michigan. *Address:* 2865 E. Rock Road, Clare, MI 48617, USA.

MEEK, Jay, b. 23 Aug. 1937, Grand Rapids, Michigan, USA. Professor; Writer. m. Martha George, 29 Aug. 1966, Syracuse, New York, 1 daughter. *Education:* BA, University of Michigan; MA, Syracuse University. *Literary Appointments:* Guest member, Writing faculty, Sarah Lawrence College, Bronxville, New York, 1980–82; Associate professor, Massachusetts Institute of Technology, Cambridge, Massachusetts, 1982–83; Writer in Residence, Memphis State University, Tennessee, 1984; currently, Professor, University of North Dakota, Grand Forks, North Dakota. *Publications:* The Week the Dirigible Came, 1976; Drawing on the Walls, 1980; Earthly Purposes, 1984. *Contributions to:* Poetry: The Paris Review; The Yale Review; The Virginia Quarterly Review; numerous others. *Honours:* Award, National Endowment for the Arts, 1972–73; Preliminary Judge, Associated Writing Programmes, 1981; Judge, American Book Awards, 1983. *Memberships:* American Poets, Playwrights, Editors, Essayists and Novelists. *Address:* University of North Dakota, University Station 8237, Grand Forks, ND 58202, USA.

MEEKS, Esther MacBain, b. 17 Feb. 1921, Council Bluffs, Iowa, USA. Writer. m. Wilkison Winfield Meeks, 23 Feb. 1946, New York, 2 daughters. *Education:* BA, University of Iowa, 1942. *Appointments:* Scriptwriter, Radio OWI, Omaha, 1943, Radio Station WSAY, Rochester, 1944–45; Director, Radio Broadcasting, Western Maryland College, 1948–49; Freelance Writer for Children, 1950–. *Publications:* Jeff and Mr James' Pond, 1962; Web of Winter, 1967; 1972; 1983; 1985. Canticles for Christmas, 1968. *Contributor to:* Fifth Summer Anthology, 1976. *Honours:* Junior Literary Guild Selection, 1962; Honorable Mention Recipient, Distinguished Writing for Children award, 1963. *Memberships:* Children's Reading Round Table of Chicago; Society of Children's Book Writers. *Address:* 2911 Oak St, Terre Haute, IN 47803, USA.

MEGGED, Aharon, b. 10 Aug. 1920, Wloclavec, Poland. Writer. m. Eda Zirlin-Zoritte, 11 May 1944, Tel Aviv, 2 sons. *Appointments:* Editor, Literary Bi-Weekly, Massa, 1952–55; Literary Editor, Lamerhav Daily, 1953–68; Cultural Attache, Israel Embassy, London, England, 1968–71; Columnist, Davar Daily, 1971–. *Publications:* Fortunes of a Fool, 1960; Living on the Dead, 1965; The Short Life, 1971; Evyater's Notebooks, 1973; Asahel, 1978; The Flying Camel and the Golden Hump, 1982. *Contributor to:* Atlantic Monthly; Encounter; Midstream; Partisan Review. *Honours:* Ussishkin Literary Prize, 1955; Brenner Literary Prize, 1957; Shlonsky Literary Prize, 1963; Bialik Literary Prize, 1973; Fichman Prize, 1979; K B Smilen Award, 1983. *Memberships:* Israel Writers Association; Israel PEN Centre, President; The Hebrew Academy. *Literary Agent:* Gloria Stern, New York, USA. *Address:* 26 Rupin St, Tel Aviv 63457, Israel.

MEGGITT, Mervyn John, b. 20 Aug. 1924, Warwick, Australia. Anthropologist. m. Joan Alice Lillistone, 1 Jan. 1949, Brisbane. *Education:* BA Honours 1953, MA Honours 1955, PhD 1960, Anthropology, University of Sydney. *Publications:* Desert People, 1962; The Lineage System of the Mae Enga of New Guinea, 1965; Gods, Ghosts and Men in Melanesia, (co-editor), 1965; Gadjari Among the Walbiri Aborigines, 1966; Pigs, Pearlshells and Women, (co-editor), 1969; Studies in Enga History, 1974; Blood is Their Argument, 1977; Law and Order in the New Guinea Highlands, (co-author), 1985. *Contributions to:* Professional anthropological journals and collections. *Address:* Department of Anthropology, Queens College, City University of New York, Flushing, NY 11367, USA.

MEHAFFY, Robert Eugene, b. 4 Dec. 1935, French Camp, California, USA. Educator. m. Irene M Carpenter, 13 June 1964, Carmichael, California. *Education:* AA, Sacramento City College, 1962; BA, 1964, MA, 1967, State University, Sacramento. *Publications:* Writer's Workshop, 1972; Survival, 1975; Writing for the Real World, 1980; Words on Words, 1981; Writer's Guidebook, 1982. *Contributions to:* Educational Technology; Teaching English at the Two-Year College;

49 magazine articles in various boating publications. *Membership:* American Society of Journalists and Authors. *Address:* 6326 Palm Drive, Carmichael, CA 95608, USA.

MEHRABIAN, Albert, b. 17 Nov. 1939, Iran. Psychologist. *Education:* BS 1961, MS 1961, Mechanical Engineering, Massachusetts Institute of Technology, USA; PhD Psychology, Clark University, 1964. *Literary Appointments:* Division 8 editor, APA Proceedings, 1969; Consulting editor, Journal of Psycholinguistic Research, 1971–; Consulting editor, Journal of Personality and Social Psychology, 1973–76; Consulting editor, Perceptual and Motor Skills, 1973; Consulting Editor, Sociometry, 1974–77; Member of Editorial Board, Environmental Psychology and Nonverbal Behaviour, 1975–. *Publications:* An Analysis of Personality Theories, 1968; Language Within Language: Immediacy, a Channel in Verbal Communication, (with M Wiener), 1968; Tactics of Social Influence, 1970; Silent Messages, 1971; Nonverbal Communication, 1972; A Theory of Affiliation, (with S Ksionzky), 1974; An Approach to Environmental Psychology, (with J A Russell), 1974; A Manual for the Mehrabian Measures of Achieving Tendency, 1975; Public Places and Private Spaces: The Psychology of Work, Play, and Living Environments, 1976; Manual for the Questionnaire Measure of Stimulus Screening and Arousability, 1976; Basic Behavior Modification, 1978; Nonverbal Communication, film, 1978; Manual for the Child Language Ability Measures, (with C Moynihan), 1979; Administration Booklet for the Child Language Ability Measures (CLAM); Inflection Production, Grammar Imitation, Grammar Formedness Judgment, and Grammar Equivalence Judgment, (with C Moynihan), 1979; Basic Dimensions for a General Psychological Theory; Implications for Personality, Social, Environmental, and Developmental Studies, 1980; Silent Messages: Implicit Communication of Emotions and Attitudes, 2nd edition, 1981. *Contributions to:* Numerous learned journals. *Address:* 9305 Beverlycrest Drive, Beverly Hills, CA 90210, USA.

MEHROTRA, Sri Ram, b. 23 June 1931, Etawah, UP, India. Professor. Writer on History & Politics. *Education:* BA 1948, MA 1950, Allahabad University; PhD, University of London, England, 1960, *Major Publications:* India & The Commonwealth 1885–1929, 1967; The Emergence of the Indian National Congress, 1971; The Commonwealth & The Nation, 1978; Towards India's Freedom & Partition, 1970. *Contributor to:* Journal of Commonwealth & Comparative Politics; Journal of Imperial & Commonwealth History; Journal of Development Studies; Indian Economic & Social Historical Review; and others. *Address:* Department of History, H P University, Simla 171005, India.

MEHTA, Purnima Vinay, b. 28 May 1947, Vagpur, India. Teacher, English Language & Literature. m. Vrindaran, 13 June 1981, 1 daughter. *Education:* Certificate, Teaching English; Diploma, Journalism; PhD, Indo Anglian Literature. *Appointment:* President, Salihya Sangam, 1975–. *Publication:* Woman in the Indo Anglian Novels, 1985. *Contributor to:* Various periodicals. *Membership:* Literary Association of Bharnagar. *Address:* 1777 Sai Akhibesh, Sardarmagar, Bhavragar 364001, India.

MEHTA, Ved Parkash, b. 21 Mar. 1934, Lahore, India. Naturalised Citizen of USA. Staff Writer. m. Linn Fenimore Cooper Cary, 17 Dec. 1983, New York, 1 daughter. *Education:* BA, Pomona College; BA, MA, Oxford University, England; MA, Harvard University, USA. *Appointment:* Visiting Professor, Bard College, 1985; Staff Writer, The New Yorker Magazine. *Publications:* Face to Face, 1957; Walking the Indian Streets, 1960; Fly and the Fly-Bottle, 1963; The New Theologian, 1968; Delinquent Chacha, 1967; Portrait of India, 1970; John is Easy to Please, 1971; Mahatma Gandhi and his Apostles, 1977; The New India, 1978; Photographs of Chachaji, 1980; A Family Affair: India under Three Prime Ministers, 1982; Daddyji, 1971; Mamaji, 1979; Vedi, 1982; The Ledge Between the

Streams, 1984; Sound-Shadows of the New World, 1986. *Honours:* Phi Beta Kappa; Hasen Fellowship, 1956–59; Harvard Prize Fellow, 1959–60; Guggenheim Fellow, 1971–72, 1977–78; Ford Foundation Travel and Study Grantee, 1971–76; Public Policy Grantee, 1979–82; MacArthur Prize Fellow, 1982–; Visiting Scholar, Case Western Reserve, 1974; Beatty Lecturer, McGill University, 1979. *Literary Agents:* A P Watt, London, England; Georges Borchardt, New York, USA. *Address:* c/o The New Yorker Magazine, 25 W 43rd Street, New York, NY 10036, USA.

MEIDINGER, Ingeborg Lucie, b. 16 March 1923, Berlin. Writer. *Education:* Studies of History and German Literature; D Phil. *Publications:* 40 works of novels, poetry, stories, radio plays, essays and critiques including: Welterlebnis in deutscher Gegenwartsdichtung 1956; Der Mond von Gestern (novel) 1963; Ordentliche Leute (stories), 1976; Zukunfts-chornik (poetry), 1978. *Contributor to:* ORF, Vienna; Die Presse, Vienna; Zeitwende; Die Welt; Nurnberger Zeitung and others. *Honours include:* Hans Sachs Drama Prize, 1976; Max Dauthenday Plaque, 1979; International Molle Literary Prize, Sweden, 1979. *Meberships:* PEN Club, Federal German Republic; European Authors' Association Die Kogge (Chairman 1967); Association of German Writers. *Address:* Schobertweg 1 a, D 8520 Erlangen, Federal Republic of Germany.

MEIER, Gerald Marvin, b. 9 Feb. 1923, Tacoma, Washington, USA. Matsushita Professor of International Economics and Policy Analysis. m. Gilda Avis Slote, 24 Oct. 1954, 4 sons. *Education:* BA, Reed College, 1947; BLitt, Oxford, 1952; PhD, Harvard, 1953. *Appointments:* General Editor, Economic Development Series, 1977–78; Editor, Pioneers in Development, 1984. *Publications:* Economic Development, 1957; International Trade & Development, 1963; Leading Issues in Economic Development, 1984; International Economics, 1986; Princing Policy for Development Management, 1982; Problems of a World Monetary Order, 1982; Emerging from Poverty, 1984. *Contributor to:* 56 articles in learned journals. *Honour:* MA, honoris causa, Wesleyan University, 1959. *Address:* 774 Santa Ynez, Stanford, CA 94305, USA.

MEIER, Joel F, b. 18 Jan. 1940, Minden, Nebraska, USA. Professor, Recreation Management. m. Patricia Dee Schmadeke, 22 Aug. 1965, Lincoln, Nebraska. *Education:* BS, MS, University of Nebraska; PhD, Indiana University. *Publications:* Backpacking, 1980; High Adventure Outdoor Pursuits: Organization and Leadership, 1980; Camp Counselling: Leadership and Programming for the Organized Camp, 1983. *Contributions to:* Parks and Recreation Magazine; Trends; Journal of Physical Education, Recreation and Dance; Journal of Leisure Research; Leisure Today. *Honour:* Fulbright Scholar to New Zealand, 1980. *Membership:* American Association for Leisure and Recreation (Past President, 1979–80). *Address:* 9615 Old Mill Trail, Missoula, MT 59802, USA.

MEIJER, Mia. *Education:* Graduate in Dutch Language and Literature, University of Amsterdam, Holland. *Appointments:* Dramaturge for Stage and Television, Holland to 1976; Freelance author for Theatre and Television, 1976–present. *Publications include:* Professor Stranger, 1977 (TV serial); Schreber, (Theatre Play), 1977; Your Bed Your Cupboard, (TV Play), 1978; Caviar and Red Herring, (TV play), 1978; ZENO/SVEVO Confessions, (TV documentary), 1978; Tasso in Weimar, (theatre play), 1979; A Little Seducing, (TV film), 1979; George Sand, (Music Theatre play), 1980; Cecile, (theatre play), 1980; Eva and Henne, (theatre play), 1981; Eva and Sandra, (theatre play), 1981; Eva and Freek, (VARA), 1981; Asper, (theatre play), 1982; I Don't Like You, (TV film), 1982. *Honour:* Albert von Dalsum Award, 1977. *Address:* Oude Zijds Voorburgwal 326/11, 1012 GM Amsterdam, The Netherlands.

MEINERS, Roger Evert, b. 28 Dec. 1948, Walla Walla, Washington, USA. Economics Professor. m. Cary O'Keefe Brown, 28 Nov. 1981, Floydada, Texas, USA, 1 daughter. *Education:* BA, Washington State University; MA, University of Arizona; JD, University of Miami; PhD, Virginia Polytechnic Institute. *Publications:* Victim Compensation, 1977; Barriers to Corporate Growth, 1979; Legal Environment of Business, 1st Edition, 1981, 2nd Edition, 1985. *Contributions to:* Policy Review; International Review of Law and Economics; Public Finance Quarterly; Business Horizons; Public Choice; Social Science Review; Management Review. *Address:* Department of Economics, Clemson University, Clemson, SC 29631, USA.

MEINHARDT, Günther, b. 22 Jan. 1925, Blankenburg, Federal German Republic. Writer; Historian. m. Susanne Meylahn, 28 July 1970, Heidelberg. *Education:* Universities of Halle and Gottingen; PhD, 1958. *Literary Appointment:* Publisher of Lower Saxonia and Prussia district historical and anecdotes, animal stories and history books for young people. *Publications:* Muenz-u. Geldgeschichte des Herzogtume Preussen, 1959; Gottinger Originale, 1962; 4th edition, 1982; Bullerjahn, Göttinger Studenten-Anekdoten, 1974; Die Universitat Gottingen, 1977; Gemuenzt zu Konigsberg, 1977; Aus Brombergs Vergangenheit, 1973; Der Admiral der Hanse, 1976; Der Weltkrieg in alten Ansichten, 1979; Gottingen in alten Ansichten, 1970; Garnisonstadt Gottingen, 1981; Eduard von Simson, Preussens Parlamentspraesident, 1981; 750 Jahre Kulm, 1983. *Contributor to:* Gottinger Tageblatt; Der Westpreusse; Duisburger Journal (more than 1000 articles); Animal stories in Der Deutsche Kleintierzuchter (more than 500). *Honours:* Internationaler Buchpreis fur Geschichte und Landeskunde, 1981; Needle of Gold of Honour of German Animal Friends, 1983; President, der Prussia-Gesellschaft, 1983–; Founder of Dr. Günther Meinhardt Foundation, 1983. *Memberships:* German Authors Association; Heinrich Berth Society. *Address:* Über den Höfen 12, 3401 Waake, Federal Republic of Germany.

MEINKE, Peter, b. 29 Dec. 1932, Brooklyn, New York, USA. Writer; Teacher. m. Jeanne Clark, 14 Dec. 1957, 2 sons, 2 daughters. *Education:* BA, Hamilton College, Clington, New York, 1955; MA, University of Michigan, 1961; PhD, University of Minnesota, 1965. *Literary Appointments:* Poet-in-Residence: Hamlin University, 1973; Hamilton College, 1980; Jenny McKean Moore Lecturer, George Washington University, 1981–82. *Publications:* Howard Nemerov, 1968; Lines from Neuchatel, 1974; The Night Train and the Golden Bird, 1977; The Rat Poem, 1978; Trying to Surprise God, 1981. *Contributions to:* The New Yorker; Yankee; The Atlantic; The New Republic; The Virginia Quarterly; Poetry; The Georgia Review; various others. *Honours:* Creative Writing Fellowship, National Education Association, 1974–75; Gustav Davidson Memorial Award, 1976, Lucille Medwick Memorial Award, 1984, Poetry Society of America; O'Henry Award, 1983. *Memberships:* Poetry Society of America; Poets, Playwrights, Editors, Essaysist and Novelists International; Florida Colleges English Association. *Address:* 147 Wildwood Lane South East, St Petersburg, FL 33705, USA.

MEISLER, Stanley, b. 14 May 1931, New York, USA. Journalist. m. Elizabeth Fox, 21 Jan. 1984, Paris, 5 sons, 1 daughter. *Education:* BA English Literature, City College of New York; Graduate studies, University of California at Berkeley. *Literary Appointments:* Paris Correspondent, Los Angeles Times. *Contributions to:* Atlantic; Nation; Foreign Affairs and others. *Literary Agent:* Emilie Jacobson, Curtis Brown Limited, New York. *Address:* Los Angeles Times, 73 Champs-Elyseés, 75008 Paris, France.

MELCHIOR, Ib Jorgen, b. 17 Sep. 1917, Copenhagen, Denmark. Author. m. Cleo Baldon, 18 Jan. 1964, Los Angeles. 1 son, previous marriage. *Education:* Cand Phil, University of Copenhagen. *Publications:* Order of Battle, 1972; Sleeper Agent, 1975; The Haigerloch Project, 1977; The Watchdogs of Abaddon, 1979; The Marcus Device, 1980; The Tombstone Cipher, 1983; Eva, 1984; V-3, 1985. *Contributions:*

Approximately 100 articles & stories, numerous periodicals; 12 feature motion picture scripts; Over 100 documentary & TV scripts; 3 legitimate plays. *Honours:* Golden Scroll, Best Writing, Academy of Science Fiction, 1976; Hamlet Award, Shakespeare Society of America, 1982. *Memberships:* PEN: Authors Guild; Writers Guild of America. *Address:* 8228 Marmont Lane, Los Angeles, CA 90069, USA.

MELE, Jim, b. 16 July 1950, New York City, USA. Writer. m. Joan Fiedler, 9 June 1974, United National Chapel, 1 son. *Education:* BA, English, Stony Brook University, 1972; MA, Creative Writing, City College of New York, 1974. *Appointments:* Assistant Editor, Sea-farers Log; Associate Editor, Container News; Reporter, Journal of Commerce; General Manager, New York State Small Press Association; Executive Editor, DES; News Editor, Fleetowner. *Publications:* An Oracle of Love, 1976; The Sunday Habit, 1978; Sonnets & Other Dead Forms, 1980; Isaac Asimov, with Jean Fiedler, 1982; The Calculation of Tow, 1982. *Contributor to:* Numerous magazines and journals including: An Argument for New Romantics, Cross Country; The Art of Discovery, Cross Country, No. 16. *Address:* 32 Haviland Road, Ridgefield, CT 06877, USA.

MELFI, Mary, b. 10 June 1951, Italy. Writer. m. George Nemeth, 17 May 1975, Montreal, Canada, 2 sons. *Education:* BA cum laude, Loyola College, Concordia University, 1973; MLS first class honours, McGill University, 1977. *Publications:* The Dance, The Cage and the Horse, 1976; A Queen is Holding a Mummified Cat, 1982; A Bride in Three Acts, 1983; A Dialogue with Masks, 1985. *Contributions to:* Emile; The Canadian Author and Bookman; Matrix; Waves; Ariel; Room of One's Own; The Antigonish Review; Canadian Forum; The Alchemist; Germination; Toronto Life; Moosehead Review; Prism International; Descant; The New Quarterly; Event; Pierian Spring; Next Exit; Earth and You; Poetry Canada Review. *Honours:* Poetry grants, 1980–81, Short story grants, 1981–82, Canada Council. *Membership:* League of Canadian Poets. *Address:* 5040 Grand, Montreal, Quebec, Canada H3X 3S2.

MELIKIAN, Souren, b. 5 Dec. 1936, Paris, France. Art Historian. *Education:* Degrees in classical Arabic and Persian, Paris School of Oriental Languages, 1962; MA, Arabic and Persian literature, 1966; Doctorate in Persian Literature, 1968, Doctorate in Islamic Art History, 1972, Sorbonne. *Literary Appointments:* Art critic, Realites Magazine, 1965–70; Art market columnist, International Herald Tribune, 1969–; Art market Columnist, Art and Auction, 1985–. *Publications:* Le Roman de Varge et Golsah, 1970; Islamic Metalwork from the Iranian World, 1982; The Kitab Sulwan al Mutafi Udwan Al Atba, A rediscovered masterpiece of Arab literature and Art, *Contributions to:* Over 40 studies dealing with cultural history of Iranian world and Arab world in English and French (Journal Asiatigue, Metropolitan Museum of Art Journal and others); Hundreds of art historical essays in Realites, English and French; Articles in dailies and weeklies in English and French (Art News, The Connoisseur and others). *Membership:* Societe Asiatique, Paris. *Address:* 18 rue de la Jonquiere, Paris 75017, France.

MELIS, Godelieve Philomena Josephina Maria, b. 21 Sep. 1930, Hasselt. m. Mathe Gustaaf Melis, 20 Sep. 1952, Antwerp, 5 sons, 2 daughters. *Education:* Academy of the Arts, Art History & Child Psychology. *Publications:* 18 Fairy-tale books; 5 poetry books; Spookjes en Verhalen, 1949; Toetssteen, 1976. *Honours:* Prize, Province of Antwerp, 1953; Prize, Flemish Provinces, 1954; Premium for Toetssteen, 1978. *Memberships:* Association of Limburger Authors; Association of Flemish Literature; Scriptures Christiani; Writers for Youth. *Address:* Antoon van Dyckstraat 58, 2018 Antwerpen, Belgium.

MELLANBY, Kenneth, b. 26 Mar. 1908, Barrhead, Renfrewshire, England. Scientific Research Worker; Research Station Director; University Principal and

Professor. *Education:* BA, DSc, Kings College, Cambridge University; PhD, London University. *Publications including:* The Mole, 1971; The Biology of Pollution, 1972; Can Britain Feed Itself, 1975; Talpa, 1976; Farming and Wildlife, 1982. Editor, International Journal of Environmental Pollution. *Contributions to:* Various professional and other journals. *Membership:* Past President, Institute of Biology. *Honours:* Honorary DSc; Universities of Ibadan, Nigeria, Bradford, Leicester, Sheffield and Essex, England; OBE, 1945; CBE, 1954. *Address:* 38 Warkworth Street, Cambridge CB1 1ER, England.

MELLICHAMP, Josephine (Weaver), b. 30 Sep. 1923, Helton, North Carolina, USA. Writer. m. Stiles A Mellichamp, 16 Dec. 1961, Ringgold, Georgia, USA. *Education:* AB, Emory & Henry College, 1943; Graduate School, Division of Journalism, Emory University, 1950–51. *Publications:* Senators from Georgia (model book in series for Strode Publishers), 1976; Georgia Heritage. *Contributor to:* Atlanta Journal and Constitution Magazine; Birmingham News Magazine; Georgia Magazine; Grit; Modern Woodmen. *Honours:* Recipient, Dixie Council of Authors & Journalists, 1976; Award, to Georgia Author of the Year in Non-Fiction (for Senators from Georgia), 1977. *Memberships:* Dixie Council of Authors & Journalists Inc; SE Writers Association Inc; Atlanta Writers Club; International Platform Association; Atlanta Historical Society. *Address:* 1124 Reeder Circle NE, Atlanta, GA 30306, USA.

MELLOR, John Leigh, b. 11 Nov. 1928, London, England. Barrister. m. Mavis Yvonne Patricia Edwards, 1955, Hendon, England, 1 son, 1 daughter. *Education:* LLB, London. *Publications:* The Law – A Teach Yourself Book, 1955; Income Tax, 1961. *Contributions to:* Taxation, Simon's Taxes. *Address:* 24 Sherwood Road, Hendon, London NW4, England.

MELLOWN, Elgin Wendell, b. 29 Dec. 1931, Selma, Alabama, USA. University Professor. m. Muriel Jackson, 22 June 1957, Rawmarsh, 1 son, 1 daughter. *Education:* BA, Emory University; MA, Queen Mary College, PhD, King's College, University of London, England. *Appointments:* Faculty, University of Alabama, 1958–65, Duke University, 1965–. *Publications:* Bibliography of Writings of Edwin Muir, 1964, 1966; Checklist of Writings about Edwin Muir, with Peter Hoy, 1971; Descriptive Catalogue of Bibliographies of 20th Century British Writers, 1972, 1978; Dedwin Muir, 1979; Jean Rhys, Descriptive and Annotated Bibliography, 1984. *Contributor to:* Articles and reviews in various Scholarly Journals. *Membership:* Modern Language Association. *Address:* English Department, Duke University, Durham, NC 27706, USA.

MELLY, Alan George Heywood, b. 17 Aug. 1926, Liverpool, England. Writer. *Publications:* I Flook, 1962; Owning Up, 1965; Revolt Into Style, 1970; Flook Bytrog, 1970; Rum, Bum and Concertina, 1977; Media Mob, 1980; Scouse Mouse, 1984. *Contributor to:* Observer; Sunday Times; Guardian; New Statesman; Punch; New Society. *Honour:* IPC Award for Critic of the Year, 1971. *Agent:* A M Heath Limited. *Address:* 33 St Lawrence Terrace, London W10 5SR, England.

MELONE, Albert Philip, b. 25 Apr. 1942, Chicago, Illinois, USA. Political Scientist. m. Peggy Harles, 26 Aug. 1971, Fargo, North Dakota, 2 sons, 1 daughter. *Education:* AA, Mount San Antonio College, 1962; BA, 1964, MA, 1967, California State University at Los Angeles; PhD, University of Iowa, 1972. *Publications:* Lawyers, Public Policy and Interest Group Politics, 1977; Primer on Constitutional Law, 1982; Research Essentials of Administrative Law, 1983; Bridges to Knowledge in Political Science: A Handbook for Research, 1984. *Contributions to:* Journal of Politics; The Western Political Quarterly; Policy Studies Journal; Judicature; Journal of Legal Education; Washington University law Quarterly; North Dakota Law Review. *Address:* 109 Rod Lane, Carbondale, IL 62901, USA.

MELTON, David Gordon, b. 10 Apr. 1934, Springfield, Missouri, USA. Author, Illustrator. m. Nancy Ruth Thatch, 15 Sep. 1954, Springfield, Missouri, USA, 1 son, 1 daughter. *Education:* BA, Southwest Missouri State University, Springfield, Missouri, 1956. *Major Publications:* Todd, 1968; I'll Show You the Morning Sun, 1971; When Children Need Help, 1972; Images of Greatness, 1978; Theodore, 1978; Harry S Truman – The Man Who Walked with Giants, 1980; Written & Illustrated by, 1985. *Honours:* Outstanding Young Men of America, 1969; Benjamin Franklin Freedom Award, 1978; Thorpe Menn Award for literary achievement, 1979. *Address:* 7422 Rosewood Circle, Prairie Village, KS 66208, USA.

MELZACK, Ronald, b. 19 July 1929, Montreal, Canada. Professor of Psychology. m. Lucy Louise Birch, 7 Aug. 1960, Montreal, 1 son, 1 daughter. *Education:* BA; MSc; PhD. *Publications:* The Day Tuk Became a Hunter, and other Eskimo stories, 1967; Raven, Creator of the World, and other Eskimo Legends, 1970; The Puzzle of Pain, 1972; Why The Man In The Moon Is Happy, and other Eskimo Creation Stories, 1973; The Challenge of Pain (with P D Wall), 1983; Pain Measurement and Assessment, 1983; Textbook of Pain (with P D Wall), 1984. *Honour:* Fellow, Royal Society of Canada. *Address:* 51 Banstead Road, Montreal West, Quebec H4X 1P1, Canada.

MENARD, Orville D, b. 4 Apr. 1933, Omaha, Nebraska, USA. Professor of Political Science, m. E. Darlene Book, 9 Apr. 1954, Omaha. *Education:* BA, MA, PhD. *Publications:* The Army and the Fifth Republic, 1967; Civil Military Relations, 1977. *Contibutions to:* Military Affairs; Midwest Quarterly; Magazine of the Midlands; Teaching Politics. *Address:* Department of Political Science, University of Nebraska at Omaha, NE 68182, USA.

MENASHE, Samuel, b. 16 Sep. 1925, New York, USA. *Education:* BA, Queens College; Doctorat d'Universite, University of Paris, France. *Publications:* The Many Named Beloved, 1961; No Jerusalem But This, 1971; Fringe of Fire, 1973; To Open, 1974. *Contributor to:* Poems in, The Times Literary Supplement; Temenos; Poetry National Review; Proteus; etc. *Honour:* Longview Foundation Award, 1957. *Membership:* PEN. *Address:* 75 Thompson Street, New York, NY 10012, USA.

MENNELL, Stephen John, b. 1 May 1944, Huddersfield, England. Academic. m. Barbara Vivien Farncombe, 3 Sep. 1971. *Education:* BA, Economics, Cambridge University, 1966; Frank Knox Fellow, Harvard University, 1966–67; Dr Soc Sc, University of Amsterdam, 1985. *Literary Appointments:* Assistant Lecturer 1967–70, Lecturer 1970–78, Senior Lecturer 1978–; University of Exeter, Department of Sociology; Project Director, Council of Europe, 1975–79; Co-Director, Western European Studies Centre, University of Exeter, 1979–85; Senior Associate Member, St Anthony's College, Oxford, 1980–81. *Publications:* Sociological Theory: Uses and Unities, 1974, 2nd edition 1980; Leisure, Culture and Local Government, with F M M Lewes, 1976; Cultural Policy in Towns, 1976 (and in 6 other languages); Alexis de Tocqueville on Democracy, Revolution and Society, editor with J Stone, 1980; All Manners of Food, 1985; Also two translations: G Rocher, Talcott Parsons and American Sociology, 1975, N. Elias, What is Sociology? 1978. *Address:* 7 Wheatsheaf Way, Alphington, Exeter, Devon EX2 8QQ, England.

MERCHAND, Leslie A(lexis), b. 13 Feb. 1900, Bridgeport, Washington, USA. Professor (retired); Writer. m. Marion Hendrix, 8 July 1950, Washington, DC. *Education:* BA, 1922, MA, 1923, University of Washington; PhD, Columbia University, 1940. Honorary Degrees: Dr of Humane Letters, University of Alaska, 1976; Litt D, Rutgers University, 1981. *Literary Appointments include:* Instructor, Rutgers University, 1937–42; Assistant Professor, 1942–46; Associate Professor, 1946–53; Professor, 1953–66; Emeritus,

1966–; Visiting Professor Greece and Universities in USA. *Publications:* The Athenassum: A Mirror of Victorian Culture, 1941; Byron: A Biography, 1957; Byron's Poetry: A Critical Introduction, 1965; Byron: A Portrait, 1970; Editor, Letters of Thomas Hood, 1945; Selected Poetry of Lord Byron, 1951; Lord Byron: Don Juan, 1958; Byron's Letters and Journals, Volumes 1-12, 1973–82. *Contributions to:* Professional journals. *Honours:* James Russell Lowell Prize, 1974; Ivan Sandrof Award, National Book Critics Circle, 1982. *Memberships:* Keats-Shelley Association of America, Member, Board of Directors; Byron Society: PEN; Fellow, Royal Society of Literature; Phi Beta Kappa. *Address:* 1551 Beach Road, Apt 301, Englewod, FL 33533, USA.

MERGEN, Bernard Matthew, b. 30 Mar. 1937, Reno, Nevada. University Professor. m. 3 Sep. 1960, Reno, Nevada, 1 son, 1 daughter. *Education:* BA, University of Nevada; PhD, University of Pennsylvania. *Literary Appointments:* Lektor, English Department, University of Goteborg, Sweden; Instructor, Community College of Philadelphia, 1965–66; Assistant Professor, Grinnell College, Grinnell, Iowa, 1968–70; Assistant Professor – Professor, George Washington University, 1970–. *Publications:* Play and Plaything, 1982; Secreational Vehicles and Travel, 1985. *Contributions to:* American Quarterly; Industrial and Labor Relations Review; Journal of Popular Culture; Journal of American Culture; American Studies International Senior Editor, 1979–. *Honours:* Woodrow Wilson Fellowship 1959–61; Fulbright Lecturer, University of Goteborg, 1962–65; Fulbright Professor, Free University of Berlin, 1982. *Memberships:* American Studies Association; The Association for the Anthropological Study of Play (President 1984–85); Washington Independent Writers; Oral History Middle Atlantic Region. *Address:* George Washington University, Washington, DC 20052, USA.

MERHOTTEIN, Walter T E, b. 16 July 1934, Antwerp, Belgium. Municipal Chamber Theatre Director. m. Danielle Van Beeck, 26 June 1985, 1 stepson. *Education:* Teacher, 1954; Actor-director, Royal Flemish Academy for Dramatic Arts, 1968; Higher Degree, Poem reciter, 1969. *Literary Appointments:* Founder, Merksems-Kamer Theater (Municipal Chamber Theatre of Merksem-Antwerp) and of Puppet Theatre Kiekeboe-Pats. *Publications:* Author of several theatre play translations and original puppet plays for children (with the cartoons of Kiekeboe and his family), screenplays for television. *Honours:* Ministry of Flemish Culture, 1963; Award as Stage director, 1968, 69. *Memberships:* Flemish Authors Guild; British Puppet and Model Theatre Guild; ONEPP (Professional puppeteers). *Address:* Nieuwdreef 116 G2, B–2060 Merksem Antwerp, Belgium.

MERILUOTO-PAAKKANEN, Aila Marjatta, b. 10 Jan. 1924, Pieksa Maki, Finland. Writer. m. (1) Lauri Viita, 10 Nov. 1948, (2) Jouko Paakkanen, 1 Nov. 1980, 2 sons, 2 daughters. *Education:* Studies in literature, physchology, art history, Helsinki University, 1943–48; Zurich University, Switzerland, 1947. *Publications:* Author of 10 books of poetry including: Latimaaians, 1946; Pahat unet, 1958; Silmanitta, 1969; Varokaa putoileviia enkeleita, 1977; Talvikaupubki, 1980. Childrens books: Peter-Peter, 1971; Vishrea tukka, 1982; Laura Viita, 1974, biography and others. Translations include: Aniaia by Martinson, 1963; Rilke'ss Duineser Elegien, 1974. *Honours:* State Literary Awards, 1947, 53, 59, 75; Kalevi Fantte prize, 1947; Siilanpaa Prize, 1958; Koslenniemi prize, 1961; Pro Finandia Medal, 1962. *Memberships:* Suomen Kirjailijaliitto; PEN. *Literary Agent:* WSOY, Helsinki. *Address:* Topelinksenkatu 2 A 8, 00250 Helsinki, 25, Finland.

MERKLE, Ludwig, b. 28 Mar. 1928, München, Federal Republic of Germany. Travel Journalist; Writer. m. Dr Elli Röckl, 20 Dec. 1949, Munich, 3 sons. *Education:* PhD. *Publications:* Breissn dratzn, 1971, 8th edition 1984; Sonntagssegein, 1974, 3 edition 1977; Bairische Grammatik, 1973, 2nd edition 1984;

Vornamen in Bayern, 1981. *Contributor to:* Gute Fahrt; Die Schöne Welt; Literator in Bayern; Berge; etc. *Address:* Perlacher Bahnhofstrasse 9, D–8000 Munich 83, Federal Republic of Germany.

MERRILL, Jean Fairbanks, b. 27 Jan. 1923, Rochester, New York, USA. Writer. *Education:* BA, Allegheny College, 1944; MA, Wellesley College, 1945; Fulbright Scholar, University of Madras, India, 1952–53. *Literary Appointments:* Feature Editor, Scholastic Magazines, 1947–50; Editor, Literary Cavalcade, 1956–57; Writer, consultant, Bank Street College of Education, 1964–65. *Publications include:* Henry, the Hand-Painted Mouse, 1951; Boxes, 1953; The Travels of Marco, 1956; A Song for Gar, 1960; The Superlative Horse, 1961; The Pushcart War, 1964; Red Riding, 1968; Mary, Come Running, 1970; The Toothpaste Millionaire, 1972; Maria's House, 1974. Libretto for chamber opera, Mary, Come Running, 1982. *Contributions to:* Vermont Life; Scholastic Magazines. *Honours:* Lewis Carroll Shelf Award, 1963, 1965; Junior Book Award, Boys Club of America, 1965; Dorothy Canfield Fisher Memorial Book Award, 1975–76; Seguoyah Award, 1977. *Memberships:* Authors Guild; Dramatists Guild; Vermont League of Writers; Society of Childrens Book Writers. *Address:* Angel's Ark, 29 S Main Street, Randolph, VT 05060, USA.

MERRILL, John C, b. 9 Jan. 1924, Mississippi, USA. Professor of Journalism. m. Dorothy Lee Jefferson, 9 Sep. 1948, Inverness, Mississippi, 2 sons, 3 daughters. *Education:* BA English, Mississippi Delta State University; MA Journalism, Louisiana State University; MA Philosophy, University of Missouri; PhD Mass Communication, University of Iowa. *Publications:* The Elite Press; The Imperative of Freedom; Existential Journalism; The World's Great Dailies; Philosophy and Journalism. *Contributions to:* Many journals dealing with journalism and mass communication. *Address:* 2425 Cottonwood Avenue, Baton Rouge, LA 70808, USA.

MERRY, Peter James, b. 11 Feb. 1947, Berkhamsted, Hertfordshire, England. Journalist. m. Eva Margareta Skärvik, 28 Aug. 1976, London, England, 1 daughter. *Education:* BSc (Pharmacy), Portsmouth Polytechnic, England. *Appointments:* Founding Editor, Hospital Doctor, newspaper, 1978–81; Editor, Health and Social Service, Journal, 1982–. *Memberships:* Medical Journalists' Association; Association of British Science Writers. *Address:* Yew Trees, Southview Road, Crowborough, East Sussex TN6 1HF, England.

MERTON, Robert K, b. 5 July, 1910, Philadelphia, Pennsylvania, USA. University Professor Emeritus. *Education:* AB, Temple University, USA, 1931; MA, Harvard University, USA, 1932, PhD, 1936. *Publications include:* Science, Technology and Society in 17th Century England, 1938, 1970; Social Theory and Social Structure, 1949, new editions, 1957 and 1968; Sociology Today, 1959, 1967; On the Shoulders of Giants, 1965, 1985; Contemporary Social Problems, 1961, 4th edition, 1976; The Sociology of Science in Europe, 1977; Editor, Toward a Metric of Science: The Advent of Science Indicators, 1978; The Sociology of Science: An Episodic Memoir, 1979; Editor, Qualitative and Quantitative Social Research; Social Research and the Practicing Professions, 1982; Papers in honour of Paul F Lazarfield, 1979. *Contributor to:* Numerous professional journals. *Honours:* Guggenheim Fellow, 1962; Prize, Distinguished Scholarship in the Humanities, American Council of Learned Societies, 1962; Talcott Parsons Prize in Social Sciences, American Academy of Arts and Sciences, 1979; Commonwealth Award, American Sociological Association, 1979; Career Distinguished Scholarship Award, ASA, 1980; First Who's Who of America Achievement Award in the Social Sciences, 1984; numerous honorary degrees. *Memberships include:* National Academy of Sciences, 1968; Founder Member, Royal Swedish Academy of Sciences, 1976; American Sociological Association (President, 1957); Eastern Sociological Society (President), 1969.

Address: 415 Fayerweather, Columbia University, New York, NY 10027, USA.

MERTZ, Barbara Gross, b. 29 Sep. 1927, Canton, Illinois, USA. Writer. (div.) 1 son, 1 daughter. *Education:* PhD, University of Chicago, 1952. *Publications include:* As Barbara Mertz: Temples, Tombs & Hieroglyphs, 1964; Red Land, Black Land, 1966; Two Thousand Years in Rome, 1968. As Barbara Michaels: 20 novels including The Master of Blacktower, 1966; The Crying Child, 1971; House of Many Shadows, 1974; The Wizard's Daughter, 1980; Be Buried in the Rain, 1985. As Elizabeth Peters: 19 novels including: The Jackal's Head, 1968; The Seventh Sinner, 1972; Legend in Green Velvet, 1976; Summer of the Dragon, 1979; Die for Love, 1984. *Contributions to:* The Writer (articles); Washington Post (reviews); Baltimore Sun (reviews); Encyclopaedia Britannica, Americana, World Book (articles). *Memberships:* Authors Guild; Mystery Writers of America. *Literary Agent:* Dominick Abel. *Address:* c/o Dominick Abel, 498 West End Avenue, New York, NY 10024, USA.

MESA-LAGO, Carmelo, b. 11 Aug. 1934, Havana, Cuba. University Professor. m. Elena Gross, 3 Sep. 1966, Miami, 3 daughters. *Education:* Bachelor in Law, University of Havana, Cuba, 1956; Doctor in Law, Labour, University of Madrid, Spain, 1958; Diploma, Social Security Specialist, OISS, 1958; MA Economics, University of Miami, Florida, USA, 1965; PhD Industrial and Labour Relations, Cornell University, USA, 1968. *Literary Appointments:* Editor, Cuban Studies/Estudios Cubancs; Editorial Board; Latin American Research Review, Journal of Inter-American Studies and World Affairs, Caribbean Review. *Publications:* Planificacion de la Seguridad Social, 1959 and 1960; The Labor Sector and Socialist Distribution in Cuba, 1968; Revolutionary Change in Cuba, 1971 and 1973; The Labor Force, Employment, Unemployment and Underemployment in Cuba; 1899–1970, 1977; Cuba in the 1970's, 1974, 1976 and 1978; Comparative Socialist Systems, 1975; Social Security in Latin America, 1978; Cuba in the World, 1979; The Economy of Socialist Cuba, 1981; Cuba in Africa, 1982; El desarrols de la seguridad social en America Latins, 1985; The Crisis of Social Security and Health Care, 1985. *Contributions to:* Numerous magazines and journals. *Honours include:* Numerous grants. *Memberships include:* American Economic Association; Association for Comparative Economic Studies; Past President, Latin American Studies Association. *Address:* Center for Latin American Studies, University of Pittsburgh, AE04 Forbes Quadrangle, Pittsburgh, PA 15260, USA.

MESERAULL, Elaine Amalia, b. 19 Apr. 1943, Springfield, Illinois, USA. Editor-in-Chief. m. Fred D Meseraull, 12 July 1964, Springfield, 1 Son, 1 daughter. *Education:* BA, Andrews University; Graduate studies in English, Biology and Communications. *Literary Appointments:* Scriptwriter, Your Story Hour, radio; Multi-Image Scriptwriter, Lake Union Conference; Editor-in-Chief, Clubhouse, Your Story Hour, Berrien Springs, Michigan. *Contributions to:* Clubhouse, numerous stories articles and puzzles. *Address:* c/o Your Story Hour, Box 15, Berrien Springs, MI 49103, USA.

MESSERLI, Douglas John, b. 30 May 1947, Waterloo, Iowa, USA. Publisher; Poet. *Education:* BA, University of Wisconsin, University of Maryland; MA, PhD, University of Maryland. *Literary Appointments:* Assistant Professor of English, Temple University, 1979–84; Director, Contemporary Arts Educational Project, 1984–; Publisher, Sun & Moon Press, 1978–. *Major Publications:* Djuna Barnes: A Bibliography, 1974; Dinner on the Lawn (poems), 1979; Some Distance (poems), 1982; River to Rivet: A Manifesto, 1984; River to Rivet: A Poetic Trilogy (in 3 volumes), 1984; Contemporary American Fiction (editor), 1982. *Contributor to:* Paris Review; Conjunctions; Washington Review; Mississippi Review; Boundary 2; Credences; Zone; Art Quarterly 1; The Pushcart Prize VI, 1981; Contemporary Literature; Sagetrieb 3. *Honour:* Coordinating Council of Literary Magazines Editor's Award,

1979. *Membership:* Modern Language Association. *Address:* c/o Sun & Moon Press, 6363 Wilshire Boulevard Suite 115, Los Angeles, CA 90048, USA.

METHOLD, Kenneth, b. 23 Dec. 1931, Sussex, England. Author; Dramatist; Broadcaster. m. Chustana Chulasathiera, 8 July 1962. *Education:* Teachers Certificate, Institute of Education, London University. *Publications:* Three novels, one collection of radio plays, three plays, one biography, three collections of short stories, over a dozen radio plays, over 100 educational books, mostly published by Longman and its associated companies. Contributor to British educational journals, Australia's major newspapers and journals, ABC radio Books and Writing programme and reviewer of SF for The Australian and Omega Magazine. *Memberships:* Chairman, Australian Society of Authors, 1982 to present; Director, Copyright Agency Limited, 1985; Executive Member, National Book Council, 1985. *Honour:* Australian Writer's Guild AWGIE Award for best radio adaptation, 1980. *Address:* c/o Australian Society of Authors Limited, POB 450, Milson's Point, New South Wales, Australia, 2061.

METODIEV, Dimitar, b. 11 Sep. 1922, Belovo, Bulgaria. Writer. *Education:* Agronomy, Sofia University; The Moscow, Maxim Gorki Literary Institution. *Literary Appointment:* Editor-in-Chief of the Nasha Rodina magazine. *Publications:* Poetry: The Clan of Dimitrov, novel in verse, 1951; The Land of Dreams 1956; I'll Die This Way, 1961; About the Time and About Myself, 1963; A Song for Russia, 1967; The Great Migration, 1970: And All Will Be Repeated Again, 1975. *Contributor to:* All main Bulgarian literary editions. *Honours:* Dimitrov Prize, 1952 and 1964; A People's Worker of Culture, 1974; A Hero of Socialist Labour, 1982. *Membership:* Union of Bulgarian Writers. *Address:* bloc 73, complex Lenin, Sofia, Bulgaria.

METZEMAEKERS, René, b. 29 Oct. 1932, Antwerp, Belgium. Author; Radio Drama Director/Producer. Widower. *Education:* Higher Pedagogical. *Publications:* 3 books for children. *Contributions to:* Radio, Television, Magazines. *Honours:* 3rd Award, 1950, 1st Award 1952, National Radio Drama Contest; 1st Award, Short Story, Literary Magazine Boulevard, 1976; Ministerial Award for Translation (Caught on the Hop by Derek Benfield), 1979. *Memberships:* Vlaamse Vereniging voor Toneelauteurs; Vereniging van Vlaamse Letterkundigen; Vereniging van Schrijvers voor de Jeugd; Vereniging van Journalisten van de Periodieke Pers. *Literary Agent:* N V Verba, Belgium. *Address:* c/o N V Verba, Fazantenlaan 8, B–2610 Elsdonk – Antwerp, Belgium.

MEUDT, Edna Kritz, b. 14 Sep. 1906. Homemaker; Writer; Teacher. *Education:* Academy of the Sacred Heart, Edgewood, Madison, Wisconsin, USA. *Appointments:* Teaching Staff, Rhinelander School of the Arts since 1964; Continuing Staff, The Valley Studio; Judge and Modertor, Poetry Wis; HS Supervisor; Workshops Colleges in Idaho, Louisiana, Western Virginia, etc. *Publications:* Round River Canticle, 1960; No Strange Lane, 1964; No One Sings Face Down, 1969; The Ineluctable Sea; An Uplands Reader, 1979; Plain Chant, (poems), 1980; Selected poems, (in press), 1986. *Contributions to:* numerous journals and magazines; Editor, Uplands Reader II, 1982; Editor, Country Poet magazine, 1983–. *Honours:* Numerous, including the Governor's award for Creativity in the Arts, 1971; 1st Prize for, Plain Chant for a Tree, North American Mentor magazine, 1979; Honorary distinction University of Wisconsin, USA Department of Agriculture and Life Sciences, 1979; Christopher Scholes Award from the Council of Wisonsin Writers for, Extraordinary Inspiration and Help to Writers; Honorary Member of 1 State Organisation and 1 State National. *Memberships:* Chairman, Creative Writing, Wisconsin Arts Foundation and Council; Charter Member and former Board Member, Wisconsin Regional Writers' Association; Charter Member, 1st Secretary and President, 2 terms, Wisconsin Fellowship of Poets; State Chairman, National Poetry Day, 1958–; President, National Federation of State Poetry Societies Inc; Vice-President, NLAPW; Vice-President, Academy of Sciences, Arts and Letters; International Poetry Society, UK, (Hon US Edit Advisor). *Address:* Route 3, Dodgeville, WI 53533, USA.

MEWS, Sibylle, b. 17 May 1927, Clausthal, Harz. Author of Children's Books. m. 1 Nov. 1952, Berlin, 2 sons, 1 daughter. *Publications:* Flusterkuchen,1967; Apfelsim Schlafrock, 1968; Das Haus Mit Den Vielen Feustern, 1972; Was da Gurkenfass Nacht; Macht, 1973; Otto Kommtmit Allen Klar, 1977; Zwitsch, 1980; Kennst Den Dominikus Munk?, 1981; Dubist su Dick, Isabella?, 1982.*Contributions to:* Anthologies and children's journals; 15 plays for radio. *Membership:* Bodecker-Kreis, Hannover. *Address:* Ain Miller Strasse 33, 8000 Munich 40, Federal Republic of Germany.

MEYER, Charles Robert, b. 30 Sep. 1920, Chicago, Illinois, USA. Educator. *Education:* MA, Religion, St Mary of the Lake Seminary, 1945; BS, Library Science, Rosary College, 1948; STD, St Mary of the Lake Seminary, 1952; Post-doctoral Research, Gregorian University & Vatican Library, Rome, Italy, 1948–49. *Publications:* The Thomistic Concept of Justifying Contrition, 1949; A Contemporary Theology of Grace, 1971; The Touch of God: A Theological Analysis of Religious Experience, 1972; Man of God: A Study of the Priesthood, 1974; What a Modern Catholic Believes about the Holy Spirit, 1974; Religious Belief in a Scientific Age, 1983. *Contributor to:* Concilium; Chicago Studies; American Ecclesiastical Review; Homiletic and Pastorial Review; New Catholic Encyclopedia; etc. *Memberships:* Catholic Theological Society of America; American Catholic Historical Association; American Society for Church History; Catholic Biblical Association of America. *Address:* St Mary of the Lake Seminary, Mundelein, IL 60060, USA.

MEYER, E Y, b. 11 Oct. 1946, Leistal, Switzerland. Writer. *Publications:* Ein Reisender in Sachen Umsturz, 1972; In Trubschachen, 1973; Eine entfernte Aehnlichkeit, 1975; Die Ruckfahrt, 1977; Die Halfte der Erfehrung, 1980; Playdoyer, 1982; Sundaymorning, 1984. *Contributions to:* Numerous periodicals. *Honours:* Literature Prize of the Province of Basel, 1976; Gerhart-Hauptmann-Prize, 1983; Prize of the Swiss Schiller-Foundation, 1984; Welti-Prize for the Drama, 1985. *Memberships:* Swiss Author Group OLTEN; Swiss-German PEN Centre. *Address:* Brünnen-Gut, CH 3027 Berne, Switzerland.

MEYER, Michael Leverson, b. 11 June 1921, London, England. Author, Translator. *Education:* MA, Christ Church, University of Oxford, England. *Major Publications include:* (editor) Eight Oxford Poets, 1941; (editor) Collected Poems of Sidney Keyes, 1945; The End of the Corridor (novel), 1951; The Ortolan, 1967; Henrik Ibsen: The Makaing of a Dramatist, 1967; Henrik Ibsen: The Farewell to Poetry, 1971; Henrik Ibsen: The Top of a Cold Mountain, 1971; Lunatic and Lover, 1981; (editor) Summer Days, 1981; Strindberg: A Biography, 1985; Numerous translations of plays by Ibsen & Strindberg. *Contributor to:* Times Literary Supplement; The Times; The Sunday Times. *Honours:* Gold Medal, Swedish Academy, 1964; Whitbread Biographical Prize, 1971; Knight Commander, Order of the Polar Star (Swedish), First Class, 1976. *Memberships include:* Fellow, Royal Society of Literature. *Literary Agent:* David Higham Associates. *Address:* 4 Montagu Square, London W1H 1RA, England.

MEYER, Peter Barrett, b. 15 Feb. 1950, Salem, Oregon, USA. Journalist. m. Janet Kathleen Kealy, 5 Oct. 1985, New York City. *Education:* MA, University of Chicago; BA, Portland State University, Oregon; Institute for American Universities, Certificate of Study, Aix-en-Provence, France. *Publications:* James Earl Carter: The Man and The Myth, 1978; The Yale Murder, 1982; Death of Innocence, 1985. *Contributions to:* Harper's Magazine; New York Magazine; GEO Magazine; Universal Press Syndicate. *Honour:* Award for Excellence in Reporting on the National Economy, University of

Missouri School of Journalism, 1979. *Membership:* American Society of Journalists and Authors. *Address:* 309 West 57th Street, New York, NY 10019, USA.

MEYER, Yvonne, SSM, b. St Louis, Missouri, USA. Editor. *Education:* BS, St Louis University, St Louis, Missouri, 1949; MEd, St Louis University, 1952.*Literary Appointments:* Editorial Board & Bibliographer, 1954–55, 1959, American Association of Medical Record Administrators, Editor, Highlights, St Mary's Hospital, Kansas City, 1956–60; Editor, Rambling Rose, Mount St Rose Hospital, St Louis 1968–76; Editor, SSM Links, Sisters of St Mary, St Louis, 1974–; Editor, Ad On, Advertising Women of St Louis, St Louis, 1977–78; Director, Publication Services, Sisters of St Mary, St Louis, Missouri, 1974–. *Major Publications:* Time & Cost Study of Medical Record Library Procedures, 1950; An Administrative Manual for Medical Records, 1958; History of St Mary's School of Nursing, Kansas City, Missouri, 1977; A Woman for All Times, 1980. *Contributor to:* Numerous National Journals. *Address:* Sisters of St Mary, 1100 Bellevue Avenue, St Louis, MO 63117, USA.

MEYER-CLASON, Curt, b. 19 Sep. 1910, Ludwigsburg, Germany. Writer. m. Christiane Thye, 10 Apr. 1959, 2 daughters. *Publications include:* 100 translations of Latin-American prose and poetry from 1960 to present; a series of anthologies of Latin American short stories, poems and essays from 1965 to 1985; Erstens die Freiheit (travel notes), 1978; Portugiesische Tagebücher, 1980; Eaquator, 1986. *Contributions to:* Süddeutsche Zeitung; Stuttgarter Zeitung; Die Zeit; Merkur; Akzente. *Honours:* Award of Akademie für Sprache und Dichtung; Gold Medal Brazilian Academy of Letters. *Address:* Lucile-Grahn-Strasse 48, 8000 München 80, Federal Republic of Germany.

MEYERS, Carol L, b. 26 Nov. 1942, Wilkes Barre, Pennsylvania, USA. University Professor; Archaeologist. m. Eric M Meyers, 25 June 1964, Wilkes Barre, Pennsylvania, 2 daughters. *Education:* AB, Biblical History, Wellesley, 1964; MA, Near Eastern and Judaic Studies, 1966, PhD, 1975, Brandeis University. *Literary Appointments:* Committee on Publications, American Schools of Oriental Research, 1977–; Editorial Committee, Dissertation Series, American Schools of Oriental Research, 1978–; Editorial Committee, Biblical Archaeologist, 1982–; Editorial Advisory Board, Social World of Biblical Antiquity Series, Almond Press, 1983–. *Publications:* The Tabernacle Menorah: A Synthetic Study of a Symbol from the Biblical Cult, 1976; Excavations at Ancient Meiron, Upper Galilee, Israel 1971–72, (with E M Meyers, J F Strange), 1981; The Word of the Lord Shall Go Forth, (Editor with M O'Connor), 1983; Haggai and Zecharish 1-8, (with E Meyers), 1986. *Contributions to:* Professional publications (articles and book reviews). *Honours include:* Grants and Fellowships including: Visiting Scholar, Oxford Centre for Postgraduate Hebrew Studies, 1982–83; Visiting Research Fellow, Queen Elizabeth House, Oxford, 1982–83; Regular Grant, Research Council, Duke University, 1983–84, 1985–86. Howard Foundation Fellow, 1985–86. *Memberships:* Office holder and member of several professional organizations, such as Society of Biblical Literature. *Literary Agent:* United Media Productions. *Address:* Department of Religion, PO Box 4735, Duke University, Durham, NC 27706, USA.

MEYERS, Eric Mark, b. 5 June 1940, Norwich, Connecticut, USA. Professor. m. Carol Lyons, 25 June 1964, Wilkes-Barre, Pennsylvania, 2 daughters. *Education:* A B, Dartmouth College; MA, Brandeis University; PhD, Harvard University; Attended University of Vienna and Hebrew University. *Literary Appointments:* Editor, Biblical Archaeologist; Vice-President for Publications, American Schools of Oriental Research. *Publications:* Jewish Ossuaries, 1981; Xhirbet Shema, 1976; Meiron, 1981; Archaeology, The Rabbis and Early Christianity, 1981; Anchor Bible Commentary. Haggai Zechariah 1-8, (with C L meyers), 1986. *Contributions:* Approxi-

mately 100 articles, reviews and encyclopedia entries. *Literary Agent:* United Media, 200 Park Avenue, New York City. *Address:* P O Box 4735 Duke Station, Durham, NC 27706, USA.

MICHALSKI, Jozeff Ozga, b. 8 Mar. 1919, Bieliny, Poland. Writer; Poet; Politician. m. 13 June 1944, Stanislaw Maj, 1 son, 2 daughters. *Education:* Political University. *Publications:* (Poetry) Poemat nowosielski, 1947; Lutnia wiejska, 1954; Czernek i Anna, 1956; Kartki partyzanckie, 1957; Bolska, 1958; Swiatowid, 1959; Druga strona kiezyca, 1961; Walc karnawalowy, 1963; Pelnia, 1965; Do najjasniejszej pani, 1968; Taka badz, 1973; Poezje wybrane, 1975; Rajski oset, 1977; Hejnal na pogode, 1979; Powrot z litwya, 1980; (Prose) Mlodzik, 1969; Sowizdrzal Swietokrzyski, 1972; Sklepienia niebieskie, 1974; Smutne i wesole, 1956; Krajobraz rodzinny, 1973; W kogo trafigrom, 1978; Piolun i popiol, 1979; etc. *Honours:* Literary Award, 1 degree, 1985, Minister of Culture PRL; Order of the White Rose, Finland. *Memberships:* Presidency Literary Society PRL; PEN; Chairman, Literary Society Popular Writers, Poland; Board of Culture, Polish Parliament. *Address:* A1 1-ej Armii, WP 16 m 27, 00-582 Warsaw, Poland.

MICHAUD, Stephen Gage, b. 7 Mar. 1948, Burlington, Vermont, USA. Writer. m. Susan Denise Harper, 11 June 1983, Dallas, Texas. *Education:* AB, History, Stanford University, 1970. *Literary Appointments:* Newsweek Magazine, 1970–77; Business Week Magazine, 1977–79. *Publications:* The Only Living Witness, co-author; 1983; Witness to War, ghost writer, 1984. *Contributions to:* Smithsonian; Esquire; Venture; People. *Memberships:* National Association of Science Writers; Authors Guild. *Literary Agent:* Kathy Robbins, New York City. *Address:* c/o Kathy Robbins, 866 Second Avenue, 12th Floor, New York, NY 10017, USA.

MICHEL, Henri, b. 27 Apr. 1907, Vidauban, Var, France. Professor; Historian. *Education:* DLit, University of Paris, Sorbonne. *Publications:* Les Courants de Pensee de la Resistance, 1962; Jean Moulin, 1964; La Seconde Guerre Mondaile, 1968; Vichy, Annee Quarante, 1966; La Guerre de l'Ombre, 1970; La Drole de Guerre, 1972; Le Proces de Riom, 1979; Paris allemand, 1982; Paris resistant, 1984. *Contributions to:* Revue Historique; Les Annales; Revue d'Histoire de la Seconde Guerre Mondiale. *Memberships:* Society of Contemporary History; President, Historical Committee of the Second World War; Superior Commission of Archives; Commission of Military Archives; Royal Historical Society. *Address:* 12 Rue de Moscou, 75008 Paris, France.

MICHEL, Markus, b. 18 Sep. 1950, Bern, Switzerland. Writer. 1 son. *Publications:* Immer nur lächeln, 1979; Jean und die Andern, 1981; Hilde Brienz, 1984; Tanz der Krähen, 1982; Bürgertherapie, 1984. *Honours:* Drama Convocation at St Gallen City Theatre: Half of 1st Prize for, Tanz der Krähen, 1980; Prix Suisse, Swiss Radio Prize for Radio Play, Jean und die Andern, 1981. *Memberships:* Swiss Authors Group, Olten; Bern Writers' Association. *Literary Agent:* Stefani Hunzinger Bühnenverlag, Bad Homburg, Federal Republic of Germany. *Address:* Chutzenstr. 27, CH 3007, Bern, Switzerland.

MICHEL, Scott, b. 23 Oct. 1916, New York, USA. Writer. m. Rita White, 30 July 1940, Yonkers, 1 son, 1 daughter. *Education:* New York University, School of Journalism. *Publications:* The X-Ray Murders, 1942; Sweet Murder, 1943; The Psychiatric Murders, 1944; The Black Key, 1945; Dear Dead Harry!, 1946; Journey into Limbo, 1963; 4 plays produced, 2 on Broadway; Documentaries, Warner Brothers. *Contributor to:* The Writer; Anthology, Writing Detective Fiction; Writer's Year Book. *Address:* 80 Broome Avenue, Atlantic Beach, NY 11509, USA.

MICHELMORE, Peter, b. 11 Dec. 1930, Australia. Writer. m. Nanette West, 2 Feb. 1952, Adelaide, 2 sons, 1 daughter. *Publications:* Einstein: Profile of the Man,

1962; Dr Mellon of Haiti, 1964; The Swift Years, Robert Oppenheimer Biography, 1969; Arson!, 1974. *Contributor to:* Biographies to Encyclopedia Britannica; Articles to Readers Digest, Roving Editor. *Membership:* Author's Guild of America. *Literary Agent:* Loomis-Watkins Agency, New York. *Address:* 75 Hickory Lane, Closter, NJ 07624, USA.

MICHELSON, William, b. 26 Jan. 1940, Trenton, New Jersey, USA. Professor of Sociology. m. Ellen-Rachel Brause, 17 June 1962, Mount Vernon, 4 sons, 2 daughters. *Education:* AB, Princeton University; AM, PhD, Harvard University. *Publications:* Man and his Urban Environment, 1970; Behavioral Research Methods in Environmental Design, editor, 1975; Environmental Choice, Human Behavior, and Residential Satisfaction, 1977; Public Policy in Temporal Perspective, editor, 1978; The Child in the City, (co-author and co-editor), 1979; From Sun To Sun: Daily Obligations and Community Structure in the Lives of Employed Women and their Families, 1985. *Contributions to:* American Journal of Sociology; Social Forces; Journal of the American Institute of Planners; Social Issues; Mazingira; etc. *Address:* Centre for Urban and Community Studies, University of Toronto, 455 Spadina Avenue, Toronto, Ontario, M5S 2GB, Canada.

MICKWITZ, Camilla, b. 22 Sep. 1937, Helsinki, Finland. Graphic Artist; Author; Cartoon maker. m. Erik Mickwitz, 17 Aug. 1960, 1 son, 2 daughters. *Education:* University of Industrial Arts, Helsinki, 1955–58. *Publications:* Jason, 1975; Jason's Summer, 1976; Jason & Angry Agnes, 1977; Jason Abroad, 1978; Emily & Oscar, series, 5 parts, 1979–81; Mimosa, 1983; ...And You Will Be A Clown, 1984; Mimosa's Birthnight, 1985. Picture books, stories & drawings own work. *Honours:* State Award, 1973, 1975; Arvid Lydecken Award, 1979; Swedish Literary Society Award, 1979; Publishers Award, 1979, 1981; Finnish Picture Book Award, 1982; Rudolf Koivu Award, 1984. *Memberships:* Finlands Svenska Författarförening; Nuorisokirvaillijat. *Publisher:* Weilin & Göös, Helsinki. *Address:* Observatoriegatan 4 A 11, 00140 Helsingfors, Finland.

MIDDLEBROOK, Martin, b. 24 Jan. 1932, Boston, England. Military Author. *Publications:* The First Day on the Somme, 1971; The Nuremberg Raid, 1973; Convoy, 1976; Battleship, 1977; The Kaiser's Battle, 1978; The Battle of Hamburg, 1980; The Bomber Command War Diaries 1939–1945, with Chris Everitt, 1985; Operation Corporate – The Falklands War, 1985. *Agent:* A P Watt Ltd. *Address:* c/o A P Watt Ltd, 26/28 Bedford Row, London WC1R 4HL, England.

MIDDLETON, Christopher, b. 10 June 1926, Truro, Cornwall, England. University Professor. *Education:* BA, 1951, MA, D Phil, 1954, Oxford University. *Publications:* Torse 3, 1962; Nonsequences, 1965; Our Flowers and Nice Bones, 1969; The Lonely Suppers of W V Balloon, 1975; Carminalenia, 1980, III Poems, 1983 Essays: Bolshevism in Art, 1977; The Pursuit of the Kingfisher, 1983. *Honours:* Sir Geoffrey Faber Memorial Prize, 1964; Guggenheim Poetry Fellowship, 1974–75; National Endowment for the Arts Poetry Fellowship, 1980. *Address:* c/o Department of Germanic Languages, University of Texas at Austin, Austin, TX 78712, USA.

MIDDLETON, Katharine. *Publications:* Frog Paperweight, 1974; Water Lane, 1976. *Contributions to:* Poetry Review; Bananas; Samphire; Southern Arts; Poetry Dimension Annual. *Honour:* First Prize, Stroud International Poetry Competition, 1974. *Memberships:* The Poetry Society; Ver Poets. *Address:* 35 The Drive, Hailsham, East Sussex BN27 3HW, England.

MIDDLETON, Osman Edward, b. 25 Mar. 1925, Christchurch, New Zealand. Writer; Author. Divorced, 1 son, 1 daughter. *Education:* University of Auckland, 1946, 1948; University of Paris, France, 1955–56. *Appointments:* Robert Burns Fellow, University of Otago, 1970–71; Visiting Lecturer, University of

Canterbury, 1971; Visiting Writer, Karolyi Foundation, Vence, France, 1983; Visiting Lecturer, Commonwealth Literature, Universities of Zurich, Frankfurt, Giessen, Kiel, Erlangen, Regensburg, Turin, Venice, Bologna, Pisa, Rome, 1983. *Publications:* The Stone and Other Stories, 1959; A Walk on the Beach, 1964; The Loners, 1972; Selected Stories, 1973; Confessions of an Ocelot, 1979. *Contributor to:* Landfall; Mate; New Zealand Listener; Here and Now; Pilgrims; Islands; Arena; Monthly Review. *Honours:* Award of Achievement, Katherine Mansfield Award, 1959; Hubert Church Award, 1965; Scholarship in Letters, 1966; New Zealand Fiction Award, Joint Winner, 1976. *Membership:* PEN, 1959–82. *Address:* 20 Clifford Street, Dunedin, New Zealand.

MIDDLETON, Richard, b. 4 Feb. 1945, Wakefield, Yorkshire, England. University Teacher. *Education:* BA Music 1966, MA 1970, Clare College, Cambridge; D Phil, University of York, 1970. *Publications:* Pop Music and the Blues, 1972; Popular Music volumes 1 – 5, (editor with David Horn). *Contributions to:* Music and Letters; Music Review; Popular Music; Musica/Realta. *Address:* Arts Faculty, The Open University, Milton Keynes, England.

MIDDLETON, Stanley, b. 1 Aug. 1919, Bulwell, Nottingham, England. Novelist. *Education:* BA, London University, 1940; MEd, Nottingham University, 1952. *Publications:* A Short Answer, 1958; Harris's Requiem, 1960; A Serious Woman, 1961; The Just Exchange, 1962; Terms of Reference, 1964; The Golden Evening, 1966; Wages of Virtue, 1968; Brazen Prison, 1970; Cold Gradations, 1971; A Man Made of Smoke, 1972; Holiday, 1974; Distractions, 1975; Still Waters, 1976; Ends and Means, 1977; Two Brothers, 1978; In a Strange Land, 1979; The Other Side, 1980; Blind Understanding, 1982; Entry into Jerusalem, 1983; The Daysman, 1984; Valley of Decision, 1985; An After Dinner's Sleep, 1986. *Honours:* Booker Prize, (with Nadine Gordimer), 1974; Honorary MA, Nottingham University, 1975. *Memberships:* PEN; WAG; Writers Guild of Great Britain. *Literary Agent:* Hutchinson Publishing Group. *Address:* 42 Caledon Road, Sherwood, Nottingham NG5 2NG, England.

MIESEL, Sandra, b. 25 Nov. 1941, New Orleans, Louisiana, USA. Writer. m. John Miesel, 20 June 1964, 1 son, 2 daughters. *Education:* BS, College of St Francis, Joliet, Illinois, 1962; MS 1965, MA 1966, University of Illinois. *Major Publications:* Myth, Symbol & Religion in the Lord of the Rings, 1973; Against Time's Arrow: The High Crusade of Paul Anderson, 1978; Dreamrider, 1982. *Contributor to:* Amazing; Asimov's SF Magazine; Extrapolation; National Catholic Register; SF Chronicle; Algol Starship; Galileo; SF Monthly; Riverside Quarterly. 20th Century Science Fiction Writers. *Honours:* Nomination as Best fan writer for Hugo Award of World SF Society, 1973, 1974, 1975; Nomination for John W Campbell Award as Best New SF Writer, 1983. *Memberships:* Science Fiction Writers of America; The Fantasy Association. *Address:* 8744 N Pennsylvania Street, Indianapolis, IN 46240, USA.

MIHAJLOV, Mihajlo, b. 26 Sep. 1934, Pancevo, Yugoslavia. University Professor/Author. *Education:* BA, Comparative Literature, Zagreb University, 1959; MA, Modern Russian Literature, Zagreb University, 1961. *Literary Appointments:* Editorial Board Member, Kontinent 1975–84; Forum (Munich) 1982–, Tribuna (Paris) 1983–. *Contributor/Editor,* Religion in Communist Dominated Areas (New York) 1979–. *Publications:* Moscow Summer, 1965; Russian Themes, 1968; Underground Notes, 1976; Unscientific Thoughts, 1979; Planetary Consciousness, 1982; Yugoslav Paradox and Tyranny and Freedom, to be published. *Contributions to:* New York Review of Books; The New Leader; Kontinent; Sihtaxis; Forum; Counterpoint; Survey; Cerani; St Croix Review; The Nation; The Washington Quarterly etc. *Honours:* Annual Award, International League for Human Rights 1978; Ford Foundation Award for Humanistic Perspectives on Contemporary Society, 1980. *Memberships:*

International PEN Club (French Branch); International PEN Club (American Branch); Honorary Member, Free German Authors' Organisation. *Address:* 3921 Fifth Street, North #2, Arlington, VA 22203, USA.

MIHALIK, John Michael, b. 4 May 1955, Tachikawa, Japan. Medical Student. m. Catherine Lynne Bise, 28 Dec. 1980, California, USA, 2 daughters. *Education:* BA, Philosophy, Gonzala University; BSN, Seattle University School of Nursing; MD, University of Washington School of Medicine. *Publications:* 35 Amazing Games for Your Commodore 64, 1984; 35 Ausgesuchte Spiece fur Ihren Commodore 64, 1984; 35 Amazing Games for Your Commodore 128, 1986. *Contributor to:* Waking; Loyola-Marymount University Literary Journal, 1975. *Literary Agent:* Theodore DiSante. *Address:* 2428 E Miller St, Seattle, WA 98112, USA.

MIKES, George, b. 15 Feb. 1912, Siklos, Hungary. Writer. m. Lea Hanak, 2 Jan. 1948, 1 son, 1 daughter. *Education:* LLD, Budapest University. *Literary Appointments:* President, PEN in Exile, 1974–81. *Publications include:* How to be an Alien, 1946; Milk & Honey, 1950; The Hungarian Revolution, 1957; The Spy Who Died of Boredom; 1973; How to be Poor; 1983; How to be a Guru, 1984; etc. *Contributions to:* Encounter; Times Literary Supplement; Observer; Sunday Times. *Membership:* Executive Committee 1962–66, PEN Club. *Address:* 1B Dorncliffe Road, London SW6, England.

MILES, Elton Roger, b. 25 May 1917, Coryell, Texas, USA. Professor of English, (Retired: Professor Emeritus). m. Lilian Neale, 19 July 1941, Denton, Texas, 1 son, 1 daughter. *Education:* BA, Baylor University, Waco, Texas, 1939; MA, North Texas State University, Denton, 1946; PhD, University of Texas at Austin, 1952. *Publications:* Lucky Seven: Autobiography of a Cowman, (Editor), 1957; The Way I Heard It, (Editor), 1959; Southwest Humorists, 1969; Tales of the Big Bend, 1977. *Contributions to:* Publications of the Texas Folklore Society; Southwestern American Literature. *Honours:* Border Regional Library Association Award for the Best Book of Non-Fiction. *Memberships:* Texas Folklore Society (President); Southwestern American Literature Society (President). *Address:*) 505 E Hendryx Avenue, Alpine, TX 79830, USA.

MILGRAM, Gail Gleason, b. South Amboy, New Jersey, USA. Professor, Center of Alcohol Studies, Rutgers University. m. William H Milgram, 6 Aug. 1966, 2 daughters. *Education:* BS, Georgian Court College, 1963; M Ed 1965, Ed D 1969, Rutgers University. *Literary Appointments:* Editorial referee, Journal of Studies on Alcohol; Editorial Board, Alcoholism Treatment Quarterly, 1983. *Publications:* The Teenager and Alcohol, (with Albert Ayers), 1970; The Teenager and Smoking, 1972; Alcohol Education Resource Unit, (with Paul Weber), 1973; The Teenager and Sex, 1974; Alcohol Education Materials, 1950–1973; An Annotated Bibliography, 1975; What is Alcohol and Why Do People Drink?, pamphlet, 1975; A Discussion Leader's Guide for Hollywood Squares; Beverage Alcohol Use and Misuse, 1975, revised edition 1981; Your Career in Education, 1976; Coping With Alcohol, 1978; Alcohol Education Materials, 1973–1978; An Annotated Bibliography, 1980; What, When and How To Talk to Your Children About Alcohol and Other Drugs, 1983; What, When and How to Talk to Students About Alcohol and Other Drugs: A Guide for Teachers, (with Thomas Griffin), in press. *Contributions to:* Journal of Alcohol and Drug Education; Alcoholism Treatment Quarterly; Alcoholism; Journal of Drug Education; Focus; Journal of Studies on Alcohol; US Journal of Alcohol and Drug Dependence; The Alcoholism Digest; The Journal of School Health; New Jersey Adult Educator; NJEA Review; Chapters in books; Several papers. *Honours:* Faculty Merit Award, Rutgers University, 1983; Distinguished Service Award, Middlesex County Alcohol Association, 1983. *Address:* Center of Alcohol Studies, Rutgers University, New Brunswick, NJ 08903, USA.

MILHAVEN, John Giles, b. 1 Sep. 1927, New York, USA. Professor. m. Anne Teresa Lally, 21 May 1970, New York, 1 daughter. *Education:* AB, 1949, MA, 1951, Woodstock College, Baltimore, USA; Lic Theol, Theological Faculties of Enghien, Belgium, 1957; PhD (Philosophy), University of Munich, Germany, 1962. *Literary Appointments:* Assistant Professor of Philosophy, Canisius College, Buffalo, New York, 1951–53; Assistant Professor of Philosophy, Fordham University, 1961–66; Associate Professor of Theology, Woodstock College, 1966–70; Associate Professor of Religious Studies, 1970–76, Professor of Religious Studies, 1976–,Brown University. *Publications:* Towards a New Catholic Morality, 1970; Vers une Nouvelle Théologie Morale Catholique, 1972. *Contributions to:* Journal of Religious Ethics; Theological Studies; Annual of the Society of Christian Ethics; Thought; America;a Echanges. *Memberships:* American Academy of Religion; Catholic Theological Society of America; Society of Christian Ethics. *Address:* 20 Penrose Avenue, Providence, RI 02906, USA.

MILHOUSE, Paul William, b. 31 Aug. 1910, Illinois, USA. Clergyman. m. Mary Frances Noblitt, 29 June 1932, Ogilvile, 1 son, 2 daughters. *Education:* AB, Indiana Central University, 1932; BD, 1939, ThD, 1946, American Theological Seminary. *Publications:* Enlisting and Developing Church Leaders, 1946; Come With Me, 1946; Doorways to Spiritual Living, 1950; Christian Worship in Symbol and Ritual, 1953; Laymen in the Church, 1957; Except the Lord Build the House, 1949; Life Up Your Eyes, 1955; As Life's Crossroads, 1959; Nineteen Bishops of the Evangelical United Bretheren Church, 1974; Organizing for Effective Ministry, 1980; Theological and Historical Roots of United Methodists, 1980; Detours Into Yesterday, 1984; Oklahoma City University; Miracle at 23rd and Blackwelder, 1984. *Contributor to:* Associate Editor, Telescope Messenger, 1950–59. *Honours:* Recipient, Numerous honours and awards. *Membership:* Mark Twain Writers Guild. *Address:* Oklahoma City University, Bishop in Residence, 2501 N. Blackwelder, Oklahoma City, OK 73106, USA.

MILLER, Brent Carlton, b. 11 Jan. 1947, Logan, Utah, USA. University Professor. m. Kevon Costley, 11 Sep. 1969, Logan, 2 sons, 1 daughter. *Education:* BS, Weber State College, 1971; MS, Utah State University, 1972; PhD, University of Minnesota, 1975. *Literary Appointments:* Associate Editor: The Family Coordinator, 1977; Journal of Marriage and the Family. Consulting Editor and Guest Reviewer: Family Process; Social Psychology Quarterly; Child Development and others. *Publications:* Family Studies Review Yearbook, with David Olsen, volumes 1-3, 1983–85; Marriage and Family Development, with Evelyn Durall, 6th Edition, 1985; Family Research Methods: A Primer, 1986. *Contributions to:* Journal of Marriage and the Family; Advances in Consumer Research; Journal of Comparative Family Studies; Contemporary Sociology; The Family Coordinator; Stress and the Family; Handbook of Marriage and Family, and numerous others. *Honours:* Academic Scholarship, 1969–71, Outstanding Academic Achievement Award, Psychology, 1971, BS cum laude, 1971, Phi Kappa Phi, Student body Vice President, 1971, Weber State College; Graduate Fellowship, Utah State University, 1971–72; Fellowship, National Institute of Mental Health, 1972–75; Researcher of the Year, Utah State University, 1981, 1985. *Memberships:* National Council on Family Relations (Publications Vice President, Board of Directors). *Address:* Department of Family and Human Development, Utah State University, Logan, UT 84322–2905, USA.

MILLER, Casey Geddes, b. 26 Feb. 1919, Toledo, Ohio, USA. Writer. *Education:* AB, Smith College, 1940; School of Art and Architecture, Yale University. *Publications:* Words and Women, with Kate Swift, 1976; The Handbook of Nonsexist Writing, with Kate Swift, 1980. *Contributor to:* New York Times Magazine; Washington Post; New York; Ms; etc. *Memberships:* Women's Institue for Freedom of the Press; Authors League. *Literary Agent:* Virginia Barber Literary Agency, New

York City. *Address:* PO Box 94, East Haddam, CT 06423, USA.

MILLER, Clement A, b. 29 Jan. 1915, Cleveland, Ohio, USA. Musicologist. *Education:* B Mus, M Mus, Cleveland Institute of Music; MA, Western Reserve University; PhD, University of Michigan. *Publications include:* Franchinus Gaffurius; Practica Musicae, 1968; Johannes Cochlaeus; Tetrachordum Musices, 1970; Sebald Heyden; De Arti Canendi, 1971; Hieronymus Cardanus; Writings on Music, 1973; Franchinus Gaffurius; De Harmonia Musicorum Instrumentorum Opus, 1977; The Chansons of Le Gendre, Maille, and Morpain, 1980; Nicolaus Burtius; Musices Opusculum, 1983. *Contributions to:* Musical Quarterly; Musica Disciplina; Journal of American Musicology Society. *Honour:* Guggenheim Fellowship Award, 1974-75. *Memberships:* American Musicology Society; Royal Music Association; The Renaissance Society of America. *Address:* 7922 Bremen Avenue, Parma, OH 44129, USA.

MILLER, Donald George, b. 30 Oct. 1909, Braddock, Pennsylvania, USA. Professor of the New Testament. m. Eleanor Chambers, 21 July 1937, Ventnor, New Jersey, 2 sons, 1 daughter. *Education:* AB, Greenville College, 1930; STB, 1933, STM, 1934, Biblical Seminary in New York; MA, 1934, PhD, 1935, New York University. *Literary Appointments:* Co-editor of, Interpretation: A Journal of Bible and Theology, 1947-62; New Testament Editor of, The Layman's Bible Commentary. *Publications:* Conqueror in Chains: A Story of the Apostle Paul, 1951; Fire in Thy Mouth, 1954; The Way to Biblical Preaching, 1957; The Nature and Mission of the Church, 1957; The Gospel According to Luke, 1959; The Authority of the Bible, 1972; Exegesis (translator from French), 1978; P T Forsyth (Editor and Contributor), 1981. *Contributions to:* Interpretation; Theology Today; Christianity Today; Presbyterian Life; The Presbyterian Outlook; The Presbyterian Survey; The Princeton; Seminary Bulletin; The Scottish Journal of Theology; The Pulpit; Eternity; and others. *Membership:* Society of Biblical Literature and Exegesis. *Address:* 401 Russell Avenue, Apartment 405, Gaithersburg, MD 20877, USA.

MILLER, Douglas Taylor, b. 27 May 1937, Orange, New Jersey, USA. Professor; Author. m. Susanne E Nielsen, 22 May 1982, 1 son, 1 daughter. *Education:* BA, Colby College, 1958; MA, Columbia University, 1959; PhD, Michigan State University, 1965. *Publications:* Jacksonian Aristocracy, 1967; The Birth of Modern America, 1970; Editor, The Nature of Jacksonian America, 1972; Then was The Future, 1973; The Fifties, co-author, 1977; America Since the War, in press. *Contributions to:* American Historical Review; American Quarterly; Journal of American History; Educational Theory; Michigan History; New York History; New York Historical Society Quarterly; Pennsylvania Magazine of History & Biography; Pacific Northwest Historical Quarterly. *Literary Agent:* Virginia Barber, New York City. *Address:* Department of History, Michigan State University, East Lansing, MI 48824, USA.

MILLER, E Ethelbert, b. 20 Nov. 1950, New York, USA. Administrator. m. Denise King, 25 Sep. 1980, Washington, DC, 1 daughter. *Education:* Graduate, Howard University, 1972. *Literary Appointments:* Director, Afro-American Studies Resource Center, Howard University, 1974-; Board, PEN/Faulkner Award for Fiction, 1985-. *Publications:* Andromeda, 1974; The Land of Smiles and The Land of No Smiles, 1974; Synergy, 1975; Women Surviving Massacres and Men, 1977; Migrant Worker, 1978; Season of Hunger: Cry of Rain, 1982. *Contributor to:* Essence; Greenfield Review; Washingtonian; Caliban; Obsidian; Black America Literary Forum; Praxis; Black Scholar; Yardbird Reader; The Unrealist; South and West; Aleph; The Painted Bride Quarterly; Gargoyle; Circus Maximus. *Honours:* Achievement Award, Institute for Arts and Humanities, Howard University, 1978; E Ethelbert Miller Day proclaimed by Mayor of Washington, DC, 28 Sep. 1979.

Memberships: Poets & Writers; Institute for Preservation and Study of African American Writing; PEN; National Writers Union, Member, Executive Board. *Address:* PO Box 441, Howard University, Washington, DC 20059, USA.

MILLER, Frederick Walter Gascoyne, b. 19 Sep. 1904, Hastings, New Zealand. Journalist. m. Ngaire Malcolm, 11 Sep. 1928, Dunedin, 1 son, 4 daughters. *Literary Appointment:* Member, State Literary Grants Advisory Committee, 1964-70. *Publications:* Golden Days of Lake County, 3 editions from 1949; Gold in the River, 1946; Beyond the Blue Mountains, 1954; West to the Fiords, 1954; Hokonui, The School and the People, 1982; Waikaia, The Golden Century, 1966; Ink on My Fingers, 1967; Story of the Kingston Flyer. *Honour:* OBE 1975. *Address:* 156 Venus Street, Invercargill, New Zealand.

MILLER, Hugh, b. 27 Apr. 1937, Wishaw, Scotland. Author. m. Annette Elizabeth Slater, 18 May 1981, Warwick, England. 1 son, 2 daughters from previous marriages. *Education:* Stow College; London Polytechnic; University of Glasgow. *Publications:* The Open City, 1973; Kingpin, 1974; Ambulance, 1975; The Dissector, 1976; The Rejuvenators, 1978; Victims, 1981; The Silent Witnesses, 1984. *Membership:* Mark Twain Society USA. *Literary Agent:* Fraser and Dunlop Limited, 91 Regent Street, London W1, England. *Address:* 40 St John's Court, Warwick, CV34 4NL, England.

MILLER, J Maxwell, b. 20 Sep. 1937, Kosciusko, Mississippi, USA. University Teacher. m. Alice Julene King, 2 sons. *Education:* PhD, Emory University, 1964; Post-doctoral studies at Biblisch-archaologisches Institut of the University of Tübingen, Tübingen, West Germany. *Literary Appointments:* Editorial Board, Society of Biblical Literature Monograph Series, 1969-75; Editorial Board, Journal of Biblical Literature, 1985-. *Publications:* Joshua, with Gene M Tucker, Cambridge Commentary Series, 1975; The Old Testament and the Historian, 1976; Israelite and Judean History, co-edited with John Hayes, Old Testament Library Series, 1977; Introducing the Holy Land, 1982. *Contributions to:* The Elisha Cycle and the Accounts of the Omride Wars, Journal of Biblical Literature, 1966; The Moabite Stone as a Memorial Stela, Palestine Exploration Quarterly, 1974; Archaeology and the Israelite Conquest of Canaan: The Present Status of the Debate, PEQ, 1977. *Honour:* Honorary DD, Millsaps College, Jackson, Mississippi, 1984. *Memberships:* Society of Biblical Literature, Vice-President of SE section 1969-70, President 1970-71, National Chairman, History of Israel section 1975-; American Schools of Oriental Research; Palestinian Exploration Society; International Society for Old Testament Studies; Der Deutsche Verein zur Erforschung Palastinas. *Address:* Candler School of Theology, Emory University, Atlanta, GA 30322, USA.

MILLER, Jane Judith, b. 6 Oct. 1925, Sydney, Australia. Freelance Photographer; Author. *Publications:* Foxglove Farm, 1975; Birth of a Foal, 1977; Lambing Time, 1978; A Calf is Born, 1981, German translation, 1981; Farm Alphabet Book, 1981, reprinted, 1982, 1984, paperback edition, 1981, reprinted, 1983, 1984; Farm Counting Book, 1983, reprinted, 1984, paperback, 1986, Danish Translation, 1983, German translation, 1984, Swedish translation, 1986; Birth of Piglets, 1984; German translation, 1984; Seasons on the Farm, 1986, Danish, German and Swedish translations. *Contributor to:* books, magazines, newspapers, greeting cards and calendars. *Honours:* National Book League, Best Children's Book of the Year, 1985 for Birth of Piglets; Outstanding Science Book for Children (National Science Teachers Association, Children's Books Council, Joint Committee, USA); Awards for Birth of a Foal, 1977, Lambing Time, 1978; Fellowship, Royal Photographic Society, 1985. *Literary Agent:* Jonathan Clowes. *Address:* 14 Dealtry Road, London, SW15 6NL, England.

MILLER, Jim Wayne, b. 21 Oct. 1936, Leicester, North Carolina, USA. Teacher. m. 17 Aug. 1958, Willard,

2 sons, 1 daughter. *Education:* AB, English, Bera College, 1958; PhD, German & American Literature & Language, Vanderbilt University, 1965. *Appointments:* Staff Member, Hindman Settlement School Writers Workshop, 1978–; Writer in Residence; Centre College, Danville, 1984, East Tennessee State University, 1985. *Publications:* (Poems) Copperhead Cane, 1964; Dialogue with a Dead Man, 1974, 1978; The Mountains Have Come Closer, 1980; Vein of Words, 1984; (Ballards) The More Things Change the More They Stay the Same, 1971. *Contributor to:* Journal of Kentucky Studies; Appalchian Heritage; New York Times Literary Magazine; etc. *Honours:* Appalachian Writers Association Award for best book of 1981; Thomas Wolfe Literary Award for, The Mountains Have Come Closer, 1980. *Membership:* Kentucky State Poetry Society. *Address:* IWFAC 272, Western Kentucky University, Bowling Green, KY 42101, USA.

MILLER, Jordan Yale, b. 2 Sep. 1919, Manhattan, Kansas, USA. Professor of English. m. Elaine Elizabeth Graham, 31 Dec. 1945, New Haven, Connecticut, 2 daughters. *Education:* BA, Yale University, 1942; PhD, Columbia University, 1957. *Publications:* American Dramatic Literature, 1961; Eugene O'Neill and the Critics, 1965; 20th Century Views of a Streetcar Named Desire, 1971; Heath Introduction to Drama, 1976 and 1983. *Contributions to:* Georgia Review; Kansas Quarterly; Modern Drama; American Literature; 19th Century Theatre Research; Series of critical anthologies on the 20's 30's and 40's and the black American writer; Field Editor, G K Hall Publishers for T Wayne Critical History of American Drama (4 vol), 1986–87. *Memberships:* Modern Language Association; Secretary, Eugene O'Neill Society. *Address:* 23 Locust Drive, Kingston, RI 02881, USA.

MILLER, Lily Poritz, b. 7 June 1938, Cape Town, Republic of South Africa. Editor, Playwright. m. Stephen Harris Miller, 6 Aug. 1966, New York City, USA, (divorced). *Education:* Fay School, Boston, Massachusetts, USA; American Academy of Dramatic Arts, New York, USA; New School for Social Research, New York. *Literary Appointments:* Editor, Collier-Macmillan and McGraw-Hill, New York; Teacher of Creative Writing, City University of New York; Presently Senior Editor, McClelland & Stewart Publishers, Toronto, Canada. *Major Publications:* My Star of Hope (play), 1962; The Proud One, (play) 1974. *Contributor to:* American Scene; New Voices. *Honour:* The Proud One, received Samual French Award, 1974. *Memberships:* Playwright Union of Canada; Dramatists; Guild of Authors League of America. *Literary Agent:* Bertha Klausner, New York, USA. *Address:* c/o Playwrights' Union of Canada, 8 York Street, 6th Floor, Toronto, Ontario M5J 1R2, Canada.

MILLER, Maureen Ann, b. 20 Feb. 1942, England. Publisher; Editor; Director. m. Philip E New, 1979, 1 stepson, 1 stepdaughter. *Education:* Information Science Diploma, Oslo University, Norway. *Literary Appointments:* Publisher, Discovery Press and World Viewdata Services. *Contributions to:* Editor, North America Travel Market Directory, Business in View; Managing editor and contributor, Holiday USA and Canada Magazine; Editor, Englands Seaside Resorts, new magazine to appear 1986. *Address:* 5 Ashburnham Close, Stanley Road, London N2, England.

MILLER, Merl K, b. 17 July 1942, Cheyenne, Wyoming, USA. Author. m. Patricia Hayward, 8 Oct. 1976, Champaign, 1 son, 2 daughters. *Education:* BSc, Engineering. *Publications:* 24 Books including: Computers for Everybody; Things to do with Your Apple Computer; How to MAke Money with Your Microcomputer; Managements Guide to Computers; Presenting the Macintosh; 1985 Computer's for Everybody Buyers Guide. *Contributor to:* Over 300 articles in, Byte; Infoworld; Interface Age; Creative Computing; etc. *Address:* PO Box 367, Lake Oswego, OR 97034, USA.

MILLER, Naomi, b. 28 Feb. 1928, New York City, New York, USA. Art Historian. *Education:* BA, City College New York, 1948; MA, Columbia University, 1950; MA New York University, 1960; PhD, 1966. *Publications:* French Renaissance Fountains, 1977; Heavenly Caves, 1982. *Literary Appointments:* Book Review Editor, 1974–80, Editor 1980–84, Journal Society Architectural Historians. *Contributions to:* Articles and catalogues. *Honour:* Fellow, National Endowment for the Humanities, 1972–73; Dumbarton Oaks, 1976–77, 1983–; I Tatti, 1984–85. *Memberships:* College Art Association; Society of Architectural Historians. *Address:* Art History Department, Boston University, 725 Commonwealth Avenue, Boston, MA 02115, USA.

MILLER, Rob Hollis, b. 2 Oct. 1944, Colfax, Washington, USA. Writer. m. Kathleen Edvalson, 4 sons. *Education:* BA, Eastern Oregon State College; MA, Washington State University. *Publications:* Ghrist Mill II, 1970; Shanghai Creek Fire, 1974; The Boy Whose Shoesocks Ran Away, 1982. *Contributions to:* Rolling Stone; Christian Science Monitor; Beloit Poetry Journal; Oregon East; Dialogue; Sunstone; Measare; Trends (Scotland); Eureka (Sweden); Urthkin; St Andrews Review; The Phoenix; West Coast Review; Riverside Quarterly; Fortean Times; Durak; International Poetry Review, etc. *Address:* PO Box 669, Union, OR 97883, USA.

MILLER, Robinder Rahoula, b. 21 Mar. 1961, Madras, South India. Photojournalist, Tourist Guide. *Literary Appointment:* Apprentice Photojournalist, Indian Express. *Membership:* New Poetry Workshop Press, UK. *Contributor to:* Indian Express; Aside. *Address:* The Frogs, Madras 600 109, South India.

MILLER, Sandra (Sandy) Kay, b. 25 Dec. 1948, Horton, Kansas, USA. Author. m. 18 May 1968, Mounds, Oklahoma, 4 sons, 2 daughters. *Education:* Tulsa Junior College. *Publications:* Two Loves for Jenny, 1982; Smart Girl, 1982; Lynn's Challenge, 1984, Chase the Sun, 1983; Freddie The Thirteenth, 1985; A Tale of Two Turkeys, 1985; This Song is For You, 1985. *Contributions to:* Humpty Dumpty's Magazine; Sunshine Magazine; Pentecostal Evangel; Straight; Wonder Time; Discovery; Nursery Days; The Outpost, etc; 30 poems 5 short stories; articles. *Honours:* IRA/CBC Award for, Two Loves for Jenny, 1983. *Memberships:* Tulsa Tuesday Writers, former Vice-President and President, 1981–82; Oklahoma Writers Federation Incorporated; Tulsa Christian Writers, Vice-President, 1982. *Literary Agent:* Merrilee Heifetz, Writers House Incorporated. *Address:* PO Box 311, Mounds, OK 74047, USA.

MILLER, Stuart Creighton, b. 2 June 1927, New York City, USA. University Professor, Author. m. Naomi Esterowitz, 11 June 1955, 1 son, 1 daughter. *Education:* BA, Colgate University; MA, PhD, Columbia University. *Literary Appointments:* Instructor in History, Columbia University, 1959–62; Assistant Professor of Social Science & History, 1962–66, Associate Professor, 1966–71, Professor, 1971–, San Francisco State University; Visiting Associate Professor of History, Smith College, 1968. *Major Publications:* The Unwelcome Immigrant; American Images of the Chinese 1785–1882, 1969; Benevolent Assimilation: The American Conquest of the Philippines 1899–1903, 1982; Ends & Means: The Protestant Missionary Justification of Force in 19th Century China, 1974. *Contributor to:* Pacific Historical Review; Historian; Trans Action; Amerasia Journal; Journal of American Ethnic History; Journal of American History; Pacific Studies; Social Education; American Historical Review; Societas; New York Times; New York Times Book Review; San Francisco Chronicle; Los Angeles Times; San José Mercury News. *Honour:* National Endowment for the Humanities Faculty Research Award, 1968. *Address:* 181 San Carlos Avenue, Sausalito, CA 94965, USA.

MILLER, Teresa Lynn, b. 23 Nov. 1952, Tahlequah, Oklahoma, USA. Writer. *Education:* BA, 1973, MEd,

1975, Northeastern Oklahoma State University. *Publication:* Remnants of Glory, 1981. *Membership:* Authors Guild. *Literary Agent:* Virginia Barber Literary Agency. *Address:* P O Box 395, Tahlequah, OK 74465, USA.

MILLER, Vassar, b. 19 July 1924, Houston, Texas, USA. Writer. *Education:* BS, MA, University of Houston. *Literary Appointments:* Writer-in-Residence, Saint Thomas University, 1975–76; Alternative Poet Laureate of The State of Texas, 1983. *Publications:* Adam's Footprint, 1956; Wage War on Silence, 1957; My Bones Being Wiser, 1960; Onions and Roses, 1963; If I Could Only Sleep Deeply Enough, 1968; Small Change, 1976; Approaching Nada, 1977; Selected and New Poems, 1981; Struggling to Swim on Concrete, 1984; Despite This Flesh: The Handicapped in Stories and Poems, 1985. *Contributions to:* Sewanee Review; Georgia Review; Poetry; Poetry Now; New Letters; Latitudes; Kaleidescope; Poetry Northwest. *Honours:* Pulitzer Prize Nomination, 1962, 84; Voertman Award, Texas Institute of Letters, 1956, 62. *Memberships:* PEN, Poetry Society of America. *Address:* 1615 Vassar, Houston, TX 77006, USA.

MILLHAUSER, Steven Lewis, b. 3 Aug. 1943, New York City, USA. Novelist. m. Cathy Allis, 16 July 1984, Larchmont, New York. *Education:* BA, Columbia College, 1965; 3 years Graduate Study, Brown University. *Major Publications:* Edwin Mullhouse: The Life & Death of an American Writer 1943–54, 1972; Portrait of a Romantic, 1977; Stories: In the Penny Arcade, 1986. *Contributor to:* The New Yorker; Antaeus; Hudson Review; and others. *Honour:* Prix Médicis Etranger (for translation of Edwin Mullhouse), Paris, France, 1975. *Literary Agent:* McIntosh & Otis Inc, New York. *Address:* 515 Wagner Avenue, Mamaroneck, NY 10543, USA.

MILLHISER, Marlys, b. 27 May 1938, Charles City, Iowa, USA. Writer. m. David R Millhiser, 25 June 1960, 1 son, 1 daughter. *Education:* BA, University of Iowa, 1960; MA, University of Colorado, 1963. *Publications:* Michael's Wife, 1972; Nella Waits, 1974; Willing Hostage, 1976; The Mirror, 1978; Nightmare Country, 1981; The Threshold, 1984. *Contributions to:* Denver Post; The Writer Magazine. *Honours:* Top Hand Award for Adult Fiction, for Nela Waits, 1975, for The Threshold, 1985, Colorado Authors League. *Memberships:* Authors League of America; Mystery Writers of America; Western Writers of America; Colorado Authors League. *Literary Agent:* Roberta Kent. *Address:* 1743 Orchard Avenue, Boulder, CO 80302, USA.

MILLINGTON, Terence Alario, b. 2 Aug. 1922, England. University Lecturer. 4 sons. *Education:* BSc, Kings College, University of London, 1948; DipEd, University of London Institute of Education, 1949. *Literary Appointments include:* Editorial Board, Education for Teaching, 1958–66; Scriptwriter, Yorkshire Television. *Publications include:* Dictionary of Mathematics, 1966, 1972, 1979 and 1980; Living Mathematics, 1967–74; Introduction to Sets, 1971; History of Mathematics, 1972; Joy of Knowledge and Random House Encyclopedia (co-author), 1976 and 1981; Academic American Encyclopedia, 1977; Never A Dull Moment, (co-author), 1982. *Contributions to:* Education for Teaching; The Teacher; UNESCO Reports; Indian Journal of Mathematics Teaching. *Honours:* Fellow, Institute of Mathematics and its Applications, 1967; Recognised Teacher of the University of London, 1969; Certificate of Honours, Thailand, 1976. *Memberships include:* Society of Authors. *Address:* 10 Creswick Walk, Hampstead Garden Suburb, London NW11 6AN, England.

MILLIS, Christopher, b. 27 May 1954, Hartford, Connecticut, USA. Poet. m. Nina Davis, 30 July 1977, Wesleyan Univ. *Education:* BA, Wesleyan University, 1976; MA, New York University, 1982. *Productions:* The Shining House, dance opera (with Jean Erdman and Paul Jenkins), 1980; Poems For The End of the World theatre work of poetry and dance, (with June Anderson) Merce Cunningham Dance Studio, 1982; The Magnetic Properties of Moonlight theatre work of music, dance, poetry and scenic design, 1984. *Contributions to:* Monitor's Anthology of Magazine Verse and Year Book of American Poetry; The Kansas Quarterly; The Greenfield Reviews; Poet Love College English; The Bellingham Review; The Croton Review; Stone Country; Sotheby's International Poetry Competition Anthology; Casa El Salvador; San Diego Poets Press; Nimrod; others. *Honours:* Award, Academy of American Poets, 1976; Yaddo Fellowships, 1981, 1985; Writer in residence grant, New York Arts Council Fellowship, Virginia Centre for the Creative Arts, 1984; First Prize Phoenix International Poetry Competition, 1985. *Memberships:* Poets and Writers; The Poetry Society of America; The Dramatists Guild. *Address:* 366 Savin Hill Avenue #3L, Dorchester MA 02125, USA.

MILLS, Claudia, b. 21 Aug. 1954, New York City, USA. Writer; Editor. *Education:* BA, Philosophy, Wellesley College, 1976; MA, Philosophy, Princeton University, 1979. *Publications:* Luisa's American Dream, 1981; At the Back of the Woods, 1982; The Secret Carousel, 1983; All the Living, 1983; Boardwalk with Hotel, 1985. *Memberships:* Authors Guild; Washington children's Book Guyild (Recording Secretary, 1984–85); Society of Children's Book Writers. *Address:* 7302 Birch Avenue, Takoma Park, MD 20912, USA.

MILLS, Daniel Quinn, b. 24 Nov. 1941, Houston, Texas, USA. Educator. m. Joyce A Smith, 2 Jan. 1970, Northboro, Massachusetts, 2 daughters. *Education:* BA, Ohio Wesleyan University, 1963; MA, Economics, 1965; PhD, Economics, 1968, Harvard University. *Publications:* Industrial Relations and Manpower in Construction, 1972; Labor, Government and Inflation, 1975; Labor-Management Relatives, 1982; The Construction Industry: Balance Wheel of the Economy (with Julian Lange), 1979; Work Decisions in the 1980s, 1981; Managing Human Assets (with Michael Beer), 1984; Industrial Relations in Transition (with Janice McCormick), 1984; Human Resources Management (with Michael Beer, et al), 1985; The New Competititors: A Report from the Harvard Business School on American Management, 1985. *Contributions to:* Harvard Business Review; Monthly Labor Review; Bell Journal of Economics and Management Science; Organizational Dynamics; Industrial Relations; US Industrial Relations, 1950–80: A Critical Assessment; Toward a New US Industrial Policy? Government, Technology and the Future of the Automobile; Federal Policies and Worker Statue Since the Thirties; US Competitiveness in the World Economy. *Memberships:* Phi Beta Kappa; American Economic Association; Industrial Relations Research Association. *Address:* 40 Westland Avenue, Winchester, MA 01890, USA.

MILLS, John, b. 23 June 1930, London, England. Academic. m. Elaine Hyde, 10 Dec. 1983, Vancouver, Canada, 1 son, 1 daughter. *Education:* BA, University of British Columbia, 1964; MA, Stanford University, USA, 1965. *Publications:* The Land of Is, 1972; The October Men, 1973; Shevington's Daughter, 1978; Lizard in the Grass, 1981; Robertson Davies, 1985. *Honour:* Woodrow Wilson Fellow, 1965. *Address:* 3850 West 8th Avenue, Vancouver, British Columbia, Canada.

MILNE, Antony Alexander, b. 25 Apr. 1942, Tring, Hertfordshire, England. Science Writer. m. Ayshea Tomris, 30 May 1970, London, 1 son, 1 daughter. *Education:* B Sc Economics, London University, 1971–74; Research Fellow in environmental economics, NATO sub-committee, 1976–78. *Publications:* Noise Pollution, 1979; London's Drowning, 1982; Floodshock forthcoming 1986. *Contributions to:* Freethinker; New Humanist; Ego. *Membership:* Association of British Science Writers. *Address:* 13 Howarth Road, Abbey Wood, London SE2 OUL, England.

MILNE, Christopher, b. 21 Aug. 1920, London, England. Author. m. Lesley de Selincourt, 24 July 1948, London, 1 daughter. *Education:* BA(Hons), English Literature, Cambridge University. *Publications:* The

Enchanted Places, 1974; The Path Through the Trees, 1979; The Hollow on the Hill, 1982; The Windfall, 1985. *Membership:* PEN *Literary Agent:* Curtis Brown. *Address:* Embridge Forge, Dartmouth, Devon TQ6 OLQ, England.

MILNE, David Ross, b. 23 Feb. 1934, Dundee, Scotland. Medical Journalist (Writing, Photography, Broadcasting). m. Lu Pi Yun, Tokyo, 1 daughter. *Education:* AB, Honours, Biology, Washington & Jefferson College, 1960. *Literary Appointment:* Editorial Research Associate, Department of Surgery, Medical College of Ohio, 1978. *Contributions to:* Journal of the American Medical Association; Medical Tribune; Medical News; Readers Digest; Sports Illustrated; China News; Health Herald; Medical Post; Medical World News; Emergency Department News; Oncology Times; Surgical Practice News; Cardiovascular News; Health Care News; Selecta; Praxis Kurier; Arztliche Praxis; Le Concours Medical; Critical Care Monitor; Female Patient; Medizinische Klinik; On Call; Pulse; etc. *Honours:* Award, Japan Medical Association, 1969; Award, Japan Atherosclerosis Foundation, 1969 (preparation, manuscripts, medical congresses). *Memberships:* American Medical Writers Association; National Association of Science Writers, USA. *Address:* 1626 Circular Drive, Toledo, OH 43614, USA.

MILNE, Robert Scott, b. 3 Sep. 1917, Dighton, Massachusetts, USA. Travel Writer; Publisher, Newsletter for Travel Writers. m. Gaby Kuranda, 30 June 1957, New York, 1 son, 1 daughter. *Education:* AB, Clark University. *Publications:* Opportunities in Travel Careers, 1976, 3rd edition, 1984. *Contributor to:* Numerous articles in professional journals, magazines and newspapers. *Honours:* Silver Tankard Trophy, Freelance Council of the Society of American Travel Writers in appreciation of his Newsletter, Travelwriter Marketletter. *Memberships:* Council of Writers Organizations, Secretary; Freelance Council, Society of American Travel Writers; Travel Journalists Guild, Vice President; New York Travel Writers Association; Authors Guild; Media Alliance; Newsletter Association; Naval Intelligence Professor. *Address:* The Plaza Hotel – Room 1723, New York, NY 10019, USA.

MILNE, William Gordon, b. 17 Mar. 1921, Massachusetts, USA. Teacher. *Education:* AB, Brown University, 1941; MA, 1947, PhD, 1951, Harvard University. *Appointments:* Instructor, University of Kansas City, 1948–49; Assistant Professor, Massachusetts Institute of Technology, 1951; Assistant Professor, 1951–53, Associate Professor, 1953–57, Professor, 1957–, Lake Forest College; Fulbright Guest Professor, Wurzburg University, Germany, 1958–59. *Publications:* George William Curtis and the Genteel Tradition, 1956; The American Political Novel, 1966; The Sense of Society: A History of the American Novel of Manners, 1977; Stephen Crane at Brede: An Anglo-American Literary Circle of the 1890's, 1980. *Contributor to:* American Literature; Die Neueren Sprachen; University of Kansas City Review. *Memberships:* American Studies Association; Modern Language Association; American Association of University Professors; United Chapters of Phi Beta Kappa, Member, Nominating Committee, 1982–. *Address:* 501 Green Bay Road, Lake Bluff, IL 60045, USA.

MILNER, Ian Frank George, b. 6 June 1911, Oamaru, New Zealand. University Professor of English Literature. m. Jarmila Fruhaufová Maranová, 24 July 1958, Prague. *Education:* MA English 1st class honours, Canterbury University, New Zealand; BA 1st class honours Philosophy, Politics, Economics, Oxford University; Commonwealth Fellow, University of California, University of Columbia, USA; Dr Sc Literature, Charles University, Prague, Czechoslovakia. *Literary Appointments:* Lecturer and Associate Professor of Modern English Literature, Charles University, Prague, 1951–76; Visiting Professor in English, University of Otago, New Zealand, 1971; Research Fellow, Alexander Turnbull Library, Wellington, New Zealand, 1980. *Publicatons:* New Zealand's Interests and Policies in the Far East,

1940; The Structure of Values in George Eliot, 1968; Dickens Centennial Essays, (contributor), 1971; Milner of Waitaki – Portrait of the Man, 1983; Translations from the Czech: Miroslav Holub – Selected Poems (with G Theiner), 1967; Vladimir Holub – Selected Poems (with Jarmila Milner), 1971; M Holub, Although (with J Milner), 1971; M Holub, Notes of a Clay Pigeon (with J Milner), 1977 and 1985; Vladimír Holan, A Night with Hamlet (with J Milner), 1980. *Contributions to:* Nineteenth Century Fiction; Studies in English Literature, USA; Notes and Queries; Philogica Pragensis; Prague Studies in English; Landfall, New Zealand; Islands, New Zealand; Translations in Times Literary Supplement, London Magazine, New Statement, etc. *Honour:* Petr Bezrul Prize, 1967; *Memberships:* Circle of Modern Philology, Prague; Friends of the Turnbull Library, New Zealand. *Address:* Lopatecka lla, Prague 4 Podoli, 147 00 Czechoslovakia.

MILSOM, Charles Henry, b. 29 Dec. 1926, Liverpool. England. Journalist. m. Brenda Ashford, 1953, Wirral, England, 2 daughters. *Publications:* Guide to the Merchant Navy, 1968; The Coal Was There for Burning, 1975; The Competitive Swimmers' Handbook, 1982. *Address:* 110 Manor Drive, Upton, Wirral, Merseyside, England.

MILTON, David Q, b. 19 June 1952, Pittsburgh, Pennsylvania, USA. Psychiatric Technician; M H Program Specialist. *Education:* BS, California State University, Dominguez Hills; MS, California Polytechnic State University, San Luis Obispa. *Publications:* Electrobiochemical Stew, 1980; Poems of Our Civilization, 1981; Images of Dust and Stone, 1983. *Contributions to:* Environment, 1976; Ouija Madness, 1980; Earth's Advocate, 1980; Three River's Network, 1983; Not Man Apart, 1984; Phone-a-Poem, 1984; Audio-Visual Poetry Foundation, 1985. *Address:* 12525 Santa Lucia, Atascadero, CA 93422, USA.

MILTON, John R. b. 24 May 1924, Anoka, Minnesota, USA. Professor of Western American Literature; Editor. m. Leonharda A Hinderlie, 3 Aug. 1946, St. Paul, 1 daughter. *Education:* BA, MA, University of Minnesota, Minneapolis; PhD, University of Denver, Colorado. *Publications include:* Conversations with Frank Waters, 1971; Oscar Howe: The Story of an American Indian, 1972; The Tree of Bones and Other Poems, 1973; The Blue Belly of the World, 1974; Crazy Horse, 1974; The Literature of South Dakota, 1976; Notes to a Bald Buffalo, 1976; South Dakota: A Bicentennial History, 1977; The Novel of the American West, 1980. *Contributions to:* South Dakota Review, Editor; Several other Western American journals. *Honours include:* Governor's Award for Achievement in the Arts, 1978; Western America Award, 1984. *Memberships:* Member and Officer, Literary and Poetry organisations. *Address:* 630 Thomas Street, Vermillion, SD 57069, USA.

MINARIK, John Paul, b. 6 Nov. 1947, McKeesport, Pennsylvania, USA. Engineer; Poet. m. Marcia M(argaret) Tarasovic, 8 Sep. 1979, Pittsburgh, Pennsylvania, 2 daughters. *Education:* BA, Mechanical Engineering, Carnegie-Mellon University, 1970; BA, Magna Cum Laude, English and Psychology, University of Pittsburgh, 1978. *Literary Appointment:* Editor, Academy of Prison Arts, 1973–. *Publications:* A Book, 1974, Second Editon 1977; Patterns in the Dusk, 1977; Past the Unknown, Remembered Gate, 1980; Kicking Their Heels With Freedom (Editor), 1980; The Light From Another Country: Poetry from American Prisons (Advisory Editor), 1984. *Contributions to:* Poetry Society of America Bulletin; New Orleans Review; Prison Writing Review; Journal of Popular Culture; Small Pond; Interstate; Backspace; Gravide; Joint Conference; Nitty Gritty and others. *Honour:* Honorable Mention, International PEN, 1976–77. *Address:* PO Box 99901, Pittsburgh, PA 15233–0901, USA.

MINEAR, Richard Hoffman, b. 31 Dec. 1938, Evanston, Illinois, USA Professor of History. m. Edith Murray Christian, 25 Aug. 1962, New Haven, 2 sons. *Education:* BA, Yale College, 1960; MA, 1962, PhD,

1968, Harvard University. *Literary Appointments:* Assistant Professor of History, Ohio State University 1967–70; Associate Professor of History, 1970–75, Professor of History, 1975–, University of Massachusetts. *Publications:* Japanese Tradition and Western Law, 1970; Victors' Justice; The Tokyo War Crimes Trial, 1971; Through Japanese Eyes (Editor), 1974; Requiem for Battleship Yamato, by Yoshida Mitsuru (Translated and Editor), 1985. *Contributions to:* Harvard Journal of Asiatic Studies; Journal of Asian Studies; Monumenta Nipponica; The Progressive; and others. *Honours:* Literary Book Club alternate selection for, Victors, Justice; Military Book Club Alternate selection for, Requiem for Battleship Yamato. *Membership:* Association for Asian Studies. *Address:* Department of History, University of Massachusetts, Amherst, MA 01003, USA.

MINER, Ward Lester, b. 22 Mar. 1916, Wallman, Iowa, USA. University Professor (retired). m. Thelma M Smith, 27 Oct. 1950, Carlisle, Pennsylvania. *Education:* BA, University of Colorado, 1938; MA, University of Chicago, 1940; PhD, University of Pennsylvania, 1951. *Literary Appointments:* English Departments: South Dakota State College, 1941–42; Colorado School of Mines 1945–46; Temple University, 1946–51; University of Kansas, 1956–57; Youngstown State University, 1957–76. *Publications:* The World of William Faulkner, 1952; Transatlantic Migration: The Contemporary American; Novel in France (with Thelma M Smith) 1955; William Goddard Newspaperman, 1962. *Contributor to:* Numerous magazines and journals. *Honours:* ACLS Fellow 1951–52; American Philosophical Society grant 1954; Fulbright Lecturer, Finland 1955–56, Denmark 1960–61, Iceland 1966–67. *Address:* Box 96, Harborside, ME 04642, USA.

MINES, Samuel, b. 4 Oct. 1909, New York City, USA. Writer; Science Writer. m. Susan Wanderman, 16 Aug. 1936, New York, 1 daughter. *Education:* Columbia University, New York. *Publications include:* The Best From Startling Stories, science fiction, 1953; Moment Without Time, 1956; Coyote Gulch (as Peter Field), 1936; The Last Days of Mankind, 1971; The Conquest of Pain, 1974; Pfizer: An Informal History, 1978; All About Depression, in preparation. *Contributions:* Over 350 stort stories in magazines; articles on ecology, environment, medicine, health, opinion columns, book reviews, Washington Post, 1971–76; Staff writer, American Cyanamid Company, 1955–61; Senior Science Writer, Pfizer Inc, 1961–75. *Membership:* National Association of Science Writers, 1934–75. *Literary Agent:* (Former) Curtis Brown Ltd. *Address:* 881A Heritage Village, Southbury, CT 06488, USA.

MINETT, Pamela Mary, b. 9 Oct. 1928, Gorleston-on-Sea, Norfolk, England. Writer. m. Stanley Charles Minett, 4 Apr. 1953, Caister-on-Sea, Norfolk, 1 son, 3 daughters. *Education:* BSc Honours, Nottingham. *Publications:* Concise Human Biology and Hygiene, 1974; Child Care and Development, 1985. *Address:* Stokesby House, Stokesby, Great Yarmouth, Norfolk, NR29 3ET, England.

MINGAY, Gordon Edmund, b. 20 June 1923, Long Eaton, Derbyshire, England. University Professor. m. Mavis Tippen, 20 Jan. 1945. *Education:* BA 1st Class Honours 1952, PhD 1958, University of Nottingham. *Literary Appointments:* Editor, Agricultural History Review, 1972–84; Editor, Volume VI Agrarian History of England and Wales. *Publications:* English Landed Society in the Eighteenth Century, 1963; The Agricultural Revolution 1750–1880 (with J D Chambers), 1966; The Gentry, 1976; Rural Life in Victorian England, 1977; The Victorian Countryside (Editor), 1981. *Contributions to:* Economic History Review; Agricultural History Review; Agricultural History; Times Literary Supplement. *Honours:* Fellow Royal Historical Society.

MINKOWSKI, Aleksander, b. 27 Feb. 1933, Warsaw, Poland. Novelist. m. Grazyna Zalewska, 2 Dec. 1956, 2 sons. *Education:* MA, Warsaw University, Poland. *Appointments:* Associate in Polish and Russian Literature, Columbia University, New York, USA, 1969–70 and 1971–72. *Publications:* Blekitna Milosc, 1958; Nigdy na Swiecie, 1959; Urlopna Tahiti, 1962; Gruby, 1966; Odmieniec, 1983; Zmartwychwstane Pudrycego, 1984; Dolina Swiatla, 1985. *Contributions to:* Pokolenie; Po prostu; Swiat; Tu i Teraz. *Honours:* The Warsaw Youth Literary Award, 1958; The National Award, 1976; Christian Andersen Honour List, 1980; Prime Ministers Literary Award, 1982. *Address:* Zwiazek Litertow Polskich, Krakowskie Przedmiescie 85/87, Warsaw, Poland.

MINKOWSKI, Helmut, b. 19 Sep. 1908, Duisberg, Germany. Retired Teacher. m. Ilse Rannacher, 20 Feb. 1937, 1 son. *Education:* D Phil, Konigsburg University, Berlin, Germany, 1932. *Appointment:* Editor, Der Turmer/Deutsche Monatshefte, to 1945. *Publications include:* JC Smuts: Holism and Evolution (translator), 1938; Kepler, Life and Letters (translator), 1953; Keplen, Leben und Briefe (co-author), 1953; Der Turm zu Babel, 1960; Mystik und Wissenschaft, Philos (Essays, co-author), 1963; Horizons of a Philosopher (Co-editor), 1963; Das grosste Inawkr, 1965, 14th edition, 1983. *Contributions to:* Turris Babel. *Honours:* Kant Preis, Konigsberg University 1929 and 1930; Royal Jugoslav Sv. Sava Order, 1939. *Address:* Berlin-Zehlendorf, Eggepfad 32, Federal Republic of Germany.

MINNEMANN, Joachim, b. 30 July 1949, Hamburg, Federal Republic of Germany. Teacher. *Education:* 1 and 2, Staatsexamen. *Appointments:* Lecturer, Hamburg. *Publications:* gute aussicht aus meinem fenster, 1976; der friede ist eine frau, 1978; Kleines Kinderbuch, 1978; sehusüchte stark wie gewissheit, 1979; der tagtägliche tag. Poem, 1981; der atlas reisegedichte; ich unterhalte mich gern über den frieden, 1981; das blane erfinden essays, 1987; weisse wiese, 1987; etc. *Contributor to:* Numerous professional journals. *Memberships:* Verband deutscher Schriftsteller, Literaturzentrum Hamburg, Board of Directors, 1980–83; International Association for the Study of Dialectical Philosophy; Foundation Member, International Bloch Association. *Literary Agent:* Carolin Emcke, Hamburg. *Address:* Eulenstr. 81, 2000 Hamburg 50, Federal Republic of Germany.

MINNIUM, Edward W(headon), b. 28 Nov. 1917, Alameda, California, USA. University Professor of Psychology. m. Juanita Elizabeth Pico, 3 July 1941, Alameda, 2 daughters. *Education:* AB, Stanford University, 1939; PhD, University of California, Berkeley, 1951. *Publications:* Statistical Reasoning in Psychology of Education, 1970 and 1978; Elements of Statistical Reasoning, (with Robert B Clarke), 1982. *Contributions to:* Various psychological and educational journals. *Address:* 2281 Lansford Avenue, San Jose, CA 95125, USA.

MINOGJE, Kenneth Robert, b. 11 Sep. 1930, University Professor. m. Valerie Pearson Hallett, 16 June 1954, 1 son, 1 daughter. *Education:* BA, University of Sydney, Australia, 1949; B Sc Economics, London School of Economics, University of London, England, 1955. *Publications:* The Liberal Mind, 1961; Nationalism, 1967; The Concept of a University, 1974; Alien Powers: The Pure Theory of Ideology, 1985. *Contributions to:* Encounter; Philosophy; Political Studies; Times Literary Supplement; American Spectator; Times Higher Education Supplement; Quadrant. *Address:* 16 Buckland Crescent, London NW3 5DX, England.

MINOT, Stephen, b. 27 May 1927, Boston, Massachusetts, USA. Writer. m. (1) 1 son, (2) Virginia M Stover, 18 Feb. 1955, Portland, Maine, 2 sons. *Education:* AB, Harvard, 1951; MA, The Johns Hopkins University, 1955. *Literary Appointments:* Bowdoin College, 1955–58, University of Connecticut, Hartford, 1958–59; Trinity College, Hartford, 1959–61. *Publications:* Three Genres, 1965, 3rd edition 1982; Chill of Dusk, 1964; Crossings, 1975; Ghost Images, 1979; Surviving The Flood, 1981; Reading Fiction, 1984. *Contributions to:* Magazines and journals including: Atlantic; Harpers; The Kenyon Review; The Virginia

Quarterly Review; Redbook; Playboy; The Sewanee Review; Paris Review; Carleton Miscellany; The North American Review; Missouri Review; American Poetry Review. *Honours:* Saxton Memorial Fellowship, 1963; National Endowment for the Arts Fellowship for Writing, 1976-77 and 1981-82. *Membership:* The Authors Guild. *Literary Agent:* Miss Emilie Jacobson, Curtis Brown Limited, 10 Astor Place, New York, NY 10003. *Address:* 69 Hickory Hill Road, Simsbury, CT 06070, USA.

MINSKY, Betty Jane L, b. 16 Feb. 1932, Calumet County, Wisconsin, USA. Writer; Author; Behaviour Consultant. m. John A Minsky, 27 May 1952, Green Bay, 3 sons, 1 daughter. *Education:* Currently studying behaviour science, psychology, Lansing Community College. *Publications:* Gimmicks Make Money in Retailing, 1963, revised 1977; A History of Clinton County, co-author. *Contributor to:* Various trade, business publications including, Supermarket News; Footwear News; Women's Wear Daily; Daily News Record; Metalworking News; Electronic News;Home Furnishings Daily; Drug News Weekly; Ford Times; Popular Gardening; Outdoor Life; Field & Stream Collectors Quarterly; Bird Watcher's Digest; East Michigan Tourist Council Guidebooks; Michigan Correspondent, Religious News Service of New York. *Address:* N.U.S. 27, Rt 3, St Johns, MI 48879, USA.

MINWEGEN, Hiltrud, b. 2 June 1929, Essen, Germany. Writer. m. Dr Erwin Minwegen, 14 Feb. 1953, 2 sons, 1 daughters. *Education:* PhD, University of Bonn. *Publications:* Mario, 1983; Hinter Spiegeln, 1985; Besuch in Rom; Die Macht der schwarzen Bande; Der Ritter mit der Angst; Im Netz der Schmuggler; Tschau Roma; Sizilianischer Sommer. *Address:* Via Delfini 16, 00186 Rome, Italy.

MIRVISH, Robert Franklin, b. 17 July 1921, Washington DC, USA. Author. m. Lucille A Racciopi Di Giglio, 1 June 1963, Las Vegas Nevada, USA, 2 sons. *Education:* University of Toronto, Toronto, Canada. *Publications:* Novels: A House of Her Own, 1953; The Eternal Voyagers, 1953; Texana, 1954; The Long Watch, 1954; Red Sky at Midnight, 1955; Woman in a Room, 1959; Two Women, Two Worlds, 1960; Dust on the Sea, 1960; Point of Impact, 1961; Cleared Narvik 2000, 1962; The Last Capitalist, 1963; There You Are But Where Are You, 1964; Holy Loch, 1964; Non-Fiction: Business is People, 1963. *Contributor to:* Many major magazines and journals. *Membership:* Author's League of America.*Literary Agent:* Laurence Pollinger Ltd, London. *Address:* 32 Salonica Road, Don Mills, Ontario, Canada.

MISSELWITZ, Anna, b. 30 May 1901, Mährisch Rothwasser, Austria. Writer. m. (1) Robert Eisenberg, 1920, (2) Erich Misselwitz, 1956, 1 son, 2 daughters. *Education:* 22 terms, University; Guest Student, Hamburg, 1964-78. *Literary Appointments:* Poetry, short stores in anthologies and books. *Publications:* Ein Liedercyklus von Nina Wostall, Liebeslieder, 1935; Der Weg ins Unendliche, poetry, 1936; Goralen, Lieder aus den Beskiden, 1964. *Contributions to:* Prager Tagblatt, Bohemia; Ostrauer Morgenzeitung; Deutsche Zeitung; 3 papers in Czechoslovakian; Permanent correspondent, Mein Beskidenland, Journal for Refugees; Poetry contributed to, Landshuter Zeitung, and Tsar Post. *Honours:* Batia Award, 1938. *Memberships:* VS, Association of German Writers in Czechoslovakia; Ostrau Authors Association; Gedok; Esslingen Artists Guild; Association of Sudeten-German Writers. *Address:* Thumsee Strasse 9, Senidrenheim, 8230 Bad Reichenhall, Democratic Republic of Germany.

MISSFELDT, Joehen, b. 26 Jan. 1941, Satrup, Federal Republic of Germany. Writer. m. Ruth Finckh, 8 Apr. 1967, Sussen, 3 daughters. *Literary Appointments:* Hohwacht-Verlag, Bonn, 1975; Langewiesche-Brandt, Ebenhausen, 1979. *Publications:* Gesammelte Angste, poems, 1975; Mein Vater war Schneevogt, poems, 1979; Zwischen Oben zwischen Unten, novel, 1982; Capo Frasca und andere Fliegergeschichten, short

stories, 1984. *Honours:* Advancement Award, Friedrich Hebbel Foundation, 1980. *Memberships:* Federkiel; Past Chairman, Schleswig-Holstein section, Association of German Writers. *Address:* Lauacker 10, D-2262 Stadum, Federal Republic of Germany.

MITCHELL, Adrian, b. 24 Oct. 1932, London, England. Writer. *Education:* Christ Church, Oxford University. *Publications include:* Novels: If You See Me Comin; The Bodyguard; Wartime; Man Friday. Stage Shows: Tyger; Man Friday; Mind Your Head; Uppendown Mooney; Hoagy, Bix & Wolfgang Beethoven Bunkhaus; A Seventh Man; The Wild Animal Song Contest; etc. Adaptations of foreign plays: Marat/Sade; The Criminals; The Major of Zalamea; The Government Inspector; Life's a Dream; The Great Theatre of the World. Lyrics for National Theatre's Animal Farm, Royal Shakespeare Company's, Us. Books of Poetry: Poems, 1964; Out Loud, 1968;Ride the Nightmare, 1971; The Apeman Cometh, 1975; Collected Poems 1953-79, 1982; On the Beach at Cambridge, 1984; Nothingmas Day, 1984. *Honours:* Granada Fellow in the Arts, Lancaster University, 1967-69; Fellow, Centre for the Humanities, Wesleyan University, 1973; Resident Writer, Sherman Theatre, Cardiff; Visiting Writer, Billericay School, Essex, 1978-80; Judith M E Wilson Fellow, Cambridge University, 1980-81; Resident Writer, Unicorn Theatre for Children, 1982-83. *Literary Agent:* Fraser & Dunlop (Scripts) Ltd. *Address:* c/o Fraser & Dunlop (Scripts) Ltd, 91 Regent Street, London W1R 8RV, England.

MITCHELL, Benjamin (Ben) David, b. 29 Aug. 1941, Brighton, Victoria, Australia. Editor; Writer. m. 29 Nov. 1968, Kensington, London, 2 daughters. *Publications:* Summer City, 1979. *Contributions:* In-depth personality features on celebrities and showbusiness performers in UK, South Africa, Australia. Editor, TV Soap, Australia's first magazine covering TV serials & Series. Interviews for Australian provincial newspapers, Fleet Street dailies. BBC documentary, Land of Fire; Show Business stories for City Magazines, London. Reporter, ADS 7 Adelaide, hosting panel show, presenting sports news. Assistant Editor, Pix, magazine. Worked in Africa as a columnist for the Argus, Cape Town; Investigative stories, Angolan War. TV Week, Australia; Features, Pix/People; Script writer, The Young Doctors. *Literary Agent:* Curtis Brown Australia P/L. *Address:* 28 Barclay Street, Waverley, New South Wales 2024, Australia.

MITCHELL, Cynthia Eugenie, b. 10 Aug. 1922, Sharlston, Yorkshire. Retired Infant Teacher. m. Dennis Hardie Mitchell, 2 daughters. *Education:* Teaching Certificate, Balls Park College of Education, Hertford. *Publications:* Time for School – A Practical Guide for Parents of Young Children, 1973; Haloweena Hecatee and other rhymes to Skip to, 1978; Playtime, 1978; Hop-Along Happily and Other rhymes for the Playground, 1979; Compiler, Under the Cherry Tree, 1979; Here a Little Child I Stand, 1985. *Contributor to:* The Guardian; Times Educational Supplement; Where; The Best of Where; Books for Your Children; Verse for BBC Schools Radio Programme Poetry Corner; Scripts for BBC Schools Radio Programme Poetry Corner. *Address:* 32 Barnsley Road, Ackworth, Pontefract, West Yorkshire, England.

MITCHELL, David John, b. 24 Jan. 1924, London, England. Freelance writer. m. Cecilia Milwidsky, Feb. 1955 (divorced 1976), 1 son. *Education:* MA Modern History, Oxford University. *Publications:* Women on the Warpath (Monstrous Regiment – USA), 1965; The Fighting Pankhursts, 1967;1919 Red Mirage, (L'Annata Rossa dell'Europa – Italy, 1972), 1970; Pirates, 1976; Queen Christable, 1977; The Jesuits, 1980; The Spanish Civil War, 1982. *Contributions to:* Times; Times Literary Supplement; Times Educational Supplement; History Today; New Stateman; New Society; London magazine. *Honours:* Pirates; US Literary Guild alternate choice, UK History Guild selection, 1976; The Jesuits; UK History Guild selection, 1980; The Spanish Civil War; UK History Guild selection, 1982. *Membership:*

Society of Authors. *Address:* 20 Mountacre Close, Sydenham Hill, London SE26 6SX, England.

MITCHELL, Donald Earl, b. 15 Oct. 1947, Chicago, USA. Author; Farmer; Carpenter. m. Cheryl Warfield, 29 Nov. 1969, Princeton, 1 son, 1 daughter. *Education:* BA, Swarthmore College, 1984. *Appointments:* Visiting Faculty, Middlebury College, Winter 1985. *Publications:* Thumb Tripping, 1970; Four-Stroke, 1974; The Souls of Lambs, 1979; Moving Upcountry: A Yankee Way of Knowledge, 1984. *Contributor to:* Monthly column, RRFD, for Boston Magazine, 1979–84. *Honour:* Book of the Month Club Writing Fellowship, 1969. *Memberships:* Author's Guild, USA; League of Vermont Writers, Board of Directors, 1984–. *Literary Agent:* Blanche G Gregory, New York. *Address:* RD 2, Box 264, Vergennes, VT 05491, USA.

MITCHELL, Karen, b. 27 Nov. 1952, Jackson, Mississippi, USA. Director of Editorial Services & Program Development. 1 son. *Education:* BSN, University of Mississippi; MSN, St Louis University; PhD, University of Missouri, Kansas City. *Literary Appointments:* Editor, Pediatric Nursing, 1983; Editor, Community Nursing Newsletter, 1984; Editor, Nursing Economics, 1985. *Contributions to:* Pediatric Nursing; Nursing Economics; Child Care Newsletter. *Honours:* Phi Kappa Phi, 1973; Faculty Award, Top Graduating Student, 1974; Summa Cum Laude, (BSN), Graduated with Special Distinction, 1974; University of Mississippi School of Nursing; Full Federal Academic Traineeship, St Louis University School of Nursing, Master's Program; Pi Lambda Theta, 1982; Recognition Award for Young Scholars, 1983; Nominated for American Association of University Women, 1984–85. *Memberships:* Truman Medical Center Clinical Research Review Board, 1981–83; Consultant, Mississippi House of Representatives and Senate Insurance Committees to develop Bill providing 3rd party reinbursement to nurse practitioners, 1979; Mississippi Board of Nursing Committee, 1978; University of Missouri Committee for Distribution of Health Professionals, 1979–81; Advisory Board to University of Missouri, Kansas City Women's Center. *Address:* c/o Anthony J Jannetti, Inc, N Woodbury Road, Box 56, Pitman, NJ 08071, USA.

MITCHELL, Marcia Louise, b. 31 May 1942, Walla Walla, Washington, USA. Author. m. Fred L Mitchell, 6 Feb. 1961, Pendleton, 2 daughters. *Education:* Graduated, Walla Walla High School, 1960. *Publications:* Jenny, 1983; Spiritually Single, 1984. *Contributor to:* Northwest Magazine; Evangel; Family Life Today; Trails; Herald of Holiness; others. *Honours:* Writer of the Year, Victorious Living, Christian Writers Conference, Warner Pacific College, 1984. *Memberships:* Speakers and Writers Ink; Washington Christian Writers Fellowship. *Address:* 835 Valencia, Walla Walla, WA 99362, USA.

MITCHELL, Raymond Walker, b. 21 June 1919, Sydney, Australia. Freelance Journalist and Television Commentator; Boxing Referee; Speaker. m. Mavis Grace Hutton, 21 July 1945, Parramatta, Australia, 3 sons. *Literary Appointments:* Editor, Cavalcade and Adam, 1952–55; Editor, Australian Ring, 1956–66; Editor, The Square Ring, 1982–. *Publications:* Great Australian Fights, 1965; The Fighting Sands, 1965; Ray Mitchell's Boxing Quiz Book, 1966; Fight For Your Life, 1967; Boxing Rule Book, 1966; Several boxing record books. *Contributions to:* World Book Encyclopaedia; Australian Encyclopaedia; The Ring, USA; The Square Ring; Ampol Australian Sporting Records; Various newspapers. *Honours:* Queen's Silver Jubilee Medal, 1977; MBE, for services to Boxing and to sports journalism, 1978. *Address:* 23 Milburn Road, Gymea, NSW 2227, Australia.

MITCHELL, Robby Koons, b. 2 Apr. 1916, Kelton, Texas, USA. Real Estate Manager, Investor. m. Glenn Mitchell, 8 Dec. 1934, Denton, Texas, 2 sons, 2 daughters. *Literary Appointments:* Poet Laureate of Texas, 1970–71. *Publications:* A Texas Sampler, anthology, 1942; World's Fair Anthology, 1943;

Mockingbird's Song in the Night, 1956; Fire and Frost, 1963; And Burn My Brand, 1970; Splinter of Bone, 1977; Anthology: First Flight, 1978; Anthology: Feathers on the Wind, 1982; From Hide and Horn, anthology, 1985. *Contributions to:* Facets; Allenspark Wind; Feature poem in, Forefathers of the Panhandle, 1984. *Honours:* Poet Laureate of Texas, 1970–71; 1st Place Award, Texas Contest-The Old South Prize; 34 places, including 10 first places, in contests, 1980–85. *Memberships:* Councillor, Red River Area, State of Texas 1970–,President Mockingbird chapter 1970 and 1978, Treasurer Mockingbird chapter 1983–85, Poetry Society of Texas; National Federation of Poetry Societies. *Address:* 405 N Waddill, McKinney, TX 75069, USA.

MITCHELL, Sally, b. 8 Oct. 1937, San Antonio, Texas, USA. English Professor. 2 daughters. *Education:* BA, University of Colorado, 1959; MA, University of Wisconsin, Milwaukee, 1971; D Phil, Oxford (Linacre), 1977. *Appointments:* Lecturer, English, University of Wisconsin; Reviewer, Library Journal; Assistant Professor, English & Women's Studies, Temple University; Editor in Chief, Victorian Britain. *Publications:* The Fallen Angel: Chastity, Class and Women's Reading, 1835–1880, 1981; Dinah Mulock Craik, 1983; Essays in: A Widening Sphere, 1977; American Women Writers, 1979–82; etc. *Contributor to:* Victorian Studies; Victorian Periodicals Review; etc.*Honour:* Fulbright Scholar, Oxford, 1972–73. *Address:* English Dept, Temple University, Philadelphia, PA 19122, USA.

MITCHELL, (Sibyl) Elyne Keith, b. 30 Dec. 1913, Melbourne, Australia. Author. *Publications:* Adult books: Australia's Alps, 1942; Speak to the Earth, 1945; Soil and Civilization, 1946; Images in Water, 1947; Flow River, Blow Wind, 1953; Black Cockatoos Mean Snow, 1956; Light Horse, The Story of Australia's Mounted Troops, 1978; The Snowy Mountains, 1983; Discoverers of the Snowy Mountain, 1985. Novelization of the film, Man from Snowy River, 1982; Chauvel Country, 1984; children's books: Silver Brumby, 1958; Silver Brumby's Daughter, 1960; Kingfisher Feather, 1962; Winged Skis, 1964; Silver Brumbies of the South, 1965; Silver Brumby Kingdom, 1966; Moon Filly, 1968; Jinki, Dingo of the Snow, 1970; Light Horse to Damascus, 1971; Silver Brumby Whirlwind, 1973; The Colt at Taparoo, 1975; Son of the Whirlwind, 1976; The Colt from Snowy River, 1979; Snowy River Brumby, 1980; Brumby Racer, 1981. *Membership:* Australian Society of Authors. *Literary Agent:* Curtis Brown Ltd. *Address:* Towong Hill, Corryong, Victoria 3707, Australia.

MITCHELL, Tean Jane, b. 5 July 1952, Cornwall, England. Journalist/Publisher. *Literary Appointments:* Sub-Editor, Fishing News; Hon. Editor, BVCG News; Assistant Editor, BVA Publications; Publisher, Brevet Publishing, (current). *Contributions to:* numerous journals. *Address:* 128 Cranworth Gardens, London SW9, England.

MITCHISON, Rosalind Mary, b. 11 Apr. 1919, Manchester, England. University Teacher. m. John Murdoch Mitchison, 21 June 1947, Oxford, 1 son, 3 daughters. *Education:* MA, Oxford. *Publications:* Agricultural Sir John, 1962; A History of Scotland, 1970; British Population Change Since 1860, 1977; Life in Scotland, 1978; Lordship to Patronage: Scotland 1603–1745, 1983. *Contributions to:* Historical journals including: Past and Present; Economic History Review; Historica; Journal; London Review of Books. *Membership:* President 1981–84, Scottish History Society. *Address:* Great Yew, Ormiston, East Lothian, Scotland EH35 5NJ.

MITRU, Alexandru, b. 6 Nov. 1914, Craiova, Romania. Writer; Literature Teacher. *Education:* University of Bucharest. *Publications include:* Muntele der Aur, 1954, 4th edition, 1974; In tara legendelor, 1956, 3rd edition, 1973; Povesti cu tilc, 1956, 4th edition, 1973; Legendele Olimpului, 2 volumes 1960–62, 5th edition, 1978; Marile legende ale lumii, 2 volumes, 1963–65; Sageata capitanului Ion, 1967, 2nd edition, 1969; Pvestiri despre Pacala si Tindala, 1975; Legenda Valaha, 1979 *Contributor to:* numerous literary and children's journals. *Honours include:* Short Story Prize, Ministry of Culture, 1949; Romanian Writers' Union Prize, 1968; Prize, Romanian Academy, 1972; Readers Trphy Cup, 1974. *Memberships:* Bucharest Writers Association; Romanian Writers Union, etc. *Address:* 20 str. Visinilor 2, Bucharest II, Romania.

MIX, Sheldon Alfred, b. 9 Nov. 1927, Chicago, USA. Writer; Editor. m. Joyce Eitel, 19 June 1954, Chicago, 2 sons, 2 daughters. *Education:* BSc, Journalism, University of Illinois. *Contributor to:* Inland; American Way; Chicago Tribune; Christian Science Monitor; Baseball Digest; Milwaukee Journal; Wall Street Journal. *Address:* 18 South Home Avenue, Park Ridge, IL 60068, USA.

MOAT, John, b. 1936, Mussoorie, India. Writer. *Education:* MA, University of Oxford, England. *Publications:* Heorot, novel, 1968; A Standard of Verse, 1969; Thunder of Grass, 1970; The Tugen and the Toot, 1973; The Ballad of the Leaf, verse, 1974; Fiesta and the Fox Reviews His Prophecy, poems, 1979; Bartonwod, novel, 1978; Mai's Wedding, 1983; Skeleton Key, verse, 1983. The Way to Write, with John Fairfax, 1981. *Contributions to:* Listener; British Broadcasting Corporation. Co-Founder, Arvon Foundation. *Address:* c/o A D Peters and Company, 10 Buckingham Gate, London WC2, England.

MOBERG, Verne, b. 6 July 1938, East Moline, Illinois, USA. Teacher. *Education:* BA, English, University of Illinois, 1960; MA, Germanic Languages & Literature, State University of New York, 1976; PhD, Scandinavian Studies, University of Wisconsin, 1984. *Literary Appointments:* Assistant Editor, Harper's Magazine, 1961–65; Editor, Pantheon Books, 1968–71; Vice President, Feminist Press, 1971–74. *Translations include:* As Others See Us, Göran Palm, 1967; Homunculus, Sven Delblanc, 1968; I'm Like Me, Siv Widerberg, 1973; Stories in, Modern Swedish Prose, 1979; Sexism, Marie Louise Janssen-Jurreit, 1982. Into Swedish: Vid dödsstunden, Karlis Osis & Erlendur Haraldsson (with Marianne Lindström), 1980. *Contributions to:* Numerous journals including: Small Press Review; Edda. *Honours:* Translator's grants to Sweden & Norway, 1979–84. *Memberships:* Modern Languages Association; Society for the Advancement of Scandinavian Studies. *Address:* 1640 Monroe Street, Apt G, Madison WI 53711, USA.

MÖCKEL, Klaus, b. 4 Aug. 1934, Kirchberg, Germany. Writer. m. 19 Dec. 1964, 1 son. *Education:* D Phil, University Romanitik, Germany. *Publications:* Ohne Lizenz des Königs, 1973; Die Einladung, 1976; Drei Flaschen Tokaier, 1976; Die Gläserne Stadt, 1980; Die Mackende Ursula, 1980; Hass, 1981; Kopfstand der Farben, 1982; Hoffnung fur Dan, 1983. *Address:* 1071 Berlin, Wisbyer Street 28, Democratic Republic of Germany.

MOERSCH, Karl, b. 11 Mar. 1926, Calw, Wurttemberg, Federal Republic of Germany. Journalist; Former Minister of State. *Education:* Training as Editor. *Publications:* Kursrevision (Deutsche Politik nach Adenauer), 1978; Europa fur Anfanger (Fakten sur Volljahrigkeit), 1979; Bei uus im Staate Beitelsbach, 1984; Ein Unterthau das ist ein Tropf, 1985. *Contributions to:* Radio stations including: Sudwestfunk and Deutschlandfunk. *Address:* Aalenerstrasse 10, 714 Ludwigsburg-Ossweil, Federal Republic of Germany.

MOFFAT, Gwen, b. 3 July 1924, Brighton, England. Author. m. (1) Gordon Moffat, 1948, 1 daughter, (2) John Lees, 1956. *Publications:* Space Below My Feet, 1961; Lady With a Cool Eye, 1973; Deviant Death, 1973; The Corpse Road, 1974; Miss Pink at the Edge of the World, 1975; Hard Option, 1975; Over The Sea To Death, 1976; Persons Unknown, 1978; Hard Road West, 1981; The Buckskin Girl, 1982; Die Like a Dog, 1982; Last Chance Country, 1983; Grizzly Trail, 1984. *Contributions to:* Publications including: Guardian;

Sunday Telegraph; Sunday Times; Homes and Gardens; She; Scotsman; Glasgow Herald. *Honours:* Welsh Arts Council Bursary, 1978. *Memberships:* Crime Writers' Association; Society of Authors. *Literary Agent:* A M Heath. *Address:* Porth Moddfa, Clwt Y Bont, Caernarfon LL55 3DL, Wales.

MOFFETT, Samuel Hugh, b. 7 Apr. 1916, Pyongyang, Korea. Missionary; Educator. m. Eileen Flower, 15 Sep. 1956, Seoul, Korea. *Education:* AB, Wheaton College, 1938; ThB, Princeton Theological Seminary, 1942; PhD, Yale University, 1945; Former Member, Fitzwilliam College, Cambridge. *Appointments:* Henry Winters Luce Professor, Ecumenics and Mission; Chairman, Church History, Princeton Theological Seminary. *Publications:* The Christians of Korea, 1962; Joy for an Anxious Age, 1966; Asia & Missions, in Korean, 1976; First Encounters: Korea 1880–1910, Co-author, 1982. *Contributor to:* Journals & Concise Dictionary of Christian World Mission. *Memberships:* President, Royal Asiatic Society, Korea Branch, 1968. *Honours:* Citation & Prize, Ministry of Education, Republic of Korea, 1977; Litt D, Yonsei University, Seoul, 1981; Order of Civil Merit, Peony Medal, Republic of Korea, 1981; Medal of Aaron and Hur, US Army Chaplains Corps, 1982; DD, King College, Tennessee, 1985. *Address:* Princeton Theological Seminary, CN 821, Princeton, NJ 08542, USA.

MOFFITT, John, b. 27 June 1908, Harrisburg, Pennsylvania, USA. Poet; Author; Editor. *Education:* AB, English, Princeton University, 1928; Graduate, Composition, Curtis Institute of Music, 1932; Novice, Order of Ramakrishna, India, 1949, Monk, 1959, Left Order, 1963. *Appointments:* Copy Editor, 1963–70, Poetry Editor, 1963–, America, Magazine. *Publications:* This Narrow World, 1958; The Living Seed, 1962; Adam's Choice, 1967; Editor, Contributor: A New Charter for Monasticism, 1970; Journey to Gorakhpur, 1972; Escape of the Leopard, 1974; The Road to Now, 1982; Signal Message, 1982. *Contributor to:* The Atlantic; Saturday Review; Sewanee Review; Kenyon Review; Antioch Review; Virginia Quarterly Review; New Yorker; Prairie Schooner; America; Theological Studies; Journal of Ecumenical Studies; Cross Currents; Christian Century; Vita Monastica; Italy, etc. *Address:* Route 1, Box 728, Unionville, VA 22567, USA.

MOFFITT, Phillip William, b. 11 Sep. 1946, Kingsport, Tennessee, USA. Magazine Editor. *Education:* MS, Economics, 1971, BS, Political Science, 1968, University of Tennessee. *Literary Appointments:* Co-Founder, 1971, Editor, 1971–, President, 1976–, 13-30 Publishing Group, Knoxville, Tennessee; President, Esquire Associates, New York City, 1979–; Editor in Chief, Esquire Magazine, 1979–. *Contributor to:* Monthly Columnist, Esquire Magazine, Backstage, 1979–84; Monthly Columnist, Esquire Magazine, Esquire Journal, 1984–. *Membership:* Board of Directors, Magazine Publishers Association, Associated Investment Ltd, London. *Address:* 2 Park Avenue, New York, NY 10016, USA.

MOGGACH, Deborah, b. 28 June 1948, London, England. Novelist. m. Anthony Moggach, 21 Nov. 1971, Lake District, 1 son, 1 daughter. *Education:* BA, English, Bristol University. *Publications:* You Must Be Sisters, 1978; Close to Home, 1979; A Quiet Drink, 1980; Hot Water Man, 1982; Porky, 1983; To Have and To Hold, 1986. *Contributions to:* Over 21; Sunday Times; The Observer; The Times; Daily Mail; Cosmopolitan; Sunday Express Magazine. *Literary Agent:* Curtis Brown, Rochelle Stevens. *Address:* 28 Gloucester Crescent, London NW1, England.

MOHER, Francis (Frank) Anthony, b. 14 Sep. 1955, Edmonton, Alberta, Canada. Writer. m. Diana Hart, 2 Oct. 1982, 1 son. *Appointments:* Literary Manager, Northern Light Theatre, Edmonton, 1977–80; Books Editor, Alberta Report Magazine, 1983–; Playwright in Residence, Workshop West Theatre, Edmonton, 1984–85. *Publications:* Plays: Pause, 1975; Down for the Weekend, 1981; The Broken Globe, 1980. *Contributor* *to:* Contributing Writer to, Interface Magazine; Senior Editor, Books Editor, Alberta Report Magazine.; *Honours:* Alberta Culture Playwriting Award, 1974; Edmonton Journal Literary Award, 1974; Clifford E Lee Award Scholarship, 1979. *Memberships:* Playwrights Union of Canada. *Address:* 12326 91 Street, Edmonton, Alberta, T5B 4C6, Canada.

MOHLER, James Aylward, b. 22 July 1923, Toledo, Ohio, USA. Professor. *Education:* Litt B, Xavier University, Cincinnati, Ohio, 1946; PhL 1949, STL 1956, Jesuit School of Theology of Loyola University, Chicago; MSIR, Loyola University, Chicago, 1959; PhD, University of Ottawa, Canada, 1964; STD, University of St Paul, Canada, 1966. *Publications:* Speaking of God, (co-author), 1967; Man Needs God, 1967; The Beginning of Eternal Life, 1968; Dimensions of Faith, 1969; Origin and Evolution of the Priesthood, 1970; The Héresy of Monasticism, 1971; The School of Jesus, 1973; Cosmos, Man, God, Messiah, 1973; Dimensions of Love, 1975; Sexual Sublimation and the Sacred, 1978; The Sacrament of Suffering, 1979; Dimensions of Prayer, 1981; Love, Marriage and the Family, 1982. *Honours:* Post-doctoral research and fellowships including: Union Theological Seminary, New York, 1966; Ecumenical Institute of the World Council of Churches, Celigny, Switzerland, 1968; Institute Saint Serge, Paris, France, 1968. *Memberships:* Association for Asian Studies; American Academy of Religion; Catholic Theological Society; American Association of University Professors. *Address:* Rodman Hall, John Carroll University, Cleveland, OH 44118, USA.

MOHR, Steffen b. 24 July 1942, Leipzig, Democratic Republic of Germany. Writer. *Education:* Diplomas, Theatre-University Leipzig, Institut of Literature, Leipzig. *Publications:* At the Beginning of this Travel, 1975; Andy, Set the Fashion, 1975; A Day Full of Music, 1976; Interrogation without Order, 1979; Strange Causes of Captain Merks, 1980; Today I'll Kill 10 past 12, 1980; Flowers from the Heaven-meadow, 1982; (Films): 5 Animation Films, 1973; Women with and Without, TV film, 1985. *Membership:* Writers Union, Democratic Republic of Germany. *Address:* Liechtensteinstr 25, 7030 Leipzig, Democratic Republic of Germany.

MOINEAU, Guy, b. 17 May 1950, Montreal, Quebec, Canada. French Teacher in Montreal. *Education:* General Certificate of Education, advanced level in Literature, Quebec University. *Publications:* Poems: Falaises sur fables, 1976; Traverse de Figures, 1976; La Fuite et la Conversation, 1978; Aucune Intention de Bonheur, 1984; Chien, 1985; Nous Ne Serons Jamais Intacts, 1985. *Contributor to:* magazines including: Cul Q, Montreal; Hobo-Quebec, Montreal; Head Building, Montreal; La Nouvelle Barre du Jour, Montreal, 25 Mensuel, Belgium. *Memberships:* Union des Écrivains Québécois; Société Littéraire de Laval, Vice-President on Board of Directors. *Address:* 1767 Jacques-Lemaistre, Montreal, Quebec, Canada H2M 2C7.

MOL, Johannis J(acob) Hans, b. 14 Feb. 1922, Netherlands. University Professor. m. L Ruth McIntyre, 14 Feb. 1953, 2 sons, 2 daughters. *Education:* BD, Union Theological Seminary, New York, 1955; MA, 1956, PhD, Sociology, 1960, Columbia University. *Publications:* Race and Religion in New Zealand, 1966; The Breaking of Traditions, 1966; Christianity in Chains, 1969; Religion in Australia, 1971; Western Religion, Editor, 1972; Identity and the Sacred, 1976; Identity and Religion, Editor, 1976; Wholeness and Breakdown, 1978; The Fixed and the Fickle, 1982; The Firm and the Formless, 1982; Meaning and Place, 1983; Faith and Fragility, 1985; How God Hoodwinked Hitler, forthcoming; The Faith of Australian, 1984. *Contributor to:* Numerous professional journals. *Honours:* Kenneth Edwards Prize, 1951; McFadden Fellowship, 1955–56; Canada Council Leave Fellowship, 1977, 1983–84; Paine Lecturer, University of Missouri, Columbia, 1978; Best Feature Award, Canadian Church Press Association, 1983. *Memberships:* Convener, 1st Conference, Sociological Association of Australia & New Zealand,

1964, Secretary/Treasurer, 1963–69, Delegate, 1966–70; Chairman, Sociological Research in Religion, VIIth World Congress of Sociology, Varna, 1970; Director, Board of Directors, Religious Research Association, 1972–74; Editorial Advisory Board, Studies in Religion, 1984; Advisory Committee, Concilium, Revue Internationale de Theologie, 1984; etc. *Address:* Dept of Religious Studies, McMaster University, Hamilton, Ontario, Canada.

MOLDENHAUER, Hans, b. 13 Dec. 1906, Mainz, Germany. Musician and writer. *Education:* BA, Whitworth College, Spokane, USA, 1945; Doctor of Music, Boguslawski College of Music, Chicago, USA, 1945; Doctor of Fine Arts, Musicology, Roosevelt University, Chicago, USA, 1951. *Appointments include:* Founder-Director, Spokane Conservatory, 1942, President, 1946–present; Chairman, American Musicological Society, NW Chapter, 1958–60; Lecturer, University of Washington, 1961–64. *Publications:* Duo Pianism, 1950; Anton von Webern; Perspectives, 1966; Anton von Webern; Sketches (1926–1945), 1968; Der Tod Anton von Webern, 1970; Anton von Webern: A Chronicle of his Life and Work, 1978; Anton von Webern: Chrenik seines Lebens und Werkes, 1980; Catalogue of the Modeldenhauer Archives, (in preparation). *Contributions:* Numerous articles in German and English in various publications and journals including, The New York Times; Saturday Review; The musical Times; Neus Zeitschrift fur Musik; Osterreichisohe Musikzeitschrift. *Honours:* ASCAP Deems Taylor Award for biography, 1980; Officer's Cross of the Order of Merit of the Federal Republic of Germany, 1980; Goldernes Verdienstzeichen des Landes Wien, 1981. *Memberships:* Spokane Rotary Club; American Alpine Club. *Address:* 1001 Comstock Court, Spokane, WA 99203, USA.

MOLLENKOTT, Virginia Ramey, b. 28 Jan. 1932, Philadelphia, Pennsylvania, USA. College Professor, English Language & Literature. m. Friedrich H. Mollenkott, 17 June 1954, Philadelphia, (div. 1973), 1 son. *Education:* BA, Bob Jones University; MA, Temple University; PhD, New York University. *Literary Appointments:* Professor, Chair of English, Shelton College, 1955–63, Nyack College 1963–67; Professor of English, William Paterson College, 1967–, Department Chair 1972–76; Inclusive Language Lectionary Committee, National Council of Churches, 1982–; International Education Board, Studies in Mystical Literature, 1983–. *Publications include:* Adamant & Stone Chips: A Christian Humanist Approach to Knowledge, 1967; In Search of Balance, 1969; Adam Among the Television Trees, 1971; Women, Men & the Bible, 1976; Is the Homosexual my Neighbour?, 1978; Speech, Silence, Action: The Cycle of Faith, 1980; The Divine Feminine: Biblical Imagery of God as Female, 1983; Views from the Intersection, 1984; An Inclusive Language Lectionary Year A 1983, Year B, 1984, Year C, 1985. *Contributions to:* Books: Studies in Formative Spirituality, 1984; Journal of English & Germanic Philology, 1981. Journals including, Bucknell Review, etc. *Honours:* Penfield Fellowship, 1963; Andiron Award, 1964; Integrity Award, 1979; Virginia E Bailey Medallion for outstanding preaching, 1983. *Memberships:* Steering Committee, Milton Society of America; Regional delegate, executive committee, religion & literature section, Modern Language Association; Chief bibliographer, director, Conference on Christianity & Literature. *Address:* 11 Yearling Trail, Hewitt, NJ 07421, USA.

MÖLLER, Ingrid (Ulla Ursula), b. 12 Oct. 1934, Rostock, German Democratic Republic. Scientist of Art. m. Bruno Möller, 29 Mar. 1955, Grabow, 2 sons, 1 daughter. *Education:* Dipl phil; Dr phil, history of art. *Publications:* Der Bauer in der Kunst, 1973; Das Haus der Voldersgracht. Ein Vermeer-Roman, 1977, 3rd edition 1980; Vermeer van Delft Eletregenye, 1983; Meister Bertram. Ein Künstlerroman, 1981 and 1982; Introduction to The Playing Cards by I.M.F. 1617, 1979; The La Fontaine Taroc Cards, 1980; The Copperplate Pack of Cards by Virgil Solis, 1981. *Contributions to:*

Bildende Kunst; Lexikon der Kunst; Neue Museumskunde; Catalogues from the museums Schwerin and Berlin; Schweriner Blatter. *Membership:* Schriftstellerverband der DDR. *Address:* DDR 2711 Seehof, Schwerin Dorfstraße 14, Democratic Republic of Germany.

MOLLO, Victor, b. 17 Sep. 1909, St Petersburg, Russia. Journalist and Author. m. Jeanne Victoria Forbes, 21 Feb. 1952. *Education:* Brighton College; London School of Economics, London, England. *Publications:* Streamlined Bridge, 1947; Card Play Technique, (with N Gardener), 1955; Bridge For Beginners, (with N Gardener), 1956; Bridge Psychology, 1958; Will You Be My Partner?, 1959; Bridge: Modern Bidding, 1961; Success at Bridge, 1964; Bridge in the Menagerie, 1964; Confessions of an Addict, 1966; The Bridge Immortals, 1967; Victor Mollo's Winning Double, 1968; Bridge: Case for the Defence, 1970; Defence at Bridge, (with Aksel J Nielsen); Best of Bridge, (with Eric Jannersten), 1973; Bridge Unlimited, 1976; Bridge Course Complete, 1977; The Finer Arts of Bridge, 1979; Masters and Monsters, 1979; Streamline Your Bidding, 1979; Streamline Your Card Play, 1981; Bridge à le Carte, 1982; Winning Bridge, 1983; You Need Never Lose at Bridge, 1983; I Challenge You, 1984; The Other Side of Bridge, 1984; Tomorrow's Textbook, 1985; Pocket Guides: Winning Bidding, 1955; WinningDefence, 1964; Winning Convenience, 1970. *Contributions to:* Bridge International; American Contract League's Bulletin; Popular Bridge, USA. Bridgetidnigen, Sweden; Le Bridgeur, France; Bridge d'Italia; Bridge, Spain. *Memberships:* Society of Authors; International Bridge Press Association; St James's Bridge Club. *Address:* 801 Grenville House, Dolphin Square, London SW1, England.

MOLLOY, Martha Bankhead, b. 31 Dec. 1916. Art Teacher. *Education:* BS, Home Economics, Teachers Certificate in Art and Home Economics. *Contributions to:* Numerous anthologies, newspapers, magazines and journals, USA, France, UK, Italy, Belgium and Canada including: The Spring Anthology; Anthology of American Poetry; Modern American Muse; Fragments of Faith; Literary Gold; Blue Book of American Poetry; Bouquets of Poems; Wisconsin Poetry Magazine; American Poetry League Bulletin; American Bard; Midwest Chaparral; The Muse; Orphic Lute; Seydell Quality; Prairie Poet Anthology; From Sea to Sea in Song; English Grammar and Literature Appreciation; American Poets' Best. *Honours include:* US Congressional Citation for Literature, 1962; Religious Poetry Exhibition at Lambert Castle, International Poets Shrine, 1964; Medal of Honour for Literature, Centro Studi e Scambi International, 1966; Book dedication, Centro Studi e Scambi, 1973; Honorary Doctorate. *Memberships:* Executive Board Member, 2 terms, Alabama Writers Conclave; Executive, Centre Studi e Scambi International; Alabama Chairman, World Poetry Day; Regent, Chaparral South East; National League of American Pen Women; American Poetry League. *Address:* 505 Vernon Street, PO Box 304, Sulligent, AL 35586, USA.

MOLNAR, Miklos, b. 28 Oct. 1918, Budapest, Hungary. Professor. m. Eva Rudas, 26 Mar. 1949, Budapest, 2 sons. *Education:* MA, Budapest, Hungary, 1956; PhD, Geneva, Switzerland, 1963. *Publications:* A History of the Hungarian Revolution, 1960; Marx, Engels et la politique internationale, 1975; Short History of the Hungarian Communist Party, 1978; Fanaticism, A Historical and Psychoanalytical Study, co-author, 1983. *Address:* 42 rue de Vermont, CH-1202, Geneva, Switzerland.

MOLSON, Kenneth Meredith, b. 30 Oct. 1916, Montreal, Canada. m. Frances Lillian Cowie, 24 Aug. 1946, Toronto, Canada. *Education:* Diploma from Boeing School of Aeronautics, Oakaland, California, 1938. *Publications:* Pioneering in Canadian Air Transport, 1974; Canadian Aircraft since 1909, co-author, 1982; 125 Years of Canadian Aeronautics – A Chronology 1840–1965, co-author, 1983.

Contributions to: Canadian Aviation Historical Society's Journal; American Aviation Historical Society's Journal; Aircraft (Canada); Canadian Aeronautics and Space Journal; Canadian Aircraft Operator; Cross and Cockade; Cross and Cockade (Great Britain). *Honours:* Willis Nye Award, American Aviation Historical Society, 1972; Research Award, Canadian Aviation Historical Society, 1980; C Don Long Award, Canadian Aviation Historical Society, 1982. *Address:* 20 Ridgevalley Crescent, Islington, Ontario, Canada M9A 3J6.

MONCURE, Jane Belk, b. 16 Dec. 1926, Orlando, Florida, USA. Educator; Author; Consultant. *Education:* BS, Virginia Commonwealth University, 1952; MA, Columbia University, 1954. *Publications include:* Pinny's Day at Playschool, 1955; Bunny Finds a Home, 1962; Flip, the True Story of a Dairy Farm Goat, 1964; Try on a Shoe, 1973; (series of 5) Play With Me Alphabet Books, 1973; How Do You Fell?, 1974; Winter is Here, 1975; Spring is Here, Summer is Here, Fall is Here, 1975; Wait! Says His Father, 1975; Our Easter Book, 1976; Our Valentine Book, 1976; Just the Right Place, 1976; One Little World, 1976; Rhyme me a Rhyme, 1977; Riddle me a Riddle, 1977; Barbara's Pony Buttercup, 1977; Sound Box Books, (series of 20), 1976–79; My Baby Brother Needs a Friend, 1978; The Gift of Christmas, 1979; Wishes, Whispers & Secrets, 1979; Elfin Magic, 1980; Word Bird Books, (series of 24), 1982–86; Now I Am...Books, (series of 4), 1985; First Steps to Math (series of 10), 1984–86; The Five Senses, (series of 5), 1983–86. *Honours:* Award, Virginia Association for Early Childhood Education, 1979. *Address:* 1046 Briarcliff Road, Burlington, NC 27215, USA.

MONETTE, Madeleine, b. 3 Oct. 1951, Montreal, Canada. Writer. m. William R. Leggio, 27 Dec. 1979, Ridgefield, New Jersey, USA. *Education:* MA, Literature, University of Quebec, Montreal. *Publications:* Le Double Suspect, 1980; Petites Violences, 1982; Amandes et Melon, in preparation. *Contributions to:* Québec francais; Possibles; Arcade; Le Devoir; Canadian Broadcasting Corporation. (Short stories, self-portraits). Pending: New York, Sun; Ecrits du Canada Francais. *Honours:* Robert-Cliche Award, Quebec City International Book Fair, 1980; Grants, Canadian Council of Arts, 1981, 1984. *Membership:* Quebec Writers Union. *Literary Agent:* Deborah Karl, for Sanford Greenburger Associates. *Address:* 2 Charlton Street, 11K, New York, NY 10014, USA.

MONEY, David Charles, b. 5 Oct. 1918, Oxford, England. Author. m. Madge Dorothy Matthews, 30 Nov. 1945, 1 son. *Education:* Honours degree Chemistry, Honours degree Georgraphy, St John's College, Oxford, 1937–47. *Publications:* Human Geography, 1954; Australia and New Zealand, 1958; South America, 1961; Climate, Soils and Vegetation, 1965, last edition 1978: The Earth's Surface, 1970; Man the Homemaker, 1973; Patterns of Settlement, 1972; Man's Environment, 1975; Environmental Systems, 6 book series, 1980–82; China, The Land and the People, 1984. *Contributions to:* Film strips for Longmans and Woodmansterne. *Memberships:* Fellow, Royal Geographic Society; Geographical Association. *Address:* 52 Park Avenue, Bedford, MK40 2NE, England.

MONEY, Keith. *Publications:* Salute The Horse, 1960; Florian's Farmyard (with Pat Smythe), 1962; The Equestrian World, 1963; The Horseman in Our Midst, 1963; The Art of The Royal Ballet, 1964, 2nd Ed. Revised 1967; The Art of Margot Fonteyn, 1965, 1975; The Royal Ballet Today, 1968; Fonteyn: The Making of a Legend, 1973; John Curry, 1977; With Peter Beales: Georgina and Regency Roses, Early Victorian Roses, 1978, Late Victorian Roses, Edwardian Roses, 1979. Anna Pavlova, Her Life and Art, 1982; The Bedside Book of Old-fashioned Roses, 1985; Forthcoming: Paintings Out of Africa, limited edition, 1986; By Some Other Sea: The true story of Rupert Brooke, 1986/87; The Art of A J Cummings, 1987/88. *Contributions to:* Articles and illustrations in publications including: The British Racehorse; Horse and Hound; Stud and Stable;

Tatler; Dancing Times; The Field; IPC magazines in general. *Agent:* Anne Harrel Agency. *Address:* Carbrooke Hall Farm, Thetford, Norfolk, England.

MONK, Robert C, b. 7 July 1930, Holly Grove, USA. Professor of Religion. m. Carolyn Parker, 31 Aug. 1952, Amarillo, 2 daughters. *Education:* BA, Sociology, Texas Technological College, 1951; BD, Theology, Southern Methodist University, 1954; MA, 1960, PhD, 1963, Religion, Princeton University. *Appointments:* Methodist Campus Minister, Texas A & M, 1954–58; Associate Director, Texas Methodist Student Movement, 1961–64; Professor of Religion, McMurry College, 1964–. *Publications:* John Wesley, His Puritan Heritage, 1966; Exploring Religious Meaning, Co-author, 1973; Exploring Christianity, co-author, 1984; The Methodist Excitement in Texas, 1984. *Contributor to:* Unity and Diversity Among 18th Century Methodists and Anglicans, Historical Magazine of the Protestant Episcopal Church, 1969. *Honours:* Danforth Campus Ministry Grant, 1958–59; Lilly Foundation Grant, 1960–61; Bishop Baker Memorial Award, 1959–61; Outstanding Educators of America, 1970. *Address:* McMurry College, Abilene, TX 79697, USA.

MONSARRAT, Ann Whitelaw, b. 8 Apr. 1937, Walsall, Staffordshire, England. Writer. m. Nicholas Monsarrat (d. 1979), 22 Dec. 1961, Bromley Kent. *Literary Appointments:* Journalist, West Kent Mercury, 1954–58; Journalist, Daily Mail, London, 1958–61; Assistant Editor, Stationery Trade Review, 1961. *Publications:* And the Bride Wore....., The Story of the White Wedding, 1973; An Uneasy Victorian: Thackeray the Man, 1980. *Contributor to:* Since 1962 occasional contributor to Daily Mail; The Sun (London); The Times; Telegraph Magazine. *Literary Agent:* John McLaughlin, Campbell Thomson and McLaughlin Ltd, 31 Newington Green, London N16 9PU. *Address:* San Lawrenz, Gozo, Malta.

MONTAGU OF BEAULIEU, Edward John Barrington Douglas-Scott-Montagu, (Lord), b. 20 Oct. 1926, London, England. Museum Director. *Publications:* The Motoring Montagus, 1959; Lost Causes of Motoring, 1960; Jaguar: A Biography, 1961; The Gordon Bennett Races, 1963; Rolls of Rolls-Royce, 1966; The Gilt and The Gingerbread, 1967; Lost Causes of Motoring, volume 1 1969, volume 2 1971; More Equal Than Others, 1970; The Horseless Carriage, 1975; Early Days on the Road, 1976; Behind The Wheel, (with Wilson McCoomb), 1977; Royalty on the Road, 1980; Home, James, 1982. *Contributions to:* Books and Bookmen. *Memberships:* Chairman, Motor Museum Trust; Chairman, Historic Buildings and Monuments Commission; Guild of Motoring Writers; Past President, Historic Houses Association; Founder, Trustee, National Motor Museum, Beaulieu. *Literary Agent:* Curtis Brown, London. *Address:* Palace House, Beaulieu, Hampshire, England.

MONTARDIT, Teresa Grifoll, b. Tarragona, Spain. Writer on Drama, History and Philosophy. *Education:* Arts Degree; French Teacher. *Publications:* Poetry: Rimas con ruada mirada desde una ventana sin cristal, 1971. Drama 1973–80: Diogenes y Platon; Los Poetas, los otros y el paso de la noche; Vivir amar y llevar el luto; Promenteo; La Cibeles castiga a; hijo Triopas; Herakles; Clitemnestra; Loki; El suicidio de Neron; Andronico Conmeno; Julian conde de las Gomeras y el ultimo rey godo; Platon y la voz de Socrates; Saulo de Tarso a Roma; El rapto de Martin Lutera; Oliver Cromwell, Lord Protector; El proceso de Danton; Napoleon Buonaparte a la conquista del poder; Crimen inutil y morir a Venecia; Don Juan de Austria y Margarita de Valois. Novel: La imposible verdad. Other works: Muerte de Seneca, Ramon Llull; Rudolfo de Austria principe heredoro; Abdicacion de Nicolas II de Russia; Theatro Moderno: Todos le acusaban; Ana Mara sola en la cuidad; Eficacia del impacto; La Venganza de la nina; Historia de la Filosofic y Diccionario filosofica. Various works in preparation. *Address:* Calvet 51-53, Barcelona 21, Spain.

MONTGOMERIE, William, b. 1904, Glasgow, Scotland. Poet; Former Editor. *Education:* Universities of Glasgow and Edinburgh; MA; PhD. *Literary Appointments:* Editor, Lines Review, Edinburgh, 1977–82. *Publications:* Via; Squared Circle; New Judgements, Robert Burns; Scottish Nursery Rhymes, 1985; From Time to Time, Selected Poems, 1985; Well at the World's End. *Contributions to:* Review of English Studies; Hibbert Journal; Scottish Studies; Scottish Literary Journal; Folk-Lore; Journal of Folk Dance and Song Society; New British Poets; Radios 3 and 4, British Broadcasting Corporation. Editor: Burns Chronicle, 1950; Scots Chronicle, 1951. *Address:* 131 Warrender Park Road, Edinburgh EH9 1DS, Scotland.

MONTGOMERY, David John, b. 6 Nov. 1948, Bangor, Co Down, Northern Ireland. Editor, News of the World. m. 12 Apr. 1971, Helen's Bay. *Education:* BA, Queen's University, Belfast. *Address:* 30 Bouverie Street, London EC4, England.

MONTGOMERY, John, b. 14 Apr. 1916, Edinburgh, Scotland. Author. *Publications include:* Mr Sparrow; Foxy; Village Green; My Friend Foxy; Your Dog; Abodes of Love; Royal Dogs; Toll for the Brave; The Twenties; The Fifties; 1900: The End of an Era; The Christmas Cat; Foxy and the Badgers; Looking After Your Cat; Comedy Films; The World of Cats; Florence Nightingale; Arthur, The Television Cat; Caring For Cats and Kitens; Editor: Pan Book of Animal Stories; Editor: Pan Book of Cat Stories; West Sussex: Brighton in Old Picture Postcards. *Contributor to:* Guardian; Sunday Times; Observer; Evening Standard; Women's Own; Saturday Book. *Literary Agent:* A D Peters, London. *Address:* c/o A D Peters, 10 Buckingham Street, London WC2, England.

MONTGOMERY, Marion, b. 16 Apr. 1925, Tomaston, Georgia, USA. Teacher; Writer. *Education:* BA, MA, University of Georgia. *Publications include:* Novels: The Wandering of Desire, 1962; Darrell, 1964; Ye Olde Bluebird, novella, 1967; Fugitive, 1974. Poetry: Dry Lightning, 1960; Stones from the Rubble, 1965; The Gull and Other Georgia Scenes, 1969. Ezra Pound: A Critical Essay, 1970; T S Eliot: An Essay on the American Magus, 1970; The Reflective Journey Toward Order; Essays on Dante, Wordsworth, Eliot and others, 1973; Eliot's Reflective Journey to the Garden, criticism, 1979. Trilogy: The Prophetic Poet and the Spirit of the Age (Why Flannery O'Connor Stayed Home, 1981; Why Poe Drank Liquor, 1983; Why Hawthorne Was Melancholy, 1984). *Address:* Box 115, Crawford, GA 30630, USA.

MONTI, Laura Virginia, b. 12 June 1930, Argentina. Librarian (Rare Books). *Education:* Professor of Literature, Universidad Nacional de Buenos Aires; Librarian Diploma, Museo Libre Social Argentino; Archivist Diploma, American University and National Archives, USA; PhD, Literature, Catholic University of Buenos Aires. *Publications:* Sor Juana Ines de la Cruz, 1958; List of French Pamphlets in the University of Florida, 1971; Calendar of the Rochambeau Papers, 1972; Selected Letters of Marjorie Kinnan Rawlings (co-Editor), 1983. *Contributions to:* Revista Literarie Universidad de la Plata; Annals of the American Philosophical Society; The Journal of Caribbean Studies. *Membership:* National Association of Women Writers. *Address:* Boston Public Library, Copley Square, Boston, MA 02117, USA.

MOODIE, Graeme Cochrane, b. 27 Aug. 1924, Dundee, Scotland. Professor of Politics. *Education:* MA, University of St Andrews, 1943; Harkness Fellow, Princeton University, USA, 1949–51; MA, Oxford University, England, 1953. *Publications:* Some Problem of the Constitution (with Geoffrey Marshall), 1959, 5th edition, 1971; The Government of Great Britain, 1961, 3rd edition, 1971; Opinions, Publics and Pressure Groups, (with G Studdert Kennedy), 1970; Power and Authority in British Universities, (with Rowland Eustace), 1974; Editor, Standards and Criteria in Higher Education, 1986. *Contributor to:* Studies in Higher Education; Political Studies; Parliamentary Affairs;

Times Higher Educational Supplement. *Address:* Department of Politics, University of York, Heslington, York YO1 5DD, England.

MOODY, Henry Laurence, b. 1 Mar. 1907, Whitehead, County Antrim, Northern Ireland. Author. *Education:* Royal Belfast Academy. *Publications:* The Lantern Men, 1951; The Young Kings, 1960, 62; Some Must Die, 1964; No More to the Woods, 1967; Comet in a Red Sky, 1968; The Ruthless Ones, 1969, 72; Conquistador, 1969; The Small War, 1970; The Roxton Kibbutz, 1971; The Dark-Eyed Client, 1974; The Austrian Butterfly, 1975; The Golden Princess, 1976; The Greatest Tudor, 1977; What Became of Jack and Jill, film, 1972. *Contributions to:* Century of Historical Stories; Evening News; Belfast Telegraph. *Address:* 44 Bawnmore Road, Belfast, Northern Ireland.

MOODY, Peter Richard Junior, b. 13 Oct. 1943, San Francisco, California, USA. Teacher. m. Margaret Shahan, 18 June 1966, New Haven, Connecticut, 4 sons, 2 daughters. *Education:* BA, Vanderbilt University, 1965; MA, 1967, PhD, 1971, Yale University. *Publications:* The Politics of the Eighth Central Committee of the Communist Party of China, 1975; Opposition and Dissent in Contemporary China, 1977; Chinese Politics After Mac, 1983. *Contributions to:* China Quarterly; Asian Survey; World Politics; International Philosophical Quarterly; Survey; Pacific Affairs; Review of Politics' and others. *Address:* Department of Government and International Studies, University of Notre Dame, Notre Dame, IN 46556, USA.

MOODY, Ronald, b. 8 Jan. 1924, London, England. Actor, Writer. *Education:* B Sc Economics 1950, London School of Economics and Political Science, London University, 1948–53. *Publications:* Musicals – book, music and lyrics : Joey, Joey, 1966; Saturnalia, 1971; Move Along Sideways, 1976; The Showman, 1977; Novels: My LSE, 1978; The Devil You Don't, 1979; Very, Very Slightly Imperfect, 1983. *Honours:* Oscar nomination, 1968; Hollywood Golden Globe Award, 1969; Moscow Golden Bear, 1969; Variety Club of Great Britain, 1969; Tony Award nomination, 1984; Theatre World Award, 1984. *Literary Agent:* Eric Glass. *Address:* c/o Eric Glass, 28 Berkeley Square, London W1, England.

MOON, John Frederick, b. 13 Aug. 1929, Shipley, Yorkshire, England. Technical Journalist. m. Caroline Bowden Headley, 27 Apr. 1956, 2 sons, 1 daughter. *Publications:* Rudolf Diesel and the Diesel Engine, 1974. *Literary Appointments:* Technical Staff, Commercial Motor, 1954–64; Executive Editor, Diesel and Gas Turbine Worldwide, USA and High Speed Diesel Report, USA. *Contributions to:* Various enginering and transport magazines in United Kingdom, Europe and USA, 1964–75. *Address:* 19 Buckingham Street, London WC2N 6EW, England.

MOORCROFT, Marilyn, b. 23 July 1942, Cedar Rapids, Iowa, USA. Freelance Writer, Editor, Translator. *Education:* MA, German, New York University, 1984; BA, German, University of Iowa, 1966. *Publication:* Investigative Reporting, 1981. *Contributor of:* Floundering with Grass, to, Commonwealth Journal, 1977. *Honours:* Books for the Teenage, 1982, New York Public Library. *Membership:* Society of Children's Book Writers. *Address:* PO Box 425, Village Station, New York, NY 10014, USA.

MOORE, Brian, b. 25 Aug. 1921, Belfast, Northern Ireland. Novelist. *Publications:* Judith Hearne, 1955; The Feast of Lupercal, 1957; The Luck of Ginger Coffey, 1960; An Answer from Limbo, 1962; The Emperor of Ice Cream, 1965; I Am Mary Dunne, 1968; Fergus, 1970; Catholics, 1972; The Great Victorian Collection, 1975; The Doctor's Wife, 1976; The Mangan Inheritance, 1979; The Temptation of Eileen Hughes, 1982; Cold Heaven, 1983; Black Robe, 1985. *Honours:* Authors Club of Great Britain First Novel Award, 1956; Quebec Literary Prize, 1958; US National Institute of Arts and Letters Award, 1961; Fiction Award, Governor General of Canada, 1961; 1975; W H Smith Award, 1973; James Tait Black Memorial Award, 1975; Scottish Arts Council International Fellowship, 1982. *Literary Agent:* Percy Knowlton, Curtis Brown, 10 Astor Place, New York, NY 10003, USA. *Address:* 33958 Pacific Coast Highway, Malibu, CA 90265, USA.

MOORE, Brian Leslie Dean, b. 21 Apr. 1957, Ashburton, New Zealand. Magazine Editor. *Publications:* Editor, Australasian Stamp Catalogue, 22nd edition, 1985. *Contributions to:* Stamp News, magazine (editor, feature writer). *Membership:* International Philatelic Press Club, New York. *Address:* 35 Margaret Crescent, Dubbo, New South Wales 2830, Australia.

MOORE, David Moresby, b. 26 July 1933, Barnard Castle, Co Durham, England. University Professor of Botany. m. Ida Elizabeth Shaw, 26 July 1957, Carlisle, 2 sons. *Education:* BSc, Hons, Botany, 1954, PhD, 1957, DSc, 1984, University College and Botany Department, Durham University. *Publications:* The Vascular Flora of the Falkland Islands, 1968; Flora Europaea, Vols 1-5, co-editor with T G Tutin et al, 1964–80; Plant Cytogenics, 1976; Citogenetica Vegetal, 1979; Flora Europaea Check-List and Chromasome Number Index, 1982; Green Planet, editor, 1982; Flora of Tierra del Fuego, 1983; Current Concepts in Plant Taxonomy, co-editor with V H Heywood, 1984; Transecta Botanica de Patagonia Austral, co-editor (with O Boelcke and F A Roig) 1985. *Contributions to:* 80 scientific papers in scientific journals published in Britain, USA, Spain, Argentina, Chile, Portugal and Sweden. *Address:* Department of Botany, The University, Whiteknights, Reading RG6 2AS, England.

MOORE, E Garth, b. 6 Feb. 1906, London, England. Ecclesiastical Judge; Barrister; Priest; Fellow. *Education:* MA, Cantab, Trinity College Cambridge; Fellow of Corpus Christi College, Cambridge; of Gray's Inn, Barrister-at-Law. *Publications:* 8th Edition Kenny's Criminal Cases; Moore's Introduction to English Canon Law, 1966, (2nd Edition 1985); Believe it or Not: Christianity and Psychical Research, 1977; The Church's Ministry of Healing; (jointly), Ecclesiastical Law in Halsbury, (3rd Edition). *Contributions to:* Numerous legal and theological journals. *Address:* Corpus Christi College, Cambridge, England.

MOORE, John Michael, b. 12 Dec. 1935, Kent, England. Headmaster. *Publications:* The Manuscript Tradition of Polybius, 1965; Res Gestae Divi Augusti, with P A Brunt, 1967; Variorum, with J J Evans, 1969; Timecharts, 1969; Aristotle and Xenophon on Democracy and Oligarchy, 1974. *Address:* 9 College Green, Worcester WR1 2LH, England.

MOORE, Linda Perigo, b. 25 Nov. 1946, Evansville, Indiana, USA. Writer. m. 12 Aug. 1967, Evansville, Indiana, 1 son. *Education:* BS, Miami University, Oxford, Ohio; MEd, University of Louisville, Kentucky. *Publications:* Does This Mean My Kid's a Genius, 1981; You're Smarter Than You Think, 1985; Collaborator with Bart Conner for Bart Conner's Winning the Gold, 1985; Collaborator with Richard Simmons for Reach for Fitness, 1986. *Literary Agent:* Amy Berkower, Writers House, 21 W.26 New York, 10010, USA. *Address:* PO Box 489, Boonville, IN 47601, USA.

MOORE, Nicholas, b. 16 Nov. 1918, Cambridge, England. Writer. m. (1) Priscilla Craig, 1940, (2) Shirley Putnam, 25 July 1953, 1 son, 2 daughters. *Education:* BA, Cambridge University, 1940. *Publications:* A Wish in Season, 1941; The Island and the Cattle, 1941; The Cabaret, the Dancer, the Gentleman, 1942; The Glass Tower, Poems 1936–43, 1944; 35 Anonymous Odes, 1944 (published anonymously); The War of the Little Jersey Cows, 1945; Recollections of the Gala, Selected Poems 1943–48, 1950; Resolution and Identity, 1970; Spleen, 1973. *Honours:* Patrons Prize from, Contemporary Poetry, 1945; Harriet Monroe Memorial Prize, 1947. *Address:* 89 Oakdene Road, St Mary Cray, Kent, England.

MOORE, Rayburn Sabatzky, b. 26 May 1920, Helena, Arkansas, USA. University Professor. m. Margaret Elizabeth Bear, 30 Aug. 1947, 1 son, 1 daughter. *Education:* AA, Hendrix College, 1940; BA, 1942, MA, 1947, Vanderbilt University; PhD, 1956, Duke University. *Literary Appointments:* Research and Graduate Assistant, Duke University, 1952–54; Assistant Professor, Hendrix College, 1954–59; Associate Professor of English, 1959–65, Director of Graduate Studies in English, 1964–69, Professor of English, 1965–, Chairman, American Studies Program, 1968–, Chairman, Division of Language and Literature, Arts and Sciences, 1975–, University of Georgia. *Publications:* Constance Fenimore Woolson, 1963; For the Major and Selected Short Fiction of Constance Fenimore Woolson, 1967; Paul Hamilton Hayne, 1972; A Man of Letters in the Ante-Bellum South: The Selected Letters of Paul Hamilton Hayne, 1982; Senior Editor: The History of Southern Literature, 1985. *Contributor to:* Over 100 articles, notes and reviews in scholarly and professional journals. *Honours:* Phi Beta Kappa; Blue Key. *Memberships:* Modern Language Association of America (Executive Committee, General Topics VI, 1972–74); South Atlantic Modern Language Association (Executive Committee 1974–77); Society for the Study of Southern Literature (Executive Council 1968, 1974–80, Vice President 1980–82, President 1982–84); South Atlantic Graduate English Co-operative Group 1969–78 (Chairman 1972–73; Virginia Historical Society; Poe Society; Henry James Society; Philological Society of the Carolinas. *Address:* Department of English, University of Georgia, Athens, GA 30602, USA.

MOORE, Ruth Nulton, b. 19 June 1923, Easton, Pennsylvania, USA. Writer. m. Carl Leland Moore, 15 June 1946, Easton, 2 sons. *Education:* BA, Bucknell University; MA, Columbia University. *Publications:* Frisky The Playful Pony, 1966; Hiding The Bell, 1968; Peace Treaty, 1977; Ghost Bird Mystery, 1977; Mystery of the Lost Treasure, 1978; Tomas and the Talking Birds, 1979; Wilderness Journey, 1979; Mystery at Indian Rocks, 1981; The Sorrel Horse, 1982; Danger in the Pines, 1983; In Search of Liberty, 1983; Mystery of the Missing Stallions, 1984; Mystery of the Secret Code, 1985. *Contributions to:* Jack and Jill: Children's Activities. *Honours:* C S Lewis Honor Book Medal, 1983; Religion in Media. Silver Angel Award, 1984. *Membership:* Children's Authors and Illustrators of Philadelphia. *Literary Agent:* McIntosh and Otis. *Address:* 3033 Center Street, Bethlehem, PA 18017, USA.

MOORE, Wilfred George, b. 8 May 1907, Burton-on-Trent, England. Author. m. Gwenfra Marian Williams, 10 Aug. 1934, Burton-on-Trent, 1 son. *Education:* BSc, London University. *Publications:* Penguin Dictionary of Geography, 1949; Penguin Encyclopedia of Places, 1971, 78; The World's Wealth, 1947; New Visual Geography, 17 books, 1959–72; Fundamental Geography of the British Isles, 1981. *Address:* 34 Copsewood Way, Northwood, Middlesex HA6 2UA, England.

MOORE-RINVOLUCRI, Mina Josephine, b. 1 Sep. 1902, Liverpool, England. Retired University Lecturer. m. Dr Giuseppe Rinvolucri, 29 July 1938, Cardiff, 2 sons. *Education:* BA Honours, 1923, MA, 1925, French, Liverpool University; Doctorate, Strasbourg, 1934. *Publications:* Bernard Shaw et la France, 1933; Charme de Province, 1940; Oral Work in Modern Languages, 1955; Education in East Germany, 1974. *Contributor to:* Dublin Review; Irish Ecclesiastical Review; Times Educational Supplement; Modern Languages; etc. *Honours:* Médaille de Vermeil, Académie Française, 1937; Palmes Accadémiques, 1947. *Address:* 45 Lon Tywysog, Myddleton Park, Denbigh, Clwyd LL16 4AE, Wales.

MOOREHEAD, Caroline Mary, b. 28 Oct. 1944, London, England. Journalist; Writer. m. Jeremy Swift, 27 May 1967, Tarquinia, Italy, 1 son, 1 daughter. *Education:* BA, Honours, Psychology & Philosophy. *Publications:* Fortune's Hostages: A Study of Kidnapping in the World Today, 1980; Editor, Letters of

Freya Stark, 1983; Sidney Bernstein: A Biography, 1984; Freya Stark: A Biography, 1985. *Contributions to:* New Society; Spectator; Tatler; London Review of Books; in Britain; Departures. *Honour:* Valiant for Truth, media award, 1984. *Literary Agent:* Anthony Sheil. *Address:* 36 Fitzroy Road, London NW1, England.

MOORHOUSE, Frank, b. 21 Dec. 1938, Nowra, Australia. Writer. *Education:* External Student, University of Queensland. *Literary Appointments include:* 1979–82, President, Australian Society of Authors; 1985, Chairman, Copywright Council of Australia. *Publications:* Futility and Other Animals, 1969; The Americans, Baby, 1972; The Electrical Experience, 1974; Conference-Ville, 1976; Tales of Mystery & Romance, 1977; Everlasting Secret Family and Other Secrets, 1980; Days of Wine and Rage, 1980. *Contributions to:* Bulletin; National Times, Australia, Tabkid Story. *Honours:* Henry Lawson Short Story Prize, 1970; National Award for Fiction, 1975 (The Electrical Experience); Winner, ANGIE Award, Best Script (Conference-Ville). *Memberships:* Australian Journalists' Association, 1966–70; Vice President, Australian Society of Authors, 1978–80; President, Australian Society of Authors, 1979–82; Member of the Order of Australia, 1985; Chairman, Copywright Council of Australia, 1985. *Literary Agent:* Rosemary Creswell. *Address:* c/o Rosemary Cresswell, P O Box 161 Glebe, NSW 2037, Australia.

MOORHOUSE, Geoffrey, b. 29 Nov. 1931, Bolton, Lancashire, England. Author. m. Marilyn Isobel Edwards. 1 sons, 1 daughter, previous marriage. *Publications:* The Other England, 1963; Against All Reason, 1969; Calcutta, 1971; The Missionaries, 1973; The Fearful Void, 1974; The Diplomats, 1977; The Boat & the Town, 1979; The Best Loved Game, 1979; Lord's 1983; India Britannica, 1983; To the Frontier, 1984. *Contributions to:* The Guardian; The Times; Observer; London Magazine; Books & Bookmen; etc. *Honours:* Fellow, Royal Geographical Society, 1972; Fellow, Royal Society of Literature, 1982; Cricket Society Literary Award, 1979; Thomas Cook Literary Award, 1984. *Literary Agent:* A P Watt Ltd, 26-28 Bedford Row, London WC1R 4HL. *Address:* Park House, Gayle, Near Hawes, North Yorkshire DL8 3RT, England.

MOORMAN, (Rt Rev), John Richard Humpidge, b. 4 June 1905, Leeds, England. Clergyman. m. Mary Caroline Trevelyan, 29 Sep. 1930, Cambridge. *Education:* BA, 1927, MA, 1931, BD, 1941, Dr Divinity, 1945, Emmanuel College, Cambridge. *Publications:* Sources for the Life of Saint Francis, 1940; A History of the Church in England, 1953; Vatican Observed, 1966; A History of the Franciscan Order, 1968; Church Life in 13th Century, 1945; The Grey Friars in Cambridge, 1952; Medieval Franciscan Houses, 1983; Anglican Spiritual Tradition, 1983; Publisher, Cambridge University Press. *Contributor to:* Various publications. *Honours:* LittD, University of Leeds, 1964; LittD, Saint Bonaventure, USA, 1966. *Memberships:* Fellow, Society of Antiquaries. *Address:* 22 Springwell Road, Durham DH1 4LR, England.

MOOSDORF, Johanna Elsa Charlotte, b. 12 July 1911, Leipzig, Germany. Writer. m. Paul Bernstein, 11 Nov. 1932, Berlin, died, Auschwitz 1945, 1 son, 1 daughter. *Education:* Senior Girls' School; Gottschedschule, Leipzig. *Appointments:* Serial Editor, Leipzig, 1946–47; Editor in Chief, März, Leipzig, 1947–48; Freelance Writer, 1950–. *Publications:* Das Bildnis, 1947; Flucht nach Afrika, 1952; Nebendn, 1961; Die Andermanns, 1969; Die Freundinnen, 1977; Poetry published in Berlin, Munich, St Michael. *Contributor to:* Reviews, Short Stories, poems in, Leipziger Volkszeitung; Die Zeit; Die Welt; Neue Deutsche Hefte. *Honours:* Thomas Mann Award of Advancement, 1950; Zuckmayer Prize, 1952; Cultural Prize, Dortmund, 1963; Honorary Scholarship, Villa Massimo, Rome, 1963. *Membership:* Federal Republic of Germany PEN Centre. *Address:* Kastolnieu allee 27, 1000 Berlin 19, Federal Republic of Germany.

MOOTE, A Lloyd, b. 22 Mar 1931, Hamilton, Ontario, Canada. University Professor. m. Barbara Brown, 27 Dec 1956, Toronto, Canada, div, 2 sons, 2 daughters. *Education:* BA, University of Toronto, 1954; MA, 1956, PhD, 1958, University of Minnesota. *Literary Appointments:* Lecturer, University of Toronto, 1958–61; Assistant Professor, University of Cincinnati, 1961–62; Assistant Professor, 1962–65, Associate Professor, 1965–71, Professor, 1971–, University of Southern California. *Publication:* The Seventeenth Century: Europe in Ferment 1970; The Revolt of the Judges: the Parliament of Paris and the Fronde 1642–1652, 1971. *Contributions to:* The Parliamentary Fronde and Seventeenth Century Robe Solidarity, French Historical Studies, 1962; Law and Justice under Louis XIV in J C Rule ed. Louis XIV and the Craft of Kingship, 1969; Seventeenth Century Peasant Faries (co-author) Past and Present 1971, The Preconditions of Revolution in Early Modern Europe Canadian Journal of History, 1972; The Annales Historians' Queen's Quarterly, 1978; 33 signed articles, Academic American Encyclopedia, 1980; Louis XIII, Richelieu and Two-Headed Monarchy Proceedings of Western Society for French History, 1983. *Honours:* American Philosophical Society Grant 1962; National Endowment for the Humanities Award 1969–70; University of Southern California Creative Scholar Award, 1972; Guggenheim Fellow, 1976–77. *Membership:* President, Society for French Historical Studies, 1985. *Address:* Department of History, University of Southern California, Los Angeles, CA 90089–0034, USA.

MORACE, Robert Anthony, b. 22 Sep. 1947, Rockville Centre, New York, USA. Educator. m. Barbara G Horan, 28 June 1970, Pocantico Hills, New York, 1 son. *Education:* BA, MS English Education, State University of New York, Cortland; PhD, University of South Carolina. *Literary Appointments:* Teaching Associate, University of South Carolina, 1976–77; Assistant Professor 1977–81, Associate Professor of English 1981–, Daemen College; Fulbright Lecturer, University of Warsaw, 1985–86. *Publications:* John Gardner: Criticial Perspectives (with Kathryn Van Spanckeren), 1982; John Gardner: An Annotated Secondary Bibliography, 1984. *Contributions to:* Essays in numerous scholarly journals and literary reviews including: Modern Fiction Studies; Critique; Fiction International; Studies in the Novel; The Literary Review; Journal of Modern Literature; Journal of American Culture. *Honour:* Distinguished Faculty Achievement Award, Daemen College, 1979. *Memberships:* Modern Language Association; Northeast Modern Language Association; American Culture Association. *Address:* 56 Highgate, Buffalo, NY 14214, USA.

MORALES, Goldie Pearl Laden, b. 29 Aug. 1909, USA. Educator. *Education:* BA, University of California, Los Angeles, USA, 1957; MA, California State University, 1960; MA, University of Southern California, 1962. *Appointments include:* Instructor, English, East Los Angeles College, 1964–67; Assistant Professor, English, 1967–69, Philosophy, 1969–72, Professor of Philosophy, 1972–75, Professor Emeritus, 1975– East Los Angeles College. *Publications:* Dreams of Youth, 1927; Eternal Etching, 1977; Star Journey, 1978; Moving Image, 1978. *Contributions to:* American Poet; Bardic Echoes; Bitterroot; Arizona Quarterly; Western Poetry Quarterly; California State Poetry Quarterly; Creative Review, and others. *Honours include:* Best of Issue Award, Tiotis, 1979. *Memberships:* Founder, Fellow, International Academy of Poets; World Poetry Society; Life Member, New York Poetry Forum; President, East Los Angeles chapter, California State Poetry Society; American Poetry League. *Address:* 1340 College View Drive, Apt 3, Monterey Park, CA 91754, USA.

MORAN, Thomas Francis, b. 5 Dec. 1943, Philadelphia, Pennsylvania, USA. Writer. m. Marilyn Groch, 24 June 1978, Los Angeles, California, USA, 1 daughter. *Education:* BSME, California State Polytechnic University, 1965; MSME, California State University at Long Beach, 1968. *Major Publications:* The Photo Essay, 1974; Fantasy By The Sea, 1979; Roller Skating is for Me, 1981; BMX is for Me, 1982; Frisbee Flying is for Me, 1982; River Thrill Sports, 1983; Canoeing is for Me, 1984; Kite Flying is for Me, 1984; BMX, 1985. *Contributor to:* Los Angeles; L A; California Living; Quinto Lingo; Chic; Big Table; Magazine. *Address:* 218 Rowland Canal, Venice, CA 90291, USA.

MORATINOS IGLESIAS, José-F, b. 10 Mar. 1944, Tetuán, Morocco. University Tutor in Educational Sciences. *Education:* Arts degree; Graduate in Tourism. *Publications:* Nuevo Concepto de Escuela, 1977; La Disciplina en la Comunidad Escular, Co-author, 1979; La Co-Gestión en la Empresa Educativa, 1981; La Tecnologia en la Escuela, 1983; La Dirección de la Empresa Educativa, 1984; La Escuela de Padres, 1985. *Contributions to:* La Escuela en Acción; Vida Escolar; Revista Española de Pedagogia; Bordón; Revista de Ciencias de la Education; Información; La Verdad, and others. *Honours:* National Essay Prize, 1974; San José de Calasanz Essay prize, 1976, Luis Vives Education Prize, 1980; Ceyr Investigation Prize, 1985. *Memberships:* Asociación Colegial de Escritores de España; Spanish Society of Comparative Education; Twentieth Century Spanish Association of America. *Address:* c/avda Aguilera 48-2-D, Alicante 03006, Spain.

MORDI, Sigrid, b. 24 May 1942, Merseburg, Federal Republic of Germany. Pre-school teaching/councelling. m. Obi Mordi, 24 Aug. 1965, Heidelberg, 2 sons, 3 daughters. *Education:* Kindergarten teacher; Montessori Diploma. *Publications:* Roland mag nicht, stories, 1974; Dreckigsein ist Schön, stories, 1975; Mini und Maxi, stories, 1977; Spiele in der Vorschulzeit, 1978 and 1980; Ike in the Evil Bush, 1978; The White Snake and other stories, 1981. *Contributions to:* Spielen und Lernen; Zeitschrift fur Eltern und Kinder. *Membership:* Verwertungsgesellschaft. *Address:* Riverside Nursery School, PO Box 9043, Enugu, Nigeria.

MOREAU, David Merlin, 9 Oct. 1927, Cairo, Egypt. Company Chairman; Broadcaster. m Elizabeth M. Rees (dec. 1980), High Wycombe, 22 Dec. 1956, 1 son, 1 daughter. *Education:* BA, Modern Languages, 1950, Law Tripos 1951, Jesus College, Cambridge; 1st Class Pass, Spanish 5th Year, London Polytechnic. *Literary Appointments:* Motoring & Flying correspondent. The Director, 1970. *Publications:* The Simple Life, 1962; That Built-in-Urge, 1963; Summer's End, 1966; Look Behind You, 1973. *Contributions to:* Guardian; Bedside Guardian; Sunday Times; Financial Times; New Scientist; Listener; Penthouse; Director; Pharmaceutical Journal; Manufacturing Chemist; Ideal Home; Vogue; Australian Financial Review, etc. Own series, BBC Radio, 1984, 1985. *Membership:* Society of Authors. *Address:* Rowley Cottage, Langley Park, Buckinghamshire SL3 6DT.

MOREY, Robert Albert, b. 13 Nov. 1946, Orlando, Florida, USA. Clergyman; Author; Lecturer. m. Anne V Smadbeck, 3 June 1972, New York City, USA, 1 son, 1 daughter. *Education:* BA Philosophy; M Div. Theology; D Min. Apologetics. *Publications:* The Bible and Drug Abuse, 1972; The Dooyeweendian Concept of the Word of God, 1974; An Examination of Exclusive Psalmody, 1974; A Christian Handbook for Defending the Faith, in English 1979, in Chinese 1985; How To Answer A Jehovah's Witness, 1980, in Spanish; Is Sunday The Christian Sabbath, 1980; The Saving Work of Christ, 1980; Reincarnation and Christianity, 1981; Horoscopes and the Christian, in English 1981, in German 1985; How to Answer a Mormon, 1982; Outlines For Living, 1985; Death and the Afterlife; Worship is All of Life, 1984; When Is It Right To Fight, 1985; Modern Atheism and Unbelief, 1986. *Contributions to:* Christianity Today; Eternity; Baptist Reformation Review; Commentary; Personal Freedom Outreach; Perry County Times. *Honours:* Significant Book of the Year, Christianity Today, 1974; Book of the Year nomination, Cornerpost, 1984; 2 times listed in The Best of the Good Books, 1985. *Address:* RDI Box 637, Shermans Dale, PA 17090, USA.

MORGAN, Fidelis, b. 8 Aug. 1952, Salisbury Plain, England. Actress. *Education:* BA Honours Drama and Theatre Arts, Birmingham University. *Publications:* Plays/Adaptations: Scandal a series for television, (with Lynda La Plante); Pamela (Richardson) for Shared Experience, (with Giles Havergal); Madonna and Child; Wedlock/Deadlock from Bickerstaff's Burying by Centlivres; Books: The Female Wits, 1981; Autobiography of Mrs Manley forthcoming; History of the English Actress, in preparation. *Contributions to:* Observer. *Literary Agent:* Patricia Robertson, Hughes Massie. *Address:* c/o Hughes Massie, 31 Southampton Row, London WC1, England.

MORGAN, Helen Louise, b. 11 Apr. 1921, Ilford, Essex, England. Author. m. Tudor Meredydd Morgan, 15 May 1954, Maidstone, Kent, 3 daughters. *Major publications:* The Little Old Lady, 1961; Tales of Tigg's Farm, 1963; Meet Mary Kate, 1963; A Dream of Dragons, 1965; Satchkin Patchkin, 1966; Mary Kate & The Jumble Bear, 1967; Mrs Pinny & The Blowing Day, 1968; Mrs Pinny & The Sudden Snow, 1969; Mary Kate & The School Bus, 1970; Mother Farthing's Luck, 1971; Mrs Pinny & The Salty Sea Day, 1972; Two in the House, 1965; Two by The Sea, Two on The Farm, 1967; Two in The Garden, 1968; The Tailor and The Sailor and The Small Black Cat, 1954; A Mouthful of Magic, 1964; The Sketchbook of Crime, 1980. *Contributor to:* Various Literary journals and magazines. *Membership:* Society of Authors. *Literary Agent:* Juvenilia Literary Agency, Winchester. *Address:* c/o Faber & Faber, 3 Queen Square, London WC1N 3AU, England.

MORGAN, John Smith, b. 20 Mar. 1921, Cleveland, Ohio, USA. Author. m. 15 Feb. 1947, Cleveland, 3 daughters. *Education:* BA, Yale University. *Publications:* Getting Across to Employees, 1964; Improving Your Creativity on the Job, 1968; Managing Change, 1972; Noah Webster – A Biography, 1975; Robert Fulton – A Biography, 1977; You Can't Manage Alone, 1985.*Membership:* The Authors Guild. *Address:* 302 Fox Chapel Road, Apt 516, Pittsburgh, PA 15238, USA.

MORGAN, Robert, b. 17 Apr. 1922, South Wales. Artist; Poet. m. Jean E F Loveday, 19 Dec. 1953, Portsmouth, 2 daughters. *Education:* Teaching Diploma, Bognor College of Education, 1952; Advanced Diploma, Special Education, University of Education, 1970. *Publications include:* The Night's Prison, 50 poems & verse play, 1967; Poems & Extracts, 1968; The Storm, poems, 1974; On the Banks of the Cynon, poems, 1975; Voices in the Dark, verse play; My Lamp Still Burns, autobiography, 1981; The Light in the Dark, short stories, 1985. 2 verse plays broadcast, BBC, 1967, 1974. *Contributions:* Many poems, short stories in magazines & journals, UK & USA, including: Anglo Welsh Review; Blackfriars Magazine; Hibbert's Journal; London Welsham; Poetry Review; Poetry Wales; Review of English Literature; Dublin Review; Tablet; Transatlantic Review; Tribune; Poetry India; New Statesman; Fine Madness; Panache; Hubbub; etc. *Membership:* Welsh Academi. *Address:* 72 Anmore Road, Denmead, Hampshire PO7 6NT, England.

MORGAN, Roberta E, b. 1 May 1953, New York, USA. m. Dr Brian Leslie Gordon Morgan, 8 Apr. 1973, New York. *Education:* BA, New York University, 1973. *Literary Appointments:* Instructor, Writing and Publishing, the New School, 1979. *Publications:* Main Event, 1979; Disco, 1980; How to Break into Publishing, 1980; The Guinness Book of College Records, 1982; Nutrition and the Brain, 1985. *Contributions to:* American Health Magazine; Self Magazine; Family Circle Magazine; Seventeen; Come Alice. *Honours:* Kappa Tau Alpha, Honoury Journalism Society, 1973; Lena Kastle Award for scholarship in Literature, New York University, 1973; Phi Beta Kappa, 1973. *Membership:* Kappa Tau Alpha. *Literary Agent:* Bleekerstreet Associates Inc. *Address:* 16 West 16th Street, #10RS, New York, NY 10011, USA.

MORGAN, William, b. 13 June 1944, Princeton, New Jersey, USA. Architectural Historian. m. Carolyn Johnson Morrill, 28 Dec. 1978, Louisville, 2 sons. *Education:* AB, Dartmouth College, 1966; MA, Certificate in Architecture, Columbia University; PhD, University of Delaware, 1971. *Appointments:* Architecture Critic, The Courier-Journal, Louisville, 1975–80; Book Review Editor, Landscape Architecture, 1976–78. *Publications:* Bucks County: Photographs of Early Architecture, with Aaron Siskind, 1974; Louisville: Architecture and the Urban Environment, 1979; Portals: Photographs by William Morgan, 1981; The Almighty Wall: The Architecture of Henry Vaughan, 1983. *Contributor to:* Historical New Hampshire; Progressive Architecture; Places; New York Times; etc. *Honour:* Nominee, Pulitzer Prize in Criticism, 1980. *Membership:* Society of Architectural Historians. *Address:* Hite Art Institute, University of Louisville, Louisville, KY 40292, USA.

MORGAN-WITTS, Max, b. 27 Sep. 1931, Detroit, USA. Author; Producer, TV & Film Documentaries. m. Pauline Lawson, 4 Jan. 1958, Westminster, London, England, 1 son, 1 daughter. *Education:* Academy of Radio & TV Arts, Honours, University of Toronto. *Publications:* The Day the World Ended, 1969; The San Francisco Earthquake; Shipwreck – The Strange Fate of the Morro Castle; Voyage of the Damned; The Day Guernica Died; Ruin From the Air; The Day the Bubble Burst; Trauma – the Search for the Cause of Legionnaires' Disease; Pontiff; The Year of Armageddon, 1984. *Contributor to:* Reader's Digest; The Listener. *Honours:* Edgar Allan Poe Award; Mark Twain Award, 1978. *Memberships:* Royal Society of Literature; Authors Guild. *Literary Agent:* Jonathan Clowes. *Address:* c/o Jonathan Clowes, 22 Prince Albert Road, London NW1 7ST, England.

MORLEY, Don, b. 28 Jan. 1937, Derbyshire, England. Photographer/Journalist. m. Josephine Mary Munro, 17 Sep. 1961, Mickleover, Derbyshire, 2 sons. *Education:* National Certificates Electrical Engineering and Photography. *Literary Appointments:* Former Picture Editor, The Guardian; Former Chief Photographer, Sports World magazine, British Olympic Association; Chief Photographer, MotoCourse. *Publications:* Action Photography, 1975; Motorcycling, 1977; Everyone's Book of Photography, 1981; Everyone's Book of Motorcycling, 1981; The Story of the Motorcycle, 1983; Motorbikes, 1983; Classic British Trials Bikes, 1984; Classic British Moto Cross Machines, 1985. *Contributions to:* Magazines and journals worldwide. *Honours:* 17 times national and international photography award winner. *Memberships:* Founder 5 years Chairman, currently committee member, Professional Sports Photographers Association. *Address:* 132 Carlton Road, Reigate, Surrey RH2 OJF, England.

MORLEY, Hilda Auerbach, b. 19 Sep. 1921, New York, USA. Writer. m. Stefan Wolpe, 18 Sep. 1952, New York City. *Education:* BA, Hons, English, University College, London; MA, English, Wellesley College, Wallesley, Massachusetts, USA. *Publications:* A Blessing Outside Us, 1976; What Are Winds and What Are Waters; To Hold in My Hand: Selected Poems, 1955–83. *Contributions to:* The Nation; The Window (London); Black Mountain Review; Mail; New Letters; Endymion Ironwood; Hudson Review; New Directions Annual; Trellis; American Poetry Review; Chicago Review; Partisan Review Conjunctions, etc. *Honours:* Guggenheim Fellowship 1983–84; Capricorn Award for best poetry of poet over 40. *Memberships:* Poets and Writers USA; Poetry Society of America; PEN, American Branch. *Address:* 463 West Street, New York, NY 10014, USA.

MORLEY, Patricia Marlow, b. 25 May 1929, Toronto, Canada. Writer and Teacher. m. Laurence Whitaker Morley, 17 June 1950, Toronto, Canada, 3 sons, 1 daughter. *Education:* BA (Hon.) University of Toronto, Canada, 1951; MA, Carleton University, 1967; PhD, University of Ottawa, 1970. *Appointments:* Lecturer, University of Ottawa, Canada, 1971–72; Assistant Professor, Sir George Williams University, 1972–75; Associate Professor, Concordia University, 1975–79;

Professor, 1980–present. *Publications include:* The Mystery of Unity: Theme and Technique in the Novels of Patrick White, 1972; The Immoral Moralists, 1972; Robertson Davies, 1976; The Comedians, 1977; Morley Callaghan, 1978; Margaret Laurence, 1981; Kurelek; A Biography, 1986. *Contributions:* Numerous book reviews and articles in newspapers, magazines and academic journals including, James Joyce Quarterly; Canadian Literature; Canadian Forum; Saturday Night; University of Toronto Quarterly. *Honours:* Social Sciences and Humanities Research Council research grants for William Kurelek biography, 1981–83 and 1985–86. *Memberships:* Association of Canadian University Teachers of English; The Writers Union of Canada; Association of Canadian and Quebec Literatures; Commonwealth Language and Literature Studies. *Address:* Box 137, Manotick, Ontario K0A 2N0, Canada.

MORLEY, Sheridan Robert, b. 5 Dec. 1941, Ascot, Berkshire, England. Drama Critic and Arts Editor, Punch; London Drama Critic, International Herald Tribune. m. Margaret Gudejko, 1965, 1 son, 2 daughters. *Education:* MA Honours, Merton College, Oxford, 1964. *Literary Appointments:* Newscaster, reporter and scriptwriter, ITN, 1964–67; Interviewer, Late Night Line Up, BBC2, 1967–71; Presenter, Film Night, BBC2, 1972; Deputy Features Editor, The Times, 1973–75; Presenter, Kaleidoscope, BBC Radio 4; Presenter, Meridian, BBC World Service; Frequent radio and television broadcasts on the performing arts; Narrator, Side by Side by Sondheim, Guildford and Norwich, 1981–82; Member of Drama Panel, British Council, 1982–; Devised and narrated, Noel and Gertie, Coward anthology, King's Head, London 1983. *Publications:* A Talent To Amuse: The Life of Noel Coward, 1969; Review Copies, 1975; Oscar Wilde, 1976; Sybil Thorndike, 1977; Marlene Dietrich, 1977; Gladys Cooper, 1979; Noel Coward and His Friends, (with Cole Lesley and Graham Payn), 1979; The Stephen Sondheim Songbook, 1979; Editor of a series of theatre annuals and film and theatre studies including: Punch at the Theatre, 1980; Gertrude Lawrence, 1981; The Noel Coward Diaries, (edited with Graham Payn), 1982; Tales From the Hollywod Raj, 1983; Shooting Stars, 1983; The Theatregoer's Quizbook, 1983; Katherine Hepburn, 1984; The Other Side of the Moon, biography of David Niven, 1985. *Contributions to:* The Times; Evening Standard; Radio Times; Mail on Sunday; Playbill, New York; High Life; The Australian. *Literary Agent:* Curtis Brown, 162 Regent Street, London W1. *Address:* c/o Punch, 23 Tudor Street, London EC4, England.

MORRESSY, John, b. 8 Dec. 1930, USA. Writer, Educator. m. Barbara Ann Turner, 11 Aug. 1956, St Vincent Ferrer. *Education:* MA, New York University, 1961. *Literary Appointments:* Writer-in-Residence, Worcester Consortium for Higher Education, Worcester, Massachusetts, 1977; Visiting Lecturer in Creative Writing and Lloyd C Elliott Professor of English. University of Maine, Orono, 1977–78; Writer-in-Residence and Professor of English, Franklin Pierce College, Rindge, New Hampshire, 1978–. *Publications:* The Blackboard Cavalier, 1966; The Addison Tradition, 1968; Starbrat, 1972; Nail Down The Stars, 1973; A Long Communion, 1974; Under a Calculating Star, 1975; Frostworld and Dreamfire, 1977; Ironbrand, 1980; Graymantle, 1981; Kingsbane, 1982; The Mansions of Space, 1983; Other Stories, 1984; The Time of the Annihilator, 1985. *Contributions to:* TheMagazine of Fantasy and Science Fiction; New Orleans Review; Omni; Playboy; Isaac Asimov's Science Fiction Magazine; Twilight Zone; Harpers; National Review. *Honours:* Balrog Award for best short fantasy fiction, 1984; Pandora Award for Science Fiction, 1984. *Memberships:* Author's Guild; Science Fiction Writers of America. *Literary Agent:* Perry Knowlton, Curtis Brown Limited. *Address:* c/o Perry Knowlton, Curtis Brown Limited, 10 Astor Place, New York, NY 10003, USA.

MORRILL, George Percival, b. 14 May 1920, Montclair, New Jersey, USA. Author: Editor. *Education:*

BA, MA, Wesleyan University, Middletown, Connecticut, USA. *Publications:* Dark Sea Running, 1960; The Multi-millionaire Straphanger. The Biography of John Emory Andrus, 1971; Snow, Stars and Wild Honey, 1975. *Contributions to:* Saturday Evening Post; Cosmopolitan; McCall's; Colliers Argosy; Vermont Life; Readers Digest and others. *Memberships:* Socratic Literature Society. *Honour:* Colliers Star Story, 1949. *Literary Agent:* Brandt and Brandt. *Address:* Thayer Road, Higganum, CT 06441, USA.

MORRIS, Benjamin Stephen, b. 25 May 1910, Sherborne, Dorset, England. University Teacher. m. Adeline Margaret Lamont, 2 July 1938, East Newport, Fife, Scotland, 2 sons, 1 daughter. *Education:* BSc Honours Organic Chemistry 1933, MEd Honours Education and Psychology 1937, University of Glasgow. *Publications:* Objectives and Perspectives in Education, 1972; Some Aspects of Professional Freedom of Teachers, an international pilot enquiry, 1977. *Contributions to:* Chapters in books including: The Study of Education Edited by Tibble, 1966; Towards Community Mental Health Edited by Sutherland, 1971; The Sciences, the Humanities and the Technological Threat Edited by Niblett, 1975. *Address:* 7 Howcroft, Churchdown, Gloucester GL3 2EP, England.

MORRIS, Brian Robert, b. 4 Dec. 1930. Principal of St David's University College, Lampeter, Wales. m. Sandra Mary James, 1955, 1 son, 1 daughter. *Education:* MA, DPhil; Worcester College, Oxford. *Literary Appointments:* Fellow of Shakespeare Institute, University of Birmingham, 1956–58; Assistant Lecturer, 1958–60, Lecturer, 1960–65, University of Reading; Lecturer, 1965–67, Senior Lecturer, 1967–71, University of York; Professor of English Literature, University of Sheffield, 1971–80; General Editor, New Mermaid Dramatists, 1964–; British Library Board, 1980–; Trustee, National Portrait Gallery, 1977–; Welsh Arts Council, 1983, Member, Literary Committee, 1976–; Yr Academi Gymreig, 1979–; National Heritage Memorial Fund, 1980–; Broadcaster, scriptwriter and presenter of telelvision programmes. *Publications:* John Cleveland: A Bibliography of his Poems, 1967; The Poems of John Cleveland (with Eleanor Withington), 1967; Editor, New Mermaid Critical Commentaries I-II, 1969–72; Mary Quant's London, 1963;Editor, Ritual Murder, 1980; Edited Plays: Ford's The Broken Heart, 1965; Tis Pity She's a Whore, 1968; (With Roma Gill) Tourneaur's, The Atheist's Tragedy, 1976; Shakespeare's The Taming of the Shrew, 1981; Poetry: Tide Race, 1976; Stones in the Brook, 1978. *Contributions to:* Journals. *Address:* Bryn, North Road, Lampeter, Dyfed SA48 7HZ, Wales.

MORRIS, Christopher Hugh, b. 28 March, 1938, Luton, England. Journalist. m. Georgina Reda, 31 March, 1962, Pirton, England, 1 daughter. *Education:* Diploma, National Council Training of Journalists. *Appointments:* Reporter, Daily Sketch, London, England, 1958–62; Freelance Correspondent, Spain, 1962–72; Reporter, BBC Radio News, London, 1972–74; Special Correspondent, BBC TV News, 1974–present. *Publication:* The Day They Lost the H-Bomb, 1967. *Contributions:* Numerous articles in worldwide publications. *Honours:* Silver Award, New York International TV Festival, 1983; Golden Nymph, Monte Carlo, 1984. *Address:* Oakdell, Firs Drive, Gustard Wood, Wheathampstead, Hertfordshire, England.

MORRIS, Colin, b. Liverpool, England. Writer; Producer; Director; Actor; Interviewer, BBC Television and ITV. *Publications:* Stage play productions: Desert Rats, 1945; Italian Love Story, 1945; Reluctant Heroes, 1950; Television plays: The Unloved, 1954; Who Me, 1959; Jacks and Knaves, 1960; Women in Crisis, 1963; The Newcomers, 1965; King of the River, 1967; Walk With Destiny, 1974; Television serials: Reluctant Bandit, 1966; The Dragon's Opponent, 1973; Television series: The Carnforth Practice, 1974; Heart to Heart; Turning Point; My Way; Women of Today; My Life; My Marriage; My Family, 1986; Numerous dramatized documentaries, 1954–74. *Contributions to:* Evening

Standard; Sunday Mirror. *Honours:* Atlantic Award in Literature, 1946; 4 Best Scripts Awards, 1955, 1956, 1958 and 1961. *Address:* 75 Hillway, London N6, England.

MORRIS, Desmond, b. 24 Jan. 1928, Purton, Wiltshire, England. Author; Zoologist; Painter; Formerly, TV Presenter, Zoo Curator & Director, Institute of Contemporary Arts, London. *Education:* BSc, Birmingham University; DPhil, Oxford University. *Publications include:* Curious Creatures, 1961; The Biology of Art, 1962; The Mammals, A Guide to the Living Species, 1965; Primate Ethology, Editor, 1967; The Naked Ape, 1967; The Human Zoo, 1969; Patterns of Reproductive Behaviour, 1970; Intimate Behaviour, 1971; Manwatching, a Fieldl-Guide to Human Behaviour, 1977; Gestures, their Origins & Distribution, with P Collett, P Marsh & M O'Shaughnessy, 1979; (Autobiography) Animal Days, 1979; The Giant Panda, 1981; The Soccer Tribe, 1981; Inrock (fiction), 1983; The Book of Ages, 1983; The Art of Ancient Cyprus, 1985; Bodywatching, A Field-Guide to the Human Species, 1985; The Illustrated Naked Ape, 1986; Men & Snakes, 1965, Men & Apes, 1966, & Men & Pandas, 1966, (these with Ramona Morris); several children's books. *Contributor to:* Scientific journals. *Address:* c/o Jonathan Cape, 32 Bedford Square, London WC1B 3EL, England.

MORRIS, Jan, b. 2 Oct. 1926. Author. *Education:* MA Oxon. *Publications:* Venice, 1960; Spain, 1964; Oxford, 1965; The Pax Britannica Trilogy, 1965–70; Conundrum, 1974; The Matter of Wales, 1984; Among the Cities, 1985; Last Letters from Hav, 1985. *Honour:* Heinemann Award, 1961. *Membership:* Fellow, Royal Society of Literature. *Literary Agent:* A P Watts. *Address:* Trefan Morys, Llanystumdwy, Gwynedd, Cymru, Wales.

MORRIS, Joan Ursula, b. 14 Apr. 1901, Hove, Sussex, England. Church Art Historian, Church Historian, Film Producer. *Education:* MA Liturgical Research, University of Notre Dame, Indiana, USA. *Literary Appointments:* Editor, Art Notes, 1937–47; Editor of review Catholic Citizen, St Joan's International Alliance; Director, Vrai Publishers, London. *Publications:* Novecento Sacro, 1937 (translation: Modern Sacred Art, 1938); The Decorative Arts of the Christian Church, co-author, 1972; The Lady Was a Bishop, 1973 (UK version: Against Nature and God, 1974); Storia Nascosta di Donne, in Italy; Pope John VIII; An English Woman; Alias Pope Joan. *Contributions to:* The New Catholic Encyclopedia; The Times; The Catholic Herald; The Catholic Citizen; Women Speaking; The Month; Blackfriars. *Honours:* Award, Women Today, Chicago, USA; Cambridge Dictionary of Bibliography. *Memberships include:* Ecclesiastical Historical Society. *Address:* 27 Red Lion Street, London WC1R 4PS, England.

MORRIS, Leon Lamb, b. 15 Mar. 1914, Lithgow, New South Wales, Australia. m. Mildred Dann, 4 Jan. 1941, Campsie, New South Wales. *Education:* BSc, University of Sydney, 1934; Th L, Australian College of Theology, 1937; HBD, 1943, M Th, 1946, University of London; PhD, University of Cambridge, 1952; MSc, University of Melbourne, 1966. *Publications:* The Apostolic Preaching of the Cross 1955; The Lord from Heaven 1958; The Cross in the New Testament 1965; Studies in the Fourth Gospel 1969; The Gospel According to John 1971; Apocalyptic 1972; Testaments of Love 1981; The Atonement 1983. *Contributor to:* Many magazines and journals. *Honours:* Hey Sharp Prize, 1937; ThD, honoris causa, Australian College of Theology, 1980. *Address:* 17 Queen's Avenue, Doncaster, Victoria 3108, Australia.

MORRIS, Stephen, b. 14 Aug. 1935, Smethwick, Staffordshire, England. Senior Lecturer. m. Michèle Madeliene, 31 Aug. 1963, Exeter, Devon, 1 son, 2 daughters. *Education:* Universities of Cardiff and Leicester; Fircroft College, Marieborgs Folkhighschool, Sweden. *Publicatons:* Poetry: The Revolutionary, 1972; The Kingfisher Catcher, 1974; Death of a Clown, 1976;

The Moment of Truth, 1978; Too Long at the Circus, 1980; Widening Circles, anthology of 5 poets, 1977, Lord of Death, play, 1963 and The Umbreallas of Mr Parpluie, childrens stories, 1985. *Contributions to:* Sunday Times; The Observer; International Times; Tribune; The Medalist; The Western Mail; Daily Mirror; Peace News. *Honours:* Toured India and Far East, British Council; toured USA, Holland, Belgium, Sweden, Denmark and Malaysia, presenting work at universities, colleges and literary societies; 25 exhibitions of visual poetry and paintings, 1969–85. *Literary Agent:* J Moon, Ludlow, Shropshire. *Address:* c/o J Moon, 23 Bell Lane, Ludlow, Shropshire, England.

MORRIS, Thomas Baden, b. 30 Apr. 1900, Godstone, Surrey, England. Novelist; Playwright. *Publications include:* (Novels) Blind Bargain, 1957; So Many Dangers, 1960; Murder on the Loire, 1964; Wild Justice, 1965; Orchids With Murder, 1966; Shadows on Abu Simbel, 1967; Undying Serpent, 1970; The Muddy Leaf Mystery, 1971; The Horns of Truth, 1972; Third Time Unlucky, 1973; (3 Act Plays), The Beautiful One, 1938; Murder Without Men, 1944; The Song of the Morning, 1949; Frost on the Rose, 1951; The Nine Days, 1953; Island of Sirens, 1957; Deserted Night, 1961; The Crooked Tree, 1963; (Plays for BBC) Nefertiti's Daughter; Too Dear for My Possessing; Bitter Beauty. *Address:* 6 Sion Hill Place, Lansdown, Bath, BA1 5SJ, England.

MORRIS, Thomas Dean, b. 1 Nov. 1938, Eugene, Oregon, USA. Professor of History. m. Sally Scholz, Nov. 1977, Portland, Oregon, 2 sons, 1 daughter. *Education:* BA, MA, PhD, University of Washington. *Publications:* Free Men All: The Personal Liberty Laws of the North, 1780–1861, 1974; A chapter in David Bodenhamer and James W Ely, Jr, editors, Ambivalent Legacy: A Legal History of the South, 1984. *Contributions to:* Law and Society Review, 1981–82; South Carolina Historical Magazine, 1982. *Address:* History Department, Portland State University, Portland, Oregon 97207, USA.

MORRIS, William Edward, b. 11 Sep. 1913, Granity, New Zealand. Journalist. m. Ruve Frances Cross, 24 Aug. 1946, Tauranga, 1 daughter. *Education:* Westport Technical College; Victoria University, Wellington; Diploma of Merit, Accademia Leonardo da Vinci, Rome, 1981; Diploma D'Onore 1982; Diploma of Recognition 1983; Diploma D'Onore, Palme D'Oro Accademiche 1984; Masters of Contemporary Poetry, Prince of Poets 1985; Certificate of Merit IWWP 1971; DSC World Poetry Society 1978. *Literary Appointments include:* Oceanian Editor, Poet, World Poetry Society 1972; Poet Laureate of New Zealand (United Poets Laureate International); Diploma Poet Laureate, World Academy of Arts and Culture 1981; Cultural Doctorate in Literature, World University Roundtable, Arizona USA; Executive Vice-President UPLI 1979; Annual Associate American Biographical Institute 1984. *Publications:* Silent Touches of Time, 1971; Alchemy of Time, 1973; Children of Zero, 1974; Journey into Yesterday (History), 1976; Crucible, 1981. *Contributions to:* Columnist for Bay of Plenty for the new National Art Journal New Zealand Art News. *Honours:* Distinguished Service Citation, World Poetry Society, 1978; Diploma of Merit Universati Delle Arti, Italy, 1982; Founder Fellow International Academy of Poets, 1977; Founder Fellow International Poetry Society 1973. *Memberships:* Patron, International Poetry Organisation, India; Board Member, The Centre for Studies and Research in Indian Writing in English, India. *Address:* 50 Harvey Street, Tauranga, Bay of Plenty, New Zealand.

MORRISH, (Ernest) Ivor (James), b. 8 Feb. 1914, London, England. Lecturer; Author; Editor. *Education:* BD, BA, Acad Dip Ed, London University; BA, Bristol University; FRSA. *Publications include:* The Background of Immigrant Children, 1971; The Sociology of Education, 4th edition 1975; Brazilian Translation, 1973; Aspects of Emotional Change, 1976; Obeah, Christ & Rastaman, 1982; The Dark Twin: A Study of Evil and Good, 1980. *Contributor to:* The British Journal of Sociology; Academic Editor, Unwin Educational Books, Geo. Allen & Unwin Ltd, 1969–. *Memberships include:* FRSA; The Oxford Society. *Address:* Starboard, 15A Victoria Road South, Bognor Regis, West Sussex PO21 2NA, England.

MORRISH, (Ernest) Ivor (James), b. 8 Feb. 1914, London, England. Lecturer; Author; Editor. *Education:* BD, BA, Academic diploma in education, London University; BA, Bristol University; Post graduate, St Catherine's College, Oxford University. *Literary Appointments:* Academic Editor, Unwin Education Books, George Allen and Unwin Limited, 1969–79. *Publications:* Disciplines of Education, 1967; Education Since 1800, 1970; The Background of Immigrant Children, 1971; The Sociology of Education, 1972; Aspects of Educational Change, 1976; The Dark Twin, 1980; Obeah, Christ and Rastaman, 1982. *Honours:* Fellow, Royal Society of Arts. *Memberships:* Fellow, Royal Society of Arts; Oxford Society. *Address:* Starboard, 15a Victoria Road South, Bognor Regis, West Sussex PO21 2NA, England.

MORRISON, Anthony James, b. 5 July 1936, Gosport, Hampshire, England. Writer;TV Film Maker. m. Elizabeth Marion Davies, 1965, 1 daughter. *Education:* BSc, Zoology; Certificate of Education–Post Graduate Diploma. *Publications:* Steps to a Fortune, with Mark Howell, 1964; Animal Migration, 1973; Land Above the Clouds, 1974; Pathways to the Gods, 1976; The Andes–Time Life, 1976; Editor and writer: Lizzie, with Ann Brown and Ann Rose, 1984. Contributor of chapters to edited volumes. *Contributor to:* Sunday Telegraph Magazine; Observer and many others especially Natural History magazines or those on fringe science and archaeology. *Memberships:* Fellow, Royal Geographical Society; Explorer's Club, New York. *Literary Agent:* Anita Diamant, New York. *Address:* 48 Station Road, Woodbridge, Suffolk IP12 4AT, England.

MORRISON, James Frederic, b. 4 Oct. 1937, Grinnell, Iowa, USA. University Professor. m. Eveline d'Angremond Morrison, 2 sons, 2 daughters. *Education:* AB, Stanford University, 1958, MA, 1963, PhD, 1969; Warsaw University, 1960–61, 1964–65. *Literary Appointments:* Associate Professor, University of Florida since 1966; Visiting Professor, Adam Mickiewicz University, Poznan, Poland, 1974–75, 1981–82. *Major publications:* Integration & Community Building, 1968; The Polish People's Republic, 1968; Politics & the International System, (with K R Legg), 1971. *Honours:* Phi Beta Kappa, 1958; Pi Sigma Alpha, 1958; Wilson Fellowship, 1965–68. *Address:* Department of Political Science, University of Florida, Gainesville, FL 32611, USA.

MORRISON, Kristin, b. 22 Apr. 1934, Los Angeles, California, USA. Professor. m. Robin Popplestone, 29 Sep. 1985, Edinburgh. *Education:* BA, IHC, 1957; MA, St. Louis University, 1960; PhD, Harvard University, 1966. *Publications:* A Handbook of Contemporary Drama, co-author with Michael Anderson, Jacques Guicharnaud, Jack Zipes, 1971, New York, 1972 London; In Black and White, 1972; Canters and Chronicles; The Use of Narrative in the Plays of Samuel Beckett and Harold Pinter, 1983. *Contributions to:* Texas Studies in Literature and Language; Nineteenth Century Fiction; Quarterly Journal of Speech; Western Humanities Review; American Imago; Comparative Drama; Modern Drama; and others. *Address:* Department of English, Boston College, Chestnut Hill, MA 02167, USA.

MORRISON, (Philip) Blake, b. 8 Oct. 1950, Burnley, Lancashire, England. Poet, Literary Critic. m. Katherine Drake, 15 July 1976, Brentwood, Essex, 1 son, 1 daughter. *Education:* BA, Nottingham University, 1972; MA, McMaster University, 1973; PhD, University College, London, 1978. *Literary Appointments:* Poetry and Fiction Editor, Times Literary Supplement, 1978–81; Deputy Literary Editor, Observer, 1981–. *Publications:* The Movement: English Poetry and Fiction of the 1950's, 1982; The Penguin Book of Contemporary British Poetry, (co-editor), 1982; Seamus Heaney, 1982; Dark Glasses, 1984. *Contributions to:* Grants; London Review of Books; Times Literary Supplement; Encounter; New Stateman; Poetry Review; London Magazine; PM Review; Delta; Outposts; and others. *Honours:* Eric Gregory Award, 1980; Somerset Maughan Award, 1985; Dylan Thomas Award, 1985; UK-Europe nomination, Commonwealth Poetry Prize, Best First Book, 1985. *Memberships:* General Council and Executive, Poetry Society, 1980–84; Chairman, Poetry Book Society, 1984–. *Literary Agent:* A D Peters. *Address:* 4 Macartney House, Chesterfield Walk, London SE10, England.

MORRISON, Robert Hay, b. 11 May 1915, Melbourne, Victoria, Australia. Author. m. Anna Dorothea Booth, 20 Sep. 1939, Adelaide, Australia, 1 son, 1 daughter. *Major publications:* Poetry: Lyrics from Pushkin, 1951; Lyric Images, 1954; A Book of South Australian Verse, 1957; Opus 4, 1971; Australia's Russian Poets, 1971; Some Poems of Verlaine, 1972; Australia's Ukrainian Poets, 1973; 1976; In the Ear of Dusk, 1977; The Secret Greenness and Other Poems, 1978; One Hundred Russian Poems, 1979; Ancient Chinese Odes, 1979; Sonnets from the Spanish, 1980; For the Weeks of the Year, 1981; The Cypress Chest, 1982; Poems for an Exhibition, 1985; (Prose:) Valentina Georgievnaa Szobovits: A Memoir, 1984. *Contributor to:* Numerous magazines and Anthologies in Australia, India, USA, UK. *Address:* 6 Bradfield Street, Burnside, SA 5066, Australia.

MORRISON, Robert Haywood, m. 27 Mar. 1927, Hickory, North Carolina, USA. Writer; President, Investors Corporation of South Carolina. *Education:* AB, University of North Carolina, Chapel Hill; MA, ibid. *Literary Appointments:* Managing Editor, The Davidsonian; Davidson, North Carolina; Editor, The Daily Tar Heel, Chapel Hill, North Carolina; Editor and Publisher, The Daily New-Enterprise, Newton, North Caroline; Professor of Journalism, Winthrop College, Hock Hill, South Carolina. *Publications:* A Guide to Bank Correspondence, 1949; Problems and Cases in Business Writing, 1951; Better Letters, 1952; Bank Correspondence Handbook, 1964. *Contributor to:* Many publications; some hundreds of articles. *Honour:* Paul Harris Fellow, 1982. *Memberships:* Phi Beta Kappa; Philanthropic Literary Society, President (University of North Carolina); Speaker, Dialectic Literary Society, University of North Carolina, Chapel Hill. *Address:* Suite 6, 1373 East Morehead Street, Charlotte, NC 28207, USA.

MORRISS, Frank, b. 28 Mar. 1923, Pasadena, California, USA. Writer; Teacher. m. Mary Rita Moynihan, 11 Feb. 1950, Denver, Colorado, 1 son, 3 daughters. *Education:* BS (magna cum laude) 1943, Regis, Denver; JD, 1948, Georgetown University; Litt D, 1953; Register College of Journalism. *Literary Appointments:* News Editor, National Catholic Register, 1963–67; Founding Editor, Twin Circle, 1967; Contributing Editor, The Wanderer, 1969; Editor, Forum, Newsletter, Wanderer Forum Foundation Affiliate program, 1984. *Publications:* Boy of Philadelphia, 1955; Adventures of Broken Hand, 1957; Alfred of Wessex, 1959; Submarine Pioneer, 1961; Saints for the Small, 1964; Forgotten Revelation, 1964; The Conservative Imperative, 1969; The Divine Epic, 1973; Abortion, (co-author), 1979; The Catholic as Citizen, 1979; A Christmas Celebration, (editor and contributor), 1983. *Contributor to:* Wanderer, weekly column since 1968. *Honour:* George Washington Freedom Medal, Freedom Foundation, for newspaper writing, 1951, 1953. *Address:* 3505 Owens Street, Wheat Ridge, CO 80033, USA.

MORRISSEY, Michael James Terence, b. 22 Mar. 1942, Auckland, New Zealand. Writer. *Appointments:* Writer-in-Residence, University of Canterbury, 1979; Artist in Residence, Northcote College, Auckland, 1985; Participant, International Writing Programme, Iowa University, USA, 1985. *Publications:* Poetry: Make Love in all the Rooms, 1978; Closer to the Bone, 1981;

She's not the Child of Sylvia Plath; Dreams, 1981; Taking in the View, 1986; Short Stories: The Fat Lady & the Astronomer, 1981; Jane's Balloons and Other Stories, (publication pending); Mona Lisa Meets the Phantom, 1986; Editor: The New Fiction, 1985; The Globe Tapes, 1985. Contributor to: Landfall; Islands; Climate; New Zealand Listener; Metro; Jetway; etc; Anthologies include, All the Dangerous Animals are in Zoos; New Zealand Writing since 1945; New Zealand Short Stories; Listener Short Stories; etc. Honours: Writer's Bursary, 1977–78; Macmillan Brown Prize, 1978; Tom Gallon Award, 1978; Te Awamutu Rose Festival of Arts Prize, 1979; Best First Book of Prose, PEN, New Zealand, 1982; Fulbright Cultural Travel Award, 1981; Auckland Star Short Story Prize, 1985. Memberships: PEN, New Zealand; Writers Guild. Address: Box 39-288 Auckland West, Auckland, New Zealand.

MORROW, Bradford, b. 8 Apr. 1951, Baltimore, Maryland, USA. Writer; Editor. Education: BA, University of Colorado; MA, Yale University. Publications: A Bibliography of the Writings of Wyndham Lewis, 1978; A Bibliography of the Black Sparrow Press, 1981; Posthumes, 1982; Blast, editor, 1982; The Selected Poems of Kenneth Rexroth, editor, 1984; Conjunctions: Bi-Annual Volumes of New Writing, editor issues 1-7 of continuing serial, 1981–85. Contributions to: Paideuma; Ark; Ploughshares; Sulfur; Correspondences; Tamarisk; Sagetrieb; Conjunctions; Bomb; 2 Plus 2; New Directions Anthology; Temblor; Tyuonyi. Honours: Amigos de las Americas Foundation Award for study in Honduras, 1967; American Field Service Scholarship, Italy, 1968–69; Danforth Fellowship, 1973; CCLM Editor's Award, 1984. Membership: Phi Beta Kappa. Literary Agent: Roslyn Targ Literary Agency. Address: 33 West 9th Street, New York, NY 10011, USA.

MORROW, Felix, b. 3 June 1906, New York City, USA. Publisher, Psychoanalytic Books. m. Gloria Pugliese, 5 Mar. 1950, New York City, 1 son, 2 daughters. Education: BA, New York University. Literary Appointments include: Former: Executive Vice President, British Book Center Inc; Editor, Fourth International, magazine; Editor, Psychological Studies, Dialogue House Library, New York; Current: Publisher, Felix Morrow, Publishing and Healing Tao Books. Publications: Author, Revolution & Counterrevolution in Spain, 1938, enlarged edition 1974; General Editor, University Books series, Comparative Religion, 1954–68. Contributions to: Journal of Humanistic Psychology, 1984–85. Address: 13 Welwyn Road, Great Neck, NY 11021, USA.

MORROW, John Howard, b. 27 May 1944, Trenton, New Jersey, USA. Professor, History. m. Diane Batts, 14 June 1969, Philadelphia, 1 son, 1 daughter. Education: BA, Honours, History, Swarthmore College, 1966; PhD, History, University of Pennsylvania, 1971. Appointments: Assistant Professor, 1971–77, Associate Professor, 1977–83, Professor, 1983–, Head, 1983–, History Dept, University of Tennessee. Publications: Building German Airpower, 1909–1914, 1976; German Airpower in World War I, 1982. Contributor to: Aerospace Historian; Journal of Economic History. Honours: Phi Kappa Phi; Lindsay Young Professorship, University of Tennessee, 1982–83; University of Tennessee National Alumni Association Outstanding Teacher, 1983. Address: 103 Greenbriar Dr, Knoxville, TN 37919, USA.

MORTIMER, John Clifford, b. 23 Apr. 1923, London, England. Writer. m (1) Penelope Fletcher, (2) Penelope Collop, 1 son, 3 daughters. Education: BA, Oxon. Publications include: Novels: Charade, 1947; Rumming Park, 1948; Answer Yes or No, 1950; Like Men Betrayed, 1953; The Narrowing Stream, 1957; Plays include: The Wrong Side of the Park, 1960; The States for Comfort, 1962; Come As You Are, 1969; Voyage Round My Father, 1970; Collaborations, 1972; Books: Rumpole of the Bailey, 1978; The Trials of Rumpole, 1979; Rumpole's Return, 1980; Rumpole For The Defence, 1981; Rumpole and the Golden Thread,

1983; Clinging to the Wreckage, autobiography, 1982; Paradise Proposed, 1985. Translations: The Boulevarde Farces; Captain of Konernic. Contributions to: Numerous publications. Honours: Italia prize, 1957; Screen Writers Guild Award, 1969; British Academy Writers Award, 1979; Honorary D Litt, Susquehanna University, Pennsylvania, USA. Memberships: Chairman, Union of Dramatists; National Theatre Board UK; Fellow, Royal Society of Literature. Literary Agent: A D Peters. Address: c/o A D Peters, 10 Buckingham Street, Strand, London WC2, England.

MORTIMER, Penelope Ruth, b. 19 Sep. 1918, Rhyl, North Wales. Writer. m. (1) Charles Dimont, 6 Nov. 1939, Salisbury, (2) John Clifford Mortimer, 27 Aug. 1949, London. 1 son, 5 daughters. Education: University College, London. Literary Appointments: Visiting Professor, Boston University, USA, 1975–77. Publications: Johanna, 1947; A Villa in Summer, 1954; The Bright Prison, 1956; Daddy's Gone A-Hunting, 1958; Saturday Lunch With The Brownings, 1960; The Pumpkin Eater, 1962; My Friend Says It's Bulletproof, 1967; The Home, 1971; Long Distance, 1974; About Time, autobiography, 1979; The Handyman, 1983. Contributions to: Publications including: New Yorker; Film Critic, Observer, 1967–70; Observer. Honours: Whitbread Prize for, About Time, 1979. Membership: FRSL. Literary Agent: Curtis Brown, 163-168 Regent Street, London W1H, 5TA, England. Address: The Old Post Office, Chastleton, Moreton in Marsh, GL56 OAS, England.

MORTIMER, Peter John Grenville, b. 17 Dec. 1943, Nottingham, England. Writer. 1 son. Education: BA, Economics, Sheffield University, 1968. Literary Appointments: Editor, IRON Literary Magazine, 1973–; Writer-in-Residence, North Tyneside, 1980; Theatre Critic, Northern Echo, 1975–. Publications: Waiting for History, 1979; Utter Nonsense, 1980; The Shape of Bricks, 1981; The Oooosquidal, 1982. Contributions to: The Newcastle Journal, Weekly Columnist, 1977–81; Northern Life Magazine, Monthly Columnist, 1978–83. Membership: Northern Playwrights Society. Literary Agent: Cecily Ware, London. Address: 5 Marden Terrace, Cullercoats, North Shields, Tyne & Wear NE30 4PD, England.

MORTON, Arthur Leslie, b. 4 July 1903, Hengrave, England. Writer. Education: BA, Peterhouse, Cambridge University, 1924. Publications: A People's History of England, 1938; The English Utopia, 1952; The Life & Ideas of Robert Owen, 1962; The Matter of Britain, 1966; The World of the Ranters, 1970; Freedom in Arms, 1976; Collected Poems, 1976. Contributor to: Criterion; Twentieth Century; Listener; Modern Quarterly; Science & Society; Marxism Today. Honours: Recipient, PhD, Rostock University, 1975. Membership: Writers Guild of Great Britain. Agent: Lawrence & Wishart. Address: The Old Chapel, Clare, Suffolk, England.

MORTON, Brenda Neish, b. Stirling, Scotland. Author. Major Publications: Make Your Own Soft Toys, 1957; Hobbies for the Housebound, 1961; Brownie Handwork, 1964; Needlework Puppets, 1964; Mascot Toys, 1969; Floppy Toys, 1971; Toys Without Gussets, 1972; The Woodland Book for Guides & Brownies, 1972; Your Book of Knitted Roys, 1973; Do-it-Yourself Dinosaurs, 1973; Cuddly Dolls & How to Dress them, 1976; Sleeve Puppets, 1978; Toys from Knitted Squares, 1982. Address: 11 Chisholm Avenue, Dunblane, Perthshire, Scotland.

MORTON, Frederic, 5 Oct. 1924, Vienna, Austria. Author. m. Marcia Colman, 28 Mar. 1957, Salsburg, 1 daughter. Education: BS, College of the City of New York; MA, Graduate Faculty, the New School for Social Research, New York. Literary Appointments: Lecturer on Modern Literature and Creative Writing at University of Utah, University of Southern California, Johns Hopkins University, New York University. Publications: Novels: The Hound, 1947; The Darkness Below, 1949; Asphalt and Desire, 1952; The Witching Ship, 1960;

The Schatten Affair, 1965; Snow Gods, 1969; An Unknown Woman, 1976; The Forever Street, 1984. Non-Fiction: the Rothschilds, 1962; A Nervous Splendour – Vienna 1888–9, 1979. *Contributions to:* The New York Times; Playboy; Esquire; Atlantic Monthly; New York Magazine; The Nation; Hudson Review; Village Voice (columnist); Harper's Magazine etc. *Honours:* Dodd, Mead Intercollegiate Literary Fellowship Award, 1948; Columbia University Fellowship, 1955; Author of the Year Award, National Anti-Defamation League, 1962; Nominee, National Book Award, 1962; Nominee, American Book Award, 1980; Honorary title of Professor, by the Republic of Austria, 1981. *Memberships:* Executive Board Member, PEN Club (American); Council Member, Authors' Guild of America. *Literary Agent:* Sterling Lord Agency, New York. *Address:* 110 Riverside Drive, New York, NY 10024, USA.

MORTON, Henry Albert, b. 20 July 1925, Gladstone, Manitoba, Canada. Writer; Retired Associate Professor of History. *Education:* BA, BEd, University of Manitoba; MA, University of Cambridge, England; PhD, University of Otago, New Zealand. *Publications:* And Now New Zealand, 1969; The Wind Commands, 1975; Which Way New Zealand, 1975; Why Not Together, 1978; The Whale's Wake, 1982. *Honour:* Sir James Wattie Award for, The Wind Commands, (Book of the Year), 1976. *Memberships:* Blenheim Club; PEN, New Zealand. *Agent:* Ray Richards. *Address:* 23 Mountain View Road, Blenheim, Marlborough, New Zealand.

MORTON-EVANS, Michael David, b. 13 Jan. 1942, Windsor, Berkshire, England. Writer. m. Christine Margaret Williams, 14 July 1975, Sydney, Australia, 2 sons, 2 daughters. *Publications:* The Australian Book of Lists, 1980; The Book of Gifts, 1981; Todler Taming (in association with Dr Christopher Green), 1984. *Membership:* Australian Society of Authors. *Address:* 14 Muston Street, Mosman, NSW 2088, Australia.

MORZFELD, Erwin Wilhelm, b. 1 Oct. 1923, Wattenscheid, Germany. Headmaster, Secondary School. m. Karin Lotz, 13 Oct. 1962, Bochum, 2 sons, 1 daughter. *Education:* Abitur; 3 state examinations. *Publications:* Ich weiss nichts von dem Mord, 1954; Er flog an meiner Seite, 1957. *Contributions to:* Ruhrfolk (Die Zeit); Westfälische Rundschau; WAZ; WDR; Westfalenpost; Die Sonnenuhr. *Honours:* Novelists Prize, German Coalfield Directorate, 1948; Literary Prize, Town of Wattenscheid, 1949. *Address:* Eppendorfer Strasse 69, 4630 Bochum 6, Federal Republic of Germany.

MOSBERGER, Cathérine, b. 1 Jan. 1940, Muttenz by Basel, Switzerland. Writer. *Education:* D Psy. *Publications:* Mit Dir und Mir, 1971; Die Nachtäugigen, 1984; Die Bewährung, 1984; Die Bestimmung, 1985; Die Nebelweber, 1985. *Address:* Apartado de Correos, Puerto de Andraitx, Mallorca/Baleares.

MOSBY, Aline, b. 27 July 1922, Missoula, Montana, USA. Journalist. *Education:* BA, University of Montana; Graduate work, Columbia University. *Literary Appointments:* Journalist, Time Magazine, 4 months; Journalist, foreign correspondent, United Press International, 37 years; Feature Writer, New York Times, 1985. *Publication:* The View From No. 13 People's Street, 1962. *Contributions to:* Saturday Review of Literature; Art News; Antique World. *Honours:* Cabanes Prize, International Wire Service Competition, 1980; Honorary Doctorate, University of Montana, 1985. *Membership:* Board of Directors, 6 years, Anglo-American Press Club, Paris. *Literary Agent:* Roberta Miller, United Media Enterprises, 200 Park Avenue, New York, NY 10166, USA. *Address:* 1 Rue Maitre Albert, Paris 75005, France.

MOSCOVITCH, Allan Stanley, b. 29 Dec. 1946, Montreal, Canada. University Teacher. m. Julie White, 1978, Ottawa, 1 son, 1 daughter. *Education:* BA, Carleton University; MA, Essex University. *Appointments:* Editorial Board, Studies in Political Economy,

1978–; Editorial Board, Perception, 1981–. *Publications:* Inequality: The Political Economy of Social Welfare, 1981; The Welfare State in Canada: A Selected Bibliography 1840–1978, 1983. *Contributor to:* Numerous articles in professional journals, newspapers and magazines. *Honours:* Recipient, various honours and awards. *Address:* 165 Holmwood Avenue, Ottawa K1S 2P3, Canada.

MOSELEY, Virginia Douglas, b. 31 Jan. 1917, Texas, USA. Retired University Professor. *Education:* BA, English, 1938, MA, 1948, University of Oklahoma; PhD, Columbia University, 1958. *Appointments:* Assistant Professor, English, Southeastern State University, 1947–55; Professor, English, Northern Illinois University, 1955–65; Professor, English, Texas Crossmans University, Denton, 1965–69; Professor, English, University of Ottawa, Canada, 1969–81. *Publications:* Joyce and the Bible, 1967; Those Americans co-trans from Russia, 1964.*Contributor to:* Numerous professional journals including, MidWest Quarterly; College English; etc. *Honours:* Recipient various honours and awards. *Membership:* James Joyce Foundation. *Address:* 821 North Humboldt (406), San Mateo, CA 94401, USA.

MOSER, Norman Calvin, b. 15 Oct. 1931, Durham, North Carolina, USA. Writer. m. (1) Hadassah Haskale, 1966 (deceased 1971); (2) Yolanda de Jesus Chitinos, 1978, San Pedro Sula, Honduras, 1 son. *Literary Appointments:* Contributing Editor, Grand Ronde Review, 1969–72; Magazine Editor, 1972–74; Staff Writer, North Carolina, Anvil, 1974–75; Teacher, Modern Art History, University of Maryland, Ulm, Germany, 1956; Teacher, Contemporary Literature, University of California, Berkeley, 1967–68; Teacher, French, University of Arizona, Tucson, 1969. *Publications:* Shorter Plays and Scenarios, 1981; El Grito del Morte, Stories and Tales, 1984. *Contributions to:* Manas; Oakland Tribune; Berkeley Works; Blue Unicorn; Abraxas; The Sun; Galley Sail Review; Athena Incognito; Cloud-Hidden Friends. *Literary Agents:* Jane Walker; Joyce Cole. *Address:* Illuminations Press, 2110–9th Street, Apt B, Berkeley, CA 94710, USA.

MOSES, Claire Goldberg, b. 22 June 1941, Hartford, Connecticut, USA. Professor. m. Arnold Moses, 11 Sep. 1966, 2 daughters. *Education:* Institut de Sciences Politiques, Paris, France, 1960–61; Columbia University, 1963–64; AB, Smith College, 1963; M Phil 1971, PhD 1978, George Washington University. *Publications:* Nineteenth Century French Feminism, 1984. *Contributions to:* French Women and the Age of Enlightenment, 1984; Journal of Modern History. *Honours:* Graduate Teaching Fellowship in History, George Washington University, 1968–71; Faculty Research Grant, General Research Board, University of Maryland, 1981. *Address:* 11658 Mediterranean Court, Reston, VA 22090, USA.

MOSES, Elbert Raymond Jr, b. 31 Mar. 1908, Concord, Ohio, USA. Professor Emeritus, Education: m. (1) Mary M Sterrett (d.1984), 21 Sep. 1933, Pittsburgh, 1 son; (2) Caroline M Chambers, 19 June 1985, Prescott Valley, Arizona. *Education:* AB, University of Pittsburgh; MSc, PhD, University of Michigan. *Publications:* A Guide to Effective Speaking, 1956, 1957; Phonetics: History & Interpretation, 1964; Three Attributes of God, 1983. *Contributions to:* American Speech & Hearing Magazine; Journal of American Speech; Speech Monographs; Veterans' Voices (works of hospitalised veterans in cooperation with Veterans Administration). *Honours include:* Paul Harris Fellow, Rotary, 1971; Certificate, Humanitarian Services, Nicaraguan Government, 1974; Phi Delta Kappa Service Key, 1978, Certificate for services to education, 1981; Citation, House of Representatives, Pennsylvania; Life Patron, American Biographical Institute, 1985; Statue of Victory, World Culture Prize, Centro Studi e Richerche delle Nazioni, Italy, 1985. *Address:* 2001 Rocky Dells Drive, Prescott, AZ 86301, USA.

MOSIER, John, b. 9 July 1944, Bentonville, Arkansas, USA. University Professor. *Education:* BA, MA, PhD, Tulane University. *Literary Appointments:* North American Editor, Iste e Espectaculo; Film Editor, New Orleans Review; Contributing Editor, Americas Magazine; Editor in Chief, New Orleans Review. *Publications:* Institutional Research to 1970, 1972; Women and Men Together, 1978; Handbook of Popular Culture in Latin America, 1985. *Contributions to:* Studies in Latin American Popular Culture; Americas; America; New Orleans Review; Publications of Modern Language Association; Kino; Variety; Iste a Cinema; Audio Brandon-MacMillan International Film Catalog. *Address:* 6363 Saint Charles Avenue, New Orleans, LA 70118, USA.

MOSS, Robert Alfred, b. Nuneaton, Warwickshire, England. Author. m. Joyce Nancy Green, Cheltenham, 1 son, 1 daughter. *Literary Appointments:* Chief Editor, Purnell Books, London & Midsomer Norton. *Major Publications:* ABC in Real-Life Pictures, 1943; The House of the Hundred Heads, 1939; Jenny of the Fourth, 1953; Jenny's Exciting Term, 1954; Shy Girl at Southdown, 1956; Mystery at Gull's Nest, 1956; The School on the Precipice, 1954; Susan's Stormy Term, 1955; Strange Quest at Cliff House, 1956; The Riddle of Cliff House, 1957; The Cliff House Monster, 1958; The Golden Bar Book of Brownie Stories, 1961; The Golden Ladder Book of Brownie Stories, 1963; The Challenge Book of Brownie Stories, 1968; The Wild White Pony & other Girl Guide Stories, 1976; The Second Challenge Book of Brownie Stories, 1981; The Brownie Storybook, 1986. *Contributor to:* Many popular childrens weeklies, radio & television. *Address:* Green Acres, Kidnappers' Lane, Cheltenham, Gloucestershire GL53 ONP, England.

MOTSCHMANN, Klaus Simon Markus, b. 4 Mar. 1934, Berlin, Germany. Professor. m. Dagmar Sell, 4 June 1962, 2 sons, 1 daughter. *Education:* Diplom-Politologe, 1960; Dr phil, 1969. *Literary Appointments:* Editor, Konservativ-heute, 1972–; Editorial Staff, Criticon, 1980. *Publications:* Evangelische Kirche und preußischer Staat in den Anfangsjahren der Weimar Republik, 1970; Sozialismus – Das Geschäft mit der Lüge, 1977; Oskar Brüsewitz – Sein Tod, sein Prostest, seine Mahnung, 1978; Sozialismus und Nation, 1979; Herrschaft der Minderheit, 1983. *Contributions to:* Konservativ-heute; Criticon; Deutsche Tagepost; Evangelische Sammlung; Erneuerung und Abwehr. *Memberships:* Berliner Autoren-Vereinigung; Managing board, Bundersverband Deutscher Autoren. *Address:* Ahrweilerstraße 12, D-1000 Berlin–Federal Republic of Germany.

MOTT, Michael Charles Alston, b. 8 Dec. 1930, London, England. Writer. m. Margaret Ann Watt, 8 May 1961, London, 2 daughters. *Education:* Diploma, Central School of Arts & Crafts, London; Intermediate Law Degree, Law Society, London; BA, History of Art, Courtaulds & Warburg Institutes, London; Honorary Doctor of Letters, St Mary's College, Notre Dame, 1983. *Literary Appointments:* Assistant Editor, Adam International Review, (research on Brecht & Proust), 1956–66; Editor, Fine Art Books, Thames & Hudson, 1961–64; Assistant Editor, The Geographical Magazine, 1964–66; Poetry Editor, The Kenyon Review, 1967–70; Visiting Professor, Writer-in-Residence, Kenyon College, State University of New York at Buffalo, Concordia University (Montreal), Emory University; The College of William & Mary; Bowling Green State University; Currently Professor of English, Creative Writing Program, Bowling Green State University. *Major Publications include:* The Notebooks of Susan Berry (novel), 1962; Helmet and Wasps, (novel), 1966; Absence of Unicorns, Presence of Lions, (poetry), 1976; Counting the Grasses, (poetry), 1980; The Seven Mountains of Thomas Merton, (biography), 1984; and others. *Contributor to:* Encounter; Poetry Chicago; The Sunday Times, (London); The Kenyon Review; Southern Review; Sewanee Review; Iowa Review; Pearl, (Denmark); Reviews in, The Sunday Times, Baltimore Sun, Poetry, and many others. *Honours:* Governor's

Award in Fine Arts, State of Georgia, 1974; Guggenheim Fellowship, 1979–80; The Christopher Award, 1984; Ohiona Book Award, 1985; Olscamp Research Award, 1985; Nancy Dasher Book Award, 1985; Runner-up Pulitzer Prize in Biography, 1984. *Memberships:* Art Club; Fellow, Royal Geographical Society, 1953–; Associated Writing Programs; Author's Guild; Amnesty International. *Literary Agents:* A D Peters (UK); Harold Matson (USA). *Address:* 128 North Maple Street, Bowling Green, OH 43402, USA.

MOTTO, Anna Lydia, b. New York City, New York, USA. Professor and Chairman, Department of Classics, University of South Florida. *Education:* BA, Queens College, New York, 1946; MA, New York University, 1948; PhD, University of North Carolina, 1953. *Publications include:* Seneca Sourcebook: Guide to the Thought of Lucius Annaeus Seneca, 1970; Seneca, 1973; Satire-That Blasted Art, Editor, 1973; Seneca: Moral Epistles, 1985; Senecan Tragedy, 1986. *Contributions to:* Scholarly journals of 60 articles on Seneca and other classical and modern topics. *Honours:* Vice President, Classical Association of the Atlantic States, 1972; President, Classical Association of the Middle West and South, 1982–83; Invited Resident, Institute for Advanced Study, Princeton, Summers, 1979,80. *Memberships:* American Philogical Association; American Classical League; Classical Society of the American Academy in Rome; Modern Language Association; New York Classical Club; Vergilian Society of Cumae. *Address:* Department of Classics, University of South Florida, Tampa, FL 33620, USA.

MOUAT, Kit, b. 1 Mar. 1920, England. Writer. 1 son. *Publications:* What Humanism is About, translation German, 1963; Leben in dieser Welt, 1964; Time Smoulders and Other Poems, 1971; Poems of an Angry Dove, 1975; Fighting for Our Lives – Introduction to Living with Cancer, 1984; I'm Staying – More Poems, 1985. *Contributions to:* Publications including: World Medicine; General Practitioner; Freethinker; New Humanist; Tribune; Guardian. *Address:* Mercers, High Street, Cuckfield, West Sussex, England.

MOULD, Daphne Desiree Charlotte Pochin, b. 15 Nov. 1920, Salisbury, England. Author & Photographer. *Education:* BSc Geology, University of Edinburgh, Scotland, 1943; PhD Geology, University of Edinburgh, 1946. *Major Publications:* The Roads from the Isles, 1950; West-over-Sea (The Outer Hebrides), 1953; Scotland of the Saints, 1952; Ireland of the Saints, 1953; Irish Pilgrimage (the ancient pilgrimages), 1955; The Rock of Truth, 1953; The Irish Dominicans, 1957; The Celtic Saints (Celtic Spirituality), 1956; Peter's Boat, 1959; The Angels of God, 1960; The Irish Saints (critical biographies), 1964; St Brigid, 1964; The Aran Islands, 1972; Ireland from the Air, 1972; The Mountains of Ireland (2nd edition), 1976; The Monasteries of Ireland, 1976; Valentia: Portrait of an Island, 1978; Discovering Cork: An Exploration of the County, 1986. *Contributor to:* Numerous publications including: Irish Times; Ireland of the Welcomes; Cara; The Countryman; US Catholic; The Furrow; and others. *Address:* Aherla House, Aherla, Co Cork, Republic of Ireland.

MOULE, Charles Francis Digby, b. 3 Dec. 1908, Hangchow, People's Republic of China. University Professor, Anglican Clerk in Holy Orders; Canon. *Education:* Classical tripos part i and ii, first class MA, Emmanuel College, University of Cambridge, 1934. *Publications:* An Idiom Book of New Testament Greek, 1953 and 1959; Commentary on Colossians and Philemon, 1957; The Birth of the New Testament, 1962. 3rd edition 1981; The Phenomenon of the New Testament, 1967; The Origin of Christology, 1977. *Contributing to:* Technical journals including: The Journal of Theological Studies; New Testament Studies; Theology; The Expository Times. *Honours:* Evans Prize 1931, Jeremie Septuagint Prize 1932, Crosse Scholarship 1933, in Theology, University of Cambridge; Honorary DD, University of St Andrews, 1958; Fellow 1966, Burkitt Medal 1970, British Academy; Honorary Fellow, Emmanuel College, Cambridge, 1972; Collins

Biennial Prize, 1977; CBE, 1985. *Memberships:* Fellow, Clare College, Cambridge, 1944–; Fellow, British Academy; President 1967–68, Studiorum Novi Testamenti Societas; Honorary member, Society of Biblical Literature, USA. *Address:* King's Houses, Pevensey, East Sussex, BN24 5JR, England.

MOULT, Edward Walker. Farmer; Broadcaster. m. Marie Rose. *Appointments:* Self-employed. *Publications:* Down to Earth, 1973; In the Country, co-author, 1980. *Address:* Scaddows Farm, Ticknall, Derby, England.

MOURÉ, Erin, b. 17 Apr. 1955, Calgary, Canada. Poet. *Publications:* Empire, York Street; The Whisky Vigil; Wanted Alive; Domestic Fuel. *Contributions to:* The Malahat Review; Prism International; Saturday Night and many others. *Honour:* National Magazine Award for Poetry, 1983. *Membership:* League of Canadian Poets (Quebec Representative 1985–86). *Address:* 3550 Jeanne Mance #211, Montreal, Quebec, Canada.

MOUSSA, Pierre Louis, b. 5 Mar. 1922, Lyon, France. Banker. m. Anne Marie Trousseau, 1957. *Education:* Ancien Eleve, l'Ecole Normale Superieure; Agrege des Letters; Inspecteur des Finances. *Publications:* Les Chances Economiques de la Communaute Franco-Africaine, 1957; Les Nations Proletairs 1959; LL'Economie de la Zone Franc, 1961; Les Etats-Unis et les Nations Proletaires, 1965. *Honours:* Officer: Legion of Honour, 1976; Ordre National du Merite. *Address:* Dillon Read Limited, Devonshire House, Mayfair Place, London, W1X 5FH, England.

MOWAT, Farley McGill, b. 12 May 1921, Ontario, Canada. Writer. m. Claire Wheeler. *Education:* BA, University of Toronto; Honorary Degrees: University of Toronto; University of Lethbridge, Alberta; Laurentian University; University of Prince Edward Island; University of Victoria. *Publications:* (Fiction), Lost in the Barrens, 1957; The Black Joke, 1963; The Curse of the Viking Grave, 1966; Owis in the Family, 1963; (Short Stories), The Snow Walker, 1977; (Plays) TV Scripts: Sea Fare, 1964; Diary of a Boy on Vacation, 1964; etc.; (Other), People of the Deer, 1952; The Regiment, 1955; The Dog Who Wouldn't be, 1957; The Grey Seas Under, 1959; The Desperate People, 1960; The Serpent's Coil, 1962; Never Cry Wolf, 1964; Westviking: The Ancient Norse in Greenalnd and North America, 1965; Canada North, 1967; This Rock Within the Sea: A Heritage Lost, 1969; The Boat Who Wouldn't Float, 1970; Sibir: My Discovery of Siberia, 1970; A Whale for the Killing, 1973; Wake of the Great Sealers, 1973; Snow Walker, 1975; And No Birds Sang, 1979; Canada North Now, 1976; Sea of Slaughter, 1984; My Discovery of America, 1985. *Contributor to:* Numerous journals, magazines, newspapers etc. *Honours:* University of Western Ontario President's Medal, 1952; Auisfeld-Wolf Award for non-fiction, 1952; Governor-Generals Award, 1957; Canadian Library Association Book of the Year Medal, 1958; Leacock Medal, 1970; Order of Canada, 1981. *Memberships:* PEN International; Writers Union of Canada. *Literary Agent:* Herta Ryder. *Address:* c/o McClelland & Stewart Ltd, 25 Hollinger Road, Toronto, Ontario, Canada M4B 3G2.

MOWERY, Dorothy May, b. Hammond, Indiana, USA. Journalist, Teacher. m. William Byron Mowery, Aug. 1935, Chicago, Illinois, USA, 1 daughter. *Education:* MED, University of Florida. *Literary Appointments:* Teacher, Creative Writing, Florida Junior College, Jacksonville; Teacher, Dawn Writing Couse, Jacksonville University. *Major Publications:* Swamp Shadows, 1948; War Chant, 1954; Seminole Trail, 1956. *Contributor to:* St Nicholas; Boys Life; Childs Life; Florida Times Union. *Memberships:* Jacksonville Poetry Society; League of American Penwomen, President, Jacksonville Branch, 1972–73. *Literary Agent:* Ruth Cantor, New York. *Address:* 1273 Menna Street, Jacksonville FL 32205, USA.

MOWSHOWITZ, Abbe, b. 13 Nov. 1939, Liberty, New York, USA. Computer Scientist. m. Harriet A Hobson, 1 Feb. 1964, West Hartford, Connecticut, 2 sons. *Education:* BS, Mathematics, University of Chicago, 1961; MS, Mathematics 1966, PhD, Computer Science 1967, University of Michigan. *Literary Appointments:* Editor, Proceedings, 2nd Conference on Human Choice & Computers, International Federation of Information Processors, 1979; Member, Editorial Boards, Computers & the Social Sciences, 1984, Future Computing Systems, 1984. *Publications:* The Conquest of Will: Information Processing in Human Affairs, 1976; Inside Information: Computers in Fiction, author/editor, 1977; Human Choice & Computers 2, editor/contributor, 1980. *Contributions to:* Various journals, books, proceedings including: Communications of the Association for Computing Machinery; Human Systems Management; Behavioural Sciences; Journal of Mathematical Biophysics; Journal of Combinatorial Theory; Computers & People; Colloquium Mathematicum; Bulletin of the London Mathematical Society. *Address:* 212 Hessian Hills Road, Croton-on-Hudson, NY 10520, USA.

MOYNIHAN, John Dominic, b. 31 July 1932, London, England. Journalist; Author. 1 son, 2 daughters. *Education:* Felsted School; Chelsea School of Art. *Literary Appointments:* Bromley Mercury, 1953–54; Evening Standard, 1954–63; Daily Express, 1963–64; The Sun, 1964–65; The Sunday Telegraph, 1965– (Assistant Literary editor, Sports correspondent). *Publications:* The Soccer Syndrome, 1966; Not All a Ball, autobiography, 1970; Park Football, 1970; Football Fever, 1974; Soccer, 1974; The Chelsea Story, 1982; The West Ham Story, 1984. *Contributions to:* Sunday Telegraph Magazine; New Statesman; Spectator; Harpers and Queen; The Observer; The Melbourne Age; Sunday Supplement, Australia; The Radio Times; Now Magazine; Evening Standard; Daily Express. *Memberships:* Sports Writers Association; Football Writers Association; Lawn Tennis Writers Association; Chelsea Arts Club; Scribes. *Literary Agent:* Irene Josephy, London. *Address:* 102 Ifield Road, London SW10, England.

MUDRICK, Marvin, b. 17 July 1921, Philadelphia, Pennsylvania, USA. Writer. m. Jeanne Ilda Little, 1 Nov. 1946, Los Angeles, 1 son, 3 daughters. *Education:* BA, Temple University, 1942; MA, 1947, PhD, 1949, University of California, Berkeley. *Publications:* Jane Austen, 1952; On Culture and Literature, 1970; The Man in the Machine, 1977; Books Are Not Life But Then What Is?, 1979; Nobody Here But Us Chickens, 1981. *Contributor to:* Human Review; New York Review of Books; Harper's. *Honour:* Guggenheim Fellow, 1959–60. *Memberships:* PEN, American Centre. *Address:* 1716 Hillcrest Road, Santa Barbara, CA 93103, USA.

MUELLER, Harald Waldemar, b. 18 May 1934, Memel, USSR. Playwright. m. Ingrid Mueller-Wegener, 17 Nov. 1974, 3 daughters. *Publications:* Plays: Grosser Wolf; Halbdeutsch; Stille Nacht; Strandgut; Winterreise; Frankfurter Kreuz; Henkersnachtmahl; Die Trasse; Kohlhaas; Der Tolle Bomberg; Rosel; Totenfloss. *Honours:* Gerhart-Hauptmann-Preis, 1969; Suhrkamp-Förderstipendium, 1970. *Membership:* Verband Deutscher Schriftsteller (VS). *Literary Agent:* Ute Nyssen, Merowingerstrasse 21, 5000 Köln 1, Federal Republic of Germany. *Address:* Borkumer Strasse 18, 1000 Berlin 33, Federal Republic of Germany.

MUELLER, Robert Emmett, b. 3 Apr. 1925, St Louis, Missori, USA. Artist; Writer. m. Diana Eva Lobl, New York City, 1 son, 1 daughter. *Education:* BS, EE, Boston; BA, Philosophy, New York City; New School for Social Research; Brooklyn Museum Art School. *Publications:* Inventivity, 1963; The Science of Art, 1967; Eyes in Space, 1965; Investor's Notebook, 1964. *Contributor to:* Art in America; Creative Computing; Leonardo; Art Com. *Address:* Britton House, Roosevelt, NJ 08555, USA.

MUENZER, Paul Johann, b. 18 Dec. 1928, Kehl-am-Rhein, Federal Republic of Germany. Writer & Decipherer. *Education:* Diplom-Ingenieur, Institute of

Technology, Munich, Federal Republic of Germany, 1957. *Literary Appointments:* Lecturers on deciphering of Mincan Linear A & the Phaistos Disk for Greek cultural societies in Germany & Switzerland. *Major Publications:* Die keltischen Viereckschanzen in Baden-Württemberg and Bayern,1979; Dichten und Denken,1980; Spiralförmige Inschriften auf Scheiben und Schalen von König Minos bis Knud den Groben, 1981. *Contributor to:* Numerous archaeological publications in Federal Republic of Germany, Switzerland, Austria & USA. *Honour:* Third Prizefor dialect prose, Freiburg, Federal Republic of Germany, 1976. *Address:* Erzgießereistraße 26, D–8000 Munich 2, Federal Republic of Germany.

MUESING-ELLWOOD, Edith Elizabeth, b. 18 Sep. 1947, Manhattan, New York, USA. Freelance Writer. m. William A G Ellwood, P E 15 Sep. 1980, New York City, 1 son, 1 daughter. *Education:* BA, Fordham University, 1969 (Regents Scholar): MA, New York University, 1971. *Publications:* Non-Fiction: The Alternative to Technological Culture, 1983; United States Democracy: Myth Versus Reality, 1985. *Contributions to:* Dragonfly; Orphic Lute; Wind Chimes; Piedmont Literary Review; Ram the Letterbox; Poets Pride. *Honours:* Readers Vote for Best of the Issue, Dragonfly/East West Haiku Quarterly, 1985; Presentation of Nonfiction paper, International Conference of the Society for Philosophy and Technology, The Netherlands, 1985; Listed in various biographical works. *Address:* 128 Dean Street, Brooklyn, NY 11201, USA.

MÜHRINGER, Doris Agathe Annemarie, b. 18 Sep. 1920, Graz, Austria. Writer. *Major Publications:* Gedichte 1, 1957; Das Märchen von den Sandmännlein, (Kinderbilderbuch), 1961; Gedichte II, 1969; Staub öffnet das Auge, (Gedichte III), 1976; Mein Tag, mein Jahr, (Lyrik-Photo-Buch) (with H Valencak), 1983; Vögel, die ohne Schlaf sind, (Gedichte IV), 1984; Tanzen unter dem Netz, (Kurzprosa), 1985. *Contributor to:* Numerous literary magazines in 9 countries.*Honours:* Georg Trakl Prize, 1954; Award of Achievement, Vienna, 1961; Lyrics Prize of Steiermark, 1973; Austrian State Scholarship, 1976; Award of Achievement, Board of Austrian Literar-Mechana, 1984. *Memberships:* PEN; Association of Austrian Writers; Podium; Kogge. *Address:* Goldeggasse 1, A–1040, Vienna, Austria.

MUIR, Allan Thompson, b. 7 Nov. 1917, Glasgow, Scotland, Editor. m. Doris Louise, 1 May 1974, Rutland, Vermont, 1 son, 2 daughters. *Education:* Local Certificate, Oxford; School of Navigation Royal Technical College, Glasgow, Scotland; 1st prize, Mathematics, Navigation and Nautical Astronomy, Royal Society of Arts, 1932; Master Mariner. *Literary Appointments:* Editor, Canadian Fisherman; Editorial Director, National Business Publications Limited; Editor, Founding Publisher, Log Home Guide for Builders and Buyers, Chairman of the Board, Muir Publishing Company, Ltd. *Publications:* Building the Chateau Montebello, with Doris Muir, 1980; Editor, Your Log House, 1981, The Energy Economics and Thermal Performance of Log Houses, 1981, The Energy Economics and Thermal Performance of Log Houses, 1981 and The Handbook of Canadian Log Building, 1985. *Contributions to:* Men Only; Singapore Straits Times, Nautical Magazine; Liberty; London Times, and numerous trade publications. *Honours:* Best Editorial, Kenneth R Wilson Memorial Award, Canadian Business Press, 1967. *Literary Agent:* Larry Pihera. *Address:* Log Home Guide Information Center, Exit 447 1-40, Hartford, TN 37753, USA.

MUIR, Doris Louise, b. 14 July 1935, Harrisburg, Pennsylvania, USA. Publisher; Editor, m. Allan Muir, 1 May 1974, West Rutland, Vermont, 1 son, 2 daughters. *Education:* Student, James Madison University, George Washington University and Howard University. *Literary Appointments:* Founding Editor, Log Home Guide for Builders and Buyers; President, Muir Publishing Company Ltd. *Publications:* Building the Chateau Monetbello,1980; Energy Economics and Thermal Performance of Log Homes, 1982. *Contributions to:*

Log Home Guide for Builders and Buyers; Log Home Design; Log Home Decor. *Literary Agent:* Larry Pihera. *Address:* Log Home Guide Information Center, Exit 447 Interstate 40, Hartford, TN 37753, USA.

MUIR, Kenneth, b. 5 May 1907, London, England. University Teacher. m. Mary Ewen, July 1936, Crossby, 1 son. *Education:* BA, MA, Dip Ed, Oxford University. *Literary Appointments:* Editor, Shakespeare Survey, 1965–80; Chairman, International Shakespeare Association, 1974–85. *Publications include:* Macbeth, 1951; King Lear, 1952; Five Plays of Jean Racine, translation, 1960; Unpublished Poems by Sir Thomas Wyatt, 1961; Life and Letters of Sir Thomas Wyatt, 1963; Othello, editor, 1968; Collected Poems of Sir Thomas Wyatt, (edited with Patricia Thomson, 1969; The Comedy of Manners, 1970; A New Companion to Shakespeare Studies, (with S Schoenbaum), 1971; Shakespeare's Tragic Sequence, 1972; Shakespeare The Professional, 1973; The Singularity of Shakespeare, 1977; The Source's of Shakespeare's Plays, 1977; Shakespeare's Comic Sequence, 1979; Shakespeare's Sonnets, 1979; Four Comedies of Calderon, translation, 1980; Troilus and Cressida, editor, 1982. *Honours:* Honorary doctorates: Rouen 1967, Dijon 1976; FBA, 1970; FRSL, 1978. *Membership:* President, Liverpool Shakespeare Society. *Address:* 6 Chetwynd Road, Oxton, Birkenhead, Merseyside, L43 2JJ, England.

MUIR, Richard, b. 18 June 1943, Yorkshire, England. Author; Photographer. *Education:* 1st class honours in Geography, Aberdeen, Scotland, 1967; PhD, Aberdeen, 1970. *Literary Appointment:* Editor, National Trust Regional Histories and Countryside Commission National Park Series. *Publications:* Modern Political Geography, 1975; The English Village; Shell Guide to Reading the Landscape; Lost Villages of Britain; History from the Air; National Trust Guide to Prehistoric and Roman Britain, with Humphrey Welford; Visions of the Past, with C Taylor; East Anglian Landscapes, with J Ravensdale; Shell Countryside Book, with E Duffey; Reading the Celtic Landscape; National Trust Guide to Dark Age and Medieval Britain; Landscape and Nature Photography; National Trust Book of Rivers, (with M Muir). *Contributions to:* Geographical Magazine; Sunday Times Magazine; Observer Magazine; various academic articles. *Honour:* Yorkshire Arts Literary Prize, 1982–83. *Address:* Waterfall Close, Station Road, Birstwith, Harrogate, Yorkshire, England.

MUIRDEN, Bruce Wallace, b. 31 May 1928, Melbourne, Australia. Journalist. m. June Margaret Erickson, Deniliquin, Australia, 2 Dec. 1954, 1 son, 1 daughter. *Education:* Universities of Melbourne & Adelaide. *Publications:* The Puzzled Patriots, 1968; When Power Went Public, 1978. *Editor:* Austrovert Literary journal, 1949–52; The Australian Humanist, 1965–75. *Contributions to:* Flinders History of South Australia, 1986. *Address:* 219 Kensington Road, Kensington, Adelaide, SA 5068, Australia.

MUI[TK]ZNIEKS, Sarma Gundega, b. 10 Sep. 1960, Kalamazoo, Michigan, USA. Freelance Poet, Editor, Translator. m. Janis Liepins, 18 Aug. 1984, 1 son. *Education:* BA Art and Public Policy, Kalamazoo College; Western Michigan University. *Literary Appointments:* Literary programme coordinator and lecturer, 2x2 Latvian Youth Summer Seminars, 1979–85; Editor, A Kaugars manuscripts, 1983–84; Director, BUDA publishing house for limited edition manuscripts, 1984–. *Publications:* Izgerbies. *Contributions to:* Various magazines and newspapers including: Jauna Gaita, Canada; Pédéjais Laiks, Canada; Afisas, Federal Republic of Germany; Australijas Latvietis, Australia; Latvija (Vacija), Federal Republic of Germany. Laras Lapa, USA. *Honours:* George Errington Prize in Art, 1982; Kalamazoo Art Council Grant, 1982. *Membership:* American Latvian Writers Association. *Address:* 23 Highland Road, Boxford, MA 01921, USA.

MUJAHID, Sharif, b. 1 July 1926, Madras, India. Professor. m. Shakila Khanum, 7 Apr. 1967, 4 daughters. *Education:* MA, History, Madras University, 1950; MA,

Journalism, Stanford University, 1952; MA, Islamics, McGill University, 1954. *Literary Appointments include:* Associate Professor, and Head of Department of Journalism, University of Karachi, Pakistan, 1962–72; Visiting Asian Professor, Bradley University and State University of New York, 1964; Professor of Journalism, University of Karachi, 1972–; Director, Quaid-i-Azam Academy, Karachi, 1976–. *Publications:* Haquq-i-Insani, 1959; Indian Secularism: A Case Study of the Muslim Minority, 1970; The Poet of the East, 1961; Pakastani Nationalism, 1961; Ideological Orientation of Pakistan, 1976; Founder of Pakistan, 1976; Quaid-i-Azam Jinnah: Studies in Interpretation, 1981. *Contributions to:* Numerous professional journals, including, Collier's Encyclopedia. *Honours:* Fulbright Scholar, Stanford University, 1951–52; Research Fellow,Islamic Institute, McGill University, 1952–54; Pakistani Representative at UNESCO Seminar, 1961; Nominating Member,Magasasay Award, Manila,1960–61; President's Award – Quaid-d-Azam Jinnah : Studies in Interpretation, 1981. *Memberships include:* Member, Executive Committee, Pakistan Historical Society; Pakistan Institute of International Affairs; Asian Mass Communication Research and Information Centre, Singapore; Consultant Mass Media. Planning Commission, Government of Pakistan. *Address:* Quaid-i-Azam Academy, 297 M A Jinnah Road, Karachi 5, Pakistan.

MUKHOPADHYAYA, Uma Prasad, b. 12 Oct. 1902, Calcutta, India. Formerly Professor, Calcutta University Law College and Advocate, Calcutta High Court. *Education:* MA, LLB. *Publications:* Gangabataran; Himalayer Pathé Pathé; Kuari Giripathe Manimahesh; Trilokenather Pathé; Kaveri Kahini; Pancha Kedar; Sherpader Deshe; Afridi Muluké; Kailas ó Mánassarovar; Vaishnodevi ó annyánya káhini; Pálámaur jangalay; Muktináth; Saratchandra Prasanga; Alochháyar Pathé, (all in the Bengali language). *Contributor to:* Desh; Jugantar; Amrita; Katha Sahitya etc. *Honour:* Sahitya Akademi Award, 1972. *Address:* 126 Asutosh Mookerjee Road, Calcutta 700 025, West Bengal, India.

MULGRUE, George Edward, b. 11 June 1911, Geraldton, Western Australia. Writer; Drama Critic; International Civil Servant. *Education:* Private Studies of Engineering. *Publications:* Throw Back the Little Ones, 1962; Mo Chridhe: Songs for Three Lost Loves, 1984. *Contributor to:* POL; Cleo Magazine; Australian Women's Weekly Magazine; Australian House and Garden; Craft Australia; Reader's Digest; Australian Playboy; Belle Bride. *Honours include:* 1st Prize, Australia Wide Radio Play Competition, WA Drama Festival, 1937; Honorary LLD, University of Portland, 1969. *Memberships:* Western Australia Branch, Fellowship of Australian Writers, Secretary, 1939–40; Australian Writers Guild; Australian Journalists Association. *Literary Agent:* J Stewart, New York City, USA. *Address:* 498 Gt Eastern Highway, Greenmount, WA 6050, Australia.

MULLANEY, Marie Marmo, b. 21 Sep. 1953, Newark, New Jersey, USA. College Professor. m. Kenneth F Mullaney Junior, 27 Aug. 1977, Orange, New Jersey. *Education:* BA, Seton Hall University, 1975; MA, 1977, PhD, 1980, Rutgers University. *Publications:* Revolutionary Women: Gender and the Socialist Revolutionary Role, 1983. *Contributions to:* Journal of Psychohistory; Historical reflections/Réflexions Historiques; Maryland Historian; Journal of Rutgers University Libraries; International Social Science Review; Social Science Journal; Red River Historical Journal of World History; Alternative Futures: The Journal of Utopian Studies. *Honour:* Danforth Fellow, 1975–80. *Address:* Department of History and Political Science, Caldwell College, Caldwell, NJ 07006, USA.

MULLARD, Christopher Paul, b. 23 Nov 1944, Britain. University Professor. *Education:* MA, Sociology, PhD, Sociology, University of Durham. *Publications:* Black Britain 1973; Aborigines in Australia Today, 1974; On Being Black in Britain, 1975; Race, Power and Resistance, 1985. *Contributions to:* Race Today, 1973;

Sociology; Case Studies on Human Rights and Fundamental Freedoms: A World Survey, 1976; British Journal of Sociology; Journal of Contemporary Asia, 1978; Acid, 1979; Plural Societies; Educational Analysis, 1981; Educational Policy Bulletin, 1982; Journal of World Studies Education, 1983. *Address:* Race Relations Policy and Practice Research Unit, University of London Institute of Education, 57 Gordon Square, London WC1H ONT, England.

MULLEN, Harryette Romell, b. 1 July 1953, Florence, Alabama, USA. Writer; Teacher. *Education:* BA, English (Hons), University of Texas at Austin, 1975; Doctoral Studies in Literature at University of California, Santa Cruz. *Literary Appointments:* Writer-in-Residence, Galveston County Cultural Arts Center; Writer-in-Residence, Beaumont Independent School District. *Publications:* Tree Tall Woman, 1981; Washing the Cow's Skull (anthology), 1982; Her Work: Short Fiction by Texas Women, 1982; South by Southwest (fiction anthology), forthcoming 1985 or 1986. *Contributions to:* Obsidian; Nimrod; Hoo-Doo; Hambone; Callaloo; Praxis; The Greenfield Review; Poetry Texas; Cedar Rock; Black American Literature Forum; South and West; Phosphene; Open Places; Sunbury; The Black Collegian; Black Expressions; Texas Observer; Methula; River Styx; Hubris; New Life News; Grassroot Struggle; A Journal of Contemporary Literature; Essence; The Universal Black Writer; Metis; Mexos; WIN; Artist Alliance News. *Honours:* Phosphane Poetry Prize; Dobie-Paisano Fellowship; The Helene Wurlitzer Foundation of New Mexico Residence Grant. *Membership:* Texas Institute of Letters. *Address:* c/o A A Mullen, 2329 Linda Lane, Fort Worth, TX 76119, USA.

MULLER, Peter O, b. 10 May 1942, England. Professor of Geography. m. Nancy L Kohler, 11 June 1966, Rahway, New Jersey, USA, 1 daughter. *Education:* BA, City College of New York, 1963; MA, 1966, PhD, 1971, Rutgers University. *Literary Appointments:* Editorial Review Boards: The Southeastern Geographer; Urbanism Past and Present. *Publications:* Contemporary Suburban America, 1981; Economic Geography (co-author), 1981; Geography: Regions and Concepts, 4 revised editions (co-author), 1985; Human Geography: Culture, Society and Space, 3 revised editions (co-author) 1986. *Contributions to:* Progress in Geography; Economic Geography; The Professional Geographer; American Quarterly; Urbanism Past and Present, several other book chapters and articles. *Memberships:* Association of American Geographers (Councillor); National Council for Geographic Education; American Geographical Society; Phi Beta Kappa. *Address:* Department of Geography, University of Miami, Coral Gables, FL 33124–8152, USA.

MULLER-FELSENBURG, Alfred, b. 26 Dec. 1926, Bochum, Federal German Republic. Author; Educator. m. 27 Dec. 1951, 1 son, 2 daughters. *Education:* Teacher Training Colleges, Hofheim/Taunas 1941–43; Grosskrotzenburg/Main, 1943–44; Educational Padagogische Akademie, Essen-Kupferdreh, 1949–51; State Teaching Examinations 1951, 1954. *Publications include:* Die Abenteuer der Heiligen, 1964; In Metz der Gewalt, 1980; Ich will nicht zum lieben Gott, 1982; Das Tagebuch des Fabian Molitor, 1982; Gefahrlicher Wind– Oder: 1984 und kein Ende, 1983; Klasse IV in Aufruhr, 1984; Der Kupferesser, 1984; Morgen ist Vergangenheit, 1984; Guten Tag! Texte zum Nachdenken, 1985; Architekt Gottes/Leben und Werk des Bruders Joh. Hopfer SVD (1856–1936) Steyler Missionar und Baumeister in Togo/Afrika, 1985; and many others. *Honours:* Prize for, Die Abenteuer der Heiligen, 1964, Paris; 3rd Prize for competiton, Wann entfaltete sich die Rose..., 1974; Witten; 2nd Prize for competition, Kathetrale zu Reims, 1975; Aschen; 2nd Prize for competition, Zwei Menschen, 1976, Witten; Stipend for work from the Ministre for Culture in Nordhein-Westfalen for the book, In Nets der Gewalt, Dusselforf, 1979; Hugo-Carl-Jungst-Medaille for fortschrittliche Literatur, Hagen, 1979; 2nd Prize for competition, Rosa Mystica, Herna/Witten, 1981. *Memberships:* Autorenkreis, Ruhr-Mark; Verband Deutscher Schriftsteller in der Industrie Gewerkschaft Druck und Papier; Arbeitsksreis, Das gute Jugendbuch; Inklings-Gesellschaft fur Literatur und Aesthetik. *Address:* Lahnstrasse 10, D–5800 Hagen 1, Federal Republic of Germany.

MÜLLER-HENNING, Margarete, b. 8 July 1924, Kiev, Germany. Interpreter. m. Felix Müller, deceased, 1 son, 1 stepson and 2 stepdaughters. *Education:* Diploma, Interpreter School. *Publications:* Am Hang, 1974; Anfang des Kreises, 1980; Siehst du Dien Santis?, 1984; So Viel Himmel, 1984; Das Jahr Macht Seinen Weg, 1985. *Contributions to:* Silhouette, Berlin-Israel; Evengelische Nachricthen, Regensburg; Die Oberpfalz; Sovremennik, Russian literature journal, Canada; Anthologien der RSGI. *Membership:* RSGI (Regensburger Schriftstellergruppe International). *Address:* Boessnerstrabe 3 d, 8400 Regensburg, Federal Republic of Germany.

MULLINGS, Peter Coningsby, b. 17 Dec. 1928, Ashton-upon-Mersey, England. Television Producer and Director. m. Barbara Greenhalgh, 11 Jan. 1965, London, 1 daughter. *Education:* St Bede's College, Manchester. *Literary Appointment:* Faculty Member, Pennsylvania State University, USA, 1971–72. *Publications:* Chapter: Lighting The Stage in, Handbook for the Amateur Theatre, 1957. *Contributions to:* Society of Film and Television Arts Journal; Amateur Photographer; Coins; Television in the University. *Honours:* Award, What The Papers Say, 1977; Member of the Order of the British Empire (MBE), 1981. *Memberships:* Association of British Science Writers; Royal Institution of Great Britain; British Academy of Film and Television Arts; Savage Club; Cinema and Television Veterans; Chairman 1973–, Manchester and District CTBF. *Address:* 2 Penrith Avenue, Sale, Cheshire M33 3FN, England.

MULLINS, Carolyn (Holt) Johns, b. 29 Apr. 1940, Worcester, Massachusetts, USA. Professor. m. Nicholas Creed Mullins, 21 June 1962, Tampa, Florida, USA, 2 sons, 1 daughter. *Education:* BA Literature, Cornell University, 1962; MRE, Andover Newton Theological School, 1967. *Literary Appointments:* Joint appointment to Computing Centre & Associate Professor of English, Virginia Polytechnic Institute & State University, 1983–. *Major Publications:* A Guide to Writing & Publishing in the Social & Behavioural Sciences, 1977; The Complete Writing Guide, 1980; The Complete Manuscript Preparation Style Guide, 1982; The Office Automation Primer, 1982; A Parents Guide to Youth Soccer, 1983; Harnessing Information Technologies, 1984; Word-Processing on the TI Professional, 1985. *Contributor to:* Various trade, popular & computer magazines. *Honours:* Various awards for writing and for software. *Memberships:* NCTE Committee on Instructional Technology; Working Group on Standards for USA Documentation Technical Committee on Software Engineering, Institute of Electrical & Electronic Engineers (1984–86). *Address:* 1509 Hoyt Street, Blacksburg, VA 24060, USA.

MULLINS, Edwin, b. 14 Sep. 1933, London, England. Writer. 1 son, 2 daughters. *Education:* MA, Oxford University. *Publications:* Alfred Wallis, 1967; Braque, 1968; The Pilgrimage to Santiago, 1974; Angels on the Point of a Pin, 1979. Great Paintings, 1981; Sirens, 1983; The Arts of Britain, 1983; The Painted Witch, 1985; A Love Affair with Nature, 1985. *Literary Agent:* Curtis Brown, London. *Address:* 7 Lower Common South, London SW15 1BP, England.

MULLINS, Helene, b. 12 July 1899. Writer. m. Linne Johnson, deceased. *Publications:* Earthbound, 1929; Balm in Gilead, 1930; Streams from the Source, 1938; The Mirrored Walls, 1970. *Contributions to:* Scribners Magazine; Harper's Magazine; American Scholar; New Leader; New York Times; The Nation; Saturday Review; Liberation; Commonweal; Georgia Review; New Orleans Anthology; New Yorker, and others.

Membership: Poetry Society of America. *Address:* 16 West 16th Street, New York City, NY 10011, USA.

MULTER, Rita, b. 21 Jan. 1930, Larsbach, Federal Republic of Germany. Elementary School Headmistress. m. Friedrich Multer, 6 Aug. 1956, 3 daughters. *Education:* Examined elementary teacher. *Publications:* Nur aus einer Rippe, 1968; Liebe mich mit treuem Sinn, 1980; Die Landshuter Fürstephochzeit, 1983. *Contributions to:* Newspapers and journals concerning womens rights and magazines concerning education and teaching.

MULVILLE, Frank, b. 1 Jan. 1924, Dinard, France. Writer. *Publications:* Terschelling Sands, 1968; In Granma's Wake, 1970; Rustler on the Beach, 1976; Schooner Integrity, 1979; Single Handed Cruising and Sailing, 1982. *Contributions to:* Sunday Times; Observer; Guardian; Yachting Monthly; Motor Boat and Yachting; Yachts and Yachting; Sail (USA); Cruising World (USA). *Literary Agent:* Watson, Little Ltd. *Address:* 20 Downs Road, Maldon, Essex, England.

MUNDELL, Matt, b. 17 Jan. 1936, Annan, Scotland. Journalist. m. Anne McL, Jackson, 1959, 2 daughters. *Publications:* Country Diary, 1981. *Contributions to:* various publications, including fiction. *Address:* Norwood, Abercromby Road, Castle Douglas, Kirkcudbrightshire, Scotland.

MUNDSTOCK, Karl, b. 26 Mar. 1915, Berlin, Germany. Writer. m. 10 July 1943, Berlin, 1 son, 1 daughter. *Publications:* Ali und die Bande vom Lauseplatz, 1956, 13 editions; Gespenster-Edes Tod und Auferstehung, 1959; 8 editions; Tod an der Grenze, 1961, 7 editions; Meine tausend Jahre Jugend, 1981, 2 editions; Zeit der Zauberin, 1985. *Honours:* FDGB Literature Prize, 1982; Goethe Prize, City of Berlin, 1984; National Prize of German Democratic Republic, 1985; Fighters against Facism Medal, 1958; Fatherland Order of Merit in Silver, 1974. *Memberships:* Writers Association of German Democratic Republic, Revision Commission; PEN, Centre of German Democratic Republic, (Praesidium). *Address:* Wolfshagenerstr. 75, 1100 Berlin–PanKow, Democratic Republic of Germany.

MUNFORD, William Arthur, b. 27 Apr. 1911, London, England. Retired Librarian. m. Hazel Despart Wilmer, 25 Aug. 1934, Stoke Newington, 2 sons, 1 daughter. *Education:* B Sc Economics, PhD, London School of Economics, 1929–32. *Literary Appointments:* City Librarian, Cambridge. 1945–53; Director-General, National Library for the Blind, 1954–82. *Publications:* Penny Rate, 1951; William Ewart, M P, 1960; Edward Edwards, 1963; James Duff Brown, 1968; A History of the Library Association, 1877–1977, 1976. *Contributions to:* Librarianship journals. *Honours:* MBE, 1946; Honrary Fellow, The Library Association, 1977; Librarian Emeritus, National Library for the Blind, 1982. *Membership:* Society of Bookmen. *Address:* 11 Manor Court, Pinehurst, Grange Road, Cambridge CB3 9BE, England.

MUNRO, John Murchison, b. 29 Aug. 1932, Wallasey, England. Writer and University Professor. m. Hertha Ingrid Bertha Lipp, 10 Aug. 1956, Paris, France, 2 sons, 2 daughters. *Education:* BA, Durham University, England; PhD, Washington University, St Louis, Missouri, USA. *Appointments:* Instructor, Washington University, USA, 1956–60; Instructor, University of North Carolina, 1960–63; Assistant Professor, University of Toronto, Canada, 1963–65; Professor, American University of Beirut, Lebanon, 1965–present. *Publications:* English Literature in Transition, 1968; Arthur Symons, 1969; The Decadent Poetry of the 1890's, 1970; Selected Poems of Theo Marzials, 1974; James Elroy Flecker, 1976; A Mutual Concern, 1977; The Nairn Way, 1980. *Contributions:* Some 50 articles and reviews in various journals. *Address:* Department of English, American University of Beirut, Beirut, Lebanon.

MUNSON, Kenneth George, b. 17 Oct. 1929, London, England. Aviation Author; Editor. *Literary Appointments:* Assistant Editor, Jane's All the World's Aircraft, 1973–; Editor, The Rolls-Royce Magazine, 1979–81. *Publications:* Approx. 40 books on aircraft and aviation, including, Aircraft of World War II, 1962, 2nd edition, 1975; Pocket Encyclopaedia of World Aircraft in Colour, (14 vols.), 1966–72; Aircraft of World War I, 1967; Pictorial History of BOAC and Imperial Airways, 1970; Famous Aircraft of All Time, 1976. *Contributor to:* Contributing Editor, Jane's Defence Weekly; 1984–. *Honours:* Literary Award, Aéro-Club de France, 1970. *Memberships:* Associate Member, Royal Aeronautical Society; Associate Royal Historical Society. *Address:* Briar Wood, 4 Kings Ride, Seaford, East Sussex BN25 2LN, England.

MUNSON, Thomas Nolan, b. 26 Jan. 1924, Chicago, Illinois, USA. Professor. *Education:* AB Classics & English; MA Philosophy; PhL, STL, PhD Philosophy. *Major Publications:* The Essential Wisdom of George Santayana, 1962; Reflective Theology: Philosophical Orientations in Religion, 1968; Religious Consciousness and Experience, 1975; The Challenge of Religion: A Philosophical Approach, 1985. *Contributor to:* Philosophy Today; The Review of Metaphysics; The Monist; Philosophy & Phenomenological Research; Listening; Journal of Religion; Archives de Philosophie; Chicago Studies; and others. *Honours:* Rockefeller Foundation Grant, 1962–63; Cross-discipline Fellowship, Society for Values in Higher Education, 1965–66. *Address:* Department of Philosophy, 2323 N Seminary, Chicago, Il 60614, USA.

MUNZ, Peter, b. 12 May 1921, Chemnitz, Germany. University Professor. m. Keelah Anne Vickerman, 18 Sep. 1950, Wellington, New Zealand, 1 son. *Education:* MA, Canterbury University; PhD, Cambridge University. *Publications:* The Place of Hooker in the History of Thought, 1952; Problems of Religious Knowledge, 1959; Origin of the Carolingian Empire, 1960; Relationship and Solitude, 1964; Life in the Age of Charlemagne, 1969; Frederick Barbarossa, 1969; Boso's Life of Pope Alexander III (with G Ellis), 1973; When the Golden Bough Breaks, 1973; The Shapes of Time, 1977; Our Knowledge of the Growth of Knowledge, 1985. *Contributor to:* Dozens of Journals including: English Historical Review; Philosophical Quarterly; Numen; Journal of the Philosophy of the Social Sciences. *Literary Agent:* D Elworthy, Shoal Bay Press, Auckland, New Zealand. *Address:* 128 Ohiro Road, Wellington, New Zealand.

MUNZER, Martha E, b. 22 Sep. 1899, New York City, USA. Writer. m. Edward M Munzer, 15 June 1922, Woodmere, New York, 1 son, 2 daughters. *Education:* BS Electrochemical Engineering, Massachusetts Institute of Technology. *Publications:* Teaching Science Through Conservation: A Sourcebook for Teachers, (with Dr Paul Brandwin), 1960; For young readers: Unusual Careers; From Solar Science to Land Use Planning, 1962; Planning Our Town: A Primer on City Planning, 1964; Pockets of Hope: Studies of Land and People, 1966; Valley of Vision; The TVA Years, 1969; Block by Block: Rebuilding City Neighbourhoods, (with Helen Vogel), 1973; New Towns: Building Cities From Scratch, (with John Vogel), 1974; Full Circle: Rounding Out a Life, 1978; The Three R's of Ecology, 1986. *Contributions to:* Various magazines and journals. *Honours:* Chemistry Teachers Club of New York, 1947; Salute to Women, Governor Rockefeller, New York, 1950's; Key Award, Conservation Education Association, 1960's. *Address:* 4411 Tradewinds Avenue East, Lauderdale by the Sea, FL 33308, USA.

MURATA, Kiyoaki, b. 19 Nov. 1922, Ono, Hyogo, Japan. Author. m. Minako Iesaka, 26 March, 1960, Tokyo, 2 sons, 1 daughter, divorced March 1981. *Education:* BA, Carleton College, MN, USA; MA, Columbia University, NY, USA. *Publications:* Japan's New Buddhism–an Objective Account of Soak Gakkai, 1969; Japan–The State of the Nation, 1979; Saigo no Ryugakusei (The Last Student to Study Abroad), 1981;

Kikuren Nikki–Suppon Wan no Kaiso (UN Diary–Recollections of Turtle Bay), 1985. *Honours:* Vaughn Prize, Japan Newspaper Publishers Association, 1957; Honorary LLD, Carleton College. *Address:* 19–12 Hiroo 2-chome, Shibuya-ku, Tokyo, Japan 150.

MURCH, Edward (William Lionel), b. 20 Apr. 1920, Plymouth, Devon, England. Playwright. *Publications include:* Numerous one-act plays including: The Poet of Goosey Fair, 1946; Things That Go Bump; No Name in the Street; The Last Blue Mountain; Journey of the Star; Tell It to the Wind; The Dipper; Beggars of Bordeaux; Caroline; Bethlehem Boy; The Revival, 1982. *Honours:* Fellowships: Royal Society of Arts; International Institute of Arts and Letters. *Literary Agent:* Walter H Baker Company. *Address:* Heatherdene, Dousland, Yelverton, Devon, England.

MURDIN, Paul Geoffrey, b. 5 Jan. 1942, Croydon, England. Astronomer. m. Lesley Carol Milburn, 8 Aug. 1964, Maidstone, 2 sons, 1 daughter. *Education:* BA, Wadham College, Oxford, 1963; PhD, University of Rochester, New York, 1970. *Publications:* The Astronomer's Telescope, 1963; Radio Waves from Space, 1965; The New Astronomy, 1975; Catalogue of the Universe, 1981; Colours of the Stars, 1984. *Contributions to:* Yearbook of Astronomy; Popular Astronomy; Observatory; Astrophysical Journal; Nature; Physics Bulletin; Quarterly Journal and Monthly Notices of the Royal Astronomical Observatory. *Address:* Royal Greenwich Observatory, Herstmonceux Castle, Hailsham, East Sussex BN27 1RP, England.

MURDOCK, Eugene Converse, b. 30 Apr 1921, Lakewood, Ohio, USA. College Professor. m. Margaret B McColl, 7 Oct. 1950, Cleveland, Ohio, 1 son, 1 daughter. *Education:* BA, 1943, Wooster College, Ohio; MA, 1948, PhD, 1951, Columbia University. *Academic Appointments:* Professor of History, Rio Grande (Ohio) College, 1952–55; Professor of History 1986–, Department Chair, 1972–, Marietta College, Ohio. *Publications:* Ohio's Bounty System in the Civil War 1963; Patriotism Limited 1967; One Million Men 1971; Fenton Glass (with William Heacock) two volumes 1978, 1980; Ban Johnson; Czar of Baseball 1982; Mighty Casey, All-American 1984. *Contributor to:* Professional journals of over 60 articles and reviews. Choice, 1963–69; America, History and Life, 1964–77; Encyclopedia of Southern History, 1979; Insider Baseball 1983. *Address:* 415 Columbia Avenue, Williamstown, WV 26187, USA.

MURDY, Louise, b. 28 Sep. 1935, Dover, New Hampshire, USA. Associate Professor of English. m. William George Murdy, 23 Aug. 1958, Gainesville, Florida, 1 son, 1 daughter. *Education:* BA(Hons), 1957, PhD, 1962, University of Florida; MA, University of North Carolina, 1958. *Literary Appointments:* Instructor in Humanities, Florida State University, 1962–63; Part-time Assistant Professor of English, 1963–70, Part-time Associate Professor of English, 1970–76. Tenured Associate Professor of English, 1976–, Winthrop College, South Carolina. *Publications:* Sound and Sense in Dylan Thomas's Poetry, 1966. *Contributions to:* Encyclopedia Americana, 1971–. *Memberships:* South Atlantic Modern Language Association; Southeastern 19th Century Studies Association. *Address:* Department of English, 333 Kinard Building, Winthrop College, Rock Hill, SC 19730, USA.

MURPHY, Clive (Hunter), b. 28 Nov. 1935, Liverpool, England. Writer; Recorder/Editor. *Education:* BA, LL B, Trinity College, Dublin; Solicitor, Incorporated Law Society of Ireland. *Publications:* (Novels) Freedom for Mr Mildew, 1975; Nigel Someone, 1975; Summer Overtures, 1976; (Tape Recorded and Eited Autobiographies), The Good Deeds of a Good Woman, by Beatrice Ali, 1976; Born to Sing, by Alexander Hartog, 1978; Four Acres and a Donkey, by S.A.B. Rogers, 1979; Love, Dears!, by Marjorie Davison, 1980; A Funny Old Quist, by Evan Rogers 1981; Oiky, by Len Mills, 1984. *Contributor to:* Short Stories in, Books & Bookmen; Over 21; Cara; PEN Broadsheet. *Honour:*

Joint Winner, Adam International Review, 1st Naval Award for abridged original version of, Summer Overtures, 1968. *Memberships:* Authors' Club; Society of Authors. *Address:* 132 Brick Lane, London E1 6RU, England.

MURPHY, Emmett Jefferson, b. 2 July 1926, Thomasville, Georgia, USA. Educational Administrator. m. Mildred T Blackman, 7 Mar. 1954, Washington DC, 1 son, 2 daughters. *Education:* AB, MA, Emory University; PhD, University of Connecticut. *Publications:* Understanding Africa, 1969; History of African Civilization, 1972; Teaching Africa Today, 1973; The Bantu Civilization of Southern Africa, 1974; Creative Philanthropy: Carnegie Corporation and Africa, 1975; Understanding Africa, revised 1978. *Address:* 83 Crossbrook Road, Amherst, MA, USA.

MURPHY, Gordon John, b. 16 Feb. 1927, Milwaukee, Wisconsin, USA. Professor of Electrical Engineering and Computer Science. m. Dorothy F Brautigam, 26 June 1948, Milwaukee, 1 son, 1 daughter. *Education:* BS, 1949, Milwaukee School of Engineering; MS, 1952, University of Wisconsin; PhD, 1956, University of Minnesota. *Publications:* Basic Automatic Control Theory, 1957, 2nd Edition, 1966; Control Engineering, 1959. *Contributions to:* Numerous technical and engineering journals. *Address:* 638 Garden Court, Glenview, IL 60025, USA.

MURPHY, John William, b. 3 Nov. 1948, Youngstown, Ohio, USA. University Professor. m. Karen Calaghan, 10 Oct. 1981, 1 daughter. *Education:* BA, Psychology, Kent State University, Kent, Ohio, 1972; MA, Sociology, Ohio University, Athens, Ohio, 1974; PhD, Sociology, Ohio State University, Columbus, Ohio, 1981. *Literary Appointments:* Research Assistant, Kent State University, 1970–71; Research Assistant, Sociology Department, Ohio University, 1972–74; Instructor of Sociology (part-time) Cuyahoga Community College, Cleveland, Ohio, 1977–79; Teaching Associate, Ohio State University, 1979–81; Director, Research and Program Evaluation, Community Action Against Addiction, Cleveland, Ohio, 1976–79; Research Assistant, The Academy for Contemporary Problems, Columbus, Ohio, 1979–80; Research Associate, Assessing Non-Integrative Law in the Black Community, 1979–82; Assistant Professor of Sociology, Muskingum College, New Concord, Ohio, 1981–82; Director, Program Evaluation, Health Careers Opportunity Program, Ohio State University, May-Aug 1982; Assistant Professor of Sociology Capital University, Columbus, Ohio, Summer 1982; Assistant Professor of Sociology, Arkansas State University, Jonesboro, Arkansas. *Publications:* The Social Philosophy of Martin Buber, 1982; Qualitative Methodology: Theory and Practice, A Guide to the Social Practitioner, 1983. *Contributions to:* Numerous articles and book reviews in Evaluation News; Human Studies; Diogenes; East European Quarterly; New Orleans Review; Listening; The Churchman; American Journal of Theology and Philosophy; The American Journal of Economics and Sociology; Canadian Community Law Journal; The International Journal of the Additions; Philosophy Today; History of European Ideas; Studies in Soviet Thought and many others. *Memberships include:* North Central Sociology Association; National Institute of Drug Abuse, Program Evaluation Task Force, 1978, 1979; North American Society for Social Philosophy, Chairman, Sociology Division, 1983–; Consultant, Franklin County Community mental Health Board, Ohio, 1983–. *Address:* 2216 Hamilton Avenue, Poland, OH 44514, USA.

MURPHY, Rhoads, b. 13 Aug. 1919, Philadelphia, Pennsylvania, USA. Professor of History and Asian Studies. m. Eleanor Albertson, 12 Jan. 1952, Burlington, New Jersey, 2 sons, 2 daughters. *Education:* AB magna cum laude 1941, MA History 1942, MA China 1948, PhD History and Geography 1950, Harvard University. *Literary Appointments:* Editor, Journal of Asian Studies, 1959–65; Editor, Michigan Papers in Chinese Studies, 1967–72. *Publications:* Shanghai: Key To Modern China, 1953; Approaches to Chinese History, 1968; The

Outsiders: Westerners in India and China, 1977; The Mozartian Historian, 1976; The Fading of the Naoist Vision, 1980. *Contributions to:* Scholarly journals. *Honours:* SSBC Fellow, 1948–50; Ford Fellow, 1955–56; Guggenheim and ACLS Fellow, 1966–67; NETH Fellow, 1972–73; JSPS Fellow, 1978–79; Best Book of the Year Award, 1979. *Address:* Department of History, University of Michigan, Ann Arbor, MI 48109, USA.

MURPHY, Richard, b. 6 Aug. 1927, Republic of Ireland. Poet. 1 son, 1 daughter. *Education:* Scholar 1945, BA Honours English 1948, MA 1968, Magdalen College, Oxford, England. *Literary Appointments:* Visiting Lecturer, Reading University, England, 1968; Compton Lecturer in poetry, Hull University, 1969; Visiting O'Connor Professor of Literature, Colgate University, 1971; Visiting Professor; Bard College 1972, Princeton University 1974, Iowa University 1976, Syracuse University 1977; Distinguished Visiting Poet, Catholic University, Washington DC, 1983; Distinguished Writer in residence, Pacific Lutheran University, Tacoma, Washington, 1985. *Publications:* The Archaeology of Love, 1955; Sailing To An Island, 1963; The Battle of Aughrim, 1968; High Island, 1974; High Island: New and Selected Poems, 1975; Selected Poems, 1979; Care, 1982; The Price of Stone, 1985; The Price of Stone and Earlier Poems, 1985. *Contributions to:* The Times Literary Supplement; Irish Literary Supplement; New York Review of Books; Grand Street; Poetry; Sewanee Review; Massachusetts Review; Yale Review; The Reporter; New Statesman; Listener; Irish Times; Poetry Australia; Digraphe, Paris; Ramp, Netherlands; Helix, Australia. etc. *Honours:* A Memorial Award for Poetry, Ireland, 1951; First Prize, Guinness Awards, Cheltenham, England, 1962; 2 British Arts Council Awards, 1967 and 1976; Marten Toonder Award, Ireland, 1980; American Irish Foundation Literary Award, 1983. *Memberships:* Fellow, Royal Society of Literature; Acsdana, Ireland. *Address:* Knockbrack, Glenalua Road, Killiney, County Dublin, Republic of Ireland.

MURPHY, Richard Thomas, b. 23 Nov. 1908, Minneapolis, Minnesota, USA. Roman Catholic Priest, Professor. *Education:* STD; SSD. *Publications:* History of Israel 1-11, translator, 1955; The Sunday Gospels/Epistles, 1960–61; The Passion of Christ, translation and commentary, 1965; Background To The Bible, 1978; Days of Glory, 1980. *Honour:* Master in Sacred Theology, 1960. *Membership:* Catholic Biblical Association. *Address:* 775 Harrison Avenue, New Orleans, LA 70124, USA.

MURPHY, Thomas, b.23 Feb. 1937, Tuam, County Galway, Republic of Ireland. Playwright. m. Mary Hamilton Hippisley, 14 Nov. 1966, Palma, Majorca, 2 sons, 1 daughter. *Education:* Vocational Engineering Teachers Diploma, 1957. *Literary Appointments:* Writer in association, Druid Theatre Company, Galway, 1983–. *Publications include:* Stage plays: On The Outside, 1959; A Whistle in the Dark, 1961; Famine, 1966; The Orphans, 1968; The Fooleen: A Crucial Week in the Life of a Grower's Assistant, 1969; The Morning After Optimism, 1971; The White House, 1973; On The Inside, 1974; The Vicar of Wakefield, adaptation, 1974; The Sanctuary Lamp, 1975; The J Arthur Maginni, Story, 1976; Epitaph Under Ether, 1968; The Blue Macushla, 1980; The Informer, adaptation, 1981; She Stoops to Conquer, adaptation, transplantation, 1982; The Gigli Concert, 1983; Conversations on a Homecoming, 1985; Bailegangaire, 1985; Bailegangaire II (A Thief of a Christmas), 1985; Television plays for BBC, Thames and RTE. *Honours:* Irish Academy of Letters Award for Distinction in Literature, 1973; Harvey's and Independent Newspaper Awards for Play of the Year, 1983–84. *Memberships:* Irish Academy of Letters; Acadana; Writer's Guild of Great Britain; Society of Irish Playwrights; Board of Directors, Irish National Theatre, The Abbey Theatre, 1972–83; International Committee on English in the Liturgy, 1972–75; Founder member, Moli Productions, 1974. *Literary Agents:* Fraser and Dunlop Scripts Ltd, London; ICM, 46 West 57th Street, New York, NY

10019, USA. *Address:* 46 Terenure Road West, Dublin 6, Republic of Ireland.

MURPHY, Walter Francis, b. 21 Nov. 1929, Charleston, South Carolina, USA. Professor; Writer. m. Mary Therese Dolan, 28 June 1952, Davenport, Iowa, 2 daughters. *Education:* BA, University of Notre Dame, 1950; MA, George Washington University, 1954; PhD, University of Chicago, 1957. *Literary Appointments:* McCormick Professor, Princeton University, New Jersey. *Publications:* Congress and the Court, 1962; Elements of Judicial Strategy, 1964; Wiretapping on Trial, 1965; The Vicar of Christ, 1979; The Roman Enigma, 1981. Co-Author: The Study of Public Law, 1971; Public Evaluation of Constitutional Courts, 1973; American Democracy, 10th edition, 1983. Co-Author and Co-Editor: Modern American Democracy, 1969; Basic Cases in Constitutional Law; Comparative Constitutional Law, 1977; Courts, Judges and Politics, 4th Edition, 1986; American Constitutional Interpretation, 1986. *Contributions to:* Numerous professional publications. *Honours:* Birkhead Award, 1958; Adolphe Menjou Award, American Civil Liberties, 1963; Award, Chicago Foundation for Literature, 1980. *Membership:* Authors Guild. *Literary Agent:* Robert Lantz, New York. *Address:* 240 Western Way, Princeton, NJ 08540, USA.

MURRAY, Steven T, b. 7 Oct. 1943, Berkeley, California, USA. Publisher, Translator. m. Tiina K. Nunnally, Copenhagen, Denmark, 5 Oct. 1985. *Education:* Stanford University, 1961–64, 1968; BA English, California State University, Hayward, 1972; Graduate School of Scandinavian Studies, University of California, Berkeley, 1981–82. *Literary Appointment:* Publisher, Fjord Press, 1981–. *Major Publications:* Translations of: The Sardine Deception by Leif Davidsen; Witness to the Future by Klaus Rifbjerg. *Contributor to:* Scandinavian Review; Translation; Berkeley Fiction Review. *Honour:* Award of Translation Centre, Columbia University for work on translating Rifbjerg. *Membership:* American Literary Translators Association. *Address:* PO Box 16501, Seattle, WA 98116, USA.

MURRAY, William Hutchison, b. 18 Mar. 1913, Liverpool, England. Author. m. Anne Burnet Clark, 1 Dec. 1960. *Publications:* Author of 21 books including: Mountaineering in Scotland, 1947; Undiscovered Scotland, 1951; Scottish Himalayan Expedition, 1951; The Story of Everest, 1953; The Hebrides, 1966; Companion Guide to West Highlands, 1968; The Western Islands of Scotland, 1973; The Scottish Highlands, 1976; Rob Roy MacGregor, biography, 1982. *Contributions to:* Numerous publications. *Honours:* Mungo Park Medal, Royal Scottish Geographical Society, 1950; Literary award, US Education Board, 1954; OBE, 1966; Honorary Doctorate, University of Sterling, Scotland, 1975. *Address:* Lochwood, Loch Goil, Argyll, Scotland.

MURRAY-SMITH, Stephen, b. 9 Sep. 1922, Melbourne, Australia. University Teacher; Wrtier. m. Nita Bluthal, 6 Feb. 1948, Melbourne, 1 son, 2 daughters. *Education:* BA, BEd, PhD, University of Melbourne. *Appointment:* Founder, Editor, Overland, 1954–. *Publications:* Henry Lawson, 1962, 1975; An Overland Muster, 1965; Marcus Clark: His Natural Life, 1970; Mission to the Islands, 1979; Indirections, 1981; The Dictionary of Australian Quotations, 1984. *Contributor to:* Numerous professional journals and magazines. *Honour:* Member of the Order of Australia, 1981. *Address:* PO Box 249 Mount Eliza, Victoria 3930, Australia.

MURTI, Kotikalapudi Venkata Suryanarayana, b. 9 May 1925, Parlakemidi, India. Reader in English; Teacher; Research Guide. *Education:* MA, English Language & Literature, 1963, PhD, English, 1972, Andhra University; Certificate in Linguistics, Central Institute of English and Foreign Languages, Hyderabad, 1969. *Publications include:* The Allegory of Eternity, 1975; The Triple-Light, 1975; Sparks of the Absolute, 1976; Spectrum, 1976; Symphony of Discords, 1977; Waves of Illumination, 1978; Thamlo Param, 1979;

Lilahela, 1981; Araku, 1982; The Sword & the Sickle: A Study of Mulk Raj Anand's Novels, 1983. *Contributor to:* Numerous journals including: Poet, Indian Editor; World Literature Today, Review Committee. *Memberships include:* International Academy of Poets; World University Round Table, Tucson, USA. *Honours:* Recipient of Numerous Honours including Honorary DLitt, University Asia, 1970; World University, 1977. *Address:* Andhra University, Visakhapatnam 530 002, (AP), India.

MUSE, Benjamin, b. 17 Apr. 1898, Durham, North Carolina, USA. m. Beatrig de Regil, 3 Sep. 1926, London, 2 sons, 3 daughters. *Education:* Trinity College (now Duke University); George Washington University. *Publications:* Virginia's Massive Resistance, 1961; Ten Years of Prelude, 1964; The American Negro Revolution 1968. *Contributor to:* Washington Post; Harper's; Nation; Reporter; New Republic. *Honours:* James Hoey Award for Interracial Justice, 1962. *Address:* 11400 Washington Plaza West, Reston, VA 22090, USA.

MUSETTO, Andrew P, b. 6 Feb. 1945, Morristown, New Jersey, USA. Psychologist. m. dissolved, 2 daughters. *Education:* BA, Seton Hall University, 1966; MA, 1972, PhD, 1973, Temple University, Philadelphia, Pennsylvania. *Major Publication:* Dilemmas in Child Custody: Family Conflicts & Their Resolution, 1982. *Contributor to:* Review of Religious Research; Journal of Marriage & Family Counseling; Family Therapy; Journal of Contemporary Psychotherapy; Journal of Divorce; Journal of Clinical Child Psychology; Family Relations; USA Today. *Address:* c/o Psychological Service Associates, 49 Grove Street, Suite C, Haddonfield, NJ 08033, USA.

MUSGRAVE, Susan, b. 12 Mar. 1951, Santa Cruz, California, USA. Writer. *Appointments:* Writer in Residence: University of Waterloo, 1983–85; University of New Brunswick, Summer 1985. *Publications include:* (Fiction), The Charcoal Burners, 1980; Hag Head, 1980; (Poetry) Songs of the Sea-Witch, 1970; Entrance of the Celebrant, 1972; Grave-Dirt and Selected Strawberries, 1973; Gullband, 1974; The Impstone, 1976; Kiskatinaw Songs, 1977; Becky Swan's Book, 1978; A Man to Marry, a Man to Bury, 1979; Tarts and Muggers: Poems New and Selected, 1982; Cocktails at the Mausoleum, 1985; Numerous Phamphlets and Broadsides, etc. *Contributor to:* Numerous Anthologies; Saturday Night; Toronto Life; Exile; Malahat Review; Canadian Forum; Queen's Quarterly; West Coast Review; Second Aeon; Ambit; Poetry Review; Helix; Poetry Australia, and many other magazines; Poems broadcast on CBC, and Poetry Now, Radio 3, BBC, London. *Agent:* Lucinda Vardy, Toronto, Canada. *Address:* 2407 Tryon Road, RR #3, Sidney, BC V8L 3X9, Canada.

MUSIKER, Reuben b. 12 Jan. 1931, Johannesburg, South Africa. Librarian. m. Naomi Messroch, 9 Apr. 1961, Johannesburg, 1 son, 2 daughters. *Education:* MA; BSc; H Dip Lib; FSAILIS. *Publications:* South Africa, 1979; South African Bibliography, 2nd edition, 1980; Companion to South African Libraries, 1985. *Contributor to:* 150 articles in various journals. *Honours:* Ad Hominem Professorship, University of the Witwatersrand, 1980; Award for Bibliography, South African Institute for Librarianship and Information Science, 1985. *Address:* University of the Witwatersrand Library, Private Bag 31550, Braamfontein 2017, South Africa.

MUSKE, Carol Anne, b. 17 Dec. 1945, St Paul, Minnesota, USA. Writer. m. David Dukes, 31 Jan. 1983, 1 daughter. *Education:* MA, State University of California, San Francisco, 1970. *Literary Appointments:* New York University; Columbia University; University of California, Irvine; Iowa Writers Workshop; University of Southern California. *Publications:* Camouflage, 1975; Skylight, 1981; Wyndmere, 1985. *Contributions to:* Poetry: The New Yorker; APR; Field; Esquire; Ms and Others. Critical reviews: New York Times; Los Angeles Times Book Review. *Honours:* Dylan Thomas Poetry

Award, 1972; Alice Fay Di Castagnola Award, Poetry Society, 1979; John Simon Guggenheim Foundation Fellowship, 1981; National Endowment for the Arts, 1984. *Memberships:* Poets, Playwrights, Editors, Essayists and Novelists; Authors Guild; Poets and Writers; Poetry Society of America.

MUSOLF, Lloyd Daryl, b.14 Oct. 1919, Yale, South Dakota, USA. University Professor. m. Berdyne Peet, 20 June 1944, Minneapolis, Minnesota, 1 son, 2 daughters. *Education:* BA, Huron College, 1941; MA, University of South Dakota, 1946; PhD, Johns Hopkins University, 1950. *Publications:* Federal Examiners and the Conflict of Law and Administration, 1953; Public Ownership and Accountability: The Canadian Experience, 1959; Promoting The General Welfare: Government and the Economy, 1965; Legislatures in Developmental Perspective, 1970; Malaysia's Parliamentary System: Representative Politics and Policymaking in a Divided Society, 1979; Mixed Enterprise: A Developmental Perspective, 1972; Legislatures in Development: Dynamics of Change in New and Old States, 1979; Uncle Sam's Private, Profitseeking Corporations: Comsat, Fannie Mae, Amtrak and Conrail, 1982. *Contributions to:* American Political Science Review; Public Administration Review; Western Political Quarterly; Legislative Studies Quarterly; George Washington Law Review; Journal of Comparative Administration; Policy Studies Jurnal; International Review of Administrative Sciences; Asian Survey; Public Personnel Review. *Address:* 3215 Bermuda Avenue No 13, Davis, CA 95616, USA.

MUSSELL, John William, b. 9 July 1942, Salisbury, Wiltshire, England. Publisher; Editor. m. Mary Rose Moody, 18 May 1964, Bishopstone, 2 sons. *literary Appointment:* 1982 Editor, Coin & Medal News; Editor, The Searcher, 1985. *Contributions to:* Art & Antiques Weekly; Equilibrium, magazine, International Society of Antique Scale Collectors; Coin & Medal News. *Address:* Chestnut Cottage, Bowcott Hill, Headley, Bordon, Hampshire, England.

MUSTO, Gordon Barry, b. 18 Jan. 1930, Birmingham, England. Public Relations. m. Jean Mackie, 29 Apr. 1954, Birmingham, 1 son. *Publications:* The Lawrence Barclay File; Storm Centre; The Sunless Land; The Fatal Flaw; Codename Bastille; No Way Out; The Weighted Scales; The Lebanese Partner. *Contributions to:* BBC Morning Story; Technical Journals; Enginering media. *Memberships:* Crime Writers Association; Past Chairman, Birmingham Writers Group. *Address:* Thistles, Little Addington, Kettering, Northamptonshire, England.

MUTO, Susan Annette, University Professor. *Education:* BA, Journalism and English; MA, English Literature; PhD, English Literature. *Publications:* Approaching the Sacred, 1973; Steps Along the Way, 1975; A Practical Guide to Spiritual Reading, 1976; The Journey Homeward, 1977; Renewed At Each Awakening, 1979; Celebrating the Single Life, 1982; Blessings That Make Us Be, 1982; Pathways of Spiritual Living, 1984. *Contributions to:* Envoy; Studies in Formative Spirituality; The Catholic Woman; Contemplative Review; Sign; The Annals of St Anne de Beaupre; Proceedings of the Fourteenth and Fifteenth General Assemblies Consortium Perfectae Caritatis; Catholic Library World; Cross and Crown; Spiritual Life; Praying; Our Lady of Fatima Magazine; Humanitas. Managing Editor of Envoy and Studies in Formative Spirituality. *Honour:* Phi Kappa Phi Honor Society. *Address:* Institute of Formative Spirituality, Rockwell Hall, Duquesne University, Pittsburgh, PA 15282, USA.

MUUSS, Rolf Eduard, b. 26 Sep. 1924, Tating, Germany. Professor; Director, Special Education. m. Gertrude Kremser, 22 Dec. 1953, Santa Monica, USA, 1 son, 1 daughter. *Education:* Teaching Diploma, Padagogische Hochschule, Flensburg, Germany, 1951; University of Hamburg, 1951; Central Missouri State College, USA, 1951–52; Teachers College, Columbia University, USA, 1952; MEd, Western Maryland College, 1954; PhD, University of Illinois, 1957. *Appointments:* Graduate Assistant, University of Illinois, 1954–57; Research Assistant, Professor, State University of Iowa, 1957–59; Associate Professor, 1959–64, Professor, 1964–, Director, Special Education, 1977–, Goucher College. *Publications include:* First Aid for Classroom Discipline Problems, 1962; Adolescent Behavior and Society: A Book of Readings, 3rd edition 1980; Theories of Adolescence, 4th edition, 1982; Grundlagen der Adoleszentenpsychologie, 1982; Chapters in Books; Scientific papers; etc. *Contributor to:* Pedagogiska Forum; MEA Journal; Adolescence; Journal of Verbal Learning and Verbal Behavior; Journal of Experimental Education; Journal of Personality; Many other professional and scholarly journals. *Honours:* Mary Wilhelm Williams Felowship, Social Sciences, 1972, 1973; Andrew Mellon Foundation Grant for Faculty Development, 1976–77; Goucher College Award for Distinguished Scholarship, 1979; Elizabeth C Todd Distinguished Professorship, endowed Chair, 1980–85. *Memberships:* Fellow, American Psychological Association; Treasurer, 1971–73, Maryland Psychological Association; Vice President, 1970–71, Baltimore Psychological Association; Society for Research in Child Development; Council for Exceptional Children; Phi Delta Kappa; Kappa Delta Pi, Chapter Vice President, 1956–57. *Address:* Goucher College, Towson, MD 21204, USA.

MWANJA, Geoffrey Daniel, b. 10 Nov. 1949, Bupigu, Chitipa. Senior Administrative Officer. m. Emily Ndagha Mushani, 2 Sep. 1978, Lilongwe, 2 sons, 2 daughters. *Contributor to:* Odi; University Magazine; Sandcutters Magazine, USA; Tantam Magazine, India; The Other Poetry Book, USA; World Anthology of Poetry, USA. *Membership:* Malami Writers Group. *Address:* c/o Office of the President & Cabinet, PB 301, Capital City, Lilongwe, S E Africa.

MYCUE, Edward Delehant Benedict, b. 21 Mar. 1937, Niagara Falls, New York, USA. Poet. *Education:* BA, North Texas State University, 1959. *Literary Appointments:* MacDowell Fellow, 1974. *Publications:* Damage Within The Community, 1973; Root, Route and Range: The Song Returns, 1979; The Singing Man My Father Gave Me, 1980; Briefing The Wave, 1986; Village, 1986. *Contributions to:* Magazines and journals including: Antigonish; Meanjin; Stand; Gypsy; Frank; Mockersatz; Yellow Silk; No Apologies; Fag Rag; Pearl; European Judaism; Littack Supplement; Box of Rain; Moorlands; Akros; My Best Friend; Green's; Ally; Poetry Now; Contant II; M: Gentle Men for Gender Justice; Androgeny; RFD; Real Fiction. *Honours:* MacDowell Fellow, 1974. *Memberships:* Poetry Society of America; National Writers' Union; PEN; Small Press Writers' Workshops. *Address:* PO Box 640543, San Francisco, CA 94164–0543, USA.

MYERS, Arthur, b. 24 Oct. 1917, Buffalo, New York, USA. Writer. *Education:* BA, Hobart College. *Publications:* Safety Last: An Indictment of the Auto Industry, 1965; Careers for the Seventies: Journalism, 1970; The Ghost Hunters, 1980; Kids Do Amazing Things, 1980; Sea Creatures Do Amazing Things, 1981; Why You Feel Down and What You Can Do About It, (co-author), 1982. *Contributions:* Over 50 short stories and 100 articles published. *Honours:* 3 Press Awards in the 1950's. *Memberships:* American Society Of Journalists and Authors; PEN; Society of Children's Books Writers. *Literary Agent:* Adele Leone. *Address:* 315 Boston Post Road, Weston, MA 02193, USA.

MYERS, Burton James, b. 3 Feb. 1949, Toronto, Canada. Editor. m. Anna Zeilinski, 8 Sep. 1970, Toronto, 1 son, 1 daughter. *Education:* Journalism Diploma, Centennial College of Applied Arts and Technology. *Literary Appointments:* Editor, Ontario Out of Doors, magazine. *Honours:* Greg Clark Outdoor Editorial Writing Award, 1978; Outdoor Writers of Canada Photo Contest Award of Merit, 1984 and 1985. *Membership:* President 1984–85, Outdoor Writers of Canada. *Address:* RR I, Brooklin, Ontario, LOB 1C0, Canada.

MYERS, Jack Elliott, b. 29 Nov. 1941, Lynn, Massachusetts, USA. Professor of English. m. Willa Naomi Robins, 15 Aug. 1980, Atlanta, 3 sons. *Education:* BA, University of Massachusetts, 1970; MFA, University of Iowa, 1972. *Publications:* Black Sun Abraxas, 1970; Will It Burn, 1974; The Family War, 1977; I'm Amazed That You're Still Singing, 1981; A Trout in the Milk, 1982; New American Poets of the '80's, 1984; The Longman Dictionary & Handbook of Poetry, 1985; As Long as You're Happy, 1986. *Contributor to:* Esquire; American Poetry Review; Antaeus; Poetry: A Magazine of Verse; Iowa Review; Minnesota Review; Virginia Quarterly Review; Georgia, Missouri, and Southern Poetry Reviews; Ploughshares; Southwest Review; Fiction International; The Nation, etc. *Honours:* Texas Institute of Letters Poetry Award, 1978; Elliston Book Award, 1978; National Endowment for the Arts Fellowship, 1982. *Memberships:* PEN; Associated Writing Programs; Texas Institute of Letters; Texas Association of Creative Writing Teachers. *Address:* Dept of English, Southern Methodist University, Dallas, TX 75275, USA.

MYERS, John Myers, b. 11 Jan. 1906, Northport, Long Island, New York, USA. Writer. m. Charlotte Shanahan, 15 Jan. 1943, Louisville, Kentucky, USA, 2 daughters. *Education:* St Stephens College; Middlebury College; University of New Mexico. *Literary Appointments:* Special Lecturer & Writer's Conference Director, Arizona State University, 1948–49. *Publications include:* The Harp and the Blade, 1941; Out on Any Limb, 1942; The Wild Yazoo, 1947; The Alamo, 1948; Silverlook, 1949; The Last Chance, 1950; Maverick Zone, 1961; Doc Holliday, 1955; Dead Warrior, 1956; I, Jack Swilling, 1961; Maverick Zone, 1961; The Deaths of the Bravos, 1962; Pirate, Pawnee and Mountain Man: The Saga of Hugh Glass, 1963; Building a State in Apache Lane, 1963 (Editor); San Francisco's Reign of Terror, 1966; Print in a Wild Lane, 1967; The Westerners: A Roundup of Pioneer Reminiscences, 1969, (Editor); The Border Wardens, 1971; The Moon's Fire Eating Daughter, 1981. Poems: The Ballad of Shotgun Ed, 1951; Pete Kitchen Cashes In, 1953; The Sack of Calahassas, 1958. *Contributions to:* Numerous Western publications. *Membership:* Western Writers of America. *Address:* 6515 East Hermosa Vista Drive, Mesa, A2 85205, USA.

MYERS, Ramon H, b. 31 Aug. 1929, Toledo, Ohio, USA. Scholar of East Asian International Relations and Modern History. m. Edna L Bellah, 15 Mar. 1980, San Jose, California, 1 son, 1 daughter. *Education:* BA, Far Eastern Studies, 1954; MA, Economics, 1956; PhD, Economics, 1960. *Literary Appointments:* Curator, Scholar, East Asian Collection, Hoover Institution, Stanford, California, 1975–. *Publications:* The Chinese Peasant Economy: Agricultural Development of Hopei and Shantung Provinces from 1895–1949, 1970; Two Chinese States; United States Foreign Policy and Interests, 1978; The Chinese Economy: Past and Present, 1980; I A US Foreign Policy for Asia; The 1980s and Beyond, 1982; The Economic Development of Manchuria, 1932–45, 1982; The Japanese Colonial Empire, 1984; Understanding Communist China, 1986. *Contributions to:* Asian Survey, Volume 28 No. 4, Apr. 1983; The China Quarterly, No.99, 1984. *Address:* East Asian Collection, Hoover Institution, Stanford, CA 94305, USA.

MYERS, Robert Manson, b. 29 May 1921, Charlottesville, Virginia, USA. University Professor. *Education:* BA, Vanderbilt University, 1941; MA 1942, PhD

1948, Columbia University; MA, Harvard University, 1943. *Literary Appointments:* Instructor in English, Yale University, 1945–47; Assistant Professor of English, College of Williamand Mary, 1947–48; Assistant Professor of English, Tulane University, 1948–53; Assistant Professor of English 1959–63, Associate Professor 1963–68, Professor 1969–. University of Maryland. *Publications:* Handel's Messiah: A Touchstone of Taste, 1948; From Beowulf to Virginia Woolf, 1952, revised and enlarged edition 1984; Handel, Dryden and Milton, 1956; Restoration Comedy, 1961; The Children of Pride, 1972, abridged edition 1984; A Georgian at Princeton, 1976. *Contributions to:* Publications of the Modern Language Association; Harvard Theological Review; The Musical Quarterly. *Honours:* Fulbright Research Fellow, University of London, 1953–54; Fulbright Lecturer, Rotterdam, The Netherlands, 1958–59; National Book Award, 1973. *Memberships:* Jane Austen Society; Jane Austen Society of America. *Address:* 2101 Connecticut Avenue NW, Washington, DC 20008, USA.

MYNOTT, Roger Jeremy, b. 15 Feb. 1942, Colchester, Essex, England. Publishing. *Education:* MA 1961–64, PhD 1965–68, Corpus Christi College, Cambridge. *Literary Appointments:* Various editorial positions 1968–, currently Editorial Director of Humanities and Social Sciences, Director of Publishing Development 1982–, Cambridge University Press. *Address:* Lavender Cottage, Little Thurlow, Suffolk, CB9 7LA, England.

MYRSIADES, Kostas John, b. 21 May 1940, Samos, Greece. Comparative Literature. m. Linda Suny Myrsiades, 6 June 1965, Philadelphia, 1 son, 1 daughter. *Education:* BA, Iowa University, 1963; MA, 1965, PhD, 1972, Indiana University. *Appointments:* Instructor, English, Homer Institute, Athens, Greece, 1965–66; Assistant Professor, English, Westchester University, USA, 1969–73; Assistant Professor, Modern Greek, Degree College, Athens, Greece, 1973–74; Associate Professor of English, Westchester University, 1974–76; Professor, English, Comparative Literature, Westchester University, 1976–. *Publications:* Takis Papatsonis, 1974; Scripture of the Blind, 1979. *Contributor to:* Numerous professional journals. *Honours:* Dissertation Grant, 1967; Research Grants, Westchester University, 1976, 1980, 1982; Lily Fellow, University of Pennsylvania, 1981; Philadelphia Council of the Humanities Grant, 1983; Faculty merit Award, Westchester University, 1984. *Memberships:* Modern Language Association; Modern Greek Studies Association; American Literary Translators Association; National Association of Self-Instructional Programmes; Association of Pennsylvania State Colleges and Universities Faculty; Hellenic-American League. *Address:* 370 N Malin Road, Newtown Square, PA 19073, USA.

MYSS, Walter, b. 22 Sep. 1920, Kronstadt (Brasov), Transylvania. Writer and Publisher. m. Eva Lubinger, 7 Oct. 1952, 2 sons. *Education:* Dr Phil *Appointments:* Owner Wort und Welt Verlag, Austria, 1972–present. *Publications:* (selection): St Paulus auf der Schaukel, 1963; Kaiser, Künstler, Kathedralen, 1972; Hat Europas Kunst Zukunft, (4 volumes), 1978–85. *Honours:* Dehio Preis Esslingen, 1968; Prof. h.c. Austria, 1975; Silbernes Ehrenzeichen, Republik Osterreich, 1982; Ehrenzeichen für Kultur, Innsbruck, 1983. *Membership:* PEN Austria. *Literary Agent:* Wort und Welt Verlag, Innsbruck. *Address:* Lindenbühelweg 16, 6020 Innsbruck Austria.

N

NA'AMAN, Shlomo, b. 10 Nov. 1912, Essen, Germany. Professor of Social History. *Education:* BA; MA; PhD; Jerusalem. *Publications include:* Die Konstituierung der deutschen Arbeiterbewegung 1862–63, 1975; (in Hebrew) The Birth of a Civilization, the first Millenium of Latin Europe, 1975; Von der Arbeiterbewwegung zur Arbeiterpartei, 1976; Lassalle, 1970; Emanzipation und Messianismus. Leben und Werk des Moses Hess, 1982; Der Deutsche Nationalverein die politische Konstituierung des deutschen Burgertums, 1986. *Contributions to:* International Review of Social History; Jahrbuch fur Sozialgeschichte; International Wissenschaftliche Korrespondenz; Jahrbuch des Instituts fur deutsche Geschichte, University of Tel-Aviv. *Address:* Tagorestreet 42, Tel-Aviv/Ramath-Aviv, Israel.

NAGAYAMA, Mokuo, b. 14 Dec. 1929. Teacher. *Education:* Doshisha College of Foreign Affairs, Japan, 1950. *Publications:* Snow Bridge, 1976; Mist on the Ridge, 1985. *Contributions to:* Poetry Nippon; Mundus Artium, USA; International Poetry, USA; New Muses, USA; Counterpoint, England; The Field, England; Iron, England; Orbis, England; Little Word Machine, England; Poet, India; Amber, Canada; Noreal, France; Poesie Sonore, Switzerland; Monthly Review, New Zealand; Poems Convidado, USA; Inky Trails; USA; Success, England, India. *Honours:* 2nd prize, Sangamon Writers International Poetry Contest, USA, 1983; 1st prize, Japalish Review Poetry Contest, Japan, 1984; 1st prize, American Poetry Association Contest, USA, 1985. *Memberships:* Poetry Society of Japan; Japan Poets Club; World Poetry Society. *Address:* 1168 Ouchi, Kurashiki, Okayama Prefecture, Japan.

NAGEL, Stuart S, b. 29 Aug. 1934, Chicago, Illinois, USA. Professor; Lawyer. m. Joyce Golub, 1 Sep, 1957, Chicago, 1 son, 1 daughter. *Education:* BS, 1957, JD, 1958, Northwestern University; PhD, Northwestern University, 1961. *Appointments:* Instructor, Pennsylvania State University, 1960–61; Assistant Professor – Professor, University of Illinois, 1962–; Assistant Counsel, US Senate Subcommittee, Administrative Practice and Procedure, 1966–67; Director, Attorney, OEO Legal Services Agency, Champaign County, 1967–70, *Publications include:* Legal Process from a Behavior Perspective, 1969; Rights of the Accused, 1972; Environmental Politics, 1975; Policy Studies and the Social Sciences, 1975; Policy Studies in America and Elsewhere, 1975; Improving the Legal Process, 1975; Operations Reseach Methods, 1976; Modeling the Criminal Justice System, 1977; Legal Policy Analysis: Finding an Optimum Level or Mix, 1977; the Legal Process: Modelling the System, 1977; Policy Studies Review Annual, 1977; Policy Analysis in Social Science Research, 1978; Decision Theory and the Legal Process, 1979; Improving Policy Analysis, 1980; Policy Studies Handbook, 1980; Encyclopedia of Policy Studies, 1982; The Political Science of Criminal Justice, 1982; Policy Evaluation: Making Optimum Decisions, 1982; Public Policy: Goals means and Methods, 1983; Contemporary Public Policy Analysis, 1983. *Contributor to:* Numerous professional journals and magazines. *Honours:* Recipient, numerous honours and awards. *Memberships include:* Policy Studies Organisation, Secretary, Treasurer, Co-Founder; Law and Society Associaton, Editorial Board; American Politicial Science Association; Programme Committee; American Bar Association; etc. *Address:* Political Science Dept, 361 Lincoln Hall, University of Illinois, 702 S Wright Street, Urbana, IL 61801, USA.

NAKOVSKI, Atanas, b. 31 Aug. 1925, Sofia, Writer. *Education:* Economic Faculty, Sofia University. *Literary Appointment:* Vice Editor-in-Chief of literary magazine, Septemvri. *Publications:* Prose: An Endless Street, 1968; Without Shadows, 1970; The Boards of the River, 1971; The World in the Morning, The World in the Evening, 1973; Selected Works, 1975. *Contributor to:*

All main Bulgarian literary editions. *Honour:* An Honoured Worker of Culture, 1980. *Membership:* Union of Bulgarian Writers. *Address:* 48 Boul, Sofia, Bulgaria.

NAMGALIES, Ursula Bautze, b. 15 June 1915, Berlin, Germany. Writer; Painter. m. Bruno Namgalies, 31 May 1936, Tanzania, 3 sons, 3 daughters. *Education:* Abitur, Afrikanistik, University of Berlin, 1934–35. *Publications:* Der junge Bwana, 1955; Afrikanische Weihnachtsgeschichten, 1957, 58; Schwarzer Bruder in Tanganyika, 1960; Wolken über Afrikas Steppen, 1960; Freiheit am Kilimanjaro, 1965; Auf der Brücke von Avignon, 1964; Südafrika zwischen Schwarz und Weiss, 1963; Anweisung zum glucklichen Leben, 1970; Weihnacht in Nord und Süd, 1971; Das Geheimnis von Kilimani Gedi, 1979. *Contributions to:* Numerous booklets on Christian Youth, Senior literature and adventure; Contributions to Christian journals. *Honours:* Gold Medal and Diploma de Maitrise de l'Ordre de Saint Fortunat. *Memberships:* Die Künstlergilde; Federation Internationale Culturelle Feminine, France. *Address:* Coupiac, Brissac, 34 190 Ganges (Herault), France.

NANCEKIVELL, Judith Mary, b. 13 May 1952, Toronto, Canada. Editor. *Education:* BA Hons, University of Toronto, 1979. *Literary Appointments:* Editor, Canadian Plastics, Southam Communications Limited 1981–; Editor, Corpus Plastics Report, Southam Communications Limited, 1982–85. *Honour:* Tom Turner Editorial Award, 1985; President's Award: Best Newsletter. *Membership:* Membership Chairman, National Editors & Writers Society, Toronto. *Address:* 195 Carlton Street, Toronto, Ontario M5A 2K7, Canada.

NARAIN, Laxmi, b. 2 Feb. 1930, Delhi, India. Professor and Principal, University College of Commerce and Business Management, Osmania University. m. Nirmala Devi, 11 Nov. 1951, Delhi, 1 son, 2 daughters. *Education:* B Com Honours, M Com, LL B, Delhi University; PhD, London University, England. *Publications:* Public Enterprise in India: A Study of Public Relations and Annual Reports, 1967; Efficient Audit of Public Enterprise in India, 1972; Managerial Compensation and Motivation in Public Enterprises, 1973; Parliament and Public Enterprise in India, 1979; Principles and Practice of Public Enterprise Management, 1980; Organization Structure in Large Public Enterprises, 1981; Autonomy of Public Enterprises, editor, 1982; Workers Participation in Management in Public Enterprises, 1984; Public Enterprises and Fundamental Rights, co-editor, 1984. *Contributions to:* Over 40 papers to national and international journals. *Honour:* Meritorious Teacher Award for University Teachers, Andhra Pradesh State Government, 1979–80. *Memberships:* Vice-President 1976–77, Indian Association for Management Development; Life member, Indian Institute of Public Administration; Member of Governing Body, Institute of Public Enterprise. *Address:* Department of Business Management, Osmania University, Hyderabad 500 007, India.

NARPATI, B, b. 1920. Belgian National. Financial Journalist. m. Cornelia van Dorp, 1971. *Memberships:* The Institute of Journalists, London; The Society of Authors, London; Royal Economic Society, Cambridge; The American Economic Association, Nashville, Tennessee, USA; The English Centre of International PEN; London Press Club. *Address:* c/o The Institute of Journalists, Bedford Chambers, Covent Garden, London WC2E 8HA, England.

NASH, Andrew John, b. 21 Oct. 1954, Bath, England. Writer; Editor; Publishing Consultant. *Education:* BSc, Honours, Biological Sciences. *Appointment:* Writer in Residence, West End Centre, Aldershot, Hampshire, part-time, 1985. *Publications:* Co-Author, School & College Textbooks, Manuals, Reference Books, etc; An Introduction to Microcomputers in Teaching, with Derek Ball, 1982. *Contributor to:* Microcomputers – for you?, Educational Computing, 1983; Not Quite a Writer, The Author, 1984. *Memberships:* Society for Authors, Committee Member, Educational Writers' Group, 1984–

, Committee Member, Technical Writers' Group Society of Literature; Associate Member, Association of British Science Writers. *Address:* 46 Church Avenue, Farnborough, Hampshire GU14 7AT, England.

NASH, Gerald David, b. 16 July 1928, Berlin, Germany. Historian; University Professor. m. Marie Louise Norris, 19 Aug. 1967, 1 daughter. *Education:* BA, New York University, 1950; MA, Columbia University, 1952; PhD, University of California, Berkeley 1957. *Literary Appointments:* Instructor in History, Stanford University, 1957–58; Assistant Professor of History, N Illinois University, 1958–59; Visiting Assistant Professor of History, Stanford University, 1959–60; Post-Doctoral Fellow, Harvard University, 1960–61; Assistant Professor, 1961–63, Associate Professor, 1963, Professor of History, Chair, 1974–80, Presidential Professor 1985–, University of New Mexico; Visiting Professor, University of Maryland, University of California and New York University. *Publications:* State Government and Economic Development in California, 1964; Ed: Issues in American Economic History, 1964, revised editions 1972, 1980; Ed: F D Roosevelt, 1967; US Oil Policy, 1968; The Great Transition, 1971; Perspectives on Administration, 1971; The American West in the 20th Century, 1973; The Great Depression and World War II, 1979; The American West Transformed, 1985. *Contributor to:* Professional journals of more than 40 articles and 150 book reviews. Editor, The Historian, 1974–1984. *Honours:* Phi Beta Kappa, 1950; Newberry Library Fellow, 1959; Huntington Library Fellow, 1979; National Endowment for Humanities Fellow, 1981. *Memberships:* American Historical Association, Organisation of American Historians; Phi Alpha Theta; Western History Association; Organisation of American Historians; Phi Alpha Theta; Western History Association. *Address:* Department of History, University of New Mexico, Albuquerque, NM 87131, USA.

NASH, Paul, b. 2 Sep, 1924, England. Writer. m. Anne Steere, 27 June 1957, Radnor, Pennysylvania, USA, 1 son, 1 daughter. *Education:* BSc Economics, London School of Economics, England; MEd, Toronto University, Canada; EdD Harvard University, Cambridge, Massachusetts. *Literary Appointments:* Consulting Editor, Random House, 1962–68; Consulting Editor, John Wiley, 1968–75; Editorial Boards of Various Journals. *Major Publications:* The Educated Man, 1965; Authority & Freedom in Education, 1966; Models of Man, 1968; Culture & The State, 1968; History & Education, 1970. *Contributor to:* Various publications – some 100 articles. *Address:* Rhode Island School of Design, Providence, RI 02903, USA.

NASKILA, Marja, b. 20 July 1946, Pori, Finland. Author, m. Heikki Naskila, 19 Mar. 1973. *Education:* MA. *Publications:* Awake in the Dark, 1976; Woman's Life, 1978; At Our Farm in the Country, 1981; A Farmer's Wife in Finland, 1982; The Rebuilding Time (Post-World War II), 1985. *Contributions to:* Various journals and newspapers. *Honours include:* 12 awards, 1976–85, including Information Award, 1983, Award, Cultural Treasury of Finland, 1985, etc. *Memberships:* Association of Writers in Finland; Writers of Salpausselkä. *Literary Agent:* Otava, 1976–78; Kirjayhtymä, 1979–. *Address:* 12100 Oitti, Finland.

NASSAR, Eugene Paul, b. 20 June 1935, Utica, New York, USA. Professor of English. m. Utica, New York, 1 son, 2 daughters. *Education:* BA, Kenyon College, Ohio, 1957; MA, Worcester College, Oxford University, England, 1960; PhD, Cornell University, Ithaca, New York, USA, 1962. *Literary Appointments:* Professor of English, Utica College of Syracuse University, New York, 1971–. *Publications:* Wallace Stevens: An Anatomy of Figuration, 1965, 68; The Rape of Cinderella: Essays in Literary Continuity, 1970; Selection from a Prose Poem: East Utica, 1971; The Cantos of Ezra Pound: The Lyric Mode, 1975; Essays: Critical and Metacritical, 1983. *Contributions to:* College English; Renascence; Essays in Criticism; Piadeuma; Masaic; American Oxonian; Melus; Wallace Stevens Journal;

Syracuse Scholar; New York Folklore; Modern Age; Bulletin of Research in the Humanities. *Honours:* Recipient of grants; Rhodes Scholarship; Cornell Graduate Fellowship; Woodrow Wilson Fellowship; Phi Beta Kappa; Summer grant, 1967, Fellowship, 1975, National Endowment for the Humanities. *Address:* 704 Lansing Street, Utica, NY 13501, USA.

NATANSON, Wojciech, b. 7 July. 1904, Krakow, Poland. Writer. m. Kazimiera Zaczkiewicz, 20 Oct. 1934, 1 son. *Education:* Master and Doctor of International Law, Jagiellonian University; French Literature, Sorbonne, Paris, France. *Appointments:* Literary Advisor, Teatr Stary, Krakow, Poland, 1945–47, Theatre in Katowice, 1947–50, Teatr Rozmaitosci, Warsaw, 1985–present. *Publications:* Wyspianski, 1965; Z Róza Czerwoną Przez Paryz, 1970; Szczęście Syzyfa, 1980. *Contributions to:* Listy z Teatnu, (Editor in chief), 1946–49; Teatr, (Sub-Editor), 1952–71. *Honours:* Nagroda im Pietrzaka, 1973; Nagroda Zycia Literackiego, 1975; Order of Chevalier des Arts et Lettres, France, 1985; Order of Polonia Restituta (Poland, 1979). *Memberships:* PEN; Societe Europenne de Culture. *Address:* Ul Jaracza 10131, 00378 Warsaw, Poland.

NATCHEZ, Gladys, b. 13 Nov. 1915, New York City, New York, USA. Psychotherapist. *Education:* MA, Teachers College, Columbia University; PhD, New York University; Postdoctoral Degree Psychoanalysis and Psychotheraphy, Adelphi University. *Publications:* Personality Patterns; Reading Disability: Diagnosis and Treatment, 1964, 2nd edition 1971; Children with Reading Problems, 1968; Gideon: A Boy who Hates Learning at School, 1975; The Guru Therapist's Notebook by Kenneth Fisher, editor, 1976; Reading Disability: A Human Approach to Learning, 3rd edition 1977. *Contributions to:* New York Times Magazine; Voices. *Membership:* Authors Guild. *Address:* 263 West End Avenue, New York City, NY 10023, USA.

NATHAN, Edward Leonard, b. 8 Nov. 1924, Los Angeles, California, USA. Teacher; Poet. m. Carol G Nash, 27 June 1949, Los Angeles, 1 son, 2 daughters. *Education:* BA, Magna Cum Lauda, 1950; MA, 1951; PhD, 1961. *Publications:* Western Reaches, 1958; Glad and Sorry Seasons, 1963; The Day the Perfect Speakers Left, 1969; Returning Your Call, 1975; Dear Blood, 1980; Holding Patterns, 1982; Carrying On: New & Selected Poems, 1985. *Contributor to:* Salmagundi; New Yorker; New Republic; Kenyon Review; Massachusetts Review; Poetry; Quarterly Review of Literature; Shenandoah; Perspective; Prairie Schooner; Antaeus Review; Eopch; Commentary; The Nation; Georgia Review; etc. *Honours:* Guggenheim Fellowship, 1976–77; Nominee, National Book Award, 1975; National Institute of Arts and Letters Award for Creative Literature, 1971; American Institute of Indian Studies Fellowship, 1965–66; Creative Arts Fellowship, UCB, 1973–74, 1963–64. *Address:* 40 Beverly Road, Kensington CA 94707, USA.

NATHAN, Norman, b. 19 Nov, 1915, USA. Professor of English. m. Frieda Agin, 21 July 1940, Washington DC, 3 daughters. *Education:* BA, 1936, MA 1938, PhD 1947, New York University. *Publications:* Though Night Remain, 1959; Judging Poetry, 1961; The Right Word, 1962; Writing Sentences, 1964; Short Stories, 1969; Prince William B, 1975. *Contributor to:* Over 500 articles including Shakespeare Quarterly; Oui; Saturday Review; Saturday Evening Post; Critical Quarterly; Names; Ladies' Home Journal; New York Times; Malahat Review. *Address:* 1189 S W Tamarind Way, Boca Raton, FL 33432, USA.

NATHUSIUS, Marie-Sophie, b. 19 June 1906, Amsterdam, Netherlands. Writer. 1 daughter. *Education:* Dancing & Theatrical studies. *Publications:* De Partner, 1954; Meneer Goed; Fout in het Kadaster; etc. Het Manuscript, 1984. *Contributions to:* Numerous magazines & journals. *Honours:* Municipal Prize, Town of Amsterdam; Van der Vies Prize; Minor awards for young people's stories. *Memberships:* PEN; Maatschappy der Letterkunde; Die Kogge, Europäische Literatur Verein.

Literary Agent: International Drama Agency, Elpermeer 26b, 1025 AP Amsterdam, Netherlands.

NATUSCH, Sheila Ellen, b. 14 Feb. 1926, Invercargill, New Zealand. Writer. m. Gilbert G Natusch, 28 Nov. 1950, Stewart Island. *Education:* MA Otago University, New Zealand. *Publications:* Animals of New Zealand, 1967; Hell and High Water, 1977; Brother Wohlers, 1969; On the Edge of the Bush; The Cruise of the Acheron, 1978; Southward Ho!, 1985. *Honours:* Hubert Church Award, PEN, New Zealand, 1969; South Island Writers Association and Christchurch Press newspaper feature article competition, 1st prize, 1984. *Address:* 46 Ohiro Bay Parade, Wellington 2, New Zealand.

NATWAR-SINGH K, b. 16 May, 1931, Bharatpur, India. Diplomat; Politician, Minister. m. Heminder Kaur, 1967, 1 son, 1 daughter. *Publications:* E M Forster: A Tribute, 1964; The Legacy of Nehru, 1965; Tales From Modern India, 1966; Stories From India, 1971; Maharaja Suraj Mal, 1981; Curtain Raiser, 1984. *Contributions to:* New Statesman, London; Financial Times, London; Sunday Times, London; Illustrated Weekly of India; Times of India; Hindustan Times. *Honour:* Awarded Padma Bhushan, Government of India, 1984. *Memberships:* Garrick, London; Royal Overseas League, London; Gynkhana, New Delhi. *Address:* 9 Safdarjung Road, New Delhi, India.

NAUMAN-TODD, Sheila, b. 6 Jan. 1957, Dubugue, Iowa, USA. Writer; Publisher. m. 28 Dec. 1984, Zephyr Cove, Lake Tahoe, Nevada, 1 step-daughter. *Education:* BA American Studies & Medical Sociology, Hamline University, St Paul; BA Small Business Management & Communications, Metropolitan State University, St Paul. *Literary Appointments:* Staff Writer, Telegraph Herald, Dubugue, Iowa, 1973–75; Independent Professional Writer, 1975–79; Senior Editor, Nutrition & Health, University of Minnesota School of Public Health, 1979–82; Editor/Publisher, True-to-Form Press & The Health Literature Review, St Paul, 1982–; Director of Publications, American Medical Writers Association, Bethesda, Maryland, 1983–85. *Memberships:* North Central Chapter Representative, Board of Directors, American Medical Writers' Association, 1983–. *Address:* True-to-Form Press & The Health Literature Review, 1330 Conwed Tower, St Paul, MN 55101–2110, USA.

NAVARRE, Yves Henri Michel, b. 24 Sep. 1940, Condom, France. Writer Novels and Plays. *Education:* Spanish, English and Modern literature degrees, Business School, University of Lille, France. *Publications:* Author of 35 novels (17 unpublished) including: Lady Black, 1970; Les Loukoums; Killer, 1975; Niagarak, 1976; Je Vis ou je m'Attache, 1978; Le Temps Voulu, 1979; Biographie, 1981; Romances Sans Paroles, 1982; Premieres Pages; L'Esperance des Beaux Voyages Ete/Automne, 1984; L'Esperance des Beaux Voyages Hiver/Printemps, 1984; Louise, 1986. Numerous works for theatre including: Champagne; Les Valises; Histoire d'Amour; September Song; Happy End. Numerous translations of novels and plays published in Europe, Poland. Roumania and Bulgaria, Scandinavia. *Contributions to:* Numerous works. *Honour:* Prize Goncourt, for, Le Jardin d'Acclimatation, 1980. *Memberships include:* SACD; SEDL; SELF. *Address:* Petit Pont, 84220 Lioux, France.

NAVROZOV, Andrei, b. 26 Oct. 1956, Moscow, USSR. m. Kathleen Spencer Kilpatrick, 30 May 1981, Litchfield, Connecticut, USA. *Education:* BA, 1978, Yale University. *Literary Appointments:* Editor, The Yale Literary Magazine, 1978–; Contributing Editor, Harper's, 1984–. *Publication:* Transport of Elements, 1978. *Contributions to:* The Wall Street Journal, 1983–. *Membership:* Director, American Literary Society 1980– . *Address:* c/o The Yale Literary Magazine, Box 243–A Yale Station, New Haven, CT 06520, USA.

NEAL, Alfred C(larence), b. 23 June 1912. Economist. m. Marguerite Stephenson, 15 June 1937, London, England. *Education:* AB, University of California, 1934; PhD, Brown University, 1941, Honorary LL D, Brown University, 1957. *Major Publications:* Industrial Concentration & Price Inflexibility, 1942; Modern Economics, (with Burns & Watson), 1948; The New England Economy, (with others), 1951; Introduction to War Economics, (author/editor), 1942; Business Power & Public Policy, 1981. *Contributor to:* Harvard Business Review; Foreign Affairs; and others. *Address:* 222 Osborn Road, Harrison, NY 10528, USA.

NEAL, Berniece Marie, b. 26 July 1914, Elsinore, Missouri, USA. Writer and book reviewer. m. (1) George Leo Roer (deceased), 2 sons, (2) Harry Edward Neal, 1965. *Publications:* How To Write Articles; Chicken. *Contributions to:* New York Times, Washington Post; Woman's Day; Optimist International; Writer's Digest; The Writer; Chicago Tribune; Baltimore Sun; Life and Health; Marriage; Halrequin; Guideposts; Family Circle; Children's Playmate; Dynamic Graphics; Culpeper News; National Research Bureau and others. *Honours:* 1st Place Award in Article Writing, Missouri Writers Guild, 1965; 1st Place in Article Writing, Virginia Press Women, 1970; Outstanding Merit in Non-Fiction Writing, Techinical Writers and Publishers, St Louis chapter, 1965. *Memberships:* Newsletter publication committee member, American Society of Journalists and Authors; National Federation of Press Women; St Louis Writers Guild. *Address:* 210 Spring Street, Culpeper, VA 22701, USA.

NEAL, Ernest Gordon, b. 20 May 1911, Boxmoor, Hertfordshire, England. Teacher. m. Helen Elizabeth Thomson, 30 Apr. 1937, Boxmoor, Hertfordshire, 3 sons. *Education:* BSc, MSc, PhD, London University. *Publications:* Exploring Nature with a Camera, 1946; The Badger 1948; Woodland Ecology, 1953; Topsy and Turvey, My Two Otters, 1961; Uganda Quest 1971; Biology for Today (with K R C Neal) 1974; Badgers, 1977; Badgers in Close up, 1983; Natural History of Badgers, 1986 (in press). *Contributor to:* Field; Country Life; Illustrated London News; Times; Sunday Times; Living Countryside; Wildlife Magazine. *Honours:* Stamford Raffles Award for Zoology, Zoological Society of London, 1965; Fellow, Institute of Biology, 1968; Wildlife Photographer of the Year, Wildlife Magazine, 1969; MBE, 1976. *Memberships:* Society of Authors; Mammal Society (Past Chairman, Past President); Vice President, Somerset Trust for Nature Conservation (Past Chairman). *Address:* Mansell House, Milverton, Taunton, Somerset TA4 1JU, England.

NEAL, Fred Warner, b. 5 Aug. 1915, Northville, Michigan, USA. Professor of International Relations. m. Mary Caroline Hall, 20 Jan. 1982, Claremont, California, USA, 1 son, 1 daughter. *Education:* PhD, University of Michigan, 1955. *Major Publications:* Titoism in Action, 1968; US Foreign Policy & the Soviet Union, 1961; Yugoslavia & the New Communism, 1962; War and Peace and Germany, 1962; A Survey of Détente – Past, Present & Future, 1977; Détente or Débâcle, 1979. *Contributor to:* Atlantic Monthly; Center Magazine; Current History; Progressive Nation; International Studies Quarterly; American Slavic & East European Review; East European Quarterly; Bulletin of the Atomic Scientist; American Political Science Review; Western Political Quarterly; New York Times; Los Angeles Times. *Address:* 210 E Foothill, Claremont, CA 91711, USA.

NEAL, Harry Edward, b. 4 May, 1906, Pittsfield, Massachusetts, USA. Writer. m. (1) Helen Grafton Armstrong (deceased) at Washington DC, 8 May 1929, 1 son, 1 daughter. (2) Berniece Raymer Roer, 1965, 2 stepsons. *Education:* Graduate, Shields Business College, Bristol, Connecticut; Fellow, Kansas City, Missouri, Academy of Medicine. *Publications:* Writing and Selling Fact and Fiction, 1949; Nature's Guardians, 1956; The Telescope, 1958; Skyblazers, 1958; Six Against Crime, 1959; Disease Detectives; Communication: From Stone Age to Space Age, 1960; Also 24 others. *Contributions to:* Esquire; Coronet;

Cosmopolitan; Changing Times; The Woman; Family Circle; American Girl; The Writer; Saturday Evening Post; Collier's; Liberty; Argosy; Saga; Christian Herald; Civil War Times; Popular Photography; People's Almanac; Scandinavian Review; Writer's Digest. *Honours:* Exceptional Civilian Service Medal, US; Treasury Department, Washington, DC, 1957; For achievement in the communication of writing skills, Georgetown University, Washington DC, 1969. *Memberships:* The Author's Guild; The Children's Book Guild; Association of Former Agents of the US Secret Service. *Address:* 210 Spring Street, Culpeper, VA 22701, USA.

NEAL, Marie Augusta, b. 22 June 1921, Brighton, Massachusetts, USA. Teacher and Researcher. *Education:* AB, Emmanuel College, Boston, 1942; MA, Boston College, 1953; PhD, Harvard University, 1963. *Literary Appointments:* Professor, Sociology, for research and teaching, Emmanuel College, Boston, 1963; Visiting Professor, Sociology, University of California, Berkeley, 1968; Harvard Divinity School, 1973; Ford Foundation Grant to study women's roles in society, 1975; Research Associate, Women's Studies in Religion, Harvard Divinity School, 1982. *Publications:* Values and Interests in Social Change, 1963; A Socio-Theology of Letting Go, 1977; Catholic Sisters in Transition from the 1960's to the 1980's, 1984; Essays in Socio-Theology, 1986. *Contributions to:* Journal for the Scientific Study of Religion, Social Justice and Right to Use Power, 1984; Religious Education, Reaching Out and Letting Go: Societal Transformation, 1984; International Schools Journal, Altruism and Social Justice, 1984. *Honours:* Honorary Doctor of Laws degree, Notre Dame University, 1985; John XXXIII Award New Rochelle College, 1985. *Memberships:* President, Association for the Sociology of Religion, 1972; President, Society for the Scientific Study of Religion, 1982–84. *Address:* Emmanuel College, 400 The Fenway, Boston, MA 02115, USA.

NEAMAN, Judith S, b. 20 Sep. 1936, Syracuse, New York, USA. Scholar. *Education:* BS, University of Michigan, USA, 1958; MA, 1960; PhD, 1968, Columbia University. *Publications:* The American Vision, (with Rhoda B Nathan), 1973; Suggestion of the Devil, 1978; Insanity in the Middle Ages and the Twentieth Century, 1978; Kind Words; A Thesaurus of Euphemisms, 1983. *Contributor to:* Phjilol. Quarterly; Bulletin of the History of Medicine; Fourteenth Century English Mystics Newsletter; Res Publica Literarum. *Memberships:* Medieval Academy of America; MLA of America; Int Courtly Lit Soc; Inst for Research in His. *Honour:* Summer Fellowship, National Endowment for the Humanities. *Address:* 230 Riverside Drive, New York, NY 10025, USA.

NEATE, Frank Anthony, b. 11 Apr. 1928, Plympton, Devon, England. Journalist. m. 29 Feb. 1960, Christchurch, New Zealand, 1 son, 2 daughters. *Publications:* The Hour-Glass Girl, 1966; Shell Guide to New Zealand, Contributing Editor, 1968; various short stories. *Contributor to:* Short stories, articles, historical material etc, to professional journals and magazines. *Membership:* PEN International. *Address:* P O Box 3, Greymouth, New Zealand.

NEDDEN, Otto C A zur, b. 18 Apr. 1902, Trier, Germany. University Professor. m. Irma Bentner, 12 Sep. 1936, 2 daughters. *Education:* Abitur; Dr phil habil; Professorship. *Appointments:* Director, Musicology, Theatrical Sciences, Institute University Jena, 1938; Director, Studio-Buhne, University of Cologne, 1957; Quellen und Studien, Upper Rhineland Musicology in 15th and 16th Centuries, 1931; Reclams Schauspielfuhrer, 1954, 16th Edition 1983. *Publications:* Das Testament des Friedens, 1973; T E Lawrence, 1958; Die Kunst der Fuge des Theaters, 1982. *Contributor to:* Europaische Akzente, 1950–65 Duisburg, Dusseldorf 1982, Tokyo 1984. *Honour:* Honorary Member, Studio-Buhne, University of Cologne. *Membership:* Schopenhauer Society, Frankfurt am Main. *Address:* Gyrhofstrasse 4, D-5000 Köln 41, Federal Republic of Germany.

NEEDHAM, Joseph, b.1900, Clapham, London, England. Director, East Asian History of Science Library, Cambridge; Emeritus Sir William Dunn Reader in Biochemistry; Senior Fellow, Caius College. *Education:* Caius College, Cambridge University. *Publications:* Science and Civilisation in China, 7 volumes in 20 parts; Heavenly Clockwork; The Development of Iron and Steel Technology in China; Celestial Lancets; Chemical Embryology, 3 volumes; Biochemistry and Morphogenesis; The Sceptical Biologist; Time, the Refreshing River; Within the Four Seas; The Grand Titration; Moulds of Understanding. *Memberships:* Fellow; Royal Society; FBA. Honorary FRCP. *Address:* 42 Grange Road, Cambridge, England.

NEEDHAM, Richard, b. 16 Jan. 1939, Cleveland, Ohio, USA. Editor. *Education:* AB, Denison University, 1961; MA, University of Missouri, 1967. *Literary Appointments:* Copy Editor, Saturday Review, 1967–69; Editor-in-Chief, Preview International, 1969–71; Editor, Institutions magazine, Service World International, 1971–72; Editor, Ski Magazine, 1976–80; Editor in Chief, Ski Business, 1978–80. *Publications:* Ski Magazine's Encyclopedia of Skiing, 1978. *Honour:* Lowell Thomas Award for Excellence in Journalism. *Memberships:* Overseas Press Club; American Society of Magazine Authors. *Address:* 115 Old Post Road North, Croton-on-Hudson, NY 10520, USA.

NEEDLE, Jan, b. 8 Feb. 1943, Holybourne, Hampshire, England. Writer. *Education:* Graduate in Drama, University of Manchester, England, 1971. *Major Publications:* Albeson & The Germans, 1977; My Mate Shofiq, 1978; A Fine Boy for Killing, 1979; Brecht (with Peter Thomson), 1980; A Pitiful Place, 1984; A Game of Soldiers, 1985; also television, radio & stage plays. *Contributor to:* Numerous publications. *Literary Agents:* David Highams, Curtis Brown, London; Rochelle Stevens, London (for Drama). *Address;* Rye Top, Gellfield Lane, Uppermill, Oldham, Lancashire, England.

NEELD, Elizabeth Harpey Cowan, b. 25 Dec. 1940, Brooks, Georgia, USA. Writer. m. Jerele Neeld, 29 Oct. 1983, Bryan, Texas. *Education:* PhD, University of Tennessee. *Publications:* Options for the Teaching of English: The Undergraduate Curriculum, 1974; Writing, 1980; 2nd edition, 1986; Writing Brief, 1982; Readings for Writing, 1983. *Contributions to:* Writers on Writing; English Journal; Change Magazine; and others. *Honours:* Various biographical listings. *Memberships:* Director, English Programme, Modern Language Association. *Literary Agent:* Al Lowman. *Address:* 2608 Melba Circle, Bryan, TX 77802, USA.

NEELY, Richard, b. 2 Aug. 1941, USA. Chief Justice of West Virginia. m. Carolyn Elmore, 21 Apr. 1979, Palm Beach, 1 son. *Education:* AB, Dartmouth College, Hanover, New Hampshire, LLB, Yale University Law School, New Haven, Connecticut. *Publications:* How Courts Govern America, 1981; Why Courts Don't Work, 1983; The Divorce Decision, 1984. *Contributions to:* The Politics of Crime, cover article, The Atlantic Monthly, August 1982. *Literary Agent:* Nat Sobel Associates, 146 East 19th Street, New York, NY 10003, USA. *Address:* West Virginia Supreme Court of Appeals, 306-E State Capitol, Charleston, WV 25305, USA.

NEF, Ernst, b. 4 Aug. 1931, Basel, Switzerland. College Professor. m. Nadine Pignat, 27 May 1977, 1 son. *Education:* PhD, University of Zurich. *Publications:* Das Werk Gottfried Benns, 1958; Der Zufall in der Erzählkunst, 1970. *Contributions to:* Die Zeit; Neue Zürcher Zeitung (Regular contributions, literary criticisms). Films about: Wolfgang Hildesheimer; Rolf Hörler; Gerhard Meier, for Swiss television. *Membership:* Schweiz Schriftstellerverein. *Address:* Nordstrasse 127, 8037 Zürich, Switzerland.

NEGGERS, Carla Amalia, b. 8 Sep. 1955, Massachusetts, USA. Writer. m. Joe B Jewell, 23 July

1977, Massachusetts, 1 daughter. *Education:* BS, magna cum laude, Journalism, Boston University. *Publications:* 15 novels of contemporary and historical romance and romantic suspense including: Matching Wits, 1983; Outrageous Desire, 1983; Heart on a String, 1983; The Venus Shoe, 1984; The Knotted Skein, 1984; Southern Comfort 1984, The Uneven Score, 1985. *Honour:* Publicity Club of Boston Award for Excellence in Journalism, Communications and Public Relations, 1976. *Memberships:* International Women's Writing Guild; Romance Writers of America. *Literary Agent:* Denise Marcil, New York City. *Address:* 6 Mayfield Road, Gardner, MA 01440, USA.

NEILAN, Sarah, b. Newcastle-upon-Tyne, England. m. London, 1 son, 3 daughters. *Education:* Ma, Oxford University. *Publications:* The Braganza Pursuit, 1976; An Air of Glory, 1977; Paradise, 1981. *Contributions to:* British Book News; The Bookseller; The Observer, etc. *Honours:* Mary Elgin Prize, 1976; Daughter of Mark Twain, 1977. *Membership:* PEN. *Literary Agent:* A D Peters, 10 Buckingham Street, London WC2. *Address:* c/o Hodder & Stoughton Ltd, 47 Bedford Square, London WC1.

NEILSEN, Niels C, b. 6 June 1921, Long Beach, California, USA. Professor of Philosophy and Religious Thought. m. Erika Kreuth, 10 Aug. 1958, Vienna, Austria, 1 son, 1 daughter. *Education:* BA, 1942, George Pepperdine College, BD 1946; PhD, 1951, Yale. *Publicationa:* A Layman Looks at World Religions, 1962; Solshenitzyn's Religion, 1976; The Religion of President Carter, 1977; The Crisis of Human Rights, 1978; Religions of the World, (Editor); 1983; Religions of Asia, (Editor), 1983. *Contributions to:* Religion in Latin American Life and Culture; Review of Mataphysics; Bulletin of the Houston Museum. *Honours:* Kent Fellow of Society for Religion and Higher education; Fulbright Grant for Research at Madras, India, 1965–66; AMAX Visiting Professor of Humanities, Colorado School of Mines, 1982–83. *Membership:* Executive Secretary, American Society for the Study of Religion. *Address:* Department of Religious Studies, Rice University, P O Box 1892, Houston, TX 77251, USA.

NEILSON, Andrew, b. 15 Nov. 1946, Ordsall, Nottinghamshire, England. Writer. m. Sally, 19 July 1980, Bix, Oxon, 1 son, 1 daughter. *Education:* BA (Hons), Liverpool University, 1968. *Publications:* Braking Point, 1983; Dead Straight, 1984; The Monza Protest, 1985. *Literary Agent:* Julian Friedmann, Blake Friedmann Agency. *Address:* Las Nayas, Partida Lluca, Javea (Alicante), Spain.

NEITZEL, Renate, b. 3 Feb. 1947, Reutlingen, Germany. Secretary. m. Lothar Neitzel, 5 July 1968, 1 daughter. *Education:* Certificate, Commercial School; Certificate, Special Course for Secretaries. *Publications:* ed Schempfa – blooss bruddla, book of poems in Swabian Dialect. *Contributor to:* Anthologies: Horch, edds pfeifd a andrar Weed, 1980; Poetry broadcast. *Membership:* Werkkreis Schwabische Mundart. *Address:* Grünewaldstr. 37, D 7440 Nürtingen, Federal Republic of Germany.

NELIDA, Pinon, b. 3 May 1938, Rio, Brazil. Author. *Education:* University Catholic of Rio de Janeiro. *Publications include:* Guia Mapa de Gabriel Arcanjo, 1961; FundadoR, 1969; The House of Passion, 1972; The Republic of Dreams, 1984. *Contributions to:* Various national and international publications. *Honours include:* Mario de Andrade Prize, 1973; APCA, 1985. *Literary Agent:* Carmen Balcells. *Address:* Avenue Rodolfo Amoedo, 418 apt 201 Barra, 22620 Rio de Janeiro, Brazil.

NELLESSEN, Bernhard, b. 13 Dec. 1958, Bad Ems, Federal Republic of Germany. Journalist. m. Ursula Kohl, 26 Sep. 1981, Kocherbach, 1 daughter. *Education:* MA, History, Philosophy, Comparative literature. *Literary Appointments:* Co-Editor, Müncher Edition, Schneekluth-Verlag. *Publications:* An den Wassern von

Rhein und Ruhr, poems, 1981; Neu leuchten die Zäune, poems, 1984. *Honour:* Scholarship of Literarisches Colloquim Berlin, 1981. *Address:* Am Kocherbach 25, 6948 Wald-Michelbach, Federal Republic of Germany.

NELMS, Sheryl Lynne, b. 3 Dec. 1944, Marysville, Kansas, USA. Insurance Examiner/Writer. 2 sons, 1 daughter. *Education:* BA, Child Development and Family Relations, South Dakota State University. *Literary Appointments:* Writer in the Schools South Dakota Arts Council, 1979–80; Writer in the Schools Texas Arts Council, 1984; Head of Humanities Division, Trinity Arts Council, Bedford, Texas, 1982–84; Vice President, Oklahoma Writers Federation, 1984–86; Contributing editor to Byline, and Streets. *Publications:* Their Combs Turn Red in the Spring, 1984. *Contributions to:* Reader's Digest; Modern Maturity; Kansas Quarterly; Webster Review; Spoon River quarterly; Abraxas; Poetry Now; Farm Wife News; Capper's Weekly; Byline; Southern Exposure; San Jose Studies; Naked Man; Black Jack; Black Willow; Poets on Surviving; Cedar Rock; Smoke Signals; Salome; Confrontation; The Laurel Review; Progressive Farmer; Buffalo Spree and Mendicino Review. *Honours:* 1st Place Schultz-Wyarth Research Award SDSU, 1978. *Memberships:* Western Writers of America; Oklahoma Writers Federation; President and Vice President, Dallas/Fort Worth Writers Workshop; National Writers Club; Southwest Writers; Texas Arts Council; South Dakota Arts Council; Trinity Arts Council. *Address:* PO Box 14180, Ft Worth, TX 76117, USA.

NELSON, Cordner Bruce, b. 6 Aug. 1918, San Diego, California, USA. Writer. m. Mary Elizabeth Kenyon, 4 Feb. 1941, 3 daughters. *Education:* AB, 1940, University of the Pacific; Oklahoma University, 1946–47. *Publications:* The Jim Ryun Story, 1967; The Miler, 1969; Track & Field; The Great Ones, 1970; Runners & Races: 1500/Mile, 1973; Advance Running Book, 1984; How To Train, 1985; The Milers, 1985. *Contributor to:* Various publications. *Honour:* US Track & Field Hall of Fame, 1976. *Address:* Box 6476, Carmel, CA 93921, USA.

NELSON, Ed(win) P, b. 6 Nov. 1925, USA. Journalist. m. Norma J Johanson, 24 June 1965, Chicago, Illinois, 1 daughter. *Literary Appointments:* Features Editor, Science and Mechanics Monthly; Automotive Editor, Popular Mechanics Monthly; Senior Editor, World Book, Science Year and Year Book annuals; Publications Director, Institute on the Church in Urban-Industrial Society. *Contributions to:* Numerous publications. *Membership:* American Society of Journalists and Authors. *Address:* 938 North Austin Boulevard, Oak Park, IL 60302, USA.

NELSON, Geoffrey Kenneth, b. 8 Aug. 1923, Dereham, Norfolk, England. Lecturer. m. Irene Griggs, 31 July 1955, Walsoken, 2 sons, 2 daughters. *Education:* Certificate in Social Science, Liverpool University, 1950; Teachers Certificate 1954, BSc Sociology 1958, MSc Economics 1961, PhD 1968, London University. *Publications:* Spiritualism and Society, 1969; Mobility and Religious Commitment, 1971; History of Modern Spiritualism, study notes, 1975; World Religions, study notes, 1976; Butterflys Eye, poetry, 1980; Report of Parliamentary Group Video Violence Study, (with C Hill, et al), 1984; The Fountain of Youth, A Study of Religious Creativity, forthcoming; The Third Alternative, The Life and Work of V Branford, forthcoming. *Contributions to:* 40 articles in learned journals including: Sociological Review; Social Compass; Review of Religious Research; Journal for the Scientific Study of Religion; Articles on sociology, religion, local history and poetry in magazines. *Address:* 32 Clun Road, Northfield, Birmingham B31 1NU, England.

NELSON, Jack E, b. 15 Sep. 1940, Washington DC, USA. President, Metrotec Inc. m. Mollie Sayers, 24 Apr. 1977, Washington DC, 2 daughters. *Education:* AB, Howard University; BA, Pennsylvania State University. *Publications:* Equal Employment Opportunity in Trucking: An Industry at the Crossroads, 1971; The Impact of

Corporate Suburban Relocations on Minority Employment Opportunities, 1974; An Analysis of the Federal Policy Requiring Drug Abuse Treatment Centres to Maximize the Capture of Third Party Reimbursements, 1975; Equal Employment Opportunity and the AT&T Case, 1976; Guide to Drug Abuse Research Terminology, co-editor, 1982; Public Health Issues and Drug Abuse Research, co-editor, 1982; Alcoholism Treatment Assessment Research Instruments, co-author, 1985. *Contributor to:* Various publications. *Memberships:* Vice President, Board Member, Association of Editorial Business, 1983–. *Address:* Metrotec Inc, 1623 Connecticut Ave, NW Washington DC 20009, USA.

NELSON, Joseph Bryan, b. 14 Mar. 1932, Shipley, England. University Reader. *Education:* BSc, St Andrews University, 1959; DPhil, Oxford University, 1963. *Publications:* Galapagos, Islands of Birds, 1968; Azraq, Desert Oasis, 1974; The Sulidae Gannets and Boobies, 1978; The Gannet, 1978; Seabirds, Ecology and Biology, 1980; Living with Seabirds, 1986. *Contributor to:* Over 50 journals. *Honour:* Fellow, Royal Society, Edinburgh, 1981. *Address:* Balkirk, Glenlochar, Castle Douglas DG7 2LU, Scotland.

NELSON, Kenneth Davies, b. 3 Aug. 1921, Llandebie, South Wales. Civil Engineer. *Education:* BSc, University of Wales, Cardiff. *Publications:* Dictionary of Applied Geology, 1967; Dictionary of Water and Water Engineering, 1973; Water Resources, 1979; Investigation and Design of Small Earth Dams, 1985. *Contributor to:* Colliery Guardian; Canada Mining Journal; Victoria Resources; Victoria Year Book. *Honours:* ED, 1971. *Memberships:* PEN; Australian Society of Authors; Fellowship of Australian Writers. *Address:* 151 Domain Park, 193 Domain Road, South Yarra, Victoria 3141, Australia.

NELSON, Kent, b. 21 Apr. 1943, Cincinnati, Ohio, USA. Fiction Writer. *Literary Appointments:* Guest Lecturer, University of Colorado, Boulder, 1983; Guest Lecturer, University of Texas, Austin, 1983–84; Guest Lecturer, University of the South, Sewanee, Tennessee, 1985. *Publications:* The Tennis Player (stories), 1978; Cold Wind River (novel), 1981. *Contributions to:* Mademoiselle; Mid-American Review; Virginia Quarterly Review; Southern Review; Arizona Quarterly; PEN Syndicated Fiction Project also 35 other stories in literary reviews. *Membership:* Authors Guild. *Address:* c/o Hastie, Rt 4, Ravenswood, Charleston, SC 29407, USA.

NELSON, Ray Faraday, b. 3 Oct. 1931, Schenectady, New York, USA. Science Fiction Novelist. m. Kirsten Enge, 4 Oct. 1957, Paris, France. 1 son. *Education:* BA, University of Chicago, Illinois, 1960; Programmers Certificate, Automation Institute, Oakland, California, 1961. *Publications:* The Ganymede Takeover, 1967; Blakes Progress, 1975; Then Beggars Could Ride, 1976; The Ecolog, 1977; Revolt of the Unemployables, 1977; Dimension of Horror, 1978; The Prometheus, 1983; Time Quest, 1985. *Contributions to:* Fantasy and Science Fiction Magazine; Amazing Stories; Fantastic Adventures; Weird Tales; Science Fiction Review; Nova; Nugget; Different Worlds; Just for Laughs; Sluth; Berkeley Gazette; Berkeley Barb; Richmond Independent; Writers Connection; various others. *Honours:* Featured in Best Science Fiction of the Year Anthology, 1965 and Best from Fantasy and Science Fiction Anthology, 1965; Philip K Dick Citation, 1983; Jack London Award, 1983; Ina Coolbrith Poetry Award, 1979. *Memberships:* Past twice President, California Writers Club; Bloodbank Chairman, Science-Fiction Writers of America; Mystery Writers of America; Writers Connection; Ina Coolbrith Poetry Society. *Address:* 333 Ramona Avenue, El Cerrito, CA 94530, USA.

NELSON, Sharon H, b. 2 Jan. 1948, Montreal, Canada. Editor. *Education:* BA, Sir George Williams University; MA, Concordia. *Publications:* A Broken Vessel, 1972; Sayings of my Fathers, 1972; Seawreck, 1973; Blood Poems, 1978; Problem Solving and Computer Programming, 1982; Mad Women and Crazy Ladies, 1983. *Contributions to:* Poems and articles to publications including: The Radical Reviewer; Broadside; Fireweed; This Magazine; Atlantis; Critical Quarterly; Europeam Judaism; The Fiddlehead; Poetry Canada Review; Poetry Review London; Prism; Room of One's Own; Shirim; Stuffed Crocodile; Tree; Viewpoints. *Memberships:* The Writer's Union of Canada; The League of Canadian Poets; Freelance Editors Association of Canada. *Address:* c/o Metonymy Productions, 4125 Beaconsfield Avenue, Montreal, Quebec H4A 2H4, Canada.

NELSON-HUMPHRIES, Tessa, b. Yorkshire, England. Professor of English Literature; Lecturer; Writer. m. (1) Kenneth Nelson Brown, 1 June 1957, London, (dec. 1962); (2) Cecil H Unthank, 26 Sep. 1963, New Mexico, (dec. 1979). *Education:* BA, MA, University of North Carolina, USA; PhD, University of Liverpool, 1973. *Contributions to:* Michigan Quarterly Review; Southern Folklore Quarterly; Dalesman; Let's Live; Cats Magazine; Bulletin of Society of Children's Book Writers; Child Life; Vegetarian Times; Bulletin Society Women Writers and Journalists; The Lookout; Joycean Literary Arts Guild Magazine; Alive; The British Vegetarian; Blue Unicorn; Candles and Lamps; Outposts. *Honours:* Short Story Prize, Society of Women Writers, UK, 1975; Silver Trophy (Julia Cairns Trophy) for Poetry, UK, 1978; Mellon Award for Writing/Travel in China, 1981; James Still Fellowship in Humanities at the University of Kentucky for work on a biography of L E Landon, 1983; others include Danforth, Fulbright and AAUW awards; Article Prize, SWWJ, 1985. *Memberships:* Society of Children's Book Writers, USA; Society of Women Writers and Journalists, UK. *Address:* York Cottage, Rt 4, Box 944, Williamsburg, KY 40769, USA.

NEMMERS, Erwin Esser, b. 6 Oct. 1916, Milwaukee, Wisconsin, USA. Professor of Management, Attorney. *Education:* MusB, MusM, Wisconsin Conservatory of Music; AB Magna cum laude, Marquette University; AM, University of Chicago; LLB, Harvard University; PhD, SJD, University of Wisconsin, BE Aero Engineering, State University of Iowa; CPA, Wisconsin; Member of the Bar, Wisconsin, Illinois, US Supreme Court, 7th Circiut Court of Appeals, Federal District Courts of Wisconsin and Illinois. *Publications:* Breviloquim of Bonaventure, 1946; Twenty Centuries of Catholic Church Music, 1948; Hobson and Underconsumption, 1956; Dictionary of Economics and Business, 1959, 19th edition, 1985; Cases in Finance, 1963; Business Research, Text and Cases, 1966; Managerial Economics, 1972; Basic Management Finance, 1975; Managerial Finance Essentials, 1976. *Contributions to:* Columbia Law Review; Harvard Law Reviw; Virginia Law Review; Marquetta Law Review; Wisconsin Law Review. *Honours:* Austin, Lehman and University Fellow, Harvard, 1941–42; Ford Foundation Faculty Research Fellow, Wisconsin, 1942; Professional Research Fellow, Case Western Reserve University, 1967–68. *Address:* 2936 N Hackett Avenue, Milwaukee, WI 53211, USA.

NEPHTALÍ DE LEÓN, b. 9 May 1945, Laredo, Texas, USA. Poet; Writer. 2 daughters. *Literary Appointments:* Artist in Residence for The State of Texas, USA, 1982. *Publications:* Chicanos: Our Background & Our Pride, 1972; Chicano Poet, 1973; 5 Plays, 1974; I Color my Garden, 1974; I Will Catch The Sun, 1974; Tequila Mockingbird, 1980; Segundo de Febrero, 1983. *Contributions to:* Contributor to various journals including, Texas Observer; Zez; New Blood; Poetry International; Trinity Review. Major Anthologies, We Are Chicanos, 1974; Festival de Floricanto, 1975; El Quetzal Emplumece, 1976; Dale Gas, 1978; Hispanics in The United States, Creative Literature, 1980; Chicanos: Antologia Historica y Literaria, 1981; Les Fils de Soleil, 1980; Patterns in American Literature, 1985. *Honour:* Fellowship Ford Foundation Association for Bilingual Education. *Membership:* Hispanic Writer's Guild. *Address:* PO Box 3573, San Antonio, TX 78211, USA.

NETTLER, Gwynne, b. 7 July 1913, New York, USA. Emeritus Professor of Sociology and Psychology. *Education:* AB, UCLA: MA, Claremont Colleges; PhD, Stanford University. *Publications:* Explanations, 1970; Social Concerns, 1976; Explaining Crime, 3rd Edition, 1984; Criminal Careers, (4 volumes), 1982. *Honours:* E H Sutherland Award from the American Society of Criminology, 1982; Alberta Achievement Award, 1982. *Address:* 12862 Circulo Dardo, San Diego, CA 92128, USA.

NEUGEBOREN, Jay, b. 30 May 1938, Brooklyn, New York, USA. Writer. 2 sons, 1 daughter. *Education:* Ba, Columbia College, 1959; MA, Indiana University, 1963. *Publications:* Big Man, 1966; Listen Ruben Fontanez, 1968; Corky's Brother, 1969; Parentheses: An Autobiographical Journey, 1970; Sams Legacy, 1973; An Orphans Tale, 1976; The Stolen Jew, 1981; Before My Life Began, 1985. *Contributor to:* The Atlantic; The American Scholar; Ploughshares, etc. *Honours:* Bernard DeVito Fellowship, 1966; Transatlantic Review Novella Award, 1967; NEA Fellow, 1973–74; Guggenheim Fellow, 1978; Present Tense/Similer Prise to The Stolen Jew, Best Novel, 1981; etc. *Literary Agent:* Curtis Brown Ltd. *Address:* English Department, University of Massachusetts, Amherst, MA 01003, USA.

NEUMEYER, Kathleen Marshall, b. 11 June 1944, Indianapolis, Indiana, USA. Journalist. 1 son, 1 daughter. *Education:* BSJ, Northwestern University, 1966. *Appointments:* Freelance Writer, 1972–; Contributing Editor, Los Angeles Magazine, 1976–; Correspondent, Los Angeles, The Economist, 1977–; Instructor, California State University, 1974–. *Contributor to:* Los Angeles Magazine; The Economist; Los Angeles Lawyer; US Magazine; etc. *Memberships:* American Society of Journalists and Authors; Sigma Delta Chi, President, Los Angeles Chapter, 1980; SDX Distinguished Service Awards, Co-Chair National Awards, 1983; Judge, 1981, 1982, 1984. *Address:* 9796 Burnley Place, Beverly Hills, CA 90210, USA.

NEUSNER, Jacob, b. 28 July 1932, Hartford, Connecticut, USA. University Professor. m. Suzanne Richter, 15 Mar. 1964, 1 son, 3 daughters. *Education:* AB, Harvard College, 1953; Jewish History, Lincoln College, Oxford University, 1953–54; MHL, Jewish Theological Seminary, 1960; PhD, Religion, Columbia University, 1960. *Appointment:* Professor, Judaic Studies, Brown University, 1968–. *Publications include:* A Life of Yohanan ben Zakkai, 1962; A History of the Jews in Babylonia, 1965–70; Development of a Legend: Studies on the traditions Concerning Yohanan ben Zakkai, 1970; Aphrahat and Judaism: The Christian Jewish Argument in Fourth Century Iran, 1971; The Rabbinic Traditions about the Pharisees before 70, 1971; Eliezer ben Hyrcanus: The Tradition and the Man, 1973; The Idea of Purity in Ancient Judaism, 1973; A History of the Mishnaic Law of Purities, 1974–77; The Tosefta, translated from the Hebrew, 1977–80; The Glory of God is Intelligence, 1978; A History of the Michnaic Law of Holy Things, 1979; Form Analysis and Exegesis: A Fresh Approach to the Interpretation of Mishnah, 1980; A History of the Mishnaic Law of Women, 1979–80; A History of the Mishnaic Law of the Appointed Times, 1981–83; History of the Michnaic Law of Damages, 1983–85; Judaism: The Evidence of the Mishnah, 1981; The Mishnah: A New Translation, 1986; etc. *Contributor to:* Numerous professional and scholarly journals. *Honours:* University Medal for Excellence, Columbia University, 1974; LHD, 1978; PhD, h c, 1979, University of Chicago, University of Cologne; Distinguished Humanitarian Award, Melton Centre for Jewish Studies, Ohio State University, 1983; Recipient numerous Fellowships. *Address:* Programme in Judaic Studies, Brown University, Providence, RI 02912, USA.

NEVILLE, Jill Adelaide, b. 29 May 1942, Sydney, Australia. Freelance Writer. m. David Leitch, 5 Nov. 1970, Marylebone Registry Office, London, 1 son, 1 daughter. *Literary Appointments:* Fiction Critic, Sunday Times, 1974–78; Freelance for: T.L.S; London Magazine; Evening Standard, Book Page etc. *Publications:* Fall Girl, 1966; The Girl who played Gooseberry, 1968; The Love Germ, 1970; The Living Daylights, 1974; Last Ferry to Manly, 1984. *Contributor to:* Literary Articles to: Harpers; Times Literary Supplement; The London Magazine; The Sunday Times; Good Housekeeping; The Evening Standard, etc. *Literary Agent:* Tessa Sayle. *Address:* 63A Belsize Park Gardens, London NW3, England.

NEW, Anthony Sherwood Brooks, b. 14 Aug. 1924, London, England. Architect. m. Elizabeth Pegge, 11 Apr. 1970, Portsmouth, England, 1 son, 1 daughter. *Education:* Diploma in Architecture, Northern Polytechnic, London. *Publications:* Observer's Book of Postage Stamps, 1967; Observer's Book of Cathedrals, 1972; A Guide to the Cathedrals of Britain, 1980; PSA Historic Buildings Register, 1983; A Guide to the Abbeys of England and Wales, 1985. *Contributions to:* Stamp Collecting; Gibbons Stamp Monthly; Netherlands Philately; Essex Countryside; Hertfordshire Countryside; Thames Valley Countryside. *Address:* 26 Somerset Road, New Barnet, Hertfordshire, England.

NEWBY, (George) Eric Newby, b. 1919. Writer. *Literary Appointments:* With Secker and Warburg Limited, Publishers, 1956–59; Travel Editor, The Observer Newspaper, London and General Editor, Time Off Books, 1963–73. *Publications:* The Last Grain Race, 1956; A Short Walk in the Hindu Kush, 1958; Something Wholesale, 1962; Time Off Guide to Southern Italy, 1966; Slowly Down the Ganges, 1966; My Favourite Stories of Travel,1967; Grain Race (in USA as, Windjammer), 1968; (with D Petry) Wonders of Britain, 19687; Wonders of Ireland, 1969; Love and War in the Apennines, 1971; When the Snow Comes They Will Take You Away; Ganga, 1973; World Atlas of Exploration, 1975; Great Ascents, 1977; The Big Red Train Ride, 1978; A Traveller's Life, 1982; On the Shores of the Mediterranean, 1984; A Book of Traveller Tales, 1985. *Contributions to:* Numerous publications. *Address:* West Bucknowle House, Bucknowle, Wareham, Dorset BH20 5BQ, England.

NEWBY, James Richard, b. 8 July 1949, Minneapolis, Minnesota, USA. Executive Director, Yokefellow Institute and Academy. m. Elizabeth Salinas, 21 Dec. 1969, Wichita, Kansas, 1 daughter. *Education:* BA, Friends University, 1971; MDiv, Earlham School of Religion, 1977; Honorary DDiv, William Penn College, Iowa, 1985. *Publications:* Reflections from the Light of Christ, 1980; The Best of Elton Trueblood, 1980; The Creation of a Future, 1982; Between Peril and Promise, 1984. *Contributions to:* The Christian Ministry; Ministry; Proclaim; The Christian Bookseller; Eternity; Quaker Life. *Honour:* Staley Distinguished Christian Scholar Lecturer. *Address:* 230 College Avenue, Richmond, IN 47374, USA.

NEWCOMB, Duane, b. 12 Feb. 1924, Oklahoma City, Oklahoma, USA. Author, Lecturer. m. Karen L Ball, Reno, Nevada, 1 son. *Education:* BS Forestry, MS Botany, University of Washington. *Publications:* Mobile Home Gardening Guide, 1962; Trailering in Canada, 1964; Trailer Owner's Driving Guide, 1965; How To Make Big Money Freelance Writing, 1970; The Wonderful World of Houseboating, 1974; Spare Time Fortune Guide, 1974; Word Power Makes The Difference, 1974; A Complete Guide to Marketing Magazine Articles, 1975; The Postage Stamp Garden Book, 1975; The Poor Man's Road to Riches, 1975; The Apartment Farmer, 1976; Georgie Clark – Thirty Years of River Running, 1977; The Complete Vegetable Gardener's Sourcebook, 1980; The Owner Built Adobe, 1980; $10 Can Make You Rich, 1980; Growing Vegetables The Big Yield/Small Space Way, 1981; RX For Your Vegetable Garden, 1982; Fast Fortune Secrets of the Super Rich, 1983; The Underground Shopper, 1984. *Contributions to:* Family Circle; Better Homes and Gardens; American Home; Field and Stream. *Memberships:* American Society of Journalists and Authors; Associate Business Writers of America;

Author's Guild; Vice-President, California Writers. *Literary Agent:* Jane Jordan Browne, Multimedia Product Development Inc, Suite 724, 410 South Michigan Avenue, Chicago, IL 60605, USA. *Address:* 18293 Crystal Street, Grass Valley, CA 95945, USA.

NEWCOMBE, Park Judson, b. 14 Dec. 1930, Grand Rapids, USA. Professor. *Education:* BA, Western Michigan University; MA, PhD, Northwestern University. *Publications:* Co-Editor, New Horizons for Teacher Education in Speech Communication, 1974; Teaching Speech Communication, with Karl F Robinson, 1975; Communicating Message and Meaning, 1982. *Contributor to:* The Speech Teacher; Today's Speech; Communication. *Memberships:* Vice President, President, Florida Speech Communication Association, Pacific Speech Association, Hawaii Association for Student Teaching; American Theatre Association; TESOL; International Council on Education for Teaching; AAUP; Speech Communication Association; World Communication Association. *Address:* Communication Department, University of South Florida, Tampa, FL 33620, USA.

NEWCOMER, James William, b. 14 Mar. 1912, Ohio, USA. m. Ruth Salisbury, 17 Aug, 1946, Wheaton, 1 son, 2 daughters. *Education:* PhB, Kenyon College, 1933; MA, University of Michigan, 1938; PhD, University of Iowa, 1952. *Publications:* Liberal Education and Pharmacy, 1960; Maria Edgeworth the Novelist, 1967; Maria Edgeworth, 1973; Celebration, libretto, 1973; The Merton Barn Poems, with Ruth Newcomer, 1981; The Grand Duchy of Luxembourg: The Evolution of Nationalhood, 1984; The Resonance of Grace, 1984; Lady Morgan the Novelist, in press. *Contributor to:* Numerous professional journals and magazines including: College English; Studies in Short Fiction; Scots Magazine; Nineteenth Century Fiction; Texas Review; etc. *Memberships:* Creative Writing Teachers of Texas; Texas Poets; Academy of American Poets. *Address:* 1100 Elizabeth Boulevard, Fort Worth, TX 76110, USA.

NEWELL, Arlo Frederic, b. 22 Feb. 1926, Stafford, Kansas, USA. Clergyman. m. Helen Louise Jones, 1 Aug. 1947, Hutchinson, 1 son, 2 daughters. *Education:* AB, Anderson College, 1950; MRE, 1964, M Div, 1967, Eden Theological Seminary; DD, Gulf Coast Bible College, 1970. *Appointments:* Editor in Chief, Warmer Press Inc, 1977. *Publications:* Receive the Holy Spirit, 1978; The Church of God Revealed in Scripture, 1981; Revision Editor, Christian Theology, by R R Byrum. *Contributor to:* Pathways to God; Vital Christianity; Herald of Holiness. *Memberships:* Society of Professional Journalists; Evangelical Press Association. *Address:* 1927 Mark Lane, Anderson, IN 46012, USA.

NEWHOUSE, Joseph Paul, b. 24 Feb. 1942, Waterloo, Iowa, USA. Economist. m. Margaret Locke, 22 June 1968, Cambridge, Massachusetts, USA, 2 sons. *Education:* BA, 1963, PhD, 1969, Harvard University. *Major Publications:* An Economic Analysis of Public Library Services, 1972; The Economics of Medical Care: A Policy Perspective, 1978. *Contributor to:* American Economic Review; New England Journal of Medicine. *Honours:* Institute of Medicine, National Academy of Sciences, 1977; David N Kershaw Award & Prize, 1983. *Address:* 1700 Main Street, Santa Monica, CA 90406–2138, USA.

NEWLIN, Margaret Rudd, b. 27 Feb. 1925, New York City, New York, USA. Poet; Critic. m. Nicholas Newlin, 2 Apr. 1956, New York City, 4 sons. *Education:* BA, Bryn Mawr, 1947; PhD, Reading, 1951. *Publications:* Divided Image: A Study of Blake and Yeats, prose, 1953; Organized Innocence: The Story of Blake's Prophetic Books, prose, 1956; Poetry: The Fragile Immigrants, 1971; Day of Sirens, 1973; The Snow Falls Upwards: Collected Poems, 1976; The Book of Mourning, 1982; Collected Poems 1963–1984, 1985. *Contributions to:* Critical Quarterly; Southern Review; Essays in Criticism; Poetry Nation; PNR. *Honours:* AAUW and American Philosophical Association Fellowships; Greenwood Prize, 1969 and 1971; National

Endowment of the Arts Fellow, 1976; National Book Award nominee for Poetry, 1977; Honorary D Litt, Washington College, 1980. *Memberships:* Poetry Society of America; Poetry Society, London; Academy of American Poets. *Address:* Shipley Farm, Secane, PA 19018, USA.

NEWLOVE, John Herbert, b. 13 June 1938, Regina, Saskatchewan, Canada. Poet. m. Susan Mary Phillips, 9 Aug. 1966, Vancouver, British Columbia, 1 stepson, 1 stepdaughter. *Literary Appointments:* Writer-in-Residence, Loyola College, Montreal, Quebec 1974–75, University of Western Ontario, London, Ontario 1975–76, University of Toronto 1976–77, Regina, Saskatchewan, Public Library 1979–80; Instructor, David Thompson University Centre, Nelson, British Columbia, 1982–83. *Publications:* Moving In Alone, 1965; Black Night Window, 1968; The Cave, 1970; Lies, 1972; The Fat Man: Selected Poems, 1977; The Green Plain, 1981; The Night The Dog Smiled, 1986. *Contributions to:* Magazines and Journals worldwide. *Honours:* Governor-General's Award, 1972; Saskatchewan Writers' Guild Founders Award, 1984. *Memberships:* Saskatchewan Writers' Guild; League of Canadian Poets. *Address:* 923 Vernon Street, # 1, Nelson, British Columbia VIL 4G7, Canada.

NEWMAN, Andrea, b. 7 Feb. 1938, England. Writer. *Education:* BA 1960, MA 1972, London University. *Publications:* A Share of the World, 1964; Mirage, 1965; The Cage, 1966; Three Into Two Won't Go, 1967; Alexa, 1968; A Bouquet of Barbed Wire, 1969; An Evil Streak, 1977; Another Bouquet, 1977; Mackenzie, 1980. 38 Television Plays, including series. *Contributions to:* She; Woman's Own; Woman's Realm; Options. *Literary Agent:* A D Peters. *Address:* c/o A D Peters, 10 Buckingham Street, London WC2, England.

NEWMAN, Daisy, b. 9 May 1904, Southport, England. Author. m. George Selleck, 18 Mar. 1978, Framingham, 1 son, 1 daughter. *Publications:* Timothy Travels, 1928; Sperli the Clockmaker, 1932; Now That April's There, 1945; Diligence in Love, 1951; The Autumn's Brightness, 1955; Mount Joy, 1968; A Procession of Friends, 1972; I Take Thee, Serenity, 1975; The Wondrous Gift, (Novella); Indian Summer of the Heart, 1982. *Contributor to:* Ladies Home Journal; New Yorker; Saturday Review of Literature; New York Times. *Membership:* Author's Guild. *Literary Agent:* Curtis Brown. *Address:* c/o Houghton Mifflin, 2 Park Street, Boston, MA 02155, USA.

NEWMAN, Paul Baker, b. 12 May 1919, Chicago, Illinois, USA. Professor of English. *Education:* BS, 1940, PhD, 1958, University of Chicago; MFA, University of Iowa, 1951. *Publications:* The Cheetah and the Foundation, 1968; Dust of the Sun, 1969; The Ladder of Love, 1970; Paula, 1975; The House on The Saco, 1978; The Light of the Red House, 1981. *Contributions to:* Massachusetts Review; Literary Review; Antioch Review; Virginia Quarterly; Southern Poetry Review; Carolina Quarterly; Chicago Review; Poetry; Southern Humanities Review; College English; Minnesota Review. *Honours:* Williams Billings Fiske Award for poetry, University of Chicago, 1955; Roanoke-Chowan Award, 1968, 71; Crucible Award, 1969, 75; Award, North Carolina Poetry Society, 1978. *Membership:* Sigma Upsilon. *Address:* 2215 Hassell Place, Charlotte, NC 28209, USA.

NEWMAN, Peter Charles, b. 10 May 1929, Vienna, Austria. Author; Journalist. m. Camilla Jane Turner, 1978. *Education:* BA, MBA, University of Toronto. *Literary Appointments:* Assistant Editor, The Financial Post, 1951–55; Ottawa Editor, Maclean's 1955–64; Ottawa Editor, Toronto Daily Star, 1964–69; Editor-in-Chief, Toronto Daily Star, 1969–71; Editor-in-Chief, Maclean's 1971–82; Director, Macleans Hunter Ltd, 1972–83; Director, Key Radio Ltd, 1983–; Senior Contributing Editor, Maclean's 1982–; Host, weekly TV show on Global Network, 1981–. Publications: Flame of Power, 1959; Renegade in Power, 1963; The Distemper of Our Times, 1968; Home Country, 1973; The

Canadian Establishment: volume I, 1975; Bronfman Dynasty: The Rothschilds of the New World, 1978; The Acquisitors – The Canadian Establishment, volume II, 1981; The Establishment Man, 1982; True North – Not Strong and Free 1983; Debrett's Illustrated Guide to the Canadian Establishment, 1983; Company of Adventurers, 1985. *Honours include:* Honorary Doctor of Laws, Brock University, 1974; Honorary Doctor of Letters, York University, 1975; Quill Award as Journalist of the Year, 1977; Appointed Officer in the Order of Canada, 1978; Awarded Knighthood in the Order of St Lazarus, 1980; Best Television Programme of the Year, ACTRA Awards for two Canadian Establishment programmes, 1981; Promoted to Knight-Commander in the Order of St Lazarus, 1983; Honorary Doctor of Laws, Wilfred Laurier University, 1983; Governor, Shaw Festival, 1984; Director, Saskatchewan Indian Federated College, 1984; Visiting Professor, Creative Writing, University of Victoria, 1985. *Address:* 4855 Major Road, Victoria, BC, Canada V8Y 2L8.

NEWMAN TURNER, Roger, b. 29 Apr. 1940, Radlett, Hertfordshire, England. Acupuncturist; Naturopath; Osteopath. *Education:* Diplomas, Osteopathy and Naturopathy, British College of Naturopathy and Osteopathy; Licenced Acupuncturist, Bachelor of Acupuncture, British College of Acupuncture. *Publications:* First Aid – Natures Way, 1969; Diets to Help Asthma and Hay Fever, 1970; Diets to Help Heart Disease, 1971; Slimmers Guide to Calories, 1974; Self Help for Gallbladder Troubles, 1977; Diets to Help Control Cholesterol, 1978; Principles and Practice of Moxibustion, 1981; Naturopathic Medicine, 1984. *Contributions to:* Various professional journals. *Memberships include:* British Acupuncture Association; British Naturopathic and Osteopathic Association. *Address:* 111 Norton Way South, Letchworth, Hertfordshire, England.

NEWMARK, Leonard, b. 8 Apr. 1929, Attica, Indiana, USA. Professor of Linguistics. m. Ruth Broessler, 16 Sep. 1951, Michigan City, Indiana, 1 son, 1 daughter. *Education:* AB, University of Chicago, 1947; MA 1951, PhD 1955, Indiana University. *Major Publications:* Structural Grammar of Albanian, 1957; Using American English, 1964; A Linguistic Introduction to the History of English, 1963; Spoken Albanian, 1980; Reference Grammar of Albanian, 1982. *Address:* 2643 St Tropez Place, La Jolla, CA 92037, USA.

NEWSOME, George Lane Jr, b. 5 Oct. 1923, Bessemer, Alabama, USA. College Professor. Philosophy of Education. m. Martha Cornelia Merchant, 8 June 1947, Bessemer, 1 son, 2 daughters. *Education:* BS, 1949, MA 1950, University of Alabama; PhD, Yale University, 1956. *Literary Appointments:* Professor, Department of Curriculum & Supervision; Editor, Journal of Research & Development in Education. *Contributions to:* Educational theory; Proceedings of 38th Annual Meeting, Philosophy of Education Society. *Honour:* Outstanding Teaching, Honours Day, University of Georgia, 1982. *Memberships:* President 1981–82, Philosophy of Education Society; Advisory Board, Museum & Archives of Education in Georgia, 1975–. *Address:* 323 Aderhold Hall, University of Georgia, Athens, GA 30602, USA.

NEWTON, Robert Parr, b. 31 July 1929, San Antonio, Texas, USA. Professor. m. Katharina Fides Unteutsch, 1 Aug. 1959, Freiburg, Federal Republic of Germany, 2 sons. *Education:* BA Physics, 1950, MA German, 1958, Rice University; PhD German, John Hopkins University, 1964. *Literary Appointments:* Assistant Professor of German, University of Pennsylvania, 1965–70; Associate, then Full Professor of German, University of North Carolina at Greensboro, 1970–. *Major Publications:* Form in the Menschheitsdämmerung, 1971; Vowel Undersong, 1981; Your Diamond Dreams Cut open my Arteries, (poems by Else Lasker-Schüler), translated, 1983. *Contributor to:* Modern Language Notes; Colloquia Germanica; Scholarly articles in various journals. *Memberships:* Modern Language Association; American

Association of Teachers of German. *Address:* 114 East Brentwood, Greensboro, NC 27403, USA.

NEY, Norbert, b. 30 June 1951, Eutin/Holstein, Federal Republic of Germany. Writer; Translator. *Education:* Translating Diploma, 1973. *Literary Appointments:* Various. *Publications:* Tendenzwendgedichte, 1975; Dankeman lebt, Gedichte, 1978; Nichtsdestotrotz, 1980; Tumult & Traume, 1985; Liebe Laster Leid & Lust, 1983; Nicht mit dir und nicht ohne dich, Lesebuch für schlaflose Nächte, 1984; Sie haben mich zu einen Auslander gemacht – ich bin einer geworden, 1985; Lasst mich bloss in Frieden, Lesebuch, 1981; Ich bin sterilisiert, 1981; Ratgeber Sterilisation, 1986; Traumberufe, 1985; Das andere Junggesellenkochbuch, Rezepte für alle Lebenslagen, 1985. *Contributions to:* About 100 publications. *Honours:* Numerous. *Memberships:* Verband deutscher Schriftsteller; VS-Hamburg. *Address:* Käthnerort 59, D-2000 Hamburg 76, Federal Republic of Germany.

NIBLETT, William Roy, b. 25 July 1906, Keynsham, Somerset, England. University Professor. *Education:* BA, University of Bristol; MLitt, University of Oxford. *Publications:* Education and the Modern Mind, 1954; Christian Education in a Secular Society, 1960; Editor, Moral Education in a Changing Society, 1963; Universities Between Two Worlds, 1974; Editor, The Sciences, The Humanities and the Technological Threat, 1975; The University Connection, with D W Humphreys, 1975. *Contributions to:* Times Higher Education Supplement; Universities Quarterly; Guardian; Fortnightly; Modern Churchman. *Honour:* CBE, 1970. *Address:* 7 Blenheim Road, Bristol BS67 7JL, England.

NICHOLS, Elizabeth L, b. 26 May 1937, Chase City, Virginia, USA. Geneology Writer. *Education:* Secretarial Degree, Howard Business College, Shelby NC, 1959; Accredited Researcher (Genealogist), The Genealogical Department of The Church of Jesus Christ of Latter-day Saints, 1976, 1982; Brigham Young University, Provo, Utah. *Literary Appointments:* Professional Helper editor for the Genealogical Helper, Logan, Utah, 1969–70; Writer and Editor, The Church of Jesus of Latter-day Saints, 1970–; Associate Editor, Genealogical Journal (Utah Genealogical Association, SLC, Utah) 1977–78. *Publications:* The Genesis of YOUR Genealogy 1st ed 1969, 2nd ed 1973; Help is Available 1st ed 1972, 2nd ed 1979. Both Simplified Step-by-Step Instruction Books for the Beginner in Genealogy. *Contributions to:* New England Historical Genealogical Register (Boston, Massachusetts); The Genealogical Journal (Salt Lake City, Utah); The Genealogical Helper (Logan, Utah); The Ensign (Church of Jesus Christ of Latter-day Saints); The New Era, (Church of Jesus Christ of Latter-day Saints); Proceedings of the 1980 World Conference on Records; Today's Greatest Poems; Our Twentieth Century's Greatest Poems. *Honour:* Scholarship to Brigham Young University, 1955. *Memberships:* National Genealogical Society, member, Computer Interest Group; Secretary, Board of Directors, Utah Genealogical Association; International Platform Association; Daughters of the American Revolution (Chapter Insigma Chairman); National Writers Club. *Address:* 28 Hillside Avenue # 2, Salt Lake City, UT 84103, USA.

NICHOLS, John Treadwell, b. 23 July 1940, Berkeley, California, USA. Writer. m. (1) Ruth Harding, 9 Apr. 1965, New York (2) Juanita Wolf, 13 Sep, 1985, Taos, New Mexico, 1 son, 1 daughter. *Education:* Ba, Hamilton College, Clinton, New York, USA. *Major Publications:* The Sterile Cuckoo, 1965; The Wizard of Loneliness, 1966; The Milagro Beanfield War, 1974; The Magic Journey, 1978; If Mountains Die, 1979; A Ghost in the Music, 1979; The Nirvana Blues, 1981; The Last Beautiful Days of Autumn, 1982; On The Mesa, 1986. *Honour:* Governor's Award for Excellence in Literature, New Mexico, 1981. *Literary Agent:* Curtis Brown Ltd, New York. *Address:* P O Box 1165 Taos, NM 87571, USA.

NICHOLS, Peter R, b. 31 July 1927, Bristol, England. Playwright. *Education:* Bristol Old Vic Theatre School;

Trent Park Training College. *Publications include:* (TV Plays) Promenade; Ben Spray; The Gorge; (Stage Plays) A Day in the Death of Joe Egg; The National Health; Forget-me-Not Lane; Chez Nous; The Freeway; Privates on Parade; Born in the Gardens; Passion Play; (Stage Musical) Peppy; (Autobiography) Feeling You've Behind. *Honours:* 3 Evening Standard Drama Awards; John Whiting (shared); Plays & Players; Variety Critics; Society of West End Theatres; Ivor Novello Award; 2 SWET Awards; 1 Tony Award. 1985. *Memberships:* Arts Council, Drama Panel, 3 years; Governor, Greenwich Theatre, 5 years. *Agent:* Dr Jan Van Loewen. *Address:* 60 Albert St, London NW1, England.

NICHOLS, Roger David Edward, b. 6 Apr. 1939, Ely, England. Writer. m. Sarah Anne Edwards. 11 Apr. 1964, Lisvane, Cardiff, Wales, 2 sons, 1 daughter. *Education:* MA, Music, Oxford University; Fellow of Royal College of Organists. *Publications:* Debussy, 1973; Through Greek Eyes (with K McLeish), 1974; Messiaen, 1975; Through Roman Eyes (with K McLeish), 1976; Ravel, 1977; Greek Everyday Life (with Sarah Nichols), 1978; Livy, Stories of Rome, 1982. *Contributions to:* Articles and reviews in Musical Times, Music and Letters, Times Literary Supplement. *Address:* West End, Docklow, Leominster, Herefordshire HR6 0RU.

NICHOLSON, Geoffrey, b. 11 Apr. 1929, London, England. Journalist. m. Mavis Mainwaring, 16 Aug. 1952, Kensington, London, 3 sons. *Education:* BA English, University College, Swansea, Wales, 1949–52. *Literary Appointments:* Sports Features Editor, The Sunday Times, 1964–65; Sports Editor, The Observer, 1976–78. *Major Publications:* Report on Rugby (with W John Morgan), 1959; The Professionals, 1964; The Great Bike Race, 1977. *Contributor to:* The Observer; The Sunday Times; The Times; The Guardian; The Spectator; Time & Tide; Management Today; and others. *Literary Agent:* David Higham Associates. *Address:* Aber-Rhaeadr Farmhouse, Llanrhaeadr-ym-Mochnant, Powys SY10 0AX, Wales.

NICHOLSON, Norman, b. 8 Jan. 1914. Millom, Cumbria, England. Author. m. Yvonne Gardner, 6 July 1956, Millum, deceased 1982. *Publications:* Five Rivers, 1944; The Old Man at the Mountainside, 1945; Cumberland and Westmoreland, 1947; The Pot Geranium, 1954; The Lakers, 1954; Greater Lakeland, 1968; A Local Habitation, 1971; Wednesday Early Closing, 1975; Sea To The West, 1982. *Contributions to:* Times Literary Supplement; Stand; Church Times. *Honours:* Heinemann Prize, 1965; Honorary MA, Manchester, 1958; Cholmondeley Award, 1967; Honorary MA, Open University, 1975; Queen's Medal for Poetry, 1977; Honorary Litt D, Liverpool, 1980; OBE, 1981; Honorary D Litt, Lancaster, 1984. *Membership:* Fellow, Royal Society of Literature. *Literary Agent:* David Higham Associates. *Address:* 14 St George's Terrace, Millom, Cumbria, England.

NICK, Dagmar, b. 30 May 1926, Breslau, German Republic. Writer. *Education:* Studies of Psychology and Graphology, Munich, 1947–50. *Publications:* (Poetry) Martyrer, 1947; Das Buch Holofernes, 1955; In den Ellipsen des Mondes, 1959; Zeugnis und Zeichen, 1969; Fluchtlinien, 1978; Gezahlte Tage, 1986; (Prose), Einladung nach Israel, 1963; Rhodos, 1967; Israel gestern und haute, 1968; Sizilien, 1976; Gotterinseln der Agais, 1981. *Contributor to:* Zeit; Frankfurter Allgemeine Zeitung; Akzente; Merian; Westermanns Monatshefte; Horen. *Honours:* Liliencron Prize, Hamburg 1948; Eichendorff-Prize 1966; Honorary Award, Gryphius Prize, 1970; Roswitha Medal, 1977. *Memberships:* PEN Club; Association of German Writers. *Address:* Kuglmüllerstrasse 22, D 8000 Munich 19, Federal Republic of Germany.

NICKELL, Joe, b. 1 Dec. 1944, Lexington, Kentucky, USA. Investigative Writer. *Education:* BA, 1967, MA, 1982, University of Kentucky. *Publication:* Inquest on the Shroud of Turin, 1983. *Contributions to:* Popular Photography; Canada West; Journal of Police Science and Administration; Law Enforcement Technology; Virginia Magazine of History and Biography; Indiana Folklore; Performing Arts in Canada; Fate; Skeptical Inquirer; Identification News; Appalachian Heritage; The Fire and Arson Investigator; Filson Club History Quarterly. *Honour:* Farquhar Award for Poetry, University of Kentucky, 1967. *Address:* PO Box 67, West Liberty, KY 41472, USA.

NICOL, Eric Patrick, b. 28 Dec. 1919, Kingston, Ontario, Canada. Writer. m. Mary Helen Heselton, 13 Sep. 1955, Vancouver. 1 son, 2 daughters. *Education:* BA, 1941, MA, 1948, University of British Columbia. *Publications Include:* Sense and Nonsense, 1948; The Roving I; Twice Over Lightly; Shall We Join the Ladies; Girdle Me a Globe; In Darkest Domestica; An Uninhibited History of Canada; Say, Uncle; A Herd of Yaks; Russia, Anyone?; Space Age Go Home!; 100 Years of What?; A Scar is Born; Vancouver; Don't Move; Still a Nicol; One Man's Media; Letters to my Son; There's a Lot of It Going Around; Cancelled Because of the Lack of Interest; The Joy of Hockey; The Joy of Football; Golf-The Agony and the Ecstacy; Tennis-It Serves You Right; Canadide; How To..., 1985. *Contributions to:* Numerous publications including: British Broadcasting Corporation comedy series, writer; The Province, columnist, Vancouver, Canada. *Honours:* Winner of Stephen Leacock Award for Humour, 1950, 55, 57. *Address:* 3993 West 36th Avenue, Vancouver, British Columbia, Canada V6N 2S7.

NICOLSON, James Robert, b. 10 July 1934, Shetland, Scotland. Author; Journalist. m. Violet Sinclair, 6 Sep. 1965, Lerwick, 1 son, 2 daughters. *Education:* Anderson Institute, Lerwick, BSc, MA, Aberdeen University. *Literary Appointments:* Editor, Shetland Life, 1980. *Publications:* Shetland, 1972; Traditional Life in Shetland, 1978; Food From The Sea, 1979; Shetland Folklore, 1981. *Contributions to:* The Shetland Times (weekly column, 1976–); Fishing News, *Address:* Fairhaven, Castle Street, Scalloway, Shetland ZE1 0TP, Scotland.

NIELSEN, Frederik W, b. 21 Sep. 1903, Stuttgart, Federal Republic of Germany. Writer; Lecturer. m. (1) Elfriede Wunderlich, 29 Nov. 1948, Birmingham, deceased. 31 Oct. 1982, (2) Irene Schulz, 2 Mar. 1984, Freiburg. *Education:* Evangelical Theology Seminary in Schöntal and Urach; Theatrical & Directing Pupil, Berlin. *Publications:* Kleiner Zyklus Deutschland, 1935; Peter Bohnenstroh, 1935; Kniha v plamenech, 1936; Ernte, 1936; Dank dem Geiste T G Masaryks, 1937; Appell an die Welt, 1938; Kleine Stadt Wozu?, 1964; Nachlese 1933–39, 1971; Eleonora Duse, 1974; Emigrant für Deutschland, 1977; Protest gegen einen Buchmord, 1978; Reminiszenzen 1934–79, 1980; Rückblick, poetry 1983; Krieg dem Mord, 1983; Eleonora Duse – Josef Kainz, 1984; Es begann in Prag, 1984; Translator of: Havlícek – Tiroler Elegien, 1936; Neruda – Nachdichtungen, 1936; Herben-Masaryks Familienleben, 1937. *Contributor to:* various newspapers. *Address:* Sundgauallee 19, 7800 Freiburg, Federal Republic of Germany.

NIELSEN, Helen Berniece, b. 23 Oct, 1918, Roseville, Illinois, USA. Writer. *Publications:* The Kind Man, 1951; Gold Coast Nocturne, 1951; Detour 1953; The Woman on the Roof, 1954; Stranger in the Dark, 1955; Borrow the Night, 1956; False Witness, 1956; The Fifth Caller, 1959; The Crime is Murder, 1960; Verdict Suspended, 1964; After Midnight, 1966; Darkest Hour, 1969; Shot on Location, 1972; The Severed Key, 1973; The Brink of Murder, 1976; etc, together with Teleplays. *Contributions to:* Ellery Queen Magazine; Alfred Hitchcock Magazine; Toronto Star. *Honours:* Best Detective Stories – David Cooke Anthologies, 1955; Ellery Queen Anthologies, 1962, 1972; Best Legal Stories – Welcome, 1970; Alfred Hitchcock Anthologies, etc. *Membership:* The Authors' Guild. *Literary Agent:* Ann Elmo, New York. *Address:* 2622 Victoria Drive, Laguna Beach, CA 92651, USA.

NIELSEN, Herluf, b. 23 Dec. 1922, Naestved, Denmark. Editor. *Education:* MA, University of Copenhagen, 1948; Certificate for Teaching, 1948. *Publications:* Diplomatarium Danicum, 3rd series, volumes I-IX, 1958–82; Danish Translation, Danmarks Riges Breve and Volume I 789-1052, Volume III, 1170–1199 of 1st series, with C A Christensen, 4th series, volume I, 1984; Kronologi, 1962, 2nd edition, 1967; Ein papstliches Formellbuch aus der Zeit des [el] Schismas, 1979. *Honours:* Munksgaardsprisen, 1966. *Memberships:* Danish Society of Language and Literature; Kungliga Samfundet for Utgivande av handskrifter rorande Skandinaviens historia. *Address:* Norsvej 32, 2920 Charlottenlund, Denmark.

NIELSON, Roger Charles, b. 29 Feb. 1952, Omaha, Nebraska, USA. Writer; Poet; Printer. m. Christine Marie Beckenhauer, 23 Oct. 1982, Omaha, 2 sons. *Education:* Graduate Information Specialist, DINFOS, DOD, 1977; BFA, Writers Workshop, College of Fine Arts, University of Nebraska, 1984. *Literary Appointments:* Foundry Worker: Cummington Press; Abattoir Press: Fine Art Press, University of Nebraska, Omaha. Associate Editor or Editor: Smackwarm/Nebraska Review Magazine, University of Nebraska, 1979–84. Proprietor, Dutchess Press, 1979–. *Publications:* Cattails and Sandbars, 1976; If It's Friday, Then You're in Omaha, 1976; The Whiteness Was all Around Me, 1976; We Parted Arms Southwest of Galveston, 1976; The Guardian of Coppenbrugge, 1979; Towering, 1983; Bid the Banns, 1983; 6514 Franklin, 1985. Assisted in the production and publication of numerous works for Abattoir Editions and for University of Nebraska. Various emphemera and errata for Dutchess Press, 1979–. *Contributions to:* Various magazines and journals; Editor, Head Start Development Corporation Newsletter; Editor and Media Relations, Douglas County Health Department, 1985–. *Honours:* Diploma di Merito, University of Art, Italy, 1982; Honorable Mention, Maxim's Regional High Plains Art Exhibit, Greely, Colorado, 1980. *Membership:* Former Member and Office Holder, Nevbraska Poets Association. *Address:* PO Box 4221, Omaha, NE 68104, USA.

NIEMINEN, Kai Tapani, b. 11 May 1950, Helsinki, Finland, Poet; Translator. Divorced, 1 daughter. *Publications:* Joki vie ajatukseni, 1971; Syntymästä, 1973; Kiirreettä, 1977; Tie jota oli kuljettava, 1979; Vain mies, 1981; Elämän vouteessa, 1982; Oudommin kuin unessa, 1983; En Min[im]a tiedä, 1985. Translations from Japanese include: Joutilaan mietteitä, 1978; Kapea tie phojoiseen, 1981; Harhojenmaja, 1984; Genji monogatari; Kokoro, 1985. *Contributions to:* Numerous translations of Japanese poetry, essays on Japanese literature and culture. *Honours:* National Literary Awards for translations, Ministry of Educations, 1978, 82. *Memberships:* Finnish Authors Society; Eino Leinon Seura Society. *Literary Agent:* Tammi Publishers. *Address:* Baggböle, 07740 Gammelby, Finland.

NIEMINEN, Kaiho Kalervo, b. 20 Dec. 1941, Viipuri, Finland. Writer. m. Tellervo Lapatto, 12 Nov. 1967, 1 son, 1 daughter. *Major Publications:* Locistoori, 1972; Tavallinen Impi, 1973; Valtakunta, 1976; Isat, 1978; Saalistajat, 1982; AidItön mies, 1985. *Honours:* 1st Prize, Weilin Göös Centenary Competition, 1972; J H Erkko Prize, 1972; State and Cultural awards. *Memberships:* Finnish Literary Society; Writers of Helsinki; Eino Leino Society. *Literary Agent:* Werner Söderström. *Address:* Merikorttitie 4 B 634, 00960 Helsinki, Finland.

NIEMINEN, Matti Johannes, b. 19 Apr. 1948, Tampere, Finland. Dramaturge. m. 24 Feb. 1971. *Education:* MA. *Publications:* Plays: Aikataikarauta, 1971; Sirkus Sorkys, 1972; Prinssi ja Supermies, 1979; Pimeat rahat, 1985. *Contributions to:* Ryhma 84; Kaltio. *Membership:* Finnish Dramatists' Society. *Address:* Lehtokatu 16 c, 94100 Kemi 10, Finland.

NIGRO, Felix Anthony, b. 8 Aug. 1914, Brooklyn, New York, USA. Teacher; Author; Arbitrator. m. Edna Helen Nelson, 28 July 1938, Henderson, Kentucky, 1 son, 1 daughter. *Education:* AB, 1935, AM, 1936, PhD, 1948, University of Wisconsin. *Publications:* Public Administration: Readings and Documents, 1951; Public Personel Administration, 1959; Modern Public Administration, 1969, 6th edition with Lloyd G Nigro, 1984; Management Employee Relations in Public Service, 1969; Readings in Public Administration, with L G Nigro, 1983; Public Personnel Administration, with L G Nigro, 1976, 3rd edition, 1986. *Contributor to:* 70 articles in professional journals. *Address:* 199 Westview Drive, Athens, GA 30606, USA.

NIKAUS, Robert, b. 18 July 1910, London, England. Professor of French. m. (1) Thelma Elinor Florence Jones, 25 July 1936 (deceased 1970) 2 sons, 1 daughter. (2) Kathleen Anne Folta, 27 Jan. 1973. *Education:* BA, PhD, London: L es L, Lille, France. *Publications:* Jean Moreas, poete lyrique, 1936; A Literary History of France: The Eighteenth Century, 1970; Le Barbier de Seville, 1968; Le Mariage de Figaro, 1983; Numerous critical editions of French texts for French and English publishers; General Editor, Textes Francais Classiques et Modernes. *Contributions to:* Encyclopedia Britannica; Chamber's Encyclopaedia of Philosophy; The Year's Work in Modern Language Studies; The Romanic Review; The Contemporary Review; Studies on Voltaire and the Eighteenth Century; The British Journal for Eighteenth-Century Studies; The Revie d'histoire litteraire de la France; Etudes Anglaises; Reviews in European History; Revue Internationale de Philosophie; French Studies. *Honours:* Dr Honoris cause, University of Rennes, 1963; Officer de l'ordre National du Merite, 1973; Emeritus Professor of French, University of Exeter, 1976; Hon D Litt, Exon, 1981. *Memberships:* President 1968–70, Society for French Studies; Treasurer 1968–79, International Society for Eighteenth Century Studies. *Address:* 17 Elm Grove Road, Topsham, Exeter, EX3 0EQ, England.

NIKLANDER, Hannu Kustaa, b. 16 Mar. 1951. Writer; Critic; Journalist; Teacher. *Education:* MA, Finnish Literature, Political History, Altaic Philology, History of Art, University of Helsinki, 1983. *Appointments:* Editor in Chief, Journal of Students of Literature, 1973–74; Columnist, Helsingin Sanomat Newspaper, 1984–; Columist, Kirjastolehti, 1983–. *Publication:* Kotiinpäin, 1974; Maakuntalaulu, 1979; Kauniisti niiaava tytär, 1983; Redactor for an Anthology of Young Short Stories, Kenkää enolle, 1983. *Contributor to:* Kaltio; Kulttuurivihkot; Kanava; Newspapers and Magazines in Sweden, Norway, Soviet Union, Bugaria, Romania, India. *Honours:* 1st Prize, Poetry Competition, Nuoren Vioman Liitto, 1972. *Memberships:* Eino Leino Society; PEN Club, Finland; Union of Provincial Writers; Union of Finnish Critics. *Address:* Ollila, Vihti, Finland.

NIKULA, Karl Oscar, b. 31 May 1907, Vasa, Finland. University Professor Emeritus of History. *Education:* MA, 1928; PhD, 1934; Abo Akademi. *Literary Appointment:* With Civic Administration in Finland. *Publications:* Svenska skargardsflottan 1756–91, 1933; Tenala och Bromarf socknars historia, 1938; Augustin Ehrensvard, 1960; Abo stads historia 1721–1809, 1972; Abo stads historia 1809–1856, 1974. *Honours:* Falckenska priset, 1939; Hedvig von Schantz pris, 1961; Eklund-Modeenska priset, 1974; Svenska litt. sallskapet i Finland; Svenska Akademiens Finlandia pris, Stockholm, 1982. *Memberships:* Research Member, Finska historiska samfundet, 1952; Societas Scientiarum Fennica, 1953; K Hum Vetenskapssamfundet i Lund, 1965; 1 K Hum. Vegenskapssamfundet i Uppsala, 1975; Research Member, Tunn hist. Yhdistys, 1967. *Address:* Slottsg 28A, 20100 Abo 10, Finland.

NILSEN, Aileen Pace, b. 10 Oct. 1936, Phoenix, Arizona, USA. University Professor. m. Don L F Nilsen, 21 Mar 1958, Phoenix, Arizona, 2 sons, 1 daughter. *Education:* BA, Brigham Young University, 1958; MEd, American University, 1961; PhD, University of Iowa, 1973. *Literary Appointments:* Instructor of English, Highland Park Junior College, 1961; Instructor of English, Eastern Michigan University, 1964; Assistant Professor of Teaching, Northern Iowa University, 1971; Assistant Professor of Education, 1975, Associate

Professor of Education, 1978, Professor of Education, 1981–, Arizona State University. *Publications:* Pronunciation Contrasts, (with Don L F Nilson) 1971; Sexism and Language, 1977; Language Play (with Don L F Nilsen) 1978; Changing Words in a Changing World, 1980; Literature for Today's Young Adults, (with Ken Donelson), 1980, 1985; Dust in our Desks, 1985. *Contributions to:* Winning the Great He/She Battle, College English, 1984; The Adult as Critic vs the Child as Reader, Language Arts, 1980; Children's Literature and Mass Media School Library Journal, 1977; Sexism in English: A Feminist View, Female Studies VI, 1972; Women in Children's Literature, College English, 1971. *Memberships:* National Council of Teachers of English; Rocky Mountain Modern Language Association; Assembly on Literature for Adolescents, NCTE (President 1976). *Address:* 1884 E Alameda, Tempe, AZ 85282, USA.

NILSEN, Mary Ylvisaker, b. 1 Cot. 1938, Fargo, North Dakota, USA. m. Roy C Nilsen, 2 Apr. 1960, Moorhead, Minnesota, USA, 2 sons, 3 daughters. *Education:* BA, Concordia College, Moorhead, Minnesota; MA Expository Writing, University of Iowa. *Literary Appointments:* Teacher, Freshmen Rhetoric, 1982–85; Editor, Iowa Woman, quarterly journal of information, literature & Art, 1983–85. *Major Publications:* Real Living (study of St Luke's Gospel), 1977–79; Our Family Shares Advent, 1980; Tending the Family Tree, 1980; The Story of Our Church, 1983; When a Bough Breaks, 1985. *Contributor to:* The Other Side; Iowa Woman. *Address:* 2710 East Court, Iowa City, IA 52240, USA.

NILSSON, Bo Sigvard, b. 11 Nov. 1942, Gotenberg, Sweden. Author. *Publications:* Undinas Horn, 1968; Forlorare, 1969; Domsucusua flichorug 1970; Dagsens Sanning, 1972; Den raa Styrhan, 1974; Min Mootar Egen, 1984. *Memberships:* Swedish Union of Playwrites; Swedish Writers Union. *Address:* Lutagardsvägen 40, 44300 Lerum, Sweden.

NILSSON, Nic, b. 1 Nov. 1933, Lund, Sweden. Ombudsman. *Education:* The Geneva School, Switzerland; University of Manchester, England. *Publications:* Space for Play, 1969; The Bugbears in the playground Debate, 1970; ABC Adventure Playgrounds, 1972; High-Rise or Low-Rise Housing, 1974; Play for Everybody, 1975; Together in the Block, 1978; War is No Game, 1981; Education for Peace, 1982; Our Leisure, 1986. *Contributions to:* Miljospegein (Editor); Var Bostad; Att Bc; Tiden; Aktuellt; Byggmastaren; Byggnadsarbetaren; Aftonbladet; Arbetet; Ny Tid; Stockholms-Tidningen. *Membership:* Swedish Union of Authors. *Agent:* Tidens Forlag, Stockholm. *Address:* Norrtullsgatan 12 B, S–11327 Stockholm, Sweden.

NIMMO, Kurt, b. 18 Nov. 1952, Detroit, Michigan, USA. Writer. *Publications:* Confederate Jasmine, 1975; Waves in the Sun, 1977; Midnight Shift in Detroit, 1978; Message From Phobos, 1979; Notes on a Condition, 1984; Aura, 1985; Destined for Oblivion, 1985; The Hostage Notes. *Contributions to:* Samisdat; Cumberland Journal; A Smudge on the Window; Gypsy; Poetry Motel; Thunder Sandwich; Random Wierdness; Gargoyle; Planet Detroit; Mockersatz; Verse and Universe. Numerous others. *Honour:* Editor of the Year Award, Pig in a Pamphlet, 1984. *Address:* P O Box 28414, Detroit, MI 48228, USA.

NIMNICHT, Nona, b. 17 Mar. 1930. Legal Secretary. *Education:* BA, University of Colorado, 1952; MA, Colorado State University, 1966; MA, University of California, Berkeley, 1969. *Literary Appointments:* English Instructor, Colorado State University, 1966–67, Chapman College, 1973–76, Merritt College, 1973–78; Legal Sectretary, Oakland, California, 1978–. *Major Publication:* In the Museum Naked, 1978. *Contributor to:* Numerous literary periodicals including: Bay Guardian; Blue Unicorn; California Quarterly; Colorado State Review; Contemporary Women Poets; Poetry Flash; Poetry Now; Quarterly West; San Francisco Review of Books. *Honours:* Residency, Helene Wurlitzer Foundation of the Arts, Taos, New Mexico, 1980; James

D Phelan Award, Montalvo Centre for the Arts, California, 1981; National Endowment for the Arts Creative Writing Fellowship, 1984–85. *Address:* 303 Adams, apt 210, Oakland, CA 94610, USA.

NIMS, John Frederick, b. 20 Nov. 1913. Professor; Editor, Poetry Chicago. m. Bonnie Larkin, 1 son, 2 daughters. *Education:* AB, 1937, MA, 1939, University of Notre Dame; PhD, University of Chicago, 1945. *Literary Appointments:* Professor of numerous universities including: University of Notre Dame, University of Florence, University of Illinois, Harvard University, Williams College; Editor, Poetry, Chicago. *Publications:* The Iron Pastoral, 1947; A Fountain in Kentucky, 1950; The Poems of St John of the Cross, translation, 1958, 3rd edition 1979; Knowledge of the Evening, 1960; Of Flesh and Bone, 1967; Sappho to Valery; Poems in Translation, 1971; The Harper Anthology of Poetry, 1980; The Kiss: A Jambalaya, poems, 1982; Selected Poems, 1982; A Local Habitation: Essays on Poetry, 1985. *Contributions to:* Numerous magazines, journals and reviews including: Poetry; Hudson Review; Atlantic; Harpers; Time Literary Supplement; Saturday Review. *Honours include:* National Institute of Arts and Letters Award, 1967; Creative Arts Poetry Award. Brandeis University, 1972; Fellowship, Academy of American Poets, 1982. *Address:* 3920 Lake Shore Drive, Chicago, IL 60613, USA.

NINEHAM, Dennis Eric, b. 27 Sep. 1921, Southampton, England. University Teacher; Clerk in Holy Orders. m. Ruth Corfield Miller, 13 Aug. 1946, Oxford, 2 sons, 2 daughters. *Education:* BA, Lit Hum, 1943, BA, Theology, 1945, MA, 1947, BD, 1964, DD, Oxford University, 1977, BD, Cambridge University, 1964. *Publications:* Studies in the Gospels, (Editor) 1956; A New Way of Looking at the Gospels, 1961; The Church's Use of the Bible, (Editor), 1963; The Gospel of St Mark, 1963; The Use and Abuse of the Bible, 1976; Explorations in Theology, 1977. *Contributor to:* Journal of Theological Studies; Theology; Epworth Review; Times Literary Supplement; Expository Times; Theol; Biblica. *Honours:* DD, Birmingham University; DD, Berkeley Divinity School, Yale University, USA. *Address:* 4 Wootten Drive, Iffley Turn, Oxford OX4 4DS, England.

NISBET, Dennis John, b. 17 Apr. 1920, Southend-on-Sea, Essex, England. Administrative Officer (retired); Essex County Councillor. m. Joy Holman, Hendon, England, 2 Mar. 1951, 2 sons. *Major Publications:* Compiler of indexes to numerous published works. *Memberships:* Society of Indexers. *Address:* 1 Ash Road, Benfleet, Essex SS7 2BA, England.

NIVEN, Alastair Neil Robertson, b. 25 Feb. 1944, Edinburgh, Scotland. Lecturer; University Administrator; Formerly Director General, Africa Centre, 1978–84. m. Helen Margaret Trow, 22 Aug. 1970, Chelmsford, 1 son, 1 daughter. *Education:* MA, University of Cambridge; MA, University of Ghana; PhD, University of Leeds. *Publications:* The Commonwealth Writer Overseas, Editor, 1976; D H Lawrence: The Novels, 1978; The Yoke of Pity: The Fiction of Mulk Raj Anand, 1979; D H Lawrence: The Writer and his Work, 1980. *Contributor to:* Journal of Commonwealth Literature; Ariel; Times; Literature Half-Yearly; etc. *Honours:* Honorary Lecturer, School of Oriental & African Studies, 1979–85; Honorary Fellow, Institute of Commonwealth Studies, University of London, 1985–. *Memberships:* Chairman, Greater London Arts Association Literature Panel, 1981–84; Executive Committee, United Kingdom Council on Overseas Student Affairs. *Address:* Eden House, 28 Weathercock Lane, Woburn Sands, Buckinghamshire MK17 8NT, England.

NIVEN, Sir (Cecil) Rex, b. 30 Nov. 1901, Japan. Retired Administrator. m. Dorothy Marshall Mason, 9 June 1925, London, 2 daughters (1 deceased). *Education:* MA, Balliol College, Oxford. *Publications:* 12 titles including: Short History of Nigeria, 1937 (13 editions to 1966); Outline of a Colony, 1945; How Nigeria is Governed, 1950; Nine Great African, 1964; War of Nigerian Unity, 1970; Nigerian Kaleidoscope, 1968.

Contributions to: Royal Geographical Journal; Colonial and Nigerian Journals, etc. Honours: Knight Bachelor, 1960; CMG, 1954; MC, 1968. Memberships: Council Member, Royal Society of Art; Royal Geographical Society; Royal African Society. Address: 12 Archery Square, Walmer, Kent CT14 7HP, England.

NOAKES, Vivien, b. 16 Feb. 1937, England. Writer. m. Michael Noakes, 9 July 1960, Reigate, 2 sons, 1 daughter. Publications: Edward Lear: The Life of a Wanderer 1968, US 1969, 1985; For Lovers of Edward Lear, 4 volumes, editor, 1978; Edward Lear 1812–1888, English 1985, US 1986. Contributor to: The Times; The Times Literary Supplement; The New Scientist; The Harvard Magazine. Literary Agent: Watson, Little Ltd. Address: 146 Hamilton Terrace, London NW8 9UX.

NOBES, Christopher William, b. 20 Mar. 1950, Portsmouth, England. University Professor. m. Diana Jane Harris, 27 Mar. 1982, Exeter, England. Education: BA Economics 1968–71, PhD Accounting 1982, Exeter University; Fellow, Chartered Association of Certified Accountants, 1973. Literary Appointments: Journals committee, Institute of Chartered Accountants in England and Wales, 1981–82; Editorial board, Accounting and Business Research, 1980–; Associate Editor, Accounting and Business Research, 1982–. Publications: The Economics of Taxation (with S R James), 1978 and 1983; Introduction to Financial Accounting, 1980 and 1983; Comparative International Accounting (with R H Parker), 1981 and 1985; Becoming an Accountant, 1983; The Development of Double Entry, 1984; International Classification of Financial Reporting, 1984; The Pocket Accountant, 1984; Accountants Liability in the 1980's (with E P Minnis), 1985. Contributions to: Accounting and Business Research; Journal of Business Finance and Accounting; Accounting Review; Abacus; British Tax Review; Journal of Business Law; Accountancy; The Accountant; Journal of Business Law. Address: Department of Accounting and Finance, University of Strathclyde, Glasgow G4, Scotland.

NOBLE, William Charles, b. 19 Mar. 1935, London, England. Professor, Microbiology. Education: BSc, London; MSc, London; PhD, London; DSc, London; FRCPath. Publications: Coli, Great Healer of Men – Biography of Dr L Colebrook, 1974; Microbiology of Human Skin, 2nd edition 1981; Microbial Skin Disease, 1983; Prevent Infection, 1983. Contributor to: More than 100 articles in scientific journals. Address: Institute of Dermatology, Homerton Grove, London E9 6BX, England.

NOCK, Oswald Stevens, b. 21 Jan. 1905, Sutton Coldfield, Warwickshire, England. Chartered Engineer. m. Olivia Hattie Ravenall, 15 May 1937, Bushey, Hertfordshire, 1 son, 1 daughter. Education: BSc Engineering, DIC, FCGI, Imperial College, London University. Literary Appointments: Honorary Editor, Journal of Institution of Railway Signal Engineers. Publications: Author of 131 books on engineering and railways, biography, 1945–, most recently British Locomotives in the 20th Century, 3 volumes, 1983–85. Contributions to: The Engineer; Railway Gazette; Railway Magazine. Honours: Fellow, Institution of Civil Engineers, Institution of Mechanical Engineers; Fellow and Past President, Institution of Railway Signal Engineers. Address: 28 High Bannerdown, Batheaston, Bath, Avon BA1 7JY, England.

NOELLE-NEUMANN, Elisabeth, b. 19 Dec. 1916, Berlin, Federal Republic of Germany. Head, Instiut für Demoskopie Allensbach; Director, Institut fur Demoskopie Allensbach; Professor Emeritus, Institut fur Publizistik, University of Mainz; Visiting Professor, University of Chicago, 1978–. Education: Graduate, University, Berlin 1940. Publications include: Umfrageforschung in der Rechtspraxis, with Carl Schramm, 1961; Umfragen in der Massengesellschaft Einführung in die Methoden der Demoskopie, 1963, 7th edition, 1976, translated into French, Dutch, Czech, Spanish, Russian; Öffentlichkeit als Bedrohung,

Beiträge zur empirischen Kommunikationsforschung, 1977, 2nd edition 1979; Werden Wir alle Proletarier? Wertewandel in unserer Gesellschaft, 1978; Die Schweigespirale, öffentliche Meinung – unserer soziale Haute, 1980, Paperback editor with new introduction 1982, English Edition, 1984; Eine Generation Spaeter, (with co-author), 1983; Eine Demoskopische Deutschstunde, 1983; Macht Arbeit Krank: Macht Arbeit Glueclkich?, 1984; Editor, Several books. Contributor to: Numerous books; Publizistik; Politische Vierteljahresschrift; Public Opinion Quarterly; Journal of Communication. Honours include: Honorary Doctor, St Gallen College, 1978; Commander's Cross of the Order of Merit of the Federal Republic of Germany. Memberships: World Association for Public Opinion Research, (President 1978–80, Council Member 1980–); Editorial Board, Public Opinion Quarterly. Address: Institut für Demoskopie Allensbach, Radolfzeller Str 8, D-7753 Allensbach 1, Federal Republic of Germany.

NOGEE, Joseph Lippman, b. 16 June 1929, Schenectady, New York, USA. Political Scientist. m. Jo Nabors, 17 Dec. 1960. Fresno, 1 son, 1 daughter. Education: BSFS, Georgetown School of Foreign Service, Washington DC; MA, University of Chicago; PhD, Yale University. Publications: Soviet Policy Toward International Control of Atomic Energy. 1961; The Politics of Disarmament, co-author, 1962; Man, State and Society in the Soviet Union, editor, 1972; Congress, the Presidency and American Foreign Policy, co-editor, 1981; Soviet Foreign Policy since World War II, co-author, 1984; Soviet Politics, Russia After Brezhnev, Editor, 1985. Contributor to: International Conciliation; Conflict Resolution; Anals of the American Academy of Political and Social Science; World Affairs; Orbis; Vital Issues; Journal of Inter-American Studies and World Affairs, Parameters. Address: 8735 Link Terrace, Houston, TX 77025, USA.

NOLAN, Patrick, b. 1 Feb. 1933, Bronx, New York, USA. Teacher. m. Karen Ursula O'Connor, 10 May 1969, St John Neuman, 3 sons. Education: MA, English Literature, University of Detroit, 1969; PhD, English Literature, Bryn Mawr College. Appointments: Instructor, University of Detroit; Professor, Villanova University. Publications: Films: The Hourglass Moment, 1968; The Jericho Mile, 1978. Contributor to: The Origin of Fear in The Emporer Jones, O'Neill Newsletter, 1980; A Jungian View of Desire Under the Elms, O'Neill Newsletter, 1981. Honours: Emmy Award, Academy of Television Arts & Sciences, 1979; Citation for Teaching Excellence, Philadelphia Magazine, 1980. Membership: Writers Guild of America, West. Address: English Dept, Villanova University, Villanova, PA 19087, USA.

NOLAND, Patricia Hampton, Poet. Education: University of Houston, Texas, USA, 1963–69. Publications: Poems, 1960; Editor, Whoever Heard a Birdie Cry? (collection of juvenile poetry by Lottie Catherine Robinett). Contributor to: New Orleans Times-Picayune: Houston Post; Boise Daily Statesman; Jackson Daily News; River Oaks Times; Buffalo Courier Express; Newsletter of International Poetry Institute; SW Gardener. Honours: Honorary International Poet Laureate International, Mahila, Philippines, 1969; Honorary Doctorate, International Academy of Leadership, Cuezon City, Manila, Philippines, 1969; DHL, Free University, University of Asia, Karachi, Pakistan, 1973; Diploma of Merit, Accademia Italia, University Delle Arti, 1986. Memberships: Founder, International Poetry Institute, Houston, Texas; Iowa Poetry Day Association. Address: PO Box 53087, Houston, TX 77052, USA.

NOONAN, Lowell Gerald, b. 11 Feb. 1922, San Francisco, USA. Professor of Political Science. m. Mary Joan Westfall, 2 Sep. 1949, Oakland, 2 daughters. Education: AB, San Francisco State University, 1944; MA, Political Science, Stanford University, 1946; PhD, Political Science, University of California, Berkeley. Publications: European Politics and Government (co-author), 1962; France; The Politics of Continuity in Change, 1970; European Political Party Systems (co-author), 1980. Contributions to: Journal of Political, The

Decline of the Liberal Party in British Politics, 1954; Western Political Quarterly, French Politics Today: Rebirth or Devaluation, 1959; Some Aspects of the Fifth French Republic, 1960. *Honours:* Fellow, Fund for Advancement of Education, 1952–53; Senior Fulbright Research Professor, Institut d'etudes politiques, Paris, 1957–58; Senior Fulbright Lecturer, University of Innsbruck, Austria, 1966–67. *Address:* Department of Political Science, California State University, 18111, Nordhoff St, Northridge, CA 91330, USA.

NORA, James Jackson, b. 26 June 1928, Chicago, Illinois, USA. Physician; Writer. m. Audrey Hart, 9 Apr. 1966, Houston, Texas, 1 son, 4 daughters. *Education:* AB, Harvard University; MD, Yale University; MPH California (Berkeley). *Publications:* 9 Books: Medical Genetics, 1st edition 1974, 2nd edition, 1981, with F C Fraser; Genetic Counseling, with A H Nora, 1978; The Whole Heart Book, 1980; Congenital Heart Disease, with A Takao; etc. *Contributor to:* Over 150 articles in professional journals. *Memberships:* Authors Guild; Authors League; Academy of American Poets. *Address:* 6135 E.6th Avenue, Denver, CO 80220, USA.

NORITIS, Rudolfs-Pauls, b. 6 May 1920, Riga, Latvia. Landscape Architect. 2 sons, 1 daughter. *Education:* Diploma, State Horticulture College, Latvia, 1940; Various courses, Univerity of Guelf, Canada. *Literary Appointments:* Editor, Latvia America, 1967–72; Editor various Latvian Almanacs in Canada; Staff reporter, Latvian newspapers including Latvia America, and Latvian Times, USA. *Contributions to:* Satires and humourous short stories in various Latvian newspapers and magazines. *Honours:* Award for Excellent News Coverage, Ethnic Press Association of Ontario, Canada, 1969. *Memberships:* President, Latvian Press Association of Canada; Board of Directors, Ethnic Press Association of Ontario; Board of Directors, Ethnic Press Federation of Canada. *Address:* 159 Goldhawk Trail, Scarborough, Ontario M1V 1X1, Canada.

NORMAN, John, b. 20 July 1912, Syracuse, New York, USA. Professor. m. Mary Lynott, 28 Dec. 1948, Pittsburgh, Pennsylvania, 4 daughters. *Education:* BA 1935, MA 1938, Syracuse University; PhD Clark University, 1942. *Major Publications:* Edward Gibbon Wakefield: A Political Reappraisal, 1963; Labor & Politics In Lybia & Arab Africa, 1965. *Contributor to:* Funk & Wagnall's Encyclopedia Yearbook; Encyclopedia Americana; Industrial & Labour Relations Review; Far Eastern Historical Review. *Address:* John's Pond, Cooper Road, Ridgefield, CT 06877, USA.

NORRIS, Leslie, b. 21 May 1921, Merythr Tydfil, Wales. m. 31 July 1948, Merthyr Tydfil. *Education:* Diploma in Education, PhM, University of Southampton. *Literary Appointments:* Theodore Roethke Visiting Professor, Unviersity of Washington, Seattle, Washington, USA, 1973, 80, 81; Visiting Poet, Eton College, England, 1978; P A Christensen Fellow, Brigham Young University, Utah, USA. 1984–85. *Publications:* Tongue of Beauty, poems, 1941; Poems, 1942; The Loud Winter, poems, 1959; Finding Gold, poems, 1960; Ransoms, poems, 1964; Mountains, Polecats, Pheasants, 1968; Glyn Jones, criticism, 1974; Merlin and the Snake's Egg, 1975; Sliding and other stories, 1976; Water Voices, 1978; Walking the White Fields, 1980. *Contributions to:* New Yorker; Atlantic Monthly; London Magazine; London Review of Books; Audubon; Poetry Wales; New Criterion; British Broadcasting Corporation. *Honours:* Alice Hunt Bartlett Award, Poetry Society, 1963; Welsh Arts Council Award, 1963; Arts Council of Great Britain Award; Chomondeley Poetry Prize, 1974; Welsh Arts Council Prize, 1977; Katherine Mansfield Prize, 1982. *Memberships:* Fellow, Royal Society of Literature; Welsh Academy. *Literary Agent:* David Higham Associates Limited. *Address:* Plas Nant, Northfields Lane, Aldingbourne, Chichester, West Sussex PO20 6UH, England.

NORTH, Joan Marian, b. 15 Feb. 1920, Hendon, England. Writer. m. C A Rogers, 23 Feb. 1952, St Johns Wood, London, 2 daughters. *Publications:* Emperor of

the Moon, 1956; The Cloud Forest, 1965; The Whirling Shapes, 1968; The Light Maze, 1972. *Contributions to:* Various publications. *Membership:* Society of Authors. *Address:* 8 Grey Close, London NW11 6QG, England.

NORTON, Augustus Richard, b. 2 Sep. 1946, New York, USA. College Professor; Army officer, m. Deanna J Lampros, 27 Dec. 1969. Fort Bragg, North Carolina, 1 son. *Education:* BA cum lauda, MA, University of Miami, Florida; PhD, University of Chicago. *Publications:* Co-editor, Studies in Nuclear Terrorism, 1979, International Terrorism, 1980, NATO, 1984, Touring Nam, 1985; Co-author, The Emergence of a New Labanon? 1984; Harakat Amal and the Shi'a of Lebanon, 1986. *Contributions to:* New Leader; New Outlook; Middle East Insight; American-Arab Affairs; National Defense; The Middle East Journal and numerous others. *Honours:* Outstanding Academic Book of the Year for, International Terrorism, Choice Magazine, 1980. *Address:* Department of Social Sciences, United States Military Academy, West Point, NY 10996, USA.

NORTON, Charles Albert, b. 18 Oct. 1920, Cincinnati, Ohio, USA. Author. m. Harriet Schetter, 18 Apr. 1942, Cincinnati, 3 sons, 2 daughters. *Education:* University of Cincinnati, 1942–65, 1984. *Publications:* Melville Davisson Post: Man of Many Mysteries, 1973; Writing Tom Sawyer: The Adventures of A Classic, 1983. *Contributor to:* Mark Twain Bulletin; The Twainian; Missouri Life; Armchair Detective. *Membership:* Queen City Writers, President, 1982, 1983. *Address:* 9882 Prechtel Rd, Cincinnati, OH 45247, USA.

NORWICH, (Viscount) John Julius (Cooper), b. 15 Sep. 1929, London, England. Writer; Broadcaster. *Education:* Upper Canada College, Toronto, Canada; University of Strasbourg, France; New College, Oxford. *Publications:* Mount Athos, with Rereseby Sitwell, 1966; The Normans in the South, 1967; Sahara, 1968; The Kingdom in the Sun, 1970; Great Architecture of the World, General Editor, 1975; A History of Venice, Volume 1 – The Rise to Empire, 1977, Volume 2 – The Greatness and the Fall, 1981; Christmas Crackers, 1980; The Architecture of Southern England, 1985; Fifty Years of Glyndbourne, An Illustrated History, 1985; A Taste for Travel, 1985. *Memberships:* FRSL; Literary Society. *Agent:* Spokesmen. *Address:* 24 Blomfield Road, London W9, England.

NOSTBAKKEN, Janis Elizabeth, b. 29 Sep. 1949, Windsor, Ontario, Canada. Magazine Editor; TV Producer. m. David Vinge Nostbakken, 6 Aug. 1971, Burlington, 1 son, 1 daughter. *Education:* BA, English, Trent University, Peterborough, Ontario. *Publication:* The Canadian Inventions Book, 1976. *Contributor to:* Founding Editor, Chickadee Magazine; Article, TV Guide; Front Row Centre Magazine. *Address:* 104 Lawrence Ave, East Toronto, Ontario M4N 1S7, Canada.

NOTAR, Stephen, b. 11 Aug. 1926, Montreal, Canada. Advertiser. m. Shirley Joan Holmes, 24 July 1954, 2 daughters. *Education:* Bachelor of Commerce: Honours Economics, Political Science. *Publication:* The St James Quest, 1976. *Contributions to:* Hobby, Publication, 1951; Cyclic Magazine, 1965; The New Quarterly, University of Waterloo, 1981. *Address:* 1320 Montpellier, St Laurent, Quebec, Canada, H41 4R4.

NOVAK, Maximillian Erwin, b. 26 Mar 1930, New York City. University Professor. m. Estella Gershgoren, 21 Aug 1966, Los Angeles, 2 sons, 1 daughter. *Education:* PhD, University of California Los Angeles, 1958; DPhil, St John's University of Oxford, 1961. *Literary Appointments:* Assistant Professor, University of Michigan, 1958–62; Assistant Professor – Professor, University of California, Los Angeles, 1962–. *Publications:* Economics and the Fiction of Daniel Defoe, 1962; Defoe and the Nature of Man, 1963; Congreve, 1970; Realism, Myth and History in the fiction of Daniel Defoe, 1983; Eighteenth Century English Literature, 1983; Editor: The Wild Man Within, 1970; English Literature in the Age of Disguise, 1977; Calif., Dryden Vols X and XIII, 1971, 1984 etc. *Contributions to:* Essays in Criticism; PMLA; JEGP; MP; PQ; SEL; Kenyon Review; SP; Studies in the Literary Imagination; MLR; TSLL etc. *Honours:* Fulbright Fellowship, 1955–77; Guggenheim Fellowship 1965–66, 1985–86; National Endowment for the Humanities, 1981–82. *Memberships:* Modern Language Association; American Society for Eighteenth-Century Studies. *Address:* Department of English, University of California, Los Angeles, Los Angeles, CA 90024, USA.

NOVAK, Michael, b. 9 Sep. 1933. Pennsylvania, USA. Writer; Scholar. m. Karen Ruth Laub, 29 June 1963, 1 son, 2 daughters. *Education:* AB (summa cum laude), Stonehill College, 1956; BT (cum laude) Gergorian University, Rome, Italy, 1958; MA Harvard University, 1956. *Publications:* The Tiber Was Silver, 1961; A New Generation, 1964; The Experience of Marriage, 1964; The Open Church, 1964; Belief and Unbelief, 1965; A Time to Build, 1967; A Theology for Radical Politics, 1969; The Experience of Nothingness, 1970; Story in Politics, 1970; Politics: Realism and Imagination, 1971; All the Catholic People, 1971; The Rise of the Unmeltable Ethnics, 1972; Choosing our King, 1974; The Joy of Sports, 1976; The Guns of Lattimer, 1978; The American Vision, 1978; The Spirit of Democratic Capitalism, 1982; Moral Clarity in the Nuclear Age, 1983; Confession of a Catholic, 1983; Freedom with Justice, 1984. *Contributions to:* National Review; The New Republic; Commentary; Harpers; The Atlantic; This World; Catholicism in Crisis. *Honour:* Newspaper Column, Illusions & Realities nominated by Jury for Pulitzer Prize, 1979. *Membership:* PEN. *Literary Agent:* Sterling Lord Agency. *Address:* American Enterprise Institute, 1150 17th Street NW, Washington DC, 20036, USA.

NOWAK, Kurt, b. 28 Oct. 1942, Leipzig, Germany. Church Historian; Writer. m. Gisela Nowak, 6 June 1971, 1 son. *Education:* Dr Theology, University of Leipzig and Jena, 1971; Dr sc Theol, 1978; Dr Phil, 1984. *Publications:* (Novels), Eintreffe heute abend, 1971; Der Tod des Studenten Lothar Dahl, 1974; Stechow, 1978; Schöner Ubermut des Herbstes, 1982; (Scientific Works), Euthanasie und Sterilisierung im Dritten Reich, 1977; Evangelische Kirche und Weimarer Republik, 1981; Schleiermacher und die Fruhromantik, 1985. *Contributor to:* Numerous scientific journals edited in Switzerland, and Germany. *Honours:* Prize, Leipzig University, 1971, 1982. *Membership:* Authors Association of Democratic Republic of Germany. *Address:* August Bebel Strasse 51, 7030 Leipzig, Democratic Republic of Germany.

NOVELLI, Florence, b. 6 Aug. 1931, Liverpool, England. Playwright; Director. 1 son, 2 daughters. *Literary Appointments:* Dramatist & Artistic Director, Community Children's Theatre, Seneca College, Toronto, Canada, 1978–79; Co-founder & Artistic Director, Renaissance Theatre, Toronto, 1972–84. *Publications:* Peppercorn's Magic; Misty the Little Lost Cloud, Itchy Snithy & Boo, Mrs Perriwinkle's Cosmic Dream, 1980; Mrs Oodle-Noodle & Crumdum, Mrs Oodle-Noodle & Santa, Santa & the King, 1982; Queen Cat of Furbit, Spindlerion & the Princess, 1983; Twinkle & the Cosmic Pirate, Freeky the Pretty Witch, 1984. *Contributions to:* Toronto Sun; Canadian Jewish News; Toronto East End Express; Belleville Intellingencer; Port Colborne News; Stouffville Sun; Classical Guitar Magazine (UK). *Honours:* Grant 1973, Award 1980, Ontario Arts Council. *Membership:* Playwrights Union of Canada. *Address:* 18A Gloucester Street, Clifton Village, Clifton, Bristol, Avon, England.

NOYES, Stanley (Tinning), b. 7 Apr. 1924, San Francisco, USA. Writer; Teacher. m. Nancy Black, 12 Mar. 1949, Berkeley, California, 2 sons, 1 daughter. *Education:* AB, English, 1950, MA English, 1951, University of California, Berkeley, USA. *Major Publications:* No Flowers for a Clown (novel), 1961; Shadowbox (novel), 1970; Faces and Spirits (poems), 1974; Beyond the Mountains Beyond the Mountains,

(poems), 1979; The Commander of Dead Leaves, (poems), 1984. *Contributor to:* Numerous literary journals, including: San Francisco Review; Le Coeland (France); Trace; New Mexico Quarterly; Sumac; Greenhouse Review; Blue Unicorn; Greenfield Review; Don Quichotte (Switzerland); Contact II. *Honours:* MacDowell Fellow, 1967. *Memberships:* Rio Grande Writers Association, Board of Directors 1976–78; PEN American Center; Santa Fe Writers' Cooperative. *Address:* 634 East Garcia, Santa Fe, New Mexico 87501, USA.

NUNN, William Curtis, b. 2 June 1908, Georgetown, Texas, USA. Emeritus Professor of History. m. Thelma Inez Petsick, 25 June 1940, Brownwood, Texas, 1 son, 1 daughter. *Education:* BA, Southwestern University, 1928; MA 1931, PhD 1938, University of Texas, Austin. *Literary Appointments:* Editor in chief, Southwestern magazine, 1927. *Publications:* Texas, Story of the Lone Star State (with George C Hester and Rosa M Henson), 1948; Escape From Reconstruction, 1956; Texas Under The Carpetbaggers, 1962; Peace Unto You, 1970, under penname of Will Curtis; Somervell, Story of a Texas County, 1975; Ten Texans in Gray, 1968; Ten Other Texans in Gray, 1980; Marguerite Clark, America's Darling of Broadway and the Silent Screen, 1981. *Contributions to:* Southwestern Historical Quarterly; Fort Worth Press; Waco News Tribune; Dallas Times Herald. *Honours:* Andrew Carnegie Grant for Advancement of Teaching, 1950; TCU Research Grants, 1953, 1953 and 1965; Davis Award, 1978; Hillcrest Foundation Grants, 1978, 1980 and 1981. *Membership:* American Historical Association. *Address:* 3801 South Drive, Fort Worth, TX 76109, USA.

NURNBERG, Walter, b. 18 Apr. 1907, Berlin, Germany. Photographer; Author. m. Ilse Rita, 25 Oct. 1941, London, 1 son, 1 daughter. *Appointment:* Contributing Editor, British Journal of Photography. *Publications:* Author, various books, many articles including 2 standard textbooks on Lighting, 1 in its 18th English Printing; over 20 British Museums showed his industrial work including The Science Museum, London; Kodak Museum, London. *Honours:* OBE; Hon. FBIPP. *Address:* 18 Cornwall Close, London N2 0HP, England.

NUTT, Kathleen Cecilia, b. London, England. Author. *Education:* BA, Somerville, Oxford University Journalism Diploma, London University. *Publications:* Poems: Landscapes and Departures, 1947; Poems From The North, 1956; Creatures and Emblems, 1961; Elegies and Other Poems, 1982; Novels: Mile End, 1938; Theory Deluge, 1947; Private Fires, 1960; An Elderly Retired Man, 1962; Philosophy and Criticism: The Emperor's Clothes, 1953; Philosophy and Human Nature, 1969; A Soul in the Quad, 1970; The Good Want Power, 1977; General: A Clean Well-Lighted Place, Sweden, 1960. *Contributions to:* Observer; Times Literary Supplement; Times; Commentary; BBC. *Honour:* FRSL, 1977. *Memberships:* President 1974–75, Vice-President, PEN; Society of Authors. *Address:* 5 Limpsfield Avenue, Thornton Heath, Surrey, CR4 6BG, England.

NUTTALL, Jeff, b. 8 July, 1933, Clitheroe, Lancashire, England. Artist. m. Jane Couch, 1954 (divorced), 3 sons, 1 daughter, Amanda Porter, 2 sons. *Literary Appointments:* Senior Lecturer in Fine Arts, Leeds Polytechnic 1970–81; Head of Fine Art, Liverpool Polytechnic 1981–84. *Education:* National Diploma in Design Painting; Art Teachers' Diploma. *Appointment:* Chairman, National Poetry Society, 1976–78. *Publications:* Penguin Modern Poets 12, 1968; Bomb Culture, 1968; Poems – 1964–69, 1970; The Gold Hole, (Quartet), 1977; King Twist – A Portrait of Frank Randle, 1978; Performance Art – Memoirs and Scripts, 1979. *Contributions to:* The Guardian, (Poetry Critic), 1979–81. *Address:* 392 Halifax Road, Todmordon, Lancashire OL14 5ST, England.

NYE, Joseph Samuel, b. 19 Jan. 1937, New Jersey, USA. Professor. m. Molly Harding, 10 June 1961, 3 sons. *Education:* AB, Princeton University; BA, Oxford University; PhD, Harvard University. *Publications:* Power and Interdependence, co-author, 1977; Energy and Security, co-author 1980; Living with Nuclear Weapons, co-author, 1983; The Making of America's Soviet Policy, editor and co-author, 1984; Hawks, Doves and Owls, Editor and co-author, 1985; Nuclear Ethics, 1986. *Contributions to:* Member, Editorial Boards of: Foreign Policy, International Security, International Organisation; Policy articles in, The New York Times; The Washington Post; The Los Angeles Times; The Boston Globe; The Christian Science Monitor; The Atlantic Monthly; The New Republic; many articles in various professional journals. *Honours:* Rhodes Scholar, 1958–60; Distinguished Honor Award, US State Department, 1979. *Literary Agent:* Maxune Groffsky. *Address:* Center for Science and International Affairs, The John F Kennedy School of Government, 79 John F Kennedy Street, Cambridge, MA 02138, USA.

NYE, Nelson C, b. 28 Sep. 1907, Chicago, Illinois, USA. Novelist; Columnist; Critic. *Education:* Academy of Art, Cincinnati, Ohio. *Publications:* (95) novels, and 6 non-fiction horse books with A S Barns, including, Pistols for Hire, 1941; Wild Horse Shorty, 1944; Riders by Night, 1950; The Red Sombrero, 1954; Long Run, 1959. *Contributor:* Over 700 articles to numerous magazines etc, including, Texas Livestock Journal, formerly Horse Editor; New York Times Book Review, Columnist; Cincinnati Enquirer, reviewer; Oakland Tribune, Reviewer. *Honours:* Spur Award, Best Western Critic, 1954; Spur Award, Best Western Novel of 1959; Levi Straus Golden Saddleman Award, 1968; Editorial Award, Quarter Racing Owners of America, 1972. *Membership:* Western Writers of America, Co-Founder, twice President, twice Director. *Address:* 2165 Silverbell Road, Tucson, AZ 85745, USA.

NYLUND, Gunnar Isak Georg, b. 2 June 1916, Nykarleby. Teacher. m. Anna, 25 Aug. 1947, Vasa, 2 daughters. *Publications:* Alla de Dagar, 1978; Sasom Blommor Pa Rod Jord, 1981; Solvarv, 1982; Dandlighetens Eftermiddag, 1984; Var by vid Alven: Ytterjeppo, 1985. *Contributions to:* Horisont (poems). *Memberships:* Svenska Osterbottens Litteraturforening; Finlands Svenska Forfattareforening. *Address:* Strandgatan 7B, 65100 Vasa, Finland.

NYLUND-KARLSSON, Harriet Linnea, b. 9 Feb. 1944, Helsinki, Finland. Dramatist. m. Bert Christian Karlsson, 1 son, 1 daughter. *Education:* Dramatist examination from Dramatiska Institutet in Stockholm, Sweden. *Publications include:* Don't Cry Sam, (TV play), 1974; Johnny Be Good, 1978. *Contributions to:* Various magazines and journals in her capacity as a journalist, 1965–73. *Honours include:* Several scholarships from the Finnish Ministry of Education. *Membership:* Societedes Auteurs Dramatiques de Finlande. *Address:* c/o Suomen Kirjailijalii Ho, Runeberginkatu 32C 28, 00100 Helsinki, Finland.

NYSTROM, Carolyn, b. 22 May 1940, West Union, Ohio, USA. Writer. m. J Roger Nystrom, 26 Aug. 1961, Xenia, Ohio, 2 sons, 2 daughters. *Education:* BA, Wheaton College, Illinois, USA. *Publications include:* The Holy Spirit in Me, 1980; Why Do I Do Things Wrong? 1981; What Happens When We Die? 1981; What is the Bible? 1982; Growing Jesus's Way, 1982; Jesus is No Secret, 1983; Lord, I Want to Have a Quiet Time, 1984; Before I Was Born, 1984; Angels and Me, 1984; People in Turmoil: A Woman's Workshop on 1 Corinthians, 1985; Characters and Kings: A Woman's Workshop on the History of Israel, 1985; At the Starting Line, Beginning New Life, 1985; Behold Your Christ, A Woman's Workshop on Jesus, 1986; Relationships: Face to Face, 1986; Mike's Lonely Summer, 1986. *Address:* 38W566 Sunset, St Charles, IL 60174, USA.

NYTCZENKO, Dmytro, b. 21 Feb. 1905, Zinkiv, Ukraine. Institute Lecturer; Storeman. m. Mariya Drobiazko, 15 May 1930, Kharkiv, 2 daughters. *Education:* BA, Kharkiv State Pedagogical Institute, 1940. *Appointments:* State Publishing House of Ukraine, 1929–34; Secretary, Translator, Ukrainian News, 1945–49; Literary Worker, Journalist; President, Ukranian School Committee in Australia, 1950–62. *Publications:* This Happened in Australia, 1953; In the Forest Near Viazma, 1958, 83; Shevchenko The Man, 1963, English, 1985; Ukrainian Orthographic Dictionary, 1968, 85; People With Big Hearts, 1981; In the Mirror of Life and Literature, 1982; West of Moscow, 1983; So This is Australia, 1980. Contributor to magazines and other publications. *Memberships:* Slove, Ukrainian Writers in Exile; President, Ukranian Arts Club, Melbourne; Association of Literary Workers for children and Youth, Canada; Shevchenko Scientific Society. *Honours:* Book Club (Ukranian), West Australia, 1982; OPLDM Canada, 1982; Special Mention, Ivan Franko Club, Chicago. *Address:* 36 Percy Street, Newport, Victoria 3015, Melbourne, Australia.

O

OAKES, Philip, b. 31 Jan. 1928, Burslem, Staffordshire, England. Writer. m. Stella Fleming, 9 Sep. 1950, 1 son, 2 daughters. *Publications:* Unlucky Jonah, 1954; Exactly What We Want, 1962; The Godbotherers, 1969; From Middle England, 1980; Dwellers All in Time & Space, 1982; At the Jazz Band Ball, 1983. *Contributions to:* The Times; Times Literary Supplement; Sunday Times; New Society. *Membership:* Society of Authors. *Literary Agent:* Elaine Green. *Address:* c/o Elaine Green, 31 Newington Green, London N16 9PU, England.

OAKGROVE, Artemis, b. USA. Publisher of fiction. *Education:* Community College of Denver, Colorado; Colorado State University, Horticulture & Botany. *Major Publications:* The Raging Peace, 1984, Dreams of Vengeance, 1985 (two volumes of The Throne Trilogy). *Address:* P O Box 10037, Denver, CO 80210–0037, USA.

OAKMAN, Henry Octave, b. 4 Apr. 1906, Sydney, Australia. Landscape Architect. *Education:* Technical College, Sydney, Newcastle, Brisbane, Canberra; Queensland University. *Publications:* Colourful Trees, 1967, 3rd edition, 1979; Gardening in Queensland, 3rd edition, 1967; Trees of Australia, 4th edition, 1970, 5th edition 1975; Tropical & Subtropical Gardening, 3rd edition & 4th edition, 1979. *Contributor to:* various professional journals, etc. *Honours:* Recipient, Australian Award in Park Administration, 1973. *Memberships:* Fellow, Landscape Institute; Fellow, Australian Institute of Landscape Architects. *Address:* 95 Priors Pocket Road, Moggill, Queensland 4070, Australia.

OANDASAN, William, b. 17 Jan. 1947, Santa Ros, California, USA. Poet; Editor; Publisher. m. Georgiana, 28 Oct. 1973, Santa Rosa, California, 2 daughters. *Education:* BA, University of California, Santa Cruz, 1974; MA, University of Illinois, Chicago Circle Campus, 1981; MFA, Vermont College, Norwich University, 1984. *Publications:* A Branch of California Redwood, 1981; Moving Inland, 1984; Round Valley Songs, 1984. *Contributions to:* Journal of Contemporary Literature; American Indian Culture and Research Journal (UCLA); New America (University of New Mexico); Southern California Anthology, (University of Southern California), 1984; The Beloit Poetry Journal; Electrum. *Honour:* 1985 American Book Award for Round Valley Songs (Minneapolis): West End Press, 1984, from the Before Columbus Foundation. *Memberships:* Modern Language Association; Rocky Mountain Modern Language Association; National Indian Education Association; National Association of Ethnic Studies; A Writers Circle. *Address:* 2852 Sawtelle Boulevard #42, Los Angeles, CA 90064, USA.

O'BALLANCE, Edgar, b. 17 July 1918, Dublin, Republic of Ireland. Author. *Publications:* The Language of Violence; Terror in Ireland; Tracks of the Bear; No Victory, No Vanquished; Wars in Vietnam; The Arab – Israeli War 1948–49; Arab Guerilla Power; The Indo – China War 1946–54; The Sinai Campaign 1956; The Third Arab – Israeli War 1967; The Electronic War in the Middle East 1968–70; The Kurrdish Revolt 1961–70; The Malayian Insurrection 1948–60; The Red Army of China; The Red Army (of Russia); The Korean War 1950–53; The French Foreign Legion; The Algerian Insurrection 1954–62; The Secret War in the Sudan 1955–72; The Greek Civil War 1944–49. *Contributions to:* Various international and national magazines of over 700 in-depth features on statistical and international defence affairs. *Address:* Wakebridge Cottage, Wakebridge, Matlock, Derbyshire DE4 5HD, England.

OBERG, James Edward, b. 7 Nov. 1944, New York City, USA. Aerospace Engineer. m. Alcestis Demetra Ritsos, 30 Aug. 1969, Chicago, 2 sons. *Education:* MS, Astrodynamics, Northwestern University, 1970; MS,

Computing Sciences, University of New Mexico, 1972. *Publications:* Red Star in Orbit, 1981; New Earths, 1981; Mission to Mars, 1982; Outer Space Mysteries, 1982; New Race for Space, 1984; Pioneering Space, 1986; The Great Galactic Ghoul and Other Space Legends, 1986. *Contributions to:* OMNI; Science Digest; Spaceflight; Senior Editor for Space, Aviation/Space Magazine. *Honours:* Goddard History Award, 1975 & 1977; NASA Area Engineering Man of the Year Award, 1984. *Memberships:* Phi Beta Kappa; National Association of Science Writers. *Address:* Rt 2 Box 350, Dickinson, TX 77539, USA.

OBERHOLTZER, Donna, b. 15 Apr. 1941, Illinois, USA. Editor; Writer. *Education:* BA English, San Francisco State College, 1966; MA English, Bryn Mawr College, 1972. *Literary Appointments:* Editor (manuscript, production), F A Davies Co, Philadelphia, Pennsylvania, 1973–76; Editor (production), Wadsworth Publishing Co, Belmont, California, 1980–81; Editor/Writer, Northern California Cancer Program, Palo Alto, California, 1981–82; Biomedical Writer/Editor, Biospherics Inc, Rockville, Maryland, 1982–85. *Major Publication:* The Road to Recovery for the Heart Patient, 1983. *Membership:* American Medical Writers Association. *Address:* 13903 Castle Boulevard, Silver Spring, MD 20904, USA.

OBERLAENDER, Gerhard, b. 12 Sep. 1907, Berlin, Federal Republic of Germany. Illustrator. *Education:* Reiman-Schule, Berlin; Accademie of Arts, Berlin. *Publications:* Illustrations: Andersens Fairy Tales (4 volumes), 1964–67; J Chr von Grimmelshausen: der abenteuerliche Simplicius Simplicissimus, 1961; Brother Grimm Fairy Tales (3 volumes), 1958–61; M de Cervantes Saavedra: Don Quijote (2 volumes), 1969; A Daudet: Tartarin, 1974; Le petit chose, 1977; Lettres de mon moulin, 1984; Text and illustrations for 13 children's books. *Contributions to:* Frankfurter Allgemeine Zeitung; Mainpost; Mannheimer Morgen; Frankfurter Rundschau; Scala International; Stern. *Honours:* 13 books amongst, the Most Beautiful Books of the Year, Federal Republic of Germany; Premio Grafico, Bologna, Italy, 1967; Silver Medal, Schönste Bücher der Welt, Leipzig, 1970. *Address:* Clemensstrasse 3, 8000 München 40, Federal Republic of Germany.

OBERMEIER, Siegfried Ludwig Karl, b. 21 Jan. 1936, Munich, Federal Republic of Germany. Writer. m. Gertrude Schott, 1962, 1 daughter. *Education:* Secondary School. *Appointments:* Bavarian Editor, Artis, 4 years; etc. *Publications:* Lago Maggiore, Comer See, Luganer See, 1972; 2nd edition 1978; Die Kunst, co-author, 1972; Karnten, 1975, 2nd edition 1980; Munchens Goldene Jahre, 1976; Freuz und Adler, 1978; Walther von der Vogelweide – Der Spielmann des Reiches, 1980; Richard Lowenherz, 1982; Starb Jesus in Kaschmir, 1983;, 3 editions; Munchen Leuchter ubers Jahr, 1985; Mein Kaiser – Mein Herr, 1986. *Memberships:* VDS; Association of German Writers. *Awards:* Littera Medaille, 1986. *Address:* 8042 Oberschleissheim, Munchen, Hirschplanallee 7, Republic of Germany.

OBERRECHT, G Kenneth (Kenn), b. 11 Jan. 1943, Hamilton, Ohio, USA. Magazine Writer; Photojournalist; Book Author. m. Patricia Ann Connaughton, 2 Sep. 1967, Hamilton, Ohio. *Education:* AA, Humanities 1967, BSc English 1970, University of Cincinnati; BA, Journalism, University of Alaska, 1972; MA, English and Journalism, University of Alaska, 1974. *Appointments:* Lecturer, Colleges and Universities in Alaska and Oregon. Outdoor Editor, The Scoreboard, 1973–74; Staff Writer and Photographer, Alaska Construction & Oil, 1972–74; Fairbanks Representative and Consultant, Alaska Media Services Incorporated, 1972–74, etc. *Publications:* The Great Outdoors Catalog, 1977; The Practical Angler's Guide to Successful Fishing, 1978; The Outdoor Photographer's Handbook, 1979; The Apartment Workshop, 1980; The Angler's Guide to Jigs and Jigging, 1982; Plywood Projects Illustrated, 1983. Contributor to more than 60 magazines, newspapers, annuals, anthologies, etc. *Memberships:* Society of Professional Journalists, Sigma Delta Chi; Ka Alpha Mu. *Honours include:* Reader's Digest Foundation travel grant, 1971; Graduate Fellowship in English, University of Alaska, 1970–72. *Literary Agent:* Jane Jordan Browne. *Address:* 1911 Ash Court, PO Box C, North Bend, OR 97459, USA.

O'BRADY, Frederic Michel, b. 11 Dec 1903, Budapest. Actor. m. Colette Fleurent, 13 Dec. 1960, New York. *Publications:* French Novels: Exterieurs à Venise, 1950; Le ciel d'en face, 1954; Romarin pour le souvenir, 1958. All Told, autobiography in English, 1970; Propos Pertinents et Impertinents, French textbook for colleges, 1973. *Honour:* French Knighthood of Arts and Letters, 1981. *Address:* 1077 East Avenue, Rochester, NY 14607, USA.

O'BRIEN, James Aloysius, b. 7 Apr. 1936, Cincinnati, Ohio, USA. Professor of Japanese Literature. m. Rumi Matsumoto at Cincinnati, 26 Aug. 1961. *Education:* BA, St Joseph's College, 1958; MA, University of Cincinnati, 1960; PhD, Indiana University, 1969. *Publications:* Dazai Osamu, 1975; Dazai Osamu: Selected Stories and Sketches, 1983; Three Stories by Muro Saisei, 1985. *Address:* Department of East Asian Languages and Literature, University of Wisconsin, Madison, WI 53706, USA.

O'BRIEN, Katharine Elizabeth. Educator. *Education:* BA, Bates College, USA; MA, Cornell University; PhD, Brown University; Honorary ScD Ed, University of Maine, 1960; Honorary LHD, Bodwoin College, 1965; Deborah Morton Award, Westbrook College, 1985. *Publications:* Excavations and Other Verse, 1967; Sequences, 1966. *Contributions to:* Saturday Review; Christian Science Monitor; New York Times; Ladies Home Journal; New York Herald Tribune; Poet; India; Poetry Chapbook; Boston Herald; Rotarian; Survey; American Mathematics Monthly; Mathematics Magazine; Scripta Math; Mathematics Teacher; Science Monthly and various others; Numerous Anthologies including: The Golden Year; The Phoenix Nest; The Diamond Year; Maths and Humour. *Memberships:* Phi Beta Kappa; Sigma Xi; Mathematics Association of America; Poetry Society of America; New York Academy of Sciences; Founder Fellow, International Academy of Poets. *Address:* 130 Hartley Street, Portland, ME 04103, USA.

O'BRIEN, Lawrence Francis, b. 7 July 1917, Massachusetts, USA. Politics; Government; Sports. m. Elva Brassard, 30 May 1944, Springfield, 1 son. *Education:* LL D, Northeastern University, 1942; Honorary Degrees: LL D, Western New England College, 1962, Villanova University, 1966, Loyola University, 1967, Xavier University, 1971, LHD, American International College, 1971, Wheeling College, 1971, St Anselms College, 1966; DPA, Northeastern University, 1965, Seton Hali University, 1967; DS in BA, Bryant College, 1978; D Humanics, Springfield College, 1982. *Publications:* O'Brien Manual, 1960, 4th edition 1972; No Final Victories, 1974. *Contributor to:* Numerous articles in various magazines and journals including, New York Times. *Honours:* Named Man of Year, Basketball Weekly, 1976; Sports Man of Year, Sporting News, 1976; Recipient, Spl. Victor Award, 1977; Brotherhood Award, NCCJ, 1977; Israel Prime Minister's Medal for Distinguished Service to Democracy and Freedom, 1978; John W Bunn Award, Basketball Hall of Fame, 1984; NBA World Championship Trophy designated Larry O'Brien Trophy, 1984. *Address:* 860 United Nations Plaze, New York, NY 10017, USA.

O'CEIRIN, Cyril, b. 9 Feb. 1934, Dublin, Republic of Ireland. Teacher. *Education:* BA, University of Dublin; Higher Diploma in Education. *Publications:* My Story, 1970; An toilithreach Gaelach, 1973; Wild and Free, 1979; 1980. Editor: Breith (Cloan chuirt Eigse) 1974. *Contributor to:* Maynooth Review; Irish Times; Poetry Ireland; Innti 4; Comhar; Stony Thursady Book; New Irish Writing; various collections. *Memberships include:* Poetry Ireland. *Honours:* Feile na Maighe, 1975;

Oireachtas na Gaeilge, 1977. *Address:* dochas, Bothar na Cathrach, Mungairit, Co Luimni, Republic of Ireland.

OCHSNER, Jeffrey Karl, b. 25 Sep. 1950, Milwaukee, Wisconsin, USA. Architect. m. Sandra Lynn Perkins, 5 Aug. 1979, Boothbay Harbor, Maine. *Education:* BA 1973, Master of Architecture 1976, Rice University, Houston, Texas. *Publications:* H H Richardson: Complete Architectural Works, 1982. *Contributions to:* Texas Architect; Journal of the Society of Architectural Historians; Architectural Review; Architectural Record; Cite; Sallyport. *Honours:* AIA School Award, 1975; James Chillman Prize for architecture portfolio, 1973; Phi Beta Kappa; Tau Sigma Delta. *Memberships:* American Institute of Architects; Society of Architectural Historian; National Trust for Historic Preservation. *Address:* 2825 Quenby, Houston, TX 77005, USA.

O'CONNOR, Anthony Michael, b. 5 June 1939, London, England. University Teacher. m. Angela Templeman, 1 Jan. 1964, Bournemouth, 1 son, 1 daughter. *Education:* BA, 1960, PhD, 1963, Cambridge University. *Publications:* Railways and Development in Uganda, 1965; An Economic Geography of East Africa, 1966, 1971; The Geography of Tropical African Development, 1971, 1978; The African City 1983. *Contributor to:* Various magazines and journals. *Address:* Department of Geography, University College, 26 Bedford Way, London WC1H 0AP, England.

O'CONNOR, Francine Marie Provost, b. 8 Apr. 1930, Springfield, Massachusetts, USA. Editor. m. John F O'Connor, 29 Dec. 1951, 1 son, 2 daughters. *Literary Appointments:* Editorial Assistant, Associate Editor, Managing Editor, Liguorian Magazine, Liguori, Missouri. *Publications:* Growing Up With Jesus, 1977; God and You, 1979; Following Jesus, 1979; The Ten Commandments, 1980; The Seven Sacraments, 1981; The Stories of Jesus, 1982; Stories of God and His People from the Old Testament, 1984; Jesus Loves You; The ABC's of the Rosary, 1984. *Contributions to:* Liguorian Magazine, Columnist, 1976–; Major Catholic publications, USA, Canada, England and Ireland; Explaining God's Word, Sunday leaflet for children in primary grades; Explaining God's Word, Sunday leaflet for children in primary grades; Exploring Our Faith, Bulletin for children in middle grades; First Penance and First Communion, Bulletins for Sacrament preparation. *Address:* 1 Liguori Drive, Liguori, MO 63057, USA.

O'CONNOR, Garry Peter, b. 31 Jan. 1939, Edgware, London, England. Author, Playwright. m. Victoria Meredith-Owens, 25 May 1970, Kensington, London, 4 sons, 1 daughters. *Education:* BA, Kings College, Cambridge University; Ecole Jacques Lecoq, Paris, France. *Literary Appointments:* Television Critic, Queen Magazine, 1964–66; Theatre Critic, Finacial Times, 1966–74. *Publications:* Le Théâtre en Grande-Bretagne, 1966; The Musicians, play, 1969; I Learned in Ipswich How to Poison Foowers, play, 1970; Different Circumstances, play, 1974; Semmel-weiss, play, 1975; French Theatre Today, 1975; Dialogue Between Friends, play, 1976; The Persuit of Perfection: A Life of Maggie Teyte, 1979; Ralph Richardson: An Actor's Life, 1982; Darlings of the Gods: Laurence Olivier and Vivien Leigh, 1984. *Contributions to:* Sunday Times; The Observer; Financial Times; Times Literary Supplement; and others; British Broadcasting Corporation radio and television; Translator of several plays. *Honours include:* 1st Prize, Playwriting Competition, 1974; Arts Council Literary Award, 1979. *Memberships:* Society of Authors; Critics Circle. *Literary Agent:* Deborah Rogers, London. *Address:* c/o Hodder and Stoughton, 47 Bedford Square, London WC1B 3DP, England.

O'CONNOR, Patricia W, b. 26 Apr. 1931, Memphis, Tennessee, USA. Professor. m. Anthony Pasquariello, 11 Feb. 1978, Newport, Kentucky, 1 son, 1 daughter. *Education:* PhD. *Publications:* Women in the Theater of Gregorio Martinez Sierra, 1967; Gregorio and Maria Martinez Sierra, 1977; Contemporary Spanish Theater, (with A M Pasquariello), 1977; Plays of Protest from the

Franco Era, 1981; Contemporary Spanish Plays: The Social Comedies, 1983. *Contributions to:* Hispania; Hispanic Review; Spain Today; Modern International Drama; Hispanofila; Theater Survey; Revista de Estudios Hispanicos; Journal of Spanish Studies; Estreno; Critics Hispanica; Hispanic Journal; The American Hispanist; Educational Theatre Journal. *Honours:* Phi Beta Kappa, 1961; Taft Grants, 1965, 1972, 1978, 1981; American Philosophical Society Grant, 1971; Rieveschel Award for Creative and Scholarly Work, 1982. *Address:* Department of Romance Languages and Literatures, University of Cincinnati, OH 45221, USA.

O'CONNOR, Patrick Joseph, b. 28 Aug. 1947, Chicago, USA. Professor, Senior Professor, De Vrey Institute of Technology. m. Leah Rachel Gurrie, 12 July 1969, Chicago, 2 daughters. *Education:* BS, Physics, Northern Illinois University, 1968; MS, National College of Education, 1983. *Publications:* Digital and Microprocessor Technology, 1983; Understanding Digital Electronics – How Microcomputers and Microprocessors Work, 1984; Voice and Data Telecommunications, 1986. *Contributor to:* Contributing Editor: Interface Age, 1979–83, Tandy/Radio Shack Computer User, 1983–84, Chicago Computer People, 1984–. *Honour:* Sigma Pi Sigma Physics National Honours Society, 1974. *Membership:* Authors Guild. *Address:* 6315 West Raven Street, Chicago, IL 60646, USA.

O'CONNOR, Raymond Gish, b. 6 June 1915, St Louis, Missouri, USA. Professor of History. m. Sally Sayles, 23 Aug 1941, San Francisco, 3 sons. *Education:* MA; PhD. *Publications:* Perilous Equilibrium, 1962; American Defense Policy in Perspective, 1965; Presidential Powers in Foreign Affairs, 1966; Diplomacy for Victory, 1971; Force and Diplomacy, 1972; War, Diplomacy and History, 1979. *Contributor to:* Journal of American History; Pacific Historical Review; Military Affairs; Diplomatic History; US Naval Institute Proceedings; Naval War College Review; Journal of Peace Research; Australian Journal of Politics and History; Virginia Quarterly Review. *Honours:* Grants from Social Science Research Council, 1956–57; American Council of Learned Societies, 1962; Ford Foundation, 1964–65. *Memberships:* American Military Institute, Trustee; American Historical Association; Organization of American Historians; Society for Historians of American Foreign Relations. *Address:* 212 Claudius Drive, Aptos, CA 95003, USA.

O'CONNOR, Robert Patrick, b. 27 Sep. 1937, Kilgore, Texas, USA. Playwright. *Publications:* Robert Patrick's Cheep Theatricks, 1972; Kennedy's Children, 1974; Golden Circle, 1975; Play-by-Play, 1975; One Man, One Woman, 1977; Judas, 1978; Mercy Drop, 1980; Mutual Benefit Life, 1979; My Cup Ranneth Over, 1979. *Contributions to:* Other Stages; Gaysweek; Soho Weekly News; Dramatics; New York City News and many others. *Honours:* Rockefeller Grant, 1973; NYSCAPS Grant, 1974; Glasgow Citizens World Playwrights Award, 1973; International Thespians Founders Award. 1978. *Address:* c/o La Mama, 74A E 4th Street, New York, NY 10003, USA.

O'CONNOR, William E, b. 26 Mar. 1922, Boston, Massachusetts, USA. Writer. *Education:* AB, Brown University, 1942; MA, George Washington University, 1947; PhD, American University, School of International Service, 1970. *Publications:* Economic Regulation of the World's Airlines: A Political Analysis, 1971; An Introduction to Airline Economics, 1978, 3rd edition 1985. *Contributor to:* Air Law; Aviation Research Journal; Book Reviews: American Journal of International Law; Antitrust Bulletin; Journal of Air Law and Commerce; American Political Science Review. *Address:* Sandy Park Apartments, No 619, 1049 Brentwood Drive, Daytona Beach, FL 32017, USA.

ODAGA, Bole Asenath, b. 5 July 1938, Kenya. m. James Charles Odaga, 27 Jan. 1957, Kisumu, 2 sons, 3 daughters. *Education:* BA Honours; Diploma of Education; MA. *Literary Appointments:* Editor, Lake Publishers and Enterprises, Kisumu; Editorial Committee, Voice of Women. *Publications:* Thu Tinda: Stories from Kenya; Yesterdays Today: The Study of Oral Literature; The Shade Changes; Luo-English; English-Luo Dictionary; Between the Seasons. *Contributions to:* Viva Magazine; E A Journal. *Memberships:* Secretary, Writers Association of Kenya; International Board on Books for Young People; African Association of Science Editors; East African Association for Commonwealth Literature and Language Studies. *Address:* PO Box 1743, Kisumu, Kenya.

O'DALY, William Anthony, b. 13 Nov. 1951, Santa Monica, California, USA. Assistant Professor; Editor.*Education:* BA, English, California State University, 1976; MFA, Poetry and Translation, Eastern Washington University, 1981.*Literary Appointment:* Editor, Willow Springs (magazine, literary and art) 1970–. *Publications:* The Whale in the Web, poems, 1979; translation of poems: Still Another Day (Aun), by Pablo Neruda, 1984; translation of poems: The Separate Rose (La rosa Separada) by Pablo Neruda, 1985. *Contributions to:* Poetry and articles in Poetry Now; Another Chicago Magazine; Northwest Review; Borrowed Times; Silver Vain; Valley Grapevine; Willow Springs; Cafeteria; Tailwind; Literary Magazine Review; Dalmo'ma Anthology; Rain in the Forest, Light of the Trees; etc. *Honour:* Award by The Bloomsbury Review One of The Four Best Translations Published by a Literary Press in 1984 for 'Still Another Day'. *Address:* c/o Willow Springs, Pub P O Box 1063, Eastern Washington University, Cheney, WA 99204, USA.

ODELL, Robin Ian, b. 19 Dec. 1935, Totton, near Southampton, England. Editor; Publications Manager. *Publications:* Jack the Ripper in Fact and Fiction, 1965; Humanist Glossary, (with T Barfield), 1967; Exhumation of a Murder, 1975; Murderers' Who's Who, (with J H H Gaute), 1979; Lady Killers, (with J H H Gaute), 1980; Muder, Whatdunit, (with J H H Gaute), 1982. *Contributor to:* Crimes and Punishment. *Honours:* F C C Watts Membership Prize, 1957; International Humanist and Ethical Union Prize, 1960. *Memberships:* Society of Authors; Crime Writers Association. *Address:* 15 Churchill Crescent, Sonning Common, Reading RG4 9RU, England.

O'DELL, Scott, b. 23 May, 1898, Los Angeles, California, USA. Writer. *Education:* Student, Occidental College, University of Wisconsin, Stanford University and University of Rome. *Publications include:* Woman of Spain, 1934; Hill of the Hawk, 1947; Man Alone, 1953; Country of the Sun, 1957; The Sea is Red, 1958; Island of the Blue Dolphins, 1960; The King's Fifth, 1966; The Black Pearl, 1967; The Dark Canoe, 1968; Journey to Jericho, 1969; Sing Down the Moon, 1970; The Cruise of the Arctic Star, 1973; Child of Fire, 1974; Zia, 1976; The 290, 1976; Carlotta, 1977; Kathleen, Please Come Home, 1978; The Captive, 1979; The Feathered Serpent, 1981; The Spanish Smile, 1982; The Amethyst Ring, 1983; The Castle in the Sea, 1983; Alexandra, 1984; The Road to Damietta, 1985. *Contributions to:* Psychology Today, 1968; Horn Book, 1982. *Honours:* Newbery Medal, 1961; Rupert Hughes Award, 1960; Hans Christian Andersen Award of Merit, 1960; William Allen White Award, 1963; Jugend buchpreis, 1963, 69; Nene Award, 1964; Hans Christian Andersen Medal, 1972; DeGrummond Medal, 1976; Regina Medal, 1978. *Membership:* Authors Guild. *Address:* c/o Houghton Mifflin Company, 1 Park Street, Boston, MA 02107, USA.

O'DONNELL, Kevin Jr, b. 29 Nov. 1950, Cleveland, Ohio, USA. Writer. m. Lillian Kia Chou 'Kim' Tchang, 14 Sep. 1974, Yonkers, New York. *Education:* BA, Chinese Studies, Yale University, 1972. *Literary Appointments:* Managing Editor, Empire For The SF Writer, 1979-81; Publisher, 1981–83. *Publications:* Novels: Bander Snatch, 1979; Mayflies, 1979; Caverns: Journeys of McGill Feighan, Book I, 1981; Reefs: The Journeys of McGill Feighan, Book II, 1981; War of Omission, 1982; Lava: The Journeys of McGill Feighan, Book III, 1982; Oracle, 1984; Cliffs: The Journeys of McGill Feighan,

Book IV, 1986; Non-Fiction: The Electronic Money Machine (with the Haven Group), 1984. *Contributions:* Short stories and articles to various magazines including: Analog, Alfred Hitchcock's Mystery Magazine; Galaxy; Cavalier; Orbit 19; Isaac Asimov's SF Magazine; Empire; OMNI; Amazing SF. *Membership:* Science Fiction Writers of America. *Literary Agent:* Howard Morhaim, New York City. *Address:* c/o Howard Morhaim Literary Agency, 501 Fifth Avenue, New York, NY 10017, USA.

O'DONOVAN, Joan Mary, b. 31 Dec. 1914, Mansfield, Nottinghamshire, England. Former Educationalist; Currently Writer. 1 son. *Education:* Furzedown Training College; London University Certificate of Education. *Publications:* Dangerous Worlds, 1958; The Visited, 1959; Shadows on the Wall, 1960; The Middle Tree, 1961; The Niceties of Life, 1964; She, Alas, 1965; Little Brown Jesus & Other Stories, 1970. *Contributor to:* Punch; The Guardian; Good Housekeeping; Seventeen, USA, etc. *Membership:* Society of Authors. *Literary Agent:* Rivers Scott, Scott-Ferris Agency. *Address:* 98 (B), Banbury Road, Oxford, OX2 6JT, England.

OESTERREICH, Hans Guenther, b. 29 July 1910, Charlottenburg. Author; Film Producer. m. Ingeborg Von Schneidewind, 7 May 1945, Berlin, 1 son. *Publications include:* Eine Weltreise, 1947; Familie Meierdierks, 1953, 2nd edition 1980; Soldatensender, Lili Marleen, 1985; Geschichte und Geschichten, 1958; Der Wolfspelz, 1985. *Contributor to:* Pariser Tageblatt; Kolo, Belgrade; Konkret; etc; several German newspapers; over 100 screenplays, TV scenarios and radio plays. *Honour:* Die Schlacht, Bundes-Filmpr. *Membership:* Verwertungsgesellschaft WORT, Munich. *Address:* Lueder-von-Bentheimstr. 43, D2800 Bremen 1, Federal Republic of Germany.

OEYEN, Edith Clothildis, b. 31 May 1945, Heppen, Belgium. Housewife; Author. m. Bijloos Ivo Theophiel, 15 July 1965, Heppen, 2 sons. *Literary Appointments:* Various journals. *Publications:* Glimlach van een Zonnebloem, poetry, 1981; Neveldraden en Morgendauw, poetry, 1983; Leila Muggelyn, children's story, 1983; Het oog Parelt, artistic poetry album, 1984; 1000 Jaar Jericho (with André Smeets), poetry, 1985; Ook dit Gebeart, Christmas play, 1985; Rabarber, children's play, 1985. *Contributions to:* t Kofschip; Oostland; Plinius (editor); t Kandelarteje (committee member). *Honours:* Honorable Wabo Prize, 1984; Final selection, Bernescot poetry, Verloren Paradijs, 1985; Charter, Municipality Beringen; Charter, Opglabbeek. *Memberships:* Ooostland; t Kofschip; Plinius, Bries Kruispunt; Vlaanderen; Kreatief; Creare; Handen Lift; Iambe; Appel; Muzisch Meerdaal; etc. *Address:* Hanebergstraat 75, B-3960 Beringden-Beverlo, Belgium.

O'FAOLAIN, Anna Julia, b. 6 June 1932, London, England. Writer. m. Lauro Rene Martines, 1957, Florence, Italy, 1 son. *Education:* BA and MA, National University of Ireland; Post Graduate at Universita di Roma, Italy and Sorbonne, Paris. *Publications:* We Might See Sights and Other Stories, 1968; Godded and Codded, 1970; As Three Lovers, 1971; Man in the Cellar, 1974; Woman in the Wall, 1975; No Country for Young Men, 1980; Daughters of Passion, 1982; The Obedient Wife, 1982; The Irish Signorina, 1984; Not in God's Image (with Lauro Martines), 1973. *Contributions to:* Internationally, to numerous publications. *Honours:* Short listed for Booker Prize, 1980; Arts Council Bursary, 1981. *Literary Agent:* Deborah Rogers Ltd. *Address:* 49 Blenheim Crescent, London W11 2EF, England.

OFFEN, Yehuda, b. 4 Apr. 1922, Journalist; Writer. *Education:* BA, London University, England; MA, Hebrew University, Jerusalem, Israel. *Literary Appointments include:* Senior Editor, Daily Guardian, Al Hamishmar, 1961–. *Publications:* L'lo L'an, 1961; Har Vakhol, 1963; Shirim Lirfua, translation, 1965; Lo Agadat Khoref, 1969; Nofim P'nima, 1979; Bema'gal Sagur, In a Closed Circle, Short stories of 4 continents,

1979; N'Vilat Vered, 1983; Shirim Bir'Khov Ayee, Poems, in a Tired Street, 1984; P'Gishot Me'ever Maz'man, 1986; Massekhet Av, 1986. *Contributions to:* Most Israeli newspapers and periodicals, anthologies including: Poet; Coarina. Various recordings. *Honours:* ACUM Literary Prizes, for L'lo L'an, 1960, for A Collection of Short Stories, 1976; Talpir Literary Prize, 1979. *Memberships:* Hebrew Writers Association, Tel Aviv; ACUM Society of Authors, Composers and Editors of Music, Tel Aviv; World Poetry Society; International Academy of Poets, England. *Address:* 8 Gazit Street, Tel Aviv 69417, Israel.

OFFERLE, Mildred Gladys Goodell, b. 3 Jan. 1912, Barnum, Minnesota, USA. Teacher. *Education:* Diploma, Duluth Teacher's College, 1932; BS, Mankato State University, 1966. *Publications:* Poetry: Crystal Wells, 1950; Moods and Thoughts, 1970; Novel: The Long Cry, 1960; Co-editor, The Turning Wheel, 1982; Co-editor, Prairie Bread, 1985. *Contributions to:* Premier Poets; Great American World Poets; Outstanding Contemporary Poets; Sea to Sea in Song; American Bard; Cresset; Independent Woman. *Honours include:* Margaret Miller Pettingill Memorial Award, 1950. *Memberships:* World Poetry Society Intercontinental; Centro Studi e Scambi Int; American Poetry League; League of Minnesota Poets. *Address:* 105 3rd Street SW, Madelia, MN 56062, USA.

O'FIANNACHTA, Padraig, b. 20 Feb. 1927, Dingle, Republic of Ireland. Professor of Modern Irish, St Patrick's College, Republic of Ireland. *Education:* BA, Celtic Languages, 1947; Higher Diploma in Education, 1949; MA, 1955. *Publications:* Dictionary of Royal Irish Academy, Co-Editor, 1966–74; Life of E De Valera, 1968, 70; Catalogue of Irish Manuscripts in Maynooth Library. Volumes II-VIII, 1966–74; Tain Bo Cuailnge, 1966; An Barantar, 1978. Original Poetry: Ponc, 1969; Ruin, 1972; Feoirlingi Fileate, 1974; Doun Bo, 1978; Spaisteoireacht, 1982; Leas ar ar Letriocht, 1974; Leas Eile ar ar Litriocht, 1982. *Contributions to:* Eigse; Erui; Studia Celtica; Maynooth Review; Irish Review; An Sagent, Editor; New Irish Bible, Editorial Translator, 1981. *Honours:* Douglas Hyde Prize for Irish Literature, 1972. *Memberships:* Cymmrodorion Society; Royal Irish Academy. *Address:* St Patrick's College, Maynooth, Republic of Ireland.

O'FLAHERTY, James Carneal, b. 28 Apr. 1914, Henrico Co, Virginia, USA. Professor of German Emeritus, Wake Forest University. m. Lucy Maupin Ribble, 4 Feb. 1936, Wytheville, Virginia, 1 son. *Education:* BA, College of William and Mary, Georgetown College, 1939; MA, University of Kentucky, 1941; PhD, University of Chicago, 1950. *Literary Appointments:* Instructor in History and Religion, Georgetown College, 1939–41; Instructor to Full Professor, Wake Forest University, 1947–84. *Publications:* Unity and Language: A Study in the Philosophy of Hamann, 1952, reprinted 1966; Hamann's Socratic Memorabilia, 1967; Studies in Nietzsche and the Classical Tradition, 1976, reprinted 1979; Johann Georg Hamann, 1979; Studies in Nietzsche and the Judaeo-Christian Tradition, 1985. *Contributions to:* German Quarterly; Germanic Review; Harvard Theological Review; Journal of English and Germanic Philology; American Scientist; Bulletin of the American Association of University Professors. *Honours:* American Philosophical Society Grant, 1958; Fulbright Research Scholar, University of Heidelberg, 1960–61; Friendship Award of the Federal Republic of Germany, 1984. *Address:* 2164 Faculty Drive, Winston-Salem, NC 27106, USA.

ÖGMUNDSSON, Karvel, b. 30 Sep. 1903, Beruvik, Snaefellsnesi, Iceland. Director; Ship Owner. m. Anna Margret Olgeirsdottir, 14 Apr. 1928, Olafsvik, Snaefellsnesi, 2 sons, 5 daughters, 1 other son. *Publications:* Sjomannsaefi, Volume 1, 1981, Volume 2, 1982, Volume 3, 1985. *Contributions to:* Faxi; Sjomannabladid Vikingur; Morgunbladid. *Honours:* Honorary Citizen, Njardvik town, 1978; Decorated, Icelandic Government, 1979. *Memberships:* Rithofundasamband Islands. *Literary Agent:* Orn and

Orlygur hf, Reykjavik. *Address:* Bjargi, Ytri-Njardvik, 260 Njardvik, Iceland.

OGNIBENE, Peter John, b. 9 Dec 1941, Washington DC, USA. Writer. m. Brigid Ann Selz, 7 Apr. 1984, Washington DC. *Education:* BS, United States Air Force Academy, 1963; MSE, Aerospace Engineering, University of Michigan, 1965; MA, Government and Politics, University of Maryland, 1967. *Appointments:* Freelance Writer, 1970–; Contributing Editor, The New Republic, 1972–77. *Publications:* Scoop: The Life and Politics of Henry M Jackson, 1975; The Big Byte, 1984. *Contributor to:* Omni; National Journal; Science Digest; Rocky Mountain Magazine; Saturday Review; Parade; Playboy; Smithsonian; Horizon; Psychology Today; New York Times; Los Angeles Times; Washington Post; St Louis Post-Dispatch; Boston Globe; Chicago Tribune; The Baltimore Sun; Philadelphia Inquirer' Newsday. *Honours:* National Press Club Award for Excellence in Consumer Journalism, 1979. *Membership:* Washington Independent Writers, Advisory Board Member. *Literary Agent:* Elaine Markson, New York, USA. *Address:* Silver Spring, MD, USA.

O'GRADY, Desmond James Bernard, b. 27 Aug. 1935, Limerick, Ireland. Poet; Translator. 1 son, 1 daughter. *Education:* PhD, Celtic Languages and Literatures and Comparative Literatures, Harvard University. *Literary Appointments:* Teaching Fellow, Harvard University; Visiting Professor and Poet in Residence, American University in Cairo; Visiting Professor, Alexandria University, Alexandria, Egypt. *Publications:* Chords and Orchestrations, 1956; Reilly and Other Poems, 1961; Profesor Kelleher and the Charles River, 1964; The Dark Edge of Europe, 1967; Separazioni, 1968; Off Licence (Translations from Irish, Italian and Armenian poetry), 1968; The Dying Gaul, 1968; Hellas, 1971; Separations, 1973; Stations, 1976; Sing Me Creation, 1977; The Gododdin (translation from Welsh), 1977; A Limerick Rake (translation from Irish); His Skaldcrane's Nest, 1979; The Headgear of the Tribe, 1979; Grecian Glances (translation), 1982; These Fields in Springtime, 1985. Poems included in following anthologies: The Norton Anthology of Modern Poetry; The Faber Book of Irish Poetry; The Penguin Book of Irish Verse; The New Irish Poetry; The Castle Poets; The Sphere Books of Modern Irish Poetry; Choice; The Patrick Kavanagh Anthology; Soundings 72; Irish Poets 1924–1974. *Contributor to:* The Transatlantic Review; Botteghe Oscure; McCalls; Atlantic Monthly; Poetry Ireland; City Lights journal, and many others. *Honours:* Irish Representative, Congress of the Community of European Writers at Florence, Italy, 1962; Premio Taormina for Anna Akmatova at Sicily, 1964; Congress of the Community of European Writers at Rome, 1965; Congress of European Literary Editors and Publishers, Belgrade, 1966. *Memberships:* Aosdana, Ireland; Irish Academy of Letters; European Community of Writers. *Address:* Rincurran Cottage, Ardbrack, Kinsale, Co Cork, Republic of Ireland.

O'GRADY, Francis Dominic, b. 24 Apr. 1909, Sydney, Australia. Retired Town Clerk. m. Doris Joyce Byrne, 17 Oct. 1936, Waverley, deceased, 4 sons, 2 daughters. *Education:* Diploma, School of Applied Advertising, Sydney; Certificate, Local Government Clerk. *Publications:* The Golden Valley, 1955; Goonoo Goonoo, 1956; Hanging Rock, 1957; No Boundary Fence, 1960; Wild Honey, 1961; The Sun Breaks Through, 1964; Francis of Central Australia, 1977. *Contributor to:* Australian Dictionary of Biography; Annals Australia; Catholic Weekly. *Honours:* Fellow, Association of Local Government Clerks; Guy Kable Memorial Award, 1948; Fellow, Royal Australian Historical Society. *Address:* 21 Karilla Ave, Lane Cove, NSW, Australia.

O'GRADY, Tom, b. 26 Aug. 1943, Teacher; Poet; Vintner. *Education:* BA, University of Baltimore, USA, 1966; MA, Johns Hopkins University, 1967; Advanced studies of English and American Literature, University of Delaware, 1972–74. *Literary Appointments:* Lecturer in English, Johns Hopkins University, 1966–67; Catonsville College, 1969–71; University of Delaware, 1972–74; Hampden-Sydney College, 1974–76; Adj. Professor of English and Poet-in-Residence, Hampden-Sydney College, 1976–. *Publications:* Unicorn Evils, (pamphlet), 1973; Establishing a Vineyard, (sonnet sequence), 1977; Photographs, 1980; Co-Founder and Editor, The Hampden-Sydney Poetry Review; Translation of, Jaroslav Siefert, (1984 Nobel Laureate in Literature); The Casting of Bels; Mozart in Prague; Eight Days. *Contributor to:* Newsletters; Dryad; Enoch; Delaware Literary Review; Contemporary Literary Scene; Pyx; Nimrod; New Laurel Review, etc. *Honours include:* Leache Prize for Poetry, Chrysler Museum, Norfolk, Virginia, 1975; National Endowment for the Arts Poetry Residency, 1976–77; Impact Book Award, 1980. *Membership:* Coordinator, Council of Literary Magazine COSMEP South. *Address:* Rte 3 Box 252, Farmville, VA 23901, USA.

O'HEITHIR, Breandán, b. 18 Jan. 1930, Aran Island, Galway, Republic of Ireland. *Education:* Colaiste Einde and University College, Galway. *Publications:* Willie the Plain Pint agus an Papa, 1977; Lead Us into Temptation, 1978; Over the Bar, 1984. *Contributions to:* Irish Radio and Television, Scriptwriter; The Irish Times, weekly columnist. *Honours:* Irish-American Foundation Award, 1975; Gradam an Oireachtais, 1977; Bursary, Irish Arts Council, 1978. *Literary Agent:* Chris Green, London, England. *Address:* 54 Taney Road, Dundrum, Dublin 14, Republic of Ireland.

Ó HEARN, Peter Joseph Thomas, b. 2 Jan. 1917, Halifax, Nova Scotia, Canada. Judge. m. Mary Margaret McCormick (now deceased), 8 Sep. 1944, Halifax, Nova Scotia, 1 son. *Education:* BA, 1937; Superior A Teaching Certificate, 1938; LLb, 1947; M Th, 1973. *Publication:* Peace, Order and Good Government: A New Constitution for Canada, 1964. *Contributions to:* McGill Law Journal; Criminal Law Quarterly; Canadian Bar Review; Revue de Droit dell'Universitie de Sherbrooke; Studio Canonica; University of Toronto Law Journal; Ottawa University Law Review. *Honour:* Knight Commander of the Order of Saint Gregory the Great, 1969. *Address:* 6369 Berlin Street, Halifax, Nova Scotia B3L 1TA, Canada.

O'HIGGINS, James (Reverend), b. 21 Aug. 1915, Birstall, Leeds, England. Tutor for Graduates and Modern History. *Education:* MA, PhD, Oxford University; Lic Phil, STL, Meythrop College. *Literary Appointments:* Casual Review, Crime, Spectator, 1983; Reviewer, The Catholic History, 1983. *Publications:* Anthony Collins, The Man and His Works, 1970; Determinism and Freewill, 1976; Yves de Vallone, The Making of an Esprit Fort, 1982. *Contributions to:* Journal of Theological Studies; The Meythrop Journal. *Memberships:* Fellow, Royal Historical Society; British Historical Association; American Catholic Association. *Literary Agent:* Curtis Brown Limited, London. *Address:* Campion Hall, Oxford OX1 1QS, England.

O'HIGGINS, Paul, b. 5 Oct. 1927, Hersham, England. University Professor. m. Rachel Elizabeth Bush, 1 son, 3 daughters. *Education:* MA, LLB, PhD, Fellow, Christ's College, Cambridge, England from 1959. *Appointments:* Book Review Editor, Industrial Law, Journal, 1972; Joint General Editor, Mansell's Studies in Labour and Social Law, 1977; Joint General Editor, Encyclopaedia of Labour Relations Law; Member of Advisory Board, Northern Ireland Legal Quarterly, 1977; Editorial Board, Human Rights Review, 1979–82; General Editor, Law at Work, series, 1980–81. *Publications:* Bibliography Periodical Literature Irish Law, 1966, supplements, 1975, 1983; Public Employee Trade Unionism in UK: Legal Framework, 1971; Censorship in Britain, 1972; Workers' Rights, 1976; Cases and Materials on Civil Liberties, 1980; Bibliography of Irish Social Security Law, 1986; Bibliography of Irish Trials and Other Legal Proceedings, 1986. *Contributions:* Numerous, including, British Yearbook International Law; Cambridge Law Journal; Criminal Law Review; Human Rights Review; Industrial Law Journal; International and Comparative

Law Quarterly; Modern Law Review. *Honours:* Gilbert Murray Prize (shared), 1968; Hon Member Grotian Society, 1968; Vice President, Institute of Shops, Health and Safety Acts. *Membership:* Society of Authors. *Address:* Christ's College, Cambridge CB2 3BU, England.

OISTEANU, Valery, b. 3 Sep. 1943, Russia. Writer; Poet. m. Ruth Friedman, 3 Dec. 1973, NYC, USA. *Education:* MA, University of Bucharest, Romania. *Literary Appointments:* Columnist, Cultural News Weekly, Bucharest, Romania; Writer for Broadcasting, Bucharest; Freelance Writer, Journalist, USA. *Publications:* Prothesis, 1970; Underground Shadows, 1977; Underwater Temples, 1979; Do Not Defuse, 1980; Vis A Vis Bali, 1985. *Contributor to:* Literary Magazine, Bucharest; Anthology of Literature and Critic, Vienna, 1968; International Anthology of Poetry, Naples, 1970; Assembling Press, New York Press, QUOZ? San Francisco; International Poetry Letter, Mele, University of Hawaii, 1975–80; Poetry Coast to Coast, 1977; The Voyeur, New York; Free for All Anthology, New Jersey, 1979; Dream Helmet Anthology, New Jersey, 1984; Various others. *Membership:* Poets and Writers Inc, New York. *Literary Agent:* Ruth Friedman. *Address:* 170 2nd Avenue #2A, New York City, NY 10003, USA.

OJALA, Ossi Arne Atos, b. 22 Mar. 1933, Savonlinna, Finland. Amateur Theatre Director, Teacher, Copywriter. *Education:* BA, University of Helsinki, Finland. *Major Publications:* Saarella Tapahtuu (The Island), 1963; Valkoinen Vaara (The White Danger), 1966; Kahvila Sinuhe (The Café named Sinuhe), 1967; Toisenlainen Rakkaustarina (The Different Love Story), 1981; Ja Aika Pysähtyi (The Time Stopped), 1985; Ennen Hiljaisuutta Minä Huudan (Before Stillness I will cry out), 1985; Suolintu (The Crane), 1966; 30 other plays for broadcasting. *Contributor to:* Theater; Itä-Häme; Kaleva; Kainuun Sanomat; Opistolehti; and others. *Honours:* Saarella Tapahtuu Otava Prize, 1964; Suolintu – 1st Prize in competition, 1966; Kahvila Sinuhe, Best Finnish Novel for young people, 1967. *Memberships:* Suomen Kirjailijaliitto (Helsinki); Suomen Nöytelmäkirjailijaliitto (Helsinki); Salpausselän Kirjailijat (Lahti); Pirkkalaiskirjailijat (Tampere). *Literary Agent:* WSOY Helsinki; Kustannusoy Pohjoinen, Oulu. *Address:* Paasikivenkatu 32 B 23, 38700 Kankaanpää, Finland.

OKAZAKI, Tadao, b. 7 Apr. 1943, Tokyo, Japan. Physician; Editor in Chief. *Education:* Prefectural Medical School of Fukushima, Japan. *Literary Appointment:* Editor-in-Chief, New Cicada Haiku Poetry Magazine, 1984–. *Contributions to:* Cicada; The Modern Haiku; Frogpond, Haiku Society of America; New Cicada Haiku Magazine; Various medical journals. *Honours:* The Cicada Prize, 1976; Special Mention Award, Modern Haiku, 1979. *Memberships:* The Haiku Society of America; Western World Haiku Society; Haiku Canada. *Address:* 13 Shimizu, Fushiguro, Date, Fukushima 960-05, Japan.

OKE, Janette Lorene, b. 18 Feb. 1935, Alberta, Canada. Writer. m. Edward L Oke, 13 May 1957, Champion, Alberta, 3 sons, 1 daughter. *Education:* Diploma, Mountain View Bible College, Didsbury, Alberta. *Publications:* Love Comes Softly, 1979; Love's Enduring Promise, 1980; One Upon a Summer, 1981; Love's Long Journey, 1982; Spunky's Diary, 1982; When Calls the Heart, 1983; Love's Abiding Joy, 1983; New Kid in Town, 1983; Quite Places, Warm Thoughts, 1983; Love's Unending Legacy, 1984; The Prodigal Cat, 1984. *Contributor to:* Emphasis, 1980, 1981; The Christian Writer, 1983; Emphasis, 1984; Regular column in Spirit of Michiana. *Honours:* Gold Medallion Book Award, Fiction Category, Love's Long Journey, Evangelical Christian Publishers Association, 1983. *Membership:* Christian Writer's Club of Michiana. *Address:* 55136 E. Lori Lane, Mishawaka, IN 46545, USA.

OKSANEN, Aulikki, b. 19 July 1944, Karvia, Finland. Writer. m. Alpo Halonen, 1972, 1 son, 1 daughter.

Publications: Hevosen Kuolema, prose, 1966; Tykleimiehen syli, novel, 1968; Isosisko ja pikkuveli, novel, 1973; Kirsikkavarleat, short stories, 1976; Kultivoidut rikokset, short stories, 1978; Seitsemän rapua seitsemän skorpionia, poetry, 1979; Alumiinipaita, novel, 1984. *Contributions to:* Kulthurivihkot. *Honours:* J H Erkko-price, 1966; The Scandinavian drama-prize, 1974; The State's Literary Prize, 1974 and 1980. *Membership:* Finnish Writers Union. *Literary Agent:* Kirjayhtymä. *Address:* Valleotie IE, 01620 Vantaa 62, Finland.

OKSENBERG, Michel, b. 12 Oct. 1938, Brussels, Belgium. Professor. m. Lois Elinor Clarenbach, June 1962, 1 son, 1 daughter. *Education:* BA, Swarthmore College, 1960; MA 1963, PhD 1969, Columbia University. *Literary Appointments:* Acting Assistant Professor of Political Science, Stanford University, 1966–68; Assistant Professor of Political Science, Research Associate, East Asian Institute, Columbia University, 1968–71; Associate Professor, Columbia University, 1971–74; Associate Professor, 1974–77, Professor of Political Science, 1977–, University of Michigan; Senior Staff Member, National Security Council, 1977–80; Editorial Board, Journal of Asian Studies, 1977; Advisory Board for Chinese Language edition, Encyclopaedia Britannica. *Major Publications:* Bibliography of Secondary English Language Literature on Contemporary Chinese Politics, 1970; China: The Convulsive Society (pamphlet), 1970; China's Developmental Experience (editor), 1973; The Provinces of the Peoples' Republic of China: Political & Economic Bibliography (with Emerson, Field & Yuan), 1976; China & America: Past & Future (pamphlet, with R Oxnam), 1977; Dragon & Eagle (co-editor with R Oxnam), 1978; A Research Guide to, The Peoples' Daily, Editorials (with Gail Henderson), 1982. *Contributor to:* Numerous scholarly & political journals on Far Eastern & chinese Affairs. *Honours:* Amoco Good Teaching Award, 1982. *Memberships include:* American Political Science Association; Council on Foreign Relations; Board of Directors, Committee on Scholarly Communication with the Peoples' Republic of China; Board of Directors, National Committee on US/China Relations. *Address:* 1322 Granger, Ann Arbor, MI 48104, USA.

OLAFSSON, Einar, b. 11 Sep. 1949, Reykjavik, Iceland. m. Gudbjörg Sveinsdóttir, 1983, 1 son, 1 daughter. *Education:* BA, Literature and History. *Publications:* Oll rettindi askilin, poetry, 1972; Drepa drepa, poetry, 1974; Augu vid gangstett, poetry, 1983. *Memberships:* Writers Union of Iceland. *Address:* Solheimar 27 1OB, 104 Reykjavik, Iceland.

OLDS, Sharon, b. 19 Nov. 1942, USA. Poet. *Education:* MA, Stanford University, 1964; PhD, Columbia University, 1972. *Literary Appointments:* Manhattan Theater Club, 92nd Street Y Poetry Center; 1982; Poetry Society of America, 1983; NYU, Sarah Lawrence College, 1984; NYU, Goldwater Hospital, Roosevelt Island, NYC, 1985; Columbia University, Brandeis University, 1986. *Publications:* Satan Says, 1980; The Dead and the Living, 1984. *Contributor to:* The New Yorker; The Ameerican Poetry Review; Poetry; The Paris Review; Missouri Kenyon Review; Antioch Review; Yale Review. *Honours:* Guggenheim Fellowship, 1981; NEA Fellowship, 1982; The Lamont Award, (The Academy of American Poetry), 1984; The National Book Critics Circle Award, 1984. *Memberships:* Freedom-to-Write Committee, PEN American Center; Authors Guild; Poetry Society of America. *Literary Agent:* William Thompson, Lordly and Dame. *Address:* c/o A A Knopf, 201 East 50, New York City, NY 10022, USA.

OLDSEY, Bernard, b. 18 Feb. 1923, Wilkes-Barre, Pennsylvania, USA. Professor; Editor; Writer. m. Ann Marie Re, 21 Sep. 1946, New York City, 1 son, 1 daughter. *Education:* BA, 1948, MA, 1949, PhD, 1955, Pennsylvania State University. *Appointments:* Instructor to Associate Professor, English, Pennsylvania State University, 1951–69; Senior Fulbright Professor,

American Literature, Universidad de Zaragoza, Spain, 1964–65; Professor, English, West Chester University, 1969–; Editor, College Literature, 1974–. *Publications:* From Fact to Judgement, 1957; The Art of William Golding, 1965; The Spanish Season, novel, 1970; Hemingway's Hidden Craft, 1979; Ernest Hemingway: Papers of a Writer, 1981; British Novelists, 1930–1960, 1983; Critical Essays on George Orwell, 1985. *Contributor to:* Nation; American Literature; Modern Fiction Studies; Studies in American Fiction; College English; etc. *Honours:* Senior Fulbright Appointment, Universidad de Zaragoza, 1964–65; Distinguished and Academic Service Award, Pennsylvania State Colleges and Univesities Award, 1978. *Memberships:* Modern Language Association, Council of Editors of Learned Journals; Hemingway Society; Literary Fellowship of Philadelphia. *Address:* 1003 Woodview Lane, West Chester, PA 19380, USA.

O'LEARY, Liam, b. 25 Sep. 1910, Youghal, County Cork, Eire, Television Film Viewers; Film Historian. *Education:* University College, Dublin. *Literary Appointments:* Editorial staff, Ireland Today, 1936–37. *Publications:* Invitation to the Film, 1945; The Silent Cinema, 1965; Rex Ingram, Master of the Silent Cinema, 1980; International Dictionary of Films and Filmmakers, 1985; Cinema Ireland: A History, in progress. *Contributions to:* Ireland Today, film critic; Irish Times; Films and Filming; Kosmorama; The Leader; Irish Press; Envoy; The Bell. *Honours:* Medal for services in film section, Brusells International Film Fair, 1958; Medal for contribution to Irish Film Industry, National Film Studios of Ireland. *Address:* The Garden Flat, 74 Ranelagh Road, Dublin 6, Republic of Ireland.

OLECK, Howard L, b. 6 Jan. 1911, New York City, USA. Writer; Law Professor. m. Helen Eugenie Gemeiner, 21 Dec. 1941, New York, 2 daughters. *Education:* BA, University of Iowa; JD, New York Law School. *Literary Appointments:* Historian, Editor, US Army War Department; Editorial Assistant, New York Law Journal; Columnist, syndicated newspapers; Editor, various publications. *Publications include:* Military Histories, 1945–; Law Books, 1950–; Novels, 1950–. Approximately 34 books to date. *Contributions to:* Numerous magazines & journals. *Honours include:* President, Scribes Society, 1966; Numerous plaques, cups, certificates etc; Various honorary degrees & diplomas. *Membership:* Scribes. *Literary Agent:* Ann Elmo, New York City. *Address:* 1440 Sea Gull Drive South, St Petersburg, FL 33707, USA.

OLIVER, Covey Thomas, b. 21 Apr. 1913, Laredo, Texas, USA. Jurisconsult; Publicist; Professor of International Law. m. Barbara Frances Hauer, 28 Dec. 1946, Walnut Creek, California, 2 sons, 3 daughters. *Education:* BA, Summa cum laude, University of Texas, 1933; MA, University of Pennsylvania; J D Summa cum laude, University of Texas, 1936; Doctor of Juridical Science, 1954. *Literary Appointments:* Associate Editor-in-Chief, Texas Law Review, Columbus University 1935–36; Member of Board of Editors, American Journal of International Law, 1950–; (except for periods of Government service); a Member of various other publications boards. *Publications:* Law and Politics in the World Community, with co-authors, 1951; Restatement of the Foreign Relations Law of the USA, with co-authors, 1965; The International Legal System, 1st edition 1973, 2nd edition 1981. *Contributions to:* Numerous articles etc, published in USA and abroad. *Honours:* Most Significant Publication of the Year, American Society of International Law for, Restatement of the Foreign Relations Law of the USA, 1966; Order of Boyaca, Grand Cross, Colombia, 1966; LL D Southern Methodist University, 1978. *Memberships:* Council on Foreign Relations; International Law Association; American Society of International Law; American Council of Learned Societies; President, American Society of International Law. *Address:* Thomas Cottage, Ingleton-on-Miles, RFD 1 Box 194, Easton, MD 21601, USA.

OLIVER, Francis Richard, b. 5 June 1932, Nairobi, Kenya. University Teacher of statistics. *Education:* BA, MA, St John's College, Cambridge University, England, 1950–53; Diploma in Statistics, D Phil 1959, Balliol and Nuffield Colleges, Oxford. *Publications:* The Control of Hire Purchase, 1961; What Do Statistics Show, 1964; An Index of House Prices, 1983. *Contributions to:* Economic and statistical professional journals. *Address:* Department of Economics, The University, Exeter EX4 4RJ, England.

OLIVER, John Edward, b. 21 Oct 1933, Dover, Kent, England. University Professor. m. Sylvia Oberholzer, 18 Aug 1957, Newport, Gwent, 2 daughters. *Education:* BSc, London University, 1956; MA, 1966, PhD, 1969, Columbia University. *Literary Appointments:* Associate Editor, Journal of Human Ecology; Editor, Physical Geography. *Publications:* A Geography of Bermuda, 1964; Climate and Man's Environment, 1973; Perspectives on Applied Physical Geography, 1977; Physical Geography, 1980; Climatology: Selected Applications, 1981; Climatology: An Introduction, 1984. *Contributions to:* Annals Association of American Geography; Professional Geographer; Journal of Geography; Geographical Review; etc. *Address:* Department of Geography and Geology, Indiana State University, Terre Haute, IN 47809, USA.

OLIVER, Kenneth Arthur, b. 17 Feb, 1912, Sweet Home, Oregon, USA. University Professor. m. Madaline Schmidt, 18 Aug. 1935, Salem, Oregon, 2 sons. *Education:* BA, Willamette University, Salem, Oregon, 1935; MA, University of Washington, 1939; PhD, University of Wisconsin, 1947. *Literary Appointments:* Professor of Literature (Comparative and English), University of Wisconsin, 1947–48; Professor, Occidental College, 1948–77; Fulbright Professor of English Literature, University of Salonika, Greece, 1956–57. *Major Publications:* Our Living Language, 2nd edition, 1962; Words Every College Student Should Know, 3rd edition, 1983; Mr Privilege to Live, 1985; Guide to World Literature (Associate Editor and contributing author), 1980. *Contributor to:* Several literary journals. *Honours:* First Faculty Award Lecture, 1958; 2nd Prize, PEN International Short Story competition, 1972. *Address:* 1742 Drescher Street, San Diego, CA 92111, USA.

OLIVER, Richard, b. 9 Aug. 1945, Etterbeek, Belgium. Playwright; Film Producer. m. Monique Licht, 16 Sep. 1967, 1 son. *Education:* Institut des Arts et Diffusion. *Publications:* Amin Dada Ier Empereur de Belgique, 1980; Adaptation of Gulliver for children's television; Films include: Leurs Trucs en Plumes; Le Charme de l'Ambiguite; Strip School; Black Paris; Marvin Gaye Transit Ostende; La Chanson Rebelle; Le Buteur Fantastique; Musical Comedy: King Singer; Big Dady Dada; L'Irresistible Ascension de John Travol'rat. *Contributions to:* Le Soir Illustre; Pourquoi Pas?; Moustique. *Honours:* Prix Ondas, Spain, 1974; Prix RTBF? La Louviere, 1969; Prix Label of Quality CNC, 1977, 1981 and 1983; Prix du Jury de Festival Automoto, Paris, 1980; Prix Belgian Authors Write SABAM, 1982, 1984; Prix BNP, Rennes, 1984. *Memberships:* Administrateur de la commission Audio-visuelle SABAM. *Address:* 27 rue Joseph Stallaert, 1060 Brussels, Belgium.

OLIVER, Roland Anthony, b. 30 Mar. 1923, Srinagar, Kashmir. University Professor. m. Caroline Florence (deceased), 1947, 1 daughter. *Education:* MA, PhD, King's College, Cambridge. *Literary Appointments:* Lecturer, School of Oriental and African Studies, 1948–59; Reader in African History, University of London, 1958–63; Francqui Professor, University of Brussels, 1961; Visiting Professor, Northwestern University, Illinois, 1962; Visiting Professor, Harvard University, 1967; Travelled in Africa 1949–50 and 1957–58; Organised International Conferences in African History and Archaeology, 1953–61; Professor of History of Africa, London University, 1963–. *Publications:* The Missionary Factor in East Africa, 1952; Sir Harry Johnston and the Scramble for Africa, 1957; Editor: The

Dawn of African History, 1961; A Short History of Africa (with J D Fage), 1962; (with Gervase Mathew), A History of East Africa, 1963; Africa since 1800 (with A E Atmore), 1967; The Middle Age of African History, 1967; (with J D Fage), The Journal of African History, 1960–73; (with B M Fagan) Africa in the Iron Age, 1975; (with A E Atmore) The African Middle Ages, 1981; General Editor (with J D Fage) Cambridge History of Africa, 8 volumes, 1975–86. *Honour:* Haile Selassie Prize Trust Award, 1966. *Memberships:* President, African Studies Association, 1967–68; British Institute in Eastern Africa, 1981–; Member Permanent Bureau, International Congress of Africanists, 1973–78; Council, Royal African Society; Chairman, Minority Rights Group; Corresponding Member, Académie Royale des Sciences d'Outremer, Brussels. *Address:* 7 Cranfield House, Southampton Row, London WC1, England.

OLMSTED, Robert Walsh, b. 15 Mar. 1936, Washington, District of Columbia, USA. Editor/Publisher. m. Elaine Bennett, 6 May, 1958, Laurens, South Carolina, USA, 1 son, 3 daughters. *Education:* BA, Mansfield State University, Pennsylvania; BS, MS, Bemis State University, Minnesota; MA, University of Maine; PhD, University of Massachusetts. *Literary Appointments:* Editor, Northwoods Press. *Publications:* Northern Lights, poetry, 1969; First Christmas Ever, juvenile, 1972; Shadows and Casseopeia, poetry, 1976; Wild Strawberries at 3,000 feet, poetry, 1985. *Contributions to:* Numerous. *Address:* PO Box 88, Thomaston, ME 04861, USA.

OLNEY, James, b. 12 July 1933, Marathon, Iowa, USA. University Professor. 1 son. *Education:* BA, University of Iowa, 1955; MA, 1958, PhD, 1963; Columbia University. *Literary Appointment:* Editor, The Southern Review, 1983–. *Publications:* Metaphors of Self: The Meaning of Autobiography, 1972; Tell Me Africa: An Approach to African Literature, 1973; The Rhizome and the Flower: The Perennial Philosophy – Yeats and Jung, 1980; Editor: Autobiography: Essays Theoretical and Critical, 1980. *Address:* The Southern Review, 43 Allen Hall, Louisiana State University, Baton Rouge, LA 70803, USA.

OLOFSSON, Tommy, b. 22 May 1950, Karlshamn, Sweden. Poet; Critic; Lecturer. m. Marianne Olofsson, 21 Sep. 1982, Lund, 4 daughters. *Education:* Fil Dr, University of Lund, 1981. *Literary Appointments:* Secretary, James Joyce Society of Sweden and Finland. *Publications:* SMå Pratologier, 1970; Kärlekens nya Kläder, 1975; Elementära Dikter, 1977; Sol Utan Datum, 1979; Frigörelse Eller Samman Brott? (with Stephen Dedalus, Martin Birch), 1981; Samtal med min Skugga, 1982; Joyce I Sverige, 1986; Mina Känner inte Varandra, 1986. *Contributor to:* Critic, Svenska Dagbladet; Contributor of essays to anthologies and literary magazines. *Honours:* Various Awards and Stipendiums. *Memberships:* Swedish PEN; Swedish Union of authors. *Address:* Måsvägen 106, Uppåkra, S–22248 Lund, Sweden.

OLSEN, Theodore Victor, b. 25 Apr. 1932, Rhinelander, Wisconsin, USA. Freelance Writer. m. Beverly Butler, 25 Sep. 1976, Sun Prairie. *Education:* BSC, English. *Publications:* 43 books including, Haven of the Hunted, 1956; High Lawless, 1960; Canyon of the Gun, 1965; The Hard Men, 1966; Blizzard Pass, 1968; A Man Named Yuma, 1971; There Was a Season, 1972; Summer of the Drums, 1972; Starbuck's Brand, 1973; Run to the Mountain, 1974; Track the Man Down, 1975; Day of the Buzzard, 1976; Rattlesnake, 1979; Roots of the North, 1979; Our First Hundred Years, 1981; Birth of a City, 1983; Red is the River, 1983; Lazlo's Strike, 1983; Lonesome Gun, 1985. *Honour:* Award of Merit, State Historical Society of Wisconsin, 1983. *Literary Agent:* Ray Puechner, Milwaukee, Wisconsin, USA. *Address:* T V Olsen, P O Box 856, Rhinelander, WI 54501, USA.

OLSEN, Violet Mae, b. 5 Aug. 1922, Spencer, Iowa, USA. Writer. m. William D Olsen, 28 Jan. 1950,

Davenport. *Education:* BA, Art, English. *Publications:* The Growing Season, 1982; Never Brought to Mind, 1985. *Contributor to:* Spiritual Life; Reader's Digest; Our Family; Scope; Your Church; The Key; Lutherna Women. *Honours:* Quad City Writer of the Year, 1982; Writers Studio Writer of the Year, 1985. *Membership:* National League of American Pen Women. *Address:* 1010 W 15th St, Davenport, IA 52804, USA.

OLSON, David John, b. 18 May 1941, Brandford, North Dakota, USA. Professor and Chairman, Political Science. m. Sandra Jean Crabb, 11 June 1966, West Bend, Wisconsin, 1 daughter. *Education:* BA, Concordia College, 1963; MA, 1966, PhD, 1971, University of Wisconsin. *Publications:* Black Politics, 1971; Theft of the City, 1974; To Keep the Republic, 1975; Commission Politics, 1976; Governing The United States, 1977. *Contributor to:* Journal of Politics; Transactions; American Political Science Review. *Honours:* Rockefeller Fellow, 1964; Vilas Fellow, 1966; Brookings Predoctoral Fellow, 1968; Frederick Bachman Lieber Distinguished Teaching Award, 1973. *Memberhips:* Western Political Science Association, Vice President 1984, President 1985; American Political Science Association; Midwest Political Science Association; Southern Political Science Association. *Address:* 6512 E Green Lake Way North, Seattle, WA 98103, USA.

OLSON, Toby, b. 17 Aug. 1937, Berwyn, Illinois, USA. Poet and Novelist. m. Miriam Meltzer Olson, 27 Nov. 1966, New Haven, Connecticut, USA. *Education:* BA, Occidental College, California, USA, 1965; MA, Long Island University, 1968. *Appointments:* Associate Director, Aspen Writers; Workshop, Aspen, Colorado, USA, 1965–69; Member of the Faculty, The New School for Social Research, New York City, 1968–73; Assistant Professor of Long Island University, USA, 1968–74; Professor of English, Temple University, Philadelphia, USA. 1975–present. *Publications:* The Life of Jesus, 1976; Seaview, 1982; We Are The Fire, 1984; The Woman Who Escaped From Shame, 1986. *Contributions to:* Numerous magazines, including: Arts in Society; New Directions in Prose and Poetry; American Book Review; Inside Outer Space; The American Experience: A Radical Reader; The Nation; The Ohio Review; The Minnesota Review; The New York Quarterly; The New York Times; Choice; Sun; Catepillar; The American Poetry Review; Boundary 2; Conjunctions; Sun and Moon. *Honours:* CAPS Award in Poetry, 1974; Pennsylvania Council in the Arts Fellowship in Fiction, 1983; The PEN/Faulkner Award for the Most Distinguished World of American Fiction, 1983; National Endowment for the Arts Fellowship in Fiction, 1985; Guggenheim Fellowship in Fiction, 1985. *Memberships:* Guggenheim Fellowship in Fiction, 1985; PEN; Poets and Writers, CCLM. *Literary Agent:* Ellen Levine. *Address:* 329 South Juniper Street, Philadelphia, PA 19107, USA.

O'MEARA, John Joseph, b. 18 Feb. 1915, County Galway, Republic of Ireland. University Professor. m. Odile de Barthes de Montfort, 24 July 1947, Dublin. 1 son, 2 daughters. *Education:* BA, 1938, MA, 1939, National University of Ireland; D Phil, Oxford University, 1945. *Literary Appointments:* Editorial Board, Irish University Review, 1954–; Academic Adviser, Irish University Press, 1968–73. *Publications:* The Young Augustine, 1954; Pornhyry's Philosophy from Oracles in Augustine, 1959; Charter of Christendom, 1961; The Voyage of St Brendan, 1976. *Contributions to:* Journals specializing in St Augustine, Neo-platonism and Eriugena. *Honour:* Croix de la Legion d'Honneur, 1985. *Address:* 15 Maple Road, Dublin 14, Republic of Ireland.

OMOLEYE, Mike, b. 26 Jan. 1940, Oye-Ekiti, Ondo State, Nigeria. Journalist; Publisher. m. M A Omoleye, 1970, Ibadan, 4 sons, 3 daughters. *Education:* Diploma in Journalism. *Literary Appointments:* Freelance Journalist, 1960–63; Reporter, Morning and Sunday Post, 1964–69; Special Roving Features Writer, Daily and Sunday Sketch, 1969–71; News editor, 1972–73, Assistant Editor, 1974–76, Daily and Sunday Sketch;

Managing Director, Omeleye Publishing Company Limited, 1976–. *Publications:* You Can Control Your Destiny, 1974; Fascinating Folktales, 1976; Great Tales of the Yorubas, 1977; Mystery World Under the Sea, 1979; Awo As I Know Him, 1982; The Book of Life, 1982; Self Spiritual Healing, 1982; Issues at Stake, 1983. *Contributions to:* numerous articles in Nigerian newspapers; Former columnist, Sunday Post, Daily Sketch, Sunday Sketch; Sunday Tribune. *Literary Agents:* Helios Books, Somerset, England. *Address:* GPO Box 1265, Ibadan, Oyo State, Nigeria.

O'MORRISON, Kevin, b. 25 May 1916, St Louis, Missouri, USA. Playwright. m. Linda Soma, 30 Apr. 1966, New York City, New York. *Education:* Illinois Military Schools. *Publications:* The Long War, 1967; The Morgan Yard, 1975; Ladyhouse Blues, 1979; Stage Plays: Requiem, 1969; Three Days Before Yesterday, revised, 1970; The Morgan Yard, 1971; Ladyhouse Blues, 1975; A Party for Lovers, 1978; Report to the Stockholders, 1980; Dark Ages, 1979; The Old Missouri Jazz, musical, 1985. Television Plays: The House of Paper, 1959; And Not A Word More, 1960; A Sign for Autumn, 1962; Pompeii...One Day Before Yesterday. *Honours:* Creative Artists Public Service Fellow, 1975; Fellow, National Endowment for the Arts, 1980. *Memberships:* Dramatist Guild; Authors League of America; Writers Guild of America. *Literary Agent:* Samuel Liff, William Morris Agency, New York. *Address:* 20 East 9th Street, New York City, NY 10003, USA.

O'NEILL, Judith Beatrice, b. 30 June 1930, Melbourne, Australia. Writer. m. John Cochrane O'Neill, 17 Apr. 1954; Melbourne, 3 daughters. *Education:* MA, University of Melbourne, PGCE, University of London, England. *Publications:* Martin Luther, 1975; Transported to Van Diemen's Land, 1977; Jess and the River Kids, 1984; Stringy Bark Summer, 1985. *Honours:* Rigby/Australian 3rd prize for Jess and the River Kids, Festival of Arts, Adelaide, Australia, 1982; Short listed for The Observer Teenage Fiction Prize, 1984. *Literary Agent:* A P Watt. *Address:* c/o Professor J C O'Neill, New College, The Mound, Edinburgh, EH1 2LX, Scotland.

O'NEILL, Nena, b. 29 Nov. 1923, St Lawrence, Pennsylvania, USA. Writer. m. George C O'Neill, 14 Apr. 1945, 2 sons. *Education:* BA, Barnard College; Graduate course in Psychology, New School for Social Research; Graduate courses in Anthropology, Graduate Center, City University of New York. *Publications include:* Open Marriage, 1972 and Shifting Gears, 1974 (with George O'Neill); The Marriage Premise, 1977. *Contributions to:* Newsday; Readers Digest; New York; Family Circle; Working Woman; Woman's Day; The New York Times; Comprehensive Textbook of Psychiatry (editors Freedman, Kaplan and Sadock); and others. *Honours:* National Organization of Women Positive Image of Women Award in Books for 1972. *Memberships:* American Society of Journalists and Authors; Authors Guild. *Address:* M Evans and Company, 216 East 49th Stret, New York, NY 10017, USA.

ONG, Walter Jackson, b. 30 Nov. 1912, Kansas City, Missouri, USA. University Professor; Priest of the Society of Jesus; Author. *Education:* BA, Rockhurst, 1933; PhL, 1940, MA, 1941, STL, 1948, St Louis University; PhD, Harvard University, 1955; various honourary degrees. *Literary Appointments:* Instructor in English and French, Regis College, Denver; Instructor in English, 1953–54, Assistant Professor, 1954–57, Associate Professor, 1957–59, Professor, 1959, Professor of Humanities in Psychiatry, 1970–, University Professor of Humanities, 1981–, St Louis University; Visiting Professor or Lecturer to various universities, North America, Europe, East Asia, Middle East, Africa. *Publications:* Frontiers in American Catholicism, 1957; Ramus, Method, and the Decay of Dialogue, 1958; Ramos and Talon Inventory, 1958; American Catholic Crossroads, 1959; The Barbarian Within, 1962; In the Human Grain, 1967; The Presence of the Word, 1967; Rhetoric, Romance, and Technology, 1971; Interfaces of the Word, 1977;

Fighting for Life: Contest, Sexuality,and Consciensness, 1981; Orality and Literacy, 1982. *Contributions to:* Over 300 articles. *Honours:* Guggenheim Fellow, 1949–50, 1951–52; Fellow, Center for Advanced Studies, Wesleyan University, Middletown, Connecticut, 1961–62; Fellow, Center for Advanced Studies in Behavioral Sciences, Stanford, California, 1973–74; William Riley Parker Award, Modern Language Association of America, 1975. *Memberships:* President, Modern Language Association of America, 1978; President, Milton Society of America, 1967; Fellow, American Academy of Arts and Sciences; Chevalier dans l'Ordre des Palmes Academiques, France; Academy of Literary Studies, USA. *Address:* St Louis University, St Louis, MO 63103, USA.

OPFERMANN, Hans-Carl, b. 26 Apr. 1907, Altdorf, Germany. Writer. 2 daughters. *Education:* University Chemical Engineering Graduate; Law Court Expert Photography and Film. *Publications:* Die Neue Schmalfilmschule, 1938; Ein Weg zum Meisterfilmer, 1976; Vom Drehbuch zum Filmkunstwerk, 1976; Die Neue Schachschule, 1971; Die Spielgeheimnisse der grossen Schachkämpfer, 1978; Die Leistung der grossen Schach-Denker, 1980; Spielen mit dem Schach-Computer, 1980; Schach für Fortschrittene Schach-Gestalt-Scrategie; Meistøohaft kochen Schritt für Schritt; H C Opfermann's Film – Video-kurs. *Contributions to:* Foto-Magazin. *Honours:* 1st Prize, Bavarian Radio Commentator's Competition, 1936; Honorary Member, German Society of Photography, 1967; Selected Film Expert, German Pavilion, World Exhibition, Montreal, Canada, 1967. *Memberships:* Lifetime Member, L C München-Altschwabing; Honorary President, Honorary Member, L C München Nymphenburg and L C Lower Hutt, New Zealand, 1985; District Governor, 1971–, Lions International. *Agent:* Horst G Kliemann; Dr Stephen S Taylor. *Address:* Winzererstrasse 31, D–8000 Munich 40, Federal Republic of Germany.

OPIE, Iona Margaret Balfour, b. 13 Oct. 1923, Colchester, England. Folklorist. *Education:* Honours MA, Oxon. *Publications:* (all with Husband, Peter Mason Opie): The Oxford Dictionary of Nursery Rhymes, 1951; The Oxford Nursery Rhyme Book, 1955; The Lore and Language of Schoolchildren, 1969; Children's Games in Street and Playground, 1969; The Oxford Book of Children's Verse, 1973; The Classic Fairy Tales, 1974; A Nursery Companion, 1980; The Oxford Book of Narrative Verse, 1983; The Singing Game, 1985. *Honours:* (jointly with Peter M Opie): Coote-Lake Medal, 1960; Chicago Folklore Prize, 1969. *Address:* Westerfield House, West Liss, Hants, England.

OPIE, June, b. 27 June, 1926, New Zealand. Writer, Broadcaster, Lecturer and Educational Psychologist. *Education:* Auckland and Christchurch Universities, New Zealand. *Publications:* Over My Dead Body; Portrait of an Artist (BBC Programme). *Contributions to:* New Zealand Listener; Journal of RSA; ADP Quarterly (editor). *Honour:* FRSA. *Membership:* PEN. *Address:* 1 Trelawney Avenue, St Ives, Cornwall TR26 1AR, England.

OPPENHEIMER, Joel L, b. 18 Feb. 1930, Yonkers, New York, USA. Poet. *Education:* Cornell University; University of Chicago; Black Mountain College. *Publications:* The Dutiful Son, 1956; The Love Bit, 1961; In Time, 1969; On Occasion, 1973; The Woman Poems, 1975; Names, Dates and Places, 1979; Just Friends/Friends and Lovers, 1981; At Fifty, 1983; New Spaces, 1985. *Contributor to:* Village Voice and numerous Sunday and literary magazines. *Honours:* CAPS Award (NYSCA), 1971; NEA Grant in Poetry, 1980. *Memberships:* PEN; Authors Guild; Poetry Society of America. *Address:* 463 W Street, New York, NY 10014, USA.

ORANEN, Raija Helena, b. 2 Aug. 1948, Hyrynsalmi, Finland. Writer. m. 18 Apr. 1973, 2 sons. *Education:* MAG, Social Sciences. *Appointments:* Secretary Helsinkin Kirjailijat RY. *Publications:* Nainen Joka Soi

Jurnssa Appelsiinin, Short stories, 1972; Valomerkki, 1978; 2 Childrens Novels, 1979, 1984; Dramas for Theatre, TV and Radio. *Contributor to:* Several journals & magazines. *Memberships:* Suomen Kirjailjaliitto; Suomen Naytezmakirjailjalitto; Helsingin Kirjailijat RY. *Address:* Japaninkatu 9, 00560 Helsinki, Finland.

ORDONA, Alex Alejo, b. 9 Nov. 1950, The Philippines. Industrial Engineer. m. Mariam Formento, 20 May 1979; Manila, The Philippines, 1 son, 1 daughter. *Education:* BSc, Electrical Engineering, Feati University, Philippines, 1973; One year Masters in Business Administration, Ateneo de Manila University, 1977–78; Graduate Diploma in Management, Royal Melbourne Institute of Technology, Australia, 1982. *Apointments:* Managing Editor, The Philippine Mabuhay, 1983, Editor, The Philippine Mabuhay, 1983; Co-Editor, Silangan International Magazine, 1985. *Publications:* Editorial articles. *Address:* 482 Springvale Road, Glen Waverley, Victoria, Australia 3150.

ORDWAY, Sally, b. Lafayette, Alabama, USA. Playwright. *Education:* BA, Hollins College; MA, Hunter College. *Publications:* Plays: There's a Wall Between Us, Darling, 1968; 3 plays in, Scripts, 1971; Family Family, 1974. *Honours:* ABC Fellowship, Yale University, 1968; NEA Grant, 1978; CAPS Grant, 1978. *Memberships:* Dramatists Guild; PEN; Women in Film. *Literary Agent:* Charles Hunt, Fifi Oscard Agency, New York City. *Address:* 344 West 38th, 10B, New York, NY 10018, USA.

O'REILLY, Donald Edmund, b. 1 May 1913, Attleboro, Massachusetts, USA. Magazine and Newspaper Writer-Photographer. m. Edith Lillian Macomber, 9 July 1938, Mansfield, Massachusetts, 1 son (deceased). *Literary Appointments:* Report, Photographer, 1937–47; Editor and Publisher, Speed Age Magazine, 1947–53; Manager, NASCAR News Bureau, Florida, 1953–59; Public Relations Director, Atlanta, Georgia International Raceway, 1959–64; Manager, Automotive Division, Dynamic Films Inc, 1964–68; Self-syndicated Newspaper Column, 1956–; Award-winning Freelance Writer and Broadcaster, 1968–; Bureau Chief, Daytona Beach News-Journal, 1976–80; Feature Writer for Circle Track Magazine, 1980–. *Publications:* Complete Book of Motor Camping, 1971; Mr Hockey: The World of Gordie Howe, 1975. *Contributor to:* Flagler Palm Coast News-Tribune; Dayton Beach News-Journal; Circle Track Magazine; Racing Pictorial. *Honours:* Burt Williams Award, National Press Photographers Association; several other awards. *Memberships:* American Auto Racing Writers and Broadcasters Association (former Vice-president); Society of Professional Journalists; International Motor Press Association; Florida Freelance Writers Association, etc. *Literary Agent:* Dominick Abel, New York City. *Address:* 198 Sea Pines Circle, Indigo Lakes, Daytona, Beach, FL 32014, USA.

OREL, Harold, b. 31 Mar. 1926, Boston, Massachusetts, USA. Professor of English. m. Charlyn Hawkins, 25 May 1951, Ann Arbor, Michigan, 1 son, 1 daughter. *Education:* BA, 1948, University of New Hampshire, MA, 1949, PhD, 1952, University of Michigan, USA. *Literary Appointments:* Teaching Fellow, University of Michigan, 1948–52; Instructor, University of Maryland, 1952–56; Associate Professor, 1957–63; Professor of English, 1963–74; Distinguished Propfessor, 1974–, University of Kansas, USA. *Major Publications Include:* The World of Victorian Humor (editor), 1961; Thomas Hardy's Epic-drama: A Study of 'The Dynasts', 1963; The Development of William Butler Yeats 1885–1900, 1968; The Nineteenth-Century Writer and his Audience (co-editor with G J Worth), 1969; Irish History and Culture: Aspects of a Peoples' Heritage, 1976; The Scottish World (co-editor), 1981; Rudyard Kipling: Interviews and Recollections (2 volumes), 1983; The Literary Achievements of Rebecca West, in preparation. *Contributor to:* Numerous literary and scholarly journals. *Honours:* Vice-President, President, American Committee on Irish Studies, 1967–72; Vice-President, Thomas Hardy Society, 1968–; Lecturer in Japan, 1974, India, 1985. *Memberships:* Modern

Language Association; International Association of University Professors of English; International Association for the Study of Anglo-Irish Literature; Association for Scottish Studies. *Address:* 713, Schwarz Road, Lawrence, KS 66044, USA.

ORESICK, Peter Michael, b. 8 Sep. 1955, Ford City, Pennsylvania, USA. Teacher. m. Stephanie Flom, 26 Nov. 1977, Pittsburgh, Pennsylvania, USA, 3 sons. *Education:* Diploma, Ford City High School; BA, University of Pittsburgh; MFA, University of Pittsburgh. *Literary Appointments:* Poet, Pennsylvania Council on the Arts, Poets in the Schools Program, 1977–. *Publications:* The Story of Glass, 1977; Other Lives, 1985; An American Peace, 1985. *Contributions to:* The Christian Century; Michigan Quarterly Review; Minnesota Review; Poetry East; Poetry Northwest; Slow Loris Reader. *Honours:* Academy of American Poets Prize, 1980; Fellowship, Pennsylvania Council on the Arts, 1984. *Memberships:* Associated Writing Programmes; National Writer's Union. *Address:* 1424 Mellon Street, Pittsburgh, PA 15206, USA.

ORGA, Hüsnü Ates D'arcy, b. 6 Nov. 1944, Kingston, Surrey, England. Lecturer; Writer. m. Josephine Prior, Sough, 23 Nov.1974, 1 son, 1 daughter. *Education:* BMus, University of Durham, 1968; ATCL, piano, 1964, TCL, teaching, 1966, FTCL, composition, 1972, Trinity College of Music, London. *Literary Appointments:* BBC Music Division, 1971–75; University of Surrey Music Department, 1975–; Artistic Consultant, Institute of Armenian Music, 1976–80; Artistic Consultant, Sutton Place Heritage Trust, 1983–. *Publications:* The Proms, 1974; Chopin: His Life & Times, 1976, 1980, 1983; Beethoven: His Life & Times, 1978, 1980, 1983. *Contributions to:* Journals including: International Music Guide; Hi-Fi News; Records & Recording; Music & Musicians; Listener; Radio Times; Composer; Books & Bookmen; etc. Programmes Annotator for: Philharmonia Orchestra; London Symphony Orchestra; City of London Sinphonia; London Sinfonietta; Sutton Place. Sleeve Notes for various recording companies. *Membership:* Chairman, Music Panel, South East Arts. *Address:* Music Department, University of Surrey, Stag Hill, Guildford, Surrey GU2 5XH, England.

ORGAN, Troy Wilson, b. 25 Oct. 1912, Edgar, Nebraska, USA. University Professor. m. Vinita McMullin, 10 June 1979, Dayton, 1 son, 1 daughter, by previous marriage. *Education:* BA, Hastings College, 1934; BD, McCormick Theological Seminary, 1937; MA, 1939, PhD, 1941, University of Iowa; Post Graduate Studies, University of Hawaii, University of Chicago, Oxford University, England. *Appointments:* Parsons College, 1941–45; University of Akron, 1945–46; Chatham Colege, 1946–54; Ohio University, 1954–. *Publications:* Index to Aristotle, 1949; Self in Indian Philosophy, 1964; Art of Critical Thinking, 1965; Hindu Quest for Perfection of Man, 1970; Hinduism: Its Historical Development, 1974; Western Approaches to Eastern Philosophy, 1975. *Contributor to:* 64 articles in professionaljournals. *Honours:* Ford Foundation Fellowship, 1952; Fulbright to India, 1958, 1965; Distinguished Profesor Award, 1965, Baker Fund Award, 1966, Ohio University; Outstanding Educators of America, 1970. *Memberships:* American Philosophical Association; Indian Philosophical Congress; Ohio Philosophical Association, President, 1961–64. *Address:* Department of Philosophy, Ohio University, Athens, OH 45701, USA.

ORIARD, Michael Vincent, b. 26 May 1948, Spokane, Washington, USA. University Professor. m. Julie Ann Voelker, 14 June 1971, Spokane, Washington, USA, 2 sons. *Education:* BA, University of Notre Dame, Indiana, USA, 1970; PhD, Stanford University, California, USA, 1976. *Literary Appointments:* Editorial Board, Arete: The Journal of Sport Literature. *Publications:* Dreaming of Heroes: American Sports Fiction, 1868–1980, 1982; The End of Autumn: Reflections on my Life in Football, 1982. *Contributions to:* Critical articles in, Modern Fiction Studies; Southern Literary Journal; Studies in American Fiction; Critique;

Journal of American Culture; Journalism in,the New York Times; Sports Illustrated. *Honours:* Phi Beta Kappa, 1970; Damforth Fellowship, 1970; Phi Kappa Phi, 1979; National Endowment for the Humanities Fellowship, 1984. *Memberships:* Modern Language Association; American Studies Association; North American Society for Sport History; Sport Literature Association. *Address:* Department of English, Oregon State University, Corvallis, OR 97331, USA.

ORIZET, Jean Germain, b. 5 Mar. 1937, Marseilles, France. Journalist; Publisher. m. Isabelle Constantin, 22 June 1968, Paris, 2 daughters. *Education:* Interpreter School, University of Geneva, Switzerland; Political Science School, University of Paris, France. *Literary Appointments:* Lecturer, Alliance Francaise and Cultural Department, Ministry of Foreign Affairs, France, 1975–. *Publications:* En Soi le Chaos, 1975; Niveaux de Survie, 1978; Le Voyageur Absent, 1982; Errance, 1961; L'Humour des Poetes, 1981; Dits d'un Monde en Miettes, 1982; Histoire de l'Entretemps, 1985. *Contributions to:* Poesie I; Figaro Magazine; Demeures and Chateaux. *Honours:* Prix Marie Noel, 1966; Prix Charles Vildrac, 1982; Prix Max Jacob, 1975; Prix Apollinaire, 1982. *Memberships:* Secretary General, Academie Mallarme; Committee of French, PEN Club; Societe des Gens de Lettres. *Address:* 35 rue de Verneuil, 75007 Paris, France.

ORLEN, Steven Leslie, b. 13 Jan. 1942, Holyoke, Massachusetts, USA. Poet. m. Gail Barbara Marcus, 11 Aug. 1968, 1 son. *Education:* BA, University of Massachusetts, USA, 1964; MFA Creative Writing, Writer's Workshop, University of Iowa, USA, 1967. *Literary Appointments:* Professor of English, University of Arizona, Tucson, Arizona, USA. *Publications:* Permission to Speak, 1978; A Place At The Table, 1981. *Honours:* George Pillon Award, Poetry Magazine, 1971; National Endowment for the Arts Award, 1974, 1980. *Membership:* Poetry Society of America. *Address:* 436 South Fifth Avenue, Tucson, AZ 85701, USA.

ORTHWEIN, Laura Rand, b. 2 Nov. 1940, St Louis, Missouri, USA. Director, Women's History Research Centre/Executive Director, National Clearinghouse on Marital Rape. *Education:* BA, University of California, Berkeley, 1971. *Publications:* Women's Songbook; Female Artists Past and Present; Films By and/or About Women, Internationally Past and Present; Women and Health/Mental Health, Microfilm, 1974; Women and Law, Microfilm, 1974; Herstory Microfilm. *Contributor to:* Producer/Editor/Publisher/Distributor: Women in World History: International Women's Day, 1969; Spazm, 1969; Only National Women's Liberation Newsletter of this period; It Ain't Me Babe, first newspaper of the current women's movement; Bibliographies on Women; Bibliographies on Rape; Women's Studies Course Outlines; Socio-Legal Chart of cases where Marital Rape is a Crime. *Honours:* Unanimous Commendation by the American Library Association, 1972; Woman of Achievement Award, Mademoiselle, 1974; First World Congress of Victimology Award for starting the National Clearinghouse on Marital Rape, 1980; Soroptomists Honorarium; Diana Award. *Memberships:* American Historical Association; American Library Association; Association of College and Research Libraries. *Address:* Women's History Research Center, 2325 Oak, Berkeley, CA 94708, USA.

ORTIZ, Antonio Gilberto, b. 5 Mar. 1946. Writer. *Education:* AA, Los Angeles City College, USA, 1967; BA, 1969, MA, 1971, University of California, Los Angeles. *Appointments include:* Instructor, Santa Ana City College, California; Instructor, Santa Monica City College; Instructor, Pepperdine University. *Contributor to:* Various Anthologies including: Flor y Canto, I and II, Chicano Poetry Anthologies; Metaforas Verdes; Chicano Poetry Anthology; NM Magazine; Urbis Magazine; La Opinion Newspaper. *Honours:* Writers Guild Open Door Awards, 1975, 1976. *Memberships:* Writers Guild of America; Vice Chairman, Latin Writers

Commission; Freedom of Speech & Censorship Committee; Welcoming Committee and Conference Planning Committee. *Address:* 3620 Faris Dr, Los Angeles, CA 90034, USA.

ORTON, Clive Robert, b. 5 July 1944, Dorking, Surrey, England. Archaeologist. m. Jean Lesley Sturgess, 17 Aug. 1968, Hampstead, 1 son, 1 daughter. *Education:* MA, Cambridge, 1967; Diploma, Mathematical Statistics, Cambridge; Certificate, Field Archaeology, London Extra-Mural. *Appointment:* Editor, the London Archaeologist, 1976–. *Publications:* Spatial Analysis in Archaeology, 1976, with I R Hodder; Mathematics in Archaeology, 1980. *Contributor to:* Statistical News; World Archaeology; British Poultry Science; Journal of the Royal Statistical Society; Animal Farmer and Vegetable Grower; British Journal of Nutrition; Bulletin of the Institute of Archaeology; Science in Archaeology; London Archaeologist; British Archaeological Reports; Surrey Archaeological Collections; etc. *Membership:* Society of Authors. *Address:* 39A Benhill Wood Road, Sutton, Surrey SM1 3SL, England.

OSBORN, Neil Frank, b. 24 Oct. 1949, Hertford, England. Financial Journalist. *Education:* BA, MA, Modern History, Worcester College, Oxford University. *Appointments:* Senior Editor, Institutional Investor, magazine, 1978–83; US Editor 1983–. Editor 1985, Euromoney, magazine. *Honours:* Runner up 1980, Business Journalism Award 1982, University of Missouri. *Address:* c/o Euromoney, 677 5th Avenue, New York, NY 10022, USA.

OSBORNE, Chester Gorham, b. 18 Sep. 1915, Portsmouth, New Hampshire, USA. Writer, Composer. m. Mary E Rooney, 26 Apr. 1943, Center Moriches, New York, 2 sons, 3 daughters. *Education:* B Mus, New England Conservatory; M Mus, Northwestern University. *Major Publications:* The First Bow & Arrow, 1951; The First Puppy, 1953; The First Lake Dwellers, 1956; The First Wheel, 1959; The Wind & The Fire, 1959; The Silver Anchor, 1967; The Memory String, 1984; Plays: The Twenty-Fourth Candle, 1952; Handel: The Boy and the Music, 1985; Mozart's Magic Ring, 1986. *Contributor to:* Childrens Playmate; Educational Music; Etude; Instructor; Journal of New York Conference for Brass Scholarships; Junior Natural History; Long Island Forum; Music Educators Journal; The School Musician; and others. *Honour:* Gold Medal, Boys Club of America, 1956 (for The First Lake Dwellers). *Membership:* American Society of Composers, Authors and Publishers. *Literary Agent:* McIntosh & Otis, Inc. *Address:* P O Box 517, Center Moriches, NY 11934, USA.

OSBORNE, Harold, b. 1 Mar. 1905, London, England. Writer. *Education:* MA, Cambridge. *Publications:* Foundations of the Philosophy of Action, 1933; Indians of the Andes, 1952; USA, 1973; Bolivia: A Land Divided, 1954, 3rd edition, 1964; Aesthetics & Criticism, 1955; Ed. Aesthetics & The Modern World, 1968; Aesthetics & Art Theory, 1968; USA, 1970; Portuguese translation, 1970; South American Mythology, 1968; The Art of Appreciation, 1970; Ed. The Oxford Companion to Art, 1970; Ed. Aesthetics, 1972; Ed. The Oxford Companion to the Decorative Arts, 1975; Oxford Companion to Contemporary Art, 1976; Abstraction and Artifice in Twentieth-Century Arts, 1979; Former Ed. British Journal of Aesthetics. *Contributions to:* Various aesthetics journals. *Memberships:* Athenaeum Club; President, British Society of Aesthetics. *Literary Agent:* Curtis Brown. *Address:* Kreuzstrasse 12, 8640 Rapperswil SG, Switzerland.

OSBORNE, Mary Pope, b. 20 May 1949, Fort Sill, Oklahoma, USA. Writer. m. Will Osborne, 16 May 1976, New York City. *Education:* BA, University of North Carolina. *Publications:* Run, Run As Fast As You Can, 1982; Love Always, Blue, 1983; Best Wishes, Joe Brady, 1984; Mo To The Rescue, 1985; Last One Home, publication pending. *Literary Agent:* Sheldon Fogelman,

Esq. *Address:* c/o Dial Books, E P Dutton Inc, 2 Park Avenue, New York, NY 10016, USA.

OSBORNE, Robin Hamilton, b. 21 June 1947, Sydney, Australia. Journalist; Writer. m. Anne Schillmoller, 21 Dec. 1983, Sydney, 1 son. *Education:* BA Communications, Sydney Institute of Technology. *Major Publication:* Indonesia's Secret War: The Guerilla Struggle in Iranian Jaya, 1985. *Contributor to:* The Guardian; The Australian; National Times (Australia); Tempo (Indonesia); Times of Papua New Guinea. *Address:* Dateline, SBS-TV, 4 Cliff Street, Milson's Point, Sydney, New South Wales, Australia, 2061.

OSERS, Ewald, b. 13 May 1917, Prague, Czechoslovakia. Freelance Translator; formerly Broadcasting Executive. *Education:* Charles University Prague; BA Honours, University of London, England. *Publications:* (volume of poetry) Wish You Were Here, 1977; (translations of over 90 books including) The Correspondence Between Richard Strauss and Hugo von Hofmannsthal, 1961; The Secret Conferences of Dr Goebbels, 1939–1943, 1970; Three Caech Poets, 1971; Contemporary German Poetry, 1976. *Contributor to:* London Magazine; Modern Poetry in Translation; Times Literary Supplement; etc. *Honours:* Schlegel-Tieck Translation Prize, 1971; CB Nathhorst International Translation Prize, 1977; Fellow, Royal Society of Literature. *Memberships:* PEN; Poetry Society; International Poetry Society; Writers & Scholars International; Radiowriters Association; Institute of Linguistics, Fellow, Council Member 1973–, Vice Chairman, 1975–80; Translation Association, Chairman, 1971, 1980–81, 1983–84; Translators Guild, Chiarman, 1975–79; International Federation of Translators, Vice President. *Address:* 33 Reades Lane, Sonning Common, Reading RG1 9LL, England.

O'SHEA, Martin Lester, b. 6 Dec. 1938, San Francisco, California, USA. Partner, Real Estate Investment Company. m. (1) Barbara Ann Behn, 2 Aug. 1969, San Francisco (div. 1984) 3 daughters. (2) Camille de Campos, 28 July 1984, Reno, Nevada. *Education:* BA, Economics, Stanford University, 1959; Graduate work, Oxford University, UK, 1959–61; MSA, Harvard Business School, 1963. *Publication:* Tampering with the Machinery: Roots of Economic & Political Malaise, 1980. *Address:* 235 Montgomery Street, San Francisco, CA 94104, USA.

OSMAN, Nixar Gunal, b. 20 Feb. 1936, Cyprus. Economist. m. Elizabeth Ann, 14 July 1973, Woking, Surrey, England, 2 sons, 1 daughter. *Education:* BSc, University of Ankara, Turkey; MSc, University of Arkansas, USA. *Literary Appointments:* Editor, World Sugar Journal, 1978; Editorial Board, Tate and Lyle Sugar Industry Abstracts, 1980; Publisher, Golf Club Management, 1984; Executive editor, World Sugar Directory, 1984. *Publications:* Factors Affecting the Estimated Future Foreign Demand for Soyabeans, 1966; World Sugar, Capacity, Cost and Policy, 1977; World Sugar Directory, 1985. *Contributions to:* Arkansas Farm Research; World Sugar Journal; Golf Club Management. *Address:* 1 Murdoch Road, Wokingham, Berks RG11 2DL, England.

OSTRANDER, Fred, b. 23 Apr. 1926, Berkeley, California, USA. Appraiser. m. Nancy Majors, 2 sons. *Education:* BA, University of California, Berkeley, 1948. *Publications:* Accent on Barlow: a commemorative anthology, 1962; The Hunchback and the Swan, 1978. *Contributions to:* The Blue Unicorn; Works, a Quarterly Review; Ishmael; Galley Sail Review. *Membership:* Associated with Activist Group of Writers in San Francisco Bay Area. *Address:* 2741 Woolsey Street, Berkeley, CA 94705, USA.

OSWALD, Roy Lee, b. 20 July 1944, Montgomery, Alabama, USA. Investor. m. Lynda F Knight, 26 Mar. 1983, Montgomery. *Education:* BS, Troy State University; Diploma, John Patterson Technical College. *Publications:* After the Storm – The Rainbow, 1977; Venture Inward, 1978; Fruitful Thoughts, 1981; Inner

Echoes, 1982. *Contributor to:* Over 1,000 poems published in 60 literary publications. *Honours:* Recipient numerous prizes and awards. *Memberships:* Society of Christian Poets; Academy of American Poets. *Address:* 1136 Lombard Drive, Montgomery, AL 36109, USA.

OTAMBO, Mary Emily Inda, b. 25 Dec. 1941. separated, 1 son. Writer; Editor; Publisher. *Education:* BA, Huston Tillotson College, Austin, Texas, 1966. *Literary Appointments:* Information Officer, Ministry of Information and Broadcasting, Government of Kenya, 1966–76. *Publications:* Blue Ribbon, 1973; Instant Fad I, 1973; Instant Fad II and III, 1974; A Child's Fun Poetry; Myriad Mythos, (booklet), 1982. *Contributor to:* International Poetry Society's Anthology; Gems of Modern British Poetry; Havens of the Muse; Target; Ghala; Inside Kenya Today; Herald; Poet; Ipso Facto; Ocarina; Coast Week. *Honours:* Diploma of Merit, for Myriad Mythos, Italian University of Arts, 1982; DLit, World Academy of Arts and Culture, affiliated to World Congress of Poets, 1984. *Address:* PO Box 86047, Nairobi, Kenya.

OTTEN, Terry Ralph, b. 15 Apr. 1938, Dayton, Kentucky, USA. Chairman and Professor, Department of English, Wittenberg University. *Education:* BA, Georgetown College, 1959; MA, University of Kentucky, 1961, PhD, Ohio University, 1966. *Publications:* The Deserted Stage: The Search for Dramatic Form in 19th Century English Literature; After Innocence: Visions of the Fall in Modern Literature, 1982. *Contributions to:* Southern Humanities Review; Journal of American Fiction; Journal of Aesthetics and Art Criticism; South Atlantic Quarterly; Comparative Drama; Research Studies; Bucknell Review; Illinois Quarterly; Studies in the Humanities; College Literature and others. *Honours include:* Distinguished Teacher Award, Wittenberg University, 1975. *Memberhips:* Modern Language Association; NCET; College English Association of Ohio; Byron Society. *Address:* English Department, Wittenberg University, Springfield, OH 45501, USA.

OTTEN, Willem Jan, b. 1951, Amsterdam, The Netherlands. Playwright. *Education:* Study of Philosophy and English. *Appointments:* Theatre critic, Vrij Nederland, 1975; Dramaturg, Baal Company, Holland, 1982; Full time playwright, 1984–present. *Publications:* Henry II (theatre play); A Snow (theatre play); three novels. *Address:* Turfpoortstraat 51, 1411 EE Narden, The Netherlands.

OTTENHOF, Jan, b. 26 Aug. 1952, Amsterdam, Holland. *Appointments:* Freelance writer for theatre, television and films, 1978–present. *Publications:* The Wolfsting (film scenario), 1978; Wings of Wax, (theatre play), 1981; Mezcal (theatre play), 1983; Between Chaos and Hangovers, (theatre play), 1983; Transport (TV play), 1983. *Honour:* 1st prize for The Wolfsting, in a film scenario contest, 1978. *Address:* Keizersgracht 24A II 1015 CR Amsterdam, The Netherlands.

OTTLEY, William Henry, b. 7 Mar. 1929, New York, USA. Aviation. *Education:* BA, Yale University, 1950; Georgetown University School of Foreign Service, 1953. *Publications:* Wall Street Twentieth Century, 1957. *Contributor to:* Private Pilot Magazine, 1967–77; Editor, National Pilots Association News, 1967–77; Associate Editor, Yale Alumni Magazine, 1950–51, Yale Daily News, 1947–50; Contributing Editor, Parachutist Magazine, 1964–78; Publisher, Parachutist Magazine, 1978–. *Honours:* Dr of Aeronautical Science, Honoris Causa, Embry Riddle Aeronautical University, 1979; Consultant, Centre for the Study of Human Factors in Aviation, 1975–77. *Address:* 1440 Duke Street, Alexandria, VA 22314, USA.

OVERHOLSER, Wayne D, b. 4 Sep. 1906, Pomeroy, Washington, USA. Teacher, Writer. m. Evaleth Miller, 21 Apr. 1934, Yakima, Washington, 3 sons. *Education:* BSc, Oregon. *Publications:* The Violent Land, 1954; The Sweet and Bitter Land, 1950; Cast A Long Shadow, 1955; Sun On The Wall, 1973; Law Man, 1953.

Contributions to: Approximately 400 publications including: The Law Abiding Outlaw; Matt Seery's Town; Book L'Arnin' and the Equalizer; The Patriarch of Gunsight Flat. *Honours:* Best Adult Fiction Book, Colorado Authors League, 1950 and 1960; Best Western Novel, 1953 and 1954, Best Western Juvenile Novel (co-author with Lewis B Patten) 1969, Western Writers of America. *Literary Agent:* John Payne. *Address:* 500 Mohawk Drive, Boulder, CO 80303, USA.

OVERTON, Jenny Margaret Mary, b. 22 Jan. 1942, Cranleigh, Surrey, England. *Education:* MA Honours English Literature, Cambridge. *Publications:* Creed Country, 1969; The Thirteen Days of Christmas, 1971; The Night-Watch Winter, 1972; The Ship From Simnel Street, 1986. *Address:* Crest Hill, Peaslake, Guildford, Surrey, England.

OWEN, Charles, b. 14 Nov. 1915, England. Author; Management Consultant; Royal Navy Officer (retired). m. Felicity, 14 Feb. 1950, London, 1 son, 1 daughter. *Education:* Royal Naval Colleges, Dartmouth and Greenwich, England. *Major Publications:* Independent Traveller, 1966; Britons Abroad, 1968; The Opaque Society, 1970; No More Heroes, 1975; The Grand Days of Travel, 1979; Just across the Channel, 1983. *Contributor to:* Various magazines & journals. *Honour:* Distinguished Service Cross, 1943. *Memberships:* Society of Authors; Writers Guild of Great Britain; PEN; West Country Writers Association. *Address:* 25 Montagu Street, London W1H 1TB, England.

OWEN, David Elystan, b. 27 Feb. 1912, Kingston-on-Thames, England. Museum Curator. m. Pearl Jennings, 2 Apr. 1936, Leicester, 1 son, 1 daughter. *Education:* BSc, PhD, Kings College, London University. *Publications:* Water Highways, 1967; Water Rallies, 1969; Water Byways, 1973; Canals to Manchester, 1977; Cheshire Waterways, 1979; The Manchester Ship Canal, 1983; Exploring England by Canal, 1986. *Contributions to:* Waterways journals; Papers in Paleontological journals and in archeological journals. *Honour:* CBE, 1972. *Address:* 9 Carleton Road, Poynton, Stockport, Cheshire SK12 1TL, England.

OWEN, Eileen, b. 27 Feb. 1949, Concord, New Hampshire, USA. Editor; Writer. m. John D Owen, 19 June 1971, Chichester, New Hampshire. *Education:* BA, Spanish, University of New Hampshire, 1971; BA, English, University of Washington, 1979; MA, Creative Writing, University of Washington, 1981. *Publication:* Facing the Weather Side, 1985. *Contributions to:* Poetry Northwest; Dark Horse; Tar River Review of Poetry; Passages North; Sojourner; Walter; The Seattle Review; Mississippi Mid; Hollow Springs Review; Arts and Artists; and other publications. Articles in Signpost Magazine. *Honours:* Artist-in-Residence, Ucross Foundation, Wyoming, 1984; Poems selected in competition Seattle Arts Commission, 1983; Poems selected King County Arts Commission, 1983; Honorable Mention, Washington Poets Association, 1981. *Address:* 18508 90th Avenue W, Edmonds, WA 98020, USA.

OWEN, John Gareth, b.15 Mar. 1936, Ainsdale, Lancashire, England. Writer. *Education:* Certificate, Education, Bretton Hall College; Goldsmith's College, University of London. *Publications:* 19 Fragments, 1974; Salford Road, 1979; Song of the City, 1985; 3 Poets -5, 1986; (Novel) The Final Test, 1985. *Membership:* Poetry Society. *Agent:* Deborah Rogers. *Address:* 48 King Edwrad Road, Moseley, Birmingham B13 8HR, West Midlands, England.

OWEN, Maude Lurline, b. 26 Dec. 1956, Fort Hood, Texas, USA. Teacher. *Education:* BA, 1978; MA, 1985; North Texas State University, Denton. *Literary Appointments:* Society, Food and Entertainment editor, The Independent, Gallup, New Mexico, 1978–80; Currently studying at l'Alliance Francaise, Paris, France. *Publications:* Anthologies include: DHS Poetry Magazine; The Minstrel, 1973; Chrysalis, 1974, 75; Young America Sings; Reg Anthologies, 1973, 75; Creative Writing Awards Editor, 1973; 75; Special Awards Editor, 1976. *Honours:* Second Place, HS Grades General Category, Poetry Society of Texas, 1974; Certificate of Acceptance, National H S Poetry Press, 1975; Third Place, Dumas HS Annual Poetry Contest, 1975. *Membership:* DHS Poetry Club, 3 years. *Address:* 1800 Scripture #6, Denton, TX 76201, USA.

OWEN, Warwick Jack Burgoyne, b. 12 May 1916, Auckland, New Zealand. University Teacher. m. Betty Isabel Drummond, 20 Dec. 1945, London, 1 son, 1 daughter. *Education:* MA, New Zealand; MA, Oxford; PhD, Wales. *Literary Appointments:* Assistant Lecturer/Lecturer/Senior Lecturer, English, University College of North Wales, UK, 1946–65; Professor of English, McMaster University, Canada, 1965–81; Professor Emeritus, 1981–. *Publications Include:* Wordsworth's Preface to Lyrical Ballads, 1957; Editor, Wordsworth & Coleridge, Lyrical Ballads, 1798, 1967; Wordsworth as Critic, 1969; Editor with J W Smyser, Prose Works of William Wordsworth, 1974; Editor, Wordsworth's Literary Criticism, 1974; Editor, Wordsworth, The Fourteen-Book Prelude, 1985. *Contributions:* 46 articles, mainly on Edmund Spenser & William Wordsworth. *Honours:* Canada Council Leave Fellow, 1973–74; Fellow, Institute for Advanced Studies in Humanities, University of Edinburgh, Scotland, 1973–74; John Simon Guggenheim Fellow, 1980–81. *Memberships:* Modern Language Association of America; Modern Humanities Research Association; Association of Canadian University Teachers of English; International Association of University Professors of English; Fellow, Royal Society of Canada (Secretary, Academy II, 1983–86). *Address:* Department of English, McMaster University, Ontario, Canada L8S 4L9.

OWIREDU, Peter Augustus, b. 22 Aug. 1926, Cape Coast, Ghana. Headmaster. *Education:* Intermediate BA, 1949; BA, 1952; Postgraduate Certificate in Education, 1953. *Publications include:* Some Reflections on Education in the Gold Coast, 1955; Nine Years at Apam, 1967; The Tenth Year at Apam, 1968; Apass Comes of Age, 1974; At Fifty One, 1977; Apass Hits Silver, 1980. *Contributions to:* Ghana News-Papers: Daily Graphic; Evening News; Ghanaian Times; Ashanti Pioneer; Ashanti Times; School Star; Africa Affairs, 1957, 59; West African Review, 1958, 59; various book reviews. *Honours include:* Tour of 14 educational institutions, UK, 1959, 63; Prize for devotion to duty, Ghana United Nations Association, 1974. *Memberships include:* Patron, Ghana United Nations Association; Central Regional President; Ghana Volunteer Workcamps Association; National President, VOLU, Volunteer Workcamps Association of Ghana, 1978. *Address:* PO Box 1474, Kumasi, Ghana.

OXLEY, William, b. 23 Apr. 1939, Manchester, England. Writer. m. Patricia Holmes, 13 Apr. 1963, Middleton, Lancashire, 2 daughters. *Education:* Fellow, Institute of Chartered Accountant. *Literary Appointments:* Visiting Poet, University of Salzburg, Austria. *Publications:* The Dark Structures and other poems, 1967; Mirrors of the Sea, 1973; The Mundane Shell, 1975; Notebook of Hephaestus, 1981; Poems of a Black Orpheus, 1981; The Idea and its Imminence, 1982; The Cauldron, of Inspiration, 1983; A Map of Time, 1984; The Inner Tapestry, 1985. *Contributions to:* Salzburg Studies in English Literature; The Scotsman; New York Times; Encounter Littack; Critical Quarterly; The Countryman; Words Magazine; Orbis; Delta; Anglo Welsh Review; Poetry Wales; Akros; Contemporary Review; Poetry Survey; Iron; Dublin Magazine, Tribune, Poetry Review; Chapman; Bananas; Acumen. *Honours:* 1st prize, Forest Poets Anthology Award, 1974; 3rd prize, Outposts Poetry Competition, 1984. *Memberships:* Yorkshire Poets Association; Poets Workshop; Workshop; Poetry Society of Great Britain; Founder, Vitalists Poets Group; West Country Writers Association. *Address:* 6 The Mount, Furzeham, Brixham, South Devon TQ5 8QY, England.

OXNARD, Charles Ernest, b. 9 Sep. 1933, Durham City, England. Registered Medical Practitioner; Dean,

Professor, University of Southern California, USA. *Education:* BSc, 1955, MD CHB, 1958, PhD, 1962, DSc, 1975, University of Birmingham, England. *Publications:* Form and Pattern in Human Evolution, 1973; Primate Locomotion, with J Stern, 1973; Uniqueness and Diversity in Human Evolution, 1975; Human Fossils: The New Revolution, 1977; Beyond Biometry: Holistic Views of Biological Structure, 1981; The Order of Man, 1983; Humans, Apes and Chinese Fossils, 1985; Whence Man? Whence Woman? 1986; Fossils, Teeth and Sex, 1986. *Contributions to:* Scientific journals of 200 articles, chapters to 18 books. Associate Editor, American Primatology, 1974–78. *Honours:* Ciba Foundation Lecturer, UK, 1966; Lo Yuk Tong Foundation Lecturer, Hong Kong, 1974; Illinois Christian Science Lecture, USA, 1976; President, Phi Kappa Phi, University of Southern California, USA, 1980; S T Chan Medal (Gold), University of Hong Kong, 1980. Fellow: American Association for Advancement of Science, 1983; New York Academy of Science, 1983. Hong Kong Government Award for Best Book, 1984; Phi Kapp Phi Book Award, 1984; Distinguished Faculty Lecturer, University of Southern Carolina, 1985; President, Sigma Xi, 1985; Britannica Book of the Year, Science, 1985. *Literary Agent:* Mrs E M Oxnard. *Address:* 820 Oak Knoll Circle, Pasadena, CA 91106, USA.

OZ, Amos, b. 4 May 1939, Jerusalem, Israel. Writer. m. Nily Zuckerman, 5 Apr. 1960, Hilda, 1 son, 2 daughters. *Education:* BA, Hebrew University, Jerusalem, 1963; MA, St Cross College, Oxford University, England, 1970. *Literary Appointments:* Editor, The Seventh Day, and anthology Stories from the Kibbutz, 1968; Visiting Fellow, St Cross College, Oxford University, England, 1969–70; Author in Residence, Hebrew University, Jerusalem, Israel, 1975. *Publications:* Where the Jackals Howl, 1965, 83; Elsewhere Perhaps, 1966, 85; My Michael, 1968, 82; Unto Death, 2 novellas, 1971, 83; Touch the Water, Touch the Wind, 1973, 80; Different People, anthology, 1974; The Hill of Evil Counsel, 1976, 81; Sumchi, 1978, 83; Under this Blazing Light, 1979; A Perfect Peace, 1982, 85; In the Land of Israel, 1983, 84. *Contributions to:* Keshet, and numerous others. *Honours:* Several. *Membership:* Pen International. *Literary Agent:* Deborah Owen Ltd. *Address:* c/o Deborah Owen Ltd, 78 Narrow Street, London E14, England.

OZER, Mark Norman, b. 17 Jan. 1932, Cambridge, Massachusetts, USA. Physician. m. Martha Ross Redden, 13 Aug. 1979, Washington DC, 1 son, 4 daughters. *Education:* AB cum laude; MD. *Publications include:* A Cybernetic Approach to the Assessment of Children, 1979; Solving Learning & Behavior Problems of Children, 1980; The Ozer Method, 1982; The What Works Method for Learning in Children, 1985. *Contributions to:* Various journals in fields of neurology, psychiatry, child development. *Literary Agent:* Regina Ryan. *Address:* 1919 Stuart Avenue, Richmond, VA 23220, USA.

P

PAANANEN, Eloise K, b. 12 Apr. 1923, Seattle, Washington, USA. Writer. m. Lauri A Paananen, 1 Oct. 1973, Virginia, 1 son, 1 daughter. *Education:* BA, Foreign Affairs. *Literary Appointments:* Teacher of Writing, Northern Virginia Community College, 1972–76. *Publications:* Sea Challenge, 1962; Princess of Paradise, 1962; Countdown for Cindy, 1962; Sea of the Bear, 1964; Pararescue, 1964; Escape, 1965; Sky Rangers, 1966; Earthquake, 1966; Medic, 1969; The House That Half-Jack Built, 1971; Parachutes – How They Work , 1972; Do's and Don'ts of Delightful Dieting, 1972; National Governments Around the World, 1974; The Winter War, 1973, 85; America's Maritime Heritage, 1975; Finns in North America, 1975; The Finns in America, 1977; Man in Flight, 1979; Tremor, 1982; Of Cabbages and the King, 1984; Baltimore One-Day Trip Book, 1985. *Contributions to:* Washington Post; Washington Times; Exxon Air World; Dossier; Woman's World; VFW; Flying; Marine Corps Gazette; Catholic Digest; Cobblestone; FAA General Aviation News; Alexandria Gazette; Romantic Dining and Travel; Medical World News; National Forum; Ladycom; Yankee; Career World; American Scandinavian Review and numerous others. *Honours:* Outstanding Science Books for Children, 1972; Cindy Award for Film, More Than Shelter; Best Book Award, for Winter War, National Federation of Press Women and for America's Maritime Heritage and Man in Flight; Order of the White Rose of Finland, 1981. *Membership:* Past National Secretary, Society of Women Geographers. *Address:* 6348 Cross Woods Drive, Falls Church, VA 22044, USA.

PACEY, Philip Kay Rutherford, b. 12 Apr. 1946. Art Librarian. m. Gill Pacey. *Education:* Corpus Christi College, Cambridge University, England. *Literary Appointments:* Tutor Librarian, Hertfordshire College of Art and Design; Art Librarian, Preston Polytechnic. *Publications:* A Sense of What is Real, 1977; Charged Landscapes, 1978; In the Elements Free, 1983; David Jones and other Wonder Voyages, 1982; If Man, 1984. *Contributions to:* Akros; Critical Quarterly; Outposts; Palantir; Phoenix; Poetry Review; Scotsman; Sesheta; Stand; Tracks; Transatlantic Review; Anglo Welsh Review; Poetry Wales; 2nd Aeon, Anthologies including Poems, 1971; Found Poems, 1972; The Happy Unicorns, 1971; Poetry Dimension, 2 and 4, 1974, 76; PEN New Poems, 1974; New Poetry, 1 and 3, 1975, 77. *Honours:* 1st Prize, Pernod National Young Poets Competition, 1971; Runner-Up, New Poets Award, 1972; Gregory Award, 1973; Poets Yearbook, 1979. *Address:* 21 Cadley Avenue, Fulwood, Preston, Lancashire PR2 2LT, England.

PACHE, Jean, b. 4 Mar. 1933, Teacher. *Education:* Licence-ès-Lettres, University of Lausanne, Switzerland. *Literary Appointments include:* Teacher of French Literature, Gymnase de Lausanne (currently); Editor, literary series, editions l'Aire, Lausanne, 1970–75, Literary Chronicle for 24 Heures. *Major Publications include:* Les Fenêtres simultanées (poems), 1955; Poèmes de l'Autre (poems), 1960; Analogies (poems 1958–61), 1966; Repères (poems 1962–66). 1969; Rituels (poems 1966–69), 1971; Anachroniques (récit), 1973; L'oeil cérémonial (poems 1970–74), 1975; Le Corps Morcelé (poems 1975–76), 1977; La Parodie (fiction), 1980; Lacunaires (poems 1975–78), 1980; Les Corps Imaginaires (poems), 1983; Baroques (fictions), 1983. *Contributor to:* Les Cahiers du Sud; La nouvelle Revue Française; DU; La Revue de Belles-Lettres (Editor-in-chief 1959–62); Pays du Lac (ed comm 1953–55); Gazette de Lausanne; 24 Heures, 1967–. *Honours include:* Prix Follope de Poésie, Université de Lausanne, 1959; Prix de la Fondation Schiller, 1967, 1978. *Memberships include:* PEN Club; Association des Ecrivains de la Langue Française; Association des Ecrivains vaudois; Association internationale des Critiques littéraires. *Address:* 14 Route du Signal, CH–1018 Lausanne, Switzerland.

PACKARD, Jerrold M, b. 14 May 1943, Orange, California, USA. Writer. *Education:* BA, Political Science. *Publications include:* The Queen & Her Court: A Guide to the British Monarchy Today, 1981; American Monarchy: A Social Guide to the Presidency, 1983; Peter's Kingdom: Inside the Papal City, 1985. *Membership:* Authors Guild. *Literary Agent:* Frederick Hill Associates, San Francisco. *Address:* San Francisco, California, USA.

PACKARD, Vance Oakley, b. 22 May 1914, Granville Summit, Pennsylvania, USA. Author. m. Virginia Mathews, 25 Nov. 1938, 2 sons, 1 daughter. *Education:* BA, Pennsylvania State University; MS. Columbia University; Litt D, Monmouth College. *Literary Appointments:* Centre Daily Times, State College, PA; Boston Record; Feature Service of Associated Press; American Magazine; Collier's Magazine. *Publications:* Animal IQ, 1949; The Hidden Persuaders, 1957; The Status Seekers, 1959; The Waste Makers, 1960; The Pyramid Climbers, 1962; The Naked Society, 12964; The Sexual Wilderness, 1968; A Nation of Strangers, 1972; The People Shapers, 1977; Our Endangered Children, 1983. *Contributions to:* Atlantic; NY Times Magazine; Readers Digest; Collier's; American Magazine. *Honours:* Distinguished Alumni Awards, Columbia University and Penn State University; Notable Book Award, American Library Association, 1977. *Memberships:* Author's Guild; President, Society of Magazine Writers; Member, National Board, the National Book Committee; PEN; American Sociology Association. *Address:* 87 Mill Road, New Canaan, CT 06840, USA.

PACKER, James Innell, b. 22 July, 1926, Twyning, Gloucestershire, England. Christian Educator. m. Ethel Mullett, 17 July, 1954, Birmingham, England, 1 son, 2 daughters. *Education:* BA, MA, DPhil, Oxford University, England; DD Conwell Seminary, Massachusetts, USA. *Appointments:* Professor of Theology, Regent College; Senior Editor, Christianity Today, 1984–. *Publications:* Fundamentalism and the Word of God, 1958; Evangelism and the Sovereignity of God, 1961; God has Spoken, 1964; Knowing God, 1973; I Want to be a Christian, 1977; Under God's Word, 1980; God's Words, 1982; Keep in Step with the Spirit, 1984; Christianity, the True Humanism, (with T Howard), 1985. *Address:* Regent College, 2130 Wesbrook Mall, Vancouver, British Columbia, Canada.

PACKETT, Charles Neville, b. 25 Feb. 1922, Bradford, Yorkshire, England. Insurance Broker. *Publications include:* Guide to the Republic of San Marino, 1958 and 1964; Story of the Green Order of St Dennis of Zante, 1962; Diamond Jubilee History of the Ionic Lodge No. 3210, 1966; Travel and Holiday Guide to Tongatapu Island, Kingdom of Tonga, 1969, 4th edition 1981; The Orders of Knighthood of the Most Serene Republic of San Marino, 1970; Guide to the Republic of Mauru, 1971 and 1978; A History and A to Z of her Majesty's Lieutenancy of Counties (1547–1972) with Particular Reference to the West Riding of Yorkshire, 1973; The County Lieutenancy in the United Kingdom (1547–1975), 1975; Association of Lieutenants of Counties and Custodes Rotulorum – A Brief History (1907–1977), 1977; The St John Ambulance-Midland Area Directory, 1977; The Texas Navy – A Brief History, 1983. *Honours include:* Justice of the Peace, 1964–; Member of the Order of the British Empire, 1974; Knight, Order of St John, 1985; Honours from San Marino, Greece, Tonga and USA. *Memberships:* Fellow, Royal Society of Arts; Fellow, Royal Geographical Society; Master, Worshipful Company of Women of London, 1979–80; Master, Worshipful Company of Tin Plate Workers, 1986–87. *Address:* Lloyds Bank Chambers, Hustlergate, Bradford, West Yorkshire, BD1 1PA, England.

PACKIE, Susan, b. 5 Oct. 1946, Maplewood, New Jersey, USA. Writer. *Education:* BA, Columbia University, (Cum laude and departmental honours); MA, New School for Social Research. *Literary Appointments:* Associate Editor, Pandora Literary Magazine; Staff Writer, Inside Joke. *Publication:* Yanticaw, 1985.

Contributions to: About 150 publications including: North American Mentor Magazine; Black Fly Review; Rebirth of Artemis; San Fernando Poetry Journal; The Thomas Wholfe Review; Piedmont Literary Review; The Old Red Kimono; Hemlocks and Balsaams; The Ecphoriser; Antithesis; The Artful Codger; Home Planet News; Samisdat; Planet Detroit. *Honours:* 1st Prize, New Jersey Artfrom Magazine Poetry Contest, 1982; Certificate of Merit, Poetry Contest, North American Mentor Magazine, 1983–85; Honorable Mention, Hoosier Challenger, 1984. *Address:* 10-D Belleview Court, Belleview, NJ 07109, USA.

PADFIELD, Peter Lawrence Notton, b. 3 Apr. 1932, Calcutta, India. Author. m. Dorothy Jean Yarwood, 23 Apr., 1960, Dodleston, Chester, 1 son, 2 daughters. *Publications:* The Titanic and the California, 1965; An Agony of Collisions, 1966; Aim Straight: A Biography of Admiral Sir Percy Scott, 1966; Broke and the Shannon: A Biography of Admiral Sir Philip Broke, 1968; The Battleship Era, 1972; Guns at Sea: A History of Naval Gunnery, 1973; The Great Naval Race; Anglo-German Naval Rivalry 1900–1914, 1974; Nelson's War, 1978; Tide of Empires: Decisive Naval Campaigns in the Rise of the West, Volume I 1481–1654, Volume II 1654–1763, 1979 and 1982; Rule Britannia: The Victorian and Edwardian Navy, 1981; Beneath The Houseflag of the P & O, 1982; Dönitz, The last Führer, 1984; Novels: The Lion's Claw, 1978; The Uniquiet Gods, 1980; Gold Chains of Empire, 1982; Salt and Steel, 1986. *Literary Agent:* Anne Harrel. *Address:* Westmoreland Cottage, Woodbridge, Suffolk, England.

PADGETT, Ron, b. 17 June 1942, Tulsa, Oklahoma, USA. Writer. m. Patricia Mitchell, 21 June 1963, Miami, Oklahoma, 1 son. *Education:* BA, Columbia College, 1964. *Publications:* Great Balls of Fire, poetry, 1969; An Anthology of New York Poets, anthology editor, 1970; Tourjours l'Amour, poetry, 1976; Tulsa Kid, poetry, 1979; Triangles in the Afternoon, poetry, 1979; The Poet Assassinated and Other Stories, by Guillaume Apollinaire, translation, 1984. *Contributions to:* Magazines and journals including: The New Yorker; Poetry; C; Art and Literature; Sulfur; Adventures in Poetry; Les Lettres Nouvelles; MS; Big Sky. *Honours:* Gotham Bookmart Avant-Garde Poetry Prize, 1964; Fulbright Fellowship, 1965; Translation Fellowship, National Endowment for the Arts, 1983; Translation Grant, New York State Council on the Arts, 1985. *Membership:* Blaise Cendrars International Society. *Literary Agent:* Robert Cornfield. *Address:* Apartment 6, 342 East 13 Street, New York, NY 10003, USA.

PADMANABHAN, Neela, b. 26 Apr. 1938, Trivandrum, India. Executive Engineer; Writer. m. U Krishnammal, 3 July 1963, Trivandrum, India, 1 son, 3 daughters. *Education:* BSc, BSc Engineering, MIE. *Appointments include:* Junior Engineer, 1963–70; Assistant Executive Engineer, 1971–81, Executive Engineer, 1981, Kerala State Electricity Board, India; Member, Board of Studies, Kerala University for Tamil. *Major Publications:* Thalaimuraigal (novel) 1968; Moham Muppathathuaandu (short stories) 1969; Pallikonda Puram (novel) 1970; Mondravathunaal (short stories) 1974; Uravugal (novel) 1975; Neela Padmanabhan Kavithigal (poems) 1975; Irandavathumugham (short stories) 1978; Sidhariya Chinthanaikal (essays), 1978; Surrender and Other poems, 1982; Naa Kaakka (poems) 1983. *Contributor to:* Ezhutthu; Ilakkia Vattam Nadai; Gnanaratham; Zha; Thamarai; Deepam; Kanaiyazhi; Indian Literature; Indian Writing Today; Triveni; Caravan; Kalki; Sathangai; Kekala Kavitha; Mirror; Fiction Today; Prathibha India; Indian Author; Poetry Time; and others. *Honours:* 1st Prize, Intervarsity Radio Play Competition, 1962; Rajah Sir Annamalai Chettair Award, 1977; Novelarasu, 1981, Bharathi National Forum. *Memberships:* Authors Guild of India; PEN. *Address:* Nilakant, Manacaud PO, Trivandrum 695009, India

PAGANO, Margareta, b. 28 Aug. 1955, Oslo, Norway. Financial Journalist. m. Jugurtha Yadi, 26 Oct. 1979, London, 1 son. *Education:* BSc Economics and Politics, School of Oriental and African Studies, London University. *Literary Appointments:* City Correspondent, The Guardian, 1984. *Contributions to:* The Times; The Guardian. *Address:* City Office, The Guardian, 119 Farringdon Road, London EC1, England.

PAGE, Charles Hunt, b. 12 Apr. 1909, New York, USA. Sociologist. m. Leonora McClure, 15 June 1936, New York. *Education:* AB, University of Illinois, 1931; PhD, Columbia University, 1940. *Appointments:* Consulting Editor, Doubleday & Co, 1952–54; Random House-Knopf, 1954–80; Press Committee, University of Massachusetts, Press, 1969–75. *Publications:* Class and American Sociology, 1940; Society: An Introductory Analysis, with R M MacIver, 1949; Freedom and Control in Modern Society, 1954, co-editor; Sociology and Contemporary Education, co-author, co-editor, 1964; Sport and Society, with S T Talamini, 1973; Fifty Years in the Sociological Enterprise: A Lucky Journey, 1982. *Contributor to:* American Sociological Review; American Journal of Sociology; Social Forces; Society; Isis; Science; New Republic; etc. *Honours:* Honorary Fellow, Alder E Stevenson College, 1968; Outstanding Educators in American, 1972; Merit Award, Eastern, Sociological Society, 1975. *Address:* 7 Hampton Terrace, Northampton, MA 01060, USA.

PAGE, Patricia Kathleen, b. 23 Nov. 1916, Swanage, Dorset, England. Writer. m. W Arthur Irwin, 16 Dec. 1950. *Publications:* The Sun and the Moon, 1944; As Ten as Twenty, 1946; The Metal and the Flower, 1954; Cry Ararat, 1967; The Sun and the Moon and Other Fictions, 1973; Poems, Selected and New, 1974; To Say The Least (Editor), 1979; Evening Dance of the Grey Flies, 1981; The Glass Air, 1985. *Contributions to:* The Observor; Encounter; Ariel; Artscanada; Canadian Forum; Canadian Literatures; Contemporary Verse, Preview; Saturday Night; Tamarack Review; Tuatara; Voices; The White Pelican; Ellipse; Malahat Review; Queen's Quarterly; The Ontario Review; Poetry Australia, and others. *Honours:* The Bertram Warr Award, 1940; Oscar Blumenthal Award, 1944; Governor General's Award, 1954; Received as a poet by the Academia Brasileira de Letras 1959; Officer of the Order of Canada, 1977; National Magazine Awards, 1985; D Litt, University of Victoria, 1985. *Membership:* League of Canadian Poets. *Address:* 3260 Exeter Road, Victoria, British Columbia, V8R 6H6, Canada.

PAGELS, Heinz Rudolf, b. 19 Feb. 1039, Brooklyn, New York, USA. Theoretical Physicist. m. Elaine L Hiesey, 7 June 1969, New York, 1 son. *Education:* BS, Magna Cum Laude, Physics, Princeton University, 1960; PhD, Physics, Stanford University, 1965. *Publications:* The Cosmic Code, 1983; Perfect Symmetry: The Search for the Beginning of Time, 1985. *Contributor to:* Book Reviews, New York Times; Articles, The Sciences; Natural History. *Honour:* AIP Scientific Book Award, 1983. *Membership:* PEN. *Literary Agent:* John Brockman, New York. *Address:* 2 East 63rd Street, New York, NY 10021, USA.

PAHLOW, Mannfried Otto Siegfried, b. 21 Jan. 1926, Martinshagen, Pommern, Federal Republic of Germany. Chemist. *Education:* Studies of pharmacies, Braunschweig. *Publications include:* Chemische Lehrversuche für Apothekerpraktikanten, 1956; Botanishc-pharmakognostische Lehrversuche für Apothekerpraktikanten, 1957; Physikalische Lehrversuche für Apothekerpratikanten, 1957; Drogenkunde für Apothekerpraktikanten und PTA, 1958; 25 Jahre Apotheker, 1974; Pilze und Beeren, 1975; Richtig würzengenesunder leben, 1976; Heilpflanzen heute, 1976; Natur – das gesündeste Hobby, 1976; Beeren und andere Wildfrüchte, 1976; Das grosse Buch der Heilpflanzen, 1979; Kampfergeist und Anisol, 1979; Thymian und Lindenblüten, 1983; Tausendgüldenkraut, 1984; Hopfen und Baldrian, 1985. *Honours:* Sertürner Medal, Pharmaceutical Society of Germany, for important scientific work in field of pharmacies, 1962; Medal of Stadt Bogen, gold, 1983; AWMM Buckpreis, 1985. *Address:* Stadtplatz 58, D-8443 Bogen, Federal Republic of Germany.

PAINTER, Charlotte, b. Louisiana, USA. Writer. m. 1962, 1 son. *Education:* MA, Stanford University. *Literary Appointments:* Stanford University; University of California – Berkeley and Santa Cruz; Eastern Washington University; Associate Professor, San Francisco State University. *Publications:* Who Made the Lamb, 1965; Confession from the Malaga Madhouse, 1971; Seeing Things, 1975, 1982; Revelations: Diaries of Women (co-editor), 1975; Gifts of Age, 1985. *Contributions to:* (stories) New Yorker; Redbook; Hawaii Review; Massachusetts Review; Mediterranean Review. Poetry and essays in little magazines. *Honours:* Wallace Stegner Award, 1961–62; Radcliffe Institute Fellow, 1968–69; National Endowment for the Arts Grant, 1972; Fulbright Fellowship, 1985. *Memberships:* PEN; MacDowell Colony. *Address:* San Francisco State University, 1600 Holloway, San Francisco, CA 94132, USA.

PAINTER, Raymond, b. 2 July 1934, London, England. Freelance Financial Journalist. m. Shirley Tickner, 6 Apr. 1957, West Wickham, Kent, 2 sons, 1 daughter. *Literary Appointments:* City reporter, Daily Express, 1950–66; Editor, Investment, 1966–67. *Publications:* Fortunes To Be Made, 1970; Your Money & You, 1972; Money Matters, 1982. *Contributions to:* Extensive freelance contributor since 1967 to a wide range of publications including: Woman & Home; Weekend; The Scotsman; What Mortgage; Weekly News; Doctor; Harpers Wine & Spirit Gazette; The Dentist; Carpet & Floorcoverings Review; What Investment. *Honour:* Insurance Writer of the Year, 1973. *Literary Agent:* Rupert Crew Ltd, King's Mews, London WC2N 2JA (Mrs Doreen Montgomery). *Address:* 12 Alexander Close, Aldwick, Bognor Regis, West Sussex, PO21 4PS, England.

PALLISTER Janis L, b. 12 Jan. 1926. University Professor of Romance Languages. *Education:* BA, cum laude, 1946, MA, 1948, PhD, 1964, University of Minnesota, USA. *Literary Appointments include:* Black Hills College, 1948–50; University of Minnesota, 1955–59; Colby College, 1959–61; Instructor, Assistant Professor, Associate Professor, Professor, University Professor, Bowling Green State University, Ohio, 1961–. *Publications:* The World View of B de Verville, 1971; Mon Autre Lyre, 1971, 2nd edition, 1974; The Planting, 1972; Green Balloon, 1974; Confrontations, 1976, Esanzo, 1977; The Bruised Reed, 1978; Sursum Corda, 1982; Pares Monsters and Marvels, 1982; At the Eighth Station, 1983; Interanimations, 1984; Waiting for Death (co-author), 1979. *Contributor to:* North American Mentor Magazine; En Passant/Poetry; Poetry Now; Greenfield Review; Mr Cognito; Invisible City; Poesie USA, etc. *Honours:* Certificates of Merit, North American Mentor; Columbia University Trans Center Award. 1978. *Memberships:* African Literary Association; MLA, etc. *Address:* 211 State Street, Bowling Green, OH 43402, USA.

PALMÁSON, (Kristófer) Baldur, b. 17 Dec. 1919, Húnavatnasýsla, N Iceland. Writer. *Publications:* Hrafninn flýgur um aftaninn (The Raven Flies at Eventide) (poems), 1977; Björt mey og hrein (Fair Maiden and Pure) (poems), 1979, Icelandic translation of book by Albert Schweitzer, 1965. *Membership:* Rithöfundasemband Ísland (Writers Association of Iceland). *Address:* Egilsgata 14, Reykjavík, PO Box 1204, Iceland.

PALMEN, Aili Inkeri, b. 18 Oct. 1917, Jyväskyä, Finland. Author/Writer. m. Professor Eino E Suolahti, 24 Mar. 1940, divorced 1947. *Education:* MA, University of Helsinki. *Literary Appointments:* The Otava Book Publishing Co, Helsinki. *Publications:* Ystäväni, Miehet, Naiset, 1978; Kirjeitä, Kohtaloita, 1980; Se Toivon Tähti, 1983. *Contributor to:* Professional journals. *Honours:* P E Svinhufvudin Muistosäätion Kirjallisuuspalkinto, 1978. *Memberships:* Suomen Kirjailijaliitto; Suomalaisen Kirjailisuuden Seura. *Address:* Ulvilantie 2 C.19, 00350 Helsinki, Finland.

PALMER, Alan Warwick, b. 28 Sep. 1926, Ilford, Essex. England. Schoolmaster. m. Veronica Mary Cordell, 1 Sep. 1951, London. *Education:* MA, M Litt, Oxford University. *Publications include:* Dictionary of Modern History, 1962; Yugoslavia; 1964; The Gardeners of Salonika, 1965; Napoleon in Russia, 1967; The Lands Between, 1970; Life and Times of George IV, 1972; Metternich, 1972; Russia in War and Peace, 1972; Alexander I, 1974; Frederick the Great, 1974; Bismark, 1976; The Kaiser, 1978; Prince of Wales, 1979; Dictionary of 20th Century History, 1979; The Chancelleries of Europe, 1983; Encyclopedia of Napoleon's Europe, 1984; Crowned Cousins, 1985. Co-Autorships: Independent Eastern Europe, 1962; Quotations in History, 1976; Who's Who in Shakespeare's England, 1981; Royal England, A Historical Gazetteer, 1983. *Contributions to:* Oxford Slavonic Papers; History Today; History of World War I; The Times. *Membership:* Fellow, Royal Society of Literature. *Literary Agent:* Campbell Thomson and McLaughlin Limited. *Address:* 4 Farm End, Woodstock, Oxford, England.

PALMER, M John, b. 13 May 1943, Sydney, Nova Scotia, Canada. Writer. *Education:* BA, English, Carleton University, Ottawa. *Appointments:* Dramaturge, Factory Lab, 1970–72; Literary Manager, Toronto Free Theatre, 1972–74; Resident Playwright, Juilliard School, New York City, USA, 1980–81, Canadian Rep Theatre (T O), 1985–. *Publications:* Bland Hysteria, 1971; Memories for my Brother, Part 1, 1971; A Touch of God in the Golden Age, 1972; The end, 1972; Henrik Ibsen on the Necessity of Producing Norwegian Drama, 1976; The Man Behind the News, 1973. *Contributor to:* Canadian Theatre Review; This Magazine, volume II; Notes on a Production of Tango, Drama at Calgary, volume III; Canadian Playwrighting Crisis: The Twelfth Hour, Performing Arts in Canada, 1971. *Memberships:* Founding Member, Founding Co-Chairman, East, Playwrights Union of Canada. *Literary Agent:* Great North Artists Management, Toronto; Joyce Ketay, New York. *Address:* 80 Wellesley St E, #701, Toronto, Ontario M4Y 1H3, Canada.

PALMER, Pamela Lynn, b. 29 May 1951. Special Collections Assistant. *Education:* BA, MA, Stephen F Austin State University; Doctoral Candidate, Texas A&M University. *Appointments include:* Cataloguing Clerk, University of Texas, Austin, Texas, 1976; Humanities Assistant, 1976–78; Special Collections Assistant, 1979–, Stephen F Austin State University, Nacogdoches. *Publications:* Rain is for Dreaming, 1968; A Book of Visions, 1979; The Women of Knossos, 1981, poems. *Contributions to:* The Texas Quarterly; Quartet; Bitterroot; Houston Chronicle; Book of the Year, Texas Poetry Society; Pennsylvania Poetry Society Prize Poems; Louisiana Poets; The Texas Anthology and others. *Honours:* Winner of about 120 awards from various poetry societies, conferences, Bitterroot, International Poetry Institute; Outstanding Young Woman of America Award, 1977, 78, 80. *Memberships:* Life Member, Poetry Society of Texas; International Poetry Institute; Texas Folklore Society. *Address:* 304 Davis Nacogdoches, TX 75961, USA.

PALOMINO, Angel, b. 2 Aug. 1929, Toledo, Spain. Novelist; Journalist; Television Writer. *Education:* Studies of Linguistics, Science and Chemistry, Central University, Madrid; Technician in Management. *Publications:* Numerous works of poetry, short stories, essays and novels including: El Cesar de Papel, 1957; Zamora y Gomora, 1968; Torremolinos Gran Hotel, 1971; Memorias de un Intelectual Antifranquista, 1972; Un Jaguar y una Rubia, 1972; Madrid Costa Fleming, 1973; Todo Incluido, 1975; Divorcio Para una Virgen Rota, 1977; La Luna se Llama Persez, 1978; Plan Marshall para 50 Munutos, 1978; Las Otras Violaciones, 1979. *Contributions to:* Estafeta Literaria; ABC; Semana. *Honours:* Numerous Literary prizes including: Miguel de Cervantes National Literary Prize, 1971; Finalist, Planeta Prize, 1977; International Prize, Press Club, 1968; others. *Memberships:* Royal Academy of Fine Arts and Historical Sciences; National Academy of Gastonomy;

Spanish Association of Book Writers; International Federation of Tourism Writers; International Association of Literary Critics. *Literary Agent:* Editorial Planeta and Carmen Balcells, Barcelona. *Address:* Conde de Penalver 17, 28006 Madrid, Spain.

PALSSON, Sigurdur, b. 30 July 1948, Skinnastadur, Iceland. Writer, translator, stage director, TV director. *Education:* DUEL, Maîtrise Spécialisée, Diplôme d'Etudes Approfondies Théâtre, Sorbonne, Paris, France; Diploma Conservatoire Libre du Cinéma Francais, Cinema Direction. *Publications:* Ljod vega salt, 1975; Undir Sudvesturhimni, 1976; Hlaunvidd Sex, 1977; Ljod vega menn, 1980; Ljod vega gerd, 1982; Midjardarfor, 1983; Ljod namu land, 1985. *Memberships:* President 1976–77, Alliance Francaise Iceland; Member of the direction, PEN Club of Iceland, 1983; Director's Association of Iceland; President, Writers' Union of Iceland, 1984–. *Address:* Postholf 1160, 121 Reykjavik, Iceland.

PAMA, Cornelis, b. 5 Nov. 1916, Rotterdam, The Netherlands. Editor; Author; Armorist. m. Heather Myfanwy Woltman, 1 Mar. 1976, Cape Town, 1 son, 2 daughters from previous marriage. *Education:* PhD, h.c. *Literary Appointments:* Managing Director, Modern Books Limited, 1955–69; Director. A A Balkema Limited, Publishers, 1969–74; Editor, Tafelberg Publishers Limited, 1974–80; Editor in Chief, Nederlandse Post, Arma, Familia and Chairman, Historical Publication Society, current. *Publications:* Handbook der Wapenkunde, 4 editions, 1938–66; Lions and Virgins, Heraldic State Symbols in South Africa 1487–1962; Genealogies of old South African Families 3 volumes 1966; Heraldry of South African Families, 1968; Groot Afrikaanse familienaamboek, 1983; author of 24 other books on history, genealogy and heraldry in Dutch, English and Afrikaans. *Contributions to:* Some 800 in the fields of history, genealogy and heraldry. *Honours:* Extraordinary Gold Medal, South African Akademie v Wetensk and Kuns, 1966; Medal Pro Merito Genealogia, Germany, 1970; Braken-Lee Award, Salt Lake City, Utah, USA, 1967; Van Riebeeck Gold Medal, 1983. *Memberships:* Committee member, PEN Club; SA Skrywersking; Honorary secretary, Friends of the South African Library. *Address:* PO Box 4839, Cape Town 8000, Republic of South Africa.

PAMPEL, Martha Maria, b. 4 Apr. 1913, Muhlheim, Ruhr, Federal German Republic. Author. m. Adolf Pampel, 1 June 1936, 1 daughter. *Education:* Business Training; Correspondence course, English; Organist Examination; International Famous Writers School. *Publications:* Die Tur steht offen, 1965, 76; Heilige mit kleinen Fehlern, 1977; Land der dunklen Walder, 1977; Wer in der Liebe bleibt, 1978; Ein Streiter vor dem Herrn, 1979; Das Freuen lernen, 1979 (also recorded on tape, 1983); Seven small volumes in the series: Die Feierabendstunde, and some little books: Die Kleinen Freuden des Alltags, 1986; Calendars and Children's devotions book. *Honours:* Diploma of Merito, Universite delle Arti, Italy, 1982; Albert Einstein Academy Bronze Medal Award for Peace Proposition, Universal Intelligence Data Bank of America, 1986. *Address:* Lortzingstrasse 9 (3423) Bad Sachsa, Federal Republic of Germany.

PANICHAS, George Andrew, b. 21 May 1930, Springfield, Massachusetts, USA. Educator, Literary Critic, Scholar. *Education:* BA, American International College, 1951; MA, Trinity College, Hartford, Connecticut, 1952; PhD, Nottingham University; England, 1962. *Literary Appointments include:* Instructor in English 1962, Assistant Professor 1963, Associate Professor 1966, Professor 1968–, University of Maryland; Member of Editorial Advisory Board 1971, Associate Editor 1978, Editor 1984, Modern Age: A Quarterly Review; Advisory Editor, Continuity: A Journal of History, 1984–. *Publications:* Adventure in Consciousness: The Meaning of D H Lawrence's Religious Quest, 1964; Epicurus, 1967; The Reverent Discipline: Essays in Literary Criticism, Culture, 1974; The Burden of Vision: Dostoevsky's Spiritual Art, 1977 and 1985; The

Courage of Judgment: Essays in Literary Criticism, Culture and Society, 1982; As editor: Renaissance and Modern Essays: Presented to Vivian de Sola Pinto in Celebration of his Seventieth Birthday, (with George R Hibbard and Allan Rodway), 1966; Mansions of the Spirit: Essays in Literature and Religion, 1967; Promise of Greatness: The War of 1914–1918, 1968; The Politics of Twentieth Century Novelists, 1971 and 1974; The Simone Weill Reader, 1977; Irving Babbitt: Representative Writings, 1981; Irving Babbitt In Our Time, (with Claes G Ryn). *Contributions to:* Books, anthologies and journals. *Honours:* Earhart Foundation grantee, 1982; Honorary D Litt, American International College, 1984. *Memberships:* Richard M Weaver Fellowship Award Committee; Co-Director, Conference on Irving Babbitt: Fifty Years Later, 1983; Academic Board, National Humanities Institute. *Address:* 4313 Knox Road, Apartment 402, College Park, MD 20740, USA.

PANIKER, Ayyappa, b. 12 Sep. 1930, Kerala, India. Professor of English. m. Sreeparvathy, 9 Sep. 1961, Haripad, India, 2 daughters. *Education:* BA (Hons), 1951; MA, 1959; AM, PhD, 1971; CTE, 1966. *Literary Appointments:* CMS College, Kottayam; MG College, Trivendrum; Mahraja's University College, Trivandrum; University Institute of English, Trivendrum. *Publications:* Ayyappa Panikerude Kritikal, 1974, 1982; Ayyappa Panikerude Lekhanangal, 1981; A Short History of Malayalam Literature, 1978; Seven Poems, (Ezhukavitakal), 1983. *Contributor to:* Mathrubhumi; Indian Literature; Tenor; Vagartha; Minnesota Review; Sameeksha; Kerals Kavita; Kamadhenu; Indian Verse; Bhashaposhini; Thilakam; Kalakaubudi; Malayalamanorama; Malayalanadu; Kerala Spectrum. *Honours include:* Kerala Sahitya Akademi Award, 1975; Kalyani Krishna Menon Prize, 1977; Sahitya Pravartaka Coop. Society Award, 1979; Central Sabitya Akademi Award, 1984; National Lecturer, 1985–86; Represented India at Struge Poetry Festival, 1975. *Memberships:* Executive Committee, Authors Guild of India; Life Member, Ali-Kerala Sahitya Parishath; Sahitya Prevartske Coop. Society; Kavita Samiti; Trivandrum Indian Association for english Studies; American Studies Research Center. *Address:* 111 Gandhi Nagar, Trivandrum 695014, India.

PANIKER, Salvador, b. 1 Mar. 1927, Barcelona, Spain. Publisher; Writer. *Education:* Lic. Philos; Dr Indl. Engrng. *Publications:* Conversaciones en Cataluna, 1966; Los Signos y las Cosas, 1968; Conversaciones en Madrid, 1969; La Difficultad der Ser Espanol, 1979; Approximacion al Origen, 1982; Primer Testamento, 1985. *Contributor to:* La Vanguardia; El Pais; Convivum; Revista de Occidente; Ciencia y Pensamiento. *Honour:* International Press Prize, 1969. *Address:* Numancia 110, Barcelona 29, Spain.

PAPADEMETRIOU, Peter Constantine, b. 1 May 1943, Newark, New Jersey, USA. Architect and Architectural Historian. 1 daughter. *Education:* BA, Architecture (cum laude), Princeton University, 1965; M Arch, Yale University, 1968. *Literary Appointments:* Correspondent, Architectural Forum, 1973–75; Correspondent, Progressive Architecture, 1975–; Contributing Editor, Texas Architect, 1976; Executive Editor, Journal of Architectural Education, 1982–85. *Publications:* Perspecta 12, The Yale Architectural Journal, 1969; Houston: An Architectural Guide, 1972; The Museums of Fine Arts, Houston, 1972; Transportation and Urban Development in Houston 1830–1980, 1982. *Contributions to:* Architecture Review; Supplement 7, Dictionary of American Biography; Global Architecture Book 7: Office Buildings, 1981; Global Architecture Book 9: Museums, 1981; The Yale Architectural Journal; Architectural Design; Tung Hai Jien Chu; AIA Journal; Architectural Forum; Texas Architect; Domus; Progressive Architecture; Design Quarterly; Houston Home & Garden and many other publications. *Membership:* Society of Architectural Historians, Board of Directors, 1984–87. *Address:* c/o PO Box 1892, School of Architecture, Rice University, Houston, TX 77251, USA.

PARADIS, Adrian Alexis, b. 3 Dec. 1912, Brooklyn, New York, USA. Editor; Writer. m. Grace Dennis, 8 Oct. 1938, Eatontown, 2 sons, 1 daughter. *Education:* AB, Dartmouth College, 1934; BS, Columbia University, 1942. *Publications:* Numerous books including, From High School to a Job, 1956; Librarians Wanted: Careers in Library Service, 1959; The New Look in Banking, 1961; Business in Action, 1962; Labor in Action, 1963; From High School to a Job, 1964; Government in Action, 1965; Reference Handbook, 1966; Toward a Better World, 1966; Economics in Action Today, 1967; Jobs to Take You Places, Here and Abroad, 1968; Job Opportunities for Young Negroes, 1969; Gold: King of Metals, 1970; Reclaiming the Earth, 1971; Labour Reference Book, 1972; International Trade in Action, 1973; Social Security in Action, 1975; Opportunities in Banking, 1980; Opportunities in Aviation, 1981; Opportunities in Military Service, 1984; Opportunities in Your Own Service Business, 1985; etc. *Address:* Box 83, Sugar Hill, NH 03585, USA.

PARANAGUA, Paulo Antonio, b. 19 Nov. 1948, Rio de Janeiro. Journalist. *Education:* Licence en Sociologie, University of Paris VIII, 1970; Diplome de L'Ecole des Hautes Etudes en Sciences Sociales, Paris, 1981. *Publications:* Cinema na America Latina, 1985; La Historie Y El Cine, 1983; Cinema Bresilien, 1983. *Contributions to:* Numerous professional journals. *Literary Agent:* Ana Maria Santeiro. *Address:* 49 Rue de l'Ermitage, 75020 Paris, France.

PARATTE, Henri-Dominique, b. 19 Mar. 1950, Berne, Switzerland. Writer; Translator. 1 son. *Education:* Licence ès lettres 1969, Maîtrise 1970, Strasbourg; Doctorat IIIe cycle, Lille, 1974. *Literary Appointments include:* Editorial Board, various journals; Editor, Swiss-French Studies, 1980–85; Jury member, Prix littéraire Suisse-Canada, 1980–85. *Publications:* Virgée Tantra Non Arpadar, 1972; La Mer Ecartelée, 1979; Jura-Acadie, 1980; Dis-Moi La Nuit, 1982; Cheval Des Iles, 1984; Alexandre Voisard, 1985. *Contributions to:* Poesie-USA; Eloizes; Ecriture; Pottersfield Portfolio; Cavaliers Sculs; Osiris; Coinidences; Sur Parole; Alpha; Reenbou; Jura Pluriel; Cahiers Ramuz; Etudes Irlandaises; Swiss-French Studies; Ecriture Francaise; Books in Canada, etc. *Honours:* Literary awards, Canton de Berne, Switzerland, 1972, 1979; Honorable Mention, John Glassco Award, 1985. *Memberships:* Writers Council; Writers Federation of Nova Scotia (executive, 1979–82); Executive, Association des Ecrivains Acadiens, 1980–83, 1984–85; President, ibid, 1985–87; Numerous other literary memberships. *Address:* 23 Highlands Avenue, Wolfville, Nova Scotia, Canada BOP 1X0.

PARAYRE, Sylvie M, b. 19 Jan. 1953, Montreal, Canada. Editor; Writer. *Education:* BA, Communications. *Contributor to:* Writing & Editing for 'infirmière Canadienne; Writing, for The Canadian Nurse. *Memberships:* American Medical Writers' Association; International Association of Business Communicators; World Association of Women Journalists and Writers. *Address:* 48 Prud'Homme Street, Hull, Quebec J8Y 5V5, Canada.

PARES, Marion Stapylton, b. 7 Nov. 1914, W Farleigh, England. Housewife; Writer. *Publications:* Family Pony, 1962; The Queen Rides, 1965; Horses in the Sun, 1966; Police Horses, 1967; World of Horses, 1969; Anne, Portrait of a Princess, 1970; Elizabeth and Philip, 1972; Royalty on Horseback, 1974; The World of the Horse (USA), 1975; Anne and Mark, 1976; Your Own Pony Club, 1979; Queen Elizabeth II, 1979; The Mutant, 1980; Charles, A Prince of Our Time, 1981; The Royal Partners, 1982; Royal Horses, 1983; Ponies and Palaces, pending. *Contributor to:* Field; Woman's Own; Woman; Woman's Realm; Riding; Pony. *Literary Agent:* A M Heath. *Address:* c/o A M Heath, 40-42 William IVth Street, London WC2N 4DD, England.

PARHAM, William Thomas, b. 11 July 1913, London, England. Writer. m. Helena Pilkington, 29 Apr. 1944, Bromyard, England, 1 daughter. *Education:* Kingston upon Thames Technical College. *Publications:* Books: Von Tempsky-Adventurer, 1969; Island Volcano, 1973; The Colonial New Zealand Wars, with T C Ryan, 1986. Monographs: Man at Arms, 1977; Away from it all, 1977; John Roberts – A Man in His Time, 1984; James Francis Fulloon – A Man of Two Cultures, 1985. *Contributions to:* The New Zealand Herald; The Auckland Star; The Christchurch Press; Historical Review; Historical Record; The Volunteer; Te Rama; Forest and Bird; Rotorua Post and numerous other journals. *Honour:* Nicholson-London trophy for history writing, 1978, 84. *Address:* 19 Lincoln Avenue, Tawa, Wellington, New Zealand.

PARIS, Bernard Jay, b. 19 Aug. 1931, Baltimore, Maryland, USA. University Professor. m. Shirley Helen Freedman, 1 Apr. 1949, Baltimore, 1 son, 1 daughter. *Education:* AB, 1952, PhD, 1959, The Johns Hopkins University. *Literary Appointments:* Instructor, Lehigh University, 1956–60; Assistant Professor, 1960–64, Associate Professor, 1964–67, Professor of English and Comparative Literature, 1967–81, Michigan State University; Professor of English, University of Florida, 1981–; Director, Institute for Psychological Study of the Arts, 1985–. *Publications:* Experiments in Life, George Eliot's Quest for Values, 1965; A Psychological Approach to Fiction: Studies in Thackeray, Stendhal, George Eliot, Dostoevsky and Conrad, 1974; Character and Conflict in Jane Austen's Novels, 1978; Editor: Third Force Psychology and the Study of Literature, 1985. *Contributions to:* Numerous essays in scholarly and literary journals. *Honours:* Phi Beta Kappa, 1952; Fellow, National Endowment for the Humanities, 1969; Fellow, John Simon Guggenheim Foundation, 1974. *Memberships:* Modern Language Association of America; South Atlantic Modern Language Association; Shakespeare Association of America; Honorary Member, Association for the Advancement of Psychoanalysis. *Address:* Department of English, University of Florida, Gainesville, FL 32611, USA.

PARIS, Matthew, b. 9 Apr. 1938, Brooklyn, New York, USA. Author; Playwright; Musician; Poet; Cultural Producer; Composer. m. Marion Palm, 4 May 1985, Anpanolis, 4 sons, 1 daughter. *Education:* BA Honors program, University of Michigan, 1959; MA, Brooklyn College, 1967. *Literary Appointments:* Adjunct Professor, LIU, 1980–83. *Publications:* Mystery, 1973; The Holy City, 1979; Off Broadway productions of plays: Bedpan; Jughead; The Night They Raided Pinsky's; Solomon and His Thousand Wives; David and Bathsheba; Judas Machabeus; Ruth; Aaron. *Contributions to:* December; Pulpsmith; Village Voice; Home Planet News; Brooklyn Literary Review (editor); Prospect Park Anthology (editor). *Address:* 850 E 31st Street Apt C-6, Brooklyn, NY 11210, USA.

PARIZEAU, Alice, b. 1930, Poland. Author. *Education:* Licence en droit, Paris, France. *Appointment:* Delegate, Salon du Livre, Paris, 1983. *Publications:* Les lilas fleurissent a Varsovie, volume 1, 1981; La Charge des sangliers, volume 2, 1982; Cote-des-Neiges, 1983; The Lilacs Blossom in Warsaw, 1985; Ils se sont connus a Lwow, 1985. *Contributor to:* La Presse, Montreal; Le Devoir, Montreal; Chatelaine, Montreal; Radio-Canada. *Honours:* Canadian Women's Press Club, Montreal, 1966; prix European de l'Association des ecrivans de langue francaise, Paris, 1982. *Membership:* Union of Authors. *Literary Agent:* Richard Balkin, New York, USA. *Address:* 40 Avenue Robert, Outremont, Quebec H35 2P2, Canada.

PARK, Chung I, b. 25 Aug. 1938, Korea. Librarian. m. Jung Yol Yoo, 30 Aug. 1969, Chicago, Illinois, USA, 1 son, 2 daughters. *Education:* BA, Yonsei University, Seoul, Korea, 1961; MSLS, University of Southern California, USA, 1971; Post MLS courses, University of Illinois, 1975–76. *Publications:* Advertisement Digest; Library and Information Services, 1979; Best Sellers and Best Choices, 1980; Best Books by Consensus, 1983–84; Best Microcomputer Hardware, 1985; Best Microcomputer Software, 1985. *Contributions to:* The Coint Reports, (Communication and Information

Technology: A Multidisciplinary Approach), bi-monthly research reports. *Address:* 9302 Parkside Avenue, Morton Grove, IL 60053, USA.

PARKER, Barrett, b. 12 Oct. 1908, South Orange, New Jersey, USA. USA Foreign Service (retired). m. Pamela Mary Smeeton, 6 June 1959, Kabul, Afghanistan, 1 son. *Education:* AB, Haverford College, USA, 1932; MA, Harvard University, 1935; University College, University of London, England, 1949–50. *Literary Appointments:* Assistant Editor, Harvard University Press, 1940; Managing Editor, Army Talks, US Army, 1943–44. *Publications:* On The Idea of an International University, 1945; Selection of American Historical Documents, 1945; Famous British Generals, (editor), 1952; U S and Vietnam, 3 volumes, 1966–67; Canadian-American Relations, 3 volumes, 1968; A Collection of Afghan Legends, (with A Javid), 1970; Selected Poems, 1974; Sassvez de Champlain, monograph, 1983. *Contributions to:* Book Review Section, Boston Evening Transcript, 1935–39; Encyclopedia Americana, 1940–41; Encyclopedia Britannica, 1941; Royal Air Force Journal; Yank Magazine; Stars and Stripes, 1943–44; Times Record, Brunswick, Maine, 1977–83. *Membership:* Assocation of American Historians, 1981–84. *Address:* 57 McKeen Street, Brunswick, ME 04011, USA.

PARKER, Barry Richard, b. 15 Apr. 1935, Penticton, British Columbia, Canada. University Professor. m. Gloria, 1960, Vernon, British Columbia, 1 son. *Education:* BA Honours, M Sc, University of British Columbia; PhD, Utah, State University, USA. *Publications:* Concepts of the Cosmos, 1984. *Contributions to:* Astronomy; Star and Sky; Fly Fisherman; Fishing World; Encyclopaedia Britannica; Science Year Book, 1981. *Honour:* 1st Prize, McDonald Observatory Science Writing Contest, 1984. *Literary Agent:* Arthur Schwartz, New York. *Address:* 750 Fairway Drive, Pocatello, ID 83201, USA.

PARKER, Catherine E, b. 20 Sep. 1912. Writer. m. Allen F Parker. *Education:* BA cum laude, Mount Mary College, Milwaukee, Wisconsin, USA. *Literary Appointments include:* Writer for President, Illinois Bell Telephone Company, Chicago, Illinois. *Contributions to:* Over 80 newspapers, magazines and anthologies including: Modern Maturity; Rancho Bernardo Magazine; Hallmark; Chicago Tribune; From Sea to Sea in Poetry; Bernardo News; Ideals; Playboy; American Poetry – Old and New; The New World; Haiku Highlights; Horizons; Konkani Sahitya Prakashan, India; The Irish World; The Tattler. *Honours include:* Annual Contest, San Diego Poets, 1979; Rancho Bernardo Magazine, 1980; Golden Poet Award, world of Poetry; various others. *Memberships:* Past President, New World Poets Club; Workshop Director, Poets and Patrons Club; Planning Committee, Farr Horizons Poetry Club; Moderator, Rancho Bernardo World News Forum; Vice President, Rancho Bernardo Scribblers. *Address:* 16826 Acebo Drive, San Diego, CA 92128, USA.

PARKER, David Owen, b. 6 Mar. 1941, Salisbury, Wiltshire, England. Journalist. *Education:* Certificates in General Agriculture Stage III, Business Management and Organisation. *Publication:* (privately) Tales of a Carter's Daughter, 1984. *Contributions to:* Technical journals. *Membership:* Guild of Agricultural Journalists. *Address:* Home Close, Teffont, Salisbury SP3 5QY, Wiltshire, England.

PARKER, (James) Stewart, b. 20 Oct. 1941, Belfast, Northern Ireland. Playwright. *Education:* BA, 1964, MA, 1966, Queens University, Belfast. *Publications:* Spokesong, 1980; Catchpenny Twist, 1980; Nightshade, 1980. Numerous other plays produced in theatre, radio and television and the cinema. *Honours:* Most Promising Playwright Award, Evening Standard, 1976; Christopher Ewart-Biggs Memorial Prize, 1979; Giles Cooper Award, 1980. *Literary Agent:* Marc Berlin, London Management. *Address:* c/o Marc Berlin, London Management, 235/241 Regent Street, London W1A 2JT, England.

PARKER, John, b. 1906, Bristol, England. Politician. *Education:* MA, St John's College, Oxford. *Publications:* Independent Worker & Small Family Business, 1931; New Trends in Socialism, 1936; 42 Days in the Soviet Union, 1946; Labour Marches On, 1948; The Newfoundland, 1950; 12 Modern Yugoslave Novels, Editor, 1958; Harold Wilson, 1964; Willy Brandt, 1966; Father of the House, 1982. *Contributor to:* Public Enterprise; Political Quarterly; New Statesman; etc. *Honours:* CBE, 1965; Yugoslav Red Star, 1975. *Memberships:* Fabian Society, General Secretary 1939–45, Honorary Secretary, 1954–71. Chairman, 1950–53, Vice President 1971, President 1980. *Address:* 4 Essex Ct, Temple, London EC4, England.

PARKER, Marion Dominica Hope (Sister Mary Dominic of the Cross), b. 29 June 1914, Christchurch, New Zealand. Eremitical Contemplative of the Order of Preachers. *Education:* BA, MA, Canterbury University New Zealand; BLitt, Oxford University, England. *Publications include:* Language and Reality, A Course in practical criticism, 1949; The Slave of Life, A Study of Shakespeare and the Idea of Justice, 1955; Media of Communication: Art and Morals, 1970; (transls.) Latourelle, Theology, Science of Salvation, 1969; Danielou, The Crisis in Intelligence, 1970; Laurentin, Has Our Faith Changed?, 1972. *Contributor to:* New Zealand New Writing, 1944, 1945. *Honours:* Recipient, Hilda Mathieson Prize, 1948. *Address:* 27 Grosvenor Road, Richmond, Surrey TW10 6PE, England.

PARKER, Thomas Henry Louis, b. 28 Sep. 1916, Hayling Island, Hampshire, England. Clerk in Holy Orders; University Teacher. m. Mary Angwin, 14 June 1940, Gulval, 2 sons, 1 daughter. *Education:* Emmanuel College, Cambridge, 1935–38, MA 1942, BD 1952, DD 1961. *Literary Appointments:* Editorial Board, Lutterworth Press, 1962–71; Assistant editor for English translation of K Barth: Kirchliche Dogmatik; Editorial Committee: Supplementa Calviniana and Calvini Editio Secunda. *Publications:* The Oracles of God, 1947; Calvin's Doctrine of the Knowledge of God, 1952; 1959, 1969; Portrait of Calvin, 1954, 1961; Karl Barth, 1970; Calvin's New Testament Commentaries, 1971; John Calvin, 1975, 1977, 1982; Calvin's Old Testamant Comentaries, 1986; Commentaries on Romans 1532–1542, 1986; Editor: Calvin's Sermons on Isaiah 53, 1956; English Reformers, 1966; Calvini Commentaries in Epistolam ad Romanos, 1981; Essays in Christology for Karl Barth, 1956; Service in Christ, 1966. *Contributions to:* Numerous articles and reviews especially in Scottish Journal of Theology; Journal of Theological Studies; Zeitschrift für Kirchengeschichte; Erasmus, *Address:* 72 Windsor Road, Cambridge, England.

PARKER, Watson, b. 15 June 1924, Chicago, Illinois, USA. Professor of History; Writer. m. Olga Massel Glassman, 9 Sep. 1950, Warren, Pennsylvania, 2 sons, 1 daughter. *Education:* AB, University of Chicago, 1948; BS, Cornell University, 1951; MA 1962, PhD 1965, University of Oklahoma. *Literary Appointments:* Editorial Boards, Journal of the West, The Old Northwest. *Publications:* Black Hills Ghost Towns & others, 1964; Gold in the Black Hills, 1966; Black Hills Bibliography, 1970; Black Hills Ghost Towns, with Hugh K Lambert, 1974; Deadwood: The Golden Years, 1981. *Contributions to:* Great Plains Journal; The American West; Brandbook, Chicago Corral of Westerners; Journal of the West; South Dakota History. *Honour:* Woodrow Wilson Dissertation Scholarship, 1963. *Memberships:* Chicago & Black Hills Corrals of Westerners. *Address:* PO Box 638, Hill City, SD 57745, USA.

PARKES, Roger Graham, b. 15 Oct. 1933, Chingford, Essex, England. Novelist; Scriptwriter. m. Tessa Isabella McLean, 5 Feb. 1964, London, 1 son, 1 daughter. *Education:* National Diploma of Agriculture; Member, Royal Agricultural College. *Literary Appointments:* Editor, Farming Express, 1963. *Publications:* Death Mask, 1970; Line of Fire, 1971; The Guardians, 1973; The Dark Number, 1973; The Fourth Monkey, 1978; Alice

Ray Mortons Cookham, 1981; Them and Us, 1985. *Contributions to:* Daily Express; Sunday Express; Farming Express and Scottish Daily Express, staff writer, 1959–63; Staff script editor, drama, British Broadcasting Corporation television, London, 1964–70. *Honours:* Grand Prix de Literature, Paris, France, for The Dark Number, 1974; Runner Up, Prix Jeunese, with television play Secrets, Munich, Germany. *Memberships:* Writers Guild of Great Britain. *Literary Agent:* Cecily Ware, London. *Address:* Cartlands Cottage, Kings Land, Cookham Dean, Berkshire Sl6 9AY, England.

PARKHURST, Louis Gifford, b. 13 Aug. 1946, Broken Arrow, Oklahoma, USA. Minister; Author. m. Patricia Ann Kirkham, 8 June 1968, Tulsa, Oklahoma, USA, 1 son, 1 daughter. *Education:* BA 1969, MA 1974, Philosophy, University of Oklahoma; M Div in New Testament, Princetown Theological Seminary, 1973. *Publications:* Principles of Prayer, (with C G Finney), 1980; Principles of Victory, (with C G Finney), 1981; Principles of Liberty, (with C G Finney), 1983; Answers to Prayer, (with C G Finney), 1983; Principles of Holiness, (with C G Finney), 1984; Principles of Union with Christ, (with C G Finney), 1985; Francis Schaeffer: The Man and His Message, 1985; Principles of Sanctification, (with C G Finney), 1986; Pilgrim's Prayerbook, (with John Bunyan), 1986. *Contributions to:* Fundamentalist Journal; The Expository Times. *Address:* Christian Life Study Center, PO Box 7024, Rochester, MN 55903, USA.

PARKINSON, Thomas Francis, b. 24 Feb. 1920, USA. Professor. m. Ariel Reynolds, 23 Dec. 1948, Piedmont, California, 2 daughters. *Education:* AB 1945, MA 1946, PhD 1948, University of California, Berkeley. *Literary Appointments:* Instructor 1948, Professor 1960, University of California. *Publications:* Letter To A Young Lady, verse, 1947; W B Yeats, Self Critic, 1951; Men, Women, Vinces, verse, 1959; A Casebook of the Beat, Editor, 1960; Masterworks of prose, Editor, 1961; W B Yeats, The Later Poetry, 1964; Thanatos, verse, 1965, enlarged edition 1976; Robert Lowell, A Collection of Critical Essays, Editor, 1969; Protect The Earth, verse and prose, 1970; Homage to Jack Spicer, Verse, 1970; What The Blindman Saw, verse drama, 1974; The Canters of T P, Verse, 1978; Hart Crane and Yvor Winters: Their Literary Correspondence, 1978, paperback 1982; From The Grande Chartreuse, pamphlet, 1980. *Contributions to:* Magazines and Journals including: Nation; New York Times; Southern Review; Sagetrieb; Modern Philology; Yeats Annual; Critical Inquiry. *Honours include:* Honorary Fellow, St Peter's College, Oxford, 1969; Senior Fellow, National Endowment for the Humanities, 1984–85; Visiting Senior Research Fellow, St John's College, Oxford, 1984–85. *Memberships:* PEN; Modern Language Association. *Address:* Department of English, University of California, Berkeley, CA 94720, USA.

PARKKINEN, Pekka Kustas, b. 4 June 1940, Helsinki, Finland. Writer; Poet; Translator. m. Eija Bastman, 28 May 1977, Helsinki, 1 daughter. *Publications:* The Moon Is Still Glowing, 1965; If I Loved My Country, poetry, 1967; The Shell, novel, 1969; So It Is, poetry, 1970; Little Rider, novel, 1971; One Winter It Then Happened Something, novel, 1972; A Town Called Lotto, poetry, 1972; A Three Which Vawes the Winds, poetry, 1973; Usu Caption, poetry, 1974; Selected Poems, 1975; With A Rose Stamped Sleeping Partner, poetry, 1976; Joy, novel, 1977; Scarfs, poetry, 1977; Is It So, poetry, 1981; Selected Poems – completed edition, 1981; Distant Shore, poetry, 1983; The Time of Little Hearts, poetry, 1985; The Wind of Freedom, novel, 1985; Translations include: Max Jacob; Henry Michaux; Rimbaud. *Honours:* Weilin and Göös Award, 1965, 1971, 1983. *Membership:* The Finnish Writers Association. *Address:* Weilin and Göös, Abertajantie 2, 02100 Espoo, Finland.

PARKS, Douglas Richard, b. 28 Aug. 1942, Long Beach, California, USA. Linguist; Anthropologist. *Education:* AB, University of California, Berkeley, 1964; PhD, Linguistics, University of California, Berkeley,

1972. *Publications:* A Grammar of Pawnee, 1976; An Introduction to the Arikara Language, 1979; Ceremonies of the Pawnee, 1981. *Contributions to:* Nebraska History; articles in professional publications. *Honours:* Post-Doctoral Fellow, Smithsonian Institution, 1973–74; Fellow, American Council of Learned Societies, 1982. *Address:* 8275 East State Road 46, Bloomington, In 47401, USA.

PARLAND, Oscar Percival, b. 20 Apr. 1912, Kiev, Writer; Psychiatrist. m. Heidi Runeberg, 24 Sep. 1941, Helsingfors, 1 son, 1 daughter. *Education:* Licenciate of Medicine, Specialisation in Psychiatry and Neurology. *Publications:* Forvandlinger, Metamorphoses, 1945, Norwegian edition, 1947, Finnish edition, 1964; Den Fortrollade vagen, The Enchanting Way, 1953, Finnish editions, 1955, 83; Tjurens ar, The Year of the Bull, 1962, Finnish editions, 1963, 85. *Contributions to:* Finnish and Swedish scientific and cultural journals, newspapers and magazines of articles on art, psychiatry and literature. *Honours:* Literature Prize, Finnish State, 1946, 54, 63; Prize, Swedish Literature Society, 1946, 54, 63; Literature Prize, Svenska Dagbladet, Sweden, 1953; Literature Prize, Langman, Sweden, 1968. *Memberships:* PEN Club, Finnish Section; Swedish Writers Society in Finland; Semiotical Society of Finland; Aestetic Society of Finland. *Literary Agent:* Holger Schildt. *Address:* Munksnasallen 7A8, 00330 Helsingfors 33, Finland.

PARLETT, David, b. 18 May 1939, London. Writer. m. Barbara Hoare, 26 Mar. 1966, Kingston-upon-Thames, England, 1 son, 1 daughter. *Education:* BA, Modern Languages, University of Wales. *Publications:* A Short Dictionary of Languages, 1967; The Penguin Book of Card Games, 1979; The Penguin Book of Patience, 1979; The Penguin Book of Word Games, 1981; Selections from the Camina Burana, 1986. *Contributor to:* Games and Puzzles Magazine, Former Editor. *Membership:* Society of Authors. *Literary Agent:* John McLaughlin, Campbell Thomson McLaughlin Ltd. *Address:* 1 Churchmore Road, Streatham, London SW16 5UY, England.

PAROISSIEN, David Harry, b. 24 Oct. 1939, Middlesbrough, England. Professor of English Literature. m. Miriam Shinkle, 19 Dec. 1963, Turin, Italy, 1 son, 2 daughters. *Education:* PhD, University of California, Los Angeles, USA, 1968. *Literary Appointments:* Staff 1968–, Associate Director of Graduate Studies English Department 1984, University of Massachusetts, Amherst; Book Review Editor, Dickens Studies Newsletter, 1979–82; General Editor, Dickens Quarterly, 1983–. *Publications:* Dickens's Pictures From Italy, (editor, with introduction and notes), 1973; Selected Letters of Charles Dickens, 1985; Oliver Twist: An Annotated Bibliography, 1985. *Contributions to:* The Dickensian; Dickens Studies Newsletter; Victorian Studies; English Language Notes; English Miscellany; Studi Americani; Hartford Studies in Literature; Film and Literature Quarterly. *Membership:* Trustee, The Dickens Society, 1982–85. *Address:* Department of English, University of Massachusetts, Amherst, MA 01003, USA.

PARRACK, Richard M, b. 6 Oct. 1927, Whitley Bay, England. Managing Editor, News of the World, London, England. m. Kathleen Scott, 1951, Whitley Bay, 1 son, 1 daughter. *Address:* News of the World, 30 Bouverie Street, London EC4, England.

PARRISH, William Earl, b. 7 Apr. 1931, Garden City, Kansas, USA. University Professor., m. Helen Sue Stoppel, 2 June 1972, Fulton, 1 son, 1 daughter. *Education:* BS, Honours, Kansas State University; MA, PhD, University of Missouri, *Appointments:* Harry S Trueman Professor of American History, Westminster College, Fulton, 1955–78, Dean, 1973–75; Professor, History, Mississippi State University, 1978–, Head, History, 1978–85. *Publications:* David Rice Atchison of Missouri: Border Politician, 1961; Turbulent Partnership: Missouri and the Union, 1861–1865, 1963; Missouri Under Radical Rule, 1865–1879, 1965; Editor, The Civil War: A Second American Revolution, 1970,

1978; A History of Missouri, Volume III 1860–1875, 1973; Missouri: The Heart of the Nation, co-author, 1980. *Contributor to:* Civil War Times Illustrated, 1964; Journal of the West, 1968; Civil War Times Illustrated, 1978; Missouri Life, 1979. *Honours:* Award of Merit, American Association for State and Local History, 1974; Proclamation by Governor Joseph P Teasdale, 1978. *Memberships:* Phi Alpha Theta, International Vice President, 1983–85, International President, 1985–; Organization of American Historians; Southern Historical Association; Western Historical Association; National Trust for Historic Preservation. *Address:* Department of History, Mississippi State University, MS 39762, USA.

PARSONS, Christopher James, b. 5 Aug. 1941, Epsom, Surrey, England. Lecturer. m. Janelle Mary Cooper, 7 Sep. 1979, 2 daughters. *Education:* BA, PhD, Diploma in Management Studies. *Major Publications:* Written Communication for Business Students, 1970; Library Use in Further Education, 1973; Theses & Project Work, 1973; How to Study Effectively, 1976; Problems in Business Communication, 1977; Communication for Business Students, 1978; Getting the Right Job, 1979; Work for Yourself, 1980; English for Business Studies, 1981; Assignments in Communication, 1982. *Membership:* Society of Authors. *Literary Agent:* Tessa Sayle, London. *Address:* 12 Berber Road, London SW11 6RZ, England.

PARSONS, Edward, b. 9 Dec. 1900, Burwash Common, Sussex, England. Retired Officer, Royal Marines & New Zealand Regular Force. *Publications include:* Owning, Training and Racing Horses, 1974; Bible-back, 1974; Once a Marine – Always a Marine, 1984; The Kipling I Knew, 1985. *Contributor to:* Cookery & Catering Reviews & Magazines, United Kingdom and New Zealand; various racing and cricket articles, short stories, etc. *Honours:* Recipient , The Queen's Silver Jubilee Medal. *Memberships:* PEN, Past Chairman, New Zealand Division; The Cookery & Food Association, Life Member. Silver Medalist, UK & New Zealand Cookery & Food Association. *Address:* 48 Bollard Avenue, Avondale, Auckland 7, New Zealand.

PARSONS, Jack, b. 6 Dec. 1920, Greasely, Nottinghamshire, England. Author; Lecturer. m. Barbara Jean Barker, 4 Apr. 1960, London, 1 son, 1 daughter. *Education:* BA Honours Philosophy and Politics, Keele University, 1955. *Publications include:* Population v Liberty, 1971; The Economic Transition, 1975; Population Fallacies, 1977. *Contributions to:* Environment and Industrial Society, 1976; Britain's Crisis in Sociological Perspective, 1977; Human Fertility Control: Theory and Practice, 1979; New Statesman and Nation; The Times Guardian; People; Population and Development Review; Social Biology and Human Affairs; The Humanist; New Scientist; Journal Biosocial Science. *Membership:* Conversation Society. *Address:* Treferig Cottage Farm, Llantrisant, Mid Glamorgan CF7 8LQ, Wales.

PARTAIN, Floydene, b. 26 May 1924, Lamesa, Texas, USA. Writer. m. George Everet Couch (deceased), 11 Oct. 1942, Seagraves, Texas, USA, 3 daughters. *Education:* BA, Wayland University, USA, 1954. *Appointments:* Teacher, Creative writing, Seminole Public Schools, USA, 1962–63; Teacher, Creative Writing, Broward County Schools, Fort Lauderdale, Florida, USA. 1963–65. *Publications:* Crying in the Wilderness (volume 1 of The Caribbean Chronicles), 1983. *Contributions to:* Texas Outlook; Florida Eucation; The Student Writer; Dude; Florida Features Syndicate. *Memberships:* Book Group of South Florida; Writers Guild. *Literary Agent:* Richard Kahlenberg. *Address:* Anacaona Caribbean Inc, 617 Southeast 8th Street, Fort Lauderdale, FL 33316, USA.

PARTRIDGE, Frances Catherine, b. 15 Mar. 1900, London, England. Writer; Translator. m. Ralph Partridge, 2 Mar, 1933, London, 1 son. *Education:* Honours Degree English Literature and Moral Sciences,

Newnham College, Cambridge, 1921. *Literary Appointments:* Staff, Antiquarian bookshop Birrell and Garnett, 1922–28; Assistant to editor Ralph Partridge, The Greville Memoirs, 8 volumes, 1938. *Publications:* A Pacifist's War, 1978; Memories, 1982; Julia – A Portrait of Julia Strachey, 1983; Everything To Lose, 1986; Over 20 translations from Spanish and French including works by Blasco Ibañez, Miguel Asturias and 4 books on Napoleon by G Martineau. *Contributions to:* Reviews in literary magazines including: The New Statesman; The Times Literary Supplement; The Spectator. *Memberships:* Felow, Royal Society of Literature; International PEN. *Literary Agent:* Gill Coleridge, Messrs Anthony Sheil, Doughty Street, London W1. *Address:* 16 West Halkin Street, London SW1X 8JL, England.

PARVIN, Betty, b. 10 Oct. 1916, Cardiff, South Wales. Writer. m. Daniel Frederick McKenzie-Parvin, 5 May 1941, Nottingham, England, 1 son. *Education:* Nottingham College of Art; Honorary Litt D, University of Danzig, 1977. *Appointments:* Competitions Secretary, Nottingham Writers' Club, England, during 1960's; Secretary, Nottingham Poetry Society, 1960's – 70's, Life President, 1980–present. *Publications:* Astone My Star, 1961; The Bird with the Luck, 1968; Sketchbook from Mercia, 1969; A Birchtree with Finches, 1976; Country Matters, 1979; The Book of Daniel, 1980; Prospect, 1981; The Book of Oliver, 1984; Editor, It's All Ours, 1985. *Contributions:* Numerous but include, The Listener; Encounter; Punch; New Statesman; Chicago Tribune; Country Life; Countryman; Poetry Review; Poetry Nottingham; Outposts. *Honours:* Albert Ralph Korn Award for Poetry; Manifold Scholarship Award, 1968; Hon Litt D, Danzig University, 1977; 1st Prize Scotish Open Poetry, 1979; Life Presidency, Nottingham Poetry Society, 1980; Lake Aske Memorial Awards – several, but most recent 1980; 1st Prize, South Wales Eisteddfod, 1983. *Memberships:* Leicester Poetry Society; East Midlands Arts Literary Panel; Nottingham Writers' Club; Nottingham Poetry Society. *Address:* 'Bamboo', Bunny Hill Top, Costock, Nr Loughborough, Leicestershire, LE12 6UX, England.

PASAMANIK, Luisa, b. 16 Dec. 1930, Buenos Aires, Argentina. Poet; Writer; Journalist; Translator. *Education:* Professor of Foreign Languages. *Publications:* Poetry: Poemas al hombre del manana, 1953; Plegaria grave, 1958; Vacio para cuerdas, 1960; El angel desterrado, 1962, published USA as The Exiled Angel, 1973 and as The Banished Angel, 1979; Sinfonia de las esferas, 1963; Metal y vidrio, 1967; Sermon negro, 1968; Tlaloke, 1970; Primero el fuego, 1972; Sinfonia alucinada, 1973; various translations into Portuguese. Various short stories and plays. *Contributions to:* Argentinian and Foreign anthologies of poetry, various publications in Latin America and Spain. Readings: Organisation for International Promotion of Culture, Foreign Ministry of Mexico, Argentina and Mexico City, Mexico. Translator: International News Agency, Reuters; International Congresses. *Honours include:* Several prizes for short stories, Argentina and Spain, 1957–58, 1969; Band of Honour, Argentine Writers Association, 1961; Panero Prize for Poetry, Madrid, Spain, 1968; Boscan Prize for Poetry, Barcelona, 1972; Special Distinction for Poetry, Martorell City, 1979. *Memberships:* Including: Argentine Writers Association. *Address:* Casilla de Correo Nro 153, Sucursal 1 (Av.de Mayo), 1401 Buenos Aires, Argentina.

PASK, Gordon Andrew Speedie, b. 28 June 1928, Derby, England. Professor and Director of Research; Author; Inventor; Artist; Consultant. m. Elizabeth Poole, Jan. 1956, Chelsea, London, 2 daughters. *Education includes:* MA, Cambridge University; PhD, London University; DSc, Open University. *Literary Appointments:* Editor or editorial board member of numerous organisations including, Behavioural Science, Instructional science, Ideas in Psychology and Advances in Cybernetics. *Publications include:* The Cybernetics of Human Learning and Performance, 1955; Conservation, Cognition and Learning, 1975; Conservation Theory: Applications in education and Episticology, 1976; Micromaw with S Currow, 1981,

82, 84; Edges of Mind; Journeys in the Park. *Contributions to:* numerous learned journals and book chapters, popular technical journals and magazines. *Honours include:* Fellow, Columbia Pacific University, 1983; Honorary Fellow, Cybernetic Society, UK, 1982; Weiner Gold Medal, American Society for Cybernetics, 1984. *Memberships include:* Past Chairman, Cybernetic Society, UK; The Athenaeum; Chelsea Arts Club. *Literary Agent:* Curtis Brown. *Address:* 35a Kings Road, Richmond, Surrey TW10 6EX, England.

PASK, Raymond Frank, b. 27 May 1944, Australia. Teacher. *Education:* BA, Dip Ed, Monash University. *Publications:* Over 12 books including: People and Places, 1970 and 1974; Australia and New Zealand, 1976 and 1980; China's Changing Landscapes, 1979; China, 1982; Using The Earth, 1982 and 1983; The Changing Earth, 1985; The World Now, 1986. *Contributions to:* Geographical magazine, London. *Address:* 41 Yarra Street, Abbotsford 3067, Australia.

PASSES, Alan, b. 12 Jan. 1943. Writer. m. Jame Burnett Darling, 1 Apr. 1972, London, 1 son, 1 daughter by previous marriage. *Publications:* Big Step, 1977; The Rembrandt Diary, 1985; Bits, 1986. *Contributor to:* New Worlds; Bananas Literary Review; Calabash. *Literary Agent:* Deborah Rogers Ltd, London. *Address:* 50 Hamilton Road, London SW19, England.

PASSOW, A(aron) Harry, b. 9 Dec. 1920, Liberty, New York, USA. University Professor. m. Shirley Siegal, 2 July 1944, Chicago, Illinois, USA, 1 son, 2 daughters. *Education:* BA, State University of New York at Albany, 1942; MA, State University of New York, 1947; Ed D, Columbia University, 1951; MA, Columbia University, 1979. *Major Publications:* Education in Depressed Areas (editor), 1963; Secondary Education for All: The English Approach, 1961; Developing Programs for the Educationally Disadvantaged (editor), 1968; Reaching the Disadvantaged Learner (editor), 1970; Urban Education in the 1970s (editor), 1971; Secondary Education Reform: Retrospect & Prospect, 1976; American Secondary Education: The Conant Approach, 1977; The Gifted & The Talented: Their Education & Development (editor), 1979; Reforming Schools in the 1980s, 1984. *Contributor to:* Various professional educational journals. *Address:* Teachers College, Columbia University, 525 West 120th Street, New York, NY 10027, USA.

PATAI, Raphael, b. 22 Nov. 1910, Budapest, Hungary. Writer on Cultural Anthropology. 2 daughters. *Education:* PhD, University of Budapest, 1933. *Literary Appointment:* Editor, Herzel Press, USA, 1956–71; Advisory Editor Judaism, Encyclopedia Americana, 1959–. *Publications include:* Shire R Yisrael Berekhya Fontanella, 1933; Ha Mayim, 1936; Ha Sapanut ha'lvrith, 1938; Mivbar haSippur haArtzisraeli, 2 volumes, (edited with Z Wohlmuth), 1938; Adam waAdama, 2 volumes, 1942–43; Masorot Historiyot, 1945; Edoth, 3 volumes, (edited with J J Rivlin), 1945–48; Studies in Folklore and Ethnology, 5 volumes, (edited with J J Rivlin), 1946–48; Social Studies, 2 volumes, (edited with R Bachi), 1946–48; Mada'ha Adam, 2 volumes, 1947–48; Man and Temple in Ancient Jewish Myth and Ritual, 1947 and 1967; Israel Between East and West: A Study in Human Relations, 1953 and 1970; The Hashemite Kingdom of Jordan, 1956; The Republic of Lebanon, 2 volumes, (editor), 1956; The Kingdom of Jordan, 1958; Current Jewish Social Research, 1958; Cultures in Conflict, 1958 and 1961; Herzl Year Book, 7 volumes, (editor) 1958–71; The Complete Diaries of Theodor Herzl, 5 volumes, 1960; Studies in Biblical and Jewish Folklore, (edited with F Utley and D Noy), 1960; Golden River to Golden Road; Society, Culture and Change in the Middle East, 1963, 3rd edition, 1969; Hebrew Myths, (with R Graves), 1964; The Hebrew Goddess, 1967 and 1978; Encyclopedia of Zionism and Israel, Editor, 1971; Tents of Jacob: The Diaspora Yesterday and Today, 1971; The Arab Mind, 1973 and 1983; The Myth of the Jewish Race, (with Jennifer Wing), 1975; The Jewish Mind, 1977; The Messiah Texts, 1979; Gates to the Old City, 1980 and 1981; The Vanished Worlds of Jewry, 1980; On Jewish Folklore, 1983. *Address:* 39 Bow Street, Forest Hills, NY 11375, USA.

PATERSON, (James Edmund) Neil, b. 31 Dec. 1915, Greenock, Scotland. Author; Screenwriter. m. Rosabelle MacKenzie, 7 July 1939, Aberdeen, 2 sons, 1 daughter. *Educaton:* MA, Edinburgh University. *Literary Appointments:* Chairman, Literature Committee, Scottish Arts Council, 1967–76. *Publications:* The China Run, 1948; Behold Thy Daughter, 1950; And Delilah, 1951; Man on the Tightrope, 1953; The Kidnappers, 1957. *Honours:* Atlantic Award in Literature, 1946; American Academy Award (Oscar), 1959. *Literary Agent:* H N Swanson Inc, 8523 Sunset Boulevard, Los Angeles, USA. *Address:* St Ronans, Crieff, Perthsire, Scotland.

PATERSON, Ronald William Keith, b. 20 Sep. 1933, Arbroath, Scotland. University Lecturer in Philosophy. m. Angela Thackery Marr, 2 Apr. 1964, York. *Education:* MA 1955, Dip Ed 1958, B Phil 1962, University of St Andrews; PhD, University of Hull, 1972. *Publications:* The Nihilistic Egoist: Max Stirner, 1971; Values, Education, and the Adult, 1979. *Contributions to:* Adult Education; International Journal of Lifelong Education; Journal of Philosophy of Education; Philosophical Quarterly; Philosophy; Ratio; Religious Studies; Rewley House Papers; Studies in Adult Education. *Address:* 215 Boroughbridge Road, York, England.

PATINKIN, Don, b. 8 Jan. 1922, Chicago, Illinois, USA. Professor of Economics. m. Deboraha Trossman, 17 June 1945, Chicago, 1 son, 3 daughters. *Education:* Chicago Yeshiva, 1933–43; BA 1943, MA 1945, PhD 1947, University of Chicago. *Major Publications:* Money, Interest & Prices: An Integration of Monetary & Value Theory, 1956, 2nd edition 1965; The Israel Economy: The First Decade, 1959; Keynes' Monetary Thought: A Study of its Development, 1976; Essays on & in the Chicago Tradition, 1981; Anticipations of the General Theory? & other essays on Keynes, 1982. *Contributor to:* Scientific Journals on monetary, employment, price theory & history of economic thought. *Honours:* Phi Beta Kappa, 1943; Rothschild Prize (in the Social Sciences), 1959; Israel Prize (same) 1970; Econometric Society 1974, Fellow; Honorary Member, American Economic Association, 1975; President, Israel Economic Association, 1976; Member, Israel Academy of Sciences & Humanities, 1963; Foreign Honorary Member, American Academy of Arts & Sciences, 1969; Honorary DHL, University of Chicago, 1976; Honorary LI.D, University of Western Ontario, Canada, 1983. *Address:* Hebrew University of Jerusalem, Mount Scopus, Jerusalem 91905, Israel.

PATITZ, Dolores R, b. 12 Apr. 1931. Business Manager; Accountant. *Education:* Business College Diploma; Various College credits, seminars, Business and Drama, Public Speaking, Creative Writing. *Contributions to:* North American Mentor Magazine (poetry), 1972–84. *Honours:* Certificate of Merit, North American Mentor Magazine, 1975, 76, 77; Honours Award, 1977; Certificate of Merit, 1978, North American Mentor Magazine; Poetry used for local, district and state Forensic Contest, 1976–80. *Address:* R R 1, Box 189, Glidden, WI 54527, USA.

PATON, Alan Stewart, b. 11 Jan. 1903, Pietermaritzburg, Natal, South Africa. Writer (originally Teacher). *Education:* BSc, BEd, University of Natal. *Publications:* Cry, The Beloved Country, 1948; Too Late the Phalarope, 1953; Land and People of South Africa, 1955; Tales from a Troubled Land, 1960; Hofmeyr, 1965; Instrument of Thy Peace, 1968; Kontakion for You Departed, 1969; Apartheid and the Archbishop, 1973; Knocking on the Door, 1975; Towards the Mountain, (autobiography) 1980; Ah But Your Land is Beautiful, 1981. *Contributor to:* Numerous magazines, newspapers etc. *Honours:* Honorary Doctorates from Kenyon College and Universities of Yale, Natal, Harvard, Trent, Edinburgh, Rhodes, Willamette, Witwatersrand, Michigan (Flint); Freedom Award, USA, 1960; Free

Academy of Hamburg, 1961; CNA Literary Awards, 1965 and 1973. *Memberships:* Society of Authors; Dramatists Guild of America; FRSL. *Address:* PO Box 278, Hillcrest, 3650 Natal, Republic of South Africa.

PATTEN, Brian, b. 7 Feb. 1946, Liverpool, England. Poet. *Publications:* Little Johnny's Confesion, 1967; Penguin Modern Poets no. 10, 1968; Notes to the Hurrying Man, 1969; The Irrelevant Song, 1971; Vanishing Trick, 1976; Mr Moon's Last Case, 1975; The Elephant and the Flower, 1970; Grave Gossip, 1979; Love Poems, 1981; Gargling with Jelly, 1985; Gangsters, Ghosts and Dragon Flies, editor, 1981. Plays for Children: The Pig and the Junk Hill, 1975; The Man Who Hated Children, 1979; Plays for Adults: Blind Love, 1982; The Mouth Trap, with Roger McGough, 1982. *Contributions to:* Numerous publications including: The Sunday Times; Times Literary Supplement; The Observer; Poetry Review; Ambit. *Literary Agent:* Anthony Sheil Associates. *Address:* Allen and Unwin Publishers, 40 Museum Street, London WC1, England.

PATTEN, Robert L, b. 26 Apr. 1939. 2 daughters. *Education:* BA High Honours, Swarthmore College, 1960; MA 1962, PhD 1965, Princeton University; Bedford College, University of London, England, 1963–64. *Literary Appointments include:* Lecturer 1964–66, Assistant Professor 1966–69, Bryn Mawr College; Assistant Professor 1969–71, Associate Professor 1971–76, Professor 1976–, Rice University; Editor, Dickens Studies Newsletter, 1969–72; Editor, The Flyleaf, 1971–73; Sub Editor, Dickens Studies Annual, 1970–79; Editor, SEL: Studies in English Literature 1500–1900, 1978–84; Reader, consultant and advisory editor. *Publications include:* Charles Dickens, The Pickwick Papers, (editor, with introduction), 1972, 8th edition 1978; George Cruikshank: A Revaluation, (editor), 1974; Charles Dickens and His Publishers, 1978. *Contributions to:* SEL; NCF; ELH; Dickens Studies Annual; Nature and the Victorian Imagination; Approaches to Victorian Autobiography; Art Journal. *Honours include:* Fulbright Scholar, Bedford College, University of London, England, 1963; NEH Younger Scholar Fellow, 1968–69; NEH Fellowship for Independent Study and Research, 1977–78; Guggenheim Foundation Fellowship, 1980–81. *Memberships:* Modern Language Association; American Association of University Professors; South Central Modern Language Association; Victorian Society in America; The Dickens Fellowship; The Dickens Society Inc; Phi Beta Kappa; PEN. *Address:* Apt 17G, 1400 Mermann Drive, Houston, TX 77004, USA.

PATTERSON, Orlando Horace, b. 5 June 1940, Jamaica, West Indies. Professor of Sociology. m. Nerys Thomas, 4 Sep, 1965, Caernarfon, Wales, 2 daughters. *Education:* BSc Honours Economics, London University (External), 1962; PhD Sociology, London School of Economics, 1965. *Publications include:* The children of Sisyphus, fiction, 1964; An Absence of Ruins, fiction, 1967; The Sociology of Slavery, 1967; Die The Long Day, fiction, 1972; Ethnic Chauvinism: The Reactionary Impulse, 1977; Slavery and Social Death, 1982. *Contributions to:* Magazines and journals including: The Times Literary Supplement; New Society; The New Statesman; The Listener; The British Journal of Sociology, New Left Review. *Honours:* Honorary AM 1971, Walter Channing Cobat Prize Fellowship 1984, Harvard University; Jamaica Government Exhibition Scholar, University of West Indies, 1959–62; Commonwealth Scholar, Great Britain, 1962–65; Research Grants, National Endowment for the Humanities, 1973–74, 1978, 1981 and 1984; Guggenheim Fellow, 1978–79; Distinguished Contribution to Scholarship Award of American Sociological Association, 1983; Ralphe Bunche Award, American Political Science Association, 1983. *Memberships:* Caribbean Artists Movement, 1964–69; American Sociological Association. *Address:* Department of Sociology, Harvard University, William James Hall 520, Cambridge, MA 02138, USA.

PAUK, Walter, b. 1 may 1914, New Britain, USA. Professor. m. Esther Florian, 27 July 1944, Savannah, 1 son, 1 daughter. *Education:* BA, University of Connecticut, 1949; Philosophy, 1949–51, PhD, 1955, Cornell University. *Appointments:* Editorial Board: Journal of Reading; Reading Improvement; Journal of the Reading Specialist; Education; College Student Journal; Reading World. *Publications:* How to Study in College, 1962, 3rd edition, 1984; How to Take Tests, 1969; Six-Way Paragraphs, 1974, A Skill-at-a-Time, 10 books, 1975; Jamestown Classics, 12 booklets, 1976; Essential Skills, 20 books, 1976; Six Way Paragraphs, Middle & Advanced Levels, 1983; Single Skills, 60 books, 1985. *Contributor to:* American Journal of Psychology; Educational & Psychological Measurement; Seventh Mental Measurements Yearbook; Reading Teacher; Journal of Reading; Reading World. *Membership:* Phi Kappa Phi. *Address:* Reading Research Centre, 147 Olin Hall, Cornell University, Ithaca, NY 14853, USA.

PAUL, Barbara Jeanne, b. 5 June 1931, Maysville, Kentucky, USA. Writer. divorced, 1 son. *Education:* BA, Bowling Green State University; MA, University of Redlands; PhD, University of Pittsburgh. *Publications:* An Exercise for Madmen, 1978; Bibblings, 1979; The Fourth Wall, 1979; Liars and Tyrants and People Who Turn Blue, 1980; Under the Canopy, 1980; First Gravedigger, 1980; The Renewable Virgin, 1984; Prima Donna at Large, 1985; Kill Fee, 1985. *Contributions to:* Fantasy; Fantasy and Science Fiction; Science Fiction. *Membership:* Science Fiction Writers of America. *Literary Agent:* Scott Meredith. *Address:* c/o Scott Meredith, 845 Third Avenue, New York City, NY 10022, USA.

PAULEY, Barbara Anne, b. 12 Jan. 1925, Nashville, Tennessee, USA. Novelist. m. Robert Reinhold Pauley, 22 June 1946, Pound Ridge, New York, USA, 3 sons, 2 daughters. *Education:* Wellesley College, Massachusetts, USA. *Major Publications:* Blood Kin, 1972; Voices Long Hushed, 1976. *Membership:* Mystery Writers of America. *Literary Agent:* Blassingame, McCauley & Wood. *Address:* P O Box 288, Wenham, MA 01984, USA.

PAULSON, Ronald Howard, b. 27 May 1930, Bottineau, North Dakota, USA. 18th Century Scholar, Divorced, 1 son, 1 daughter. *Education:* BA, MA, PhD, Yale University. *Appointments:* University of Illinois, 1958–63; Rice University, 1963–67; Johns Hopkins University, 1967–75, 1984–; Yale University, 1975–85; John Hopkins University 1985–. *Publications:* Theme and Structure in Swift's, Tale of a Tub, 1971; Hogarth's Graphic Works, 2 volumes 1965; The Fictions of Satire, 1967; Satire and the Novel in Eighteenth Century England, 1967; Hogarth: His Life, Art and Times, 2 volumes 1971; Rowlandson: A New Interpretation, 1972; Emblem and expression: Meaning in English Art of the Eighteenth Century, 1975; The Art of Hogarth, 1975; Popular and Polite Art in the Age of Hogarth and Fielding, 1979; Literary Landscape: Turner and Constable, 1982; Representations of Revolution 1789–1820, 1983; Book and Painting: Shakespeare, Milton and the Bible, 1983. *Contributor to:* Numerous professional journals. *Address:* Dept of English, Johns Hopkins University, Baltimore, MD 21218, USA.

PAULU, Burton, b. 25 June 1910, Pewaukee, Wisconsin, USA. Public Broadcaster; Mass Media Scholar and Teacher (retired). m. Frances Tuttle Brown, 19 June 1942, Hastings, Minnesota, 1 son, 2 daughters. *Education:* BA, cum laude, 1931, BS, 1932, MA, 1934, University of Minnesota; PhD, New York University, 1949. *Appointments:* Manager, Radio Station, KUOM, University of Minnesota, 1938–57; Professor and Director, Radio and Television, 1957–72, Professor and Director, Media Resources, 1972–78, University of Minnesota. *Publications:* A Radio and Television Bibliography, 1952; Lincoln Lodge Seminar on Educational Television, 1963; British Broadcasting; Radio and Television in the United Kingdom, 1956; British Broadcasting in Transition, 1961; Radio and Television Broadcasting on the European Continent, 1967; Radio and Television Broadcasting in Eastern Europe, 1974; Television and Radio Broadcasting in the United Kingdom, 1981. *Contributor to:* Articles and book reviews over many years in EBU Review; Public Telecommunications Review; Americana Encyclopedia; Journalism Quarterly; NAEB Journal; Quarterly of Film, Radio and Television; Telecommunications Journal; Journal of the Association for Education by Radio; Musci Educators Journal; Education on the Air; Minneapolis Star and Tribune. *Honours include:* Sigma Delta Chi Award for Research about Journalism, 1962; Citation of Radio and Television Broadcasting on the European Continent, National Journalism Society, 1967; Pioneering Award, International Broadcasting Society, Netherlands, 1968; Broadcast Preceptor Award, San Francisco State University, 1968 and 1982. *Memberships:* Board Member, Minnesota Fulbright Alumni Association, 1985; Phi Beta Kappa; Phi Kappa Phi; Phi Delta Kappa; Kappa Delta Pi; Phi Alpha Theta; Sigma Delta Chi; Member of Board of Directors, President, Past President, 1981–85, University of Minnesota Retirees Association; Campus Club, University of Minnesota; American Association of University Professors. *Address:* 5005 Wentworth Avenue, Minneapolis, MN 55419, USA.

PAUST, Marian Pier, b. 5 Feb. 1908, Richland Center, Wisconsin, USA. Poet. m. Martin A Paust, 10 July 1928, 4 daughters. *Education:* BS, University of Wisconsin, Madison, Wisconsin. *Literary Appointments:* Regional Vice President, State Secretary, State Vice President, State Historian (for 25 years), elected Honorary Member 1980, Wisconsin Fellowship of Poets. *Publications:* Honey to be Savored, 1968; Everybody Beats a Drum, 1972; Personal Poems, 1977; North Country, 1979; New Poems Hung Up To Dry, 1980; The Green Webb, 1982. *Contributions to:* Country Poet; Heartland Journal; PEO Record; PEN Woman; Midwest Chaparral; Different; Alura; WRWA Poetry Quarterly; Poet and many more. *Honours:* Jade Ring Award and Bard's Chair, 1967; Jade Ring Award and Bard's Chair, 1969; State Writer's Cup, 1970. *Memberships:* Wisconsin Fellowship of Poets; Wisconsin Regional Writers Association; National League of American PEN Women; Academy of American Poets; National Affiliated Poetry Societies; Council of Wisconsin Writers. *Address:* PO Box 677, Richland Center, WI 53581, USA.

PAVEY, Donald Adiar, b. 25 July 1922, Wandsworth, England. Art Researcher. *Education:* Royal College of Art, ARCA, Medal of Special Distinction; Art Postgraduate Research, London University and Royal College of Art. *Literary Appointments:* Editor, Methuen Handbook of Colour and Colour Dictionary, 1961, 1967, 1978; editor, Athene, Journal of the Society for Education through Art, 1972–80. *Publications:* Art-Based Games, 1975; Colour, 1980; Juegos de Expression Plastica, 1982; The Artists' Colourmen's Story, 1985. *Contributions to:* Journal of the Royal College of Art, 1958; Athene, 1972, 1976, 1985. *Honours:* Painting School Prize, Royal College of Art, 1946; Architecture Prize, Royal College of Art, 1945. *Address:* 30 Wayside, Sheen, London SW14 7LN, England.

PÅWALS, Per-Hakon Wilhelm, b. 12 May 1928, Helsingfors, Finland. Author. m. Oili Makinen, 27 May 1956, 1 son, 3 daughters. *Publications:* Glas Emallan, 1956; Solkatt, 1957; Minnet ar en Vinge, 1960; Snuviga Gatlyktor, 1960; Om Vintern och om Varen, 1962; Min Salladsgrona Alskarinna, 1967; En Del au Varldsrymden, 1973; Jag Sjunger for Bertrand Russell, 1976; Ovala Rutor, 1979; Keskiviikko Syyskuu Syksy, 1981; Du Vet inte att du ler, 1983; Mägna àr livets dròmmar, 1985. *Address:* Dalvagen 11 a 10, 02700 Grankulla, Finland.

PAWLIKOWSKI, John Thaddeus, b. 2 Nov. 1940, Chicago, USA. Professor of Social Ethics; Roman Catholic Priest. *Education:* PhD, University of Chicago; Ordination, St Mary of the Lake Seminary; AB, Loyola University; Additional study, University of Wisconsin, Oxford University, Spertus College of Judaica. *Publications include:* What Are They Saying About Christian-Jewish Relations?; Christ in Light of the Christian-Jewish Dialogue; Sinai & Calvary; The Chalenge of the Holocaust for Christian Theology; Housing Project for the Inner City: A Case Study; etc. *Contributions to:*

Various edited volumes including: The Holocaust; Ideology, Bureaucracy & Genocide, ed. H Friedlander & S.Milton; Formation of Social Policy in the Catholic & Jewish Traditions, ed. E J Fisher & D F Polish; Antisemetism & The Foundations of Christianity, ed. A T Davies; Auschwitz: Beginning of a New Era?, ed. E. Fleischner; Selected Papers 1979: The American Society of Christian Ethics, ed. M.L. Stackhouse. *Honours:* Interfaith Award, American Jewish Committee, 1972; Founders Citation, National Catholic Conference for Interracial Justice, 1973. *Address:* Catholic Theological Union, 5401 South Cornell Avenue, Chicago, IL 60615, USA.

PAXAL, Tom Roger, b. 23 Sep. 1947, Helsinki, Finland. Author. 1 son. *Appointments:* Cabaret Ekollon, 1977; Plays: Break, 1981, Livstycken, 1979; Radioplay, Simpparn, 1981. *Publications:* Vannerna, 1977; Rodbergen, 1981. *Honours:* Literary Award, Short Story, Violininsten, Helsinki, 1984. *Memberships:* Finlands Svenska Forfattareforeningen RF; Finlands Dramatikerforbund. *Agent:* Soderstroms & Forlags AB; Finlands Dramatikerforbund. *Address:* Vesatie 3 A 6, 04200 Kerava, Finland.

PAXTON, John, b. 1923. Editor, The Statesman's Yearbook. *Literary Appointment:* Consultant Editor, The New Illustrated Everyman's Encyclopaedia, 1981–84. *Publications include:* Everyman's Dictionary of Abbreviations, 2nd Edition, 1986; The Statesman's Yearbook World Gazetter, 1975, 3rd edition 1986; The Developing Common Market, 1976; A Dictionary of the European Communities, 1977; A Calendar of Creative Man, (with S Fairfield), 1980; Commonwealth Political Facts, (with C Cook), 1980; Companion to Russian History, 1983. *Contributions to:* Keesing's Contemporary Archives; Times Literary Supplement. *Memberships:* Society of Authors; PEN. *Address:* c/o Coutts and Co, 188 Fleet Street, London EC4A 2HT, England.

PAYES, Rachel Cosgrove, b. 11 Dec. 1922. Westernport, Maryland, USA. Writer. *Education:* BS, W Va, Wesleyan College, 1943. *Publications include:* Hidden Valley of Oz, 1951; The Deathstones, 1964; Planet of Death; The First Immortals, 1965; Mystery of Echo Caverns, 1966; O Charitable Death, 1968; Peace Corps Nurse, 1967; Malverne Hall, 1970; Forbidden Island, 1972; The Sapphire Legacy, 1976; Moment of Desire, 1978; The Coach to Hell, 1979; Bride of Fury, 1980; Satan's Mistress, 1981; Playing for Keeps, (as Joanne Kaye), 1982; Lady Alicia's Secret, 1986. *Contributor to:* Numerous magazines and anthologies. *Memberhips:* Science Fiction Writers of America; Authors Guild and Authors League. *Address:* 3589 Frost Road, Shrub Oak, NY 10588, USA.

PAYNE, Donald Gordon, b. 3 Jan. 1924, London, England. Author. m. Barbara Back, 20 Aug. 1947, Warblington, 4 sons, 1 daughter. *Education:* MA History, Oxford. *Publications:* Walkabout, 1959; A River Ran Out of Eden, 1963; The Island At The Top Of The World, 1970; To The Farthest Ends of the Earth, History of the Royal Geographical Society, 1980; Mountains of the Gods, 1984. *Literary Agent:* David Higham Associates Limited. *Address:* Pippacre, Westcott Heath, Dorking RH4 3J2, England.

PAYNE, James Richmond, b. 1 June 1921, Australia. Anglican Clergyman; Bible Society National Secretary. m. Joan Elliot, 16 Jan. 1943, Sydney, 3 sons. *Education:* Matriculation, Sydney University; Th L, Australian College of Theology. *Publication:* Around the World in Seventy Days, 1965. *Honour:* MBE, 1982. *Address:* 10/42 Jinka Street, Hawker, ACT, Australia 2614.

PAYNE, Peggy, b. 8 Jan. 1949, Wilmington, North Carolina, USA. Writer. m. Dr Bob Dick, 8 Dec. 1983, Raleigh, North Carolina. *Education:* AB, English, Duke University. *Contributions to:* Cosmopolitan; Ms; Family Circle; Travel and Leisure; New York Times; Washington Post; McCall's. *Honours:* Annual Fiction Award given by Crucible, 1978; NEH Fellowship, 1979. *Memberships:* Society of American Travel Writers; American

Society of Journalists and Authors. *Literary Agent:* Julian Bach. *Address:* 611 West North Street, Raleigh, NC 27603, USA.

PAYNE, Rhonda C, b. 15 June 1949, Newfoundland, Canada. Writer; Theatre Director. *Education:* BA, York University, Toronto, Canada. *Publications:* East End Story (co-author) Stageplay, 1974; IWA Strike (co-author) stageplay, 1975; They Club Seals Don't They? (co-author) Stageplay, 1976; Stars in the Sky Morning, stageplay, 1978. *Contributions to:* Various journals and magazines on freelance basis. *Address:* 3 Monroe Street, St John's, Newfoundland, Canada A1C 1X7.

PEABODY, Richard Myers Jr, b. 14 Mar. 1951, Washington DC, USA. Writer; Editor. *Education:* BA, English, University of Maryland; MA, Literature, American University. *Literary Appointment:* Fiction Writing, St John's College, Annapolis, Maryland. *Publications:* I'm In Love With The Morton Salt Girl, poetry, 1979; D C Magazines: A Literary Retrospective, editor, 1982; Mavericks: Nine Independent Publishers, editor, 1983; Echt & Erzatz, poetry, 1985. *Contributions to:* Kuchibashi; Best Sellers; University of Windsor Review; Jeopardy; Bogg; Washington Review; Washingtonian; Northeast Rising Sun; Library Quarterly; New Pages; Poetry East; etc. *Membership:* Charter member, American Association of Australian Literary Studies. *Address:* P O Box 3567, Washington DC 20007, USA.

PEACOCK, Ronald, b. 22 Nov. 1907, Leeds, England. University Professor. m. Ilse Gertrud Eva Freiwald, 26 Dec. 1933. *Education:* BA, MA, Litt D, Leeds University, England; D Litt (Hon), Manchester University, England. Dr Phil, Marburg, Germany. *Publications:* Das Leitmotiv bei Thomas Mann, 1944; Hölderlin, 1938, 1973; The Poet in the Theatre, 1946, reproduced with additions 1960; The Art of Drama, 1957, 1959; Goethe's Major Plays, 1959, 1970; Criticism and Personal Taste, 1972. *Contributions include:* The Times Literary Supplement; The Listener; Manchester Guardian; Modern Language Review; German Life and Letters; Euphorion. *Honours:* Gold Medal, Goethe-Institut, Munich, Germany; Hon Fellow, Bedford College, University of London, England. Hon President, Modern Humanities Research Association, 1983. *Address:* Greenshade, Woodhill Avenue, Gerrards Cross, Buckinghamshire, England.

PEAKE, Pamela, b. 17 Sep. 1940, New Zealand. Designer, Writer. m. John Fordyce Peake, 2 Apr. 1963, London, England. 2 daughters. *Education:* BSc, MSc Honours 1st Class, Victoria University, New Zealand; Postgraduate work, Glasgow University, Scotland. *Publications:* Creative Soft Toy Making, 1974; How To Make Dinosaurs and Dragons, 1976; Complete Book of Soft Dolls, 1979; Catcraft, 1984. *Contributions to:* Nature; Golden Hands; Mother; HCAA Bulletin. *Literary Agent:* Watson Little, 26 Charing Cross Road, London. *Address:* Spring Cottage, Ightham, Sevenoaks, Kent, TN15 9HN, England.

PEARCE, Ann Philippa, b. Great Shelford, Cambridgeshire, England. Freelance Writer of Childrens books. m. Martin James Graham Christie, 9 May 1963, Hampstead, 1 daughter. *Education:* MA, Cambridge University. *Literary Appointments:* Script Writer, Producer, School Broadcasting, radio, 1945–58; Children's Editor, Andre Deutsch Limited, 1960–67. *Publications:* Minnor on the Say, 1954; Tom's Midnight Garden, 1958; A Dog So Small, 1962; What the Neighbours Did and other stories, 1972; The Shadow Cage and other stories of the Supernatural, 1977; The Battle of Bubble and Squeak, 1978; The Way to Sattin Shore, 1983; Lion at School and other stories, 1985. *Contributions to:* Times Literary Supplement and The Observer, Childrens book reviewer, 1960–75. *Honours:* Carnegie Medal, for Tom's Midnight Garden, 1959; New York Herald Tribune Spring Festival Prize, for A Dog So Small; Whitbread Prize, for Battle of Bubble and Squeak, 1979. *Memberships:* Society of Authors. *Literary Agent:* Laura Cecil. *Address:* c/o Laura Cecil, 17 Alwyne Villas, London N1 2HG, England.

PEARCE, Brian Louis, 4 June 1933, Acton, London, England. Poet; Author; Librarian. m. 1 daughter. *Education:* MA (London); FLA; FRSA. *Appointment:* Member, Greater London Arts Writes in Schools Scheme. *Publications include:* The Eagle and the Swan, play 1966; Requiem for the Sixties, 1971; Selected Poems 1951–1978, 1978; The Vision of Piers Librarian, 1981; Office Hours, 1983; Browne Study, 1984; Bond Street Snatches, experimental fiction 1984; Dutch Comfort: poetry, prose, translations, 1985; Palgrave; Selected Poems. Edited with a biographical and critical introduction, 1985; Gwen John Talking, 1985. *Contributor to:* Numerous journals; Arts Council and PEN Anthologies. *Memberships:* Chairman, Richmond Poetry Group, 1974–84; Poetry Society; PEN; Elder, URC. *Address:* 72 Heathfield South, Twickenham, Middlesex TW2 7SS, England.

PEARCE, Francis James Charles, b. 3 Oct. 1909, Plymouth, England. Writer. m. Vera Alice Hodder, 15 Apr. 1933, Truro, 1 son. *Publications:* The Ship That Torpedoed Herself, 1975; Along The Fal, 1975; Brandy for The Parson, 1976; Mayday, Mayday, Mayday, 1977; Potrait of a Cornish Village, 1977; Last Call for HMS Edinburgh, 1982; A View From The Sea, 1985. *Address:* Trees, No. 7 Cosawes Park, Perranarworthal, Truro, Cornwall, England.

PEARCE, Mary Emily, b. 7 Dec. 1932, London, England. Writer. *Publications:* Apple Tree Lean Down, 1973; Jack Mercybright, 1974; The Sorrowing Wind, 1975; Cast a Long Shadow, 1977; The Land Endures, 1978; Seedtime and Harvest, 1980; Polsinney Harvest, 1983. *Memberships:* Society of Authors; National Book League. *Address:* Owls End, Shuthonger, Tewkesbury, Gloucestershire, England.

PEARSALL, Derek Albert, b. 28 Aug. 1931, Birmingham, England. University Professor. m. Joy Rosemary Elvidge, 31 Aug. 1952, Kings Lynn, 2 sons, 3 daughters. *Education:* BA 1951; MA 1952, University of Birmingham. *Literary Appointments:* Lecturer, Kings College, London, 1959–65; Lecturer 1965; Senior Lecturer 1968; Reader 1971, Professor 1976, University of York; Visiting Professor, Harvard University, USA, 1985–87. *Publications:* John Lydgate, 1970; Old English and Middle Poetry, 1977; Piers Plowman, An Edition of the C-Text, 1978; The Canterbury Tales, 1985. *Address:* University of York, Centre for Medieval Studies, The King's Manor, York YO1 2EP, England.

PEARSON, Frederic Stephen, b. 3 Sep, 1944, Detroit, USA. Professor, Political Science. m. Melvadean McIntosh Pearson, 20 Jan. 1980, St Louis, 1 son, 2 daughters. *Education:* BA, Oakland University, 1965; MA 1966, PhD, 1971, University of Michigan. *Appointments:* Associate Director, Centre for International Studies, Professor, University of Missouri, St Louis. *Publications:* The Weak State in International Crisis: The Case of the Netherland in the German Invasion Crisis of 1939–40, 1981; International Relations: The Global Condition in the Late Twentieth Century, with J M Rochester, 1984. *Contributor to:* Orbis; Arms Control; International Affairs. *Honours:* Fulbright Senior Research Awards to Netherlands, 1977, United Kingdom, 1985; Ford Foundation Grant, University of Lancaster, United Kingdom, 1981–82; National endowment for Humanities and F Thyssen Foundation Grants for Research in Federal Republic of Germany, 1984. *Memberships:* American Political Science Association; International Studies Association; Regional Board; International Political Science Association. *Address:* Centre for International Studies, University of Missouri, 8001 Natural Bridge Road, St Louis, MO 63121, USA.

PEARSON, Keith David, b. 23 Aug. 1925, Perth, Australia. Minister of Religion. m. Daphne Daisy Jones, 23 Feb. 1957, Sydney, Australia. 2 sons, 1 daughter. *Education:* BSc; Ed M. *Publications:* Why Do We Baptise Our Children? 1961; The Meaning of Church Membership, 1962; The Minister's Handbook, 1962; A Programme for Church and Home, 1964; The Elder Serving the Church (Ed.), 1964; Introduction to Group

Dynamics, 1968; Introduction to Organisation Development, 1973; RAP Groups (Rapport and Personal Relationships), 1977; Understanding the Uniting Church, 1978; Introduction to Systems Thinking, 1979; Worship in the Round, 1981; Praying the Bible, 1983; Worship in the Wide Red Land, 1985. *Address:* 73, Walpole Street, Kew, Victoria 3101, Australia.

PEARSON, Scott Roberts, b. 13 Mar. 1938, Madison, Wisconsin, USA. Professor. m. Sandra C Anderson, 12 Sep. 1962, Lagos, Nigeria, 2 daughters. *Education:* BS, American Institutions, University of Wisconsin, 1961; MA, Johns Hopkins University, 1965; PhD, Economics, Harvard University, 1969. *Publications:* Petroleum and Nigerian Economy, 1970; Commodity Exports and African Development, 1974; Rice in West Africa: Policy and Economics, Co-author, 1981; Food Policy Analysis, 1983; co-author; Cassava Economy of Java, 1984. *Contributor to:* Numerous journals. *Honours:* Dean's Award for Teaching, Stanford University, 1978; Award for Professional Excellence, American Agricultural Economics Association, 1984. *Address:* c/o Food Research Institute, Stanford University, Stanford, CA 94305, USA.

PEARSON, William Harrison, b. 18 Jan. 1922, Greymouth, New Zealand. University Teacher. Writer. *Education:* MA, New Zealand, 1948; PhD, London, 1952. *Publications:* Coal Float, 1963; Henry Lawson among Maoris, 1968; Fretful Sleepers amd other essays, 1974; Rifled Sanctuaries, 1984. *Contributions to:* Landfall, Islands; Journal of the Polynesian Society; Journal of Pacific History. *Honours:* Landfall Readers' Prose Award for Non-fiction, 1960; New Zealand Prose Award for Non-fiction, 1974. *Membership:* PEN New Zealand Centre. *Address:* English Department, University of Auckland, Auckland, New Zealand.

PECK, Robert McCracken, b. 15 Dec. 1952, Philadelphia, Pennsylvania, USA. Museum Administrator; Writer. *Education:* BA, History of Art/Archaeology, Princeton University, 1974; MA, Winterthur Program in American Cultural History, University of Delaware, 1976. *Literary Appointments:* Managing Editor, Frontiers, annual publication of the Academy of Natural Sciences of Philadelphia, 1979–; Editorial Board Member, Explorers Journal, quarterly publication of the Explorers Club, New York, 1984–. *Publications:* William Bartram's Travels, Introduction and Notes, 1980; A Celebration of Birds: The Life and Art of Louis Agassiz Fuertes, 1982, 1983; The Birds of America – John James Audubon, Foreword, New York; Macmillan, 1985, London: Collier Macmillan, 1985. *Contributions to:* Laessle, American Art Review, 1976; Steichen, Image, 1977; Eakins, Arts Magazine, 1979; Yellowstone, Rod and Reel, 1981; Harriman, Audubon, 1982; Fuertes, National Wildlife, 1983; Fuertes, Southwest Art, 1983; Fuertes, Terra, 1984; Collections, Antiques, 1985. *Address:* 27 West Springfield Avenue, Philadelphia, PA 19118, USA.

PECKENPAUGH, Angela Johnson, b. 21 Mar. 1942, Richmond, USA. Assistant Professor, Creative Writing. m. C W Peckenpaugh, 1970, divorced 1981. *Education:* BA, English Literature; Denison University; MA, 20th Century Literature, Ohio University; MPA, Writing, University of Massachusetts. *Appointments:* Instructor, English, Ohio University, 1966–67; Lecturer, English, UW Milwaukee, 1968–74; Instructor, Creative Writing, Milwaukee School of Arts, 1967–77; Director, Writing Programme for Adults, UW Milwaukee, 1978–82; Assistant Professor, English, UW Whitewater, 1982–. *Publications:* Letters from Lee's Army, 1979; Discovering the Mandala, 1981; A Book of Charma, 1983. *Contributor to:* Margins; Greenfield Review; Milwaukee Journal; Abraxas; Virginia Quarterly Review; Southern Poetry Review; Wind; Panache; Louisville Review; etc. *Honours:* All University Fellowship, University of Massachusetts 1977–78; Sackbut Review, received grants from CCLM, National Endowment for the Arts, Wisconsin Arts Board, while she was Editor. *Memberships:* Feminist Writers Guild; Wisconsin Regional Writers; Council for Wisconsin Writers. *Address:* 2513 E Webster Pl, Milwaukee, WI 53211, USA.

PEDLER, Frederick Johnson (Sir), b. 10 July 1908, London, England. African Trader. m. Esther Ruth Carling, 11 June 1935, Mombasa, 2 sons, 1 daughter. *Education:* MA, Gonville & Caius College, Cambridge. *Publications:* Post-War England (England und Frankreich in Wort und Bild), Teubner, Leipzig, 1932, 1935; West Africa (Home Study Books), Methuen, 1951, 1959; Economic Geography of West Africa; Longmans, 1955; The Lion & The Unicorn In Africa: The United Africa Company 1787–1931, Heinemann, 1974; Main Currents of West African History, Macmillan, 1979; A Pedler Family History, Phillimore, 1984. *Contributions to:* Numerous journals. *Honours:* Goldsmith Exhibition, 1928; Schuldham Prize, Gonville & Caius College, 1931; Knight Bachelor, 1969; Honorary Fellow, London School of Oriental & African Studies, 1979. *Address:* 36 Russell Road, Moor Park, Northwood HA6 2LR, England.

PEEL, Bruce Braden, b. 11 Nov. 1916, Ferland, Saskatchewan, Canada. Librarian. *Education:* BA, 1944, MA, 1946, University of Saskatchewan; BLS, University of Toronto, 1946. *Publications:* The Saskatoon Story 1882–1952, with Eric Knowles, 1952; Bibliography of the Prairie Provinces, 1956, 2nd edition, 1973; Librarianship in Canada 1946–67, Editor, 1968; Steamboats on the Saskatchewan, 1972; Early Printing in the Red River Settlement, 1974; Rossville Mission Press, 1974. *Honours:* Award, Historical Society of Alberta, 1969; Tremaine Medal, Bibliography Society of Canada, 1975. *Address:* 11047 83rd Avenue, Edmonton, Alberta, Canada.

PEEL, Hazel Mary, b. 26 May 1930, London, England. m. Roy Peel, 24 Oct. 1953, Brisbane, Australia. *Publications:* Fury, Son of the Wilds, 1959; Pilot the Hunter, 1962; Pilot the Chaser, 1964; Easter the Showjumper, 1965; Jago, 1966; Night Storm, Flat Racer, 1966; Dido and Rogue; 1967; Gay Darius, 1968; Untamed, 1969; Land and Power, 1967; Low of the Wilds, 1976; Pocket Dictionary of the Horse, 1978. *Contributions to:* Courier; She; Riding; Elizabethan; Honey; Petticoat; Animal Ways; Reveille; Argosy; The Australian Herald. *Membership:* Society of Authors. *Address:* c/o The Society of Authors, 84 Drayton Gardens, London SW10, England.

PEEL, Lynnette Jean, b. 8 Oct. 1938, Geelong, Victoria, Australia. Historian, Agriculutural Scientist. *Education:* B.Agr. Sc., M.Agr.Sc., University of Melbourne, Australia, PhD (History), Monash University. *Major Publications:* Contributor to: The Pastoral Industries of Australia, 1973, 1986; Rural Industry in the Port Phillip Region, 1835–1880, 1974; Contributor to: History of Technology: The Twentieth Century, 1978; Joint editor: Domestication, Conservation and Use of Animal Resources, 1983; Editor, The Henty Diaries, 1834–1889, 1985. *Contributor to:* Various historical and agricultural journals. *Honours:* International Federation of University Women Research Grant, 1972; Visiting Fellow, University of Reading, England, 1972; Visiting Research Fellow, University of Melbourne, 1975, 1984. *Memberships:* Society of Authors; Institute of Biology; Fellow of the Royal Historical Society; Vice-President, The Royal Institution, 1984–85. *Address:* 49 Oaklands, Hamilton Road, Reading RG1 5RN, England.

PEEL, Malcolm L, b. 12 June 1936, Jeffersonville, Indiana, USA. Professor of Religious Studies. m. Ruth Ann Nash, 18 June 1960, Cincinnati, Ohio, 1 son, 1 daughter. *Education:* BA, Indiana University, 1957; M Divinity, Louisville Presbyterian Seminary, 1960; MA, 1960, PhD, 1966, Yale University; Universitaet Utrecht/Theologische Institut; Post-Doctoral, Universities of Chicago, Harvard, Vanderbilt, Claremont. *Literary Appointments:* Research Associate, Institute for Antiquity and Christianity, University of Claremont, 1967–. *Publications:* The Yale Gnosticism Seminar; Spring, 1964, co-editor C. Colpe, 1964!; The Epistle to

Rheginos: Valentinian Letter on the Resurrection, introduction, translation, commentary, 1969; Gnosis und Auferstehung, 1974; The Teachings of Silvanus; Introduction, Translation, Commentary, 1983; Viewer Guide: Journey into Faith Television Series, 1984. *Contributions include:* 48 articles published; 3 Translations from Coptic originals of texts in, The Nag Hammadi Library in English, 1977; Gnostic Eschatology and the New Testament, Novum Testament (Journal) Vol XXI, No 2, 1970; Teachings of Silvanus from the Library of Nag Hammadi, Novum Testamentum, XIV, 3, 1972 (with J Zandee); Resurrection, Treatise on, The Interpreter's Dictionary of the Bible, 1976. *Honours:* Yale University Scholar, 1962–63; United Presbyterian Graduate Fellow, 1962–65; John Simon Guggenheim Fellow, 1971–72; Fulbright Travel Grant to Netherlands, 1972; Mellon-University House Fellowship, 1977, 1981; Lilly Faculty Fellowship, 1981. *Memberships:* American Academy of Religion; Society of Biblical Literature Section Chairman and the Bible; Institute for Antiquity and Christianity Claremont University. *Address:* 3918 Wenig Road, NE, Cedar Rapids, IA 52402, USA.

PEGGE, Cecil Denis, b. 7 Dec. 1902, Briton Ferry, Wales. Author; University teacher; Film maker; Researcher in film. m. (1) Adelaide Mary Keane, 1 son, (2) Brenda Margaret Barnett. *Education:* MA, Engineering tripos, Cambridge University, England. *Literary Appointments:* Judge of poetry including for Crabbe Memorial Prize; Lecturer in Literature and Poetry. *Publcations:* Contruction, novel, 1930; Bombay Riots, film scenario, 1932; Obsidian, poems, 1934; The Fire, poems, 1943; The Flying Bird, poems, 1955; Tribute, poems, 1966; Night View, selected poems, 1979. *Contributions to:* Blackwoods Magazine; Contemporary Review; Times Literary Supplement; New Statesman; Poetry Review; Poetry Australia; Outposts; Scrip; Envoi; Orbis; The New Humanist; Cambridge Review; Asimov's Science Fiction Magazine; Sight and Sound; University Film Journal; Quarterly of Film Radio and Television; Audio Visual Communication Review; Journal of Mental Science; Nature; Fear No More, anthology; British Broadcasting Corporation broadcasts. *Membership:* Society of Authors, UK. *Address:* c/o Barclays Bank PLC, Senet Street, Cambridge, England.

PEKARIK, Andrew Joseph, b. 8 Nov. 1946, Lebanon, Pennsylvania, USA. Museum Director. m. Julia Baldwin Meech, 4 Aug. 1972, Tokyo, Japan. *Education:* BA, Fordham University; MA, MPhil, PhD, Columbia University. *Publications:* Japanese Ceramics from Prehistoric Times to the Present, 1978; Japanese Lacquer, 1600–1900, 1980; Ukifune: Love in The Tale of Genji, editor/contributor, 1982. *Contributions:* The Cave Temples of Dunhuang, in, Archaeology, 1983. *Address:* The Asia Society, 725 Park Avenue, New York, NY 10021, USA.

PELLERIN, Gilles, b. 26 Apr. 1954, Shawinigan, Quebec, Canada. Editor of Nuit blanche (magazine). *Education:* Master in French Literature, Université Laval, Quebec. *Appointments:* Secretary of redaction Livres et auteurs quebecois, 1978–80; Secretary of redaction, Estuaire, 1981–82; Editor, Nuit blanche, 1985 to present; Secretary, Editions de l'Instant, 1985 to present. *Publication:* Les Sporadiques Adventures de Guillaume Untel, 1982. *Contributor to:* Nuit blanche; Livres et auteurs quebecois; Lettres quebecoise; La Nouvelle Barre du jour; Estuaire; Solaris; Imagine; Moebius; Jungle and Etudes francaise. *Address:* Gilles Pellerin, 444 rue Latourelle, app.3, Quebec, Canada G1R 1E2.

PELTON, Joseph N, b. 29 Oct. 1943, Tulsa, Oklahoma, USA. Expert, Satellite Communications. m. Eloise Christine Janssen, 10 Sep. 1965, Tulsa, 1 son, 2 daughters. *Education:* BS, Physics, University of Tulsa, 1965; MA, International Relations, New York University, 1967; PhD, Political Science, Georgetown University, 1972. *Literary Appointments:* Vice Chairman, Pacific Telecommunications Council Publications Committee; Editorial Boards, Space Policy, Telematics & Informatics. *Publications include:* Books written or edited: Global Communications Satellite Policy, 1974; Economic & Policy Problems in Satellite Communications, 1977; Global Talk, 1981; The INTELSAT Global Satellite System, 1984; In progress, Telepower: Life in the Future, Global Electronic Nerves: The East/West Telematics Reports. *Contributions to:* Books: Communications & The Future, 1982; The 1983 Satellite Communications Directory, 1983; Telecommunications in the Year 2000, 1983; Wideband Communications, 1983; World Communications: A Handbook, 1984; etc. Journals: Columbia Journal of World Business; English Education; Intermedia; Telematics & Informatics; etc. *Honours:* Literary Award, American Astronautics Society, 1982; Nomination, Pulitzer Prize, 1981. *Literary Agent:* Carol Mann. *Address:* c/o Carol Mann, 174 Pacific Street, Brooklyn, NY 11201, USA.

PENDER, Lydia (Kathleen), b. 29 June 1907, London, England. Writer for Children. m. Walter (Gatling Banks) Pender, 5 Mar. 1932, Sydney, Australia, 2 sons, 2 daughters. *Education:* Sydney University. *Publications:* Marbles in my Pocket (Verse) 1957; Barnaby and the Horses, 1961; revised 1980; Dan McDougall and the Bulldozer, 1963; Sharpur the Carpet Snake, 1967, revised 1982; Brown Paper Leaves (Verse), 1971; Barnaby and the Rocket, 1972; The Useless Donkeys, 1979; Morning Magpie (Verse), 1984. *Contributions to:* School Magazine, Education Department of New South Wales and similar papers in other States. Represented in over two dozen anthologies of verse and/or stories in Australia and overseas, and also in school readers, TV and radio. Verse often chosen for recitation at Eisteddfods and festivals; talks at seminars, sometimes published. *Honours:* Children's Book Council of Australia Book of the Year Awards: Sharpus the Carpet Snake – Highly Commended, 1968, Barnaby and the Rocket – Commended 1973, The Useless Donkeys – Commended 1980. *Memberships:* Australian Society of Authors; Children's Book Council of Australia (New South Wales Branch). *Address:* 10 Blenheim Road, Lindfield, New South Wales 2070, Australia.

PENEN, Virginie-Marguerite, b. 5 Dec. 1909, Uccle, Brussels, Belgium. Journalist, divorced, 1 son, 1 daughter. *Literary Appointments:* Founder and President, Founder and Bulletin Editor, Union Mondiale de las Presse Feminine; President, Association for Cultural and Tourism Documentation and Information; Board member, Trustee, Association of Belgian and Overseas Periodical Journalists; Active Member, French Section, Consultative Commission for Provision of Documents and Identification Passes for Members of Specialised Information Press. *Publications:* Petales de...Marguerite, poems; Cour de...Marguerite, poems. *Contributions to:* La Propriete Terrienne; La Lanterne; Bonnes soirees; Chez-nous; Libelle; La vie au Foyer; La semaine d'averbode; Femmes d'aujourd 'h[sc]oui; Quick. *Honours:* Chevalier, French Social Merit; Honorary member, Arts and Letters Section, University of Toronto; Chevalier de la Route, Via Secoura. *Memberships:* Association of Tourism Writers; Association of Walloon Writers; French-Speaking Writers; Honorary member, La Plume Libre. *Address:* 32 avenue de la Floride, 1180 Brussels, Belgium.

PENFOLD RAQUET, Bonita Susan, b. 19 Mar. 1950, Buffalo, New York, USA. Montessori teacher; Nanny. 2 daughters. *Education:* BA Communications and the Arts, Empire State College, Buffalo, New York, 1984; Currently studying for MA Writing, Lesley College Graduate School, Cambridg, Massachusetts, due 1986. *Publications include:* Anthologies: Lyrical Treasures: Classic and Modern, 1983; The American Muse, 1984; Lyrical Fiesta: A Poetry festival in Print, 1985; The Poet's Job: To Go Too Far, 1985. *Contributions to:* Earth's Daughters; Buffalo Spree; Arachne; Pudding; Slipstream; Common Ground; New Voices; Pure Light; Voices for Peace; Wayward Wind; Yellow Butterfly; Women's Quarterly Review; The Friend; Up Against The Wall, Mother. *Honours:* Special Recognition, Looking

Glass Poetry Chapbook Competition, Pudding Magazine, 1983; Honourable Mention, Editor's Choice Awards, Up Against The Wall, Mother, 1983. *Memberships:* Poets and Writers; Assistant programme coordinator, Niagara-Erie writers, 1984; Earth's Daughters Poetry Collective. *Address:* c/o 11385 Big Tree Road, East Aurora, NY 14052, USA.

PENMAN, Margaret Elizabeth, b. Toronto, Ontario, Canada. Writer/University Teacher. *Education:* BA, MA, Toronto University; PhD, University College, London, UK. *Publications:* Wheelchair, a burlesque play in Women Writers for Theatre, 1976; A Century of Service: History of the Toronto Public Library 1883–1983, 1983; New faces, chapter in Loyal She Remains, Bicentennial History of Ontario, 1984. *Contributions to:* Numerous articles and reviews in Canadian newspapers and magazines e.g. Toronto Star; Macleans; Chatelaine; Canadian Forum, French language theatre critic for, The Toronto Star, 1981–. *Honours:* Two Canada Council creative writing grants, 1969–70; Winner of Women Writers for Theatre Competition, 1976 sponsored by Playwrights Canadian International Women's Year. *Membership:* Playwrights Union of Canada. *Address:* Apt 17E 20 Prince Arthur Avenue, Toronto, Ontario, Canada M5R 1B1.

PENN, Emily Josephine. Teacher of Singing and Piano; Speaker. *Education:* College for the Visually Handicapped, Gipsy Hill, London, England; Royal Norma College graduating with LRAM Music and Board of EDucation's Certificate for Elementary School Teachers; Poetry Course, Hadley College, Ill, USA. *Appointments include:* Teacher of Singing and Piano; Speaker, various guilds and unions in neighbourhood. *Contributor to:* Lancashire Life; Sunday Companion; various braille magazines; two anthologies; Methodist Calendars. *Honours include:* Pomfrett Cup, 1972, 1973; McKenzie Cup, twice, both Preston Poets; Batty Cup, 1962, 1963, also 1979 with Simon Diamond Jubilee Award, both Lancashire Authors; City of Bradford Metropolitan Councils Cultural Activities Trophy, most outstanding poem in Wharfedale Music Festival, 1978; numerous Certificates and small prizes, Poetry. *Memberships:* International Poetry Society; Lancashire Authors' Association; Preston Poets Society. *Address:* Hertford House, Tarleton, Near Preston, Lancashire, England.

PENZI, James, b. 17 July 1952. *Publications:* Salt Rever, 1976; Cadences, 1981; C(air)ns, 1984; Fragments, 1985. *Contributions:* Poem-cards, Caligula Press, Strawberry Press; Anthologies including, Blues 10, ed. C H Ford & K Boyle 1981; Magazines, journals including, After Dark; Bitter Oleander; Contact II; Dodeca; Dream Helmet; Hydrant; Image; Kayak; Isthmus; Magic Changes; Montana Gothin; Mouth of the Dragon; Mundus Artium; Painted Bride; Thunder Mount Review; Whetstone. *Honours:* 1st Prize, Poetry, Philadelphia Writers Conference, 1972; Lila Acheson Fellowship, Playwriting, Juilliard, 1980; Pennsylvania Council Special Projects Grant, 1984; Award, Iolaire Arts Foundation Poetry Chapbook Competition, 1985; Fellowship, Playwriting, Pennsylvania Council, 1985. *Memberships:* Poets & Writers; Academy of American Poets; Dramatists Guild; Authors League of America. *Address:* 1326 Spruce Street, Apt 1905, Philadelphia, PA 19107, USA.

PENZIK NARELL, Irena, b. 17 Sep. 1923, Poland. Writer; Lecturer. m. Murray Narell, 29 June 1945, New York, USA, 2 sons. *Education:* BA English and Creative Writing, Columbia University. *Literary Appointments:* Editorial Board, Western States Jewish Historical Quarterly. *Publications:* Ashes To The Taste, autobiography, 1961; The Invisible Passage, short story collection, 1969; Joshua, Fighter for Bar Kochba, historical novel, 1978; Our City: The Jews of San Francisco, Historical non-fiction, 1981. *Contributions to:* Women's American ORT Magazine; Present Tense; Hadassah; Sh'ma; The Jewish Digest; Western States Jewish Historical Quarterly. *Honours:* Agnon Prize, 1956; National Jewish Book Award, 1979. *Memberships:* National Writers

Union; Institute for Historical Study. *Literary Agent:* McIntosh and Otis Inc, New York. *Address:* 5949 Estates Drive, Oakland, CA 94611, USA.

PEPER, George Frederick, b. 25 Jan. 1950, Nyack, New York, USA. Editor, Golf Magazine. m. Elizabeth Marshall White, 20 May 1978, Kansas City, Missouri, 2 sons. *Education:* BA, English, Princeton University; Graduate Work, Comparative Literature, Yale University Graduate School. *Publications:* Scrambling Golf, 1977; Golf's Supershots, 1982; Masters Annual, 1983, 84, 85; The PGA Championship, 1916–1984, 1985; Golf Courses of the PGA Tour, 1986. *Contributions to:* Golf Magazine. *Honour:* Nominated for National Magazine Award, 1984. *Membership:* American Society of Magazine Editors. *Address:* 159 River Road, Grandview, NY 10960, USA.

PEPPE, Rodney Darrell, b. 24 June 1934, Eastbourne, Sussex, England. Author: Artist. m. Tordis Tatjana Tekkel, 16 July 1960, London, 2 sons. *Education:* National Diploma in Art and Design, Illustration, London County Council Central School of Arts and Crafts. *Publications include:* The Alphabet Book, 1968; Circus Numbers, 1969; The House That Jack Built, 1970; Hey Riddle Diddle!, 1971; Simple Simon, 1972; Cat and Mouse, 1973; Odd One Out, 1974; Humpty Dumpty, 1975; The Henry Books, 4 titles, 1975; Picture Stories, 1976; Puzzle Book, 1977; Humphrey the Number Horse, 1978; Ten Little Bad Boys, 1978; Rodney Peppe's Moving Toys, 1980; Indoors and Outdoors, 1980; The Mice Who Lived in a Shoe, 1981; Run Rabbit Run, 1982; The Kettleship Pirates, 1983; The Little Toy Board Books, 5 titles, 1983; Make Your Own Paper Toys, 1984; Hello Henry and Hurrah for Henry, 1984; Rodney Peppe Block Books, 4 titles, 1985; The Mice and the Flying Basket, 1985. All books self-illustrated. *Contributions to:* Books for Your Children-Cover Artist Profiles, 1973, 81; Making First Books, 1978; Radio Times; Observer; Accent; Homes and Gardens. *Membership:* Society of Authors. *Address:* Cotchford House, Bramshott Chase, Hindhead, Surrey GU26 6DG, England.

PERCY, Herbert Roland, b. 6 Aug. 1920, Burham, Kent, England. Writer. m. Mary Davina James, 28 Mar. 1942, Neath, Glamorgan, Wales, 2 sons, 1 daughter. *Education:* RCN Preparatory School, Esquimalt, British Columbia, Canada; RN Engineering College, Manadon, Devon, England. *Literary Appointments:* Editor, Canadian Author and Bookman, 1963–65. *Publications:* The Timeless Island & Other Stories, 1960; Flotsam, 1978; Painted Ladies, 1983; A Model Lover, 1986. *Contributions to:* Numerous publications, including, Books in Canada; Heritage Canada; New Quarterly; Atlantic Insight; Ottawa Journal; Chitty's Law Journal; Canadian Army Journal; Nova Scotia Times. *Honours:* Nova Scotia Novel Award, 1975; Nominated for Governor General's Award, (Fiction), 1983; Canada Council Senior Arts Grant, 1985. *Memberships:* Writers' Union of Canada, (Membership Chairman); Writers' Federation of Nova Scotia, (Founding Chairman); Canadian Authors' Association; PEN International. *Literary Agent:* Bella Pomer. *Address:* The Moorings, Granville Ferry, Nova Scotia, BOS 1KO, Canada.

PEREIRA, Samuel Joseph, b. 17 Apr. 1949, Los Banos, California, USA. Store Manager. *Education:* BA, California State University, Fresno, 1971; MFA, University of Iowa, 1975. *Publications:* The Marriage of the Portuguese, 1978. *Contributor to:* Missouri Review; Poetry; Antioch Review; Ironwood; Telescope; Porch; Chowder Review; Raccoon; Sonora Review. *Address:* 1548 Canal Farm Lane # 1C, Los Banos, CA 93635, USA.

PEREIRA, Teresinha, b. 1 Nov. 1934, Writer. Professor of Literature and Theatre. *Education:* Faculdade de Filsofia de Minas Gerais, Brazil, 1953; PhD, Spanish, University of New Mexico, USA, 1972. *Literary Appointments include:* Visiting Assistant Professor of Portuguese, Georgetown University, Washington DC, 1973–74; Assistant Professor of Spanish and

Portuguese, University of Colorado, 1975–. *Publications:* As Lagrimas dos Mortos, 1973; Torre de Mitos, 1973; A Rosa no Tempo dans Cerejeiras em Flor, 1974; The Falcons Swoop in, 1975; Mauvais Sang, 1975; La Alegria esta en huelga, 1978; Sotto la Luna, 1979. *Contributions to:* Sin Nombre, Puerto Rico; Chasqui, USA; Vida Universitaria, Mexico; Jornal de Letras, Brazil; Comunidad, Mexico; International poetry Society Magazine, UK; Vendaval, Argentina; Real Poetry, Australia; Numerous others. *Honours include:* Poet of the Year, Canadian Society of Poets, 1977; Personalidade Literaria do Ano, Brazil, 1979. *Memberships include:* World Poetry Society; Associacion de Escritores de Mexico; Canadian Society of Poets; Society Argentina de Letras, Artes & Ciencias; Uniao Brasiliera de Trovadores. *Address:* Department of Spanish and Portuguese, University of Colorado, Boulder, CO 80309, USA.

PERKIN, Harold James, b. 1 Nov. 1926, Stoke-on-Trent, England. Social Historian. m. Joan Griffiths, 3 July 1948, Stoke-on-Trent, 1 son, 1 daughter. *Education:* BA, MA, Jesus College, University of Cambridge, England. *Literary Appointments:* Professor of History, Northwestern University, Evanston, Illinois, USA; (Concurrently) Honorary Visiting Professor of Social History, University of Lancaster, England. *Major Publications:* The Origins of Modern English Society 1780–1880, 1969; Key Profession, 1969; New Universities in the UK, 1969; The Age of the Railway, 1970; History: An Introduction for the Intending Student, 1970; The Age of the Automobile, 1976; The Structured Crowd, 1981. *Contributor to:* Various Journals. *Honours:* Gold Medal, Research Institute for Education, Tokyo, Japan. *Memberships:* Fellow, Royal Historical Society, 1969, Founding Chairman, Social History Society of UK, 1976, (Honorary Vice President, 1985). *Address:* Department of History, Northwestern University, Evanston, IL 60201, USA.

PERKINS, David Dodd, b. 25 Oct. 1928, Philadelphia, Pennsylvania, USA. Educator. *Education:* AB, Harvard, 1951; MA, 1952; PhD 1955. *Publications:* The Quest for Permanence: the Symbolism of Wordsworth, Shelley & Keats, 1959; Wordsworth & the Poetry of Sincerity, 1964; English Romantic Writers, 1967; A History of Modern Poetry in England & America, (Vol I), 1976; Editorial Advisor, Keats-Shelley Journal, 1962–. *Memberships:* MLA; Cambridge Science Club; Keats-Shelley Association; Byron Society. *Address:* Department of English, Harvard University, Cambridge, MA 02138, USA.

PERKINS, Dwight Heald, b. 20 Oct. 1934, Chicago, USA. Professor, Economics. m. Julie Anne Rate, 15 June 1957; Iowa City, 2 sons, 1 daughter. *Education:* BA, Cornell University, 1956; MA, 1961, PhD, 1964, Harvard University. *Publications:* Market Control and Planning in Communist China, 1966; Agricultural Development in China 1368–1968, 1969; China's Modern Economy in Historical Perspective, Editor, 1975; The Economic and Social Modernisation of Korea, co-author, 1980; The Economics of Development, co-author, 1983; Rural development in China, with S Yusuf, 1984. *Contributor to:* Over 50 journal articles, contributor to books, etc. *Address:* 64 Pinehurst Road, Belmont, MA 02178, USA.

PERKINS, George Burton, b. 16 Aug. 1930, USA. University Professor. m. Barbara Miller, 9 May 1964, Philadelphia, Pennsylvania, USA, 3 daughters. *Education:* AB, Tufts College, 1953; MA, Duke University, 1954; PhD, Cornell University, 1960. *Literary Appointments:* Teaching Assistant, Cornell University, 1955–57; Instructor, Washington University, 1957–60; Assistant Professor, Baldwin-Wallace College, 1960–63; Assistant Professor, Farleigh Dickinson University, 1963–66; Lecturer in American Literature, Edinburgh University, 1966–67; Professor, Eastern Michigan University 1967–; General Editor, Journal of Narrative technique, 1970–. *Publications:* Writing Clear Prose, 1964; The Theory of the American Novel, 1970; Realistic American Short Fiction, 1972; American

PoeticTheory, 1972; The American Tradition in Literature (with Bradley, Beatty, Long), 4th, 5th, 6th editions, 1974, 1981, 1985; The Practical Imagination (with Frye, Baker), 1981; The Harper Handbook to Literature (with Frye, Baker) 1985. *Contributions to:* Essays and reviews in Nineteenth-Century Fiction; Journal of American Folklore; The Dickensian, The New England Quarterly and other journals. Fiction in Descant. *Honours:* Duke University Fellow, 1953–54; Cornell University Fellow, 1954–55; Phi Kappa Phi, 1956; Distinguished Faculty Award, Eastern Michigan University, 1978; Fellow, Institute for Advanced Studies in the Humanities, Edinburgh University, 1981. *Memberships:* Modern Language Society of America; Founding Member, The Society for the Study of Narrative Literature. *Address:* 1316 King George Boulevard, Ann Arbor, MI 48104, USA.

PERKINS, Michael, b. 3 Nov. 1942, Lansing, Michigan, USA. Writer. m. Renie McCune (died June 1968), 20 June 1960, 1 son, 2 daughters. *Education:* BA, Ohio University at Athens, USA. *Literary Appointments:* Editor, Tompkins Square Press, Croton Press Ltd, Milky Way Productions; Ulster Arts Magazine. *Major Publications:* Evil Companions, 1968; The Secret Record, 1976; The Persistence of Desire, 1977. *Contributor to:* The Nation; The Village Voice; Mother Jones; and others. *Honours:* Poetry Panelist, 1985; Artists Fellowship, New York Foundation for the Arts; Poet-in-Residence, Crandall Library, Glens Falls, New York, 1985. *Memberships:* Authors Guild; National Book Critics Circle. *Literary Agent:* John Brockman Associates. *Address:* RR1 Box 56, Ohayo Montain Road, Glenford, NY 12433, USA.

PERRACHON, Alix Gudefin, b. 30 Apr. 1956, New York, USA. Freelance Writer; Editor. m. Jean Bernard Perrachon, 16 Sep. 1978, New York, 1 daughter. *Education:* Publishing Procedures Course, Harvard University, 1977; BA, International Relations, French Literature, University of Pennsylvania, 1977. *Appointments:* American Associate Editor, 1981–83, Contributing Editor, 1984–, Hali; Contributing Editor, The Oriental Rug Magazine, 1983–. *Publications:* Book Prefaces Etc. *Contributor to:* Numerous professional journals and magazines including: Antiques Monthly; Antique Collector; Antiques World; House & Garden; New York Times; The Vogue of the Chinese Carpet – The Peking and Tientsin Era Rediscovered, 1983, Romanian Kilims – A Decorative Blend of Trends Past and Present, 1983; Modern Chinese Carpets A Decorative Tour de Force, 1984, all in Hali – The International Journal of Oriental Carpets and Textiles'. *Honours:* Magna Cum Laude, University of Pennsylvania, 1977; Phi Beta Kappa, 1977. *Membership:* Editorial Freelancers Association. *Address:* 340 East 80th St – 9B, New York, NY 10021, USA.

PERREAU-SAUSSINE, Gerald, 1 Apr. 1938, Tokyo, Japan. Author. *Education:* BA, University of California at Los Angeles, USA; University of Fribourg; Georgetown University. *Major Publications:* That Cold Day in the Park, 1965; Angel Loves Nobody, 1967; The Moonbathers, 1974; Drink & Sing, 1980; The Prints of Paul Jacoulet, 1984. *Contributor to:* Poetry London – New York; Poetry Chicago; Odyssey. *Memberships:* American Academy of Poets; Writers Guild of America. *Honours:* W Recipient, Samuel Goldwyn Award, 1972, 1973. *Address:* 268 N Bowling Green Way, Los Angeles, CA 90049, USA.

PERRETT, Bryan, b. 9 July 1934, Liverpool, England. Author; Military Historian. m. Anne Catherine Trench, 13 Aug. 1966, Burscough. *Education:* Liverpool College. *Literary Appointments:* Defence Correspondent, Liverpool Echo, 1982 (Falklands War). *Publications include:* Author of some 24 books on armaments including: NATO Armour, 1970; The Churchill, 1973; Allied Tank Destroyers, 1979; Wavell's Offensive, 1979; The Panzerkampfwagen, III, 1980, IV, 1980; The Czar's British Squadron, 1981; The Tiger Tanks, 1981; Weapons of the Falklands Conflict, 1982; German Light Panzers, 1983; A History of Blitzkrieg,

1983, paperback edition as Lighting War, 1985; Mechanised Infantry, 1984; The Hawks – A Short History of the 14th/20th King's Hussars, 1984; Allied Tanks Italy World War II, 1985. *Contributions to:* Army Quartely; US Army Defence Review; Battle; War Monthly; Military Modelling; Born in Battle; Defence Update; War in Peace; The Elite; Military History. Chapters contributed: Elite Fighting Units, 1984; The Korean War-History and Tactics, 1984. Fiction scripts for IPC Battle Library. *Honours:* Territorial Decoration, 1970; Served in Royal Tank Regiment as Captain. *Memberships:* Royal United Services Institute; Royal Instituton of Great Britain. *Literary Agent:* Watson Little Limited. *Address:* 7 Maple Avenue, Burscough, nr Ormskirk, Lancashire, England.

PERRIN, Jim, b. 30 Mar. 1947, Manchester, England. Author. m. 2 sons, 1 daughter. *Literary Appointments:* Literary Editor, Diadem Books, 1981–82; Consultant Editor, High magazine, 1982. *Publications:* Cwm Silyn and Cwellyn, 1970; Wintour's Leap, 1971; Mirrors in the Cliffs, 1983; Menlove, 1985; On and Off the Rocks, 1986. *Contributions to:* The Guardian; The Observer; The New Statesman; The Countryman; 7 Days High; The Great Outdoors; Climber and Rambler; Crags; Mountain; Rocksport; Climbers' Club; Journal. *Honours:* Lewis Jones Prize, 1978; Boardman Tasker Prize, 1985. *Literary Agent:* Anthony Sheil (Anthony Sheil Associates Limited). *Address:* 1 College Road, Buxton, Derbyshire, SK17 9DZ, England.

PERRINE, Laurence, b. 13 Oct. 1915, Toronto, Canada. Retired University Teacher. m. Catherine Lee Stockard, 17 Sep. 1948, Dallas, Texas, USA, 2 sons. *Education:* BA 1937, MA 1939, Oberlin College; PhD, Yale University, 1948. *Publications:* Sound and Sense: An Intro to Poetry, 1956, 6th edition 1982; Story and Structure, 1959, 6th edition, 1983; Literature: Structure, Sound and Sense, 1970, 4th edition 1983; The Art of Total Relevance: Papers on Poetry, 1976. *Contributions to:* Notes, articles and poems in magazines and journals including: PMLA; American Literature; College English; Victorian Poetry; Philological Quarterly; Studies in Short Fiction; College Literature: The Explicator; Poetry; The Saturday Review; The New York Times: The Arlington Quarterly; Laurel Review; CEA Critic; Light Year '85 and '86. *Memberships:* The Texas Institute of Letters; President 1970–71, South Central Modern Language Association; President 1973–74, The (Texas) Conference of College Teachers of English. *Address:* 7617 Royal Place, Dallas, TX 75230, USA.

PERRY, Alan, b. Mar. 1942, Swansea, Wales. Teacher. m. Jean Morgan, 21 Aug, 1965, Cyrant, 2 sons. *Literary Publications:* Characters, 1969; Live Wires, 1970; Fires on the Common, 1975; Road Up and Other Stories, 1977; 55999 and other stories, 1979; Winter Bathing, 1980; Three Swansea Poets, 1985; Upside Down Roses, 1985; Rhyme, Wine and Worse, 1985; Time Pieces, 1985; U Turns, 1985; Messiah, 1985. *Contributions to:* Sunday Times; Poetry London/Apple Magazine; Urban Gorilla; Grosseteste Review; Honest Ulsterman; 2 Plus 2. *Honours:* Eric Gregory Award for Poetry, 1970; Welsh Arts Council Writer Bursary, 1977; Leslie Moore Award for Painting, 1978. *Address:* 76 Terrace Road, Mount Pleasant, Swansea, Wales.

PERRY, Erma, b. Winthrop, Massachusetts, USA. Journalist. m. Irving Chester Perry, 29 Apr. 1939, Wyncote, Pennsylvania, 1 son. *Education:* BA, Boston University; Postgraduate in Art, The Barnes Foundation, Merion, Pennsylvania. *Contributor to:* New York Times; Chicago Tribune; Los Angeles Times; Miami Herald; Amtrak Express; Prevention; Better Homes and Gardens; Copley News Syndicate, etc. *Honours:* Photojournalism awards: Egypt, 1979; Canada, 1980; Northern Ireland, First Prize, 1981; Canada, Grand Prize, 1983. *Memberships:* Society of American Travel Writers; American Society of Journalists and Authors; Bucks County Writers (President, 1970). *Address:* 134 Greenwood Avenue, Jenkintown, PA 19046, USA.

PERRY, Grace, b. 26 Jan. 1927, Melbourne, Australia. Poet; Editor; Publisher; Paediatrician; Livestock Breeder. m. Harry Kronenberg, 1951, 1 son, 2 daughters. *Education:* MB, BS (Sydney), 1950; ATCL, 1943. *Appointments:* Medical Practitioner, 1953–; Senior Paediatrician, Fairfield District Hospital, 1955–63; Physician, Renwick Hospital for Infants; Honorary Paediatrician, South Sydney Women's Hospital; Founder Head Press, 1964–; Founder, Editor, Poetry Australia, 1964–; Established Eidolon Stud, Berrima, 1972–. *Publications:* Red Scarf, 1963; Frozen Section, 1967; Two Houses, 1969; Black Swans at Berrima, 1972; Berrima Winter, 1974; Journal of a Surgeon's Wife, 1975; Snow in Summer, 1980. *Honours:* Literary Fellowship, 1973; Special Literary Grant, 1981. *Memberships:* ASA, Founder Member; Australian Simmental Breeders Association. *Address:* Eidolon, Berrima, NSW 2577, Australia.

PERRY, Marion J H, b. 2 June 1943, Takoma Park, Maryland, USA. Poet. m. Franklyn A H Perry, 17 July 1971, 1 son, 1 daughter. *Education:* MA 1966, MFA 1969, University of Iowa; MA Reading Specialist, 1979, PhD Eng. Inst. 1986, State University of New York at Buffalo. *Literary Appointments:* Instructor, Erie Community College; Associate Faculty, Empire State College. *Major Publications:* Icarus, 1980; The Mirror's Image, 1981; Establishing Intimacy, 1982. *Contributor to:* Intrepid; Buckle; Earth's Daughters; A Different Drummer; Poetry Section, Buffalo Evening News; Golden Fleece; The Coffee House; Black Mountain II Review. *Honours:* College Arts Contest, 1967; All Nations Poetry Contest, 1980, 1981; Serendipity, The Poem Finds its Place Contest, 1980. *Memberships:* Poets & Writers; Poetry Society of America. *Address:* Erie Community College, 4140 Southwestern Boulevard, Orchard Park, NY 14127, USA.

PERRY, Robin, b. 27 Dec. 1917, New York City, USA. Writer; Author. *Education:* US Army Command & General Staff College; Industrial College of the (US) Armed Forces; USAR Command School. *Publications include:* Over 250 articles and short stories, 8 books. The Woods Rider, 1973; The Road Rider, 1974; Creative Color Photography, 1975; The Trails Motorcyclist, 1975; Welcome for a Hero, novel, 1976; Photography for the Professionals, 1976; Creative Professional Photography, 1979; Shadows of the Mind, short stories, in press; The Toy Soldiers, in press. Works in progress: How to Build Your Own Home; The Creative Fiction Writer; How To Buy A Computer; Videography. *Contributions to:* Numerous magazines including: The New York Times; Popular Photography; Flying; Camara 35; Woman's Day; Time; Fortune; Life; Art Direction; Ad Art Techniques; Hasselblad; The Professional Photographer; International Photo Taknik, Germany; Foto, Germany, Italy; Writer's Digest, etc. Over 175 monthly articles for the, Dexter Bulletin. *Lectures:* Almost all national, regional, state photographic associations in Canada, USA & Europe. Taught writing workshops, own Creative Color Workshops. *Honours:* FIIP; FNPP; FRPS. *Address:* 30 Niantic River Road, Waterford, CT 06385, USA.

PERSEN, Richard Donald, b. 25 Jan. 1947, Suffern, New York, USA. Director, Communications. *Education:* BS, MS. *Literary Appointments:* Advertising Copy, Associate Creative Director, Stuart Williams Associates, Stamford, Connecticut, USA; Director, Communications, Analytical Assessment & Marketing Communications, Saddle Brook, New Jersey, USA. *Contributor to:* Medical Laboratory Observer; Diagnostic Medicine; Clinical Lab Products; Laboratory Medicine; Laboratory Management; American Clinical Products Review; Medical Economics; International Clinical Products Review; Clinical Chemistry; Clinical Chemistry News, with advertising copy and technical articles. *Honours:* Excellence in Medical Communication, Medical Economics Company; Associate Creative Director, Damon Diagnostics Reference Laboratories; Biomedical Marketing Association, 1985; Awards, 1st Place: Campaigns; 2nd Place: Collateral Materials. *Memberships:* American Medical Writers' Association. *Literary Agent:*

Analytical Assessment & Marketing Communications. *Address:* 147-A S, Main Street, New York City, NY 10956, USA.

PERSICO, Joseph E, b. 19 July, 1930, USA. Writer. m. Sylvia la Vista, 23 March, 1959, Gloversville, New York, USA. 2 daughters. *Education:* BA, State University of New York, USA. *Publications:* My Enemy, My Brother: Men and Days of Gettysburg, 1977; Piercing the Reich, 1979; The Spider Web, 1980; The Imperial Rockefeller, 1982. *Contributions to:* American Heritage; Parade. *Honour:* Best Book on Intelligence, National Intelligence Society, 1979. *Memberships:* PEN; Authors' Guild. *Literary Agent:* Clyde Taylor, Curtis Brown Ltd. *Address:* PO Box 108, Albany, NY 12260, USA.

PERSSON, (Nils) Bertil (Alexander), b. 10 Nov. 1941, Trelleborg, Sweden, Professor; Headmaster; Author. *Education:* MA, 1965; LittB, 1970; EdM, 1972; DD (USA), 1974; ODhc (Nigeria), 1974; DDSC (USA); DDhc, 1982; D TH hc (India), 1985. *Publications:* Cults, Sects, Congregations, 1970; Voices of the East: Anthology on the struggle of the believers in USSR, 1974; Religious Minorities in the Soviet Union, 1974; From the Language of Jesus, 1975; Christian Faith and Way of Life, 1975; The Life and You, 1976; Editor-in-Chief, Religion and Culture; Assyriernas kyrktillhorighet, 1977; Religionsboken, 1978, 82, 86; Aramaic Idioms of Eshop (Jesus) Explained, 1978; Världsreligionerhas gudsbegrepp, 1985. *Memberships:* Swedish Union of Authors; St Ephrem's Institute, Switzerland; Syriac Academy, iraq, 1976; Norwegian Orientalic Fellowship, 1980; Aramaic Bible Centre, 1977; Odd Fellow Order, 19700; European Secretary, The Vilatte Guild, 1979; Knight Sovereign order of St John of Jerusalem, 1980; Senato of High Court of Justice for World Security International Tribunal of International Parliament for Safety and Peace, 1981; National Chancellor, International Association of Education for World Peace; New York Academy of Science, 1982; Fellow Royal Society of Arts, London, 19082; Academic Adviser, Centre International de Recherches Universitaires, Belgium, 1984; Representative for Northern Europe of International University, 1984; Professor, Central School of Religion, England, 1984; Headmaster, Enskilde Gymnasisth Carlssons Hogstadieskola, Stockholm, 1983. *Address:* P O Box 7048, S 17107, Solna, Sweden.

PERTWEE, Michael H R, b. 24 Apr. 1916, London, England. Screenwriter; Playwright; Author. *Publications:* Name Dropping, autobiography, 1974; Plays: Death on the Table, (with Guy Beauchamp), 1938; The Paragon, (co-author), 1948; It's Different for Men, 1953; Four Musketeers, (co-author), 1967; She's Done It Again, 1969; Don't Just Lie There, Say Something, 1971; A Bit Between The Teeth, 1973; Birds of Paradise, (adaptor, 1973; Sextet, 1978; Find The Lady, 1979; A Bit on the Side, 1984; Look No Hans, (co-author), 1984; Films: Laughter in Paradise; Happy Ever After; The Naked Truth; Strange Bedfellows; A Funny Thing Happened On The Way To The Forum; Salt and Pepper; One More Time. *Literary Agent:* Richard Stone. *Address:* 34 Aylestone Avenue, London NW6 7AA, England.

PESETSKY, Bette, b. 16 Nov. 1932, Wisconsin, USA. Writer. m. Irwin Pesetsky, 25 Feb. 1956, Iowa City, 1 son. *Education:* BA, Washington University; MFA, State University of Iowa. *Publications:* Stories Up to A Point, 1982; Author from a Savage People, 1983; Digs, 1984. *Contributor to:* Vogue; Vanity Fair; Ontario Review; Ms; Antaeus. *Honours:* Literary Fellowship, National Endowment for the Arts, 1979–80; CAPS Fellowship, New York State Council for the Arts, 1980. *Memberships:* PEN; Author's Guild. *Literary Agent:* Goodman Associates. *Address:* Hilltop Park, Dobbs Ferry, NY 10522, USA.

PESSEN, Edward, b. 31 Dec. 1920, New York, USA. Historian, Author. m. Adele Barlin, 25 Nov. 1940, Brooklyn, New York, 2 sons, 3 daughters. *Education:* BA, 1947, MA, 1948, PhD, 1954, Columbia University, New York, USA. *Literary Appointments:* City College of New York, 1948–54; Fisk University, Nashville, Tennessee, 1954–56; Staten Island Community College, 1956–70; Baruch College and Graduate School & University Centre, City University of New York, 1970–. *Major Publications:* Most Uncommon Jacksonians, 1967; Jacksonian America: Society, Personality & Politics, 1969, revised edition, 1978; Riches, Class & Power before the Civil War, 1973; Three Centuries of Social Mobility in America, 1974; The Log Cabin Myth: Social Backgrounds of the Presidents, 1984. *Contributor to:* Journal of American History; American Historical Review. *Honours:* National Book Award Finalist, 1974; Guggenheim Foundation Fellowship, 1977; Rockefeller Foundation Fellow, 1978; Fulbright Lecturer, Moscow State University, USSR, 1985. *Memberships:* President, Society of Historians of the Early American Republic, 1985–86; American Historical Association; American Antiquarian Society; Organisation of American Historians; Southern Historical Association. *Address:* City University of New York, 17 Lexington Avenue, New York, NY 10010, USA.

PETERKIEWICZ, Jerzy, b. 1916, Poland. Professor of Polish Language and Literature, University of London, England. *Education:* Dlugosz School, Wloclawek; Universities of Warsaw and St Andrews, Kings College, University of London, England. *Publications:* The Knoted Cord, 1953; Loot and Loyalty, 1955; Polish Prose and Verse, 1956, 70; Antologia liryki angielskiej, 1958; Future to Let, 1958; Isolation, 1959; Five Centuries of Polish Poetry, 1960; OUP, 1970, 79; Quick and the Dead, 1961; That Angel Burning at My Left Side, 1963; Inner Circle, 1966; Poematy londynskie, 1965; Green Flows the Bile, 1969; Other Side of Silence, 1970; Third Adam, 1975; Easter Vigil and Other Poems, Editor and translator of work by Karol Wojtyla, 1979; Kula Majiczna, Selected Poems 1934–54, 1980; Collected Poems, by Karol Wojtyla (Pope John Paul II), Editor and translator, 1982. *Contributions to:* Sunday Times; Times Literary Supplement; London Magazine; The Listener; Slavonic Review; 20th Century; Encounter; Botteghe Obscure; New Lit History; Kultura. *Address:* 7 Lyndhurst Terrace, London NW3, England.

PETERS, Anne Mary, Poet. *Education:* Literary courses, Universities of New York and Oklahoma, USA. *Appointments:* Director, Allied Forces Contre, Salisbury, Wiltshire, England during World War II; Owner & Manager, Speciality Department Store, Boston, Massachusetts, USA. *Major Publications:* Poetry included in anthologies, including: Poetry Today (USA), 1964; Gardener's Book of Verse (USA), 1966; Collected poems in Rings of Green, 1982. *Contributor to:* Irish Press; Spirit Magazine; America Magazine, Manifold. *Memberships:* Poetry Society of America; Craftmen's Group, New York, USA; Poetry Society, United Kingdom; Poetry Society, Ireland. *Address:* 5 William Orchard Close, Old Headington, Oxford OX3 9DR, England.

PETERS, Margot McCullough, b. 13 May 1933, Wausau, Wisconsin, USA. Biographer; Professor of English, University of Wisconsin-Whitewater. m. Peter Ridgway Jordan. *Education:* BA, MA, PhD, University of Wisconsin, Madison, 1969. *Publications:* Charlotte Bronte: Style in the Novel, 1973; Unquiet Soul: A Biography of Charlotte Bronte, 1975; Bernard Shaw and the Actresses, 1980; Mrs Pat: The Life of Mrs Patrick Campbell, 1984. *Contributions to:* Southwest Review; The Chronicle of Higher Education; Journal of Communication; British Studies Monitor; Language and Style; Biography; The Annual of Bernard Shaw Studies; Harvard Magazine. *Honours:* Award for Best Work of Prose, Friends of American Writers, 1000, 1975; Fellow, American Council of Learned Societies, 1976–77; Best Theatre Book, Freedley Award, 1980, 84; Banta Award, 1980, 85. *Memberships:* Shaw Society; Authors Guild; Modern Language Association; Womens Caucus for the Modern Languages; Bronte Society. *Address:* 511 College Street, Lake Mills, WI 53551, USA.

PETERS, Robert Louis, b. 20 Oct. 1924, Wisconsin, USA. Poet; Critic; Actor; Professor of Literature. 3 sons, 1 daughter. *Education:* BA, 1948; MA, 1949; PhD, 1952. *Literary Appointments:* Fellowships to Yaddo and MacDowell Colonies. *Publications:* The Crowns of Apollo: Swinburne's Principles of Literature and Art, 1965; Songs for a Son, 1967, (Poems); The Gift to be Simple, 1975, (Poems): The Great American Poetry Bake-Off: First and Second Series, 1979, 1985; What Dillinger Meant to Me, 1984; Hawker, 1984; Brueghel's Pig, 1985; The Peters Black and Blue Guide to Current Literary Periodicals, 1983, 1985. *Contributions to:* American Book Review; Sulfur; Poetry Now; Contact II; Electrum; New Letters; Pulpsmith; Prairie Schooner; Gay Sunshine; Western Humanities Review; and numerous others. *Honours:* Guggenheim Fellow, 1966–67; NEA Fellowship, 1974; Alice Faye de Castagnoca Prize, 1984; Larry P Fine Award for Criticism, 1985. *Memberships:* PEN; Authors' Guild; Poetry Society of America. *Address:* Department of English, University of California, Irvine, CA 92717, USA.

PETERSEN, P(eter) J(ames), b. 23 Oct. 1941, Santa Rosa, California, USA. Writer; Teacher. m. Marian Braun, 6 July 1964, San Mateo, 2 daughters. *Education:* AB, Stanford University; MA, San Francisco State University; PhD, University of New Mexico. *Appointment:* English Instructor, Shasta College. *Publications:* Would you Settle for Improbable, 1981; Nobody Else Can Walk It For You, 1982; The Boll Weevil Express, 1983; Here's to the Sophomores, 1984; Corky & the Brothers Cool, 1985. *Honour:* Fellow, National Endowment for the Humanities, 1976–77. *Membership:* Society of Children's Book Writers. *Literary Agent:* Ellen Levine Inc. *Address:* 1243 Pueblo Court, Redding, CA 96001, USA.

PETERSON, Bruce Henry, b. 21 Sep. 1918, Sydney, Australia. Consultant Psychiatrist. *Education:* MB, BS, Sydney University, 1941; Dip Psych Med, Sydney University, 1952; Fellow, Royal Australian and New Zealand College of Psychiatrists, 1963. *Publications:* The Voices of Conscience (intervarsity Fellowship), 1967; Understanding Psychosexual Development (Family Life Movement), 1970; Growing in Love and Sex, (Family Life Movement), 1981. *Contributor to:* Australian Journal of Sex, Marriage & Family, Editor 1980; Medical Journal of Australia; Australian and New Zealand Journal of Psychiatry. *Memberships:* Royal Australian and New Zealand College of Psychiatrists, President 1972, Treasurer 1963–70; Family Life Movement of Australia, President 1963–65. *Address:* 5 Aspinall Pl, Woolwich, NSW 2110, Australia.

PETERSON, Edward Norman, b. 27 Aug. 1925, St Joseph, Missouri, USA. Professor. m. Ursula Martha Schmidt, 29 Aug. 1946, Hersfeld, 2 sons. *Education:* BA, 1950, MA, 1951, PhD, 1953, University of Wisconsin. *Appointments:* Professor, History, University of Wisconsin, River Falls, 1954–. *Publications:* Hjalmar Schacht – For and Against, Hitler, 1954; Limits of Hitler's Power, 1969; US Occupation of Germany, 1978. *Contributor to:* Social Research; Der Staat; Book Reviews: American Historical Review; Journal of Contemporary History. *Honours:* Phi Beta Kappa, 1950; Alexander V Humboldt Graht 1963–74, 1966, 1970; National Endowment of Humanities Award, 1969; Social Science Research Council Award, 1970. *Address:* 936 W Maple St, River Falls, WI 54022, USA.

PETERSON, Franklynn, b. 25 May 1938, Phillips, Wisconsin, USA. Communicator (Computers). 2 sons, 1 daughter. *Education:* BS, Sociology, University of Wisconsin. *Publications:* Handbook of Lawn Mower Repair, 1973, 78; The Build-It-Yourself Furniture Catalog, 1976; How to Fix Damn Near Everything, 1977; Co-author Judi Kesselman-Turkel: The Do-It-Yourself Custom Van Book, 1977; Eat Anything Exercise Diet (co-author Dr Frank Konishi), 1979; Handbook of Snowmobile Maintenance and Repair, 1979; Good Writing, (textbook), 1980; Test-Taking Strategies, 1981; Study Smarts, 1981; Homeowner's Book of Lists, 1981; How To Improve Damn Near

Everything Around Your Home, 1981; Research Shortcuts, 1982; Magazine Writer's Handbook, 1982; Author's Handbook, 1982 and many others. For Children: Vans, 1979; I Can Use Tools, 1981. *Contributions to:* Magazines, etc. including: True; Ramparts; Mankind; Science and Mechanics; Holiday Inn Magazine; Writer's Digest; Popular Science; Omni; Fortune; Parade; Numerous newspaper articles; Author of continuing internationally syndicated computer column, The Business Computer, in more than 85 newspapers, 1983–. *Honours:* National Conference of Christians and Jews Brotherhood in Media Award, 1968; American Optometric Association, Journalism Award, 1971; Jesse H Neal Award of American Business Press Association; Citation for Excellence in Consumer Journalism, National Press Club, 1984–. *Memberships:* American Society of Journalists and Authors (Vice-President, 1974–75; Co-Chair, Annual Nonfiction Writers Conference, 1978–82); Authors Guild. *Address:* P/K Associates Incorporated, 4343 West Beltline Highway, Madison, WI 53711, USA.

PETERSON, Kenneth Curtis Jr, b. 20 May, 1941, St Paul, Minnesota, USA. Editor. m. Deborah Ann Swan, 8 Apr. 1961, 2 sons, 1 daughter. *Literary Appointments:* Editor, Contact, 1977; Editor, Marriage Encounter, 1984. *Memberships:* Treasurer, International Association of Business Communicators, 1981. *Literary Agent:* Kethleen Kelley. *Address:* Forest Lake, MN, USA.

PETERSON, Levi Savage, b. 13 Dec. 1933, Snowflake, Arizona, USA. Professor of English, Weber State College. m. Althea Sand, 31 Aug. 1958, Orem, Utah, 1 daughter. *Education:* BA, English, 1958, MA, English, 1960, Brigham Young University; PhD, English, University of Utah, 1965. *Publications:* The Canyons of Grace, (short stories), 1982; Greening Wheat: Fifteen Mormon Short Stories, (Edited with Introduction), 1983. *Contributions to:* Western American Literature; Journal of Mormon History, Sunstone. *Honours:* First Prize, collection of short stories, The Confessions of Augustine, 1978; Short Story Award for The Canyons of Grace, Association for Mormon Letters, 1982; Special Editing Award for Greening Wheat, Association for Mormon Letters, 1983. *Address:* 1561 25th Street, Ogden, UT 84401, USA.

PETERSON, Lorraine Joyce, b. 10 July 1940, Red Wing, Minnesota, USA. Teacher. *Education:* BA, History, North Park College, Chicago; Certificate, Teaching as a Second Language, Institute Cultural Guadalajara, Mexico. *Publications:* If God Loves Me, Why Can't I Get My Locker Open? 1980; Falling Off Cloud Nine and Other High Places, 1981; Why Isn't God Giving Cash Prizes?, 1982; Teacher's Guide: If God Loves Me Why Can't I Get My Locker Open? 1983; Real Characters in the Making, 1985. *Honour:* Gold Medallion Book Award of 1984 for Why Isn't God Giving Cash Prizes? presented by the Evangelical Christian Publishers Association. *Literary Agent:* Bethany House Publishers, Minneapolis, Minnesota. *Address:* c/o Bertil Peterson, 2465 Londin Lane, Maplewood, MN 55119, USA.

PETESCH, Natalie L M, b. Detroit, Michigan, USA. Author, University Professor. m. Donald Anthony Petesch, 30 Aug. 1959, Austin, Texas, 1 son, 1 daughter. *Education:* BS magna cum laude, Boston University, 1955; MA, Brandeis University, 1956; PhD, University of Texas at Austin, 1962. *Literary Appointments:* University of Texas at Austin, 1959–60; San Francisco State University, 1961; Distinguished Visiting Professor, University of Idaho, 1982. *Publications:* After The First Death There Is No Other, 1974; The Odyssey of Katinou Kalokovich, 1974 and 1979; Seasons Such As These: 2 novels – The Long Hot Summers of Yasha K, and The Leprosarium, 1979; Soul Clap Its Hands and Sing, 1981; Duncan's Colony, 1982; Wild With All Regret, 1986. *Contributions to:* Anthologies and journals including: Different Drummers: A College Anthology, 1973; Fiction Omnibus; California Quarterly. *Honours:* The Iowa School of Letters Award for Short Fiction, 1974; Kansas Quarterly Fiction Award, 1976; The New Letters

Summer Prize Book Award, 1978; The Louisville Review First Prize for Fiction, 1978; Fellowship in Literature, Pensylvania Council on the Arts, 1980; Twice nominated for a Governor's Award for Excellence in the Arts; Winner 1984, Swallow's Tale Short Fiction for, Wild with All Regret. *Address:* 6320 Crombie Street, Pittsburgh, PA 15217, USA.

PETIT, Gaston, b. 16 Aug. 1930, Shawinigan, Quebec Province, Canada. Catholic Priest (Dominican); Artist. *Education:* Degrees in Philosophy and Theology. *Publications:* 44 Modern Japanese Print Artists, 1973; Gendai Hanga, 1974; Japanese Woodblock Printmaking: Evolving Techniques, 1977; Publisher: Kodansha International; QWERTYUIOPLKJHGFDSA-ZXCVBNM; editor, Chikus bin Shuppan, Tokyo, 1979. *Contributor to:* Nouvelles de l'Estampe; Paris; Nibliotheque Nationale; Hemisphere (Asian-Australian Monthly); Asian Pacific Quarterly; Seoul; Hanga Geijustus, Tokyo; Solidaridad, Manila. *Address:* 13 18 Nampeidai, Shibuya-Ku, Tokyo 150, Japan.

PETRAS, John William, b. 17 Feb. 1940, Ashland, Wisconsin, USA. Professor and Counselor. m. Laura C Gourlay, 4 Oct, 1984, New York State, 1 son, 1 daughter. *Education:* BA, Northlands College, Ashland, 1962; MA 1964, PhD 1966, University of Connecticut, Storrs, Connecticut; MA, Central Michigan University, Mount Pleasant, Michigan, 1982. *Literary Appointment:* Editor, Sociological Focus, 1971–74. *Publications:* George H Mead Essays, 1968; Sociology of Knowledge, 1970; Sexuality in Society, 1972; Seximale/Gender: Masculine, 1975; Symbolic Interactionism, 1975; Social Meaning of Human Sexuality, 1978; Learning About Sex, 1978; Learning About Sexual Abuse, 1985. *Contributions to:* Numerous magazines and journals. *Honour:* Outstanding Science Trade Book for Children, National Science Teachers Association, 1978. *Address:* 3021/2 E Chipperon Street, Mount Pleasant, MI 48858, USA.

PETRIDES, Avra, b. New York City, USA. Actress; Producer. *Publications:* Author, Series of 8 Plays; Plays Produced in New York 1970–77 include: On the Rocks; The Bloom is off Mr Rose; The Dirty Old Man; High Time; In the Dark; The Tree Piece Band; Phoebus; Luminous Grey. *Membership:* New Dramatists. *Literary Agent:* Charles Hunt, New York City. *Address:* 101 W 78th St, New York, NY 10024, USA.

PETROSKI, Catherine, b. 7 Sep. 1939, St Louis, Missouri, USA. Writer. m. Henry Petroski, 15 July 1966, Urbana, Illinois, 1 son, 1 daughter. *Education:* BA, MacMurray College; MA; University of Illinois. *Literary Appointments:* Writer-in-Residence, Illinois Arts Council, 1976–78. Fellow: Corporation of Yaddo, 1980, 84; Bread Loaf Writers Conference, 1982. *Publications:* Gravity and Other Stories, 1981; Beautiful My Mane in the Wind, 1982; Lady's Day, 1983; The Summer That Lasted Forever, 1984. *Contributions to:* North American Review; Prairie Schooner; Ms Magazine; New Directions in Poetry and Prose; numerous other magazines, anthologies and newspapers. *Honours:* Berlin Prize, 1961; John Crowe Ransom Prize, 1974; Texas Institute of Letters Prize, 1976; Creative Writing Fellowship, National Endowment for the Arts, 1978–79, 1983–84; DLit, MacMurray College, 1984, American Association University Women Literature Prize, 1985. *Membership:* Authors Guild Incorporated. *Literary Agent:* Ellen Levine Literary Agency Incorporated. *Address:* 2501 Perkins Road, Durham, NC 27706, USA.

PETROVSKA, Marija, b. Yugoslavia. Professor of French, Italian, & Comparative Literature. *Education:* Diploma, Institut des Hautes Etudes d'Interprétariat, Milan, Italy; MA, French, University of Tennessee, USA; PhD, French, University of Kentucky. *Publications:* Victor Hugo: l'Ecrivain engagé en Bohême, 1977; Prague Diptych, novel, 1980; Merope: The Dramatic Impact of a Myth, 1984; A Brief Anthology of French Poetry, editor, 1985. *Contributions to:* Various French & US literary journals. *Honours:* Fulbright Nominee, 1984;

Various university research grants; Invited lecturer, University of Ghent, Belgium, 1978; Visiting Professor of Italian, Indiana University of Pennsylvania, 1984–85. *Address:* 3617 Southwood Drive, Knoxville, TN 37920, USA.

PETRY, Ann, b. 12 Oct. 1908, Old Saybrook, Connecticut, USA. Author. m. George D Petry, 22 Feb. 1938, Old Saybrook, USA, 1 daughter. *Education:* PhS, School of Pharmacy, University of Connecticut, USA, 1931; Honorary Doctor of Letters, Suffolk University, 1983. *Publications:* The Street, 1946; Country Place, 1947; The Narrows, 1953; Harriet Tubman, 1955; Tituba of Salem Village, 1964; Miss Muriel and Other Stories, 1971. *Contributions to:* The New Yorker; Red Book. *Honours:* Houghton Mifflin Literary Fellowship, 1946. *Memberships:* Authors' League; Authors' Guide; American PEN. *Literary Agent:* Russell and Volkening Inc. *Address:* 113 Old Boston Post Road, Old Saybrook, CT 06475, USA.

PETRY, Carl F, b. 29 June 1943, Camden, New Jersey, USA. University Professor. *Education:* BA, Carleton College, Minnesota, 1965; MA, 1966, PhD, 1974, The University of Michigan. *Literary Appointments:* Assistant Professor, 1974–80, Associate Profesor, 1980–, Department of History, Northwestern University, Evanston, Illinois. *Publication:* The Civilian Elite of Cairo in the Later Middle Ages, 1981. *Contributions to:* Geographic Origins of the Civil Judiciary of Cairo during the Fifteenth Century, Journal of the Economic and Social History of the Orient, 1978; three subsequent articles in this series in the same journal, A Paradox of Patronage under the Mamluks, The Muslim World. *Honours:* Phi Beta Kappa, 1965; Woodrow Wilson Graduate Fellowship, 1966; National Science Foundation Dissertation Grant, 1972; Research Grants from the American Research Center in Egypt, 1970, 1980 (funded by the NEH) 1985 (funded by the USIA). *Memberships:* Medieval Academy of America; Middle East Studies Association (program committee 1979, 1983); American Historical Association; American Research Center in Egypt, (Islamic studies editor, Journal of American Research Center in Egypt). *Address:* Department of History, Northwestern University, Evanston, IL 60201, USA.

PETTIFER, James Milward, b. 6 Apr. 1949, Hereford, England. Playwright. m. Susan Ann Comely, 1 June 1974, Oxford, 1 son, 1 daughter. *Education:* BA, Honours, English Language and Literature, Hertford College, Oxford University, 1970. *Publications:* Stage Plays: The Blood on the Marsh; Bad Dream in an Old Hotel, 1978; The Wally, 1981; The Other Side, 1981; Go Go; The Bezzle, 1984; The Pale Horseman, 1984; God Keep Lead Out of Me, with Oliver Ford Davies; Novel, The Escape from Sleen House. *Contributor to:* The Stage; Screen; New Statesman; Cork Examiner; Sanity. *Memberships:* Writers Guild of Great Britain, Theatre Committee Member, Campaign for Nuclear Disarmament; Greenpeace. *Literary Agent:* Judy Daish Associates. *Address:* c/o Judy Daish Associates, 83 Eastbourne Mews, London W2 6LQ, England.

PETTIT, Stephen Lewis Ingham, b. 25 Feb. 1921. Retired Company Director; Ex-RAF Volunteer Reserve Wartime Flying Officer (Pilot). *Education:* Brighton College, Sussex, England; RAF College, Cranwell. *Literary Apointments:* Writer; Antologist; Poet; Adjunctor; Lecturer, *Publications:* The Peregrine Instant, 1967; In The Desert of Time, 1969; For a Moment of Time, 1971; Arthur, King of the Britons, 1971; Anthology of the Wye Valley, 1973. *Contributor to:* Poesia Vivante, Geneva; Quill; Breakthru; Platform; The Pilot; Contrasts; Pause; Mofussil; Paperway-Oyster; Dean Forest Guardian; Anglo-Welsh Review; Envoi; Scrip; Rainbow; Viewpoints; various other anthologies and magazines. *Honours include:* Numerous Certificates of Merit; Sovereign's Commendation for Valuable Service in the Air, 1945; Known as The Poet of the Wye Valley; First Prize, Wilfrid M Appleby Silver Cup, Cheltenham, 1971; First Prize, Dr O.Lamming Memorial Award, Isle of Man, 1973 and First Prize,

1984. *Memberships:* Poetry Society of Cheltenham, President; International Poetry Society, Founder, Fellow; The Royal Institute of Philosophy, London; Isle of Man Literary Society. *Address:* The Old Vicarage, May Hill, Ramsey, Isle of Man, British Isles.

PETZOLD, Paul Marcus, b. 12 Sep. 1940, Epsom, Surrey, England. Publishing Director. *Education:* Polytechnic; Regent School of Photography. *Publications:* All in One Cine Book, 1969; Light on People, 1971; Work of the Motion Picture Cameraman (with Freddie Young), 1972; Effects & Experiments in Photography, 1973; Photoguide to Movie Making, 1975; Filming for Television (with A A Englander), 1976; Photoguide to Low Light Photography, 1976; Photoguide to Lighting, 1977; Focal Book of Practical Photography, 1980. *Contributions to:* Photoguide Magazine, (editor, 1962–64); Focal Pictorial Cyclopaedia of Photography, (joint editor, 1967); Cinematography books, Focal Press (editor, 1968–); Petzold/Element, Director, 1981–. *Address:* 4a Alexandra Mansions, West End Lane, London NW6 1LU, England.

PEYTON, Kathleen Wendy, b. 2 Aug. 1929, Birmingham, England. Writer. m. Michael Peyton, 2 Sep. 1950, London, 2 daughters. *Education:* ATD. *Publications:* Numerous books including: Flambards (Trilogy), 1967; The Edge of the Cloud, 1969; Flambards in Summer, 1969; A Midsummer Night's Death, 1978; Marion's Angels, 1979; Flambards Divided, 1981; Dear Fred, 1981; Going Home, 1983; Foggetts Revenge, 1985. *Honours:* Carnegie Medal, 1969; Guardian Award, 1970. *Membership:* Society of Authors. *Address:* Rookery Cottage, North Fambridge, Chelmsford, Essex CM3 6LP, England.

PFEFFER, Jeffrey, b. 23 July 1946, St Louis, Missouri, USA. Professor. *Education:* BS 1968, MS 1968, Carnegie-Mellon University; PhD, Stanford University, 1972. *Publications:* Organizational Design, 1978; The External Control of Organizations: A Resource Dependence Perspective (with G R Salancik), 1978; Power in Organizations, 1981; Organizations & Organization Theory, 1982. *Contributions:* Over 60 articles, book chapters. *Honour:* George R Terry Book Award, Academy of Management, 1984. *Address:* Graduate School of Business, Stanford University, Stanford, CA 94305, USA.

PFEIFER, Luanne, b. 27 Nov. 1928, Tampa, Florida, USA. Journalist. m. James Wayne Pfeifer, 13 Aug. 1955, Malibu, 1 son, 2 daughters. *Education:* BSc, Seattle University; Fellowship, Tuffs University. *Appointments:* Sports Columnist, Santa Monica Evening Outlook; Sports Writer, Los Angeles Times; Senior Editor, World Travel Magazine; Stringer, Times-Mirror Magazines. *Publications:* Ski California, 1980; The Malibu Story, 1985. *Contributor to:* Westways; Teen; Intro; Valley; Sports Illustrated; West; Ski; Ski Business; Western World; Inflight; Travel Sections, Metropolitan Newspapers. *Honours:* United States Ski Writers Award, 1968; William B Berry Writing Award, 1967 and 1983; National Endowment of Humanities Journalism Fellowship Recipient, 1978. *Memberships:* Ski Writers Association of Southern California; United States Ski Writers Association; American Society of Journalists & Authors. *Address:* Atelier 1032, Sun Valley, ID 83340, USA.

PFEIFFER, Hans, b. 22 Feb. 1925, Schweidnitz, German Democratic Republic. Professor of Drama. *Education:* Graduate in Philosophy (Diplom-Phil), Karl Marx University, Leipzig, German Democratic Republic. *Major Publications:* Begriff und Bild: Heines philosophische und ästhetische Ansichten, 1958; Die Mumie im Glassarg: Bemerkungen zur Kriminalliteratur, 1960; Plädoyers, 1970; Die Sprache der Toten, 1968; Die Spuren der Toten, 1977; Thomas Müntzer: Ein biografischer Roman, 1975; Phantasiemorde, 1985; Numerous television films and Radio Plays. *Honours:* Arts Prize, City of Leipzig; Golden Laurel Award, GDR Television; Theodor Körner Prize; National Prize for Art & Literature. *Membership:* Writers' Association of the

GDR. *Address:* 7010 Leipzig, Straße des 18. Oktober 15, Democratic Republic of Germany.

PHELAN, James, b. 25 Jan. 1951, Flushing, New York, USA. University Professor. m. Elizabeth Menaghan, 10 June, 1972, Maywood, New Jersey, USA., 1 son, 1 daughter. *Education:* BA, Boston College, USA, 1972; MA, University of Chicago, 1973, PhD, 1977. *Appointments:* Assistant Professor, Ohio State University, 1977–83; Associate Professor, 1983–present. *Publications:* Worlds From Words: A Theory of Language in Fiction, 1981. *Contributions to:* Diacritics; College English; Semiotica, and others. *Memberships:* Society for the Study of Narrative Literature; Society for Critical Exchange; Modern Language Association; Midwest Modern Language Association. *Address:* Department of English, Ohio State University, Columbus, OH 43210–1370, USA.

PHELPS, Gilbert Henry, b. 23 Jan. 1915, Gloucester, England. Writer; Former BBC Third Programme Producer and Chief Instructor, BBC Staff Training Department. m. Kay Batchelor, 23 Oct. 1972, Fulham, London, 1 son, 1 daughter (by previous marriage), 3 stepsons. *Education:* BA, First Class Hons, English Literature, Fitzwilliam House, Cambridge, 1937; Research and Training, St John's College, Cambridge, 1937–48; MA, 1941. *Literary Appointments:* Editor, Latin American Series (Charles Knight), 1971–76; Editor, Makers of Empire, Series (Charles Knight), 1972–77. *Publications:* The Dry Stone (novel), 1953; The Heart in the Desert (novel), 1954; A Man on His Prime (novel), 1955; The Russian Novel in English Fiction, 1956; The Centenarians (novel), 1958; The Love Before the First (novel), 1960; The Winter People (novel), 1963; The Last Horizon: Travels in Brazil, 1964; A Survey of English Literature, 1965; The Byronic Byron, 1971; The Old Believer (novel), 1973; The Tragedy of Paraguay, 1975; The Loz Roads, 1975; Squire Waterton, 1976; The British Monarchy, 1977; An Introduction to Fifty British Novels, 1960–1900, 1979; The Prose of Browne and Donne; Varieties of English Gothic; Letters and Journals of the Romantic Revival; The New Literature from Africa, etc. *Contributions to:* Numerous magazines, newspapers, etc. *Honours:* Arts Council Awards, 1968, 78. *Memberships:* Fellow, Royal Society of Literature; Society of Authors (various committees); Southern Arts Association (various offices). *Address:* The Cottage, School Road, Finstock, Oxford DX7 3DJ, England.

PHILIPP, Elliot Elias, b. 20 July 1915, London, England. Gyneacological Surgeon. m. Lucie Hackenbroch, 22 Mar. 1939, London, 1 son, 1 daugter. *Education:* BA, 1936, MA, 1942, MB, BCh, 1947, University of Cambridge; Member, Royal College of Surgeons, London Royal College of Physicians, 1939; Fellow, Royal College of Surgeons of England, 1951; Fellow, Royal College of Obstetricians & Gynaecologists, 1962. *Literary Appointments:* Formerly Medical Correspondent, News Chronicle, The Sunday Times. *Major Publications:* Obstetrics & Gynaecology for Students, 1970; Scientific Foundations of Obstetrics & Gynaecology (editor), 3rd edition, 1985. Hiltons Rest and Pain, 1950 (editor); Overcoming Childlessness, 2nd edition, 1984. *Contributor to:* British Medical Journal; British Journal of Obstetrics & Gynaecology; Numerous 'glossy' magazines, some 300 articles. *Honour:* Chevalier de la Legion d'Honneur, 1971. *Memberships:* Society of Authors, 1950; Committee Member, Medical Writers Group, 1980–. *Literary Agent:* Caradoc King of A J Watt. *Address:* 78 Nottingham Terrace, York Gate, London NW1 4QE, England.

PHILLIPS, David Lindsay, b. 27 Nov. 1914, Dundee, Scotland. Writer. *Publications:* The Lichty Nichts, 1962; The Exploits of Wiselike Ned, 1963; Hud Yer Tongue, 1964; My Dundee, 1971; No Poets Corner in the Abbey, 1971; Our, Dundee, 1972; McGonagall and Tommy Atkins, 1973; Jimmy Shand, 1976; The Lichty Nichts Omnibus, 1976; Pictorial Dundee, 1977; Up T'the Knees in Can'le Grease, 1979; Pictorial Dundee 2, 1979; I Never Fell Into a Midden, 1978; Dundee, with Douglas Phillips, 1980; Tea Aff the Bunker, 1981; The Hungry

Thirties, 1981; Eh'll Hae a Peh, 1983. *Contributions to:* Scots Magazine; People's Journal; various others Scottish periodicals. *Address:* 8 Quarryside, Dundee, Scotland.

PHILLIPS, Dewi Zephaniah, b. 24 Nov. 1934, Swansea, Wales. Professor of Philosophy. m. Margaret Monica Hanford, 2 Sep. 1959, 3 sons. *Education:* BA 1956, MA 1958, Wales; B Litt, Oxon, 1961. *Publications:* The Concept of Prayer, 1965; Moral Practices, (with H O Mounce), 1970; Faith and Philosophical Enquiry, 1970; Sense and Delusion, (with Ilham Dilman), 1971; Religion Without Explanation, 1976; Through a Darkening Glass, 1981; Dramau Gwenlyn Parry, 1981; Belief, Change and Forms of Life, 1985; R S Thomas: Poet of the Hidden God, 1985. *Contributions to:* Mind; Philosophy; Philosiphical Quarterly; Analysis; Philosophical Investigations. *Membership:* Aristotelian Society. *Address:* 45 Queen's Road, Sketty, Swansea, Wales.

PHILLIPS, Glenly Roy Elliott, b. 21 Feb. 1936, Southern Cross, Western Australia. Tertiary Education Lecturer. *Education:* Teachers Certificate, Claremont Teachers College, 1957; BEd (Hons) 1957, MEd 1967, MA (Prelim) 1971, University of Western Australia; University for Foreigners, Perugio, Italy, 1980; Certificate of Proficiency, Foreign Languages (Italian), Perth Technical College, 1982. *Literary Appointments include:* English teacher, 1958–61; Lecturer, Teachers College, 1962–69; Head, Department of Speech & Drama, Mount Lawley Teachers College, 1970–73; Assistant Vice Principal, ibid, 1974–78; Assistant Director, Mount Lawley College of Advanced Education, 1979–81; Associate Dean, West Australian College of Advanced Education, 1982–. *Publications:* Intersection, 1972; Writing Essays & Dissertations (co-author); Seedtime, 1976; Umbria Green; Australian Gold (co-author), 1985. *Contributions to:* Various Poetry Anthologies, Australia, Italy; Poems, Australian, American journals; Articles, reviews, various Australian journals including, Artlook, Westerly, Poetry Australian, Australian Book Review. *Honours:* Bertha Houghton Prize (education studies), University of Western Australia, 1957; Equal 2nd, Tom Collins Poetry Prize, 1980; Highly Commended, New South Wales Bilingual Book Competition, 1982. *Memberships:* President 1978–9, 1982, Fellowship of Australian Writers, and other offices; Australian Society of Authors; Perth Branch, 1985; PEN; Societá Italiana di Studi Australiani (associate member). *Address:* 23 Clifton Crescent, Mount Lawley, WA 6050, Australia.

PHILLIPS, Margaret Mann, b. 23 Jan. 1906, Rotherham, England. Writer; Lecturer. m. Charles William Phillips, 3 July 1940, Stainton-in-Cleveland, 1 son, 1 daughter. *Education:* BA, 1927, MA, 1932, Somerville College, Oxford University; Docteur d'Université, Sorbonne, Paris, France, 1934; D Litt, Oxford University, 1979. *Literary Appointments:* Lecturer, Manchester University, 1934–36; Lecturer, Director of Studies, Newnham College, Cambridge University, 1936–45; Lecturer, Reader in French, Kings College, London University, 1959–68; Honorary lecturer, University College, London University, 1975–. *Publications:* Erasme et les débuts de la Réforme française, 1934; Outgoing, 1936; Within the City Wall, 1943; Erasmus and the Northern Renaissance, 1949, 81; The Adages of Erasmus, 1964; Collected Works of Erasmus, volume 23, 1978, volume 31, 1982. *Contributions to:* Modern Language Review; Moreana; Erasmus of Rotterdam Yearbook; Humanisme et Renaissance. *Honours:* Prix Bordin, Académie des Belles Lettres, Paris, France; Medal, Collège de France, Paris; President, Erasmus of Rotterdam Society, USA. *Address:* 57 Hampton Road, Teddington, Middlesex TW11 0LA, England.

PHILLIPS, Meredith Bowen, b. 5 July 1943, Oshkosh, Wisconsin, USA. Editor. m. Peter F C Phillips, 5 Aug. 1972, Santa Cruz, California, 3 sons. *Education:* BA, Stanford University, 1965. *Publications:* The Child's Peninsula, 1979; Death Spiral, Murder at the Winter

Olympics, 1984. *Contributor to:* Better Homes and Gardens; Accent; The Menlo-Atherton recorder; The Real Food Places; Women's Sports ; Writers Connection; Miniature Gazette; Modern Maturity. *Memberships:* Mystery Writers of America; Crime Writers Association. *Address:* P O Box 384, Menlo Park, CA 94026, USA.

PHILLIPS, Michael R, b. 13 Dec. 1946, Arcata, California, USA. Writer. m. Judy Carter, 24 Oct. 1971, Arcata, 3 sons. *Education:* BS, Physics, Humboldt State University, 1969; currently studying for MA in History. *Publications:* A Christian Family in Action, 1976; Growth of a Vision, 1977; Does Christianity Make Sense, 1977; Blueprint for Raising a Child, 1978; A Survival Guide for Tough Times, 1978; A Vision for the Church, 1979; Building Respect, Responsibility & Spiritual Values in Your Child, 1981; Control Through Planned Budgeting, 1979; Getting More Done in Less Time, 1982; In Quest of Gold, 1984; Heather Hills of Stonewycke, 1985; Flight from Stonewycke, 1985; Lady of Stonewycke, 1986. *Honour:* Magna Cum Laude Graduate, Humboldt State University, 1969. *Address:* 1707 E. St., Eureka, CA 95501, USA.

PHILLIPS, Robert A J, b. 19 Apr. 1922, Toronto, Canada. Writer. m. Mary Anne Cochrane, 15 June 1946, Toronto, 3 daughters. *Education:* BA, University of Toronto, 1942. *Major Publications:* Canada of the North, 1965; The Yukon & Northwest Territories, 1966; Canada's North, 1967; The East Block of the Parliament Buildings, 1967; Canada's Railways, 1968. *Contributor to:* Numerous journals in Canada and elsewhere. *Address:* P O Box 319, Cantley, Quebec, J0X 1L0, Canada.

PHILMUS, Robert M, b. 3 Sep. 1943, New York City, University Professor. m. Maria Rita Rohr, 12 June 1967, Berkeley, USA. *Education:* BA, Brown University, 1964; PhD, University of California, San Diego, 1968. *Literary Appointments:* Instructor of English, Carleton College, Northfield MN, 1967–68; Assistant Professor of English, Loyola College, Montreal, 1968–72; Associate Professor of English, 1972–76, Professor of English, 1976–, Concordia University, Montreal; Editor, Science Fiction Studies, 1978–. *Publications:* Into the Unknown: The Evolution of Science Fiction from Francis Godwin to H G Wells, 1970, 2nd edition 1983; H G Wells: Early Writings in Science and Science Fiction (editor with D Y Hughes) 1975; H G Wells and Modern Science Fiction (associate editor with D Suvin) 1977; H G Wells's Literary Criticism (editor with P Parrinder) 1980. *Contributor to:* PMLA; ELH; Texas Studies in Literature and Language; Science Fiction Studies of essays on various subjects. *Honours:* Academy of American Poets' Prize, Brown University, 1964; Phi Beta Kappa, Brown University, 1964. *Memberships:* Modern Language Association; Science Fiction Research Association. *Address:* c/o English Department, Concordia University, 7141 Sherbrooke Street West, Montreal, Quebec, Canada H4B 1R6.

PHIPPS, William Eugene, b. 28 Jan. 1930, Waynesboro, Virginia, USA. Professor of Religion and Philosophy. m. Martha Ann Swezey, 21 Dec. 1954, Waynesboro, Virginia, 1 son, 2 daughters. *Education:* BS, Davidson College; M Div, Union Theological Seminary in Virginia; MA, University of Hawaii; PhD, University of St Andrews. *Publications:* Was Jesus Married?, 1970; Influential Theologians on Wo/Man, 1980; Paul Against Supernaturalism, 1986; Before and After Death, 1986. *Contributions to:* Numerous publications, including, Theology Today; New York Times; Journal of the American Academy of Religion. *Address:* Davis and Elkins College, Elkins, WV 26241, USA.

PICARD, Barbara Leonie, b. 4 Dec. 1917, Richmond, Surrey, England. Author. *Publications:* The Odyssey of Homer, 1952; Ransom for a Knight, 1956; The Illiad of Homer, 1960; Lost John, 1962; One is One, 1965; The Young Pretenders, 1966; Twice Seven Tales, 1968; Three Ancient Kings, 1972; Tales of Ancient Persia,

1972. *Address:* Oxford University Press, Walton Street, Oxford, England.

PICARDIE, Michael, b. 13 Aug. 1936, Johannesburg, South Africa. University Lecturer; Playwright. m. Hilary Garnett, 20 Oct. 1960, Hampstead, London, 2 daughters. *Education:* BA, BA, Hons, Witwatersrand University; MA, Oxford University; MA, Leicester University; Diploma of Applied Social Studies, Liverpool. *Literary Appointments:* Directorial Adviser to production of, Shades of Brown, at Kings Head Theatre, London, 1970, Fagel Bla Theatre, Stockholm amd Rogasland Theatre, Stavenger, 1982, New Federal Theatre, New York City, 1983, Cincinnati Playhouse, 1984. *Publication:* Play: Shades of Brown, in Theatre Three: Market Plays, 1985. *Contributions to:* Numerous contributions to Social Work; Social Work Today; British Journal of Psychiatric Scoial Work; British Journal of Social Work. *Membership:* Theatre Writers Union. *Literary Agent:* Margaret Ramsay, 14a Goodwins Court, St Martin's Lane, London WC2N 4LL. *Address:* Pant-Teg, St Mellon's Road, Llanedeyrn, Cardiff CF3 9YG, Wales.

PICK, Christopher Charles, b. 13 July 1948, Watford, England. Writer; Editorial Consultant. m. Jennifer Mary Trehern née Try, 23 July 1983, 1 daughter. *Education:* BA, University of Kent, 1969; MA, University of East Anglia, 1970. *Literary Appointments:* Editor, Thames and Hudson, 1970–73; Chief editor, MacMillan, 1973–75; Freelance writer, editorial consultant and editor, 1975–. *Publications:* Encyclopedia of Transport, co-author, 1982; What's What in the 1980s, General editor, 1982; The Election Book, 1983; Off the Motorway, 1984; Children's London, 1985; Ageing Today and Tomorrow, 1985; Numerous information books for children. *Contributions to:* Junior Education; Good Housekeeping and to others. *Memberships:* Society of Authors; National Union of Journalists. *Literary Agent:* John Parker of Campbell, Thomson McLaughlan. *Address:* 41 Chestnut Road, London SE27 9EZ, England.

PICK, John Barclay, b. 26 Dec. 1921, Leicester, England, Author. m. Gene Atkinson, 2 Oct. 1943, Ilkeston, 2 sons. *Education:* Emmanuel College, Cambridge University. *Publications:* Under the Crust, 1946; Out of the Pit, 1950; Phoenix Dictionary of Games, 1952; The Lonely Aren't Alone, 1952; Spectator's Handbook, 1956; A Land Fit for Eros, with John Atkins, 1957; The Last Valley, 1959; The Strange Genius of Davis Lindsay, with Wilson, Visaik, 1970; Neil M Gunn: A Highland Life, with F R Hart, 1981. *Contributions to:* The Scotsman; Glasgow Herald; News Chronicle; Times Literary Supplement; Punch; John Bull; Everybodys; Hibbert Journal; Studies in Scottish Literature; Housewife; Life and Letters Today; Adelphi; New English Review; New English Weekly; Scots Review' Adam; New Directions; Modern Reading and others. *Honours:* Book Award for, A Highland Life, The Scottish Arts Council, 1982. *Membership:* Scottish PEN. *Address:* Hollins, Balmaclellan, Castle Douglas, Kirkcudbrightshire DG7 3QH, Scotland.

PICKARD, Thomas Mariner, b. 7 Jan. 1946, Newcastle upon Tyne, England. Writer. m. Joanna Voit, 21 July 1978, London, 1 son. *Publications:* High on the Walls, 1967; Order of Chance, 1972; Guttersnipe, 1972; Hero Dust, 1979; Jarrow March, 1981; Custom and Exile, 1985. *Contributions to:* New Socialist; New Departures; The World; Ink; North Dakota Quarterly; Scipsi. *Honours:* Fellowships: C D Lewis, 1976–77; Arts Council Creative Writing, Warwick University, 1978–79. *Membership:* Writers Guild of Great Britain. *Literary Agent:* Judy Daish Associates. *Address:* c/o Judy Daish Associates, 83 Eastbourne Mews, London W2 6LQ, England.

PICKARD, Willis Ritchie Sturrock, b. 21 May 1941, Dunfermline, Scotland. Journalist. m. Ann Marie MacNeil, 27 Dec. 1969, Edinburgh, 2 daughters. *Education:* MA Honours, St Andrews University. *Literary Appointments:* Literary Editor, The Scotsman, 1971–

77; Editor, Times Educational Supplement, Scotland, 1977–; Member Literature Committee, Scottish Arts Council. *Contributions to:* Many newspapers and magazines including: The Scotsman; The Times; Sunday Times; Scottish Review. *Address:* 4 Strathfillan Road, Edinburgh, Scotland.

PICKERING, Paul Granville, b. 9 May 1952, Rotherham, England. Writer. m. Alison Beckett, 11 Dec. 1983, Mahé, Seychelles. *Education:* Royal Masonic Schools, BA (Hon), Psychology, Leicester University. *Publication:* Wild About Harry, 1985, 86. *Contributor to:* Punch; New Society; The Times. *Membership:* The Society of Authors. *Literary Agents:* A D Peters (UK); Literistic (USA). *Address:* 12 Ladbroke Square, London W11 3NA, England.

PIDOUX, Edmond, b. 25 Oct. 1908, Hornu, Belgium. Professor; Writer. m. Lise Payot, Lausanne, 2 sons, 1 daughter. *Education:* Licence Degree, Arts, University of Lausanne. *Publications:* (Drama) L'Arche de Jonc; L'Histoire de Jonas; Le Masque et la Rose; Le Vendredi de Robinson; Mademoiselle de Roannez ou l'Ombre de Blaise; (Poetry) Charmes pour la Male heure; Africaines; De David a Jonas; L'Espace d'Un Moment; Des Trous dans le mur; (Essays) L'Afrique a l'age ingrat; Madagascar maitre a son bord; Voir la Montague; Chillon; Le Langage des Romards; (Novels) Une île nommée; Newbegin; La Journée de Dreuze; Malices et Merveilles. *Contributor to:* Les Alpes; Le Protestant, Geneva. *Honours:* Many awards for drama, poetry, short stories, novels; Vaud Book Prize for total work, 1982. *Memberships:* Swiss Society of Writers; Vaud Association of Writers; PEN; Society of Authors & Dramatists. *Address:* 3 Coin d'En-Bas, 1092 Belmont-sur-Lausanne, Switzerland.

PIEDISCALZI, Nicholas, b. 10 Apr. 1931, Chicago, Illinois, USA. Professor of Religion. m. Sibyl Hale Carter, 3 Sep. 1976, Dayton, Ohio, 3 sons, 3 daughters. *Education includes:* BA, Grinnel College; MDiv, Yale University; PhD, Boston University. *Literary Appointments:* Visiting Professor, St Martin's College, Lancaster, England, 1985. *Publications:* Contemporary Religion and Social Responsibility, 1973, Co-Editor and Co-Author; From Hope to Liberation: Towards a New Marxist-Christian Dialogue, co-editor and co-author, 1974; Teaching about Religion in Public Schools, Co-editor and Co-author, 1977; Public Education Religion Studies: AN Overview, Associate Editor and Author, 1981; The Bible in American Education, Co-Editor, 1982; Three Words of Marxist-Christian Encounters, Co-Editor and Co-Author, 1985. *Contributions to:* Youth Department News Sheet; Journal for the Scientific Study of Religion; Here and Now; Yale Alumni Magazine; Religion and Public School Curriculum; Journal of Religion and Health; Intellect; Southwestern Journal of Social Education; Bucknell Review. Church and State; Ateismo e Dialogo; Peace and the Sciences; Numerous others. *Honours include:* Stipends, grants and fellowships, National Endowment for the Humanities; Distinguished Alumni Award, Grinnel College, 1977; American Delegate, 6th International Marxist-Christian Symposium, USSR, 1978; Summer Faculty Fellowship, Free Enterprise Foundation and Syracuse University, 1978; WSU Research Council Grants, 1981, 84, 85. *Memberships include:* President, National Council on Religion and Public Education; Editor, Christin-Marzist Encounter Newsletter; Society for Scientific Study of Religion; American Society of Christian Ethics; various offices, American Academy of Religion. *Address:* Department of Religion, Wright State University, Dayton, OH 45435, USA.

PIERCE, Meredith Ann, b. 5 July 1958, Seattle, Washington, USA. Novelist. *Education:* AA Liberal Arts 1976, BA English 1978, MA English 1980, University of Florida. *Publications:* The Darkangel, 1982; A Gathering of Gargoyles, 1984; Birth of the Firebringer, 1985; The Woman Who Loved Reindeer, 1985. *Contributions to:* Scholastic Magazine; Mythlore XXXI. *Honours:* National First Prize, Scholastic Creative Writing Awards

Contest, Scholastic Magazine, 1973; Graduate Teaching Assistant Award, University of Florida English Department, 1979–80; The Darkangel: International Reading Association's Children's Book Award, Listed on American Language Association's Best Books for Yung Adults Roster, ALA Best of the Best Books List, Chosen for New York Times Notable Children's Book List, Appeared on Parents' Choice Award Book roster, 1982; Jane Tinkham Broughton Fellow in Writing for Children, Bread Loaf Writers' Conference, 1984. *Memberships:* Phi Beta Kappa; Secretary-Treasurer, Children's Literature Association's annual convention, 1982; The Author's Guild Inc; Science Fiction Writers of America. *Address:* 703 NW 19th Street, Gainesville, FL 32603, USA.

PIERCE, Richard Austin, b. 26 July 1918, Manteca, California, USA. Historian. m. Vera Hilda Morris, 5 Jan. 1955, Birmingham, England, 1 daughter. *Education:* BA, 1940, MA, 1952, PhD, 1956, University of California. *Publications:* Russian Central Asia, 1867–1917: A Study in Colonial Rule, 1960; Russia's Hawaiian Adventure, 1815–1817, 1965; Editor, Alaska History Series, Volumes 1-27, 1972–85; Translator, with A S Donnelly, of P A Tilchmenev, History of the Russian American Company, 1978. *Contributor to:* The Alaska Journal; Pacific Northwest Quarterly. *Honours:* Fulbright Fellowship, University of Hamburg, Germany, 1953; Guggenheim Fellowship, 1965. *Address:* 237 Yonge Street, Kingston, Ontario, Canada K7M 1G2.

PIERCE, Roy, b. 24 June. 1923, New York, New York, USA. Professor of Political Science. m. Winnifred Poland, 19 July 1947, Winchester, Massachusetts. *Education:* BA 1947, MA 1948, PhD 1950, Cornell University. *Publications:* Contemporary French Political Thought, 1966; French Politics and Political Institutions, 1968 and 1973; Political Representation in France (with Philip E Converse), 1986. *Contributions to:* American Journal of Political Science; Comparative Politics; Legislative Studies Quarterly; Political Behaviour. *Address:* Department of Political Science, University of Michigan, Ann Arbor, MI 48109, USA.

PIERMAN, Carol J, b. 16 Oct. 1947, Lima, Ohio, USA. Writer. *Education:* BA 1969, MFA 1972, PhD 1980, Bowling Green University. *Publication:* The Naturalized Citizen, 1981. *Contributions:* Poems in: Ascent; Carolina Quarterly; Southern Poetry Review; St Andrews Review; Open Places; Three Rivers Poetry Journal; Poetry Now; Centenniel Review. *Honours:* Devine Fellowship, 1972; Artist's Fellowship, Illinois Arts Council, 1980. *Address:* Box 324, Ottawa, OH 45875, USA.

PIERSON, George Wilson, b. 22 Oct. 1904, New York, USA. Historian. m. Mary Laetitia Verdery, 10 Sep. 1936, 2 daughters. *Education:* BA, 1926, PhD, 1933, Yale University. *Appointments:* Instructor to Professor of History, 1926–27, 1929–30, 1933–44, Learned Professor of History, Yale, 1946–73, Emeritus, 1973–; Historian, Yale University, 1938–. *Publications:* Tocqueville and Beaumont in America, 1938 abridged Tocqueville in America, 1959; Yale College 1871–1921, 1952; Yale: The University College, 1921–37, 1955; The Education of American Leaders, 1969; The Moving American, 1973; Gustave de Beaumont: Lettres d'Amerique, 1973; Yale: A Short History, 1976, 2nd edition 1979; A Yale Book of Numbers: Historical Statistics of the College and University, 1983. *Contributor to:* Historical and Educational Publications. *Honours:* John Addson Porter Prize, Yale, 1933; Wilbur Lucas Cross Medal, Yale, 1973; BK Medal, Yale, 1974; Yale Medal, 1975; American Academy of Arts and Sciences. *Memberships:* President, Yale Chapter, BK; Elizabethan Club, Yale; Acorn Club, Connecticut; Century Association. *Address:* 176 Ives Street, Mount Carmel, CT 06518, USA.

PIERSON, Robert, b. 3 Jan. 1911, Brooklyn, New York, USA. Retired Minister, Church Administrator. m. Dollis Mae Smith, 2 Sep. 1931, Ocala, Florida, USA, 2 sons. *Education:* Doctor of Divinity, Andrews University, Berrien Springs, Michigan; Ordained Minister, 1933. *Publications:* Your Bible Speaks, 1943; Wonderful Jesus, 1948; Road To Happiness, 1948; Triumps of the Cross, 1951; Paddles Over The Mamarang, 1953; Secret of Happiness, 1958; Give Us This Day, 1959; Road To True Riches, 1965; 501 Illustrations, 1965; What Shall I Speak About? 1966; So You Want To Be A Leader! 1966; Final Countdown, (co-author), 1966; Faith on Tiptoe, 1967; Though The Wind Blows, 1968; Heart to Heart, 1970; Bible Answers to Today's Questions, 1973; Faith Triumphant, 1974; We Still Believe, 1975; Angels Over Elisabethville, 1975; Goodbye, Planet Earth, 1976; In Step With Jesus, 1977; Beloved Leaders, 1978; How To Be A Successful Christian Leader, 1978; What's Just Ahead, 1978; Miracles Happen Every Day, 1982; Here Comes Adventure, 1984. *Address:* 127 Fulton Drive, Hendersonville, NC 28739, USA.

PIES, Ronald William, b. 12 June 1952, Rochester, New York, USA. Psychiatrist. *Education:* BA, Cornell University, 1974; MD, State University of New York, Upstate Medical Center, 1978. *Literary Appointments:* Senior Editorial Staff, The Psychiatric Times. *Publications:* Inside Psychotherapy: The Patient's Handbook, 1983; Lean Soul, Poetry, 1985. *Contributions to:* Archives of General Psychiatry; Archives of Internal Medicine; American Journal of Social Psychiatry; Hospital and Community Psychiatry; Journal of Clinical Psychiatry; Psychosomatics; American Family Physician; Journal of Nervous and Mental Disease; Literature and Medicine. Numerous editorial and letters to editors. Poetry contributed to: The Literary Review; Kailiope; An Anthology of Contemporary Poetry. *Honours:* BA with distinction, Cornell University, 1974; Commendation, American Cancer Society, 1975; Laughlin Fellowship, American College of Psychiatrists, 1980. *Membership:* National Association of Poetry Therapy. *Literary Agent:* Susan Protter, New York. *Address:* Department of Psychiatry, Box 1007, Tufts University School of Medicine, 171 Harrison Avenue, Boston, MA 02111, USA.

PIFER, Ellen I, b. 26 June 1942, New York, USA. University Professor. m. Drury L Pifer, 30 Dec. 1962, San Mateo, California, 1 daughter. *Education:* BA, English, 1964, MA, Comparative Literature, 1969, PhD, Comparative Literature, 1976, University of California, Berkeley. *Literary Appointments:* Acting Instructor, Comparative Literature, University of California, Berkeley, 1974–76; Theatre Critic, The Berkeley Gazette, 1975–76; Colimnist, New West Magazine, 1976–77; Assistant Professor, English, 1977–81, Associate Professor, English and Comparative Literature, 1981–, University of Delaware; Consultant, various university presses and professional journals, 1979–; Consultant and panelist, seminar series, Delaware Theatre Company, 1980–81. *Publication:* Nabokov and the Novel, 1980. *Contributions to:* Articles and reviews in professional journals including, Modern Fiction Studies; Mosaic; Studies in American Fiction; Slavic and East European Review; Modern Language Quarterly; The Russian Review; Slavic Review. Essays in several volumes of collected criticism. *Honours:* George Stewart Prize in Creative Writing 1962; Phi Beta Kappa award 1962; Nominated, Woodrow Wilson Fellowship 1964; Various grants and fellowships, 1960–62, 1968–71, 1978, 1979, 1981. *Memberships:* Vladimir Nabokov Society; Modern Language Association; American Association of Teachers of Slavic and East European Languages. *Address:* English Department, University of Delaware, Newark, DE 19716, USA.

PIGUET, Suzanne, b. 16 Apr. 1926, Yverdon, Switzerland. m. Jean-Francois Piguet, 4 May 1949, 3 sons. *Education:* 1/2 licence Theology; licence Mathematics. *Publications:* Corinne, 1961; San Domenico, 1964; L'Enfant et La Mort, 1968; Pour Dormir sans Reves, 1981; L'Homme n'est Jamais Seul, 1983; Les 7 Vies de Louis Moraz, 1985. *Contributions to:* Articles and short stories in French language newspapers and magazines. *Honours:* Prix du Lyceum, 1963; Prix Charles Veillon, 1969; Prix Pro Helvetia, 1981. *Memberships:* Pen Club;

SSE (Zurich); SACD (Geneva-Paris); SGLF (Paris); AECEF (Paris). *Address:* 11 rte de Lausanne, 1096 Cully, Switzerland.

PIGUET-KNIGHT, Marie-Jos[sc]e b. 21 Apr. 1941, Lausanne, Switzerland. m. Lionel John Knight, Painter, 16 Dec. 1972, Truro, Cornwall. *Publications:* Reviens ma Douce, 1974; Jean Fantoche: Portrait bouffon d'une auguste famille, 1981. *Contributions to:* Ecriture 8 Ecriture 13 (Swiss literary magazines); La Femme d'aujourd'hui, Geneva; Tribune de Lausanne, Gazette de Lausanne; Journal de Genève; Samedi Litteraire. *Honours:* Georges Nicole Prize for novels, Lausanne, 1974; Alpes-Jura Prize, Paris, 1975; Schiller Prize, Switzerland, 1982; Grants, Pro Helvetia, Pro Arte. *Memberships:* Vaudoise Association of Writers, Lausanne; Association of French Speaking Writers, Paris; Swiss Society of Writers. *Literary Agent:* Editions Bertil Galland, Vevey, Switzerland. *Address:* Caroline Place, 2 Chudleigh Road, Exeter EX2 8TU, England.

PIKE, Glenville, b. 11 Sep. 1925, Toowoomba, Queensland, Australia. Writer. m. Carolyne Dewhurst Kuri, Brisbane, 7 Dec. 1980. *Literary Appointment:* Feature writer (historical), North Queensland Register, 1947. *Publications include:* Frontier Territory, 1972; An Untamed Land, 1974; Pioneers Country, 1976; Roads of Yesterday, 1977; Queensland Frontier, 1978; Queen of the North, 1979; The Golden Days; 1981; Campfire Tales, 1982; The Last Frontier, 1983; Conquest of the Ranges, 1984. *Contributions:* Editor & Publisher, North Australian Monthly, 1954–65. Freelance articles on northern Australian life & history, Christian Science Monitor; Chambers Journal; Wide World Magazine; Walkabout; This Australia; Up North, etc, 1943–84. *Honours:* Fellow, Royal Geographical Society of Australasia, 1949, Royal Historical Society of Queensland, 1978; Litchfield Literary Award, 1972; Foxwood Literary Award, 1976. *Address:* P O Box 822, Mareeba, North Queensland 4880, Australia.

PIKOULIS, John, b. 21 Jan. 1941, Rhodesia. Senior Lecturer in English Literature. m. Lorraine Maxine Whiteman, 9 June 1969, Cardiff, Wales, 1 son, 2 daughters. *Education:* BA, BA Honours, Cape Town University. Republic of South Africa; Dip Ed, Oxford University, England; MA, Leicester; PhD, Wales. *Publications:* The Art of William Faulkner, 1982; Alun Lewis, A Life, 1984; Alvia Lewis, A Miscellany of His Writings, (editor), 1984. *Contributions to:* Articles on various aspects of 19th and 20th century literature in English and American journals. *Address:* 16 Station Road, Dinas Powys, South Glamorgan, Wales.

PIKUNAS, Justin, b. 7 Jan. 1920, Lithuania. Professor of Psychology. m. Regina Liesunaitis, 8 Aug. 1953, Montreal, Canada, 1 son, 2 daughters. *Education:* PhD, University of Munich, Federal Republic of Germany, 1949. *Appointments:* Assistant Professor, 1952–56, Associate Professor, 1956–61, Professor, 1961–, University of Detroit, USA; Director, Children's Psychodiagnostic Centre, 1970–. *Publications:* Human Developmental Child Psychology, 1957, 1965; Human Development: An Emergent Science, 1961; Manual for the Pikunas Graphosopic Scale, 1953, 4th edition, 1982. *Contributor to:* Science Education; Journal of Clinical Psychology; Journal of Personality Assessment; Academic; Psychology Bulletin; etc. *Honours:* Outstanding Service Award, University of Detroit, 1981. *Memberships:* American Psychological Association; American Association for the Advancement of Science; Michigan Academy of Science Arts and Letters. *Address:* 8761 W Outer Dr, Detroit, MI 48219, USA.

PILCHER, Rosamunde, b. 22 Sep. 1924, Lelant, Cornwall, England. Freelance writer. m. Graham Pilcher, 7 Dec. 1946, Lelant, 2 sons, 2 daughters. *Publications:* Sleeping Tiger; Another View; The End of the Summer; Snow in April; The Empty House; The Day of the Storm; Under Gemini, 1975; Wild Mountain Thyme, 1978; The Carousel, 1980; Voices in Summer, 1983; The Blue Bedroom & Other Stories, 1985. *Contributions to:* USA: short stories; Good Housekeeping; McCalls; Redbook.

UK: short stories; Woman & Home; Woman's Weekly; Woman; Woman's Own; Woman's Realm; Woman's Journal. *Literary Agent:* Curtis Brown, 62/68 Regent Street, London W1, England. *Address:* Over Pilmore, Invergowrie, by Dundee, Scotland.

PILISUK, Marc, b. 19 Jan. 1934, New York, USA. Professor of Public Health. *Education:* BA, Queens College, 1955; MA, University of Michigan, 1956; PhD, 1961; Licensed Clinical Psychologist. *Publications:* The Triple Revolution Emerging: Social Problems in Depth (with R Perrucci), 1971; Poor Americans: How the White Poor Live (with P Pilisuk), 1971; How We Lost the War on Poverty (with P Pilisuk), 1971; International Conflict and Social Policy, 1972; The Healing Web: Social Networks and Human Survival (with Susan H Parks), 1986. *Contributions to:* Numerous professional magazines and journals, *Honours include:* Award for Essay (with T Hayden), 1965; Various Professional awards. *Memberships include:* Fellow, American Orthopsych. Association; Member of Committee, Mental Health Aspects of War, Violence and Aggression, Committee on Social Issues. *Address:* 494 Cragmont, Berkeley, CA 94708, USA.

PILLIAWSKY, Monte Eddy, b. 6 Feb. 1944, New Orleans, Louisiana, USA. College Teacher. *Education:* BA, Hons, University of New Orleans, 1965; MA, Tulane University, 1968; PhD Tulane University, 1970. *Publication:* Exit 13, Oppression and Racism in Academia, 1982. *Contributions to:* High Black Turnout Re-elects Morial, In These Times, 1982; From Black Agenda to National Policy: A Few Proposals, Southern Changes, 1982; The Limits of Power, Dutch Morial, Mayor of New Orleans Southern exposure, 1984; Racial Equality in the United States: From Institutionalized racism to, Respectable Racism, Phylon, 1984; The Hidden Message in the 1984 American Presidential Election: White Racism Talking Drums, 1985. *Address:* 708 Desire Street, New Orleans, LA 70117, USA.

PILON, Jean-Guy, b. 12 Nov. 1930, Saint-Polycarpe, Quebec, Canada. Writer; Radio Producer & Broadcaster. *Education:* Graduate, Law, University of Montreal, 1954. *Literary Appointments:* Founder 1959, Director 1959–79, review, Liberté; Head, Cultural Broadcast Service, 1970–85, Producer, Radio Canada. *Publications include:* Poetry: La Fiancée du Matin, 1953; Les Cloitres de l'Eté, 1955; L'Homme et le Jour, 1957; La Mouette et le Large, 1960; Recours au Pays, 1961; Por Saluer une Ville, 1963; Comme eau retenue, 1969; Saisons pour la Continuelle, 1969; Silences pour une Souveraine, 1972; Comme eau retenue, revised, 1985. *Contributions to:* La Presse Devoir, 1960–80. Articles of tourism, litrature, writers, poets. Frequently a member of many national juries (Prix David, etc), & International juries (Prix Gilson, Prix Canada-Belgique etc). *Honours include:* Quebec Poetry Prize, Prix David, 1956; Louise Labé Prize, 1969; France-Canada Prize, 1969; Van Lerberghe Prize, Paris, 1969; Prize. Governor-General of Canada, 1970; Athanase David Prize, 1984. *Memberships:* President, International Quebec Writers Reunion; President, l'Académie Canadienne-Franaise; Royal Society of Canada. *Address:* 5724 Cote Saint-Antoine, Montreal, Quebec, Canada H4A 1R9.

PINCHER, Chapman, b. 29 Mar. 1914, Ambala, India. Author. m. Constance Sylvia Wolstenholme, 1965, 1 son, 1 daughter. *Education:* BSc Honours, London, 1953; Fellow, King's College, 1979; D Litt, (Honorary), Newcastle upon Tyne, 1979. *Publications:* Breeding of Farm Animals, 1946; A Study of Fishes, 1947; Into the Atomic Age, 1947; Spotlight on Animals, 1950; Evolution, 1950; Sex in Our Time, 1973; Inside Story, 1978; Their Trade is Treachery, 1981; Too Secret Too Long, 1984; The Secret Offensive, 1985; Novels: Not with a Bang, 1965; The Giantkiller, 1967; The Penthouse Conspirators, 1970; The Skeleton at the Villa Wolkonskil, 1975; The Eye of the Tornado, 1976; The Four Horses, 1978; Dirty Tricks, 1980; The Private World of St John Terrapin, 1982. *Contributor to:* Numerous Scientific and Defence Journals; Scientific and Defence Correspondent, Daily Express, 1946–79.

Honours: Carter Gold Medallist, London 1935; Granada Award, Journalist of the Year, 1964; Reporter of the Decade, 1966. *Address:* Church House, Kintbury, Newbury, Berkshire, England.

PINCHOT, Ann, b. New York City, USA. Novelist. m. Ben Pinchot, 1 daughter. *Publications:* Shrine of Fair Women, 1932; Talk of the Town, 1941; Hear This Woman, 1955; Hagar, 1957; 52 West, 1960; Vanessa, 1978; Certain Rich Girls, 1979; Doctors and Wives, 1980; Luck of the Linscotts, 1982; A Moment in the Sun. *Contributor to:* Short stories, novels and serials in Cosmopolitan; Good Housekeeping; McCall's American Magazine; Woman's Home Companion; Woman's Day; Christian Herald; Guideposts; and others. Also in magazines and newspapers abroad. Selections in Guideposts anthologues and anthologies for junior high school English students. *Honour:* Christopher Award for Best Short Story of the Year in McCall's Magazine, 1959. *Literary Agent:* Julian Bach, 747 Third Avenue, New York City, USA. *Address:* 88 Maltbie Avenue, Stamford, CT 06902, USA.

PINCKARD, Terri Ellen, b. 24 May 1930, Asbury Park, New Jersey, USA. Writer. m. G Thomas Pinckard, 14 July 1961, 1 son, 3 daughters. *Education:* AS, Monmouth Junior College, 1948; University of California, Los Angeles, 1949–51. *Literary Appointments:* Art Layout Copy Editor, Lynn-Western Inc, Los Angeles; Teacher, Adult Education, Professional Writing Tips Course (Mentally Gifted Minors) Righetti High School, 1977–79; Lecturer, Freelance writer, 1950–; Founder, Creator, with husband of The Pinkard Science Fiction Writer's Salon, 1963–. *Publications:* Collaborator, several Weird Tales, 1955, CBS TV series; Author, Centennial Musical, The American Spirit, 1976: Official Biographer with husband of Forrest J Ackerman, Mr Science Fiction. *Contributor to:* Non-fiction Magazine and Newspaper feature articles, etc. *Honours include:* Best Horror Story of the Year (England and American Editions, 1971; Solar Pons Society, Praed Street, Penny Mistery Award, 1971; Count Dracula Gothic Literature Society Mrs Ann Radcliffe Award, 1971. *Memberships:* Madame Severance Society; Academy of Science Fiction and Fantasy; Count Dracula Gothic Literature Society; Science Fiction Writers of America; The World Science Fiction Writers Association. *Address:* Far Horizons, 2340 Lake Marie Drive, Santa Maria, CA 93455, USA.

PINE, Leslie Gilbert, b. 22 Dec. 1907, Bristol, England. Author. m. Grace Violet Griffin, 20 Aug, 1948, London, 1 son. *Education:* BA Honours, London University, 1931; D Litt, 1985, Central School of Religion; Barrister at Law, Inner Temple, 1953; Fellow, Institute of Journalists; FSA Scot; FRGS; D Fell, American College of Heraldry. *Literary Appointments:* Managing Editor, Burke's Peerage and other works, 1946–60, Managing Editor, Shooting Times, 1946–64. *Publications include:* 35 books including: A Dictionary of Mottoes; A Dictionary of Nicknames, 1984; Teach Yourself to Trace Family History, 1984. *Contributions to:* Numerous newspapers and magazines. *Memberships:* Institute of Journalists; Royal Geographical Society; American College of Heraldry. *Address:* Hall Lodge Cottage, Brettenham, Ipswich, Suffolk, England.

PINION, Francis Bertram, b. 4 Dec. 1908, Glinton, Peterborough, England. Retired Reader and Sub-Dean, University of Sheffield. *Education:* MA, Cambridge University; Diploma in Education, Oxford University. *Publications include:* A Hardy Companion, 1968, 4th edition, 1978; A Jane Austen Companion, 1973, 3rd edition, 1985; A Bronte Companion, 1975, 85; Commentary on the Poems of Thomas Hardy, 1976, 85; Thomas Hardy: Art and Thought, 1977, 79; A D H Lawrence Companion, 1978, 84; A George Eliot Companion, 1981, 83; A Wordsworth Companion, 1984, 2nd edition, 1984; A Tennyson Companion, 1984; A TS Eliot Companion, 1986. Editor of various works including: (with Evelyn Hardy),One Rare Fair Woman, 1972;; Thomas Hardy and the Modern World, 1974; Hardy's Two on a Tower, 1975; Budmouth

Essays on Thomas Hardy, 1976; Hardy's Short Stories, 3 volumes, 1977; A George Eliot Miscellany, 1982; The Thomas Hardy Society Review, 1975–84. *Contributions to:* Reviews: The Review of English Studies; British Book News. *Honours:* LittD, Cambridge University, 1981; Mid-American State Universities Distinguished Foreign Scholar, 1981–82; Vice President, Thomas GHardy Society; Honrary Member, Victorian Studies Association of Western Canada. *Memberships:* Thomas Hardy Society; D H Lawrence Society; George Eliot Fellowship. *Address:* 65 Ranmoor Crescent, Sheffield S10 3GW, England.

PINSKER, Sanford, b. 28 Sep. 1941, Washington, Pennsylvania, USA. College Professor. *Education:* BA, Washington and Jefferson College, 1963; PhD, University of Washington, 1967. *Publications:* The Schlemial as Metaphor, 1971; The Comedy That Hoits: An Essay on the Fiction of Philip Roth, 1975; The Languages of Joseph Conrad, 1978; Critical Essays on Philip Roth, 1981; Memory Breaks Off, 1984; Conversations with Contemporary American Writers, 1985. *Contributor to:* New York Times; Harper's Salmagundi; Kan Quarterly; Dissent; Southern Review etc. *Honour:* National Endowment for the Humanities Fellowship. *Address:* 700 N Pine Street, Lancaster, PA 17603, USA.

PINSKY, Robert, b. 20 Oct. 1940, Long Branch, New Jersey, USA. Writer. m. Ellen Bailey, 30 Dec. 1961, New Jersey, 3 daughters. *Literary Appointments:* Poetry Editor, The New Republic, 1978–85. *Major Publications:* Landor's Poetry, 1967; Sadness & Happiness, 1974; The Situation of Poetry, 1977; An Explanation of America, 1979; History of my Heart, 1984; The Separate Notebooks: Poems of Czeslaw Milosz (translation), 1984; Mindwheel: An Electronic Novel. 1985. *Contributor to:* New Yorker; Threepenny Review; Hudson Review; New Republic; and others. *Honours:* Guggenheim Fellowship, 1979; American Academy Prize, 1977; William Carlos Williams Prize, 1984. *Address:* Department of English, University of California at Berkeley, Berkeley, CA 94720, USA.

PINTER, Harold, b. 10 Oct. 1930, London, England. Playwright; Director. *Plays include:* The Room, 1957; The Birthday Party, 1957; The Dumb Waiter, 1957; The Hothouse, 1958; A Slight Ace, 1958; A Night Out, 1959; The Caretaker, 1959; Night School, 1960; The Dwarfs, 1960; The Collection, 1961; The Lover, 1962; Tea Party, 1964; The Homecoming, 1964; The Basement, 1966; Landscape, 1967; Silence, 1968; Old Times, 1970; Monologue, 1972; No Man's Lane, 1974; Betrayal, 1978; Family Voices, 1980; A Kind of Alaska, 1982; Victoria Station, 1982; One for the Road, 1984. *Screenplays:* The Caretaker, 1962; The Servant, 1962; The Pumpkin Eater, 1963; The Quiller Memorandum, 1965; Accident, 1966; The Birthday Party, 1967; The Go-Between, 1969; The Homecoming, 1969; Langrishe Go Down, 1970; A La Recherche du Temps Perdu, 1972; The Last Tycoon, 1974; The French Lieutenant's Woman, 1980; Betrayal, 1981; Turtle Diary, 1984. *Publications include:* Various plays; Mac, 1968; Joint editor, New Poems, 1967; Landscape & Silence, 1969; Poems & Prose 1949–1977, 1978; Family Voices, 1981; Other Places, 1982. *Honours include:* Honorary DLitt, Reading, Birmingham, Glasgow, East Anglia, Stirling, Brown (US) Universities; Numerous literary & drama awards including Austrian State Prize for European Literature, 1973; Madrid Critics Award, Best Foreign Play, 1974; Pirandello Prize, Sicily, 1980; Commonwealth Award for Dramatic Arts, Washington DC, 1981; Donatello Prize, Italy, 1982; Ennio Flaiano Award for Screenwriting, 1982; Companion, Order of the British Empire (CBE), 1966. *Address:* c/o Judy Daish Associates Ltd, 83 Eastbourne Mews, London W2 6LQ, England.

PIRIE, Henry Ward, b. 13 Feb. 1922, Edinburgh, Scotland. Crossword Compiler; Journalist; Broadcaster. Formerly Sheriff Court Bench, Glasgow. *Education:* MA,

LLB, Ebinburgh University. *Contributions to:* Contributor of numerous crossword puzzles to various publications; Legal articles to newspapers; Talks on Scottish legal issues to radio and TV. *Address:* 16 Poplar Drive, Lenzie, Glasgow G66 4DN, Scotland.

PIRINEN, Marja-Leena, b. 18 Mar. 1939, Salo, Finland. Writer. *Education:* Candidate of Philosophy, Helsinki University, Finland, 1963. *Publications:* Naisia, 1962; Raskas Puuvilla, 1971; Laakarin Rouva, 1972; Anni Manninen, 1977; Maailman Virrassa, 1981; Jalkeen Kelo Kymmenen, 1964. *Contributions to:* Parnasso, Finalnd; Kultuurivihkot. *Honours:* Eino Leino Award, 1968; State Prize for Literature, 1971, 1972, 1977, 1984. *Membership:* Finnish Writers' Union. *Literary Agent:* Otava, Helsinki. *Address:* Kalvervonk 12.C.16, 00610 Helsinki, Finland.

PITCHER, Harvey John, b. 26 Aug. 1936, London, England. Writer. *Education:* BA, 1st class honours in Russian, Oxford University. *Publications:* Understanding the Russians, 1964; The Chekhov Play: A New Interpretation, 1973, 85; When Miss Emmie was in Russia, 1977, 84; Chekhov's Leading Lady, 1979; Chekhov: The Early Stories 1883–1888, with Patrick Miles, 1982; The Smiths of Moscow, 1984. *Contributions to:* Times Literary Supplement. *Literary Agent:* Tessa Sayle. *Address:* 37 Bernard Road, Cromer, Norfolk NR27 9AW, England.

PITCHES, Douglas Owen, b. 6 Mar. 1930, Exning, Suffolk, England. Poet. m. Barbara Joyce Budgen, 7 Aug. 1954, Horsham. *Education:* Bognor Regis Teacher Training College, 1950–52; BA, Honours, Open University, 1979. *Appointments include:* Teacher, Holdsworth Valley CP School, Newmarket; Teacher, Queen Edith CJ School, Cambridge; Teacher, Bourne CP School, Eastbourne. *Publications:* Poems, 1965; Prayer to the Virgin Mary, 1965 (Chaucer Translation); Man in Orbit and Down to Earth, 1981. *Contributor to:* Various Anthologies including Responding, New Voices; Man, It's World That Makes the Low Go Round, Laudamus Te; Magazines including: Outposts; Envoi; Scrip; Tribune; Weyfarers; Manifold; Breakthru; Expression One. *Address:* 14 Linkway, Westham, Pevensey, Sussex, England.

PITKÄNEN, Paavo, b. 13 Jan. 1908, Uusikirkko, Vpl, Finland. Bank Manager. m. Aura Maria Huttunen, 11 Dec. 1932, Vierema, 2 sons, 3 daugters (1 deceased). *Education:* Juridical Studies, Helsinki University. *Publications:* Lemmemlenkilla Lapissa, 1948; Noita ja Neljatoista, 1963; Kultaa ja Kivikirveita, 1968; Puhava Tunturi, 1972; Kavalkadi ja Purppuri, 1973; Tapahtui Lapissa, 1974; Kuurtaneen Jattilainen, 1975; Librett to the opera, Haavruuva composed by Akti Sonninen, 1970; M S to the, Kultalan Kruunun Stationi, television series in six parts, prospective director Ake Lindman; Editor, The Ivalojoen Kultalat, 1984. *Contrubutions to:* Suomen Kuvalehti and several other journals. *Honours:* Several Military and Civil Decorations. *Membership:* Suomen Kirjailijaliitto RY. *Literary Agent:* WSOY, Weilin & Goos OY, SULASOL. *Address:* Laajalahdentie 22 A 2, 00330 Helsinki 33, Finland.

PITTENGER, (William) Norman, b. 23 July 1905, Bogota, New Jersey, USA. Professor of Theology and Priesthood. *Education:* Princeton University, USA; Oxford University, England; Columbia University, USA; General Theological Seminary, STB; M Div; ThD; STD. *Publications:* 86 books including: Lure of Divine Love, 1980; After Death, 1981; Picturing God, 1982; The Pilgrim Church, 1985; The Word Incarnate, 1959; Time For Consent, 1967. *Contributions to:* Many theological and religious publications. *Memberships:* Vice President for England, Modern Churchmen's Union. *Address:* King's College, Cambridge CB2 1ST, England.

PLANER, Nigel, b. 22 Feb. 1953, London, England. Actor; Comedian; Writer. *Publication:* Neil's Book of the Dead, with Terence Blacker, 1984. *Membership:* Writers Guild. *Literary Agent:* Mark Lucas, Fraser & Dunlop.

Address: c/o Fraser & Dunlop Ltd, 91 Regent Street, London W1, England.

PLANO, Jack Charles, b. 25 Nov. 1921, Merrill, Wisconsin, USA. Author and University Professor. m. Ellen Louise Ruehlow, 25 June 1954. Oshkosh, Wisconsin, USA, 2 sons, 1 daughter. *Education:* AB, Ripon College, USA, 1949; MA, University of Wisconsin, 1959, PhD, 1954. *Publications:* The American Political Dictionary, 1962, 1967, 1972, 1976, 1979, 1982, 1985; Forging World Order, 1967, 1971; The Latin-American Politial Dictionary, 1980; The International Relations Dictionary, 3rd edition, 1982; Dictionary of Political Analysis, 1982; The Public Administration Dictionary, 1982. *Honours:* Pi Gamma Mu, Social Science Honour Society, 1954; Phi Beta Kappa, 1981; Hubert Herring Award for Best Reference Book on Latin America, 1981. *Address:* 705, Weaver Circle, Kalamazoo, MI 49007, USA.

PLATTS, Beryl, b. Buckhurst Hill, Essex, England. Author; Journalist. *Publications:* A History of Greenwich, 1973; Origins of Heraldry, 1980; Scottish Hazard, 1985. *Contributor to:* Short stories and articles to many leading journals. *Memberships:* Society of Authors; Institute of Journalists. *Address:* 9 Crooms Hill, Greenwich, London SE10, England.

PLEASANTS, Henry, b. 12 May 1910, Wayne, Pennsylvania, USA. Music Critic; Author; Translator of books on musical subjects. m. Virginia Duffey, 31 Aug. 1940, Paoli, Pennsylvania. *Literary Appointments:* Music Critic, Philadelphia Evening Bulletin, 1930–42; London Music Critic, International Herald Tribune, 1967–. *Publications:* The Agony of Modern Music, 1955; The Great Singers, 1966; Serious Music – And All That Jazz!, 1969; The Great American Popular Singers, 1974. Translations of Edward Hanslick, Louis Spohr, Robert Schumann, Hugo Wolf and Friedrich Wieck. *Contributions to:* Modern Music; High Fidelity; Stereo Review; Opera; Opera News; New York Times; JazzQuarterly; Down Beat; Saturday Review; Punch; Hibernia etc. *Honours:* Doctor of Music (Hon) Crutis Institute of Music, Philadelphia, 1977. *Literary Agent:* Oliver G Swan, Collier Associates, 875 Avenue of the Americas, New York, NY 10001, USA. *Address:* 95 Roebuck House, London SW1E 5BE, England.

PLEIJEL, Agneta Christine, b. 26 Feb. 1940. Writer. m. M Bielawski, 27 Nov. 1982, Stockholm, Sweden. 1 daughter. *Education:* Dr Phil, Gothenburg, 1973. *Literary Appointments:* Vice President Swedish PEN Club; Editor, Ord & Bild, 1972–75; Literary Critic of, Aftonbladet, 1968–80; Editor, Hotel Ornskold. *Publications:* Order Reigns in Berlin, 1970; Happy Lisa, 1979; Kollontay, 1979; Angels, Dwarfs, 1981; Eyes Out of a Dream, 1984; The Hill on the Dark Side of the Moon, 1984; Some Summer Nights, 1984. *Contributions to:* Various Swedish daily papers and literary magazines. *Memberships:* Swedish Writers' Union; Swedish Playwrights' Union. *Literary Agent:* Folmer Hansen, Lundgaten 4, Solna, Sweden. *Address:* Tantogatan 45, 117 42 Stockholm, Sweden.

PLEZIA, Marian, b. 26 Feb. 1917, Cracow, Poland. Classical Scholar, Professor. *Education:* PhD, Cracow University, 1944. *Publications:* De Andronici Rhodii Studiis Aristoteliciis, 1946; De Commentariis Isagogicis, 1949; Cronica Petri Comitis Poloniae, 1951; Aristotelis Epistularum Fragmenta, 1960; Lettre d'Aristote a Alexandra sur la Politique, (with J Bielawski), 1970; Lexicon Mediae et Infirmae Latinitatis Polonorum I-V, 1953–; Aristotelis Privatorum Scriptorum Fragmenta, 1977. *Contributions to:* Numerous journals. *Honours include:* Officer of the Cross, Polonia Restituta; A Jurzykowski Award, 1980. *Memberships include:* Academia Latinitati Inter Omnes Gentes Fovendae, Rome, italy; Corresponding member, Polish Academy of Sciences. *Address:* Friedleina 28c/4, 30-009, Cracow Poland.

PLISCHKE, Elmer, b. 15 July 1914, Milwaukee, Wisconsin, USA. University Professor Emeritus; Author. m. Audrey Alice Siehr, 30 May 1941, Milwaukee, 1 son,

1 daughter. *Education:* PhB, Marquette University, 1937; MA, American University, 1938; PhD, Clark University, 1943; Certificate, International Law, University of Michigan, 1938; Certificate, Naval School of Military Government & Administrtion, Columbia University, 1943. *Literary Appointments:* Trustee 1960–64, President 1961–63, Institute for Documentary Research on Foreign Nations; Editorial Board, Journal of Politics, 1966–68. *Publications include:* Summit Diplomacy, 1958; Contemporary Governments of Germany, 2nd edition 1969; Government & Politics of Contemporary Berlin, 1963; Foreign Relations Decisionmaking: Options Analysis, 1973; US Diplomats & Their Missions: A Profile of American Diplomatics Emissaries since 1776, 1975; Modern Diplomacy: The Art & The Artisans, 1979; US Foreign Relations: A Guide to Information Sources, 1980; Presidential Diplomacy: Chronology of Summit Visits, Trips & Meetings, 1985; Diplomat-in-Chief: The President at the Summit, in press. *Contributions to:* Numerous professional & literary journals including, American Journal of International Law; American Political Science Review; International Studies Quarterly; World Affairs; etc. *Honours:* Dedication, Foreign Policy & Public Policy, ed. Don C Piper & Ronald J Terchek, 1983; Member, five honour societies. *Address:* 227 Ewell Avenue, Gettysburg, PA 17325, USA.

PLOOIJ, Jean-Pierre Etienne, b. 13 July 1945, Amsterdam, The Netherlands. Writer. 1 daughter. *Education:* Political Science and French Literature, University of Amsterdam. *Publications:* Duvelsmoer, (Devils mother), 1981; Patience, 1984; 15 Radio Plays for KRO, Holland, WDR, Germany, France Culture, France, BRT, Belgium. Text for Rolf Orthel's TV documentary about William Sandberg for NOS Holland. NRC-Handelsblad; Avenue; Dramatisch Accoord. *Literary Agent:* Jan Michael. *Address:* Lindengracht 69 II, 1015 KD Amsterdam, The Netherlands.

PLUM, Thomas Schunior, b. 8 Sep. 1945, Washington DC, USA. Author & Trainer. m. Joan Hall, 16 Sep. 1975, Lincoln, Nebraska, USA. *Education:* BA Mathematics, Rice University, Houston, Texas, 1965; PhD Computer & Communication Science, University of Michigan, Ann Arbor, Michigan, 1972. *Major Publications:* Learning to Program in C, 1982; C Programming Guidelines, 1984; Reliable Data Structures in C, 1985; Efficient C, (with J Brodie), 1985. *Honour:* Phi Beta Kappa, 1964. *Address:* 1 Spruce Avenue, Cardiff, NJ 08232, USA.

PLUMB, John Harold (Sir), b. 20 Aug. 1911, Leicester, England. Historian, Professor of Modern English History at University of Cambridge. *Education:* University College, Leicester; Christ's College, Cambridge; BA; PhD; LittD. *Literary Appointments:* Editor, History of Human Society, 1959–; European advisory editor, Horizon, 1959–; Historical advisor, Penguin Books. *Publications include:* England in the Eighteenth Century, 1950 and 1953; Sir Robert Walpole volume I 1956, volume II 1960, both reprinted 1972; The First Four Georges, 1956; The Renaissance, 1961; Crisis in the Humanities, 1964; The Growth of Politcal Stability in England 1675–1725, 1967; Death of the Past, 1969; In the Light of History, 1972; The Commercialisation of Leisure, 1974; Royal Heritage the book of the BBC television series, advisor and co-author with Huw Wheldon, 1977; New Light on the Tyrant, George III, 1978. *Honours include:* Knight; Several honorary degrees. *Memberships include:* Fellow, British Academy; Fellow, Royal Historical Society; Fellow, Society of Antiquaries; Fellow, Royal Society of Literature; Honorary foreign member, American Academy of Arts and Sciences. *Address:* Christ's College, Cambridge, England.

PLYMTON, Bill, b. 30 Apr. 1946, Portland, Oregon, USA. Cartoonist. *Education:* BA, Graphic Design, Portland State University, 1969. *Publications:* Tube Strips, 1976; Medium Rare, 1978; Polls Apart, with Kathi Paton, 1984. *Contributions:* History of Censorship, (Penthouse); Kisses, (Rolling Stone); Hair

Styles, (National Lampoon).. *Honours:* 1st Prize, Pacific Northwest Film Festival, 1984, 1st Prize, Brazilian Film Festival 1984, Winner, Black Maria Film Festival, New Jersey 1984, animated film, Boomtown. *Literary Agent:* Kris Dahl. *Address:* 153 1st Avenue, New York, NY 10003, USA.

POBO, Kenneth George, b. 24 Aug. 1954, Elmhurst, Illinois, USA. English Teacher. *Education:* BA, English, Wheaton College, 1976; MA, 1979, PhD, 1983, English, University of Wisconsin. *Publications:* Musings from the Porchlit Sea, 1979; Billions of Lit Cigarettes, 1981. *Contributor to:* Indiana Review; Hanging Loose; Poet & Critic; Poem; Tendril; Poetry Row; Roanoke Review; etc. *Honours:* Winner, Mae E Galen Prize, 1979; Winner, Phillips Award, 1985. *Address:* c/o English Dept, University of Tennessee, Knoxville, TN 37919, USA.

POCOCK, Tom, b. 18 Aug. 1925, London, England. Author; Journalist. m. Penelope Casson, 26 Apr. 1969, 2 daughters. *Publications:* Nelson and His World, 1968; Chelsea Reach, 1970; Fighting General, 1973; Remember Nelson, 1977; The Young Nelson in the Americas, 1980; 1945: The Dawn Came Up Like Thunder, 1983. *Contributions to:* Numerous national magazines and newspapers. *Address:* 22 Lawrence Street, London SW3 5NF, England.

PODHORETZ, Norman, b. 16 Jan. 1930, Brooklyn, New York, USA. Editor and Author. m. Midge Decter, 21 Oct. 1956, New York, 1 son, 3 daughters. *Education:* AB, Columbia, 1950; BHL, Jewish Theological Seminary, 1950; BA, Clare College, Cambridge, England, 1952; MA, Cambridge, 1957. *Literary Appointment:* Editor, Commentary magazine, 1960–. *Publications:* Doings and Undoings, 1964; Making It, 1967; Breaking Ranks: A Political Memoir, 1979; The Present Danger, 1980; Why We Were in Vietnam, 1982; The Bloody Crossroads: Where Literature and Politics Meet, 1986. *Contributions:* Numerous magazines and journals. *Honours:* Various honorary degrees. *Literary Agent:* George Borchardt. *Address:* c/o Commentary, 165 E 56th Street, New York, NY 10022, USA.

PODLECKI, Anthony Joseph, b. 25 Jan. 1936, Buffalo, New York, USA. University Educator. *Education includes:* BA, 1960, MA, 1963, Oxford University, England; MA, 1961, PhD, 1963, University of Toronto, Canada. *Publications include:* The Political Background of Aeschylean Tragedy, 1966; Aeschylus, The Persians, Verse translations with Commentary, 1970; The Life of Themistocles: A Critical Survey of the Literary and Archaeological Evidence, 1975; Age of Glory: Imperial Athens in the Time of Pericles, 1975; The Early Greek Poets and Their Times, 1984. *Contributions to:* Various journals. *Honours include:* Fulbright Scholarship, 1957–59. *Memberships include:* Classical Association of Canada. *Address:* 4024 West 18th Avenue, Vancouver, British Columbia, Canada V6S 1B8.

POEN, Monte M, b. 25 Nov. 1930, Lake City, Iowa, USA. Historian. m. Kathryn Walker, 22 May 1982, Las Vegas, Nevada, 4 sons, 2 daughters. *Education:* BA; MA; PhD. *Literary Appointments:* Editor, Albert D Lasker, Foundation, New York, 1967; Northern Arizona University, Flagstaff, Arizona, 1966–, currently Professor of American History. *Publications:* Harry S Truman versus the Medical Lobby: The Genesis of Medicare, 1979; Editor: Strictly Personal and Confidential: The Unmailed Letters of Harry S Truman, 1982; Editor: Letters Home by Harry Truman, 1984. *Contributions to:* Contributor to various magazines and journals. *Honours:* Outstanding Educator of America, 1972; President's Award (NAU) 1982; Distinguished Faculty Award (NAU) 1982. *Memberships:* Organization of American Historians; Oral History Association; Center for the Study of the Presidency; Arizona Authors' Association. *Literary Agent:* Ann Elmo, New York. *Address:* 3703 N Grandview Drive, Flagstaff, AZ 86001, USA.

POERNER, Artur José, b. 1 Oct. 1939, Rio de Janeiro, Brazil. Writer; Journalist. m. Rita de Cassia da Frota, 4 Mar. 1984, Rio de Janeiro. *Education:* Naval Academy,

Rio de Jeneiro, 1959–60; BA, Law, University of Rio de Janeiro, 1968; German for Foreigners, Free University, Berlin, 1972. *Publications:* Argelia: O Caminho da Independencia, 1966; Essay, O Poder Jovem, 1968; Essay, En lo Profundo del Infierno, 1978; Novel. *Contributions to:* Numerous journals including: Cadernos do Terceiro Mundo, 1985; Encontros com a Civilizacao Brasileira, 1980–81; Iberoamericana, 1980; Der Spiegel, 1971–80; Exempla, University of Tübingen, 1977; New Society, 1969–71; Polityka, Belgrade, 1969; Istoé, 1981–84; Pasquim, 1971–84; Correio da Manha, 1963–70; Folha da Semina, 1965–66. *Honours:* Premio Letterario Verrina-Lorenzon, Cosenza, Italy, 1978: Premio de Leitura do Servico Nacional de Teatro, Brazil, 1981. *Literary Agent:* Carmen Balcells, Barcelona, Spain. *Address:* Rua Gustavo Sampaio, 621-Apt 1001, Leme, CEP 22. 010, Rio de Janeiro-RJ, Brazil.

POGREBIN, Letty Cottin, b. 9 June 1939, New York City, USA. Author. m. Betrand B Pogrebin, 1963, 1 son, 2 daughters. *Education:* BA, cum laude, Brandeis University, 1959. *Publications:* Having Friends, Being Friends, 1986; Family Politics, 1983; Growing Up Free, 1980; Getting Yours, 1975; How to Make it in a Man's World, 1970; Stories for Free Children, Editor, 1982; Editor, Ms Magazine 1971–; Contributor to numerous Anthologies, 1974–85. *Contributor to:* Columnist: The New York Times, 1983; Ladies Home Journal, 1971–81; Articles in, New York Times; Moment Magazine; TV Guide; McGill Journal of Education; Boardroom reports; etc. *Honours:* Recipient numerous honours and awards including, Poynter Fellow, Yale University, National Honorary Life Member, Pioneer Women, 1984; Emmy Award, 1974; Clarion Award, Women in Communiation; etc. *Memberships:* Founding Member, National Women's Political Caucus; Charter Member, The Liberty Club; Women's Forum; Anthor's League; National Commission for Women's Equality of the American Jewish Congress; UJA-Federation Task Force on Women; New York Network; Board of Directors: Action for Children's Television, Child Care Action Campaign, Public Action Coalition on Toys, Women's Action Alliance, Jewish Fund for Justice International Center for Peace in the Middle East; Board of Trustees, Public Education Association; etc. *Address:* c/o Ms Magazine, 119 W 40th Street, New York, NY 10018, USA.

POIRIER, Richard, b. 9 Sep. 1925, Gloucester, Massachusetts, USA. Literary Critic. *Education:* University of Paris, France, 1946; BA, Amherst College, USA, 1949; MA, Yale University, 1950; Fulbright Scholar, Cambridge University, England, 1952; PhD, Harvard University, Massachusetts, USA, 1960. *Literary Appointments:* Williams College, 1950–52; Harvard University, 1955–62; Rutgers University, 1962–; Vice President, Library of America, 1980–. Editor; Partisan Review, 1963–71; Raritan Quarterly, 1980–. *Publications:* Comic Sense of Henry James, 1960; A World Elsewhere, 1966; The Performing Self, 1971; Norman Mailer, 1976; Robert Frost: The Work of Knowing, 1977. In Defense of Reading, co-Editor, 1962. *Contributions to:* Daelalus; New Republic; Partisan Review; New York Review; London Review of Books; various others. *Honours:* Phi Beta Kappa, 1949; Fulbright Fellow, 1952; Gugenheim Fellow, 1967; National Endowment for the Humanities Fellow, 1972; HHD, Amherst College, 1978; Award, American Academy of Arts and Letters, 1980. *Memberships:* Poets, Playwrights, Editors, Essayists and Novelists; American Academy of Arts and Sciences; Century Club. *Address:* 104 West 70th Street, 9B, New York, NY 10023, USA.

POLAK, Maralyn Lois, b. Long Branch, New Jersey, USA. Journalist; Poet. *Education:* BS, Temple University. *Literary Appointments:* Assistant Editor, Temple University, Alumni Review; Instructor, Writing, Community College of Philadelphia; Poetry Workshop Instructor, Glassboro State College, Miquon School, Merion Mercy Academy, Norristown Middle School; Curent, Contributing Editor, Philadelphia Inquirer Magazine. *Publication:* Facing the Music, poetry, 1985; The Writer as Celebrity, interviews, 1986. *Contributions:*

Poetry: Painted Bride Quarterly; Village Voice; Electricity; South Street Star; Woman Poet; Metropolitan Magazine; Philadelphia Magazine; Friday. Articles: Philadelphia Inquirer Sunday magazine; Andy Warhol's Interview. *Honours:* Awards from: Poets in the Schools, Pennsylvania; Poetry on Wheels, Pennsylvania. *Membership:* Pen & Pencil Club. *Literary Agent:* Blanche Schlessinger, Philadelphia. *Address:* 132 South 18th Street, Philadelphia, PA 19103, USA.

POLAND, Dorothy Elizabeth Hayward, b. 3 May 1937, Barry, South Glamorgan, Wales. Writer. *Publications include:* The Admiral's Lady, 1978; Secret of Petherwick, 1982; The Massingham Topaz, 1982; Beware the King's Enchantess, 1983; Moon in Aries, 1984; Eagle's Talon, 1984; Death in the New Forest, 1984; Ghost from the River; Woman from Beyond the Tamar; Santa Cruz. *Address:* 95 Dock View Road, Barry, South Glamorgan, Wales.

POLE, Jack Richon, b. 14 Mar. 1922, London, England. Historian; Rhodes Professor of American History & Instititions, Oxford University. m. 31 May 1952, Pittsburgh, USA, 1 son, 2 daughters. *Education:* BA, 1949, MA, 1978, Oxon; PhD, Princeton, USA, 1953; MA, Cantab, 1963. *Publications:* Political Representation in England & the Origins of the American Republic, 1966; Foundations of American Independence, 1972; The Pursuit of Equality in American History, 1978; Paths to the American Past, 1979; The Gift of Government: Political Responsibility from the English Restoration to American Independence, 1983. *Contributor to:* American Historical Review; William and Mary Quarterly; Journal of Southern History; Times Literary Supplement; The Spectator; The New Republic; etc. *Honours:* New Jersey Prize, Princeton, 1953; Radall Award, Southern Historical Association, 1959; Honorary Fellow, Historical Society of Ghana, 1967; Knight of Mark Twain, FRHist S; FBA. *Address:* 20 Divinity Road, Oxford OX1 4LJ, England.

POLITELLA, Dario, b. 12 Aug. 1921, Lawrence, Massachusetts, USA. Professor of Journalistic Writing & Public Relations. m. Frances Charlotte O'Neal, 24 Oct. 1942, Camp Hood, Texas, USA, 1 son, 2 daughters. *Education:* BA, University of Massachusetts, 1947; MA Journalism, Syracuse University, 1949; PhD, Mass Communication, Syracuse University, 1965. *Literary Appointments:* Bureau Manager, Geneva New York Daily Times, 1949–50; Assistant Professor of Journalism, Kent State University, Ohio, 1950–55; Senior Instructor, Syracuse University, 1955–57; Managing Editor, Skyways Magazine, 1957; writer, CBStv, 1958; Senior Publicity Accountant Executive, OS Tyson Agency, New York City, 1958–60; Associate Editor, Flying Magazine, 1957–58; Public Relations Representative, Lockhead Corporation, 1960–62; Assistant Professor of Journalism, Ball State University, 1962–65; Associate Professor, Professor of English and Journalism Studies, University of Massachusetts, Amherst, USA, 1965–. *Major Publications:* Operation Grasshopper, 1958; Illustrated Anatomy of Campus Humor, 1971; 5 editions of Directory of the College Student Press in America, 1967–81. *Contributor to:* Numerous articles on many subjects. *Honours:* Gold Key Award, Columbia University, 1984. *Memberships:* Vice-President (East), Society of Collegiate Journalists; Board of Trustees, 1969–, Chairman, 1973–85, Graves Memorial Library, Sunderland Masachusetts; Association for Education in Journalism; Society for Professional Journalists. *Address:* 178 N Main Street, Sunderland, MA 01375, USA.

POLITO, Mary Elaine, b. 26 Feb. 1949, Ontario, Canada. Children's Musical Theatre Playwright; Piano Teacher. m. 1971, (div) 2 daughters. *Education:* Associate of the Western Ontario Conservatory of Music-Piano Teacher. *Publications:* No Wonder It's Thunder, 1983; The Fair and Square Fair, 1984; Teri and the River Crystal, 1985; (all Plays for Children with Musical Scores). *Membership:* Vice-Chairman, Ontario Board of Directors, Jeunesses Musicale. *Literary Agent:*

Playwrights' Union of Canada. *Address:* 23 Wolfe Street, Lindsay, Ontario K9V 2J3, Canada.

POLKING, Dorothy, b. 21 Dec. 1925, USA. Director, Writer's Digest School. *Education:* University of Cincinnati. *Literary Appointments:* National Headliner, Women in Communications Inc, 1970. *Publications:* How to Make Money In Your Spare Time by Writing, 1971; Artists Market, 1975; The Writer's Encyclopedia, 1983; Oceans of the World: Our Essential Resource, 1983; Freelance Jobs For Writers, 1984; Beginning Writer's Answer Book, 1984; Law and the Writer, 1985; The Private Pilot's Dictionary and Handbook, 1985; Children's Books: Let's Go with Lewis and Clark, 1963; Let's Go With Henry Hudson, 1964; Let's Go See Congress at Work, 1966; Let's Go to an Atomic Energy Town, 1968. *Contributions to:* Writer's Digest magazine; Writer's Yearbook; Quill magazine; The Press Woman; various consumer and trade magazines. *Memberships:* Author's Guild; National Federation of Press Women; President Cincinnati branch, Ohio State President, National League of American Pen Women; Women in Communications. *Address:* 529 Constitution Square, Cincinnati, OH 45230, USA.

POLLAND, Madeleine Angela, b. 31 May 1918, Kinsale, County Cork, Ireland. Writer. m. Arthur Joseph Polland, 10 June 1946, Letchworth, England, 1 son, 1 daughter. *Publications:* Children of the Red King, 1960; The Town Across the Water, 1961; Born the Proud, 1961; Fingal's Quest, 1961; The White Twilight, 1962; Chuiraquimba and the Black Robes, 1962; City of the Golden House, 1963; The Queen's Blessing, 1964; Flame over Tara, 1964; Mission to Cathay, 1965; Queen Without Crown, 1965; Deirdre, 1967; To Tell My People, 1968; Straner in the Hills, 1968; To Kill a King, 1970; Alhambra, 1970; A Family Affair, 1971; Daughter to Poseidon, 1972; Prince of the Double Axe, 1976; Adult Novels: Thicker Than Water, 1964; The Little Spot of Bother, 1967; Random Army, 1970; Package to Spain, 1971; Double Shadow, 1977. *Contributor to:* Numerous journals and magazines including, Woman; Woman's Realm. *Honours:* Recipient, numerous honours and awards. *Literary Agent:* Hilary Rubinstein, A P Watt Ltd, London, England. *Address:* Edihicio Hercules 406, Avda Gamonal, Arroya de la Miel, Malaga, Spain.

POLLEY, Judith Anne, b. 15 Sep. 1938, London, England. Writer. m. 28 Mar. 1959; Kenton, Middlesex, England, 1 son. *Major Pubications:* The Countess, 1967; Maria Elena, Journey into Love, Master of Karatangi, A Pride of Macdonalds, 1968; Slightly Scarlet, 1969; Children of the Devil, The Flowering Desert, A Man for Melanie, Madelon, 1970; The King's Cavalier, 1971; Dangerous Deception, Castle of the Mist, 1972; The King's Shadow, 1975; Francesca, Keeper of the Flame, 1977; Laird's French Bride, The Captive Heart, Place of Happiness, 1978; To Touch the Stars; Beloved Enemy, 1980; Don't run from Love, Moonshadow, Prince of Deception, 1981; Beloved Adversary, 1981; Shadow of the Eagle, Silver Salamander, The Wind of Change, 1982; The Measure of Love, The Peacuful Homecoming, 1983; The Valley of Tears, Moonflower, Elusive Flame of Love, Mistress of Tanglewood, 1984; Black Ravenswood, The Lord of Darkness, Devil of Talland, 1985; Passionate Pirate, 1986; Where The Heart Leads, 1986. *Contributor to:* Several English magazines, serialised in Woman's Weekly Library. *Membership:* Founder Member of English Romantic Novelists' Association. *Address:* Calcada, 8150 Sao Braz de Alportel, Algarve, Portugal.

POLLINI, Francis, b. 9 Sep. 1930, West Wyoming, Pennsylvania, USA. Author. m. Gloria Ann Swann, 12 Sep, 1959, 2 daughters. *Education:* BA, Liberal Arts & Psychology, Pennsylvania State University, 1951. *Publications include:* Novels: Night, 1960; Glover, 1965; Excursion, 1965; The Crown, 1967; Pretty Maids All In A Row, 1969; Dubonnet, 1974; The Hall, 1975. Plays: Three Plays, 1967. *Membership:* Society of Authors, UK. *Literary Agent:* Georges Borchardt, New York.

Address: c/o UPB, 983 Wyoming Avenue, Forty Fort, PA 18704, USA.

POLLOCK, John Charles, b. 1923, London, England. Clergyman, Writer. *Education:* MA, Trinity College, Cambridge; Ridley Hall, Cambridge. *Publications include:* A Cambridge Movement, 1953; Earth's Remotest End, 1960; Hudson Taylor and Maria, 1962; Moody Without Sankey, 1963; The Keswick Story, 1964; The Christians From Siberia, 1964; Billy Graham, 1966, revised edition 1969; The Apostle, 1969; A Foreign Devil in China, USA 1971, UK 1972; George Whitefield and The Great Awakening, USA 1972, UK 1973; Wilberforce, UK 1977, USA 1978; Billy Graham Evangelist To The World, 1979; The Siberian Seven, UK 1979, USA 1980; Amazing Grace: John Newton's Story, 1981; The Master A Life of Jesus, UK 1984; USA 1985; Billy Graham: Highlights of the Story, 1984; In USA 1985 as, To All The Nations; The Cambridge Seven, revised centenary edition, 1985; Shaftesbury: The Poor Man's Earl, UK 1985, USA 1986. *Contributions to:* Churchman; Church of England Newspaper; Christianity Today; Sunday Telegraph. *Membership:* English Speaking Union. *Literary Agent:* Curtis Brown Limited. *Address:* Rose Ash House, South Molton, Devon EX36 4RB, England.

POLLOCK, Sharon. Writer. *Appointments:* Head, Playwriting Division, University of Alberta, Canada, 1976–77; Director, Playwrights' Colony, Banff Centre of Fine Arts, 1977–80; Playwright in Residence, Alberta Theatre Projects, Calgary, 1977–79; Artist in Residence, National Arts Centre, 1979–82; Visiting Lecturer, numerous universities and colleges. *Publications:* Stage Plays: A Compulsory Option; Walsh; And Out Goes You?; The Komagata Maru Incident; One Tiger to a Hill; Generations; Blood Relations; Whiskey Six Cadenzaa; Family Trappings; Wudjesay?; New Canadians; Superstition Through the Ages; The Rose and the Nightingale, adaptation; The Magic Prince, adaptation; Starchild, adaptation; The Great Drag Race; A Lesson in Swizzlery; The Wreck of the National Line; Chautaulua Spelt Energy; Radio Plays: Split Seconds in the Death of; 31 for 2; We to the Gods; Waiting; In memory of; Intensive Care; Mrs Yale and Jennifer, 7 episode series; etc; TV Plays include: Portrait of a Pig; The Larsens; Ransom; The Person's Case; Country Joy, episodes 16,19,22,28,31,35. *Honours include:* Governor General's Literary Award for Drama, 1981; Nellie Award for Best National Radio Drama, 1981; Golden Sheaf Award for Human Drama, Television, 1979; Senior Artist's Award, Canada Council, 1985; etc. *Memberships:* Advisory Arts Panel, Chairman, Canada Council, 1979–80; Secretary, ACTRA Regional Council, Southern Alberta, 1983; Judge, ACTRA National Awards, 1984; various other professional organisations. *Address:* 319 Manora Drive NE, Calgary, Alberta, Canada T2A 4RZ.

POLOMA, Margaret M, b. 27 Aug. 1943, Los Angeles, California, USA. University Professor. m. T Neal Garland, 3 July 1970, Cleveland, Ohio, USA. *Education:* BA, Notre Dame College of Ohio, 1965; MA, 1967, PhD, 1970, Case Western Reserve University. *Publications:* Contemporary Sociological Theory, 1979; The Charismatic Movement: Is there a New Pentecost? 1982; Social Problems: Christian Perspectives, edited with Charles F DeSanto, 1985. *Contributions to:* Former co-editor, Sociological Forms; Editor of the Newsletter, Christian Sociological Society. *Memberships:* Christian Sociological Society; Association for the Sociology of Religion; Society for the Scientific Study of Religion. *Address:* Department of Sociology, The University of Akron, Akron, OH 44325, USA.

POLUNIN, Nicholas, b. 26 June 1909, Checkendon, Oxfordshire, England. Biological Environmentalist; Former University Professor. m. Helen Eugenie, 3 Jan. 1948, Montreal, Canada, 2 sons, 1 daughter. *Education:* MS, Yale University, USA; MADPhil, DSc, Oxford University, England; various Fellowships. *Literary Appointments:* Founding editor, Biological Conservation,

1968–74; Founding Editor, Environmental Conservation, 1974–; Editor, series, Plant Science Monographs, and World Crops Books, 1954–78; currently, Convener and General Editor, Environmental Monographs and Symposia and Chairman of Editorial Board of Complementary Environmental Policy Series. *Publications include:* Botany of the Canadian Eastern Arctic, 3 volumes, 1940–48; Arctic Unfolding, 1949; Circumpolar Arctic Flora, 1959; Introduction to Plant Geography and some related sciences, 1960; Editor, The Environmental Future, 1972, Growth Without Ecodisasters?, 1980, Ecosystem Theory and Application, 1986; about 40 other books written, edited, or planned and convened. *Contributions to:* Numerous publications. *Honours include:* Canadian Medaille Marie-Victoria; United States Order of Polaris (twice); CBE; FLS, life; FRGS, life; FRHS, life; Fellowships and life memberships including Harvard Club of New York City, Reform Club of London, and New College, Oxford; Vice President, Oxford University Exploration Club. *Address:* Environmental Conservation, 7 Chemin Taverney, 1218 Grand-Saconnex, Geneva, Switzerland.

POMEROY, Elizabeth Wright, b. 31 July 1938, San Francisco, California, USA. Library Administrator and Scholar. m. Charles W Pomeroy, 25 June 1966, San Marino, California, 1 son, 1 daughter. *Education:* BA, Stanford University; MAT, Harvard University; MA, University of California, Berkeley; PhD, University of California, Los Angeles. *Literary Appointments:* Visiting Scholar, Center for Medieval and Renaissance Studies, University of California at Los Angeles, 1985–86. *Publications:* The Elizabethan Miscellanies, 1973; The Huntington Library, Art Gallery and Botanical Gardens, 1983. *Contributions to:* Modern Fiction Studies, Explicator; Twentieth Century Literature; Wilson Library Bulletin. *Memberships:* Phi Beta Kappa; Modern Language Association; British Studies Association; President 1981, Southern California Renaissance Conference. *Address:* 420 South Parkwood Avenue, Pasadena, CA 91107, USA.

POND, Lily, b. 30 Sep. 1947, Detroit, Michigan, USA. Publisher; Writer; Editor; Designer. *Education:* BA, California State University, San Francisco, 1979. *Literary Appointments:* Originator, Publisher, Editor and Designer, Yellow Silk: Journal of Erotic Arts, 1981–. *Contributions to:* Coordinating Council of Literary Magazines, Editors Award, 1984. *Membership:* Coordinating Council of Literary Magazines. *Address:* P O Box 6374, Albany, CA 94706, USA.

PONIEWAZ, Jeff, b. 28 Sep. 1946, Milwaukee, Wisconsin, USA. Poet; Teacher. *Education:* BA, 1970; MA, 1973; University of Wisconsin, Milwaukee. *Literary Appointments:* Teacher, Creative Writing, University of Wisconsin, Milwaukee, 1971–73; 1976, 1983–86; Poets-in-the-Schools Programme, Wisconsin, 1973–83. *Publications:* Dolphin Leaping in the Milky Way, 1985; Anthologies: New Poetry Out of Wisconsin, 1969; Brewing: 20 Milwaukee Poets, 1972; Gathering Place of the Waters: 30 Milwaukee Poets, 1983. *Contributor to:* Earth First; Greenpeace Chronicles; Blake Times; Los Angeles Times; New Age; Mickle Street Review; Beloit Poetry Journal; New American and Canadian Poetry; Minnesota Review; Wisconsin Review; The World; Hanging Loose; Height-Ashbury Literary Quarterly, etc. *Honour:* First Prize, Academy of American Poets Poetry Contest, 1973. *Address:* 4540 S 1st Street, Milwaukee, WI 53207, USA.

POOLE, Mildred Ferguson, b. 27 Sep. 1916, United States. Writer. m. Leland Dwight Poole, 20 Apr. 1943, Hollywood, 1 son, 2 daughters. *Contributor to:* Today's Health; Cancer Journal; Institute for Research; Chronicle Guidance; National Enquirer; Mother Earth News; Biomedical News; The Answer. *Memberships:* Mystery Writers of America (Affiliate); Writers' Workshop West. *Literary Agent:* David Rose. *Address:* 313 Koogler Drive NW, Roanoke, VA 24017, USA.

POOLLA, Tirupati Raju, b. 3 Sep. 1904, B K Palli. Educator; Author. 1 son. *Education:* BA; MA; PhD;

SASTRI. *Appointments:* Lecturer, Reader, Andhra University; Professor, Philosophy and Psychology, University of Rajasthan; Professor, Philosophy, Indian Studies, The College of Wooster, Ohio, USA; Visiting Professor, California, Illinois, Hawaii, New York, Mainz, etc. *Publications:* Thought and Reality, 1937; Comparative Studies in Philosophy, 1951; Idealistic Thought of India, 1953; Introduction to Comparative Philosophy, 1962; The Concept of Man, 1966; Philisophical Traditions of India, 1971; Spirit, Being and Self, 1982; The Structural Depths of Indian Thought, 1985. *Contributor:* More than 200 articles in Indian, British, German and American Philosophical Journals. *Honour:* Order of Merit, Padma Bhushan, Government of India, 1958. *Memberships:* Numerous professional philosophical associations in India and USA. *Address:* The College of Wooster, Wooster, OH 44691, USA.

POPE, Katherine Victoria, b. 8 May 1939, Springfield, Missouri, USA. English Professor. m. Will Marshall, 3 Mar. 1980, Fort Worth, 2 stepsons, 1 stepdaughter. *Education:* BA, Smith College, 1961; PhD, Rice University, 1971. *Publications:* Who Am I This Time? Female Portraits in British and American Literature, (with Carol Pearson), 1976; The Female Hero in American and British Literature, (with Carol Pearson), 1981. *Contributions to:* Literary and psychological journals including: Journal of Mental Imagery; Imagination, Cognition and Personality. *Address:* English Department, Bel Mar College, Baldwin and Ayers, Corpus Christi, TX 78403, USA.

POPESCU, Christine, b. 1 Oct. 1930, Wimbledon, London, England. Author. m. Julian Popescu, 6 Oct. 1954, Henley-on-Thames, 2 sons, 2 daughters. *Publications:* 82 books including Phantom Horse, 1956; Pony Patrol Series, 1970's; Black Pony Series, 1970's; Father Unknown, 1980; No Home For Jessie, 1986. *Contributor to:* Daily Telegraph; Pony; Horse and Rider. *Memberships:* PEN; Society of Authors. *Address:* The Old Parsonage, Mellis, Eye, Suffolk, England.

POPOVSKY, Mark Aleksandr, b. 8 July 1922, Odessa. Author. m. Lilya Grinberg, 4 Nov. 1969, 1 son, 2 daughters. *Education:* MA, Moscow State University, 1952. *Appointments:* Freelance Writer, Russia, 1946–77; Deputy Editor, Grani (Quarterly), 1984–. *Publications:* Kogda Vrach mechtaet, 1957; Put' k Serdtsu, 1960; Po Sledam Otstupaiushtshich, 1963; Vtoroe Sotvorenie Mira, 1960; Razorvannaia Pautina, 1962; The Story of Dr Haffkine, 1963; Kormil'tsy Planety, 1964; Piat'Dnei Odnoi Zhizni, 1965; Dorozhe Zolota, 1966; Nado Speshit, 1968; Nad Kartoy Tshelovetshesich Stradanij, 1971; Liudi Sredi Ludei, 1972; Pantatseia-Doch'Eskulapa, 1973; Iun'skie Novosti, 1978; Manipulated Science, 1979; Upravliaemaia Nauka, 1978; Zhizn' i zhitie Voinolasenetskogo arkiepiskopa i khirurga, 1979; Science in Chains, 1980; The Vavilob Affairs, 1984; Delo Akademika Vavilova, 1983; Russkie Muzhiki Rasskazivaiut, 1983; Tretii Lishnii.On, Ona i Sovetskii Rezhim, 1985. *Contributor to:* Numerous professional journals, magazines and newspapers, including, Novoye Russkoye Slovo; Panorama; New York City Tribune, etc. *Memberships:* Union of Soviet Journalists, 1957–77; Union of Soviet Writers, 1961–77; PEN; Vice President, Writers in Exile, American Branch. *Address:* 65 Hillside Ave, Apt 5H, New York, NY 10040, USA.

POPPER, Frank James, b. 26 Mar. 1944, Chicago, Illinois, USA. City Planner. m. Deborah Epstein, 9 Aug. 1968, New York City, 1 son, 1 daughter. *Education:* BA, Haverford College, 1965; MPA, 1968, PhD, 1972, Harvard University. *Publications:* The President's Commissions, 1970; Urban Nongrowth, 1976; The Politics of Land-Use Reform, 1981; Land Reform, American Style, 1984. *Contributor to:* Numerous City Planning, Political Science and Medical Journals; Major Newspapers. *Honour:* Gilbert F White Fellowship, 1982–83. *Address:* Urban Studies Department, Rutgers University, New Brunswick, NJ 08903, USA.

POPPER, (Sir) Karl (Raimund), b. 28 July 1902, Vienna, Austria. Author. m. Josefine Anna Henninger, 11 Apr. 1930, Vienna. *Education:* PhD, University of Vienna, 1928; MA, University of New Zealand, 1937; D Litt, University of London, England; Honorary Doctorates from 14 Universities in USA, Britain, Germany, Austria, Canada and New Zealand. *Major Publications:* Logik der Forschung, 1934; The Open Society & Its Enemies, 1945, 14th edition 1984; The Poverty of Historicism, 1957, 11th edition 1984; The Logic of Scientific Discovery, 1959, 11th edition, 1983; Conjectures & Refutations, 1963, 9th edition 1984; Objective Knowledge, 1972, 7th edition 1984; Unended Quest (autobiography), 1926, 6th edition 1982; Postcript to The Logic of Scientific Discovery, ed. W W Bartley, Volume 1 Realism & The Aim of Science, Volume 2 The Open Universe, Volume 3 Quantum Theory & the Schism in Physics, 1982–83. *Contributor to:* Over 100 Philosophical and scientific journals. *Honours:* Knighthood, 1965; Companion of Honour, 1982; Grand Decoration of Honour in Gold (Austria), 1976; Gold Medal, American Museum of Natural History, New York, 1979; Ehrenseichen fr Wissenschaft und Kunst (Austria), 1980; Order Pour le Mérite (Germany), 1980; Grand Cross with Star (Germany), 1983; and others. *Memberships:* Académie Internationale de Philosophie des Sciences, 1949; Fellow of the British Academy, 1958; Fellow of the Royal Society, 1976; Membre de l'Institut de France; Accademia Nazionale dei Lincei (Rome); Foreign Honorary Member, American Academy for Arts & Sciences; 6 other national and international academies. *Address:* Fallowfield, Manor Close, Manor Road, Penn, Buckinghamshire, HP10 8HZ, England.

POPPINO, Rollie Edward, b. 4 Oct. 1922, Portland OR, USA. University Professor. m. Lois Lamberson, 17 June 1950, Berkeley CA, 2 sons, 1 daughter. *Education:* AB, International Relations, 1948, MA, History, 1949, PhD, History, 1953, Stanford University. *Literary Appointments:* Instructor, History, Stanford University, 1953–54; Intelligence Research Specialist, Office of Research and Analysis, US Department of State, 1954–61; Lecturer, American University, 1959–61; Assistant Professor to Professor, University of California, Davis, 1961–. *Publications:* International Communism in Latin America, 1964; A History of Modern Brazil, 1889–1964 (co-author) 1966; Brazil: The Land and People 1968 and 1973; Feira de Santana 1968. *Contributions to:* Numerous articles and reviews since 1949, chiefly on Brazilian History, in Mid-America, Hispanic American Historical Review, The Americas, American Historical Review, Current History, Yearbook of International Communist Affairs, Revista Brasileira de Estudos Politicos, Revista do Instituto Histórico e Geográfico Brasileiro and others. *Honours:* Henry L and Grace Doherty Foundation Fellowship 1950–51; Social Science Research Council grants 1963, 1967–68; National Endowment for the Humanities, Senior Fellowship, 1967–68; Fulbright-Hays Lectureship in History, to Brazil, 1974; Colar D Pedro I, Awarded by São Paulo Historical Institute, 1972. *Memberships:* Conference on Latin American History; American Historical Association; Instituto Histórico e Geográfico Brasileiro. *Address:* Department of History, University of California, Davis, CA 95616, USA.

POPPLE, James, b. 12 May 1927, Bacup, Lancashire, England. Teacher. m. Margaret Joan O'Brien, 25 Sep. 1950, Salesbury, Lancashire, 1 son, 1 daughter. *Education:* BA 1952, Diploma in Education 1953, MA 1960, University of Sheffield, England, MEd, 1981, University of Victoria British Columbia, Canada. *Major Pubications:* The Landscape of Europe: Four Geographic Studies, 1966; The Landscape of Japan: A Geographic Study, 1973. *Contributor to:* Various magazines, articles of geographic and social issues. *Membership:* Fellow, Royal Society of Arts, 1957–. *Address:* 2490 Holyrood Drive, Nanaimo, British Columbia, V9S 4K8, Canada.

PORAY-BIERNACKI, Janusz, b. 11 July 1907. Writer; Journalist; former Lawyer. *Education:* LLM,

Warsaw University, Poland. *Publications:* Po Narviku by Tobruk, short stories, 1945. Novels: Walter 7.65, 1951; Brunatne i Czerwone, 1953; Finger on the Trigger, Translation of Walter 7.65, 1952–53; Slowo O Bitwie, 1955; Gwiazdzisty Szalik, 1974. Literary Essay: Z Przekonania, 1979. *Contributions to:* Wiadomosci; Dziennik Polski and others. *Honours:* Literary Prize. Veritas, Publishing House, London, England, 1952. Honorary Awards, Radio Free Europe, Munich, Germany, 1953, 54. *Memberships include:* Association of Polish Writers Abroad. *Address:* Flat 3, 47 Bramham Gardens, London SW5 0HQ, England.

PORTEOUS, Leslie Crichton, b. 22 May 1901, Leeds, England. Journalist; Author. m. Ruth Elizabeth Marchington, 5 July 1927, Chaple-en-le-Frith, Derbyshire. *Publications include:* Farmer's Creed, 1938, Teamsman, 1939, Land Truant, 1940, Autobiography; The Cottage, novel, 1941; The Farm By The Lake, 1942; The Snow, novel, 1944; The Earth Remains, novel, 1945; Sons of the Farm, novel, 1948; Changing Valley, novel, 1950; Wild Acres, 1951; Man of the Moors, 1954; Broken River, 1956; Lucky Columbell, 1959; Toad Hole, 1960; Strike, 1962; Chuckling Joe; Derbyshire; Peakland, topographic; The Beauty and Mystery of Well Dressing. *Contrubutions to:* Manchester Guardian; London Mercury; Countryman; Argosy; The Field; Life and Letters; Farmer's Weekly; Picture Post; Penguin Parade; others. *Literary Agent:* Curtis Brown, London. *Address:* Hawkshaw, 18 The Parkway, Darley Dale, Matlock, Derbyshire DE4 2FW, England.

PORTER, Bernard Harden, b. 14 Feb. 1911, Porter Settlement, Maine, USA. Author. *Education:* BS, Colby College, 1932; ScM, Brown University, 1933; DSc, Institute of Advanced Thinking, 1959. *Publications:* Author of 71 books including: Fitzgerald Bibliography, 1960; Aphasia, 1964; Scigraffiti, 1964; Henry Miller, 1965; Mathematics for Electronics, 1965; Moscow, 1966; Dieresis, 1969; Henry Miller Bibliography, 1970; The Book of Dos; Here Comes Everybody's Don't book; My My Dear Me; Sweet Ever Sometime; Sweet End The Last Acts of Saint Fu; The Porter. *Contrubutor to:* Around 200 assorted technical and nontechnical magazines and journals. *Honours:* Carnegie Authors Award, 1976; PEN Award, 1976; National Endowment of Arts, 1981. *Memberships:* Fellow, Society Technical Writers and Publishers; Maine Writers and Publishers Alliance. *Address:* 22 Salmond Way, Belfast, ME 04915, USA.

PORTER, Bernard John, b. 5 Feb. 1941, Hornchurch, Essex, England. University Lecturer. m. Deirdre O'Hara, 1 son, 2 daughters. *Education:* BA, 1963, MA and PhD, 1967, Corpus Christi College, Cambridge. *Literary Appointments:* Research Fellow, Corpus Christi College, Cambridge, 1966–68; Lecturer and Senior Lecturer in History, University of Hull, 1968–; Editor, Journal of Imperial and Commonwealth History, 1980–83. *Publications:* Critics of Empire, 1968; The Lion's Share, 1976 2nd edition 1984; The Refugee Question in Mid-Victorian Politics, 1979; Britain, Europe and the World 1850–1982, 1982. *Contributions to:* Contributions to academic historical journals. *Address:* History Department, The University, Hull HU6 7RX, England.

PORTER, Burton F, b. 22 June 1936, New York, USA. Professor of Philosophy. m. Barbara Metcalf, 31 Dec. 1980, Darien, 1 son, 1 daughter, 1 step-daughter. *Education:* BA, Philosophy, University of Maryland, 1959; PhD, Philosophy, University of St Andrews and University of Oxford, 1962. *Publications:* Deity and Morality: With Regard to the Naturalistic Fallacy, 1968; Philosophy, A Literary and Conceptual Approach, 1980; Personal Philosophy: Perspectives on Living, 1976; The Good Life: Alternatives in Ethics, 1980; Reasons for Living, 1986. *Literary Agent:* Gene Lovitz, Porter & Lovitz. *Address:* 90 First Street, Troy, NY 12180, USA.

PORTER, David Lindsey, b. 18 Feb. 1941, Holyoke, Massachusetts, USA. Professor of History of Political Science. m. Marilyn Platt, 28 Nov. 1970, Lansing, Michigan, 1 son, 1 daughter. *Education:* BA, Franklin

College, Indiana, 1963; MA, Ohio University, 1965; PhD, Pennsylvania State University, 1970. *Literary Appointments:* Assistant Professor of History, Rensselaer Polytechnic Institute, 1970–75; Educational Administrative Assistant, Troy Civil Service, New York, 1975–76; Associate Professor, Profesor of History and Political Science, William Penn College, Iowa, 1977–. *Publications:* The Seventy-Sixth Congress and World War II 1939–1940, 1979; Congress and the Waning of the New Deal, 1980; Biographical Dictionary of American Sport, 4 volumes, Editor. *Contributions to:* Numerous professional journals including: American Heritage; AHA Perspectives; Sunday Register, Des Moines; Nahaska County History; Foundations; Tennessee Historical Quarterly; West Virginia History; Filson Club History; The Palimpsest; Books at Iowa; The Annals of Iowa; Senate History and various others. Book Chapters contributed to numerous books including: The Book of Lists, 1983; The Hero in Transition, 1983; The Rating Game in American Politics; Biographical Dictionary of American Sport; The FDR Encyclopedia; Sports Encyclopedia North America, 1985. *Honours include:* Presidents Scholar, Franklin Scholar, Alpha, Kappa Depta Pi, Phi Alpha Theta, Magna cum laude, Franklin College, 1959–63; Wilson Fellow, 1963–65; National Science Foundation Grant, 1967; Faculty Travel grants; National Endowment for the Humanities grant, 1979; Eleanor Roosevelt Institute grant, 1981. *Memberships:* Numerous. *Address:* 616 Fourth Avenue East, Oskaloosa, IA 52577, USA.

PORTER, Joshua Roy, b. 7 May 1921, Godley, Cheshire, England. Clerk in Holy Orders; University Professor, Theology. *Education:* BA, MA, Merton College, Oxford. *Publications:* World in the Heart, 1944; Moses & Monarchy, 1963; Proclamation and Presence, 1963, 2nd revised edition, 1985; The Extended Family in the Old Testament, 1967; The Non-juring Bishops, 1973; Leviticus, 1976; The Crown & The Church, 1978; Folklore & the Old Testament, 1979; Leviticus, Japanese Edition, 1984; *Contributor to:* Promise and Fulfilment, 1963; The Journey to the Other World, 1975; Tradition and Interpretation, 1979; A Basic Introduction to the Old Testament, 1980; Divination and Oracles, 1981; Folklore Studies in the 20th Century, 1981; The Folklore of Ghosts, 1981; Israel's Prophetic Tradition, 1982; Tracts for Our Times, 1983; The Hero in Tradition & Folklore, 1984; Harper's Bible Dictionary, 1985; Arabia and the Gulf: From Traditional Society to Modern States, 1986. *Honours:* Ethel M Wood Lecturer, 1979; Michael Harrah Wood Memorial Lecturer, 1984. *Memberships:* President, Society for Old Testament Study, 1983; Vice-President, Folklore Society, 1979–; Society for Biblical Literature; Association of British Orientalists. *Address:* 36 Theberton Street, London N1 0QX, England.

PORTIS, Charles McColl, b. 28 Dec. 1933, El Dorado, Arkansas, USA. Writer. *Education:* BA, University of Arkansas, 1958. *Publications:* Norwood, 1966; True Grit, 1968; The Dog of the South, 1979; Masters of Atlantis, 1985. *Literary Agent:* Lynn Nesbit, ICM, New York. *Address:* 7417 Kingwood, Little Rock, Ar 72207, USA.

PORTWAY, Christopher, b. 30 Oct. 1923, Halstead, Essex, England. Travel Journalist; Author; Novelist; Travel Editor. m. Jaroslava Anna Krupickova, 4 Apr. 1957, Halstead, Essex, 1 son, 1 daughter. *Publications:* Journey to Dana, 1955; The Pregnant Unicorn, 1969; All Exits Barred, 1971; Corner Seat, 1972; Lost Vengeance, 1973; Double Circuit, 1974; The Tirawa Assignment, 1974; The Anarchy Pedlars, 1976; The Great Railway Adventure, 1983; Journey Along the Spine of the Andes, 1984; The Great Travelling Adventure, 1985. *Contributions to:* Travel Editor, Annabel magazine; Times; Daily Telegraph; Times Educational Supplement; Guardian; Country Life; The Lady; Railway Magazine; In-Flight Magazines; Various Holiday and Travel Magazines. *Honours:* TD; FRCS. *Literary Agent:* Peterborough Literary Agency (Daily Telegraph). *Address:* 22 Tower Road, Brighton, Sussex BN2 2GF, England.

POSEY, L Michael, b. 22 Aug. 1955, Albany, Georgia, USA. Pharmacist-Editor. *Education:* BS Pharmacy, BS Microbiology, University of Georgia, 1979. *Literary Appointments:* Editorial staff, American Journal of Hospital Pharmacy, Clinical Pharmacy, American Society of Hospital Pharmacists' Newsletter, American Society of Hospital Pharmacists' Signal, 1980–85; Editor, The Communicator (of Phi Delta Chi Pharmacy Fraternity), 1983–85. *Membership:* American Medical Writers' Association. *Address:* Pharmacy Association Services, PO Box 5770, Bethesda, MD 20814, USA.

POSPISIL, Leopold Jaroslav, b. 26 Apr. 1923, Olomouc, Czechoslovakia. University Professor of Anthropology and Law. m. Zdenka Smydova, 31 Jan. 1945, Olomouc, 2 daughters. *Education:* UUC, Charles University, Prague, 1947; BA, Willamette University, Salem, Oregon, USA, 1950; MA, University of Oregon, Eugene, 1952; PhD, Yale University, New Haven, Connecticut, 1956. *Publications:* Kapauku Papuansand Their Law, 1958; Kapauku Papuan Economy, 1963; The Kapauku Papuans of West New Guinea, 1963; Anthropology of Law, 1972; Anthropologie des Rechts, 1982. *Contributions to:* Journals including: American Anthropology; Transactions New York Academy of Sciences; Oceania; Nature; Ethnology. *Honours include:* Honorary ScD, Willamette University, Salem, Oregon, 1969; Various Fellowships. *Memberships:* American Anthropological Association; National Academy of Sciences; Fellow, New York Academy of Sciences; Sigma Xi; President 1980–84, Czechoslovakian Society of Arts and Sciences; American Association for the Advancement of Science; Vice-President, Association for Political and Legal Anthropology. *Address:* 175 Whitney Avenue, New Haven, CT 06520, USA.

POTOK, Chaim, b. 17 Feb. 1929, Bronx, New York, USA. Writer. m. Adena Sara Mosevitzky, 8 June 1958, Brooklyn, New York, USA, 1 son, 2 daughters. *Education:* BA, Yeshiva University, 1950; MHL, rabbinic ordination, Jewish Theological Seminary, 1954; PhD Philosophy, University of Pennsylvania, 1965. *Literary Appointments:* Visiting Professor, University of Pennsylvania, 1982; Visiting Lecturer, Bryn Mawr College, 1985. *Major Publications:* The Chosen, 1967; The Promise, 1969; My Name is Asher Lev, 1972; In The Beginning, 1975; Wanderings, 1978; The Book of Lights, 1981; Davita's Harp, 1985. *Contributor to:* New York Times Magazine; Commentary; Saturday Review; Esquire; Seventeen; McCall's; and others. *Honours:* National Book Award Nomination (for The Chosen); Athenaeum Award (for The Promise); Wallant Award (for The Chosen). *Memberships:* PEN; Authors Guild. *Address:* 20 Berwick Road, Philadelphia, PA 19131, USA.

PÖTRY, Mauno-Olavi, b. 17 Jan. 1946, Lappeenranta, Finland. Playwright. m. Meeri Jelekäinen, 5 May 1973, Lappeenranta. *Publications:* Muuttolintu, 1974; Hymyileva potilas, 1974; Tyo ja taistelu, 1975; Ruumisarkkukauppiaan Konkurssi, 1980; Meidän Herramme teatteriseurue, 1984. *Contributions to:* Numerous journals and cultural magazines. *Honours:* Tampereen teatterikesä, 1974; Kymeenläänin taidepalkinto, 1975; Lappeenrannan kaupungin taidepalkinto, 1977. *Memberships:* Suomen Kirjailijaliitto; Suomen Näytelmäkirjailijalii tio; Kymenläänin Kirjailijayndistys Paltta. *Literary Agent:* Kirjailijoiden näytelmätoimisto. *Address:* Asemakatu 8-10 C 19, 53300 Lappeenranta, Finland.

POTTER, Eloise Lillian Fretz, b. 17 Feb. 1931, Norfolk, Virginia, USA. Editor, divorced, 2 sons, 2 daughters. *Education:* Meredith College, Raleigh, North Carolina, 1949–50. *Literary Appointments:* Editor: The Chat (Quarterly journal of Carolina Bird Club), 1963–; North Carolina Biological Survey, 1981–; Director of Publications, North Carolina State Museum of Natural History, 1985–. *Publications:* Birds of the Carolinas, 1980; Rackley: A Southern Colonial Family, 1984. *Contributions to:* The Auk; Journal of Field Ornithology; The Living Bird. *Honours:* Honorary Life Member, Little River Historical Society, 1982. *Address:* North Carolina

State Museum of Natural History, P O Box 27647, Raleigh, NC 27611, USA.

POTTER, Margaret, b. Harrow, England. Writer. m. Jeremy Potter, 11 Feb. 1950, 1 son, 1 daughter. *Education:* MA, St Hugh's College, Oxford. *Publications include:* The Last of the Lorimers, (Anne Melville), 1983; Lorimer Loyalties (Ann Melville), 1984; The Boys Who Disappeared, 1985. *Contributor to:* New Statesman; Homes & Gardens; Good Housekeeping, etc. *Honour:* Major Award, Romantic Novelist Association, 1966. *Membership:* Society of Authors. *Literarly Agent:* A D Peters. *Address:* c/o A D Peters, 10 Buckingham Street, London WC2N 6BU, England.

POULET, George Eugene, b. 29 Nov. 1902, Chenee, Belgium. Professor (retired). m. Elisabeth Gregoire, 31 Mar. 1928, Liege, Belgium. *Education:* PhD, University of Liege, Belgium. *Literary Appointments:* Reader, University of Edinburgh, Scotland; Professor of French, Johns Hopkins University, USA; Professor of French Literature, University of Zurich; Professor of French, University of Nice. *Publications:* Etudes sur le temps humain; 4 volumes, 1950–68; Les metamorphoses du cercle, 1961; La conscience critique, 1972; L'espace pronstien, 1963. *Contributor to:* Nouvelle Revue francaise. *Honours:* Docteur Honoris Causa, Universities of Geneva, 1959, Nice, 1966, Edinburgh, 1971. *Memberships:* Academie Royale de Belgique, 1970; Accademia Arcadia, 1972; American Academy of Arts and Sciences, USA, 1950. *Address:* 119 Avenue de Brancolar, Nice, France.

POULIN, Gabriella, b. 21 June 1929, St Prosper, Quebec, Canada. Writer. *Education:* BA, University Montreal; Lic Letters; Dip Higher Studies; D.Litt, University Sherbroke. *Publications:* Les Miroirs d'un poets: image et reflets de Paul Eluard, 1969; Cogne la caboche, 1979; L'Age de l'interrogation, 1937–52, 1980; Romans du pays, 1968–79, 1980; Un cri trop grand, 1980; Les Mensonbes D'Isabella, (novel), 1983; All the Way Home, originally published as, Coena la Caboche, translated by Jane Pentland, 1984. *Contributor to:* Vois et images; Lettres quebecoises; Relations. *Honours:* Prize, Swiss Embassy, 1967; Grant, Arts Council of Canada on 7 occasions, 1969, 70, 71, 72, 73, 79, 80; Press Lit. prize, 1979; Champlain Lit. Prize, 1979; Grant, Arts Council of Canada on 10 occasions, 1968, 70, 71, 72, 73, 79, 80, 82, 83, 85. *Memberships:* Union Quebecois Writers; Union of Artists; Association of French-Speaking Writers (home and abroad). *Literary Agent:* Rene Dionne, Lettres Francaises, University of Ottawa. *Address:* 1997 Avenue Quincy, Ottawa, Ontario, Canada K1J 6B4.

POULIN, Jacques, b. 23 Sep. 1937, St Gédéon, Quebec, Canada. Writer. *Education:* Degrees in Psychology, Literature, Université Laval, Quebec. *Publications:* Mon Cheval pour un Royaume, 1967; Jimmy, 1969; Le coeur de la baleine bleue, 1971; Faites de beaux réves, 1974; Les Grandes marées, 1978; Volkswagen Blues, 1984. *Honours:* Prix de l'Editeur La Presse, 1974; Prize, Governor General, 1978. *Membership:* Quebec Writers Union. *Literary Agent:* John C Goodwin, Montréal. *Address:* 4041 Chemin St Louis, Cap-Rouge, Quebéc G1Y 1V7, Canada.

POUNDS, Norman John Greville, b. 23 Feb. 1912, Bath, England. Professor of History. m. Dorothy J Mitchell, 30 July 1938, Bath. *Education:* BA, 1934, MA, 1940, Fitzwilliam College, Cambridge University; BA, 1944, PhD, 1946, London University. *Publications:* The Ruhr, 1952; The Earth and You, 1962; Poland, with V L Benes, 1970; An Historical Geography of Europe, Volume 1, 1973, Volume 2, 1979, Volume 3, 1985; An Economic History of Medieval Europe, 1974; Eastern Europe, 1969. *Contributor to:* Geographical Journal; Economic History Review; Archaeological International; Annals; etc. *Honours:* State of Indiana Award for best general non-fiction book, 1963. *Memberships:* Fellow, Society of Antiquaries; Royal Archaeological Institute, Vice President. *Address:* Department of History, Indiana University, Bloomington, IN 47405, USA.

POUPLIER, Erik, b. 16 June 1926, Svendborg, Denmark. Writer. m. Analise Hansen, 28 Sep. 1947, 1 daughter. *Education:* Trained as Journalist. *Publications:* In Danish: Lend Me Your Wife, 1957; My Castle in Ardeche, 1968; The Gentle Revolt, 1970; The Discreet Servant of the Death, 1972; The Adhesive Pursuer, 1973; Murder, Mafia and Pastis'er, 1974; My Castle in Provence, 1979; The Old Man in Provence, 1980; The Clumsy Kidnappers, 1981; The World of Annesisse, 1982; The Galic Cock, 1984; My Own Provence, 1984; The Cuisine of Provence, 1985. *Contributions to:* JyllandsPosten, Denmark. *Memberships:* Danish Authors Society; Danish Press Association. *Address:* Les Charmettes, Chemin de Plateau, 83550 Vidauban, France.

POWE, Bruce Allen, b. 9 June 1925, Canada. Vice-President, Public Affairs, Canadian Life & Health Insurance Association. m. Alys Maude Brady, 30 June 1949, Edmonton, Canada, 1 son, 1 daughter. *Education:* MA Economics, University of Alberta, Edmonton. *Major Publications:* Expresso 67, 1966; Killing Ground: The Canadian Civil War, 1968; The Last Days of the American Empire, 1974; The Aberhart Summer, 1983. *Contributor to:* The Idler, *Membership:* The Writers' Union of Canada. *Address:* 158 Ridley Boulevard, Toronto, Ontario, M5M 3M1, Canada.

POWELL, Geoffrey Stewart, b. 25 Dec. 1914, Scarborough, England. Retired Army Officer. m. Felicity Wadsworth, 7 July 1944, Angelsey, 1 son, 1 daughter. *Education:* BA, Open University. *Publications:* The Green Howards, 1969; The Kandyan Wars, 1973; Men at Arnhem, (with Tom Angus), 1976; Suez: The Double War, (with Roy Fullick), 1979; The Book of Campden, 1982; The Devil's Birthday: The Bridges to Arnhem, 1984. *Contributions to:* History Today; The Army Quarterly; Royal United Services Institute; Journal; British History Illustrated; Various Academic Journals. *Honour:* Military Cross. *Literary Agent:* A M Heath and Company Limited. *Address:* 2 North End Terrace, Chipping Campden, Glos GL55 6AE, England.

POWELL, Lester, b. 14 June 1912, London, England. Writer. m. Hazel Mary Heath, 10 Sep. 1952, Hove, Sussex, 1 son, 1 daughter. *Publications:* A Count of Six, 1948; Shadow Play, 1949; Spot the Lady, 1950; Still of Night, 1952; The Black Casket, 1953; The Big M, 1973. *Contributions to:* 50 short stories and numerous articles. *Membership:* Past Regional Chairman, Writers Guild of Great Britain. *Literary Agent:* Harvey Unna. *Address:* 3/4 Fairfax Place, Dartmouth, Devon TQ6 9AD, England.

POWELSON, John P, b. 3 Sep. 1920, New York City, USA. Professor of Economics. m. Alice Roberts, 31 May 1953, Moorestown, New Jersey, 2 sons, 3 daughters. *Education:* AB, Economics, Harvard University, 1941; MBA, Accounting, Wharton School, University of Pennsylvania, 1942; AM, Economics, 1947; PhD, Economics, Harvard University, 1950; CPA, State of New York, 1950. *Literary Appointements:* Editorial Boards: Journal of Energy and Developement and Land Use Policy. *Publications include:* Threat to Development: Pitfalls of the NIED (with William Loehr), 1983; The Economics of Development and Distributions (with William Loehr), 1981; Institutions of Economic Growth: A Theory of Conflict Management in Developing Countries, 1972; Latin America: Today's Economics and Social Revolution, 1964; National Income and Flow of Funds Analysis, 1960; Economic Accounting, 1964; Books in Progress: The Peasant Betrayed: Agriculture and Land Reform in the Third World (with Richard Stock); The Story of Land: A History of Land Tenure and Agrarian Reform; A History and Theory of Economic Development. *Contributions to:* Books and professional journals; Book Reviews. *Honours include:* Fellowships; Grants and Prizes. *Memberships:* American Economic Association; Latin American Studies Association. *Address:* 45 Bellevue Drive, Boulder, CO 80302, USA.

POWER, Patrick Victor, b. 16 Oct. 1930, Dublin, Ireland. Professor; Writer. m. Marybel Killian, 4 Nov. 1968, Rock Island, Illinois, USA, 1 son, 2 daughters. *Education:* MA, Journalism, 1968; MFA, Creative Writing, 1970; University of Iowa, USA; PhD, Coursework completed, 1971. *Literary Appointments:* Shubert Playwriting Fellow, University of Iowa, 1968; Norman Felton Playwriting Fellow, 1969; Chicago Council on Fine Arts, 1976–79; Artist-in-Residence, Body Politic Theater, Chicago, 1978; Professor, Cochise College, 1982. *Publications:* Translation: Apple on the Treetop, by Richard Power, 1980; The Town of Ballymuck, (collection of short stories), 1984; The Escape, (polay), 1984; Johnnie Will, (play), 1986. *Contributor to:* Triquarterly; Best of Triquarterly; Bananas; Firebird 2; North American Review; Literary Review; Antigonish Review; Ireland of the WElcomes CARA; Capuchin Annual; Iowa State Liquor Store; Short Story International; Ohio Review; Irish Heritage; Long Story; The Arizona Literary Magazine; The Yearbook of Discovery. *Honours:* Direachtes Gaelic Literary Prize, 1959, 61; All Ireland Drama Prize, 1964,66; Story Award for Drama, 1969; Story Award for Fiction, 1970; Illinois Arts Council WTTV-TV Award for Drama, 1974; Illinois Arts Council Creative Writing Fellowship for FIction, 1980; Artist in residence Body Politic, 1978; Columbia University Prize for translation, 1980; Swallow's Tale Press First Award for collections of short fiction, 1983. *Memberships:* Poets and Writers; Associated Writing Programs; Sigma Delta Chi; Dramatists Guild; Kappa Tau Alpha. *Address:* 108 La Cholla, Bisbee, AZ 85603, USA.

POWERS, Anne, b. 7 May 1913, Cloquet, Minnesota, USA. Novelist; Housewife. *Education:* University of Minnesota. *Publications:* The Gallant Years, 1946; Ride East! Ride West!, 1947; No Wall So High, 1948; The Ironmaster, 1951; The Only Sin, 1954; The Thousand Fires, 1957; No King But Caesar, 1960; Rachel, 1974; The Royal Consorts, 1978; The Young Empress, 1979; Eleanor, The Passionate Queen, 1980. *Memberships:* Bookfellows of Milwaukee; Allied Authors; Fictionears. *Literary Agent:* Larry Sternig Literary Agency. *Address:* 3800 N Newhall Streert, Milwaukee, WI 53211, USA.

POWERS, Robert M, b. 9 Nov. 1942, USA. Author. m. Patricia Bungdorf, divorced, 1 daughter. *Education:* BA, University of Arizona, USA; Certificate, University of Edinburgh, Scotland. *Publications:* Planetary Encounters, 1978; Shuttle: Worlds First Space Ship, 1979; The Coattails of God, 1981; Other Worlds Than Ours, 1983; Mars, 1986. *Contributions to:* Major magazines in USA including, Geo, Readers Digest, Saturday Review, Smithsonian. *Honours:* Best Space Book, Aviation Space Writers, 1979; Best Book, Literary Journals, 1984; Best Space Book, AWA, 1978. *Memberships:* Authors League and Guild: Aviation Space Writers Association; Fellow, Royal Astronomical Society, UK. *Literary Agent:* Adole Leone, Scarsdale, New York, USA. *Address:* P O Box 12158, Denver, CO 80212, USA.

POYER, Joseph b. 30 Nov. 1939, Battle Creek, Michigan, USA. Author. m. Susan Pilmore, 17 June 1961, 2 sons. *Education:* BA. (Communications). *Literary Appointments:* Former Editor, Multiphasic Health Screening Newsletter; Field Editor, International Combat Arms – Journal of Defense Technology. *Publications:* Operation Malacca, 1968; North Cape, 1969; Balkan Assignment, 1971; Chinese Agenda, 1972; Shooting of the Green (Hellshot), 1973; Day of Reckoning, 1976; The Contract, 1978; Tunnel War, 1979; Vengeance 10, 1980; Devoted Friends, 1982; A Time of War – (1), The Transgressors, 1983, (2) Come Evil Days, 1985. *Literary Agent:* Diane Cleaver. *Address:* 5744–66 Creekside, Orange, CA 92669 USA.

POZZETTA, George Enrico, b. 29 Oct. 1942, Massachusetts, USA. Professor. m. Sandra Gail Magdalenski, 16 Sep. 1966, Housatonic, Massachusetts, 1 son, 1 daughter. *Education:* BA 1964, MA 1965, Providence College; PhD, University of North Carolina, Chapel Hill, 1971. *Major Publications:* America & the New Ethnicity, 1979; Pane E Lavoro: The Italian American Working Class, 1980; Reform & Reformers in the Progressive Era, 1983. *Contributor to:* Journal of Ethnic Studies; Journal of Urban History; Florida Historical Quarterly. *Honours:* Cavaliere dell'Ordine al Merito della Repubblica Italiana, 1984; Phi Alpha Theta (National History Honor Society), 1970. *Memberships:* Immigration History Society (Executive Council), 1982–84; Southern Historical Association, membership committee 1982–84; American Historical Association; Organization of American Historians. *Address:* Department of History, University of Florida, Gainesville, FL 32611, USA.

PRANCE, Claude Annett, b. 28 June 1906, Portsmouth, Hampshire, England. Bank Manager, (Retired). *Education:* Associate, Institution of Bankers; Associate, Chartered Institute of Secretaries. *Publications:* Peppercorn Papers, 1965; The Laughing Philosopher, 1976; Index to the London Magazine, with Frank P Riga, 1978; Companion to Charles Lamb: A Guide to People and Places 1760–1847, 1983. *Contributor to:* Times Literary Supplement; Book Handbook; Book Collector; Charles Lamb Bulletin; Private Library; American Book Collector; Journal of the Institute of Bankers; Sunday Times of Malta; Crowell's Readers Encyclopedia of English Literature; British Literary Periodicals. *Honour:* Elected Vice President, Charles Lamb Society, 1983. *Memberships:* Charles Lamb Society; Private Libraries Association; Keats-Shelley Association of America; Society for Theatre Research; Selborne Society. *Address:* 16 Alleyne Close, MacGregor, Canberra, ACT 2615, Australia.

PRATER, Donald Arthur, b. 6 Jan. 1918, London, England. Member of Her Majesty's Foreign Service; University Lecturer (German); Translator with CERN, Geneva. m. Patricia Gardner, 30 June 1945, Colombo, Sri Lanka, 2 sons, 1 daughter. *Education:* MA Corpus Christi College, Oxford, 1939. Army Service: 8th Army; W Desert, Italy, 1941–44; Allied Land Forces SE Asia, Brigadier GS, Inteligence, 1945. *Publications:* European of Yesterday: A Biography of Stafan Zweig, 1972 (revised German edition: Des Leben eines Ungeduldigen, 1981, 84; Stefan Zweig: Leben u. Werk in Bild, 1981; A Ringing Glass: The Life of Rainer Maria Rilke, 1986 (German edition, 1986); Ihre mir so lieb gegebene Gegenwart! Rilke u. Zweig in Briefen und Zeugnissen, 1987. *Contributor to:* German Life and Letters; Reviews for TLS and NZBC; Die Neue Welt; Modern Austrian Literature; AJR Information, London; Exile: The Writer's Experience, 1982. *Honour:* OBE, 1945; *Memberships:* Rilke-Gesellschaft, Bale, Committee Member. *Address:* Pré de la Ferma, CH–1261 Gingins, Switzerland.

PRATLEY, Gerald Arthur, b. 3 Sep. 1923, London, England. Director, Ontario Film Institute. *Education:* Queen's University, Kingston, Ontario. *Literary Appointments:* Seneca College; University of Toronto; York University. *Publications:* Cinema of John Frankenheimer, 1969; Cinema of Otto Preminger, 1971; Cinema of David Lean, 1974; Cinema of John Huston, 1977; Torn Sprockets: The Uncertain Projection of the Canadian Film, 1985. *Contributor to:* International Film Guide; International TV and Video Guide; Variety, Tribute, Films and Filming; Films in Review, etc. *Honour:* Order of Merit, Poland, 1980; Member, Order of Canada, 1984. *Memberships:* University Film Association; St George's Society; Arts and Letters Club, Toronto. *Address:* Ontario Film Institute, 770 Don Mills Road, Don Mills, Ontario, Canada M3C 1T3.

PRATT, James Norwood, b. 27 Mar. 1942, Winston-Salem, North Carolina, USA. Writer. m. Charlot Alleta Saunders, 1 May 1979, San Francisco, 1 son. *Education:* University of North Carolina, Chapel Hill; Heidelberg University, Germany. *Publications:* The Wine Bibbers Bible, 1971; Rodin's Sculpture (Translation), 1977; The Tea Lover's Treasury, 1982. *Contributor to:* Paris Jazz; Carolina Quarterly; Cosmopolitan; Viva; Ms; Wine World; Parade; New Orleans Times-Picayune; Contributing Editor: Wine New, Epicure, Wine Editor: California

Critic. *Memberships:* WGAW; LA; CA; Commonwealth Club, San Francisco; Jargon Society, Highland, North Carolina; Cast-Iron Lawn Deer Owners of America. *Address:* 103 W President Street, Greenwood, MS 38930, USA.

PRATT, John Clark, b. 19 Aug. 1932, St Albans, USA. Writer; Educator. m. (2) Doreen Goodman, 28 June 1968, Colorado Springs, USA, 1 son, 5 daughters. *Education:* BA, University of California, 1954; MA, Columbia University, New York, 1960; PhD, Princeton University, New Jersey, 1965. *Appointments:* Instructor of English, United States Air Force Academy, 1960–66; Assistant Professor, 1965–69, Associate Professor, 1969–73, Professor, 1973–75; Professor, Colorado State University, 1975–present. *Publications:* The Meaning of Modern Poetry, 1962; John Steinbeck, 1970; One Flew Over the Cuckoo's Nest, (editor), 1973; Middlemarch Notebooks, 1978; Vietnam Voices, 1984; The Laotian Fragments, 1985. *Contributions to:* Vietnam War Literature; Vietnam Perhasie. *Honours:* Fulbright Lecturer, University of Lisbon, Portugal, 1974–75; Fulbright Lecturer, Leningrad State University, USSR, 1980. *Address:* Department of English, Colorado State University, FG Collins, CO 80523, USA.

PRATT, Willis Winslow, b. 20 Aug. 1908, Los Angeles, California, USA. Professor of English Literature, m, 1 June 1932, 1 daughter. *Education:* BA, MA, PhD, Cornell University, Ithaca, New York. *Literary Appointments:* Instructor, University of Texas, Austin, Texas, 1932–38; Associate Professor, 1945–50; Professor, 1950–76. *Publications:* Byron at Southwell, 1948; Galveston Island, The Journal of Francis Sheridan 1839–1840, 1954; Byron's Don Juan, 1957; Modern Drama, 1963; Lord Byron: Don Juan, Editor, 1973. *Contributions to:* Various literary publications. *Memberships:* Executive Committee, Byron Society of America; Keats-Shelley Association of America. *Address:* 3001 West 35th Street, Austin, TX 78703, USA.

PREBBLE, John Edward Curtis, b. 1915, Edmonton, England. Writer. *Publications include:* Where the Sea Breaks, 1944; The Edge of Darkness, 1948; Age Without Pity, 1950; The Mather Story, 1954; The Brute Streets, 1954; The High Girders, 1956; My Great Aunt Appearing Day, 1958; The Buffalo Soldiers, 1959; Culloden, 1961; The Highland Clearances, 1963; Glencoe, 1966; The Darien Disaster, 1968; The Lion in the North, 1971; Spanish Stirrup, 1973; Mutiny Highland Regiments in Revolt, 1975; John Prebble's Scotland. 1984. *Honours:* Fellow, Royal Society of Literature. *Memberships:* Poets, Playwrights, Editors, Essayists and Novelists; Society of Authors; Writers Guild. *Literary Agent:* Curtis Brown. *Address:* Hill View, The Glade, Kingswood, Surrey KT20 6LL, England.

PRÉMONT, Henri, b. 8 July 1933, Braine-L'Alleud, Belgium. Records: Electronics. *Education:* Electronics A1. *Appointments:* Theatre, Radio and TV Plays, 1958–; SF Short stories, 1974; Adaptor from Latin-American Dramatists. *Publications:* Mieux Comprendre ses Reves Par La Parapsychologie, 1985. *Contributor to:* Le Magazine De L'Evenement; Realities-Psi-Magazine; Octa Magazine; Fortean Times, London. *Memberships:* PEN Club; Societaire De La Societe Des Gens De Lettres De France, Paris. *Address:* 26 Avenue Léon Jourez, 1420 Braine-L'Alleud, Belgium.

PRESCOTT, John Robert Victor, b. 12 May 1931, Newcastle upon Tyne, England. Lecturer. m. Dorothy Francis Allen, 12 Sep. 1953, Newcastle upon Tyne, 1 son, 1 daughter. *Education:* BSc, MA, Dip Ed, Durham University; PhD, London; MA, Melbourne. *Publications:* The Geography of Frontiers and Boundaries, 1965; The Geography of State Policies, 1968; The Evolution of Nigeria's International and Regional Boundaries, 1861–1971, 1971; Political Geography, 1972; The Political Geography of the Oceans, 1975; The Map of Mainland Asia by Treaty, 1975; Our Fragmented World: An Introduction to Political Geography, with Professor Emeritus W G East, 1975; The Frontiers of Asia and South East Asia, co-author, 1979;

Editor, Contributor, Australia's Continental Shelf, 1979; Maritime Jurisdiction in Southeast Asia: A Commentary and Map, 1981; Australia's Maritime Boundaries, 1985. *Contributor to:* Numerous professional journals. *Address:* Dept of Geography, University of Melbourne, Parkville 3052 Victoria, Australia.

PRESPER, Mary Lenore, b. 29 May 1914, Philadelphia, Pennsylvania, USA. Writer, Photographer. *Education:* AB, Elmira College, 1937; MS, Penn State University, 1939. *Publications:* The Joys of Woodstoves and Fireplaces, 1980. *Contributions to:* American Dietetics Journal; American Home; Today's Woman; Bride's; Family Health, and others. *Memberships:* Authors Guild of the Authors League of America; Poetry Society of America. *Literary Agent:* Elizabeth Marton. *Address:* 8 Oakwod Road Terraces, Rocky Point, NY 11778, USA.

PRESS, Charles, b. 12 Sep. 1922, St Louis, Missouri, USA. Professor of Political Science. m. Nancy Miller, 10 June 1950, Chicago, Illinois, USA. 3 sons, 1 daughter. *Education:* BJ University of Missouri, 1948; MA, PhD, University of Minnesota, 1951–53. *Publications:* When One Third of a City Moves to the Suburbs, A Report on the Grand Rapids Metropolitan Area, 1959; Convention Report, (with Charles Adrian), 1962; Main Street Politics; Democracy in Urban America, (co-editor with O P Williams), 1964; The American Political Process, (with Charles R Adrian), 1965; Empathy and Ideology, (editor with Alan Adrian), 1966; Democracy on the Fifty States, (co-editor with O P Williams), 1966 and 1968; Governing Urban America, (with Charles R Adrian), 1974; State and Community Governments in the Federal System, (with Kenneth VerBerg), 1979 and 1982; Policy Boxes for American Government Courses, (with Kenneth VerBerg), 1981; The Political Cartoon, 1983; States and Communities in a Federal System, 1982. *Contributions to:* Numerous professional journals; Syndicated newspaper column with Kenneth VerBurg, Pros and Cons Politics. *Honours:* Ford Foundation Fellowship, University of Minnesota, 1953–54; Distinguished Faculty Award, MSU, 1980; Canadian Government Grants, 1982 and 1985. *Address:* 987 Lantern Hill, East Lansing, MI 48823, USA.

PRESS, Simone Naomi Juda, b. 14 Apr. 1943, Cambridge, Massachusetts, USA. Playwright. m. Steven Eric Press, 14 June 1969, New York City, New York, 2 daughters. *Education:* BA, Bennington College, 1965; MA, Columbia University, 1967. *Literary Appointments:* Apprentice Director and Playwright, University of Michigan; Playwright in Residence, New Playwrights Forum; Coordinator, Arts and Education Coordinator, Attic Theatre; Artistic Director, Young Peoples Theater. *Publications:* Poetry: Thaw, 1974; Lifting Water, 1979. Childrens Play: How Does Your Garden Grow? 1981; Play: Willing, produced, Attic Theater, 1983, Off-Broadway, 1984. *Contributons to:* Boston After Dark; Greenhouse; Quadrille; New York Times; Ann Arbour News. *Honours:* Creative Writers in Schools, 1974–, Confined Audience Grant, Artist Apprenticeship, Creative Artist Grant, Michigan Education Association. *Memberships:* Dramatists Guild. *Address:* 1109 West Washington, Ann Arbor, MI 48103, USA.

PRESTON, Ivy Alice, b. 11 Nov. 1913, Timaru, New Zealand. Writer. m. Percival Edward James Preston, deceased, 2 sons, 2 daughters. *Publications:* The Silver Stream, autobiography; 37 romance novels published in hardback and paperback and translated into 9 languages. *Contributions to:* New Zealand Woman's Weekly; Home Journal; Dairy Exporter; Farmer; Inflight Magazine; Femina; South Canterbury Journal; Australian Parade; Pix; various newspapers. *Memberships:* President and Secretary, South Canterbury Writers Guild; PEN New Zealand; New Zealand Woman Writer; South Island Writers Association; Romance Novelists Association, England; Romance Writers of America. *Literary Agent:* John Hale, London, England. *Address:* 95 Church Street, Timaru, New Zealand.

PRESTON, James J, b. 12 Jan. 1941, Los Angeles, California, USA. University Professor. m. Carolyn Marie Pastore, 11 Feb. 1967, San Francisco, 2 sons, 1 daughter. *Education:* BS, California State University, San Francisco, 1967; MEd, University of Vermont, 1970; PhD, The Hartford Seminary Foundation, 1974. *Publications:* Community, Self and Identity: Styles of Communal Living in World Cultures, editor with B Misra, 1978; Cult of the Goddess: Religious Change in a Hindu Temple, 1980; Mother Worship: Theme and Variations, Editor, 1982. *Contributions to:* Numerous articles and book reviews in, Gandhi Marg; Science News; Human Organization; Intellect; International Review of Cross-Cultural Studies; Mankind Quarterly; Multiverse; Journal of the Institute of Oriental and Orissan Studies; The Journal of Psychological Anthropology; The Journal of Psychoanalytic Anthropology; Choice. *Honours:* Visiting Scholar, Department of Religion, University of North Carolina, Chapel Hill Fellowship from the National Endowment for the Humanities, 1977; Director, Community Program on Coping with Death (SUCO). Federal Grant from New York State Office for the Aging, 1978; Travel Grant from the American Council of Learned Societies to deliver invited paper at Xth International Congress on Anthropological and Ethnological Sciences in New Delhi, India, 1978; Outstanding Young Man of the Year Award, 1978; Visiting Lecturer and Resource Consultant, The National Science Foundation Anthropology/Education Workshop, SUNY Plattsburgh, 1979; Walter B Ford Professional Development Grant to develop new interdisciplinary oriented course, Alternative Life Styles for the 1980's, 1982. *Memberships:* American Anthropological Association, 1970–80; Life Member, The N K Bose Foundation for Anthropological Research. *Address:* Department of Anthropology, State University of New York College at Oneonta, NY 13820, USA.

PRESTON, Richard Arthur, b. 4 Oct. 1910, England. Retired Professor of History. m. Marjorie Fishwick, 2 Sep. 1939, 2 sons, 1 daughter. *Education:* BA, MA, DipEd, University of Leeds, UK; PhD, Yale University, USA. *Literary Appointments:* Lecturer, Assistant Professor, University of Toronto, Canada; Assistant Lecturer, University College, Cardiff, Wales; Professor, Royal Military College of Canada; W K Boyd Professor, Duke University; Honorary Professor, History, Royal Military College of Canada. *Publications include:* Gorges of Plymouth Fort, 1953; Men in Arms, 4th edition, 1979; Canada in World Affairs, 1959–51, 1965; Canada & 'Imperial Defence', 1967; Canada's RMC, 1969; For Friends at Home, 1964; The Squat Pyramid, 1980; The Defence of the Undefended Border, 1977. *Honours:* Donner Medal, Promotion of Canadian Studies in USA, 1975; Telecom Gold Medal, Promotion of Canadian Studies, 1982. *Membership:* Fellow, Royal Historical Society. *Address:* Department of History, Duke University, Durham, NC 27705, USA.

PRESTWICH, Michael Charles, b. 30 Jan. 1943, Oxford, England. University Teacher. m. Margaret Joan Daniels, 11 May 1973, St Andrews, Scotland, 2 sons, 1 daughter. *Education:* BA, 1964, MA, D Phil 1968; University of Oxford. *Major Publications:* War, Politics & Finance under Edward I, 1972; The Three Edwards, 1980. *Contributor to:* Bulletin of the Institute of Historical Research; English Historical Review; Economic History Review; Parliamentary History Yearbook; Parliaments, Estates & Representation; and others. *Memberships:* Fellow, Royal Historical Society; Fellow, Society of Antiquaries. *Address:* Department of History, 43-46 North Bailey, Durham, DH1 3EX, England.

PRICE, Anthony Alan, b. 16 Aug. 1928, Hertfordshire, England. Journalist. m. Ann Stone, 29 June 1953, Willingdon, Sussex, 2 sons, 1 daughter. *Education:* MA, Merton College, Oxford University. *Publications:* The Labyrinth Makers, 1970; The Alamut Ambush, 1971; Colonel Butler's Wolf, 1972; October Men, 1973; Other Paths to Glory, 1974; War Game, 1975; Our Man in Camelot, 1977; The '44 Vintage, 1978; Tomorrow's Ghost, 1979; The Hour of the Donkey, 1980; Soldier, No More, 1981; The Old

Vengeful, 1982; Gunner Kelly, 1983; Sion Crossing, 1984; Here Be Monsters, 1985. *Honours:* Silver Dagger, for The Labyrinth Makers, 1970, Gold Dagger, for Other Paths to Glory, 1974, Crime Writers Association; Award for Other Paths to Glory, Swedish Academy of Detection, 1979. *Memberships:* Crime Writers' Association; Detection Club. *Literary Agent:* Hilary Rubinstein Esq, A P Watt Limited. *Address:* Wayside Cottage, Horton-cum-Studley, Oxford OX9 1AW, England.

PRICE, Cecil John Layton, b. 14 June 1915, Swansea, Wales. Professor of English. m. Ceinwen Daniel Lloyd, 19 Aug. 1940, Carmarthen. *Education:* MA 1939, Phd 1953, D Litt 1969, University College Swansea, University of Wales, 1934–39. *Literary Appointments:* Lecturer in English Literature, 1949–59, Senior Lecturer 1959–61, University College of Wales, Aberystwyth; Professor 1961–80, Emeritus Professor 1980–, University College, Swansea. *Publications:* The English Theatre in Wales in the Eighteenth and Early Nineteenth Centuries, 1948; Cold Caleb, 1956; The Letters of Richard Brinsley Sheridan, 3 volumes, editor, 1966; The Dramatic Works of..., 2 volumes, editor, 1973; Theatre in the Age of Garrick, 1973. *Contributions to:* Review of English Studies; National Library of Wales Journal; Times Literary Supplement. *Honours:* Research Fellowship, Folger Shakespeare Library, 1960; Research Fellowship, Huntington Library, San Marina, 1971; Grantee: British Academy 1957, Leverhulme Fund 1958, Newberry Library Chicago 1971; Research Fellowship, Humanities Centre, Australian National University, Canberra, 1976. *Address:* 86 Glanbrydan Avenue, Swansea SA2 0JH, Wales.

PRICE, Edgar Hoffmann, b. 3 July 1898, Fowler, California, USA. Author. m. 3 times, 1 son, 1 daughter. *Education:* ScB, United Stated Military Academy, West Point, New York. *Publications:* Strange Gateways, 1867; Far Lands, Other Days, 1975; Devil Wives of Li Fong, 1979; Operation Misfit, 1980; Jade Enchantress, 1982; Operation Longlife, 1983. *Contributions to:* Magazines of the Pulp Era: Adventure Magazine; Short Stories; Argosy; Western Story Magazine; Black Mask; Top Notch; Complete Stories; also from 1924–52, various miscellaneous items, including 10 serials. *Literary Agent:* Scott Meredith, Inc.

PRICE, Kingsley, b. 24 Aug. 1917, Salem, Indiana, USA. Professor. *Education:* BA; MA; PhD, University of California, Berkeley. *Literary Appointments:* Assistant Professor, University of Nevada, 1947–48; Assistant Professor, Sarah Lawrence College, 1948–51; Assistant Professor, University of Washington, 1951–53; Assistant Professor, The Johns Hopkins University, 1953; Associate Professor, 1957; Professor, 1962; Visiting Professor at the following: Ohio State University; Columbia University; Stanford University; University of California, Berkeley. *Publications:* Education and Philosophical Thought, 1962, revised 1967; On Critiicizing Music: Five Philosophical Perspectives, 1981. *Contributions to:* Numerous professional journals, including, The Philosophical Review; Encyclopaedia of Philosophy; The British Journal of Aesthetics. *Memberships:* American Philosophical Association; President, 1973; Executive Board 1974–75, Philosophy of Education Society; American Association of University Professors; American Society for Aesthetics; Philosophy of Education Society; Washington Philosophy Club; British Society of Aesthetics. *Address:* Department of Philosophy. The Johns Hopkins University, Baltimore, MD 21218, USA.

PRICE, Roger David, b. 7 Jan. 1944, Port Talbot, Wales. University Lecturer. m. Heather Lynne, Port Talbot, 1 son, 3 daughters. *Education:* BA Modern History & Politics, University College of Wales, Swansea, 1965; D Litt, University of East Anglia, 1985; Lecturer, 1968, Senior Lecturer, 1983, Reader, 1984, European Social History, University of East Anglia, England. *Major Publications:* The French Second Republic: A Social History, 1972; 1848 in France, 1975; Revolution & Reaction, 1975; The Economics

Modernisation of France, 1975; An Economic History of Modern France, 1981; The Modernisation of Rural France, 1983. *Contributor to:* Historical Journal; European Studies Review; Journal of European Studies; European History Review. *Membership:* Fellow, Royal Historical Society. *Address:* School of Modern Languages & European History, University of East Anglia, Norwich NR4 7TJ, England.

PRICE, Sally, b. 16 Sep. 1943, Boston, Massachusetts, USA. Anthropologist. m. Richard Price, 22 June 1963, Cincinnati, Ohio, 1 son, 1 daughter. *Education:* BA, Harvard University, 1965; PhD, Johns Hopkins University, 1982. *Publications:* Afro-American Arts of the Suribame Rain Forests, with Richard Price, 1980; Co-Wives and Calabashes, 1984; Caribbean Contours, Edited with Sidney W Mintz, 1985. *Contributions to:* Ethnology; American Ethnologist; New West Indian Guide; Caribbean Review; Natural History; Anthropologica; Names; Man; Southwestern Journal of Anthropology. *Honour:* Alice and Edith Hamilton Prize, University of Michigan, 1982. *Address:* 215 Overhill Road, Baltimore, MD 21218, USA.

PRICE, Stanley, b. 12 Aug. 1931, London, England. Writer. m. Judy Fenton, 5 July 1957, New York, USA, 1 son. *Education:* MA, University of Cambridge, England. *Major Publications:* Crusading for Kronk, 1960; A World of Difference, 1961; Just for the Record, 1962; The Biggest Picture, 1964; Plays: Horizontal Hold, 1967; The Starving Rich, 1972; The Two of Me, 1975; Moving, 1980; Why Me?, 1985; also television plays (BBC & ITV). *Contributor to:* The Observer; Sunday Telegraph; New York Times; Los Angeles Times; Punch; Plays & Players; The New Statesman; Town. *Memberships:* The Writers' Guild, Chairman of Film Committee 1977–80; The Dramatists; Club. *Address:* 17 Cranley Gardens, London N10, England.

PRIES, Johannes Heinrich, b. 20 Feb. 1920, Flensburg, Germany. Vocational Teacher; Lecturer, Chambre of Handicraft, Flensburg. m. 6 May 1944, Flensburg. 1 son, 1 daughter. *Education:* Vocational Pedagogy, Pedagogical Academy, Frankfurt/Main, 1948–51. *Publications:* Grosse Servierkunde, 1967, 7th edition 1984, translated into Turkish, 1984. *Contributor to:* Magazine of Hotel Business, Switzerland, 2 years. *Honours:* Silver Medal, International Cookery Exhibition, Frankfurt/Main, 1968; Gold Medal, GAD, Literary Competition Book Mess, 1981; Honorary Master of Handicraft, 1980; Cultural Doctor, Philosophy of Education, WUR, Tucson, USA, 1984. *Membership:* International Biographical Association, Cambridge, England. *Literary Agent:* Carl Gerber Verlag. *Address:* Karolinenstr, 10, D–2390 Flensburg, Federal Republic of Germany.

PRIEST, Christopher, b. 14 July 1943, England. Author. *Publications:* A Dream of Wessex, 1977; An Infinite Summer, 1979; The Affirmation, 1981; The Glamour, 1984. *Literary Agent:* A P Watt Limited. *Address:* c/o Jonathan Cape Limited, 32 Bedford Square, London WC1, England.

PRIEST, Robert John, b. 10 July 1951, England. Poet; Composer. m. Marsha Kirzner, 1 son. *Publications:* The Visible Man, 1979; Sadness of Spacemen, 1980; The Man Who Broke out of the Letter X, 1984. *Contributor to:* Tamerack Review; Waves; Descant; Dalhousie Review; Rampike; Canadian Forum; The Literary Half-Yearly, India. Record Albums: The Robert Priest EP, 1982; Summerlong, children's record, wrote lyrics, 1984. *Membership:* The League of Canadian Poets. *Address:* 100 Bain Avenue, #7, The Aberdeens, Toronto, Ontario M4K 1E8, Canada.

PRIESTLAND, Gerald Francis, b. 26 Feb. 1927, Berkhamstead, England. Radio/TV Broadcaster. m. Sylvia Rhodes, 1949, London, 2 sons, 2 daughters. *Education:* BA, Oxford. *Literary Appointments:* News Staff of BBC 1949–82, including Foreign Correspondent in Paris, 1954; New Delhi, 1954–58; Washington, 1958–60; Beirut, 1960–61; Washington,

1965–69; Religious Affairs Correspondent, 1976–82. *Publications:* America, The Changing Nation, 1968; Frying Tonight, 1972; The Future of Violence, 1974; Yours Faithfully, 1979; Dilemmas of Journalism, 1979; West of Hayle River, 1980; Priestland's Progress, 1981; Yours Faithfully 2, 1981; Gerald Priestland at Large, 1983; Priestland Right and Wrong, 1983; The Case Against God, 1984. *Contributions to:* Numerous professional publications. *Honours:* Hon. Fellow Manchester Polytechnic, 1977; Hon. Master The Open University, 1985; Sandford St Martin Award, 1983. *Membership:* West of England Writers' Association. *Literary Agent:* Campbell, Thomson & McLaughlin, London, England. *Address:* 4 Temple Fortune Lane, London NW11 7UD, England.

PRIME, Derek James, b. 20 Feb. 1931, London, England. Minister of the Gospel, Charlotte Baptist Chapel, Edinburgh. m. Betty Kathleen Martin, 9 Apr. 1955, West Norwood, London, 2 sons, 2 daughters. *Education:* MA, Emmanuel College, Cambridge, 1954; S Th, Lambeth Diploma in Theology, 1959. *Publications:* A Christian's Guide to Prayer, 1963; A Christian's Guide to Leadership, 1964; Questions on the Christian Faith, 1967; This Way to Life, 1968; Tell me the Answer, books for children, 1965–67; Bible Guidelines, 1979; Created to Praise, 1981; From Trials to Triumphs, 1982. *Literary Agent:* Edward England. *Address:* 11 Midmar Gardens, Edinburgh EH10 6DY, Scotland.

PRINCE, Frank Templeton, b. 13 Sep. 1912. University Teacher. *Education:* Balliol College, Oxford, England; D Litt, Southampton; D University of York. *Appointments:* Professor, English, University of Southampton, 1957–74; Professor, English, University of the West Indies, Mona, Jamaica, 1975–78; Hurst Visiting Professor, Brandeis University, Boston, USA, 1978–80; Visiting Professor, Washington University, St Louis, USA, 1980–81; Visiting Professor, Sana's University, North Yemen, 1981–83. *Publications:* Poems: Poems, 1938; Soldiers Bathing, 1954; The Doors of Stone, 1963; Memoirs in Oxford, 1970; Drypoints of the Hasidim, 1975; Afterword on Rupert Brooke, 1977; Collected Poems, 1979; Later on, 1983. *Contributor to:* Professional journals. *Memberships:* President, English Association, 1985–86. *Address:* 32 Brookvale Road, Southampton SO2 1QR, England.

PRING, John Lambert, b. 29 July 1923, Exeter, England. Indexer. m. Hildred Mary Carlisle, 24 Oct. 1951, Westminster, London, England, 2 sons. *Education:* 4B Wartime degree, Trinity College, Cambridge, 1942. *Publications:* Indexes for: Professional Studies – Law, 1984; Matrimonial Conveyancing 2nd edition 1985; Essential Law For Journalists, 9th edition 1985; Recovery of Interest Practice and Procedures; US Investment in Latin America and the Caribbean. *Membership:* Society of Indexers. *Address:* Wynnards Mead, Tiverton, Devon EX16 5NE, England.

PRING, Martin John, b. 27 Feb. 1943, Bristol, England. Publisher; Author. m. Anne M T Fayne, 18 Sep. 1965, 1 son, 1 daughter. *Education:* BSc, Economics, Honours, Southampton. *Publications:* Technical Analysis Explained, 1980, 2nd Edition 1985; International Investing Made Easy, 1980; How to Forecast Interest Rates, 1981; The McGraw Hill Commodity & Futures Handbook, 1985. *Address:* RR1, Box 83, Washington Depot, CT 06794, USA.

PRIOR, Allan, b. 13 Jan. 1922, Newcastle on Tyne, England. Author. *Publications:* Novels: A Flame in the Air, 1951; The Joy Ride, 1952; The One Eyed Monster, 1958; One Away, 1961; The Interrogators, 1965; The Operators, 1967; The Loving Cup, 1968; The Contract, 1970; Paradiso, 1973; Affair, 1976; Never Been Kissed, 1979; Theatre, 1981; A Cast of Stars, 1981; The Big March, 1983. *Honours:* Critic's Award CWA, 1961 and 1966; Writers Guild of Great Britain Award, 1962 and 1965; Grand Prix de Litterature Policiere, 1963; British Academy Award, Television, 1974. *Literary Agent:* Ed Victor. *Address:* c/o Ed Victor, 162 Wardour Street, London W1, England.

PRITCHARD, Hilary Kathleen, b. 8 Dec. 1944, New York, USA. Scientific Editor. m. Stephen Hohl, 18 Dec. 1964, San Mateo, California, 2 daughters. *Education:* BA, English 1978, MA English 1980, San Francisco State University. University of California, Santa Barbara, 1962-64. *Appointments:* Principal Editor, Department of Restorative Dentistry, University of California, San Francisco, School of Dentistry, 1969 to present; Poetry Editor, Transfer magazine, San Francisco, 1979, 80. *Publications:* Proceedings, International Workshop on Biocompatibility (in press), 1985. Articles in magazines, etc, include: A Fan's Plea to Pro Tennis, World Tennis, 1984; Kudos for Rules Column — And for Officials, International Tennis Weekly, June 1984. *Memberships:* American Medical Writers Association; Council of Biology Editors. *Address:* Restorative Dentistry D-3212, University of California, 707 Parnassus Avenue, San Francisco, CA 94143, USA.

PRITCHARD, R(obert) John, b. 30 Nov. 1945, Los Angeles, California, USA. Historian. m. Sonia Magbanna Zaide, 15 Aug. 1969, Manila, Philippines, divorced 1984, 1 son, 1 daughter. *Education:* AB, History, University of California, 1967; MA, History, 1968, PhD, Economics in International History, 1980, London School of Economics, England. *Publications:* The Reichstag Fire: Ashes of Democracy, 1972; The Tokyo War Crimes Trial: The Complete Transcripts of the Proceedings of the International Military Tribunal for the Far East, with S M Zaide, 22 volumes, 1982; The Tokyo War Crimes Trial: Index and Guide, with S M Zaide, 5 volumes, 1981-86; Contributor, Kotusai Shinposiuma Tokyo Saiban wa tou, 1984; General History of the Philippines, V:1; The American Half-Century 1898-1946, with Lewis E Gleeck et al, 1984; Total War: Causes and Courses of the Second World War, with Peter Calvocoressi, Guy Wint. *Contributor to:* Numerous professional journals. *Honours:* California Stage Graduate Fellowship, 1967; University of California Teaching Assistantship, 1968-70; Zeitlin & Ver Brugge Book Collection Prize, 1969, 1970; Social Science Research Council Research Grants, 1974-76, 1976-77, 1977, 1977-78; Japan Foundation Endowment Committee Research Grant, 1978-79; International Centre for the Study of Economics and Related Disciplines, Research Grants, 1978-79, 1979-80, 1980-82; Japan Foundation Research Grant, 1981-82; Twenty-seven Foundation Research Grant, 1981-82; British Academy Research Grant, 1982-83; Nuffield Foundation Research Grant, 1983; Recipient many other Grants. *Memberships:* American Historical Association; Association of Contemporary Historians; British Association for Japanese Studies; British Institute of Management. *Address:* 28 Star Hill, Rochester, Kent ME1 1XB, England.

PRITCHARD JONES, Harris Elwyn, b. 3 Oct. 1933, Dudley, England. Writer. m. Lenna Harries, 20 Sep. 1965, 2 sons, 1 daughter. *Education:* LRCP, MRCS, Trinity College, Dublin, Republic of Ireland. *Publications:* Troeon, (Ch. Davies), 1966; Dychwelyd, (Gomer), 1972; Storiau Tramor, (Gomer); Pobl, (Gomer), 1978; Freud, 1982. *Contributor to:* Taliesin; Former Deputy Editor, Barn; Planet; Irish Times; for Television, a film, 'Sglyfaethe, 1984; Y Clown, 1985. *Honours:* Short Story, Eisteddford of Wales, 1965; Prose, Welsh Arts Council, 1977. *Memberships:* Yr Academi Gymreig. *Literary Agent:* David Higham Associates Limited. *Address:* 9 Heol Wingfield, Eglwys Newydd, Caerdydd, CF4 1NJ, Wales.

PROCHNOW, Herbert V, b. 19 May 1897, Wilton, Wisconsin, USA. Banker. Author. m. Laura Stinson, 12 June 1928 (deceased 1977), 1 son. *Education:* BA, MA, Honorary LL.D, University of Wisconsin; PhD, Honorary LL.D, Northwestern University; Honorary doctorate degrees from Millikin University, Ripon College, Lake Forest University, Monmouth College, University of North Dakota and Thiel College. *Publications:* Books include: The Complete Toastmaster, 1982; Speaker's Book of Illustrations, 1960; 1400 Ideas for Speakers and Toastmasters, 1964; Tree of Life, 1972; A Speaker's Treasury for Educators, Convocation Speakers, 1973; Toastmaster's Quips and Stories and How to Use Them, 1982. Editor: Dilemmas Facing the Nation, 1979; Bank Credit, 1981; Co-author with Herbert V Prochnow Junior: The Toastmaster's Treasure Chest, 1979; A Treasure Chest of Quotations for All Occasions, 1983. Co-author: Practical Bank Credit, 1939, revised 1963; Co-author with Everett M Dirksen: Quotation Finder, 1971. *Contributions to:* Magazines, journals, etc. *Honours include:* Order of VASA, Sweden; Commanders Cross of Order of Merit of Federal Republic of Germany; Silver Plaque, Highest Award, National Conference of Christians and Jews. *Address:* 2950 Harrison Street, Evanston, IL 60201, USA.

PRONZINI, Bill, b. 13 Apr. 1934, Petaluma, California, USA. Writer. *Major Publications:* 40 novels, 2 collections of short stories, 2 non-fiction works, 1971–; Editor, Co-editor, 45 anthologies of mystery/suspense, Western, Fantasy & Science Fiction. *Contributor to:* Cosmopolitan; Ellery Queen's Mystery Magazine; Analog Science Fiction; Argosy; Adventure; The Writer; The Armchair Detective and some 250 other short stories, articles, essays, book reviews especially, San Francisco Chronicle. *Honours:* Shamus Award for Best Novel, 1981; Best short story, 1983. *Memberships:* Mystery Writers of America, Regional Vice-President; Western Writers of America, Chairman, Grievance Committee; Writers Guild West. *Literary Agent:* Curtis Brown Ltd, New York. *Address:* P O Box 27368, San Francisco, CA 94127, USA.

PROSE, Francine, b. 1 Apr. 1947, New York, USA. Writer. m. Howard Michels, 24 Sep, 1976, 2 sons. *Education:* BA, Radcliffe College; MA, Harvard University. *Publications:* Judah the Pious, 1973; The Glorious Ones, 1974; Household Saints, 1981; Hungry Hearts, 1983. *Contributions to:* Stories in: The Atlantic; Mademoiselle; Commentary; Tri-Quarterly; Massachusetts Review. Articles and Criticism: The New York Times; The New York Times Book Review; The Village Voice. *Honours:* National Endowment Grant, 1979-80; New York State CAPS Grant, 1975-76, 1982. *Memberships:* Poets, Playwrights, Editors, Essayists and Novelists. *Literary Agent:* Georges Borchardt. *Address:* c/o Georges Borchardt, 136 East 57th Street, New York City, NY 10022, USA.

PROSSER, Harold Lee, b. 31 Dec. 1944, Springfield, Missouri, USA. Sociologist, Writer. m. Grace Eileen Wright, 4 Nov. 1971, Bakersfield, California, 2 daughters. *Eduation:* AA English, Santa Monica College, 1968; Advanced Narrative Writing, CSUN 1969-69; BS Sociology 1974, MSED Social Science (Sociology) 1982, Southwest Missouri State University. *Publications include:* Dandelion Seeds: Eighteen Stories, 1974; The Capricorn and Other Fantasy Stories, 1974; The Cymric and Other Occult Poems, 1976; The Day of the Grunion and Other Stories, 1977; Spanish Tales, 1977; Goodbye, Lon Chaney, Jr, Goodbye, 1978; Summer Wine, 1979; The Alien and Other Fantasy Poems, (with W R Wilkins), 1980; A Gathering of Secret Places, autiobiographical sketches, 1981; Charles Beaumont, 1986; Robert Bloch: The Man Who Walked Through Mirrors, 1986; Frank Herbert: Prophet of Dune, 1986; Poul Anderson, 1986. *Contributions to:* Magazines and journals including: Nitty-Gritty; Ozarks Mountaineer; Fate; Antaeus; Dialogue; Fantasy and Horror Journal. *Honour:* Manuscripts permanently housed at Archives of Contemporary History, University of Wyoming, Laramie. *Memberships:* Science Fiction Research Association; Founder and Director, Capricorn Seven Reasearch Society. *Address:* 1313 South Jefferson Avenue, Springfield, MO 65807, USA.

PRYBYLA, Jan S, b. 21 Oct. 1927, Poland. Professor of Economics. m. Jacqueline Meyer, 29 Nov. 1958, Montreal, 1 son, 1 daughter. *Education:* BComm, MEcon Sc, PhD, National University of Ireland; Diploma, Higher European Studies, University of Strasbourg. *Publications:* The Political Economy of Communist China, 1970; The Chinese Economy: Problems and Policies, 1978, 1981; Issues in Socialist

Economic Modernization, 1980; The Bird in the Cage; Marker and Plan Under Socialism, 1986. *Contributions to:* Numerous professional journals, including The Chine Quarterly; Asian Survey, Slavic Review; Journal of Industrial Economics. *Honours:* Distinction in the Social Sciences Award, College of the Liberal Arts, 1978. *Address:* 523 Kern Building, University Park, PA 16802, USA.

PRYCE-JONES, David Eugene Henry, b. 15 Feb. 1936, Vienna, Austria. Author. m. 29 July 1959, Alltmawr, 1 son, 2 daughters. *Education:* BA, MA, Oxford University. *Literary Appointments:* Literary editor, Time and Tide, 1960–61, Spectator, 1964–65. *Publications:* Owls and Satyrs, 1961; The Sands of Summer, 1963; Next Generation, 1964; Quondam, 1965; The Stranger's View, 1967; The Hungarian Revolution, 1969; Running Away, 1971; The Face of Defeat, 1972; The England Commune, 1975; Unity Mitford, 1976; Shirley's Guild, 1979; Paris in the Third Reich, 1981; Cyril Connolly, 1983. *Contributions to:* Spectator; Encounter; Commentary; Sunday Telegraph Magazine; New Republic; Financial Times and others. *Membership:* Royal Society of Literature. *Literary Agent:* A D Peters. *Address:* c/o A D Peters, 10 Buckingham Street, London WC2, England.

PRYNNE, Jeremy Halvard, b. 24 June 1936, Kent, England. Poet. *Publications:* Force of Circumstance and Other Poems, 1962; Kitchen Poems 1968; Day Light Songs, 1968; Aristeas, 1968; The White Stones, 1969; Fire Lizard, 1970; Brass, 1971; Into the Day, 1972; A Night Square, 1973; Wound Response, 1974; High Pink on Chrome, 1975; News of Warring Clans 1977; Down where changed, 1979; Poems 1982; The Oval Window, 1983.

PRYTZ, Kjeld Jan, b. 27 June 1934, Hellerup, Denmark. Editor. *Education:* Higher Commercial Examination; Merkonom in Finance. *Contributor to:* Forsikring, Danish Insurance Review. *Membership:* Danish Publishing Society. *Address:* Horsekildevej 38, st. tv, DK–2500 Valby, Denmark.

PRZYPKOWSKI, Andrzej Jozef, b. 9 July 1930, Wolomin, Poland. Writer. m. Halina Sienska, 17 Mar. 1980, Warsaw, 1 daughter. *Education:* University of Warsaw, 1952. *Publications include:* Zwykly Rejs, 1962; Gdzies we Francji, 1966; Oni Byli wszedzie, 1967; Ulica Milosierdzia, 1968; Gdy Wrocisz de Montpellier, 1969; Nie ma Jutra w Saint-Nazaire, 1971; Ksiezyc nad Sierra Leone, 1972; Arena, 1973; Odwrot, 1976; Przestapie prog, 1977; Taniec Marihuany, 1977; Palm City, 1978; Victoria, 1980; Opetani, 1985. *Contributions to:* Nike; Argumenty. *Honours:* Polinia Restituta, 1980; Literary Award, Minister of National Defense, 1980. *Membership:* Vice-president of Warsaw branch, Union of Polish Writers. *Literary Agent:* Author's Agency Limited, POB 133, 00-950 Warszawa. *Address:* Graniczna 62, 05-540 Zalesia Gorne, Poland.

PUGH, Patterson David Gordon, b. 19 Dec. 1920, Carshalton, Surrey, England. Naval Orthopaedic Surgeon (retired). m. Eleanor Margery Jones, 20 May 1967, Cardiff, Wales. *Education:* MA; MB B Chir; Fellow, Royal College of Surgeons, England. *Publications:* Practical Nursing, 1945–69; Nelson and His Surgeons, 1968; Staffordshire Portrait Figures and Allied Subjects, of the Victorian Era, 1969; Naval Ceramics, 1971; Heraldic China Mementoes of the First World War, 1972; Pugh of Carshalton, 1974; Boer War Ceramics – A History of the War and the Cermaics it Inspired, 1986. *Contributions to:* Journals including: Journal of the Royal Naval Medical Service; British Medical Journal. *Honours:* OBE, 1968; C St J, 1975. *Membership:* Society of Authors. *Address:* 14 Hove Road, Camps Bay 8001, Cape Town, Republic of South Africa.

PUJOL, Carlos, b. 17 Apr. 1936, Barcelona, Spain. Publishing Adviser. m. Marta Lagarriga, 31 Dec. 1962, Barcelona, 3 sons, 1 daughter. *Education:* Doctor of Philosophy, 1962. *Publications:* Balzac y la Comedia Humana, 1974; Leer a Saint-Simon, 1979; La sombra del tiempo, 1981; Un viale a Aspaña, 1983; El lugar del aire, 1984; Es otoño en Crimea, 1985. *Contributor to:* La Vanguardia; El Ciervo. *Literary Agent:* Ute Korner de Moya. *Address:* Avenida de República Argentina 279, 6°2a, 08023 Barcelona, Spain.

PULASKI, Mary Ann Spencer, b. 9 Sep. 1916. Psychologist; Author; Lecturer. *Education:* BA, Wellesley Coll, 1938; MA, Queens Coll, 1958; PhD, CUNY, 1968. *Publications include:* Understanding Pieage: An Introduction to Children's Cognitive Development, 1971; Step by Step Guide to Correct English, 1974; Your Baby's Mind and How it Grows, 1978. *Contributor to:* Child Dev; Psychol Today; Educational film strips etc; The Child's World of Make-Believe (ed J Singer), 1974; The International Encyclopedia of Neurology, Psychiatry, Psychoanalysis and Psychology, (ed B Wolman), 1977. *Honours:* Fellow, American Psychol, Association, 1974; Durant Scholar, Wellesley College, 1937. *Memberships include:* Nassau Co Psychol Association (President and Treasurer); New York State Psychological Association (Member Executive Board); Board of Directors, Jean Piaget Society. *Address:* 19 Lynn Road, Port Wash, NY 11050, USA.

PULLEIN-THOMPSON, Josephine Mary Wedderburn, b. Wimbledon, England. Author. *Publications:* 39 books for children, numerous others for adults including: Gin and Murder; They Died in the Spring; Murder Strikes Pink; Race Horse Holiday; All Change; Historical Anthology; Horses and their Owners, 1970; A Place with Two Faces, 1972; Proud Riders, 1973; Ride Better and Better, 1974; Black Beauty's Clan, 1975; Star Riders of the Moor, 1976; Fear Treks the Moor, 1978; Ride to the Rescue, 1979; Mystery on the Moor, 1984; Pony Club Trek, 1985. *Honours:* Recipient, Ernest Benn Prize, 1961; MBE 1984. *Memberships:* Crimewriters' Association; General Secretary, English Centre of International PEN, 1976–; Society of Authors; British Horse Society. *Address:* 16 Knivet Road, London SW6 1JH, England.

PUNDEFF, Marin V, b. 7 Nov. 1921, Sofia, Bulgaria. Professor of History. m. Janet Ziegler, 21 Jan. 1979, Pacific Grove, California, USA, 1 son, 1 daughter (by previous marriage). *Education:* Law, University of Sofia; International Relations, University of Southern California; MA Government, George Washington University; PhD History, University of Southern California. *Literary Appointments:* Consultant to the Library of Congress, 1952, 1963. Fellow, American Council of Learned Societies, 1966; Fellow, Centre d'Etudes des Institutions Religious, Geneva, Switzerland, 1966–70. *Major Publications:* History in the USSR, 1967; Bulgaria: A Bibliographic Guide, 1968; Co-author: Nationalism in Eastern Europe, 1969, Leaders of the Communist World, 1971, Religion and Atheism in the USSR & Eastern Europe, 1975 and others. *Contributor to:* Slavic Review; American Historical Review; Südost-Forschungen (Munich); Revue des Etudes Slaes (Paris); Österreichische Osthefte (Vienne); Harvard Educational Review; Osteuropa (Stuttgart); Libri (Copenhagen); Slavic East European Journal; East European Quarterly; Annals of the American Academy of Political & Social Science; and others. *Honour:* Medal 1300 Years Bulgaria (Council of State of Bulgaria), 1984. *Memberships:* American Association for the Advancement of Slavic Studes; Western Slavic Association (Secertary & Treasurer); Bulgarian Studies Association. *Address:* Department of History, California State University, Northridge, CA 91330, USA.

PUNNER, Helen Walker, b. 18 June 1915, New York City, USA, Writer; Educator; Editor. m. Samuel Paul Puner, 6 July 1936, New York City, 1 son, 2 daughters. *Education:* Graduated, Honours, Barnard College, 1934. *Publications:* Freud: His Life and His Mind, 1947; Not While You're a Freshman, 1964; 5 Childrens Books, 2 of which are still in print. *Contributor to:* Numerous articles and light verse in Harper's Magazine, The New York Times Magazine, many others. *Honours:* A Stay at Yaddo, Saratoga Springs; 2 Stays at Ossabaw

Foundation, 1970's; A Stay at Ragdale Foundation. *Memberships:* Authors League; Poetry Society of America. *Address:* 157 Pinesbridge Road, Ossining, NY 10562, USA.

PUPUTTI, Marja-Liisa, b. 28 Aug. 1941, Kauhajoki, Finland. Writer & Leader of Children. m. Pertti Kalevi Puputti, 24 June 1961, Kaihajoki, Finland, 1 son, 1 daughter. *Major Publications:* Tiniiamarain matka aurinkoon; Missä Timo; Meidän pihan mustanaamat; Raukkis; Tuli palaa, Apua; Posliinikissa; Mä olen kummitus; Koiruuksia; Pikku siili piikkipallo; Ravunkäyntiä; Hassina. *Contributor to:* Päiväkerholehti; Joulupuu; various anthologies. *Honours:* Publishers' Prize, 1975; Tauno Karilas Prize, 1981. *Memberships:* Suomen Kirjailijaliitto ry; Suomen Nuorisokirailijat ry; Lounais-Suomen Kirjailijat ry; Suomen Maakuntakirjailijat ry. *Literary Agent:* Werner Söderström oy & Lasten Keskus Oy. *Address:* Riutojankatu 1 B M 87, 20350 Turku, Finland.

PURCELL, Sally Anne Jane, b. 1 Dec. 1944, England. Writer. *Education:* LMH, Oxford, 1863; BA, 1966; MA, 1970. *Literary Appointments:* Honorary Secretary, Foundation for Islamic Culture, Oxford, 1969–; Joint General editor, Fyfield Books, Oxford and Cheadle, Cheshire, 1969–. *Publications:* The Devil's Dancing Hour, 1968; Provinçal Poems, translator, 1969; The Happy Unicorns: Poetry of the Under-25's, editor with L Purves, 1971; The Holly Queen, 1972; George Peele, editor, 1972; Monarchs and the Muse: Poems by Monarchs and Princes of England, Scotland and Wales, editor and translator, 1972; The Exile of James Joyce by Hélène Cixous, translator, 1972; Charles d'Orléans, editor, 1973; Dark of Day, 1977; By The Clear Fountain; Guenever and the Looking Glass, 1984–85; The Early Italian Poets, by D G rossetti, editor, 1981; Gaspara Stampa, 1984–85; Lake and Labyrinth, 1985. *Contributions to:* Magazines and journals including: Carcanet; New Measure; Oxford Poetry. *Honour:* Arts Council Grant. *Address:* c/o Anvil Press, 69 King George Street, London SE10 8PX, England.

PURDEN, Roma Laurette (Laurie), b. 30 Sep. 1928, Tunbridge Wells, Kent, England. Journalist; Magazine editor. m. John Keith Kotch (dec), 26 June 1957, London, 2 daughters. *Literary Appointments:* Fiction editor, Home Notes, 1948–51; Assistant Editor, ibid, 1951–52, Woman's Own, 1952; Senior Assistant Editor, Girl, 1952–54; Editor, Housewife, 1954–57, Home, 1957–62; House Beautiful, 1963–65, Good House-keeping, 1965–73; Editor-in-chief, Good Housekeeping and Womancraft, 1973–77; Editor-in-chief, Woman's Journal, 1978–, Woman & Home, 1982–83. *Honours:* Member, Order of the British Empire, 1973; Magazine Editor of the Year, British Society of Magazine Editor, 1979; PPA voted Woman's Journal, 'Consumer Maga-zine of the Year', 1985. *Address:* IPC Magazines, King's Reach Tower, Stamford Street, London SE1 9LS, England.

PURDY, James, b. 17 July 1923, Ohio, USA. Writer. *Publications:* 63 books including, Dream Palace, 1956; Malcolm, 1959; The Nephew, 1960; Eustace Chisholm and the Works, 1967; The House of the Solitary Maggot, 1974; In A Shallow Grave, 1976; Narrow Rooms, 1978; Mourners Below, 1982; On Glory's Course, 1985. *Contributions to:* Esquire; Harper's Bazaar; Nuovi Argomenti (Rome); The London Magazine. *Honours:* National Academy of Arts and Letters Fellowship, 1958; Guggenheim Fellowship, 1958 and 1962; Ford Fellowship, 1963; Rockefeller Foundation Fellowship, 1965. *Membership:* PEN. *Literary Agent:* William Morris Associates Inc, 1350 Avenue of the Americas, New York. *Address:* c/o Ned Leavitt, William Morris Associates Inc, 1350 Avenue of the Americas, New York, NY 10019, USA.

PURKEY, William Watson, b. 22 Aug. 1929, Shenandoah, Virginia, USA. University Professor. m. Imogene Hedrick, 8 May 1951, Roanoke, Virginia, 1 son, 1 daughter. *Education:* BS, 1957, MEd, 1958, EdD, 1964, University of Virginia. *Publications:* Self-Concept

and School Achievement, 1970; Helping Relationships, with A Combs and D Avila; Inviting School Success, 1978, 2nd edition 1984; The Inviting Relationship, forthcoming. *Contributions to:* Over 80 articles in professional journals. *Honours:* University of Florida Student Award for Instructor Excellence; Good Teach-ing Award, Standard Oil Foundation; Outstanding Teacher Award, Omicron Delta Kappa, National Leadership Honor Society; Ralph F Berdie Memorial Research Award, American Personnel and Guidance Association, 1979; Distinguished Alumnus Award, School of Education, University of Virginia, 1980; Distinguished Service to the Field of Education Award, Alumni Council, School of Education, Lehigh University, 1981. *Address:* 4407 Williamsburg Road, Greensboro, NC 27410, USA.

PURSCHKE, Hans Richard, b. 29 July 1911, Olmutz, Moravia, Austria (now CSSR). Administrative Officer (retired). *Education:* Dr juris, German University of Prague, 1940. *Publications include:* Das ABC des Handpuppenspiels, 1951; Puppenspiel in Deutschland, 1957 (5 languages); Liebenswerte Puppenwelt, 1962; Das allerzierlichste Theater, 1968; Das Deutsche Puppentheater heute, 1979 (5 languages); Die Anfange der Puppenspielformen und ihre vermutlichen Ursprunge, 1979; Puppenspiel und verwandte Kunste in der Freien Reichs-Stadt Frankfurt am Main, 1980; Uber das Puppenspiel und seine Geschichte, 1983; Die Entwicklung des Puppenspiels in den klassichen Ursprungslandern Europas, 1984; Die Puppenspieltraditionen Europas, Bd 1, 1985; many publications on historical puppetry. *Contributor to:* Perlicko-Perlacko (puppetry journal), Publisher and Editor. *Honours:* Honorary Citizen of Tennessee, 1971; Honorary member, Union International de la Marionnette, 1980; Federal Cross of Merite, 1983. *Address:* PF 550135, D–6000 Frankfurt/Main, Federal Republic of Germany.

PURSER, John Whitley, b. 10 Feb. 1942, Glasgow, Scotland. Writer, Composer. 1 son, 1 daughter. *Educa-tion:* D R S A M; MA Honours. *Publications:* The Counting Stick, 1976; A Share of the Wind, 1980; Amoretti, 1985. *Contributions to:* Scottish International Words; The Scotsman; Aquarius; The Times Educational Supplement; Akros; The Glasgow Herald; Stretto; Craftwork. *Honours:* Scottish Arts Council New Writing Award, 1976; Buchanan Prize, 1977. *Address:* 29 Banavie Road, Glasgow G11 5AW, Scotland.

PUSA, Timo Tapani, b. 9 Oct. 1951, Kotka, Finland. Writer. *Publications:* Tuulessa hymyileva puu, collection of poems, 1978, 2nd edition, 1978; Yövuiro, collection of poems, 1979; Opporits ja muita novelleja, collection of short stories, 1982. Plays: Kummallinen metsa, play for children, together with Juhani Pusa, 1978; Kaukkalan jokijuhlat, with Juhani Pusa, 1979; Könys ja Miranda, play for children, 1981; Conributions pf poetry to school textbooks and anthologies. Joint Exhibition of poems with Olavi Heino, Painter, 1984; Kulttuurivihkot, poems, 1979; Uusi nainen, short story, 1981; Peilaaja, poems, narratives of journeys, etc, 1982–84; Runous poems, 1983. *Honours:* Jyväskylän Talvi, writing com-petitions, First Prize for poems, 1978; J H Erkko, Playwriting competition, divided First Prize, 1979; Loviisa Youth-Play Writing Competition, First Prize, 1980; Latvijas Padomju Rakstnieku Savieniba, Medal of the Latvian Writers Union, 1983. *Memberships:* Paltta, Writers Association of Kymi-county, 1976; Writers Union of Finland, 1980; Board Member, Paltta, 1981–, Chairman, 1983–84. *Literary Agent:* Kirjayhtymä Oy. *Address:* Vähäpellonpolku 11, 48400 Kotka, Finland.

PUSEY, Merlo John, b. 3 Feb. 1902, Woodruff, Utah, USA. Journalist; Author. m. Dorothy Richards, 5 Sep. 1928, Salt Lake City, USA, deceased, 3 sons, *Education:* AB, University of Utah; Doctor of Letters, Hon Degree, Brigham Young University, 1952; Doctor of Laws, Hon Degree, University of Utah, 1975. *Major Publications:* Big Government: Can we Control it?, 1945; Charles Evans Hughes, 1951; Eisenhower the President, 1956; The Way we Go to War, 1969; Eugene Meyer, 1974;

Ripples of Intuition (verse), 1985. *Contributor to:* Saturday Evening Post; Harper's; American Mercury; and others. *Honours:* Pulitzer Prize for Biography, 1952; Bancroft Prize for Biography, 1952; Tamiment Book Award 1952; Kappa Tau Alpha Book Award, 1974. *Address:* 19410 Martinsburg Road, Dickerson, MD 20842, USA.

PUTTNER, Mario, b. 7 Jan. 1916, Pralitz, Germany. Retired Pharmacology Assistant. m. Johanne Lange, 1 Aug. 1952, 1 son, 1 daughter. *Education:* Studies of Arts and Crafts, Academy of Art, Graz, Austria. *Literary Appointments:* Poetry: Im Abendwind; Satire, Und lach mal druber, Es lebt der Mensch; Short story, Xandi Filsers Briefwechsel. *Publications:* Song: Olympiade; 1972. Shanty Song: O Fare Ye Well; 36 songs and hit song; 3 records with the Shanty-Chor, Aurich. *Contributions to:* Ostfriesen Zeitung; Playboy; Various newspapers and journals. *Honours:* Award, Dietz Verlag, Regensburg; Award, Fackel-Verlag, Hanover; Award, Austrian Touring, Hamburg. *Memberships:* GEMA, Berlin. *Address:* Ringstr 41, D-2955 Bunde, Federal Republic of Germany.

PUYDT, Raoul Maria de, b. 22 Feb. 1944, Gistel, Belgium. Lawyer. m. Kristine van Cauwelaert, 2 Feb. 1970, Brussels. 2 sons, 2 daughters. *Education:* Doctor of Laws; Licentiate of International Law. *Publications include:* Een menselÿke revolutie, 1973; Liefdesvuur, 1978; Made in Flanders, 1981; Liefdessprokkels, 1982; Signalen uit het Paradÿs, 1985. *Contributions to:* t Kofschip (editor-in-chief); Vlaanderen (editor). *Honours:* Silvergilt Medal of Arts, Sciences & Letters, Paris, 1979; P P Rubens Memorial Medal, Antwerp, 1979. *Memberships:* Vice President, Association of Flemish Writers; President, Kofschip-Kring. *Literary Agent:* Kofschip-Kring. *Address:* Ninoofsesteenweg 153, B-1080 Brussels, Belgium.

PYBUS, Rodney, b. 5 June 1938, Newcastle upon Tyne, England. Writer. m. Ella Johnson, 24 June 1961, Villars, Switzerland, 2 sons. *Education:* BA, Classics, English, Gonville & Caius College, Cambridge, 1960: Ma, Classics, English, Cantab. *Appointments:* Literature Officer for Cumbria, 1979–82; Arts Council Creative Writing Fellow, Great Cornard Upper School, Suffolk, 1982–84; Arts Council Writer-in-Residence, Parkside Community College & Homerton Centre, Cambridge, 1985. *Publications:* In Memoriam Milena, 1973; Bridging Loans, 1976; At the Stone Junction, 1978; The Loveless Letters, 1981; Talitha Cumi, 1983; Adam's Dream: Poems from Cumbria, Editor with W Scammell, 1981. *Contributor to:* Poetry in Times Literary Supplement; Stand; Encounter; Poetry Review; Quarto; New Statesman; PN Review; Honest Ulsterman; Kenyon Review, USA; Equivalencias, Spain; Southerly, Australia; Helix, Australia; etc. *Honours:* Alice Hunt Bartlett Award, Poetry Society, 1974; National Poetry Competition Prizewinner, 1984; Basil Bunting Poetry Competition Prizewinner, 1985. *Membership:* Writers' Guild. *Address:* 21 Plough Lane, Sudbury, Suffolk CO10 6AU, England.

PYLKKONEN-SUOMI, Maila Annikki, b. 9 June 1931, Helsinki. Freelance Author. m. Olli Suomi, 13 Oct 1971, Helsinki, 2 sons. *Education:* Student of Philosophy, Finnish folklore, Pedagogics, Psychology, Genetics. *Publications:* Klassilliset Tunteet, 1957, Poems: Jeesuksen Kyla, 1958, Poems; Arvo, 1959 Dramatic Monologue; Valta, 1962 Dramatic Monologues; Virheita, 1965, stories; Tarinatappelkusta, 1970, Stories and Poems; Mustista, 1972, Stories and Poems; Mariamies Naisenmuistiinpanoja, 1975, Stories and Poems; Onkesavain, 1977, Collected Poems 1983. *Honour:* Finnish State Prize for Literature, 1973. *Membership:* The Union of Finnish Writers. *Address:* Naurulokinpolku 2C1, 00960 Helsinki 96, Finland.

Q

QUAGGIN HARKIN, Alison Margaret, b. 26 Apr. 1958, Douglas, Isle of Man. Medical Journalist. m. Michael Eugene Harkin, 21 Aug. 1984, Scarborough, Ontario, Canada. *Education:* BA Honours English, Trinity College, University of Toronto, 1981. *Contributions to:* Canadian Family Physician. *Address:* 11 Dervock Crescent, No 204, Willowdale, Ontario M2K 1A6, Canada.

QUAN, Michael John, b. 26 Sep. 1927, Cholsey, Oxfordshire, England. Science Journalist. m. Dorothy Collier, 9 Aug. 1952, Weston-Super-Mare. *Education:* HNC Electrical Engineering, Radio Communications; Endorsement in Physics; Graduate, Institute of Electronic and Radio Engineers; Various City & Guilds certificates in radio. *Literary Appointments:* Technical Author, 1961; Press officer, 1964; Industrial Reporter, 1973; Editor, Spectrum, COI, 1974. *Contributions to:* Numerous to British trade press and overseas newspapers and science, technology and medical journals. *Membership:* Association of British Science Writers. *Address:* 35 Bramley Crescent, Bearsted, Kent ME15 8JZ, England.

QUANDT, Richard E, b. 1 June 1930, Hungary. Professor of Economics. m. Jean H Briggs, 6 Sep. 1955, 1 son. *Education:* BA, Princeton University, 1952; MA 1955, PhD 1957, Harvard University. *Publications:* Microeconomic Theory, with J M Henderson, 1958, 1971, 1980; The New Inflation, with W Thorp, 1959; Strategies and Rational Decisions in the Securities Options Market, with B G Malkiel, 1969; Nonlinear Methods in Econometrics, with S M Goldfield, 1972; The Demand for Travel, Editor, 1970; Studies in Nonlinear Estimation, Editor with S M Goldfield, 1976. *Contributor to:* Quarterly journal of Economics; Econometrica; Journal of Political Economy; Economic Journal; etc. *Honours:* Fellow, Econometric Society; Fellow, American Statistical Association; Guggenheim Fellow, 1959. *Address:* Department of Economics, Princeton University, Princeton, NJ 08544, USA.

QUAYLE, Eric, b. 14 Nov. 1921, Liverpool, England. Author. m. Sachiko Kitahara, 26 May 1979, Zennor, 1 son, 2 daughters. *Publications:* Ballantyne the Brave, 1967; The Ruin of Sir Walter Scott, 1968; The Collector's Book of Books, 1971; The Collector's Book of Children's Books, 1971; The Collector's Book of Detective Fiction, 1972; Old Cook Books – An Illustrated History, 1978; Early Childrens Books – A Collector's Guide, 1983; The Magic Ointment, and other Cornish Legends, 1986. *Memberships:* Arts Club, London; Bibliographical Society, London. *Address:* Carn Cobba, Zennor, Cornwall TR26 3BZ, England.

QUEBEDEAUX, Richard (Anthony), b. 16 Oct. 1944, Los Angeles, California, USA. Author & Consultant on Religion. *Education:* BA History, University of California at Los Angeles, 1966; MA History, 1970; BD, 1968, Harvard University, Cambridge, Massachusetts. *Major Publications:* The Youngs Evangelicals, 1974; The New Charismatics, 1976; The Worldly Evangelicals, 1978; I Found it!: The Story of Bill Bright & Campus Crusade, 1979; By What Authority: The Rise of Personality Cults in American Christianity, 1982; The New Charismatics II, 1983. *Contributor to:* Various Religious Magazines & Journals. *Memberships:* American Society of Journalists & Authors. *Address:* 2236 Channing Way, Berkeley, CA 94704–2164, USA.

QUELLER, Donald E, b. 14 Jan. 1925, St Louis, Missouri, USA. Professor of History. m. Marilyn L Queller, 12 June 1949, Grosse Pointe Woods, Michigan, 2 sons, 3 daughters. *Education:* AB 1949, MA 1951, University of Michigan; PhD, University of Wisconsin. *Major Publications:* Early Venetian Legislation on Ambassadors, 1966; The Office of the Ambassador in the Middle Ages, 1967; The Fourth Crusade, 1977; The Venetian Patriciale: Myth vs Reality, 1986. *Contributor*

to: American Historical Review; Revue Belge de Philologie et d'histoire; Speculum; Le Moyen Age; Medievalia et Humanistica; English Historical Review; Studies in the Renaissance; Explorations in Economic History; and others. *Memberships:* American Historical Association; Medieval Academy of America. *Honours:* Guggenheim Fellow; Institute of Advanced Study; Several Academic Awards. *Address:* 2406 South Prospect, Champaign, IL 61820, USA.

QUENZER, Gerlinde Schreiber, b. 28 Jan. 1924, Uberlingen, Bodensee, Germany. Translator. *Publications:* Translations from French: Bidault Meoiren, 1966; Colette Autobiografie, 1967; Simone Signoret Memoiren, 1977. Translations from English: Dorthy Sayers, 12 Kriminalgeschichten, 1964; Der Fall Harrison, 1967; Walter Strauss, Lebenszeichen, 1982; Herman Dicker, Bilder aus Wurttembergs judischer Vergangenheit, 1984. Translations from Yiddish: Katzektnik, Hollen fahrt, 1980. *Honours:* Scheffelpreis fur besondere Leistungen im Fach Deutsch, Abitur, 1941. *Memberships:* Various literary organisations. *Address:* Fürstenbergstr 12, D–776 Radolfzell, Federal Republic of Germany.

QUESTER, George Herman, b. 14 July 1936, Brooklyn, New York, USA. Professor of Government and Politics. m. Aline Marie Olson, 20 1964, Rockford, Illinois, 1 son, 1 daughter. *Education:* AB History, Columbia College, 1958; MA 1964, PhD 1965, Political Science, Harvard University. *Publications:* Deterrence Before Hiroshima, 1966; Nuclear Diplomacy: The First Twenty-Five Years, 1970; The Politics of Nuclear Proliferation, 1973; The Continuing Problem of International Politics, 1974; Offense and Defense in the International System, 1977; American Foreign Policy, The Lost Consensus, 1982. *Contributions to:* Academic journals including; World Politics, Foreign Affairs, International Security; American Political Science Review; Foreign Policy; Armed Forces and Society; Policy Studies Journal. *Address:* 5124 North 37th Street, Arlington, VA 22207, USA.

QUIGLEY, (Margaret) Ellen, b. 18 Apr. 1955, Toronto, Canada. Editor. *Education:* BA, Hons. University of Toronto. *Publications:* Canadian Writers and Their Works, co-editor with Lecker, Robert, Jack David, Fiction Series, Vol I 1983, Vol VIII 1985; Canadian Writers and Their Works, co-editor with Lecker, Robert, Jack David, Poetry Series, Vol II 1983, Vol V 1985. *Contributions to:* Poems: Fireweed; Erindale Review; Pink Ink. Articles: Studies in Canadian Literature; Essays on Canadian Writing. Reviews: The Fiddlehead; Quill and Quire. *Honours:* Harold Sonny Ladoo Literary Award for Creative Writing, Erindale College, University of Toronto, 1976, 1978 and 1979; Writers' Workshop (Toronto) Scholarship, 1978; English Students' Association Award for Critical Achievement, Erindale College, University of Toronto, 1979; Ontario Arts Council Writer-Inspiration Grant (through Fireweed) 1984. *Address:* 67 Constance Street, Toronto, Ontario, Canada M6R 1S5.

QUINN, David Beers, b. 24 Apr. 1909, Dublin, Ireland. Emeritus Professor of History. m. Alison Moffat Robertson, 30 Oct, 1937, Southampton, 2 sons, 1 daughter. *Education:* BA 1931, MA 1957, DLit 1958, Queen's University, Belfast; PhD, King's College, University of London, 1934. *Literary Appointments Include:* Professor of History, University College of Swansea, 1944–57; Professor of Modern History, University of Liverpool, 1957–76; Visiting Professor, US Universities. *Publications include:* Raleigh & the British Empire, 1947; Roanoke Voyages, 1955; The Discovery of North America, 1971, co-author; The Elizabethans & the Irish, 1966; The Hakluyt Handbook, 1974; North America From First Discovery to Early Settlements, 1977, co-author; English New England Voyages, 1983; Set Fair for Roanoke, 1985; etc. *Contributions to numerous journals including:* Times Literary Supplement; Library Journal; Economist; History; Proceedings of the American Philosophical Society; Proceedings of the Royal Irish Academy; Proceedings of the Royal Historical

Society; History Today; etc. *Honours include:* Member, Royal Irish Academy, 1943; President, Historical Association Branches, various 1935–68; President, 1982–, Hakluyt Society; Various offices, Royal Historical Society; Past & Present Society; Society for Nautical Research; Society for Historical Archaeology; Secretary, 1939–44, Ulster Society for Irish Historical Studies; Honorary Fellow, British Academy, etc. *Address:* 9 Knowsley Road, Liverpool L19 0PF, England.

QUINN, John Patrick, b. 6 Mar. 1943, Albany, Oregon, USA. University Professor. *Education:* BA English Literature 1969; MFA Creative Writing 1971, University of Oregon. *Publications:* The Wolf Last Seen, 1980; Easy Pie, 1984. *Contributions to:* Hudson Review; Cutbank; Gray's Sporting Journal; Yarrow; Greensboro Review; Asiaweek; Mss; Writer's Forum; Nebo; Three Rivers Poetry Journal; Northwest Review. *Address:* 2109-355 Togoku, Kamishidami, Moriyama-ku, Nagoya 463, Japan.

QUINNELL, A J, Author. *Publications:* Man on Fire, 1981; The Mahdi, 1982; Snap Shut, 1983; Blood Ties, 1984. *Honour:* Edgar – Mystery Writers of America. *Literary Agent:* Christopher Little. *Address:* c/o Christopher Little, 49 Queen Victoria Street, London EC4N 4SA, England.

QUINNETT, Paul Guthrie, b. 17 Nov. 1939, Los Angeles, California, USA. Clinical Psychologist. m. Pamela Nye, 3 June 1970, Pocatello, Idaho, 3 sons. *Education:* BA, Utah State University; MS, PhD, Washington State University. *Publications:* The Troubled People Book: A Comprehensive Guide to Getting Help, 1982. *Contributions to:* Numerous national magazines including: Audubon; Sports Afield; Outdoor Life; New Age Journal; American Forests; Outdoor America; Gray's Sporting Journal; Gun Dog, and others. *Address:* Route 2 Box 291-D, Cheney, WA 99004, USA.

R

RABB, Theodore K, b. 1937. Professor of History, Princeton University, USA. 3 children. *Education:* BA 1958, MA 1962, Queen's College, Oxford University, England; MA 1960, PhD 1961, Princeton University, USA. *Literary Appointments:* Board of Editors, Computers and the Humanities, 1969–73; Board of Editors, Computer Studies in the Humanities and Verbal Behaviour, 1968–74; Founder and Co-Editor, The Journal of Interdisciplinary History, 1970–; Editor, The Community College Humanist, 1978–80; Board of Editors, Climatic Change, 1980–; Editor, The Mid-Career Fellowship Program Bulletin, 1980–. *Publications include:* The Thirty Years War: Problems of Motive, Extent and Effect, 1964. revised/enlarged 1972; Enterprise and Empire: Merchant and Gentry Investment in the Expansion of England, 1575–1630, 1967; The Family in History: Interdisciplinary Essays, (co-edited with Robert Rotberg), 1973; Gunpowder and the Transformation of Europe, audio-visual teaching aid, 1973; The Western Experience, (co-author), 1974; Marriage and Fertility, (co-edited with Robert Rotberg), 1980; Consultants Handbook, (co-author), 1981; Climate and History, (co-edited with Robert Rotberg), 1981, Italian Edition 1984; Industrialization and Urbanization, (co-edited with Robert Rotberg), 1981; The Origins of Modern Nations, 1981; Peoples and Nations, (with Anatole G Mazour and John M Peoples), 1982; The New History: The 1980's and Beyond, (with Robert Rotberg), 1983; Sir Edwin Sandys (1561–1629): A Life and Times. *Contributions to:* Numerous journals. *Honours include:* American Council of Learned Societies, 1969 and 1976; Guggenheim Foundation, 1970. *Memberships include:* Fellow, Royal Historical Society. *Address:* Department of History, Princeton University, Princeton, NJ 08540, USA.

RABBEN, Michael, b. 31 Jan. 1908, Philadelphia, Pennsylvania, USA. Writer; Oral Medicine (Clinical Nutrition). m. (1) Mary Blatt, 2 Mar. 1937, Philadelphia, 3 daughters. *Education:* Pre-Dental Certificate, La Salle College Philadelphia; DMD, Temple University, Philadelphia; Various Post-Graduate Courses at several colleges. *Literary Appointments:* Associate Editor, Temple Dental Review Journal; Science Writer. Daily Republican (Phoenixville, Pa); Correspondent for Ocala Star-Banner, Ocala, Florida; Former editor of the Emergency Medical Service Educators of Florida, Newsletter; Free-lance Writer. *Publication:* In process of writing a book on How to Stay Healthy through Nutrition and Exercise; How to Survive in this Poisoned World. *Contributions to:* Dental Digest; Dental Survey; Bucks County Panorama; Omaha (The Chronicle); Lions of Florida Journal; Pennsylvania Dental Journal; Massachusetts Dental Journal; Mexican Dental Journal; Prevention Magazine; Oral Hygiene (Latin America Edition); Modern Nutrition; American Medical Writer's Newsletter (Florida Chapter); American Dental Association Dental Association Journal; World Congress on Acupuncture. *Honours:* Honorable Mention for one and First Prize for magazine Article at Writer's Seminar, Sep. 1984; Pierre Fauchard Academy (Honorary Society for Scientific Contributions); Fellow of Royal Society of Health; Fellow of American Academy of Oral Medicine. *Memberships:* American Medical Writer's Association; National Writer's Club; Florida Freelance Writer's Association; Writer's Digest. *Address:* 10139, N Citrus Springs Boulevard, Citrus Springs, FL 32630, USA.

RABE, Berniece Louise, b. 11 Jan. 1928, Parma, Missouri, USA. Author. m. Walter H Rabe, 30 July 1946, 3 sons, 1 daughter. *Education:* BS, National College, Evanston, Illinois; Graduate Work in psychology, Roosevelt University, Northern Illinois University. *Publications:* Rass, 1973; Naomi, 1975; The Girl Who Had No Name, 1977; The Orphans, 1978; Who's Afraid, 1980; The Balancing Girl, 1981. *Contributions to:* The Friend; The Ensign; Cricket; Childcraft; Encyclopedia Britannica. *Honours:* Golden Kite Award, National

Society of Childrens Book Writers, 1976, 78; Outstanding Contribution to Children's Literature, State of Missouri, 1977; Outstanding Book of the Decade, School Library Journal, 1970s. *Memberships:* Executive positons: Society of Midland Authors; Fox Valley Writers; Off Campus Writers. *Address:* 860 Willow Lane, Sleepy Hollow, IL 60118, USA.

RABINOVITZ, Rubin, b. 18 July 1938, New York, USA. College Professor. m. Margit Johansson, 6 June 1974, 1 son, 1 daughter. *Education:* BA, Rutgers College, 1959; MA, 1961, PhD, 1966, Columbia University. *Literary Appointments include:* Reader, 1965–66, Instructor in English 1966–68, Assistant Professor of English, 1968–74, Columbia University; Associate Professor of English, 1974–79, Professor of English, 1979–, University of Colorado, Boulder. Editorial Board, English Language Notes; Chairman (1976–80) and Trustee, Colorado Seminars in Literature. *Publications:* The Reaction Against Experiment in the English Novel, 1950–60, 1967, three excerpts of this book appear in Contemporary Literary Criticism, vol 4 1975, vol 5 1976; Iris Murdoch, 1968, Excerpt appears in Contemporary Literary Criticism, vol 1 1973; The Development of Samuel Beckett's Fiction, 1984. *Contributions to:* Contributor to numerous articles, essays and reviews to journals, magazines and edited volumes. *Honours:* Numerous honours, most recently: Research Grant-in-Aid, University of Colorado, 1981–82; Winner, Kayden Faculty Manuscript Award, University of Colorado, for The Development of Samuel Beckett's Fiction, 1982; University of Colorado Faculty Research Fellowship 1984–85; Winner, Colorado Seminars Award in Literature for The Development of Samuel Beckett's Fiction, 1985. *Memberships:* Modern Language Association; Samuel Beckett Society. *Address:* Department of English, Campus Box 226, University of Colorado, Boulder, CO 80309, USA.

RABINOWICZ, Mordka Harry, b. 8 July 1919, Warsaw, Poland. Rabbi. *Education:* BA, Jews College, 1943; PhD, London University, 1948; Min's Cert, 1945; Rabbi, 1954. *Publications:* The Ethical Will of the Biala Rabbi, 1947; Guide to Hasidism, 1960; The Slave Who Saved the City, 1960; The Jewish Literary Treasures of England and America, 1960; A Guide to Life, 1964; The Legacy of Polish Jewry, 1965; The World of Hasidism, 1970; Treasures of Judaica, 1970; Hasidic Story Book. *Contributor to:* Encyclopedia Judaica; Editor, Encyclopedia of Hasidism; Jewish Chronicle; Times Literary Supplement, Journal of Jewish Studies. *Honours:* Recipient various Fellowships and Scholarships. *Address:* 151 Anson Road, London NW2, England.

RABORG, Frederick Ashton Jr, b. 10 Apr. 1934, Richmond, Virginia, USA. Writer; Editor; Publisher. m. Eileen Mary Bradshaw, 19 Oct. 1957, Las Vegas, 4 sons, 2 daughters. *Education:* AA, Bakersfield College, 1970; BA, California State College, Bakersfield, 1973; Graduate studies 1974–75. *Literary Appointments:* Liaison Editor, The Oildale News, 1968–70; Editor, Pantry, 1963–65; Book reviewer, drama critic, The Bakersfield Californian, 1970–78; Columnist, Bakersfield News Bulletin, 1969–71; Editor, publisher, Amelia, 1983–. *Publications:* Gin Street Rhythms, 1971; Why Should the Devil Have All the Good Tunes?, 1972; Posing Nude, 1985. *Contributions to:* Numerous magazines & journals including Ladies' Home Journal; Tendril; Westways; Cuisine; Prairie Schooner; Poetry Australia; Sports Afield; Ohio; Cavalier; Portland Review; Japanophile; Educational Studies; Statesman; Old Hickory Review.*Honours include:* 1st prize, Class, International Intercollegiate Creative Writing Competition (short story), 1969–70; 1st prize, Netherlands – USA 200 Foundation Award (essay), 1982; 1st prize, Guideposts, award (article), 1973; Hundreds of poetry awards in magazines. *Memberships:* Authors Guild; Authors League of America; Dramatists Guild; Poetry Society of America; Poets & Writers Inc; Various state poetry societies. *Address:* P O Box 2385, Bakersfield, CA 93303, USA.

RABUZZI, Kathryn Allen, b. 3 June 1938, New York, New York, USA. College Teacher. m. Daniel D Rabuzzi, 11 June, 1958, Pawling, New York, 3 sons. *Education:* Radcliffe College, 1958–60; AB English 1970, MA English 1971, PhD Humanities 1976, Syracuse University. *Publication:* The Sacred and the Feminine; Toward a Theology of Housework, 1982. *Literary Appointments:* Founder and editor, 1982–85, Editorial Board 1985–, Literature and Medicine. *Contributions to:* Anima; Alumni Journal, Syracuse Medical Alumni Association; American Baptist Quarterly. *Honours:* Syracuse Univesity Scholar, 1971–73; Lemoyne College Faculty Research Grant, 1977. *Membership:* Theta Chi Beta. *Address:* Department of English, Syracuse University, Syracuse, NY 13210, USA.

RACHLIN, Harvey Brant, b. 23 June 1951, Philadelphia, Pennsylvania, USA. Author. *Education:* BA, Hofstra University, Hempstead, New York, 1973. *Publications:* The Songwriter's Handbook, 1977; The Encyclopedia of the Music Business, 1981; Love Grams, 1983; The Money Encyclopedia, 1984; The Kennedys: An Almanac, 1986. *Contributions to:* High Fidelity Magazine; Music Management and International Promotion Magazine; Songwriter Magazine; Songwriter's Review; County Music World; Vibes. *Honours:* ASCAP Deems-Taylor Award, 1982; Outstanding Reference Book of the Year Award, American Library Association, 1982 and 1985; Encyclopedia of the Music Business recommended 1984 Grammy Awards, internationally televised. *Membership:* American Society of Composers, Authors and Publishers. *Literary Agent:* Julian Bach Literary Agency, New York City. *Address:* 252 Robby Lane, Manhasset Hills, NY 11040, USA.

RADAVICH, David Allen, b. 30 Oct. 1949, Boston, Massachusetts, USA. University Professor. *Education:* BA, 1971; MA, 1974; MPhil, 1976; PhD, 1978; University of Kansas. *Literary Appointments:* Assistant Instructor, English, University of Kansas, 1973–74, 1975–79; Lecturer, American History, University of Stuttgart, West Germany, 1979–81; Instructor of English, Iowa State University, 1982–84; Professor of English, Eastern Illinois University, 1984–. *Publications:* Five chapbooks of poems published in England and USA, 1975–77; Slain Species, (book of poems), 1980; Unpublished plays: Time's Daughter, 1981; The Life of Bonneur, 1983; Nevertheless, 1985. *Contributor:* (poems): Counterpoint; Orbis; Outrigger; Poetry Nottingham; Success; Trends; Wayfarers, UK; Eureka, Sweden; Funnel, W Germany; Kansas Quarterly; Louisville Review; Lyrical Iowa; New Magazine; Poets On, USA, etc; Newspaper Review; Academic and Informal articles and satire; included in German anthology, Die weiten Horizonte: Amerikanische Lyrik 1638 bis 1980, 1985. *Honours:* First Prize, Tell Tale Poetry Competition, Bolton, England, 1978; First Prize, International Verse Competition, Coventry, England, 1982; Third Prize, Sucess Poetry Competition, Peterborough, England, 1983; Consolation Prize, International Peace Competition, Barcelona, Spain, 1984; Several other prizes and awards. *Memberships:* The Dramatists Guild; Poets and Writers; Illinois Writers; Associate Writing Programs; Phi Beta Kappa. *Address:* 1304 Fourth Street, Charleston, IL 61920, USA.

RADDALL, Thomas Head, b. 13 Nov. 1903, Hythe, Kent, England. Author. m. Edith Freeman, 9 June 1927, Milton, Canada, 1 son, 1 daughter. *Education:* Honorary LLD, Dalhousie University, Canada, St F x University, Nova Scotia; Honorary DCL, Kings College, Halifax; Honorary DLitt, St Mary's University, Halifax. *Publications:* His Majesty's Yankees, 1942; Pride's Fancy, 1946; The Nymph and the Lamp, 1950; Tidefall, 1953; The Path of Destiny, 1957; The Governor's Lady, 1963; Hangman's Beach, 1966; In My Time, 1976. *Contributions to:* Blackwood's Magazine, UK; Maclean's Magazine, Canada; Saturday Evening Post, USA; Colliers Magazine, USA. *Honours:* Governor General's Award, Canada, 1944, 49, 58; Fellow, Royal Society of Canada, 1953; Lorne Pierce Medal, Canada, 1956; Officer, Order of Canada, 1970. *Memberships:*

Honorary member, Writers Union of Canada. *Address:* P O Box 459, Liverpool, Nova Scotia, Canada B0T IK0.

RADER, John Trout, b. 23 Aug. 1938, Corpus Christi, Texas, USA. Economics Professor. m. 30 July 1966, 1 son, 3 daughters. *Education:* BA, Honours, Economics, University of Texas, 1959; MA, 1960, PhD, 1963, Economics, Yale University. *Appointments:* Research assistant, Yale University, 1961–62; Assistant Professor, University of Missouri, 1962–64; Assistant Professor, Economics, University of Illinois, Urbana, 1964–65; Associate Professor, 1965–70, Professor, 1970–, Economics, Washington University, St Louis. *Publications:* Economics of Feudalism, 1971; Theory of Microeconomics, 1972; Theory of General Economic Equilibrium, 1972. *Contributor to:* 29 articles to professional journals including, The New Palgrave; Journal of Mathematical Economics; Journal of Economic Theory; Econometrica; etc. *Honours:* Fellow, Econometric Society, 1978. *Address:* Department of Economics, Washington University, St Louis, MO 63130, USA.

RADER, Rosemary, b. 11 Apr. 1931, Saint Leo, Minnesota, USA. University Professor, Prioress of Saint Paul's Priory. *Education:* BA Latin and History, College of Saint Catherine; MA Latin and Classical History, Univesity of Minnesota; PhD Religious Studies and Humanities, Stanford University. *Publications:* A Lost Tradition: Women Writers of the Early Church, co-author, 1981; The Continuing Quest for God; Monasticism in Tradition and Transition, co-author, 1982; Rader, Rosemary, Breaking Boundaries; Male/Female Friendship in Early Christian Communities, 1983; Dictionary of Christian Spirituality (editor: G Wakefield), Contributor, 1983. *Contributions to:* Religious Studies Review; Journal of the College Theology Society. *Honours:* American Classical League Fellowship, 1962; Fulbright Fellowship to Itlay, 1966–67; Graduate Fellowship, Stanford University, 1972–76; Whiting Award for Reasearch in the Humanities, 1976–77. *Address:* Saint Paul's Priory, 2675 East Larpenteur, Saint Paul, MN 55109, USA.

RADFORD, John Kirby, b. 23 Mar. 1931, Stockport, England. Psychologist. *Education:* BA, BA Honours, PhD, University of London. *Publications:* Co-author: Thinking: Its Nature and Development, 1974; The Person in Psychology, 1975; Individual Differences, 1976; Thinking in Perspectives, 1978; The Teaching of Psychology, 1980; A Textbook of Psychology, 1980; Your Introduction to Psychology, 1984; Psychology Teaching: Information and Resources, 1984. *Contributions to:* Numerous journals of scientific or popular nature. *Membership:* Society of Authors. *Address:* 38 Cephas Avenue, London E1 4AT, England.

RADITCHKOV, Yordan, b. 24 Oct. 1929, Kalimanitza, Bulgaria. Writer. m. Souzy Markova, 1954, 2 sons 2 daughters. *Publications:* Short stories: A Furious Mood; Last Summer; The Obscure Yards; A Gunpowder Primer; A Hot Noon; A Small Northern Saga; A Tender Spiral. *Contributor to:* All main Bulgarian magazines. *Honours:* People's Worker of Culture; Dimitrov Prize, 1972. *Membership:* Union of Bulgarian Writers. *Address:* 22 Oborishte Street, Sofia, Bulgaria.

RADLEY, Paul John, b. 28 Feb. 1962, Newcastle, New South Wales, Australia. Barman. *Literary Appointments:* Writer-in-Residence, St Andrews University, Fife, Scotland, 1983. *Publications:* Jack Rivers and Me, 1981; My Blue-Checker Corker and Me, 1982; Good Mates!, 1985. *Contributions to:* Overland Quarterly, (Australia); Platform, (St Andrews University, Fife, Scotland); Cencrastus, (Edinburgh, Scotland). *Honours:* Vogel, Australian Literary Award, 1980; Young Australian of the Year, 1981; Australian Arts Council Grant, 1982; Fellowship Creative Writing Scottish Arts Council, 1983. *Literary Agent:* Elise Goodman, Goodman Associates, 500 West End Avenue, NY, USA. *Address:* Crown and Anchor Hotel, Hunter Street, Newcastle, New South Wales 2300, Australia.

RADTKE, Günter, b. 23 Apr. 1925, Berlin. Federal Republic of Germany. Author. *Education:* Trainee journalist. *Publications:* Davon Kommst du Nicht Los, 1971; Die Dünne Haut Der Luftballons, 1975; Der Krug Auf Dem Weg Zum Wasser, 1977; Glück aus Mangel an Beweisen, 1978; Suchen Wer Wir Sind, 1980. *Contributions to:* Numerous literary magazines, newspaper and broadcasting stations. *Honours:* German Short Story Prize, 1971; George Mackensen Prize, 1973; The First Roman Literature Prize, 1975; Literature Prize, Markische Culture Conference, 1979. *Memberships:* Die Kogge; Association of German Writers; NGL, Hamburg and Berlin, PEN. *Literary Agent:* Deutsche Verlags-Anstalt. *Address:* Postfach 209, Stuttgart, Federal Republic of Germany.

RAE, Hugh Crauford, b. 22 Nov. 1935, Glasgow, Scotland. Novelist. m. Elizabeth Dunn, 3 Sep. 1960, Glasgow, 1 daughter. *Literary Appointments:* Scottish Arts Council, 1975–80. *Publications include:* Skinner, 1965; Night Pillow, 1966; A Few Small Bones, 1968; The Saturday Epic, 1970; Harkfast, 1976; Sullivan, 1978; Haunting at Waverley Falls, 1980; Privileged Strangers, 1982. As Jessica Stirling: The Spoiled Earth, 1974; The Hiring Fair, 1976; The Dark Pasture, 1978; The Deep Well at Noon, 1980; The Blue Evening Gone, 1982; The Gates of Midnight, 1983; Treasures on Earth, 1985. As James Albany: Warrior Caste, Mailed Fist, Deacons's Dagger, 1982; Close Combat, Matching Fire, 1983; Last Bastion, Borneo Story, 1984; etc. *Membership:* Scottish Association of Writers, President. *Address:* Drumore Farm Cottage, Balfron Station, Stirlingshire, Scotland.

RAE, John Malcolm, b. 20 Mar. 1931, London, England. Director, Laura Ashley Foundation. *Education:* MA, Sidney Sussex College, Cambridge University, 1955; PhD, King's College, London University. *Publications:* The Custard Boys, 1960; Conscience and Politics, 1970; The Golden Crucifix, 1974; The Treasure of Westminster Abbey, 1975; Christmas is Coming, 1976; Return to the Winter Palace, 1979; The Third Twin: A Ghost Story, 1980; The Public School Revolution, 1981. *Contributions to:* Encounter; Times Literary Supplement; Times Educational Supplement; The Times; Sunday Telegraph. *Honour:* Recipient of United Nations Award for film script, Reach for Glory, 1962. *Literary Agent:* A D Peters and Company Limited. *Address:* 26 Balliol House, Manor Fields, Putney Hill, London SW15 3LL, England.

RAE, Margaret Doris, b. Jan. 1907, Newcastle upon Tyne, England. Author. *Publications:* The Whispering Ward, 1958; The Rowans are Red, 1960; The Constant Star, 1965; The Golden Hours, 1968; Honeysuckle in the Hedge, 1973; Duet in Low Key, 1974; Awake to the Dawn, 1975; Summer Noon, 1976; Spring Song, 1977; Mist on the Moors, 1979; The Spell of Solitude, 1981; Rich the Treasure, 1984. *Membership:* Society of Authors. *Address:* 79 Cheviot View, Ponteland, Northumberland NE20 9BH, England.

RAÉL, Leyla, b. 9 Nov. 1948, Miami Beach, Florida, USA. Astrological Consultant. m. Dane Rudhyar, 21 Mar. 1977, Redwood City, California. *Publications:* Lunation Process in Astrological Guidance, 1979; Astrological Aspects: A Process-Oriented Approach, 1980; Shambhala Astrological Calendar, 1980–85. *Contributions to:* Horoscope: The Astrological Journal. *Address:* 1639 Eighth Avenue, San Francisco, CA 94122–3717, USA.

RAFAEL, Gideon, b. 5 Mar. 1913, Berlin, Germany. Diplomat; Ambassador. m. Nurit Weisberg, 1940, Haifa, Israel, 1 son, 1 daughter. *Education:* University of Berlin. *Publications:* Black Book of Nazi Atrocities, 1945; Destination Peace – Three Decadeas of Israel Foreign Policy, 1981; Foreign Policy from Bengurion to Begin (German) Ullstein Berlin 1984. *Contributions to:* Jerusalem Post; various Hebrew newspapers in Israel; Weltwoche, Switzerland; Weit am Sonntag, Germany; New York Times, USA; Washington Post; Los Angeles Times; International Herald Tribune; Times, London,

England; Telegraph. *Memberships:* Member of Board: International Peace Academy and Israel Cancer Association. *Honour:* Steven Wise Award. *Address:* 36 Hantke Street, Jerusalem 96 629, Israel.

RAGHUBIR SINH, b. 23 Feb. 1908, Laduna, Sitamau, Central India. Author; Historian; Former Member of Parliament and State Administrator; Chairman and Honorary Director, Shri Natnagar Shodh-Samsthan, 1975–. m. Princess Mohan Kumari of Partabgarh, 1929, 2 sons (1 deceased), 2 daughters. *Education:* BA, 1928, LLB, 1930, MA, 1933; DLitt, Agra University. *Pubalications:* In Hindi: Purva-Madhyakalin Bharat, history, 1932; Malwa men Yugantar, 1938; Shesh Smrityan, Essays, 1939, 4th edition, 1966; Purva Adhunik Rajasthan, history, 1951; Maharana Pratap, biography, 1973. In English: Malwa in Transition, 1936; Indian States and New Regime, 1938; Durga Das Rathor, biography, 1975. *Contributions to:* Sarswati; Nagari Pracharini Patrika. *Honours:* Mangla Prasad Prize, 1945; Uttar Pradesh Government Prize, 1954; Sahitya Vachaspati, Non-Official Academy, Literary Association of Hindi Writers. *Memberships include:* PEN Indian Branch; Life Member, Royal Asiatic Society, UK. *Address:* Raghubir Niwas, Sitamau (Malwa-MP) 458-990, India.

RAGNARS, Aslaug, b. 23 Apr. 1943, Reykjavik, Iceland. Writer. m. Jon Isleifsson, 16 Nov. 1985, Fellsmuli, 2 sons. *Literary Appointments:* Journalist, Morgunbladid, 1973–83. *Publications:* Haustvika, 1980; Sylvia, 1982. *Contributions to:* Morgunbladid, freelance writer. Director, programme on arts and culture, Icelandic Television, 2 years. *Membership:* Icelandic Writers Union. *Address:* Flyorugrandi 10, Reykjavik, Iceland.

RAGUIN, Yves Emile, b. 9 Nov. 1912, St Catherine de Fierbois, France. Missionary, Professor. *Education:* Lic. ès Lettres, Sorbonne University, Paris; Lic. de Théologie, Institut Catholique, Paris, France. *Major Publications include:* Chemins de la Contemplation, 1970; Missionary Spirituality, 1972; Bouddhisme/Christianisme, 1973; Célibat pour notre temps, 1972; God is my Life, 1973; La Profondeur de Dieu, 1973; L'Esprit sur le Monde, 1975; Sixteen Lessons on Buddhism, 1975; The Christ et son mystère, 1979; Leçons sur le Taoïsme, 1981; Le Livre de Marie, Attention to the Mystery, 1982. Dictionnaire français de la langue Chinoise, 1976 (in collaboration); most books translated into various languages, including English, Spanish, Italian, German, Dutch and Chinese. *Contributor to:* Christus (Paris); Axes (Paris); Numerous articles in Religious & learned journals. *Memberships:* Director, Ricci Institute for Chinese Studies, Taiwan, Republic of China; American Oriental Society; Ecole Française d'Extrême-Orient. *Address:* Hsin Hai Road, Section 1, No 24 8 F, Taipei 10718, Taiwan, Republic of China.

RAINA, Peter, b. 10 June 1935, Srinagar, Kashmir. Historian. *Education:* MA, PhD, Warsaw University, Poland. *Publications:* Krise der Intellektuellen, 1968; Gomulka: Politische Biographie, 1970; Zur Entstehung des polnischen Reformkommunismus, 1976; Gomulka (in Polish) 1969; Polish-German Relations 1937–39, 1975; Political Opposition in Poland, 1954–77, 1978; Kardynal Wysznski, 1979; John Paul II, the Primate and the Polish Episcopate on the State of War in Poland (in Polish), 1982; The Church in Poland, 1981–84 (in Polish), 1985; Poland 1981;Towards Social Renewal, 1985; Kardynal Wyszynski, volume II, 1986. *Contributor to:* Various publications. *Memberships:* Canadian Association of Slavists; Life Member, Clare Hall, Cambridge, England. *Address:* Moerchinger Str. 54, D–100 Berlin 37, Federal German Republic.

RAINE, Craig Anthony, b. 3 Dec. 1944, Shildon. Poet. m. Ann Pasternak Slater, 27 Apr. 1972, Oxford, England, 2 sons, 1 daughter. *Education:* PhB Honours, Oxford University, 1966. *Literary Appointments:* Books Editor, New Review; Poetry Editor, New Statesman and Faber and Faber, London. *Publications:* The Onion Memory, 1978; A Martian Sends a Postcard Home, 1979; Rich,

1984; The Electrification of the Soviet Union, 1986. *Contributions to:* Times Literary Supplement; New Statesman; London Review of Books; The Listener; Encounter; Literary Review. *Honours:* Kelvs Prize, 1978; Southern Arts Literature Award, 1979; Cholmondeley Award, 1981. *Membership:* Fellow, Royal Society of Literature. *Address:* c/o Faber and Faber Limited, 3 Queen Street, London WC1N 3AU, England.

RAINOV, Bogomil, b. 19 June 1919, Sofia, Bulgaria. Writer. *Education:* Degree in Philosophy. *Literary Appointment:* Corresponding Member, Bulgarian Academy of Science. *Publications:* Night's Boulevards, 1963; The Inspector and The Night, 1964; Ways To Nowhere, 1966; Mister Nobody: Selected Poems, 1969; The Big Boredom, 1971; This Peculia Job, 1976; The Third Way, 1977; Only For Men, 1981. *Contributor to:* All main Bulgarian literary editions. *Honours:* Dimitrov Prize, 1952 and 1969; People's Worker of Culture, 1971. *Membership:* Vice President, Union of Bulgarian Writers. *Address:* 10, Rouski Boulevard, Sofia, Bulgaria.

RAINWATER, Dorothy Thornton, b. 14 Sep. 1918, Ardmore, Oklahoma, USA. Writer. *Education:* BA, University of Oklahoma, USA; Graduate work, University of Hawaii and Honolulu Academy of Arts. *Publications:* American Silver Manufacturers, 1966; American Spoons, Souvenir and Historical, 1968; American Silverplate, 1972; Sterling Silver Holloware, 1973; Encyclopedia of American Silver Manufacturers, 1975; A Collector's Guide to Spoons Around the World, 1976. *Contributions to:* Antiques; Antiques Journal; Antiques Trader; Jewelers Circular-Keystone; The Magazine of Silver; The Spinning Wheel; Western Collector. *Memberships:* National Science Fair International Council; Chairman, Inter-Society of Science Education Council, Hawaii Academy of Science; Hawaii State Science Fair; American Association of University Women; American Silver Collectors' Society, Board of Directors. *Address:* 2805 Liberty Place, Bowie, MD 20715, USA.

RAJAN, Tilottama, b. 1 Feb. 1951, New York City, USA. University Professor. *Education:* BA (Hons) English, 1972, MA, English, 1973. PhD, English, 1977, University of Toronto. *Literary Appointments:* Teaching Assistant and Instructor, Victoria College, University of Toronto. *Literary Appointments:* Teaching Assistant and Instructor, Victoria College, Univeristy of Toronto, 1974–75; Assistant Professor, Huron College, University of Western Ontario, 1977–80; Assistant and Associate Professor, Queen's University, Kingston, Canada, 1980–85; Visiting Professor, University of California at San Diego, 1984; Professor, University of Wisconsin, at Madison, 1985–. *Publications:* Myth in a Metal Mirror, poems, 1967; Dark Interpreter: The Discussion of Romanticism, criticism, 1980, paperback edition forthcoming in 1986. *Contributor to:* Literary criticism in English Literary History, Studies in Romanticism, Yeats-Eliot Review, University of Toronto Quarterly, New Literary History, Wordsworth Circle; Lyric Poetry: Beyond New Criticism, 1985. Approaches to Teaching Wordsworth, forthcoming 1986. Poems in New Voices of the Commonwealth; Commonwealth Poems of Today; The Shell and the Rain, and in some journals. *Memberships:* Association of Canadian Univeristy Teachers of English; Modern Language Association of America; member of Division Executive for non-fictional prose 1985–88, Chairman of the Division for 1986. *Address:* 1008 Spaight Street, Madison, WI 53704, USA.

RAJPUT, A B, Author; Journalist; Public Relations Executive; Former Press and Cultural Attache, Iran; Editor in Chief. *Education:* BA, University of Punjab, India; MA, Nagpur University; Certificate in Training in Journalism, British Council, London, England. *Publications:* Iran Today, 1945, 3rd edition, 1953; The Punjab Crisis and Cure, 1946; The Cabinet Mission, 1945; The Struggle for Freedom, 1946; The Constituent Assembly, 1947; The Muslim League Yesterday and Today, 1948;

Architecture of Pakistan, 1963, 3rd edition, 1965; The Tribes of Chittagong Hill Tracts, 1963, 3rd edition, 1965; Social Customs and Practices in Pakistan, 1978. *Contributions to:* Over 1200 articles to numerous newspapers and journals in various countries. *Honours:* Colombo Plan Fellowship, 1964; Imperial Iranian OM, Nishan-I-Sipas, for book Iran Today, 1952. *Memberships:* Archaeological Survey of India; Fellow, Royal Anthropological Institute, London, England. *Address:* 23-R Block 2, Pech Soc, Karachi 29, Pakistan.

RAKEL, Robert Edwin, b. 13 July 1932, Cincinnati, Ohio, Physician. m. Margaret Ann Klare, 20 Aug. 1955, 1 son, 3 daughters. *Education:* BS, 1954, MD, 1958, University of Cincinnati, USA. *Major Publications:* Principles of Family Medicine, 1977; Family Practice (with H F Conn & T W Johnson), 2nd edition, 1978; Textbook of Family Practice, 3rd edition, 1984; Conn's Current Therapy (editor), annual publications since 1984, all published by W B Saunders, Philadelphia; Year Book of Family Practice, annually since 1977, Year Book Medical Publishers, Chicago, USA. *Contributor to:* Various medical journals, including: Journal of the American Medical Association; Archives of Internal Medicine; Family Practice News. *Address:* Department of Family Medicine, Baylor College of Medicine, One Baylor Plaza, Houston, TX 77030, USA.

RALPH, Wayne Douglas, b. 18 June 1946, St Johns, Newfoundland, Canada. Civil Aviation Inspector, Transport Canada. *Education:* BA, Memorial University of Newfoundland, 1967; MA, University of Calgary, 1983. *Literary Appointments:* Editor: Wings Magazine of Canada, 1976–81; Helicopters in Canada, 1980–81; Beaufort Magazine, 1981–83; Canada's Air Force Commemorative Issue, 1984; Aviation Safety Letter, Transport Canada, 1986. *Contributions to:* Quest; Canadian Defence Quarterly; International Defence Review; Energy; Alberta Inc.; Air Transport World; Armed Forces and Society. *Honours:* Department of National Defence Strategic Studies Scholar, for studies in weapons procurement, 1981–82. *Memberships:* Aviation/Space Writers Association. *Address:* Suite 806, 221 Lyon Street, Ottawa, Ontario, Canada K1R 7X5.

RALSTON, Anthony, b. 24 Dec. 1930, New York City, USA. University Professor. m. Jayne M Rosenthal, 14 Feb. 1958, New Jersey, 3 sons, 1 daughter. *Education:* SB, 1952, PhD, 1956, NIT. *Publications:* Mathematical Methods for Digital Computers, Co-editor; A First Course in Numerical Analysis, 1965; Mathematical Methods for Digital Computers, Volume II, co-editor, 1967; An introduction to Programming and Computer Science, 1971; Fortran IV Programming – A Concise Exposition, 1971; Editor, Encyclopedia of Computer Science, 1976; Statistical Methods for Digital Computers, Volume III, co-editor, 1977; A First Course in Numerical Analysis, co-author, 2nd edition, 1978; Taxonomy of Computer Science and Engineering, Editor, 1980; Editor, Encyclopedia of Computer Science and Engineering, 2nd edition 1982; The Future of the First Two Years of College Mathematics, Co-editor, 1983. *Contributor to:* Numerous professional journals and magazines. *Honours:* Distinguished Service Award, Association for Computing and Machinery, 1982. *Address:* Department of Computer Science, 226 Bell Hall, Amherst, NY 14260, USA.

RALYA, Jerry Alan, b. 13 July 1943, Lansing, Michigan, USA. Writer. m. Cheryl Ann Stabb, 9 Apr. 1976, Stuttgart, Federal Republic of Germany, 1 son. *Education:* BA Humanities, Michigan State University, 1965; MA English (Creative Writing), Stanford University, USA, 1969. *Major Publications:* The Gimmick Reading Series, Flammarion, 1978; Understanding Computers and Data Processing – Study Guide (with C S Parker & D S Long), Holt, Rinehart & Winston, 1984; Systems Analysis, Design and Development: Study Guide, Holt, Rinehart & Winston, 1985; Computers and Information Systems: A Working Approach (with J Burstein), Holt, Rinehart & Winston,

1986. *Contributor to:* Falmouth Review (By the Window, Short story), 1967; Fountains Aixen-Provence, France, The Promise, short story, 1979. *Literary Agent:* Theron Raines. *Address:* 318 West 100th Street, 8–A, New York, NY 10025, USA.

RAMANUJAN, A K b. 16 Mar. 1929, Mysore, India. Professor. *Education:* BA, 1949; MA, 1950; Mysore University, PhD, Indiana University, USA, 1963. *Publications include:* (poetry), The Striders, (Oxford University Press), 1966; The Interior Landscape, (translation from Classical Tamil), Indiana), 1967, 1975; Relations, (Oxford University Press), 1971; Speaking of Siva (translations from medieval Kannada), (Penquin Classics), 1972; Selected Poems, (Oxford University Press), 1977; Mattu Itara Padyagalu, (Dharwar), 1977; Hymns for the Drowning, (translation from Medieval Tamil), (Princeton University Press), 1981; Poems of Love and War, (translation from classical Tamil), (Colombia University Press), 1985; Second Sight, (Oxford University Press), 1986. *Honours include:* Awarded title Padma Sri, Government of India, 1976; MacArthur Prize Fellowship, 1983–89. *Address:* Foster Hall, University of Chicago, 1130 East 59th Street, Chicago, IL 60637, USA.

RAMEY, James Walter, b. 29 June 1928, Louisville, USA. Medical Professor. m. Betty Morrison, 1 Aug. 1969, New City, 2 sons, 2 daughters. *Education:* BA, University of Chicago, 1951; MA, 1957, PhD, 1958, Decision Theory, Columbia University. *Appointments:* Chief Executive Officer, Director, H F Enterprises, 1979–. *Publications:* Television in Medical Teaching and Research, 1965; Mechanization of the Library and Information Centre, 1969; Intimate Friendships, 1976; Talking With Your Child About Sex, Questions and Answers for Children from Birth to Puberty, co-author, 1983. *Contributor to:* Numerous professional journals and magazines including, Journal of Experimental Education; Career Briefs; Personal Efficiency; Health Sciences TV Bulletin; Journal of Chemical Documentation; Education for Librarianship; TV in Psychiatry; Forum; Family Coordinator; etc. *Honours:* Research Assistant, 1st Simulation Project in USA, 1957–58; NDCC Fellow, 1958; Research Grant, Esso Foundation, 1958; Kellogg Scholar, Columbia University, 1958. *Memberships:* President, Kappa Chapter, Kappa Delta Pi, 1958; Historian, Beta Chapter, Phi Delta Kappa, 1958. *Literary Agent:* Lorna Brown. *Address:* c/o Lorna Brown, 185 Charter Oak Drive, New Canaan, CT 06512, USA.

RAMIREZ-DE-ARELLANO, Diana, b. 3 June 1919. University Professor; Writer. *Education:* BA, Univeristy of Puerto Rico, 1941; MA, Columbia University, 1946l PhD, University of Madrid, Spain, 1952. *Appointments:* Professor of Spanish Literature, City University, New York, 1958–. *Publications:* Yo soy Ariel, 1947; Albatross sobre el Alma, 1955; Angeles de Ceniza, 1958; Umvuelo casi humano, 1960; Privilegio, 1963; Del Senalado oficio de la Muerte, 1975; La Comedia Genealogica de Lope de Vega, 1952; Camino de la Creacion Poetica en Pedro Salinas, 1984; Poesia contemporanea en Lengua espanola, 1958. *Contributions to:* Numerous magazines including: El Mundo; Inter-American Review; El Telegrafo, Ecuador. *Honours include:* Gold Medal, Ateneo de San Juan, Puerto Rico, 1958; 1st Prize in Literature, IPR Lit, 1958; Poetry Prize, Ministry of Education, Bolivia, 1961, Ecuador; Order of Merit, Ecuador, 1967; Laurel Clara Lair, APE Poets and Writers Association, 1985; Poetry Prize Loca Rodriquez de Tio, Rev Al Marger Agosto, 1985. *Memberships:* President, Josefino Romo Arregia Memorial Foundation; PEN Club International, Puerto Rico Chapter; Puerto Rican Writers Association; Puerto Rican Ateneo in New York; Hispanic Society of America. *Address:* 23 Harbour Circle, Centerport, NY 11721, USA.

RAMON, Renaat, b. 17 Oct. 1936, Bruges, Belgium. Sculptor. *Education:* Academies of Bruges & Amsterdam. *Publications:* Oogseizoen, poems, 1976; Ansichten, poems, 1980; Flandria Fabulata, poems, 1983; Vallen (In-, Uit-,), aphorisms, 1983.

Contributions to: Betoel, 1971–73; Radar, 1975–82; De Tafelronde; De Nieuwe; Diogenes, Editor-in-Chief. *Honour:* Trap Award, 1981. *Membership:* Society of Flemish Writers. *Address:* Betferkerklaan 187, 8200 Bruges, Belgium.

RAMSDEN, E H, Art Historian. *Publications:* An Introduction to Modern Art, 1940, 2nd edition, 1949; Twentieth Century Sculpture, 1949; Sculpture: Theme and Variations, 1953; The Letters of Michelangelo, Translator, Annotator, Editor, 2 volumes, 1963; Michelangelo, Masters series, 1966; Michelangelo, 1971; Come Take this Lute: A Quest for Identities in Italian Renaissance Portraiture, 1983. Contributor to Studi in onoredi Luigi Grassi in Prospettiva, 1985. *Contributions to:* Numerous journals including: Appollo; Country Life; Burlington; Polemic; Horizon; Studio; World Review; Werk. *Memberships include:* Society of Authors. *Address:* 30 Mallord Street, London SW3, England.

RAMSEY, Gordon Clark, b. 28 May 1941, Hartford, Connecticut, USA. Writer; Organist; Fundraiser; Teacher. *Education:* BA American Studies, Yale University, 1963. *Literary Appointments:* Instructor in English (Adjunct), University of Hartford, Connecticut, 1985. *Publications:* Agatha Christie: Mistress of Mystery, 1967; These Fields and Halls, prayerbook, 1974; An Undertaking Sett Forward: The History of the Yale Alumni Fund, 1976; Aspiration and Perseverence: The History of Avon Old Farms School, 1984; Nullas Horas Nisi Aureas: The History of The Ethel Walker School, 1986. Recording: Behold What Manner of Love: Scriptural Songs of James G MacDermid (1875–1960); *Contributions to:* New York magazine; New York Times Book Review; HiFi Stero Review; The American Organist; Hartford Courant Sunday Magazine; New Haven Register Sunday Magazine; The Generator and Distributor; The Educational Register. *Address:* 58 Mountain View Avenue, Avon, CT 06001, USA.

RAMSEY, Jarold William, b. 1 Sep. 1937, Bend, Oregon, USA. Professor of Literature; Poet. m. Dorothy Anne Quinn, 16 Aug. 1959, Madras, Oregon, USA, 1 son, 2 daughters. *Education:* BA, Hons, University of Oregon, 1959; PhD, University of Washington, 1966. *Literary Appointments:* Acting Instructor, University of Washington, 1963–65; Assistant Professor of English, 1965–69, Associate Professor of English, 1970–81, Professor of English, 1982–, University of Rochester; Visiting Professor, Univeristy of Victoria, Canada, 1974, 1975–76. *Publications:* Love in an Earthquake, poems, 1973; The Lodge of Shadows, A Cantata, with Samuel Adler, 1976; Coyote Was Going There, Indian Literature, 1977; Coyote Goes Upriver: A Cycle for Story Theater and Mime, 1981; Dermographia, poems, 1982; Reading the Fire, studies in Indian Literature, 1983. *Contributions to:* Since 1960 poems and essays in The Atlantic; PLMA; Sports Illustrated; Shakespeare Quarterly; Iowa Review; Poetry Northwest; Northwest Review; Ohio Review; Journal of American Folklore; Alcheringa; Massachusetts Review, etc. *Honours:* Borestone Mountain Awards 1972, 1975, 1976; Lillian Fairchild Award, 1973; Librettist Award, National Endowment for the Arts, 1974; National Endowment for the Arts Writing Fellowship, 1976; Ingram Merril Writing Grant, 1976; Pushcart Prize selections 1977–78, 1982–83; Don Walker Award 1978; Helen Bullis Poetry Prize, 1985. *Memberships:* Modern Language Association; American Folklore Association; Association for the Study of American Indian Literature (President 1980–81). *Address:* c/o English Department, University of Rochester, Rochester, NY 14627, USA.

RAMSEY, Norman Foster, b. 27 Aug. 1915, Washington DC, USA. professor of Physics. Research Association President. *Education:* AB 1935, MA 1939, PhD 1940, Columbia University, New York, USA; BA 1937, MA 1940, ScD 1954, University of Cambridge, England; MA 1973, ScD 1973, University of Oxford, England. *Major Publications:* Experimental Nuclear Physics, 1953; Nuclear Moments, 1953; Molecular Reams, 1956; Nuclear Interaction in Molecules

(Science in Progress 13); Quick Calculus, 1965. *Contributor to:* Physics Review; Various scientific journals. *Honours include:* 3 Honorary Degrees; Davisson-Germer Prize, 1974; Medal of Honour, Institute of Electrical & Electronic Engineers, 1983; Karl Compton Medal, 1985; Rumford Premium, 1985. *Memberships:* President, American Physics Society; 1978–79; Board of Trustees, Carnegie Endowment for International Peace, Rockefeller University; Sigma Xi; Phi Beta Kappa; American Philosophical Society. *Address:* Lyman Laboratory of Physics, Harvard University, Cambridge, MA 02138, USA.

RAMSEY, Paul, b. 26 Nov. 1924, Atlanta, Georgia, USA. Teacher & Writer. m. Betty Miller, 23 June 1951, Rossville, Georgia, 2 sons, 2 daughters. *Education:* University of Tennessee at Chattanooga, 1941–43; BA 1947, MA 1949, University of North Carolina; PhD, University of Minnesota, 1956. *Literary Appointments:* Instructor of English, 1948–50, Assistant Professor of English, 1953–57, University of Alabama; Assistant Professor of English, Elmira College, New York, 1957–62; Assistant Professor of English, University of the Pacific, Stockton, California, 1962–64; Associate Professor of English, University of the South, Sewanee, Tennessee, 1964–66; Professor of English, 1966–71, Almuni Distinguished Service Professor, 1971–81, Guerry Professor of English, 1981–, University of Tennessee at Chattanooga. *Major Publications:* The Lively & The Just (with S Kahn & J Taylor), 1962; Tryptych (poems), 1964; In an Ordinary Place, (poems), 1965; A Window for New York (poems), 1968; The Doors (poems, 1968; The Art of John Dryden, 1969; No Running on the Boardwalk (poems), 1975; Eve, Singing (poems), 1977; The Fickle Glass: A Study of Shakespeare's Sonnets, 1979; The Keepers (poems), 1984; The Truth of Values: A Defence of Moral & Literary Judgement, 1985. *Contributor to:* Various literary magazines and anthologies. *Honours include:* English-Speaking Union Bicentennial Poetry Prize, 1976; Newberry Fellowship, 1978; Research Fellow, Yale University, 1981; National Humanities Faculty, 1984. *Memberships:* Academy of American Poets; Bibliographical Society of America; Bibliographical Society of London; National Council of Teachers of English; Milton Society; Modern Language Association (Co-founder, metrics seminar); Poetry Society of America (Judge). *Literary Agent:* Duleslin Agency, New York. *Address:* University of Tennessee at Chattanooga, Chattanooga, TN 37402, USA.

RANA-BENGTSSON, Frida Christina, b. 22 May 1908, Sweden. Teacher of Retarded Children; Author; Actor. *Education:* High School for Teachers; Scholarship for study of creative dramatics and retarded children, USA, 1963. *Publications:* Cocktail Party, 1967; My Child is Just Showing Off, 1973; With 'Kaik' in the Temple of Balder; I Can if You Like; Give Me a Chance; The World Has Been Robbed; Fallen Angels and Human Beings; Under the Same Moon; A Brilliant Roll for You (2 plays about August Strindberg). *Memberships:* Society of Actors; Society for Authors; Society for Dramatic Authors. *Address:* Brantings gatan 36, 115 35 Stockholm, Sweden.

RANDALL, Belle, b. 25 Jan. 1940, Ellensburg, Washington, USA. Writer, Teacher. m. Joseph Edwards, 3 Mar. 1977, Indiana, Pennsylvania, USA, 1 son. *Education:* MA English, Stanford University; MA English, University of Washington; Currently in PhD Programme, University of Washington. *Literary Appointments:* Lecturer, Stanford University, 1971–74; Assistant Professor of English, Indiana University of Pennsylvania, 1974–77; Writer-in-Residence, Indiana Central University, Indianapolis, Indiana, 1977; Fiction Writer-in-Residence, Centrum Foundation, 1981; Writer-in-Residence, Oregon State College, 1982. *Major Publications:* 101 Different Ways of Playing Solitaire and Other Poems, 1973; The Prpheus Sedan, 1980. *Contributor to:* Poetry Chicago; Southern Review; PN Review (England). *Honour:* Wallace Stegner Fellowship, Stanford University. *Address:* 959 N Motor Place, Seattle, WA 98103, USA.

RANDALL, Bob, b. 20 Aug. 1937, New York City, USA. Writer. *Education:* BA, New York University, 1958. *Publications:* (Books) The Fan, 1975; The Next, 1977; The Calling, 1980; (Broadway Plays) 6 RMS Riv vu, 1972; The Magic Show, 1973; (TV) On Our Own, 1975–76; Kate & Allie, 1984–. *Honours:* Edgar Allan Poe Award, 1975; Writers Guild Award, 1973; 3 Emmy Nominations. *Memberships:* Writers Guild of America; Dramatists Guild. *Address:* Box 236, Bloomington, NY 12411, USA.

RANDALL, Dale Bertrand Jonas, b. 18 Mar. 1929, Cleveland Heights, Ohio, USA. Professor of English. m. Phyllis Rosanna Link, 25 June 1955, Johnstown, Pennsylvania, 1 son, 1 daughter. *Education:* BA, Adelbert College, Western Reserve University, 1951; MA, Rutgers University, 1953; PhD, University of Pennsylvania, 1958. *Literary Appointments:* Teaching Assistant, Rutgers University, 1951–53; Teaching Assistant, 1953–55, 1956–57, University of Pennsylvania; Instructor, 1957–60, Assistant Professor, 1960–65, Associate Professor, 1965–70, Professor, 1970–, Duke University. *Publications:* The Golden Tapestry: A Critical Survey of Non-chivalric Spanish Fiction in English Translation (1543–1657), 1963; Joseph Conrad and Warrington Dawson: The Record of a Friendship, 1968; Johnson's Gypsies Unmasked: Background and Theme of The Gypsies Metamorphos'd, 1975; Gentle Flame: The Life and Verse of Dudley, Forth Lord North (1602–1677), 1983. *Contributions to:* English Language Notes, The Roman Vibrations of Julia's Clothes; Studies In Philology, The Ironing of George Herbert's Collar; English Literary Renaissance, Some Observations on the Theme of Chastity in The Changeling. *Honours:* Harrison Fellowship, 1955–56; Guggenheim Memorial Foundation Fellowship, 1970–71; Senior Fellow, Southeastern Institute of Medieval and Renaissance Studies, 1978; Folger Shakespere Library Senior Fellow, 1986. *Memberships:* Medieval and Renaissance Drama Society; Society for Theatre Research; Renaissance Society of America; Southeastern Renaissance Conference (Co-editor of the Conference's Renaissance Papers). *Address:* 325 Allen Building, Duke University, Durham, North Carolina 27706, USA.

RANDALL, Rona, b. Birkenhead, Cheshire, England. Novelist, Non-fiction Writer. m. Frederick Walter Shambrook, 1 son. *Education:* Pitmans College, London, Royal Society of Arts Diploma in English Literature; Birkenhead School of Art.*Literary Appointments:* Sub-editor & journalist, Amalgamated Press; Assistant Editor, George Newnes Ltd; Short Story Writer, novelist, non-fiction writer. Simon & Schuster, Coward McCann & Geoghegan (USA). *Major publications:* Jordan & The Holy Land, 1968; Dragonmede, 1974; Watchman's Stone, 1975; Eagle at the Gate, 1978; The Mating Dance, 1979; Ladies of Hanover Square, 1981; Curtain Call, 1983; The Drayton Legacy, 1985. *Contributor to:* Woman's Own; Woman; Woman & Home; Good Housekeeping; Homes & Gardens; Woman's Journal; Mother & Home; Daily Telegraph; Annabel; and others. *Honours:* Joint Major Award Winner, Romantic Novelists' Association of Great Britain, 1969; Various selections for US Literary Guild, Doubleday Book Club; Book Club Associates (UK) and Australia, Book Club selections in Canada, Germany, Italy & Holland. *Memberships:* Fellow, International PEN; Crime Writers' Association of Great Britain; Society of Women Writers & Journalists; Society of Sussex Authors; Kent Writers Association; Associate, South East Arts; Former Chairman, Womens' Press Club, London. *Literary Agent:* Curtis Brown Ltd. *Address:* c/o Curtis Brown Ltd, 168 Regent Street, London W1R 5TA, England.

RANDHAWA, Mohinder Singh, b. 2 Feb. 1909. Administrator. m. Smt Iqbal Kaur, Narangwal, Dist Ludhiana, India, 2 sons, 1 daughter. *Education:* FSc, Hons, Forman Christian College, Lahore, 1926; BSc, Hons, Botany, 1929, MSc, Hons, 1930, Government College Lahore; DSc, Punjab University, 1955. *Literary Appointments:* President, Punjabi Sahitya Akademi Ludhiana; Chairman, Punjab Arts Council; President, All India Fine Arts and Crafts Society, New Delhi; President,

Punjab Lalit Kala Akademi Chandigarh; Chairman, Museum Advisory Committee, Chandigarh. *Publications include:* Indian Painting With Professor J K Galbraith, 1968; The Kumaon Himalayas 1971; Kangra Ragmala Paintings, 1973; Travels in Wetern Himalayas, 1974; Gardens through the Ages, 1976; Kishangarh Painting, 1980; Indian Minature Paintings, 1980; History of Agriculture in India, 1981; Indian Sculpture, 1985. *Contributions to:* Illustrated Weekly of India, Bombay; Indian Farming. *Honours:* Robe of Honour, Punjab Government for Services to Punjab Literature, 1968; Fellowship of Indian Standards Instition, 1968; Grant Gold Medal, Royal Agri-Horticultural Society of India, Calcutta, 1971; Padam Bhushan Award by President of India for services to Indian Administration, Art and Agriculture, 1972; Honorary Doctor of Science, Ohio State University, Columbus, Ohio; Plaque, Punjab State Co-operative Fruit Development Federation; Honorary Doctor of Science, University of Udaipur, Udaipur, Rajasthan, 1977; Honorary Doctor of Science, Punjabi University of Patiala, 1978; Vadyawati Dharam Vira Award, Delhi Horticultural Society, 1982; Felowship Award, Lalit Kala Akademi, New Delhi, 1982; Distinguished Punjabi Award by 3rd World Punjabo Conference, Bankok 1983; Award of Honour, Punjab State Horticultural Society. 1983. *Memberships:* Chairman, Punjab Arts Council, Chandigarh; President, All India Fine Arts and Crafts Society, New Delhi; Chairman, Punjabi Sahitya Akademi Ludhiana. *Address:* Garden House, Garden Colony, Kharar, Near Chandigarh, India.

RANSFORD, Oliver Neil, b. 25 Apr. 1914, Bradford, Yorkshire, England. Anaestheologist. m. Doris Irene Galloway, 17 July 1985, Zomba, 1 son 2 daughters. *Education:* MD, London; D Phil; FFARCS (Eng); DA. *Publications:* Livingstone's Lake; The Battle of Maguba Hill; The Rulers of Rhodesia; Bulawayo; The Battle of Spion Kop; The Slave Trade; Historia Rhodesia; David Livingstone; Bid the Sickness Cease. *Honours:* Book Centre of Rhodesia Award; 1973; Kingstones Literary Award; Gold Medal, Rhodesiana Society. *Literary Agent:* David Higham, London. *Address:* 8 Heyman Road, Bulawayo, Zimbabwe.

RANSLEY, Peter, b. 10 Dec. 1931, Leeds, England. Writer. m. Cynthia Harris, 14 Dec. 1974, Hammersmith, 1 son, 1 daughter. *Publications include:* Numerous television plays including, Plays for Today, Minor Complications, Kate the Good Neighbour; Series, Bread with Blood, BBC, 1982, The Price (Channel 4, 1985). Book: The Price, based on series. Theatre: Runaway, Royal Court, 1974; Ellan & Disabled, Hampstead Theatre Club, 1972. *Honours:* Gold Medal, Kate, 1st Commonwealth TV Film Festival, 1980; Award, Royal Television Series Writers, Minor Complications, 1981. *Literary Agent:* Sheila Lemon, 21 Pottery Walk, London W11, UK (plays). *Address:* c/o Sheila Lemon.

RANSOM, Jay Ellis, b. 12 Apr. 1914, Missoula, Montana, USA. Author; Technical Writer and Editor; Educator (Science and Mathematics Teacher). m. (1)Barbara E Callarman, 31 July 1936, Seattle, Washington; (2) Wilhelmina J Buitelear, 28 Dec. 1960, Las Vegas, Nevada, 3 sons, 2 daughters. *Education:* BA, 1935, Graduate College,1936–41, University of Washington, Seattle; MA, Education, level, University of California, Los Angeles, 1943, 47. *Publications include:* Petrified Forest Trails, 1955; The Rock Hunter's Range Guide, 1962; A Range Guide to Mines and Minerals, 1964; Fossils in America, 1964; The Gold Hunter's Field Book, 1975; Gems and Minerals of America, 1975; Complete Field Guide to North American Wildlife, 1981; Writing for Publication, 1982; Anthropology and Native American Linguistics at the University of Washington, 1934–41, 1982; Scientific Monograph: Archaeolinguistics and Peleoethnography of Ancient Rock Structures in Western North America, 1984. *Contributions:* 360 feature articles in magazines and some 3,000 feature stories in newspaper journalism. *Literary Agent:* Ann Elmo Agency Incorporated, New York City. *Address:* 1821 East 9th Street, The Dalles, OR 97058, USA.

RAPHAEL, Adam Eliot Geoffrey, b. 22 Apr. 1938, London, England. Journalist. m. Caroline Rayner Ellis, 15 May 1970, 1 son, 1 daughter. *Education:* MA Honours History, Oxford University. *Literary Appointments:* London 1965–68, Foreign Correspondent in Washington USA 1969–73, The Guardian; Political Correspondent 1976–82, Political Editor 1982–, The Observer. *Honours:* Investigative Journalist of the Year, Granada Awards, 1973; Journalist of the Year, IPC Awards, 1973. *Address:* c/o The Observer, 8 St Andrew's Hill, London EC4, England.

RAPHAEL, Frederic Michael, b. 14 Aug. 1931, Chicago, USA. Writer. m. Sylvia Betty Glatt, 17 Jan. 1955, London, England, 2 sons, 1 daughter. *Education:* MA, St John's College, Cambridge. *Publications include:* Novels: Earlsdon Way, 1956; The Limits of Love, 1960; Lindmann, 1963; Orchestra & Beginners, 1967; Like Men Betrayed, 1970; April, June & November, 1972; California Time, 1975; The Glittering Prizes, 1976; Richard's Things, 1973; Heaven & Earth, 1985. Short stories: Sleeps Six, 1979; Oxbridge Blues, 1980; Think of England, 1986. Biography: Somerset Maugham & His World, 1977; Byron, 1982. Essays, translations, screenplays. *Contributions to:* Numerous magazines & journals including: New York Times; New Statesman; Vogue; Cosmopolitan; Saturday Review; Sunday Times; etc.*Honours:* Lippincott Prize, 1961; US Academy Award, 1966; Royal Television Society Award, 1976. *Membership:* Fellow, Royal Society of Literature. *Literary Agent:* A P Watt Ltd. *Address:* Lagardelle, St Laurent-la-Vallée, 24170 Belves, France.

RAPOPORT, Janis, b. 22 June 1946, Toronto, Ontario, Canada. Writer/Editor/Teacher. m. 1. Dr. D Seager, 22 Dec. 1966 (divorced Feb. 1980), 2. Douglas Donegani, 20 May 1980, 1 son, 3 daughters. *Education:* BA, Philosophy, New College, University of Toronto, 1967. *Literary Appointments include:* Assistant Editor, Bellhaven House (Division of Heinemann Educational Books) 1971–73; Story Editor, CBC TV Drama, 1973–74; Playwright-in-Residence, Tarragon Theatre, 1974–75; Playwright-in-Residence, Banff Centre, summer 1976; Freelance editor, writer and broadcaster 1975–; Associate Co-ordinator, Words Alive reading series, 1980–84; Editor, Ethos magazine, 1983–; Part-time Teacher, Sheridan College, 19840–. *Publications:* Within the Whirling Moment (poetry) 1967; Jeremy's Dream (poetry) 1974; Co-editor, Landscape (poetry) 1977; Winter Flowers (poetry) 1979; Dreamgirls (drama) 1979; Imaginings (co-author) 1982. Plays produced: And She Could Eat No Lean, Toronto, Tarragon Theatre, 1975 and Detroit, Wayne State University, 1976; Gilgamesh, Toronto, Theatre Balagan, 1976; Dreamgirls, Toronto, Theatre Passe Muraille, 1979 and subsequently in British Columbia, Alberta, Rural Ontario and Prince Edward Island; Telecast, in part, TV Ontario, 1985. *Contributor to:* Poetry, plays and critical writing in magazines, anthologies and newspapers also broadcast on CBC radio. *Honours:* Canada Council Arts Award 1981–82; New York Art Directors' Club Award of Merit for, Imaginings, 1983; New York Art Directors' Club Award of Merit for poem on University of Guelph poster, 1983; American Institute of Graphic Arts, Certificate of Excellence for, Imaginings, 1983. *Memberships:* League of Canadian Poets; Writers' Union of Canada; Playwrights Union of Canada; PEN International; ACTRA.

RASCH, Aiga, b. 9 July 1941, Stuttgart, Germany. Graphic designer. *Education:* Studies of German Philology, Psychology and Art. *Publications:* Abraxas (book & playing cards), 1976; Der schwarz-weisse Tiger, 1975; Pipapo im Fehlerzirkus, 1977; Der Kampf um den Molar, 1979 (all illustrated by author); Designer of approximately 400 book covers and 5000 illustrations for numerous publishers in Europe, including the series Hitchcock/Die drei??? 1969–, and Doyle/Sherlock Holmes, 1981–. *Contributor to:* IWZ, Supplement of Stuttgarter Zeitung and numerous local Newspapers. *Memberships:* Verband Bildender Kuenstlei; Verwertungsgesellschaft Bild/Kuenst. *Address:* Im Wispelwald, D-7022 Leinfelden-Oberaichen, Federal Republic of Germany.

RASKY, Harry, b. 9 May, 1928, Toronto, Canada. Writer. m. Arlene Rurth Workhoven, 20 Mar. 1965, New York, 1 son, 1 daughter. *Education:* BA 1949, LLD 1983, University of Toronto. *Literary Appointments:* Features Editor, The Varsity U of T; Editor, Northern Daily News; Writer, Saturday Night Magazine, CBS, NBC, ABC, BBC, CBC. *Publications:* Nobody Swings on Sunday, 1980; Tennessee Williams' SOUTH-The Laughter and Lamentation of a Film Friendship, 1986. *Contributions to:* The Nation; Saturday Night; Televison-world wide; 200 Films. *Honours:* More than 200 International Prizes and Nominations for TV and Films, including Academy Awards in TV and Film in Canada and USA; chiefly for, Homage to Chegall- the Colours of Love; Strata Sphere, Hall of Kings. *Memberships:* Writers Guild of America; Writers Guild of Canada, (ACTRA). *Literary Agent:* Lucinda Vardey. *Address:* c/o Box 500, Terminal A, Toronto, Canada.

RASOF, Henry, b, 16 Nov. 1946, Santa Monica, California, USA. Editor. *Education:* BA, Music, University of California, Los Angeles; MFA, Creative Writing, Brooklyn College. *Publications:* The Dubrovnik Massacre, co-author, 1982; The Folk, Country & Bluegrass Musician's Catalgue, 1983. *Contributions to:* Partisan Review; Kansas Quarterly; Gallimaufary; Black Box; Bachy; Brooklyn College Literary Review; Zone; Modularist Review; Salome; Third Rail; Gone Soft; Beatitude; Contact; Dodeca; Junction; Riverrun, Wilmore City. *Membership:* Poets & Writers. *Address:* 44 Prospect Park West, Brooklyn, NY 11215, USA.

RASS, Rebecca Rivka, b. 9 Dec. 1936, Israel. Writer. 1 daughter. *Education:* BA, 1976–77, Empire State College, New York; MFA, 1977–79, Brooklyn College. *Literary Appointments:* New York Art Critic, Zero Magazine, Amsterdam, 1978–80; English Department, The City College of New York, 1971–78; Pace University, Queens College, Hofstra University, 1979–84; Assistant Professor, Pace University, Manhattan Community College, Queens College, 1985–. *Publications:* From A to Z, 1969; Word War I and Word War II, 1973; From Moscow to Jerusalem, 1976; The Fairy Tales of My Mind, 1978; The Mountain, 1982; From A to Z & Word War I and Word War II, (Hebrew and English), 1985. *Contributions to:* San Francisco Chronicle; Aftenposten; Rotterdam Courant; Zero Magazine; Tat-Rama; Yedioth Ahronoth. *Honour:*CAPS Award, fiction, 1981. *Membership:* Poets and Writers. *Address:* 355 Clinton Avenue Apt. 5F, Brooklyn, NY 11238, USA.

RATCLIFF, Gerald Lee, *Education:* BA magna cum laude, Georgetown, USA, 1967; MA, University of Cincinnati, 1970; PhD, Bowling Green State University, 1975. *Literary Appointments include:* Associate Professor, Chair, Department of Speech and Theatre, Montclair State University, 1975–; Associate editor, Communications Quarterly, 1978–81; Editorial Staff, Reader's Theatre News, 1981–84; Editorial Board, Liberal and Fine Arts Review, 1981–; Associate Editor Education Supplement, Communication Quarterly, 1982–; National Editor, Secondary School Theatre Journal, 1983–; National Editor, The Cue, 1979–82 and 1983–. *Publications include:* Beginning Scene Study: Aristophanes to Albee, 1980; Beginning Reader's Theatre: A Primer for Classroom Performance, 1981; Speech and Drama Club Activities, 1982; Oedipus Trilogy, 1984; Combating Stagefright, 1985; Playscript Interpretation and Production, 1985; The Prince, 1985; Introduction to the Musical Comedy, (with Suzanne Trauth), 1986. *Contributions to:* Numerous journal; including: Secondary School Theatre Journal; Theatre Journal' The Cue; Liberal and Fine Arts Review; Theatre News; College English Notes; Eugene O'Neill Newsletter. *Memberships include:* Fellow, American Film Institute; Fellow, International Academy of Poets; American Theatre Association. *Address:* Montclair State College, Upper Montclair, NJ 07043, USA.

RATCLIFFE, Barrie M, b. 30 July 1940, Rainhill, Lancashire, England. History Professor. m. Cheryl Lynne Daniere, 21 Dec. 1980, Corona, 1 son. *Education:* BA, 1st Class Honours, Modern History, University of Manchester, 1963; PhD, University of Manchester, 1970. *Appointments:* Lecturer, History, University of Manchester, 1967–75; Associate Professor, History, 1976–80, Professor, Later Modern European History, 1980–, Université Laval, Québec, Canada. *Publications:* Great Britain and Her World 1750–1914, 1975; Essays in Trade and Transport, 1977, with W H Chaloner; A French Sociologist, 1977, with W H Chaloner. *Contributor to:* 80 articles in learned journals and dictionaries in Britain, France, Italy, USA, Canada. *Memberships:* Society for French Historical Studies, President 1985–86; Canadian Historical Association, Chair Ferguson Prize, 1980–82. *Address:* 20 Rue Mont-Carmel, Québec, Canada G1R 4A4.

RATHBONE, (Christopher) Julian, b. 10 Feb. 1935, London. Writer. *Education:* Magdalene College, Cambridge, English degree. *Literary Appointments:* Southern Arts Bursary, 1976; Literature Consultant to Berkshire Libraries, 1983–84. *Publications:* King Fisher Lives, 1976; Joseph, 1979; A Last Resort, 1980; A Spy of the Old School, 1982; Nasty, Very, 1984; Wellington's War, 1984; Lying in State, 1985. *Contributions to:* The Literary Review; The Guardian. *Honours:* Runner-up for the Booker Prize, 1976 and 1979. *Literary Agent:* Margaret Hanbury, 27 Walcot Square, London SE11. *Address:* Sea View, School Road, Thorney Hill, Nr Christchurch, Dorset BH23 8DS, England.

RATTEE, Michael Dennis, b. 27 Feb. 1953, Holyoke, Massachusetts, USA. Design Painter. m. Hannelore Quander, 4 Sep. 1977, Randolph, Vermont, 1 son, 1 daughter. *Education:* University of Vermont. *Publications:* Mentioning Dreams, 1985; Calling Yourself Home, (book of Poems) forthcoming, 1986. *Contributions to:* (Poems) Blue Unicorn; Brush Fire; Contact II; Cedar Rock; dodeca; New Kauri; Modus Operandi; Negative Capability; Phantasm; Pikestaff Forum; Pinch Penny; Poet Lore; Prickly Pear, Tucson; Pteranondon; Salome; Small Pond; Third Eye; Topo; Cut Bank. *Honour:* Fellowship Grant, Poetry, National Endowment for the Arts, 1984. *Address:* 2833 E.Kaibab Vista, Tucson, AZ 85713, USA.

RAUBENHEIMER, George Harding, b. 26 June 1923, Pretoria, Republic of South Africa. Ceramics Manufacturer; Writer. m. Shirley Hall, 26 Apr. 1958, Johannesburg, 2 sons, 1 daughter. *Education:* Matriculation. *Publications:* North of Bushman's Rock, 1965; Dragon's Gap, 1967; The Gun Merchants, 1969; The Skytrap, 1972; Crossfire, 1980; Screenplay: Mr Kingstreets War, (co-writer), 1970; TV Scripts: Taskforce, 1981; Tilly, 1985; Currently working on TV Scripts for SATV. *Memberships:* South African Military History Association; South African Air Force Association. *Address:* 19 Lystanwold Road, Saxonwold 2196, Johannesburg, Republic of South Africa.

RAUCH, Basil, b. 6 Sep. 1908, Dubuque, Iowa, USA. Historian and Professor of History, Barnard College, Columbia University. *Education:* BA, University of Notre Dame, 1929; Yale University, 1929–33; PhD, Columbia University, 1946. *Publications:* History of the New Deal, 1944; American Interest in Cuba, 1947; Roosevelt: From Munich to Pearl Harbor, 1950; The Roosevelt Reader, 1957; Empire for Liberty, 2 volumes (with D Malone), 1960 and 1965. *Contributions to:* Yale Review, and others. *Honour:* Edmund Campion Award, 1972. *Memberships:* American Studies Association; Century Association; Yale Club, New York; Lawn Club, New Haven. *Address:* 140 RMH Road, Killington, CT 06417, USA.

RAUCH, Leo, b. 9 July 1927, Berlin, Federal Republic of Germany. College Professor. m. Gila Ramras, 24 June 1969, 2 sons. *Education:* BA, City University of New York, 1951; MA, Columbia University, New York, 1954; PhD, New York University, 1968. *Appointments:* Senior Lecturer, Philosophy, Haifa University, Israel, 1970–77; Research Associate, Boston University, 1977–78; Associate Professor, Philisophy, University of Texas, 1978–79; Ohio State University, 1979–81, University of

Cincinnati, 1981–82, Babson College, 1982–. *Publications:* Faith and Revolution, in Hebrew, 1978; The Political Animal, 1981; Hegel and the Human Spirit, 1983; Readings in Contemporary Analytic Philosophy, Anthology, edited, introductions, in Hebrew, 1983; Hegel's Philosophical Propaedeutic, forthcoming, *Contributor to:* Numerous professional journals including, Journal of Critical Analysis; Independent Journal of Philosophy; Thought; The Owl of Minerva. *Memberships:* American Philosophical Association; Hegel Society of America. *Address:* Babson College, Wellesley, MA 02157, USA.

RAVEN, Ronald William, b. 29 July 1904, Coniston, Cumbria, England. Consulting Surgeon. *Education:* St Bartholomew's Medical College, University of London, St Bartholomew's Hospital, MRCS (Eng); LRCP, (Lond) .1928; FRCS (Eng) 1931. *Literary Appointments:* former Assistant Editor, Post-Graduate Medical Journal; Former Senior Editor, Journal of Clinical Oncology. *Publications:* Treatment of Shock (translated into Russian) 1942; Surgical Care, 1942; Cancer in General Practice, co-author, 1952; Surgical Instruments and Appliances, co-author, 1952; Handbook for Nurses and Health Visitors, 1953; Editor and Contributor, Cancer, 7 vols, 1957–60; Cancer Pharynx, Larynx, Oesophagus and its Surgical Treatment, 1958; Editor and Contributor: The Dying Patient (translated into Japanese and Dutch), 1975, Modern Trends in Oncology, 2 vols, 1973; Foundations of Medicine, 1978; Editor and Contributor, Principles of Surgical Oncology, 1977, and many others. *Contributor to:* Numerous articles relating to Surgery and Cancer in British and foreign journals. *Honours:* MD (Hon) Cartegena; OBE, 1946; OSCJ, 1946; Chevalier Legion d'Honneur, 1952; TD, 1953; Court of Patrons, Royal College of Surgeons of England (former Council Member) 1976–; Chairman and Vice-President, Epsom College, 1954–. *Memberships:* Ruskin's Association; Turner's Society; Foreign Member, Academy of Athens; Master of Worshipful Company of Barbers, 1980–81. *Address:* 29 Harley Street, London W1N 1DA, England.

RAVENTOS, Antolin, b. 3 June 1925, Wilmette, Illinois, USA. Medical Professor. m. Anne Patricia Gray, 23 July 1976, San Francisco. *Education:* BS, 1946, MD 1947, University of Chicago; MSc, University of Pennsylvania, 1955. *Literary Appointments:* Assistant Instructor – Professor, University of Pennsylvania, 1950–70; Professor University of California – Davis, 1970–; Associate Editor, CANCER, 1964–. *Contributor to:* 88 contributions to medical and scientific journals. *Memberships:* American Medical Writers Association, President, North California Chapter, 1984–86; Council of Biology Editors. *Address:* 3216 Country Club Drive, P O Box 3136, El Macero, CA 95618, USA.

RAVITCH, Norman, b. 22 Nov. 1936, New York, USA. Professor of History. m. Sara Ann Silva, 24 Mar. 1972, 1 son. *Education:* BA, Queens College, 1957; MA 1959, PhD, 1962, Princeton University. *Appointments:* Instructor, Philadelphia Museum College, 1961–62; Assistant Professor, Associate Professor, Professor, University of California, Riverside, 1962–. *Publications:* Sword and Mitre, 1966; Images of Western Man, 3 volumes, 1973. *Contributor to:* Encounter; Commentary; Church History; Historical Journal; Journal of the American Academy of Religion; Cahiers d'histoire; Catholic Historical Review; International Journal of Economic and Social History. *Honours:* Phi Beta Kappa, 1956; Fulbright Fellowship, 1960–61. *Memberships:* American Historical Association; Western Society for French History. *Address:* Department of History, University of California, Riverside, CA 92521, USA.

RAWCLIFFE, John Michael, b. 2 Apr. 1934, Blackpool, England. Teacher. m. Hilary Miles, 12 Oct. 1957, Ilford, Essex, 2 sons, 1 daughter. *Education:* BA Honours in History, Nottingham University, 1955; Postgraduate Certificate in Education, 1959, Academic Diploma in Education, 1961, Institute of Education, London University; MA, University of Kent, 1976.

Literary Appointments: Joint General Editor, Finding Out Series, Batsford Press, 1982–. *Publications:* F D Rossevelt, 1980; Victorian Towns, 1982; Bromley: Kentish Market Town to Victorian Suburb, in, The Rise of Suburbia, 1982; Victorian Country Life, 1984; Victorian London, 1985; Victorian Public Health and Housing, 1986; Victorian Social Reformers, 1987. *Contributions to:* American Historical Association History Education Project, Historical Sources for Use in Schools, 1974; The Use of Maps in Schools, 1975. *Address:* 9 Copley Dene, Bromley, Kent BR1 2PW, England.

RAWORTH, Thomas Moore, b. 19 July 1938, London. Writer. m. Valarie Murphy, 4 sons, 1 daughter. *Education:* University of Essex, MA, 1967–70. *Literary Appointments:* Poet in Residence, Department of Literature, University of Essex, 1969–70; Fellowship, Yaddo, New York State, USA, 1971; Teaching, Bowling Green State University, Ohio, USA, 1972–73; Resident Poet, North Eastern Illinois University, Chicago, USA, 1973–74; Teaching University of Texas, USA, 1974–75; Poet in Residence, King's College, University of Cambridge, Ewngland, 1977–78. *Major Publications:* The Relation Ship, 1966, 1969; The Big Green Day, 1968; A Serial Biography, 1969, 1977; Lion Lion, 1970; Betrayal, 1970; Moving, 1971; Act, 1973; Ace, 1974, 1977; Cloister, 1975; Common Sense, 1976; The Mask, 1976, Logbook, 1977; Nicht wahr, Rosie?, 1980; Writing, 1982; Tottering State: Selected Poems 1963–83, 1984. *Contributor to:* Various publications in some 10 countries. *Honours:* Alice Hunt Bartlett Prize, 1970; Cholmondely Award, 1971; Committee on Poetry Award (New York), 1972. *Address:* 132 Ditton Fields, Cambridge, CB5 8QL, England.

RAWSON, Claude Julien, b. 8 Feb. 1935, Shanghai, China. University Professor. m. Judith Ann Hammond, 14 July 1959, Reading, 3 sons, 2 daughters. *Education:* MA, B Litt, Oxford University. *Literary Appointments:* Editor, Yearbook of English Studies, 1974–: English and American Editor, Modern Language Review, 1974–; General Editor, Unwin Critical Library, 1975–; Co-editor, Cambridge History of Literary Criticism, 1984–. *Publications:* Focus Swift, 1968; Henry Fielding, 1971; Henry Fielding and the Augustan Ideal Under Stress, 1972; Gulliver and the Gentle Reader, 1973; Fielding: A Critical Anthology, 1973; The Character of Swift's Satire, 1983. English Satire and the Satiric Tradition, 1984; Order From Confusion Sprung: Studies in 18th Century Literature From Swift to Cowner, 1985. *Contributions to:* Times Literary Supplement; London Review of Books; New York Times Book Review; Poetry Review; Observer; Essays in Criticism; Essays and Studies; Sewanee Review; Review of English Studies; Journal of English and Germanic Philology; Modern Philology; Modern Language Review. *Memberships:* Committee, Modern Humanities Research Association, 1974–; President 1974 and 1975, British Society for 18th Century Studies; American Society for Eighteenth Century Studies. *Literary Agent:* A D Peters. *Address:* Department of English, University of Warwick, Coventry CV4 7AL, England.

RAY, Cyril, b. 16 Mar. 1908. Journalist. m. Elizabeth Mary Brocklehurst, 25 May 1953, London, 1 son. *Education:* Open History Scholar, Jesus College, Oxford University. *Literary Appointments:* War Correspondent, Manchester Guardian and British Broadcasting Corporation, 1940–45; Moscow Correspondent, Sunday Times, 1949–56; Assistant Editor, The Spectator, 1958–62; The Observer, 1962–74; Editor, Compleat Imbiber Annual, 1956–71. *Publications:* Author of numerous books including: Merry England, 1960; The Gourmet's Companion, 1963; The Wines of Italy, 1966; In a Glass Lightly, 1967; Bollinger, 1971; Cognac, 1973; Wine With Food, 1975; The Wines of France, 1976; The Wines of Germany, 1977; The Complete Book of Spirits and Liqueurs, 1978; The Saint Michael Guide to Wines, 1978; Ray on Wine, 1979; Vintage Tales, 1984; Robert Mondavi of the Napa Valley, 1984. *Contributor to:* Punch, 1978–, and others. *Honours include:* Chevalier du Merite Agricole, France, 1974; Cavaliere, Italian Order of Merit, 1972; Chevalier, French Order of Merit,

1985; Andre Simon Prize, International Wine and Food Society, 1964; Bologna Trophy, 1967; Glenfiddich Medallist 1970; Glenfiddich Wine Book of the Year, 1979; Glenfiddich Wine and Food Writer of the Year, 1979; Glenfiddich Wine and Food Writer Special Award, 1984. *Memberships:* Honorary Life Member, National Union of Journalists; Founder, Past President, Honorary Life member, Circle of Wine Writers; Society of Authors. *Address:* Albany, Piccadilly, London W1V 9RQ, England.

RAY, David Eugene, b. 20 May 1932, Sapulpa, USA. Writer; Teacher; Editor. m. Suzanne Judy Ray, 21 Feb. 1970, Richmond, 1 son, 3 daughters. *Education:* BA, 1952, MA, 1957, University of Chicago. *Appointments:* Instructor, English, Wright Junior College, Chicago, 1957–58; Instructor, English, Northern Illinois University, 1958–60, Cornell University, 1960–64; Assistant Professor, Reed College, Oregon, 1964–66; Lecturer, University of Iowa, 1969–70; Visiting Associate Professor, Bowling Green State University, 1970–71; Professor, English, 1971–; Editor, New Letters, 1971–85, University of Missouri, Kansas City; Visiting Professor, English, Syracuse University, 1976–79, University of Rajasthan, India, 1981–82. *Publications include:* X-Rays, 1965; Dragging the Main and Other Poems, 1968; A Hill in Oklahoma, 1972; Gathering Firewood: new Poems and Selected, 1974; Enough of Flying: Poems Inspired by the Ghazals of Ghalib, 1977; The Mulberries of Mingo and other Stories, 1978; The Tramp's Cup, 1978; The Touched Life, 1982; Not Far from the River, 1984; Elysium in the Halls of Hell, 1984; On Wednesday I Cleaned Out My Walet, 1985; Editor, numerous books including, The Chicago Review Anthology, 1959; New Asian Writing, 1979; New Letters Readers I and II, 1984; etc. *Contributor to:* Many professional journals. *Honours:* Recipient, numerous honours and awards, msost recent, National Endowment for the Arts Fellowship, 1983; Faculty Fellowship, University of Missouri, Kansas City, 1984; Associated Writing Programmes Poetry Contest, 2nd Prize, 1985; PEN Syndicated Fiction Award for Story, Sanctuary, 1985. *Memberships:* PEN; AAUP; Poetry Society of America; etc. *Address:* 5517 Crestwood Drive, Kansas City, MO 64110, USA.

RAY, Mary Eva Pedder, b. 14 Mar 1932, Rugby, England. Writer. *Education:* Diploma of Social Science, London University; Certificate of Religious Knowledge, Cambridge University. *Publications:* The Voice of Apollo, 1964; The Eastern Beacon, 1965; Standing Lions, 1968; Spring Tide, 1969; Living in Earliest Greece, 1969; Shout Against the Wind, 1970; A Tent for the Sun, 1971; The Ides of April, 1974; Sword Sleep, 1975; Beyond the Desert Gate, 1977; Song of Thunder, 1978, Rain from the West, 1980; The Windows of Elissa, 1982; The Golden Bees, 1984. *Address:* 24 Richmond Drive, Herne Bay, Kent CT6 6RT, England.

RAY, Suzanne Judy, b. 21 Aug. 1939, Petworth, Sussex, England. Radio Producer; Writer. m. David Eugene Ray, 21 Feb. 1970, Richmond, Indiana, USA, 1 son, 3 daughters. *Education:* BA Honours, University of Southampton, England, 1960. *Literary Appointments:* Secretary to Editor, Transition Magazine, Kampala, Uganda, 1965–67; Editorial Assistant, New Letters Magazine, Kansas City, Missouri, USA, 1971–; Radio Producer, New Letters on the Air, weekly radio programme, 1977–. *Publications:* Pebble Rings, poems, 1980, Co-Editor, New Asian Writing, 1979. *Contributions to:* The Chariton Review; 1981 Yearbook of American Periodical Verse; Getting from Here to There; Voices from the Interior; Missouri Poets; Assembling; The Poetry Review; Rajasthan Journal of English Studies; Studia Mystica. Various poetry readings, USA and India. Photographs used as covers and published in journals. Several exhibitions of photographs, USA. *Honours:* Prizes for Sedokas and Sestina, World Order of Narrative Poets, 1983; Prize for Sedokas, World Order of Narrative Poets, 1984. *Membership:* Poetry Society of America. *Address:* 5517 Crestwood Drive, Kansas City, MO 64110, USA.

RAYL, Harris Ashton, b. 23 March 1953, Hutchinson, Kansas, USA. Newspaper Editor. m. Shannon Drews, 6 Jan. 1979, Kansas, USA. *Education:* BGS, English; MS, Journalism, University of Kansas. *Literary Appointments:* Reporter, Ottawa Herald, Ottawa, Kansas, 1978; Reporter, 1980; Associate Editor, 1981, Olathe Daily News, Olathe, Kansas; Editor, 1982; Editor and Publisher, 1985, Salina Journal, Salina, Kansas. *Memberships:* American Society of Newspaper Editors; International Press Institute. *Address:* 333 S Fourth, Salina, Kansas MO 67401, USA.

RAYNER, Claire Bernice, b. 22 Jan. 1931, London, England. Writer. m. Desmond Rayner, 23 June 1957, London, 2 sons, 1 daughter. *Education:* SRN; CMB Part 1. *Literary Appointments include:* Acknowledged as leading Agony Aunt having written columns for leading publications including, as Ruth Martin, 1966–75, under own by-line, 1975–, Woman's Own Magazine; The Sun, 7 years; currently writing for The Sunday Mirror; Numerous radio and television appearances in one-off programmes, series or as guest in long running topical programmes. *Publications include:* Mothers and Midwives, 1962; Your Baby, 1965; For Children 1967; 101 Key Facts of Practical Baby Care, 1967; Day Lady Mislaid, 1968; The Meddlers, 1970; Woman's Medical Dictionary, 1971; Nurse in the Sun, 1972; The Burning Summer, 1972; The Performers, 12 volume family saga, 1973–; Where Do I Come From?, 1974; Claire and Keith's Kitchen Garden, with Keith Fordyce, 1978; Related to Sex, 1979; Reprise, 1980; The Running Years, 1981; Growing Pains, 1984; The Getting Better Book, 1985; The Virus Man, 1985. Numerous of her 70 titles printed worldwide. *Contributions to:* The Lancet; Medical World; Nursing Times; Nursing Mirror; also to most leading national newspapers, UK. *Honour:* Freedom of City of London, 1981. *Literary Agent:* Desmond Rayner. *Address:* Box 125, Harrow, Middlesex, England.

REA, Kenneth Wesley, b. 20 July 1944, Ruston, Louisiana, USA. University Professor. m. Rebecca E Sanders, 28 June 1964, El Dorado, 2 sons. *Education:* BA, Louisiana Technical University, 1966; MA, University of Colorado, Boulder, 1968; PhD, University of Colorado, 1970. *Appointments:* Professor, History, Louisian Technical University, 1968–. *Publications:* Co-Editor, China: An Analytic Reader; Editor, Canton in Revolution, 1977; Early Sino-American Relations 1841–1912; Co-Editor, The Forgotten Ambassador: The Reports of John Leighton Stuart 1943–49. *Contributor to:* Asian Forum; Chinese Culture; Chinese Scholar; Asian Profile; Asian Affairs; etc. *Honours:* Louisiana Technical University, College of Arts and Science Outstanding Research Award, 1979; Professorship Award, 1984. *Memberships:* Association of Asian Studies; Society of Ching Studies; American Associaton of Chinese Studies. *Address:* 3103 Lakeview Place, Ruston, LA 71270, USA.

READ, Anthony, b. 21 Apr. 1935, Staffordshire, England. Writer. m. Rosemary E Kirby, 29 Mar. 1958, Great Barr, West Midlands, 2 daughters. *Education:* Central School of Speech & Drama, London, 1952–54. *Publications:* The Theatre, 1964; Operation Lucy (with David Fisher), London & USA, 1980; Colonel Z, (with David Fisher), London 1984, USA, 1985. Also well over 100 television films, plays, serials. *Honours:* Pye Colour TV Award, 1983. *Membership:* Trustee, Chairman 1981–82, Writers Guild of Great Britain. *Literary Agent:* Books, Murray Pollinger; TV & Film, Stephen Durbridge, Harvey Unna & Stephen Durbridge Ltd. *Address:* 7 Cedar Chase, Taplow, Buckinghamshire, England.

READ, Brian Ahier, b. 19 Jan. 1927, Jersey, Channel Islands. Writer. m. Beryl Austin, 1951, 2 sons, 1 daughter. *Publications:* 12 books for young children, 1963–85. *Literary Agent:* Laurence Pollinger Ltd. *Address:* c/o Laurence Pollinger Ltd, 18 Maddox Street, London W1R OEU, England.

READ, David Haxton Carswell, b. 2 Jan. 1910, Cupar, Fife, Scotland. Minister of the Presbyterian

Church. *Education:* MA Honours, University of Edinburgh, 1932; BC with Distinction in Dogmatics, New College, Edinburgh, 1936; Ordained, Church of Scotland, 1936. *Literary Appointments:* Reviewer, The Religious Book Club, and others. *Publications include:* Giants Cut Down to Size, 1970; Religion Without Wrappings, 1970; Overheard, 1971; Curious Christians, 1972; Good News in the Letters of Paul, 1975; Go and Make Disciples, 1978; Unfinished Easter, 1978; The Faith is Still There, 1980; This Grace Given, autobiography part 1, 1984; Grace Thus Far, autobiography part 2, 1985. *Contributions to:* Numerous magazines and journals including: A.D. Magazine; America; The Atlantic Monthly; Theology; In collected editions including: Best Sermons, edited by G Paul Butler; Preaching The Resurrection. *Honours include:* Wallace Award, The American-Scottish Foundation Inc, New York City, 1976; Clergyman of the Year Award, Religious Heritage of America, St Louis, 1980; Clergyman of the Year Award, Society of the Family of Man, Council of Churches of the City of New York, 1980; 10 Honorary Degrees. *Memberships include:* Director, Foundation for the Arts, Religion and Culture; Vice-President, The Appeal of Conscience Foundation. *Address:* Madison Avenue Presbyterian Church, New York City, NY 10010, USA.

READ, Donald, b. 31 July 1930, Manchester, England. Professor of Modern English History. *Education:* MA, Blitt, University College, Oxford University; PhD, University of Sheffield, 1961. *Publications include:* Peterloo: The Massacre and its Background (Manchester University Press), 1958; Press and the People (Arnold), 1961; Cobden and Bright, A Victorian Political Partnership (Edward Arnold), 1967; Edwardian England (Harrap), 1972; England 1868–1914, The Age of Urban Democracy (Longman), 1979. *Contributor to:* Chartist Studies (Macmillan), 1959; Various professional journals. *Memberships:* Fellow, Royal Historical Society; President, Historical Association. *Literary Agent:* Curtis Brown Academy Limited. *Adress:* Darwin College, University of Kent, Giles Lane, Canterbury, Kent CT2 7NY, England.

READ, Gardner, b. 2 Jan. 1913, Evanston, Illinois, USA. Composer, Writer, Teacher. m. Vail Payne, 17 Sep. 1940, Chicago, Illinois, USA, 1 daughter. *Education:* BN, MM, Eastman School of Music, Rochester, New York, USA. *Major Publications:* Thesaurus of Orchestral Devices, 1953; Music Notation, 1964; Contemporary Instrumental Techniques, 1976; Modern Rhythmic Notation, 1978; Style & Orchestration, 1979. *Contributor to:* Music Journal; Music News; New York Times; Christian Science Monitor; American String Teacher; Notes; Boston Globe; Mexican Life; Journal of Music Theory; Arts in Society; College Music Symposium; World of Music; MusicEducators Journal; The Composer Magazine; Music Clubs Magazine; American Peoples Encyclopaedia Yearbook. *Honours:* Doctor of Music (honoris causa) Doane College, 1964. *Address:* 47 Forster Road, Manchester, MA 01944, USA.

READ, Peter Graham, b. 11 Jan 1948, Renmark, Republic of South Austraila. Newspaper Editor. m. Bronwyn, 1970, Adelaide, 2 daughters. *Publication:* Dust, Sweat and Tears, 1981, (with Gordon Beer). *Address:* Box 832, Renmark, Republic of South Australia 5341.

READ, Piers Paul, b. 7 Mar. 1941, Beaconsfield, England. Writer. m. Emily Boothby, 27 July 1967, Strasbourg, 2 sons, 2 daughters. *Education:* MA, St John's College, Cambridge University. *Literary Appointments:* Fellow, Royal Society of Literature. *Publications:* Game in Heaven With Tussy Marx, 1966; The Junkers, 1969; Monk Dawson, 1970; The Professor's Daughter, 1971; The Upstart, 1973; Alive, 1974; Polonaise, 1976; The Train Robbers, 1978; A Married Man, 1980; The Villa Golitsyn, 1982. *Contributions to:* Various journals. *Honours:* Geoffrey Faber Memorial Prize, 1966; Somerset Maugham Award, 1971; Hawthornden Prize. *Membership:* Society of Authors. *Literary Agent:* Gillon

Aitken. *Address:* 50 Portland Road, London W11, England.

REANEY, James Crerar, b. 1 Sep. 1926, South Easthope Township, Ontario, Canada. Professor of English. m. Colleen Thidaudeau, Dec. 1951, Ontario, Canada, 2 sons, 1 daughter. *Education:* BA 1948, MA 1949, University of Toronto: PhD, 1957. *Publications include:* Poetry: Poems, 1972; Imprecations, The Art of Swearing, 1984; Drama: The Killdeer and other plays, 1962; Masks of Childhood, 1972; Listen To The Wind, 1973; Baldoon, 1976; The Dismissal, 1978; Wacousta!, 1979; Gyroscope, 1982; The Donnelly Trilogy, 1983; The Canadian Brothers, 1984; Juvenile: Apple Butter and other plays, 1973; The Boy With An R In His Hand, 1965; Take The Big Picture, 1985; Non-Fiction: 14 Barrels From Sea to Sea, 1977. *Contributions to:* Canadian Art; Canadian Literature; University of Toronto Quarterly. *Honours include:* Governor General's Award for: Poetry, 1949, 1958, Drama 1969; Chalmers Awards, for Best Canadian Plays, 1974, 1975 and 1976. *Memberships include:* President 1959–60, Association of Canadian University Teachers: League of Canadian Poets. *Literary Agent:* Sybil A Hutchinson. *Address:* c/o Sybil A Hutchinson, Apt 409 Ramsden Place, 50 Hillsboro Ave, Toronto, Ontario M5R IS8, Canada.

REARDON, Bernard Morris Garvin, b. 9 Apr. 1913, London, England. University Teacher. *Education:* MA, Oxford University. *Publications:* Henry Scott Holland, 1962; Religious Thought in the 19th Century, 1966; Liberal Protestantism, 1968; Roman Catholic Modernism, 1970; From Coleridge to Gore: A Century of Religious Thought in Britain, 1971; Liberalism and Tradition: Aspects of Catholic Thought in 19th Century France, 1975; Hegel's Philosophy of Religion, 1977; Religious Thought in the Reformation, 1981; Il pensiero religioso della Riforma, 1984; Religion in the Age of Romanticism: Studies in Nineteenth Century European Thought, 1985. *Contributions to:* Nineteenth Century Religious Thought in the West, volume II, 1985; Religious Studies, 1985; Numerous reviews in, Journal of Theological Studies, Journal of Ecclesiastical History, Religion and Life; Anglican Theological Review (USA), Theology BBC Radio, London Weekend Television. *Address:* 2 The Grove, Newcastle-upon-Tyne, NE12 9PE, England.

REARDON, Janet Elizabeth Mauk, b. 26 June 1914, Toledo, Ohio, USA. Writer. m. Albert F Reardon, 23 Apr. 1937, Washington, DC, 1 daughter. *Education:* AB cum laude. *Contributions to:* Poet and Critic; Poem; Poet Lore; America; New Renaissance; Voices International; Song; Passages North; Encore; WEID and many others. *Honours:* First Prize for subjective poetry published in Poet Lore, 1968; Second Prize for Subjective poetry published in Poet Lore, 1970; Second Prize in Poetry, Writers Digest Contest, 1970. *Memberships:* Poetry Society of America; Poets and Writers Society Incorporated. *Address:* 8273 Anderson Drive, Fairfax, VA 22031, USA.

REBERT, M Charles, b. 10 May 1920, Hanover, Pennsylvania, USA. Teacher; Writer; Antiquarian. *Education:* AB, Western Maryland College, Westminster, Maryland, Graduate, Penn State, York College, Shippensburg University. *Publications include:* American Majolica 1850–1900, 1981. *Address:* 140 Meade Avenue, Hanover, PA 12331, USA.

RECHEIS, Käthe, b. 11 Mar. 1928, Engelhartszell, Austria, Freelance Writer of Children's and Young People's Literature. *Publications:* Gen heim und vergiss Alles, 1964; Professor, du siehst Gespenster, 1973; Fallensteller am Bibersee, 1972; London 13 Juli, 1974; Der weite Weg des Nataiyu, 1978; 99 Minutenmarchen, 1978; Wo die Wolfe glucklich sind, 1980; Der Weisse Wolf, 1982; Weisst du, dass die Baume reden, 1983. *Honours:* Austrian State Prize for Childrens and Young Peoples Literature. 1961, 63, 64, 67, 71, 72, 75, 76, 79, 80, 84; Hans Christian Andersen Certificate of Honour for Der weite Weg des Nataiyu and for Der Weisse Wolf.

Memberships: Austrian Writers Association; PEN Club, Austria. *Address:* Rembrandtstrasse 1/28, A–1020 Vienna, Austria.

RECK, Andrew Joseph, b. 29 Oct. 1927, New Orleans, USA. University Professor. *Education:* BA, 1947, MA, 1949, Tulane University; University of St Andrews, 1952–53; PhD, Yale University, 1954. *Appointments:* Editorial Advisory Board: Tulane Studies in Philosophy, 1969–; Southern Journal of Philosophy, 1973–; Philosophical Topics, 1972–; Paragon House Publishers, 1982–85; Dialogue, 1984–. *Publications:* Recent American Philosophy, 1984; Introduction to William James, 1967; New American Philosophers, 1968; Speculative Philosophy, 1972; Selected Writings of George Herbert Mead, 1981. *Contributor to:* Over 100 articles in professional Journals; 50 reviews. *Honours:* Fulbright Scholar, 1952–53; American Council of Learned Societies Grantee, 1960–61; Howard Foundation Fellow, 1962–63; American Philosophical Society Grantee, 1971; Huntington Library Fellow, 1972; Liberty Fund Fellow, 1982. *Memberships:* Southwestern Philosophical Society, President, 1973–74; Southern Society for Philosophy and Psychology, President, 1976–77; Metaphysical Society of America, President, 1977–78. *Address:* Dept of Philosophy, Tulane University, New Orleans, LA 70118, USA.

REDAY, Ladislaw, b. 22 June 1913, Frederick, Maryland, USA. Travel and Feature Writer. m. Marjorie Gladys Sullivan, 12 Jan. 1946, Sydney, Australia, 3 daughters. *Education:* BS, Massachusetts Institute of Technology; University of Cincinnati; Fishers Art School. *Literary Appointment:* Contributing Editor, Orange County Illustrated. *Publications:* How to Organize a Community Arts Festival, 1974; Relax and Get Rich, 1979; Making It Rich in the 1980's, 1980; Fifty-Two Steps to Adventure, 1985. *Contributions to:* Over 50 magazines and newspapers including: Los Angeles Times; World Travelling; Oceans Waterfront; Sea Frontiers; Allied Pub; Halsey Pub Rotarian; Boating; Easy Times; Airfair; Pacific Skipper; Air California; PSA; Westworld; Cavalier. *Honour:* Orange County Book Award, 1980. *Membership:* Friends of Library. *Address:* 359 Via Lido Soud, Newport Beach, CA 92663, USA.

REDFERN, Roger Andrew, b. 9 Nov. 1934. Teacher; Photojournalist. *Education:* Derby College of Agriculture, England; Worcestershire College of Education. *Literary Appointments:* Cowman; Mountaineering Tutor; Teacher. *Publications:* Ramables in Peakland, 1965; Rambles in the Hebrides, 1966; Rambles in North Wales, 1968; Portrait of the Pennines, 1969; Peakland Days, 1970; The Dukeries of Nottinghamshire, 1974; Verses from my Country, 1975; Walking in England, 1976; South Pennine Country, 1979. *Contributions to:* Country Life; The Lady; Mountaineering Press. *Memberships:* International Poetry Society. *Address:* The Cottage, Old Brampton, Chesterfield, Derbyshire, England.

REDFERN, Walter David, b. 1936, Liverpool, England. Professor, Reading University. *Education:* MA, PhD, Cambridge University; Ecole Superieure, Paris, France. *Publications:* The Private World of Jean Giono, 1967; Paul Nizan, 1972; Puns, 1984; Georges Darien, 1985. *Contributions to:* Romantic Review; French Review; Symposium; Times Literary Supplement; Nouvelle Revue, Francaise; Europe; Journal of European Studies; Panurge. *Address:* 8 Northcourt Avenue, Reading, Berkshire, England.

REDGROVE, Peter, b. 2 Jan. 1932. Poet; Novelist; Playwright; Psychologist. *Education:* Open and State Scholarships, Natural Sciences, Queens College, Cambridge. *Literary Appointments:* Reviews for Times Literary Supplement, 1956–; Guardian, 1975–; Scientific Journalist and Editor, 1954–61; Visiting Poet, Buffalo University, NY, 1961; Gregory Fellow in Poetry, Leeds University, 1962–65; Resident Author and Senior Lecturer, Complementary Studies, Falmouth School of Arts, Cornwall, England, 1966–83; O'Connor Professor

of Literature, Colgate University, NY, 1974–75; Freelance Writer, present. *Publications include:* (novels) In the Country of the Skin, 1973; The Terrors of Dr Treviles, (with Penelope Shuttle), 1974; The Glass Cottage, 1979; The God of Glass, 1979; The Sleep of the Great Hypnotist, 1979; The Beekeepers, 1980; The Facilitators, or Madam Hole-in-the-Day, 1982; The Sin Doctor, pending; The Wise Wound, (with Penelope Shuttle), 1978, German and Dutch editions, updated edition, (with introduction by Margaret Drabble), 1986; (playbooks) Miss Carstairs Dressed for Blooding and Other Plays, 1976; In the Country of the Skin, 1973. Numerous radio and TV dramas including: Florent and the Tuxedo Millions, Martyr of the Hives, Memorial (TV film); Anthologies; Reviews; Recordings and Discs; Broadcasts; 900 poems in journals and anthologies, since 1960. *Contributor to:* Various literary journals such as Times Literary Supplement, The Spectator, New Statesman, Observer, Listener; contributor to anthologies of poetry and prose; Lectures and Committees. *Honours:* Numerous Literary Awards including Guardian Fiction Prize; Giles Cooper Award For Radio Drama, 1982; Cholmondeley Award, 1985. *Memberships include:* Writer's Guild; Authors Society. *Literary Agent:* David Higham Associates. *Address:* c/o D Higham Associates Limited, 5-8 Lower John Street, Golden Square, London W1R 4HA, England.

REECE, Benny Ramon, b. 7 Dec. 1930, Asheville, North Carolina, USA. Professor, Classical Languages. m. Ethel Van Dyke, 4 June 1960, Macon, Georgia, USA, 1 son. *Education:* BA, Duke University, 1953; MA, 1954, PhD, 1957, University of North Carolina. *Publications include:* Learning in the Tenth Century, 1968; Sermones Ratherii Episcopi Veronensis, 1969; The Role of the Centurion in Ancient Society, 1974; A Bibliography of First Appearances of the Works by A Conan Doyle, 1975; Diocletian's Edict on Prices, 1985. *Contributions to:* Professional journals and magazines. *Honours include:* Fulbright Scholar, University of Munich, 1957–58. *Memberships:* American Philological Association; Classical Association of Middle West and South; American Philosophical Society. *Address:* Rte 7, Roeford Road, Greenville, SC 29609, USA.

REECE, Paul Charles, b. 20 June 1960, Ashton, Lancs, England. Meter Agent/Poet. *Literary Appointments:* Invited to read poetry at several meetings including National Peace Foundation Poetry Prize Giving. *Contributions to:* Approximately 60 poems published worldwide in newspapers and magazines including Poetry of Love (Denmark), Folio International, New Hope International, Peace and Freedom, Writers Own Magazine etc. *Honours:* In top 20 National Peace Foundation Poetry Competiion; Winner of Foilio International Poetry Competition, 1985; Recipient of several small prizes for invididual works, namely Orions and Dandelions; The Barbed Wire Rainbow; Children of the Wilderness; Mirage of Reality, etc. *Address:* 50 Town Lane, Denton, Greater Manchester M34 1AE, England.

REEDY, Penelope Michal Croner, b. 5 June 1947, Everett, Washington State, USA. Farmer's Wife, Writer. m. Jim Reedy, 2 Oct. 1971, Everett, Washington, USA, 2 sons, 2 daughters. *Education:* Laboratory Institute of Fashion Merchandise, New York City, Brooklyn College, New York, 1965–69; Correspondence, University of Washington, Seattle, 1975; Workshop with Robert Stone, Idaho, 1977. *Literary Appointments:* Founder, Editor & Publisher, The Redneck Review of Literature, 1975–. *Contributor to:* Sun Valley Magazine; Mountain Express; Twinfalls Times News; and others. *Membership:* Association for the Humanities in Idaho. *Address:* Route 1, Box 1085, Fairfield, ID 83327, USA.

REES, Barbara Elizabeth, b. 9 Jan. 1934, Worcester, England. Writer. m. Larry Herman, 1 Sep. 1967, London, Divorced 1978, 1 daughter. *Education:* BA, Hons, English Language and Literature, University of Oxford; MA. *Literary Appointments:* Arts Council of Great Britain Creative Writer in Residence at North London Polytechnic, 1976–78. *Publications:* Try Another

Country three short novels, 1969; Diminishing Circles, UK 1970, USA 1971, Netherlands 1972; Prophet of the Wind, USA 1973, UK 1975, 1976; George and Anna, 1976; The Victorian Lady, 1977; Harriet Dark, UK and USA 1978, USA 1980. *Contributor to:* Short stories published in many magazines in UK and abroad including: Good Housekeeping; Melbourne Herald; Annabella; Det Nye; Woman's Own. *Honour:* Arts Council Award 1974. *Membership:* Writers' Guild of Great Britain. *Address:* 2-B Willes Road, London NW5 3DS, England.

REES, David Bartlett, b. 18 May 1936, London, England. Freelance writer. m. Jenny Watkins, 23 July 1966, London, (divorced), 2 sons. *Education:* BA 1958, MA 1961, Cambridge University. *Publications:* Storm Surge, 1975; Quintin's Man, 1976; The Missing German, 1976; Landslip, 1977; The Spectrum, 1977; The Ferryman, 1977; Risks, 1977; The Exeter Blitz, 1978; The House That Moved, 1978; In The Tent, 1979; Silence, 1979; The Green Bough of Liberty, 1980; The Lighthouse, 1980; The Marble in the Water, 1980; The Night Before Christmas Eve, 1980; Miss Duffy is Still With Us, 1980; A Reason for the Romans, 1981; Holly, Mud and Whisky, 1981; The Milkman's On His Way, 1982; The Mysterious Rattle, 1982; Waves, 1983; The Estuary, 1983; Painted Desert, Green Shade, 1984; Out of the Winter Gardens, 1984; Islands, 1985; A Better Class of Blond, 1985. *Contributions to:* Children's Literature in Education: The School Librarian; San Jose Studies; The Horn Book; Top of the News; Children's Book Bulletin. *Honours:* Library Association Carnegie Medal, 1978; The Other Award, 1980. *Address:* 49 Sandford Walk, Exeter, Devon EX1 2ET, England.

REES, Ioan Bowen, b. 13 Jan. 1929, Dolgellau, Wales. County Secretary; Solicitor; Chief Executive. *Education:* MA, Queen's College, Oxford. *Publications:* (books on mountaineering in Welsh language), Galwad y Mynydd, 1961; Dringo Mynyddoedd Cymru, 1965; Mynyddoedd, 1975; The Welsh Political Tradition, 1962, 2nd edition, 1975; Celtic Nationalism, (co-author), 1967; Government By Community, 1971; the Mountains of Wales, (anthology of prose and verse), 1986. *Contributor to:* Planet: Barn; Taliesin; New Law Journal; Public Administration; Local Government Chronicle; JP; Local Government Review; Publius (Philadelphia). *Honour:* Recipient, Haldane Medal, 1968. *Address:* Tal-Sarn, Llanllechid, Bangor Gwynedd, Wales.

REES, Lucy, b. 21 Dec. 1943, Birkenhead, England. Writer. *Education:* BSc Honours, Zoology, University College, London University; University of Sussex. *Publications:* Wild Pony, 1975, 3rd edition, 1977; Horse of Air, 1980; Take It to the Limit, 1981, 82; The Horse's Mind, 1984. *Contributions to:* Proceedings of the Royal Society, 1969; Out of This World, science fiction anthology; New Internationalist; various horse magazines. *Honours:* 1st Buchpreis Des Deutschen Alpenvereins, for Take It to the Limited, 1984. *Literary Agent:* P Kavanagh, A D Peters. *Address:* Penygraig, Croesor, Penrhyndevdraeth, Gwynedd, Wales.

REEVE, F(ranklin) D(olier), b. 18 Sep. 1928, Philadelphia, Pennsylvania, USA. Writer. *Education:* PhD, Columbia University, 1958. *Literary Appointments:* Adjunct Professor of Letters, Wesleyan University, 1970-; Visiting Lecturer, English, Yale University, 1972-. *Publications include:* In the Silent Stones, 1968; The Red Machines, 1968; Just Over the Border, 1969; The Brother, 1971; The Blue Cat, 1972; White Colors, 1973. Editor, Poetry Review, 1982-74. *Contributions to:* Poems, essays, stories in American Poetry Review; New England Review; Yale Review; Sewanee Review; Manhattan Poetry Review; Confrontation; New Yorker; Kansas Quarterly; North American Review; etc. *Honour:* Literature Award, American Academy - National Institute of Arts and Letters, 1970; PEN, Syndicated Fiction Award, 1985. *Memberships:* PEN, American Centre, Vice President 1982-84, Poetry Society of America; Board of Directors, Poets House. *Address:* Turco Road, Mount Holly, VT 05758, USA.

REEVES, Clement, b. 13 Mar. 1940, Limerick, Ireland. University Professor, Philosophy. m. Fionnuala Reeves, 1965, 2 daughters. *Education:* BA, Honours, Double 1st, Philosophy 1965, MA Honours 1967, National University of Ireland, Cork; PhD, Philosophy, University of Ottawa, Canada, 1974. *Publications:* The Psychology of Rollo May, 1977. *Honours:* University Postgraduate Scholar, 1966-67; Canada Council Doctoral Fellowship, 1971; Queen Elizabeth II Doctoral Scholarship, 1971-72; Canada Council Postdoctoral Leave Fellowship, 1982. *Address:* Department of Philosophy, University of Guelph, Guelph, Ontario, Canada N1G 2W1.

REEVES, Fionnuala A, b. 10 Apr. 1943, Limerick, Ireland. Novelist. m. Dr Clement Reeves, 1965, 2 daughters. *Education:* BA, Double First, Modern Languages, 1963, MA, Honours, Spanish, 1967. National University of Ireland. *Publications:* Deadly Inheritance, New York, Toronto, 1983, German translation 1984-85; Second and third novels forthcoming. *Honours:* University Scholar, 1960-63; Peel Memorial Prize, 1963; French Essay Prize, 19th Century Literature, 1962; Postgraduate Scholarship, 1963; French Government Gold Medal, 1963; Postgraduate Scholarship, 1964. *Literary Agent:* McIntosh & Otis Inc, 475 Fifth Avenue, New York, NY 10017, USA.

REEVES, Marjorie Ethel, b. 17 July 1905, Bratton, Wiltshire, England. University Teacher. *Education:* BA, St Hugh's College; DLitt, Oxford University; PhD, Westfield College, London University. *Publications:* The Influence of Prophecy in the Later Middle Ages, 1969; The Figurai of Joachim of Fiore, 1972; Joachim of Fiore and the Prophetic Future, 1976; Sheepbell and Ploughshare, 1978; Why History, 1980. *Contributor to:* Times Educational Supplement; Minerva; Speculum; Traditio; Medievalia et Humanistica; Mediaeval and Renaissance Studies; Recherches de Theologie ancienne medievale, Sophia. *Memberships:* Fellow British Academy; Corresponding Fellow, Medieval Academy of America; Fellow, Royal Historical Society. *Address:* 38 Norham Road, Oxford OX2 6SQ, England.

REEVES, Thomas C, b. 25 Aug. 1936, Tacoma, Washington, USA. University Professor. m. Kathleen Garrison, 1 Feb. 1958, Portland, Oregon, 3 daughters. *Education:* BA, Pacific University; MA, University of Washington; PhD, University of California, Santa Barbara. *Literary Appointments:* University of Colorado, 1966-70; University of Wisconsin - Parkside, 1970-. *Publications:* Freedom and the Foundation: The Fund for the Republic in the Era of McCarthyism, 1969; Gentleman Boss, The Life of Chester Alan Arthur, 1975; The Life and Times of Joe McCarthy: A Biography, 1982. *Contributions to:* Political Science Quarterly; The Historian; The Wisconsin Magazine of History; The Nation; Pacific Historical Review; New York History; Hayes Historical Journal; The Living Church; The Christian Challenge, etc. *Honours:* Grants from: NEH; University of Colorado; University of Wisconsin; American Philosophical Society; Eleanor Roosevelt Institute; Lilly Endowment. Awards from: State Historical Society of Wisconsin; Council for Wisconsin Writers. *Memberships:* American Historical Association; Organisation of American Historians; The National Episcopal Historians' Association. *Address:* 5039 Cynthia Lane, Racine, WI 53406, USA.

REGENSTREIF, Samuel Peter, b. 9 Sep. 1936, Montreal, Canada. Professor/Political Consultant. m. Donna Lorraine Irony (div), 2 sons, 2 daughters. *Education:* BA, McGill University, 1957; PhD, (Government), Cornell University 1963. *Literary Appointments:* Editorial Consultant, Toronto Star, 1968-82. *Publications:* The Diepenbaker Interlude: Parties and Voting in Canada, 1965. *Contributions to:* Toronto Star, 1963-82; Canadian Journal of Political Science; American Political Science Review; Western Political Quarterly; Current History; International Journal; Public Opinion; Dalhousie Review. *Address:* Department of Political Science, University of Rochester, Rochester, NY 14627, USA.

REGIN, Deric Wagenvoort, b. 23 Aug. 1915, Amsterdam, The Netherlands. Author. *Education:* MA, Yale University, Connecticut, USA, 1954; PhD, Columbia University, New York, 1964. *Publications:* Job, The Man of the Rubble, Poems, 1950; Freedom and Dignity, 1965; Culture and the Crowd, 1968; Reflections from a Prison, Poems, 1971; Traders, Artists, Burghers, 1976. *Contributions to:* Groot Nederland; Elzeviers Maandblad; Helikon; Gulden Wincket; Palaestra; Het Toonell; Keroniek Voor Kunst Enkultuur Erasme; Poetry, England; Outposts. *Honours include:* 1st Prize, Nationwide Drama Contest, Netherlands, 1949; Fulbright Fellowship, 1952. *Address:* 601 West 115th Street, Apt 93a, New York City, NY 10025, USA.

REICH, Richard, m. Lilly Joss Reich. *Publications:* Plays: House Without Windows, New Lindsey Theatre Club, London, Theatre Royal, Windsor and in over 100 regional theatres in the USA; Girls are the Funniest, over 400 performances in Buenos Aires in Spanish, Also in Mexico City; Orchester, in Vienna; Norland, Akademie Theatre, Vienna; Pets, Provincetown Playhouse, New York, also a Hollywood film. Plays on Television in USA, Canada, England, Switzerland, Austria and Argentina. *Membership:* The Dramatists Guild, New York. *Address:* 875, West End Avenue, New York, NY 10025, USA.

REICHART, Walter A, b. 15 Nov. 1903, Pressburg, Austria. Professor of Germanic Languages and Literatures. m. Ruth Oakman, 8 June 1929, Detroit. *Education:* AB, AM, PhD, 1930. *Publications:* Storm's Pole Poppenspäler (editor), 1934; Stehr's Geigenmacher, 1935; Hauptmann und Shakespeare, 1938; Hauptmann's Der arme Heinrich, 1936; Hauptmann's Die Dinsternisse, 1947; Washington Irving and Germany, 1957; Gerhart Hauptmann Bibliographie, 1969; Washington Irving: Journals and Notebooks 1819–1827, 1970; Washington Irving: Journals and Notebooks 1807–1822, 1981. *Contributions to:* Numerous journals and encyclopedias, over 50 scholarly articles dealing with German, English and American Literature. *Honours:* Distinguished Faculty Award. *Memberships:* Modern Language Association, 1929–; Gerhart Hauptmann Gesellschaft, 1962; Thomas Mann Gesellschaft, 1963–; American Association of Teachers of German, 1930–, President, 1951. *Address:* 2106 Londonderry Road, Ann Arbor, MI 48104, USA.

REICHE, Dietlof, b. 31 Mar. 1941, Dresden, Germany. Writer. *Education:* Engineering Studies; Diploma, Engineering. *Publications:* Der Bleisiegelfalscher, 1977; Der Verlorene Fruhling, Die Geschichte von Louise Goith und dem Lokomotivheizer Hannes Buhn, der zum Barrikadenbauer wurde, Frankfurt, 1884, 1979; Wie Spreu vor dem Wind, 1981; Der Einzige, 1986. Historical Novels for Readers from 14 years. *Honours:* Oldenburg Children's and Young Peoples' Book Prize, 1977; German Young Peoples, Book Prize, 1978. *Memberships:* Association of German Writers in the Press Trade Union. *Address:* Hermannstrasse 17, D–6000 Frankfurt am Main 1, Federal Republic of Germany.

REID, Clyde Henderson, b. 13 Dec. 1928, Peoria, Illinois, USA. Spiritual psychotherapist/educator in private practice. *Education:* BS, Bradley University, 1949; MA and MTh, Pacific School of Religion, 1952, 1953; ThD, Boston University, 1960; Postdoctoral Fellow in Religion and Psychiatric Theory, The Menninger Foundation, 1964–65. *Literary Appointments:* Assistant Dean of Students, Bradley University, 1949–50; Assistant Professor, Union Theological Seminary, New York, 1960–64; Associate Director, Institute of Advanced Pastoral Studies, 1967–70; Associate Professor of Interpersonal Ministries, Iliff School of Theology, 1971–74; Director, Center for New Beginnings, Denver, 1974–80. *Publications:* The God-Evaders, 1966; The Empty Pulpit, 1967; Groups Alive; Church Alive, 1969; Help, I've Been Fired, 1971; 21st Century Man Emerging, 1971; Celebrate the Temporary, 1972; Die Leere Kanzel, Oncken Verlag Wuppertal, 1973; Let it Happen, with Jerry Kerns, 1973; The Return to Faith, 1974; You Can Choose Christmas, 1975; Dreams:

Discovering Your Inner Teacher, 1983. *Contributor to:* About 30 published articles in, The Christian Century; International Journal of Religious Education; Journal of Religion and Health; Bulletin of the Association for Past-Life Research and Therapy; Union Seminary Quarterly; Pastoral Psychology; Bulletin of the Colorado Institute for Transpersonal Psychology; and others. *Honours:* Pindell Trophy for Journalism Excellence, Bradley University, 1946; Man of the Month, Pastoral Psychology magazine, 1967. *Memberships:* American Association of Pastoral Counselors (Diplomate); Associations of Humanistic Psychology (President of Colorado Chapter); Jung Society of Colorado (co-founder and board member); Association of Past-Life Research and Therapy (board member). *Address:* 1035 Tantra Park Circle, Boulder, CO 80303, USA.

REID, Helen Evans, b. 3 Sep. 1911, Calabogie, Ontario, Canada. Physician, Journalist. m. Andrew Lawrence Chute, 6 Oct. 1939, Toronto, 1 son, 1 daughter. *Education:* MD, University of Alberta, 1935; Fellow of the Royal College of Physicians (Canada), Royal College of Physicians & Surgeons, 1947. *Literary Appointments:* Columnist, Canadian Home Journal, 1953; Maclean's Magazine, 1965; Director, Medical Publications, Hospital for Sick Children. Toronto, 1967–74. *Major Publications:* A World Away, 1965; All Silent, All Damned, 1969. *Contributor to:* Canadian Home Journal; Maclean's Magazine. *Honours:* Outstanding Achievement Award for distinguished service in medicine, University of Alberta, 1977. *Address:* RR #1, Loretto, Ontario, LOG 1LO, Canada.

REID, Hilary Fay, b. 13 May 1928, Auckland, New Zealand. Housewife. m. John Graeme Sinclair Reid, 19 Aug. 1950, Auckland, 1 son, 2 daughters. *Education:* MA, Auckland University, 1951. *Publications:* A Century in Commerce, 1969; St Mark's Remnera; 1847–1981, 1982. *Contributor to:* Historic Buildings of New Zealand North Island, Chapter on Inner City Churches, Auckland, Cassell New Zealand in conjunction with New Zealand Historic Places Trust, 1979. *Honour:* Queen's Service Medal, 1980. *Membership:* New Zealand Women Writers Society. *Address:* 117 Arney Road, Auckland 5, New Zealand.

REID, John Kelman Sutherland, b. 31 Mar. 1910, Leith, Scotland. University Professor. m. Margaret Winifrid Brookes, 4 Jan. 1950, Corrie, Isle of Arran. *Education:* MA, BD, University of Edinburgh; Universities of Heidelberg, Marburg, Basel, Strasbourg. *Literary Appointments:* Joint Editor, Scottish Journal of Theology, 1948–80, Editor Emeritus 1980–; Honorary Secretary, New English Bible, 1949–82. *Publications include:* The Authority of Scripture, 3rd edition, 1981; Our Life in Christ, 1963; Presbyterians & Unity, 1965; Christian Apologetics, 1969. Translations: Calvin's Theological Treatises, 1965; Concerning the Eternal Predestination of God, 2nd edition, 1982. *Contributions to:* Scottish Journal of Theology. *Honours:* Honorary degrees: DD, Edinburgh, 1957; TD, 1961. CBE, 1971. *Memberships:* Society N T Studiorum; Society for the Study of Theology; President, Church Service Society, 1978–80; President, Scottish Church Society, 1963–65. *Address:* 1 Camus Park, Edinburgh, Scotland EH10 6RY.

REID, Loren, b. 26 Aug. 1905, Gilman City, Missouri, USA. Author; Publisher. m. 28 Aug. 1930, Des Moines, Iowa, 3 sons, 1 daughter. *Education:* BA, Grinnall College, Iowa, 1927; MA, 1930, PhD, 1932, University of Iowa. *Literary Appointments:* Instructor of Retoric and Public speaking, University of Missouri, 1935–39; Assistant professor, Syracuse University, 1939–44; Professor, 1939–75, Professor Emeritus, 1975–, University of Missouri-Columbia; Interim visiting professorships, University of Southern California, University of Hawaii, University of Maryland (overseas, London, England), University of Michigan and Louisiana State University. *Publications:* Teaching Speech, 4 editions, 1952–71; Speaking Well, 4 editions, 1960–81; Charles James Fox, 1969; Hurry Home Wednesday, 1978; Finally It's Friday, 1981. *Contributions to:* Quarterly Journal of Speech; Speech Monographs; The

Speech Teacher; History Today; Parliamentary History; School and Society; Missouri Heritage. *Honours:* Winans Award and Golden Anniversary Award for Charles James Fox, 1969, 70; Literary awards for Hurry Home Wednesday, Missouri Writers Guild and Missouri Library Association, 1979; Distinguished Service Award, University of Missouri-Columbia, Central States Speech Association, Speech Communication Association, New York Speech Association and Speech and Theatre Association of Missouri, 1967–83. *Membership:* Missouri Writers Guild. *Address:* 200 East Brandon Road, Columbia, MO 65203, USA.

REID, William Stanford, b. 13 Sep. 1913, Montreal, Quebec, Canada. Professor Emeritus of History. *Education:* BA, 1934, MA, 1935, McGill University; ThB, ThM, 1938, Westminster Theological Seminary, Philadelphia, Pennsylvania, USA; PhD, University of Pennsylvania, 1941. *Publications include:* The Church of Scotland in Lower Canada: Its Struggle for Establishment, 1936; Skipper from Leith: The Life of Robert Barton of Over Baynton, 1962; Trumpeter of God: A Biography of John Know, 1974; John Calvin: His Influence in the Western World, Editor, 1983; The Scottish Tradition in Canada, Editor, 1976. *Contributions to:* Various religious and historical journals. *Honours include:* Honorary Degrees: DHL, Wheaton College, Illinois, USA, 1976; DDiv, Presbyterian College, Montreal, Canada, 1979. Numerous grants. *Memberships include:* Royal Historical Society; American and Canadian Historical Associations; Scottish Historical Society. *Address:* Department of History, University of Guelph, Guelph, Ontario, Canada N1G GWI.

REILLY, Noel Marcus Prowse (Peter), b. 31 Dec. 1902, Pinner, Middlesex, England. Government Servant; Economist. m. (1) Dolores A Pratten, 17 Sep. 1927, Kensington, (2) Dorothy A Rainsford, 1 son, 1 daughter. *Education:* BA, 1924, MA, 1927, Cambridge University; BSc, Economics, 1st Class Honours, 1946, PhD, 1972, University of London. *Publication:* The Key to Prosperity, 1931. *Contributor to:* The Spectator; Christian Science Monitor; Numerous letters in The Times; New York Times, local US Newspapers. *Honour:* CMG, 1958. *Address:* North Sandwich, NH 03259, USA.

REILLY, Patrick, b. 6 Jan. 1932, Glasgow, Scotland. University Lecturer. m. Rose Fitzpatrick, 2 Mar. 1957, 3 sons, 3 daughters. *Education:* MA Honours, University of Glasgow; DLitt, Pembroke College, University of Oxford. *Major Publications:* Catholics & Scottish Literature, in, Modern Scottish Catholicism (edited D McRoberts), 1979; Jonathan Swift: The Brave Desponder, 1982; Swift Our Contemporary, in, Literary Criticism from 1400 to 1800, (edited D Poupard), 1984; Fielding's Magisterial Art, in, Henry Fielding: Justice Observed, (edited K G Simpson), 1985; George Orwel: The Age's Adversary, 1986. *Contributor to:* Critical Quarterly; Innes Review; Clergy Review; WAS (Hefte für Kultur und Politik), Graz, Austria; articles on Orwell, Joyce, Scottish Literature, Education, Religion etc. *Address:* Department of English, The University, Glasgow G12 8QQ, Scotland.

REILLY, Robert Thomas, b. 21 July 1922, Lowell, Massachusetts, USA. Teacher; Writer. m. Jean Marie McKenzie, 9 June 1945, Omaha, Nebraska, 3 sons, 3 daughters. *Education:* BA Cum Laude, Boston College, Creighton University, Suffolk University, 1947; MA, 1948, PhD candidate, 1948–50, Boston University. *Publications:* Red Hugh, Prince of Donegal, 1957; Christ's Exile, 1957; Massacre at Ash Hollow, 1960; Rebels in the Shadows, 1962; Irish Saints, 1964; Come Along to Ireland, 1968; Public Relations in Action, 1980; Travel and Tourism Marketing Techniques, 1980; Handbook of Tour Management, 1982; What Can Go Wrong with a Speech, 1985. *Contributions to:* Over 100 publications including: Reader's Digest; Saturday Evening Post; U S Catholic; Jubilee; The Critic; Salt; Sign; American Airlines. Author of over 100 scripts for television and films. *Honours:* Fonda-McGuire Best

Actor Award, 1954; American College PR Hall of Fame, 1965; Henderson Medal, 1968; Boss of the Year, 1969; Midland's Journalist of the Year, 1977; Irish Saints selected for Thomas More Book Club, 1964; Writers Grant, American Irish Foundation, 1965; Jameson Hibernia Award, 1981; Kayser Chair of Journalism, 1979–85; Nebraska Professional of the Year, PRSA, 1985. *Memberships:* Vice President, Nebraska Writers Guild. *Address:* 9110 North 52nd Avenue, Omaha, NE 68152, USA.

REIMANN, Arnold Luehrs, b. 3 July 1898, Adelaide, Australia. Teacher of Physics/Researcher (retired). m. 11 June 1927, Wembley, 1 son, 1 daughter. *Education:* BSc, 1919, Hons BSc, 1922, Adelaide; Dr of Philosophy, Berlin University, 1926; DSc, Adelaide, 1936. *Publications:* Thermoinic Emission, 1934; Vacuum Technique, 1952; Physics, 2 volumes, 1971; Modern Physics, 1973. *Contributions to:* Several articles in journals and magazines. *Address:* 52 Lucinda Street, Taringa, Queensland 4068, Australia.

REIMERS, Emil, b. 2 June 1912, Emden, Ostfriesland, Writer; Journalist. *Education:* Philosophy, University of Hamburg (8 terms). *Literary Appointments:* Writer for publishers Heyne-Verlag, Munchen, Sudwest-Verlag, Nelson, London; Journalist for magazines. *Publications:* Meditationen uber fernostliche Symbole; Der kalten Kuche Kostlichkeit; Alles Vom Ei; Dia echte japanische Kuche, (with Eigenan Schriftmalereien); Probleme der Dritten Welt; Kostliches aus der Pilzkuche; Chinesische Kochkunst; Kostliches aus Fluss und Meer; Aus dem Munsterland; Leckere Diatrezepte. *Contributor to:* Nein aagen zu allen Ubeln und Ungerechtigkeiten; Die selbstgedrehte Papiertute als Handwarkszeug; Darwins schopferische Hypothese; Nachdankliche Warendorfer Emswanderungen; Geht es nicht ohne standige Superlative; In China deutsche Speisen kochen, and many others. *Honours:* Gold Medal for, Meditationen uber fernostliche Symbole, 1965; Silver Medal for, Echte japanische Kuche, 1966; Bronze Medal for, Die Kunst den Flambierens. *Membership:* Deutscher Schriftsteller-Verand. *Address:* Postfach 504, 4410 Warendorf, Federal Republic of Germany.

REIN, Karl (Carolus) Hilding Gabriel, b. 14 May 1935, Turku, Finland. Author. *Education:* Student, Grankulla Samskola, 1953; Candidate in humanistic sciences, University of Helsinki, 1966; PhM, Åbo Akademi, 1970. *Publications:* Poetry collections: Färd genom verkligheter, 1954; Syskon till ingen, 1955; Dansens yta, 1956; Vårsvart, 1958; Seende, 1960; Världen ar endast du, 1963; Det obesegrades röst, 1967; Vågbrytningar, 1971; Eros och logos, 1975; Stigar mellan Elysion och Hades, 1978; Mellanstationer, 1981; Amor et Apocalypsis, 1984. Novel: Erinnyerna, 1976. *Contributions to:* Hufvudstadsbladet, 1958–72; Nya Argus, 1958–73.*Honours:* Extra Scholarship, Svenska Litteratursällskapet i Finland, 1959; part of a s c Lybeckian prize, 1968; s c Wasastjerna Prize, 1982. *Memberships:* Finlands Svenska Författareförening; International Academy of Poets; Almquist-sällskapet, Sweden. *Literary Agent:* Södeerstrom and Company. *Address:* Thurmansallén 14, A, 02700 Grankulla, Finland.

REINECKE, Ian, b. 3 Apr. 1945, Australia. Writer. *Education:* BA, Honours, University of Melbourne. *Publications:* Micro Invaders, 1982; The Phone Book, with Julianne Schultz, 1983; Micro Computers, 1984; Electronic Illusions, 1984. *Address:* 391 Lawrence Hargrave Drive, Scarborough, NSW 2511, Australia.

REINHARDT, Madge, b. 29 Nov. 1925, Grand Forks, North Dakota, USA. m. Rolland R Ritter, 9 Sep. 1951, Lincoln, Nebraska, 1 son, 2 daughters. *Education:* BA, University of Nebraska, 1947. *Publications:* You've Got to Ride the Subway, 1977; The Year of the Silence, 1978; The Voice of the Stranger, 1982. Features to Scripps-Howard Syndicate, The Minneapolis Star and Tribune and The Christian Science Monitor. *Address:* 1803 Venus Avenue, St Paul, MN 55112, USA.

REINOWSKI, Werner, b. 13 Oct. 1908, Bernburg a/Saale, Democratic Republic of Germany. Author. m. 20 July 1953, Saale, 2 sons. *Publications:* Der kleine Kopf, 1952; Zwei Brüder, 1959; Unbequeme Freundin, 1973; Goldenweise, 1975; Hoch-Zeit (Schreibweise titelbedingt) am Honigsee, 1985. *Honours:* Kuntstpreis, Stadt Halle, 1956; Bezirk Halle, 1957; Waterländischer Verdienstorden, Bronze 1959, Silver 1968, Gold 1978. *Memberships:* Authors' Association of the Democratic Republic of Germany; Bezirksverband Halle, Saale. *Literary Agent:* Mitteldeutschen Verlag. *Address:* 4714 Rottleberode, Mülfleck 5, Democratic Republic of Germany.

REISS, Alvin Herbert (Skip), b.15 June 1930, New York, USA. Writer. m. Ellen Komoroff, 26 Aug. 1956, New York City, 3 sons. *Education:* MA, 1953, BA, 1952, University of Wisconsin. *Appointments:* Arts Management, Editor, Publisher, 1962–; Columnist, Cultural Affairs Magazine, 1967–70; Consulting Editor, Museums New York, 1979–80; Columnist, Vantage Point Magazine, 1984–85; Columnist, Fund Raising Management Magazine, 1985–. *Publications:* The Arts Management Handbook, 1970, 2nd edition, 1974; Culture & Company, 1972; The Arts Management Reader, 1979. *Contributor to:* American Way; Art News; Coronet; Creative Living; Cue, Cultural Post; Dance; Diversion; Drama Review; Esquire; Family Health; Mainline; Newsday; New York Times; etc. *Memberships:* American Society of Journalists and Authors, Executive Committee Member, 1974–75, Executive Vice President, 1980–81; Music Critics Association, 1973–; Authors Guild. *Address:* 408 West 57th Street, New York, NY 10019, USA.

REISS, Steven Allan, b. 26 Aug, 1947, New York City, USA. Professor of History. m. Tobi E Epstein, 4 Aug. 1980, Chicago, 2 daughters. *Education:* BA, New York University, 1968; MA 1969, PhD 1974, University of Chicago. *Appointments include:* Lecturer, Social Sciences, University of Michigan, Dearborn, 1975–76; Assistant Professor, 1976–80, Associate 1980–84, Professor 1984–, Northeastern Illinois University. *Publications:* Touching Base: Professional Baseball & American Culture in the Progressive Era, 1980; The American Sporting Experience: A Historical Anthology of Sport in America, editor, 1984. *Contributions to:* Journal of Sport History; Journal of Interdisciplinary History; Journal of Social History; Journal of Ethnic Studies. *Honours include:* Various Scholarships, Study Grants; UNI Presidential Merit Award, 1985; Fellowship, National Endowment for the Humanities, 1983–84. *Memberships:* American Historical Association; Organization of American Historians; North American Society for Sport History (editor, Journal of Sport History); Society of American Baseball Researchers. *Address:* Department of History, Northeastern Illinois University, 5500 St Louis, Chicago, IL 60625, USA.

REJAI, Mostafa, b. 11 Mar. 1931, Tehran, Iran. Professor; Writer. *Education:* BA, 1959, 1961, PhD, 1964, University of California, Los Angeles. *Appointments:* Assistant Professor, 1964, Associate Professor, 1967, Professor, 1970, Distinguished Professor, 1983–, Miami University. *Publications:* Democracy: The Contemporary Theories, Editor, Contributor, 1967; Ideologies and Modern Politics, Co-Author, 1971; Decline of Ideology, Editor, Contributor, 1971; The Strategy of Political Revolution, 1973; The Comparative Study of Revolutionary Strategy, 1977; Leaders of Revolution, 1979; World Revolutionary Elites, 1983; Comparative Political Ideologies, 1984. *Contributor to:* Numerous articles in professional journals. *Honours:* Faculty Summer Research Fellowship, 1967, 1970, 1976, 1979, Outstanding Teacher Award, 1970, Distinguished Professor, 1983, Miami University. *Memberships:* American Political Science Association; American Sociological Association; International Society of Political Psychology; International Studies Association; etc. *Address:* Dept of Political Science, Miami University, Oxford, OH 45056, USA.

REKOLA, Mirkka Elina, b. 26 June 1931, Tampere, Finland. Writer, Poet. *Education:* University of Helsinki, 1954–57. *Publications:* Vedessa Palaa, 1954; Tunnit, 1957; Syksy Muuttaa Linnut, 1961; Ilo ja Epasymmetria, 1965; Anna Paivan Oila Kaikki, 1968; Muistikirja, 1969; Mina Rakastan Sinua, Mina Sanon Sen Kaikille, 1972; Fuulen Viime Vuosi, 1974; Kohtaamispaikka Vuosi, 1977; Maailmat Lumen Vesistoissa, 1978; Runot, 1954, 1978, 1979; Kuutamourakka, 1981; Puun Syleilemaila, 1983; Silmarkantama, 1984. *Contributions to:* Parnasso, and Suomalainen Suomi. *Honours:* Finnish State Awards for Writers, 1965, 1968, 1972, 1982; Prize Eino Leino, 1979. *Membership:* Society of Finnish Writers. *Literary Agent:* Werner Soderstrom Oy. *Address:* Huvilakatu 22 A 10, 00150 Helsinki 15, Finland.

REMSBERG, Bonnie Kohn, b. 1 Apr. 1937, Cleveland, Ohio, USA. Journalist. 1 son, 1 daughter. *Education:* BS, Speech, Northwestern University. *Publications:* Radio and TV Spot Announcements for Family Planning, 1978; The Stress-Proof Child, A Loving Parent's Guide, 1985. *Contributions to:* Readers Digest; Family Circle; Ladies Home Journal; Woman's Day; Seventeen; Redbook; Success; New York Times Magazine; Good Housekeeping; etc. *Honours:* Sidney Hillman Award, 1968; Penney-Missouri Award, 1974; American Society of Journalists and Authors Outstanding Magazine Article of the Year, 1984. *Membership:* American Society of Journalists and Authors, Board of Directors, Midwest Representative. *Address:* 1521 Kirk St, Evanston, IL 60202, USA.

RENAUD, Bernadette, (Marie Elise), b. 18 Apr. 1945, Quebec, Canada. Writer; Scriptwriter for television films. *Education:* Diploma for elementary teaching. *Publications:* Emilie La Baignoire A Pattes, 1976; Le Chat de L'Oratoire, 1978 (English version, The Cat in the Cathedral, 1983, Braille 1984); La Revolte de la Courtepointe, 1979, Braille 1983; La Maison Tete de Pioche, 1979; La Depression de L'Ordinateur, 1981 (English version, The Computer Revolts, 1984); La Grande Question de Tomatelle, 1982, Comment on Fait un Livre?, 1983; 21 albums for young children; 12 scripts for children's television; 1 full length film, Bach Et Bottine, 1986. *Honours:* Canadian Council of Arts Award, 1976; Alvine Belisle's Award, 1977. *Memberships:* Board member, Communications-Jeunesse, 1970–82 and 1985–; Board 1982–85, Societe de Gestion des Droits d'Auteurs; Union des Ecrivains Quebecois. *Address:* PO Box 1103, Contrecoeur, Quebec, JOL ICO, Canada.

RENAUD, (Ernest) Jacques, b. 10 Nov. 1943, Montreal, Canada. Writer, Screenwriter. 2 sons, 1 daughter. *Education:* High School Degree, 1960. *Appointments:* Teacher, Creative Writing Workshop, Quebec University, Montreal, 1980–83. *Publications:* Electrodes, 1962; Le Cassé, 1964; Clandestines, 1980; La Colombe et la brisure Eternite, 1979; La Race Orange (SF Feature Screenplay), 1985; etc. *Contributor to:* Le Devoir; Jonathan; Radio-Canada; Forces; Perspectives; Liberte; La Barre du Jour; Moebius, etc. *Memberships:* Quebec Writer's Union. *Address:* 3909 Saint-Hubert, Montreal, Quebec, H2L 4A6, Canada.

RENDELL, Joan, b. Launceston, Cornwall, England. Author; Lecturer. *Publications:* Collecting Matchbox Labels, 1963; Flower Arrangement with a Marine Theme, 1967; Matchbox Labels, 1968; Collecting Natural Objects, 1972; Collecting Out of Doors, 1976; Your Book of Corn Dollies, 1976; Country Crafts, 1977; Along the Bude Canal, 1979; Lundy Island, 1979; Hawker Country, 1980; Gateway to Cornwall, 1981; Cornish Churches, 1982; The Match, The Box and the Label, 1983; Your Book of Pressed and Dried Flowers, 1978; North Cornwall in the Old Days, 1983; Around and About Bude and Stretton, 1985. *Contributions to:* Flora; Cornish Life; Devon Life; Somerset and Avon Life; This England; Country Life; The Field; Manx Life; Popular Gardening and others. *Honours:* MBE, 1958; Queen's Silver Jubilee Medal, 1977; Bard of the Cornish

Gorseth, 1980. *Literary Agent:* Dieter Klein, London. *Address:* Tremarsh, Launceston, Conrwall, England.

REPLANSKY, Naomi, b. 23 May 1918, Bronx, New York, USA. Poet. *Education:* BA, University of California at Los Angeles. *Literary Appointments:* Poet-in-Residence, Pitzer College, Claremont, California, 1981. *Publications:* Ring Song, 1952. *Contributions to:* Various magazines including, Poetry; The Nation; Missouri Review; Feminist Studies; Frank; various anthologies including, No More Masks; Geography of Poets; Bread and Roses. *Honours:* nominated for National Book Award for Poetry, 1952; Fellow, Djerassi Foundation, Woodside, California, 1984. *Memberships:* PEN American Center; Poetry Society of America. *Address:* 146 West 76th St, New York, NY 10023, USA.

RESTIVO, Sal, b. 22 Sep. 1940, Brooklyn, New York, USA. Professor of Sociology and Science/Technology Studies. *Education:* BA, Honours, City College of New York, New York, 1965; MA, 1966, PhD with Distinction, 1971, Michigan State University. *Literary Appointments:* Instructor, Michigan State University, 1967–70. Assistant Professor: Wellesely College, 1970–74; University of Hartford, Connecticut, 1972–74. Assistant to Full Professor, Rensselaer Polytechnic Institute, Troy, New York, 1974–. *Publications:* Comparative Studies in Science and Society, Co-Editor and Contributor, 1974; The Social Relations of Physics, Mysticism and Mathematics, 1983. *Contributions to:* Social Studies of Science; Science, Technology and Human Values; Sociological Quarterly; The Centennial Review; Social Science Information. Book Chapters in: Science Observed, 1983; Sociological Theory, 1983; and other books. *Honours:* National Science Foundation Award, 1966, 1968–70; Phi Kappa Phi, 1967; US Office of Education Grant, 1975–76; National Endowment for the Humanities Fellowship, 1985–86. *Memberships:* Council member, Society for Social Studies of Science, 1983–85. *Address:* Department of Science and Technology Studies, Rensselaer Polytechnic Institute, Troy, NY 12181, USA.

REUPKE, Michael, b. 20 Nov, 1936, Potsdam, Germany. Journalist. m. Helen Elizabeth Restrick, 14 Sep. 1963, London, 1 son, 2 daughters. *Education:* MA, Cambridge; Diploma in European Studies, College of Europe, Bruges. *Literary Appointments:* Editor-in-Chief, Reuters, 1978–. *Address:* c/o Reuters Limited, 85 Fleet Street, London EC4P 4AJ, England.

REVELL, John Robert Stephen, b. 15 Apr. 1920, Tunbridge Wells, Kent, England. Retired University Professor of Economics. m. Patricia Hiatt, 23 Feb. 1946, Liverpool, 1 son, 2 daughters. *Education:* BSc, London School of Economics, 1950; MA, University of Cambridge, 1960. *Publications:* The Wealth of Nation, 1967; The British Financial System, 1973; Solvency and Regulation of Banks, 1975; Costs and Margins in Banking, 1980; A Study of the Spanish Banking System, 1980; Banking and Electronic Fund Transfers, 1983. *Contributions to:* Various economic and banking journals of about 50 articles. *Address:* 12 Rustat Road, Cambridge CB1 3QT, England.

REWALD, John b. 12 May, 1912, Berlin, Germany. Writer; Distinguished Professor Emeritus. *Education:* Docteur es-lettres, University of Paris, France, 1936. *Publications include:* Paul Cezanne, Letters, Editor, 1941, 76; Georges Seurat, 1943, 46; The History of Impressionism, 1946, 4th edition, 1973; Post-Impressionism – From Van Gogh to Gauguin, 1956. 3rd edition, 1982; Camille Pissarro, 1963; Giacomo Manzu, 1967; Paul Cezanne, The Watercolours, 1984. *Contributions to:* Armour del Art; Art News, Art in America; Gazette des Beaux-Arts, Member of Committee of Direction. *Honours:* Gold Medal, Honorary Citizenship, Aix-en-Provence, France, 1984; Honorary Trustee, Museum of Modern Art, New York, USA. *Address:* 1075 Park Avenue, New York City, NY 10128, USA.

REY, Margret E, b. 16 May 1906, Hamburg, Federal Republic of Germany. Writer. m. Hans Augusto Rey, Sep. 1935. *Education:* Art School, Hamburg. *Publications:* Curious George; Curious George Takes a Job, Curious George Rides a Bike; Curious George Gets a Medal; Curious George Flies a Kite; Curious George Learns the Alphabet; Curious George Goes to the Hospital; Cecily G and the Nine Monkeys; Katy No-Pocket; Where's My Baby?; Anybody at Home?; Feed the Animals; See The Circus; The Stars – a New Way to See Them; Find the Costellations; Elizabite; Pretzel; Spotty; Billy's Picture; The Park Book. *Contributor to:* Numerous journals and magazines throughout the World. *Literary Agent:* A P Watts Limited, London, England. *Address:* 14 Hilliard St, Cambridge, MA 02138, USA.

REY, Michael Stephen, b. 23 Mar. 1946, Nottingham, England. Writer. m. Laurie Jane Kanester, 1 July 1982, Victoria, 1 son (former marriage). *Education:* Notre Dame University; University of Calgary; BA, History, 1970; BEd First Class Honours, 1974; Postgraduate Work Experimental Psychology, University of Victoria, 1979; Post-Graduate Fellowship in Educational Foundations. *Publications:* Clowns (one act play), 1981, Photo-illustrated Edition, 1981; Talisman (poetry), 1983; Awaiting publication: The Butterfly (novel); Invisible Footprints (Haiku poetry and Sumi-e Sketches); Sixty Percent Chance of Rain (novel); If All the World's A Stage...? (three-act play); Victims (three-act play); Amateur Standing (Poetry Collection). *Honours:* Play, Clowns, nominated for Governor General's Award, 1981 and Canadian Literary Award, 1981; Novel, Indian Roulette, written for Pulp Press Annual Three-Day Novel Competition. *Membership:* Playwrights Canada. *Literary Agent:* Rajab Breibish. *Address:* 1585 West Shawnigan Lake Road, RR1, Shawnigan Lake, British Columbia, V0R 2W0, Canada.

REYES, Carlos, b. 2 June 1935. Marshfield, Missouri, USA. Poet. m. (1) Barbara Hollingsworth, Portland, Oregon, 1958 (2) Karen Stoner, 1978; 1 son 3 daughters. *Education:* BA, University of Oregon, 1961; MA, 1965, ABD, 1965, University of Arizona. *Literary Appointments:* Member, Governor's Advisory Committee on the Arts in Oregon, 1974–75; Poet, City of Portland, 1976; Board Member, Portland Poetry Festival, 1980–81, 1983–84. *Major Publications:* Poetry: The Prisoner, 1973; The Shingle Weaver's Journal, 1980; At Doolin Quay, 1982; Nightmarks, forthcoming. *Contributor to:* Antioch Review; Chealsea; Porch; Minessota Review; Poetry Review; Poet Lore; Poetry Now; and others. *Honours:* National Endowment for the Arts Grant, 1970; Oregon Arts Commission Travel Grant to Ireland, 1982; Fellowship to YADDO, 1984. *Address:* 2754 SE 27th Street, Portland, OR 97202, USA.

REYNOLDS, Barrie Gordon Robert, b. 8 July 1932, London, England. University Professor, Dean of Arts. m. 27 Dec. 1953, Meopham, Kent, England, 1 son, 1 daughter. *Education:* BA, Hons, Anthropology and Archaeology, 1954, MA, Anthropology, 1958, Cambridge University; AMA Diploma of Museums Association, London 1961; MSc, Anthropology, Cambridge University, 1963; D Phil, Anthropology, Oxford University, 1968. *Publications:* Magic, Divination and Witchcraft Among the Barotse of Northern Rhodesia, 1963; Material Culture of the Peoples of Gwembe Valley, 1968; Material Anthropology: Contemporary Approaches to Material Culture, (co-editor with Margaret Stott) 1986. *Contributor to:* Various professional journals. *Honours:* Fellow, Museums Association, 1967; Fellow, Museums Association of Australia, 1984. *Address:* James Cook University of North Queensland, Townsville 4811, Queensland, Australia.

REYNOLDS, Bonnie Lea, b. 5 Aug. 1943, Erie, Pennsylvania, USA. Ad Compositor. *Education:* University of Arkansas, Fayetteville, 1964, 65, 67; Arkansas Technical University, Russellville, 1967, 68. *Literary Appointments:* Co-Editor, Spindrift Words; Anthology, annual, 1979; Editor, Where Have They

Gone?, anthology, sponsored by Garland County Animal Welfare Association, 1984; Editor, Poetry Column, Reflections, in LaVille Newspaper; Hot Springs Village, Arkansas, 1982–85; Editor, newsletter of Fairdale Baptist Church, Hot Springs, 1985–; Editor, newsletter of Poets Roundtable of Arkansas, 1981–82; 1984–. *Publications:* A Touch of Wonder, (poetry anthology), 1976; Hurry Dawn, (poetry anthology), 1986. *Contributor to:* Voices International; Christian Poetry Journal; Country Poet; Mountain View Digest; Newspaper poetry columns in Arkansas and anthologies including: Listen to the Valley, 1976; Bible Based Poetry by Arkansas Poets, 1979; Valley of the Water of Life, 1981; Poetry of Love, Past and Present, 1982; The American Muse, a Treasury of Lyric Poetry, 1984; Poems by Poets Roundtable of Arkansas. *Honours:* Arkansas Award of Merit, presented for outstanding service in encouraging poets in the art, 1985; various 1st, 2nd and 3rd prizes and honorable mentions on local, state and national levels. *Memberships include:* Poets Roundtable of Arkansas, 3rd Vice-President, 1985–87; Roundtable Poets of Hot Springs; Founder, Hot Springs Chapter, Arkansas Authors, Composers and Artists Society, etc. *Address:* 107 Euclid, Hot Springs, AR 71901, USA.

REYNOLDS, Brian James, b. 22 Apr. 1938, London, England. Financial Journalist. *Contributions to:* Provincial newspapers, UK and Eire; Most leading family and consumer magazines; various financial publications; currently writing for Express Money, Daily Express, London. *Address:* Aikten House, 121 Fleet Street, London EC4, England.

REYNOLDS, Ernest Randolph, b. 13 Sep. 1910, Northampton, England. Lecturer, Writer. *Education:* BA, London University, 1930; Cambridge Diploma in Education, 1931; PhD, Cambridge University, 1934. *Publications:* Early Victorian Drama, 1936; Mephistopheles and the Golden Apples, 1943; Modern English Drama, 1949; Collecting Victorian Porcelain, 1966; The Plain Man's Guide to Antiques, 1963; The Plain Man's Guide to Opera, 1964; Northamptonshire Treasures, 1972; Northampton Repertory Theatre, 1976; 5 Portuguese plays, Lisbon, 1940's; The Three Musketeers, Royal Theatre, Northampton (play); Queens of England, Norwegian Television, Oslo, (play); Candlemas Night, BBC Radio 3. *Contributions to:* The Monthly Musical Record; Northampton Chronicle and Echo; Northampton Independent. *Honours:* BA 1st Class honours English. *Literary Agent:* Curtis Brown, London. *Address:* 43 Wantage Road, Abington Park, Northampton, England.

REYNOLDS, Graham, b. 10 Jan. 1914, Highgate, London, England. Writer; Art Historian. *Education:* BA Honours, Queens College, Cambridge University. *Publications:* Nicholas Hilliard and Isaac Oliver, 1947, 71; English Portrait Miniatures, 1952; Painters of the Victorian Scene, 1953; Catalogue of the Constable Collection, Victoria and Albert Museum, 1960, revised, 1973; Constable, The Natural Painter, 1965; Victorian Painting, 1966; Turner, 1969; Concise History of Watercolour Painting, 1972; Catalogue of Portrait Miniatures, Wallace Colection, 1980; The Later Paintings and Drawings of John Constable, 2 volumes, 1984. *Contributions to:* Burlington Magazine; Apollo; New Departures; Palindromes and Anagrams, anthology; H W Bergerson, Editor, 1973. *Literary Agent:* A M Heath & Company Limited. *Address:* The Old Manse, Bradfield St George, Bury St Edmunds, Suffolk IP30 OAZ, England.

REYNOLDS, (Marjorie) Moira Davison, b. 22 June 1915, Bangor, Northern Ireland. Writer; Retired Biochemist. m. Orland B Reynolds, 4 Sep. 1954, Quincy, Massachusetts, USA, 1 son. *Education:* BA, Dalhousie University, Nova Scotia, Canada; MA, PhD, Boston University, Massachusetts, USA. *Publications:* Clinical Chemistry for the Small Hospital, 1969; Aim for a Job in the Medical Laboratory, 1972, 82; The Outstretched Hand/Modern Medical Discoveries, 1980; Margaret Sanger, 1981; Uncle Tom's Cabin and Mid-Nineteenth Century United States/Pen and Conscience, 1985. *Contributions to:* Great Lakes Gazette; Luthern Journal;

Maine Life; Midwest Roto; The Atlantic Advocate; South Jersey Living; Cadence. *Honours:* President's Award for Distinguished Citizenship, Northern Michigan University, 1979. *Address:* 225 East Michigan Street, Marquette, MI 49855, USA.

REYNOLDS, Sydney, b. 22 Jan. 1939, Richmond, Surrey, England. Journalist. m. Jennifer Knapp, 26 Jan. 1963, Kensington Register Office, London 4 sons. *Literary Appointments:* Night Editor, Associated Iliffe Press, 1962–65; Sub-Editor, Daily Telegraph, 1965–84; Art Editor, Sunday Telegraph, 1984–. *Contributor to:* The Artist; Daily Telegraph; The Lady; Scottish Field; American in Britain; Majesty; Music & Musicians; Art & Antiques; Universe; Woodworker; Melbourne Herald/Sun; Drum; Ulster Tatler; Almost every Country Magazine in Britain; Sunday Times of Ceylon. *Membership:* Press Club. *Address:* 113 Bridgewater Road, Berkhamsted, Hertfordshire, England.

RHOADS, Jonathan Evans, b. 9 May 1907, Philadelphia, Pennsylvania, USA. Surgeon. m. Teresa Folin, 4 July 1936, Cambridge, Massachusetts, 5 sons, 1 daughter. *Education:* BA, Haverford College, 1928; MD, Johns Hopkins University, 1932; D.Med.Sc., University of Pennsylvania, 1940. *Literary Appointments:* Editorial Board, Annals of Surgery, 1947, Chairman 1971–73; Editorial Board, Journal of Surgical Research, 1960–71; Editor, Cancer, 1972–; Editorial Committee, Transactions and Studies of the College of Physicians of Philadelphia, 1979–. *Publications:* Surgery: Principles and Practice, 1957, 4th edition 1970; The Chemistry of Trauma, (with J M Howard), 1963; The Impact of the Natural Sciences upon Natural Selection, in Trends in Modern American Society, 1962. *Contributor to:* American Journals Medical Science; Surgery; Journal of the American Dietetic Association; New Physician; Journal of the Royal College of Surgeons, Edinburgh; Laryngoscope; Journal of Medical Ethics; many other professional journals. *Honours:* Phi Beta Kappa; Alpha Omega Alpha; Sigma Xi; DSc, Swarthmore College, 1969; DSc, Hahnemann University, 1978; LLD University of Pennsylvania, 1960; DSc, Haverford College, 1962; DSc, Duke University, 1979; D Litt, Thomas Jefferson University, 1979; DSc, Georgetown University, 1981. *Membership:* Philomathian Society. *Address:* 131 W Walnut Lane, Philadelphia, PA 19144, USA.

RHODAS, Virginia, b. Rhodes, Greece. Free Lance Journalist; Writer. *Education:* Journalism, Human and Public relations, East and West Philosophy, Argentina and Europe. *Literary Appointments:* Journalist, Newspaper corrector, Secretary of Redaction, several magazines and journals; Director, International Poetry Letter, magazines and journals; Director, International Poetry Letter Will Come a Day... and other poems, 1968; Brother Century XXI, Open Letter to Humanity, Listen to Me, Humanity, 1985; From the Greece's Nucleous...To Your Heart; 6 theatre plays, short stories, essays, children's stories. *Contributions:* Work translated into English, Italian, Portuguese, Arabian, Hebrew, Armenian, Korean, Hindi and several Indian dialects and published in many magazines and journals, Latin America, North American, Canada, Australia, Europe and Asia. *Honours:* Poetry and Essay, Orthodox Church, Argentina, 1968; World Poetry Society, 1975; Academy of Arts and Culture, 1981; Doctor Honoris Causa in Literature, World University, USA, 1984. *Memberships:* Youth Women Christian Association; Christian Committee for World Prayer; Argentine Society for Writers; Latin American Regent, World Poetry International Society. *Literary Agent:* International Poetry Letter. *Address:* Rivadavia 2284 PB-J, 1034 Buenos Aires, Argentina.

RHODES, Anthony, b. 24 Sep. 1916, Plymouth, Devon, England. Writer. m. Rosaleen Forbes, 9 Apr. 1956, Geneva, Switzerland. *Education:* Rugby; Royal Military Academy, Woolwich; MA, Trinity College, University of Cambridge, England; Licence ès Lettres, University of Geneva, Switzerland. *Major Publications:* Sword of Bone, 1942; The Uniform, 1949; A Sabine

Journey, 1952; A Ball in Venice, 1953; The General's Summer-House, 1954; The Dalmation Coast, 1955; Where the Turk Trod, 1956; The Poet as Superman: A Life of Gabriele D'Annunzio, 1959; The Prophet's Carpet, 1969; Propaganda in the Second World War, 1976; Rise & Fall of Louis Renault, 1966; The Vatican in the Age of the Dictator, 1922–45, 1973; Princes of the Grape, 1970; Art Treasures of Eastern Europe, 1971; The Vatican in the Age of the Liberal Democracies, 1983; 15 book-length translations from French, Italian and German. *Contributor to:* Encounter; Sunday Telegraph; and others. *Honour:* Cavaliere Commendatore del'Ordine di San Gregorio Magno (Papal Title). *Memberships:* Society of Authors; PEN. *Literary Agent:* Anthony Sheil. *Address:* 46 Fitzjames Avenue, London W14, England.

RHODES, Philip, b. 2 May 1922, Sheffield, England. Postgraduate Dean of Medicine. m. Mary Elizabeth Worley, 26 Oct. 1946, Barrowden, England, 3 sons, 2 daughters. *Education:* Clare College, Cambridge and St Thomas Hospital, London, MA, MB, B Chir (Cantab), FRCS (Eng), FRCOG, FRACMA, *Publications:* Fluid Balance in Obstetrics, 1960; Preparing for your Baby, 1961; Expecting a Baby, 1967; Woman: A Biological Study, 1969; Reproductive Physiology, 1969; The Value of Medicine, 1977; Dr John Leake's Hospital, 1978; Letters to a Young Doctor, 1983; An outline History of Medicine, 1985. *Contributions to:* Lancet; British Medical Journal; Practitioner; British Journal of Obstetrics and Gynaecology. *Honour:* Prize of the Bronte Society, 1972. *Membership:* Committee Member, Medical Writers' Group, Society of Authors. *Address:* Fairford House, Lyndhurst Road, Brockenhurst, Hants SO4 7RH, England.

RIASANOVSKY, Nicholas Valentine, b. 21 Dec. 1923, Harbin, China. Historian. *Education:* BA, University of Oregon, USA, AM, Harvard University; DPhil, Oxford University, England. *Publications:* Russia and the West in the Teaching of the Slavophiles: A Study of Romantic Ideology, 1952; Nicholas I and Official Nationality in Russia, 1825–1855, 1959; A History of Russia, 4th edition; California Slavic Studies, 1960, 2nd edition 1979; The Teaching of Charles Fourier, 1969; A Parting of Ways: Government and the Educated Public in Russia, 1801–1855, 1976; The Image of Peter the Great in Russian History and Thought, 1985. *Contributions to:* 24 scholarly periodicals and encyclopaedias; Russian Review; American Oxonian; American Slavic and East European Review; Russian Thought and Politics; and others. *Honours:* Various Fellowships. *Address:* Department of History, University of California, Berkeley, CA 94720, USA.

RICARD, André, b. 18 Oct. 1938, Quebec, Canada. Writer. m. Mary Eleanor Brennan, 18 May, 1972, Quebec, 1 son. *Education:* Licence degree on Arts, Laval University; Conservatory of Dramatic Art, Quebec. *Translations:* Absurd Person Singular by Alan Ayckbourn, 1980; The Crucible by Arthur Miller, 1983. *Authorships:* La Vie exemplaire d'Alcide Ier, le pharamineaux et de sa proche descendance, 1973; La Gloire des Filles a Magloire, 1975; Le Casino Voleur, 1878; La Tir a blanc, 1983; La longue Marche dans les Avents, 1984. *Contributions to:* Les Ecrits du Canada francais; Liberte; Le Devoir. *Honours:* Award for short piece, 1976. *Memberships:* Board of Directors: Quebec Writers Union; Trident Theatre. Society of Authors, Researchers, Documentalists and Composers, Montreal; Experimental Centre for Dramatic Authors, Montreal. *Address:* 841 avenue de Bienville, Quebec, Canada G1S 3B9.

RICCHIUTI, Paul B(urton), b. 4 July 1925, Redford Township, Michigan, USA. Writer. *Education:* Andrews University, 1949–52; Loma Linda University, 1953. *Literary Appointments:* Layout and Design Artists, Pacific Press Publishing Association, Nampa, Idaho, 1955–. *Publications:* For children: I Found a Feather, 1967; Whose House Is It?, 1967; Up in the Air, 1967; When You Open Your Bible, 1967; Jeff, 1973; Amy,

1975; Five Little Gifts, 1975; Let's Play Make Believe, 1975; My Very Best Friend, 1975; Elijah Jeremiah Phillip's Great Journey, 1975; Yankee Dan, 1976; General Lee, 1978; Mandy, 1978; Mike, 1978; Jimmy and the Great Balloon, 1978, Ellen (adult biography of Ellen G White), 1977. *Contributions to:* Work represented in anthologies including, The Family Album, 1975 and 1976. Contributor of articles, stories and poems to magazines including: Signs of the Times; Our Little Friend; Primary Treasurer; These Times; Adventist Review, and to newspapers. *Address:* 5702 E Powerline, Nampa, ID 83651, USA.

RICE, James William Junior, b. 10 Feb. 1934, Coleman County, Texas, USA. Illustrator; Author; Professor of Art. m. Martha Eulene Oustad, 4 June 1955, Brownwood, Texas, 3 sons, 2 daughters. *Education:* MFA, Stephen F Austin State University; MEd, Howard Payore University; BFA, University of Texas. *Publications:* Gaston the Alligator, 1974; Lyn and the Fuzzy, 1975; Cajun Alphabet, 1975; Prairie Christmas, 1976; Cowboy Alphabet, 1976; Gaston Goes to Mardi Gras, 1976; Gaston Goes to Texas, 1977; Gaston Lays an Offshore Pipeline, 1978; Gaston Drills an Offshore Oilwell, 1979; Nashville 98; Gaston Goesto Nashville, 1985; Texas Night Before Christmas, 1986; Texas Honky Tonk Music, 1986. Illustrator: Cajun Night Before Christmas, 1973; Cajun Columbus, 1974; Hillbilly Night Before Christmas, 1982. *Honours:* Award for Excellence in Design, for Gaston Goes to Texas, Printing Industries of America, 1979. *Literary Agent:* Andrea Brown. *Address:* Pelican Publishing Company, 1101 Monroe Street, Gretna, LA 70053, USA.

RICH, Elaine Sommers, b. 8 Feb. 1926, Plevna, Indiana, USA. Writer. m. Dr Ronald L Rich, 14 June 1953, 3 sons, 1 daughter. *Education:* BA, Goshen College, 1947; MA, Michigan State University, 1950. *Appointments:* Contributing Editor, Japan Christian Quarterly, Tokyo, Japan, 1970's. *Publications:* Breaking Bread Together, 1958; Hannah Elizabeth, 1964; Tomorrow, Tomorrow, Tomorrow, 1966; Am I This Countryside, 1980; Mennonite Women: A Story of God's Faithfulness 1683–1983, 1983. *Contributor to:* Fortnightly Column, Thinking With, Mennonite Weekly Review; Book Reviews; Provident Book Finder. *Membership:* Bluffton Creative Writers. *Address:* 112 S Spring St, Bluffton, OH 45817, USA.

RICHARDS, Alun, b. 27 Oct. 1929, Pontypridd, Wales. Author. m. Helen Howden, 8 July 1956, 3 sons, 1 daughter. *Education:* Diploma in Social Science and Education, University of Wales. *Literary Appointments:* Editor, Penguin Book of Welsh Short Stories and Penguin Book of Sea Stories, volumes 1-11. *Publications:* The Elephant You Gave Me, 1963; The Home Patch, 1966; A Woman of Experience, 1969; Home to An Empty House, 1974; Ennal's Point, 1979; Dai Country, 1979; The Former Miss Merthyr Tydfil and other stories, 1980; Barque Whisper, 1982. *Contributor to:* Guardian; Planet; Western Mail. *Honours:* Arts Council Prize for Collected Short Stories, 1974; Royal National Lifeboat Institution Public Relations Award, 1983.*Memberships:* Writers Guild of Great Britian. *Literary Agent:* Harvey Unwin and Stephen Durbridge Limited. *Address:* 326 Mumbles Road, Swansea SA3 5AA, Wales.

RICHARDS, Christine Louise, b. 11 Jan. 1910, Radnor, Pennsylvania, USA. Artist; Composer; Pianist; Publisher. *Education:* Piano and Private Schools; Art School. *Publications:* The Blue Star Fairy Book of Stories for Children, 1950; The Blue Star Fairy Book of More Stories for Children, 1969; The Blue Star Fairy Book of New Stories for Children, 1980; Branches, 1983; Lyrics for Songs, 1950. *Honours:* 2 Silver Medals, IBC; 2 Gold Medals, Prize of Golden Centaur, Accademia Italia; Master of Painting, Accademia Italia; Honorary Silver Medal of Honor, and International Hall of Fame, American Biographical Institute. *Address:* Springslea, PO Box 188, Morris, NY 13808, USA.

RICHARDS, Denis, b. 1910, London, England. Writer. *Education:* BA, 1931, MA, Trinity Hall, Cambridge, 1935. *Publications:* Portal of Hungerford; Royal Air Force, 1939–45, (with H St G Saunders), 3 volumes; Modern Europe; Modern Britain (with J W Hunt); Britain Under the Tudors and Stuarts; Britain 1714–1851, (with Anthony Quick); The Modern Age, (with Evan Cruikshank); Offspring of the Vic; A History of Morley College; Britain and the Ancient World (with J A Bolton); Britain 1851–1945, (with Anthony Quick), 1967; Twentieth Century Britain, 1968; Medieval Britain, (with A E Ellis), 1973. *Contributor to:* various journals. *Honour:* Recipient, C P Robertson Membership Trophy, 1954 for Royal Air Force 1939–45. *Memberships include:* PEN; Arts Club; Society of Authors; Garrick Club. *Address:* 16 Broadlands Road, London N6, England.

RICHARDS, Ronald Charles William, b. 15 Apr. 1923, London, England. Writer; Journalist. *Publications:* The Great Brain Robbery, 1965; Gilt Edge, 1966; Talking Turkey, 1968; Betty, 1974; Stage Plays: All Basic Comforts, 1977; Wizz and Worm; Children's Books; The King and Queen, series; Mr Wizz; The Relay Race; Jerry and the Monsters; Smudger's Seaside Spectacular; 20 radio plays broadcast on BBC; TV: The Concert Party, (with Doris Richards). *Contributions:* Drama Critic, The Guardian; Plays and Players; Plays; Plays International; Feature Writer, The Guardian; Sunday Times Magazine; The Observer Magazine; Time Out; Daily Telegraph; Columnist, Western Morning News; Editor, Western Front Westward Look; BBC Radio 3; Western Morning News; BBC Radio research for BBC TV and radio 3. *Memberships:* Writers' Guild; (Chairman, West Country Branch, 1974–77); National Union of Journalists; Drama Panel, SW Arts Association. *Literary Agent:* Dawn Arnall Hope, Leresche and Sayel. *Address:* 6 South Street, Totnes, Devon, TQ9 5DZ, England.

RICHARDS, (Sir) James, b. 13 Aug. 1907, London, England. Editor; Journalist; Writer; Historian. *Education:* Diploma, Architectural Association School of Architecture, London, 1929; Associate, Royal Institute of British Architects, 1930. *Publications:* High Street, 1938; Introduction to Modern Architecture, 1940; The Castles on the Ground, 1946; The Functional Tradition, 1958; Editor, The Anti-Rationalists, 1973; Editor, Who's Who in Architecture, 1977; Eight Hundred Years of Finnish Architecture, 1978; Memoirs of an Unjust Fella, 1980; Goa, 1981; National Trust Book of English Architecture, 1981. *Contributor to:* Architectural Review; Architects Journal; Times; Times Literary Supplement; Listener; New Statesman; Country Life; Editor, Architectural Review, 1937–71; Architectural Correspondent, The Times, 1947–71. *Honours include:* CBE, 1959; Bicentenary Medal, Royal School of Architects, 1971; Knight, 1972; Honorary Fellow, American Institute of Architects, 1984; Commander, Order of the White Rose of Finland, 1985. *Agent:* Curtis Brown Limited. *Address:* 29 Fawcett Street, London SW10, England.

RICHARDS, William Leslie, b. 28 May 1916, Capel Isaac, Llandeilo, Wales. Retired Schoolmaster. *Education:* BA, MA, Diploma in Education, University of Wales. *Publications include:* Yr Etifeddion, 1956; Telyn Teilo, 1957; Llanw a Thrai, 1958; Cynffon o Wellt, 1960; Gwaith Dafydd Llwyd o Fathafarn, 1964; Dail yr Hydre, 1968; Adledd, 1973; Cymraeg Heddiw, Co-Author, 4 volumes, 1965–69; Y Cawr o Rydcymerau, Co-Editor, 1970; Cerddi'r Cyfnos, 1986. *Contributions to:* Various Welsh language journals. *Honours:* T E Ellis Essay Prize, 1939; Sir Ellis Griffith Memorial Prize, University of Wales, 1964–65; Honorary Druid, Gorsedd of Bards, 1971. *Membership:* Cymmrodorion Society. *Address:* Heulfryn, Thomas Street, Llandeilo, Dyfed SA19 6LB, Wales.

RICHARDSON, Alan, b. 4 Dec. 1923, England. University Reader in Psychology. m. Faith May Clayton, 22 Aug. 1953, Perth, Western Australia, 2 daughters. *Education:* BA, Hons, Diploma in Clinical Psychology,

University of Western Australia; PhD, London University. *Literary Appointments:* Assistant Lecturer in Psychology, Bedford College, University of London, 1953–56; Senior Lecturer in Psychology, 1957–69, Reader in Psychology, 1970–, University of Western Australia. *Publications:* Mental Imagery, 1969; Man in Society, 1974; British Immigrants and Australia, 1974; The Experimental Dimension of Psychology, 1984. *Contributions to:* Over 50 publications in Psychological Journals and Books. A Note on A Neil Lyons (1880–1940) in English Literature in Transition: 1880–1920, 1980. *Honours:* Carnegie Commonwealth Travel Grant, 1963; Visiting Fellowship, Australian National University, 1966; Foundation Fellow of the Australian Psychological Society, 1967; Deutscher Akademischer Austauschdienst Grant, 1978; Fellow of the Academy of the Social Sciences in Australia, 1981. *Address:* 75, Beatrice Road, Dalkeith 6009, Western Australia.

RICHARDSON, Dorothy, b. 8 Nov. 1922. Republic of Ireland. Writer of Children's Books. m. Bernard Allen Richardson, 10 Sep. 1960, Harpenden, Hertfordshire. *Publications:* The Secret Brownies, 1979; The Brownie Venturers, 1982; The Brownie Explorers, 1983; The Brownie Rescuers, 1984; The Brownie Entertainers, 1985. *Contributions to:* Brownie magazine; Girls' Annuals; D C Thomson's Children's publications. *Membership:* Society of Women Writers and Journalists. *Address:* 11 Hawthorne Court, Joel Street, Northwood, Middlesex HA6 1LR, England.

RICHARDSON, George Barclay, b. 19 Sep. 1924, London, England. Publisher. m. Isabel Alison Chalk, 2 sons. *Education:* BSc Mathematics and Physics, University of Aberdeen, Scotland, 1944; MA Philosophy, Politics and Economics, Corpus Christi College, Oxford, 1949. *Literary Appointments:* Fellow, St John's College, Oxford, 1951–; Secretary to the delegates and Chief Executive, Oxford University Press, 1974–. *Publications:* Information and Investment, 1960; Economic Theory, 1964. *Honours:* Commander of the British Empire, 1978. *Address:* Cutts End, Cumnor, Oxford OX2 9QH, England.

RICHARDSON, Ian Francis, b. 16 Oct. 1922, Dublin, Republic of Ireland. Journalist; Editor. m. Molly Van Loo, 1957, 2 sons, 1 daughter. *Education:* MA, Merton College, Oxford University. *Literary Appointments:* Member, Royal Commission on the Press, 1973–77; Financial Editor, Birmingham Post, 1955–. *Honours:* Wincott Award for Provincial Financial Journalist of the Year, 1972; Wincott National Award, shared, 1982. *Address:* 4 Granville Park, London SE13 7EA, England.

RICHARDSON, Midge Turk, b. 26 Mar. 1930, Los Angeles, California, USA. Editor. *Education:* BA, 1951, MA, 1956, Immaculate Heart College. *Publications:* The Buried Life, A Nun's Journey, 1971; UK, 1972; Gordon Parks, A Biography for Children, 1971. *Contributions to:* Glamour; Seventeen, Editor, 1979–. *Memberships:* Board of Directors, Girl Scouts Council of Greater New York; Board of Trustees, Timothy Dwight School, New York International House; River Club, New York; Fashion Group, New York. *Literary Agent:* Sterling Lord Agency. *Address:* 920 Park Avenue, New York City, NY 10028, USA.

RICHARDSON, Miles, b. 22 Jan. 1932, Palestine, Texas, USA. Professor, Anthropology. m. Valerie Thorn Woodger, 19 Dec. 1959, 2 sons, 1 daughter. *Education:* BS, Biology & History, Stephen F Austin University, Texas, 1957; PhD, Anthropology, Tulane University, Louisiana, 1965. *Publications include:* San Pedro, Columbia, 1970; Editor, The Human Mirror, 1974; Editor, Place: Experience & Symbol, 1984. *Contributions to:* Anthropologist: The Myth Teller, American Ethnologist, Volume II, 1975; The Southern, Review, fiction, 1984; Anthropology & Humanism Quarterly, 1984. *Honour:* 2nd Place, short story, Deep South Writers Conference, 1984. *Memberships:* Several anthropological associations including: American Anthropological Association; Society for Humanistic Anthropology; Southern Anthropolopical Society. Philological Association of Louisiana. *Address:* Department of Geography & Anthropology, Louisiana State University, Baton Rouge, LA 70803, USA.

RICHES, Brenda, b. 20 Jan. 1942, Jubbulpore, India. Editor; Writer. 1 son, 2 daughters. *Education:* MA, Cambridge University. *Literary Appointments:* Fiction Editor, 1980, Editor-in-Chief, 1983, Grain Literary Magazine. *Publications:* Dry Media, 1981. *Contributions to:* Stories and poems in a number of Canadian magazines including, Grain; The Capilano Review; Event; Prism International; also Canadian anthologies including, More Saskatchewan Gold; West of Fiction; Canadian Short Fiction Anthology. *Honours:* 1st Prize, Saskatchewan Writers Guild Poetry Contest, 1977; Grant from Saskatchewan Arts Board, 1977, 1981; Regina City Writers Grant, 1983; Grant from the Canadian Council, 1983. *Membership:* President, The Saskatchewan Writers' Guild, Council, 1983. *Membership:* President, The Saskatchewan Writers' Guild, 1979–80. *Address:* 2025 Edward Street, Regina, Saskatchewan, Canada S4T 4N3.

RICHLER, Mordecai, b. 27 Jan. 1931. Author. m. Florence Wood, 1960, 3 sons, 2 daughters. *Education:* Sir George Williams University, Montreal, Canada. *Literary Appointments:* Writer in Residence, Sir George Williams University, 1968–69; Visiting professor, English department, Carleton University, Ottawa, 1972–74; Editorial Board, Book of the Month Club, New York. *Publications:* Novels Include: The Acrobats, 1954; A Choice of Enemies, 1955; Son of a Smaller Hero, 1957; The Apprenticeship of Duddy Kravitz, 1959, 1972; The Incomparable Atuk, 1963; Cocksure, 1968; St Urbain's Horseman, 1971; Joshua Then and Now, 1980. Essays: Hunting Tigers Under Glass, 1969; Shovelling Trouble, 1973; The Street, autobiography, 1972. Childrens Books: Jacob Two-Two Meets the Booded Fang, 1975. Editor, The Best of Modern Humour, anthology, 1983. *Contributions to:* Encounter; Commentary; New York Review of Books, and others. *Honours:* Canada Council Senior Arts Fellowship, 1960; Guggenheim Fellowship, Creative writing, 1961; Governor-General's Award for Literature, 1969, 72; Paris Review Humour Prize, 1969; Film of The Apprenticeship of Duddy Kravitz received Golden Bear Award, Berlin Film Festival, 1974, Writers Guild of America Annual Award, 1974 and Academy Award nomination, 1974. *Address:* Apt 80C, 1321 Sherbrooke Street West, Montreal, Quebec, Canada H3G 1J4.

RICHMOND, Anthony Henry, b. 8 June 1925, Ilford, Essex, England. University Professor. m. 29 Mar 1952, 1 daughter. *Education:* BSc, Economics; MA; PhD; FRSC. *Literary Appointments:* Editor (Sociology) Pergamon Press, 1962–74; Editorial Boards of various academic journals. *Publications:* Colour Prejudice in Britain, 1954; 1971; The Colour Problem, 1955, 1961; Post-War Immigrants in Canada, 1967, 1970; Migration and Race Relations in an English City, 1973; Factors in the Adjustments of Immigrants and their Descendants, 1980. *Contributions to:* Various journals – more than 50 articles, reports and monographs. *Honours:* Elected Fellow of the Royal Society of Canada, 1980. *Membership:* International Union for the Scientific Study of Population. *Address:* Department of Sociology, York University, 4700 Keele Street, North York, Ontario, Canada M3J 1P3.

RICHMOND, Douglas, b. 21 Feb. 1946, Walla Walla, Washington, USA. University Professor. m. Belinda González Martinez, 29 Dec. 1979, Mexico City, 1 daughter. *Education:* BA, 1968, MA, 1971, PhD, 1976, University of Washington. *Literary Appointments:* Assistant Professor of History, 1976; Associate Professor of History, 1982. *Publications:* Co-editor, Essays on the Mexican Revolution: Revisionist Views of the Leaders, 1979; Venustiano Carranza's Nationalist Struggle, 1893–1920, 1983. *Contributions to:* Factional Political Strife in Coahuila, 1910–1920, in Hispanic American

Historical Review, 1980; Confrontation and Reconciliation; Mexicans and Spaniards During the Mexican Revolution, 1910–1920 in The Americas, 1984. *Memberships:* American Historical Association; Conference on Latin American History; Southwestern Council of Latin American Studies. *Address:* Department of History, Box 19529, University of Texas at Arlington, Arlington, TX 76019, USA.

RICHMOND, Roaldus Frederick, b. 19 Jan. 1910, Barton, Vermont, USA. Writer. m. Evelyn d'Este, 1931, West Glover, 1 son. *Education:* BA, University of Michigan, 1933. *Appointments:* State Editor; Assistant Director; Director, Vermont Writers Project, WPA Programme. *Publications:* Consetoga Cowboy, 1949; Maverick Heritage, 1951; Riders of Red Butte, 1951; Mojave Guns, 1952; Island Fortress, 1952; Death Rides the Dondrino, 1954; Montana Bad Man, 1957; Lash of Idaho, 1958; Wyoming Way, 1958; The Kansan, 1960; The Deputy, 1960; Forced Gigolos, 1960; The Wild Breed, 1961; Web of Evil, 1962; The Blazing Star, 1963; War in the Panhandle, 1979; The Lashtrow Series, 10 titles, 1979–82; An End to Summer, 1980; The Blaze of Autumn, 1980; Kelleway's Luck, 1981; El Paso del Norte, 1982. *Contributor to:* Published over 350 stories in national magazines including, Story; American Prefaces; Catholic World; Good Taste; Yankee; etc. *Honours:* Short Story, Thanks for Nothing, reprinted in O'Briens Best Short Stories, 1936; 1st Prize, story in College Life, 1953; 2nd Prize, national contest for WPA Writers, 1937. *Membership:* Charter Member, Western Writers of America, 1952. *Address:* 7 Fayette Street, Concord, NH 03301, USA.

RICHTER, Derek, b. 14 Jan. 1907, Bath, Avon, England. Medical Researcher. *Education:* BSc, MA, Oxford University, 1926–29; PhD, Munich University, Germany, 1932; MRCS; MRCP; PRCPsych, St Bartholomew's Hospital, London, England, 1943–45. *Publications:* Perspectives in Neuropsychiatry, 1950; Schizophrenia: Somatic Aspects, 1957; Metabolism of the Nervous System, 1957; Comparative Neurochemistry, 1964; Aspects of Learning and Memory, 1966; The Challenge of Violence, 1972; Schizophrenia Today, 1976; Addiction and Brain Damage, 1980; Women Scientists, 1982; Research in Mental Illness, 1984. *Contributions to:* Several scientific journals. *Honours:* Chapman Research Prize, Oxford University, 1933; Semmelweiss Medal, Budapest, Hungary, 1971. *Memberships:* Society of Authors; Past Secretary, Scientific Publications Council. *Address:* Deans Cottage, Walton-on-the-Hill, Tadworth, Surrey KT20 7TT, England.

RICHTER, Hans Peter, b. 28 Apr. 1925, Cologne, Germany. Professor. m. Elfriede Feldmann, 20 May 1952, Mainz, 1 son, 3 daughters. *Education:* Universities of Cologne, Bonn, Mainz, Tubingen; Prof Dr rer pol. *Publications include:* Karussell und Luftbailon (Uncle & His Merry-go-Round), 1958; Das Pferd Max (Hengist the Horse), 1959; Damals war es Friedrich (Friedrich), 1961, 25th edition 1985; Wir waren Dabei, 1962; Saint-Just, 1975; Die Zeit Der jungen Soldaten (The Time of the Young Soldiers), 1980; Wissenshcaft von der Wissenschaft, 1981. *Contributor to:* Numerous magazines and journals, radio & TV. *Honours:* Jugenbuchpreis, 1961, Auswahlliste, 1962; Cité Internationale des Arts, Paris, 1965–66; Mildred-Batchelder Book Award, 1971; Best Book, Japanese Library Association, 1984. *Address:* 58 Franz-Werfel-Str, D–6500 Mainz 1, Federal Republic of Germany.

RICHTER, Harvena, b. 13 Mar. 1919, Reading, Pennsylvania, USA. Writer; Teacher. *Education:* BA, University of New Mexico, 1934; MA, 1955, PhD, 1967, New York University. *Publications:* The Human Shore, (novel), 1959, 60; Virginia Woolf: The Inward Voyage, (criticism), 1970, 78; Editor: The Rawhide Knot & Other Stories, by Conrad Richter, 1978. *Contributor to:* Journals and newspapers etc. including: New Yorker; Atlantic; Saturday Evening Post; University publications.*Honours:* AAUW Fellowship, 1964–65; Writing Fellowships at Yaddp, MacDowell Colony and

Wurlitzer Foundation, 8 summers, 1962–75. *Memberships:* Authors' Guild; MLA; AAUW; Kappa Kappa Gamma. *Literary Agent:* Ray Lincoln, Philadelphia, USA. *Address:* 1932, Candelaria Road NW, Albuquerque, NM 87107, USA.

RICHTER, Melvin, b. 6 Apr. 1921, Revere, Massachusetts, USA. University Professor. m. Michaela Wenninger, 1976, 2 sons. *Education:* BA, Harvard College, 1943; PhD, Harvard University, 1953. *Publications include:* The Politics of Conscience, 1964; Essays in Theory & History, editor, 1970; The Political Theory of Montesquieu, 1977; Political Theory & Political Education, editor. *Honour:* Triennial Prize, Conference on British Studies, 1966. *Literary Agent:* Richard Balkin. *Address:* City University of New York Graduate School, 33 West 42nd Street, New York, NY 10036, USA.

RIDGWAY, Judith Anne, b. 10 Nov. 1939, Stalybridge, England. Writer. *Education:* BA, Class II Division I, Keele University, 1962. *Publications:* The Vegetarian Gourmet, 1979; Salad Days, 1979; Home Preserving, 1980; The Seafood Kitchen, 1980; The Colour Book of Chocolate Cookery, 1981; Mixer, Blender, Processor Cookery, 1981; The Breville Book of Toasted Sandwiches, 1982; 101 Fun Foods to Make, 1982; Waitrose Book of Pasta, Rice and Pulses, 1982; Home Cooking for Money, 1983; Booklets: Making the Most of Rice, 1983; Making the Most of Pasta, 1983; Making the Most of Potatoes, 1983; Making the Most of Bread, 1983; Making the Most of Eggs, 1983; Making the Most of Cheese, 1983; The Little Lemon Book, 1983; Barbecues, 1983; Cooking Round the World, 1983; Cooking With German Food, 1983; The Little Bean Book, 1983; Frying Tonight, 1984; Running Your Own Wine Bar, 1984; Sprouting Beans and Seeds, 1984; Man in the Kitchen, 1984; The Little Rice Book, 1984; Successful Media Relations, 1984; Running Your Own Catering Company, 1984; Festive Occasions, 1986; The Vegetable Year, 1985; Nuts and Cereals, 1985; Cooking Without Gluten, 1986. *Contributions to:* Woman's World, Cookery Editor; Woman and Home, Wine Columnist. *Memberships:* Society of Authors; Circle of Wine Writers. *Address:* 124 Queens Court, Queensway, London, W2 4QS, England.

RIDLER, Anne Barbara, b. 30 July 1912, Rugby, England. Poet; Editor. m. Vivian Ridler, 2 July 1938, Little Gaddesden, England, 2 sons. *Education:* Diploma in Journalism, King's College, London. *Publications:* Poetry: Poems, 1939; A Dream Observed, 1941; The Nine Bright Shiners, 1943; The Golden Bird, 1951; A Matter of Life and Death, 1959; Selected Poems, 1961; Some Time After, 1972. Plays: Cain, 1943; The Shaddow Factory: A Nativity Play, 1946; Henry Bly and Other Plays, 1950; The Trial of Thomas Cranmer, 1956; Who is My Neighbour?, 1963; The Jesse Tree, 1970; The King of the Golden River, 1975. Editor: A Little Book of Modern Verse, 1941; Best Ghost Stories, 1945; Supplement to Faber Book of Modern Verse, 1951; The Image of the City and Other Essays by Charles Williams, 1958; Shakespeare Criticism, 1935–60, 1963; Poems of James Thomson, 1963; Thomas Traherne, 1966; Edited Poems of George Darley, 1979. *Contributions to:* Chiefly poems to Delta; Seven; The Listener; The Times Literary Supplement; Purpose; Horizon; New Writing; The New Statesman; The Critical Quarterly; The Sunday Times; The New Yorker; The New York Times; Poetry (Chicago); Poetry (London). *Address:* 14 Stanley Road, Oxford, England.

RIDLEY, Jasper Godwin, b. 25 May 1920, West Hoathly, Sussex. Author. m. Vera Pollakova, London, 1 Oct. 1949, 2 sons, 1 daughter. *Education:* Sorbonne University, Paris; Magdalen College, Oxford. *Publications:* Nicholas Ridley, 1957; Law of Carriage of Goods, 1957; Thomas Cranmer, 1962; John Knox, 1968; Lord Palmerston, 1970; Mary Tudor, 1973; Garibaldi, 1974; The Roundheads, 1976; Napoleon III & Eugenie, 1979; History of England, 1981; The Statesman & the Fanatic, 1982; Henry VIII, 1984. *Contributions to books:* The Prime Ministers, Volume 2, 1975 (Viscount Palmerston); Garibaldi Generale della Libertà, Rome,

1982 (Le ripercussioni internazionali della spedizione di Garibaldi del 1860). *Honour:* James Tait Black Memorial Prize for non-fiction, 1971. *Memberships:* Fellow, Royal Society of Literature; Vice-President, English Section of International PEN; Society of Sussex Authors; Kent Writers. *Literary Agent:* Curtis Brown. *Address:* 6 Oakdale Road, Tunbridge Wells, Kent TN4 8DS, England.

RIDLEY, Matthew White, b. 7 Feb. 1958, Newcastle, England. Journalist. *Education:* BA, PhD, Oxford University. *Literary Appointments:* Science Correspondent, The Economist, 1983–; Science and Technology Editor, The Economist, 1984–. *Contributions to:* The Economist; New Scientist. *Honour:* Glaxo Science Writers Award, 1983. *Address:* 10 Clifton Gardens, London W9, England.

RIDOUT, Ronald, b. 23 July 1916, Farnham, Surrey, England. Author. m. 10 Feb. 1940, Woking, 1 son, 2 daughters. *Education:* BA, Honours, Oxon. *Publications:* 482 titles, 1st English Today, 1948; most recent: Ronald Ridout's Children's Dictionary, 1983; Now I Can Write, 1984; Now I Can Spell, 1984; Ronald Ridout's English A-Z, 1985; Ronald Ridout's Puzzle Boxes, 1985. *Membership:* Society of Authors, 1st Chairman, Educational Writers Section. *Literary Agent:* A P Watt & Co. *Address:* St Lucia, West Indies.

RIDPATH, Ian, b. 1 May 1947, Ilford, Essex, England. Writer; Broadcaster. *Publications:* Worlds Beyond, 1975; Encyclopedia of Astronomy and Space, Editor, 1976; Messages From The Stars, 1978; Stars and Planets, 1978; Young Astronomer's Handbook, 1981; Hamlyn Encyclopedia of Space, 1981; Life Off Earth, 1983; Collins Guide to Stars and Planets, 1984; Gem Guide to the Night Sky, 1985; Secrets of the Sky, 1985; A Comet Called Halley, 1985. *Address:* 48 Otho Court, Brentford Dock, Brentford, Middlesex TW8 8PY, England.

RIEBS, Gunnar Ilse Gustav, b. 10 Apr. 1960, Louvain, Belgium. Teacher. *Education:* Degree, Dutch, History & Religion, Heilig Hartinstituut, Heverlee, 1983. *Literary Appointments:* Lectures in Belgium, 1975–, Netherlands, 1981–, Austria 1982–, Switzerland 1984–. Lecturer in poetry at exhibitions. *Publications:* Hulde ann componist Jan De Middeleer, 1978; Zie-zo Tremelo, 1983; De leidende stilte – de lijdende stilte, 1984. *Contributions to:* De Nieuwe Echo, 1983–. *Honours:* Cruz al Mérito Belgo-Hispanica, 1984; Decoration, Minister of Culture, 1984; Knight, Order of Jerusalem, 1985. *Memberships:* SABAM: Vereniging van Vlaamse letterkundigen. *Literary Agent:* Jos Braes, Stationsstrat 10, 3140 Ramsel-Herselt. *Address:* Kardinaal Mercierstraat 27, 3220 Aarschot, Belgium.

RIELY, John, b. 27 Aug. 1945, Philadelphia, Pennsylvania, USA. University Professor. m. Elizabeth Dumesnil Gawthrop, 23 Aug. 1969, West Chester, Pennsylvania, 2 sons. *Education:* AB English cum laude, Harvard College, 1967; Diploma, Exeter College, Oxford University, 1967; MA 1968; PhD 1971, University of Pennsylvania. *Literary Appointments:* Assistant Research Editor, 1971–72, Associate Research Editor, 1973–79, Yale Edition of Horace Walpole's Correspondence; Assistant Professor of English, Columbia University, 1979–80; Visiting Assistant Professor of English, University of Minnesota, 1980–81; Assistant Professor of English, 1981–85, Associate Professor 1985–, Boston University. *Publications:* The Age of Horace Walpole in Caricature, 1973; Rowlandson Drawings from the Paul Mellon Collection, 1977; Horace Walpole's miscellaneous Correspondence, 3 volumes, 1980; English Caricature, 1620 to the Present, (exhibition organized with Richard Godfrey), 1984. *Contributions to:* History Today; Eighteenth-Century Studies; Festschriften. *Honours:* Nominated for Louis Gottschalk Prize, American Society for Eighteenth-Century Studies, 1980. *Memberships:* Modern Language Association; American Society for 18th-Century Studies; Modern Humanities Research Association; The Johnsonians, USA; Walpole Society, UK; College Art

Association; American Association of University Professors. *Address:* Department of English, Boston University, 236 Bay State Road, Boston, MA 02215, USA.

RIEWALD, Jacobus Gerhardus, b. 15 Aug. 1910, Doesburg (Gld.), Netherlands. Professor of English & American Literature, University of Groningen. *Education:* Degrees in English, French & German; Graduate Study, University of Michigan, USA, 1951; Diploma, US Office of Education, 1951; PhD, English Literature, University of Nijmegen, Netherlands, 1953. *Publications:* Sir Max Beerbohm, 1953; A Book of English & American Literature (with L Grooten & T Zwartkruis), 4 volumes, 1953–55; Word Study, 4 volumes, 1957–71; Max in Verse, 1963; Reynier Jansen of Philadelphia, 1970; Nieuw Engels Woordenboek, 1974; The Surprise of Excellence, 1974; Perspectives in British and American Literature, (with L Grooten), 1974; Beerbohm's Literary Caricatures, 1977; The Critical Reception of American Literature in the Netherlands, (with J Bakker), 1980. *Contributor to:* Professional journals and encyclopedias including: De Katholieke Encyclopaedie, (Editor, English & American Literature), 25 volumes, 1949–55. *Memberships:* Official, Professional and Literary organisations including Dutch MLA; MLA of America; Maatschappij der Nederlandse Letterkunde. *Literary Agent:* Author Aid Associates, New York City. *Address:* Froonacker, Westerse Drift 35, 9752 LB Haren (Gr), Netherlands.

RIFFEL, Herman H, b. 25 July 1916, Saskatchewan, Canada. Minister. m. Lillie Hoover, 17 Oct. 1942, Detroit, 2 sons, 1 daughter. *Education:* AB, Wheaton College, USA; C G Jung Institute, Zurich, Switzerland; Multnomah School of the Bible, Portland, USA. *Publications:* Christian Maturity and the Spirit's Power, 1974; Voice of God, 1978; Your Dreams: God's Neglected Gift, 1981. *Address:* 6619 Flamingo Road, Melbourne, FL 32904, USA.

RIFKIN, Shephard, b. 14 Sep. 1918, New York City, USA. Writer. *Publications:* What Ship? Where Bound?, 1961; The Murderer Vine, 1969; McQuaid, 1974; The Snow Rattlers, 1977; McQuaid in August, 1979. *Honours:* Atlantic Monthly First, 1961; Fellowship, MacDowell Colony; Fellowship, YADDO. *Membership:* Authors' League. *Literary Agent:* Knox Burger, 391/2 Washington Square South, New York, NY 10012, USA. *Address:* 105 Charles Street, New York, NY 10014, USA.

RIGELHOF, Terrance Frederick, b. 24 Apr. 1944, Regina, Saskatchewan, Canada. College Lecturer; Novelist. m. Ann Harley Johnson, 11 June 1968, Hamilton, Ontario. *Education:* BA, University of Sasketchewan, 1965; BTh, University of Ottawa, 1967; MA, McMaster University, 1968. *Publications:* A Beast With Two Backs, 1981; The Education of J J Pass, Canada, UK, 1983. *Contributions to:* The Compass; Descant; The Gadfly; Grain; Journal of Canadian Fiction; Matrix; Montreal Review; Waves. (Stories). *Membership:* Writers Union of Canada. *Address:* c/o Writers Union of Canada, 24 Ryerston Avenue, Toronto, Ontario, Canada M5T 2P3.

RIGONI, Orlando Joseph, b. 27 Dec. 1917, Mercur, Utah, USA. Writer. m. (3) Maria Stella Ludwig, 18 July 1974, Santa Maris, California, 1 son, 1 daughter. *Publications:* Numerous gothic and western novels. *Contributions to:* Education Magazine; Short stories, novelettes, plays and poetry. *Membership:* Fictioneers. *Literary Agent:* Donald McCampbell, New York. *Address:* 2900 Dogwood Avenue, Morro Bay, CA 93442, USA.

RIJNDERS, Gerardjan, b. 2 June 1949. *Education:* Law student; Stage-management, School of Theatrical Arts *Literary Appointments:* Stage-manager, Baal, Nieuwe Comedie, Fact, Projecttheatre and Globe, where since 1977 he is leading artistic-manager. *Publications:* Theatre plays: Dollie or Avocado's at Lunch, at Projekttheatre, 1977; The Rhinestone Queen, original

title Rosemary Clooney's Baby, at Independent Theatre, 1978; Eczema, at Globe 1982 – plays published at ERIS under title 'Collective Work, part one: Comedies. Plays written with other playwrights: Schreber, with Mia Meijer at Fact 1976; Tasso At Weimar at Baal 1978; Snow Above Moscow, with Bert Edelenbos, Academic Society, 1982; Ovomaltine, Globe, 1983/84. *Address:* William de Zwijgerstraat 49, 5616 AC Eindhoven, The Netherlands.

RILEY, Edward Calverley, b. 5 Oct. 1923, Mexico City. University Professor. m. Judith Mary Bull, 1 son, 1 daughter. *Education:* MA, Queens College, Oxford University. *Publications:* Cervantes's Theory of the Novel, 1962; Suma Cervantina, co-editor, 1973; Don Quixote, 1986. *Contributor to:* Numerous Articles, Reviews in Bulletin of Hispanic Studies; Modern Language Review; Journal of Hispanic Philology; Modern Language Notes; Times Literary Supplement; etc. *Memberships:* International Association of Hispanists; Cervantes Society of America. *Address:* Department of Hispanic Studies, University of Edinburgh, David Hume Tower, George Square, Edinburgh 8, Scotland.

RILEY, Jocelyn Carol, b. 6 Mar. 1949, Minneapolis, Minnesota, USA. Writer (fiction, non-fiction, reviews, scripts). m. Jeffrey Allen Steele, 4 Sep. 1971, Northfield, Minnesota, 2 sons. *Education:* BA, English Literature, Carleton College, Northfield, 1971. *Publications:* Only My Mouth Is Smiling, 1982; Crazy Quilt, 1984; Page Proof, forthcoming. *Contributions to:* Publishers Weekly; Society of Childrens Book Writers; Contemporary Literary Criticism Writer; Book Review Digest. *Honours:* Huntington Poetry Prize, Carleton College, 1970; Best Books for Young Adults, American Library Association 1982; Arthur Tofte Memorial Award, Council for Wisconsin Writers, 1982; Writers Cup, 1985. *Memberships:* President, Madison Professional Chapter, 1984–85, Women in Communications; Authors Guild; Society for Childrens Book Writers. *Literary Agent:* Jane Gelfman, John Farquharson Ltd, 250 West 57th Street, New York, NY 10107, USA. *Address:* PO Box 5264, Madison, WI 53705, USA.

RILEY, John, b. 26 May 1940, Grand Rapids, Michigan, USA. Screenwriter; Journalist. m. Judith Ann Hartman, 7 Sep. 1962, Mansfield, Ohio, 1 son, 1 daughter. *Education:* BSc, Journalism, Northwestern University, Illinois, 1962; Certificate in Russian, Defense Language Institute, Monterey, California, 1964. *Literary Appointments:* Reporter, City News Bureau; Reporter, Chicago's American Correspondent, Time, Life, Newseek. *Films produced include:* For Ladies Only, Catalina-Viacom-NBC, 1981. Number 1 best-selling American movie for television in worldwide cassette sales. *Contributions to:* Esquire; Playboy; Human Behavior; Penthouse; People; Oui; Look; Los Angeles; Playgirl; California; New West; True; West. Book Reviewer: Los Angeles Times; Los Angeles Herald-Axaminer. *Memberships:* Writers Guild of America, West, Incorporated; American Society of Journalists and Authors; Time-Life Aliumni Society. *Literary Agent:* Roberta Kent. *Address:* Suite 223, Writers & Artists Building, 9507 Santa Monica Boulevard, Beverly Hills, CA 90210, USA.

RILEY, Madeleine Veronica, b. 9 Apr. 1933, London. Writer. m. Norman Riley, 31 July 1954, Oxford. 4 sons, 1 daughter. *Education:* BA Hons. *Publications:* Spot Bigger Than God, 1967; Brought to Bed, 1968; Dairy for Two, 1970; Ideal Friend, 1976. *Literary Agent:* David Higham. *Address:* The Manor House, Wolston, Coventry, Warwickshire, England.

RIMM, Virginia Mary, b. 18 July 1933, Staten Island, New York, USA. Editor; Publisher. m. Charles B. Rimm, 26 May 1957, Katonah, New York, 3 sons, 4 daughters. *Education:* 2 years' pre-nursing, Elmira College, New York; BSc, RN, Columbia Presbyterian Medical Center/Presbyterian Hospital School of Nursing. *Literary Appointment:* Publisher, New England Sampler.

Contributions: Freelance articles, photographs in: Yankee Magazine; Maine Life; Christian Herald; Upcountry; Maine Organic Farmer & Gardener; Woman's National Farm & Garden; Evangel; various children's publications. Served as publicity writer, Maineport Council, to Maine Development Foundation for port development. *Honours:* New England Sampler, rated among Top Ten in its class, as market for fiction writers, Writer's Digest, surveys, 1983, 1984, 1985. *Address:* RFD 1, Box 2280, Brooks, ME 04921, USA.

RINALDI, Nicholas Michael, b. 2 Apr. 1934, Brooklyn, New York, USA. Writer; College Professor. m. Jacqueline Tellier, 29 Aug. 1959, Eastchester, 3 sons, 1 daughter. *Education:* AB, Classics, Shrub Oak, 1957; MA, 1960; PhD, 1963, English Literature, Fordham. *Appointments:* Instructor, Assistant Profesor, St John's University, 1960–66; Lecturer, City University of New York, 1966; Associate Professor, Columbia University, Summer 1966; Professor, University of Connecticut, Summer 1972; Assistant Professor, Professor, Fairfield University, 1966–. *Publications:* The Resurrection of the Snails, 1977; We Have Lost our Fathers, 1982; The Luftwaffe in Chaos, 1985; Bridge Fall Down, Novel, 1985. *Contributor to:* Yale Review; New American Review; Prairie Schooner; Carolina Quarterly; etc. *Honours:* Joseph P Slomovich Memorial Award for Poetry, 1979; All Nations Poetry Award, 1981, 1983; AWP Award Series Publication, We Have Lost Our Fathers, 1982; New York Poetry Forum Award, 1983; Eve of St Agnes Poetry Award, 1984; Charles Angoff Literary Award, 1984. *Memberships:* Associated Writing Programme; Poetry Society of America. *Literary Agent:* International Creative Management. *Address:* 190 Brookview Avenue, Fairfield, CT 06432, USA.

RIND, Sherry, b. 29 Mar. 1952, Seattle, Washington, USA. Writer. m. John Welliver, 15 July 1984, Seattle, Washington. *Education:* BA English, 1973, MA English, 1977, University of Washington. *Major Publications:* The Whooping Crane Dance, 1981; The Hawk in the Back Yard, 1985. *Contributor to:* Poetry Northwest; Seattle Review; The Written Arts; Akross; Southern Poetry Review, Seattle Arts; Georgia Review; and others. *Honours:* Dearborne Award, 1972; William Stafford Award, 1974; Louisa Kern Award, 1982; Anhinga Prize for Poetry, 1984. *Address:* 6509 210th Avenue N E Redmond, WA 98053, USA.

RIORDAN, (Edward) Michael, b. 3 Dec. 1946, Massachusetts, USA. Scientist and Writer. m. Linda Michele Goodman, 8 Apr. 1979, Stanford, California. *Education:* SB 1968. PhD, Physics, 1973, Massachusetts Institute of Technology. *Publications:* The Solar Home Book, with Bruce Anderson, 1977; The Day After Midnight, editor, 1982. *Contributions:* Thermal Storage in Solar Age, 1978; Numerous book reviews in Technology Review, San Francisco Chronicle, New Scientist. Editor/Publisher, Cheshire Books (energy, environment, ecology, architecture, science, technology). *Honour:* Sigma Xi, 1968. *Membership:* Authors Guild. *Literary Agent:* John Brockman Associates, New York. *Address:* Post Office Box 130, La Honda, CA 94020, USA.

RÍOS, Juan, b. 28 Sep. 1914, Barranca, Lima, Peru. Poet and Dramatist. m. Rosa Saco, 16 Sep. 1946, Lima, 1 daughter. *Education:* Writer's Fellowship, United Nations Educational, Scientifc and Cultural Organisation, Europe and Egypt, 1960–61. *Publications:* Canción de Siempre, 1941; Malstrom, 1941; La Pintura Contemporánea en el Perú, 1946; Teatro (I), 1961; Ayar Manko, 1963; Primera Antología Poética, 1982. *Honours:* 5 National Prizes for Playwriting, 1946–60; National Poetry Prize, 1948 and 1953. *Membership:* Academia Peruana de la Lengua, Corespondiente a la Real Academia Española. *Address:* Bajada de Baños 109, Barranco, Lima, Peru.

RIOUX, Helene, b. 12 Jan. 1949, Montreal, Canada. Author, Divorced, 1 son, 1 daughter. *Education:* BA, Russian Studies. *Publications:* Suite pour un visage, 1970; Finitudes, 1972; Yes, Monsieur, 1973; Un sens a

ma vie, 1975; J'Elle, 1979; Une Histoire Gitane, 1982. *Contributor to:* 2 short stories in Moebius, Les visions d'Eleonore, 1985; Appel anonyme, 1985. *Membership:* Union of Quebec Writers. *Address:* 865 Rue Champagneur, Outremont, Quebec, Canada H2V 3R2.

RIPLEY, S Dillon, b. 20 Sep. 1913, New York City, USA. Zoologist; Museum Director; Author. *Education:* BA, Yale University, USA, 1938; PhD, Harvard University, 1943; MA, Yale University, 1961; ScD, 1974. *Publications:* Trail of the Money Bird, 1942; Search for the Spiny Babbler, 1952; A Paddling of Ducks, 1957; Ornithological Books in Yale Library, (with L Scribner), 1961; A synopsis of the Birds of India and Pakistan, (with Salim Ali) volumes 1-X, 1968–74; The Sacred Grove, 1969; The Paradox of the Human Condition, 1975; A Monograph of the Family of Rails, 1976; Rails Portfolio, (editor), 1985. *Contributor to:* Wildlife and Am; Smithsonian Magazine; new York Times Book Review; Journal of World History; International Zoo Yearbook; Am. Sci.; Auk; Ibis; Condor, etc. *Honours:* Officier, Ordre Francais des Arts et Lettres, 1972; Hon DSc, Cambridge University, 1973; Hon KBE. *Agent:* Russell and Volkening Inc. *Address:* 2324 Massachussetts Avenue, NW, Washington DC 20008, USA.

RITCHIE, Elisavietta Artamonoff, b. Kansas City, Missouri, USA. Writer; Poet. m. Lyell Ritchie, divorced, 2 sons, 1 daughter. *Education includes:* Degree Superieur cours de Civilisation Francaise. Sorbonne, Paris, 1951; BA, University of California, 1954; MA, American University, 1976. *Literary Appointments include:* Multiple work as freelance writer, translator, teacher, editor and public relations person, 1954–; Instructor, Writer's Center, Bethseda, Maryland; Lecture Tour, sponsored by United States Information Agency for various countries, 1971, 1977, 1979; Poet-in-Schools, 1970–; Translator and editor, US Government and private clients, 1960–; Instructor and Graduate Teaching Fellow, French Department American University, 1968–74; President, Founder, Wineberry Press, 1983; President, Washington Writers Publishing House, 1984–. *Publications:* Timbot, 1970; Tightening the Circle Over Eel Country, 1974; A Sheath of Dreams and Other Games, 1976; Moving to Larger Quarters, 1977; Raking the Snow, 1982. Editor: Finding the Name, 1983; Tide Turning: An Anthology of Poems on Endangered Marine Species, 1985; The Problem with Eden, 1985. *Contributions to:* Various publications including: New York Times; Washington Post; Christian Science Monitor; New Republic; Washingtonian National Geographic; Miami Herald. *Honours include:* Graduate Fellowship, American University, 1970–74; Various awards from Poetry Society of Americana and Poetry Society of Georgia; New Writers Award, Great Lakes Colleges Association, 1975–76; Winner, Washington Writers Publishing House competition, 1981; Syndicated Fiction Project selection, PEN/NEA, 1983; Amelia's Fiction Prize, 1985. *Memberships:* Numerous. *Literary Agent:* Leona Schecter. *Address:* 3207 Macomb Street, Washington, DC 20008, USA.

RITTER, Alan, b. 19 Feb. 1937, New York City, USA. College Teacher. *Education:* BA, Yale University, 1958; PhD, Political Science, Harvard University, 1966. *Publications:* The Political Thought of Pierre-Joseph Proudhon, 1969; Anarchism: A Theoretical Analysis, 1980. *Address:* University of Connecticut School of Law, 65 Elizabeth St, Hartford, CT 06103, USA.

RITTER, Erika, Elizabeth, b. Regina, Canada. Writer. *Education:* BA McGill University, Montreal, Canada; MA Drama Centre, University of Toronto. *Literary Appointments:* Writer-in-Residence: Banff Centre, Banff, Alberta, 1981, Concordia University, Montreal, 1984; Playwright-in-Residence: Smith College, Massachusetts, USA, 1985, Stratford Festival, Stratford, Ontario, Canada, 1985. *Major Publications:* Plays: A Visitor from Charleston, 1975; The Splits, 1978; Winter, 1979; Automatic Pilot,1980; Urban Scrawl (essays), 1984. *Contributor to:* Chatelaine; Saturday Night; The Fiddlehead; Canadian Fiction Magazine; Toronto Life;

Regular Column in City Woman Magazine. *Honours:* Chalmers Canadian Play Award, 1980; ACTRA Radio Writer Award, 1982. *Memberships:* Playwrights Union of Canada; Alliance of Canadian Cinema & Television Artists; Writers Union of Canada. *Address:* c/o Playwrights Union of Canada, 8 York Street, Toronto, Ontario, Canada.

RIVENBURGH, Viola Lenore, b. 15 Mar. 1897, Albert Lea, Minnesota, USA. Professor. m. Bertram Gardenier Rivenburgh, 25 Nov. 1926, Cheyenne, 1 daughter. *Education:* University of Wyoming; BA, University of Nebraska, 1919; MA, Columbia University, 1923; Unfinished PhD, University of Washington. *Appointments:* University of Alaska, 1922; University of Hawaii; Creative Writing, University of Washington, 1942–67. *Publications:* Princess Kadulani, 1960; Words at Work, 1965; Hawaii from Monarchy to Annexation, 1970; Aeolus Sings, Collected Poems, 1978; On the Threshold: Alaska 1922, 1985. *Contributor to:* College Magazine; Medical Nursing World; Penwen's National Magazine; Poetry; Poetry Magazines, etc. *Honours:* Phi Beta Kappa; Woman of the Year, Owl Award, National League of American Penwomen; Crescent Award, Woman of the Year, Crescent Award, Gamma Phi Beta, 1968. *Memberships:* Phi Beta Kappa, Founder, Honolulu, Treasurer; University Faculty Clubs; National League of American Penwomen, National Board; etc. *Address:* Padelford Hall, University of Washington, Seattle, MA 98105, USA.

RIX, Timothy John, b. 4 Jan. 1934, England. Publisher. m. Gillian Greenwood, 1 son, 2 daughters. *Education:* BA, Clare College, University of Cambridge, England, 1957; Mellon Fellow, Yale University, USA, 1957–58. Literary Appointments: Chief Executive, Longman Group, 1967–; Chairman, Longman Group, 1984–; President, Publishers' Association of Great Britain, 1983–84; British Library Advisory Council, 1982–; Arts Council of Great Britain Literature Panel, 1983–; Director, Yale University Press, London, England, 1984–. *Contributor to:* Various book trade journals. *Honour:* Companion, British Institute of Management. *Memberships:* National Book League; Executive Committee, 1979–, Deputy Chairman, 1984–. *Address:* 24 Birchington Road, London N8 8HP, England.

ROADS, Curtis Bryant, b. 9 May 1951, Cleveland, USA. Composer; Researcher; Editor. *Education:* California Institute of the Arts, 1972–74; BA, Highest Honours, University of California. *Publications:* Proceedings of the 1977 International Computer Music Conference, 1978; Proceedings of the 1978 International Computer Music Conference, 1979; Foundations of Computer Music, 1985; Composers and the Computer, 1985; Computer Music Tutorial, 1986. *Contributor to:* Numerous professional magazines and journals. *Honour:* ASCAP Composer's Award, 1984–85; 1985–86. *Address:* Computer Music Journal, E15-487, MIT, Cambridge, MA 02139, USA.

ROBBINS, Christopher, b. 19 Nov. 1946, Bristol, England. Writer. *Major Publications:* Assassin, 1974; Air America, 1979; The Invisible Air Force, 1979. *Contributor to:* The Observer; The Sunday Times; Die Zeit (Federal Republic of Germany); Panorama (Netherlands); Los Angeles Magazine (USA). *Literary Agent:* Mark Lucas. *Address:* c/o Dunlop & Fraser, 91 Regent Street, London W1, England.

ROBBINS, Doren Richard, b. 20 Aug. 1949, Los Angeles, California, USA. Poet. m. Emily Lang, 29 July 1979, Los Angeles, California, 1 daughter. *Literary Appointments:* Editor, Publisher, Third Rail Press, 1975–82. *Publications:* Detonated Veils, 1976; The Roots and the Tower, 1980; Seduction of the Groom, 1982; Sympathetic Manifesto, 1985. *Contributions to:* Kayak; North Dakota Review; Alcatraz; Contact II; Floating Island; Greenfield Review; Momentum; Thirdrail; Amorotica; One Mind; Japan; Vie, Japan; Will, Japan; Hawaii Review; Bitter Oleandor; Poema Convidado, Brazil; Poetry International 78; Poets Voices; Bachy;

Alembic; The Ark; Lamp in the Spine, etc. *Address:* 12540 Rubens Avenue, Los Angeles, CA 90066, USA.

ROBBINS, J Albert, b. 5 Dec. 1914, Knoxville, Tennessee, USA. Professor. m. Simone Bassett, 8 July 1950, Chapel Hill, 1 daughter. *Education:* BA, 1937, MA 1938, University of Florida; PhD, University of Pennsylvania, 1947. *Appointments:* Instructor, English, Duke University, 1946–50; Professor, English, Professor Emeritus, Indiana University, 1950–85; Fulbright Lecturer, American Literature, Universities of Lyon & Clermont-Ferrand, France, 1955–56. *Publications:* Editor, American Literary Manuscripts, 2nd edition 1977; Contributor, Editor, American Literary Scholarship, 1968–72, 1976, 1978, 1980, 1984; Editor, Interlude with Robert Frost, 1982. *Contributor to:* Studies in Bibliography; Indiana University Bookman; Modern fiction studies; Poe Newsletter; American Transcendental Quarterly; Poe Studies; etc. *Memberships:* Modern Language Association of America; American Literature Section of Modern Language Association. *Address:* 1011 S Hawthorne Drive, Bloomington, IN 47401, USA.

ROBBINS, John William, b. 21 Oct. 1948, Honesdale, Pennsylvania, USA. Writer; Consultant. m. Linda Kaye Stephens, 3 Nov. 1973, Maryland, 3 daughters. *Education:* AB, cum laude, Grove City College,1969; MA, 1970, PhD, 1973, Johns Hopkins University. *Publications:* Answer to Ayn Rand, 1974; Scripture Twisting in the Seminaries, 1985; Truth and Love, 1986. *Contributor to:* Numerous articles in professional journals and magazines including, Intercollegiate Review; Journal of Christian Reconstruction; The Trinity Review, 1985. *Address:* 3606 Coolcrest Drive, Jefferson, MD 21755, USA.

ROBBINS, Richard Leroy, b. 27 Aug, 1953, Los Angeles, California, USA. College Professor. m. Candace L Black, 8 Sep. 1979, Missoula, Montana, 1 son. *Education:* AB, San Diego State University, 1975; MFA, University of Montana, 1979. *Literary Appointments:* Writer-in-Residence, Montana Arts Council, 1979–81; Assistant Professor, Creative and Technical Writing, Montana State University, 1984. *Publications:* Towards New Weather, 1979; The Invisible Wedding, 1984. *Contributions to:* More than 30 magazines including The Nation; The North American Review; Poetry Northwest (Poems). *Honours:* First Prize, Brandford P Millar Award from Portland Review, 1978; Winner, Frontier Award, University of Montana Foundation, 1978. *Memberships:* Poetry Society of America; Associated Writing Program; Modern Language Association; Academy of America Poets. *Address:* Department of English, Mankato State University, Mankato, MN 56001, USA.

ROBERSON, William Howard, b. 3 Mar. 1952, Mount Vernon, New York, USA. Librarian, Bibliographer. m. Jean Allison Rowehl, 16 May 1976, Mattituck, New York, 1 son, 1 daughter. *Education:* BA, Art, 1974; State University of New York at Stony Brook; MS, Library Science, 1976, Long Island University; Advanced Certificate in Library and Information Studies, 1979, St John's University; MA, English, 1984, State University of New York at Stony Brook. *Publications:* Louis Simpson: A Reference Guide, 1980; George Washington Cable: An Annotated Bibliography, 1982; Robert Bly: A Primary and Secondary Bibliography, 1986. *Contributions to:* RQ; Bulletin of Bibliography; The Great Lakes Review. *Address:* Library, Long Island University, Southampton, NY 11968, USA.

ROBERT, Guy, b. 7 Nov. 1933, Quebec, Canada. Art Writer and Consultant. m. Louise Labelle, 24 June 1970, Montreal, 3 sons. *Education:* MA Literature, PhD Studies in Literature, Montreal; Doctorate in Aesthetics, Paris. *Literary Appointments:* Director of Series, CPP, Montreal, 1962; Literary Director, Librairie Deom, Montreal; Director of Book, Man and His World, Expo 67, Montreal; Publisher, Editions Goglin 1959–, Editions du Songe 1968–75, Editions Iconia 1975–. *Publications include:* Over 50 books including: Ecole de Montreal,

1964; Borduas, 1972; L'Art au Quebec Depuis 1940, 1973; La Peinture au Quebec Depuis ses Origines: Riopelle, Chasseur d'Images, 1981; Art Actuel au Quebec, 1983; Art et Non Finito, 1984. *Contributions to:* Magazines and journals including: Vie des Arts, Montreal; Culture Vivante, Quebec; Le Devoir, Montreal; La Revue d'Esthetique, Paris; Liberte, Montreal. *Honour:* Grand Prix Litteraire de Montreal, 1976. *Memberships:* Union des Ecrivains Quebecois; Association Internationale des Critiques d'Art. *Address:* 242 Stanstead Avenue, Mount-Royal, Quebec, H3R 1X3, Canada.

ROBERT, Suzanne, b. 14 Mar. 1948, Montréal, Canada. Book Reviewer; Editor. *Education:* Masters Degree in Physical Anthropology, Université de Montréal, 1975. *Appointments:* Books Reviewer, Radio-Canada; Editor, Liberté. *Publications:* La Dame Morte, 1973; Les Trois Soeurs de Personne, 1980; Vulpera, 1983. *Memberships:* Union des Écrivains québécois; Editing Committee, literature magazine Liberté since 1984. *Honours:* 1 of 3 finalists for Prix du Journal de Montréal, 1981; 1 of 5 finalists Prix du Gouverneur Général, 1984. *Address:* 7070, rue Louis-Hémon , Montréal, Québec, Canada H2E 2T5.

ROBERTIELLO, Richard Candela, 20 June 1923, Brooklyn, New York, USA. Psychiatrist and Psychoanalyst. Divorced, 1 son. *Education:* BA, Harvard University, 1943; MD, Columbia University, 1946; Certified Psychoanalyst, New York Medical College, 1954. *Publications:* Voyage From Lesbos, 1959; A Handbook of Emotional Illness and Treatment, 1961; Sexual Fulfillment and Self-Affirmation, 1963; The Analyst's Role, 1964; Hold Them Very Close – The Let Them Go, 1975; Big You, Litle You, 1977; Your Own True Love, 1978; A Man in the Making, 1979; A Psychoanalyst's Quest, 1986. *Contributions to:* Popular magazines and professional journals. *Literary Agent:* Don Croydon, 177 East 70th Street, New York, NY 10021. *Address:* 49 East 78th Street, New York, NY 10021, USA.

ROBERTS, Benjamin Charles, b. 1 Aug. 1917, Leeds, England. Professor of Industrial Relations. m. 28 Sep. 1945, Hampstead, 2 sons. *Education:* London School of Economics; MA, New College, Oxford. *Publications:* Trade Union Government and Administration in Great Britain, 1956; Trades Union Congress 1868–1921, 1958; Towards Industrial Democracy, 1979; Industrial Relations in Europe: Imperatives of Change, 1985. *Contributions to:* Editor, British Journal of Industrial Relations. *Address:* 28 Temple Fortune Lane, London, NW11 7UD, England.

ROBERTS, Brian, b. 19 Mar. 1930, London, England. Writer. *Education:* St Mary's College, Twickenham; London University. *Literary Appointments:* Contributor and Consultant to Dictionary of South African Biography. *Publications:* Ladies in the Veld, 1965; Cecil Rhodes and Princess, 1969; Churchills in Africa, 1970; The Diamond Magnates, 1972; The Zulu Kings, 1974; Kimberley: Turbulent City, 1976; The Mad Bad Line: The Family of Lord Alfred Douglas, 1981; Randolph: A Study of Churchill's Son, 1984. *Contributions to:* South African newspapers and magazines; British magazines. *Literary Agent:* John Farquharson Ltd, 162-168 Regent Street, London. *Address:* North Knoll Cottage, 15 Bridge Street, Frome, BA11 1BB, Somerset, England.

ROBERTS, Edward Adam, b. 29 Aug. 1940. Penrith, England. University Teacher. m. Frances Primrose Dunn, 16 Sep. 1966, London, 1 son, 1 daughter. *Education:* BA, History, Oxford University, 1962. *Literary Appointments:* Assistant Editor, Peace News Ltd, 1962–65. *Publications:* The Strategy of Civilian Defence: Non-violent Resistance to Aggression, 1967; Csechoslovakia, 1968 (with P Windsor), 1969; Nations in Arms, 1976; Documents on the Laws of War (with R Guelff), 1982. *Contributions to:* New Society; The Times; The Guardian; The World Today; Survival etc. *Honour:* Stanhope Historical Essay Prize, Oxford

University, 1961. *Memberships:* Council Member, Royal Institute of International Affairs, 1985–. *Address:* St Antony's College, Oxford, OX2 6JF, England.

ROBERTS, Eirlys Rhiwen Cadwaladr, b. 3 Jan. 1911, England. Journalist. *Education:* BA Honours, Classics, Cambridge, University, *Literary Appointments:* Editor, Which? Magazine, Research Director, Consumers' Association, England, 1958–73. *Publications:* Consumers, 1966. *Contributions to:* Numerous Publications. *Honour:* CBE, 1977. *Address:* 8 Lloyd Square, London, WC1, England.

ROBERTS, Eric, b. 5 Apr. 1914, London, England. Writer; Broadcaster. m. Stella Margaret Smith, 22 Aug. 1940, Northampton, 1 daughter. *Publications:* Adventure in the Sky, 1960; Oddities of Animal Life, 1962; Animal Ways and Means, 1963. *Contributions to:* Punch; BBC Radio and Television; Daily syndicated column in the Countryside. *Address:* 53 Sywell Road, Overstone, Northampton, NN6 0AG, England.

ROBERTS, Francis Warren, b. 3 Dec. 1916, Menard, Texas, USA. Educator. *Education:* AB, Southwestern University, USA, 1938; DLitt, (Hon) ibid, 1972; PhD, University of Texas, 1956. *Publications:* General Editor, with Professor James T Boulton, Cambridge University Press, Citical Edition of the Works of D H Lawrence; Bibliography of D H Lawrence, 1962; Complete Poems of D H Lawrence, (with V de Sola Pinto), 1964; D H Lawrence and His World, (with H T Moore), 1966; Phoenix II, (with H T Moore), 1968. *Contributor to:* Texas Quarterly; Journal of Modern Literature; Renaissance and Modern Studies. *Honours:* Theta Sigma Chi Award for Bibliography of D H Lawrence, 1963. *Memberships include:* Texas Institute of Letters (Secretary, 1976–77). *Literary Agent:* Lawrence Pollinger Limited, London. *Address:* 2305 Windsor Road, Austin, TX 78703, USA.

ROBERTS, John Morris, b. 14 Apr. 1928, Bath, England. Historian. m. 1 son, 2 daughters. *Education:* BA 1949, MA 1953, D Phil 1954, Oxford University. *Publications:* Europe 1880–1945, 1967; The Mythology of the Secret Societies, 1972; Revolution and Improvement, 1976; The History of the World, 1976; The French Revolution, 1978; The Penguin Illustrated History of the World, 1978; The Triumph of the West, 1985. *Contributions:* Various magazines and journals. *Literary Agent:* A D Peters. *Address:* Merton College, Oxford, OX1 4JD, England.

ROBERTS, Leonard Robert, b. 13 Mar. 1947, Cohoes, New York, USA. Professor. m. Nancy Crane, 31 Dec. 1982, St Stephens's, 2 sons, 1 daughter. *Education:* BA, Siena College, Loudonville, New York; MA, University of Dayton, Ohio; PhD, Lehigh University, Bethlehem, Pennsylvania. *Literary Appointments:* Poet-in-the-Schools, Pennsylvania, 1975–. *Major Publications:* Cohoes Theatre, 1980; From the Dark, 1984; The Driving, 1986. *Contributor to:* Ohio Review; Missouri Review; Poetry Australia; Virginia Quarterly Review of Literature; Seattle Review; California Quarterly; Carolina Quarterly; Mississippi Review; Southern Poetry Review; Poetry Now; and many others. *Honours:* Pennsylvania State Poetry Fellowship, 1981 and 1986. National Endowment for the Arts Creative Writing Fellowship, 1984; Anthology of Magazine Verse: Yearbook of American Poetry, 1983, 1984, 1985, 1986. *Address:* 1791 Wassergass Road, Hellertown, PA 18055, USA.

ROBERTS, Nancy Elizabeth, b. 21 Feb. 1958, Yorkshire, England. Editor, Pony Magazine. *Education:* BA, Joint Honours, English and American Studies, University of Hull. *Publications:* The Pony Book, 1984. *Contributor to:* Pony, and Horse & Rider Magazine, 1979–. *Address:* 23 Woodside, Wimbledon, London SW19, England.

ROBERTS, Richard Dale, b. 26 May 1939, St Louis, Missouri, USA. Editor, Writer. m. Patricia F Nehring, 2 May 1964, St Louis, Missouri, 2 sons, 1 daughter.

Education: BS, St Louis University, 1961; Certificate, Writers Institute, St Louis University. *Literary Appointments:* United Press International; Assistant Editor, St Louis Light; Editor, St Louis University Magazine; Editor, Universitas Magazine. *Major Publication:* Healing with Hypnosis (in preparation). *Contributor to:* New York Times; Washington University Magazine; Commerce Magazine; Fleur-de-Lys; Universitas; and others – some 200 articles & short stores. *Literary Agent:* Ducas/Elek, New York City. *Address:* 1410 Bluefield Drive, Florissant, MO 63033, USA.

ROBERTS, Selyf, b. 20 May 1912, Corwen, Gwynedd, Wales. Retired Bank Officer. m. 28 Aug. 1945, Bridgend, S Wales, 1 daughter. *Publications:* Translations into Welsh: Alice in Wonderland, (abridged), 1951, (full translation), 1982; Through the Looking Glass, 1984; Essays: Deg o'r Diwedd, 1958; Mesur Byr, 1977; Hel Meddyliau, 1982; Imaginary Biography; Dr R P Howells, 1974; Autobiography: Tocyn Dwyffordd, 1984; Novels: Cysgod yw Arian, 1959; Helynt er Hoelion, 1960; A Eilw ar Ddyfnder, 1962; Wythnos o Hydref, 1965; Ymweled ag Anwiredd, 1975; Iach o'r Cadwynau, 1977; Tebyg Nid Oes, 1981; Teulu Meima Lloyd, 1986. *Contributor:* Essays and Short Stories to: Y Llenor; Yr Eurgrawn; Taliesin; Genhinen; Various anthologies. *Honours:* Honorary Member, Gorsedd of Bards; Winner of Prose Medal National Eisteddfod of Wales, Pwllheli, 1955. *Memberships:* Yr Adademi Gymreig (Welsh Academy); Chairman, Undeb Awduron Cymru (Union of Welsh Authors), 1975–86. *Address:* Hefod Les, Trefonen Road, Oswestry, Shropshire SY11 2TW, England.

ROBERTS, Willo Davis, b. 29 May 1928, Michigan, USA. Writer. m. David Roberts, 20 May 1949, Portland, Oregon, USA, 2 sons, 2 daughters. *Publications:* Adult books include: The Search for Willie, 1980; The Face at the Window, 1981; A Long Time to Hate, 1982; The Gallant Spirit, 1982; Days of Valor, 1983; Sniper, 1984; Keating's Landing, 1984; The Annalise Experiment, 1985; Books for juveniles include: The Girl with the Silver Eyes, 1980; The Pet Sitting Peril, 1983; No Monsters in the Closet, 1983; Eddie and the Fairy Godpuppy, 1984; Baby Sitting is a Dangerous Job, 1985; The Magic Book, 1985. Books for young adults include: House of Fear, 1983; Elizabeth, 1984; Caroline, 1984; Victoria, 1985. *Honours:* Evansville Book Award, 1980; Young Hoosier Award, 1980; Western Australian Young Readers, 1981; Georgia Children's Book Award, 1982; Mark Twain Award, 1984. *Memberships:* Science Fiction Writers of America; Seattle Free-Lances; Pacific Northwest Writers Conference. *Literary Agent:* Curtis Brown, New York City. *Address:* 12020 Engebretson Road, Granite Falls, WA 98252, USA.

ROBERTSON, Denise, b. 9 June 1933, Sunderland, England. Writer. m. (1) Alexander Robertson, 19 Mar. 1960, Sunderland; (2) John Tomlin, 3 Nov. 1973, Seaham. 5 sons. *Publication:* Land of Lost Content, 1985. *Honour:* Constable Fiction Trophy, 1984. *Literary Agent:* Carol Smith, 25 Hornton Court East, Kensington High Street, London W8 7RT. *Address:* 17 Maureen Terrace, Seaham, County Durham, England.

ROBERTSON, James Andrew Irvine, b. 14 May 1945, Stirling, Scotland. Writer. m. Gilda Bailey, 1 May 1971, London, England, 1 son, 1 daughter. *Publications:* Any Fool Can Be a Dairy Farmer, 1979; Any Fool Can Be a Yokel, 1985. *Contributions to:* Numerous publications. *Literary Agent:* Curtis Brown. *Address:* Lower Mill, Dulverton, Somerset, England.

ROBERTSON, James I, b. 18 July 1930, Danville, Virginia, USA. Professor of History. m. Elizabeth Green, 1 June 1952, Danville, Virginia, 2 sons, 1 daughter. *Education:* BA, LittD, Randolph-Macon College; MA, PhD, Emory University. *Literary Appointments:* Associate Professor of History, University of Montana, 1965–67; Professor and Head, History Department, 1967–75, C P Miles Professor of History, 1976–, Virginia Polytechnic Institute and State University. *Publications:* The Stonewall Brigade, 1963; Civil War Books: A Critical

Bibliography, 1965–67; The Civil War Letters of General Robert McAllister, 1965; Recollections of a Maryland Confederate Soldier, 1975; Four Years in the Stonewall Brigade, 1978; The 4th Virginia Infantry, 1980; Civil War Sites in Virginia: A Tour-Guide, 1982; The 18th Virginia Infantry, 1983; Tentinting Tonight: The Soldiers' View, 1984. *Contributions to:* More than 150 Articles in Historical Journals and History Magazines. *Honours:* The Harry St Truman Historical Award, 1962; The Centennial Medallion of the US Civil War Centennial Commission, 1965; Nevins-Freeman Award, 1980; Bruce Catton Award, 1982; A P Andrews Memorial Award, 1985; James Robertson Award of Achievement, 1985. *Memberships:* Board of Trustees, Virginia Historical Society; Organisation of American Historians; Southern Historical Association; Confederate Memorial Society. *Address:* Department of History, Virginia Polytechnic Institute and State University, Blacksburg, VA 24061, USA.

ROBERTSON, Marion Gordon, b. 22 Mar. 1930, Lexington, Virginia, USA. Broadcaster. m. Adelia Elmer, 1954, 2 sons, 2 daughters. *Education:* BA, Washington & Lee University, 1950; JD, Yale University, 1955; MDiv, New York Theological Seminary, 1959. *Major Publications:* Shout it from the Housetops, 1972; My Prayer for You, 1977; The Secret Kingdom, 1982; Beyond Reasons, 1984; Answers: To 200 of Life's Most Probing Questions, 1984. *Contributor to:* Christian Life; Decision; Destiny. *Honours:* Various Humanitarian awards. *Address:* CBN Center, Virginia Beach, VA 23463, USA.

ROBERTSON, William P, b. 29 May 1950, Bradford, Pennsylvania, USA. Teacher. *Education:* BS English, Mansfield University, Pennsylvania. *Major Publications:* Poems: Burial Grounds, 1977; gardez au froid, 1979; Animal Comforts, 1981; Life after Sex Life, 1983. *Contributor to:* Over 80 literary periodicals in USA, Canada & UK. *Honours:* Various awards for poetry. *Memberships:* Poets & Writers; National Writers Club; and others. *Address:* P O Box 293, Duke Center, PA 16729–0293, USA.

ROBINOWITZ, Joe R, b. 13 Dec. 1950, Houston, Texas, USA. Editor. m. Elizabeth Beekman, 28 June 1975, 2 daughters. *Education:* BSc, Medill School of Journalism, Northwestern University, Evanston, Illinois. *Literary Appointment:* Editor, The Boston Herald. *Address:* The Boston Herald, One Herald Square, Boston, M A 02106, USA.

ROBINS, Robert Henry, b. 1 July 1921, Broadstairs, England. University Teacher. m. Sheila Marie Fynn, 29 Aug. 1953, deceased, 3 Oct. 1983. *Education:* MA Oxon, New College Oxford, 1948. *Publications:* Ancient and Mediaeval Grammatical Theory in Europe, 1951; The Yurok Language, 1958; General Linguistics: An Introductory Survey, 1946; A Short History of Linguistics, 1967; Diversions of Bloomsbury: Selected Writings on Linguistics, 1970; Ideen – und Problemgeschichte der Sprachwissenschaft, 1973; System and Structure in Sudanese, 1983. *Contributions to:* Various learned journals in the field on linguistics. *Honours:* D Litt, London, 1968. *Memberships:* Honorary member 1980–, member, Linguistics Society of America, 1951–; Honorary Secretary 1961–, Philological Society, President, 1974, Societas Linguistica Europaea. *Address:* School of Oriental and African Studies, University of London WC1E 7HP, England.

ROBINSON, (Donald) Julian, b. 16 Sep. 1931, London, England. Designer; Author; Lecturer; Journalist. 1 son, 2 daughters. *Education:* DesRCA, Royal College of Art, England. *Publications:* The Penguin Book of Sewing, 1972, 1974, 1976; Fashion in the 1940's, 1975, 1978, 1981; The Golden Age of Style, 1976, 1981, 1983, 1985; Fashion in the Thirties, 1977, 1982; La Mode Art Deco/Arte E Moda Nel'900, 1977, 1983; Grande Chic, 1982. *Contributions to:* Golden Hands; Harpers Bazaar; Tatler; Art & Illustration; Art & Design; House & Gardens; Cleo; Mode; Advertising Art; Antique Collector; etc. *Honours:* Royal Scholar, Royal

College of Art, 1957; Essex Art Travelling Scholarship, 1958. *Address:* 252 Liverpool Street, East Sydney, NSW 2010, Australia.

ROBINSON, Dorothy Anderson, b. 30 May 1924. Librarian. *Education:* BA, Michigan State University, USA, 1948; MS Library Science, University of Kentucky, 1954. *Literary Appointments:* Public Schools, 1948–53; Walnut Hills High School, Cincinnati, Ohio, 1954–57; Kentucky Wesleyan College, Owensboro, Kentucky, 1957–59; Marion County Schools, Fairmont, 1959–60 and 1969–70; Fairmont State College, West Virginia, 1960–61 and 1963–64. *Contributions to:* Anthologies: A Bouquet of Flowers, Poetry, St Peterburg, Florida Branch, American Association of University Women; News When the World is Quiet; (editor: Peter Meinke); National Poetry Anthology for Teachers and Librarians; Echoes of the West Virginia Poetry Society; Unity; West Virginia Garden News; Poetic License, St Petersburg; The West Virginian. *Membership:* Poetry Group, St Petersburg Branch, American Association of University Women. *Address:* 5949 15th Avenue South, Gulfport, FL 33707, USA.

ROBINSON, Fred Colson, b. 23 Sep. 1930, Birmingham, Alabama, USA. Professor. m. Helen Caroline Wild, 21 June 1959, Wyoming, Delaware, 1 son, 1 daughter. *Education:* BA, MA, PhD. *Literary Appointments:* Instructor & Assistant Professor of English, Stanford University, 1960–65; Associate Professor, Cornell University, 1965–67; Professor, Stanford University, 1967–72; Douglas Tracy Smith Professor of English, Yale University, 1972–. *Major Publications:* Old English Literature: A Selective Bibliography, 1970; (with S Greenfield) A Bibliography of Publications on Old English Literature, 1980; (with B Mitchell) A Guide to Old English, 1983; Beowulf & the Appositive Style, 1985. *Contributor to:* Literary & scholarly journals & books 0 over 100 articles. *Honours:* Haskins Medal, Medieval Academy of America, 1984; Honorary D. Lett, 1985; Fellow, American Academy of Arts & Sciences, 1976; and others. *Memberships:* President, Medieval Academy of America, 1984; President, Connecticut Academy of Arts & Sciences, 1980–85; President, New England Medieval Conference, 1983. *Address:* Department of English, Yale University, New Haven, CT 06520, USA.

ROBINSON, Judith Isobel, b. 11 June 1955, Espanola, Ontario, Canada. Writer, Teacher, Journalist. *Education:* BA English, Wilfred Laurier University, 1977; BEd, English, Music, University of Toronto, 1979; M Fine Arts, Creative Writing, Currently studying, University of British Columbia. *Major Publication:* Course Countdown 1973–80: A Study in the Use of Canadian Literature in Canadian High Schools, 1982. *Contributor to:* Quill & Quire (reviews of poetry); United Church Observer; Globe & Mail; Halton Hills Herald; Numerous poems published in literary journals. *Honours:* Scholarships to Banff Centre School of Fine Arts, 1982, 1984. *Memberships:* League of Canadian Poets, Associate Member 1980–85; Member, Centre for Investigative Journalism. *Address:* P O Box 388, Espanola, Ontario, POP 1C0, Canada.

ROBINSON, Kenneth Ernest, b. 9 Mar. 1914, London, England. University Teacher and Administrator. *Education:* MA, Hertford College, Oxford; London School of Economics. *Publications:* Editor, Five Elections in Africa, (with W J M MacKenzie), 1960; Editor, Essays in Imperial Government, (with A F Madden), 1963; The Dilemmas of Trusteeship, 1965; Co-Editor, A Decade of the Commonwealth, 1966. *Contributor to:* University Co-operation and Asian Development; l'Europe du XIX et XX Siecle, tome 7; Perspectives on Imperialism and Decolonisation, 1984; International Affairs; Political Studies; Public Administration; American Political Science Review; African Affairs; Listener; Economist. *Honours:* LLD, Chinese University of Hong Kong, 1979; CBE, 1971; DLitt, University of Hong Kong, 1972; DUniv, Open University, 1978; Hon Fellow, Nuffield College, Oxford, 1984. *Memberships:*

Fellow, Royal Historical Society; Corresponding member, Academie des Sciences d'outre mer, Paris; Vic President, Royal Commonwealth Society, 1983. *Address:* The Old Rectory, Westcote, Oxford OX7 65F, England.

ROBINSON, Linda Jane Rookwood, b. 4 Dec. 1914, Professor of English. *Education:* Queensland Teachers College, Australia; University of Queensland; BA, MA, University of Texas, USA; PhD, Tulane University, Louisiana, USA. m. Paul G Robinson. *Literary Appointments:* Teacher; Captain, Australian Women's Army Service; Copywriter; Editor; Newspaper Reporter; University Professor. *Contributor to:* Southwest Heritage; Liberal Arts Review; Rocky Mountain Review; National Society of Published Poets Anthology. *Membership:* Literary Club. *Address:* PO Box 635, Portales, NM 88130, USA.

ROBINSON, Noel Mary, b. Melbourne, Australia. Writer. *Education:* BA, Sydney University. *Publications:* Playwright, Film Scriptwriter; Stage Plays: Glasstown, 1973; Family Matter, 1976. *Contributor to:* Many contributions to British and Australian TV & Radio. *Memberships:* Writers Guild of Great Britain; Australian Writers Guild. *Literary Agent:* Curtis Brown. *Address:* 14/6 Wyargine St, Mosman, NSW 2088, Australia.

ROBINSON, Sheila Mary, b. 18 Nov. 1928, Cogenhoe, Northamptonshire, England. Writer. *Education:* BA, University of London. *Publications:* Death & the Maiden, 1978; The Chief Inspector's Daughter, 1981; A Talent for Destruction, 1982; Blood on the Happy Highway, 1983; Fate Worse Than Death, 1985. *Literary Agent:* Curtis Brown. *Address:* c/o Curtis Brown, 162-168 Regent Street, London W1R 5TB, England.

ROBISON, Mary, b. 14 Jan. 1949, Washington, District of Columbia, USA. Fiction Writer, Assistant Professor of English. m. James Robison, 2 daughters. *Education:* MA English with honours, Johns Hopkins University, 1977. *Literary Appointments:* Ohio University, Athens, Ohio, 1979–80; Harvard University, Cambridge, Massachusetts, 1981–87; Oberlin College, Oberlin, Ohio, 1984–85. *Publications:* Days, short story collection, 1979; Oh!, novel, 1981; An Amateurs Guide To The Night, short story collection, 1983. *Contributions to:* The New Yorker. *Honour:* Guggenheim, 1980–81. *Memberships:* PEN; Author's Guild. *Literary Agent:* Andrew Wylie, Andrew Wylie Agency. *Address:* 17 Clark Road, Brookline, MA 02146, USA.

ROBITAILLE, Gerald, b. 27 May 1923, Outremont, Quebec, Canada. Writer. m. Diane Nelder, 25 Jan. 1950, Montreal, Quebec. *Literary Appointments:* Secretary, American Writer Henry Miller. *Publications:* The Book of Knowledge, 1964; Un Huron a la recherche de l'art, 1967; Images, 1969, 71; Le Pere Miller, 1971, 80; Pays perdu et retrouve, 1980. Various translations. *Contributions to:* Liberte; Nouvelles Litteraires; Int H M Letter; Synthese, Belgium; Hoama, Caracas; El Corno Emplumado, Mexico; Svetova Literatura; Biographie de Henry Miller, in Encyclopedie Universalis. *Address:* CP 583, Les Hauts-de-Morin, Quebec, Canada J0R 1H0.

ROBSON, Derek Ian, b. 26 Sep. 1935, Leeds, England. Teacher. m. Margaret, 17 May 1958, Melbourne, Australia, 1 son, 1 daughter. *Education:* BA; DipEd; BEd; MEd. *Appointments:* Editor, Staff Development Association Journal, 1974–; Editor, Studies in Administration, 15 volumes, 1977–. *Publications include:* A Student's British History, 1964; A Student's Asian History, 1968; Indonesia – A Brief Survey, 1968; The Use of Sources, co-author, 1969; Evaluation, co-author, 1974; co-author, Booklets including, History Co-Ordinator's Handbook; History Teacher's Handbook; Survival Lessons for History Teachers. *Contributions to:* Numerous professional journals and magazines including; Historian; Senior Staff Association Journal; Studies in Administration; Staff Development Journal; etc. *Honour:* Member Australian College of

Education, 1983. *Address:* 2 Apple Court, East Burwood, Melbourne, Australia 3151.

ROCES, Alfredo, b. 29 Apr. 1932, Manila, Philippines. Writer-Painter; Editor. m. Irene Pineda, 28 May 1957, Manila, 3 daughters. *Education:* BFA, University of Notre Dame, USA. *Literary Appointments:* Daily Columnist, Daily Mirror, 1958; Daily Columnist, Manila Times, 1959–72; Editor-in-Chief, Filipino Heritage, 10 Volume Encyclopedia, 1972–78; Editor, Geo, Australasia's Geographical Magazine, 1978–. *Publications:* The Story of the Philippines, 1968; Amorsolo, 1975; Sanso, 1976; Drawings, 1974; Filipino Nude, 1977; Culture Shock, Philippines, 1985; Philippine Cartoons, political cartoons of the American Era, 1985. *Contributions to:* Hemisphere (Australia); La Revue Francais: Asian Pacific Quarterly; Arts of Asia; Orientations; Sunday Times Magazine; Philippine Studies; Veritas; Mr and Mrs; Solidaridad. *Honours:* Ten Outstanding Young Men (TOYM) of the Philippines, 1961; Arawng Pasay Heritage Award in Journalism, 1970; Citizen Council for Mass Media Columnist of the Year, 1971. *Address:* 2 Furber Place, Davidson, New South Wales, Australia.

ROCHA, Nuno, b. 13 Feb. 1933. Porto, Portugal. Journalist. m. Maria do Sameiro Souto, 2 Sep. 1958, 2 daughters. *Education:* Faculty of Letters, Lisbon. *Literary Appointments:* Editor, Tempo Weekly, Lisbon, 1975–. *Publications:* Franca – Emigracao Dolorosa; Guerra em Mocamique; Memorias de um Ano de Revolucao – 1975; O Jornalismo como Romance. *Memberships:* International Press Institute, England; Freedom House, USA. *Literary Agent:* Editora Nova Nordica/Tempo. *Address:* Av dos Estados Unidos da America 107-60, 1700 Lisbon, Portugal.

ROCHER, Gregory David de, b. 21 Dec. 1943, Valparaiso, Indiana, USA. Professor, Romance Languages and Classics. m. Françoise Blanche Simon Bierge, 16 Apr. 1966, Michigan, 2 sons, 1 daughter. *Education:* Certificat d'Aptude à l'enseignement du français à l'estranger; Certificat d'Etudes françaises, Université de Poitiers, France, 1965, AB, University of Detroit, 1966; MA, PhD, 1967, 1972, University of Michigan. *Publications:* Rabelais's Laughers and Joubert's Traité du Ris, 1979; Treatise on Laughter, Editor, Annotator, 1980; Options: Aperçus de la France, co-author, 1980. *Contributor to:* Bibliothèque d'Humanisme et Renaissance; Revue de Philologie et d'Histoire; The French Review; French Forum; Kentucky Romance Quarterly; Journal of the Faculty of Arts and Sciences of the Royal University of Malta; Renaissance Papers. *Honour:* Grand Prix du poème du Cercle Français, Prix Jean Moréas, 1977. *Memberships:* Modern Language Association; Renaissance Society of America; American Association of Teachers of French; Southeastern Renaissance Conference; Association International des Seiziernistes. *Address:* 220 Pelham Loop Road, Tuscaloosa, AL 35405, USA.

ROCK, Maxine Arlene, b. 29 Apr. 1940, New York City, USA. Journalist; Author. m. David F Rock, 3 Sep. 1963, New York, 1 son, 1 daughter. *Educations:* BS, Journalism, New York University; MA, Journalism & Science, University of Michigan. *Appointments include:* Instructor, University of Maryland, 1967; Professor, Georgia State University, 1975. *Publications:* Gut Reactions, 1980; Fiction Writer's Help Book, 1982. *Contributor to:* New York Times; Smithsonian; McCalls; Travel & Leisure; Inc; The South; Southern Accents; Atlantic Business Atlanta. *Honours:* Recipient, various scholarships; Sigma Delta Chi Gold Key Award, New York University, 1960; Motar Board, Woman of the Year, Georgia State University, 1975; 2nd Place, Nonfiction, Readers Digest Foundation, 1981; Woman of the Year, Journalism, Davidson's of Atlanta, 1982; 1st Prize, non-fiction, Writers Digest, 1982; etc. *Literary Agent:* Libby Mark, New York City. *Address:* 370 Valley Green Drive, NE, Atlanta, GA 30342, USA.

RODAHL, Kaare, b. 17 Aug. 1917, Brönnöysund, Norway. Scientist; Author. m. Joan Hunter, 6 Apr. 1946, Oslo, 1 son, 1 daughter. *Education:* MD, 1948, DSc,

1950; Oslo University. *Appointments:* Special Consultant, US Air Force, 1949; Chief, Physiology, Artic Aeromedical Laboratory, Alaska, 1950–52; Assistant Professor, Physiology, Oslo University, 1952–54; Director, Research, Artic Aeromedical Laboratory, Alaska, 1954–57; Director, Research, Lankenau Hospital, Philadelphia, USA, 1957–65; Director, Institute of Work Physiology, Oslo, 1965; Professor, Norwegian College of Physical Education, Oslo, 1966–. *Publications:* Numerous books including: North, 1953; The Last of the Few, 1963; Be Fit for Life, 1966; Stress, 1972. *Contributor To:* Numerous scientific and popular journals and magazines; Co-author, Textbook of Work Physiology, 1985. *Address:* Måltrostveien 40, Holmenkollen, 0390 Oslo 3, Norway.

RODDICK, Nicholas James, b. 27 July 1945, Cheshire, England. Magazine Editor. m. Joanna Elizabeth Hayes, 15 Nov. 1984, London, 2 sons, 1 daughter. *Education:* MA, Honours, Oxon, 1966; BA, 1968, PhD, 1976, Bristol. *Appointments:* Film Editor, Stills Magazine, 1983–85; Editor, Cinema Papers, 1985–. *Publications:* A New Deal in Entertainment: Warner Brothers in the 1930's, 1983; British Cinema Now, 1985. *Contributor to:* Sight & Sound; Monthly Film Bulletin; Times Literary Supplement; Los Angeles Times. *Address:* c/o Cinema Papers, 644 Victoria Street, North Melbourne, Victoria 3051, Australia.

RODES, Robert Emmet, b. 29 May 1927, New York, New York, USA. Professor of Law. m. Jeanne Emily Cronin, 29 Aug. 1953, Belmont, Massachusetts, 5 sons, 2 daughters. *Education:* AB, Brown University, 1947; LLB (changed to JD), Harvard University, 1952. *Publications:* The Legal Enterprise, 1976; Ecclesiastical Administration in Medieval England, 1977; Lay Authority and Reformation in the English Church, 1982. *Contributions to:* Legal and theological publications. *Address:* Notre Dame Law School, Notre Dame, IN 46556, USA.

RODGERS (Sir) John Charles, b. 5 Oct. 1906, York, England. Company Chairman/Author. m. Betsy Aiken-Sneath, 23 Dec. 1930, London, 2 sons. *Education:* MA, Keble College, Oxford. *Publications:* Mary Ward Settlement – A History, 1931; Old Public Schools of England, 1938; English Woodland, 1941; English Rivers, 1947; Tobias and Raphael, 1949; York, 1951; Thomas Gray – edited; One Nation, 1950; Atlantic Community, 1963; Industry looks at the New Order. *Honour:* Fellow of the Royal Society of Arts. *Address:* The Dower House, Groombridge, Kent, England.

RODRIGUEZ, Judith Catherine, b. 13 Feb. 1936, Perth, Western Australia, Australia. Writer; Teacher; Editor. m. (2) Thomas William Shapcott, 11 Oct. 1982. *Literary Appointments include:* Poetry Reader, Freemantle Arts Centre Press, 1983; Consultant, Western Australia Arts Council, 1984; Consultant, Literature Board, Australia Council for the Arts, 1985. *Publications include:* Witch Heart, poems, 1982; Mrs Noah and the Minoan Queen, Editor, poems by 6 Australian women poets, 1983; Noela Hjorth, monograph with Vicki Pauli, 1984; Poems selected from The Australian's 20th Anniversary Competition, edited with Andrew Taylor, 1985. *Contributions to:* Sydney Morning Herald, Poetry column, 1984. *Memberships:* Past Executive Committee Member, Melbourne Centre, PEN International; Past Management Committee Member, Australian Society of Authors. *Address:* 62 Cremorne Road, Cremorne, NSW 2090, Australia.

ROEMER, Kenneth Morrison, b. 6 June 1945, East Rockaway, New York, USA. University Professor. m. Claire M Roemer, 15 June 1968, East Rockaway, New York, 1 son, 1 daughter. *Education:* BA, Hons, English, Harvard University, 1967; MA, American Civilization, 1968, PhD, American Civilization, 1971, University of Pennsylvania. *Publications:* The Obsolete Necessity: America in Utopian Writings, 1888–1900, 1976; America as Utopia, 1981; Build Your Own Utopia, 1981. *Contributions to:* Approximately 50 reviews and essays on Utopian and Indian Literature in journals such as

American Literature; College English; American Quarterly; American Historical Review and the Japan Times. *Honours:* Exxon Foundation Grant, 1977; National Endowment for the Humanities Grant, Texas Committee for the Humanities, 1985. *Memberships:* Chairman, Executive Committee on late 19th Century and early 20th Century American Literature 1981, Modern Language Association; Chairman, Native American Literature Discussion Group 1981; Chairman, Publicity Committee, Society for Utopian Studies. *Address:* Department of English, Box 19035, University of Texas at Arlington, Arlington, TX 76019, USA.

ROES, Nicholas A, b. 26 Dec. 1952, Jersey City, New Jersey, USA. Writer. m. Nancy Bennett, 26 Nov. 1977, Massapequa. *Education:* BS, 1974, MA, 1983, University of Bridgeport. *Publications:* America's Lowest Cost Colleges, 1977, 5th edition 1985; Helping Children Watch TV, 1979, 2nd edition 1983. *Contributor to:* Syndicated columnist; Editor, Teacher Update Newsletter; Wall Street Casino, Regular Feature. *Membership:* EDPRESS. *Agent:* Theron Raines, Raines & Raines, New York, USA. *Address:* PO Box 205, Saddle River, NJ 07458, USA.

ROESCH, Ronald, b. 25 May 1947, New Jersey, USA. Professor. m. Kathy, 13 Nov. 1976, Champaign, USA, 2 sons. *Education:* Phd, Psychology, University of Illinois, 1977. *Appointments:* Professor, Psychology, Simon Fraser University. *Publications:* Competency to Stand Trial, with S L Golding, 1980; Evaluation and Criminal Justice Policy, with R Corrado, 1981. *Contributor to:* 35 articles amd chapters published. *Honours:* Social Issue Dissertation Award, 1977; Consulting Psychology Research Award, 1977; American Bar Association Travel Award Certificate of Merit, 1981. *Address:* Simon Fraser University, Dept of Psychology, Burnaby, BC V5A 1S6, Canada.

ROESELER, Wolfgang Guenter Joachim, b. 30 Mar. 1925, Berlin, Germany. Educator; Professor, Urban Planning, Texas A & M University; Director, Texas A & M University Center for Urban Affairs. m. Eva Maria Jante, 12 Mar. 1947, Marburg, Federal Republic of Germany, 1 son, 2 daughters. *Education:* PhD, Economics & Sociology, University of Hesse at Marburg; Post-doctoral studies, University of Wisconsin, Madison, USA. *Literary Appointments:* Chairman, Publication Advisory Council, American review of Public Administration, 1982. *Publications:* EMR Publications: General Policies & Principles for Prototype Zoning Regulations, 1976; Alternative Goals of Urbanization for America, 1977; US Department of Transportation: Impact of Technological Changes in Transportation on Productivity and Development, 1981; Lexington Books, Successful American Urban Plans, 1981; Institute of Transportation Engineers, Synthetic Fuels and other Petroleum Substitutes – Impacts on Transportation, 1982; Ekistics, 1985: Advanced Industrial Technology and Settling the Desert: Examination of Recent Saudi Desert Settlement Projects. *Contributor to:* Bruecke und Strasse; Western City; American City; Kansas City Law Review; Journal of Housing; Traffic Quarterly; ASCE Journal of Urban Planning; Urban Lawyer; Midwest Review of Public Administration; etc. *Address:* 2508 Broadmoor, Bryan, TX 77801, USA.

ROETTGER, Dorye, b. 22 Oct. 1932, Utica, New York, USA. Musician, Journalist. *Education:* BMus, University Extension Conservatory, Chicago, Illinois, USA, 1955; PhD, University of East Florida, 1972. *Literary Appointments:* Founder, Director, Festival Players of California; Creator, Artistic Apprenticeship, a project within Festival Plaques; Editor, Independent News Bureau; Syndicated Columnist, Bridging the Culture Gap. *Contributor to:* Herald Dispatch; Music Educators Journal; Sounding Board; Overture; Los Angeles Times; and others. *Memberships:* National Writers Club; Los Angeles Press Club. *Address:* 3809 De Longpre Avenue, Los Angeles, CA 90027, USA.

ROGALA, Stanislaw Joseph, b. 9 Oct. 1948, Zrecze Chalupczanskie, Poland. Writer. m. Wanda Teresa

Kargulewicz, 19 Aug. 1972, Ozarow, 1 son, 1 daughter. *Education:* MA, Polish Philolgy. *Publications:* Modlitwa o Grzech, 1978; Zreczaki, 1979; Pisarze Kielecczyzny, 1981; Nocne Czuwanie, 1982; Vcieczki, 1984; Piotrowe Pole, 1985. *Contributor to:* Przemiany; Okolice; Akcent; Zeszyty Kieleckie-Slowo. *Honours:* 3rd Prize, Literary Competition, 30th Anniversary of LSW, 1978; 3rd Prize, Literary Competition, Robotnicy, 1978; Award, Ministry of Education, 1979; 1st Prize, 40th Anniversary of the Peoples Republic of Poland, 1984; 34d Prize, Drama Competition, 1985. *Memberships:* Chairman, Kielce Centre, Correspondence Writers' Club, 1976–80; President, Kielce Branch, Polish Writers' Union, 1981–. *Address:* 05 Stoneczne Wxgorze 8 m 13, 25–480 Kielce, Poland.

ROGER-HENRICHSEN, Gudmund, b. 16 Mar. 1907, Copenhagen, Denmark. Literary Critic; Literary Historian. *Education:* MA, University of Copenhagen; Queens College, University of Cambridge, UK. *Publications include:* De tålte ikke tvang (They Could't Bear Tyranny), 1948; Vejen går om Grøonland (Greenland – A Long Passage Out & Back To Civilization), 1955; England genskabes 1945–60 (The Restoration of England After The War), 1961; Digtere i vort Samfund 1900–60 (Great Danish Writers in the Middle of our Society), 1963; A Decade of Danish Literature, 1960–70 (English & German translations), 1971. *Contributions to:* Various journals & newspapers. Literary tour of UK, 1984; BBC broadcasts; The Committee of Exchange of Literature between countries in the World, inside The Ministry of Culture in DK. *Memberships include:* Dansk Forfatterforening; PEN V. *Honours:* Prizes, Swedish Fund, Clara Lachmann, 1965; Danish Carlsberg Fund, 1978. *Literary Agent:* Gyldendals Forlag. *Address:* Rymarksvej 16, DK 2900 Hellerup Denmark.

ROGERS, Jane Rosalind, b. 21 July 1952, London, England. Novelist/Teacher. 1 son, 1 daughter. *Education:* BA, Hons, English Literature, New Hall, Cambridge, 1974; Post-Graduate Certificate of Education, Leicester University, 1976. *Literary Appointment:* Writer-in-Residence, Northern College, Barnsley, South Yorkshire, 1985–86. *Publications:* Separate Tracks, 1983, 1984; Her Living Image, 1984, 1986. *Contributions to:* Occasional reviewing for local arts paper and Times Literary Supplement. *Honours:* North West Arts Writers' Bursary, 1984; Somerset Maugham Award for, Her Living Image, 1985. *Membership:* The Writers' Guild. *Literary Agent:* Pat Kavanagh, A D Peters and Co Ltd. *Address:* c/o Pat Kavanagh, A D Peters and Co Ltd, 10 Buckingham Street, London WC2N 6BU, England.

ROGERS, Pattiann, b. 23 Mar. 1940, Joplin, Missouri, USA. Poet. m. John Robert Rogers, 3 Sep. 1960, Joplin, Missouri, 2 sons. *Education:* BA, English Literature, University of Missouri, Columbia; MA, Creative Writing, University of Houston. *Publication:* The Expectations of Light, 1981. *Contributions to:* Poetry; Poetry Northwest; Georgia Review; Iowa Review; Virginia Quarterly Review; Prairie Schooner; New Yorker; Massachusetts Review; Southern Review. *Honours:* Bess Hokin Prize from Poetry, 1982; Voertman Poetry Award, Texas Institute of Letters, 1982; NEA Grant, 1982; Guggenheim Fellowship, 1984–85. *Memberships:* PEN American Center; Texas Institute of Letters; Modern Poetry Association. *Address:* 11502 Brookmeadows Lane, Stafford, TX 77477, USA.

ROGERS, Thomas Hunton, b. 23 June 1927, Chicago IL, USA. Teacher/Writer. m. 16 June 1956, Chicago, 2 daughters. *Education:* MA, PhD, University of Iowa. *Publications:* The Pursuit of Happiness, 1968; The Confession of a Child of the Century, 1972; At the Shores, 1980. *Contributions to:* Short stories in The American Review, Esquire; Reviews in Commentary, Book Week, New Republic, Chicago Sun Times. *Honours:* Friends of American Literature Prize for The Pursuit of Happiness, 1969, and The Confession of a child of the Century; Rosenthal Foundation Award from the National Institute of Arts and Letters for The

Confession of a Child of the Century; Guggenheim Fellowship, 1969–70. *Memberships:* PEN Club; Institute for the Arts and Humanistic Studies, Penn State University. *Literary Agents:* Georges Borchardt, Michelle Lapautre. *Address:* 502 E Foster State College, PA 16801, USA.

ROGGEMAN, Willem Maurits, b. 9 July 1935, Brussels, Belgium. Journalist. m. 8 Jan. 1975, Brussels, 1 son, 1 daughter. *Education:* Economic sciences, University of Ghent. *Publications:* Poetry: Rhapsody in Blue, 1958; Baudelaire Verliefd, 1964; Memoires, 1985; Een leegte die Verdwijnt, 1985. Novels: De Centauren, 1963; De Verbeelding, 1966. Essays: Cesare Pavese, 1961; Beroepsgeheim, 1975. *Contributions to:* De Vlaamse Gids; Nieuw Vlaams Tijdschrift; Avenue; De Gids. *Honours:* Dirk Martensprize, 1963; Louis Paul Boon Prize, 1974; Prize, City of Brussels, 1975. *Memberships:* Vereniging van Vlaamse Letterkungigon; Secretary, Flemish PEN Centre. *Address:* Albert Heyrbautlaan 48, 1710 Dilbee, Belgium.

ROHNER, Ronald P, b. 17 Apr. 1935, Crescent City, California, USA. Professor of Anthropology. m. Nancy D Rohner, 9 June 1984, Manchester, 1 son, 1 daughter. *Education:* BS, Psychology, 1958; MA, Anthropology, 1960; PhD, Anthropology, 1964. *Publications:* The People of Gilford: A Contemporary Kwakiutl Village, 1967; The Ethnography of Franz Boas: Letters and Diaries of Franz Boas written on the Northwest Coast from 1886 to 1931, 1969; The Kwakiutl: Indians of British Columbia, 1970; They Love Me, They Love Me Not: A Worldwide Study of the Effects of Parental Acceptance and Rejection, 1975; Parental Acceptance and Rejection: A Review and Annotated Bibliography of Research and Theory, 2 volumes, 1978; Worldwide Tests of Parental Acceptance-Rejection Theory,Co Editor, 1980; Handbook for the Study of Parental Acceptance and Rejection, 1980; The Warmth Dimension; Foundations of Parental Acceptance-Rejection Theory, 1986; Palashpur: Family Interaction and Child Socialization in a West Bengal Village (under review for publication). *Contributor to:* 41 Articles, 21 Reviews and other publications. *Honours:* Recipient, numerous honours and awards including NIMH Research Grant, 1980–84; Fellow, American Psychological Association, 1980; National Science Foundation Travel Grant to India, 1981. *Memberships:* American Anthropological Association; American Psychological Association; Society for Cross-Cultural Research; International Association for Cross-Cultural Psychology; Society for Psychological Anthropology; etc. *Address:* Centre for the Study of Parental Acceptance & Rejection, University of Connecticut, Storrs, CT 06268, USA.

ROHRBACH, Peter Thomas, b. 27 Feb. 1926, New York City, New York, USA. Writer. m. Sheila Sheehan, 21 Sep. 1970, Washington, District of Columbia, 1 daughter. *Education:* BA, MA, Catholic University of America. *Publications:* Author of 15 books including: Conversation with Christ, 1981; Stagecoach East, 1983; American Issue, 1985. *Contributions to:* Time-Life; Washington Star; America; Aviation News; PAMA News; AIA Journal; and various encyclopedias. *Memberships:* Authors Guild of America; Poets, Playwrights, Editors, Essayists and Novelists; Washington Independent Writers. *Literary Agent:* Gloria Mosesson, New York. *Address:* 9609 Barkston Court, Potomac, MD 20850, USA.

ROHWER, (Franz) Jurgen, b. 24 May 1924, Friedrichrode, Thuringia, Germany. Director, Library of Contemporary History. *Education:* History, Hamburg University, 1947–53; Dr.phil. 1954. *Publications include:* Seemacht heute, 1957; Entscheidungaschlachten Zweiten Weltkrieges, 1960 (English edition, Decisive Battles of World War II, 1965, Italian, Spanish editions); Die U-Booterfolge der Achsenmachte, 1964 (English edition, Axis Submarine Successes 1939–45, 1983); Ed. Piterskij, Die Sowgetflotte im Zweiten Weltkrieg, 1966; Chronik des Seekrieges 1939–45, 1968 (English edition, Chronology of the War at Sea, 2 volumes, 1972–74);

Seemacht, Von der Antike bis zur Gegenwart, 1974, 82; The Confrontation of Superpowers at Sea, 1975; Geleitzugschlachten im Marz, 1943, 76 (English edition, Critical Convoy Battles of March 1943, 1977); Die Funkaufklarung und ihre Rolle in Zweiten Weltkrieg, 1979; Kriegswende Dezember 1941, 1984; Der Mord an den Juden in Zweiten Weltkrieg, 1985; Neue Forschungen zur Geschichts des Ersten Weltkrieges, 1985. *Contributor to:* and Editor of several historical series and magazines including: Marine-Rundschau! Editor, 1958–; Jahresbibliographie der Bibliothek fur Zeitgeschichte; Editor, 19590; Brassey's Defence Annual; US Naval Institute Proceedings and Naval Review; Review Maritime; Defence Journal; Karachi. *Memberships:* Member, National International and foreign professional organisations including: Arbeitskreis fur Wehrforschung, President; Commission Internationale d'Histoire Militaire, Vice President. *Address:* Bibliothek für Zeitpeschichte, Konrad Adenauer Stc 8, D–7000 Stuttgart 1, Federal Republic of Germany.

ROKEBY-THOMAS, Anna Elma, b. 10 May 1911, Crieff, Ontario, Canada. Registered Nurse (retired); Housewife, *Education:* Guelph General Hospital School of Nursing; Anglican Woman's College. *Publications:* Ningiyuks Igloo World, 1972, 1973, German Translation, 1977; Ning's Igloo Romance, 1975, Swedish translation, 1978. *Contributions to:* North Magazine; Family Herald; Jack and Jill; Young World; Discovery; Golden Book; Canadian Nurse. *Honour:* Ningiyuk's Igloo World, in exhibition of Notable Canadian Children's Books, National Library of Canada, 1973. *Address:* 74 Jackson Ave, Kitchener, Ontario, Canada N2H 3P1.

ROLAND, Charles Gordon, b. 25 Jan. 1933, Winnipeg, Canada. University Professor, History of Medicine. *Education:* B Sc Med 1958, MD, 1958, University of Manitoba. *Publications:* Scientific Writing, (with Lester S King), 1968; William Osler: The Continuing Education, (with J P McGovern), 1969; An Annotated Checklist of Osleriana, (with E Nation and J P McGovern), 1976; An Annotated Bibliography of Canadian Medical Periodicals, 1979; Health, Disease and Medicine: Essays in Canadian History, (Editor), 1983; Secondary Sources in Canadian Medical History: A Bibliography, 1984. *Contributions to:* Journals including: Annals of Allergy; New England Journal of Medicine; Books, Manuscripts and the History of Medicine. *Honours:* Hannah Visiting Lecturer, Universities of Western Ontario, Toronto and Ottawa and Queen's University, 1976; Squibb Lecturer, Cardiff, Wales, 1978; Sid W Richardson Visiting Professor of Medical Humanities, University of Texas, USA, 1984; Visiting Fellow, Huntington Library, San Marino, California, 1984. *Memberships:* Chicago Literary Society; Bibliographical Society of Canada; President 1970, American Medical Writers Association. *Address:* 3N10–HSC, McMaster University, Hamilton, Ontario, L8N 3Z5, Canada.

ROLFE, Bari, b. 20 July 1916, Chicago, Illinois, USA. Teacher; Writer. *Publications:* Behind the Mask, 1977; Commedia dell-Arte, A Scene Study Book, 1977; Mime Bibliography, 1978; Farces, Italian Style, 1978; Mimes on Miming, 1980. *Contributor to:* Quarterly Journal of Speech; Educational Theatre Journal; Impulse; Los Angeles Times; San Francisco Chronicle; Drama Review; Chicago Tribune; Mime Journal Number One; Mime Journal Number 2; Dance Magazine; Mime Mask and Marionette; Mime News; etc. *Address:* 434–66th Street, Oakland, CA 94609, USA.

ROLL, Eric (Sir), Lord Roll of Ipsden, b. 1907. Former Professor of Economics and Commerce, University of Hull. *Education:* BCom, PhD, University of Birmingham. *Publications:* An Early Experiment in Industrial Organisation, 1930; Spotlight on Germany, 1933; About Money, 1934; Elements of Economic Theory, 1935; The Combined Food Board, 1957; The World After Keynes, 1968; A History of Economic Thought, 1973; The Uses and Abuses of Economics, 1978; Crowded Hours, 1985. *Contributor to:* Economic

Journal; Economica; American Economic Review. *Honours: KCMG; CB.* Address: 33 King William Street, London EC4 R9AS, England.

ROLLINS, Wayne Gilbert, b. 24 Aug. 1929, Detroit, Michigan, USA. Professor of Religious Studies. m. Donnalou Myerholtz, 30 Aug. 1953, Oak Harbor, 3 sons. *Education:* BA, Capital University, 1951; BD, Yale Divinity School, 1954; MA, 1956, PhD, 1960, Yale University. *Appointments:* Instructor, Princeton University, 1958–59; Assistant Professor, Wellesley College, 1959–66; Professor, Hartford Seminary Foundation, 1966–74; Professor, Coordinator, Graduate Programme, Religious Studies, Assumption College, 1974–. *Publications:* The Gospels: Portraits of Christ, 1964; Jung and the Bible, 1983. *Contributor to:* Assumption Quarterly; Canadian Forum; Choice; Hartford Quarterly; Journal of American Academy of Religion; Journal of Biblical Literature; Journal for the Scientific Study of Religion; New Testament Studies; etc; Contributor to, Festschrift Volume, Interpreter's Dictionary of the Bible. *Honours:* The Gospels; Portraits of Christ, January 1964 Selection, Religious Book Club; University Fellow, Yale University, 1955; American Association of Theological Schools Fellow, 1970. *Memberships:* American Academy of Religion, President, New England Section, 1984–85; Society of Biblical Literature; Studiorum Novi Testamenti Societas. *Address:* 75 Craigmoor Road, West Hartford, CT 06107, USA.

ROLLS, Eric Charles, b. 25 Apr. 1923, Grenfell, New South Wales, Australia. Author; Farmer. m. Joan Stephenson, 27 Feb. 1954, Newcastle, New South Wales, 2 sons, 1 daughter. *Publications:* Sheaf Tosser, 1967; They All Ran Wild, 1969; Running Wild, 1973; The River, 1974; The Green Mosaic, 1977; Miss Strawberry Verses, 1978; A Million Wild Acres, 1981; Celebration of the Senses, 1984. *Contributions to:* The Bulletin; Overland; National Times; The Age; Sydney Morning Herald; and various others. *Honours:* David Myer Trust Award for Poetry, 1968; Captain Cook Bicentennial Award for Non-Fiction, 1970; John Franklin Award, for Children's Book, 1974; Braille Book of the Year, 1975; The Age Book of the Year, 1981; Talking Book of the Year, 1982; Fellow, Australian Academy of the Humanities, 1985. *Memberships:* Australian Society of Authors; National Book Council. *Literary Agent:* Curtis Brown Pty Limited. *Address:* Cumberdeen, Baradine, NSW 2396, Australia.

ROLSTON, Holmes II, b. 19 Nov. 1932, Staunton, Virginia, USA. Educator. m. Jane Irving Wilson, 1 June 1956, Richmond, 2 son, 1 daughter. *Education:* BS, Davidson College, 1953; BD, Union Theological Seminary, Richmond, 1956; MA, University of Pittsburgh, 1968; PhD, Theology, University of Edinburgh, Soctland, 1958. *Appointments:* Professor, Philosophy, Colorado State University, 1968–; Visiting Scholar, Harvard University Center for the Study of World Religions, 1974–75. *Publications:* John Calvin versus the Westminster Confession, 1972; Religious Inquiry – Participation and Detachment, 1985. *Contributor to:* Ethics; Environmental Ethics; Natural History; Inquiry; Zygon; Journal of Medicine and Philosophy. *Honours:* University Award, Distinguished Teaching and Outstanding Service (Pennock Award), 1983. *Memberships:* American Academy of Religion; American Philosophical Association. *Address:* Dept of Philosophy, Colorado State University, Fort Collins, CO 80523, USA.

ROMANO, Deane Louis, b. 4 Jan. 1927, El Paso, Texas, USA. Author; Screenwriter; Novelist. *Education:* Art Institute of Chicago, 1 year; Various courses, New York University, University of California (Berkeley, Los Angeles). *Publications:* Posh, 1968; The Town That Took a Trip, 1968; Flight from Time One, 1972. *Memberships:* Writers Guild of America; Science Fiction Writers of America. *Address:* 4612 Fern Place, Los Angeles, CA 90032, USA.

ROMANO, Louis George, b. 1 Jan. 1921, Milwaukee, Wisconsin, USA. Professor. m. Shirley Mae Stevens, 20 Feb. 1943, Milwaukee, 2 daughters. *Education:* BS, Milwaukee State Teachers College, 1943; MS, 1946, PhD, 1955, University of Wisconsin-Madison. *Publications:* Author of over 100 books including, Exploring Wisconsin, 1957; Events in the Life of Thomas Jefferson, 1966; A Guide to Successful Parent–Teacher Conferences, 1966; The History of Our Nation's Capital, 1968; Wisconsin Historical Sites, 1968; Famous Black Leaders, 1969; Evaluation of Teacher Competancy, 1968; Selective Readings on General Supervision, 1970; The Management of Educational Personnel, 1973; A Guide to an Effective Middle School, 1984. *Contributions to:* Educational Leadership; National Middle School Journal; Michigan Middle School Journal; Clearing House. *Honour:* Hall of Fame (Michigan Association of Middle School Educators). *Memberships:* Michigan Association of Middle School Educators (Executive Director); Phi Delta Kappa (Vice-President); National Middle School Association (Former President). *Address:* 4453 Manitou Okemos, MI 48864, USA.

ROME, Margaret, b. 20 Sep. 1929, Carlisle, England. Romantic Novelist. m. Ronald Rome, 30 Sep. 1950, Carlisle, 1 son. *Education:* Secretarial skills, business studies. *Publications include:* 36 novels, many reprints, 1968–85. Majority translated into many languages including Japanese & Serbo-Croat; numerous bestsellers; first novel still in print. *Memberships:* Society of Authors; Romantic Novelists Association; Authors Lending & Copyright Society. *Address:* Rome Publications Ltd, 202 Dalston Road, Carlisle, Cumbria CA2 6DY.

ROMERO, Luis, b. 24 May 1916, Barcelona, Spain. Writer. *Education:* Perito Mercantil. *Publications:* Novels: La Noria, 1952, Los Otros, 1956, El Cacique, 1963; Stories: Esas sombras del trasmundo, 1957; Art books: Todo Dali en in rostro, 1975; Histories: Tres dias de julio, 1967; Cara y Cruz de la Republica, 1980; Further publications: Poetry: Cuerda Tensa; Novel: Carta de Aver, Las Viejas voces, La Noche buena, La Corriente; Stories: Tuda; Histories: Desastre em Cartagena, El final de la guerra; Two short novels: in Catalan: La Finestra & El Carrer; Two books on Spanish wine shops; Two illustrated books: Barcelona and Costa Brava; Recent publication: Aquel Dali, illustrated with photographs. *Contributions to:* La Vanquardia; Historia y Vida etc. *Memberships:* Corresponding Member, Hispanic Society of America; Society of Spanish and Spanish American Studies. *Honours include:* Premio Nadal, 1951; Premio Planeta, 1963. *Address:* calle Calabria 152, Barcelona 15, Spain.

ROMINE, Aden Foster, b. 6 Oct. 1940, Gainesville, Texas, USA. Aerospace Quality Control Engineer. m. Mary Cox Romine, 14 Apr. 1978, Grand Prairie, Texas. *Education:* Hume Financial Institute, 1985; BA, Psychology, Columbia Pacific University, 1985. *Literary Appointments:* Editor, High School Newspaper; Editor, Company Newspaper. *Publications:* The Eternity Stone, 1980; The Fellowship, 1984. *Contributor to:* Popular Boating; Skin Diver; Ranch Romances; Planets Stories; Lake Texoma News. *Honours:* 3rd Prize, Texas Poetry Society, Troy, 1972; 1st Prize, National Poetry Day, My Brother's Name is Legion, 1973. *Memberships:* Fort Worth Poetry Society, Vice President; Texas Poetry Society; National Writer's Club. *Literary Agent:* Ellen Lively Steele & Associates. *Address:* 511 S. Bowen Road, #F, Arlington, TX 76013, USA.

ROMO, Ricardo, b. 23 June 1943, San Antonio, Texas, USA. History Professor. m. Harriett Durr, 1 July 1967, Pasadena, Texas, 1 son, 1 daughter. *Education:* BA, University of Texas at Austin; MA, Loyola University, Los Angeles, California, Los Angeles. *Publications:* New Directions in Chicano Scholarship, (with Raymond Paredes), 1978; East Los Angeles: History of a Barrio, 1983 and 1984. *Contributions to:* The Texas Humanist; Aztlan; Texas Books in Review; Western Historical Quarterly; Hispanic American Historical Review; Pacific Historical Review; Reviews in American History. *Honour:* Chancellor's Distinguished

Lectureship, University of California, Berkeley. *Address:* History Department, University of Texas at Austin, Austin, TX 78712, USA.

ROMTVEDT, David, b. 6 June 1950, Portland, Oregon, USA. Writer. *Education:* BA, Reed College; MFA, Iowa Writers' Workshop. *Publications:* Writing from the World. (assistant editor), 1976; Loaf of Bread and a Bus Ticket Home, (play), 1982; Moon, (poems), 1984; Free and Compulsory for All, (fiction), 1984. *Contributions to:* Numerous publications, including, American Poetry Review; Paris Review; The Arts, and others. *Honours:* NEA Writer-In-Residence Fellowship, 1979; King County Arts Commission Publication Award, 1983; UCross Foundation Residency Fellowship, 1984. *Address:* 457 N Main, Buffalo, NY 82834, USA.

RONAN, Colin Alistair, b. 4 June 1920, London, England. Author. *Education:* BSc, Astronomy; MSc, History and Philosophy of Science. *Literary Appointments:* Editor, Journal of the British Astronomical Association, 1965–85; Project Co-Ordinator, East Asian History of Science Trust, Cambridge, 1965–. *Publications:* Edmond Halley, Genius in Eclipse, 1969; Galielo, 1974; The Shorter Science and Civilisation in China, volume I, 1978, volume II, 1981; The Cambridge Illustrated History of the World's Science, 1983. *Contributions to:* Journal of British Astronomical Association; Interdisciplinary Science Reviews; Nature. *Memberships:* Royal Astronomical Society; British Astronomical Association; British Society for the History of Science. *Literary Agent:* Watson and Little, London. *Address:* 13 Acorn Avenue, Bar Hill, Cambridge CB3 8DT, England.

RONEY, Alice Lorraine (Mann), b. 6. Dec. 1926, Michigan, USA. Homemaker. m. Robert Kenneth Roney, 1 son, 1 daughter. *Education:* BA, UCLA, 1950. *Literary Appointments:* Technical Writer, Hughes Aircraft Company, 1949–52; Correspondence Secretary, Ebell Juniors, The Ebell of LA, 1958–59; Chairman, Ebel Jr Blind Recording, 1959–63; Librarian, St Augustine by-the-sea Episcopal Day School, 1961–68; Member School Board, St Augustines Day School, 1964–76; Correspondence Secretary, Assistance League of Santa Monica, 1966–68; Alter Guild Directress, St Augustine by-the-sea Episcopal Church, 1969–71; President, PEO Chapter QB, CA, 1969–71, 1976–78; Treasurer, Episcopal Churchwomen, LA, 1970–73; Cottey College Area Chairman, California State Chapter, PEO, 1972–74; Vice President Inglewood Reciprocity PEO, 1973–74, President, 1974–75; First Vice President, 1980–82, President, 1982–84, Second Vice President, 1984–86, Santa Monica Bay Women's Club. *Publications:* Those Treasured Moments, 1972; The Seeds of Love, 1975; Psalms for My Lord, 1975. *Contributions to:* Yearbook of Modern Poetry, 1971; Lyrics of Love, 1972; Outstanding Contemporary Poetry, 1972, 1973; Melody of the Muse, 1973; Poet; Major Poets; United Poets; Premier Poets Anthology, 1972, 1976, 1978, 1980, 1982, 1984. *Honours:* Recipient honorary mention in poetry contests; Freelance Writers Newsletter Contest, 2nd Place, 1975; Creative Writing Awards, California Federation of Women's Clubs, Marina District, GFWC, Poetry 2nd place, Inspirational Poetry 3rd place, 1979, Light verse 3rd place, 1980, Inspirational poetry 2nd and 3rd places, 1981, 2nd place 1982, Inspirational prose, 1st place, 1982, Children's story 1st place, 1983, 1985. *Memberships:* Member of several poetry societies. *Address:* 1105 Georgina Avenue, Santa Monica, CA 90402, USA.

RÖNNBÄCK, Ingegerd, b. 1 Sep. 1946, Vinslöv, Sweden. Author; Dramatist. m. Sture Rönnbäck, 12 July 1980, 2 sons, 1 daughter. *Education:* High School for Journalists, Gothenburg; University degree in music, information, radio and televisions. *Publication:* Tandaren, 1985. *Honours:* Scholarship, Swedish Government, 1981; Scholarship as author of book on old ship-building yard, 1985. *Membership:* Swedish Dramatist Society. *Address:* Box 108, 430–93 Hälsö, Sweden.

RONSLEY, Joseph, b. 3 June 1931, Chicago, Illinois, USA. Professor of English. m. Joanne Paschen, 30 June 1956, Milwaukee, USA, 1 son, 1 daughter. *Education:* BS, 1953, MA, 1962, PhD, 1966, Northwestern University. *Appointments:* McGill University, Montreal, Canada, 1965–67, 1969–; University of Wisconsin, Madison, USA, 1967–69. *Publications:* Yeats's Autobiography: Life as Symbolic Pattern, 1968; Editor: Myth & Reality in Irish Literature, 1977; Denis Johnston: A Retrospective, 1981; Selected Plays of Denis Johnston, 1983; Broadcast Plays of Denis Johnston, in press. *Honours:* Social Sciences & Humanities Research Council of Canada Leave Fellowships, 1975–76, 1982–83; SSHRCC Publication Grant, 1977; SSHRCC, Research Grants, 1975, 1980, 1982, 1985; Canada-Japan Bilateral Cultural Exchange, 1982. *Memberships:* Canadian Association for Irish Studies, President 1981–84; International Association for Study of Anglo-Irish Literature; Association of Canadian University Teachers of English. *Address:* Department of English, McGill University, Montreal, Quebec M3A 2T6, Canada.

ROOD, Ronald, b. 7 July 1920, Torrington, Connecticut, USA. Lecturer, Author. m. Margaret Lines Bruce, 21 Dec. 1982, Stamford, Connecticut, 2 sons, 2 daughters. *Education:* BS 1941, MS 1946, University of Connecticut. *Publications include:* 24 books including: Land Alive; Animals Nobody Loves; How Do You Spank a Porcupine; Loon In My Bathtub; Elephant Bones and Lonely Hearts; Several children's books. *Contributions to:* Magazines including: Coronet; Audubon magazine; National Wildlife; Reader's Digest; New York Times; Vermont Life; Christian Herald. *Memberships:* President 1965 and 1971–73, League of Vermont Writers; Outdoor Writers Association of America. *Literary Agent:* Toni Mendez Inc, New York. *Address:* Rt 1 Box 131, Lincoln via Bristol, VT 05443, USA.

ROOK, Pearl Lucille Newton, b. 26 Mar. 1923, Poetry Editor, Author. *Education:* Mt Vernon Seminary, Washington, District of Columbia, USA, 1941–42; Hobart and William Smith, Geneva, new York, 1946–48. *Literary Appointments include:* Piano Music Teacher; Poetry Editor, 1966–81, Social Editor 1967–68; Newark Courier Gazette; Poetry Editor, Rochester Democrat and Chronicle, 1973–82. *Publications:* Shifting Sands, 1971; Hidden Universe, 1974; The Sound of Thought, (with husband), 1977. *Contributions to:* Cyclo Flame; Encore; Legend; North American Mentor; Poetry Society of New Hampshire Newsletter; Poet (International); Quoin; Bitterroot. *Honours include:* Numerous honours and awards. *Memberships include:* Numerous professionals organisations. *Address:* 126 Williams Street, Newark, NY 14513, USA.

ROOKE, Daphne Marie, b. 6 Mar. 1914, Boksburg, Transvaal, South Africa. Novelist. m. Irvin Rooke, 1 June 1937, Johannesburg, 1 daughter. *Publications:* The Sea Hath Bounds, 1946; Mittee, 1951; Ratoons, 1953; Wizards' Country, 1957; Beti, 1959; Diamond Jo, 1965; Boy on the Mountain, 1969; Margaretha dela Porte, 1974; A Grove of Feber Trees; A Lover for Estelle, 1961; The Greyling, 1963; Juvenile: The South African Twins, 1953; The Australian Twins, 1954; The New Zealand Twins, 1957; Double Ex!, 1971; A Horse of His Own, 1976. *Contributor to:* The Woman; John Bull; South African Stories; etc. *Honour:* 1st Prize, Afrikaanse Pers Bpk Novel Competition, 1946. *Literary Agent:* John Farquharson Ltd, London, England. *Address:* 34 Bent Street, Fingal Bay, NSW 2315, Australia.

ROOKE, Leon, b. 11 Sep. 1934, North Carolina, USA. Author. *Literary Appointments:* Writer-in-Residence, University of North Carolina, 1965–66; Writer-in-Residence, University of Victoria, 1972–73; Writer-in-Residence, University of Southwest Menniota, 1974–75; Visiting Professor, University of Victoria, 1980–81; Writer-in-Residence, University of Toronto, 1984–85. *Publications:* Last One Home Sleeps in the Yellow Bed, 1968; The Broad Back of the Angel, 1977; Fat Woman, 1980; Death Suite, 1982; The Birth Control King of the Upper Volta, 1983; Shakespeare's Dog, 1983; Sing Me No Long Songs I'll Say You No Prayers, 1984; A Bolt of

White Cloth, 1984. *Contributions to:* Approximately 150 short stories in leading North American journals. *Honours:* Canada/Australia Literary Prize, 1981; Best Paperback Novel of the Year (Fat Woman), 1981; Governor General's Award for Fiction (Shakespeare's Dog), 1984. *Memberhips:* PEN; Writers' Union of Canada. *Literary Agent:* Liz Darhansoff. *Address:* 1019 Terrace Avenue, Victoria BC, Canada V8S 3V2.

ROOM, Adrian Richard West, b. 27 Sep. 1933, Melksham, England. Writer. *Education:* Honours degree in Russian, University of Oxford, England, 1957; Diploma in Education, University of Oxford, 1958. *Major Publications Include:* Place-names of the World, 1974; Great Britain: A Background Studies English-Russian Dictionary (Russian Language), Moscow, 1978; Room's Dictionary of Confusibles, 1979; Place-name Changes since 1900, 1980; Naming Names 1981; Room's Dictionary of Distinguishables, 1981; Dictionary of Trade Name Origins, 1982; Room's Classical Dictionary, 1983; Dictionary of Cryptic Crossword Clues, 1983; A Concise Dictionary of Modern Place-names in Great Britain and Ireland, 1983; Guide to British Place-names, 1985; Dictionary of Confusing Words and Meanings, 1985; Dictionary of Translated Names and Titles, 1985; Dictionary of Irish Place-names, 1986; Dictionary of Britain, 1986. *Contributor to:* Everyman's Encyclopedia, 1978; Journal of Russian Studies; Britain – USSR (on Marie Bashkirtseff). *Memberships:* Society of Authors; Fellow, Royal Geographical Society; Vice-President, Names Society; American Name Society; Great Britain – USSR Association. *Address:* 173 The Causeway, Petersfield, Hants, GU31 4LN, England.

ROOT, William Pitt, b. 28 Dec. 1941, Austin, Minnesota, USA. Writer; Poet. m. Judith Carol Bechtold, 1965 (divorced 1970) 1 daughter. *Education:* BA, University of Washington, Seattle, 1964, 1964; MFA, University of North Carolina, Greensboro, 1966. *Literary Appointments:* Visiting Writer-in-Residence: Amherst College, 1971; Wichita State University, 1976; University of Southwest Louisiana, 1976; Interlochen Arts Academy, 1979; University of Montana, 1977, 1980, 1983–86. *Publications:* The Storm and Other Poems, 1969; Striking the Dark Air for Music, 1973; Coot and Other Characters, 1977; Fireclock, 1981; In the World's Common Grasses, 1981; Reasons for Going It On Foot, 1981; Invisible Guests, 1984; Selected Odes of Pablo Neruda (translations) 1986; Faultdancing, 1986. *Contributions to:* The New Yorker; The Atlantic; Harpers; Nation; Poetry; American Poetry Review; New Letters; Sewanne Review; Hudson Review; One Earth (Scotland); Stzemez (Jugoslavia); Poetry Kanto (Japan) Cafe Existens (Sweden) etc. *Honours:* Academy of American Poets University Prize, 1966; Orpheus Award (International Poetry Film Festival), 1976; Pushcart Prize, 1977, 1982, 1984; Stanley Kunitz Poetry Award, 1982; Guy Owen Poetry Prize, 1984. Also Stegner Fellowship, 1968; Rockefeller Grant, 1969; Guggenheim Grant, 1970; NEA Grant, 1973; US/UK Exchange Fellowship, 1978. *Address:* c/o Bruce McGrew, Box E – Rancho Linda Vista, Oracle, AZ 85623, USA.

ROOTHAM, Jasper St John, b. 21 Nov. 1910, Cambridge, England. Banker. m. Joan McClelland, Chelsea, 1 son, 1 daughter. *Education:* Senior Scholar, Major Scholar, 1st class classical tripos parts 1 and 11, MA, St Johns College, Cambridge. *Publications:* Miss-Fire, 1946; Demi-Paradise, 1960; Verses 1928–72, 1973; The Celestial City, 1975; Reflections from a Crag, 1978; Selected Poems, 1980; Stand Fixed in Steadfast Gaze, 1981; Affirmation, 1982; Lament for a Dead Sculptor and other poems, 1985. *Contributions to:* Occasional contributor to professional publications. *Literary Agent:* W Hoade, Wimborne Bookshop, wimborne, Dorset. *Address:* 30 West Street, Wimborne Minster, Dorset BH21 1JS, England.

ROPER, David, b. 30 Nov. 1954, Hessle, Yorkshire, England. Theatre Critic. *Education:* MA, AKC, King's College, London. *Literary Appointments:* Editor of,

Square One, 1978; Editor of, Gambit, 1978–85; Joint-editor of, Platform, 1981–82; Drama Editor of, Event, 1981–82; Assistant Theatre Critic of, The Guardian, 1981–82; Theatre Critic of, The Daily Express, 1982–; Editor of, Plays and Players, 1983–84. *Publications:* The Pineapple Dance Book, 1983; The Dictionary of Musicals, 1986. *Contributions to:* Plays and Players; Plays; Gambit; Platform; Tatler; Event; Time Out; Journal of Semiotics; Campaign; The Movie; Cosmopolitan; The Stage and BBC Radio. *Literary Agent:* Clarke, Conway-Gordon, 213 Westbourne Grove, London W11. *Address:* 24a Pavilion Terrace, Wood Lane, London W12, England.

ROSA, Nicholas Alfred Anthony, b. 15 Jan, 1926, Stamford, Connecticut, USA. Writer. 1 stepson, 1 stepdaughter. *Education:* Physics, Yale University 1943–44, 1947–48; BS, Social Science (History & Government), Fairfield University, 1952. *Publications:* Atronautics for Science Teachers, ed John G Meitner, 1965; What's Ecology? with L W McCombs, 1972, revised 1977; Life Science: A Laboratory Approach, John G Marean et al, 1972; Small Computers for the Small Businessman, co-author with Sharon Rose Wood, 1980; Management's Guide to Desktop Computing, contributing author, 1982. *Contributions to:* Various journals including; Electronics World; Electronics Illustrated; Reporter; Oceans (Contributing Editor); Science World. Occasionally to Atlantic Monthly; Science; Various newspapers. Reviews, science books & films, American Association for the Advancement of Science. *Literary Agent:* Susan Zeckendorf, New York. *Address:* 2200 Curtner Avenue, No 77, Campbell, CA 95008–5626, USA.

ROSAND, David, b. 6 Sep. 1938, Brooklyn, New York, USA. Art Historian and Critic. m. Ellen Fineman, 18 June 1961, New York, 2 sons. *Education:* AB, Columbia College, 1959; MA, 1962, PhD, 1965, Columbia University. *Publications:* Titian and the Venetian Woodcut (with Michelangelo Muraro) 1976; Titian, 1978; Painting in Cinquecento Venice: Titian, Veronese, Tintoretto, 1982. *Contributions to:* Articles in Art Bulletin; Art News; Burlington Magazine; Master Drawings; New Literary History; The New Criterion; Times Literary Supplement; Renaissance Quarterly etc. *Honours:* Fulbright Travel Fellowship, 1971–72; National Endowment for the Humanities Fellowship, 1971–72; John S Guggenheim Memorial Foundation Fellowship, 1974–75; National Endowment for the Humanities Fellowship, 1985–86. *Address:* Department of Art History and Archaeology, Columbia University, New York, NY 10027, USA.

ROSARIO-BRAID, Florangel, b. 17 Sep. 1931. Lecturer. m. Dr Andrew F Braid, 1 son. *Education:* BSE, English, 1951; Graduate work Education & Psychology, 1953–55, University of the Philippines; MS, Mass Communication, Syracuse University; Graduate work, University of California, 1961; PhD, Mass Communication, Syracuse University, 1967–70. *Literary Appointments:* Include Coordinator of Production. Metropolitan Educational Television Association, Director for Programming, Philippine Broadcasting Service, 1962–65; Director, Information and Publications; Special Assistant to the President, Silliman University, Philippines, 1965–67; Research Associate. East-West Population and Communication Institutes; Assistant Professor, University of Hawaii, 1970–74; UNESCO Advisor, Communication Strategy Project, 1974–76; Fellow, Development Academy of the Philippines, 1976–79; Fellow, Head, Communication Development Academy of the Philippines, 1976–80; Director Asian Institute of Journalism, Professional Lecturer, University of the Philippines, Diliman and Los Banòs, 1980–. *Publications:* Include, Communication Strategies for Productivity Improvement, 1979, 2nd Edition, 1983; A Survey of Social-Psychological Variables in Family Planning Research, 1971. *Contributions to:* Numerous professional journals. *Honours:* E W Hazen Foundation Fellowship Grant, 1967–69; Syracuse University Scholarship Grant, 1970, 1960–61. *Memberships:* Association for Education in Journalism; International

Communication Association; Television Committee; Citizens Council for Mass Media; Mass Communication Committee, UNESCO; Asian Mass Communication Research and Information Centre; Bishops-Businessmen's Conference; Concerned Women of the Philippines. *Address:* 7 Matipuno Street, Horseshoe Village, ACPO Box 423, Quezon City, Philippines.

ROSE, Al, b. 3 Feb. 1916, New Orleans, USA. Author; Artist; Recording Director; Composter; Consultant. m. Diana Beals, 14 Apr. 1970, Hallandale, 3 sons. *Appointments:* Board of Advisors, Tulane University Archive of New Orleans Jazz; Director, Tulane Hot Jazz Classic, 1983, 1984. *Publications:* New Orleans Jazz: A Family Album, 1967; Storyville, New Orleans, 1974; Eubie Blake, 1980; Born in New Orleans, 1983; I Remember Jazz, 1986. *Contributor to:* The Role of the Plectrum Banjo in New Orleans Jazz, Pickin; Blue Notes and Red Lights, Merian, Germany; The Second Line; etc. *Honours:* Louisiana Library Association Literary Award, 1967; Book, Storyville, was the basis of Paramount Film, Pretty Baby. *Memberships:* Consultant, Time-Life Books; National Geographic. *Literary Agent:* Roslyntaro Literary Agency, New York. *Address:* 350 E Ocean Ave, Hypoluxo Island, FL 33462, USA.

ROSE, Ernst Andreas Gottlieb, b. 18 June 1899, Sangerhausen. College Professor. m. Hildegard Martha Schmidt, 27 Nov. 1929, New York, USA, 2 daughters. *Education:* PhD, Leipzig University, 1922. *Appointments:* New Yorker Staatszeitung, 1922–24; Brearley School, New York, 1924–25; New York University, 1925–66, Professor, 1949, Chairman, 1948–65, Head, Germanic Languages & Literatures, 1958–66, Emeritus, 1966; University of California, Davis, 1967–68. *Publications:* Deutsche Kulturkunde, with C M Purin, 1926; Contemporary German Literature, 1930; Fliessend Deutsch, 1951; A History of German Literature, 1960; Faith from the Abyss, 1965; Grosse Vergangenheit, with F Semmler, 1969; Blick nach Osten, 1981. *Contributor to:* Germanic Review, 1929; German Quaterly, 1943; Germanic Review, 1943; Review of National Literatures, 1971; Theatrum Mundi, 1980; Yearbook of German-American Studies, 1984; Neue deutsche Biographie; Dizionario Critico della Letteratura Tedesca; Columbia Dictionary of Modern Literature; Cassell's Encyclopedia of World Literature. *Honours:* E Rose – C G Schuchard Anniversary Prize established by Students and alumni, German Department, New York University, 1950; Recipient, Medal, 37 Years Service, New York University, 1962; New York University Studies in Germanic Languages and Literatures, ed. in Ernst Rose's Honour by Robert A Fowkes and Volkmar Sander, 1967. *Address:* 16 Ramapo Terrace, Fair Lawn, NJ 07410, USA.

ROSE, Marilyn Gaddis, b. 2 Apr. 1930, Fayette, Missouri, USA. University Professor. *Education:* AB, Central Methodist College; MA, University of South Carolina; PhD, University of Missouri. *Major Publications:* Axel, (translation), 1969; Julian Green, Gallic-American Author, 1970; Jack B Yeats, Painter & Poet, 1972; Katherine Tynan, 1974; (Editor), Translation in the Humanities, 1977; (translation monograph issue), Paintbrush, 1978; (translation monograph issue), Pacific Quarterly, 1980; (translation), Spectrum, 1981; (translation), Eve of the Future Eden, by Villiers de l'Isle-Adam, 1981; (editor & contributor), Translation Perspectives, 1984; (translation), A View of Him, (lui) by Louise Colet, 1986. *Contributor to:* Academic Journals; Edited, series of American Translators Association. *Memberships:* PEN USA; American Translators Association; American Literature Translators Association. *Honour:* Senior Fellowship, Australian National University, 1977. *Address:* 4 Johnson Avenue, Binghamton, NY 13905, USA.

ROSE, Norman Anthony, b. 29 Dec. 1934, London, England. University Professor. m. Tslilla Kuper, 21 Feb. 1959, Rehovoth, Israel, 1 daughter. *Education:* B Sc Economics Honours 1965, PhD 1968, London School of Economics. *Publications:* The Gentile Zionists, 1973; Baffy. The Diaries of Blanche Dugdale, 1973; Vansittart.

Study of a Diplomat, 1978; Letters of Chaim Weizmann, 1979; Lewis Namier and Zionism, 1980; Chaim Weizmann. A Biography, 1986. *Contributions to:* Middle Eastern Studies; The Historical Journal; Journal of Modern History; Weiner Library Bulletin. *Address:* c/o Dept of International Relations, The Hebrew University, Mount Scopus, Jerusalem 91905, Israel.

ROSE, Paul, b. 26 Dec. 1935, Manchester, England. Barrister at Law. m. Eve Lapu, 13 Sep. 1985, Bury, 2 sons, 1 daughter. *Education:* LlB, Honours, Manchester University; Barrister at Law, Grays Inn. *Publications:* Law Relating Industrial & Provident Societies; Weights & Measures Law; The Manchester Martyrs; Backbencher's Dilemma; The Moonies Unmasked; History of the Fenians in England. *Contributor to:* Numerous political, legal and general article to Newspapers, magazines and journal in England and abroad; Regular contributor and book reviewer, Contemporary Review. *Address:* 10 King's Bench Walk, Temple, London EC4, England.

ROSE, Peter Isaac, b. 5 Sep. 1933, Rochester, New York, USA. Professor of Sociology and Anthropology; Writer. *Education:* BA, Syracuse University, 1954; MA, 1957, PhD, 1959, Cornell University. *Publications include:* They and We, 1964, 3rd edition, 1981; The Study of Society, 1967, 4th edition, 1977; The Ghetto and Beyond, 1968; The Subject is Race, 1969; Nation of Nations, 1970; Americans from Africa, 1970; Seeing Ourselves, 1972, 75; Inquiring Into Society, 1976; Strangers in Their Midst, 1977; Views from Abroad, 1978; Socialisation and the Life Cycle, 1979; Mainstream and Margins, 1983; Working with Refugees, 1983. *Contributions to:* Numerous publications. General Editor, Ethnic Groups in Comparative Perspective; Consulting Editor, Human Behavior. *Memberships include:* Past Council Member, American Sociological Association; Past Vice President, Society for Study of Social Problems; Past Vice President, Eastern Sociological Society; Past President, Massachusetts Sociological Society. *Address:* 66 Paradise Road, Northampton, MA 01060, USA.

ROSE, Phyllis, b. 26 Oct. 1942, New York City, USA. Writer. Divorced 1975, 1 son. *Education:* BA, summa cum laude, Radcliffe College, 1964; MA, Yale University, 1965; PhD, Harvard University, 1970. *Literary Appointments:* Assistant Professor of English, Wesleyan University, 1969–76; Associate Professor, 1976–81; Professor, 1981–; Visiting Professor of English, University of California, Berkeley, 1981–82. *Publications:* Woman of Letters: A Life of Virginia Woolf, 1978; Parallel Lives: Five Victorian Marriages, 1983; Writing of Women, 1985. *Contributor to:* The New York Times; The New York Times Book Review; The Nation; The Atlantic; Vogue; The Yale Review; Washington Post Book World. *Honours:* NEH Fellow, 1973–74; Rockefeller Foundation Fellow, 1984–85; Guggenheim Fellow, 1985. *Memberships:* PEN; National Book Critics Circle. *Literary Agents:* Georges Borchardt, New York; Richard Scott Simon, London. *Address:* 74 Wyllys Avenue, Middletown, CT 06457, USA.

ROSE, Richard, b. 9 Apr. 1933, St Louis, Missouri, USA. Professor of Public Policy; Director, Centre for Study of Public Policy; University of Strathclyde. m. Rosemary J Kenny, 14 Apr. 1956, Whitstable, Kent, England, 2 sons, 1 daughter. *Education:* BA, Johns Hopkins University; DPhil, Oxford University, England, 1960. *Literary Appointments:* Reporter, St Louis Post-Dispatch, USA, 1955–57; Freelance contributor to American and British publications 1955–. *Publications:* Politics in England, 1964, 4th edition, 1985; Governing without Consensus; An Irish Perspective, 1971; Electoral Behaviour, 1974; International Almanac of Electoral History, with T T Mackie, 1974–1982; Problem of Party Government, 1974; Managing Presidential Objectives, 1976; Can Government Go Bankrupt? with B G Peters, 1978; Do Parties Make a Difference? 1980; Presidents and Prime Ministers, co-editor, 1980; Understanding Big Government, 1984; Understanding the United Kingdom, 1982; Nationwide Competition for Votes,

1984; Public Employment in Western Nations, 1985; Journal of Public Policy, 1984. *Contributions to:* Times; Telegraph; New Society; Economist; various television stations. *Honours:* Guggenheim Fellowship, 1974; Woodrow Wilson International Centre Fellow, Washington, USA, 1974; Japan Foundation Fellow, 1984; Honorary Foreign Member, Finnish Academy of Arts and Sciences. *Address:* CSPP, University of Strathclyde, Glasgow G1 1XQ, Scotland.

ROSE-NEIL, Wendy, b. 24 July 1941, Bristol, England. Editor; Journalist. *Education:* BA, Honours, Psychology. *Literary Appointments:* Editor, Healthy Living Magazine, 1975–78; Deputy Editor, Parents Magazine, 1978–80; Editor, Parents Magazine, 1980–. *Publicatiaons:* A Visual Encyclopaedia of Unconventional Medicine (consultant editor), 1978; The Complete Handbook of Pregnancy (consultant editor), 1984. *Contributions:* Numerous articles on health, women's issues, relationships, nutrition, childcare; Healthy Living; Parent. *Address:* 5 Franconia Road, London SW4 9NB, England.

ROSEN, Gerald, b. 24 Dec. 1938, New York City, USA. Novelist. m. Marijke Wittkampf, 20 Feb. 1982, San Francisco, USA, 1 son. *Education:* BEE, Rensselaer Polytechnic Institute, 1960; Master of Business Administration, Wharton Graduate School, 1962; MA, University of Pennsylvania, 1966; PhD, University of Pennsylvania 1969. *Literary Appointments:* University Writer in Residence, California State University, 1971–. *Major Publications:* Blues for a Dying Nation, 1972; Zen in the Art of J D Salinger, 1977; The Carmen Miranda Memorial Flagpole, 1977; Dr Ebenezer's Book & Liquor Store, 1980; Growing Up Bronx, 1984. *Contributor to:* San Francisco Review of Books; San Francisco Bay Guardian; Parisian Review; American Quarterly; and others. *Address:* California State University, Sonoma, Rohnert Park, CA 94928, USA.

ROSEN, Michael J, b. 20 Sep. 1954, Columbus, Ohio, USA. Writer. Literary Director. *Education:* BS, Ohio State University, 1976; MFA Poetry, Columbia University, 1981. *Literary Appointment:* Literary Director, The Thurber House, 1983–. *Publications:* A Drink at the Mirage, (poetry), 1984; Traveling in Notions, (poetry), 1966; Permanent Damage, (sport stories), 1986; Seeing Things, (novel), 1986. *Contributions to:* The New Yorker; The Nation; Grand Street; The Atlantic; Prairie Schooner; Georgia Review; Epoch; Chicago Review. *Honours:* Ingram Merrill Foundtion Fellowship, 1982 and 1983; Ohio Arts Council, 1982 and 1985; National Endowment for the Arts Fellowship, 1984; Gustav Davidson Award, Poetry Society of America, 1985; Ohiona Book Award, 1985. *Memberships:* Poetry Society of America; PEN, American Centre; Academy of American Poets. *Address:* 1312 East Broad Street 7a, Columbus, OH 43205, USA.

ROSEN, Robert Charles, b. 29 Dec. 1947, Brooklyn, New York, USA. College English Teacher. m. Barbra Apfelbaum, 12 June 1983, Philadelphia, Pennsylvania. *Education:* BS, Massachusetts Institute of Technology, 1970; MA, 1975, PhD, 1978, Rutgers University. *Literary Appointments:* Assistant Professor, 1978–85, Associate Professor, 1985–, English, William Paterson College, Wayne, New Jersey. *Publications:* John Dos Passos: Politics and the Writer, 1981. *Contributions to:* Arizona English Bulletin; College Literature; Modern Fiction Studies; Review of Education; Journal of Technical Writing and Communication; American Journal of Education; Modern Fiction Studies; The Modern Amerian Novel and the Movies, 1978; Editorial Board Member and Editor of Teaching Notes column, Radical Teacher. *Honours:* National Endowment for the Humanities Fellowship to Summer Seminar for College Teachers, University of Massachusetts, 1980. *Membership:* National Coucil of Teachers of English. *Address:* Department of English, William Paterson College, 300 Pompton Road, Wayne, NJ 07470, USA.

ROSEN, Sidney, b. 5 June 1916, Boston, Massachusetts, USA. Professor Emeritus, Astronomy.

Education: AB, University of Massachusetts, 1939; MA, 1952, PhD, 1955, Harvard University. *Publications:* Galilee and The Magic Numbers, 1958; Doctor Paracelsus, 1959; The Harmonious World of Johann Kepler, 1961; Wizard of the Dome, 1969; (textbook), Concepts in Physical Science, (with Wiegfrued and Dennison), 1965, Death and Blintzes, with D Rosen 1985. *Contributor to:* World Book Encyclopedia; various academic journals. *Honours include:* Clara Ingram Judson Memorial Award for children's Literature, 1970. *Memberships include:* Fellow, AAAS; Past Associate, Editor, Journal National Association for Research in Science Teaching; Authors Guild; History of Science Society; Mystery Writers of America. *Address:* 1417 Mayfair Road, Champaign, IL 61820, USA.

ROSENAU, Anita H, b. 25 Aug. 1923. Philadelphi, Pennsylvania, USA. Playwright. m. Gary Rosenau, 24 Apr. 1945, Inlet, New York, USA, 1 son, 1 daughter. *Education:* LA, University of Pennsylvania, 1945; MA Playwriting, Temple University, 1956. *Publications:* Lancelot & Guinevere (trilogy in blank verse for Master's thesis), 1956; Strangers, Islands (first 2 parts of modern trilogy); Future Murder; Mandate for Murder; Screenplay for, Murder for Love; Journey into Murder (in progress); Various children's books on Christian themes. *Contributor to:* Christian Science Monitor; Christian Science Journal; Christian Science Sentinel; Herald of Christian Science. *Memberships:* National Writers' Club; Poetry Society of America; Dramatists' Guild. *Literary Agent:* Bertha Klausner. *Address:* 424 Sinclair Road, Box 5667, Snowmass Village, CO 81615, USA.

ROSENBERG, Bruce Alan, b. 27 July 1934, New York City. Professor. m. Ann Harleman Stewart, 20 June 1981, Seattle, Washington, USA, 3 sons, 1 daughter. BA, 1955, Hofstra University; MA, 1962, Penn State University; PhD, 1965, Ohio State University. *Literary Appointments:* University of California, Santa Barbara, 1965–67; University of Virginia, 1967–69; Penn State University, 1969–77; Brown University, 1977–. *Publications:* The Art of the American Folk Preacher,1970; Custer and the Epic of Defeat, 1975; The Code of the West, 1982. *Contributions to:* More than 60 journals and publications. *Honours:* ACLS, Fellow, 1966–67; James Russell Lowell Prize, 1970; Second Prize, Chicago Folklore Competition, 1970; Newberry Library Fellow, 1971; Guggenheim Fellow, 1982–83. *Memberships:* Modern Language Association; Medieval Academy of America. *Address:* 199 Vaughn Hill Road, Bolton, MA 01740, USA.

ROSENBERG, Dorothy Louise, b. 25 Dec. 1906, Waverly, Washington, USA. Author. *Education:* Reed College, Portland, Oregon, 1937–39; University of Washington, Seattle, 1956–57, 1962. *Children's Books Published Include:* Mystery of Steamboat Rock, 1956, 1984; Series of six, Readers for Slow Learners, 1962–74; Danger in Sagebrush Country, 1984; Trouble on the Blue Fox Islands, 1985; Poison Ring Mystery, in press. *Contributions to:* Architectural Digest. *Honours:* National Gold Biennial, NLAPW, 1978; 2 awards for good writing, NLAPW; Owl Award, outstanding achievement, NLAPW Seattle Branch, 1984. *Membership:* National League of American Pen Women (NLAPW), Seattle Branch (President 1984–86). *Address:* 3506 NE 95th Street, Apt. 306, Seattle, WA 98115, USA.

ROSENBERG, Marvin, Writer. *Education:* AB, MA, PhD. *Publications:* The Masks of Othello, 1968; The Masks of King Lear, 1973; The Masks of Macbeth, 1978. *Contributions to:* PMLA; Shakespeare Quarterly; Journal of English and Germanic Philology; Studies in Philology; Philological Quarterly; English Studies; Journal of Aesthetics and Art Criticism; Hamlet Studies Theatre Journal; Modern Drama; Shakespeare Studies etc. *Address:* Department of Dramatic Art, University of California, Berkeley, CA 94720, USA.

ROSENBERG, Morris, b. 6 May 1922, New York City, USA. Sociologist. m. Florence Rafman, 14 Aug. 1949, Brooklyn, 1 son. *Education:* BA, Brooklyn College,

1946; MA, 1950, PhD, 1953, Columbia University. *Publications:* Occupations and Values, 1957; Society and the Adolescent Self-Image, 1965; The Logic of Survey Analysis, 1968; Conceiving the Self, 1979; Social Psychology: Sociological Perspectives, 1981; Social Psychology of the Self-Concept, co-author, 1982. *Contributor to:* Social Forces, 1953; Public Opinion Quarterly, 1954; American Sociological Review, 1956. *Honours:* Co-Winner, American Association for the Advancement of Science Sociopsychological Prize, 1963; American Sociological Association Distinguished Contribution to Scholarship Award, 1981. *Address:* Department of Sociology, University of Maryland, College Park, MD 20742, USA.

ROSENBERGER, Francis Coleman, b. 22 Mar. 1915, Virginia, USA. Attorney-at-Law. m. Astra Lazdins Brennan, 12 Dec. 1966, Virginia. *Education:* University of Virginia; J D George Washington University, USA. *Literary Appointments:* Book reviewer, Richmond Times – Dispatch, 1938–40; Washington Post, 1940–43; New York Herald Tribune, 1945–62; Washington Star, 1967–71; occasional reviewer, New York Times, Virginia Quarterly Review, and others. Editor, Columbia Historical Society, 1960–79, 8 volumes. *Major Publications:* The Virginia Poems, 1943; XII Poems, 1946; One Season Here (poems), 1976; An Alphabet (poems), 1978; The Visit (poems), 1984. Editor, Virginia Reader: A Treasury of Writings from the First Voyages to the Present, 1948, reprinted 1972; Jefferson Reader: A Treasury of Writings about Thomas Jefferson, 1953; Washington and the Poet, 1977 and others. *Contributor to:* Poetry, Southern Poetry Review, Southwest Review, Laurel Review, Arizona Quarterly, Poetry Quarterly Review of Literature, University Review and 40 others. Poems in anthologies: Best Poems of 1942, 1943, American Writing 1944, Cross Section, 1943 etc. to Light Year, 1985. *Honours:* University of Virginia Poetry Award, 1936; National Poetry Centre Award, New York World Fair, 1939; Adviser, US delegations to International Conferences, Geneva, 1955, 1956, Vienna, 1973. *Memberships:* Poetry Society of America; Poetry Society of Virginia; Guest Scholar, Brookings Institution, Washington DC, 1979–80. *Address:* 6809 Melrose Drive, McLean, VA 22101, USA.

ROSENBLOOM, Bert, b. 2 Feb. 1944, Philadelphia, USA. College Professor. m. Pearl Rosenbloom, 1 son, 1 daughter. *Education:* BS, 1966, MBA, 1968; PhD, 1974, Temple University. *Appointments:* Consulting Editor, Marketing, Random House, 1977; Editorial Boards: Journal of the Academy of Marketing Science, 1976, Journal of Consumer Marketing, 1984. *Publications:* Marketing Channels: A Management View, 1978; Retail Marketing, 1981; Marketing Channels: A Management View, 2nd edition, 1983. *Contributor to:* Journal of Marketing; Journal of Retailing; Business Horizions; Journal of Academy of Marketing Science; Industrial Marketing Management; Long Range Planning; Journal of Consumer Marketing. *Honour:* Beta Gamma Sigma. *Address:* Dept of Marketing, College of Business and Administration, Drexel University, Philadelphia, PA 19104, USA.

ROSENBLOOM, Noah H, b. 29 Sep. 1915, Radom. University Professor. m. Pearl, 16 June 1946, Brooklyn, New York, USA. 2 daughters. *Education:* BRE, Yeshiva University, 1942; Ordination, Riets Theological Seminary, Yeshiva University, 1942; MA, Columbia University, 1945; DHL, Yeshiva University, 1948; PhD, New York University, 1958. *Academic Appointments:* Hunter College, 1949–54; Professor, Yeshiva University, 1954–80. *Publications:* Luzzatto's Ethico – Psychological Interpretation of Judaism, 1965; Tradition in an Age of Reform, 1976; The Threnodist and the Threnody of the Holocaust, 1980; The Exodus Epic of the Enlightenment and Exegesis, 1983. *Contributions to:* Judaism; Historia Judaica; Revue des Eduded Juives; Mabua; Bitzaron, Sura; P'rakim; G'nazim. *Honours:* Horeb Award, Yeshiva University, 1965; Abraham Friedman Award for The Exodus Epic of the Enlightenment by the Histadrut Ivrit of America, 1983.

Membership: Editorial Board Member of Tradition. *Address:* 1066E 85th Street, Brooklyn, NY 11236, USA.

ROSENBLUM, Martin Jack, b. 19 Aug. 1946, Appleton, Wisconsin, USA. Academic Counselor/ Admissions Specialist; Poet/Musician. m. Maureen Rice, 6 Sep. 1970, Chicago, Illinois, 1 daughter. *Education:* BS English, 1969, MA Literature and Creative Writing, 1971, PhD Modern Poetry, 1980, University of Wisconsin. *Literary Appointments:* Lecturer in English and American Literature, University of Wisconsin–Milwaukee, 1970–80; Lecturer in Irish Literature, Marquette University, Milwaukee, 1970; Guest Lecturer in American Literature, University of East Anglia, Norwich, England, 1976. *Publications:* Settling Attention and other poems, 1970; Home, 1971; The Werewolf Sequence, 1974; Brewing 20 Milwaukee Poets, (editor), 1974; As I Magic, 1976; Divisions One, 1979; Brite Shade, 1984; Still Life, 1985. *Contributions to:* Journal of Popular Culture; Wisconsin Review; Pricesely; Road Apple Review; John Berryman Studies; Abraxas; Hey Lady; Images; Pembroke Magazine. *Honours:* Academy of American Poets Award, 1970; University of Wisconsin-LaCrosse Collections Award, 1971; Yale University Sterling Library selection as one of America's promising younger poets, 1977. *Address:* 2521 East Stratford Court, Shorewood, WI 53211, USA.

ROSENDAHL, Tony Harry, b. 30 Aug. 1936, Stockholm, Sweden. Author; Journalist. *Education:* MA, Uppsala University. *Publications:* Brev, 1972; Handbook for Rattslosa, 1975; Television and Teacher plays. *Contributions to:* Aftonbladet. *Memberships:* Swedish Union of Authors; Swedish Association of Playwrights; Swedish Association of Journalists; Secretary General, Swedish Writers Center; Publicistklubben. *Address:* Reykjaviksgatan 100, 752 63 Uppsala, Sweden.

ROSENFELD, Albert Hyman, b. 31 May 1920, Philadelphia, Pennsylvania, USA. Science Writer. m, 24 Aug. 1948, Philadelphia, 1 son, 1 daughter. *Education:* BA, History & Social Science, New Mexico State University. *Literary Appointments include:* Associate Editor 1956–58, Senior Science Editor, 1958–69, Life; Managing Editor, Family Health, 1969–71; Senior Science Editor, Saturday Review, 1973–80; Contributing Editor, Geo 1979–81, Science, 1980–82. *Publications include:* The Quintessence of Irving Langmuir, 1962; The Second Genesis: The Coming Control of Life, 1969; Prolongevity, 1976; Mind & Supermind, editor, 1977; Science, Invention & Social Change, editor, 1978; Responsible Parenthood, with G W Kliman, 1980; Prolongevity II, 1985. *Contributions to:* Life; Time; Fortune; Sports Illustrated; McCall's Redbook; Harper's Readers Digest; Think; Saturday Review; Better Homes & Gardens; Physicians World; Horizon; Geo; Prime Time; Science Digest; etc. *Honours include:* Aviation/Space Writers Award, 1964; Westinghouse Writing Award, AAAS, 1966; Lasker Award, medical journalism, 1967; Claude Bernard Science Journalism Award, 1974; National Magazine Award, service to the individual, 1975; James P Grady Medical, American Chemical Society, 1981; Honorary DLett, New Mexico State University; etc. *Memberships:* 3 times president, Council for the Advancement of Science Writing; National Association of Science Writers; American Medical Writers Association; Authors Guild; Sigma Delta Chi; Deadline Club, New York. *Literary Agent:* Ann Elmo Agency Inc, New York. *Address:* 25 Davenport Avenue, New Rochelle, NY 10805, USA.

ROSENFELD, Sybil Marion, b. 20 Jan. 1903, London, England. Theatre Historian. *Education:* BA 1st Class Honours, 1922, MA, 1924, King's College, London University; Honorary DLitt, Western College, Oxford, Ohio, USA. *Literary Appointments:* Editor, Theatre Notebook, 1945–85; Editor, Essays and Studies, 1965. *Publications include:* Strolling Players and Drama in the Province 1660–1765, 1939, reprinted 1970; The Theatre of the London Fairs, 1960; A Short History of Scene Design in Great Britain, 1973; Temple of Thespis, 1978; Georgian Scene Painters and Scene Painting, 1981; The Georgian Theatre of Richmond, Yorks, 1984.

Editor, Letterbook of Sir George Etherege, 1928. *Contributions to:* British Museum Quarterly; Essays and Studies, English Association; PLMA; Shakespeare Surgery, and others. *Honours:* Rosemary Crawshay Prize, British Academy, 1942. *Memberships include:* Past Joint Secretary, Conn, Member, The Society for Theatre Research; English Association. *Address:* 103 Ralph Court, Queensway, London W2 5HU, England.

ROSENFIELD, Patricia Byrne, b. 6 June, 1925. Educator; Writer. *Education:* BS, English, Boston University, USA, 1972; MA, Regis College, Weston, Massachussets, 1984. *Appointments Include:* Teacher, Wellesley High, 1972; Assistant to Director, MAT. Programme, Harvard University, 1970–72; Director, Language Evaluation and Learning Laboratory, Newton Junior College, 1967–70. *Contributor to:* Southern Poetry Review; Quoin; Phylon; Folio; Spring Anthology (London): Among the Once Loved Things (Anthology): Cardinal Poetry Quarterly: Pyramid; Haiku Highlights; and others. *Honours:* 1st Mary F Lindsley Award, New York Poetry Forum, 1969; Hon Mention, Ky Poetry Society, 1970. *Memberships:* N E Poetry Society; American Academy of Poets; Yeats Society; New York Poetry Forum. *Address:* 42 Wessex Road, Newton Centre, MA 02159, USA.

ROSENMEYER, Thomas G, b. 3 Apr. 1920, Hamburg, Germany. University Teacher. m. Lieselotte H Hannes, 7 Sep. 1951, Cataumet, Massachusetts, USA, 2 daughters. *Education:* BA, McMaster University, 1944; MA, University of Toronto, 1945; PhD, Harvard University, 1949. *Literary Appointments:* University of Iowa, 1947–52; Smith College, 1952–55; University of Washington, 1955–66; University of California, Berkeley, 1966–; Princeton University, Autumn, 1975; Harvard University, Autumn, 1984. *Publications:* Bruno Snell: The Discovery of the Mind (translation), 1953; The Masks of Tragedy, 1963; The Green Cabinet, 1969; The Art of Aeschylus, 1982. *Contributions to:* Numerous publications (articles and reviews). *Address:* c/o Department of Comparative Literature, University of California, Berkeley, CA 94705, USA.

ROSENSTIEL, Leonie, b. New York City, New York, USA. Writer; Editor; Publisher. *Education:* BA, Barnard College; MA, PhD, Columbia University, New York. *Literary Appointments:* Editor and Special Projects Editor, Current Musicology, 1969–74; Consulting Editor, Association of University Presses, Da Capo Press, 1975; Correspondent, Carribean Network Systems, 1976; Co-Founder, Editor, president, Research Associates International, 1981–. *Publications:* Music Handbook, Translation, 197; The Life and Works of Lili Boulanger, 1978; Schirmer History of Music, 1982; Nadia Boulanger: A Life in Music, 1982. Editor, Freelances of North America, 1983–; Co-Editor, Literary Agents of North America, 1983–. *Contributions to:* Current Musicology, Translations, Articles and Book reviews; Virtuoso Magazine; American Music, Book reviews. *Honours:* Diploma, Instituto Nacional de Ballas Artes, mexico, 1975; Grants and Fellowships, Rockefeller Foundation, American Council of Learned Societies and American Philosophical Society, 1977–78. *Memberships:* Authors Guild of America. *Literary Agent:* Author Aid Associates. *Address:* c/o Research Associates International, 340 East 52nd Street, New York City, NY 10022, USA.

ROSENTHAL, Abraham Michael, b. 2 May 1922, Sault St Marie, Ontario, Canada. Executive Editor. m. Ann Marie Burke, 12 Mar. 1949, New York City, New York, USA, 3 sons. *Education:* BS, New York City College, 1944; Honorary LLD, City College of City University of New York, 1974. *Literary Appointments:* Executive Editor, The New York Times. *Publications:* 38 Witnesses; One More Victim, co-author, 1967; The Sophisticated Traveler, Co-Editor, 1984, 85. *Contributions to:* Colliers; Saturday Evening Post; Foreign Affairs; New York Times Magazine, and others. *Honours:* Citation for work in India, Overseas Press Club, 1956, for work in India and Poland, 1959, for 2 foreign affairs magazine articles, 1965; for International Reporting, Pulitzer Prize, 1960; Number One Award, Overseas Press Club, 1960; George Polk Memorial Award, 1960, 65; Page One Award, Newspaper Guild of New York, 1960. *Address:* c/o The New York Times, 229 West 43rd Street, New York City, NY 10036, USA.

ROSENTHAL, Barbara Ann, b. 17 Aug. 1948, The Bronx, New York City, USA. Literature and Art. 2 Daughters. *Education:* Numerous courses, various Universities and Colleges; BFA, Carnegie Melon University, 1970; MFA, CUNY, 1975. *Publications include:* Clues to Myself, 1981; Notes on the Structure and Meaning of Clues to Myself, 1982; Sensations, 1984; Homo Futurus, Version I, 1984; Old Address Book, 1985; Homo Futurus, Version II, 1986. *Contributor to:* Numerous professional journals and magazines; Editor in Chief, Patterns, 1967–69; Editor, Parsons College Council Faculty Affairs Committee Newsletter, 1985. *Honours:* Recipient, various honours and awards, *Address:* 727 Avenue of the Americas, New York, NY 10010, USA.

ROSENTHAL, Edwin Stanley, b. 18 June 1914, Far Rockaway, New York, USA. Journalist. *Education:* Yale University 1932–33; University of Arizona, 1933–35; BA, University of Wisconsin, 1936. *Publications:* Articles in Newspapers & magazines. *Contributor to:* Yank (World War II); Illustrated. *Membership:* Overseas Press Club of America. *Address:* Springfield, Witnesham, Ipswich, Suffolk, England.

ROSENTHAL, Harold David, b. 30 Sep. 1917, London, England. Editor; Author; Critic. m. Lillah Phyllis Weiner, 7 Aug. 1944, London, 1 son, 1 daughter. *Education:* BA; Dipl Ed. *Publications:* Two Centuries of Opera at Covent Garden, 1958; Concise Oxford Dictionary of Opera (with John Warrack), 1964, revised 1980, 1983; Covent Garden; A Short History, 1967; Annals of Opera 1940–80, 1985; My Mad World of Opera, 1982. *Honours:* Cavaliere Ufficiale of the Order Al Merito della Reppublica Italiana, 1977; OBE, 1984. *Memberships:* Critics Circle of Great Britain; Society of Authors. *Address:* 6 Woodland Rise, London N10 3UH, England.

ROSENTHAL, Trudy Tappan, b. 25 Nov. 1947, Norfolk, Virginia, USA. University Faculty. m. Samuel Lee Rosenthal, 25 Mar, 1972, New Orleans, Louisiana. *Education:* BSN, Virginia Commonwealth University, 1970; MA, Villanova University, Pennsylvania, 1975; MS, Virginia Commonwealth University, 1980; Currently PhD Candidate, Virginia Commonwealth University. *Literary Appointments:* Editorial Review Panel, Virginia Nurse and Nursing Economics. *Publication:* Administrative Handbook for Virginia LPN Directors (in press). *Contributions include:* Over 30 articles published in professional publications including: Health Values; Nursing Management; Nursing Life; Nursing Economics; Focus on Critical Care. *Honours:* American Legion Public Speaking Award, 1966; American Journal of Nursing Excellence in Writing Award, 1980; Temple Memorial Award, 1980; Outstanding Young Women of America, 1982. *Memberships:* Virginia Nurses Association (Publications Committee Member, 1980–84, Chairman, 1984); Phi Kappa Phi; Sigma Theta Tau; Phi Delta Kappa. *Address:* 2708 Fillmore Road, Richmond, VA 23235, USA.

ROSENZWEIG, Roy Alan, b. 6 Aug. 1950, New York, USA. Professor of History. m. Deborah Kaplan, 9 Aug. 1981, Portland, Connecticut. *Education:* BA, Columbia University, 1971; Kellet Fellow, Cambridge University, 1971–73; PhD, Harvard University, 1978. *Publications:* Experiments in History Teaching, (edited with S Botein, W Leon, M Novak and G B Warden), 1977; Mission Hill and the Miracle of Boston, historical documetary film, (co-producer with R Broadman, J Grady and J Pennington, 1979; Water and the Dream of the Engineers, historical documentary film, co-writer and researcher 1983; Eight Hours For What We Will: Workers and Leisure in an Industrial City, 1870–1920, 1983; Presenting The Past; Essays on History and the Public, (co-editor with S P Benson and S Brier), 1986.

Contributions to: Labor History; Radical History Review; Journal of Social History; ILWCH; International Journal of Oral History. *Honours:* Kellet Fellow, 1971–73; Stoutter Fellow, 1976–78; Mellon Fellow, 1980–81; NEH Fellow, 1984. *Address:* Deparment of History, George Mason University, Fairfax, VA 22030, USA.

ROSHWALD, Mordecai Marceli, b. 26 May 1921, Drohobycz, Poland. Professor of Social and Political Philosophy. m. 25 Aug. 1945, Tel Aviv, Israel, 1 son. *Education:* MA, 1942; PhD, 1947, Hebrew University of Jerusalem. *Publications:* Adam Ve'hinukho, (Man and Education), 1954; Humanism in Practice, 1955; Level Seven, 1959; A Small Armageddon, 1962; Moses: Leader, Prophet, Man, (with Miriam Roshwald), 1969. *Contributions to:* Numerous philosophical and sociological journals. *Honours:* United Nations Essay Contest Prize, 1954; United World Federalist Essay Competition Prize, 1955; McKnight Foundation Humanities Award, 1962, 1963. *Address:* G-2 Glacier Drive, Nashua, NH 03062, USA.

ROSKAM, Karel Lodewyk, b. 7 Mar. 1931, Amsterdam, The Netherlands. Foreign Commentator, Radio. m. Annelies Wymenga, 7 Apr. 1964, Hoofddorp, 2 daughters. *Education:* LLD, Free University, Amsterdam. *Publications:* Apartheid and Discrimination, 1960; Alleen voor Blanken, 1961; Dekolonisatie van Afrika, 1975, 2nd edition, 1982; Zwart Afrika, 1975; Honger-Een Zwartboek, 1975; Mobutu, 1976; Zuid-Afrika: De Toekomst degon Gisteren, 1981; Afrika/Politiek, 1982; Frony Lynstaten, with N Kussendrager, 1985. *Contributions to:* Winkler Prins Encyclopedia; Winkler Prins Year Book, 1969–; Editor Kroniek van Afrika, 1966–71; African Social Research Documents, 1970–71; Vry Nederland; Samsam-Magazine. *Memberships:* Jury, Dick ScherPenzeez Prys; PEN Netherlands Centre. *Address:* Meidoornstraat 14, Bussum, the Netherlands.

ROSKILL, Mark Wentworth, b. 10 Nov. 1933, London, England. Art Historian and Critic. *Education:* BA 1956, MA 1961, University of Cambridge; MA, Harvard University, USA, 1957; MFA, PhD, Princeton University, 1961. *Publications:* English Painting from 1500 to 1865, 1959; The Letters of Vincent Van Gogh, editor, 1963; Dolce's Aretino and Venetian Art-Theory of the Sixteenth Century, 1968; Van Gogh, Gauguin and the Impressionist Circle, 1970; What Is Art History, 1976; Truth and Falsehood in Visual Images, (with David Carrier), 1984; The Interpretation of Cubism, 1985. *Contributions to :* Art News; Arts Magazine; Art International; Listener; Burlington Magazine; Oud Holland; Victorian Studies; Paris Review; Counter-/Measures. *Honours:* Fellowships, American Council of Learned Societies, 1956–66 and 1974–75. *Membership:* College Art Association of America. *Address:* Department of Art History, Bartlett Hall, University of Massachusetts, Amherst, MA 01002, USA.

ROSNER, Fred, b. 3 Oct, 1935, Berlin, Germany. Physician. m. Saranne Eskolsky, 24 Feb. 1959, New York City, USA, 2 sons, 2 daughters. *Education:* BA, Yeshiva College, 1955; MD, Albert Einstein College of Medicine. *Publications:* The Medical Writing of Moses Maimonides, 1969; The Medical Aphorisms of Moses Maimonides, 1973; Modern Medicine & Jewish Law, 1978; Sex Ethics in the Medical Writing of Moses Maimonides, 1974; Moses Maiamonides Commentary on the Mishnah, 1975; Editor, Proceedings of the Association of Orthodox Jewish Scientist, 1976; Medicine in the Bible and the Talmud, 1977; Julius Preuss Biblical-Talmudic Medicine, Translator, Editor, Proceedings of the Association of Orthodox Jewish Scientists, 1979; Moses Maimonides' Glossary of Drug Names, 1979; Co-Author, Jewish Bioethics, 1979; Practical Medical Halachah, 1980; Editor, Proceedings of the Association of Orthodox Jewish Scientists, 1980; Mamonides' Commentary on the Mishnah, 1981; Moses Maimonides; Treatise on Resurrection, 1982; Co-Editor, Compendium of Medical Ethics, 1984; Medicine in the Mishneh Torah of Mamonides, 1984. *Contributions to:* 500 articles in professional journals. *Honours:* Mosby Company Scholarship Book Award,

1957; Schering Pharmaceutical Company Medical Student Essay, Honorable Mention, 1957; Maimonides Hospital Research Society Award, 1965; Michael Reese Hospital and College of Jewish Studies, Chicago, Maimonides Award, 1969; Bernard Ravel Memorial Award, Yeshiva College Alumni Association, 1971; Maimonides Award of Wisconsin, 1977. *Address:* 82-68 164 Street, Jamaica, NY 11432, USA.

ROSS, Alan, b. 6 May 1922, Calcutta, India. Author, Journalist, Publisher. *Literary Appointments:* The Observer, 1953–72; Editor, London Magazine, 1961–. *Publications:* Australia 55, 1955; Poems 1942–67, 1968; The Taj Express, 1973; Open Sea, 1975; Death Valley, 1980; Ranji, 1983; Colours of War, 1983; Blindfold Games, 1986. *Contributions to:* Magazines and journals including: New Statesman; Spectator; Times Literary Supplement. *Honours:* FRSL, 1970; CBE, 1983. *Membership:* PEN. *Address:* 4 Elm Park Lane, London SW3, England.

ROSS, Angus, b. 19 July 1911, Otepopo, New Zealand. Lecturer, Former Professor of History. *Education:* MA, University of New Zealand; ED, 1951; PhD, University of Cambridge, England. *Publications:* 23 Battalion, 1959; New Zealand's Aspirations in the Pacific in the 19th Century, 1964; New Zealand's Record in the Pacific Islands in the 20th Century, 1969. *Contributions to:* New Zealand's Heritage; Dictionary of National Biography; An Encyclopaedia of New Zealand; Historical Journal; Journal of Imperial and Commonwealth History; The Press. *Honours include:* Military Cross, 1943; Bar to Military Cross, 1944; Commonwealth Fellow, St John's College, Cambridge, 1962; Smuts Fellow, University of Cambridge, 1970–71; Order of the British Empire, 1980. *Address:* 134 Cannington Road, Maori Hill, Dunedin, New Zealand.

ROSS, Dave Hugh, b. 2 Apr. 1949, Schenectady, New York, USA. Author; Illustrator. m. Kathleen Shannon, 25 June 1983, Clifton Park, 2 sons, 2 daughters. *Education:* BS, Art Education, State University College at Buffalo, 1971; MS, Curriculum and Instruction, State University of New York, Albany, 1974; Advanced Graduate Study, SUNY, 1974–78. *Publications:* (Author and Illustrator): Mummy Madness, 1979; Book of Hugs, 1980; How To Keep Warm in Winter, 1980; Making Robots, 1980; Making Space Puppets, 1980; Making UFU's, 1980; Space Monster, 1980; Mr Terwilliger's Secret, 1981; A Book of Kisses, 1982; Gorp and The Jelly Sippers, 1982; Rat Race and Other Rodent Jokes, 1983; Gorp and the Space Pirates, 1983; Gorp and the Run Away Computer, 1984; How to Prevent Monster Attacks, 1984; More Hugs, 1984; Baby Bear's Christmas 1985; Little Mouse's Valentine, 1986; (Illustrator): Illustrated Soccer Dictionary for Young People, James B Gardner, 1976; The Little Book of Big Riddles, Marion Meade, 1976; The Little Book of Big Tongue Twisters, Foley Curtis, 1977; Ghastly Ghostly Riddles, Gloria Milkowitz, 1977; Surfing, Basic Techniques, Arnold Madison, 1979; Win, Lose or Wear a Tie, Gloria Milkowitz, 1980; The Roller Coaster Ghost, Jane and Joyce Milton O'Connor, 1983, etc. *Honours:* Two Children's Choirs Awards, 1982. *Membership:* Author's Guild, New York City. *Literary Agent:* Andrea Brown. *Address:* 41 Warner Road, Clifton Park, NY 12065, USA.

ROSS, David, b. 26 Sep. 1929. Poet. *Education:* Champlain College, New York, USA; Syracuse University, New York. *Literary Appointments:* Teacher: New School for Social Research, New York; Antioch College, West Los Angeles; Poetry Workshops. *Publications:* Three Ages of Lake Light, 1962. *Contributions to:* The Nation; Poetry; Kulchur; The New Yorker; The Michigan Quarterly, Review; The Transatlantic Review; Advance. Reviews: New York Times Book Review; Kulchur; Michigan Quarterly Review; Advance. Anthologies including: The New Yorker Book of Poems, 1969; The Golden Horses; Poetry for a New Civilisation, 1976. *Address:* c/o Helen Ross, 170 East Hartsdale Avenue, 3E, Hartsdale, NY 10530, USA.

ROSS, Kenneth Graham, b. 4 June 1941, Melbourne, Australia. Writer; Playwright. *Major Plays Produced:* Don't Piddle Against the Wind, Mark; Breaker Morant (also as film); The Right Man; The Sound of Silence; Norman Lindsay & His Push in Bohemia; The Death of Dan Ko; Sorry, Sold Out. Also television & film plays. *Contributions to:* Theatre Australia; Melbourne Age; etc.*Honours:* Nominated, Writers AGIE Award, 1978, 1982. *Membership:* Australian Writers Guild. *Literary Agent:* Curtis Brown. *Address:* c/o Curtis Brown (Aust) Pty Ltd, 27 Union Street, Paddington, NSW, Australia.

ROSS, Marilyn, b. 3 Nov. 1939, San Diego, California, USA. Writer; Publishing Consultant. m. Tom Mulvane Ross, 25 May 1977, 3 sons, 1 daughter. *Education:* San Diego State College. *Publications:* Finding Your Roots, 1977; Creative Loafing, 1978; Discover Your Roots, 1978; Co-author, The Encyclopedia of Self-Publishing, 1979; Be Tough or Be Gone, 1984; Co-author, The Complete Guide to Self-Publishing, 1985, plus other ghostwritten books. *Contributions to:* Modern Maturity; Essence; Office Systems '85; The Toastmasters; NRTA Journal; Executive Female; National Enquirer; The Bureau of Business Practices Publications; Complete Woman; Southwest Airlines Magazine; COSMEP Newsletter, and numerous trade journals. *Honours:* First Place, non-fiction book for Creative Loafing, California Press Women, 1978; First Place, non-fiction book for The Encyclopedia of Self-Publishing, California Press Women, 1979. *Memberships:* Authors Guild; National Writers Club (professional division); San Luis Valley Writers Guild (co-founder); COSMEP. *Address:* PO Box 538, Saguache, CO 81149, USA.

ROSS, Ralph Gilbert, b. 27 Aug. 1911. Alexander Professor of Humanities Emeritus, Scripps College; Professor of Philosophy Emeritus, Claremont Graduate School. *Education:* BA, University of Arizona, USA, 1933; MA, 1935, PhD, 1940, Columbia University, New York. *Publications include:* The Fabric of Society, with Ernest van den Haag, 1957; The Art of Reading, with John Berryman and Allen Tate, 1960; Symbols and Civilization, 1963; Obligation: A Social Theory, 1970; Former book review Editor, Journal of the History of Philosophy; Former Advisory Editor, The Journal of Existentialism. *Honours include:* Distinguished Teacher Award, University of Minnesota, 1963. *Memberships include:* American Philosophy Association. *Address:* 429 Baughman, Claremont, CA 91711, USA.

ROSS, Robert N, b. 24 Feb. 1941, New York City, USA. Medical-Science Writer. 1 son, 2 daughters. *Education:* BA, Williams College, 1963; MA, 1965; PhD, 1967, Cornell University. *Literary Appointments:* Assistant Professor, Literature, University of Pennsylvania, 1968–71; Director, Science Communication Program, Boston University, 1981–82; Editor, Cutis Magazine, 1981–85; Editor, Tufts Medical Bulletin, 1985. *Publications:* Clinical Chemistry for Medical Technologists, 1978; The Enchanted Ring: The Untold Story of Penicillin, 1982; Handbook of Clinical Psychobiology and Pathology, 1982; The Clinical Use of Nasal Cromolyn Sodium, 1983; Medicine in International Almanac of Science and Technology, 1985. *Contributions to:* Journal of History of Ideas; Brain and Language; Medical Costs, 1981; Quest, 1984; Clinical Dependency and Mental Illness, 1985; Mast Cell Stabilizers, 1986. *Honour:* Exceptional Achievement Award; American Association for the Advancement of Science, Council for the Advancement and Support of Education, 1983. *Memberships:* Phi Beta Kappa; American Medical Writers Association; Semiotic Society of America; American Association for the Advancement of Science. *Literary Agent:* Katinka Matson, New York. *Address:* 24 Stedman Street, Brookline, MA 02146, USA.

ROSS, Sam, b. 10 Mar. 1912, Russia. Writer. m. Charlotte Bergman, 2 May 1941, Chicago, Illinois, USA. 1 son. *Education:* BS, Journalism, Northwestern University, USA. *Publications:* He Ran All the Way, 1947; Someday, Boy, 1948; The Sidewalks Are Free,

1950; Port Unknown, 1952; The Tight Corner, 1956; Ready for the Tiger, 1955; Hang-Up, 1958; The Fortune Machine,1970; Solomon's Palace, 1973; Windy City, 1979. *Literary Agent:* Ann Elmo. *Address:* 11433 Rochester Avenue, Los Angeles, CA 90025, USA.

ROSS, Veronica, b. 7 Jan. 1946, Hanover, Federal Republic of Germany. m. Roger Ross, 22 June 1965, Liverpool, Nova Scotia, 1 daughter, separated 1984. Writer. *Education:* Credits, Mount Allison University, New Brunswick, Canada. *Literary Appointments:* Writer in Community, Nova Scotia, 1981. *Publications:* Goodbye Summer, short stories, 1980; Dark Secrets, short stories, 1983; Fisherwoman, novel, 1984. *Contributionms to:* Chatelaine; Redbook; Cosmopolitan; Canadian Forum; Antigonish Review; Dalhousie Review; Canadian Author – Bookman; and others. *Honours:* Benson Hedges Magazine Writing Award, for Where Are You Susannah Brown, 1977; Award for Whistling, 1979, for God's Blessings, 1984, Canadian Periodical Publishers; Award for the Last Night of the Circus, Okanagan Fiction Award, 1985. *Memberships:* Writers Union of Canada; Writers Federation of Nova Scotia. *Literary Agent:* Nancy Colbert. *Address:* 234 Mansions Street, Apt 1, Kitchener, Ontario, Canada N2H 2K6.

ROSS, William Edward Daniel, b. 16 Nov. 1912, Saint John, N B, Canada. Author. m. Marilyn Ann Clark, 2 July 1960, Barrington, New Hampshire, USA. *Education:* University of Oklahoma; University of Chicago; University of Michigan. *Publications include:* 319 published books to date. Most recent: Denver's Lady; Shadows Over Briarcliff; Smiles of Summer. *Contributions to:* Daily News; London Evening News; This Week; Mike Chayne Mystery; Alfred Hitchcock; The Saint; etc. More than 600 short stories. Play: Murder Game. *Honours include:* Dominion Drama Festival Award; Queen's Jubilee Medal; Papers collected by Boston University, N B Legislative Library. *Memberships:* Former President, N B Branch, National Executive of Canadian Authors; Society of Authors; Authors League of America; Crime Writers Mystery Writers, Playwrights of Canada. *Literary Agent:* Richard Curtis. *Address:* 80 Horton Road, East Riverside, Saint John, N B, Canada E2H 1P8.

ROSSNER, Judith, b. 31 Mar. 1935, New York City, New York, USA. Novelist. m. twice, divorced twice, 1 son. *Publications:* To the Precipice, 1966, Nine Months in the Life of an Old Man, 1969; Any Minute I Can Spit, 1972; Looking for Mr Goodbar, 1975; Attachments, 1977; Emmeline, 1980; August, 1983. *Contributions to:* Stories, essays and reviews in magazines and journals. *Literary Agent:* Wendy Weil, Julian Bach Agency. *Address:* c/o W Weil, Julian Bach Agency, 747 Third Avenue, New York, NY 10017, USA.

ROSTON, Murray, b. 10 Dec. 1928, London, England. University Professor. *Education:* MA, Queen's College, University of Cambridge; MA, Queen Mary College, London; PhD, University of London. *Major Publications:* Prophet & Poet, 1965; Biblical Drama in England from the Middle Ages to the Present Day, 1968; The Soul of Wit: A Study of John Donne, 1974; Milton & The Baroque, 1979; Sixteenth Century English Literature, 1982; Renaissance Perspectives in Literature & the Visual Arts, 1986. *Address:* 51 Katznelson Street, Kiryat Ono, Israel.

ROSZKO, Janusz, b. 4 Nov. 1932, Lwow, Poland. Writer. m. Anna Kopczyńska, 12 Aug. 1967, 1 son, 1 daughter. *Education:* Degree in History, University of Cracow, 1954. *Literary Appointments:* Lecturer/Contract Professor, University of Cracow, 1972–84; Vice President, Polish Writers Union, 1983–. *Publications:* 18 books including: Pogański książę, silny wielce, 1970; Kolebka Siemowita, 1974; Ostatni Rycerz Europy, biography of Casimir Pułłaski, 1984. *Contributions to:* Życie literackie; Kontrasty. *Honours:* Literary Award of Cracow Town, 1979; Literary Award 1st degree of Minister of Culture in Poland, 1983.

Membership: Polish Writers Union. *Address:* 32–082 Bolechowice k, Krakowa, Poland.

ROTEN, Iris von, b. 2 Apr. 1917, Basel Switzerland. Lawyer; Author. m. Dr iur Peter von Roten, 25 July 1946, Marly, Canton Fribourg, 1 daughter. *Education:* Doctor iuris utriusque, University of Bern, Switzerland, 1941; Zürcher Rechtanwalt, Zürich, Switzerland, 1946. *Literary Appointments:* Editor, Schweizer Frauenblatt; Writer for Schweizer Speigel Verlag; Editorial work for Heim und Leben with J C Bucher AG, Lucerne. *Major Publications:* Frauen im Laufgitter, 1958–59, the first and largest strictly feminist book in Switzerland; Frauenstimmrecht-Brevier, 1959; Von Bosporus zum Euphrat, Türken und Türkei, 1964. *Contributor in the forties, fifties and sixties to:* Schweizer Spiegel, Zürich; Heim und Leben, Lucerne; Neue Zürcher Zeitung; Weltwoche, Zürich; Elle, Zürich. *Address:* Heuberg 12, CH–4051 Basel, Switzerland.

ROTH, Andrew, b. 23 Apr. 1919, New York, USA. Political Journalist and Biographer. m. Mathilda Anna Friederich, 30 June 1949, Hong Kong, divorced 1984, 1 son, 1 daughter. *Education:* Bachelor of Social Science BSS, City College of New York; MA, Columbia University; Certificate in Japanese, Harvard University. *Publications:* Japan Drives South, 1941; French Interests and Policies in the Far East, 1942; Dilemma in Japan, 1945; Business Background of MP's, 1959, 7th edition 1980; The MP's Chart, 1967, 5th edition 1979; Enoch Powell, Tory Tribune, 1970; Can Parliament Decide?, 1971; Heath and Heathmen, 1972; Lord on the Board, 1972; Sir Harold Wilson, Yorkshire Walter Mitty, 1977; Parliamentary Profiles, volumes I-IV, 1984–85. *Contributions to:* Lobby Correspondent, New Statesman, 1984–. *Literary Agent:* Judy Tench. *Address:* 3-14 Palace Chambers, Bridge Street, London SW1A 2JT, England.

ROTH, Audrey J, b. 4 Feb. 1927, Newark, New Jersey. USA. English Teacher. m. Raymond N Roth, 26 June 1947, Dayton, Ohio, USA, 1 son, 1 daughter. *Education:* BA, MA, Ohio State University; PhD, Union Graduate School. *Literary Appointments:* Youngstown (Ohio) College; University of Miami, 1958–63; Miami-Dade Community College, 1963–. *Publications:* Prose As Experience, co-editor, 1965; Writing Step By Step co-author, 1969; Words People Use, co-author, 1972; The Research Paper: Process, Form and Content, 5th edition, 1986. *Contributions to:* College English; Florida English Journal; College English Association Forum; College Composition and Communications, etc. *Memberships:* President, Florida College English Association; President, Florida Council of Teachers of English, and other offices in other organisations. *Address:* Department of English, Miami-Dade Community College, 11011 S W 104 Street, Miami, FL 33176–3393, USA.

ROTH, Charles Edmund, b. 14 Jan. 1934, Danbury, Connecticut, USA. Environmental Educator. m. Betty Jane King, 22 Dec. 1956, Greenwich, Connecticut, 2 sons, 2 daughters. *Education:* AB Zoology, University of Connecticut; MS Conservation Education, Cornell University. *Publications:* The Most Dangerous Animal in the World, 1971; Man and Environment, volume 1 1972, volume 2 1974; Walking Catfish and other Aliens, 1973; The Farm Book, 1975; Then There Were None, 1977; An Introduction to Massachusetts Mammals, 1978; The Wildlife Observers Guidebook, 1982; The Plant Observers Guidebook, 1984; The Sky Observer's Guidebook, 1986. *Contributions to:* Britannica Junior; Audubon; Sanctuary; Curious Naturalist; Ranger Rick; KIND; The Environmentalists; Journal of Mammalogy; Junior Natural History. *Address:* 39 Mill Road, Littleton, MA 01460, USA.

ROTH, June Doris Spiewak, b. 16 Feb. 1926, Haverstraw, New York, USA. Author, Syndicated Newspaper Columnist. m. Frederick Roth, 7 July 1945, 1 son, 1 daughter. *Education:* Pennsylvania State University, 1942–44; Tobe-Coburn School, 194405; BA, Thomas Eidson College, 1981; MS, University of Bridgeport, 1982. *Major Publications:* The Freeze & Please Homefreezer Cookbook, 1963; The Rich & Delicious Low-Calorie Figure Slimming Cookbook, 1964; Thousand Calorie Cookbook, 1967; How to Use Sugar to Lose Weight, 1969; Fast & Fancy Cookbook, How to Cook Like a Jewish Mother, The Take Good Care of My Son Cookbook for Brides, 1969; The Indoor-Outdoor Barbecue Book, The Pick of the Pantry Cookbook, 1970; Let's Have a Brunch Cookbook, 1971; Edith Buner's All in the Family Cookbook, The On-Your-Own Cookbook, Healthier Jewish Cookery, The Unsaturated Fat Way, 1972; Elegant Desserts, 1973; Old-Fashioned Candy-Making, 1974; Walt-free Cooking with Herbs and Spices (tastemaker award), 1975; The Troubled Tummy Cookbook, 1976; Cooking for your Hyperactive Child, 1977; The Gallery Cookbook, 1977; The Food-Depression Connection, 1978; Aerobic Nutrition, 1981; The Pasta-Lover's Diet Book, 1984. *Contributor to:* Harper's Bazaar Magazine; Family Circle. *Memberships:* American Society of Journalists & Authors, President 1982–83; Authors League of America, National Federation of Press Women; Newspaper Food Editors & Writers Association; Newspapere Features Council; National Press Club. *Literary Agent:* Anita Diamant. *Address:* 1057 Oakland Court, Teaneck, NJ 07666, USA.

ROTHCHILD, Kurt Wilhelm, b. 21 Oct. 1914, Vienna, Austria. University Professor Emeritus. m. Valerie Kunke, 10 Aug. 1938, Vienna, 1 son, 1 daughter. *Education:* DrJur, University of Vienna, 1938; MA, Economics, University of Glasgow, Scotland, 1940. *Academic Appointments:* Lecturer, Economics, University of Glasgow, 1940–47; Senior Research Worker, Austrian Institute of Economic Research, Vienna, 1947–66; Professor of Economics, University of Linz, Austria, 1966–85. *Publications:* The Austrian Economy, 1947; Theory of Wages, 1954; Economic Forecasting, 1969; Economics of Power, 1971; Disequilibrium Economics, 1981. *Contributions to:* Numerous journals. *Honours:* Social Science Award, City of Vienna, 1978; Science Award, City of Linz, 1980. *Address:* Döblinger Hauptstrasse 77a, A1190 Vienna, Austria.

ROTHENBERG, Jerome (Dennis), b. 11 Dec. 1931, New York City, USA. Poet. m. Diane Brodatz, 25 Dec. 1952, New York, 1 son. *Education:* BA, City College, City University of New York, 1942; MA, University of Michigan, 1953. *Publications:* New Young German Poets, 1959; White Sun Black Sun, 1960; Sightings 1-1X, 1964; The Gorky Poems, 1966; Between, 1967; Poems 1964–67, 1968; Technicians of the Sacred, 1968; Poems for the Game of Silence, 1971; Shakeing the Pumpkin, 1972; America a Prophecy, 1973; Revolution of the Word, 1974; Poland/1931, 1974; A Big Jewish Book, 1977; A Seneca Journal, 1978; Vienna Blood, 1980; Pre-Faces, 1981; Symposium of the Whole, 1983; That Dada Strain, 1983. *Contrubutor to:* Numerous professional journals. *Honours:* Longview Foundation Award, 1960; Wenner-Gren Foundation, 1968; Guggenheim Foundation Fellowship, 1974; National endowment for the Arts Grant, 1976; Before Columbus Foundation American Book Award, 1982; New York State Writers Institute Distinguished Writer in Residence, 1986. *Memberships:* PEN International; New Wilderness Foundation. *Address:* c/o New Directions, 80 Eighth Avenue, New York, NY 10012, USA.

ROTHENSTEIN, John Knewstub Maurice, (Sir), b. 11 July, 1901. Director of the Tate, 1938–64 and other Art Galleries; University Professor. *Education:* MA, Oxford University, 1927; PhD, University College, London, 1931. *Publications include:* An introduction to English Painting, 1934; Augustus John, 1944; Modern English Painters, 3 vols, 1952–74; Turner, 1960; Sickert, 1961; Paul Nash, 1961; Francis Bacon, 1967; (autobiog in 3 vols): Summers Lease, 1965; Brave Day, Hideous Night, 1966; Time's Thievish Progress, 1970; Edward Burra, 1972; Stanley Spencer, The Man, 1979; Modern English Painters, updated edition, 1984; Robert Buhler, 1986. *Honours include:* Knight, 1952; CBE, 1948; Knight Commander, Order Aztec Eagle, Mexico,

1953; Honorary Fellow, Worcester College, Oxford, 1953; Fellow, University College, London, 1976–; Knight Commander, Order St Gregory the Great, 1977. *Memberships include:* Athenauem Club. *Address:* Beauforest House, Newington, Dorchester-on-Thames, Oxford OX9 8AG, England.

ROTHFORK, John Gilbert, b. 18 Dec. 1946, Holstein, Iowa, USA. Professor. m. Sandra Jepson, 22 July 1966, Sioux City, 1 son. *Education:* BA; MA; PhD. *Appointment:* Founding Editor, New Mexico Humanities Review, 1978. *Publications:* Watermelon Mountain, 1984; Indians, 1980; Messages from a Typewriter, 1980. *Contributor to:* 100 articles to professional journals including, Philological Quarterly; Illustrated Weekly of India; Southwest Review; Northwest Review; Journal of General Education; Descant; Charlton; Studia Mystica; Concerning Poetry; Texas Review; Great Plains Poetry Anthology, etc. *Honours:* BA Comprehensive Honours, English, Morning Side College; NEA Grant, 1979, 1980, 1983, 1984; NM Arts Division Grant, 1981, 1983; Coordinating Council of Literary Magazine Grant, 1979; Senior Fulbright Professor to India, 1981–82, to Japan 1984–85. *Memberships:* NEH Fellowship, 1978; American Phililogical Association Fellowship, 1974; Board of Directors, Rio Grande Writers Association. *Address:* 1008 Lopezville Road, Socorro, NM 87801, USA.

ROTHROCK, George Abel, b. 11 Nov. 1932, Wilmington, Delaware, USA. Professor of History. *Education:* BA, University of Delaware, 1954; University of Grenoble, France, 1954–55; MA 1956, PhD 1958, University of Minnesota, USA. *Major Publications:* Vauban, Sebastien Le Prestre de, A Manual of Siegecraft & Fortification (translated), 1968; Europe, a Brief History, 1971, 2nd edition with Tom B Jones, 2 volumes, 1975; The Huguenots: A Biography of a Minority, 1979. *Contributor to:* Various professional journals. *Honours include:* Canadian Council Research Grant, 1968–69; Fellow, Royal Historical Society, 1966–. *Address:* Briarcliffe, 2715 124th street, Edmonton, Alberta, T6J 4T2, Canada.

ROTHSCHILD, Joseph, b. 5 Apr. 1931, Fulda, Federal Republic of Germany. Professor. m. Ruth Deborah Nachmansohn, 19 July 1959, New York City, 1 son, 1 daughter. *Education:* AB summa cum laude, 1951, AM, 1952, Columbia University; D Phil, Oxford University, England, 1955. *Publications:* The Communist Party of Bulgaria, 1959; Communist Eastern Europe, 1964; Pilsudski's Coup d'Etat, 1966; East Central Europe Between the Two World Wars, 1974; Ethnopolotics, 1981. *Contributions to:* Scholarly journals and edited volumes. *Honours:* Social Science Research Council Fellow, 1963–64; John Simon Guggenheim Fellow, 1967–68; American Council of Learned Societies Fellow, 1971–72; National Endowment for the Humanities Fellow, 1978–79; Ford Foundation – ACLS Research Fellow, 1985–86. *Membership:* Phi Beta Kappa. *Address:* 445 Riverside Drive, New York, NY 10027, USA.

ROTHSTEIN, Samuel, b. 12 Jan. 1921, Moscow, Russia. University Professor. m. Miriam Ruth Teitelbaum, 26 Aug. 1921, Vancouver, BC, Canada, 2 daughters. *Education:* BA, 1939, MA, 1940, University of British Columbia; Graduate Studies, University of California, Berkeley, 1941–42; Graduate Studies, University of Washington, Seattle, 1942–43; BLS, University of California, Berkeley, 1947; PhD, University of Illinois, 1954. *Publications:* The Development of Reference Services, 1955; As We Remember It, co-editor, 1970; The Library – The University, co-author, 1972; A Century of Service, co-author, 1976. *Contributions to:* Library Quarterly; Library Journal; College and Research Libraries; Canadian Library Journal; A L A World Encyclopedia of Library and Information Services; Encyclopeadia of Library and Information Science. *Honours:* The Dr Helen Gordon Stewart Award (BC Library Association) 1970; Doctor of Letters (Honorary) York University, Toronto, 1971. *Address:* School of Library, Archival and Information Studies, The University of British Columbia, 831–1956 Main Mall, Vancouver, BC, Canada V6T 1Y3.

ROTHWELL, Kenneth Sprague, b. 26 May 1921, Bay Shore, New York, USA. Professor of English. m. Marilyn Gregg Rothwell, 26 June 1954, Cortland, New York, 2 sons, 2 daughters. *Education:* BA, University of North Carolina, Chapel Hill, 1948; MA, 1949, PhD, 1956, Columbia University. *Literary Appointments:* Instructor, University of Rochester, 1952–55; Instructor, University of Cincinnati, 1955–57; Assistant Professor then Professor, University of Kansas, 1957–70; Professor, University of Vermont, 1970–. *Publications:* Question of Rhetoric, 2nd edition, 1974; A Mirror for Shakespeare, 2nd printing, 1982; Co-editor; Shakespeare on Film Newsletter, 1976–. *Contributor to:* Articles and Reviews to Shakespeare Quarterly; CEA Forum; American Literature; Kansas Quarterly; Modern Language Note; Literature/Film Quarterly. *Honours:* Grant-in-aid, American Philosophical Society, 1968. *Memberships:* MLA; Shakespeare Association of America. *Address:* 324 Old Mill, Department of English, University of Vermont, Burlington, VT 05405, USA.

ROUECHE, John Edward, b. 3 Sep. 1938, Statesville, North Carolina, USA. Professor; Author; Lecturer. m. Susanne Davis, 28 May 1976, Dallas Texas, USA. 1 son, 2 daughters. *Education:* AA, Mitchell College, 1958; BA, Lenoir-Rhyne College, 1960; MA, Appalachian State University, 1961; PhD, Florida State University, 1964. *Literary Appointments:* Editor for Community College, Jossey-Bass Publishers, 1971–83; Editorial Advisor, Prentice-Hall Publishers, 1973–75; Editor and Co-ordinator, Series on Creative Teachings, Harcourt-Brace/Media Systems, Publishers, 1977–; Member of National Editorial Boards for five national educational journals in higher education. *Publications:* More than a dozen books including: A Modest Proposal; Students Can Learn, 1972; Catching Up: Remedial Education, 1973; Overcoming Learning Problems, 1977; Holistic Literacy in College Teaching; Beaconms for Change; Community College Leadership in the 1980's; America's Best Schools: A National Study; Access with Excellence in the Open Door College: A National Study. *Contributor to:* More than 100 articles in national journals and chapters in books. *Honours:* More than a dozen Distinguished Research and Writing Awards since 1980, including the University of Texas Distinguished Researcher Award, 1985 and the Distinguished Research Publication Award from the Council of Universities and Colleges, 1985. *Memberships include:* President, Council of Universities and Colleges, 1977–78; Phi Beta Kappa; Phi Delta Kappa. *Address:* EdB 348, University of Texas at Austin, Austin, TX 78712, USA.

ROUGEMONT, Denis de, b. 8 Sep. 1906, Neuchâtel, Switzerland. Author. m. Anahite Repond, 2 Feb. 1952, Geneva, 1 son, 1 daughter. *Education:* Universities of Neuchatel, Geneva, Vienna; Degrees in Letters and Philosophy, 1931; Honorary Doctorate, University of Geneva. *Publications include:* Author of some 33 books most recently: Lettre ouverte aux Europeens, 1970; L'Un et le Divers, 1970; Le Cheminement des Esprits, 1970; Les Dirigeants et les Finalités de la Societe occidentale, 1972; L'Avenir est notre Affairs, 1977; Raport au Peuple europeen sur l'Etat de l'Union de l'Europe, 1979. *Honours:* Schiller Prize, Zurich, Switzerland, 1934, 46, 60; Gottfried Keller Prize, 1947; Eve Delacroix Prize, 1956; Monaco Literary Prize, 1958; Literary Prize, City of Geneva, 1967; Paul Tillich Award, New York, USA, 1969; Robert Schuman Prize, Bonn, Germany, 1970; Grand Prix, Swiss Schiller Foundation, 1982; Corresponding member, Academy of Moral and Political Sciences, Paris and Academy of Athens. *Membership:* Society of Swiss Writers. *Address:* F-01630 Saint-Genis Pouilly, France.

ROULSTON, Donald Lovell, b. 2 Nov. 1937, Clearfield, Pennsylvania, USA. Writer; Editor. m. Sandra Louise Parker, 15 Feb. 1981, North Salem, New Hampshire, USA, 1 son. *Education:* US Coast Guard Academy; Duke University; Harvard; Doctor of Divinity, Church of Gospel Ministry. *Publications:* Collaborator on medical texts and anthologies. *Contributions include:* Archive Magazine; Nexus magazine; New Hampshire Profiles; Infoworld; Survive magazine; The Observer; Manchester Union Leader. *Honours:* H H Rumpot Dubiel Award, 1958. *Memberships:* American Medical Writers Association; Society for Technical Communication; National Association for Government Communicators. *Literary Agent:* T'Ai Honda. *Address:* 20 Alfred Drive, Salem, NH 03079, USA.

ROUSSEAU, George Sebastian, b. 23 Feb. 1941, New York City, New York, USA. Educator. *Education:* BA, Amherst College, Amherst, Massachusetts, 1962; Diploma, American School of Classical Studies, Athens, Greece, 1963; MA 1964, PhD 1966, Princeton University, Princeton, New Jersey, USA. *Literary Appointments:* Instructor of English, Harvard University, 1966–68; Assistant Professor of English 1968–70, Professor of English 1970–79, Professor of 18th Century Studies 1980–, University of California, Los Angeles. *Publications:* This Long Disease My Life: Alexander Pope and the Sciences, (with Marjorie Hope Nicolson), 1968; English Poetic Satire (with N Rudenstein), 1969; The Augustan Milieu: Essays Presented to Louis A Landa, (editor with Eric Rothstein), 1970; Tobias Smollett: Bicentennial Essays Presented to Lewis M Knapp, (editor with P G Bouce), 1971; Organic Form: The Life of an Idea, (editor), 1972; Goldsmith: The Critical Heritage, 1974; The Ferment of Knowledge: Studies in the Historiography of Science, (with Roy Porter), 1980; The Letters and Private Papers of Sir John Hill, 1982; Tobias Smollett: Essays of Two Decades, 1982. *Contributions to:* Numerous magazines and journals. *Honours:* Osgood Fellow in Literature, Princeton University, 1965–66; American Council of Learned Societies Fellow – ACLS, 1970; Visiting Fellow Commoner, Trinity College, Cambridge University, 1982; Senior Fulbright Research Professor, Sir Thomas Browne Institute, 1983. *Memberships:* American Society for 18th Century Studies; Modern Language Association; History of Science Society; American Historical Association. *Address:* 2424 Castilian Drive, Outpost Estates, Los Angeles, CA 90068, USA.

ROUSSEV, Nikola, b. 13 July 1932, Berkovitza, Bulgaria. Writer. *Education:* High Theatre School, Krastyou Sarafov, Sofia. *Publications:* Plays: Look How Many Poppies, 1965; A Tobacco Case 18 Carats, 1967; The Brave Fellows, 1968; From Earth to Heaven, 1978. *Contributor to:* The, Theatre, magazine. *Honour:* An Honoured Worker of Culture, 1978. *Membership:* Union of Bulgarian Writers. *Address:* 33 A, Nezabravka Street, Sofia, Bulgaria.

ROUTH, Francis John, b. 15 Jan. 1927, Kidderminster, England. Composer; Pianist; Writer. m. Virginia Anne Raphael, 1 Sep. 1956, St John's Wood, London. England. 2 sons, 2 daughters. *Education:* MA, Kings College, Cambridge, England, 1954; LRAM FRCO, Royal Academy of Music, 1953. *Literary Appointments:* Ed Composer magazine. *Publications:* The Organ, 1958; Contemporary Music – an Introduction, 1968; Contemporary British Music, 1972; Early English Organ Music, 1973; Stravinsky, 1975; co-author of section in: The Patronage and Presentation of Contemporary Music, 1970; Patronage of the Creative Artists, 1974; Stravinsky (in Makers of Modern Culture), 1981. *Contributions to:* Performing Right; Records and Recording; Music Teacher; Composer; Performance; Musique et Loisirs; Musical Times; Redcliffe Concerts anniversary programme books. *Literary Agent:* Formerly Curtis Brown (Academic) Ltd. *Address:* Arlington Park House, Sutton Lane, London W4 4HD, England.

ROVEN, Milton Dean, b. 25 Feb. 1916, New York, USA. Doctor of Podiatric Medicine and Surgery. m. Ruth Katz, 18 Dec. 1955, New York City, 1 son, 1 daughter. *Education:* Doctor of Podiatric Medicine; Fellow, Academy of Podiatric Medicine; Fellow, Academy of Ambulatory Foot Surgery; Diplomate, American Board of Ambulatory Foot Surgery. *Literary Appointments:* Associate Editor, Journal of American Association of Hospital Podiatrists; Contributing Editor, Journal of Podiatric Medicine; Editorial Consultant in Podiatric Surgery Current Podiatry Journal. *Publications:* Contributing author to textbook Modern Foot Therapy, 1948; Author of textbook, Non-Disabling Surgical Rehabilitation of the Forefoot, 1976; Questions and Answers on Foot Care, 1981. *Contributions to:* Papers summarized in Popular Science Magazine; Health Care News; Ladies Home Journal; Family Circle; Midnight Globe; New York Magazine; Glamour Magazine. *Honours:* Recipient of 20 awards on foot care research including 7 gold medal first prize awards for the Journal of American Podiatric Medicine, Current Podiatry Journal, Academy of Podiatric Medicine and International Academy of Ambulatory Foot Surgery. *Address:* 63 Marlborough Road, Brooklyn, NY 11226, USA.

ROWAT, Donald C, b. 1921, Somerset, Manitoba, Canada. University Professor. m. 2 children. *Education:* BA, Toronto University, 1943; MA, 1946, PhD, 1950, Columbia University. *Literary Appointments include:* Council and Executive Committee, Social Science Research Council of Canada, 1974–77, Vice President 1978–79 and Chairman, Committee on the Freedom of Communication of Social Scientists, 1980–82; NATO Fellow studying access to information laws, summer 1977; Appraisals Committee, Ontario Council on Graduate Studies, 1977–80, 1983–; National Archives Advisory Council of Public Records, 1977–; Carleton Senate, 1979–81; HRC Leave Fellow to study and lecture on access and ombudsmen in France, India, Japan and Sweden, 1981–82; Board of Directors, Canadian Civil Liberties Association, 1981–; Editorial Board, International Review of Administrative Sciences, 1983–; Chairman, Academi Advisory Board of Ombudsman Forum, International Bar Association, 1984–. *Publications:* The Reorganization of Provincial-Municipal Relations in Nova Scotia, 1949; Your Local Government, 1955 2nd edition, 1975; Editor: Basic Issues in Public Administration, 1961; Editor: The Ombudsman: Citizen's Defender, 1965, 2nd edition 1968; The Canadian Municipal System: Essays on the Improvement of Local Government, 1969; The University, Society and Government, 1970; Joint editor: Studies on the University, Society and Government, 1970; Editor: The Government of Federal Capitals 1972; The Ombudsman Plan: Essays on the Worldwide Spread of an Idea, 1973; The Finnish Parliamentary Ombudsman, editor and author of foreword, 1973; The Provincial Political System joint editor, 1976; Political Corruption in Canada, joint editor, 1976; Public Access to Government Documents: A Comparative Perspective, 1978; Administrative Secrecy in Developed Countries, editor, 1979; International Handbook on Local Government Reorganization, editor 1980; Also editor of 9 books of graduate student essays published by Carleton's Department of Political Science. *Address:* Department of Political Science, Carleton University, Ottawa, Canada K1S 5B6.

ROWBOTHAM, Sheila, b. 27 Feb. 1943, Leeds, England. Writer. *Education:* BA History, University of Oxford, England. *Literary Appointments:* Visiting Professor in Womens' Studies, University of Amsterdam, 1982–83; Visiting Lecturer US & Canadian Universities, Teacher in Schools & Further Education. Co-Editor, Jobs for a Change, Industry & Employment Branch, Greater London Council. *Major Publications:* Women's Resistance & Revolution, 1972; Woman's Consciousness, Man's World, 1973; Hiden from History, 1973; A New World for Women, 1977; Socialism and the New Life (with Jeff Weeks) 1977; Dutiful Daughters (with Jean McCrindle), 1977; Beyond the Fragments, (with Lynne Segal & Hilary Wainwright), 1979; Dreams and Dilemmas, 1983. *Contributor to:* New Society; The Guardian; New Socialist; Socialist Worker; Times Literary Supplementary; New York Times; Granta; The Miner; Spare Rib;Corridor; Islington Guter Press; Hackney People's Press; New Statesman; Marxism Today; The Chartist. *Address:* 97 Powerscroft Road, London E5, England.

ROWE, John Carlos, b. 11 Dec. 1945, Los Angeles, California, USA. University Professor. m. Kristin Hornor, 15 June 1968, San Francisco, 3 sons. *Education:* BA, Hons, The Johns Hopkins University, 1967; PhD, State University of New York, Buffalo, 1972. *Literary Appointments:* Assistant Professor of English, University of Maryland, 1971–75; Assistant Professor, 1975–77, Associate Professor, 1977–80, Professor of English, 1980–, Chairman, English Department, 1979–82, University of California, Irvine, *Publications:* Henry Adams and Henry James: The Emergence of a Modern Consciousness, 1976; Through the Custom-House: Nineteenth-Century American Fiction and Modern Theory, 1982; The Theoretical Dimensions of Henry James, 1984. *Contributions to:* Scholarly essays and reviews in: ELH; MLN; ESQ; Glyph; Criticism; Cultural Critique; Genre; Nineteenth-Century Fiction; Delta; Boundary 2; Modern Philology, etc. *Honours:* University Fellowship, State University of New York, Buffalo, 1970–71; Fulbright Senior Lectureship, University dea Saarandes, 1974–75; Rockefeller Foundation Fellowship, Humanities, 1982–83; Director, National Endowment for Humanities, Summer Seminar, 1986. *Memberships:* Modern Language Association; Henry James Society; Humanities Institute, California; Focused Research Program, Critical Theory, University of California, Irvine. *Address:* Department of English and Comparative Literature, University of California at Irvine, Irvine, CA 92717, USA.

ROWELL, George Rignall, b. 6 June 1923, Mansfield, Nottinghamshire, England. Reader in Theatre History, University of Bristol. m. Elspeth Nancy Noble, 5 Sep. 1959, Bristol. *Education:* BA 1st Class Honours Modern History 1947, B Litt 1950, Hertford College, Oxford. *Literary Appointments:* General Editor, Theatre Research, 1961–64. *Publications:* Nineteenth Century Plays, collection, 1953, new edition, 1972, 5th Impression, 1985; The Victorian Theatre, 1956, revised edition 1978; Engaged! comic opera, (with Kenneth Mobbs), 1963; Sixty Thousand Nights, play, (with Julian Slade), 1967; Late Victorian Plays, collection, 1968 and 1972; Victorian Dramatic Criticism, collection, 1971; Trelawny, play, (with Julian Slade and Aubrey Woods), 1973; Queen Victoria Goes To The Theatre, 1978; Theatre in The Age of Irving, 1981; Plays By W S Gilbert, collection, 1982; The Repertory Movement, (with Anthony Jackson), 1984. *Contributions to:* Theatre Notebook; Nineteenth Century Theatre Research; Theatre Research International. *Memberships:* Vice Chairman, Society for Theatre Research, 1985–; Society of Authors; Vice-President, Gilbert and Sullivan Society, *Literary Agent:* Curtis Brown Academic. *Address:* 11 Stoke Paddock Road, Bristol BS9 2DJ, England.

ROWEN, Herbert Harvey, b. 22 Oct. 1916, New York, New York, USA. Historian. m. Mildred Ringel, 28 June 1940, New York, 1 son, 2 daughters. *Education:* BSS, City College of New York, 1936; MA 1948, PhD 1951, Columbia University, *Publicatons:* The Ambassador Prepares for War: The Dutch Embassy of Arnauld de Pomponne, 1668–1671, 1957; A History of Early Modern Europe, 1500–1815, 1960; A History of the Western World, (co-author), 1969 and 1974; John de Witt: Grand Pensionary of Holland, 1625–1672, 1978; The King's State: Proprietary Dynasticism in Early Modern France, 1980; Johan de Witt: Staatsman van de Ware Vrijheid, 1985. *Contributions to:* Journal of Modern History; American Historical Review; French Historical Studies; Encyclopedia Britannica. *Memberships:* Phi Beta Kappa; Foreign Member, Royal Netherlands Academy of Arts and Sciences. *Address:* Department of History, Rutgers University, New Brunswick, NJ 08903, USA.

ROWEN, Ruth Halle, b. New York City, USA. University Teacher; Professor, CUNY. *Education:* Barnard College; Columbia University; BA; MA; PhD. *Publicatons:* Early Chamber Music; Co-Author, Hearing – Gateway to Music; Music Through Sources & Documents, 1979. *Contributor to:* Musical Quarterly; Piano Quarterly; Music Library Association Notes. *Memberships:* American Musicology Society; National Federation of Music Clubs. *Address:* 115 Central Park W, Apt 25D, New York, NY 10023, USA.

ROWLAND-ENTWISTLE, (Arthur) Theodore (Henry), b. 30 July 1925, Clayton-le-Moors, Lancashire, England. Writer. *Education:* BA, Open University. *Publications:* Teach Yourself the Violin, 1967; Winston Churchill, 1972; Napoleon, 1973; Famous Composers, with Jean Cooke, 1974; Famous Explorers, with J Cooke, 1974; Animal Worlds, with J Cooke, 1975; Facts & Records Books of Animals, 1975; The World You Never See: Insects, 1976; Famous Kings & Emperors, with J Cooke, 1976; Our Earth, 1977; Editor, Concise Encyclopedia of the Arts, 1979; Editor, Pictorial Encyclopedia of Nature, 1980; Natural Wonders of the World, 1980; Atlas of the Bible Lands, 1981; Granada Guide to Insects, 1983; Granada Guide to Heraldry, 1984; Houses, 1985. *Contributor to:* Various encyclopedias. *Memberships:* FRGS; FZS. *Agent:* Rupert Crew Ltd. *Address:* West Dene, Stonestile Lane, Hastings, Sussex TN35 4PE, England.

ROWLEY, Gordon Douglas, b. 31 July 1921, London, England. Retired University Lecturer in Horticultural Botany. *Education:* BSc, University of London, 1942. *Publications:* Flowering Succulents, 1959; Illustrated Encyclopedia of Succulents, 1978; Name That Succulent, 1980; Adenium and Pathypodium Handbook, 1983; The Haworthia Drawings of John Thomas Bates, 1985. Editor of various botanical publications and contributor to journals on succulents and roses. *Honours:* Veitch Memorial Gold Medal, Royal Horticultural Society, 1980; Cactus d'Or de Monaco from Princess Grace of Monaco, 1982 (for services to horticulture). *Memberships:* President, British Cactus and Succulent Society; Fellow, Cactus and Succulent Society of America. *Address:* Cactusville, 1 Ramsbury Drive, Reading, Berkshire RG6 2RT, England.

ROWSE, Alfred Leslie, b. 4 Dec. 1903, St Austell, Cornwall, England. Writer. *Education:* MA, DLitt, Gouis College, Oxford. *Literary Appointments:* President, English Association, 1951–52; President, Shakespeare Club, Stratford-upon-Avon, 1970–71. *Publications Include:* The England of Elizabeth; Tudor Cornwall; The Churchills; Shakespear the Man; A Life: Collected Poems; The Cornish in America. *Contributions to:* New York Times; Financial Times; Books & Bookmen; English Historical Review. *Honours:* Honorary DLitt, Exeter; Honorary DCL; etc. Benson Medal, Royal Society of Literature. *Memberships:* Royal Society of Literature; British Academy. *Address:* Trenarren, St Austell, Cornwall PL26 6BH, England.

ROY, Lucille Thérèse, b. 24 Apr. 1943, Thunder Bay, Ontario, Canada. Professor; Writer. m. Joseph Hewitson, 16 July 1966, Kingston, 3 sons, 1 daughter. *Education:* BA, Honours, Queens University, Kingston, 1965; University Doctorate, University of Strasbourg, France, 1968; Third Cycle Doctorate, University of Bordeaux, France, 1979. *Publications:* Harmonies d'un songe, 1979; L'Impasse, 1980; Entre le lumiere et l'ombre, 1984; L' Appasionata, 1985. *Contributor to:* Liberte; Voix et Images; French Review; Ecriture franciase; Etudes francaises. *Honours:* Gold Medal, French, Queen's University, 1965; Canada Council Fellowship, 1966–67. *Memberships:* Association of Teachers of French in Canadian Universities; Association of French Speaking Writers; American Association of Teachers of French. *Address:* 377 Windermere Road, Beaconsfield, Quebec, Canada H9W 1W8.

ROY, Marcelle, b. 7 Apr. 1935, Nicolet, Canada. Editorial Assistant. Divorced, 2 sons, 1 daughter. *Education:* BA; Studies in Architecture. *Publications:* VLB Editeur, Traces, 1982. *Contributor to:* Le Devoir; Arcade; l'Interdit; Questions de culture; Chatelaine; Decormag. *Membership:* Union des écrivains québécois. *Address:* 708A Avenue de l'Epee, Montreal, Quebec, Canada H2V 3T9.

ROYCE, Joseph Russell, b. 19 Aug. 1921, New York City, USA. Professor of Psychology, University of Alberta. m. Lilye B Summerlin, 3 Apr. 1944, 1 son, 1 daughter. *Education:* AB, Denison University, 1941; PhD, University of Chicago, 1951. *Publications:* 10 books including: The Encapsulated Man, 1964; Toward Unification in Psych, editor, 1970; Multivaraite Analysis and Psychology Theory, Editor, 1973; Humanistic Psychology, (with L P Mos), 1980; Theory of Personality and Indicidual Differences, (with A D Powell), 1983. *Contributions to:* 50 chapters in books; Over 130 articles in major American Psychology journals including: American Psychologist; Psychological Bulletin; Contemporary Psychology; Journal of Comparative and Physiological Psychology; Behaviour Genetics and Multivariate Behavioral Research; Canadian Journal of Psychology; Canadian Psych; Science; American Scientist. *Address:* Center for Advanced Study in Theoretical Psychology, University of Alberta, Edmonton, Alberta, Canada.

ROYCE, Kenneth, b. 11 Dec. 1920, Croydon, Surrey, England. Novelist. m. Stella Parker, 16 Mar. 1946, Northampton. *Publications:* My Turn To Die, 1958; The Soft Footed Moor, 1959; The Long Corridor, 1960; No Paradise, 1961; The Night Seekers, 1962; The Angry Island, 1963; The Day The Wind Dropped, 1964; Bones in the Sand, 1967; A Peck of Salt, 1968; A Single To Hong Kong, 1969; The XYY Man, (also adapted for television), 1970; The Concrete Boot, (also adapted for television) 1971; The Miniatures Frame, (also adapted for television) 1972; Spider Underground, 1973; Trapspider, 1974; Man on a Short Leash, 1974; The Woodcutter Operation, (also adapted for television) 1975; Bustillo, 1976; Assissination Day, 1976; Autumn Horoes, 1977; The Satin Touch, (also adapted for television) 1978; The Third Arm, 1980; 10,000 Days, 1981; Channel Assault, 1982; The Stalin Account, 1983; The Cryptic Man, 1984; The Mosley Receipt, 1985; Breakout, 1986. *Memberships:* Society of Authors; Crime Writers Association. *Literary Agent:* David Higham Associates. *Address:* 3 Abbotts Close, Abbotts Ann, Andover, Hants SP11 7NP, England.

ROYCE, Robert Bernard, b. 5 December 19844, Berkhamstead, England. Publisher. m. Jane, 1973, London, 1 son, 1 daughter. *Education:* MA, Cambridge University. *Literary Appointments:* Commissioning Editor, Macmillan Education, 1966–74; Managing Director, Ward Lock Educational 1974–80; Director, Muller 1980–81; Director, Evans 1981–83; Managing Director, Robert Royce, 1984–. *Address:* 93 Bedwardine Road, London SE19 3AY, England.

ROYCE, The Revd James E, b. 20 Oct. 1914, Spokane, Washington, USA. Professor of Psychology. *Education:* BA 1939, MA 1940, Philosophy, Gonzaga University, Spokane, Washington, USA; PhD Psychology, Loyola University, Chicago, Illinois, 1945. STL (theology), Alma College, University of Santa Clara, California, USA, 1948. *Literary Appointments:* Book Reviewer, America, 1948–; Chairman, Editorial Board, Alcoholism: The National Magazine; Reviews in numerous journals of psychology, philosophy & Alcoholism. *Major Publications:* Personality & Mental Health, 1955, 1964; Man & His Nature, 1961; Man & Meaning, 1969; Alcohol Problems & Alcoholism, 1981; chapter on, Alcohol & Drug Dependency, (in Clinical Handbook of Pastoral Counseling), 1985. *Contributor to:* Over 25 periodicals, including: Journal of Historical & Behavioural Science; American Psychologist; Journal of Drug Issues; Voices: The Art & Science of Psychotherapy; Education. *Honours:* Governor's Distinguished Service Award, Washington State, 1965; Outstanding Achievement Award, National Association of Alcoholism Counselors, 1981; Bier Award, American Psychological Association, 1984. *Memberships:* Fellow, American Psychological Association; President, Division 24 (Philosophical Psychology), 1964–65; Charter Member, Academy of Religion & Nental Health; Alpha Sigma Nu (1982 award); Delta Epsilon Sigma. *Address:* Seattle University, Seattle, WA 98122, USA.

ROZOVSKY, Lorne Elkin, b. 13 Sep. 1942, Timmins, Canada. Lawyer. m. Fay Adrienne Frank, 16 Dec. 1979, Saint John, New Brunswick, 1 son. *Education:* BA, University of New Brunswick, 1963; LLB, University of Toronto, 1966. *Publications:* Canadian Hospital Law: A Practical Guide, 1974; Canadian Manual on Hospital By-Laws, 1976; The Canadian Patient's Book of Rights, 1980; Legal Sex, with Wife, 1982; The Canadian Law of Patient Records, with Wife, 1984; Canadian Health Facilities Law Guide, with monthly supplements, with Wife, 1983. *Contributor to:* Co-Author, with wife, regular column, Canadian Doctor; Canadian Operating Room Nursing Journal; Canadian Critical Care Nursing Journal; Health Care; Regular Columnist; Oral Health. *Honour:* QC, 1984. *Membership:* Writers' Federation of Nova Scotia, Council Member, Former Member, executive. *Address:* 2044, Armcrescent Avenue, Halifax, Nova Scotia, B3L 3C5, Canada.

RUBEL, Toby Gloria, b. 22 Sep. 1926, New York, USA. Medical Writer. m. Stanley J Rubel, 19 June 1955, New York City, 1 son. *Education:* BA, Hunter College, 1947. *Publications:* Fibrinolytic Enzyme Manufacture, 1969; Vitamin E Manufacture, 1969; Optical Brighteners: Technology and Application, 1972; Antifoaming and Defoaming Agents, 1972. *Contributor to:* Numerous articles in medical journals; Associate Editor, Medical Economics, 1969. *Memberships:* American Medical Writers Association. *Address:* 11 Jill Drive, West Nyack, NY 10994, USA.

RUBENS, Bernice Ruth, b. 26 July 1928, Cardiff. Author. m. 1947, Cardiff, 2 daughters. *Education:* BA Honours, English, Cardiff. *Publications:* Set on Edge, 1960; Madame Sousatzka, 1962; Mate in Three, 1965; The Elected Member, 1969; Sunday Best, 1971; Go Tell the Lemming, 1973; I Sent a Letter to My Love, 1975; The Ponsonby Post, 1977; A Five Year Sentence, 1978; Spring Ssonata, 1980; Birds of Passage, 1981; Brothers, 1983; Mr. Wakefield's Crusade, 1985. *Honours:* Booker Prize, 1970; Fellow of University of Wales (Cardiff), 1981. *Literary Agent:* AD Peters Ltd. *Address:* 89 Greencroft Gardens, London NW6, England.

RUBIN, Abraham (Abe), b. 14 Aug. 1911, Winnipeg, Canada. Professional Education; Podiatrist. m. Doris Sylvia Miller, 8 July 1938, Chicago, 1 son, 1 daughter. *Education:* University of Manitoba, 1928–32; DPM, Illinois College of Podiatry, 1937; All requirements for PhD, except thesis defense, University of Chicago, 1951–54. *Appointments:* Editor, Journal of American Podiatry Association, 1955–70; Contributing Editor: Current Medical Digest, 1959–61, Editorial Advisory Boards: JAPA, 1970–76, Nation's Health, APHA, 1972–74; Medical Communications, AMWA, 1972–74. *Publications:* Accreditation in Higher Education, 1959; The Podiatry Curriculum Blauch, 1970. *Contributor to:* Numerous professional journals including: Chiropody Record; Journal of the National Association of Chiropodists; Journal of American Podiatry Association; Current Medical Digest; etc. *Honours:* Gold Medal, Stickel Awards Research Paper, 1954; DLitt, Honoraris Causa, Ohio College of Podiatry. *Memberships:* Fellow, American Medical Writers Association. Treasurer, President, Mid-Atlantic Chapter. *Address:* 29501 Cedar Road, Mayfield Heights, OH 44124, USA.

RUBIN, Larry Jerome, b. 14 Feb. 1930, Bayonne, New Jersey, USA. Professor of English, Georgia Technical Institute. *Education:* BA 1951, MA 1952, PhD 1956, Emory University. *Literary Appointments:* Smith-Nundt Fellow, University of Krakow, Poland, 1961–62; Fulbright Lecturer, University of Bergen, Norway 1966–67, Free University of West Berlin 1969–70, University of Innsbruck, Austria 1971–72. *Publications include:* 3 books of poetry: The World's Old Way, 1963; Lanced in Light, 1967; All my Mirrors Lie, 1975. *Contributions:* Poetry to various literary journals including: New Yorker; Poetry; Saturday Review; Yale Review; The Nation; Esquire; Transatlantic Review; London Magazine; etc; *Honours:* Reynolds Lyric Award, Poetry Society of America, 1961; Literary Achievement Award, Georgia Writers Association, 1963; Sidney Lanier

Award, Oglethorpe University, 1964; Georgia Poet of the Year, Dixie Council of Authors & Journalists, 1967, 1975; Annual Award, Poetry Society of America, 1973. *Membership:* Poetry Society of America. *Address:* Box 15014, Druid Hills Branch, Atlanta, GA 30333, USA.

RUBIN, Nancy (Ruth) Zimman, b. 25 Nov. 1944, Boston, Massachusetts, USA. Journalist; Author. m. Peter H Rubin, 9 July 1967, Boston, 2 daughters. *Education:* BA, Tufts University, 1966; MAT, Brown University, 1967. *Literary Appointments:* Co-Director, Media Unit, Bush Center in Child Development and Social Policy, Yale University, 1981–85. *Publications:* Books: The New Surburban Woman: Beyond Myth and Motherhood, 1982; The Mother Mirror: How a Generation of Women is Changing Motherhood in America. *Contributions to:* The New York Times; Chatelaine; Institute for Socioeconomic Studies; Ladies Home Journal; McCall's Parents Magazine; Working Mother; Newsday; Los Angeles Times; Success Magaine. *Honours:* Time Incorporation Scholar, Bread Loaf Writers Conference, 1979; Fellow, MacDowell Colony, 1981. *Memberships:* American Society of Journalists and Authors; Authors Guild; Women Ink; National Writers Union. *Literary Agent:* Ellen Levine, New York. *Address:* 35 Broadfield Road, New Rochelle, NY 10804, USA.

RUDAKOFF, Judith D, b. 8 Jan. 1953, Montreal, Canada. Dramaturge. m. E Myles Warren, 1978. *Education:* BA, McGill University; MA, University of Alberta; PhD, University of Toronto. *Literary Appointments:* Dramaturge, Nightwood Theatre, Toronto, 1984; Dramaturge, 45.3 Company, 1985; Dramaturge, Toronto Free Theatre, Toronto, 1985. *Publications:* Shaping the Canadian; The Plays of David French, David Freeman and David Fennario, 1986; Michel Tremblay, 1986. *Contributions to:* Numerous professional publications. *Honours:* Canada Council Doctoral Fellowship, 1980; Ontario Arts Council Grant (Playwrighting); 1985; Ontario Arts Council Grant (Writing), 1985. *Memberships:* Playwrights' Union of Canada; Association of Canadian Theatre History. *Address:* Box 2251, Gravenhurst, Ontario, Canada POC 1GO.

RUDINGER, Joel Douglas, b. 12 Dec. 1938, Cleveland, Ohio, USA. Professor. m. 24 Sep. 1983, (div), 2 daughter. *Education:* MA, University of Alaska, 1964; MFA, University of Iowa, 1966; PhD Bowling Green State University, 1971. *Publications:* First Edition: 40 Poems, 1975; Lovers & Celebrations, 1985. *Contributions to:* Folk Ogres of the Firelands: Narrative Variations of a North Central Ohio Community (Indiana Folklore, 1976); The Snake (Fiction from Firelands, 1980); The Bed, poem (Colorado North Reveiw, 1984); Yesterday I Fed the Fish in City Park (New York Quarterly, 1979); etc. *Memberships:* Academy of American Poets; Popular Culture Association; National Association for the Preservation and Perpetuation of Storytelling. *Address:* 901 Rye Beach Road, Huron, OH 44839, USA.

RUDKIN, James David, b. 29 June 1936, London, England. Dramatist. m. Alexandra Margaret Thompson, 3 May 1967, 2 sons, 2 daughters. *Education:* MA, Oxford University. *Publications:* Afore Night Come, Penguin Books: New English Dramatists vol 7, 1963; Moses and Aaron translation of libretto by Schoenberg, Friends of Covent Garden, 1965; The Sons of Light, Eyre Methuen 1981; The Grace of Todd, libretto for opera by Gordon Crosse, Oxford University Press, 1969; Burglars, Hutchinson; Prompt vol 2, 1976; Cries from Casement as his Bones are Brought to Dublin, BBC Publications 1974; Ashes, Samuel French, 1974; Pluto Press, 1978 and Talon Books Canada. Penda's Fen, Davis-Poynter, 1975; The Triumph of Death, Eyre Methuen, 1981. Hippolytus, translation of Euripides, Heinemann 1980; Peer Gynt, translation of Ibsen, Eyre Methuen, 1982. *Contributor to:* Tempo; Drama; Encounter etc. *Honours:* Evening Standard Drama Award, London 1962; Arts Council John Whiting Award, London 1974; OBIE, New York, 1977. *Literary Agent:* M

Ramsay Ltd, 14A Goodwin's Court, London WC2. *Address:* c/o M Ramsay Ltd, 14A Goodwin's Court, London WC2, England.

RUDOLF, Anthony, b. 6 Sep. 1942, London, England. Writer and Publisher. Divorced, 1 son, 1 daughter. *Education:* BA, Cantab. *Literary Appointments:* London Editor, Stand, 1969–72; Literary Editor, European Judaism, 1970–72; Advisory Editor, Modern Poetry of Translation, 1973–82. *Publications:* The Same River Twice, poems, 1976; After The Dream, poems, 1980; Voices Within The Ark anthology, 1980; Things Dying Things Newborn translation of Yves Bonnefoy, 1985. *Contributions to:* Poetry Review; Stand; Times Literary Supplement; New Statesman; PNR; Temenos; Literary Review. *Honours:* 2 ACGB Grants; Juror on Neustadt Prize, Oklahoma, 1986. *Memberships:* General Council, Poetry Society, 1970–76. *Address:* Menard Press, 8 The Oaks, Woodside Avenue, London N12 8AR, England.

RUDOLPH, Lee, b. 28 Mar. 1948. Mathematician. *Education:* BA, Princeton University, 1969; PhD, Massachusetts Institute of Technology, 1974. *Publications:* The Country Changes, 1978; Curses and Songs and Poems, 1974. *Contributions to:* Kayak; Quarterly Review of Literature; The Troy Sun; Counter-Measures and others. *Honours:* Bainswigget Memorial Award, Krull Memorial, Academy of American Poets, 1966–69; Book of the Month Club; College English Association, Writing Fellowship, 1969–70. *Memberships:* Past Treasurer, Alice James Poetry Cooperative. *Address:* PO Box 251, Adamsville, RI 02801, USA.

RUDY, Willis, b. 25 Jan. 1920, New York City, New York, USA. Historian. *Education:* Bachelor of Social Science, City College of New York, 1939; MA, 1940, PhD, 1948, Columbia University. *Publications:* A History of the College of the City of New York, 1949; The Liberal Arts College Curriculum: A Historical Review, 1960; Schools in an Age of Mass Culture, 1965; Higher Education in Transition; A History of American Higher Education, 1958, 3rd edition, 1976; The Universities of Europe 1100–1914: A History, 1984. *Contributions to:* American Historical Review; Mississippi Valley Historial Review; National Education Association Journal; Christian Science Monitor. *Memberships:* American Historical Association; Society of American Historians; Gamma Chapter, Phi Beta Kappa. Recipient, Cromwell Medal in History and Belles Lettres, 1939. *Address:* 161 West Clinton Avenue, Tenafly, NJ 07670, USA.

RUE, Leonard Lee III, b. 20 Feb. 1926, Paterson, New Jersey, USA. Wildlife Photographer; Author; Lecturer. m. Beth Castner, 6 May 1945, divorced, 3 sons. *Publications include:* Animals in Motion, 1957; Tracks and Tracking, 1958; The World of the White Tailed Deer, 1962, now in 14th printing; The World of the Beaver, 1963; Pictorial Guide to Mammals, 1967; Sportsman's Guide to Game Animals, 12 printing, 1968–, enlarged and revised as Game Animals of North America, 4 printings; Game Birds of North America, 1973; The Deer of North America, 1978; How I Photograph Wildlife and Nature, 1984. Collaborator on various books. *Contributions to:* Columnist: American Hunter; Turkey; Deer and Deer Hunting; Archery World; Outdoor Photographer. Photos published in over 1200 books and magazines in 42 countries. *Honours:* 14 Awards for Excellence, New Jersey Association of Teachers of English, 1964–; Charter Member, New Jersey Literary Hall of Fame. *Address:* RD3 Box 31, Blairstown, NJ 07825, USA.

RUEGER, Russ A, b. 11 Dec. 1954, New York, USA. Author. *Education:* AS, BA, MA, PhD, JD, DD (all earned). *Literary Appointments:* Universities of California, Oklahoma, Southern Mississippi, Columbia; Westwinds Learning Institute, New York; East-West Centre for Holistict Studies, New York. *Major Publications:* Biography of a Renaissance Man, Towards a Unified Theory of Language, Book of the Strange, 1979; Frauds, Deceptions and Hoaxes, 1980; The Joy of Touch, 1981; The Pleasure Book, 1982; Speelse

Massage (Dutch, 1983), The Joy of Touch (German, 1983); Ask Dr Russ Rueger about Sex, 1984; The Joy of Success, 1985. *Contributor to:* Penthouse; Ms; The Star; Sherwood Forest; New University Review; High Society; Cosmopolitan; Seed; Renaissance Review; Phenomenological Sociology; Interviu (Spanish); CU Student (Chinese); Los Angeles Times; New YorK Times; Time Magazine; WIN; Psychology Today; Human Behaviour and others. *Honours:* Outstanding Graduate in Social Sciences, 1970; Title IV Federal Fellowship, 1970–74; Bread Loaf Writers' Conference Fellowship, 1973; Columbia University Writers' Program Scholarship, 1974; Maine Writers' Conference Scholarship, 1981. *Memberships:* American Society of Journalists and Authors; American Association for the Advancement of Sciences; International Platform Speakers' Association; New York Academy of Sciences; Human Services Unlimited (President). *Literary Agent:* Dr Anthony Sala. *Address:* PO Box 81, Staten Island, NY 10301, USA.

RUFFELL, Ann Morag, b. 2 Feb. 1941, England. Writer. m. 14 July 1981, Wolverhampton, 1 son, 2 daughter. *Education:* BA Honours, English; Certificate of Education; Piano Teaching Licentiate, Royal Academy of Music. *Literary Appointments:* Writer-in-Residence, Renfrew District Council, 1980–82. *Publications:* The Cuckoo Genius, 1978; Firebird, 1979; Blood Brother, 1981; The Black-Sand Miners, 1985. *Address:* 46 St Judes Road West, Wolverhampton, West Midlands, England.

RUHEN, Olaf, b. 24 Aug. 1911, Dunedin, New Zealand. Author. m. (1) Claire Stickland, 22 May 1936, Sydney, 1 son, (dec). (2) Madeleine Thompson, 31 Mar. 1959. *Literary Appointments:* Director, School of Creative Writing, Adelaide, Australia, 1963; School of Creative Writing, Papua, New Guinea, 1965. *Publications:* Land of Dahori, 1957; Naked Under Capricorn, 1958; Minerva Reef, 1963; Tangaro's Godchild, 1963; The Broken Wing, 1965; Beneath Whose Hand, with R Williams, 1985. *Contributions to:* Numerous magazines, Australia, New Zealand, USA and UK. *Honour:* Douglas Prize, 1971. *Membership:* Founding Committee member, Australian Society of Authors. *Address:* 9 Cross Street, Mosman, NSW 2088, Australia.

RULE, Jane, b. 28 Mar. 1931, Plainfield, NJ, USA. Writer. *Education:* BA, Mills College, California. *Publications:* (novels), The Desert of the Heart, 1964; This Is Not For You, 1970; Against the Season, 1971; The Young in One Another's Arms, 1977; (literary criticism), Lesbian Images, 1975; (stories), Theme for Diverse Instruments, 1975; Inland Passage, 1985; (novel), Contract With the World, 1980; (stories and essays), Outlander, 1981; A Hot-eyed Moderate, 1985. *Contributor to:* magazines and journals including Body Politic; Branching Out; Canadian Literature; Chatelaine. *Honours:* Canadian Council Grants, 1970–71, 1971–72; Canadian Authors' Association Awards for Best Novel of 1978 and Best Short Story of 1978; Gay Academy Union Literary Award, 1978; The Fund for Human Dignity Award of Merit, 1983. *Literary Agents:* Georges Borchardt Incorporated (USA); Tessa Sayle (UK). *Address:* The Fork, Route 1, Galiano, BC, Canada VON IPO.

RUNCIMAN, Alexander, b. 13 Feb. 1951, Portland, Oregon, USA. College Teacher. m. Deborah Jane Berry, 11 Sep. 1971, Los Angeles, California, USA, 2 daughters. *Education:* BA, University of Santa Clara, California, 1973; MFA, University of Montana, 1977; PhD, University of Utah, 1981. *Literary Appointments:* Teaching Fellow, University of Utah, 1978–81; Editor, Quarterly West Magazine, 1981; Instructor, Department of English, Oregon State University, 1981–; Editor, Arrowood Books, Inc, 1985. *Major Publications:* Where we Are: The Montana Poets Anthology, (editor), 1978; Luck (poems), 1981. *Contributor to:* Antaeus; Northwest Review; and others. *Honour:* Clarice Short Teaching Award, University of Utah, 1981. *Memberships:*

Poetry Society of America; Associated Writing Programs. *Address:* C S C Writing Lab, Oregon State University, Corvallis, OR 97331, USA.

RUSCH, John Jay, b. 8 Apr. 1942, Manitowoc, Wisconsin, USA. Professor of Science Education. m. Carole R Vasey, 14 Aug. 1965, Crystal Lake, Illinois, 2 sons. *Education:* BS, Carroll College, 1963; MAT, 1968, EdD, 1970, Indiana University. *Publications:* The Physical Sciences: Inquiry and Investigation, co-author, 1977; Science Teaching and the Development of Reasoning, series of 5 books, 1977; Physical Science, co-author, 1979; Science and Social Issues: A Guide for Science Teachers, co-author, 1981; Teaching Science Grades 5 to 9, co-author, 1982. *Contributions to:* The Science Teacher, 1975; American Biology Teacher, 1976, 78, 82; School Science and Mathematics, 1978; Viewpoints in Teaching and Learning, volume 55, 1979; report, Undergraduate Teaching Improvement Council, 1983. *Honours:* Fellowship, AYI, Indiana University, National Science Foundation, 1967–68, Indiana University, 1969; Gustav Ohaus Award, 1977, Max Levine Award, 1977, 78, 79, with Dr C R Barman, University of Wisconsin; Gustav Ohaus Award, NSTA, 1981; Ron Gibbs Award for Outstanding Wisconsin Science Educator 1984. *Memberships:* Wisconsin Academy of Sciences, Arts and Letters. *Address:* 905 East 9th Street, Superior, WI 54880, USA.

RUSH, Michael David, b. 29 Oct. 1937, Kingston-upon-Thames, Surrey, England. Head, Politics Dept, University of Exeter. m. Jean Margaret Telford, 25 July 1964, Longwood, 2 sons. *Education:* BA, 1962, PhD, 1966, University of Sheffield. *Publications:* The Selection of Parliamentary Candidates, 1969; The Member of Parliament & His Information, with Anthony Barker, 1970; An Introduction to Political Sociology, with Phillip Althoff, 1971; The House of Commons: Services & Facilities, Joint Editor with Malcolm Shaw, 1974; Parliament & the Public, 1976; Parliamentary Government in Britain, 1981; The House of Commons: Services and Facilities 1972–82, 1983; The Cabinet and Policy Formation, 1984; Parliament and the Public, 2nd revised edition, 1986. *Contributor to:* Party Affairs; Political Studies. *Honours:* Recipient, Gilbert Campion Award, Hansard Society, 1965–66. *Memberships:* Former Joint Secretary, Study of Parliament Group. *Address:* Dept of Politics, University of Exeter, Exeter, Devon EX4 4RJ, England.

RUSH, Paul A, b. 19 Dec. 1938, Toronto, Canada. Editor. m. Regina Sask, 25 July 1959, 1 son, 2 daughters. *Education:* BA Honours, University of Western Ontario. *Publications:* Life of the Harp Seal, editor, 1977; Children of the North, editor, 1979. *Contributions to:* Regina Leader-Post; Canadian Press; Toronto Star; Weekend magazine; Financial Post magazine; Folio; Star Weekly; Report on Confederation; World Press Review; Biz. *Honours:* Saskatchewan Legislature Press Gallery. *Memberships:* Magazines Canada; University of Western Ontario Honour Society. *Address:* 777 Bay Street, Toronto, Ontario M5W IA7, Canada.

RUSH, Peter Geffrey Brian, b. 26 July 1937, London, England. Illustrator; Model Maker. 3 sons, 1 daughter. *Publications:* Papier Mache, 1980; Travellers Tales, 1981; Balloonatrics, 1982; Illustrator of numerous childrens books. Numerous television programmes for British Broadcasting Corporation including, Jackanory; 26 programmes in, Heggerty Haggerty, series for Yorkshire Independent Television, 1983–85. *Contributions to:* Sunday Telegraph Magazine, papier mache caracature models, 1979. *Honour:* British Book Design Award for Travellers Tales, 1984. *Address:* 45 Caster Street, Canterbury, Kent CT1 2PY, England.

RUSHDIE, Ahmed Salman, b. 19 June 1947, Bombay, India. Writer. m. Clarissa Luard, 22 May 1976, London, 1 son. *Education:* MA (Hons), History, King's College, Cambridge (1965–68). *Literary Appointment:* Executive Member, National Book League, 1983–84. *Publications:* Grimus, 1975; Midnight's Children, 1981;

Shame, 1983. *Contributions to:* The Times; The Guardian; Observer; Sunday Times; London Review of Books; New Statesman; Grants; New York Times; Washington Post; Atlantic Monthly, etc. *Honours:* Booker McConnel Prize, 1981; Arts Council Literature Bursary, 1981; English Speaking Union Award, 1982; James Tait Black Prize, 1982. *Memberships:* International PEN; Fellow, Royal Society of Literature, 1983. *Literary Agent:* Deborah Rogers. *Address:* c/o Deborah Rogers Limited, 49 Blenheim Crescent, London W11, England.

RUSHTON, John Philippe, b. 3 Dec. 1943, England. University Professor. m. Doylene Gabrielle Sack, 2 Dec. 1961, (div.) Toronto, Canada, 1 son. *Education:* BSc Psychology, 1970, PhD Psychology, 1973, University of London, England. *Literary Appointments:* Assistant Professor of Psychology, York University, Toronto, Canada, 1974–76; Assistant Professor of Psychology, University of Toronto, 1976–77; Professor of Psychology, University of Western Ontario, London, Canada, 1977–. *Major Publications:* Altruism, Socialization & Society, 1980; Altruism & Helping Behavior, (with R M Sorrentino), 1981; Psychology, (with H L Roediger, E D Capaldi & S G Paris), 1984. *Contributor to:* Numerous scholarly journals & edited books, mostly in social psychology. *Memberships:* British Psychological Society, elected Fellow 1982; Canadian Psychological Association, elected Fellow 1985; American Psychological Association, elected Fellow 1982; American Association for the Advancement of Science. *Address:* Department of Psychology, University of Western Ontario, London, Ontario, N6A 5C2, Canada.

RUSS, Lawrence, b. 18 Aug. 1950, USA. Attorney. m. Mary Margaret Long. *Education:* Sloan Scholar in Humanities, 1968–72, BA, 1972, University of Michigan, USA; Master of Fine Arts, University of Massachusetts, 1974; JD, School of Law, University of Michigan, 1977. *Major Publication:* The Burning-Ground (chapbook), 1981. *Contributor to:* The Nation; The Iowa Review; The Virginia Quarterly Review; Ironwood; Yankee; Beloit Poetry Journal; Chelsea; and others; poetry included in various anthologies. *Honours:* Hopwood Awards for Poetry, 1970, 1971, 1975; Hopwood Award for Essay, 1976; Academy of American Poets Award, 1970; Writing Fellow in Poetry, University of Massachusetts, 1972–. *Address:* c/o Trager & Trager, 1305 Post Road, Fairfield, CT 06430, USA.

RUSSELL, David Seager, b. 12 June 1940, Wolverhampton, England. Teacher. m. Elisabeth M Brooks, 9 Jan. 1965, 1 daughter. *Education:* University of Durham, England, 1959–62; Postgraduate Diploma, Chelsea College, University of London, 1973–74. *Literary Appointments:* Free-lance work, Mid-Century Authors, 1965–66; Lecturer in Liberal Studies, Guildford County Technical College, 1967–68; Technical Publishing, 1969–; Sub-editor, British Safety Council, currently. *Major Publications:* Exacting Modality of the World Web, 1970; A Chip off the Old Block, 1973; Nothing Hero, 1984. *Contributor to:* New Leaf Magazine; Cread Poetry Poster; Use of English, 1980. *Honours:* Jubilee Essay Prize, University of Durham, 1962. *Address:* 8 McGregor Road, London W11 1DE, England.

RUSSELL, Diana Elizabeth Hamilton, b. 6 Nov. 1938. University Professor; Writer. *Education:* BA, University of Capetown, South Africa, 1959; Postgraduate Diploma, London School of Economics and Political Science, 1961; MA, 1967, PhD, 1970, Harvard University. *Appointments include:* Research Assistant, Harvard University, 1967; Research Associate, Center of International Studies Princeton University 1967–68; Assistant Professor of Sociology, 1969–75, Associate Professor of Sociology, 1975–83, Professor of Sociology, 1983–, Mills College, Oakland, California. *Publications:* Rebellion, Revolution and Armed Forces: A comparative study of fifteen countries with special emphasis on Cuba and South Africa, 1974; The Politics of Rape: The Victim's Perspective, 1975; Crimes Against Women: the proceedings of the International Tribunal, 1976, (with N Van de Ven); Editor with R Linden, D Pagano, L Star, Against Sadomasochism: A radical feminist analysis, 1982; Rape in Marriage, 1982, paperback 1983; Sexual Exploitation: Rape, child sexual abuse and workplace harassment, 1984. *Contributor to:* Articles in numerous magazines and journals and chapters and introductions in many edited volumes. *Honours:* Research Consultant on sexual violence for the California Commission on Crime Control and Violence Prevention 1981–82; Recommended as a Fellow of the Center for Advanced Study in the Behavioral Sciences, 1979; Harvard Fellowships 1963–64, 1965–66; Mostyn Lloyd Memorial Prize for best student studying for Postgraduate Diploma at London School of Economics, 1961. *Address:* Department of Social Sciences, Mills College, Oakland, CA 94613, USA.

RUSSELL, Donald Andrew Frank Moore, b. 13 Oct. 1920, London, England. University teacher. m. Joycelyne Gledhill Dickinson, 22 July 1967, at Oxford. *Education:* MA, Balliol College, University of Oxford, England, 1947. *Literary Appointments:* Fellow of St John's College, Oxford; University Reader in Classical Literature. *Major Publications:* Longinus On the Sublime, 1964; Plutarch, 1972; Criticism in Antiquity, 1981; Greek Declamation, 1983; Criticism in Antiquity (with M Winterbottom), 1972; Menander Rhetor (with N G Wilson), 1981. *Contributor to:* Various classical journals, including: Journal of Roman Studies, Journal of Hellenic Studies, Greece & Rome, Mnemosyne and others; also articles in Oxford Classical Dictionary, and other reference works and volumes of essays. *Honour:* Fellow of the British Academy, 1971. *Address:* St John's College, Oxford, England.

RUSSELL, Douglas Andrew, b. 9 Feb. 1927, Berkeley, California, USA. Professor of Drama. m. Marilyn Carol Nelson, 26 Dec. 1953, 1 son, 1 daughter. *Education:* BA, 1949; MA, 1950; Stanford University; MFA, Yale University, 1961. *Publications:* Stage Costume Design, 1973; Theatrical Style: A Visual Approach to Theatre, 1976; Period Style for the Theatre, 1980; An Anthology of Austrian Drama, 1982; Costume History and Style, 1982; Stage Costume Design, 2nd edition, 1984. *Exhibitions:* Theatrical Designs, Mandeville Center, University of California, San Diego, 1975; Organizer, Lee Simonson Design Exhibit for US Institute of Theatre Technology Conference, Oakland, California, 1986. *Contributor to:* Theatre Crafts; Educational Theatre Journal; Players Magazine; Modern Austrian Literature. *Honours:* Fulbright Grant, 1954–55; Danforth Grant, 1959–60; Research and Development Grants, Stanford University, 1972, 84; Feminist Studies Grant, Stanford University, 1985. *Memberships:* Common Cause; United Scenic Artists of America; American Theatre Association; United States Institute of Theatre Technology; Museum Society of San Francisco; American Association of University Professors. *Address:* 765 Mayfield Avenue, Stanford, CA 94305, USA.

RUSSELL, Francis, b. 12 Jan. 1910, Boston, USA. Writer. m. Rosalind Lawson, 16 Mar. 1984, Boston, 1 daughter, by previous marriage. *Education:* AB, Bowdoin; AM, Harvard. *Publications:* Three Studies in 20th Century Obscurity, 1953; Tragedy in Dedham: The Story of the Sacco-Vanzetti Case, 1962; The Shadow of Blooming Grove, 1968; A City in Terror: The 1919 Boston Police Strike, 1973; President Makers from Mark Hanna to Joseph P Kennedy, 1974; Sacco-Vanzetti: The Case Resolved, 1986, etc. *Contributor to:* Times; Observer; Countryman; Queens Quarterly; Christian Science Monitor; New York Times; Antioch Review; Yale Review; Harvard Magazine; etc. *Honours:* Edgar of Mystery Writers of America, 1962; Guggenheim Fellow, 1964, 1965; Fellow, American Society of Historians; Friendship Award, Federal Republic of Germany. *Memberships:* Harvard Club of Boston; Goethe Society of New England, (Director). *Address:* The Lindens, Sandwich, MA 02563, USA.

RUSSELL, Helen Diane, b. 8 Apr. 1936, USA. Historian. *Education:* AB, Vassar College, 1958; PhD, The Johns Hopkins University, 1970; Member, Institute for Advanced Study, 1980–81. *Literary Appointments:* Curator, National Gallery of Art, 1964–; Assistant Head, Department of Prints and Drawings, 1981–; Professional Lecturer, The American University, 1966–72, 1978; Adjunct Professor, 1983; Faculty, The Folger Institute of Renaissance and Eighteenth Century Studies, 1985. *Publications:* Rare Etchings by Giovanni Battista and Giovanni Domenico Tiepolo, 1972; Jacques Callot, Prints and Related Drawings, 1975; Claude Lorrain 1600–1682, Paris, 1983. *Contributions to:* Art Bulletin; Art News; Signs; Studies in the History of Art. *Honours:* Wilson Fellowship, 1958–59; Johns Hopkins Fellwoship, 1961063; Kress Foundation Fellowship, 1973; National Endowment for the Arts Fellowship, 1980–81; Alfred H Barr Jr Award, College Art Association of America, 1984. *Memberships:* College Art Association; American Society for Aesthetics; Print Council of America; Societe Civile des Auteurs Multimedia, Paris. *Address:* Department of Prints & Drawings, National Gallery of Art, Washington, DC 20565, USA.

RUSSELL, (Irwin) Peter, b. 16 Sep. 1921, Bristol, England. Poet; Translator. m. Lana Sue Long, British Columbia, Canada, 1 son, 2 daughters. *Literary Appointments:* Poet in Residence, University of Victoria, British Columbia, Canada, Purdua University, Indiana, USA, Farah Pahlavi University, Tehran, Iran; Associate Professor, Damavand College, Tehran; Fellow, Imperial Academy of Philosophy, Iran; Visiting Professor, Unviersity of Florence, Italy. *Publications include:* Selected Poems 1947–75; All For the Wolves; Elemental Discourses, 140 long poems, 1982; Malice Aforethought, 150 epigrams, 1982; Africa: A Dream, narrative poem, 1982; Theories, lyrical poems, 1978; Acts of Recognition, 1980; The Elegies of Quintilius, translation & criticism, 1975; The Golden Chain, poems 1963–70; etc. *Contributions to:* Numerous journals in USA, UK, Europe, Middle East, India. *Address:* 52026 Pian di Sco, Prov Arezzo, Italy.

RUSSELL, Kenneth Victor, b. 11 Nov. 1929, Brierley Hill, England. Principal Lecturer in Law. *Education:* Certificate of Education; Diploma of Education; Diploma of Religious Education; MEd, PhD. *Appointments include:* Principal Lecturer in Law; Visiting Professor, University of Nevada, Las Vegas, Nevada, USA. *Publications:* Learning to Give. 1967; Crime Is Our Business, 1973; Projects in Religious Education, 1974; Complaints Against the Police: A Sociological View, 1976; Complaints Against the Police: The Police Complaints Board, The First Six Months, 1979. *Contributions to:* Sunday Times; Sunday Telegraph; Police Review; Police Journal. *Honour:* Odhams Literary Award, 1976. *Address:* 6 St Peter's Close, Glenfield, Leicester LE3 8QB, England.

RUSSELL, Lawrence Wells, b. 17 Feb. 1941, Northern Ireland. Professor of Creative Writing. m. Diana Olson, 3 Oct. 1966, Victoria, 1 son, 1 daughter. *Education:* BA, University of Victoria; MA, California. *Literary Appointments:* Professor of Creative Writing, University of Victoria, 1968–. *Publications include:* Penetration, 1972; Mystery of the Pig Killer's Daughter, 1975. *Contributions to:* Canadian Fiction magazine; Malahat Review; Prism International; Quarry; Random Thought; Canadian Theatre Review; The Journal of Canadian Literature; DNA Stereo magazine. *Honours:* CBC Radio Drama prize, 1983. *Membership:* Playwright's Union of Canada. *Address:* Creative Writing Department, University of Victoria, P O Box 1700, Victoria BC, V8W YZY, Canada.

RUSSELL, Lois Ann, b. 17 Sep. 1931, New Brunswick, New Jersey, USA. Professor of French. *Education:* BA, Douglass College; MA, Fordham University; PhD, Bryn Mawr College. *Literary Appointments:* Consultant for, Choice; Lily-Penn Fellow; Visiting Fellow Romance Languages, Princeton University. *Publications:* Robert Challe: A Utopian Voice in the Early Enlightenment,

1979. *Contributions to:* Nineteenth-Century French Studies; Eighteenth-Century Life; Revue d'Histoire Littéraire de la France; Stesndhal Club; Studies on Voltaire and the Eighteenth Century; Journal of the Western Society for French History. *Honours:* American Council Learned Societies, 1979; American Philosophical Society, 1979; Newberry Library Fellow, 1980; Folger Library Fellow, 1981; NEH Seminar Dartmouth College, 1981. *Memberships:* Executive Board (Current) EC/American Society for Eighteenth Century Studies; ISECS: AATF: Alliance Francaise; PS/MLA. *Address:* 4 Morris Circle, Wayne, PA 19087, USA.

RUSSELL, Martin James, b. 25 Sep. 1934, Bromley, Kent, England. Writer. *Publications:* No Through Road, 1965; The Client, 1975; Mr T, 1977; Death Fuse, 1980; Backlash, 1981; The Search for Sara, 1983; A Domestic Affair, 1984; The Darker Side of Death, 1985. *Memberships:* Crime Writers' Association; Detection Club. *Literary Agent:* Curtis Brown. *Address:* 21 Cromarty Court, Widmore Road, Bromley, Kent BR1 3BX, England.

RUSSELL, Norman H, b. 28 Nov. 1921, Big Stone Gap, Virginia, USA. Professor of Biology. *Education:* BA, Slippery Rock College, Pennsylvania, 1946; PhD, University of Minnesota, 1951. *Publications include:* 26 Books including: Introduction to Plant Science, 1975; Indian Thoughts; My Journey, 1980; The Longest March, 1980. *Contributions to:* Northeast; Poetry Northwest; Prairie Schooner; Trends, Scotland; Kansas Quarterly; Virginia Quarterly; Massachusetts Quarterly; Nimrod; Cimarron Review; Denver Quarterly. *Address:* Biology Department, Central State University, Edmond, OK 73034, USA.

RUSSELL, Peter Edward, b. 24 Oct. 1913, Christchurch, New Zealand. Emeritus Professor of Spanish Studies, Oxford University, England. *Education:* MA, Queen's College, Oxford; D Litt, Oxford, 1979. *Publications:* As fontes de Fernão Lopes, 1941; Hispanic Manuscripts and Books in the Bodleian and Oxford College Libraries, (with D M Rogers), 1963; The nglish Intervention in Spain and Portugal in the time of Edward III and Richard II, 1955; Prince Henry the Navigator, 1966; Spain: A Companion to Spanish Studies, 1973; Temas de La Celestine y otros estudios: del Cid al Quijote, 1978; Prince Henry the Navigator: The Rise and Fall of a Culture Hero, 1984; Cervantes, 1985; Traducciones y traductores en la Peninsular Iberica (1400–1550), 1985; Editor, Iberian and Latin American series. *Contributions to:* Various professional journals. *Memberships:* British Academy; Portuguese Academy of History; Royal Historical Society; Real Academia de Buenas Letras de Barcelona; Instituto de Estudios Canarios. *Address:* 23 Belsyre Court, Woodstock Road, Oxford OX2 6HU, England.

RUSSELL, Roy, b. 7 Aug. 1918, Blackpool, Lancashire, England. Author; Dramatist. *Publications include:* Television: No Hiding Place; Fothergale; The Saint; The Troubleshooters; A Man of Our Times; Champion House; Sexton Blake; Dixon of Dock Green; Doomwatch; Crime of Passion; Crown Court; A Family at War; The Onedin Line; Intimate Strangers; A Family at War: Towards Victory, 1971; A House in Regent Place, 4 plays; Tales of the Unexpected; The Woodcutter Operation; Last Video and Testament; The Irish RM; British Broadcasting Playhouse. Childrens television dramas and radio plays. Documentary Films: The Lonely Sea and Sky; Prince Bernard, Pilot Royal; Prince Charles, Pilot Royal. Stage Plays: The Eleventh Commandment. *Contributions to:* Various magazines of articles on drama. *Honours:* Laurel Award for distinguished services to writers, Writers Guild of Great Britain. *Memberships:* Writers Guild of Great Britain; Society of Authors; Guild of Drama Adjudicators. *Literary Agent:* Harvey Unna and Stephen Durbridge Ltd. *Address:* c/o Harvey Unna and Stephen Durbridge Ltd, 24 Pottery Lane, Holland Park, London W11 4LZ, England.

RUSSETT, Bruce Martin, b. 26 Jan. 1935, Massachusetts, USA. Dean Acheson. Professor of International Relations and Political Science. m. Cynthia Eagle, 18 June 1960, 2 sons, 2 daughters. *Education:* BA magna cum laude, Williams College, 1956; Diploma in Economics, King's College, Cambridge University, 1957; MA 1959, PhD 1961, Yale University. *Literary Appointments:* Editor, Journal of Conflict Resolution, 1972–. *Publications include:* Community and Contention: Britain and America in the Twentieth Century, 1963; World Handbook of Political and Social Indicators, 1964; Trends in World Politics, 1965; International Regions and the International System, 1967; What Price Vigilance? The Burdens of National Defense, 1970; The Prisoners of Insecurity, 1983, Power and Community in World Politics, 1974; World Politics: The Menu for Choice, (co-author), 1981 and 1985. *Contributions to:* Over 100 articles in book and journals. *Honours:* Guggenheim Foundation Fellowship, 1969 (1977 declined): Fulbright-Hays Fellowship, 1969; German Marshall Fund Fellowship, 1977; Several research grants. *Memberships:* Council member 1985–87, American Political Science Association; President 1977–79, Peace Science Society (International); Chairman 1977–81 North American Advisory Council, International Political Science Association; President 1983–84, International Studies Association. *Address:* Political Science Department, Box 3532 Yale Station, New Haven, CT 06520, USA.

RUSSO, Albert, b. 26 Feb. 1943, Kamina, Zaire. Writer (English & French). Claudine, 31 May 1978, at Paris, 1 son, 1 daughter. *Education:* Abschluß-Diplom, Heidelberg, Federal Republic of Germany; BSc, General Business Administration, University of New York, USA. *Literary Appointment:* Member, Jury of the Prix de l'Europe (with Ionesco), 1982–. *Major Publications:* Incandescences, 1970; Eclats de malachite, 1971; La Pointe du diable, 1973; Mosaïque Newyorkaise, 1975; Your Son Léopold, Princess and Gods and Triality, excerpts of which have appeared in reviews in North America, Great Britain, India and Africa. *Contributor to:* Various periodicals in North America, Great Britain, Europe, Australia, India, Sri Lanka and Africa: Short Story International; The International Herald Tribune; Chapman; Orbis; Stories Magazine, Indian Literature; Chandrabhaga; The Island (Colombo); Prize Africa Magazine; Words & Visions (Australia); Confrontations; L'Espérance (Belgium); Tribune poétique and others. *Honours:* Various awards for books; New York Poetry Forum awards; Writers' Digest award; Society of American Writers' fiction Award; Volcano Review International fiction award (California, USA). *Memberships:* PEN (American & Belgian centres); Authors Guild of America; Writers & Poets (USA); Association of French-speaking Writers (France). *Address:* BP 573, 75826 Paris Cedex 17, France.

RUSSO, Vito, b. 11 July 1946, New York City, USA. Writer. *Education:* BA, Fairleigh Dickinson University; MA, New York University. *Publication:* The Celluloid Closet, 1981. *Contributions to:* Funk and Wagnall's Encyclopedia 1984; Esquire; Rolling Stone; New York; Moviegoer; The Advocate; The New York Native. *Honours:* Gay Book Award, American Library Association, 1982; Writer of the Year Award, Stonewall Foundation, 1983; Human Rights Award, Human Rights Campaign Fund, 1984; Lambda Legal Defense Award, 1983. *Literary Agent:* Jed Mattes, International Creative Management, New York City. *Address:* 401 West 24th Street, New York, NY 10011, USA.

RUTHERFORD, Gordon Malcolm, b. 21 Aug. 1939, Newcastle upon Tyne, England. Journalist. m. Elizabeth Claude Rosemary Maitland Pelen, 24 Feb. 1970, 3 sons. *Education:* Balliol College, Oxford. *Literary Appointments:* Arts Editor, Spectator, 1962; Founding Editor, Latin America, 1966; Assistant Editor, Financial Times, 1977. *Publications:* Can We Save The Common Market?, 1981. *Address:* 89 Bedford Gardens, London W8, England.

RUTSALA, Vera, b. 5 Feb. 1934, McCall, Idaho, USA. Writer, Professor. m. Joan Colby, 6 Apr. 1957, Aiken, South Carolina, 2 sons, 1 daughter. *Education:* BA, Reed College; MFA, University of Iowa. *Literary Appointments:* Professor of English, Lewis & Clark College, 19610; Visiting Professor, University of Minnesota, 1968–69; Visiting Professor, Bowling Green University, 1970; Writer-in-Residence, Redlands University, 1979. *Major Publications:* The Window, 1964; Laments, 1975; The Journey Begins, 1976; Paragraphs, 1978; Walking Home from the Icehouse, 1981, Backtracking, 1985. *Contributor to:* Poetry; The New Yorker; Atlantic; American Poetry Review; New Statesman; Times Literary Supplement; Hudson Review; Poetry Northwest; and others. *Honours:* Guggenheim Fellowship, 1982; National Endowment for the Arts Fellowships, 1974, 1979; Northwest Poets Prize, 1975. *Memberships:* PEN; Poetry Society of America. *Address:* Department of English, Lewis & Clark College, Portland, OR 97219, USA.

RUTT, Theodor, b. 5 May 1911, Cologne, Federal Republic of Germany. Professor. *Education:* State Teachers Examinations for Primary and Secondary Stages, I and II; PhD. *Publications:* Sparchenfaltung und Buch, 2nd edition, 1961; Muttersprachschule, part 1, 2nd edition, 1966, part 2, 3rd edition, 1966; Didaktik der Muttersprache, 2nd edition, 1968; Adalbert Stifter der Erzieher, 2nd edition, 1970; Chronil des Rheinisch; Bergischen Kreises, 3rd edition, 1972; Katholoscher Religionsunterricht heute, 1975, 1975; Katechese aus dem Glauben, 1979; Antropos Pad, 1983; Fr Wester, Verfolgterdes Nationalsozialismus, 1983; Petersueschule heute, 1983; P Petersen, Leben u Werk, 1984. Editor: die Quelle zur historischen, empirischen und Vergleichenden Erziehungswissenschaft, 70 volumes to date, 1956–. *Honours:* Knight, Gregoriusorden. *Memberships:* Corresponding Member, Adalbert Stifter Institut; Gorresgesellschaft. *Address:* Werthmannstrasse 13, 5 Cologne 41, Federal Republic of Germany.

RUTTER, Michael Llewellyn, b. 15 Aug. 1933, Brummanna, Lebanon. Professor of Child Psychiatry, University of London. m. Marjorie Heys, 27 Dec. 1958, 1 son, 2 daughters. *Education:* MB ChB, University of Birmingham medical School, 1950–55; Academic DPM, University of London 1961; MD, University of Birmingham, 1963; Fellow, Royal College of Psychiatrists, London 1971; Fellow, Royal College of Physicians, London 1972. *Major Publications include:* Children of Sick Parents: An Environmental & Psychiatric Study, 1966; A Neuropsychiatric Study in Childhood, (with P Graham & W Yule), 1970; Education, Health & Beaviour, (edited with J Tizard & K Whitmore), 1970; The Child with Delayed Speech, (edited with J A M Martin), 1972; Helping Troubled Children, 1975; Cycles of Disadvantage, (with N Madge), 1976; Autism: A Reappraisal of Concepts & Treatment, (edited with E Schoppier), 1978; Changing Youth in a Changing Society, 1979; Stress, Coping & Development, (edited with N Garmezy), 1983; Developmental Neuropsychiatry, (edited), 1983; Juvenile Delinquency: Trends & Perspectives, (with H Giller), 1983; A Measure of Our Values: Goals & Dilemmas in the Upbringing of Children, 1983; Child & Adolescent Psychiatry: Modern Approaches, 2nd edition (edited with L Hersov), 1985; Depression in Young People: Developmental & Clinical Perspectives, (with C Izard & F Read), 1986. *Contributor to:* Numerous professional & medical/psychiatric journals. *Honours:* Nuffield Medical Travelling Fellowship, 1961–62; Belding Travelling Scholar, 1963; Coulstonian Lecturer, Royal College of Physicians, 1973; American Association on Mental Deficiency Research Award, 1975; Honorary Fellow, British Psychological Society, 1978; Rock Carling Fellow of the Nuffield Provincial Hospitals Trust, 1979; Salmon Lecturer, New York; Fellow, Centre for Advanced Study in the Behavioural Sciences, California, 1979–80; Honorary Doctorate, University of Leiden, Netherlands, 1985; Numerous Memorial Lectures & Visiting Professorships. *Address:* Department of Child & Adolescent Psychiatry, Institute of Psychiatry, De

Crespigny Park, Denmark Hill, London SE5 8AF, England.

RYAN, John Gerald Christopher, b. 4 Mar. 1921, Edinburgh, Scotland. Artist; Illustrator; Writer. m. Priscilla A Ryan, 3 Jan. 1950, London, 1 son, 2 daughters. *Publications:* 14 Picture Storybooks on Captain Pugwash, 1965–; 12 Picture Storybooks on, Noah's Ark, 1979–; various other childrens books. *Contributor to:* Eagle Magazine, 1950–1960; Cartoonist, Catholic Herald, 1965–. *Membership:* Society of Authors. *Address:* 12 Airlie Gardens, London W8 7AL, England.

RYAN, Paul Brennan, b. 19 Apr. 1913, Burlington, Vermont, USA. Historian; Writer; Retired Captain, US Navy. *Education:* BS, US Naval Academy, 1936; MA, Stanford University, California, 1964, San Jose State University, 1965. *Literary Appointments:* Research Fellow, Hoover Institution, Stanford, California, 1975–. *Publications:* The Panama Canal Controversy, 1977; First Line of Defense: The US Navy since 1945, 1981; The Iranian Rescue Mission: Why It Failed, 1985. Co-Author: The Lusitania Disaster, with Thomas A Bailey, 1975; Hitler vs Roosevelt: The Undeclared Naval War, with Thomas Bailey, 1979. *Contributions to:* American Neptune; US Naval Institute Proceedings; Sea Power; New York Times; This World. *Memberships:* US Naval Institute; North American Society for Oceanic History; Naval Submarine League; Navy League; Association of Naval Aviation. *Address:* Hoover Institution, Stanford, CA 94305, USA.

RYAN, Paul Ryder, b. 5 Jan. 1932, Mineola, New York, USA. Writer, Editor. m. Ruthann Tobin, 12 Aug. 1958, Salem, New Hampshire, 2 sons, 2 daughters. *Education:* BA, Harvard University, USA. *Literary Appointments:* Executive Editor, Drama Review, 1970–75; Editor, Oceanus Magazine, 1976–. *Contributor to:* Various magazines & journals. *Honours:* Member, New York Academy of Sciences, 1985; Academy Award for Best Foreign Film (The War Game) 1967; Pulitzer Prize, 1962. *Memberships:* Society for Scholarly Publishing; Council of Biological Editors. *Address:* PO Box 637, Woods Hole, MA 02543, USA.

RYAN, Peter Allen M M, b. 4 Sep. 1923, Melbourne, Australia. Publisher. m. Gladys A Davidson, 1947, 1 son, 2 daughters. *Education:* BA, University of Melbourne. *Publications:* Fear Drive My Feet, 1959; The Preparation of Manuscripts, 1966; General Editor, Encyclopaedia of Papua and New Guinea, 1972; Redmond Barry, 1973. *Contributor to:* Various newspapers and magazines. *Honour:* Military Medal, 1943. *Membership:* Australian Society of Authors. *Address:* 932 Swanston Street, Carlton, Vicotira 3053, Australia.

RYCHLAK, Joseph Frank, b. 17 Dec. 1928, Cudahy, Wisconsin, USA. Professor of Psychology. m. Lenora Pearl Smith, 16 June 1956, Columbus, Ohio, 1 son, 1 daughter. *Education:* BS, University of Wisconsin, 1953; MA, 1954, PhD, 1957, The Ohio State University. *Publications:* A Philosophy of Science for Personality Theory, 1968; Introduction to Personality and Psychotherapy, 1973; The Psychology of Rigorous Humanism, 1977; Discovering Free Will and Personal Responsibility, 1979; Personality and Life Style of Young Male Managers: A Logical Learning Theory Analysis, 1982. *Contributions to:* Over 125 Philosophical and Scientific Journal articles. *Address:*

Maude C Clarke Professor of Humanistic Psychology, Department of Psychology, Loyola University of Chicago, 6525 North Sheridan Road, Chicago, IL 60626, USA.

RYDER, Michael Lawson, b. 24 July 1927, Leeds, England, Research Biologist. m. Mary Nicholson, 1952, Leeds, 2 sons. *Education:* BSc, 1951, MSC, 1954, PhD, 1956, Leeds University; Fellow of the Institute of Biology, 1965. *Publications:* Wool Growth (with S K Stephenson), 1968; Animal Bones in Archaeology, 1969; Hair, 1973; Sheep and Wool for Handicraft Workers, 1978; Sheep and Man, 1983. *Contributor to:* Various journals. *Memberships:* Formerly member of Scottish PEN (committee); Society of Authors (Scottish committee). *Address:* 23 Swanston Place, Edinburgh EH10 7DD, Scotland.

RYKEN, Leland, b. 17 May 1942, Pella, Iowa, USA. College Teacher. m. Mary Graham, 22 Aug. 1964, St Louis, Missouri, 1 son, 2 daughters. *Education:* BA, Central College, Iowa, 1964; PhD, University of Oregon, 1968. *Publications:* The Apocalyptic Vision in Paradise Lost, 1970; The Literature of the Bible, 1974; Triumphs of the Imagination: Literature in Christian Perspective, 1979; The Christian Imagination, 1981; Milton and Scriptural Tradition: The Bible into Poetry, 1984; The New Testament in Literary Criticism, 1984; How To Read The Bible As Literature, 1984; Windows to the World: Literature in Christian Perspective, 1985. *Contributions to:* Huntington Library Quarterly; The Explicator; Journal of English and Germanic Philology; Milton Quarterly; Christian Today; Christianity and Literature; Christian Scholar's Review; Tennessee Studies in Literature. *Memberships:* Board of Directors 1977–80, Conference on Christianity and Literature. *Address:* Department of English, Wheaton College, Wheaton, IL 60187, USA.

RYTTEN, Jack Edward, b. 23 Sep. 1914, Port Chester, New York, USA. Investigator and Criminologist. *Publications include:* An Investigator's View of Crime and Punishment, 1973; An Investigator's View of the Liberal Press, 1974; Private vs Public Education, 1975; Law and the Western Values, 1975; Socialized Misery, 1975; Lower Standards in Higher Education, 1975; Public Relations and The Engineering Community, 1975; Problems of Personnel and Pre-Employment Investigation, 1975; Pre-Trial Accident Investigation, 1978; Regulation Man and His Invisible Victims, 1979; Correcting The Media, 1979; National Security at Death's Door, 1979; Labor Unions in a Free Market, 1979; The Liberal Mentality and the Malpractice Mess, 1979; The Family Circle and America's Future, 1979; Investigative Photography as Evidence, 1985; Traffic Accident Investigation for Attorneys, 1985; Traffic Accident Investigation for Police, 1985. *Contributions to:* Book review editor/Feature writer to various publications including: Courier-Journal, Louisville, Kentucky; The Jeffersonian, Towson, Maryland; Baltimore Engineer; Maryland Trooper; The Investigator's Notebook; Daily Record, Baltimore. *Honours include:* Liberty Award, Congress of Freedom, 1969; Citation, 95th Congress of the United States; Special Recognition Award, American Security Center and Pentagon Education Center, 1979. *Memberships:* President 1965–69, Professional Forum of Baltimore; Maryland Historial Society. *Address:* 8415 Bellona Lane, Baltimore, MD 21204, USA.

S

SAAB, Ann Pottinger, b. 18 Dec. 1934, Boston, Massachusetts, USA. College Professor. m. Elie Georges Saab, 23 July, 1966, Kornet Chehwan, Lebanon, 2 sons. *Education:* MA 1957, PhD, 1962, Harvard University; BA, Wellesley College, 1955. *Publications:* Napoleon III and the German Crisis 1865–66, 1966; The Origins of the Crimean Alliance, 1977; Translation and Introduction Winfried Baumgart, Der Friede Von Paris (The Peace of Paris, 1981). *Contributions to:* Journals. *Honour:* Caroline I Wilby Thesis Prize, 1962. *Address:* 5003 Beale Avenue, Greensboro, NC 27407, USA.

SABATO, Ernesto, b. 24 June 1911, Rojas, Argentina. Writer. *Education:* PhD, University of La Plata, Argentina, 1937; Postgraduate, Laboratory Curie, Paris, France, 1938, Massachusetts Institute of Technology, USA, 1939. *Publications:* Novels: El Tunel, 1947; Sobre Heroes y Tumbas, 1961; Abaddon, 1974. Essays: Uno y el Universo, 1945; Hombres y Engranjes, 1951; Heterodoxia, 1953; El Escritor y sus Fantasmas, 1963; Tres Aproximaciones a la Literature de Nuestro Tiempo, 1969. *Contributions to:* Various Argentinian and foreign magazines and journals. *Honours include:* Prize, Institute for Foreign Relations, Stuttgart, Germany, 1973; Grand Prize, Argentinian Writers Society, 1974; Premio Consgracion Nacional de la Argentina, 1975; Grand Cross, Spanish Royarme, 1979; Chevalier, Commandeur, 1983, Arts et Lettres, France; Prix au Meilleur, Livre, Paris, France, 1976; Chevalier, Legion d'Honneur, France, 1979; Prize Gab Mistral, Washington, USA, 1984; Prize M de Cervantes, Spain, 1984; Comm Merito Civile, Italy, 1982. *Memberships include:* Club of Rome; Comite pour l'Universalite de UNESCO, Paris; Jerusalem Committee. *Address:* 1676 Santos Lugares, Argentina.

SABINE, Ellen S, b. 23 Feb. 1908, Brooklyn, New York, USA. Artist, Illustrator, Author. m. 2 July 1937, London, England. *Education:* New York School of Fine and Applied Arts; Pratt Institute of Fine and Applied Arts, New York. *Publications:* American Antique Decoration, 1956; American Folk Art, 1958; Early American Decorative Patterns, 1962. *Memberships:* Historical Society of Early American Decoration Inc, Esther Stevens Brazer Guild, New York. *Address:* 9 D Sterling Street, Lakehurst, NJ 08733, USA.

SABLE, Martin Howard, b. 24 Sep. 1924, Haverhill, Massachusetts, USA. Library Science Educator. m. Minna Gibbs, 5 Feb. 1950, 2 sons. *Education:* Student, Northeastern University, 1942–43; BA, 1946, MA, 1952, Boston University; Dr en letras, National University of Mexico, 1952; MLS, Simmons College, 1959. *Literary Appointments:* Bibliographer, Reference Librarian, Northeastern University, 1959–63; Research Librarian, Harvard, 1962–63; Language Librarian, California State College, Los Angeles, 1963–64; Assistant research professor, Latin American Centre, University of California, Los Angeles, 1965–68; Associate professor, 1968–72, Professor, 1972–, School Library and Information Science, University of Wisconsin, Milwaukee. *Publications:* Master Directory for Latin America, 1965; A Guide to Latin American Studies, 1-11, 1967; Communism in Latin America, 1968; A Bio-Bibliography of the Kennedy Family, 1969; Latin American Studies in Non-Western World, 1970; Latin American Urbanisation, 1971; International and Area Studies Librarianship, 1973; The Guerrilla Movement in Latin America since 1950, 1977; Exobiology, A Research Guide, 1978; Latin American Studies Directory 1981; The Protection of the Library and Archive 1984; Advisory editor on Latin America, Encyclopaedia Americana, 1967–. *Contributions to:* Professional journals of articles on librarianship. *Memberships:* American Library Association; Latin American Studies Association; American Association of University Professors; Midwest Association for Latin American Studies; Pacific Coast Council of Latin American Studies (newsletter editor 1965–68); Conference on Latin American History.

Address: 4518 North Larkin Street, Milwaukee, WI 53211, USA.

SACHS, Marilyn, b. 18 Dec. 1927, USA. Writer. m. Morris Sachs, 26 Jan. 1947, New York City, 1 son, 1 daughter. *Education:* BA, Hunter College, New York; MS, Library Science, Columbus University, New York. *Publications:* Fiction: Amy Moves In, 1964; Veronica Ganz, 19687; The Bears' House, 1971; The Truth About Mary Rose, 1973; A Pocket Full of Seeds, 1973; Dorrie's Book, 1975; A Summer's Lease, 1979; Class Pictures, 1980; Call Me Ruth, 1982; Fourteen, 1983; The Fat Girl, 1984; Underdog, 1985; Baby Sister, 1986; many other books. *Honours:* Outstanding Book of the Year, 1971; National Book Award Nominee, 1972; Austrian Children's Book Prize, 1977; School Library Journal, Best Books of the Year, 1973; Silver Slate Pencil Award, 1974; Jane Addams Children's Book Honour Award, 1974; Garden State Children's Book Award for Younger Fiction; Association of Jewish Libraries' Award, 1983; etc. *Memberships:* Jane Austen Society, Great Britain; Jane Austen Society of North America. *Address:* 733 – 31st Avenue, San Francisco, CA 94121, USA.

SACHS, Mendel, b. 13 Apr. 1927, Portland, Oregon, USA. Professor of Physics. m. Yetty Herman, 22 June 1952, Los Angeles, California, USA, 3 sons, 1 daughter. *Education:* AB Physics, 1949; MA Physics, 1950, PhD Physics, 1954, University of California at Los Angeles. *Major Publications:* Solid State Theory, 1963; 1974; The Search for a Theory of Matter, 1971; The Field Concept in Contemporary Science, 1973; Ideas of the Theory of Relativity, 1974; Ideas of Matter, 1981; General Relativity and Matter, 1982. *Contributor to:* Il Nuovo Cimento; Foundations of Physics; Annales de la Foundation L de Broglie; La Recherche. *Address:* Department of Physics & Astronomy, State University of New York at Buffalo, Buffalo, NY 14260, USA.

SACKS, Karen Brodkin, b. 21 Nov. 1941, New York City, USA. Anthropologist. m. William Sacks, 9 June 1961, New York City, 2 sons. *Education:* AB, Brandies University, 1963; MA, Harvard University, 1964; PhD, University of Michigan, 1971. *Literary Appointments:* Instructor, Assistant Professor, Oakland University, 1968–75; Visiting Assistant Professor, Social Sciences, Fordham University, Lincoln Center, 1975–76; Assistant Professor, Sociology, Anthropology, Clark University, 1976–80; Reasearch Associate, Anthropology, Duke University, 1981–85; Research Director, Business and Professional Women's Foundation, 1981–. *Publications:* Sisters and Wives, 1978, paperback, 1982; My Troubles are Going to Have Trouble With Me (co-editor), 1984. *Contributions to:* Monthly Review; American Anthropologist; American Ethnologist; Jewish Currents; Signal; Ms; The Woman's Annual, 1983. *Honour:* NIMH Pre-doctoral Fwp, Harvard University, 1963–66; Rackham Prize Fwp, University of Michigan, 1968–70; NIMH Post-doctoral Fwp, Duke University (Public Policy), 1978–80; NSF Research Grant, Anthropology, 1982–84; Editorial Board, Signs, 1984–. *Memberships:* National Women's Studies Association; American Anthropological Association; American Ethnological Society; American Sociological Association, Capitol Area Sociologists for Women and Society. *Address:* 8718 Geren Road, Silver Spring, MD 20901, USA.

SADDLEMYER, Eleanor Ann, b. 29 Nov. 1932, Prince Albert, Sasketchewan, Canada. University Professor. *Education:* BA, University of Sasketchewan, 1953; MA, Queen's University of Kingston, 1956; PhD, University of London, 1961. *Literary Appointments:* Professor of English, University of Victoria, Victoria BC, 1960–71; Professor of English, Victoria College, University of Toronto, 1971 and Professor of Drama, Graduate Centre for Study of Drama, 1971; Director of Graduate Centre for Study of Drama, 1972–77 and 1985–86; Visiting Professor, Berg Chair, New York University, 1975. *Publications:* The World of Yeats, 1965; In Defence of Lady Gregory, Playwright, 1966; Synge and Modern Comedy, 1968; The Plays of J M Synge, 2 volumes, 1968; The Plays of Lady Gregory, 4

606 INTERNATIONAL AUTHORS AND WRITERS WHO'S WHO

volumes, 1970; Letters to Molly, 1971; Co-Editor, Theatre History in Canada, 1980–86; Theatre Business, 1982; The Collected Letters of John Millington Synge, 2 volumes, 1983–84; Lady Gregory Fifty Years After, (with Colin Smythe), 1986. *Contributions to:* Numerous journals and magazines, including Journal of Irish Literature; English Studies in Canada; Modern Drama; Canadian Journal, of Irish Studies. *Honours:* John Simon Guggenheim Fellowships, 1965, 1977; Fellow of the Royal Society of Canada, 1976; LLD, Queen's University in Kingston, 1977; Japan Society for Promotion of Science, Canada Exchange, 1984. *Memberships:* Chairman, International Association for Study of Anglo-Irish Literature, 1973–76; Executive, Canadian Association for Irish Studies; President, Association for Canadian Theatre History, 1976–77. *Address:* 297 Watson Avenue, Oakville, Ontario L6J 3V3, Canada.

SADEH, Pinhas, b. 17 June 1929, Lwow, Poland (now USSR). Writer. *Publications:* Life as a Parable, (autobiography) 1958; Notes on Man's Condition, (novel) 1967; The Death of Abimelech and his Ascent to Heaven in his Mother's Arms, (novel) 1969; Collected Poems, 1970; Journey, (Travel diary) in Europe, 1971; Journey in the Land of Israel and Meditations on God's Disappointed Love, 1974; To Two Honourable Young Ladies, (poems) 1977; The Diary of the Writing of Life as a Parable, 1980; The Mending of the Heart, (stories, dreams and pensees of Rabi Nachman of Bratzlav), 1981; The Book of the Imaginings of the Jews, (Jewish folktales), 1983; The Book of Yellow Pears, (stories, poems and pensees), 1985; Seven University Lectures on the Poetry of ch. n. Bialik, 1985, books originally published in Hebrew, some translated into various languages. *Literary Agent:* Rosica Colin Ltd, London, England. *Address:* Hahagana 138, Tel-Aviv, 67422, Israel.

SADIE, Stanley (John), b. 30 Oct. 1930, London, England. Writer on Music; Editor. m. (1) Adèle Bloom, 10 Dec. 1953, London, 2 sons, 1 daughter. (2) Julie Anne McCormack, 18 July 1978, London, 1 son, 1 daughter. *Education:* MA, PhD, BMus, Gonville and Caius College, Cambridge University. *Literary Appointments:* Music Critic, The Times, 1964–81. Editor: The Musical Times, 1967–; The New Grove Dictionary of Music and Musicians, 1970–. *Publications:* Handel, 1962; Pan Book of Opera, 1964, 2nd edition, 1984, with A Jacobs; Mozart, 1966; Beethoven, 1967; Handel, 1968; Handel Concertos, 1972; The New Grove Dictionary of Music and Musicians, Editor, 20 volumes, 1980; The New Grove Mozart, 1982; The New Grove Dictionary of Musical Instruments, 3 volumes, 1984; The Cambridge Music Guide, with A Latham, 1985; Mozart Symphonies, 1986. *Contributions to:* Musical Times; Gramaphone; Opera. *Honours:* Honorary DLitt, Leicester University, 1982; Honorary RAM, Royal Academy of Music, 1982; CBE, 1982. *Memberships:* Vice President, Royal Musical Association; International and American Musicological Societies; Critics Circle. *Address:* 12 Lyndhurst Road, Hampstead, London NW3 5NL, England.

SADKOWSKI, Waclaw, b. 19 May 1933, Torun, Poland. Literary Critic. m. Danuta Kwiecinska, 26 Sep. 1953, Warsaw. *Education:* BA, MA, University of Warsaw. *Literary Appointment:* Fellow at International Writing Program, University of Iowa, Iowa City, USA, 1976. *Publications:* Catholic Literature in Poland, 1963; Roads and Crossroads of Western Literature, 1968, 2nd edition 1978; Cercles of Community, 1972; James Baldwin, 1985. *Contributions to:* Editor-in-Chief, Literatura Na Swiecie, monthly magazine, 1972–. *Memberships:* PEN Club; Association Internationale des Critiques Littéraires; Societe Européene de Culture. *Address:* Madalinshiego 50/52 m 18, 02-581 Warszawa, Polska.

SADOFF, Ira, b. 7 Mar. 1945, New York, USA. Writer. m. Dianne Fallon, 29 July 1968. *Education:* BS, Cornell University, 1966; MFA, University of Oregon, 1968. *Appointments:* Co-Founder, Co-Editor, The Seneca Review, 1968–74; Poetry Editor, The Antioch Review,

1973–77. *Publications:* Settling Down, 1975; Palm Reading in Winter, 1978; Uncoupling, 1982; A Northern Calender, 1982. *Contributor to:* New Yorker; Poetry; American Poetry Review; Esquire; Partisan Review; Paris Review; Antaeus; Transatlantic; The Hudson Review; The Iowa Review; Tri-Quarterly; Antioch Review. *Honours:* National Endowment for the Arts Creative Arts Fellowship, 1981–82. *Memberships:* Poetry Society of America; PEN. *Literary Agent:* Georges Borchardt. *Address:* English Dept, Colby College, Waterville, ME 04901, USA.

SAFRAN, Claire, b. New York City, USA. Writer; Editor. m. John Hilton Williams, 8 June 1958, Brooklyn, New York, 1 son. *Education:* BA Cum laude, Brooklyn College, 1951. *Literary Appointments:* Editor-in-Chief, Coronet Magazine, 1968–71; Contributing Editor, 1974–77, Executive Editor, 1977–78, Contributing Editor, 1979–81, Redbook Magazine; Contributor to major national and international magazines, 1972–; Roving Editor, Reader's Digest, 1983–. *Publications* New Ways to Lower Your Blood Pressure, 1984. *Honours:* Media Awards: American Psychological Foundation, 1977; Odyssey Institute, 1979, 80. Finalist, Penney-Missouri, Magazine Awards, 1977; Merit Award in Journalism, 1977; Merit Award in Journalism, Religious Public Relations Council, 1978; Journalism Award, American Academy of Pediatrics, 1979; Matrix Awards, Women in Communications, 1982–84; 1st Place Magazines, William Harvey Award, 1984; Outstanding Magazine Article of the Year, American Society of Journalists and Authors, 1984; Journalism Award, American Academy of Family Physicians, 1984. *Memberships:* American Society of Journalists and Authors; Women in Communications. *Literary Agent:* Julian Bach. *Address:* 53 Evergreen Avenue, Westport, CT 06880, USA.

SAFRAN, William, b. 8 July 1930, Dresden, Germany. Political Science Professor. m. Marian Celia Folk, 25 Mar. 1961, Scranton, Pennsylvania, USA. 1 son, 1 daughter. *Education:* BA, 1953, MA, 1955, City University of New York; PhD, Columbia University, 1964. *Appointment:* Professor of Political Science, University of Colorado, Boulder. *Publications:* Veto-Group Politics, 1967; The French Polity, 1977, 79, 85; Ideology and Politics: The Socialist Party of France (co-author), 1979; Comparative Politics (co-author), 1983. *Contributions to:* American Political Science Review; Western Political Quarterly; East European Quarterly; German Studies Review; Tocqueville Review; International Studies Notes; French Politics and Society; Ethnic and Racial Studies (London); Comparative Politics. Chapters in 8 books. *Honours:* History Honors, City University of New York, 1953; Faculty Research Grantee, University of Colorado. 1966, 1969–70; Social Science Foundation Fellow, 1966; National Endowment for Humanities Grantee, 1980–81. *Memberships:* American Political Science Association; Western Political Science Association; Conference Group on French Politics and Society; American Academy of Political Science; International Studies Association; Tocqeville Society; Association Francaise de Science Politique; International Political Science Association. *Address:* University of Colorado, Department of Political Science, Boulder, CO 80309, USA.

SAGGS, Henry William Frederick, b. 2 Dec. 1920, Weeley, Essex, England. Professor, Semitic Languages. m. Joan Butterworth, 21 Sep. 1946, Elmstead, 4 daughters. *Education:* BD; MA; MTh; PhD. *Appointments:* Lecturer, then Reader, Akkadian, School of Oriental and African Studies, University of London, 1953–66; Professor, Semitic Languages, University College, Cardiff, University of Wales, 1966–83. *Publications:* The Greatness that was Babylon, 1962; Everyday Life in Babylonia and Assyria, 1965; The Encounter with the Divine in Mesopotamia and Israel, 1978; The Might That Was Assyria, 1984. *Contributor to:* Articles in Iraq; Journal of Theological Studies; Journal of Semitic Studies; Archiv für Orientforschung; Journal of Cuneiform Studies; Revue D'Assyriologie; Sumer. *Address:*

Eastwood, Bull Lane, Long Melford, Suffolk CO10 9EA, England.

SAHGAL, Nayantara, b. 10 May 1927, Allahabad, India. Novelist; Political Journalist. m. (1) Gautam Sahgal, 2 Jan. 1949, 1 son, 2 daughters. (2) E N Manget Rai, 17 Sep. 1979. *Education:* BA History, Wellesley College, Massachusetts, USA. *Literary Appointments:* Advisory Board for English, Sahitya Akademi, 1972–76; Writer-in-Residence, Southern Methodist University, Dallas, Texas, USA, 1973, 77. *Publications:* Prison and Chocolate Cake, 1954; A Time to Be Happy, 1958; This Time of Morning, 1965; From Feart Set Free, 1962; Storm in Chandigarh, 1969' History of the Freedom Movement, 1970; The Day in Shadow, 1971; A Situation in New Delhi, 1977; Indira Gandhi's Emergence and Style, 1978; A Voice for Freedom, 1977; Indira Gandhi: Her Road to Power; Rich Like Us, 1985; Plans for Departure, 1985. *Contributions to:* Indian magazines and newspapers, foreign magazines notably British and American; Indian Express, monthly columnist. *Honours:* A Time to Be Happy, Books Society Recommendation, 1958; Rich Like Us, Winner of Sinclair Prize, 1985. Fellow, Woodrow Wilson International Center for Scholars, Washington, DC, USA, 1981–82; National Humanities Center, North Carolina, 1983–84. *Literary Agent:* A L Hart, New York, USA. *Address:* 181-B Rajpur Road, Dehra Dun, Uttar Pradesh 248009, India.

SAINI, Balwant Singh, b. 6 Feb. 1930, Simla, India. Architect; Educator. m. Elizabeth Morgan, 9 July 1978, Brisbane, Australia, 2 daughter. *Education:* BA; BArch; PhD. *Publications:* Architecture in Tropical Australia, 1970; Building Environment, 1973; Building in Hot Dry Climates, 1980; The Australian House, 1982. *Contributons to:* (Australian Regional Editor): Man Environment Systems, New York and Ekistics, Athens, 1973–. *Honour:* Book Award, Building Science Forum of Australia, 1974. *Membership:* World Society of Ekistics. *Address:* 11 Montrose Road, Taringa, Queensland 4068, Australia.

SAINT, Dora Jessie, b. 17 Apr. 1913, London, England. Writer. m. Douglas Edward John Saint, 26 July 1940, Ealing, 1 daughter. *Education:* Homerton College, Cambridge. *Publications include:* Village school, 1955; Thrush Green, 1958; 30 more, mainly about these 2 villages. *Contributions to:* Punch; Times Educational Supplement; Countryman; The Lady, etc. *Membership:* Society of Authors. *Address:* c/o Michael Joseph Ltd, 44 Bedford Square, London WC1B 3DU, England.

ST. AUBYN, Giles (Hon.), b. 11 Mar. 1925, London, England. Writer. *Education:* Wellington College; MA, Trinity College, Oxford University; FRSL. *Publications:* Lord Macaulay, 1952; A Victorian Eminence, 1958; The Art of Argument, 1958; The Royal George, 1963; A World to Win, 1968; Infamous Victorians, 1971; Edward VII, Prince and King, 1979; The Year of Three Kings, 1983. *Honour:* LVO, 1977. *Memberships:* Fellow, Royal Society of Literature; Society of Authors. *Address:* Cornwall Lodge, Cambridge Park, St Peter Port, Guernsey, Channel Islands.

SAINT CHRISTOL, Irene de, b. 23 May 1914, Cambrai, France. Teacher. Divorced, 1 son, 1 daughter. *Education:* Higher Certificate; Certificate of Teaching. *Appointments:* Poet; Songwriter; Literary & Fine Arts Critic; Preface Writer; Editor, Inter-Muses. *Publications:* Les Messes de Soleil, 1974; Horizon brule, 1977; Au temps ou la femme, 1980; Visions desincarness, 1980; Angles d'ecoute, 1983; La vallee de l'eveil' 1986. *Contributor to:* Articles, poems, lectures in numerous French, Spanish, Italian, Portuguese magazines; Scientific books; etc. *Honours:* Grand Prix for free poetry, French Syndicate of journalists & writers, 1978; Poetry Prize, Academie Francaise, 1981, 1983; Silver-gilt Medal, City of Paris, 1983; Grand Prix de Fondation, Association French Poets, 1984; Silver-gilt Medal of Arts, Sciences, Letters. *Memberships:* Vice President, International Academy of Lutece; Assistant Principal, Scientific Section, Academy of Lutece; Association French Poets; Numerous Boards of Examiners for Literature & Fine Arts, France, Italy; French Syndicate of Journalists & Writers. *Address:* Boite Postale 14, 94701 Maisons-Alfort, France.

ST CLAIR, Margaret, b. 17 Feb. 1911, Kansas, USA. Writer. m. Eric St Clair, 25 May 1932, Berkeley. *Education:* MA, Greek, University of California, 1934. *Publications:* Agent of the Unknown, 1956; The Green Queen, 1956; The Games of Neith, 1960; Sign of the Labrys, 1963; Message from the Eocene, 1964; The Worlds of Futurity, 1964; The Dolphins of Altair, 1967; The Shadow People, 1969; The Dancers of Noyo, 1973; Change the Skys & Other Stories, 1974; The Best of Margaret St Clair, 1985. *Contributor to:* More than 100 pieces of short fiction published in various journals and magazines. *Memberships:* Former Member, Authors League of America; Science Fiction Writers of America. *Literary Agent:* Julie fallowfield, McIntosh & Otis, New York City. *Address:* Star Route, Manchester, CA 95459, USA.

ST CLAIR, William, b. 7 Dec. 1937, London, England. Assistant Secretary, Her Majesty's Treasury. *Education:* Oxford University. *Publications:* Lord Elgin and the Marbles, 1967, Revised, 1983; That Greece Might Still Be Free: The Philhellenes in the War of Independence, 1972; Trelawny's Adventures of a Younger Son, Editor, 1974; Trelawny, The Incurable Romancer, 1977. *Contributions to:* Sunday Telegraph; Financial Times; Times Literary Supplement. *Honours:* Fellow: Royal Society of Literature; Huntington Library, California, USA, 1985. Visiting Fellow, All Souls College, Oxford University, 1981–82; Heinemann Prize, 1973. *Address:* 52 Eaton Place, London SW1, England.

ST. CYR, Napoleon J, b. 8 May 1924, Franklin, New Hampshire, USA. Editor/Publisher. *Education:* BA, University of New Hampshire, CT; MA & Certificate of Advance Study, Fairfield University, CT, USA. *Literary Appointments:* Literary Advisor, Stratford Cultural Commission, 1975–80; Final Judge in poetry and history, National Book Awards; Advisory Board of Consultants, Small Press Review of Books, 1985–. *Publications:* Pebble Ring, 1966, (poems); Stones Unturned, 1967, (poems). *Contributions to:* Over 60 journals in the form of poetry. *Honour:* Sherrard Short Story Prize/Honours Convocation, University of New Hampshire, CT, USA. *Membership:* Academy of American Poets. *Address:* POB 664, Stratford, CT, 06497, USA.

SAINT-DENIS, Janou, b. 6 May 1930, Montreéal, Canada. Actress, Poet. m. Jean Saint-Denis (deceased 1956), 1 son, 1 daughter. *Education:* Diploma-ès Lettres et Sciences, Couvent d'Hochelaga-Montréal, 1946; Diploma, Conservatoire Lassalle (theatre), 1950; Diploma, Université du Théâtre des Nations, Paris, France, 1962. *Literary Appointments:* Established poetry readings in Montréal, 1959, Paris 1961–71, Nuits de la Poésie, the University of Québec, Montréal, Place Aux Poètes, Montréal, 1975–85. *Major publications:* Mots à dire, Maux à dire, 1972; Place aux poètes, 1977; Claude Gauvreau, le Cygne, 1978; Dollars Désormais, Poème à l'anti-gang et l'escouade vlimeuse, Mise à part, 1981; La Roue Dufeu Secret, 1985. *Contributor to:* Moebius; Canton s'met à faire de la poésie; Les Cahiers de la femme; Atelier littéraire de la Maurice; Revue de l'université d'Ottawa; Sorcières; Femme Plurielle; Xceteras; Cahier des arts visuels; Arcade. *Memberships:* CAPAC; Union des écrivains québecois; Union des Artistes; Les Satellites de Montréal (Theatre Company). *Address:* 4445 rue St-Dominique, Montréal, Québec, H2W, 2B4, Canada.

ST JACQUES, Elizabeth Joyce Gloria, b. 9 Apr. 1939, Ontario, Canada. Freelance Writer and Photographer. m. Rene Maurice, 25 May 1957, Kirkland Lake, Ontario, Canada, 2 sons. *Literary Appointments:* Poetry Comments Editor, Pegasus, 1972–74; UAP: Historian, 1972–73, Vice-President 1973–74, Prose Laureate Judge 1972–73; Trans-Atlantic Competitions Judge, Patterned Poetry, 1973–74; Columnist: Lifeline 1977–

80, Canadian Biker 1985. *Publications:* Diary of Thoughts, poetry, 1967; Silver Sigh and Shadows Blue, poetry 1978; Canadian Poets and Friends, anthology 1975–80, editor and publisher; Canadian Encounter, writers' anthology, 1981, editor and publisher. *Contributions to:* Canadian Living; Farm Woman News; Coup de Pouce; Our Family; Purpose; Ssunday Digest; Venture Road; Road Rider; Rider; Canadian Biker; Canadian Author and Bookman: The Inkling; Amber; White Wall Review (Ryerson Literary Society); South West Ontario Poetry; Glory (India); New Day (Ireland); Higginson Journal etc. *Honours:* Numerous awards including: Poem of the Year Award, Inky Trails, 1970; Poet of the Month Award, Friendship Ferry, 1971; Star of the Month Award, The Unkown Poet, 1975; National Writers Contest, H M (poetry) 1976; Mainichi Daily News, Annual Haiku Contest, HM 1985 (Japan). *Memberships:* Scotian Guild 1970; Laurel Symposium, Honorary Member, 1975; National Writers Club 1975–76. *Address:* 406 Elizabeth Street, Sault Ste Marie, Ontario, Canada P6B 3H4.

ST. JOHN, John, b. 7 Feb. 1917, Gillingham, Kent, England. Author. m. Diana Sinnott, 10 Oct. 1952, London, 1 son, 3 daughters. *Literary Appointments:* Editor & Director, William Heinemann Ltd, retired 1983. *Major Publications:* Roast Beef & Pickels, 1955; A Trick of the Sun, 1956; The Small Hours (with Diana St John), 1957; Surgeon at Arms (with Daniel Paul), 1958; Probation – The Second Chance, 1961; Alphabets & Reading (with James Pitman), 1969; To the War with Waugh, 1973; Travels in Inner Space, 1977; Religion & Social Justice, 1985. *Memberships:* Society of Authors; PEN. *Address:* 40 Arkwright Road, London NW3 6BH, England.

SAINT PHALLE, Thérèse de, b. 7 Mar. 1930, New York, USA. Novelist. m. Baron Jehan de Drouas, 30 Dec. 1950, Paris, 1 son. *Education:* Baccalauréat. *Literary Appointment:* Assistant General Manager, Stock Publisher, Paris. *Major Publications:* La Mendigote; La Chandelle; Le Tournesol; Le Souverain; La Clairière; Le Métronome, finishing Le Programme. *Contributor to:* Le Monde; Interventions; Psychologie; Lu. *Honours:* Works translated and published in USA, Great Britain, Spain, Italy, Germany, Denmark, Holland, Czechoslovakia, Japan and Roumania. *Memberships:* PEN Club; Associations des écrivains croyants d'expression Les amis d'Alexandre Dumas. *Literary Agent:* Gallimard Publishers, Paris, France. *Address:* 46 Boulevard Emile Augier, 75116 Paris, France.

SAINT PHALLE, Thibaut de, b. 23 July 1918, New York City, USA. International Consultant; Lawyer; Professor; Writer. (1) Rosamond Frame (deceased 1960); (2) Elene Cannobert (divorced 1983); (3) Mariana Mann, 4 sons, 5 daughters. *Education:* Harvard University, 1935–37; AB, 1939, JD, 1941, Columbia University. *Literary Appointments:* Professor, International Law and Finance, International Management Institute, 1971–76; Professor of International Economics and William Scholl Chair in International Business, Georgetown University, Washington, DC, 1981–83. *Publications:* The Dollar Crisis, 1963; Multinational Corporations (co-author); Trade Inflation and the Dollar, 1981 (Revised Edition, 1984); The Federal Reserve: An International Mystery, 1985. *Contributions to:* Euromoney; Business Week, Washington Post. *Literary Agent:* Scott Meredith, New York City. *Address:* 3227 Reservoir Street NW, Washington, DC 20007, USA.

SAINT-PIERRE, Paul, b. 23 Apr. 1920, Outremont, Quebec, Canada. Chartered Administrator. m. Yvonne Vautheir, 27 Sep. 1949, St Lambert, 2 sons, 1 daughter. *Education:* BA, College Jean-de-Brebeuf, Montreal; MBA, University of Montreal; MA, Fordham University, New York. *Literary Appointments:* Assistant Financial Editor, La Presse; Copywriter, J Walter Thompson Ltd; Editor, Le Bureau, Maclean Hunter Ltd. *Publications:* Le Pétrole au Vénézuela, 1946; Vocabulary of Office Terms, 1972; Lexique anglais-français des affaires, 1976. *Contributions to:* Magazines: Commerce; Le Temps; Le

Samedi; Bâtiment (editor 1972–73); Sono; Men's Wear; L'Homme et la Mode; Forêt et Papier (editor 1975–84). Chief, editorial services. Maclean-Hunter; Editor, Le Bureau, 1965–86. *Honours include:* 1st Award for best editorial, award for best technical report, Cercle de la Presse d'Affaires du Quebec, 1970; Kenneth R Wilson Memorial Award, Business Press Editors Associaiton, 1972, best professional article, 1972; Awards for best cover, best editorial, Association des Journalistes de la Press spécialisée du Québec, 1977, 1978, 1979. *Memberships:* President, Cercle de la Presse d'Affaires du Quebec, 1972; Director, Business Press Editors Association, 1974; President, Association des Journalistes de la Presse spécialisée, 1978. *Address:* 80 Lorne Avenue, Apr 508, St Lambert, Quebec, Canada J4P 3R6.

ST PIERRE, Paul, b. 14 Oct. 1923, Chicago, Illinois, USA. Television Scriptwriter; Former Editor, Politician, Police Commissioner. m. Melanie Ann McCarthy, 17 Nov. 1978, 1 son, 2 daughters from previous marriage. *Publications:* Boss of the Namko Drive, 1965; Breaking Smith's Quarter Horse, 1966; Sister Balonika, Play, 1969; Chilcotin Holiday (columns), 1970; British Columbia: Our Land, photographs, 1981; Smith and Other Events: Tales of the Chilcotin, 1983; Stageplays: How to Run the Country, 1967; Teleplays: The Education of Phylisteen; Antoine's Wooden Overcoat; How to Break a Quarter Horse; Kaleshnikoff; Cabin Fever; Justice on the Jawbone; The Strong People; All Indian; The White Mustang; The Window at Namko; Sarah's Copper; Hunt at Happy Ann, and others; Author, Scripts, Cariboo Country. *Contributor to:* Numerous magazines and journals; Author, Column, Vancouver Sun, 1965–68, 1972–79. *Honours:* Wilderness Award, CBC, 1966; Spur Award, WWA, 1985. *Address:* Box 911, Fort Langley, BC, Canada VOX 1J0.

SAINTE CROIX, Geoffrey Ernest Maurice de, b. 8 Feb. 1910, Macao, China. University teacher (retired), Ancient Historian. m. Margaret Knight, 3 Sep. 1959, Oxford, England, 2 sons. *Education:* BA, University College, London; DLitt, MA, Oxford University. *Publications:* Studies in the History of Accounting, (co-author), 1956; The Crucible of Christianity, (co-author), 1969; The Origins of the Peloponnesian War, 1972; Debits, Credits, Finance and Profits, (co-author), 1974; Studies in Ancient Society, (co-author), 1974; The Class Struggle in the Ancient Greek World, From the Archaic Age to the Arab Conquests, 1981, revised edition 1983. *Contributions to:* Scholarly journals. *Honour:* Honorary Fellow, New College, Oxford. *Memberships:* Association of University Teachers; Fellow, British Academy. *Address:* Evenlode, Stonesfield Lane, Charlbury, Oxford, OX7 3ER, England.

SALAFF, Janet W, b. 15 Dec. 1940, New York, USA. University Professor. m. Stephen Salaff, 6 Sep. 1964, 1 daughter. *Education:* BA, Sociology, 1963, MA, Sociology, 1966, PhD, Sociology, 1972, University of California, Berkeley. *Publications:* Working Daughters of Hong Kong: Female Filial Piety or Power in the Family, 1981; Lives: Chinese Working Women, edited with Mary Sheridan. *Contributions to:* Institutional Factors Affecting Fertility in the People's Republic of China, Population Studies, 1973. *Address:* 563 Spadina Avenue, Toronto, Ontario, Canada M5S 1A1.

SALAMAN, Raphael Arthur, b. 24 April, 1906, Barley, Hertfordshire, England. m. 11 May 1934, London, 1 son 3 daughters. *Education:* Emmanuel College, Cambridge, Engineering and Law. *Publications:* Dictionary of Woodworking Tools 1975; Dictionary of Leather-working Tools 1986; Tradesmen's Tools c. 1500–1850 a chapter in Vol III A History of Technology, 1954. *Contributions to:* Journal of the Tools And Trades Historical Society; Journal of the Early American Industries Association (USA); Journal of Folk Life; Journal of Physics (Italy). *Membership:* Society of Antiquaries; Newcomen Society. *Address:* 21 Kirkdale Road, Harpenden, Hertfordshire AL5 2PT, England.

SALCEDO, Ernesto Abao, b. 31 Jan. 1931, Balingasag, Mis Or Philippines. Writer; Novelist; Mediaman; Lecturer; Orator. m. Herminia Ocate, 8 Aug. 1963. *Literary Appointments:* Editor: The Reporter and Bulawan Magazine. Newswriter, GMA, TV-12. *Publications:* Hara Maginda, Comic novel, 1984. *Contributions to:* Various publications of short stories entitled: Valentines Day; The Thief; The Uniform; Underwater Fire; Ang Panudya; Unvaluable Money; Tahas; That First Good Friday; Santa Claus is Coming; Saudi Arabia; Kilumkilom; Ang Masinahon and others. *Honours:* Certificate of Appreciation, Literature, FISLA/DAVAO Savings and Land Bank of the Philippines. *Memberships:* Vice President, Oro LUDABI chapter, LUDABI Incorporated; Founder and President, BARKADA Incorporated. *Address:* Gumamela-Caimito Street, Carmen, Cagayan de oro City 8401, The Philippines.

SALE, Richard Townsend, b. 26 Mar. 1942, New York City, New York, USA. Journalist; Author. m. Haida Shapurian, Aug. 1967, Washington, District of Columbia, 1 son, 1 daughter. *Education:* Columbia College; BA History with Honours, Principia College. *Literary Appointments:* Reporter: Life Magazine, 1968–71; Iran and Middle East, Washington Post, 1976–78; State Department, Aerospace Daily, Washington, 1982–. Free lance Journalist, 1973–76; Editor and Publisher, The Courier, 1978–82. *Publications:* The Blackstone Rangers, 1872, 73; The Prudent Lion: Germany in tte 1980's, 1985. *Contributions to:* Life; Show; National Geographic; Washington Post; Dallas Times-Herald; National Public Radio; British Broadcasting Corporation, England; numerous other major publications including foreign policy journals such as: The Washington Quarterly of CSIS and John Hopkins SAIS Review. *Honours:* Nominated for short story O'Henry Award, Carolina Quarterly, 1964, 65. *Literary Agent:* Elizabeth Knappman, New England Publishers Incorporated. *Address:* 2123 California Street North West, Washington, DC 20008, USA.

SALES, Joan, b. 10 Nov. 1912, Barcelona, Spain. Writer; Publisher. m. Nuria Folch i Pi, 8 Feb. 1933, Barcelona, 1 daughter. *Education:* Lic Law. *Publications:* Viatge D'un Moribund, 1952; Incerta Gloria, 1956; En Tirant Lo Blanc A Grecia, 1972; El vont de la Mit, 1981; Cartes a Marius torres. *Contributions to:* Quaderns de l'Exili, Mexico, Editor, 1943–47; Full Catala, Mexico, 1941–42. *Honours:* Premi Joanot Martorell, 1955; Ramon Llull, 1968; Ciutat de Barcelona, 1970; Creu de S Jordi. *Address:* Mare de Deu del Pilar (Carmel) 2, 08032 Barcelona, Spain.

SALINGER, Pierre, b. 14 June 1925, San Francisco, California, USA. Journalist. m. Nicole Gillman, 3 sons, 1 daughter. *Education:* BS History, University of San Francisco, California. *Publications:* With Kennedy, 1966; On Instruction of my Government, 1971; Je suis un American, 1975; La France et le Nou veau Monde, 1976; American Held Hostage, 1981; Above Paris, with Robert Cameron, 1985; The Dossier, with Leonard Gross, 1984. *Contributions to:* L'Express, roving editor, 1973–78; 50 magazines and newspapers in USA, France, UK, Switzerland, Germany and Italy. *Honours:* Overseas Press Club Award, for best reporting with American Held Hostage, 1982. *Memberships:* President, Ritz Hemingway Award; Association des Francais en Amerique; President, Board of Trustees, American College, Paris. *Literary Agent:* Sterling Lord. *Address:* 22 avenue d'Eylau, 75116 Paris, France.

SALLAH, Tijan M, b. 6 Mar. 1958, Gambia. Economist. *Education:* BS Economis, BS Business Management, Berea College, USA, 1982; MA Economics, Economics Doctoral Candidate, Virginial Technical College. *Literary Appointments:* Literary editor, Silent Runner, Rabun Gap School, 1977; Africa representative, World Poetry Society. *Publications:* When Africa Was A Young Woman, poems, 1980; The Land Comes to Consciousness; Let My Continent Awake, poems; What Are Children For?, play. *Contributions to:* Atlanta Gazette; Africa Woman; Mountain Review; Cumberlands; Black Scholar; New African; Greenfield Review; Pegasus; Oconee Review; Poet; Obsidian; Callaloo; Linear B; Onyx; Wind Literary Journal; Social Science; Radio Gambia; BBC; Presence Africaine; West Africa, Ba Shiru; Ufahamu. *Honours include:* Dubois-Nyerere Award, Berea College, 1979; Francis S Hutchins Award in Literature, Berea College, 1980; D Litt, World Academy of Arts and Culture. *Memberships include:* President 1980, African Studies Association; Vice-President 1980, Tau Kappa Alpha chapter, Delta Sigma Rho, Berea College; World Poetry Society; Kentucky State Poetry Society; Poetry editor, Onyx, Berea Creative Writers; African Literary Association. *Address:* PO Box 124, Banjul, The Gambia, West Africa.

SALMONSON, Jessica Amanda, b. 6 Jan. 1950, Seattle, USA. Novelist; Anthologist. *Publications include:* Amazons I, 1979; Amazons II, 1981; Tomoe Gozen, 1980; The Golden Naginata, 1981; The Swordswoman, 1982; Heroic Visions, 1983; Thousand Shrine Warrior, 1984; Ou Lu Khen & the Beautiful Madwoman, 1985; Tales by Moonlight, 1985; Heroic Visions II, 1985; A Silver Thread of Madness, 1986; Innocent of Evil, 1984; etc. *Honour:* World Fantasy Award, 1980. *Memberships:* Horror & Occult Writers League; Science Fiction Writers of America. *Literary Agent:* Susan Cohen, Literistic, New York. *Address:* Box 20610, Seattle, WA 98102, USA.

SALOMONE, A William, b. 18 Aug. 1915, Italy. University Professor; Historian. m. Lina Palmer, 13 Sep. 1941, 1 daughter. *Education:* BA, La Salle College, Philadelphia, 1938; MA, 1940, PhD, 1943, University of Pennsylvania. *Literary Appointments:* Member, Editorial Board, The Journal of Modern History, 1965–68; Member, Editorial Board, The Italian Americana, 1972–; Member, Editorial Board, The Italian Quarterly, 1974–. Wilson Professor of European History, University of Rochester, New York, 1962–. *Publications:* Italian Democracy in the Making, University of Pennsylvania, 1945; L'Eta giolittiana, la Nouva Italia, 1949; Readings in 20th Century European History, co-editor, Appleton-Century-Crifts 1950; Italy in the Giolittian Era, University of Pennsylvania, 1960; Italy from the Risogimento to Fascism, Doubleday-Anchor 1970, David and Charles, England, 1971. *Contributions to:* Journal of Central European Affairs; The American Historical Review; The Italian Quarterly etc. Recent articles include: Momenti di storia, frammenti di ricordi, in Archivio Trimestrale, 1982; Introduction and article, Italian Antifascism in America, in A Varsori ed. L'antifascismo italiano negli Stati Uniti, 1984; Federalism and Centralism in Italian and American History: An Epilogue, in Regionalism and Centralization, 1985. *Honours:* Social Science Research Council Fellowships, 1942–43, 1955–56; Herbert Baxter Adams Prize in European History, American Historical Association, 1946; Guggenheim Fellowship 1951–52; Order of Merit of the Italian Republic, 1960; Citation for Distinguished Achievement, Society for Italian Historical Studies, 1967; Senior Fellowship, National Foundation for the Humanities, 1967–68; Symposia and Conferences held in his honour at University of Rochester, AHA Congress and Columbia University. *Memberships:* American Historical Association; Societa Dagli Storici Italiani; Renaissance Society of America; Society for Italian Historical Studies; Academy of Political Science.

SALTER, Owen Robert, b. 22 Nov. 1954, Melbourne, Australia; Editor; Writer. m. Jane Valerie Arnold, 11 Apr. 1981, Hawthorn, 1 son, 1 daughter. *Education:* BA; Diploma of Education. *Appointments:* Editor, On Being Magazine, 1977–. *Conributor to:* Staff Writing, On Being Magazine; Occasional contributor to specialist religious journals. *Address:* On Being Magazine, 2 Denham Street, Hawthorn, Victoria 3122, Australia.

SALVADORI, Max William, b. 16 June 1908, London. Teacher. m. Joyce Woodforde Pawle, Lilliput, Poole, 7 May 1934, 1 son, 1 daughter. *Education:* Licencié ès Sciences Sociales, University of Geneva, Switzerland, 1929; Dr. Sci. (Pol), University of Rome, Italy, 1930. *Academic Appointments:* Lecturer,

University of Geneva, 1937–39; Assistant Professor, St Lawrence University, Canton, New York, 1939–41; Professor, Social Science, Bennington College, Vermont, USA, 1945–62; Professor, History, Smith College, Northampton, Massachusetts, 1949–75. *Publications include:* La Colonisation Européene au Kenya, 1938; Problemi di Liberta, 1949; Resistenza ed Azione, 1951, rewritten as The Labour & The Wounds, 1958; The Rise of Modern Communism, 1952, 1953; Liberal Democracy, 1957, 1958; Locke & Liberty, 1959; Western Roots in Europe, 1961; A Pictorial History of the Italian People, 1972; Breve Storia della Resistenza Italiana, 1974; The Liberal Heresy, 1977; Numerous pamphlets, papers, book chapters, etc. *Contributions to:* Numerous journals. *Honours include:* Honorary Litt.D., American International College, 1959. *Address:* 36 Ward Avenue, Northampton, MA 01060, USA.

SALVAGE, Jane Elizabeth, b. 6 Aug. 1953, Brighton, England. Journalist and Nurse. *Education:* BA (Honours), English Literature, Newnham College, University of Cambridge, England, 1976; State Registered Nurse, 1979. *Literary Appointments:* Editorial Trainee, Nursing Mirror, News Editor, Features Editor, Nursing Times, Editor, Senior Nurse. *Major Publication:* The Politics of Nursing, Heinemann, London 1985. *Contributor to:* Nursing Mirror; Nursing Times; Senior Nurse; Nursing Standard; The Health Services; International Nursing Review; Marxism Today; and others. *Membership:* Medical Journalists' Association; Royal College of Nursing; National Union of Journalists. *Address:* 19 Brownlow Road, Hackney, London E8 4NS, England.

SAMBROOK, Arthur James, b. 5 Sep. 1931, England. University Teacher. m. Patience Ann Crawford, 25 Mar. 1961, Finchingfield, England. *Education:* BA 1955, MA 1959, Worcester College, Oxford; PhD, University of Nottingham, 1957. *Publications include:* A Poet Hidden: The Life of Richard Watson Dixon, 1833–1900, 1962; The Scribleriad 1742 & The Difference Between Verbal & Practical Virtue 1742, Editor, 1967; James Thomson's The Seasons & The Castle of Indolence, editor, 2nd edition 1984; William Cobbett, an author guide, 1973; Pre-Raphaelitism, critical essays, Editor, 1974; English Pastoral Poetry, 1983; etc; Editor, James Thomson's The Seasons, 1981; The Intellectual and Cultural Context of English Literature, 1700–1789; 1986; Editor, Liberty, The Castle of Indolence and Other Poems, 1986. *Contributions to:* Books: The Rosettis & Contemporary Poets in The Sphere History of Literature, 1970; Pope & the Visual Arts, in Alexander Pope, ed Peter Dixon, 1972; Biographical critical, bibliographical articles on various English writers in numerous reference books. Over 100 articles & Reviews in, Church Quarterly Review; 18th Century Life, 18th Century Studies; English; English Language Notes; Garden History; Journal of English & German Philology; Library; Modern Language Review; Times Literary Supplement; etc. *Address:* Department of English, Southampton University, England.

SAMPSON, Geoffrey Richard, b. 27 July 1944, Broxbourne, Hertfordshire, England. University Professor. m. Vera van Rijn, 1975, France, 2 daughters. *Education:* 1st class honours Chinese Studies, St John's College, Cambridge; MA, PhD, Cambridge; MA, Yale; MA, Oxford. *Publications:* The Form of Language, 1975; Liberty and Language, 1979; Making Sense, 1980; Schools of Linguistics, 1980; An End to Allegiance, 1984; Writing Systems, 1985. *Contributions to:* The Spectator; Times Literary Supplement; Free Life; Inquiry, San Francisco; Academic journals of linguistics, philosophy and political theory. *Honours:* Visiting Professor, University of Geneva, 1980–81; Visiting Professor, University of Cape Town, 1982. *Literary Agent:* A D Peters and Co Ltd. *Address:* Greenburn Laitre, Cowling Hill, near Keighley, Yorkshire BD22 OLP, England.

SAMS, Eric, b. 3 May 1926, London, England. Retired Civil Servant. m. Enid Mary Tidmarsh, 30 June 1952, London, 2 sons. *Education:* BA, 1950, PhD, 1970,

Cambridge University. *Publications:* Songs of Hugo Wolf, 1961; Songs of Robert Schumann, 1969; Songs of Brahms, 1972; Shakespeare's Lost Play: Edmund Ironside, 1986. *Contributions to:* Musical Times; Sunday Times; Times Literary Supplement; New Grove. *Address:* 32 Arundel Avenue, Sanderstead, Surrey CR2 8BB, England.

SANCHEZ DRAGO, Fernando, b. 2 Oct. 1936, Madrid, Spain. Writer. 1 son, 2 daughter. *Education:* Degrees, Romance Philology, Modern Languages, University Complutense, Madrid. *Publications:* Gárgoris y Habidis, (4 volumes), 1978 La Espana Magica, 1983; Eldorado, novel, 1984; Finisterre, travel book, 1984; Ideas para una nueva Politica Cultural, 1984; Las Fuentes Del Nino, (Novel), 1986. *Special Envoy to:* Japan, India, Germany, Indonesia, Kenya, Chile, Venezuela, Mexico. *Contributions:* Editor, Disidencais, cultural supplement; Comment & literary criticism to various journals including Diaro 16, Madrid. *Honour:* Premio Nacional de Literatura, 1979. *Memberships:* Press Association, Madrid; Official College of Doctors of Philosophy, Madrid. *Address:* Jesus del Valle 8, Madrid 28004, Spain.

SANCHEZ-PUIG, Maria, b. 27 Apr. 1940, Jarkov, USSR, Professor of Russian Language and Literature. *Education:* Lic Philol, Madrid University; Diploma, Geneva University; Dr Philol. *Publications:* Lecciones de Ruso (for Spanish speaking students), 3 volumes with cassettes, 1975; Textos Rusos (selection, adaptation, notes), 1985; Translations; Poesias en prosa by I Turguenev (with prologue), 1976; Historia de un Caballo by L Tolstoy (play), 1979; Los huevos fatales by M Bulgakov, 1986. *Contributor to:* Publication of International Association of Russian Language and Literature Teachers; Russki Yazyk za Rubezhom, 1986; Bulletin of the International Association Slavic Cultures, UNESCO. *Honour:* Gold Medal of International Association of Russian Language and Literature Teachers, 1985. *Address:* Castellana 159, 28046 Madrid, Spain.

SANDAUER, Artur, b. 14 Dec. 1913, Sambor, Poland. Writer; University Professor. m. Erna Rosenstein, 1956, 1 son, 1 daughter. *Education:* Doctor of Polish Literature, 1946, Professor 1963. *Literary Appointment:* Director, Warsaw Literary Weekly, 1948–49. *Publications:* The Death of the Liberal, short stories, 1946; Poets of Three Generations, essays on poetry, 1955; My Deviations, essays and polemics, 1956; 2,000 Years Later, 1956; About the Unity of Form and Contents, 1957; Without Reduced Tariff, 1959; Suicide of Mithridates, 1967; Lyrics and Logics, 1969; God, Satan, Messiah and...? 1977 translated into English 1981; Complete Critical Works, 1979; Translations of Greek, French, German and Russian poetry. *Contributions to:* Temps Modernes; Lettres Nouvelles; Diogene; Dialectics and Humanism and Polish literary weeklies; Odrodzenie; Kuznica; Kultura; Polityka. *Honour:* Laureate of the Polish Ministry of Culture, 1975. *Membership:* Polish Writers' Society. *Address:* Karlowicza 20/1, 02-552 Warsaw, Poland.

SANDBURG, Helga, b. 24 Nov. 1918, Maywood, Illinois, USA. Writer. *Publications:* Novels: The Wheel of Earth, 1958; Measure My Love, 1959; The Owl's Roost, 1962; The Wizard's Child, 1967. Non-Fiction: Sweet Music, 1963; Above and Below, with George Crile Junior, 1969; A Great and Glorious Romance: The Story of Carl Sandburg and Lilian Steichen, 1978. Poetry: The Unicorns, 1965; To A New Husband, 1970. Young Adult Novels: Blueberry, 1963; Gingerbread, 1964. Childrens Books: Joel and the Wild Goose, 1963; Bo and the Old Donkey, 1965; Anna and the Baby Buzzard, 1970. Short Story Collections: Children and Lovers: Fifteen Stories By Helga Sandburg, 1976. *Contributions to:* Numerous newspapers and magazines. *Honours:* Prize for Best Short Story, Virginia Quarterly Review, 1959; Borestone Mountain Poetry Award, 1962; Poetry Award, Chicago Tribune, 1970; All National Poetry Contest, Triton College, 1975, 76. *Memberships:* Poetry Society of America. *Address:* 2060 Kent Road, Cleveland Heights, OH 44106, USA.

SANDELIN, Carl Fredrik, b. 26 Nov. 1925, Jakobstad, Finland. Author; Journalist. m. Sirp Norri, 1 Sep. 1975, 1 son, 1 daughter, 4 children from 1st marriage. *Appointment:* Journalist, Executive, Finnish News Agency, 1953–84. *Publications:* Short stories, 1947; Novels, 1950, 1953, 1969, 1973, 1981, 1985; Collection of Poems, in Swedish, 1979. *Contributor to:* Book Reviews in Magazines and Newspapers in Finland. *Honours:* 1 Year State Scholarship for Authors, 1953; Recipient, various grants, 1969. *Memberships:* Secretary 1953–60, Chairman 1961–72, Honorary Member 1974, Finland's Swedish Authors Society. *Address:* 32730 Keikyä, Finland.

SANDERLIN, Owenita Harrah, b. 2 June 1916, Los Angeles, California, USA. Writer/Teacher. m. George William Sanderlin, Washington, 2 sons, 2 daughters. *Education:* BA, summa cum laude, The American University, 1937; Postgraduate, University of Maine, 1939–40; University of California, Santa Barbara, 1967; Teaching Certificate, San Diego State University, 1969; University of California, San Diego, 1974. *Literary Appointments:* Creative Writing Teacher, University of Maine, 1942–46; Maine Writers' Conference, 1945; Academy of Our Lady of Peace, San Diego, California, 1961–68. *Publications:* Jeanie O'Brien, 1965; Johnny, 1968, paperback 1967 and 1978; Creative Teaching, 1971; Teaching Gifted Children, 1973; Tennis Rebel, 1978; Match Point, 1979; Gifted Children: How to Identify and Teach Them, with Ruthe Lundy, 1979. *Contributor to:* Freelance writer 1941–, poems, stories and articles in Saturday Evening Post; Ladies' Home Journal; Parents; Catholic World; Catholic Digest; Readers Digest Reading Progress, short stories; The Writer; Writer's Digest; Seventeen; Jack and Jill; Irish Digest; Today's Family; Plays; Retirement; Living. *Honours:* Radcliffe Book Award for Outstanding Junior Girl, 1932; Alpha Chi Omega Poetry Award, 1936; Mortarboard, 1937; Double Ruby Award, National Forensic's League, 1966. *Address:* 997 Vista Grande Road, El Cajon, CA 92021, USA.

SANDERS, David John, b. 3 August 1930, Luton, England. Editor. m. Sheila Mary Ball, 21 June 1956, St Albans, 2 sons, 1 daughter. *Education:* Sir John Cass College, London; Extra Master's Certificate. *Literary Appointments:* Journal of Commerce and Shipping Telegraph, London Office 1960–61, Newcastle-upon-Tyne Office, 1960–63; Shipping & Shipbuilding Editor of Fairplay Shipping Journal, London, 1963–74; Founder Editor of Financial Times World Shipping Year Book, 1974–80; Editor, Seaways – The Journal of the Nautical Institute, 1980–. *Major Publications:* Going to Sea – The Merchant Navy, 2nd edition, 1977; Financial Times World Shipping Year Book (editor); Major Contributor to Financial Times International Year Books on Mining, Oil & Gas and World Insurance, 1983–85. *Contributor to:* Wirtschafts- Correspondent (Federal Republic of Germany), 1968–73; Navy, 1969–73; Navy Year Book, 1970–72; Maritime Survey, (annual) 1973–76; British Columbia Newsletter 1974–85. *Address:* 33 Laurel Close, Mepal, Ely, Cambridgeshire CB6 2BN, England.

SANDERS, Lewis, b. 22 May 1945, Parsons, Tennessee, USA. Writer; Publisher; Editor. *Appointments:* Publisher and editor of The Red Pagoda (a journal of Haiku). *Publications include:* Shadows on the Empty Road (a chapbook of Haiku) *Contributions to:* Frogpond; Dragonfly; East West Journal of Haiku; Virtual Image; Orphic Lute; Jean's Journal; Windchimes; Brussel Sprouts; Piedmont Literary Journal; Prophetic Voices; Mainichi Daily News; Newsletter of the American Association of Haikuists. *Memberships:* Haiku Society of America; Co-founder of the American Association of Haikuists. *Address:* 125 Taylor Street, Jackson, TN 38301, USA.

SANDERS, Ronald, b. 7 July 1932, New Jersey, USA. Writer. m. Beverly Helen Gingold, 19 Mar. 1967, Great Neck, New York. *Education:* BA, Kenyon College, Ohio, 1954; MA, Columbia University, 1957. *Literary Appointments:* Associate Editor 1965–73, Editor 1973–75,

Midstream, magazine. *Publications:* The Downtown Jews, 1969; Reflections on a Teapot, 1972; Los Tribes and Promised Lands, 1978; The Days Grow Short: The Life and Music of Kurt Weill, 1980; The High Walls of Jerusalem, 1984. *Contributions to:* Magazines and journals including: The New York Times; New Republic; Washington Post; Commentary; Nation; New Leader; Commonweal. *Honours:* Fulbright Fellowship, Paris, 1960–61; B'Nai B'Rith Book Award, 1970. *Membership:* PEN Club. *Literary Agent:* Georges Borchardt, New York City. *Address:* 49 West 12th Street, New York, NY 10011, USA.

SANDFORD, Cedric Thomas, 21 Nov. 1924, Basingstoke, Hampshire, England. University Professor. m. (1) Evelyn Belch, 1 Dec. 1945 (Deceased 19 Mar. 1982), 1 son, 1 daughter. (2) Christina Katarin Privett, 21 July 1984. *Education:* BA Honours, MA, Economics, Manchester University; BA Honours History, London University. *Publications:* Economies of Public Finance, 1969; Taxing Personal Wealth, 1971; Hidden Costs of Taxation, 1973; An Accessions Tax (co-author), 1973; An Annual Wealth Tax, (co-author), 1975; Social Economics, 1977; Costs and Benefits of VAT, (co-author), 1981; Tax Policy – Making in the United Kingdom, (co-author), 1983; The Irish Wealth Tax: A Case Study in Economics and Politics, (co-author), 1985. *Contributions to:* Journals including: Accountancy; British Tax Review; Financial Times. *Membership:* President, Economics Association, 1983–. *Literary Agent:* A D Peters. *Address:* Old Coach House, Fersfield, Perrymead, Bath, Avon, BA2 5AR, England.

SANDLER, Corey, b. New York, USA. Writer. m. Janice Keefe, 3 May 1982, Half Moon, 1 son. *Education:* BS, Journalism, Graduate studies, Syracuse University. *Publications:* Desktop Graphics for the IBM PC, 1984; Guide to the IBM PC-AT, 1985; Telecommunications for the Business User, 1985. *Contributor to:* PC Week; PC Magazine; PCjr Magazine; Creative Computing; Smart Living; Publishers Weekly; PC Technical Journal; etc. *Literary Agent:* Dominick Abel, New York. *Address:* 22 Pelham Ave, Nanuet, NY 10954, USA.

SANDRICK, Karen Marie, b. 21 Mar. 1944, Whiting, Indiana, USA. Writer. m. Michael J Foley, 15 Mar. 1975, Chicago. *Education:* BS, Biology, Loyola University. *Literary Appointment:* Media Consultant, American College of Surgeons. *Publications include:* Co-author: Care Communications ADRG & Prospective Pricing Action Plan for Social Work, 1984; Care Communications for Rehabilitation Services, 1984. Editor: Home Pharmacy, 1979; The Vitamin Book, 1979; Caring for Your Child, 1979; Measuring & Improving Productivity, 1982; QA Agenda Planner, 1982. *Contributions to:* Woman Magazine; Senior Writer; Private Practice; Regular contributor, American Medical News; Hospitals; Multis; Trustee; Quality Review Bulletin; The Coordinator; Health Industry Yellow Pages. *Memberships:* American Medical Writers Association; National Writers Club; Council of Biology Editors. *Address:* 1242 Henderson, Chicago, IL 60657, USA.

SANDRY, Ellen Sue, b. 29 Nov. 1945, Bronx, New York, USA. Teacher. *Education:* BA (Psychology), Hunter College, New York, USA; MSc (Education), Yeshiva University, New York. *Literary Appointment:* Regular Columnist in Sovereign Gold Literary Magazine. *Major Publications:* Porpoises and Purposes, 1981; A is for Aardvark, 1982; Tamarins and Tetons, 1983; Nature's Nonconformists, 1984; Wildlife only please, 1985. *Contributor to:* Some 20 journals, including: Inky Trails; Modern Images; Sovereign Gold; Amateur Writer's Journal; Poetic Moods Quarterly; Parnassus. *Honours:* Inky Trails Book of the Year Award, 1981; other awards from Amateur Writer's Journal and Hoosier Challenger Magazine. *Address:* 2481 S W 82nd Avenue (Apt 204), Fort Lauderdale, FL 33324, USA.

SANDY, Stephen, b. 2 Aug. 1934, Minneapolis, Minnesota, USA. Writer; University Teacher. m. Virginia Scoville, 11 Oct. 1971, New York, 1 son, 1 daughter.

Education: BA, Yale University, 1955; MA, Harvard University, 1958; PhD, Harvard University, 1963. *Literary Appointments include:* Chautauqua Institution, Poetry Workshop, Director, 1975, 1977; Johnson State College, Green Mountains Workshop, Poetry Director, 1976, 1977; Bennington Writing Workshop, Poetry Workshop Founder and Director, 1978–80; Wesleyan University Writers Conference, Poetry Director, 1981; Bennington College, Member of Literature Faculty 1969–, Member of Faculty with Tenure, 1975–. *Publications:* Riding to Greylock, 1983; The Raveling of the Novel, Studies in Romantic Fiction from Walpole to Scott, 1980; Roofs, 1971; Stresses in the Peaceable Kingdom, 1967. *Contributions to:* Numerous studies, Notices and Reviews in Michigan Quarterly Review; The Yale Review; Salmagundi; The Berkshire Eagle; The Virgina Quarterly Review; The New Leader; The New York Times Book Review; The Harvard Advocate; The Providence Journal-Bulletin; Booklist (American Library Association); Publishers Weekly; American Literary Scholarship etc. *Honours:* Ingram Merril Foundation, 1985; Vermont Council on the Arts Fellowship, 1974; Huber Foundation Fellowship, 1973; Fulbright Teaching Fellowship, Toyko, Japan, 1967–68; Dexter Fellowship (Harvard University), 1961. *Address:* Box 524, North Bennington, VT 05257, USA.

SANDYS, Elspeth Sandilands, b. 18 Mar. 1940, Timaru, New Zealand. Writer. 1 son, 1 daughter. *Education:* MA, Auckland, New Zealand; LTCL (Music); FTCL (Speech, Drama). *Publications:* Catch a Falling Star, 1978; The Broken Tree, 1981; Love and War, 1982. *Contributions to:* Landfall, New Zealand; PEN, England; Writer, Numerous radio plays, BBC. *Membership:* Writers Guild. *Literary Agent:* Deborah Rogers, Stephen Burbridge, London. *Address:* 31 West Street, Osney, Oxford OX2 0BQ, England.

SANFORD, Geraldine Agnes Jones, b. 1 Aug, 1928, Sious Falls, USA. Teacher. m. Dayton M Sanford, 28 Aug, 1948, Sioux Falls, 4 sons, 1 daughter. *Education:* BA, English, Psychology, Augustana College, 1971; MA, English, University of South Dakota, 1977. *Appointments:* University of Minnesota, 1979–82; University of South Dakota, Spring 1979, Spring 1978, 1975–77; Editorial Assistant, South Dakota Review, 1983–. *Publications:* Four Poems, Spirits from Clay, 1982; Alex, in Horizons: The South Dakota Writers Anthology, 1983. *Contributor to:* Various Magazines, Journals and Newspapers. *Honours:* Graduate Poetry Contest Award, University of South Dakota, 1976; Gladys Haase Poetry Prize, University of South Dakota, 1977; Outstanding English Graduate Student, 1977. *Memberships:* Poets and Writers. *Address:* 306 West 36th Street, Number 25, Sioux Falls, SD 57105, USA.

SANGER, Marjory Bartlett, b. 11 Feb. 1920, Maryland, USA. Writer. *Education:* BA, Wellesley College. *Literary Appointments:* Founder, Rollins College Writers Conference, 1964; Lecturer, Rollins College, Winter Park, Florida. *Publications:* The Bird Watchers, 1957; Greenwood Summer, 1958l Mangrove Island, 1963l Cypress Country, 1965; World of the Great White Heron, 1967; Checkerback's Journey, 1968; Billy Bartram, 1972; Escoffier, 1976; Forest in the Sand, 1983. *Contributions to:* Book Reviews: Audubon Magazine; Florida Historical Quarterly. Class notes, Wellesley Magazine. Column, Focus on Food for local newspapers. *Honours:* Jacqueline Award in English, 1942; Charlton Tebeau Award, Florida Historical Society; Award, American and Local History Association. *Address:* P O Box 957, Winter Park, FL 32790, USA.

SANGUINETI, Edoardo, b. 9 Dec. 1930, Genoa, Italy. Former Professor of Italian Literature. m. Luciana Garabello, 30 Sep. 1954, Turin, 3 sons, 1 daughter. *Education:* BA, University of Turin, 1956. *Publications:* Poems: Laborintus, 1956; Opus Metricum, 1960; Triperuno, 1964; Wirrwarr, 1972; Catamerone, 1974; Postkarten, 1978; Stracciafoglio, 1980; Scartabello, 1981; Segnalibro, 1982; Novels: Capriccio Italiano, 1963; Il Guioco dell'Oca, 1967; Theatre: Teatro, 1969;

Storie Naturali, 1971; Faust, un Travestimento, 1985; Essays: Interpretazione di Malebolge, 1961; Tre Studi Danteschi, 1961; Tra Liberty e Crepuscolarismo, 1961; Alberto Moravia, 1961; Ideologia e Linguaggio, 1965; Il Realismo di Dante, 1966; Guido Gozzano, 1966; Poesia Italiana del Novecento, 1969; Giornalino, 1976; Giornalino Secondo, 1979; Scrinnilli, 1985; Translations: La Baccanti di Eurpide, 1968; Fedra di seneca, 1969; Le Troiane di Euripde, 1974; Le Coefore di eshilo, 1978; Edipo Tiranno di Sofocle, 1980. *Address:* Via Pergolesi 20, 16159 Genova, Italy.

SANN, Paul, b. 7 Mar. 1914, Brooklyn, New York, USA. Editor; Author. m. Bertha Pullman, 28 Aug. 1934, Bronx, New York, 1 son, 1 daughter. *Literary Appointment:* Executive editor, New York Post, 1949–77. *Publications:* Pictorial History of the Wild West, (with James D Horan), 1954; The Lawless Decade, 1957; Red Auerbach: Winning The Hard Way, (with Arnold Red Auerbach), 1967; Fads, Follies and Delusions of the American People, 1967; Kill the Dutchman! The Story of Dutch Schultz, 1971; Dead Heat: Love and Money, 1974; The Angry Decade: The Sixties, 1979; American Panorama, 1980; Trial in the Upper Room, 1981. *Contributions to:* Anthologies: A Century of Journalism, 1943; More Post Biographies, 1947; These Were Our Years, 1959; Ain't We Got Fun, 1980; Magazines and journals including: Reader's Digest; Saturday Evening Post; Nation. *Membership:* Authors Guild. *Literary Agent:* Carl D Brandt, Brandt and Brandt, New York City. *Address:* 12 Springbrook Avenue, Rhinebeck, NY 12572, USA.

SANT, Andrew John, b. 16 Sep. 1950, London, England. Writer; Editor. 2 daughters. *Education:* BA. *Appointment:* Editor, Island Magazine, 1979–; Writer-in-Residence, University of Adelaide, 1985. *Publications:* Lives, 1980; The Caught Sky, 1982; The Flower Industry, 1985. *Contributor to:* The Age Monthly Review; The Age; The Australian; The Bulletin; Meanjin; Quadrant; Southerly; Poetry; Australia; Overland; Westerly; The Australian Broadcasting Corporation, etc; Criticism: Helix; The Age Monthly Review; Australian Book Review; etc. *Honours:* 2 Grants, and 1 Fellowship, Literature Board of the Australia Council, 1981–85. *Address:* 4 Davenport Street, Glebe, Tasmania, Australia.

SANTARRITA, Marcos Antonio, b. 16 Apr. 1941, Sergipe, Brazil. Journalist. Separated, 1 son. *Education:* Social sciences studies, Philosophy College, Bahia State University. *Publications:* Novels: Danacao dos Justos, 1977; A Solidao do Caveleiro no Horizonte, 1979; A Juventude Passa, 1983; Lady Luana savage, 1985. A Solidao dos Homens, short stories, 1986. Numerous Translations from English, French, Spanish and Italian works including books by Joseph Conrad, Charlotte Bronte, Standhal, Carson McCullers, Raymond Chandler, Dashiel Hammet and Ira Levin. *Contributions to:* Jornal da Bahia; A Tarde; Diario de Notocias; Revista da Bahia; Jornal do Brasil; Corrieo da manha; O Globo; Jornal do Comercio; Cadernos Brasileiros; Leitura; Isto E; Folha de San Paulo. *Membership:* Sindicato dos Escriteroes do Rio de Janeiro. *Literary Agent:* Carmen Balcells, Barcelona, Spain. *Address:* Rua Nascimento Silva 284/101, 22421 Ipanema, Rio de Janeiro, Brazil.

SANTOS, Jose Abel Royo dos, b. 29 Nov. 1938, Itajuba, Brazil. University Professor. *Education:* Electrical and Mechanical Engineer, Itajuba Federal Institute of Technology, 1961; MSc, Electrical Engineering, Federal University of Rio de Janeiro, 1968; Doctor, Itajuba Federal Institute of Technology, 1974. *Publications:* Computacao Analogiea, 1974; Minicalculadoras Electronicas, 2nd edition, 1979; Processamento de Dados, 1980; Microcomputadores e Minicalculadoras, 1982. *Contributions to:* Various magazines. *Memberships include:* Itajuba Literary Academy, Brazil; Institute of Electrical and Electronic Engineers, USA; American Society of Engineering Education. *Address:* Rua Silverstre Ferraz 361, 37500 Itajuba MG, Brazil.

SANTSCHI-ROTH, Suzanne, b. 26 Sep. 1936, Basle, Switzerland. Writer. m. Albert Santschi-Roth, 10 Apr. 1954, La Réchesse, Jura, 2 sons, 4 daughters. *Publications:* Lettres à Maman, 1970; Une Graine de Malheur, 1974; Le Chant du Noisetier, poems, 1976; Marie de mes Douleurs, poems, 1978; Le Livre de la Bonté, poetic essay, 1982; Italie-Porrentruy Aller-retour, novel, 1983; L'Homme et l'Arbre un Jour..., poems, 1985. *Contributions to:* Le Pays, regional newspaper, articles, poetry. *Honours:* Premier Prix des Poètes Suisses de Langue Française, 1976; 2nd Prize, Jeux Floraux Académie Provençale, Tarascon, France, 1976; Médaille d'Argent, Académie de Lutèce, Paris, 1979, 1983; 2nd Prize, Jeux Floraux Académie, 1985. *Memberships:* Society of Swiss Writers; Association des Ecrivains Paysans de France. *Literary Agent:* Jean-Michel Queloz, 2900 Porrentruy, Switzerland. *Address:* Editions du Faubourg, 2900 Porrentruy, Switzerland.

SAPERGIA, Barbara, b. 15 May, 1943, Saskatchewan, Canada. Writer. m. Geoffrey Ursell, 8 July 1967, Sasketchewan, Canada. *Education:* BA, University of Sasketchewan; MA, University of Manitoba. *Literary Appointments:* Playwright-in-Residence, Persephone Theatre, Saskatoon, Saskatchewan. *Publications:* Dirt Hills Mirage (poetry), 1980; Lokkinen (play), 1984; Foreigners (novel), 1984. *Contributions to:* Poems; Grain; Newest Review; Salt; Short Fiction: Journal of Canadian Fiction; Canadian Ethnic Studies. *Honours:* Major Award for Drama, Saskatchewan Writers Guild, 1985. *Memberships:* Playwrights Union of Canada; Saskatchewan Writers Guild; ACTRA. *Address:* c/o Persephone Theatre, 2802 Rusholme Road, Saskatoon, Saskatchewan, Canada S7L 0H2.

SAPPOR, Josephine Adjoh, b. 16 Nov. 1936, Lagos, Nigeria, (Ghanaian). Journalist. *Education:* Ghana Institute of Journalism, 1960–62; Diploma in Journalism, Ghana, 1962; Advanced course in Journalism, Federal Republic of Germany, 1963–64; various courses, German Democratic Republic News Agency and Reuters Library, 1974. *Literary Appointments:* Staff reporter, 1962–64, Sub-editor, 1964–68, Chief Sub-editor, 1968–72, Editor, 1972–76. Senior Editor, 1977–84, Chief Editor, 1984–, Ghana News Agency, Accra, Ghana. *Publications:* Ghana News Agency Information Classification List, 1974; Ghana Assembly of Women Leadership Training Manual, co-Editor; Ghanaian Women, Quarterly magazine, co-Editor. *Contributions to:* Ghanaian newspapers on topic of womens issues, 1960–; Columnist, West German newspaper, 1963, Ruhr Nachrichten. *Honours:* Scholarship to study journalism, Federal Republic of Germany, sponsored by Fredrich-Ebert Foundation, 1963–64; Guest, Canadian Women Press Club, 1967; International Visitor, US Information Agency, 1963; United Nations Fellowship to Womens Decade Conference, Nairobi, Kenya, 1985. *Memberships:* Ghana Journalists Association; Vice President, Association of Women in the Media, Ghana. *Address:* P O Box 9289, Airport, Accra, Ghana.

SARGEANT Winthrop, b. 10 Dec. 1903, San Francisco, USA. Writer. m. Jane Sargeant, 22 Dec. 1955, Laredo, Texas. *Appointments:* Time Magazine, 1930; Life Magazine, 1945; The New Yorker, 1955. *Publications:* Geniuses, Godesses and People, 1940; Divas, 1949; In Spite of Myself, 1960; Jazz: Hot & Hybrid, 1975; The Bhagauad Gita, translated from the Sanskrit, 1979. *Contributor to:* Countless journals. *Membership:* Century Club. *Address:* Box 755, Salisbury, CT 06068, USA.

SARGENT, Colin Wendell, b. 5 Nov. 1954, Portland, Maine, USA. Poet; Editor. m. Nancy Davis, 22 Nov. 1980, Annapolis, Maryland, USA, 1 son. *Education:* BS English, US Naval Academy, Annapolis, Maryland, 1977. *Literary Appointments:* Editor, Approach magazine, U S Navy's monthly flying magazine, 1981–83; Associate Editor, Flight Crew, New York; Editor, Greater Portland magazine, 1983–. *Publications:* Luftwaffe Snowshoes, poetry, 1984; Blush, 1985. *Contributions include:* Poet Lore; Samisdat; Gargoyle; Dog River Review; US Naval Institute Proceedings; Maine Sunday Telegram; Maine Times; Approach; Port Folio; Greater Portland; Flight Crew; Brunswick Times Record; Window; Taurus. *Honours:* Academy of American Poets Prize, US Naval Academy, 1976; Open Poetry Prize, Virginia Poetry Society, 1983; Naval Achievement Medal for Approach, 1983; National Endowment Grant Funds for Luftwaffe Snowshoes, 1984. *Memberships:* Board of Directors, Maine Writers and Publishers Alliance, 1984–; Writer's Center; COSMEP; Director, MWPA. *Address:* Greater Portland Magazine, 142 Free Street, Portland, ME 04101, USA.

SARGENT, Lyman Tower, b. 9 Feb. 1940, Rehoboth, Massachusetts, USA. University Professor. m. (1) Patricia McGinnis, 27 Dec 1961, Minneapolis, Minnesota, (divorced 1969), 1 son, (2) Mary T Weiler, 14 Aug. 1985, St Louis, Missouri. *Education:* BA, Macalester College, 1961; MA, 1962, PhD, 1965, University of Minnesota. *Literary Appointments:* Instructor, University of Wyoming, 1964–65; Assistant Professor, 1965–70, Associate Professor, 1970–75, Professor, 1975–, University of Missouri – St Louis; Visiting Professor, Department of Politics, University of Exeter, England, 1978–79; 1983–84; Member, School of Historical Study, Institute for Advanced Study, Princeton, New Jersey, 1981–82; Visiting Professor, Department of Government, London School of Economics and Political Science, 1985–86. *Publications:* Contemporary Political Ideologies: A Comparative Analysis, 1969; Revised edition 1972, 1975, 1978, 1981, 1984; Techniques of Political Analysis: An Introduction (with Thomas A Zant) 1970; New Left Thought: An Introduction, 1972; British and American Utopian Literature 1516–1975. An Annotated Bibliography, 1979; Editor: IVR Northam IV Consent: Concept, Capacity, Conditions, Constraints 1979. *Contributor to:* Minnesota Review; Minus One; Anarchy; Annals of Iowa; Futurist; Comparative Literature Studies; Political Theory; Extrapolation; Journal of General Education; Science-Fiction Studies; Nomos; Personalist; Polity; History of Political Thought; The Wellsian; Archiv fur Rechts-und Sozialphilosophie. *Honours:* Phi Kappa Delta; De Witt Wallace Graduate Fellowship 1961–62; Fellow, Wilton Park, England, 1972; Member, School of Historical Studies, Institute for Advanced Study, 1981–82.*Memberships include:* American, Canadian and International Political Science Association; Political Studies Association of the United Kingdom; American Association of University Professors; Association of Members of the Institute for Advanced Study. *Address:* Department of Political Science, University of Missouri–St Louis, 8001 Natural Bridge Road, St Louis, MO 63121, USA.

SARJEANT, William Antony Swithin, b. 15 July 1935, Sheffield, England. Professor of Geological Sciences. m. (2) Ann Margaret Crowe, 4 Apr. 1966, Leeds, 3 daughters. *Education:* BSc, Honours, PhD, 1959, Sheffield University; DSc, University of Nottingham, 1972. *Literary Appointments:* 1st Editor, The Sorby Record, Sorby Natural History Society, Sheffield, 1958–59; Editor, Darts, University of Sheffield, 1956–59; Founder and 1st Editor, Mercian Geologist, 1964–70; Board of Directors, Micropaleontology Press, 1981–84; Editorial Boards, Geoscience Canada and Modern Geology, 1984–. *Publications:* Fossil and Living Dinaflagellates, 1974; Geologists and the History of Geology: An International Bibliography, from the origins to 1978, 1980. Editor: Terrestrial Trace Fossils, 1983. Co-Author: Palynology I Spores and Pollen, 1977; Palynology II, Dinaflagellates, arcitarchs and other microfossils, 1977; Saskatoon: A Century in Pictures. Co-editor: History of Concepts in Precambrian Geology, 1979. *Contributions to:* 206 academic articles, 12 translations, 8 poems and songs; 41 book reviews, 16 essays, 11 historical and environmental publications, 23 folk music articles, 16 articles on detective fiction and 110 newspaper articles. *Address:* Department of Geological Sciences, University of Saskatchewan, Saskatoon, Saskatchewan, Canada S7N 0W0.

SARNAT, Marshall, b. 1 Aug. 1929, Chicago, USA. University Professor. m. Carmela Shenker, 17 Jan. 1956,

Israel, 2 sons, 1 daughter. *Education:* BA, Hebrew University, Jerusalem; MBA, PhD, Northwestern University, USA. *Publications:* Inflation and Capital Markets, 1978; International Finance and Trade, 1979; Capital Investments and Financial Decisions, (with H Levy) 1982; Portfolio and Investment Selection, (with H Levy) 1984. *Contributions to:* American Economic Review; Journal of Finance. *Address:* Nayot 34, Jerusalem, Israel.

SARNO, Ronald Anthony, b. 26 Sep. 1941, Jersey City, USA. Professional Fund Raiser. m. Una McGinley, 26 July 1975, New York, 1 daughter. *Education:* AB, MA, Boston College; M Divinity, Woodstock College; PhD, New York University. *Publications:* Achieving Sexual Maturity, 1969; Let Us Proclaim the Mystery of Faith, 1970; The Story of Hope, 1972; Liturgical Handbook for CLC's (with Stan Gogol), 1974; The Cruel Caesars, 1975; Morality: How to Live it Today, (with Len Badia), 1979; Modern Communication and Religious Education: Theory and Practice, 1986; Modern Communication Theory and Catholic Religious Education, 1950–1980, (PhD Thesis), 1984. *Contributions to:* Clergy Review; Chicago Studies; Bible Today; Classical Bulletin; Annals of Science; Messenger; Sign; The Priest; NJ News; and others. *Honours:* IPA Previews Speaker at National Convention, 1973. *Address:* 52 Charles Street, Little Ferry, NJ 07643, USA.

SARNOFF, Dorothy, b. New York City, USA. Chairman, Speech Dynamics Inc, an Ogilvy & Mather Co, Speech and Image Consultant. m. Milton H Raymond, 15 Mar. 1957. *Education:* BA, Public Speaking and Drama, Cornell University. *Publications:* Speech Can Change Your Life; Make the Most of Your Best; Never Be Nervous Again, (Crown) to be published, 1986. *Contributor to:* Numerous magazines and journals. *Honour:* Woman of Achievment Award, Albert Einstein Medical College. *Membership:* Authors' Guild. *Address:* Speech Dynamics Inc, 111 West 57th Street, New York, NY 10019, USA.

SAROYAN, Aram, b. 25 Sep. 1943, New York City, New York, USA. Writer. m. Gailyn McClanahan 9 Oct. 1968, New York City, 1 son, 2 daughters. *Education:* University of Chicago, Illinois; New York and Columbia Universities, New York. *Publications:* Aram Saroyan, 1968; Pages, 1969; Words and Photographs, 1970; The Street: An Autobiographical Novel, 1974; Genisis Angels: The Saga of Lew Welch and the Beat Generation, 1979; Last Rites: The Death of William Saroyen, 1982; Trio: Portrait of an Intimate Friendship, 1985. *Contributions to:* The New York Times Book Review; The Nation; The Village Voice; Mother Jones; Paris Review. *Honour:* Poetry Award, National Endowment for the Arts, 1967, 68. *Membership:* Authors Guild. *Literary Agent:* Erica Spellman, William Morris Agency. *Address:* 26 Stonecrest Road, Ridgefield, CT 06877, USA.

SARRAUTE, Nathalie, b. 18 July 1900, Ivanowo, Russia. Writer. *Education:* Sorbonne; Parish School of Law; Oxford University, England. *Publications include:* Tropismes, 1939; Tropisms, England, 1964; Portrait d'un Inconnu, 1948, England 1959; Martereau, 1953, England, 1964; Le Planetarium, 1959, England, 1962; Les Fruits d'Or, 1963, England, 1965; Entre la Vie & la Mort, 1968, England, 1969; (Plays) Le Silence, Le Mensonge, 1967, England, 1969; Isma, 1970; Vous Les Entendez?, 1972, England, 1972; C'est beau, 1973; Fools Say, 1976; The Age of Suspicion, 1956; Theatre, 1979; L'usage de la parole, 1980, England, 1983; Enfance, 1983, England, 1984; Pour un oui ou pousun nom, 1982. *Honour:* Recipient, Prix International de Literature, 1964. *Address:* 12 Ave Pierre I de Serbie, Paris 16, France.

SARRI, Margareta Irja, b. Lo Dce. 1944, Stockholm. Author. m. Nils Sarri, 13 Apr. 1968, (div. 1979), 1 son, 2 daughters. *Education:* BA, University of Stockholm, 1983. *Publications:* (novels) Då Simon Fjallborg m. fl. kom till insikt, (When Simon Fjallberg Among with others Arrived at the Truth), 1971; Man Borde Hänga sig i en Tall (Hang Myself Now), 1972; Ta dej en slav, (Slave Trade), 1975; Mor ror, åran är trasig, (Jill went up the hill, there's a hole in the Pail), 1978; Under Hallonträdet, (Under the Raspberry Tree), 1980; Du fjällhöga Nord, (Mountainous North) 1983; Konfetti, (Confetti), 1986. *Honours:* Northlandic Society of Authors, 1977; The County of Norrbotten, 1981; The County of Uppsala, 1983; Uppsala Municipality, 1984. *Memberships:* Swedish Union of Authors; Northlandic Society of Authors. *Address:* Apelsinv 46, S–74100 Knivsta, Sweden.

SARRI, Rosemary C, b. 13 Sep. 1926, St Paul, Minnesota, USA. Professor. m. Romilos Sarri, 6 Sep. 1961, Faribault, 2 daughters. *Education:* BA, 1946, MSW, 1955, University of Minnesota; PhD, University of Michigan, 1962; Honorary DHL, Western Maryland College, 1981. *Publications:* The School and the Community, 1972; Individual Change Through Small Groups, 1974; Under Lock and Key, 1974; Brought to Justice: Juveniles, The Court and the Law, 1976; The Management of Human Services, 1978; Issues in the Evaluation of Human Services, 1980; Disruptive Youth in School, 1980; Women in Prison in Michigan 1968–78, 1981. *Contributions to:* Crime and Delinquency; Child Welfare; Administration in Social Work; Signs; numerous others. *Honours:* Honorary DHL, 1981; Fulbright Senior Scholar, Australia, 1977–78; Distinguished Faculty Achievement Award, University of Michigan, 1984. *Address:* 2730 Daleview Drive, Ann Arbor, MI 48103, USA.

SARTON, May, b. 3 May. 1912, Wondelgem, Belgium. Writer. *Literary Appointments include:* Danforth Visiting Lecturer, College Arts Programme, 1960–61; Lecturer, Creative Writing, Wellesley College, 1960–64; Poet-in-Residence, Lindenwood College, 1965; Writer-in-Residence, Colby College, 1982. *Publications include:* Encounter in April, 1937; The Inner Landscape, 1939; The Lion & the Rose, 1948; A Shower of Summer Days, 1952; Faithful Are the Wounds, 1955; I Knew a Phoenix, 1959; Joanna & Ulysses, 1963; A Private Mythology, 1966; Plant Dreaming Deep, 1968; A Grain of Mustard Seed, 1971; AS We Are Now: Journal of a Solitide, 1973; Crucial Conversations, 1975; The House by the Sea, 1977; Halfway to Silence, 1980; A Winter Garland, 1982; At Seventy, 1984; The Magnificent Spinster, 1985; etc. *Contributions:* Verse & prose to numerous periodicals including: Atlantic Monthly; Beloit Poetry Hournal; Family Circle; Harpers; Kenyon Review; New York Times Book Review; Transatlantic Review; Vogue; Yale Literary Magazine; etc. *Honours include:* Edward Bland Memorial Prize for Poetry, 1945; Golden Rose, New England Poetry Society, 1945; Honorary Doctorates, various universities & colleges, 1959–; Human Dignity Award, 1984; American Book Award, 1985; etc. *Memberships:* Fellow, American Academy of Arts & Sciences, 1958–; Academy of American Poets. *Literary Agents:* A M Heath & Company, London, UK; Russell & Volkening, New York City. *Address:* Box 99, York, ME 03909, USA.

SARTORI, Eva Maria, b. Subotica, Yugoslavia. Nationality British. Author. *Education:* Academy of Dramatic Art, Dresden. *Publications:* Pierre, mon amour, 1967; Wie eine Palme im Wind, 1968; Oh, diese Erbschaft, 1969; Karriere ist Silber: Heiraten Gold, 1977; Die Rheinhagens, 1980; Damals in Dahlem, 1982; Streite nicht mit dem Wind, 1985. *Contributions to:* Neie Welt; die Aktuelle; Frau Aktuell; Sieben tage; Frau mit Herz; Frau im Spiegel, Neies Blatt; TV Sehen & Hören; Bella; Echo der Frau; etc. *Honour:* DLitt, World University, USA. *Membership:* Freier Deutscher Autorenverband, München. *Literary Agent:* Grit Peters, D–2161 Estorf. *Address:* Berliner Platz 3, D–8263 Burghausen, Federal Republic of Germany.

SARTORI, Franco, b. 30 Dec. 1922, Crocetta del Montello, Italy. University Professor of Ancient History. *Education:* Degree in Literature, University of Padua, 1947. *Publications include:* Problemi di storia costituzionale italiota, 1953; Platone, Republica,

1970; Una pagina di storia ateniese in un frammento dei Demi eupolidei, 1975. *Contributor to:* Aquileia nostra; Atane e Roma; Athenaeum; Atti dell'Istituto Veneto di Scienze; Letters ed Arti, etc. *Honours include:* Honorary Degree, University of Besancon, France, 1965; Gold Medal, Ministry of Education, Rome, 1968; Gold Medal, University of Padua, 1970; Honorary Degree, University of Torun, Poland, 1985. *Memberships include:* Osterreichische Akademie der Wissenschaften; Deutsches Archaologisches Insta; Pontificia Accademia Romana di Archeologia, Citte del Vaticano, The Vatican City, 1985; Society of the European Historians, Rome, 1984. *Address:* Via Seminario 16, 35122 Padua, Italy.

SAUL, George Brandon, b. 1 Nov. 1901, Shoemakersville, Pennsylvania, USA. Professor Emeritus. m. (1) Dorothy M Ayers, 28 June 1925, deceased 1937, (2) Eileen S Lewis, 3 July 1937, Philadelphia, 2 sons, 1 daughter. *Education:* AB, 1923, AM, 1930, PhD, 1932, University of Pennsylvania. *Appointments:* Professor Emeritus, English, University of Connecticut. *Publications:* The Wild Queen, 1967; Hound and Unicorn: Collected Verse – Lyrical, Narrative and Dramatic, 1969; Traditional Irish Literature and its Backgrounds, 1970; In Praise of the Half-Forgotten, 1976; Adam Unregenerate: Selected Lyrical Poems, 1977. *Contributor to:* LTLS; Notes and Queries; College English; MLN; Bulletin of New York Public Library; Arizona Quarterly; Twentieth Century Literature; Colby Library Quarterly; etc. *Honours:* Recipient, Prizes, Contemporary Verse and Poet Lore; Harrison Scholar in English, University of Pennyslvania, 1930–31; Awards, University of Connecticut for Research in Ireland, 1967, 1970. *Memberships:* American Committee, Irish Studies; MLA; Poetry Society of America. *Address:* Owls' Watch, 136 Moutton Road, Storrs, CT 06268, USA.

SAUNDERS, Ann Loreille, nee Cox-Johnson, b. 23 May 1930, London, England. Historian. m 4 June 1960, Hampstead, 1 son. *Education:* BA, University College, London; PhD, Leicester University. *Publications:* Handlist to the Ashbridge Collection on the History and Topography of St Marylebone, 1959; John Bacon R A – 1740–1799, 1961; Handlist of Painters, Sculptors and Architects associated with St Marylebone 1760–1900, Editor, 1963; Regent's Park, 1969, revised edition, 1981; Arthur Mee's King's England: London North of the Thames, except the City and Westminster, Editor, 1972; London, The City and Westminster, 1975; The Art and Architecture of London: An Illustrated Guide, 1984. *Contributions to:* Burlington; Geological Magazine. *Honours:* Winner, Best Specialist Guide Book of the Year with The Art and Architecture of London, British Tourist Board, 1984. Fellow, Society of Architecture. *Address:* 3 Meadway Gate, London NW11 7LA, England.

SAUNDERS, Jean b. 8 Feb. 1932, London. Author. m. Geoffrey Thomas Saunders, 20 Sep. 1952, Clevedon, Avon, 1 son, 2 daughters. *Publications:* 42 novels, including contemporary romance, historical romance, teen-age novels, most recent: Willow Harvest 1984; Scarlet Rebel 1985; Non-fiction The Craft of Romantic and Historical Fiction 1986. *Contributor to:* Most UK Women's Magazines over past 20 years, short stories. *Memberships:* Honorary Member/Secretary, Romantic Novelists Association; Romance Writers of America; West Country Writers Association. *Literary Agent:* Imogen Parker, Curtis Brown, London. *Address:* The Paddocks, Broadway, Oldmixon, Weston-Super-Mare, Avon BS24 9ET, England.

SAVAN, Bruce, b. 11 July 1927, Portland, Oregon, USA. Theatrical Agent. *Education:* Bachelor of Music, University of Southern California. *Publication:* Your Career in the Theater, 1961. *Address:* 26 West 38th Street, New York, NY 10018, USA.

SAVERY, Constance Winifred, b. 31 Oct. 1897, Froxfield, Wiltshire, England. Author. *Education:* MA, Honours, School of English Literature, Oxford University. *Publications:* Forbidden Doors, 1929; Green Emeralds for the King, 1938; Enemy Brothers, 1943; The Good Ship Red Lily, 1944; The Reb and the Redcoats, 1961. *Contributions to:* The Times: Times Literary Supplement; Child Life; Sunday at Home; Methodist Magazine; Classmate; Girls Today; Woman; Everybody's. *Honours:* Junior Gold Seal, for Good Ship Red Lily, Bowkers Literary Prizes. *Membership:* Life member, Bronte Society. *Address:* Cherry Trees, 5 Garden Close, Dumbleton, Evesham WR11 6TT, England.

SAVINO, Thomas, b. 17 Aug. 1950, Brooklyn, New York, USA. Writer. *Education:* BFA, Communication Arts. *Literary Appointments:* Critic for Brooklyn Today, 1972; Writer of, Dead Air, weekly radio drama, 1974–76; Writer of, Idiotorials, weekly radio drama, 1975–78; Writer of, Adventurers of Mel and Collie Baby, 1975–77; Writer of, Fat Tuesday Literary Press, 1981–. *Contributions to:* The Relationship – Fat Tuesday; Neo-Prick Song – Fat Tuesday; Poor Poor Pepperon – Fat Tuesday. *Address:* 3935 Berry #9, Studio City, CA 91604, USA.

SAVOIE, Paul, b. 11 Jan. 1946, St Boniface, Manitoba, Canada. Writer/Musician. *Education:* MA, English Literature, Carleton University, Ottowa, Canada; MA, French Litrature, University of Manitoba, Canada. *Literary Appointments:* Lecturer in French Literature, 1968–72, Lecturer in English Literature, 1974–75, St Boniface College, Manitoba; Program Officer, Canada Arts Council, 1982–. *Publications:* Salamandre, 1974; Nahanni (Poetry) 1976; La Maison sans murs, 1979; Acrobats (Poetry) 1982; A la façon d'un charpentier, 1984. *Contributions to:* ARC; Prairie Fire; Reenbou; Anthos; Les moissons; Concerning Poetry etc. *Memberships:* League of Canadian Poets; Union des écrivains québecois. *Address:* 5–467 Laurier West, Ottawa, Ontario, Canada K1R 5C7.

SAVVAS, Minas, b. 2 Apr. 1939. Professor. *Education:* BA, 1963, MA 1964, University of Illinois, USA; PhD, University of California at Santa Barbara, 1970. *Literary Appointments include:* Professor of English & Comparative Literature, San Diego State University, California, 1968–. *Major Publications:* Scars & Smiles, 1975; Chroncile of Exile, 1976; Subterranean Horses, 1980. *Contributor to:* Los Angeles Times; New York Review of Books; Tri-quarterly; Chicago Review; Yale Review; Colorado Quarterly; Michigan Quarterly Review; Journal of Hellenic Diaspora; Minnesota Review; College English; Translation; Language Quarterly; Texas Quarterly; Hellenic Journal; Quarterly Review of Literature; Poetry Venture; California Quarterly; The Z Anthology; Praxis; Greek World; Calendar; Cafeteria; San Diego Union; World Literature Today; Books Abroad; Comparative Literature. *Memberships:* Modern Language Association; Poets & Writers; Modern Greek Studies Association. *Address:* Department of English & Comparative Literature, San Diego State University, San Diego, CA 92182, USA.

SAWAI, Gloria Ostrem, b. Minneapolis, Minnesota, USA. Writer, 1 son, 1 daughter. *Education:* BA, Augsburg College; MFA, The University of Montana. *Publications:* Neighbour, play; Three Times Five, anthology of short stories. *Contributions to:* NE West Review; Aurora; Best Canadian Stories; Short Stories By Canadian Women. *Memberships:* President 1985–86, The Writer's Guild of Alberta; Playwrights Union of Canada. *Address:* 4403 52 A Street, Camrose, Alberta T4V 1W2, Canada.

SAX, Joseph Lawrence, b. 3 Feb. 1936, Chicago, Illinois, USA. Professor of Law. m. Eleanor Charlotte Gettes, 17 June 1958, Boston, 3 daughters. *Education:* AB, Harvard University, 1957; JD, University of Chicago, 1959. *Publications:* Water Law, Cases and Commentary, 1965; Water Law, Planning and Policy, 1968; Defending the Environment, 1971; Mountains without Handrails, 1980; Legal Control of Water Resources, 1986. *Honours:* Environmental Quality Award, US Environmental Protection Agency, 1976; American Motors Conservation Award, 1976; Elizabeth

Haub Award, Free University of Brussels Gold Medalist, 1977; Distinguished Faculty Achievement Award, University of Michigan, 1979; Resource Defense Award, National Wildlife Federation, 1981; Conservationist of the Year, Audubon Society, Detriot, 1981; Biennial Book Award, University of Michigan Press, 1981; William O Douglas Legal Achievement Award, The Sierra Club, 1984; Environmental Law Institute Award, 1985. *Address:* University of Michigan Law School, Ann Arbor, MI 48109, USA.

SAYERS, Edward Stuart, b. 27 Dec. 1923, Melbourne, Australia. Journalist. m. Gladys E Mateer, 11 Nov. 1950, London, 1 son, 3 daughters. *Literary Appointments:* Literary Editor, The Age, Melbourne, 1966–. *Publications:* By Courage and Faith: The First Fifty Years at Carey Baptist Grammar School, 1973; Ned Herring: A Life of Sir Edmund Herring, 1980. *Contributor to:* The Age – numerous articles and reviews; Papers in The Journal of the Royal Historical Society of Victoria; Contributor to The Australian Dictionary of Biography. *Memberships:* Australian Society of Authors; Victorian Fellowship of Australian Writers. *Address:* c/o "The Age", Box 257C, G P O, Melbourne 3001, Victoria, Australia.

SAYLOR, J Galen, b. 12 Dec. 1902, Carleton, Nebraska, USA. Educator. m. Helen R Smith, 1 June 1927, Carleton, Nebraska, 1 son, 2 daughters. *Education:* BA, McPherson College, 1922; MA, 1934, PhD, 1941, Columbia University. *Publications:* Factors Associated with Participation in Co-operative Programs of Curriculum Development, 1941; Secondary Education: Basic Principles and Practices, with W M Alexander, 1950; Curriculum Planning for Better Teaching and Learning, 1954; Modern Secondary Education: Basic Principles and Practices, 1959; Curriculum Planning for Modern Schools, 1966; The High School Today and Tomorrow, 1971; Curriculum Planning for Schools, 1974; 1981; Antecedent Developments in the Movement to Competency-Based Teacher Education, 1976; Who Planned the Curriculum: A Curriculum Plans Reservoir Model with Historical Examples, 1983; A History of the Department of Secondry Education, University of Nebraska, Lincoln 1871–1980, 1982; A Saylor Lineage: A Brief History and Genealogical Record of One Line of Descendants of Joseph Saylor (circa 1670–1680), 1983; A Smith Lineage: A Brief History and Genealogical Record of One Line of Descendants of Robert Smith 1623, 1985. *Contributor to:* Scores of magazine articles, booklets and chapters in books and contributions to encyclopedias. *Address:* 3300 South 39 Street, Lincoln, NE 68506, USA.

SCAGLIONE, Aldo D, b. 10 Jan. 1925, Torino, Italy. University Professor. m. Jeanne Daman, 14 June 1952, Chicago, USA. *Education:* Doctorate, Modern Letters, University of Torino, 1948. *Literary Appointments:* Lecturer, University of Toulouse, France, 1949–51; Instructor, University of Chicago, 1951–52; Assistant, Associate, Full Professor, University of California, Berkeley, 1952–68; W R Kenan Professor, University of North Carolina, 1968–. *Publications include:* Edition of M M Boiardo, 2 volumes, 1951; Nature & Love in the Late Middle Ages, 1963; Ars grammatica, 1970; Classical Theory of Composition, 1972; The Theory of German Word Order, 1983; The Liberal Arts & The Jesuit College System, 1986; Francis Petrarch Six Centuries Later, 1975. *Contributions to:* 65 articles, 110 book reviews, in: Romance Philology; Studi Francesi; Comparative Literature; Italica; Journal of Aesthetics, etc. *Honours:* Fulbright Fellowship, 1951; J Simon Guggenheim Fellowship, 1958; Newberry Library Senior Fellowship, 1964; H Johnson Distinguished Fellowship, University of Wisconsin, 1981; etc. *Memberships:* Executive Council 1980–84; MLA; Vice President 1980–83, American Association for Italian Studies; Council 1974–76, AATI Renaissance Society of America; Medieval Society of America. *Address:* Department of Romance Languages, University of North Carolina, Chapel Hill, NC 27514, USA.

SCAGNETTI, Jack, b. 24 Dec. 1924, Piney Fork, Ohio, USA. Magazine Writer; Author. m. Doris Jean Woolford, 19 July 1952, Dearborn, Michigan, 1 son, 1 daughter. *Literary Appointments:* Managing Editor: Allen Park, Michigan Reporter; Popular Hot Rodding Magazine. Editorial Director, Argus Publishers, Los Angeles, California. *Publications:* Intimate Life of Rudolph Valentino; The Life and Loves of Gable; Laurel and Hardy Scrapbook; The Joy of Walking; Bee Pollen; Racquetball Made Easy; Soccer; Bicycle Motocross. Co-Author: Golf for Beginners; Cars of the Stars; Famous Custom and Show cars; Five Simple Steps to Perfect Golf. *Contributions to:* Motor Trend Magazine, 5 part series; Motor Trend; Golf Magazine, monthly columnist; Golf Score Magazine, 400 instruction articles; The People's Almanac, contributing Editor. *Memberships:* Licensed Literary Agent, State of California. *Address:* 5258 Cartwright Avenue, North Hollywood, CA 91601, USA.

SCALAPINO, Robert Anthony, b. 19 Oct. 1919, Leavenworth, Kansas, USA. Professor; Political Scientist. m. Ida-Mae (Dee) Jessen, 23 Aug. 1941, 3 daughters. *Education:* BA, Santa Barbara College, 1940; MA, 1943, PhD, Political Science, 1948, Harvard University. *Literary Appointments:* Lecturer, Santa Barbara College, 1940–41; Instructor, Harvard University, 1948–49; Assistant Professor, 1949–51, Associate Professor 1951–56, Professor 1956–77, Robson Research Professor of Government, University of California, Berkeley 1977–; Editor, Asian Survey, 1962–. *Publications:* Parties and Politics in Contemporary Japan, with J Masumi, 1962; The Japanese Communist Movement 1920–66, 1967; Communism in Korea, with C S Lee, 1972; Elites in the People's Republic of China, editor, 1972; Asia and the Road Ahead: Issues for the Major Powers, 1975; The Foreign Policy of Modern Japan, 1977; The Early Japanese Labor Movement, 1984; Modern China and Its Revolutionary Process (1), with G T Yu, 1985. *Contributions to:* Scholarly articles published in such journals as: Orbis; Journal of Asian Studies; Politique Internationale; Problems of Communism; Korea Observer; Foreign Affairs; Korea and World Affairs; The American Spectator; Asian Survey; Survey. *Honours:* Guggenheim Fellowship, 1965–66; Elected to American Academy of Arts and Sciences, 1972; Woodrow Wilson Foundation Award (American Political Science Association) for best book published in 1973 on government, politics or international affairs (with C S Lee) 1974; HonoraryLLD, China Academy, Taiwan, 1976. *Memberships:* American Academy of Arts and Sciences 1972–; Council on Foreign Relations, Member, Board of Directors, 1982–; Editorial Advisory Board, numerous journals. *Address:* Institute of East Asian Studies, 2223 Fulton Street, University of California, Berkeley, CA 94720, USA.

SCARFE, Wendy Elizabeth, b. 21 Nov. 1933, Australia. m. Allan John Scarfe, 1 son, 3 daughters. *Education:* BA, Melbourne University; Associated Teachers Training Certificate. *Publications:* Shadow and Flowers: Poems, 1964, enlarged edition, 1984; The Lotus Throne, 1976; Neither Here Nor There, 1984; With Allan Scarfe: A Mouthful of Petals, 1967; Tiger on a Rein, 1969; People of India, 1972; Victims or Bludgers, 1974 and 1981; J P His Biography, (also Hindi translation) 1975; Labor's Titan: The Story of Percy Brookfield, editors. *Honour:* Awarded Special Purpose Grant, Australian Council, 1980. *Membership:* Fellowship of Australian Writers. *Address:* 8 Bostock Street, Warrnambool, Victoria, Australia.

SCARRY, Richard, b. 5 June 1919, Boston, Massachusetts, USA. Writer; Illustrator of Children's Books. m. New York, 1 son. *Publications:* Between 200 and 300 publications including: Tinker and Tanker, series 7 vols, 1960–78; Best Ever, series 7 vols 1963–79; Busy, Busy World, 1965; Storybook Dictionary, 1966; What Do People Do All Day, 1968; Look and Learn Library, 1971; Great Big Air Book, 1971; ABC Workbook, 1971; Funniest Storybook Ever, 1972; Great Big Mystery Book, 1972; Please and Thank You Book,

1973; Find Your ABC's, 1973; Cars and Trucks and Things That Go, 1974; Animal Nursery Tales, 1975; Look-Look Books, 1976; Color Books, 1976, Early Words, 1976; Busiest People Ever, 1976; Best Make-It Book Ever, 1977; Postman Pig, 1978; Toy Book, 1978; Lowly Worm, series, 1979; Easy to Read Books, 1981. *Contributor to:* Many US magazines. *Address:* Gstaad, Switzerland.

SCHACHT, Richard Lawrence, b. 19 Dec. 1941, Racine, Wisconsin, USA. Professor of Philosophy. m. Marsha Ruth Clinard, 17 Aug. 1963, Madison, Wisconsin, USA, 2 sons. *Education:* BA, Harvard University, 1963; MA, 1965, PhD, 1967, Princeton University; Studies at University of Tbigen, Federal Republic of Germany, 1966–67. *Major Publications:* Alienation, 1970; Hegel and After, 1975; Nietzsche, 1983; Classical Modern Philosopher, 1984. *Contributor to:* Numerous Philosophical Journals. *Memberships:* American Philosophical Association; North American Nietzsche Society; International Sociological Association. *Address:* Department of Philosophy, University of Illinois at Urbana-Champaign, 105 Gregory Hall, 810 South Wright Street, Urbana, IL 61801, USA.

SCHAFER, Edward Hetzel, b. 23 Aug. 1913, Seattle, Washington, USA. University Professor. m. Phyllis Brookh, 7 Sep. 1971, California, 2 sons, 1 daughter from previous marriage. *Education:* AB, (Anthropology), 1938, University of California; MA, (Oriental Studies), 1940, University of Hawii; PhD, (Oriental Language), University of California, 1947. *Literary Appointments:* Agissiz Professor of Oriental Languages and Literature, University of California, 1969–. *Publications:* The Empire of Min, 1954; Tu Wan's Stone Catalogue of Cloudy Forest, 1961; The Golden Peaches of Samarkand, 1963; Ancient China, 1967; The Vermillion Bird, 1967; Shore of Pearls, 1970; The Divine Woman, 1970; Pacing the Void, 1977; Mirages on the Sea of Time, 1985. *Contributions to:* Numerous magazines and journals. *Honours:* Editor, Journal of the American Oriental Society, 1958–64; President, American Oriental Society, 1974–75; Inaugral Lecturer, Department of Oriental Languages and Literatures, University of Colorado, 1982; Hill Distinguished Visiting Professor, Department of East Asian Languages, University of Minnesota, 1983. *Address:* 60 Avis Road, Berkeley, CA 94707, USA.

SCHALEKAMP, Jean, b. 26 June 1926, Rotterdam, Netherlands. Author; Literary Translator. m. Muriel Hess, 27 Feb. 1985, Palma, 2 sons, 1 daughter. *Education:* University of Paris, France. *Literary Appointments:* Writer-in-Residence, University of Minnesota, USA, 1977–78. 1978–79. *Publications:* De Dolle Trams, 1964; Bedankt voor Alles, 1966; Alles onder Handbereik, 1970; Van een Eiland kun je Niet vluchten, 1980; De Una Isla no se puede Escapar, 1980; De Sneeuwvrouw wacht (novel), 1985. *Contributor to:* Literair Paspoort; Maatstaf; Vrij Nederland; Alg Handelsblad; De Nieuwe Linie; Insula; El Urogallo; Cuadernos del Norte, Spain. *Memberships:* PEN; Vereniging van Litterkundigen, *Address:* Apartado 777, Palma de Mallorca, Spain.

SCHALK, Adolph Francis, b. 17 Jan. 1923, St Louis, Missouri, USA. Publicist. *Education:* St Louis University; Marquette University; Notre Dame University; MA. *Literary Appointments:* Reporter, Sun Herald, Kansas City, Missouri, USA, 1951; Editor, Today, Chicago, Illinois, 1953; Editor, The Bridge, Hamburg, Federal Republic of Germany, 1957; Publisher, Arlecchino Publishing Company, Indemini, Switzerland, 1983–. *Publications:* Eyes on the Modern World, with John Deedy, 1964; The Germans, 1971. *Contributions to:* Religious News Service, USA; Catholic News Service, Washington; Commonweal; National Catholic Reporter; Time; Neue Zuercher Zeitung; Die Weltwoche; Catholic Herald; radio scripts for Swiss and German studios; television appearances on Swiss and German television. *Honours:* 1st Prize, for best article, 1958, for best editorial, 1959, for best article, 1969,

Catholic Press Association, USA. *Memberships:* American, Federal Republic of German and Swiss Press Associations; American Authors Guild. *Address:* Casa Arlecchimo, CH–6579 Idemini, Ticino, Switzerland.

SCHAPPES, Morris Urman, b. 3 May. 1907, Kaminets-Podolsk, Ukraine. Historian; Editor; Educator. m. Sonya Laffer, 6 Apr. 1930, New York. *Education:* BA, College of the City of New York, 1928; MA, Columbia University, 1930. *Appointments:* English Department, College of the City of New York, 1928–41; Editorial Board, Jewish Life, New York City, 1946–58; Editor in Chief, Jewish Currents, New York, 1958–; Adjunct Professor, History, Queens College, City University of New York, 1972–76. *Publications:* Editor: Selections from Prose and Poetry of Emma Lazarus, 1944, 5th Edition, 1982; Letters of Emma Lazarus, 1949; A Documentary History of the Jews in US 1654–1875, 1950, 3rd edition, 1971; The Jews in the USA 1654–1954, 1958; An Epistle to the Hebrews by Emma Lazarus, 1986. *Contributor to:* Articles in Learned Journals including, American Literature; American Jewish History; New York History; Journal of Ethnic Studies; The Symposium; Poetry; New York Post; Chicago Jewish Forum; Jewish Life; Jewish Currents; Yiddishe Kultur; etc. *Honours:* Tercentenary Award, Emma Lazarus Federation of Jewish Women's Clubs, 1954; Award, Haim Zhitlovsky Foundation for Jewish Secularism, 1969; Holocaust Memorial Award, New York Society of Clinical Psychologists, 1979; Award, Leadership Council of Secular and Humanist Jews. *Membership:* Presidium, Yiddisher Kultur Farband. *Address:* 700 Columbus Ave, 8E, New York, NY 10025, USA.

SCHARF, Lauren Ileene Barnett, b. 9 May 1956, Chicago, Illinois, USA. Editor; Publisher; Writer. m. Craig Allen Scharf, 8 Apr. 1979, Newport Beach, California. *Education:* BA, State of Connecticut Board for State Academic Awards. *Literary Appointments:* Editor & Publisher, Lone Star Publications of Humor, 1981–. *Publications include:* Stand-up Poems: A Comic Book of Poetry, 1975. Comedy material for cartoonists, disc jockeys, comedians, public speakers, etc. *Contributions to:* Journal of Irreproducible Results; Innverview; Woman's World; Computer World, etc. *Memberships:* Association of Comedy Writers; Committee of Small Magazine Editors & Publishers, San Francisco. *Address:* c/o Lone Star Publications of Humor, P O Box 29000, Suite 103, San Antonio, TX 78229, USA.

SCHEELE, Roy (Martin), b. 10 Jan. 1942, Houston, Texas, USA. Educator. m. Frances McGill Hazen, 26 June 1965, Lincoln, Nebraska, 2 sons. *Education:* AB Classical Greek 1965, MA English 1971, University of Nebraska; Graduate study, English, University of Texas, 1965–66. *Publications:* Accompanied, chapbook-poems, 1974; Noticing, chapbook–poems, 1979; The Sea-Ocean, poems, 1981; Pointing Out the Sky, poems, 1985. *Contributions to:* Poems in magazines and journals including: The Bloomsbury Review; The Christian Century; Commonweal; The Countryman; The Greenfield Review; The Hollins Critic; Kansas Quarterly; The North American Review; Poetry; Poetry Northwest; Prairie Schooner; The Sewanee Review; Southern Humanities Review; Three Rivers Poetry Journal; Essays and reviews in: Papers on Language and Literature; The South Carolina Review; Southwest Review. *Honours:* Scholarship, Rocky Mountain Writers' Conference, 1960; BreadLoaf Writers' Conference, 1960; Ione Gardner Noyes Poetry Awards, University of Nebraska, 1962 and 1964; Finalist, Walt Whitman Poetry Award, Academy of American Poets, 1980; 1st Prize, John Neihardt Poetry Competition, 1983. *Address:* 2020 S 25th Street, Lincoln, NB 68502, USA.

SCHEFFER, Victor B(lanchard), b. 27 Nov. 1906, Manhattan, Kansas, USA. Zoologist–wildlife research. m. Mary Elizabeth MacInnes, 12 Oct. 1935, Puyallup, Washington, 1 son, 2 daughters. *Education:* BS 1930, MS 1932, PhD 1936, University of Washington, Seattle. *Publications:* The Year of the Whale, 1969; The Year of the Seal, 1970; The Seeing Eye, 1971; A Voice For Wildlife, 1974; A Natural History of Marine Mammals, 1976; Adventures of a Zoologist, 1980; The Amazing Sea Otter, 1981; Spires of Form: Glimpses of Evolution, 1983. *Contributions to:* Popular articles to: Alaska Geographic; American Fabrics; Animal Kingdom; Audubon; Defenders; McCall's; National Geographic; Natural History; Wilderness; Wildlife, London; Scientific articles in journals including: Journal of Mammalogy; Journal of Wildlife Management; Proceedings Zoological Society London. *Honours:* Distinguished Service Award, US Department of the Interior, 1965; Medal, John Burroughs Memorial Association, 1970; Joseph Wood Krutch Award,Humane Society, USA, 1975; Alumnus Summa Laude Dignatus, University of Washington, 1977. *Address:* 14806 SE 54th Street, Bellevue, WA 98006, USA.

SCHEIBER, Harry N, b. 1935, USA. Educator; Legal Historian. *Education:* AB, Columbia University; MA, PhD, Cornell University. *Literary Appointment:* Professor of Law and History, University of California, Berkeley. *Publications:* Wilson Administration and Civil Liberties, 1960; Ohio Canal Era, 1969; Old Northwest, 1969; American Economic History, (co-author), 1976; American Law and the Constitutional Order, (co-editor), 1978. *Contributor to:* Law and Society Review; The Atlantic Monthly; Journal of Economic History; American Historical Review; California Law Review; Political Science Quarterly; Journal of American History; Stanford Law Review and others. *Honours:* Moses Coit Tyler Prize, Cornell University, 1960; Ohio University Press Award, 1970; CHOICE Best Academic Books List, 1970. *Memberships:* Law and Society Association, Past Trustee; Agricultural History Society, Past President; Economic History Association, Past Trustee, Present Board of Editors. *Literary Agent:* Gerard McCauley, New York City. *Address:* School of Law, Boalt Hall, University of California, Berkeley, CA 94720, USA.

SCHELL, Orville Hickok III, b. 20 May 1940, New York CIty. Writer/Rancher. *Education:* BA (magna cum laude), Harvard; MA, PhD, University of California, Berkeley. *Literary Appointments:* Research Associate, University of California Center for Chinese Studies. *Publications:* In The People's Republic, 1946; The China Reader, 1967; Modern China: The Story of a Revolution, 1972; Brown, 1979; Watch Out for the Foreign Guests: China Encounters the West, 1981; Modern Meat, 1984; To Get Rich is Glorious – China in the 80's, 1985. *Contributions to:* Numerous national and international publications. *Honours:* University of California Center for Chinese Studies Fellowship, 1979; Alicia Patterson Foundation Fellowship, 1981. *Memberships:* Authors' Guild; PEN. *Literary Agent:* Amanda Urban. *Address:* Box 56 Overlook Road, Bolinas, CA 94924, USA.

SCHENKEL, Barbara Carolina, b. Warsaw, Poland, Retired Teacher of Drama and Health, Social Worker, Writer, Broadcaster, Actor, Editor. m. Leon Theodore Schenkel. *Literary Appointments include:*Writer in native polish, Australia, 1949–; Editor, Children's Page, Polish Newspaper. *Publications:* English and Other Than English, anthology, 1979; Israel, Impressions from a Journey, poetry, 1981; Anthology of Ethnic Australia, 1981; The Anniversary, short story, 1981; The Aliens and Ethnic Australia, poems, 1981; Anthologies: World Poetry, 1983; World Poetry, Poetry Australia, 1983; Indo-Australian Flowers, 1984; Joseph's Coat, anthology, 1985. *Contributions to:* Oziennik Baltycki; Polish Weekly, formerly Glos Polski and Tygodnik Katolicki; Polish News; Melbourne Chronicle; 3EA Radio Station Magazine; Open Channel Magazine; PHS School Magazine; Open Journal. *Honours:* Decorated by Polish Government in Exile, London, England; Silver Cross of Merit, 1977. *Memberships include:* Fellowship of Australian Writers; Victorian Association of Ethnic Radio Co-ordinators, Broadcasters and Telecasters; Poets Union of Australia; Executive member, Polish Cultural and Artistic Circle; Australian Journalists Association; Actors Equity of Australia; Co-ordinator, International

Poets Club. *Address:* 2/225 Glen Eira Road, East St Kilda, 3183 Victoria, Australia.

SCHENKER, Eric, b. 24 Feb. 1931, Vienna, Austria. University Dean, Economist. m. Virginia, Martha Wick, 14 Apr. 1963, Milwaukee, Wisconsin, 3 sons. *Education:* BBA, City College of New York, 1952; MS, University of Tennessee, 1955; Phd, University of Florida, 1957. *Literary Appointments:* Assistant Professor, Michigan State University, 1957–59; Member of Faculty, University of Wisconsin, 1959–, Professor of Economics, 1965–, Dean, 1976–, Director, Urban Research Centre, 1974–76. *Major Publications:* The Port of Milwaukee: An Economic Review, 1967; (co-author) Port Planning & Development as Related to Problems of US Ports & the US Coastal Environment, 1974; The Great Lakes Transportation System, 1976; Port Developement in the US, 1976; Maritime Labour Organisations on the Great Lakes – St Lawrence Seaway System, 1978; The Great Lakes Transportation System in the 80s (co-author), 1986. *Contributor to:* Various periodicals, articles & monographs. *Honours:* Phi Kappa Phi; Alpha Kappa Psi. *Memberships:* Governor's Council of Economic Advisors; American Economic Association; Financial Executives Institute; Rotary Club. *Address:* 2254 West Dunwood Road, Milwaukee, WI 53209, USA.

SCHERUBL, Gabriele Maria, b. 24 Mar. 1959, Mayo, Yukon, Canada. Editor. *Education:* Bachelor of Journalism, Carleton University, Ottawa, Ontario, Canada. *Literary Appointments:* Assistant Editor 1983–84, Editor 1984–85, Skyword. *Contributions to:* Skyword; Westin; Okanagan; Seasons. *Address:* Skyword Marketing, 2802 30th Street, Vernon, BC V1T 8G7, Canada.

SCHEVILL, James, b. 10 June 1920, Berkeley, California, USA. Poet; Playwright. m. Margot Blum, 2 Aug. 1966, 2 daughters by previous marriage. *Education:* BS, Music, Harvard University, USA, 1942; MA, Brown University. *Appointments:* California College of Arts and Crafts, 1951–58, elected President of the Faculty Assembly, 1956; San Francisco State University, 1959–68, Professor, 1968; Professor, of English, Brown University, 1968 to date. *Publications include:* 24 volumes of plays and poems including: Lovecraft's Follies, (play, 1969; Violence and Glory, (Poems), 1969; The Buddhist Car and Other Characters, (poems), 1973; Breakout: In Search of New Theatrical Environments, 1973; Pursuing Elegy: A poem about Haiti, 1974; Cathedral of Ice, (play), 1975; The Arena of Ants, (novel), 1976; The Mayan Poems, 1978; Fire of Eyes: A Guatamalan Sequence, (poems), 1979; The American Fantasies: Collected Poems, 1945–1981, 1983; Editor: Six Histories, by Ferdinand Schewill, 1956; Co-Editor: Wastepaper Theatre Anthology, 1976; Recording: Performance Poems, performed by James and Margot Schewill, 1984; numerous play productions, translations, readings, etc. *Honours include:* Ford Foundation for Education grant in Poetic Drama, 1954; Office for Advanced Drama Reasearch, Rockefeller Foundation, 1957; Guggenheim Fellowship in Poetry, 1981; McKnight Fellowship in Playwriting, 1984. *Memberships:* Director, The Poetry Centre, San Francisco, 1961–68; Board Member, Trinity Square Repertory Company, Providence, Rhode Island, 1975–date; President, Rhode Island Playwrights Theatre, 1984. *Literary Agent:* Helen Merrill. *Address:* English Department, Brown University, Providence, RI 02912, USA.

SCHIAPPA, Barbara D, b. 3 Dec. 1943, Murray, Kentucky, USA. Writer. m. Charles F Schiappa, 28 Sep. 1974, Medford, Massachusetts. *Education:* Murray State University, 1967–69; Accredited Medical Record Technician, 1971. *Publication:* Mixing: Catholic-Protestant Marriages in the 1980s, 1982. *Contributions to:* Sports Illustrated; Boston Magazine; Business Computer Sustems; Parents Choice and Others. *Memberships:* The Authors Guild Inc; Authors League of America; PEN – New England. *Address:* 135 Stearns Street, Carlisle, MA 01741, USA.

SCHICK, Joel Warren, b. 27 May 1945, Chicago, Illinois, USA. Illustrator. m. Alice Raffer, 20 June 1967, Lawrence, New York, 1 son. *Education:* BA, Psychology, Roosevelt University, Chicago, 1968. *Publications:* (about 40 books): The Gobble Uns'll Git You Ef You Don't Watch Out!, 1975; Santaberry and the Snard, 1976; Joel Schick's Christmas Present, 1977; Just This Once, 1978; Frankenstein, 1980; Dracula, 1980; Doggy Drama: The Maltese Maltese/Snow Ruff and the Seven Dwarfs; DOGGY DRAMAS: The Done Ranger/A G The Alien Guy, 1983. *Honours:* Society of Illustrators Exhibition (Gobble Uns), 1975; Various Best Book of the Year Lists, School Library Journal, National Science Foundation, etc; Biennale of Illustrations Bratislava, 1981 (Frank and Drac). *Address:* PO Box 101, Monterey, MA 01245, USA.

SCHIFFHORST, Gerald, b. 13 Oct. 1940, St Louis, Missouri, USA. Professor of English. *Education:* BS, 1962, MA, 1963, St Louis University; PhD, Washington University, 1973; Postdoctoral Fellow, Duke University, 1974. *Literary Appointments:* Instructor, University of Missouri-St Louis, 19661-67; Assistant Professor, 1970-77, Associate Professor, 1977-85, Profesor, 1985-, University of Central Florida. *Publications:* The Triumph of Patience: Medieval and Renaissance Studies, editor and co-author, 1978; Short English Handbook, co-author, 1979, 3rd edition 1986. *Contributions to:* Milton Studies, 1982; Christianity and Literature, 1984; South Atlantic Review, 1984; College Composition and Communication, 1976. *Honours:* Ford Foundation Honours Fellowship 1962-63; NEH Postdoctoral Fellowship, Duke University, 1974; NEH Shakespeare Institute (Co-Director), 1979; English Speaking Union Scholarship, Oxford, 1980. *Memberships:* Modern Language Association; South Atlantic Modern Language Association; Milton Society of America; Conference on Christianity and Literature. *Address:* Department of English, University of Central Florida, Orlando, FL 32816, USA.

SCHILPP, Paul Arthur, b. 6 Feb. 1897, Dillenburg, Germany. Univeristy Professor; Philosopher; Author; Editor. m. (1) Louise Gruenholz, Terre Haute, 16 Sep. 1918, 2 sons, 2 daughters. (2) Madelon Golden, Evanston, Illinois, 27 July 1950, 1 son, 1 daughter. *Education:* AB, Baldwin-Wallace College, Ohio, 1916; MA, Northwestern University, 1922; BD, Garrett Theological Seminary, 1922; PhD, Stanford University, 1936. *Academic Appointments include:* Professor of Philosophy, Northwestern University, 1936-65; Distinguished Research Professor of Philosophy, Southern Illinois University, 1965-82; Emeritus Professor, both universities. *Publications include:* Do We Need A New Religion?, 1929; Higher Education Faces the Future (ed), 1931; The Quest for Religious Realism, 1938; Kant's Pre-Critical ethics, 1938; Human Nature & Progress, 1940; The Crisis in Science & Education, 1963; Founder, Editor, The Library of Living Philosophers, 17 volumes to date. *Contributions to:* Most technical philosophical journals of magazines in the English-speaking world. *Honours include:* Honorary degrees; Litt D, Baldwin-Wallace College, 1946; LHD, Springfield College, 1963; LHD, Kent State University, 1975; Litt D, Southern Illinois University, 1982. *Memberships:* Vice President, President, American Philosophical Association (Western Division), 1957-59; Consultant in Philosophy, Encyclopedia Britannica, 1961-; Kant-Gesellschaft, Germany (contributing editor, Kant-Studien); Bertrand Russell Society (recipient, 1st Distinguished Service Medal, 1980). *Address:* 9 Hillcrest Drive, Carbondale, IL 62901, USA.

SCHINDLER, Regine, b. 26 May 1935, Berlin, Germany. Author. m. Alfred Schindler, Zürich, 7 Apr. 1959, 2 sons, 3 daughters. *Education:* Dr phil, German Literature, 1962; Dr theol hc, 1985. *Publications:* Grosse Gott – singst Du im Wind?, 1973; Herr Langfuss, 1975; Erziehen zur Hoffnung, 1977; Gott, ich kann mit dir reden, 1982; Der Weihnechtsclown, 1982; Starche Gott, Du bisch min Fründ, 1984; Die lachende Katze, 1984; Series, Religion für kleine Leute, 11 volumes, 1979-85. *Contributions to:* Schritte ins Offene etc.

Honours: Dr hc, University of Zürich, Schweiz, Jugendbuchpreis, Katholischer Kinderbuchpreis, 1985. *Memberships:* Schweiz. Schriftsteller-Verband; Executive Board, Berner Schriftstellerverein, 1983-. *Address:* Waldhöheweg 29, CH–3013, Bern, Switzerland.

SCHIRMER, Karl-Heinz, b. 22 Jan. 1926, Stendal, Germany. *Education:* PhD, University of Greifswald, 1954; Habilitation, University of Hamburg, 1966. *Appointments:* Professor, Hamburg University, 1971; Full Professor and Director of Seminars of German Language and Literature, Kiel University, 1974. *Publications:* Die Strophil Walthers von der Vogelweide, 1956; Die Mittelhochdeutsche Versnovelle, 1969; Das maere, Die Unterhaltungsdichtung des spaeteren Millelalters, 1983. *Contributions to:* Numerous publications. *Memberships:* International Association of Germanists; International Society for History of Rhetoric. *Address:* 23a Dueppelstr, D–2300 Kiel 1, Federal Republic of Germany.

SCHISGAL, Murray, Musician; Lawyer; Writer. m. Marrie Reene Schapiro, 1958, 1 son, 1 daughter. *Education:* Brooklyn Conservatory of Music; Long Island University; LLB, Brooklyn Law School, 1953; BA, New School for Social Research, 1959. *Publications include:* Most Recent: Popkins, produced at Margo Jones Theatre, Dallas, 1978; The Pushcart Peddlers, produced Off-off Broadway, 1979; Nights of a French Horn Player, Novel, 1980; Walter and the Flatulist, 1980; The Downstairs Boys, 1980; Twice Around the Park, 2 one act plays, 1983; Screenplays, Co-Author, Tootsie, 1982; Luv and Other Plays, 1983; Closet Madness and Other Plays, 1984; Old Wine in a New Bottle, 1985; The Rabbi and the Toyota Dealer, Mayfair Theatre, 1985. *Honours:* Vernon Rice Award, Outer Circle Award, Saturday Review Critics Poll Award for, The Typists and the Tiger; Luv, nominated for Critics Circle and American Theatre Wing's Tony Awards; The Love Song of Barnet Kempinski, nominated for Outstanding Dramatic Programme by National Academy of TV Arts and Sciences; Recipient, LA Film Critics Award, Writers Guild of America Award, National Society of Film Critics Award, New York Film Critics Award, Nominated by Academy of Motion Picture Arts and Sciences for Oscar, Nominated by British Academy of Film and TV Arts for, Tootsie. *Address:* International Creative Management, 40W 57th Street, New York, NY 10019, USA.

SCHLESINGER, Benjamin, b. 20 July, 1928, Berlin, Germany. Professor, Social Work, University of Toronto. m. Rachel Clara Aber, 29 Mar. 1959, Ithaca, 3 sons, 1 daughter. *Education:* BA, Sir George Williams University; NSW, University of Toronto; PhD, Cornell University. *Publications:* Poverty in Canada and the United States, 1966; The Multi-Problem Family: A Review and Annotated Bibliography, 3rd edition, 1970; The Jewish Family: A Survey and Annotated Bibliography, 1971; Family Planning in Canada: A Source Book, 1974; The Chatelaine, Guide to Marriage, 1975; Families: A Canadian Perspective, 1975; Sexual Behaviour in Canada: Patterns & Problems, 1977; The One Parent Family: Perspectives and Annotated Bibliography, 4th edition, 1978; Families: Canada, 1979; Sexual Abuse of Children: A Resource Guide and Annotated Bibliography, 1982; The One Parent Family in the 1980's: Perspectives and Annotated Bibliography, 1985; One in Ten: One-Parent Families in Canada, 1979; Booklets: What About Poverty in Canada, 4th printing 1977; One-Parent Families in Canada, 2nd printing 1975. *Contributor to:* About 250 articles in professional journals and magazines. *Address:* Faculty of Social Work, University of Toronto, 246 Bloor St West, Toronto, Ontario M5S 1A1, Canada.

SCHLICHTING, Harold Eugene, b. 19 Mar, 1926, Detroit, Michigan, USA. Professor of Botany, m, Mary Louise Southworth, 20 Aug, 1949, Lansing, Michigan, 5 sons, 1 daughter. *Education:* BS Zoology, University of Michigan, Ann Arbour; MS Biological Science, PhD Botany, Michigan State University. *Publications:* Algae; Ecology, (with Mary S Schlichting); Pollution, (with

Mary S Schlichting); The Food Crisis, (with Mary S Schlichting). *Contributions to:* 80 scientific publications concerning Dispersal of Algae, Airborne Algae and Protozoa, Biological Monitoring of Water Quality and Algal Ecology. *Address:* 151 S Ridge Street, Port Sanilac, MI 48469, USA.

SCHLOSSBERG, Dan, b. 6 May 1948, New York City, New York, USA. Freelance Travel Writer; Freelance Baseball Writer. 1 daughter. *Education:* BA, Syracuse University, 1969. *Publications:* Hammerin' Hank: The Henry Aaron Story, 1974; Barons of the Bullpen, 1975; The Baseball Catalog, 1980; Baseballaffs, 1983; The Baseball Book of Why, 1984; Baseball Stars 1985, 1985; Baseball Stars 1986, 1986. *Contributions to:* Travel-Holiday; Chevron/USA; Vista/USA; Goodlife; Diversion; Ford Fair Lanes; Grit; Encyclopedia America Yearbook; Numerous inflight and baseball team publications; Street and Smith's Official Baseball Yearbook; Official World Series Program; various baseball periodicals; New York Post; Charlotte Observer; Boston Herald; San Diego Tribune; Copley News-Service. *Honours:* Former President: Sigma Delta Chi, Syracuse University; New Jersey Chapter, International Association of Business Communicators. The Baseball Catalog, Book-of-the-Month Club Alternative, 1980. *Memberships:* National Writers Club; Society for American Baseball Research. *Literary Agent:* Basil Kane, Burns Sports Celebrity Service, Chicago, Illinois. *Address:* D-13 77 Brook Avenue, Passaic, NJ 07055, USA.

SCHLOSSBERG, Edwin Arthur, b. 19 July 1945, New York City, USA. Designer. *Education:* BA 1967, MA, Science & Literature 1969, Columbia College; PhD, Science & Literature, Columbia University, 1971. *Literary Appointments:* Editor, Encyclopedia of Science & Technology, 1977; Editor, Quest Magazine, 1967–70. *Publications include:* Books: Co-author, The Home Computer Handbook, 1978; The Philosopher's Game, 1977, The Pocket Calculator Game Book, 1975, etc; 1st Annual Report of Trustees of Earth, 1971; Bohr/Stevens Letters: Imaginery Letters Between Niels Bohr & Wallace Stevens, 1970; A Catalog of Films for the Study of Science in Human Affairs, 1969; etc. *Contributions to:* Art on the Marketplace, 1984; New Perspectives on our Lives with Companion Animals, co-author, 1983; Cities; Cybernetics Forum; About Bateson, by E P Dutton, 1977; One Liners, 1975; Architectural Design, 1979; Los Angeles Free Press, 1968, 1969. *Address:* 20 West 20th Street, New York, NY 10011, USA.

SCHMIDT, Frank H (Friedel Heinrich), b. 23 Dec. 1931, Syke, Bremen, Federal Republic of Germany. Journalist. m. Adelaide Runnacles, 2 Nov. 1962, 2 sons. *Education:* Matriculation, University of Adelaide, Australia, 1963. *Literary Appointments:* Editor, Highway, 1960–69; Editor, Local Government in South Australia, 1963–76; Editor, Modern Administration, 1967–69; Editor, Highway Engineering in Australia, 1969–; Editor, Municipal Engineering in Australia, 1973–; Editor, Waste Disposal and Water Management in Australia, 1973–. *Contributions to:* Highway; Local Government in South Australia; Modern Administration; Highway Engineering in Australia; Municipal Engineering in Australia; Waste Disposal and Water Management in Australia. *Literary Agent:* Editorial and Publishing Consultants Pty Limited, 29 First Avenue, Klemzig, South Australia 5087, Australia. *Address:* 29 First Avenue, Klemzig, South Australia 5087, Australia.

SCHMIDT, Karl M, b. 19 Mar. 1917, Utica, New York, USA. University Professor. m. Mary Erma Murphy, 3 Apr. 1943, New York City, 1 son, 1 daughter. *Education:* AB, magna cum laude, Colgate University, Hamilton, New York, 1948; MA, 1950, PhD, 1951, The Johns Hopkins University, Baltimore Maryland. *Publications:* Henry & Wallace: Quixotic Crusade 1948, 1960; Papers from the Staff College, editor, 1962; American Government in Action, editor, 1965; American State and Local Government in Action, editor, 1966; American Government in Action: National, State and Local, editor, 1967. *Contributions to:* American Political Science

Review, Choice. *Honour:* Phi Beta Kappa, 1948. *Address:* 100 Cutler Drive, Syracuse, NY 13219, USA.

SCHMIDT, Marlene Ruth, b. Chicago, Illinois USA. Motion Picture Producer and Writer. m. Howard Adevid, 6 May 1974, 3 step daughters. *Education:* BA, Communications, University of Washington; Graduate Courses in Cinema and Law at UCLA and USC. *Literary Appointments:* Casting Department, Columbia Pictures Television; Producer of daily hour show, CBS TV; Actress in leading roles in films in Europe for five years; Producer and co-writer of screenplays of following films: The Stepmother Crown International Pictures, 1972; The Teacher Crown International Pictures, 1974; Scorchy American International Pictures Inc (Orion) 1976, Video – Vestron; Texas Detour Cinema Shares International, 1977, Video – Prism; The Fifth Floor, Film Ventures International 1978, Video – Media Home Ent, TV – CBS Network; Separate Ways, Crown International Pictures, 1979, Video – Vestron; Mortuary, Artists Releasing Corporation through Film Ventures International, Video – Westron, 1982; Playing with Fire, New World Pictures, 1984, Video – Thorn EMI. *Honour:* Academy Award Nomination for, The Stepmother, 1972. *Address:* Hickmar Productions Inc, The Burbank Studios, 4000 Warner Boulevard, Burbank, CA 91505, USA.

SCHMIDT, R Marilyn, b. 2 Mar. 1929, New Brunswick, New Jersey, USA. Writer; Pharmacologist. *Education:* BS Degree. *Publications:* Harper's Handbook of Therapeutic Pharmacology, 1980; The Simply Seafood Cook Book...of East Coast Fish, 1981, 84; The Simply Seafood Cook Book...of East Coast Shellfish, 1981; Seafood Secrets: A Nutritional Guide to Seafood, 1982; All About Monkfish (booklet), 1982; Everything You Always Wanted to Know About Tilefish, (booklet); Fresh Tuna (booklet); Blue Fish: A Cookbooklet; Mussels: A Cookbooklet. *Memberships:* New Jersey Press Women; PEN Women. *Address:* 7 Wynnewood Drive, Cranbury, NJ 08512, USA.

SCHMIDT, Stanley Albert, b. 7 Mar. 1944, Cincinnati, Ohio, USA. Editor. m. Joyce Mary Tokarz, 9 June 1979, Shelby, Ohio. *Education:* BS, University of Cincinnati, Ohio, 1966; MA, 1968, PhD, 1969, Case Western Reserve University. *Literary Appointments:* Editor, Analog Science Fiction/Science Fact, 1978–. *Publications:* Newton and the Quasi Apple, 1975; The Sins of the Fathers, 1976; Lifeboat Earth, 1976; Tweedlloop, 1985. *Contributions to:* Analog Science Fiction/Science Fact, short stories, articles and serialised novels; Isaac Asimov's Science Fiction Magazine; The Magazine of Fantasy and Science Fiction; Rod Sterling's The Twilight Zone; Rigell; Camping Journal; Writers Market. *Memberships:* Science Fiction Writers of America. *Literary Agent:* Scott Meredith Literary Agency. *Address:* c/o Analog, 380 Lexington Avenue, New York City, NY 10017, USA.

SCHMITTHOFF, Clive Macmillan, b. 24 Mar. 1903, Berlin, Germany. Professor of Law, Barrister. m. Ilse (Twinkie) Auerbach, 25 Oct. 1940. *Education:* University of Berlin; University of Freiburg in Breisgau; London School of Economics, England. *Literary Appointment:* General Editor of the Journal of Business Law, London, 1957–. *Major Publications:* The English Conflict of Laws, 3rd edition 1954; Schmitthoff's Export Trade – The Law & Practice of International Law, 8th edition 1986; Charlesworth's Mercantile Law, 14th edition 1984 (co-editor); Commercial Law in a Changing Economic Climate, 2nd edition 1981; International Commercial Arbitration, 3rd edition, 1985; Palmer's Company Law 24th edition 1986 (general editor). *Address:* 29 Blenheim Road, Bedford Park, London W4 1ET, England.

SCHODER, Raymond Victor, b. 11 Apr. 1916, Battle Creek, MI, USA. Jesuit priest/University Professor. *Education:* AB, 1938, MA, 1940, Loyola University, Chicago; PhD, St Louis University, Missouri, 1944; STL, West Baden Pontifical University, Indiana, 1948. *Literary Appointments:* Teacher of Latin, Greek, English

Literature, University of Detroit High School, 1943–44; Lecturer of Graduate Courses in Latin and Greek literature and art and archaeology, 1951–81, Professor Emeritus, 1982–, Loyola University, Chicago. *Publications:* Reading Course in Homeric Greek 3 vols (with V C Horrigan) 1947; Immortal Diamond, Studies in G M Hopkins (with N Weyand) 1948; Masterpieces of Greek Art 1960; Ancient Greece from the Air, 1974; Landscape and Inscape; Poems of G M Hopkins (with P Milward) 1975; Readings of the Wreck (with P Milward) 1976. *Contributions to:* Artistry of Pindar's First Pythian Ode, Classical Journal, 1943; Poetic Imagination vs Didacticism in Lucretius Classical Journal, 1949; Ancient Cumae, Scientific American, 1963; Vergil's Poetic Use of the Cumae Area, Classical Journal, 1972; The Significance of St Augustine, American Ecclesiastical Review, 1946; Spelt from Sibyl's Leaves, Thought, 1944. *Honours:* Alumni Merit Award, St Louis University, 1963; Outstanding Faculty Member of the Year, Loyola University, 1974; Latin Ovatio for achievements, Classical Association USA, 1979. *Memberships:* Catholic Biblical Association; Vergilian Society of American; Manresa Educational Corporation (President 1974–86); Classical Association Midwest and South. *Address:* Loyola University, 6525 N. Sheridan Road, Chicago, IL 60626, USA.

SCHOECK, Richard, b. 1920, New York, USA. University Professor. m. Megan S Lloyd, 1977. *Education:* MA, PhD, 1949, Princeton University. *Major Publications:* The Achievement of Thomas More, 1976; Intertextuality & Renaissance Texts, 1984; (editor) Acta Bononiensis, 1985. *Contributor to:* Numerous scholarly journals; poetry in journals such as Queen's Quarterly, Dalhousie Review, and others. *Honours:* FRSC; Fellow, Royal Historical Society; and others. *Membership:* International Association for Neo-Latin Studies, President, 1976–79. *Address:* 4628 Tanglewood Trail, Boulder, CO 80301, USA.

SCHOEN, Barbara, b. 4 July 1924, New York, USA. Writer, College Professor. m. Donald R Schoen, 9 Nov. 1946, New York, 2 sons, 2 daughters. *Education:* BA Bryn Mawr College, 1946; MA, University of Boston, 1948. Further Study towards doctorate, University of Boston, 1950–55. *Literary Appointments:* Teacher, 1970–73; Assistant Professor, Language Arts, 1973–78, Associate Professor, 1978–, State University of New York, USA. *Major Publications:* A Place and a Time. 1967; A Spark of Joy, 1969. *Contributor to:* Various literary & professional journals, including: Review Press – Reporter; New York Times; Journal of Development & Remedial Education. *Memberships:* Authors Guild, New York; National Council of Teachers of English. *Literary Agent:* Francis Collin. *Address:* 101 Park Avenue, Bronxville, NY 10708, USA.

SCHOENBERGER, Nancy Jane, b. 3 Dec. 1950, Oakland, California, USA. *Education:* MFA, Columbia University School of the Arts, NYC, 1981; MA 1974, BA, Louisiana State University, 1972. *Literary Appointments:* Teaching Assistant, Stonecoast Writing Seminars, University of Southern Maine, 1981; Instructor, Academy of American Poets Poetry Writing Workshop, 1983–86; Writer's Residency, Centrum, Port Townsend, WA, 1984, Writer's Residency, Study and Conference Center in Bellagio, Italy, 1985. *Publications:* The Taxidermist's Daughter, 1979; Girl on a White Perch, 1987. *Contributor to:* Poems published in Antaeus, American Poetry Review, Poetry, The Southern Review, The Senora Review, Ploughshares, Cutbank; Columbia, a magazine of poetry and prose; Interviews in the Three Penny Review; Cutbank. *Honours:* First Book Award, Montana Arts Council, 1979; National Endowment of the Arts Fellowship, 1984; Editor's Choice Award, Columbia Review, 1985; The Richard Hugo Memorial Award, poetry, Cutbank, 1985. *Memberships:* Poetry Society of America, 1984–. *Address:* 406 E 83rd Street #4B, New York, NY 10028, USA.

SCHOENBRUN, David Franz, b. 15 Mar. 1915, New York City, USA. Radio/TV Correspondent. m. Dorothy Scher, 28 Sep. 1938, New York City, 1 daughter.

Education: BA, CCNY, 1930; NHon Dr Humane Letters, New School Social Research. *Publications:* As France Goes, 1957; The 3 Lives of Ch de Gaulle, 1965; The New Israelis, 1973; Triumph in Paris, 1976; Soldiers of the Night, 1980; America Inside Out, 1984. *Contributor to:* Harper's New Republic; New York Times; Life; Colliers; Saturday Evening Post; Le Figaro; VSD; many other journals and newspapers world wide. *Honours:* Best Book, Foreign Affairs, Overseas Press Club, As France Goes, 1958. *Memberships:* Author's Guild; PEN. *Literary Agent:* Scott Meredith. *Address:* N S Bienstock, 10 Columbus Circle, New York, NY 10019, USA.

SCHOENFELD, Maxwell Philip, b. 15 June 1936, Erie, Pennsylvania,. USA. University Professor. *Education:* BA, Allegheny College, 1957; MA, 1959, PhD, 1962, Cornell University. *Publications:* The War Ministry of Winston Churchill, 1972; Sir Winston Churchill: His Life & Times, 1973; Charles Vernon Gribley: A Naval Career, 1983. *Contributions to:* Churchill & Calais, 1940: Tragic Necessity or Unnecessary Tragedy, Wisconsin Dialogue, 1982. *Address:* Department of History, University of Wisconsin, Eau Claire, WI 54701, USA.

SCHOEPFER, Virginia Barbara, b. 17 Mar. 1934, Queens, New York. Writer. 1 daughter. *Education:* Pace University, New York City, 1951–52; New York University, 1958–60. *Publications:* Author of textbooks including: Legal Stenospeed Book for Speedwriting Inc. 1967; Desk Companion for Legal Secretaries 1970; Legal Textbooks and Dictionary 1973; Legal Typewriting and Dictation Course 1974. *Address:* 128-8 Birch Drive, Bricktown, NJ 08723, USA.

SCHOLBERG, Henry, b. 29 May 1921, Darjeeling, India. Librarian. m. Phyllis Nelson, 16 June 1951, Brainerd, 2 sons, 1 daughter. *Education:* BA, University of Illinois, USA. 1943; BS, 1954, MA, 1962, University of Minnesota. *Appointments:* Librarian, Columbia Heights High School, 1954–61; Librarian, Ames Library of South Asia, University of Minnesota, 1961–. *Publications:* The District Gazetteers of British India: A Bibliography, 1970; Bibliographie des Francais dans l'Inde, 1973; Bibliography of Goa and the Portuguese in India, 1982. *Contributor to:* Numerous professional journals. *Address:* 195 Windsor Lane, St Paul, MN 55112, USA.

SCHOLEFIELD, Alan, b. 15 Jan. 1931, Cape Town, Republic of South Africa. Author. m. Anthea Goddard, 3 daughters. *Education:* BA English Literature. *Publications:* A View of Vultures, 1966; Great Elephant; The Eagles of Malice; Wild Dog Running; The Young Masters; The Hammer of God; Lion in the Evening; The Alpha Raid; Venom, (filmed); Point of Honour; Berlin Blind; The Stone Flower; The Sea Cave; Fire in the Ice; King of the Golden Valley, 1985; The Dark Kingdoms, history; River Horse Lake, 13 part television series; Jock of the Bushveld, 8 part television series. *Literary Agent:* Elaine Greene Limited. *Address:* c/o Elaine Greene, 31 Newington Green, London N16 9PU, England.

SCHOLEY, Arthur (Edward), b. 1932, England, Writer of Plays, Children's Fiction, Libretti. *Publications:* The Song of Caedmon (with Donald Swann), 1971; Christmas Plays and Ideas for Worship, 1973; The Discontented Dervishes, 1977; Sallinka and the Golden Bird, 1978; Wacky and his Fuddlejig, (with Donald Swann), 1978; Singalive, (with Donald Swann), 1978; Herod and the Rooster, (with Ronald Chamberlain), 1979; The Dickens Christmas Carol Show, 1979; Twelve Tales for a Christmas Night, 1979; Baboushka, (with Donald Swann), 1979; Five Plays for Christmas, 1982; Four Plays about People, 1983; Martin the Cobbler, 1983; The Hosanna Kids, 1986. *Address:* 1 Cranbourne Road, London N10 2BT, England.

SCHON, Isabel, b. 19 Jan. 1940, Mexico. Professor of Library Science. m. R R Chalquest, 7 Oct. 1977, 1 daughter. *Education:* BS, Mankato State College; MA, Elementary Education, Michigan State University; PhD, Education, University of Colorado. *Publications:* Books in Spanish for Children and Young Adults (in press); A

Hispanic Heritage: A Guide to Juvenile Books About Hispanic People and Cultures, Series II, 1985; Dona Blanca and Other Hispanic Rhymes and Games, 1983; Books in Spanish for Children and Young Adults, 1983; A Hispanic Heritage: A Guide to Juvenile Books About Hispanic People and Cultures, 1980; Books in Spanish for Children and Young Adults, 1978. *Contributions to:* Top of the News, 1984; School Library Journal, 1984; Hispania, 1984, etc. *Address:* Department of Educational Technology/Library Science, FLS/College of Education, Arizona State University, Tempe, AZ 85287, USA.

SCHONFIELD, Hugh Joseph, b. 17 May, 1901, London, England. Author. m. Hélène Cohn, 27 July 1927, London, 3 daughters. *Education:* Doctor of Sacred Literature, University of Glasgow. *Publications:* According To The Hebrews, 1927; The Suez Canal, 1939; The Passover Plot, 1965; These Incredible Christians, 1968; The Politics of God, 1970; The Pentecost Revolution, 1974; The Essene Odyssey, 1984; The Authentic New Testament, editor and translator, 1955. *Contributions to:* Encyclopedia Britannica. *Honours:* Nominated for Nobel Peace Prize, 1952. *Memberships:* Vice-President, H G Wells, Society; Society of Authors; Fellow, International Society for Arts and Letters. *Literary Agent:* Mark Paterson. *Address:* 1033A Finchley Road, London NW11 7ES, England.

SCHOULTZ, Solveig Von, b. 5 Aug. 1907, Borga, Finland. Author. m. Erik Bergman, 7 July 1961, Aarhus. *Education:* Teacher's Qualification. *Publications:* Poetry: Eko av ett rop, 1946; Natet, 1956; Sank ditt ljus, 1963; De fyra flojtspelarna, 1975; Bortom traden hors havet, 1980; En enda minut, 1981; Short Novels: Ingenting ovanligt, 1948; Narmare nagon, 1951; Den blomstertid, 1958; Aven dina Kameler, 1965; Rymdbruden, 1970; Somliga mornar, 1976; Kolteckning, ofullbordad, 1983; Ingen dag forgaves, 1984; Plays for TV & Radio. *Honours:* The State Literary Prize, 1953, 1957, 1959, 1982; Svenska Litteratursallskapets Big Prize, 1959, 1981; Svenska Akademiens Big Literary Prize, 1972; The Church's Literary Prize, 1981; Edith Sodergran Prize, 1984; Honorary Member, Svenska Litteratursalliskapet, 1976; Pro Finlandia Medal, 1980. *Memberships:* Pen Club; Board Member, Finland's Svenska forfattareforening, 1947–69, 1982–. *Address:* Berggatan 22C, Helsinki 10, Finland.

SCHRADER, Ludwig, b. 11 Mar. 1932, Dresden, Germany. Professor of Romance Philology. m. Gidela Buechler, 26 July 1958, Zetel, 3 sons. *Education:* Universities of Hamburg, Murcia (Spain), Bonn; DPhil, Bonn University, 1958. *Publications:* Panurge und Hermes, 1958; Sinne und Sinnesverlnüpfungen, 1969, Spanish edition, 1975; Editor, Rabelais, Gargantua und Pantagruel German translation by Regis, with Commentary, 1964. *Contributor to:* Romanistisches Jahrbuch; Archiv fur das Studium der neueren Sprachen und Lit; Romanische Forchungen: Deutsches Dante-Jahrbuch, etc. *Memberships:* Assn Int de Hispanistes; Inst Int de Lit Iberoamericans. *Address:* Gleiwitzer Strasse 20 D–4-44 Kaarst 2, Federal Republic of Germany.

SCHREIBER, Hermann Otto Ludwig, b. 4 May 1920, Vienna, Austria. Writer. divorced, 1 son, 1 daughter. *Education:* PhD, University of Vienna, Austria, 1944; Professor honoris causa, Fed President of Austrian Republic, 1968. *Publications:* Die Hummen, The Huns, 1976; Auf den Spuren der Goten, On traces of the Goths, 1978; The Ship from Stone, History of Venice, 1982; The Versailles Novels, 6 volumes, 1977–84; various others. *Contributions to:* Damals; Berge. *Honours:* Several citations; Order of Merit, Arts and Letters, Austria. *Memberships:* Austrian section, PEN Club; Journalists Union, Western Germany. *Literary Agent:* Ava, Seeblickstrasse 46, Herrsching, Bavaria. *Address:* Schleissheimerstrasse 274, D–8000, Munich 40, Federal Republic of Germany.

SCHREIBER, Jan Edward, b. 31 July 1941, Wisconsin, USA, Social Scientist. m. Frances Nason, 23 June 1984, Boston, Mass, USA, 1son. *Education:* BA, Stanford University, USA, 1963; MA, University of Toronto, Canada, 1969; PhD, Brandeis University, USA. 1972. *Literary and Professional Appointments include:* Editor, University of Toronto Press, 1965–70; Editor, Godine Press, 1972–74; Research Director, Radcliffe Institute Programmes in Health Care, 1974–75; Research Associate, Harvard Ctr for Criminal Justice, 1976–78; President, Social Science Research Institute, 1978–83; Editor, Canto Mag, 1976–81; Research Scientist, Lincoln Institute, Cambridge, Mass, 1983–. *Publications:* Digressions, 1970; A Stroke upon the Sea, 1984; Godine Poetry Chapbooks, First Series (editor), 1974. *Contributions to:* Southern Review; Hudson Review; Modern Occasions; Agenda; Chowder Review; Counter/Measures; The Far Point; Canto. *Honours:* Carey Thomas Award for Creative Publishing, 1974. *Memberships:* Poets and Writers Incorporated; Associated Writing Programmes; PEN. *Literary Agent:* John Brockman Associates, NY, USA. *Address:* 210 Reservoir Road, Brookline, MA 02167, USA.

SCHROEDER, Andreas Peter, b. 26 Nov. 1946, Hoheneggelsen, Federal Republic of Germany. Writer. *Education:* BA, 1969, MA, 1971, University of British Columbia, Canada. *Major Publications:* The Ozone Minotaur (poetry), 1969; File of Uncertainties (poetry), 1971; The Lat Man (fiction, 1972; Universe (poetry, 1973; Shaking it Rough (non-fiction), 1976; Toccata in D (novella), 1985; Dustbowl mariner (novel), 1986. *Contributor to:* Numerous poetry & literary magazines including: Canadian Forum; Capilano Review; Poetry Chicago. *Memberships:* PEN Club; Writers Union of Canada; League of Canadian Poets; Canadian Periodical Publishers Association. *Honours include:* Canadian Film Development Corporation Grant, 1971. *Address:* P O Box 3127, Mission, British Columbia, V2V 4J3, Canada.

SCHUFF, Karen Elizabeth, b. 1 June 1937. Housewife; Poet. *Publications:* Barefoot Philosopher, 1968; Come, Take My Hand, 1968; Of Rhythm and Cake, 1970; Of June I Sing, 1979. *Contributions to:* Jean's Journal; Bardic Echoes; Pegasus; Cyclo-Flame; Circus Maximus; Dragon Fire; Dancing Dogs; Dangling Dreams; Outstanding Contemporary Poetry; APL Bulletin; Driftwood; Modern Haiku; Forty Salutes to Michigan Poets; Haiku Highlights; From Sea to Sea in Song; American Poet; Major Poets; Prairie Poet; Poet; American Bard; Golden Quill Press Anthology; Seneca Press; Modern Images; Moon Age Poets; Inky Trails; Happy Landing; Friendship Trail; Sixty-Eight Poets; Golden Song; Convergence and various others. *Honours include:* Writer's Digest Annual Poetry Contest, 1971, 75, 76, 78, 79; Poetry Society of Michigan Contest, 1977, 78, 81; Kentucky State Poetry Society, 1975, 76, 80; 1st Prize, 81 Non-Fiction, Piedmont Literary Contest Review. *Memberships:* Avalon World Arts Academy; Poetry Societies of Michigan and New Hampshire; Kentucky State Poetry Society; Piedmont Literary Society. *Address:* 15310 Windermere Avenue, Southgate, MI 48195, USA.

SCHULER, Carol Ann. b. 29 Jan. 1946, Bethlehem, Pennsylvania, USA. Technical Writer. *Education:* BA, Economics, Muhlenberg College, Allentown, Pennsylvania, 1968. *Publications:* The Vibes Book, with Ellin Dodge Young, 1979; Love Numbers, with Sandra Kovacs Stein, 1980. *Address:* 405 East 51st Street, New York City, NY 10022, USA.

SCHULLER, Robert Harold, b. 16 Sep. 1926, Alton, Iowa, USA. Minister/Motivational Speaker/Author. m. Arvella DeHaan, 15 June 1950, Newkirk, Iowa. 1 son 4 daughters. *Education:* BA, Hope College, Holland, Michigan, 1947; BD, Western Theological Seminary, Holland, Michigan, 1950. *Publications:* Your Future Is Your Friend, 1964; Move Ahead with Possibility thinking, 1967; SelfLove: The Dynamic Force of Success 1969; Power Ideas for a Happy Family, 1972; You Can Become the Person You Want To Be, 1973; The

Greatest Possibility Thinker That Ever Lived, 1973; Your Church Has Real Possibilities, 1974; Positive Prayers for Power-Filled Living, 1976; Reach Out For New Life, 1977; Peace of Mind Through Possibility Thinking, 1977; Daily Power Thoughts Volume 1, 1978; It's Possible, 1978; Discover Your Possibilities, 1978; The Courage of Carol, 1978; Turn Your Stress Into Strength, 1978; The Peak to Peek Principle, 1980; Self-Esteem: The New Reformation, 1982; Tough Times Never Last, But Tough People Do!, 1983; Tough Minded Faith for Tender Hearted People, 1984; The Power of Being Debt Free, with Paul David Dunn, 1985; The Be Happy Attitudes, 1985. *Contributor to:* Christianity Today; Family Circle; Saturday Evening Post; Guide Posts; Reader's Digest; USA Today. Compiled 1st topical and scriptural index of, The Institutes of the Christian Religion, by John Calvin. *Honours:* Honorary Doctorates from Asusa Pacific College, 1970; DD, Hope College, 1973; Pepperdine University, 1976; Barrington College (RI) 1977 and Hanyang University, Seoul, Korea, 1982; Recipient of The Freedoms Foundation of Valley Forge's Principal Award (the highest award for a sermon) 1973; Clergyman of the Year by Religious Heritage of America. *Address:* 12141 Lewis Street, Garden Grove, CA 92640, USA.

SCHULLERY, Paul David, b. 4 July 1948, Middletown, Pennsylvania, USA. Writer; Research Consultant. m. Dianne Patricia Russell, 11 June 1983, Lancaster, Ohio, USA. *Education:* BA, American History, Wittenberg University, Springfield, Ohio, 1970; MA, American History, Ohio University, Athens, Ohio, 1977. *Literary Appointments:* Editor, The American Fly Fisher, 1978–83 (journal of the American Museum of Fly-fishing, Manchester, Vermont). *Major Publications:* (editor) Old Yellowstone Days, 1979; The Bears of Yellowstone, 1980; (editor) The Grand Canyon: Early Impressions, 1981; (editor) American Bears: Selections from the Writings of Theodore Roosevelt, 1983; (with J D Varley) Freshwater Wilderness: Yellowstone Fishes and their World, 1983; Mountain Time, 1984; The National Parks (editor), 1986; Theodore Roosevelt: Wilderness Writings (editor), 1986. *Contributor to:* Country Journal; American West; Field & Stream; Newsweek; Early American Life; Outdoor Life; National Parks; and other fishing magazines; Scholarly historical articles for Montana; The Magazine of American History; The New York Times Book Review; and others. *Honours:* 2 Printing Industries of America Awards as co-designer & editor of, The American Fly-fisher; 2 awards from National Parks Cooperative Associations Competition, for Freshwater Wilderness. *Address:* PO Box 1004, Livingston, MT 59047, USA.

SCHULTZ, Joseph, b. 2 Dec. 1928, Chicago, Illinois, USA. Professor. m. Bella Intrater, 2 Aug. 1955, 1 son, 2 daughters. *Education:* BA, Yeshiva University, 1951; Rabbinic Ordination, Masters of Hebrew Literature, Jewish Theological Seminary, 1955; PhD, Brandeis University, 1962. *Appointments:* Lecturer, 1963, Instructor, 1964, Modern Languages, Professor, Religion, 1968, Boston University; Associate Profesor, History, Director, Danciger Judaic Studies, 1973, Oppenstein Brothers Distinguished Professor, Judaic Studies, 1978, University of Missouri. *Publications:* From Destruction to Rebirth: The Holocaust and the State of Israel, with Carla Klausner, 1978; From My Father's Vineyard, 1978; Judaism and the Gentile Faiths: Comparative Studies in Religion, 1981; Mid-American's Promise: A Profile of Kansas City Jewry, 1982. *Contributor to:* Jewish Quarterly Review; Journal of Ecumenical Studies; Journal of Religious Ethics; etc. *Honours:* Cyrus Adler Scholarm Jewish Theological Seminary, 1954; Lemmelein-Buttenweiser Prize, Excellence in Rabbinic Literature, Jewish Theological Seminary, 1955; Hyman G Enelow Award, Jewish Theological Seminary, 1976. *Memberships:* American Academy of Religion; American Academy for Jewish Research. *Address:* University of Missouri, Dept of History, 5100 Rockhill Road, Kansas City, MO 64110, USA.

SCHULTZ, Julianne, b. 2 Jan, 1956, Hamilton, New Zealand. Journalist. *Education:* BA, University of Queensland, Australia. *Publications:* The Phone Book; Australia's Communications Future on the Line (with Ian Reineccke), 1983; Steel City Blues: The Human Cost of Industrial Crisis, 1985. *Contributions to:* Australian newspapers & magazines including The National Times, The Age, Australian Society. Journals: Media; Culture & Society; Telecommunications Policy. *Address:* 391 Lawrence Hargrave Drive, Scarborough, New South Wales 2511, Australia.

SCHULTZ, Samuel Jacob, b. 9 June 1914, Mountain Lake, Minnesota, USA. Educator. Author. m. Eyla June Tolliver, 17 June 1943, 1 son, 1 daughter. *Education:* BA, John Fletcher College, 1940; BD, Faith Theological Seminary, 1944; MST 1945, Th D 1949, Harvard Divinity School. *Publications:* The Old Testamanet Speaks, 1960, 3rd edition 1980, translated into 15 languages; The Prophets Speak, 1968; Deuteronomy – Gospel of Love, 1971; The Gospel of Moses, 1974; Leviticus – God Dwelling Among His People, 1983; Message of the Old Testament, 1986. *Literary Appointments:* Editor, Journal of the Evangelical Theological Society, 1961–74. *Honours:* New York Univesity Study Grant, 1966; The Living and Active Word of God, Essays in honour of Samuel J Schultz, 1983. *Memberships:* Phi Sigma Tau; Wheaton College Scholastic Honors Society; Phi Alpha Chi – Gordon Conwell Theological Seminary. *Address:* 18 Lois Lane, Lexington, MA 02173, USA.

SCHUTZ, Susan Polis, b. 23 May 1944, New York City, USA. Writer. *Education:* BA, English, Biology. *Publications:* Come Into the Mountains, 1972; I Want to Laugh, I Want to Cry, 1972; Someone Else to Love, 1975; Love, Live and Share, 1980; Find Happiness in Everything You Do, 1982; Don't Be Afraid to Love, 1984. *Contributions to:* All major magazines (poems). *Honour:* Best-Selling Poet. *Address:* Blue Mountain Arts, P O Box 4549, Boulder, CO 80306, USA.

SCHUYLER, James Marcus, b. 9 Nov. 1923, Chicago, Illinois, USA. Poet. *Education:* Bethany College, West Virginia; University of Florence, Italy. *Publications:* Freely Espousing, 1969; The Crystal Lithium, 1972; Hymn to Life, 1974; The Morning of the Poem, 1981; A Few Days, 1985. *Contributions to:* Contributing Editor of Art News, New York, 1955–61; Poetry in Times Literary Supplement and in numerous American magazines including The New Yorker. *Honour:* Pulitzer Prize for, The Morning of the Poem, 1981. *Membership:* Fellow, Academy of American Poets. *Literary Agent:* Maxine Groffsky. *Address:* c/o Maxine Groffsky, 2 Fifth Avenue, New York, NY 10003, USA.

SCHUYLER, Keith C, b. 10 June 1919, Berwick, Pennylvania, USA. Writer. m. Eloise Jean Helt, 17 Jan. 1942, Berwick, 3 sons. *Appointments:* President, Pennsylvania Outdoor Writers Association; Board Member, Outdoor Writers of America Association. *Publications:* LURES – The Guide to Sport Fishing, 1955; Elusive Horisons, 1968; Archery from Golds to Big Game, 1971; Bow Hunting for Big Game, 1974; A Last Time to Listen, 1977; Flyrod Fishing, 1979. *Contributor to:* Columnist, Press-Enterprise Newspaper, 1938–, Veterans of Foreign Wars Magazine, 28 years, Pennsylvania Game News, 1963–; Freelance, Outdoor Life; Sports Affield; Field & Stream; Toronto Star; Farm Journal; Sports Illustrated; Police Gazette; etc. *Membership:* Authors Guild. *Address:* Box 3120–D, RD 3, Berwick, PA 18603, USA.

SCHWAB, Laurie, b. 26 Apr. 1947, West Germany. Journalist; Broadcaster. m. Helen Briggs, 20 Nov. 1982, Melbourne, Australia, 2 sons, 1 daughter. *Publications include:* The Socceroos & Their Opponents, 1979. *Contributions to:* Penthouse; Pix-People; Walkabout; Club; Game; The Age; Parade; etc. *Address:* 9 Vincent Avenue, St Albans, Victoria 3021, Australia.

SCHWAB, Peter, b. 15 Nov. 1940, USA. Professor of Political Science. *Education:* MA, 1966, PhD, Political Science, 1969, New School for Social Research, New York City, New York. *Publications:* Decision Making in Ethiopia, 1972; John F Kennedy, 1974; Haile Selassie, 1979; Human Rights, 1979; Towards a Human Rights Framework, 1982; Ethiopia, 1985. *Contributions to:* African Affairs, 1978; Journal of Modern African Studies, 1976; Marxist Government, Volume 2, 1981; Current History, 1985. *Honour:* Fulbright Scholar, 1967. *Address:* Department of Political Science, State University of New York, College at Purchase, Purchase, NY 10577, USA.

SCHWAGER, Edith,. b. 16 Dec. 1916, Trenton, New Jersey, USA. Editor. Divorced. 1 son, 1 daughter. *Appointments:* Editor, Medical Communications, 1977–81, 1983–. *Publications:* Editor, more than 1,000 medical articles, 1964–; Copy Editor, Executive Editor, 32 books including, Emergency Room Care, 1972; Cardiac Arrhythmias, 1973; Endrocrinology and Diabetes, 1975; Gastrointestinal Emergencies, 1976; Antibiotic Prophylaxis in Surgery, 1984. Author of: Regular Columnist, Dear Edie, Medical Communications, 1978–; Clarity Begins at Home, 1976, Writer vs Editor: Why Not Allies, 1976, The Redactor's Responsibility, 1977, articles in Medical Communications; Guest Editorial (Fishbein issue), Medical Communications, 1977; Continuing Self-Education of Medical Editors and Writers, Connecticut Medicine, 1979; etc. Teacher of workshops on medical writing and editing. *Honours:* Fellow, American Medical Writers Association, 1975; President's Award, AMWA, 1981; McGovern Honor Lectureship Award, 1983; Super Communicator Award, Women in Communications, 1984; Delaware Valley Chapter President's Award, 1985. *Memberships:* American Medical Writers Association, President, Delaware Valey Chapter, 1974–77, Chair, National Editors Section, 1977; Women in communications. *Address:* 4404 Sherwood Road, Philadelphia, PA 19131, USA.

SCHWARTS, Jeffrey, b. 29 Feb. 1952, Cleveland, Ohio. Teacher. m. Betsy Bowen, 19 Aug. 1984, Rumson, New Jersey, USA. *Education:* BA, English, Boston University, 1974; MA, English, University of Massachusetts, 1977; Doctor of Arts, English, Carnegie-Mellon University, 1985. *Publication:* Contending with the Dark, 1978. *Contributions to:* Poems in Agni Review; Aspects; Poetry Now; The Little Magazine; The Minnesota Review; The Cincinnati Review; Hanging Loose; Three Rivers Poetry Journal; The Greenfield Review; The Nantucket Review; Spirit That Moves Us. *Honours:* Academy of American Poets Prize, 1977; Adamson Awards for Writing, 1982, 1983, 1984. *Address:* 365 South Atlantic Avenue, Pittsburgh, PA 15224, USA.

SCHWARTZ, Eli, b. 2 Apr. 1921, New York City, USA. Professor of Economics. m. Renee Kartiganer, 29 Aug. 1948. Poughkeepsie, New York, 1 son, 1 daughter. *Education:* BC, Denver University, 1943; Special Student, University of Manchester, UK, 1945; MA, University of Connecticut, 1949; PhD, Brown University, 1952. *Publications:* Corporate Finance, 1961; Management Policies in Local Government Finance, 1945; Trouble in Eden: A Comparison of the British & Swedish Economies, 1980. *Contributions to:* Various academic & professional journals. *Address:* Department of Economics, LeHigh University, Bethlehem, PA 18015, USA.

SCHWARTZ, Kessel, b. 19 Mar. 1920, Kansas City, Missouri, USA. Professor of Hispanic Literature; Literary Historian. m. Barbara Lewin, 1947, New York, 3 sons, 1 daughter. *Education:* BA, with Distinction, 1940, MA, 1941, University of Missouri; PhD, University of New York, 1953. *Literary Appointments:* Hofstra College, 1949; Hamilton College, 1950; Colby College, 1951–53; University of Vermont, 1953–57; University of Arkansas, 1957–62; University of Miami, 1962–. *Publications:* A New History of Spanish Literature, with R Chandler, 1961; Fiestas, 1964; A New Anthology of Spanish Literature, with R Chandler, 1967; Introduction

to Modern Spanish Literature, 1968; Vincente Aleix Andre, 1969; The Meaning of Existence in Contemporary Hispanic Literature, 1970; Juan Goytislo, 1970; A New History of Spanish American Fiction, 1972; Studies on Twentieth Century Spanish and Spanish American Literature, 1983. *Contributions to:* Various magazines and journals including, Hispanic Review; Hispania; Revista Iberoamericana; Hispanofila; Kentucky Language Quarterly; Folio; Romance Notes; Journal of InterAmerican Studies; Revista de Estudio Hispanicos; Norte; Caribbean Studies; Southern Quarterly. *Honours:* American Association of College and Research Libraries, Academic book of the Year, 1972; Don Quijote Medal awarded by Sigma Delta Pi, National Spanish Honor Society, to outstanding American Hispanists. *Memberships:* Modern Language Association, Twentieth Century Spanish Literature Section, Secretary, 1964, Chairman, 1965; Associate Editor, of Hispania, Journal of the American Association of Teachers of Spanish and Portuguese, 1965–84; American Association of Teachers of Spanish and Portuguese, Peninsular Literature Section, Secretary; 1971, Chairman, 1972; President of Phi Beta Kappa Chapter of South Florida, 1977; Darien Action Committee, 1977; Hispanic Heritage Week Committee of Dade County, 1978; Phi Beta Kappa; Phi Sigma Iota; Pi Delta Phi; Sigma Delta Pi; Delta Phi Alpha; Omicron Delta Kappa. *Address:* University of Miami, Coral Gables, FL 33124, USA.

SCHWARTZ, Lloyd, b. 29 Nov, 1941. New York City, USA. Poet; Critic; Teacher. *Education:* BA, Queens College (CUNY), 1962; MA, 1963, PhD, Harvard University, 1976. *Appointments:* Classical Music Editor, Boston Phoenix, 1978–; Co-ordinating editor, Ploughshares, 1979; Director, Creative Writing Program, University of Massachusetts/Boston, 1982/1983, 1984–; Executive Committee, PEN, New England, 1983. *Publications:* These People, 1981; Elizabeth Bishop and Her Art, 1983. Contributor of reviews, articles to magazines and journals. *Honours:* ASCAP-Deems Taylor Award, 1981; Daniel Varoujan Prize, 1984; Nomination by Boston Phoenix for Pulitzer Prize, 1984 and 1985. *Memberships:* Poetry Society of America; New England Poetry Club; PEN/New England, Executive Comittee; MLA. *Address:* 27 Pennsylvania Avenue, Somerville, MA 02145, USA.

SCHWARTZ, Michael H, b. 9 May 1942, New York, USA. Sociologist. 1 son, 2 daughters. *Education:* BA, Highest Honours, University of California; PhD, Sociology, Harvard University. *Appointments:* University of California, 1969–70; University of Edinburgh, Scotland, 1975–76; State University of New York, 1970–75, 1976–. *Publications:* Radical Protest and Social Structure, 1976; The Power Structure of American Business, with B Mintz, 1985; The Business Elite as a Ruling Class, co-author, 1986; The Structural Analysis of Business, Editor with M Mizruchi, 1986. *Contributor to:* Social Problems; American Sociological Review; Science for the People; Social Problems; Nature; etc. *Honours:* National Science Foundation Grants, 1974, 1983; Chancellor's Award for Excellence in Teaching, State University of New York, 1975; Guggenheim Fellow, 1980. *Memberships:* American Sociological Association; Society for the Study of Social Problems. *Agent:* Richard Balkin, New York City. *Address:* Dept of Sociology, State University of New York at Stony Brook, Stony Brook, NY 11790, USA.

SCHWARTZ, Sheila Ruth, b. 15 Mar. 1936, New York City, USA. Professor, Author, Lecturer. Divorced, 1 son, 1 daughter (1 deceased). *Education:* BA, Adelphi University, 1956; MA, Teachers College, Columbia, 1958; Ed D, New York University, 1964. *Publications:* How People Lived in Ancient Greece and Rome, (with Reuben), 1966; How People Live in Mexico, 1967; Teaching the Humanities, 1970; Earth in Transit, 1971; Growing Up Guilty, 1978; Like Mother, Like Me, 1978; Teaching Adolescent Literature, 1979; Solid Gold Circle, 1980; Hollywood Writers' Wars, 1981; One Day You'll Go, 1982; Jealousy, 1983; Sororoity, 1986. *Contributions to:* Numerous magazines and journals.

Honours: Fulbright Fellow, University College, Cork, Republic of Ireland, 1977; Excellence in Letters, Excellence in Teaching, New York State, 1979; Contributions to Adolescent Literature, 1982; Research Award, State University of New York, 1984. *Memberships:* PEN; Authors' Guild; Past President, New York State English Council; Past President, Adolescent Literature Association. *Literary Agent:* Harvey Klinger. *Address:* State University College, New Paltz, NY 12561, USA.

SCHWARTZ, Steven, b. 3 May 1950, Chester, Pennsylvania, USA. University Professor. m. Emily Hammond, 25 May 1985, Tucson, Arisona, USA. *Education:* BA, Psychology, University of Colorado, 1973; MFA, Creative Writing, University of Ariszona, 1981. *Literary Appointments:* Founding Editor, Sonora Review, 1980–82; Fiction Editor, Colorado Review, 1984–. *Publications:* To Leningrad in Winter, 1985. *Contributions to:* The Virginia Quarterly Review; Antioch Review; Epoch; Mid-American Review; Cimarron Review; The New Mexico Humanities Review, Columbia. *Honours:* Pobert C S Downs Alumni Award in Fiction, 1981; Best American Short Stories, 1983; Distinguished Short Story Citation; O Henry Award, 1983; Breakthrough Award Competition, University of Missouri Press, 1983; PEN Syndicated Fiction Award, 1985. *Membership:* Associated Writing Programs. *Address:* English Department, Colorado State University, Fort Collins, CO 80523, USA.

SCHWARZ, Henry Guenter, b. 14 Dec. 1928, Berlin, Germany. Professor; Editor, Studies on East Asia, 1971–. *Education:* BA, 1954, MA, 1958, PhD, 1962, University of Wisconsin, USA. *Publications include:* China: Three Facets of a Giant, 1966; Liu Shao-ch'i and, People's War, 1969; Chinese Policies Toward Nationalities, 1971; Monogolian Short Stories, 1974; Studies on Mongolia, 1979; The Minorities of Northern China, 1984; Mongolian Publications of Western Washington University, 1984. *Contributions to:* Central Asiatic Journal; Zentralasiatische Studien; China Quarterly; Journal of Politics; Military Review; Journal of Asian Studies; Survival; China Report; Asian Studies; Orbis, and others. *Address:* Center for East Asian Studies, Western Washington University, Bellingham, WA 98225, USA.

SCHWEITZER, N Tina, b. 1941, Hartford, Connecticut, USA. Writer, Public Relations, Counselor. *Education:* BS, Emerson College, Boston, Massachusetts, USA. *Literary Appointments:* First business columnist, Hartford Woman newspaper, 1984, Freelance writer, Boston and Washington, 1965–67; Editor, Chief of Production Press/Information staff, Embassy of the Republic of Indonesia, Washington, 1969–70; Director of Public Relations, Greater Hartford Office of US Committee for UNICEF, 1984–. *Major Publication:* A Woman's John-hunting Guide, 1984; Numerous articles for Federal Government and private organisations. *Contributor to:* Television Stations WFSB, 1977, VCIT, 1983; WFSB, 1984. *Memberships:* American Mensa Ltd; Sigma Delta Chi, National Press Photographers Association, Inc; Elected Delegate, White House Conference on Small Business, 1986. *Address:* Schweitzer Associates, 30 Woodland Street Apt. #9b, Hartford, CT 06105, USA.

SCHWEMER, Erna Anna Helene, b. 30 Dec. 1915, Rüstringen, Oldenburg, Federal Republic of Germany. Secretary, Interpreter. m. 3 May 1944, at Wilhelmshaven, 1 son. *Education:* Interpreting School Diploma. *Major Publications:* Viel Vergnügen mit meinen Pferden (13 horse stories), 1959; Königreich Lasum (novel), 1961; Ferien mit Pferden (booklet), 1966; Zwei silberne Dosen (novel), 1969; Ponyferien auf der Schlattenburg (Youth Book), 1972; Der Fluß der Zeit steht niemals still (novel), 1974; Katrin und Fella (Youth Book), 1976; Zom Erfolg verurteilt (novel), 1981; Die Ablösung (novel), 1985. *Contributor to:* Horse-magazines (horse stories); Harburger Auzeigen und Nachrichten (novel); Rhapsody in Blue, 1975–76); some 35 papers with short stories and articles about

every-day life. *Literary Agent:* Robert Mölich-Verlag, Berlin. *Address:* Am Försterland 36, 2105 Seevetal 2– Fleestedt, Federal Republic of Germany.

SCHWENGER, Hannes, b. 26 Dec. 1941, Meiningen, Federal Germany Republic. Writer. *Education:* Studies, Psychology, Literature, Political Science; PhD. *Publications:* Antisexuelle Propaganda, Sexualpolitik in der Kirche, 1969; Das Ende der Unbescheidenheit, 1974; Schritsteller und Gewerkschaft, 1974; Solidaritat mit Rudolf Bahro, Editor, 1978; Literaturproduktion Zwishchen Selbstverwicklichung und Vergesellschaftung, 1979; Im Jahr des Grossen Bruders, 1983; Menschen im Buro, Editor, 1984. *Contributor to:* Vorwarts; Die Zeit; German Radio; Stuttgarter Zeitung. *Memberships:* Association German Writers, Berlin Chairman, 1973–78. *Address:* Pommersche Strasse 12a, 1000 Berlin 31, Federal Republic of Germany.

SCHWERNER, Armand, b. 5 Nov. 1927, Antwerp, Belgium. Poet. 2 sons. *Education:* MA, Columbia University, 1964. *Publications include:* Seawood, 1969; The Tablets I-XV, 1971; Redspell, from the American Indian, 1975; Bacchae Sonnets, 1977; The Work, the Joy and the Triumph of the Will, 1978; Sounds of the River Naranjana and The Tablets I-XXIV, 1983. *Contributions to:* Numerous magazines and journals including The Nation: San Francisco Review; Conjunctions; Kulcher; Bluefish; Caterpillar; Origin. *Honours:* Numerous Grants and Fellowships including: Faculty Research Fellowship, SUNY, 1970, 1972; Creative Artists Public Service Program Creative Writing Fellowship, 1973; National Endowment for the Humanities Summer Seminars, Princeton, 1978, Fordham, 1981. *Memberships:* PEN; Poetry Society of America. *Address:* 30 Catlin Avenue, Staten Island, New York, NY 10304, USA.

SCOBIE, Ilka, b. 5 Aug. 1950, Brooklyn, New York, USA. Writer; Teacher. 1 daughter. *Education:* School of Visual Arts, New York City; Arts and the Ageing, New School of Social Research, New York City; Poetry Classes with E Field, New York City. *Literary Appointment:* New York State Poets in the School, 1979–. *Publication:* There for the Taking, 1978. *Contributions to:* Letters; Country Women; Stroker; Mati; Coldspring Journal; Home Planet News; Cathartic; Gone Soft; Woodstock Review; Cats Eye; Woodstock Times; Snakeroot; Sunbury Rocky Mountain Creative Arts Journal; The Fred! London, England; Voicefree, Dublin, Ireland. *Address:* 20 Desbrosses Street, New York, NY 10013, USA.

SCOTT, Amoret Tanner, b. 27 Mar. 1930, Vancouver, British Columbia, Canada. Writer. m. Dr Ralph Tanner, 13 Aug. 1985, Hook, Hampshire, England. *Publications:* A-Z of Antique Collecting, 1963; Collecting Bygones, 1964; Tobacco and the Collector, 1966; Dummy Board Figures, 1966; Antiques as an Investment, 1967; The Collecting Book, for children, 1968; Discovering Staffordshire Figures, 1969, 86; Discovering Smoking Antiques, 1970, 81; Treasures in Your Attic, 1971; Wellington, 1973; Discovering Stately Homes, 1973, 3rd edition, 1981; Hedgerow Harvest, 1979; A Murmur of Bees, 1980; Parrots, 1982. *Contributions to:* The Saturday Book; British Council, book reviews; various antique press publications. *Membership:* The Ephemera Society. *Address:* The Malthouse, Heckfield, Basingstoke, Hampshire RG27 OLN, England.

SCOTT, Andrew, b. 10 May 1955, Edinburgh, Scotland. Science Writer. m. Margaret Wright, 6 Aug. 1977, Edinburgh. *Education:* BSc, Biochemistry, Edinburgh University, 1977; PhD, Darwin College, Cambridge University, 1981. *Publications:* Pirates of the Cell – the Story of Viruses from Molecole to Microbe, 1985. *Contributor to:* Numerous scientific articles, New Scientist; etc; Broadcasts of BBC External Service Writers. *Address:* 104 Duke Street, Edinburgh EH6 8HL, Scotland.

SCOTT, Charlotte Mary, b. 18 July 1907, Leicester, England. Journalist. m. Kenneth Stott, 19 Feb. 1937,

Salford, 1 daughter. *Publications:* Forgetting's No Excuse, 1973; Organization Woman, 1978; Ageing For Beginners, 1981; Before I Go, 1985. *Contributions to:* Guardian; Sunday Telegraph; Good Housekeeping. *Honours:* Honorary Fellow, Manchester Polytechnic, 1974; OBE, 1975. *Address:* Flat 4, 11 Morden Road, Blackheath, London SE3 0AA, England.

SCOTT, David Aubrey (Sir), b. 3 Aug. 1919, London, England. Retired Diplomat. m. Vera Kethleen Ibbitson, Sutton Coldfield, 21 Jan, 1941, 2 sons, 1 daughter. *Literary Appointments:* Leader writer, Egyptian Gazette, Cairo, 1946–47. *Publication:* Ambassador in Black & White, 1981. *Contributions to:* Egyptian Gazette, 1946–47; The Aeroplane, 1946–49. *Honour:* GCMG, 1979. *Membership:* PEN. *Literary Agent:* Peterborough Literary Agency, The Daily Telegraph. *Address:* Wayside, Moushill Lane, Milford, Godalming, Surrey GU8 5BQ, England.

SCOTT, Elizabeth Patricia, b. 20 Feb. 1938, Hendon, Middlesex, England. Clerical Officer. m. Alan G D Scott, 1 July 1961, divorced 1974. *Education:* Hornsey College of Arts, UK. *Literary Appointments:* Clerk/Typist; Clerical Officer, Stocktender; Horticulturalist; Clerical Officer Law Society. *Contributor to:* Poetry Today; Living Poetry; Poetic Moods; Editor Choice; Little Children. *Honours:* Finalist, Living Poetry, 1974; Diploma, International Academy of Poets, 1976; Diploma and Plaque, International Who's Who in Poetry, 1977; Honourable Mention and Reading, NY Shelley Society, 1977; 1st Honourable Mention and Reading, New York, 1984. *Memberships:* Founder Fellow, Internaitonal Academy of Poets; Fellow, International Biographical Association; Honorary Advisor, American Biographical Institute; Honorary Member, Shelley Society of New York; International Poetry Society; Byron Society. *Address:* 24 Martins Walk, Muswell Hill, London N10 1JT, England.

SCOTT, George Peter, b. 1 Aug. 1946, Newcastle upon Tyne, England. Journalist. m. Cherill Andrea Williams, 28 Dec. 1968, 1 daughter. *Education:* BA Modern History, Merton College, University of Oxford; Visiting Scholar, School of Public Policy, University of California, Berkeley, USA. *Literary Appointments:* The Times, 1969–71 and 1974–76; Deputy Editor 1971–73, Editor 1976–, The Times Higher Education Supplement. *Publications:* Strategies for Post Secondary Education, 1976; The Crisis of the University, 1984. *Contributions to:* Journals in educational studies; Edited collections of essays. *Address:* The Times Higher Education Supplement, Priory House, St John's Lane, London EC1, England.

SCOTT, John Anthony, b. 20 Jan. 1916, London, England. Historian. m. Maria Hahar, 28 Aug. 1940, Wales, Massachusetts, USA, 2 sons, 1 daughter. *Education:* BA Modern Greats 1st class Honours summa cum laude 1937, MA 1945, Trinity College, Oxford University; MA 1947, PhD 1950, History and Political Science, Columbia University, USA. *Literary Appointments:* General editor, Living History Library, Alfred A Knopf Inc, 1965–76; Co-editor, Folksong in the Classroom Magazine, 1980–. *Publications include:* Introduction to Contemporary Civilisation in the West, co-editor, 1946; Republican Ideas and the Liberal Tradition in France 1870–1914, 1951 and 1966; Living Documents in American History, 2 volumes, 1964 and 1968; The Ballad of America: The History of the United States in Song and Story, 1966 and 1983; Hard Trials on my Way: Slavery and the Struggle Against It, 1800–1860, 1974 and 1978; Fanny Kemble's America, 1973 and 1975; Woman Against Slavery: The Life of Harriet Beecher Stowe, 1978; The Story of America, 1984. *Contributions to:* Journal including: Journal of Negro History; The Nation; Rutgers Law Review; Journal of the Early Republic; Perspectives. *Memberships include:* American Historical Association; Organisation of American Historians; Association for the Study of Negro History. *Address:* School of Law, Rutgers University, 15 Washington, Newark, NJ 07102, USA.

SCOTT, John Somerville, b. 22 Feb. 1915, Jullundur, India. Writer; Translator. m. Maria Gabriele Steiner, 1960, London, England. 3 sons, 2 daughters. *Education:* BSc Mining Engineering; Fellow, Institute of Linquistics; (Russian); Member, Institute of Linguistics (French & German); Chartered Structural Engineer. *Major Publications:* Penguin Dictionary of Civil Engineering, 3rd Edition, 1981; Penguin Dictionary of Building, 3rd edition, 1984; Longman's Civil Engineering Reader for Engineers Learning English, 1968; Butterworth's Dictionary of Waste & Water Treatment (Pollution), (with P Smith), 1983. *Address:* 74 Park Avenue South, London N8 8LS, England.

SCOTT, Lowell Kendrick, b. 4 May 1943, Glasgow, Kentucky, USA. Educator. m. Elizabeth Carroll, 20 Aug. 1966, Bowling Green, 2 daughters. *Education:* BA, 1966, MA, 1969, Western Kentucky University; EdD, University of Kentucky, 1976. *Contributions to:* Educational Administration Quarterly; Medical Education; ERIC Clearinghouse on tests, Measurement and Evaluation; Journal of Educational Psychological Measurement; Journal of Medical Education; Journal of Psychiatric Education; Southern Medical Journal; KSBA Agenda; Kentucky School Board Journal; Government Union Review (and Special education edition, 1982); Journal of Chronic diseases. Author, Selecting a Superintendent, for Kentucky School Boards Association, 1983. Editor, Policy Reference manual, 1983. *Address:* 29 Ryswick Lane, Frankfurt, KY 40601, USA.

SCOTT, Nathan A Jnr, b. 24 Apr. 1925, Cleveland, Ohio, USA. University Professor. m. Charlotte Hanley, 21 Dec. 1946, New York City, 1 son, 1 daughter. *Education:* BA, University of Michigan, 1944; BD, Union of Theological Seminary (New York) 1946; PhD, Columbia University, 1949. *Literary Appointments:* Instructor, Assistant Professor, Associate Professor of Humanities, Howard University, 1948–55; University of Chicago, 1955–76; Assistant Professor, Associate Professor and Professor of Theology and Literature, University of Virginia, 1976–. *Publications include:* Albert Camus in the series, Studies in Modern European Literature and Thought, 1962; Samuel Beckett in the series, Studies in Modern European Literature and Thought, 1965; The Broken Center: Studies in the Theological Horizon of Modern Literature, 1966; Craters of the Spirit: Studies in the Modern Novel, 1969; Negative Capability: Studies in the New Literature and the Religious Situation, 1969; The Wild Prayer of Longing: Poetry and the Sacred, 1971; Three American Moralists – Mailer, Bellows, Trilling, 1973; The Poetry of Civic Virtue – Eliot, Malraux, Aude, 1976; Mirrors of Man in Existentialism, 1979; The Poetics of Belief: Studies in Coleridge, Arnold, Pater, Santayna, Stevens and Heidegger, 1985. *Contributions to:* The Chicago Review; The Centennial Review; The London Magazine; The Kenyon review; The Denver Quarterly Review; The American Scholar; Boundary 2; New Literary History; The Carleton Miscellany; The Journal of the American Academy of Religion; Cross Currents; The Journal of Religion and many others. *Honours:* Litt D, Ripon College, 1965; LHD, Wittenberg University, 1965; DD, Philadelphia Divinity School, 1967; STD, General Theological Seminary, 1968; Litt D, St Mary's College, Notre Dame, 1969; Litt D, Denison University, 1976; Litt D, Brown University, 1981; Litt D, Northwestern University, 1982; DD, Virginia Theological Seminary, 1985. *Memberships:* Modern Language Association; American Philosophical Association; American Academy of Religion (President 1986). *Address:* Department of Religious Studies, University of Virginia, Charlottesville, VA 22903, USA.

SCOTT, Roy Vernon, b. 26 Dec. 1927, Wrights, Illinois, USA. College Professor. m. Jane A Brayford, 9 July 1959, Collinsville, 1 son, 2 daughters. *Education:* BS, Iowa State University, 1952; MA, 1953; PhD, 1957, University of Illinois. *Appointments:* Asitant Professor, University of Southwestern Louisiana, 1957–58; Associate, Business History Foundation, 1958–59; Assistant Professor, University of Missouri, 1959–60; Assistant

Professor, 1960–62, Associate Professor, 1962–64, Professor, 1964–78, Distinguishged Professor, 1978–, Mississippi State University. *Publications:* The Agrarian Movement in Illinois, 1880–1896, 1962; The Reluctant Farmer: The Rise of Agricultural Extension to 1914, 1970; The Public Career of Cully A Cobb: A Study in Agricultural Leadership, 1973; Editor, Southern Agriculture since the Civil War, 1979; Railroad Development Programs in the Twentieth Century, 1985. *Contributor to:* Journal of transport History; Agricultural History; etc. *Honours:* Edwards Award in Agricultural History, 1958; American Philosophical Society Grants, 1962, 1969, 1970, 1976; Certificate of Communication, American Asociation of State and Local History, 1977. *Memberships:* Agricultural History Society, Vice President, 1977–78, President, 1978–79; American Historical Association; Organization of American Historians; Southern Historical Association; American Associaiton of University Professors; etc. *Address:* Dept of History, Mississippi State University, Mississippi State, MS 39762, USA.

SCOTT STOKES, Henry, b. 15 June 1938, Glastonbury, Somerset, England. Writer. m. Akiko Sugiyama, 27 Apr. 1974, 1 son. *Education:* MA, Oxford University. *Publications:* The Life and Death of Yukio Mishima, 1974. *Literary Agent:* Roger Straus. *Address:* Wick Hollow, Glastonbury, Somerset, England.

SCOVILLE, James Griffin, b. 19 Mar. 1940, Amarillo, Texas, USA. Professor. m. Judith Nelson, 11 June 1962, Oberlin, Ohio, 1 son. *Education:* AB, Oberlin College, 1961; AM 1963, PhD 1965, Harvard University. *Publications:* The Job Content of the US Economy, 1940–70, 1969; The Internaitonal Labour Movement in Transition, (with Adolf Sturmthal), 1972; Concepts and Measurements for Occupational Analysis, 1973. *Contributions to:* Numerous scholarly articles in publications including: Industrial Relations; Economic Development and Cultural Change; Review of Economics and Statistics. *Address:* 4849 Girard Avenue South, Minneapolis, MN 55409, USA.

SCRIMGEOUR, James Richard, b. 29 July 1938, Holden, Massachusetts, USA. Associate Professor of English. m. Christine Xanthakos, 13 Oct. 1963, Southbridge, Massachusetts, 2 sons, 1 daughter. *Education:* BA, Clark University, 1963; MA 1968, Phd 1972, University of Massachusetts, Amherst. *Literary Appointments:* Assistant Professor of English, Illinois State University, 1971–78; Assistant/Associate Professor of English, Western Connecticut State University, 1978–; Co-editor, Pikestaff Publications, 1977–. *Publications:* What Is That Country Standing Inside You, poetry anthology, (editor), 1976; Sean O'Casey, 1979; Dikel, Your Hands and other poems, 1979. *Contributions to:* Modern Drama; Scandinavian Studies; Sean O'Casey Review. *Address:* 36 Caldwell Drive, New Milford, CT 06776, USA.

SCRUGGS, Charles Eugene, b. 16 Nov. 1937, Cullman, Alabama, USA. University Professor. m. La Donna Kathryn Loesher, 13 June 1959, Ohio, 2 daughters. *Education:* BA, Transylvania University, Lexington, Kentucky, 1959; MA 1962; PhD French Language and Literature, 1968, University of Kentucky. *Literary Appointments:* Instructor in French, University of Kentucky, 1962; Instructor in French, Appalachian State University, 1963–65; Assistant Professor of French, Eastern Kentucky University, 1967–72; Associate Professor of French, University of South Florida, 1972–. *Publication:* Charles Dassoucy: Adventures in the Age of Louis XIV, 1984. *Contributions to:* Kentucky Romance Quarterly; USF Language Quarterly; Revue de l'Université d'Ottawa. *Memberships:* American Association of Teachers of French; American Translators Association; North American Society for Seventeenth Century French Literature; South Atlantic Modern Language Association. *Address:* 501 San Jose Place, Temple Terrace, FL 33617, USA.

SCRUTON, Roger, b. 27 Feb. 1944, Buslingthorpe, England. Professor of Aesthetics. *Education:* BA, MA,

PhD, Jesus College, Cambridge; Inner Temple Bar. *Publications:* Art and Imagination, 1974; The Aesthetics of Architecture, 1979; The Meaning of Conservationism, 1980; The Politics of Culture, 1981; Fortnight's Anger, 1981; A Short History of Modern Philosophy, 1981; A Dictionary of Political Thought, 1982; The Aesthetic Understanding, 1983; Thinkers of the New Left, 1985; Sexual Desire, 1986. *Contributions to:* The Times; Times Literary Supplement; Encounter; Spectator; Salisbury Review; Public Interest; American scholar; P N Review. *Literary Agent:* Curtis Brown. *Address:* Department of Philosophy, Birbeck College, Malet Street, London WC1, England.

SCULLY, James, b. 23 Feb. 1937, New Haven, Connecticut, USA. Teacher. m. Arlene Steeves, 10 Sep. 1960, 2 sons, 1 daughter. *Education:* BA High Honours 1959, PhD 1964, University of Connecticut. *Publications:* Modern Poetrics, 1965; The Marches, 1967; Avenue of the Americas, 1971; Santiago Poems, 1975; Prometheus Bound, by Aeschylus, (translated with C J Herington), 1975; Quechua Peoples Poetry, (translated with Maria Proser), 1977; Scrap Book, 1977; De Repente/All of a Sudden, (translated with Maria Proser and Arlene Scully), 1979; May Day, 1980; Apollo Helmet, 1983. *Contributions to:* Minnesota Review; Fiction International; The Nation; Alcatraz; The Poetry Review; Compages; Harvard Magazine; Left Curve; Jump/Cut; The Unrealist; New Yorker; Praxis; The Radical Teacher; Arion; Massachusetts Review; Leviathan; Critical Quarterly; Poetry. *Honours:* Ingram Merrill Foundation Felowship, 1962–63; Lamont Poetry Award, 1967; Guggenheim Fellowship 1973–74; National Endowment for the Arts Fellowship, 1976–77; Islandsand Continents Translation Award, 1980; Bookbuilders of Boston Award, 1983. *Memberships:* PEN; Poetry Society of America. *Address:* 250 Lewiston Avenue, Willimantic, CT 06226, USA.

SCUPHAM, John Peter, b. 24 Feb. 1933, Liverpool, England; Teacher; Publisher. m. Carola Nance Braunholtz, 10 Aug. 1957, Harpenden, 3 sons, 1 daughter. *Education:* Honours Degree, English, Emmanuel College, Cambridge University. *Publications:* The Snowing Globe, 1972; Prehistories, 1975; The Hinterland, 1977; Summer Palaces, 1980; Winter Quarters, 1983. *Contributor to:* Reviews for Times Literary Supplement; Poems broadcast by BBC; Poems in most leading British Journals & Magazines, and Contemporary Penguin Anthologies. *Address:* 2 Taylor's Hill, Hitchin, Hertfordshire, SG4 9AD, England.

SEAGERS, Ralph W, b. 3 Nov. 1911, Geneva, NY, USA. Professor, Emeritus of English. *Education:* University of California; Berkeley, 1950–51; LittD, Keuka College, 1970. *Publications:* (verse) Songs from a Willow Whistle, (Wake-Brook House), 1956; Beyond the Green Gate, (Wake-Brook House), 1958; Christmas Chimes in Rhyme (Judson Press), 1962; Cup, Flagon and Fountain, (Wake-Brook House), 1965; A Choice of Dreams, (Partridge Press), 1970; Wheatfields and Vineyards, (Christian Herald House), 1975; The Manger Mouse and Other Christmas Poems, (Judson Press), 1977; (Prose) The Sound of an Echo, (Wake-Brook House), 1963; Little Yates and the United States (Tillman Press), 1976; (Verse) Hiding in Plain Sight (Tillman Press), 1982; The Love Tree (The Dundee Observer), 1985. *Memberships include:* Poetry Society of America. *Address:* Penn Yan, NY 14527, USA.

SEALE, Jan Epton, b. 28 Aug, 1939, Pilot Point, Texas, USA. Writer. m. Carl Seale, 4 Apr. 1958, 3 sons. *Education:* BA, University of Louisville; MA, North Texas State University. *Publications:* Bonds, 1978, 2nd edition 1981; Sharing the House, 1982. *Contributor to:* Chicago Tribune; San Francisco Chronicle; Kansas Chronicle; Kansas City Star; Hartford Courant; Arizona Republic; New America; Wind; New Mexico; Humanities Review; Calyx; Kalliope; Latitude 30°18; Nimrod Pikestaff; Forum; Aileron; Cedar Rock; Newsday. *Honour:* NEA Creative Writing Fellowship, 1982. *Address:* 400 Sycamore, McAllen, TX 78501, USA.

SEALEY, Leonard George William, b. 7 May 1923, London, England. Education Author & Consultant. m. Nancy Verre, 29 Aug. 1972, Lewes, England, 1 son, 4 sons from previous marriage. *Education:* Loughborough College of Advanced Technology; Teachers Certificate, Peterborough College; DipEd, MEd, University of Leicester. *Publications:* Creative Use of Mathematics, 1961; Communication & Learning, co-author, 1962; Exploring Language, 1968; Basic Skills in Learning, 1970; Lively Reading, 1973; General Editor, Macmillan Children's Encyclopaedia, 1974; Open Education: A Study of Selected American Elementary Schools, 1977; Children's Writing, co-author, 1979. *Contributions to:* Teachers College Record. *Memberships:* FRSA: Phi Delta Kappa. *Address:* 11 Chilton Street, Plymouth, MA 02360, USA.

SEALFON, Peggy, b. 3 Mar. 1949, New York City, USA. Writer; Author. m. Gerald Ilowite, 17 Feb. 1984, New York. *Education:* BS, New York University. *Publication:* The Magic of Instant Photography. *Contributions to:* McCalls; Newsweek International; Science Digest; Better Homes & Gardens; American Way; Travel & Leisure; Zoom (France); Camera (UK); Popular Photography; New York Times; etc. *Memberships:* Authors Guild; Authors League; American Society of Journalists & Authors. *Address:* PO Box 3527, Princeton, NJ 08540, USA.

SEALTS, Merton M, Jr. b. 8 Dec. 1915, Lima, Ohio, USA. Emeritus Professor of English. m. Ruth Louise Mackenzie, 17 Nov. 1942, Franklin, Massachusetts, USA. *Education:* BA, College of Wooster, 1937; PhD Yale University, 1942; DLitt, College of Wooster, 1974. *Literary Appointments:* Instuctor in English, University of Missouri, 1941–42; Instructor in English, Wellesley College, 1946–48; Assistant Professor, 1948–51, Associate Professor 1951–58, Professor of English, Lawrence College, University; Appleton, Wisconsin, 1958–65; Professor of English, 1965–75; Henry A Pochmann Professor of English, 1975–82, Emeritus Professor, 1982–, University of Wisconsin, Madison. *Major Publications:* Melville as Lecturer, 1957, 1970; Billy Bud, Sailor, (co-editor), 1962; The Journals & Miscellaneous Notebooks of Ralph Waldo Emerson, volumes 5 (1965) & 10 (1973) (editor); Melville's Reading: A Check-list of Books Owned & Borrowed, 1966; Emerson's Nature: Origin, Growth, Meaning (co-editor), 1969, 1979; The Early Lives of Melville..., 1974; Pursuing Melville, 1940–80; Chapters & Essays, 1982. *Contributor to:* Many periodicals. *Honours:* Fellow, Fund for the Advancement of Education (Ford Foundation), 1953–54; Fellow, Guggenheim Memorial Foundation, 1962–63; Senior Fellow, National Endowment for the Humanities, 1975. *Memberships:* Modern Language Association of America; Nathaniel Hawthorne Society; Poe Studies Association; The Melville Society, President, 1953; The Thoreau Society. *Address:* 4006 Mandan Crescent, Madison, WI 53711, USA.

SEARCY, Ronald L, b. 18 Apr. 1930, Los Angeles, California, USA. Medical Writers. m. Yvonne Vandergriff, 25 Aug. 1951, Las Vegas, Nevada, USA, 1 son, 1 daughter. *Education:* BA, 1952, Whittier College, California; PhD, 1957, University of Southern California. *Literary Appointments:* Director of Diagnostic Research, Hoffman-LaRoche, 1966–70; Director of Diagnostic Research, Searle/US, 1970–74; Director of Advertising and Promotion, Sigma Diagnostics, St Louis, Missouri, 1974–. *Publications:* Lipoprotien Chemistry in Health and Disease, (Charles C Thomas), 1962; Diagnostic Biochemistry, (McGraw-Hill), 1969; Lipopathies, (Charels C Thomas), 1971. *Contributions to:* New England Journal of Medicine; Lancet; Journal of the American Medical Association; American Journal of Clinical Pathology; Clinical Chemistry; Clinica Chimica Acta; Journal of Medical Technology; Analytical Biochemisty; American Journal of Gastroenterology; Metabolism; Clinical Biochemistry; Journal of Atheroschlerosis Research; Journal of Lipid Research, and others. *Membership:* American Medical Writers' Association. *Address:* 293 Oakleigh Woods Drive, Ballwin, MO 63011, USA.

SEARLS, Henry H Jr, b. 10 Aug. 1922, San Francisco, USA. Author. m. Berna Ann Cooper, 19 Dec. 1959, Copenhagen, Denmark, 2 sons, 1 daughter. *Education:* University of California, Berkeley; USNA, Annapolis, Maryland. *Publications include:* Big X; Crowded Sky; Pilgrim Project; The Penetrators; The Hero Ship; The Lost Prince: Young Joe, the Forgotten Kennedy; Pentagon; Overboard; Jaws II; Firewind; Sounding; Blood Song. *Memberships:* Authors League; Writers Guild. *Literary Agent:* Scott Meredith. *Address:* Scott Meredith Agency, 845 3rd Avenue, New York, NY 10022, USA.

SEARS, David O'Keefe, b. 24 June 1935, Urbana, Illinois, USA. Professor, Psychology and Political Science; Dean, Social Sciences. 3 daughters. *Education:* BA, Stanford University, 1957; MS, 1959, PhD, 1962, Yale University. *Publications:* Public Opinion, with R E Lane, 1964; Social Psychology, with J L Freeman, J M Carlsmith, 1970, 4th edition 1981, 5th edition with J L Freedman, L A Peplau, 1985; The Politics of Violence: The New Urban Blacks & The Watts Riot, with J B McConahay, 1973; Tax Revolt: Something for Northing on California, with J Citrin, 1982, 2nd edition 1985. *Honours:* Edward L Bernays Foundation Psychology and Social Issues Book Issues Book Award, 1975; Gordon Allport Intergroup Relations Prize. *Memberships:* Fellow, American Psychological Association; American Political Science Association. *Address:* Office of the Provost, College of Letters and Science, University of California, Los Angeles, CA 90024, USA.

SEBEOK, Thomas A, b. 9 Nov. 1920, Budapest. University Professor. *Education:* BA University of Chicago, 1941; MA 1943, PhD 1945 Princeton University. *Literary Appointments:* Distinguished Professor of Linguistics 1967–78; Distinguished Professor of Linguistics and Semiotics 1978–, Professor of Anthropology; Professor of Uralic and Altaic Studies, Indiana University. Visiting Professor to numerous Universities throughout the world. Executive Editor, Advances in Semiotics 1976–; Co-editor, Studies in Animal Communication 1979–; General Editor, Nonverbal Behaviour, 1979–85; Co-Editor, Topics in Contemporary Semiotics, 1979–; Co-Editor, Topics in Languages and Linguistics 1979–. *Publications:* Author of executive publications in the field of Linguistics and Semiotics. Most recent include: Classics of Modern Semiotics (co-author); Contributions to the Doctrine of Signs; Encyclopedic Dictionary of Semiotics (editor-in-chief); The Semiotic Sphere (co-editor). *Contributions to:* American Journal of Semiotics; International Semiotics Spectrum; Times Literary Supplement; American Scientist; The Skeptical Inquirer; Poetics Today and many others. *Honours:* Recipient of numerous Fellowships, major grants and special appointments since 1943, most recently; Regents Fellow, Smithsonian Institution, 1983–84; Research Associate, Office of Symposia and Seminars, Smithsonian Institution 1984–87; Adjunct Fellow, Woodrow Wilson International Center for Scholars 1983–84; Fellow, The Committee for the Scientific Invetigation of Claims of the Paranormal, 1983–; Councilor, Society for Scientific Exploration, 1983–85; Distinguished Service Award, American Anthropological Association, 1984. *Memberships:* Committee of Presidents, Linguistic Society of America; President, Semiotic Society of America; Member of numerous other scientific societies and associations. *Address:* 1104 Covenanter Drive, Bloomington, IN 47401, USA.

SEBESTYEN, Ouida Dockery, b. 13 Feb. 1924, Texas, USA. Writer of Fiction for Young Adults. divorced, 1 son. *Publications:* Words By Heart, 1979; Far From Home, 1980; IOU's, 1982; On Fire, 1985. *Contributions to:* The ALAN Review (National Council of Teachers of English); Short stories in American magazines and anthologies. *Honours:* Children's Book Award, International Reading Association, 1979; American Book Award (Childrens Fiction), 1982; Silver Pencil, Holland, 1984. *Membership:* Authors League of America. *Address:* 115 South 36th Street, Boulder, CO 80303, USA.

SEE, Carolyn, b. 13 Jan. 1934, California, USA. Writer. m. (1) Richard See, 18 Feb. 1954, (2) Tom Sturak, 30 Apr. 1960, 2 daughters. *Education:* PhD, University of California at Los Angeles, 1953. *Literary Appointments:* Professor of English, University of California at Los Angeles. *Major Publications:* The Rest is Done with Mirrors, 1970; Blue Money, 1974; Mothers Daughters, 1977; Rhine Maidens, 1980; Golden Days, 1985; (under pseudonym): Lotus Land, 1983; 1-10 Shanghai Road, 1985. *Contributor to:* Esquire; McCalls; Atlantic; Sports Illustrated; California Magazine; Contributing Editor, Book reviews, Los Angeles Times. *Honours:* Samuel Goldwyn Award, 1963; Sidney Hillman Award, 1969; National Endowment for the Arts, Grant, 1974. *Literary Agent:* Elaine Markson. *Address:* P O Box 107, Topanga, CA 90290, USA.

SEE, Lisa Lenine, b. 18 Feb. 195, Paris, France. Writer. m. Richard Becker Kendall, 18 July 1981, Los Angeles, USA, 1 son. *Education:* BA, Loyola Marymount University. *Publications:* Lotus Land (as Monica Higland), 1983; Day on the Life of Hawaii (text, as Lisa See), 1984. *Contributions to:* Publisher's Weekly; TV Guide; USA Today; Dynamic Years; Twin Circle; Sporting Times; Women's Sports. *Honour:* Proclamation, City of Los Angeles, 1983. *Membership:* ASJA. *Literary Agent:* Elaine Markson. *Address:* 17975 Porto Marina Way, Pacific Palisades, CA 90272, USA.

SEEBOHM, Caroline, b. 14 Sep. 1940, Nottinghamshire, England. Writer. m. Walter H Lippincott, 6 June 1974, London, 1 son, 1 daughter. *Education:* BA, Oxford University. *Publications:* 20th Century Decorating, Architecture & Gardens, 1980; The Man Who Was Vogue, 1982. *Contributor to:* House & Garden; Vogue; New York Times; Wall St Journal; New Statesman; Connoisseur; Vanity Fair; Village Voice. *Address:* 106 Iroquois Place, Ithaca, NY 14850, USA.

SEED, Cecile Eugenie, b. 18 May 1930, Cape Town, Republic of South Africa. Writer. m. Edward Robert Seed, 31 Oct. 1954, Pietermartitzburg, Natal, 3 sons, 1 daughter. *Publications:* The Voice of the Great Elephant, 1968, 85; The Prince o the Bay, 1969; The Broken Spear, 1972; Strangers in the Land, 1975; The Great Thirst, 1971, 85; Cancas City, 1968, 3rd edition, 1983; The Spy Hill, 1984. *Address:* 10 Pioneer Crescent, Northdene, Natal 4093, Republic of South Africa.

SEELEY, Ivor Hugh, b. 8 July 1924, Petersfield, Hampshire, England. Emeritus Professor; Chartered Surveyor. m. Gladys Lilian Bensley, 27 Mar. 1947, Martham, 2 daughters. *Education:* BSc, London University; MA, PhD, Nottingham University; FRICS; CEng; FICE; MCIOB. *Literary Appointments:* Editor, Building and Surveying Series, Macmillan Press; Book Reviewer, The Contruction Surveyor. *Publications:* Building Quantities Explained; Civil Engineering Quantities; Civil Engineering Specification; Building Economics; Building Technology; Building Maintenance; Advanced Building Measurement; Quantity Surveying Practice; Building Surveys, Reports and Dilapidations. *Contributions to:* Professional and technical journals of various articles. *Memberships:* General Council, Royal Institution of Chartered Surveyors. *Address:* 36a Mapperley Hall Drive, Mapperley Park, Nottingham NG3 5EW, England.

SEELY, Norma Yvonne, b. 12 Oct. 1942, Tillamook, Oregon, USA. Writer. m. Lloyd Seely, Jr, 15 May 1965, Reno, Nevada, USA, 2 daughters. *Education:* BA History, Lewis & Clark College, Portland, Oregon, USA. *Major Publications:* The Treasure of Seacliff Manor, 1977; Leaves on the Wind, 1978; The Depths of Love, 1982; Love in the Wind, 1985. *Memberships:* Authors Guild. *Literary Agent:* Kidde, Hoyt & Picard. *Address:* 842 South 5th Street, Lakeview, OR 97630, USA.

SEGAL, David R, b. 22 June, 1941, New York City, USA. Professor of Sociology. m. Mady Wechsler, 25 Dec. 1966, New York City, 1 daughter. *Education:* BA, Harpur College, 1962; MA, 1963, PhD 1967, University of Chicago. *Literary Appointments:* Associate Editor: American Sociologist 1973-75, Sociological Focus 1973-79, Journal of Political & Military Sociology, 1974-77 & 1981-83, Western Sociological Review, 1977-81, Armed Forces & Society, 1980-82; Guest editor, Youth & Society, 1978; Editor, Armed Forces & Society, 1982-. *Publications:* Society & Politics, 1974; The Social Psychology of Military Service, with Nancy L Goldman, 1976; The All-Volunteer Force, with Jerald Bachman & John Blair, 1977. *Contributions to:* Various sociology journals, titles include, Observations from the Sinai, 1985; Institutional & Occupational Models of the Army, 1984; Paratroopers as Peacekeepers, 1984. *Honours:* Ruth M Sinclair Memorial Award, University of Michigan, 1970; Distinguished Scholar/Teacher, University of Maryland, 1980-81. *Address:* Department of Sociology, University of Maryland, College Park, MD 20742, USA.

SEGALL, Anne Celia, b. 20 Apr. 1948, Zimbabwe. Journalist. m. David Howard Evans, 15 June 1973, 2 sons. *Education:* Honours degree in Politics, Philosophy & Economics, Oxford University. *Contributions include:* Economics & Banking Correspondent, Investors Chronicle, 1971-76; Banking Correspondent, The Economist 1976-79, Daily Telegraph 1981-. *Honour:* Wincott Prize for Financial Journalists, 1975. *Address:* 24 Pembroke Gardens, London W8, England.

SEGALLER, A(rthur) Denis, b. 31 Jan. 1915, London. England. Writer; Newspaper Subeditor. m. (1) Joyce Alice Westwood, 27 Sep. 1942, Great Malvern, 2 sons, (2) Laddawan Jaroonchol, 26 Dec. 1973, Bangkok, Thailand. *Education:* BSc, 1st Class Honours, University College, London University, 1935. *Literary Appointments:* Staff Member, Post Publishing Company Limited, Bangkok, Thailand, 1974-86. *Publications:* Thai Ways, 1981; More Thai Ways, 1982, 85. *Contributions to:* Sawasdee, Inflight Magazine, 1978-; The Observer Magazine; Holiday Time in Thailand, official magazine of Tourism Authority of Thailand; Living in Thailand; Orientations; Bangkok World, weekly column. *Address:* c/o Post Publishing Company Limited, U Chuliang Foundation Building, 968 Rama IV Road, Bangkok 10500, Thailand.

SEGERS, Gerd, b. 9 Jan. 1938, Berchem, Antwerp, Belgium. Writer; Poet. m. Carol Theijssens, 12 July 1960, 1 daughter. *Education:* Library School of Antwerp. *Literary Appointments:* Member of Review HET KAHIER X, 1962-66; Editor of Review REVOLVER, 1968-; Member of Review HAM, 1985-. *Publications:* Poetry: Veltro, 1965; Clothing-cyclus, 1966; Dagboekje Intiem, 1966; Een Belg in Zwitserland, 1972; Verdwaald ben je er precies pas geweest, 1975; Topografie van een vrouw, 1983; Criticism: Jan Vanreit, painter, 1975; Bibliography: Lode Monteyne, 1960; Du Cafe, 1961; Guide: (historical) Luchtbal 50 jaar, 1975; Luchtbal 60 jaar, 1985. *Contributions to:* Newspapers: Volksgazet; De Nieuwe Gazet. Magazines: Revolver; Kreatief; H A M; HET Kahier X; Heibel; Yang. *Memberships:* Pen Club, Belgium; Sabam, Belgium; Honest Arts Movement. *Address:* Ludwig Burchardst 35 - B, 2050 Antwerp, Belgium.

SEGHERS, Pierre Paul, b. 5 Jan. 1906, Paris, France. Author; Editor. *Education:* DLitt, University of Paris X. *Publications:* La Resistance et ses poetes, 1940-45; La Resistance, ses chants et ses poetes (2 records); Le Livre d'or de la poesie; Le Temps des marveilles, Poemes 1938-78. *Contributor to:* Numerous reviews and literary and artistic magazines of poetry and art critiques; Radio & TV Productions. *Honours:* Apollinaire Prize, 1959; Grand Record Prize, 1975; Christo Botev Grand Poetry Prize, Sofia, 1977; Grand Prize, City of Paris, 1979; Prix Blaise Cendrars, 1984; Gd. Prix SACEM, Paris, 1984; Officer of the French Legion of Honour; Commander, French Order of Arts & Letters; Vice President, Maison de La Poésie, Paris; Director of the Review Poésie 75. *Memberships:* Society Men of Letters, France; PEN Club; Academy Mallarme. *Address:* 228 Blvd Raspail, 75014 Paris, France.

SEIDEL, Kathleen Gilles, b. 20 Oct. 1951, Lawrence, Kansas, USA. Writer. m. Larry R Seidel, 14 Apr. 1973, Lawrence, Kansas. *Education:* AB, Unversity of Chicago; MA, PhD, The Johns Hopkins University. *Publications:* The Same Last Name, 1983; A Risk Worth Taking, 1983; Mirrors and Mistakes, 1984; After All These 1984; When Love Isn't Enough, 1984; Don't Forget to Smile, 1986. *Honours:* Romantic Times, Best Harlequin American Romance, 1983; Romance Writers of America, Best Non-Series Romance, 1984. *Memberships:* Romance Writers of America; Washington Romance Writers, Chairman, 1983–85. *Literary Agent:* Heide Lange, Sandford J Greenburger Associates. *Address:* c/o Heide Lange, Sandford J Greenburger Associates, 55 Fifth Avenue, New York, NY 10003, USA.

SEIDLER, Edouard, b. 23 Mar. 1932, Brno, Czechoslovakia. Journalist. m. Rhoda Madden, 20 Oct. 1958, New York, USA, 2 daughters. *Education:* School of Political Sciences, Paris, France; MBA, University of California, Los Angeles, USA. *Publications:* Labor in Virginia, 1954; Dictionaire des Sports, 1963; Le Sport et La Presse, 1964; Lea Grandes Voix de l'Automobile, 1970; Champion of the World, 1974; The Romance of Renault, 1974; Let's Call it Fiesta, 1976; The Renault Challenge, 1982; Sport a la Une, 1986. *Contributor to:* Action Automobile, Paris; Autocar, London; Car Graphic, Tokyo, etc. *Honours:* Harold Pemberton Trophy, British Guild of Motoring Writers; Trophee de Liedekerque-Beaufort of the Automobile Club de France, 1974; Knight of the Legion of Honor; Knight of the National Order of Merit. *Address:* 104 Rue Brancas, F 92310, Sevres, France.

SEIDMAN, Hugh, b. 1 Aug. 1940, USA. Writer; Poet. *Education:* BA, Polytechnic Institute of Brooklyn; MS, University of Minnesota; MFA, Columbia University. *Literary Appointment:* Member of Faculty, New School for Social Research, New York City. *Publications:* Collecting Evidence, 1970; Blood Lord, 1974; Throne/Falcon/Eye, 1982. *Honours:* Yale Series of Younger Series of Younger Poets Prize, 1969; NEA Fellowship, 1970, 1972–73, 1985; CAPS Fellowship, 1971; Writer's Digest Prize, 1982. *Memberships:* American PEN; Author's League and Author's Guild; Poetry Society of America. *Address:* 463 West Street, New York, NY 10014, USA.

SEIFERT, Anne Martha, b. 1 Jan. 1943, New York, USA. Author; Public Health Advocate. m. Fred Willis Hoyt IV, 17 Sep. 1969, Reno, Nevada. *Education:* BA, Psychology, Hofstra University, New York; MA, Psychology, Smith College, Northampton, Massachusetts; MPH, PhD, Epidemiology, University of California, Berkeley. *Publications:* His, Mine & Ours: A Guide to Keeping Marriage from Ruining a Perfectly Good Relationship, 1979; The Intelligent Women's Diet: The Practical Way to Keep Trim, Relax & Stay Well the Rest of Your Life, 1982. *Contributions:* Newspaper Columnist, restaurant reviews: Times Advocate; Escondido, California; Scientific journals. *Address:* P O Box 9655, Marina del Rey, CA 90295, USA.

SEIFMAN, Eli, b. 4 Aug. 1936, New York, USA. Professor, Social Science. *Education:* BA, 1957, MS, 1959, Queens College, City University of New York; PhD, New York University. *Publications:* A History of the New York State Colonization Society, 1966; The Social Studies: Structure, Models and Strategies, 1969; The Teachers Handbook, 1971; Toward a New World Outlook; A Domumentary History of Education in the People's Republic of China, 1976. *Contributor to:* Numerous professional journals. *Honours:* Pi Lamba Theta Award, 1973; University Honours Scholar, New York University, 1963; Department of History Prize, Queens College, 1957; Phi Beta Kappa, 1956. *Address:* P O Box 211, Stony Brook, NY 11790, USA.

SEILER, Alexander J, b. 6 Aug. 1928, Zurich, Switzerland. Film and Television Director and Writer. *Education:* Universities of Basle, Zurich, Paris-Sorbonne, Munich; PhD, University of Vienna, Austria. *Publications:* Casals, Olten and Frieburg, 1956; Siamo italiani/Die Italiener, 1965. *Contributions to:* Films in der Schweiz, 1978; Francesco Rosi, 1983; Die Weltwoche; Tages Anzeiger Magazin; Cinema. *Honours:* Palme d'Or, for short films, Cannes, 1963; Documentary Award, Bilbao, 1965; Zurich Film Prize, 1965, 77; Swiss Federal Film Awards, 1963, 1965–69, 77, 82. *Membership:* Swiss Authors Group of Olten. *Address:* Tannsberg, CH–8627 Grunigen, Switzerland.

SEKLER, Eduard Franz, b. 30 Sep. 1920, Vienna, Austria. Professor of Architecture. m. Mary Patricia May, 21 July 1962, Vienna. *Education:* Dipl Ing, Architecture, Technical University of Vienna, 1945; PhD, Warburg Institute, London University, 1946. *Appointments:* Editorial Board, Series Zeitwende, Eine Oesterreichische Bibliothek. *Publications:* Point Houses in European Housing, 1952; Wren and His Place in European Architecture, 1956; Master Plan for the Conservation of the Cultural Heritage in the Kathmandu Valley, 1977, Editor, co-Author; Le Corbusier at Work, co-author, 1978; Josef Hoffman, the Architectural Work, 1985. *Contributor to:* Daedalus; Der Aufbau; Connection; Architectural Review; Alte und Moderne Kunst; Canadian Collector; etc. *Honours:* Cross of Honour, Science and Art, 1st Class, Austrian Republic, 1970; Prize, City of Vienna for the Humanities and Social Sciences, 1983. *Memberships:* Fellow, American Academy of Arts & Sciences; Signet Society. *Address:* Carpenter Centre for the Visual Arts, Harvard University, 24 Quincy Street, Cambridge, MA 02138, USA.

SELBOURNE, David, b. 4 June 1937, London, England. Playwright; Political Journalist. *Education:* Balliol College, Oxford. *Literary Publications:* The Play of William Cooper and Edmund Dew-Nevett, 1968; The Two-Backed Beast, 1969; Dorabella, 1970; Samson, 1971; Alison Mary Fagan, 1971; The Damned, 1971; An Eye to India, 1977; An Eye to China, 1978; Through the Indian Looking Glass, 1982; Against Socialist Illusion, 1985; Moving On, 1986. *Contributor to:* Guardian; New Statesman; New Society; Harper's; Tribune; etc. *Honour:* Aneurin Bevan Membership Fellowship. *Literary Agent:* Xandra Hardie. *Address:* Ruskin College, Oxford, England.

SELDEN, Neil Roy, b. 20 Mar. 1931, New York City, USA. Writer. m. Lee Morris Imbrie, 23 July 1960, Lawrenceville, New Jersey, 1 son. *Education:* BA, New York University, 1952. *Publications:* Great Lakeside High Experiment, 1982; Secrets, 1983; Last Kiss in April, 1984; Drawing the Dead, 1984. *Honours:* Wisconsin Library Poetry Award, 1953; Audrey Wood Award, Playwriting, 1972. *Membership:* Phi Beta Kappa. *Literary Agent:* William Morris Agency, Steve Weiss, California. *Address:* 40 Tamara Drive, Roosevelt, NJ 08555, USA.

SELDES, George Henry, b. 10 Sep. 1890, Alliance New Jersey, USA. Writer. m. Helen Larkin Wiesman, 1932. *Publications:* You Can't Print That, 1929; World Panorama, 1933; Sawdust Caesar, 1935; The Great Quotations, 1960; The Great Thoughts, 1985. *Contributor to:* The Nation; The New Republic; Esquire and various other magazines. Published weekly newsletter, In Fact 1940–50, first regular publication devoted entirely to press criticism and publication of suppressed news in US press. *Honours:* Annual Award for Professional Excellence from Association for Education in Journalism, 1980; The Spacial Polk Award, 1981; The Sigma Delta Chi Award of the Society of Professional Journalists, Temple University, 1982. *Literary Agent:* Russell and Volkening, 50 West 29th Street, New York City, NY 1001, USA. *Address:* Hartland-4-Corners, Rural Route 1, Windsor, VT 05089, USA.

SELLMAN, Hunton Dade, b. 20 May 1900, Maryland, USA. University Professor. m. Priscilla Morrison, 22 July 1933, 2 daughters. *Education:* BS, MS, Yale University. *Publications:* Stage Scenery and Lighting, 1930; Modern Theatre Practice, 1936, 1973; Essentials of Stage Lighting, 1972, 1980. *Address:* 5015 Campanile Dr, San Diego, CA 92115, USA.

SELLMAN, Roger Raymond, b. 24 Sep. 1915, London, England. Schoolmaster, Lecturer, Devon County Inspector of Schools (retired). m. Minnie Coutts, 10 Aug. 1938, Hastings. *Education:* MA, Dip Ed, Oxford University, PhD, Exeter University. *Publications:* Methuen's Outline Series: Castles and Fortresses, 1954; The Crusades, 1955; Roman Britain, 1956; English Churches, 1956; The Vikings, 1957; Elizabethan Seamen, 1957; Prehistoric Britain, 1958; Civil War and Commonwealth, 1958; The Anglo-Saxons, 1959; Ancient Egypt, 1960; Norman England, 1960; Medieval English Warfare, 1960; The First World War, 1961; The Second World War, 1964; Garibaldi and the Unification of Italy, 1973; Bismarck and the Unification of Germany, 1973; The Prairies, 1974; Historical Atlases and Textbooks: Outline Atlas of Eastern History, 1954; Outline Atlas of World History, 1970; Modern World History, 1972; Students Atlas of Modern History, 1973; Historical Atlas for First Examinations, 1973; Modern British Economic and Social History, 1973; Modern European History, 1974; Local History: Illustrations of Dorset History, 1960; Illustrations of Devon History, 1962; Devon Village Schools in the Nineteenth Century, 1968; Aspects of Devon History, 1985. *Contributions to:* The Victorian Countryside, 1981; The Devon Historian; Devon and Cornwall Notes and Queries. *Address:* Pound Down Corner, Whitestone, Exeter EX4 2HP, England.

SELTER, Leon F, b. 9 Aug. 1940, Philadelphia, Pennsylvania, USA. Psychotherapist. m. Maxine Wolfson, 17 Aug. 1975, Cleveland, Ohio, USA. *Education:* BA English, Temple University, 1962; MA English, University of Illinois, 1964; PhD English, State University of New York, Buffalo, 1967; MA Psychology, 1980, PhD Psychology 1983, University of Cincinnati. *Literary Appointments:* Assistant Professor of English, Cleveland State University, 1970–78. *Major Publications:* The Vision of Melville & Conrad: A Comparative Study, 1970; Paradoxical Strategies in Psychotherapy: A Comprehensive Overview & Guidebook, 1986. *Contributor to:* Numerous periodicals. *Membership:* American Psychological Association; Academy of San Diego Psychologists, San Diego Psychology – Law Society. *Address:* 14195 Mango Drive, Del Mar, CA 92014, USA.

SELTZER, Joanne, b. 21 Nov. 1929, Detroit, Michigan, USA. Poet; Writer. m. Stanley Seltzer, 10 Feb. 1951, Detroit, Michigan, 1 son, 3 daughters. *Education:* BA, University of Michigan; MA, College of Saint Rose. *Publication:* Adironack Lake Poems, 1985. *Contributions to:* Blueline; Waterways; The Village Voice; Small Press Review; The Minnesota Review; Studia Mystica; The Glens Falls Review; Poetry Now; Primavera; Earth's Daughters; The Greenfield Review; Galliope. *Honours:* A Winner, Fifth Annual All Nations Contest, 1978; Honorable mention, Robert Browning Award, World Order of Narrative Poets, 1984. *Memberships:* The Poetry Society of America; Associated Writing Programs; The Feminist Writers' Guild; International Women's Writing Guild. *Address:* 2481 McGovern Drive, Schenectady, NY 12309, USA.

SELZER, Richard Alan, b. 24 June 1928, Troy, New York, USA. Surgeon. m. Janet White, 13 Feb, 1955, New Haven, Connecticut, USA, 2 sons, 1 daughter. *Education:* BS, Union College, 1948; MD, Albany Medical College, 1953; Surgical Residency, Yale, 1960. *Major Publications:* Rituals of Surgery, 1974; Mortal Lessons, 1976; Confessions of a Knife, 1979; Letters to a Young Doctor, 1982. *Contributor to:* Vanity Fair; and others. *Honour:* College of Pennsylvania. *Literary Agent:* Georges Borchardt. *Address:* 6 St Ronan Terrace, New Haven, CT 06511, USA.

SENELICK, Laurence Philip, b. 12 Oct. 1942, Chicago, USA. University Professor; Director; Actor. *Education:* BA, Northwestern University, 1964; AM, 1965, PhD, 1972, Harvard University. *Publications:* A Cavalcade of Clowns, 1978; British Musichall, 1840–1923; A Bibliography and Guide to Sources with a Supplement on European Musi=hall (with D Cheshire

and U Schneider), 1981; Russian Dramatic Theory from Pushkin to the Sumbolists, 1981; Gordon Craig's Moscow Hamlet: A Reconstruction, 1982; Serf Actor: The Life and Art of Mikhail Shchepkin, 1984; Anton Chekov, 1985. *Contributions to:* Theatre; History of Photography; Nineteenth Century Theatre Research; Cuisine Theatre Survey; Performing Arts Journal Theatre Studies; Essays in Theatre; Theatre Quarterly; Theatre Research International; Theatre Journal; New Boston Review; Victorian Studies; After Dark; Dickensian; Modern Drama; Dickens Studies; Poe Studies; Drama Critique. *Honours:* Woodrow Wilson Fellowship, 1964; Dissertation Fellowship, 1965; Susan Anthony Potter Prize, Harvard, 1971; John Simon Guggenheim Foundation Fellow, 1979–80; George Freedley Award of Theatre Library Association, 1983; Fellow, Institute of Advanced Study, Berlin, 1984/85. *Memberships:* Russian Research Center, Harvard; International Federation for Theatre Research; American Society for Theatre Research; Society for Theatre Research; British Music Hall Society; Society for Cultural Relations with USSR. *Literary Agent:* Jed Mattes, International Management Corporation. *Address:* 117 Mystic Street, West Medford, MA 02155, USA.

SENIOR, Michael, b. 14 Apr. 1940, Llandudno, Noth Wales. Writer. *Education:* BA, 1st Class Honours, Open University. *Publications:* Portrait of North Wales, 1973; Portrait of South Wales, 1974; Greece & Its Myths, 1978; Myths of Britain, 1979; Sir Thomas Malory's Tales of King Arthur, editor, 1980; The Life & Times of Richard II, 1981; Who's Who in Mythology, 1985. *Contributions to:* New Scientist; Ecologist; Anglo-Welsh Review. *Literary Agent:* David Higham Associates. *Address:* Bryn Eisteddfod, Glan Conwy, Colwyn Bay, North Wales.

SENNETT, Richard, b. 1 Jan. 1943, Chicago, Illinois, USA. Writer. *Education:* BA, University of Chicago, 1964; PhD, Harvard University, 1969. *Publications:* The Uses of Disorder, 1970; The Hidden Injuries of Class, 1972; The Fall of Public Man, 1977; Authority, 1980; The Frog Who Dared to Croak, 1982; An Evening of Brahams, 1984. *Contribtions to:* New Yorker; New York Review of Books; Times Literary Supplement, England; New York Times Book Review Partisan Review; Esprit, France; Tel Quel, France; Kenyon Review. *Honours:* Guggenheim Award, 1973; Fellowship, Institute for Advanced Study, 1974; Award, National Endowment for the Humanities, 1976; Ingram-Merrill Award for Fiction, 1983. *Memberships:* Vice President, PEN; Century Association; Signet Society, Harvard. *Literary Agent:* Lynn Nesbit International Creative Management. *Address:* 44 Washington Mews, New York City, NY 10003, USA.

SERENYI, Peter, b. 13 Jan. 1931, Budapest, Hungary. University Profesor of Art. *Education:* Baccalaureate Degree, French-Hunagrian Lyceum, Innshbruck, Austria, 1949; BA, Dartmouth College, USA, 1957; MA, Yale University, 1958; PhD Washington University, St Louis, Missouri, 1968. *Literary Apointments:* Editorial Consultant, Architectural History Foundation, New York City, New York, 1979–81. *Publications:* Le Corbusier in Perspective, Editor and Contributor, 1975. *Contributions to:* Art Bulletin; Journal of Society of Architectural Historians; Harvard Architectural Review; Perspecta, Yale Architectural Review; Architecture Plus Design, 1985; Technique et Archtecture, 1985. *Honours:* Fulbright Senior Research Grant to India, 1974–75; Smithsonian Institution Grant to India, 1984–85. *Memberships include:* Various offices, Society of Architectural Historians; Director, Massachusetts Committee for the Preservation of Architectural Records; Society for Preservation of New England Antiquities; Victoria Society of America. *Address:* 79 Greenough Street, Brookline, MA 02146, USA.

SERGEANT, Herbert Howard, b. 6 May 1914, Hull, England. Freelance Writer, Poet, Editor. m. Jean Crabtree, 27 Mar. 1953, London, 1 son, 3 daughters. *Education:* College of Commerce, Hull; Metropolitan

College; School of Accountancy; FCIS; FCAA. *Appointments:* Founder, Editor, Outposts Poetry Quarterly, 1943–. *Publications include:* Poetry; The Leavening Air, 1946; The Headlands, 1954; Selected Poems, 1980; Travelling Without a Valid Ticket, 1982; Fairground Familiars, 1985; Criticism: The Cumberland Wordsworth, 1950; Tradition in the Making of Modern Poetry, 1952; A Critical Survey of South African Poetry, 1958. *Contributor to:* Ambit; Anglo-Welsh Review; Argo; Books and Bookmen; Contemporary Review; Country Life; Countryman; Daily Telegraph; Encounter; The Field; London Magazine; New Statesman; Observer; Orbis; Poetry Review; Spectator; Times Educational Supplement; Times Literary Supplement; etc. *Honours:* MBE, 1978; Henry Shore Award for Poetry, 1979; Dorothy Tutin Award for Poetry, 1980. *Memberships:* Society of Authors; PEN, former Member Executive Committee Twice, Ex Chairman, Poetry Subcommittee; Ver Poets, Vice President. *Address:* 72 Burwood Road, Walton-on-Thames, Surrey KT12 4AL, England.

SERLE, Alan Geoffrey, b. 10 Mar. 1922, Melbourne, Australia. *Education:* BA, University of Melbourne; DPh, Oxford University, England. *Literary Appointments:* General Editor, Australian Dictionary of Biography, Editor, Historical Studies, Australia and New Zealand, 1955–62. *Publications:* The Golden Age, 1963; The Rush To Be Rich, 1971; From Deserts the Prophets Come, 1973; John Monash: A Biography, 1982. *Honours include:* Ernest Scott Prize, 1964 and 1971; National Book Council Award, 1974 and 1982. *Memberships include:* Council 1976, Australian Society of Authors; Fellowship of Australian Writers; Australian Academies of the Humanities and Social Sciences. *Address:* 31 Lisson Grove, Hawthorn, Victoria 3122, Australia.

SERNINE, Daniel, b. 7 Nov. 1955, Montréal, Canada. Writer. *Education:* BA, History, 1975, MA, Library Science, 1977, Université de Montreal. *Publications:* Les contes de l'ombre, 1979; Légendes du vieux manoir, 1979; Organisation Argus, 1979; Le trésor du 'Scorpion', 1980; Le vieilhomme et l'espace, 1981; L'épée Arphal, 1981; La cité inconnue, 1982; Argus intervient, 1983; Les méandres du temps, 1983; Ludovic, 1983; Quand vient la nuit, 1983; Le cercle violet; 1984; Les Envoûtements, 1985; Aurores boréales 2, 1985. *Contributor to:* Numerous professional journals including 25 short stories, science-fiction and fantasy in magazines, 19750; Requiem; Solaris; La Nouvelle Barre du Jour, Antarès; etc. *Honours:* Prix Dragon, for story, Exode 5, 1977; Prix Solaris, short story, Loin des vertes prairies, 1982; Canada Council's Award for Children's Literature, for novel, Le cercle violet, 1984. *Address:* 6675 Avenue Darlington, Apt 9, Montréal, Quebec H3S 2J6, Canada.

SERRAILLIER, Ian Lucien, b.24 Sep. 1912, London, England. Author; Editor. m. Anne Margaret Rogers, Stourbridge, England, 1 son, 3 daughters. *Education:* MA, Oxford University. *Literary Appointment:* Joint Editor with Anne Serreillier of The New Series, Heinemann Educational Books, London. *Publications:* Prose; Numerous titles include – They Raced for Treasure, 1946; Flight to Adventure, 1947; There's No Escape, 1950; The Silver Sword, 1956; The Ivory Horn, 1960; The Way of Danger, 1962; Fight for Freedom, 1965; Havelock the Dane 1967; Heracles the Strong, 1970; Have You Got Your Ticket? 1972; Pop Festival, 1973. Verse includes: The Ballad of St Simeon, 1970; A Pride of Lions, 1971; The Bishop and the Devil, 1971; Marko's Wedding, 1972; I'll Tell You A Tale, 1973; The Robin and the Wren, 1973; Suppose You Met A Witch, 1974. *Membership:* The Society of Authors. *Address:* Singleton, Chichester, Sussex PO18 0HA, England.

SERVADIO, Gaia Cecilia Metella, b. 13 Sep. 1938, Padoua, Italy. Writer; Journalist. m. William Mostyn-Owen, 28 Sep. 1960, London, England, 2 sons, 1 daughter. *Education:* Liceo Classico, Degree in Graphic Design and Typography, St Martins School of Art, London, England. *Literary Appointments:* Vice President, Foreign Press Association, London, England;

President, Emigrazione e cultura, London. *Publications:* Meumba, 1968; Dom Juan-Salome, 1969; A Siberian Encounter, 1972; A Profile of a Mafia Boss, 1973; Mafioso, 1975; Insider, Outsider, 1977; To a Different World, 1978; Luchino Viscomti, 1981. *Contributions to:* Il Monde; La Stmampa; Europea; The Observer; The Sunday Times; The Times; Evening Standard. *Honour:* Cavalieze Ufficiale della Republica Italiana. *Membership:* Accademia degli Informi, Italy. *Literary Agent:* Ed Victor Limited, London. *Address:* 31 Bloomfield Terrace, London SW1, England.

SERVAN-SCHREIBER, Jean-Jacques, b. 13 Feb. 1924, Paris, France. Author. m. 11 Aug, 1960, 4 sons. *Education:* Bachelor. Mathematics, Lycee Jeanson de Sailly, Paris; Graduate Engineer, Ecole Polytechnique of France. *Publications:* Lieutenant in Algeria, 1957; The American Challenge, 1967; Radical Manifesto, 1971; Regional Power, 1972; The World Challenge, 1981. *Contributions to:* Le Monde, Editorial writer, 1948–53; L'Express, Publisher and editor, 1953–70. *Address:* 49 Boulevard de Courcelles, Paris 75008, France.

SERVIEN, Louis-Marc, b. 8 Jan. 1934. Economic and Finance Writer; Editor and Journalist. *Education:* Licentiate, Law Economics and Commercial Sciences, University of Lausanne, Switzerland; University of London, England; University of Cologne, Germany; Dr Acc, Rome, Italy. *Publications include:* Les Fonds de Placement Collectif en Suisse, 1964; I Fondi Communi di Investimento: Una Nuova Forma di Risparmio, 1967; Investment Trusts: Moderne Kapitalanlage, 1968; Mutual Funds, Why Not? A Survey of International Investment Funds, 1968; Quelques Réflexions à propos du Nouveau Statut Juridique des Fonds de Placement Suisses, 1969; Fondos de Inversion, Una Nueva Formula de Ahorro, 1970; Fondi Comuni di Investimento in Svizzera, 1972; Gibraltar: Tax on the Rock, 1986. *Memberships include:* Union Internationale des Journalistes et de la Presse de Langue Francaise, Paris; Syndicat des Journalistes et Ecrivains, Paris, France. *Honours:* Commendatore of the Concordia Order, Sao Paulo, Brazil; Gold Medal, Arts, Sciences et Lettres, Paris, France. *Address:* 23 Ch du Levant, 1005 Lausanne, Switzerland.

SETH-SMITH, Leslie James, b. 12 Jan. 1923, Kampala, Uganda. Writer; Producer, Film and Television. m. (1) Elizabeth Marka Webb, London, England, 1 son, 3 daughters. (2) Margaret L Lord, 22 June 1974, Manchester. *Education:* Sidney Sussex College, Cambridge University, 1939–40; BA Honours, London University, 1944. *Literary Appointments:* Story Editor, British Broadcasting Corporation Television, 1963–68. *Publications:* Albert Schweitzer, biography, 1975; Dorothy L Sayers, biography, 1981. *Honour:* Fellow, Royal Society of Literature, 1977. *Memberships:* Society of Literature. *Literary Agent:* David Higham Associates. *Address:* 36 Kingswood Road, Chiswick, London W4 5ET, England.

SETHNA, Minocher Jehangirji, b. 1 Nov. 1911, Bombay, India. Jurist; Professor of Law, Author. m. Khorshed Jamshedji Anklesaria, 26 Jan, 1940, Bombay, 1 son. *Education:* PhD, Bombay University; Barrister-at-Law, Middle Temple, London, UK. *Academic Appointments:* Professor, Government Law College, Bombay, 1952–60; Professor, Postgraduate Faculty, Bombay University, 1960–1976; Visiting Professor, 1976–80. *Publications include:* Indian company Law, 9th edition, 1983; Mercantile Law, 10th edition, 1982; Jurisprudence, 3rd edition, 1973; Society & the Criminal, 4th edition, 1980; Photography, encyclopaedic work, 1970; Art of Living, 1973; Health & Happiness, 1975; The Beauty That Is Kashmor, 1982. *Contrubutions to:* Essays in Honour of Dean Roscoe Pound; Numerous articles in Law journals. *Honours:* Appointed as Emeritus Professor to deliver the Chief Justice Dr P B Gajendragadkar Memorial Lecture, Bombay University, 1985; Other invited lectures. *Memberships:* Former member, Bombay Bar Association; Fellow, Royal Economic Society, UK. *Address:* 251 Sethna House, Tardeo Road, Bombay 7, India.

SETHURAMAN, Arugathurai Ramakrishna Sasthri, b. 11 Oct. 1945, Tiruvottiyur, South India. Assistant Administration Manager. m. Uma Sethuraman, 16 Apr. 1971, Mayuram, Tamilnadu, 1 son, 2 daughters. *Education:* MA Economics; MCom; Dr.D.Litt., World University, USA. *Thesis:* Industrial Administration. *Honours:* Fellowship, United Writers Association of India; Fellowship, Management Studies Promotion Institute. *Membership:* United Writers Association of India; Accredited Member, British Institute of Management, London. *Address:* 18 Second Main Road, Nanganallur, Madras – 600 061, Tamilnadu, India.

SETON, Anya, b. New York, USA. Writer. 1 son, 2 daughters. *Education:* Spence School, New York, USA, Oxford, England, Private Tutors. *Publications:* Dragonwyck; The Turquoise; The Hearth and Eagle; Fox Fire; Avalon; Biographical novels: My Theodosia; Katherine; The Winthrop Woman; Devil Water; Books for teenagers: The Mistletoe and Sword; The Life of Washington Irving. etc. *Contributor to:* Numerous contributions to magazines and journals. *Memberships:* Pen and Brush; English Speaking Union; National League of American Penwomen Inc. *Address:* 61 Binney Lane, Old Greenwich, CT 06870, USA.

SEVERIN, Tim, b. 25 Sep. 1940, Jorhat, Assam. Author. *Education:* MA, B Litt, Oxford University. *Publications:* Tracking Marco Polo, 1964; Explorers of the Mississippi, 1967; Golden Antilles, 1970; The African Adventuree, 1973; Vanishing Primitive Man, 1974; The Oriental Adventures, 1976; The Brendon Voyage, 1978; The Sinbad Voyage, 1982; The Jason Voyage, 1985. *Contributor to:* National Geographic Magazine. *Honours:* Book of the Sea, 1979; Christopher Award, 1979; Thomas Cook Prize, 1982; Book of the Sea, 1982; Sir Percy Sykes Medal, 1983; Literary Medal, Academia de Marine, 1985. *Agent:* Anthony Shiel Associates. *Address:* Countmacsherry, Co Cork, Republic of Ireland.

SEWARD, Deborah Gordon, b. 26 Aug. 1956, USA. Journalist. *Education:* BA, History, University of North Carolina; Certificat d'Etudes Politiques, Institut d'Etudes Politiques, Paris, France, 1979. *Literary Appointments:* Researcher, 1982, Reporter, Paris Bureau, 1983, Reporter, Bonn Bureau, 1983, Newsweek. *Honours:* Rotary International Fellowship, 1978–79; Fellowship for Journalists in Europe, 1983. *Address:* Newsweek, Winston Churchill Strasse 1A, Bonn 5300, Federal Republic of Germany.

SEWART, Alan, b. 26 Aug. 1928, Bolton, Lancashire, England. Writer. m. Dorothy Teresa Humphreys, 13 Oct. 1962, Blackburn, 2 sons, 1 daughter. *Education:* LLB, University of London. *Publications include:* Tough Tontine, 1978; A Ribbon for my Repute, 1978; The Salome Syndrome, 1979; The Women of Morning, 1980; In That Rich Earth, 1981; Smoker's Cough, 1982; Death Game – Five Players, 1982; If I Should Die, 1983; Dead Man Drifting, 1984; The Educating of Quintin Quinn, 1984; etc. As Alan Stewart Well: Mr Crumblestone's Eden, 1980; Where Lionel Lies, 1984; Candice is Dead, 1984; etc. As Padder Nash: Grass, 1982; Coup de Grass, 1983; Wayward Seeds of Grass, 1983; Grass & Supergrass, 1984; ect. Others in press. *Contributions to:* Police Review. *Membership:* Crime Writers Association. *Address:* 7 Knott Lane, Easingwold, York YO6 3LX, England.

SEXAUER, Arwin Garellick, b. 18 Aug. 1921, Richford, Vermont, USA. Author, Composer, Poet, Lyricist, Editor, Retired Librarian. m. and widowed 3 times, 1 son, 1 daughter. *Education:* Studied piano, drama and journalism under private tutelage; Library Science, State University of New York; PhD; D.Litt. *Literary Appointments:* Assistant Librarian, 1966–73, Head Librarian, 1974–76, Kellogg Hubbard Library, Montpelier, USA; Society Reporter, Times-Argus, 1964–65; First Woman editor, Vermont Oddfellows Magazine, 1959–70; Radio/Theatre Monologist, 1939–53; Vice-President (International Affairs), Marquis G

Scicluna International University Foundation for Promotion of Literature, Science and Fine Arts. *Major Publications:* Remembered Winds (poetry) 1963; The Tastevin (poems), 1984; Music Mission Story and Songs from La Casa de Paz, 1985; 14 award-winning musical pageants, 1956–84; poetry in 45 anthologies; numerous dramatic works. *Contributor to:* Numerous poetry journals in Europe, India and America including: Poet; Hoosier Challenger; Pegasus; Hellenic Light; Troubador; Poetical Rainbow; Congressional Record. *Honours:* Some 330 International and National Honours & Awards, including: 3 George Washington Medals, 1957, 1959, 1973; 3 Virgilio-Mantegna Silver Medals, 1982–84; President Reagan Gold Medal of Merit, 1984; National League of American Pen Women Music Award, 1985; various honorary degrees, including PhD (Music), World University, Tucson, USA; Leonardo da Vinci Poet Laureate, 1984; da Vinci Princess of Poetry, 1985; Vice President, Music, Accademia Leonardo da Vinci, Rome, Academic Senate, 1985; World Peace Award for Poetry. *Memberships:* Gospel Music Association; Songwriters Hall of Fame; Composers Guild; Life Fellow, International Academy of Poets; Academy of American Poets; Life Fellow, Shelley Society of New York & London; International Platform Association Poets' Academy; International Press Association; Vermont Library Association; World Poetry Society; National League of American Pen Women. *Literary Agent:* ASCAP. *Address:* Music Mission, Inc, La Casa de Paz, Dewey Street, Richford, VT 05476, USA.

SEXTON, Virginia Staudt, b. 30 Aug. 1916, New York City, USA. Professor of Psychology. m. Dr Richard J Sexton, 21 Jan. 1961, New York City. *Education:* BA, cum laude, Classics, Hunter College 1936; MA, Psychology, 1941, PhD, 1946, Fordham University; Honorary LHD, Cedar Crest College, 1980; Postdoctoral Training, Psychology, Fordham University, 1949–51; Psychology and Neuroanatomy, Columbia University, 1952–53. *Literary Appointments:* Lecturer; University Professor. *Publications:* Co-author: Catholics in Psychology: A Historical Survey, 1954 Translated into Spanish: Los Catolicas y La Psicologia: Anotaciones Historicas, 1955; Co-author: History of Psychology: An Overview, 1966; Historical Perspectives in Psychology Readings, 1971; Phenomenological, existential and Humanistic Psychologies: A Historical Survey, 1973; Psychology Around the World, 1976; History and Philosophy of Science: Selected Papers, 1983. Monograph: Clincial Psychology: An Historical Survey: Genetic Psychology Monographs, 1965; Publications in press: existential Psychology in, The Social Science Encyclopedia; Autobiographical Sketch in, Introductory Psychology. *Contributions to:* The New Catholic Encyclopedia; Dictionary of Behavioral Science; International Encyclopedia of Neurology, Psychoanalysis, Psychiatry and Psychology; Numerous professional journals, etc. *Memberships include:* Phi Beta Kappa; Eta Sigma Phi; Sigma Xi; Psi Chi; Delta Kappa Gamma; Fellow: New York Academy of Sciences; American Association for Advancement of Science; American Psychological Association and Member of professional organizations. *Address:* 188 Ascan Avenue, Forest Hills, NY 11375, USA.

SEYMOUR, Arthur James, b. 12 Jan, 1914, Guyana. Civil Servant. m. Elma Edith Bryce, 31 July 1937, Georgetown, 3 sons, 3 daughters. *Literary Appointments:* Editor, Kykoveral, 1946–62; Joint-Editor, Kykoveral, Revived, 1984. *Publications:* My Lovely Native Land, with Elma Seymour, 1971; New Writing in the Caribbean, 1972; Dictionary of Guyanese Folklore, 1975; Cultural Policy in Guyana (UNESCO), 1977; Images of Majority (poems), 1978; Making of Guyanese Literature, 1980; Dictionary of Guyanese Biography Vol I, 1984. *Contributions to:* Numerous contributions to magazines and journals. *Honours:* Golden Arrow of Achievement (B G Government), 1970; Hon D Litt, University of West Indies, 1983. *Memberships:* Former President, B G Writers' Association; Former President, Guyana PEN. *Address:* 23 North Road, Bourda, Georgetown, Guyana.

SEYMOUR, Gerald William Herschel Kean, b. 25 Nov. 1941, Surrey, England. Writer. m. Gillian Mary Roberts, 2 May 1964, Sutton, Surrey, 2 sons. *Education:* BA, Modern History, University College, London. *Publications:* Harry's Game, 1975; Glory Boys, 1976; Kingfisher, 1977; Red Fox, 1979; The Contract, 1980; Archangel, 1982; In Honour Bound, 1984; Field of Blood, 1985. *Literary Agent:* A D Peters. *Address:* c/o A D Peters and Company Limited, 10 Buckingham Street, London WC2N 6BU, England.

SEYMOUR-SMITH, Martin, b. 24 Apr. 1928. Poet; Writer. m. Janet de Glanville, 18 Sep. 1953, Palma de Mallorca, 2 daughters. *Education:* BA Hons, MA, St Edmund Hall, Oxford. *Literary Appointments:* Poetry Editor of Truth 1956–58; Poetry Editor of the Scotsman 1963–67; Visiting Professor of English and Writer-in-Residence, University of Wisconsin, 1971–72. *Publications:* Poetry: Tea with Miss Stockport; Reminiscences of Norma, 1971; Guide to Modern World Literature, 1973, revised and rewritten 1985; Sex and Society, 1975; Who's Who in Twentieth Century Literature, 1976; Poets Through Their Letters; Robert Sheves and 34 other publications. *Contributor to:* Times; Telegraph; Spectator; Statesman; New Criterio; New Yorker; Encounter; London Magazine; Financial Times etc. *Honours:* Wightman Prize for a Satirical Poem, 1972; Travelling Scholarship, Authors' Society, 1984. *Membership:* Committee of Management, Authors' Society. *Literary Agent:* Anthony Sheil Associates Ltd. *Address:* 36 Holliers Hill, Bexhill-on-Sea, East Sussex TN40 2DD, England.

SEYS, Raf (Rafaël Jozef), b. 17 Mar. 1928, Koekelare, Belgium. Retired Teacher. m. Astrid Provoost, 14 July 1955, Diksmuide. *Education:* Teacher Training School, Blankenberge, 1947. *Publications:* Ballade van het Misverstand, 1956; De Dichter van de Rozen. Level en Werk van de Gezelliaan dr, Karel de Gheldere, 1958; De Apostel van het Heilig Hart. P J Aernoudt s j 1962; Michiel de Swaen, Gelijk de Zonnebloem, 1964; Käthe Kollwitz in Vlaanderen, 1964; De Slag aan de Peene, 1967, 1977; Guido Gezelle en Koekelare, 1981. *Contributions to:* Der Spiegel: Gezellekroniek; VWS-Cahiers/Bibliotheek van de Westvlaamse Letterer, founder in 1966; Vlaandered; Boek en Bibliotheek; Coclariensia; CVV-Kroniek; Lexicon van Westvlaamse Schrijvers. *Honours include:* Vlaamse Poëziedagen, 1955; Prijs van het Guido Gezelle Museum, 1958; Joris Eeckhoutpriss, 1958; Cultuurprijs De Gouden Feniks, 1983; Erkentelijk-heidmedaille van het Ministerie van de Vlaamse Gemeenschap, 1985. *Memberships include:* Secretaris-penningengmeester 1962–82, Vereniging van Westrlaamse, Commissie voor Taal en Letterkinde; Bibliotheekcommissie van het Willemsfonds; Centrum voor Vlaamse Volkscultuur te Brussel; Koninklijke Commissie voor Plaatsnaamgouing, to Brussel. *Address:* Ringlaan 1, B 8280 Koekelare, Belgium.

SHACK, William Alfred, b. 19 Apr. 1923, Chicago, Illinois, USA. Professor, Anthropology. m. Dorothy Calhoun Nash, 1 Sep. 1960, Atlanta, 1 son. *Education:* BAE, 1955; MA, 1957; PhD, 1961. *Publications:* The Gurage, 1966; Gods and Heroes, 1974; The Central Ethiopians, 1974; Politics and Leadership, 1979; Strangers in African Societies, 1979. *Contributor to:* Africa; Man. *Address:* Dept of Anthropology, University of California, Berkeley, CA 94720, USA.

SHACKLETON, (Lord) Edward Arthur Alexander, b. 15 July 1911, London, England. Former Explorer; Politician & Cabinet Minister; Deputy Chairman, RTZ Corporation Ltd. *Education:* MA, Magdalen College, Oxford; DSc, University of Warwick; PhD, University of Newfoundland. *Publications:* Artic Journeys; Nansen, The Explorer; Borneo Jungle, co-author. *Memberships include:* President, 1969 & 1979, Artic Club; President, 1976–80, Parliamentary & Science Committee; President, 1960–64, British Association of Industrial Education; President, British Standards Institution; Chairman, East European Trade Council. *Honours include:* Knight of the Garter; Privy Councillor; OBE; Cuthbert Peek Award, 1933; Ludwig Medallist, Munich Geological Society, 1938; Honorary LLD, University of Newfoundland. *Address:* 6 St James's Square, London SW1, England.

SHAFFER, Dale Eugene, b. 17 Apr. 1929, Salem, Ohio, USA. Library Consultant/Writer/Library Director. *Education:* BS, Kent State University, Kent, Ohio, 1955; MA. Economics, Ohio State University, Columbus, Ohio, 1965; MALS, Library Science, Kent State University, Kent, Ohio, 1960. *Publications:* 20 books and monographs for librarians and educators including: Criteria for Improving the Professional Status of Librarianship 1980; The Educator's Sourcebook of Posters – Mostly Free; For Teachers and Librarians 1981; A Guide to Writing Library Job Descriptions; Examples Covering Major Work Areas 1981; Sourcebook of Teaching Aids – Mostly Free; Posters and Pamphlets for Educators 1984. Books on Salem history: Marbles – A Forgotten Part of Salem History, 1983; Some Remembrances of Salem's Past, 1983; Reflections of Salem's Past, 1984; Views of Salem History, 1985. *Contributor to:* Numerous articles published in education journals. *Address:* 437 Jennings Avenue, Salem, OH 44460, USA.

SHAFFER, Harry George, b. 28 Aug. 1919, Vienna, Austria. University Professor. Divorced, 3 sons, 1 daughter. *Education:* BA, 1947, MA, 1948, PhD, 1958, New York University, USA. *Appointments:* Professor, Economics, Soviet and East European Studies, University of Kansas. *Publications:* The Soviet Economy, 1963, 2nd edition 1969; The Soviet System, 1965, 2nd edition, 1984; The Communist World, 1967; From Underdevelopment to Affluence, 1968; The Soviet Treatment of Jews, 1974; The US Conquers the West, booklet, 1974; Periodicals on the Socialist Countries and on Marxism, 1977; Soviet Agriculture, 1977; Women in the Two Germanies, 1981. *Contributor to:* 60 articles to professional journals, periodicals, magazines, newspapers. *Address:* Department of Economics, University of Kansas, Lawrence, KS 66045, USA.

SHAFFER, Olive Charlotte, b. 13 July 1896, Masonville, West Virginia, USA. Elementary school teacher. *Education:* BA, Shepherd College, WV, USA; MA, West Virginia University, Morgantown. *Literary Appointments include:* Teacher, one-room schools; Teacher, Graded Schools; Principle of Elementary School. *Publications:* The Arm That is Stronger Than Mine, (song), 1953; Music of the Hills, 1975. *Memberships:* American Poetry League. *Honours:* Certificate of Merit, 1971, 1973. *Address:* 127 Mt View Street, Petersburg, WV 26847, USA.

SHAH, Idries, b. 16 June 1924. Author. *Literary Appointments:* Adviser, Harcourt Brace Jovanovich, publishers, USA, 1975–79. *Publications include:* Oriental Magic, 1956; Destination Mecca, 1957; The Sufis, 1964; Exploits of the Incomparable Mulla Nasrudin, 1966; Tales of the Dervishes, 1967; Caravan of Dreams, 1968; The Book of the Book, 1969; The Dermis Probe, 1970; Ten Texts, 1971; The Magic Monastery, 1972; Subtleties of the Inimitable Mulla Nasrudin, 1973; The Elephant in The Dark, 1974; Neglected Aspects of Sufi Study, 1977; The Hundred Tales of Wisdom, 1978; World Tales, 1979; Letters and Lectures, 1981; Seeker After Truth, 1982; Kara Kush, 1986; Darkest England, 1986; Melon City, 1986; Nail Soup, 1986. *Honours:* 5 First Prizes, UNESCO World Book Year, 1972; Gold Medal, Distinguished Services to Poetry, 1973; Award for Outstanding Contributions to Human Thought, USA, 1975. *Memberships:* Society of Authors; PEN, London; Authors Club, London. *Address:* PO Box 457, London NW2 4BR, England.

SHAHANE, Vasant Anant, b. 18 Dec. 1923, Parbhani, India. Professor; Principal, University College. *Education:* BA, 1944, LLB, 1946, MA, 1947, University of Bombay; PhD, University of Leeds, England, 1958. *Publications:* E M Forster A Reassessment, 1962; Perspectives in E M Forster's A Passage to India, 1968;

Perspectives in E M Forster's A Passage to India, 1968; Khushwant Singh, 1972; Notes on Walt Whitman's Leaves of Grass, 1972; Rudyard Kipling Activist & Artist, 1972; E M Forster A Study in Double Vision, 1975; Focus on a Passage to India, 1975; Ruuth Prawer Jhabvala, 1976; A Passage to India: A Study, 1977; Indian Poetry in English A Critical Assessment, 1980; The Flute and the Drum: Studies in Sarojini Naidu's Poetry and Politics, 1980; Modern Indian Fiction, 1981; Approaches E M Forster, 1981; A Passage to India E M Forster, 1982; T S Eliot's The Waste Land a Study, 1982; Prajapati: God of the People [ND] A Novel, 1984. *Memberships:* Indian PEN; Poetry Society, London. *Address:* English Dept, University College of Arts, Osmania University, Hyderabad, Andhra Pradesh, India 500007.

SHAIN, Merle, b. 14 Oct. 1935, Toronto, Ontario, Canada. Author. 1 son. *Education:* BA, University College, 1957; BSW, School of Social Work, University of Toronto, 1959. *Publications:* Some Men Are More Perfect Than Others, 1973; When Lovers Are Friends, 1978; Hearts That We Broke Long Ago, 1983. *Contributions to:* Toronto Telegram; Globe and Mail; Chatelaine; Toronto Life. *Literary Agent:* Mort Janklow. *Address:* 50 Chestnut Park Road, Toronto, Ontario M4W 1W8, Canada.

SHALES, Melissa Jane, b. 10 Dec. 1958, Croydon, England. Magazine Editor. *Education:* BA, Hons, History and Archaeology, Exteter University, 1980. *Literary Appointments:* Assistant Editor, Catering and Hotel Management; Editor, The Traveller. *Publications:* The Traveller's Handbook Editor, 1985; 100 Gold Inside Tips for the Business Traveller, 1985. *Contributor to:* Editor: The Traveller, Catering and Hotel Management, The Artist. Also articles for Central Office of Information, The Guardian, Going Places. *Memberships:* Guild of Travel Writers; Fellow, The Royal Geographical Society. *Address:* 121 Brixton Hill Court, Brixton Hill, London SW2, England.

SHALLCRASS, John James, b. 11 Sep. 1922, Auckland, New Zealand. Teacher. *Education:* MA, Victoria University; Diploma of Education, University of New Zealand; Advanced Diploma of Teaching, New Zealand Department of Education. *Publications:* Educating New Zealanders, 1967; Introduction to Maori Education, with K J L Ewing, 1970; Secondary Schools in Change, 1973; Spirit of an Age, with J L Robson, 1975; Forward to Basics, 1978; Recreation Reconsidered, with R Larkin and R Stothart, 1980; No Stone Unturned, with P Wilson, 1982; Civil Liberties in a Changing New Zealand, Editor, 1985. *Contributions to:* New Zealand Listener; Landfall; American Journal of Educational Psychology; National Education; New Zealand Journal of Educational Studies; Australian Education Magazine; Comment; National Business Review. *Honour:* Mobil Radio Award, 1980. *Memberships:* PEN International. *Address:* 18 Simla Crescent, Wellington 4, New Zealand.

SHAMBAUGH, Joan Dibble, b. 14 Mar. 1928. Writer; Teacher; Moderator, Creative Writing Workshops. *Education:* AB, Sociology; Educational Teaching Certificates, Secondary and Elementary, Women's College, Duke University, USA. Med, Lesley College, 1980. *Appointments include:* Assistant Professor, Harvard Ext Advanced English Composition, 8 years; Moderator-Teacher, Creative Writing Workshops, Adult Continuing Programmes, Lincoln-Sudbury, Lexington, Concord, Weston Lib. *Publications:* Poems Given, 1975; from the Dream Outward, 1980; Book of Stones or Stone Songs, 1983; Two Anthologies forthcoming in American Anthol amd Poets and Fiction Writers. *Contributions:* Professional papers; The Lincoln Review; The Sheba Review; Origins, Ont; The Alchemist; Montreal; Folio; Bones; Fish; Stony Hills; Trees; Pyramid and various others. *Honours:* American Directory of Poets and Fiction Writers, 1977 and 1980; Prof papers to be preserved in Manuscript Department, William Perkins Library, Duke University. *Membership:*

Poetry Society of America. *Address;* 185 Merriam Street, Weston, MA 02193, USA.

SHANKARAN, T S, b. 4 July, 1932, Tirunelveli, India. Bank Officer. m. Parvathy 12 Apr. 1961, Cape Comorin, 1 son. *Education:* Graduate in Economics; Certified, Associate of Indian Institute of Bankers; Diploma in Industrial Financal; Diploma in Co-Operation; Cultural Doctorate in Literature, World University, USA. *Literary Appointments:* Editor, Childrens magazine; Editor, College magazine; Honorary Editor, Conflict Monthly and Weekly Observer. *Contributions to:* Most daily newspapers (letter columns); author 50 anecdotes under heading, Life's L'i Tears, Weekly magazines; Panorama of Life column; Little Known Facts, column; author of numerous articles. *Honours:* DLitt, World University; Currently working for Dimploma in Mass Communcation and Journalism. *Memberships:* Past Assistant Secretary, Literary Society of Bank; Fellow, United Writer Association, Madras. *Address:* No 16-D Sree Ramaprasada, 37th Cross, Jayanagar 8th Block, Bangalore, 560 082, India.

SHANKLAND, Peter Macfarlane, b. 15 June 1901, London, England. Author. m. 3 sons, 1 daughter. *Publications:* Malta Convoy, 1961; Dardanelles Patrol with Anthony Hunter, 1963; The Phantom Flotilla, 1968; Byron of the Wager, 1975; The Royal Baccarat Scandal, 1977; Murder with a Double Tongue, with Sir Michael Havers, 1978; Tragedy in Three Voices, with Sir Michael Havers, and A Barrett, 1980; Death of an Editor, 1981. *Address:* Bowden House, 9 Market Street, Poole, Dorset, England.

SHAPIRO, Cecile Peyser, b. 6 Feb. 1925, New York City, USA. Writer. m. David Shapiro, 18 June 1944, 2 daughters. *Education:* BA, Adelphi University; MA. Columbia University. *Publications:* Co-author with David Shapiro: Fine Prints, 1976; American Images in 20th Century Art, in press. *Contributions to:* House & Garden Guides; Americana; American Artist; Art News; Chronicle of Higher Education; Publishers Weekly; Saturday Review. *Memberships:* Director-at-Large 1984–87, Chair, Awards Committee 1984–85, Secretary 1977–78, American Society of Journalists & Authors. *Address:* RFD Box 77, Cavendish, VT 05142, USA.

SHAPIRO, Harvey, b. 27 Jan. 1924, Chicago, Illinois, USA. Poet Journalist. m. Edna Kaufman, 23 July 1953, New York, USA, 2 sons. *Education:* BA, Yale University, 1947; MA, Columbia University, 1949. *Major Publications:* Poetry: The Eye, 1953; Mountain, Fire, Thornbush, 1961; Battle Report, 1966; This World, 1971; Lauds & Nightsounds, 1978; The Light Holds, 1984. *Address:* 43 Pierrepont Street, Brooklyn, NY 11201, USA.

SHAPIRO, Robert, b. 23 Nov. 1935, New York, New York, USA. Professor of Chemistry. m. Sandra Milstein, 5 Apr. 1964, Yonkers, New York, 1 son. *Education:* BS, City College of New York, 1956; AM 1957, PhD 1959, Harvard University. *Publications:* Life Beyond Earth, (with Gerald Fienberg), 1980; Origins: A Skeptic's Guide to the Genesis of Life, 1986. *Contributions to:* Scientific and popular science journals. *Literary Agent:* Joh Brockman Associates. *Address:* 23 Ridge Drive East, Great Neck, NY 11021, USA.

SHARKANSKY, Ira, b. 25 Nov. 1938, USA. Professor of Political Science and Public Administration. m. Varda Horn, 28 Sep. 1982, 2 sons. *Education:* BA, Wesleyan University, 1960; PhD, Unversity of Wisconsin, 1964. *Publications:* The Routines of Politics, 1970; The United States: A Study of a Developing Country, 1976; Wither the State?, 1979; What Makes Israel Tick?, 1985. *Address:* Department of Political Science, Hebrew University, Jerusalem, Israel.

SHARKEY, Jack, b. 6 May 1931, Chicago, Illinois, USA. Playwright; Composer. m. Patricia Walsh, 14 July 1962, Chicago, Illinois, 1 son, 3 daughters. *Education:* BA English in Creative Writing, St Mary's College,

Winona, Minnesota, 1953. *Literary Appointments:* Editor, Aim, (later, Good Hands) magazine, Allstate Insurance Corporation, 1964–75. *Publications:* Muder, Maestro, Please, 1960; The Secret Martians, 1960; Death for Auld Lang Syne, 1962; The Addams Family, 1965; Jack Sharkey's Audition Pieces and Classroom Exercises, 1984; 55 plays and musicals including: Honestly, Now, play; Musical version of Wilde's, The Picture of Dorian Gray. *Contributions to:* Hundreds of magazines and journals including: Fantastic; Amazing; Galaxy; Worlds of Tomorrow; Fantasy and Science Fiction; Dude; Gent; Alfred Hitchcock's Mystery Magazine; Playboy; Rogue; If; Sir Kay; Cavalier. *Honours:* Best Editorial of 1967, American Association of Industrial Editors, 1968; Key to the City, Garden Grove, California, 1981; Best Play of 1983 Season, Inland Theatre League, California, 1984. *Memberships:* Dramatists Guild and Authors League of America; Nu Delta Chapter, Alpha Psi Omega National Dramatic Fraternity. *Literary Agent:* M Abbott Van Nostrand, 45 W 25th, New York, New York. *Address:* Orange County, California, USA.

SHARLAND, Michael (Mike) Reginald, b. 4 July 1943, London, England. Screenwriter. m. Lady Alice Z, 16 July 1967, 2 sons, 1 daughter. *Education:* MA. *Publication:* Nervestorm, 1974. *Contributions to:* Television series; Theatre plays; Films. Over 600 to date. *Membership:* Television & Film Committee, Executive Councillor, Chairman Technical Committee, Writers Guild of Great Britain; ACTTC, Film Section. *Literary Agent:* Jon Thurley, 79 New Bond Street, London W1, England. *Address:* c/o Writers Guild of Great Britain, 430 Edgware Road, London W1 1EH, England.

SHARMA, Jagdish Saran, b. 29 Apr. 1924, Gazzalpur, India. Professor-Head-cum-Librarian, University of Jammu. *Education:* MA, St Stephen's College, 1947; Dip Lib Sci, University of Delhi, 1948; MA, 1949, PhD, 1954, University of Michigan, USA. *Publications include:* India's Struggle for Freedom, 3 volumes 1965; India Since the Advent of the British, 1971; National Biographical Dictionary of India, 1972; Sources of Indian Civilization: Bibliography of works by World Orientalists other than Indian, 1974; Encyclopaedia Indica, 1975, 2 volumes, 2nd edition 1981; Fundamentals of Bibliography with Special Reference to India, 1976; Fundamentals of Library Science, 1978; Library Organization: A Modern Approach, 1978; Knowledge Its Origin & Growth from the Earliest times to the Present, 1978; Descriptive Bibliographies: Mahatma Gandhi, 2nd edition 1969; Jawaharial Nehru, 1969; Indian National Congress, revised edition, 1970; Library Movement in India and Abroad – Observations of a Librarian. *Contributor to:* Professional journals. *Honours:* Recipient, Meritorious Library Service Award, Punjab Library Association; International Library Movement Award; University of Jammu Library, Jammu-Tawi, J & K State, India. *Memberships:* Former Member, Authors Guild of India. *Address:* University of Jammu Library, Bahu Wali Rakh, New Campus, Jammu 180001, India.

SHARMA, Ravindra Nath, b. 22 Oct. 1944, Kartarpur, Panjab, India. Library Adminstrator. m. Mithlesh Joshi, 7 July 1972, Toronto, Canada, 2 daughters. *Education:* BA Honours, 1963, MA History, 1966, University of Delhi, India; MLS, North Texas State University, Denton, Texas, USA, 1970; PhD Library Studies and Higher Eduation, State University of New York, Buffalo, 1982. *Literary Appointments:* Editor, Library Times International, 1984–; Contributing Editor, International Librarian, 1984–. *Publications:* India and Indians: A Bibliography, 2 volumes, 1974; Indian Librarianship: Perspectives and Prospects, 1981; Indian Academica Libraries Since 1800 and contributions fo Dr S R Ranganathan: A Critical Study, 1985. *Contributions to:* Various library journals in Europe, India and USA. *Honour:* Consultant, National Endowment for the Humanities, 1983–. *Memberships:* Chairman of South Asia for International Relations Round Table, American Library Association, 1983–; Secretary Asian/African Section, Association of College and Research Libraries,

1985–88; Treasurer 1982–84, Asian/ Pacific American Librarians Association; Indian Library Association. *Literary Agent:* MS M Joshi. *Address:* Libraries and Learning Resources, University of Wisconsin-Oshkosh, Oshkosh, WI 54901, USA. The Pennsylvania State University, Beaver Campus, Brodhead Road, Monaca, PA 15061, USA.

SHARMAT, Marjorie Weinman, b. 12 Nov. 1928, Maine, USA. Writer. *Education:* Graduate, Westbrook Junior College, 1948. *Publications include:* Rex, 1967; 51 Sycamore Lane, 1971; A Visit With Rosalind, 1972; Nate the Great, 1972; Sophie and Gussie, 1973; Morris Brookside, a Dog, 1973; Morris Brookside is Missing, 1974; Nate the Great Goes Undercover, 1974; I'm Not Oscar's Friend Any More, 1975; Walter the Wolf, 1975; Nate the Great and the Lost List, 1975; Burton and Dudley, 1975; Maggie Marmelstein for President, 1975; Edgement, 1976; The Lancelot Closes at Five, 1976; Mooch the Messy, 1976; The Trip and Other Sophie and Gussie Stories, 1976; I Don't Care, 1977; I'm Terrific, 1977; Nate the Great and the Phoney Clue, 1977; The Story of Bentley Beaver, 1984; How to Have a Gorgeous Wedding, 1985; Get Rich Mitch! 1985; One Terrific Thanksgiving, 1985; Helga High-Up, 1986; Hooray for Mother's Day, 1986; Marjorie Sharmat's Sorority Sisters, (series), 1986; Go to Sleep, Nicholas Joe, 1986, etc. *Contributor to:* Various magazines. *Honours include:* Tower Award, 1975. *Memberships include:* Authors' Guild. *Address:* Tucson, AZ, USA.

SHAROT, Stephen Andrew, b. 5 Aug. 1943, England. University Professor. m. 7 July 1968, 1 son, 1 daughter. *Publications:* Judaism: A Sociology, 1976; Messianism, Mysticism, and Magic: A Sociological Analysis of Jewish Religious Movements, 1982. *Contributions to:* Comparative Studies in Society and History; British Journal of Sociology; Jewish Journal of Sociology; Journal for the Scientific Study of Religion; Religion; Ethnic and Racial Studes. *Honours:* Harkness Fellowship, 1968–70; Kenneth B Smilen/President Literary Award, 1983. *Address:* Department of Behavioural Sciences, Ben-Gurion University of the Negev, Beer-Sheva, Israel.

SHARP, Buchanan, b. 25 Sep. 1942, Dumbarton, Scotland. University Teacher. m. Jeannine Blazzard, 15 Aug. 1964, San Francisco, California, USA. 1 son, 1 daughter. *Education:* BA 1964, PhD 1971, University of California, Berkeley, USA; MA, University of Illinois, 1965. *Publications:* In Contempt of All Authority: Rural Artisans and Riot in the West of England 1586–1660, 1980; Popular Protest in Seventeenth Century England, in Barry Read (editor), Popular Culture in Seventeenth Century England, 1985. *Contributions to:* Theory and Society; American Historical Review; Albion. *Honours:* Fellowship in the Social Sciences 1966–67, Fellowship in History 1967–68, University of California. *Memberships:* American Historical Association; Economic History Society; Past and Present Society; Scottish History Society. *Address:* Stevenson College, University of California, Santa Cruz, CA 95064, USA.

SHARP, Harold Wilson, b. 29 Jan. 1914, War Eagle, Arkansas, USA. Writer, Artist, Illustrator, Painting Photographer. *Education:* Chouinard Art Institute, Los Angeles, California. *Literary Appointments:* Introduced syndicated column on hunting and fishing, now appearing in 600 newspapers, 1950. *Major Publications:* Sportsman's Digest of Hunting, 1952; Sportsman's Digest of Fishing, 1954; Spin-fishing, 1954. *Contributor to:* Mechanics Illustrated during 1950s. *Honours:* Award of Merit, American Artists of the West, 1953; Award of Achievement, Historical Photograph exhibition, 1973, 1974. *Memberships:* Outdoor Writers' Association; Press Club, Las Vegas, Nevada during 1960s. *Literary Agent:* Toni Mendez, New York. *Address:* 1545 N Hobart Boulevard apt 307, Hollywood, CA 90027, USA.

SHARPE, Thomas Ridley, b. 20 Mar. 1928, London, England. Novelist. m. Nancy Anne Looper, 6 Aug. 1969, Cambridge, 3 daughters. *Education:* MA, Pembroke

College, Cambridge, 1948–51; Post-graduate Certificate of Education, 1962–63. *Publications:* Riotous Assembly, 1971; Indecent Exposure, 1973; Porterhouse Blue, 1974; Blott on the Landscape, 1975; Wilt, 1976; The Great Pursuit, 1977; The Throwback, 1978; The Wilt Alternative, 1979; Ancestral Vices, 1980; Vintage Stuff, 1982; Wilt on High, 1984. *Literary Agent:* Richard Scott Simon, 32 College Cross, London N1 1PR. *Address:* Martin Secker and Warburg, 54 Poland Street, London W1V 3DF, England.

SHARR, Francis Aubie, b. 5 Oct 1914, Manchester, England. Retired Librarian. m. Florence McKeand, 1962. *Education:* BA, London University; Postgraduate Diploma in Librarianship. *Publications:* County Library Practice 1950; County Library Transport 1952; The Library Needs of Northern Nigeria 1963; Western Australia Plant Names and their meaning; a glossary, 1977. *Contributor to:* Numerous Magazines and Journals. *Honours:* OBE 1977; HCL Anderson Award, 1980. *Address:* 58 The Avenue, Nedlands, WA 6009, Australia.

SHARROCK, John Timothy Robin, b. 6 Dec. 1937, Alfington, Devon, England. Ornithologist. m. Erika Marion Otte, 4 Aug. 1961, Hampstead, 1 son, 1 daughter. *Education:* BSc, 1st Class Honours; PhD. *Literary Appointment:* Managing Editor, Journal British Birds, 1976–. *Publications include:* The Natural History of Cape Clear Island, 1973; Scarce Migrant Birds in Britain and Ireland, 1974; The Atlas of Breeding Birds in Britain and Ireland, 1976; Rare Birds in Britain and Ireland, 1976; Frontiers of Bird Identification, 1980; The RSPB Book of British Birds, 1982; The British Birds Mystery Photographs Book, 1983; The Shell Guide to the Birds of Britain and Ireland, 1983; A First Book of Birds, 1984. *Contributions to:* British Birds; Bird Study; Cape Clear Bird Observatory Reports; Ardeola; etc. *Address:* Blunham, Bedford, England.

SHARROCK, Roger Ian, b. 23 Aug. 1919, Robin Hood's Bay, Yorkshire, England. m. Gertrude Elizabeth Adams, 24 Dec. 1940, Hawick, Scotland, 1 son, 2 daughters. University Professor; Editor; Author; MA, BLitt, St John's College, Oxford, England. *Publications include:* John Bunyan, 1954; (Editor) Bunyan, The Pilgrim's Progress, 1960; (Editor) Bunyan, Grace Abounding, 1962; (Editor) Oxford Standard Authors, Bunyan, 1966; (Editor) Pelican Book of English Prose, 1970; Casebook on Pilgrim's Progress, 1976; English Short Stories of Today, 1976; (General Editor) Oxford Edition of Bunyan's Miscellaneous Works. *Contributions to:* Blackfriars; Durham University Journal; Essays in Criticism; Modern Language Review; Notes and Queries; Reviews of English Literature; Review of English Studies; Tablet; Times Literary Supplement. *Memberships:* Chmn. English Association; Management Committee World Centre for Shakespeare Studies. *Literary Agent:* Curtis Brown Academic. *Address:* 12 Plough Lane, Purley, Surrey, England.

SHAW, Bynum Gillette, b. 10 July 1923, Alamance County, North Carolina, USA. Professor of Journalism. m. (1) Louise N Brantley (dec) 30 Aug. 1948; (2) Emily P Crandall, (dec) 19 June 1982; 2 daughters. *Education:* BA 1951, Wake Forest College. *Publications:* The Sound of Small Hammers, 1962; The Nazi Hunter, 1968; Divided We Stand: The Baptists in American Life, 1974; Days of Power, Nights of Fear, 1980; W W Holden: A Political Biography, (with Edgar E Folk), 1982. *Contributions to:* Esquire; The New Republic; Moneysworth; The New York Times. *Honour:* Sir Walter Raleigh Award in Fiction, 1969. *Memberships:* Board of Directors, North Carolina Literary and Historical Association; North Carolina Writers' Conference. *Literary Agent:* Scott Meredith. *Address:* 2700 Speas Road, Winston-Salem, NC 27106, USA.

SHAW, Charles Thurstan, b. 27 June 1914, Plymouth, England. Archaeologist. m. Gilian Ione Maud Magor, 21 Jan. 1939, St Tudy, 2 sons, 3 daughters. *Education:* BA, MA, PhD, Sidney Sussex College, Cambridge; Teacher's, Postgraduate Diploma, London University Institute of Education. *Publications:* Excavations at Dawn, 1961; Archaeology & Nigeria, 1964; Igbo-Ukwu: An Account of Archaeological Discoveries in Eastern Nigeria, 1970; Africa & The Origins of Man, 1973; Discovering Nigeria's Past, 1975; Why Darkest Africa?, 1975; Unearthing Igbo-Ukwu, 1977; Nigeria: Its Archaeology and Early History, 1978; Filling Gaps in Africa Maps: Fifty Years of Archaelogy in Africa, 1984. *Contributor to:* Various scholarly journals. *Honours:* CBE 1972; Amaury Talbot Prize, Royal Anthropoligical Institute, 1970, 1978; Honorary DSc., University of Nigeria, 1982. *Memberships:* FSA; Vice President, Panafrican Congress on Prehistory; Committee, Union International des Scis. Pre-et Proto-Historiques. *Address:* 37 Hawthorne Road, Stapleford, Cambridge CB2 5DU, England.

SHAW, Howard, b. 16 Sep. 1934, Clifton, England. Head of History, Harrow School. m. Elizabeth Du Heaume, 26 Dec. 1958, Taunton, Devon, 2 sons. *Education:* MA, Oxford University. *Publications:* The Levellers, 1968; Killing No Murder, 1972; Death of a Don, 1981. *Contributions to:* The Listener; A History Today. *Membership:* Crime Club. *Literary Agent:* Laurence Pollinger. *Address:* Syon, Harrow Park, Harrow on the Hill, Middlesex, England.

SHAW, Ronnie Glen, b. 26 Aug. 1958, Fort Worth, Texas, USA. Managing Editor of the Choral Journal. m. Laquita Jenise Fisher, 10 Aug. 1985, Chattanooga, OK. *Education:* BM, Hardin-Simmons University, Abilene, Texas, USA. *Literary Appointments:* Managing Editor, The Choral Journal. *Memberships:* Educational Press Associates of America, New Jersey. *Address:* The Choral Journal, PO Box 6310, Lawton, OK 73506, USA.

SHAW, Timothy M, b. 27 Jan. 1945, England. University Professor. m. Jane L Parpart, 2 Sep. 1983, Halifax, Nova Scotia, 1 son, 3 daughters. *Education:* BA, Sussex, 1967; MA, East Africa, 1969; MA, Princeton, 1971; PhD, ibid, 1975. *Literary Appointments:* General Editor, International Political Economy Series, Macmillan, 1984–; Co-editor, Dalhousie African Studies Series, University Press of America, 1984–. *Publications:* The Politics of Africa; Dependence & Development, 1979; Zambia's Foreign Policy; Studies in Diplomacy and Dependence, 1979; Alternative Futures for Africa, 1982; Nigerian Foreign Policy: Alternative Perceptions and Projections, 1983; The Political Economy of African Foreign Policy, 1984; Africa Projected: From Recession to Renaissance by the year 2000, 1985; Towards a Political Economy for Africa: The Dialectics of Dependence, 1985; Southern Africa in the 1980's, 1985. *Contributions to:* Africa Today; Alternatives; Canadian Journal of African Studies; International Political Science Review; Journal of Modern African Studies; Millenium; Review of Black Political Economy; Third World Quarterly; West Africa. *Address:* Centre for African Studies, Dalhousie University, 1444 Seymour Street, Halifax, Nova Scotia, Canada B3H 4H6.

SHAWN, Wallace Michael, b. 12 Nov. 1943, New York, USA. Playwright. *Education:* BA, Harvard College; BA, MA, Magdalen College, Oxford. *Publications:* Marie and Bruce 1980; My Dinner with Andre, (with Andre Gregory) 1982; The Hotel Play, 1982; Aunt Dan and Lemon, 1985. *Literary Agent:* Luis Sanjurjo. *Address:* c/o Luis Sanjurjo, I.C.M., 40 West 57th Street, New York, NY 10019, USA.

SHEAFFER, Louis, b. 18 Oct. 1912, Louisville, Kentucky, USA. Writer. *Education:* University of North Carolina, 1930–31. *Publications:* O'Neill, Son and Playwright, 1968; O'Neill, Son and Artist, 1973. *Honours:* Guggenheim Fellowships, 1959, 62, 69; Grant-in-Aid, American Council of Learned Societies, 1960, 62, 82; Fellowship, National Endowment for the Humanities, 1971; Award for O'Neill Son and Playwright, best theatre book, Theatre Library Association, 1968; for O'Neill, Son and Artist, The Pulitzer Prize, 1974. *Membership:* Authors Guild. *Literary Agent:* Lescher and Lescher, New York, USA. *Address:* 5 Montague Terrace, Brooklyn, NY 11201, USA.

SHELBY, Graham, Writer. *Publications:* The Knights of Dark Renown, 1969; The Kings of Vain Intent, 1970; The Villains of the Piece, 1972; The Devil is Loose, 1973; The Wolf at the Door, 1975; The Cannaways, 1978; The Cannaway Concern, 1980. *Literary Agent:* Deborah Rogers Ltd, London. *Address:* c/o Deborah Rogers Ltd, 49 Blenheim Crescent, London W11 2EF, England.

SHELDON, Walter James, b. 9 Jan. 1917, Philadelphia, Pennsylvania, USA. Civil Servant (retired). m. Yukiko Aida Sheldon, 6 Aug. 1953, Tokyo, Japan, 3 sons. *Education:* Pennsylvania Museum School of Industrial Art. *Publications:* Troubling of a Star, novel, 1952; The Man Who Paid His Way, novel, 1955; Dust Devil, novel 1957; Enjoy Japan, Travel, 1961; The Key to Tokyo, Travel, 1962; The Honorable Conquerors, Non-fiction, 1965; Hell or High Water, Non-fiction, 1968; Tigers in the Rice, Non-fiction, 1969; The Dunes, novel 1974; Boating without Going Broke, non-fiction, 1975; The Beast, novel, 1980; Rites of Murder, novel, 1984. *Contributor to:* Numerous magazines and journals including: Saturday Review of Literature; Esquire; Cosmopolitan; Collier's etc. *Literary Agent:* Scott Meredith, 845 Third Avenue, New York, NY 10022, USA. *Address:* 1611 Oriental Avenue, Bellingham, WA 98226, USA.

SHELLEY, Louise Isobel, b. 13 Mar. 1952, New York City, USA. Associate Professor, American University. m. Donald E Graves, 26 June 1975, 1 son, 1 daughter. *Education:* BA, Cornell University, 1972; MA, 1973, PhD, 1977, University of Pennsylvania. *Publications:* Crime and Modernization, 1981; Reading in Comparative Crimonolgy, 1981; Lawyers in Soviet Work Life, 1984. *Contributions to:* Law and Society; American Sociological Review; Journal of Criminal Law and Criminology; Slavic Review; International Herald Tribune. *Honours:* IREX Fellowship, 1975; Fulbright-Hays Fellowship, NEH Fellowship, 1984; Guggenheim Fellowship, 1984. *Address:* 4538 Cathedral Avenue NW, Washington, DC 20016, USA.

SHELTON, Regina Maria, b. 29 July 1927, Weisstein, Germany. Library Technical Assistant. m. Clarence Wilson Shelton Jr, 24 July 1948, Nordenham, Germany (div 1968), 5 dons. *Education:* BA, Southern Illinois University, 1971. *Publication:* To Lose a War: Memories of a German Girl, 1982. *Contributions to:* Adaption: A One-Year Survey of Reserve Photography (Journal of Academic Librarianship, 1980); The Lure of the Browsing Room (Library Journal, 1982). *Honour:* Delta Award, Friends of Morris Library, 1983. *Address:* Route 1, Box 500, Carbondale, IL 62901, USA.

SHELTON, William Roy, b. 9 Apr. 1919, Rutherfordton, North Carolina, USA. Journalist, Author, Motion Picture Writer/Producer. m. Mary Jackson, Winston-Salem, Aug. 1981, 1 son, 3 daughters. *Education:* AB, Rollins College, 1948. *Publications include:* Countdown, 1960; Flights of the Astronauts, 1963; American Space Exploration, The First Decade, 1967; Man's Conquest of Space, 1972; Stowaway to the Moon, novel 1973, television motion picture scriptwriter and technical advisor 1975; Soviet Space Exploration, The First Decade, 1973; New Hope For the Dead, poetry, 1977; Houston, Supercity of the Southwest, (with Ann Kennedy), 1978; Love and other Miracles, play, 1983. *Contributions to:* Magazines and journals including; Fortune; Atlantic; Time. *Honours include:* Book of the Year Award, Aviation/Space Writers Association, 1969; Atlantic Metro Goldwyn Mayer First Prize, 1949; O Henry prize Stories Collection, 1950. *Memberships:* Author's Guild; Writers Guild of America. *Literary Agent:* Aaron Priest, New York. *Address:* 861 Kenwick Drive, Winston-Salem, NC 27106, USA.

SHENK, Lois Elaine Landis, b. 30 May 1944, Ephrata, Pennsylvania, USA. Housewife. m. John Barge Shenk, 12 June 1966, Ephrata, 2 sons. *Education:* BA English, Eastern Mennonite College, Virginia, 1966; M Sc Education, Temple University, Philadelphia, Pennsylvania, 1984. *Literary Appointments:* English Mistress,

Githumu Secondary School, Kenya, 1966–68; English teacher, Kraybill's Junior High, Mount Joy, Pennsylvania, USA, 1976–77; Editorial work, Mennonite Central Committee, Akron, 1977; Religious News Correspondent, Gospel Herald Scottdale, 1978–82. *Publications:* Out of Mighty Waters, 1982; Drama: A House for David, in, Swords into Plowshares, edited by Rogers, 1983. *Contributions to:* Poems, stories and features in magazines and journals including: Purpose; Gospel Herald; Christian Living; On The Line; Health Quarterly. *Honours:* National Merit Certificate of Commendation, 1961; Award of Excellence, Religion Media, Los Angeles, California, 1983. *Address:* 2478 Horseshoe Road, Lancaster, PA 17601, USA.

SHENTON, Joan Alicia, b. 16 Mar. 1943, Antofagasta, Chile. Television Producer and Reporter. *Education:* MA Spanish and French, Modern Languages, Oxon. *Publications:* Director, Meditel Productions making science/medical documentaries for television. *Honours:* A Silver Award, 8th International Consumer Film Competition, Berlin, for documentary on health foods. *Agent:* Geoffrey Irvine, The Bagenal Harvey Organisation. *Address:* 18 St Ann's Road, London W11 4SR, England.

SHEPARD, Leslie Alan, b. 1917, West Ham, London, England. Overseas Consultant, Gale Research Company, Detroit, USA; Former Film Producer; Editor; Scriptwriter. *Publications:* The Broadside Ballad; A Study in Origins and Meaning, UK and USA, 1962; John Pitts, Ballad Printer of Seven Dials, London 1765–1844, UK and USA, 1970; the History of Street Literature, UK and USA, 1973; How to Protect Yourself Against Black Magic and Witchcraft, 1978; (ED), The Dracula Book of Great Vampire Stories, USA 1977; (ED.), The Dracula Book of Great Horror Stories, USA, 1981; (ED.) Encyclopedia of Occultism and Parapsychology, USA, 3 volumes, 1984–85. *Contributor to:* Palm and TV Technician; New Society; Mountain Life and Work; Folk Scene; etc. *Memberships include:* International Council for Traditional Music; College of Physic Studies; English Folk Dance and Song Society; Bibliographical Society; British Society of Dowsers; Printing Historical Society; Pvte. Libs. Association; Society for Psychical Research. *Address:* 1 Lakelands Close, Stillorgan, Blackrock, Co Dublin, Republic of Ireland.

SHEPARD, Valerie Ann, b. 8 Aug. 1948, Lincolnshire, England. Editor. m. Michael Brian Shepard, 6 Sep. 1969, London, 1 son, 1 daughter. *Education:* BA, 1st Class Honours, English, University of London, 1971. *Literary Appointments:* Editor, The Museums Association 1974–75, Paper & Paper Procedure ITB 1975–79, Local Council Review 1979–. *Contributions:* Numerous. *Membership:* British Association of Industrial Editor. *Address:* 18 Stone Park Drive, Forest Row, East Sussex RH18 5DG, England.

SHEPHARD, Bruce Dennis, b. 21 Apr. 1944, San Francisco, USA. Physician. m. Carroll Swanson 22 June 1969, 2 sons, 1 daughter. *Education:* MD, University of California, San Francisco, 1970. *Major Publication:* The Complete Guide to Women's Health (with Dr Carroll Shephard), Mariner Publishing Company, 1982, revision in paperback, New American Library, 1985. *Honour:* Phi Beta Kappa, University of California, Berkeley, 1966. *Address:* Suite B, 2901 St Isabel Street, Tampa, FL 33607, USA.

SHEPHARD, Roy Jesse, b. 8 May 1929, London. Medical Scientist. m. Muriel Neve, 18 Aug. 1956, Hornsey, 2 daughters. *Education:* BSc, Physiology, MBBS, PhD, MD, FFIMS, FACSM, Guy's Hospital, Medical School, London University. *Literary Appointments:* Section Editor, Medicine and Science in Sports, 1972–76; Editorial Board: Human Biology, 1976–, Ergonomics, 1981–, European Journal of Applied Physiology, 1983–, J Cardiac Rehab, 1983–, Sports Medicine 1984–. *Publications:* Endurance Fitness, 1969; Frontiers of Fitnees, 1972; Men At Work 1974; Fit Athlete, 1978; Human Physiological Work Capacity, 1978; Physical Activity and Aging, 1978; Physical And

Growth, 1982; Ischemic Heart Disease and Exercise, 1982; Risks of Passive Smoking, 1982; Physiology and Biochemistry of Exercise, 1982; Carbon Monoxide – The Silent Killer, 1983; Biochemistry of Exercise, 1983; Fitness and Health in Industry, 1985. *Contributor to:* Over 600 articles published in scientific literature. *Honours:* University of London Post Graduate Scholar 1952–53; Fulbright Scholar 1956–58; Philip Noel Baker Research Prize (UNESCO) 1976; Citation by Province of Ontario 1983; MRC and CNRS Travelling Professor 1985–86; First Recipient CASS Honour Award, 1985. *Memberships:* Member of 15 professional societies. Former President, American College of Sports Medicine; Former President, Canadian Association of Sport Sciences. *Address:* 42 Tollerton Avenue, Willowdale, Ontario, Canada M2K 2H3.

SHEPHERD, Arthur Anderson, b. 27 May 1932, Blackpool, Lancashire, England. Writer; Photographer. m. Mary Elizabeth Lawson, 29 Nov. 1958, Reading, 1 daughter. *Education:* BSc, Agriculture, Reading University. *Contributions:* Regular features to: Shooting Magazine; Airgun World. Occasional articles to: Pig Farming; Farmers Weekly; Shooting Times; Country Magazine. *Address:* 1 Norwood Avenue, Southmoor, Abingdon, Oxfordshire, England.

SHEPPARD, David, b. 6 Mar. 1929, Reigate, Surrey, England. Bishop. m. Grace Isaac, 19 June 1957, Lindfield, 1 daughter. *Education:* MA, Trinity Hall, Cambridge University. *Publications:* Parson's Pitch, 1964; Built as a City, 1974; Bias to the Poor, 1983. *Contributions to:* Woman's Own, columnist, 1957–74; Occasional contributor to various other publications. *Honours:* Honorary LLD, Liverpool University, 1981. *Address:* Bishop's Lodge, Woolton Park, Liverpool L25 6DT, England.

SHERE, Charles, b. 20 Aug. 1935, Berkeley, California, USA. Composer; Art, Music Critic. m. Lindsey Remolif, 11 June 1957, Berkeley, 2 sons, 2 daughters. *Education:* AB, University of California, Berkeley, 1960. *Publications:* Contributor to: Storia Universale della Musica, 1982. *Contributor to:* Arts Canada; New Performance; Images and Issues; Art News; Threepenny Review; Editor, Publisher, Ear, 1973–78; Staff Art, Music Critic, Oakland Tribune, 1972–. *Honours:* National Endowment of the Arts Composers' Fellowship, 1977, Art Critics Grant, 1977; Manufacturers Hanover Trust Co, Art World Award for Distinguished Newspaper Art Criticism, 1982. *Memberships:* Association International des critiques d'art; Music Critics Association. *Address:* 1824, Curtis St, Berkeley, CA 94702, USA.

SHERMAN, Arthur, b. 5 Dec. 1920, New York City, USA. Writer; Actor; Director. m. Margery Ruth Frost, 16 June 1974, 1 son, 1 daughter. *Education:* Bachelor of Music; Master of Music Education; Doctoral equivalency City University of New York; Director of Performing Arts. *Publications:* include: Plays, Musical Comedies and Screenplays. In the USA: Not While I'm Eating, sketches and lyrics, produced at Madison Avenue Playhouse, New York City, 1961; Lenore and the Wonder House, book and lyrics, 1963; So What, lyrics and choral work, 1963. In Australia: TV Series, Number 96, 1973; TV Comedy, The Unmarried Marrieds, 1973; Stage includes: Seeds Upon the Wind, 1983; The Walls, 1984; Once Upon a...Crime, musical comedy, book and lyrics, 1985. Screen includes: Thistle and Thorn, 1984–85; Dazzle and Barrel, 1985. *Memberships:* American Society of Composers, Authors and Publishers; Australia Performing Rights Association. *Honour:* A Comparative Analysis of Western and Eastern Ethos, made part of collection: State University of New York, USA, New Delhi University, India, presented at Indian Cultural Conference, Colgate University, New York, 1970; Not While I'm Eating, made part of permanent collection, New York City Public Library. *Literary Agent:* June Cann. *Address:* 111 Cook Street, Forestville, New South Wales, Australia.

SHERMAN, Kenneth Jeffrey, b. 3 July 1950, Toronto, Canada. Teacher. *Publications:* Snake Music, 1978; The Cost of Living, 1981; Words for Elephant Man, 1983; Black Flamingo, 1985; Relations, 1986. *Address:* 10 Romney Road, Downsview, Ontario, Canada M3H 1H2.

SHERMAN, Roger, b. 10 Sep. 1930, Jamestown, New York, USA. Professor, Economics. m. Charlotte Ann Murphy, 4 Apr, 1953, Glenview, 2 sons. *Education:* BS, Grove City College, 1952; MBA, Harvard University, 1959; MS, 1965, PhD, 1966, Carnegie-Mellon University. *Publications:* Oligopoly: An Empirical Approach, 1972; The Economics of Industry, 1974; Antirtust Policies and Issues, 1978. *Contributor to:* Numerous professional journals including, Rate-of-Return Regulation and Two-Part Tariffs, with Michael Visscher, Quarterly Journal of Economics; Nonprice Rationing and Monopoly Price Structure when Demand is Stochastic, with Michael Visscher, Bell Journal of Economics, 1982; Pricing Behaviour of the Budget Constrained Public Enterprise, Journal of Economic Behavior and Organization, 1983; The Price and Profit Effects of Horizontal Merger: A Case Study, with David Barton, Journal of Industrial Economics, 1984; Author, Chapters in books. *Memberships:* American Economic Association; American Finance Assocation; Econometric Society; Royal Economic Society; Southern and Western Economic Associations. *Address:* 1858 Field Road, Charlottesville, VA 22903, USA.

SHERMAN, William David, b. 24 Dec. 1940, Philadelphia, Pennyslvania, USA. Writer; Poet. *Education:* AB, Temple University, 1962; MA, 1964, PhD 1968, State University of New York. *Literary Appointments:* Lecturer, Film Studies, State University of New York, Buffalo, 1967; Lecturer, American Studies, University of Hull, UK, 1967–68; Lecturer, American Literature, University College of Wales, UK, 1969–72; Tutor/Counsellor, Open University, London, UK, 1976–79; Lecturer, Literary Criticism, University of Maryland, London, 1981–82. *Publications include:* The Springbok, 1973; The Hard Sidewalk, 1975; The Horses of Gwyddno Garanhir, 1976; Duchamp's Door, 1982; Mermaids, 1985; Heart Attack & Spanish Songs, 1981. *Contributions:* Editor/Publisher, Branch Redd Review, Branch Redd poetry chapbooks, 20 years of poems & essays, various journals including Anglo-Welsh Review, 1970; Anthologised in, Fool's House, 1980, Don Quixote (Switzerland), In Hui 19 (France). *Address:* P O Box 3171, Margate, NJ 08402, USA.

SHERRIN, Edward George (Ned), b, 18 Feb. 1931, Lowham, Somerset, England. Director; Producer; President; Writer. *Education:* MA, Oxford University; Barrister-at-Law. *Publications:* Cindy-Ella (with Caryl Brahms), 1962; Rappel (with C B), 1984; Benbow Was His Name (with C B), 1967; Ooh La La (with C B), 1973; After You Mr Feydeau (with C B), 1975; A Small Thing Like An Earthquake, 1983; Song by Song (with C B), 1948; Cutting Edge, 1984; 1956 & All That (with Neil Shand), 1984; The Metropolitan Mikado (with Alistair Beaton), 1985. *Literary Agent:* Margaret Ramsay Ltd. *Address:* c/o Margaret Ramsay, 14A Goodwin's Court, St Martin's Lane, London WC3, England.

SHERRY, Dulcie Sylvia, b. Newcastle upon Tyne, England. Writer. m. Norman Sherry, Newcastle upon Tyne. *Education:* BA, Honours, English, (Dunelm); Certificate of Education. *Publications:* Street of the Small Night Market, 1966; Frog in a Coconut Shell, 1968; A Pair of Jesus-Boots, 1970; The Loss of the Night Wind, 1970; Snake in the Old Hut, 1971; Dark River Dark Mountain, 1975; Mat the Little Monkey, 1977; Girl in a Blue Shawl, 1978; South of Red River, 1981; A Pair of Desert-Wellies, 1985. *Literary Agent:* Jonathan Clowes Ltd. *Address:* 6 Gillison Close, Melling, Carnforth, Lancashire LA6 2RD, England.

SHERRY, James, b. 30 Dec. 1946, Philadelphia, Pennsylvania, USA. Writer. m. Lee Sahlins, 13 June 1968, Tarrytown, New York. *Education:* BA, Reed

College. *Literary Appointments:* Editor, Roof Magazine, 1976. *Publications:* Part Songs, 1979; In Case, 1981; Coverses, 1983; Popular Fiction, 1985. *Contributions to:* Paris Review; Partisan Review; L-A-N-G-U-A-G-E; Roof. *Honours:* Literary Fellowship, CAPS. 1984. *Memberships:* Poets and writers; Alliance of Literary Organisations; Segue Foundation. *Address:* 300 Bowery, New York City, NY 10012, USA.

SHERWIN, Richard Elliott, b. 21 Aug. 1933, Malden, Massachesetts, USA. Professor of English Literature, Poet. m. Rachel Domke, Aug. 1958, 1 son, 2 daughters. *Education:* BA, University of California at Los Angeles, 1955–59; MA, 1959–60, PhD 1960–63, Yale University. *Literary Appointments:* Lecturer, Carleton College, Minnesota, 1962–64; Senior Lecturer, Bar-Ilan University, Israel, 1964–79; Visiting Lecturer, Tel Aviv University, Israel, 1965–80, University of California at Los Angeles, 1971–72; Chairman, Department of English, 1972–76, Dean, Faculty of Humanities, 1976–78, Associate Professor, Chairman of Department of English, 1979–83, 1984–, Bar-Ilan University; Visiting Research Fellow, Australian Studies Institute, University of Queensland, Australia; Visiting Fellow, Oriental Studies, University of California at Berkeley, USA, 1983–84. *Major Publications:* A Strange Courage, 1978 (poems); Various poems & reviews. *Memberships:* Phi Beta Kappa; Woodrow Wilson, Fellow; Society for Religion in Higher Education; Poetry Society, London; Modern Language Association; Association of University Teachers of English, Israel; English Committee, Israel Ministry of Education; Secretary, Assistant Chairman, Israel Union of Writers in English; Treasurer, Israel American Studies Association. *Address:* Department of English, Bar-Ilan University, Ramat-Gan, Israel.

SHERWOOD, Hugh Clements, b. 9 Feb. 1928, Boston, Massachusetts, USA. Editor; Writer, Divorced. *Education:* BA, Yale, 1948; MS, Columbia University School of Journalism, 1950. *Appointments:* Associate editor, Medical Economics, 1955–59; Freelance Writer, 1960–62, 1970–77; Associate, Senior, Managing Editor, Business Management, 1963–69; Assistant Managing Editor, Finance, 1969; Editorial Services Officer, Irving Trust Company, 1977–. *Publications:* Author, The Journalistic Interview, 1969; How to Invest in Bonds, 1974; How Corporate and Municipal Debt is Rated: The Inside Story of Standard & Poor's Rating System, 1976. *Contributor to:* Over 2000 articles in, Industry Week; Town & Country; Nation's Business; Harper's Bazaar; Physician's Management; Dental Management; Woman's Day; New York Times Sunday Magazine; Family Circle; American Medical News, etc. *Honours:* George Washington Honour Medal, National Media Award, 1st Prize, Family Association of America, 1965. *Membership:* American Society of Journalists and Authors. *Address:* 109 North Broadway, White Plains, NY 10603, USA.

SHERWOOD, John H M, b. 14 May 1913, Cheltenham, Gloucestershire, England. Author. m. Joan Yorke, 29 June 1952, Bridgewater, 1 daughter. *Education:* Open Classical Scholar, Oriel College, Oxford. *Literary Appointments:* Scriprwriter 1946–73, Head of French Service, 1963–73, BBC External Services, 1946–73. *Publications:* 17 detective stories including: Dr Bruderstein Vanishes, 1949; Undiplomatic Exit, 1958; The Half Hunter, 1961; A Shot in the Arm, 1982; A Botanist at Bay, 1984; No Golden Journey: A Biography of James Elroy Flecker, 1973. *Memberships:* Detection Club; Crime Writers Association: *Literary Agent:* A P Watt and Company. *Address:* 4 Surrenden Dering, Pluckley, Ashford, Kent, England.

SHEVILL, Ian, b. 11 May 1917, Broken Hill, New South Wales, Australia. Bishop. m. Dr June Stephenson, 12 Dec. 1960, Brisbane, 2 sons. *Education:* MA, Sydney and London; ThD (A.C.T). *Publications:* New Dawn in Papua, Cheshire, 1949; Pacific Conquest, 1949; God's World in Prayer, S P G, 1951; Orthodox Churches in Australia; Half Time, 1966; Going It With God, Boolarong, 1971; One Man's Meditations, Queensland

Newspapers. *Contributions to:* Weekly contribution to The Sunday Mail, Queensland, Australia. *Honour:* Order of Australia. *Address:* 13 Cottesmore Street, Fig Tree Pocket, Brisbane, Queensland 4069, Australia.

SHIBLES, Warren, b. 10 July 1933, Hartford, Connecticut, USA. University Professor; Author; Publisher. m. Carolyn Foster, 26 Jan. 1977, Wisconsin, USA, 2 sons, 1 daughter. *Education:* BA, University of Connecticut; MA, University of Colorado; PhD Work, Indiana University. *Major Publications:* Wittgenstein, Language & Philosophy, 1970; Mataphor: An Annotated Bibliography & History, An Analysis of Mataphor, Philosophical Pictures, Models of Ancient Greek Philosophy, 1971; Essays on Metaphor, 1972; Death: An Interdisciplinary Analysis, Emotion, 1974; Rational Love, Humor: A Comprehensive Classification & Analysis, 1978; Teaching Young People to be Critical (series of 5 volumes), 1978; Lying: A Critical Analysis, 1985. *Contributor to:* Numerous professional journals.*Address:* Department of Philosophy, University of Wisconsin, Whitewater, WI 53190, USA.

SHIBUTANI, Tamotsu, b. 15 Oct. 1920, Stockton, California, USA. Professor of Sociology. m. Sandra J Gettman, 25 Nov. 1981. *Education:* AB, University of California, Berkeley, 1942; AM, 1944, PhD, 1948, University of Chicago. *Appointments:* Instructor, 1948–51, Assistant Professor, 1951–57, Associate Professor, Professor, 1961–, Sociology, University of Chicago. *Publications:* Society and Personality, 1961; Ethnic Stratification, with K M Kwan, 1965; Improvised News: A Sociological Study of Rumor, 1966; The Derelicts of Company K, 1978; Social Process, 1986; Editor, Human Nature and Collective Behaviour: Papers in Honor of Herbert Blumer, 1970. *Contributor to:* Articles, Reviews, American Journal of Sociology; American Sociological Review; Articles in International Encyclopedia of the Social Sciences. *Honours:* Fellow, Social Science Research Council, 1946–48; Fellow, American Association for the Advancement of Science, 1984. *Memberships:* American Sociological Association; American Association for the Advancement of Science. *Address:* 136 Olive Mill Road, Santa Barbara, CA 93108, USA.

SHIELDS, Barbara, b. 26 May 1945, Brooklyn, New York, USA. Editor. m. Kevin Sheilds, 12 Aug. 1967, Brooklyn, New York, 1 son, 1 daughter. *Education:* BS, Marymount Manhattan College. *Publications:* Research Abstracts published on Medical Insurance, Materials Management, Investment Recovery, Remote Meter Technology, The Private Sector, 1981–85. *Contributor to:* New York Times. *Honour:* Quill and Scroll Award, 1962. *Membership:* Editorial Freelancers Association. *Address:* c/o McGraw Hill Inc, 1221 Ave of Americas, New York, NY 10020, USA.

SHIELDS, Carol Ann, b. 2 June 1935, Oak Park, Illinois, USA. Writer; Professor. m. Donald Hugh Shields, 20 July 1957, Oak Park, 1 son, 4 daughters. *Education:* BA, Hanover College, 1957; MA, University of Ottawa, 1975. *Publications:* Small Ceremonies, 1976; The Box Garden, 1977; Happenstance, 1980; A Fairly Conventional Woman, 1982; Various Miracles, short stories, 1985. *Contributor to:* Numerous Canadian Magazines and Journals. *Honours:* CBC Prize, Poetry, 1965; Canadian Authors' Association Prize, 1977; CBC Drama Prize, 1983; CBC Short Story Prize, 1984; National Magazine Award, 1985. *Memberships:* Writers Union of Canada; Manitoba Writers Guild. *Agent:* Bella Pomer. *Address:* 701-237 Wellington Cr, Winnipeg, Manitoba, Canada, R3M OA1.

SHIELDS, Michael Joseph, b. 29 Oct. 1938. *Literary Appointments include:* Head of Information Services, Motor Industries Research Association, England; Associate Editor, Here Now, 1970–73; Editor, Orbis Magazine, 1980–. *Publications:* Helix, 1970. *Contributor to:* Orbis; Here Now; Outposts; Littack; The Writer; New Headland. *Honours:* A F Cross Award, Nuneaton Festival of Arts, 1974, 1979; George Eliot Fellowship Trophy, NFA, 1975, 1977, 1979. *Memberships:* Member, Society of Authors; Fellow, Institute of Information

Scientists; Chairman, Translators Association, 1984–85. *Address:* 199 The Long Shoot, Nuneaton, Warwickshire CV11 6JE, England.

SHIFFERT, Edith Marion, b. 19 Jan. 1916, Toronto, Canada. Writer. m. (1) Steven R Shiffert, 1940; (2) Minoru Sawano, 1981. *Education:* Asian Studies, Creative Writing, Anthopology, University of Washington, 1956–63. *Appointments:* Retired Professor, English, Kyoto, 1963–83. *Publications:* Poetry: In Open Woods, 1961; For a Return to Kona, 1964; The Kyoto Years, 1971; A Grasshopper, 1976; New & Selected Poems, 1979; A Way to Find Out, 1979; Translations from Japanese Poetry (with others) include: Anthology of Modern Japanese Poetry, 1971; Chieko, 1974; Haiku Master Buson, 1978; Included in several anthologies including: The Woman Poets in English, 1972. The New York Times Book of Verse, 1970; The Contemporary World Poets, 1976; Books: The Story in the Bell, 1983; This Fair Port, 1983; The Woman in the Mountains, 1983; Clean Water (Haiku with Minoru Sawano), 1983. *Contributor to:* Poetry, Essays, reviews in USA, Canada, Japan, Australia, Europe. *Address:* c/o Sugimoto, 60 Yamanomoto-cho, Kitashirakawa, Sakyo-ku; Kyoto, Japan 606.

SHIGA, Yoshio, b. 8 Jan. 1901, Kita-Kyushu City, Japan. Journalist. m. 1 Apr. 1925. *Education:* Tokyo University. *Publications:* 18 Years in Tenno Prison, 1945; The Portraits of Japanese Revolutionaries, 1948; On State, 1949; World and Japan, 1949; Why Rice Cake is Round, 1949; Japan (by Max, Engels and Lenin), 1961; Appeal to Japanese, 1971; Creators of Present Day Japan, 1971; Kurils and Collective Securities, 1971; Japanese Imperialism before and after the War, 1972; Notes on CPJ, 1978. *Contributor to:* Marxism; APKA-HATA; Nihon no Koe (The Voice of Japan); Heiwa to Shakaishugi (Peace and Socialism). *Membership:* President, Heiwato Shakai-Shugi. *Address:* 26-15 Manami-cho 3, Kichijoji, Musashino City, Tokyo, Japan.

SHILLINGLAW, Gordon, b. 26 July 1925, Albany, New York, USA. University Professor. m. Barbara Ann Cross, 24 June 1950, Averhill Park, New York, 1 son, 1 daughter. *Education:* AB magna cum laude, Brown University, 1945; MS, University, 1945; MS, University of Rochester, 1947; PhD, Harvard University, 1952. *Publications:* Managerial Cost Accounting (first published as, Cost Accounting: Analysis and Control), 1961, 5th edition, 1982; Accounting: A Management Approach, (with Philip E Meyer), 8th edition, 1986. *Contributions to:* Encyclopedia Britannica; Harvard Business Review; Accounting Review; Journal of Business; Journal of Accounting Research; Journal of Industrial Economics; Accountancy; Management Accounting; Cost and Management; The Engineering Economist, etc. *Address:* 196 Villard Avenue, Hastings-on-Hudson, NY 10706, USA.

SHILOH, Ailon, b. 5 Sep. 1924, USA. Professor of Anthropology. m. Cynthia Amias, 31 Aug. 1952, London, 2 sons, 1 daughter. *Education:* BA; MA; PhD; MAR, Yale University. *Publications:* The Total Institution: Profiles of Mental Patient Perception and Adaptation, 1966; People and Cultures of the Middle East, 1969; Studies in Human Sexual Behaviour: The American Scene, 1970; Altenative to Doomsday; Considerations of the Population/Pollution Syndrome, 1971; By Myself I'm a Book: An Oral History of the Early Jewish Experience in Pittsburgh, 1 972; Ethnic Groups of America: Their Morbidity, Morality and Behaviour Disorders (edited with I C Selavan), 2 volumes, 1973; Christianity Against Jesus, 1977; Faith Healing: The Religious Experience as Therapeutics Process, 1981. *Address:* Department of Anthropology, College of Social and Behavioral Sciences, University of Southern Florida, Tampa, FL 33620, USA.

SHIMBERG, Elaine Fantle, b. 26 Feb. 1937, Yankton, South Dakota, USA. Writer. m. Mandell Shimberg, 1 Oct. 1961, Tampa, Florida, 3 sons, 2 daughters. *Educations:* BS, Northwestern University. *Publications:* How to be a Successful Housewife/Writer, 1979; Two for the Money: A Woman's Guide to a Double Career Marriage, co-author, 1981; The Complete Guide to Writing Non-Fiction, contributor, 1983; Teenage Drinking and Driving: A Deadly Duo, 1985; Coping with Kids & Vacations, co-author, 1986. *Contributions to:* Numerous magazines and journals including: Womans Day; Seventeen; Glamour; Lady Circle; Screen Star; Mother, UK; Rotatian; Writers Digest; Ladycom. *Honour:* Citation, American Cancer Society, 1982. *Memberships:* American Society of Journalists & Authors; Authors Guild; American Medical Writers Association; Women in Communication. *Address:* 1013 South Shokie, Tampa, FL 33629, USA.

SHIMKHADA, Deepak, b. 5 Sep. 1945, Darkha, Nepal. Teacher. m. Kanti Koirala, 5 July 1970, Kathmandu, 2 daughters. *Education:* BFA (Painting), 1968, MFA (Art Criticism), MS University of Baroda, India; MA (Art History), University of Southern California, USA, 1975; PhD (Art History), Ohio State University, Colombus, Ohio, USA, expected 1985. *Literary Appointments:* Teaching Associate, Ohio State University, 1977–81; Visiting Professor, Scripps College, 1981–82; Adviser, Institute of Fine Arts, Tribhuban University, Kathmandu, Nepal, 1971; Head Librarian, Buckeye Village College of Ohio State University, 1980–81; Microfiche Project Coordinator, Claremont Graduate School, Claremont, California, 1982–. *Major Publications:* God, Man, Woman, and Nature in Asian Art, 1982; Popular Buddhist Mantras in Sanskrit (co-author), Mahayana Buddhist Vihara, Taiwan, Republic of China, 1984. *Contributor to:* Oriental Art; Artibus Asiae; Arts of Asia; Himalayan Research Bulletin; Orientations. *Honours:* Cultural Fellow, Government of India, 1962–68, 1969–71; Fulbright Fellow, US Department of State, 1972–74; Junior Research Fellow, American Institute of Indian Studies, 1978–79. *Memberships:* College Art Association of America; Art Historians of Southern California; South Asian Club, University of Wisconsin, Madison, USA; Vice-President, America-Nepal Society of California; American Committee on South Asian Art; Nepalese Studies Association, Cornell University. *Address:* Claremont Graduate School, 160 East 10th Street, Claremont, CA 91711, USA.

SHINE, Frances Louise, b. 8 Jan. 1927, Worcester, Massachusetts, USA. Author. *Education:* BA, Radcliffe College, 1948; MA, Cornell University, 1952. *Publications:* Novels: The Life-Adjustment of Harry Blake, 1968; Johnny Noon, 1973; Conjuror's Journal, 1978. *Contributions to:* Grecourt Review, short story; New York Times and Catholic World, poetry. *Honours:* National 5-Arts Fellowship Award for short story, The Exile 1952. *Membership:* Authors' Guild. *Literary Agent:* Curtis Brown Ltd. *Address:* 17 Clark Street, Framingham, MA 01701, USA.

SHINER, Sandra Miriam, b. 12 June 1936, Toronto, Ontario, Canada. University Lecturer; Writer; Counsellor. m. Irwin Huck Shiner, 30 July 1957, Toronto, 3 sons, 3 daughters. *Education:* BA (Hons); MA, Education; PhD, Psychology Education: University of Toronto; Diploma in Child Study (Counselling), Institute of Child Study, University of Toronot. *Publications:* Communications; Communication in Writing, 1975; Be Informed A Handbook on Special Education, Toronto Board of Education, 1978; Gifted and talented children, 1981; The arts in guidance therapy for the gifted in Creative Drama in a Development Context, editor, J K Lanham, 1985. *Contributor to:* Chatelaine Magazine; Weekend Magazine; Orbit; Curriculum Implications of the Profiles of gifted High School Students (doctoral dissertation), 1978; The Gifted and talented in the Arts in The Face of the Future, Canadian Conference of the Arts, Ottawa, 1980; (Films): How Do the Gifted Grow? TV Ontario, 1980; Pearls in the Alphabet Soup, TV Ontario, 1980. *Honours:* J S McLean Scholarship for English, History, French, Jacob Goldblatt Memorial Scholarship Award, 1954; Portia Trophy for Debating, University of Toronto, 1955; Ontario Institute for

Studies in Education Assistantships, 1974–78. *Memberships:* Founder and Past President, Association for Bright Children, Chairmam, National Task Force on Arts and Education, Canadian Conference of the Arts; National and World Association for Gifted Children; Humanistic Psychology. *Literary Agents:* Matie Molinaro, Toronto; Carter and Woods, Nashville, USA. *Address:* 11 Ava Road, Toronto, Ontario M5P 1X8, Canada.

SHINKMAN, Elizabeth Benn, b. 10 May 1907, Bexley, Kent, England. Freelance Writer. m. Paul A Shinkman, 30 July 1935, Tandridge, Surrey, 3 sons. *Education:* Graduated Roedean, 1925; French Literature, Piano and Voice tuition, Paris, 1926–27. *Literary Appointments:* Book Reviewer for Time & Tide 1931; Reality, 1932; The Independent, 1933–35; Washington Correspondent, Benn Journals, 1957. *Major Publications:* Is this Tomorrow?, a book of children's verses, Ernest Benn Ltd, 1949; So Little Disillusion – An American Correspondent in Paris and London, 1924–31, EPM Publications, 1983. *Contributor to:* The Fruit Grower; Etude; Nursery World; The American Travellers' Gazette; Parents Magazine; The Horn Book; National Capital Garden Club League Bulletin; National Council of State Garden Clubs Bulletin; Garden Club of America. *Memberships:* Founder, Dogwood Children's Library, Bethesda, Maryland, 1946; President, Evermay Club of Georgetown, 1967–69. *Literary Agent:* Nick Lyons, New York, USA. *Address:* 3040 Dent Place NW, Washington, DC 20007, USA.

SHIPLEY, Joseph Twadell, b. 19 Aug. 1893. New York, USA. Author; Editor. m. Shirley Hector, 3 sons, 1 daughter. *Education:* BA, City College of New York, 1912; MA 1914, PhD 1931, Columbia University. *Literary Appointments:* Drama Critic, New Leader, 1918–62; Editor, American Bookman, 1945; Drama Critic, Radio EVD, 1940–82. *Publications:* Editor, Modern French Poetry, 1945, 1980. Author, 26 Books including: In Praise of English, 1977; Origins, discursive dictionary, Indo-European Roots, 1984; Crown Guide to the World's Great Plays, 1984. *Contributions to:* Numerous periodicals, USA, UK, France, Pakistan. *Honours:* College Alumni Class President, 1969–; Townsend Harris Medal, distinguished career, 1977. *Literary Agent:* Shirley Hector. *Address:* 29 W 46th Street, New York, NY 10001, USA.

SHIPMAN, David, b. 4 Nov. 1932, Norwich, England. Writer. *Major Publications:* The Great Movie Stars: The Golden Years, 1970; The Great Movie Stars: The International Years, 1972; The Story of Cinema (two volumes), 1982 & 1984; The Good Film & Video Guide, 1984; A Pictorial History of Science Ficton Films, 1985; Caught in the Act: Sex & Eroticism in the Cinema, 1985. *Contributor to:* Films & Filming; Radio Times. *Literary Agent:* Frances Kelly. *Address:* c/o Frances Kelly, 111 Clifton Road, Kingston-upon-Thames, Surrey, England.

SHIPPEY, Thomas Alan, b. 9 Sep. 1943, Calcutta, India, Professor. m. Susan Margaret Vgale, 27 Dec. 1966, 1 son, 2 daughters. *Education:* BA 1964; MA 1967; Queen's College, Cambridge, 1961–64. *Publications:* Old English Verse, 1972; Poems of Wisdom and Learning in Old English, 1976; Beowulf, 1978; The Road to Middle-Earth, 1982. *Contributions to:* Comparative Literature; Modern Language Review; English Historical Review; Times Literary Supplement; Times Higher Education Supplement; Guardian; and others. *Literary Agent:* A P Watt. *Address:* 22 Falkland Court, Harrogate Road, Leeds LS17 6JE, England.

SHIRER, William L, b. 23 Feb. 1904, Chicago, Illinois, USA. Author, Journalist. *Education:* AB, Coe College, 1925; College de France, Paris, France, 1925–27. *Publications:* Non-fiction: Berlin Diary, 1941; End of a Berlin Diary, 1947; Mid-Century Journey, 1952; The Challenge of Scandinavia, 1955; The Rise and Fall of the Third Reich, 1960; The Collapse of the Third Republic, 1969; 20th Century Journey – A Memoir of a Life and the Times, 1976, volume 2 1984; Gandhi – A Memoir, 1979; 20th Century Journey Volume 2, The Nightmare

Years, 1984; Fiction: The Traitor, 1950; Stranger Come Home, 1954; The Consul's Wife, 1956; Juveniles: The Rise and Fall of Adolf Hitler, 1961; The Sinking of the Bismarck, 1962. *Contributions to:* Harper's Atlantic; New Republic; Nation. *Honours include:* Honorary LittD, Coe College, 1941; Honorary LittD, University of Hartford, 1952. *Memberships:* Authors Guild of America; PEN; Century Club. *Literary Agent:* Don Congdon. *Address:* PO Box 487, Lenox, MA 01240, USA.

SHOCKLEY, Ann Allen, b. 2 June 1927, Louisville, Kentucky, USA. Librarian. 1 son, 1 daughter. *Education:* BA, Fisk University; MSLS, Case Western Reserve University. *Publications:* Living Black American Authors, (with Sue P Chandler), 1973; Loving Her, novel, 1974; A Handbook of Black Librarianship, (with E J Josey), 1977; The Black and White of It, short stories, 1980; Say Jesus and Come to Me, novel, 1982. *Contributions to:* New Letters; Black World; Freedomways; Phylon; Negro Digest; Essence; Feminary; Library Journal; College and Research Libraries; English Journal; Northwest Journal of Africa and Black American Studies; CLA Journal; Negro History Bulletin. *Honours:* American Association of University Women Short Story Award, 1962; ALA Black Caucus Award for Editing BC Newsletter, 1975; Hatshepsut Award for Literature, 1981; Martin Luther King Black Author's Award, 1982. *Memberships:* The Author's Guild; Feminist Writers Guild; National Women's Studies Association; Association of Black Women Historians; American Library Association; Association for the Study of Afro-American Life and History; Society of American Archivists. *Literary Agent:* Carole Abel. *Address:* 5975 Post Road, Nashville, TN 37205, USA.

SHORT, Geoffrey Philip, b. 13 Aug. 1938, Sydney, Australia. Investment Consultant; Editor. m. Janette Buckle, 16 Dec. 1967, Sydney, 2 sons, 2 daughters. *Education:* Diploma of Publication Typography. *Literary Appointments:* Financial Journalist, The Sun (Sydney), 1955–61, The Times (London), 1961–63, Sydney Morning Herald, 1963–66; Deputy Financial Editor, The Australian, 1966–72; Finance Editor, Daily Mirror, 1972–77. *Major Publications:* The Productivity Secret, 1981. *Memberships:* Australian Journalists Association; Society of Business Communicators. *Address:* 42 Trafalgar Avenue, Lindfield, New South Wales 2070, Australia.

SHORT, Philip, b. 17 Apr. 1945, Bristol, England. Journalist. m. Christine Victoria Baring Gould, 9 Aug. 1969, Blawtyre, 1 son. *Education:* BA, Cambridge. *Publications:* Banda, 1974; The Dragon and the Bear, 1982. *Literary Agent:* David Higham. *Address:* c/o Lloyds Bank, Downend, Bristol, England.

SHRAPNEL, Norman, b. 5 Oct, 1912, Grimsby, England. Journalist; Critic. m. Mary Lilian Myfanwy Edwards, 27 Apr. 1940, Birmingham, 2 sons. *Publications:* A View of the Thames, 1977; The Performers: Politics as Theatre, 1978; The Seventies: Britain's Inward March, 1980. *Contributions to:* The Guardian; Times Literary Supplement. *Honour:* Political Writer of the Year Award, 1969. *Address:* 27A Shooters Hill Road, London SE3, England.

SHREEVE, Caroline Mozelle, b. 25 Oct. 1943, St Neots, Huntingdon, England. Medical Author and Journalist. m. David Shreeve, 23 May 1981, Epsom Registry Office. *Education:* MB; BS, London; LRCP, London; MRCS, England; Member, National Council of Psychotherapists. *Literary Appointments:* Assistant Editor, Medicine Journal, 1976,; Doctor writer, Living magazine, 1985. *Publications:* The Premenstrual Syndrome – The Curse That Can Be Cured, 1983; Divorce, 1984; The Healing Power of Hypnotism, (with David Shreeve), 1984; Depression, 1984. *Contributions to:* Doctor; G.P.; Over 21; Options; Living; Parents; She. *Honour:* Silver Medallist in Biology, Royal College of Surgeons in Ireland, 1965. *Memberships:* The Society of Authors. *Literary Agent:* Barbara Levy, The Carol Smith

Agency. *Address:* Avalon, 1-4 Fronfedw Row, Tegryn, Near Glogue, Dyfed SA36 OEE, Wales.

SHRIMSLEY, Bernard, b. 13 Jan. 1931, London, England. Journalist. *Literary Appointments:* Editor, The Daily Post, Liverpool 1968–69, The Sun, 1972–75, News of the World, 1975–80, The Mail on Sunday, 1982. *Publications:* The Candidates, 1968; Lion Rampant, 1984. *Literary Agent:* John Farquharson Limited. *Address:* c/o John Farquharson Limited, 162-168 Regent Street, London W1R 5TB, England.

SHTERN, Israel Hersh, b. 11 Oct. 1913. Professor. *Education:* BSc, Sir George Williams College; MA, Educational Psychology, New York University, USA; MSc, Pure Mathematics, PhD, McGill University, Canada. *Literary Appointments include:* Lecturer, Mathematics, Assistant Professor, Pure Mathematics, McGill University, Canada; Associate Professor, Pure Mathematics, Loyola College, 1966–69. *Publications:* Out of the Burning Bush, 1968; Va Yehi BiYemey (And It Came to Pass in the Days of[el]), in Yiddish, 1976; Avrom Reyzen, 1974; Mani Leyb, 1975. *Contributions to:* Numerous literary journals and anthologies in English; numerous in Yidish, 1976; Avrom Reyzen, 1974; Mani Leyb, 1975. *Contributions to:* Numerous literary journals and anthologies in English; numerous in Yiddish. *Honours include:* International Rizal Poet Laureate; Numerous other literary awards and honours. *Memberships include:* United Poets Laureates International; World Poetry Society; Intercontinental; International Poetry Society; Canadian Authors and Bookmen; Jewish Writers Association of Montreal; Centro Studi e Scambi Int; International Vice President, Tagare Academy. *Address:* 6741 Baily Road, Montreal, Quebec, Canada H4V 1A4.

SHU, Wang, b. Oct. 1924, Jiangsu Province, China. Ambassador of the Chinese Peoples Republic in Vienna. *Education:* University Graduate. *Literary Appointments:* Journalist, Editor of Xinhua News Agency, China; Correspondent for Xinhua News Agency in Karachi, Accra, Kontary, Banako, Havana and Bonn; Councillor at Embassy of People's Republic of China in Federal German Republic; Extraordinary and Plenpotentiery Ambassador of People's Republic of China in Federal German Republic; editor-in-Chief, Hongqui Newspaper (Red Flag); Vice Foreign Minister of People's Republic of China; Extraordinary and Plenipotentiary Ambassador of People's Republic of China in the Republic of Austria. *Address:* Ambassador of the Chinese People's Republic in Vienna, Vienna, Austria.

SHUBIN, Seymour, b. 14 Sep. 1921, Philadelphia, Pennsylvania, USA. Author. m. Gloria Amet, 27 Aug. 1957, 1 son, 1 daughter. *Education:* BA, Temple University. *Literary Appointments:* Managing Editor: Official Detective Stories Magazine; Psychiatric Reporter. *Publications:* Anyone's My Name, 1953; Manta, 1958; Wellville USA, 1961; The Captain, 1982; Holy Secrets, 1984; Voices, 1985. *Contributions to:* Saturday Evening Post; Reader's Digest; Redbook; Family Circle; Story; Ellery Queen's Mystery Magazine; Emergency Medicine; Official Detective Stories Magazine; Perspectives in Biology and Medicine; numerous others. *Honours:* Jesse H Neal Award, 1978; Edgar Allan Poe Special Edgar Award, 1983; Special Citation for Fiction, Athenaem, 1984; Fellowship in Literature, Pennsylvania Council on the Arts. *Memberships:* Poets, Playwrights, Editors, Essayists and Novelists American Center; American Society of Journalists and Authors; Mystery Writers of American. *Address:* 122 Harrogate Road, Overbrook Hills, PA 19151, USA.

SHUFORD, Cecil Eugene, b. 21 Feb. 1907, Fayetteville, Arkansas, USA. Professor of Journalism (retired). m. Catherine Brooks, 27 June 1937, Fayetteville, 2 sons, 1 daughter. *Education:* BA, University of Arkansas; MSJ, Northwestern University, USA. *Literary Appointments:* Fellowships at the MacDowell Colony, Peterboro, New Hampshire, 1929 & 1930. *Major Publications:* The Red Bull, 1964; Selected Poems, 1933–71, 1972; 1300 Main Street, 1980; Flowering

Noose, 1985. *Contributor to:* Scribner's; Frontier and Midland; The New Republic; Saturday Evening Post; Southwest Review; Kaleidograph; Quicksilver; Voices; South and West; New Mexico Quarterly; Arlington Quarterly; Cedar Rock; Thicket; and numerous yearbooks of the Poetry Society of Texas and Anthologies. *Honours:* More than 60 awards for poetry; Honor Professor North Texas State University, 1974. *Memberships:* Poetry Society of Texas; Poetry Society of America. *Address:* 2910 East McKinney, Denton, TX 76205, USA.

SHUKER, Ronald H, b. 4 June, 1939, Alert Bay, British Columbia. Canada. Journalist; Editor. m. Birthe Lis (Jill) Rasmussen, 10 July 1963, Revelstoke, British Columbia, 1 son, 2 daughters. *Education:* Diploma, Journalism, Ryerson Polytechnical Institute, Toronto. *Editor/Writer for:* Heating, Plumbing & Air Conditioning; Furniture & Furnishings; Foodservice & Hospitality; Engineering Times; Canadian Wood Products; Canadian Forest Industries. Several other political, business, consumer magazines. *Honours:* Kenneth R Wilson Memorial Awards (Canadian business writing), Honorable Mention 1972, 1981, 1st Award 1974; Tom Turner Awards, Winner 1978, 7 Awards of Merit, 1975–82. *Memberships:* Founding President 1982–83, National Editors & Writers Society for Business Media; Past President, Director, Business Press Editors Association. *Address:* RR 1, Cedar Valley, Ontario, Canada L0G 1EO

SHULTIS, Elizabeth W, b. 30 Jan. 1952, Syracuse, New York. Science Editor and Writer. *Education:* BA, 1975, Hobart & William Smith Colleges, Geneva, New York. *Literary Appointments:* Science Writers, University of Idaho News Bureau, Moscow, Idaho, 1977–78; Assistant Editor, Westview Press, Boulder, Colorado, 1978–81; Medical Writer, Editor, Department of Radiology, University of Massachusetts Medical Center, Worcester, Massachusetts, 1982–85; Teaching Assistant in Technical Writing, University of Montana, Young Woman of America, 1982. *Memberships:* American Medical Writers' Association; Council of Biology Editors. *Address;* School of Forestry, University of Montana, Missoula, MT 59812, USA.

SHULVASS, Moses, b. 29 July 1909, Plonsk, Poland. Professor. m. Celia Cemach, 4 Apr. 1935, Warsaw, 2 daughters. *Education:* Ordained as Rabbi, Tachkemoni Rabbinical Seminary, Warsaw, Poland; MA; PhD magna cum laude, University of Berlin. *Literary Appointments include:* Lecturer, Author and Editor, Israel, 1935–47; Profesor of Rabbinic Literature and Jewish History, Baltimore Hebrew College, USA, 1948–51; Editor: Jewish Historical Texts Series, 1948–52; Italy (Quarterly for Culture and History of Jews in Italy), 1945; Perspectives in Jewish Learning, Volume 2, 1966. *Publications:* Author of 12 books including: The Jews in Wuerzburg during the Middle Ages, in German, 1934; Rome and Jerusalem, in Hebrew, 1944; In the Grip of Centuries, in hebrew, 1960; From East to West, 1971; The Jews in the World of the Renaissance, Hebrew version, 1955, English Version, 1973; Jewish Culture in Eastern Europe: The Classical Period, 1975; The History of the Jewish People, volume 1, 1982, volume 2, 1982, volume 3, 1985. *Contributions to:* Scholarly and Literary journals in English, Hebrew, Yiddish and German. *Honours:* LaMed Prize, 1956; Doctor of Hebrew Letters, Spertus College of Judaica, 1974; Solomon Goldman Creativity Award, 1981. *Memberships:* Hebrew and Yiddish PEN Clubs. *Address:* 2733 West Greenleaf Avenue, Chicago, IL 60645, USA.

SHUMAKER, (Charles) Wayne, b. 8 Feb. 1910, Indianapolis, Indiana, USA. University Teacher. m. (1) Estella Grace Smith, 22 Dec. 1940, Boulder, 1 son, 1 daughter, (2) Helen McLinn, 12 Sep, 1981, Winter Park, Florida. *Education:* BA, DePauw University, 1931; MA, Harvard University, 1932; University of California, Berkeley, 1943. *Appointments:* University Teacher; Editor, various University Presses. *Publications:* English Autobiography, 1952; Elements of Critical Theory, 1951; Literature and the Irrational, 1960; An Approach to Poetry, 1965; Unpremeditated Verse, 1969; The

Occult Sciences in the Renaissance, 1972; John Dee on Astronomy, with John Heilbronn, 1978; Renaissance Curiosa, 1982. *Contributor to:* Numerous journals including, Criticism; Hudson Review; Milton Quarterly; Thought; Journal of Aesthetics; etc. *Memberships:* Modern Language Association of America; Renaissance Society of America; etc. *Address:* 778 Contra Costa Ave, Berkeley, CA 94707, USA.

SHUTTLE, Penelope, b. 1947, Middlesex, England. Writer; Poet. m. Peter Redgrove, 1 daughter. *Publications include:* (Novels): An Excusable Vengeance, 1967; All the Usual Hours of Sleeping, 1969; Wailing Monkey Embracing a Tree, 1974; Rainsplitter in the Zodiac Garden, 1977; The Mirror of the Giant, 1980; (With Peter Redgrove): The Terrors of Dr Treviles, 1974; The Glass Cottage, 1976; (Poetry): Autumn Piano, 1974; Songbook of the Snow, 1974; Webs on Fire, 1975; The Lion from Rio, 1986; (Collections): The Orchard Upstairs, 1980; The Child-Stealer, (with Peter Redgrove), 1983; The Hermaphrodite Album, 1972; (Psychology and Sociology); The Wise Wound: Menstruation and Everywoman (with Peter Redgrove), 1980; (Radio Drama): The Girl Who Lost Her Glove, 1974; The Dauntless Girl, 1978; (Recordings): Poems recorded for Harvard Poetry Room, Poems Broadcast on BBC Radio 3's Poetry Now and Westward. Look programmes; Several public readings of her work. *Contributor to:* Anthologies, magazines, journals, etc. including: The Times Literary Supplement; The Poetry Review; Harper's and Queen; The Scotsman, etc. *Honours:* Joint third prize in Radio Times Drama Bursaries Competition, 1974; Three Arts Council Awards, 1969, 72, 85; Greenwood Poetry Prize, 1972; E C Gregory Award for Poetry, 1974. *Address:* c/o D Higham Associates Limited, 5-8 Lower John Street, Golden Square, London W1R HHA, England.

SICOTTE, Sylvie Marie Diane Michelle, b. 13 Oct. 1936, Montréal, Canada. Writer. Divorced, 2 sons, 1 daughter. *Education:* BA, 1956, Arts degree, 1971, MA Literature, 1975, University of Montreal. *Literary Appointments:* Jury Member, Prix littéraire de la Ville de Montréal and Prix littéraire du Journal de Montréal, 1982. *Publications:* Poems: Pour appartenir, 1968; Infrajour, 1973; Femmes de la forêt, 1975; Sur la pointe des dents, 1978. Essay: L'Arbre dans la poésie de Rina Lasnier, 1977. Short Stories: Non, je n'ai pas dansé nue, 1984. *Contrubutions to:* La Presse, Montreal, reporter and contributor; Le Devoir; Vioxet Images. *Honours:* Prix Anik, for teleplay Entre le soleil et l'eau, Radio-Canada, 1980. *Memberships:* Past Administrator, Quebec Writers Union; Administrator, Societe des auteurs, recherchistes et documentalistes, *Address;* 314 Girouard, P O Box 145, Oka, Quebec, Canada J0N 1E0.

SIDNELL, Michael John, b. 29 Sep. 1935, London, England. Professor. m. Felicity A Burridge, 6 Sep. 1958, Surrey, 2 sons, 2 daughters. *Education:* BA 1st Class Honours 1956, MA with Distinction, 1961, PhD 1967, University of London. *Literary Appointments:* Editorial Boards: Canadian Forum, 1964–69; Modern Drama, Toronto, 1969–84; Themes in Drama, Cambridge, 1979–; Yeats Annual, London, 1983–. *Publications:* Druid Craft, (with D Clark and G Mayhew), 1971; Yeat's The Secret Rose: A Vanorum Edition, (with P Marcus and W Gould), 1981; Dances of Death: The Group Theatre of London in the Thirties, 1984. *Contributions to:* Books, magazines and journals including: Litters From Aloft, 1971; Modern Drama; Yeats and the Occult, 1976; Yeats: An Annual, 1985. *Memberships:* Canadian Association for Irish Studies; International Federation for Theatre Research; Society for Theatre Research; MLA; American Theatre Association. *Address;* Trinity College, Toronto, Canada M5S 1HB.

SIEGAL, Aranka, b. 10 June 1930, Czechoslovakia (became Hungary, now USSR). Author; Social Anthropologist. m. Gilbert Siegal, 3 Feb. 1952, New York, 1 son, 1 daughter. *Education:* Empire State University, New York, USA, 1977. *Major Publication:* Upon the Head of the Goat, 1981; Grace in the Wilderness, 1985. *Honours:* Newberry Honor Book, 1981; School Library Journal, One of Best Books 1981; 1st Prize, B'nai Brith Janusz Korchak Literary Competition, 1981; The Boston Gobe Hornbook Award, 1st Prize Non-fiction, 1982. *Membership:* The Authors' Guild. *Literary Agent:* Jean V Naggar. *Address:* 390 Carrollwood Drive, Tarrytown, NY 10591, USA.

SIEGEL, Benjamin, b. 22 Sep 1914, New York, USA. Novelist. m. Frances Zeluck, 1948, 1 son, 1 daughter. *Education:* A + T, Columbia, CCNY. *Publications:* The Sword and the Promise, 1959; A Kind of Justice, 1960; The Principal, 1963; Doctors and Wives, 1970; Case History, 1971; Jurors, 1973; Four Doctors, 1975; Private Practice, 1975; Richard O'Boy, 1980. *Literary Agent:* Greenburg Associates. *Address:* Pine Hill Road, Tuxedo, NY 10987, USA.

SIEGEL, Mary-Ellen, b. 12 Feb. 1932, New York City, USA. Social Worker; Author. m. (1) Edgar Kulkin, 11 Apr. 1951 (div), (2) Walter Siegel, 24 Aug. 1980, New York City, 1 son, 2 daughters. *Education:* BA, City University of New York; MS, Columbia University School of Social Work, *Publications:* Her Way, revised edition 1984; What Every Man Should Know About His Prostate, 1983; More Than A Friend: Dogs With A Purpose, 1984; Revising Hair Loss, 1985; The Cancer Patient's Handbook, 1986. *Contributions to::* Cancer News (American Cancer Association); Chemotheraphy Foundation Newsletter. *Memberships:* American Medical Writers Association; Authors Guild; American Society of Journalists & Authors. *Literary Agent:* Connie Clausen. *Address:* 75-68 195th Street, Fresh Meadows, NY 11366, USA.

SIEGEL, Robert Harold, b. 18 Aug. 1939, Oak Park, Illinois, USA. University Professor. m. Roberta Ann Hill, 19 Aug. 1961, Arlington Heights, Illinois, USA. 3 daughters. *Education:* BA, Wheaton College, Illinois, 1961; MA, John Hopkins University, 1962; PhD, Harvard University, 1968. *Literary Appointments:* Instructor of English, Trinity College, 1962–63; Teaching Fellow, Harvard University, 1965–67; Assistant Professor of English, Dartmouth College, 1967–1975; Visiting Lecturer in Creative Writing, Princeton University, 1975–76; Poet-in-Residence and Visiting Professor, Wheaton College, 1976; Assistant & Associate Professor, University of Wisconsin-Milwaukee, 1976–79, 1979–82; Professor of English, University of Wisconsin-Milwaukee, 1983–. *Publications:* The Beast & The Elders, Poetry 1973; In A Pig's Eye, Poetry, 1980; Alpha Centuarim (Fiction), 1980; Whalesong, (Fiction), 1981; The Kingdom of Wundle, (Fiction), 1982. *Contributions to:* Contributor of poems to various journals and anthologies including, Colorado Quarterly; Georgia Review; Poetry; New York Quarterly; The Best Poems of 1976; The Yearbook of American Poetry. *Honours:* Foley Award, 1970; The Cliff Dwellers Award, 1974; Glatstein Memorial Prize, 1977; Prairie Schooner Poetry Prize, 1977; Society of Midland Authors Poetry Prize, 1974, 1981; National Endowment for the Arts Poetry Fellowship, 1980; Ingram Merril Poetry Award, 1979; ECPA Gold Medallion, 1981; Matson Award, Friends of Literature, 1982. *Memberships:* Authors Guild; Council of Wisconsin Writers. *Literary Agent:* Marian Young, Nat Sobel Associaties. *Address:* English Department, University of Wisconsin-Milwaukee, WI 53201, USA.

SIEGER, Hermann Walter, b. 6 Apr. 1928, Schwäbisch Gmünd, Federal Republic of Germany. Kaufmann. m. Giesla geb Mangolf, 11 Aug, 1972, 1 son, 2 daughters. *Education:* Abitur. *Literary Appointments:* Numerous specialised philatelic publications including handbook and catalogue of Zepplin Mail covers, House magazine, Siergerpost. *Honours:* Hermann Oberth Medal; Ring, Hermann-Oberth Society; Ring, Werbher von Braun; Decoration. Deutsches Rotes Kreuz; Silver decoration, Deutsche Sporthlfe; Gold Medal, Federation International d Societes Aerophilateliques; Badge of Honour, German Red Cross. *Memberships:* Philatelic Press Club; Association des Journalistes Philateliques; Association Internationa Editeurs des catalogues.

Address: 32-34 Venusberg, D–7073, Loch Württemberg, Federal Republic of Germany.

SIGAL, Leon Victor, b. 20 Aug. 1942, New Haven, Connecticut, USA. University Professor of Government. m. Meg Fidler, 16 Apr. 1983, New York. *Education:* BA, Yale University, 1964; PhD, Harvard University, 1971. *Literary Appointments:* Assistant Professor of Government, 1974–77, Associate Professor of Government, 1977–83, Professor of Government, 1983–, Wesleyan University. *Publications:* Reporters and Officials: The Organization and Politics of Newsmaking, 1973; Alliance Security: NATO and No-First-Use Question, with John Steinbruner, 1983; Nuclear Forces in Europe: Enduring Dilemmas, Present Prospects, 1984. *Contributions to:* The Rational Policy, Model and the Formosa Straits Crises' International Studies Quarterly, 1970; Official Secrecy and Informal Communications in Congressional-Bureaucratic Relations Political Science Quarterly, 1975; Re-Thinking the Unthinkable Foreign Policy, 1979; Warming to the Freeze Foreign Policy, 1981. *Honours:* Carnegie Teaching Fellowship, Yale University, 1954–65; Rockefeller Younger Scholar in Foreign Policy Studies, The Brookings Institution, 1972–73; International Affairs Fellowship, The Council of Foreign Relations, 1979. *Memberships:* International Institute for Strategic Studies; Council on Foreign Relations. *Address:* 250 West 88th Street, Apt 804, New York, NY 10024, USA.

SIGFUSDOTTIR, Greta, b. 20 Feb, 1910, Reykjavik, Iceland. Writer. *Education:* Studies art with Rikardur Jonsson, 1925–28; Commerical School, Norway. *Publications:* Bak vi byrga Glugga, Behind the Blinds, 1966; I Skugga Jaroar, In the Shadow of Earth, 1969; Fyrir Opnum Tjoldum, The Curtain Goes Up, 1972; The Sun Rises in the West, 1977; The Flight of Arrows, 1978. *Contributions to:* Various magazines and newspapers of short stories, poems and articles. *Honour:* Annual Grant, Icelandic Government, 1970–. *Memberships:* Writers Association of Ireland, *Address:* Furugerdi 1, Flat 706, 108 Reykjavik, Iceland.

SIGURDARDÓTTIR, Frída Á, b. 11 Dec. 1940, Hesteyri, Iceland. Writer. m. Gunnar Ásgeirsson, 2 Aug. 1959, Keflavík, Iceland, 2 sons. *Education:* Cand. mag. in Icelandic Literature, University of Iceland. *Publications:* Thetta er ekkert alvarlegt, short stories, 1980; Sólin og skugginn, novel, 1981; Vid gluggann, short stories, 1984. *Contributions to:* Einkenni nútíma I ljodum Thorgeirs Sveinbjarnarsonar, Skírnir, 1973; Leikrit Jökuls Jakobssonar, Studia Islandica, 1980; Hugleidingar um stödnun, Tímarit Máls og menningar, 1984. *Membership:* Writers' Association of Iceland. *Address:* Eyktarás 12, Reykjavík 110, Iceland.

SIGURDSSON, Adalsteinn Ásberg, b. 22 July 1955, Husavik, Iceland. Writer; Folksinger; Songwriter. m. Anna Palina Árnadottir, 16 Aug 1985. Bessastadir, Iceland. *Education:* Commerical Degree, 1974; Matriculation 1976, The Commerical College of Iceland. *Publications:* Ósánar lendur (Virgin Soil) poems 1977; Förunótt (Wandering Night) poems, 1978; Ferð undir fjögur augu (A Journey Eye to Eye) novel 1979; Gálgafrestur (Waiting at the Gallows) poems 1980; Fugli (Birds) poems 1982; AEvintýri úr Nykurtjörn (Adventure from Kelpytarn) a story for children with grammaphone record, 1984. Jarðljóð (Earth poems) 1985. *Contributions to:* Short stories, articles and translation of poetry for several Icelandic magazines *Membership:* Writer's Association of Iceland. *Address:* Eiriksgata 13, 101 Reykjavik, Iceland.

SIGURDSSON, Ólafur Jóhann, b, 26 Sep. 1918, Iceland. Writer. m. Anna Jónsdóttir, 22 Apr. 1943, 2 sons. *Education:* Columbia Unniversity, New York, 1944. *Publications:* Author of 23 books including: Vio Álftavatn (At Swans Lake) 1934 collection of stories for children; Litbrigði jarðaronnar short novel published in 10 foreign languages, 1947, 1959, 1968, 1979; Fjallið og draumurinn, 1944, 1979 and Vorkold jöro, 1951, 1979, a novel in 2 vols; Gangvirkið, 1955, 1979, Seiður og hélog, 1977, 1982 and Drekar og smáfuglar, 1983, a

novel in 3 volumes. Hreiðrið, 1972, 1979, novel; Bréf séra Böðvars, 1965, 1979, short novel published in 7 foreign languages; Poetry: Að laufferjum, 1972, 1976, Að brunnum, 1974, 1976; Virki Og vötn. 1978; Five books of short stories widely translated some into 15 languages. *Honours:* Silver Horse, Icelandic Critics for novel Hreiorio, 1973; Nordic Council Literary Award for, Að Laufferjum and Að brunnum, 1976; Annual pension of honour, Icelandic Parliament 1982–. *Membership:* Writers' Union of Iceland (Elected Honorary Fellow 1985). *Address:* Suðurgötu 15, PO Box 838, 121 Reyjavik, Iceland.

SIKS, Geraldine Brain, b. 11 Feb. 1912, Thorp, Washington, USA. Educator in Drama, Author. Playwright. m. Charles J Siks, 26 July 1941, Evanston, Illinois. 2 sons. *Education:* BA, Central Washington State College, Ellensburg, 1935; MA, Northwestern University, Evanston, Illinois, 1940. *Publications include:* Creative Dramatics: An Art for Children 1958, Japanese translation 1979; Children's Literature for Dramatization: an Anthology, 1964; The Sandalwood Box, 3 act play, 1975, Arabic translation 1979; Drama with Children, 1977 and 1983, Japanese translation 1983. *Contributions to:* Educational Theatre Journal; Children's Theatre Review; Children and Drama, 1985. *Honours include:* Creative Drama Award, Children's Theatre Association, 1977; Theta Alpha Phi Medallion of Honor, 1979; Distinguished Alumnus Award, Central Washington University, 1982; American Theatre Association Award of Merit, 1982. *Memberships include:* Fellow, American Theatre Association; Delta Kappa Gamma; Zeta Phi Eta. *Address:* 1754 N E 90th Street, Settle, WA 98115, USA.

SILBERSACK, John Walter, b. 8 Dec. 1954, New York City, New York, USA. Publisher. m. Elionora van Tyen Wilking, 29 June 1985. *Education:* AB, Brown University. *Literary Appointments:* Publisher and Editor, Hellcoal Press, 1974–77; Editor, G P Putnam's Sons, 1977; Senior editor, Berkley Publishing Group, 1978–81; Freelance consultant, 1982–. *Publications:* Rogers's Rangers, 1983; No Frills Science Fiction Novel, 1981. Compiler: Fritz Leiber's The Change War, 1978; Avram Davidson's Collected Fantasies, 1982. Editor: A Sampler of Caribbean Poetry, 1983; The Little Magazine, volumes 11-13, 1977–82; The Berkley Showcase: New Writings in Science Fiction and Fantasy, volume 1, 1980, volume 2, 1980, volume 3, 1980, volume 4, 1981. *Contributions to:* Quantum Leap to Consciousness in Foundation 31, 1984. Contemporary Literary Criticism, 1984; Columnist: Speculation, Science fiction Digest, 1980–82; Dossier, Heavy Metal magazine, 1982–84. *Memberships:* Science Fiction Writers of America; Committee of Small Press Editors and Publishers; Editorial Freelancers Association. *Literary Agent:* Henry Morrison. *Address:* 44 South 4th St, Locust Valley, NY 11560, USA.

SILBEY, Paula Jane, b. 11 Dec. 1946, Washington, District of Columbia, USA. Writer. *Education:* BFA, Ithaca College, Ithaca, New York, 1968; Certificate in Journalism, Price School of Advertising and Journalism, Philadelphia. Pennsylvania, 1970. *Contributions to:* House Beautiful; Stagebill; Feeling Great; Dance; Dance Magazine; Musical America; Weight Watchers; Brewers Digest; Food and Beverage Marketing; Art & Antiques; Stories; Shopping Centres Today; Hair and Beauty Guide; In-Bound Traffic Guide; Chamber Music Magazine; The Travel Agent. *Memberships:* Woman in Communication, former Vice-President, S E Wisconsin Chapter; American Society of Journalists and Authors; Editorial Freelancers Association. *Address:* 19 Barrow Street, New York, New York, NY 10014, USA.

SILITCH, Clarissa Silence MacVeagh, b. 18 Dec. 1930, New York City, USA. Editor. m. Nicholas E Silitch, 25 Dec. 1959, Cambridge, Divorced, 2 sons. *Education:* BA, Bryn Mawr College, 1952. *Appointments:* Translations Editor, Scipta Technica; Assistant Editor, Yankee Magazine; Editor, Yankee Books; Acquisitions Editor, Yankee Books, Dublin, New Hampshire. *Publications:* Editor/Anthologist of: 1973, Mad and Magnificent

Yankees; Danger, Disaster & Horrid Deeds, 1974; A Treasury of N E Short Stories, 1974; Yankees Remember, 1976; The Colonial Cookbook; OFA Book of Old Fashioned Puzzles; A Little Book of Yankee Humor, 1977; Making Old Fashioned Jams, Jellies, etc, 1977; Making Old Fashioned Pickles, Relishes, 1978; The Church Supper Cookbook, 1980; The Heritage Cookbook, 1982; The Perilous Sea, 1985; Good Neighbours USA Cookbook, 1985. *Address:* Dublin, NH 03444, USA.

SILK, Joseph Ivor, b. 12 Mar. 1942, London, England. Astronomer. m. Margaret Wendy Kuhn, 11 Aug. 1968, 2 sons. *Education:* MA, University of Cambridge, England; PhD, Harvard University, USA. *Major Publications:* The Big Bang, 1980; The Left Hand of Creation, 1983. *Contributor to:* New Scientist; Scientific American; Nature; and others. *Address:* 3074 Buena Vista Way, Berkeley, CA 94720, USA.

SILKIN, Jon, b. 2 Dec. 1930, London, England. Poet, Playwright, Editor. m. Lorna Tracy, 1974, 2 sons, 1 daughter. *Education:* BA Honours English, University of Leeds, 1962. *Literary Appointments Include:* Founder, Editor, Stand Magazine, 1952–; Visiting Lecturer and poet to USA, Australia and Israel. *Publications include:* The Peaceable Kingdom, 1954 and 1975; The Two Freedoms, 1958; The Re-ordering of the Stones, 1961; Nature With Man, 1965; Poems New and Selected, 1966; Amana Grass, 1971; Out of Battle: Criticism on the poets of WWI, 1972; Poetry of the Committee Individual: Anthology of Poetry from Stand, 1973; The Principle of Water, 1974; The Little Time Keeper, 1976; The Penguin Book of First World War Poetry, (editor), 1979; The Psalms with their Spoils, 1980; Selected Poems, 1980; Gurney: a play in verse, 1985; The War Poems of Wilfred Owen, (editor), 1985; The Penguin Book of First World War Prose, (editor with John Glover), 1986; The Ship's Pasture, poems, 1986. *Honours include:* Gregory Fellowship in Poetry, University of Leeds, 1958–60; Geoffrey Faber Memorial Prize, 1966. *Address:* 19 Haldane Terrace, Newcastle, NE2 3AN, England.

SILLITOE, Alan, Author. *Publications:* Three Plays, 1978; Novels include: Saturday Night and Sunday Morning, 1958; The General, 1960; Key to the Door, 1961; The Death of William Posters, 1965; A Tree on Fire, 1967; Raw Material, 1972; The Widower's Son, 1976; The Storyteller, 1979; Her Victory, 1981; The Lost Flying Boat, 1983; Down from the Hill, 1984; Life Goes On, 1985; (Poetry), The Rats & other Poems, 1960; A Falling Out of Love, 1964; Love in the Environs of Varonesh, 1968; Snow on the North Side of Lucifer, 1979; Sun Before Departure, 1984; Tides and Stone Walls, with Victor Bowley, 1986; (Childrens Books), The City Adventures of Marmalade Jim, 1968; Big John & the Stars, 1977; The Incredible Fencing Fleas, 1977; Marmalade Jim on the Farm, 1980; numerous stories including: The Loneliness of the Long Distance Runner, 1959; The Second Chance, 1981; Marmalade Jim and the Fox, 1985; (Travel): Nottinghamshire, with David Sillitoe, 1986. *Honours:* Recipient, Honorary Degree, Manchester Polytechnic, 1976; Hawthornden Prize, Literature, 1960. *Member:* Savage Club. *Agent:* Hope Leresche & Sayle. *Address:* c/o Hope Leresche & Sayle, 11 Jubilee Place, London SW3 3TE, England.

SILLO-SEIDL, Georg, b. 19 Jan. 1925, Budapest, Hungary. Physician; Writer. *Education:* MD. *Publications:* Empfangnis und Verhutung, 1963, also in Spanish & Flemish; Frauenreport, 1969; Die Frau und ihre Gesundheit, 1973, also in Italian; Six Sense of the Surgeon, 1979; My Most Interesting Cases, 1981; 25 Births, 1981; Bathing and Drinking Cures, 1984; The Affair Semmeboeis, 1985; To Health with Cells, 1985. *Contributor to:* Numerous German & other medical & popular journals. *Honours:* Recipient, several awards from the Hungarian National Theatre, Budapest, for dramaturgy. *Memberships:* Deutscher Schritstellerverband Frier. *Address:* Thorwaldsen Str. 17, D–6 Frankfurt am Maine, Federal Republic of Germany.

SILMAN, Roberta, b. 29 Dec. 1934, Brooklyn, New York. Writer. *Education:* BA, English Literature, Cornell University, 1956; MFA, Writing, Sarah Lawrence College, Bronxville, NY, 1975. *Publications:* (children's book) Somebody Else's Child, 1976 (paperback), 1979; (stories) Blood Relations, 1977; (novel) Boundaries, 1979, UK, 1980. *Contributions to:* Numerous magazines in USA and UK including: Atlantic Monthly; New Yorker; McCall's Redbook; Family Circle; Hadmassah. *Honours:* Child Study Asociation, Award for Best Children's Book (Somebody else's Child), 1976; Honorable Mention, Hemingway Award, 1978; Honorable Mention, Janet Kafka Prize, 1978, 1980; Guggenheim Fellowship, 1979; National Endowment for the Arts Fellowship, 1983; National Magazine Award, Fiction, 1984; PEN Syndicated Fiction Project Award, 1983–84. *Memberships:* PEN (Freedom to Write Committee); Authors Guild; Poets and Writers; Phi Beta Kappa. *Literary Agent:* Philippa Brophy, Sterling Lord Agency. *Address:* 18 Larchmont Street, Ardsley, NY 10502, USA.

SILVA, David B, b. 11 July 1950, Carmel, California, USA. Writer. *Education:* Associate of Arts; BS Recreation. *Major Publications:* Masques, 1984, Cold Sweat, 1985 (anthologies). *Contributor to:* The Horror Show. *Address:* Star Route 1, Box 151-T, Oak Run, CA 96069, USA.

SILVA, João da, b. 21 Dec. 1927, Funchal, Madeira. Professor. m. Maria Alzira de Brito Figueiroa, 12 Aug. 1957, 2 sons, 1 daughter. *Education:* Human/Classical Learning, Philosophy & Theology, Seminary, Funchal; Vacation Courses, University of Lisbon, Madeira; Intensive course, Ontology, Epistemology, Anthropology, Ethics, Catholic University of Portugal. *Publications include:* Caterdral dos Meus Sonhos, 1967, Madeira, Terra de Encantos, 1967; Oratório da Saudade, 1968; Sortilégios do Sol-Pôr, 1969; Melopeias Insulares, 1970; Lucubrações, dum Poeta, 1970; Rimas dum Ilhéu, 1971; Aguarelas da Madeira, 1972; A Mulher – Estrela, Flor ou Anjo Tutelar? 1983; Camões, Grande Camoes, 1984; Redondilhas Ditadas por Lucina, 1985. *Contributions to:* Presencias, Buenos Aires; Eeo do Funchal, Madeira; Journal de Madeira; Diário da Madeira; Madeira Popular; Voz da Madeira; Journal dos Poetas e Trovodores. *Honours:* Silver Crown, Academia Internationale di Pontzen, di Lettere, Scienze ed Arti, Italy, 1984. *Memberships:* Accademia Internazionale di Pontzen, di Lettere, Scienze ed Arti; Academie Internationale de Lutecè, France; Académie Européenne des Arts, Belgium; L'Amicale des Anciens Membres du Club des Intellectuelles Français; Institute Argentino. *Address:* Rua de Santa Maria No 115, 9000 Funchal, Maderia, Portugal.

SILVER, Abraham Jack, b. 3 Aug. 1917, London, England. Journalist. m. Pauline Mary Bennett, 5 May 1961, Liberal Jewish Synagogue, 1 son, 2 daughters. *Education:* London Chamber of Commerce; Royal Society of Arts; Accountancy, Mercantile Law, Business Studies. *Literary Appointments:* Editor: The Licensed Bookmaker, 1962, Greyhound Express, 1965, The Trader, 1981. *Publications:* How I Won A Thousand Pounds on the Pools, 1946; Capitos – the Secret of Success, 1961; Making The Game Pay, 1966. *Address:* 31a Camden Mews, London NW1, England.

SILVER, Daniel Jeremy, b. 26 Mar. 1928, Cleveland, Ohio, USA. Rabbi. m. Adele Zeidmen, 19 July 1956, 2 sons, 1 daughter. *Education:* AB, Harvard University, 1948; MHL Rabbi, Hebrew Union College, 1952; PhD, University of Chicago, 1962. *Publications:* Maimonidean Criticism and the Maimonidean Controversy 1180–1240, 1965; A History of Judaism – From Abraham to Maimonides, Volume 1, 1974; Images of Moses, 1982. *Contributor to:* Jewish Quarterly Review; In the Time of Harvest; Movement and Issues in Contemporary Judaism; Central Conference of American Rabbis Yearbook; Journal of Jewish Law; Jewish Reflections of Death; Judaism; Encyclopedia Judaica; Midstream; etc; Book Reviews in: Judaism; Journal of Reform Judaism; Journal of Biblical Literature; etc.

Address: 2841 Weybridge Road, Shaker Heights, OH 44120, USA.

SILVER, Marc, b. 26 Dec. 1951, USA. Editor. m. Marsha Dale, 8 June 1980. *Education:* BA University of Maryland, 1973. *Contributor to:* Baltimore Jewish Times; Baltimore Sunpapers; Present Tense. *Honours:* Smolar Award for Excellence in North American Journalisn, 1984; 2nd Place, Simon Rockower Award for Distinguished Feature Writing, 1985. *Address:* c/o Jewish Monthly, 1640 Rhode Island Avenue, NW, Washington, DC 20036, USA.

SILVERMAN, Hershel, b. 17 Apr. 1926, Candystore Owner-Operator. m. Laura. *Education:* Seton Hall Part-time College, 2 years. *Literary Appointment:* Editor-Publisher, Beehive, A Magazine of Contemporary Poetry, 1984. *Publications:* Krishna Poems, 1970; Nite Train Poems, 1975; Vietnam Newreels After the Times, 1975; Elegies, 1979; 80 Romona, 1983; Humm, 1983; Jazz and the Changes, 1984. *Contributions to:* Nomad Magazine; El Corno Emplumado; N E ; The Small Pond; Pavan; Maine Ed; Journal of New Jersey Poets; Nostoc; New Magazine; New Jersey Poetry Monthly; Dimension. *Honour:* New Jersey Council on the Arts Fellowship, 1980–81. *Membership:* New Jersey Poetry Society. *Address:* 47 E 33 Street, Bayonne, NJ 07002, USA.

SILVERMAN, Jason Howard, b. 26 May 1952, Brooklyn, New York, New York, USA. Historian; Educator. *Education:* BA, with Distinction, University of Virginia, 1974; MA, Colorado State University, 1976; PhD, University of Kentucky, 1981. *Publications:* The Frederick Douglass Papers, volumes 2 & 3, (with John W Blassinggame); 1982–1985; Unwelcome Quests: Canada West's Response to American Fugitive Slaves, 1980–1985, 1985; The War of the Confederacy, (with John R McKivigan), 1987; Beyond The Melting Pot In Dixie: Ethnicity & Immagination In Southern History, 1988. *Contributions to:* Over 20 articles, reviews & essays to scholarly journals including Canadian Historical Review; Journal of American Ethnic History; Civil War Times Illustrated; The Filson Club History Quarterly. *Honours:* Phi Alpha Theta International Historical Honour Society, 1974; Phi Kapp Phi National Honour Society, 1976; A D Kirwan Award in History, University of Kentucky, 1980; National Historical Papers and Records Commision Editing Fellowship, 1980; Winthrop College Outstanding Junior Professor Award. 1985; Research Fellow; Institute for Southern Studies, University of South Carolina, 1985. *Memberships:* American Historical Association; Organization of American Historians; Southern Historical Association. *Address:* Department of History, Wintrop College, Rock Hill, SC 29733, USA.

SILVERMAN, Jerry, b. 26 Mar. 1931, New York, USA. Author, Teacher. m. Tatiana Cherniacoski, 23 June 1967, Paris, France, 3 sons. *Education:* BS, Music, City College of New York; MA Musicology, New York University. *Publications:* Folk Blues, 1958; Folksinger's Guitar Guide, 1962; Beginning Blues Guitar, 1964; Folksinger's Guide to Note Reading and Music Theory, 1966; The Chord Player's Encyclopedia, 1967; How to Play the Guitar, 1968; Folksong Encyclopedia, 1975; Ragtime Guitar, 1975; Play Old-Time Country Fiddle, 1975; The Young Guitarist, 1982; The Yiddish Song Book, 1983. *Contributions to:* Sing Out; Guitar Player. *Address:* 160 High Street, Hastings on Hudson, NY 10706, USA.

SILVERSTEIN, Josef, b. 15 May 1922, Los Angeles, California, USA. Professor of Political Science. *Education:* BA, UCLA, 1952; PhD, Cornell University, 1960. *Publications:* Southeast Asia in World War II: Four Essays, 1966: The Political Legacy of Aung San, 1972; The Future of Burma in Perspective, 1974; Burma: Military Rule and the Politics of Stagnation, 1977; Burmese Politics and the Dilemma of National Unity, 1980. *Contributor to:* Journal of Asian Studies: Pacific Affairs; Asian Survey; China Quarterly; Journal of S E Asian History; Journal of S E Asian Studies: Public

Opinion Quarterly; etc. *Address:* 93 Overbrook Drive, Princeton, NJ 08540, USA.

SILVESTRI, Richard, b. 11 June 1944, New York City, USA. Clinical Psychologist. *Education:* BS, CONY, 1967; PhD, Kent State University, 1973. *Publications:* CT: The Astounding New Confrontation Theraphy, 1978; The Treatment of Children's Disorders Using Confronation Therapy, forthcoming. *Contributor to:* Magazines and professional journals including: Cosmopolitan (British & American editions); Australian Weekly; Journal of Clinical & Consultant Psychology; Behavior Research & Theraphy. *Agent:* Ms Lisa Collier. *Address:* 590 Doremus Ave, Glen Rock, NJ 07452, USA.

SIM, Katharine Phyllis, b. 28 June 1913, Teddington, London, England. Author; Artist; Freelance Journalist. m. Alexander Woodrow Stuart Sim, 2 July 1938, Chalfont St Peter, 2 sons. *Education:* Silver Medal Portraiture, Diploma Malay Language, Malaysia, 1952; London Arts Schools, 1930–35. *Appointments:* Regular Freelance Journalist, various periodicals & syndicates, including, The Straits Echo; Malay Mail; The Straits Times; Dyfed County Life etc. *Publications:* Malayan Landscape, 1946; Black Rice, 1961; Malacca Boy, 1957; Desert Traveller: The Life of Jean Louis Burckhardt, 1969; Jean Louis Burckhardt – A Biography, 1981; David Roberts R A – A Biography, 1984; etc. *Contributor to:* Numerous professional journals and magazines including: The Western Mail; She; Homes & Gardens; The Times; The Daily Telegraph; The Guardian; etc. *Honours:* Ratna Kebudayaan, Kuala Lumpur, Malaysia, 1959. *Memberships:* PEN; Society of Authors. *Address:* Pencarreg, Llanybydder, Dyfed SA40 9QJ, Wales.

SIMENON, Georges, b. 13 Feb. 1903, Liege, Belgium. Novelist. *Education:* College St Servais. *Publications:* Over 200 novels including 80 Maigret Novels & 131 non-detective novels; (non-fiction), When I Was Old; Letter to My Mother; 21 volumes of daily recordings of thoughts, memoirs, souveniers; most recent autobiographical book, Intimate Memoirs, 1984; Works translated into 57 languages & published in 40 countries. *Address:* Secretariat de George Simenon, Avenue du Temple 19B, 1012 Lausanne, Switzerland.

SIMIONESCU, Mircea Horia, b. 23 Jan. 1928, Tirgoviste, Romania. Writer. m. Teodora Dinca, 26 Feb. 1953, Bucharest, 2 daughters. *Education:* BA, Literature, Bucharest University, 1964. *Publications:* The Well Tempered Ungenious Man, Vol I 1969, II 1970, III 1980, IV 1983; After 1900, About Noon, 1974; Ganymede's Kidnapping, 1975; Half Plus One, 1976; Endless Dangers, 1978; Advice for the Dauphin, 1979; Ulysse and the Shadow, 1982; The Banquet, 1982; The Cutaway, 1984; Sale by Auction, 1985. *Contributor to:* Most major magazines and newspapers and radio and TV programmes in Romania. *Honours:* Prize for Prose, Writers Union of Romania; Journalists Union of Romania. *Address:* 3 Belgrad Str, Bucharest 63, CD 71.248 Romania.

SIMMIE, James Martin, b. 18 July 1941, Oxford, England. Lecturer. *Education:* BSc, Economics, PhD, London University; M.Phil, Southampton University. *Appointments:* Editor, Town Planning Discussion papers, University College, London; Editor, Sociology, Politics and Cities, Macmillan; Lecturer, Urban Sociology, University College London. *Publications:* The Sociology of Internal Migration, 1971; Citizens in Conflict, 1974; Power, Property and Corporatism, 1981; Planning and the Decline of London, 1983. *Contributor to:* International Journal of Urban and Regional Research, 1985; Journal of the American Planning Association, 1983; Urban Studies. *Address:* University College, London, Wates House, 22 Gordon Street, London WC1H OQB, England.

SIMMONDS, Sam (Andrew Samuel Garriock), b. 25 July 1938, Hampstead, London, England. Film and Television Programme Producer/Director; Journalist. m.

(1) Patricia Daphne Matthews (nee Whessell), 11 May 1963, Hampstead, London, 1 daughter; (2) Beth Lorraine Langridge, 7 Mar. 1981, Chapel-en-le-Frith, Derbyshire. *Publications:* Contributor to Everybody's Magazine, 1950's; Original material and translations (from the French) for Mountview Theatre School, 1959–73; Various TV programs and series in UK for Rediffusion, HTV, Grampian, London Weekend and Granada. In Australia for Grundy TV Organization and The Dunera Story for Special Broadcasting Service, 1961–85; Documentaries and Feature Film Screenplays for independent producers, 1983–85. *Membership:* Australian Writers Guild. *Address:* 1/6 Vista Street, Greenwich, New South Wales 2065, Australia.

SIMMONS, Anthony, b. 16 Dec. 1922, London, England. Film director; Screen Writer. m. Maria St Clare, 18 Dec. 1981, Bodmin, Cornwall, 4 sons. *Education:* LLB, Barrister at Law. *Publications:* The Optimist of Nine Elms, 1964. Screenplays: The Passing Stranger; Four in the Mourning; The Optimist of Nine Elms; Black Joy; On Giant's Shoulder. Radio: Oil Rig; Two Days in Love. *Honours:* Vice Chairman, Director Guild of Great Britain, *Memberships:* Writers Guild of Great Britain. *Literary Agent:* Hatton and Baker, London. *Address:* c/o West One Film Productions Limited, 2 Lower James Street, London W1, England.

SIMMONS, James Stewart Alexander, b. 14 Feb. 1933, Londonderry, Northern Ireland. Writer. m. (1) Laura Stinson, (2) Imelda Foley, 1 son, 5 daughters. *Education:* BA Honours, Leeds University, England, 1958. *Literary Appointments:* Lecturer, English, Ahmadu Bello University, Nigeria, 1963–67; Lecturer, Senior Lecturer, English, Chairman, Department of English, 1968–73. *Publications include:* Poetry: Late but in Ernest, 1967; In the Wilderness, 1969; Energy to Burn, 1971; The Long Summer Still to Come, 1973; West Strand Visions, 1976; Judy Garland and the Cold War, 1976; The Selected James Simmons, 1978; Constantly Singing, 1981. Plays: An Exercise in Dying, 1970; Black Eye, 1975; The Death of Herakles, 1978. *Anthologies:* Editor, Out on the Edge, 1958, New Poems from Ulster, 1971, Ten Irish Poets, 1974, Soundings 3, 1976. Various recordings and settings of poems. *Contributions to:* The Spectator; New Statesman; New England Review; Paris Review; Observer and others. Founder Editor, The Honest Ulsterman, 1968. *Honours:* Gregory Award; Cholmondelly Award; Subject of British Broadcasting Corporation television programme, 1976. *Address:* c/o Northern Ireland Arts Council, 181a Stranmillis Road, Belfast, Northern Ireland.

SIMMS, George Otto, b. 4 July 1910, Dublin, Eire. Anglican Archbishop (Church of Ireland). m. Mercy Felicia Gwynn, 2 Sep. 1941, Dublin, 3 sons, 2 daughters. *Education:* Moderator, Classics & Ancient History BA, 1932; MA 1935; BD 1936; PhD 1950; Trinity College, Dublin University. *Contributions to:* Facsimile edition, Book of Kells, Urs Graf Verlag, Bern, 1950; Book of Durrow, 1960. Articles in: Hermathena; Theology; Crane Bag; Aquarius. Reviews in: Journal of Theological Studies; Studies; New Divinity; Search; Irish Times; Irish Press. *Honours:* DD (iure dignitatis), Dublin University, 1952; DD, honoris causa, Huron College, Ontario, Canada, 1963; DCL, honoris causa, Kent University, UK, 1978; DLitt, honoris causa, New University of Ulster, 1981. *Address:* 62 Cypress Grove Road, Dublin 6, Republic of Ireland.

SIMON, Edward John, b. 1 May 1931, Hamburg. Author. m. Teresa Francesca King, 9 Mar. 1979, Islington, London, 1 son. *Publications:* The Chequered Year, 1971; Jupiter's Travels, 1979; Riding Home, 1984. *Contributions to:* Numerous contributions to magazines and journals. *Literary Agent:* Gillon Aitken. *Address:* East Lane, Covelo, CA 95428, USA.

SIMON, Karl Günter, b. 9 Feb. 1933, Ludwigshafen, Federal Republic of Germany. Journalist. *Education:* Studies in Romance Languages and Journalism; PhD, Free University, Berlin. *Major Publications:* Jean Cocteau, 1958; Pantomime, 1960; Die Kronprinzen, 1969; Millionendiener, 1973; Comedies and Musicals with brother Saul Simon. *Contributor to:* Stern; Geo; Playboy; Theater heute; and others; Radio and television broadcasts, journalistic works, especially in France, Spain, South America and Arab countries. *Address:* Post Box 9, D6903 Dilsberg bei Heidelberg, Federal Republic of Germany.

SIMON, Michael Arthur, b. 20 Dec. 1936, New Jersey, USA. Professor. m. Shannon Slon, 23 Feb. 1964, Cambridge, Massachusetts, 1 son, 1 daughter. *Education:* AB, Amherst College; AM, PhD, Harvard University. *Publications:* The Matter of Life, 1971; Understanding Human Action, 1982. *Contributions to:* Numerous magazines and journals. *Address:* 320 N Village Avenue, Rockville Centre, NY 11570, USA.

SIMON, Sheldon Weiss, b. 31 Jan. 1937, Minnesota, USA. University Professor. m. Charlann Scheid, 23 Apr. 1962, Tempe, Arizona, 1 son. *Education:* BA, PhD, University of Minnesota; MA, Princeton University; Doctoral research, University of Geneva, Switzerland. *Literary Appointments include:* Professor of Political Science, Director, Center for Asian Studies, Arizona State University. *Publications include:* The Broken Triangle: Peking, Djakarta & the PKI, 1969; War & Politics in Cambodia: A Communications Analysis, 1974; Asian Neutralism & US Policy, 1975; The Military & Security in the Third World, 1978; The Asean States & Regional Security, 1982. *Contributions to:* Numerous journals including: Journal of Conflict Resolution; Asian Survey; China Quarterly; Pacific Affairs; Current History; Australian Outlook; Orbis; etc. *Honours:* Research grants; US Information Agency & Earhart Foundation, 1972, 1979, 1981, 1982, 1984; American Enterprise Institute, 1974; Hoover Institution, 1981, 1984. *Memberships:* American Political Science Association; International Studies Association; Association for Asian Studies. *Address:* Center for Asian Studies, Arizona State University, Tempe, AZ 85287, USA.

SIMONS, Elwyn LaVerne, b. 14 July 1930, Lawrence, Kansas, USA. Academic Professor of Anthropology and Anatomy, Primatologist, Paleontologist. m. Friderun Annursel Aukel, 2 Dec. 1972, New Haven, Connecticut, 2 sons, 1 daughter. *Education:* BS, Rice University, 1953; MA 1955, PhD 1956, Princeton University; D Phil, University College, Oxford University, 1959; MA, Yale University, 1967. *Publications:* The Paleocene Pantodonta, 1960. *Contributions to:* Numerous journals including: American Journal of Primatology; American Journal of Physical Anthropology; Nature; Transactions of American Philosophical Society; Annals of the New York Academy of Science; Science; Proceedings National Academy of Science; Scientific American; Folia Primatologica; American Science; Medical Opinion and Review; Discovery; Natural History. *Honours:* Anadale Memorial Medal, The Asiatic Society of Calcutta, 1973; Alexandere von Humboldt Senior Sccientists Award, Federal Republic of Germany, 1976; National Academy, 1981; James B Duke Professor, Duke University, 1982. *Address:* Duke University Primate Center, 3705 Erwin Road, Durham, NC 27705, USA.

SIMONSUURI, Kirsti Katariina, b. 26 Dec. 1945, Helsinki, Finland. Professor. *Education:* Fil Kand, MA, University of Helsinki, 1971; PhD, Cambridge University, England, 1977; Postgraduate Diploma in English Literature, University of Edinburgh, Scotland, 1969. *Literary Appointments:* Professor of Literature, University of Oulu, Finland, 1978–81; Senior Researcher, Academy of Finland, 1981–. *Publications:* Including: Homer's Original Genius, 1979; Murattikaide, poems, 1980; Pohjoinen Yokirja, prose, 1981; Juntematon Tekija, poems, 1982; Euroopan Ryosto, 1984. *Contributions to:* Kaleva, columnist, 1979–82; World Literature Today; Parnasso; Helsingin Sanomat; BFB French Studies. *Honours:* Osk Huttunen Century Award, 1971; J H Erkko Award, for best 1st book, 1980; British Academy Wolfson Award, 1981; Fulbright Reseach Award, USA, 1984. *Memberships:* International Pen; Finland's Writers Association.

Address; Ruusulankatu 2 c 35, 00260 Helsinki 26 Finland.

SIMPSON, Dick W, b. 8 Nov. 1940, Houston, Texas, USA. University Professor; Elected Government Officer; Ordained Minister *Education:* BA, 1963, University of Texas; MA, 1964, PhD, 1968, Indiana University; MDiv, McCormick Theological Seminary, 1984. *Publications:* Who Rules? Introduction to the Study of Politics, 1970; Wining Election: A Handbook in Participatory Politics, 1972; Chicago's Future: An Anthology of Reports, Speeches and Scholarship Providing and Agenda for Change, 1976; Strategies for Change: How to Make the American Political Dream Work, with George Beam, 1976; Blueprint of Chicago Government, with Charles Williams, 1983; Political Action: The Key to Understanding Politics, with George Beam, 1984; Justice Ministeries, with Clinton Stockwell, 2 volumes, 1985. *Films:* with Bill Mahin: By the People, 1970; In Order to Change, 1973; Neighbourhood Government in Chicago's 44th Ward, with J Stephens and R Kohnen, 1979. *Contributions to:* Focus Midwest Magazine; Saturday Evening Post; Chicago Tribune; Perspectives; and others. *Honours:* Several awards and grants including: Ford Foundation Foreign Area Fellowship, 1966–67; Wieboldt Foundaiton Grant, 1974; MacDonald's Corporation Grant, 1976; Fellow, University of Illinois Humanities Institute, 1985–86. *Memberships:* American Political Science Association; Midwest Political Science Association; Committee on Foreign and Domestic Affairs; Independent Precinct Organisation, Founder and Former executive Director; Independent Voters of Illinois. *Address:* Department of Political Science, University of Illinois, Box 4348, Chicago, IL 60680, USA.

SIMPSON, Ervin Peter Young, b. 13 May 1911, New Zealand. Ordained Minister of American Baptist Churches, Retired Professor of History. m. Lilian Eileen Andrew, 30 June 1937, Christchurch, 2 sons. *Education:* Diploma of Theology, New Zealand Baptist Theological College; BA, MA, University of New Zealand; BD, ThM, ThD, Berkeley Baptist Divinity School, USA; M Div, American Baptist Seminary of the West, Berkeley, California; FRAI, London, England; FSA, Edinburgh, Scotland. *Publications:* How the Church Got There, edited by Alan Brash, 1947; History of the New Zealand Baptist Missionary Society, 1948; History of the Baptists in New Zealand, 1950; Factors in the Doctrine of the Ministry, 1952; The Doctrine of the Church, 1965; Ordination and Christian Unity, 1966; A Study Guide on Medieval History, 1968; A Study Guide on Renaissance-Reformation History, 1969; A Plan for the Development of an Indian University at Bacone College, 1980; History of Alderson-Broaddus College, 1812–1951, 1983. *Contributions to:* Numerous magazines and journals. *Honours:* Fulbright Fellow, 1949–50; Faculty Fellow, American Association of Theological Schools, 1957–58. *Memberships include:* Secretary, Past-President-elect of Pacific Coast Branch, American Society of Church History; Royal Society of New Zealand. *Address:* Box 82, Alderson-Broaddus College, Philippi, WV 26416, USA.

SIMPSON, Jacqueline Mary, b. 25 Nov. 1930, Worthing, West Sussex, England. Author. *Education:* BA Honours, 1952, MA 1955, D Litt 1980, London. *Literary Appointments:* Honorary Editor, Folklore, the journal of the Folklore Society, London, 1979–. *Publications:* Penguin English Dictionary, (with G N Garmonsway), 1964; The Northmen Talk, 1965; Everyday Life in the Viking Age, 1967; Beowulf and its Analogues, (with G N Garmonsway), 1968; Folktales and Legends of Iceland, 1971; The Folklore of Sussex, 1973; The Folklore of the Welsh Border, 1976; The Viking World, 1980; British Dragons, 1980. *Contributions to:* Folklore; Antiquity; Fabula: The Journal of the American Folklore Society; Revue Celtique; The Saga-Book of the Viking Society; Shirnir. *Memberships:* Committee member, Folklore Society, 1966–; The Viking Society for Northern Research. *Address:* 9 Christchurch Road, Worthing, West Sussex BN11 1JH, England.

SIMPSON, Louis Aston Marantz, b. 27 Mar. 1923, Jamaica, West Indies. Writer. m. Miriam Bachner, 23 June 1985, New York, USA, 2 sons, 1 daughter from previous marriage. *Education:* PhD, 1959, Columbia University, New York. *Literary Appointments:* Editor, Bobbs-Merrill Publishing Company, 1950–59; Instructor, Columbia University, New York. *Literary Appointments:* Editor, Bobbs-Merril Publishing Company, 1950–59; Instructor, Columbia University, 1955–59; Professor, University of California at Berkeley, 1959–67; Professor, State University of New York at Stony Brook, 1967–. *Publications:* The Arrivistes: Poems 1940–49, 1949; At the End off the Open Road, 1963; Three on the Tower: the Lives and Works of Ezra Pound, T S Eliot, and William Carlos Williams, 1975; A Company of Poets, 1981; People Live Here, 1983; The Best Hour of the Night, 1983. *Contributions to:* The Hudson Review; The Virginia Quarterly Review; The Ohio Review; The Listener; The Critical Quarterly, and others. *Honours:* Guggenheim Foundation Fellowship, 1962, 1970; Pulitzer Prize for poetry, 1964; Medal, Excellence, Columbia University, 1965. *Memberships:* Phi Beta Kappa, 1980; Vice-President, Poetry Society of America, 1985. *Address:* P O Box 91, Port Jefferson, NY 11777, USA.

SIMPSON, Lucy Picco, b. 11 Sep. 1940, Berwyn, Illinois, USA. Publisher; Writer; Editor. m. Barry Simpson, 14 Aug. 1965, Cicero, Illinois, 1 daughter. *Education:* BA, Park College, Parkville, Missouri; MA, Teaching, Wesleyan University, Connecticut. *Contributions to:* Editor, TABS: Aids for Ending Sexism in School, 1977–84; Numerous Articles for Above journal. *Address:* 744 Carroll Street, Brooklyn, NY 11215, USA.

SIMPSON, Myrtle Lillias, b. 5 July 1931, Aldershot, Hampshire, England. Writer. m. Dr Hugh Simpson, 21 Mar. 1959, Edinburgh, Scotland, 3 sons, 1 daughter. *Literary Appointments:* Lecturer, Extra Mural Department, Aberdeen University, Scotland, 1970–; Lecturer, Writer at large scheme, Scottish Arts Council. *Publications include:* White Horizen, 1965; Due North, 1969; Sisters, 1983; Greenland Summer, for children, various others. *Contributions to:* National Geographic; Observer; Daily Telegraph; She; Woman; various Danish and American periodicals including Politician and Christian Science Monitor. *Membership:* Committee member, PEN. *Literary Agent:* Wymant Towers. *Address:* Farletter, Kincraig, Invernesshire, Scotland.

SIMPSON, Nancy, b. 16 Dec. 1938, Miami, Florida, USA. High School Teacher of Exceptional Students. *Education:* BS Education, Western Carolina University, 1978; MFA Writing, Warren Wilson College, 1981. *Literary Appointments:* Poetry Instructor, North Carolina Writer's Network Poetry Workshops; Teacher, Hayesville, North Carolina and at State University of New York at Brockport. *Publications:* Across Water, poetry, 1983; Night Student, poetry, 1985. *Contributions to:* Anthology of Magazine Verse and Yearbook of American Poetry, 1980, 1981, 1984, 1985 and 1986 editions; Magazines and journals including: The Georgia Review; Florida Review; Southern Poetry Review; Indiana Review; Confrontation; Nimrod; Negative Capability; Appalachian Journal; Georgia Journal; Texas Review. *Honours:* Nomination for Pushcart Award, 1986. *Memberships:* Board of Trustees, North Carolina Writer's Network. *Address:* Route 2, Cherry Mountain Road, Hayesville, NC 28904, USA.

SIMPSON, Roger John, b. 13 Aug. 1944, Dunedin, New Zealand. Writer. 1 son, 1 daughter. *Education:* LL B, University of Auckland, New Zealand. *Major Publications:* Hunters Gold, 1976; The Trial of Ned Kelly, 1977; Gather Your Dreams, 1978; Children of Fire Mountain (with Graeme Farmer), 1983. *Contributor to:* The film & television world, with: Division 4 & Young Ramsey; Power Without Glory; Players to the Gallery; I Can Jump Puddles; Squizzy Taylor. *Honours:* Australian Writers' Guild 'Awgie' Awards: Best Drama series, 1974, Best Documentary 1975, Best Children's Drama 1977, Best Drama series, 1980, Best Original work for television

1980; New Zealand 'Feltex' Awards for best script of the Year, 1978, 1979. *Memberships:* Australian Writers Guild (Past Chairman, Victorian Branch); New Zealand Writers Guild. *Address:* c/o Simpson Le Mesurier Films, Suite 2, 69 Davis Avenue, South Yarra, 3141, Australia.

SIMPSON, Ronald Albert, b. 1 Feb. 1929, Melbourne, Victoria, Australia, Lecturer in Art, Chisholm Institute of Technology. m. Pamela, 2 children. *Education:* Associatie Diploma of Art, Melbourne Institute of Technology; Primary Teachers' Certificate, Melbourne Teachers College, 1951. *Literary Appointments:* Poetry Editor: The Bulletin, Sydney, 1963–65; The Age, Melbourne, 1969–. *Publications:* Verse: The Walk along the Beach, 1960; This Real Pompeii, 1964; After the Assissination and Other Peoms, 1968; Diver, 1972; Poems from Murrumbeena, 1976; The Forbidden City, 1979; Poems from The Age, 1979; Selected Poems, 1981; Critical Study: The Literature of Australia (editor; Geoffrey Dutton), 1976; Manuscript Collection: National Library of Australia, Canberra. *Honour:* Australian Arts Council Travel Award, 1971. *Address:* 29 Omama Road, Murrumbeena, Melbourne, Victoria 3163, Australia.

SIMS, Bernard John, b. 13 May 1915, London, England; Solicitor. m. Elizabeth Margaret Eileen Endicott, 27 Apr. 1963, Eastbourne. *Education:* Law Society's School of Law; University of London. *Appointments:* Consultant Editor, Taxation Matters, Encylopaedia of Forms and Precedents, 4th Edition and Service; Senior Member, Editorial Board, Simon's Taxes; Capital Taxes Encyclopaedia. *Publications:* Sergeant and Sims on Stamp Duties (Including Capital Duty), 8th edition, 4th Cum. Supp., 1985. *Honours:* LL.B Honours, 1937. *Address:* 89 Dovehouse Street, Chelsea, London SW3 6JZ, England.

SIMS, Thomas Courtney, b. 25 Jan. 1944, Spokane, Washington, USA. Free-lance Writer. m. Judith Rixford, 15 Mar. 1975, 2 daughters. *Education:* BA, Psychology, University of Minnesota, 1966; Defense Language Institute, Monterey, California. *Contributions to:* Guidepost, English language magazine for tourists, Spain. *Memberships:* Vladimir Nabokov Society; Henry James Society, Dickens Society; Hemingway Society. *Address:* 1315 Overhill Road, Golden, CO 80401, USA.

SIMS, Watson Shedrick, b. 9 July 1921, Pembroke, California, USA. Journalist. m. Elisabeth Mann Strudivant, 10 Sep. 1948, Nashville, Tennessee, 1 son, 1 daughter. *Education:* Bachelor of Naval Science, Tufts University; MA, Columbia University. *Publications:* Contributor: History of American Society of Newspaper Editors, 1973; Telecommunications in Year 2000, 1983; Importance of a Tree Press to America, 1984. *Contributions to:* Nieman Reports; Bulletin of American Society of Newspaper Editors; APME News; Gannetteer; Quill. *Honours:* Nieman Fellow, Harvard University, 1953; Chairman, Pulitzer Prize Jury, 1978; Pulitzer Prize Juror, 1973, 79. *Address:* 7 Lemore Circle, Rocky Hill, NJ 08553, USA.

SINASON, Valerie Elaine, b. 17 Dec. 1946. Child Psychotherapist, Tavistock Clinic, Nathanial Heckford EBD School. London Hospital. m. Dr Michael Sinason. *Education:* BA (Hons), English Language and Literature, London University, England; Postgraduate Diploma in Teaching English Drama, double distinction, Goldsmith's College, University of London; Child Psychotherapy Training, Tavistock Clinic, London. *Appointments include:* Group Worker, William Tyndale Junior School, London, 1977–80; Child Psychotherapist, Adolsescent Department, Tavistock Clinic, London, 1979–. *Contributor to:* Ambit; Omens; Outposts; Little World Machine; The Teacher; Jewish Chronicle; New Statesman; Arts Council; New Poetry, volumes 1, 2, 4 and 5; PEN; Contemporary Women Poets; Voices of the 70's; One Foot on the Mountain; Britains's First Feminist Anthology; Exiles; Arts in London; Thames TV; BBC; Radio London, etc. *Honours include:* Goldsmith's College Arts Festival 2nd poetry prize, 1968. *Memberships:* Poetry Society, London;

Cockpit Theatre, London., 1974–77; Co-director, Outscan Foundation; Member, Prodicagal Daughters, 1976–78. *Address:* 3 Honeybourne Road, London NW6 1HH, England.

SINCLAIR, Andrew (Annandale), b. 21 Jan. 1935, Oxford, England. Writer; Publisher; Film Director. *Education:* BA, 1958, PhD, Trinity College, Cambridge, England; Commonwealth Fellow, Harvard University, USA, 1959–61. *Publications include:* The Breaking of Bumbo, 1959; The Hallelujah Bum, 1963; Gog, 1967; Magog, 1972; Patriot for Hire, 1977; Jack London, 1977; The Facts in the Case of A E Poe, 1979, (nonfiction); Prohibition, 1962; The Emancipation of the American Woman, 1965; The Available Man, 1965; Guevara, 1970; The Savage, 1977; John Ford, 1979; The Red and the Blue, 1986; Plays and Screenplays: Before Winter Comes, 1968; Martin Eden, 1979. *Honour:* Maugham Award, 1967. *Memberships:* Fellow, Society of American Historians; FRSL. *Agent:* Gillan Aitken. *Address:* 16 Tite Street, London SW3, England.

SINCLAIR, Olga Ellen, b. 23 Jan. 1923, Norfolk, England. Writer. m. Stanley George Sinclair, 1 Apr. 1945, Watton, Norfolk, 3 sons. *Publications:* Gypsies, 1967; Hearts By The Tower, 1968; Bitter Sweet Summer, 1970; Dancing in Britain, 1970; Children's Games, 1972; Toys, 1974; My Dear Fugitive, 1976; Never Fall in Love, 1977; Master of Melthorne, 1979; Gypsy Girl, 1981: Ripening Vine, 1981; Lord of Leet Castle, 1984; The Gretna Bride, 1985. *Memberships:* Society of Authors; Romantic Novelists Association; Society of Women and journalists; Vice-President, Norwich Writers' Circle. *Address:* Dove House Farm, Potter Heigham, Norfolk NR29 5LJ, England.

SINGER, J David, b. 7 Dec. 1925, New York, USA. Professor of Political Science. m. (1) 2 sons, 2 daughters, (2) Kathleen Manninen, 23 July 1983, Ann Arbor, Michigan. *Education:* AB, Duke University, 1946; PhD, New York University, 1956. *Literary Appointments:* Editor or advisor to several journals. *Publications include:* Financing International Organization: The United Nations Budget Process, 1961; Deterrence, Arms Control, and Disarmament: Toward a Synthesis in National Security Policy, 1962 and 1984; The Wages of War, 1816–1965; A Statistical Handbook, (with Melvin Small), 1972; Beyond Conjecture in International Politics: Abstracts of Data-Based Research, (with Susan Jones), 1972; The Study of International Politics: A Guide to Sources for the Student, Teacher, and Researcher, (with Dorothy LaBarr), 1976; Resort to Arms: International and Civil War, 1816–1980, (with Melvin Small), 1982; Several anthologies including: Cumulation in International Relations Research, (with P Terry Hopman and Dina Zinnes), 1981; Quantitive Indicators in World Politics: Timely Assurance and Early Warning, (with Richard Stoll), 1984; International War: An Anthology, (with Melvin Small). *Contributions to:* Numerous journals. *Honours include:* Honorary Doctor of Laws, Northwestern University, 1983. *Address:* Department of Political Science, University of Michigan, Ann Arbor, MI 48109, USA.

SINGER, Marcus George, b. 4 Jan. 1926, New York City, USA. Professor of Philosophy. m. Blanche Ladenson, 10 Aug. 1947, Chicago, 2 daughters. *Education:* AB, University of Illinois, 1948; PhD, Cornell University, 1952. *Publications:* Generalization in Ethics, 1961; Morals and Values, editor, 1977; American Philosophy, editor, 1986. *Contributions to:* Philosophy; The Philosophical Quarterly; Proceedings of the Aristotelian Society; The Philosophical Review Mind; The Monist; Philosophia; American Philosophical Quarterly; Ethics; Philosophical Studies; Etyka; Journal of Value Inquiry; Philosophy of Science; Zygon; The Encyclopedia of Philosophy; Academic Encyclopedia; World Book. *Honours:* American Philosophical Association Fellowship, 1956–57; Guggenheim Fellowship, 1962; Institute for Research in the Humanities Fellowship, 1984. *Membership:* President 1975–86, American Philosophical Association Central Division.

Address: 5021 Regent Street, Madison, WI 53705, USA.

SINGERMAN, Robert L, b. 19 Dec. 1942, Los Angeles, California, ISA. Librarian; Curator, Price Library of Judaica, University of Florida Libraries. m. Claudia Davis, 25 June 1972, Cincinnati, Ohio, 1 son, 1 daughter. *Education:* MSLS, University of Southern California, 1970; MA, History, Xavier University, 1975. *Literary Appointments:* Judaica Librarian, Hebrew Union College, Cincinnati, 1970–76; Coordinator, Cataloguing and Classification, Hebrew Union College, 1976–79; Chairman, Price Library of Judaica, University of Florida, Gainesville, 1979–. *Publications:* The Jews in Spain and Portugal: A Bibliography, 1975; Jewish and Hebrew Onomastics: A Bibliography, 1976; Antisemitic Propaganda: An Annotated Bibliography and Research Guide, 1982. *Contributions:* Cecil Roth Bibliography: Supplement, Miscellanies of the Jewish Historical Society of England, 1977; American-Jewish Reactions to the Spanish Civil War, Journal of Church and State, 1977; The American Career of the Protocols of the Elders of Zion, American Jewish History, 1981–82. *Address:* 2622 S W 14th Drive, Gainesville, FL 32608, USA.

SINGH, Khushwant, b. 2 Feb. 1915, Hadali, West Punjab, India. Freelance Journalist; Author; Member of Indian Parliament. m. Kaval Khushwant Singh, 1 son, 1 daughter. *Education:* Kings College, London, England; LLB, London. *Literary Appointments:* Editor, Illustrated Weekly of India, 1969–78; Editor in Chief, National Herald, 1978–79; Chief Editor, New Delhi, 1979–80; Editor, Hindustan Times, 1980–83. *Publications:* Author of 11 books on Sikh history and religion including: A History of the Sikhs, 2 volumes, 1964; Sacred Writings of the Sikhs, co-author; Fall of the Kingdom of the Punjab; Sikhs Toady; Hymns of Nanak the Guru; Sikhism Through the Hymns of the Gurus, 2 Long playing recordings. Author of 6 works of fiction and 10 other works including: I Shall Not Hear the Nightingales; The Voice of God and Other Stories; A Bride for Sahib and Other Stories; Shri Ram, a Biography; War and Peace in India, Pakistan and Bagladesh; Gurus, Godmen and Good People; Indira Ghandi Returns; The Sikhs, 1984; Punjab Tragedy, 1984. Various translations. *Contributions to:* Most national daily newspapers and foreign journals including: New York Times; Observer, England; New Statesman; Harpers; Evergreen Review; London Magazine; Encyclopedia Brittanica, entries on Sikhism. *Honours include:* Award for best fiction work, Grove Press; Award and Robe of Honour for contribution to Sikh literature, Punjab Government; S Mahan Singh Award; Distinguished Journalist Award, Rotary Club, Cochin; Padma Bhushan awarded by President of India, 1974. *Address:* 49–E Sujan Singh Park, New Delhi 110 003, India.

SINGHAL, Damodar Prasad, b. 24 Sep. 1925, India. History Professor. m. Maniktaia Devahuti, 18 May 1950. *Education:* BA, 1946, MA, 1949, University of Punjab; PhD, University of London, 1955; PhD, 1972, D Litt, 1974, University of Queensland. *Appointments:* Lecturer, History, University of Malaya, Singapore; Faculty Member, 1950–56; General Editor, Asia Library, Sidgewick & Jackson, London, 1969–72, 1972–74. *Publications:* The Annexation of Upper Burma, 1960; India and Afghanistan: A Study in Diplomatic Relations, 1963; Nationalism in India and other Historical Essays, 1967; India and World Civilization, 2 volumes, 1969; Modern India Society and Culture, 1981; Gypsies; Indians in Exile, 1982; A History of the Indian People, 1983; Buddhism in East Asia, 1984. *Address;* University of Queensland, Department of History, St Lucia, Queensland 4067, Australia.

SINGLETON, Frederick Bernard, b. 13 Oct. 1926, Hull, England. University Lecturer (Retired)/Visiting Research Fellow. m. Elizabeth Anne Croft Andrew, 23 Feb. 1957, Brompton, North Yorkshire, England, 2 sons, 2 daughters. *Education:* BA, Hons, Geography, 1950, MA, 1951, Leeds University. *Publications:* History of Yorkshire (with W E Tate) 1960; Yugoslavia (with M

Heppell) 1961; Background to Eastern Europe 1965; Industrial Revolution in Yorkshire 1970; Twentieth Century Yugoslavia 1976; The Economy of Yugoslavia with B Carter, 1982; Short History of the Yugoslav Peoples 1983. *Contributions to:* International Affairs; The World Today; Geographical Magazine; Times Higher Educational Supplement; Osteuropa; Co-existence. *Membership:* Authors Society. *Address:* 21 Eaton Road, Ilkley, West Yorkshire LS29 9PU, England.

SINGLETON, Richard Fred, b. 13 June 1926, Provo, Utah, USA. Writer; Producer. *Education:* Brigham Young University, 2 years; US Naval School. *Publications:* Two Movie stories: The Last Round; One Alone; Four records: Lisa; Day and Night; Let Me Be Your Escort; Little Dipper. *Honours:* Dancing Contests and Awards, 1953–59; American Film Institute, Assistant to Producer and Director, Northwest Motion Picture Company. *Memberships:* American Film Institute; Producers Club Universal Studios; President and Owner, M-3 Production. *Literary Agent:* Richard G Twayne. *Address:* Richard G Twayne. *Address:* 396 West 300 South, Provo, UT 84601, USA.

SINKANKAS, John, b. 15 May 1915, Paterson, New Jersey, USA. Author; Captain, US Navy Retired. *Education:* BS, William Paterson State University College, New Jersey, 1936. *Publications include:* Gem Cutting, A Lapidary's Manual, 1955, 3rd edition, 1984; Gemstones and Minerals, How and Where to Find Them, 1961; Gemstones of North America, volume 1, 1959, volume 2, 1976; Mineralogy for Amateurs, 1964; Mineralogy: A First Course, 1966; Van Nostrand's Strand Catalog of Gems, 1968; Prospecting for Gemstones and Minerals, 1970; Gemstones and Minerals, 1970; Gemstones and Minerals Data Book, 1972; Mineralogy, 1975; Emerald and Other Beryls, 1983. *Contributions to:* Principla gemmological and mineralogy journals. *Honour:* Honorary PhD, William Paterson College, New Jersey, 1982. *Memberships include:* Authors Guild of New York; Fellow, Mineralogical Society of America. *Address:* 5372 Van Nuys Court, San Diego, CA 92109, USA.

SIRC, Ljubo, b. 19 Apr. 1920, Kranj, Yugoslavia, Director. Centre for Research into Communist Economies, London. m. Susan Powell, 18 Sep. 1976, Glasgow, 1 daughter. *Education:* dipl iur, University of Ljubljana, 1943; Dr rer pol. University of Fribourg, 1961. *Publications:* Nonesense and Sense, autobiography (in Slovene) 1968; Economic Devolution in Eastern Europe, 1969; The Yugoslav Economy under Self-Management, 1979. *Contributions to:* The Journal of Economic Affairs; Revue d'Etudes Comparative Est-Ouest; Ordo-Jahrbuch; Scottish Journal of Political Economy; Economica Internazionale; Soviet Studies. *Address:* 41A Westbourne Gardens, Glasgow G12 9XQ, Scotland.

SIRCH, P Bernhard Anton, b. 26 Apr. 1943, Günzberg, Bavaria, Federal Republic of Germany. Director of Publishing and Printing of EOS Verlag, Writer, Clergyman. *Education:* Diploma Theology, 1970; DTh, 1973; Staatlich Auerkannter Erzieher. *Publications:* Der Ursprung der Bischöflichen Mitra und Päpstlichan Tiara, 1975; Mein Marien-album, 1977; Mein Jesusalbum, 1978; Das Immerwährende Gebet bei Johannes Cassianus, 1983. *Membership:* Benedictine Order. *Address:* EOS Verlag, Erzabtei St Ottilien, D 8917 St Ottilien, Federal Republic of Germany.

SIREN, Eero, b. 2 June 1946, Helsinki, Finland. Actor/Director. m. Leena Lotvonen-Siren, 7 Aug, 1981, 1 daughter. *Education:* Theatre High School of Finland. *Literary Appointments:* Editor, Magazine Repliiki, Dramaturg, City Theatre of Kemi. *Publications:* Livari Kiivastuu, 1971; Aapeli Kiipelissa, 1972; Sipuliretki: Merilevàsuvannossa, 1974; Rieskaa Afrikkaan, 1985 screenplay for film; Translation of Romeo and Juliet into Finnish, 1975. *Membership:* The Finnish Dramatists' Society. *Literary Agent:* The Finnish Dramatists' Society. *Address:* Ilmarinkatu 7A6, 94100 Kemi, Finland.

SIROLA, Harri Erkki William, b. 28 May 1958, Helsinki, Finland. Writer. m. Laitila Riitta Hannele, 1 Jan. 1985, 1 daughter. *Education:* Studied Medicine, Physics, Philosophy, Literature and Astronomy, University of Helsinki. *Publications:* Abiturientti (High School Student), novel, 1980; Anna palaa (Let it Burn), novel, 1983; Translated Henry Miller's Opus Pistorum from English to Finnish, 1984; Wrote manuscript for Finnish movie Apinan vuosi (The Year of the Ape), directed by Janne Kuusi, 1983. Five short stories in Finnish magazines: Aiti (Mother), Ylioppilaslehti, 1980; Susikoirani uutena ja vanhana vuonna (My Shepherd Dog in the New and Old Year, 1984), Kiima, 1981; Linnut (The Birds), Kiima; 1983; Tulevaisuudenkuva (The Vision of Future), Me, 1984; Venalainen tytto keskella Aasiaa (A Russian Girl in Middle Asia), Jaana, 1984; Two essays about Henry Miller, Hemingway and Mike Waltari. *Memberships:* Suomen Kirjailijaliitto; Suomen Pen. *Honour:* Kalevi Jantti Prize (shared with Annika Idstrom), 1981. *Literary Agent:* Werner Soderstrom Oy (WSOY). *Address:* WSOY, Bulevardi 12, 00120 Helsinki 12, Finland.

SISSON, Charles Hubert, b. 22 Apr. 1914, Bristol, England. Poet; Translator; Critic. m. 19 Aug. 1937, Bristol, 2 daughters. *Education:* BA Philosophy and English Literature, University of Bristol, 1934; Travelling scholarships, Berlin and Freiburg, 1934–35, Paris 1935–36. *Publications:* The Spirit of British Administration, 1959; Christopher Homm novel, 1965; English Poetry 1900–1950, 1971; In The Trojan Ditch collected poems and selected translations, 1974; Lucretius, translation, 1976; The Avoidance of Literature, collected essays, 1978; The Divine Comedy of Dante translation,1979; The Regrets of Du Bellay translation, 1984; Collected Poems, 1984. *Contributions to:* Times Literary Supplement; London Review of Books; Spectator; Poetry Nation Review; Agenda; others. *Honours:* FRSL, 1975; Honorary D.Litt, Bristol University, 1980. *Literary Agent:* A D Peters. *Address:* Moorfield Cottage, The Hill, Langport, Somerset TA10 9PU, England.

SITWELL, Nigel Degge Wilmot, b. 23 Aug, 1935, Alverstoke, Hampshire, England. Writer. *Appointment:* Editor, Wildlife Magazine; Special Writer, Now Magazine. *Publications:* The Shell Guide to Britain's Threatened Wildlife, 1984; many books edited. *Contributor to:* New Scientist; Illustrated London News; Sunday Times Magazine; Observer Magazine; High Life; Smithsonian, USA; Sceince Digest, USA; International Wildlife, USA; Das Tier, Germany; etc. *Honours:* Order of the Golden Ark, Netherlands, 1979; Arbor Day Award, USA, 1985. *Membership:* Association of British Science Writers. *Address:* 243 King's Road, London SW3 5EL, England.

SJOBERG, Leif T I, b. 15 Dec. 1925, Boden, Sweden. Educator; Scandinavian Studies Specialist. *Education:* Fil kand, 1952, Fil Mag, 1954, Fil lic, 1968, Uppsala University. *Publications:* Dag Hammarskjold: Markings, translation with W H Auden, 1964; Gunnar Ekelof: Selected Poems, translation with W H Auden, 1971; A Reader's Guide to Gunnar Ekelof's A Molna Elegy, 1973; Par Lagerkvist, 1976; Artur Lundkvist: Agadir, translation with William Jay Smith, 1979; G Ekelof: A Molna Elegy, with M Rukeyser, 1980. *Contributions to:* Numerous journals. *Honours include:* Honorary Fil Dr, Uppsala University, Sweden, 1980. *Memberships include:* Executive Committee, New York University Colloquia on Comparative Literature. *Literary Agent:* Curtis Brown Limited. *Address:* 50 Morningside Drive, New York City, NY 10025, USA.

SKELTON, Geoffrey David, b. 11 May 1916, Springs, Republic of South Africa. Writer, Translator, Broadcaster. m. Gertrude Klebac, 4 Sep. 1947, Velden, Austria, 2 sons. *Publications:* Wagner at Bayreuth : Experiment and Tradition, 1965 and 1976; Wieland Wagner: The Positive Sceptic, 1971; Paul Hindemith: The Man Behind the Music, 1975; Richard and Cosima Wagner: Biography of a Marriage, 1982; Translations from German include: The Marat/Sade play (with Adrian Mitchell), 1964; Frieda Lawrence (biography by Robert

Lucas), 1973; Cosima Wagner's Diaries 2 volumes, 1978–80. *Honours:* PEN Translation Prize, with Adrian Mitchell, 1966; Schlegel-Tieck Translation prize, 1973; Yorkshire Post Music Award, 1976. *Memberships:* Executive Committee 1969–81, Chairman 1974, Vice-Chairman 1980–81, Translators Association. *Literary Agent:* David Higham Associates, London. *Address:* 49 Downside, Shoreham, West Sussex, BN4 6HF, England.

SKELTON, Peter, b. 29 Dec. 1929, Amsterdam, Netherlands. Author. m. Lady Doreen Fox-Strangways, 23 Sep. 1959, 1 daughter. *Education:* Tripos, Law & Economics, Cambridge University. *Literary Appointments include:* Publisher's reader; Art editor; Magazine editor; Film script writer; etc. *Publications include:* The Charm of Hours, 1954; Animals All, 1956; All About Paris, Paris By Night, 1959; The Promise of Days, 1962; The Room of Overnight (play), 1963; The Blossom of Months (novel, 5 columes), 1973; Tiger Kub & The Royal Jewel, 1983; The Flowering of Seasons, 1985; etc. *Contributions to:* Daily Telegraph (book reviews); Sunday Times (science fiction); News of the World (features, as Edward Trevor); Holland Herald (features); Daily Express (contributor, William Hickey column). *Honour:* Fellow, International Institute of Arts & Letters, 1962. *Membership:* South Devon Literary Society (honorary secretary). *Address:* St Anthony, Higher Woodfield, Torquay, Devon, England.

SKEMP, Joseph Bright, b. Bilston, Staffordshire, England. University Teacher. m. Ruby James, 6 Sep. 1941, Cardiff, Wales. *Education:* MA Cambridge; PhD Edinburgh. *Appointments:* Editor Durham University Journal, 1953–58; Joint Editor Phronesis, 1957–64. *Publications:* The Theory of Motion in Plato's Later Dialogues, 1942 reprinted and enlarged, 1967; Plato's Statesman, 1952 now being reprinted with postscript. *Contributions to:* Several volumes of Proceedings of Symposium Aristotelicum. *Address:* 6a Westfield Park, Bristol BS6 6LT, England.

SKENE, Anthony, b. England. Television Playwright. *Television Plays include:* Square on the Hypotenuse; What's In It For Me? A Walk Through the Forest; Blunt Instrument. *Contributions to:* Numerous Television series including: The Prisoner; The Name of the Game; Upstairs, Downstairs. *Address:* 5a Furlong Road, London N7 8LS, England.

SKIBBE, Eugene Moritz, b. 16 July 1930, Minneapolis, Minnesota, USA. College Professor, Clergyman, American Lutheran Church. m. 1 Aug. 1953, Northfield, 2 sons, 2 daughters. *Education:* BA, St Olaf College, Northfield, 1952; M Div, Luther Theological Seminary, St Paul, 1956; ThD, University of Heidelberg, Germany, 1962. *Publications:* Protestant Agreement on the Lord's Supper, 1968. *Contributor to:* Kergyma und Dogma; Lutherische Monateshefte; Dialog; Lutheran Quarterly; The American Ecclesiastical Review; Una Sancta; etc. *Address:* Augsburg College, Minneapolis, MN 55454, USA.

SKIMIN, Robert Elwayne, b. 30 July 1929, Belden, Ohio, USA. m. Claudia, 1 May, 1974, El Paso. *Publications:* The Booze Game, 1976; The Thodesian Sellout, 1977; Soldier for Hire, Volumes 1, 2, 3, 4, 1980–81; Chikara, 1984–85. *Contributor to:* Several professional journals. *Honours:* Major (Retired) US Army, BSM; Al Paso Arts Alliance Literary Arts Award, 1984; The Ohioana Book Award for Fiction, 1985. *Membership:* Authors Guild; Authors League of America. *Literary Agents:* Freya Manston, New York; Abner Stein, London; Rosemary Buckman, Oxford; Robert Fouques Durparc, Paris, Irene Webb, Hollywood. *Address:* 8409, W H Burges, El Paso, TX 79925, USA.

SKINNER, June Margaret O'Grady, b. 23 July 1922, Vancouver, British Columbia, Canada. Author. m. Frederick Snowden Skinner, 5 Mar. 1948, Vancouver, 1 son, 2 daughters. *Publications:* O'Houlihan's Jest, 1961; Pippin's Journal, 1962; Let's Kill Uncle, 1963; Bleak November, 1970; The May Spoon, 1981. *Literary Agent:* A L Hart, Fox Chase Agency, 419E 57th Street,

New York NY 10022, USA. *Address:* The Classic, Suite 204, 1350 View Crescent, Delta, British Columbia, Canada V4L 2K3.

SKINNER, Knute (Rumsey), b. 25 Apr. 1929, St Louis, Missouri, USA. Poet. m. Edna Faye Kiel, 25 Mar. 1978, Bellingham, Washington, 3 sons (by previous marriages). *Education:* Culver-Stockton College, 1947–49; BA, Speech & Drama, University of Northen Colorado, 1951; MA, English, Breadloaf School of English, Middlebury, Middlebury College, 1954; PhD, English, University of Iowa, 1958. *Literary Appointments:* Founder and President of the Signpost Press Incorporated. In connection with this press, Editor and Publisher of eighteen issues of, The Bellingham Review, a literary magazine and fice poetry collections in the Signpost poetry series; Professor of English, Western Washington Unviersity, 1973. *Publications include:* Poetry: Stranger With a Watch, 1965; A Close Sky Over Killaspuglonane, 1968; In Dinosaur Country, 1969; The Sorcerers, 1972; A Close Sky Over Killaspuglonane, 2nd Edition, 1975; Hearing of the Hard Times, 1981; The Flame Room, 1983; Selected Poems, 1985. *Contributions to:* Numerous publications of articles, reviews, short stories, poetry; Recordings, radio broadcasts and TV Films. *Honours:* Tuition Scholarship, Middlebury College, 1985; Huntington Hartford Foundation Fellowship to write poetry, 1961; Governor's Invitational Writers' Day Certificate of Recognition, State of Washington, 1968; Fellowship in Creative Writing from National Endowment for the Arts, 1975; Millay Colony for the Arts Fellowship 1976; Residency, Tyrone Guthrie Centre, 1985. *Memberships:* Poetry Society of America; Washington Poets Association (Board Member); American Committee for Irish Studies. *Address:* 412 N State Street, Bellingham, WA 98225, USA.

SKLAR, Dusty, b. 11 Mar. 1928, Poland. Writer. m. David Sklar, 27 Nov. 1949, New York City, USA, 2 sons, 1 daughter. *Publication:* Gods & Beasts: The Nazis & the Occult, 1977. *Contributions to:* Cosmopolitan; Self; Virginia Quarterly Review; Nation; Family Weekly; Modern Maturity; Mendocino Review Playgirl; American Legion Magazine. *Memberships:* American Society of Journalists & Authors; Women's Ink; International Women's writing Guild (Board of Directors). *Address:* 1043 Wilson Avenue, Teaneck, NJ 07666, USA.

SKOGLUND, John Egnar, b. 1 Apr. 1912, San Diego, California, USA. Professor of Theology. m. Daisy Winnifred Nelson, 3 Nov. 1934, Oakland, California, 6 daughters. *Education:* BA, University of California, Berkeley; MA, BD, Berkeley Baptist Divinity School; PhD, Yale University. *Literary Appointments:* Editor, Foundations, a Baptist Journal of History and Theology (now American Baptist Quarterly) 1967–73; Editor, Colgate Rochester Quarterly, 1964–67. *Publications:* The Spirit Tree, 1951; They Reach for Life, 1955; Come and See, 1956; To the Whole Creation, 1958; Fifty Years of Faith and Order, (with J R Nelson) 1964; The Baptists, 1965; Worship in the Free Churches, 1965; Worship and Renewal, editor 1965; Worship in a Secular Age, editor, 1967; A Manual of Worship, 1968. *Contributions to:* An Approach for Christian Missions Religion in Life, 1949; Making Dialogue Preach, The Pulpit, 1961; The Map of Christian Preaching, the Rochester Heritage, The Pulpit, 1964; Unity, Union and the Church Crusader, 1966; Articles on Baptist Worship in A Dictionary of Liturgy and Worship, 1986 (new edition). *Address:* 1909 San Antonio Avenue, Berkeley, CA 94707, USA.

SKUTCH, Alexander Frank, b. 20 May 1904, Baltimore, Maryland, USA. Naturalist; Writer. m. Pamela Joan Lankester, 27 Apr. 1950, San José, Costa Rica, 1 (adopted) son. *Education:* AB, 1925, PhD Botany, 1928; John Hopkins University. *Major Publications:* Life Histories of Central American Birds (3 volumes), 1954–69; Life Histories of Central American Hiughland Birbs, 1967; The Golden Core of Religion, 1970; A Naturalist in Costa Rica, 1971; Studies of Tropical American Birds, 1972; The Life of the Humming-Bird,

1972; Parent Birds & their young, 1976; A Birdwatcher's Adventures in Tropical America, 1977; Aves de Costa Rica, 1977; The Imperative Call: A Naturalist's Adventures in Temperate & Tropical America, 1979; A Naturalist on a Tropic Farm, 1980; New Studies of Tropical American Brids, 1981; Birds of Tropical America, 1983; Nature Through Tropical Windows, 1983; Life Ascending, 1985; Life of the Woodpecker, 1985. *Contributor to:* Animal Kingdom; Audobon; Aryan Path; GeoMundo; Nature Magazine; Natural History; Scientific Monthly; Various ornithological Journals, Botanical Journals; and others. *Honours:* Brewster Award of American Ornithologists' Union, 1950; John Burroughs Medal, 1983; Arthur A Allen Award, Cornell University Laboratory of Ornithology, 1983. *Memberships:* Honorary Member, American Ornithologists Union; British Ornithologists Union; Cooper Ornithological Society. *Address:* Quizarrá, 8000 san Isidro de El General, Costa Rica, Central America.

SLATE, Libby, b. 14 Oct. 1954, Los Angeles, California, USA. Writer. *Education:* BA, 1975, Graduate work, 1975–77, University of California, Los Angeles. *Publications:* Critiques of films, Magill's Survey of Cinema, 1980 and Magill's Cinema Annual, 1981, 83, 84, 85. *Contributions to:* Los Angeles Times; Performing Arts; Emmy; Us; California; American Premiere; Skating; Essence; Canadian Skater. *Honours:* National 1st place Winner, Senior Scholastic Magazine Creative Writing Awards, 1971; Graduate, Phi Beta Kappa, Magna Cum Laude, Deans List, Honours Programme, University of California, Los Angeles, 1975. *Memberships:* Sigma Delta Chi; Independent Writers of Southern California. *Address:* 6316 West 6th Street, Los Angeles, CA 90048, USA.

SLATER, Ian David, b. 1 Dec. 1941, Toowoomba, Australia. Author; Lecturer. m. Marian Johnston, 18 Dec. 1968, Vancouver, Canada, 1 son, 1 daughter. *Education:* BA, 1972, MA, 1973, PhD, 1977, University of British Columbia, Vancouver, Canada. *Publications:* Firespill, 1977; Sea Gold, 1979; Air Glow Red, 1981; Orwell: The Road to Airstrip One, 1985. *Contributions to:* Orwell, Marcuse and the Language of Politics, Political Studies, 1975. *Honours:* Royal Institution Scholarship in Arts, University of British Columbia, 1970; Mack Eastman United Nations Essay Award, 1971 (Vancouver). *Memberships:* The Writers' Union of Canada; Authors' Guild of America. *Address:* 4074 West 17th Avenue, Vancouver, British Columbia, Canada V6S 1A6.

SLATER, Joyce Ann, b. 12 Aug. 1941, Detroit, Michigan, USA. Freelance Writer. m. Robert A Slater, 13 Aug. 1966, Carmel, California, 1 daughter. *Education:* BA, English; MA, English (summa cum laude); California State University, Sacramento. *Contributions to:* Book Reviewer for The Atlanta Journal-Constitution; Library Journal; People Magazine; Atlanta Magazine. *Memberships:* Village Writers, Atlanta, Georgia. *Literary Agent:* Katherine Kidde, Kidde, Hoyt and Picard, New York City. *Address:* 181 Shiloh Road, Kennesaw, GA 30144, USA.

SLATER, Lydia Elizabeth, b. 21 Mar. 1902. Biochemist; Writer; Poet; Translator; Performer at Poetry Recitals. m. 4 children. *Education:* University of Moscow, UUSR; Dr phil, Berlin, Germany. *Publications:* Poems by Boris Pasternak (translations), 1958, 59, new enlarged edition, 1986; Before Sunrise (poems), 1971, 73, 79; Eighteen Contemporary Russian Poems (translations), 1973l 2 small records: B Pasternak (poems), 1960, 61; 2 tapes: The Poetry of B Paternak, 1973; Pasternak, Brother and Sister, 1973; Vypyshki Magnija (Russian poems), 1974–75; Forthcoming: Russian Salad (translations) and Songs of Joy, Despair and Hope (poems). *Contributor to:* Times Literary Supplement; Oxford Mail; Isis; Scotsman; John O'London's; New York Herald; Spring Anthology; Poesie Vivante; Hungarian Poetry in Translation; Expresison; First International Poetry Society Anthology; Candelabrum; Poet; Ipse; Orbis, etc. *Memberships:* World Poetry Society Intercontinental; Founder, Fellow,

International Poetry Society. *Address:* 20 Park Town, Oxford OX2 6SH, England.

SLATTERY, Bradley, b. USA. Writer; Owner, Brad Lee Publications. m. Barbara Redka, 1 daughter. *Education:* BS Economics, New York University; MA, Sociology, New School. *Literary Appointments include:* Owner, Brad Lee Publications, 1951–. *Contributions to:* Numerous anthologies including: Poetry Parade, 1963; Melody of the Muse, 1964; Golden Harvest, 1967; Yearbook of Modern Poetry, 1971; Outstanding Contemporary Poetry, 1972, 73; Sweet Seventies Anthology, 1974; Of Thee I Sing, 1975. Numerous journals including: Major Poets; East Hampton Star; Journal of Contemporary Poets, Titanic Commutator; A Distant Drummer. *Honours include:* Biographical entries. *Memberships:* Past President and Past Programme Chairman, New York Chapter, National Writers Club; Voluntary Critic, Denver Chapter, National Writers Club. *Address:* Box 8, Forest Hills, NY 11375, USA.

SLAUGHTER, Frank Gill, b. 25 Feb. 1908, Washington, District of Columbia, USA. Freelance Author; Retired Surgeon. *Education:* AB, Duke University, 1926; MD, John Hopkins Medical School, 1930. *Publications:* Author of over 50 books including: That None Should Die, 1941; Air Surgeon, 1942; Battle Surgeon, 1944; The New Science of Surgery, 1946; The Golden Isle, 1947; Medicine for Moderns, 1948; East Side General, 1952; The Galileans, 1953; The Scarlet Cord, 1956; Sword & Scalpel, 1957; Daybreak, 1958; The Crown & the Cross, 1959; Epidemic, 1961; David, Warrior & King, 1962; Upon this Rock, 1963; The Purple Quest, 1965; Surgeon, USA, 1966; Doctor's Wives, 1967; Countdown, 1970; Code Five, 1971; Convention MD, 1972; Women in White, 1973; Stonewall Brigade, 1975; Plague Ship, 1974; Devil's Gamble, 1977; The Passionate Revel, 1979; Doctor's Daughters, 1981; Gospel Fever, 1982; Doctor at Risk, 1983; No Greater Love, 1984. *Contributor to:* Colliers; Cosmopolitan; Family Weekly; The Writer, Advisory Board. *Honours:* DHL, Jacksonville University, 1978. *Memberships:* Fellow, several professional medical associations. *Address:* Box 14 Ortega Stn, Jacksonville FL 32210, USA.

SLAVIN, Stephen L, b. 29 July 1939, Brooklyn, USA. Professor of Economics. *Education:* BA, Brooklyn College; MA, PhD, Economics, New York University. *Publications include:* The Einstein Syndrome: Corporate Anti-Semitism in America Today, 1982; Jelly Bean Aconomics, 1984. Pamphlet, The Truth Anout Inflation, 1979. *Contributions to:* Studies in Family Planning; Patterns of Prejudice; Journal of Biosocial Science; Business & Society Review; Jewish Currents; Public Management; Better Investing; Focus Midwest; Jewish Spectator; Northwest Investment Review; etc. Various newspapers throughout USA. *Address:* 225 Prospect Park West, Brooklyn, NY 11215, USA.

SLIWINSKI, Wincenty Piotr, b. 18 Jan. 1915, P[ls]lock, Poland. Poet; Painter; Graphic artist; Constructor of Violins; Metal worker; Scientist. m. Eugenia Barbara Dwigwbska, 24 Feb. 1945. *Education:* Teachers Seminary, P[ls]lock, 1930–36; University and Engineering College, Warsaw, 1936–39; Academy of Fine Arts, Warsaw, 1936–39, 1948. *Publications include:* Author of over 2500 poems published in USA, India, Italy, Philippines, 1965– including: Sad Song, Tale on the Human Fate; Book of Dreams; Book of Lamentations; Song of Fields; Songs of Joy and Songs of Sadness. *Contributions to:* International Anthology on World Brotherhood and Peace, 1980; World Poetry, Poetry Europe, World Anthology; Voices International, An Anthology of World Poetry; Poet International, USA; Journal Poetry International, India. *Honours include:* Honorary DLitt, World University, USA, 1981; Gold Medal, International Parliament for Safety and Peace, USA, 1982; Statue of Victory, World Culture for Letters, the Arts and Sciences, Centro Studi e Ricerche delle Nazioni, Italy, 1983; Medaille d'Argent, Grand Concours Internationale, Paris, France, 1983; Albert Einstein Prize, International Academy Foundation, Delaware, USA,

1984; Oscar d'Italia statue, Accademia Italia, lettres, Arts Sciences, Italy, 1985. *Memberships include:* World Poetry Society Intercontinental, USA; World University; International Academy of Poets, England; Accademia Internazionale Leonardo da Vinci, Italy; Accademia Internazionale Tumasso Campanella, Italy; Arts, Sciences, Lettrés, France; International Editorial Board, India. *Literary Agents:* Dr Krishna Srinivas and Professor Dr Syed Ameeruddin, Madras, India. *Address:* 4/78 Tatrzanska St, 00–742 Warsaw, Poland.

SLOANE, Peter James, b. 6 Aug. 1942, Cheshire, England. Profesor of Political Economy. m. Avril Mary Urquhart, 31 Jylu 1969, Aberdeen, 1 son. *Education:* BA Economics, University of Sheffield, 1961–64; PhD, University of Strathclyde, 1964–66. *Publications:* Discrimination in the Labour Market, (with B Chiplin), 1976; Women and Low Pay, (editor), 1980; Equal Employment Issues (with H C Jain), 1981; Tackling Discrimination at the Workplace, (with B Chiplin), 1982; Labour Economics, (co-author), 1985. *Contributions to:* Economic Journal; Economics; Bulletin of Economic Research; Applied Economics; Scottish Journalof Political Economy; Management and Decision Economics; International Labour Review; British Journal of Industrial Relations: Industrial Relations Journal; and others. *Address:* The Eaves, Kincardine Road, Torphins, near Banchory, Aberdeenshire AB3 4HH, Scotland.

SLOCOMBE BOUCHON, Joan Tamara, b. 14 Jan. 1917, London, England. Journalist. m. Bouchon, 28 Aug. 1940, Limoges, France, died 1971. *Literary Appointments:* Paris Office, News Chronicle; Paris Office, Reuters; BBC French Service during war years; Reuters; Fleet Street then Paris Office; AFP Franch News Agency. *Contributions to:* Sunday Express; Daily Mail, Sunday Graphic. *Membership:* Anglo American Press Association, Paris. *Address:* 65 rue Violet, 75015 Paris, France.

SLOMAN, Albert Edwrad, b. 14 Feb. 1921, Launceston, Cornwall, England. Vice-Chancellor, University of Essex. m. Bernadette Bergson, 3 daughters. *Education:* BA Medieval & Modern Languages, 1941, MA, 1946, PhD, 1948, Wadhan College, University of Oxford; MA, University of Dublin, Ireland. *Literary Appointments:* Lecturer in Spanish, University of California at Berkeley, USA, 1946–47; Reader in Spanish, University of Dublin, Republic of Ireland, 1947–53; Gilmour Professor of Spanish, University of Liverpool, England, 1953–62, Dean, Faculty of Arts, 1961–62; Vice-Chancellor, University of Essex, 1962–; Editor, Bulletin of Hispanic Studies, 1953–62; Reith Lecturer, 1963 (BBC Radio). *Major Publications:* The Sources of Calderon's 'El Principe Constante', 1950; The Dramatic Craftsmanship of Calderon, 1958l A University in the Making, 1964. *Contributor to:* Modern Language Review; Bulletin of Hispanic Studies; Hispanic Review; Romance Philology; and others. *Honours:* CBE, 1980; Top Exhibitioner, 1939; Honorary Fellow, 1983, Wadham College, Oxford. *Memberships include:* Board of Governors, Centre for Information on Language Teaching, 1979–; Committee for International Cooperation in Higher Education, 1985–; Vice-Chairman, Association of Commonwealth Universities, 1985–; Committee of Management, British Institute in Paris, 1982–; Commonwealth Scolarships Commission, 1984–; British Council Board, 1985–; Chairman, Committee of Vice-Chancellors & Principles of the Universities of the United Kingdom, 1979–81, Member, 1981–83. *Address:* University of Essex, Wivenhoe Park, Colchester, Essex, England.

SLONIM, Reuben, b. 27 Feb. 1914, Winnipeg, Manitoba, Canada. Rabbi; Writer. m. Rita Short, 21 June 1936, New York, USA, 1 daughter. *Education:* BS, Arts & Sciences, Illinois Institute of Technology; MHL, Jewish Seminary, New York; Rabbi, Teacher, Preacher; Jewish Theological Seminary. *Publications:* In the Steps of Pope Paul, 1965; Both Sides Now, 1972; Family Quarrel, 1977; Grand To Be An Orphan, 1983. *Contributor to:* Editor, Toronto Telegram, 1955–71; Toronto

Star; Toronto Globe and Mail. *Honours:* Chaplain, Variety Club, Toronto; Co-Chairman, Interfaith Committee, United Way of Metro, Toronto; President, Association of the Living Jewish Spirit, 1985. *Address:* 625 Roselawn Ave, Suite 1105, Toronto, Ontario M5N 1K7, Canada.

SLOVENKO, Ralph, b. 4 Nov. 1927, New Orleans, Louisiana, USA. Profesor, Law, Psychiatry. *Education:* BA 1948, LLB 1953, MA 1960, PhD 1965, Tulane University, New Orleans; Fulbright Scholar, Aix-en-Provence, France. *Appointments:* Editor, Behavioral Sciences and Law; Profesor, Law, Psychiatry, Wayne State University; Board of Editors: Bulletin of American Academy of Psychiatry and Law, Behavioural Sciences and Law; Journal of Psychiatry and Law. *Publications:* Handbook of Criminal Procedure, 1967; Sexual Behaviour and the Law, 1965; Psychotheraphy, Confidentiality and Privileged Communication, 1966; Psychiatry and Law, 1973. *Contributor to:* New York Times; Wall Street Journal; Journal of Psychiatry and Law. *Honour:* Manfred Guttmacher Award, American Psychiatric Association. *Membership:* Order of Golf. *Address:* Wayne State University School of Law, Detroit, MI 48202, USA.

SLOVES, David Howard, b. 20 Nov. 1957, New York, USA. Public Relations Account Executive. m. Janice Lynn Perzley, 26 Aug. 1984, Verona, New Jersey, USA. *Education:* BA, Journalism, minor, Political Science, Rider College, Lawrenceville, New Jersey. *Literary Appointments:* Former Associate Editor, World Construction, World Mining Equipment. *Contributions to:* Printed Circuit Design; Western Electronics; Graphic Arts Monthly; Editors Only; etc. *Memberships:* Treasurer, New York Business Press Editors; New York Press Club; Deadline Club; National Writers Club. *Address:* 249 White Birch Road, Edison, NJ 08837, USA.

SLY, Ridge Michael, b. 3 Nov. 1933, Seattle, Washington, USA. Physician. m. Ann Turner Jennings, 12 June 1957, Floydsburg, Kentucky, 2 daughters. *Education:* AB, magna cum laude. Kenyon College, Ohio, 1956; MD, Washington University School of Medicine, St Louis, 1960; Junior Assistant Resident and Assistant Resident in Pediatrics, St Louis Children's Hospital, 1960–62; Chief Resident in Pediatrics, University of Kentucky Medical Center, 1962–63; Fellow in Allergy & Immunology, UCLA Medical Center, 1965–67. *Literary Appointments:* Editorial Boards: Annals of Allergy, 1982–; Clinical Reviews in Allergy, 1982–; Journal of Asthma, 1982–. *Publications:* Pediatric Allergy, 1977, Second Edition, 1981; Textbook of Padiatric Allergy, 1985. *Contributions to:* Journal of Allergy and Clincial Immunology; Annals of Allergy; Drug Therapy; Pediatric Annals, and some 76 other publications. *Honours:* Louisiana Plaque of American Lung Association of Louisiana, 1978; N Murray Peshkin Memorial Award of Association for the Care of Asthma, 1983. *Memberships:* Phi Beta Kappa; American Medical Writers Associaiton. *Address:* 111 Michigan Avenue NW, Washington, DC 20010, USA.

SMALL, Margaret Genevieve, b. 26 May 1950, Montgomery, Alabama, USA. Writer; Editor. *Education:* BA, Rollins College, Florida, MA, North Texas State University, Denton, Texas. *Publications:* Editor, Current Controversies in Breast Cancer, 1984. *Contributions to:* Pipeline and Gas Journal, contributor and assistant editor, 1975–77; Editor, Oncologia Report to Physicians, 1983–85; Writer, Medical Tribune, 1984–. *Honours:* Distinguished Technical Communication Award, 1985. *Membership:* American Medical Writers Association. *Address:* 3918 Crestridge, San Antonio, TX 78229, USA.

SMALLEY, Stephen Stewart, b. 11 May, 1931, London, England. Clerk in Holy Orders. m. Susan Jane Paterson, 13 July 1974, Manchester, 1 son, 1 daughter. *Education:* BA 1955, MA 1958, PhD 1979, Jesus College, Cambridge; BD, Eden Theological Seminary, USA, 1957. *Publications:* Christ and Spirit in the New Testament, editor (with B Lindars) and contributor,

1973; John: Evangelist and Interpreter, 1978, USA edition, 1984; 1, 2, 3 John, 1984. *Contributions to:* 24 artcles in learned journals and Festschriften; several articles in 5 Theological Dictionaries and 1 encyclopedia. *Honours:* Foundation Scholarship, Jesus College, Cambridge, 1948; Lady Kay Scholarship, 1955; Select Preacher, University of Cambridge, 1963–64. *Memberships:* Archbishops Doctorine Commission of the Church of England; Studorium Novi Testamenti Societas. *Address:* 35 Morningside, Coventry CV5 6PD, England.

SMARIO, Tom, b. 5 Mar. 1950, Oakland, California, USA. Orthopedic Technician. m. 6 Dec. 1979, California, USA. 2 sons, 1 daughter. *Education:* Associate of Arts, Associate of Science, Lancy College, Oakland, California. *Literary Appointment:* Poet in Residence, Oregon, 1976–78. *Publications:* The Soles of My Shoes, 1975; Lines, 1978; Luckynuts and Real People, 1979; The Cat's Pajamas, 1982; Spring Fever, 1984. *Contributions to:* 149 poems published, magazines include, Dog River Review; The Lunatic Fringe; Catalyst; The Oregonian; Aura; Poetry of The Poor. *Memberships:* President Oregon State Poetry Association; Poets & Writers Inc; Portland Poetry Festival; The Academy of American Poets. *Address:* 11900 SE Foster Place, Portland, OR 97266, USA.

SMART, Elizabeth, b. 27 Dec. 1913, Ottawa, Ontario, Canada. Writer. 2 daughters. *Education:* Kings College, London University, England; London Theatre Studio. *Literary Appointments:* Writer-in-Residence, University of Alberta, Edmonton, Alberta, Canada, 1982. *Publications:* By Grand Central Station I Sat Down and Wept, 1945; A Bonus, 1977; The Assumption of the Rogues and Rascals, 1978; 11 Poems, 1982; In The Meantime, 1985; Necessary Secrets: Journals, 1986. *Contributor to:* House and Garden; Tatler; Queen; Harpers and Queen; Cyphers, Dublin; Botteghe Oscure, Rome, *Honours:* Recipient, Arts Council Grant, 1966; Major Canada Council Grant, 1983–84. *Address:* The Dell, Flixton, Bungay, Suffolk, England.

SMART, Ninian, b. 6 May 1927, Cambridge, England. University Professor. m. Libushka Clementina Baruffaldi, 19 July 1985, 2 sons, 2 daughters. *Education:* MA, B Phil, Oxon; Hon LHD, Layola, Chicago; Hon D Litt, Glasgow, 1969; Hon Doctorate, University of Stirling, 1986. *Publications:* Reasons & Faiths, 1958; A Dialogue of Religion, 1960; Doctrine and Augment in Indian Philosophy, 1964; The Religious Expereience of Mankind, 1969, 3rd edition 1983; The Science of Religion, 1973; Beyond Ideology, 1981; World News, 1983; Saved Texts of the World, 1983; Concept & Empathy, 1986. *Contributions to:* Mind; T.H.E.S.; Encounter; The Listener; Observer; etc. *Honour:* Gifford Lecturer, Edinburgh, 1979–80. *Literary Agent:* Michael Sissons, A D Peters, London. *Address:* Westbourne House, Lancaster LA1 5EF, England.

SMELSER, Neil Joseph, b. 22 July 1930, Kahoka, Missouri, USA. University Professor. m. (1) Helen Thelma Margolis, 10 June 1954, divorced 1965; (2) Sharin Fateley, 20 Dec. 1967, 2 sons, 2 daughters. *Education:* BA, Harvard University, 1952; BA 1954, MA 1959, Magdalen College, Oxford, England; PhD, Harvard University, 1958; Graduate, San Francisco Psychoanalytic Institute, 1971. *Publications:* Economy and Society, with T Parsons, 1956; Social Change in Industrial Revolution, 1959; Theory of Collective Behaviour, 1962; The Sociology of Economic Life, 1963, 2nd edition 1975; Essays in Sociological Explanation, 1968; Sociological Theory: A Contemporary View, 1971; Comparative Methods in the Methods in the Social Sciences, 1976; The Changing Academic Market, with R Content, 1980; Sociology, 1981, 2nd edition 1984. *Contributor to:* 52 articles to professional journals. *Honours:* Junior Fellow, Society of Fellows, Harvard University, 1955–58; Fellow, American Academy of Arts and SCiences, 1968. *Membership:* American Philosophical Society. *Address:* Dept of Sociology, University of California, Berkeley, CA 94702, USA.

SMIL, Vaclav, b. 9 Dec. 1943, Pilsen, Bohemia. University Professor. m. Eva Fidler, 14 Dec. 1967, 1 son. *Education:* RNDr, Faculty of Natural Sciences, Carolinum University, Prague, Czechoslovakia, 1965; PhD, College of Earth and Mineral Sciences, Pennsylvania State University, USA, 1972. *Publications:* China's Energy, 1976; Energy in the Developing World, editor, 1980; Energy Analysis in Agriculture, principal author, 1983; The Bad Earth, Environmental Degradation in China, 1984; Carbon Nitrogen Sulfur Human Interference in Grand Biosperic Cycles, 1985. *Contributions to:* Numerous journals including: Ambio; American Scientist; Bulletin of the Atomic Scientist; Current History; Energy Policy; Environmental Management; Food Policy; Far Eastern Economic Review; The China Quarterly; Power Engineering; Scientific American. *Address:* Department of Geography, University of Manitoba, Winnipeg, Maitoba, Canada R3T 2N2.

SMILEY, Charles Wesley, b. 18 Dec. 1940, Kirkland Lake, Ontario, Canada. Social Worker; Teacher. m. Glenys Marie Spangler, 12 June 1960, 1 son, 2 daughters. *Education:* BA Humanities, Abilene Christian University, Abilene, Texas, USA, 1962; Master of Social Work, Portland State University, Portland, Oregon, 1965; MA Drama, Angelo State University, San Angelo, Texas, 1985. *Publications:* George Johnson is a Son-of-a-bitch, 1973; The Horticulturalist, 1974; The Valedictorian, 1975; The Distant Cry of a Drunken Leprechaun, 1979; Shawn Victor O'Casey – The One and Only, 1981; The Royal Erin, 1983; Anthology: Transitions I – Short Plays, A sourcebook of Canadian literature, 1978. *Contributions to:* Professional journals in the field of social work. *Membership:* Playwright's Union of Canada. *Address:* Post Office Box 2, Carlsbad, TX 76934, USA.

SMITH, Alice Upham, b. 4 Apr. 1908, Duluth, USA. Landscape Architect. m. Eastman Smith, 26 Aug. 1933, Duluth. *Education:* Landscape architecture, University of Minnesota, 1 year; University of Edinburgh, 1 year; Cambridge School of Architecture and Landscape, 2 years. *Publications:* Trees in a Winter Landscape, 1969; Patios Terraces Desks and Roof Gardens, 1969; A Distinctive Setting for Your House, 1973. *Contributor to:* New York Times Sunday Garden Page; Flower and Garden; House and Garden; Nursery Business; Landscape Industry; Horticulture; Woman's Day; Pen and Ink Illustrations in Hunt Institute for Botanical Documentation, Carnegia Mellon University, Pittsburg, etc. *Honours:* Missouri Writers Guild Springfield Chapter Award for Best Article, 1965; Named Fellow of Garden Writers Association of America, 1984. *Memberships:* Garden Writers Association of America; Ozark Writers League. *Agent:* Marilyn Marlow, Curtis Borwn Ltd, New York, USA. *Addres:* Cranfield Circle, Rt 4, Box 460, Mountain Home, AK 72653, USA.

SMITH, Anthony Charles, b. 31 Oct. 1935, Kew, England. Writer. *Education:* MA, Cambridge University. *Publications:* The Crowd, 1965; Zero Summer, 1971; Orghast at Persepolis, 1972; Paper Voices, 1975; Treatment, 1976; The Jericho Gun, 1977; Edward and Mrs Simpson, 1978; Extra Cover, 1981; The Dark Crystal, 1982; Wagner, 1983; Sebastian the Navigator, 1985; Lady Jane, 1985; Labyrinth, 1986. *Contributions to:* New Society; Transatlantic Review; Listener; Times; Telegraph Magazine; Sunday Times; Observer; British Broadcasting Corporation and Independent Television. *Honours:* Writing Awards, Arts Council, 1970–71, 1974–75, 1980. *Memberships:* Writers Guild of Great Britain; Literary Advisory Panel, Southwest Arts, 1972–75; Director, Cheltenham Festival of Literature, 1978–79; Executive, Playwrights Company, 1979–83. *Address:* 21 West Shrubbery, Bristol BS6 6TA, England.

SMITH, Anthony John Francis, b. 30 Mar. 1926, Buckinghamshire, England. Writer. m. 1956, London, 1 son, 2 daughters. *Education:* MA, Zoology Oxford University. *Publications:* Blind White Fish in Persia, 1953; Throw Out Two Hands, 1963; The Body, 1968; The Human Pedigree, 1975; The Mind, 1984; Smith and Son, 1984; The Body, revised, 1985. *Contributions to:*

Various publications. *Honours:* Glaxo Science Writers Travelling Fellowship, 1977. *Literary Agent:* Curtis Brown. *Address:* 10 Aldbourne Road, London W12, England.

SMITH, Arnold Cantwell, b. 18 Jan. 1915, Toronto, Canada. Secretary-General of the Commonwealth 1965–75; Retired international politician, Ambassador, Professor, Writer. m. Evelyn Hardwick Stewart, 8 Sep. 1938, London, 2 sons, 1 daughter. *Education:* BA Political Science & Economics, University of Toronto, 1935; Rhodes Scholar for Ontario, 1935; MA Jurisprudence, Christ Church, University of Oxford, England, 1937; BCL, 1938; Boulter Exhibitioner in Law, Gray's Inn, London. *Literary Appointments:* Editor The Baltic Times, Tallinn, Estonia, 1939–40; Editor-in-Chief, The War in Pictures, Images de la Guerre, Akhbar el Harp, Aera, Cephe (all published in Cairo, Egypt), 1941–43; Member, Editorial Board, The Round Table, (London), 1975–. *Major Publications:* Stitches in Time – The Commonwealth in World Politics, André Deutsch, London and others, 1981; My Canada (with K Cowan), 1984; International Negotiation and Mediation – Instruments and Methods, (with Arthur Lall) Pergamon, New York, 1985; The We – They Frontier: From International Relations to World Politics (with A Lall), 1983. *Contributor to:* Numerous articles in learned and other journals on international affairs, Soviet affairs, Canada, especially Siberia – Soviet Land of Promise, Geographical Magazine, 1965. *Honours:* Companion of Honour, 1975; R B Bennett Commonwealth Prize, Royal Society of Arts, 1975; Zimbabwe Independence Medal, 1980; Order of Canada, 1984; Various honours and honorary degrees, American, Canadian and English Universities. *Address:* 260 Metcalfe Street, Apt 4-8, Ottawa K2P 1R6, Canada.

SMITH, Barbara A (Atkeson), b. 21 Mar. 1932. Educator. *Education:* BA, Carroll College, Wisconsin, USA; MA, University of Wisconsin; Studied various universities. *Literary Appointments include:* Associate Professor of Literature and Writing, 1960–, Chairman, Division of Humanities, 1975, Alderson-Broaddus College, Philippi, West Virginia; Editor, Grab-a-Nickel Publications, Barbour County Writers Workshop; Co-Host, Weekly Public radio Broadcast, West Virginia; Poetry Consultant, Appalachian Writers Workshop and University of Kentucky. *Publications:* Six Miles Out, 1981; Never Tell a Miner Goodbye: A Testimony to Coal Miners' Wives, 1986; Winner: An Anthology of West Virginia Writers, editor, 1986. *Contributions to:* Numerous anthologies and literary journals including: North American Mentor Magazine; Mountain Review; Appalachian Journal; Kansas Quarterly; Cimmaron Review; Laurel Review; Appalachian Heritage; Illustrated Appalachian Intelligence; Poet Lore; Ohio Journal. *Honours include:* Various reading; Various biographical listings. *Memberships include:* West Virginia Writers Incorporated; Southern Appalachian Writers; Cooperative; Director, Barbour County Writers Workshop; Society of Technical Communication; Appalachian Writers Association Director. *Address:* Box 2158, Alderson-Broaddus College, Philippi, WV 26416, USA.

SMITH, Barbara Herrnstein, b. 6 Aug, 1932, New York, USA. Educator. m. (1) Richard J Herrnstein, 28 May 1951, divorced 1961, 1 daughter, (2) Thomas H Smith, 21 Feb. 1964, divorced 1974, 1 daughter. *Education:* BA, 1954, MA, English and American Literature, 1955, PhD, English and American Litertaure, 1965, Brandeis University. *Literary Appointments:* Member of Faculty, Division of Literature and Language, Bennington College, 1961–73; Visiting Lecturer in Communications, Annenberg School, University of Pennsylvania, 1973–74; Professor of English and Communications, 1974–80, University Professor of English and Communications, 1980–, Member Graduate Group Comparative Literature Theory, 1979–, Director Center for the Study of Art and Symbolic Behaviour, 1979–, University of Pennsylvania. *Publications:* Discussions of Shakespeare's Sonnets editor, 1964; Poetic Closure: A Study of How Poems End 1968; Shakespeare's Sonnets editor and introduction, 1960; On the Margins of Discourse: The Relation of Literature to Language,

1978. *Contributions to:* Numerous lectures and articles including: Fixed Marks and Variable Constances: A Parable of Literary Value, in Poetics Today, 1979; Narrative Versions, Narrative Theories, in Critical Inquiry, 1981, reprinted in On Narrative, 1981; Contingencies of Value, in Critical Inquiry, 1983. *Honours:* Christian Gauss Award for Poetic Closure, 1968; Explicator Award for Poetic Closure 1968; Fellowship, National Endowment for the Humanities, 1970–71; Guggenheim Fellowship 1977–78; Rockefeller Foundation Fellowship 1981; Fellow, Center for Advanced Study in Behavioural Sciences, 1985–86. *Memberships:* President, Academy of Literary Studies; Modern Language Association Division on Philosophical Approaches to Literature; Associate editor, Poetics Today; Member Editorial Board, Critical Inquiry. *Address:* 412 Williams Hall, University of Pennsylvania, Philadelphia, PA 19104, USA.

SMITH, Bertie Reece, b. 16 Nov. 1913, Monroe, North Carolina, USA. Retired Senior Service Reviewer. m. Reginald Lowell Smith, 24 Dec. 1932, Chester, SC, USA, 2 sons. *Education:* Diploma, Ideal Business School; Continuing education, Queen's College. *Literary Appointments:* Reader to numerous groups. *Publications:* Lace and Pig Iron, 1931; A Time for Poetry, 1966; Quaderni Di Poesia, 1976; Award Winning Poems, 1976; Colannades, 1981; Masters of Modern Poetry, 1981; Soundings in Poetry, 1981; Rainbows, 1985. *Honours:* Honourable Mention, Carl Sandburg Category, NCPS Annual Contest, 1976; Gold Medal, Accademia Leonardo Da Vinci, Rome, Italy, 1981. *Memberships:* Past Treasurer, North Carolina Poetry Society; National Federation of Poetry Societies; American Academy of Poets. *Address:* 1012 Keystone Court, Charlotte, NC 28210, USA.

SMITH, Charles Leeman, b. 1 June 1946, Knoxville, Tennesse, USA. Technical Writer. 2 sons. *Education:* BA, English, University of Tennessee, 1966. *Literary Appointments:* Publications Assistant, Biology Division, Oak Ridge National Laboratory, 1970–74; Lecturer, Technical Writing, Oak Ridge Graduate School of Biomedical Sciences, 1971–75; Technical Reports Analyst, Info Division, Oak Ridge National Laboratory, 1974–75; Educational and Scientific Materials Editor, Medical University of South Carolina, 1975–81; Editorial Assistant, Clinical Immunology and Immunopathology, 1976–82; Instructor, Science Writing, Medical University of South Carolina, 1981–82; Technical Writer, Science Applications International Corporation (Consultant, US Department of Energy), Washington, DC, 1982–. *Contributions to:* Comparative Immunology, Microbiology and Infectious Disease; Journal of Immunology; Rivista Immunologia e Immunofaracologia; Scandinavian Journal of Immunology; Annals of Clincial and Laboratory Science; Clinical Cellular Immunology: Molecular and Therapeutics Reviews; Technical Communications. *Memberships:* Phi Eta Sigma; Phi Kappa Phi; Phi Beta Kappa; American Association for the Advancement of Science; American Medical Writers Association; Council of Biology Editors; New York Academy of Sciences. *Address:* Box 9513 Friendship Station, Washington, DC 20016, USA.

SMITH, Christopher Upham Murray, b. 27 Dec. 1930, Brixham, England. University Lecturer. *Education:* BSc Zoology, University of Birmingham; BSc Physics, University of London; Diploma in Biophysics University of Edinburgh, Scotland. *Publications:* The Architecture of the Body, 1964; Molecular Biology: A Structural Approach, 1968; The Brain: Towards an Understanding, 1970; The Problem of Life: An Essay in the Origins of Biological Thought, 1976. *Contributions to:* Journals including: Nature; School Science Review; Adult Education; Journal of History of Biology; Studies in History and Philosophy of Science; Journal of Social and Biological Structures. *Address:* Department of Biological Sciences, University of Aston, Birmingham B4 7ET, England.

SMITH, David Fay, b. 6 July 1939, San Francisco, California, USA. Consultant. m. Anne Rush Mollegen, 3 Nov. 1962, Alexandria, Virginia, 1 daughter. *Education:* BA, University of Pennsylvania, 1961. *Publications:* A Computer Dictionary for Kids and Other Beginners, 1984. *Contributions to:* Publishers Weekly, Contributing Editor; Working Woman; Dial Magazine. *Literary Agent:* F Joseph Spieler. *Address:* 451 West 24th Street, New York, NY 10011, USA.

SMITH, David Jeddie, b. 19 Dec. 1942, Portsmouth, Virginia, USA. Professor of English. m. Deloras Mae Weaver, 31 Mar. 1966, Camden, North Carolina, USA, 1 son, 2 daughters. *Education:* BA English, University of Virginia, 1965; MA English, Southern Illinois University, 1968; PhD English, Ohio University, 1976. *Major Publications:* Poems: The Fisherman's Whore, 1974; Cumberland Station, 1977; Dream Flights, 1981; Goshawk, Antelope, 1979; Homage to Edgar Allen Poe, 1981; Oniliness (novel), 1981; In the House of the Judge, 1983; The Roundhouse Voice: Selected and New Poems, 1985. *Contributor to:* New Yorker; Antlantic Magazine; Poetry; Sewanee Review; Southern Review; The New Republic; Yale Review; Hudson Review; and many others. *Honours:* National Endowment for the Arts Poetry Fellowships, 1976, 1982; Guggenheim Fellowship in Poetry, 1982; Award for Literature, American Academy & Institute for Arts & Letters, 1979. *Memberships:* PEN; Associated Writing Programs (Vice-President, 1978); Poetry Society of America; Poetry Society of Virginia. *Literary Agent:* Timothy Seldes (Russell & Volkenning). *Address:* 1935 Stonehenge Drive, Richmond, VA 23225, USA.

SMITH, Dexter Jerome, b. 12 Feb. 1958, Slough, England. Journalist and Author; College Lecturer. *Education:* BSc, Economics, Honours, University of London; Certificate in Education, Distinction, Garnett College. *Literary Appointments:* Strategic Affairs Consultant, Defence, 1983–85; Special Correspondent, Defensa Latino Americana, 1983–, Defence Africa, 1984–. Miltronics, 1984–; Strategic Affairs Editor, Defence, 1985–. *Publication:* Why Yes to SDI, 1985. *Contributions to:* Defence; Defensa Latino Americana; Defence Africa; Miltronics; A Job of Work – Defence Looks at the Falklands; Teaching Politics; Journal of the Foreign Affairs Research Institute; Jane's Military Reveiw. *Address:* Whitegates, 124 Upton Court Road, Slough, Berkshire SL3 7ND, England.

SMITH, Dorothy Batton Rodriguez, b. 30 Nov. 1945, Minden, Louisiana, USA. Enterostomal Therapy Nurse. m. Harold E Smith, 20 Mar. 1982, Houston, Texas, 1 daughter. *Education:* BS, University of Northwest Louisiana; MSC, University of Colorado, *Publication:* Sexual Rehabilitation of the Urologic Cancer Patient, 1981. *Contributions to:* Journal of Enterostomal Theraphy; Nursing Clinics of North America; Clinics of Gastroenterology; Journal of Urology; Cancer Bulletin (34 articles and book chapters). *Honours:* IMWA Honourable Mention, Sexual Rehabilitation, 1982; EAET-ET Foundation Manuscript Award, 1984. *Membership:* American Medical Writers Association. *Address:* 5814 Immogene, Houston, TX 77074, USA.

SMITH, Duane Allen, b. 20 Apr. 1937, San Diego, California, USA. Professor of History. *Education:* BA, 1959, MA, 1961, PhD, 1964, University of Colorado, USA. *Publications include:* A Colorado History (with Ubbelohde and Benson), 1972; Editor Centennial, 1976; Horace Tabor, 1973; Silver Saga: Story of Caribou Colorado, 1974; Colorado Mining, 1977. *Honours:* American Association for State and Local History Certificate of Commendation for Horace Tabor, 1974; Little Joe Award, Colorado Mining Westerners Int, 1978. *Memberships:* Western Historical Association; Colorado Historical Society. *Address:* 2911 Cedar Avenue, Durango, CO 81301, USA.

SMITH, Dudley Gordon (Sir), b. 14 Nov. 1926, Cambridge. Member of Parliament. m. Catherine Miriam Amos, London, 11 June 1976, 1 son, 2 daughters by previous marriage. *Publications:* They Also Served,

1945; Harold Wilson: a Critical Biography, 1964. *Contributions:* Articles, mostly as member of parliament, for various newspapers & journals. Weekly column, Medical News, for several years. Regular contributor to industrial publications over 10-year period. *Honour:* Knight Bachelor, 1983. *Address:* Church Farm, Weston-under-Wetherley, Nr Leamington Spa, Warwickshire, England.

SMITH, Elsdon Coles, b. 25 Jan. 1903, Virginia, Illinois, USA. Retired Lawyer, Onomatologist. m. Clare Irvette Hutchins, 23 Dec. 1933, Chicago, 1 daughter. *Education:* BS, University of Illinois, 1925; LLB, Harvard, 1930. *Publications:* Naming Your Baby, 1943; The Story of Our Names, 1950; Personnal Names: An Annotated Bibliography, 1952; New Dictionary of American Family Names, 1972; Treasury of Name Lore, 1967; American Surnames, 1969; The Book of Smith, 1978. *Contributions to:* Names: Journal of American Name Society. *Memberships:* President 1951–54 and 1970, American Name Society; International Committee on Onomastic Sciences. *Address:* 8001 Lockwood Avenue, Skokie, IL 60077, USA.

SMITH, Emma, b. 21 Aug. 1923, Newquay, Cornwall, England. Writer. m. Richard Llewellyn Stewart-Jones (d. 1957), 31 Jan. 1951, Chelsea, 1 son, 1 daughter. *Publications:* Maiden's Trip, 1948; The Far Cry, 1949; Emily, 1959; Out of Hand, 1963; Emily's Voyage, 1966; No Way of Telling, 1972; The Opportunity of a Lifetime, 1978. *Contributions to:* Various magazines. *Honours:* Atlantic Award, short stories, 1948; John Llewellyn Rhys Memorial Prize, 1948; James Tait Black Black Memorial Prize, 1949. *Literary Agent:* Curtis Brown. *Address:* c/o Curtis Brown, 162-168 Regent Street, London W1R 5TB, England.

SMITH, Frederick Escreet, b. 4 Apr. 1922, Hull, Yorkshire, UK. Author; Playwright. m. 11 July 1945, Hull, 2 sons. *Publications include:* Novels: Of Masks & Minds, 1954; Laws Be That Enemy, 1955; Lydia Trendennis, 1957; The Grotto of Teberius, 1962; The Storm Knight, 1966; The Wider Sea of Love, 1968; A Killing for the Hawks, 1967; Waterloo, 1969; The Tormented, 1974; The War God, 1980; A Crossing of Stars, 1986; etc. Series of 633 Squadron novels, 1956–82; The Obsession 1984; Saffron's War, 1975, Saffron's Army, 1976. Plays: The Glass Prison; A House Divided. Screen Credits: 633 Squadron; The Devil Doll. Over 80 short stories, novels published in 25 countries. 6 other novels as D Farrell. *Honours:* Mark Twain Award, USA, 1967; Shortlisted, Winston Churchill Fellowship. *Memberships:* Writers Guild; Committee, early '70's Crime Writers Association. *Address:* 3 Hathaway Road, Southbourne, Bournemouth, Dorest BH6 3HH, England.

SMITH, H(arold) Wendell, b. 26 Sep. 1923, Topeka, Kansas, USA. Educator. m. (1) Virginia Lee Howson, 15 April 1946, Glendale, California, 1 son, 3 daughters. (2) E Nadine Andrews, 29 Mar. 1969, Santa Monica, California. *Education:* BA, 1948, MA, 1952, University of California, Los Angeles, USA. *Major Publications:* Modern English (with A L Lazarus & A MacLeish), 1971; On Paper: A Course in College Writing, Wadsworth, 3rd edition, 1982; The Craft of Prose (with R H Woodward), 1976; Elements of the Essay, 3rd Edition, 1983; A Glossary of Literature and Composition (with A L Lazarus), 1983; Readable Writing: Revising for Style, 1985; The Belmont Reader: Essays for Writers, 1986. *Memberships:* Modern Language Association; International Society for General Semantics. *Address:* Box 7522, Canyon Lake, CA 92380, USA.

SMITH, Hedrick Lawrence, b. 9 July 1933, Kilmacolm, Scotland. Journalist & Author. m. Ann Bickford, 27 June 1957, 1 son, 3 daughters. *Education:* BA Williams College, 1955; Balliol College, University of Oxford, England, 1955–56; Nieman Fellow, Harvard University, USA, 1969–70; D Litt Williams College, 1975; D Litt, Wittenberg University, 1984. *Major Publications:* The Pentagon Papers (co-author), 1972; The Russians, 1976; Reagan, The Man, The President,

1980. *Contributor to:* New York Times, Atlantic. *Honours:* Pulitzer Prize for International Reporting, 1974; Member of Reporting Team, Pultizer Prize for Public Services, 1972; Overseas Press Club Non-fiction Award, 1976. *Membership:* Gridiron Club, Washington DC, USA. *Literary Agent:* Julian Bach. *Address:* 3502 Shepherd Street, Chevy Chase, MD 20815, USA.

SMITH, H(orace) Bernard, b. 8 Mar. 1933, Walsall, England. Author, Writer and Freelance Journalist. m. (1) Veronica Bullows, 29 Sep. 1956, King's Norton, dissolved 1972 (2) Rosaline Sarah Haywood, 9 July 1973, Aldridge, England, 1 son, 2 daughters. *Education:* King's College, University of London; University of Aston, Birmingham; PhD; FAAI; FISTC; MBIM; MInstM; MJI; LBIPP. *Literary Appointments:* Editor, MCPF News; Editor, Microindexer. *Major Publications:* Architectural Photography, 1965; A Slight Lack of Definition, 1979; Quarrymen's Hospital, 1979; What Price the Rural Life? 1979; Better Letters, 1985. *Contributor to:* Reader's Digest; Sunday Express; Amateur Photographer; Practical Photography; Practical Motorist; and others; Scripts for BBC Television and Radio, and Independent Television. *Memberships:* Society of Authors; Writers' Guild of Great Britain; Institute of Journalists; Royal Society of Literature; PEN. *Literary Agent:* Murray Pollinger, London, England. *Address:* Lleifior, Malltraeth, Bodorgan, Isle of Anglesey, Gwynedd, LL62 5AF, Wales.

SMITH, Howard Everett Jr, b. 18 Nov. 1927, Gloucester, Massachusetts, USA. Writer. m. Louanne Norris, 1 June 1953, Dawson, Georgia, 1 son, 1 daughter. *Education:* BA, English, Colorado College, 1952. *Literary Appointments:* Editor/Writer, Basic Books Inc, 1962; Editor, McGraw Hill Book Company, 1967–75. *Publications include:* From Under the Earth, 1967; Giant Animals, 1977; A Complete Beginner's Guide to Mountain Climbing, 1977; An Oak Tree Dies & Journey Begins, with Louanne Norris, 1979; Killer Weather, 1982; A Naturalists Guide, 1985. *Contributions:* Articles, nature & science, published by American Museum of Natural History, 1965–66. *Honours:* 2 citations, Children's Book Council/National Science Teachers Association. *Literary Agent:* Don Congdon. *Address:* 128 Willow Street, Apt 2C, Brooklyn, NY 11201, USA.

SMITH, Howard Markell, b. 29 Dec. 1939, New Brighton, Pennsylvania, USA. Scientific writer/editor. m. Josephine Grogan Mellon, 13 June 1970, Baltimore, Maryland, 2 daughters. *Education:* BA, Thiel College; MA, University of Virginia. *Literary Appointments:* Editor, Jeffersonia: A Newsletter of Virginia Botany, 1974–79; Book Review Editor, Medical Communications, Journal of the American Medical Writers Association, 1978–81; Editor, Medical Communications, 1981–83. *Publications:* Partial Flora of the Society Islands: Ericaceae to Anocynaceae, (with M L Grant and F R Fosberg), 1974. *Contributions to:* Plant Life; Journal of Cell Science; Neuropharmacology; Journal American Podiatry Association; Jeffersonia; Virginia Journal of Science; Journal Pacific History; Elementary Genetics. *Memberships:* Director, Department of Education, American Medical Writers Association; Council of Biology Editors. *Address:* A H Robins Company, 1211 Sherwood Avenue, PO Box 26609, Richmond, VA 23261–6609, USA.

SMITH, Howard Ross, b. 6 July 1917, Iowa, USA. Retired Profesor of Management. m. 20 Feb. 1943, Athens, Georgia, 2 sons, 1 daughter. *Education:* BA, Simpson College, 1938; MA 1940, PhD 1945, Louisiana State University; Studies at University of Iowa, Stanford University and Harvard Graduate School of Business Administration. *Publications include:* Statistical Abstract of Georgia, editor, 1953; Economic History of the United States, 1955; Government and Business, 1958; Democracy and Public Interest, 1960; The Capitalist Imperative, 1975; Management: Making Organizations Perform, (with Professors Carroll, Kefalas and Watson), 1980; Management: Making Organizations Perform – A Book of Readings, (with

Professors Carroll, Kefalas and Watson), 1980; Numerous monographs and papers. *Contributions to:* Several journals including: Management Review; California Management Review; Collegiate Forum; Training and Development Journal; Journal of Business Research. *Memberships:* Phi Kappa Phi; Beta Gamma Sigma; Delta Sigma Pi; Pi Gamma Mu; Sigma Iota Epsilon; Secretary-Treaurer 1951–56, Vice President 1956–57; President 1958, Southern Economic Assocation; American Academy of Management; American Society of training and Development; Southern Management Association. *Address:* 382 West View Drive, Athens, GA 30606, USA.

SMITH, Iain Crichton, b. 1 Jan. 1928, Glasgow, Scotland. Author. m. Donalda Gillies Barnett, 16 July 1977, Perth, 2 step-sons. *Education:* MA (Hons), Aberdeen University. *Publications:* Consider the Lilies (Novel), 1968; A Field Full of Folk (Novel), 1982; Selected Poems, 1982; Selected Poems, 1984. *Contributions to:* Encounter; The Times Literary Supplement, Spectator, and many other publications. *Honours:* OBE, 1980; LL D, Dundee University, 1983; D Litt, Glasgow University, 1984. *Memberships:* Fellow, Royal Literary Society; Scottish Arts Council; Literary Committee. *Address:* Tigh NA Fuaran, Taynuilt, Argyll, Scotland.

SMITH, Julie, b. 25 Nov. 1944, Annapolis, Maryland, USA. Writer. *Education:* BA, University of Mississippi, 1965. *Publications:* Death Turns a Trick, 1982; The Sourdough Wars, 1984; True-Life Adventure, 1985. *Memberships:* Mystery Writers of America, Regional Vice-President, Northern California Chapter; Red-Headed League; Private Eye Writers of America. *Literary Agent:* Maureen Walters, Curtis Brown Ltd. *Address:* 5684 Ocean View Drive, Oakland, CA 94618, USA.

SMITH, Ken, b. 4 Dec. 1938, Rudston, East Yorkshire, England. Writer. m. 1. Ann Minnis, 1 August 1960, 2. Judi Benson, 4 July 1981, 2 sons, 2 daughters. *Education:* BA, Leeds University. *Literary Appointments:* Visiting Writer, Clark University, Worcester, Massachusetts, USA, 1972–73; Yorkshire Arts Writer in Residence, Leeds University, 1976–78; Writer in Residence, Kingston Polytechnic, Surrey, 1979–81; Writer in Residence, H M Prison Wormwood Scrubs, 1985–86. *Publications:* The Pity, 1967; Work Distances, 1972; Burned Books, 1981; The Poet Reclining, 1982; Terra, 1986; Chinese Whispers, 1986. *Contributions to:* London Magazine; Stand; London Review of Books, Literary Review; Poetry Review etc. *Honours:* Gregory Award 1964; Arts Council Bursary 1975. *Address:* 78 Friars Road, London E6 1LL, England.

SMITH, Ken Edward, b. 18 July 1944, Leeds, Yorkshire, England. University Lecturer. m. Wendy Marilyn Barber, 27 July 1968, 1 son, 1 daughter. *Education:* MA, B Phil, New College, Oxford; Phd, Wales. *Appointments include:* Lecturer in English, University College Wales, Aberystwyth, 1968–73; Lecturer in Literature 1973–83, Senior Lecturer, 1983–, University of Bradford, England. *Publications:* Outcrop, poetry, 1976; The Dialect Mine, Critical Study, 1979; Slight Damage, poetry, 1980; Instress, limited edition, 1980; West Yorkshire Dialect Poets, critical study, 1982; On Wilsden Hill, poetry, 1984. *Contributions to:* Pennine Platform; Orbis; Poetry and Audience; Poetry Wales; New Hope; editor, Transactions of the Yorkshire Dialect Society. *Memberships:* Pennine Poets; Bronte Society; President, Bradford University Poetry Society. *Address:* The Old Manse, Chapel Row, Wilsden, Bradford, Yorkshire BD15 OEQ, England.

SMITH, Larry, b. 11 Feb. 1943, Steubenville, Ohio, USA. Professor. m. A Ann Zaben, 3 July 1965, 1 son, 2 daughters. *Education:* BA, Muskingum College, 1965; MA 1969, PhD 1974, Kent State University. *Literary Appointments:* Professor of English & Humanities, Bowling Green State University; Director, Firelands writing Center, Editor of Publications; Editor, The Plough: North Coast review; Publisher, Bottom Dog Books. *Major Publications:* Growth: Poems & Sketches,

1976; Kenneth Patchen, 1978; Echo Without Sound (poems, with S Smigocki), 1981; Scissors, Paper, Rock, 1982; Lawrence Ferlinghetti: Poet-at-Large, 1983; Across these States, 1984. *Contributor to:* Poetry Now; Dictionary of Literary Biography; Wormwood Review; Chariton Review; and others. *Memberships:* Poets & Writers Inc; North Central Ohio Arts Council. *Address:* Department of English, Firelands College, Bowling Green State University, Huron OH 44839, USA.

SMITH, Margery, b. 21 March 1916, Nottingham, England. Teacher, Poet, Editor, Secretary. *Education:* Charlotte Mason College, Ambleside, PNEU Teacher. *Literary Appointments:* Poetry Board, Manifold Journal, 1963–69; Organiser, Portfolio of Story & Verse (PNEU), 1964–72; Executive Council, Charlotte Mason College Association, 1971–84; Editor, L'Umile Pianta (for association), 1972–79; Co-editor (with Hannah Kelly) 5th & 6th Anthologies of the Camden Poetry Group, 1979 & 1982. *Major Publications:* Poems: In Our Time, Favil, 1941; Still in my Hand, Outposts, 1964; In Transit, Outposts, 1981; Contributor to various anthologies, including: Poems of This War, Northern Contemporary Poets, 1947; Mitre, Kentucky Harvest, 1967; Without Adam, 1968; Laudamus Te; Doves for the Seventies, 1969; Look through a Diamond, 1971; Chaos of the Night, 1984. *Contributor to:* Poetry Review; Anglo-Welsh Review; Yoga Today; Outposts; The Glass; PNEU Journal; N A Mentor; South & West; and others. *Honours:* Poetry Review, Premium Awards, 1939, 1940; Rosanna Webb, 1967; 1st prizes for Sonnets Lucia Markham, Manifold, Anglo-Welsh Review, 1968. *Memberships:* Poetry Society UK, 1937–; General Council, 1967–69; Poetry Society of America, 1967–; Co-Founder, Honorary Secretary and Treasurer, Nottingham Poetry Society, 1941–42; Founder Fellow, International Poetry Society; Camden Poetry Group; Byron Society; Honorary Member, Shelley Society of New York, USA. *Address:* 12 Springfield Crescent, Horsham, West Sussex, RH12 2PP, England.

SMITH, Mark Power, b. 14 May 1958, Augusta, Georgia, USA. Medical Writer. *Education:* AA, Young Harris College, Georgia, 1978; BA, Emory University, Atlanta, 1980; MSc, Auburn University, Alabama, 1986; studied, University of California at Los Angeles and University of Southern California, 1983. *Literary Appointments:* Editorial associate, American Journal of Sports Medicine, 1981–82; Medical writer, Centinela Hospital Medical Center, Inglewood, California, 1983–84. *Contributions to:* Corn Creek Review, poetry; Young Harris College Literary Magazine; Emory Archon, poetry; Emory University Literary Magazine; assistant to various authors of articles in American Journal of Sports Medicine. *Honours:* Phi Theta Kappa, 1977; Annual Young Harris College Poetry Award, 1978; Ashmore Academic Scholarship, Emory University. *Membership:* American Medical Writers Association. *Address:* PO Box 65, Pine Mountain Valley, GA 31823, USA.

SMITH, Mark Richard, b. 19 Nov. 1935, Michigan, USA. Writer; Professor. m. Anthea Eatough, 1963, Newfoundland, Canada, 4 daugters. *Education:* BA, Northwestern University, 1960. *Literary Appointments:* Professor of English, University of New Hampshire, 1966–; Writer in Residence, Hollins College, 1981; Thornton Writer in Residence, Lynchburg College, 1984; Senior Fulbright Lecturer to Yugoslavia, 1985. *Publications:* Toyland, 1965; The Middleman, 1967; The Death of the Detective, 1974; The Moon Lamp, 1978; The Delphinium Girl, 1980; Doctor Blues, 1983; Smoke Street, 1984. *Honours:* Rockefeller Grant, 1965; Guggenheim Fellowship, 1968; Ingram Merrill Foundation Grant, 1976, 77; National Endowment for the Arts Fellowship, 1976. *Memberships:* Board member, Associated Writing Programmes, 1983–86. *Literary Agent:* Harriet Wasserman. *Address:* English Department, Hamilton-Smith, University of New Hampshire, Durham, NH 03824, USA.

SMITH, Michael Townsend, b. 5 Oct. 1935, Kansas City, Missouri, USA. Author. m. Michele Marie Hawley, 22 June 1974, Denver, Colorado, 2 sons. *Literary*

Appointments: Associate Editor, Theatre Critic, The Village Voice, New York, 1959–74; Arts Editor, The Taos (New Mexico) News, 1977–78; Music Critic, The (New London, Connecticut) Day, 1981–. *Publications:* Eights Plays from Off-Off-Broadway, with Nick Orzel, 1966; Theatre Trip, 1969; More Plays from Off-Off-Broadway, 1972; also numerous plays. *Honours:* Brandeis University Creative Arts Citation, 1965; Obie Award, 1971; Rockefeller Foundation Award, 1976. *Address:* 86 Main Street, Westerly, RI 02891, USA.

SMITH, Richard Paul, b. 9 Mar. 1949, Bremerton, Washington. Writer, Photographer. m. Lucy J La Faive, 15 May 1976. *Education:* BS degree. *Major Publications:* Deer Hunting, 1978; Animal Tracks and Signs of North America, 1982; The Book of the Black Bear, 1985; Hunting Rabbits and Hares, 1986. *Contributor to:* Innumerable periodicals. *Honours:* Conservation Communicator of the Year, Michigan United Conservation Clubs, 1978; Writer of the Year Award, Upper Peninsula of Michigan Writers, 1978; Bass'N Gal Writing Award in magazine category, 1982; 3rd Prize, Eagle Rare Writing Award in magazine category, 1983. *Memberships:* Outdoor Writers Association of America; Michigan Outdor Writers Association (Board of Directors). *Address:* 814 Clark Street, Marquette, MI 49855, USA.

SMITH, Robert Dickie, b. 13 Aug. 1928, Framingham, Massachusetts, USA. Catholic Priest. *Education:* BA, Harvard University, 1949. *Publications:* The Mark of Holiness, 1961; Comparative Miracles, 1965; The Elegance of Catholic Faith, 1978. *Contributions to:* The Wanderer, columnist. *Address:* 6 Cottage Street, Haverhill, MA 01830, USA.

SMITH, Robert Wayne, b. 3 Jan. 1926, Kokomo, Indiana, USA. College Professor. *Education:* Indiana State University; AB 1950, MA 1951, University of Southern California; PhD, University of Wisconsin, 1957; University of Michigan. *Publications:* Christ & the Modern Mind, editor, 1972; Art of Rhetoric in Alexandria, 1974; Over 200 biographical enitries, Ancient Greek & Roman Rhetoricians, 1968. *Contributions to:* Quarterly Journal of Speech; Western Speech; American Speech; Christianity Today; Parliamentary Journal; Journalism Quarterly; Central States Speech Journal; etc. *Honour:* Research Grant, Old Dominion Fund, University of Virginia, 1961. *Memberships:* Speech Communication Association; Southern Speech Association; Central States Speech Association. *Address:* 632 Wright Avenue, Alma, MI 48801, USA.

SMITH, Rodney Robert Templeton, b. 19 Dec. 1946, Edinburgh, Scotland. Journalist; Broadcaster. m. Margaret Sheridan Besford, 1 May 1982, London, 1 daughter. *Education:* BSc, Mining Engineering, Witwatersrand University, South Africa. *Contributions to:* Financial Times; Observer; Various magazines. *Address:* 1 South Rise, St George's Fields, London W2, England.

SMITH, Rodney Theodore, b. 13 Apr. 1948, Washington DC, USA. Teacher; Writer. *Education:* BA, Philosophy, University of North Carolina; MA, English Literature, Appalachian State University. *Literary Appointments:* Editor, Cold Mountain Review; Editor, Open House; Poetry Editor, Southern Humanities Review; Managing Editor, Caesura. *Publications:* Waking Under Snow, 1975; Good Water, 1979; Rural Route, 1981; Beasts Did Leap, 1982; From the High Dive, 1983; Finding the Path, 1983; Roosevelt Unbound, 1984. *Contributions to:* Southern Poetry Review; International Poetry Review; Kansas Quarterly; Texas Review; Florida Review; South Carolina Review; Kentucky Poetry Review; Memphis State Review; Seattle Review; Georgia Journal; Sou'wester. *Honours:* Miscellany Poetry Prize, 1973; John Masefield Poetry Award, 1982; Birminghamn Literary Festival Award, 1982. *Literary Agent:* F N Stewart. *Address:* 1709 2nd Avenue, Opelika, AL 36801, USA.

SMITH, Roger William, b. 28 Nov. 1938, London, England. Journalist. m. Terry Jaqueline, 7 Feb. 1976, Richmond, North Yorkshire, 2 daughters. *Publications:* The Winding Trail anthology (editor), 1981; Walking in Scotland (editor), 1981; Penguin Book of Orienteering, 1982; Outdoor Scotland, 1982; Weekend Walking, 1982; Guide to the Scottish Borders, 1983; Jet Guide to Scotland's Countryside, 1985. *Literary Appointments:* Editor, The Great Outdoors. *Contributions to:* Scottish Field; Climber and Rambler. *Memberships:* Member of Council, National Trust for Scotland; Chairman, Scottish Wild Land Group; Member of Council, Scottish Conservation Projects Trust; Honorary Vice-President, Habitat, Scotland. *Address:* St Ronan's, 93 Queen Street, Alva, Clackmannan, FK12 5AH, Scotland.

SMITH, Thomas (Broun), b. 3 Dec. 1915, Glasgow, Scotland. General Editor, Laws of Scotland; Stair Memorial Encyclopaedia. m. Ann Dorothea Tindall, 3 Feb. 1940, Exmouth, 1 son deceased, 2 daughters. *Education:* BA, MA, BCL, DCL, Oxford University; LL.D, Edinburgh University. *Publications:* Doctrines of Judicial Precedent in Scots Law, 1952; Scotland: The Development of its Laws and Constitution, 1955; British Justice: The Scottish Contribution, 1961; Studies Critical and Comparative, 1962; A Short Commentary on the Law of Scotland, 1962; Property Problems in Sale, 1978; Basic Rights and Their Enforcement, 1979; Holy Willie, 1984. *Contributor to:* Many professional journals including Acta Juidica; Virginia Law Review; Tulane Law Review. *Honours:* Queens Counsel, 1956; Fellow, British Academy, 1958, Royal Society of Edinburgh, 1977; Honorary LLD, Capetown, 1959, Aberdeen, 1969, Glasgow, 1978; Knight Bachelor, 1981. *Memberships:* British Academy; Royal Society of Edinburgh. *Address:* 18 Royal Circus, Edinburgh, EH3 6SS, Scotland.

SMITH, Thomas Henry, b. 19 Mar. 1933, Schenectady, New York, USA. Professor of Literature; Poet. m. Virginia DeAngelis, 27 Jan. 1965, Highland Park, New Jersey, 2 sons. *Education:* BA, State University of New York, Albany, 1956; MA, Rutgers University, 1958; ABD, Rutgers University, 1962. *Literary Appointments:* Professor of Literature, Castleton State College, 1964–; Instructor in Poetry, Cape Cod Writer's Conference, Aug. 1985. *Publications:* Singing the Middle Ages, 1982; Traffic, 1984. *Contributions to:* American Scholar; Audience; Bay Windows; Deloit Poetry Journal; Beyond Baroque; Caroline Quarterly; Chicago Review; Dark Horse; Epoch; Far Point; Minnesota Review; Northern New England Review; Pulpsmith; Satire Newsletter; Swallow's Tale; Truck; Virginia Quarterly Review; Haiku in Dragonfly; Frogpond; Gusto; RED; Pagoda; Wind Chimes (poems). *Honour:* New Book Award from Beyond Baroque Foundation for chapbook Some Traffic, 1976; *Memberships:* Poetry Society of America; Academy of American Poets; Poets & Writers Incorporated; Haiku Society of America; Lewis Carroll Society of North America. *Address:* Box 223, Castleton, VT 05735, USA.

SMITH, V Kerry, b. 11 Mar. 1945, Jersey City, New Jersey, USA. Centennial President of Economics. m. Pauline, 10 May 1969, 1 son, 1 daughter. *Education:* PhD, Economics, Rutgers University, 1970. *Literary Appointments:* Board of Editors: Land Economics, Quarterly Review of Economics and Business; Editor, Advances in Applied Micro-Economics (annual series published by JAI Press). *Publications:* Monte Carlo Methods: Their Role for Econometrics, 1973; Technical Change, Relative Prices and Environmental Resource Evaluation, 1974; The Costs of Congestion: An Econometric Analysis of Wilderness Recreation, (with C J Cichetti), 1976; Structure and Properties of a Wilderness Travel Simulator: An Application to the Spanish Peaks Area, (with J V Krutilla), 1976; The Economic Consequences of Air Pollution, 1976; Scarcity and Growth Reconsidered, (Editor and Contributing Author), 1979; Explorations in Natural Resource Economics, (Co-Editor and Contributing Author with J V Krutilla), 1982; Environmental Policy Under Reagan's

Executive Order: The Role of Benefit-Cost Analysis, (Editor and Contributing Author), 1984; Benefit Measurement and Water Quality Improvements: An Econometric Analysis, (with W H Desvousges), 1986. Several Monographs. *Contributions to:* professional journals, etc. *Memberships:* American Economic Association; American Statistical Association; Econometric Society; Southern Economic Association; Association of Environmental and Resource Economists (holder of several offices including President, 1985–87), several other organizations. *Address:* Department of Economics, Campus Box 52B, Vanderbilt University, Nashville, TN 37235, USA.

SMITH, Virginia Everett, b. 12 Feb. 1909, Niskayuna, New York, USA. Advertising Copywriter. Divorced, 1 son, 1 daughter. *Education:* AB, Bryn Mawr College, 1931; New York University School of Commerce, 1946; UCI Creative Writing, 1975. *Publications:* Lion Rugs from Fars, 1982; Inhale, Exhale, Hold, 1985. *Contributor to:* (reviews) Southwest Review; Piedmont Literary Society. *Honours:* First Prizes, Inaugural Issue, Western Poetry Quarterly, for, June Legend; California State Poetry Contest for Trompe l'Oeil, 1975; Book Prize, California State Poetry Contest for, Grass, 1975; Best Poem of 1981, Yearbook of American Poetry for, Daysleep; Honorable Mention, 1979 Laguna Hills Writers and Publishers contest for, Russian Ways and Ours, in book, Siberians Picnic Hip-Deep in Snow; Third Prize, Laguna Hills Contest, 1982, a sonnet on Edna St Vincent Millay Stamp, Commemorative; Second Prize, Florida State Poetry Contest, 1982 for Balcony; Third Prize, Blue Unicorn Annual Contest, 1985 for, Lens Implant. *Address:* 2286–Q Via Puerta, Laguna Hills, CA 92653, USA.

SMITH, Vivian Brian, b. 3 June 1933, Hobart, Tasmania. University Lecturer. m. Sybille Maria, 12 Feb. 1960, 1 son, 2 daughters. *Education:* MA, Tasmania; PhD, Sydney. *Publications:* The Other Meaning (Poems) 1956; Tide Country (Poems) 1982; Selected Poems, 1985; Vance and Nettie Palmer (Critical Biography) 1975. *Contributions to:* Quadrant; Meanjin; Southerly etc. *Honours:* New South Wales Premiers Award, 1982; Grace Leven Prize, 1982. *Membership:* Australian Society of Authors. *Address:* 19 McLeod Street, Mosman, New South Wales, Australia 2088.

SMITHER, Elizabeth Edwina, b. 15 Sep. 1941, New Plymouth, New Zealand. Librarian; Freelance Journalst. m. Michael Duncan Smither, 31 Aug. 1963, New Plymouth, 2 sons, 1 daughter. *Education:* University student; NZLA Certificate. *Literary Appointments:* Writing Bursary, 1977; Literary Fellow, Auckland University, 1984. *Publications:* Tug Brothers, 1983, for children; First Blood, 1983; Brother Love, Sister Love, 1986. Poetry collections: Here Come the Clouds, 1975; You're Very Seductive William Carlos Williams, 1978; The Sarah Train, 1980; Casanova's Ankle, 1981; The Legend of Marcello Mastroianni's Wife, 1981; Shakespeare Virgins, 1983; Professor Musgrove's Canary, 1985. *Contributions to:* Listener; Landfall; Islands; Meanjin; Poetry Australia; PN Review; Times Literary Supplement; London Magazine and numerous others. *Honours:* Freda Buckland Award, 1983. *Membership:* PEN, New Zealand. *Address:* 19a Mount View Place, New Plymouth, New Zealand.

SMITHSON, Alison Margaret, b. 22 June 1928. Architect. m. Peter Denham Smithson, 18 Aug. 1949, London, 1 son, 2 daughters. *Education:* Dip Arch (dist), Department of Architecture, Newcastle-upon-Tyne, University of Durham, 1949. *Publications include:* Without Rhetoric, 1975; The Tram Rats 1976; Calendar of Christmas, 1976; The Christmas Tree, 1976; Places Worth Inheriting, 1978; Anthology of Christmas, 1979; 24 Doors to Christmas, 1979; Anthology of Scottish Christmas, and Hogmanay, 1980; Heroic Period Modern Architecture, 1981; The Shift, 1982; Team 10 Out of Ciam, 1982; The 1930's, 1985. *Contributor to:* Before 1975: Architectural Design and others; After 1975; International Architecture magazines. *Address:* Cato Lodge, 24 Gilston Road, London SW10 9SR, England.

SMITHYMAN, Kendrick, b. 9 Oct. 1922. Senior Tutor. m. (1) Mary Stanley Smithyman, deceased 1980, 3 sons, (2) Margaret Ann Edgcumbe, 1981. *Education:* Seddon Memorial Technical College, Auckland, New Zealand; Auckland Teachers College; Auckland University College. *Literary Appointments:* Visiting Fellow in Commonwealth Literature, University of Leeds, England, 1969; Currently Senior Tutor, Department of English, University of Auckland. *Publications:* Seven Sonnets, 1946; The Blind Mountain, 1951; The Gay Trapese, 1955; The Night Shift: Poems on Aspects of Love, (co-author), 1957; Inheritance, 1962; Flying to Palmerston, 1968; Earthquake Weather, 1974; The Seal in the Dolphin Pool, 1974; Dwarf With a Billiard Cue, 1978; Stories about Wooden Keybourds, 1985. *Contributions to:* Anthologies including: A Book of New Zealand Verse, 1951; New Zealand Poetry Yearbook, 1951–54; An Anthology of New Zealand Verse, 1966; Recent Poetry on New Zealand, 1965; Commonwealth Poems of Today, 1967; Poetry New Zealand, 1971–; Fifteen Contemporary New Zealand Poets, 1980; Oxford Book of Contemporary New Zealand Poetry, 1982; The Penguin Book of New Zealand Verse, 1985. *Address:* Deparment of English, University of Auckland, Auckland, New Zealand.

SMUTS, Dene, b. 13 July 1949, South Africa. Editor. m. Dr Steve Louw, 16 July 1977, Cape Town, 1 son, 1 daughter. *Education:* BA, English, Honours, University of Stellenbosch. *Appointments:* Assistant editor, Sarie, 1976–77; Editor, Fair Lady, 1983–. *Honours:* Stellenbosch Farmers Wineries Awards for Enterprising Journalism, 1978, 1981. *Address:* Fair Lady, P O Box 1802, Cape Town 8000, South Africa.

SMYRL, Frank Herbert, b. 16 Feb. 1938, Tyler, Texas, USA. College Teacher. m. Carolyn Janet McWilliams, 3 June 1961, Tyler, Texas, 1 son, 1 daughter. *Education:* BA, 1959, MA, 1961. University of Texas at Austin, USA; PhD, 1968, University of Oklahoma. *Literary Appointments:* Instructor, San Antonio College, 1961–64; Assistant Professor, Associate Professor, East Texas State University, 1967–73; Professor, University of Texas at Tyler, 1973–. *Major Publications:* Poley Morgan: Son of a Texas Scalawag, 1982; The Twenty Eighth Star: Texas during the period of Early Statehood 1846–61, 1983; Texas in Gray: The Civil War Years 1861–65, 1983. *Contributor to:* Southwestern Historical Quarterly; Chronicles of Smith County, Texas. *Honours:* Distinguished Alumnus, Tyler Junior College, 1976; Hudnall Professor of American Affairs, University of Texas at Tyler, 1984. *Address:* 3900 University Boulevard, Tyler, TX 75701, USA.

SMYTHE, Colin Peter, b. 2 Mar. 1942, Maidenhead, Berkshire, England. Publisher. *Education:* BA, 1963, MA, 1966, Trinity College, Dublin University, Republic of Ireland. *Publications include:* A Guide to Coole House, The Home of Lady Gregory, 1973, revised 1983. General Editor: The Coole Edition of Lady Gregory's Writings, 14 volumes published of planned 21 volumes, 1970; Collected Works of G W Russell, with Henry Summerfield, 1977. Editor: The Coole Edition of Lady Gregory's Writings, volumes 13 and 19; Bibliography of the Writing of W B Yeats. Various volumes of poetry. *Honours:* Knight of Merit with Star, Sacred and Military Constantinian Order of St George, 1985; Gold Cross of Merit, Polish Republic, 1984. *Memberships include:* Past Chairman, Bibliography Sub-committee, Executive committee member, International Association for Study of Anglo-Irish Literature. *Address:* P O Box 6, Gerrards Cross, Buckinghamshire SL9 8XA, England.

SNAPE, Christopher Paul, b. 30 Dec. 1948, Chester, England. Playwright. m. Judith Mary Gibbs (Norman), 30 Dec. 1978, Shaldon, Devon, 2 daughters. *Education:* Royal Military Academy, Sandhurst; Drama Centre, London. *Membership:* Writers Guild of Great Britain. *Address:* Pyt House Farmhouse, Tisbury, Salisbury, Wiltshire, England.

SNAPES, Joan, b. 25 July 1925, Treales, Lancashire, England. Writer; Illustrator, Childrens books. m. 18 Sep.

1948, London, 2 sons. *Publications:* Another Pet for Peter, 1978; The Kick that Went Wild, 1978; Mr Tuckett Moves to Town, 1978; Just the Place for a Cat, 1979; Buffy, 1981. *Address:* Wayside, Little Preston, Northamptonshire, England.

SNELLGROVE, Laurence Ernest, b. 2 Feb. 1928, London, England. Author. m. Jean Hall, 5 Apr. 1951, Oxford, 1 son. *Education:* BA; Associate of College pf Preceptors. *Publications:* From Kitty Hawk To Outer Space, 1960; From Steamcarts to Minicars, 1961; From Coracles to Cunarders, 1962; From Rocket to Railcar, 1963' Suffragettes and Votes For Women, 1963; Franco and the Spanish War, 1964; Modern World Since 1870, 1968; Ancient world, (with R J Cootes), 1971; Early Modern Age, 1972; Picture The Past, 5 volumes, 1978-81; Wide Range History Stories, 1978-80; History Around You, 1982-83; Storyline History, 1985. *Contributions to:* Storyteller. *Address:* 23 Harvest Hill, East Grinstead, West Sussex RH19 4BU, England.

SNIDER, Jerry Don, b. 14 Nov. 1952, Lexington, Missouri, USA. Publisher; Editor. *Publications:* Editor, The Architecture of St Charles Avenue, 1977. Editor, regular contributor to, Magical Blend Magazine. *Address:* P O Box 11303 San Francisco, CA 94101, USA.

SNIDER, Richard Michael (Rick), b. 19 July 1960, Washington, District of Columbia, USA. Editor; Writer. m. Lisa Marie Koscheka, 20 Dec. 1980, Waldorf, Maryland, 1 daughter. *Education:* BS Journalism, University of Maryland, College Park, 1982. *Appointments:* Sports Reporter, The Washington Times; Editor, Football Forecast (national weekly tabloid); Correspondent for Reuters and Sports Network; Editor, Gaming International. *Publications:* Ghost Writer: Johnny Unitas Rating the Pros, 1983; currently working on book involving horse racing. *Contributor to:* Weight Watchers, Flex, Gaming International, Turf and Sport Digest, Football Forecast and Betting Sports. *Membership:* White House Press Association. *Address:* 1843 Aberdeen Circle, Crofton, MD 21114, USA.

SNODGRASS, Ann Arlene, b. 5 May 1958, Iowa, USA. University Instructor. *Education:* Certificate, New York University Book Publishing Workshop, 1979; BA, University of Iowa, USA, 1980; Certificate, University of Vienna, Austria, 1980; MA, The Johns Hopkins University, USA, 1981; PhD Candidate, University of Utah. *Literary Appointments:* Poetry reader, Ploughshares, 1981-82; Poetry Editor, 1983-85, Editor, 1985-86, Quarterly West. *Contributor to:* Paris Review; New Letters (translations); Quarterly West (reviews); Carolina Quarterly; Police Beat; RUNE; Antioch Review; Sonora Review; Telescope; Black Warrior Review (poetry). *Honours:* Resident, Yaddo Arts Colony, 1982; Honorable Mention, Academy of American Poets Prize, 1984, 1985; Renato Poggioli Award for translation (PEN American Center), 1985. *Address:* 1121 1st Avenue apt 3, Salt Lake City, UT 84103, USA.

SNOW, Helen Foster, b. 21 Sep. 1907. Author; Researcher; Genealogist. m. Edgar Snow, 25 Dec. 1932, Tokyo, Japan. *Education:* University of Utah, 1925-27; Yenching University, Peking, China, 1934-35. *Appointments:* Foreign Correspondent, Scripps-Canfield Newspaper League, Seattle, Washington, 1931; Correspondent, China Weekly Review, Peking, 1935-37; Associate Editor, Democracy Magazine, Peking, 1937; Book Reviewer, 1941-46, Saturday Review of Literature, New York; Co-founder 1938, Chinese Industrial Cooperatives, with Edgar Snow and Rewi Alley, revived in China, 1983. *Publications:* Inside Red China, 1939; China Builds for Democracy, 1941; Song of Ariran, 1941; The Chinese Labor Movement, 1945; The Chinese Communists, 1952; Fables and Parables, 1952; Women in Modern China, 1967; My China Years (Brought by CBS for TV Series), 1984; etc. *Contributor to:* China Weekly Review; New Republic Asia; Saturday Review of Literature; Readers Digest; Ladies Home Journal; many others. *Honours:* International Institute of Arts and Letters, Lindau-Bodensee, 1960; Honorary

Doctorate of Letters, St Mary of the Woods College, Indiana, 1981; One of 66 Nominees for Nobel Prize for Peace, 1981-82. *Literary Agent:* Peter Pampack, New York. *Address:* 148 Mungertown Road, Madison, CT 06443, USA.

SNOW, Philip Albert, b. 7 Aug. 1915, Leicester, England. Author. m. Anne Harris, 2 May 1940, Suva, Fijian Islands, 1 daughter. *Education:* Open Exhibitioner in history, Christs College, 1934-37, MA Honours, Colonial Administrative Service Course, 1937-38, Cambridge. *Publications:* Civil Defence Services, 1943; Fijian Customs, with G K Roth, 1944; Cricket in the Fiji Islands, 1949; Report of Visit of Three Bursars to United States and Canada, co-author, 1965; Best Stories of the South Seas, 1967; Bibliography of Fiji, Tonga and Rotuma, 1969; The People from the Horizon, with Stefanie Waine, 1979; Stranger and Brother: A Portrait of C P Snow, 1982. *Contributions to:* Sunday Times; Daily Telegraph; Times Literary Supplement; Dictionary of National Biography; Times; Discovery; Go; American Anthropologist; Journal of Polynesian Society; Journal of Royal Anthropological Institute; Société des Océanistes; Wisden's Cricketers Almanac. *Honours:* MA, 1940; FRAI, 1952; Justice of the Peace, Warwickshire, 1967-76, West Sussex, 1976-; MBE, 1979; FRSA, 1984; OBE, 1985; Foreign Specialist Award, USA Government, 1964; Vice Patron, Fiji Cricket Association, 1946-; President, Bursars Association of Great Britain and Commonwealth, 1962-65; Honorary Life Member, MCC, 1970-; Chairman, Associate Member Countries, International Cricket Conference, 1982-; Captain, Fiji Cricket Team touring New Zealand, 1948. *Memberships:* Vice President, Fiji Society, 1944-52; President, Worthing Society 1982-. *Address:* Gables, Station Road, Angmering, Sussex BN16 4HY, England.

SNOWDEN, Alan, b. 14 Dec. 1920, London, England. Editor. m. Kathleen, 18 July 1943, Finchley, 1 son, 1 daughter. *Education:* London College of Printing. *Literary Appointments:* RAF Signals Security Press, 1939-46; Daily Sketch, 1947-61; Daily Telegraph, 1961-85; Editor, The Magic Circular 1972-. *Contributor to:* British and American Magic Magazines. *Address:* 5 Folkington Corner, Woodside Park, Finchley, London N12 7BH, England.

SNOWMAN, Daniel, b. 4 Nov. 1938, London, England. Producer. m. Janet Linda Levison, 17 Dec. 1975, Hove, Sussex, 1 son, 1 daughter. *Education:* BA, 1st class honours, Cambridge University, 1961; MA, Cornell University, USA, 1963. *Literary Appointments:* Producer of talks, features and documentaries, British Broadcasting Corporation, 1967-. *Publications:* USA: The Twenties to Vietnam, 1968, reprinted as America Since 1920, 1984; Eleanor Roosevelt, 1970; Kissing Cousins: An Interpretation of British and American Culture 1945-1975, 1977; If I Had Been....Ten Historical Fantasies, 1979; The Amadeus Quartet: The Men and the Music, 1981; The World of Placido Domingo, 1985. *Contributions to:* The British General Election of 1966, 1966; Since 1945: Aspects of Contemporary World History, 1966, 71; The American Destiny: An Illustrated Bicentennial History of the United States, 1976; Introduction to American Studies, 1981; numerous American newspapers and British journals including, Denver Post, Amerillo Globe-News; The Economist, English Historical Review, Jewish Chronicle, Journal of American Studies, Listener, New Society, New Statesman, Over 21, Political Studies, Sunday Times, Tribune. *Honours:* Invited speaker and lecturer at various universities and professional organisations, USA, Canada and UK. *Address:* 47 Wood Lane, Highgate, London N6 5UD, England.

SNYDER, Francis Gregory, b. 26 June 1942, Madison, Wisconsin, USA. University Teacher. m. Sian Miles, 23 Aug. 1967, Clynnog, North Wales, 1 son. *Education:* BA Honours, Yale, 1964; Fulbright Scholar, Institut d'Etudes Politiques de Paris, 1964-65; JD, Harvard Law School, 1968; Doctorat de Spécialité, Universié de Paris, 1973. *Publications:* One Party

Government in Mali, 1965; Law and Population in Senegal, 1977; Capitalism anf Legal Change, 1981; Law of the Common Agricultrual Policy, 1985; The Political Economy of Law, (co-editor), 1985. *Contributions to:* Law and Society Review; Social Anthropology and Law; British Journal of Law and Society. *Honours:* Charles Washburn Clark Prize, 1964; Wrexham Prize, 1964; Fulbright Grant, 1964–65; SSRC-ACLS Foreign Area Fellowship, 1968–70; Wenner-Gren Foundation Fellowship, 1970; Travel and Research Grant in International Development, IDRC; Herskovits Prize nominee, 1981. *Memberships:* Phi Beta Kappa; Massachusetts Bar Association; Society of Public Teachers of Law; Editorial boards: Law and Society Review, Review of African Political Economy, Journal of Legal Pluraliam. *Address:* School of Law, University of Warwick, Coventry CV4 7AL, England.

SNYDER, Howard Albert, b. 9 Feb. 1940, Santo Domingo, Dominican Republic. Author. m. Janice Marian Lucas, 18 Aug. 1962, Marysville, Michigan, USA, 3 sons, 1 daughter. *Education:* BA, Greenville College, Greenville, Illinois; BD, Asbury Theological Seminary, Wilmore, Kentucky; PhD, University of Notre Dame, Notre Dame, Indiana. *Publications:* 100 Years at Apring Arbor, 1973; The Problem of Wineskins, 1975; The Community of the King, 1977; The Radical Wesley and Patterns for Church Renewal, 1980; Liberating the Church: The Ecology of Church and Kingdom, 1983; A Kingdom Manifesto, 1985. *Contributions to:* Christianity Today; The Witenburg Door; Sojourners; The Other Side; United Evangelical Action; Light and Life; Presbyterian Journal; etc. *Honours:* Honorary Doctor of Divinity, Asbury Theological Seminary, 1976. *Memberships:* American Society of Missiology; Wesleyan Theological Society. *Address:* 4918 North Whipple St Chicago, IL 60625, USA.

SNYDER, Leslie, b. 26 July 1945, Newark, New Jersey, USA. Author. m. George J Conway, 14 June 1973, Malibu, 3 sons. *Publications:* Why Gold?, 1974; Gold and Black Gold, 1974; Justice or Revolution, 1979. *Contributor to:* The Freeman. *Address:* 30070 NE 82nd Avenue, Battle Ground, WA 98604, USA.

SOCOLOFSKY, Homer Edward, b. 20 May 1922, Tampa, Kansas, USA. Professor of History. m. Helen Margot Wright, 23 Nov. 1946, Westmorland, Kansas, 4 sons, 2 daughters. *Education:* BA 1944, MS 1947, Kansas State University; PhD, University of Missouri, 1954. *Literary Appointments:* History Editor, Kansas Quarterly, 1969–; Book Review Editor, Journal of the West, 1978–. *Publications:* Arthur Capper, Publisher, Politican, Philanthropist, 1962; Historical Atlas of Kansas, (with Huber Self), 1972; Landlord William Scully, 1979. *Contributions to:* Over 40 articles in journals and anthologies. *Honours:* RS: Award of Merit, American Academy for State and Local History, 1963; Westerners International Co-Founder Award, 1973; Edgar Langsdorf Award for Excellence in Writing, 1983. *Memberships:* President 1975–76, Board of Directors, Executive Committee, Kansas State Historical Society; President 1969, Agricultural History Society; Executive Council 1979–81, Western History Association. *Address:* Department of History, Kansas State University, Manhattan, KS 66506, USA.

SODERSTROM, Edward Jonathan, b. 17 Nov. 1954, Grand Rapids, Michigan, USA. Director, Office of Technology Applications, Oak Ridge National Laboratory. m. Gail Louise DeWitt, 25 June 1977, Grand Rapids, 2 daughters. *Education:* BA, Psychology, Hope College; PhD Psychology, Northerstern University, Evanston. *Appointments Include:* Head, Office of Technology Applications, 1984–, Leader, Technology Transfer Research Group, Energy Division, 1984–, Oak Ridge National Laboratory. *Publications:* Social Impact Assessment: Experimental Methods and Approaches, 1981; The Psycho-social Impacts of Restarting Three Mile Island Unit 1, 1986; Book Chapters in various books. *Contributor to:* Evaluation Review; Energy; Energy Systems and Policy; Risk Analysis, etc. *Honours:* Presidential Scholar, Hope College, 1972; Psi Chi,

1974; Sigma Chi Senior Research Award, Hope College, 1976; Phi Beta Kappa, 1976; Graduated, Magna Cum Laude, Hope College, 1976. *Address:* Oak Ridge National Laboratory, P O Box X, Oak Ridge, TN 37831, USA.

SODERSTROM, Neil D, b. 31 Mar. 1943, Duluth, Minnesota, USA. Editor; Book Producer. m. Hannelore Pfiz, 3 Feb. 1968, Alexandria, Virginia, 1 son. *Education:* BA. *Literary Appointments:* Managing Editor, Camping Journal, 1970–71; Senior Editor, Popular Science and Outdoos Life book clubs, Times Mirror Magazines Inc, 1973–84; President, Soderstrom Publishing Group Inc, 1984–. *Publications:* How To Drive To Prevent Accidents, (with E D Fales), 1971; Heating Your Home with Wood, 1978; Chainsaw Savvy, 1981. *Contributions to:* Popular Science; Home Mechanix; Family Handyman; Outdoor Life; Harrowsmith; Camping Journal; Backpacking Journal; Travel; Outdoor Life; Consumer's Research; American Forests; Small World. *Membership:* Officer, National Association of Home and Workshop Writers. *Address:* P O Box S, Shenorock, NY 10587, USA.

SODUMS, Dzintars, b. 13 May 1922, Riga, Latvia. Pensioner. m. Skaidrite Kronbergs, 2 sons. *Education:* Riga University, Latvia, 1942–43; Numerous correspondence courses; Courses, International Typographical Union Training Center, Colorado Springs, USA. *Appointments include:* War Correspondent, German-led International war Correspondents Platoon (later Company), Latvian Legion (drafted), 1943–44; Typographer, Stockholm, Sweden, 1945–63, Boston, Massachusetts, USA 1964–73. *Publications:* Poetry Tris Autori (Three Authors), with Velta Snikers & Ojars Jegens, Stockholm, 1950; novel, Taisam Tilty par Plasu, juru (Build a Bridge Over the Wide Sea), New York, 1957; Latvian translation of James Joyce's Ulysses, Vasteras, Sweden, 1960. *Contributions to:* Latvian exile literary magazines, Cela Zimes, London, UK & 'Juana Gaita', Canada, 1950's. *Memberships include:* Swedish Typographical Union, Stockholm, 1960–63; Boston Typogr Union Nr 13, 1964–73; International PEN Latvian Centre, Stockholm, Sweden, 1979–; LARA (Latvian Writers Association in Exile), 1984–. *Address:* 66 Bassett Street, Apt 63, Lynn, MA 01902, USA.

SOESBE, Douglas, b. 22 Sep. 1948, Portland, Oregon, USA. Motion Picture Story Analyst. *Education:* BA, MA, Portland State University. *Publications:* Children in a Burning House, 1986. *Literary Agent:* Stephen Blackwelder, J & S Literary Services, New York, USA. *Address:* 3269 Rowena Avenue, Los Angeles, CA 90027, USA.

SOETE, Gerard Andre, b. 29 Jan. 1920, Pittem, Belgium. Inspector General of Police (retired). m. Liliane Desprez, 15 Aug. 1948, Maniema, 5 daughters. *Education:* Teachers' College, Germanic Languages, Philosophy, Criminology and Police Techniques etc. *Publications:* De Achterhoede (The Rear Guard), 1967; Negropolis, 1971; Keerverbod, (No U Turn) 1976; De Stroom (The River) 1976; De Arena 1978; De Afrekening (The Summing Up), 1980; Hotel 'roze uren' (Hotel Rosy Hours), 1985. *Contributions to:* Reporting and articles in local weekly and some cultural magazines. *Honours:* Commandeur Ordre de la Couronne 1974; Literary Award for novel, Stad van bordelen en kathedralen, (Town of Brothels and Cathedrals), 1980; Prize, Provincial literary contest, West Flanders. *Memberships:* Christian Flemish Society of Artists; Society of Writers of Occidental Flanders. *Address:* Bos en Lommer 14, 8310 Sint-Kruis, Brugge, Belgium.

SOHL, Jerry, b. 2 Dec. 1913, Los Angeles, California, USA. Author; Screenwriter. m. Jean Gordon, 28 Oct. 1943, Salt Lake City, 1 son 2 daughters. *Publications:* Hardcover books include: The Lemon Eaters, 1967; The Spun Sugar Hole, 1971; Underhanded Chess, 1975; The Resurrection of Frank Borchard, 1973; Underhanded Bridge, 1975; Night Wind, 1981 (also in paperback). Paperbacks include: Mamelle, the Goddess, 1977; Kaheesh, 1983; Death Sleep, 1983; Black Thunder,

1985. Television: Staff writer for Star Trek, Alfred Hitchcock Presents, The New Breed; writer of episodes of The Twilight Zone, Naked City, Route 66, M-Squad, G E Theater, Markham, Border Patrol, The Invaders, The Outer Limits, Target, The Corruptors, Man From Atlantis and The Next Step Beyond. Movies: Twelve Hours to Kill (20th Century Fox); Die, Monster, Die (American International); Night Slaves (ABC Movie of the Week). *Contributions to:* Playboy; Galaxy; If; Magazine of Fantasy and Science Fiction; Science Fiction Adventures; Imagination; Space; Infinity plus stories in anthologies such as, The New Mind, Future Corruption, and the, Whisper, series. *Memberships:* Charter Member, Science Fiction Writers of America Inc; Writers Guild of America, West, Inc; Mystery Writers of America; The Authors Guild; Authors League of America. *Literary Agent:* Joseph Elder. *Address:* 3020 Ash Ct, Thousand Oaks, CA 91360, USA.

SOHRE, Helmut, b. 21 May 1915, Zwönitz, German Republic. Writer; Journalist. *Education:* University Studies of Sports, German Philology, Geography, Publicity; Certified Sports Teacher. *Publicaitons include:* Weltmacht Fussball, 1966; Gespielen des Windes, 1977; Triumph der Technik, 1979; Gefahr in den Wolken, 1978; Die grossen Abenteuer am Berg, 1979; Spass am Judo, 1979; Gut Freund mit Pferden, 1974; Alles über Fussball, 1974; Die siegreiche Elf, 1982; Fussball Zauber, 1983; Fussball total, 1981; Fussball Kalender, 1983; Sorveist die Hufetrager, 1985. *Contributor to:* Nordpress; Kicker Olympisches Feuer. *Address:* 76 Offenburg, Föhrenstrasse 10, Federal Republic of Germany.

SOKOLOW, Jayme Aaron, b. 3 Oct. 1946, USA. Educator. m. Judy Shapiro, 10 Dec. 1968, 1 daughter, marriage dissolved. *Education:* BA Social Studies Secondary Education, Trenton State College, 1968; MA History 1970, PhD History, 1972, New York University. *Literary Appointments:* Public Schools, New York City, 1971–76; Texas Tech University, 1976–81; National Endowment for the Humanities, Washington DC, 1982–. *Major Publication:* Eros and Modernization: Sylvester Graham, Health Reform, and the Origins of Victorian Sexuality in America, 1983. *Contributor to:* Southwestern Historical Quarterly; Journal of American Studies; Journal of Ethnic Studies. *Honours:* Graduate Fellowships, Trenton State, 1968, New York University, 1968. *Memberships:* American Historical Association; Society for Historians of the Early American Republic; Society for Utopian Studies. *Address:* National Endowment for the Humanities Education Division, Old Post Office, 1100 Pennsylvania Avenue NW, Washington, DC 20506, USA.

SOLOMON, Goody L, b. 1 June 1929, Brooklyn, New York, USA. Syndicated Newspaper Columnist and Consumer Writer; Author; Educator. *Education:* BA, Brooklyn College, New York, 1950; MA, New York University, 1955. *Literary Appointment:* Editor, Nutrition Policy (Monthly newspaper), 1985–. *Publications:* The Radical Consumer's Handbook, 1972. *Contributions to:* Washington Star; Money; Women's World; Changing Times; Barron's Weekly; Ladies Home Journal; Redbook; Stories; Modern Textiles; US Consumer; Family Circle; The Washington Women; Gannett News Service. *Honours:* Writing Awards, National Federation of Press Women, 1975–78; Special Citiation for excellence in consumer reporting, National Press Club, 1980; 1st place in 2 categories, Capitol Press Women, 1984. *Memberships:* American Society of Journalists and Authors; Society of Professional Journalists; American Newspaper Women's Club; Capitol Press Women. *Literary Agent:* Toni Mendez. *Address:* 1712 Taylor Street, North West, Washington, DC 20011, USA.

SOLOMON, Petre, b. 15 Feb. 1923, Bucharest, Romania. Writer. *Education:* MA, University of Bucharest. *Publications include:* Verse: Relief, In High Relief, 1965; Intre Foc Si Cenusa, In Between Fire and Ashes, 1968; Umbra Necesara, The Necessary Shadow, 1971; Exercitt de Candoare, Exercises in Candor, 1974;

Culoarea Antotimpurilor, The Colour of the Seasons, 1977; Timpul Neprobabil, The Improbable, 1985. Literary Criticism and Biographies: Fielding, A Forerunner of Realism, 1954; Mark Twain, or the Adventures of Humour, 1958, 60; John Milton, Monograph, 1962; Mark Twain, at the Sources of the River, 1976; Rimbauld: O Calatorie Spre Centrul Cuvintului, Rimbauld, A Voyage to the Center of the World, 1980. Translations: Works by Shelley, Shakespeare, Walter Scott, Gragham Greene, Mark Twain, Paul Celan and Melville. *Contributions to:* The Times Literary Supplement; Spectator; Literary Review; Adam. Numerous Romanian and other journals. *Honours include:* Several awards for translations of Flemish Literature, Belgian Minister of Culture; Prize for Translation from World Literature, Romanian Union of Writers, 1982. *Address:* Str Bozianu 23, Bucharest 75271, Romania.

SOLOMON, Robert C, b. 14 Sep. 1942, Detroit, Michigan, USA. Professor; Writer. *Education:* BA, Molecular Biology, University of Pennsylvania, 1963; MA, 1965, PhD, 1967, Philosophy, Psychology, University of Michigan. *Appointments:* Teaching Fellow, University of Michigan, 1965–66; Lecturer, Princeton University, 1966–67, Winter 1967–68; Assistant Professor, CUNY, 1971–72; Associate Professor, 1972, Professor, 1977–, University of Texas, Austin. *Publications:* From Rationalism to Existentialism, 1972; The Passions, 1976; History and Human Nature: A Philosophical Review of European History and Culture 1750–1850, 1979; Introducing Philosophy: Problems and Perspectives, 1981; editor: Nietsche, 1973; Existentialism, 1974; What is an Emotion? with C Calhoun, 1984. *Contributor to:* Existentialism, 1974; What is an Emotion?, with C Calhoun, 1984. *Contributor to:* Over 100 articles in professional journals; regular columnist, Austin American Statesman, Texas Observer; Occasional columns: Newsweek; Los Angeles Times; etc. *Honours:* Danforth Foundation Nominee, 1969; Standard Oil Outstanding Teaching Award, 1973. *Memberships:* American Philosophical Association; Society for Phenomenology & Existential Philosophy. *Literary Agent:* Melanie Jackson, New York. *Address:* Dept of Philosophy, University of Texas, Austin, TX 78712, USA.

SOLOMON, Samuel, b. 20 Sep. 1904, Calcutta, India. Author, Indian Civil Servant (retired). m. Moselle Solomon, London, England, 16 Sep. 1937, 1 son, 2 daughters. *Education:* BA Modern Languages, King's College, University of Cambridge, England, 1926; MA, University of Cambridge. *Major Publications:* Poems from East and West, 1927; The Saint and Satan, 1930; The Complete Plays of Jean Racine, 1968; Pierre Corneille's Seven Plays, 1969; Franz Grillparzer – Plays on Classic Themes, 1970; Hawaii and other poems, 1983; Memories with Thoughts on Gandhi, 1984; The Fall of Hitler, or, Where is Thy Peace?, 1985. *Contributor to:* Contemporary Review; Civil Service Opinion; London Magazine; Tulane Drama Review; Hudson Review; World Jewry; The Times; and others. *Address:* 51 Hollycroft Avenue, London, NW3 7QJ, England.

SOLTOW, James Harold, b. 1 July 1924, Chicago, Illinois, USA. Historian. m. Martha Jane Stough, 14 Sep. 1946, Carlisle. *Education:* AB, Dickinson College, 1948; AM, 1949, 1954, University of Pennsylvania. *Appointments:* Lecturer, Hunter College, 1952–55; Research Associate, Colonial Williamsburg, 1955–56; Instructor, Russell Sage College, 1956–58; Assistant Professor of Professor, Michigan State University, 1959–85. *Publications:* Economic Role of Williamsburg, 1965; Origins of Small Business, 1965; Evolution of the American Economy, co-author, 1979; Essays in Economic & Business History: Selected Papers from the Economic & Business Historical Society, 1976, 1977, 1978, 1979; Essays in Economic & Business History 1979, 1981. *Contributor to:* Numerous professional journals. *Honours:* Business History Fellowship, Harvard University, 1958–59; Fulbright Research Fellowship, University of Louvian, Belgium, 1965–66. *Memberships:* Economic History Association; Business History Conference, Trustee, 1980–; Economic & Business

Historical Society, President, 1982, Chief Editor, 1978–84. *Address:* 32 Marsh Island, Isle of Palms, SC 29451, USA.

SOLWITZ, Sharon, b. 10 Dec. 1945, Pittsburgh, Pennsylvania, USA. Writer. m. Barry Silesky, 13 June 1982, Chicago, Illinois. *Education:* BA, English, Cornell University, 1968; MFA, Printmaking, University of Illinois, Chicago, 1980; MFA. Creative Writing, University of Illinois, Chicago, 1981. *Literary Appointments:* Lecturer in English, University of Illinois, Chicago, 1981–84; Visiting Lecturer in English, School of the Art Institute of Chicago, 1984–; Fiction Editor, Another Chicago Magazine, 1984–. *Contributions to:* Playgirl; Another Chicago Magazine; Kansas Quarterly; Telescope. *Honours:* University Fellowship, University of Illinois, Chicago, 1980–81, 1985–86; First Prize for Documentary K-A M, Chicago International Film Festival, 1969; Literary Award for, High Horse, Illinois Arts Council, 1984. *Address:* 2215 N Orchard Street (rear house), Chicago, IL 60614, USA.

SOMARJAI, Gabor A, b. 4 May 1935, Hungary. Professor of Chemistry. m. Judith K, 2 Sep. 1957, 1 son, 1 daughter. *Education:* PhD, Chemistry, University of California, Berkeley, 1960. *Publications:* Principles of Surface Chemistry, 1972; Chemistry in Two Dimensions Surfaces, 1981; Structure of Absorbed Monolayers, 1982. *Contributions to:* Over 400 articles in scientific journals. *Honours:* Kokes Award, John Hopkins University, 1976; Emmett Award, American Catalysis Society, 1978; Surface Chemistry Award, American Chemistry Society, 1980. *Memberships:* National Academy of Sciences; American Academy of Arts and Sciences. *Address:* Department of Chemistry, Unversity of California, Berkeley, CA 94720, USA.

SOMCYNSKY, Jean-François, b. 20 Apr. 1943, Paris, France. Diplomat, Canadian Foreign Service. m. Micheline Beaudry, Ottawa, Canada, 22 Aug. 1968. *Education:* MEcon, University of Ottawa, 1970. *Publications:* Les Rapides, novel, 1966; Encore Faim, novel, 1971; Les Grimaces, short stories, 1975; Le Diable du Mahani, novel, 1978; Les Incendiaires, novel, 1980; Peutêtre à Tokyo, short stories, 1981; Trois Voyages, poems, 1982; La Planète Amoureuse, novel, 1982; Vingt Minutes D'Amour, Novel, 1983; La Frontière du Milieu, novel, 1983; J'ai Entendu Parler D'Amour, short stories, 1984. *Contributions:* Short stories to Solaris; Imagine; Antares; Fiction, etc; Various anthologies. Occasional poems, various magazines. *Honours:* Prix international Solaris, science fiction, 1981; Prix Boréal, best short stories, science fiction & fantasy, 1982; Prix littéraire Esso du Cercle du Livre de France, 1983. *Membership:* Union des écrivains québécois. *Address:* 5 avenue Putman, Ottawa, Ontario, Canada K1M 1Y8.

SOMERVILLE-LARGE, Peter, b. 23 Apr. 1928, Dublin, Eire. Writer. m. Gillian Somerville-Large, July 1958, 1 daughter. *Publications:* Tribes & Tribulations, 1967, 1968; Coast of West Cork, 1972; From Bantry Bay to Leitrim, 1974; Eagles Near the Carcasx, 1974; Irish Eccentrics, 1975; Couch of Earth, 1975; Dublin, 1979; Living Dog, 1981; Grand Irish Tour, 1982; Cappaghglass, 1983; Hangglider, 1985. *Contributions to:* Various journals. *Literary Agent:* Anthony Sheil. *Address:* Leamcon House, Leamcon, Schull, County Cork, Republic of Ireland.

SOMMER, Edith (Schwab), b. 28 Jan. 1927, Vienna, Austria. Writer; Former Librarian. m. Dr Viktor Mrázek, 16 Apr. 1966, Vienna, 1 son. *Education:* Dr phil. *Publications:* Immer noch Hoffnung, 1983; Begegnung in Wort, editor, 1984; Ein Sommer ohne Wiederkehr, 1985; Neonlicht und Kerzenschimmer, co-author, 1985. *Contributions to:* Aufschreiben, anthology, 1981; Mutter und Ich, anthology, 1984; Jahrbuch katholischer Schriftsteller Osterreichs, 1984; IGdA-Almanach, 1985–86; Aktuell, & other journals, poems, short stories. Book reviews, Aktuell, Germany, Schrifttum aus Osterreich, Austria. *Honours:* Poetry Prize, Austrian Youth Culture Week, Innsbruck, 1951, 1953. *Memberships:* AKM; Industrial Trade Union of Austrian Authors;

Industrial Trade Union of German-Speaking Authors (IGdA); Austrian Writers Association; Catholic Writers Association; Kreis; Authors' Section, Association of the Spiritually Creative. *Address:* Tallesbrunngasse 6/2, A–1190 Vienna, Austria.

SOMMER, Piotr, b. 13 Apr. 1948, Walbrzych, Poland. Writer. m. Jolanta Piasecka, 28 Oct. 1972, Otwock, Poland, 1 son. *Education:* MA, English Literature, University of Warsaw, 1973. *Literary Appointments:* Visiting Professor, Washington & Lee University, Lexington, Virginia, USA, 1983. *Publications include:* Poetry: W Krzesle, 1977; Pamiatki Po Nas, 1980; Kolejny Swiat, 1983; Czynnik Liryczny, 1986. Other: Przed Snem, poems for children, 1981; Antologia Nowej Poezji Brytyjskiej, editor, 1983; Zapisy Rozmow: Wywiady z Poetami Brytyjskimi, interviews with British poets, 1985; Numerous translations, contemporary American, English, Irish poetry. *Contributions:* In Poland: Odra; Tworczosc; Literatura na Swiecie; Studio; Akcent; Punkt; Wezwanie; Res Publica; etc. Abroad: Zeszyty Literackie, Paris; Oficyna Poetow, London; The Honest Ulsterman, Belfast; Shenandoah, USA; The Prairie Schooner, USA; Threepenny Review, USA; International Portland Review, USA; Quarto, London; etc. *Memberships:* Polish Writers Union, 1981–83 (union dissolved 1983); Honorary member, Poetry Book Society, UK. *Address:* Ul.Szekspira 4 m.24, 01-913 Warszawa, Poland.

SOMMES, Robert Thomas, b. 6 Aug. 1926, Baltimore, Maryland, USA. Editor. m. Helen Louise Ray, 19 Oct. 1952, 1 son, 1 daughter. *Education:* BS, University of Maryland, College Park, 1950. *Publication:* The US Open: Golf's Ultimate Challenge, 1986. *Literary Agent:* Kenneth Bowden. *Address:* RD2 Box 230B, Basking Ridge, NJ 07920, USA.

SOPER, Eileen Louise Service, b. 14 Dec. 1900, Sydney, Australia. Writer. m. Frederick George Soper, 14 Feb. 1938, Dunedin, New Zealand. 1 stepson, 1 stepdaughter. *Education:* BA, Otago University, New Zealand. *Literary Appointments:* Eitor, Notes for Women, Otago Daily Times, 1924; Associate Editor, Otago Witness, 1924–32; editor, Notes for Woman, Otago Daily Times, 1932–38. *Publications:* The Otago of Our Mothers, 1948, 78; Young Jane, 1955; The Green Years, 1969; The Month of the Brittle Star, 1971; The Leaves Turn, 1973. *Contributions to:* New Zealand Listener; Otago University Review. *Address:* 6 Howard Street, Macandrew Bay, Dunedin, New Zealand.

SORESTAD, Glen Allan, b. 21 May 1937, Vancouver, Canada. Writer. m. Sonia Diane Talpash, 17 Sep. 1960, Buchanan, Canada, 3 sons, 1 daughter. *Education:* Master of Education, University of Saskatchewan 1975. *Literary Appointments:* Member, Board of Directors, Thistledown Press, 1975–; Advisory Board, Poetry Canada Review, 1983–85. *Publications:* Prairie Pub Poems, 1976; Ancestral Dances, 1979; Jan Lake Poems, 1984; Hold the Rain in Your Hands, 1985. *Contributions to:* Numerous magazines and journals. *Memberships:* Founding Member, Saskatchewan Writers' Guild, Member, 1969–; Member, League of Canadian Poets, Executive Member, 1978–84. *Address:* 668 East Place, Saskatoon, Saskatchewan, Canada S7J 2Z5.

SORINE, Stephanie Riva, b. 3 Sep. 1954, New York, USA. Copywriter. m. Daniel S Sorine, 1 July 1977. *Education:* Hunter College; New York University; School of Visual Arts. *Publications:* Dancershoes, 1979; Imagine That! It's Modern Dance, 1981; At Every Turn: It's Ballet, 1981; Our Ballet Class, 1981; That's Jazz, 1982; Doll Friends, 1982; The French Riviere Body Book, 1983; Stretchout, 1984. *Contributor to:* Family Circle; Ladies Home Journal; Harper's Bazaar; Woman's Day; Redbook; Mademoiselle.

SORLEY WALKER, Kathrine, b. Aberdeen, Scotland. Author; Journalist. *Education:* King's College, University of London; University of Besancon, France.

Literary Appointments: Geographical Magazine, London, England, 1953–57; Ballet and dance critic, critic of mime and puppetry, Daily Telegraph, London, 1965–. *Publications:* Robert Helpmann, 1958; The Heart's Variety, verse, 1960; Eyes on the Ballet, 1963, 65; Eyes on Mime, 1969; Dance and Its Creators, 1972; Saladin-Sultan of the Holy Sword, 1971; Joan of Arc 1972; Ballet for Boys and Girls, 1979; Emotion and Atmosphere, verse, 1979; The Royal Ballet: A Picture History, 1981, 82; De Basil's Ballets Russes, 1982, 83; Editor, Raymond Chandler Speaking, 1962 and Writings on Dance by A V Coton 1938–68, 1975. *Contributions to:* International Encyclopedia of Dance; Encyclopedia Britannica; Enciclopedia dello Spettacolo; Encyclopedia of the Dance and Ballet; Dance Encyclopedia, UK Editor; The Dancing Times; Dance Gazette; Dance Chronicle, New York, USA; Hemisphere; Australia; The Lady; The Stage; Sunday Telegraph and others. *Membership:* Critics Circle, London. *Address:* 60 Eaton Mews West, London SW1W 9ET, England.

SOROCZYNSKI, Tadeusz. b. 29 Jan. 1942, Busk, USSR. Teacher. m. Maria Kasprzyk, 3 Aug. 1968, Prudnik, Poland, 1 son, 1 daughter. *Literary Appointments:* Literary Debut, a poem in a local paper, The Trynuna Opolska, 1961; Column of poems in, Odra, 1965; Poem in 'Zycie Literackie', 1966. *Publications:* (Poetic volumes), Daruje ci Sad, 1967; Blizej Sadu, 1967; Sploty, 1973; (Poetic folder) Krajobraz Serdeczny, 1977. *Contributor to:* Zycie Literackie; Odra; Poezja; Tygodnik Kultualny; Opole; The Trybuna Opolska. *Honours:* Laureate, poetic competition Zeota Strzecha, Raciborz, 1965, 1966, 1967. *Memberships:* Member, Candidate of the Society of Polish Writers; Correspondence Club of Young Writers; Literary Club of Polish Teachers' Association. *Address:* ul Wroclawska 20c/23, 45-707 Opole 7, Poland.

SOUDEYNS, Maurice (Alexandre), b. 9 Aug. 1944, Montreal, Canada. Writer. *Publications:* L'Oree de l'Eternite, 1972; La Trajectoire, 1974; Chas, 1974; Valmer, 1984. *Membership:* Union of Quebec Authors. *Address:* C P 608, Succ N, Montreal, Quebec H2X 3M6, Canada.

SOULE, Maris Anne, b. 19 June 1939, Oakland, California, USA. Writer. m. William L Soule, 11 May 1968, Santa Barbara, 1 son, 1 daughter. *Education:* BA, Secondary Teaching Credential, University of California, Davis and Berkeley. *Publications:* First Impressions, editions in 3 languages, 1983; No Room for Love, editions in 2 languages, 1984; Lost and found, editions in 2 languages, 1985; Sounds Like Love, 1986. *Memberships:* Romance Writers of America; Chapter Adviser, Mid-Michigan Chapter, Romance Writers of America. *Literary Agent:* Denise Marcil Literary Agency. *Address:* 16269 T S Avenue East, Fulton, MI 49052, USA.

SOUTHALL, Ivan Francis, b. 8 June 1921, Australia. Writer. m. (1) Joy Blackburn, 1954, London (divorced) 1 son, 3 daughters; (2) Susan Westerland Stanton, 1976, Sydney. *Literary Appointments:* Whittall Poetry and Literature Lecturer, US Library of Congress, 1973; May Hill Arbuthnot Honor Lecturer, American Library Association, 1974; Writer in Residence, Macquarie University, 1980 etc. *Publications:* Fifty-five books published between 1942 and 1985. *Honours:* DFC, 1944; Australian Children's Book of the Year, 1966, 1968, 1971, 1976; Australian Picture Book of the Year, 1969; Japanese Children's Welfare and Culture Encouragement Award, 1969; Silver Griffel, Holland, 1972; Carnegie Medal, 1971; Member, Order of Australia, 1981. *Address:* PO Box 25, Healesville, Victoria 3777, Australia.

SPACKS, Barry, b.21 Feb. 1931, Philadelphia, Pennsylvania, USA. Teacher; Writer. *Education:* BA Honours, University of Pennsylvania, 1952; MA, Indiana University, 1956; Fulbright Scholar, Cambridge University, England. 1956–57. *Literary Appointments:* Teacher, Literature and Creative Writing; Indiana University, 1954–56; University of Florida, 1957–59;

Massachusetts Institute of Technology, 1960–78; University of Kentucky, 1978–79; University of California, Berkeley, 1980; Santa Barbara, 1981–. *Publications:* Novels: The Sophomore, 1969; Orphans, 1972. Poetry: The Company of Children, 1968; Something Human, 1972; Teaching the Penguins to Fly, 1975; Imagining a Unicorn, 1978; Spacks Street: New and Selected Poems. 1982. *Contributions to:* Numerous journals and magazines. *Honours:* St Botolph's Arts Award for fiction and poetry, 1971; Poetry medal, Commonwealth Club of California, 1983. *Literary Agent:* Lynn Nesbit, ICM. *Address:* 1111 Bath Street, Santa Barbara, CA 93101, USA.

SPACKS, Patricia Meyer, b. 17 Nov. 1929, San Francisco, California, USA. College Teacher; Writer. *Education:* BA, Rollins College, 1949; MA, Yale University, 1950; PhD, University of California, Berkeley, 1955. *Publications:* The Varied God, 1959; The Insistence of Horror, 1962; The Poetry of Vision, 1967; An Argument of Images, 1971; The Female Imagination, 1975; Imagining a Self, 1975; The Adolescent Idea, 1982; Gossip, 1985. *Contributions to:* Prose Studies; Soundings; Hudson Review; Modern Language Quarterly; South Atlantic Quarterly. *Honours include:* Guggenheim Fellowship, 1969–70; NEWH Senior Fellowship, 1974; National Humanities Institute, 1976–77; ACLS Fellowship, 1978–79. *Literary Agent:* Maxine Groffsky. *Address:* Department of English, Yale University, New Haven, CT 06520, USA.

SPAENS – de VRIEZE, Gerda Jozefa Francina, b. 13 July 1946, Etterbeek, Brussels, Belgium. Journalist/Poet. m. Eric Spaens, 12 Apr 1966, 3 daughters. *Publications:* Het Kleurrijke wit, 1983; Wat de dag me brengt, vertel ik jou Altiora, Averbode, 1981; Het Verschijnsel Man Gottmer, Nijmegen, Orion, Brugge, 1978; Van Aap tot Schapen Van In, Lier, 1977; Rood licht, Yang Poeziereeks, Gent, 1974. Documentary films: The French Flanders: Langs de schreve 1984; The French Flanders; Menschen lyk wieder, part 2, 1982; Terra Nova, 1982; Alpenhirt 1981; Mariakerke, kleurig puzzelstukje van Oost-Vlaanderen, 1980; The French Flanders: De Westhoek, groenende parel van Vlaanderen, part 1 1978; Poëzie en kleur, 1975; Te voet doorheen Mariakerke, 1974. *Contributions to:* Top magazine voor tieners, G-P Altipra Averbode(Belgium); Zonneland, G-P Altiora, Averbode. Freelance theatre critic. *Honours:* Prijs voor Poëzie Vlaams Brussel, 1976; Prijs, Achtste Jong-Nederlands-Literaire Dagen, St-Martens-Latem 1965. *Memberships:* SABAM; Vereniging van Vlaamse Letterkundigen (Flemish authors). *Address:* Henri Storystraat 20, 9910 Gent (Mariakerke), Belgium.

SPALDING, Keith, b. 15 May 1913, Darmstadt, Federal Republic of Germany. University Professor. m. A Phyllis Card, 24 Dec. 1946. *Education:* Universities of Frankfurt and Vienna; BA, 1937, MA, 1938, PhD, 1940, University of Birmingham. *Literary Appointment:* Associate Editor, Muret-Sanders Encyclopedic Dictionary English-German/German-English, 1952–74. *Publications:* Kultur oder Vermichtung, 1933; Introduction to German through Lyric Poetry, 1940; Der weite Weg, 1946; Historical Dictionary of German Figurative Usage, since 1952, still in progress; German Word Patterns 1962; Editor: Ackermann aus Böhmen 1950, Selections from Stifter, 1952, Grillparzer's Sappho, 1965, Stifter's Abdias, 1966; Goethe's Herman und Dorothea 1968. *Contributions to:* Modern Language Review; German Life and Letters; Archivum Linguisticum; Modern Languages; Gwerin; Muttersprache; Erasmus; Revue Belge de Philologie et d'Histoire. *Honours:* Honorary D Phil, University of Tübingen, 1972; Grand Cross of Merit of the Federal Republic of Germany, 1976. *Address:* Gower House, Llanfairpwll, Gwynedd LL61 5NX, Wales.

SPARK, Muriel Sarah, b. Edinburgh. Writer. m. 1937 (marriage dissolved) 1 son. *Education:* James Gillespie's School for Girls, Edinburgh; Heriot Watt College, Edinburgh, FO, 1944. *Literary Appointments:* General Secretary, the Poetry Society; Editor, The Poetry Review, 1947–49. *Publications:* Critical and biographical: Joint editor, Tribute to Wordsworth, 1950; Editor, Selected Poems of Emily Bronte, 1952; Child of Light a Reassessment of Mary Shelley, 1951; Joint editor, My Best Mary, the Letters of Mary Shelley, 1953; John Masefield, 1953; Joint editor, Emily Bronte her Life and Work, 1953; Editor, The Bronte Letters, 1954; Joint editor; Letters of John Henry Newman, 1957. Poems: The Fanfarlo and Other Verse, 1952; Collected Poems 1, 1967; Going Up to Sotheby's and Other Poems, 1982. Fiction: The Comforters, 1957; Robinson, 1958; The Go-Away Bird, 1958; Momento Nori, 1959 (adapted for stage 1964); The Ballad of Peckham Rye, 1960; The Bachelors, 1960; Voices at Play, 1961; The Prize of Miss Jean Brodie, 1961 (adapted for stage 1966, filmed 1969 and BBC TV 1978); Doctors of Philosophy, (play) 1963; The Girl of Slender Means, 1963 (adapted for radio 1964 and BBC TV 1975); The Mandelbaum Gate, 1965; Collected Stories 1, 1967; Bang Bang You're Dead and other stories, 1982. Collected Poems 1 1967; The Public Image 1968; The Very Fine Clock, (for children) 1969; The Driver's Seat, 1970 (filmed 1974); Not to Disturb, 1971; The Hothouse By the East River, 1973; The Abbess of Crewe 1974 (filmed 1977); The Takeover, 1976; Territorial rights, 1979; Loitering with Intent, 1981; The Only Problem, 1984. *Honours:* OBE 1967; FRSL 1963; Honorary Member, American Academy of Arts and Letters 1978; Hon D Litt, Strathclyde University; Italia Prize for dramatic radio for The Ballad of Peckham Rye, 1962; James Tait Black Memorial Prize for, The Mandelbaum Gate. *Address:* c/o Macmillan London Ltd, 4 Little Essex Street, London WC2, England.

SPARKES, Ivan George, b. Stratton St Margaret, Wiltshire, England. Librarian, Curator. *Major Publications include:* The Windsor Chair, 1975; Stage Coaches & Carriages, 1975; Dictionary of Group Terms & Collective Nouns, 1975; High Wycombe as it was, 1975; Victorian & Edwardian Photographs of Buckinghamshire (with M Lawson), 1976; Old Horse Shoes, 1976; The Book of Wycombe, 1979; English Domestic Furniture, 1979; English Windsor Chairs, 1985; High Wycombe in Old Picture Postcards, 1983; Dictionary of Group Terms, 1985. *Contributor to:* Essex Review; Furniture Historian. *Honours:* Sir Evelyn Wrench Travelling Fellowship for Librarian, 1965; Nature Librarian's Award. Librarians Association, 1974. *Memberships:* Librarians Association; Royal Historical Association; Museums Association. *Address:* 124 Green Hill, High Wycombe, Buckinghamshire, England.

SPARKS, James Allen, b. 31 May 1933, Mays Lick, Kentucky, USA. University of Wisconsin Extension Professor. m. Pauline Lenore Zahrte, 13 Aug. 1955, Milwaukee, Wisconsin, 1 daughter. *Education:* BA, Transylvania University, Lexington, Kentucky, 1955; M Div, Pittsburgh Theological Seminary, 1958; MS, University of Wisconsin, 1972. *Publications:* Potshots at the Preacher, 1977; Friendship After Forty, 1980; Living the Bad Days, 1982; If This Pew Could Talk, 1985. *Contributions to:* The Clergy Journal (Columnist writing on continuing education issues of clergy). *Honour:* Merit Certificate for Friendship After Forty, given by The Council for Wisconsin Writers Incorporated, 1980. *Membership:* The Council of Wisconsin Writer Incorporated. *Address:* 610 Langdon Street, Madison, WI 53703, USA.

SPARSHOTT, Francis Edward, b. 19 May 1926, Chatham, Kent, England. University Teacher. m. Kathleen Elizabeth Vaughan, 7 Feb. 1953, Mimico, Ontario, 1 daughter. *Education:* MA, 1950, Oxon. *Publications:* An Enquiry Into Goodness, 1958; The Structure of Aesthetics, 1963; A Divided Voice, 1965; The Concept of Criticism, 1967; A Cardboard Garage, 1969; Looking for Philosophy, 1972; The Naming of the Beasts, 1979; The Rainy Hills, 1979; The Theory of the Arts, 1982; The Cave of Trophonius, 1983; The Hanging Gardens of Etobicoke, 1983; Storms and Screens, 1985. *Honour:* First Prize, Poetry, CBC Radio Literary Awards, 1981. *Membership:* League of Canadian Poets, President 1977–78. *Address:* 50 Crescentwood Road, Scarboro, Ontario M1N 1E4, Canada.

SPEAIGHT, George Victor, b, 6 Sep. 1914, Bishops Hatfield, England. Publisher, puppeteer. *Literary Appointments:* Bookseller, J and E Bumpus; Editor, Odhams Press; Editorial Director, Rainbird Publishing Group. *Publications:* Juvenile Drama: the History of the English Toy Theatre, 1946; The History of the English Puppet Theatre, 1955; Punch and Judy: a History, 1970; The Book of Clowns, 1980; A History of the Circus, 1980; Bawdy Songs of the Early Music Hall, editor, 1975; The New Shell Guide to Britain, editor, 1985. *Contributions to:* Theatre Notebook; Nineteenth Century Theatre Research; Animations; King Pole; Le Cirque dans l'univers; Circo. *Memberships:* Fellow, Royal Society of Arts; Past Chairman, Society for Theatre Research; Member of Honour, Union International de la Marionnette. *Address:* 6 Maze Road, Kew Gardens, Richmond, Surrey TW9 3DA, England.

SPEED, Frederick Maurice, b. 18 Oct. 1911, London, England. Film Critic; Editor. m. (2) 16 Sep. 1979. *Literary Appointments:* Editor, What's On in London, (Later as Managing editor), 1937–80. *Publications:* Film Review Annual, 1945–; Western Film and TV Annual; They Rubbed Him Out, thriller; Movie Cavalcade; The Moviegoers Quiz Book, 1985. *Contributions to:* News of the World; Los Angeles Times; Topic; Jersey Sun; various other magazines and periodicals. *Membership:* Critics Circle. *Address:* 39 Hollytree Close, Inner Park Road, Wimbledon, London SW19 6EA, England.

SPEIDEL, Michael P, b. 25 May 1937, Pforzheim, Baden. Professor, History. m. Gisela Stahlberg, 21 Aug. 1967, Heidelberg, 1 son, 1 daughter. *Education:* PhD, Freiburg in Breisgau, 1962. *Publications:* Die equites singulares Augusti, 1965; Guards of the Roman Armies, 1978; The Religion of Iuppiter Dolichenus, 1978; Mithras-Orion, 1980; Roman Army Studies I, 1984. *Contributor to:* 100 papers on Roman Army. *Honour:* Studienstiftung des Deutschen Volkes, 1960. *Membership:* American Society of Papyrologists. *Address:* Dept of History, 2530 Dole Street, University of Hawaii, Honolulu, HI 96822, USA.

SPENCE, Donald P, b. 8 Feb. 1926, New York City, USA. Psychologist; Psychoanalyst. m. Mary N Cross, 2 June 1951, Bernardsville, New Jersey, 1 son, 3 daughters. *Education:* BA, Harvard College; PhD, Columbia University. *Literary Appointments:* Editorial Board: Journal of the American Psychoanalytic Association, Journal of Abnormal Psychology, Psychoanalysis and Contemporary Thought. *Publications:* Editor: The Broad Scope of Psychoanalysis: The Collected Papers of Leopold Bellak, 1967; Psychoanalysis and Contemporary Science, Volume IV, 1976; Author: Narrative Truth and Historical Truth, 1982. *Contributions to:* Journal of Abnormal and Social Psychology; Journal of Personality; Psychological Reports; Psychosomatic Medicine; Behavioral Science; Journal of Nervous and Mental Disease; Perceptual and Motor Skills; Journal of Verbal Learning and Verbal Behavior; Transactions of the New York Academy of Science; Handbook of Psychotherapy and Behavior Change; Psychoanalysis and Contemporary Science, Volumes I, II, V; Social Science and Medicine; Psycholinguistic Research; Past, Present and Future; British Journal of Psychology; International Journal of Psycho-Analysis; Handbook of Stress; Theoretical and Clinical Aspects; The Denial of Stress. Numerous Book Reviews. *Address:* 9 Haslet Avenue, Princeton, NJ 08540, USA.

SPENCER, Charles Samuel, b. 28 Aug. 1925, London, Writer; Lecturer; Exhibition Organiser. *Education:* Courtauld Institute, London; University of Rome. *Literary Appointments:* Editor, Art and Artists London; Editor, Editions Alecto, London; Art Critic, New York Times European Edition; Art Critic, Daily Mail, London. *Publications:* Erte, 1970; A Decade of Print Making, 1972; The Aestetic Movement, 1973; Leon Nakst, 1973; The World of Serge Diaghilev, 1974; Cicil Beaton Stage and Film Designs, 1975. *Contributions to:* Studio International; Apollo; Connoisseur; Arts Review etc, and notably journals in Italy, Israel and United States.

Literary Agent: Gloria Ferris. *Address:* Flat 11, 44 Grove End Road, London NW8 9NE, England.

SPENCER, Elizabeth, b. Carrollton, Mississippi, USA. Fiction Writer. m. John A B Rusher, 29 Sep. 1956, Cornwell. *Education:* AB, Belhaven College, Jackson, Mississippi; MA, Vanderbilt University, Nashville, Tennessee. *Literary Appointments:* Donnelly Fellow and residence, Bryn Mawr, 1962; Residency, University of North Caroline, 1969; Writer in residence, Hollins College, Virginia, 1973; Writer in residence, 1977–78, Visiting Professor, 1976–81, Adjunct Professor, 1981–, Concordia University, Montreal, Canada. *Publications:* Novels: Fire in the Morning, 1948; This Crooked Way, 1952; The Voice at the Back Door, 1956; The Light in the Piazza, 1960; Knights and Dragons, 1965; No Place for an Angel, 1968; The Snare, 1972; The Salt Line, 1984; Short story collections: Ship Island and other stories, 1969; The Stories of Elizabeth Spencer, 1981; Marilee, 1981. *Contributions to:* The New Yorker; Atlantic; The Southern Review; Journal of Canadian Fiction; New York Times Sunday Book Review; and others. *Honours include:* Recognition Award, 1952, First Rosenthal Award 1957, Award of Merit Medal 1983, American Academy of Arts and Letters; Honorary LL D, Southwestern University, 1968; Various grants and fellowships. *Memberships:* Department of Literature, American Academy/Institute of Arts and Letters; International PEN; Canadian and New York Centre; Author's Guild, New York. *Literary Agent:* Virginia Barber, 353 West 21st St, New York, NY 10011, USA. *Address:* c/o Rusher, Apt 610, 2300 St Matthew, Montreal, Quebec H3H 2J8, Canada.

SPENCER, William, b. 1 June 1922, Erie, Pennsylvania, USA. Writer; University Professor. m. Elizabeth Bouvier, 18 May 1969, Tallahasse, 1 son, 2 daughter. *Education:* AB, Princeton University, 1948; AM, Duke University, 1950; PhD, International Relations, American University, Washington, 1965. *Appointments:* English Instructor, St Lawrence University, 1950; Fellow, US Information Agency, Turkey, 1953; Assistant Editor, Middle East Journal, 1956. *Publications:* Political Evolution in the Middle East, 1962; The Land and People of Turkey, 1970; Algiers in the Age of the Corsairs, 1976; Historical Dictionary of Morocco, 1980; The Islamic States in Conflict, 1983; The Middle East: Global Cultures, 1985. *Contributor to:* Travel; Landscape; Africa Report; Mideast; Middle East Journal; Venture; New York Times Travel; Regular book reviewer, various journals, many years. *Honour:* Carnegie and Lippincott Literary Awards, 1960. *Address:* P O Box 1702 – Suite 52, Gainesville, FL 32602, USA.

SPERLING, Daniel Lee, b. 22 Dec. 1949, New York City, USA. Writer. *Education:* BA, Psychology, Duke University, 1971. *Publications:* A Spectator's Guide to Baseball, 1983; A Spectator's Guide to Football, 1983; A Spectator's Guide to Basketball, 1983. *Contributions:* of articles and reviews to: The Washington Post; Geo; Rolling Stone; The Manchester Guardian; Eastern Review; Us Magazine; Success Magazine; USA Today. *Literary Agent:* Audrey Wolf. *Address:* Washington, DC, USA.

SPIEGEL, Marcia Cohn, b. 16 Oct. 1927, Chicago, Illinois, USA. Lecturer; Writer. m. Sidney Lawrence Spiegel, 4 Sep. 1949, 2 sons, 3 daughters. *Education:* BA, Rockford College; Certificate, University of Southern California; MA, Hebrew Union College, Jewish Institute of Religion. *Literary Appointment:* Faculty Member, University of Judaism. *Publications:* The Heritage of Noah: Alcoholism in the Jewish Community Today, 1979; In Her Own Words, 1980; Women of the Bible 1984; Women Speak to God, 1985–86. *Contributions to:* Hadassah Magazine; British Journal of Alcoholism; Present Tense; International Congress of Drugs and Alcohol; Women Writers West Anthology; Women's League Outlook; Judaica Book News; Reconstructionist Magazine. Poetry Translations included in: Directions; 5th World Congress of Poetry; SHIRIM, SHMA; Reconstructionist; Women Writers West. *Honours:* Woman of Merit, Temple Menorah,

1973; Francis Henry Scholarship Award, 1978, Outstanding Alumni, 1982, Hebrew Union College; Centennial Award, National Federation of Temple Sisterhoods, 1978; Alimni of Distinction, Rockford College, 1984. *Memberships:* President, Founder, Women Writers West and Creative Jewish Womens Alliance; National Writers Conference; Leader and Organiser, Great Books. *Address:* 4856 Ferncreek Drive, Rolling Hills Estates, CA 90274, USA.

SPIEGLER, Charles G, b. 14 Mar. 1911, New York City, USA. Teacher; Writer. m. Evelyn Weiser, 4 Dec. 1948, 1 son. *Education:* BA, City College, 1932; Teachers College, Columbia University, 1933. *Appointments include:* Teacher, Speech, English, New York City High Schools, 1934–54; Instructor to Assistant Professor, English, Baruch College, 1947–75; Supervisor, English, New York City High Schools, 1954–76. *Publications:* If You're Not Going to College, co-author, 1959; Adventures for Americans, Co-Editor, 1962; Striving, Co-Editor, 1967; Editor, Merrill Mainstream Series, 5 volumes, 1968; What to Do After High School, co-author, 1971; Yes, We Can, co-author, 1972; On My Mind, Co-author, 1973; A Matter of Judgement, co-editor, 1979. *Contributor to:* New York Times Magazine; Parents Magazine; This Week Magazine; TV Guide; Chicago Jewish Forum; High Points; Reading Teacher; Clearing House; English Record; English Journal; Scholastic; Education; NEA Journal. *Memberships:* International Reading Association, President Manhattan Chapter; Overseas Press Club; Author's Guild. *Literary Agent:* Sanford Greenburger Associates. *Address:* 67-65 Fleet Street, Forest Hills, NY 11375, USA.

SPIESSENS, Raymond François Philomène, b. 15 Mar. 1928, Antwerp, Belgium. Author. m. Irene de Lombaert, 27 May 1958, 1 son. *Education:* Cand civil engineer, Licentiate sciences, University of Ghent; Indian philosophies and religions, University of Utrecht. *Publications:* De Witte kardinaal, novel, 1969; Juan doorheen de spiegel, 3 tales, 1970; Het ultimatum, 3 tales, 1971; De Verminkten, 1972. *Contributions to:* Vereniging van Vlaamse Letterkundigen; PEN Club. *Address:* Leopold de Vriesstraat 36, 2600 Brechem-Antwerpen, Belgium.

SPIKE, Paul Robert, b. 3 Aug. 1947, Newark, Ohio, USA. Writer. m. Maureen Freely, 26 Mar. 1976, London, 1 son, 1 daughter. *Education:* AB, Columbia University, USA; St Catherine's College, University of Oxford, England. *Literary Appointments:* Editor, The Columbia Review, 1969–70; Visiting distinguished Professor, University of Texas (El Paso), USA. *Major Publications:* Bad News, 1970; Photographs of my Father, 1973; The Night Letter, 1979; Last Rites, 1981. *Contributor to:* The Paris Review, Evergreen Review, International Herald Tribune, Penthouse, New American Review. *Honours:* Paris Review Humour Prize, 1969; National Endowment for the Arts Fellowship, 1974. *Memberships:* Authors' Guild; Mystery Writers of America; PEN. *Address:* c/o St Catherine's College, Oxford, OX1 3UJ, England.

SPILLEMAECKERS, Werner Lodewijk, b. 3 Dec. 1936, Antwerp, Belgium. Author. *Education:* BA, History of Art & Archaeology, Institute for Art History, Antwerp, 1965. *Literary Appointments:* Founder & Editor, magazines Mandragora, 1954, Artisjok 1968–69; Editor, magazine, Diogenes, 1984–. *Publications include:* Ik ben Berlijn, 1961; Tekst in Tekst Asbest, 1964; Fuga Magister, 1970; Veranda, 1974; Blad na Blad, 1983; Vanaf Alfa, 1970; Verzamelde Gedichten 1954–1974, collected poems, 1974. *Contributions to:* Numerous journals including: Mandragora; Frontaal; De Tafelronde; Artisjok; Album Poëziemarkt Wetteren; Het Kahier X; Avenue; Nieuw Vlaams Tijdschrift; Diogenes. *Honours:* Signaal-prize, 1969; Trap-price, 1975; Knight, Order of the Crown, 1975; Knight, Order of Leopold, 1980; Officer, Order of the Crown, 1985. *Membership:* Association of Flemish Authors. *Address:* Molenstraat 57, B–2018 Antwerp, Belgium.

SPINDLER, George Dearborn, b. 28 Feb. 1920, Wisconsin, USA. University Professor. m. Mary Louise

Schaubel, 29 May 1942, Bessemer, Michigan, 1 daughter. *Education:* BA 1940, MS 1947, University of Wisconsin; PhD, University of California, Los Angeles, 1952. *Publications:* Menominee Acculturation, 1955; Transmission of American Culture, 1959; Anthropology and Education, 1955; Education and Culture, 1963; Education and Cultural Process, 1974; The Making of Psychological Anthropology, 1978, 1980; Doing The Ethnography of Schooling, 1982; Toward An Interpretive Ethnography of Education, 1986; Editor (with wife), over 200 case studies in cultural anthropology. *Contributions to:* Various magazines and journals. *Honours:* Fellowship, Center for Advanced Study in the Behavioral Sciences, Stanford, 1956–57; Distinguished Alumnus, University of Wisconsin, 1972; Dinkelspiel Award for Distinguished Teaching, Stanford, 1978; Distinguished Service Award, Third World Anthropologists and Association for International Diplomacy, 1984. *Memberships:* Journal Editor, American Anthropological Association; President 1982; Council for Education and Anthropology; President, 1963, Southwestern Anthropological Association. *Address:* Ethnographics, P O Box 38, Calistoga, CA 94515, USA.

SPINGARN, Lawrence Perreira, b. 11 July 1917, USA. Emeritus Professor of English; Publisher. m. Sylvia Georgina Wainhouse, 19 June 1949, 1 son, 1 daughter. *Education:* BS, English, Boedoin College; MA, English, University of Michigan. *Publications include:* Rococo Summer & Other Poems, 1947; The Lost River: Poems, 1951; Letters From Exile: Poems, 1961; Madame Bidet: Poems, 1968; Freeway Problems: Poems, 1970; The Blue Door: Stories, 1977; The Dark Playground: Poems, 1979; Moral Tales: Fictions, 1983. *Contributions to:* Numerous periodicals including: The European; Harper's; Kenyon Review; Modern Age; New Yorker; New York Times; Paris Review; Poetry; Western Humanities Reviews; Yale Review; etc. *Honours:* Bread Loaf Fellowship, 1941, 1942; MacDowell Colony Fellowships 1946, 1981; Huntington Hartford Award & Fellowships, 1950, 1955, 1956; Yaddo Fellowship, 1958; Best Poem, Poetry Society of America, 1975; Best Poem of Year, Yankee Magazine, 1981. *Memberships:* International Institute of Arts & Letters; PEN; Poetry Society of America; Poetry Society (UK). *Address:* c/o Perivale Press, 13830 Erwin Street, Van Nuys, CA 91401, USA.

SPINK, John Stephenson, b. 22 Aug. 1909, Pickering, Yorkshire, England, deceased 4 June 1985. Former University Teacher. m. Dorothy Knowles, 27 July 1940, Liverpool. *Education:* BA 1930, MA 1932, Universities of Leeds and Paris; Docteur de l'Univerité de Paris, 1934. *Literary Appointments:* Assistant, Lycée Henri IV, Paris 1930–33; Lecturer, Sorbonne, 1931; Assistant Lecturer, University of Leeds, 1933–36; Lecturer, King's College, University of London, 1937–50; Professor of French, University College, Southampton, 1950–52; Professor of French, Bedford College, University of London, 1952–74; Editorial Board, French Studies, 1985–. *Publications:* J-J Rousseau et Geève, 1934; The Tanker Derbent, translation of Krimov, 1944; Critical Edition of J-J Rousseau Les Rêveries du Promeneur solitaire, 1948; Literature and the Sciences in the Age of Molière, 1953; French Free-Thought From Gassendi to Voltaire, Several foreign Langauge translation, 1960; Critical Edition of Rousseau's Educational Writings in Pléiade Oeuvres Complètes, Vol VI, 1969; Diderot Oeuvres Complètes, Vol II, Joint Editor, 1975. *Contributions to:* Annales J-J Rousseau; Mercure de France; Revue d'Histoire Littéraire; Modern Language Review; Revue e Littérature Comparée; Problèmes des Genres Littéraires; Cahiers de l'Association Internationale des Etudes Françaises; Dix-huitième Siècle; Actes du Colloque Diderot, 1984; W H Barber Festschrift, 1985. *Honours:* Lauréat de l'Académie Française, 1935; Officier de l'Ordre National du Mérite, 1973; Emeritus Professor of French, London University, 1974. *Address:* 48 Woodside Park Road, London N12 8RS, England.

SPINK, Reginald (William), b. 9 Dec. 1905, York, England. Journalist; Translator. *Publications:* The Land and People of Denmark, 1953; Fairy Tales of Denmark, retellings, 1961; The Young Hans Andersen, 1962; Hans Christian Andersen and His World, 1972; Hans Christian Andersen: The Man and His Work, 1972; 40 aar efter (memoirs), 1983; England bygger op, with Jenns Otto Krag, 1947, Swedish edition, 1948. Translations include: Ludvig Holberg: Three Comedies, Carl Nielson: My Childhood; Living Music; Palle Lauring: The Roman; Poul Borchsenius: Behind the Wall; Land of the Tollund Man; Hans Christian Andersen: Fairy Tales and Stories; Bengt Danielsson: Gauguin in the South Seas. *Contributions to:* Several leading journals. *Memberships:* Society of Authors; Translators Association, Executive Committee. *Honours:* Knights Cross of Danish Order of the Dannebrog, 1966. Ebbe Munck Memorial Award, 1983. *Address:* 6 Deane Way, Eastcote, Ruislip, Middlesex HA4 8SU, England.

SPIRES, Elizabeth, b. 28 May 1952, Lancaster, Ohio, USA. Writer; Poet. *Education:* BA, Vassar College, 1974; MA, Johns Hopkins University, 1979. *Publications:* Globe, poems, 1981; Swan's Island, poems, 1985. *Contributions:* Poetry to: New Yorker; New Republic; Poetry; American Poetry Review; American Review; Paris Review; Partisan Review; Yale Review; Antaeus; Antioch Review; New Criterion; Ploughshares. *Honours:* W K Rose Fellowship, Creative Arts, 1976; Creative Writing Fellowship, National Endowment for the Arts, 1981; Ingram Merrill Foundation Award, 1982; Individual Artist's Grant, Maryland State Arts Council, 1982. *Memberships:* Poetry Society of America; Academy of American Poets. *Address:* 3005 Cresmont Avenue, Baltimore, MD 21211, USA.

SPITZ, Lewis William, b. 14 Dec. 1922, Nebraska, USA. University Professor. m. Edna Huttenmaier, 14 Aug. 1948, Lincoln, Nebraska, 2 sons. *Education:* AB, Concordia College; MDiv, Concordia Seminary; MA, University of Missouri, PhD, Harvard University. *Literary Appointments:* Assistant to Associate Professor, University of Missouri, 1953–59; Associate to Full Professor, Stanford University, 1960–. *Publications:* Conrad Celtis, The German Arch-Humanist, 1957; The Religious Renaissance of the German Humanists, 1963; Life in Two Worlds – A Biography of William Sihler, 1968; The Renaissance and Reformation Movements, 1980; The Protestant Reformation, 1517–1559, 1985. *Contributions to:* Archive for Reformation History; Church History; over 70 Chapters in theological and scholarly journals. *Honours:* Harbison Award for Outstanding College Teaching, 1965; DD, Concordia Theological Seminary, 1977; LLD, Valparaiso University, Indiana, 1978; LittD, Wittenberg University, Ohio, 1983. *Memberships:* President, Central Renaissance Conference, Renaissance Society of America; President, Northern California Renaissance Conference; President, American Society for Reformation Research; President, American Society of Church History. *Address:* History Department, Stanford University, Stanford, CA 94305, USA.

SPITZER, Lyman Junior, b. 26 June 1914, Toledo, Ohio, USA. Professor Emeritus of Astronomy. m. Doreen D Canaday, 29 June 1940, 1 son, 3 daughters. *Education:* BA, Yale University, 1935; MA, 1937, PhD, 1938, Princeton University, New Jersey. *Publications:* Physics of Sound in the Sea, Editor, 1946, 69; Physics of Fully Ionized Gases, 1956, 62; Diffuse Matter in Space, 1968; Physical Process in the Interstellar Medium, 1978; Searching Between the Stars, 1982. *Contributions to:* Astrophysical Journal; Monthly Notices of Royal Astronomical Society; The Physical Review; Physics of Fluids. *Honours include:* DSc: Yale University, 1958; Case Instute of Technology, 1961; Harvard University, 1975; Princeton University, 1984. LLD, University of Toledo, 1963; Henry Norris Russell Lecturer, 1953; Rittenhouse Medal, Franklin Institute, 1957; Exceptional Scientific Achievement Medal, NASA, 1972; Bruce Gold Medal, Astronomical Society of the Pacific, 1973; James Clerk Maxwell Prize, American Physical Society, 1975; Gold Medal, Royal Astronomical Society, England, 1978; National Medal of Science, 1980; Jules Medal, Societe Astronomique de France, 1980; Franklin Medal, Franklin Institute, 1980; Crafoord Prize, Royal Swedish Academy of Science, 1985. *Address:* Princeton University Observatory, Peyton Hall, Princeton, NJ 08544, USA.

SPITZER, Robert James, b. 12 Sep. 1953, Utica, New York, USA. College Professor of Political Science. *Education:* BA Summa cum laude, State University of New York, 1975; MA, 1978, PhD, 1980, Cornell University. *Publications:* The Presidency and Public Policy, 1983; New York State Today, chapter, 1985; The Right to Life Movement and Third Party Politics, 1986; Moral Controvosies and Public Policy, chapter. *Contributions to:* American Political Science Review; Journal of Politics; Presidential Studies Quarterly; National Civic Review; Perspective; Administrative Science Quarterly; America. *Address:* 29 Clinton Street, Homer, NY 13077, USA.

SPIVACK, Charlotte, b. 23 July 1926, Schoharie, New York, USA. University Professor. m. Bernard Spivack, 17 Oct. 1956, 1 son, 1 daughter. *Education:* BA, State University of New York, Albany, 1947; MA, Cornell University, 1948; PhD, University of Missouri, Columbia, 1954. *Major Publications:* Early English Drama (co-author), 1966; George Chapman, 1967; The Comedy of Evil on Shakespeare's Stage, 1978; Ursula K Le Guin, 1984. *Contributor to:* The Centennial Review, *Address:* Department of English, University of Massachusetts, Amherst, MA 01003, USA.

SPIVEY, Ted Ray, b. 1 July 1927, Fort Pierce, Florida, USA. University Professor. m. Julia Douglas, 30 June 1962, 1 son, 1 daughter. *Education:* BA, Emory University; MA, PhD, University of Minnesota. *Publications:* A Manual of Style, with Kenneth England, 1960; The Renewed Quest, 1969; The Coming of the New Man, 1971; The Journey Beyond Tragedy, 1980; Revival: Southern Writers in the Modern City, 1986. *Contributions to:* The Southern Review; Studies in the Literary Imagination; The Southern Quarterly. *Address:* 3181 Frontenac Court North East, Atlantic, GA 30319, USA.

SPRACKLING, Michael Thomas, b. 6 Nov. 1934, Tewkesbury, England. University Lecturer. m. Brenda Riches, 30 July 1960, Nunhead, London, England, 5 sons. *Education:* BSc, 1955, PhD, 1959, University of Bristol. *Publications:* The Mechanical Properties of Matter, 1970; The Plastic Deformation of Simple Ionic Crystals, 1976; Liquids and Solids, 1985. *Contributions to:* Several papers in Philosophical Magazine; Journal of Photographic Science; Journal of Physics. *Address:* 35 Princes Gardens, Acton, London W3 OLX, England.

SPREADBURY, Frank George, b. 18 Aug. 1908, London, England. Lecturer. *Education:* Senior Member, MIEEE; MASEE. *Publications:* Aircraft Electrical Engineering, 1943; Electric Discharge Lighting, 1946; Electronics, 1947; Permanent Magnets, 1949; Fractional Horse Power Electric Motors, 1951; Electrical Ignition Equipment, 1954; Electronic Measurements and Measuring Instruments, 1956; Electricity in Aircraft, 1958; Electronic Rectification, 1962; Electronic Invertors, 1967; Non Mechanical Energy Conversion, 1968; Principles and Characteristics of Electron Devices, 1973. *Contributions to:* The American Academic Encyclopedia; translator of French and Spanish scientific literature, Institute of Electrical Engineers. *Honours:* Silver Medallist, London College of Music, 1925; Associate, London College of Music (A Mus LCM), 1929. *Address:* 15 Melrose Avenue, Cricklewood, London NW2 4LH, England.

SPREIREGEN, Paul David, b. 12 Dec. 1931, Boston, Massachusetts, USA. Architect. m. Rose-Helene Bester, 6 Mar. 1961. *Education:* B Arch, MIT, 1954; Fulbright Scholar, Italy, 1954–55. *Publications:* Urban Design: The Architecture of Towns and Cities, 1965; The Modern Metropolis: Selected Essays of Hans Blumenfeld, (editor) 1967; On the Art of Designing Cities: Selected Essays of Elbert Peets, (editor) 1968; Building a New Town: The Story of Finland's City,

Topiola, with Heikki von Hertzen, 1971, 1973; Metropolis and Beyond: Selected Essays of Hans Blumenfeld (editor) 1978; Design Competitons, 1979. *Contributor to:* The Development of Skyscrapers, in Encyclopedia Britannica 1986 Yearbook of Science and the Future. *Honour:* Fellow, American Institute of Architects, 1977. *Address:* 2215 Observatory Place N W, Washington, DC 20007, USA.

SPRENT, Peter, b. 28 Jan. 1923, Hobart, Australia. Writer. m. Janet Irene Findlater, 9 Apr. 1955, Stoke Poges. *Education:* BSc, University of Tasmania, 1946; PhD, University of London, 1966. *Literary Appointments:* Editor, Notes & Queries, Biometrics; Associate Editor, Journal of American Statistical Association; Editor, Applied Statistics. *Publications:* Models in Regression, 1969; Statistics in Action, 1977; Quick Statistics, 1981. *Contributions:* Numerous scientific & technical papers in various statistical journals; Popular articles on science & aviation. *Honour:* Fellow, Royal Society of Edinburgh, 1973. *Membership:* Society of Authors. *Address:* 32 Birkhill Avenue, Wormit, Fife, DD6 8PW, Scotland.

SPRIGGE, Timothy Lauro Squire, b. 14 Jan. 1932, London, England. University Professor. m. 4 Apr. 1959, London, 1 son, 2 daughters. *Education:* MA, PhD, Cantab. *Publications:* Correspondence of Jeremy Bentham, volumes I and II, (editor), 1968; Facts, Words and Beliefs, 1970; Santayana: An Examination of his Philosophy, 1974; The Vindication of Absolute Idealism, 1983; Theories of Existence, 1984. *Contributions to:* Learned journals including: Mind; Philosophy; Inquiry; Nous. Reviews for: learned journals; Times Literary Supplement; Times Higher Education Supplement; and others. *Address:* 14 Great Stuart Street, Edinburgh EH3 7TN, Scotland.

SPRINGER, Haskell Saul, b. 18 Nov. 1939, New York City, USA. Professor of English. m. Marlene Jones, 8 June 1964, Louisville Kentucky, USA, 2 daughters. *Education:* BA, Queen's College, City University of New York, 1961; MA 1965, PhD 1968, Indiana University. *Literary Appointments:* Professor of English, University of Kansas. *Major Publications:* Studies in Billy Budd, 1970; Rip Van Winkle & The Legend of Sleepy Hollow, 1975; Washington Irving: A Reference Guide, 1976; The Sketch Book of Geoffrey Crayon, Gent, 1978; Plains Woman: The Diary of Martha Farnsworth, 1985. *Contributor to:* Ohio History; South Atlantic Bulletin; Modern American Poetry; American Transcendental Quarterly; Resources for American Literary Study; New England Quarterly. *Honours:* Fulbright Professorship, Rio de Janeiro, 1975–76; Visiting Professor of American Literature, The Sorbonne, Paris, France, 1985–86. *Memberships:* Modern Language Association; American Culture Association; Midcontinent American Studies Association; President 1982–83; Melville Society. *Address:* Department of English, University of Kansas, Lawrence, KS 66045, USA.

SPRINGER, Otto, b. 18 Mar. 1905, Aalen, Wurttemberg, Germany. University Professor of Germanic Languages and Literatures. m. Herta Fischer-Colbrie, 26 Mar. 1959, Philadelphia, USA, 2 sons, 1 daughter. *Education:* Gymnasium Heilbronn, Germany; Evangelical Theological Seminary Maulbronn, 1919–21; Evangelical Theological Seminary Blaubeuren, 1921–23. *Literary Appointments:* Assistant Professor of German, Wheaton College, Norton, Massachusetts, USA; Professor and Chairman, Germanics Department, University of Kansas, Lawrence, Professor of Germanic Language and Literature, University of Pennsylvanie, Philadelphia. *Publications:* Die Flussnamen Wurttembergs und Badens, 1930; Die nord Renaissance in Skandinavien, 1936; A German Conscript with Napoleon, 1938; Langenscheidts enzykl, Wb d engl & dt Sprache, I, 1, 2 and II, 1 2, 1963–75; Arbeiten z germ Phlogie and z Literatur des Mittelalters, 1975; (in preparation) Wtymol Worterbcuh des Althochdeutschen. *Contributor to:* Language journals, etc. *Honours:* Honorary Degree of doctor of Humane Letters, 1984; Destschrift; Germanic Studies in Honor of Otto Springer, 1978. *Memberships:*

Modern Langauge Association of America; Fellow, Medieval Academy of America; Correspondierendes Mitflied des Institute fur Duetsche Sprache, Mannheim. *Address:* 1311 Pine Road, Rosemont, PA 19010, USA.

SPULBER, Nicolas, b. 1 Jan. 1915, Brasov, Romania, Professor of Economics. *Education:* MA, PhD, 1952, New School for Social Research, New York City, New York, USA. *Publications:* The Economics of Communist Eastern Europe, 1957, 76; The Soviet Economy Structure, Principles, Problems, 1962, 69; The State and Economic Development in Eastern Europe, 1966; Socialist Management and Planning, 1971; Quantitive Economic Policy and Planning, Co-Author, 1976; Organizational Alternatives in Soviet Type Economics, 1979. *Contributons to:* Journal of Economic Literature; Kylos; Review of Economics and Statistics; Weltwitschaftliches Archiv; Challenge and others. *Honours:* Title of Distinguished Professor of Economics, 1974. *Memberships:* Amrican Economics Association; Royal Economic Society. *Address:* Department of Economics, Indiana University, Bloomington, IN, 47405, USA.

SPURLING, (Susan) Hilary, b. 25 Dec. 1940, Manchester, England. Writer. m. John Spurling. 4 Apr. 1961, Bristol, 2 sons, 1 daughter. *Education:* BA, Somerville College, University of Oxford. *Literary Appointments:* Theatre Critic, The Spectator, 1964–70; Literary Editor, The Spectator, 1966–70. *Major Publications:* Ivy When Young: The Early Life of Ivy Compton-Burnett 1884–1919, 1974; Handbook of Anthony Powell's Music of Time, 1977; Secrets of a Woman's Heart: Later Life of Ivy Compton-Burnett 1920–69, 1984. *Contributor to:* The Observer (book reviews). *Honours:* Rose Mary Crawshay Prize, 1974; Duff Cooper Memorial Prize, 1985; Heinemann Literary Award (jointly), 1985; *Literary Agent:* David Higham, London. *Address:* c/o David Higham, 5-8 Lower John Street, Golden Square, London W1R 4HH, England.

SPURNEY, Nicole, b. 26 Jan. 1930, Alés, France. Writer. m. Alan B Spurney, 1 son, 1 daughter. *Education:* BA, Wellesley College, USA; Certificate Propedeutique, Piaget Institute, University of Geneva, Switzerland. *Publications:* Reina The Galgo, 1981. *Contributor to:* Weekly Column, Looking at Galleries, Geneva Weekly Tribune, Switzerland, 1967–68; Swiss Correspondent, Pictures in Exhibit, New York, 1966–68; Articles in Washington Star; Alexandria Gazette; Brides Magazine; Americas. *Address:* c/o J M Dent & Sons Ltd, Aldine House, 33 Welbeck Street, London W1M 8LX, England.

SQUIRE, Susan Beth, b. 17 Oct. 1950, Connecticut, USA. Writer. m. James Lee Rahman, 1 May 1976, Los Angeles. *Education:* BA, English Literature, Pomona College, Claremont, California. *Publication:* The Slender Balance, 1983. *Contributions to:* Hollywood Extras, New York Times Magazine; The Doctor's Dilemma: Practising Defensive Medicine, New York Magazine; Who's In Charge Here?, Playboy; Sexual Midlife Crisis, Redbook. *Literary Agent:* Kathy P Robins. *Address:* c/o The Robbins Office Inc, 866 Second Avenue, New York, NY 10017, USA.

STAAL, Jan, b. 1925. Playwright. *Education:* School of Dramatic Art. *Publications:* Theatre Plays: Customers Can't Wait; Ashes from Tjiparan; Wrong Start; Deliver Us From All Evil; Back to Warschau; Mother, Can I Go To The Office?; A Day Like All the Others. Television Plays: The Last Train; I Thought To Be On Time. Cabaret series for Television called Adventures in the French Manner. Series for Youngsters, Bart Boudewjin. An adaptation of, The Knock On the Door, originally by Ina Boudier Bakker. Original comedy series, My Aunt Victoria. The Persijn Family, published for 700 year commemoration of city of Amsterdam. Two adaptations from Simenon's series, Maigret. *Address:* Prinsengracht 571/I, 1016 HT Amsterdam, The Netherlands.

STAAR, Richard Felix, b. 10 Jan. 1923, Warsaw, Poland. Political Scientist. m. Jadwiga Ochota, 28 Mar. 1950, Wyandotte, 2 daughters. *Education:* BA,

Dickinson College; MA, Yale University; PhD, University of Michigan. *Appointments:* Editor, Yearbook on International Communist Affairs, 1969–; Member, Editorial Boards, Current History, 1980–; Orbis, 1984–; Strategic Review, 1985–. *Publications:* Poland 1944–62, 1962, 1975; Communist Regimes in Eastern Europe, 1967, 1971, 1977, 1982; Arms Control: Myth vs Reality, 1984, Editor; USSR Foreign Policies After Detente, 1985; Societ Military Policy Since World War II, Co-author, 1986. *Contributor to:* Journal Central European Affairs; American Slavic and East European Review; Military review; Etudes Slaves & East-Europeennes; Mid West Journal of Political science; New Leader; Il Politico; Marine Corps Gazette; Wehrkunde; Journal Public Law; Current History; Revista de estudois politicos; Naval War College Review; East Europe; US Naval Institute Proceedings; Temoignages; Communist Affairs. *Address:* Hoover Institution on War, Revolution & Peace, Stanford University, Stanford, CA 94305, USA.

STABILE, Toni (Antoinette D), b. New York City, USA. Writer. *Education:* AB Journalism, University of Kentucky; Post-graduate Study, Columbia University. *Major Publications:* Cosmetics: Trick or Treat?, 3rd edition, 1969; Cosmetics: The Great American Skin Game, revised edition 1979; Everything you Want to Know about Cosmetics, 1984. *Contributor to:* The Nation; Reader's Digest; Redbook; Today's Health; Drug & Cosmetic Industry; Field Newspaper Syndicate; and other national & international magazines & newspapers. *Honour:* WPIX-TV award for Service to Consumers, 1974. *Memberships:* Authors Guild; American Society of Journalists & Authors; Deadline Club; Society of Professional Journalists; Women in Communications; National Association of Television Arts & Sciences; National Press Club. *Address:* 411 East 53rd Street, New York, NY 10022, USA.

STACEY, Margaret, b. 27 Mar. 1922, London, England. University Professor of Sociology. m. Frank Arthur Stacey, 20 May 1945, 3 sons, 2 daughters. *Education:* BSc, Economics, London University. *Publications:* Tradition and Change: A Study of Banbury, 1960, Reprinted 1964. This impression and paperback edition 1970. Methods of Social Research, 1969; Editor: Hospitals, Children and their Families: A Study of the Welfare of Children in Hospital, 1970; Power, Persistence and Change: A Second Study of Banbury, co-author with Eric Batstone, Colin Bell and Anne Murcott, 1975; Editor, The Sociology of the National Health Service, 1976; Beyond Separation: Further Studies of Children in Hospital, joint editor with David Hall and author of one chapter, 1979; Women, Power and Politics, joint author with Marion Price, 1981. *Contributions to:* Articles and reviews in Sociology, Sociological Review, Feminist Review, Social Science and Medicine. *Honour:* Fawcett Prize (with Marion Price) for Women, Power and Politics, 1982. *Membership:* Honorary Secretary, Chairperson, President, british Sociological Association. *Literary Agent:* Curtis Brown, London, England. *Address:* 8 Lansdowne Circus, Leamington Spa, Warwickshire CV32 4SW, England.

STACEY, Tom, b. 11 Jan. 1930, Bletchingley, England. Author. *Education:* Oxford University. *Publications:* The Hostile Sun, 1953; The Brothers M, 1960; Summons to Ruwenzori, 1964; Today's World, 1968; The Living & the Dying, 1975; The Pandemonium, 1979; The Worm in the Rose, 1985. *Contributions to:* Numerous journals. *Honours:* Fellow, Royal Society of Literature, 1977; Llewellyn Rhys Memorial Prize, 1954; Granada Award, 1961. *Literary Agent:* Curtis Brown. *Address:* 128 Kensington Church Street, London W8, England.

STACK, George Joseph, b. 8 Nov. 1932, New York, USA. Professor of Philosophy. m. 8 Sep. 1962, Claire Joan Avena (deceased), 1 son, 1 daughter. *Education:* BA, Pace University, New York, 1960; MA, 1962, PhD, 1964, Pennsylvania State University. *Major Publications:* Berkeley's Analysis of Perception, 1970; On

Kierkegaard: Philosophical Fragments, 1976; Kierkegaard's Existential Ethics, 1977; Sartre's Philosophy of Social Existence, 1978; Lange & Nietzsche, 1983. *Contributor to:* Professional journals and periodicals throughout the world (some 350 articles & reviews). *Address:* Department of Philosophy, State University of New York, Brockport, NY 14420, USA.

STACK, Neville Maurice, b. 2 Sep. 1928, Manchester, England. Editor. m. Molly Rowe, 19 Oct. 1953, Tipton, 1 son, 1 daughter. *Literary Appointment:* Editor, Leicester Mercury. *Publication:* The Empty Palace, 1976. *Literary Agent:* John Johnson. *Address:* 34 Main Street, Belton-in-Rutland, Oakham, Leicestershire LE15 9LB, England.

STADE, George Gustav, b. 25 Nov. 1933, New York City, USA. Professor, English; Writer. m. Dorothy Fletcher, 16 Dec. 1956, New York, 2 sons, 2 daughters. *Education:* BA, St Lawrence University, 1955; MA, 1958, PhD, 1965, Columbia University. *Appointments:* Bernard Baruch School of Business, 1957–58; Brooklyn Polytechnic Institute, 1958–59; Rutgers in Newark, 1960–62; Columbia University, 1962–. *Publications:* Editor: Selected Letters of E E Cummings, 1968; Six Modern British Novelists, 1974; Six Contemporary British Novelists, 1976; Columbia Essays on Modern Writers 1964–76, 74 Volumes; European Writers 1983–, in progress; Robert Graves, 1967; Confessions of a Lady-Killer, 1979. *Contributor to:* Over 100 articles and reviews in Journals such as, Partisan; Hudson; Nation; New Republic; New York Times Book Review; College English; Chronicle of Higher Education; etc. *Memberships:* PEN; New York Book Critics Circle; MLA; CCCC; Popular Culture Association. *Literary Agent:* Russell and Volkening. *Address:* English Dept, Columbia University, New York, NY 10027, USA.

STADTLER, Bea, b. 26 June 1921, Cleveland, Ohio, USA. College Registrar (retired)/Writer. m. Dr Oscar Stadtler, 31 Jan. 1945, Cleveland, 1 son, 2 daughters. *Education:* Religious School Teacher's Diploma; Bachelor of Jewish Studies; MS in Religious Education. *Publications:* Once Upon a Jewish Holiday, 1965; The Adventures of Gluckel of Hameln, 1967; The Story of Dona Gracia, 1969; Saviour from the Sky, in Hebrew, 1971; The Holocaust: A History of Courage and Resistance, 1974. *Contributions to:* Western Reserve Magazine; Young Judaean; Shofar; World Over; Olomeinu; Our Age; Methodist Update; Linn's Stamp News; Israel Philatelist; Jewish Education Magazine; Davka Magazine; New Book of Knowledge, published by Grolier; Weekly columns for Youth in many Jewish weeklies for past 20 years. *Honour:* National Jewish Book Award for Outstanding Jewish Juvenile, 1975. *Address:* 24355 Tunbridge Lane, Beachwood, OH 44122, USA.

STAFF, Frank William, b. 9 Mar. 1908, Kirn, Argyll, Scotland. Private Courier. m. Alison M Hay, 3 Feb. 1937, Weymouth, 2 sons. (1 deceased). *Publications:* The Transatlantic Mail, 1956; The Penny Post 1680–1918, 1964; The Valentine and its Origins, 1969; Picture Postcards and Travel, 1979. *Contributions to:* Articles on Postal History, Valentines and Picture Postcards to English and American journals. *Honours:* Fellow, Royal Geographical Society. *Address:* West Cliff, West Bay, Bridport, Dorset, England.

STAGG, Frank, b. 20 Oct. 1911, Eunice, Louisiana, USA. Minister; Professor. m. Evelyn Owen, 19 Aug. 1935, Alexandria, Louisiana, 2 sons, 1 daughter. *Education:* BA, Louisiana College, 1934; THM, 1938, PhD, 1943, The Southern Baptist Theological Seminary; LLD, Louisiana College, 1955. *Literary Appointment:* Managing Editor, Review and Expositor, 1965–71, 1974–75. *Publications:* The Book of Acts, The Early Struggle for an Unhindered Gospel, 1955; Exploring the New Testament, 1961; New Testament Theology, 1962; Studies in Luke's Gospel, 1967; Glossolalia, Tongue Speaking in Biblical, Historical and Psychological Perspective, with Wayne E Oates and E Glenn Hinson, 1967; Commentary on Matthew, in Broadman Bible Commentary, 1969; Commentary on, Philippians, in Broadman Bible Commentary, 1971; The Holy Spirit Today, 1973; Polarities of Man's Existence in Biblical Perspective, 1973; Woman in the World of Jesus, with Evelyn Stagg, 1978; Galatians/Romans, in Knox Preaching Guides, 1980; The Bible Speaks on Aging, 1981; The Doctrine of Christ, 1985. *Contributor to:* Review and Expositor; The Journal of Biblical Literature; The Southwestern Journal; The Theological Educator. *Memberships:* Society of Biblical Literature; The Academy of Religion. *Address:* 5610 Ahuawa Place, Diamondhead, Bay St Louis, MS 39520, USA.

STAICAR, Thomas Edward, b. 30 May 1946, Detroit, Michigan, USA. Writer. m. 27 Apr. 1975, Detroit, Michigan. *Educations:* BA Political Science, Wayne State University, Detroit. *Literary Appointments:* Science Fiction General Editor, Frederick Ungar Publishing Co, 1980–82; Book Review Columist, Amazing Stories Magazine, 1979–82, Fantastic Stories Magazine 1982. *Major Publications:* Fritz Leiber, 1983; Critical Encounters II (essays) editor, 1982; The Feminine Eye (essays) editor, 1982. *Contributor to:* New Magazine Review; Science Fiction Review; SF & Fantasy Book Review; New England Senior Citizen; An Arbor News; Twilight Zone Magazine; and others. *Address:* 1515 Pine Valley Boulevard, Apt 2B, Ann Arbor, MI 48104, USA.

STALDER, Heinz, b. 1 July 1939, Allenlüften, Switzerland. Teacher. *Education:* Business School, Lucerne. *Publications:* Ching hei si gnue, 1969; Angu, 1970; 96 Liebesgedichte und 20 Pullover, 1974; (Novels): Das Schweigende Gewicht, 1981; Marschieren, 1984; Das Bild on Ende des Ganges, 1986; (Plays): Wi Unghuur Us Amerika, 1978; Ein Pastalozzi, 1979; Lerchenfeld, 1981; Chatz u Muus, 1983; Der Todesfahrer, 1986; (Lyric Poetry); Features for Radio and TV. *Honours:* Art Prize, Lucerne, 1976; First Prize, Drama Competition, 10 Swiss Cities, 1978; Welti Prize for Drama, 1979; Literary Prizes for the novels, Das Scweigenda Gewicht, and Marschieran, Berne and Lucerne. *Membership:* Swiss Authors Group, Olten. *Literary Agent:* Nagel and Kimche, Zurich. *Address:* Erlenweg 4, CH–6010 Kriens, Switzerland.

STAMBLER, Peter Lane, b. 17 Nov. 1944, Washington DC, USA. Professor. m. 27 Oct. 1984, Green Bay, 1 son, 2 daughters, 2 stepdaughters. *Education:* BA, Yale University, 1966; MFA, Carnegie Mellon, 1968; PhD, Syracuse University, 1974. *Publications:* Wilderness Fires, 1981; Witnesses, 1984; Clara's Husband, drama, 1984. *Contributor to:* Beloit Poetry Journal; Kansas Quarterly; Shenendoah; Carolina Quarterly; Willow Springs, etc. *Honours:* Leonard Crown Poetry Prize, 1972I Ingram Merrill Foundation grant, 1979; Council for Wisconsin Writers Best Book Award, 1982; CWW Best Play Award, 1984; Wisconsin Public Radio Drama Award, 1983. *Address:* University of Wisconsin, Green Bay CC 331, Green Bay, WI 54302, USA.

STAMP, Roger, b. 28 June 1913, Glasgow, Scotland. Engineering Design Draughtsman (retired). m. Nelly Edith Chevalley, 9 Jan. 1973, Bromley, London. *Education:* Advanced Mathematics Diploma, Advanced Applied Mathematics Diploma. *Major Publications:* Oil Weight Tables, 1954; Ten Days to the Moon, 1955. *Memberships:* Society of Authors; The Authors' Lending and Copyright Society; The Penman Club; Books at Stationer's Hall, London. *Address:* Au Verger, 1812 Rivaz, Canton Vaud, Switzerland.

STAMPP, Kenneth M, b. 12 July 1912, Milwaukee, Wisconsin, USA. University Professor. m. Isabel Macartney Filgate, 4 July 1962, Oxford, England, 1 daughter, 1 son, 1 daughter, by previous marriage. *Education:* PHB, 1935; MA, 1937, PhD, 1942, University of Wisconsin; MA, Oxford, 1961. *Appointment:* Professor Emeritus, History, University of California, Berkeley. *Publications:* Indiana Politics during the Civil War, 1949; And the War Came: The North and the Secession Crisis 1860–1861, 1950; The

Peculiar Institution: Slavery in the Ante-Bellum South, 1956; The Causes of the Civil War, 1959; Co-Author, The National Experience, 1963; The Era of Reconstruction, 1964; The Imperiled Union, 1980. *Contributor to:* American Historical Review; Journal of American History; Journal of Southern History; Journal of Negro History; etc. *Honours:* Silver Medal, Commonwealth Club, 1981; Honorary Doctor of Humane Letters, University of Wisconsin, Milwaukee, 1981; Award of Merit, Confederate Memorial Literary Society, 1981. *Memberships:* Organization of American Historians, President, 1978; American Historical Association; American Antiquarian Society; American Academy of Arts and Sciences. *Address;* 682 San Luis Road, Berkeley, CV 94707, USA.

STANDER, Siegfried, b. 26 Aug. 1935, Rieteron, Republic of South Africa. Author. m. Jo, 1 son, 1 daughter. *Publications:* Fiction: This Desert Place, 1961; The Emptiness of the Plains, 1965; Strangers, 1965; The Journeys of Josephine, 1968; The Horse, 1969; The Fortress, 1972; Leopard in the Sun, 1973; The Unwanted, with Professor Barnard, 1976; Flight from the Hunter, 1977; In the Night Season, with Professor Barnard, 1978; Into the Winter, 1983; The Faith, with Professor Barnard, 1984. Non-Fiction: Tree of Life, 1983; Like the Wind, 1985. *Contributions to:* Various publications. *Honours:* CNA Literary Award, 1961, 68. *Memberships:* Poets, Playwrights, Editors, Essayists and Novelists; Authors League. *Literary Agent:* A M Heath and Company. *Address:* Cliff Cottage, Plettenberg Bay, Republic of South Africa.

STANFORD, Barbara Lynn, b. 4 Sep. 1943, California, USA. Writer; Consultant. m. Gene Stanford, 26 July 1969, Edwardsville, Illinois, USA, 1 son. *Education:* BA, University of Illinois; MA, Teachers' College, Columbia University; PhD, University of Colorado, 1973. *Publications:* Learning Discussion Skills Through Games, 1969; Myths and Modern Man, 1972; On Being Female: An Anthology, 1974; Peacemaking, 1976; Black Literature for High School Students, 1978; Thinking Through Language, 1985. *Contributions to:* Various professional journals. *Address:* 12406 Colleen Drive, Little Rock, AR 72212, USA.

STANFORD, Derek, b. 11 Oct. 1918. Poet; Journalist; Teacher; Editor. *Appointments include:* Lecturer in English Literature and Poetry Writing, City Literary Institute, London, England, 1960–79. *Publications include:* The Freedom of Poetry, 1947; Music for Statues, 1948; A Romantic Miscellany, with J Bayliss, 1946; The Traveller Hears the Strange Machine – Selected Poems, 1980; The Vision and Death of Aubrey Beardsley, 1985. Critical Books including: John Betjeman: A Study, 1961; Dylan Thomas, A Literary Study, 1964; Anne Bronte: Her Life and work, with A Harrison, 1959; Emily Bronte: Her Life and Work, with M Spark, 1963; Tribute to Wordsworth, with M Spark, 1950. Critical Anthologies including: Poets of the Nineties, 1965; Writing of the Nineties, 1971; Pre-Raphaelite Writing, 1976; Inside the Forties: Literary Memoirs, 1936–1956, 1977. *Contributions to:* William Kiraber Supernatural Anthology, 6 editions; studies in Contemporary Verse, 1947; various anthologies and journals including: Scotsman; Books and Bookmen; Times Literary Supplement: Orbis; Tribune; Outposts. *Address:* c/o National Westminster Bank, Law Courts Branch, Chancery Lane, London WC2, England.

STANFORD, Donald Elwin, b. 7 Feb. 1913, Amherst, Massachusetts, USA. Alumni Professor Emeritus of English; Editor Emeritus, Southern Review. m. Maryanna Peterson, 14 Aug. 1953, Reno, Nevada. *Education:* BA, 1933, PhD, 1953, Stanford University; MA, Harvard University, 1934. *Literary Appointments:* Instructor to Alumni Professor of English, Louisiana State University, 1949–83; Visiting Professor, Duke University, North Carolina, 1961–62; Editor, The Southern Review, Louisiana State University, 1963–83; Alumni Professor Emeritus, Louisiana State University, 1983–; Visiting Professor, Texas A&M University, College Station, 1984. *Publications:* New England

Earth, (poems), 1941; The Traveler, (poems), 1955; The Poems of Edward Taylor, 1960; Edward Taylor, 1965; Selected Poems of Robert Bridges, 1974; Selected Poems of S Foster Damon, 1974; In the Classic Mode, The Achievement of Robert Bridges, 1978; Revolution and Convention in Modern Poetry, 1983; Selected Letters of Robert Bridges, (2 volumes), 1983, 84; John Masefield: Letters to Margaret Bridges, 1984; John Masefield: Selected Poems, 1984; Editor, Dictionary of Literary Biography, volumes 19 and 20, 1983; The Cartesian Lawnmower and Other Poems, 1984. *Contributor to:* Southern Review; Hudson Review; Sewanee Review; Michigan Quarterly Review; Hopkins Quarterly, etc. *Honours:* Guggenheim Fellowship, 1959–60; Distinguished Faculty Fellowship, 1973; Distinguished Research Master, 1982. *Memberships:* Phi Beta Kappa; Phi Kappa Phi; PEN; MLA; SAMLA; SCM:A. *Address:* 776 Delgado Drive, Baton Rouge, LA 70808, USA.

STANGER, Frank Bateman, b. 31 Aug. 1914, Cedarville, New Jersey, USA. m. Mardelle Amstutz, 2 June 1937, 1 son, 2 daughters. *Education:* AB, Asbury College, 1934; ThB, Princeton Theological Seminary, 1937; STM, Temply University, 1940; STD, Temply University, 1942. *Publications:* A Workman That Needeth Not To Be Ashamed, 1958; The Pauline Doctrine of Conscience, 1940; Life and Work of the Reverend Joseph Pilmore, 1942; Would You Be Made Whole?, 1967; He Healed Them, 1968; God's Healing Community, 1978; Spiritual Formation in the Local Church, (publication in process). *Contributions to:* Christianity Today; Asbury Seminarian; Methodist History; Good News Magazine; United Methodist Curriculum Series; Denominational Periodicals; Theological Education. *Honours:* DD, Philathea College, 1953; LLD, Houghton College, 1962; LHD, Asbury College, 1970; DSL, Asbury Theological Seminary, 1982; Festschrift, A Celebration of Ministry, Asbury Theological Seminary, 1982. *Address:* 3367 Ridgecane Road, Lexington, KY 40513, USA.

STANHOPE, Henry Seymour, b. 8 May 1934, Newtown, Powys, Wales. Journalist. m. Alison Thomas, 1 Feb. 1964, Chelsea, 1 son. *Education:* BA, London University, 1955. *Literary Appointments:* Defence Correspondent, 1970–82, Diplomatic Correspondent, 1982–, The Times, London; Director, Brassey's Military Publishers Ltd. 1978–. *Publication:* The Soldiers: An Anatomy of the British Army, 1979. *Contributions to:* Various magazines and journals and also to broadcasting. *Literary Agent:* A D Peters. *Address:* The Times, London WC1X 8EZ, England.

STANKIEWICZ, Wladyslaw Jozef, b. 6 May 1922, Warsaw, Poland. Professor of Political Science. *Education:* MA, University of St Andrews, Scotland, 1944; PhD, London School of Economics and Political Science, London, England, 1962. *Publications:* Politics and Religion in 17th-Century France, 1960; Political Thought Since World War II, editor, 1964; In Defence of Sovereignty, editor, 1969; Relativism: Thoughts and Aphorisms, 1972; Canada-US Relations, 1973; Aspects of Political Theory, 1976; A Guide to Democratic Jargon, 1976; Approaches to Democracy: Philosophy of Government at the Close of the Twentieth Century, 1980; The Tradition of Polish Ideals, editor, 1981. *Contributions to:* Political Studies; Political Science Quarterly; Political Science, (New Zealand); Politikon; Proceedings of the American Philosophical Society; Proceedings of the Huguenot Society of London; Canadian Slavonic Papers; Canadian Forum; Contemporary Review; etc. *Honours:* Canada Council Fellow, 1966–69, 1974–75; I W Killam Senior Fellow, 1969–70, 1971–72, 1977–78; SSHRC Fellow, 1979–80. *Address:* Department of Political Science, University of British Columbia, Vancouver V6T 1W5, British Columbia, Canada.

STANLEY, Diane, b. 27 Dec. 1943, Abilene, Texas, USA. Author; Illustrator, Children's Book. m. Peter Vennema, 8 Sep. 1979, Houston, 1 son, 2 daughters. *Education:* BA, Trinity University, San Antonio, Texas,

1965; MA, Johns Hopkins University, 1970. *Publications include:* Story & Pictures: The Conversation Club, 1983; A Country Tale, 1985; Birdsong Lullaby, 1985. Illustrations to: The Farmer in the Dell, 1978; Little Mouse Nibbling, Tony Johnston, 1979; Onions, Onions, Toni Hormann, 1981; Sleeping Ugly, Jane Yolen, 1981; Little Orphant Annie, James Whitcombe Riley, 1983. *Honours:* Children's Choice, American Reading Association, 1979; Best Books, School Library Journal, 1983; Notable Children's Trade Books in field of social studies, 1983; Ann Martin Book Mark Award, Catholic Library Association, 1984. *Address:* 2120 Tangley Street, Houston, TX 77005, USA.

STAPLES, Reginald Thomas, b. 26 Nov. 1911, London, England. Author; Company Director. m. Florence Anne Hume, 12 June, 1937, Sanderstead, Surrey, 1 son. *Publications:* The Summer Day is Done, 1976; Flight from Bucharest, 1977; Appointment in Sarajevo, 1978; Woman of Cordova, 1979; Warrior Queen, 1979; Canis the Warrior, 1980; Fields of Yesterday, 1982; Shadows in the Afternoon, 1983; The Hostage, 1985. *Literary Agent:* Sheila Watson, Watson Little Ltd. *Address:* 52 Dome Hill, Caterham, Surrey CR3 6EB, England.

STAPLES, Robert Eugene, b. 28 June 1942, Roanoke, Virginia, USA. University Professor. *Education:* AA 1960; AB 1964; MA 1965; PhD 1970. *Literary Appointments:* Bethune Cookman College, 1967–68; California State University, Hayward, 1968–70; University of California, Irvine, 1970–71; Howard University, 1971–73; University of California, San Francisco, 1973–. *Publications:* The Lower Income Negro Family in Saint Paul, 1967; The Black Family: Essays and Studies, 1971; The Black Woman in America, 1973; Introduction to Black Sociology, 1976; The World of Black Singles, 1981; Black Masculinity, 1982. *Honours:* Distinguished Achievement, Howard University, 1979; Distinguished Achievement, National Council on Family Relations. *Memberships:* National Council of Family Relations; American Sociological Association; Association of Black Sociologists. *Address:* Graduate Program in Sociology, University of California, San Francisco, CA 94143, USA.

STARKE, Roland, b. Cape, Republic of South Africa; United States resident. Novelist, Screenwriter, dramatist. *Major Publications:* Freedom Ceremony; Something Soft; I never touched you; The 14; Films: The Burning, The 14, and others; Stage: Goodbye Mr Chips (musical, with Leslie Bricusse); Girlie. *Honour:* International Writers' Guild Best Screenplay Award for The 14. *Membership:* Writers' Guild of America (West). *Literary Agents:* Robin Dalton, Fraser & Dunlop (London); Oscard Agency, New York. *Address:* c/o Robin Dalton, Fraser & Dunlop Ltd, 91, Regent Street, London W1, England.

STAROBINSKI, Jean, b. 17 Nov. 1920, Geneva, Switzerland, University Professor. m. Jaqueline Sirman, 15 Aug. 1954, Geneva, 3 sons. *Education:* Licence ès Lettres 1942, Doctorat ès Lettres, 1958, Université de Genève; Doctoriate en medisin MD, Universités de Genève et Lausanne, 1960. *Literary Appointments:* Professor of Literature, Johns Hopkins University, 1954–56; Professor of Literature, University of Geneva, 1958–85. *Publications:* Jean-Jacques Rousseau, 1957; L'Oeil Vicant, 19612; L'Invention de la Liberté, 1964; La Relation Critique, 1970; Portrait de l'artiste en Saltimbanque, 1971; Les Emblèmes de la Raison, 1974; Montaigne en Mouvement, 1982. *Contributions to:* Magazines and journals including: Times Literary Supplement; New York Review of Books; Daedalus; Diogenes; Ke Débat; Critique; La Nouvell Revue Francaise; Vuelta; Neue Rundschau Schweizer Monatsheffer. *Honours:* Honorary Fellow: Accademia dei Lincei, British Academy; American Academy of Arts and Sciences; Accademia delle Scienze di Torino; Prix Européen de L'essai, 1982; Balzan Prize, 1984; Chevalier de la Légion d'honneur, 1980. *Memberships:* President, Société J J Rousseau, Geneva, 1964–.

Address: 12 Rue de Candolle, CH 1205, Geneva, Switzerland.

STARR, Joan Elizabeth, b. 1 Apr. 1927, Tenterfield, New South Wales, Australia. Journalist, Writer. m. David Shearston Thompson, 11 Sep. 1948, Tenterfield, Australia, divorced 1965, 1 son, 1 daughter. *Education:* University Extension courses in advanced English, English Literature; Institute of Modern Languages, Italian. *Literary Appointments:* Roving Reporter, Hoofs and Horns, Country Magazine, Outdoors, 1948–63; Editor, Tenterfield Star, 1963–64; Journalist, Subeditor, The Cairns Post, 1967–71; Cable Subeditor, The Queensland Times, 1971–72; News Editor, Twin Towns Star, 1972; Senior editorial Officer, QHEC, 1972–76; Journalist, Public Relations Section, Australia Post, Brisbane 1976–80; Assistant Manager (Public Relations), Victoria, 1980–83. *Major Publications:* Pioneering New England, Rigby, 1978; Settlers on the Marthaguy, Macquarie, 1979; Wines and Wineries of the Granite Belt, Research, 1982; The Wellington Caves – a Treasure-trove of Fossils, Macquarie, 1985; Melton, Plains of Promise, Melton Shire Council, 1985. *Contributor to:* Roofs and Horns; People; Australasian Post; New Idea; Silver dKisdis; Australian Women's Weekly; Outdoors; Country Magazine; Sunday Mail Colour Magazine; Queensland Country Life; The Northern Daily Leader; and others. *Memberships:* Former Member, Scriptwriters of Brisbane; Committee, Freelance Section, Australian Journalists' Association. *Address:* Arakoon, via Tenterfield, New South Wales, 2372, Australia.

STATLER, Oliver, b. 21 May 1915, Chicago, USA. Writer. *Education:* BA, University of Chigaco. *Publications:* Modern Japanese Prints: An Art Reborn, 1956; Japanese Inn, 1961l The Black Ship Scroll, 1963; Shimoda Story, 1971; Japanese Pilgrimage, 1983, *Literary Agent:* William Morris Agency. *Address:* 1619 Kamamalu Avenue, Apartment 302, Honolulu, HI 96813, USA.

STAUDACHER, Rosemarian V, b. 8 Mar. 1918, Cincinnati, Ohio, USA. Journalist; Teacher. m. Lucas George Staudacher, 4 Sep. 1948, Madeira, 1 son, 1 daughter. *Education:* BA, Edgecliff College; MA, Journalism, Marquette University. *Appointments:* Associate Editor, Pflaum Publishers, Dayton; Literary Critc, Writer's Digest, Cincinnati; Assistant to Public Relations Director, Xavier University, Cincinnati; Reporter, Marquette University News Bureau; Teacher, Messmer High School, Marquette University. *Publications:* Modern Crusaders, 1957; Catholic Campuses, 1958; Chaplains in Action, 1962; Children Welcome, 1963; In American Vineyards, 1966. *Contributor to:* Numerous newspapers, and magazines in US, Canada, India, Ireland. *Honours:* Thomas More Award for Excellence in Journalism, 1940. *Memberships:* Society of Professional Journalists; Council of Wisconsin Writers; Crossroads Poetry Society. *Address:* 2023 East Olive St, Shorewood, WI 53211, USA.

STAUFFER, Heinz, b. 25 Aug. 1942, Wattenwil/Bern, Switzerland. Author. m. Monique Kobel, 9 May 1964, Wattenwil, 2 sons, 1 daughter. *Education:* Gymnasium, Bern; VDM, Universität Bern. *Publications:* 's Geit mi ja Nut a, 1978; Die da Obe, 1979; Zwätschgiebei, 1981; We si nid gschtorbe si, de schtärbe Sino, 1982; Vo nüt chunut eifach nüt, 1985. *Contributions to:* Bund, Bern; Leben und Glauden; Laupenj Der Schweizerische Beobachter, Glattbrugg; Bieler Tagblatt, Biel; Berner Zeitung, Bern. *Memberships:* Berner Schriftsteller-Verein; Schweizerischer Schriftstaller-Verband. *Address:* Bifangweg 3, 3270 Aarberg, Switzerland.

STAVAUX, Michel, b. 6 May 1948, Brussels, Belgium. European Commission Administrator. m. Danielle Lurquin, 18 Aug. 1972, at Nivelles, 2 daughters. *Education:* LLD. *Major Publications:* Cheval d'Ivoire, 1964; La Promenade Rue Voliére, 1970; Le Maître du Hazard, 1977. *Honours:* Polak prize, Royal Academy of French Language and Literature of Belgium.

Membership: PEN Club. *Address:* Au Saint Gérard De Stave, Clos des Chênes, 64, 1170 Brussels, Belgium.

STAVE, Bruce M, b. 17 May 1937, New York City, New York, USA. Professor of History and Chairman. m. Sondra T Astor, 16 June 1961, New York City, 1 son. *Education:* BA, Columbia College, 1959; MA, Columbia University, 1961; PhD, University of Pittsburgh, 1966. *Publications:* The New Deal and the Last Hurrah, 1970; Urban Bosses, Machines and Progressive Reformers, 1970, 84; The Discontented Society, with Leroy Ashby; Socialism and the Cities, 1975; The Making of Urban History, 1977; Modern Industrial Cities, 1982. *Contributions to:* Journal of Urban History and various other journals and newspapers. *Honours:* Harvey Kantor Memorial Award for outstanding work in oral history, 1977; Fulbright Professor, India, 1968–69, Australasia, 1977; People's Republic of China, 1984–85. *Memberships:* Organization of American Historians; American Historical Association; Oral History Association. *Address:* Department of History, University of Connecticut, Storrs, CT 06268, USA.

STAVIS, Barrie, b. 16 June 1906, New York City, USA. Playwright and Historian. m. Bernice Coe, 7 May 1950, 1 son, 1 daughter. *Education:* Columbia University 1924–27. *Literary Appointments:* Lectured and/or gave Seminars at: Wisconsin University, University of Minnesota, Menninger Foundation, Pennsylvania State University, The Swedish Dramatic Institute, Stockholm, Brigham Young University, Syracuse University, University of Kansas, University of Oregon; Visiting Fellow, Institute for the Arts and Humanistic Studies, Pennsylvania State University. *Publications:* Fiction: The Chain of Command 1945; Home Sweet Home!, 1949. Plays: Refuge, 1938; Lamp at Midnight, 1948; The Man Who Never Died, 1954; Harper's Ferry, 1967; Coat of Many Colors, 1968; History: Notes on Joe Hill and His Times, 1954; John Brown: The Sword and the Word, 1970; Song Book: Songs of Joe Hill, edited with Frank Harmon, 1955. Opera: Joe Hill, with music by Alan Bush, 1970. Oratoriio: Galileo Galilei, with music by Lee Hoiby, 1975. *Contributor to:* Saturday Evening Post; Colliers; Ladies Home Journal; This Week; Drama Survey; Folk Music. *Honours:* National Theatre Conference, 1948 and 1949; YADDO Fellowship, 1939; Fellow of the College of Fellows of the American Theatre Association, 1982. *Memberships:* American Theatre Association; National Theatre Conference; PEN; ASCAP; US Institute for Theatre Technology (Co-Founder and Board Member); Dramatists Guild; Authors Guild. *Address:* 70 East 96th Street, New York, NY 10128, USA.

STAVRIANOS, Leften Stavros, b. 5 Feb. 1913, Vancouver, Canada. Professor of History. m. Bertha Kelso, 20 July 1940, 1 son, 1 daughter. *Education:* BA, 1933, MA, 1934, PhD, 1937. *Literary Appointments:* Lecturer, Queens University, Kingston, Canada, 1937; Instructor and Assistant Professor, Smith College, 1939–46; Associate Professor and Professor, Northwestern University, 1946–73; Adjunct Professor, University of California, San Diego, 1974–. *Publications:* Balkan Federation, 1944; Greece: American Dilemma and Opportunity, 1952; Balkans Since 1453, 1958; World Since 1500, 1966; World to 1500, 1970; The Promise of the Coming Dark Age, 1976; Global Rift: The Third World Comes of Age, 1981. *Contributions to:* Approximately 50 popular and professional journals. *Honours:* Royal Society of Canada Travelling Fellowship, 1938–39; Guggenheim Fellowship, 1951–52; Rockefeller Foundation Fellowship, 1967–68; Fellow at Center for Advanced Study in the Behavioural Sciences, 1972–73. *Address:* Department of History, University of California, La Jolla, CA 92093, USA.

STEAD, Thistle Yolette, b. 29 July 1902, Sydney, Australia. Writer; Retured Lecturer. m. David George Stead, 30 June 1951, Sydney. *Education:* BSc, Dip Ee, University of Sydney, 1923; Dip Landscape Design, University of New South Wales, 1969; BEd, MEd, University of Melbourne, 1946; DSc, Honoris causa, University of Woolongong, 1985. *Publications:*

Wildflowers of Australia, 1938; Nature Problems, 1945; Handbook of Nature Study for Teachers, 1945; Australian Plants for the Garden, 1953; Teaching of Nature Study, 1954; Eastern Australian Wildflowers, 1962; Plants without Flowers, 1967; Alpine Plants of Australia, 1970; Gardening with Australian Plants, Trilogy, Shrubs, 1977; Small Plants and Climbers, 1979; Trees, 1980; Editor, Arranger: Naturecraft in Australia, 1956. *Contributor to:* Numerous professional journals including, Australian Wildlife; Wildlife Research News; The Australian Naturalist; Journal of Sex Education, London; New Horizons in Education; etc. *Honours:* Natural History Medallion, Field Naturalists' Club, Victoria, 1963; Benefactor's Medallion, National Trust, 1964; Member Order of Australia, 1980, etc. *Memberships include:* Association for Environmental Studies; Australian Society of Authors; Australian Systematic Botany Society; Wildlife Preservation Society of Australia; Australian Society of Authors; etc. *Address:* 14 Pacific Street, Watson's Bay, NSW 2030, Australia.

STEADMAN, John Marcellus, III, b. 25 Nov. 1918, Spartenburg, South Carolina, USA. Research Scholar; University Professor. *Education:* AB, 1940, MA, 1941, Emory University; MA, 1948, PhD, 1949, Princeton University; LHD, Emory University, 1976. *Publications:* Milton and the Renaissance Hero, 1967; Milton's Epic Characters, 1968; The Myth of Asia, 1969, 70; Disembodied Laughter, 1972; The Lamb and the Elephant, 1974; Nature into Myth: Medieval Renaissance Moral Symbols, 1979; Editor, Huntington Library Quarterly, 1962–81; Epic and Tragic Structure in Paradise Lost, 1976; Milton's Biblical and Classical Imagery, 1984; The Hill and the Labyrinth: Discourse and Certitide in Milton and His Near-Contemporaries, 1984; The Wall of Paradise, Essays on Milton's Poetics, 1985; Co-editor, A Milton Encyclopedia, 1978–83. *Contributor to:* Milton Studies, Editorial Board; Complete Prose Works of John Milton, Editorial Board; Variorum Commentary on the Poetry of John Milton, Editorial Board; Renaissance Quarterly, numerous other professional journals. *Memberships:* Milton Society of America, President, 1973, etc. *Address:* 250 South Oak Ave, Apt 109, Pasadena, CA 91101, USA.

STEAHLY, Vivian Eugenia Emrick, b. 10 July 1915, Wapakoneta, Ohio, USA. Retired Professor Emeritus. m. Frank Lester Steahly, 17 Oct. 1936, deceased 1967, 1 son. *Education:* BA, BS, Ohio State University, 1936; MA, University of Cincinnati, 1941; Postgraduate, University of Virginia, Michigan State University. *Publications:* Seven Steps to Sensible Structure and Styule, 1970; I Always Wanted to Live in the Chicken Yard, 1973; The Gift and Other Tales, 1974; Stories for Little People, 1976; Eldon, My Very Own Elf, 1983; Seek and Find, 1984; Lydia and Other Tales, 1985. *Contributions to:* Magazines and journals including: Early American Life; Missouri English Bulletin; NHA Journal; West Viorginia School Journal; Christian Science Monitor; Hartford Courant; Illinois Schools Journal. *Memberships:* Phi Beta Kappa; Pi Lambda Theta; Eta Sigma Phi. *Address:* 206 Stinebaugh Drive, Wapakoneta, OH 45895, USA.

STECKLER, Larry, b. 3 Nov. 1933, Brooklyn, New York, USA. Magazine Publisher & Editor. m. Catherine Coccozza, 6 June 1959, 1 son, 3 daughters. *Education:* City University of New York, 1951. *Literary Appointments include:* Associate Editor, Radio-Electronics, 1957–62; Electronics editor, Popular Mechanics, 1962–65; Associate Editor, Electronic Products, 1965–67; Editor, Radio-Electronics, 1967–; Editorial Director, Merchandising, 2-Way Radio, 1975–77; Vice President, Director, Gernsback Publications, New York City, 1975–; Publisher, Radio-Electronics, 1980–; Publisher, Editorial Director, Special Projects, 1980–. *Honours:* Award, National Alliance, TV & Electronic Services Association, 1974, 1975; Man of the Year, National Electronics Service Dealers association, 1975. *Memberships include:* American Society of Business Press Editors. *Address:* 158 Whitewood Drive, Massapequa Park, NY 11762, USA.

STEEGMULLER, Francis, b. 3 July 1906, New Haven, Connecticut, USA. Writer. *Education:* BA, 1927, MA, 1928, Columbia University. *Publications include:* Novels: The Musicale, 1930; A Matter of Iodine, 1940; States of Grace, 1947; The Christening Party, 1960. Short Stories: Stories and True Stories, 1972; Silence at Salerno, 1978. Non-Fiction: O Rare Ben Jonson, 1928; Flaubert and Madame Bovary, 1939, various subsequent editions; Maupassant, 1950; Apollinaire, 1963; Cocteau, 1970; Your Isadora, 1974. Translations: Le Hibou et la Poussiquette, 1961; various editions and translations of Flaubert. *Honours include:* Chevalier, Legion of Honour; National Book Award, 1971. *Memberships:* National Institute of Arts and Letters; University Club, New York. *Address:* 200 East 66th Street, New York City, NY 10021, USA.

STEEL, David Robert, b. 29 May 1948, Oxford, England. Administrator. m. Susan Elisabeth Easton, 12 Apr. 1977, Strathblane, 1 son, 1 daughter. *Education:* BA, 1969, MA 1975, D Phil, 1975, Oxford University. *Appointment:* Lecturer, Politics, University of Exeter, 1972–84. *Publications:* The Administrative Process in Britain, with R G S Brown, 1979; Privatising Public Enterprises, with D. Heald, 1985. *Contributor to:* Public Administration; Political Quarterly; British Journal of Political Science; Public Money. *Address:* 14 Meadow Hill Road, Birmingham B38 8DD, England.

STEEL, Ronald, b. 25 Mar. 1931, Morris, Illinois, USA. Author. *Education:* BA, Northwestern University, 1953; MA, Harvard University, 1955. *Publications:* The End of Alliance: America and the Future of Europe, 1964; Pax Americana, 1967; Imperialists and Other Heroes, 1971; Walter Lippmann and the American Century, 1980. *Contributor to:* Contributing Editor, New Republic; New York Review; Articles in, Harper's; Atlantic; Esquire; New York Times. *Honours:* Sidney Hillman Award, 1967; Guggenheim Fellowship, 1973; National Book Critics Circle Award, 1980; Bancroft Prize in American History, 1981; American Book Award, 1981. *Membership:* PEN International. *Literary Agent:* Morton Janklow Inc. *Address:* c/o Morton Janklow Inc, 598 Madison Ave, New York, NY 10021, USA.

STEEL, Rt Hon David Martin Scott, b. 31 Mar. 1938, Scotland. Member of Parliament. m. Judith Mary Macgregor, Oct. 1962, 3 sons, 1 daughter. *Education:* MA, 1960, LLB, 1962, Edinburgh University. *Publications:* No Entry, 1969; A House Divided, 1980; Partners in One Nation, editor, 1985; Border Country, (with Judy Steel), 1985. *Contributor to:* Various articles to The Times; The Guardian; Sunday Times; Observer; Daily Telegraph; Scotsman. *Honour:* Privy Counsellor, 1977. *Address:* House of Commons, London SW1A OAA, England.

STEELE, John Gladstone, b. 20 July 1935, Brisbane, Queensland, Australia. Lecturer. *Education:* BSc, PhD, University of Queensland; ThL, Australian College of Theology; Associate, Securities Institute of Australia; Member, Australian Institute of Physics; Postdoctoral Study & Research, Stanford University, California & MIT, USA, Queen's University, Kingston, Ontario, Canada, Hydraulics Research Station, Wallingford, Oxford, England. *Publications:* The Explorers of the Moreton Bay District 1770–1830, 1972; Brisbane Town in Convict Days 1824–1842, 1975; The Brisbane River, 1976; Conrad Martens in Queensland, 1978; Aboriginal pathways in Southeast Queensland and the Richmond River, 1984. *Contributor to:* Queensland Heritage. *Honours:* Special Grant, Literature Board, Australia Council, 1974, 1980; ANZ Bank Award for non-fiction 1975, 1979; J P Thomson Medal, Royal Geographical Society of Australasia, 1985. *Address:* 7/48 Dunmore Terrace, Auchenflower, Queensland, 4066, Australia.

STEELE, Peter, b. 5 May 1935, London, England. Physician. m. Sarah Fleming, 20 May 1961, Denston, Suffolk, 1 son, 2 daughters. *Education:* MA, Cambridge University; MB BChir; FRCS, Edinburgh, Scotland. *Publications:* Two and Two Halves to Bhutan, 1970; Doctor on Everest, 1982; Medical Care for Mountain Climbers, 1976. *Contributions to:* Alpine Journal; World Medicine! England; The Medical Post, Canada. *Address:* 11 Sunset Drive North, Whitehorse, Yukon, Canada Y1A 4M7.

STEELE, Peter Adrian, b. 5 Nov. 1961, Gloucester, England. Semi-trained Photographer. Author of many unpublished novels and childrens books. *Literary Agent:* Penman Literary Service. *Address:* 101a Quedgeley Court Park, Greenhill Drive, Tuffley, Gloucestershire GL2 6NZ, England.

STEFANILE, Felix (Neil), b. 13 Apr. 1920, Long Island City, New York, USA. Professor. m. Selma Epstein, 17 Jan. 1953. *Education:* BA English, City College of New York, 1944. *Literary Appointments:* Editor & Publisher, Sparrow Press, 1954–; Board Chairman, Purdue University Press, 1964–69; Advisory Editor, Italian Americana, (State University of New York), 1972–. *Major Publications:* A Fig Tree in America, 1970; East River Nocturne, 1978; Umberto Saba: 31 Poems (translations from Italian), 1980; The Blue Moustache: Some Italian Futurist Poets, (translations), 1981; In that Far Country (sonnets), 1982. *Contributor to:* Virginia Quarterly Review; Saturday Review; New York Times Sunday Book Review; Tri-Quarterly; Centennial Review; Parnassus; and others. *Honours:* Various awards for poems. *Memberships:* Poetry Society of America; American Literary Translators Association. *Address:* Department of English, Heavilon Hall, Purdue University, West Lafayette, IN 47907, USA.

STEFANOVA, Lilyana, b. 17 Apr. 1929, Sofia. Writer. *Education:* The Moscow, Maxim Gorki, Literary Institution. *Literary Appointment:* Editor-in-Chief of the, Obzor, literary magazine. *Publications:* Poetry: The World That I Love, 1958; Love and Pain, 1967; The Sun Kissed Me, 1970; A Southern Coast, 1972; A Magnetic Field, 1978. *Contributor to:* All main Bulgarian literary editions. *Honours:* A People's Worker of Culture, 1978; Dimitrov Prize, 1971. *Memberships:* Vice President, Union of Bulgarian Writers; Chairman, Bulgarian PEN club. *Address:* bloc 73, complex Lenin, Sofia, Bulgaria.

STEFANSSON, Thorsteinn, b. 1 Dec. 1912, Lodmundarfjoerdur, Iceland. Author; Editor. *Publications include:* Fra oedrum hnetti, 1935; Dalen, 1942; Dalurinn, 1944; Mens Nordlyset danser, 1949; Den gyldne Fremtid, 1958; The Golden Future, 1974; Wo sich die Wege kreuzen, 1976; Dybgroenne Tun, 1976; Pa lovens grund, 1977; Forlovelsesringem, 1977; Du, Som Kom, collection of poems, 3 volumes, 1979–81; The Wind Blows..., 1985; Men det Koster (But you will have to pay for it), 1986. Numerous translations of Icelandic authors into Danish including works by: Fridjon Stefansson, Kristmann Kudmundsson, Olafur Johann Sigurdsson. *Contributions to:* Datskaya Novella XIX-XX Vekov, 1967; Anthology of Scandinavian Short Stories, 1978; Anthology of Icelandic Short Stories, 1980. Various Literary magazines in UK, USA, Germany, Switzerland, Scandinavia and Iceland. *Honour:* Hans Christian Andersen Medal and Prize, 1942. *Memberships:* Dansk Forfatterforening. *Address:* Teglgardsvej 531, DK 3050 Humlebaek, Denmark.

STEFFLER, John Earl, b. 13 Nov. 1947, Toronto, Canada. Poet. m. Shawn O'Hagan-Steffler, 30 May 1970, Toronto, 1 son, 1 daughter. *Education:* BA, English Language and Literature, University of Toronto; MA, English Language and Literature, University of Guelph. *Publications:* An Explanation of Yellow, 1981; The Grey Islands, 1985. *Contributions to:* many Canadian Literary Journals, including: Queen's Quarterly; Descent; The Fiddlehead; CV/II; Quarry; Canadian Forum. *Honour:* First Prize, Norma Epstein Competiton, 1971. *Membership:* The League of Canadian Poets. *Address:* Department of English; Memorial University of Newfoundland, Sir Wilfred Grenfell College, Corner Brook, Newfoundland, Canada A2H 6P9.

STEIGER, Otto, b. 4 Aug. 1909, Thun, Switzerland. Author. m. Rosemarie Salber, 1949, Zurich, 1 son, 1 daughter. *Education:* Universities of Zurich and Paris, France. *Publications:* Portrat eines angesehenen Mannes, 1955; Lornac ist uberall, novel, 1980; Spurlos vorhanden, novel, 1981; Die Unreifeprufung, 1984. *Contributions to:* Numerous journal articles. *Honours include:* Schweizer Jungenbuchpreis, 1980. *Membership:* Swiss Authors Association. *Address:* Regensdorferstrasse 179, CH–8049 Zurich, Switzerland.

STEIN, Bruno, b. 19 July 1930, Vienna, Austria. Professor of Economics. m. Judith A Paris, 1969, 1 daughter. *Education:* AB, AM, PhD, New York, University, USA. *Publications:* On Relief, 1971; Incentives & Planning in Social Policy, co-editor, 1973; Work & Welfare in Britain & the USA, 1976; Social Security and Pensions in Transition, 1980. *Contributor to:* Numerous articles in learned journals. *Address:* c/o Dept of Economics, 269 Mercer St, New York University, New York, NY 10003, USA.

STEINBERG, Erwin Ray, b. 15 Nov. 1920, New Rochelle, New York, USA. College Professor. *Education:* BS, 1941, MS, 1942, State University, New York; PhD, New York University, 1956; *Literary Appointments include:* Consultant, Coordinator, Project English, US Office of Education, 1963, 64; Chairman, Examiners for General Examination in English Composition, 1963–67; currently, Thomas S Baker Professor of English and Interdiscipliniary Studies, Carnegie-Mellon University. *Publications include:* Needed Research in the Teaching of English, 1963; The Stream of Consciousness and Beyond, 1973; Communication in Business and Industry, co-author, 1960, 83. Editor: The Rule of Force, 1962; The Stream of Consciousness Technique in the Modern Novel, 1979; La Tecnica del fluir de la conciencia en la novela moderna, 1982. Co-Editor of various works. *Contributions to:* Literature and Psychology; Modern Fiction Studies; Journal of Modern Literature; James Joyce Review; D H Lawrence Review; Style; Studies in Short Fiction; College English; Management Review; American Banker; American Journal of Orthopsychiatry, and numerous others. *Honours:* Carnegie Teaching Award, 1956; Distinguished Alumnus, State University of New York, Albany, 1969; Alumnus of the Year, State University of New York College, Plattsburgh, 1971. *Address:* Department of English, Carnegie-Mellon University, Pittsburgh, PA 15213, USA.

STEINER, Kurt, b. 10 June 1912, Vienna, Austria. Professor Emeritus, Political Science. m. Josepha Eisler, 26 Aug. 1939, Cleveland. *Education:* JD, University of Vienna, 1935; PhD, Stanford University, USA, 1955. *Publications:* Local Government in Japan, 1965; Politics in Austria, 1972; Political Opposition and Local Politics in Japan, co-editor, co-author, 1980; Modern Austria, Editor, 1981; Tradition and Innovation in Contemporary Austria, 1982, Editor. *Contributor to:* Far Eastern Quarterly; Washington Law Review; Far Eastern Survey; American Journal of Comparative Law; Economic Development and Cultural Change; American Political Science Review; Journal of Asian Studies; Pacific Affairs. *Honour:* Austrian Cross of Honour for Science and Arts, 1981. *Address:* 832 Sonoma Terrace, Stanford, CA 94305, USA.

STEINKE, Ann E, b. 5 Nov. 1946, River Falls, Wisconsin, USA. Writer. m. William P Steinke, 28 Oct. 1967, Penn Yan, New York, 1 son, 1 daughter. *Major Publications:* An Ocean of Love, (as E Reynolds), 1982; The Rare Gem, (as A Williams), 1982; Love for the Taking, (as B Christopher), 1983; Sailboat Summer, 1983; Jeff's New Girl, 1984. *Membership:* Charter Member of Romance Writers of America, 1982–. *Literary Agent:* Denise Marcil, New York. *Address:* 17 Sutton Park Road, Poughkeepsie, NY 12603, USA.

STEINMAN, Lisa Malinowski, b. 8 Apr. 1950, Willimantic, Connecticut, USA. Professor of English/Poet. m. James Shugrue, 23 July 1984, Portland, Oregon, USA. *Education:* BA, Comparative Literature, 1971, MFA, Poetry, 1973, Cornell University;

PhD, Nineteenth-Twentieth Century American/ British Poetry, 1976. *Literary Appointment:* Associate Professor, Department of English, Reed College, Portland, Oregon, 1976–. *Publication:* Lost Poems, 1976. *Contributions to:* Articles on nineteenth and twentieth century American and British poetry in ELH; Wallace Stevens Journal; Twentieth Century Literature; Approaches to Teaching Wordsworth; Romanticism Past and Present and others. Poems in over forty literary magazines and anthologies including Ironwood; Chicago Review; Epoch; Threepenny Review; Tendril; MSS. *Honours:* Danforth Fellow, 1971–74; Academy of American Poets Mention, 1975; Bread Loaf Writers Conference (Scholar) 1981; Oregon Arts Commision Poetry Fellowship, 1983; National Endowment for the Arts (USA) Poetry Fellowship, 1984. *Memberships:* Poets and Writers; Modern Language Association; Board of Directors, Portland Poetry Festival. *Address:* Department of English, Reed College, Portland, OR 97202, USA.

STEINMETZ, Lawrence L, b. 26 Sep. 1938, USA. Speaker. m. Sally Wismer, 27 Dec. 1958, Lawrence, 1 son, 2 daughters. *Education:* BS, MS, University of Missouri; PhD, University of Michigan. *Publications:* Grass Roots Approach to Industrial Peace, 1966; Labor Law, 1967; Interviewing Skills for Supervisory Personnel, 1971; Art and Skill of Delegation, 1976; Human Relations: People and Work, 1979; Managing the Small Business, 1982; First Line Management, 3rd edition, 1982; Nice Guys Finish Last, 1983; Managing the Marginal and Unsatisfactory Performer, 1985. *Address:* 3333 Iris Ave, Boulder, CO 80301, USA.

STELTENKAMP, Michael Francis, b. 14 Nov. 1952, Detroit, Michigan, USA. Counsellor; Writer; Chaplain. *Education:* BA, University of Detroit; MA, Indiana University; MDiv, Loyola University, Chicago; PhD, Michigan State University. *Publication:* The Sacred Vision: Native American Religion & Its Practice Today, 1983. *Contributions:* A Vision of the Sacred, in, Bear & Co: The Little Magazine of Personal & Social Transformation. *Contributor:* Plains Authropologist, journal. *Address:* 327 M A C Avenue, East Lansing, MI 48823, USA.

STENROOS, Merja-Riitta, b. 5 Oct. 1963, Helsinki, Finland. Writer. *Major Publications:* Guldrävarens tarar, 1981; Fri marknad, 1983; Kanariefagel blues, 1985 (all poetry). *Contributor to:* Runous (Finnish Poetry), 1983–84; BLA (annual cultural magazine), 1985; Chief Editor, KLO (young people's magazine), 1985–; Arbetarbladet; Ny Tid; and others. *Honour:* Edith Södergran Prize, 1985. *Address:* Bollvägen 41, 01280 Vanda, Finland.

STENSON, Frederick Thomas, b. 22 Dec. 1951, Pincher Creek, Alberta, Canada. Writer. m. Susan Leigh Palmer, 29 Mar. 1980, Clagary, 1 son, 1 daughter. *Education:* BA, Economics, University of Calgary, 1972. *Publications:* Lonesome Hero (novel), 1974; 3 x 5 (short fiction), 1984; Waste to Wealth (non-fiction), 1985. *Contributions to:* Arlene (short story) in Saturday Night Dec 1980–Jan 1981; Delusions of Agriculture (short story) in Saturday Night, 1981; Teeth (short story) in Edmonton Magazine, 1981; Round and Smooth (short story) in Chatelaine, 1982. *Honours:* Canadian Authors' Association Silver Medal for Fiction, 1975; Author's Award, Magazine Fiction, 1980; Alberta Motion Picture Industry Association, Non-Dramatic Screen Play Award, 1984. *Memberships:* Writers Guild of Alberta; Writers Union of Canada. *Address:* 2639 Lougheed Drive SW, Calgary, Alberta, Canada T3E 5T7.

STEPHAN, John Jason, b. 8 Mar. 1941, Chicago, USA. Professor of History, University of Hawaii. m. Barbara Brooks, 22 June 1963, Greenwich, Connecticut, USA. *Education:* BA, 1963, MA, 1964, Harvard University, Cambridge, Massachusetts, USA; PhD, University of London, England, 1969. *Literary Appointments:* Far Eastern Editor, The Harvard Review, 1962; Visiting Fellow, St Antony's College, University of Oxford, England, 1977; Member, Board of Editors,

University of Hawaii, Press, 1980–. *Major Publications:* Sakhalin: A History, 1971; The Kuril Islands: Russo-Japanese Frontier in the Pacific, 1974; The Russian Fascists, 1978; Hawaii under the Rising Sun, 1984; Soviet-American Horizons in the Pacific, 1986 (with V P Chichkanov). *Contributor to:* Modern Asian Studies; American Historical Review; Pacific Affairs; Pacific Community; Journal for Asian Studies; and others. *Honours:* Fulbright Fellowship, 1967–68; Japan Culture Translation Prize, 1973; Japan Foundation Fellowship, 1977; *Memberships:* Authors' Guild; PEN Club; International House of Japan (Life member); Association for Asian Studies (Life member); American Association for the Advancement of Slavic Studies. *Literary Agent:* Paul R Reynolds, Inc. New York, USA. *Address:* Department of History, University of Hawaii, 2530 Dole Street, Honolulu, HI 96822, USA.

STEPHENS, Alan, b. 19 Dec. 1925, Greeley, Colorado, USA. Professor of English Literature. m. Frances Jones, 26 Dec. 1948, Tulsa, Oklahoma, 3 sons. *Education:* BA; MA; PhD. *Publications:* The Sum, 1958; Between Matter and Principle, 1963l The Heat Lightning, 1967; Tree Meditation and others, 1970; White River Poems, 1976; In Plain Air, 1982. *Contributions to:* Poems included in: Southern Review; Denver Quarterly; Poetry; New Mexico Quarterly; Willow Springs magazine; Little Square Reviews; Spectrum; Paris Review; The Nation. *Address:* 326 Canon Drive, Santa Barbara, CA 93105, USA.

STEPHENS, Meic, b. 23 July 1938, Pontypridd, Wales. Literature Director, Welsh Arts Council. *Education:* BA, University of Wales, 1961; Dip, University of Rennes, France, 1960. *Publications:* Triad, 1962; The Lilting House, 1969; Exiles All, 1973; The Welsh Language Today, 1973; A Reader's Guide to Wales, 1973; Artists in Wales I-III, 1971–77; Linguistic Minorities in Western Europe, 1976; Green Horse, 1978; The Arts in Wales, 1950–75, 1979; Writers of Wales, 65 vols, 1969 nh. Ed: Poetry Wales, 1965–73; The Oxford Companion to the Literature of Wales, 1986. *Memberships:* Gorsedd of Bards (White Robe). *Address:* 42 Church Road, Whitchurch, Cardiff, Wales.

STEPHENS, Robert Oren, b. 2 Oct. 1928, Corpus Christi, Texas, USA. m. Carey Virginia Jones, 8 Sep. 1956, Norfolk, Virginia, 1 son, 2 daughters. *Education:* BA, Texas College of Arts & Industries, 1949; MA 1951, PhD 1958, University of Texas, Austin. *Literary Appointments:* Instructor, English, University of Texas, Austin, 1957–61; Assistant Professor, 1961–66, Associate Professor 1966–68, Professor of English 1968–, Chairman, English Deparment 1981–, University of North Carolina, Greensboro. *Publications include:* Hemingway's Nonfiction: The Public Voice, 1968; Ernest Hemingway: The Critical & colonial writers, George Washington Cable, Texas oil folklore. *Honour:* Fellow in the Humanities, Cooperative Programme, University of North Carolina – Duke University, 1965–66. *Memberships:* Modern Language Association; South Atlantic Modern Language Association; Southeastern American Studies Association; Society for the Study of Southern Literature. *Address:* Department of English, University of North Carolina, Greensboro, NC 27412, USA.

STEPHENS, William Peter, b. 16 May 1934, Penzance, Cornwall, England; Methodist Minister; Lecturer, Church History. *Education:* MA, BD, Cambridge University; Docteur Es Sciences Religieuses, Strasbourg. *Appointments:* Assistant Tutor, Hartley Victoria College, Manchester; Ranmoor Chair, Church History, Hartley Victoria College; Randles Chair, Historical and Systematic Theology, Wesley College, Bristol; Lecturer, Church History, The Queen's College, Birmingham. *Publications:* The Holy Spirit in the Theology of Martin Bucer, 1970; The Theology of Huldrych Zwingli, 1986; other books, chapters in symposia, etc. *Contributor to:* Various articles and reviews in, Epworth Review; Expository Times; Scottish Journal of Theology; Worship and Preaching; Symposia. *Honours:* Fernley Hartley Lecturer, 1972;

James A Gray Lecturer at Duke University, 1976; Hartley Lecturer, 1982. *Membership:* Society for the Study of Theology, Secretary 1963–77. *Address:* The Queen's College, Somerset Road, Birmingham B15 2QH, England.

STEPHENSON, Hugh, b. 18 July 1938, Simla, India. Journalist. *Education:* BA, Oxford University. *Literary Appointments:* Editor, The New Statesman, 1982–. *Publications:* The Coming Clash, 1972; Mrs Thatcher's First Year, 1980; Claret and Chips, 1982. *Literary Agent:* Curtis Brown Limited. *Address:* c/o The New Statesman, 14-16 Farringdon Lane, London EC1, England.

STEPHENSON, Ralph, b. 3 Sep. 1910, New Zealand. Accountant; Writer. m. Jane Hoover, 5 Feb. 1940, 2 sons, 1 daughter. *Education:* MA, Economics, New Zealand; Postgraduate, London School of Economics. *Literary Appointments:* Assistant Secretary, British Film Institute, 1959–67; Director, Paris Pullman Cinemas, 1967–79. *Publications:* The Cinema as Art, 1965/69/70/71/73/74/78; Festival Death, 1966 (and 4 other thrillers); The Animated Film, 1973/77; 500 Miles in a Catamaran 1974; Small Boats and Big Seas (anthology) 1978. *Contributor to:* Encyclopedia Britannica, The Art of Motion Pictures, 1974. *Address:* 66 Cheriton Square, London SW17 8AE, England.

STEPHENSON, Raymond Meadows, b. 8 Apr. 1904. Retired Chartered Engineer. *Education:* Salford University, England. *Appointments include:* Export Director; Company Director. *Publications:* (Poems), Along the Shingle Shore, 1978. *Contributor to:* Time & Tide; Spectator; Writers of East Anglia; Suffolk Fair; BBC. *Honours:* Various East Anglian Awards, 1970–80. *Address:* 2 Marlborough Ct, Southwold, Suffolk IP18 6LR, England.

STERN, Barbara Lang, b. New York City, USA. Writer. m. Ernest L Stern, 15 Sep. 1968. *Education:* BA, Cornell University. *Publications:* Woman's Doctor, with Dr W J Sweeney, 1973; Making of a Woman Cop, with M E Abrecht, 1976; Stages, with Dr L J Singer, 1980. *Contributor to:* Monthly Columnist, Your Well-Being, Vogue, 1978–; How to Start Loving Instead of Leaving, McCall's, 1984. *Membership:* Authors Guild. *Address:* 445 East 86 St, Apt. 12-C, New York, NY 10028, USA.

STERN, Edith B, b. 7 Jan. 1949, New Rochelle, New York, USA. Medical Editor. *Education:* BA Music History, Washington Square College, New York University, 1968–71. *Literary Appointments:* Instructional Developer 1978–80, Project Editor 1980–, The Johns Hopkins University School of Medicine, Baltimore, Maryland. *Publications:* Slide-tape continuing education series: Patient Care and Digestive Disease: An Update in Gastroenterology, 1979; The Johns Hopkins Postgraduate Course in Internal Medicine, 1980–81, The Johns Hopkins Medical Grand Rounds, 1981–, (project editor). *Membership:* American Medical Writers Association. *Address:* Office of Continuing Education, 61 Turner Auditorium, The Johns Hopkins University School of Medicine, 720 Rutland Avenue, Baltimore, MD 21205, USA.

STERN, Ellen Norman, b. 10 July 1927, Hannover, Germany. Writer. m. Harold H Stern, 7 Oct. 1956, Louisville, USA, 2 sons. *Education:* University of Luoisville, 1950. *Publications:* Embattled Justice – The Story of Louis D Brandeis, 1971; Dreamer in the Desert – A Profile of Nelson Glueck, 1980; Elie Wiesel: Witness for Life, 1982. *Contributor to:* Louisville Courier-Journal; Philadelphia Evening Bulletin; Jewish Digest; World Over Magazine; Inside. *Address:* 135 Anbury Lane, Willow Grove, PA 19090, USA.

STERN, James Andrew, b. 26 Dec. 1904, Kilcairne, County Meath, Ireland. Author. m. Tania Kurella, 9 Nov. 1935, London, England. *Education:* Eton College, RMC, Sandhurst, UK. *Appointments:* Assistant Editor, The London Mercury, 1929–31; Art Critic, Time Incorporated, 1942–43. *Publications:* The Heartless Land, 1932; Something Wrong, 1938; The Hidden Damage, 1947;

The Man Who Was Loved, 1952; The Stories of James Stern, 1968. Contributor to short stories to: London Mercury, Penguin Parade, New Statesman and Nation, Penguin New Writing, Harper's Bazaar, Esquire, Dublin Magazine, London Magazine, New Writing and The News Chronicle. *Membership:* Royal Society of Literature, Fellow, 1953. *Honours:* National Institute of Arts & Letters Grant, 1949; British Arts Council Award, 1966. *Literary Agent:* Elaine Greene. *Address:* Hatch Manor, Tisbury, Salisbury SP3 6PH, England.

STERN, Jay Benjamin, b. 17 Feb. 1929, New York City, USA. Writer; Consultant. m. Suzanne Cutler, 13 Aug. 1950, Brooklyn, New York, 1 son, 2 daughters. *Education:* BA, Brooklyn College; BD, MRE, DRE, DPed (hon), Jewish Theological Seminary of America. *Publications:* Comparative Religious Literature, 1977; What's a Nice God Like You Doing in a Place Like This. 1986; A Curriculum for the Afternoon Jewish School, 1978. *Contributions to:* American Jewish Historical Society Quarterly; Catholic Biblical Quarterly; Journal of Jewish Communual Service; Jewish Spectator; New York History; Religious & Theological Abstracts; HaDoar (in Hebrew); Shavilei HaHinukh (in Hebrew). *Address:* 10802 Cavalier Drive, Silver Sping, MD 20901, USA.

STERN, Madeleine B, b. 1 July 1912, NY, USA. Writer; Business Partner in Rare Books. *Education:* BA, Barnard College, 1932; MA, Columbia University, 1934. *Publications include:* The Life of Margaret Fuller, 1942; Louisa May Alcott, 1950; Purple Passage: The Life of Mrs Frank Leslie, 1953; Imprints on History: Book Publishers and American Frontiers, 1956; We the Women: Career 1st's of 19th Century America, 1963; So Much in a Lifetime; The Story of Dr Isabel Barrows, 1964; Queen of Publishers' Row; Mrs Frank Leslie, 1965; The Pantarch: A Biography of Stephen Pearl Andrew, 1968; Heads and Headlines: The Phrenological Fowlers, 1971; The Victoria Woodhall Reader, 1974; Behind a Mask: The Unknown Thrillers of Louise May Alcott, 1975; Old and Rare: Thirty Years in the Book Business, (with Leona Rostenberg), 1975; Plots and Counterplots; More Unknown Thrillers of Louisa May Alcott, 1978; Books and Book People in 19th Century America, 1978; Publishers for Mass Entertainment in 19th Century America, 1980; Phrenological Dictionary of 19th Century Americans, 1982; Critical Essays on Louisa May Alcott, 1984; Antiquarian Bookselling in the United States: A History from the Origins to the 1940's, 1985. *Contributor to:* Sewanee Review; New England Quarterly; PMLA; American Notes and Queries; AB Bookman's Weekly; American Book Collector; Papers of the Bibliographical Society of America etc. Phi Beta Kappa, 1932; Guggenheim Fellowship, 1945–47; Medalie Award, Barnard College, 1982; Co-recipient, with Dr Leona Rostenberg, American Printing History Association Award, 1983. *Memberships:* MLA, Authors League; Past Government Antiquarian Booksellers Association of America Incorporated; Trustee, Manuscript Society; American Printing History Association. *Address:* 40 East 88 Street, New York, NY 10128, USA.

STERN, Richard, b. 25 Feb. 1928, New York, USA. Writer/University Professor. m. (1) Gay Clark, 1950, divorced 1978, 3 sons, 1 daughter, (2) Alane Rollings, 1985. *Education:* BA, University of North Carolina; MA, Harvard University; PhD, University of Iowa. *Publications:* Golk 1960; Europe of Up and Down with Baggish and Schreiber, 1961; In Any Case, 1962; Teeth, Dying, 1964; Stitch, 1965; 1968: A Short Novel etc, 1970; Other Men's Daughters, 1973; Natural Shocks, 1978; Packages, 1980. *Contributor to:* Numerous magazines and journals. *Honours:* Longwood Award, 1959; Friends of Literature, 1962; National Institute of Arts and Letters, 1968; Guggenheim Award, 1973; Sandburg Award for Novel, 1979; Award of Merit Medal for the Novel, 1985. *Membership:* PEN. *Literary Agent:* Arbor House. *Address:* Department of English, University of Chicago N50 E59, Chicago, IL 60637, USA.

STERN, Richard Martin, b. 17 Mar. 1915, California, USA. Writer. m. Dorothy Helen Atherton, 20 Dec. 1937, Los Angeles, California, USA. 1 (adopted) daughter. *Education:* Harward College. *Literary Appointments:* Editorial Board, The Writer. *Major Publications:* The Bright Road to Fear, 1958; Suspense, 1959; The Search for Tabatha Carr, 1960; Unlucky Deeds, 1961; High Hazard, 1962; Cry Havoc, 1963; Right Hand Opposite, 1964; I Hide, We Seek, 1964; The Kessler Legacy, 1967; Merry Go Round, Brood of Eagles, 1969; Manuscript for Murder, Murder in the Walls, 1971; You Don't Need An Enemy, 1972; Stanfield Harvest, 1972; Death in the Snow, 1973; The Tower, 1973; Power, 1974; The Will, 1976; Snowbound Six, 1977; Flood, 1979; The Big Bridge, 1982; Wildfire, 1985. *Contributor to:* Saturday Evening Post; Collier's; McCalls; American; Liberty; Redbook; Cosmopolitan; Good Housekeeping; Argosy; Bluebook; and others. *Honour:* Mystery Writers of America Edgar Award, 1958. *Memberships:* Mystery Writers of America, President, 1971; Crime Writers Association; Literary Guild; The Press Club (London, England). *Literary Agent:* Brandt & Brandt, New York. *Address:* Santa Fe, New Mexico, USA.

STERNLICHT, Sanford, b. 20 Sep. 1931, New York City, USA. University Professor. *Education:* BA, State University of New York, Oswego, 1953; MA, Colgate University, 1955; PhD, Syracuse University, 1962. *Publications:* Gull's Way, 1961; Love in Pompeii, 1967; The Black Devil of the Bayous, 1971; McKinley's Bulldog, 1977; John Masefield, 1977; C S Forester, 1981; USF Constellation: Yankee Racehorse, 1982; The Selected Short Stories of Padraic Colum, 1985; Padraic Colum, 1985. *Contributor to:* New York Times; New York Herald Tribune; Saturday Evening Post; Harvard Magazine; College English; Papers on Language and Literature, United States Naval Institute Proceedings; etc. *Honours:* New Poets Award, Writer Magazine, 1960; Fellow, Poetry Society of America, 1964. *Address:* 100 Buckingham Ave, Syracuse, NY 13210, USA.

STEVEN, Stewart Gustav, b. 30 Sep. 1935, Hamburg, Federal Republic of Germany. Journalist. m. Inka Sobien, 1 son. *Literary Appointments:* Journalist, Daily Express; Journalist, Daily Mail; Editor, The Mail on Sunday. *Publications:* Operation Splinter Factor, 1974; The Spymasters of Israel, 1981; The Poles, 1982. *Contributions to:* Daily Express; Daily Mail; Mail on Sunday. *Literary Agent:* George Greenfield, John Farquharson. *Address:* The Mail on Sunday, Northcliffe House, Tudor Street, London EC4, England.

STEVENS, Christopher Anthony, b. 17 Aug. 1948, Bournemouth, England. Economist. m. Cindy Margaret Emms, 29 June 1969, Watford, England, 4 sons. *Education:* BSC (Hons) Economics, University of Wales; MA, University of London (SOAS), PhD, University of London (LSE). *Literary Appointments:* Research Officer, Overseas Development Institute, 1975–79; Joint Senior Research Officer, ODI, and Research Fellow, Institute of Development Studies, 1979–89; Joint Research Fellow, Centre for European Policy Studies, Brussels, ODI and IDS, 1984–. *Publications:* The Soviet Union and Black Africa 1976; Food Aid and the Developing World 1979; Nigeria; Economic Prospects to 1985, 1982; The Political Economy of Nigeria, 1984; Editor: EEC and the Third World: A Survey Vol 1 1981, Vol 2 1982, Vol 3 1983, Vol 4 1984, Vol 5 1985. *Contributor to:* Numerous Magazines and Journals. *Address:* Centre for European Policy Studies, Rue Ducale 33, 1000 Brussels, Belgium.

STEVENS, James Richard, b. 11 June 1940, Stratford, Ontario, Canada. Writer. *Education:* BSc, 1964, MA, 1966, Cornell University, Ithaca, New York, USA. *Major Publications:* Sacred Legends of the Sandy Lake Cree, 1971; Paddy Wilson's Gold Fever, 1976; Legends from the Forest, 1984; Killing the Shamen, 1985. *Contributor to:* Winnipeg Free Press; Books in Canada; In Review; Northward Journal. *Honours:* Canada Council Award, 1971, 1974; Ontario Arts Council

Award, 1982, 1984. *Membership:* Canadian Authors Association. *Literary Agent:* Pamela Buckmaster, Carnell Literary Agency, Little Hallingbury, Essex, England. *Address:* RR # 13, Thunder Bay, Ontario, P7B 5E4, Canada.

STEVENS, Lauren Rogers, b. 3 May 1938, Philadelphia, Pennsylvania, USA. Writer; Editor. m. Beverly Decker, 20 June 1964, 1 son, 2 daughters. *Education:* BA, Princeton University; MA, University of Iowa. *Appointments:* Editor, Berkshire Review, 1965–70; Planning for the Moosic, 1980; Williamstown Advocate, 1981–; 20003: A Study of Williamstown, 1984; Berkshire Environmental Report, 19840. *Publication:* The Double Axe, 1961. *Contributor to:* The Advocate; The Berkshire Eagle; Berkshires' Week; numerous other magazines and journals. *Honours:* Maxwell E Perkins Comemorative 1961; Aetheaeum of Philadelphia Literary Award, 1961. *Address:* 1192 Main Street, Williamstown, MA 01267, USA.

STEVENSON, Anne Katharine, b. 3 Jan. 1933, Cambridge, England. Writer; Poet. m. Michael John Guy Farley, (3rd marriage), 2 sons, 1 daughter. *Education:* BA, MA, University of Michigan, USA. *Literary Appointments:* Compton Fellow in Writing, University of Dundee, 1973–75; Fellow, Lady Margaret Hall, Oxford, 1975–77; Fellow in Writing, Balmersh College, Reading, 1977–78; Northern Arts Literary Fellow, Newcastle, Durham, 1981–82, 1984–85. *Publications:* Living in America (poems), 1965; Elizabeth Bishop (criticism), 1966; Reversals (Poems), 1969; Correspondences (poems), 1974; Travelling Behind Glass (selected poems), 1974; Enough of Green (poems), 1977; Minute by Glass Minute (poems), 1982; The Fiction-Makers (poems), 1985; Selected Poems (Forthcoming), 1986. *Contributions to:* The Listener; The TLS; The New Yorker; Encounter; The New Stateman; Stand; Pn Review; Poetry Review; Poetry Chicago; Outposts; Other Poetry; Country Life; The Scotsman; Other Poetry; Poetry Reviewer for The Listener, 1973–75; Arts North, 1984–85; Reviews in TLS and New York Times. *Honours:* Hopwood Awards, University of Michigan, 1952, 54; Scottish Arts Award for Poetry, 1975; Poetry Book Society Recommendation for Minute by Glass Minute, 1982; Poetry Book Society Choice for The Fiction Makers, 1985. *Memberships:* FRSA; Advisory Panel, Arts Council of Great Britain (Literature), 1983–85. *Address:* 30 Logan Street, Langley Park, Durham DH7 9YN, England.

STEVENSON, David, b. 30 Apr. 1942, Largs, Ayrshire, Scotland. University Lecturer. m. Wendy Beatrice McLeod, 15 July 1972, Stonehaven, 2 sons. *Education:* BA, Trinity College, Dublin; PhD, University of Glasgow. *Publications:* The Scottish Revolution, 1973; Revolution and Counter Revolution in Scotland, 1977; Alasdair MacColla and the Highland Problem, 1980; Scottish Covenanters and Irish Confederates, 1981; Government under the Covenanters, 1982. *Contributions to:* Historical journals. *Memberships:* Honorary Secretary 1976–84. Scottish History Society; Royal Historical Society. *Address:* Department of History, University of Aberdeen, Old Aberdeen AB9 2UB, Scotland.

STEVENSON, Elizabeth, b. 13 June 1919, Ancon, Panama Canal Zone. Biographer; University Professor; Historian. *Education:* BA, Agnes Scott College, Decatur, GA. *Publications:* The Crooked Corridor: A Study of Henry James, 1949; paperback, 1961; Henry Adams: A Biography, 1955, (Bancroft Award), paperback, 1961; Babbitts and Bohemians: The American 1920s, 1967, paperback, The American 1920, 1970; (anthology), A Henry Adams Reader, 1958, reprint 1968: (biography) Lafeadio Hearn, 1961; Park-Maker: A Life of Frederick Law Olsted, 1977. *Contributor to:* South Atlantic Quarterly; Vancouver Quarterly Review, Nation; Commentary; Montana Magazine; Landscape Journal. *Honours:* Recipient, several academy and literary awards including Bancroft Award, 1956; NEH Summer Stipend, 1974; ACLS Award, 1975; 5 Emory University

Research Grants; 2 Guggenheim Fellowships; 1 Rockefeller Foundation Grant. *Memberships:* Authors Guild; Consultant, National Endowment for the Humanities; Board Member, Frederick Law Olmsted Association; American Studies Association. *Address:* 532 Daniel Avenue, Decatur, GA 30032, USA.

STEVENSON, Florence, b. Los Angeles, California, USA. Writer. *Education:* BA English, MA Drama, University of Southern California. *Literary Appointments:* Editorial Assistant, Mademoiselle, magazine, 1958; Assistant Editor, 1959, Contributing Editor 1960, Opera News; Contributing Editor, FM Magazine, 1962; Contributing Editor, Weight Watchers Magazine, 1964; Contributing Editor, New Ingenue. *Publications include:* Child's Play, play, 1951; The Price of Apples, play, 1961; Ophelia, 1968; The Curse of the Concullens, 1971; The Horror from The Tombs, 1977; Julie, 1978; Call Me Counselor, (with Sara Halbert–autobiography), 1979; The Golden Galatea, 1979; Moonlight Variations, 1980; The Wicked Cousin, 1980; Athena's Airs, 1980; Witness, play, 1980, Bold Pursuit, 1981; Tiffany's True Love, 1981; Pretender to Love, 1981; The Chadbourne Luck, 1982; An Adverse Alliance, 1982; The Mourning Bride, 1982; Queen of Hearts, 1982; The Dashing Guardian, 1982; Cactus Rose, 1982; Splendid Savage, 1982; A Novel Alliance, 1984; Lord Caliban, 1985; The Irish Heiress, 1985; The Dangerous Doctor Langhorne, 1985. *Contributions to:* Mademoiselle; Cosmopolitan; Weight Watchers; New Ingenue; Opera News; Music Journal; Musical America; FM Magazine; Ventura Magazine; Theater Arts Magazine; Dance Magazine; Applause Magazine; Youth Beat; Los Angeles Times Mirror; Signature Magazine; Libretto; Bravo Magazine; SteroReview. *Honours:* Best Script of the Year, Theatre-Americana, 1951; Award, WaldenBooks, 1982. *Membership:* Associate member, Dramatist's Guild. *Literary Agent:* Phyllis Westberg, Harold Ober, Associates. *Address:* 227 E 57th Street, New York, NY 10022, USA.

STEVENSON, Robert Benjamin (III), b. 13 Feb. 1950, Topeka, Kansas, USA. Prosthodontics; Dentistry. m. Barbara J Sulick, 9 June 1975, Cleveland, Ohio, USA, 1 son, 1 daughter. *Education:* BS, Biology, University of Miami, 1972; DDS, Ohio State University, 1975; MS, Prosthodontics, Ohio State University, 1980; MA, Journalism, Ohio State University, 1980. *Literary Appointments:* Editor, Ohio State University, Disclosing Tabloid, 1973–1975 Editor, Columbus Dental Society, Bulletin, 1980–; Editor, O S U Dental Alumni, Quarterly, 1981–; Editor, Ohio Sec, Am Col Prosthodontists, Denture, 1982–; Editor, Ohio Valley Sec Am Medical Writer's Assoc, Amwire, 1984–; Advisor, O S U, Odontos Yearbook, 1984–. *Contributions to:* Contributor to numerous articles to professional journals including, Odontos; Ohio Dental Journal; Psi Omega Frater; Dental Student Magazine; Columbus Dispatch. *Honours:* Special Citation, International College of Dentists Journalism Awards Competition, 1976. *Memberships:* American Association of Dental Editors; American Medical Writer's Association; Treasurer, Editor, Ohio Valley Chapter; Council of Biology Editors. *Address:* 3600 Olentangy River Road, Suite D-3, Columbus, OH 43214, USA.

STEVROID, Lionel Laertes, b. 26 Jan. 1940, Oslo, Norway. Author. *Literary Appointments:* Staff Writer, Le Couteau, Lyons, France, 1958; Playwright-in-Residence, Beaufort Theatre, Marseilles, France, 1964; Editor, Writer, Bootstench, New York, USA, 1969; Editor, Writer, Dolomite Journal, Toronto, Canada, 1974; Assistant Editor, Fat Tuesday, Los Angeles, California, 1983. *Major Publications:* Jesus & Me, 1974; The Snail Remembers Nothing, 1975; Thero – Dynamics & The History of Love, 1979; Of William Bendix, 1981; Waiting for Goudreau, 1981. *Contributor to:* Bootstench; Dolomite Journal; Fat Tuesday. *Address:* 808 3/4 N Detroit, Los Angeles, CA 90046, USA.

STEWART, Angus J M, b. 22 Nov. 1936, Adelaide. Author. *Education:* MA, Christ Church, Oxford. *Publications:* Sandel, 1968; Snow in Harvest, 1969; Sense and Inconsequence, Verses, Foreword by W H Auden, 1972; Tangier: A Writer's Notebook, 1977. *Contributions to:* Short stories in London Magazine, Transatlantic Review; Various anthologies; Contributor to New Statesman, TLS. *Honours:* Richard Hillary Award, University of Oxford, 1963; Writer's Grant, Arts Council of Great Britain, 1976. *Membership:* Society of Authors. *Address:* Fawler Copse, Fawler, Wantage, Oxon OX12 9QJ, England.

STEWART, Bruce Robert, b. 4 Sep. 1927, Auckland, New Zealand. Writer. m. Ellen Noonan, 16 Oct. 1950, Sydney, Australia, 3 sons, 3 daughters. *Education:* BA, Auckland. *Publications include:* A Disorderly Girl, 1980; The Hot and Copper Sky, 1982; The Turning Tide, 1980; The Hallelujah Boy, play; Shadow of a Pale Horse, play; The Devil, Makes Sunday, Television play; Jungle, television play; The Daedalus Equations, television plays; Stars in my Hair, radioplay; Hector's Fixed Idea, radioplay. *Contributions to:* Film Criticism, The Month, 1970–80; Reviews and Criticisms in publications including: The New Statesman; Times Literary Supplement; The Tablet. *Honours:* Edgar Allen Poe Award, USA, 1963; Charles Henry Foyle Award, UK, 1968. *Memberships:* Writers Guild of Great Britain; Writers Guild of Australia; British Film Institute; Co-Chairman, WGGB, 1978–80. *Literary Agent:* Harvey Unna. *Address:* c/o Harvey Unna, 24 Pottery Lane, Holland Park, London W11, England.

STEWART, Daniel Kenneth, b. 14 July 1925, East Lansing, Michigan, USA. Professor of Advertising and Marketing. m. Joyce Margaret Theisen, 5 Aug. 1947, Lansing, 1 son, 3 daughters. *Education:* BA Mathematics 1949, MA Philosophy 1952, PhD Biological Science 1959, Michigan State University. *Literary Appointments:* Editor in Chief, Journal of Advertising, 1972–75. *Publications:* The Psychology of Communication, 1968, Spanish edition 1970; Advertising and Consumer Behavior: Basic Considerations of Advertising evaluation, 1979. *Contributions to:* Various scholarly journals. *Honours:* Research Grant, NIMH, 1960–62; Felowship, Advertising Age, 1972; Special Award, First Editor, Journal of Advertising, 1975. *Membership:* Executive Committee, American Academy of Advertising. *Address:* 14 Gold View Place, DeKalb, IL 60115, USA.

STEWART, Donald Charles, b. 24 June 1930, Kansas City, Missouri, USA. College Professor of English. m. Patricia Louise Pettepier, 3 June 1955, St Joseph, Missouri, 2 daughters. *Education:* BA 1952, MA 1955, University of Kansas; PhD, University of Wisconsin, 1962. *Literary Appointments:* Instructor 1962, Assistant Professor, 1963, University of Illinois; Assistant Professor, 1968, Associate Professor, 1975, Professor, 1981, Kansas State University. *Major Publications:* The Authentic Voice, 1972; The Versatile Writer, 1985. *Contributor to:* Various scholarly & literary journals. *Memberships:* President, Conference on College Composition and Communication, 1983; National Council of Teachers of English, Modern Language Association of America; Kansas Association of Teachers of English, President 1984–85. *Address:* Department of English – Denison Hall, Kansas State University, Manhattan, KS 66506, USA.

STEWART, James Alexander, b. 30 Jan. 1948, Glasgow, Scotland. Poet; Musician; Composer. m. Martha Jane Macdonald, 16 Aug. 1974, Saint John, New Brunswick, Canada, 1 son, 2 daughters. *Education:* University of New Brunswick, Canada. *Publications include:* Cormorant's Rock, 1973; The Mute's Song, 1975; So the Night World Spins, 1975; East of Canada: An Atlantic Anthology, co-editor, 1976. *Poems published in:* The Fiddlehead; Canadian Review; Wascana Review; Alpha; Event; Descent; Grain; Dandelion; etc. *Honour:* Canada Council Grant, 1975. *Address:* 102 Shore Road, Renforth, Saint John, New Brunswick, Canada E2H 1K8.

STEWART, John, b. 5 Mar. 1952, England. Writer. m. Susan Kramer, 2 Nov. 1981, Chelsea Town Hall. *Publications:* Encyclopedia of Australian Film, 1984. *Membership:* Australian Society of Authors. *Address:* The Connaught, 187 Liverpool Street, Sydney 2000, Australia.

STEWART, Mary Elizabeth, b. 11 Apr. 1933, Stoke-on-Trent, England. Yoga Teacher. m. 7 May 1954, 2 sons, 1 daughter. *Publications:* Stretch and Relax, 1985; The Yoga Book, 1986. *Literary Agent:* Carol Smith. *Address:* 10 Foster Road, London W4 4NY, England.

STEWART, Michael James, b. 6 Feb. 1933, Leeds, England. Economist. m. Frances Kaldor, 23 June 1962, Cambridge, 1 son, 2 daughters, 1 daughter deceased. *Education:* BA, 1955, MA, 1964, 1st Class Honours, Philosophy Politics and Economics, Magdelen College, Oxford. *Publications:* Keynes and After, 1967; The Jekyll and Hyde Years: Politics and Econoimc Policy since 1964, 1977; Controling the Economic Future, 1983. *Contributor to:* Numerous professional journals. *Literary Agent:* Curtis Brown. *Address:* 79 South Hill Park, London NW3 2SS, England.

STEWART, Michael (Lord Stewart of Fulham), b. 6 Nov. 1906, Bromley, London, England. Politician. m. Mary, Baroness Stewart (deceased). *Education:* MA, Oxford University. *Publications:* The British Approach to Politics, 1st edition, 1928, last edition 1965; Modern Forms of Government, 1969; Life and Labour, autobiography, 1980. *Contributions to:* New Statemen; Washington Quarterly; Fabian Society Pamphlets. *Address:* 11 Felden Street, Fulham, London SW6, England.

STEWART, Robert Michael Maitland, (Lord Stewart of Fulham), b. 6 Nov. 1906, Bromley, Kent, England. Politician. m. Mary Birkinshaw, July 1941, Holborn. *Education:* BA, 1929; MA 1835, St John's College, Oxford. *Publications:* The British Approach to Politics, 1928, (latest edition, 1965); Modern Forms of Government, 1958; Life and Labour, 1980. *Contributions to:* The Times; The New Statesman; The Spectator. *Address:* 11 Felden Street, Fulham, London SW6 5AE, England.

STEWART, William Alexander Campbell, b. 17 Dec. 1915, Glasgow, Scotland. University Professor. m. Ella Elizabeth Burnett, 27 Sep. 1947, Aberdeen, 1 son, 1 daughter. *Education:* MA, PhD, University College and Institute of Education, University of London. *Publications:* Quakers and Education, 1953; Systematic Sociology (with Karl Mannheim and John Erös), 1957; An Introduction to the Sociology of Education, (with Karl Mannheim), 1962; The Educational Innovators, Volume II 1968; Progressives and Radicals in English Education, 1973. *Contributions to:* Learned journals in sociology and education. *Honours:* Deputy Lieutenant, Staffordshire, 1973; Hon D Litt, Ulster and Keele. *Address:* 42 Dean Court Road, Rottingdean, Brighton BN2 7DJ, England.

STICKLER, John Cobb, b. 18 July 1937, Washington DC, USA. Public Relations Officer. m. Lu Han, 6 Dec. 1964, Seoul, Korea, 2 sons. *Education:* BA, Honours, Sociology, Yale University, 1959; Peace Corps Diploma, Penn State University, 1961. *Publications:* Editor & publisher, Advertising in Korea, Volumes I & II, 1973, 1975; Growing up Afraid, Poems of The Atomic Age, 1985. *Contributions to:* Advertising Age; Asia Mail; Asia Magazine; Business Week; Editor & Publisher; Journal of Applied Management, (publisher 1976–81); New York Times; Response; Travel & Holiday; Media. *Honours:* CLIO Advertising Finalist, 1975; 2 Poetry Awards. *Memberships:* American Society of Journalists & Authors; Royal Asiatic Society; Director, Yale Club of Tucson; Society of Southwestern Authors; Newsletter Editor, Tucson Press Club; Past President, IABC Tucson; PRSA. *Address:* 8300 N La Cholla Boulevard, Tucson, AZ 85741, USA.

STIERLIN, Helm, b. 13 Mar. 1926, Mannheim, Germany. Professor, University of Heidelberg. m. Satuila Zanolli, 15 June 1965, Washington, DC, USA, 2 daughters. *Education:* PhD, 1951, MD, 1953, University of Heidelberg. *Publications include:* Der gewalttatige Patient: Eine Untersuchung uber die von Geisteskranken an Arzten und Pflegepersonen verubten Angriffe, 1956; Conflict and Reconciliation, 1969; Das Tun des Einen ist das Tun des Anderen, 1971; 4th German edition, 1985; Separating Parents and Adolescents, 1974, enlarged edition, 1981; Adolf Hitler, A Family Perspective, 1975, various foreign editions; Psychoanalysis and Family Therapy, 1975, Italian, Swedish, Spanish and English editions; The First Interview with the Family, co-author, 1977, 3rd enlarged German edition, 1985; Delegation und Familie, 1978, Norwegian edition, 1984; Krankheit und Familie, co-author, 1982; Die Christen in der Weltfamilie: Auserwahlt zur Friedensstiftung, 1982; Die Sprache der Familientherapie 'Ein Vokabular,' 1984. *Contributions to:* Editor and Founder, Familiendynamik; Editor, Texte zur Familiendynamik; Associate Editor or Editorial Board member of numerous professional journals including: Praxis der Psychotherapie und Psychosomatik; Family Process; Journal of Family Therapy. *Honours:* Distinguished Professional Contributions to Family Therapy Award, American Association for Marriage and Family Therapy. *Memberships include:* Corresponding Member, American and Finnish Psychiatric Associations; American and International Psychoanalytic Associations. *Address:* Mönchhofstr 15a, D–6900 Heidelberg 1, Federal Republic of Germany.

STILLINGER, Jack, b. 16 Feb. 1931, Chicago, Illinois, USA. Educator; University Professor. m. Nina Baym, 21 May 1971, Urbana, Illinois. *Education:* AB, University of Texas at Austin, 1953; AM, Northwestern University, 1954; PhD, Harvard University, 1958. *Literary Appointments:* Teaching Fellow in English, Harvard University, 1955–58; Assistant Professor of English, 1958–61, Associate Professor of English, 1961–64, Professor of English, 1964–, University of Illinois; Editor, Journal of English and German Philology, 1961–72. *Publications include:* The Hoodwinking of Madeline and Other Essays on Keat's Poems, 1971; The Texts of Keat's Poems, 1974; The Poems of John Keats, 1978. *Contributions to:* Various learned Journals and Literary Magazines; about 10 articles, reviews and poems. *Honours:* Woodrow Wilson Fellowship, 1953–54; Guggenheim Fellowship, 1964–65; Permanent Membership, University of Illinois Center for Advanced Study, 1970–. *Address:* Department of English, University of Illinois, 608 S Wright Street, Urbana, IL 61801, USA.

STILLMAN, Richard Joseph, b. 20 Feb. 1917, Lansing, Michigan, USA. Writer. m. Ellen Darlene Slater, 2 sons, 1 daughter. *Education:* BA, University of Southern California; Postgraduate, 1938–39, Harvard University; MS, 1950, PhD, 1955, Syracuse University; Graduate Army War College, 1960; Graduate NATO Defense College, 1961. *Literary Appointments:* Professor of Business Administration, Director Management Development Programs and Director, Center for Economic Opportunity, Ohio University, 1965–67; Professor of Management, 1967–82, Professor Emeritus, 1982–; University of New Orleans. *Publications:* The US Infantry: Queen of Battle, 1965; Bitter Victory: A History of Black Soldiers in World War I, (with Florette Henri), 1970; Guide to Personal Finance: A Lifetime Program of Money Management, 1972, 2nd Edition 1975, 3rd Edition 1979, 4th Edition, 1984; Do It Yourself Contracting to Build Your Own Home: A Managerial Approach, 1974, 2nd Edition, 1981; Personal Finance Guide and Workbook: A Managerial Approach to Successful Household Recordkeeping, 1977; Moneywise: The Prentice-Hall Book of Personal Money Management, 1978; More For Your Money: Personal Finance Techniques to Cope With Inflation and the Energy Shortage, 1980; Your Personal Financial Planner: A Sourcebook of Tools to Beat Inflation and the Energy Shortage, 1981; Small Business Management: How To Start and Stay in Business, 1983; Dow Jones Industrial Average: History and Role In An Investment Strategy, 1986; How To Use Your Personal Computer to Manage Your Personal Finances (with John Page), 1986. *Contributions to:* Numerous military publications. *Honours:* Bronze Star, 1945; Luxembourg Order of the Crown, 1945; Maxwell Scholar, Syracuse University, 1949; Scouter's Award, 1955; Legion of Merit, 1965; US Naval Institute Writing Prize, 1966. *Memberships:* Authors Guild Inc; Authors League of America Inc; Academy of Management; Financial Management Association; American Finance Association. *Address:* 2311 Oriele Street, New Orleans, LA 70122, USA.

STINCHCOMBE, William Charles, b. 30 May 1937, Farwell, Michigan, USA. Professor of History. m. Jean Evera Lovelace, 17 Aug. 1963, 2 sons, 1 daughter. *Education:* BA, San Francisco State College, 1960; MA, 1962, PhD, 1967, University of Michigan. *Appointments:* Consultant, The Papers of John Marsall, Institute for Early American History and Culture, 1971; Editor, The Papers of John Marshall, 1972–79. *Publications:* The French Alliance and the American Revolution, 1969; Republicanism and World Diplomacy, 1978; The Papers of John Marshall, Volume III, editor, 1979; The XYZ Affair, 1980, *Contributor to:* Journal of American History; William and Mary Quarterly; Proceedings of the American Philosophical Society. *Honours:* Gilbert Chinard Prize, 1969l Fellow, American Council of Learned Societies, 1970; Fellowship, American Philosophical Society. *Memberships:* Institute for Early American History and Culture; Organization of American Historians; American Historical Association; Society for American Diplomatic Historians. *Address:* 110 Poole Road, DeWitt, NY 13214, USA.

STINI, William Arthur Anthony, b. 9 Oct. 1930, Wisconsin, USA. University Professor. m. Mary Ruth Kalous, 11 Feb. 1950, Oshkosh, Wisconsin, USA, 3 daughters. *Education:* BBA, 1960; MS, 1967; PhD, 1969, University of Wisconsin. *Literary Appointments:* Field Editor for Physical Anthropology, American Anthropologist, 1979–82; Editorial Board, Nutrition and Cancer, 1981–; Editor in Chief, American Journal of Physical Anthropology, 1983–; Editorial Board, Collegium Antropologicum (Zagreb) 1984–. *Publications:* Ecology and Human Adaptation, 1975; Nature, Culture and Human History, (with Davydd Greenwood) 1977; Physiological and Morphological Adaptation and Evolution, Edited volume, 1979. *Contributions to:* More than 60 articles, chapters, reviews etc. in various serial publications and edited volumes in Europe, Asia and the United States. *Honour:* Fellow of New York Academy of Science, 1983. *Membership:* International Society of Editors in Anthropology. *Address:* Department of Anthropology, University of Arizona, Tucson, AZ 85721, USA.

STINSON, Kathy, b. 22 Apr. 1952, Toronto, Canada. Children's Author. 1 son, 1 daughter. *Publications:* Red is Best, 1982; Big or Little?, 1983; Mom and Dad Don't Live Together Anymore, 1984; Those Green Things, 1985. *Contributor to:* The Campout, Chickadee, 1985. *Honours:* Iode Award, for Red is Best, 1982. *Memberships:* Writer's Union of Canada; Canadian Society for Children's Authors; Illustrators, and Performers. *Address:* 49 Blantyre Avenue, Scarborough, Ontario M1N 2R3, Canada.

STOCKHAM, Peter Alan, b. 7 July 1928, Birmingham, England. Bookseller; Publisher; Consultant. *Education:* BA, University of Keele. *Publications include:* (author) British Local History, Bibliography, 1963; University Bookselling, 1965; Publishers Catalogues: A Standard for Essentials of Content and Format, 2nd edition, 1972, forthcoming edition, 1986; (Editor with introduction), Chapbook Riddles, 1974; Chapbooks ABC's, 1974; The Mother's Picture Iphabet, 1974; Little Book of Early American Crafts and Trades, 1976; Life and Death of A Apple Pie, 1978; Old Aunt Elspa's ABC, 1978; Numerous reprints 18c and 19c children's books, chapbooks, printed ephemera with additional notes of a literary and bibliographic nature. *Contributor to:* Various literary journals and magazines including The Bookseller; British Book News; British Journal of Aesthetics. *Memberships include:* Honorary Treasurer, National Book League, 1970–76; Honorary Chairman, British Library, British National Bibliography Research Fund, 1975–80; Library Committee Chairman, Mark Longman Library, NBL, 1974–76. *Address:* 16 Cecil Court, London WC2, England.

STOCKS, John Bryan, b. 17 July 1917, Baildon, Yorkshire, England. Freelance Writer; Poet; Broadcaster. *Education:* University of Leeds, England. *Publications:* (Plays); Trouble on Helicco,-best one-act plays of 1963–64, new edition, 1972; After You've Gone, 1969, 1972; Zodiac and Other Adventures in Platform Drama, 1983. *Contributor to:* More Poems from the Forces; Northern Aspect; Poems from Hospital; I Burn for England; Sunday Times; Yorkshire Life; Yorkshire Post; Stage and TV Today; radio programmes. *Honour:* Co-recipient, 1st prize, Wharfedale Festival, 1962. *Membership:* Life Member, Arts Theatre Club, London. *Address:* Bradda, 11 Halstead Drive, Menton-in-Wharfedale, Ilkley, West Yorkshire LS29 6NT, England.

STODDARD, Ellwyn R(eed), b. 16 Feb. 1927, Garland, Utah, USA. Professor of Sociology and Anthropology. m. Elaine Kirby, 5 sons, 4 daughters. *Education:* BS, Utah State University, 1952; MS, Brigham Young University, 1955; PhD, Michigan State University, 1961. *Publications include:* Mexican Americans, 1973 and 1981; The Borderlands Sourcebook, (editor with R L Nostrand and J P West), 1983; Booklets and major reports including: Conceptual Models of Human Behavior in Disaster, 1968; Patterns of Poverty Along The US-Mexican Border, 1978; El Paso-Ciudad Juárez Relations and the Tortilla Curtain: A Study of Local Adaptation to Federal Border Policies, (co-editor), 1979. *Contributions to:* International regional and regional conferences and to books, encyclopaedias and professional journals including: Dictionary of Chicano History; Academic American Encyclopedia; Social Science Journal. *Honours include:* Graduate Fellowships, Brigham Young and Michigan State Universities; Borderlands Sourcebook, 1983; Southwest Book Award, Border Regional Library Association, 1984. *Memberships include:* American Sociological Association; Founder, Association of Borderlands Scholars; International Rural Sociology Society. *Address:* Department of Sociology, University of Texas at El Paso, El Paso, TX 79968, USA.

STOEV, Gentocho, b. 5 Feb. 1925, Harmanli, Bulgaria. Writer. *Education:* Philosophy, Sofia University. *Publications:* Novels: A Bad Day, 1965; The Price of the Gold, 1965; Like Swallows, 1970; The Cyclop, 1973; A Return, 1976. *Contributor to:* All main Bulgarian literary editions. *Honours:* An Honoured Worker of Culture, 1974; Dimitrov Prize. *Membership:* Union of Bulgarian Writers. *Address:* 33A Nezabravka Street, Sofia, Bulgaria.

STOLOFF, Carolyn, b. 14 Jan. 1927, New York City, USA. Poet; Painter; Teacher. *Education:* BS, Painting, Columbia School of General Studies; Further art studies – Xavier Gonzales, Eric Isenburger, Hans Hofmann; further poetry studies – Poetry workshops with Stanley Kunitz. *Literary Appointments:* Teacher of Painting and Drawing, 1957–74 and also taught Seminar in Writing (poetry) for 5 years, Manhattanville College; Teacher of English and Creative Writing, Baird House, 1973; Visiting Writer, Stephens College, 1975; Numerous residence grants including: MacDowell Colony 1961, 62, 70, 76; Ossabaw Island Project 1976; Michael Karoly; Memorial Foundation, 1983; Virginia Center for the Creative Arts, 1985. *Publications:* Stepping Out, 1971; Dying to Survive, 1973; In the Red Meadow, 1973; Lighter-Than-Night Verse, 1977; Swiftly Now, 1982; A Spool of Blue, New and Selected Poems, 1983. *Contributions to:* Poems in The New Yorker; The Nation; Partisan Review; Yankee; Poetry Northwest; Chelsea; Choice; Carleton Miscellany; Antioch Review; Prairie Schooner; Kayak; The Little Magazine; Porch; Open Places; The Agni Review and many other magazines. Poems also in anthologies: The New Yorker

Book of Poems; Our Only Hope is Humor; Rising Tides; A Carpet of Sparrows; Alcatraz. *Honours:* Theodore Roethke Award from Poetry Northwest, 1967; National Council on the Arts Award for Achievement, 1968; First Prize for Poetry from The Miscellany, 1972; Travel Grant from Manhattanville College, 1972; Third place Conrete Poetry Competition from Gamut, 1983. *Memberships:* Poetry Society of America; Authors Guild. *Address:* 24 West 8th Street, New York, NY 10011, USA.

STONE, Lowell, b. 7 Sep. 1915, Lorain, Ohio, USA. Professional Ghostwriter. m. Katherine Pfaff, 25 July 1936, Elyria, Ohio, 2 daughters. *Education includes:* Graduate, School of Commerce, 1935, Institute of Applied Science, 1942, Newspaper Institute, 1975. *Literary Appointments include:* President, Stone-Kalo Incorporated and Kalo Features, 1945–; Vice President and General Manager, Independent Weekly Newspaper, 1979–80; Associate editor, Dance Digest, 10 years; Writer, various science fiction magazines and Belmont Division of Ridge Tool Corporation; Writer, Illustrator, Stone's Strange World; Teleplay writer, Once Upon a Time, childrens television series; Instructor: State certified Adult education programme, Writing for Profit, Indian River Community College, Creative Writing; Programmer and speaker, Sailfish Writers Seminar and various research organisations; Instructor, seminars on writing techniques. *Contributions to:* Dance Digest, DMA Editor; National Writers Club, volunteer critic. Professional critic of fiction and non-fiction. *Memberships:* Honorary member, Florida Freelance Writers Association; Associate member, Florida Press Association (Educator classification); National Writers Club. *Address:* Conquistador 7–107, Stuart, FL 33494, USA.

STONE, Merlin David, b. 29 July 1948, London, England. Management Consultant. m. Ofra Sharon, 16 Nov. 1975, Brighton, 2 daughters. *Education:* BA, Economics, 1st Class Honours, 1969, DPhil, 1975, Sussex University. *Publications:* Product Planning, 1976; Marketing and Economics, 1980; How to Market Computers and Office Systems, 1984; Field Service Management, 1985. *Contributor to:* Planning Marketing; Computing Press. *Address:* 31 Guildford Avenue, Surbiton, Surrey KT5 8DG, England.

STONE, Morton B, b. 16 Aug. 1929, New York City, USA. Writer; Editor. m. Ilasue, 5 July 1985, 1 son, 1 daughter. *Education:* BA, Journalism, University of Oklahoma. *Publications:* Editor, Ghost Writer (not listed as author): Take Charge of Your Diabetes, 1980; Self Blood Glucose Monitoring, 1984; Education Management, 1973. *Contributions to:* Diabetes in the News (bi-monthly news magazine), Editorial Director, 1972–. *Memberships:* Society of Professional Journalists; American Medical Writers Association. *Address:* 1165 N Clark Street 311, Chicago, Il 60610, USA.

STONE, Peter H, b. 27 Feb. 1930, Los Angeles, California, USA. Playwright; Scenarist. *Education:* BA, DLitt, Bard College, new York; MFA, Yale University. *Publications:* Plays: Kean; Skyscraper; 1776; Two by Two; Sugar; Full Circle; Women of the Year; My One and Only, (Broadway musical), 1983; Films: Charade; Mirage; Father Goose; Sweet Charity; Arabesque; 1776; The Taking of Pelham 1-2-34; Who's Killing the Great Chefs of Europe? *Honours include:* Academy Award (Oscar), 1964; Tony Award, 1969; New York Drama Critics Award, 1969; TV Academy Award (Emmy), 1962; London Theatre Critics Award, 1970; Second Tony Award for, Woman of the Year, 1981. *Memberships:* President, Dramatists Guild of America; Authors League of America; Motion Picture Academy Award; TV Academy Award; American Film Institute Award. *Literary Agent:* William Morris Agency. *Address:* 160 E 71st Street, New York, NY 10021, USA.

STONEHOUSE, John Thomson, b. 28 July 1925, Author. m. Sheila Black, 31 Jan 1981, Bishops Walltown, 1 son, 3 daughters, 1 son by previous marriage. *Education:* BSc. *Publications:* Gangrene, (co-author), 1959; Prohibited Immigrant, 1960; Death of an Idealist, 1975; My Trial, 1976; The Ultimate, 1976;

Ralph, 1982; The Baring Fault, 1976. *Address:* c/o Jonathan Cape Limited, 30 Bedford Square, London WC1 3EL, England.

STONER, Oliver, b. 3 July 1903, Teddington, Middlesex, England. Writer; Journalist. *Publications include:* 7 novels, 1932–48; Blake's Hayley, 1951, USA, 1972; 20 other volumes concerned with S T Colderidge, Shelley, Boswell, Samuel Rogers, James Smetham, George Gising; Forthcoming, Fragments from Morebath; Table Talk of Arthur Machen. *Contributor to:* New Statesman; Times; Times Literary Supplement; John o'London Weekly; Books and Bookmen; Sunday Telegraph, etc. *Membership:* FRSL. *Address:* Velthams, Morebath, Tiverton, Devon EX16 9AL, England.

STOREY Anthony, b. 10 Nov. 1928, Wakefield, Yorkshire, England. Writer; Lecturer. m. Anne-Marie Gulude, 22 Apr. 1970, Bury St Edmunds, Suffolk, 2 sons 1 daughter. *Education:* BA, Hons, Psychology, MA, Cambridge University. *Literary Appointment:* Visiting Distinguished Professor of English, University of Delaware, 1985. *Publications:* Jesus Iscariot, 1967; Graceless Go I, 1968; The Rector, 1970; Platinum Jag, 1972; The Centre Holds, 1973; Platinum Ass, 1975; Brothers Keepers, 1977; Stanley Baker: Portrait of an Actor, 1977; The Saviour, 1978. *Address:* Beyton Cottage, Bury St Edmunds, Suffolk IP30 9AL, England.

STOREY, Elizabeth Margaret Carlton, b. 27 June 1926, London, England. English Teacher. *Education:* MA (Cantab). *Publications:* Pauline, 1963; Kate & the Family Tree, 1963; Timothy & Two Witches, & series, 1965; The Smallest Doll, & series, 1967; Wrong Gear, 1974; Keep Running, 1975. *Address:* c/o Faber & Faber, 3 Queen Square, London WC1N 3AU, England.

STOREY, Robin Lindsay, b. 25 July 1927, Newcastle-upon-Tyne, England. Professor of Medieval History, Nottingham University. m. Sheila Bredon Challenger, 16 June 1956, Poole In Wharfedale, 1 son, 1 daughter. *Education:* BA 1951, MA 1955, New College, Oxford, 1948–51; PhD, Durham University, 1954. *Publications:* The end of the House of Lancaster, 1966; The Reign of Henry VII, 1968; The Study of Medieval Records, co-editor, and contributor, 1971; Chronology of the Medieval World, 1973. *Address:* 19 Elm Avenue, Beeston, Nottingham NG9 1BU, England.

STOVER, Leon E, b. 9 Apr. 1929, Lewiston, Pennsylvania, USA, University Professor. m. Takeko Kawai, 12 Oct. 1965, New York City, 1 daughter from first marriage. *Education:* BA, English, Western Maryland College, 1950; PhD, Anthopology and China Studies, Columbia University, 1962. *Literary Appointments:* Science editor, Amazing Stories, 1967–69; First Chairman, John W Campbell Memorial Award 1972; Commissioned by American Studies Program at the Sorbonne to write textbook on Science Fiction entitled, La Science Fiction Americain, 1972. *Publications:* The Cultural Ecology of Chinese Civilization, 1974; China: An Anthopological Perspective, 1976; Stonehenge and the Origins of Western Culture, 1979; The Shaving of Karl Marx, 1982; Stonehenge, Where Atlantis Died, 1985; The Prophetic Soul: A Reading of H G Wells's Things to Come, 1986. *Contribor to:* Numerous articles for academics journals in fields of anthropology, Far Eastern studies and science fiction studies, also short stories for science fiction magazines. Contributor to Contemporary Authors (on H G Wells) and to Twentieth Century Science Ficiton Writers (on John Campbell, George R Stewart, Harry Harrison and Jules Verne). *Honours:* Honorary Doctor of Letters from Western Maryland College, 1980. *Memberships:* Science Fiction Writers of America; science Fiction Research Association; The H G Wells Society. *Literary Agents:* (for science fiction works only) Nat Soble Associates, New York; A P Watt Ltd, London. *Address:* 3100 S Michigan, Apt #602, Chicago, IL 60616, USA.

STOWE, David Metz, b. 30 Mar. 1919, Council Bluffs, Iowa, USA. Clergyman. *Education:* BA, University of California, USA, 1940; BD, 1943, ThD, 1953, Pacific School of Religion, California. *Publications:* The Church's Witness in the World, 1963; When Faith Meets Faith, 1963; Partners with the Almighty, 1966; Ecumenicity and Evangelism, 1970. *Contributions to:* Christian Century; Religion in Life. *Honours include:* DD, Pacific School of Religion, Berkeley, California, 1966. *Memberships include:* Financial and Investment Committee, US Conference, World Council of Churches; Governing Board, National Council of Churches. *Address:* 54 Magnolia Avenue, Tenafly, NJ 07670, USA.

STRAHAN, Bradley Russel, b. Sep. 1937, Boston, Massachusetts, USA. Editor; Poet. m. Shirley G Sullivan, 17 Oct. 1981, Alexandria, Virginia, 1 son, (2 sons, 1 daughter by previous marriage). *Education:* BA, History, 1960, MA, Social Science, 1963I, University of City of New York. *Literary Appointments:* Director, Washington Poets Workshop, Fall 1977–; Editor, Publisher, Black Buzzard Press, Summer 1979–; Editor, Visions, The International Magazine of Illustrated Poetry, 1979–; Poetry Coordinator for the Art Barn Gallery, Washington, DC, 1980–. *Publications:* Love Songs for an Age of Anxiety, (poetry), 1981; Poems, 1982; Anthologies: The 1981 and 1985 editions of The Anthology of Magazine Verse, Blood to Remember, (Avon Books), Snow Summits in the Sun and Outer Space Anthology, 1986. *Contributions to:* Christian Science Monitor; Tribune (UK); The Southwestern Review; Midstream; Wind; Trends (UK); Orbis (UK); Poetry Australia; Lips; Song; New Laurel Review; North Dakota Quarterly; Soundings East; Krax (UK); West Hills Review; American Man; American Forests; Hollins Critic; Poetry Today; Bogg; Negative Capability; Bitterroot; Pulpsmith; Gargoyle; Stone Country; Kudos. *Honours:* Chosen to read at The Folger Shakespeare Library Poetry Series, 1982; Winner of Alexandria NLAPW Poetry Contest $100 prize for traditional verse, 1983; Selected to Lecture and read own poetry at The University of Tübingen, Germany, 1985. *Memberships:* Co-ordinating Committee of Little Magazines, New York City; The Washington Area Writers Center, Bethesda, Maryland. *Address:* 4705 South 8th Road, Arlington, VA 22204, USA.

STRAND, Mark, b. 11 Apr. 1934, Summerside, California, USA. Writer. m. Julia Garretson, 15 Mar. 1976, San Mateo, California, USA, 1 son, 1 daughter. *Education:* BA, Antioch College; BFA, Yale University. *Major Publications:* Sleeping with One Eye Open (poems), 1964; Reasons for Moving (poems), 1968; Contemporary American Poets Anthology, 1969; Darker, 1970; The Story of Our Lives (poems), 1973; The Late Hour (poems), 1973; The Late Hour (poems), 1978; The Monument (prose) 1978; Selected Poems, 1980; Mr & Mrs Baby (short stories), 1985; Editor: Art of the Real, 1983. *Contributor to:* New Yorker; Antaeus; Vogue. *Honours:* Various grants & fellowships. *Memberships:* American Academy & Institute of Arts & Letters; Fellow, American Academy of Poets. *Literary Agent:* Robert Cornfield. *Address:* 1408 Yale Avenue, Salt Lake City, UT 84105, USA.

STRANGER, Joyce, b. Forestgate, London, England. Writer. m. Kenneth Bruce Wilson, 28 Feb, 1944, 2 sons, 1 daughter. *Education:* BSc, University College, London. *Publications:* The Running Foxes, 1965; A Day In A Million, 1984; The Hounds of Hades, 1985; The Family at Fool's Farm, 1985. *Contributions to:* Gwynedd Leader; Dog and Country; Western Mail; Cat World; Off Lead, USA. *Honours:* Shortlisted for Trento Award, Italy, 1978. *Memberships:* Society of Authors; Institute of Journalists; Society of Women Writer's and Journalists; Welsh Union of Writers. *Literary Agent:* Brian Stone, Hughes Massie/Gillon Aitken. *Address:* c/o Brian Stone, Hughes Massie/Gillon Aitkin, 29 Fernshaw Road, London SW10 0TG, England.

STRASMA, Ellen Louise, b. 5 May 1946, Indianapolis, Indiana, USA. Magazine/Newsletter Editor; Librarian; Teacher. m. James Frederick Strasma, 22 Aug. 1970, Bloomington, 1 son. *Education:* BA, DePauw University; MLS, Indiana University. *Appointments:* Co-Editor: Midnite Software Gazette, 1980–,

Church Computer Users Network Newsletter, 1982–; Instructor, Library Science, Western Illinois University. *Publications:* Jointly with her Husband: PET Personal Computer Guide, 1982; CBM Professional Computer Guide, 1982; Whole PET Catalog, 1982; Best VIC/Commodore Software, 1983; User's Guide to Commodore 64 and Vic 20, 1983; Time-Life Step-by-Step Guide to the Commodore 64, 1984; 1541 Disk Drive User's Guide, 1984. *Honours:* Graduated, Honours, DePauw and Indiana Universities. *Address:* PO Box 6100, Macomb, IL 61455, USA.

STRASMA, James Frederick (Jim), b. 31 Dec. 1948, Kankakee, Illinois, USA. United Methodist Minister. m. Ellen Louise Spencer Strasma, 22 Aug. 1970, Bloomington, 1 son. *Education:* BA, DePauw University; MTh, Boston University; enrolled, MCS Programme, Western Illinois University. *Appointments:* Co-Editor: Midnite Software Gazette, 1980–, Church Computer Users Network Newsletter, 1982–; Associate Editor: Micro, Magazine, 1980–84, Run Magazine, 1983–; Computer Editor, Your Church Magazine, 1984–; Assistant Professor, Computer Science. *Publications:* PET Personal Computer Guide, 1982; CBM Professional Computer Guide, 1982; Whole PET Catalog, 1982; Best VIC/Commodore Software, 1983; User's Guide to Commodore 64 and VIC 20, 1983; Time-Life Step-by-Step Guide to the Commodore 64, 1984; 1541 Disk Drive User's Guide, 1984; Microcomputer Handbook, Chapter 12, Systems, 1984, all jointly with his wife Ellen Strasma. *Contributor to:* Numerous professional journals including, Microcomputing; Christian Ministry; Interpreter; Evangelical Newsletter; Light and Life. *Honours:* Rector Scholar, ODE Economics Honorary, DePauw University, 1968–71; Graduated Honours, Boston University, 1974. *Address:* PO Box 6100, Macomb, IL 61455, USA, 1238 Richland Ave, Lincoln, IL 62656, USA.

STRAUB, Peter Francis, b. 2 Mar. 1943, Milwaukee, Wisconsin, USA. Novelist. m. Susan Bitker, 27 Aug. 1966, Milwaukee, 1 son, 1 daughter. *Education:* BA, University of Wisconsin, 1965; MA, Columbia University, 1966. *Publications:* Open Air, poetry, 1972; Marriages, novel, 1973; Julia, novel, 1975; If You Could See Me Now, novel, 1977; Ghost Story, novel, 1979; Shadowland, novel, 1980; Floating Dragon, novel, 1983; Leeson Park & Belsize Square, poetry, 1983; The Talisman, novel (with Stephen King), 1984; Blue Rose, novella, 1985. Reviewer for: Times Literary Supplement, The New Statesman, 1970–72. *Memberships:* Writers & Authors Guild, 1970–72; PEN: Authors League; Authors Guild. *Literary Agent:* Kirby McCauley. *Address:* PO Box 395, Greens Farms, CT 06436, USA.

STREATFEILD, (Mary) Noel, b. 24 Dec. 1895, Sussex, England. Author. *Publications include:* Whicharts, 1931; Tops and Bottoms, 1933; Ballet Shoes, 1936; Wisdom Teeth, play, 1956; Tennis Shoes, 1937; Luke, 1940; House in Corneall, 1940; Winter is Past, 1942; Myra Carrol, 1944; Curtain Up, 1944; Party Frock, 1946; Grass in Piccadilly, 1947; Mothering Sunday, 1950; Years of Grace, Editor, 1950; White Boots, 1951; By Special Request, Editor, 1953; The Fearless Treasure, 1953, 63; The First Book of Ballet, 1953, USA (revised edition, UK 1963); The Bell Family, 1954; Judith, 1956; Wintles Wonders, 1957; Bertram, 1959; The Royal Ballet School, 1959; The Ballet Annual, 1960; Christmas with the Crystals, 1960; Look at the Circus, 1960; Queen Victoria, 1961; Lisa Goes to Russia, 1963; The Children on the Top Floor, 1964; Enjoying Opera, 1966; The Growing Summer, 1966; The Thames, 1966; The Barrow Lane Gang, 1968; The First Book of Shoes, 1971; The Boy Pharoah, Tutankhamen, 1972; Far To Go, 1976; Meet the Maitlands, part 1, 1978; The Maitlands: ALI Change at Cuckley Place, 1979. Editor: Growing Up Gracefully, 1955; The Day Before Yesterday, 1956; Nicholas, 1968. Autobiographical: A Vicarage Family, 1963; Away From the Vicarage, 1965; Beyond the Vicarage, 1971. *Honours:* For, The Circus is Coming, Carnegie Gold Medal, 1938; OBE, 1983. *Literary Agent:* A M Heath

and Company Limited. *Address:* Vicarage Gate House, Vicarage Gate, London W8 4AQ, England.

STREET, Julia Lilly Montgomery, b. 19 Jan. 1898, Concord, USA. Teacher; Writer. m. Claudius A Street MD, 13 Sep. 1924, Raleigh, 1 son, 1 daughter. *Education:* AB English, University of North Carolina, 1923; Graduate Work, University of North Carolina, Chapel Hill. *Appointments:* Secretary, North Carolina Writers Conference, 1969; Teacher, Creative Writing, NWCA, Winston-Salem, 1972–78. *Publications:* Fiddler's Fancy, 1955; Moccasin Tracks, 1958; Drover's Gold, 1961; Dulcie's Whale, 1963; Candle Love Feast, 1959; North Carolina Parade, 1966, 1981, 1984; Judaculla's Handprint, 1972–75. *Contributor to:* Many stories, poems for children in Sunday School Papers; over 25 articles in professional journals; about 100 Radio Scripts for in-school history. *Honours:* AAUW Award, Best Juvenile Book of Year, North Carolina, 1956, 1963, 1967; Alumni Service Award, University of North Carolina, 1967. *Memberships:* American Association of University Women; North Carolina Writer's Conference, Secretary 1969; Winston-Salem's Writers Group. *Address:* 545 Oaklawn Ave, Winston-Salem, NC 27104, USA.

STREET, Lucie, b. Sussex. Author; Educationist. *Education:* MA, Manchester University; John Bright Fellowship; Postgraduate; study Comparative Literature, Sorbonne, University of Paris, France, *Publications:* Penn of Pennsylvania (play), 1945; E William Penn, 1947: Tomorrow's Continent, (with Lt-Col. P Penn), 1950; Editor, I Married a Russian, Czech and Danish transls.; Spoil the Child, 1961; The Tent Pegs of Heaven: (novels) The Wind on the Morfa; Good Morning, Mirand; (poems) Autumn Phoenix. *Contributor to:* Bell, A Choice of Modern Prose, 1967. *Honours:* Trust Award for Historical Research. 1974–75. *Memberships include:* Society of Authors; PEN; Sussex Authors. *Address:* Warminghurst, High Hurstwood, Uckfield, Sussex, England.

STREETEN, Paul Patrick, b. 18 July 1917, Vienna, Austria. Economist. m. Ann H Palmer, 9 June 1951, Woodstock, Vermont, USA. 1 stepson, 2 daughters. *Education:* MA, Aberdeen University; BA, MA, DLitt, Oxford University. *Publications:* Value in Social Theory (ed) by Gunnar Myrdal, 1958; Economic Integration, 1961, 2nd ed 1964; Unfashionable Economics (ed) 1970; The Frontiers of Development Studies, 1972; Foreign Investment, Transnationals and Developing Countries (with S Lall) 1977; Development Perspectives, 1981; First Things First (with others) 1981. *Contributions to:* Editor; World Development; The Limits of Development Research, World Development, 1974; Conflicts between Output and Employment Objectives (with F Stewart) Oxford Economic Papers, 1971; New Strategies for Development (with F Stewart) Oxford Economic Papers, 1976. *Honours:* Honorary Fellow Institute of Development Studies, 1977; Honorary LLD, Aberdeen University, 1980. *Address:* World Development Institute, Boston University, 270 Bay State Road, Boston, MA 02215, USA.

STREHLOW, Kathleen Stuart, b. 10 Apr. 1936, Western Australia. Research Director. m. Theador George Henry Strehlow, 25 Sep. 1972, Adelaide, 2 sons, 1 daughter. *Education:* BA, University of Adelaide, 1969; MA, University of Toronto, Canada, 1985; Teachers' Certificate, Claremont Teacher's College, 1954. *Literary Appointments:* Research Assistant, University of Adelaide, 1974–75; Research Director, The Strehlow Research Foundation, Inc, 1975–. *Major Publications:* Aboriginal Central Australia in Songs of Central Australia, 1971; Aboriginal Land Ownership in Central Australia, 1985. *Contributor to:* The Australasian Nurses' Journal; GEO Magazine; and others. *Honour:* Certificate of Merit for Service to the Community, 1984. *Memberships:* Fellow, Australian Fellowship of Writers; Foundation Member, Australian Stockman's Hall of Fame; Australian Society of Authors. *Address:* The

Strehlow Research Foundation, Inc, 30 Da Costa Avenue, Prospect, 5082, South Australia.

STREHLOW, Loretta Jean, b. 14 Jan. 1933, Omro, Wisconsin, USA. Writer; Teacher. m. Roland Paul Strehlow, 20 June 1953, Berlin, Wisconsin, 1 son. *Education:* 2 Years, University Wisconsin-Madison. *Publications:* Short Stories in many Anthologies. *Contributor to:* Redbook; Good Housekeeping; Family Circle; Woman's World; Alfred Hitchcock's Mystery Magazine; Farm Wife News; True Confessions; Harlequin Magazine; numerous regional, denominational newspapers and magazines, in USA and abroad; Juvenile and Teen Fiction and Non-Fiction in, American Girl; Young Miss; Jack & Jill; The Friend; Highlights for children. *Honours:* Winner, Jade Ring and Bard's Chair for Poetry; Short Fiction Awards, both Council for Wisconsin Writers and Wisconsin Regional Writers Association. *Memberships:* Wisconsin Fellowship of Poets, Vice President; Wisconsin Regional Writers Association; Council for Wisconsin Writers, Inc; Byliners; Fictioneers. *Literary Agent:* Larry Sternig. *Address:* N76 W7292 Linden St, Cedarburg, WI 53012, USA.

STREIT, Clarence K, b. 21 Jan. 1896, California, Missouri, USA. Journalist. *Education:* Universities of Montana and Oxford. *Publications:* Where Iron Is: There is the Fatherland, 1920; Hafiz: The Tongue of the Hidden, 1928; Union Now, 1939; Union Now with Britain, 1941; The New Federalist, with others, 1950; Freedom Against Itself, 1954; Freedom's Frontier-Atlantic Union Now, 1961; Freedom and Union, Editor, 1946-. Partner, Federal Union Incorporated, 1939-. President, International Movement for Atlantic Union, 1959-. *Honour:* Kefauver Union of the Free Award, 1968. *Address:* Ontario Apartments, 2853 Ontario Road North West, Washington, DC 20009, USA.

STREITWIESER, Andrew, b. 23 June 1927, Buffalo, New York, USA. Chemistry Professor. m. Suzanne Cope Beier, 29 July 1957, Berkeley, California, 1 son. *Publications:* Molecular Orbital Theory in Organic Chemistry, 1961; Solvolytic Dispslacement Reactions, 1962; Dictionary of πElectron Calculations, (with C A Coulson), 1965; Supplemental Tables of Molecular Orbital Calculations, (with J I Brauman, 1965; Orbital and Electron Density Diagrams, (with P H Owens), 1973, Introduction to Organic Chemistry, (with C H Heathcock), 1976, 3rd edition 1985; Student Solution Supplement for Introduction to Organic Chemistry, (with C H Heathcock), 1976 and 1981. *Contributions to:* Journal American Chemical Society; Journal Organic Chemistry; Tetrahedron; Tetrahedron Letters; Journal Chemical Society; Journal Computational Chemistry; Computers in Chemistry; Progress in Physical Organic Chemistry; Journal Organometallic Chemistry; Organometallics; Imorganic Chemistry; Acta Chemica Inorgana. *Address:* Department of Chemistry, University of California, Berkeley, CA 94720, USA.

STRENG, Frederick John, b. 30 Sep. 1933, Seguin, Texas, USA. University Professor. m. Bette Sue Deane, 23 May 1981, Dallas, Texas, 2 sons, 2 daughters. *Education:* BA, Texas Luteran College, 1955; MA, Southern Methodist University, 1956; BD, School of Chicago Divinity School, 1960; PhD, University of Chicago, 1963. *Appointment:* Editor, Religious Life of Man Series, 1967. *Publications:* Emptiness A Study of Religious Meaning, 1967; Senior Editor, Ways of Being Religious, 1973; Understanding Religious Life, 3rd edition 1985. *Contributor to:* 36 articles including, Buddhist-Christian Studies, Volume 2; Philosophy East & West. *Honour:* Outstanding Professor Award, Southern Methodist University. *Address:* Dept of Religious Studies, Southern Methodist University, Dallas, TX 75272, USA.

STRESHINSKY, Shirley, b. 7 Oct. 1934, Alton, Illinois, USA. Writer. m. Ted Streshinsky, 16 June 1966, San Francisco, California, 1 son, 1 daughter. *Education:* BA, University of Illinois. *Publications:* And I Alone Survived, 1978; Hers The Kingdom, 1981; A Time

Between, 1984. *Contributions to:* Over 100 articles in Journals and Magazines, including: Red Book; Ms; Glamour; Ladies Home Journal; McCalls. *Honours:* Best human interest article, Society Magazine Writers Association, 1968; Educational Press Award, 1968. *Memberships:* Author's Guild. *Literary Agent:* Claire Smith, Harold Ober Associates, New York. *Address:* PO Box 674, Berkeley, CA 94701, USA.

STRICKLAND, Margot Teresa, b. 5 Mar. 1927, Madrid, Spain. Author. m. Arthur Herbert Strickland, 26 Sep. 1946, St Leonards on Sea, Sussex, 1 son, 1 daughter. *Publications:* The Byron Women, 1974, USA, 1975; Angela Thirkell: Portait of a Lady Novellist, 1977; I Want a Hero, fiction, 1981. *Contributions to:* Country Life; The Times; Woman's Realm; Parents Voice, Mencap publication; Hertfordshire Countryside; Suffolk Fair; The Literary Review; Australian Byron Journal. *Memberships:* Executive Committee. The Byron Society; Angela Thirkell Society. *Address:* c/o Duckworth Publishers, The Old Piano Factory, 43 Gloucester Crescent, London NW1 7DY, England.

STROM-PAIKIN, Joyce Elizabeth, b. 25 Oct. 1946, Syracuse, New York, USA. Psychiatric Nurse; Marriage and Family Therapist. m. Lester Paikin, 26 June 1982, Ft Lauderdale, Florida, USA, 2 sons, 1 daughter. *Education:* AAS Nursing; BS Community Mental Health; MS Counseling Psychology; Certified Psychiatric Nurse; Graduate, Newspaper Institute of America. *Publications:* Pending: Medical Treason; Through The Fight. *Contributions to:* Lapidary Journal; Messenger of St Anthony; Nursing Life; American Journal of Nursing; Florida Nursing News; Condo Courier. *Honour:* Winner in Articles and Features Category, Writers Digest, 1981. *Memberships:* National Writers Club; Florida Freelance Writers Association. *Address:* 6112 N W 1st Street, Margate, FL 33063, USA.

STRONG, Douglas Hillman, b. 7 Oct. 1935, San Francisco, California, USA. Professor of History. m. Karlan Styler, 14 June 1982, Santa Barbara, California, 1 son, 2 daughters by previous marriage. *Education:* MA History, University of California at Berkeley, 1958; PhD Social Science, Syracuse University, 1964. *Major Publications:* Trees – or Timber ?, The Story of Sequola & Kings Canyon National Parks, 1973; The Conservationists, 1971; These Happy Grounds: A History of the Lassen Region, 1973; Tahce: An Environmental History, 1984. *Contributor to:* Southern California Quarterly; California Historical Society Quarterly; Environmental Affairs; Arizona & The West; Journal of Forest History; California History. *Address:* Department of History, San Diego State University, San Diego, CA 92182–0380, USA.

STRONG, Leah Audrey, b. 14 Mar. 1922, Buffalo, New York, USA. Professor, American Studies. *Education:* AB, Allergheny College, 1943; AM, Cornell University, 1944; PhD, Syracuse University, 1953. *Literary Appointments:* English Departments, University of Bridgeport, 1946–47, Syracuse University 1947–52, Cedar Crest College, 1953–61; American Studies Department, Wesleyan College, Macon, Georgia, 1961–. *Publications:* Joseph Hopkins Twichell: Mark Twain's Friend & Pastor, 1966. *Contributions to:* American Literature; Pacific Northwest Quarterly; North Carolina Folklore; St Andrew's Review; Mississippi Quarterly; New York Folklore Quarterly; etc. *Memberships:* Modern Language Association; South Atlantic Modern Language Association; Former President & Exective Secretary, Southern Humanities Conference; American Studies Association; Past Studies Association; Past President, Southeastern American Studies Association. *Address:* Department of American Studies, Wesleyan College, Macon, GA 31297, USA.

STRONG, Milton V, b. 12 Apr. 1926, Los Angeles, California, USA. Publisher. *Education:* Graduate, Electronics Engineering, Cogswell Polytechnical College, 1951. *Literary Appointments:* Technical Writer, aerospace industry; International publisher/writer, Square Dance Books. *Publications include:* Square Dancing for

Learners; Basic Calls for Advanced & Challenge Square Dancing; Mainstream Plus Square Dance Calls; Extended Challenge C-2 Square Dance Calls; Round Dance Cues for Callers. *Address:* PO Box 1023, Garden Grove, CA 92642, USA.

STROUD, Andrea Diane, b. 15 July 1942, New York City, USA. Journalist. m. Dr Franklin Lyle Stroud, 14 Dec. 1968, St Ignatius, Loyola, 2 sons, 1 daughter. *Education:* BA, English, Newton College, 1963. *Publications:* How Jimmy Won, 1977. *Contributor to:* New York Times; New York Times Magazine; Washington Star; Ladies Home Journal; McCalls; New York Magazine; Womens Wear Daily. *Literary Agent:* William Adler. *Address:* 3121 0 Street NW, Washington, DC 20007, USA.

STROZIER, Charles Burnett, b. 16 Feb. 1944, Athens, Georgia, USA. University Professor. m. Cathryn C Compton, 25 Jan. 1985, Springfield, Illinois, 3 sons. *Education:* BA, Harvard, 1966; MA, 1967, PhD, 1971, University of Chicago. *Publications:* Public and Private Lincoln, 1979; Lincoln's Quest for Union 1982; The Leader: Psychohistorical Essays, 1985; Self Psychology and The Humanities, 1985. *Contributions to:* Articles on Psychohistory, Lincoln and Civil War Period. Editor, The Psychohistory Review, 1972–. *Honours:* BA, Magna cum laude, Harvard; Lincoln Library Writer of the Year, 1983. *Membership:* Executive Officer, Group for the Use of Psychology in History. *Address:* History Program, Sangamon State University, Springfield, IL 62708, USA.

STRUGATSKY, Boris Natanovich, b. 15 Apr. 1933, Leningrad, USSR. Writer. m. 16 Nov. 1957, 1 son. *Education:* Faculty of Mathematics & Mechanics, University of Leningrad, USSR. *Appointments:* Astronomer. *Major Publications:* (with Arkady Strugatsky): Noon: 22nd Century, Escape Attempt, 1962; Far Rainbow, Hard to be a God, 1964; Monday begins on Saturday, The Final Circle of Paradise, 1965; The Snail on the Slope, 1966; The Second Martian Invasion, 1968; Prisoners of Power, 1971; Roadside Picnic, 1972; Definitely Maybe, 1976; Beetle in the Anthill, 1979. *Membership:* Union of Soviet Writers. *Literary Agent:* VAAP, USSR. *Address:* st Pobeda 4 ap 186, 196070 Leningrad M–70, USSR.

STUART, Carole, b. 22 Feb. 1941, New York City, New York, USA. Book Publisher. m. (2) Lyle Stuart, 4 Feb. 1982, Kingston, Jamaica, West Indies, 1 daughter. *Education:* BA, Magna cum Laude, Brooklyn College, City University of New York, 1968. *Publications:* To Turn You On: 39 Sex Fantasies for Women, 1975; Why Was I Adopted, 1978; I'll Never Be Fat Again, 1980; Why Am I Going to the Hospital?, with Claire Ciliotta, 1981; How to Lose 5 Pounds Fast, 1984. *Membership:* Authors League of America. *Address:* 120 Enterprise Avenue, Secausus, NJ 07094, USA.

STUART, Dabney, b. 4 Nov. 1937, Richmond, Virginia, USA. Professor of English. m. Sandra Westcott, 20 Jan, 1983, Arlington, Virginia, 2 sons, 1 daughter. *Education:* AB, Davidson College, North Carolina, USA; AM, Harvard University, Massachusetts. *Literary Appointments include:* McGuffey Lectureship in Creative Writing, Ohio University, 1975; Visiting Poet, Trinity College, 1978; Visiting Poet, University of Virginia, 1981. *Publications:* The Diving Bell, 1966; A Particular Place, 1969; The Other Hand, 1974; Friends of Yours, Friends of Mine, 1974; Round and Round, 1977; Nabokov: The Dimensions of Parody, 1978; Rockbridge Poems, 1981; Common Ground, 1982. *Contributions to:* Numerous publications. *Honours:* Dylan Thomas Prize, 1964; Summer Stipend, National Endowment for the Humanities, 1968; Literary Fellowship, National Endowment for the Arts, 1975; First Governor's Award for the Arts, Virginia, 1979; Literary Fellowship, National Endowment for the Arts, 1982. *Membership:* Authors' Guild of America. *Literary Agent:* Anne Elmo. *Address:* 30 Edmonson Avenue, Lexington, VA 24450, USA.

STUART, Forbes Darvall, b. 14 Aug. 1924, Cape Town, Republic of South Africa. Author & Guide-Lecturer. Divorced, 1 daughter. *Education:* BA, University of Cape Town, Republic of South Africa. *Major Publications:* Horned Animals Only, 1966; The Magic Bridle, 1970; A Medley of Folksongs, 1971; The Boy on the Ox's Back, 1971; Stories of Britain in Song, 1972; The Magic Horns, 1974; The Danger of Burton Flair, 1976; The Mermaid's Revenge, 1979. *Contributor to:* Great Britain Now (Spanish edition). *Literary Agent:* Watson & Little. *Address:* 7 Bath Road, London E7 8QQ, England.

STUART, Vivian Alex (née Finlay), b. 2 Jan. 1914, Rangoon, Burma. Novelist. *Education:* University of London, England; University of Budapest, Hungary. *Major Publications:* Some 78 books, including: Fiction: The Captain's Table, 1954; Life is the Destiny, 1956; Heroic Garrison, Shannon's Brigade, Sailors on Horseback, 1975–76; Captain of Cavalry, Mutiny at Dawn, Massacre at Cawnpore, 1976; Escape from Hell, 1976; The Exiles, 1980; The Settlers, 1981; The Traitors, 1982; The Explorers, 1983; The Adventurers, 1983; The Colonists, 1984; The Goldseekers, 1985; Non-fiction: The Beloved Little Admiral: A Biography of Admiral of the Fleet Sir Henry Keppel, 1967; His Majesty's Sloop-of-War Diamond Rock, with George Eggleston, 1978; Autobiographical: Life is the Destiny, 1958, Large print, 1984. *Memberships include:* Society of Authors; WAG; Past Chairman, currently Vice-Chairman, Writers' Summer School. *Literary Agents:* Aidan Ellis, Henley-on-Thames, England; Book Creations Inc, New York, USA. *Address:* 461 Malton Road, York YO3 9TH, England.

STUBBS, Jean, b. 23 Oct. 1926, Denton, Lancashire, England. Writer. m. (1) 1 son, 1 daughter. (2) Roy Oliver, 5 Aug. 1980, Helston. *Education:* Manchester School of Art. *Literary Appointments:* Writer in residence for Avon, 1984. *Publications:* The Rose Grower, 1962; The Travellers, 1963; Hanrahan's Colony, 1964; The Straw Crown, 1966; My Grand Enemy, 1967; The Passing Star, 1970; The Case of Kitty Ogilvie, 1970; An Unknown Welshman, 1972; Dear Laura, 1973; The Painted Face, 1974; Kit's Hill, 1979; The Ironmaster, 1981; The Vivian Inheritance, 1982; The Northern Correspondent, 1984; 100 Years Around the Lizard, 1985. *Contributions to:* Women's magazines including: Good Housekeeping; Woman's Journal; Homes and Gardens; Reviewer, Books and Bookmen, 1966–80. *Honour:* Daughter of Mark Twain, 1973. *Memberships:* Past committee member, Crime Writers Association; PEN; Society of Women Writers and Journalists; Lancashire Authors Association; Detection Club; Romantic Novelists Association. *Literary Agent:* Macmillan (London) Ltd, 4 Little Essex Street, London WC2R 3LF, England. *Address:* Trewin, Nancegollan, Helston, Cornwall, TR13 OAJ, England.

STUBBS, Peter Charles, b. 4 Aug. 1937, Manchester, England. Economist. m. Rosemary Mackenzie, 8 Sep. 1962, Edinburgh, Scotland, 4 sons. *Education:* BA, Cambridge, England 1960, MA 1964; PhD. Melbourne, Australia, 1967. *Publications:* Innovation and Research, 1969; The Australian Motor Industry, 1972; The History of Dorman Smith, 1972; Technology and Australia's Future, 1980; Transport Economics, 1980 (revised 1984); Australia and the Maritime Industries, 1983. *Contributions to:* Various academic journals. *Address:* Department of Economics, University of Manchester, Manchester M13 9PL, England.

STUBER, Florian, b. 1 Mar. 1947, Buffalo, New York, USA. Writer; Professor. *Education:* BA cum laude, Columbia College, 1968; MA, Highest Honours, 1969, MPhil, Highest Honours, 1971, PhD, Distinction, 1980, Columbia University. *Literary Appointments:* Instructor/Preceptor, Columbia College, 1970–75; Lecturer/Instructor, Barnard College, 1979–85; Instructor/Adjunct Assistant Professor, Fashion Institute of Technology, 1977–. *Publications include:* Small Comforts for Hard Times: Humanists on Public Policy, 1977; Los humanistas y la política, 1984; Clarissa: A theater Work, (Part 1), with Margaret Doody, produced Manhattan, 1984; Pamela's Wedding Day at F.T.T., viedotape, with Margaret Doody, 1985. *Contributions:*

On Original & Final Intentions, or Can There Be an Authoritative Clarissa? (Text 2, 1986); On Fathers & Authority in Clarissa, (Studies in English Literature, 1985); Clarissa Censored; with Margaret Doody (Modern Language Studies, 1986). *Honours:* Woodrow Wilson Fellow, 1968–69; Columbia University Faculty Fellow, 1968–72; Grants, Axe-Houghton Foundation, 1984, 1985. *Memberships:* Dramatists Guild; Dance Theater Workshop; American Society for 18th-Century Studies; Northeast American Society for 18th-Century Studies; Society for Textual Scholarship. *Literary Agent:* Richard Horner, Richard Horner Associates Ltd, 165 West 46th Street, No. 710, New York, NY 10036. *Address:* 134 West 93rd Street, 3B, New York, NY 10025, USA.

STUHLMUELLER, Carroll, b. 2 Apr. 1923, Hamilton, Ohio, USA. Professor of Old Testament Studies. *Education:* Licentiate in Sacred Theology (STL), Catholic University Washington, 1952; Licentiate in Sacred Scriptures (SSL), 1954, Doctorate in Sacred Scripture (SSD), 1968, Pontifical Biblical Institute, Rome. *Literary Appointments:* Associate Editor, Catholic Biblical Quarterly, 1973–77; Associate Editor, Testamant Reading Guide, 1974–79; President, Catholic Biblical Association, 1978–79; Associate Editor and Book Review Editor, The Bible Today, 1965–80, Editor, 1965–80, Editor in Chief, 1980–85; President, Chicago Society of Biblical Research, 1982–84. *Publications:* Creative Redemption in Deutero-Isaiah, 1970; Books of Jeremiah and Barch, 1973; Thirsting for the Lord, 1977; Biblical Meditations, 6 volumes 1978–85; The Psalms, 2 volumes, 1983; Biblical Foundations for Mission (with Donald Senior), 1983. *Contributions to:* Jerome Biblical Commentary, 4 chapters, 1968; Theology of Creation, Catholic Biblical Quarterly, 1959; Yahweh-King and Deutero-Isaiah, Biblical Research, 1970; Repentance for Original Sin Communio, 1974; History as Revelation of God, Chicago Studies, 1977. *Honour:* Doctor of More Humane Letters, St Benedict College, Atchison, Kansas, 1969. *Membrships:* Catholic Biblical Assocation; Chicago Society of Biblical Research; Catholic Theological Society of America. *Address:* Catholic Theological Union, 5401 S Cornell Ave, Chicago, IL 60615, USA.

STUPAK, Ronald Joseph, b. 28 Nov. 1934, Allentown, USA. Professor; Consultant; Manager. m. Dolores Barbara Sarmir, 14 June 1958, Allentown, 1 daughter. *Education:* BA, Moravian College, 1961; MA, 1964, PhD, 1967, Ohio State University. *Appointments:* Visiting Professor, National Security Studies, Ohio State University, 1969; Scholar-in-Residence, International Studies Seminar, Southwestern at Memphis; Served, numerous department and university committees, Miami University, 1966–75; Chair, Reader, numerous Masters Theses and Doctoral Dissertations, Miami University, 1966–75; Visiting Professor, Western College, 1972. *Publications:* The Shaping of Foreign Policy : The Role of the Secretary of State as Seen by Dean Acheson, 1969; American foreign Policy: Assumptons, Processes, and Projections, 1976; Understanding Political Science: The Arena of Power, co-author, 1977; Inside the Bureaucracy: The View from the Assistant Secretary's Desk, co-author, 1979. *Contributor to:* Numerous professional journals. *Honours:* Mid-Atlantic Honorary Designation, Sigma Xi; Comenius Award, Outstanding Achievement in Liberal Education, Bethlehem, Pennsylvania. *Memberships:* Director, The Bureaucrat, 1977–84; Board of Directors, Advisory Boards: Alfa Consulting Firm, 1980–83; BJS Consulting Assoc, 1983–85; Appropriate Solutions Inc. 1984–85. *Literary Agent:* Barbara J. Salmi Associates. *Address:* University of Southern California, School of Public Administration, Washington Public Affairs Centre, 512 Tenth St, NW, Washington DC 20004, USA.

STUPPLE, Gwen E, b. 1 May 1924, Hamilton, Ontario, Canada. Magazine Publisher. m. John A Stupple, 11 May 1946, Hamilton, Ontario, 4 sons, 1 daughter. *Contributions to:* Gardenland Magazine; Grower Talks Magazine; Landscape Canada Magazine. *Honour:* Landscape Ontario Garden Writers' Award, 1974.

Address: 43 Glen Road, Hamilton, Ontaraio, Canada L8S 3M6.

STURMAN, John Rollin, b. 15 May 1952, New York, USA. Editor. *Education:* BA Columbia College, New York, USA, 1975; MA, University of North Carolina, Chapel Hill, North Carolina, 1975. *Major Contributions:* The Bedside, Bathtub & Armchair Companion to Agatha Christie (edited Riley & McAllister), 1979; The DuMont Guide to Paris and the Ile de France, 1985; Roadside Food, 1986; The DuMont Guide to the French Riviera, 1986; The DuMont Guide to the Loire Valley, 1986. *Contributor to:* ARTnews. *Honour:* Seymour Brick Memorial Prize for Playwriting, 1973. *Address:* P O Box 20135, London Terrace Station, NY 10011, USA.

STURMTHAL, Adolf F(ox), b. 10 Sep. 1903, Vienna, Austria. University Professor. m. Hattie Ross, 25 July 1940, Leesburg, Virginia, USA, 3 daughters. *Education:* Doctor rerum politicarum, University of Vienna, Austria; Diploma renewed, Honorary, 1975. *Literary Appointments:* Bard College, Columbia University, 1940; Cornell University, 1952–54; Philip Murray Professor, Roosevelt University, 1955–60; Yale University, 1962–63; University of Illinois, 1960–. *Publications:* Author of numerous works including: The Tragedy of European Labor 1918–1939, 1943–1951; Workers Council, a Comparative Study of Workplace organisations on both sides of the Iron Curtain, 1964; Unity and Diversity in European Labor, 1953, White Collar Trade Unions, Contemporary Developments in Industrialised Societies, 1966; Comparative Labor Movements: Confrontation and Accomodation, 1972; Left of Center: European Labor since World War II, 1983. *Contributions to:* Labor and Nation; Forum; Industrial and Labor Relations Review; Journal of Political and Labor Relations Review; Journal of Political Economy; American Perspective; World Politics; Wirschaftsdienst; Encyclopedia Britannica; International Encyclopedia of Social Sciences; and various others. *Honours:* Doctor of Humane Letters, Honoris causa, Bard College, New York, 1985. *Address:* 61 Greencroft Drive, Champaign, IL 61821, USA.

STUTTARD, John Corrie, b. 4 November 1916, Hebden Bridge, England. Civil Servant (retired); Librarian. m. Eleanor Sandes, London, 19 June 1957, 2 sons, 3 daughters. *Education:* BA, University of London, MSc, University of Cambridge, England. *Major Publications:* Indo-China, 1943; Various contributions to Chamber's Encyclopaedia on Far East Countries, and to Encyclopaedias on Mountains Rivers and Lakes; History of Leatherhead (with others), 1986. *Contributor to:* Society of Indexers. *Address:* 6 Orchardleigh, St Nicholas' Hill, Leatherhead, Surrey, England.

STYAN, John Louis, b. 6 July 1923, London, England. University Professor. m. Constance Winifred Maude Roberts, 17 Nov. 1945, 2 sons, 2 daughters. *Education:* BA, 1947, MA, 1948, Department of Education Certificate, 1948, Cambridge University English Tripos. *Appointments:* Staff Tutor, then Senior Staff Tutor, Literature, Drama, Adult Education, University of Hull, 1950–65; Professor, Chairman, English, University of Michigan, USA, 1965–74; Andrew W Mellon Professor, English, University of Pittsburg, 1974–77; Franklyn Bliss Snyder Professor, English Literature, Northwestern University, 1977–; Professor Theatre, 1984–. *Publications:* The Elements of Drama, 1960; The Dark Comedy, 1962; The Dramatic Experience, 1965; Shakespeare's Stagecraft, 1967; Chekhov in Performance, 1971; Drama, Stage and Audience, 1975; The Shakespeare Revolution, 1977; Modern Drama in Theory and Practice, 3 volumes, 1981; Max Reinhardt, 1982; All's Well That Ends Well, 1984; The State of Drama Study, 1984; Restoration Comedy in Performance, in press. *Contributor to:* About 70 articles in, Studies in English Literature; Theatre Journal; Shakespeare Quarterly; Modern Drama; Comparative Drama; College Literature; Educational Theatre Journal; Modern Language Quarterly; Speech and Drama; Costerus; Genre; British Book News; Adult Education; Plays and Players; Divadlo, etc. *Honours:* Visiting Professor, University of

Michigan, 1963; University of Iowa, 1971; Northwestern University, 1977; Columbia University, 1982; Kathleen Robinson Lecturer, Drama, University of Sydney, 1983; Fellowships: National Endowment for the Humanities, 1978; Guggenheim Foundation, 1983; etc. *Memberships:* Modern Language Association of America, Drama Division Chair, 1984; Shakespeare Association of America; International Shakespeare Association; Advisory Council, Shakespeare Globe Centre, North America, Chair, 1981–. *Address:* 1414 Ridge Avenue, Evanston, IL 60201, USA.

SUGITA, Yutaka, b. 13 July 1930, Ohmiya City, Saitama prefecture, Japan. Author; Illustrator of Children's Picture Books; Graphic Designer. m. Sadako Sugita, 12 Nov. 1954, Ohmiya City, 2 sons. *Education:* BA, Arts, 1953; Graduate, Tokyo University of Education. *Literary Appointments:* Author, Illustrator, Children's Picture Books; Graphic Designer, Various fields; Professor, Art and Design, Tsukuba University. *Publications:* Children's Picture Books: When we Dream, 1965; Where is My Mother? 1966; Runaway James and the Night Owl, 1968; Good Morning, 1969; Good Night, 1971; My Dog, 1972; My Name is Blackie, 1974; My Hoops, 1976; Little Angel's Visit, 1977; Hippo and Turtle, 1978; The Mouse's Feast, 1978; Do You Know What I Like?, 1980; Hide and Seek, 1982; The Joyful Journey, 1982; Blackie and HIs iesta, 1984. Author of Various other childrens books, many published in foreign editions. *Contributions to:* Newspapers: Asahi, The Childrens Library, Jury Member and Critic; Yomiuri, Jury Member; Talks on Tokyo FM Radio. Appeared at Japan national Broadcasting Programme. *Honours:* Office Chretien du Livre, France, 1974; Winner, Poster of the Year, Childrens Year, Bologna Book Fair, 1979, Bologna '79 Graphic Prize, 1979; BRNO Graphic Design Biennale, Special Award, 1984 and numerous others. *Memberships:* Modern Art Society; Tokyo Design Space; Japan Graphic Designers Association; Artists Union for Juvenile Illustrated Publications; Japanese Board on Books for Young People, Special Committee. *Literary Agents:* Shiko-Sha Company and Kodansha Limited. *Address:* Azuma-cho 1-42, Ohmiya City, Saitama Prefecture, Japan 330.

SUHOR, Mary Lou, b. 11 July 1929, New Orleans, Louisiana, USA. Editor, The Witness Magazine. *Education:* BA, Education, Loyola University, New Orleans, 1949; MA, Sociology, The Catholic University of America, Washington DC, 1960. *Literary Appointments include:* Instructor, Journalism, Loyola University, New Orleans, 1952–55; Assistant Editor, North Central Louisiana Register, 1956–58; Staff Editor, The Queen's Work, Catholic Publishing House and Lecturer, Summer Schools of Catholic Action, 1960–63; Managing Editor, The Witness Magazine, 1976–80; Editor, The Witness Magazine, 1981–. *Publications:* Co-Editor, Struggling With the System, Probing Alternatives, 1979–80; One of 5 editors, Volume I, Christian Commitment for the 1980s: Must We Choose Sides?, Co-Editor of Volume 2, Which Side Are We on?, 1985; Editorial Board Member, Ordinary Women, Extra-ordinary Lives: My Story Is On. *Contributor to:* The Progressive Magazine; Christianity and Crisis; National Catholic Reporter, etc. *Honours:* Catholic Press Association Award, Best Series in the Public Interest, 1957; Catholic Press Association Award, Best Feature Story, 1958; Associated Church Press Award of Merit, Best Feature Story, 1984; Best Editorial, Episcopal Communicator Polly Bond Award, 1984. *Memberships:* Women's Institute for Freedom of the Press; Associated Church Press. *Address:* 174 S Bethlehem Pike, Ambler, PA 19002, USA.

SUINN, Richard M, b. 8 May 1933, Honolulu, Hawaii, USA. Head of Department of Psychology, Colorado State University. m. Grace Toy, 1958, 2 sons. *Education:* BA Summa cum laude, Ohio State University, 1955; PhD, Stanford University, 1959. *Literary Appointments:* Past Editor; Behavior Therapy, Behavior Counseling Quarterly; Currently Editor: Journal Consulting and Clinical Psychology, Journal Counseling Psychology, Journal Behavior Medicine, Journal Sports Psychology. *Publications:* Predictive Validity of Projective Measures,

1969; The Innovative Psychological Therapies; The Innovative Medical-Psychiatric Therapies, 1976; Psychology in Sports, 1980; Fundamentals of Behavior Pathology, 1975; Fundamentals of Abnormal Psychology, 1984. *Contributions to:* Psychological journals. *Membership:* Phi Beta Kappa. *Address:* Department of Psychology, Colorado State University, Fort Collins, CO 80523, USA.

SUKENICK, Ronald. Teacher; Writer. *Education:* BA, Cornell University, 1955; PhD, Brandeis University, 1962. *Appointments:* Professor, English Literature, University of Colorado, 1975–. *Publications:* Out, 1973; Inform: Digressions on the Act of Fiction, 1985; Blown Away, 1985; Endless Short Story, 1986. *Contributor to:* Founder, American Book Review; Partisan Review; New Literary History; Studies in American Fiction. *Honours:* Fulbright Fellowship, 1958; Guggenheim Fellowship, Fiction, 1977–78; National Endowment for the Arts Fellowship in Writing, 1980; Butler Chair, State University of New York, Buffalo, 1981; Fulbright Fellowship, Israel, 1984; Editors Grant, CCLM, 1985. *Memberships:* Chairman, Board of Directors, Coordinating Council of Literary Magazines, 1975–77; Founding Member, Board Member, Fiction Collective. *Address:* Dept of English, University of Colorado, Boulder, CO 80309, USA.

SULIEMAN, Michael W, b. 1934, Tiberias, Palestine (American Citizen). Professor of Political Science. m. 2 children. *Education:* BA, Bradley University, 1960; MS, 1962, PhD, 1965, University of Wisconsin. *Literary Appointments:* Editorial Board: International Journal of Middle East Studies, 1982–; Arab Studies Quarterly, 1979–; Journal of Arab Affairs, 1980–. Reviewer of Manuscripts for professional journals. *Publications:* Political Parties on Lebanon: The Challenge of a Fragmental Political Culture, 1967; American Images Middle East Peoples: Impact of the High School, 1977. *Contributions to:* International Journal of Middle East Studies; Preface, Arab-American Almanac; Journal of Palestine Studies; Political Behaviour of the Arab States, Editor Tawfic E Farah, 1983; Journal: Institute of Muslim Minority Affairs; Split Vision; Journal of Social Sciences, etc. Book reviews. Contributor to newspapers, radio and television stations of papers, articles etc; Guest Lecturer and Conference Participant. *Honours include:* Fulbright Hayes Fellowship, 1983–84; American Philosophical Society Travelling Fellowship, 1974; Scott Goodknight National Scholarship, Phi Eta Sigma, 1960; Ford Faculty Research Fellowship, 1969–70 and several other fellowships, grants, etc. *Memberships:* American Political Science Association; Middle East Studies Association; The Middle East Institute; International Association for Mass Communication Research. *Address:* Department of Political Science, Kansas State University, Manhattan, KS 66506, USA.

SULLIVAN, Clara K, b. 4 Apr. 1915, Brooklyn, New York, USA. Public Finance Analyst. m. 7 Feb. 1948, Yonkers, New York. *Education:* Columbia University, MA 1943, PhD 1959. *Literary Appointments:* Economics Editor, Hougton Mifflin Co, 1967–69. *Major Publications:* The Tax On Value Added, 1965; The Search for Tax Principles in the European Economic Community, 1963; Two Chapters in, Fiscal Harmonization in Common Markets, edited Carl Shoup, 1967. *Address:* 336 Pensacola Road, Venice, FL 33595, USA.

SULLIVAN, Eleanor Regis, b. 19 Oct. 1928, Cambridge, Massachusetts, USA. *Education:* BS, Salem State College, Salem, Massachusetts. *Publications:* A Biblio-Bio-Anecdotal Memoir of Rederic Dannay, 1984. *Contributions to:* Ellery's Queen's Mystery Magazine; Alfred Hitchcock's Mystery Magazine; Mystery Writers' Handbook; New York Times; National Lampoon; San Francisco Chronicle. *Memberships:* Secretary, 1974–76, Director 1974–77, 1982–85, Mystery Writers of America; Member 1974–, Dramatists Guild; Member 1983–, American Film Institute. *Literary Agent:* Emilie Jacobson. *Address:* 236 East 49th Street, New York, NY 10017, USA.

SULLIVAN, Patrick Sean James, b. 21 Apr. 1961, Fayetteville, North Carolina, USA. Publisher. *Education:* BA, Sociology, Honours, 1984. *Contributor to:* Founding Co-Editor, Publisher, Ceilidh, 1981–; Editor in Chief, Monday Morning Blues, 1981; Poetry Editor, Unicorn, 1981; Production Manager, Reed, 1982. *Address:* 986 Marquette Lane, Foster City, CA 94404, USA.

SULLIVAN, Scott, b. 9 May 1937, Cleveland, USA. Journalist. m. Betty Hillman, 15 May 1983, Paris, 1 son, 3 daughters. *Education:* BA, Yale College, USA, 1958; BA, MA, Saint Catherine's College, Cambridge, England. *Literary Appointments:* European Editor, Newsweek. *Publications:* The Shortest, Gladdest Years. *Contributions to:* The Baltimore Sun; Newsweek. *Address:* 24 Boulevard de Latour-Maubourg, Paris 75007, France.

SULTAN, Stanley, b. 17 July 1928, New York City, USA. University Professor. m. Betty Hillman, 15 May 1965, Nashua New Hampshire, USA, 1 son, 1 daughter. *Education:* AB, Cornell University, 1949; MA, Boston University, 1950; PhD, English Literature, Yale University, 1955. *Literary Appointments:* Assistant Editor, National Lexicographic Board Ltd; currently: Professor of English Literature, Clark University. *Publications:* The Argument of Elysses, 1965; Ulysses, The Waste Land and Modernism, 1977; Rabbi: A Tale of the Waning Year, novel, 1978. *Contributions to:* Literary Studies: Massachusetts Review; Journal of Modern Literature; University Review; Journal of English and Germanic Philology; Southern Review; James Joyce Quarterly; Midstream. Fiction: Pequod; A Shout in the Street; Brown Review; University Review; Epoch; Kenyon Review; West Branch etc. *Honours:* Inclusion in Best American Short Stories, 1953; Best American Short Stories Honor Roll 1956; Fellowship to Yaddo, Saratoga, New York, 1958; Broadcast Reading, contemporary fiction series, WBAI-FM, Pacifica Radio, New York, 1981. Inclusion in, Current Authors, section of A Critical Survey of Short Fiction, Salem Press 1981. *Address:* 25 Hardwick Street, Brighton P O, Boston, MA 02135, USA.

SULTANA, Donald Edward, b. 20 Oct. 1924, Malta. Honorary Fellow, University of Edinburgh; Formerly Reader in English Literature. m. Myriam Vella, 31 Oct. 1964, Malta. *Education:* BSc, MD, Royal University of Malta; MA, DPhil, University of Oxford. *Literary Appointments:* Lecturer in English, Royal University of Malta; Lecturer, Senior Lecturer, Reader, Literature, University of Edinburgh; Honorary Fellow, University of Edinburgh. *Publications:* Samuel Taylor Coleridge in Malta and Italy 1804–1806, 1969; Benjamin Disraeli in Spain, Malta and Albania, 1979; The Siege of Malta Rediscovered: An Account of Sir Walter Scott's Mediterranean Journey and His Last Novel, 1977; New Approaches to Coleridge: Biographical and Critical Essays, 1981; The Journey of Sir Walter Soctt to malta, 1986. *Contributor to:* Times Literary Supplement; British Book News; Times of Malta; Sunday Times of Malta. *Honours:* Rhodes Scholar at St John's College, Oxford, 1946–50; Carnegie Visiting Fellowship, 1957; Specialist Lecturer for British Council, 1970. *Memberships:* Oxford Union; Royal Commonwealth Society. *Address:* 5 Howe Street, Edinburgh 3, Scotland.

SUMMERFIELD, Henry, b. 3 Nov. 1935, Newcastle-on-Tyne, England. University Teacher. *Education:* BA 1959, MA 1963, Exeter College, Oxford; MLitt, University of Durham, 1965. *Publications:* That Myriad-Minded Man: A Biography of George William Russell A E, 1975; An Introductory Guide to The Anathemata and the Sleeping Lord, Sequence of David Jones, 1979; Collected Works of A E (George W Russell 1967–1935), (co general editor). *Contributions to:* Blake: An Illustrated Quarterly; Nineteenth Century Fiction; Trivium; The Malahat Review. *Address:* Department of English, University of Victoria, British Columbia V8W 2Y2, Canada.

SUMMERS, Hal (Henry Forbes), b. 18 Aug. 1911. Civil Servant (retired). *Education:* Fettes College, Edinburgh, Scotland; Trinity College, University of Oxford, England. *Appointments include:* Under-Secretary, Department of the Environment. *Major Publications:* Smoke after Flame, 1944; Hinterland, 1947; Visions of Time, 1951; Tomorrow is my Love, 1978; The Burning Book, 1982. *Contributor to:* The Listener; Various other periodicals. *Address:* Folly Fields, Linden Gardens, Tunbridge Wells, Kent TN2 5QV, England.

SUMMERS, Joseph Holmes, b. 9 Feb. 1920, Louisville, Kentucky, USA. Professor of English. m. U T Miller Summers, 24 Sep. 1943, Washington DC, USA, 1 son, 2 daughters. *Education:* BA, 1941, MA, 1948, PhD, 1950, Harvard University, Cambridge, Massachusetts. *Literary Appointments:* Bard College, University of Connecticut; Washington University, St Louis; Amherst College (visiting); University of Oxford (visiting); Michigan State University; University of Kent (visiting); University of Rochester. *Major Publications:* George Herbert: His religion & Art, 1954; The Muse's Method: An Introduction to, Paradise Lost, 1962; The Lyric & Dramatic Milton (editor), 1965; The Heirs of Donne & Jonson, 1970; Dreams of Love & Power: On Shakespear's Plays, 1984. *Contributor to:* Publications Modern Language Association; Massachusetts Review; Studies in English Literature; Modern Language Quarterly; University of Toronto Quarterly. *Honours:* Visiting Fellow, All Souls College, Oxford, England; Senior Fellow, Folger Shakespear Library; Fellow, New Huntington Library; Fellow, Americam Academy of Arts & Sciences; Honoured Scholar of Milton Society of America.*Memberships:* Milton Society of America, Vice-President, 1981, President, 1982; International Association of University Professors of English; Shakespeare Association of America; Modern Language Association of America; Renaissance Society of America. *Address:* Department of English, University of Rochester, Rochester, NY 14627, USA.

SUMMONS, John Graham, b. 6 Sep. 1952, Sydney, Australia. Playwright; Teacher. *Education:* BA, University of New South Wales; Diploma in Education, University of New South Wales. *Literary Appointment:* Playwright-In-Residence, Ensemble Theatre, Sydney, Australia. *Publications:* Lamb of God, 1978, (Stage Play); The Coroner's Report, 1977, (Stage Play); The Sower and the Reaper, 1980, (Stage Play). *Membership:* Australian Writers Guild. *Address:* 63 Short Street, Balmain, Sydney, Australia 2041.

SUMNER, (Edith) Aurea, b. 28 Mar. 1913, Goole, Yorkshire, England. Retired Schoolmistress. *Education:* Student, Bishop Grosseteste College, Teaching Certificate, Archbishops Certificate, Religious Studies. *Publications:* Listen and Do, 1958; More Listen and Do, 1959; The Hand, 1982. *Contributor to:* Treasure Trail; Bible Trail; Bible Highway; Junior Concise Guides; Partners in Learning; Church Teacher. *Address:* Galatea, 535 Main Road, Dovercourt, Harwich, Essex CO12 4NH, England.

SUNDERLAND, Eric, b. 18 Mar 1930, Ammanford, Dyfed, Wales. University Principal. m. Jean Patricia Watson, 1957, 2 daughters. *Education:* BA, Geography with Anthropology, 1950, MA, Anthropology, 1951, University College of Wales Aberystwyth; PhD, Anthropology, University College London, 1954. *Publications:* Elements of Human and Social Geography; some anthropological perspectives, 1973; Genetic Variation in Britain (co-editor) 1973; The Operation of Intelligence, biological pre-conditions for the operation of intelligence (co editor) 1980; Genetic and Population Studies in Wales (co-editor) 1986. *Contributions to:* Approximately 80 papers written for journals plus approximately 50 book reviews. *Membership:* Honorary Treasurer, Royal Anthropological Institute; Secretary General, International Union of Anthropological and Ethnological Sciences (IUALES). *Address:* Byrn, Ffriddoedd Road, Bangor, Gwynedd LL57 2EH, North Wales.

SUOMELA, Erkki Kalevi, b. 18 Nov. 1929, Sippola, Finland. Writer. m. Päivi Liljeblad, 7 May 1959, 1 son, 1 daughter. *Publications:* Vieras Kesä, 1973; Kirppu, 1974; Muu Maa Mustikka, 1976; Moi Suoimi, 1977; Oravapoika, 1979; Simppa ja Salsaiset Kaupat, 1981; Tosi Mesta, 1983; Henkka, 1985. *Honours:* State Literary Prize, 1974, 1984. *Membership:* Suomen Kirjailijalitto. *Literary Agent:* K J Gummerus Oy, PL 479, 00101 Helsinki, Finland. *Address:* Kuusikuja A 3, 10420 Pohjankuru, Finland.

SUPER, Robert Henry, b. 13 June 1914, Wilkes-Barre, Pennsylvania, USA. University Professor. m. Rebecca Ragsdale, 25 Jan. 1953, Brooklyn, New York, USA, 2 sons. *Education:* BA, Princeton University, 1935; B Litt, University of Oxford, England, 1937; PhD, Princeton University, 1941. *Literary Appointments:* Instructor in English, Princeton University, 1938–42; Assistant Professor of English, Michigan State Normal College, Ypsilanti, 1942–47; Assistant Professor to Professor of English, University of Michigan, 1947–84, retired. *Major Publications:* Walter Savage Landor: A Biography, 1954; Matthew Arnold's Complete Prose Works (editor), 11 volumes, 1960–77; The Time-Spirit of Matthew Arnold, 1970; Trollope in the Post Office, 1981; Anthony Trollope's, Marions Fay (editor), 1982. *Honours:* The Manners Prize, Princeton University, 1935; The University of Michigcan Press Prize, 1967, 1982. *Address:* 1221 Baldwin Avenue, Ann Arbor, MI 48104, USA.

SURTEES, Virginia, b. London, England. Author. m. (1) Sir Ashley Clarke, GCMG (div); (2) David Craig, OBE (div). *Publications:* D G Rossetti, A Catalogue raisonné, 1971; Sublime & Instructive, 1972; Charlotte Canning, 1975; The Beckford Inheritance, 1977; Reflections of a Frienship, 1979; The Diary of Ford Madox Brownm 1981; The Ludovisi Goddess, 1984. *Contributions to:* Burlington Magazine; Apollo; Princeton University Library Chronicle. *Membership:* Fellow, Royal Society of Literature. *Address:* c/o Royal Bank of Scotland, 43 Curzon Street, London W1, England.

SUSILO, Richard Yani, b. 15 Mar. 1961, Jakarta, Indonesia. Philatelic Journalist; Reporter. *Education:* Doctorate standard, Mass Communication. *Literary Appointment:* Chief Editor, Indonesia Philatelic News Bulletin. *Publications:* Mengenal Philateli Di Indonesia, 1982; Bunga Rampai Filateli, 1984. *Contributions to:* Sinar Harapan newspaper, especially philatelic column. *Memberships:* Society of Philaticians, New York; Writers Unit 30, American Philatelic Society: Journalists, Authors & Poets on Stamps, a special ATA study unit, USA. *Address:* Jalan Jambu 4 Pav, Jakarta 10350, Indonesia.

SUSILUOTO, Laura Rebecka, b. 17 Aug. 1913, Hämeenlinna. Playwright. m. 3 Sep. 1939, 3 sons, 1 daughter. *Education:* Degree in Didactics, Sibelius Academy. *Publications:* 21 TV Plays including: Father Christmas Slips Up, 1961; Santa Claus and the Conjurer, 1962; The Secret of Doll. 19 Theatre Plays including: Song of Sixpence, 1978 and Titulus, musical for children, 1982. Books: Lasten Satunäytelmiä, 1964; Jänka-Jaanan taika, 1965; Tinanappi ja muita näytelmiä, 1967; Noidanlukon salaisuus, 1970; Teltta metsän keskellä, 1972. *Honours:* Various awards from the Ministry of Education 1970–85; Award from Central Council of Arts 1982. *Address:* Lapinrinne 4 B 12, 00180 Helsinki 18, Finland.

SUTCH, Richard Charles, b. 8 Dec. 1942, St Paul, Minnesota, USA. Educator: Professor of Economics. m. Susie Olive Speakman, 31 Oct. 1968, Padenarum, Massachusetts, 1 daughter. *Education:* BA, Economics, University of Washington, 1963; PhD, Economics, Massachusetts Institute of Technology, 1968. *Literary Appointment:* Board of Editors, Journal of Economic History, 1980–83. *Publications:* Reckoning With Slavery: A Critical Study in the Quantitative History of American Negro Slavery, (co-author), 1976; One Kind of Freedom: The Economic Consequences of Emancipation, (co-author), 1977; Explorations in the New Economic History: Essays in Honor of Douglass C North, (co-editor), 1982. *Contributions to:* Professional journals including, Journal of Economic History, Quarterly Review of Economics and Business; Journal of Business and Economic Statistics; Contributions to Books including: Reckoning with Slavery; Race and Slavery in the Western Hemisphere; Quantitative Studies, 1975. *Honours include:* Distinguished Teaching Award, Academic Senate, University of California, Berkeley, 1980; Guggenheim Fellowship, 1984–85. *Memberships:* Agricultural History Society; American Economic Association; American Economic History Association; American Historical Association; Cliometric Society; Economic History Society; Organization of American Historians; Population Association of America; Social Science History Association. *Address:* Department of Economics, University of California, Berkeley, CA 94720, USA.

SUTCLIFF. Rosemary, b. 14 Dec. 1920, East Clandon, Surrey, England. Writer. *Publications:* The Eagle of the Ninth, 1955; The Lantern Bearers, 1959; Sword at Sunset, 1962; The Flowers of Adonis, 1977; Frontier Wolf, 1981 and about 40 other books. *Honours:* Carnegie Award, 1959; OBE for Service to Children's Literature, 1975; Phoenix Award, 1985 and several others. *Membership:* Fellow, Royal Society of Literature. *Literary Agent:* Murray Pollinger. *Address:* Swallowshaw, Walberton, Arundel, Sussex BN18 0PO, England.

SUTHERLAND, Margaret, b. 16 Sep. 1941, Auckland, New Zealand. Author. Separated, 2 sons, 1 daughter. *Education:* Studying, Asian Language Degree; Registered Nurse. *Appointments:* Literary Fellow, Auckland University, 1981; Scholarship in Letters, New Zealand Government, 1984. *Publications:* The Fledgling, 1974; The Love Contract, 1976; Getting Through, 1977; Dark Places, Deep Regions, 1980; The Fringe of Heaven, 1984; Childrens Books: Hello I'm Karen, 1974. *Contributor to:* Literary & Popular New Zealand Magazines and Journals. *Honours:* Recipient, Katherine Mansfield Short Story Award, *Membership:* PEN, New Zealand. *Address:* 22 Kaurilands Road, Titirangi, Auckland, New Zeland.

SUTHERLAND, Norman Stuart, b. 26 Mar. 1927, London, England. University Professor. m. Jose Louise Fogden, 30 June 1956 (separated), 2 daughters. *Education:* BA Literae Humaniories, 1949, BA Psychology, Philosophy and Physiology, 1953, D Phil Experimental Psychology, 1957, Oxford University. *Publications:* Shape Discrimination by Animals, 1959; Animal Discrimination Learning, (with R N Gilbert), 1969; Mechanisms of Animal Discrimination Learning, (with N J Mackintosh), 1971; Breakdown: Personal Crisis and a Medical Dilema, 1976; Discovering the Human Mind; Tutorial Essays in Psychology, volume 1, 1977, volume 2, 1979; The Price of Everything, novel, 1986. *Contributions to:* Sunday Times; Observer; Times Literary Supplement; Times Higher Education Supplement; Sunday Telegraph; Nature; New Scientist; New York Times Review of Books; Technical journals on psychology and philosophy. *Literary Agent:* Deborah Rogers, London. *Address:* Laboratory of Experimental Psychology, University of Sussex, Brighton BN1 9QG, England.

SUTHERLAND, Robert D, b. 4 Nov. 1937, Blytheville, Arkansas, USA. Professor of English. m. Marilyn F Neufeldt, 25 July 1959, 2 sons. *Education:* BA, Wichita State University, 1959; MA, 1961, PhD, 1964, University of Iowa. *Literary Appointment:* Editor, The Pikestaff Forum, Literary magazine, 1977–. *Publications:* Language and Lewis Carroll, 1970; Sticklewort and Feverfew, novel, 1980. *Contributions to:* College English; Children's Literature in Education, 1985; various articles, poems, book reviews in magazines and journals. *Honours:* Juvenile Book Merit Award for Author/Illustrator, Friends of American Writers, 1981.

Membership: Illinois Writers Incorporated. *Address:* 501 East Willow, Normal, IL 61761, USA.

SUTTON, Bridie, b. 27 Feb. 1928, Rawtenstall, Rossendale, Lancashire, England. Housewife. m. Arthur Edwin Breeze Sutton, 4 Dec. 1950, Newchurch, 5 sons, 1 daughter. *Contributions to:* A Pot Pourri of Verse (Preston Poets); Articles, stories numerous poems to BBC Radio Lancashire; ITV (Poetry Competition); Family Care Magazine; Shropshire Cauldron, (British Rail Magazine); Thwaites Brewery Magazine; Currently writing book to benefit parents or guardians of autistic children. *Honour:* Recipient of Rose Bowl from Preston Poets, 1985. *Membereships:* Life Patron, IBA; Lancashire Authors Association; Preston Poets; Blackburn Writers Circle; Fellow Member of World Literary Academy, IBA. *Address:* 22 Irving Place, Blackburn, Lancashire BB2 6LR, England.

SUTTON, Denys Miller, b. 10 Aug. 1917, London, England. Author. m. Cynthia Sassoon, 1960, 1 son and 1 daughter by previous marriage. *Education:* BA, BLitt, Exeter College, Oxford University. *Literary Appointments:* Art expert, United Nations Educational, Scientific and Cultural Organisation, 1948; Visiting Lecturer, Yale University, USA, 1949; editor, Apollo, 1962–. *Publications:* Andre Derain, 1959; Whistler, 1963; Rodin, 1966; Sickert, 1976; Letters of Roger Fry, 1972. *Contributions to:* Apollo; Burlington Magazine; Connoisseur; Gazette des Beaux Arts; Country Life. *Honour:* Legion d'Honneur; CBE, 1985. *Address:* 22 Chelsea Park Gardens, London SW3, England.

SUTTON, Louise Weibert, b. 22 Apr. 1920, Evansville, Indiana, USA. Writer; Poet. *Publications:* Through Lense of Poetry, 1967 Songs from the April Hills, 1967; The Voice of Verse, 1968; A Pen of Stars, 1968; The Emerald Quill, 1969; Poetry from the Heart. 1978. *Contributions to:* Canadian Pet Magazine; Northwestern Farmer; Gems of Faith; family album. Numerous local newspapers, Canadian Ideals, Poetry and Religious publicsitons; Garden and pet magazines. *Honours include:* Eagle Feather Awards for Writing, 1950–65; 3rd National Poetry Contest, 1967; Best Poet of the Year Award, UAPAA, 1969. *Memberships include:* NAPA. *Address:* 203 South Bosse Avenue, Evansville, IN 47712, USA.

SUTTON, Margaret Rachel Irene, b. 22 Jan. 1903, Odin, Pennsylvania, USA. Writer for Young People. m. (1) William H Sutton, 3 Nov. 1924. Coudersport, Pennsylvania, 1 son, 4 daughters; (2) Everett C Hunting, 19 Oct. 1975, Freeport, New York. *Education:* Graduate, Rochester Business Institute, 1920. *Literary appointments:* Teacher, Writing and Lecturer, several Universities including University of California, Berkeley. *Publications include:* Judy Bolton mystery series (38 titles), 1932–67; The Magic Makers, 1936; Jemina, Daughter of Daniel Boone, 1942; Gail Gardner Wins Her Cap, 1944; Who will Play With Me? 1953; Papaoe Wagon Family, 1957; The Weed Walk, 1965; work in progress: historical novel, the 39th Judy Bolton Mystery and an autobiographical novel Jupiter Girl. *Contributor to:* Child Life; Picture World; Boys and Girls; Publishers Weekly; Writer Magazine; Teen Magazine, several Sunday School papers including Sunshine and Calling All Girls. *Honours:* Recipient of several honours. *Memberships:* Authors League (Life Member); Everett Club; California Writers; Women's National Book Association. *Literary Agent:* Helen McGrath, Concord, California. *Address:* 1312 Jospehine Street #7, Berkeley, CA 94703, USA.

SVAFÁR, Jónas Einarsson, b. 8 Sep. 1925, Reykjavik, Iceland. Fisherman. *Education:* Heradsskolinn Laugarvatni. *Publications:* (Poetry) Thad blaedir ur morgunsarinu, 1952; Geislavirk tungl, 1957; Klettebelti fjalikonunnar, 1968; Staekkunargler undir smasja, 1978; Sjostjarnan i meyjarmerkinu, 1986. *Contributor to:* Icelandic Writing Today; New World's Writing; many other professional journals and magazines. *Honours:* Honorary Award, Writer's Fund of Iceland, 1978, 1985. *Memberships:* Writer's Union of Iceland. *Literary Agent:*

Vaka/Helgafell, Iceland. *Address:* Thingholtsstraeti 25, IS-101 Reykjavik, Iceland.

SVENDSEN, Kari Anne, b. 8 Mar. 1928, Oslo, Norway. Author. m. Alf B Svendsen, deceased, 1 daughter. *Education:* Junior College, Oslo, 1946; BA, American Literature, University of California, Berkeley, California, USA. 1948. *Publications:* 12 Fables, 1956; Golda, Cat of the Artic, 1977; Fabian, The Magic Cat, 1981; Rabian Goes to Lapland, 1985; Tales of the Norsemen, Norwegian folktales and fairy-tales retold in English, also appearing as a talk-book, 1986. *Contributions to:* The Norsemen; Travel Trade, USA; Major newspapers in Norway; Norwegian radio and television. *Honours:* Literary Prize, Norway Cultural Department, 1965; work Scholarship, Norwegian Society of Childrens and Youth Literature, 1980. *Memberships:* Norwegian Society of Children's and Youth Literature; New York Press Club. *Address:* Sven Brunsgate 2, 0166, Oslo 1, Norway.

SVENNINGSEN, Poul Flłoe, b. 23 May 1919, Vejle, Denmark. Journalist; Illustrator. *Publications:* Little Stranger, 1951; Little Nuisance, 1952; Anglers Angle, 1953; Snooze, 1954; Little Angel, 1961; Jagt og Tone, on hunting, 1975; Sejlads mellem ŁOerne, on yachiting, 1977; Mille – A Very Special Dog, 1979; Dear Lord Fieldmouse, novel, 1979. *Contributions to:* Berlingske Tidende, Copenhagen. *Memberships:* Danish Journalists Association; Society of Danish Authors. *Address:* Dämringsvej 15, 2900 Hellerup, Denmark.

SWAIM, Alice Mackenzie, b. 5 June 1911, Craigdam, Scotland. Writer, Consultant, Contest Judge. m. William Thomas Swaim, 27 Dec. 1932, Pittsburgh, Pennsylvania, 2 daughters. *Education:* BA, Wilson College, 1930, 32.*Literary Appointments:* Newspaper Columnist, Cornucopia, Tejas, Carlisle, Pennsylvania Evening Standard, 1953–70; Newspaper Columnist, Touchstone, New Hampshire, 1970–85; National Contest Judge, 1954–85; Poetry Therapy Consultant, 1971–75; Public Relations Director, 2nd World Congress of Poets; Writer, Concordia Greeting Card Company, 1981–82. *Publications:* Let The Deep Song Rise, 1952; Up To The Stars, 1954; Sunshine in a Thimble, 1958l; Crickets are Crying Autumn, 1960; The Gentle Dragon, 1962; Pennsylvania Profile, 1966; Scented Honeysuckle Days, 1966; Here On The Threshhold, 1966; Beaneth a Dancing Star, 1968; Beyond My Catnip Garden, 1970; 5 brochures, 1974–80; And Miles To Go, 1981; Unicorn and Thistle, 1982; Children in Summer, 1983. *Contributions to:* Radio programmes in USA, Canada, Germany, United Kingdom; Numerous poems published. *Honours include:* Over 800 awards and citations including: Medals from Philippines, Italy and USA; American Heritage Award, JFK Library for Minorities, 1974. *Memberships:* Poetry Society of America; Academy of American Poets; National Federation of State Poetry; Marketing Editor, Poetry Society of New Hampshire; Poetry Society of Pennsylvania, Kentucky and Californis. *Address:* 322 North Second Street, Apt 1606, Harrisburg, PA 17101, USA.

SWAIN, Dwight Vreeland, b. 17 Nov. 1915, Rochester, Michigan, USA. Writer. m. Joye Raechel Boulton, 12 Feb. 1969, Las Vegas, Nevada, 2 sons, 2 daughters. *Education:* BA, University of Michigan, 1937; MA, University of Oklahoma, 1954. *Literary Appointments:* Member of editorial staffs of daily & weekly newspapers in Michigan, Pennsylvania, California & Oklahoma; also, Flying Magazine, 1940–41;Script-writer for Motion Picture Unit, University of Oklahoma, 1949–65; Professor of Professional Writing, School of Journalism, 1952–74, Professor Emeritus, 1974–, University of Oklahoma. *Major Publications:* The Transposed Man, 1955; How to Write Better Home Study Text Materials, 1968; Tricks & Techniques of the Selling Writer, revised as, Techniques of the Selling Writers, 1974; Film Scriptwriting: A Practical Manual, 1976; Scripting for Video & Audiovisual Media, 1981. *Contributor to:* Amazing Stories; Fantastic Adventure; Imagination; Imaginative Tales; Giant; Western; True; Labor Today;

Writers Digest; Sunday Oklahoman; and many others. *Honours:* Various Awards for writing on television and film work. *Memberships:* Science Fiction Writers of America; Mystery Writers of America; Oklahoma Writers Federation; American Medical Writers Association; and others. *Address:* 1304 McKinley Avenue, Norman, OK 73069, USA.

SWALES, Martin William, b. 3 Nov. 1940, Victoria, British Columbia, Canada. Professor of German. *Education:* BA, MA, Cambridge University, England; PhD, Birmingham University. *Publications:* Arthur Schnitzler – A Critical Study, 1971; The German Novelle, 1977; The German Bildungsroman from Wieland to Hesse, 1978; Thomas Mann, 1980, Adalbert Stifter – A Criutical Study, with Wrika Swales, 1985. *Contributions to:* German Life and Letters; Modern Language Review; Germanic Review; Times Literary Supplement. *Memberships:* Modern Humanities Research Association; English Goethe Society. *Address:* Department of German, University College of London, Gower Street, London WC1E 6BT, England.

SWALLOW, Norman, b. 17 Feb. 1921, Eccles, England. Television Producer. m. Constance Madeline Naylor, Worsley, England, 8 Sep. 1945. *Education:* Degree, Modern History, Keble College, Oxford, 1942. *Publications:* Factual Television, 1965; Eisenstein, 1978. *Contributions to:* Numerous journals, including: The Listener; Spectator; New Statesman; Televisual; Radio Times; Penguin New Writing; Times Educational Supplement; New Commonwealth; Tribune; Music & Musicians; Sight & Sound. *Membership:* Society of Authors. *Address:* 36 Crooms Hill, London SE10, England.

SWARD, Robert, b. 23 June 1933, Chicago, Illinois, USA. Writer, Professor. m. Irina, 28 Aug. 1975, Califoornia, 2 sons, 3 daughters, separated 1985. *Education:* BA Honours, University of Illinois, 1956; MA, University of Iowa, 1958; Postgraduate, University of Bristol, England. *Literary Appointments:* Instructor in English, Connecticut College, 1958–59; Instructor in English, Editorial Board, Epoch magazine, Cornell University, 1962–64; Poet-in-Residence, University of Iowa, 1966–67; Poet-in-Residence, Aspen Writers Workshop; Assistant Professor of English, University of Victoria, 1969–73; Editor and Publisher, Soft Press, 1970–78; Editor, Hancock House Publishers, 1976–79; English Teacher, Mount Madonna School, 1985–. *Publications include:* Advertisements, poetry, 1956; Uncle Dog and Other Poems, 1962; Kissing The Dancer, poetry, 1964; Thousand-Year-Old Fiancée, poetry, 1965; The Jurassic Shales, novel, 1975; The Iowa Poems, 1975; Six Poems, 1980; The Toronto Islands, 1983; Poems New and Selected (1957–1983); Half-A-Life's-History, 1983; Poet Santa Cruz, 1985. *Contributions to:* Anthologies including: A Controversy of Poets, 1965; Magazines including: Poetry Chicago;p Art Magazine. *Honours include:* Guggenheim Fellowship in Poetry, 1964–65; D H Lawrence Fellowship, 1965–66; National Writers Union, USA; Canada Council Grants, 1981–83. *Memberships:* League of Canadian Poets; Writers Union of Canada. *Address:* PO Box 7062, Santa Cruz, CA 95001, USA.

SWARD, Robert Stuart, b. 23 June 1933, Chicago, Illinois, USA. Poet; Writer; Teacher. m. Irine, 28 Aug. 1975, 2 sons, 3 daughters. *Education:* BA (Hons), English, University of Illinois; MA, English, University of Iowa; Postgraduate work: University of Bristol, England; Middlebury College; Bread Loaf School of English. *Literary Appointments:* Poet-in-Residence, Cornell University, 1962–64; Guggenheim Fellowship for Poetry, 1964–66; D H Lawrence Fellowship, Taos, New Mexico, 1966–67; Poet-in-Residence, University of Victoria, Canada, 1969–73; Poet-in-Residence, Aspen Writers/workshop, 1967; Canada Council and Ontario Arts Council Grants, 1981, 1982–83; CBC Radio Broadcaster for, Anthology, 1983–85. *Publications:* Uncle Dog and Other Poems, 1962; Kissing the Dancer, 1964; Thousand Year Old Fiancee, 1965; Horgbortom Stringbottom. I Am Yours, You Are History, 1970; Half a

Life's History, Poems, New and Selected 1957–83, 1983; The Toronto Islands, 1983; The Jurassic Shales (novel), 1975; The Three Roberts, Premiere Performance (with Robert Priest and Robert Zend), 1984; The Three Roberts on Love and The Three Roberts on Childhood, 1985. *Contributions to:* Magazines, etc. in Canada, USA and England.*Honours:* Fulbright Grant for Study in England, 1960–61; Poetry Fellowships, Bread Loaf School of English and Writers Workshop, 1959–61; Yaddo and MacDowell Colony Fellowships, 1959–83. *Memberships:* National Writer's Union, USA; Writers Union of Canada, Chairman, Newsletter Committee; Chairman, Canada Writers Committee, Book of Members, League of Canadian Poets. *Address:* Mt Madonna Center, 445 Summit Road, Watsonville, CA, 95076, USA.

SWARTHOUT, Glendon Fred, b. 8 Apr. 1918, Pinckney, Michigan, USA. Author. m. Kathryn Blair Vaughn, 28 Dec. 1940, Albion, Michigan, 12 son. *Education:* AB, AM, PhD. *Major Publications:* They Came to Cordura, 1958; Where the Boys Are, 1960; The Eagle & The Iron Cross, 1966; Bless the Beasts and Children, 1970; The Tin Lizzie Troop, 1972; The Shootist, 1975; The Melodeon, 1977; Skeletons, 1979; The Old Colts, 1985. *Contributor to:* Esquire; Saturday Evening Post; New World Writing. *Honours:* Theatre Guild Award in Playwriting, 1947; Gold Medal, National Society of Arts & Letters, 1972; Spur Award, Best Western Novel, 1975. *Address:* 5045 Tamanar Way, Scottsdale, AZ 85253, USA.

SWARTZ, Jon David, b. 28 Dec. 1934, Houston, Texas, USA. University Administrator; Professor, Education & Psycholohy. m. Carol J Hampton, 20 Oct, 1966, Austin, 2 sons, 1 daughter. *Education:* BA 1956, MA 1961, PhD 1969, University of Texas; Senior Postdoctoral Fellowship, ibid, 1973–74. *Literary Appointments include:* Assistant/Associate/Editor/Editorial Board, various professional journals, newsletters including: Consulting Editor, Journal of Personality Assessment, 1982–. *Publications include:* Inkblot Perception & Personality, 1961; Mental Retardation, 1969; Multihandicapped Mentally Retarded, 1973; Personality Development on Two Cultures, 1975; Exceptionalities Through the Lifespan, 1982; Holtzman Inkblot 1956–82: An Annotated Technique, 1956–82: An Annotated Bibliography, 1983. *Contributions to:* Numerous scientific professional journals. *Honours include:* Member, 6 honour societies; US Office of Education Fellow, 1964–66; Franklin Gilliam Prize, Humanities Research Centre, University of Texas, 1965; Spencer Fellow, National Academy of Education, 1972–74; Faculty Fellowship, Southwestern University, 1981. *Memberships:* Fellow or Member, various academic & professional associations. *Address:* Office of the Associate Dean, Cody Memorial Library, Southwestern University, Georgetown, TX 78626, USA.

SWARTZ, Roberta Teale (Chalmers), b. 9 June 1903, Brooklyn, New York, USA. Teacher. Writer. m. Gordon Keith Chalmers, 3 Sep. 1929, Brooklyn, New York, 3 sons, 1 daughter. *Education:* BA magna cum laude, Mount Holyoke College, 1925; MA, Radcliffe College, 1926; B Litt, Oxford University, England, 1929. *Publications:* Lilliput, 1926; Lord Juggler, 1932. *Contributions to:* Oxford Review; Poetry, a Magazine of Verse; The Atlantic; Kenyon Review; The New Yorker. *Honours:* D Litt, Mount Holyoke College, 1937; D Litt, Kenyon College, 1960; Alderman Sydney Sullivan Award, Queens College, Charlotte, North Carolina. *Address:* 6 Haven Road, Welesley, MA 02181, USA.

SWEDE, George, b. 20 Nov. 1940, Riga, Latvia. Teacher. *Education:* BA, University of British Columbia, Canada, 1964; MA, Dalhousie University, Canada, 1965. *Literary Appointments:* Poetry Editor, Poetry Toronto, 1980–81; Children's Book Review Editor, Writers' Quarterly, 1982–84; Poetry Review Editor, Writers' Quarterly, 1984–. *Major Publications:* Unwinding, 1974; Tell-Tale Feathers, 1978; Endless Jigsaw, 1978; Wingbeats; Canadian Haiku Anthology, A Snowman, Headless, As far as the Sea can Eye,

Moonlit Gold Dust, Quillby the Porcupine, all 1979; Missing Heirloom, This Morning's Mockingbird, 1980; Seaside Burglaries, Eye to Eye with a Frog, The Modern English Haiku, 1981; Undertow, Downhill Theft, All of her Shadows, 1982; Flaking Paint, Tick Bird, Frozen Breaths, 1983; Bifids, Night Tides, Time is Flies, 1984. *Contributor to:* More than 225 Periodicals, in Australia, Canada, England, Holland, Japan, USA; Some 40 periodicals with scientific and literary articles, papers and reviews. *Honours:* Golden State Bank Award, 1979; Haiku Society of America Merit Book Award, 1980; Yuki Teikei Haiku Society Award, 1980; Museum of Haiku Literature Award, 1983, 1985; Children's Book Centre of Canada Our Choice Award, 1984, 1985; *Memberships:* Canadian Authors Association, Canadian Psychological Association, Canadian Society of Children's Authors, Illustrators & Performers; League of Canadian Poets; PEN International; Writers Union of Canada; International Academy of Poets. *Address:* Department of Psychology, Ryerson Polytechnical Institute, 350 Victoria Street, Toronto, Ontario, Canada, M5B 2K3.

SWEET, George Elliott, b. 26 Sep. 1904, Denver, Colorado, USA. Geophysicist; Author. m. Mildred Robison 13 Sep. 1932, 1 son. *Education:* BS, MS, University of Oklahoma, USA; Graduate Studies, Harvard University, Cambridge, Massachusetts, 1940–41. *Major Publications:* Shakespeare, The Mystery, 1956, enlarged edition, 1963; Gentleman in Oil, 1966; The History of Geophysical Prospecting, volume 1, 1966, volume 2, 1969; The Petroleum Saga, 1971, Seven Dramas from Seven Centuries, 1978; Beginning of the End, 1982; Murder by Guess, 1985. *Honour:* Valedictorian, Class of 1927, University of Oklahoma. *Memberships:* Phi Beta Kappa; American Association of Petroleum Geologists; Society of Exploration Geophysicists; National President of Blue Pencil, 1928–29. *Literary Agent:* Carol Sue Lipman. *Address:* 502 Georgina Avenue, Santa Monica, CA 90402, USA.

SWEETSER, Wesley Duaine, b. 25 May 1919, California, USA. Professor Emeritus. n. Marceine la Dickfos, 21 Dec. 1942, Brisbane, Australia, 2 sons, 2 daughters. *Education:* BA 1938; MA 1946; Phd 1958, University of Colordo. *Literary Appointments:* Instructor, English, University of Colorado, 1945–48; Assistant Professor, English, Peru State Teachers' College, 1948–50; Associate Professor, English, Air Force Academy, 1959–63; Visiting Professor, English, Nebraska Wesleyan, 1966–67; Professor of English, State University at Oswego, New York, 1967–82. *Publications:* Arthur Machen, 1964; Substantial contribution to, Thomas Hardy: An Annotated Bibliography of Writing About Him, Editor E Gerber and W Eugene Davis, 1973; Ralph Hodgson: A Bibliography, 1974; Ralph Hodgson: A Bibliography, 1980. *Contributions to:* Numerous literary publications. *Membership:* Arthus Machen Society. *Address:* RD5, Box 74, Oswego, NY 13126, USA.

SWENSON, Karen, b. 29 July 1936. Professor. *Education:* BA, Barnard College, USA, 1959; MA, New York University, USA, 1971. *Appointments include:* Poet in Residence, Clark University, USA, 1976; Assistant Professor, Skidmore College, 1977–78; Read Tour of Montana, Idaho, Colorado, 1978–79; Poet in Residence, Universities of Idaho and Colorado, 1979–80; Poet in Residence, Scripps College, Claremont, California, 1980–81. *Publications:* An Attic of Ideals, 1974; East–West, 1980. *Contributor to:* New Yorker; Saturday Review; Texas Quarterly; Bennington Review; Salmagundi; Denver Quarterly; Paris Review; Poetry; Prairie Schooner; The Nation; New York Quarterly; Carolina Quarterly; Virginia Quarterly Review. *Honour:* Transatlantic Fellowship, 1974. *Memberships:* PEN; Poetry Society of America. *Address:* 430 State Street, Brooklyn, NY 11217, USA.

SWIERENGA, Robert Peter, b. 10 June 1935, Chicago, Illinois, USA. Professor of History. m. Joan Boomker, 16 June 1956, Oak Park, 2 sons, 3 daughters. *Education:* BA, Calvin College, 1957; MA, Northwestern University, 1958; PhD, University of Iowa, 1965. *Appointments:* Professor, Calvin College, 1960–61, 1965–68; Professor, Kent, State University, 1968–. *Publications:* Pioneers and Profits, 1968; Quantification in American History, 1970; Beyond the Civil War Synthesis, 1975; Acres for Cents, 1976; A Bilateral Bicentenial, 1982; History and Ecology, 1984; The Dutch in America, 1985; Netherlanders in America, 1985. *Contributor to:* 50 articles in professional journals. *Honours:* American Council of Learned Societies Fellowship, 1967; Fulbright-Hays Silver Oppertunity Research Fellowship, The Netherlands, 1976; American Council of Learned Societies Fellowship, 1981; Fulbright-Hays Research Fellowship, The Netherlands, 1985. *Memberships:* Social Science History Association; Organisation of American Historians; Economic History Association; Business History Society; Agricultural History Society; Immigration History Society; etc. *Address:* Dept of History, Kent State University, Kent OH 44242, USA.

SWIFT, Kate, b. 9 Dec. 1923, Yonkers, New York, USA. Writer. *Education:* AB, University of North Carolina, Chapel Hill, 1944. *Publications:* Words and Women, with Casey Miller, 1976; The Handbook of Nonsexist Writing, with Casey Miller, 1980. *Contributor to:* New York Times Magazine; Washington Post; New York; Ms; etc. *Memberships:* National Association of Science Writers; Women's Institute for Freedom of the Press. *Literary Agent:* Virginia Barber, 353 W. 21st St, New York. *Address:* PO Box 94 East Haddam, CT 06423, USA.

SWIFT, Mary Grace, b. 3 Aug. 1927, Bartlesville, Oklahoma, USA. Professor of History. *Education:* BA, MA, Creighton University; PhD, University of Notre Dame. *Publications:* The Art of the Dance of the USSR, 1968; A Loftier Flight; The Life & Accomplishments of Charles-Louis Didelot, Balletmaster, 1974; With Bright Wings: A Book of the Spirit, 1976; Belles & Beaux on Theor Toes: Dancing Stars in Young America, 1980. *Contributions to:* Dance Magazine; Dancing Times; Modern Drama; Thought; New Orleans Review; Cincinnati Historical Society Bulletin; Missouri Historical Review; Revue de Louisianne; The Bible Today; Louisiana History; etc. *Honour:* De la Torre Bueno Award, best manuscript on dance, 1973. *Address:* Box 192, Loyola University, New Orleans, LA 70118, USA.

SWIHART, Thomas Lee, b. 29 July 1929, Indiana, USA. Professor of Astronomy. m. Merna L Connelley, 10 Oct. 1951, Indiana, 1 son, 2 daughters. *Education:* AB, 1951, AM, 1952, Indiana University; PhD, Astronomy, University of Chicago, 1955. *Publications:* Astrophysics & Steller Astronomy, 1968; Steller Atmospheres, 1971; Steller Interiors, 1972; Journey Through the Universe, 1978; Radiation Transfer and Stellar Atmospheres, 1981. *Contributor to:* Professional journals; Encyclopedia. *Address:* Steward Observatory, University of Arizona, Tucson, AZ 85721, USA.

SYERS, William Edward, b. 20 Dec. 1914, Jackson, Tennessee, USA. Advertising and Public Relations Executive. m. 25 June 1938, 1 son, 2 daughters. *Education:* BA, University of Texas at Austin. *Publications:* Seven, Navy Subchasers, 1960; Texas – Off The Beaten Trail (3 vols) 1963–65, 1971; Texas – The Beginnings, 1973; The Devil Gun, 1975; Backroads of Texas, 1979; Ghost Stories of Texas, 1981; Balefire Watch, forthcoming 1986. *Contributor to:* Numerous contributions to magazines and journals. *Membership:* Sigma Delta Chi. *Address:* 322 Thompson Drive, Kerrville, TX 78028, USA.

SYLVESTER, Doreen Rosalie Mammatt, b. 21 Jan. 1947, Brigg, Lincolnshire, England. Freelance Artist. m. R J Sylvester, 10 July 1983, Ashby. *Education:* Diploma, London Art College (Press Art, Cartooning). *Literary Appointments:* Founder Fellow, International Poetry Society. *Major Publications:* Anthologies, Poetry, Poetry Magazines, Lincolnshire Life; The Small

Poetry Magazines, 1979; Mitre Press Anthologies, 1968–69. *Memberships:* Fellow of Poetry in Orbis Magazine. *Honours:* International Poetry Day Second Place, 1967; Runner-up, Arnold Vincent Bowen Competition, 1981. *Address:* 32 St Paul's Road, Ashby, Scunthorpe, South Humberside DN16 3DJ, England.

SYLVESTRE, Jean Guy, b. 17 May 1918, Sorel, Quebec, Canada. Librarian. *Education:* BA 1939, BPh 1940, LPh 1941, MA 1942, University of Ottawa. *Publications include:* Poètes Catholiques de la France Contemporaine, 1944; Sondages, 1945; Impressions de Théâtre, 1950; Amours, Délices et Orgues, 1953; Panoroma des Lettres Canadiennes-Francaises, 1964; Canadian Writers 1964; Canadian Writers, 1964; Literature in French Canada, 1967; A Century of Canadian Literature, 1967; Editor of numerous works. *Honours:* Commander, International Order Public Good; Commander, Order OM, Poland. *Memberships:* Fellow, Past President, Royal Society of Canada; French-Canadian Academy; Society of Canadian Writers; Director, President 1960–61, Canadian Writers Foundation. *Address:* 2286 Bowman Road, Ottawa, K1H 6V6, Canada.

SYMANSKI, Richard, b. 7 Jan. 1941, San Francisco, California, USA. Writer. m. Nancy Burley, 3 July 1975, Austin, Texas, 1 daughter. *Education:* BS, Accounting & Finance, San Jose State University; MA, PhD, Geography, Syracuse University, New York. *Publications:* Order & Skepticism (with John Agnew), 1981; The Immoral Landscape: Female Prostitution in Western Societies, 1981; Wild Horses and Sacred Cows, 1985. *Contributions:* Over a dozen articles in social science journals: Peasants in Latin America; Philosophy; Hobos; Wild horses; Prostitution. *Literary Agent:* Gunther Stuhlmann. *Address:* Department of Ecology, Ethology and Evolution, University of Illinois, Urbana, IL 61801, USA.

SYMMONS-SYMONOLEWICZ, Konstantin, b. 18 Aug. 1909. Retired College Professor. m. Krystyna M Wiczynski, 1 Feb. 1951, 1 daughter. *Education:* Mag phil, University of Warsaw, Poland, 1931; PhD, Columbia University, USA, 1955. *Publications:* Modern Nationalism: Toward a Consensus in Theory, 1968; Nationalist Movements: A Comparative View, 1970; National Consciousness in Poland: Origin & Evolution, 1983; Essays in Sociology of Nationhood, in press. *Contributions to:* Polish Review; Current Anthopology; Comparative Studies in Society & History; Canadian Review of Studies in Nationalism; etc. *Address:* 540 Deissler Court, Meadville, PA 16335, USA.

SYMONDS, Pamela Maureen Southey, b. 11 Jan. 1916, Waterlooville, Hampshire, England. Teacher. m. Ronald Charters Symonds, 20 Nov. 1939, Bedford, 2 sons, 1 daughter. *Education:* MA, Honours, Oxford; Diploma of Education. *Publications:* Let's Speak French, 2 volumes, 1962–63; Let's Read French, 5 volumes, 1965–73; French Through Action, 2 volumes, 1967–69; French from France, 1975–76, 5 volumes; A L'Ecoute, 1982. *Membership:* Society of Authors. *Address:* 10 Bisham Gardens, London N6 6DD, England.

SYMONDS, Richard, b. 2 Oct. 1918, Oxford, England. Writer; Former United Nations Official. m. Ann Spokes, 30 Dec. 1980, Oxford, 2 sons from previous marriage. *Education:* MA, Oxford University. *Publications:* The Making of Pakistan, 1950; The British and Their Successors, 1966; International Targets for Development, editor, 1970; The United Nations and the Population Question, with M Carder, 1973; Oxford and Empire – The Last Lost Cause?. *Contributions to:* Times; Guardian; New York Times; Oxford; Round Table and others. *Membership:* Society of Authors. *Address:* 43 Davenant Road, Oxford OX2 8BU, England.

SYMONS, Leslie John, b. 8 Nov. 1926, Reading, Berkshire, England. University Professor. m. 24 Mar. 1954, Kingston on Thames, 2 daughters. *Education:* BSc Econ, London; PhD, Belfast. *Publications:* Land Use in Northern Ireland, editor, 1963; Agricultural Geography, 1867 and 1978; Russian Agriculture, 1972; Russian Transport, (editor with C White), 1975; The Soviet Union, A Systematic Geography, editor, 1983; Soviet and East European Transport Problems, co-editor, 1985. *Contributions to:* Geographical, Soviet Studies and Aviation journals and to books edited by others. *Memberships:* Institute of British Geographers; Section Committee member, Royal Aeronautical Society; National Association of Soviet and East European Studies. *Address:* 17 Wychwood Close, Langland, Swansea SA3 4PH, Wales.

SYRJÄ, Juhani Volevi, b. 7 June 1943, Juupajoki, Finland. Author. m. Leena-Kaija Salojärvi, 5 June 1966, Jyväskylä, 1 son, 1 daughter. *Publications:* Neitsytpoika, 1970; Pakenijat, 1972; Perinto, 1978; Ihmisen Ääni, 1979; Kivinen Tiuku, 1980; Portti, 1981. *Contributor to:* Parnasso. *Memberships:* Suomen Kirjailijalitto; Pirkkalaiskirjailijat. *Literary Agent:* K J Gummerus Oy. *Address:* Leppahammas, 35300 Orivesi, Finland.

SYROP, Konrad, b. 9 Aug. 1914, Vienna, Austria. Writer; Broadcaster; Translator. m. Dr Sara Joelson, 6 Apr. 1940, 1 son, 3 daughters. *Education:* LLB, University of Warsaw, Poland. *Literary Appointments:* Head, Central Talks & Features, BBC External Services, 1956–73. *Publications:* Spring in October, 1957; Poland Between the Hammer & the Anvil, 1968; Poland in Perspective, 1982. *Contributions to:* Numerous journals. *Memberships:* Committee of Management 1981–84, Society of Authors; Treasurer 1983–, Authors Lending & Copyright Society; Chairman 1983–, Copyright Licensing Agency. *Literary Agent:* Watson, Little Ltd. *Address:* 7 Great Spilmans, Dulwich, London SE22 8SZ, England.

SZANTO, George Herbert, University Professor. *Education:* BA, German and French, Dartmouth College, Geothe Universitaet, Frankfurt, Germany, Universite d'Aix-en-Prevence, France, PhD, Comparative Literature: German, English and French, Harvard University. *Literary Appointments:* 1976–, The Writer's Union of Canada: 1977–84 Member, Grievance Committee, 1978–79 Quebec representative, 1977–, The Guild of Canadian Playwrights: 1977 Quebec Delegate and Member Founding Convention, Calgary. *Publications:* Narrative Consciousness (criticism) 1972; Sixteen Ways to Skin a Cat (stories), 1978; After the Ceremony (play) 1978; Theater and Propaganda (criticism), 1978; The Next Move (play), 1981; The New Black Crook (play), 1981; Not Working (novel), 1982, 1983, 1984; The Great Chinchilla War (play with Milton Savage) 1983; Narrative Taste and Social Perspectives: The Matter of Quality (criticism), 1986. *Contributions to:* Texas Quarterly; Critique; Kansas Quarterly; Bucknell Review; Massachusetts Review; Canadian Comparative Literature Review and many others. *Address:* 3712 Avenue Laval, Montreal, Quebec, Canada H2X 3C9.

SZASZ, Thomas Stephen, b. 15 Apr. 1920, Budapest, Hungary. Professor of Psychiatry, State University of New York. USA. *Education includes:* BA, 1941, MD, 1944, University of Cincinnati. Diplomate: National Board of Medical Examiners, 1945I; American Board of Psychiatry and Neurology, 1951. *Publications include:* Pain and Pleasure: A Study of Bodily Feelings, 1957, expanded 1975; The Myth of Mental Illness: Foundations of a Theory of Personal Conduct, 1961, 74; Psychiatric Justice, 1965; The Second Sin, 1973; Heresies, 1976; Schizopherenia: The Sacred Symbol of Psychiatry, 1976; Sex by Prescription, 1980, UK editions as Sex: Facts, Frauds and Follies, 1981; The Theraputic State: Psychiatry in the Mirror of Current Events, 1984. *Contributions to:* Author of 400 articles, book reviews, letters to editors and newspaper columns. Editorial Board Memberships Include: Contemporary Psychoanalysis; International Journal of Addictions; Journal of Law and Behavior; Journal of Mind and Behaviour, Consulting Editor: Syracuse Scholar; Inquiry; Free Inquiry. Advisory Board: Corporation for Economic Education. *Honours include:* C P Snow

Lectureship, Ithica College, 1970; Honorary DSc, Allegheny College, Pennsylvania, 1975, Universided Francisco Marroquin, Guatemala, 1979; Knight of Mark Twain, 1973; Honorary Member, Mark Twain Society, 1973; Mencken Award, Free Press Association, 1981. *Address:* Department of Psychiatry, State University of New York, Upstate Medical Center, 750 East Adams Street, Syracuse, NY 13210, USA.

SZEKELY, Endre, b. 9 Sep. 1922, Budapest, Hungary. Clinical Psychologist. m. Frances Vivian Finkelsen, 6 Jan. 1961, Sydney, 1 son. *Education:* Diploma, University of Budapest, 1942; PhD, University of Budapest, 1944; MA, 1955, Ad eundem statum (PhD), 1955, University of Queensland, Australia. *Publications:* Basic Analysis of Inner Psychological Functions, 1965; Functional Laws of Psychodynamics, 1979. *Contributor to:* Australian Journal of Psychology; Australian Psychologist; Australian Nurses Journal. *Memberships:* Associate, British Psychological Society; Australian Psychological Society; Board of Clinical Psychologists, A.Ps.S. *Address:* 67 Ronald Avenue, Lane Cove, Sydney, NSW 2066, Australia.

SZIRTES, George Gabor Miklos, b. 29 Nov. 1948, Budapest, Hungary. Poet; Teacher; Artist. m. Clarissa Upchurch, 11 July 1970, West Drayton, 1 son, 1 daughter. *Education:* BA (First Hons), Fine Art; ATC. *Publications:* The Slant Door, 1979 (poems); November and May, 1981 (poems); Short Wave, 1983 (poems); The Photographer in Winter, 1986 (in press). *Contributions to:* New Statesman; TLS; Encounter; Quarto; Literary Review; Poetry Review, etc. (reviews and articles; Poems in The Observer, The Listener, BBC and many others. Edited Literature section of, Eastword, 1983. *Honours:* Co-Winner, Faber Memorial Prize for The Slant Door, 1980; Poetry Book Society Choice for Short Wave, 1983. *Memberships:* Fellow, Royal Society of Literature; International PEN. *Address:* 20 Old Park Road, Hitchin, Hertfordshire SG5 2JR, England.

SZMAGLEWSKA, Seweryna, b. 11 Feb. 1916, Przyglow, Poland. Writer. m. Withold Wisniewski, 10 Mar. 1946, Lodz, 2 sons. *Education:* Diploma, Warsaw Open University. *Publications:* Dymy nad Birkenau, 1945; Prosta droga Lukasza, 1955; Zapowiada sie piekny dzien, 1960; Czarne stopy, 1960; Nowy slad czarnych stop, 1975; Odcienie milosci, 1969; Niewinni w Norymberdze, 1972; Wilcza jagoda 1976; Biala roza, 1983; Dwoje smutnych ludzi, 1985. *Contributions to:* Po prostu; Zycie literackie; Nowe ksiazki; Argumenty; Odrodzenie; Przeglad kulturalny. *Honours:* Zloty krzyz zaslugi (Golden Order of Merit) 1954; Polonia Restituta, Commender's Cross, 1960; 1st class prize for whole literary output, Ministry of Culture, 1975; Sztandar Pracy (Banner of Labour) 1st Class, 1978; Krays Oswiecimski (the Auschwitz Cross) 1985. *Memberships:* Polish Writers' Union, General Board Member, Chairman of Lodz Branch 1950–52; PEN Club; ZAIKS (Union of Writers, Artists and Composers). *Literary*

Agent: Agencja Wydawnicza, (Authors' Agency). *Address:* ul. Bajonska 5, 03-946 Warszawa, Poland.

SZUCSANY, Désirée Carole Anna, b. 14 Feb. 1955, Montreal, Canada. Writer, Translator, Journalist. *Education:* Certificate in Spanish Studies, University of Madrid, Spain. *Major Publications:* La Chasse-Gardée (novel), 1980; Le Violon, 1981; La Passe (short novels), 1981; L'Aveugle (poetry), 1983; Les Filets (short novels), 1984. *Contributor to:* Feminin-Pluriel; La Vie en Rose; Sabord; 200 Scientific articles in, Le Courier Médical & Santé. *Memberships:* Quebec Writers Union; Association of Literary Translators. *Address:* 5836 9è Avenue, Montreal, Quebec H1Y 2K2, Canada.

SZUMIGALSKI, Anne Howard (neé Davis), b. 3 Jan. 1922, London, England. Writer. m. Jan W Szumigalski, 28 Apr. 1946, Wunsdorf, Germany, 2 sons, 2 daughters. *Literary Appointments:* Writer-in-Residence, Saskatoon Public Libraries, 1981–82. *Major Publications:* Woman Reading in bath, 1974; Wild Man's Butte, 1979; A Game of Angels, 1980; Doctrine of Signatures, 1983; Risks, 1983; Instar, 1985. *Contributor to:* Numerous Canadian Journals, including: Wascana Review; Grain; Salt; Dandelion; Malahat; Canadian Literature; NeWest Review Events; Canadian Forum; Waves. *Memberships:* Saskatchewan Writers Guild; League of Canadian Poets; ACTRA Writers Guild. *Address:* #9 Connaught Place, Saskatoon, Saskatchewan, S7L 1C7, Canada.

SZUPROWICZ, Bohdan Olgierd, b. 20 May 1931, Grondo, Poland. High Technology Market Researcher & Investor. m. Maria Hendris-Oszczakiewicz, 21 Nov. 1961, Las Vegas, USA. *Education:* BSc Aeronautical Engineering, Imperial College of Science & Technology, London, England, 1957. *Major Publications:* Doing Business with the People's Republic of China, 1978; How to Avoid Strategic Materials Shortages, 1981; How to Invest in Strategic Metals, 1982. *Contributor to:* Supergrowth Technology USA (in 20 countries); Barron's; High Technology; Christian Science Monitor; Atlanta Constitution; Denver Post; New Scientist; The Bulletin; Finance Week; Bull & Bear; Newsweek International; Usine Nouvelle; and others. *Address:* 8200 Boulevard East, North Bergen, NJ 07047, USA.

SZYSZKOWITZ, Gerald, b. 22 July 1938, Graz, Austria. Head of TV Drama Department, ORF, Vienna. *Education:* Dr Phil, University of Vienna. *Publications:* Genosse Bruggemann; Commander Carrigan; Kainiten-Der Fladnitzer; Waidmannsheil, all theatre-plays at the Thomas Sessler-Verlag; Der Thaya; Seitenwechsel; Osterschnee; Furlani oder Die Zartlichkeit des Verrats, four novels in the Paul Zsolnay-Verlag. *Contributor to:* (Ed.), Fernsehspiel-Biblothek (Residenz-Verlag, Salzburg); Member, Maske und Kothurn, History of TV Drama; PEN Club. *Address:* Maria Enzersdorf near Vienna, Liechtensteinstrasse 18a, Austria.

T

TABOR, Bruce Lyle, b. 13 Nov. 1948, New York City, New York, USA. Writer. m. Maureen Mileski, 27 Nov. 1983, New York City, New York. *Education:* BFA, New York University School of the Arts. *Contributions to:* Co-Founder and Fiction Editor, Fat Tuesday, (contributor of numerous short scripts.)

TABORSKI, Boleslaw, b. 7 May 1927, Torun, Poland. Writer; Translator; Broadcaster. m. Halina Junghertz, 20 June 1959, London, England, 1 daughter. *Education:* BA, MA, Bristol University. *Publications:* Poetry: Times of Passing, 1957; Grains of Night, 1958; Crossing the Border, 1962; Lesson Continuing, 1967; Voice of Silence, 1969; Selected Poems, 1973; Web of Words, 1977; For the Witnesses, 1978; Observer of Shadows, 1979; Love, 1980; A Stranger's Present, 1983; Observer of Shadows, 1979; Love, 1980; A Stranger's Present, 1983; Art, 1985. Criticism: New Elizabethan Theatre, 1967; Polish Plays in English Translations, 1968; Byron and the Theatre, 1972. Co-Author: Crowell's Handbook of Contemporary Drama, 1971; Polish Plays in Translation, 1983. Major translations into English of works by Jan Kott, Wiktor Wororzyklski, Karol Wojtyla and others. Translations into Polish of works by Grahame Greene, Robert Graves, Harold Pinter and others. *Contributions to:* Oxford Companion, 1957; Gambit; Stand; Theatre Research; Theatre Quarterly; Literacki; Tulane Drama Review; Slavic and East European Arts; Polish Review; Kultura, France; Dialog, Poland; Odra; Wiez and others. *Honours:* Polish Writers Association Abroad Award, 1954; Jurzykowski Foundation Award, New York, USA, 1968; Merit for Polish Culture Badge and Diploma, Warsaw, Poland, 1970; Koscielski Foundation Award, Geneva, Switzerland, 1977. *Address:* 66 Esmond Road, Bedford Park, London W4 1JF, England.

TABORSKY, Edward Joseph, b. 18 Mar. 1910, Praha, Czechoslovakia. Professor. m. 15 Oct. 1943, 1 son, 2 daughters. *Education:* Doctorate, State Science and Law, Charles University, Praha. *Publications:* The Czechoslovak Cause, 1944; Czecholsovak Democracy at Work, 1945; Pravda Zvitezila, 1947; Communism in Czecholovakia, 1948, 1960; Communist Penetration of the Third World, 1973; President Edward Benes between East and West, 1938–48, 1981. *Contributor to:* Numerous professional journals including, Foreign Affairs; American Political Science Review; Orbis; Current History; Journal of Politics; etc. *Honours:* 1st Prize, Literary Contest, Publishing House Druzstevni Praoe, Praha, 1946; Guggenheim Fellowship, 1960. *Memberships:* Czechoslovak Society of Arts and Sciences in America. *Address:* 4503 Parkwood Road, Austin, TX 78722, USA.

TAGAMI, Marshal L, b. 18 Nov. 1949. Producer, Writer for television, film, video and radio. *Education:* Industrial apprenticeships on television, film, video and radio. *Literary Appointments:* Producer, writer, host, KPOO-AM/FM Radio; Producer, Writer, Asian Women's Film Team; Producer, writer, host, KTVU Channel 2, Cox Broadcasting; Media Director, Youth Advocates Inc; Executive Producer, Christ Kobayashi and Associates; Executive Director, Minorities and Women Telecommunications Network Inc. *Contributions to:* Third World Women, anthology; Time to Greeze, anthology; Bridge magazine; Ayumi, anthology; Networks, anthology; Local publications in Hawaii and San Francisco. *Honour:* California Arts Council Artist-in-Residence, 1977–78. *Address:* 298 Coleridge Street, San Francisco, CA 94110, USA.

TAGGART, John P, b. 5 Oct. 1942, Guthrie Center, Iowa, USA. Professor. *Education:* BA, Earlham College; MA, University of Chicago; PhD, Syracuse University. *Publications:* To Construct a Clock, 1971; The Pyramid is a Pure Crystal, 1974; Prism & The Pine Twig, 1977; Dodeka, 1979; Peace on Earth, 1981; Dehiscence, 1983. *Contributions to:* Origin; Boundary 2; Poetry Journal; Chicago Review; Massachusetts Review;

Northwest Review; and others. *Honours:* Ford Foundation Fellowship, 1965–66; Distinguished Academic Service Award, (Pa Department of Education), 1976; NEA Writing Fellowship, 1976; Chicago Review Poetry Prize, 1980; Ironwood Poetry Prize, 1982. *Membership:* Melville Society. *Address:* 210 S Washington, Shippensburg, PA 17257, USA.

TAGLIABUE, John, b. 1 July 1923, Cantu (Como), Italy. Writer; College Professor. m. Grace Ten Eyck, 11 Sep. 1946, 2 daughters. *Education:* BA, MA, Columbia University. *Literary Appointments:* Poet in Residence, Bennett College, Greensborough, North Carolina, USA; Poet in Residence, University of Rio Grande do Norte, Natal, Brazil; Poet in Residence, Anatolia College, Thessaloniki; Professor of English, Bates College, Maine, USA. *Publications:* Poems, 1959; A Japanese Journal, 1966; The Buddha Uproar, 1970; The Doorless Door, 1970; The Great Day, 1984. *Contributions to:* Poems, essays & parts of travel journals published in, Atlantic Monthly; Boundary Z; Chelsea; The Centennial Review; Carolina Quarterly; Chicago Review; Epoch; Greenfield Review; The Hudson Review; Harpers; Kayak; Kenyon Review; Literature East & West; Massachusetts Review; Minnesota Review; New York Quarterly; Poetry; Virginia Quarterly. *Honours:* Phi Beta Kappa, 1945; 2 Fulbright Grants to Italy; 2 Fulbright Grants to Japan, 1958–1960; Rockefeller Grant to Italy, 1981; Fulbright Grant to The People's Republic of China. *Memberships:* PEN; Poetry Society of America. *Address:* 12 Abbott Street, Lewiston, ME 04240, USA.

TAIT, George E, b. 19 July 1910, Sarnia, Canada. University Professor. m. Reginae M Stapleford, 31 Aug. 1938, Watford, Ontario, 1 son. *Education:* BA, University of Western Ontario; Bachelor of Pedagogy, Doctor of Education, University of Toronto. *Publications:* Saddle of Carlos Perez, 1949; The Silent Gulls, 1950; Wake of the West Wind, 1952; Famous Canadian Stories, 1953; Breastplate and Buckskin, 1953; The World was Wide, 1954; The Upward Trail, 1956; Proud Agnes, 1958; Fair Domain, 1960; One Dominion, 1962; Young Teacher's Handbook, 1967; The Eagle and the Snake, 1968; The Unknown People, 1974. *Contributor to:* Educational journals of miscellaneous articles. *Honours:* Award of Merit by Design Canada on behalf of Canadian Government for 'The Unknown People: Indians of North America', 1974; The McGraw-Hill Ryerson Award, 1978. *Address:* 105 Golfdale Road, Toronto, Canada M4N 2B8.

TALBOT, Godfrey Walker, b. 8 Oct. 1908, Walton, Yorkshire, England. Author; Broadcaster; Lecturer; Journalist. m. Bess Owen, 7 Oct. 1933, Wigan, Lancashire, 2 sons (1 dec.). *Literary Appointments:* Editorial staff, Yorkshire Post, 1928; Editor, Manchester City News, 1932–34; Editorial staff, Daily Dispatch, 1934–37; Joined BBC, 1937; BBC War correspondent overseas, 1941–45; Organised BBC Reporting Unit (Chief Reporter) after war; Official BBC correspondent to Buckingham Palace, 1948–69; BBC Commentator, major Royal occasions and world tours, 1947–70. *Publications:* Speaking from the Desert, 1944; Ten Seconds from Now, 1973; Royalty Annuals, 1952–56; Queen Mother, 1973; Permission to Speak, 1976; Our Royal Heritage, 1977; Country Life Book of the Queen Mother, 1978; Country Life Book of the Royal Family, 1980, 1983; Country Life, Queen Mother, new edition 1983. *Contributions:* Articles on British Royal family and monarchy, journals, broadcasting, television. *Honours:* OBE, Mention In Despatches, 1942, 1946; MVO 1960; LVO 1985. *Membership:* President, Queen's English Society. *Literary Agent:* David Higham Associates. *Address:* Holmwell, Hook Hill, Sanderstead, Surrey, England.

TALBOT RICE, Tamara, b. 2 July 1904, St. Petersburg, Russia. Art Historian. m. David Talbot Rice, 31 Dec. 1927, Paris, 1 son, 2 daughters. *Education:* Oxford; Paris. *Publications include:* Russian Art, 1949; The Scythians, 1957; Icons, 1959; The Seljuks, 1961; A Concise History of Russian Art, 1963; Finding Out About the Early Russians, 1963; Russian Icons, 1963;

Ancient Arts of Central Asia, 1965; Everyday Life in Byzantium, 1967; Byzantium, 1969; Csars and Csarinas of Russia, 1968; Elizabeth, Empress of Russia, 1970; Icons & Their Dating, 1974. *Contributions:* Numerous, including Times Literary Supplement; Speculum; Architectural Review; Apollo; etc. *Membership:* The Author. *Address:* 13 Calcot, Northleach, Gloucestershire GL54 3JZ, England.

TALESE, Gay, b. 7 Feb. 1932, Ocean City, New Jersey, USA. Writer. m. Nan Ahearn, 10 June 1959, 2 daughters. *Education:* BA, University of Alabama. *Literary Appointments:* Writer, The New York Times, 1955–65; Writer, Editor, Esquire magazine and other publications. *Publications:* New York – A Serendipiter's Journey, 1961; The Overreachers, 1962; The Bridge, 1964; The Kingdom and the Power, 1969; Fame and Obscurity, 1970; Honor Thy Father, 1971; Thy Neighbor's Wife, 1979. *Contributions to:* Magazines including, Esquire Magazine. *Membership:* Vice-President, PEN, New York. *Address:* 109 East Sixty-First Street, New York, NY 10021, USA.

TALIAS, Angela, b. 14 Nov. 1948, Atlanta, Georgia, USA. Author. m. Nicholas Talias, 6 June 1970, 2 daughters. *Education:* Georgia State University (one year). *Publications:* The Treacherous Heart, 1980; Sometimes A Stranger, 1981; The Velvet Thorn, 1982; More Than Yesterday, 1984. *Honours:* National League of American Pen Women Fiction Award for, Sometimes A Stranger, and, The Velvet Thorn, 1981, 82; Honorable Mention Award for, The Velvet Thorn, (historical novel), from Romance Writers of America, 1982. *Memberships:* National League of American Pen Women, (Historian, Chairman of Juvenile Events Committee); Romance Writers of America, (Georgia State President, 1985). *Literary Agent:* Denise Marcil. *Address:* 301 Lakeshore Drive, Marietta, GA 30067, USA.

TALMADGE, Jeffrey, b. 18 Feb. 1953, Attorney-at-Law. *Education:* BA, Duke University, USA, 1975; JD, University of Texas, 1980. *Literary Appointments:* Editorial Staff, Archive; Texas Quarterly; Staff, Texas Law Review, 1978–80; Articles Editor, Review of Litigation, 1979–80. *Contributor to:* Greensboro Review; Archive; Texas Quarterly; Thicket; Gargoyle; Sulphur River; Res Scriptae; Analacta; Academy American Poets Anthology. *Honours:* Honorary Mention, Academy of American Poets Award, 1974; Academy of American Poets Award, 1975; Grant, Mary Roberts Rhinehart Foundation, 1975; Third Place, Anne Flexner Memorial Writing Award, 1974, 75; Second Place, Christopher Morley Writing Award, 1978, 79; Hon. Mention, Annie Irvine Prize, 1979. *Membership:* Austin Writers League. *Address:* PO Box 2598, Austin, TX 78768–2598, USA.

TALMON, Shemaryahu, b. 28 May 1920, Skierniwice, Poland. Professor of Bible Studies. *Education:* MA, PhD, Hebrew University, Jerusalem, Israel. *Major Publications:* Qumran & the History of the Biblical Text, (edited with F M Cross), 1975; Religion and Politik, (edited with G Siefert), 1978; Editor, Hebrew University Bible Project, & Textus (Annual of Project). *Contributor to:* Numerous journals, including: Annual of the Swedish Theological Institute; Bulletin of the American Schools of Oriental Research; Biblica; Ecumenical Review; Freiburger Rundbrief; Harvard Theological Review; Vetus Testamentum. *Honours:* Romano Guardini Medal, 1976. *Memberships:* Society of Biblical Studies; American Oriental Society; Society of Old Testament Studies, Great Britain; Israel Archaeological Society; Israel Society of Bible Studies; Advisory Committee, Vetus Testamentum; Editorial Committee, Tehologisches Wörterbuch zum Alten Testament; Editorial Board, Judaism; Editorial Board, Jewish Quarterly Review. *Address:* 5 Jan Smuts Street, 93108 Jerusalem, Israel.

TAMARI, Moshe, b. 20 May 1910, Warkowicze, Poland (now USSR). Editor, Books & Periodicals (retired). m. Miriam Gefel, 31 Dec. 1937, Tel Aviv, 1 son, 1 daughter. *Education:* Biblical & Literary Studies,

1920–28. *Literary Appointments include:* Judges Committee, Association of Writers, Composers & Editors of Music, 1958; Editorial Secretary, Hapoel Hazair weekly; Column of literary criticism, Davar (workers daily). *Publications include:* Voice of Life, 1941; From Scene to Scene, 1951; Days Gone By, Hebrew 1972, English translation 1984, Two Brazilian Books, 1963; The Mirror of our Conscience, 1984. Translations. *Contributor to:* Various journals including Davar; Atidoth; Gazith. Israel, USA, Poland, Argentina. *Honour:* Grant, Lamdan Promotion Fund, 1961. *Memberships include:* Hebrew Writers Association, 1944–; Control Commission, 1954–55, 1958–62. *Literary Agent:* Book Publishers Association of Israel, International Promotion & Literary Rights Department, Tel Aviv. *Address:* 4 Pineless Street, PO Box 21488, Tel Aviv, 62 265 Israel.

TAN, Lek Hor, b. 10 Mar 1944, Cambodia. Journalist. m. Meriem Kasdarli, 30 Aug. 1983, London. *Education:* Bachelor of Arts. *Publication:* Cambodia in the South East Asian War (with Malcolm Caldwell) 1973. *Contributor to:* Index on Censorship Magazine; South Magazine; The Guardian. *Address:* Flat 5, 35 Mount Pleasant Road, London N17, England.

TANGERMAN, Elmer John, b. 8 Aug. 1907, Hammond, Indiana, USA. Author, Editor, Woodcarver. m. Mary Christopher, 7 Sep. 1929, Hammond, Indiana, 1 son (deceased), 2 daughters. *Education:* BSME, 1929, ME, 1937, Purdue University. *Literary Appointments:* Technical Editor, McGraw-Hill Publishing Company, 1929–69. *Major Publications:* Whittling and Woodcarving, 1936; Design and Figure Carving, 1939; Horizons Regained, 1964; The Modern Book of Whittling and Woodcarving, 1973; 1001 Designs for Whittling and Woodcarving, 1976; Build Your Own Doll House, 1977; Carving Wooden Animals, 1979; Carving Faces and Figures in Wood, Carving Religious Motifs in Wood, 1980; Carving Flora and Fables in Wood, Carving Personality in Wood, 1981; Relief Wood Carving, Carving the Unusual, 1982; Basic Whittling and Woodcarving, 1983; Carving Birds in Wood, The Complete Guide to Woodcarving, 1984; The Woodcarver's Library, 1985; Woodcarving Pattern Guide, 1986. *Contributor to:* Popular Mechanics; Popular Science Monthly; Scouting; Chip Chats; World of Wood; Woodworking Crafts; and others. *Honours:* Freedom Foundation of Valley Forge Medal, 1955; Jesse Neal Award of Merit, 1958, 1960, 1961; Honorary Member, Guild of Mastercraftsmen (England). *Memberships:* Various technical and Engineering Societies. *Address:* 111 Ivy Way, Port Washington, NY 11050, USA.

TANNAHILL, Reay, b. Glasgow, Scotland. Author. *Education:* MA, University of Glasgow. *Publications:* Food in History, 1973; Sex in History, 1980; Fiction – A Dark and Distant Shore, 1983. *Literary Agent:* Campbell Thomson & McLaughlin. *Address:* c/o Campbell Thomson & McLaughlin Ltd, 31 Newington Green, London N16 9PU, England.

TANNEN, Mary, b. 2 June 1943, New London, Connecticut, USA. Writer. m. Michael Tannen, 25 Sep. 1965, Cold Springs Harbor, New York, USA, 1 son, 1 daughter. *Education:* BA, Barnard College. *Major Publications:* Wizard Children of Finn, 1981; Lost Legend of Finn, 1982; Huntley Nutley & the Missing Link, 1983. *Contributor to:* Family Circle; Company; (UK). *Literary Agent:* Elaine Markson. *Address:* 90 Riverside Drive, New York, NY 10024, USA.

TANNER, Jacqueline, b. 23 June 1943, Geneva, Switzerland. Laborantine. *Education:* Certificat d'Etudes. *Literary Appointments:* May Littéraire, 1978–79; Maison de la Poésie, Paris, 1984; Journée Littéraires de Soleure, 1984; Rencontre Internationales Poétiques d'Yverdon, 1984; Grande Fête des Lettres à Fribourg, 1985. *Publications:* Aurore Petrifiée, poetry, 1979; Melanie la Nuit, poetry, 1980; Hommage à Robert Favarger, collected works, 1982; La Maryssée, novel, 1984. *Contributions to:* Journal du Jura; Journal de Genève; Poésie 1984; Revue poétique; Pierre Seghers,

Paris; Entailles; etc.*Honours:* Prix Schiller, 1981; Prix Michel Dentan, 1984. *Memberships:* Swiss Society of Writers; Association Vaudoise des Ecrivains; Association des Ecrivains Francais & d'Outre-Mer. *Address:* Editions de l'Aire, Avenue Jean-Jacques Mercier 2, Lausanne, Switzerland.

TANSELLE, George Thomas, b. 29 Jan. 1934, Lebanon, Indiana, USA. Professor of English; Author; Editor; Vice President, John Simon Guggenheim Memorial Foundation, New York. *Education:* BA, Yale University, 1955; MA, 1956, PhD, 1959, Northwestern University. *Publications:* Royal Tyler, 1967; Guide to the Study of United States Imprints, 1971; Selected Studies in Bibliography, 1979. *Contributions to:* Studies in Bibliography; American Literature; New England Quarterly; 19th Century Fiction; Book Collector; Harvard Library Bulletin; Modern Language Review, and various others. Bibliography Editor, The Writings of Herman Melville, 1968–. *Honours include:* Jenkins Prize in Bibliography, 1973. *Memberships include:* President, Bibliography Society of America; Council Member, American Antiquarian Society; Bibliography Society, England; Private Library Association; Modern Language Association of America; Grolier Club; Caxton Club. *Address:* 90 Park Avenue, New York City, NY 10016, USA.

TANSLEY, Richard Charles, b. 7 Feb. 1938, Leicester, England. Agricultural Journalist. *Education:* Social Anthropology, London School of Economics; Graphic Design Diploma; Agricultural Marketing Diploma, Harper Adams College. *Literary Appointments:* Editor, Leicester Graphic; Technical Journalist, Agricultural Machinery Journal; Acting Editor, Vet Drug; PR Writer, John Deere. *Contributions to:* Agricultural Machinery Journal, 1979–83; Farming press, freelance and PR articles, 1983–85; Travelogues, trade and industrial press, Europe/Mexico, 1960's. *Honour:* Harper Adams Magazine, Best Article, 1978. *Memberships:* Guild of Agricultural Journalists; Leicester Literary and Philosophical Society. *Address:* Thatched Roofs, 45 Main Street, Newtown Linford, Leicester LE6 OAE, England.

TAPPE, Eric Ditmar, b. 8 July 1910, London, England. University Professor. *Education:* BA, Oxford University, 1932, MA, 1935. *Publications:* Rumanian Prose and Verse, 1956; Documents Concerning Rumanian History, (1427–1601) collected from Britsh Archives, 1964; I L Caragiale (Twayne's World Author's Series), 1974 (translation); M Eliade and M Nicelescu Fantastic Tales 1969, (translation); I L Caragiale Sketches and Stories, 1979. *Contributions to:* Revue des Etudes Roumaines; Revue des Etudes Sud Est Europeenes; Slavonic and East European Review. *Address:* 24 Markwick Terrace, St Leonards on Sea, Sussex TN38 ORF, England.

TARGET, George William, b. 12 Sep. 1924, England. Freelance Writer. *Publications include:* The Evangelists, 1958; The Teachers, 1960; The Missionaries, 1961; Watch With Me, 1961; The Shop Stewards, 1962; The Americans, 1964; We The Crucifiers, 1964; The Scientists, 1966; Evangelism Inc, 1968; Under the Christian Carpet, 1969; Unholy Smoke, 1969; The Young Lovers, 1970; Tell it the Way it is, 1970; Confound Their Politicks, 1970; The Patriots, 1974; Bernadette Devlin, 1974; Dear Dirty Dublin, 1974; The Nun in the Concentration Camp, 1974; The Triumph of Vice, 1976; Out of this World, 1985; How to Stop Smoking, 1985. *Contributions:* Chiefly to the religious press. *Address:* Sea House, Coast Road, Trimingham, Norfolk NR11 8DZ, England.

TARKKA, Pekka Sakari, b. 4 Dec. 1934, Helsinki, Finland. Books and Arts Editor. m. Leena Majender, 2 Sep. 1983, Helsinki, 1 daughter. *Education:* PhD, 1978. *Literary Appointments:* Literary Critic in Helsingin Sanomat, 1958–61, 1969–84; Docent (Finnish Literature), University of Helsinki, 1978–85; Lecturer, Finnish Literature, University of London, 1980–81; Books and Arts Editor, Helsingin Sanomat, 1984–.

Publications: En roman och dess publik, 1970; Salama, 1973; Putkinotkon tausta, 1977; Otavan historia, 1980; Finnische Literatur der Gegenwart, 1983; Sanat sanoista, 1984. *Contribution to:* Books from Finland, 1977–. *Honour:* State Literature Prize for translation, 1973. *Membership:* Eino Leino Society, Vice-President, 1972–83. *Address:* Katajanokanranta 17 B, Helsinki, Finland.

TARLING, Peter Nicholas, b. 1 Feb. 1931, Iver, England. University Professor. *Education:* BA, MA, PhD, LittD, Cambridge University. *Publications:* British Policy in the Malay Peninsula and Archipelago 1824–1871, 1957; Anglo-Dutch Rivalry in the Malay World 1790–1824, 1962; Piracy and Politics in the Malay World, 1963; A Concise History of Southeast Asia, 1966; Britain, the Brookes and Brunei, 1971; Imperial Britain in Southeast Asia, 1975; Sulu and Sabah, 1978; The Burthen, the Risk and the Glory, 1982. *Contributions to:* About 50 articles mainly on Southeast Asian History. *Honour:* Queen's Jubilee Medal 1978. *Address:* University of Auckland, Private Bag, Auckland, New Zealand.

TARNAWSKY, Ostap, b. 3 May 1917, Lviv, Ukraine, USSR. Poet; Essayist; Translator. *Education:* Diploma, Polytechnic, Lviv & Graz; MA, Drexel University, Philadelphia, USA; PhD, Ukrainische Freie University, Munich, Germany. *Publications include:* Shakespeare's Hamlet on the Ukrainian Stage, 1943, 2nd edition 1973; Slova i Mriyi, Poetry, 1948; Zhyttia, (sonnets sequence), 1952; Mosty, (Poetry), 1956; Samotnie Derevo, (Poetry), 1960; Tuha za Mitom, (Essays), 1966; Brat Bratovi, 1971; Kaminni Stupeni, (short stories), 1975; T S Eliot & P Tychyna: A Comparative Study, 1976; A Hundred Sonnets, 1984; Literary Lviv in the War-time, 1986. *Contributor to:* Various literary journals. *Honours:* Recipient, various honours. *Memberships:* President, Ukrainian Writers Association; Slovo; PEN; ALA. *Address:* 6509 Lawnton Ave, Philadelphia, PA 19126, USA.

TARR, Joel Arthur. b. 8 May 1934, Jersey City, New Jersey, USA. Professor. m. Tova Brafman, 17 Aug. 1978, Israel, 1 son, 3 daughters. *Education:* BS, 1956; MA, 1957, Rutgers University; PhD, 1963, Northwestern University. *Literary Appointments:* California State University, Long Beach, 1961–66; Santa Barbara, 1966–67; Carnegie-Mellon University, 1967–. *Publications:* A Study in Boss Politics, 1971; Retrospective Technology Assessment, 1977, (Editor); Transportation Innovation and Spatial Change in Pittsburgh, 1850–1934; 1978. *Contributions to:* Numerous professional journals. *Address:* Department of Social Sciences, Carnegie-Mellor University, Pittsburgh, PA 15213, USA.

TARSKY, Susan, b. 26 July 1946, New York City, USA. Children's author and Editor. *Education:* Cedar Crest College, Allentown, Pennsylvania, BA. *Major Publications:* The Nature Trail Book of Wild Flowers, 1977; The Children's Book of the Countryside (with M Hart and I Selberg), 1978; Taking a Walk in the Town, Taking a Walk in the Park, Taking a Walk in the Countryside, Taking a Walk at the Seashore, 1978; The Prickly Plant Book, The Window Box Book, The Potted Plant Book, 1980; Apple and Pear, Cup and Bowl, Doll and Drum, Table and Chair, 1983 ('Look and Say' Zebra Books series); Playtime, Shopping, 1983 ('Time to Talk' Zebra Books series); Who goes Moo?, Open the Door, I Can, Who Goes Splash? 1985 ('Chatterbox' Zebra Books Series); The Spectrum Book of Subroutines (with Michael Raine), 1985; Sindy At the Studio, Sindy and the Royal Visit, 1985. *Honour:* The Prickly Plant Book award for one of the outstanding books for children 1981, National Teachers' Association/Children's Book Council Joint Committee, USA.

TASCA, Jules E, b. 10 Dec. 1938, Philadelphia, USA. Professor; Writer. m. Beatrice Hartranft, 28 Jan. 1962, 2 sons, 1 daughter. *Education:* BA, 1961, Pennsylvania State University; MA, 1964, Villanova University; DFA,

1983, Heed University, Hollywood. *Literary Appointments:* 1963–, Associate Professor, Gwynedd Mercy College, Gwynedd Valley, Pennsylvania. *Publications:* Tear Along the Dotted Line; Subject to Change; Tadpole; The Mind with the Dirty Man; Chip Off Olympus; Five One Act Plays By Mark Twain, (Adaptation); Susan B; Alive and Kicking; The Amazing Einstein; Guy de Maupassant; The Necklace and Other Stories. *Contributor to:* George S Kaufman – An Intimate Portrait, Howard Teichman's Biography. *Honours:* Joseph Jefferson Award nomination for Best New Play, Chicago Area Theatre, 1972–73; Grand Prize, Performing Arts Repertory Company, New York, 1983. *Memberships:* Dramatists' Guild; Authors' League of America; Screen Writers' Guild. *Literary Agent:* Charles Hunt. *Address:* 313 Heston Avenue, Morristown, PA 19403, USA.

TATAY, Sándor, b. 6 May 1910, Bakonytamási, Hungary. Writer. m. Mária Takacs, 6 Dec. 1944, 1 daughter. *Education:* Evangelical Theology, Sopron; Pécs University. *Literary Appointment:* Journalist, Kelet Nepe, 1937–. *Publications:* Thunderstorm, 1941; The Simeon Family, 5 volumes, 1955–59; White Carriage, 1960; The House Under the Rocks, film, 1958; Lyuk a teton, novel, 1980; Meglepeteseimkonyve, Lodorgesek kora, 1983; Bakonyi kronika, 1985; Palacsinta aproban, short stories, 1986; Kinizsi Pal, 1954, novel for children; Puskak es galambok, 1958. *Contributions to:* Kortars; Jalenkor; Elet es Irodalam. *Honours:* Jozsef Attila Prize; Gold Degree of Munka Erdemrend; Magyar Nephoztarsasag Zaszlorendje; Golden Gate Prize for film script, San Francisco, California, USA. *Memberships:* Member of Presidency, Association of Hungarian Writers; Hungarian PEN. *Address:* Gyöngyösi ut 53, H-1131 Budapest, Hungary.

TATELBAUM, Brenda Loew, b. 1 Apr. 1951, Boston, USA. Publisher; Editor. m. 1 son, 1 daughter. *Education:* BA, English Language & Literature, Boston University, 1971; MA, Linguistic Science, Brown University, 1973. *Publications:* Eden Poems, 1982; Live Evolves from Living, 1983; Boston Collection of Women's Poetry, Volume 1, 1983. *Contributor to:* Pudding Magazine; Language, Speech, Hearing Services in Schools; Our Little Friend. *Membership:* Poetry Club of New England. *Address:* c/o Eidos Magazine, PO Box 96, Boston, MA 02134, USA.

TAVEL, Ronald, b. USA. Writer. *Education:* MA, University of Wyoming. *Literary Appointments:* Screenwriter, Andy Warhol Films Inc, 1964–66; First Artist-in-Residence, Yale Divinity School, 1975–77; First Playwright-in-Residence, Cornell University, 1980–81; Annual Summer Writers Conference Workshop Teacher, Hofstra University, 1984; Drama Critic, Stages magazine, 1984–; Instructor in Playwrighting, East Meadow Union Free School District, 1985; Commissioned Playwright, Theatre For The New City, 1983–87. *Publications:* Street of Stairs, novel, 1968; Theatre of the Ridiculous, plays, 1978; Wordplays, plays, 1981; Bigfoot, play, 1985; My Foetus Lived on Amboy Street, play, 1984. *Contributions to:* Stages magazine; Brooklyn Literary Review; The Village Voice. *Honours:* Awards 1969 and 1973, Nomination 1985, Obie Award for Playwriting. *Memberships:* Founding member, New York Theatre Strategy, 1971–; American Theatre Association. *Literary Agent:* Helen Merrill, 337 West 22nd Street, New York City, NY 10011, USA. *Address:* 438 West Broadway, Apartment 1, New York, NY 10012, USA.

TAYLOR, Andrew John Robert, b. 14 Oct. 1951, Stevenage, Hertfordshire, England. Writer; Freelance Sub-Editor. m. Caroline Jane Silverwood, 6 Sep. 1979, Littleton. *Education:* BA, MA, 1976, Emmanuel College, Cambridge, 1970–73; Diploma in Library, Archive and Information Studies, 1979; MA in Librarianship, 1980, University College, London. *Publications:* Caroline Minuscule, 1982; Waiting for the End of the World, 1984; Our Fathers' Lies (scheduled for mid 1985). *Honours:* John Creasey Memorial Award for Best Crime Novel 1982 for, Caroline Minuscle, Crime Writers'

Association; Scroll-winner for Mystery Writers of America's Edgar for Best First Novel, 1983, Caroline Minuscule. *Membership:* Crime Writers Association. *Address:* 19 Cinderhill, Coleford, Gloucestershire GL16 8HJ, England.

TAYLOR, Charles Alfred, 14 Aug. 1922, Hull, Yorkshire, England. University Professor of Physics. m. Nancy Truefitt, 22 Apr. 1944, Scarborough, 2 son, 1 daughter. *Education:* BSc, Queen Mary College, London, 1942; PhD 1951, DSc 1959, Manchester. *Publications:* Fourier Transforms & X Ray Diffraction, (with H Lipson), 1958; Optical Transforms, (with H Lipson), 1964; The Physics of Musical Sounds, 1965; An Atlas of Optical Transforms, (with G Harburn and T R Welberry), 1975; Sounds of Music, 1976; Images, 1978. *Contributions to:* Grove 6 Dictionary of Music; Learned Journals including: Proceedings of the Royal Institution; Interdisciplinary Science Reviews; Unesco Impact. *Honours:* Bragg Medal and Prize, Institute of Physics, 1983. *Memberships:* Fellow, Royal Society of Arts. *Address:* 9 Hill Deverill, Warminster, Wiltshire BA12 7EF, England.

TAYLOR, Conciere Mariana, b. 30 Oct. 1950. Writer; Arts Administrator. *Education:* AA, Queensborough Community College, USA, 1971; BFA, C.W. Post College, Long Island University, 1974; MA candidate, ibid. *Literary Appointments:* Business Manager, Ronald Arthur's Int. Theatre, 1974; Literary Assistant, Queens Council on the Arts, 1976–79; Director, Literary Arts Division, ibid, 1979–; Personal Manager, Chris Glen & Z/MO Rock Group, 1979–81; Business Manager, Tips & Tours Magazine, 1980–82. *Contributions to:* New York Times; New York Quarterly; Source; Poetry Nippon; Whetstone; Earth's Daughters; Washout Review; Wings Anthology; New Worlds Anthology; Vega; Unicorn; Rapunzel, Rapunzel; etc. *Honours include:* Eminent Mention, Poets of the Vineyard, 1979; 1st Prize, Today Category, New Worlds Anthology, 1980. *Memberships:* Word Guild; Poets & Writers of America. *Address:* 67-08 Parsons Boulevard, Apt. 6B, Flushing, NY 11365, USA.

TAYLOR, Donald Leslie, b. 20 Sep. 1948, Old Kilpatrick. Journalist. *Education:* Dip Ag Sci, Royal Agricultural College; National Diploma in Agriculture; Member, Royal Agricultural College. *Literary Appointments:* Deputy Business Editor, Farmers Weekly, 1980; Business Editor, Farming News, 1982; Assistant Editor, Farming News, 1985–. *Contributions to:* Various and many publications. *Membership:* Guild of Agricultural Journalists. *Address:* 18 St Johns Villas, Friern Barnet Road, London N11 3BU, England.

TAYLOR, Elisabeth Russell, b. 14 May 1930, London, England. University Lecturer. Divorced. 1 son. *Education:* BA Honours English. *Publications:* Wish You Were Here, 1976; London Lifelines, 1977; The Gifts of the Tarns, 1977; The Loadstone, 1978; Tales from Barleymill, 1978; The Potted Garden, 1980; The Diabetic Cookbook, 1981; Turkey in the Middle, 1983; Marcel Proust and his Contexts, 1983. *Contributions to:* The Observer; The Sunday Times; The Times; New Library World; Bulletin of Bibliography; Forfatteren; Books and Bookmen; Assistant Librarian; She magazine; Amateur Gardening; Ideal Home; Medical News; Library Association Record. *Honour:* Friends of Israel Writer's Bursary, 1984. *Literary Agent:* Margaret Hanbury, 27 Walcot Square, London SE11. *Address:* 21 Steeles Road, London NW3 4SH, England.

TAYLOR, Gordon Clifford, b. 24 Oct. 1915, Wigan, Lancashire, England. Clerk in Holy Orders; Rector, St Giles-in-the-Fields, London. m. Audrey Constance Rowse, 10 Apr. 1948, London, 2 daughters. *Education:* BA, 1937, MA, 1941, Christ's College, Cambridge University; Ripon Hall, Oxford University, 1937–38. *Publications:* The Sea Chaplains, 1978; London's Navy, 1983. *Contributions to:* Ritual Murder, 1980; Editor, St Giles Newsletter, 1953–. *Honours:* Volunteer Reserve Decoration; chaplain, Royal Naval Reserve. *Memberships:* Fellow, Society of Antiquaries; Member, Society for Nautical Research; MCC. *Address:* St Giles-in-the-

Fields Rectory, 15a Gower Street, London WC1, England.

TAYLOR, Ian, b. 25 Mar. 1938, St Helens, Lancashire, England. Playwright. m. Patricia Ann, 24 June 1958. *Literary Appointments:* Resident Playwright: Victoria Theatre, Stoke, 1973–74; Bristol Old Vic, 1974–75. *Publications:* Tarantara! Tarantara!, 1976; Hungry Times, 1985; Cocks and Hens, 1986. *Honours:* Award to New Playwrights, Thames Television, 1974; Arts Council Bursary, 1976; Nomination, for Hungry Times, British Academy of Film and Television Award, 1984. *Memberships:* Theatre Writers Union; Writers Guild of Great Britain. *Literary Agent:* Valerie Hoskins. *Address:* 2 Meadow View, Radstock, Bath BA3 3QS, England.

TAYLOR, Ina Margaret Kathleen, b. 5 Feb. 1949, Odiham, Hampshire. Writer. m. Colin Harvie Taylor, 1970, Odiham, Hampshire, 1 daughter. *Education:* BEd (Hons). *Literary Appointment:* Writer-in-Residence for Telford, West Midlands Arts, 1983–84. *Publication:* The Edwardian Lady: The Story of Edith Holden, 1980. *Contributions to:* Pins and Needles; New Library World; Family Circle. *Literary Agent:* Barbara Levy, Carol Smith Literary Agency. *Address:* Spring Cottage, Spout Lane, Leighton, Shrewsbury, Shropshire, England.

TAYLOR, John Gerald, b. 18 Aug. 1931, London, England. Mathematical Physicist. *Education:* Mid-Essex Technical College, Chelmsford, Essex, 1948–50; BSc Chemistry Physics Mathematics 1st Class Honours 1950, BSc Mathematics 1st Class Honours 1952, London Extension; BA 1st Class Honours 1953, MA 1955, PhD 1956, Christ's College, Cambridge, 1950–56. *Publications:* Quantum Mechanics: An Introduction, 1969; The Shape of Minds To Come, 1971; The New Physics, 1972; Black Holes: The End of the Universe, 1973; Superminds, 1975; Special Relativity, 1975; Science and The Supernatural, 1980; The Horizons of Knowledge, 1982. *Contributions to:* Physical Review; Physics Letters; Journal of Mathematical Physics; Journal of Physics; Proceedings of the Royal Society; Nature; Vogue; The Listener. *Literary Agent:* Andrew Best, Curtis Brown, London. *Address:* c/o Department of Mathematics, Kings College, The Strand, London WC2R 2LS, England.

TAYLOR, John Vernon, b. 11 Sep. 1914, Cambridge, England. Retired Bishop. m. Peggy Wright, 5 Oct. 1940, Oxford, 1 son, 2 daughters. *Education:* BA, St Catherines, Oxford University; MA, Trinity College, Cambridge University; Dip. Ed, London University Institute of Education. *Publications:* Christianity and Politics in Africa, 1955; The Growth of the Church in Buganda, 1958; The Primal Vision, 1963; The Go-Between God, 1972; Enough is Enough, 1975. *Honours:* Honorary Doctor of Divinity, Toronto, 1983; Collins Religious Book prize, 1974. *Address:* 65 Aston Street, Oxford, OX4 1EW, England.

TAYLOR, John William Ransom, b. 8 June 1922, Ely, Cambridgeshire, England. Author; Editor. m. Doris Alice Haddrick, 7 Sep. 1946, Southall, 1 son, 1 daughter. *Education:* FRACS; FRHistS; FSLAET; AFAIAA(USA). *Appointments:* Air Correspondent, Meccano Magazine, 1943–72; Editor, Air BP Magazine, 1956–72; Editor, Jane's All the World's Aircraft, 1959–; Contributing Editor: Air Force Magazine (USA), 1971–, Jane's Defence Weekly, 1984–. *Publications:* Spitfire, 1946; Spies in the Sky, 1972; History of Aviation, 1973; History of Aerial Warfare, 1974, and 225 others; Pictorial History of the Royal Air Force, 3 volumes, 1969–73; CFS – Birthplace of Air Policy, 1959. *Contributor to:* Most aviation journals in Europe & USA. *Honours:* C P Robertson Memorial Trophy, Air Public Relations Association, MOD, 1959; Certificate of Honour, Committee of Bibliography, History and Arts, Aero Club De France, 1971; Freeman, Guild of Air Pilots and Master Navigators, London, 1983; Order of Merit, World Aerospace Education Organisation, 1981; Member, French National Academy of Air and Space, 1985. *Address:* 36 Alexandra Drive, Surbiton, Surrey KT5 5AF, England.

TAYLOR, Kent, b. 8 Nov. 1940, Poet; Medical Research Associate. *Education:* BA, Ohio Wesleyan University, Delaware, OH, USA, 1962. *Literary Appointments:* Cinema Usher; Merchant Seaman; Longshoreman; Several Hospital Research Technical Posts; Currently, Medical Research Associate, University of California, San Francisco, California, USA. *Publications:* Driving Like the Sun, 1976; Empty Ground, 1976; Shit Outside When Eating Berries, 1971; Cleveland Dreams, 1971; Torn Birds, 1969; Late Stations, 1966; Selected Poems, 1963; 2 books concrete poetry. *Contributions to:* Vagabond; Living Underground; Free Lance; 2nd Aeon; Poetmeat; Invisible City; Tampa Poetry Review; Ann Arbor Review; Scree; Vagabond Anthology; Potpourri; Moonstones; Wormwood Review; Grist; Congress; The Willie; Cronk; Runcible Spoon; Shaded Room; Upjut; Podium; Glass Onion; 87 paper; Fine Arts; Earth; Kauri; Mother; Little Magazine; Gooseberry; Assassinators Broadsheet; Panama Gold; Ampersand; Ole Anthology; Ole; Alleheny Star Route; Cream City Review; Taproot; Ally; Planet Detroit Anthology; American Freeway (anthology); Limberlost Review; Quixote; Telegrams from Central Control; etc. *Address:* 1450 10th Avenue, San Francisco, CA 94122, USA.

TAYLOR, Laurie Aylma, b. 3 Sep. 1939, Tappan, New York, USA. Writer. m. Allen H Sparer, 17 July 1971, Pittsburgh, Pennsylvania, USA, 2 daughters. *Education:* BA, Mathematics. *Major Publications:* Changing the Past (poetry), 1981; Mystery Fiction: Footnote to Murder, 1983; Only Half a Hoax, 1983; Deadly Objectives, 1984; Shed Light on Death, 1985. *Contributor to:* Various literary magazines (short stories, mystery & science fiction and poetry). *Honours:* Minnesota Voices Project publication award for poetry, 1981; 1st prize in, Plainswoman, magazine short story competition for, Storm Watch, 1984. *Membership:* Mystery Writers of America. *Literary Agent:* Gouverneur & Co, New York. *Address:* c/o Gouverneur & Co, 220 East 85th Street, New York, NY 10028, USA.

TAYLOR, Margaret Stewart, b. Coventry, England. Former Librarian and Museum Curator. *Education:* MA, Oxon; FLA. *Publications:* Handbook of Classification and Cataloguing, 1948; The Crawshays of Eyfartha Castle, (biography), 1967; St Helena: Ocean Roadhouse (travel), 1969; Focus on the Falkland Islands, (travel), 1971; (fiction as Margaret Stewart Taylor) 2 dealing with modern Wales, 1964; 11 historical romances, 1967–80; (as Margaret Collier), The Mangrove Swamp, 1978; The Bell Stone, 1979. *Contributor to:* Various journals. *Memberships:* Society of Authors; Soroptimist International; Romantic Novelists Association; Merthyr Historical Association. *Address:* Flat 36, St Tydfil's Court, Caedrew Road, Merthyr Tydfil, Wales.

TAYLOR, Michael, b. 15 May 1937, Little Lever, Bolton, Lancashire, England. Editor, Methodist Recorder. m. 3 sons. *Previous Appointments include:* Sub-editor, The Guardian, Manchester; Chief Sub-editor, Daily Mail, Manchester; Assistant editor, Lancashire Evening Post, Preston; Editor, Evening Post & Chronicle, Wigan. *Address:* 122 Golden Lane, London EC1, England.

TAYLOR, Richard W(arren), b. 8 Dec. 1924, Hollywood, California, USA. Missionary Professor. m. Mary Lynn Seasholes, 20 Aug. 1948, Dayton, Ohio, 5 sons. *Education:* AB, University of California at Los Angeles, 1947; STB, Boston University, 1950; AM, University of Southern California, 1951. *Publications:* Mud Walls and Steel Mills, (with M M Thomas), 1963; Tribal Awakening, (editor with M M Thomas), 1965; The Changing Pattern of Family in India, (reviser), 1966; The Contribution of E Stanley Jones, 1973; Jesus in Indian Paintings, 1976; Society and Religion (editor), 1976; Religion and Society, 1953–1978; The First 25 Years, (editor), 1981; A Remembered Parish: St Mark's Cathedral, Bangalore, 1986. *Contributions to:* Co-editor, Religion and Society Quarterly, Bangalore. *Address:* Christian Institute for the Study of Religion and Society, 14 Jangpure B, Mathura Road, New Delhi 110 014, India.

TAYLOR, Samuel A, b. 13 June 1912, Chicago, Illinois, USA. Playwright. m. Suzane Combes, 4 June 1940, New York, 2 sons 1 daughter. *Education:* University of California, Berkeley. *Publications:* Plays: The Happy Time, 1950; Sabrina Fair, 1954; The Pleasure of his Company, 1958; First Love, 1961; No Strings, 1962; Beekman Place, 1965; Avanti!, 1968; Perfect Pitch, 1974; A Touch of Spring, 1975; Legend, 1976. *Memberships:* Authors' League of America; Dramatists & Guild of America; Writers' Guild of America; Dramatists' Guild Council 1955–70; Chairman of the Board, Dramatists Play Service; Century, New York (Club). *Address:* Meadow Rue, East Blue Hill, ME 04629, USA.

TAYLOR, Theodore Langhans, b. 23 June 1921, Statesville, North Carolina, USA. Writer. m. (1) Gwen Goodwin, 25 Oct. 1946, Bluefield, 2 sons, 1 daughter, (2) Flora Gray, 18 Apr. 1982, Laguna Beach. *Publications:* The Magnificent Mitscher, 1954; Fire on the Beaches, 1957; The Cay, 1968; The Children's War, 1971; The Maldonado Miracle, 1973; Teetoncey, 1974; Jule, 1979; The Trouble with Tuck, 1981; Battle Off Midway Island, 1982; HMS Hood vs Bismarck, 1983; Battle In The English Channel, 1984; Sweet Friday Island, 1984; The Cats of Shambala, 1985. *Contributor to:* Saturday Evening Post; McCall's; Ladies Home Journal; Saturday Review of Literature; Argosy; etc. *Honours:* Lewis Carroll Shelf Award; Jane Addams Peace & Freedom Foundation Award; Western Writers of America Award; George G Stone Center Award. *Literary Agent:* Gloria Loomis, Watkins-Loomis, New York City. *Address:* 1856 Catalina Street, Laguna Beach, CA 92651, USA.

TAYLOR, Walter Harold, b. 2 Dec. 1905, Melbourne, Australia. Civil Engineering and Concrete Technology. m. Esma Jean Ainslie, 1 Feb. 1957, East Kew, Victoria. *Education:* Royal Melbourne Institute of Technology, 1921–25; RMIT Diplomate, 1928; Local Government Engineer, 1928; Trinity College and University of Melbourne, 1928–31; Bachelor of Civil Engineering, 1931; Master of Civil Engineering, 1937. *Publication:* Concrete Technology and Practice, 1965, 4th edition 1977. *Contributions to:* Over 20 professional periodicals including: ASTM Bulletin; American Concrete Institute Journal; Magazine of Concrete Research; RILEM Bulletin; Constructional Review; Nature; Chemical Industry; Zement Kalk Gipps. *Honours:* The Argus and Simon Fraser Engineering Awards, University of Melbourne, 1928–31; Building Science Forum of Australia Book Award, 1968; Honorary Life Membership, Concrete Institute of Australia, 1979. *Memberships:* Fellow, Branch Chairman 1961–62, Institution of Engineers Australia; Fellow, Branch Chairman, 1969–70, Institution of Civil Engineers, UK; Australian Institute of Management; Standards Association; Cement and Concrete Association; Council of Engineering Institutions, Britain. *Address:* 19 Lawson Street, Hawthorn East, Victoria 3123, Australia.

TEHAN, Joan Mary, b. 8 July 1945, Melbourne, Australia. Journalist; Editor. m. Anthony O'Hara Tehan, 1966, Victoria, 1 son, 3 daughters. *Literary Appointments:* Journalist, Sun Newspaper, Melbourne, Australia, 1964–66; Co-owner, Mansfield Courier, Victoria, 1971–; Editor, Mansfield Courier, 1974–. *Membership:* Victoria Country Press Association. *Address:* Blackheath, Mansfield 3722, Victoria, Australia.

TEKEYAN, Charles, b. 15 Apr. 1936, New York, USA. Writer. *Publications:* The Passionate Tennis Player and Other Stories; Hot Boys and Cold Girls; New York Is All Ours; The Revelations of a Disappearing Man. *Contributor to:* Stories and articles in several publications. *Literary Agent:* Mavis McIntosh. *Address:* Box 416, Cathedral Sta, New York, NY 10025, USA.

TELFER, Ross Alexander, b. 17 Sep. 1937, Newcastle, Australia. University Professor. m. Bronwyn Edwards, 9 Jan. 1960, Boolaroo, 3 daughters. *Education:* Teachers Certificate, Newcastle Teachers' College, Australia, 1956; BA, University of New South Wales,

1964; Diploma in Educational Administration, 1968, Master of Educational Administration, 1972, University of New England; PhD, University of Newcastle. *Major publications:* Sailing Small Craft, 1964; How to Sail Small Boats, 1968; Australian Sailing, 1984; Teacher Tactics, 1975, The Process of Learning, 1981, Psychology and Flight Instruction, 1985 (joint publications). *Contributor to:* Numerous professional educational, instructional journals, many international (over 60 articles). *Honour:* New South Wales Public Service Board Fellow, 1971. *Address:* 20 MacQuarrie Street, Bolton Point, New South Wales 2283, Australia.

TELLECHEA IDIGORAS, Jose Ignacio, b. 13 Apr. 1928, San Sebastian, Spain. Professor of Church History, Pontifical University of Salamanca. *Education:* Priest, Seminary of Vitoria; DTh, Licentiate in Church History, University Gregoriana; Licentiate in Philosophy and Letters, University of Madrid. *Publications include:* Fray Bartolome Carranza, Documentos historicos, 6 volumes, 1962–81; El Arzobispo Carrenza y su tiempo, 2 volumes, 1968; El Obispo ideal en el siglo de la Reforma, 1963; Obras del P Larramendi, 3 volumes, 1969–83; Cathechismo Christiano, de Crranza, 2 volumes, 1972; La Reforma Tridentina en San Sebastian, 1972; Las Hermanas de la Caridad y el Hospital de Zaragoza, 4 volumes, 1967–86; Guia espiritual de Miguel Molinos, 1976; Tiempos recios, Inquisicion y heterodoxias, 1977; Fray Bartolome Carranza y el Cardenal Pole, 1977; Anclas de Hernani, 1977; Hernan Perez de Yarza, alcaide de Behobia, 1979; La polemica entre el Cardenal Mendoza y el Abed Maluenda, 1980; Mosen Bonal, 2 volumes, 1974–80; Melanchton y Carranza, Prestamos y afinidades, 1979. *Contributions to:* Numerous theological and historical journals. *Address:* Usandizaga 27 5°, 20002 San Sebastian, Spain.

TELLER, Walter Magnes, b. 10 Oct. 1910, New Orleans, USA. Writer. m. Jane Simon, 7 Apr. 1933, New York, 4 sons. *Education:* BS, Haverford College; PhD, Columbia University. *Publications:* An Island Summer, 1951; The Search for Captain Slocum: A Biography, 1956; Area Code 215: A Private Line in Bucks County, 1963; Cape Cod and the Offshore Islands, 1970; Joshua Slocum, 1971; Twelve Works of Naive Genius, 1972; Walt Whitman's Camden Conversations, 1973; On the River: A Variety of Canoe & Small Boat Voyages, 1976. *Contributor to:* New York Times Book Review; Saturday Review; American Scholar; Atlantic; Canadian Geographic. *Honour:* Fellow, John Simon Guggenheim Memorial Foundation, 1953. *Memberships:* Authors Guild; PEN, American Centre. *Address:* 200 Prospect Avenue, Princeton, NJ 08540, USA.

TELSER, Lester G, b. 3 Jan. 1931, Chicago, USA. Professor of Economics. m. Sylvia Ruth Trossman, 24 June 1956, Chicago, 1 son, 1 daughter. *Education:* AB, Roosevelt University, 1951; Graduate Student, Harvard University, 1951–52; AM, 1953, PhD, 1956, University of Chicago. *Publications:* Competition, Collusion and Game Theory, 1972; Functional Analysis in Mathematical Economics, 1972; Economic Theory and the Core, 1978. *Contributions to:* Various economic journals. *Honours:* Fellow, American Statistical Association, 1968; Fellow, Econometric Society, 1968. *Address:* Department of Economics, University of Chicago, 1126 E, 59th Street, Chicago, IL 60637, USA.

TEMKO, Florence. Author; Craft Designer. *Education:* London School of Economics, England; New School for Social Research, New York, USA. *Publications:* Paper: Folded, Cut, Sculpted, 1974; Folk Crafts for World Friendship, 1976; The Big Felt Burger and 27 Other Craft Projects to Relish, 1977; The Magic of Kirigami: Happenings with Paper and Scissors, 1978; Paperworks; Let's Take a Trip, Come to My House, Guess Who, 1982; Chinese Papercuts: Their Story, How to Use Them and Make Them, 1982; Elementary Art Games and Puzzles, 1982; New Knitting, 1984; Chinese Ducks and 55 Other Things to Fold with Paper, 1985. *Contributor to:* New York Sunday Times; Boston Globe; Crafts; Creative Crafts; The Instructor; Faces Children's Magazine. *Honour:* Citation for Excellence of Books.

Memberships: Authors' Guild; ASJA; American Pen Women; San Diego Press Club. *Address:* 1855 Diamond Street, Suite 5–324, San Diego, CA 92109, USA.

TEMPERLEY, Alan, b. 12 Sep. 1936, Sunderland, England. Teacher; Author. 1 son. *Education:* BA, Manchester University, England, 1964; Dip Ed Edinburgh University, Scotland, 1965; Teaching Diploma Primary/Secondary, Moray House College, Edinburgh, Scotland, 1965. *Publications:* Tales of the North Coast, 1977; Tales of Galloway, 1979; North Coast Boy, 1986; Silas and the Mermaid, (pending), 1987; Short stories published by Penguin, Pan, Collins, SAC, Octopus, Heinemann, Hamlyn, etc. *Contributions to:* BBC; Scottish Magazine; Words; Scottish Field; Times Educational Supplement; Glasgow Herald, etc. *Honour:* Major Bursary, Scottish Arts Council, 1977. *Memberships:* Society of Authors; Scottish PEN. *Address:* c/o Schoolhouse, Rhonehouse, Castle Douglas, Kirkudbrightshire DG7 1SA, Scotland.

TEMPERLEY, Harold Neville Vazeille, b. 4 Mar. 1915, Cambridge, England. Retired University Professor. m. Geraldine Howard la Coste Bartrop, 6 Feb. 1940, West Hoathly, Sussex, 3 sons, 2 daughters. *Education:* BA 1937, MA 1941, SCD 1958, King's College, Cambridge. *Publications:* Properties of Matter, 1953; Changes of State, 1956; A Scientist Who Believes in God, 1961; The Physics of Simple Liquids, 1968; Liquids and Their Properties, 1978; Graph Theory and Applications, 1982. *Contributions to:* About 75 original papers; Reviews; articles; Journal of Physics; Physical Review; Proceedings Cambridge Philosophical Society, etc. *Honours include:* College Studentship, 1938 and 1939 Smiths Prize, 1939; Fellow, Kings College, 1941–54; Smithson Research Fellow, Royal Society, 1947–48. *Memberships:* Institute of Physics. *Address:* Thorney House, Thomey, Langport, Somerset, TA10 ODW, England.

TEMPLE, Nigel Hal Longdale, b. 21 Jan. 1926, England. Painter; Architectural Historian; Lecturer. m. Judith Tattersill, 1 son, 1 daughter. *Education:* National Diploma in Design (NDD) 1951; Art Teachers Diploma (ATD) Sheffield 1953; M Litt in Architecture, Bristol, 1978; PhD, Keele, 1985. *Publications:* Farnham Inheritance, 1956, 1965; Farnham Buildings and People, 1963, 1973; Seen and Not Heard, 1970; John Nash and the Village Picturesque, 1979; Looking at Things, 1968. *Contributions to:* Country Life; Architectural Review; Journal of Garden History etc. *Honours:* Fellow, Royal Society of Arts, 1955; Fellow, National Society for Art Education, 1964; Member, Royal West of England Academy, 1983. *Address:* 4 Wendover Gardens, Christchurch Road, Cheltenham, Gloucestershire GL50 2PA, England.

TEMPLE, Robert Philip, b. 20 Mar. 1939, Yorkshire, England. Author. m. Daphne Evelyn Kenn, 12 June 1965, Invercargill, New Zealand, 1 son, 1 daughter. *Literary Appointments:* Associate Editor, Landfall, 1972–75; Judge, New Zealand First Book of Prose Award, 1978; New Zealand Authors Fund Advisory Committee, 1985–. *Publications:* Nawok!, 1962; The Sea and the Snow, 1966; The World at Their Feet, 1969; Mantle of the Skies, 1971; Christchurch, 1973; Castles in the Air, 1973; Patterns of Water, 1974; South Island, 1975; Ways to the Wilderness, 1977; New Zealand Explorers, 1985; Moa, 1985; Shell Guides to New Zealand Walking Tracks, 1976–86; Novels: The Explorer, 1975; Stations, 1979; Beak of the Moon, 1981; Sam, 1984. *Contributor to:* New Zealand Listener. *Honours:* Wattie Award, 1970; New Zealand Literary Fund Grant 1972; New Zealand Literary Fund Bursary 1976; Katherine Mansfield Memorial Fellowship, Menton, 1979; Robert Burns Fellowship, University of Otago, 1980. *Memberships:* PEN (New Zealand), Vice President 1978–79; Australian Society of Authors; New Zealand Writers Guild. *Address:* Post Office, Little Akaloa, Banks Peninsula, New Zealand.

TEMPLE, Wayne Calhoun (Lt General), b. 5 Feb. 1924, Delaware County, Ohio, USA. Archivist; Author;

Military Officer. m. Sunderine Wilson, 9 Apr. 1979, Springfield. *Education:* AB, History, 1949, AM 1951, PhD, 1956, University of Illinois; Lincoln Diploma of Honour, Lincoln Memorial University, 1963. *Appointments:* Editor in Chief, 1958–73, Associate Editor, 1973–; Guest Lecturer, US Military Academy, West Point, 1975; The Lecturer, Illinois Lodge of Research, 1985. *Publications:* Indian Villages of the Illinois Country: Historic Tribes, 1958, 3rd edition 1977; Campaigning with Grant, 1961; Stephen A Douglas: Freemason, 1982; By Square and Compasses: The Building of Lincoln's Home and Its Saga, 1984, and many others. *Contributor to:* Numerous professional journals. *Honours:* Recipient, Bronze Star Medal for action under fire, Rhine River, 1945; Lincoln Medallion, 1960; Award of Achievement, US Civil War Centennial Commission, 1965; Algernon Sydney Sullivan Medallion, 1969; Distinguished Service Award, Illinois State Historical Library, 1969, 1977; Distinguished Service Award, Civil War Round Table Chicago, 1983; Sigma Tau Delta Gold Honour Key; 3 Books, Book Club Selections. *Memberships:* Board of Directors, Vachel Lindsay House; Phi Alpha Literary Society; Life Fellow, Royal Society of Arts, London, England. *Address:* 1121 S 4th Street Court, Springfield, IL 62703, USA.

TEMPLETON, Edith, b. 7 Apr. 1916, Prague. m. Dr Edmund Ronald, 24 Sep. 1955, London, England, 1 son. *Major Publications:* Summer in the Country, 1950; Living on Yesterday, 1951; The Island of Desire, 1952; The Surprise of Cremona, 1954; This Charming Pastime, 1955; Gordon (as Louise Walbrooke), 1966; Three, 1971. *Contributor to:* The New Yorker; Vogue; Harpers; Housewife; Transatlantic Monthly. *Honour:* Book Society Choice 1954 (for Surprise of Cremona). *Membership:* PEN. *Address:* 55 Compayne Gardens, London NW6, England.

TENE, Benjamin, b. 10 Dec. 1914, Warsaw, Poland. Writer; Author. m. Sarah, 1937, Tel-Aviv, 1 son, 1 daughter. *Literary Appointment:* Editor, Michmar L'Iladim. *Publications:* Mehora, 1939; Massa Begalil, 1949; Beheret Hadwai, 1945; Tmolin Al Hasaf, 1947; Hazamir, 1963; Shirim Upoemot, 1967; Ktsir Hapele, (for children), 1957; Translation Poems and Ballads by Itzik Manger; Mizmor Lehag, (for children), 1973; (Prose books): In the Shade of the Chestnut Tree, 1973; Schoolboys Before the Storm, 1976; The Story of Mor, 1977; City of My Youth, 1979; A Friend inNeed, 1981; The Third Courtyard, 1982. *Honours:* Alfred Jurzykowski Foundation Award, 1970; Zew Award, 1974; Lamden Award, 1980; Zew Award, 1981. *Memberships:* Association of Hebrew Writers in Israel; PEN Club. *Address:* Karni 8, 69025 Tel-Aviv, Israel.

TENNANT, Emma Christina, b. 20 Oct. 1937, London, England. Writer. 1 son, 2 daughters. *Publications:* Hotel de Dream, 1976; The Bad Sister, 1978; Wild Nights, 1979; Woman Beware Woman, 1983. *Contributions to:* Guardian; Vogue; Granta; Literary Review, etc. *Membership:* Fellow, Royal Society of Literature. *Address:* c/o Faber & Faber, 3 Queen Square, London WC1, England.

TENNANT, Kylie, b. 12 Mar. 1912, Manly, New South Wales, Australia. Author. m. Lewis Charles Rodd, Nov. 1932, Coonabarabran, Australia, 1 son (dec), 1 daughter. *Publications:* Tiburon, 1935 & 1981; Foveaux, 1939 & 1946, 1968, 1981. The Battlers, 1941 & 1946, 1961, 1965, 1967; Ride on a Stranger, 1943 & 1979, 1980; Time Enough Later, 1943, 1945, 1961; Lost Haven, 1946, 1947, 1968; The Joyful Condemned, 1953; The Honey Flow, 1956, 1974; Tell Morning This, 1968, 1970; Tantavallon, 1983. *Honour:* Order of Australia. *Literary Agent:* Judy Barry. *Address:* Cliff View Orchard, Shipley, New South Wales, Australia.

TENNANT, Roger, b. 8 Apr. 1919, Tasmania. Priest, Anglican Church. m. Agnita Myong Hong, 6 Feb. 1964, Lutterworth, England, 1 son, 1 daughter. *Education:* PhD, 1974, Open University. *Publications:* Born of a Woman, 1961; Litany of St Charles, 1968, (USA title, Cast on a Certain Island); Joseph Conrad, a Biography,

1981; Editor, World's Classics Edition, Conrad's Secret Agent, 1983. *Literary Agent:* A M Heath. *Address:* Bitteswell Vicarage, Lutterworth, Leicestershire, England.

TENNISON, Patrick Joseph, b. 16 July 1928, Brisbane, Australia. Journalist. m. Olga Massey, 17 Mar. 1955, Brisbane, 1 son, 1 daughter. *Publications:* Meet the Gallery, 1968; The Marriage Wilderness, 1972; Defence Counsel, 1975; Lucky Country Reborn, 1976; Heyday or Doomsday – Australia 2000, Editor, 1977; Family Court: The Legal Jungle, 1983; Melbourne Press Club. *Contributions to:* The Australian; The Age; The Herald; The Sun; The Bulletin; Forum; National Times. *Memberships:* Australian Society of Authors; Australian Journalists Association. Fellowship of Australian Writers; Mastering the Interview, 1985. *Address:* 375 High Street, Ashburton, Victoria 3147, Australia.

TEPLITZ, Paul Victor, b. 31 Aug. 1940, New Orleans, Louisiana, USA. Management Consultant. m. Katherine J Kent, 11 May 1973, Cambridge, Massachusetts, 1 son, 2 daughters. *Education:* SB, Massachusetts Institute of Technology, 1962; MS, Carnegie-Mellon University, 1963; SM, MIT Sloan School of Management, 1965; DBA, Harvard University, 1969. *Publications:* Urban Analysis, co-author, 1970; Trends Affecting the US Banking System, 1976; Baseball Economics and Public Policy, with Professor Jesse Markham, 1981; Alternative Tax Proposals – How The Numbers Add Up, 1986. *Contributor to:* Management Science; American Banker. *Honours:* Recipient various honours. *Memberships:* North American Society for Corporate Planning; Planning Executives Institute; Institute of Electrical and Electronic Engineers. *Address:* Cambridge Research Institute, 44 Brattle Street, Cambridge, MA 02138, USA.

TERPSTRA, Vern, b. 20 Aug. 1927, Michigan, USA. Professor. m. Bonnie Lou Fuller, 18 Sep. 1950, Grand Rapids, Michigan, 2 sons, 2 daughter. *Education:* BA, 1950, MBA, 1951, PhD, 1965, University of Michigan. *Literary Appointments:* Assistant Professor, University of Pennsylvania, 1963–66; Professor, University of Michigan, 1966–. *Publications:* American Marketing in the Common Market, 1967; International Marketing, 1972, 1983; Cultural Environment of Int'l Business, 1985. *Contributions to:* Int'l Product Policy, Columbia Journal of World Business, 1977; Appropriate Products for Developing Countries, Journal of International Business Studies; American Challenge in International Advertising, Journal of Advertising, 1984. *Address:* Business School, University of Michigan, Ann Arbor, MI 48109, USA.

TERRY, Carolyn Mary, b. 18 June 1940, Bristol, England. Writer, m. Roy Terry, 1969, Nelspruit, Republic of South Africa. *Publications:* King of Diamonds, 1983; The Fortune Seekers, 1985. *Membership:* Society of Authors. *Literary Agent:* Christopher Little. *Address:* c/o Christopher Little Literary Agency, 49 Queen Victoria Street, London EC4N 4SA, England.

TERRY, Megan, b. Washington, USA. Playwright. *Education:* B Ed, University of Washington; Graduate work, University of Alberta and Banff School of Fine Arts, Canada; Theatre training, Seattle Repertory Playhouse, USA. *Literary Appointments:* Cornish Players of Seattle; Founding member, Open Theatre, New York Theatre Strategy and The Women's Theatre Council, New York; Playwright-in-residence and Literary Manager, Omaha Magic Theatre, Omaha, Nebraska, 1974–. *Publications include:* Over 50 plays including: Comings and Goings, Viet Rock – 4 plays, 1967; The Gloaming, Oh My Darling, Viet Rock – 4 plays, 1967; Keep Tightly Closed in a Cool Dry Place, Viet Rock – 4 plays, 1967; The Magic Realists in Best One Act Plays of 1968, Edited by Stanley Richards, 1969; The People Vs Ranchman, 1970; Megan Terry's Home: Or Future Soap, 1972; Sanibel and Captiva, 1972; Massachusetts Trust, 1972; Hothouse, 1975; Calm Down Mother, one act, 1975; Brazil Fado musical, 1979; Ex-Miss Copper Queen on a Set of Pills, one act, 1979; Approaching

Simone, 1980; Babes in the Bighouse, 1983. *Honours include:* Stanley Drama Award; Dramatists Guild Annual Award, 1983; Various fellowships and grants. *Literary Agent:* Elizabeth Marton. *Address:* c/o E Marton, 96 Fifth Avenue, New York, NY 10011, USA.

TERRY, Sarah Meiklejohn, b. 16 July 1937, Newton, Massachusetts, USA. University Professor. m. Robert Cushing Terry, 14 May 1966. *Education:* BA, Distinction, Cornell University, 1959; MA, Soviet Studies, 1961, PhD, Political Science, 1974, Harvard University. *Appointments:* Associate Dean, Lecturer, Political Science, Tufts University, 1976–78; Visiting Lecturer, Government, Harvard University, 1977, 1983; Assistant Professor, 1978–84, Associate Professor, 1984–, Political Science, Adjunct Associate Professor, Diplomacy, 1984–, Fletcher School of Law & Diplomacy, Tufts University. *Publications:* Poland's Place in Europe: General Sikorski & The Origin of the Oder Neisse Line 1939–1943, 1983; Soviet Policy in Eastern Europe, Editor, Contributor, 1984. *Contributor to:* Numerous articles on contemporary Polish Politics, East European Political Economy, and Soviet-East European Relations. *Honours:* Phi Beta Kappa, 1958; Phi Kappa Phi, 1959; Graduate Fellowships: Woodrow Wilson Foundation, Radcliffe Graduate School, Ford Foundation, National Defence Foreign Language Programme; Postgraduate Fellowships: American Council of Learned Societies, National Endowment for the Humanities; International Research & Exchanges Board. *Memberships:* American Association for the Advancement of Slavic Studies, Board of Directors, 1983–86; American Political Science Association; New England Slavic Assocation; Fellow, Harvard University's Russian Research Centre. *Address:* Dept of Political Science, Tufts University, Medford, MA 02155, USA.

TESELLE, Eugene Arthur, b. 8 Aug. 1931, Ames, Iowa, USA. Professor. m. Penelope Saunders, 6 Mar. 1978, Nashville, 4 sons, 1 daughter. *Education:* BA, University of Colorado, 1952; BD, Princeton Theological Seminary, 1955; MA 1960, PhD 1963, Yale University. *Publications:* Augustine the Theologian, 1970; Augustine's Strategy as an apologist, 1974; Christ in Context, 1975. *Contributions to:* Recherches Augustiniennes; Augustinian Studies. *Honours:* Presbyterian Graduate Fellow, 1958; Rockefeller Fellow, 1960; Kent Fellow, 1961. *Memberships:* Phi Beta Kappa; Society for Values in Higher Education; American Academy of Religion; American Society of Church History. *Address:* Divinity School, Vanderbilt University, Nashville, TN 37240, USA.

TESSIER, Thomas Edward, b. 10 May 1947, USA. Writer. m. Alice Audietis, 15 June 1968, USA, 1 son, 1 daughter. *Publications:* Novels: The Fates, 1978; The Nightwalker, 1980; Shockwaves, 1981; Phantom, 1982; Finishing Touches, 1986. *Literary Agent:* Carol Smith. *Address:* c/o Carol Smith, 25 Hornton Court, Kensington High Street, London W8 7RT, England.

TESSLER, Sandra Rubin, b. 26 Mar. 1944, Detroit, Michigan, USA. Journalist. m. Martin Edward Tessler, 3 Aug. 1964, 2 daughters. *Education:* Bachelor of Science. *Literary Appointments:* The Detroit News. *Contributions to:* Newspapers and magazines including: Time; Monthly Detroit; Private Practice, a Physician's Journal. *Honours:* Nomination for Scripps Award for excellence in journalism, Nomination for Pulitzer Prize. *Memberships:* American Medical Writers Association; Women in Communications; The Society of Professional Journalists. *Address:* The Detroit News, 615 Lafayette Boulevard, Detroit, MI 48231, USA.

TEYE, Nicholas, b. 12 June 1939, Manya Krobo, Ghana. Film-Maker, Screenplay Scriptwriter, Poet, Critic. *Education:* Diploma, Drama and Theatre Studies; Diploma, Film-Making. *Publications:* Collection of Poetry (forthcoming). *Contributions to:* Growth Literary Magazine. *Memberships:* Ghana Association of Writers; National Association of Writers. *Address:* Ghana Film Industry Corporation, PO Box M83, Accra, Ghana.

THACKARA, John, b. 6 Aug. 1951, Newcastle, England. Editor; Journalist. *Education:* BA Honours, Philosophy. *Literary Appointments:* Senior Editor, Granada Publishing, 1975–79; Managing Editor, NSW University Press, 1980–82; Editor, Design Magazine, 1983–. *Publications:* Architects Data, international edition, 1980; Cheap Eats in Sydney, 1st edition, 1982; Design after Modernism, 1986. *Literary Agents:* David Higham Associates. *Address:* 28 Haymarket, London SW1Y 4SU, England.

THACKRAH, John Richard, b. 31 Jan. 1947, Leeds, England. Lecturer. *Education:* BA, Geography, History, Postgraduate Certificate in Education, Leeds University, 1971; MA, International History, Birkbeck College, London University, 1972; MA, Contemporary European Studies, Reading University, 1982. *Publications:* Handbook on European History 1945–1978; The River Tweed; Oxford University and Its Colleges; The Royal Albert Hall; Contemporary Policing; A Bibliography of Malta. *Contributor to:* Poland and the Western Allies in 1945, Polish Review, 1978; Spain and the Gibraltar Question, Iberian Studies, 1979; The Invasion of Greece 1941, Army Quarterly, 1979; The Middle East Wars, in Atlas of Modern Warfare; The Palestine Liberation Organisation, War in Peace, 1984. *Honours:* Cecil Peace Prize, for work on The United Nations and the Use of Force, 1971; Reinhold Schneider Peace Prize, The Political Feasibility of Christian Peace, 1975. *Literary Agent:* Catt-Wilson Agency, London. *Address:* Flat 2 Up Green Lodge, Up Green, Eversley, Near Basingstoke, Hampshire RG27 OPB, England.

THADEN, Edward Carl, b. 24 Apr. 1922, Seattle, USA. Historian. m. Marianna Forster, 7 Aug. 1952, Seattle. *Education:* BA, University of Washington, 1944; Certificate, University of Zurich, Switzerland, 1948; PhD, Sorbonne University of Paris, France, 1950. *Publications:* Conservative Nationalism in 19th Century Russia, 1964; Russia and the Balkan Alliance of 1912, 1965; Russia Ssince 1801: The Making of a New Society, 1971; Russification in the Baltic Provinces and Finland 1855–1914, (editor and co-author), 1981; Russia's Western Borderlands 1710–1870, 1984. *Contributions to:* Journal of Baltic Studies; Russian Review; Slavic Review. *Honours:* Fulbright Fellowships, Finland, Federal Republic of Germany and Poland, 1957–58 and 1968; Visiting Research Scholar, Institute of History, Soviet Academy of Sciences, Moscow, USSR, 1975; Fellow, Wilson International Center for Scholars, 1980. *Memberships:* Executive Secretary 1980–82, American Association for the Advancement of Slavic Studies; Vice-President, Commission Internationale des Studes Slaves, 1985–. *Address:* Department of History, University of Illinois, Chicago, IL 60680, USA.

THEAR, Katie, b. 7 Apr. 1939, Tudweiliog, North Wales. Writer. m. David Thear, 14 Aug. 1964, Bootle, Lancashire, 2 sons, 1 daughter. *Education:* Teachers Certificate, University of Wales School of Education; Glamorgan Training College, Barry, Glamorgan; Curently studying for Arts Degree with Open University. *Literary Appointments:* Editor, Home Farm, Magazine, 1975–; Consultant to B T Batsford Limited, 1982–; Consultant to Channel 4 Television, 1983. *Publications:* The Complete Book of Raising Livestock and Poultry, 1981; Part-Time Farming, 1982; The Family Smallholding, 1983; Home Dairying, 1983; A Kind of Living, 1983; Practical Chicken Keeping, 1983. *Contributions to:* Home Farm; The Herbalist; Western Mail; The Field. *Membership:* The Society of Authors. *Address:* Broad Leys, Widdington, Saffron Walden, Essex CB11 3SP, England.

THEINER, George Fredric, b. 4 Nov. 1927, Prague. Editor. m. Shirley Harris, 25 Oct. 1975, Harrow, 1 son. *Literary Appointments:* English Literary Editor, ARTIA Foreign Language Publishing House, Prague, 1958–62; Assistant Editor, 1973–82, Editor, 1982–, Index on Censorship, London. *Publications:* Editor: New Writing in Czechoslovakia, 1969; The Kill Dog, 1970 (co-author); Editor: They Shoot Writers, Don't They?, 1984.

Contributor to: Times Literary Supplement; London Magazine; The Bookseller; The Encyclopaedia Britannica Book of the Year. *Honour:* Prize for translations of Czech literature into English from the Czechoslovak Writers Union, Prague, 1968. *Membership:* English PEN Club, Member and Chairman of its Writers in Prison Committee. *Address:* 154 Barry Road, Dulwich, London SE22 OJW.

THEMERSON, Stefan, b. 25 Jan. 1910. Author. *Publications:* Bayamus, 1949; The Adventures of Peddy Bottom, 1950; Wooff Wooff, 1951; Professor Mmaa's Lecture, 1953; Factot T, 1956; Kurt Schwitters in England, 1958; Cardinal Pölätüo, 1961; Semantic Divertissements, 1962; Apollinaire's Lyrical Ideograms, 1966; Tom Harris, 1967; St Francis and the Wolf of Gubbio, opera, 1972; Special Branch, 1972; Logic Labels and Flesh, 1974; On Semantic Poetry, 1975; General Piesc, 1976; The Chair of Decency, 1982; The Urge To Create Visions, 1983; The Mystery of the Sardine, 1986. *Contributions to:* Various magazines and journals in Europe. *Address:* 28 Warrington Crescent, London W9 1EL, England.

THEOBALD, Robert, b. 11 June 1929, Madras, India. Writer. m. Jeanne Scott, 8 Dec. 1951, Cambridge. *Education:* MA, Economics, Cambridge University. *Publications:* The Rich and the Poor, 1959; The Challenge of Abundance, 1961; Free Men and Free Markets, 1963; Teg's 1994, (with J M Scott) 1970; Beyond Despair, 1974; Avoiding 1984, 1983; The Rapids of Change, 1986. *Address:* Box 2240, Wickenburg, AZ 85358, USA.

THESEN, Hjalmar Peter, b. 20 June 1925. Game Farmer. m. Judith Zoe Lyn, 19 Aug. 1960, Knysna, South Africa, 2 sons, 2 daughters. *Publications:* The Echoing Cliffs, 1963; The Castle of Giants, 1969; Master of None, 1970; Country Days, 1974; A Deadly Presence, 1982. *Contributions to:* Various South African newspapers. *Membership:* PEN. *Literary Agent:* Sheila Watson, London. *Address:* Seaford, Thesen Hill, Knysna (Box 54), Republic of South Africa 6570.

THESING, William B, b. 30 Dec. 1947, St Louis, Missouri, USA. College Professor. m. Jane Ann Isley, 17 July 1976, Bloomington, Indiana, USA, 1 daughter. *Education:* BA, University of Missouri-St Louis, 1969; MA 1970, PhD 1977, Indiana University, Bloomington. *Literary Appointments:* Associate Instructor of English, Indiana University, 1975–77; Instructor of English 1977–79, Assistant Professor 1979–83, Associate Professor of English 1983–, University of South Carolina. *Publications:* The London Muse: Victorian Poetic Responses to the City, 1982; English Prose and Criticism, 1900–1950: A Guide to Information Sources, (with Christopher C Brown), 1983. *Contributions to:* Victorian Poetry; Tennyson Research Bulletin; Journal of the 1890's Society; CLA Journal; Scottish Literary Journal; Modernist Studies; Turn of the Century Women. *Honours:* South Atlantic Modern Language Association Studies Award, 1980; American Council of Learned Societies Travel Grant Award, 1984. *Memberships:* Association for Scottish Literary Studies; College English Association; International Hopkins Association; Modern Language Association; National Council of Teachers of English; South Atlantic Modern Language Association; The Tennyson Society; Victorians Institute; Georgia-South Carolina College English Association; Vice President 1985, President 1986, Philological Association of the Carolinas. *Address:* Department of English, University of South Carolina, Columbia, SC 29208, USA.

THÉVOZ, Jacqueline, b. 29 Apr. 1926, Estavayer-le Lac, Switzerland. Writer. divorced, 2 daughters. *Education includes:* Conservatory of Music, Lausanne; Catholic Institute; University of Lausanne; Conservatory Lausanne-Paris, France. *Literary Appointments include:* Journalist various newspapers; Teacher, Ballet Pensionnat La Chassotte, Fribourg; Founder of Studio of Zaehringen, Studio du Théâtre de Fribourg, Centre de Choregraphie. *Publications include:* La Voix Humaine,

1955; Raison vagabonde, 1959; Petit traité de danse classique, 1971; Le Cheval, 1972; La Danse, 1972; Escales vers ma mort, 1974; Mimile, 1975; Jean Dawint, l'extraordinaire châtelain de Cernex, 1977; Le Château de Paradis, 1979; Le Prince au palais dormant, 1980; Maman-Soleil, 1980; Les Termites, 1982. *Contributions to:* Tribune de Lausanne; Femmes Suisses; Nouvelle Revue de Lausanne; La Suisse; Le Républicain; La Femme d'Aujourd'hui'; Espaces; Memento-Enfants. *Honours:* Knight, Silver Star at Arts International; Gold and Silver Medals, Academy International of Lutece, Academy Arts-Sciences-Letters; Prize, Academy des Treize; Follope Prize, Faculty of Letters, University of Lausanne, 1982; Honorary Doctorate, Cultural, Literary and Arts Centre of Felgueiras. *Memberships:* Founder, Movement for Return to Former Catholic Liturgy; Swiss delegate, International Academy of Lutéce, France; Vice President, Firbourg Society of Writers; Adherent Member, Society of Persons of Letters, France; Society of Swiss Writers; Geneva Society of Writers; Society for Musical Educational Science. *Address:* Lala, 38 Whitecroft Swanley, Kent BR8 7YH, England.

THIAGARAJAN, K, b. 30 Jan. 1950, Vellore, North Arcot District, India. Journalist; Educator. m. Vaidehi Thiagarajan, 12 Apr. 1984, 1 daughter. *Education:* BSc; PGDip, Journalism, Public Relations; DLitt, World University, USA; PhD, USA; DL; DH; FBIM, London; FMSPI, India; MZSI; FUWAI. Thesis: Heritage of Indian Art Through Several Ages. *Publication:* Gandhiji's Teachings. *Contributions:* Numerous articles and Letters to several journals and periodicals, over 10-15 years. *Honours include:* Presidential Award; Mahatma Gandhi Memorial Award; Naraindoss Memorial Award; Divine Life Society Award; NIF Best Contributors Award; NIF International Award; Jawaharlal Nehru Award, etc. *Memberships:* Fellow: Royal Asiatic Society, Columbo; British Institute of Management, London; Management Studies Promotion Institute, Delhi; United Writers Association of India. *Address:* 8 Warren Road, RR Flat 17-E, Mylapore, Madras – 600 004, India.

THIELE, Margaret, b. 16 May 1901, Michigan, USA. Librarian. m. 1 J Henry White, 15 Nov. 1921, 1 son (deceased) 2 daughters (1) deceased), (2) E R Thiele, 22 July 1962. *Education:* BA, MA, San Jose State College. *Publications:* Whirlwind of the Lord, 1954; By Saddle and Sleigh, 1963; None But The Nightingale, 1967; A Home for Sulon, 1971; Girl Alive, 1980. *Contributions to:* A series of articles to Life and Health magazine; other short subjects. *Honour:* Alpha Beta Alpha. *Address:* 245 Howell Mt Road, Angwin, CA 94508, USA.

THISTLE, Melville William, b. 22 Apr. 1914, St John's, Newfoundland, Canada. Professor of Journalism. m. Lauretta Jean Finlayson, 27 Sep. 1941, Ottawa, 2 daughters. *Education:* BSc 1st Class Honours Chemistry 1936, MA, Diploma to Teach in Nova Scotia 1938, Mount Allison University, Sackville, New Brunswick. *Literary Appointments:* Editor-in-Chief, Argosy Weekly, Sackville, New Brunswick, 1935–37; Founder with R E M Anderson, National Science Film Library of Canada, 1960; Consultant on History, National Research Council of Canada, 1965–75; Professor of Journalism, Carleton University, 1969–79. *Publications:* Peter The Sea Trout, 1954; Happy Journey, by R Fraser, editor, 1958; The Inner Ring, 1966; Time Touch Me Gently, 1970; The Mackenzie-Macnaughton Wartime Letters, 1975. *Contributions to:* 18 papers to various Canadian journals of research; 200 articles to various magazines including: Saturday Night; Family Herald, and Weekly Star; Food in Canada; Articles and reviews in, Bulletin of the Society on General Samantics; Paper, on ethics of communication, Revistade Occidente. *Honours:* 2nd prize for English Poetry in Canada, Centennial Commission, 1967; Canadian editor of Communication, 1976–. *Membership:* Canadian Authors Association. *Address:* 1476 Farnsworth Avenue, Ottawa, Ontario K1H 7C3, Canada.

THIVIERGE, Renée, b. 21 May 1942, Montréal, Canada. Information Agent. *Education:* MA Education Science, University of Montréal, Canada. *Literary Appointment:* Editor, Le Littéraire de Laval. *Major Publications:* L'homme du Jardin; Être dans ta Maison; J'ai cherché. *Contributor to:* Revue Intervention; Journal Le Village (Expo '76). *Memberships:* Société Littéraire de Laval; Québec Writers' Union; Association des Auteurs-Compositeurs du Canada. *Address:* 1380 Boulevard de la Concorde Ouest app 402, Laval, Québec, H7N 5P4, Canada.

THOMAE, Betty Jane, b. 9 Sep. 1920, Columbus, Ohio, USA. Legal Secretary; Poet; Writer; Songwriter. m. 1 son, 1 daughter. *Education:* Certificate Professional Secretary, 1964; Professional Legal Secretary, 1970. *Publications:* Roses and Thorns, 1970; Legal Secretary's Desk Book – With Forms, 1973; Legal Secretary's Encyclopedic Dictionary, Editor, 1977; Stand Still, Summer, 1985. *Contributor to:* 35 articles in professional journals and Sunday magazines; 150 poems in anthologies, magazines, newspapers, etc. *Honours:* Danae, International Clover Poetry Association; Diploma of Merit, Medal of Honour, centro Studi a Scambi of Rome; Citation of Honour, World Poetry Society; 2 Citations, International Clover Poetry Association; 1st Place, Writer's Contest for The Fall; Legal Secretary of the Year, Columbus Chapter, National Association of Legal Secretaries, 1970; Golden Poet Award, World of Poetry, 1985. *Memberships:* National Association of Legal Secretaries; ASCAP; World of Poetry; Authors Guild Inc; Authors League of America Inc; Verse Writers Guild of Ohio. *Address:* 1008 Hardesty Place West, Columbus, OH 43204, USA.

THOMAS, Arthur Lawrence, b. 8 July 1952, Cleveland, Ohio, USA. Teacher. *Education:* BA, Baldwin-Wallace College, Ohio; MA, Kent State University. *Publications:* Recreational Wrestling, 1976; Sports for Me, 12 titles in series, 1977–81; Theater Publicity Handbook, 1980; Merry-Go-Round Book, 1982. *Contributions to:* Westlife, Drama Critic, 1981–; Cleveland Plain Dealer Sunday Magazine; Cleveland Magazine, and others. *Honours:* Recognised by Childrens Book Council of Chicago, Illinois, 1981. *Memberships:* International Mensa; US Institute of Theater Technology; National Council of Teachers of English; American Film Institute and others. *Address:* 12500 Edgewater Drive 1601, Lakewood, OH 44107, USA.

THOMAS, Charles Robert, b. 8 Sep. 1944, Newcastle, New South Wales, Australia. Presbyterian Minister. m. Alison Rosemary Colvin, 17 May 1971, Hornsby, New South Wales, Australia, 1 son, 1 daughter. *Education:* Teacher's Certificate. *Appointments:* Editor, Australian Presbyterian Life. *Publication:* Evangelism and the Reformed Faith (Editor), 1980. *Address:* 2 Bellbird Crescent, Blaxland, New South Wales 2774, Australia.

THOMAS, Clara McCandless, b. 22 May 1919, Ontario, Canada. University Professor m. Morley Thomas, 23 May 1942, Winnipeg, 2 sons. *Education:* BA 1941, University of Western Toronto; MA 1944; PhD 1962, University of Western Toronto. *Literary Appointments include:* York University, Professor 1969, Professor Emeritus, 1984–. *Publications:* Canadian Novelists, 1946; Love and Work Enough The Life of Anna Jameson, 1967; Margaret Laurence, 1969; Ryerson of Upper Canada, 1969; Our Nature, Our Voices, 1972; The Manawaka World of Margaret Laurence, 1975; William Arthur Deacon: A Canadian Literary Life (with John Lennox), 1982. *Contributions to:* Canadian Literature; Journal of Canadian Studies; Etudes Canadiennes. *Honours:* Canada Council Grants, 1963, 1968, 1974; Social Science and Humanities Research Council Grant 1978, 1979; Fellow of the Royal Society of Canada, 1983. *Memberships:* Association of Canadian University Teachers of English; Writers' Union of Canada; Canadian Association of Commonwealth Language and Literature. *Address:* 15 Lewes Crescent, Toronto, Canada M4N 3J1.

THOMAS, David St John, b. 30 Aug. 1929, Romford, England. Publisher. m. Georgette Zackey, 9 Sep. 1979, Vermont, USA, 1 son, 1 daughter by 1st marriage. *Appointments:* Founder, Chairman, David & Charles Publishers and Readers Union Group of Book Clubs, David & Charles Inc, Vermont, USA. *Publications:* A Regional History of the Railways of Great Britain, Volume 1, The West Country, 1960, 5th edition 1981; A Guide to Writing & Publishing, 1973; The Country Railway, 1976; many others. *Contributor to:* numerous country transport magazines, journals; Columnist, The Western Morning News. *Address:* Hylton, 26 Keyberry Park, Newton Abbot, Devon TQ12 1DF, England.

THOMAS, Denis, b. 23 July, 1922, London, England. Author; Journalist. *Education:* BA, St Edmund Hall, Oxford University, England. *Publications:* Thomas Churchyard of Woodbridge, 1966; The Visible Persauders, 1967; Concise Encyclopaedia of Antiques, 1969; The Mind of Economic Man, 1970; English Watercolours, 1750–1900, 1971; The Impressionists, 1975; Picasso and His Art, 1975; Abstract Painting, 1976; The Face of Christ, 1979; Dictionary of Fine Arts, 1981. *Contributor to:* Connoisseur; Antique Collector; The Listener. *Honour:* Freeman, City of London. *Memberships:* Society of Authors; Institute of Journalists; Association of Art Historians. *Address:* Coach House, Oakwood Close, Chislehurst, Kent, England.

THOMAS, Edward Boaden, b. 1 Mar. 1901. Retired Research Chemist. *Education:* BSc, Birkbeck College, London University. *Publications:* The Twelve Parts of Derbyshire, 4 volumes, 1969–74; Anne Clifford, 1977. *Contributions to:* Time and Tide; The Observer; Punch. *Address:* Reighton Hill House, Ashleyhay, Wirksworth, Derbyshire DE4 4AJ, England.

THOMAS, Gordon, b. 21 Jan. 1933, Capel Seion, Drefach, Cann, England. Author. m. Edith Marie Kraner, 28 Sep. 1970, London, 1 son, 1 daughter. *Appointments:* Foreign Correspondent, Daily Express, Middle East, South Africa, Korea, 1953–59; Daily Mail Diarist, 1959–61; Screenwriter, MGM, 20th Century Fox, Paramount, 1961–64; BBC Television Director and Producer, 1964–69. *Publications include:* The Day Their World Ended, 1966 (with Max Morgan Witts); The San Francisco Earthquake, 1968, (with Max Morgan Witts); Shipwreck the Strange Fate of the Morro Castle, 1971, (with Max Morgan Witts); Issels: The Biography of a Doctor, 1973, (with Max Morgan Witts); Voyage of the Damned, 1974, (with Max Morgan Witts); Guernica: The Crucible of World War Two, 1975, (with Max Morgan Witts); Enoca Gay, 1977, with Max Morgan Witts; The Day the Bubble Burst, 1979; Trauma, 1981, (with Max Morgan Witts); Pontiff, 1982, (with Max Morgan Witts); The Year of Armageddon, 1983, (with Max Morgan Witts): The Operation, 1984; Desire and Deniac, 1986. *Contributor to:* Daily Express; Sunday Express; Sunday Independent, Association of Press of America; Contributing author, Readers Digest, 1964–; Detroit Free Press; Rand Daily Mail; Diario 16 (Spain); The Australian; New York Post; Chicago Sun-Times; Irish Times. *Honours:* Critics Prize, VII International Festival, Monte Carlo, 1968; Edgar Allen Poe Award, 1972. *Literary Agent:* Jonathan Clowes Limited. *Address:* The Old Rectory, Ashford, Co Wicklow, Republic of Ireland.

THOMAS, Graham Charles Gordon, b. 20 Jan. 1942, Cardiff, Wales. Senior Assistant Archivist, National Library of Wales. *Education:* MA, University College of Wales, Cardiff, Wales. *Contributions to:* Y Drysorfa; Bulletin of the Board of Celtic Studies; National Library of Wales Journal; Economica; Scottish Slavonic Review. *Memberships:* Society of Archivists; Powysland Club; International Courtly Literary Society; Associate, Library Association. *Address:* Bryn Alaw, Banadl Road, Aberystwyth, Dyfed, Wales.

THOMAS, Graham Stuart, b. 3 Apr. 1909, Cambridge, England. Horticulturist. *Education:* Horticultural Training, Cambridge University Botanic Gardens. *Publications:* The Old Shrub Roses, 1955; Colour in the Winter Garden, 1957; Shrub Roses of Today, 1962; Climbing Roses Old & New, 1965; Plants for Ground Cover, 1970; Perennial Garden Plants, 1976; Gardens of the National Trust, 1979; Three Gardens, 1983; Trees in the Landscape, 1983; The Art of Planting, 1984; Recreating the Period Garden, General Editor, 1984. *Contributor to:* Royal Horticultural Society Journal; Royal National Rose Society Annual; Horticultural Press. *Honours:* Veitch Memorial Medal, 1966; Vic, Medal of Honour, 1968; OBE, 1975; Dean Hole Medal, 1976. *Memberships include:* Committee, Garden Historical Society. *Address:* Briar Cottage, 21 Kettlewell Close, Horsell, Woking, Surrey GU21 4HY, England.

THOMAS, Michael Charles, b. 10 Mar. 1946, Bullamakanka. Screenwriter. m. Camilla Rose Wigan, Singapore, 8 Jan. 1977, 2 sons. *Education:* University of Sydney, Australia (no degree). *Publications:* Babylon on a Thin Wire, 1979; Jah Revenge, 1982. *Contributions to:* Life; Look; Esquire; Rolling Stone (Caribbean editor); Harpers; Playboy. *Literary Agent:* Fraser & Dunlop. *Address:* 91 Regent Street, London W1, England.

THOMAS, Paul, b. 18 July 1908, Meloor, Kerala, India. Writer. m. Rose Varkey, 24 Jan. 1946, New Delhi, 1 son, 1 daughter. *Education:* Diploma in Railway Training. *Literary Appointments:* Assistant editor, Indian Literary Review; Managing Director, Horizon Publishers Limited; Publisher, Anglo-Malayalam Weekly, Kaalam; Editor, Orient Times, Kerala Shahitya Akademi's English Journal Malayalam Literary Survey. *Publications:* Women and Marriage in India, 1939; Epics Myths and Legends of India, 1941; Hindu Religion, 1946; Christianity in India, 1954; Kama Kalpa, 1956; Kama Katha, 1969; Festivals and Holidays of India, 1971; Secrets of Sorcery Spells and Pleasure Cults of India, 1982; The Death of a Harijan, 1984. *Contributions to:* World Book Encyclopedia; Illustrated Weekly of India; Sunday Standard; March of India and others; Columnist, Kaalam, Kerala Chronicle and others. *Memberships:* President, Kala Sadan; Patron, Sahridaya Vedi; Sahridaya Samithi; Authors Guild of India; Vice President, Christian Cultural Museum, Diocese of Trichur. *Address:* V1/359 East Fort, Trichur 680 005, Kerala, India.

THOMAS, William, LeRoy, b. 18 Mar. 1920, Long Beach, California, USA. University Professor of Geography and Southeast Asian Studies. *Education:* BA 1941, MA 1948, University of California at Los Angeles, PhD, Yale University, 1951. *Publications include:* Current Anthropology, (editor), 1956; Land Man and Culture in Mainland Southeast Asia, 1957; Cultural Geography: An Evolutionary Introduction to Our Humanized Earth, (with J E Spencer), 1969; Asia, East by South: A Cultural Geography, (with J E Spencer), 2nd edition 1971; Paths to Asia: Asian Studies at Australian Universities, 1974; Introducing Cultural Geography, (with J E Spencer), 2nd edition 1978. *Contributions to:* Various professional journals. *Honour:* Citation for Meritorious Contribution to the Field of Geography, for organising and editing, Man's Role in Changing the Face of the Earth, and, Man, Time and Space in Southern California, Association of American Geographers, 1961. *Memberships include:* Association of American Geographers; Association for Asian Studies; Pacific Science Association; American Geographical Society. *Address:* Geography Department, California State University, Hatward, CA 94542, USA.

THOMEY, Tedd, b. 19 July 1920, Butte, Montana, USA. Journalist; Author. m. Patricia Natalie Bennett, 11 Dec. 1943, Manassas, Virginia, 1 daughter. *Education:* BA, University of California, 1943. *Literary Appointments include:* Publicity Director, San Diego State College, California, 1941–42; Reporter, San Diego Union-Tribune, 1942; Reporter, Assistant Editorial Promotion Manager, San Francisco Chronicle, 1942–43, 45-58; News Editor, Columnist, Long Beach Press-Telegram, 1950–; Creative Writing Instructor, Long Beach City College; Guest lecturer, University of Southern California; Consultant, 20th Century Fox

Studies. *Publications:* And Dream of Evil, 1954; Jet Pilot, 1955; Killer in White, 1956; Jet Ace, 1958; I Want Out, 1959; Flight to Takla-Ma, 1961; The Loves of Errol Flynn, Biography, 1961; The Sadist, 1961; Doris Day, biography, 1962; All The Way, 1964; The Glorious Decade, 1971. Co-Author: The Big Love, biography, 1961; Hollywood Uncensored, 1965; Hollywood Confidential, 1967; The Comedians, 1970. *Contributions to:* US, Canadian and Foreign magazines and biographies of film and television personalities to national magazines. *Honours:* 1st place for distinguished newspaper feature writing, Theta Sigma Phi Journalism Society Contest, 1952; Award for Best Front Page, California Newspaper Publishers. *Literary Agent:* Scott Meredith, New York. *Address:* 7228 Rosebay Street, Long Beach, CA 90808, USA.

THOMPSON, Edgar Tristram, b. 13 Sep. 1900, Little Rock, South Carolina, USA. Teaching. m. Alma Louise Mary, 15 June 1929, Richmond, Indiana, 1 daughter. *Education:* AB, University of South Carolina, 1922; MA, University of Missouri, 1924; PhD, University of Chicago, 1932. *Appointments:* Professor of Sociology, Duke University, 1935–70; Fellowship, Rhodes University, Grahamstown, South Africa, 1956. *Publications:* Race Relations and the Race Problem, 1939; Race: Individual and Collective Behavior, 1958; Race and Region, 1970; Plantation Societies, Race Relations and the South, 1975; The Plantation: An International Bibliography, 1983. *Contributor to:* Agricultural History; American Journal of Sociology; Social Forces. *Memberships:* American Sociological Society; North Carolina Sociological Society. *Address:* 512 Baldwin Road, Richmond, VA 23229, USA.

THOMPSON, Henry Orrin, b. 23 Oct. 1931, Northwood, Iowa, USA. Teacher; Clergyman. m. Joyce Elaine Beebe, 15 June 1980, Owosso, Michigan, 2 sons from previous marriage. *Education:* BS, Iowa State University, 1953; MDiv, 1958, PhD, 1964, Drew University; MS, Education, Syracuse University, 1971; MA, Educational Psychology 1975, Diploma, School Psychology 1976, Jersey City State College; Graduate study, Rutgers University, 1978–80; Diploma, Institute for Personal & Family Relations, 1977. *Publications include:* Approaches to the Bible, 1967; Mekal, 1970; Archaeology & Archaeologists, 1972; Hidden & Revealed, 1973; Ethics in Nursing (with J E Thompson), 1981; Bioethical Decision Making for Nurses (with J E Thompson), 1985. Editor, other theological works. *Contributions to:* Biblical Archaeologist; Archaeology; Christianity Today; Journal of Ecumenical Studies; Antiquity; Negro History Bulletin; Australian Journal of Biblical Archaeology; Bulletin of the American Schools of Oriental Research; etc. *Address:* 7 University Mews, Philadelphia, PA 19104, USA.

THOMPSON, Ian Bentley, b. 2 Jan. 1936, Dewsbury, Yorkshire, England. University Professor. m. Hélène Lamérant, 11 July 1961, Douai, France, 4 daughters. *Education:* BA, Durham University; MA, Indiana University; PhD, Durham University. *Literary Appointment:* Editor: Croom Helm Industrial Geography Series, 1982–. *Publications:* Modern France 1970; Corsica 1971; Paris Basin 1973; La France, 1973; France: A Geographical Study 1973; The Lower Rhone and Marseille, 1975. *Contributor to:* Numerous magazines and journals. *Honour:* Chevalier dans l'Ordre des Palmes Académiques. *Address:* Department of Geography, The University, Glasgow G12 8QQ, Scotland.

THOMPSON, Jesse Jackson, b. 26 July 1919, Sanger, California, USA. Professor Emeritus, Communicative Disorders. m. Clara Lucile Roy, 4 Feb. 1945, Aberdeen Proving Ground, Maryland, 3 sons, 1 daughter. *Education:* BA, Santa Barbara State College, 1941; M Sc Education 1947, PhD 1957, University of Southern California. *Publications:* Talking Time, (coauthor), 1951, 2nd edition 1966; Speech Ways, (coauthor), 1955; Phonics in Listening, Speaking, Reading and Writing, (co-author), 1962; Rhymes for Fingers and Flannelboards, 1962 and 1984; Say and Sing, record albums, 1956; When a Child Speaks, filmstrip with

sound, 1962; Children with Learning Disorders, video film, author-narrator, 1983. *Contributions to:* California Parent Teacher; The Instructor; Western Speech; The Voice; Grade Teacher. *Honours:* Phi Kappa Phi Lecturer, California State University, Long Beach; Honours of the Association, California Speech and Hearing Association, 1980. *Memberships:* Fellow, American Speech, Language and Hearing Association. *Address:* 13282 Cedar Street, Westminster, CA 92683, USA.

THOMPSON, Julian Francis, b. 16 Nov. 1927, New York City, USA. Author. m. Polly Nichy, 11 Aug. 1978, South Dartmouth, Massachusetts. *Education:* BA, Princeton University; MA, Columbia University. *Publications:* The Grounding of Group 6, 1983; Facing It, 1983; A Question of Survival, 1984; Discontinued, 1985; A Band of Angels, 1986. *Memberships:* The Author's Guild; The Author's League of America. *Literary Agent:* Curtis Brown Ltd, 575 Madison Avenue, New York, NY 10022, USA. *Address:* PO Box 138, West Rupert, VT 05776, USA.

THOMPSON, Kenneth W, b. 29 Aug. 1921, Des Moines, Iowa, USA. Educator; Author. m. Beverly C Thompson, 3 sons, 1 daughter. *Education:* BA, PhD, University of Chicago. *Literary Appointments:* Northwestern University; University of Chicago; University of California, Berkeley; Columbia University; Rockefeller Foundation; University of Virginia. *Publications:* Political Realism and the Crisis of World Politics, 1952; Ethics and the Dilemmas of Foreign Policy, 1958; American Diplomacy and Emergent Patterns, 1959; Foreign Assistance, 1961; Ethics, Punctionalism and Power, 1978; Morality and Foreign Policy, 1981; Masters of International Thought, 1982; President and Public Philosophy, 1985; Winston Churchill's World View, 1984; Moralism and Morality, 1984; Toynbee's Philosophy of International Relations, 1985. *Contributions to:* Many journals of political thought including: Review of Politics; International Studies; Journal of Politics; American Political Scene Review; Reporter Magazine. *Honours:* 9 Honorary Doctorates; University of Chicago Medal, 1974; Virginia Laureate, 1978; Phi Beta Kappa Annual Prize, 1983; Virginia Book Store Award, 1983. *Memberships:* American Academy of Arts and Sciences; American Political Science Association. *Address:* Director, Miller Center Public Affairs, PO Box 5707, University of Virginia, Charlottesville, VA 22905, USA.

THOMPSON, Laurence G, b. 9 July 1920, China. Professor of East Asian Languages and Cultures. m. Grace Russell, 29 May 1943, Boulder, Colorado, USA, 3 sons, 2 daughters. *Education:* AB, University of California at Los Angeles, 1942; MA, 1947, PhD, 1954, Claremont Graduate School, California. *Publications:* Ta T'ung Shu: the One-World Philosophy of K'ang Yu-wei, 1958; German edition 1974; Chinese Religion: an Introduction, 3rd edition 1979; The Chinese Way in Religion, 1973; Studia Asiatica, (festschrift for Professor S Y Ch'en), 1975; Studies of Chinese Religion, 1976; Chinese Religion in Western Languages, (bibliography of Western-language publications through 1980–1985). *Contributor to:* Major papers include: P'eng-hu in mid-Ch'ing times according to the P'eng-hu Chi Lueh of Hu Chien-wei, Monumenta Serica XXX 1972/73; Chinese Religion, Encyclopedia Britannica 15th edition 1974; Obiter dicta on Chinese religion as play, Transactions of First International Sinological Conference, Academia Sinica, Taipei, 1981; The moving finger writes: a note on revelation and renewal in Chinese religion, Journal of Chinese Religions X; 1982. *Address:* 5515 Medea Valley Drive, Agoura Hills, CA 91301, USA.

THOMPSON, Neil, b. 19 Mar. 1929, Ceduna, West Coast, South Australia, Australia. Writer. m. Valma Ruth Byars, 8 Oct. 1955, Adelaide, 1 son, 1 daughter. *Education:* BA, Adelaide University; MA, Flinders University. *Literary Appointments:* Teacher, Primary Schools; English Teacher, High School; English Teacher and Inspector, Migrant English Classes, South Australia; Lecturer, English and Creative Writing, Flinders

University and STURT College of Advanced Education/Teachers College. *Publications:* Shadow on the Sea, 1965; Ride the Hurricane In, 1966; Ask the Wind, Ask the Sea, 1967, German and Norwegian Editions; Storm North, 1967; Elliston Incident, 1969; Written Communication, 1971; Southern Backwash, 1968; Cocos Deadline, 1972; Hiri, 1975, translated into Swedish; Colour and Chaos, 1976; Write Now, 1981; Cruising Gulfs Log, 1984; Meg Merrilees Sea Foods, Cookbook, with Val Thompson, 1985. *Contributions to:* Numerous professional journals and others. *Address:* 44 Marlborough Street, Brighton, SA 5048, Australia.

THOMPSON, Paul, b. 23 Nov. 1943, Hitchin, Hertfordshire, England. Institute Head of Directing and Playwriting. m. Veronique Bernard, 14 Feb. 1981, Paris, France, 1 daughter by previous marriage. *Education:* Actors Workshop, London, England, 1963–64; Stanislavsky Institute, London, 1964. *Literary Appointments:* Tutor in Playwriting, City Literary Institute, London, England, 1980–84; Lecturer in Playwriting, Artists University, London, 1980–84; Head, Directing and Playwriting, National Institute of Dramatic Art, University of New South Wales, Australia, 1984–. *Publications:* The Children's Crusade, 1975; The Motor Show, 1976; By Common Consent, 1976; The Lorenzaccio Story, 1978. *Honours:* Awards and bursaries, Arts Council of Great Britain, 1984, 87. *Memberships:* Theatre Writers Union; Writers Guild of Great Britain. *Literary Agent:* Michael Imison Playwrights, London. *Address:* c/o National Institute of Dramatic Art, University of New South Wales, P O Box 1, Kensington, NSW 2033, Australia.

THOMPSON, Roger Francis, b. 24 Oct. 1933, London, England. University Reader. m. Kathleen Hoey, 19 June 1963, Lakeville, Connecticut, USA, 1 son, 2 daughters. *Education:* MA, Oxon. *Publications:* The Golden Door, 1969; Women in Stuart England and America, 1974; Samuel Pepy's Penny Merriments, 1976; Contrast and Connection, with H C Allen, Editors, 1976; Unfit for Modest Ears, 1979; The Witches of Salem, 1982. *Contributor to:* Articles and Reviews in British and American historical journals. *Honour:* Fellow, Royal Historical Society, 1983. *Literary Agent:* Curtis Brown Academic. *Address:* School of English & American Studies, University of East Anglia, Norwich, Norfolk, England.

THOMPSON, Vivian L, b. 7 Jan. 1911, New Jersey, USA. Writer; Retired Teacher. m. Daniel Thompson, 17 Mar. 1951, Paauilo, Hawaii, USA. *Education:* BS, Education, MA, Guidance, Teachers College, Columbia University; Maren Elwood School of Professional Writing, Hollywood; Private Study in Juvenile Fiction, Odessa Davenport. *Literary Appointments:* Hawaii Island Library Advisory Commission; Delegate to First Governor's Conference on Libraries. *Publications:* 15 books for children including: Camp-In-The-Yard, 1961; Sad Day, Glad Day, 1962; Hawaiian Legends of Tricksters and Riddlers, 1969; Maui-Full-Of-Tricks, 1970; Hawaiian Tales of Heroes and Champions, 1971; Aukele The Fearless, 1972; The Protected One, 1981. 3 plays published: Keola's Hawaiian Donkey, 1982; Neat! Said Jeremy, 1982; The Scary Thing – Snatcher, 1982. 3 additional plays produced (Hawaiian folklore, fairy tale). *Contributions to:* Child Life; Jack and Jill, Humpty Dumpty's Magazine; Children's Activities; Highlights for Children; World Youth; Scholastic Magazines; Weekly Reader. *Honours:* Citation for, Sad Day, Glad Day, from New Jersey Associaton of Teachers of English, 1963; Junior Literary Guild Selection – Camp-In-The-Yard, 1961; Outstanding Achievement in Literature Award, YWCA, 1984. *Memberships:* Honorary Member, International Mark Twain Society; Authors Guild; Dramatists Guild. *Address:* 936, Kumukoa Street, Hilo, HI 96720, USA.

THOMSON, David, b. 17 Feb. 1914, Quetta, India. Writer. m. Martina Mayne, London, 3 sons. *Education:* BA, Oxford. *Publications:* The People of the Sea, 1954, 5th edition 1984; Daniel, 1962; Break in the Sun, 1965; Woodbrook, 1974, 6th edition 1984; Irish Journals of

Elizabeth Smith, (editor), 1980; The Leaping Hare, (with George Ewart Evans), 1972, 3rd edition 1974; Dandiprats Days, 1983; In Camden Town, 1983; For Children: Danny Fox, 1966, 6th edition 1976; Danny Fox Meets a Stranger, 1968, 4th edition 1975; Danny Fox at the Palace, 1976; Ronan and Other Stories, 1984.*Membership:* Fellow, Royal Society of Literature. *Address:* 22 Regents Park Terrace, London NW1, England.

THOMSON, June, b. 24 June 1930, Kent, England. Writer. Divorced, 2 sons. *Education:* BA, Honours, English, London University. *Publications:* Not One of Us, 1972; Death Cap, 1973; The Long Revenge, 1974; Case Closed, 1977; A Question of Identity, 1978; Deadly Relations, 1979; Alibi in Time, 1980; Shadow of a Doubt, 1981; To Make a Killing, 1982; Sound Evidence, 1984; A Dying Fall, 1985. *Contributor to:* Ellery Queen Magazine; Writers Monthly. *Honour:* Prix Du Roman d'Adventures, 1983. *Memberships:* Crime Writers' Association, Committee Member; The Detective Club; PEN. *Literary Agent:* Tessa Sayle, London. *Address:* c/o Constable & Co. Ltd., 10 Orange Street, London WC2 H7EG, England.

THORBURN, James Alexander, b. 24 Aug. 1923, Professor of English. m. June Yingling, 18 Apr. 1981, Hammond, Louisiana. *Education:* BA 1949, MA 1951, Ohio State University; PhD Linguistics, Louisiana State University, 1977. *Appointments:* Surveyor, Field Artillery, World War 2; Surveyor, International Boundary & Water Commission, US & Mexico; Head of English Department, Sheridan Rural Agricultural School, Michigan; Instructor in English, University of Missouri; Monmouth College, Illinois, Texas Western College; Instructor in English & in Charge English Programme, University of Missouri in St Louis; Instructor in English, Louisiana State University, 1961–70-. Assistant Professor of English, Southeastern Louisiana University, 1970–. *Memberships:* Avalon World Arts Asociation; Experimental Group, Modern Poetry Association (formerly); American Name Society; Phi Kappa Phi; National Council of Teachers of English; Conference of College Composition & Communication; American Association of University Professors; Book Review Editor, Experiment: An International Review; Linguistic Society of America; Linguistic Association of the Southwest; American Dialect Society. *Honours:* Sigma Delta Pi; Phi Mu Alpha Sinfonia (Music, 1985). *Contributor to:* Numerous periodicals & anthologies, including: National Poetry Anthology, 1960; Spring Anthology, 1967–69; Ardentia Verba, 1967; Laudamus Te, 1967; Poetry Dial Anthology, 1968; The Prairie Poet; Poetry Digest; Cyclotron; Flame; The Church School; Discourse; Haiku Highlights; Writers Digest; Cardinal Poetry Quarterly; Poet Lore; Translator of several Old Portuguese & Old Provencal Lyrics into modern English verse, Beowulf into modern English verse. *Address:* Box 739, Department of English, Southeastern Louisiana University, Hammond, LA 70402, USA.

THORELLI, Hans B, b. 18 Sep. 1921, Newark, New Jersey, USA. Professor of Business Administration. m. Sarah Virginia Scott, 14 May 1948, Stockholm, Sweden, 1 son, 1 daughter. *Education:* MA, 1944, LLB 1945, PhD, 1954, University of Stockholm. *Publications:* The Federal Anti-trust Policy: Origination of an American Tradition, 1955; International Operations Simulation (INTOP), 1964; Consumer Information Handbook: Europe and North America, 1974; The Information Seekers: An International Study of Consumer Information and Advertising Image, 1975; Consumer Information System and Consumer Policy, 1977; Structure + Strategy = Performance: The Strategic Planning Imperative, 1977; International Marketing Strategy 1973 and 1980: Consumer Emancipation and Economic Development, 1982. *Contributions to:* Editorial Board of the: International Marketing Review, Industrial Marketing Management Journal, Journal of Consumer Policy (Stuttgart), Journal of International Business Studies; over 60 Articles in various journals. *Honours:* E W Kelley Professorship, Indiana University, 1970–; Fellowships from the Ford Foundation, Rocker Feller Foundation;

General Electric Foundation Research Grants; Fallbeck Foundation Medal for Outstanding Treatise; Research Awards from Midwest Universities International Consortium, Hitachi Ltd. *Address:* 9250 North Buskirk Road, Gosport, IN 47433, USA.

THORHALLSSON, Thorhall, b. 9 Sep. 1946, Reykjavik, Iceland. General Manager; Writer. m. Theodora Emils, 17 May 1975, 1 son, 1 daughter. *Education:* Commercial School of Iceland. *Publications:* Translation, Peter the Fox, K Tellerup, 1978; Stay/before, poems, 1982; The Story of the Water-Basin & other Stories for Children, audio-cassette, 1984; Winter Anxiety, poems, 1984. *Contributions to:* A Review for Everything. *Membership:* Writers Association of Iceland. *Address:* Reynimelur 80, 107 Reykjavik, Iceland.

THORNTON, Donald Ray, b. 15 Dec. 1936, Winnsboro, Louisiana, USA. Educator. m. Suzannah Smith, 3 June 1961, 1 son, 1 daughter. *Education:* BA, Louisiana Polytechnic University; MA, Fine Arts, Louisiana State University; Certification in Gifted Education. *Publications:* Outcry, 1960; Sounding, 1976; A Walk on Water, 1905. *Contributions to:* Travois; Ellensburg Anthology; The Black Creek Review; The Pawn River Review; Poetry Texas; The Southwestern Review; Still; Texas Portfolio; Nexus; Cedar Rock; Dark Horse; The New York Smith; Poetic Images; The Poet; Art Beat; Mind in Motion; Crab Creek Review; Sucking on Rattlesnake Bones; Museum of Haiku Literature, Tokyo, Japan. *Honour:* Presently being nominated for Poet Laureate of Louisiana. *Literary Agent:* Bill Armentor, Cajub Publishing. *Address:* 1504 Howard Street, New Iberia, LA 70560, USA.

THORNTON, Jean Frances, b. 19 Nov. 1926, Keighley, England. Principal Tutor in Creative Writing. *Education:* BA, Honours, La Trobe University, Melbourne, Australia, 1977. *Contributions to:* Magazines & Newspapers. Editor, Luna. *Memberships:* Australian Society of Authors; Fellowship of Australian Writers; PEN. *Address:* 43 Railway Place, Williamstown, Victoria 3016, Australia.

THORNTON, John William, b. 7 May 1948, Philadelphia, Pennsylvania, USA. Local Government Administrator. m. Arlie Terry, 17 Aug. 1975, Pensacola, Florida, 1 son, 1 daughter. *Education:* BA Political Science, Pennsylvania State University, 1970; Master of Public Administration, University of West Florida, 1972. *Publications:* Believed To Be Alive (with Captain John W Thornton), 1981. *Contributions to:* Virginia Review. *Honours:* George Washington Honor Medal, The Freedoms Foundation at Valley Forge, Pennsylvania, 1982. *Address:* P O Box 27032, Richmond, VA 23273, USA.

THORPE, James, b. 17 Aug. 1915, Aiken, South Carolina, USA. Literary Research Scholar. m. Elizabeth McLean Daniells, 19 July, 1941, Toledo, Ohio, USA, 2 sons, 1 daughter. *Education:* AB The Citadel, 1936; MA, University of North Carolina, 1937; PhD, Harvard University, Cambridge Massachusetts, 1941. *Literary Appointments:* Professor of English, Princeton University, New Jersey, USA, 1946–66; Director, Huntington Library, Art Gallery and Botanical Gardens, 1966–83; Senior Research Associate, Huntington Library, 1966–. *Major Publications:* Principles of Textual Criticism, 1972; Gifts of Genius: Treasures of the Huntington Library, 1980; A Word to the Wise, 1982; John Milton: The Inner Life, 1983. *Honours:* Guggenheim Fellow, 1949–50, 1965–66; Honorary Degrees: DLitt, LLD, LHD, HHD. *Memberships:* American Antiquarian Society; American Academy of Arts & Sciences; American Philosophical Society. *Address:* Huntington Library, San Marino, CA 91108, USA.

THORSTEINSSON, Ragnar, b. 5 Sep. 1908, Isafjörour, Iceland. Bank Employee. *Education:* Captain, Fishing & Cargo Vessels. *Major Publications:* Novels: Vikingablod, 1951; Ormur i Hjarta, 1960; Morgunrodi, 1962; Thad Gefur a Batinn, 1970; Upp A Lif Og Dauda, 1972; Skjotradur Skipstjori, 1973; Med horkunni hafa

their tad, 1976; Lifid er Saltfiskur; Elias Palsson, (biography), 1977; Floskuskeytid, 1977; Skipstjorinn Okkar Er Kona, 1978. *Contributor to:* Vikan; Heima Er Bezt; Vikingur. *Memberships:* Writers Association of Iceland. *Honours:* Hon Prize, Icelandic Writers; Association; 1st Prize, Short Story Competiton in Vikingur, The Sailors' Monthly. *Address:* Brekkubbraut 21, Akranes, Iceland.

THROWER, Percy John, b. 30 Jan 1913, Winslow, Bucks, England. Horticulturist. *Education:* National Diploma in Horticulture. *Publications:* In Your Garden Week by Week, 1959; Encyclopaedia of Gardening, 1962; In Your Greenhouse, 1963; Every Day Gardening, 1969; Vegetables and Herbs from Your Garden, 1974; Vegetables and Fruit, 1977. *Contributor to:* Amateur Gardening; Daily Mail; Blue Peter, BBC TV. *Honours:* Association of Honorary Royal Horticultural Society; Victoria Medal of Honour; MBE, 1985. *Memberships:* Royal Horticultural Society. *Address:* The Magnolias, Bomere Heath, Shrewsbury, England.

THUBRON, Colin Gerald Dryden, b. 14 June 1939, London, England. Author. *Publications:* Mirror to Damascus, 1967; The Hills of Adonis, 1968; Jerusalem, 1969; Journey Into Cyprus, 1975; The God in the Mountain, 1977; Emperor, 1978; The Royal Opera House, 1982; Among the Russians, 1983; A Cruel Madness, 1984. *Contributions to:* Sunday Telegraph; The Times; Times Literary Supplement; Departures; Granta. *Honours:* Fellow, Royal Society of Literature, 1969; Silver Pen Award, 1984. *Membership:* Fellow 1969, Councillor 1982, PEN. *Address:* c/o William Heinemann Ltd, 10 Upper Grosvenor Street, London W1, England.

THUM, Gladys Ethel, b. 9 Nov. 1920, St Louis, Missouri, USA. English Professor. *Education:* BA, Journalist, MA, English, Washington University, St Louis, Missouri; Graduate work, English and Comparative Education, University of California, Berkeley; PhD, Communications, Education, St Louis University, Missouri. *Publications:* The Persuaders, (co-author with Marcella Thum), 1972; reprint, Persuasion and Propaganda, 1974; Bias Against Women in American Educational History, (dissertation), 1975; Exploring Military America, (co-author Marcella Thum), 1982; Airlift, (co-author Marcella Thum), 1986. *Contributor to:* Educational Horizons, 1977; Teaching the Middle Ages, (book of essays), 1982. *Literary Agent:* Eleanor Wood, Blassingame, McCaulley and Wood. *Address:* 6507 Gramond Drive, St Louis, MO 63123, USA.

THUM, Marcella, b. St Louis, Missouri, USA. Author. *Education:* MA, Webster College, St Louis, Missouri; MLA, University of California, Berkeley, USA. *Major Publications:* Mystery at Crane's Landing, 1964; The Persuaders: Propaganda in War & Peace, 1972; Exploring Black America, 1975; Exploring Literary America, 1979; Exploring Military America, 1982; Airlift: The Story of Military Airlift Command, 1986; The White Rose, 1980; Blazing Star, 1983; Jasmine, 1984; Wild Laurel, 1985. *Honours:* Several awards for books. *Memberships:* St Louis Writers Guild, Past President; Missouri Writers Guild; Romance Writers of America. *Literary Agent:* Eleanor Woods. *Address:* 6507 Gramond Drive, St Louis, MO 63123, USA.

THURSTON, Harry Kenneth, b. 3 Mar. 1950, Yarmouth, Nova Scotia, Canada. Writer; Freelance Journalist; Poet; Editor. m. Catherine Mary Rideout, 1 July 1972, 1 daughter. *Education:* BS, Biology. *Literary Appointments:* Editor, Publisher, Germination, A Hotbed of Verse Culture, 1977–82; Contributing editor, Equinox, 1984–. *Publications:* Barefaced Stone, 1980; Clouds Flying Before the Eye, 1985. *Contributions to:* Poetry: The Canadian Forum; The Fiddlehead; Dalhousie Review; Grain; Prism International, and others. Articles: Atlantic Insight; Audubon; Canadian Art; Equinox; National Geographic; Harrowsmith; Readers Digest, and others. *Honours:* Authors Award for Personality Profile, 1982; Authors Award for Public Affairs, 1982; Silver Medal, National Magazine Award for Science and Technology, 1983. *Memberships:* Writers Federation of Nova Scotia, Writers Council; Canadian League of Poets; Periodical Writers Association of Canada. *Address:* RR3, Southampton, Nova Scotia, Canada BOM IWO.

TIAINEN, Arja Riitta Hannele, b. 19 Oct. 1947, Seinäjoki, Finland. Writer. m. Usko Tuukko, 12 Nov. 1968, Helsinki, 1 son. (legally separated). *Publications:* Nukun silmat auki (poems), 1971; Suomi go go (novel), 1974; Palava susi (poems), 1977; Sastanan tytar (poems), 1977; Vallan Casanovat (poems), 1979; Isolde pakolainen (poems), 1981; Kalastaje Merlin (poems), 1982; Tuhkimo ja Mefisto (novel), 1983. *Contributions:* Columns and Book Reviews to several papers and dramatizations for television. *Honour:* State Prize, 1983. *Memberships:* Union of Finnish Critics; PEN Club; Association of Finnish Writers. *Literary Agent:* WSOY/V, Helsinki. *Address:* Liisankuja 2 B 30, 02230 Espoo, Finland.

TIBBETTS, Orlando Lailer, b. 9 Apr. 1919, Portland, Maine, USA. Clergyman. m. Phyllis Mae Jones, 25 June 1951, Chelsea, Massachusetts, 2 sons, 2 daughters. *Education:* BA, Gordon College; MDiv, Andover Newton Theology; STM, DMin, Andover Newton Theology; Honorary DD, Rio Grande College. *Literary Appointments:* Editor, Connecticut Baptist Magazine, 1970–81; Adjunct Professor, Writings of Miguel de Unamuno, Eastern Baptist Theological Seminary, 1981; Lecturer, Maine Writers Conference, 1983. *Publications:* The Reconciling Community, 1969; Sidewalk Prayers, 1971; More Sidewalk Prayers, 1973; The Work of Church Trustees, 1979; How to Keep Useful Church Records, 1983; The Ministers Handbook, 1986. *Contributions to:* Christian Century; Foundation Magazine; Connecticut Baptist Magazine; Upper Room Discipline; Faith for Our Times, 1973. *Honour:* Best Selling Book Award, Judson Press, 1981. *Literary Agent:* Judson Press, Valley Forge, Pennsylvania. *Address:* Box 1601, Manchester, CT 06040, USA.

TICKELL, Renée Oriana, b. 23 July 1906, London, England. Freelance Writer; British Council Officer. *Education:* BA, MA, St Hugh's College, Oxford. *Publications:* Neopolitan Ice, 1928; Immortal John, 1932; The Holy Hunger, 1935; Pan Caesar and God, 1938; Hilaire Belloc, 1953; 1958; The Hidden Springs, 1961, 1973; Philosopher King a Life of Benedict XIV, 1970; The Seeing Eye the Seeing I, 1976; The Society for Psychical Research 1882–1982, 1982. *Contributor to:* Blackfriars; Contemporary Review; Month; Punch; Tablet; Time and Tide; Times Literary Supplement; Twentieth Century; Christian Parapsychologist; various Dutch, French and USA periodicals; various anthologies etc. Editor, Journal and Proceedings, Society for Psychical Research. *Literary Agent:* AM Heath Ltd. *Address:* Garden Flat, 41 Springfield Road, London NW8 OQJ, England.

TICKLE, Phyllis A, b. 12 Mar. 1934, Johnson City, Tennessee, USA. Writer. m. Dr Samuel M Tickle, 17 June 1955, 3 sons, 4 daughters. *Education:* BA, East Tennessee State University; MA, Furman University. *Literary Appointments:* Poet-in-Residence, Memphis Brooks Museum, 1977–. *Publications:* The Story of Two Johns, 1976; American Genesis, 1976; On Beyond Koch, 1981; The City Essays, 1983; Selections, 1984; What the Heart Already Knows, 1985. *Contributions to:* The Spiscopalian; The Tennessee Churchman; The Dixie Flyer; The Feminist Digest. *Honours:* Individual Artists Fellowship in Literature, 1983. *Memberships:* Vice President, President, Tennessee Literary Arts Association; Chair, Publishers Association of the South. *Literary Agent:* Mary Jane Ross. *Address:* 3522 Lucy Road South, Lucy Community, Millington, TN 38053, USA.

TIDLER, Charles Lewis, b. 23 Apr. 1946, Bluffton, Ohio, USA. Writer; Playwright. m. Carol Lee Ewing, 28 Feb. 1970, Ganges, British Columbia, Canada, 2 sons. *Education:* BA, Purdue University, Indiana, USA, 1968. *Publications:* North of Indianapolis, 1969; Straw Things, 1972; Whetstone Almanac, 1975; Flight, 1976;

Broken Branches, 1977; Anonymous Stone, 1977; Dinosaurs, 1982; Blind Dancers, 1982; The Farewell Heart, 1983. *Radio and Stage Plays Produced:* Blind Dancers, 1979; Straight Ahead, 1981; The Monkeys Raincoat, 1982; Sleep in the Grave, 1983; The Farewell Heart, 1983; We Want What is Real, 1984; The Blue Devil, 1984; Shoot the Unicorn, 1985. *Honours:* Polymnia Prize for Traditional Poetry, 1969; Canada Council Writing Awards, 1975, 81-83; Chalmers Award for Outstanding Canadian Play, 1981. *Memberships:* Playwrights Union of Canada. *Literary Agent:* New Play Centre, Vancouver, British Columbia, Canada. *Address:* RR4 Site 420, Courtenay, British Columbia, Canada V9N 7J3.

TIDY, Michael George, b. 14 Jan. 1943, Teddington, England. Teacher. m. Anastasia Obuya, 16 Jan. 1971, Nyabondo, Kenya, 1 son. *Education:* BA, MA, Diploma of education, University of Oxford. *Publications:* The Revolutionary Years, West Africa since 1800, new edition co-author, 1980; A History of Africa 1840–1914, volume I, 1980, volume II, 1981; African History in Maps, co-author, 1982; Nationalism and New States in Africa, co-author, 1984. *Address:* Wimbledon College, Edge Hill, London SW19 4NS, England.

TIERNEY, Margaret A, b. 29 Apr. 1953. Musician; Writer; Craftsperson. *Appointments:* Law Clerk, Naas, Kildare, Republic of Ireland; Professional Musician; Writer; Arts and Craftsperson. *Contributions to:* International Poetry Guild Editor, Anthology of New Poetry, 1977; Oandas; Caritas. *Memberships:* Fellow, International Academy of Poets. *Address:* Grange Clare, Kilmeague, Naas, County Kildare, Republic of Ireland.

TIGER, Virginia Marie, b. 20 Aug. 1942, Montreal, Canada. Professor of Literature; Literary Critic. m. Lionel Tiger, 19 Aug. 1964, Vancouver, 1 son. *Education:* BA, University of Toronto, 1963; MA, 1965, PhD, 1971, University of British Columbia. *Literary Appointments:* Drama Critic, Toronto Daily Star, 1960–81; New York Times, 1984–. Various radio and television appointments, Canadian Broadcasting Corporation, 1964–67; Television Documentary, CTV Toronto, 1977. *Publications:* William Golding, 1974, 78; Everywomen, 1977; Doris Lessing, 1986. *Contributions to:* New York Times; Soho News; Columbia Forum; 20th Century Literature; Dalhousie Review; Quartz Magazine; Doris Lessing Newsletter; Contemporary Literature; American Book Review; Washington Post; Women and Literature. *Memberships:* Poets, Playwrights, Editors, Essayists and Novelists; Modern Languague Association; NWSA; Women's Ink; Doris Lessing Society; Colloquia at New York University. *Literary Agent:* Lynn Nesbitt, Entertainment Creative Management. *Address:* 17 West 9th Street, New York, NY 10011, USA.

TIGGES, John, b. 16 May 1932, Dubuque, Iowa, USA. Author. m. Kathryn E Johnson, 22 Apr. 1954, Bernard, Iowa, 3 sons, 2 daughters. *Education:* Alumnus, Loras College, Dubuque, Iowa. *Publications:* The Legend of Jean Marie Cardinal, 1976; Garden of the Incubus, 1982; They Came from Dubuque, 1983; Unto the Altar, 1985; Kiss Not the Child, 1985; Milwaukee Road Narrow Gauge – The Chicago, Bellevue, Cascade & Western – Iowa's Slim Princess, 1985; Evil Dreams, 1986; The Immortal, 1986. Playwright, No More – No Less, 1982; Television drama: An Evening With George Wallace Jones, 1983. *Contributions to:* Julien's Journal; Capper's Weekly; Treasur Magazine; Long John Latham's Treasure Magazine; Fate; Reader's Digest; Lost Treasure; Memory Lane; Cavalier; The Phoenix Gazette; Telegraph Herald; Tough Trivia Tidbits, syndicated columnist; Electronic Media Enterprises (Scripps Howard); Treasure Found; Radio station WDBQ, radio drama. *Honours:* Commissioned to write a historical novel, Bicentennial Committee; Representative work chosen and included in Governor of Iowa Library, 1978; Awarded Carnegie-Stout World of Literature diploma, 1981. *Memberships:* Fellow, World Literary Academy; National Writers Club, professional member; Charter member, Iowa Authors. *Address:* PO Box 902, Dubuque, IA 52004, USA.

TIGHE, Carl, b. 26 Apr. 1950, Birmingham, England. Writer. *Education:* BA Honours, 1973, MA, 1974, University College, Swansea, Wales; Postgraduate Diploma in English as Second Language, Leeds University, 1979. *Literary Appointments:* Writer-in-Residence, Action PIE Theatre Company, 1982. *Publications:* The Playwrights' Register, 1984, 85. *Contributions to:* Drama; Notes and Queries; Element 5; Iron; Frames; Spectrum; Arcade; The Stage. *Memberships:* Associate member, Yr Academi Gymreig; Welsh Union of Writers; Past Secretary, Wales Branch, Theatre Writers Union. *Address:* 34 Plantagenet Street, Riverside, Cardiff CF1 8RP, Wales.

TIIHONEN, Ilpo Veikko Antero, b. 1 Sep. 1950, Kuopio, Finland. Writer. *Publications:* Poems: Sarkunmäen palo (The Fire at Sarkunmäki), 1975; Antero Vipuliini ja taikatakki (Antero Vipuliini and the Magical Coat), 1976; Teille ei tarjoilla enaa (You can't take anymore), 1978; Arjen armada (Everyday's Armada), 1980; Eroikka (Eroica), 1982; Hyvät pahat ja rumat (The Good, the Bad and the Ugly), 1984. *Memberships:* Finnish Society of Authors; Finnish Dramatists Society; Finnish Literature Society. *Honours:* State Prize of Literature, 1981; Prize of K Jantti Foundation, 1983. *Literary Agent:* WSOY, Helsinki, Finland. *Address:* WSOY, Bulevardi 12, 00120 Helsinki, Finland.

TIKKA, Eeva Kaarina, b. 31 July 1939, Ristiina, Finland. Author. *Education:* MA. *Publications:* Novels: Tunturisusi (The Fell Wolf), 1975; Punainen harka (The Red Ox), 1977; Hiljainen kesa (The Quiet Summer), 1979; Jyrkanparras (The Steep), 1981; Annu, 1983. Short Stories: Alumiinikihlat, 1984; Satuja, fairy stories, 1984. *Contributions to:* Parnasso, literary magazine. *Honours:* Literary Prize, of State, 1980, of Church, 1984, of State for juvenile literature, 1985. *Memberships:* Union of Finnish Writers; PEN Club of Finland. *Literary Agent:* Gummerus Oy. *Address:* Rinnetie 6 as 9, 82200 Hammaslahti, Finland.

TIKKANEN, Märta Eleonora (Cavonius), b. 3 Apr. 1935, Helsinki, Finland. Author. m. Georg Henrik Tikkanen, 6 Feb. 1963 (deceased May 1984), 2 sons, 2 daughters. *Education:* BA (Fil.kand.), Swedish Literature & Language, English Language, University of Helsinki, 1958. *Publications include:* Novels: Nu imorron, 1970; Ingemansland, 1972; Vem bryr sej om Dpris Mihailov, 1974; Män kan inte våldtas, (Man Rape), translations, 9 languages, 1975. Poems: Arhundradets kärlekssaga (Love Story of the Century), translations 8 languages, dramatised, 1978; Mörkret som ger glädjen djup, translations 4 languages, 1981. Documentary: Sofias egen bok, translations 4 languages, 1982; Du Tror du Kuvar Mig Liv, (an anthology of Finnish women's poetry with Tua Forsstrom), 1984; Henrik, (20 essays on late husband Henrik Tikkanen by friends and colleagues), 1985. *Contributions to:* Ilta-Sanomat, Finland, 1974–76; Aftonbladet, Sweden, 1977–79; Fönstret, Sweden, 1981–84; VI, Sweden, 1984–. *Honours:* Literary Prize, Northern Women, 1979; Thanks for the Book, 1979; Information Prize of the State, 1983. *Memberships:* Board 1972–74, Författarcenrtum; Board 1980–, Vice Chairman 1984–, Finlands Svenska Författareförening r.f.; Literary Commission of the Finnish State, 1985–. *Literary Agent:* Trevi Publishers, Stockholm, Sweden. *Address:* Tölögatan 8A a, 00100, Helsingfors, Finland.

TILGHMAN, Benjamin Ross, b. 11 Jan. 1927, St Louis, Missouri, USA. Professor of Philosophy. m. Marilyn Hunter, 22 Dec. 1953, Kerville, Texas, 1 son, 1 daughter. *Education:* BA, 1950, MA, 1954, Washington University; PhD, University of Washington, 1959. *Appointments:* Instructor, Philosophy, Reed College, 1956–57; Assistant Professor, Philosophy, Western State College of Colorado, 1957–60, University of Wyoming, 1960–67; Professor, Philosophy, Kansas State University, 1967–. *Publications:* The Expression of Emotion in the Visual Arts, 1970; Language and Aesthetics, 1973; But is it Art?, 1984. *Contributor to:* Mind; Journal of Aesthetics and Art Criticism; Culture

and Art. *Address:* Dept of Philosophy, Eisenhower Hall, Kansas State University, Manhattan, KS 66506, USA.

TILLINGHAST, Richard Williford, b. 25 Nov. 1949, Memphis, Tennessee, USA. Poet and Professor. m. Mary Graves Tillinghast, 22 Apr. 1973, Corte Madera, California, 3 sons, 1 daughter. *Education:* BA, University of The South, Sewanee, Tennessee, 1963; MA 1963, PhD 1970, Harvard University. *Literary Appointments:* Assistant Professor of English, University of California at Berkeley, 1968–73; Visiting Assistant Professor, University of The South, Sewanee, Tennessee, 1979–80; Briggs-Copeland Lecturer, Harvard University, 1980–83; Associate Professor of English, University of Michigan, 1983–. *Publications:* Sleep Watch, 1969; The Knife and Other Poems, 1980; Our Flag Was Still There, 1984. *Contributions to:* Antaeus; Atlantic Monthly; Boston Globe; Boston Review; Crazy Horse; Critical Quarterly; Georgia Review; Harper's Bazaar; Harvard Advocate; The New Republic; New York Times Book Review; Paris Review; Partisan Review; Ploughshares; Poetry; Sewanee Review; Shenandoah; Southern Review; Washington Post; Yale Review. *Honours:* Woodrow Wilson Fellowship, 1962–63; Sinclair-Kennedy Travel Grant, Harvard University, 1966–67; Creative Arts Institute Grant, University of California, 1970; National Endowment for Humanities Grant, 1980; Bread Loaf Fellowship, 1982; Michigan Arts Council Grant, 1985; Millay Colony Residency, 1985. *Address:* 1317 Granger Avenue, Ann Arbor, MI 48104, USA.

TILTON, Madonna Elaine, b. 4 Oct. 1929, Laurin, Montana, USA. Writer; Journalist. Sister of St Francis, Rochester, Minnesota. *Education:* BA, College of St Teresa, Winona, MN, USA, 1959; MA, Fordham University, NYC, USA. *Literary Appointments:* Writer in Residence, Academy of Our Lady of Lourdes, Rochester, MN, 1981–82, 1983–85; Copy Editor, Minneapolis Spokesman, Minneapolis, MN. *Publications:* Isidore Finds Time to Care, 1980; The Immortal Dragon of Sylene, 1982. *Contributions to:* The Armchair Detective, Little Known Author; Religion Teachers journal, Praying by Heart; Murder in Mind, Black Sand; Mitre Press Spring Anthology, Coward, 1969; Review, Thought. *Honours:* First Prize, Stephen Y Maynard Award, Kentucky State Poetry Society, 1982; Second Prize 1983, First Prize 1984, First Prize 1985, St Paul Branch American Association of University Women Annual Poetry Contest; Second Prize, Catholic Press Association of the US and Canada, 1983; UNICEF, International Library Listing, 1983. *Memberships:* Board Member, Sing, Heavenly Muse!; The Loft, A Place for Literature and the Arts; Kentucky State Poetry Society. *Literary Agent:* Nick Ellison. *Address:* Box 4900, Rochester, MN, 55903, USA.

TIMS, Hilary, b. 18 Dec. 1938, Sydney, Australia. Journalist, Public Relations. Divorced, 2 daughters. *Literary Appointments:* Editor, Subeditor, wide range of magazines. *Contributor to:* Various magazines, Freelance; *Honour:* Monty Grover Award, Sydney Journalism, 1958. *Membership:* Australian Writers' Guild. *Address:* P O Box 2670, Darwin, Northern Territory, 5794, Australia.

TINBERGEN, Niko, b. 15 Apr. 1907, The Hague, Netherlands. Emeritus Professor of Animal Behaviour, University of Oxford, England. m. Elisabeth A Rutten, 14 Apr. 1932, Utrecht, 2 sons, 3 daughters. *Education:* D Phil, University of Leiden, Netherlands, 1932. *Publications:* Eskimoland, 1934; The Study of Instinct, 1952; The Herring Gull's World, 1953; Social Behaviour in Animals, 1953; Curious Naturalists, 1959; Animal Behaviour, 1965; Signals For Survival, 1970; The Animal in Its World, Volume I 1972, Volume II 1973; Autistic Children – New Hope For A Cure, (with E A Tinbergen), 1965. *Contributions to:* Scientific and popular journals. *Honours:* Italia Prize for TV Documentaries, 1969; Godman-Salvin Medal, British Ornithological Union, 1969; Swammersdam Medal, 1969; Nobel Prize for Physiological Medicine, 1973;

Honorary DSc, Leicester, 1974; Honorary DSc, Edinburgh, 1978. *Address:* 88 Lonsdale Road, Oxford OX2 7ER, England.

TINDALL, Gillian Elizabeth, b. 4 May 1938. Novelist; Biographer; Historian. m. Richard G Landown, 1 son.*Education:* BA 1st class, MA, University of Oxford. *Literary Appointments:* Freelance journalist: The Observer; Guardian; New Statesman; Evening Standard, 1973–; The Times, 1983–. *Publications:* Novels: No Name in the Street, 1959; The Water and the Sound, 1961; The Edge of the Paper, 1963; The Youngest, 1967; Someone Else, 1969, 75; Fly Away Home, 1971; The Traveller and His Child, 1975; The Intruder, 1979; Looking Foreward, 1983. Short Stories: Dances of Death, 1973; The China Egg and Other Stories, 1981. Biography: The Born Exile, on George Gissing, 1974. Non-Fiction: A Handbook on Witchcraft, 1965; The Fields Beneath, 1977; City of Gold: The Biography of Bombay, 1981; Rosamond Lehmann, on Appreciation, 1985. *Contributions to:* Encounter. *Honours:* Somerset Maugham Award for Fly Away Home, 1972. *Address:* c/o Curtis Brown Limited, 162-168 Regent Street, London W1, England.

TISCHLER, Hans, b. 18 Jan. 1915, Vienna, Austria. Musicologist. m. (1) Louise Hochdorf, London, England, 27 July 1938, 1 son, 1 daughter. (2) Alice Bock, 21 June 1958, Munster, Indiana, USA. *Education:* Piano Teaching Diploma 1933, Master in Conducting 1935, Composition 1936, Vienna State Academy, Austria; PhD Musicology, University of Vienna, 1937; PhD Musicology, Yale University, USA, 1942. *Publications:* A Structural Analysis of Mozart's Piano Concertos, 1966; History of Keyboard Music to 1700, by W Apel, translator and editor, 1973; The Montpellier Codex, 3 volumes, 1978; Chanter m'estuet: Songs of the Trouvères, (with S Rosenberg), 1981; The Earliest Motets (to c 1270), 3 volumes, 1982; The Style of the Early Motets, 2 volumes, 1985; The Parisian Two-Part Organa, 3 volumes, 1986. *Contributions to:* National and International journals including: Acta Musicologica; Archiv Für Musikwissenschaft; Journal of the American Musicological Society; Music and Letter. *Honours:* 4 Grants, American Philosophical Society, 1955–81; Guggenheim Fellowship, 1964–65; Grants, Chapelbrook Foundation, 1965 and 1969; ACLS Grant-in-Aid, 1970; NEH Editorial Grant, 1971; NEH Fellowship, 1975–76. *Memberships:* International Musicological Society; Past Council member and past Chapter Chairman, American Musicological Society; Mediaeval Academy of America; Past President, Medieval Association of the Midwest; Past Chapter Secretary, Association of American University Professors. *Address:* 711 East First Street, Bloomington, IN 47401, USA.

TISDELL, Clement Allan, b. 18 Nov. 1939, Taree, Australia. Professor of Economics. m. Marie-Elisabeth Eckermann, 7 Dec. 1968, Corinda, 1 son, 1 daughter. *Education:* B Com, Honours, Economics, University of New South Wales, 1961; PhD, Australian National University, 1964. *Appointment:* Professor, Economics, University of Newcastle, Australia. *Publications:* Science & Technology Policy: Priorities of Government, 1981; Microeconomics of Markets, 1982; Wild Pigs: Environmental Pest or Economic Resource, 1982; Micro-Economic Policy, co author, 1981; Economics in Our Society: New Zealand Edition, co-author, 1981. *Contributor to:* Numerous professional journals including, Environmental Conservation; Urban Studies; Journal of Agricultural Economics; Australian Habitat; etc. *Honours:* University Medal, University of New South Wales, 1961; Australian National University Research Scholarship, Commonwealth Postgraduate Award, University Fellowship & Scholarship, University of Pennsylvania, USA, 1965; Fellowships to Princeton University, Stanford University, USA, 1965; Visiting Scholar, University of York, 1975, 1979. *Memberships:* Economics Society of Australia; Royal Economics Society; American Economic Association; Australian

Agricultural Economics Society; many other professional organisations. *Address:* Department of Economics, University of Newcastle, NSW 2308, Australia.

TITLEY, David Paul, b. 8 July 1929, England. Headmaster. m. Jeanne, 24 July 1954, Dagenham, England, 1 son, 1 daughter. *Education:* BSc, Economics, Hons. *Publications:* Machines, Money and Men, 1969; Look and Remember History Books 1-6, 1969–74; Britain in History, Books 1 and 2, 1974–75; Look and Remember, People and Events, 1-4, 1976. *Address:* 7 Leahill Close, Malvern, Worcestershire, England.

TITTERTON, Ernest William, b. 4 Mar. 1916, Tamworth, England. Professor. *Education:* BSc, 1937, MSc, 1939, PhD, 1941, Birmingham University, England. *Publications include:* Facing the Atomic Future, 1956; Many papers on Low Energy Nuclear Physics, 1945; Uranium: Energy Source of the Future, 1979. *Contributor to:* Various professional journals. *Honours:* Elected FRSAS, 1952; Fellow, American Physical Society, 1952; Elected Fellow, Australian Academy of Science, 1954; CMG, 1957; Knight Bachelor, 1970. *Memberships include:* Australian Atomic Weapons Tests Safety Committee; Council, Australian Institute for Nuclear Science and Engineering; Council, Australian Academy of Science; Council, Institute of Defence Science; etc. *Address:* 8 Somers Crescent, Forrest, ACT 2603, Australia.

TIUSANEN, Timo, b. 13 Apr. 1936, Viipuri, Finland. Professor of Theatre Studies. *Education:* MA 1959, L Lit 1965, University of Helsinki; PhD, 1969. *Literary Appointments:* Theatre critic, Uusi Suomi, 1983–. *Publications:* Tapa puhua (A Way of Speaking), 1963; O'Neill's Scenic Images, 1968; Teatterimmehahmottuu (Our Theatre Finds Its Shape), 1969; Linjoja (Lines of Development), 1977; Dürrenmatt, 1978. *Contributions to:* Readers Encyclopedia of World Drama; etc. *Memberships include:* Finnish President, International PEN, 1968–69; Vice Chairman, Aleksis Kivi Society, 1969–; International Secretary, Eugene O'Neill Society, 1980–83; Chairman of the Board, Helsinki Theatre Museum, 1982–. *Honours include:* Vaaskivi Medal, University of Tampere, 1962. *Address:* 7 Vironkatu 4 C 19, 00170 Helsinki 17, Finland.

TOBIAS, Phillip Vallentine, b. 14 Oct. 1925, Durban, Natal, Republic of South Africa. Professor of Anatomy and Director, Palaeo-anthropology Research Group. *Education:* BSc, 1946, MB, BCh 1961, PhD 1953, DSc 1967, University of the Witwatersrand, Johannesburg; Postgraduate, Cambridge University, England. *Publications include:* Man's Anatomy, (with M Arnold), volumes I-II 1963, volume III 1964, 3rd edition 1977; Man's Limbs, (with M Arnold), 1968; Man's Brain (with M Arnold), 1963, 2nd edition 1974; Olduvai Gorge, Vol II: The Cranium and Maxillary Dentition of Australopithecus (Zinjanthropus) boisei,1967; The Brain in Hominid Evolution, 1971; Dart, Taung and the, Missing Link, 1984; Hominid Evolution: Past, Present and Future, 1985. *Contributions to:* American Journal of Physical Anthropology, (associate editor); Journal of Human Evolution, (co-editor); Human Biology, (editorial board member); Nature; and others. *Honours:* Numerous academic awards. *Memberships:* President 1963–64, Science Writer's Association of South Africa; Fellow, President 1970–72, Royal Society of South Africa; Royal Anthropological Institute of Great Britain and Ireland; Linnean Society of London. *Address:* University of the Witwatersrand, Medical School, York Road, Parktown, Johannesburg 2193, Republic of South Africa.

TOBIAS, Richard Clark, b. 10 Oct. 1925, Xenia, Ohio, USA. Professor of English. m. Barbara Nitche, 18 June 1949, Cincinnati, Ohio, 1 son, 2 daughters. *Education:* BSc, 1948; MA, 1951; PhD, 1957, Ohio State University, Columbus, Ohio. *Literary Appointments:* Instructor, Ohio State, 1952–53; Instructor, University of Colorado, 1953–56; Instructor/Professor, University of Pittsburgh, 1957–. *Publications:* The Art of James Thurber, 1970; Shakespeare's Last Plays, (Editor),

1974; T E Brown, the Manx Poet, 1978. *Contributions to:* Victorian Poetry; Victorian Studies. *Honour:* Charles E Merril Humanities Award, 1965. *Membership:* Chairman, Victorian Division, 1975–77, Modern Language Association. *Address:* 5846 Darlington Road, Pittsburgh, PA 15217, USA.

TOBIAS, Ronald Benjamin, b. 25 Oct. 1946, Newark, New Jersey, USA. Writer. m. Valerie Jonsson, 5 June 1982, Wylie, Texas, 1 daughter. *Education:* BA, Kansas State University; MFA, Bowling Green State University. *Literary Appointments:* Writer-in-Residence, University of Texas. *Major Publications:* Shoot to Kill, 1981; Our Man is Inside, 1982; The Sixth Seal, 1984; Kings and Desperate Men and other Stories, 1985. *Contributor to:* USA; Kansas Quarterly; Carolina Quarterly; Esquire; Canto; Sands; Penthouse; Translation Review; ,Mundus Artium; India: Indian Literature; Chandrabhaga; Canada: Antigonish Review; Descant; Also: Rimu (New Zealand); New Edinburgh Review (Scotland); Statesman (Pakistan); Helix (Australia). *Memberships:* American Literary Translators Association; Modern Language Association. *Literary Agent:* International Creative Management, New York, USA. *Address:* PO Box 1104, Wylie, TX 75098, USA.

TOBIAS-TURNER, Bessye, b. 10 Oct. 1917, Liberty, Mississippi, USA. Poet; Lecturer; Retired Educator. *Education:* AB, English, Rust College; MA, English, MA, Speech, Columbia University; PhD, Literature, World University. *Literary Appointments:* Honorary Vice President, Centro Studi Scambi International; Board, 5th World Congress of Poets, 1981; Special Guest Poet, Asian Poets Conference, Japan, 1984. *Publications:* La Librae: Anthology of Poetry for Living, 1968; Peace & Love, 1972; Laurel Leaves for Bess, 1977. *Contributions to:* Numerous poetry magazines, World Congress of Poets, Poets Conferences, worldwide. *Honours include:* Grand Prix Mediterranee, Academie d'Europa, 1983, 1984; Clover International Poetry Association, Certificate, Award, 1976; Star of Poetry, 1984; Poet Laureate International, 1977; Special Guest Poet, APE 1984. *Memberships:* Centro Studi e Scambi Internazionali; New York Poetry Forum; Board, World Congress of Poets, 1976, 1979, 1981. *Address:* 829 Wall Street, McComb, MS 39698, USA.

TOCH, Henry, b. 15 Aug. 1923. Polytechnic Lecturer. m. Margaret Schwarz, 3 April 1958, London, England. *Education:* B Com, University of London, 1950. *Major Publications:* How to Pay Less Income Tax, 4th edition, 1973; Tax Saving for the Businessman, 3rd edition, 1975; British Political & Social Institutions, 1961; Income Tax, 13th edition, 1983; Economics for Professional Studies, 3rd edition, 1979; How to Survive Inflation, 1977; Cases in Income Tax Law, 1981; How to Pass Examinations in Taxation, 1979; Essentials of British Constitution & Government, 1983; Income Tax Made Simple, 1985; Taxation 1984/85, 1984. *Contributor to:* Cooperative News. *Memberships:* Society of Authors. *Address:* Candida, 49 Hawkshead Lane, North Mymms, Hatfield, Herts AL9 7TD, England.

TODD, Ian Alexander, b. 24 Sep. 1941, West Kirby, Cheshire, England. University Teacher; Archaeologist. m. Alison Katharine South, 12 June 1981, Larnaca, Cyprus. *Education:* BA, PhD, University of Birmingham, England. *Publications:* Catal Huyuk in Perspective, 1976; The Prehistory of Central Anatolia I: The Neolithic Period, 1980. *Contributions to:* Anatolian Studies; American Journal of Archaeology; Archaeology; Archiv fur Orientforschung; Cyprus Today; Journal of Field Archaeology; Bulletin de Correspondance Hellenique; Old World Archaeology Newsletter; Antiquity; Chalcolithic Cyprus and Western Asia, 1981 and numerous others. Presenter of various major lectures and participant at numerous conferences. *Honours include:* Local Government and British Government Grants; Fellowship, British Institute of Archaeology, 1966–69; Tweedie Exploration Fellowship, University of Edinburgh, Scotland, 1968; Sachar International Programme Grant, Brandeis University, Massachusetts, USA, 1970, 75, 81; National Science Foundation

Awards, 1976–79; Senior Fulbright Award, 1979–80; National Endowment for the Humanities Award, 1982–84; Mazer Fund for Faculty Research, Brandeis University, 1982, 84. *Memberships include:* Numerous archaeological bodies. *Address:* CLORS, Rabb 141, Brandeis University, Waltham, MA 02254, USA.

TODD, James MacLean, b. 10 Apr. 1907, Melbourne, Derbyshire, England. Schoolmaster; Headmaster; Secretary, Oxford and Cambridge Schools Examination Board. m. Janet Gillespie Holmes, 1 Sep. 1944, Glasgow, Scotland, 1 son, 1 daughter. *Education:* MA, Queens College, Oxford University. *Publications:* The Ancient World, 1938. With Janet Todd: Voices From the Past, 1955, Classical Anthology, reprinted, 1956, 60; Peoples of the Past, 1963. *Address:* Foxton Lodge, Foxton Close, Oxford OX2 8LB, England.

TOEN, Alice Edmonde Nelly, b. 25 July 1924, Antwerp, Belgium. Actress; Author, Theatre Plays. *Education:* Theatre School, Mechelen, 1957; Higher Institution for Social Science, 1959. *Literary Appointments:* Partner, Sabam (Authors Society), 1952; Partner, Jeugd & Theater, 1970; Board, ITI Brussels; Board, Assitej, Brussels. *Publications include:* Mainly theatre plays for children & young people. For children: Krentenkoek met Krieken, 1959; De Gelaarsde Kat, 1969; Ventje hout, ventje glas, ventje ijzer, 1969; Bip..bip..maan. For young people & adults: Weglopen van huis, 1973; Het Gezin, 1974; Trouwen is houwen, 1978. *Contributions:* Children's stories to Belgian magazines. *Honours include:* Knight, Order of Leopold II, 1972; Awards, Holland, Yugoslavia, Belgium, Germany; Edmund Hustinx Prize, Flemish & Dutch Authors Society, 1975; Sabam Prize, Translations, 1979. *Literary Agent:* Sabam, Brussels, Belgium. *Address:* Roelandsveldstraat 24, B–1710 Dilbeek, Belgium.

TOIVOLA, Ritva Anneli, b. 26 Feb. 1942, Finland. Editor. *Education:* BA. *Publications:* Honeybears, Polarbears, 1979; Longwing of Rushmoor, 1981; Captain Copperbeard, 1983; Miiru and the Ballet Shoes, 1983; The Treasure of the Jester, 1984; Aleksi and the Magic Feather, 1985. *Honours:* State Prize for Literature, 1982; Prize of Arvid Lydecken, 1984. *Membership:* Finnish Society of Authors. *Literary Agent:* Weilin & Goos. *Address:* Weilin & Goos, Ahertajantie 5, 02100 Espoo, Finland.

TOLEDANO, Ralph de, b. 17 Aug. 1916, International Zone of Tangier. Journalist; Syndicated Columnist. m. (1) Mora Romaine (dec), 6 July 1938, New York, 2 sons; (2) Eunice Marshall, 9 Apr. 1979, Washington DC. *Education:* BA, Columbia University, 1938; Language Studies, Cornell University, 1943. *Publications:* Frontiers of Jazz; Seeds of Treason; Dupes & Diplomats; Lament for a Generation; RFK – The Man Who Would Be President; J Edgar Hoover – The Man In His Time; One Man Alone – Richard Nixon; Devil Take Him, novel; Poems: You & I; etc. *Contributions to:* American Scholar; Commentary, Reader's Digest; Yale Literary Magazine; National Review (regular music column); American Mercury; etc. Articles, verse, short stories. *Honours:* Philolexian Prize for Poetry, twice, as undergraduate at Columbia University. *Membership:* Sigma Delta Chi. *Address:* 825 New Hampshire Avenue NW, Washington DC 20037, USA.

TOLL, Robert Charles, b. 10 Sep. 1938, USA. Writer. m. Judith Ann Dirks, 15 Dec. 1962. *Education:* BA, San Jose State University, 1964; MA, 1966, PhD, 1972, University of California, Berkeley. *Publications:* Blacking Up: The Minstrel Show in 19th Century America, 1974; On With the Show: The First Century of Show Business in America, 1976; The Entertainment Machine: Show Business in 20th Century America, 1982. Co-Editor, Old Slack's Reminiscence and Pocket History of the Colored Profession from 1865 to 1891, 1974. *Contributions to:* Handbook of American Folklore, 1983; Notable American Women; American Heritage; New York Times; various others. *Honours:* Woodrow Wilson Fellow, 1965–66; George Freedley

Memorial Award, recognising, Blacking Up, as best book on live theatre, Theatre Library Association, 1974. *Memberships:* American Society for Theatre Research; 19th Century Theatre Research. *Address:* 3900 Harrison Street Apt 203, Oakland, CA 94611, USA.

TOLLIVER, Ruby Changos, b. 29 May 1922, Fort Worth, Texas, USA. Author. m. Bowers Harbert Tolliver, Jr, 4 Nov. 1944, Corpus Christi, Texas, USA, 1 son, 2 daughters. *Major Publications:* Summer of Decision, 1979; Decision at Sea, 1980; More than One Decision, 1981; Decision at Brusby Creek, 1983; A Question of Doors, 1984. *Literary Agent:* Ann Elmo Agency. *Address:* 1806 Pin Oak Lane, Conroe, Texas TX 77302, USA.

TOLSTOY, Ivan, b. 30 Mar. 1923, Germany. Scientist; Writer. m. 1964, London, 2 daughters. *Education:* Licence Es Sciences, Sorbonne, Paris, France, 1945; MA, 1947, PhD, 1950, Geophysics, Columbia University, USA. *Publications:* Ocean Acoustics, 1966; Pulse of a Planet, 1971; Wave Propagation, 1973; James Clerk Maxwell, A Biography, 1983. *Contributor to:* New Ecologist; Guardian; Man-Environmental Systems; etc; articles in scientific journals. *Membership:* Society of Authors. *Address:* Knocktower, Knockvennie, Castle Douglas, Kirkcudbrightshire, Scotland.

TOMALIN. Ruth. Writer. m. (1) 1942 (2) 1971, 1 son. *Major Publications:* Poems: Threnody for Dormice, 1947; Deer's Cry, 1952; Novels: All Souls, 1952; The Garden House, 1964; The Spring House, 1968; Away to the West, 1972; W H Hudson – A Biography, 1982; For Children: The Sea Mice, 1962; A Green Wishbone, A Stranger Thing, 1975; Gone Away, 1979; A Summer Ghost, 1986. *Address:* c/o Barclay's Bank, 15 Langham Place, London W1, England.

TOMAZOS, Criton (Plato), b. 13 Apr. 1940, Cyprus. Playwright; Poet; Film and Television Scriptwriter. *Education:* Diploma in Architecture, Central London Polytechnic, London, England, 1964; Intensive advanced theatre design, Croydon College of Fine Art and Technology, 1977; Advanced writing for television and film, London Academy of Television, 1982. *Literary Appointments:* Editor, Environmental Forum magazine, London, England, 1976–; Resident Playwright, Prometheus Theatre Company, 1982–; Part-time critic and correspondent for several Greek papers in London and abroad. *Publications:* Lovepoem, 1965; Monologue of the Ancient Hero, poems, 1970; Relationships, 1975; Poems of 1960–61; He Who Left His Fingerprints, poem, 1979; Night March Poems; Factory Back Yard, 1980; Diaphaneies (Transparencies), poems, 1982. *Contributions to:* And, magazine; Oasis; Troubador; Greek Review; Cyprus Week, magazine; Environmental Forum, magazine; Time Out; Stage; City Limits. *Honours:* 1st prize, poetry competition Modern Greek section, EDON, for poetry collection, Diaphaneies, International Youth Festival; 1st poetry prize, Socialist Youth Festival; Essay prize, Korea; Exhibiton of his work, Ministry of Education, Cyprus, 1980. *Memberships:* Writers Forum; Writers Guild; Poetry Society; Theatre Writers Union; Director and Honorary President, Environmental Forum; London Screenwriters Workship. *Literary Agent:* Environmental Forum. *Address:* c/o The Secretary, Environmental Forum, 12A Ennis Road, Finsbury Park, London N4 3HD, England.

TOMLIN, Eric Walter Frederick, b. 30 Jan. 1913, Purley, Surrey, England. Author. *Education:* MA, Oxford and Cambridge University. *Publications include:* The Western Philosophers, 1949; Living and Knowing, 1954; Simone Weil, 1954; Tokyo Essays, 1967; The Last Country, 1974; Psyche, Culture and The New Science, 1985; The Tall Trees of Marsland, 1986. *Contributions to:* Criterion; Scrutiny; Times Literary Supplement; Spectator; Economist; Universities Quarterly, and others. *Honours:* OBE, 1959; CBE, 1965. *Memberships include:* Fellow, Royal Society of Literature; Asiatic Society; Aristolelian Society; The Athenaeum; Royal Institution of Cornwall; Union Society (Oxford). *Address:* 31 Redan Street, London W14 OAB, England.

TOMLINSON, Charles, b. 8 Jan. 1927, Stoke-on-Trent, England. Professor of English Literature. *Education:* BA, Queen's College, University of Cambridge; MA, University of London. *Major Publications include:* (poems), Seeing is Believing, 1958; A Peopled Landscape, 1963; American Scenes, 1966; The Way of a World, 1969; Poems, (with A Clarke & T Connor), 1964; Poems, (with A Brownjohn & M Hamburger), 1969; The Poem as Initiation, 1968; Words & Images, 1972; Written on Water, 1972; The Way In, 1974; Selected Poems, 1951–74, 1978; The Shaft, 1978; Air Born/Hijos del Aire, (with O Paz), 1979; The Flood, 1981; Translations, 1983; Notes from New York, 1984; Eden, 1985; Collected Poems, 1985; (prose) Some Americans: A Literary Memoir, 1981; Poetry & Metamorphosis, (The Clark Lectures), 1983; Editor, The Oxford Book of Verse in English Translation, 1980; also essays on Marianne Moore & William Carlos Williams, Poetry of Williams & Octavio Paz. *Contributor to:* Various Journals etc. *Honours:* Fellow, Royal Society of Literature; D H Lawrence Fellowship, University of New Mexico, USA, 1963; National Translation Centre Award, University of Texas, 1968; Cheltenham Poetry Prize, 1976; Honorary Fellow, Queen's College, Cambridge, 1976; Arts Council Travelling Exhibition, The Graphics & Poetry of Charles Tomlinson, 1978–81; Cholmondeley Award for Poetry, 1979; Honorary DLitt, University of Keele, 1981, Colgate University, 1981. *Address:* Department of English, University of Bristol, Bristol BS8 1HY, England.

TOMPKINS, Joyce Marjorie Sanxter, b. 3 Nov. 1897, Catford, London, England. University Lecturer. *Education:* D Lit, University of London. *Publications:* Popular Novel in England 1770–1800, 1932; The Art of Rudyard Kipling, 1959. *Contributions to:* Review of English Studies. *Membership:* Kipling Society. *Address:* St Augustine's Nursing Homes, 25 Upper Maze Hill, St Leonards on Sea, Sussex, England.

TONE, Teona LaRae, b. 11 July 1944, Texas. Author. m. Wolcott Tuckerman Schley, 1 son, 1 daughter. *Education:* BA, MA, PhD, University of California. *Publications:* Lady on the Line, 1983; Full Cry, 1985; Housemates: A Practical Guide to Living With Other People, with Deanna Sclar, 1985. *Contributions to:* New West, now California; Westways; Huntington Library Journal; Eighteenth Century Studies; Los Angeles Herald Examiner. *Honour:* Dickson Memorial Fellowship, 1976. *Memberships:* Modern Language Association; Private Eye Writers of America. *Literary Agent:* Julian Bach, New York. *Address:* PO Box 1168, Santa Ynez, CA 93460, USA.

TONER, Barbara, b. 18 June 1948, Sydney. Writer. m. Chris Greenwood, 20 Oct. 1967, 3 daughters. *Publications:* Double Shift, 1975; The Facts of Rape, 1977, 2nd Editon 1982; Married Secrets: Tales From Tessa Wood, 1984; Brain Street (due summer 1986). *Contributions to:* The Times; Woman Magazine, regular columnist, 1982–. *Literary Agent:* Fraser & Dunlop. *Address:* 104 Warriner Gardens, London, SW11 4DU, England.

TONG, Raymond, b. 20 Aug. 1922, Winchester, England. Freelance Writer. m. Mariana Apergis. *Education:* BSc. Economics, Honours, Dip.Ed., London University. *Publications:* Travel: Figures in Ebony, 1958; Poetry: Angry Decade, 1950; Fabled City, 1960; A Matter of History, 1976; Crossing the Border, 1978; African Helicon, Anthology, 1954, 2nd edition, 1975. *Contributor to:* New Statesman; Encounter; Contemporary Review; New Poetry; Outposts Poetry Quarterly; PEN Broadsheet; Poetry Review; English; A Review of English Literature; Ariel; New Humanist; History Today; The Cambridge Review; British Book News; The Gadfly, etc. *Memberships:* West Country Writers Association; Poetry Society. *Address:* 1B Beaufort Road, Clifton, Bristol BS8 2JT, England.

TONOGBANUA, Francisco G, b. 1 Dec. 1900, Binalbagan, Negros Occidental, Philippines. College Dean & Professor. m. Florencia Veloso Conwi, 7 Oct. 1934, Baclaren, Philippines, 2 sons, 4 daughters. *Education:* AA 1924, PhB 1926, BSE 1928, University of the Philippines; MA 1930, University of Wisconsin, USA; PhD, University of St Tomas, 1950. *Major Publications:* Verse Trilogy: Fallen Leaves, 1951, Green Leaves, 1954, Brown Leaves, 1965; A Stone, a Leaf, a Door, 1962; Forty-One Christmases, 1959, 1965; Sonnets, 1964; My God, My Mercy, 1956, 1972; 5 prose volumes, 6 pedagogical volumes. *Contributor to:* Numerous periodicals. *Honours:* Various awards in the Philippines, including Honorary Title of Poet Laureate of Cursillo Movement. *Memberships:* Co-Founder & Member, University of the Philippines Writers' Club; Vice-President, Philippine Writers' Association. *Address:* 32 Ragang Street, Barangay Manresa, Quezon City, Metro Manila, Philippines.

TOOLEY, Michael John, b. 17 Dec. 1942, Barnstaple, England. University Lecturer. m. Rosanna Mary Mellor, 15 Sep. 1973, Crook, Cumbria, 1 son, 1 daughter. *Education:* BA, University of Birmingham; PhD, University of Lancaster. *Publications:* The Quaternary History of the Irish Sea, editor with C Kidson, 1977; Sea Level Changes, 1978; British Prehistory: The Environment, editor with I G Simmons, 1980; The Gardens of Gertrude Jekyll in Northern England, with R Tooley; Gertrude Jekyll: Artist, Gardener, Craftswoman, editor, 1984; The Climatic Scene, editor with Gillian Sheail, 1985. *Contributions to:* More than 60 contributions to Geographical Journal; Geological Journal; Garden History; Proceedings of the Geologists' Association. *Address:* University of Durham, Durham DH1 3LE, England.

TOON, Peter, (Reverend), b. 25 Oct. 1939, Yorkshire, England. Clerk in Holy Orders. m. Vita Persram, 2 Sep. 1961, 1 daughter. *Education:* MA, Liverpool; MDMth, London; DPhil, Oxford. *Publications:* Emergence of Hyper-Calvinism, 1967; God's Statesman: Life of Dr John Owen 1616–1683, 1972; Puritans, the Millennium and Future of Israel, 1972; The Development of Doctrine in the Church, 1977; Evangelical Theology, 1833–1856, 1977; Justification and Sanctification, 1983; The Ascension of Our Lord, 1984; Britain's True Creatures, 1984; Heaven and Hell, 1986. *Contributions to:* Church of England Newspaper; Editor, Home Words, (parish magazine inset). *Address:* 15 Madeley Road, Ryhill, Wakefield, West Yorkshire, England.

TOPOLSKI, Daniel, b. 4 June 1945, London. Writer. *Education:* MA, Geography, Dip Soc Anthropology, New College, Oxford. *Publications:* Muzungu: One Man's Africa, 1976; Travels with my Father, 1983; Boat Race – The Oxford Revival, 1985. *Contributor to:* Telegraph Magazine; New Society; Daily Mail; New Standard; Radio Times; The Art Magazine. *Literary Agent:* Blake Friedmann (Julian Friedmann and Carol Blake). *Address:* 25 Clifton Hill, London NW 8, England.

TORCHIANA, Donald Thornhill, b. 22 Oct. 1923, Swarthmore, Pennsylvania, USA. Professor of English. m. Rena Margarida LeSueur, 17 May 1952, Iowa City, Iowa, divorced 1972, 2 sons, 1 daughter. *Education:* BA, DePauw University, 1947; MA 1949, PhD 1953, University of Iowa. *Literary Appointments:* Instructor-Professor, Northwestern University, 1953–67. *Publications:* W B Yeats and Georgian Ireland, 1966; Backgrounds for Joyce's Publishers, 1986. *Contributions to:* 40 articles and 25 reviews in magazines and journals. *Honours:* Newberry Library Fellow, 1959; ACLS Grant, England, 1973; Fulbright Lecturer, University College, Galway, 1960–62 and 1969–70; NEH-Newberry Library grant, 1980. *Memberships:* Chairman of Celtic Section 1970–71, Executive Committee, Anglo Irish Secretary 1980, Modern Language Association; American Committee for Irish Studies; International Association for the Study of Anglo-Irish Literature. *Address:* 1220 Hinman Avenue, Evanston, IL 60202, USA.

TORO-GARLAND, Fernando de, b. 26 Dec. 1925, Santiago, Chile. Lawyer; University Professor of Literature. *Education:* Lic. Humanities, Dominican College, Chile, 1946; Bachelor of Humanities, 1947, Lic. Legal and Social Sciences, 1955, University of Chile; LLD, University of Madrid, Spain, 1957. *Publications:* Desarrollo Institucional y Politico de Chile, 1965; El Fruto Prohibido, 1968; La Angustia Infinita, 1972; Razon y Pasion de Enamorados, 1973; Cuatro Entremeses Medievales, 1973, 2nd edition, 1978; El Arca Vino del Cielo, 1963; Cantos de Todas las Voces, 1962. *Contributions to:* Numerous publications including: Revista de Literatura; Espanol Actual; Revista Iberoamericana. *Honours include:* Literary Research Grants, Canada Council, 1968, 69; Corresponding Member, Chilean Academy, Spanish Academy. *Memberships:* General Society of Authors of Spain; Iberomaerican Institute for Literary Cooperation; International Institute for Iberoamerican Literature; International Association of Literary Critics. *Literary Agent:* Skolar. *Address:* Apartado 9, 145, 28080 Madrid, Spain.

TORRES, Emmanuel, b. 29 Apr. 1932, Manila, Philippines. Poet, Teacher. *Education:* BA Education, Ateneo de Manila University, 1954; MA English, State University of Iowa, USA, 1957. *Publications:* Angels and Fugitives, poetry, 1966; Shapes of Silence, poetry, 1972; Jeepney, non-fiction, 1979; Kayamanan: 77 paintings from the Central Bank Collection, art criticism, 1981. *Contributions to:* Poems included in: Botteghe Oscure, Rome; Poetry; A Magazine of Verse, Chicago; Beloit Poetry Journal; Genre: An International Journal of the Arts; Philippines Free Press; Asia Magazine, Hong Kong; Manila Review; Caracca, Manila; Filipinas Journal. *Honours:* Mulry Award for Literary Excellence, Ateneo de Manila University, 1954; Ten Outstanding Young Men Award for Literature, 1961; Carlos Palanca Awards for Poetry, in English, 1964, 1965, 1966 and 1968. *Address:* 456 Adalla Street, Palm Village, Makati, Philippines.

TOTTEN, Caroline V, b. 18 Sept. 1940, Canton, Ohio, USA. Freelance Writer. *Education:* Kent State University. *Publications:* River of the Sacred Monkey, Ghost writer for Dimitri Krustev, 1970. *Contributions to:* New Writers; Remington Review; Lake Superior Review; Insight; Essence; St Anthony Messenger; Akron Beacon, (Sunday magazine). *Honours:* Best Manuscript, Poetry, 1972, 75, Fiction, 1973, 74, Malone College Midwest Writers Conference; Ohio Short Story Contest, Valley Views Magazine, 1968; Review and Herald National Fiction Prize, 1977; Poetry Prize (Ohio), National League of American Pen Women, 1977, 78. *Memberships:* National Writers Club; President, (4 terms), Canton Writers Club; CODA; Poets and Writers. *Address:* 350 Winston Street North East, North Canton, OH 44720, USA.

TOUGH, Allen MacNeill, b. 6 Jan. 1936, Montreal, Canada. Professor. m. (1) Anne Wood, 19 Apr 1960, I son, 1 daughter. (2) Elaine Posluns, 10 June 1981, Toronto. *Education:* BA, Psychology, 1958, MA, Education and Psychology, 1962, University of Toronto; PhD, Social Sciences, University of Chicago, USA, 1965. *Literary Appointments:* Editor-in-Chief, University of Toronto all-campus Yearbook, 1956–58; Teacher of Public Speaking, Scarborough evening class for adults, 1960–62; Professor, Ontario Institute for Studies in Education and University of Toronto, 1966–; Consulting Editor, Adult Education: A Journal of Research and Theory, 1967–73; Judge, Political Book Award, 1982–84. *Major Publications:* Learning without a Teacher 1967; Why Adults Learn, 1968; The Adult's Learning Projects (2nd edition), 1979; Expand Your Life, 1980; Intentional Changes, 1982. *Contributor to:* Adult Education (USA); Continuous Learning; Covergence; Adult Leadership; Learning Opportunities for Adults; Continuum; College and Research Libraries News; Innovation Abstracts; Library Trends. *Honours:* Honour Award for notable contribution to undergraduate life, University of Toronto Students' Administrative Council, 1958; Kellogg Fellowship, University of Chicago, 1962;

Canada Council Scholarship for Secondary School Teachers, 1963; Tuition Scholarship, University of Chicago, 1963; Honorary Member, Ontario Society for Training and Development, 1967; Various awards in Adult Education for textbooks. *Address:* Ontario Institute for Studies in Education, 252 Bloor Street West, Toronto, Ontario, Canada M5S 1V6.

TOWEY, (Brother) Augustine Denis, b.30 June 1937. Professor. *Education:* BA, 1958, MA, 1960, St John's University; PhD, New York University, New York CIty, 1973. *Literary Appointments:* Professor, English and Theatre, Niagara University, New York, 1964–; Director, Theatre Studies, 1973–; Chairperson, Festival Arts, Niagara Falls, 1968–73; Director, Artpark Repertory Theatre, Lewiston, New York, 1975–. *Contributor to:* Commonweal; Talon; Aquila; Sequia; Buffalo Evening News; Courier Sunday Magazine. *Address:* Niagara University, NY 14109, USA.

TOWNSEND, Joan, b. 23 May 1913, Darwen, Lancashire, England. Freelance Writer. *Publications:* Summat From Home, 1964; Nowt So Queer, 1969; Lancashire Evergreen, 1969; Twixt Thee and Me, 1973; Mermaids Moon, 1975. *Contributions to:* Lancashire Life; BBC, etc. *Honours:* Lancashire Authors' Association Awards, 1938, 1946, 1947, 1948, 1952, 1953, 1959, 1972; Writer of the Year, 1972; IWWP Awards 1972 and 1974; 1st prizes for dialect poems and prose, 1978; LAA Awards, 1982, 1983; Writer of the Year, 1983. *Memberships:* Lancashire Dialect Society; Preston Poets' Society (Hon Life Member); FRSA; Lancashire Authors' Association (Vice President); Great Harwood Male Voice Choir (President); Romantic Novelists' Association. *Address:* Stoops Farm, Great Harwood, Nr Blackburn, Lancashire, England.

TOWNSEND, John Rowe, b. 10 May 1922, Leeds, England. Author. *Education:* MA, Emmanuel College, Cambridge University. *Publications:* Grumble's Yard, 1961; The Intruder, 1969; Written for Children, 1974; Noah's Castle, 1975; Dan Alone, 1983; many others. *Contributor to:* The Guardian; Times Educational Supplement; NY Times Book Review; etc. *Honours:* Silver Pen Award, English Centre, PEN, 1970; Boston Globe-Horn Book Award, 1970; Edgar, Mystery Writer of America, 1970; Christopher Award (USA), 1982; Whittall Lecturer, Library of Congress, 1976. *Memberships:* Society of Authors (Chairman, Children's Writers' Group, 1978–79, Member, Management Committee, 1982–85). *Address:* 19 Eltisley Avenue, Newnham, Cambridge, CB3 9JG, England.

TOWNSEND, Peter Wooldridge, b. 22 Nov. 1914, Rangoon, Burma. Author. m. Marie-Luce Jamagne, 21 Dec. 1959, Brussels, Belgium, 1 son, 2 daughters (2 sons from 1st marriage). *Literary Appointments:* Royal Air Force College, 1933–35; Royal Air Force Staff College, 1942–43. *Major Publications:* Earth my Friend, 1960; Dual of Eagles, 1970; The Last Emperor, 1975; Time & Chance (autobiography), 1978; The Smallest Pawns in the Game, 1979–80; The Girl in the White Ship, 1982; The Postman of Magasaki, 1984. *Contributor to:* Daily Mail; Daily Express; Sunday Express; Paris Match; Journal du Dimanche (France). *Literary Agent:* Mary Kling, Paris. *Address:* La Mare aux Oiseaux, 78116, Saint Leger-en-Yuelines, France.

TÖYRYLÄ, Timo Sakari, b. 11 Aug. 1921, Asikkala, Finland, Journalist; Artist. m. Sirkka-Liisa Vuorinen, 1 Jan. 1945 (dec. 1972), 1 son, 2 daughters. *Appointments:* Teacher, Public Schools, 1948–58; Editorial and Corrector Tasks by Werner Söderström Osakeyhtio, 1945–48; Editor-in-Chief, Paijat Hame; local newspaper, 1960–85. *Publications:* Kenttaharmaa nuoruus, 1943; Nyt olen Luonasi, 1945; Laula, mustalaispoika, 1947; Kahlaajalinnut, 1959; Kun on kuin on, 1969; Parasta mita nyt tiedan, 1970; Valitut runot, 1971; Vuorten Vanhuksen veisuja, 1971; Alakulosta latvapaloon, 1972; Vaikka taivaan rantaan, 1984; Hymyilet viistoon, 1985. Contributor of articles to magazines and other publications. *Memberships:* Suomen Kirjailijaliitto R.Y.; Salpausselan Kirjailijat R.Y.

Honours: Suomen Kirjailijaliiton Vuosipalkinto (Annual Reward), 1981; Suomen Kulttuurirahaston Tunnustuspalkinto, 1982. *Address:* 17300 Vääksy, Finland.

TRAAT, Mats, b. 23 Nov. 1936, Arula, Estonia. Writer. m. Victoria Viir, 13 May 1970, Tallinn, Estonia, 1 daughter. *Education:* Gorki Literary Institute, Moscow. *Publications:* Poetry: Angular Songs, 1962; Knolly Land, 1964; Lanterns in the Fog, 1968; Cardinal Points, 1970; Sketches Intended for Starting a Fire, 1971; Late Lambs, 1976; Time of Open Lands, 1977; September Fugue, 1980. Novels: Dance around a Locomobile, 1971; A Landscape with an Apple Tree and a Diary-Chimney, 1973; Pommer's Orchard, 1974; Coffee Beans, 1974; Inger, 1975; Trees – They Were Tender Brothers, 1979; Suspension Bridge, 1980; Pasque Flower – A Remedy for Melancholy, 1982 (all written in Estonian). *Honours:* Literary Prize by the collective farm named after Ed Vilde 1967, 1971, 1980; Soviet Estonian Prize 1972; Fr Tuglas Prize 1975; Juhan Smuul Prize 1977; Literary Prize by collective farm named after A H Tammsaare 1983; Merited Writer of the Estonian SSR 1977. *Membership:* Writers' Union of the USSR. *Address:* Tallinn 200010 Oru 16, Estonia, USSR.

TRACY, Ann Blaisdell, b. 2 Jan, 1941, Bangor, Maine, USA. English Professor. *Education:* BA, Colby College, 1962; MA, Brown University, 1964; PhD, English, University of Toronto, Canada, 1974. *Publications:* The Gothic Novel 1790–1830, 1981. *Contributions to:* Anthologies: Murderess Ink, 1979; Supernatural Fiction Writers.*Honour:* Phi Beta Kappa, 1962. *Literary Agent:* Pat Hoffmann-Francis, Grace Walworth Agency. *Address:* 12 Addoms Street, Plattsburgh, NY 12901, USA.

TRACY, Honor Lilbush Wingfield, b. 19 Oct. 1913, Bury St Edmunds, England. Author. *Education:* Grove School, Highgate School, Dresden and Sorbonne, Paris, France. *Publications include:* (travel) Mind You, I've Said Nothing!, 1953; Spanish Leaves, 1964; Winter in Castille, 1973; The Heart of England, 1983: (fiction), The Straight and Narrow Path, 1956; The First Day of Friday, 1963; The Quiet End of Evening, 1972; In a Year of Grace, 1975; The Ballad of Castle Reef, 1979. *Contributor to:* Atlantic Monthly; Harpers Bazaar; Cosmopolitan; Listener; New Statesman; Travel; Daily Telegraph. *Honours include:* Book Club Recommendation, 1950; Best British Radio Feature Script Award, British Writer's Guild, 1968. *Address:* 1 Mead House, Heathfield Lane, Chislehurst, Kent, England.

TRAINOR, Francis Rice, b. 11 Feb. 1929, USA. Professor of Biology. m. Margaret Swanton, 25 Aug. 1956, Providence, Rhode Island. *Education:* BS, Providence College, Rhode Island, 1950; MA 1953, PhD 1957, Vanderbilt University, Tennessee. *Publications:* Introductory Phycology, 1958. *Contributions to:* Various scientific journals, national & international. *Honours:* Distinguished Faculty Award, University of Connecticut, 1962; Darbaker Award, Botanical Society of America, 1965; National Lecturer, Psycological Society of America, 1983–85. *Memberships:* President 1968–, Phycological Society of America; Sigma Xi; American Association for the Advancement of Science; etc. *Address:* 101 East Road, Storrs, CT 06268, USA.

TRANSTRÖMER, Tomas Gösta, b. 15 Apr. 1931, Stockholm, Sweden. Psychologist/Writer. m. Monica Blach, 1958, 2 daughters. *Education:* Degree, University of Stockholm, 1956. *Publications:* 9 books of poetry in Swedish between 1954 and 1983. *Contributions to:* Swedish: BLM; Lyrikvannen; Dagems Nyheter; Artes etc. English: Lines; Modern Poetry in Translation; Antaeus; London Magazine; Books Abroad; Times Literary Supplement, etc. German: Akzente etc. *Honours:* Swedish: Aftonbladets Litteraturpris 1958; Bellmanpriset 1966; Övralidspriset 1975; Boklotteriets pris 1981 etc. German: The Petrarca prize, 1981. American: International Poetry Forum's Award, 1971. *Memberships:* Writers' Union of Sweden;

Swedish PEN Club. *Address:* Infanterigatan 144, 72347 Vasteras, Sweden.

TRANTER, Clement John, b. 16 Aug. 1909, Cirencester, England. Emeritus Professor, Mathematics, Royal Military College of Science, Shrivenham. m. Joan Louise Hatton, 21 Aug. 1937, Cirencester. *Education:* BA, 1931, MA, 1940, DSc, 1953, Queen's College, Oxford. *Publications:* Integral Transforms in Advanced Level Pure Mathematics, 1953; Techniques of Mathematical Analysis, 1937; Differential Equations for Engineers and Scientists, co-author, 1961; Mathematics for Sixth Form Scientists, 1964; Advanced Level Mathematics (Pure & Applied), co-author, 1966; Bessel Functions with Some Physical Applications, 1968. *Contributor to:* 40 papers in mathematical journals. *Honours:* OBE, 1953, CBE, 1967. *Address:* Flagstones, Stanton Fitzwarren, Nr Swindon, Wiltshire SN6 7RZ, England.

TRANTER, John, b. 1943, Cooma, New South Wales, Australia. Teacher; Writer. m. 2 children. *Education:* BA. *Publications include:* Poetry: Parallax, 1970; Red Movie, 1972; The Blast Area, 1974; The Alphabet Murders, 1976; Crying in Early Infancy, 1977; Dazed in the Ladies Lounge, 1979; Selected Poems, 1982; Co-Translator, Recent German Poetry, 1977; Compiler, Editor, Authology, The New Australian Poetry, 1979. *Contributor to:* Numerous articles and reviews in Newspapers and Magazines; Publisher's Editor, Senior Editor, Education, Angus & Robertson Publishers, Singapore, 1971–73; Associate Editorial Work, various magazines including, Transit; Aspect Art and Literature; New Poetry; Poetry Australia; etc. *Honours:* Recipient numerous honours and awards including: Senior Writing Fellowships, Literature Board, Australia Council, 1974, 1978, 1979, 1980, 1982, 1984, 1985, 1986; Visiting Fellow, Faculty of Arts, Australian National University, 1981; Writer in residence, School of Humanities and Social Science, New South Wales Institute of Technology, 1983; etc. *Address:* 74 Corunna Road, Stanmore 2048, Australia.

TRAVERS, Basil Holmes, b. 7 July 1919, Sydney, Australia. Schoolmaster (retired). m. Margaret Emily Marr, 14 Sep. 1942, Sydney, 3 daughters. *Education:* BA, Sydney University; MA, B Litt, Oxford University. *Publications:* Let's Talk Rugger, 1950; The Captain General, 1953. *Contributions to:* Various articles in educational journals and magazines. *Honours:* OBE, 1943; psc, 1944; AM, 1983, Fellow of College of Education; Fellow of Royal Society of Arts; FAIM. *Address:* 17 Malo Road, Whale Beach, New South Wales 2107, Australia.

TRAWICK, Leonard M, b. 4 July 1933. Professor. *Education:* BA, University of South Sewanee, Tennessee, USA, 1955; MA, University of Chicago, Illinois, 1956; PhD, Harvard University, Cambridge, Massachusetts, 1961. *Appointments:* Assistant Professor of English, Columbia University, New York City, USA, 1961–69; Associate Professor, Professor of English, Cleveland State University, Cleveland, Ohio, 1969–; Editor, The Gamut, Journal, 1980–. *Publications:* Comm and Ed Poetry Book series, Cleveland State University Poetry Centre; Beast Forms, 1971; Severed Parts, (chapbook), 1981. *Contributions to:* Poetry; Poetry Now; Sewanee Review; Antioch Quarterly; Chicago Review; Greensboro Review; Little Mag Quarterly W; Everyman; Cornfield Review; Assembling; Dark Tower; Whiskey Island Quarterly; Anthologies: Poetry, Cleveland, 1971; Forum: Ten Poets of W Reserve, 1977; 73 Ohio Poets, 1979; Tendril: Poems 1978–1983, 1984; Poems read on radio and syndicated for national broadcast. *Honours:* 1st Place, Bicentennial Poetry Competition, Cleveland Area Arts Council, 1975. *Memberships:* Trustee, Poets League, Greater Cleveland. *Address:* Department of English, Cleveland State University, Cleveland, OH 44115, USA.

TREACY, Maura, b. 3 July 1946, Kilkenny, Republic of Ireland. Writer. *Publications:* Sixpence in Her Shoe and Other Stories, 1977; Scenes from a Country Wedding, novel, 1981. *Contributions to:* New Irish Writing; Best Irish Short Stories; Bodley Head Book of Irish Short Stories. *Honour:* Short Story Award, Writers' Week in Listowel, 1974. *Address:* Rathduff, Ballyragget, Co Kilkenny, Republic of Ireland.

TREADGOLD, Donald Warren, b. 24 Nov. 1922, Silverton OR, USA. University Professor, m. Alva Granquist, 24 Aug. 1947, Eugene OR, 1 son 2 daughters. *Education:* BA Hons, University of Oregon, 1943; AM. Harvard University, 1947; D Phil, Oxford University, England, 1950. *Publications:* Lenin and His Rivals, 1955; The Great Siberian Migration, 1957; Twentieth Century Russia, 1959, 5th Edition 1981; The West in Russia and China, 2 vols 1973, reprint 1985; A History of Christianity, 1979. *Contributor to:* New Leader; New Republic; National Review; Modern Age; New Oxford Review; Slavic Review; American Historical Review; Slavonic and East European Review etc. Editor: Slavic Review, 1961–65 and 1968–75. *Honours:* Rhodes Scholar (Oregon and Queen's 1947); Ford Fellow, Harvard University, 1954–55; Guggenheim Fellow, 1964–65; E Harris Harbison Award for Distinguished Teaching, 1968; Phi Beta Kappa Visiting Scholar, 1974–75; AAASS Award for Distinguished Service, 1975; University of Washington Annual Faculty Lecturer, 1980; Fellow, American Academy of Arts and Sciences, elected 1983. *Memberships:* American Association for the Advancement of Slavic Studies, Member of Board of Directors, 1962–65, 1968–75; Publications Committee, Honors and Awards Committee, President 1977–78. *Address:* 4507 52nd Avenue NE, Seattle, WA 98105, USA.

TREADWELL, Harry, b. 29 Sep. 1925, Merseyside, England. Journalist, Editor, Publisher. m. 20 Aug. 1949, Newton-le-Willows, 2 sons, 1 daughter. *Literary Appointments:* Reporter, Runcorn Weekly News; Sports Sub editor, Warrington Guardian Series; Feature writer, Sussex Daily News; Reporter, Westminster Press; Full-time national daily freelance reporter and broadcaster; Founder-Publisher of Sussex Business Times; Editor, Cat World. *Major Publications:* Editor, The First Rotarian: The Life and Times of Paul Percy Harris, Founder of Rotary, by James Walsh, first and major biography of Harris; Publisher of Pet Trade Association Year Book; History and Management series of dog breeds; Several Biographies, including Banner Headlines: The Story of the News of the World, by S Somerfield. *Contributor to:* Numerous British and overseas newspapers; Consumer, Business and Professional magazines; Script writer for Television news. *Address:* Michaelmas, The Walled Garden, Southwick Street, Southwick, Brighton, BN4 4TE, England.

TREASE, (Robert) Geoffrey, b. 11 Aug. 1909, Nottingham, England. Author. m. Marian Haselden Granger Boyer, 11 Aug. 1933, Guyharn, Cambridgeshire, 1 daughter. *Education:* Scholar, Queen's College, Oxford, 1928–29. *Publications include:* Bows Against the Barons, 1934, first of many children's books including Cue For Treason, 1940; No Boats On Bannermere, 1949; The Cormorant Venture, 1984. Adult books: Tales out of School, 1949; Snared Nightingale, 1957; The Italian Story, 1963; A Whiff of Burnt Boats: An Early Autobiography, 1971; Laughter at the Door: A Continued Autobiography, 1974; Portrait of a Cavalier, 1979. *Contributions To:* Times Literary Supplement; Times Educational Supplement; The Author. *Honour:* New York Herald Tribune Award, 1966. *Memberships:* Chairman 1972–73, Council Member 1974–, Society of Authors; Fellow, Royal Society of Literature, 1979; PEN. *Address:* The Croft, Old Church Road, Colwall, Malvern, Worcestershire, WR13 6EZ, England.

TREAT, Lawrence Arthur, b. 21 Dec. 1903, New York City. Writer. m. Rose Ehrenfreund, 7 May 1943. *Education:* BA, Dartmouth College; LLB, Columbia University. *Publications:* Vasin Victim, 1945; Big Shot, 1951; Venus Unarmed, 1961; Crime and Puzzlement, 1981. *Contributions to:* Various publications and anthologies. *Honours:* Edgar Allan Poe Award, 1965, 1971; International Crime Writers', Prize Story, 1981.

Membership: President, Director, Mystery Writers of America. *Literary Agent:* John K Payne. *Address:* RFD Box 475A, Edgartown, MA 02539, USA.

TREBY, Ivor, b. Devenport, England. Biochemist. *Education:* MA, Hons School of Biochemistry, Exeter College, Oxford, England. *Publications:* Warm Bodies, now seeking a publisher; Foreign Parts, in preparation. *Contributor to:* The Honest Ulsterman; Argo; Kunapipi; Labrys; No Apologies; Poesis; Southwest Review; 2 Plus 2; The Literary Review; Anglowelsh Review; The Present Tense; Outposts; Straight Lines; Another Jerusalem; UK Am; Angel Exhaust; Sepia; Poetry Nottingham; Caprice; Image; Sapopho; The Gay Journal; Direction One; Magma, etc. *Honours:* Verse Cycle, Woman with Camellias, was a prizewinner in Redcliffe National Poetry Competition, 1983; as a song cycle (music Robin Bone) performed by Jane Manning and Endymion Ensem le in 1985, Piccadilly Festival. The poem, Miz Pretty, chosen as pilot for a set of poems. *Membership:* Schools' Poetry Association, 1983. *Address:* Flat 10, 30 Gloucester Terrace, City of Westminster, London W2 3DA, England.

TREFOUSSE, Hans Louis, b. 18 Dec. 1921, Frankfurt, Federal Republic of Germany. Professor of History. m. Rashelle Friedlander 26 Jan. 1947, Brooklyn, New York, USA, 1 son. *Education:* BA, City College of New York, 1942; MA 1947, PhD, 1950, Columbia University, USA. *Major Publications:* Germany & American Neutrality 1939–41, 1951; Ben Butler: The South Called him Beast, 1956; Benjamin Franklin Wade, 1963; The Radical Republicans, 1969; Impeachment of a President, 1975; Carl Schurz, 1982. *Contributor to:* Mississippi Valley Historical Review; Civil War History; Lincoln Herald; Prospects; Yearbook of German American Studies; Ohio History; New York History; Great Plains Quarterly; and others. *Honours:* Guggenheim Fellowship, 1977–78; ACLS Fellowship, 1984; Brooklundian Professor, 1985. *Memberships:* American Historical Association; OAH, SHA (Membership Committee). *Address:* Brooklyn College, Brooklyn, NY 11210, USA.

TREGIDGO, Philip Sillince, b. 3 Mar. 1926, Portsmouth, England. Writer of Educational Textbooks. m. Vera Williams, 19 Aug. 1950, Treforest, Glam, 2 sons, 1 daughter. *Education:* BA, (Oxon); Dip Ed,(Oxon); MA, (Reading). *Publications:* Practical English Usage, 1969; Background to English, 1961; Practical English 1-5, 1965–66; English for Tanzanian Schools, 1966–68; Longman New Ghana English Course 1-2, 1970–71; English Grammar in Practice, 1979; Advance with English 6-8, 1979–81; New Practical English 1-6, 1985–. *Contributor to:* Ghana Teachers Journal; English Language Teaching Journal; Lingua; Member Society of Authors; International Association of Teachers of English as a Foreign Language, Linguistics Association of Great Britain. *Address:* 11 The Avenue, Petersfield, Hampshire, GU31 4JQ, England.

TREGLOWN, Jeremy Dickinson, b. 24 May 1946, Anglesey, North Wales. Editor, Times Literary Supplement, 1982–. m. (1) Rona Bower, 1970, 1 son, 2 daughters (div. 1982). (2) Holly Urquhart, 1984. *Education:* MA, BLitt, St Peter's College, Oxford University; PhD, London. *Literary Appointments:* Lecturer, English Literature, Lincoln College, Oxford, 1973–76, University College, London, 1976–79; Assistant Editor, Times Literary Supplement, 1979–81. Editor 1982–. *Publications:* Editor, The Letters of John Wilmot, Earl of Rochester, 1980; Spirit of Wit, 1982. *Contributions to:* Plays & Players; The Guardian; Sunday Times; etc. General Editor, Plays in Performance Series, 1981–85; Articles on poetry & drama in various learned journals. *Address:* 102 Savernake Road, London NW3, England.

TRELFORD, Donald Gilchrist, b. 9 Nov. 1937, Coventry, England. Editor; Journalist. m. (1) Janice Ingram, 1963, 2 sons, 1 daughter; (2) Katherine Louise Mark, 1978, 1 daughter. *Education:* MA, Selwyn College, Cambridge. *Literary Appointments:* Judge,

British Press Awards, 1982–; Committee, Olivier Awards, Society of West End Theatre, 1984–. *Publications:* Siege, 1980; Sunday Best, 1981, 1982 and 1983; County Champions, 1982. *Contributions to:* The Listener; Literary Review; and others. *Honours:* Newspaper of the Year, Granada Television Awards, 1982; Commended, International Editor of the Year, World Press Review, 1984. *Memberships:* British Executive Committee, International Press Institute; Committee, Media Society; Committee, Journalists in Europe. *Literary Agent:* Curtis Brown. *Address:* c/o The Observer, 8 St Andrews Hill, London EC4V 5JA, England.

TREMAYNE, Sydney, b. 15 Mar. 1912, Ayr, Scotland. Poet; Retired journalist. m. (1) Lily Hanson, 1931, Knaresborough, 2 sons; (2) Constance Lipop, London, 1946. *Publications:* Time & The Wind, 1948; The Hardest Freedom, 1951; The Rock & the Bird, 1955; The Swans of Berwick, 1962; The Turning Sky, 1969; Selected & New Poems, 1973; As I Remember (with others), 1979. *Contributions to:* Numerous journals, including Life & Letters; The Windmill; Spectator; New Statesman; Listener; More than 40 anthologies. *Address:* 4 Peterburn, Gairloch, Ross-shire, Scotland IV21 2DX.

TREMBLAY, Gail, b. 15 Dec. 1945, Buffalo, New York, USA. College Professor. *Education:* BA, Drama, University of New Hampshire, 1967; MFA, Writing, University of Oregon, 1969. *Publications:* Night Gives Women the Word, 1979; Talking to the Grandfathers, 1981. *Contributor to:* Northwest Review; Denver Quarterly; Calyx; Maize; Many Smokes; Anthologies include: 1981 Anthology of Magazine Verse and Yearbook of American Poetry; A Nation Within; Sandhills and Other Geographies; Annex 22. *Honours:* Alfred E Richards Poetry Prize, University of New Hampshire, 1967; Annex 21, American Poetry Series, 1981. *Address:* Library 1402, The Evergreen State College, Olympia, WA, 98505, USA.

TRENGOVE, Alan, b. 1 July 1929, London, England. Writer; Publisher. m. Joan Eloise Moss, 21 June 1952, Wagga Wagga, Australia, 1 son, 2 daughters. *Publications:* The Golden Mile, 1961; John Grey Gorton, 1969; What's Good for Australia: The Story of BHP, 1975; Adventure in Iron, 1976; Menzies: A Pictorial Biography, 1978; Discovery: Stories of Modern Mineral Exploration, 1979. *Honour:* Moomba Award for Local History, 1976. *Memberships:* Fellowship of Australian Writers; Australian Society of Authors. *Literary Agent:* George Greenfield, John Farquharson Ltd. *Address:* 31 Trafalgar St, Mont Albert, Victoria 3127, Australia.

TREPP, Leo, b. 4 Mar. 1913, Mainz, Germany. Professor of Philosophy and Humanities. *Education:* Universities of Frankfurt, Berlin and Würzburg, 1931–35; PhD, 1935; Yeshivar Frankfurt Rabbi Seminar, Berlin, 1931–36; Ordained Rabbi, Rabbiner Seminar, Berlin, 1936; Harvard University, USA, 1944–45; University of California, Berkeley, 1951. *Publications include:* Eternal Faith, Eternal People, 1962; Die Landesgemeinde der Juden in Oldenburg, 1965; Judaism, Development and Life, 1966, 3rd revised edition 1984; Das Judentum, Geschichte und Lebendige Gegenwart, 1966, 4th revised edition 1979; Die Oldenburger Judenschaft, 1973; A History of the Jewish Experience, 1974; Una Historia de la Experiencia Judia, 1980; The Complete Book of Jewish Observance, 1980; Judische Ethik, 1984. *Contributions to:* The Experience of Religious Diversity, 1985; Contributing editor, Reconstructionist, 1944–50; Liberal Judaism; Conservative Judaism; Central Conference of American Rabbis Journal; Sh'ma. *Honours include:* Great Seal, City of Oldenburg, 1971; George Washington Honorary Medal Award, Freedoms Foundation, 1979; Doctor of Divinity honoris causa, Hebrew Union College of Jewish Institute of Religion, 1985; Doctor of Philosophy honoris causa, University of Wurzburg, 1985. *Memberships:* American Philosophical Association; Rabbinical Association; CCAR. *Address:* 295 Montecito Boulevard, Napa, CA 94558, USA.

TRESIDDER, Argus John, b. 9 Jan. 1907, Buffalo, New York, USA. University Professor; Foreign Service Officer. m. Nancy Blair Palmer, 4 May 1949, Louisville, Kentucky, USA, 1 daughter. *Education:* AB, 1928, MA, 1932, PhD, 1935, Cornell University. *Literary Appointments:* Instructor in English, Universities of Kansas and Tennessee; Professor of English, Madison College, Virginia, Northwestern University; Visiting Professor, College of the City of New York and several universities in Ceylon, Turkey, South Africa and Sweden. *Publications:* Reading to Others, 1940; Writing and Speaking, 1942; Myths of Turkey, 1955; Ceylon: An Introduction to the Resplendant Land, 1960; Article on Sri Lanka in Encyclopedia, current edition, Effective Communication, 1975; Watch-Word! A Glossary of Gobbledygook, Cliches and Solocisms,1981. *Contributions to:* Numerous articles in Madison Quarterly; American Speech; Journal of National Association of Teachers of Speech; Lank Quarterly; Sewanee Review; Saturday Review; Marine Corps Gazette; Cornell Alumni News. *Honour:* Phi Beta Kappa, 1927. *Address:* 4206 Cordell Street, Annandale, VA 22003, USA.

TREVELYAN, Raleigh, b. 6 July 1923, Port Blair, Ross Island, Andamans. Writer & Publisher. *Education:* Winchester College. *Literary Appointments:* Editor, Collins Publishers, 1948–58; Hutchinson 1958–61 (Director, New Authors, Arrow Books); Penguin Books, 1961–62; Director, Michael Joseph, 1962–75, Hamish Hamilton, 1975–80; Literary Advisor, Jonathan Cape, 1980–. *Major Publications:* The Fortress, 1956; A Hermit Disclosed, 1960; The Big Tomato, 1966; Princes under the Volcano, 1972; The Shadow of Vesuvius, 1976; A Pre-Raphaelite Circle, 1978; Rome '44, 1982; Shades of the Alhambra, 1985. *Contributor to:* The Listener; The Guardian; London Review of Books; Times Literary Supplement; Apollo; Connoisseur; John Rylands Bulletin; Pre-Raphaelite Review; The Sunday Times; The Observer; The Spectator. *Honour:* John Florio Prize for Translation from the Italian, 1967. *Memberships:* Royal Society of Literature (Fellow); International PEN (Members of English Committee). *Literary Agent:* A M Heath. *Address:* 18 Hertford Street, London W1Y 7DB, England.

TREVELYAN, Sir George Lowthian Bt, b. 5 Nov. 1906, London, England. Teacher in Adult Education. m. Editha Helen Lindsay-Smith, 6 Aug. 1940, 1 daughter. *Education:* Honours Degree 1928, MA 1955, Trinity College, Cambridge. *Publications:* A Vision of the Aquarian Age, 1977 (USA 1984); Operation Redemption, 1980 (USA 1985); Magic Casements, 1980; Translations: Eine Vision Des Wassermann-Zeitalters, 1980; Unternehmen Erlosung, 1983; Doorbraak Naar Nieuw Inzicht. *Honour:* Right Livelihood Award, Stockholm, 1982. *Address:* The Old Vicarage, Hawkesbury, Badminton, Avon GL9 1BW, England.

TREVER, John Cecil, b. 26 Nov. 1915, Milwaukee, Wisconsin. Professor of Religion/Ordained Minister. m. Elizabeth Signe Burman, 29 Aug. 1937, Los Angeles, California, 2 sons. *Education:* AB, 1937, University of Southern California; BD, 1940, Yale Divinity School; PhD, 1943, Yale Graduate School. *Literary Appointments:* Monthly articles for, International Hournal of Religious Education, 1948–53; 100 Entries on, Flora of the Bible, for the, Interpreter's Dictionary of the Bible, 1962. *Publications:* The Dead Sea Scrolls of St Mark's Monastery, (with Millar Burrows and William Brownlee), vol 1, 1950, vol II 1951; Cradle of our Faith, 1954; Untold Story of Qumran, 1965; (German edition: Das Abeneuer Von Qumran, 1967; Arabic edition, 1969); Scrolls from Qumran Cave I, 1972; The DSS: A Personal Account, 1978. *Contributions to:* The Biblical Archaeologist; Smithsonian Report; Revue de Qumren; and others. *Honours:* Phi Beta Kappa, 1936; Tew Prize in Hebrew, Yale Divinity School, 1940; Thayer Fellowship, 1947; John F Lewis Prize, American Philosophical Society, 1955. *Memberships:* Society of Biblical Literature; American Academy of Religion.

Address: 369 Radcliffe Drive, Claremont, CA 91711, USA.

TREVES, Ralph, b. 16 July 1906, New York State, USA. Journalist. m. Estelle Hennefeld, 2 daughters. *Education:* BS, New York University. *Publications:* Basements and Rec Rooms, 1957; Home Protection Book, 1968; Your Recreation Room, 1969; Kitchen Remodelling, 1976; The Cleaning Book, 1978. *Contributions to:* Some 560 articles in: Philadelphia Inquirer; Los Angeles Times; Family Handyman; Popular Science. *Honours:* President, National Association of Home Workshop Writers, 1979–84. *Memberships:* National Association of Science Writers; American Medical Writers Association. *Literary Agent:* Klausner Literary Agency. *Address:* 311 Lake Evelyn Drive, West Palm Beach, FL 33411, USA.

TREVISAN, João Silvério, b. 23 June 1944, Ribeirão Bonito, Brazil. Writer. *Education:* Faculty, Lorena/Pontificia Universidad Catolica, Sao Paulo, Brazil. *Publications:* Testamento de Jonatas deixado a David, short stories, 1976; As incriveis aventuras de El Condor, novel for young adults, 1980; Em nome do desejo, novel, 1983; Vagas noticias de Melinha Marchiotti, novel, 1984; Perverts in Paradise, essay, 1986. *Contributions to:* Khipu, Germany; Gay Sunshine, USA; Eros, Mexico; Cinema Trois, Rabat; Cine Olho, Brazil; Films Cultura; Movimento; Opiniao; Lampiao; Almanaque; Ficcao; Istoe; Folhetim. *Honours:* 1st Prize, 1957, 2nd Prize, 1961, National Short Story Competition, O Seminario Magazine; Honorable Mention, IV Latin American Short Story Competiton, 1975; Honorable Mention, 11 Erotic Short Story Competition, Status Magazine, 1976. *Memberships:* Writers Association of Brazil; Playwrights Association ofBrazil. *Address:* Rua Desembargador Euclides de Campos 32, 05030 São Paulo, Brazil.

TREVOR, William, b. 24 May 1928, Mitchelstown, Co Cork, Ireland. Author. *Education:* BA, Trinity College Dublin. *Publications include:* The Old Boys, 1964; The Bounding House, 1965; The Love Department, 1966; The Day We Got Drunk on Cake, 1967; Mrs Eckdorf in O'Neill's Hotel, 1969; Miss Gomez and the Brethren, 1971; The Ballroom of Romance, 1972; Elizabeth Alone, 1973; The Children of Dynmouth, 1976; Lovers of Their Time, 1978; Other People's Worlds, 1980; Angels at the Ritz, 1982; Beyond the Pale, 1983; Fools and Fortune, 1984. *Contributor to:* Journals including, Nova; Encounter; London Magazine; New Yorker; Atlantic Monthly; The Listener. *Honours include:* Hawthorden Prize, 1965; CBE; 1977; Whitbread Prize, 1976, 1984; Royal Society of Literature Award, 1976; Allied Irish Banks' Literary Award, 1976; Honorary Doctorates, Exeter University, 1984; Trinity, Dublin, 1986. *Memberships:* Irish Academy of Literature. *Literary Agent:* A D Peters. *Address:* c/o Bodley Head, 30 Bedford Square, London, England.

TRIBE, David Harold, b. 17 Dec. 1931. Public Relations and Scientific Officer. *Education:* Fellowship, Medicine, University of Queensland, 1949–54. *Literary Appointments:* Freelance Author, Poet, Editor, Critic, Artist, Lecturer, Broadcaster, Journalist and Public Relations Consultant, London, England, 1955–72; Publicity Officer, 1976–. *Publications:* Why Are We Here? (verse), 1965; 5 books: 100 Years of Freethought, 1967; President Charles Bradlaugh, MP, 1971; Nucleopethics: Ethics in Modern Society, 1972; Questions of Censorship, 1973; The Rise of the Mediocracy, 1976; many booklets, poems, pamphlets, articles, reviews. *Contributor to:* London Sunday Times; Punch; New Statesman; Tribune; 20th Century; BBC; New Poetry; Poetry Australia; Australian Broadcasting Corporation; Meanjin, etc. *Honours:* Recipient several honours and awards. *Memberships:* Poets Union of Australia; Australian Society of Authors; Poets in Schools Scheme, Arts Council of Great Britain; London Poetry Secretariat, Greater London Arts Association; Poets Workshop; Commonwealth Writers Club, Vice-President. *Address:* 10 Griffiths Street, Fairlight, New South Wales 2094, Australia.

TRIFFIN, Robert, b. 5 Oct. 1911, Flobecq, Belgium. Emeritus Professor. m. Lois Brandt, 30 May 1940, New York, 3 sons. *Education:* Bachelor in Philosophy, Licencié in Political and Diplomatic Science, Licencié in Economics, Louvain University; PhD Economics, Harvard University, USA. *Publications:* Monopolistic Competition and General Equilibrium Theory, 1940; Europe and the Money Muddle, 1957; Gold and the Dollar Crisis, 1960; The World Money Maze, 1966; Our International Monetary System: Yesterday, Today and Tomorrow, 1968. *Contributions to:* More than 300 to magazines and journals. *Honours include:* Dr honoris causa, Louvain 1970, New Haven and American College of Switzerland; Gold Medal of European Merit; Commandor of various national orders: Belgium, Guatemala, Paraguay; Wells Prize in Economics, Harvard, 1940; Prizes in Belgium. *Memberships include:* World Academy of Art and Science; American Academy of Arts and Sciences; Council of Foreign Relations, New York; Academie Royale de Belgique. *Address:*IRES, 3 Place Montesquieu, Louvain-la-Neuve, B 1348, Belgium.

TRILLING, Diana, b. 21 July 1905, New York City, USA. Literary Critic. m. Lionel Trilling, 12 June 1929, New York, 1 son. *Education:* AB, Radcliffe, USA. *Literary Appointments:* Fiction Critic, The Nation, 1941–49; Editorial page column, New York Herald Tribune; Column, Here & Now, The New Leader. *Major Publications:* Editor: The Viking Portable D H Lawrence, 1947; The Letters of D H Lawrence, 1958. Author: Claremont Essays, 1964; We Must March My Darlings, 1977; Reviewing the Forties, 1978; Mrs Harris: The Death of the Scarsdale Diet Doctor, 1981. *Contributor to:* New York Times Book Review; Partisan Review; Redbook; Commentary; Vogue; Harper's; The Atlantic; Harper's Bazaar; Esquire; The Scotsman; The Times Literary Supplement (London); Mademoiselle; Encounter; The American Scholar; The New Republic. *Honours:* Guggenheim Fellowship, 1950; Joint Fellowship, National Endowment for the Humanities/Rockefeller Foundation,1977–79; Honorary Membership, Phi Beta Kappa (Radcliffe Chapter). Fellow, American Academy of Arts & Sciences. *Address:* 35 Claremont Avenue, New York, NY 10027, USA.

TRILLING, Ossia, b. 22 Sep. 1913, Belstock, England. Performing Arts Critic. m. Marie-Louise Fock, 11 July 1951, London. *Education:* BA, Oxford University. *Literary Appointments:* Television Dramatist, 1937; Editor, Various performing arts periodicals, 1946. Special Arts Correspondent: The Times, 1956–70; The Guardian, 1960–71; Financial Times, 1971–84. *Publications:* International Theatre, 1946; Dobson's Theatre Yearbook, 1947. *Contributions to:* The Times; Times Educational Supplement; The Scotsman; The Guardian; Financial Times; Theatre Newsletter; Theatre; Plays and Players; Plays and Plays International; Drama Magazine; Contemporary Review; Music and Musicians; Classical Music; Scanorama; Sweden Now; Look at Finland; Canadian Theatre Review; Various USA and European magazines and journals. *Honours:* Officer: 1st Class, North Star, Sweden, 1981; 1st class, Lion of Finland, 1983. *Address:* 9a Portland Place, London W1N 3AA, England.

TRIPODI, Tony, b. 30 Nov. 1932. University Professor. 3 sons, 1 daughter. *Education:* AB, 1954, MSW, 1958, University of California, Berkeley; DSW, Columbia University, New York City, 1963. *Literary Appointments:* Editorial Boards, Social Work Abstracts, 1963–64, Social Work, 1974–78, Journal of Social Service Research, 1978–80, 1985–, Evaluation and Program Planning, 1978–, Urban and Social Change Review, 1978–, Encyclopaedia of Social Work, 1984–. Editor-in-Chief, Social Work Research and Abstracts, 1980–84. *Publications:* Clinical and Social Judgment, 1966; Assessment of Social Research, 1969; Exemplars of Social Research, 1969; Social Program Evaluation, 1971; Social Workers at Work, 1972; Uses and Abuses of Social Research in Social Work, 1974; Research Techniques for Program Planning, Monitoring and Evaluation, 1977; Differential Social Program Evaluation, 1978; Research Techniques for Clinical Social Workers, 1980; Evaluative Research for Social Workers, 1983; Social Work Research and People of Colon, 1984. *Contributions to:* Numerous articles, book reviews, editorials and research notes in a dozen journals in social work, public health and psychology. *Address:* School of Social Work, University of Michigan, Ann Arbor, MI 48109, USA.

TRIPP, Miles, b. 5 May 1923, Ganwick Corner, Barnet, England. Writer. *Literary Appointment:* Chairman, Crime Writers Association, 1968–69. *Publications include:* Faith is a Windsock, 1952; Kilo Forty, 1963; The Chicken, 1966; The Eighth Passenger, 1969; A Man Without Friends, 1970; Woman at Risk, 1974; The Wife-Smuggler, 1978; Cruel Victim, 1979; High Heels, 1980. *Contributions to:* Various journals. *Memberships:* Crime Writers Associaton; Detection Club; Society of Authors. *Literary Agent:* A D Peters. *Address:* c/o A D Peters & Co., 10 Buckingham Street, London WC2, England.

TROJAN, Judith Lynn, b. 7 July 1947, New Jersey, USA. Film Critic, Magazine Editor. *Education:* BA Fine Arts, Fairleigh Dickinson University, New Jersey, 1969; MA Cinema Studies, New York University, 1972; Certificate in Concepts in Film Criticism. The British Film Institute, London, England, 1973; Certificate in Film/Television Documentation, The American Film Institute, Beverly Hills, California, USA, 1979. *Literary Appointments:* Copywriter, WMTR Radio, Morris Plains, New Jersey, 1969–70; Editorial Coordinator, Educational Film Library Association, 1972–; Managing Editor 1972–82, Senior Editor 1982–84, Editor in Chief 1984–, Sightlights' magazine; Film/television columnist, Wilson Library Bulletin, 1980–; Contributing Editor, Media and Methods, 1976–80. *Publications:* Aging: A Filmography, 1974; 16mm Distribution, co-editor and author, 1977; American Families in Transition, 1980; American Family Life Films, 1981. *Contributions to:* Autobiography: Film/Video/Photography, 1978; Mass Media Newsletter; Take One; Film Library Quarterly; Feminist Art Journal; Media and Methods; Sightlights; Wilson Library Bulletin. *Honours include:* Pre-screening juror, Student Academy Awards, Academy of Motion Picture Arts and Sciences. *Memberships:* Educational Press Association of America; New York Film/Video Council; Association of Independent Video and Film makers. *Address:* 17 Cottage Lane, Clifton, NHJ 07012, USA.

TROTT, Elizabeth Anne, b. 16 Aug. 1943, London, Ontario, Canada. Teacher of Philosophy. m. Stephen Gregory, 19 July 1972, Toronto, Canada, 1 son. *Education:* BA; MA; BEd; PhD. *Appointment:* Teacher, Trinity College, Toronto, Canada (currently). *Publications:* The Faces of Reason, (an essay on philosophy and culture in English speaking Canada, 1850–1950), 1981 (co-author with Leslie Armour); The Industrial Kingdom of God, (introduction and notes by L Armour and E A Trott), 1982. *Contributor to:* Executive Magazine, 1983, (Ethics and the Executive); Profiles in Canadian Literature, 1986; Articles and entries in, New Canadian Encyclopaedia 1985, on Canadian Philosophy. *Membership:* Canadian Editor of, Journal of Ultimate Reality and Meaning. *Address:* 297 Bessborough Drive, Toronto, Ontario M46 3K9, Canada.

TROW, Martin A, b. 21 June 1926, New York City, USA. University Teacher and Researcher. m. Katherine Berahardi, 9 Sep. 1960, Berkeley, California, 2 sons, 1 daughter. *Education:* ME, Stevens Instiute of Technology, 1947; PhD, Sociology, Columbia University, 1957. *Publications:* Union Democracy, with S M Lipset and James Coleman, 1956; Right-Wing Radicalism and Political Intolerance, 1957, 1980; The British Academics, with A H Halsey, 1971; Students and Colleges: Interaction and Change, with B R Clark et al, 1972; Editor: Teachers and Students, 1975; The University in the Highly Educated Society: From Elite to Mass Higher Education (in Japanese) 1976; Essays in Higher Education, forthcoming. *Contributor to:* Leadership and Organization: The Case of Biology at Berkeley, in, Change, 1983; Higher Education as a

Stratification System: The Analysis of Status, in Perspectives in Higher Education: Eight Disciplinary and Comparative Views, edited by Burton R Clark, 1984; Problems in the Transition from Elite to Mass Higher Education, in, Policies for Higher Education, from General Report on the Conference on future Structures of Post-Secondary Education, Paris, 1974. *Honours:* Fellow, Center for Advanced Study in the Behavioral Sciences, Palo Alto, 1965–66; Visiting Fellow, Institute for Advanced Study, Princeton, 1976–77; DHL (HC) Carltton College, Minnesota, 1980; Fellow, American Association for the Advancement of Science, 1981–. *Address:* Center for Studies in Higher Education, South Hall Annex, University of California, Berkeley, CA 94720, USA.

TROY, Leonie Fuller Adams, b. 9 Dec. 1899, USA. Teacher; Writer. m. William E Troy. *Education:* BA, Barnard College. *Appointments include:* Poetry Consultant, Library of Congress, 1948–49; Visiting Professor, Poetry, University of Washington, 1959–69; Teacher, Purdue University, 1971–72. *Publications:* Those Not Elect, 1925; High Falcon, 1929; Poems: A Selection, 1954, 2nd edition 1959. *Contributions to:* New Republic; Poetry Chicago; Scribner's New Masses; Saturday Review of Literature; Literary Review, New York Evening Post; This Quarter. *Honours include:* Honorary Doctorate of Literature, New Jersey College for Women, 1950; Hollingen Prize, Yale, 1955; Fellowship, American Academy of Poets, 1959, 1974; Harriet Monroe Award, 1954; Shelley Memorial Award, 1954; Mark Rothke Foundation Award, 1973. *Memberships:* Fellow, American Academy of Letters; Secretary, 1959–61, National Institute of Arts & Letters; PEN. *Address:* Candlewood Valley Care Center, 30 Park Lane East, New Milford, CT 06776, USA.

TROY, Una, b. County Cork, Ireland. Writer. m. Joseph Walsh, 1 daughter. *Publications:* We Are Seven; Maggie; The Workhouse Graces; The Benefactors; Stop Press, etc. *Contributor to:* The Bell; Ireland Today; Madamoisell; Woman's Realm; Our Boys, etc. *Honours:* 1st Prize, New Playwrights Competition, Abbey Theatre, Dublin, 1938. *Membership:* PEN. *Literary Agent:* David Higham Associates, London. *Address:* 6 Osborne Terrace, Bonmahon, Co Waterford, Ireland.

TROYANOVICH, Stephen John, b. 18 Dec. 1947, Wheeling, West Virginia, USA. Correctional Education Supervisor. m. Magdalena del Rosario Coronel, 15 Apr. 1972, Iberra Ecuador, 1 son. *Education:* MA, Corrections, Montclair State; Currently working on doctoral dissertation, Rutgers University School of Criminal Justice. *Publication:* Dream Dealers and Other Shadows, 1978. *Contributions to:* (Poetry): Quarry; Stone Country; Abraxas; Wormwood Review; Blue Unicorn; Canadian Encounter; Weirdbook; Tweed; Fantasy Crossroads, The Yellow Butterfly; Mundus Artium, etc. *Memberships:* Poetry Society of America; Poets and Writers Incorporated. *Address:* Florence Tollgate 38-1, Florence, NJ 08518, USA.

TRUCHANOWSKI, Kazimierz, b. 9 Oct. 1904, Romanow na Wolyniu, Poland. Writer. m. Zofia Urbanska, 15 Jan. 1928, 1 daughter. *Education:* Gimmazjum w Zytomierzu 1922, Studia Lesne przerwane we wrzesmiu 1939. College at Zytomierz, Faculty of Forestry –1939. *Literary Appointments:* Redaktor pisma literackiego 1947. Editor, 1947, Nowiny Literackie, (Literary News). *Publications:* Ulica wszystkich swietych, (All Saints' Road); Apteka pod sloncem, (The Pharmacy under the Sun); Zmowa demiurgow, (Demiurges; Plot); Droga do nieba, (On the Way to Heaven); Oratoria nocne, (Night Oratorio); Piekny warkocz Bereniki, (The Fine Braid of Berenice); Mlyny bozr, 5 vols (God's Mills); Calowanie ziemi, (Kissing the Ground); Dzwony piekiel, (The Hell Bells); Totenhorn, (Totenhorn); Grajaca pusska, (Singing Box); and numerous translations from Russian and German. *Honours:* Cross of Polonia Restitute; First Class Literary Award, Minister of Culture and Fine Arts; Special Literary Award granted by PAX. *Memberships:* Literary Union 1936–39; Polish Literary Society 1945–;

PEN, 1950–. *Address:* ul. Koszykowa 3 m.63, 00-564 Warszawa, Poland.

TRUEBLOOD, Paul Graham, b. 21 Oct. 1905, Macksburg, Iowa, USA. University Professor of English Literature. m. Helen Churchill Trueblood, 19 Aug. 1931, Roseburg, Oregon, USA, 2 daughters. *Education:* BA, 1928, Willamette University; MA, 1930; PhD, 1935, Duke University. *Literary Appointments include:* University of Washington, 1947–52; University of Oregon, 1954–55; Visiting Professor, University of British Columbia, 1963; Willamette University, 1955–71; Professor Emeritus, 1971. *Publications:* Flowering of Byron's Genius: Studies In Byron's Don Juan, 1945; Lord Byron, 1969, 2nd Edition, 1977; Byron's Political and Cultural Influence in Nineteenth Century Europe, 1981. *Contributions to:* Numerous literary journals. *Honours:* Pendle Hill Fellow, 1934–35; Fellow of the American Council of Learned Societies, 1952–53; Participant in International Byron Seminars, 1974, 1976, 1979; First American Citizen to address the Byron Society in House of Lords, 1975; Distinguished Alumni Citation, Willamette University, 1975; Honorary Doctor of Letters, Willamette University, 1984. *Memberships:* Life Member, Modern Language Association of America; Keats-Shelley Association of America; Philological Association of the Pacific Coast; Founding Member, American Byron Society; The Byron Society. *Address:* 2635 Bolton Terrace S, Salem, OR 97302, USA.

TRUEMPER, David George, b. 1 Feb. 1939, Aurora, Illinois, USA. Professor of Theology. m. Joanna Ruth Mitschke, 29 June 1963, St Louis, Missouri, USA, 2 daughters. *Education:* BA, Concordia Senior College, Fort Wayne, Indiana, 1961; MDiv, Concordia Seminary, St Louis, Missouri, 1965; STM. Concordia Seminary, St Louis, 1969; STD, Lutheran School of Theology, Chicago, Illinois, 1974. *Literary Appointments:* Director, Institute of Liturgical Studies, Valparaiso University, 1985–. *Major Publications:* Chapters in Profiles in Belief II (by A C Piepkorn), Harper & Row, 1977; Keeping the Faith, Fortress, Philadelphia, 1981. *Contributor to:* Various religious journals, including: The Seminarian; The Cresset; Confession and Congregation; Currents in Theology and Mission. *Membership:* Executive Secretary, North American Academy of Liturgy, 1983–. *Address:* Valparaiso University, Valparaiso, IN 46383, USA.

TRUITT, Gloria Ann, b. 26 Aug. 1939, Laruium, Michigan, USA. Childrens Author. m. John Truitt, 1 June 1963, Marquette, 1 son, 1 daughter. *Education:* North Michigan University. *Literary Appointments:* Various Board appointments, Young Authors; Speaker at various writers conferences; Panelist, Women in the Arts; Conducted workshops. *Publications include:* Nature Riddle Coloring Book, series, 1982; People of the New Testament, 1983; People of the Old Testament, 1983; The Ten Commandments: Learning About God's Law, 1983; Events of the Bible, 1984; Places of the Bible, 1984; Cheerful Chad and Other Children of God, 1985; Noah and God's Promise, 1985. Included in numerous anthologies including: The Peanut Butter Hamster and Other Animal Tails, 1979; Halloween Handbook, 1984; The Incompetent Cat and Other Animal Tails, 1985. *Contributions to:* Action; Christian Living; Connect; Discovery; Explore; The Friend; Guide; Happy Times; Moody Monthly; On the Line; Power for Living; Say; Story Mates; Teen Power; Texas Methodist Reporter; Touch; War Cry; Wow; Young Ambassador, and numerous others. *Memberships:* Presbyterian Writers Guild; PEO Sisterhood. *Address:* 332 East Ohio Street, Marquette, MI 49855, USA.

TRYPANIS, Constantine Athanasius, b. 22 Jan. 1909, Chois, Greece. University Professor. m. Aliki Macris, 6 Apr. 1942, Athens, Greece, 1 daughter. *Education:* D Phil, University of Athens; MA, D Litt, University of Oxford. *Literary Appointments:* Lecturer in Classics, University of Athens, 1939–47; Professor of Medieval and Modern Greek, University of Oxford, 1947–69; University Professor of Classics, University of

Chicago, 1969–74. *Publications:* Medieval and Modern Greek Poetry, 1951; Callimachi Fragmenta, 1958; Penguin Book of Greek Verse, 1971; Greek Poetry, From Homer to Seferis, 1980. *Contributions to:* Times Literary Supplement; Classical Review; Hermes; Rheinisches Museum; Classical Quarterly; Gnomon Encounter; Kathimerine; New Yorker; New York Times. *Honours:* Koraes Prize, Academy of Athens; Heinemann Award, Royal Society of Literature; Gottfried-von-Herder Prize, University of Vienna. *Memberships:* British Royal Society of Literature; President, Academy of Athens; Honorary Fellow, British Academy. *Address:* 3 Georgiou Nikolaow, Kifisia-Athens, Greece.

TSAMBIRAS, Sotiris, b. 13 Oct. 1924, Athens, Greece. International Civil Servant. m. Micheline Rose Blanche Chevalier, 16 June 1964, Paris, 1 son, 1 daughter. *Education:* BD, University of Commercial and Economic Studies, Athens, 1952; Athens Free University of Athens; Studied, Sorbonne, Paris University. *Appointment:* Literary Correspondent, ORTF-Greek Broadcast, 1962–67. *Publications:* In Greek: Poetry ; Squalls, 1953; The Apples of Hesperides, 1964; Diaspora, 1971; The Songs of Elias and Other Poems, 1974; Odes to a Tupamaros and Other Poems, 1978; Travel Books: France, 1975; Short Stories: El Aniversariso and Other Stories, 1978; It Should Never Rain, 1985; In French: Poetry – Lettres de Colchide, 1980; Errances, 1983. *Contributor to:* Numerous professional journals, magazines and newspapers. *Honours:* Prix de la Ville de Sarlat, for Book of Poems, Errances, 1984; Recipient, various other honours and awards. *Memberships:* PEN Club of Belgium; Academie des Lettres et des Arts du Perigord; European Association for the Promotion of Poetry; Association Jane Tonny-Les Poetes de la Fleur, Brussels; Writers Union, Greece, Founding Member. *Address:* 3 Ave Albert Bechet Bte 2, 1950 Kraainem, Belgium.

TSCHUMI, Raymond Robert, b. 27 Nov. 1924, Saint Imier, Switzerland. Professor. m. Julita Lozano Paz, 1952, 2 sons, 1 daughter. *Education:* Grad. Brown University, 1947; Docteur de Lettres, Geneva, 1951. *Publications:* Thought in Twentieth Century English Poetry, 1951 (Octagon Books 1972); Science, Philosophy and Literary Critcism, 1961; A Philosophy of Literature, 1961; Theory of Culture, 1978; In French: L'Arche, 1950; Regards Voraces, 1952; Renouveau, 1953; Concert d'Ouvertures, 1967; De Dante à Milton, 1967; De la Pensée Continue, 1968; Signal de Cime, 1973; Poèmes Choisis, 1973; Jean Vincent Verdonnet, 1973; Théorie de la Culture, 1976; Grange de Veilleur, 1982; La Crise Culturelle, 1983. *Contributions to:* several literary magazines and journals including, Erasmus; English Studies; Formes et Langages; Le Temps Parallele. *Memberships:* President PEN Suisse Romande; Alliance Culturella Romande; Societé des Gens de Lettres de France; Societé des Ecrivains Suisses; Society des Ecrivains Neuchatelois et Jurassiens; Recontres Poétiques Internationales en Suisse Romande. *Address:* Quellenstr. 9, CH–9016 St Gallen, Switzerland.

TSIPIS, Kosta Michel, b. 12 Feb. 1934, Athens, Greece. Professor of Physics. m. Judith Ebel, 20 Dec. 1970, Cambridge, Massachusetts, USA, 3 sons. *Education:* BSc; MSc, Rutgers University; PhD, Columbia University. *Publications:* The Future of the Sea-Based Deterrent, 1972; Tactical and Strategic Anti-Submarine Warfare, 1975; Review of Military Research and Development, 1983; Arsenal, 1983; Review of Military Research and Development, 1984. *Contributions to:* 62 publications. *Address:* Massachusetts Institute of Technology, Cambridge, MA 02139, USA.

TSODZO, Thompson Kumbirai. Lecturer. *Education:* BA, Special Honours, University of Zimbabwe, 1980; Certificate, Project Planing and Management, Dalhousie University, Canada, 1983. *Publications:* Rurimi Rwaamai I-IV, 1979–83; Chishuma Chakauaka I-VII, 1984–85; Tsano, 1981; Rugare, 1982; Shandliko, 1983. *Memberships:* Zimbabwe Group of Authors, President; Zimbabwe Writers Union, Vice Chairman. *Address:* Dept of English, Box MP 167, Mt Pleasant, Harare, Zimbabwe.

TUBB, E(dwin) C(harles), b. 15 Oct. 1919, London, England. Writer. *Literary Appointments:* Editor, Authentic Science Fiction magazine, London, 1956–57. *Publications include:* Over 100 under various pseudonyms: Science Fiction/Fantasy: Saturn Patrol, 1951; Argentis, 1952; Planetoid Disposals Ltd, 1953; The Living World, 1954; Alien Dust, 1955; The Space-born, 1956; Touch of Evil, 1959; Moon Base, 1964; Ten From Tomorrow short stories, 1966; Death Is A Dream, 1967; C O D Mars, 1968; STAR Flight, 1969; The Jester at Scar, 1970; Lallia, 1971; Century of the Manikin, 1972; Mayenne, 1973; Veruchia, 1973; Zenya, 1974; Atilus the Slave, 1975; Jack of Swords, 1976; Haven of Darkness, 1977; Incident on Ath, 1978; Stellar Assignment, 1979; The Luck Machine, 1980. Suspense and Western novels: The Fighting Fury, 1955; Scourge of the South, 1956; Wagon Trail, 1957; Target Death, 1961; Too Tough To Handle, 1962; Airbourne Commando, 1963. *Contributions to:* 230 stories to magazines and journals. *Literary Agent:* Carnell Literary Agency. *Address:* 67 Houston Road, London SE23 2RL, England.

TUBBS, Douglas Burnel, b. 27 Mar. 1915, London, England. Writer; Translator. m. Penelope Bird, 4 Aug. 1962, Maidstone, England, 3 daughters. *Education:* BA (Cantab), Christ's College; Harvard University, USA. *Literary Appointments:* Staff, The Motor, London, 1941; Joint Sports Editor, 1945–62; Columnist, Kingpin, 1945–58. *Publications:* Vintage Cars, 1959; Kent Pubs, 1964; Lancaster Banker, 1972; Zeiss-Ikon Cameras, 1977; Art and the Automobile, 1978; Translations include: The Technique of Motor Racing, Works Driver; The Age of Motoring; Golden Age of Toys; History of Photography; Bugatti; History of Le Mans 24 Hours Race; Romantic America. *Contributor:* Articles on Motoring, Photography, Aviation, Art to various publications including, The Times; Motor; Autocar; The Car; Interdisciplinary Science Reviews, etc. *Honour:* Guild of Motoring Writers Montagu Trophy, 1979. *Membership:* Chelsea Arts Club. *Literary Agent:* Watson, Little Limited. *Address:* Winfield House, Crouch, Borough Green, Sevenoaks TN15 8PZ, England.

TUCHMAN, Barbara, b. 30 Jan. 1912, New York City, USA. Writer. m. Lester R Tuchman, 18 June 1940, New York, 3 daughters. *Education:* AB, Radcliffe; Honorary D Litt. *Publications:* Bible and Sword, 1956; The Zimmerman Telegram, 1958; The Guns of August, 1962; The Proud Tower, 1966; Stilwell and the American Experience in China, 1971; Notes from China, 1972; A Distant Mirror, 1978; Practising History, 1981; The March of Folly, 1984. *Contributions to:* Foreign Affairs; Atlantic Monthly; American Heritage; Harper's; New York Times; American Scholar; Christian Science Monitor. *Honours:* Pulitzer Prize for, The Guns of August, and for, Stilwell and the American Experience in China; Honorary D Litt from numerous colleges and universities. Honorary PhD, Ben-Gurion University, 1984. First Alumni Award, Walden School, 1964; Woman of the Year 1966, American Association of University Women; Hadassah Myrtle Wreath Award, 1974; Berkeley Citation, University of California, 1974; l'Ordre de Leopold, Belgium, 1975; Excellence Award, American Society of Journalists and Authors, 1980; City of New York Mayors Award for Honor for Arts and Culture, 1981; The Constance Lindsay Skinner Award, The Women's National Book Association, 1982; Gold Medal for History, American Academy/Institute of Arts and Letters, 1982; Annual Book Award, National Association of Independent School, 1985; Cosmos Club Award, 1983; Regents Medal of Excellence, University of the State of New York Education Department, 1984; Sarah Josepha Hale Award, 1984; Union League Club Award, 1984. *Memberships:* Radcliffe College, Trustee 1962–72; National Institute of Arts and Letters; Society of American Historians, President 1971–75; Smithsonian Council; American Academy/Institute of Arts and Letters, President 1979–81; Royal Society of Literature, London, Fellow; New York Public Library,

Trustee and Vice President, 1980–; The Athenaeum of Philadelphia, Life Fellow; New York Society Library, Trustee 1982–; Author's Guild, Treasurer; Authors Guild and League, Council Member and Officer. *Literary Agent:* Russell and Volkening Inc, 50W 29th Street, New York, NY 10001. *Address:* 83 Orchard Street, Cos Cob, CT 06807, USA.

TUCKER, Martin, b. 8 Feb. 1928, Philadelphia, Pennsylvania, USA. Professor of English, Writer. Divorced. *Education:* BA 1949, PhD 1963, New York University; MA, University of Arizona, 1954. *Literary Appointments:* Poet in Residence, Cavio American College, Egypt, 1983. *Publications:* Africa in Modern Literature, 1967; Joseph Conrad, 1976; Hornes of Locks and Mysteries, poems, 1982; The Critical Temper, editor, 4 columes. *Contributions to:* Confrontation Literary Journal; The New York Times Book Review; The New Republic; The Nation; The Saturday Review; The Commonweal; Commentary; American Scholar; Epoch; Village Voice; West Africa Review; Research in African Literature; Present Tense; New Letters. *Honours:* Editors Fellowship, National Endowment for the Arts, 1980; Trustees Award for Distinguished Achievement, Long Island University, 1981; Book of poems selected for the Books Across the Sea Program, English Speaking Union, 1983. *Memberships:* Editor PEN Newsletter 1973–78, Executive Board 1973–, PEN American Centre; Governing Board, Poetry Society of America, 1984; Modern Language Association; African Literature Association. *Address:* C W Post of L I U, English Department, Greenvale, NY 11548, USA.

TUCKER, Melvin Jay Francis, b. 3 Mar. 1931, Easthampton, Massachusetts, USA. Historian. m. N Evelyn Rapalus, 27 June 1953, Easthampton, Massachusetts, 1 son, 2 daughters. *Education:* BA, 1953, MA, 1954, University of Massachusetts; PhD, Northwestern University, 1962. *Literary Appointments:* Instructor in History, Colby College, 1959–60; Instructor in Humanities, Massachusetts Institute of Technology, 1960–63; Assistant Professor, 1963–66, Associate Professor of History, State University of New York at Buffalo, 1966–. *Major Publications:* The Life of Thomas Howard, Earl of Surrey & 2nd Duke of Norfolk, 1443–1524, 1964; (with S G Laurie), Centering: Your Guide to Inner Growth, 1978. *Contributor to:* English Historical Review; English Language Notes; Huntington Library Quarterly; History Today; Renaissance Quarterly; Moreana. *Honours:* Various Scholarships & Awards, including Fulbright Award for Research, Queen Mary College, University of London, England, 1958–59. *Memberships:* American Historical Association; Association for Bibliography of History, Council Member 1982–83; Conference of British Studies, Placement Secretary, Anglo-American Association, 1971–73. *Address:* 707 Willow Green Drive, Tonawanda, NY 14150, USA.

TUCKER, Robert Charles, b. 29 May 1918, Kansas City, Missouri, USA. Political Scientist & Historian. m. Evgenia Pestretsova, 21 Aug. 1946, Moscow, USSR, 1 daughter. *Education:* BA 1939,MA 1941, PhD Philosophy 1958, Harvard University, Cambridge, Massachusetts, USA. *Literary Appointments:* Attaché & Editor, American Embassy, Moscow, USSR, 1944–53; Researcher, Social Science Division, RAND Corporation, 1954–58; Associate Professor of Government, 1958–60, Professor, 1960–62, Indiana University, USA; Professor of Politics, 1962–84, Director, Russian Studies, 1962–68, IBM Professor of International Studies, 1982–84, Professor of Politics Emeritus, 1984–, Princeton University, New Jersey. *Major Publications:* Philosophy & Myth in Karl Marx, 1961; The Soviet Political Mind, 1963; The Marxian Revolutionary Idea, 1969; Stalin as Revolutionary, 1973; Politics as Leadership, 1981; The Marx-Engels Reader (editor), 1972; The Lenin Anthology, 1975; Stalinism: Essays in Historical Interpretation, 1977. *Contributor to:* Numerous professional & scholarly journals. *Honours:* Numerous Fellowships and endowment awards in USA & USSR. *Memberships include:* American Political Science Association, Chairman, Conference on Soviet &

Communist Studies, 1963–64; American Association for the Advancement of Slavic Studies; Member, Governing Council, International Society of Political Psychology. *Address:* 44 Hartley Avenue, Princeton, NJ 08540, USA.

TUCKER, William Edward, b. 22 June 1932, Charlotte, North Carolina, USA. Educator; University Chancellor. *Education:* East Carolina University, 1949–51; AB, Atlantic Christian College, 1953; BD, Texas Christian University, 1956; MA, PhD, Yale University, 1956–60. *Publications:* J H Garrison and Disciples of Christ, 1964; Journey in Faith: A History of the Christian Church, (Disciples of Christ) (with Lester G McAllister), 1975. *Contributor to:* The Word We Preach; Westminster Dictionary of Church History; Dictionary of American Biography 1941–45; Encyclopedia of Southern History, USA. *Memberships:* Phi Beta Kappa; American Society of Church History; Disciples of Christ Historical Society; American Academy of Religion; American Historical Association. *Address:* Office of the Chancellor, Texas Christan University, Fort Worth, TX 76129, USA.

TUCKMAN, Bruce W, b. 24 Nov. 1938, New York, USA. University Professor, Administrator. m. Darby Godwin, 24 July 1980, New York, 1 son, 1 daughter. *Education:* BS, Psychology, Rensselaer Polytechnic Institute, 1960; MA, 1962, PhD, 1963, Psychology, Princeton University. *Appointments:* Professor, Director, Educational Research, Rutgers University, 1965–78; Dean, Professor, Education, City University of New York, 1978–83, Florida State University, 1983–. *Publications:* Preparing to Teach the Disadvantaged, 1969; Conducting Educational Research, 1972, 2nd edition 1978; Measuring Educational Outcomes, 1975; Analyzing & Designing Education Research, 1979; Evaluating Educational Outcomes, 1979, 2nd edition 1985. *Contributor to:* Numerous professional journals. *Honours:* Authors Award, New Jersey Association of Teachers of English, 1969; Phi Delta Kappa Research Award, 1973. *Memberships:* Fellow, American Psychological Association; American Educational Research Association. *Address:* College of Education, Florida State University, Tallahassee, FL 323036, USA.

TUFTY, Barbara Jean,b. 28 Dec. 1923, Iowa City, Iowa, USA. Science Writer. m. Harold Guilford Tufty, 29 Dec. 1948, Chevy Chase, District of Columbia, USA, 2 sons, 2 daughter. *Education:* Vassar Duke, BA in Botany; Post-Graduate courses, School for Social Research, University of Colorado, USA, Sorbonne University, Paris, France. *Literary Appointments:* Science Writer: Science Service, 1948–68; National Academy of Sciences, 1970–72; National Science Foundation, 1972–84; Audubon Naturalist Society, 1985–. *Major Publications:* 1001 Questions Answered about Natural Land Disasters, 1969; 1001 Questions Answered about Storms, 1970; Cells, Units of Life, 1973; Crafts in the Ivory Coast, (translated from B Holas), 1967. *Contributor to:* Science Year 1980: The World Book; Women in Science, 1979; The Book of Biology, 1985; The Womens' Book of World Records & Achievements, 1979; Baltimore Sun; New York Times; Houston Chronicle; Minneapolis Tribune; Science News; American Forestry; Bombay Natural History Society Journal; and others. *Honours:* Chi Delta Phi, 1944; Bombay Natural History Society, Honorary Life Member 1956; Various Writing fellowships. *Memberships:* National Association of Science Writers; Washington Independent Writers; Authors Guild. *Address:* 3812 Livingston Street NW, Washington DC 20015, USA.

TUNLEY, Roul, b. 12 May 1912, Chicago, Illinois, USA. Writer; Editor. *Education:* BA, Yale University, 1934. *Appointment:* Faculty Member, Yale University, 1947–48. *Publications:* Kids Crime and Chaos, 1962; The American Health Scandal, 1966; Ordeal by Fire, 1967. *Contributor to:* Editor, Saturday Evening Post, Arizona Magazine; Woman's Home Companion; New York Herald Tribune; Writer, numerous magazines including, Reader's Digest, 30 years. *Memberships:*

Elizabethen Club, Yale; Council member, Author's Guild. *Literary Agent:* Paul Reynolds & Co Inc. *Address:* Box T, Stockton, NJ 08559, USA.

TUOMINEN, Pirjo Marja-Liisa, b. 6 Feb. 1939, Lappeenranta, Finland. Author. m. Rauno Juhani Tuominen, 20 Oct. 1962, 1 son, 1 daughter. *Education:* BA Economics. *Major Publications:* Mariaana, 1978; Sinisilmä, 1979; Tuuliajolla, 1980; Arvoisa Rouva Marie, 1981; Myrttiseppeleet, 1982; Keskeneräinen elämä, 1983; Puhtaana käteen, 1984; Nukkeleikki, 1985. *Membership:* Finnish Society of Authors. *Literary Agent:* Kirjayhtymä Oy. *Address:* Kurkelankatu 36, 30300 Forssa, Finland.

TURBOTT, Evan Graham, b. 27 May 1914, Auckland, New Zealand. Retired Museum Director. m. Olwyn Mary Rutherford, 7 Sep. 1940, Auckland, New Zealand. *Education:* MSc. *Publications:* New Zealand Bird Life, 1947; Buller's Birds of New Zealand, Editor and contributor, 1967; The New Guide to the Birds of New Zealand, Co-author, 1966, 3rd Edition, 1978. *Contributions to:* Various journals. *Honour:* QSO 1978. *Address:* 23 Cathedral Place, Auckland 1, New Zealand.

TURBOTT, Evan Graham, b. 27 May 1914, Auckland, New Zealand. Retired Museum Director. *Education:* MSc, University of New Zealand; Fellow, Art Galleries & Museums Association of New Zealand. *Publications:* New Zealand Bird Life, 1947; Buller's Birds of New Zealand (editor & contributor), 1967; The New Guide to the Birds of New Zealand (co-author), 1966, 3rd edition 1979. *Contributions to:* Ornithological & natural history journals, newspapers & magazines. *Membership:* Ornithological Society of New Zealand. *Honour:* QSO, 1978. *Address:* 23 Cathedral Place, Auckland 1, New Zealand.

TURCO, Lewis (Putnam), b. 2 May 1934, Buffalo, New York, USA. Professor of English. m. Jean Cate Houdlette, 16 June 1956, Meriden, Connecticut, USA, 1 son, 1 daughter. *Education:* BA, University of Connecticut, 1959; MA, University of Iowa, 1962. *Literary Appointments:* Bread Loaf Poetry Fellow, 1961; Yaddo Fellow, 1959, 1977; Visiting Professor of English, State University of New York (Potsdam College), 1968–69; Founding Director, Cleveland State University Poetry Centre, 1961–64; Faculty Fellow, Research Foundation, State University of New York, 1966, 1967, 1969, 1971, 1973, 1978; Bingham Poet in Residence, University of Louisville, 1982; Faculty Exchange Scholar of State University of New York, 1975– (Life appointment). *Major Publications:* First Poems, 1960; Awaken, Bells Falling, 1968; The Book of Forms, 1968; The Inhabitant, 1970; The Literature of New York, (Bibliography), 1970; Pocoangelini: A Fantography, 1971; Poetry: An Introduction through Writing, 1973; Seasons of the Blood, 1980; American Still Lifes, 1981; The Compleat Melacholick, 1985; Visions and Revisions, of American Poetry, 1986. *Contributor to:* Sewanee Review; New Yorker; Atlantic; Nation; Yale Review; New Republic; Hudson Review; Poetry; Tri-Quarterly; Ploughshares; Ontario Review; and others; Collier's Encyclopaedia, Dictionary of Literary Biography Yearbooks, etc. *Honours:* Various Poetry Awards and prizes in USA. *Membership:* PEN American Centre. *Literary Agent:* Arthur Orrmont, New York. *Address:* P O Box 362, Oswego, NY 13126, USA.

TURCOTTE, Elise, b. 26 June 1957, Sorel, Canada. Writer. 1 daughter. *Education:* Master's Degree. *Publications:* Navires de guerre, 194; Dans le delta de la nuit, 1982; La Mer a boire, 1980. *Contributor to:* Nouvelle Barre du Jour; Moebius; Lévres Urbaines; Estuaire; Montreal Now. *Memberships:* Union of Quebec Authors. *Address:* 966 St Joseph Est #5, Montreal N2J 1K8, QC, Canada.

TURECAMO, Dorrine, b. 22 June 1930, Pittsburgh, Pennsylvania, USA. Writer; Lecturer. m. Charles Turecamo, 2 Jan. 1974, New York City, 2 sons. *Education:* Honorary Degree, Drama. *Appointments:* Editor, Caldwell Communications, 1974; Playwright,

Artistic Promotions, 1976; Radio/TV Commercials, Management Training Tapes, Training Programmes, 1974–78; Teacher, Journalism, Long Island University, 1977–78; Teacher, Metropolitan State University, 1984–. *Contributor to:* Over 2,000 articles in national Magazines; Nationally syndicated column on business management. *Honours:* International Self Development Teacher of the Year, 1964, 1965. *Memberships:* American Society of Journalists & Authors; Press Club. *Address:* 6400 Barrie Road, #611, Edina, MN 55435, USA.

TURK, Frances Mary, b. 14 Apr. 1915, Huntingdon, England. Novelist. *Education:* Huntingdon Grammar School. *Literary Appointments:* Huntingdonshire County Library Committee, 1950–74. *Publications include:* Over 50 novels, many reissued in paper back, large print, cassette. Titles include; The Precious Hours, 1938; Paradise Street, 1939; Candle Corner, 1943 (2 editions); The Five Grey Geese, 1944 (3 editions); The House of Heron, 1946 (2 editions; The Gentle Flowers, (2 editions), 1952; Dinny Lightfoot, 1956; The White Swan, 1958; A Time to Know, 1960; The Secret Places, 1962; A Lamp from Murano, 1963; The Mistress of Medlam, 1963; Goddess of Threads, 1966; Lionel's Story, 1966; The Lesley Affair, 1968, Whispers, 1972. *Contributions to:* The Writer; Woman's Way; Home & Country; Cambridgeshire, Huntingdon & Peterborough Life; Young Writers Tales, 1974; Sunday Companion; WI Monthly News; etc. *Memberships:* Romantic Novelists Association (offices); Writers Summer School (course leader, lecturer). *Address:* Hillrise, Brampton Road, Buckden, Huntingdon, PE18 9UH, England.

TURKKA, Sirkka Annikki, b. 2 Feb. 1939, Helsinki, Finland. Author, Poet. *Education:* BA Stablemaster. *Major Publications:* The Room in the Space; In the Whale's Belly; It-s Me; The Night Opens Like a Wheel; The Man who Loved his Wife too much; Beautiful Souvering; Although it's Summer. *Honours:* State Awards, 1980, 1984. *Membership:* Finnish Literary Society. *Literary Agent:* Tammi. *Address:* Virkkalantie 2 B 11, 08100 Lohsa 10, Finland.

TURNBULL, Gael Lundin, b. 7 Apr. 1928, Edinburgh, Scotland. Medical Practitioner. Poet. m. (1) Jonnie May Draper, 1952, (2) Pamela Jill Iles, 1983, 3 daughters. *Education:* BA, Cambridge University; MD, University of Pennsylvania, USA. *Publications:* A Trampoline, 1968; Scantlings, 1970; A Gathering of Poems (1950–1980), 1983; A Year and a Day, 1985. *Contributor to:* Numerous magazines and journals. *Honours:* Hereditary Freeman of the Borough of Berwick-upon-Tweed; Alice Hunt Bartlet Award, Poetry Society, London, 1968. *Address:* 25 Church Walk, Ulverston, Cumbria LA12 7EN, England.

TURNBULL, Stephen Richard, b. 6 Feb. 1948, Redhill, Surrey. Teacher. m. Mary Josephine Arrowsmith, 14 Apr. 1973, 2 sons, 1 daughter. *Education:* MA, Psychology, Cambridge University. *Publications:* The Samurai: A Military History, 1977; Samurai Armies, 1979; Warlords of Japan, 1980; The Mongols, 1980; The Book of the Samurai, 1981; The Book of the Medieval Knight, 1985. *Contributor to:* Health Education Journal; Journal of the Institute of Health Education. *Membership:* Society of Authors. *Address:* 9 Victoria Drive, Horsforth, Leeds LS18 4PN, West Yorks.

TURNER, Alberta Tucker, b. 22 Oct. 1919, New York City, USA. College Professor of English. m. W. Arthur Turner, 9 Apr. 1943, 1 son, 1 daughter. *Education:* BA, Hunter College, 1940; MA, Welesley College, 1941; PhD, Ohio State University, 1946. *Literary Appointments include:* Professor, Cleveland State University, Ohio, 1969–; Director, Poetry Centre, ibid, 1964–; Associate Editor, Field: Contemporary Poetry & Poetics, 1970–. *Publications include:* Poems: Need, 1970; Learning to Count, 1974; Lid & Spoon, 1977; A Belfry of Knees, 1983. Text: To Make a Poem, 1982. Editor: 50 Contemporary Poets, 1977; Poets Teaching, 1980; 45 Contemporary Poems, 1985. *Contributions to:* Poetry; Iowa Review; College English; Poetry Now; Prairie

Schooner; Little Magazine; Stand; Canadian Forum; Journal of Education; etc. *Honour:* Individual Artists Grant, Ohio Arts Council, 1980. *Memberships:* PEN American Centre; Milton Society of America. *Address:* 482 Caskey Court, Oberlin, OH 44074, USA.

TURNER, Alice Kennedy, b. China. Magazine Editor. *Education:* BA, Bryn Mawr College, 1962. *Literary Appointments:* Associate editor, Publishers Weekly; Senior Editor, Ballantine Books; Senior Editor, New York; Fiction Editor, Playboy. *Publications:* Yoga for Beginers, 1972. *Contributions to:* Numerous publications. *Honours:* Judge, American Book Awards, 1985. *Memberships:* Women's Media Group; PEN America; American Society of Magazine Editors; Mystery Writers of America; Science Fiction Writers of America. *Address:* Playboy, 919 North Michigan Avenue, Chicago, IL 60611, USA.

TURNER, Bernard Charles Arthur, b. 23 Jan. 1919, Gillingham, Kent, England. Author; Lecturer. m. Mary Agnes Creed, 4 Oct. 1944, Gravesend, 3 sons, 2 daughters. *Education:* Associate, Institute of Chartered Secretaries & Administrators. *Publications include:* Winemaker's Companion, 1961; Pan Book of Winemaking, 1965; Boots Book of Home Winemaking & Brewing, 1970; Complete Home Winemaker & Brewer, 1976; St Michael, Homemade Wines & Beers, 1979; Wines From the Countryside, 1984; etc. *Contributions to:* Winemaker & Brewer; Practical Gardening; Family Circle; Woman. *Honour:* Knight of the Equestrian Order of St Gregory, Pope Paul VI, 1969. *Literary Agent:* John Pawsey. *Address:* St Jude's Cottage, 74 Bury Street, Ruislip, HA4 7TE, England.

TURNER, Ernest Sackville,b. 17 Nov. 1909, Liverpool, England. Author. *Publications:* Boys Will Be Boys, 1948; Roads to Ruin, 1950; The Shocking History of Advertising, 1952; A History of Courting, 1954; The Court of St James's, 1959; What the Butler Saw, 1962; May It Please Your Lordship, 1971; Amazing Grace, 1975; Dear Old Blighty, 1980; An ABC of Nostalgia, 1984. *Contributor to:* Punch; Listener; Sunday Telegraph; Times Literary Supplement. *Address:* 21 Woburn Court, Stanmore Road, Richmond, Surrey, England.

TURNER, Frederick, b. 19 Nov. 1943, Northants, England. Founders Professor of Arts & Humanities. m. Mei Lin Chang, 25 June 1966, Oxford, England, 2 sons. *Education:* BA (Hons), MA, Christ Church, Oxford University, England. *Literary Appointments:* Assistant Professor of English, University of California, USA, 1967–72; Associate Professor of English, Kenyon College, USA, 1972–85; Editor, Kenyon Review, 1978–82; Founders Professor, Arts and Humanities, 1985–. *Publications:* Deep-Sea Fish, 1968; Shakespeare and The Nature of Time, 1971; Between Two Lives, 1972; Counter-Terra, 1978; A Double Shadow, 1978; The Return, 1981; The Garden, 1985; The New World, 1985; Natural Classicism, 1986. *Contributions to:* Prose & Poetry to, The Kenyon Review; Southern Review; Harper's; Poetry; Chaucer Review; Ontario Review; Shenandoah; Denver Quarterly; Oral Tradition; Missouri Review; Journal of Social and Biological Structures; Bennington Review; Fantastic Stories; Yale Review. *Honours:* Levinson Poetry Prize, 1983. *Memberships:* FNLA; PEN; Science Fiction Poetry Association. *Literary Agent:* Virginia Kidd. *Address:* School of Arts and Humanities, University of Texas, Dallas, Richardson, TX 75083, USA.

TURNER, George Reginald, b. 8 Oct. 1916, Melbourne, Victoria, Australia. Writer. *Publications:* Young Man of Talent, 1959; The Cupboard Under the Stairs, 1962; Transit of Cassidy, 1978; Beloved Son, 1978; Vaneglory, 1981; In the Heart or in the Head, 1984. *Contributions to:* The Age, Review column, 1970–; Overland; SF Commentary; Foundation, England; Science Fiction and various others. *Honours:* Miles Franklin Award, for The Cupboard Under the Stairs, 1962. *Memberships:* Australian Society of Authors; Fellowship of Australian Writers. *Address:* Flat 4, 296 Inkerman Street, East St Kilda, Victoria 3183, Australia.

TURNER, Harold Walter, b. 13 Jan. 1911, Napier, New Zealand. Teacher of Religion. m. Maude Yeoman, 1 Feb. 1939, Christchurch, New Zealand, 1 son, 3 daughters. *Education:* MA, Hons, New Zealand, 1935; BD, 1943, DD, 1963, Melbourne College of Divinity. *Literary Appointments:* Positions at Universities of Sierra Leone, Nigeria, Leicester, Aberdeen, Birmingham, Emory University, Selly Oak Colleges (Birmingham). *Publications:* Halls of Residence, 1953; African Independent Church, (2 vols) 1967; Bibliography of New Religious Movements in Primal Societies, Vol 1 Black Africa (1977) Vol 2 North America (1978); Religious Innovation in Africa, 1979; From Temple to Meeting House, 1979. *Contributions to:* Tribal Religious Movements; New Encyclopaedia Britannica 1974 edition; Religion; Journal of Religion in Africa; Missiology; Numen; Archives de Sciences Sociales des Religions; International Review of Mission; Comparative Studies in Society and History; Missionalia; International Bulletin of Missionary Research etc. *Honours:* Honorary DD, Otago, 1976; Honorary Fellow, University of Birmingham, 1981–. *Address:* Centre for New Religious Movements, Selly Oak Colleges, Birmingham B29 6LQ, England.

TURNER, Henry Andrew, b. 2 Jan. 1919, King City, Gentry, Missouri, USA. Professor. *Education:* BS, North West Missouri State University, 1939; MA, University of Missouri, 1940; PhD, University of Chicago, 1950. *Publications:* Politics in the United States, (editor), 1955; The Government and Politics of California, (co-author), 4th edition 1971; American Democracy in World Perspective, 5th edition 1980; American Democracy: State and Local Government, 2nd edition 1970. *Contributuions to:* Various professional journals including: Annals of the American Academy of Politics and Social Science; Polity; Public Opinion Quarterly; The Journal of Politics; The Western Politics Quarterly; Public Administration Review; Social Science; American Psychology. *Honours:* Fulbright Lecturer, Republic of South Africa 1968, Iran 1974. *Memberships:* American Political Science Association; Western Political Science Association; Midwest Political Science Association. *Address:* Department of Political Science, University of California, Santa Barbara, CA 93106, USA.

TURNER, John Frayn, b. 9 Aug. 1923, Portsmouth, England. Writer, Editor. m. Joyce Isabelle Howson, 9 Aug. 1945, Portsmouth, 1 daughter. *Literary Appointments:* Various posts as Journalist, 1947–63; RAF Publicity, 1963–1973; Senior Editor, Central Office of Information, 1973–83; Managing Editor, Brevet Publishing Company, 1984–. *Major Publications:* Service Most Silent, 1955; Periscope Patrol, 1958; Invasion 44, 1959; Battle Stations, 1960; Highly Explosive, 1961; The Blinding Flash, 1962; A Girl called Johnnie, 1963; Destination Berchtesgaden, 1975; British Aircraft of World War 2, 1975; Famous Flights, 1978; The Bader Wing, 1981; The Yanks are Coming, 1983; Frank Sinatra, 1983; Fight for the Sky (with Douglas Bader). *Contributor to:* Art & Artists; Dance & Dancers; Films & Filming; Music & Musicians; Plays & Players (all Brevet Publishing). *Address:* 62 Defoe House, Barbican, London, EC2, England.

TURNER, Katharine Charlotte, b. 11 Mar. 1910, Normal, Illinois, USA. University Professor of English. *Education:* BEd, Illinois State Normal University; MA, PhD, University of Michigan. *Publications:* Red Men Calling on the Great White Father, 1951; Writing: The Shapes of Experience, 1966. *Contributions to:* Colorado Quarterly; Best Articles and Stories; Southern Humanities Review; Delta Kappa Gamma Bulletin. Verses: Poet Lore; Common Weal; Delta Kappa Gamma; Point West, Phoenix. *Honours:* Smith-Mundt Lectureship, Tamkang English College and National Taiwan University, Taipei, Taiwan, Republic of China, 1955–56. *Address:* 1216 South Maple Avenue, Tempe, AZ 85281, USA.

TURNER, Philip William, b. 3 Dec. 1925, Rossland, British Columbia, Canada. Writer. m. Margaret Diana Samson, 23 Sep. 1950, Loughborough, Leicestershire,

England, 2 sons, 1 daughter. *Education:* MA English Language and Literature, Oxford. *Publications:* Colonel Sheperton's Clock, 1964; The Grange at High Force, 1965; The Bible Story, 1968; Septimus and the Dane Dyke Mystery, 1971; Plays: Christ in the Concrete City, 1960; Watch of the World's End, 1980. *Honour:* Carnegie Medal for, The Grange at High Force, 1965. *Literary Agent:* Watson Little, Suite 8, 26 Charing Cross Road, London WC2H OD9. *Address:* Saint Francis, 181 West Malvern Road, Malvern, Worcestershire, England.

TURNER, Thomas Coleman, b. 28 Jan. 1927, Anniston, Alabama, USA. Writer; Real Estate Executive. Divorced, 3 sons, 1 daughter. *Education:* AB, summa cum laude, Princeton University, 1949; Special Student, University of Alabama, 1949–50. *Publication:* Buttermilk Road, novel, 1963. *Contributions to:* Short stories and articles in Harper's; The Writer; Mademoiselle; Hudson Review; Antioch Review; Southwest Review, reprinted in, Best Articles and Stories, and The Writer's Handbook. *Honour:* 3rd Prize, O'Henry Prize Stories, 1959. *Literary Agent:* McIntosh and Otis. *Address:* PO Box 1586, Anniston, AL 36202, USA.

TURNILL, Reginald George, b. 12 May 1915, Dover, Kent, England. Aerospace writer; Television Space Editor. m. Margaret Elizabeth Hennings, 10 Sep. 1938, Westminster, London, 2 sons. *Literary Appointments:* Space editor, Newsround, British Broadcasting Television. *Publications:* Moonslaught, 1969; Observer's Book of Manned Spaceflight, 1972, 78; Observer's Book of Unmanned Spaceflight, 1974; Battle for Survival of MEA, 1977; Observer's Spaceflight Directory, 1978; Space Age, 1980; Farnborough, The Story of RAE, with Arthur Reed, 1980; Jane's Spaceflight Directory, 1984. *Contributions to:* British Aerospace Incorporated Quarterly; Jane's Aviation Annual author of numerous technical magazine contributions. *Memberships:* Associate, Royal Aeronautical Society; Fellow, British Interplanetary Society. *Address:* Somerville Lodge, Hillside, Sandgate, Kent CT20 3DB, England.

TURNOCK, David, b. 19 Aug. 1938, Wigan. University Teacher. m. Edith Marion Bean, 24 July 1965, 2 sons. *Education:* MA, 1964, PhD, 1964, Cambridge University. *Publications:* Patterns of Highland Development, 1970; Scotland's Highlands and Islands, 1974; Economic Geography of Romania, 1974; Industrial Geography: Eastern Europe, 1978; Industrial Britain: The New Scotland, 1979; Historical Geography of Scotland since 1707, 1982; Railways in the British Isles, 1982. *Contributor to:* Area; GeoJournal; Scottish Geographical Magazine; Transactions Institute of British Geographers etc. *Address:* Department of Geography, The University, Leicester LE1 7RH, England.

TUROW, Joseph, b. 5 Apr. 1950, New York City, USA. Professor. m. Judith Forrest, 17 June 1979, Queens, New York, USA, 1 son. *Education:* BA, 1972; MA, 1973; PhD, 1976, University of Pennsylvania. *Literary Appointments:* Member of the following Editorial Boards: Journal of Communication; Communication Education; Journal of Broadcasting; Critical Studies in Mass Communication. *Publications:* Getting Books to Children, (American Library Association), 1979; Education, Entertainment and the Hard Sell, (Praeger), 1981; Careers in Mass Media, (SEA, 1984, an edited volume); Media Industries: The Production of News & Entertainment, (Longman), 1984. *Honours:* Phi Beta Kappa, 1971; University Fellowship, 1975–76; Russel B Nye Award, Popular Culture Association, 1983; Media Industries received, Book of the Month, designation in, Communication Booknotes, 1984. *Address:* Department of Communication, Purdue University, West Lafayette, IN 47907, USA.

TURTON, Godfrey Edmund, b. 4 Jan. 1901, Kildale, Yorkshire, England. Journalist. m. Elvira Waller Haynes, 21 Sep. 1932, Burford, 2 daughters. *Education:* BA Honours, Balliol College, Oxford. *Literary Appointments:* Editorial Staff, Truth; Staff, Oxford Latin Dictionary, Clarendon Press. *Publications:* My Lord of

Canterbury, 1967; The Emperor Arthur, 1968; The Devil's Churchyard, 1970; The Dragon's Bread, non-fiction, 1970; The Festival of Flora, 1972; The Syrian Princesses, non-fiction, 1974; The Moon Dies, 1982. *Address:* 10 Benson Place, Oxford, England.

TUSIANI, Joseph, b. 14 Jan. 1924, San Marco in Lamis, Foggia, Italy. University Professor. *Education:* DLit, University of Naples, Italy and College of Mount St Vincent, USA. *Publications include:* The Complete Poems of Michelangelo, 1960; Envoy from Heaven, 1965; Tasso's Jerusalem Delivered, 1970; Gente Mia and Other Poems, 1978; Rosa Rosarum, poems in Latin, 1984; InExilio Rezum, in Latin, 1985. *Contributions to:* Numerous journals including: New York Times; New Yorker; Catholic World; Sign; Spirit; Classical Outlook; la Paroloa. *Honours:* Greenwood Prize, Poetry Society of England, 1956; Alice Fay di Castagnola Award, Poetry Society of America, 1969; Spirit Gold Medal, Catholic Poetry Society of America, 1969. *Memberships:* Past Vice President, Poetry Society of America; Past Director, Catholic Poetry Society of America. *Address:* 2140 Tomlinson Avenue, Bronx, NY 10461, USA.

TUTT, Nigel, b. 21 June 1953, Bromley, Kent, England. Journalist. *Education:* BA (Hons), Cambridge University; ACA, Institute of Chartered Accountants. *Publication:* The Tax Raiders, 1985. *Contributions to:* Accountancy Age, Staff Writer; Daily Express; Computing. *Address:* c/o 32 Broadwick Street, London W1, England.

Tutton, Barbara Ivy Curtis, b. 6 Aug. 1914, Romford, Essex, England. Writer. m. William George Gerard Tutton, 3 Sep. 1938, Romford, 3 daughters. *Publications:* Mystery at Bracken Dale, 1960; Take Me Alive, 1961; Rich to Die, 1962; Black Widow, 1963; The Riddle of the Allabones, 1964; Plague Spot, 1965. *Contributions to:* Cat's Cradle; John Creasey Mystery Magazine. *Address:* Wall Nooks, Belper, Derbyshire DE5 2DN, England.

TYDEMAN, William Marcus, b. 29 Aug. 1935, Maidstone, Kent, England. University Lecturer. m. Jacqueline Barbara Anne Jennison, Yeovil, 29 July 1961, 2 daughters. *Education:* BA, 1st Class Honours, English, 1959, MLitt 1965, University of Oxford. *Academic Appointments:* Assistant Lecturer, Lecturer, Senior Lecturer, 1961–83, University Reader/Acting Head of Department 1983–. University College of North Wales. *Publications:* Editor, English Poetry 1400–1580, 1970; Joint Editor, Casebooks on Wordsworth, Lyrical Ballads, 1972, & Coleridge, 1973; The Theatre in the Middle Ages, 1978; Joint Editor, Joseph Hucks, A Pedestrian Tour, 1979; Editor, Plays by Tom Robertson, 1982; Casebook on Wilde's Comedies, 1982; Editor, Four Tudor Comedies, 1984; Dr. Faustus: Text & Performance, 1984; English Medieval Theatre, 1400–1500, forthcoming. *Contributions:* Articles in, Notes & Queries; Transactions of Denbigh Historical Society; Medieval English Theatre; Essays & Studies; Reviews in, Critical Quarterly; Use of English; Theatre Notebook; Prose Studies; etc; Contributor to: Thames & Hudson Cyclopedia of the Arts; Year's Work in English Studies (4 volumes); Writers of the English Language. *Address:* Department of English, University College of North Wales, Bangor, Gwynedd, LL57 2DG, Wales.

TYLER, Anne Elizabeth, b. 30 Aug. 1955, New Jersey, USA. Editor. *Education:* BA Theology (CNAA degree). *Literary Appointments:* Editor, Church of England Newspaper. *Major Publication:* My Rough Diamond, 1981. *Contributor to:* Life of Faith; Christian Woman; Christian Herald; World Vision; Daily Mail. *Address:* 146 Queen Victoria Street, London EC4, England.

TYLER, Eric John, b. 24 Apr. 1920, Tottenham, England. Writer. m. Violet D Peters, 28 July 1945, Winchmore Hill, 1 daughter. *Publications include:* European Clocks, 1968; Craft of the Clockmaker, 1973; Clocks & Watches, 1975; Black Forest Clocks, 1977;

American Clocks for the Collector, 1981; Clock Types, 1982; Clock Museums Visited, 1983; Translation, English Lantern Clocks, W F J Hana, 1980. *Contributions to:* Antique Dealer & Collectors Guide; Horological Journal; Timecraft; Clocks; Antiquerian Horology; Bulletin of the National Association of Watch & Clock Collectors, USA; Alte Uhren, Heft der Freunde Alter Uhren, West Germany; Railway Magazine; Railway World. *Honour:* Fellow, National Association of Watch & Clock Collectors, USA, 1978. *Address:* Hastings, Sussex, England.

TYLER, Robert Lawrence, b. 11 Feb. 1922, Minnesota, USA. Professor. m. (1) Molly Erlich, 22 Feb. 1947; (2) Gerry J Sack, 20 June 1971; 2 sons, 1 daughter. *Education:* AB, 1948, MA, 1949, University of Minnesota; PhD, 1953, University of Oregon. *Literary Appointments:* Contributing Editor, The Humanist, 1970–; Associate Editor, North-East Review, 1979–; Professor of History. *Major Publications:* Rebels of the Woods: The IWW in the Pacific North-West, 1968; Walter Reuther, 1972; A Hearth of Mental Rock, 1984. *Contributor to:* Various Literary Magazines (350 poems), and scholarly & literary magazines (50 essays). *Honours:* Ford Foundation Fellowship, 1951–52; Fulbright Lectureship in American Studies, University of Guyana, 1966–67. *Address:* 41 Linden Drive, Kingston, RI 02881, USA.

TYLER-WHITTLE, Michael, b. 1927. Novelist; Critic; Biographer; Writer on Botany & Horticulture. *Education:* MA (Cantab), 1951; FRSL, 1971; FLS, 1977. *Major Publications:* Spades & Feathers, 1954; The Runners of Orford, 1955; Castle Lizard, 1956; The Bullhead, 1957; As Though They Had Never Been, 1958; Heroes of Our Time (co-author), 1959; A Roll of Thunder, 1960; Tales of Many Lands, (co-author), 1960; Luke Benedict, 1961; Feet of Bronze, 1962; Young Plants & Polished Corners, 1963; Five Spinning Tops of Naples, 1964; Some Ancient Gentlemen, 1968; Common or Garden, 1970; The Last Plantagenet, 1970; The Plant Hunters, 1971; The Young Victoria, 1971; The Birth of Greece, 1972; Albert's Victoria, 1972; The World of Classical Greece, 1973; Royal & Republican Rome, 1974; Imperial Rome, 1974; The Widow of Windsor, 1974; Bertie, 1974; Edward, 1975; The Last Kaiser, 1977; Curtis, Wonderwelt der Blumen, 1979; Victoria & Albert At Home, 1980; Curtis, Flower Garden Displayed, 1981; The House of Flavell, 1982; Solid Joys & Lasting

Treasure, 1985. *Literary Agent:* Curtis Brown Ltd. *Membership:* The Athenaeum, London. *Address:* c/o Curtis Brown Ltd, 168 Regent Street, London W1R 5TB, England.

TYRRELL, R(obert) Emmett, b. 14 Dec. 1943, Chicago, Illinois, USA. Journalist. *Education;* BA 1965, MA 1967, Indiana University. *Literary Appointments:* Editor-in-Chief, American Spectator, 1967–; Nationally Syndicated Columnist, King Features, 1980–. *Publications:* The Future That Doesn't Work: Social Democracy's Failures in Britain, (editor), 1977; Public Nuisances, 1979; The Liberal Crack-Up, 1984. *Contributions to:* Harpers; Washington Post. *Honours:* American Eagle Award, 1976; Award for, greatest public service by an American under 35, American Institute for Public Service, 1976; 1 of 10 most outstanding young men, US Jaycees, 1978; 1 of 50 future leaders, Time Magazine, 1979. *Memberships:* New York Athletic Club; Council of Foreign Relations, New York. *Address:* PO Box 10448, Arlington, VA 22210, USA.

TYSDAHL, Bjøorn, Johan, b. 20 Oct. 1933, Oslo, Norway. Literary Historian. m. Bjoørg Lagset, 30 May 1959, Oslo, 2 sons, 2 daughters. *Education:* Cand philol 1959, Dr philos, 1968, University of Oslo. *Literary Appointments:* University Lecturer, 1965–72, Reader in English Literature, 1972–85, Professor of English Literature, 1985–, University of Oslo. *Publications:* Joyce and Ibsen: A Study in Literary Influence, 1968; William Godwin as Novelist, 1981. *Contributions to:* Numerous magazines and journals. *Memberships:* The James Joyce Corporation; The Oslo University Literary Society, Chairman 1985–86. *Address:* The English Department, University of Oslo, Oslo 3, Norway.

TYSON, Joseph B, b. 30 Aug. 1928, Charlotte, North Carolina, USA. Professor. m. Margaret H Helms, 12 June 1954, 1 daughter. *Education:* BA 1950, BD 1953, Duke University; STM 1955, PhD 1959, Union Theological Seminary, New York. *Publications:* A Study of Early Christianity, 1973; Synoptic Abstract, (with T R W Longstaff), 1978; The New Testament and Early Christianity, 1984. *Contributions to:* New Testament Studies; Journal of Biblical Literature; Novum Testamentum; etc. *Address:* Department of Religious Studies, Southern Methodist University, Dallas, TX 75275, USA.

U

UBBELOHDE, Alfred Rene John Paul, b. 14 Dec. 1907, Antwerp, Belgium. Research Scientist; Professor Emeritus of Thermodynamics; Senior Research Fellow, London University. *Education:* MA, DSc, Oxford University; Honorary DSc, Queens University, Belfast, Northern Ireland and University of Brussels, Belgium; Honorary Laureate, University of Padua, Italy; Honorary DSc, Nancy University, France, 1981. *Publications include:* Time and Thermodynamics, 1947; Man and Energy, 1954, revised, 1965; Graphite and Its Crystal Compounds, 1960; Melting and Crystal Structure, 1965; The Molten State of Matter, 1978. *Contributions to:* Numerous scientific research papers, articles and reviews on historical, biographical and philosophical topics. *Honours:* Numerous honorary degrees. Several academic honours including: George Skakel Award, 1975. *Memberships include:* Royal Society of Arts; Mediaeval Academy of America; Fellow, Royal Society. *Address:* Platts Farm, Fontridge Lane, Burwash, Sussex, England.

UDE, Wayne Richard, b. 23 Mar. 1946, Minneapolis, Minnesota, USA. Writer; Teacher. m. Marian Blue, 15 July 1983, Fort Collins, Colorado, USA, 1 son, 1 daughter. *Education:* BA, University of Montana, 1969; MFA, University of Massachusetts, 1974. *Literary Appointments:* Editor, Colorado State Review, Literary magazine, 1977–84; Writer-in-Residence, Mankato State University, 1984–86. *Publications:* Buffalo and other stories, 1974, fifth printing 1986; Becoming Coyote, novel, 1981, second printing 1984. *Contributions to:* Stories in Aspen Anthology; Greenfield Review; Lynx Magazine; Portland Review; Salt Cedar; Scree; Sunday Clothes; Transatlantic. Reviews and essays in American Book Review; Colorado State Review; Sunday Clothes; Western American Literature. *Memberships:* Western Literature Association; Associated Writing Programs. *Address:* Box 53, Mankato State University, Mankato, MN 56001, USA.

UEDA, Makoto, b. 20 May 1931, One-shi, Japan. Professor of Japanese and Comparative Literature. *Education:* BLitt, Kobe University, 1954; MA, University of Nebraska, USA, 1956; PhD, University of Washington, 1962. *Publications:* Literary and Art Theories in Japan, 1967; Matsoo Bashe, 1970; Modern Japanese Haiku: An Anthology, 1976; Modern Japanese Writers and the Nature of Literature, 1976. *Contributor to:* Sewanee Review; Chicago Review, etc. *Address:* Department of Asian Languages, Stanford University, Stanford, CA 94305, USA.

UHRMAN, Celia, b. 14 May 1927, New London, Connecticut, USA. Artist; Writer; Poet; Teacher. *Education:* BA, 1948, MA, 1953, Brooklyn College; PhD, University of Danzig, 1977; Postgraduate, Teachers College, Columbia University, 1961, CUNY, 1966, Brooklyn Museum Art School, 1956–57; PhD, Honorary, Litt D, 1973. *Publications:* Poetic Ponderances, 1969; A Pause for Poetry, 1970; Poetic Love Fancies, 1970; A Pause for Poetry for Children, 1973; The Chimps Are Coming, 1975; etc. *Honours:* Honorary Representative, US Centro Studi E Scambi Internazionali, Rome; Honorary Life Member, Poetry Day Committee Inc, and National Poetry Day Committee, 1977; Award, Freedoms Foundation, George Washington Medal of Honour, 1964; Diplome d'Honneur Palme d'Or des Beaux Arts Exbition, Monaco, 1969, 1972; Diploma, Gold Medal, 1972; Decorated, Order of Gandhi Award of Honour, Knight Grand Cross, 1972; Personal Poetry Certificate, WEFG Stereo, 1970; Gold Laurel Award, Esposizione Internazionale D'Art Contemporain, Paris, 1974; Named, Poetry Translator Laureate, World Academy Language and Literature, 1972; Poet of Mankind Academy, 1972; etc. *Memberships:* International Arts Guild, Monte-Carlo; World Poetry Society Intercontinental, Representative at Large, 1970–; International Academy of Poets, Founding Fellow; Brooklyn College Alumni Association, Life Member. *Address:* 1655 Flatbush Ave, Apt and Studio C106, Brooklyn, NY 11210, USA.

UHRMAN, Esther, b. 7 July 1921. Artist; Writer; Philosopher. *Education:* Traphagen School of Fashion, 1955; New York City Community College, USA, 1974; Labour Relations Studies, Cornell University, 1977; Courses: College of New Rochelle; PhD, University of Danzig, Poland, 1977. *Literary Appointments:* Self-employed Artist, Writer, 1954–; Partner, Uhrman Studio, 1973–83. *Publications:* Gypsy Logic, 1970; From Canarsie to Masada, 1984. *Contributor to:* Pub. Press; Pet Dealer; Beauty and Barber Supplier; Dietetic Foods Industry; Courier Life Publications; Fate; Inside Detective; True Detective; Life Is Tremendous; International Who's Who in Poetry Anthology; Poet Magazine, and numerous others. *Honours:* Several prestigious national and international awards for literature and art. *Memberships include:* Founding Fellow, International Academy of Poets, 1976; Honorary Vice US Representative, US Representative, Centro Studi e Scambi International; Member, International Executive Committee, Centro Studi e Scambi; Commander, International Arts Guild; World Poetry Society. *Address:* Uhrman Studio C106, 1655 Flatbush Avenue, Brooklyn, NY 11210, USA.

ULAM, Adam Bruno, b. 8 Apr. 1922, Lwow, Poland. Gurney Professor of History and Political Science, Harvard University. m. Mary Burgwin, Jan. 1963, 2 sons. *Education:* AB, Brown University, 1943; PhD, Harvard University, 1947; LLD (Honorary) Brown University, 1983. *Publications:* The Philosophical Foundations of English Socialism, 1951; Titoism and the Cominform, 1952; The Unfinished Revolution, 1960 revised 1979; The New Face of Soviet Totalitarianism, 1963; The Bolsheviks, 1965; Expansion and Coexistence, 1968; The Rivals, 1971; The Fall of the American University, 1972; Stalin: The Man and His Era, 1973; A History of Soviet Russia, 1976; In the Name of the People, 1977; Russia's Failed Revolutions, 1981; Dangerous Relations: The Soviet Union in World Politics, 1970–82, 1983. *Contributions to:* Numerous contributions to journals and magazines. *Literary Agent:* Julian Bach. *Address:* Russian Research Center, Harvard University, 1727 Cambridge Street, Cambridge, MA 02138, USA.

ULANOFF, Stanley M, b. 30 May 1922, Brooklyn, New York, USA. College Professor; Retired Brigadier General. *Education:* BA, University of Iowa; MBA, Hofstra University; PhD, University of New York. *Publications:* Illustrated Guide to US Missiles and Rockets, 1959; Fighter Pilot, 1962; MATS-The Story of the Military Air Transport Service, 1964; Ace of Aces, 1967; Flying Fury, 1968; Man in a Green Beret, 1969; Ace of the Iron Cross, 1970; Flying in Flanders, 1971: Illustrated History of World War 1 in the Air, 1971; Comparison Advertising: An Historical Retrospective, 1975; World War II Aircraft in Combat, 1976; Advertising in America: Principles of Persuasive Business Communication, 1976; American Wars and Heroes, 1984; Handbook of Sales Promotion, 1984; Fighting Israeli Air Force, 1984; Fighter Pilot, 1986. *Contributions to:* Various professional journals. *Honours include:* Legion of Merit, US Government, 1976; Chevalier dans l'Ordre des Palmes Academiques, France; Conspicuous Service Cross, State of New York. *Address:* 17 The Serpentine, Roslyn, NY 11576, USA.

ULLMANN, John Hatch, b. 29 Apr. 1945, South Bend, Indiana, USA. Newspaper Editor. m. Wendy S Tai, 9 Oct. 1984, Minneapolis. *Education:* BS, Butler University, 1968; MA, Communication, American University, 1974; PhD, Journalism & Environmental Science, University of Missouri, in progress. *Appointments:* University of Alaska, 1974–76; University of Missouri, 1976–83; Executive Director, Investigative Reporters & Editors Inc, 1979–82; Assistant Managing Editor, Projects, Minneapolis Star and Tribune, 1984–. *Publications:* The Reporter's Handbook: An Investigator's Guide to Documents and Records, 1983, Originator, co-author, co-editor. *Contributor to:* New

York Times; Washington Post; Baltimore Sun. *Honours:* Distinguished Journalism Alumnae Award, Butler University, 1985. *Membership:* Investigative Reporters & Editors, Executive Director, 1979–83. *Address:* No. 504, 1117 Marguette Avenue, Minneapolis, MN 55403, USA.

ULRICH, Betty Garton, b. 28 Oct. 1919, Indianapolis, Indiana, USA. Writer. m. Reverend Louis E Ulrich, 5 Jan. 1946, Madison, Wisconsin, 3 sons, 2 daughters. *Education:* BS, Education. *Publications:* Away We Go, 1970; Every Day With God, 1972. *Contributor to:* Co-Founder, Associate Editor, Inkling Literary Journal; Articles, short stories, poems, in over 30 publications including, Christian Herald; Eternity; Scope; The Lutheran; Readers Digest; Redbook, etc. *Address:* Box 34, Stone Lake, WI 54876, USA.

ULRICH, Elise Carolyn, b. 26 Feb. 1937, York, Pennsylvania, USA. Health, Beauty and Travel Writer. *Education:* AA, Cazenovia College, New York; Alliance Francise, Paris, France. *Contributions to:* Asia; Bestways; Cleo; Company; Frequent Flyer; Good Housekeeping; Health; L'Officiel; Mature Outlook; McCall's; Matured Health; Playboy; Redbook; Rotarian International; Sunday Women; USA Today. *Memberships:* Public Relations and Conference Committees; American Society of Journalists and Authors; Council of Writers Organization. *Address:* 330 East 49th Street, New York, NY 1017, USA.

UNDERWOOD, Gary Neal, b. 20 Oct. 1940, Piggott, Arkansas, USA. Professor. m. Sheila Anne Ross, 17 Sep. 1983, Austin, 1 son, 1 daughter. *Education:* BA, 1962, MA, 1964, Texas A & M University; PhD, University of Minnesota, 1970. *Publications:* Readings in American Dialectology, 1971; Dialect of the Mesabi Range, 1981. *Contributor to:* 28 articles in journals such as, American Speech; Bulletin of the Rocky Mountain Modern Language Association; El Guarderno; Florida Reporter; International Journal for the Sociology of Language; etc. *Honours:* Sigma Tau Delta; Phi Kappa Phi; Tozer Foundation Graduate Scholarship, 1968; American Council of Learned Societies Travel Grant, 1972; University Research Institute Summer Research Award, 1977; University Research Institute Faculty Research Assignemnt, 1985. *Memberships:* American Dialect Society; Linguistic Society of America; Modern Language Association of America; National Council of Teachers of English; Linguistic Association of the Southwest; South Central Modern Language Association; Rocky Mountain Modern Language Association. *Address:* 10021 Childress Drive, Austin, TX 78753, USA.

UNDERWOOD, Michael, b. 2 June 1916, Worthing, Sussex, England. Barrister, Government Legal Service. *Education:* MA, University of Oxford. *Publications:* Author of 40 crime novels, 1954–86. *Memberships:* Detection Club; Past Chairman, Crime Writers Association. *Address:* 100 Ashdown, Eaton Road, Hove, Sussex, England.

UNDERWOOD, Peter, b. 16 May 1923, Letchworth Garden City, England. Author. m. Joyce Elizabeth Davey, 15 July 1944, Baldock, 1 son, 1 daughter. *Education:* Private. *Education:* With J M Dent, Publishers, over 25 years; Book Reviewer: The Publisher, Books and Bookmen, Two World, Society for Psychical Research, Ghost Club, etc. *Publications:* A Gazetteer of British Ghosts, 1971; Into the Occult, 1972; A Host of Hauntings, 1973; A Gazetteer of Scottish & Irish Ghosts, 1973; Haunted London, 1973; The Ghosts of Borley, with Dr Paul Tabori, 1975; Deeper into the Occult, 1975; The Vampire's Bedside Companion, 1975; Lives to Remember – A Casebook on Reincarnation, with Leonard Wilder, 1975; Dictionary of the Supernatural, 1978; The Ghosts of Wales, 1978; Hauntings: New Light on 10 Famous Cases, 1977; Ghost Hunter's Handbook, 1980; Complete Book of Dowsing & Devining, 1980; Ghosts of Devon, 1982; Ghosts of Cornwall, 1983; Ghosts of Somerset, 1985; Ghosts of Hampshire & the Isle of Wight, 1983; Ghosts

of Kent, 1984; This Haunted Isle: Ghosts & Legends of Britain's Historic Buildings, 1984; The Ghost Hunters, 1985; Autobiography, No Common Task – the Autobiography of a Ghost Hunter, 1983; Biographies: Horror Man – the Life of Boris Karloff, 1972; Life's a Drag – a Biography of Danny La Rue, 1974. *Contributor to:* The Publisher; Local Government Chronicle; The Psychic Research, etc. *Membership:* Society of Authors. *Literary Agent:* Andrew Hewson, John Johnson (authors' Agents) Ltd. *Address:* The Savage Club, Fitzmaurice Place, Berkeley Square, London W1, England.

UNGER, Barbara, b. 10 Oct. 1932, USA. College Professor of English. *Education:* BA, MA, City University of New York. *Literary Appointments include:* Associate Professor of English, Rockland Community College, State University of New York; Writer-in-Residence New York State Council on the Arts, Rockland Center for the Arts, 1986–. *Publications include:* Basement: Poems 1959–61, 1975; Daughter, Toy Killer, 1976; The Man Who Burned Money, 1980. Fiction in, True to Life Adventure Stories, ed. J Grahn, 1980. *Contributions to:* Nation; Poetry Now; Minnesota Review; Kansas Quarterly; Thirteenth Moon; Buckle; Laurel Review; Contact II; Antigonish Review; Cottonwood Review; DeKalb Literary Arts Journal; Descant; Southern Poetry Review; Stone Country; Massachusetts Review; Beloit Poetry Journal; Nebraska Review; Frontiers; Jewish Frontier; Esprit; St Andrews Review; Abraxas; etc. *Honours include:* Faculty Research Fellowship, Creative Writing, SUNY, 1981–82; Fellow, Squaw Valley Community of Writers, 1980; Fellow, Millay Colony, 1984; Fellow, Ragdale, 1985; Numerous poetry readings. *Address:* 101 Parkside Drive, Suffern, NY 10901, USA.

UNGER, Michael Ronald, b. 8 Dec. 1943, Surrey, England. m. Eunice Dickens, 20 Aug. 1966, Henley-on-Thames, 1 son, 1 daughter. *Appointments:* Editor, Manchester Evening; Director, Guardian & Manchester Evening News plc. *Publication:* The Memoirs of Bridget Hitler, 1977. *Address:* 164 Deansgate, Manchester, England.

UNSTEAD, Robert John, b. 21 Nov. 1915, Deal, England. Author. m. Florence Thomas, 27 May 1939, Deal, 3 daughters. *Education:* Goldsmith's College, London University. *Publications:* Looking at History, 1953; People in History, 1955; Looking at Ancient History, 1959; A History of Britain, 1962–66; Castles, 1970; History of the English-Speaking World, 1971–74; A Dictionary of History, 1976; Story of Britain, 1969; A History of the World, 1983. *Contributions to:* History Today; Encyclopaedia Americana, 1985 edition. *Memberships:* Chairman, Educational Writers Group 1968–70, Society of Authors; Honorary Secretary, East Anglian Writers, 1980–. *Address:* Reedlands Thorpeness, Suffolk, England.

UNSWORTH, Walter (Walt), b. 16 Dec. 1928, Manchester, England. Author. m. Dorothy Winstanley, 1952, Abram, Lancashire, 1 son, 1 daughter. *Education:* Licentiate, College of Preceptors. *Literary Appointment:* Editor, Climber and Ramblers, 1974–. *Publications:* The English Outcrops, 1964; Portrait of the River Derwent, 1972; Encyclopedia of Mountaineering, 1975; Everest, 1981. Over 20 books including 3 novels. *Contributions to:* To a great many publications. One of the leading mountaineering, mountain, travel writers in Britain. *Memberships:* Society of Authors; Former Chairman of Authors North (the Northern Branch of the Society of Authors). *Literary Agent:* A P Watt. *Address:* Harmony Hall, Milnthorpe, Cumbria, England.

UNTERBERGER, Betty M, b. 27 Dec. 1923, Glasgow, Scotland. Professor of History. m. Robert M Unterberger, 27 July 1944, 2 sons, 1 daughter. *Education:* BA, Syracuse University, USA, 1943; MA, Harvard University, 1946; PhD, Duke University, 1950. *Literary Appointments:* Commissioner, National Historical Publications and Records Commission, 1980–84; Board of Editors, Diplomatic History, 1971–84; Editorial Advisory Board, The Papers of Woodrow

Wilson, Princeton University, 1982–; Editorial Board, Humbolt Journal of Social Relations, 1984–. *Publications:* America's Siberian Expedition: A Study of National Policy, 1969; American Intervention in the Russian Civil War, 1969; Chapter in, Woodrow Wilson and a Revolutionary World, 1982. *Contributions to:* Russian Review; Slavic Review; Pakistan Affairs; Diplomatic History; The Nation; Journal of Southern History; Pacific Historical Review; Journal of American History and others. *Honours:* Graduate Publication Award, Duke University, 1950–53; Pacific Coast Award, American Historical Association, 1956; Ford Foundation Research Grant, 1959; American Philosophical Society Research Grant, 1960–61, 66. *Memberships:* American Historical Association; American Association for the Advancement of Slavic Studies; Association for Pakistan and Indo-Islamic Studies; Association of Asian Studies; Society for Historians of American Foreign Relations, Founding member; Conference of Peace Research in History; Organisation of American Historians. *Address:* Route 3 Box 314, College Station, TX 77840, USA.

UNTERBRINK, Mary, b. 5 May 1937, Lima, Ohio, USA. Writer, Haiku Poet. m. Larry Unterbrink, 25 Aug. 1956, Ottawa, Ohio, 3 sons, 2 daughters. *Major Publications:* Jazz Women at the Keyboard, 1983; Manatees, Gentle Giants in Peril, 1984; Funny Women, 1986. *Contributor to:* Music Educators Journal; Piedmont Literary Review; Air Florida Sunshine; New York Antique Almanac; Fort Lauderdale Magazine; Black Collegian; Tallahassee Magazine; Guide to North Florida; Florida Nursing News; VW Small World; Catholic Digest; Rosicrucian Digest. *Memberships:* Florida Freelance Writers Association; Book Group (Fort Lauderdale Authors, Editors, Publishers); Florida State Poets' Association. *Address:* 625 NW 25th Street, Fort Lauderdale, FL 33311, USA.

UPWARD, Edward Falaise, b. 9 Sep. 1903, Romford, Essex, England. Schoolteacher. m. October 1936, Camberwell, London, 1 son, 1 daughter. *Education:* MA, Cambridge University. *Publications:* Journey to the Border, 1938; In the Thirties, 1962; The Rotten Elements, 1969; The Railway Accident and Other Stories, 1969; The Spiral Ascent, 1977; No Home But The Struggle, 1979. *Contributor to:* The London Magazine; Radio 3. *Honour:* The Chancellor's Medal for English Verse, Cambridge 1924. *Membership:* The Society of Authors. *Address:* c/o William Heinemann Ltd, 10 Upper Grosvenor Street, London W1X 9PA, England.

URDANG, Constance Henriette, b. New York City, New York, USA. Writer; Editor. m. Donald Finkel, 14 Aug. 1956, St Louis, Missouri, 1 son, 2 daughters. *Education:* BA, Smith College; MFA, University of Iowa. *Literary Appointments:* Co-Ordinator, The Writers Programme, Washington University, St Louis, Missouri, 1977–84; Bain-Swigett Visiting Lecturer, Princeton University, 1985. *Publications:* Charades and Celebrations, 1965; Natural History, 1969; The Picnic in the Cemetery, 1975; The Lone Woman and Others, 1980; Only the World, 1983; New and Selected Poems, 1986. *Contributions to:* Accent; American Poetry Review; Antaeus; Arts in Society; Burning Deck; Carlton Discellany; Chicago Review; Chelsea; Contact; Counter/Measures; Epoch; Focus Midwest; Harpers; New American Review; The New Republic; Poetry; Poetry Northwest; Perespective; paris Review; Pebble Quarterly; QWuarterly Review of Literature; Red Clay Quarterly; Sojourner; Texas Quarterly. *Honours:* Carlton Centennial Award for Prose, 1967; Award, National Educational Association, 1976–77; Delmore Schwartz Memorial Poetry Award, 1981. *Literary Agent:* Borchardt. *Address:* 6943 Columbia Place, St Louis, MO 63130, USA.

URQUHART, Frederick Burrows, b. 12 July 1912, Edinburgh, Scotland. Short Story Writer; Novelist. *Literary Appointments include:* Reader, various publishers, literary agency, Metro-Goldwyn-Mayer. *Publications Include:* Time Will Knit, 1938; I Fell For A

Sailor, 1940; The Clouds Are Big With Mercy, 1946; The Last GI Bride Wore Tartan, 1948; Jezebel's Dust, 1952; The Dying Stallion, 1967; The Ploughing Match, 1968; Palace of Green Days, 1979; Proud Lady in a Cage, 1980; A Diver in China Seas, 1980; The Book of Horses, 1981; Seven Ghosts in Search, 1983. *Contributions to:* New Writing; Penguin Parade; London Mercury; English Story; Story (USA); Harpers Bazaar (USA); London Magazine; Blackwoods; Tribune; Time & Tide; Spectator; Texas Quarterly (USA); Listener; Scottish Review. *Honours:* Tom-Gallon Trust Award, 1951; Arts Council grant, 1966; Scottish Arts Council grant, 1975; Arts Council bursaries, 1978; 1985; Barbara Campion Memorial Prize, 1984. *Membership:* Society of Authors. *Literary Agent:* Herta Ryder, c/o Toby Eady Associates, 55 Great Ormond Street, London WC1. *Address:* Spring Garden Cottage, Fairwarp, Uckfield, Sussex TN22 3BG, England.

URQUHART, Mary Jane, b. 21 June 1949, Canada. Writer. m. Tony Urquhart, 5 May 1976, Colborne, Ontario, 1 daughter. *Education:* BA English Literature, 1971, BA History of Art, 1975, University of Guelph, Canada. *Major Publications:* I am Walking in the Garden of His Imaginary Palace, 1982; False Shuffles, 1982; The Little Flowers of Madame de Montespan, 1984. *Contributor to:* (Fiction) Canadian Fiction Magazine; Descant; Malahat Review; (Poetry) Quarry; The New Review; Antigonish Review; Prism International; Canadian Poetry Review; Fiddlehead. *Honours:* Canada Council Award, 1983; Ontario Arts Council Award, 1982, 1983, 1984. *Memberships:* League of Canadian Poets, 1984. *Address:* 24 Water Street, Wellesley, Ontario, N0B 2T0, Canada.

URRY, Maggie, b. 5 Nov. 1955, England. Financial Journalist. *Education:* BSc Economics, London School of Economics. *Literary Appointments:* Journalist, Investor's Chronicle, 1980–83; Journalist, Standard, 1983–84; Journalist, Financial Times, 1984–. *Honours:* Young Financial Journalist of the Year, Harold Wincott Award, 1983. *Address:* Financial Times, Bracken House, Cannon Street, London EC4, England.

URSELL, Geoffrey Barry, b. 14 Apr. 1943, Saskatchewan, Canada. Writer; Composer. m. Barbara Sapergia, 8 July 1967; Regina, Canada. *Education:* BA (Hons), MA, University of Manitoba; PhD, University of London. *Literary Appointments:* Writer-In-Residence, Saskatoon Public Library, 1984–85. *Publications:* The running of the Deer, (play), 1981; Trap Lines, (poetry), 1983; Perdue; Or How the West was Lost, (novel), 1984. *Contributions to:* Grain; Saturday Night; Quarry; Canadian Forum; This Magazine; Newest Review, (poems, stories and songs). *Honours:* Clifford E Lee National Playwriting Award, 1977; Persephone Theatre National Playwriting Competition Award, 1981; Books in Canada First Novel Award, 1984. *Memberships:* Past-President, Saskatchewan Writers' Guild; Past-President, Saskatchewan Playwrights Centre; Playwrights Union of Canada; Writers Union of Canada; ACTRA. *Address:* 1610 Hilliard St E, Saskatoon, Saskatchewan, Canada S7J 0G4.

URWIN, Gregory John William, b. 11 July 1955, Cleveland, Ohio, USA. Assistant Professor of History; Historian. m. Cathy Ann Kunzinger, 31 Dec. 1982, Virginia Beach, Virginia. *Education:* BA Summa cum laude, Borromeo College of Ohio, 1977; MA, John Carroll University, 1979; MA, 1981, PhD, 1984, University of Notre Dame. *Literary Appointments:* Special Editor, Little Big Horn Associates, 1984–. *Publications:* Custer Victorious: The Civil War Battles of General George Armstrong Custer, 1983; The United States Cavalry: An Illustrated History, 1983. *Contributions to:* American History Illustrated; Military Images; Military Collector and Historian; Indiana Magazine of History; Journal of the West; Campaigns; Air Classics; Air Progress Aviation Review; Combat Illustrated; Arkansas Gazette; Western Reserve Magazine; North Jersey Highlander; Brigade Dispatch; Research Review; Air Combat. *Honours:* John W Highbarger

Memorial Award, 1981, Zahm Research Travel Grant, 1981–82, University of Notre Dame; Historical Program Research Grant, History and Museums Division, US Marine Corps, 1981–82; Research Council Grant, University of Central Arkansas, 1984–85. *Memberships:* American Historical Association; American Military Institute; Phi Alpha Theta; Company of Military Historians; Little Big Horn Associates; Custer Battlefield Historical and Museum Association. *Address:* Department of History, Box U, University of Central Arkansas, Conway, AR 72032, USA.

USBORNE, Thomas Peter, b. 18 Aug. 1937, London, England. Publisher. m. Cornelie Tuecking, 30 Oct. 1964, Munich, Germany, 1 son, 1 daughter. *Education:* BA, Oxford University; MBA, INEAD, France. *Literary Appointments:* Editor, MacDonald Educational, London. England, 1970; Publishing director, MacDonald Educational, London, 1971; Managing Director, Founder, Usborne Publishing Limited, London, 1973–. *Address:* Usborne Publishing Limited, 20 Garrick Street, London WC2, England.

USHERWOOD, Stephen Dean, b. 14 Sep. 1907, London, England. Writer. m. (1) wife deceased 1968, 1 son, 1 daughter, (2) Elizabeth Ada Beavington, 24 Oct. 1970. *Education:* MA, Oxford. *Publications:* Reign By Reign, 1960; The Bible Book by Book, 1962; Shakespeare, Play by Play, 1967; Street Names, 1969; Street Names Project Book, 1969; Place Names, 1969; Place Names Project Book, 1969; Festivals and Holidays, 1969; Festivals and Holidays Project Book, 1969; Coins, 1970; Coins Project Book, 1970; Inns and Inn Signs, 1971; Inns and Inn Signs Project Book, 1971; Britain, Century by Century, 1972; Europe Century by Century, 1972; Food, Drink and History, 1972; The Great Enterprise, 1978 and 1982; With Elizabeth Ada Usherwood: Visit Some London Catholic Churches, 1982; The Counter-Armada 1596: The Journal of the Mary Rose, UK and USA, 1983. *Contributions to:* Numerous publications. *Membership:* Society of Authors, London. *Address:* 24 St Mary's Grove, Canonbury, London N1 2NT, England.

USLANER, Eric Michael, b. 2 Feb. 1947, Passaic, New Jersey, USA. University Professor. m. Deborah Doreen Provost, 3 June 1983, London, England. *Education:* BA, Hons, Politics, Brandeis University, 1968; MA, Political Science, 1970, PhD, Political Science, 1973; Indiana University. *Literary Appointments:* Assistant Professor of Political Science, University of Florida, 1972–75; Assistant Professor of Government and Politics, 1975–78, Associate Professor of Government and Politics, 1978–, University of Maryland. *Publications:* How American Foreign Policy Is Made, co-author, 1974, 1978; Patterns of Decision-Making in State Legislation, co-author, 1977; American Foreign Policy-Making and the Democratic Dilemas, co-author, 1981, 1985; Few Are Chosen: Problems in Presidential Selection, co-author, 1984. *Contributor to:* American Political Science Review; Journal of Politics; American Journal of Political Science. *Honours:* Indiana University Fellowship, 1968–72; Faculty Enrichment Grant, Embassy of Canada (United States) 1984.

Memberships: American Political Science Association; Midwest Political Science Association; Southern Political Science Association; Public Choice Society. *Address:* Department of Government and Politics, University of Maryland, College Park, MD 20742, USA.

UTIGER, Robert David, b. 14 July 1931, Bridgeport, Connecticut, USA. Physician. m. Sally Baldwin, 1 son, 2 daughters. *Education:* William College; Washington University School of Medicine. *Literary Appointments:* Editorial Boards: Metabolism, 1970–82; Journal of Clinical Endocrimology and Metabolism, 1971–77, Journal of Clinical Investigation, 1974–79, Endocrinology, 1976–80, American Journal of Medicine, 1978–82; Editor-in-Chief, Journal of Clinical Endocrinology and Metabolism, 1983. *Publications:* Editor with R C Packman: Washington University School of Medicine Manual of Medical Therapeutics, 17th edition, 1964; Author of numerous chapters in edited scientific volumes. *Contributor to:* Numerous papers, editorials and reviews to medical journals. *Membership:* Council of Biology Editors. *Literary Agent:* D Geri Cox. *Address:* University of North Carolina School of Medicine, Department of Medicine/Division of Endocrinology, Box 501, Clinical Research Unit, North Carolina Memorial Hospital, Chapel Hill, NC 27514, USA.

UUSI-HAKIMO, Lauri Kaarle, b. 6 May 1930, Ahtari, Finland. Principal, Education Centre for Adults. m. Hilkka Tyynela, 13 mar. 1955, Helsinki, Finland, 3 sons. *Education:* Master of Political Science. *Appointments:* Chairman of Library Board, Town of Forssa, 1963–76; Member of Executive Board, Suomen Maakuntakirjailijat ry, 1976–78; Member representing literature, Committee of Arts, Hameen laani, 1980–85. *Publications:* Novels: Isalta pojalle (From Father to Son), 1974; Poika ja kesa (The Boy and the Summer), 1975; Elokuu (August), 1977; Autokauppias (Car Dealer), 1979; Punamarjapensas (The Bush with Red Berries), 1980; Kaarnavalkeat (Fires of Bark), 1982 and Sotatalvi (The Winter of War), 1985, Plays for theatre and radio. Contributor to newspaper Forssan Lehti, 1978 to present, *Memberships:* Suomen kirjailijaliitto; Suomen naytelmakirjailijaliitto. *Honours:* First Prize, Novelists Competition, 1974. Several Grants. *Literary Agent:* Kirjayhtyma Oy. *Address:* Kurkelankatu 5, 30300 Forssa, Finland.

UVALIEFF, Peter, b. 1 May 1910, Sofia, Bulgaria. Film Producer. m. Sonja Hollingswood, 13 Mar. 1960, London, 1 daughter. *Education:* LLB, St Klement University, Bulgaria; National University, Sofia, Bulgaria. *Literary Appointments:* Film Advisor, UNESCO, Paris, 1958; Scenarist, De Grunewald Productions, London, 1960; Art critic, editor, Art & Artists, London, 1962; Scriptwriter, Blow Up, Antonioni, London, 1964. *Publications include:* In Love With Leopold, novel, 1956; Escapes & Vagaries, short stories, 1958; Arabia Felix, film scenario, 1959; Socialist Realism – Soviet Aesthestics, essays, 1962. *Contributions to:* Perspectives, New York; Art News, London; L'Oeil, Paris; Tandava, Rome. *Address:* 50 Markham Street, Chelsea, London, England.

V

VADASZ, Ferenc, b. 22 June 1916, Komarom, Hungary. Journalist, Editor. *Education:* University of Political Sciences, Hungary. *Major Publications:* Szeged Goal, 1948; Battle with the Hungarian Hell, 1961; Young Men from the Remete Street, 1962; The Thirteenth Winter, 1966; The Great Optimist, 1967; The Wind Stops Blowing, 1968; Into the Light from Beneath the Earth, 1969; A Piece of the Sky, 1970; Others Die, 1972; The Lawyer, 1975; Without Legends, 1975; The Summer of Uneasiness (Trilogy, 1968, 1976, 1979 respectively); Sons of Martial Law, 1985; and others. *Contributor to:* Nepszabadsag (editor). *Honours:* SZOT (Trade Union Art Prize) 1971; Josef Attila Prize, 1976; Rósza Ference Prize. Journalists' Prize, 1981. *Memberships:* PEN; Hungarian Literary Foundation. *Address:* 1119 Budapest, Fehévári ut 153, Hungary.

VAILLANCOURT, Jean-Guy, b. 24 May 1937, Chelmsford, Ontario, Canada. Chairman and Professor of Sociology. 1 daughter. *Education:* BA, University of Sudbury, Ontario, 1957; BA, Philosophy, 1960, Licence degree, Philosophy 1961, BA, Sociology, cum laude, 1964, Jesuit Faculty of Philosophy, Montreal, Gregorian University Rome, 1967, Licence Degree Sociology, PhD, Sociology, University of California, Berkeley, 1975. *Literary Appointments include:* Full Professorship, University of Montreal; Guest Professor, various universities; Interviews, Radio & Television, ecology, peace, politics, religion; Teaching, sociology of environment, religion, etc. *Publications include:* Essais d'écosociologie, 1982; Papal Power, 1980; Les mouvements pour le désarmement et la paix, 1984; L'Etat et la société, 1983; Le processus électoral au Québec: les elections provincials de 1970 et 1973, 1976; Co-author, 3 books. *Contributions to:* Various journals, approximately 100 articles & reviews. *Honour:* Scholar, Canada Council, 1965–68. *Memberships:* Editorial Committee, Berkeley Journal of Sociology, 1969–70, Insurgent Sociologist, 1970–79; Secretary/Treasurer, Canadian Associaton of French-Speaking Sociologists & Anthropologists, 1975–77; Editor-in-Chief, Bulletin de l'ACSALF, 1975–77; CA & CEP Project Committee, Oxfam, Quebec, 1976–79; Municipal Counsellor, Dunham, Quebec Council of the Environment, 1978–. *Address:* Department of Sociology, CP 6128, University of Montreal, Quebec, Canada H3C 3J7.

VAIZEY, Marina, b. 16 Jan. 1938, New York City, USA. Art Critic. m. Lord Vaizey, 22 Sep. 1961, New York, deceased 1984, 2 sons, 1 daughter. *Education:* BA, Medieval History and Literature, Radcliffe College, Harvard University; BA, History, Girton College, Cambridge University, 1961; MA (Cantab), 1975. *Literary Appointments:* Broadcaster on National and Local BBC World Service, 1966–; Art Critic, Financial Times, 1970–74; Dance Critic, Feature Writer, Now Magazine, 1979–81; Art Critic, Sunday Times, 1974–. *Publications:* St Michael Guide to Famous Paintings, 1979; Andrew Wyeth, 1980; 100 Materpieces of Painting (UK & USA), 1980; The Artist as Photographer, 1982; Peter Blake, 1985; Narrative History of 20th Century Art (in progress). *Contributions to:* approximately 3000 articles on the visual arts, performing arts, cultural policy, Books: Oxford Magazine; Arts Review; Connoisseur; Arts News USA; Portfolio USA; New Republic USA; Antique Collector; New Statesman; Times Literary Supplement; Times Education Supplement; Tatler; British Books News, etc. *Memberships:* Arts Council, 1976–78 (Art Panel, 1973–78, Deputy Chairman, 1976–78); Paintings for Hospitals, 1974–; Committee, Contemporary Art Society, 1975–; History of Art and Complementary Studies Board, CNAA, 1978–82; Photography Board, CNAA, 1979–81; Director, Mitchell Prize for the History of Art, 1976–; Governor, Camberwell College of Arts & Crafts, 1971–; Co-Secretary. Radcliffe College of London, 1968–74. *Literary Agent:* Gill Coleridge, Anthony Sheil. *Address:* 24 Heathfield Terrace, London W4 4JE, England.

VAKKURI, Juha, b. 2 Dec. 1946, Helsinki, Finland. Author; Head of Programmes, YLE Finland. m. Catarina Doepel, 4 Aug. 1979, Tampere, 2 sons, 1 daughter. *Education:* BA, MA, Helsinki University. *Publications:* Novels: An African Afternoon, 1978; Tree of Four Generations, 1980; The Man who Turned into a Tree, 1982; Tropic of Ice, 1984; Equator, 1985; Non-fiction: Winds of Change, 1979; Gold, Islam and the Sacred Snake, 1983. *Contributor to:* Series of articles on Africa, Helsingin Sanomat, 1978–. *Honours:* National Film Award for the Script, Africa, Tarzan and I, 1979. *Memberships:* Pen Club, Finland; Eino Leinon Seura; Finnish Writers Union. *Literary Agent:* Weilen & Göös. *Address:* Weilin & Göös, Espoo, Finland.

VALA, Erik August Waldemar, b. 17 Dec. 1902, Porvoo, Finland, Journalist, Publisher. m. (1) Ursula Tesleff, 1928, Helsinki, deceased 1929; (2) Helny Wallin, 1945, Uppsala, deceased 1984, 1 son, 1 granddaughter. *Literary Appointments:* Secretary, Leader, Nuoren Voiman Liitto, 1920–30; with Kouvolan Sandmat (newspaper), 1920–22; Werner Söderström Publishers, 1924–34; Founder, Publishing firm Kirjailejain Kustannusliike, 1928; Founder & Editor, Tulenkantajat (magazine), 1928–34; with Finnish Broadcasting Company, 1945–48. *Major Publications:* Onnelliset Pessimistit (novel) 1928. *Contributor to:* Nuori Voima; Tulenkantajat; Suomen Sosiali Demokraatti; Suomen Kuvalehti; Huvudstadsbladet; Dagens Nyheter; Uusi Suomi; Kretelinit; Mustaveljeskunta; Leijonajuhlat; Finlands Tva Ansikten. *Honours:* Finnish Ministry of Education; 3 awards from Finnish Literature Society; State Pension. *Memberships:* Finnish Literary Society; PEN-Club, Finland. *Literary Agent:* Werner Söderström. *Address:* Mäntypaadentie 28, SF–00830 Helsinki, Finland.

VALENTI, Justine, b. USA. Novelist. m. Daniel Cheifetz, 31 Mar. 1985, New York. *Education:* BA, Brooklyn College. *Publications:* Lovemates, 1982; Twin Connections, 1983; No One But You, in UK, Lovesong, 1985. *Contributor to:* Gourmet Magazine, former Managing Editor. *Literary Agent:* Carole Abel, USA; David Grossman, UK. *Address:* 235 West End Ave, New York, NY 10023, USA.

VALENTIN, Knut Jakob Jack, b. 7 Dec. 1944, Solna, Sweden. Head, Department, National Institute of Radiation Protection. m. Cecilia Torudd, 29 Mar. 1985, Stockholm. *Education:* BSc, Biology, 1967; MSc, Genetics, 1968; PhD, Genetics, 1973. *Publications:* Translation into Swedish of, The Double Helix, 1968; The Andromeda Strain, 1971; others: Several education books on genetics in Swedish. *Contributor to:* Numerous translations of articles for, Readers Digest; 40 book notices and other material for GT and DN; 50 papers, in scientific journals. *Memberships:* Swedish Club of Writers, Translators Section. *Address:* National Institute of Radiation Protection, Box 60204, S–10401 Stockholm, Sweden.

VALGARDSON, William Dempsey, b. 7 May 1939, Winnipeg, Manitoba, Canada. Writer. Separated, 1 son, 1 daughter. *Education:* BA, BEd, University of Manitoba; MFA, University of Iowa, *Literary Appointments:* Assistant Professor, Department of English, Cottey College, 1970–74; University of Victoria, British Columbia, 1974–,currently Professor and Chairman of Department. *Publications:* Bloodflowers, 1973; God Is Not A Fish Inspector, 1975; In The Gutting Shed, 1976; Red Dust, 1978; Gentle Sinners, 1980. *Contributions to:* Numerous magazines and journals. *Honours:* President's Medal for Fiction, 1971; CBC Annual Literary Prize in Fiction, 1980; Books in Canada Award, best First Novel, 1981; CAA Prize in Drama, 1984. *Memberships:* The Writer's Union of Canada; Periodical Writers Association of Canada; CACLAIS; AASSC. *Address:* 3221 Doncaster Drive, Victoria, B C, Canada V8P 3V3.

VALLE, Cyro Eyer do, b. 30 Sep. 1937, Niteroi, Brazil. Engineer. *Education:* BS, Mechanical Engineering, University of Rio de Janeiro, Brazil, 1960; Scolarship in

Industrial Projects from French Government, ASTEF, Paris, 1965–66. *Major Publication:* Implantaçaõ de Industrias (in Portuguese, dealing with projects of industrial plant & complexes), 1975. *Address:* Rue Santelmo 102, 04031 São Paulo SP, Brazil.

VALTIALA, Kaarle-Juhani Bertel, b. 2 Jan. 1938, Helsinki, Finland. High School Teacher, Writer. m. 17 June 1961, Helsinki, 1 son, 1 daughter. *Education:* Fil. kand. (MA), 1962. *Publications:* Ätta noveller, 1963; Varning för människan, 1968; Notvarp i Sargassohavet, 1972; Tonga, 1974; Res våsterut unge man!; 1978; I Mark Twains hjulspår, 1982; Nationens hjälte, 1986. *Contributions to:* Nya Argus; Horisont; FBT; etc. *Honours:* First prize, shared, short story contest. Finnish Radio Corporation, 1976; First prize, shared, Fidra 84 drama contest, 1984; First Prize, shared, novel contest, Bra Böcker of Höganäs, Nationens Hjälte, 1985. *Memberships:* Finlands Svenska Författareförening rf (League of Swedish Writers in Finland); Finlands dramatikerförbund (League of Finnish Dramatists). *Address:* Parkgränden 5-7 A7, 02700 Grankulla, Finland.

VAN AMSTEL, Pamela Maree, b. 8 Dec. 1946, Western Australia. Scriptwriter. *Education:* Bachelor of Social Work, Univesity of New South Wales, Australia, 1979; General Trained Nurse, Prince of Wales Hospital, Sydney, Australia, 1971; Psychiatric Nurse, Macquarie Hospital, Sydney, 1973. *Literary Appointments:* Writer in Residence, Nimrod Theatre, Sydney, 1983; Writer's Attachment, Australian Film & Television School, 1984; Writer in Residence, TN Theatre Company, Brisbane, 1985. *Major Publications:* Are you Lonesome Tonight?, 1983; Once in a Blue Moon, 1983; Late Arrivals, 1985; Neighbourhood, 1985; Public Images, 1985. *Contributor to:* Health Media Productions (Co-writer), ABC Television. *Honours:* Australian Film Institute Nomination for Best Short Screenplay 1984 (Heads'n Tails, Co-Writer); Australian Writers' Guild Nomination for Radio Adaptation Are You Lonesome Tonight?, 1985. *Memberships:* Australian Writer's Guild (Stage Committee); Australian National Playwrights' Conference (Committee, 1984); International Young Playwrights' Festival, Sydney 1985 (Committee). *Literary Agent:* Hilary Linstead & Associates, Surry Hills, NSW. *Address:* c/o Hilary Linstead & Associates, 223 Commonwealth Street, Surry Hills, New South Wales 2010, Australia.

VAN CISE, Jerrold Gordon, b. 21 May 1910, Newark, New Jersey, USA. Attorney, New York City. m. Elizabeth Kind, 1 Dec. 1939, Garden City, new York, 1 son, 2 daughters. *Education:* BS, Princeton University, 1932; JD, Yale University, 1935. *Publications include:* Understanding the Antitrust Laws, 9th edition, 1986; The Federal Antitrust Laws, 5th edition, 1982. *Contributions:* Regulation – By Business or Government (Harvard Business Review, 1966); Aristotle & Congress (St. John's Law Review, 1970); Patents, Plowshares & Pruning Hooks (American Bar Journal, 1971); For Whom the Antitrust Bell Tolls (Harvard Business Review, 1978); Religion & Antitrust (Antitrust Bulletin, 1978); etc. *Honours:* Phi Beta Kappa, 1931; Order of Coif, 1935; McKinsey Award, Harvard Business Review, 1966; Seligson Award, Practising Law Institute, 1984; Susan Colgate Cleveland Award, Colby-Sawyer College, 1985. *Memberships:* American & New York State Bar Associations (Chairman, Antitrust Section, 1960–61, 1961–62 respectively). *Address:* New London, NH 03257, USA.

VAN DEN BERGH, Lodewyk Paulina, b. 18 June 1920, Rykevorsel, Belgium. Novelist; Professor of English. m. Nora Steyaert, 24 Dec. 1956, Ghent, 1 son. *Education:* Doctor in Philosophy and Literature. *Publications:* Dagnoek van een Missionaris (A Missionary's Journal), 1962; De Woedende Christus (The Furious Christ), 1965; Het Huis Van Mama Pondo (Mama Pondo's Home), 1972; Toen Wij Allen Samen Waren (When we were all together), 1978; Amanda, 1983. *Memberships:* Vereniging van Veeamse Letterkundigen; PEN. *Address:* Terlindenweg 122, 1700 Asse, Belgium.

VAN DIJK, Peter, b. 17 May 1949. Writer; Director. *Education:* Studies Political and Social Science at University of Amsterdam. *Literary Appointments:* Translated books (Fiction and non-fiction) and plays into Dutch. Wrote, directed and produced fringe theatre projects. Radio plays broadcast in the Netherlands and Belgium. Texts, direction and editorial work for many radio productions (satire and documentary drama). Produced material for Dutch revue and worked as copywriter for major advertising agency. *Honour:* Radio play, The New Undergrounders, was Dutch entry for Prix d'Italia, 1983. *Address:* Ceintuurbaan 366/III, 1073 El Amsterdam, The Netherlands.

VAN DIVER, Gerald R, b. 22 July 1948, St Louis, Missouri, USA. Microcomputer Researcher, Consultant and Publisher. m. Teresa Ann, 16 June 1978, St Cloud, Minnesota, 1 son, 1 daughter. *Education:* BA, Judson College, Illinois; MBA, Northern Illinois University. *Literary Appointments:* Executive Director, National Software Review Board. *Publications:* IBM PC, XT, The Software Guide, 1983; IBM PCjr Software Guide and Handbook, 1984; IBM PC, XT, PCjr Educational Software Directory, 1984; Personal Computer Software Directory for IBM, 1985; Personal Computer Software Directory for Apple, 1985. *Contributions to:* USA Today; Wall Street Journal; Publisher, PC Consumer Magazine and New Robotics Magazine. *Address:* 4730 Dakota Street South East, Prior Lake, MN 55372, USA.

VAN FRAASSEN, Bastiaan Cornelis, b. 5 Apr. 1941, Netherlands. Professor of Philosophy. *Education:* BA, University of Alberta, 1963; MA, 1965, PhD, 1966, University of Pittsburgh. *Literary Appointments:* Yale University, 1966–69; University of Toronto, 1969–82; University of Southern California, 1976–82; Princeton University, 1982–. *Major Publications:* An Introduction to the Philosophy of Time and Space, 2nd edition, 1985; Formal Semantics and Logic, 1971; The Scientific Image, 1980. *Contributor to:* Many Philosophical jounals. *Honours:* Guggenheim Fellowship, 1970–71; National Science Foundation Senior Scholar, 1982–83; Co-winner, Franklin J Matchette Prize for Philosophical Books, 1982. *Address:* Department of Philosophy, Princeton University, Princeton, NJ 08544, USA.

VAN HOUTEN Wim, b. 1939, Eindhoven, The Netherlands. *Education:* Studied English Language and Literature at Nijmegen University and Drama at Bristol University. *Literary Appointments:* Teacher of Theatre History and Literature, School of Dramatic Art, Arnhem; Dramaturg for Theatre companies in Amsterdam (Globe) and The Hague (Haagse Comedie) 1970–79; Returned to teaching in 1980. *Publication:* Play: The New Ilse Valk. *Address:* V1 van Pabststraat 30, 6814 HJ Arnhem, The Netherlands.

VAN HOUWENINGE, Chiem, b. 20 Nov. 1940. Actor; Director; Playwright. *Literary Appointments:* Acting: Nieuw Rotterdams Toneel 1969–71; Amsterdams Toneel, 1971–72; Publieks Theatre Amsterdam, 1972; played two roles every season, mainly in the classical section Sophocles, Shakespeare, Tschekov, Brecht etc. One of leading artistic figures at Publieks Theatre, 1972–81. Director of plays by Tschekov, Arrabal, Shakespeare and his own works. *Publications:* Theatre plays: Pachacamac, 1965; The Last Train, 1969 produced by Niouw Rotterdams Toneel, Northern Company Saskatchewan, Canada and Sydney, Australia. The Last Train, was reproduced in French Theatre Magazine, L'Avant Scene, translated by Michel and Marise Caillol. No 30048, 1969, Nieuw Rotterdams Toneel; The Hippy Birds of Bikini, 1971, Vieuw Rotterdams Toneel; The Dutch Crimp, 1973, Nieuw Rotterdams Toneel; The Isolated Old Lady, 1974, BWT, Antwerp; Old Toys, 1978 (new version 1982). Television Series and Plays: Weep on My Shoulder, 1968, VARA and BRT Television; Furnished, 1970, AVRO and BRT Television; Love Pet, 1970, AVRO and BRT Television; Old Toys, Television adamptation 1980 for AVRO TV; Good Riddance, 1978 NOS-Television; Every One Gets His Share, Television comedy with Alexander Pola, series in 24 parts (25 mins each) 1976–

77-78, VARA; Cassata, Television comedy, 8 parts (25 mins each) 1979, VARA; Do Say A, 1980–81, 82-83, Television comedy, VARA; Spaub Is Trump, Television comedy, NCRV, 1983. Cuddle Beasts, (Tatort) West Deutsche Rundfunk; A Good Nose, (Tatort) West Deutsche Rundfunk. Films: Scenarios (35mm cinema), The Man with a Thousand Teeth, 1967, Final examen Film Academy, director Grasveld; The Burglar, directed by Frans Weisz (Part Films); The Shopkeeper Didn't Return, Sigma Films; Sherlock Jones, Magan Films; Dear Boys, (from Gerard Reve) Sigma Films. Translations of Tschekov plays with Ton Lutz. *Address:* Broekkade 8-9, 3138 KA Vlaardingen, The Netherlands.

VAN KAAM, Adrian L, b. 19 Apr. 1920, The Hague, The Netherlands. Professor, Institute Director (Emeritus). *Education:* Philosophy, Theology Seminary, Gemert, 1947; MO, Gulemborg, 1954; Psychotherapy, University of Chicago, 1956; Personality Theory, Brandeis University, 1957; PhD, Case Western University, 1958. *Literary Appointments:* Professor, Philosophical Anthropology Seminary, Gemert, Holland, 1948–53; Assistant Professor, 1957, Associate Professor, 1960, Professor, Department of Psychology, Duquesne University, 1965–; Founder & Director, Institute of Formative Spirituality, 1963–80; Founder & Editor: Studies in Formative Spirituality; Envoy; Initiator of the Science of Formation, 1978. *Major Publications:* Religion & Personality, 1964; Existential Foundations of Psychology, 1966; The Art of Existential Counselling, 1966; Envy & Originality, 1972; Spirituality & the Gentle Life, 1974; In Search of Spiritual Identity, 1975; The Dynamics of Spiritual Self-Direction, 1976; Living Creatively, 1978; The Transcedent Self, 1979; Religion & Personality, 1980; Foundations for Personality Study, 1983; The Science of Formative Spirituality, Volume 1, Fundamental Formation, 1983, Volume 2, Human Formation, 1985, Volume 3, Formation of the Human Heart, 1986; (in preparation: Volume 4, Scientific Foundation, Volume 5, Traditional Formation). *Contributor to:* Journal of Individual Psychology; American Journal of Nursing; Review of Existential Psychology & Psychiatry; Harvard Educational Review; Insight; Journal of Humanistic Psychology; Humanitas; and others. *Honours:* Various editorial responsibilities; Visiting Professor, Institute of Psychology, University of Heidelberg, Federal Republic of Germany, 1966. *Memberships:* Felow, American Psychology Association; Society for the Scientific Study of Religion. *Address:* Institute of Formative Spirituality, Duquesne University, Pittsburgh, PA 15282, USA.

VAN LOOY, Herman, b. 22 Mar. 1922, Berchem, Belgium. Professor of Greek Literature, University of Ghent; Vice Rector of University. *Education:* Doctor of Classical Philology; Doctor of Oriental Philosophy and History. *Publications:* Demosthenes, Kransrede, 1950; Caesar, Een Monographie, 1956; Euripides, Zes verloren tragedies, 1964; Sallustius, Catilina, 1966. *Contributions to:* Antiquité Classique; Revue Belge de Philologie et d'Histoire; Ancient Society; Mus. Iond. philol. *Honour:* Laureat Kon, AK Belgie, 1962. *Memberships:* Zuidnederl; My Taal-Letterk-Gesch; Associacion des Etudes grecques, Paris, France. *Address:* Schampery 2, 9670 Horebeke, Belgium.

Van MORCKHOVEN, Paul (Lode Jozef Pauwels), b. 25 Mar. 1910, Antwerp, Belgium. Former teacher; Journalist; Playwright. 3 sons, 1 daughter. *Education:* Teacher's Diploma, 1929. *Literary Appointments Include:* Journalism; Television reporting; Founded itinerant theatrical company, 1930–33; Stage manager, avant-garde plays. *Publications Include:* Het Amerikaans Toneel (American Theatre), 1953; De Essentie van de Dramatiek (Foundations of Drama), 1959; Het Hedendaags Nederlandstalig toneel in Belgie, translated to French, German, English, 1969. Plays: Amor spant zijn boog, 1963; Draaimolen, 1938; Karel van Denemarken, 1942; Het Buitenkansje, bestselling comedy, 1955; Bartolomeusnacht, 1956; Tussen leven en dood, 1960; Vrijgesproken, 1973; De Datzja, 1977. Translations, Berthold Brecht, Bloch. *Contributions to:* De Standaard, theatre critic 1955–71;

Het Toneel, 1952–69; De Linie, 1952–64; Various Belgian & Dutch periodicals, etc. *Honours include:* Awards for plays; Honorary President, Association of Flemish Playwrights; Knight, Order of Leopold II; Medal, Flemish Cultural Council. *Membership:* Association of Flemish Writers. *Literary Agent:* SABAM & ALMO, Frankrijklei 132, Antwerp. *Address:* Lange Winkelhaakstraat 39, 2008 Antwerp, Belgium.

VAN NORTWICK, Terry Biehl, b. 8 Dec. 1948, Reading, Pennsylvania, USA. President, Publications Editing/Design Company. m. Kenneth A Van Nortwick, 12 June 1971, Gainesville, Florida. *Education:* BSc, Journalism, Public Relations, MA, Communications, University of Florida, Gainesville. *Literary Appointments:* Founder, President, Production Ink, Gainesville, Florida, 1979–; Teacher, Journalism, English, Edgewater High School, Orlando. *Contributor to:* Florida Agriculture; University of Florida, College News; various business and professional newsletters, magazines, brochures, etc. *Honours:* Recognized by Florida Public Relations Association, Florida Magazine Association, American Farm Bureau Federation, Food Trade Press, Food Industry Association Executives. *Memberships:* Florida Public Relations Association; International Association of Business Communicators; Society of Professional Journalists; Florida Magazine Association; American Advertising Federation. *Address:* Production Ink, 2826 NE Drive, Gainesville, FL 32609, USA.

VAN NOSTRAND, Morris Abbott, b. 24 Nov. 1911, New York City, USA. Publisher. m. (1) Jane Alexander, 28 Dec. 1934, New York City (Widowed Dec. 1944); (2) Julia de La Roche Eaton, 3 July 1953, New York City, 4 daughters. *Education:* BA, Amherst College, Amherst, MA, 1934. *Literary Appointments:* With Samuel French Incorporated, New York, 1934–; Secretary 1948–52, President, Samuel French Incorporated, NYC, 1952–; President, Samuel French (Canada) Limited, Toronto, 1952–; Chairman of Board, Samuel French Limited, London, 1952–; President, Walter H Baker Company, Boston and Denver, 1952–. *Memberships:* Vice President, Forest Hills Garden Association; Member, Travellers Aid Society; Trustee, Kew Forest School; Member, Council Friends of Amherts; Governor, Nassau Country Club, Glen Cove, L I; Member Chi Phi Clubs; Lambs, Amherst, Doubles; Member, Les Ambassadeurs, London; Member, The Clarmont, London. *Address:* 45 West 25th Street, New York, NY 10010, USA.

VAN OVER, Raymond, b. 29 June 1934, Long Island, New York, USA. Writer. *Education:* AA, Orange Coast University; BA, University of California, Los Angeles. Certificates: Sorbonne, Paris, France; Woolsey Hall, Oxford University, England. *Literary Appointments:* Executive Editor, Garret/Helix Press, 1964–67; Story Analyst, various film companies; Teacher, Lecturer, New York and Hofstra Universities, 1972–75; State Government Staff Writer, 1971; Freelance Writer and Editor, 1967–81; Magazine Editor, Inner Space, 1970. *Publications include:* Explorer of the Mind, 1967; I Ching, 1971; A Treasury of Chinese Literature, 1972; Unfinished Man, 1972; The Chinese Mystics, 1973; Taoist Tales, 1973; Eastern Mysticism, 2 volumes, 1977; Total Meditation, 1973; Sun Songs, 1980; Ecstasy: The Perilous Journey; Smearing the Ghost's Face with Ink, 1983; Monsters You Never Heard of, 1983; Screenwriter, documentary, 1983; Khomeini, A Biography, 1984. *Contributions to:* Publishers Weekly; New York Times; Wilson Library Bulletin; Inner Space; International Journal of Parapsychology; Technology Review, and numerous others. *Address:* 155 Bank Street, New York, NY 10014, USA.

VAN PEURSEN, Cornelis Anthonie, b. 8 July 1920, Rotterdam, Netherlands. Professor of Philosophy. m. Jeanne Marguerite Ueltschi, 17 June 1950, 1 son, 3 daughters. *Education:* Studies of law and philosophy, Doctor in philosophy, Leiden University. *Publications:* Body, Soul, Spirit, Dutch 1956 and 1978, English 1966, German 1959, Polish 1971, French 1979, Indonesian 1981, Korean 1985; Phenomena and Analytical Philosophy, Dutch 1966, German 1969, English 1972,

Korean 1979; Strategy of Culture, Dutch 1970, English 1974, Indonesian 1976, French 1976, Japanese 1977, Korean 1979; Wittgenstein, Dutch 1965, English 1968, Spanish 1973; Filosophie Orientatie, Dutch revised edition 1977, Spanish 1975, Indonesian 1979. *Contributions to:* Philosophy Today, USA; Philosophy and Phenomena Research, USA; Revue de Metaphisique et de Morale, France; Zeitschrift Philosofie Forscung, Germany; Philosofie Rundschau, Germany; Ruch Filozoficany, Poland. *Address:* A Gogelweg 39, 2517JE Den Haag, Netherlands.

VAN SANTEN, Louise, b. 15 May 1924, Amsterdam, The Netherlands. Poet; Writer. *Publications:* Poems: David zonder schild, 1964; De schaduw van de Filistijn, 1965; Eerst was er neits, 1967; Chanson (Sjanson), verses, 1971; Lang eentonig verhaal, epic poem, 1975; Laatste oprcep, 1980. Wie valt doet niet meer mee, novel, 1973. Hoor je mij, children's book, 1980. The Belle of Amherst, translation. *Contributions to:* Dutch literary magazines including: de Gids; de Tweede Ronde. *Honours:* Commission to write original poem for memorial night, Boston Cultural Centre. *Memberships:* Dutch Writers Association; PEN International. *Address:* Prinsengracht 791, 1017 KA Amsterdam, Netherlands.

VAN TIL, William, b. 8 Jan. 1911, Corona, New York, USA. Educator; Writer. m. Beatrice Blaha, 27 Aug. 1935, Corona, New York, USA, 2 sons 1 daughter. *Education:* BA, Columbia College, Columbia University, 1933; MA, Teachers College, Columbia University, 1935; PhD, Ohio State University, 1946. *Publications:* The Danube Flows through Fascism 1938; The Making of a Modern Educator, (collected essays and articles) 1961; Modern Education for the Junior High School Years, co-author, 1961, revised edition 1967; Education: A Beginning, 1971, revised edition 1974; Secondary Education: School and Community, 1978; Writing for Professional Publication, 1981 revised edition 1986; My Way of Looking at It, 1983. *Contributor to:* Author and co-author of 27 educational pamphlets; Co-editor and contributor, Democratic Human Relations, yearbook of National Council for the Social Studies, 1945; and, Intercultural Attitudes in the Making, yearbook of John Dewey Society, 1946; Editor and contributor, Forces Affecting American Education, yearbook of Association for Supervision and Curriculum Development, 1953 and, Issues in Secondary Education, National Society for the Study of Education, 1976; Contributor to 10 other yearbooks. Contributor to, Encyclopedia of Educational Research; Contributor to 27 education anthologies; Contributor of more than 170 articles, reviews, bibliographies and editorials to educational journals and other periodicals. *Honours:* For, The Making of a Modern Educator, Awards from New Jersey Collegiate Press Association and New Jersey Association of Teachers of English, 1961; Service Awards and Certificates from Association for Supervision and Curriculum Development, 1962, Associated Organizations for Teacher Education, 1973 and John Devey Society, 1977; Centennial Achievement Award, Ohio State University, 1970. *Address:* Indiana State University, Terre Haute, IN 47803, USA.

van VOGT, Alfred Elton, b. 26 Apr. 1912, Manitoba, Canada. Author. m. Lydia I Brayman, 6 Oct 1979, Los Angeles, 1 stepson, 1 stepdaughter. *Education:* University of Ottawa; University of California, Los Angeles. *Publications include:* Novel: The Violent Man, 1962; Science Fiction: The Silkie, 1969, 1973, 1982; Quest for the Future, 1970, 1971, 1972; Children of Tomorrow, 1970, 1972; The Battle of Forever, 1971, 1972, 1982; The Darkness on Diamondia, 1972, 1974, 1982; Future Glitter, 1973, 1976, as Tyranopolis, 1977; The Secret Galacrics, 1974, 1975 as Earth Factor X, 1976; The Man with a Thousand Names, 1974, 1975; The Anarchistic Colossus, 1977, 1978; Supermind, 1977, 1978; Renaissance, 1979; Cosmic Encounter, 1980; Computerworld, 1983; Null-A Three, 1985. Short stories: M–33 in Andromeda, 1971; The Book of van Vogi, 1972 as, Lost: Fifty Suns, 1979; The Gryb, 1976; Pendulum, 1978. Other Publications: The Hypnotism Handbook, 1956; The Money Personality, 1984.

Honours: Manuscripters Literature Award, 1948; Count Dracula Society Ann Radcliffe Award, 1968; Academy of Science Fiction, Fantasy and Horror Films Award, 1979; BA, Golden Gate College, Los Angeles; Guest of Honour, 4th World Science Fiction Covention 1946, European Science Fiction Convention, 1978 and Metz (France) Festival, 1985. *Address:* P O Box 3065, Hollywood, CA 90078, USA.

VANCE, John Holbrook, b. 28 Aug. 1916, San Francisco, USA. Author. m. Norma Genevieve Ingold, 24 Aug. 1946, Riverside, California, USA, 1 son. *Education:* University of California. *Major Publications:* The Dying Earth, 1950; To Live Forever, 1956; Big Planet, 1957; The Star King, The Killing Machine, 1964; The Palace of Love, 1967; The City of the Chasch, 1968; The Wankh, Emphyrio, 1969; The Dirdir, 1969; The Pnume, 1970; Bad Ronald, 1973; The Last Castle, 1975; The Face, 1979; The Book of Dreams, 1981; Lyonesse I: Suldrun's Garden, 1983; Lyonesse II: The Green Pearl, 1986. *Contributor to:* Many early pulp magazines, currently: Fantasy & Science Fiction; Galaxy; Astounding Analog. *Honours:* Various Awards for Science Fiction Writing. *Membership:* Science Fiction Writers of America. *Literary Agent:* Kirby McCauley Ltd. *Address:* c/o Kirby McCauley Ltd, 432 Park Avenue South, Suite 1509, New York, NY 10016, USA.

VANDENBROUCK, Arthur Alfred Julien, b. 31 May 1918, Louvain, Belgium. Culinary Writer, Journalist for Tourism, Divorced, 1 daughter. *Education:* Humanoria (Greek & Latin), Jesuit College of St Jean Berchman; Hotel Technology, Institut Arts et Métiers, Brussels, Belgium. *Literary Appointments:* Editor-in-Chief, Vatel (monthly magazine, Ostende), 1950–60; Writer, Pourquoi Pas? (weekly, Brussels), 1954–63; Writer, Libelle-Rosita (weekly, Antwerp) 1960–80. *Major Publications:* 1965; Marabout Flash, 1965; Marabout Service, 1970; Le Consieller en Gastronomie et Diétetique (2 volumes), 1982. *Contributor to:* Gastronomie (Canada); Hotellerie (Switzerland); and others. *Honours:* Prix Triennal du Livret d'Opérette, 1947; Gold Medal, Lauréat du Travail. *Memberships:* Belgian Society of Authors, 1947; Belgian Union of Tourist Writers, 1954; International Federation of Tourist Writers, 1957; Belgian & Foreign Journalists; Association, 1979. *Literary Agent:* Editions Le Sphinx, Brussels. *Address:* Kasteldreef 2, B.8042 Hertsberge-Oostkamp, Belgium.

VANDER GOOT, Mary Elizabeth, b. 5 Feb. 1947, Orange City, Iowa, USA. Psychologist. m. Henry Vander Goot, 12 August 1967, 2 daughters. *Education:* BA, Calvin College; MA, PhD, Princeton University. *Major Publications:* A Life Planning Guide for Women, 1983; Piaget as a Visionary Thinker, 1985. *Address:* Calvin College, Department of Psychology, Grand Rapids, MI 49506, USA.

VANDERBEKE, Clara, b. 30 March 1917, Antwerp. Journalist; Writer. *Publications:* Au Pays des Vallées d'Andorre, 1952; Costa Brava – Barcelone – Tarragone, 1964; La Grèce Touristique, 1964; La Norwege Merveilleuse, 1981. *Contributions to:* Numerous European journals. *Memberships:* Belgian Union of Journalists & Writers for Travel; International Federation of Journalists & Writers. *Address:* BP 561, 1000 Brussels, Belgium.

VANDERSEE, Charles Andrew, b. 25 Mar. 1938, Gary, Indiana, USA. Associate Professor of English. *Education:* BA, 1960, Valparaiso University; MA, 1961, PhD, 1964, University of California, Los Angeles. *Literary Appointment:* Department of English, University of Virginia, Charlottesville, Virginia, 1964–. *Publications:* Editor of John May, The Bread-Winners, 1973; Associate editor, The Letters of Henry Adams, 1858–1892, 1982. *Contributions to:* Georgie Review; Poetry; Poetry East; Sewanee Review; Cresset; American Poetry Review; Ironwood; Boundary 2; South Atlantic Quarterly; American Literary Realism; Shakespeare Survey and others. *Honour:* Fellowship, American Council of Learned Societies, 1972–73. *Address:*

Department of English, Wilson Hall, University of Virginia, Charlottesville, VA 22903, USA.

VANDERWALL, Francis William, b. 24 Apr. 1946, Colombo, Sri Lanka. University Professor. *Education:* BA 1967, MA Geography 1971, St Louis University, USA; M Div Theology and Fine Arts, GTU, Berkeley, 1976. *Publications:* Spiritual Direction: An Invitation to Abundant Life, 1981; Water in the Wilderness, 1985. *Contributions to:* Review for Religion; National Catholic Reporter; Studies in Formative Spirituality. *Honours:* Research Fellowship, Yale University, 1978; Research Fellow, Kino Institute, Phoenix, Arizona, USA, 1979; Recognized Scholar, Trinity term, Oxford University, England, 1979. *Membership:* College Theology Society. *Literary Agent:* Paulist Press, New York, USA. *Address:* Spring Hill College, 4000 Dauphin Street, Mobile, AL 36608, USA.

VANDIVER, Frank Everson, b. 9 Dec. 1925, Austin, Texas, USA. University President. m. (1) Susie Smith, 19 Apr. 1952, Dallas, Texas, (dec), (2) Renee Aubry, 21 Mar. 1980, New Iberia, Louisiana, 1 son, 2 daughters. *Education:* MA, University of Texas, 1949; PhD, Tulane University, 1951; MA, Oxford University, England, 1963; Honorary Doctorate of Humanities, Austin College, 1977. *Publications include:* Ploughshares into Swords: Josiah Gorgas and Confederate Ordinance, 1952; Mighty Stonewall, 1957; Basic History of the Confederacy, 1962; John J Pershing, 1967; Their Tattered Flags: The Epic of the Confederacy, 1970; Black Jack: The Life and Times of John J Pershing, 1977. Editor of numerous works including: The Civil War Dairy of General Josiah Gorgas, 1947; War Memories, 1960; The Idea of the South, 1964. *Contributions to:* The American Tragedy: The Civil War in Retrospect, 1959; Lincoln for the Ages, 1960; American People's Encyclopedia; Encyclopedia Americana; World Book; Encyclopedia Britannica; Encyclopedia of World Biography; The New Book of Knowledge; Encyclopedia of Southern History; over 60 articles to historical journals and over 100 reviews to, New York Times, New York Herald Tribune, Saturday Review of Literature, and other historical publications; Associate editor, Journal of Southern History, 1959–62; Chief Advisory Editor, The Papers of Jefferson Davis, 1963–; Editorial Advisory Board, The Papers of US Grant, 1977–. *Honours include:* Rockefeller Fellow, 1946–48; Guggenheim Fellow, 1955; Honorary President, Occidental University of St Louis, 1975–80; Fulbright Hays Lectureship, 1976, 79; Draugton Lectures, Auburn University, 1978; Best Book award, Editors of Texas Books in Review, 1978. *Memberships:* Member, Past and current office holder of numerous literary societie and organisations. *Address:* Office of the President, Texas A & M University, College Station, TX 77843, USA.

VANO, Gerard S, b. 26 May 1943, Hamilton, Ontario, Canada. Writer. *Education:* BA, Hons, History; MA, History. *Publications:* Neo-Feudalism: The Canadian Dilemma, 1981. *Address:* 33 Kimberley Drive, Guelph, Ontario, Canada N1H 1L3.

VANSITTART, Peter, b. 27 Aug. 1920. Writer. *Publications:* The Overseer, 1949; Broken Canes, 1951; The Tournament, 1958; The Friends of God, 1963; The Lost Lands, 1965; The Story Teller, 1968; Pastimes of a Red Summer, 1969; Quintet, 1976; Lancelot, 1978; The Death of Robin Hood, 1981; Three Six Seven, 1984; Paths From a White Horse, 1985; Aspects of Feeling, 1986; etc. *Contributions to:* Guardian; London Magazine; etc. Reviews, etc. *Honours:* Society of Authors Travelling Scholarship, 1969; Arts Council Bursaries, 1981, 1984. *Literary Agent:* Anthony Sheil. *Address:* 9 Upper Park Road, Hampstead, London NW3, England.

VANSON, Frederic. Lecturer; Journalist. *Education includes:* Whitelands College; London University. *Literary Appointments include:* Teacher and Lecturer in English, 1947–; Freelance Writer, 1945–. *Publications include:* Now Against Winter, 1952; Spring at Llyn Ogwen, 1972; The Moment Stilled, 1973; Hemingford Grey, 1980; A War Ago, 1985; The Signal Grass, 1985. *Contributions to:* Cornhill; Contemporary Review; Tablet; Country Life; London Quarterly; Cork Examiner; The Lady; Outposts; Orbis; Weyfarers; Sol; Here Now; Ore; Magma; Country Quest; Catholic Education Today; Musical Opinion; The Strad; Poetry Review; Folio; Doors Countryside Magazine; A'cumem; Moorlands Review; Prospice. Radio 1, 2, 3, and 4, British Broadcasting Corporation. *Honours:* Keats Trust Award, 1972; Gregory Memorial Prize, 1974, and others. *Memberships:* Vice Chancellor and Fellow, IAP; Fellow, Accademia Leonardo da Winci, Italy; Associate, Philosophy Society of England; Royal Musical Association. *Address:* 24 Morley Grove, Harlow, Essex, England.

VARDY, Steven Bela, b. 3 July 1936, Hungary. Historian; University Professor. m. Agnes Huszar, 3 July, 2 sons, 1 daughter. *Education:* BS, John Carroll University, USA, 1959; MA, 1961, PhD, 1967, Indiana University; Also attended University of Vienna, Austria; Western Reserve University, USA, Kent State University. *Literary Appointments:* Instructor of History, Washburn University, Kansas; Assistant Professor, Duquesne University, Pennsylvania; Professor of East European History and Chairman Department of History, Duquesne University, 1970–85; Concurrently: Adjunct Professor, University of Pittsburgh, 1979–; Visiting Scholar, Hungarian Academy of Sciences, 1969–70, 1975–76. *Publications:* History of the Hungarian Nations, (with D G Kosary), 1969; Hungarian Historiography and the Geisteegeschichte School, 1974; Modern Hungarian Historiography, 1976; Society in Change, (with A H Vardy), 1983; The Hungarian-Americans: Their History and Way of Life, 1985; Clio's Art in Hungary and Hungarian America, 1985; Louis the Great, King of Hungary and Poland, (with G Grosschmid), 1986. *Contributions to:* magazines and journals in USA, Canada, Greece, Germany, Hunrary, Italy and Belgium. *Honours:* Ford Foundation Fellowship, 1962–63; International Research and Exchanges Board Fellow (several times); Carnegie Corporation of New York Fellow, 1967–70; Hunkele Foundation Fellow (several times); Duquesne University's Excellence in Scholarship Award, 1984. *Memberships:* American Historical Association; American Association for the Advancement of Slavic Studies; American Association for the Study of Hungarian History (several offices); PEN (USA and International). *Address:* Department of History, Duquesne University, Pittsburgh, PA 15282, USA.

VARGAS-MACHUCA, Antonio, b. 20 Jan. 1933, Mancha Real, Jaén, Spain. Professor of New Testament, University Comillas, Madrid. *Education:* Classical Humanities, 1952–55, Lic Philos, Alcala de Henares and Lif. Fil y Letras, University of Madrid, 1955–58; DTh, University of Innsbruck, Austria, 1966; Lic. Biblical Sciences, Pontifical Biblical Institute of Rome, Italy, 1966–68; PhD, University of Granada, Spain, 1983. *Publications:* Escritura, Tradicion e Iglesia como reglas de fe, 1967; Introduccion a los evengelios sinopticos, 1975; 2nd edition, 1979; Tologia y mundo contemporaneo, Homenaje a K Rahner, Editor, 1975; Los evengelios sinopticos, 1976; Jesucristo en la historia y en la fe, Editor, 1977. *Contributions to:* Various professional journals including: Estudios Eclesiaticos, Director, 1975–76, 1981–. *Honours:* Recipient of several academic honours. *Memberships:* Professional organisations, Spain and England, Germany. *Address:* Universidad Comillas 7, E–28049 Madrid, Spain.

VARGYAS, Lajos Károly, b. 1 Feb. 1914, Budapest, Hungary. Ethnomusicologist; Folklorist. m. Katalin Glfi, 19 Dec. 1949, 3 sons. *Education:* University Doctorate, 1941; Academic degree, Candidate, 1952; Academic degree, DMS, 1963. *Publications:* AJ falu zenei élete, Musical Life of Aj Village, 1941; Rhythm of the Hungarian Verse, published as, A magyar vers ritmusa, 1952; Magyar vers-magyar nyelv, Hungarian Verse-Hungarian Language, 1966; Researches into the Mediaeval History of Folk Ballard, 1967; A magyar népballada és Európa, The Hungarian Folk Ballad in

Europe, 1976; Balladaskonyv, Book of Ballads, 1979; A magyarsag nepzeneje, Folkmusic of Hungarians, 1981; Hungarian Ballads and the European Ballad Tradition, 1983; Keleti hagyomany-nyugati kulture, Oriental Traditions-European Culture, Selected Essays, 1984. *Contributions to:* Magyar Osillag; Válasz; Társadalomtudomany; Ethnographia; Acta Ethnographica; Kortárs; Tiszatáj; Élet és Irodalom, and others. *Honours:* Order of Labour, Golden Degree, 1974; Erkel Prize, 1980. *Address:* Szemlohegy u 4/b, 1022 Budapest, Hungary.

VARKONYL, Mihaly, b. 25 Jan. 1931, Ujpest, Hungary. Writer. m. Julianna Landler, 17 Feb. 1963, Budapest, 1 son. *Education:* Technical University. *Publications:* Bread and Cross, (short stories), 1960; Role in the Small Hours, 1964; Divorce, 1973; On the Ground, (short stores), 1976; Legend on the Train, (novel and short stories), 1968; Least said...? (political pamphlet), 1969; The Witness, (novel), 1967; Wreath for the House's Wall, (novel), 1978; Russian Easter, (novel), 1979. *Contributor to:* Nepezabadsag; Nepszava; Magyar Hirlap; Elet es Irodalom; Uj Iraso; Kortars. *Honours:* World Youth Festival Prize, 1960; Hungarian Trade Union Prize, 1961; Moscow Film Festival 2nd Prize, 1962. *Memberships:* Hungarian Writers' Association; Society Hungarian Journalists. *Address:* Damvad u. 7, Budapest 1029, Hungary.

VARLEY, Gloria Isabel, b. 31 Mar. 1932, Toronto, Canada. Writer. m. Charles E Israel, 23 Sep. 1979, Toronto, 1 son by previous marriage. *Education:* Diploma in Journalism, Ryerson Institute, Toronto; BA, University of Toronto; Higher Certificate, Wine & Spirit Education Trust, London, England. *Major Publications:* To be a Dancer, 1971; Contributor to Peter Gzowski's Spring Tonic, 1979. *Contributor to:* Numerous periodicals, including: City Woman; Toronto Life; The Washington Post; En Route; Wine Tidings. *Memberships:* The Writers' Union of Canada; The Periodical Writers' Association of Canada; Chairman, Toronto Chapter, 1981–82. *Address:* 113 Howland Avenue, Toronto, Canada M5R 3B4.

VAS, Istvan, b. 24 Sep. 1910, Budapest, Hungary. Poet; Writer. *Publications include:* Collected Poems, I-III, 1975; Collected Essays, I-III, 1977; Collected Poetical Translations, I-III, 1982; Hard Love, I-IV, autobiographical novel, 1983–86. *Contributions to:* Most Hungarian Literary reviews. *Honours:* Recipient of numerous prizes and awards including: Kossuth Prize, 1970, 85; Pro Arts Medal, 1972; Knight, Order of Palmes Academique, 1972; Order of Banner with Wreath, 1980. *Memberships:* Committees, Hungarian Writers Union and Poets, Playwrights, Editors, Essayists and Novelists. *Address:* Groza Peter rakpart 17, 1013 Budapest, Hungary.

VAS DIAS, Robert, b. 19 Jan 1931, London, England. Writer. m. Susan McClintock, 5 May 1961, Hanover, Massachusetts, USA, 1 son. *Education:* BA, Hons, Grinnell College, Grinnell, Iowa, USA; Graduate Study, Columbia University, New York. *Literary Appointments:* Director, Aspen Writers' Workshop, Aspen, Colorado, 1964–67; Poet-in-Residence, Thomas Jefferson College, Allendale, Michigan, 1971–74; Editor/Publisher, Permanent Press 1972–; General Secretary, the Poetry Society and Director, national Poetry Centre, London, 1975–78; Joint Editor, Ninth Decade (International Literary Journal) 1983–. *Publications:* Editor: Inside Outer Space: New Poems of the Space Age, 1970; Speech Acts and Happenings (poems) 1972; Making Faces (poems) 1975; Poems Beginning: The World, 1979. *Contributions to:* Chelsea; Choice; Encounter; Maps; Mulch; The Nation; The New Yorker; Partisan Review; Poetry (Chicago); Poetry Review; Stony Brook; Sumac; Stand etc. *Honours:* CAPS Fellowship in Poetry (New York State Council on Arts) 1975; C Day Lewis Fellowship in Poetry, Greater London Arts Association, 1980. *Address:* 52 Cascade Avenue, London N10, England.

VASQUEZ, John A, b. 1 Nov. 1945, Hartford, Connecticut, USA. International Relations Scholar. m. Marie T Henehan, 8 June 1980, New Brunswick, New Jersey, 1 daughter. *Education:* BA, College of Liberal Arts, ThM, School of Theology, Boston University; MA, PhD, Syracuse University. *Publications:* Introductory Case Studies for International Relations, co-author, 1974; In Search of Theory: A New Paradigm for Global Politics, co-author, 1981; Power of Power Politics: A Critique, 1983; Classics of International Relations, editor, 1985; Evaluating US Foreign Policy, Editor, 1985. *Contributions to:* British Journal of Political Science; Journal of Peace Research; International Organization; Review of International Studies; Journal of Politics; British Journal of International Studies; Journal of Conflict Resolution; Western Political Quarterly; International Studies Quarterly. *Memberships:* International Studies Association; Peace Science Society, International World University; American Historical Association; American Political Science Association. *Address:* Department of Political Science, Rutgers University, New Brunswick, NJ 08903, USA.

VAT, Dan (Daniel Francis Jeroen) Van Der, b. 28 Oct. 1939, Alkmaar, The Netherlands. Journalist. m. Christine Mary Ellis, 30 Apr. 1962, Newcastle upon Tyne, 2 daughters. *Education:* BA Honours Classics, Durham University, England, 1960. *Publications:* The Grand Scuttle, 1982; The Last Corsair, 1983; The Ship That Changed The World, 1985. *Literary Appointments:* 8 years as foreign correspondent, The Times; Currently foreign leader-writer, The Guardian. *Honours:* Best First Work Award, Yorkshire Post, 1982; Best Book of the Sea Award, 1983. *Literary Agent:* Curtis Brown. *Address:* c/o The Guardian, 119 Farringdon Road, London EC1R 3ER, England.

VATIKIOTIS, Panayiotis Jerasimos, b. 5 Feb. 1928, Jerusalem. University Professor. m. Patricia Mary Theresa, 22 March 1958, Heidelberg, 1 son, 2 daughters. *Education:* BA, American University in Cairo, 1948; PhD, The John Hopkins University, 1954. *Literary Appointments:* Member, Editorial Advisory Board, Middle Eastern Studies, 1964–; Member, Editorial Advisory Board, Journal of Military and Political Sociology, 1978–82; Member, Editorial Advisory Board, Millennium. *Publications:* The Fatimid Theory of the State, 1957, 1981; The Egyptium Army in Politics, 1961, 1975; Politics and the Military in Jordan, 1967; The Modern History of Egypt, 1969, 1971, 1976; second revised edition as, The History of Egypt from Muhammad Ali to Sadar, 1980; third revised edition, 1985; Nasser and his Generation, 1978; Arab and Regional Politics in the Middle East, 1984; Editor: Egypt Since the Revolution, 1968; Revolution in the Middle East, 1972. *Contributions to:* Middle Eastern Studies; New Society; Encounter; The Times Literary Supplement; Bulletin of the School of Oriental and African Studies; Epikentra (Greek); Encyclopedia of Islam (2nd edition); Middle East Journal (US0; Survival. *Honour:* Guggenheim Fellow, 1961–62. *Address:* School or Oriental and African Studies, University of London, Malet Street, London WC1E 7HP, England.

VAUGHAN, Adrian Hugh, b. 10 Jan. 1941, Reading, Berkshire, England. Writer Social History. m. Susan Osullivan, 3 June 1972, Wantage, 2 daughters. *Publications:* Pictorial Record Great Western Signalling, 1972; Pictorial Record Great Western Architecture, 1974; History of Faringdon Branch and Uffington Station, 1979; Signalmans Morning, 1981; Signalman Twilight, 1983; Grub Water and Relief, 1985; Grime & Glory, 1985. *Contributions to:* BBC Historical documetaries; Steam World Series; Countryman; HTV Historical documentary; Railway World. *Membership:* Society of Authors. *Address:* 13 The Street, Barney, Fakenham, Norfolk NR21 0NB, England.

VAUGHAN, Hilda Campbell, b. 12 June 1892, Builth, Breconshire, Wales. Novelist. m. Charles Morgan, 1923, (died 1958), 1 son, 1 daughter. *Publications:* The Battle to the Weak; Here Are Lovers; The Invader; Her Father's House; The Soldier and the Gentlewoman;

A Thing of Nought; The Curtain Rises; Harvest Home; Pardon and Peace; Iron and Gold; The Candle and the Light; Plays: She, Too Was Young, (with Laurier Lister); Forsaking All Other, (with Laurier Lister); Introduction to Thomas Traherne's Centuries. *Membership:* FRSL, 1963. *Address:* c/o Roger Morgan, 30 St Peter's Square, London W6 9UH, England.

VAUGHAN BOWDEN, Vera, b. 11 July 1929, England. Magazine Editor. *Education:* Horticulture; Languages. *Literary Appointments:* Research papers, British Sugar Bureau, London; Research papers, International public relations, London; Editor, World-wide News, The Hague, Netherlands. *Publications:* Mainly cookery books 1970–. *Contributions to:* The Architect; Conference and Exhibitions; International Herald Tribune; Financial Times; Business Week; Post Monitor; Globe and Herald, Toronto and many others. *Memberships:* Foreign Correspondents Association (BPV Netherlands); Association of Journalists (NVJ Netherlands); BAIE. *Address:* Saffierhorst 200, 2592GN The Hague, Netherlands.

VAUGHAN WILLIAMS, Ursula, b. 15 Mar. 1911, Val. Writer. m. (1) Michael Forrester Wood (d.1942), 24 May 1933, London, (2) Ralph Vaughan Williams, OM (d.1958), 7 Feb. 1953, London. *Publications Include:* Verse: No Other Choice, 1941; Fall of Leaf, 1944; Need for Speech, 1946; Wandering Pilgrimage, 1952; Silence & Music, 1959; Aspects, 1984. Biography: RVW A Biography of Ralph Vaughan Williams, 1964; A Pictorial Biography of Ralph Vaughan Williams, 1971. Novels: Metamorphoses, 1966; Set to Partners, 1968; The Yellow Dress, 1984. LIBRETTI: Nine Operas, 1965–86. Choral symphony, Williamson, 1972; Songs, Cantatas, by Vaughan Williams, Anthony Milner & others, Song Cycles, 1951–83; Songs by Vaughan Williams, Finzi, Howells, etc. *Honours:* Fellow, Royal College of Music; Member, Royal Northern College of Music; Honorary Fellow, Royal Academy of Music. *Address:* 66 Gloucester Crescent, London NW1 7EG, England.

VAUTIER-FRANK, Ghislaine, b. 28 Dec. 1932, NYC, USA. Writer; Editor. m. Sylvestre Vautier, 5 Apr. 1952, Switzerland, 1 son, 2 daughters. *Education:* Diplome de Français Moderne, University of Lausanne. Switzerland. *Literary Appointments:* Founder of Editions Pierrot SA, Lausanne, Éditions les Quatre Saisons, Lausanne. *Publications:* La Toque du Chef, 1975; Au Fond du Grenier, 1976; Quand Brillent les Etoiles..., 1980; Je Te Déteste, 1980; Les Lois du Ciel, 1982; Je Démanage, 1983; Je Suce Mon Pouce, 1983; Tobor, 1983. *Contributions to:* Numerous newspapers and magazines; Television Stories for Children. Founder and writer of, Mon Ami Pierrot, Children's magazine. *Memberships:* Société des Auteures et Compositeurs Dramatiques; Société Suisse des Ecrivans; Association vaudoise des Ecrivains. *Address:* Avenue de Rumine 51, CH 1005 Lausanne, Switzerland.

VAWTER, (Francis) Bruce, b. 11 Aug. 1921, Fort Worth, Texas, USA. Professor. *Education:* BA, St Thomas College, Denver, Colorado, 1942; STL, University of St Thomas, Rome, 1950; SSL, 1952, SSD, 1958, Pontifical Biblical Institute, Rome, Italy. *Literary Appointments:* Board of Editors and Translators, New American Bible, 1963–69; Editor, Catholic Biblical Quarterly, 1965–68; Editorial Board, Concilium, 1971–76; Revised Standard Version Bible Committee, 1972–; Editor, CBQ Monograph Series, 1974–82, Old Testmant Abstracts, 1978–. *Publications:* The Conscience of Israel, 1961; The Four Gospels, 1967; This Man Jesus, 1973; On Genesis, 1977; Job and Jonah, 1983. *Contributions to:* Over 100 articles in, Journal of Biblical Literature; Catholic Biblical Quarterly; Concilium; Biblica; Colliers Encyclopedia; Dictionary of Christian Theology and others. *Honours:* Award for Distinguished Editing, Society of Biblical Literature, 1980. *Memberships:* Past Council Member, Society of Biblical Literature; Society for Old Testament Study. Past President: Catholic Biblical Association: Chicago Society of Biblical Research. *Address:* 2233 North Kenmore, Chicago, IL 60614, USA.

VAZAKAS, Byron, b. 24 Sep. 1905, New York City, USA. Poet. *Education:* Honorary Degree Doctor of Letters, Albright College, Pennsylvania, 1981. *Literary Appointments:* Various fellowships to Art Colonies Poetry in the Schools Programs. *Publications:* Poetry: Transfigures Night, 1946; The Equal Tribunals, 1961; The Marble Manifesto, 1966; Nostalgias For A House of Cards, 1970. *Contributions to:* 54 Literary periodicals and journals, etc. including poetry anthologies (Approximately 250 poems published in all). *Honours:* Honorary Degree, Doctor of Letters, Albright College, Pennsylvania, 1981; Fellowship on Poetry, Amy Lowell Foundation and Harvard University for two years abroad, mostly England. *Address:* 1623 Mineral Spring Road, Reading, PA 19602, USA.

VAZQUEZ DIAZ, Rene, b. 7 Sep. 1952, Caibarien, Cuba. Writer; Translator. *Education:* Degree in Polish Language, University of Lodz, Poland; Degree in Swedish Language, University of Lund, Sweden. *Literary Appointment:* Review Writer in Swedish journal Arbetet. *Publications:* Trovador Americano, poems, 1978; La Precocidad de los Tiempos, short stories, 1982; Tambor de Medianoche, poems, 1983; La Era Imaginaria, novel 1986. Translations of several Swedish books into Spanish. *Contributions to:* In Sweden: (Journals) Arbetet; Stockholms Tidningen; Sydsvenska Dagbladet, (Magazines) Bonniers Litterara Magazine; Artes, Fenix, Rallarros, Socialistisk Debatt, Bra Lyrik, Attiotal. In Spain: Hora de poesia. *Honours:* Fellowships from Swedish Union of Writers, 1980, 1982, 1983, 1984–89. *Memberships:* The Swedish Union of Writers; The Swedish Pen Club. *Address:* Albert Bonniers Forlag, Box 3159, 103 63 Stockholm, Sweden.

VEASEY, Jack Joseph, b. 4 Apr. 1955, Philadelphia, Pennsylvania, USA. Editor; Journalist; Poet. *Publications:* Poetry: Handful of Hair, 1975; The Truth of Blue, 1983; Tourist Season, 1984. *Contributions to:* Articles: The Philadelphia Inquirer; Philadelphia Magazine; Pennsylvania Magazine; The Courier Post; The Philadelphia City Paper. Poetry: Asphodel; Christopher Street; The Museum of Modern Art's Film Library Quarterly; Heat Magazine; The Little Word Machine; Princeton Spectrum; Tracks; Stoney Lonesome; Cassura; The South Street Star; Mouth of the Dragon; The Painted Bride Quarterly; Hot Water Review; Zone; Harbinger; The Axe Factory Review, and many other publications. *Address:* 37A West 2nd Street, Hummelstown, PA 17036, USA.

VEIGA, Jose Jacinto, b. 2 Feb. 1915, Corumba, Goias State, Brazil. Book Editor; Publisher. *Education:* Law School, Rio de Janeiro. *Publications:* (short stories) Os Cavalinhos de platiplanto, 1959, 11th edition 1979; A Maquina Extraviada, 1968, 3rd edition 1976; A Hora dos Ruminantes, 1966, 10th edition 1979; Sombras de Reis Barbudos, 1972, 6th edition 1979; Os Pecados da Tribo, 1976, 2nd edition 1978; De Jogos e Festas, 1980; Aquele Mundo de Vasabarros, 1982; Torvelinho Dia e Noite, 1985. *Contributor to:* Journal of Brazil; Ele & Ela; Status; Nova. *Membership:* PEN, Brazil. *Agent:* Carmen Balcells, Barcelona, Spain. *Address:* Rua de Gloria 122/1004, Rio de Janeiro, Brazil.

VELARDO, Joseph Thomas, b. Newark, New Jersey, USA. Biomedical Scientist; Professor; Writer; Literary Consultant. m. Forresta M Monica Power (deceased), Greeley, Colorado, USA. *Education:* AB, University of Northern Colorado, 1948; SM, Miami University, Oxford Ohio, 1949; PhD, Harvard University, Cambridge, Massachusetts, 1952. Also US Army Air Forces Western Technical Training Command, University of Northern Colorado, 1946. *Literary Appointments:* Volunteers English Instructor, Colorado Student College of Education, 1946–48; Graduate Assistant Instructor, Miami University, Oxford, Ohio, 1948–49; Research Assistant Biologist, Science-Endocrinology, Teaching Fellow, Harvard University, 1949–52; Research Associate, Harvard University & Medical School, 1953–55, Biology-Endrocrinology, Pathology, Surgery-

Endocrinology and numerous other appointments. *Major Publications:* Endocrinology of Reproduction, 1958; Essential of Human Reproduction, 1958; Contributing Author: The Uterus, 1959; The Vagina, 1961, The Trophoblast, 1960; The Ovary, 1963; Co-Author: Enzymes in the Female Genetial System, (with Prof C G Rosa), 1963; Co-Editor (with Dr B A Kasprow) Biology of Reproduction, 1973; Contributing Author, The Ureter, 2nd edition, 1982. Two radio plays, Former news writer and columnist. *Contributor to:* Numerous professional journals, books, annals, monographs and others. *Honours:* Rubin Award, American Fertility Society, 1955; Lederle Medical Faculty Award, Harvard & Yale Universities, 1955–58; Honorary Citizen, Sao Paulo, Brazil, for distinguished Scholarship, 1972. *Memberships:* Kappa Delta Phi, Sigma Xi; Phi Sigma and numerous scientific organizations. *Address:* Wilson House, 607 East Wilson Road, Lombard, IL 60148–4044, USA.

VENABLES, Roger Evelyn Cavendish, b. 4 Mar. 1911, Varna, Bulgaria. Lecturer. *Education:* MA, Christ College, Oxford University, England. *Publications:* Poems: Combe, 1942; Images of Power, 1960; The Night Comes, 1961; Leaves and Seasons, 1961. Biography: D: Portrait of a Don, 1967. Editor: Padstow Lights, by Maud Cherrill, 1949. *Membership:* Lancashire Authors Association. *Address:* Atlanta, Pendeen, Penzance, Cornwall, England.

VENDLER, Helen Hennessy, b. 30 Apr. 1933, Boston, Massachusetts, USA. Professor of English, 1 son. *Education:* AB Chemistry, Emmanuel College, Boston, Massachusetts, 1954; PhD English and American Language and Literature, Harvard University, 1960. *Literary Appointments:* Cornell University, 1960–63; Swarthmore College, Haverford College, 1963–64; Smith College, 1964–66; Boston University, 1966–65; Harvard University, 1981–. *Publications:* Yeats's Vision, and the Later Plays, 1963; On Extended Wings: Wallace Stevens' Longer Poems, 1969; The Poetry of George Herbert, 1975; Part of Nature, Part of Us: Modern American Poets, 1980; The Odes of John Keats, 1985; Wallace Stevens: Words Chosen Out of Desire, 1985; The Harvard Book of Contemporary American Poetry, editor, 1985. *Contributions to:* Magazines and journals including: Poetry Critic; The New Yorker; New York Review of Books; The New Republic. *Honours:* Lowell Prize, MLA, 1969; Award, National Academy and Institute of Arts and Letters, 1975; National Book Critics Circle Prize, 1980; Honorary Degrees: Smith College, Kenyon College, University of Hartford, University of Oslo, Norway. *Memberships:* President, 1980, MLA; Councillor, American Academy of Arts and Sciences; Trustee, English Institute. *Address:* Department of English, Warren House, Harvard University, Cambridge, MA 02138, USA.

VENDLER, Zeno, b. 22 Dec. 1921, Devecser, Hungary. University Professor. m. Semiramis Da Silva, 28 May 1965, 2 sons. *Education:* STL Maastricht, Netherlands; PhD, Harvard University. *Publications:* Linguistics in Philosophy, 1967; Res Cogitans, 1972; The Matter of Minds, 1984. *Contributions to:* Many philosophical and linguistics journals. *Honours:* Canada Council, 1969–70; N E H, 1979. *Address:* Department of Philosophy, UCSD, La Jolla, CA 92093, USA.

VENN, George Andrew Fyfe, b. 12 Oct. 1943, Tacoma, Washington, USA. Professor of English; Writer. m. Elizabeth Cheney, 1 son, 1 daughter. *Education:* BA, 1967, College of Idaho, Auditor, Central University Quito, Equador; Auditor, University of Salamanca, Spain; MFA, 1970, University of Montana, Missoula, USA. *Literary Appointments:* Instructor in English, USIS, Quito, Equador, 1964; Associate Professor of English, Eastern Oregon State College, & Writer-in-Residence, 1970–; Foreign Expert, Foreign Languages Department, Changsha Railway Institute, Changsha, Hunan, People's Republic of China, 1982–83. *Publications:* Sunday Afternoon: Grande Rone, (Prescott St Press, Portland, Oregon). 1976; Off the Main Road, (Prescott St Press), 1978; Sasquatch Looking for an Audience. *Contributions to:* Northwest Review; Poetry Northwest; American Bee Journal; Cut Bank; College Composition and Communication; Western American Literature; Portland Review; Willow Springs Journal. *Honour:* Pushcart Prize, 1980, for poem. *Address:* Department of English, Eastern Oregon State College, La Grande, OR 97850, USA.

VERBECKE, W Edwin, b. 21 July 1913. Poet; Painter; Playwright; Recitalist. *Appointments:* Teacher of Art, University of Minnesota, USA; Co-Director of Arts International of Chicago; Display Director, Sachs Interiors, New York City; Teacher, Abbey Institute, New York City. *Publications:* Line in Painting, Poems of the Spirit; Life of Virgin Mary; Story of Mary, (cassette). *Honours:* Joint Recital with Freida Hemple, San Francisco Opera House, 1952; Isadora Duncan Recital, Rutgers University, 1981; Recital, Congressional Breakfast, 1981; Lecturer, New York Engineers Club, 1982/1983; Numerous Art Exhibitions. *Address:* 840, 8th Avenue, Capitol Apartments, Suite 6M, New York, NY 10019, USA.

VERCAMMEN, Kenneth Albert, b. 7 Aug. 1959, Edison, New Jersey, USA. Attorney. *Education:* BS cum laude, University of Scranton, 1981; JD, Delaware Law School, 1985. *Literary Appointments:* Senior editor, Harvard Journal for Law and Public Policy, 1984; Casenote editor; Delaware Law Forum; Senior staff member, Delaware Law Review. *Contributions to:* DTLA Advocate; Delaware Law Forum; Pennsylvania Law Journal-Reporter; Corporation Law Review; Life Insurance Selling; Association of Trial Lawyers of America–New Jersey News; United States Justice Foundation Newsletter. *Honour:* 1st prize, Delaware/ATLA Environmental Law Essay Contest, 1984. *Address:* 12 South Heathcote Avenue, Edison, NJ 08817, USA.

VERCORS, Jean, b. 26 Feb. 1902, Paris, France. Graphic Artist; Engraver. *Publications include:* Le Silence de la Mer, 1941; La Marche a l'Etoile, 1943; Les Armes de la Nuit, 1946; Les Yeux et la Lumiere, 1948; Plus ou Moins Homme, 1950; Les Animaux denatures, 1952; Coleres, 1956; Divagations d'un Francais en Chine, 1956; Four Prendre Conge, 1957; Sur ce Rivage, Trilogy (Le Periple, 1958, Monsieur Prousthe, 1958, La Liberte de Decembre, 1960); Quota ou les Plethoriens, 1966; La Bataille du Silence, 1967; Le Radeau de la Meduse, 1969; Sillages, 1972; Sept Sentiers du Desert, 1972; Comme un Frere, 1973; Questions sur la Vie (a MM les Biologistes), 1973; Ce que je crois, 1975; 21 Recettes de Mort violente, 1977; Le Piege a loup, 1979. Plays: Zoo ou l'Assassin philanthrope, 1963; Cedipe, 1967; Le Fer et le Velours, 1969; Hamlet, 1965; Hamlet and Oedipe, 1970; College Plays, volumes 1 and 2, 1978; Assez Mentir, co-author, 1979; 100 Ans d'Histoire de France: Trology, (Moi Aristide Briand, 1981; Les Occasions perdues, 1982; Les Nouveaux Jours, 1984); Anne Boleyn, Les 40 Mois qui ont fait l'Angleterre, 1985. Numerous editions of engravings. *Memberships:* PEN; Honorary President, National Committee of Writers. *Address:* Moulin des Iles, St Augustin, 77120 Coulommiers, France.

VERCRUYSSEN, Maria-Josee, b. 25 July 1915. Teacher. *Publications:* Lente, 1964; Intuïte, 1965; Poezie Lichtbron-Mens, 1970; Stromen, 1975; Wijkindered, 1979; Blad-Zijn, 1982; Contes Poétiques; De kleine danger, 1971; De Witte Vogelen met de Wondervisjes, 1982; Avolutie van het onderwijs Vrij acteren; Aestetische opvoeding. *Contributions to:* Encyclopédie Poétique; Le Bonheur; La Mer; Koor Zomer, compositeur Jef Maes, 1973. *Memberships:* SABAM; Flemish Centre, PEN Club; Union of Flemish Authors. *Address:* Lange Leemstraat 204, Antwerp, Belgium.

VEREEKE-HUTT, June Marie, b. Brooklyn, USA. Publisher. m. Martin C Hutt, 1981, 3 children. *Literary Appointments:* Marketing Director, Marriott/Holiday Inns, Cleveland, 1970–73; President/Consultant, Organisation Resource Association, Clevelend, 1975–;

Publisher, New Cleveland Woman Journal Inc, 1983–. *Honours:* Cleveland Magazine Award, 1979; Cleveland Gazette Award, 1983. *Memberships:* American Society Training & Development; Woman's Career Network Association: Cleveland Press. *Address:* 1966; Idlewood Trail, Strongsville, OH 44136, USA.

VERMEULEN, Johan, b. 13 May 1941, Brasschaat, Belgium. Writer. *Education:* Electronics Engineer. *Major Publications:* 21 titles (in Flemish) of Juvenile Science Fiction, Thrillers and Boating. *Contributor to:* Numerous Dutch & Belgian boating magazines. *Membership:* Vlaamse Vereniging voor Letterkundigen. *Address:* Boonstraat 1/A, 2180 Kalmhout, Belgium.

VERNEY, Douglas Vernon, b. 21 Jan. 1924, Liverpool, England. Professor of Political Science. m. Dr Francine Ruth Frankel, 28 Nov. 1975, Philadelphia, USA, 2 sons. *Education:* MA, Oxford University; PhD, Liverpool University. *Literary Appointments:* Editor, Canadian Public Administration, 1970–74. *Publications:* Parliamentary Reform in Sweden 1866–1921, 1957; Public Enterprise in Sweden, 1959; The Analysis of Political Systems, 1959; Political Patterns in Today's World, 1963, 68; British Government and Politics, 1966, 76; Three Civilizations, Two Cultures, One State; Canada's Political Traditions, 1986. *Contributions to:* Journal of Commonwealth and Comparative Politics; Political Studies; India International Centre Quarterly. *Honours:* Queen's Silver Jubilee Medal, 1977; Member, Institute for Advanced Study, Princeton University, USA, 1977; Shastri Institute Senior Fellowship, 1983; Jules and Gabrielle Léger Fellowship, 1984. *Memberships:* Past President, Canadian Political Science Association. *Address:* Department of Political Science, York University, North York, Ontario, Canada M3J 1P3.

VERNEY, Peter Vivian Lloyd, b. 13 Nov. 1930, London, England. Writer. *Education:* MA, B Agriculture, Trinity College, Dublin, Republic of Ireland. *Publications include:* The Standard Bearer, 1961; The Micks: The Story of the Irish Guards, 1970; The Gardens of Scotland, 1976; The Rattle of Blenheim, 1976; Here Comes the Circus, 1978; Homo Tyrannicus, 1979; Anzio 1944, An Unexpected Fury, 1978; The Earthquake Handbook, 1979; The Weekend Athletic Fitness Chronicle, 1981. *Contributions to:* Aftenposten; Monarchist; Times; Countryman. *Literary Agent:* A P Watt and Son. *Address:* Skiveralls House, Chalford Hill, Gloucestershire GL6 8QJ, England.

VERNON, Raymond, b. 1 Sep. 1913, USA. Professor. m. Josephine Stone, 9 Aug. 1935, Washington DC, 2 daughters. *Education:* BA, 1933; PhD, Economics, 1941. *Publications:* The Regulation of Stock Exchange Members, 1941; The Changing Economic Function of the Central City, 1959; Anatomy of a Metropolis, with Edgar M Hoover, 1960; Metropolis 1985, 1960; The Dilemma of Mexico's Development, 1963; Public Policy and Private Enterprise in Mexico, Editor, 1966; The Myth and Reality of our Urban Problem, 1966; How Latin America Views the United States Investor, 1966; Manager in the International Economy, 1968, 5th edition, 1985; The Technology Factor in International Trade, Editor, 1970; Sovereignty at Bay: The Multinational Spread of US Enterprises, 1971; The Economic Environment of International Business, 1972, 4th edition 1984; Big Business and the State: Changing Relations in Western Europe, Editor; The Oil Crisis, Editor, 1976; Storm over the Multinationals: The Real Issues, 1977; State-Owned Enterprises in the Western Economics, Editor with Yair Aharoni, 1981; Two Hungry Giants: The United States and Japan in the Quest for Oil and Ores, 1983; Exploring the Global Economy: Emerging Issues in Trade and Investment, 1985. *Contributor to:* Numerous articles in professional magazines. *Address:* One Dunstable Road, Cambridge, MA 02138, USA.

VICK, Charles Patrick, b. 7 Oct. 1946, Norfolk, Virginia, USA. Technologist. *Education:* Associates, Applied Science; Mechanical Engineering Technologist.

Publications: Speaker, Various Conferences. *Contributor to:* Numerous articles of journals, magazines and newspapers including: Spaceflight; Missiles and Rockets; Aviation Week & Space Technology; China Space Report; Illustrated Encyclopedia of Space Technology; New York Times; The Sun; Journal of the British Interplanetary Society; The Observer; Papers presented include, USSR Space Programme; Large G Vehicles of the USSR; The USSR Launch Facilities; The Radar Ocean Surveillance Satellites, etc. *Honours:* Army Aviation Association of America Certificates of Acheivement, 1966, 1967; National Aeronautics and Space Administration Certificate of Outstanding Achievement; United States Air Force Award for Exhibit, Tidewater Science Congress, 1966. *Membership:* Associate, Kettering Spacecraft Monitoring Network. *Address:* 432 North Summit Avenue, Apt 201, Gaithersburg, MD 20877, USA.

VICTOR, Edward, b. 4 Mar. 1914, Boston, Massachusetts, USA. University Professor. m. Jeannette Rose Drucker, 28 Dec. 1936, Pawtucket, 1 son. *Education:* AB, Biochemistry, 1935, PhD, Science Education, 1957, Harvard University; AM, Analytical Chemistry, 1936, EdM, Science Education, 1941, Boston University. *Appointments:* Instructor, Chamistry, Boston University, 1941–44; Head, Science, Westbrook, Junior College, Portland, 1944–51; Science Supervisor, Newport Rhode Island Schools, 1951–57; Professor, University of Virginia, 1957–58; Professor, Northwestern University, 1958–78; Adjunct Professor, Arizona State University, 1978–. *Publications:* Friction, 1961; Machine, 1962; Magnets, 1962; Molecules and Atoms, 1963; Planes and Rockets, 1965; Heat, 1967; Electricity, 1967; Magnets and Electromagnets, 1967; Machines, 1969; Sound, 1969; Living Things, 1971; The Physical World, 1971; A Sourcebook for Elementary Science, co-author, 1971; Science for the Elementary, 1970, 1975, 1980, 1985. *Contributor to:* More than 50 articles in, Science and Children; Science Teacher; School Science and Mathematics. *Honours:* Outstanding Science Teacher of Rhode Island, 1953; Outstanding Teaching Recognition Award, National Science Teachers Association, 1954. *Memberships:* Life Member, National Science Teachers Association; Association for Education of Teachers in Science, President 1966–71; American Association for the Advancement of Science; National Association for Research in Science Teaching; Illinois Academy of Science. *Address:* 9819 Calico Drive, Sun City, AZ 85373, USA.

VIDGER, Leonard Perry, b. 25 Jan. 1920, Fargo, North Dakota, USA. Educator and Author. m. Alice Esther Lorentzen, 30 June 1949, Seattle, Washington, 1 son, 1 daughter. *Education:* BA, Seattle Pacific College, 1948; MEA 1950, PhD 1960, University of Washington; MS, University of South Carolina, 1954. *Publications:* Books: Selected Cases and Problems in Real Estate, 1963; Suggested Solutions to Selected Cases and Problems in Real Estate, 1963; Residential Property in San Francisco: A Study of Price Movements and Trends in Financing 1960–64, 1966; San Francisco Housing Markets: A Study of Price Movements in 1956–57 With Projections to 1976, 1969; Borrowing and Lending on Residential Property, 1981. *Contributions to:* Journals including: The Journal of Finance; Harvest Years; California Real Estate Magazine; US Naval Institute Proceedings; Land Economics. *Honours:* Several Academic honours. *Memberships:* Several professional organizations. *Address:* 2320 Whitman Way, San Bruno, CA 94066, USA.

VIDOR, Miklos Janos (Nicholas John), b. 22 May 1923, Budapest, Hungary. Writer. m. Dr Yolanda Buzas, 22 Aug. 1972. *Education:* PhD, German, Hungarian Literature and Aesthetics. *Publications:* Poetry: On the Border, 1947; Monologue, 1957; Empty Season, 1966; Meeting, 1986. Novels: Tiderace, 1954; Strangers, 1958; Pawn on the Chessboard, 1968; Hurt People, 1974; Challenge, 1975; Just One Day More, 1981. Short Stories: Guests of Baucis, 1963; Voluntary Shipwrecked Persons, 1974; Cadet with Mandoline, 1981. *Contributions to:* Nagyvilag; Ujhold; Jelenkor.

Honours: Presidium Member, Union of Hungarian Writers and Hungarian PEN; Hungarian Art Foundation; Jozsef Attila Prize, 1955. *Literary Agent:* Artisjus, Budapest. *Address:* Puskin-u 17, 1088 Budapest, Hungary.

VIERROS, Tuure Johanes, b. 20 Dec. 1927, Kankaanpaa, Finland. Senior Teacher. *Education:* Candidate, Philosophy, University of Helsinki, 1952. *Publications include:* (novels) Loukkauskivet, 1959; Harjahirsi, 1963; Lahella Kuolon rantaa, 1967; Maa oli munuun tyytyvainen, 1971; Komeetta, 1972; Tarton tanssi, 1974; Taivaasa torpan maa, 1976; various textbooks etc. approx. 30 volumes. *Honours:* Nortamo-Prize of Satakunnan Kirjallinen Kerho, 1966; Literary Prize of Pori Town, 1960, 1962. *Memberships:* Finish Society of Authors, 1962–; PEN, 1965–; Chairman, Authors in Helsinki, 1970. *Literary Agent:* Kirjayhtyma Oy. *Address:* Untuvaisentie 7 G 94, 00820 Helsinki 82, Finland.

VIERTEL, Joseph, b. 13 Aug. 1915, New York, USA. President. Public Real Estate Company. m. Janet Man, 13 Sep. 1939, New York, 2 sons, 1 daughter. *Education:* AB, Harvard, 1936; Yale School of Drama, 1937. *Publications:* So Proudly We Hail, (play), 1936; The Last Temptation, (novel), 1955; To Love and Corrupt, (novel), 1962; Monkey on a String, (novel), 1968; Lifelines, (novel), 1982. *Literary Agent:* William Morris Agency. *Address:* 36 Estate Green Cay, Christiansted, St Croix, VI 00820, USA.

VILHELMSSON, Haflidi, b. 23 Dec. 1953, Reykjavik, Iceland, Writer. divorced, 1 son, 1 daughter. *Publications:* Leid tolf –Hlemmur Fell, 1977; Helgalok, 1978; The Illustrated Story of a Black Cat, 1980; Sgan um brain, 1981; Kloi and Musny, 1984; Beygur, 1985. *Contributions to:* Several Icelandic magazines and newspapers of short stories and travel journals. *Memberships:* Writers Associaton of Iceland. *Literary Agent:* Hloougil. *Address:* Stigahlid 2, 105 Reykjavik, Iceland.

VILLA, José Garcia. Poet, Writer. *Education:* BA, University of New Mexico, USA; Postgraduate work, Columbia University. *Literary Appointments:* Associate Editor, New Directions Books, 1949–51; Instructor, Poetry Workshop, New York City College, 1952–60; Lecturer, Poetry Workshops, The New School, 1964–73; Editor, Bravo, the poet's magazine, 1981–. *Publications:* Footnote to Youth, fiction, 1933; Many Voices, 1939; Poems by Doveglion, 1941; Have Come, Am Here, poetry, 1942; Editor, E E Cummings Number, 1946; Editor, A Celebration for Edith Sitwell, 1948; Volume Two, poetry, 1949; Selected Poems and New, 1958; Poems Fifty Five, 1962; Poems in Praise of Love, 1962; Selected Stories, 1962; Editor, Doveglion Book of Philippine Poetry, 1982; The Portable Villa, 1963; The Essential Villa, 1965; Editor, new Doveglion Book of Philippine Poetry, 1975; Appassionata, 1979. *Contributions to:* Numerous books including: Best American Short Stories of 1932; Twentieth Century American Poetry; Encyclopedia of World Literature in the 20th Century; Guide to Modern World Literature; Penguin Companion to Classical and Oriental Literature. *Honours include:* Honorary D Litt, Far Eastern University, 1959; Philippines Pro Patria Award, 1961; Rockefeller Foundation Fellowship, 1963; Elected Philippines National Artist, 1973; LHD, University of the Philippines, 1973. *Address:* 780 Greenwich Street, New York City, NY 10014, USA.

VINCK, Catherine de (née Kestens), b. 20 Feb. 1922, Brussels, Belgium. Poet. m. Baron Jose M de Vinck, 1 Feb. 1945, Brussels, 4 sons, 2 daughters. *Education:* In Graeco-Latin Humanities. *Major Publications:* A Time to Gather, 1967; Ikon, 1972; A Liturgy, 1972; A Passion Play, 1975; A Book of Uncommon Prayers, 1977; Readings (John at Patmos, A Book of Hours), 1978; A Book of Eve (record & text), 1979; A Garland of Straw, 1979; A Book of Peace, 1985. *Contributor to:* Numerous publications. *Honours:* LittD, St Mary's College, Notre Dame, Indiana, 1982, St Scholastic's College, Duluth, Minnesota, 1986.

Address: 672 Franklin Turnpike, Allendale, NJ 07401, USA.

VINKS, Adriaan Jos, b. 8 Nov. 1920, Kalmthout, Belgium. Journalist. m. 11 Aug. 1951, 1 son, 2 daughters. *Education:* Teacher, School. *Publications:* Dr Borms, biography, 1974; Cyriel Verscheave, biography, 1976; Van Repressie tot Egmont, 1980; Verzamelde Gedichten, 1984; Pacifisme and Weerbaarheid, 1981; Rassisme, 1982; Dit Broos Geluid, 1985. *Contributions to:* Wij; West Magazine; Gazet van-Antwerpen; Dietsland Europa; Zuid Afrika Magazine; Medium; Junges Forum; t Pallieterke. *Honours:* Dr Snellaert Prize, 1978; Price Flanders Abroad, 1976. *Memberships:* Vereniging van Vlaamse Letterkundigen; Founder and President, Vereniging van Vlaams-Nationale Auteurs. *Address:* Ringlaan 11, 2060 Antwerp-Merksem, Belgium.

VIORST, Judith, b. 2 Feb. 1931, New Jersey, USA. Writer. m. Milton Viorst, 30 Jan. 1960, 3 sons. *Education:* BA, Rutgers University; Graduate, Washington Psychoanalytic Institute. *Publications include:* Paperback Science Books: The Natural World, 1965; The Changing Earth, 1967; Children's Books: The Tenth Thing About Barney, 1971; Rosie and Michael, 1974; Alexander, Who Used to be Rich Last Sunday, 1978; Poems: It's Hard To Be Hip Over Thirty and Other Tragedies of Married Life, 1968; People and other Aggravations, 1971; How Did I Get to be Forty and Other Atrocities, 1976; Poems for Children and Adults: If I Were in Charge of the World and Other Worries, 1981; Psychoanalytic Publications: Experiences of Loss at the End of Analysis: The Analyst's response to Termination, Psychoanalytic Inquiry, 1982, Other: The Washington Underground Gourmet, with Milton Viorst, 1970; Yes Married, 1972; Free To Be...You and Me (contributor), 1974; A Visit from St Nicholas (To a Liberated Household), 1977; Love and Guilt and The Meaning of Life, 1979; Necessary Losses, 1986. *Contributions to:* Redbook Magazine, 1985–. *Honours include:* American Academy of Pediatric Awards for article on psychological aspects of hospitalization of childen in, Redbook Magazine, 1977; American Association of University Women Award for article on older women in, Redbook Magazine, 1980. *Literary Agent:* Robert Lescher. *Adress:* 3432 Ashley Terrace NW, Washington DC, 20008, USA.

VIORST, Milton, b. 18 Feb. 1930, New Jersey, USA. Writer. m. Judith Stahl, 30 Jan. 1960, Washington, 3 sons. *Education:* BA, Rutgers University, 1951; MA, Harvard University, 1955; MA, Columbia University, 1956; Fulbright Scholar, University of Lyon, France, 1951–52. *Publications:* Liberalism: A Guide to its Past, Present and Future in American Politics, 1963; Hostile Allies: FDR and de Gaulle, 1964; The Great Documents of Western Civilization, 1965, 67; Fall from Grace: The Republican Party and the Puritan Ethic, 1968, 71; Hustlers and Heroes: An American Politicical Panorama, 1976; Fire in the Streets, 1980; Outsider in the Senate, with Senator Clinton P Anderson, 1970; An Underground Gourmet Guide to Washington DC, with Judith Viorst, 1970. *Contribution to:* Esquire; Saturday Evening Post; Harpers; Atlantic Monthly; Saturday Review; New York Times Magazine; Washingtonian; National Jewish Monthly; Paris Match; Economist; New Republican; Nation; Figaro Litteraire; Columbia Journalism Review; Progressive and others. *Memberships:* Board of directors, Washington Independent Writers, 1981–82; Past Chairman, Fund for Investigative Journalism; Past Fellow, Alicia Patterson Foundation. *Literary Agent:* Robert Lescher. *Address:* 3432 Ashley Terrace, Washington, DC 20008, USA.

VIRET, Margaret Mary-Buchanan, b. 18 Apr. 1913. Art Teacher; Poet. m. Frank I Viret. *Education:* Business College, New York City, New York, USA; Miami Art School; Terry Art School, Miami, Florida; University of Miami Extension Courses; Laramore Reader Poetry School. *Publications:* Singing in the Sun, 1965; Poetry Society of Florida Poetry Book, 1969; Affinities, 1979–80; L R P G 1980 Poetry Book. *Contributions to:* Miami

Herald; Miami News; Miami Beach Reporter Sun; New York Times. *Honours:* Poetry Award, Miami Chamber of Commerce, 1964; Laramore Rader Poetry Award, 1969–70; Poetry Award, Miami Pallette Club, 1973, Miami Womens Club, 1968; Nominee for Poet Laureate of Florida, 1980; Listed in, Julia's Daughters-Women in Dade's History, 1980. *Memberships:* Past Vice President, Florida Federation of Art; Past State Art Chairman, Florida Federation of Womens Clubs; Past Poetry Director, Miami Womens Club; Past President, currently Director, Laramore Rader Poetry Group; Founder Member, Poetry Society of Florida; Florida Federation of Womens Clubs Poets; South Florida Poetry Institute; Miami Womens Clubs Literary and Poetry Director, 1981–82. *Address:* 294 North East 55th Terrace, Miami, FL 33137, USA.

VIRTANEN, Arto Kalevi, b. 17 Dec. 1947, Helsinki, Finland. Poet; Critic. m. Ritva-Liisa Taipale, 26 Dec. 1968, Helsinki, divorced, 1974, 1 daughter. *Publications:* Kaikki liikkeessa, 1970; Junamatkan kasvot, 1973; Jumalien testamentit, 1978; Tuntematon rauha, 1981; Huimaus, 1982; Kivinen kirja, 1984. *Contributor to:* Many Newspapers; Parnasso; Suomen Sosialikemokraatti, Literature Critic. *Honours:* Tatu Vaaskivi Prize, 1984. *Memberships:* Finnish Society of Authors; Union of the Finnish Critics; Eino Leino's Club. *Literary Agent:* Werner Soderstrom oy/Ville Viksten. *Address:* Lemminkäisenkuja 3 B 33, 00100 Helsinki, Finland.

VIRTANEN, Reino, b. 26 June 1910, Ishpeming, Michigan, USA. College Professor. m. Sylvia Bornstein, 24 Apr. 1937, Albany, New York, 2 daughters. *Education:* BA, 1932, MA, 1933, PhD, 1937, University of Wisconsin. *Publications:* Claude Bernard and His Place in the History of Ideas, 1960; Anatole France, 1968; L'Imagerie scientifique de Paul Velery, 1975; Conversations on Dialogue, 1977. *Contributions to:* Kentucky Romance Quarterly; PMLA; French Review; Journal of the History of Ideas; Symposium Scandinavian Studies; Prairie Schooner. *Honours:* Markham Travelling Scholarship, 1937–38; Woods Fellowships, 1959–60,1973; Festschrift, 1978; Carmargo Foundation Fellow, 1980. *Memberships:* Editorial Board, Studies in 20th Century Literature; Phi Beta Kappa; Modern Language Association. *Address:* 1818 South 26th Street, Lincoln, NE 68502, USA.

VIVIAN, Robert W, b. 10 Mar. 1936, Elmira, New York, USA. Educator; Writer. *Education:* BA Magna cum laude, 1957; MS 1958, Syracuse University. *Literary Appointments:* Reporter, Elmira Star-Gazette, 1962–64 and 1965–67; writer, Riverside (CA) Press-Enterprise, 1968–70; Managing Editor, Palm Springs Life magazine, 1976–81. *Publications:* The Good Humor Man, 1980. *Contributions to:* Palm Springs Life; Western's World; San Francisco; PGA magazine; Chapter in, Insight Guide to Southern California, 1984. *Memberships:* Authors Guild Inc; Society of Professional Journalists; National Writers Club; California Writers Club. *Address:* PO Box 3609, Chico, CA 95927, USA.

VLEESCHOUWER-VERBRAEKEN, Maria Justina Elisabeth de, b. 26 Oct. 1913, Burcht, Antwerp, Belgium. Teacher. m. Frans de Vleeschouwer (dec.), 4 Mar. 1941. *Education:* Teacher's College. *Publications:* Wies en haar korrespondenten, 1953; Een uil vloog over, 1955; Op lange latten, 1955; Veerle, 5 parts, 1956–58; Marieke's Memoires, 3 parts, 1961–63; Marieke over de stroom, 1962; Marieke in volle zee, 1963; Zwaluwen over Hiroshima, 1966. *Honours:* Best Book for Youth, Sheed & Ward, Flanders 1955, Province of Antwerp 1957, Flanders 1959, Boekenbeurs 1963; Janusz Korczak Medal, 1983. *Memberships:* VSVJ (Society of Writers for Young People); VVL (Flemish Authors Society). *Address:* Rozenlaan 24, 2080 Kapellen, Belgium.

VLIEGHE, Piet, b. 5 June 1928, Dendermonde, Belgium. Professor. *Education:* Literary studies, Universities of Ghent & Brussels; Historical studies, Ghent. *Publications Include:* Poems, short stories, 1958–;

About 500 pages published, different subjects 15 booklets. *Contributions:* Letters to various magazines. *Honours:* Order of St Geréon, Italy. *Membership:* Club of Gastronomy (with publications). *Address:* Wautersstraat 73, B–9279 Gentbrugge, Belgium.

VOGEL, Alois, b. 1 Jan. 1922, Vienna, Austria. Writer; Professor. *Publications:* The Other Face, novel, 1959; The Song of the Cicadas, poetry, 1964; Among Parasites, poetry, 1964; Year and Day Pohanka, novel, 1964; Light in the mist, haiku, 1967; Preliminary Funeral Experience, text, 1970; Speech and Hearing, poetry, 1971; Sender Unknown, sketch, 1971; The Hour of History, radio play, 1973; Situation, poetry, 1976; Ein Unfall, Horspeil, 1976; Schlagschatten, novel, 1977; So lange du lebst, 1978; Landnahame, Lyrics, 1979; Totale Verdronkelung, novel, 1980; Das Fischergericht, 1982; Ser settene Fall, 1983; Die Sehme durchgezogen, lyric, 1983; Beobachtungen am Munhartsberg, Lyric, 1983. *Contributor to:* Classical and Modern Art; Podium; Lit. and Criticism; Vienna Art papers. *Honours:* Stimulation Prize, Vienna Art Fund, 1961; Stimulation Prize, The Korner Fund, 1962; Stimulation Prize, Vienna, 1966; Luitpold-Stern Prize, 1973; Kulturpreis d. landes Niederosterreich, 1977; Kogge-Ehrenring d. Staat Minden. 1982. *Memberships:* PEN Club; European Association of Writers; Literay Circle Podium. *Address:* Bahnstrasse 17, A3741 Pulkazi, Austria.

VOGEL, Magdalena (Katharina), b. 6 Apr. 1932, Zurich, Switzerland. Editorial Assistant. *Education:* Teaching Diploma; Secondary Diploma. *Publications:* Englische Prospekte, 1961; Linka oder Sommereiner Magd, 1964;Fluch der Scheidung, (editor of letters from Alhin Zollinger), 1965; (Poems) Kringel und Raster, 1966; Entwurf de Case, 1970; Zwischen Milchstrasse und Sackgassen, 1979; Zeicheulese, (prose) 1981; Das Eswachen im Hanm, 1982; (Poems & prose), Die Verwefung der Jahreszeiten, 1985. *Contributor to:* Tages-Anzeiger. *Honours:* Grant, STEO Foundation, 1965; Grant, Schweizerischer Schriftsteller-Verband, 1965; Donation, Pro Arte Foundation, Berne, 1977; Donation of Honour, Canton of Zurich, 1977; 2 Donations of Honour, City of Zurich, 1981, 1985. *Address:* Luegete 29, 8053 Zurich, Switzerland.

VOGT, Esther Loewen, b. 19 Nov. 1915, Collinsville, Oklahoma, USA. Freelance Writer. *Education:* AA, Tabor College, 1939. *Publications:* Cry to the Wind, 1965; The Sky is Falling, 1968; High Ground, 1970; Ann, 1971; Prairie Tales, 1971; I'll Walk Again, 1972; Eight Wells of Elim, 1974; Turkey Red, 1975; Beyond These Hills, 1977; Mystery at Red Rock Canyon, 1979; Harvest Gold, 1978; A Trace of Perfume, 1982; The Shiny Dragon, 1983; Jedediah Smsith, Trail-blazer and Trapper, 1986. *Contributions to:* Moody Monthly; Christian Life; Guideposts; Highlights for Children; Campus Life; War Cry. *Honours:* Delta Kappa Gamma; Alumni Merit Award, Tabor College, 1974; David C Cook Juvenile Book Contest Honorable Mention, 1975; 1st Place, Native Sons and Daughters Contests, Kansas, 1956, 62; Various prizes, Kansas Authors Club contests. *Memberships:* 4th district President, Kansas Authors Club; Secretary, Mentor Study Club; Historian, 4th District, Federal Womens Clubs. *Address:* 113 South Ash, Hillsboro, KS 67063, USA.

VOINOVICH, Vladimir Nikolaevich, b. 26 Sep. 1932, Dushanbe, USSR. Writer. m. Irina, 13 Nov. 1970, 1 son, 2 daughters. *Education:* Pedagogical Institute, Moscow, USSR. *Major Publications:* (in Russian): We Live Here, 1961; Two Friends, 1972; Degree of Trust, 1973; The Life and Extraordinary Adventures of Private Ivan Chonkin, 1975; Ivankiad, 1976; Pretender to the Throne, 1979. *Contributor to:* New York Times Magazine; New Republic; Partisan Review; Survey; Wall Street Journal; Index of Censorship; Times Literary Supplement; and others. *Memberships:* PEN (French Division) Paris; Bavarian Academy of Fine Arts, Munich, Federal Republic of Germany. *Literary Agent:* Georges Borchardt, New York, USA. *Address:* Hans-Carossa-Straße 5, 8035 Stockdorf, Federal Republic of Germany.

VON BALTHASAR Hans Urs, b. 12 Aug. 1905, Lucerne, Switzerland. *Education:* PhD, Munich and Lyon, 1929–38; Ordained Roman Catholic Priest. *Publications include:* Apokalypse der deutschen Seele, 3 volumes, 1937–39; Das Herz der Welt, 1945, 3rd edition, 1959; Theologie der Geschichte, 1950, 54; Das betrachtende Gebet, 1955, 5th edition, 1977; Herrlichkeit, Eine theologische Aesthetik, 7 volumes, 1961–69; Romano Guardini: Reform and dem Ursprung, 1970; In Gottes Einsatz leben, 1971; Katholisch, 1975; Henri de Lubac, Sein organisches Lebenswerk, 1976; Theodramatik 11/1 Die Personen des Spiels, Der Mensch in Gott, 1976; 11/2 Die Personen in Christus, 1978; Neue Klarstellungen, 1979; Theodramatik 111: Die Handlung, 1980; Du kronst das Jahr mit diener Huld, Radiopredigten, 1982; Theodramatik IV: Das Endspel, 1983; Unser Auftrag, 1984; Theologik 1: Wahrheit der Welt, 1985; Theologik 11: Wahrheit Gottes, 1985. Several translations. *Contributions to:* International Catholic Review; Communio. *Honours:* Recipient of several academic honours. *Memberships:* Several academic organisations. *Address:* Arnold Böcklinstrasse 42, CH–4051 Basel, Switzerland.

VON LAUE, Theodore Herman, b. 22 June 1916, Frankfurt am Main, Federal Republic of Germany. Professor of History. m. (1) Hildegarde Hunt, 23 Oct. 1943, Winchester, Massachusetts, USA, 2 daughters. (2) Angela Turner, 13 Nov. 1976, Worcester, Massachusetts. *Education:* BA, 1939, PhD, 1944, Princeton University, USA; Certificate, Russian Institute, Columbia University, 1949. *Publications:* Leopold Ranke, The Formative Years, 1950; Sergei Witte and the Industrialization of Russia, 1963; Why Lenin? Why Stalin? 1964; The Global City, 1969. *Contributions to:* Yale Review; Bucknell Review; African Affairs; American Historical Review; Slavic Review; Michigan Quarterly Review; Technology in society; Soviet Union-Union Sovietique. *Address:* c/o History Department, Clark University, Worcester, MA 01610, USA.

VON STUDNITZ, Hans Georg, b. 31 Aug. 1907, Potsdam, Federal Republic of Germany. Writer; Free-lance Journalist. *Publications:* Als Berlin brannte, 1963; While Berlin Burns, 1963; Bismarck in Bonn, 1964; Glanz und keine Gloria, 1965; Rettet die Bundeswehr, 1967; Ist Gott Mitlaufer?, 1969; Seitensprunge, 1975; Den Grossten die Ehre, 1966; Menschen aus meiner Welt, 1985. *Contributions to:* Editor-in-Chief: Hamburger Allgemeine Zeitung; Hamburger Anzeiger; Zeitbuhne. Aussenpolitik, Publisher. Criticon; Deutschland Magazin; Konservativ Heute; Adelsblatt; Bayernkurier; Welt am Sonntag. *Honours include:* Federal Cross of Merit, 1978. *Memberships include:* Luftfahrtpresseclub, Frankfurt. *Address:* Otterkring 5, 8219 Rimsting, Federal Republic of Germany.

VOORHEES, Richard J, b. 30 Sep. 1916, Toluca, Illinois, USA. Professor. m. Edna J Miller, 28 Feb. 1942, Urbana, Illinois, USA. *Education:* BA 1939, MA 1941, University of Illinois; PhD, Indiana University, 1958. *Literary Appointments:* Emeritus Professor of English, Purdue University. *Major Publications:* The Paradox of George Orwell, 1961; P G Wodehouse, 1966. *Contributor to:* S Atlantic Quarterly; Prairie Schooner; Commonweal; Canadian Forum; College English; Personalist; Queen's Quarterly; Dalhousie Review; Journal of Modern Literature; University of Windsor Review; Midwest Quarterly. *Address:* 1700 Sheridan Road, W Lafayette, IN 47906, USA.

VOSE, Ruth Hurst, b. 10 Feb. 1944, Southport, England. Author. m. James Edward Vose, 19 Sep. 1969, Aughton. *Education:* BA, Hons, Ancient and Medieval History and Archaeology of Liverpool, 1966; Diploma and Associateship of the Museums Association, London, 1971; Senior Journalistic Status, United Newspapers, London 1975; Diploma in Hypnosis and Psychology, National College of Hypnosis and Psychology, Chester and London, 1981. *Publications:* Glass, in The Connoisseur Illustrated Guides series, 1975; Glass, in The Collins Archaeology series, 1980;

Agoraphobia, 1981; From the Dark Ages to the Fall of Constantinople in, A History of Glass, 1984. *Contributions to:* Numerous contributions to newspapers, magazines and journals. *Address:* Hurleston Gate, Moorfield Lane, Scarisbrick, Near Ormskirk, Lancashire, England.

VOSS, Carl Hermann, b. 8 Dec. 1910, Pitts, Pennsylvania, USA. Author; Educator; Clergyman; Lecturer. m. (1) Dorothy K Crote, 25 Nov. 1940, Pittsburgh, PA, Divorced, 1957; (2) Phyllis MacKenzie Gierlotka, 9 May 1959, Saratoga Springs, NY, 2 daughters. *Education:* BA 1931, PhD, University of Pittsburgh, 1942; Master of Divinity, Union Theol Sem, NZC, 1935. *Publications:* The Rise of Social Consciousness in the Congregational Churches, 1965–1942, 1942; The United Nations, 1947; Two Giants in One World, (with William Loos, H A Atkinson, John R Inman), 1948; Answers on the Palestine Question, 1946, 1947, 1948, 1949; The Palestine Problem Today: Israel and Its Neighbors, 1953; The Universal God: The Eternal Quest in Which All Men Are Brothers, 1953; This is Israel: Palestine, Today and Tomorrow, 1956; Rabbi and Minister: The Friendship of Stephen S Wise and John Haynes Holmes, 1964, Paperbacks in 1968, 1980; In Search of Meaning: Living Religions of the World, 1968; Stephen S Wise: Servant of the People, selected letters, 1968; A Summons unto Men: An Anthology of the Writings of John Haynes Holmes, 1971; Quotations of Courage and Vision: A Sourcebook for Speaking, Writing and Meditation, 1972. *Contributor to:* Various religious journals such as The Christian Century; Worldview; American Judaism; A Jewish Frontier; Congress Monthly Midstream. *Honours:* Honorary Fellow, Hebrew University of Jerusalem, Israel, 1928; Honorary Degree, Doctor of Humane Letters, New York School of Hebrew Union College-Jewish Institute of Religion, 1981; National Brotherhood Award, National Conference of Christians andJews, 1978. *Address:* 7783 Point Vicente Court, Baymeadows, Jacksonville, FL 32216, USA.

VREE, Dale, b. 25 Feb. 1944, Los Angeles, California, USA. Editor. m. Elena Maria Reyes, 18 June 1965, Los Angeles, 1 son, 2 daughters. *Education:* BA 1965, MA 1967, PhD 1972, University of California, Berkeley; Humbolt University, East Berlin, Germany, 1966. *Literary Appointments:* Editor, New Oxford Review, Berkeley, California. *Publications:* On Synthesizing Marxism & Christianity, 1976; From Berkeley to East Berlin & Back, 1985. *Contributions to:* New Leader; Worldview; Commonweal; Review of Politics; Ethics; Journal of Politics; American Political Science Review; 30 Giorni, Rome; Litterae Communionis, Milan; etc. *Literary Agent:* Nancy Trichter, New York City; Mary Jane Ross, Tenafly, New Jersey. *Address:* New Oxford Review, 1069 Kains Avenue, Berkeley, CA 94706, USA.

VROMAN, Leo, b. 10 Apr. 1915. Scientist. *Education includes:* Geneeskundige Hogeschool, Jakarta, Indonesia, 1941; PhD, Rijksuniversiteit, Utrecht, Netherlands, 1958. *Publications:* Gedichten, 1946; Gedichten, Vroegere en Latere, 1949; Poems in English, 1953; Inleiding tot een Leegte, 1955; Ult Slaapwandelen, 1957; De Ontvachting, 1960; Twee Gedichten, 1961; Fabels, 1962; Manke Vliegen, 1963; 126 Gedichten, 1964; Almanak, 1965; God en Godin, 1967; 114 Gedichten, 1969; 262 Gedichten, 1974; Just One More World, 1976; Huis en Tuin, 1979; Nieuwsgierig, 1980; Het Verdoemd Carillon, 1981; Liefde, Sterk Vergroot, 1981; Avondgymnastiek, 1983; Gedichten 1946–1964, 1985. *Contributions to:* Groot Nederland; Gids; Libertinage; Tirade; Haaga Maandblad; Revisor; Parool; Poetry, Chicago. *Honours:* Lucy B and CW Van der Hoogt Award, 1950; Bijenkorf Award, 1956; Amsterdam Award, 1956 and 1961; Kunstenaars Verzet Award, 1965; PC Hooft Award, 1965; Clemsen Award for Basic Research in Biomedical Materials, 1986. *Address:* 2365 East 13th Street, Brooklyn, NY 11229, USA.

VYAS, Bhanushanker Odhavji, b. 5 Oct. 1924, Wankamer, India. Teacher; Writer. *Education:* BA, Philosophy, MA, Gujarati-Sanskrit, BT, English-

Gujarati, University of Bombay; MA, Philosophy, University of Poona. *Publications:* The Silent Thunders, 1964; The Breaking Barriers, 1974; Paul Ambroise Valéry – Through a Study of his Three Major Poems, (Gujarati) 1977; Conscience and Rural Phenomena, 1983; Soorya Surdhenuno Sahakar, 1983; Neelsalil Neerajdal Jhule, (Ed.) 1983; Untenanted Skies, 1984; Stare to Infinity, 1985. *Contributions to:* The Journal of Indian Writing in English; Bharat Protiva; Poetry; Skylark; Indian and Foreign Review; Poet; All India Radio (School Broadcasts) 1954. *Honours:* Guest Editor, Savita (India) 1958; Jagriti (Uganda) 1960; Africa Samachar (Kenya) 1959; Gujarat State Award Winner 1965/66; Editor, A Collection of Essays on Uganda (Federation of Indian Organisations, Leicester) 1979; First Prize, Short-story Competition, Gujarati Literary Academy (Britain) 1984; John Frears Scholar, Departments of Philosophy and Religion, University of Leicester, 1981–82. *Memberships:* Gujarati Literary Society, Uganda (President 1963); Gujarati Literary Academy GB (Vice President 1977); Leicester Poetry Society 1976–77; The Poetry Society, London, (Life Member); PEN for Writers in Exile, London; Life Member, Gujarati Sahitya Parishad (India); World Poetry Society Intercontinental (USA) Life Member; Gujarati Literary Conference, Leicester, 1983, Chairman. *Address:* 66 Avon Street, Leicester LE2 1BB, England.

W

WAAGE, Frederick O, b. 1 Dec. 1943, Ithaca, New York, USA. College Teacher. m. Virginia Renner, 18 June 1977, New Brunswick, 1 son, 1 daughter. *Education:* AB, 1965, PhD, 1971, Princeton University. *Appointments:* Instructor, English, Northwestern University, 1968–71; Lecture, California State University, Los Angeles, 1971–73; Assistant Professor, English, Douglass College, 1974–77; Assistant Professor, Language, Literature, College Misericordia, 1977–78; Assistant Professor, East Tennessee State University, 1978–83, Associate Professor, 1983–. *Publications:* Thomas Dekker's Pamphlets and Jacobean Popular Literature, 1977; The White Devil Discover'd: Backgrounds and Foregrounds to, Webster's Tragedy, 1984; Poetry: Minestrone, 1983; Teaching Environemntal Literature, 1985. *Contributor to:* Journal of Popular Culture; Shakespeare Studies. *Honours:* Fellow, Huntington Library, 1975, 1979; Fellow, Southeastern Instiute of Medieval and Renaissance Studies, 1975; Danforth Associate, with Virginia Renneer, 1981–86. *Memberships:* Modern Language Association, Delegate Assembly, 1977–79; Tennessee Chair, Popular Culture Association. *Address:* 2127 Sinking Creek Road, Johnson City, TN 37601, USA.

WACHS, Saul Philip, b. 24 Dec. 1931, Philadelphia, Pennsylvania, USA. Professor, Jewish Education. m. Barbara Ruth Eidelman Wachs, 27 Jan. 1957, New York City, 1 son, 3 daughters. *Education:* BA, Temple University; Hebrew Teacher's Diploma, Gratz College; Hazzan, B Sac Mus, B Rel Ed, Jewish Theological Seminary; MA, PhD, Ohio State University. *Publications:* A Theory of Practice for the Conservative Jewish School, 1967; Jewish Population Erosion, 1978; Prayer and Mitzvah Education in the Jewish School, 1978; Jewish Education and Jewish Population, 1978; Judaism, 1979; Essays in Honor of Louis Newman, 1984. *Contributor to:* Supervision in a Small School, 1962; The Congregational High School, 1968; New Models in the Training of Jewish Educators, 1974; The Kiev Synagogue, 1974, 1975; Goals for Teaching Prayers, 1982; Goals for Teaching Mitzvot, 1984; etc. *Honours:* Aaron Zacks Award, American Association for Jewish Education, 1969; Leaders in Education, 1973; Outstanding Educators of America, 1974. *Address:* 107 Maple Avenue, Bala Cynwyd, PA 19004, USA.

WADDELL, Evelyn Margaret, b. 4 May 1918, Weston, Ontario, Canada. Children's Librarian. m. Robb John Waddell, 19 Sep. 1949, Islington, 1 son, 1 daughter. *Education:* BA, English Language & Literature, BLS, University of Toronto. *Publications:* The Bells on Finland Street, 1950; The Little Magic Fiddler, 1951; Rebel on the Trail, 1953; Jady and the General, 1955; Pegeen and the Pilgrim, 1957; The Road to Kip's Cove, 1961; Samantha's Secret Room, 1963; The Brownie Handbook for Canada, 1965; The Secret of Willow Castle, 1966; The Magical Miss Mittens, 1970; Toys from the Sky, 1972; Jolly Jean-Pierre, 1973; If I Were All These, 1974; A Treasure for Tony, 1980; The Magic Pony, 1981; Sea Dreams, 1981. *Honours:* Honorary Member, Academy of Canadian Writers, Vicky Metcalf Award, 1978. *Memberships:* Writers Union of Canada; Canadian Society of Children's Authors, Illustrators and Performers. *Address:* 72 Cedarbrae Blvd, Scarborough, Ontario, Canada M1J 2K5.

WADDELL, Heather, b. 11 July 1950, Scotland. Author; Publisher; Photographer. *Education:* MA, St Andrews University, 1972; Byam Shaw School of Art, London, England, 1972–76; Certificate in Art and Design, London, 1975; Diploma in Fine Art, 1976; Leverhulme Scholar. Garnett College, London, 1976–77; Certificate of Education, London University, 1977. *Publications:* London Art and Artists Guide, 1979, 4 editions; The Artists Directory, co-editor, 1st edition, 1982, 2nd edition, 1985. *Contributions to:* The Artist, 1974; The Evening Standard, 1974; Times Educational Supplement; Art Monthly; Art and Australia; Art New

Zealand; art critic, London's Alternative Magazine, 1979–81; London Art correspondent, Glasgow Herald, 1980–84; Millions Magazine, Canada; London correspondent, Vie des Arts, 1980–; Art Line Magazine; art features writer, London Week. *Memberships:* Honorary Treasurer, International Association of Art Critics. *Address:* 28 Colville Road, London W11 2BS, England.

WADDELL, Martin, b. 10 Apr. 1941, Belfast, Northern Ireland. Author. m. Rosaleen Carragher, Dec. 1979, Belfast, 3 sons. *Literary Appointment:* Writer-in-Residence, Down District, 1983. *Publications include:* As Catherine Sefton, for children: In a Blue Velvet Dress, 1972; The Backhouse Ghosts, 1974; The Finn Gang, 1982; The Emma Dilemma, 1982; A Puff of Smoke, 1982; The Blue Misty Monsters, 1985; etc. As Martin Waddell, for children: Ernie's Chemistry Set, 1978; The Great Green Mouse Disaster, 1981; Napper, series, 3 titles, 1981–84; Mystery Squad, series, 8 titles, 1984–86; Going West, 1983; Harriet, series, 3 titles, 1982–85; etc. As Martin Waddell, for adults: Otley, 1966; Otley Pursued, 1967; Otley Forever, 1968; Otley Victorious, 1969; Come Back When I'm Sober, 1969; A Little Bit British, 1970. *Honours:* 3 bursaries, Northern Ireland Arts Council. *Membership:* Society of Authors. *Literary Agent:* Murray Pollinger, 4 Garrick Street, London WC2E 9BH. *Address:* 139 Central Promenade, Newcastle, County Down, Northern Ireland.

WADDINGTON, Miriam Dworkin, b. 23 Dec. 1917, Winnipeg, Canada. Poet; University Teacher. m. Patrick D Waddington, 5 July 1939, Montreal (divorced 1965), 2 sons. *Education:* MSW, MA, English. *Literary Appointments:* Professor, English and Canadian Literature, York University, Toronto. *Publications:* 11 books of poetry including: Driving Home, 1972; The Price of Gold, 1976; Mister Never, 1978; The Visitants, 1981; Author of critical study of A M Klein; Editor of critical work of John Sutherland and The collected Poems of A M Klein; Critical articles, reviews, short stories and translations of prose and poetry from Yiddish and German; Books include: The Glass Trumpet, 1968; Say Yes, 1969; The Dream Telescope, 1972; Driving Home, 1972; The Price of Gold, 1976; Mister Never, 1978; Summer at Lonely Beach, 1982; Collected Poems, 1986. *Contributor to:* numerous magazines, newspapers, journals, etc. *Honours:* J I Segal Prize, Montreal, 1972; Bonestone Mountain, Second Prize in Best Poems of 1974; Honorary DLitt, Lakehead University, 1975, York University, 1985. *Address:* 32 Yewfield Crescent, Don Mills, Ontario M3B 2Y6, Canada.

WADE, Graham, b. 18 Jan. 1940, Coventry, England. Senior Lecturer in Classical Guitar. m. Elizabeth Eker, 13 Jan. 1972, Boston, Lincs. *Education:* BA, 1962, MA, 1966, Jesus College, University of Cambridge, England; Licentiate, Trinity College of Music, London, England, 1973; Fellow, Trinity College of Music, 1979; Fellow, Royal Society of Arts, 1982; Fellow, College of Preceptors, 1983. *Major Publications:* Traditions of the Classical Guitar, 1980; Your Book of the Guitar, 1980; The Shape of Music, 1981; Segovia: A Celebration of the Man and his Music, 1983; The Guitarist's Guide to Bach, 1985; Guitar Method, volume 1 1974, volume 2 1978. *Contributor to:* Numerous periodicals, including: Classical Music; The Strad; Music in Education; Classical Guitar; Northern Echo; Literary Review; Private Eye; Music Teacher; Yorkshire Post; Making Music. *Literary Agent:* Barbara Levy/Carol Smith, London, England. *Address:* City of Leeds College of Music, Leeds 2, England.

WADLEY, Susan Snow, b. 18 Nov. 1943, Baltimore, USA. Professor of Anthropology, Syracuse University. *Education:* AB, Carleton College, 1965; MA 1967, PhD 1973, University of Chicago. *Major Publications:* Shakti: Power in the Conceptual Structure of Karimpur Religion, 1975; (with D Jacobson) Women in India: Two Perspectives, 1978; Powers of Tamil Women, 1980. *Contributor to:* Asian Folklore Studies; Eastern Anthropology; Pacific Affairs; Journal of Asian Studies. *Honours:* Several Honours, scholarships & grants, including: Marc Perry Galler Prize, Division of Social

Sciences, University of Chicago, 1976–74; Faculty Research Grant, American Institute of Indian Studies, 1974–75; National Endowment for the Humanities Summer Stipend for Younger Humanists, 1977; Smithsonian Project Grant, 1983–84; Fulbright Scholar, 1983–84. *Address:* 500 University Place, Syracuse, NY 13210, USA.

WADMAN, Anne Sijbe, b. 30 Nov. 1919, Langweer, Netherlands. Educator. *Education:* DLitt, University of Amsterdam, 1955. *Publications include:* Handdruk en Handgemeen, Handshakes and Close Quarters, essays and criticism, 1965; Yn'e lyste loege, In a Hole, 1960; Kugels foar in labbekak, Bullets for a Coward, Novel, 1964; By de duvel to bycht, Gone to the Wrong Shop, 1966; De feestgongers, the Merry-Makers, 1968; It rammeljen van de pels, It's of No Use, 1970; Yn Adams harnas, In Adam's Armour, 1982; De verkrachting, The Rage, 1984; Tinke oan alde tiden, Thinking About Olden Times, 1985; 16 – dei-boek 1936, 16 Diary 1936, 1985. Literary Critic, Leeuwarder Courant, 1957–71. *Honours:* Gysbert Japiks Prise for Frisian Literature, 1951. *Memberships:* Dutch Centre, PEN. *Address:* Esdoornlaan 2, 8603 CA Sneek, Friesland, The Netherlands.

WAGENKNECHT, Edward, b. 28 Mar. 1900, Chicago, Illinois, USA. Writer; Professor Emeritus, English, Boston University. *Education:* PhB, 1923, MA, 1924, University of Chicago; PhD, University of Washington, 1932. *Publications:* Author/Editor, over 60 books including: Mark Twain, The Man & His work, revised edition, 1961; The Man Charles Dickens, revised edition 1966; Merely Players, 1966; The Personality of Chaucer, 1968; The Personality of Milton, 1970; Ambassadors for Christ, 1972; The Personality of Shakespeare, 1972; Ralph Waldo Emerson, Portrait of a Balanced Soul, 1974; The Films of D W Griffith, with Anthony Slide, 1975; A Pictorial History of New England, 1976; The Letters of James Branch Cabell, Editor, 1974; (Novels, as Julian Forrest) Nine Before Forthering-hay (Mary Queen of Scots), 1966; The Glory of the Lilies (Joan of Arc), 1969; The Novels of Henry James, 1983; The Tales of Henry James, 1984. *Address:* 233 Otis St, W Newton, MA 02165, USA.

WAGER, Robin, b. 5 Nov. 1940, Bristol, England. Publisher. m. Catherine Peach, 20 June 1966, Rugby, 1 son, 1 daughter. *Education:* Fellow, Institute of Chartered Accountants. *Literary Appointments:* Assistant Editor, 1973, Publisher/Managing Director, R.F.W.W. Publications, Cirencester, 1982–; Managing Editor, Haynes Publishing Group, Yeovil, 1980; Director, ibid, 1981. *Contributions to:* Safer Motoring, 1973–; Editor & feature writer, ibid, under new title, VW Motoring, 1982–. *Address:* 30 Linden Close, Prestbury, Cheltenham, Gloucestershire GL52 3DU, England.

WAGMAN, Robert J, b. 11 Nov. 1942, Chicago, Illinois, USA. Journalist. *Education:* AB; MA; JD; St Louis University. *Literary Appointment:* Syndicated Columnist, Newspaper Enterprise Association. *Publications:* (All with Sheldon Engelmayer): Hubert Humphrey: The Man and His Dream, 1978; The Tax Revolt, 1980; Hostage, 1980; Asbestos: The Silent Killer, 1981; Lord's Justice, 1985. *Contributions to:* Various magazines, journals, etc. *Honours:* Thomas J Stokes Award for national environmental writing, 1978. *Memberships:* National Press Club; Overseas Press Club; White House Correspondents Association. *Literary Agent:* Diana Price Agency. *Address:* Suite 610, 1110 Vermont Avenue NW, Washington, DC 20005, USA.

WAGNER, Charles Abraham, b. 10 Mar, 1901, New York City, New York, USA. Journalist; Poet; Historian. *Education:* BA, Columbia College, New York City, New York, 1923; MA, Columbia University, 1925; Nieman Fellow, Harvard University, 1945. *Publications:* Poems of the Soil and Sea, 1923; Nearer the Bone: New Poems, 1929; Prize Poems, Editor, 1929; Harvard Four Centuries and Freedoms, 1950. *Contributions to:* Nation; Saturday Review; Poetry Chicago; Nieman Reports; Commonweal; Poet; India; The Listener; Poetry Review, England; various others. *Honours include:* 1st Awards

for Poetry (3), Poetry Society of America; Authors Club of New York; Harvard Club of New York. *Address:* 106 Morningside Drive, New York City, NY 10027, USA.

WAGSCHAL, Harry Goldwyn, b. 12 Oct. 1939, Trinidad, British West Indies. Teacher. m. Donna Weippert, 1 Aug. 1971, Kingston, Ontario, Canada, 2 sons, 1 daughter. *Education:* BA, Sir George Williams University; MA, McGill University; Class 1 Teachers Diploma, McGill University. *Literary Appointments:* Editor, Renaissance II, 1980; Contributing editor, Humanist-in-Canada, 1982; Member of Publications board, Canadian Humanist Publications, 1983; Board of Directors: Association for Educational Reform, Miami, Florida, 1982; Canadian Association For Future Studies. 1985; Editorial Committee, Futures Canada, 1985. *Publications:* New Society? New Education, 1979; Crisis and Creativity in Modern Education, 1983. *Contributions to:* Over 100 articles and reviews to journals and magazines, North America. *Honours:* Fellowship, Brandeis University, 1962; Arts Fellowship, Canada Council, 1969; Research Grant, Quebec Government, 1972. *Memberships:* Canadian Authors Association. *Literary Agent:* Judy McGregor-Smith. *Address:* 41 de Breslay Avenue, Montreal, Pointe Claire, Province of Quebec, Canada.

WAHLBECK, Hans Jan-Christer, b. 10 July 1948, Vasa, Finland. Psychologist; Family Therapist. m. Liisa Kaarina Ryyppö, 1 Dec. 1978, Helsinki, Finland, 1 son, 2 daughters. *Education:* MA, 1976; Diploma as Family Therapist, 1984. *Publications:* Steg På Hållplatsen (Steps on the Stop), Poetry, 1977; Bussen Stanner Bakom Hörnet (The Bus Holds Around the Corner), Poetry, 1979; Mognadens Opera (The Opera of Maturing), Poetry, 1981; Näckrosor Och Bränt Vatten (Water Lilies and Burned Water), Novel, 1983; Katastrof Efter Katastrof (Catastrophe After Catastrophe), Poetry, 1984. *Honour:* Villa Biaudet Fellowship for 1985–88 of The Finlandsswede Union of Writers. *Address:* Villa Biaudet, Östra Åsvägen 7, SF–07900, Lovisa, Finland.

WAHLUND, Per Erik, b. 24 July 1923, Stockholm, Sweden. Author. m. Ulla Britt, 23 Oct. 1948, Uppsala, 3 sons. *Education:* PhD. *Literary Appointments:* Literary Critic: Upsala Nya Tidning, 1944–50; Expressen, 1947–50; Svenska Dagbladet, 1950–69, 1971–. Manager, Swedish Radio Theatre, 1969–70; Guest Performer, Svenska teatern, Helsinki, Finland, 1968, 72, 75. *Publications:* Vakttjanst, 1942; Kammarmusik, 1944; Luftspegling, 1952; Korsbarstradet, 1954; Ressallskap, 1956; Scenvaxling, 1962; Bordssamtal, 1964; Avsiclesrepliker, 1966; Londonpromenader, 1967; Japansk dagbok, 1968; Ridafall, 1969; Kammarradinnans konterefej, 1970; Rostlagen, 1971; Lekverk, 1972; Sjalvstudier, 1974; Sverigeresan, 1976; Lovfallning, 1978; Frandskaper, 1979; Familjebok, 1980; Landkanning, 1981; Forbindelser, 1984; Melontjuven, 1985. *Honours:* Doctor, Honoris causa, University of Uppsala, 1971; Member, Gastronomical Academy of Sweden, 1979; Honorary Member, Sv Litt sallskapet i Finland, 1980; Knight Commander, Lion Order, Finland, 1985. *Memberships:* Swedish Writers Union; Pen Club. *Address:* Geijersgatan 18 A, 752 26 Uppsala, Sweden.

WAIDSON, Herbert Morgan, b. 20 June 1916, Walsall, Staffordshire, England. Emeritus Professor, German, University College of Swansea. *Education:* MA, Unviersity of Birmingham; DPhil, University of Leipzig, Germany. *Publications include:* Jeremias Gotthelf: An Introduction to the Swiss Novelists, 1953; The Modern German Novel, 1959; The Modern German Novel 1945–65, 1971; Editor, German Short Stories 1945–55, 1957; German Short Stories 1900–45, 1959; German Short Stories 1955–65, 1969; Modern German Stories, 1961; Gotthelf, Die Schwarze Spinne, 1956; Goethe, Egmont, 1960; Böll, Doktor Murkes gesammeltes Schweigen, with G Seidmann, 1963; Editor, Dürrenmatt Writings on Theatre and Drama, 1976, Anthology of Modern Swiss Literature, 1984; Translator: Goethe, Kindred by Choice, 1960; Goethe, Wilhelm Meister, 1978–82; Paquet, Prophecies, 1983.

Contributor to: Modern Language Review; German Life & Letters, etc. *Memberships:* Modern Humanities Research Association; MLA. *Address:* 29 Myrtle Grove, Sketty, Swansea SA2 0SJ, Wales.

WAINWRIGHT, John, b. 25 Feb. 1921, Leeds, England. m. Avis Wrathmell, 7 July 1941, Huddersfield. *Education:* LLB. *Publications include:* Death in a Sleeping City, 1965; The Last Buccaneer, 1971; Death of a Big Man, 1975; Landscape with Violence, 1975; The Bastard, 1976; The Jury People, 1978; Tail-End Charlie, 1978; Brainwash, 1979; Blayde R.I.P., 1982; Cul-de-Sac, 1983; The Forest, 1984; The Ride, 1984. Plus approximately 80 other crime novels, short stories. *Contributions to:* Northern Echo, Police Review. *Membership:* Detection Club. *Literary Agent:* (Publisher), Macmillan London Ltd. *Address:* 67 Albany Road, Ansdell, Lytham St Annes, Lancashire, FY8 4AT, England.

WAISER, Martin, b. 24 Mar. 1927, Wasserburg, Federal German Republic. Writer. *Education:* Theological-Philosophical College, Regensburg; PhD, University Tubingen. *Publications:* Ehen in Philippsburg, 1947; Halbzeit, 1960; Das Einhorn, 1966; Fiction, 1970; Die Gallistl'sche Krankheit, 1972; Der Sturz, 1973; Jenseits de Liebe, 1976; Ein fliehendes Pferd, 1978; Seelenarbeit, 1979; Das Schwanehaus, 1980; Brief on Lord Liszt, 1982; Members Gedanken, 1985; Brandung, 1985. *Honours:* Grp 47 Prize, 1955; Hermann Hesse Prize, 1957; Gerhart Hauptmann, 1962; Schiller Prize, 1965; Georg Buechner Prize, 1981. *Memberships:* German Academy for Language and Literature; Association German Writers; PEN Club; Academy of Arts, Berlin. *Address:* 777 Uberlingen-Nussdorf, Zum Hecht 36, Federal German Republic.

WAKOSKI, Diane, b. 3 Aug. 1937, Whittier, California, USA. Poet. m. Robert J Turney, 14 Feb. 1982, East Lansing, Michigan, USA. *Education:* BA, University of California at Berkeley, 1960. *Literary Appointments:* Writer-in-Residence: California Institute of Technology, 1972; University of Virginia, 1972–73; Wilamette University, 1974; University of California at Irvine, 1974; University of Wisconsin, Madison, 1976; Whitman College, 1976; University of Washington, 1977; University of Hawaii, 1978; Michigan State University, 1976–. *Major Publications:* Coins & Coffins, 1962; Discrepancies & Apparitions, 1966; The George Washington Poems, 1967; Inside the Blood Factory, 1968; The Magellanic Clouds, 1970; The Motorcycle Betrayal Poems, 1971; Smudging, 1972; Trilogy, 1974; Dancing on the Grave of a Son of a Bitch, 1973; Virtuosos Literature for two & four Hands, 1975; Waiting for the King of Spain, 1976; The Man who Shook Hands, 1978; Cap of Darkness, 1980; The Magician's Feastletters, 1982; The Collected Greed: Parts I-XIII, 1984. *Honours:* Guggenheim Grant, 1972; Fulbright Award for Writers, to Yugoslavia, 1984; and others. *Memberships:* PEN; Authors Guild; Poetry Society of America. *Address:* 607 Division, East Lansing, MI 48823, USA.

WALD, Richard C, b. New York City, USA. Broadcasting Executive. m. Edith May Leslie, 7 July 1953, 2 sons, 1 daughter. *Education:* BA, 1952, MA, 1953, Columbia University; BA, Clare College, Cambridge, England. *Literary Appointments include:* Columbia College Correspondent, Religion Editor, Political Reporter; Foreign Correspondent (London and Bonn), New York Herald-Tribune, 1951–66; Executive Vice-President, Whitney Communications Incorporated; Various Executive positions, NBC News, 1973–77; Assistant to Chairman of the Board, Times-Mirror Company, Los Angeles; Senior Vice-President, 1978, ABC News; Chairman of the Board, Columbia Spectator; Board of Directors, Worldwide Television News and Associated Press. *Publications:* Annotator: (with James Bellows), The World of Jimmy Breslin, 1967. *Honours:* Harry J Carman Fellow, Columbia University; Kellett Fellow, Clare College, Cambridge. *Address:* 7 West 66th Street, New York, NY 10023, USA.

WALDMAN, Guido, b. 24 Jan. 1932, Lausanne, Switzerland. Book Publisher. m. Lalage Graham, 15 Oct. 1966, London, England, 2 daughters. *Education:* BA, Brasenose College, Oxford University. *Literary Appointment:* Editor & Director, The Bodley Head Ltd, London. *Publications include:* Editor, Penguin Book of Italian Short Stories, 1969; Ariosto's, Orlando Furioso, new prose translation, 1974; The Late Flowering of Captain Latham, novel, 1979. *Contributions to:* Times Educational Supplement. *Literary Agent:* Richard Scott Simon. *Address:* c/o The Bodley Head Ltd, 30 Bedford Square, London WC1, England.

WALDROP, Rosmarie, b. 24 Aug. 1935, Kitzingen, Germany. Writer. m. Bernard Keith Waldrop, 21 Jan. 1959, Ann Arbor, USA. *Education:* PhD, Comparative Literature, University of Michigan, 1966. *Appointments:* Assistant Professor, Wesleyan University, 1964–70; Visiting Lecturer, English, Brown University, 1977–78, Tufts University, 1979–81; Visiting Associate Professor, Brown University, 1983. *Publications:* Against Language?, 1971; The Aggressive Ways of the Casual Stranger, 1972; The Road Is Everywhere or Stop This Body, 1978; When they have Senses, 1980; Nothing Has Changed, 1981; Translator, Edmond Jabes, The Book of Questions, 7 volumes, 1976, 1977, 1983, 1984. *Contributor to:* Annex; Denver Quarterly; Open Places; Grand Street; Conjunctions; etc. *Honours:* Major Hopwood Award, Poetry, 1963; Howard Fellowship, 1974–75; Columbia University Translation Centre Award, 1978; National Endowment for the Arts Fellowship, 1980. *Membership:* PEN. *Address:* 71 Elmgrove Ave, Providence, RI 02906, USA.

WALES, Robert, b. 12 July 1923, Scotland. Playwright; Short Story Writer; TV Writer; Screenplay Writer; Novelist. m. (1) 1947, Sydney, 2 sons, 3 daughters, (2) 1970, London. *Publications:* The Cell, 1971; Harry, 1985. *Contributions to:* Various publications. *Memberships:* Society of Authors; Chairman, Broadcasting Group, 1977–79. *Literary Agent:* Fraser & Dunlop. *Address:* 2 Thorne Street, Barnes, London SW13 0PR, England.

WALKE, Julia Annette, b. 9 Mar. 1908, Cedar Falls, Iowa, USA. High School Business Education Teacher. m. Delos H Walke, 30 Oct. 1938, Cedar Falls, 1 son, 1 daughter. *Education:* University of Northern Iowa; Upper Iowa University, Fayette. *Publication:* Colored Yarn, poems. *Contributions to:* North American Mentor Anthology of Poems, 1965; Uncommon Fanfare, 1985; Peo Record; The Lutheran Messenger; The Sheldon Iowa Daily; The Clayton County Register; North American Mentor Mangazine. *Honours include:* Honours Award 1964, Poetry Award cum laude 1965, Several Certificates of Merit, Contest Book Award 1972, North American Mentors; Honourable Mention General Division 1973, 1st place Harlan Miller Division 1978, Iowa Poetry Contest. *Memberships:* Iowa Poetry Association; Iowa Poetry Day Association; North American Mentor Association; The Rhymers. *Address:* 908 North Main Street, Elkader, IA 52043, USA.

WALKER, Andrew Norman, b. 19 May 1926, Cornwall, England. BBC Correspondent. m. Avril Dooley, 20 June 1956, Finchley, North London, 2 sons, 2 daughters. *Publications:* The Modern Commonwealth, 1975; The Commonwealth: A New Look, 1978; Voice for the World, 1982. *Contributions to:* Commonwealth magazine, columnist 1975–80, occasional contributor 1980–; Jane's Defence Weekly, 1985. *Memberships:* President, Diplomatic & Commonwealth Writers Association of Britain, 1980–82; Chairman, Training Committee, Commonwealth Journalists Association, 1983–. *Address:* Flat 9, Chartwell Court, Cannon Place, Brighton, Sussex, England.

WALKER, Ardis Manly, b. 9 Apr. 1901. Engineer; Poet; Writer. m. Gayle Mendelssohn. *Education:* Universities of California and Southern California. *Appointments:* Member, Technical Staff, Bell Telephone Laboratories, New York City, USA, 1927–32; Poet and Writer on American Indian Lore and early Californian history;

Lecturer. *Publications:* Wilderness Quest, verse; Quatrains, verse; From Wild Rootage, 1977; Buenavista, 1974; Wild Wonder, 1984; Muse; American Lyric Poetry; Sierra Prologue; Poets on Parade; Poetry Digest; The Winged Word; Mission Sonnets; Francisco Garces; Man and Missionary; Pioneer Padre; The Manly Story; Judas on the Kern; Sierra Sonnets; Last Gunmen; Freeman Junction; Walker Pass; Borax Smith; An Evaluation; Kern River Vignettes; The Rough and the Righteous; High Choice, verse; Vigor, verse; Haiku and Camera; West from Manhattan; The Prospectors, verse. *Address:* PO Box 37, Kernville, CA 93238, USA.

WALKER, Barbara G, b. 2 July 1930, Philadelphia, Pennsylvania, USA. Writer. m. Dr Gordon N Walker, 6 Dec. 1952, Philadelphia, 1 son. *Education:* BA, University of Pennsylvania. *Publications:* A Treasury of Knitting Patterns, 1968; A Second Treasury of Knitting Patterns, 1970; The Craft of Lace Knitting, 1971; The Craft of Cable-Stitch Knitting, 1971; Charted Knitting Designs, 1972; Knitting from the Top, 1972; The Craft of Multicolor Knitting, 1973; Sampler Knitting, 1973; Barbara Walker's Learn-To-Knit Afghan Book, 1974; Mosaic Knitting, 1976; The Woman's Encyclopedia of Myths and Secrets, 1983; The Secrets of the Tarot: Origins, History and Symbolism, 1984; The Crone: Woman of Age, Wisdom and Power, 1985. *Address:* Morristown, New Jersey, USA.

WALKER, David, b. 16 Dec. 1926, Glen Ridge, New Jersey, USA. Writing/Advertising. Divorced, 2 sons, 2 daughters. *Education:* BS Chemical Engineering, Tufts University. *Publications:* Rick Head for Soccer, 1982; Rick Goes to Little League, 1982; Rick Tees Off, 1985. *Contributions to:* Numerous magazines and journals. *Honour:* Polynian Award. *Address:* Box 996, Atlantic Beach, FL 32233, USA.

WALKER, Ida Crane, b. 3 Oct. 1909. Author, Composer, Artist. m. Roy Homer Walker (deceased). *Education:* Psychology and History, Henderson State University, Arkansas, USA, 1953; Piano, Sherwood School of Music, Chicago, Illinois, 1976. *Literary Appointments:* Author, Composer, Artist, 1976-. *Contributions to:* Poets Roundtable of Arkansas Anthology, yearly 1976-85; National Federation of State Poetry Societies Prize Winning Poems, 1980, 1982 and 1983; Pasque Petals, South Dakota State Poetry Society Anthology, 1979 and 1980; Tennessee Voices, 1978 and 1980; Haunted Visions; Spendrift Words; Hot Springs Sentinel Record; Hot Springs News. *Honours include:* Sybil Nash Abrams Award, Arkansas Poets Roundtable, 1979; National Federation of State Poetry Societies, 1980; Annual Article Competition 1979, Poetry Competiton 1980, Writer's Digest; Numerous awards in music, poetry, prose and art, Arkansas Authors', Composer's and Artists Society, 1979-85. *Memberships include:* President 1984-85, Poets Roundtable of Arkansas; Arkansas Authors', Composers and Artists Society; Poet's Study Club, Terre Haute, Indiana; Order of Eastern Star; Fine Arts Center, Hot Springs. *Address:* PO Box 26, Hot Springs, AR 71902, USA.

WALKER, Isabel Ruth, b. 2 Dec. 1953, Grimsby, Humberside, England. Freelance Journalist. m. Andrew Etchells, 25 May 1985. *Education:* BA, Hons. English Literature, Nottingham University. *Literary Appointments:* Launch Editor, Fitness Magazine; Former Medical Correspondent, Sunday Telegraph. *Contributor to:* National newspapers, Women's magazines and specialist medical and fitness publications on the subjects of Health and Fitness. *Honours:* Winner, Observer Mace Schools National Debating Competition, 1971; Special Award from Medical Journalists Association for Medico-Political Reporting, 1979. *Literary Agent:* Murray Pollinger. *Address:* Flat 1, 2 College Cross, London N1 1PP, England.

WALKER, Robert Alander, b. 30 Apr. 1912, Syracuse, New York, USA. Journalist; Editor. m. Jean Browning Clements, 1 Oct. 1937, Chicago, Illinois, 3 sons, 2 daughters. *Education:* BS 1936, MS 1941,

Journalism, Northwestern University. *Literary Appointments:* Editor, His, magazine, 1941-43; Assistant Professor, Journalism, Wheaton College, 1942-47; Editor, Christian Life, 1943-; Seminar Director, Speaker, Lecturer on Christian Writing Techniques, 1945-; Evangelical Literary Overseas Lecturer, Teaching nationals to write for publication, 1959-65; President, Christian Writers Institute, 1945-. *Publications include:* Co-author, Successful Writers & Editors Guidebook; A New Song; The Honeymoon Is Over, with Pat Boone; Finger Lickin' Good, with Colonel Harland Sanders; Leads & Story Openings. *Contributions to:* Numerous Christian periodicals. *Honours:* Award, religious journalism, Oklahoma Baptist University, 1948; Honorary Doctorates, John Brown University & Taylor University. *Address:* 515 E Oak Avenue, Wheaton, IL 60187, USA.

WALKER, Robert Wayne, b. 17 Nov. 1948, Corinth, Mississippi, USA. Writer; Novelist; Instructor. m. Cheryle Ann Ernst, 8 Sep. 1967, Benton Harbor, Michigan, 1 son. *Education:* BS, Education, MS, Graduate School of Education, Northwestern University, Evanston, Illinois. *Publications:* Novels: Sub-Zero, 1979; Daniel Webster Jackson and the Wrongway Railway, 1982; Brain Watch, 1985; Search for the Nile, series, 1986; Abaddon, 1986. Indian Brigades in the Civil War, Non-fiction, 1986-87. Spotty the Goat, Picturebook, 1985. *Address:* Route 2, Old Market Road, Potsdam, NY 13676, USA.

WALKER, Stella Archer, b. Leicester, England. Writer. *Publications:* Horses of Renown, 1954; Long Live the Horse, 1955; In Praise of Horses, In Praise of Kent, In Praise of Spring, 1952-55; The Controversial Horse, with R S Summerhays; Sporting Art England, 1700-1900, 1972; Enamoured of an Ass, 1976. *Contributions to:* Horse and Hound, Sporting Art correspondent, 1962; Editor, Summerhays Horseman's Encyclopedia, 1971; Country Life; Field; Riding; Light Horse; Pony; Art and Antiques; Chronicle of the Horse, USA; British Racehorse; Arab Horse Society News and others. *Address:* Watermill Farm, Rushlake Green, Heathfield, Sussex TN21 5PX, England.

WALKER, Ted, b. 28 Nov. 1934, Lancing, England. Writer. m. Lorna Ruth Benfell, 11 Aug. 1956, Shoreham-by-Sea, England. 2 sons, 2 daughters. *Education:* BA (Hons) St John's College, Cambridge, 1956. *Literary Appointments:* Professor of Creative Writing and English Literature, New England College (British Campus). *Publications:* Fox on a Barn Door, 1965; The Solitaries, 1967; The Night Bathers, 1970; Gloves to the Hangman, 1973; Burning the Ivy, 1978; The Lion's Cavalcade, 1980; The High Path, 1982; You've Never Heard Me Sing, 1985. *Contributions to:* Poems and Short Stories to The New Yorker; Atlantic Monthly; Audubon; Virginia Quaterly; McCall's New York Times; Spectator; Listener; Poetry Review; Observer; New Statesman etc. *Honours:* Eric Gregory Award (poetry) 1964; Cholmondeley Award (poetry) 1966; Alice Hunt Bartlett Award (poetry) 1967; Major Arts Council of Britain Award; Society of Authors Travel Bursary, 1979; J R Ackerly Award, for Literary Autobiography, 1983. *Memberships:* Society of Authors; Fellow, Royal Society of Literature. *Literary Agent:* David Higham Associates, Lower John Street, Golden Square, London. *Address:* Argyll House, The Square, Eastergate, Chichester, Sussex PO20 6UP, England.

WALL, Bengt Verner, b. 23 Jan. 1916, Boden, Sweden. Author. m. Christina Nilson, 2 Dec. 1939, Uppsala, 3 sons, 1 daughter. *Education:* BC, 1940; MA, 1944. *Publications:* De profundis, 1947; Vännen Patrik, 1948; Nakna, 1951; Ensam och kvinna, 1953; Trädgardsmästern och döden, 1956; Dikter, 1959; Desertören, 1963; Dramatik I-III, 1966-70; Rapport fran Zenotien, 1971; Världen är ingen lekplats för barn, 1973; Handbok för en ny elit, 1979; Intermezzo pa Bruno Buozzi, 1979; Dialog med kärleken, 1981; Den troilösa i Assisi, 1982; Sommaren med Maria, 1982; Noveller vid gränsen, 1983; Den svarta svanen, 1984; Här börjar ditt liv, 1984; Ascartes, 1985. *Contributions to:* Numerous magazines & journals. *Honours:* Svenska

Dagladets litteraturpris, 1948; Boklotteriets stora pris, 1966; Albert Bonniers författarfond, 1967; Sveriges Författarfond (about 20 scholarships), 1967–80; Svensk-finska kulturfonden, 1972, 1973; Italienska statens kulturstipendium, 1973, 1974; etc. *Memberships:* Sveriges Författarförbund; Swedish PEN Club; STIM; Sällskapet Stockholms Kyrkoopera (Chairman, 1968–). *Literary Agent:* Tidens förlag, Stockholm. *Address:* Gyllenstierngatan 10, S–115 26 Stockholm, Sweden.

WALL, Isabelle Louise (Woods), b. 26 Oct. 1909, Traphill, North Carolina, USA. Writer; Clergy-woman; Teacher. m. Albert S Wall, 16 Feb. 1929, 1 son, 1 daughter. *Education:* Appalachian State Teacher's College, Boone, North Carolina 1928–33; Draughn's Business College, Winston-Salem, North Carolina, 1944–45; Lee College, Cleveland, Tennessee, 1950–51; Franklin Institute, New York, 1952; High Point College, High Point, North Carolina, 1958–60, *Appointments:* Public School Teacher for several years in Surry, Randolph, Davie Counties, North Carolina; Head of Junior High Department of Miracle Valley, Arizona High School, Teacher of Visual Aids, Bible College in Arizona; Various commerical posts; various missions abroad – Delegate to International Full Gospel Fellowship of Churches, Westminster Hall, London; Preaching mission on behalf of World Conference to Southampton, England. Pastorial work in Greensboro, East Bend, Midway, Winston-Salem, North Carolina WPEC, Galix, Virginia and Rosville, Georgia. *Publications:* Spiritual Steps 2 editions, also published in Africa, India and Mexico; Sandstones of Time. *Contributor to;* Articles and poetry to journals an anthologies including Poetry of the Americas; International Clover Verse of Award Winning Poems; Winston Salem Journals; Suburbanite; Southern Republican; etc. *Honours:* Recipient of various awards for poetry; Presidential Achievement Award. *Memberships:* International Platform Association; UAP; Writer's Press; Founder and President, International Miracle Fellowship of Churches, etc. *Address:* 3231 High Point Road, Winston-Salem, NC 27107, USA.

WALL, Jerry, b. 30 Oct. 1926, Beaumont, Texas, USA. Writer; Photographer. m. Carleen Smith, 22 June 1956, Beaumont, 1 son, 2 daughters. *Education:* BBA, Management. *Contributor to:* Ford Times; Rice Farming Magazine; Soybean South; American Print Journal; Southern Florist & Nurseryman; Shooting Industry; Garden Supply Retailer; Southern Lumberman; Beaumont Guardian; Houston Chronicle; Houston Post; etc. *Memberships:* Associated Business Writers of America; National Writers Club. *Address:* 5075 Raleigh Drive, Beaumont, TX 77706, USA.

WALL, Mervyn, b. 23 Aug. 1908, Dublin, Ireland. Writer. m. Fanny Feehan, 25 Apr. 1950, Dublin, 1 son, 3 daughters. *Education:* BA, National University of Ireland. *Literary Appointments:* Book Reviewer; Radio Critic; Frequent Radio Broadcaster. *Publications:* (Fiction): The Unfortunate Fursey, 1946; The Return of Fursen, 1948; Leaves for the Burying, 1952; No Trophies Raise, 1956; Forty-Foot Gentleman Only, 1962; A Flutter of Wings, 1972; Hermitage, 1979; (Plays): Alarm Among the Clerks, 1937; The Lady in the Twilight, 1941. *Contributor to:* Many journals in Ireland, England, and USA. *Honour:* Best European Novel of the Year, Copenhagen, Denmark, 1952, *Memberships:* Irish Arts Council, Secretary, 1957–75; Irish Academy of Letters, Secretary, 1966–75; President, 1975, 76, 77; Irish Hellenic Society. *Literary Agent:* Bolt and Watson. *Address:* 16 Castlepark Road, Sandycove, Dun Laoghaire, County Dublin, Republic of Ireland.

WALL, Patrick, b. 14 Oct. 1916, Bidston, Chesire, England. Member of Parliament. *Education:* Royal Naval Staff College; Joint Services Staff College. *Publications:* Royal Marine Pocket Book, 1944; The Indian Ocean and the Threat to the West, 1975; Prelude to Delante, 1975; The Southern Oceans and the Security of the Free World, 1977. *Contributions to:* Defence; Navy International; Seapower; Defence and Foreign Affairs, USA; Strategic Review, USA; To The Point, South Africa; Brasseys Defence Yearbook. *Honours:* MC; VRD. *Address:* 8 Westminster Gardens, Marsham Street, London SW1, England.

WALLACE, K K, b. 20 Nov. 1949, Wichita, Kansas, USA. Consultant in Personnel field. *Education:* BS 1971, Masters 1974, Business Administration, University of Kansas. *Publication:* You're The Boss, 1982. *Contributions to:* The Wholesaler; St Louis Business Journal; The Executive Female; Complete Woman; The Federal Managers Quarterly; American Bookseller; Journal of American Medical Technologists; Christian Bookseller and Librarian; Nursing Life; Numerous newspapers. *Honours:* You're The Boss, 3 book club selections, 1983. *Literary Agent:* Joyce Flaherty, 186 Lynda, St Louis, Missouri. *Address:* 5 Nantucket Lane, St Louis, MO 63132, USA.

WALLACE, Ronald, b. 18 Feb. 1945. Professor of English. m. Peggy Wallace. *Education:* BA, College of Wooster, 1967; MA 1968, PhD 1971, University of Michigan. *Literary Appointments include:* Professor of English, Director of Creative Writing, University of Wisconsin, Madison. *Major Publications:* Installing the Bees, 1977; Cucumbers, 1977; The Facts of Life, 1979; Plums, Stones, Kisses & Hooks, 1981; Tunes for Bears to Dance to, 1983; God be with the Clown, 1984; The Owl in the Kitchen, 1985. *Contributor to:* New Yorker; The Nation; Poetry; Paris Review; Poetry Northwest; Prairie Schooner; Chowder Review; The Iowa Review; Yankee; North American Review; California Quarterly; New York Quarterly; Carolina Quarterly; Wisconsin Review; Southwest Review; Northwest Review; Atlantic; and others. *Honours include:* Council for Wisconsin Writers Poetry Book Award, 1977; Wisconsin Arts Board Fellowship, 1979, 1980; Poetry Miscellany Poetry Prize, 1979; Hopwood Award for Poetry, 1970. *Memberships:* Poets & Writers; Association of Writing Programmes. *Address:* Department of English, Helen C White Hall, University of Wisconsin, Madison, WI 53705, USA.

WALLACE-CARTER, Evelyn Clara, b. 26 Oct. 1940, Adelaide, South Australia. Public Relations. m. Bruce Tucker, 12 May 1984, Marino, South Australia. *Education:* Public Relations Certificate, Department of Technical & Further Education, South Australia. *Publications:* A History of the Fishing Industry in South Australia, 1986. *Contributor to:* Editor, Major Writer, SAFIC, Department of Fisheries Magazine, 1974–78; Editor, Equity, Public Service Board Publication, 1979–84. *Honour:* Australia Council Literary Board Special Purpose Grant, 1977. *Address:* 12 Shaftesbury Terrace, Marino, SA 5049, Australia.

WALLACE-CLARKE, George, b. 8 Mar. 1916, Exeter, England. Freelance Journalist; Author. m. Beatrice Murial Ridholls, 27 Jan. 1957, Plymouth. *Education:* College of Estate Management, Reading University; Professional Associate, Royal Institution of Chartered Surveyors; Fellow, Royal Society of Health; Foundation Member, Institute of Horticulture. *Literary Appointments:* Local Columnist, Ideal Home Magazine, 1975–. *Publications:* Your Rights as a Ratepayer, 1974. *Contributions to:* Ideal Home; Country Life; Horse and Hounds; Sunday Telegraph; Field; Guardian; Books and Bookmen; Architects Journal; Administrator; and many others worldwide. *Memberships:* Society of Authors; National Union of Journalists. *Address:* Sanston, Grasmere Road, Chestfield, Whitstable, Kent CT5 3LX, England.

WALLACH, Janet, b. 4 May 1942, New York City, USA. Writer. m. John P. Wallach, 9 June 1974, 2 sons. *Education:* BA, New York University. *Publications:* Working Wardrobe, 1981, 1982; The Right Look, 1985. *Contributor to:* Washington Post Magazine; Stores Magazine. *Literary Agent:* Leona Schecter, Washington DC. *Address:* 2915 Foxhall Road NW, Washington DC, 20016, USA.

WALLACH, Leah, b. 26 Nov. 1947, New York City, USA. Freelance writer. *Education:* BA, New School

College, New School for Social Research. *Literary Appointments:* Professor, Creative Writing, Young Adult Program, New School for Social Research, 1972–76; Guest Artists, Artists-in-the-School Special Project, Williamson, New York, 1980; Seminar leader, Creative Writing Workship, Ethical Culture School, 1981–82. *Contributions to:* Omni; Feeling Great; Washington Post; Metropolitan Home; Oui; Mademoiselle; Hustler; Scanorama; Women's World; TV and Radio Mirror; Cosmopolitan; Intimate; Penthouse; New York Post; New York Law Journal; Lithopinion; Holiday; Granny. *Honours:* Yaddo Fellowship, 1973; MacDowell Colony Fellowship, 1974; Ossabaw Island Project Fellowship, 1976; New York Foundation for the Arts Grant, 1980; Rhode Island Creative Arts Center Fellowship, 1984. *Memberships:* Author's Guild; American Society of Journalists and Authors. *Address:* 153 Ridge Street, New York, NY 10002, USA.

WALLER, Gary Frederic, b. 3 Jan. 1944, Auckland, New Zealand. Professor of English. m. (1) Jennifer Denham, 2 July 1966, Auckland (divorced 1980), (2) Linda Levine, 1982, Waterloo, Ontario, 2 sons. *Education:* BA, MA, Auckland; PhD, Cambridge. *Publications:* The Strong Necessity of Time, 1976; Pamphilia to Amphilanthus, 1977; The Triumph of Death, 1977; Mary Sidney Countess of Pembroke, 1979; Dreaming America, 1979; Impossible Futures Indelible Pasts, 1983; Sir Philip Sidney and the Interpretation of Renaissance Culture, 1984. *Contributions of Poetry to:* Poetry; Denver Quarterly; Carnegie-Mellon Magazine; Spirit; McGill Literary Quarterly; Quarry, etc; Literary articles: Over 100 in Review of English Studies; Assays; Dalhousie Review; Studies in English Literature, etc. *Honour:* Senior Visiting Fellow, Australian National University, 1979. *Address:* Department of English, Carnegie-Mellon University, Pittsburgh, PA 15213, USA.

WALLER, Irene Ellen, b. 8 May 1928, Birmingham, England. Artist; Lecturer. *Education:* National Diploma in Design; Art Teachers Diploma; Fellow, Royal Society of Arts. *Publications include:* Tatting a Contemporary Art Form, 1975; Knots and Metting as Contemporary Art Forms, 1976; The Craft of Weaving, 1976; Textiles Sculpture, 1977; Fine Art Weaving, 1979; Tread, An Art Form, 1973; Design Sources for Fibre Artists, 1979. *Contributions to:* Crafty Magazine; various art and craft publications, UK, USA and Canada; British Broadcasting Corporation television and Independent Television. Work illustrated in various publications. Major works in Birmingham Art Gallery. *Address:* 13 Portland Road, Edgbaston, Birmingham, England.

WALLER (Peter) Louis, b. 10 Feb. 1935, Siedlce, Poland. University Professor of Law. m. Wendy Poyser, 11 Jan 1959, Leeds, England, 2 sons, 1 daughter. *Education:* LLB, Hons, Melbourne University, 1955; BCL, Oxford University, 1958, FASSA, 1977. *Publication:* An Introduction to Law, with Sir David Denham and F K H Maber, 4th edition 1983. *Contributor to:* Numerous articles in legal and non-legal journals. Chapters in books. *Address:* 2 Hartley Avenue, Caulfield, Victoria 3162, Australia.

WALLMANN, Jeffrey M(iner), b. 1941, Seattle, Washington, USA. Novelist. *Education:* BS, Portland State University, 1963. *Major Publications:* Over 100 novels, numerous novelettes, short stories and articles, including: The Spiral Web, 1969; Judas Cross, 1974; Clean Sweep, 1976; Deathtrek (Science Fiction), 1980; The Blood and The Passion, 1980; Brand of the Damned, 1981; The Manipulator, 1982; Return to Canta Lupe, 1983; The Celluloid Kid, 1984; Business Basic for Bunglers, 1984; (as Richard Mountbatten) Spell of the Beast, 1969; (as R Van Dorne) The Desolate Cove, 1970; (as Carole Wilson) Karen & Mother, 1971; (as Bill Saxon) The Terrorists, 1972; Junkyard Rape, 1973; (as Nick Carter) Hour of the Wolf, (award), 1973; Ice Trap Terror (award), 1974; (as Leon DaSilva) (nonfiction) Green Hell, 1976; Angolan Breakout, 1976; (as Scott Sheldon) The Ikon, 1977; (as Amanda Hart Douglass) Jamaica, 1978; (as Gregory St Germain)

Resistance #1, Night & Fog, 1982; Resistance #2, Magyar Massacre, 1983; (as Wesley Ellis) Many of the Lonestar Western Series; (as William Jeffery with Bill Pronsini) Duel at Gold Buttes, 1980; Border Fever, 1982; Day of the Moon, 1983; *Contributor to:* Numerous anthologies and magazines. *Literary Agent:* Richard Curtis. *Address:* c/o Richard Curtis, 164 East 64th Street, New York City, NY 10021, USA.

WALPOLE, Ronald Noel, b. 24 Dec. 1903, Monmouthshire, England. Professor. m. Doris Gray Hoyt, 9 Aug. 1934, Llanvaches, 1 daughter. *Education:* BA, University College, Cardiff, Wales (1st class honours in French); MA, Wales; PhD, University of California, Berkeley, California, USA. *Publications:* Charlemagne and Roland, A Study of Two Middle English Metrical Romances, Roland and Vernagu and Otuel and Roland, 1944; Philip Mouskes and the Pseudo-Turpin Chronicle, 1947; The Old French Johannes Translation of the Pseudo-Turpin Chronicle, A Critical Edition, 1976; An Anonymous Old French Translation of the Pseudo-Turpin Chronicle, A Critical Edition, 1979; Le Turpin dit Le Turpin 1, Edition Critique, 1985. *Contributions to:* Speculum; Romance Philology; Travaux de linguistique et de littérature, Strasbourg University; Romania; Medium Aevum, Neophilologus. *Honours:* Guggenheim Fellow, 1949; Chevalier de la Légion d'Honneur, 1962. *Membership:* American Academy of Arts and Sciences. *Address;* 1680 La Loma, Berkeley, CA 94709, USA.

WALSH, J Michael, b. 17 Aug. 1955, Limestone, Maine, USA. Technical Writer. *Education:* BA, Temple University, Pennsylvania, 1978; MA, Colorado State University, 1983. *Literary Appointments:* Editor, Express Tilt Magazine. *Contributions to:* Poudre Magazine; Choice Magazine; Writ, University of Toronto; Fiction '84; Label; Planet Detroit. *Address:* 108 Chatam Lane, Newark, DE 19713, USA.

WALSH, John Evangelist, b. 27 Dec. 1927, New York City, USA. Editor. *Education:* Iona College, New Rochelle, New York. *Publications:* The Shroud, 1963; Strange Harp, 1967; Poe the Dectective, 1968; The Letters of Francis Thompson, 1969; The Hidden Life of Emily Dickinson, 1971; One Day at Kitty Hawk, 1975; Night on Fire, 1978; Plumes in the Dust, 1980; The Bones of St Peter, 1982. *Honour:* Edgar, for best fact-crime book, Mystery Writers of America, 1968. *Address:* 76 Davies Avenue, Dumont, NJ 07628, USA.

WALSH, John Richard, b. 21 July 1941, Sydney, Australia. Book Publisher. m. Susan Elizabeth Phillips, 18 Aug. 1966, Sydney, 2 daughters. *Education:* BA, MB, BS. *Appointments:* Co-editor, Oz Magazine, 1963–67; Founding Editor, Pol, Magazine, 1968–69; Editor, Publisher, Nation Review, 1971–78; Publisher, Chief Executive, Angus & Robertson Publishing Group, 1972–. *Publications:* No Holts Barred, 1966; On Stage Oz, 1966, play, co-author; Gough Syrup, 1967; Terror Australis, 1967, co-author, 1967; Gorton the Act, 1968. *Contributor to:* Oz; Pol; Nation Review; Sydney Morning Herald, book review; Daedalus. *Memberships:* Past Member, Literature Board of the Australia Council; Australian Society of Authors; President, Australian Book Publishers Association; Australian Paper Conversion, Printing and Publishing Industry Council. *Address:* 4/31 Waterloo Road, North Ryde, NSW 2113, Australia.

WALSH, Steve, b. 18 Oct. 1950, Glendale, California, USA. Publisher; Editor. *Education:* MBA, Pepperdine Univerity; BA, University of Southern California. *Publications:* Spud Malone – Mystery of the Golden Dog, 1984; Beyond Reason, 1985. *Contributor to:* Bakersfield Lifestyle Magazine; Verdict Magazine. *Address:* 123 Truxtun Avenue, Bakersfield, CA 93301, USA.

WALTON, Peter James, b. 14 Feb. 1947, Bloxwich, Staffordshire, England. Writer. *Education:* BA, French, German, Economics, London Extension; MSc, Accounting & Finance, London School of Economics;

FCCA, Certified Accountant. *Publications:* Bank Accounts, A World Guide to Confidentiality (J Wiley: Translation of French book by E Chambord), 1982; Modern French Financial Accounting in the Hospitality Industry, 1983. *Contributions to:* International Accounting & Financial Report, Editor 1979–84; Accountancy; The Accountant. *Address:* 10 Arlington Road, London NW1, England.

WALZER, Pierre-Olivier, b. 4 Jan. 1915, Porrentruy, Switzerland. University Professor. m. Simone Meyer, 2 Sep. 1944, 2 sons. *Education:* Universities of Lausanne, Fribourg and Paris; LittD, Lausanne, 1949; Lectureship, University of Bern, 1955. *Literary Appointments:* Director: Languages Collection, La Baconniere, Neuchtal; Collectoin Poche/Suisse i'Age d'Homme, Lausanne. *Publications:* P J Toulet, l'Oeuvre, l'Ecrivian, 1949; La Poesie de Valery, 1953; Essai sur Stephane Mallarme, 1963; Lautreamont/Nouveau, 1970; Cros/Corbiere, 1970; Anthologie jurassienne, 2 volumes, 1964–65; Les Saints du Jura, 1979; Le XXi Siecle 1898–1920, 1975. *Contributions to:* Revue d'Histoire litteraire de la France; Versants; Intervalles; Journal de Geneva. *Honours:* Prize, French Academy, Academy of Pyrenees Letters; Grand Prix, Republic and Jura Canton; Chevalier, Order of Arts and Letters, France and Legion of Honour, France. *Memberships:* Society of Swiss Writers; PEN Club. *Address:* 17 Seftigenstrasse, 307 Berne, Switzerland.

WANG, Harry (Hsi), b. 23 Apr. 1907, Chekiang, China. Education. m. Chao Lily, 24 Aug. 1932, Shanghai, 1 son, 1 daughter. *Education:* BS, 1930, MS, 1931, University of Shanghai, China; PhD, Zoology, University of Chicago, 1943. *Appointments:* Chief, Histology Division, 1949–57; Associate Professor, Anatomy, 1957–59, Professor, Anatomy, 1959–72, Loyola University Medical School, Chicago, USA; Fulbright Professor, Histology and Embryology, National Taiwan Teachers University, 1969–70; Chair Professor, Biology, Chinese University of Hong Kong, 1970–72. *Publications:* An Outline of Human Embryology, 1968. *Contributor to:* Physiological Zoology; Anatomical Record; American Journal of Physiology; Journal of Experimental Zoology; Journal Animal Science; Food Research; Journal Agriculture and Food Chemistry; American Zoologist; Nature; Canadian Journal Microbiology. *Honour:* Sigma Xi. *Memberships:* Fellow, American Association for the Advancement of Science; American Society of Zoologists; Society for Experimental Biology & medicine; American Association of Anatomists; American Society of Animal Production. *Address:* 101 Alma Street, Apt 606, Palo Alto, CA 94301, USA.

WANG, Qijian. Research Fellow; Writer. *Education:* Major in English, Central China Teachers College, 1965; MA, English and American Literature, Graduate School of the Chinese Academy of Social Sciences. *Literary Appointments:* Assistant Professor of English, Huazhong (Central China) Agricultural College; 1965–78; Assistant Research Fellow, Institute of Foreign Literature, Chinese Academy of Social Sciences, 1981–. *Publications:* Articles and chapters in numerous edited volumes including most recently: An Important Debate in Marxist Aesthetical History in Research in Arts and Literature, 1983; For A Better Understanding: Jean-Paul Sartre's Being and Nothingness, in Developments in Foreign Literature, 1983; Marx's Point of View Upon Alienation and the Reformation of Modern Western Literature, in Contemporary Literary Thought, 1983; Humanism and the Literature of the West Beijing: The Chinese Encyclopedia Publishing House, 1983; Who Was the Real Author of Wuthering Heights, World Books No 2, 1983; Modernism and Alientation in Research in Foreign Literature, 1984; On Surrealism, No 6, 1985, Literary Knowledge; The Role of Ideology in Arts and Literature, No 3 in Criticism in Arts and Literature; The Philosophic Tendency in Modern Western Literature, No 3, in Criticism in Art and Literature. *Memberships:* China Foreign Literature Academic Society; China Academic Society of Marxist Literary Theory; China Association for the Study of

American Literature; American Civilisation Association; American Studies Association. *Address:* Institute of Foreign Literature, The Chinese Academy of Social Sciences, 5 Jianguomen Nei Da Jie, Beijing, China.

WANTLAND, William Charles, b. 14 Apr. 1934, Edmond, Oklahoma, USA. Bishop of the Episcopal, Anglican, Diocese of Eau Claire. *Education:* BA, University of Hawaii, 1957; JD, Oklahoma City University, 1964; D Rel, Geneva Theological College, 1976. *Publications:* Oklahoma Probate Forms (with William Bishop and Dwaine Schmidt), 1971; Foundations of the Faith, 1983; Canon Law in the Episcopal Church, 1984. *Contributions to:* Oklahoma Bar Journal; Anglican Theological Review; St Luke's Theological Journal; The Living Church; The Evangelical Catholic; The Sceptre South Africa; Seek South Africa. *Honours:* Commendation of Merit, Oklahoma Legislature, 1967; Most Outstanding Court in USA, American Bar Association Award, 1972; Supreme Court Award for Law and Order, 1975; Outstanding Alumnus Award, Oklahoma City University, 1980. *Address:* 510 South Farwell, Eau Claire, WI 54701, USA.

WARD, Donald Edward, b. 4 Mar. 1909, Belmont, Surrey, England. Writer. m. Kathleen Philpott, 14 Sep. 1935, Canterbury, 3 sons, 1 daughter. *Publications:* The Dead Snake, 1971; A Few Rooks Circling Trees, 1975; Border Country, 1981; By The Luminous Water, 1984. *Contributions to:* Acumen; Ambit; Acquarius; Blackberry, USA; Arts Council Anthology; Caret; Gallery; Orbit; Orbis; Meridian; New Headland; Limestone; Littack; Poetry Nation; Poetry Review; Pick; Samphire; Sitting Fires; Rialto; Stand; Poet's Voice' Wheels. *Honours:* Arts Council of Great Britain Award for The Dead Snake: First Book of Poems. *Membership:* Poets Workshop, Committee Member, 70's. *Address:* 50 Daleside, Orpington, Kent BR6 6EQ, England.

WARD, Elizabeth (Biff), b. 20 Nov. 1942, Sydney, Australia. Feminist. 1 son, 2 daughters. *Education:* BA, Dip ed. *Literary Appointments:* Editorial Board, Sisters Publishing Co, 1980–845. *Publication:* Father-Daughter Rape Women's Press (UK), 1984, Grove Press (USAO 1985. *Contributions to:* Articles and poems in Mejane; Refractory Girl; ANZ Journal of Criminology. *Memberships:* Various women's writing groups. *Address:* 6 Bennett Street, Hilton SA 5033, Australia.

WARD, John Hood, b. 16 Dec. 1915, Newcastle-upon-Tyne, England. Former Senior Principal, Civil Service. m. Gladys Hilda Thorogood, 27 July 1940, Great Crosby, 1 son, 2 daughters. *Education:* Newcastle Royal Grammar School. *Publications:* A Late Harvest, 1982; The Dark Sea and Other Stories, 1983; A Kind of Likeness, 1985. *Contributor to:* Over 90 short stories, Zoo poems, various commercial and literary magazines, commercial radio and BBC radio. *Honours:* City of Westminster Arts Council Poetry Prize, 1977; Wharfedale Music Festival Open Poetry Prize, 1978; Society of Civil Service Authors Jubilee Open Short Story Prize, 1985. *Membership:* Society of Civil Service Authors. *Address:* 42 Seal Road, Bramhall, Stockport, Cheshire SK7 2JS, England.

WARE, Clyde, b. 22 Dec. 1932, Clarksburg, West Virginia, USA. Writer/Director. 1 daughter. *Publications:* The Innocents, 1969; The Eden Tree, 1972. Motion Pictures: No Drums, No Bugles (Writer/Director); When the Line Goes Through (Writer/Director). Television: Pretty Boy Floyd, Hatfields and McCoys, 300 Miles for Stephanie, (Writer/Director); The Alamo, Coward of the County, Sizzle, Silent Gun, etc. (Writer). *Honours:* Spur Award, Western Writers of America, 1969; Emmy Award, TV Academy, 1973. *Memberships:* Dramatists Guild, New York; Writers Guild of America, LA. *Literary Agent:* William Morris Agency, Beverly Hills, California, USA. *Address:* William Morris Agency, 151 El Camino Drive, Beverly Hills, CA 90212, USA.

WARLAND, Betsy B, b. 27 Dec. 1946, Fort Dodge, Iowa, USA. Writer. *Education:* BA, Luther College,

Decorah, Iowa. *Literary Appointments:* Co-Editor of In the Feminine (The Women and Words proceedings), Longspoon Press, 1985; Poetry Editor and Western Region Editor, Herizons, Winnipeg; Workshop and Readings Coordinator; Co-organizer of Landscape, A Women's Poetry Experience and Anthology, Toronto, 1977; Initiator of the Women's Writing Collective, Toronto, 1975. *Publications:* A Gathering Instinct, 1981; Open Is Broken, 1984. *Contributions to:* Waves; Island; British Columbia Monthly; The Radical Reviewer; Fireweed; Miss Chatelaine Volume 15; Room of One's Own Volume III; The Other Woman; Women: A Journal of Liberation; Branching Out. Anthologies: Women and Words: The Anthology, 1984; Femme Plurielle, 1978; Landscape, 1977. *Honour:* Canada Council Short Term Grant, 1984. *Memberships:* Writers Union of Canada; League of Canadian Poets; Federation of British Columbia Writers; West Coast Women and Words Society. *Address:* Box 65563, Station F, Vancouver, British Columbia, Canada V5N 5K5.

WARNER, Anne R, b. 6 Sep. 1928, Detroit, Michigan, USA. Public Relations Officer. m. Richard C Warner, 15 Oct. 1950, Bellevue, Ohio. *Education:* BA, Heidelberg College, Ohio; Graduate work, Pace University, Columbia University, Kent State University. *Literary Appointment:* Lecturer, Columbia University School of Public Health, 1982–. *Publications include:* Innovations in Community Health Nursing, 1978; Report on 1977 Conference on Health Womanpower, (US Department, Health, Education & Welfare), 1978; Credentialling of Health Manpower & the Public Interest (National Health Council), 1978. *Contributions to:* Compton Yearbook (Encyclopaedia Britannica), annually 1962–75; Americana Annual (Encyclopaedia Americana), annually 1962–74; Journal of Allied Health, 1974–75; Imprint, 1977; Volunteer Leader, 1980; American Journal of Nursing, 1984; etc. *Honour:* Book of the Year, American Journal of Nursing, 1978. *Memberships:* American Medical Writers Association; Women in Communications; Women Executives in Public Relations; Public Relations Society of America (President, New York Chapter 1982–83); American Society for Hospital Public Relations. *Address:* 43 Cambridge Place, Englewood Cliffs, NJ 07632, USA.

WARNER, Kenneth Wilson Jr, b. 22 Dec. 1928, Chicago, Illinois, USA. Editor. m. Deborah Ann Bollo, 28 Dec. 1982, Falls Church, Virginia, 1 son, 2 daughters from previous marriages. *Education:* BSc, Northern Illinois University, 1950. *Literary Appointments:* Assistant, Associate and Regional Editor of various business publications, 1953–60; Freelance Writer, 1960–67; Founder, Editor, Gunfacts Magazine, 1967–70; various editorial positions, National Rifle Association; Founding Editor, American Hunter Magazine; Editor, The American Rifleman; Director of Publications, 1971–79; Editor-in-Chief, 1979–, Gun Digest, Handloaders Digest, Cartridges of the World; Founding Editor, Knives, 1981– *Publications include:* Trade Books: Practical Book of Knives, 1976; Practical Book of Guns, 1978. *Contributions to:* Numerous publications over 30 year period. *Address:* Box 52, Greenville, WV 24945, USA.

WARNER, Marina Sarah. Author. m. (1) William Shawcross, (2) John Dewe Mathews, 1 son. *Publications include:* Joan of Arc, The Image of Female Heroism, 1981; The Skating Party, novel, 1983; The Impossible Day, The Impossible Night, The Impossible Bath, The Impossible Rocket, for infants, 1981–83; The Wobbly Tooth, for children, 1984; Firebird, short story, 1984; Monuments and Maidens, The Allegory of the Female Form, 1985. *Contributions to:* Sunday Times; Connoisseur; Times Literary Supplement; Listener; Vogue; Fiction Magazine. British Broadcasting Corporation. *Memberships:* Society of Authors; Poets, Playwrights, Editors, Essayists and Novelists; Fellow, Royal Society of Literature. *Address:* c/o A D Peters Limited, 10 Buckingham Street, London WC2, England.

WARNER, Philip A W, b. 19 May 1914, Warwickshire, England. Author. 2 sons, 1 daughter.

Education: MA (Cantab). *Publications:* Siege of the Middle Ages, 1968; The Medieval Castle, 1971; The SAS, 1971; The Crimean War, 1972; Distant Battle, 1973; British Battlefields: the South, the Midlands, the North, Scotland and the Borders, 1973; Dervish, 1973; The Soldier, 1975; Stories of Famous Regiments, 1975; The Battle of Loos, 1976; The Fields of War, 1977; The Best of British Pluck, 1976; Panzer, 1977; The Best of Chums, 1978; The Zeebrugge Raid, 1978; Alamein, 1979; Famous Welsh Battles, 1979; The D Day Landings, 1980; Invasion Road, 1981; Auchinleck, 1981; Phantom, 1982; The SBS, 1983; Horrocks, 1984; The British Cavalry, 1984; Kitchener, 1985. *Contributions to:* Reviews for: Daily Telegraph; Spectator; Times Literary Supplement. *Literary Agent:* J Reynolds, Dianne Coles Literary Agency. *Address:* c/o J Reynolds, Dianne Coles Literary Agency, 6 White Lion Walls, Banbury, Oxfordshire, England.

WARREN, James E(dward) Jr, b. 11 Dec. 1908, Atlanta, Georgia, USA. Teacher. *Education:* AB, MAT, Emory University. *Literary Appointment:* Teacher of English, Poet-in-Residence and School Historian, The Lovett School. *Publications:* This Side of Babylon, 1938; Against the Furious Men, 1946; The Teacher of English: His Materials and Opportunities, 1959; Selected Poems, 1967; Collected Poems, 1980; eleven chapbooks, 1964–1982 (poetry); How to Write a Research Paper, 1972; A History of The Lovett School. *Contributions to:* Poems in Atlanta Monthly; Saturday Review of Literature; New York Times; New York Herald Tribune; New York Sun; Sewanee Review; Poetry Review etc. and many little magazines. Articles in education journals. *Honours:* Annual Prize of Poetry Society of America, 1937; Literary Achievement Award, Georgia Writers Association, 1967; Writer of the YEar Award, Atlanta Writers Club, 1968; Governor's Award in Poetry, Georgia Council for the Arts etc. *Memberships:* Poetry Society of America; Georgia Poetry Society; Academy of American Poets. *Address:* 544 Deering Road N W, Atlanta, GA 30309, USA.

WARREN, Michael Joseph, b. 18 Dec. 1935, Massachusetts, USA. Professor of Religious Education. m. Constance Loos, 24 May 1980, Rye, New Hampshire. *Education:* MA, PhD, Catholic University of America. *Publications:* A Future for Youth Catechesis, 1975; Youth Ministry: A Book of Readings, 1977; Resources for Youth Ministry, 1978; Youth and the Future of the Church, 1982; The Sourcebook for Modern Catechetics, 1983. *Contributions to:* About 100 essays to: The Living Light; Religious Education; The Catechist; Concilium; New Catholic World; Liturgy. *Honour:* Award for Best Book in Religious Education Category for, Youth Ministry: A Book of Readings, Catholic Press Associaton, 1977. *Memberships:* Executive Board 1979–81, Association of Professors and Researchers in Religious Education; Executive Board, Board of Directors, Religious Education Association of the US and Canada. *Address:* Department of Theology, St John's University, Jamaica, NY 11439, USA.

WARREN, Robert Penn, b. 24 Apr. 1905, Guthrie, Kentucky, USA. Writer;Professor of English. *Education:* BA, Vanderbilt University, USA, 1925; MA, University of California, Berkeley, 1927; Yale Graduate School, 1927–38; B Litt, Oxford University, UK, 1930. *Literary Appointments include:* Professor, University of Minnesota, 1942–50; Chair of Poetry, Lib of Congress 1944–45; Lecturer, Yale University, 1950; Professor of Playwriting, ibid, 1951–56; Professor of English 1961–73 (retired 1973). *Publications include:* Brother to Dragons, 1953; Promises, 1957; You, Emporers and Others, 1960; Incarnation: Poems 1966–68, 1969; Audubon: A Vision, 1969; Selected Poems, 1923–75, 1976; Now and Then: Poems 1976–78; Being Here: Poems 1978–80; Rumour Verified: Poems 1980–81; New and Selected Poems, 1923–85, 1985. *Contributions to:* Various magazines and journals. *Honours:* Numerous honours include: Pulitzer Prize, 1947, 1958, 1979; Presidential Medal of Freedom, 1980; MacArthur Prize Fellowship, 1981; 17 honorary doctorates; Gold Medal for Poetry, American Institute and Academy of Arts and Letters, 1985. *Memberships:* American Academy of Arts and Letters; American Academy of Arts and Sciences; Chancellor, Academy of American Poets. *Literary Agent:* William Morris, 1350 Avenue of the Americas, New York, NY 10019, USA. *Address:* 2495 Redding Road, Fairfield, CT 06430, USA.

WASER, Georges Friedrich, b. 24 Mar. 1946, Schaffhausen, Switzerland. Writer, Critic. *Education:* University of London. *Contributor to:* Neue Zürcher Zeitung (cultural correspondent and columnist); Various other European publications. *Address:* Via Montefiano 13, 50014 Fiesole, Italy.

WASHINGTON, Ida Harrison, b. 19 Nov. 1924, Port Washington, New York, USA. College Professor. m. Lawrence M Washington, 26 Dec. 1948, 3 sons, 3 daughters. *Education:* AB, Wellesley College, 1946; AM, Middlebury College, 1950; PhD, Columbia University, 1962. *Literary Appointment:* Professor, Southeastern Massachusetts University. *Publications:* Co-author, Carleton's Raid, 1977; Otto Ludwigs komische Oper, Die Köhlerin, 1979; Dorothy Canfield Fisher, A Biography, 1982. *Contributions:* Articles, German & American literature & history: German Quarterly; Germanic Notes; Modern Language Journal; Modern Language Notes; Monatshefte. *Membership:* Executive Secretary 1980–83, Vice President 1984–85, President 1985–86, Northeast Modern Language Association. *Address:* Southeastern Massachusetts University, North Dartmouth, MA 02747, USA.

WASILEWSKI, Andrzej, b. 22 Sep. 1928, Radom, Poland. Writer. m. Joanna Taczynska, 10 Dec. 1977, 1 daughter. *Education:* MA, Polish Philology. *Publications:* Paszport do Wtoch, 1966; Cywilizacja i Literatura, 1969; Jacy Jestesmy, 1979; Wschod Zachod i Polska, 1985. *Contributions to:* Most important Polish literary and cultural magazines, 1949–. *Membership:* Zwiazek Literatow Polskish. *Address:* Bonifraterska 6 mf, Warszawa, Poland.

WASSREMAN, Gary Bruce, b. 1 Dec. 1944. Washington DC, USA. Writer; Consultant. m. Ann Stewart, 5 Apr. 1984, Washington DC, 1 son. *Education:* BS, Georgetown University, 1966; MA, PhD, Columbia University, 1967, 1973. *Literary Appointments:* Publisher & Editor, Mole Magazine, 1982–84. *Publications:* Politics of Decolonization, 1976; The Basics of American Politics, 4th edition, 1985. *Contributions to:* Foreign Policy; Washington Quarterly; Playboy; Washington Post; New York Times; Regardies; New Age Journal; Folio Magazine; Journal of Commonwealth Political Studies; Africa Report; etc. *Address:* National Strategies, 1919 Pennsylvania Avenue NW, Suite 704, Washington DC 20006, USA.

WÄSTBERG, Per Erik, b. 20 Nov. 1933, Stockholm, Sweden. Author. 1 son, 1 daughter. *Education:* BA, Harvard University, USA, 1955; PhD, African Literature, Uppsala University, 1962. *Publications:* 13 fiction, 22 documentary works on Africa and Stockholm including: Boy with Soapbubbles, 1949; Half the Kingdom, 1955; The Heir, 1958; Forbidden Territory, 1960; On the Black List, 1960; Single Journey, poems 1964; The Writer in Modern Africa, 1968; The Water Palace, 1968; The Air Cage, 1969; Summer Islands, 1973; African Assignments, 1976; The Moment of the Narrator, Essays: Indefinite Articles, Prose poetry, 1980; Definite Articles, 1982; A Distant affinity, 1983; The Shadow of the Fire, 1986. *Contributor to:* various journals; Chief Editor, Dagens Nykster, 1976–82. *Honours:* Swedish Academy Award, 1960; Best Novel for the Year Award, 1969; St Erik's Medal, 1969; Honorary Price, City of Stockholm, 1978; Berns Prize, 1975. *Memberships:* President, PEN, Sweden, 1967–78; President, International PEN, 1979–86; European Academy of Arts & Science. *Address:* Stora Skuggan, 115 42 Stockholm, Sweden.

WATEN, Judah Leon, b. 29 July 1911, Odessa, Russia. Novelist, Literary Critic. *Major Publications:* Alien Son, 1952; 10th edition, 1978; Distant Land,

1964, 4th edition, 1978; Shares in Murder, 1957; Time of Conflict, 1961; Season of Youth, 1966; So Far No Further, 1971; Bottle OO, 1973; The Unbending, 1974; Love and Rebellion, 1978; Scenes of Revolutionary Life, 1982. *Contributor to:* Melbourne Age; Sydney Morning Herald; Socialist; Southerly. *Honours:* Order of Australia, 1979; Commonwealth Literary Fellowships, 1952, 1970, 1975. *Memberships:* Former President, Melbourne Chapter, PEN; Former Federal & State President, Victoria Section, Fellowship of Australian Writers. *Address:* 1 Byron Street, Box Hill, 3128 Victoria, Australia.

WATERFIELD, Gordon, b. 24 May 1903, Nackington, Canterbury, Kent, England. Journalist; Author; Broadcaster. *Education:* MA, New College, Oxford University. *Publications:* Biographies: Lucie Duff Gordon, 1937; Layard of Nineveh, 1963; Sultans of Aden, biography of Captain Bettesworth Haines, 1968; Professional Dimplomat, biography of Sir Percy Loraine, 1973. Other Works: What Happened to France, 1940; Morning Will Come, 1943. *Editor:* Murray, 1967. Editor: Richard Burton's First Footsteps in East Africa, 1966; Lady Duff Gordon's Letters from Egypt, 1969. *Honours:* OBE, 1964. *Memberships:* Society of Authors, London; British Broadcasting Corporation, External Services, 1953–63. *Address:* 23 Bartholomew Lane, Saltwood, Hythe, Kent CT21 4BW, England.

WATERHOUSE, Keith Spencer, b. 6 Feb. 1929, Leeds, England. Journalist. m. Stella Bingham, 1984, 2 sons, 1 daughter (previous marriage). *Literary Appointments:* Columnist, Daily Mirror, 1970–. *Publications:* Café Royal (with Guy Deghy), 1956; There Is a Happy Land, 1957; Billy Liar, 1959; Jubb, 1963; The Bucket Shop, 1968; The Passing of the Third Floor Buck, 1974; Billy Liar on the Moon, 1975; Mondays, Thursdays, 1976; Office Life, 1978; Rhubarb, Rhubarb, 1979; Daily Mirror Style, 1980; Maggie Muggins, 1981; In the Mood, 1983; Mrs Pooter's Diary, 1983; Fanny Peculiar, 1983. *Contributions to:* Punch (member of Punch Table, 1969); High Life; Moneycare; etc. *Honours:* Granada Columnist of the Year, 1970; IPC Descriptive Writer of the Year Award, 1970; IPC Columnist of the Year Award, 1973; British Press Awards Columnist of the Year, 1978; Granada Special Quarter Century Award, 1972. *Literary Agent:* David Higham Associates Limited. *Address:* 29 Kenway Road, London SW5, England.

WATERS, John Frederick, b. 27 Oct. 1930, Somerville, Massachusetts, USA. Professional Writer. *Education:* BS, University of Massachusetts, Amherst. *Publications include:* Marine Animal Collectors (Grades 7 and Up), 1969; The Crab From Yesterday (Gades 2-5), 1970; Some Mammals Live in the Sea, 1972; Giant Sea Creatures, 1973; Exploring New England Shores, 1974; The Continental Shelves, 1975; Creatures of Darkness, 1975; Victory Chimes, 1976; Summer Seals, 1978; The Hatchlings, 1979; Crime Labs, 1979; The Sea Farmers, 1970; Green Turtle: My Stories, 1972; Camels; Ships of the Desert, 1974; Hungry Sharks, 1973; A Jellyfish is Not a Fish, 1979; The Mysterious Eel, 1973; The Royal Potwasher, 1972; Seal Harbour, 1973. *Honours:* Junior Literary Guild Book Choice (twice); Outstanding Science Books for Children Awards (six times); *Memberships include:* Past President, Southeastern Massachusetts Creative Writers Club; Organizer, Cape Cod Writers; 12 o'clock Scholars. *Address:* Box 735 Chatham, MA 02633, USA.

WATERTON, Betty Marie, b. 31 Aug. 1923, Oshawa, Ontario, Canada. Writer of Children's Book. m. Claude Waterton, 7 Apr. 1942, Vancouver, British Columbia, Canada, 1 son, 2 daughters. *Publications:* A Salmon for Simon, 1978; Pettranella, 1980; Mustard, 1983; The White House, 1984; Quincy Rumpel, 1984; Orff, 27 Dragons (and a Snarkel!), 1984; The Dog Who Stopped The War, (adaptation and translation), 1985. *Honours:* A Salmon for Simon, Co-winner, Canada Council Award for Children's Literature, 1978 and Runner-up Book of the Year Award, CACL, 1978. *Membership:* Canadian Society of Children's Authors, Illustrators and

Performers; The Writers Union of Canada. *Address:* 10135 Tsaykum Road, RR1 Sidney BC, Canada V8L 3R9.

WATKINS, Floyd C, b. 19 Apr. 1920, Cherokee County, Georgia, USA. Professor; Author; Farmer. m. Anna E Braziel, 14 June 1942, 1 son, 2 daughters. *Education:* BS, Georgia Southern, 1946; AM, Emory University, 1947; PhD, Vanderbilt University, 1952. *Literary Appointments:* Instructor, Emory University, 1949; Professor, 1961; Candler Professor of American Literature, 1980; Visiting Professor, Southeastern University, Oklahoma, Summers, 1961, 70; Visiting Professor, Texas A & M University, 1980. *Publications:* Co-editor, The Literature of the South, 1952; Thomas Wolfe's Characters, 1957; Co-author, Old Times in the Faulkner Country, 1961; The Flesh and the Word, 1971; In Times and Place, 1977; Then and Now: The Personal Past in the Poetry of Robert Penn Warren, 1982; Co-author, Some Poems and Some Talk About Poetry, 1985. *Contributions to:* The Georgia Review; The Southern Review; The South Atlantic Quarterly; The Sewanee Review; The Mississippi Quarterly; The Southern Literary Journal, etc. *Honours:* Thomas Wolfe Memorial Award, 1957; Special Achievement Award, Georgia Writers Association, 1957; Thomas Jefferson Award at Emory University, 1968; Williams Distinguished Teacher of the Year Award, 1979; Scholar Teacher of the Year, Emory University, 1984–85. *Memberships include:* Phi Beta Kappa; Modern Language Association; Society for the Study of Southern Literature, Executive Committee. *Address:* 519 Durand Drive, NE, Atlanta, GA 30307, USA.

WATKINS, James Norman, b. 16 Feb. 1952, USA. Writer. m. Lois Farra, 3 Aug. 1974, Valton, Wisconsin, USA, 1 son, 1 daughter. *Education:* BSc (Theology). *Literary Appointments:* Director, Senior High Curriculum for Aldersgate Curriculum Group. *Major Publications:* Should A Christian (fill in the blank)?, 1985. The World's Worst Date, 1985; Devotional Pursuits, 1986. *Contributor to:* Some 30 publications – over 200 articles. *Honour:* Award of Merit for 'In Touch', Evangelical Press Association. *Membership:* Evangelical Press Association. *Address:* 4201 South Washington Street, Marion, IN 46953, USA.

WATLING, Thomas Francis, b. 22 May 1926, Armagh, Northern Ireland. Project Manager. m. Audrey May Thorne, 9 Sep. 1955, Portsmouth, 1 son, 1 daugter. *Education:* BA, Honours, Open University, *Publications:* Successful Project Management, 1970, 2nd edition, 1979, The Basic Arts of Management, 1972, 2nd edition, 1985, Personal Finance for Managers, 1972, Practical Project Management, 1973, all with W J Taylor; Successful Commodity Futures Trading, with J D Morley, 1974, 2nd edition 1978; Plan for Promotion, 1977. *Contributions to:* Many articles to magazines and journals. *Honour:* MBE, 1962. *Membership:* Society of Authors. *Address:* 16 Pepys Close, Ickenham, Uxbridge, Middlesex UB10 8NL, England.

WATMOUGH, David, b. 17 Aug. 1926, London, England. Writer. *Education:* Majored, Theology, King's College, University of London. *Publications:* A Church Renascent, 1951; Ashes for Easter, 1972; Love & The Waiting Game, 1975; From a Cornish Landscape, 1975; No More into the Garden, 1978; The Connecticut Countess, 1984; Fury, 1984; The Unlikely Pioneer, 1985; The Vancouver Ficton Book, 1985. *Contributor to:* Encounter; Spectator; New York Times Book Review; San Francisco Examiner Magazine; Canadian Literature. *Honours:* Canada Council Bursary, 1967; Canada Council Senior Arts Award, 1978, 1985. *Address;* 3358 West First Avenue, Vancouver, BC, Canada, V6R 1G4.

WATSON, Derek Durant, b. 18 May 1929, Milford, Surrey, England. Agricultural Journalist. Divorced, 1 daughter. *Education:* Farm Institute, Lincolnshire. *Literary Appointments:* Agricultural Journalist, Farmer and Stockbreeder, 1951–59; Agricultural Journalist, Farming Express, 1959–63; Editor, Farmers Club

Journal 1978–. *Contributor to:* Numerous Farming magazines and journals as freelance journalist since 1963. *Honour:* Fellow of the Guild of Agricultural Journalists 1985. *Address:* Ardworth, Portsmouth Road, Milford, Godalming, Surrey GU8 5HP, England.

WATSON, James, b. 8 Nov. 1936, Darwen, Lancashire, England. Lecturer; Writer. *Education:* BA, Nottingham, University; MA, Sussex University. *Publications:* Sign of the Swallow, 1967; The Bull Leapers, 1970; Legion of the White Tiger, 1973; Liberal Studies in Further Education, 1973; The Freedom Tree, 1976; The Loneliness of Long Distance Innovation-General Studies in a College of Further Education, 1980; Talking in Whispers, 1983; A Dictionary of Communication and Media Studies, with Anne Hill, 1983; What is Communication Studies? 1985. Radio Plays: Gilbert Makepeace Lives, 1972; Venus Rising from the Sea, 1976; A Slight Insurrection, 1979. *Address:* Flat B2, Vale Towers, 58 London Road, Tunbridge Wells, Kent, England.

WATSON, Jerine P, b. 29 May 1930, Houston, Texas, USA. Writer; Editor; Ghost Writer; Poet. m. Henry Brock Watson, 27 Sep. 1951, Houston, Texas, USA, (div.), 4 sons. *Education:* BA, Southern Methodist University, Dallas, Texas. *Publications:* Wildfire, novel, 1982; The Maverick, poetry, 1984; Director, Southern California Poet's PEN. Bi-Annual Competition. *Contributions include:* Marine Military Academy Journal; Cavalier; North American Wolf Society; Seacoast Magazine; Poetry column, NWC Newsletter; Several newspaper columns and many poems. *Honours:* 2nd Poetry Competition, National Writers Club, 1979; Honorable mention, Book length Fiction Contest, National Writers Club, 1984; Many honorable mentions and runner-up awards. *Memberships:* Vice President 1983, San Diego Writers and Editors Guild; Writer's Haven Writers; Southern California Novelists; Poet's Press of La Jolla; MENSA International. *Literary Agent:* E J Pace, The Pace Company. *Address:* 2627 Wind River Road, El Cajon, CA 92020, USA.

WATSON, John Steven, b. 20 Mar. 1916, Hebburn-on-Tyne, England. University Vice Chancellor; Historian (Chairman, Scottish Academic Press and ex-Chairman Association of Commonwealth Universities; former member British Library Board). *Education:* BA, Hons, Oxford University. *Publications:* Law and Working of the Constitution 1660–1914 2 vols (with W C Costin) 1952; The Reign of George (Vol XII Oxford History of England) 1960; History of the Salters Co, 1963. *Contributor to:* History Today; Times Educational Supplement; English Historical Review; TV scripts etc. *Honours:* Honorary degrees: De Paul;, St Andrews, North Carolina, Pennsylvania, Simpson Iowa Universities; Silver Medal City of Paris, Gold Medal of American Legion. *Memberships include:* Fellow, Royal Historical Society; FRS, Edinburgh. *Address:* 37 Flask Walk, Hampstead, London NW3, England.

WATSON, Julia, b. 18 Sep. 1943, Bangor, North Wales. Author. m. 1 son, 1 daughter. *Education:* Self Taught Historian; Astrologer, Nutritionist, Professor of Nutrition Diploma. *Literary Appointments:* Consultant to Sphere, For series Golden Sovereigns, 1972–73. *Publications:* Liberty Lovers, 1980, retitled Slave Lady; Royal Slave, 1978; Scarlet Woman, 1979; Salamander, 1981; Venus Rising, 1982; Firebird, 1983; Princess and the Pagan, 1983; The Jewelled Serpent, 1984; Taboo, 1985 (HB), 1986 (PB); Desert Queen, 1986 (HB); Daughter of the Gods, 1986; Flame of the East, 1986; Pasodoble, 1986; A Kiss From Aphrodite, 1986; Castle of the Enchantress, 1986; Last 5 in Astroomance series, 7 more to follow. *Contributions to:* World of Books, article on romantic publishing and reviews; regular column in Romatic Times, reviews for the same. *Honours:* Romantic Times Award, Historical Romance, 1984; Nominated for Romantic Times Award for the most exotic book locale, 1985. *Memberships:* Romantic Novelists' Association; Crime Writers' Association, Society of Authors. *Literary Agent:* June Hall, 19 College Cross, London N1

1PT. *Address:* 4 Lansdowne Grove, Hough Green, Chester, Cheshire, England.

WATSON, Julie Vera Mather, b. 11 Nov. 1943, Banbury, Oxfordshire, England. Magazine Editor. m. John Paul Watson, 21 Sep. 1963, Brampton, Ontario, Canada, 1 son. *Literary Appointments:* Lifestyle Editor, Columnist, Guardian Patriot Newspapers, Charlottetown, Prince Edward Island, 5 years; Maritime Correspondent, Corinthian, 1980–; Editor, Walt Wheeler Publications, Charlottetown, 1983–; Preparer of feature articles for press kits, Prince Edward Island Tourism; Board Member, Prince Edward Island Arts Council. *Publications:* Seafood Cookery of Prince Edward Island, 1983; Favorite Recipes from Old Prince Edward Island Kitchens, 1985; Mussel Mania, 1986. *Contributions to:* The Corinthian; Atlantic Insight; Atlantic Advocate; Moving to and Around the Maritime Provinces; Hands; The Canadian Sportsman; Farm Focus; various others. Newsletters for Canadian Long Distance Riding Association and Prince Edward Island Writers Group. *Memberships:* President, Island Writers Association of Prince Edward Island; Periodical Writers Association of Canada; National Writers of USA. *Address:* Hillcroft, PO Box 1204, Charlottetown, Prince Edward Island, Canada C1A 7M8.

WATTENBARGER, James L, b. 2 May 1922, Cleveland, Tennessee, USA. Professor. m. Marion Swanson, 11 June 1947, Palm Beach, Florida, 3 sons. *Education:* AA, Palm Beach Junior College; BA, MA, EdD, University of Florida. *Publications:* The Community Junior College in Florida's Future, 1955; More Money for More Opportunity, 1974. *Contributions to:* Encyclopaedia of Educational Research, 1983; Articles, various journals. *Honours:* Florida Patriot, Bicentennial Commission; Distinguished Service Award, CAC, AACSC. *Address:* University of Florida, Gainesville, FL 32611, USA.

WATTS, Anthony, b. 3 Feb. 1941, Wimbeldon, Surrey, England. Library Assistant. *Major Publication:* First collection to be published, 1986. *Contributior to:* Numerous journals & anthologies, including: Thames Poetry; New Poetry; Doors; Envoi; Iron; Orbis; New Hope International; Writers Voice; Smoke; Bananas; Weyfarers; New Poetry 6; New Poetry 9 (Arts Council). *Honours:* Lake Aske Memorial Award, 1978; Michael Johnson Memorial Prize, 1979; Avon Foundation Prize, 1982; Frederick Vanson Competition for Ethiopian Famine Relief, 1st Prize (jointly), 1985. *Memberships:* International Poetry Society. *Address:* 19 Green Close, Holford, Bridgwater, Somerset TA5 1SB, England.

WATTS, Anthony John, b. 3 Apr. 1942, Frome, England. Editor, Defence Journal, Navy International. *Publications include:* The Loss of the Scharnhorst, 1970; Pictorial History of the Royal Navy, volume I, 1970, volume II, 1971; The U-Boat Hunters, 1976; Submarines and Submersibles, 1976; Submarines of World War II, 1976; Hovercraft and Hydrofoils, 1978; Battleships, 1978; Cruisers, 1979. *Memberships include:* Associate Member, US Naval Institute; Licentiate, London College of Music. *Address:* Hunters Moon, Hogspudding Lane, Newdigate, Dorking, Surrey RH5 5DS, England.

WATTS, Cuthbert Arthur Harry, b. 6 Jan. 1910, Darlington, England, Medical Practitioner. m. Dr Betty Axton, 24 Apr. 1937, 1 son, 3 daughters. *Education:* MBBS, 1934; D (Obst) RCOG, 1937; MD, Durham, 1949; FRCGP, 1969; FRC Psych, 1980; *Publications:* Psychiatry in General Practice with Betty Watts, 1952; Depressive Disorders in the Community, 1966; The Blue Plague, translated into German, 1973; Defeating Depression, 1980 Translated into Spanish. *Contributions to:* The Mild Endogenous Depression, 1957, BMJ; The Hot Line, 1971; The Art of Medical Practice, 1978 Central African Journal of Medicine; Review of Schizophrenia 1946–83, 1985, Journal of Clinical Psychology (USA). *Honour:* OBE, 1969 for services to general practice in the field of psychiatry.

Literary Agent: A P Watt. *Address:* 2 Tower Gardens, Ashby de la Zouch, Leicestershire, LE6 5GZ, England.

WATTS, Irene Naemi, b. 24 May 1931, Berlin, Federal Republic of Germany. Playwright for young audiences. 1 son, 3 daughters. *Education:* BA, Honours History and English, University College, Cardiff, Wales. *Publications:* Plays and anthologies: A Chain of Words, 1978; Martha's Magic; Tomorrow Will Be Better, A Blizzard Leaves No Footprints; Tales from Tolstoy; Beyond Belief; Seasons of the Witch. *Honour:* Achievement Award for Drama, Province of Alberta, Canada, 1976. *Membership:* Playwrights Canada. *Literary Agent:* Victoria Duncan. *Address:* Neptune Theatre, Halifax, Nova Scotia, Canada.

WAUGH, Hillary, b. New Haven, Connecticut, USA. Writer. m. Shannon O Cork. *Education:* Graduate of Yale University. *Publications:* Some 43 mystery novels including Last Seen Wearing... 1952; The Missing Man, 1964 and most recently Rivergate House, 1980; The Glenna Powers Case, 1981; The Doria Rafe Case, 1981; The Billy Cantrell Case, 1982; The Nerissa Claire Case, 1983; The Veronica Dean Case, 1984; The Priscilla Copperwaite Case, 1985. *Honours:* Last Seen Wearing... names by London Times as one of 100 best mysteries ever written. Grand Master of the Mystery Novel, Swedish Academy of Detention, Stockholm, 1981. *Membership:* Member of Board of Directors, Mystery Writers of America (Past President and Executive Vice President). *Address:* 305 West End Avenue, New York, NY 10023, USA.

WAXMAN, Herbert J, b. 19 Jan. 1913, USA. Certified Public Accountant. m. Vivian Waxman. *Education:* New York University, 1929; City College of New York, 1930–38. *Publications:* Where the Worm Grows Fat, poetry & art, 1975. *Contributions to:* New York Times; Friday (Jewish Exponent); Bitterroot; Dodeca; Speakeasy; New York Quarterly; Brotherhood; etc. *Readings at:* Great Neck Library; Chumleys; Arturo; New York Institute of Technology; REAP; etc. Radio reading, Station WBAU. *Honours include:* Poem, Letter to the Philistines, in list of 25, most proud to publish, New York Quarterly. *Memberships:* Poets & Writers; Treasurer 1978–79, New York Quarterly; Long Island Poetry Collective. *Address:* 29 Margaret Court, Great Neck, NY 11024, USA.

WAY, Brian Francis, b. 12 Sep. 1923, Norbury, England. Children's Theatre; The Arts in Education. m. Perri, 12 Mar. 1969, London, 1 daughter. *Education:* Matriculation, Cambridge, 1939. *Appointments:* Editor, Theatre in Education, England, 1950's. *Publications:* Three Plays for the Open Stage, 1959; Pinocchio, 1954; Development Through Drama, 1967; Audience Participation – Theatre for Young People, 1984; 30 additional plays; Chapter in Drama in Therapy, 1981. *Contributor to:* Creative Drama; Times Educational Supplement; The Stage; Danish Amateur Theatre Journal. *Membership:* Authors and Artists Society, England. *Literary Agent:* Walter H Baker Co, Boston, Canada. *Address:* Associate Artistic Director, Globe Theatre, 1801 Scarth Street, Regina, Saskatchewan, Canada S4P 2G9.

WEATHERS, Philip Joseph, b. 4 Nov. 1908, London, England. Theatre Director; Playwright. *Publications:* Michael Sherwood, The Weary Heart, 1938; Arms and the Woman, 1947; Philip Weathers, Madam Tic-Tac, 1951; Tell-Tale Murder, 1952; Shadow Witness, 1954; Proof of the Poison, 1955; This is My Life, 1957; Murder isn't Cricket, 1959; Once Upon A Crime, 1961; Home or Away? 1963; Sometimes it Strikes, 1968; Three Shots in the Dark, 1970; Ballet Scenario, L'Apres-midi d'un dimanche francais, 1974; Chronicle Play: The Nuns of Syon, 1975. *Memberships:* Sussex Playwrights; Crime Writers Association. *Agent:* Eric Glass. *Address:* Chaterhouse, London EC1M 6AN, England.

WEAVER, Cecelia, b. 7 Oct. 1899. Teacher. *Education:* BS, University of Minnesota, USA; Diploma, Mankato State College, 1936. *Literary Appointments* *include:* Teacher, Minnesota Lake, Mapleton, West St Paul (all Minnesota); St Paul, Minnesota, 1944–69. *Contributor to:* Yearbook of Modern Poetry, 1971; Lyrical Voices, 1979; Minnesota Education Association Journal; Christian Herald; Walker Advocate; The Moccasin; Soundings; St Paul Poets; August Poems. *Honours include:* Life Member, Southern Minnesota Poets' Society, 1983; Honoured by Parnassus Literary Journal for the poem The Last Hunt, chosen by National Subscribers as the best in 1984 editions of the journal and nominated for the Pushcart Prize; 1985. *Memberships include:* St Paul Poets; League of Minnesota Poets; Southern Minnesota Poets Society; (Co-founder and Chairman); Vice-Regent, Southern Minnesota Division, League of Minnesota Poets. *Address:* 504 Winona Street #2, Mankato, MN 56001, USA.

WEAVER, David Hugh, b. 23 Dec. 1946, Hammond, Indiana, USA. Professor of Journalism and Director of Research. m. Carol Gail Shriver, 28 June 1969, Lafayette, Indiana, 1 son, 1 daughter. *Education:* BA 1968, MA 1969, Indiana University; PhD, University of North Carolina, 1974. *Literary Appointments:* Editorial Advisory Board, Journalism Monographs; Editorial Board, Journalism Quarterly; Editorial Board, Newspaper Research Journal; Reader of Manuscripts for Longman Publishers, Indiana University Press, Journal of Communication, Communication Research, Random House Publishers. *Publications:* Newsroom Guide to Polls and Surveys, (with G C Willhott), 1980; Media Agenda-Setting in a Presidential Election, 1981; Videotex Journalism, 1983; The American Journalist. *Contributions to:* Journalism Quarterly; Gazette; Journal of Communication; Public Opinion Quarterly; Communication Research; Newspaper Research Journal; Bulletin of the Institute for Communications Research; Journal of Communication. *Honours:* Kreighbaum Under-40 Award, Association for Education in Journalism and Mass Communication, 1983. *Memberships:* Kappa Tau Alpha; International Communication Association; International Association for Mass Communication Research; American Association for Public Opinion Research; Chair of Research Committee, Head of Theory and Methodology Divison, Association for Education in Journalism and Mass Communication. *Address:* School of Journalism, Ernie Pyle Hall, Indiana University, Bloomington, IN 47405, USA.

WEAVER, II Richard L, b. 5 Dec. 1941, Hanover, New Hampshire. Professor. m. Andrea Willis, 2 sons, 2 daughters. *Education:* BA Speech, 1964, MA Speech and English, 1965, University of Michigan; PhD Speech and American Studies, Indiana University, 1969. *Literary Appointments:* Instructor, 1968–69, Assistant Professor, 1969–74, Speech Communication, University of Massachusetts; Associate Professor, 1974–79, Professor, 1979–, Speech Communication, Bowling Green St University; Director, Basic Speech Communication Course, 1974–; Visiting Professor, Speech, University of Hawaii-Manoa, 1981–82. *Major Publications:* Speech/Communication, 2nd edition (with Saundra Hybels), 1979; Speech/Communication: A Reader, 2nd edition, 1979; Speech/Communication: A Student Manual, 2nd edition, 1979; Research in Speech Communication (with R K Tucker & C Berryman-Fink), 1981; Foundations of Speech Communication: Perspectives of a Discipline, 1982; Speech Communication Skills, 1982; Understanding Public Communication, 1983; Understanding Interpersonal Communication, 3rd edition 1984; Understanding Business Communication, 1985; Understanding Speech Communication Skills, 1985; Readings in Speech Communication, 1985; Communicating Effectively, 1986. *Contributor to:* More than 50 speech, education, history, and psychological journals, including: Adult Leadership; Communication Education; The Teacher Educator; Focus on Learning; New Directions in Teaching Education; The Psychological Record; Journal of Mental Imagery; Innovative Higher Education. *Honours:* BG's Best Teacher, 1979–80. *Memberships:* World Communication Association; International Communication Association; International Society for General Semantics; International Listening Association; International Platform Association; Speech Communication Association; Central States Speech Association of Ohio; Midwest Basic Course Directors Conference. *Address:* 9583 Woodleigh Court, Perrysburg, OH 43551, USA.

WEAVER, Roger K., b. 2 Feb. 1935, Portland, Oregon, USA. English Professor. *Education:* BA, 1957, MFA, 1967, University of Oregon; MA, University of Washington, 1962. *Publications:* The Orange and Other Poems, 1978; Twenty-one Waking Dreams, 1985; Aftermath, with Joseph Bruchac, 1977. *Contributor to:* North American Review; Massachusetts Review; Nimrod; Northwest Review; Hyperion; Friends Journal; Colorado Quarterly; Poet India; College English; etc. *Honours:* 24th American Gerontological Society First Prizewinner, 1978; Poetry in Public Places Award Winner, New York State, 1980. *Memberships:* Association of American Indian Literature; Academy of American Poets. *Address:* 712 N W 13, Corvallis, OR 97330, USA.

WEBB, Colin Thomas, b. 26 Mar. 1939, Portsmouth, England. Journalist. m. Margeret Frances Cheshire, 25 Apr. 1970, Sutton Valence, Kent, 2 sons, 1 daughter. *Literary Appointments:* Editor, Cambridge Evening News, 1974–82; Deputy Editor, The Times, Oct. 1982–. *Address:* The Times, 200 Grays Inn Road, London WC2, England.

WEBB, Pauline Mary, b. 28 June, 1927, Wembley, England. Organiser of Religious Broadcasting BBC External Services, *Education:* BA, London University; AKC, Fellow of King's College; STM, Union Theol Sem, NY, USA. *Publications:* Women of Our Company, (Cargate Press), 1958; Women of Our Time, (Cargate Press), 1960; All God's Children, (Oliphants), 1964; Are We Yet Alive? (Epworth), 1966; Salvation Today, (SCM), 1973; Where Are the Women? (Epworth), 1979; Faith and Faithfulness, (WCC), 1984. *Contributor to:* Methodist Recorder; Expository Times; Guardian; Epworth Review. *Honours:* Doctor of Protestant Theology, Brussels, 1984; Doctor of Sacred Letters, Victoria Toronto, 1985. *Memberships:* Member, Board Methodist Publishing House. *Address:* BBC, PO Box 76, Strand, London WC2, England.

WEBB, Sharon Lynn, b. 29 Feb. 1936, Tampa, Florida, USA. Writer. m. Wilson Bryan Webb, 6 Feb. 1956, 3 daughters. *Education:* English, Florida Southern College, 1953–56; ADN, Miami Dade School of Nursing, 1973. *Publications:* RN, 1981; Earthchild, 1982; Earth Song, 1983; Ram Song, 1984; The Adventures of Terra Tarkington, 1985. *Contributions to:* Over 30 short stories in Isaac Asimov's Science Fiction Magazine; The Magazine of Fantasy and Science Fiction; Shadows 8; Chrysalis; Amazine; 1981 Annual World's Best Science Fiction; etc. *Honour:* Personal and business papers collected by University of Georgia, Athens, Georgia, USA; Phoenix Award, 1985, for Southern Writer of Speculative Fiction. *Memberships:* Authors Guild; Science Fiction Writers of America, Member of Board of Directors. *Literary Agent:* Merilee Heifitz, Writers House Inc. *Address:* Rt 2, Box 2600, Blairsville, GA 30512, USA.

WEBBERLEY, Maxwellyn Grant, b. 24 Sep. 1953, Hobart, Tasmania. Journal Editor. m. Jo Wiles, 2 Apr. 1983, Melbourne, Australia, 1 daughter. *Education:* LLB. *Publications:* The Nicholson Affair, 1981; Law Institute Journal, Editor, volumes 58, 59, 1984, 85. *Contributions to:* Bould's Gazette; Oh! Rourke; McMahon Magazine; numerous others. *Honours:* Paul Tonkin Prize, 1975; Dillon-Birrell Scholarship, 1980. *Memberships:* Promoter: Alsop Fun Club Timeshare Resort; Treasurer, L J J Editors Retirement Fund. *Literary Agent:* Jo Wiles. *Address:* 39 Belmont Avenue, Kew, Melbourne, Victoria, Australia.

WEBER, Hulda, b. 2 June 1909, USA. Fine Arts Artist; Author; Poet. *Education:* National Academy of Design; Scholarship, New School of Social Research, 1940–41.

Publications include: Poetry Anthologies: Blue River Anthology, 1959; Treasures of Parnassus – Best Poems, 1962; Cavalcade of Poetry Anthology – Best Poems, 1963; works included in numerous anthologies in USA and England; Children's Short Stories: Wizzie, stories; Juan and the Prize; Why the Night is Different; others in numerous magazines; Short Stories include: Daughter of Judaea; A Different Kind of Gift; Jacob The Peacemaker; etc. *Contributor to:* Poetry Digest; Flatbush Magazine; The Christian Home Magazine; The American Bard; The Explorer; Wisconsin Poetry Magazine; New York Forward English Section; Durango Herald; over 100 published poems. *Honours include:* All original manuscripts held by New York State Museum and Archives; Works held by Metropolitan Museum, The Jewish Museum and New York Public Library; 2nd Award, American Indian Contest, American Bard Magazine, 1961; Wisconsin Poetry Magazine, 1982; 1st Award, The Explorer, 1961; James Joyce Poetry Award, Poetry Society of America, 1975; International Academy of Poets Award, 1977; World Order Narrative Poets; 2nd Award, new York Poetry Forum, 1984; Life Fellow, The Metropolitan Museum of Art, Daughter of Mark Twain, Executive and Professional Hall of Fame; Hilda Katz ND Classe Nobel Academy Di Scienze Letteri Arti, 1974; Huida Weber ND, Nobel Academy Di Science, Letteri, Arti, 1975; Consigliere, Storia, Letteri Americana, 1978; holder of various life titles and names and letters. *Memberships include:* Poetry Society of America; Authors Guild Incorporated; Authors League of America; International Poetry Society, Founder Member; Founder, Fellow, International Academy of Poets; International Poets Shrine; etc. *Address:* 915 West End Avenue, Apt 5D, New York, NY 10025, USA.

WEBSTER, Brenda, b. 17 Nov. 1936, New York, USA. Writer. m. (1) Richard Webster, 3 Mar. 1961, divorced 1981, 1 son, 2 daughters, (2) Ira Lapidus, 16 Oct. 1983, 1 step-son. *Education:* MA, Columbia University, 1961; PhD, University of California, 1967. *Publications:* Yeats: A Psychoanalytical Study, 1973; Blake's Prophetic Psychology, 1984. *Contributor to:* Yeat's Shadowy Waters, American Imago, 1971; Helene Deutch – A New Look, Signs Journal of Women in Culture and Society, 1985; translations from the Italian in Penguin, Norton and Macmillan Anthologies of Women Poets. *Membership:* Poetry Society of America. *Address:* 2671 Shasta Road, Berkeley, CA 94708, USA.

WEBSTER, Joan Katherine, b. 27 Oct. 1929, Williamstown, Victoria, Australia. Writer. Divorced, 2 daughters. *Education:* State Registered Nursing Sister. *Publications:* Gate Crashed, 1976. *Contributor to:* Poetry: Overland; Melbourne Age; Linq Luna; ABC Weekly; Bohemia; Women's Mirror. Childrens Stories: Victorian School Paper. Journalism: Feature columns for Leader Associated Newspapers, Weekender, Standard Newspapers. Contributions on Australian history, nursing and medical history, investigative and general features, news and humour to various professional newspapers, journals and magazines including: Walkabout; Australian Municipal Journal; Australian Women's Weekly; Australasian Post; Cosmopolitan; Melbourne Herald and Hobart Mercury. Has given various talks on Australian Broadcasting Corporation radio. Songs and sketches for 1st Australian Broadcasting Corporation television revue, 1958 and other satirical revues; writer of 2 episodes of 1st television drama, Emergency, 1959 and 1 episode for Homicide. Writer of 2 complete satirical revuews for stage, 1956, 58, and contributor to others. Writer of lyrics for 4 songs recorded and released by W&G. Writer of lyrics for advertisng. *Honours:* Best News Story of Year, Melbourne Suburban Newspapers, 1971; Honourable mention, 1972, 79, Melbourne Suburban Newspapers. *Memberships include:* Past Secretary, Victorian branch, Australian Writers Guild; Fellowship of Australian Writers; Australian Society of Authors; Australian Journalists Association; Foundation member, Apostrophe Club. *Address:* 17 Boronia Grove, East Doncaster, Victoria 3109, Australia.

WEDDERBURN, Dorothy Enid Cole, b. 18 Sep. 1925, London, England. Principal, Royal Holloway and Bedford New College. *Education:* BA, Cambridge University, England, 1946, MA, 1950. *Appointments include:* Lecturer in Industrial Sociology, Imperial College of Science and Technology, 1965–68, Senior Lecturer, Reader, Professor, 1970–81, Director of Industrial Sociology Unit, Head of Department of Economic and Social Studies, 1976–81; Visiting Professor, Sloan School of Management, Massachussetts, USA, 1969–70; Principal, Bedford College, University of London, 1981–; Principal of Royal Holloway and Bedford New College, 1985–. *Publications include:* The Economic Circumstances of Old People (with J E G Utting), 1962; White Collar Redundancy, 1964; Redundancy and the Railwayman, 1964; The Aged in the Welfare State, 1965 (with P Townsend); Enterprise Planning for Change, 1968; Old Age in Three Industrial Societies (jointly), 1968; Workers' Attitudes and Technology (with R Crompton), 1972; Editor, Poverty Inequality and Class Structure, 1974. *Contributions to:* Journal of Royal Statistical Society; Sociological Review; New Society; Personnel Management. *Honours:* Senior Research Fellow, Imperial College of Science and Technology, 1981; Hon DLitt, Warwick University, 1984; Honorary Fellow, Ealing College of Further Education, 1985. *Address:* Flat 5, 65 Ladbroke Grove, London, W11 2PD, England.

WEHRLI, Peter, b. 30 July 1939, Zurich, Switzerland. Writer; Television Producer. *Education:* University of Zurich; University of Paris (Sorbonne) France. Aukunfte (Arrivals), 1970; Catalogue of the 134 most important observations during a long railway journey, 1974; Katalog von Allem (Catalogue of Everything) 1974; Donnerwetter das bin ja ich! 1975; Zelluloid Paradies, 1978; Tungeltangel (novel) 1982; Alles von Allem, 1985; La Farandula, 1986; Co-editor, This Books is Free of Charge; Co-founder, Thearena (Zurich); Founder: Jugendbuhne Leimbach (Switz) and Wort-Circus Bramarbasani (Switz). *Contributor to:* Magazines and journals in Switzerland, UK, USA, Italy etc. including Orte (Zurich); Manuskripte (Graz); The Poets Encyclopedia (NYC). *Honours:* Recipient of several honours: and awards including Award of the Government of Zurich; Distinguished Service Citation, World Poetry Society. *Memberships:* PEN Swiss Writers Association; Gruppe Olten; International Federation of Journalists; International Association of Art Critics. *Address:* Schifflände 16, 8001, Zurich, Switzerland.

WEIGERT, Andrew J, b. 8 Apr. 1934, New York City, USA. Professor. m. Kathleen Maas, 31 Aug. 1967, 2 daughters. *Education:* BA, 1958, PhL, 1959, Philosophy, MA, Economics, St Louis University, 1960; BTh, Theology, Woodstock College, 1964; PhD, Sociology, University of Minnesota, 1968. *Appointments:* Teacher, Athletic Coach, Colegio San Ignacio, Puerto Rico, 1960–62; Assistant Professor, 1968–72, Associate Professor, 1972–76, Professor 1976–, Sociology, University of Notre Dame; Visiting Professor, Sociology, Yale Divinity School, 1973–74. *Publications:* Family Socialization & Adolescents, 1974, Co-Author: Toward an Interpretive Sociology, co-author, 1978; Sociology of Everyday Life, 1981; Social Psychology, 1983; Life and Society: A Meditation on the Social thought of José Ortega y Gasset, 1983. *Contributor to:* Over 40 articles in professional journals, etc. *Honours:* Bobbs-Merrill Award in Sociology, University of Minnesota, 1967; NIMH Traineeship, Sociology, 1965–67; Co-Recipient, NSF Grant to study, Social Psychological Aspects of Family Interaction & Adolescent Behavior, 1969; West European Studies Programme for Study in Sociology of religion in Germany, 1970; O'Brien Fund for Parentchild Interaction & Adolescent Religiosity, 1969–70; O'Brien Fund for survey of Catholic Charismatic Renewal, 1973–74. *Address:* Dept of Sociology, University of Notre Dame, Notre Dame, IN 46556, USA.

WEINBERG, Sanford Bruce, b. 14 June 1950, USA. Professor. m. Janie Spelton, 20 May 1973, Miami, Florida, 1 son, 1 daughter. *Education:* BA, Dickinson

College; MA, University of North Carolina; Post Doctoral, University of Florida; PhD, University of Michigan. *Publications:* Communication Research, 1977; Messages, 1978; Computerphobia, 1984. *Contributions to:* Jewish Exponent; American Schools and Universities; Radio Host, Computer Talk, CBS-News. *Address:* Drexel University, Philadelphia, PA 19104, USA.

WEINBROT, Howard David, b. 14 May 1936, Brooklyn, New York, USA. Educator. *Education:* BA, Antioch College, Yellow Springs, Ohio, 1958; MA, 1959, PhD, University of Chicago, 1963. *Appointments:* Academic – Yale University, 1963–1966; University of California, Riverside, 1966–1969; University of Wisconsin, Madison, 1969; Professor, Ricardo Quintana, 1984. *Publications:* The Formal Strain: Studies in Augustan Imitation and Satire, 1969; New Aspects of Luxicography, 1972; Augustus Caesar in, Augustan, England: The Decline of a Classical Norm, 1978; Alexander Pope and the Traditions of Formal Verse Satire, 1982. Numerous Contributions to Magazines and journals. *Honours:* BA, First in class, several other university awards; MA Honours; National Endowment for the Humanities Fellowships, 1975–1976; Huntingdon Library – NEH Fellow, 1983; Newberry – British Academy Fellow, 1978; Huntingdon – British Academy Fellow, 1984. *Memberships:* American Society for 18th Century Studies: Editorial Board of journals, ECS, 1977–1980, South Atlantic Review 1982–85; Studies in Eighteenth-Century Culture, 1982–, Johnsonians (New York); Midwest American Society for 18th Century Studies, President, 1979–1980; Johnson Society of the Central Region, Secretary-Treasurer, 1970. *Address:* Department of English, 600 North Park Street, University of Wisconsin, Madison, WI 53706, USA.

WEININGER, Otto, b. Montreal, Quebec, Canada. Clinical Child Psychologist. m. Sylvia R Singer, 22 June 1954, Montreal, 2 daughters. *Education:* MA, PhD, University of Toronto. *Publications:* Play and Education, 1979; Out of the Minds of Babes, 1982; The Clinical Psychology of Melanie Klein, 1984. *Contributions to:* Over 50 articles to journals. *Honour:* Gold Medal Educator of the 1980's, Project Innovation, Chula Vista, California, USA, 1981. *Address:* Department of Applied Psychology, OISE, 252 Bloor Street West, Toronto, M5S 1U6, Canada.

WEINSTEIN, Grace W, b. New York City, New York, USA. Author. m. Stephen D Weinstein, 1 son, 1 daughter. *Education:* BA, Cornell University, Ithaca, New York. *Publications:* Children and Money, 1975, 3rd edition, 1985; A Teacher's World, 1977; Money of Your Own, 1977; People Study People, 1979; Life Plans: Looking Forward to Retirement, 1979 The Lifetime Book of Money Management, 1983. *Contributions to:* Money; McCall's; Glamour; Ladies Home Journal; and various others. Columnist, Good Housekeeping, 1979–. *Honours:* National Media Award, American Psychological Foundation, 1975; Science Writer of the Year, American Dental Association, 1979. *Memberships:* Past Vice President and Past President, American Society of Journalists and Authors; Past President, Council of Writers Organizations; Authors League. *Literary Agent:* Claire M Smith, Harold Ober Associates. *Address:* c/o Harold Ober Associates, 40 East 49th Street, New York City, NY 10017, USA.

WEIR, Joan Sherman, b. 21 Apr. 1928, Calgary, Alberta, Canada. Author; College English Instructor. m. Dr Ormond A Weir, 14 May 1955, Winnipeg, 4 sons. *Education:* BA Honours. *Literary Appointments:* Writer in Residence, Thompson-Nicola Library Systems; Instructor in English, Cariboo College, 1977–. *Publications:* Three Day Challenge, juvenile novel, 1976; Sherman, biography, 1976; The Caledonians, history, 1977; Exile at the Rocking Seven, novel, 1977; Career Girl, juvenile novel, 1979; So, I'm Different, juvenile novel, 1981; Secret at Westwind, mystery, 1982; Walhachin, history, 1984; The Buffalo Stone, juvenile novel, 1986; The Gold Rush Church that Refused to Die, history, 1986; Backdoor to the Klondike, history, 1986.

Contributions to: Discovery; The Friend; Trials; Kamloops Sentinel. *Honour:* Approved by Canada Council for giving readings and conducting creative writing workshops throughout Canada. *Memberships:* Writers Union of Canada; Federation of British Columbia Writers; Canadian Authors Association; CANSCAIP, Childrens writers. *Literary Agent:* J Kellock and Associates, Alberta. *Address:* 463 Greenstone Drive, Kamloops, British Columbia, Canada V2C 1N8.

WEIR, John Edward, b. 25 Apr. 1935, Nelson, New Zealand. Catholic Priest; College Rector. *Education:* Mount St Mary's Seminary, Hawkes Bay; BA, University of Canterbury, 1967; MA, ibid. 1969; PhD, 1974; LTCL, 1979. *Publications include:* Poems: The Sudden Sun, 1963; The Iron Bush, 1970; A Warning Against Water Drinkers, 1974; Criticism: The Poetry of James K Baxter, 1970; R A K Mason, 1977; Editor: The Labyrinth–some uncollected poems by James K Baxter, 1974; Bibliography: A Select Bibliography of New Zealand Poetry 1920–72, 1979. *Contributor to:* Numerous literary magazines and journals. *Honours:* McMillan Brown Prize for Literary Composition, 1962 and 1963. *Membership:* PEN, New Zealand. *Address:* St Patrick's College, Evans Bay Parade, Wellington 3, New Zealand.

WEIS, Jack, b. 1 Oct. 1932, Tampa, Florida, USA. Motion Picture Producer and Director; Writer; Cinematographer. *Education:* BS, Notre Dame University; Master of Psychology, University of Chicago. *Publications:* Screen Plays: Quadroon, 1970; Storyville, 1972; Crypt of Dark Secrets, 1973; Mardi Gras Massacre, 1979; You Never Gave Me Roses, 1981; The Perfect Circle, 1982; Shooting Star of Pegasus, 1985. *Address:* 6771 Marshal Foch, New Orleans, LA 70176, USA.

WEISBERG, Joseph Simpson, b. 7 June 1937, Jersey City, New Jersey, USA. Writer. m. Gloria Kobren, 21 June 1964, 1 son, 1 daughter. *Education:* BA, Jersey City State College; MA, Montclair State College; EdD, Teachers College, Columbia University. *Publications:* From Generation to Generation, 1970; Earth Science, 1971; Oceanography, 1974; Meteorology, 1976, revised 1981; InvestiGuide Series (10 books), 1967–70. *Contributions to:* Numerous journals, etc. including: Journal for Research in Teaching of Science; American Academic Encyclopedia; ACT Test Series. *Address:* Dean, School of Arts and Sciences, Jersey City State College, Jersey City, NJ 07305, USA.

WEISE, Ursula von, b. 21 Apr. 1905, Berlin, German Republic. Writer; Translator. *Education:* Dramatic Arts Studies. *Publications:* Neun in Ascona, 1933; Michel und der Elefant, 1942; Der Todessprung, 1943; Torichtes Madchen, 1944; Die Geschichte von der Sonnenblume, 1962; Andreas und der Delphin; Die Geschichte von den Zoccoli, 1976; Die Levi Strauss Sage–Jeans (with Irmalotte Masson), 1978; [el]sagte main Freundin Ernestine, 1979; Die gestohlene Sonne (with Irmalotte Masson), 1981; Wir sind schlank-Gott sei Dank, 1981; Kleine Fibel fur gutes Deutsche, 1984; Geschichte vom errotenden Papier und andere Marchen, 1985; translations of 350 books from English, French, Swedish and Danish. *Contributions to:* Neue Zurcher Zeitung. *Honours:* Award, Canton of Zurich, 1974; Pro Arte, 1978; City of Zurich, 1985. *Memberships:* PEN Club; Committee, Swiss Writers' Association; Association of German Speaking Translators. *Address:* Beckhammer 25, CH 8057 Zurich, Switzerland.

WEISS, Theodore Russell, b. 16 Dec. 1916, Reading, Pennsylvania, USA. Editor, Professor, Poet. m. Renee Karol Weiss, 6 July 1941, Philadelphia. *Education:* AB, Muhlenberg College, 1938; MA, Columbia University, 1940. *Literary Appointments include:* Instructor – Professor of English, Bard College, 1946–66; Visiting Professor of Poetry, MIT, 1961–62; Poet in Residence, Princeton University, 1966–67; Professor of English and Creative Writing, Princeton University, 1968–; Editor, Princeton University Press Poetry Series, 1974–77. *Publications:* The Catch, poems, 1951; Outlanders, poems, 1960; Gunsight, a long poem, 1962; The

Medium, poems, 1965; The Last Day and The First, poems, 1968; The World Before Us: Poems 1950–70, 1970; The Breath of Clowns and Kings: Shakespeare's Early Comedies and Histories, 1971; Fireweeds, poems, 1976; Views and Spectacles: Selected Shorter Poems, 1979; Recoveries, a long poem, 1982; The Man From Porlock: Engagements, 1944–1981, 1982; A Slow Fuse, poems, 1984. *Contributions to:* Numerous magazines and journals including: Accent: American Poetry Review; The Nation; The New Republic; The Sewanee Review; Parnassus. *Honours include:* Ford Foundation Fellow, 1953–54; Honorary Degree in Letters, Muhlenberg College, 1968; Honorary Degree in letters, Baird College, 1973, Ingram Merrill Foundation Fellow, 1974–75; Brandeis Creative Arts Award in Poetry, 1977; Paton Foundation Professor, Princeton University 1977– . *Memberships:* PEN Club; Board Member, Poetry Society of America. *Address:* 26 Haslet Avenue, Princeton, NJ 08540, USA.

WEISSTEIN, Ulrich, b. 14 Nov. 1925, Breslau, Germany. Professor of German and Comparative Literature. *Education:* BA, J W Goethe University, Frankfurt, 1950; MA, 1953, PhD, 1954, Indiana University, USA. *Publications:* Heinrich Mann: Eine historisch-kritische Einfuhrung in sein dicterishes Werk, 1962; The Grotesque in Art and Literature, translation, 1963; The Essence of Opera, 1964; Max Frisch, 1967; Einfuhrung in die Vergleichende Literaturissenschaft, 1968, English version, 1973; Expressionism as an International Literary Phenomenon, 1973; Vergleichende Literaturwissenschaft: Ein Forschungsbericht 1968–1977, 1981; Links und links gesellt sich nicht: Gesammelte Aufsatze zum Werk Heinrich Manns und Bertolt Brechts, 1985. *Contributions to:* Twayne World Authors series, Editor, German section, 87 volumes; Yearbook of Comparative and General Literature, Editor; German Studies in America, co-editor; Literature and the Other Arts, volume 111; Proceedings of the IXth ICLA Congress, Innsbruck, Austria, co-editor, 1981. *Honours include:* Guggenheim Fellow, 1972–73; Member, Executive Council, Modern Language Association, 1982; 1986; Filbright Area Commission for Austria and West Germany, 1983–85; Member, Bureau, Executive Commission for Austria and West Germany, 1983–85; Member, Bureau, 1979–85, American Secretary, 1985–88, International Comparative Literature Association; Visiting Professor, Wisconsin, Middlebury, Hamburg, Vienna, Stanford and Graz. *Memberships:* Modern Language and International Comparative Literature Association. *Address:* 2204 Queens Way, Bloomington, IN 47401, USA.

WEIXLMANN, Joseph Norman, b. 16 Dec. 1946, Buffalo, New York, USA. Professor of English. m. Sharron Pollack, 14 Mar. 1982, Terre Haute, Indiana. *Education:* AB, Canisius College, 1968; MA 1970, PhD 1973, Kansas State University. *Literary Appointments:* Instructor of English, University of Oklahoma, 1973–74; Assistant Professor of English, Texas Technical University, 1974–76; Assistant Professor of English 1976–79; Associate Professor of English 1979–83, Professor 1983–, Indiana State Univerity. *Publications:* John Barth: A Descriptive Primary and Annotated Secondary Bibliography. 1976; American Short-Fiction Criticism, 1959–1977: A Checklist, 1982; Black American Prose Theory, (co-editor), 1984; Belief Verses Theory in Black American Criticism, (co-editor), 1985. *Contributions to:* Publications including: Black American Literature Forum; Bulletin of Bibliography; American Book Review; Analytical and Enumarative Bibliography; Callaloo; CLA Journal; Critique; Modern Fiction Studies. *Honours:* New York State Regents Scholar, 1964–68; National Defense Education Act Fellow, 1970–72; National Endowment for the Humanities Fellow, 1980–81. *Memberships:* Conference Editors of Learned Journals; Modern Language Association of America; College Language Association; Conference of Small Magazine Editors and Publishers. *Address:* 1601 South Sixth Street, Terre Haute, IN 47802, USA.

WEIZMAN, Ezer, b. 15 June 1924, Tel Aviv, Israel. Minister, Israeli Cabinet. m. Reuma Shwartz, 6 June 1950, 1 son, 1 daughter. *Education:* RAF Staff College. *Literary Appointments:* Israeli Air Force, 1948–66; Former Commanding Officer, I A F Chief General Staff Branch, 1966–69; Minister of Transport, 1969–70; Minister of Defence, 1977–80; Minister, Israeli Cabinet, 1984–85. *Major Publications:* On Eagles Wings, 1975; The Battle for Peace, 1981. *Address:* 2 Hadekel Street, Cesarea, Israel.

WELBURN, Ron, b. 30 Apr. 1944, Berwyn, Pennsylvania, USA. Writer; College Instructor. m. Eileen D Millett, 1971, Brooklyn, New York, 1 son. *Education:* BA, Lincoln University; MA, University of Arizona; PhD, New York University. *Literary Appointments:* Writing Workshop Consultant, Auburn State Prison. Writer-in-Residence: Lincoln University, 1973, 74; Hartley House, New York, New York, 1982; Schenectady County Public Library, New York State Council for the Arts, New York, 1985. *Publications:* Peripheries: Selected Poems 1966–1968, 1972; Brownup, 1977; The Look in the Night Sky, 1978; Heartland, 1981. *Contributions to:* Greenfield Review; Groundswell; Contact II; Southeastern Cherokee Confederacy Incorporated Newsletter; American Poetry Review; Abraxas; Brilliant Corners; Essence; Center; Blind Alleys; High Rock Review; Valhalla; Euterpe; Magic Changes; City University of New York Community Review; Golden Isis; Sunbury; Ash Tree; Black World; Mundus Artium; Works; South and West; Chunga Review and others. *Honours:* Edward S Silvera Poetry Award, Lincoln University, 1967, 68; Fellow, Summa Institute in Jazz Criticism, Smithsonian Instition and Music Critics Association, 1975. *Memberships:* MELUS (Society for the Study of Muti-Ethnic Literature in the USA). *Address:* PO Box 692, Guilderland, NY 12084, USA.

WELCH, Ann Courtenay, b. 20 May 1917, London, England. Writer. *Publications include:* The Woolacombe Bird, 1964; The Story of Gliding, 1965; The New Soaring Pilot, 1970; Pilots Weather, 1973; Gliding, 1976; Hang Glider Pilot, 1977; The Book of Air sports, Accidents Happen, 1978; Soaring Hang Gliders, 1981; Complete Microlight Guide, 1983; Happy to Fly, Autobiography, 1984; Complete Soaring Guide, 1986. *Contributions to:* Flight International, UK; Aeroplane, UK; Editor, FAI Bulletin, Federation Aeronautique International. *Honours:* OBE; Silver Medal, Royal Aero Club; Gold, Lilienthal and Bronze Medals, Federation Aeronautique International. *Memberships:* Fellow: Royal Aeronautical Society; Royal Meterological Society. *Address:* 14 Upper Old Park Lane, Farnham, Surrey, England.

WELCH, Don, b. 3 June 1932. Professor of English. m. Marcia Zorn Welch. *Education:* BA, Kearney State College, Nebraska, USA; MA, University of Northern Colorado, Greeley; PhD, University of Nebraska, Lincoln. *Literary Appointments include:* High School Teacher, Gothenburg, Nebraska, 1958–59; Professor of English, Kearney State College, 1959–. *Publications:* Dead Horse Table, 1975; Handwork, 1978; The Rarer Game, 1980. *Contributions to:* Prairie Schooner; Nimrod; Long Pond Review; Pebble; Poetry Now; Blue Unicorn; Satire Newsletter; Kansas Quarterly; The New Salt Creek Reader; Platte Valley Review; Poet and Critic; Poets On; Cedar Rock; The Runner; Hiram Poetry Review; Pteranodon; North East Cottonwood Review; Milkwood Chronicle; Axletree; Ironwood. Various anthologies including: Anthology of American Verse and Yearbook of Poetry; A Geography of Poets; Travelling America with Today's Poets. *Honours:* Pablo Neruda Prize for Poetry, Nimrod, 1980. *Address:* 611 West 27th, Kearney, NB 68847, USA.

WELCH, Liliane, b. 20 Oct. 1937, Luxembourg. Professor, French Literature. m. Cyril Welch, 1 daughter. *Education:* BA, 1960, MA, 1961, University of Montana; PhD, Penn State University, 1964. *Appointments:* Assistant Professor, French, East Carolina University, 1965–66, Antioch College, 1966–67, Mount Allison University, 1967–71; Associate Professor,

1971–77, Professor, 1977–, French, Mount Allison University. *Publications:* Emergence: Baudelaire, Mallarme, Rimbaud, 1973; Winter Songs, 1977; Address: Rimbaud, Mallarme, Butor, 1979; Syntax of Ferment, 1979; Assailing Beats, 1979; October Winds, 1980; Brush and Trunks, 1981; From the Songs of the Artisans, 1983; Manstorna, 1985; Rest Unbound, 1985. *Contributor to:* More than 50 USA, Canadian, European, Australian Journals; Literary articles in more than 20 International journals. *Memberships:* Writers Union of Canada; Federation of New Brunswick Writers; Federation of Nova Scotia Writers; League of Canadian Poets. *Address:* Box 246, Sackville, NB EOA 3C0, Canada.

WELCH, Mary Scott (Stewart), b. Chicago, Illinois, USA. Writer. *Education:* AB University of Illinois. *Publications:* Esquire books (without by-line): Handbook for Hosts; Esquire Etiquette; The Art of Keeping Fit; Esquire Cook Book. Others: Your First Hundred Meals, 1947; Esquire's Party Book (with R Welch), 1965; What Every Young Man Should Know (with editors of Esquire), 1970; Seventeen's Guide to Travel, 1970; The Family Wilderness Handbook, 1973; Pets (for children); Paris; Networking; The Great New Way for Women to Get Ahead, 1980. *Contributions to:* Redbook; McCall's; Ladies Home Journal; etc. Numerous women's and popular magazines. *Memberships include:* Authors Guild, Authors League; American Society of Journalists & Authors; Civil Liberties Unions, America, New York; Various ecological & feminist organisations. *Literary Agent:* Alexandria Hatcher. *Address:* 30 Waterside Plaza, New York, NY 10010, USA.

WELDON, Fay, b. 22 Sep. 1931, England. Writer. m. Ronald Weldon, 1960, 4 sons. *Education:* MA, Economics and Psychology, University of St Andrews, 1954. *Literary Appointments:* Former Member, Arts Council Literary Panel; Former Member Film and Video Panel, GLA; Chairwoman of the Booker Prize, 1983. *Publications:* Novels: The Fat Woman's Joke, 1968, 1981; Down Among the Women, 1971; Female Friends, 1975; Remember Me, 1976; Little Sisters, 1977 (in US under title, Words of Advice); Praxis, 1978; Puffball, 1980; Watching Me, Watching You, 1981; The President's Child, 1982, 1983; The Life and Loves of a She-Devil, 1984; Letters to Alice (non-fiction), 1984. Writer of numerous Television plays, most recently: Little Mrs Perkins, LWT 1982 (dramatisation of Penelope Mortimer); Balkan Trilogy, BBC 8-part dramatisation of Olivia Manning; Redundant or The Wife's Revenge, BBC 1983 play; Heart of the Country, BBC drama serial; Radio plays: Spider, BBC 1973; Housebreaker, BBC Radio 3, 1973; Mr Fox and Mr First, BBC Radio 3, 1974; The Doctor's Wife, BBC Radio 4 1975; Polaris, BBC 1978; Weekend, BBC Radio 4 1979; All the Bells of Paradise, BBC Radio 4 1979; I Love My Love, BBC Radio 3 1981. Theatre Plays: Words of Advice, 1974; Friends, 1984/85; Moving House, 1976; Mr Director, 1977; Action Replay, 1978; I Love My Love, 1981; Woodworm, 1981; Watching Me, Watching You. *Honours:* SFTA Award for Best Series for Episode 1, Upstairs Downstairs; Writers Guild Award for Best Radio Play for, Spider; Giles Cooper Award for Best Radio Play for, Polaris; Booker Prize Nomination for, Praxis. *Literary Agents:* Giles Gordon, Anthony Sheil Associates, London; and, Phil Kelvin, Goodwin Associates, London. *Address:* c/o Giles Gordon, Anthony Sheil Associates, 43 Doughty Street, London WC1, England.

WELDON, John, b. 26 Feb. 1948, Evanston, Illinois, USA. Author. *Education:* BA, Sociology, California State University, San Diego, 1972; Graduate, Christian Associates Seminary, 1975; MA, Pacific College, Graduate Study, Victoria, Australia, 1982. *Appointments:* Research Editor, Christian Research Institue, El Toro, 1974–76; Research Supervisor, Robert Amram Films Inc, 1976; Instructor, Horizon School of Evangelism, 1978–85. *Publications:* UFO's What on Earth is Happening (retitled, Encounters with UFO's), 1975; The Transcendental Explosion, 1976; Is There

Life After Death, 1977; Close Encounters A Better Explanation, 1978; 1980's The Decade of Shock, 1978; Occult Shock and Psychic Forces: A Biblical View, 1980; Psychic Healing, 1982; The Holistic Healers: A Christian Perspective on New Age Health Care, 1983; Playing with Fire, 1984. *Contributor to:* Various professional journals, magazines and newspapers. *Address:* USA.

WELKER, Robert Louis, b. 26 June 1924. University Professor (retired). *Education:* Austin Peay State University; University of Connecticut; BA, George Peabody College, 1948; MA 1952, PhD 1958, Vanderbilt University. *Literary Appointments:* Teaching Fellow, 1954–55, Instructor, 1955–56, 1957–61, Assistant Professor, 1961–64, Vanderbilt University; Associate Professor, 1964–66, Professor of English, 1966–85, Chairman, Department of English, 1964–70, 1973–81, University of Alabama, Huntsville; Professor Emeritus, 1984–. *Major Publications:* Reality & Myth, 1964; The Sense of Fiction, 1966. *Contributor to:* Poem, Associate Editor, 1967–71, Editor, 1971–85. *Memberships:* President of Huntsville Literary Institute, 1971–72. *Address:* 600 Franklin Street, Huntsville, AL 35801, USA.

WELLARD, James Howard, b. 12 Jan, 1909, London, England. Freelance Writer; Former Journalist & Professor of English. *Education:* BA (honours) London; PhD, Chicago, USA. *Publications include:* A Man and His Journey, 1962; The Great Sahara, 1963; Lost Worlds of Africa, 1966; The Sun Gazers, 1968; Desert Pilgrimage, 1970; Babylon, 1972; The French Foreign Legion, 1974; The Search for Lost Worlds, 1975; Samarkand & Beyond, 1977; The Search for Lost Cities, 1980; In Search of Unknown Britain, 1982. *Contributor to:* Encounter; Times; New Society; Geographical Magazine; Horizon; etc. *Honours:* Rockefeller Fellow, 1933–35; Fulbright Fellowship, 1958–59. *Memberships:* Fellow, Royal Geographical Society; Society of Authors. *Agent:* Curtis Brown, London, New York & Melbourne. *Address:* 14 The Pryors, East Heath Road, London NW3, England.

WELLEK, René, b. 22 Aug. 1903, Vienna, Austria. University Professor. m. Nonna Dolodarenko, 21 May 1968, New haven, 1 son from previous marraige. *Education:* PhD, Charles University, Prague. Honorary degrees: D Litt, Oxford 1960, Harvard 1960, Rome 1961, Maryland 1964, Boston College 1965, Columbia 1968, Michigan 1972, Munich 1972, East Anglia 1975, SUNY 1983, CUNY 1984; D [ge]es Letters, Montreal 1970, Louvain 1970, D H L Lawrence College, 1958. *Literary Appointments:* Sterling Professor of Comparative Literature, Yale University, 1946–72. *Publications:* Immanuel Kant in England, 1931; The Rise of English Literary History, 1941; Theory of Literature, 1948; A History of Modern Criticism, 6 vols 1955, 1965, 1985; Essays on Czech Literature, 1963; Concepts of Criticism, 1963; Confrontations, 1965; Discriminations 1970; Four Critics: Croce, Valéry, Lukács, Ingarden, 1981; The Attack on Literature and Other Essays, 1982. *Contributions to:* Some 200 articles and 100 reviews listed in the bibliographies appended to Concepts of Criticism, Discriminations, The Attack on Literature and in Festschrift edited by P J Strelka, Literary Theory and Criticism, 1984. *Honours:* Guggenheim Fellow, 1961–52, 1956–57, 1966–67; Fulbright Professor 1959–60, 1969; American Council of Learned Societies Distinguished Scholar Award, 1959; Bollingen Foundation Award, 1963; Cross of Merit for Art and Scholarship, First Class, Austrian Government, 1979; Mary Peabody Waite Award, 1976. *Memberships:* International Comparative Literature Association, President 1961–64; American Comparative Literature Association, President 1962–65; Modern Humanities Research Association, President 1974; Czechoslovak Society of Arts and Sciences in America, President 1962–66. *Address;* 45 Fairgrounds Road, Woodbridge, CT 06525, USA.

WELLESLEY-COLE, Robert Benjamin Ageh, b. 11 Mar. 1907, Sierra Leone. Surgeon, m. Ajuma Josephine Wyse, 5 Aug. 1980, London, 2 sons, 2 daughters.

Education: BA, University of Durham, 1926; BA (Honours) Philosophy, University of London, 1928; MB, BS, University of Durham, 1934; MD, 1943, MS, 1944, MA, 1943, University of Durham, 1943; FRCS (England), FRCS (Edinburgh), 1944. *Literary Appointments:* Lecturer (Mathematics), Fourah Bay College, University of Durham, 1927–28; President, West African Society, 1948; Editor, Africana, 1949; Honorary Lecturer in Medicine, University of Sheffield, 1961–62; Director of Clinical Studies, Ministry of Health, Sierra Leone, 1964–74. *Major Publications:* Life According to Nature, 1929; Treatment and Control of Asthma, 1943; Kossoh Town Boy, 1960; Black Swan, 1984. *Contributor to:* Surgery in the Tropics; Problems of Unilateral Amblyopia; The Krios of Sierra Leone and their Language, etc. *Honours:* Gabbett Prize in Philosophy, University of Durham, 1929; Philipson Scholar, Dickinson Scholar, Tullock Scholar, Gibb Scholar, University of Durham. *Memberships:* President, Sierra Leone Writers' Club; Society of Authors (England); PEN International. *Address:* 30 Burghill Road, Sydenham, London SE26 4HN, England.

WELLMAN, Carl Pierce, b. 3 Sep. 1926, Lynn, Massachusetts, USA. Professor of Philosophy, Washington University. *Education:* BA, University of Arizona, 1949; MA 1951, PhD 1954, Harvard University; University of Cambridge, England. 1951–52. *Publications:* The Language of Ethics, 1961; Challenge and Response, 1971; Morals and Ethics, 1975; Welfare Rights, 1982; A Theory of Rights, 1985. *Contributions to:* Journal of Philosophy; Ethics; American Philosophical Quarterly; Journal of Value Inquiry. *Honours:* Sheldon Travelling Fellowship, 1951–52; Uhrig Distinguished Teaching Award, 1968; Senior Fellow, National Endowment for the Humanities, 1972–73; Fellow, National Humanities Center, 1982–83. *Memberships:* American Philosophical Association; International Association for the Philosophy of Law and Social Philosophy; Phi Beta Kappa. *Address:* 6334 South Rosebury, 2W, Saint Louis, MO 63105, USA.

WELLS, George Albert, b. 22 May, 1926, London, England. University Professor of German. *Education:* BA, 1947, MA, 1950, London University, England; PhD, 1954, BSc, Geology, 1963. *Publications:* Herder and After, 1959; The Plays of Grillparzer, 1969; The Jesus of the Early Christians, 1971; Did Jesus Exist?, 1975; Goethe and the Development of Science, 1750–1900, 1978; The Historical Evidence for Jesus, 1982. *Contributions to:* British Journal for Eighteenth-Century Studies; German Life and Letters; Bebbel Jahrbuch; Journal of English and Germanic Philology; Journal of the History of Ideas; Lessing Year Book; Modern Languages; Modern Language Review; New German Studies; New Humanist; Oxford German Studies; Publications of the English Goethe Society; Quinquereme; Studies on Voltaire and the 18th Century; Trivium; Wirkendes Wort. *Memberships:* Chairman, Rationalist Press Association; Council of English Goethe Society. *Address:* 35 St Stephen's Avenue, St Albans, Hertfordshire, AL3 4AA, England.

WELLS, Helen, b. 29 Mar. 1910, Danville, Illinois, USA, Deceased 10 Feb. 1986. Writer. m. 7 June 1984, New York. *Education:* BS, Honours, Philosophy, New York University, 1934. *Publications:* (for Young Readers), Cherry Ames Nurse Mysteries, series, 1942–67; Vicki Barr Flight Stewardess Mysteries, series, 1943–67; Polly French Stories, 1952, 1953, 1954; Barnum, Showman of America, 1956; Adam Gimbel, A Pioneer Trader, 1957; The Girl in the White Coat, 1958; A Flair for People, 1959; A City for Jean, 1959; Introducing Patti Lewis, 1960; Doctor Betty, 1966; Murder in Mother Goose?, 1982; Occupation, Murder, 1984. *Contributor to:* Numerous magazines and journals; Stories in, Annual of Mystery Writers of America. *Memberships:* National Arts Club; Authors' League of America; National Writers Union; Mystery Writers of America, Board of Directors, 1970–73, 1984–, Secretary, 1972, 1974, Membership Chairman, 1985–. *Address:* 345 East 57th Street, New York, NY 10022, USA.

WEMPLE, Suzanne Fonay, b. 1 Aug. 1927, Veszrem, Hungary, Historian. m. George Barr Wemple, 17 June 1957, New York, NY, USA, 2 sons, 1 daughter. *Education:* BA, University of California, Berkeley, California, USA, 1952; Master of Library Science 1955, PhD History 1967, Columbia University. *Literary Appointments:* Reference Department, Columbia University Libraries, 1955–58; Lecturer, Department of Social Sciences, Teacher's College, Columbia University, 1964–68; Assistant Professor 1968–72, Associate Professor 1972–79, Professor of History 1979–, Columbia University. *Publications:* Atto of Vercelli, Church, State and Christian Society in Tenth Century Italy, 1979; Women in Frankish Society: Marriage and Cloister, 500-900, 1981; Women in the Medieval World, (editor with Julius Kirschner), 1985. *Contributions to:* Becoming Visible: History of European Women, 1976; Cistercian Studies; Trends; Speculum; American Historical Review. *Honours:* Berkshire Historical Prize, 1981; Fellowship 1974–75, Group Research 1982–84, National Endowment for the Humanities; Fulbright Grant, 1982. *Address:* 501 East 87th Street, New York, NY 10128, USA.

WENDORF, Patricia Beatrice, b. 24 May 1928, Yeovil, Somerset, England. Author. m. Erich Karl Bernhardt Wendorf, 16 Jan. 1948, Melton Mowbray, 2 sons. *Major publications:* Peacefully in Berlin, 1983; Leo Days, 1984; Larksleve, 1985. *Honour:* Peacefully in Berlin, was runner-up for David Higham Prize for Fiction, 1983. *Literary Agent:* A M Heath & Co Ltd, London. *Address:* 7 Meadow Lane, Loughborough, Leicestershire, England.

WENDT, Albert, b. 27 Oct. 1939, Apia, Western Samoa. University Professor. *Education:* MA, University of Victoria, Wellington, New Zealand. *Literary Appointments:* Professor of Pacific Literature, University of the South Pacific, Suva, Fiji, 1982–. *Publications:* Sons For The Return Home, novel, 1973; Flying Fox in a Freedom Tree, short stories, 1974; Inside Us the Dead, Poems 1961–74, poems, 1976; Pouliuli, novel, 1977; Leaves of the Banyan Tree, novel, 1979; Shaman of Visions, poems, 1984; Birth and Death of the Miracle Man, short stories, 1986. *Contributions to:* Landfall, New Zealand; Islands, New Zealand; The Listener, New Zealand; National Daily of India; Mana, Fiji; UNESCO Courier; Australian Bulletin. *Literary Agent:* Curtis Brown (Australia) Limited. *Address:* Department of Literature and Language, University of the South Pacific, PO Box 1168, Suva, Fiji.

WENDT, Ingrid, b. 19 Sep. 1944, Aurora, Illinois, USA. Poet; Creative Writing Teacher. m. Ralph Salisbury, 23 Apr. 1969, 1 daughter. *Education:* BA, Cornell College, Iowa, 1966; MFA, University of Oregon, Eugene, 1968. *Publications:* Moving the House (poems) (BOA Eds), 1980; In Her Own Image; Women Working in the Arts (anthology), co-editor with Elaine Hedges, 1980; Starting with Little Things: A Guide to Writing Poetry in the Classroom, 1983. *Contrubtior to:* (Anthologies): Intro 1, 1968; No More Masks, 1973; (literary journals): West Coast Review: North West Review; Poetry Now; Greenfield Review; North American Review; Calyx; Feminist Studies; Poetry; Poetry Northwest; California Quarterly, etc. *Honours:* Neuberger Poetry Award, 1968; D H Lawrence Fellowship, 1982. *Memberships:* Poetry Society of America; Lane Regional Arts Council, Eugene, Oregon; Delta Chapter, Phi Beta Kappa, 1966. *Adress:* 2377 Charnelton, Eugene, OR 97405, USA.

WENDT, JoAnn, b. 7 May 1935, Oshkosh, Wisconsin, USA. Writer. m. Phillip J Wendt, 11 June 1955, Oshkosh, 2 sons. *Education:* BA, University of Maryland, 1964; MSc, Guidance, University of Wisconsin, Oshkosh, 1968. *Publications:* Beyond Surrender, 1982; Beyond the Dawn, 1983. *Contributor to:* Times Magazine; Air Force, Navy & Army Times Newspapers; Milwaukee Journal; Home Life; Ladycom; Catholic Digest; Christian Herald; etc. *Honours:* Catherine L O'Brien Award, for outstanding achievement in women's interest reporting, 1975. *Literary Agent:* Arthur

P Schwartz. *Address:* 1124 Amur Creek Court, San Jose, CA 95120, USA.

WENGER, Clara Hurt, b. 18 May 1909, Charlotte County, Virginia, USA. Teacher; Secretary and Treasurer, Screen Crafts, family owned silk-screen process printing company. *Education:* BS, Longwood College, Farmville, Virginia, 1930; University of Richmond, Virginia; Commonwealth University, Richmond. *Appointments include:* Various teaching positions 1928–46; Teacher, English and Latin, Manchester and Midlothian, Chesterfield County, Virginia, 1949–69; Secretary and Treasurer, Screen Crafts, Richmond, 1969–79. *Publications:* Hyacinths and Heather, 1973; Follow the Lark, collection of poetry, 1982. *Contributions to:* the Lyric; Prize Poems; The Poe Messenger; Richmond Times-Dispatch; Richmond News Leader; The Virginian; Rotunda; Torch of Beta Sigma Phi; Torchbearer; Various anthologies including, The American Anthology of New York Poetry Forum, 1976. *Honours include:* Prizes and Honours from various Poetry Societies. *Memberships include:* Treasurer 1980–83, Chairman of Achievements Committee 1983–85, Virginia Writers Club; Contest Committee, 1973–74, The Poetry Society of Virginia; Penn Poetry Society; New York Poetry Forum; Academy of American Poets; National Federation of State Poetry Societies. *Address:* 8710 Arran Road, Richmond, VA 23235, USA.

WERNER, Jayne Susan, b. 10 Oct. 1944, USA. Research Associate, Columbia University. m. Charles Freeman, 1969, USA, 1 son. *Education:* PhD, Cornell University, 1966. *Publications include:* Books & Monographs: Imperialism & Peasant Politics in Vietnam, in press; Peasant Politics & Religious Sectarianism: Peasants & Priests in the Cao Dai in Vietnam, 1981; Tradition & Revolution in Vietnam, edited with David G Marr, 1974. *Chapters in:* Vietnamese Communism in Comparative Perspective, ed. William Turley, 1980; US Foreign Policy in Asia: An Appraisal, ed. Yung-hwan Jo, 1978. *Contributions to:* Bulletin of Concerned Asian Scholars; Studies in Comparative Communism; Commonweal; Bulletin of Atomic Scientists. Various conference papers. *Honours:* Grant, Social Science Research Council, 1983–84; Phi Beta Kappa; NDEA Title IV Fellowship, 1966–70; Honorary Fulbright Scholarship; London-Cornell Doctoral Research Fellowship. *Address:* Southern Asian Institute, 1132 International Affairs Building, Columbia University, New York, NY 10027, USA.

WERTHMULLER, Hans, b. 23 June 1912, Burgdorf, Berne, Switzerland. Author. m. Heidi Wolf, 5 May 1945, 2 sons, 1 daughter. *Education:* Studied German philology. *Publications:* Der Weltprozess und die Farben, essay, 1950; Erleuchtete Feusterzeile, poems, 1962; Jahr des Augenblioks, poems, 1965; Der Rolladen, poems, 1972; 1000 Jahre Literatur in Basel, history of literature, 1980; Schattenwurfe, poems, 1985. *Honours:* Berner Literaturpris, 1963; Ehrengabe Schweizer Schillerstifung, 1971; Ehrengabe Stifung Pro Arte, 1973; Basler Kunstpreis, 1982. *Membership:* Schweizerischer Schriftsteller Verband. *Address:* Mischelistrasse 67, CH–4153 Reinach, Switzerland.

WESKER, Arnold, b. 24 May 1932, London, England. Playwright; Director. m. Doreen Cecilie Bicker, 14 Nov. 1958, London, 2 sons, 1 daughter. *Publications:* Chicken Soup with Barley, 1959; Roots, 1959; I'm Talking About Jerusalem, 1960; The Wesker Trilogy, 1960; The Kitchen, 1961; Chips With Everything, 1962; The Four Seasons, 1966; Their Very Own and Golden City, 1966; Fears of Fragmentation, 1970; Friends, 1970I; Six Sundays in January, 1971; The Old Ones, 1973; Love Letters on Blue Paper, 1974; Say Goodbye You May Never See Them Again, (with John Allin), 1974; The Journalists, 1975; Journey not Journalism, 1977; The Weddings Feast, 1977 and 1980; The Merchant, 1978; Said The Old Man To The Young Man, 1978; The Journalist, 1979; Caritas, 1981; Distinctions, 1985; Bluey, 1985; Annie Wobbler/Yardsale/Four Portraits (Wesker's One Woman Plays), 1986. *Honours:* Most Promising Playwright, Evening Standard Drama

Award, 1959; 1st Prize, Encylopedia Britannia Award, 1960; 3rd Prize, Encyclopedia Britannica Award, 1961; Gold Medal, prize of critics and spectators, Madrid, Spain, 1973 and 1979. *Membership:* Fellow, Royal Society of Literature. *Literary Agent:* Nathan Joseph, 10 Clorane Gardens, London NW3 7PR. *Address:* 27 Bishops Road, London N6 4HR, England.

WESSELY, Othmar, b. 31 Oct. 1922, Linz, Upper Austria. Professor of Musicology. m. Helen Kropik, 19 Sep. 1951, Vienna. *Education:* PhD, University of Vienna, 1947. *Publications:* Musik in Oberoesterreich, 1951; Arnold von Bruck, Samtliche Motetten, 1961; Die grossen Darstellungen der Musikgeschichte in Barock und Aufklaerung, 1964–; Musik, 1973; Fruehmeister des stile nuovo in Oesterreich, 1973; Johann Joseph Fux: La donna forte nella madre de'sette Maccabei, 1973. *Contributions to:* Over 250 articles on musicology and history. *Honours:* Honorary Member, Johann Joseph Fux-Gesellschaft 1978; Member, Austrian Academy of Sciences, 1982. *Address:* Waehringer Strasse 55, A–1090 Vienna, Austria.

WESSMAN, Erkki Olavi, b. 27 June 1931, Ulvila, Finland. Staff Editor, Hymy Magazine. m. Tuija Violle, 28 Aug. 1965, Pori, Finland, 1 son, 2 daughters. *Appointments:* Editor of newspaper Satakunnan Tyo, 1959–65; Freelance journalist, 1965–73; WSOY, 1965–68; Editor, Hymy Magazine, 1973 to present; Lehtimiehet Yhtyma, 1973 to present. *Publications:* Odotus (novel), 1965; Teilinummi (novel), 1967; Anna meille tana paivana (report), 1973; Ystavamme delfiinit (report), 1985. Contributor to literary publications. *Memberships:* Manuscript 63 (Founder and Chairman to 1965); Pirkkalaiskirjailijat r.y.; Suomen Kirjailijaliitto (Finnish Writers Association), 1968 to present. *Honours:* Tampere City Award, 1968; Wihuri Foundation, 1968; Ministry of Education, 1968; Vaino Linna Foundation, 1972. *Literary Agent:* WSOY, Lehtimiehet Yhtyma. *Address:* Rautatienkatu 11 A 14, 33100 Tampere 10, Finland.

WESSNER, Torbjörn, b. 1 Apr. 1948, Lund, Sweden. Translator. *Publications:* Translations: By Marin Treda (from Romanian): Den obekväme, 1975, and Vanvettets Upptakt, (Co-author Ingrid M Duke), 1980. By Jan Wolkers (from Dutch): Dronten, 1981, Dödskallefrjärilen, 1982, Odödlighetens Persika, 1983, and Snaggad, 1985. *Contributions to:* Artes (No 5/1984): Marin Sorescu; Brusten klagosångflyende stränder (from Romanian). *Honours:* Scholarships from Sveriges Författarfond, since 1982–83. *Memberships:* Sveriges Författarförbund, 1982. *Address:* Smedjevägen 9, S–191 49 Sollentuna, Sweden.

WEST, Cathcart Anthony Muir, b. 1 July 1910, County Down, Ireland. Writer. m. Olive Mary Burr, 15 Jan. 1940, London, 4 sons, 7 daugters. *Publications:* River's End and Other Stories, (short stories), USA, UK, Germany, 1957–60; The Native Moment, (novel), USA, UK, Italy, 1959–63; Rebel to Judgement, (novel), USA, 1962; The Ferrett Fancier, (novel), UK 1962, USA 1963; As Towns With Fire, UK 1968, USA 1970; All the King's Horses, (short stories), Eire, 1980; The Ferret Fancier, reprint in, Irish Classics, Eire, UK, USA, 1984; As Towns with Fire, reprint, Ireland, UK, USA, 1984. *Contributions to:* Various publications in USA, UK and Germany. *Honour:* Rockefeller Atlantic Award in Literature. *Membership:* Aosdána, Dublin. *Address:* c/o Midland Bank Limited, Castle Street, Beaumaris, Anglesey, Gwynedd, North Wales.

WEST, Donald James, b. 9 June 1924, Liverpool, England. Criminologist; Emeritus Professor, Clinical Criminology, University of Cambridge. *Education:* MA, Liverpoool University; PhD, Cambridge University; Member, Royal College of Psychs; Litt D, Cambridge, 1979. *Publications include:* The Habitual Prisoner, 1963; Murder followed by Suicide, 1965; The Young Offender, 1967; Homosexuality, 1968; Present Conduct & Future Deliquency, 1969; Who Becomes Delinquent? with D P Farrington, 1973; The Delinquent Way of Life, with D P Farrington, 1977; Homosexuality

Re-Examined, 1977; Understanding Sexual Attacks, 1978; Sexual Victimisation, 1985; Delinquency: It's Roots, Careers and Consequences, 1982. *Contributor to:* British Journal of Criminology; British Journal of Psychiatry; Journal of the Society for Psych Research. *Memberships:* British Society Criminology, President, 1975–77; Society for Psychiatric Research, Past President. *Address:* 32 Fen Road, Milton, Cambridge CB4 4AD, England.

WEST, Paul, b. 23 Feb. 1930, England. Author. *Education:* MA, Oxford and Columbia Universities, 1953. *Appointments:* Visiting Professor, University of Wisconsin, USA, 1965–66; Pratt Lecturer, Memorial University of Newfoundland, 1970; Crawshaw Professor, Colgate University, 1972; Melvin Hill Distinguished Professor, Hobart and William Smith Colleges, 1973; Distinguished Writer in Residence, Wichita State University, 1982; Writer in Residence, University of Arizona, 1984. *Publications:* Byron and the Spoiler's Art, 1960; Said the Sparrow, 1963; The Snow Leopard, 1965; Tenement of Clay, 1965; The Wine of Absurdity, 1966; Alley Jaggers, 1967; I, Expecting to Live Quite Soon, 1970; Words for a Deaf Daughter, 1970; Caliban's Filibuster, 1971; Bela Lugosi's White Christmas, 1972; Colonel Mint, 1973; Gala, 1976; The Very Rich Hours of Count von Stauffenberg, 1980; Out of My Depths: A Swimmer in the Universe, 1983; Rat Man of Paris, 1986. *Contributor to:* Numerous professional journals. *Honours:* Churton Collins Prize, 1948; Canada Council Fellow, 1959; Guggenheim Fellow, 1962; Paris Review Aga Khan Prize for Fiction, 1973; Hazlett Memorial Award for Excellence in the Arts, 1981; National Endowment for the Arts Fellowships, 1979, 1985; Award in Literature, American Academy and Institute of Arts and Letters, 1985. *Memberships:* PEN; Authors Guild; National Book Critics Circle. *Literary Agent:* Elaine Markson Agency. *Address:* 126 Texas Lane, Ithaca, NY 14850, USA.

WEST, Raeto Collin, b. 22 Oct. 1947, Lincoln, England. Author; Programmer; Publisher. m. Evelyn May Schwartz, 7 July 1977, 2 sons. *Education:* BSc. *Publications:* Programming the PET/CBM, 1982; Programming the Vic, 1984; Programming the Commodore 64, 1985. *Contributions to:* Various computer magazines. *Membership:* Society of Authors. *Address:* PO Box 438, Hampstead, London NW3 1BH, England.

WESTBURG, John Edward, b. 23 Mar. 1918. Political Scientist. *Education:* BA, English Literature, 1949, MA, Political Science & History, 1951, University of South Carolina, USA; M.For.Serv., School of International Relations, University of South California, 1954; MA, Comparative Literature, 1956, PhD, Political Science, 1958 University of Southern California; postgraduate work, various universities. *Appointments include:* Associate Professor, English, Journalism, History, St Ambrose College, Davenport, Iowa, 1964–69; Acting Postmaster, Davenport, 1969; Associate Professor, Political Science, University of Wisconsin, 1969–72; Director, Legis.Ref. Bur., Milwaukee, 1973; Director, Nutrition Project for Elderly, Grant Co, Wisconsin, 1973–78; Director, Humanities for Elders Lecturer, Political Science, University of Wisconsin, Richland Centre, 1979–82. *Publications include:* Author: States' Rights under The Federal Constitution, 1951; Constitutional Reform for Effective Government in Nevada, 1958; Politics The Queenly Art and the Model State Constitution, 1966; Editor & Publisher, North American Mentor Magazine, 1964–; Editor & Publisher, General Pols. Quarterly, 1966; Editor, Forum on Public Affairs, 1967–72; Editor & Publisher, numerous poetry and other books including, Everyman's Life of the Buddha, H C Warren, 1964; Wilderness & Gardens, An American Lady's Prospects, M L Been, 1974; Furwick Poems, 1977; Furwick Poems II, 1980; M G Christopherson: Confrontation, J Pallister, 1976; Songs of Bloody Harian, L Pennington, 1975; The Sewer Socialists: History of the Socialist Party of Wisconsin, 1897–1940, 2 volumes, Elmer Beck. *Membership:* Board of Directors, The August Derleth Society, 1983–. *Address:* 1745 Madison St, Fennimore, WI 53809, USA.

WESTBURY, John Gilbert, b. 12 Sep. 1942, Victoria, Australia. Journalist. m. Anne Loraine Draper, 7 Oct. 1978, 3 daughters. *Education:* Diploma of Journalism, C I T *Contributions to:* Various magazines and journals. *Honours:* 3 awards for ICA Bulletin; Certificate of merit, Society of Business Communicators, 1985. *Memberships:* Australian Journalists Association; Society of Business Communicators; Public Relations Institute of Australia. *Address:* 42 Molesworth Street, Seaford, Victoria 3198, Australia.

WESTCOTT, W(illiam) F(ranklin), b. 4 Sep. 1949. Toronto, Canada. Teacher. m. (1) Christine McAra, 6 June 1970 (divorced 1974); (2) Dawn Ann Jordan 17 May 1978 (divorced), 1 daughter. *Education:* Teaching Certificate Lakeshore Teachers' College, 1971; Reality Therapy Certificate, Georgian College, 1973; BA, McMaster University. 1974; Specialist Certificate in Special Education, Ontario Ministry of Education. 1976. *Literary Appointments:* Former Associate Editor, Writer's Lifeline. Assistant Editor. 1982. *Major Publications:* Small Things, Blue Heron, 1979; Basic Lessons in English Grammar, Vesta, 1980; Being, Blue Heron, 1981; Her Light was like unto Stone (poems), Blue Heron, 1981; The Old Man and the Hidden Forest (juvenile), Vesta, 1981; Captain Dreamer (poems), Vesta, 1982; So you want to be a Writer, Vesta, 1983. *Contributor to:* Numerous magazines and newspapers in Canada and elsewhere of more than 70 articles, stories and reviews. *Membership:* Canadian Authors' Association. *Address:* P O Box 1326, 103 Paris Street, Alliston, Ontario, Canada, LOM 1AO.

WESTERGAARD, Ross Grant, b. 11 June 1927, Saskatchewan, Canada. Executive, Marine Industry, Retired. m. Frances Marie Ferguson, 29 May 1953, 1 son, 1 daughter. *Education:* Various Courses. *Appointments:* Panellists, Festival of the Written Arts, Sechelt, Canada, 1985. *Publications:* The Upper Left-Hand Corner: A Writer's Guide for the Northwest, co-author, 1984. *Contributor to:* Over 50 articles, short stories in over 20 periodicals in North America; contributions to journals of Royal Naval Sailing Association, Western Canada Aviation Museum; Canadian Aviation Historical Society; editor, Newletters, Canadian Coast Guard, Western Mensa, Canada. *Honours:* Recipient, various awards, local arts councils & writers associations. *Memberships:* Federation of British Columbia Writers, membership chairman, 3 years; Burnaby Writers Society. *Address:* 3000 Jemina Road, Denman Island, BC, Canada VOR 1TO, Canada.

WESTERMEYER, Joseph, b. 8 Apr. 1937, Chicago, Illinois, USA. Psychiatrist. m. 2 children. *Education:* BS, Biology & Chemistry 1959, MD 1961, MA, Anthropology, 1969, MPH 1970, PhD, Psychiatry, 1970, University of Minnesota. *Publications:* A Primer on Chemical Dependency: A Clinical Guide to Alcohol & Drug Problems, 1976; Editor, Anthropology & Mental Health, 1976; Co-editor, Transcultural Psychiatry, 1977; Poppies, Pipes & People: A Study of Opium & Its Use in Laos, 1983; Co-author, A Manual for Substance Abuse Education, 1984; Co-author, An Update on Methadone, 1985; Co-author, Refugees & Mental Health, 1985; Clinical Guide to Diagnosis & Management of Substance Abuse, 1985. Numerous monographs, book chapters. *Contributions to:* Various professional journals. *Honours include:* Numerous research grants; Award, Meritorious service, US Agency for International Development, 1967; Ginzburg Fellow, Group for the Advancement of Psychiatry, 1969–70; NIH Summer Fellowships, 1970, 1972, 1978; Fellow, American Anthropological Association, American Association of Family Practice, American Psychiatric Association. *Address:* 1935 Summit Avenue, St Paul, MN 55105, USA.

WESTLEY, Sidney Bohanna, b. 7 Dec. 1942, Texas, USA. Writer; Editor. Divorced, 3 daughters. *Education:* BA, Smith College, USA. *Appointments:* Publications Editor, Institute for Development Studies, University of Niarobi; Editor, International Livestock Centre for Africa, Nairobi; Scientific Editor, International Laboratory for

Research on Animal Diseases. *Publications:* Editor: Education, Society & Development, 1975; Multinational Corporations in Keyna, 1977; Livestock Production in the Subhumid Zone of West Africa, 1979; Trypanotolerant Livestock in West & Central Africa, 1979; The Ruminant Immune System in Health & Disease, 1985. *Contributor to:* ILRAD (Kenya): Control of Cattle Diseases, Overseas Development, 1982; East Coast Fever: No 1 Cattle Killer in Kenya, Kenya Farmer, 1982; ILRAD's Intensive Fight Against East Coast Fever Continues, Kenya Farmer, 1984. *Honours:* Award for Excellence, for ILRAD Reports, 1984. *Memberships:* Council of Biology Editors, USA; European Association of Science editors; Agricultural Communicators in Education, USA; African Association of Science Editors, Member, Organizing Committee. *Address:* International Laboratory for Research on Animal Diseases, P O Box 30709, Niarobi, Kenya.

WESTMAN, Paul Wendell, b. 27 Oct. 1956, Minneapolis, Minnesota, USA. Attorney. *Education:* BA, University of Minnesota, Minneapolis, 1979; JD, Law, University of North Dakota School of Law, Grand Forks, North Dakota, 1984. *Publications:* Hubert Humphrey: The Politics of Joy, 1979; Alan Shepard: The First American in Space, 1979; Neil Armstrong: Space Pioneer, 1979; Ray Kroc: Mayor of McDonaldland, 1980; Walter Cronkite: The Most Trusted Man in America, 1980; John Glenn: Around the World in 90 Minutes, 1980; Jacques Cousteau: Free Flight Undersea, 1980; Jesse Jackson: I Am Somebody, 1980; Jimmy Carter: From Farm Boy to President, 1981; Billy Graham: Reaching Out to the World, 1981; Frank Borman: To the Moon and Back, 1981; John Young: Space Shuttle Commander, 1982; Thor Heyerdahl: Across the Seas of Time, 1982; Andrew Young: Champion of the Poor, 1983; Walter Mondale: Serving All the People, 1984d. *Contributions to:* Regular contributor to Current Biography, HW Wilson Co, Bronx, New York, 1978–81. *Honours:* Certificates of Merit for national achievement in creative writing, Scholastic Writing Awards, 1970, 1973; national Council of Teachers of English Award for superior performance in writing, 1974. *Address:* 905 8th Avenue Northwest, Waseca, MN 56093, USA.

WESTMAN-BERG, Karin Birgitta, b. 17 June 1915, Uppsala, Sweden. University Professor;Writer. m. Sten Berg PhD, 1 Sep. 1940, Uppsala, 1 son, 2 daughters. *Education:* PhD, History of Literature, 1962; Docent 1965. *Publications:* Studies in C J L Almqvist's Views on Women 1962; Contributing Editor, Sex Roles in Literature from Antiquity to the 1960's, 1968; Sex Discrimination Past and Present, 1972; To Analyse Texts from Sex Role Perspective, 1976; Don't Cry-Research!, 1979; Theories and Beginnings, 1980; Text-Interpretation–Valuation, 1981; Women Authors 1893–1899, Bibliography of Swedish Fiction in Sweden and Finland, 1982; Mothers–Saviours–Peacemakers, 1983. *Contributor to:* Samlaren; Hertha; Am-Scandinavian Review; Riksbankens Jubileumsfond. *Honours:* Award, Fund of Swedish Authors, 1971; Prize, Norrlandsförbundet, 1975; The Socratic Prize, Studieförbundet Vuxenskolan, 1976; A series of University lectures given annually from 1983, The Karin Westman-Berg Lectures. *Memberships:* PEN; PUG; Swedish Writers Union. *Address:* O.Slottsgatan 1o, 75235 Uppsala, Sweden.

WESTMORE, Ann Felicity, b. 7 June 1953, Melbourne, Australia. Freelance Journalist. m. David John Hill, 24 Jan. 1978, Melbourne, 1 son, 3 stepsons. *Education:* BSc, University of Melbourne, 1972. *Publications:* The Billings Method, 1980; Test-Tube Conception, 1983; The Complete Guide to Contraception and Family Planning, 1986. *Contributions:* Chapter, Clinical In-Vitro Fertilization, 1984. Journals including: Readers Digest; Australian Doctor; Herald, Newspaper, Melbourne; Diabetes in the News; IBM Quarterly; Time International. *Honours:* Best 5 New Stories, Australian Medical Association, 1975, 1977; Merit Award, ibid, 1980. *Memberships:* Australian Journalists Association; Australian Society of

Women Writers; Australian and New Zealand Association for the Advancement of Science. *Address:* 13 Laver Street, Kew, Victoria 3101, Australia.

WESTRIN, Erik Gunnar, b. 16 May 1946, Ostersund, Sweden. Teacher; Author. *Education:* BEd, Primary education, 1972. *Publications:* Hemma hos storharren, 1981, Norwegian edition, 1982; Fiske i norr, 1982; Oringnatt, 1983; Vildmarksfiske, 1984. *Contributions to:* Sportfiskaren; Jaktmarker och Fiskevatten; Fiskejournalen, Flugfiske i Norden; Der Blinker, Germany. *Honours:* The Fund of the Swedish Authors, 1982, 83. *Memberships:* Board member, Swedish Writers Union, North Swedish Writers Union. *Literary Agent:* Bokforlaget Settern, Orkelljunga, Sweden. *Address:* Overlotsvagen 2, S–955 00 Ranea, Sweden.

WETTENHALL, Roger L, b. 4 Feb. 1931, Hobart, Tasmania. Academic. m. Kathleen Lois Calvert, 25 Sep. 1955, Hobart, divorced, 1 son, 2 daughters. *Education:* MA, Dip Public Administration, University of Tasmania; PhD, Australian National University. *Publications:* A Guide to Tasmanian Government Administration 1968; Bushfire Disaster: An Australian Community in Crisis, 1975; Local Government Systems of Australia, (co-editor), 1981; Understanding Public Administration, (co-editor), 1981; Organising Government: The Uses of Ministries and Departments, 1985. *Contributions to:* Journals including: Australian Journal of Public Administration; Public Administration, London; Current Affairs Bulletin, Sydney; International Review of Administrative Sciences; Indian Journal of Public Administration. *Honours:* Haldane Silver Medal Essayist, Royal Institute of Public Administration, London, 1965; Member of Editorial Boards, International Review of Administrative Sciences and Australian Journal of Public Administration. *Membership:* President ACT Group 1973–75, Royal Australian Institute of Public Administration. *Address:* School of Administrative Studies, Canberra College of Advanced Education, Box 1, PO Beleonnen, ACT 2616, Australia.

WETTER, Gustav A(ndreas), b. 4 May 1911, Mödling, Austria. Professor Emeritus, Marxist Philosophy. *Education:* Dr Philosophy, 1932, Lic Theol 1936, Dr scientiarum ecclesiasticarum orientalium, 1943; Dr hc Theol, 1984. *Publications:* Dialectical Materialism, 1952; English Edition, 19858, 5th edition, 1960; Soviet Ideology Today, 1962, English Edition 1966. *Honours include:* Kardinal-Innitzer Preis, 1978; Österreichisches Ehrenkreuz für Wissenschaft und Kunst I Klasse, 1978; Leopold Kunschak-Preis, 1983; Das Grosse Verdienstkreuz des Verdienstordens der Bundesrepublik Deutschland, 1983. *Memberships:* American Association for Advancement of Slavic Studies; Deutsche Gesellschaft fur Osteuropakunde. *Address:* Piazza della Pilotta, 4, 1-00187 Rome, Italy.

WEXLER, Philip, b. 20 Nov. 1950, New York City, USA. Technical Information Specialist. *Education:* BS, Polytechnic Institute of New York; BA, Hunter College of City University of New York; MLS, Rutgers University. *Contributor to:* Poet Lore; Tar River Poetry; Widener Review; Mati; Still Night Writings; Kavitha, etc; Contributor, Bread Loaf Writers Conference, 1985; Public Readings at Folger Library, Writer's Center, etc. *Memberships:* Writer's Center; Poets and Writers. *Address:* 8315 Northbrook Lane, #501 W, Bethesda, MA 20814, USA.

WHALING, Frank, b. 5 Feb. 1934, Pontefract, Yorkshire, England. Methodist Minister, Religious Studies Educator. m. Patricia Hill, 6 Aug. 1960, Sheffield, 1 son, 1 daughter. *Education:* BA History, Christ's College, University of Cambridge, 1957; BA Theology, Wesley House, Cambridge, 1959; MA, University of Cambridge, 1961; ThD Comparative Religion, Harvard University, USA, 1973; FRAS, 1981; FWLA, 1985. *Literary Appointments:* Ministry at Birmingham, England, 1960–62; Faizabad and Varanas, North India, 1962–66; Eastbourne England, 1966–69; Teaching Fellow, Harvard University, 1971–73; Special Teacher, Coordinator, Religious Studies, Edinburgh, Scotland,

1973–; Visiting Professor, Indiana University, USA, 1975, 1984, Peking, China, 1982, Dartmouth College, USA, 1983, Witwatersrand, Republic of South Africa, 1984, Calcutta, India, 1985. *Major Publications:* An Approach to Dialogue: Christianity and Hinduism, 1966; The Rise of the Religious Significance of Rama, 1980; John and Charles Wesley, 2nd edition, 1982; Contemporary Approaches to the Study of Religion; The Humanities, 1984; The World's Religious Traditions: Current Perspectives in the Study of Religion, 1984; Contemporary Approaches to the Study of Religion; The Social Sciences, 1985; Religions of the World, 1985. *Contributor to:* Many theological and religious journals, including: British Journal of Religious Education; Chinese studies in World Religions; Forum; Harvard Bulletin; Indian Journal of Philosophy; Religious Education; Scottish Journal of Theology. *Honours include:* Fulbright Fellow, Harvard University, USA, 1981; British Academy Fellow to Chinese Academy of Social Sciences, 1982; Carnegie Grantee, 1982. *Memberships include:* New York Centre for Integrative Studies, USA; Chairman, President, Scottish Working Party on Religious Education in Scotland; Council Member, Christian Education Movement in Scotland. *Address:* 29 Ormidale Terrace, Edinburgh, EH12 6EA, Scotland.

WHEATCROFT, Andrew Jonathan Maclean, b. 20 July 1944, Woking, England. Author. m. Janet Margaret Wear, 25 July 1970, Chipping Warden, 2 sons, 2 daughters. *Education:* BA, MA, Christ's College, Cambridge; University of Madrid; Research Fellow, University of Edinburgh. *Publications:* The Habsburg Empire, 1972; Who's Who in Military History (with John Keegan), 1976; Russia in Original Photographs (with Marvin Lyons), 1977; The Tennyson Album, 1980; The Covent Garden Album, 1981; Arabia in Original Photographs, 1982; Dolin: Friends and Memories, 1982; The World Atlas of Revolutions 1775–1983, 1983. *Contributions to:* Cambridge Review; Spectator; London Standard. *Honour:* Gold Medal for Outstanding Atlas, Awarded to the, World Atlas of Revolutions, by the Geographical Society of Chicago, 1983. *Literary Agent:* Gill Coleridge, Anthony Sheil Associates. *Address:* Craigieburn House, by Moffat, Dumfriesshire, Scotland DG10 9LF.

WHEELER, Bonnie G, b. 12 July 1943, Charleston, West Virginia, USA. Freelance Writer; Speaker. m. Dennis R Wheeler, 14 June 1961, Fort Lauderdale, 3 sons, 2 daughters. *Publications:* Chosen Children, contributing author, 1978; Of Braces and Blessings, 1980; Wondrous Power, Wondrous Love, contributing author, 1984; Challenged Parenting, 1983; Meet the Overcomers, 1984; The Hurrier I Go, 1985. *Contributor to:* The Allianne Witness; Baptist Herald; Christian Reader; Christian Writer; Daily Blessing; Decision; Family Life; Today; Looking Ahead; Living with Children; Living With Pre-Schoolers; Lois. *Honours:* Mt Hermon Christian Writers Conference Inspirational Award, 1982. *Membership:* Co-Founder, President, Advisor, Sutter-Buttes Christian Writers Fellowship. *Address:* 887 10th Street, Box 381, Williams, CA 95987, USA.

WHEELER, Helen Rippier, b. USA. Educator. *Education:* BA Foreign Areas Studies, Barnard College; MS Library Information Science, Columbia University; MA Social Science, University of Chicago; EdD Curriculum and Teaching, Columbia University Teachers College. *Publications:* The Community College Library: A Plan For Action, 1965; Basic Collection for the Community College, 1968; Womanhood Media, 1972; Supplement, 1975; Creator of Multi-media including: Learning The Library – A Skills and Concepts series; Library Reference Information – How to Locate and Use It. *Contributions to:* Numerous books including: The Woman's Annual: 1983–84; Alternative Library Literature; 1982/1983: A Biennial Anthology; Syllabus Sourcebook on Media and Women; Principles and Practices of Teaching; Better Libraries Make Better Schools; Social and Behavioural journals including; WLW Journal; Collection Building: Studies Winter 1983/1984. *Honours include:* 1st Place, Course Proposal Contest, Women's Institute for

Freedom of the Press; Visiting Scholar, Tokyo University, Tokyo, Japan, 1964; Merritt Humanitarian Award. *Memberships include:* Pi Lambda Theta; American Library Association; California Library Association; Women Educators; American Association of University Women; National Women's Studies Association; Japan Women's Studies Society; National Organization for Women. *Address:* 2701 Durant Avenue, Suite 14, Berkeley, CA 94704, USA.

WHELCHEL, Sandra Jane, b. 31 May 1944, Denver, Colorado, USA. Freelance Writer; Author. m. Andrew Jackson Whelchel, 27 June 1965, Parker, Colorado, 1 son, 1 daughter. *Education:* BA, Elementary Education, University of Northern Colorado; Graduate work, University of California, California State University, Pepperdine College, California. *Literary Appointments:* Teacher, private writing classes, 1984–85. *Publications:* Your Air Force Academy, with O J Seiden, 1982; A Day In Blue, 1984; A Day At The Cave, 1985; ProRodeo Hall of Champions & Museum of the American Cowboy, 1985. *Contributions to:* Primary Treasure; California Horse Review: Empire Magazine; Child Life; Jack & Jill; Children's Digest. *Honours:* Biographical listings. *Membership:* National Writers Club. *Address:* 11844 N Delbert Road, Parker, CO 80134, USA.

WHELESS, E(lizabeth) Jeanine Carver, b. 6 Oct. 1950, Pinehurst, North Carolina, USA. Housewife, Mother, Freelance Medical Writer (Psychiatry). m. Don Monroe Wheless, 30 June 1974, Chapel Hill, North Carolina, 2 sons. *Education:* BA Psychology, Duke University, 1972. *Major Publications:* Psychopharmacology in the Elderly Patient: A Guide for Laymen (tentative title), to be published; Chapters in: Drug Issues in Geropsychiatry; Phenomenology and Treatment of Schizophrenia; Co-author of numerous chapters in various psychiatric works. *Contributor to:* North Carolina Mental Health; North Carolina Medical Journal; Comprehensive Psychiatry; Southern Medical Journal; Medical Digest; The Gerontologist; Weekly Psychiatry Update Series; Current Psychiatric Therapies; Directions in Psychiatry. *Membership:* American Medical Writers Association. *Address:* 1020 West Trinity Avenue, Durham, NC 27701, USA.

WHICKER, Alan Donald, b. 2 Aug. 1925. Television Broadcaster; Writer. *Publications:* Some Rise By Sin, 1948; Away – With Alan Whicker, 1963; The Best of Everything, 1978; Within Whicker's World, autobiography, 1982; Whicker's World, 1985. *Contributions to:* Sunday newspapers; various international publications. *Honours include:* Screenwriters' Guild Best Documentary Script, 1963; Personality of the Year, Guild of Television Producers and Directors, 1964; Silver Medal, Royal Television Society, 1968; Dumont Award, University of California, 1970; Best Interview Programme Award, Hollywood Festival of Television, 1973; Richard Dimbleby Award, BAFTA, 1978; TV Times Special Award, 1978. *Membership:* Fellow, Royal Society of Arts, 1970. *Address:* Le Gallais Chambers, Bath Street, St Helier, Jersey, Channel Islands.

WHINCUP, Brenda Rose. Jill of All Trades. m. Joseph William Whincup. *Appointments:* Former Nurse; Former Actress. *Publications:* Poem in Aberdeen University Press Anthology, 1985. *Contributor to:* Arts Council Anthologies (Waltham Forest), 1972, 73, 74 75, 76, 77; London Writer's Circle Anthology, 1977; Billericay Writers Word Shop, 1981; contribution to Penguin's How to be Ridiculously Well-Read, 1985. Resident Poet with Master Craftsman; Master Craftsman Magazine; Essex Countryside; Hertfordshire Countryside; Buckinghamshire Countrysdie; Essex Churchman; Capital Radio; Billericay Arts Association Poster Poems. *Honours:* 1st Pls. Contra Costa Competition, USA, 1977, 1980; Highly Commended Surrey Competition, 1980; Winner, Competition adjudicated by Ronald Blythe, 1980; Gold Medal, Cambridge Arts Festival, 1985. *Memberships:* London Writers' Circle; Brentwood Writers' Circle; Billericay Writers; Society of

Women Writers and Journalists. *Address:* 10 Frederica Road, North Chingford, London E4 7AL, England.

WHISTLER, Laurence, b. 21 Jan. 1912, Eltham, Kent, England. Writer; Glass Engraver. *Education:* MA, Oxford. *Publications:* Sir John Vanbrugh (Biography) 1938; The English Festivals, 1947; Rex Whistler, His Life and His Drawings, 1948; The World's Room (Collected Poems), 1949; The Engraved Glass of Laurence Whistler, 1952; Rex Whistler: The Konigsmark Drawings, 1952; The Imagination of Vanbrugh and His Fellow Artists, 1954; The View from this Window (poems), 1961; Engraved Glass, 1962–58; The Work of Rex Whistler, co-author, 1960; Audible Silence (poems), 1961; The Initials of the Heart: the Story of a Marriage, 1964; The Celebrate Her Living, (Poems), 1967; Pictures on Glass, 1972; Image on the Glass, 1975; Scenes and Signs on Glass, 1985; The Laughter and the Urn: Biography of Rex Whistler, 1985. *Honours:* Honorary Fellow, Balliol College; King's Gold Medal for Poetry, 1935. *Address:* Alton Barnes, Marlborough, Wiltshire, England.

WHITCOMB, Philip Wright, b. 24 Nov. 1891, Topeka, Kansas, USA. Journalist. m. (1) Valerie Gertrude McClintock, August 1914, 1 son, 2 daughters; (2) Genevieve Felicie Therese Auriol, Tarn, France, 18 Aug. 1942, 1 son, 1 daughter. *Education:* BA, Washburn University, Topeka, Kansas, 1910; BA 1914, MA 1926, Oxford University, England; M Ph 1980, PhD Scholastic Metaphysics 1981, University of Kansas, USA. *Literary Appointments:* Founder and Editor, 1st monthly publication of American Chamber of Commerce, London; Correspondent, Harper's Weekly; Correspondent, Boston Evening Transcript; Baltimore Sun war correspondent, 1939–47; Founder, editor, publisher, Euromarket News weekly; Special correspondent in France and Germany, Christian Science Monitor, 1948–78. *Publications:* In Preparation: Through a Glass Darkly; And All The Men and Women; Six Years of This and That. *Contributions include:* Harper's Weekly; Boston Evening Transcript; Baltimore Sun; Euromarket News; Christian Science Monitor. *Honours include:* D Litt honoris causa, Washburn University, 1962; Honorary Life member, American Chamber of Commerce in Germany; 2 Awards, Overseas Press Club of America-Bache, 1969 and 1975; Honorary Life Directorship, American Chamber of Commerce in France, 1968; Certificate, Kappa Tau Alpha, 1984. *Memberships:* Overseas Press Club of America; Anglo-American Press Association, Paris. *Address:* 10–bis rue Servandoni, 75006–Paris, France.

WHITE, Ivan, b. 23 May 1929, Seven Kings, Essex, England. WEA Tutor Organiser, North Lancashire and South Cumbria. divorced, 1 son, 1 daughter. *Education:* BA Honours, York Univerity, 1969; MA, Manchester University, 1971. *Publications:* Crow's Fall, 1969; Removal of an Exhibition, 1975. *Contributions to:* Poetry: Agenda; Ambit; The Aylesford Review; Arts Council Anthologies, 1, 3, 9; Barestone Mountain Awards, 1976; Brazen Voices; Brew; Envoi; Extra Verse Orbis; Outposts, Poetry Cumbria; Poet International; Writing '80, Programme of Lancaster Literature Festival; Skeletons; Raven; Socialist Commentary; Spectator; Tribune; New Voices of the Commonwealth; Adam's Dream, anthology; The Poetry Review. Home Service and Radio 3, British Broadcasting Corporation. *Honours:* 2nd Prize, Guinness Poetry Competition, Cheltenham Festival, 1964. *Memberships:* General Executive Council Past Member, Poetry Society. *Address:* Park Cottage, Tarpits Lane, Burton, Carnforth, Lancashire LA6 1HZ, England.

WHITE, James Boyd, b. 28 July 1938, Boston, Massachusetts, USA. Professor of Law. m. Mary Loiuse Fitch, 1 Jan. 1978, Chicago, Illinois, USA, 2 sons, 2 daughters. *Education:* AB, Amherst College, 1960; AM 1961, LLB 1964, Harvard Univerity, Cambridge, Massachusetts. *Major Publications:* The Legal Imagination, 1973; When Words Lose their Meaning, 1984; Heracles' Bow, 1985. *Contributor to:* Numerous Law

Reviews & quarterly journals. *Address:* School of Law, University of Michigan, Ann Arbor, MI 48109, USA.

WHITE, John Roger, b. 2 June 1929. Editor. *Education:* Collegiate Institute, Belleville, Canada. *Appointments include:* Court Reporter, JP, Hastings Company Court, Belleville, 1947–50; Assistant Editor, Hansard, Parliament Debates, Ottawa, Canada, 1951–61; Supreme Court of BC, Vancouver, 1961–68; Editor, The Baha i World, Volumes, XIV-XVII, 1971–81. *Publications:* Summer Window, 1947; Sketches of Abdu'l-Baha, 1973; Old Songs, New Songs, 1978; Different Perspectives, 1979; Another Song, Another Season, 1970; The Witness of Pebbles, 1981; Compendium of the Baha i Worlds, Volumes I-XII, 1981; One Bird, One Cage, One Flight, 1984; The Shell and The Pearl, 1985. *Memberships:* Member, Guest Editor, 1980, Voices; English Language Poets of Israel. *Address:* PO Box 155, 31001 Haifa, Israel.

WHITE, Jon Manchip, b. 22 June 1924, Cardiff, Wales. Author; Lindsay Young Professor of Humanities & Professor of English, University of Tennessee, USA. m. Valerie Leighton, 14 Jan. 1946, Cardiff, 2 daughters. *Education:* MA, University of Cambridge. *Publications include:* 14 novels; 3 biographies; 2 travel books; 4 poetry books; 2 anthropological books; 3 books, Ancient Egypt; Numerous films & television plays. *Literary Agent:* Harvey Unna. *Address:* Department of English, University of Tennessee, Knoxville, TN 37920, USA.

WHITE, June, b. 11 June 1930. Housewife. *Education:* Bangor Secretarial Training College, England. *Appointments:* Secretary, Insurance Companies, Bangor, North Wales & Kingston-upon-Thames, Surrey; Secretary, Foundry Equipment Ltd, Leighton Buzzard, Beds; Secretary to Professor D H Saunders, Cranfield Institute of Technology, Beds. *Contributor to:* Northants & Beds Life; Beds & Bucks Observer; This England; Writers Review; Tell Tale Poetry magazine; Poetry Nottingham; Salopoet Poetry Magazine; Glover Internationall, Poetry Anthology, USA, 1976; My Kind of Poetry, collected by Marjorie G Harvey; Lilac & English Tea, by Margaret Munro Gibson. *Honours include:* 1st, Writers' Review Winter Poetry Competition, 1972; John McMahon Trophy, 1979; The Joyce McKay Trophy, Poetry Anthology Eighty-Five-Published Work, The Living Land, 1982; Winner, Writer, Poetry Competition, Winter, 1983, Spring, 1983. *Address:* Sequoia, 5 Taylors Ride, Leighton Buzzard, Bedfordshire LU7 7JN, England.

WHITE, Paulette Childress, b. 1 Dec. 1948, Detroit, Michigan, USA. Homemaker, Writer. m. Bennie White, 27 Nov. 1970, Detroit, Michigan, 5 sons. *Education:* Currently Undergraduate, Wayne State University, Detroit. *Major Publications:* Love Poem to a Black Junkie, 1975; The Watermelon Dress, 1984. *Contributor to:* Redbook; Essence; Callaloo; Anthologies: Midnight Birds, 1980, Sturdy Black Bridges, 1979. *Honour:* Michigan Council for the Arts Creative Artist Award, 1984. *Address:* PO Box 32284, Detroit, MI 48206, USA.

WHITE, Robin, b. 12 July 1928, India. Author. m. Marian Biesterfeld, 3 Feb. 1948, Indiana, USA, 2 sons, 1 daughter. *Education:* BA, Yale University; Stanford University. *Literary Appointments:* Stanford Creative Writing Fellow, 1956–57; Bread Loaf Fellow, 1956; Publisher Per/Se Quarterly, 1965–69; Director, Mendocine Writing Seminar, 1984; Lecturer, Scripps College, 1984. *Publications:* House of Many Rooms, 1958; Elephant Hill, 1959; Men and Angels, 1961; Foreign Soil, 1962; All in Favor Say No, 1964, His Own Kind, 1967; Be Not Afraid, 1972; The Special Child, 1978; The Troll of Crazy Mule Camp, 1979; Moses The Man, 1981. *Contributions to:* New Yorker; Harper's New York Times; Seventeen; Mademoiselle; Ladies' Home Journal; Saturday Evening Post. etc. *Honours:* Harper Prize, 1959; O Henry Award, 1960; Distinguished Achievement Award, 1975. *Membership:* Authors Guild. *Literary Agent:* Russell and Volkening.

Address: 544 Bradford Court, Claremont, CA 91711, USA.

WHITE, Stephen Leonard, b. 1 July 1945, Dublin, Republic of Ireland. Reader in Politics. *Education:* BA, Trinity College, Dublin, 1967; PhD, University of Glasgow, Scotland, 1973. *Publications include:* Political Culture and Political Change in Communist States, co-author, 1977; Political Culture and Soviet Politics, 1979; Britain and Bolshevik Russia, 1980; Communist Political Systems, co-author, 1982; Communist Legislatures in Comparative Perspective, Co-editor, 1982; The Party Statutes of the Communist World, co-editor, 1984; The Origins of Detente, 1985. *Contributions to:* Times Higher Education Supplement; Glasgow News; Journal of Contemporary History; Slavic Review; Soviet Studies; British Journal of Political Science; International Review of Social History and others. *Address:* Department of Politics, University of Glasgow, Glasgow G12 8RT, Scotland.

WHITE, Steven F, b. 25 June 1955, Abingdon, Pennsylvania, USA. Poet, Translator. m. Nancy Ellen Pierce, Corvallis, Oregon, 21 July 1984. *Education:* BA English, Williams College; MA Spanish, University of Oregon. *Major Publications:* Poets of Nicaragua 1918–1979 (translations), 1982; Las constelaciones de la historia, (poems in Spanish), 1983; Burning the Old Year, (poems), 1984; Poets of Chile 1965–85, (translations), 1985; Culture & Politics in Nicaragua, (forthcoming). *Contributor to:* Aspen Anthology; Anthology of Magazine Verse & Yearbook of American Poetry; Another Chicago Magazine; Greenfield Review; New Orleans Review; La Prensa Literaria; Ventana; Stand; Third Rail; Bloomsbury Review; International Poetry Review; New Directions Anthology; and others. *Honours:* Academy of American Poets Prize, 1975, 1977; Hubbard Hutchinson Fellowship, 1977–79; Fulbright Fellowship, 1983. *Memberships:* Lane Literary Guild, Chairman, 1985; American Literary Translators Association; Poetry Society of America. *Address:* c/o Unicorn Press, PO Box 3307, Greensboro, NC 27402, USA.

WHITE, Theodore Harold, b. 6 May 1915, Boston, Massachusetts, USA. Author. *Education:* AB Summa cum laude, Harvard University, 1938. *Literary Appointments:* Chief, China Bureau, Time Inc, 1939–45; Editor, The New Republic, 1947; National Correspondent, The Reporter Magazine. *Publications include:* Thunder Out of China, (with A Jacoby), 1946; The Stillwell Papers, (editor) 1948; Fire in the Ashes, 1953; The View From The Fortieth Floor, 1960; The Making of the President, 1972 and 1973; Breach of Faith, The Fall of Richard Nixon, 1975; In Search of History: A Personal Adventure, 1978; America in Search of Itself, 1982; The Arch of Memory, 1984. *Honours include:* Benjamin Franklin Award, 1956; Pulitzer Prize, 1962; Sigma Delta Chi Award, 1964; Emmy Award, 1964, 1967 and 1985. *Memberships include:* Council of Foreign Relations. *Literary Agents:* J Bach, I Lazar. *Address:* 168 E 64th Street, New York, NY 10021, USA.

WHITE, William, b. 4 Sep. 1910, Peterson, New Jersey, USA. Professor; Editor; Author; Bibliographer. m. Gertrude Mason, 20 June 1951, Rhode Island, 2 sons. *Education:* BA, University of Tennessee, 1933; MA, University of Southern California, 1937; PhD, University of London, England, 1953. *Publications:* Author of 40 books including Bibliographies of: Henry David Thoreau, 1939; John Donne, 1942; D H Lawrence, 1950; John Ciardi, 1959; Wilfred Owen, 1967; Walt Whitman's Journalism, 1968; Ernest Hemingway, 1970; Nathaniel West, 1975, Author of 5 books on Hemmingway and 5 on Whitman. Latest books include: A E Houseman: A Bibliography, 1982; By-Line: Ernest Hemingway, translated into 14 languages, 1967; Dateline: Toronto – E Hemingway, 1985. Editor: Horace Traubel, With Walt Whitman in Camden, volume 6, 1985. Editor: Horace Traubel, With walt Whitman in Camden, volume 6, 1982; Walt Whitman Quarterly Review, 1955–. *Contributions to:* Numerous journals and magazines of about 2400 articles. Editor of numerous journals and periodicals including: Annual Bibliography of English Language and Literature, 1946–; Hemingway Review. *Honours include:* Distinguished Service Award, Baylor School. 1971; Distinguished Alumnus Award, University of Tennessee, Chattanooga, 1984; Various fellowships and awards. *Memberships include:* Modern Language Association; Private Libraries Association; Sigma Delta Chi; American Studies Association; Past Secretary, Cranbrook Writers Guild. *Address:* 25860 West 14 Mile Road, Franklin, MI 48025, USA.

WHITEHOUSE, Jack Edward, b. 19 June 1933, Fort Wayne, Indiana, USA. Educator; Writer. Div. 1 son, 1 daughter. *Education:* BS 1968, MS 1971, Criminology, California State University, Long Beach; PhD Government, Claremont Graduate School, California, 1974. *Literary Appointments:* Book Review Editor, Journal of Contemporary Criminal Justice. *Publications include:* Police of America, (with Dr H K Decker), 1979; A Police Bibliography, 1980; A Research Guide for Law Enforcement and the Criminal Justice System, 1983; How and Where to Find the Facts, series, 1983. *Contributions to:* Journal of California Law Enforcement; Journal of Police Science and Administration; Law and Order; Police; The Identification Officer; Quarterly Journal of the Association for Professional Law Enforcement; Journal of Contemporary Criminal Justice; Contributed chapters to 4 anthologies. *Honours include:* Citation for Distinguished Scholarship from Institute for Police Studies 1968, Citation for Excellence from School of Applied Arts and Science 1971, CSULB; Man of the Year Award, City of Artesia, 1979; Annual Award for Distinguished Service, California Youth Councelors Association, 1982, 1983 and 1984; California State Assembly Award for Merit, 1983. *Memberships include:* Mystery Writers of America Southern California Chapter. *Literary Agent:* David V Rose – Attorney at Law, Brobeck, Phleger & Harrison, 444 South Flower Street, Los Angeles, CA 90017, USA. *Address:* 16619 Graystone Avenue, Artesia, CA 90701, USA.

WHITESIDE, Thomas C, b. 16 Dec. 1901, Gentry, Arkansas, USA. Banker. m. Grayce Virginia Broyles, 28 June 1931, Bentonville, Arkansas, 1 son, 2 daughters. *Publications:* Along Sager Creek, 1982; An Inland Journey, 1983; An Ozark Odyssey, 1985. *Contributions to:* Poet India; Christian Science Monitor; Voices International; Arkansas Methodist. *Honours include:* 1st Prize, Poets Roundtable of Arkansas, 1974; 1st Prize, Ozark Creative Writers, 1978. *Memberships include:* Poets Roundtable of Arkansas; Ozark Writers & Artists Guild. *Address:* 723 West Central, Siloam Springs, AR 72761, USA.

WHITLOCK, Ralph, b. 7 Feb. 1914, Salisbury, Wiltshire, England. Author. m. Hilda Pearce, 1 Nov. 1939, Pitton Wiltshire, 1 son, 2 daughters. *Publications:* 97 to date, others in press. *Contributions to:* Farming Editor/Farming Correspondent, The Field, approx 30 years; Columnist, Western Gazette Group, 53 years, continuing; Columnist, Guardian Weekly, 4 years; Numerous series, BBC Radio & Television, over 3,000 programmes including overseas. *Honour:* Times Educational Supplement, Junior Information Award, 1975. *Literary Agent:* Laurence Pollinger Ltd, Maddox Street, London W1R 0EU. *Address:* The Penchet, Winterslow, Salisbury, Wiltshire SP5 1PY, England.

WHITNALL, Jack Rolfe, b. 9 Feb. 1916, Puyallup, Washington, USA. Forensic Photographer; Photogrammetrist; Photographic Accident Reconstructionist. m. Ethel Lesser, 16 Aug. 1946, Yakima, Washington, USA, 1 son, 1 daughter. *Education:* Business College, Yakimal Business College; American School Center, Shrivenham, England. *Contributions to:* Life magazine; Time magazine; Fortune magazine; American Fruit Growers magazine; Photomethods – Unimpeachable Witness – The Grid, 1984; National Insurance Adjuster magazine; Law Enforcement Technology, 1985; Technical papers,

American Society of Photogrammetry. *Address:* 8 N 26th Avenue, Yakima, WA 98902, USA.

WHITTEN, Kathleen Louise, b.23 Nov. 1951, Atlanta, Georgia, USA. Writer. m. Stevenson Archer Williams Richardson, 16 Apr. 1983, Columbia, South Carolina. *Education:* Summer studies, Universite de Dijon, France, 1975, Université Laval, Quebec, Canada, 1971; BA Honours in French, Winthrop College, 1972; MA, University of South Carolina, 1978. *Contributions to:* Journal of School Health; Sunday Woman Magazine; The State Magazine; Southern Educational Communications Association; Update Magazine; Sandlapper; South Carolina Educational Television Network; The Charlotte Observer; Osceola; Proceedings of Wingspread Conference; Editorial Integrity in Public Broadcasting; Public Broadcasting Governance and Management Handbook. *Honours:* WTC Bates Short Story Award, 1978. *Memberships:* Columbia Literary Exchange; Council of Biology Editors; American Medical Writers Association. *Address:* 2 Peachtree Circle, Columbia, SC 29206, USA.

WHITTEN, Leslie Hunter, b. 21 Feb. 1928, Jacksonville, Florida, USA. Reporter. *Education:* BA, Magna cum laude, Lehigh University, Pennsylvania. *Publications:* Progeny of the Adder, 1965; Moon of the Wolf, 1967; Pinion the Golden Eagle, 1968; The Abyss, 1970; F Lee Bailey, 1971; The Alchemist, 1973; Conflict of Interest, 1976; Washington Cycle, 1979; Sometimes a Hero, 1979; A Killing Pace, 1983; A Day Without Sunshine, 1985. *Contributor to:* New York Magazine; Harper's Bazaar; The Progressive; Washingtonian; Potomac; etc. *Agent:* Curtis Brown Ltd. *Address:* 114 Eastmoor Drive, Silver Spring, MD 20901, USA.

WHURR, Colin Cameron, b. 24 Apr. 1942, Edinburgh, Scotland. Publisher. m. Renata Cooke, 30 June 1973, London. *Education:* MA, Honours, Edinburgh University. *Literary Appointments:* Chairman, University College & Professional Publishers Council, The Publishers Association; Chief Executive, Services & International, The Butterworth Group, Sevenoaks, Kent. *Address:* 2 Alwyne Road, London N1 2HH, England.

WHYTE, Barbara Birkbeck, b. 17 Sep. 1913, Richards Castle, Shropshire, England. Secretary; Translator. m. Albert Whyte, 7 Sep. 1942, London, 2 sons (1 dec), 1 daughter. *Contributions to:* Cronica, and small poetry magazines in Argentina; Tower Poetry, Rikka and Vesta Publications anthology, Canada; Voices, Israel; World Poet, India; Silarus, Italy; Don Quichotte. Switzerland; Li Poetry, Tiawan, Bitterroot and Peace Anthology, USA; Galloping on Anthology, Australia; Argus, South Africa; Rhym and Rhyme, and a number of magazines in New Zealand; New Zealand News and Biographical Magazine, England. *Honours:* 1st Place, Serious Poem Penwomen's New Zealand, 1973–75; Honorary Mentions, Poets Study Club of Indiana, 1977, 1980, 1985; 2 commendations Light Verse, Light Verse Artlook, Perth Australia, 1979, 1981; World Order of Narrative Poets, USA, 1982; Honorary Merit, Mason Sonnet Sequence, 1985; Honorary Merits, Wordsworth and Fitzgerald Award; Certificate of Merit, Temple of Arts Museum, NY, 1981; Honorary Life Fellow, Arts Academy International, 1982; Honorary Professor, Temple of Arts Academy, 1985. *Memberships:* Penwomen's Club and Private Groups in Auckland; Voices, Israel; Co-founder, Secretary, Poetry Tutor, International Writers' Workshop, NZ Incorporated, NZ; Co-Founder, Co-Editor, International poetry publication, Rhythm and Thyme. *Address;* 45 Verbena Road, Birkdale, Auckland, 10, New Zealand.

WHYTE, Donald, b. 13 Mar. 1926, Newtongrange, Mid Lothian, Scotland. Consultant Genealogist; Author; Lecturer. m. Mary Burton, 3 Aug. 1950, 3 daughters. *Education:* Licentiate in Heraldry and Genealogy, Institute of Heraldic and Genealogical Studies, Canterbury, 1972; transferred to the Faculty of Fellows, 1977. *Appointments:* Lecturer in Genealogical Studies, Extra-Mural Department, Linlithgow Academy, Scotland,

1980–83, Scottish Adviser, Society for British Genealogy and Family History, 1981–present. *Publications:* Kirkliston: A Short Parish History, 1955, 3rd edition 1975; West Lothian: The Eastern District, 1970; Dictionary of Scottish Emigrants to the USA, 1972, reprinted 1981; Introducing Scottish Genealogical Research, 1978, 5th edition, 1984; Scottish Ancestry Research, A Brief Guide, 1984; Dictionary of Scottish Emigrants to Canada Before Confederation, in press, publication expected 1986. *Contributions to:* British and North American periodicals including: The Scottish Genealogist; The Genealogists' Magazine; The Irish Ancestor; Gaelic Gleanings. *Memberships:* Vice President, Scottish Genealogy Society; President, Association of Scottish Genealogists and Record Agents; Fellow of the Society of Genealogists. *Address:* 4 Carmel Road, Kirliston, West Lothian, EH29 9DD, Scotland.

WHYTE, Jon Anthony, b. 15 Mar. 1941, Banff, Alberta, Canada. Writer. *Education:* BA, MA, English, University of Alberta; MA, Communication, Stanford University. *Publications include:* Open Spaces, 1979; Homage, Henry Kelsey, 1982; Gallimaufry, 1982; Lake Louise: A Diamond in the Wilderness, 1982; Rocky Mountain Madness, with Edward Cavell, 1982; The Fells of Brightness: Some Fittes & Starts, 1983; Indians in the Rockies, 1985; The Fells of Brightness: Wenkchemna, 1985; Carl Rungius: Painter of the Western Wilderness, with E J Hart, 1985. *Contributions to:* Numerous publications including: Chicago Review; Southwest Act; Equinox; etc. *Honour:* Stephen Stephansson Award for Poetry, Writers Guild of Alberta, 1983. *Membership:* Councillor 1983–84, League of Canadian Poets. *Address:* Box 1083, Banff, Alberta, Canada TOL OCO.

WICKLEIN, John Frederick. b. 20 July 1924, Reading, Pennsylvania, USA. Journalist. m. Myra Jane Winchester, 31 July 1948, New Brunswick, New Jersey, 1 son, 2 daughters. *Education:* LittB, Rutgers University, 1947; MS, Journalism, Columbia University, 1948. *Publications:* Cable Television: A Guide for Citizen Action, 1972; Electronic Nightmare: The New Communications and Freedom, 1981, revised paperback, 1982. *Contributions:* of Articles to: The Atlantic Monthly; Washington Monthly; Progressive; Journalism Quarterly; Columbia Journalism Review; Channels of Communication, etc; Short Stories: Collier's etc. *Honours:* Venice Film Festival Award, Best documentary, 1968; George Folk Award, 1963; Armstrong (Dupont) Award, 1972. *Membership:* Phi Beta Kappa. *Literary Agent:* Frances Goldin, New York City. *Address:* Kiplinger Professor of Public Affairs Reporting, School of Journalism, Ohio State University, Columbus, OH 43210, USA.

WIDÉEN, Lennart Mauritz, b. 11 Aug. 1925, Gävle, Sweden. Author; Journalist. *Education:* Cand. Theol. *Publications:* Joseph Smith and his Prophecy, 1972; Upplandsk mystik, 1979; Ur dunkla djup, 1981; Varmlandsk mystik, 1982; Tolffors, 1984; Till forsvunnen stad, 1985. *Contributions to:* Norrtelje Tidning, and Gefle Dagblad, Literary critic, Sweden. *Memberships:* Sveriges Forfattarforbund; Finlands Svenska Forfattarforening; Norrlandska Forfattarsallskapet. *Address:* Box 45082, 10430 Stockholm, Sweden.

WIEBE, Grace Alice, b. 20 July 1922, Saskatchewan, Canada. Retired Editor, Author, Bookkeeper. m. (1) Clifford William Chubb, 12 Oct. 1942 (dec. 1967), Valor, Saskatchewan; (2) Peter Wiebe, 28 Nov. 1977, Moose Jaw. 2 sons, 2 daughters. *Education:* Diploma, Business College; Correspondence course, Creative Writing; Summer School of the Arts. *Literary Appointment:* Editor, Northern Mosaic, arts & crafts tabloid. *Contributions:* Stories, serial, poetry, articles, editorials. *Honour:* 2nd Prize, Poetry Contest, 1980. *Memberships:* United Amateur Press; Sook-Alta Scribes. *Address:* Box 1555, 2305 20th Street, Coaldale, Alberta, Canada TOK OLO.

WIEBENSON, Dora, b. 29 July 1926, Cleveland, Ohio, USA. Architectural Historian. *Education:* BA, Vassar College, 1946; MArch, Harvard University, 1951; MA, 1958, PhD, 1964, New York University. *Publications:* Sources of Greek Revival Architecture, 1969; Tony Garnier: The Cite Industrielle, 1969, Japanese translation, 1984; The Picturesque Garden in France, 1978; Architectural Theory and Practice from Alberti to Ledoux, 1982, 83, Spanish translation, 1986. *Contributions to:* Journal of Society of Architectural Historians; Art Bulletin; Art Quarterly; 18th Century Studies; Marsyas; Monuments historiques de la France. *Honours:* Fellowships: American Association of University Women, 1963–64; Yale Center for British Art, 1983; NEH, 1986–87. *Memberships include:* Past Board of Directors (2 terms) and Chairman of Education Committee, American Society of Architectural Historians; Editorial Board, American Society for 18th Century Studies. *Address:* 103 MacDougal Street, New York City, NY 10012, USA.

WIENANDT, Elwyn Arthur, b. 23 July 1917, Aniwa, Wisconsin, USA. University Administrator and Professor. *Education:* BMus, Lawrence College, Wisconsin, 1939; MMus, University of Denver, 1948; PhD, State University of Iowa, 1951. *Publications:* Musical Style in the Lute Compositions of Francesco da Milano, 1958; Choral Music of the Church, 1965; The Anthem in England and America, 1970; Opinions on Church Music, 1974; The Bicentennial Collection of American Music, 1974; Johann Pezel (1639–1694), A Thematic Catalogue of His Instrumental Music, 1983. Contributions to several composite volumes and dictionaries including: Academic American Encyclopedia, 1980. *Contributions to:* Journal of American Musicological Society; MLA Notes; Christian Century; The Diapason; Western Folklore; Music Review; The Instrumentalist; Music Journal. *Honours:* Alumni Distinguished Service Award, Lawrence University, 1974; Oustanding Faculty Member Award, Baylor University, 1982. *Memberships:* Various music associations. *Address:* 1216 Cliffview Drive, Waco, TX 76710, USA.

WIENER, Leigh Auston, b. 28 Aug. 1930, New York, USA. Photographer, 1 son. *Education:* Political Science, University of California at Los Angeles. *Literary Appointments:* Photographer, Los Angeles Times. *Major Publications:* Here Comes Me; Not Subject to Change; The Selected Letters of Robinson Jeffers; The Range of Research; How do you Photograph People? The Cliffs of Solitude. *Contributor to:* Westways Magazine, Los Angeles Times (as columnist); Life, Paris-Match, Sports Illustrated, Fortune, Time (as photographer). *Honours:* 2 Emmy Awards for TV series, Talk about Pictures. *Address:* P O Box 46278, Los Angeles, CA 90046, USA.

WIENERS, John Joseph, b. 6 Jan. 1934, Milton, Massachusetts, USA. Poet. m. 1 son. *Education:* BA, Boston College, 1954; Black Mountain College, North Carolina, 1955–56; Teaching Fellow, State University of New York, Buffalo, 1965–67. *Publications:* The Hotel Wentley Poems, 1958; Ace of Pentacles, 1964; Pressed Wafer, 1967; Asylum Poems, 1969; Nerves, 1970; Behind the State Capitol or Cinncinnati Pike, 1975; Selected Poems 1958–1984, 1986. *Contributions to:* Numerous works including: Semina; Yugen; Stylus; Floating Bear; Set; Blue Grass; Granta; Joglars; Sum; The Nation; Magazine of Further Studies; Intransit; Yale Literary Magazine; Niagara Frontier; Paris Review; Agenda; Wivenhoe Park Review; Boss; Evergreen Review; Film Culture; The World; The Emerson Review; Stone Soup; Gay Sunshine; Fag Rag; Mirage; The Boston Phoenix. *Honours:* Poet's Foundation, New York, 1961; New Hope Foundation Award, 1963; National Endowments for the Arts, 1966, 68; American Academy Award, 1968; Committee on Poetry Grant, 1970–72; Guggenheim Fellowship, 1985. *Literary Agent:* Raymond Foye, New York. *Address:* 44 Joy Street, 10, Boston, MA 02114, USA.

WIENIEWSKI, Ignacy, b. 28 Jan. 1896, Tarnopol, Poland. University Professor; Writer. *Education:* Diploma, Sorbonne University, Paris, France; PhD, Lwow University, Poland. *Publications include:* Ancient Religious Parody, 1927; Announcements of Future Events in Homer, 1928; Polish Schools Abroad, 1930; Why Do We Learn Latin, 1937; The Foundations of Polish Culture, 1946, 2nd edition, English edition, Heritage–The Foundation of Polish Culture, 1981; Back on the Via Appia (essays), 1951; Homer's Iliad (Polish translation), 1961; By the Ancient Road (essays), 1964; Kaleidoscope of Memoirs, 1970; Vergil's Aeneid (Polish translation), 1971, 2nd Edition, 1979; Selected Works, 1980. *Contributor to:* Various Literary Journals. *Honours include:* Prizes, Union of Polish Writers Abroad, 1962, 1972. *Memberships include:* Vice-Chairman, Union of Polish Writers Abroad, London; Polish Society of Arts and Sciences, London. *Address:* 50 Twyford Avenue, London W3, England.

WIGAL, Don, b. 16 Jan. 1933, Indianapolis, Indiana, USA. Writer; Editor. *Education:* BS MusEd, University of Dayton, 1955; MA, University of Notre Dame, 1965; PhD, Columbia Pacific University, 1981; Music Certification, University of State of New York, 1981. *Literary Appointments:* Executive Editor, Dell Publishing, 1975–79; Executive Editor, Lakewood Books, 1980–. *Publications:* Experience in Faith, 1970; General Knowledge, 1980; The New York Times Encyclopedia of Film, Volume 13, 1984; Smidget, 1985; Short Stories: The Peach Colored Dragon, and The Blue Grass Castle, Silver Burdett, 1979. *Contributions:* of articles to, Electronic Education; Pre-Recorded Video; New Book Review, etc. *Honours:* Publishing Hall of Fame Nomination, 1985; Distinguished Alumni Award, University of Dayton, 1985; Art Indexer of The Academic American Encyclopedia. *Memberships:* American Society of Journalists and Authors; American Society of Composers, Authors and Publishers; Editorial Freelancers Association. *Literary Agent:* World Wide Licensing, New York City. *Address:* 4 Park Avenue, New York, NY 10016, USA.

WIGHAM, Eric Leonard, b. 8 Oct. 1904, Chungking, China. Journalist. *Education:* MA, Birmingham University, England. *Publications:* Trade Unions, 1956, 1969; What's Wrong with the Unions, 1961; The Power to Manage: A History of the Engineering Employers' Federation, 1973; Strikes and the Government, 1893–1974, 1976; From Humble Petition to Militant Action: A History of the Civil and Public Services Association 1903–1978, 1980. *Contributions to:* The Times, Labour correspondent, 1946–49 and others. *Honour:* CBE. *Memberships:* Royal Commission on Trade Unions and Employers Associations, 1965–68. *Literary Agent:* Christopher Busby. *Address:* Link View, The Avenue, West Wickham, Kent BR4 0DX, England.

WILBUR, James Benjamin III, b. 21 Feb. 1924, Hartford, CT, USA. Professor of Philosophy. m. Margie M. Mattmiller, 9 July 1949, Lexington, KY, 1 son, 1 daughter. *Education includes:* MA 1951, PhD, Colombia University, 1954. *Publications include:* The Worlds of Hume and Kaut, 1967 (with H J Allen) 2nd edition, 1982; Publisher: American Book Company; The World of Early Greek Philosophers, 1979; The World of Plato and Aristotle, (with H J Allen), 1962, 2nd edition, 1970; The World of Early Greek Philosophers (with H J Allen), 1979; Editor and contributor to Cartesian Essays, 1969; Spinoza's Metaphysics, 1967; The Integration of Ethics into Business Education: Essays or the Geneseo Experience, 1984. *Contributor to:* various professional journals and publications including Journal of Value Inquiry; The Philosophy Forum: Journal of Business Ethics. *Honours:* Summer Grants, SUNY, 1969, 1970; Geneseo, 1972; NEH Pilot Grant, 1981–82; SUNY Conversations with Disciplines, 1969, 1983–; American Association of Collegiate School of Business Western Electric Fund Award, 1983; Guest Editor, The Journal of Business Ethics, 1982, 1984. *Memberships include:* Founder, Long Island Philosophy Society, 1964–; Founder, Executive Editor, The Journal of Value Inquiry, 1967–; President, Creighton Club New York Philosophy Association, 1970–72; President, American Society for

Value Inquiry, 1973–74. *Address:* 22 West View Crescent, Geneseo, NY 14454, USA.

WILBUR, Richard (Purdy), b. 1 Mar. 1921, New York City, USA. University Professor; Poet. *Education:* MA, Amherst College, Harvard University. *Publications include:* The Beautiful Changes and Other Poems, 1947; Things of this World, (poems), 1956; Tartuffe, (transl from Moliere), 1963; Loudmouse, (for children), 1963; Poems of Shakespeare (with Alfred Harbage), 1966; Walking to Sleep, (new poems and transl), 1969; School for Wives, (transl), 1971; Opposites (children's verse illustrated by the author), 1973; The Mind-Reader, 1976; Responses (essays), 1976; The Learned Ladies, (transl from Moliere), 1978; Seven Poems, 1981; The Whale (transl), 1982; Racines Andromache. (transl), 1982; Moliere Four Comedies, 1982. *Honours:* Harriet Monroe Prize, 1948; Oscar Blumenthal Prize, 1950; Prix de Rome, American Academy of Arts and Letters, 1954–55; Edna St Vincent Millay Memorial Award, 1956; Pulitzer Prize, 1957; National Book Award, 1957; Prix Henri Desfeuilles, 1971; Brandeis Creative Arts Award, 1971; Shelley Mem Prize, 1973; Harriet Monroe Poetry Award, 1983; Drama Desk Award, 1983; Chevalier, Order des Plames Academiques, 1983. *Memberships:* Chancellor, Academy of American Poets; PEN; President, American Academy of Arts and Letters; Dramatists Guild. *Literary Agent:* (theatre only) Curtis Brown. *Address:* Dodwells Road, Cummington, MA 01026, USA.

WILBY, Peter John, b. 7 Nov. 1944, Leicester, England. Journalist. m. Sandra James, 5 Aug. 1967, Derby, England, 2 sons. *Education:* BA, University of Sussex, England, 1966. *Literary Appointments:* Education Correspondent, The Observer, 1972–75; New Statesman 1975–77, The Sunday Times, 1977–. *Major Publications:* The Condition of English Schooling, (with H Pluckrose), 1979; Education 2000, (with H Pluckrose), 1980; Parents' Rights, 1981; The Sunday Times Good University Guide, 1984. *Address:* The Sunday Times, 200 Gray's Inn Road, London WC1, England.

WILCOCK, John, b. 4 Aug. 1927, Sheffield, England. Author; Editor; Cable TV Producer. Divorced. *Publications:* Greece on $20 a Day, 1964–84; Traveling in Venezuela, 1979; Magical & Mystical Sites, 1977; An Occult Guide to South America, 1976; Guide to Occult Britain, 1976; Witches Almanac, 1971–78; Witches All, 1977, both with Elizabeth Pepper; The Autobiography & Sex Life of Andy Warhol, 1971; Travel Guides for Frommer, 1960–72 on India, Japan, Mexico, California, Las Vegas, Boston, etc. *Contributor to:* New York Times; Washington Post; High Times; Penthouse; MD Magazine; Toronto Daily Star; Mainichi Daily News, Tokyo; Co-Founder, The Village Voice; Interview Magazine; Publisher: Other Scenes; Nomad. *Membership:* American Society of Journalists & Authors. *Literary Agent:* Alice Martell, New York City. *Address:* BM-Nomad, London WC1V 3XX, England.

WILCOX, Donald James, b. 29 Aug. 1938, Putnam, Connecticut, USA. College Teacher. *Education:* PhD, Harvard University, 1967. *Literary Appointments:* Assistant Professor, Harvard University, 1966–70; Associate Professor, 1970–75; Professor, 1975–, University of New Hampshire; Chair, History Department, University of New Hampshire, 1982–85. *Publications:* The Development of Florentine Humanist Historiograph during the Fifteenth Century, 1969; In Search of God and Self; Renaissance and Reformation Thought, 1975; Classical Rhetoric and Medieval Historiography (with Ward, Ray and Partner), 1985. *Contributions to:* Guicciardini and the Humanist Historians, in Annali d'Italianistica, vol 2, 1984. *Honours:* Woodrow Wilson Fellowship, 1961–62; Canaday Fellowship, 1968. *Membership:* Rennaissance Society of America. *Address:* History Department, University of New Hampshire, Durham, NH 03824, USA.

WILCOX, Earl J, b. 9 Aug. 1933, Arkansas, USA. College and University Professor. m. Elizabeth Harrison,

5 Sep. 1953, Paragould, Arkansas, 2 sons. *Education:* BA, Arkansas State University; MA, University of Texas; PhD, Vanderbilt University. *Publications:* Fundamentals of Fiction, 1975; Thomas Hardy: Annotated Bibliography, contributor, 1975; The World of Nature in...Lorca, general editor, 1980; A Casebook of Jack London's 'The Call of the Wild', editor, 1980; Robert Frost: The Man and the Poet, editor, 1981. *Contributions to:* Articles and essays in Explicator; Wilson Library Journal; Poe Studies; Hemingway Annual; Jack London Newsletter; Southern Literary Journal; Christianity and Literature; English Literature in Transition; McNeese Review; Mississippi Studies in English. Chapters in books such as Twentieth Century Views on All the King's Men; Magazines for Libraries; Critical Essays on Jack London. *Honour:* Student of Distinction, Arkansas SU, 1957. *Memberships:* South Atlantic Modern Language Association; Modern Language Association (America); Chairman, Robert Frost Society; American Studies Association; Founding President, Philological Association of the Carolinas. *Address:* Winthrop College, Rock Hill, SC 29733, USA.

WILCOX, Michael, b. 2 July 1942, Slough, Buckinghamshire, England. Writer. m. Juanita Dawar, 27 Nov. 1965, London, England, 2 sons. *Education:* Graduate Diploma, Art and Design. *Publications:* Colour Mixing System for Artists, 3 versions, Oils, Watercolour and Acrylics, 1982; Colour Theory for Artists, 2 versions, Oils and Acrylics and Watercolour, 1983. *Literary Agent:* Amina Marix Evans. *Address:* 8 Lovett Street, Scarborough, Perth, WA, Australia.

WILD, Robert Anthony, b. 30 Mar. 1940, Chicago, Illinois, USA. Roman Catholic Priest, Jesuit, Associate Professor of Theology. *Education:* BA Latin 1962, MA Classical Languages 1967, Loyola University; STL Theology, Jesuit School of Theology, Chicago, 1970; PhD Study of Religion – New Testament, Harvard University, 1977. *Publications:* Water in the Cultic Worship of Isis and Sarapis, 1981; The Sentences of Sextus, (co-editor with Richard Edwards), 1981. *Contributions to:* Aufstieg und Niedergang der römischen Welt; Biblical Archaeology Review; Catholic Biblical Quarterly. *Memberships:* Society of Biblical Literature; Catholic Biblical Association; Chicago Society for Biblical Research. *Address:* Theology Department, Loyola University, 6525 Sheridan Road, Chicago, IL 60626, USA.

WILDE, Alan, b. 26 May 1929, New York City, USA. Professor of English. *Education:* BA 1950, MA 1951, New York University; PhD, Harvard University, 1958; Fulbright, University of Paris, 1952–53. *Literary Appointments:* Teacher, Harvard University, 1954–58; Teacher, Williams College, 1958–64; Professor of English, Temple University, 1964–; Associate, Journal of Modern Literature, 1971–; Board of Review, Temple University Press, 1973–76; Board of Consultants, Contemporary Literature, 1983–; Editorial Board, Sun and Moon Press, 1983–. *Publications:* Art and Order: A Study of E M Forster, 1964; Christopher Isherwood, 1971; Horizons of Assent: Modernism, Postmodernism and the Ironic Imagination, 1981; Critical Essays on E M Forster, (editor), 1985. *Contributions to:* Journals including: Boundary 2, Arizona Quarterly; Philosophical Approaches to Literature. *Honours:* Fulbright Fellow, 1952–53; Charles Dexter Traveling Fellow, 1958; Lindback Foundation Award for Distinguished Teaching, 1975; Arizona Quarterly Annual Award for the best essay of the Year, 1984. *Memberships:* Modern Language Association; American Literature Section, MLA. *Address:* Department of English, Temple University, Philadelphia, PA 19122, USA.

WILDEN, Anthony, b. 14 Dec. 1935, London, England. Professor of Communication. *Education:* BC HS Ccorrespondence School, University of Victoria, Canada, 1959–60, 1960–61, 1963–65; PhD, Johns Hopkins University, Maryland, USA, 1968. *Publications* The Language of the Self: The Function of Speech and Language in Psychoanalysis (with Jacques Lacan), 1968, 75, reissued, Speech and Language in

Psychoanalysis, 1981; System and Structure: Essays in Communication and Exchange, 1972, 77, revised edition, 1980; Le Canada Imaginaire, 1980; The Rules are No Game: The Strategy of Communications, 1986; Man and Woman, War and Peace: The Strategists Companion, 1986. *Contributor to:* various books and journals. *Honours:* Associate, Behavior and Brain Sciences, Princeton, 1984; Member, International Advisory Board, Rechercher Semiotiques/Semiotic Inquiry, Toronto, 1980–85. *Address:* 6211 Sumas Street, Burnaby, British Columbia, V5B 2T7, Canada.

WILDER, Frederick Louis, b. 2 Jan. 1893, London, England. Art Expert. *Publications:* Print Prices Current, annually, 1918–39; Picture Prices Current, annually, 1935–37; How to Identify Old Prints, 1969; English Sporting Prints, 1972; Catalogue of English Sporting Prints c 1750–1880. *Contributor to:* Walker's Monthly; Art at Auction; Weltkunst. *Address:* 31 New Bond Street, London W1Y 9HD, England.

WILEY, Raymond A(loysius), b. 30 Oct. 1923, Flushing, New York, USA. Professor of Foreign Languages and Literatures. m. Elizabeth M Schneider, 4 Sep. 1948, Rochester, New York, 3 sons, 5 daughters. *Education:* AB, 1946, MA, 1948, Fordham College, New York City; German Certificate, Goethe Institute, Munich, German Federal Republic, 1956; PhD, Humanities, Syracuse University, New York, 1966. *Publications:* John Mitchell Kemble and Jakob Grimm, A Correspondence 1832–52, 1971; Anglo-Saxon Kemble (Life and Works of Kemble), 1979 (in Volume I of Anglo-Saxon Studies, published British Archaeological Records, 1972 UK); John Mitchell Kemble's Review of Jakob Grimm's Deutsche Grammatik, Binghamton, New York, Center for Medieval and Early Renaissance Studies, 1981; Translation: On the Origin of Language by Jakob Grimm, 1984. *Contributor to:* German Quarterly; Journal of English and Germanic Philology; German-American Studies; Pennsylvania Gazette. *Honours:* Encaenia Award, Fordham College, 1956; US Government Fulbright Hayes Award to Germany, 1956; National Endowment for Humanities Summer Seminar, Stanford University, 1980. *Memberships:* American Association of Teachers of German, Past Secretary, Vice-President, President, Central New York Chapter and former Editor of Newsletter; Foreign Language Association of Central New York; Northeast Modern Language Association. *Address:* Le Moyne College, Syracuse, NY 13214, USA.

WILFORD, John Noble, b. 4 Oct. 1933, Murray, Kentucky, USA. Journalist. m. Nancy Watts, 25 Dec. 1966, 1 daughter. *Education:* BS, University of Tennessee, 1955; MA, Syracuse University, New York, 1956; Advanced International Reporting Fellow, Columbia University, 1961–62. *Literary Appointments:* Science Correspondent, The New York Times. *Publications:* We Reach the Moon, 1969; The Mapmakers, 1981; The Riddle of the Dinosaur, 1986. Co-Author: Spaceline, 1981; The New York Times Guide to the Return of Halley's Comet, 1985. Editor: Scientists at Work, 1979. *Contributions to:* Articles: New York Times Magazine; Readers Digest; Science Digest; Saturday Review; Wilson Quarterly. Book Reviews: Science 85; Nature. *Honours:* Westinghouse Science Writing Award, American Association for the Advancement of Science. 1983; for National Reporting, Pulitzer Prize, 1984. *Memberships:* Authors Guild; Sigma Delta Chi; National Association of Science Writers; Aviation/Space Writers Association. *Address:* New York Times, 229 West 43rd Street, New York City, NY 10036, USA.

WILHELM, James J, b. 2 Feb. 1932, Youngstown, Ohio, USA. Professor of Comparative Literature. *Education:* BA, Yale University, 1954; MA, ibid. 1960; PhD, 1961. *Appointments:* Editor, Paideuma; General Editor, Garland Library of Medieval Literature and Garland Publications in Comparative Literature. *Publications:* The Cruelest Month, 1965; Seven Troubadors, 1970; Medieval Song: An Anthology of Hymns and Lyrics, 1971; Dante and Pound, 1974; The Later Cantos of Ezra Pound, 1977; Il Miglior Fabbro, 1982; Editor: The

Romance of Arthur, 1984; The American Roots of Ezra Pound, 1985. *Memberships:* American and International Comp Lit Associations; Medieval Academy; Modern Language Assocation; Elizabethan Club. *Address:* 165 E 35th Street 3E, New York NY 10016, USA.

WILKINS, Burleigh Taylor, b. 1 July 1932, Bridgetown, Virginia, USA. University Professor, 1 son, 2 daughters. *Education:* BA, Duke University, 1952; MA, Harvard University, 1954; MA, 1963, PhD, 1965, Princeton University. *Publications:* Carl Becker, 1961; The Problem of Burke's Political Philosophy, 1967; Hegel's Philosophy of History, 1974; Has History Any Meaning? 1978. *Contributions to:* Analysis; Ethics; American Historical Review; Journal of the History of Ideas; Journal of Value Inquiry etc. *Honours:* Summa cum laude, Duke University; Phi Beta Kappa. *Address:* Philosophy Department, University of California, Santa Barbara, CA 93106, USA.

WILKINS, John Anthony Francis, b. 20 Dec. 1936, Cheltenham, England. Journalist. *Education:* State scholar, Major scholar, Foundation scholar, Clare College, Classical tripos, 1959, Theological tripos, 1961, BA, 1961, Cambridge University. *Literary Appointments:* Assistant editor, Frontier, 1964–67, The Tablet. 1967–72; Features writer, British Broadcasting Corporation External Services, 1972–81; Editor, The Tablet, 1982–. *Address:* 48 Great Peter Street, London SW1P 2HB, England.

WILKINSON, Rosemary Regina Challower, b. 21 Feb. 1924. Poet, Author, Teacher of Poetry. *Education:* Undergraduate work in Literature. *Appointments include:* Hospital Administrator, 10 years. *Major Publications include:* A Girl's Will, 1973, translated into Chinese 1974–75, French, 1976; California Poet, 1976; Earth's Compromise, 1977; It Happened to Me, 1978; An Historic Epic, translated into Chinese 1975; Una Voluntad Femina, 1982 (in Spanish); Poetry & Arts (in Spanish & English), 1982; Gems Within, 1984; Nature's Guest, 1984; In The Pines, 1985. *Contributor to:* Numerous anthologies and poetry readings. *Memberships include:* Permanent Director, Ina Coolbrith Circle, San Francisco, California; Press Chairman, California Federation of Chaparral Poets, 1977–79; President, Toyon Chapter, 1973–75; California Writers Club, Peninsula Chapter; Life Member, New York Resource Center; Poetry Society, London, England; Tagore Institute of Creative Writing, India; Life Member, International Academy of Poets, United Kingdom; Honorary Life Member, Sosmosynthesis-Melbourne, Australia; Vice President, National League of American Penwomen; Vice-President, World Academy of Arts & Culture; Vice-President, World Poetry Society Intercontinental; Authors Guild, New York; Authors League of America; National Federation State Poetry Society (Fed Br Wash DC); Academie Universelle de Lausanne, Switzerland; Soroptimist International; World Jnana-Sadhak Society, West Bengal (Honorary Life Fellowship). *Honours include:* Numerous Certificates, Plaques etc; International Woman of 1975 with Laureate Honours, Philippines; President, 5th World Congress of Poets, San Francisco, 1981; Grand Dame of Merit, Knight of Malta. *Address:* 1239 Bernal Avenue, Burlingame, CA 94010, USA.

WILKS, Michael Thomas, b. 20 Mar. 1947, London, England. Author. *Publications:* Pile-Petals from St Klaed's Computer (with Brian Aldiss), 1979; In Granny's Garden (with Sarah Harrison), 1980; The Weather Works, 1983. *Literary Agent:* Carol Smith, The Carol Smith Literary Agency. *Address:* 4 North Rise, St. Georges Fields, London W2 2YB, England.

WILLCOX, Isobel, b. 27 July 1907, Long Branch, New Jersey, USA. Teacher. *Education:* BS, New Jersey State College at Trenton; MA, Political Science, Columbia University. *Publications:* Reading Aloud with Elementary School Children, 1963; Acrobats and Ping-Pong: Young China's Games, Sports and Amusements, 1981. *Contributions to:* Sicilia, Palermo; American education journals. *Honours:* Acrobats and Ping-Pong, Junior Literary Guild Selection, one of the Children's Books of the Year, Child Study Association, 1982. *Literary Agent:* Martha Millard. *Address:* 275 Engle Street J3, Englewood, NJ 07631, USA.

WILLETT, Frank, b. 18 Aug. 1925, Bolton, England. Archaeologist. *Education:* BA, University College, Oxford, 1947; Diploma in Anthropology, 1949; MA, 1951. *Publications:* Life in the History of West African Sculpture, 1967; African Art: an Introduction, 1971; Treasures of Ancient Nigeria (with Ekpo Eyo), 1980. *Contributor to:* Encyclopedia Britannica; Man; Journal of African History; Archaeometry; Journal of the Nigerian Historical Society, etc; books on African art and archaelogy. *Honours include:* Leverhulme Research Fellowship, 1964; Major Grant, National Endowment for the Humanities, Washington, DC, USA, 1970–71; Visiting Fellow, Clare Hall, Cambridge, 1970–71; Fellow, Royal Society of Edinburgh, 1979; CBE 1985. *Memberships:* Manchester Literary and Philosophy Society (Editorial Secretary 1950–58); (Editorial Boards) West African Journal of Archaeology; Journal of African Studies; Man the Journal of the Royal Anthropological Institute. *Address:* Hunterian Museum, University of Glasgow, Glasgow G12 8QQ, Scotland.

WILLIAMS, Alan Moray, b. 17 June 1915, Petersfield, Hampshire, England. Foreign Correspondent, various British newspapers for Scandinavia, USSR and others, 1948–. *Education:* MA, King's College, Cambridge University; Cand Mag in Russian, Copenhagen University, Denmark. *Publications:* Russian Made Easy, 1943; The Road to the West, 1945; Children of the Century, 1945; Copenhagen–Praise and Protest, 1965; Denmark–Praise and Protest, 1969. Translations: The Malachite Casket, by Bazhov; Sea Stories, by Stanyukovich; Soren Kierkegaard, by Peter P Rohde. *Contributions to:* Numerous British and Scandinavian newspapers and magazines. *Memberships:* Society of Authors; National Union of Journalists; Dansk Forfatterforening; Pen. *Address:* Scandinavian Features Service, Box 4, 3450 Allerod pv Copenhagen, Denmark.

WILLIAMS, Barry Edward, b. 31 Oct. 1946, London, England. Journalist. m. Gillian Crispin, 22 June 1974, Shirley, 1 son, 1 daughter. *Appointments:* Sub-Editor, The Caravan, 1968; Editor, Camping, 1973, Caravanning Monthly, 1977, Camping Sites in Britain, Caravan Sites, Continental Camping & Caravanning Sites, 1983–; Editor, Caravan Magazine, 1984. *Publications:* Caravanning, 1975; Camping, 1978. *Contributor to:* Many specialist camping & caravanning magazines in UK, Europe and USA; Features for, Sunday Times, Mail on Sunday; etc. *Membership:* Committee, Caravan Writers' Guild. *Literary Agent:* Rupert Crew. *Address:* 64 Bennetts Way, Shirley, Croydon CRO 8AB, England.

WILLIAMS, Benjamin Buford, b. 28 Apr. 1923, New York, New York, USA. University Professor. m. Marilyn Moores Simpson, 3 June 1953 Fayetteville, Tennessee, 2 sons, 2 daughters. *Education:* AB, MA, University of Alabama; PhD, Vanderbilt University. *Literary Appointments:* University Fellow in English, Vanderbilt University, 1950–52; Instructor in English, University of Alabama, 1957–68; Professor of English, Auburn University, Montgomery, 1968–. *Publications:* Sketches of Mobile, 1868 by Bernard A Reynolds, (Editor with Introduction and notes), 1971; The Role of the Senate in Alabama History, (co-author), 1978; A Literary History of Alabama: The Nineteenth Century, 1979; The Governors of Alabama, (co-author), 1984; Compiler and Editor: Our American Heritage, bicentennial pamphlet, (co-author), 1975; USAAF Credits for Destruction of Enemy Aircraft, World War II, 1978. *Contributions to:* Alabama Historical Quarterly; Alabama Review; Historical Atlas of Alabama; American History Illustrated, Montgomery Advertiser-Journal; American and British Woman Writers, 1985. *Memberships:* Modern Language Association of America; National Council of Teachers of English; Society for the Study of Southern Literature; National Historical Society. *Address:* 3813 Marie Cook Drive, Montgomery, AL 36109, USA.

WILLIAMS, David Larry, b. 22 June 1945, Souris, Manitoba, Canada. University Professor. m. Darlene Olinyk, 22 July 1967, Saskatoon, Saskatchewan, Canada, 2 sons. *Education:* Pastor's Diploma, Breircrest Bible Institute, Saskatchewan, 1965; BA (Hons) University of Saskatchewan, 1968; MA, University of Massachusetts (Amherst) 1970; PhD, University of Massachusetts, 1973. *Literary Appointments:* Lecturer 1972–73, Assistant Professor, 1973–77, Associate Professor 1977–83, Professor of English, 1983–, University of Manitoba, Winnipeg, Canada. Editorial Board Member, Canadian Review of American Studies, 1976–86. *Publications:* The Burning Wood, novel, 1975; Faulkner's Women: The Myth and The Muse Criticism, 1977; The River Horsemen, novel, 1982; Eye of the Father, novel, 1985. *Contributions to:* Chapter in Twentieth-Century Interpretations of Faulkner's SANCTUARY editor by J Douglas Canfield, 1982. Critical essays on Herman Melville, Harold Frederic, Margaret Laurence, Sinclair Ross, Rudy Wiebe, in CRevAS, DalRev, CanL, MSE. *Honours:* Woodrow Wilson Fellow, 1968–69; Canada Council Fellow, 1969–72; Canada Council Arts Grant 'B' 1977–78 for, The River Horsemen; Canada Council Arts Grant 'B' 1981–82, for, Eye of the Father; Manitoba Arts Council Grants 1975, 1979 for, The Burning Wood, and The River Horsemen; Touring Writer in Scandinavia for External Affairs, Canada, March 181. *Memberships:* The Writers' Union of Canada, 1976–, Member of National Council of Prairie Region, 1978–79, 1984–85; Chairmen, Search-for-a-New Manitoba-Novelist Competition, Manitoba Department of Cultural Affairs, 1981–83. *Address:* Department of English, St Paul's College, University of Manitoba, Winnipeg, Canada R3T 2M6.

WILLIAMS, David Ricardo, b. 28 Feb. 1923, Kamloops, British Columbia, Canada. Author. m. Laura Ella-Belle Bapty, 29 May 1948, Victoria, BC, 4 sons, 1 daughter. *Education:* BA 1948; LLB University of British Columbia, Vancouver, BC, 1949. *Literary Appointments:* Writer-in-Residence, Faculty of Law, University of Victoria, Victoria, BC, 1980–86. *Publications:* The Man for a New Country, 1977; Matthew Baillie Begbie, 1980; Trapline Outlaw, 1982; Duff–A Life in the Law, 1984. *Contributor to:* Numerous contributions to magazines and Journals including; Canadian Bar Review; Pacific Northwest Quarterly; The Advocate; The Law Society of Upper Canada Gazette; Toronto Globe and Mail. *Honours:* University of British Columbia Medal for Biography for Man for a New Country, 1978; British Columbia Book Award (non-fiction) for Dull–A life in the Law, 1984. *Memberships:* The Writers' Union of Canada; Chairman Contracts Committee. *Literary Agent:* M A *Address:* Faculty of Law, University of Victoria, PO Box 2400, Victoria, BC, V8W 3H7, Canada.

WILLIAMS, Elaine, b. 1 June 1953, Tredegar, Gwent, Wales. Journalist. m. Colin McClarence, 17 July 1976, Tredegar, 1 daughter. *Education:* Honours Degree, Electronic Engineering. *Appointments:* Assistant Editor, Electronic Engineering, 1976–77; Assistant Editor, The Engineer, 1978–79; Journalist, The Financial Times, 1979–. *Publications:* The Silicon Civilisation, 1979; Inventions That Changed the World, Contributing Author, 1981. *Contributor to:* Numerous professional journals, magazines, etc, including, Financial Times; Sunday Times; The Engineer; Radio & TV broadcasting. *Membership:* Association of British Science Writers. *Address:* 5 Clarence Road, Sidcup, Kent DA14 4DL, England.

WILLIAMS, Glanmor, b. 5 May 1920, Dowlais, Glamorgan, Wales. Professor of History. *Education:* BA, MA, University of Wales; DLitt. *Publications:* The Welsh Church, 1962; Welsh Reformation Essays, 1967; Reformation Views of Church History, 1971; Editor, Glamorgan County History, Volume III, 1971, Volume IV, 1974, Volume V, 1980; Religion, Language and Nationality in Wales, 1979; Glamorgan County History, Volume II, 1984; Henry Tudor and Wales, 1985.

Contributions to: History; English Historical Review; Economic History Review; Welsh History Review; Cambridge Journal. *Honour:* CBE, 1981. *Memberships:* Fellow, Chairman, Board of Celtic Studies, Royal Historical Society; Advisory Council on Public Records; British Library Board; Fellow, Society of Antiquaries. *Address:* 11 Grosvenor Road, Swansea SA2 OSP, Wales.

WILLIAMS, Guy Richard, b. 23 Aug. 1920, Mold, North Wales. Author; Schoolmaster. *Education:* Manchester and Hornsey (London) Colleges of Art. *Publications:* The World of Model Ships and Boats, 1971; The World of Model Aircraft, 1973; The World of Model Cars, 1976; The Black Treasures of Scotland Yard, 1973; London in the Country: The Growth of Suburbia, 1975; The Age of Agony, 1975; The Royal Parks of London, 1978; The Age of Miracles, 1981. Advisory Editor, Dramascripts Series, Macmillian. *Contributions to:* British Broadcasting Corporation radio. *Address:* 1a Earl Road, East Sheen, London SW14 7JH, England.

WILLIAMS, Hugo, b. 20 Feb. 1942. Writer. m. Hermine Demoriane, Sacy-le-petit, France, 12 Oct. 1965, 1 daughter. *Literary Appointments:* Assistant Editor, London Magazine, 1961–69; Poetry Editor & Television Critic, New Statesman, 1983–. *Major Publications:* Poetry: Symptoms of Loss, 1965; Sugar-Daddy, 1970; Some Sweet Day, 1975; Love-Life, 1979; Writing Home, 1985; Travel: All the Time in the World, 1966; No Particular Place to Go, 1980. *Contributor to:* The Review; The New Review; London Review of Books; The Times Literary Supplement; The Tatler; and others. *Honours:* Eric Gregors Award, 1965; Cholmondeley Award, 1970; Geoffrey Faber Prize, 1979. *Address:* 3 Raleigh Street, London N1, England.

WILLIAMS, Lawrence Harding, b. 10 Oct. 1933, Enfield, England. Psychotherapist. Divorced, 1 son, 2 daughters. *Education:* Recognized University Teacher, University of London; BSc Honours; BSc General, London; PGGE, London; DMS, Hatfield Polytechnic; Formerly: FRGS; AMBIM; AMIPM. *Appointment:* Principal Lecturer, Geography and Education. *Publications:* Textbooks: Introduction to Mapwork, 1968; Britain from the Air, 1970; First Interest Series, 1972; Europe from the Air, 1972; N America from the Air, 1974, Changing World, 1984; Novels: The Wolves, 1970; Copper Snare, 1980; Murder Triangle, 1982; Images of Death, 1984; Avalanche, in Press. *Contributor to:* Articles in Educational Press. *Memberships:* Society of Authors; Crime Writers Association.

WILLIAMS, Malcolm David, b. 9 Apr. 1939, Cwmllynfell, Nr Swansea, South Wales. Author. Widower, 1 daughter. *Education:* Certificate in Education, Birmingham University Institue. *Publications include:* Yesterday's Secret, 1980; Poor Litle Rich Girl, 1981; Debt of Friendship, 1981; Another Time, Another Place, 1982; My Brother's Keeper, 1982; The Stuart Affair, 1983; The Cordillera Conspiracy, 1983 (also published in large print 1984); The Girl From Derry's Bluff, 1983; Sorrow's End, 1984; A Corner of Eden, 1984. *Contributions to:* Several hundred short stories plus over 40 serial stories in magazines and newspapers in 13 different languages in UK and overseas, also poems and articles. Tele-Text to Taytel/Prestel Service. Radio Play for South African Broadcasting Service. *Honours:* First prizes in Short Story Competitions: City of Worcester College of Education, 1961; Anglo-Welsh Review, 1969. *Memberships:* West Country Writers' Association; Writers Guild of Great Britain; Fellow World Literary Academy. *Literary Agent:* Internationalt Littermert Bureau, Copenhagen. *Address:* 58 Oxbutts Park, Woodmancote, Cheltenham, Gloucestershire GL52 4HW, England.

WILLIAMS, Marian Isabele (Yost), b. 28 Jan. 1950, Cleveland, Ohio, USA. Poet; Mother; Wife. m. Ralph Arthur Williams, 9 Sep. 1967, 2 daughters. *Literary Appointments:* Honorary Editorial Advisory Board 4

years, Contributing member 3 years, Director, Committee of Membership 1 year, ABI. *Contributions:* 801 poems, 4 poetry paragraphs, various journals. *Honours:* Certificate of Merit, Nashville Newsletter, 1979; Honorable Mention, World of Poetry, 1983; Royalties, poem, 1985. *Membership:* American Biographical Association (ABI). *Address:* 13411 Madison Avenue, Lakewood, OH 44107, USA.

WILLIAMS, Michael Edward John, b. 19 Oct. 1933, Ipswich, Suffolk, England. Golf Correspondent, Daily Telegraph. m. Judith Ann Sanderson, 12 Sep. 1959, Westerfield, 1 son, 3 daughters. *Publications:* Golf Sports Facts Book, 1964; History of Golf, 1985. *Contributions to:* Golf Illustrated; Golf World. *Address:* Fairlight, Birch Lane, Stock, Essex CM4 9NB, England.

WILLIAMS, Miller. University Press Director. m. Mobile, Alabama, USA. *Education:* BS, Biology, Arkansas State College, 1950; MS, Zoology, University of Arkansas, 1952. *Literary Appointments include:* Founder and Editor, New Orleans Review, Loyola University, 1968–70; Co-Director, Program on Creative Writing, University of Arkansas, 1971–80; Executive Director, Arkansas Poetry Circuit, 1974–80; Advisory Editor, New Orleans Review, 1975–; Contributing Editor, Translation Review, 1976–80; Translation Editor, Poetry Miscellany, 1979–81; Director, University of Arkansas Press, 1980–; Member, Advisory Council, School of Classical Studies, American Academy in Rome, 1985–. *Publications:* Books include: Contemporary Poetry in America, 1972; Halfway from Hoxis: New and Selected Poems, 1973; How Does a Poem Mean? (W John Ciardi), 1974; Railroad, (with James Alan McPherson, 1976); Why God Permits Evil (poems), 1977; A Roman Collection, 1980; Sonnets of Guiseppe Belli (translation), 1981; Distraction (poems), 1981; Ozark, Ozark: A Hillside Reader, 1981; The Boys on Their Bony Mules, 1983. *Contributions to:* Letras, Peru; The Oberlin Quarterly; Saturday Review; Mississippi Quarterly and several other publications. Recording: Poems of Miller Williams (SA 1160). *Honours include:* Henry Bellaman Poetry Award, 1957; Bread Loaf Fellowship in Poetry, 1961; Fulbright Lecturer in US Literature, National University of Mexico, 1970–; Prix de Rome, American Academy of Arts & Letters, 1976; D Hum, Lander College, 1983. *Address:* University of Arkansas Press, Fayetteville, AR 72701, USA.

WILLIAMS, Raymond Henry, b. 31 Aug. 1921, Llanfihangel Crucouney, England. Writer; University Professor. *Education:* BA, MA, LittD, Hon D University (Open), Cantab. *Publications include:* Drama from Ibsen to Eliot, 1952, revised edition, Drama from Ibsen to Brecht, 1968; Drama on Performance, 1954, revised edition, 1968; Culture & Society 1780–1950, 1958; Border Country (Novel), 1960; The Long Revolution, 1961; Communications, 1962, revised edition, 1968; Second Generation (Novel), 1964; The English Novel from Dickens to Lawrence, 1970; Orwell, 1971; The Country & The City, 1973; Television: Technological & Cultural Forum, 1974; Keywords, 1976; Towards 2000, 1983; Loyalties, 1985. *Contributor to:* Various Journals. *Membership:* Society of Authors. *Address;* Jesus College, Cambridge, England.

WILLIAMS, Shirley Vivien Teresa Brittain (Right Honourable), b. 27 July 1930, London, England. Politician. m. Bernard Williams, 1955, divorced 1974, 1 daughter. *Education:* MA, Somerville College, Oxford; Columbia University, New York, USA. *Publications include:* The Common Market and Its Forerunners', pamphlet, 1958; The Free Trade Area, pamphlet, 1958, Central Africa: The Economics of Inequality, pamphlet, 1960; Politics is for People, 1981; A Job to Live, 1985. *Contributions to:* What The Human Race Is Up To, (with B A O Williams), 1962; Christian Order and World Poverty, 1964. *Honours:* Visiting Fellow, Nuffield College, Oxford, 1967–75; Honorary DEd, CNAA; Honorary Dr Pol Econ, University of Leuven, Belgium, Radcliffe College, USA; Honorary LLD, Leeds University 1979, Southampton 1981. *Memberships include:* Co-founder 1981, President 1982–, Social

Democratic Party. *Address:* c/o SDP, 4 Cowley Street, London, SW1P 3NB, England.

WILLIAMS, Thomas, b. 15 Nov. 1926, Duluth, Minnesota, USA. Writer. *Education:* BA, MA, University of New Hampshire. *Publications:* Ceremony of Love, 1955; Town Burning, 1959; The Night of Trees, 1961; A High New House, 1963; Whipple's Castle, 1969; The Hair of Harold Roux, 1974; Tsuaga's Children, 1977; The Followed Man, 1978; The Moon Pinnace, 1986. *Contributions to:* New Yorker; Esquire; Kenyon Review; Saturday Evening Post; Harpers, etc. *Honours:* Guggenheim Fellowship, 1963; Dial Fellowship for Fiction, 1963; Rockefeller Fellowship for Fiction, 1968; National Book Award, 1975. *Memberships:* Authors' Guild. *Literary Agent:* RLR Associates Ltd *Address:* 13 Orchard Drive, Durham NH 03824, USA.

WILLIAMS, Ursula Moray, b. 19 Apr. 1911, Petersfield, Hampshire, England. Writer. *Education:* Winchester College of Art. *Publications:* The Adventures of the Little Wooden Horse, 1938; Gobbolino the Witch's Cat, 1948; The Nine Lives of Island Mackenzie, 1959; Bogwoppit, 1978. *Contributor to:* Puffin Post; Cricket; USA; Lady. *Memberships:* National Book League; West Country Writers Association. *Literary Agent:* Curtis Brown Limited. *Address:* Court Farm House, Beckford, Nr Tewkesbury, Gloucestershire, England.

WILLIAMS, Wilma Dean, b. 28 Feb. 1929. Poet. *Education:* BA, Bethany-Peniel College, USA. 1952. *Literary Appointments:* Piano Accompanist, Clerk-typist, Secretary. *Contributions to:* Church School Builder; Conquest; Standard; Teens Tosay; National Federation of State Poetry Societies Prize Poems; Pen Woman; Anthology of Oklahoma Poetry Bicentennial Edition; Encore; Wildcat; Blue Grass Literary Review; Poet, India; Lyric; Major Poets; Paper Blossoms; Poet of the Month Club Anthology; Voices International; Premier Poet Anthology, India; High school Poetry Society Awards, 1978, 1980. *Memberships:* World Poetry Society; National Federation of State Poetry Societies Inc; National League of American Pen Women; Poetry Society of Oklahoma; Florida State Poets Association; Louisiana State Poetry Society; Poetry Society of Texas; South Dakota State Poetry Society; Oklahoma Writers Federation; Robert Frost Chapter, California Federation of Chapparal Poets; Random Rhyme Poetry Society of Oklahoma. *Address:* PO Box 800120, Oklahoma City, OK 73008, USA.

WILLIAMSON, Brenda Marie, b. 31 Oct. 1958, Long Branch, New Jersey, USA. Publisher. m. Robert A Williamson Jr, 27 Jan. 1979. *Education:* Graduate, Institute of Childrens Literature. *Literary Appointments:* Editor, Trouvere Company Publications. *Contributions to:* Fine Lines; Hob-Nob; Reflect; Bell's Letters; Explorer; Published; Ahoy; Parnassus Literary Journal; Archer; New Voices; Broken Streets; Black Creek Review; Dreams & Visions Anthology; Hearts On Fire Anthology; etc. *Membership:* National Writers Club. *Address:* Route 2, Box 290, Eclectic, AL 36024, USA.

WILLIAMSON, Richard Leopold Calvert, b. 1 Aug. 1935, Devon, England. Ecologist. m. Anne, 9 Mar. 1964, Bungay, Suffolk, 1 son, 1 daughter. *Publications:* Dawn is my Brother, 1959; Capreol, 1972; The Great Yew Forest, 1978. *Contributions to:* Daily Mail, 300 articles, 1960; Portsmouth and Sunderland newspapers, 20 years; Shooting Times; Thoroughbred, 8 Classic Cars; Natural World; RSPB Magazine, Man on the Island, Television play. *Honours:* Runner Up to Richard Llewellyn, Rhys Memorial Prize, 1960; Literary Prize, Civil Service, 1974. *Memberships:* West Country Writers Association; President, Henry Williamson Society. *Literary Agent:* A M Heath and Company. *Address:* Keepers, West Dean Woods, Chichester, Sussex PO18 ORU, England.

WILLIAMSON, Robin Duncan Harry, b. 24 Nov. 1943, Edinburgh, Scotland, England. Writer, Composer, Multi Instrumentalist, Record Producer. m. Janet Shankman, 20 Dec. 1970, Los Angeles, USA, 1 son. *Publications include:* Books, LP recordings; A variety of film, theatre and TV work. Incredible String Band Song Book, 1968; Home Thoughts from Abroad, 1972; Incredible String Band, A Second Songbook, 1973; Glory Trap, novel, co-author, 1976; 2 books, traditional music of British Isles: Fiddle Tunes 1976, The Penny Whistle Book, 1977; Five Denials on Merlin's Grave, 1979; Selected Writing, 1980–83, book & cassette package, 1984; Five Humourous Tales of Scotland & Ireland, Cassette, Spoken Word, 1984. Recordings include: Incredible String Band; 5000 Spirits or the Layers of the Onion; Wee Tam & The Big Huge; I Looked Up; Earthspan; Hard Rope & Silken Twine; Seasons They Change; Myrrh, solo record; American Stonehenge; Songs of Love & Parting; Music for the Mabinogi, 1983; Legacy of the Scottish Harpers; 1984; The Dragon Has Two Tongues, 1985; etc. Recent cassettes: Spoken Word, Five Celtic Tales of Enchantment, Five Bardic Mysteries, Five Legendary Histories of Britain, Five Celtic Tales of Prodigies and Marvels, 1985. *Contributions to:* Various anthologies, poetry magazines. *Memberships:* American Poetry Society; Scottish Poetry Library Association. *Address:* BCM 4797, London WC1N 3XX, England.

WILLIE, Charles V, b. 8 Oct. 1927, Dallas, Texas, USA. Harvard University Professor. *Education:* BA, Morehouse College, 1948; MA, Atlanta University, USA, 1949; PhD, Syracuse University, 1957. *Appointment:* Editorial Board, Choice and Equity. *Publications include:* Church Action in the World, 1969; Black Students in White Colleges, 1972; Racism and Mental Health, 1972; Race Mixing in Public Schools, 1973; OREO, 1975; A New Look at Black Families, 1976; Black/Brown/White Relations, 1977; Sociology of Urban Education, 1978; Black Colleges in America, 1978; The Castle and Class Controversy, 1979; Community Politics and Educational Change, 1980; The Ivory and Ebony Towers, 1981; Race Ethnicity and Socioeconomic Status, 1983; School Desegregation Plans That Work, 1984; Black and White Families, 1985. *Contributions to:* Dissent; Change; Phi Delta Kappan; Harvard Magazine; Psychology Today; Society; Integrated Education, etc. *Honours:* Distinguished Alumnus Award, Syracuse University; DHL, Berkeley Division School at Yale University; DHL, Morehouse College; DHL, Rhode Island College; DD, General Theological Seminary; MA, Harvard University. *Memberhips:* Phi Beta Kappa. *Address:* 1 Hillcrest Road, Concord, MA 01742, USA.

WILLINGS, David, b. 16 May 1932, Cambridge, England. Counselling Psychologist; Technical Director, The Centre for Innovation. m. Angela Chamberland, 23 July 1982, Portland, Maine, USA. *Education:* BA with honours, University of Durham, 1957; MA Psychology, University of London, 1962; PhD, University of Strathclyde, 1972. *Literary Appointments:* Senior Advisory Editor, STI Publishers, Halifax, Nova Scotia, Canada, 1980–; Contributing Editor, The Roeper Review, 1985–. *Publications:* The Human Element in Management, 1968; Understanding Management, 1979, 2nd edition 1985; The Creatively Gifted (also a 27 minute film on this book, written and directed by the author), 1980; Liberating Creative Potential, 1985; Enriched Career Search, due 1986. *Contributions to:* The Roeper Review; Teaching Exceptional Children; International Journal for the Advancement of Counselling; Gifted Education International; Social Service Quarterly; Glasgow Herald. *Honours:* Gold Medal for Outstanding Services, Canadian Fencing Association, 1976–1977 and 1978; Sport Canada Award for Services to Amateur Sport, 1977. *Memberships:* President 1981–84, Atlantic Association for Gifted Children and Adults; Council for Exceptional Children; World Council for Gifted and Talented Children. *Address:* The Centre for Innovation, 1 Redcliffe Place, London SW10, England.

WILLIS, Judith Laura Levine, b. 24 May 1941, Brooklyn, New York, USA. Writer; Editor. m. Ronald J

Willis, 2 May 1965, Lawrenceville, deceased, 1 daughter. *Education:* BSJ, Ohio University, 1963. *Appointments:* Reporter, Trenton (NJ) Times; Associate Editor, Metropolitan Restaurant News; Information Specialist, Public Health Service; Owner-Operator, Judith Willis, The Traveling Editor; Editor, Woodwind; Assistant Director, Public Affairs, Fairfax Hospital Association; Editor, FDA Drug Bulletin. *Contributor to:* Many articles in, FDA Consumer Magazine; Chicago Tribune; Weight Watchers Magazine; Moneysworth; Woman's Day; Poems, Prose; Womanspirit Magazine; Broomstick Magazine. *Honours:* Recipient, various honours and awards including 1st Place, Page Make-up, 1st Place, Feature Writing, 1st Place, Interviews, Virginia Press Women; 1st Place, Speeches, National Association of Government Communicators. *Memberships:* Washington Independent Writers; Writers Center; American Medical Writers Association. *Addess:* c/o FDA (HFI 42), 5600 Fishers Lane, Rockville, MD 20852, USA.

WILLOCK, Colin Dennistoun, b. 13 Jan. 1919, London, England. Television Producer; Author. *Publications include:* Sport: Come Fishing With Me, 1952; The Gun Punt Adventure, 1958; Come Fly Fishing With Me, 1953; Coarse Fishing, 1956; The Angler's Encyclopedia, 1960; Duck Shooting, 1962; 80 Crime Novels: Death at Flight, 1956; Death at the Strike, 1957; Death in Convert, 1961. Novels: The Animal Catchers, 1964; Hazanda, 1968; The Coast of Loneliness, 1971; The Fighters, 1973; Gorilla, 1976. Humour: Rod, Pole or Perch, 1958; Dudley, the Worst Dog in the World, 1977. Wildlife: Look at African Animals, 1963; The World of Survival, 1978. Autobiographies: Landscape with Solitary Figure, 1966, 80; Town Gun, 1973. Biographies: Kenzie the Wild Goose Man, 1962. Travel: The Great Rift Valley, 1974. Editor of several books including: In Praise of Fishing, anthology, 1954; The Survival Series, wildlife books, 1964–75; ABC of Shooting, 1975. *Contributions to:* As Town Gun, Shooting Times. *Literary Agent:* Curtis Brown. *Address:* Cranleigh, Ashley Drive, Walton-on-Thames, Surrey, England.

WILLS, Jean, b. 10 Feb. 1929, West London, England. Author. m. Graham Boyce Wills, 15 Nov. 1952, West London, 2 sons, 1 daughter. *Publications:* The Sawdust Secret, 1973; The Sugar Trail, 1974; Who Wants a Job?, 1976; The Hope and Glory Band, 1978; Round the Twist, 1979; Sandy's Gargoyle, 1979; Nicky and the Genius, 1980; May Day Hullabaloo, 1981; Stargazers' Folly, 1982; The Railway Computer, 1983. *Membership:* Society of Authors. *Address:* 70 Highview Road, London W13 OHW, England.

WILOCH, Thomas, b. 3 Feb. 1953, Detriot, Michigan, USA. Senior Writer. m. Denise Gottis, 10 Oct 1981, Livonia, Michigan. *Education:* BA, Wayne State University, 1978. *Literary Appointments:* Book Reviewer, SPWAO Newsletter, 1981–84; Editor, Grimoire, 1982–; Senior Writer, Gale Research Company, Detroit, Michigan. *Publications:* Poems: Stigmata Junction, 1985. Senior Writer: Contemporary Authors, Volumes 1-16, 1979–. Co-Editor: Directory of Michigan Literary Publishers, 1982. *Contributions to:* Elsewhere, volume 2 1982; Voices for Peace Anthology 1983; A Bell Ringing in the Empty Sky, 1985. Over 150 poems, reviews and articles in publications including: Croton Review; Pulpsmith; Poetry Now; University of Windsor Review; Berkeley Poets Cooperative; Bitterroot, Pinchpenny; Stride; Proof Rock; The Sun; Bogg; Nagative Capability; Minotaur; Gryphon; Zahir; Fifth Estate; Prophetic Voices. Over 200 collages featured in publications including: Kayak; New Age Journal; Telescope; Fantasy Newsletter; Cedar Rock; Wormwood Review; Velocities; Oyez Review; Milkweed Chronicle; Nyctalops. *Honour:* Poet Hunt Award, Schoolcraft College, 1985. *Address:* 43672 Emrick Drive, Canton MI 48187, USA.

WILSON, Alan G, b. 8 Jan. 1939, Bradford, Yorkshire, England. University Professor. *Education:* MA, Cambridge University. *Publications:* Entropy in Urban and Regional Modelling, 1970; Papers in Urban and Regional Analysis, 1972; Urban and Regional Models in Geography and Planning, 1964; Mathematics for Geographers and Planners (with M J Kirby), 1975; Spatial Population Analysis (with P H Rees), 1977; Models of Cities and Regions (with P H Rees, C M Leigh et al), 1977; Catastrophe Theory and Bifurcation: Applications to Urban and Regional Systems, 1981; Geography and Environment: Systems Analytical Methods, 1981; Optimisation in Locational Transport Analysis (with J D Coelho, S M Macgill, H C W L Williams), 1981; Mathematical Methods in Human Geography and Planning (with R J Bennett), 1986. *Contributor to:* Environment and Planning; Urban Studies; Journal of Transport Economics and Policy; Times Higher Educational Supplement; The Statistician; New Society, etc. *Honour:* Gill Memorial Award, Royal Geographical Society, 1978. *Literary Agent:* A D Peters & Company. *Address:* School of Geography, University of Leeds, Leeds LS2 9JT, England.

WILSON, Andrew Norman, b. 27 Oct. 1950, England. Writer. *Education:* MA, New College, Oxford, 1976. *Literary Appointment:* Literary Editor of The Spectator, 1980–83. *Publications:* Novels: The Sweets of Pimlico 1977; The Healing Art, 1980; Wise Virgin, 1982; Gentlemen in England, 1984. Biographies: John Milton, 1980; Hilaire Belloc, 1984. *Contributor to:* Regular contributor to: The Spectator, The Sunday Telegraph, The Literary Review. *Honour:* Fellow of the Royal Society of Literature, 1981. *Literary Agent:* Caroline Daunay, c/o A D Peters Ltd. *Address:* 16 Richmond Road, Oxford OX1 2JL, England.

WILSON, Arthur James Cochran, b. 28 Nov. 1914, Canada. Physicist. m. Harriett Charlotte Friedeberg, 2 sons, 1 daughter. *Education:* BSc, MSc, Dalhousie University; PhD, Massachusetts Institute of Technology, USA; PhD, Cambridge University, England; FIM; FInstP; FRS. *Publications include:* X-Ray Optics, 1949 and 1962, Russian edition 1951; Elements of X-Ray Crystallography, 1970; Structure and Statistics in Crystallography, 1985. *Contributions to:* Numerous papers in learned journals including: Acta Crystallographica; Proceedings of the Physical Society; Proceedings of the Royal Society. *Address:* University Chemical Laboratory, Lensfield Road, Cambridge CB2 1EW, England.

WILSON, Barbara, b. 13 July 1932, Hoylandswaine, Yorkshire, England. Writer. m. Colin Wilson, 19 Sep. 1953, Penistone, 1 son, 2 daughters. *Education:* Currently studying with the Open University. *Publications:* Lock up the Wind, 1964; Charged to the Account, 1966; They Conquer Love, 1967, Stubborn Clay, 1969; Before You Answer, 1970; TheRiver Within Us, 1972; The Oldest Confession, 1973; The House of Clay, 1977; The Silver Thimble, 1979; Dimity, 1980; Constant Star, 1980; A Bouquet of Irony, 1981; Tomorrow for the Roses, 1981; An Old Sweet Song, 1984. *Literary Agent:* Hughes Massie. *Address:* 30 Dig Lane, Wybunbury, Near Nantwich, Cheshire, England.

WILSON, Bryan R, b. Leeds, England. University Teacher. *Education:* BSc, PhD, London University; MA, DLitt, Oxford University. *Publications:* Sects and Society, 1961; Religion in Secular Society, 1966; Religious Sects, 1970; The Youth Culture and the Universities, 1970; Rationality, Editor, 1970; Magic and the Millennium, 1973; The Nobles Savages, 1975; Contemporary Transformation of Religion, 1976; The Social Impact of the New Religions, Editor, 1981; Religion in Sociological Perspective, 1982; Human Values in a Changing World, with Daisaku Ikeda, 1984; Values: A symposium, Editor, 1986. *Contributions to:* The Spectator; The Observer; Sunday Times; New Society; Encounter; Times; Daily Telegraph. *Honours:* Fellowships: Commonwealth Fund, Harkness, 1957–58; American Council of Learned Societies, 1966–67; Japan Society, 1975. Visiting Professor: University of Toronto, Canada, 1978; University of Louvain, Belgium, 1982, 1985–86; University of Queensland, Australia, 1986. Visiting Fellow, Ormond College, University of

Melbourne, Australia, 1981; Honorary DLitt, Soka University, Tikyo, Japan, 1985. *Membership:* Past President, Conference de Sociologie de Religions, 1971–75. *Address:* All Souls College, University of Oxford, Oxford, England.

WILSON, David Ian, b. 15 Aug. 1942, Liverpool, England. Publisher. *Education:* BA, Hertford College, Oxford. *Literary Appointments:* Editor, Monthly Film Bulletin, 1966–70; Associate Editor, Sight and Sound, 1970–80; Currently Editorial Director, BFI Publishing. *Publications:* Editor: A Fiftieth Anniversary Selection, Sight and Sound, 1982; Projecting Britain: Ealing Studios Film Posters, 1982. *Contributions to:* Sight and Sound; Time Literary Supplement; New Statesman; New Society; Stills. *Address:* Flat 1, 4 St Michaels Gardens, London W10 5SP, England.

WILSON, David MacKenzie, Sir, b. 30 Oct. 1931. Director of the British Museum. *Education:* St John's College, Cambridge, England; LittD, Lund University, Sweden. *Publications include:* The Anglo Saxons, 1960, 3rd edition 1981; Anglo Saxon Metalwork 700-1100 in British Museum, 1964; Viking Art (with O Klindt-Jensen), 1966, 2nd edition, 1980; The Vikings and their Origins, 1970, 2nd edition, 1980; The Viking Achievement (with P G Foote), 1970; The Viking Age in the Isle of Man, 1974; editor Anglo Saxon Archeology, 1976; The Northern World, 1980; Anglo Saxon Art, 1984; The Forgotten Collector, 1984; The Bayeux Tapestry, 1985. *Contributor to:* Archeologia; Antiquaries Journal, FBA, FSA, MRIA. *Honours:* Dag Stromback Prize, Royal Gustav's Adolf's Academy, 1975; Felix Neubugh Prize, 1978. *Address:* British Museum, Great Russell Street, London WC18 3DG, England.

WILSON, Delbert Ray, b. 16 Jan. 1926, Riverdale, California, USA. Daily Newspaper Editor and Publisher. m. Beatrice Joy Daffer, 5 Oct. 1947, Lebanon, Nebraska, USA, 4 daughters. *Education:* AA and AS, Elgin Illinois Community College; BS, Northern Illinois University, DeKalb, IL. *Publications:* The Folks, 1974; Fort Kearny on the Platte, 1980; Episode on Hill 616, 1981; Nebraska Historical Tour Guide, 1983; Wyoming Historical Tour Guide, 1984; Iowa Historical Tour Guide, 1985. *Honour:* Honorary Doctorate of Humane Letters; Judson College, Elgin IL, 1985. *Membership:* Sigma Delta Chi. *Address:* 1507 Laurel Court, Dundee, IL 60118, USA.

WILSON, Derek Alan, b. 10 Oct. 1935, Colchester, Essex. Author/Broadcaster. m. Marjorie Ruth Elizabeth King, 4 Apr. 1961, Harrow, 1 son, 2 daughters. *Education:* BA, 1961, MA, 1964, Peterhouse, Cambridge. *Publications:* East Africa Through a Thousand Years, 1968; A Tudor Tapestry, 1972; Sail and Steam, 1973; The People and the Book, 1974; Feast in the Morning, 1975; A History of South and Central Africa, 1975; A Time to Lose, 1976; White Gold – The Story of African Ivory, 1976; A Students Atlas of African History, 1977; The Illustrated Book of World History, 1977; A Short History of Suffolk, 1977; The World Encompassed – Drake's Voyage 1577–80, 1977; England in the Age of Thomas More, 1978; Africa – A Modern History, 1978; The Tower 1078–1978, 1978; The Bear's Whelp, 1978; The World Atlas of Treasure, 1981; Sweet Robin – Robert Dudley Earl of Leicester, 1981; Bear Rampant, 1981; Extraordinary People, 1983; Francis Frith's Travels, 1985. Numerous radio broadcasts. *Contributor to:* Numerous magazines and journals. *Honour:* Archbishop Cranmer Prize for Post Graduate Research, Cambridge University, 1964. *Membership:* Society of Authors. *Literary Agent:* J R Parker MBA, 45 Fitzroy Street, London W1. *Address:* Codecombe House, Cutcombe, Somerset TA24 7AJ, England.

WILSON, Dorothy Clarke, b. 9 May 1904, Gardiner, Maine, USA. Author. *Education:* BA, 1925, Litt D, 1946, Bates College, Maine; LHD, University of Maine, 1984. *Publications:* Author of over 70 religious plays including: Twelve Months of Drama, 1934. Novels: The Herdsman: A Story of Amos, 1946; Jezebel, 1955; The Gifts, 1956. Biographies: Take My hands, Story of Dr Mary Verghese, 1963; Ten Fingers for God, Story of Dr Paul Brand, 1965; Palace of Healing, 1968; Lone Woman, Story of Elizabeth Blackwell, the First Woman Doctor, 1970; The Big-Little World of Doc Pritham, 1971; Bright Eyes, Story of an Omaha Indian, 1974; Stranger and Traveller, Story of Dorothea Dix, 1975; Climb Every Mountain, Story of Granny Brand, 1976; American, Granny Brand, 1976; Twelve Who Cared, Autobiographical, 1977; Story of Dr Victor Rambo, 1980; Lincoln's Mother, 1981; Lady Washington, 1984. *Contributions to:* Reader's Digest; Christian Herald. *Honours include:* Westminster Religious Fiction Award, for Prince of Egypt, 1949; Alpha Delta Kappa Woman of Distinction, 1971; New England United Methodist Award, 1975. *Address:* 114 Forest Avenue, Orono, ME 04473, USA.

WILSON, Elizabeth Jane (Morfitt), b. 29 Oct. 1948, Toronto, Canada. Writer; Editor. m. George Norris Wilson, 24 Dec. 1980, Toronto, 1 son, 1 daughter. *Education:* BA, English Literature; RN (Nursing diploma). *Regular Contributor to:* Canadian Medical Associaton Journal; Canadian Nurse. Titles include: Pediatric Emergency: croup & epiglottitis; Lactose Intolerance; Ethics & the physician-nurse relationship; A new code of ethics for nursing; Political success: nurses' new goal. *Memberships:* Canadian Science Writers Association; American Medical Writers Association; Media Club of Canada. *Address:* 4 Mutchmor Road, Ottawa, Ontario, Canada K15 IL5.

WILSON, Gina, b. 1 Apr. 1943, Abergele, North Wales. Writer. m. Edward Wilson, Windermere, 22 July 1972, 1 son, 2 daughters. *Education:* MA, Honours, English Literature & Language, Edinburgh University. *Literary Appointments:* Assistant Editor, Scottish National Dictionary 1966–71, Dictionary of the Older Scottish Tongue 1971–73. *Publications:* Cora Ravenwing, 1980; A Friendship of Equals, 1981; The Whisper, 1982; All Ends Up, 1984; Family Feeling, 1986. *Contributions to:* Times Literary Supplement (poem); Anthology, Ducks & Dragons, 1980. *Literary Agent:* Patricia White at Deborah Rogers. *Address:* c/o Faber & Faber, 3 Queen Square, London WC1N 3AU, England.

WILSON, James Clyde, b. 4 Oct. 1948, Lincoln, Nebraska, USA. University Professor. m. Cynthia Buono, Alburquerque New Mexico, USA, 29 Feb. 1980, 1 son. *Education:* BA, 1971; MA, 1974, University of Nebraska; PhD, University of New Mexico, 1982. *Literary Appointments:* Editorial Assistant, Prairie Schooner, 1971–74; Editor, Saltillo, 1972–77; Assistant Professor, Department of English, 1983–; Chairman of Writing Program, 1984–, University of Cincinnati. *Publications:* Vietnam in Prose and Film, 1982; The Hawthorne-Melville Relationship, 1982; John Reed for the Masses, 1986. *Contributions to:* Prairie Schooner; Contemporary Literary Criticism; Arizona Quarterly; The Midwest Quarterly; The Wilson Quartlery; American Notes and Queries; Melville Society Extracts; ESQ. *Honours:* National Endowment for the Arts Grants, 1972, 1974, to found and Edit Saltillo; Vreeland Award for Fiction, University of Nebraska, 1974; University of Cincinnati Research Council Grants, 1984; University of Cincinnati Grant in aid of Research, 1984. *Membership:* Modern Language Association. *Address:* Department of English, McMicken Hall ML69, Univerity of Cincinnati, Cincinnati, OH 45221, USA.

WILSON, Laura Ann, b. 23 Aug. 1952, North Carolina, USA. Writer; Manager, Training and Documetation. *Education:* BA, English, with Distinction, University of Virginia; Publications Specialist Program, George Washington University. *Publications:* Young People's Yellow Pages, 1983; EPIC/JANUS User's Guide, 1985. *Memberships:* Washington Educational Association; Education Writers Association. *Address:* 8123 Kingsway Court, Springfield, VA 22152, USA.

WILSON, Norma Jean Clark, b. 30 Jan. 1946. Professor of English; Writer. m. Jerry Wayne Wilson. *Education:* BA, Tennessee Technological University,

USA, 1968; MA, Austin Peay State University, 1970; PhD, University of Oklahoma, 1978. *Literary Appointments:* Teacher, 9th and 10th grade English, Montgomery Central High, Cunningham, Tennessee, 1970–71; Instructor, Composition, Introduction to Literature, Western Oklahoma State College, Altus, 1977–78; Assistant Professor of English, 1978–; Associate Professor of English, University of South Dakota, Vermillion, 1978–. *Publication:* Wild Iris, 1978. *Contributor to:* Windmill; South Dakota Review; Best Friends; North Dakota Quarterly; Heartbeat; Within the Visionary Tradition in The Mickle Street Review, 1985; Vermillion Spring, This Morning, Monument in Boise City, in The Point Riders Great Plains Poetry Anthology, 1982; Outlook for Survival, in Denver Quarterly, 1980. *Honours:* Bush Foundation Symposium Grant, 1984; Bush Foundation Research Grant, 1984–85. *Memberships:* South Dakota Humanist; South Dakota Council of Teachers of English; Writer, Writer Reads Series, South Dakota, 1980–81; MLA; Rocky Mountain MLA; Individual Artists of Oklahoma. *Address:* RR1 Box 104, Vermillion, SD 57069, USA.

WILSON, Robert William, b. 18 Apr. 1920, Mentone, Victoria, Australia. Editor. m. Gloria Joy Norris, Pinnaroo, South Australia, 12 Aug. 1961, 1 son, 2 daughters. *Major Publications:* Land of Promise, 1961; Forth House to Bark Hut, 1985. *Address:* 2 South Terrace, Pinnaroo, South Australia, 5304.

WILSON, Sarah Elizabeth Turpin, b. 18 Oct. 1934, Syracuse, New York, USA. Artist; Illustrator. m. Herbert E Wilson, 30 Sep. 1956, Kinston, NC, 1 son, 1 daughter. *Education:* BA, Ohio University, 1956; Diploma de Estudios Hispanicos, University of Madrid, Spain, 1955. *Literary Appointments:* Medical Social Worker; Teacher, Children's Art; Co-founder, Art Workshop/West, Los Angeles; Illustrator; Toy maker. *Publications:* I Can Do It! I Can Do It!, 1976; The House at the End of the Lane, (illustrations) 1982; Beware the Dragons!, 1985. *Contributor to:* Several newspapers and magazines including: Bitterroot; The Denver Post; Laguna Beach News-Post; Pandemonium; The New York Quarterly; Waynefleet Review; Poetry. *Honour:* Don Freeman Memorial Grant, 1982. *Memberships:* The Author's Guild Society of Children's Book Writers (former Regional Advisor). *Address:* 11785 Shadow Drive, Dublin, CA 94568, USA.

WILSON, William Edward, b. 12 Feb. 1906, Evansville, Indiana, USA. Writer. m. (1) Ellen Cameron, 29 June 1929, Pittsburgh, Pennsylvania. (2) Hana Benes, 29 Sep. 1977, Bloomington, Indiana, 3 sons. *Education:* AB (cum laude), Harvard University, 1927; AM, Harvard University, 1930. *Major Publications:* The Wabash, 1940; Yesterday's Son, 1941; Big Knife, 1941; Shooting Star, 1942; Crescent City, 1947; Abe Lincoln of Pigeon Creek, 1949; The Strangers, 1952; The Raiders, 1954; Sunny Side of a One-Way Street, 1958; The Angel and the Serpent, 1962; Indiana, 1964; Every Man is my Father, 1973. *Contributor to:* American Heritage; New Yorker; Southern Review; Atlantic; and others. *Honours:* Guggenheim Fellow, 1945; Fulbright Fellow, 1956; Litt.D, University of Evansville, 1962; LHD, Indiana University, 1981; LHD Indiana State University, 1983. *Literary Agent:* Ann Elmo, New York City. *Address:* 915 Commons Drive West, Bloomington, IN 47401, USA.

WINANS, Allan Davis, b. 12 Jan. 1936, San Francisco, California, USA. Poet; Writer; Editor; Publisher. *Education:* BA, San Francisco State Unviersity. *Literary Appointments:* Editor, Writer, San Francisco Arts Commission, San Francisco, California, 1975–80; Editor, Publisher, Second Coming Press, 1972–. *Publications:* Carmel Clowns, 1972; Straws of Sanity, 1974; Org-1, 1975; Further Adventures of Crazy John, 1977; North Beach Poems, 1977; All the Graffiti on All the Bathrooms in the World Can't Hide These Scars of Mine, 1977; The Reagan Psalms, 1984. *Contributions to:* Over 350 literary and commercial magazines and journals worldwide including: Poetry Australia; Beatitude; Second Coming; Confrontation; New York Quarterly; City

Lights Journal. *Honours:* Writing Grants: Poets, Playwrights, Editors, Essayists and Novelists, 1975, 80; 85 Carnegie, 1980. Grants for Editing and Publishing: National Endowment for TLE Arts; CCLM; California Arts Council, 1975–84. *Memberships:* PEN Writing Center; COSMEP; Poetry Society of America; Board of Directors, Cosmep, 1985; Writers Club, 1985–. *Address:* P O Box 31249, San Francisco, CA 94131, USA.

WINCHELL, Wallace, b. 8 Mar. 1914, USA. College Professor. *Education:* BA, Montclair State Teachers College, USA, 1936; MDiv, Union Theological Seminary, 1944; MA, Wayne University, 1954; PhD, Hartford Seminary Foundation, 1976. *Appointments:* Field Officer, Salvation Army, 1937–43; Pastor, Congregational Churches, 1943–69; Adjunct Lecturer, University of Hartford, 1962–65; Faculty Member, Manchester Community College, 1970–. *Major Publications:* The House of Bethlehem, 1972; Century-Spanning Significance, 1974; Popping Cult Ballons: Realities to hold on to, 1985. *Contributor to:* Lyric Magazine; Antioch Review; Song & Scimitar; Christian Herald; War Cry; Hartford Courant; Chicago Sunday Tribune Magazine; The Literary Review; and others. *Honours include:* Nathan Haskell Dole Award, 1978; Dellbrook Award, 1978, 1979. *Memberships:* Charter Member, International Academy of Poets; Book Reviewer & Literary Critic, Poetry Society of America; Connecticut Poetry Society, President. *Address:* 681 Hartford Road, Manchester, CT 06040, USA.

WINDSOR, Duane, b. 27 Mar. 1947, Compton, California, USA. University Professor. m. Sandra Sue Max Windsor, 20 Apr. 1981, Houston. *Education:* BA, Rice University, 1969; AM, 1975, PhD, 1978, Political Economy and Government, Harvard University. *Appointments:* Manuscript, Grant Proposal Reviewer, National Science Foundation, Decision & Management Science Programme; Prentice-Hall Inc, Growth and Change: A Journal of Regional Development; Urban Affairs Quarterly; Journal of the American Planning Association; Southwest Journal of Business and Economics. *Publications include:* Housing Development and Municipal Costs, co-author, 1973; Fiscal Zoning in Suburban Communities, 1979; The Changing Boardroom: Making Policy and Profits in an Age of Corporate Citizenship, co-editor, 1982; The Foreign Corrupt Practices Act: Anatomy of a Statute, co-author, 1982; Numerous book chapters. *Contributor to:* Teaching Political Science; Long Range Planning; Texas Business Review; Interfaces; Human Systems Management; Scholar and Educator; Judicature: Journal of the American Judicature Society; Current Business Perspectives; etc. *Honours:* Phi Beta Kappa; Phi Delta Phi; Woodrow Wilson Fellow, 1969; NDEA IV Fellow, 1969–72; Best Paper, Business Policy & Planning Area, Southern Management Association, 1980; Best Paper, Academic Affairs and Public/Nonprofit Area, Southeast American Institute for Decision Sciences, 1981; Halliburton Education Foundation Award of Excellence, 1981. *Memberships:* Editorial Advisory Board, Journal of the American Planning Association. *Address:* Jesse H Jones Graduate School of Administration, Rice University, P O Box 1892, Houston, TX 77251, USA.

WINDSOR, Merrill Cranston Jr, b. 23 Nov. 1924, Casa Grande, Arizona, USA. Editor. m. Janice Alene Falk, 19 June 1949, Phoenix, Arizona, 2 sons (1 dec.), 2 daughters. *Education:* BA, University of Arizona, USA; BA, MA, University of Oxford, UK. *Literary appointments:* The Arizona Republic, 1951–55; Sunset Magazine, 1956–71; Special Publications Division, National Geographic Society, 1971–85; Editor Arizona Highways Magazine, 1985. *Publications include:* America's Sunset Coast, 1978; Contributing author, Peoples & Places of the Past, 1983; America's Wild Woodlands, 1985. Editor, approximately 20 publications, National Geographic Society. *Contributions to:* Sunset; American Oxonian; National Geographic Traveler; Arizona Highways. *Memberships:* Phi Beta Kappa; Phi Kappa Phi. *Address:* 12426 S. Potomac Street, Phoenix, AZ 85044, USA.

WINGFIELD DIGBY, George, b. 2 Mar. 1911, Sherborne, Dorset, England. Author; Keeper Emeritus, Victoria and Albert Museum. *Education:* Trinity College, Cambridge University; Universities of Paris and Grenoble, France. *Publications:* Work of the Modern Potter in England, 1952; Meaning and Symbol in Three Modern Artists, 1955; Symbol and Image in William Blake, 1957; Elizabethan Embroidery, 1963; The Devonshire Hunting Tapestries, with W Hefford, 1972; Tapestries Medieval and Renaissance, 1980. Co-Author: History of the West Indian Peoples, 4 volumes, 1951–56; The Bayeux Tapestry, 1957; Kei Collection of Islamic Carpets and Textiles, Introduction and Translation, 1978. *Address:* Raleigh Lodge, Sherborne, Dorset DT9 3SA, England.

WINKLER, Cornelis, b. 22 May 1927. Poet; Librarian. *Education:* MD, University of Amsterdam, Netherlands. *Literary Appointments:* Librarian. Netherlands Institute of Brain Research, Amsterdam. *Publications:* Tussen twee oorlogen, 1960; Freud is een voyeur, 1967; Gedichten, 1972; Waar nooit gemaaid wordt, 1974; Zeven x vijf gevolgd door Symfonie nr 11, 1975; Verspride momenten, 1979; Vers uit de veren, 1982; De twaalfde symfonie, 1983; Tour d'horizon, 1984; Klein Heelal, 1985; Liefde is het enige, bloemlezing, 1985. *Contributions to:* Avenue; De Gids; Hollands Maandblad; Meatstaf; NRC-Handelsblad; Tirade. *Honours:* Henriette Roland Holst Prize, 1972. *Memberships:* Vereniging voor Letterkundigen; PEN, Netherlands Centre; Maatschappij der Nederlandse Letterkunde, Leyden; Europese auterusvereniging, Die Kogge, Minden, Germany. *Address:* Van der Boechorststraat 60, 1081 BV Amsterdam, Netherlands.

WINNER, Thomas G, b. 4 May 1917, Prague, Czechoslovakia. University Professor. *Education:* BA, 1942, MA, 1943, Harvard University, USA; PhD, Columbia University, New York, 1950. *Publications:* Xazakh Literature and Oral Art, 1958; Chekhov and His Prose, 1966; Editor of 9 volumes. *Contributions to:* American Slavic and East European Review; Slavic Review; Salvonic Review, England; Semiotica; Umjetnost rijeci, Zagreb; Poetics; Slavisticna revija, Ljubljana; Studia Semiotyczne, Warsaw, Poland. *Honours include:* Honorary MA, Brown University, 1967; Various scholarships. *Memberships:* Modern Language Association; Comparative Literature Association; FILLM; Semiotic Society of America (Past President). *Address:* 19 Garden Street, Cambridge, MA 02138, USA.

WINSTON, Sarah, b. 15 Dec. 1912, New York City, USA. m. Keith Winston, 11 June 1932, deceased 1970, 2 sons. *Education:* New York University; Alumnus, Barnes Foundation. *Publications:* And Always Tommorow, 1963; Our Son Ken, 1969, 1970; Everything Happens for the Best, 1969, 1970; Not Yet Spring, 1976; V-Mail: Letters of a World War II Combat Medic, 1985. *Contributor to:* Art Journal of Barnes Foundation; Literary Review; numerous poetry journals and magazines. *Honours:* 1st Prizes, Everything Happens for the Best, And Always Tommorow, Biennial Contests, National League of American PEN Women, 1970, 1972; Both books recorded as Talking Books for the Blind & Handicapped, by Library of Congress; Our Son Ken, taped for Recording for the Blind Inc. *Membership:* National League of American PEN Women. *Address:* 1838 Rose Tree Lane, Havertown, PA 19083, USA.

WINTOUR, Charles Vere, b. 18 May 1917, Wimborne, Dorset, England. Journalist. m. Audroy Slaughter, 9 Nov. 1979, Islington, England, 2 sons, 2 daughters (by previous marriage). *Education:* MA, Cambridge University, England. *Appointments:* Assistant Editor, Sunday Express, 1952–54; Deputy Editor, Evening Standard, 1954–57; Managing Editor, Daily Express, 1958–59; Editor, Evening Standard, 1959–76 and 78-80; Managing Director, Daily Express, 1977–78; Editor, UK Press, Gazette, 1985–. *Publication:* Pressures on the Press, 1972. *Honours:* MBE, 1945; CBE, 1978. *Literary Agent:* A D Peters. *Address:* 5 Allwyns Road, London N12 2HH, England.

WIRTH, Arthur G, b. 3 Sep. 1919, Columbus, Ohio, USA. Professor of Philosophy and History of Education. *Education:* BA, 1940, MA, 1941, PhD, 1949, Ohio University. *Publications:* John Dewey as Educator, 1966; Education and the Technological Society, 1972; Logotherapy in Action, 1979; Productive Work: In Industry and Schools, 1983. *Contributions to:* Teaching and Learning, 1970; Educational Theory, Board member; Teachers College Record; History of Education Quarterly; Educational Forum; Journal of Thought; Studies in Philosophy and Education. *Honours include:* Federal Grant Award, Office of Education, USA, 1968; American Federation of Teachers Research Committee Prize; Bode Bode Centennial Memorial Lecturer (published by Ohio State University Press), 1974. *Memberships:* John Dewey Society; Philosophy of Education Society; Comparative Education Society; American Educational Research Association. *Address:* Graduate Institute of Education, Box 1183, Washington University, St Louis, MO 63130, USA.

WISBERG, Aubrey, b. London, England. Writer. Producer, Dramatist, Novelist. m. New York City. *Education:* Special Courses, New York University. *Major Publications:* Bushman at Large; This is the Life!; Patrol Boat 999; 41 films, plus stage plays, television & radio plays. *Contributor to:* Various periodicals. *Honours:* International Unity Award for film, The Burning Cross. *Memberships:* Writers Guild of America West; Directors Guild; Dramatists Guild; Authors League of America. *Literary Agent:* Paul Kohner, Los Angeles, California. *Address:* Suite 6D The Volney, 23 East 74th Street, New York, NY 10021, USA.

WISE, Charles Conrad, Jr, b. 1 Apr. 1913, Washington DC, USA. Attorney; Federal Administrator; Author. *Education:* AB, George Washington University; JD, Law School, George Washington University; Master Fiscal Administration, Columbus University. *Publications:* Windows on the Passion, 1967; Windows on the Master, 1968; Ruth & Naomi, 1971; Editor, Poems of Terry Wise, 1968; 2nd edition 1970; Picture Windows on the Christ, 1979; The Magian Gospel of Brother Yeshua, 1979; Mind Islt: Meditation Prayer, Healing and the Psychic, 1978; Thus Saith the Lord: The Autobiography of God, 1984. *Contributor to:* Spiritual Frontiers; What is Meditation?, 1974. *Address:* Solon-Lair, Cross Keys, Penn Laird, VA 22846, USA.

WISEMAN, Christopher Stephen, b. 31 May 1936, Hull, England. University Teacher. *Education:* MA, Cambridge University; PhD, University of Strathclyde. *Publications:* Waiting for the Barbarians, 1971; The Barbarian File, 1975; Beyond the Labyrinth: A Study of Edwin Muir's Poetry, 1978; The Upper Hand, 1981; An Ocean of Whispers, 1982. *Contributions to:* Poetry: Times Literary Supplement; Encounter; Critical Quarterly; Malahat Review, and others. Critical articles and reviews contributed to various journals. *Address:* Department of English, University of Calgary, Calgary, Alberta, Canada T2N 1N4.

WISEMAN, David, b. 13 Jan. 1916, Manchester, England. Writer. m. Cicely Hilda Mary Richards, 2 Sep. 1939, Cockerham, Lancashire, 2 sons, 2 daughters. *Education:* BA (Hons), History, Manchester University, 1937; Teaching Diploma, Manchester University, 1983. *Literary Appointment:* Editor, Adult Education, 1947–50. *Publications:* Jeremy Visick, 1981, USA, published as, The Fate of Jeremy Visick, 1982, UK; Thimbles, 1982, USA, 1983, UK; Blowden and the Guardians, 1933; Adam's Common, 1984. *Membership:* Society of Authors. *Literary Agent:* Mrs June Hall, London. *Address:* 21 Treworder Road, Truro, Cornwall TR1 2JZ, England.

WISEMAN, Eric, b. 5 Nov. 1933, Hetton-le-Hole, Durham, England. Journalist. m. Merrylin Grace Wright, 18 Oct. 1976, Sydney, Australia. 1 daughter by previous marriage. *Literary Appointments:* Cadet journalist, Cessnock Eagle; Regional reporter, Newcastle Sun; Senior reporter, Hertfordshire Express; Editor, Berrima Post, New South Wales; Senior reporter, Windsor

Express; chief sub-editor, Australian Broadcasting Commission, Sydney; Public Relations Officer, national Roads & Motorists Association, Sydney; Editor, Southern Star, New South Wales. *Contributions to:* Road & Track, USA; Matilda; Prime Time; Australasian Post; People; National Times, Australia; etc. Newspapers include, The Times; Canberra Times; Sydney Morning Herald. *Honours:* Editor, 2 newspapers, winners of Sommerland Awards for Journalism. *Address:* 10 Page Street, Moruya, New South Wales 2537, Australia.

WISEMAN, Timothy Peter, b. 3 Feb. 1940, Bridlington, Yorkshire, England. University Lecturer; Professor of Classics. *Education:* MA, PhD, Balliol College, Oxford University. *Publications:* Catullan Questions, 1969; New Men in the Roman Senate, 1971; Cinna the Poet and Other Roman Essays, 1974; Clio's Cosmetics, 1979; Catullus and His World, 1985. *Contributions to:* Journal of Roman Studies; Classical Quarterly; Historia; Arion, and others. *Honours:* Wolfson Scholarship in Classics, 1974. *Memberships:* Society for the Promotion of Roman Studies; American Philological Association. *Literary Agent:* Curtis Brown Limited. *Address:* Department of Classics, The University, Exeter EX4 4QH, England.

WITCOMB, Nan, b. 27 May 1928, Adelaide, South Australia. Writer; Poet. *Publications:* The Thoughts of Nanushka, Volume I, Yesterday, Today and Tomorrow, 1971; Volume II, Loving and Living, 1972; Volume III, This Moment is Forever, 1973; Volume IV, Between Love and Loneliness, 1974; Volumes I, II and III in one volume, 1975; Volume V, Pocketful of Dreams, 1976; Volume VI, The Wondere of Tomorrow, 1978; Volume I-VI with Bruce Swann sketches, 1979. *Contributor to:* Leisure Years, (national Magazine, 1st issue July 1980). *Membership:* Australian Writers Guild. *Address:* PO Box 230, Brighton 5048, South Australia.

WITHERS, Pamela A, b. 31 July 1956, Milwaukee, Wisconsin, USA. Editor/Writer. m. Stephen G Withers, 16 Mar. 1985, Vancouver, BC. *Education:* BA, Government, Beloit, Wisconsin, USA. *Literary Appointments:* Associate Editor, Runners World Magazine Co; Associate Editor, Adventure Travel Magazine; Editor, Select Homes Magazine. *Contributions to:* Numerous magazines & journals, including, Bride's; Far East Asia Traveler; The Irish Times; Seattle Times; New York Times. *Memberships:* Professional Writers Association of Canada; Freelance Editors Association of Canada. *Literary Agent:* Susan Schulman. *Address:* 3835 West 30th Avenue, Vancouver BC V6S 1W9, Canada.

WITT, Harold (Vernon), b. 6 Feb. 1923, Santa Ana, California, USA. Writer. m. Beth Hewitt, 8 Sep. 1948, Oakland, California, 1 son, 2 daughters. *Education:* BA, University of California, Berkeley, 1943; MA, University of Michigan, 1947; BLS, University of California, Berkeley, 1953. *Literary Appointments:* Co-editor, California State Poetry Quarterly, 1976; Consulting Editor, Poet Lore, 1976–; Co-editor, Blue Unicorn, 1977–. *Publications:* Family in the Forest, 1956; Superman Unbound, 1956; The Death of Venus, 1958; Beasts in Clothes, 1961; Winesburg by the Sea! A Preview, 1970; Pop. by 1940: 40,000, 1971; Now, Swim, 1974; Surprised by Others at Fort Cronkhite, 1975; Winesburg by the Sea, 1979; The Snow Prince, 1982; Flashbacks and Returns, 1985. *Contributions to:* Many anthologies and many magazines including, The New Yorker; Harper's; The Atlantic; Poetry; The Nation; The New Republic; Hudson Review; Menyon Review; Poetry Northwest; Southwest Review; New Letters; Poetry NOW; New York Quarterly; The Massachusetts Review; The Antioch Review; Carlston Miscellany. *Honours:* Hopwood Award for Poetry, 1947; Phelan Award for Narrative Poetry, 1960; First Prize, San Francisco Poetry Center Drama Competition, 1963, for, Eros on the Shield, Poetry Society of America Emily Dickinson Award, 1972; First Prizes World Order of Narrative Poets, 1982, 1983, 1984, 1985. *Membership:* Poetry Society of America. *Address:* 39 Claremont Avenue, Orinda, CA 94563, USA.

WITTE, Ann Dryden, b. 28 Aug. 1942, Oceanside, New York, USA. Professor of Economics. m. Charles Leo Witte, 2 June 1969, 1 son. *Education:* BA, High Honours, University of Florida, 1963; MA, Economics, Columbia University, 1965; PhD, Economics, North Carolina State University, 1971. *Appointments:* Economic Analyst, US Government, Washington DC, 1963–66; Systems Analyst, US Government, 1966–67; Instructor, Economics, Tougloo College, 1967–68; Instructor, Economics, North Carolina State University, 1970–72; Visiting Assistant Professor, Economics, 1972–73, Public Law & Government, 1973–74, Assistant Professor, 1974–79, Associate Professor, 1979–83, Professor, 1983–, Economics, University of North Carolina; Visiting Professor, Economics, Wellesley College, 1984–85. *Publications:* Co-Editor, Advances in Applied Micro-Economics, volume 3; An Economic Analysis of Crime and Justice: Theory, Methods and Applications, co-author, 1984; Beating the System: The Underground Economy, co-author, 1982; Basic Issues in Corrections Performance, co-author, 1982; Work Release in North Carolina, 1975; Work Release in North Carolina: The Programme and the Process, 1973. *Contributor to:* Numerous professional journals including, American Bar Foundation Research Journal; Evaluation Review; Monthly Labor Review; Journal of Urban Economics; National Tax Journal; etc. *Honours:* Selection for Residence, Rockefeller Foundation's Study & Conference, Bellagio, Italy, 1983; Recipient, Many other honours and awards. *Memberships:* American Statistical Association; Law and Society Association; American Economic Association; Trustee, Law & Society Association, 1981–83, Programme Committee, 1984; Board of Directors, Police Foundation, 1984–; many other professional organisations. *Address:* Dept of Economics, Wellesley College, Wellesley, MA 02181, USA.

WITTIG, Judith, b. 16 June 1942, Burlington, Wisconsin, USA. Writer/Freelance. m. 2 Sep. 1961, Lake Geneva, Wisconsin, USA, 2 sons. *Education:* BSc, 1981, University of Wisconsin, Madison, Wisconsin, USA. *Literary Appointments:* Editor, Wisconsin Review Literary Magazine, 1976–80, (University of Wisconsin). *Publications:* Sun-Roots, 1976; The Rose and the Bratwurst, 1978; Orange Paint on My Propellor, 1979; The Fire Next to the Firehouse, 1981. *Contributions to:* Berkeley Poetry Review; Road Apple Review; Tars & Ternes; The Nation. *Honour:* University of Wisconsin, Madison, 1977, Poetry Prize. *Address:* PO Box 4233, Woodbridge, VA 22194, USA.

WITTLIN, Thaddeus (Tadeusz), b. 1909, Warsaw, Poland. Lecturer; Radio Script Writer. *Education:* MA, LL M, University of Warsaw, Poland. *Literary Appointments:* Editor, Barber of Warsaw satirical weekly, 1931–36. *Publications:* Trail To Parnassus, poetry, 1929; The Dreamer and the Guests, Novel, 1932; The Hasbeen, novel, 1933; The Achilles Heel, short stories, 1939; The Broken Wings, novel, 1934; Happy Days, short stories and poetry, 1946; The Island of Lovers, short stories, 1950; A Reluctant Traveller in Russia, biography, English, French, Japanese and Polish versions, 1952; Modigliani–Prince of Montparnasse, biography, English, Dutch and Polish versions, 1964; Time Stopped at 6.30, historical account, 1965; Commissar, The Life and Death of Lavrenty Pavlovich Beria, biography, English, French, Spanish, Japanese versions, 1972; The Last Bohemians, 1974; The Songstress of Warsaw, 1985. *Memberships:* PEN English Centre; PEN American Centre. *Address:* 2020 F Street NW, Washington, DC 20006, USA.

WOLD, Allen Lester, b. 8 Dec. 1943. Writer. m. Diane Easterling, 24 June 1972, Altadena, California, USA. *Education:* BA, Pomona College, Claremont, California. *Publications:* The Planet Masters, 1979; Star God, 1980; Computer Science, 1984; Computers and Space, 1984; V: The Pursuit of Diana, 1985; V: The Crivit Experiment, 1985. *Contributions to:* Amazing; Sorcerers Apprentice. Contributing Editor: Softside, 1983–84; Media and Methods, 1983–85. *Memberships:* Science Fiction Writers of America. *Literary Agent:* Sharon

Jarvis. *Address;* 1710 Euclid Road, Durham, NC 27713, USA.

WOLF, Marvin Jules, b. 23 July 1941, Chicago, Illinois, USA. Writer. Divorced, 1 daughter. *Education:* AA, University of Maryland, 1974; BA California State University, 1977. *Publications:* The Japanese Conspiracy, 1983; Fallen Angels, with Katherine Mader, 1986. *Contributor to:* Reader's Digest; GEO; California; Los Angeles Magazine; Travel & Leisure; Soldier of Fortune; Boston Globe; Financial Executive; etc. *Honours:* US Marine Corps Combat Correspondents Association, 1982; Distinguished Service Award, Gold Quill International Association of Business Communcations, 1977; Los Angeles Press Club Best Story, Business Publications, 1975; Bronze Star, US Army, 1965. *Memberships:* American Society of Authors & Journalists; Independent Writers of Southern California, President. *Literary Agent:* Michael Hamilburg. *Address:* 4221 Wilshire Blvd, Los Angeles, CA 90010, USA.

WOLFF, Konrad M, b, 11 Mar. 1907, Berlin, Germany. Pianist; Musicologist. *Education:* Dr Juris, University of Berlin, 1930; MA, Columbia University, USA. 1957. *Publications:* Editor, Robert Schumann's On Music and Musicians, English transl, 1946; Erich Itor Kahn, (with Leibowitz, in French), 1958; The Teaching of Artur Schnabel, 1972, revised edition, 1979, also in Japanese and German translation; Masters of the Keyboard, 1983. *Contributor to:* Numerous professional magazines including Johann Samuel Schroeter; Musical Quarterly, 1958; Piano Quartely; American Liszt Society. *Honours:* Certificate of Merit, Peabody Conservatory, 1974. *Memberships:* AAUP; American Musicol Society; Music Teachers National Association; American Liszt Society. *Address:* 210 Riverside Drive, New York, 10025, USA.

WOLFF, Kurt H(einrich), b. 20 May 1912, Darmstadt, Germany. Professor. *Education:* Laurea Doctor, University of Florence, Italy, 1935. *Publications include:* Hingebung und Begriff, 1968; Von Einhorn zu Einhorn, Text and Illustrations, 1972; Surrender and Catch: A Palimpsest Story, 1972; Trying Sociology, 1974; Surrender and Catch: Experience and Interpretation, Today, 1976; Vorgang und immerwahrende Revolution, 1978; Beyond the Sociology of Knowledge: An Introduction and a Development, 1983. *Contributions to:* Some 50 scholarly paper, fiction, poetry in numerous scientific and professional journals and magazines. *Honours:* Grantee; Visiting Professor, Fulbright Lecturer. *Address:* 58 Lombard Street, Newton, MA 02158, USA.

WOLFMAN, Ira, b. 7 Oct. 1950, Brooklyn, New York, USA. Editor. *Education:* BA, cum laude, 1971. *Literary Appointments:* Senior Editor, Smash Magazine, 1975; Senior Editor, Circus Magazine, 1976–79; Associate Editor, 3-2-1 Contact Magazine, 1979–80; Editor, Sesame Street, Parents' Newsletter, 1980–83; Editor-in-Chief, Enter Magazine, 1983–85. *Contributions to:* New York Daily News; Ms Magazine; The Peoples Almanac II; Next Magazine; Daily American Newspaper, Rome, Italy. *Membership:* American Society of Magazine Editors. *Address:* 875 West 181 Street, New York, NY 10033, USA.

WOLLASTON, Nicholas William, b. 23 June 1926, Uley, Gloucestershire, England. Writer. *Education:* BA, Cambridge University. *Publications:* Handles of Chance, 1956; China in the Morning, 1960; Red Rumba, 1962; Winter in England, 1965; Jupiter Laughs, 1967; Pharoah's Chicken, 1969; The Tale Bearer, 1972; Eclipse, 1974; The Man in the Ice Cap, 1980; Mr Thistlewood, 1985. *Contributions to:* Sunday Times; Observer; Sunday Telegraph; New Statesman; Spectator; Times Literary Supplement; various others. *Honours:* Heinemann Award, 1969. *Memberships:* Royal Society of Literature; Society of Authors. *Literary Agent:* Gillon Aitken. *Address:* Thorington Hall, Stoke-by-Nayland, Colchester, Essex, England.

WOLSTENHOLME, Kenneth, b. 17 July 1920, Worsley, England. Journalist; Broadcaster. m. Joan Wolstenholme, 31 July 1944, Eccles, 1 daughter. *Publications:* Young England, 1959; Sports Special, 1956; The Boys Book of World Airlines, 1961; The Mirror Book of Speed, 1962; The Pros, 1968; The Wit of Soccer, 1970; The Wit of the Air, 1972; Kenneth Wolstenholme's Book of World Soccer, annually, 1961–73. *Contributor to:* Newspapers; magazines; radio; television. *Honours:* Daily Mirror Commentator of the Year, 1963; Baird Gold Medal, Services to Television; Distinguished Flying Cross and Bar, 1940–45. *Memberships:* Former Branch Chairman, National Union of Journalists; Sports Writers' Association; Football Writers' Association; Royal Automobile Club. *Literary Agent:* Essanay Limited. *Address:* 21 The Mount, Ewell, Surrey KT17 1LZ, England.

WOMBWELL, Peter Harry, b. 18 Sep. 1923, Croydon, England. Newspaper Editor. m. Fay Shaw, 5 Nov. 1949, Fremantle, Western Australia, 1 son, 2 daughters. *Appointments:* Editor, Daily Telegraph, Sydney, 1972; Editor, Sunday Mirror, Sydney, 1974; Deputy Editor, Sunday Times, Perth, Western Australia, 1975; Editor, Sunday Times, Perth, 1982; Music Critic, The Sunday Times, Western Australia. *Address:* 102A Corinthian Road, Shelley, Western Australia.

WONG, Mark Dennis, b. 21 Apr. 1957, Sydney, Australia. Clerical Assistant. *Publications:* Poetry – readings and performances; Short stories; Lyrics; Nonfictional prose; Musical comedy productions include: Brigadoon; My Fair Lady; Hello Dolly as member of stage chorus. *Honours:* Oscar recipient, 75th production, Regals Musical Society of Rockdale, 1983. *Memberships:* Sydney branch, Poets Union of Australia; Sydney branch, Fellowship of Australian Writers. *Address:* 12 Arlington Street, Rockdale, Sydney, NSW 2216, Australia.

WOOD, David Bernard, b. 21 Feb. 1944, Sutton, England. Writer, Actor, Theatre producer and director, Composer. m. Jacqueline Stanbury, 21 Jan. 1975, Sutton, 2 daughters. *Education:* BA Honours, Worcester College, Oxford. *Publications:* Musical plays for children: The Owl and the Pussycat Went to See[el], (with S Ruskin), 1970; The Plotters of Cabbage Patch Corner, 1973; Flibberty and the Penguin, 1974; Hyjack over Hygenia, 1974; The Papertown Paperchase, 1976; Larry The Lamb in Toytown, (with S Ruskin), 1976; Old Mother Hubbard, 1976; The Gingerbread Man, 1977; Old Father Time, 1977; Tickle, 1978; Babes in the Magic Wood, 1979; Nutcracker Sweet, 1979; Mother Goose's Golden Christmas, 1978; Cinderella, 1980; There Was an Old Woman, 1980; Aladdin, 1980; The Ideal Gnome Expedition, 1982; Dick Whittington and Wondercat, 1982; Meg and Mog Show, (based on the books by Jan Pienkowski and Helen Nicoll), 1985; The Selfish Shellfish, 1986; Robin Hood, (with Dave and Toni Arthur), 1985; Books: The Operats of Rodent Garden, (Illustrated by Geofrey Beitz), 1984; The Gingerbread Man, (Illustrated by Sally Anne Lamberet), 1985; The Discorats, (Illustrated by Geoffrey Beitz), 1985. *Contributions to:* Drama; Amateur Stage. *Memberships:* Society of Authors; britsh Actors' Equity Association; Green Room Club. *Literary Agent:* Margaret Ramsay Limited. *Address:* c/o Margaret Ramsay Limited, 14A Goodwin's Court, St Martin's Lane, London WC2, England.

WOOD, Derek Harold, b. 19 Mar. 1930, Croydon, England. Journalist. m. Belinda Squire, 23 July 1955, London, England, 1 son, 1 daughter. *Literary Appointments:* Editor, Aerosphere, 1948–49; Editorial Staff, British Trade Journal and Electrical Journal, 1950–53; London Editor, subsequently Managing Director, Interavia (UK) Limited, 1953–83; Air Correspondent, Liverpool Daily Post, 1952–60; Air Correspondent, Westminster Newspapers, 1954–60; Air Correspondent, Sundaya Telegraph, 1961–; Editor in Chief, Jane's Defence Weekly, 1984–. *Publications:* The Narrow Margin, 1961, revised edition 1969; Project Cancelled, 1975; Attack Warning Red, 1976; Jane's World Aircraft

Recognition Handbook, 1979, 1982 and 1985; Target England, 1980. *Contributions to:* Air Pictorial; Air Force magazine, USA; Aero Digest, USA; Aviation Week, USA; Aviation Magazine, France; Flight. *Honours:* C P Robertson Memorial Trophy, 1961; Honorary Companion, Royal Aeronautical Society. *Literary Agent:* Curtis Brown. *Address:* Stroods, Whitemans Green, Cuckfield, West Sussex, RH17 5DA, England.

WOOD, Linda Carol, b. 4 Sep. 1945, Smyrna, Tennessee, USA. Freelance Writer; Editorial Consultant. m. Joseph M Selig, 5 May 1985, LA Jolla. *Education:* BA, 1966, MA, 1969, University of California; Certificat de la Civilisation Francais, Sorbonne, Paris, France, 1967. *Literary Appointments include:* Editor, CRM Books, Del Mar, California, 1970–74; Editor, Contributing Author, The Psychology Primer, 1974; Editor, La Jolla Cancer Research Foundation Annual Reports, 1982–83, 1983–84. Editorial Director, Contemporary Western Europe: Problems and Responses, 1985; The Challenge of China and Japan: Politics and Development in East Asia, 1985. Editorial Consultant: National Media Programs, University Extension, University of California, 1979–; La Jolla Cancer Research Foundation, 1982–; Global Understanding Project, National Public Radio, 1983–84. *Publications include:* Study Guides and Faculty Manuals accompanying, Contemporary Western Europe, 1984f and, The Challenge of China and Japan, 1985. Co-Author: Sharing the Earth, 1982; Windows in Space, 1982; Understanding Space and Time, 1981; A Reader/Study Guide for Cosmos and A Viewers Guide to Cosmos, 1980; A Viewers Guide to the Body in Question, 1980. Co-Editor: Working: Changes and Choices, 1980. Editor of various other works. *Contributions to:* Science Teacher; Phi Delta Kappan; Current; Senior Scholastic. *Honours:* Distinguished Work of Nonfiction Award, Southern California Council on Literature for Children and Young People, 1983; Outstanding Science Books for Children Award, National Science Teachers Association and Childrens Book Council, 1982. *Literary Agent:* Jane Jordan Browne, Multimedia Product Development Incorporated. *Address:* 8151/2 South Coast Boulevard, La Jolla, CA 92037, USA.

WOOD, Marguerite Noreen, b. 27 Sep. 1923, Ipswich, Suffolk, England. Poet; Physiotherapist. m. Douglas James, 1 son, 1 daughter. *Education:* MCSP, school of Physiotherapy, Devonshire Royal Hospital; BA (Hons), Open University; Justice of the Peace, 1968. *Literary Appointments:* Editorial Panel, Envoi Poetry Magazine, 1974–. *Publications:* Stone of Vision, 1964; Windows Are Not Enough, 1971; Crack Me the Shell, 1975; A Line Drawn in Water, 1980; various works in preparation including Let's Write Poems Today; The Isis Tremor. *Memberships:* The Poetry Society, UK; The Suffolk Poetry Society, Chairman. *Address:* Windmill Chase, Mill Lane, Stock, Essex, England.

WOOD, Thomas J, b. 8 Oct. 1930, Hoxie, Arkansas, USA. Journalist; Aviator. *Education:* BS; MA; PhD. *Literary Appointments:* Editor/Publisher, AG-Pilot International Magazine; Editor/Publisher, Hot Props Magazine, IAAF Newsletter. *Honour:* FAA Accident Prevention Counsellor; NPA Flight Proficiency Award; Honorary Member, National Aviation Hall of Fame. *Memberships:* Aviation/Space Writers Association; VFW, American Legion; Rotary International; Universal Magazine Publishers Association; National by Aviation Association, etc. *Address:* 405 Main Street, Mount Vernon, WA 98273, USA.

WOOD, Tony, b. 14 May 1936, Epsom, Surrey. Journalist. m. Barbara Green, Wimbledon, 2 Nov. 1957, 2 sons, 3 daughters. *Major Work:* Variety of Sports publications. *Contributor to:* Fleet Street publications (Freelance); Editor, Darts World Magazine, London. *Address:* 2 Park Lane, Croydon, Surrey CR9 1HA, England.

WOODMAN, Allen, b. 21 Dec. 1954, Montgomery, Alabama, USA. Writer; Teacher; Editor. *Education:* BA, Huntingdon College, 1976; MA, PhD Candidate, Florida

State University. *Literary Appointments:* Editor, Sun Dog, 1981–84, Apalachee Quarterly, 1981–; Reader, Studies in Popular Culture, 1982, 1985; Editor, Publisher, Word Beat Press, 1982–. *Publications:* Stories Anout How Things Fall Apart & What's Left When They Do, 1985. *Contributions to:* North American Review; Epoch; Carolina Quarterly; etc. *Honours:* Award, Publications Union, Huntingdon College, 1976; Award, Alabama Poetry Society, 1976, 1977; Fellowship, Florida State University, 1983–; Florida State Student Government Scholarship, 1985; Fellowship, Ohio Valley Writers Conference, 1985. *Memberships:* President 1985, Lamda Iota Tau; Phi Kappa Phi; COSMEP; Associate Writing Programmes. *Address:* P O Box 10509, Tallahassee, FL 32302, USA.

WOODS, Aubrey Harold, b. 9 Apr. 1928, London, England. Actor/Dramatist. m. Gaynor, Stratford-upon-Avon. *Education:* Leverhulme Scholarship, Judges' Special Award, Royal Academy of Dramatic Art. *Publications:* Trelawny, book for musical play, published as Play of the Year 1971/72; BBC Radio Plays: As Long As Ye Both Shall Live, Incident at Greenwich, And On The Seventh Day, Say It Again Sam. *Literary Agent:* Fraser and Dunlop Scripts Ltd, London. *Address:* c/o Fraser and Dunlop Scripts Ltd, 91 Regent Street, London W1R 8RU, England.

WOODS, Eddie, b. 8 May 1940, New York City, USA. Writer; Editor; Journalist. Div, 2 daughters. *Literary Appointments:* Editor, In & Outs Press, Amsterdam, Netherlands. *Publications:* 30 Poems, 1973; Sale Or Return, 1982. *Contributions to:* Not Guilty, Gay Sunshine, Odalisque, The Bystander, Androgyne (USA); International Times, Iron, Anarchist Review, Libertine (UK); Ins & Outs, Crippled Warlords, P78 Anthology (Netherlands); Other World Poetry Newsletter. Literary Journalism/sole author (Netherlands); Open Road (Canada), Insight, Robert's Purple Mirror (Hongkong), The Review (Australia), etc. Eureka! (encyclopaedia, major contributor, Thames & Hudson, UK). *Membership:* London Poetry Secretariat. *Address:* PO Box 3759, Amsterdam, The Netherlands.

WOODS, Grace L, b. 19 June 1912. Clerk Typist. m. Ed Woods. *Publication:* In Retrospect, poems, 1986. *Contributions to:* Showcase, annual volume of Showcase writers Club. *Honours include:* 2nd place 1976, 1st, 2nd and 3rd places 1978, 2nd place 1979, Contra Costa County Fair; 2nd Place, San Diego Torrey Pines, 1978; 1st place 1979, 2nd place 1981, Torrey Pines chapter, Chaparral Poets. *Memberships:* Editor, Coordinator, President, Showcase Writers Club; California Federation of Chparral Poets; San Diego Torrey Pines chapter, Chapparal Poets. *Address:* 4395 Yale Avenue, La Mesa, CA 92041, USA.

WOODS, Stuart Chevalier, b. 9 Jan. 1938, Manchester, Georgia, USA. Writer. m. Judy Nicholas Tabb, 27 Dec. 1984, Atlanta, Georgia, 1 step-daughter. *Education:* BA, Sociology. *Major Publications:* Blue Water, Green Skipper. 1977; A Romantic's Guide to the Country Inns of Britain & Ireland, 1979; Chiefs (novel), 1981; Run Before the Wind (novel), 1983; Deep Lie (novel), 1986; Under the Lake (novel), due 1986; all published by W W Norton, New York, USA. *Contributor to:* Yachting; New York Times; TV Guide; Atlanta Constitution; International Portfolio. *Honour:* Edgar Allen Poe Award. *Memberships:* The Century Association; Authors' Guild National Writers' Union; New York Yacht Club; Royal Ocean Racing Club, London, England. *Literary Agent:* Morton L Janklow. *Address:* 4340 Tree Haven Drive NE, Atlanta, GA 30342, USA.

WOOTTON, Anthony, b. 11 Aug. 1935, Aylesbury, Buckinghamshire, England. Freelance Writer; Artist; Photographer. *Publications:* Ants, 1975; Beetles, 1975; Crickets and Grasshoppers, 1977; Insects Are Animals Too, 1978; All The Year Round: Essays on Nature and Country Matters, 1979; Mosquitoes, 1979; Worms, 1979; Spotter's Guide to Insects, 1979; Ingenious Insects, 1980; Spotter's Guide to Ponds and Lakes, 1980; Insects, 1980; The Amazing Fact Book of Spiders,

1980; Gorillas, 1981; Ostriches, 1981; The Life of the Ladybird, 1981; Antelopes, 1982; Spiders, 1983; Ingenious Insects, 1983; Insects of the World, 1984; Animal Myth, Legend and Folklore, in press, 1986; Consultant Editor, The Nature Trail Book of Insect Watching, 1976. *Contributor to:* Biographical Dictionary of Scientists, 1981; Entomological Consultant to BBC Wildlife Magazine; Consultant to Usborne, Blandford Press, Wayland, Dent (Publishers) etc; Book Reviewer, British Book News, Countryside (Editor 1968–80); Times Educational Supplement; BBC Wildlife; numerous professional magazines and journals including Country Life; Countryman; Sunday Express; Observer; The Living Countryside; Gardening World; etc. *Memberships:* Honorary Life Member, British Naturalists' Association. *Address:* 40 Roundhill, Stoner, Near Aylesbury, Buckinghamshire, England.

WOOTTON OF ABINGER, (Baroness) Barbara Frances, b. 1897, Cambridge, England. *Education:* MA, Girton College, Cambridge. *Publications:* (as Barbara Wootton) Twos and Threes, 1933; Plan or No Plan, 1934; London's Burning, 1936; Lament for Economics, 1938; End Social Inequality, 1941; Freedom Under Planning, 1945; Testament for Social Science, 1950; The Social Foundations of Wage Policy, 1955; Social Science and Social Pathology, 1959; Crime and the Criminal Law, 1963, 2nd edition, with postscripts, 1981; In a World I Never Made, 1967; Contemporary Britain, 1971; Incomes Policy: an inquest and a proposal, 1974; Crime and Penal Policy, 1978. *Honours include:* Companion of Honour; One US and 12 Britsh Honorary degrees. *Memberships include:* Advisory Council on Misuse of Drugs, 1971–72. *Address:* High Barn, Abinger Common, Dorking, Surrey, England.

WORNER, Philip Arthur Incledon, b. 30 Jan. 1910, Southampton, UK. Tutor in Higher Education. *Education:* University of Southampton, MA, St Edmund Hall, University of Oxford, England. *Appointments:* Languages Master, Pannal Ash College, Harrogate; Actor Member, Tonbridge Repertory Company; Languages Master, Simon Langton School, Canterbury; Exchange Teacher, Washington High School, Milwaukee, USA; Tutor, Senior Lecturer and Librarian, College of Education, Worcester, England. *Publications include:* Freedom is my Fame, verse 1943; The Cactus Hedge (play with verse), 1951; The Calling of Wenceslas, historical drama 1960; Wrack, verse 1971; Way Out, verse 1975; His Star returns (play with songs), 1978. *Contributor to:* BBC; Midland Poets; Worcester Evening News. *Memberships:* Fellow, International Poetry Society; Royal Society of Literature; Society of Authors; Writers' Guild; The Library Association, Honorary Vice-President, Worcester Writers' Circle. *Honours:* Convocation University of Southampton; Alumnus, Washington High School, Milwaukee, USA. *Address:* The Rookery, 216 Henwick Road, Worcester, WR2 5PF, England.

WORSFOLD, David Howard, b. 24 Nov. 1956, Wanstead, Essex. Journalist. m. Mariette Mason, 17 July 1982, 2 daughters. *Education:* Economics & Politics, University of East Anglia. *Literary Appointments:* Editorial Assistant, Institute of Medical Laboratory Sciences, 1978–81; Editor, Food Magazine, 1981–82; Editor, Insurance Age, 1982–. *Contributor to:* Insurance Age; The Guardian (Weekend Money); The Observer; and others. *Honour:* Runner-up, Insurance Journalist of the Year, 1983; Winner, Insurance Journalist of the Year, 1984. *Address:* 4 Terling Close, London E11 3NP, England.

WORSTHORNE, Peregrine Gerard, b. 22 Dec. 1923, London, England. Journalist. m. Claudia Bertrand de Colasse, 1950, 1 daughter. *Education:* Honours degree (2nd), History, MA, Peterhouse College, Cambridge University. *Literary Appointments:* Editorial staff, Glasgow Herald 1946, The Times 1948; Washington Correspondent 1950, Leader writer, 1952, The Times; Leader writer, Daily Telegraph, 1955; Assistant editor, Sunday Telegraph, 1961. *Publications:* The Socialist Myth, 1972; Peregrinations, 1980. *Contributions to:*

New York Times; Washington Post; Le Monde; Foerign Affairs; Encounter; Spectator; Times; Twentieth Century; Time & Tide. *Honours:* Journalist of the Year, 1981; Granada Television Award, *Address;* 6 Kempson Road, London SW6, England.

WORTH, Douglas Grey, b. 14 Mar. 1940. High School English Teacher. m. Karen. *Education:* BA, Swarthmore College, USA, 1962; MA, Columbia University, USA, 1964. *Appointments:* English Teacher, 1965–67; Rudolf Steiner School, 1967–69; Allen-Stevenson School, New York City; Friends Seminar, 1969–70; Meadowbrook Junior High School, Newton, Massachusetts, 1970–. *Publications:* Of Earth, 1974; Invisibilities, 1977; Triptych, 1979; From Dream, From Circumstance, new and Selected Poems, 1963–83, 1984. *Contributions to:* New York Times; Nation; Seventeen: Massachussetts Review; Prairie Schooner; Colo. Quarterly; (anthologies): New American Poetry, 1973; The Logic of Poetry, 1974; The Windflower Home Almanac of Poetry, 1980. *Honours Include:* Fellowship in Poetry, Artists' Foundation under sponsorship of Massachussetts Council for the Arts and Humanities; Book chosen as one of the outstanding academic books of 1977, ALA; Winner of first prize in the International Sri Chinmoy Poetry Awards for 1981; Poetry grant from the Massachussetts Arts Lottery Council in 1983. *Address:* 66 Grove Hill Avenue, Newton, MA 02160, USA.

WORTH, Helen, b. 17 July 1913, Cleveland, Ohio, USA. Food Authority. *Education:* BA, University of Michigan; New School for Social Research. *Appointment:* Instructor, Food and Wine Appreciation, University of Virginia Department of Continuing Education, 1984–. *Publications:* Down-on-the-Farm Cookbook, 1943, reissued 1983; Shrimp Cookery, 1952; Cooking Without Recipes, 1965, Paperback, 1984; Hostess Without Help, 1971; Damn Yankee in a Southern Kitchen, 1973. *Contributions to:* Talk; House Beautiful; Brides. *Honours:* Outstanding Cookbook Award, 1972; Runner-up, Cookbook Award, 1974. *Memberships include:* Authors League; American Society of Journalists and Authors; National Book Critics Circle; New York Adult Education Council; Somelior Society; Federation of Press Women; Virginia Press Women (Board Member). *Literary Agent:* Collier Associates. *Address:* 1701 Owensville Road, Charlottesville, VA 22901, USA.

WORTH, Richard, b. 13 Nov. 1945, Hartford, Connecticut, USA. Writer. *Education:* BA, 1967, MA, 1968, Trinity College, Hartford. *Publications:* Poland: The Search for National Renewal, 1982; Israel and the Arab States, 1983; The Third World Today, 1983; The American Family, 1984. *Address:* 102 Merton Street, Fairfield, CT 06430, USA.

WORTHINGTON, Barton Edgar, b. 13 Jan. 1905, London, England. Biologist. m. (1) Stella Jonson, 23 Aug, 1930, London, (2) Harriett Stockton, 6 June 1980, Sussex, 3 daughters. *Education:* MA, PhD, Gonville & Caius College, University of Cambridge, England. *Major Publications:* Fishery Surveys of East Africa, 1929 & 1932; Science in Africa, 1938; Inland Waters of Africa (with Stella Worthington), 1932; Middle East Science, 1946; Life in Lakes & Rivers, (with T T Macan), 1951; Science in the Development of Africa, 1958; The Evolution of IBP, 1975; The Ecological Century, 1983. *Contributor to:* Numerous periodicals of scientific and technical interest. *Honours:* Mungo Park Medal, Royal Scottish Geographical Society, 1938; CBE, 1964; Ridder of Golden Ark (Netherlands), 1976; Member of Honour, International Union of Nature Conservation, 1978. *Memberships:* Several Scientific (Biological) Societies; Former Councillor, Royal Geographical Society; Athenaeum Club. *Address:* Colin Godmans, Furners Green, Nr Uckfield, East Sussex TN22 3RR, England.

WORTHINGTON-WILLIAMS, Michael James, b. 30 Jan. 1938, London, England. Motoring Historian & Journalist. m. Pamela Margaret Clark, 23 July 1981,

Carmarthen, 2 sons, 1 daughter (2 sons, 1 daughter also by previous marriage). *Literary Appointments:* Editor, Veteran Car 1968–70, 1976–; Consultant, Sotheby's 1976–; Assistant Editor, Old Motor, 1977–79. *Major Publications:* Cycles & Motorcycles, 1975; Some Unusual Engines, with L J K Setright, 1975; Any Colour So Long as it's Black, 1976; Automobilia, 1979; Vintage Car Annual, 1979; Cyclecar to Microcar, 1981; Collector's Guide to Toy & Model Road Vehicles, 1985. *Contributor to:* The Automobile, The Classic Motor Cycle; Thoroughbred and Classic Cars; Classic & Sportscar; Sporting Cars; The Automobilist; Supercar Classics; The Car; Special Interest Autos. *Honours:* Dowsing Trophy, Veteran Car Club of Great Britain, 1970; Gugnot Award, Society of Automotive Historians, 1973. *Memberships:* Society of Automotive Historians, Vice-President, USA, 1973, Currently Vice-President, UK; International Society for Vehicle Preservation; Guild of Motoring Writers; Institute of Journalists; Dating Committee, Veteran Car Club of Great Britain. *Literary Agent:* Peter Roberts, Bushey Heath. *Address:* Glaspant Farmhouse, Glaspant Manor, Capel Iwan, Newcastle Emlyn, Dyfed, SA38 9LS, Wales.

WOUDSTRA, Karst, b. 1947, Leiden, The Netherlands. Dramatist; Translator; Director. *Education:* Gymnasium Examen Alpha, Doctoral degree in Scandinavian Languages and Literature. *Literary Appointments:* Dramaturge in theatres performing plays by Tschechov, Moliere, Shakespeare, Strindberg; translating plays by Strindberg, Ibsen, Marivaux, Lenz, Pohl, Noren and directing plays by Strindberg, Marivaux, Ibsen and Bernhard. *Publication:* Play: Scenes at Court about life in Don Carlos son of Philip II of Spain. Produced in 1981 by the Company Globe at Eindhoven, Holland. *Address:* Herengracht 116, 1015 Bt Amsterdam, The Netherlands.

WOUTERS, Rik, b. 2 Apr. 1956, Halle, Brussels, Belgium. Official. m. Lieve Vanderbeken, 20 Dec. 1980, 1 daughter. *Education:* Teacher's Certificate. *Publications:* Ik zeg tot je, poetry, 1979; Nauwelijks ademend verheffen woorden zich, poetry, 1982. *Contributions to:* Poetry: Literary magazines, Belgium & Netherlands; Anthologies, Belgium & Netherlands; Long-playing record, computer, non-literary magazines. Literary Criticism: Magazines, Belgium & Netherlands; Local Radio. *Honours:* Certificate of Honour, Poetry Prize; Spectraal literary magazine, 1980; 1st Encouragement Prize, poetry, Cultural council, Halle, 1983; 1st Award, Litera magazine, Poetry Prize, Beringen, 1984. *Memberships:* Editorial Staff, magazines, Vernieuwd Actietribune, 1980; t Kofschip, 1981–85; Zefier, 1985–. *Address:* Boomkwekerijstraat 67, 1610 Ruisbroek, Belgium.

WRACK, Philip, b. 24 June 1929, Retford, England. Deputy Editor. m. 2 sons, 1 daughter. *Literary Appointments:* Scunthorpe Evening Telegraph, 1943–52; Grimsby Evening Telegraph, 1952–54; Manchester Evening News, 1954–55; Chief Subeditor, London Evening News, 1955, Executive Assistant Editor, 1970; Deputy Editor, News of the World, 1970–. *Address:* 4 Crane Court, Fleet Street, London EC4, England.

WRIGHT, Celeste Turner, b. 17 Mar. 1906, St John, New Brunswick, Canada. Poet; Educator. m. Vedder Allen Wright, 26 June 1933, Berkeley, California, USA, 1 son. *Education:* BA, 1925; MA, 1926; PhD, 1928; University of California, Los Angeles and Berkeley. *Literary Appointments:* Member, Department of English, 1928–, Professor, 1948–73, Emerita, 1973–, Chairman, English Department, 1928–55, Faculty Research Lecturer, 1963–64, University of California, Davis. *Publications:* Anthony Mundy: An Elizabethan Man of Letters, 1928; Etruscan Princess and Other Poems, 1964; A Sense of Place, poems, 1973; Seasoned Timber, 1977; University Woman, memoir, 1981; Collected Poems, 1924–84, forthcoming. *Contributions to:* Proceeding of Modern Language Association of America; Modern Philology; Philological Quarterly; Studies in Philology; 20th Century Fiction; Harpers; Yale Review; Beloit Poetry Journal; Manhattan Poetry Review; Arizona Quarterly; various other magazines. Anthologies

include: The Women Poets: English; Poetspeak. *Honours include:* Reynolds Lyric Prize, 1963; Fellowship, University of California Instiute for Creative Arts, 1966–67; Silver Medal, Commonwealth Club of California, 1973; Grand Prize, Ina Coolbrith Statewide Competition, 1961, 65, 70; Several 1st prizes, World Federation of Narrative Poets, 1980–83. *Memberships:* Poetry Society of America; Academy of American Poets; Renaissance Society of America; Phi Beta Kappa. *Address:* 1001 D Street, Davis, CA 95616, USA.

WRIGHT, Dorothy, b. 4 Jan. 1910, Derbyshire, England. Playwright; Novelist; Writer on Crafts. *Publications:* The Gentle Phoenix, 1938; Queens Wilde, 1950; Advance in Love, 1953; Laurian and the Wolf, 1956; Among the Cedars, 1959; (plays): A Cradle of Willow, 1952; The Nightingale, 1954; Baskets and Basketry, 1959; A Caneworker's Book, 1970; Beginning Patchwork, 1971; The Complete Book of Baskets and Basketry, 1977, 2nd enlarged edition, 1982. *Membership:* PEN. *Literary Agent:* Curtis Brown Limited. *Address:* Long Whitstone, Bovey Tracey, South Devon, England.

WRIGHT, (Evan) Wilbur, b. 23 Aug. 1919, South Shields, England. Writer; Flying Instructor; Company Director; etc. m. Joyce Gladys Wiliams, 13 Dec. 1944, Brecon, Wales, 1 son. *Publications:* Grave of Sand, 1963; Operation Cleansweep, 1964; Down to a Sunless Sea, 1980; Sidewall, 1981; Hard Case, 1982; Carter's Castle, 1984; Seven Years to Sunset, 1985. *Literary Agent:* Christopher Little, London. *Address:* The Shrubs, Allington Lane, Southampton SO3 3HP, England.

WRIGHT, Ian W, b. 9 Mar. 1934, Paisley, Scotland. Journalist. m. Lydia Giles, 12 Oct. 1968, 1 son. *Education:* MA, Oxford University. *Literary Appointments:* Editor, Elliot Lake Standard, Ontario, Canada, 1960; Sub-editor, The Guardian, 1961; film critic, deputy features editor, ibid, 1964; Special correspondent, Sudan, Aden, ibid, 1967; Far East correspondent, war corrspondent, Vietnam, 1968; Foreign Editor, 1970; Managing Editor, Guardian, 1978. *Contributions to:* BBC; New Society; New Statesman; etc. *Honour:* David Holden Prize (joint winner), British Press Awards, 1978. *Address;* 119 Farringdon Road, London EC1 3RR, England.

WRIGHT, Mary Patricia, b. 10 May 1932, Warlingham, England. Author; County Councillor. *Education:* Associate, Royal Institute of Chartered Surveyors, 1955I; Qualified Associate, Land Agents Society, 1957; BA Honours, Modern History, University of London, 1965. *Publications:* Non-fiction: Woman's Estate, 1959; Conflict of the Nile, 1972. Fiction: Space of the Heart, 1976; Journey into Fire, 1977; Shadow of the Rock, USA, 1978; Storm Harvest, 1979; Blind Chance, written under pseudonym, 1980; This My City, (USA title, Storms of Fate), 1981; Forbidden Places, 1981; While Paris Danced, 1983; State of Fear, 1984. *Contributions to:* History Today. *Memberships:* Mark Twain Society, USA (honorary Member); PEN. *Literary Agent:* Carol Smith, London. *Address:* Whitehall House, Frant, Sussex, England.

WRIGHT, Stephen, b. 30 Nov. 1922, New York, New York, USA. Writer. m. 1954, New York, divorced. *Education:* BA, Long Island University, 1949; MA, New York University, 1950. *Literary Appointment:* Main contributor, editor, publisher, Stephen Wright's Mystery Notebook, quarterly journal, 1984–; Authors' representative, Literary agent, representing authors from Canada, UK and USA, New York. *Publications include:* Crime in the Schools, nmovel, 1959; Different anthology, (editor, author of introduction), 1974; Brief Encyclopedia of Homosexuality, 1978; The Adventures of Sandy West, Private Eye, novel, 1986. *Contributions to:* Periodicals including: Gay Literature; American Literary Journal; The Advocate; Mystery Notebook. *Memberships:* authors Guild; Authors League of America; Dramatists Guild; Mystery Writers of America; Crime Writers Association UK. *Address:* PO Box 1341, FDR Station, New York, NY 10150, USA.

WRIGHT, Theodore Paul Junior, b. 12 Apr. 1926, Port Washington, New York, USA. Professor. m. Susan J Standfast, 17 Feb. 1967, Albany, New York, 1 son, 2 daughters. *Education:* BA, Swarthmore College, 1949; MA, 1951, PhD, 1957, Yale University. *Publications:* American Support of Free Elections Abroad, 1964; Asie du Sud, Traditions et Changements, 1979. Contributing Author: Politics and Religion in South Asia, 1966; Family, Kinships and Marriage Among Muslims in India, 1976; Competition and Modernization in South Asia, 1975; Modernization and Social change among Muslims in India, 1983; Mobilization of Collective Identity, 1980; Culture, Ethnicity and Identity 1983; Islam and Public Life in Asia, 1986. *Contributions to:* American Political Science Review; Journal of Asian Studies; Pacific Affairs; Asian Survey, and others. *Honours include:* Various fellowships; Fulbright Research Professor in Pakistan, 1983–84. *Memberships:* American Political Science Association; Association for Asian Studies; Phi Beta Kappa; Past Trustee, American Institute of Pakistan Studies; Past Treasurer, South Asian Muslim Studies Association. *Address:* Graduate School of Public Affairs, State University of New York, Albany, NY 12222, USA.

WRIGHT, Thomas Lundy, b. 19 Dec. 1925, Hattiesburg, Mississippi, USA. Professor of English. m. Ruth Park Lehmann, 28 June 1972. *Education:* BA English, 1949, MA English, 1951, PhD English and European Medieval Literature, 1960, Tulane University. *Literary Appointments:* Teaching Fellow 1950–55, Instructor 1957–60, Tulane University; Associate Professor, Texas Christian University, Fort Worth, Texas, 1962–64; Assistant Professor 1960–62, Associate Professor 1964–77, Professor 1977–79, Hargis Profesor of English Literature 1979–, Auburn University; Assistant editor 1983–84, Co-editor 1984–, Southern Humanities Review, *Publications:* Malory's Originality, (co-author), editor R M Kumiansky, 1964; The Teaching of Sir Gawain and the Green Knight, (co-author), editors Jane Chance and Miriam Y Miller, 1985. *Contributions to:* Articles, reviews and poetry to: Modern Philology; Southern Humanities Review; Philological Quarterly; Speculum; Southern Quarterly; Descant. *Honours:* Carnegie Research Grant, Tulane University, 1955–56; Fulbright Scholar, University of Manchester, England, 1956–57. *Memberships:* Modern Language Association of America; Medieval Academy of America; International Arthurian Society; Southeastern Medieval Society; South Atlantic Modern Language Association; Alabama College English Teachers Associaiton. *Address:* Department of English. Auburn University, Auburn, AL 36849, USA.

WRIGHT, William Edward, b. 5 Nov. 1926, Fairfield, Alabama, USA. Professor of History. *Education:* BS, 1951, MA, 1953, University of Colorado; University of Vienna, Austria, 1954–55; PhD, University of Colorado, 1957. *Publications:* Seerf, Seigneur and Sovereign. Agrarian Reform in Eighteenth Century Bohemia, 1966; Austria Since 1945, 1982. *Contributor to:* American Historical Review; Journal of Modern History; Balkan Review; Slavic Review; Journal ofCentral European Affairs; Austrian Hist. Yearbook (Editor). *Honours:* Fulbright Graduate Fellowship, Austria, 1954–55; McKnight Foundation Humanities Award in European History, 1961; Fulbright Research Fellowship, Austria, 1962–63; Phi Alpha Theta Award, 1967. *Address:* 18200 Honeysuckle Lane, Deephaven, MN 55391, USA.

WRIGLEY, Christopher John, b. 18 Aug. 1947, Woking, Surrey, England. Reader; Economic History. *Education:* BA, University of East Anglia; PhD, University of London. *Publications:* David Lloyd George & British Labour Movement, 1976; A J P Taylor, 1980; Editor, A History of British Industrial Relations 1875–1914, 1982; William Barnes, The Dorset Poet, 1984; A History of British Industrial Relations 1914–1939, 1986; Warfare, Diplomacy and Politics, 1986; Joint Editor, The Working Class in Victorian England, 4 volumes, 1973. *Contributor to:* Economic History Review; Dorset; The Literary Review; Social History. *Memberships:*

Historical Association; Economic History Society; Dorset Archaeological Society; Leicestershire County Councillor; Charnwood District Councillor. *Address:* Department of Economics, Loughborough University, Loughborough, Leicestershire, England.

WU, Silas H L, b. 10 Mar. 1929, Shijiajuang, China. Professor of History. *Education:* AB, National Taiwan University, 1954; AB, University of California at Berkeley, 1961; MA, Yale University, 1963; PhD, Columbia University, 1967. *Literary Appointments:* Professor of History, Boston College. *Major Publications:* Communication & Imperial Control in China 1693–1735, 1970; Passage to Power: K'ang-hsi & His Heir Apparent 1661–1722, 1979. *Contributor to:* American Historical Review; Journal of Asian Studies; Boston Globe. *Memberships:* Association for Asian Studies; American Historical Association; Society for Chi'ing Studies; New England China Seminar. *Honours:* Grants from: American Council of Learned Societies, 1970; Social Science Research Council, 1973, 1974; Fulbright (Distinguished) Scholar, 1979; Committee on Scholarly Communication with People's Republic of China, 1980. *Address:* 150 Beacon Street, Chestnut Hill, MA 02167, USA.

WUCHERER, Ruth Marie. Program Assistant and Travel Writing Instructor. *Education:* BA Journalism, University of Wisconsin-Milwaukee; Currently studying for MA Journalism, Marquette University. *Publications:* How To Sell Your Crafts, 1976; Make Money Selling Your Crafts, 1977; What You should Know About Credit: With Special Reference To Women, 1977; The Fascinating World of Advertising, 1979; Travel Writing for Fun and Profit: How to Add Dollars to Your Income Writing Travel Articles and Getting them Published, 1984. *Contributions to:* Milwaukee Journal Newspaper; The Grand Rapids Press Newspaper; Good Reading magazine; Accent magazine; others. *Address:* 3045 South 9th Place, Milwaukee, WI 53215, USA.

WULFF, Thomas Fredrik, b. 24 Aug. 1953, Helsinki, Finland. Writer. m. Ann-Charlotte Wigelius, 1 Mar. 1985, 1 daugter. *Literary Appointments:* Editor-in-Chief, Fagel Fenix Magazine, 1975–76. *Publications:* Poetry: Mansten, 1973; Hjartats Stratrovare, 1976; Snapshots: Mumlade Mytologier, 1980; En Drommares Dagbok, 1982; Kirurgens Park: Kineserier, 1985; Prose: Nattens Fabler, 1974; Sumprattens Resa, 1980; Trance Dance, 1980; Utspelad i Ulan-Bator, 1983; Plays written in 1976, 79, 81. *Contributions to:* The Daily Hufvudstadsbladet (Book Reviews). *Honours:* One-year Grants from the State in 1979, 84; Grants from Svenska Kulturfonden, 1985. *Memberships:* Member of Board, Finlands Svenska Forfattareforening, 1977–79; Pen Club of Finland. *Literary Agent:* Soderstrom & Company. *Address:* Kaserngatan 8 A 6, 00140 Helsinki 14, Finland.

WURM, Franz Herbert, b. 16 Mar. 1926, Prague, Czechoslovakia. Writer. *Education:* MA (Oxon). *Literary Appointments:* Director, German-Swiss Radio's Cultural Programme, 1966–69. *Publications:* Ammeldung (poems), 1959; Anker und Unruh (poems), 1964; Acht Gedichte in Faksimile, 1973. *Contributor to:* Neue Rundshau; Akzente; Spektrum; Manuskripte; Protokolle; Neue Zurcher Ztg, etc. *Honour:* Honorary Award of State of Zurich, 1967. *Memberships:* International PEN; Holderlin Gesellschaft. *Address:* Forchstr 103, 8032 Zurich, Switzerland.

WURSTER, Michael, b. 8 Aug. 1940, Moline, Illinois, USA. Poet. *Education:* BA, Dickinson College, Carlisle, Pennsylvania, 1962. *Literary Appointments:* Founding Member and Co-Director, Pittsburgh Poetry Exchange, 1974–; Director for Poetry Programmes, The Famous Rider Cultural Centre, 1982–. *Contributor to:* Oakland Review; Ball State University Forum; Backcountry; Hyperion; Acta Victoriana; Four Quarters; Descant; SunRust; and others. *Honours:* Pittsburgh Award, Shaded Room magazine, 1970; Most Valuable Player Award, COSMEP Conference, 1980. *Address:* 159 South 16th Street, Pittsburgh, PA 15203, USA.

WÜRTH, Peter Rudolf, b. 2 Sep. 1954, Munich, Federal Republic of Germany. Journalist. *Education:* Magister Artium, Political Sciences. *Publications:* Munich for Gourmets, 1983; Munich Dream Metropolis, video guide, 1984. *Contributions to:* Abendzeitung, Munich; Süddeutsche Zeitung, Munich; Lui, Munich; Stern, Hamburg; Konkret, Hamburg; etc. *Membership:* Deutsche Journalisten-Union. *Address:* Auerfeldstrasse 4a, 8 München 90, Federal Republic of Germany.

WYATT, Rachel Evadne, b. 14 Oct. 1929, Bradford, Yorkshire, England. Writer. m. Alan Wyatt, 18 Sep. 1948, Bradford, England, 2 sons, 2 daughters. *Education:* Girls' Grammar School, Bradford. *Appointments:* Writer-in-Residence, David Thomson University Centre, Nelson, British Columbia, Canada; Playwright-in-Residence, Tarragon Theatre, Toronto. *Publications:* The String Box, 1970; The Rosedale Hoax, 1977; Foreign Bodies, 1982; Time in the Air, 1985. Radio plays for British Broadcasting Corporation and Canadian Broadcasting Corporation; Two stage plays Geometry and Chairs and Tables, produced at Tarragon Theatre in 1983 and 1984. *Memberships:* Society of Authors (Britain); Alliance of Canadian Television and Radio Artists, Member Writers Council, Ontario; Playwrights Union of Canada. *Literary Agent:* David Higham Associates Limited, London. *Address:* 40 Prince Rupert Avenue, Toronto M6P 2A7, Ontario, Canada.

WYDLER, Karl, b. 28 Apr. 1927, Zurich, Switzerland. Professor of French and Italian. m. Lily Gilgen, 25 July 1953, 1 son. *Education:* Universities of Zurich, Florence and Sorbonne-Paris, 1945–52; PhD; Masters Diploma. *Literary Appointments:* Representative with Monique Laederach of Switzerland, 1st Grand International Festival of Poetry, Paris, France, 1978; Various recitals of Poetry, Lausanne, 1981, Geneva, 1981, Paris, France, 1983; Recitals during exhibitions of his paintings at art galleries, Basle, Bern, Solothurn, 1982, 84, 85. *Publications:* Zur Stellung des attributiven adjektivs vom Latein bis zum Neufranzösischen, dissertation, 1955, (part-print); Zor Stellung des Attributiven Adjekkius Von Latein bis zum Neufranzösischen, in, Romanica Helvetica, Volume 53, 1956; Ouvertures, poems, 1974; Sub-Version Poems, 1976; Ailleurs, Poems, 1981. *Contributions to:* Almanach 81; Intermuses, 1983–85, member of Editorial Committee, 1985–; Le Cerf-Volant, short story. *Honours:* Tobler Prize, 1946, J J Rousseau Prize, 1948, University of Zurich; Paul Fort Poetry Prize, 1979, Short Story Diploma of Honour, 1979, French Poetry Circle; Golden Rose, Society of French Poets (for total work). *Memberships:* Swiss Society of Writers; Adherent member, 1979–83, Active member, 1983–, Society of French Poets. *Address:* Obere Sternengasse 27, CH–4500 Soleure/Solothurn, Switzerland.

WYMAN, Walker De Marquis, b. 7 Dec. 1907, Danville, Illinois, USA. Teacher; Author. *Education:* BEd, Illinois State University; MA, Phd, University of Iowa. *Publications include:* Nothing But Prairie and Sky, 1954, 70; The American Adventure, with M Ridge, 1964; The Lumberjack Frontier, 1969; Charles Round Low Cloud, with W Clark, 1972; Witching for Water, Oil and Precious Minerals; Centennial History of the University of Wisconsin-River Falls, with J King, 1975; Mythical Creatures of the USA and Canada, 1978; Wisconsin Folklore, 1979. *Contributions to:* various historical magazines. *Honours include:* Selection of the Lumberjack Frontier by American Library Association and English Speaking Union, 1969; Honorary LLD, Illinois State University, 1979. *Address:* 415 Crescent Street, River Falls, WI 54022, USA.

WYND, Oswald, b. Tokyo, Japan. Novelist. *Education:* Publications include: Author of 16 novels as Oswald Wynd and 14 as Gavin Black; Translator of numerous books and short stories in 10 languages. *Contributions to:* New Statesman; Spectator; Satevepost; Argosy; Woman's Day; Good Housekeeping, and others. *Honours:* Doubleday Novel prize, 1947. *Memberships:* Society of Authors; Poets, Playwrights, Editors, Essayists and Novelists. *Address:* St Adrians, Shoregate, Crail, Fife, Scotland KY10 3SU.

WYNNE-JONES, Tim, b. 12 Aug. 1948, Cheshire, England. Writer. m. Amanda West Lewis, 12 Sep. 1980, 1 son, 1 daughter. *Education:* BA, University of Waterloo, Ontario, Canada, 1974; MFA, York University, Ontario, 1979. *Publications:* Odd's End, novel, 1980; The Knot, Novel, 1982; Zoom at Sea, childrens book, 1983; Zoom Away, 1985. *Contributions to:* Books in Canada; Freefall. *Honours:* Seal First Novel Award, 1979; Book Award, Best children's book by a Toronto resident, IODE, 1983; Best Childrens Book in Canada, Ruth Schwartz Award, 1983. *Memberships:* Writers Union of Canada; Alliance of Canadian Television and Radio Artists; Composers, Authors and Publishers Association of Canada; Crime Writers Associations, Great Britain and Canada; Canadian Society of Children's Authors, Illustrators and Performers. *Literary Agent:* Lucinda Vardey, Toronto. *Address:* 142 Winona Drive, Toronto, Ontario, Canada M6G 3S9.

Y

YAFFE, James, b. 31 Mar. 1927, Chicago, Illinois, USA. Writer, Teacher. m. Elaine Gordon, 1 Mar. 1964, New York, 1 son, 2 daughters. *Education:* BA, Yale University, 1948. *Publications include:* 7 novels, 1 collection of short stories, 2 non-fiction works, 3 plays, including: Poor Cousin Evelyn, 1951; The Good-For-Nothing, 1953; What's The Big Hurry?' 1954; Nothing But The Night, 1957; Mister Margolies, 1961; Nobody Does You Any Favors, 1965; The American Jews, nonfiction, 1970; the Voyage of the Franz Joseph, 1973; So Sue Me!, 1974; The Deadly Game, play, 1968; Ivory Tower, play, (with Jerome Weidman), 1968; Cliffhanger, play, 1978. *Contributions to:* Esquire; Atlantic Monthly; Commentary; Ellery Queen's Mystery Magazine; Saturday Review; new York Times. *Honour:* National Arts Foundation Grant, 1967. *Memberships:* PEN; Writers Guild; Dramatists Guild; Phi Beta Kappa. *Literary Agent:* Robert Freedman Agency. *Address:* 1215 North Cascade, Colorado Springs, CO 80903, USA.

YAMAMOTO, Kaoru, b. 28 Mar. 1932, Tokyo, Japan. College Teacher. *Education:* BS, University of Tokyo, 1953; MA, 1960, PhD, 1962, University of Minnesota, USA. *Literary Appointments:* Editor: The American Educational Research Journal, USA, 1973–75; The Educational Forum, 1984–. Editorial Board Member, The Educational forum, 1975–78; Editorial Advisory Board Member, Youth and Society, 1975–78, 1985–. *Publications:* The Individuality: The Unique Learner, 1975. Editor, The College Student and His Culture: An Analysis, 1968. Editor and Author, Teaching: Essays and Readings, 1969. Editor and Co-Author: The Child and His Image: Self-Concept in the Early Years, 1972; Death in the Life of Children, 1978; Children in Time and Space, 1979. *Contributions to:* Professional journals in education, psychology and social sciences of some 55 single-authored and 55 co-authored papers. *Honours:* Distinguished Teaching Award, Arizona State University, USA, 1980; Landsdowne Scholar, University of Victoria, Canada, 1985; Fulbright Lecturer, University of Iceland, 1985. *Address:* c/o The Educational Forum, 400 Farmer Building, Arizona State University, Tempe, AZ 85287, USA.

YAMASAKI, Takeo, b. 1 Mar. 1905. Honami-mura, Koha-gun, Fukuoka-ken, Japan. Novelist; Critic. *Education:* Tokyo University. *Publications:* Tarukirko (Lake Tarukiri), 1940; Gichō Socrates (The Chairman Socrates), 1965; Kurohae (Black South Wind), 1966; Essay on Uno Kōzi, 1974; Sailing, 1982. *Contributions to:* Shincho; Umi. *Memberships:* Writers' Association, Japan, (Nihon Bungeika Kyokai); PEN. *Honours:* Art Encouragement Prize, 1975; Hirabayashi Taiko Prize, 1983. *Address:* 5-12-16 Naritahigashi, Suganami-ku, Tokyo, Japan.

YANKOWITZ, Susan, b. 20 Feb. 1941, Newark, New Jersey, USA. Playwright; Novelist. m. Herbert Leibowitz, 3 May 1979, Maussane, Les Alpilles, France, 1 son. *Education:* BA, Sarah Lawrence, 1963; MFA, Yale Drama School, 1968. *Publications:* Slaughterhouse Play, in New American Plays Vol 4, 1971; The Ha-Ha Play in Scripts Vol 10, 1972; Boxes, a play in Playwrights for Tomorrow, 1973; Terminal, a play in Scripts, 1971; in The Radical Theatre Notebook 1974 and in Three Works by the Open Theatre, 1975; Silent Witness, a novel 1976, 1977; Portrait of a Scientist as a Dumb Broad, screenplay in Yale/Theatre, 1984. Screenplays for Television and Films including: Charlotte Perkins Gilman: Forerunner, TV play for Red Cloud Productions WGBH, Boston, Massachusetts, 1979; The Amnesiac, screenplay for MGM; 1980 Sylvia Plath's Poetry, teleplay for Center for Visual History, 1984. Author of plays produced throughout America, Canada and France. *Contributions to:* Short stories and essays published in Yale/Theatre, African Forum, Performance, Chrysallis, Heresies, Gnosis etc. *Honours:* Joseph E Levine Fellowship in Screenwriting, 1968; Vernon Rice

Drama Desk Award for Most Promising Playwright, 1969; NEA Creative Writing Fellowship Grant, 1972; Rockefeller Foundation Grant in Playwriting, 1973; CAPS Award in Playwriting, 1974; Guggenheim Fellowship in Playwriting, 1975; NEA Creative Writing Fellowship Grant, 1979; NYSCA Playwriting Grant for work on puppet play, 1983; NEA US/Japan Grant to study puppet theatre in Japan. *Literary Agent:* Gloria Loomis, A Watkins Agency, New York. *Address:* 205 W 89th Street, New York, NY 10024, USA.

YAOS-KEST, Itamar, b. 3 Aug. 1934, Hungary. Poet, Author. m. Hanna Mercazy, 21 Aug. 1958, Tel Aviv, 1 son, 1 daughter. *Education:* BA, University of Tel Aviv. *Literary Appointments:* Founder, Eked Publishing House, 1958. *Major Publications:* Poems: Nof-Beasham, 1959; Eyes Heritage, 1966; Du-Shoresh, 1975; Toward Germany, 1980; Leshon Hanahar-Leshon Hayam, 1984; Novels: In the Window of the Travelling House, 1970; The Shadow of the Bird, 1971; The Hold of Sand, 1972; Translations: Horazius; Anthology of Jewish-Hungarian Poetry, 1960; Anthology of Hungarian Poetry, 1985. *Contributor to:* All Israeli literary magazines. *Honours:* Nordow Prize, 1961; Talpor Prize, 1969; Helzel Prize, 1972; Walenrode Prize, 1979; Chulon Prize, 1984; Werthime Prize, 1985. *Membership:* Association of Hebrew Writers, Israel. *Literary Agent:* Eked, Tel Aviv. *Address:* Nahmani 51, Tel Aviv, Israel.

YARBROUGH, Anna Nash, b. 19 Jan. 1897. Writer. *Education:* Henderson College. *Appointments include:* Poetry Editor (Formerly), Poets Forum column, Benton Courier, Denton, Arkansas; Director, Arkansas Writers Conference. *Publications:* Flower of the Field, 1962; Building with Blocks, 1965; Poetry Patterns, 1968; Lairel Branches, co-author, 1969; Syllabic Poetry Patterns, 1978. *Contributions to:* National and local magazines and newspapers. *Honours:* Numerous national and local awards for poetry and prose. *Memberships:* Pioneer Branch, Arkansas; National League of American Penwomen; Poets Roundtable, Arkansas; American Society of Composers, Authors and Publishers; National League of State Poetry Societies. *Address:* 510 South East Street, Benton, AR 72015, USA.

YARWOOD, Doreen, b. 12 Dec. 1918, London, England. Freelance Author; Artist. *Education:* Hammersmith School Arts & Crafts, London 1934–36; Clapham School of Art, 1936–39; Institute of Education, University of London, 1939–40. *Publications:* English Costume, 1952, 5th edition, 1979; Outline of English Costume, 1967, 3rd edition, 1975; The English Home, 1956; English Houses, 1966; The Architecture of England, 1963, 2nd edition, 1967; Outline of English Architecture, 1965; The Architecture of Italy, 1970; Robert Adam (biography), 1970; The Architecture of Europe, 1974; European Costume, 1975; Architecture of Britain, 1976; The Encyclopaedia of World Costume, 1978; The English Home, 1979; Architecture of Britain, 2nd edition, 1980; The British Kitchen, 1981; 500 Years of Technology in the Home, 1983; English Interiors, 1984; Costume of the Western World, 1983; Encyclopaedia of Architecture, 1985. *Contributor to:* Period Homes; Readers Digest Books; Yearbook, Macmillan Educational; World Book, Childcraft International. *Memberships include:* Costume Society; Society of Architectural Historians; Furniture History Society. *Address:* 3 Garden House Lane, East Grinstead, Sussex RH19 4JT, England.

YATES, William Edgar, b. 30 Apr. 1938, Hove, England. Professor of German, University of Exeter. m. Barbara Anne Fellowes, 6 Apr. 1963, London, 2 sons. *Education:* MA, PhD, Emmanuel College, Cambridge. *Appointment:* Germanic Editor, Modern Language Review, 1981–. *Publications:* Grillparzer: A Critical Introduction, 1972; Nestroy: Satire & Parody in Viennese Popular Comedy, 1972; Tradition in the German Sonnet, 1981; Editor, Nestroy, Stucke 12-14, 1981–82; Co-Editor, Viennese Popular Theatre: A Symposium, 1985. *Contributor to:* Modern Language Review; Forum for

Modern Language Studies; Maske und Kothurn; Germanic Review; Publications of the English Goethe Society; German Life & Letters; Renaissance & Modern Studies; Osterreich in Gaschichte und Literatur; Journal of European Studies; Neophilologus; Colloquia Germanica; Nestroyana; Hofmannsthal-Forschungen. *Honours:* J G Robertson Prize, University of London, 1975. *Memberships:* Committee Member, Modern Humanities Research Association, 1981–; English Goethe Society, Council Member, 1984–;International Nestroy Society. *Address:* 7 Clifton Hill, Exeter EX1 2DL, England.

YEH (Ye), Chun-Chan (Junjian), b. 12 Dec. 1914, Hubei, China. Professor; Writer; Translator; Editor. m. Yuan Yin, 1942, 2 sons. *Education:* BA, Wuhan University, China; Researcher, English Literature, King's College, Cambridge, England. *Appointments:* Editor, Sponsor, Chinese Literature (in English,m French), 1950–74; Council Member, Chinese Writers Union, 1953–79; Member, Secretariat, 1980–85, Standing Committee Member, 1985–, Chinese Writers Association; Vice President, China PEN Centre, 1985–. *Publications:* (In English) Forgotten People; The Ignorant and the Forgotten; The Mountain Village; They Fly South; Three Seasons; (In Chinese) New Schoolmates; The Emperor Real and False; Sketches of Two Capitals; Pioneers of the Virgin Soil; On the Steppe; Flames; Freedom; Dawn; Selected Writings; Selected Stories; Old Souvenirs and New Friends; Open Fields; On the Art of Reading, etc; (Translations) Complete Hans Andersen; Agamemnon, etc. *Contributor to:* Most major literary journals in China; New Statesmen and The Nation; Life and Letters Today; London Magazine; Politiken; London Times; Story; Berlinske Weekendavisen; etc. *Memberships:* American & English PEN Centres. *Literary Agent:* Jennifer Kavanagh, London, England. *Address:* 6 Gongjian Hutong, Di An Men, Beijing, People's Republic of China.

YELDHAM, Peter, b. 25 Apr. 1927, Gladstone, New South Wales, Australia. Playwright. m. Marjorie Crane, 27 Oct. 1948, Sydney, 1 son, 1 daughter. *Major Publications:* Birds on the Wing, 1969–70; She won't lie down, 1972; Fringe Benefits (co-author), 1973; Away Match (co-author), 1974; Feature Films include: The Comedy Man, 1963; The Liquidator, 1965; Age of Consent, 1968; Touch and Go, 1979. Television plays include: Reunion Day; Stella; Thunder on the Snowy; East of Christmas; The Cabbage Tree Hat Boys. Television series include: Run from the Morning, 1977; Golden Soak, 1978; Ride on, Stranger, 1979; The Timeless Land, 1979. Also: Levkas Man, 1980; Sporting Chance, 1981; 1915, 1982; All the Rivers Run, 1983; Flight into Hell, 1984; Tusitala, The Lancaster-Miller Affair, 1985. *Contributor to:* Numerous British television series. *Honours:* Sammy award, Best television series in Australia, 1979; Penguin Award, Best television series, 1982; Awgie Awards, Best adaptation, 1980, 1983. *Memberships:* Writers' Guild (Australia & Great Britain); Kirribilli Club; Savage Club. *Literary Agent:* Harvey Unna, London; Judy Barry Management, Australia. *Address:* 28 Wolsley Road, Mosman, Sydney, Australia 2088.

YELLAND, Philippa Margaret, b. 28 Sep. 1956, Manchester, England. Journalist; Writer. m. Ian Stuart Talbot, 13 Nov. 1982, Brisbane, Queensland, Australia. *Education:* BA, Griffith University, Queensland. *Literary Appointments:* Sub-editor, Financial Review; Editor, Powderhound Ski Magazine. *Contributions:* Fiction, short stories to: Ash Magazine, Australia; Humorous articles to: Canberra Times, Australia; Features, travel articles, Powderhound Ski Magazine. *Honour:* Selected for Australian-Japan Foundation journalists' Scholarship. *Address:* 6/29 Reiby Place, Sydney, New South Wales 2000, Australia.

YEPSEN, Roger, b. 5 Nov. 1947, Schenectady, New York, USA. Editor; Writer. m. 6 Dec. 1979, Sri Lanka, 1 son, 1 daughter. *Education:* BA, Bucknell University, Lewisburg, Pennsylvania. *Publications:* Home Food Systems, 1980; Train Talk, 1983; Encyclopedia of natural Insect and Disease Control, 1984. *Literary Agent:* Curtis Brown Ltd, New York. *Address:* RD1, Box 400, Barto, PA 19504, USA.

YERBURGH, Rhoda Carol Goldberg, b. 28 Aug, 1946, New York City, USA. English Professor. m. 27 Apr. 1983, Montpelier, Vermont. *Education:* BA, English, State University of New York, Albany, 1968; MA, English, 1970, ABD, 1972, MFA, 1973, University of Arizona, Tucson. *Literary Appointment:* Associate Professor of English, Vermont College of Norwich University, Montpellier, Vermont, *Contributions to:* Louisville review; Kansas Quarterly; Beliot Poetry Journal; En Passant Poetry Quarterly; Mati; Backbone; Jam To-Day; Blueline; Third Coast Archives and others; I Sing the Song of Myself, 1978; Anthology of Magazine Verse, 1980, 85; Strings, A Gathering of Family Poems, 1984. *Honours:* Vermont Council on the Arts Grant-in-Aid, 1978; Dana Foundation Grant, 1984. *Membership:* Vermont Council on the Arts Touring Artists Register. *Address:* Box 1030, RR1, Upper Elm Street, Montpelier, VT 05602, USA.

YEUNG, Yue-man, b. 1 Oct. 1938, Hong Kong. Professor of Geography. m. Ameda, 14 May 1967, Hong Kong, 1 son, 1 daughter. *Education:* BA Honours 1962, Dip Ed 1963, University of Hong Kong; MA, University of Western Ontario, Canada, 1966; PhD, University of Chicago, USA, 1972. *Publications:* National Development Policy and Urban Transformation in Singapore: A Study of Public Housing and the Marketing System, 1973; The Proposed Kra Canal: A Critical Evaluation and Its Impact on Singapore, (with Patrick Low), 1973; Changing South-East Asian Cities: Readings on Urbanization, (editor with C P Lo), 1976; Hawkers in Southeast Asian Cities: Planning for the Bazaar Economy, (with T G McGee), 1977; A Place to Live: More Effective Low-Cost Housing Policies in Asia, (editor), 1983; Community Participation in Delivery Urban Services in Asia, (edited with T G McGee), in press. *Contributions to:* Publications including: Bandar; Focus on Southeast Asia; Journal of Tropical Geography; Town Planning Review; Petroleum News; Insight; Profesional Geographer; Encyclopedia Britiannica; IDRC Reports. *Honours:* Hong Kong Government Scholarship, 1959–62; Canadian Government Commonwealth Scholarship, 1964–66; University Endownment Fellowship, University of Chicago, 1967–69. *Memberships:* Working Group on Market Distribution System 1973–, Working Group on Urbanisation in Developing Countries 1980–, International Geographical Union; Canadian Association of Geographers; Association of American Geographers; Regional Science Association; Society for International Development. *Address:* Department of Geography, Chinese University of Hong Kong, Shatin, NT, Hong Kong.

YLIMAULA, Anna-Maija, b. 25 June 1950, Helsinki, Finland. Writer. m. Mikko Putkonen, 15 June 1974, Oulu, Finland, 2 sons, 3 daughters. *Education:* Architect; BA; Licentiate in Technology. *Publications:* Daughter of a Priest (Papintyttö), novel, 1976; Let The Night stay, (Yö voi olla), novel, 1978; Table in the Birch Grove, (Pöytä koivikossa), novel, 1982; Idylli, (Idylli), novel, 1984; Anna!, play, 1984. *Contributions to:* Kaltio; Anthology Vuosirengas. *Honours:* Grants: Central Committee of Arts, 1980; City of O Iu, 1984. *Memberships:* Finnish Writers' Union (SKL); Finnish Playwrights; Union (SUNKLO). *Literary Agent:* Werner Söderström Oy, Helsinki. *Address:* Ravanderint 6 A 2, 90570 Oulu 57, Finland.

YOPCONKA, Natalie Ann Catherine, b. 21 July 1942, Taylor, Pennsylvania, USA. Computer Specialist. *Education:* BS, Business Administration, Personnel and Industrial Relations, University of Maryland, College Park, 1965; Numerous courses in Management, Sales and in the Computer field; MBA, Information Technology, (Computer Management), George Washington University, Washington DC, 1976. *Literary Appointments:* Information, USA, (including On Call) 1983–85; IEEE Computer Society Working Group for a Standard for Software Reviews and Audits, 1984–.

Contributor to: Federal Poet's Club Quarterly. *Honours:* Certificate of Appreciation from Association for Comuting Machinery, Washington DC Chapter, 1979, 1981, 1983; Several academic honours. *Memberships:* Federal Poet's Club; Phi Delta Gamma. *Address:* 7401 New Hampshire Avenue, Apt 1115, Hyattsville, MD 20783, USA.

YORINKS, Arthur, b. 21 Aug. 1953, Roslyn, New York, USA. Writer. m. Adrienne Berg, 23 Oct. 1983, New York City, USA. *Major Publications:* Sid & Sol, 1977; The Magic Meatballs, 1979; Louis the Fish, 1980; It Happened in Pinsk, 1983; Hey, Al, 1986. Also librettos for, Leipziger Kerzenspiel (music by Robert Moran); The Juniper Tree (music by Philip Glass & Robert Moran), 1985. *Honours:* Louis the Fish, Best Book, 1980, School Library Journal; It Happened in Pinsk, Editor's Choice, Booklist. *Literary Agent:* Marian Young, Nat Sobel Associates, New York. *Address:* 181 Thompson Street, New York City, NY 10012, USA.

YORK, William, b. 27 Sep. 1950, Tacoma, Washington, USA. Clerical. *Education:* BA, English Writing; Teaching Certificate (secondary Level). *Literary Appointments:* Editor, Assay (Washington Literary Magazine), 1970–71. *Major Publications:* Who's Who in Rock Music, 1979, Revised 1982. *Address:* 1421 N 34th Street, Seattle, WA 98103, USA.

YOUNG, Ahdele Carrine, b. 29 May 1923, Alamo, North Dakota, USA. Writer. m. Gerald W Young, 10 May 1949, Lexington, Kentucky, 1 son, 1 daughter. *Education:* BA, University of Minnesota, 1944. *Literary Appointments:* Reporter, Blue Earth Post and Fairbault County Register, Blue Earth, Minnesota, 1946; Advertising Copy Writer, Rike's Department Store, Dayton, Ohio 1948–59. *Publication:* Green Broke, 1981. *Contributions to:* Two articles in Gourmet on growing up in a Norwegian-American family on North Dakota prairies, 1983; Short story: Bank Night, Yale Review, 1984. *Honour:* Florence Roberts Head Memorial Award from Ohioana Library Association for, Green Broke, 1982. *Memberships:* Author's Guild; Authors League of America. *Address:* Rural Route 2, Tipp City, OH 45371, USA.

YOUNG, Bertram Alfred, b. 20 Jan. 1912, London, England. Journalist/Writer. *Literary Appointments:* Assistant Editor, Punch, 1949–62; Drama Critic, Punch, 1962–64; Drama Critic, Financial Times, 1964–. *Publications:* Bechuanaland 1966; Cabinet Pudding 1967; Mirror Up To Nature (collected criticism) 1982. *Contributor to:* Endless freelance writing, 1934–; about 20 plays for radio, 1938–49. *Honours:* OBE, 1980; Kentucky Colonel. *Memberships:* Drama Advisory Committee, British Council, 1973–83; President, Critics' Circle, 1978–80. *Address:* Clyde House, Station Street, Cheltenham, Gloucestershire, England.

YOUNG, David S, b. 17 July 1946, Oakville, Ontario, Canada. Novelist; Screenwriter. m. Sarah Sheard, 19 Dec. 1982, Toronto. *Education:* Degree in Literature, University of Western Ontario. *Publications:* Agent Provocateur, 1975; Incognito, 1982; Love Is Strange. 1985. *Memberships:* Writers Union of Canada; ACTRA. *Address:* 34 Marchmount Road, Toronto M6G 2A9, Canada.

YOUNG, Donald, b. 29 June 1933, Indianapolis, Indiana, USA. Editor; Writer. *Education:* BA, Indiana University; MA, Butler University. *Literary Appointments:* Senior Editor, Encyclopedia Americana, 1967–77. *Major Publications:* American Roulette, 1965; Adventure in Politics (editor), 1970; The Great American Desert (author & photographer), 1980; The Sierra Club Guides to the National Parks, Volumes 3, 4, 5 (editor), 1984–86. *Contributor to:* Numerous magazines & journals. *Address:* 166 East 61st Street, Apt 3–C, New York, NY 10021, USA.

YOUNG, Ian George, b. 5 Jan. 1945, London, England. Writer. *Publications:* Year of the Quiet Sun, 1969; Double Exposure, 1970 (enlarged edition 1974);

Curieux d'Amour (translation), 1970; Some Green Moths, 1972; The Male Muse: A Gay Anthology, editor, 1973; The Male Homosexual in Literature: A Bibliography, 1975; Common-Or-Garden Gods, 1976; Schwule Poesie, 1978; editor, On the Line: Short Stories, 1980; Editor, Overlooked and Underrated: Essays on Some 20th Century Writers, 1982; Editor, The Son of the Male Muse, 1983; Gay Resistance: Homosexuals in the Anti-Nazi Underground, 1985. *Address:* 315 Blantyre Avenue, Scarborough, Ontario, Canada M1N 2S6.

YOUNG, Jock, b. 4 Mar. 1942, Gorebridge, Midlothian, Scotland. Sociologist. *Education:* BSC, MSc, PhD, London School of Economics, London, England. *Publications include:* The Drugtakers, 1971; Contemporary Social Problems in Britain, 1972; The New Criminology, 1973; Manufacture of News, 1973; Critical Criminology, 1974; Abortion on Demand, 1976; Capitalism and the Rule of Law, 1979; Policing the Riots, 1981; What is to be done about Law and Order, 1984; Confronting Crime, 1985; Realist Criminology, 1986; Losing the Fight Against Crime, 1986, Islington Crime Survey, 1986. *Contributions to:* British Journal of Criminology; British Journal of Sociology; Issues in Criminology. *Memberships:* Executive National Deviancy Conference; Steering Committee, European Group for the Study of Deviance and Social Control. *Address:* Head, Centre for Criminology, Middlesex Polytechnic, Queensway, Enfield, Middlesex, England.

YOUNG, John Charles Edumund, b. 3 May 1934, Welland, Ontario, Canada. Newspaper Journalist. m. Elizabeth Doran, 27 Sep. 1968, Dublin, Ireland, 1 son, 1 daughter. *Literary Appointments:* Agriculture Correspondent, The Times, London. *Publications:* Two Tall Masts, 1965; The Country House in the 1980's, 1981. *Contributor to:* Regular Weekly Farming Column in, The Field; occasional articles in numerous other journals; Talks and Interviews on BBC Radio. *Address:* 37 Dewhurst Road, London W14, England.

YOUNG, Oran Reed, b. 15 Mar. 1941, New York, USA. Educator. m. Gail Osherenko, 6 Oct. 1979, Chincoteague, Virginia, 2 daughters. *Education:* AB, Harvard, 1962; MA 1964, PhD 1965, Yale University. *Publications:* The Intermediaries: Third Parties in International Crises, 1967; Systems of Political science, 1968; The Politics of Force: Bargaining During International Crises, 1968; Neutralization and World Politics, (with Cyril E Black, Richard A Falk, Klaus E Knorr), 1968; Political Leadership and Collective Goods, (with Norman Frohlich and Joe A Oppenheimer), 1971; Bargaining: Formal Theories of Negotiation, (editor and contributor), 1975; Resource Management at the International Level: The Case of the North Pacific, 1977; Compliance and Public Authority: A Theory With International Applications, 1979; Natural Resources and the State: The Political Economy of Resource Management, 1981; Resource Regimes: Natural Resources and Social Institutions, 1982. *Contributions to:* Journals including: Ocean Development and International Law; Polar Record; World Politics; Journal of Conflict Resolution. *Honours include:* Fellowship; John Simon Guggenheim Foundation, 1969–70; Grant, Resources for the Future, 1977; Distinguished Scholar/Teacher Award, University of Maryland, 1979–80. *Memberships:* American Society for Political And Legal Philosophy; International Studies Association; Public Choice Society; Cosmos Club, Washington DC. *Address:* East Hill, Wolcott, VT 05680, USA.

YOUNG, Patrick Grant, b. 19 Oct. 1946, Alberta, Canada. Actor; Director; Teacher; Playwright. *Education:* BA Honours English Language and Literature, Victoria College, University of Toronto, 1968; Elizabethan and Pre-Shakespearean Drama, University of Waterloo Graduate School, 1971–73; Acting, Directing, Theatre, History and Theory, Indiana University Graduate School, 1973–75. *Literary Appointments:* Head of Acting Progamme, Artistic Director of Dalhousie Theatre Productions, Dalhousie University, Halifax, 1982–85. *Publications:* Winnie, (Produced by

Charlottetown Festival, 1979, Filmed by Norfolk Communications, 1980–81); Aimée!, with music by Bob Ashley, (Produced by Charlottetown Festival 1981). *Honours:* Smile Company Playwriting Award, 1979; Eric Harvey Musical Theatre Award, 1980; Canada Council Writing Grant, 1982. *Memberships:* Playwrights Union of Canada; Guild of Canadian Musical Theatre Writers; ACTRA; Equity. *Address:* 432 Parliament Street, Apt 1, Toronto, Ontario, M5A 3A2, Canada.

YOUNG-JAMES, Douglas Alexander de Singleton, b. 10 July, 1914, Newport, Isle of Wight, England. Solicitor; Estate Agent; Royal Air Force Officer (retired). *Education:* Clifton College; Bristol University, England. *Publications:* Teaching of Dramatic Art – Myfany James (editor), 1962; Memoirs of an Asp (autobiography), 1962; Donald Campbell (biography), 1968. *Contributor to:* ASP Magazine. *Honours:* Grand Prior of London; Sovereign Order of St John of Jerusalem. *Memberships:* Guild of Freemen of City of London; RAF Club; Fellow, Directors' Institute, 1967; President, Aspian Society (Vice President since 1975); Vice Poresident, United Service Catholic Association; Directors' Club. *Address:* 21 Ilchester Mansions, Abingdon Road, London W8 6AE, England.

YOUNGBERG, Ruth, b. 24 Aug. 1915, Grand Rapids, Michigan, USA. Librarian. m. Chester T Youngberg, 11 Aug. 1941, San Diego, California. 4 daughters. *Education:* BA, Wheaton College, Wheaton, Illinois, 1936; BSc Library Science, University of Illinois, Champaign-Urbana, 1939. *Literary Appointments:* Librarian, Wheaton College, 1936–38, 1939–41; Catalogue Librarian, Oregon State University Library, 1962–64, 1970–76. *Major Publication:* Dorothy L Sayers: A Reference Guide, G K Hall & Co, Boston, 1982. *Address:* 841 NW Merrie Drive, Corvallis, OR 97330, USA.

YOUNGSON, Robert Murdoch, b. 13 Nov. 1926, Stirling, Scotland. Consultant Opthalmologist. m. Daphne Margaret Grant, 26 June 1950, Aberdeen, 2 sons, 3 daughters. *Education:* Bachelor of Medicine and Surgery, Diploma in Tropical Medicine and Hygiene; Diploma in Opthalmology. *Major Publications:* Everything You Need to Know about Contact Lenses, 1984; Everything You Need to Know About Your Eyes, 1985; How to Cope with Tinnitus and Hearing Loss, 1986; Shingles, 1986. *Contributor to:* Journal of the RAMC; The British Journal of Opthalmology; American Journal of Opthalmology; British Medical Journal; Studio Sound; The Tape Recorder; Wireless World; and others. *Honours:* Order of St John of Jerusalem (Officer). *Member:* Society of Authors. *Literary Agent:* Juri Gabriel, London. *Address:* c/o Williams and Glyn's Bank plc, Whitehall, London SW1, England.

YRLID, Rolf John, b. 8 Mar. 1937, Boras, Sweden. Author; Lecturer. m. Inger Ahlstedt, 14 Aug. 1965, 2 sons. *Education:* Fil.Dr. (PhD). *Publications:* Atombombstribunalen, 1972; Litteraturrecensionens anatomi, 1973; Tidsbilder, 1975; Projekt Indisk By, 1976; Vägen till Gandesa, 1982; Litteraturens villkor, 1984. *Address:* Fredsgatan 2, S–222 20 Lund, Sweden.

YUDKIN, John, b. 8 Aug. 1910, London, England. Nutritionist. *Education:* BSc, London University, 1929; Christ's College, Cambridge University, 1929–35; BA, MA, PhD, London Hospital, 1935–38; MD, Cambridge, 1943. *Publications:* This Slimming Business, 1948; Pure White and Deadly, 1972; This Nutrition Business, 1976; Penguin Encyclopedia of Nutrition, 1985. *Contributions to:* Slimming Magazine. *Address:* 20 Wellington Court, London NW8 9TA, England.

Z

ZABLOTNY, Carl Edward, b. 18 June 1952, Cleveland, Ohio, USA. Journalist; Jesuit Priest. *Education:* MA, New York University; DivM, Jesuit School of Theology, Berkeley, California; MJ, Graduate School of Journalism, University of California, Berkeley. *Literary Appointments:* Editor, National Jesuit News, USA, 1982–. *Contributions to:* Numerous religious newspapers and publications. *Honours:* Best Religious Order Newspaper, USA, 1981, 82, 83, 84; various individual awards in the Catholic Press of USA and Canada. *Address:* 5600 City Avenue, Philadelphia, PA 19131, USA.

ZACH, Natan, b. 13 Dec. 1930, Berlin. Poet; Critic; Editor; Professor of Literature. *Education:* BA, Jerusalem (Hebrew University) and Tel-Aviv, 1952–67; PhD, University of Essex, England. *Literary Appointments:* Artistic Co-Director, Ohel Theatre, Israel, 1960–65; Lector, Dvir Publishing House, Tel-Aviv, 1959–64; Co-Editor, Igre Literary Year Book, Jerusalem, 1984–. *Publications:* Poems 1960; All the Milk and the Honey (Poems) 1966; Time and Rhythm in Bergson amd Modern Poetry (Essay) 1966; North Easterly (Poems) 1979; Talks on Literature, 1983; Dancing School (Play) 1985. *Contributions to:* Atlantic Monthly; Stand (UK); Grand Street (US); All major Israeli periodicals; Caracters (France); Hortulus (Switzerland) and Many more. *Honour:* The Bialik Prize for 1981 (Israel's most prestigious Literary Award). *Address:* 64 Hazionut Avenue, Haifa 35311, Israel.

ZACHARIAS, Lela Ann, b. 1 Dec. 1944, Chicago, Illinois, USA. Writer; Teacher. m. Michael George Gaspeny, 15 Aug. 1982, 1 son. *Education:* AB, Indiana University, 1966; MA, Hollins College, 1973; MFA, University of Arkansas, 1976. *Appointments:* Lecturer, 1975–76, Assistant Professor, 1976–81, Associate Professor, 1981–, Co-ordinator, Writing Programme, 1977–, University of North Carolina; Editor, Greensboro Review, 1977–; Visiting Lecturer, Princeton University, 1980–81. *Publications:* Helping Muriel Make It Through the Night, 1976; Lessons, 1981. *Contributor to:* Redbook; Fiction International; Kansas Quarterly; South Dakota Review; New England Review; Intro; New Writers; Book Forum; Hollins Critic; The Black Warrior Review; Quartet; etc. *Honours:* National Endowment for the Arts Fellowship, 1980; Sir Walter Raleigh Award, 1982; North Carolina Arts Council Fellowship, 1985. *Memberships:* Associated Writing Programmes, Vice-President, 1980–81, President, 1981–82, Historian, 1982–83. *Literary Agent:* Rhoda A Weyr. *Address:* Dept of English, University of North Carolina, Greensboro, NC 27412, USA.

ZALKA, Miklos, b. 25 May 1928, Budapest, Hungary. Writer. *Education:* Degree by Correspondence, Zrinyi Miklos Military Academy, 1958. *Publications:* Author, many books including: A mi utcank, 1967; A borzekes, 1967; Mindenkihez, Historical Essay, 1969; A tavolban Kanaan, 1970; A dzungel vere, (Report from a Vietnamese Village), 1971; Rizs esbambusz, (short stories from Vietnam), 1971; Es felno az elefant (documents & legends on foundation of Vietnamese People's Army), 1973; Acollima Szarnya (reports from the Democratic People's Republic of Korea), 1974; Romham 03.30, (historical essay, military & political outline of the military operations during WWII in Hungary), 1975; Fustkarikak, (short stories), 1975; Az Asszony Akire Varnak, novel, 1975; Sxamuely, historical essay, 1979; Ostrom, novel, 1980; Vorosok es feherek, historical essay, 1982; Fekete karacsony, novel, 1982; Zugnak a harangok, novel, 1984; Harmadik emelet, jobbra, novel, 1985. *Honours:* Recipient, Special Prizes, 1962, 1969, 1974 (for, Fustkarikak, 1975) (for Roham 03.30). *Address:* Abonyi u.27, 1146 Budapest XIV, Hungary.

ZALLER, Robert Michael, b. 19 Mar. 1940, Brooklyn, New York, USA. Professor of History. *Education:* BA, Queens College, City University of New York, 1960; MA, 1963, PhD, 1968, Washington University. *Publications:* The Year One, 1969; The Parliament of 1621: A Study in Constitutional Conflict, 1971; Lives of the Poet, 1974; The Cliffs of Solitude: A Reading of Robinson Jeffers, 1983; Europe in Transition 1660–1815, 1984. Editor: A Casebook on Anais Nin, 1974. Co-editor: Biographical Dictionary of British Radicals in the Seventeenth Century, 3 volumes, 1982–84. *Contributions to:* New York Times; Arts in Society; Prairie Schooner; Massachusetts Review; Boston University Journal; Studies in Romanticism; Southern Literary Journal; Invisible City; Albion; Eighteenth Century Life; Journal of British Studies; Agenda. *Honours:* Prize, Phi Alpha Theta, 1972; Award, Tor House Foundation, 1984; Fellow, John Simon Guggenheim Foundation, 1985–86. *Address:* Department of History, University of Miami, Coral Gables, FL 33124, USA.

ZAMBARAS, Vassilis, b. 1 May 1944, Revmatia, Greece. Teacher of English as a Foreign Language. m. Eleni Nezi, 19 Oct. 1980, Revmatia, Greece, 1 son, 1 daughter. *Education:* BA, English 1970; MA English (Writing), 1972, University of Washington, Seattle, Washington, USA. *Major Publications:* Sentences, 1976; Aural, 1984. *Contributor to:* Assay; Mardona; Poetry Northwest; Southern Poetry Review; Wisconsin Review; The Falcon; West Coast Review (Canada); Workshop; Longhouse; Edge (New Zealand); Text; Shearsman (UK); Smoot Drive Press; Apopeira (Greece); Klinamen (Greece); Intermedio (Greece). *Honours:* Harcourt, Brace & Jovanovich Writing Fellowship, University of Boulder, Colorado USA, 1970; Prize Winner, Academy of American Poets, University of Washington, 1972. *Address:* 21 K Fotopoulou, Melighala, Messenias, Greece.

ZAREMBA, Joseph Marc, b. 27 June 1923, Bellingham, Washington, USA. College Teacher. m. Mary Jane Rigelsky, 27 June 1964, Youngstown, Ohio, 2 sons, 3 daughters. *Education:* BS, Forestry, University of Washington, Seattle, Washington, USA, 1948; MS, Forestry, College of Forestry, State University of New York, Syracuse, New York, USA. 1951; MA, Economics, 1958, PhD, Economics, 1958, Harvard University, Cambridge, Massachusetts, USA; MS, Mathematics, New York University, Courant Institute, New York, 1973. *Publications:* Economics of the American Lumber Industry, 1963; Editor: Mathematical Economics and Operations Research, 1978; Editor: Statistics and Econometrics, 1980. *Contributions to:* The Trend of Lumber Prices Journal of Forestry, 1958; Factors Influencing the Consumption of Southern Pine, Journal of Farm Economics, 1961; Estimating Health Program Outcomes Using a Markov Equilibrium Analysis of Disease Development, with J Bush and M Chen, The American Journal of Public Health, 1971; Effectiveness Measures, with J Bush and M Chen in, Operations Research in Health Care – A Critical Analyis, edited by L J Shuman, R D Speas and John P Young, 1975. *Memberships:* New York State Economics Association; Operations Research Society of America. *Address:* Home: 9 Temple Hill Acres, Geneseo, NY 14454, USA.

ZAREV, Pantelei, b. 11 Nov. 1911, Vidin, Bulgaria. Writer. *Education:* Philosophy, Sofia University. *Literary Appointments:* Academician; Member of The State Council of Bulgaria. *Publications:* A Review of Bulgarian Literature, (5 vols) 1966–76; A Transformed Literature, 1969; Literary Portraits, 1974; The Conscience Of The Writer, 1975. *Contributor to:* All main literary editions in Bulgaria. *Honours:* Dimitrov prize, 1950, 1969; A People's Worker of Culture, 1970; A Hero of Socialist Labour, 1974. *Membership:* Union of Bulgarian Writers, Chairman 1972–79. *Address:* 2 Jakobitza, Sofia, Bulgaria.

ZARINS, Christopher Kristaps, b. 2 Dec. 1943, Latvia. Vascular Surgeon. m. Zinta Zarins, 7 Aug. 1967, 1 son, 2 daughters. *Education:* BA, Lehigh University, Bethlehem, Pennsylvania, 1964; MD, Johns Hopkins University School of Medicine, Baltimore, Maryland,

1968. *Literary Appointments:* Assistant Editor, 1977–81, Associate Editor, 1981–83, Editor, 1983–, Journal of Surgical Research. *Publications:* Numerous chapters in edited medical publications. *Contributor to:* Numerous articles, book reviews and editorials to scientific and medical journals. *Honours:* Phi Eta Sigma; Omicron Delta Kappa; Phi Beta Kappa; Resident Research Award, Association of Academic Surgery, 1972. *Memberships include:* The Society of University Surgeons; The International Society of Cardiovascular Surgery; Society for Vascular Surgery; Association for Academic Surgery; American Heart Association; Fellow, American College of Surgeons; ·American Association for the Advancement of Science; American Medical Association; American Surgical Association and many others. *Address:* University of Chicago, 5841, S Maryland Avenue, Chicago, IL 60637, USA.

ZASLOW, Edmund, b. 28 Apr. 1917, New York City, USA. Poet. m. Doris Kahn, 1 Sep. 1940, New York City, 3 daughters. *Education:* BA, City College of New York, 1938; MA, New School for Social Research, 1940. *Literary Appointments:* Part-time Faculty, Adelphi University, Garden City, New York, 1977–. *Publications:* I, Too, Jehovah, poems, 1952; Dream's Navel, 1979, 81; Misapprehensions and Other Poems, 1984. *Contributions to:* American Scholar; New York Times; Saturday Review; Sewanee Review; Antioch Review; Christian Science Monitor; Denver Post; Commonweal; Judaism; Moment; Midstream; Beloit Poetry Review; Poetry Now; Poets On; Descant; Negative Capability. Anthologies: Anthology of Magazine Verse; Illustrated Treasury of Poetry for Children, and various others. *Honours:* Poetry Fellowship, Fairleigh Dickinson University, 1961; National Prize, Poetry Society of America, 1962; Hart Crane Prize, American Weave Association, 1963; Poet Lore Prize, 1967; Davies Prize, Poetry Society of America, 1982; Kreymborg Prize, PSA, 1982; Eve of St Agnes Prize, 1984; Fellow, The Macdowell Colony, 1984. *Memberships:* Past Vice President, Governing Board member, 3 terms, Poetry Society of America; Poets, Playwrights, Editors, Essayists and Novelists American Center; Poets and Writers Incorporated. *Address:* 2902 210th Street, Bayside, NY 11360, USA.

ZATKOWSKI, Linda Joyce Coscia, b. 22 Jan. 1946, Bridgeport, Connecticut, USA. Medical Editor. m. Thomas Francis Zatkowski, 2 Sep. 1967, Fairfield. *Education:* AA, Science, Bay Path Junior College, 1965; BSc, Southern Connecticut State University, 1985. *Appointments:* Editorial Assistant, Biochemical Pharmacology, 1980–84; Editor, Views, 1984–; Medical Editor, Medical Education Programs, 1984–. *Publications:* Editorial Assistant, Postoperative Disorders of the Gastrointestinal Tract, 1972; Editor: Myocardial Infarction: Complications Requiring Surgery, 1984; Cardiac and Cardiopulmonary Transplatation, 1985; Hepatitis B Infection: Effective Use of Serology and Immunoprophylaxis, 1985; Burn Injuries and the Immune Response, 1985; The Spleen: Syndromes of Disfunction, 1985; Renal and Metabolic Toxicities of Cancer Chemotherapy, 1985; etc. *Contributor to:* Numerous professional journals. *Honours:* Achievement Award, International Association of Business Communicators, 1984. *Memberships:* American Medical Writers Association; Council of Biology Editors; International Association of Business Communicators. *Address:* 103 Talcott road, Guildford, CT 06437, USA.

ZAVERI, Shantilal Mansukhlal, b. 20 Oct. 1913, Rangoon, Burma. Writer; Author; Journalist. *Literary Appointments:* Editor, Publisher, Indian vernacular monthly magazine Jindgi, 1951–56. *Publications:* The Deluge, 1944; The God's Theatre, 1978; An Age of Insanity, 1984. *Contributions to:* Magazines and journals in India, Japan, England and Australia. *Address:* Rm 508, Nissei Meguro Mansion, 3-1-7 Meguro, Tokyo 153, Japan.

ZAVRIAN, Suzanne Ostro, b. 29 Feb. 1928, Baltimore, Maryland, USA. Poet; Editor; Arts Administrator. *Education:* BA, New York University. *Publications:*

Demolition Zone, 1976; Dream of the Whale, 1982. *Contributor to:* Partisan Review; Paris Review; Center; Y'Bird; Village Voice; and many others. *Honour:* Honourable Mention, Pushcart Prize Anthology, 1980; Award for fiction finalist NYSCAPS, 1983. *Memberships:* PEN; Poets and Writers. *Address:* 321 West 94th Street, New York, NY 10025, USA.

ZEIDLER, Frank Paul, b. 20 Sep. 1912. Mediator-Arbitrator; Consultant in Public Administration. *Education:* Studied, Marquette University, Milwaukee, Wisconsin; LLD, 1958, LHD, 1983, University of Wisconsin. *Literary Appointments:* Editor: Milwaukee Turner, 1942–48; Public Enterprise Record, 1951–83. *Publications:* Bound Manuscripts in Milwaukee Public Library: A Liberal in City Government; Municipal Government and Its Improvement; Hamlet; Macbeth; Midsummer Night's Dream, Julius Caesar, all in modern verse. *Contributions to:* North American Mentor. Numerous articles on municipal government, planning, social and economic development, community organisation and democratic socialism. *Honours:* 1st Prize, for poem, I Am the Monitions Maker and I Am, American Turners Poetry, 1975. *Memberships:* President, Friends of University of Wisconsin-Milwaukee Golda Meir Library. *Address:* 2921 North 2nd Street, Milwaukee, WI 53212, USA.

ZELTINS, Teodors, b. 27 Oct. 1914, Riga, Latvia. Freelance Writer. m. Velta Linde, 30 Sep. 1939, 1 daughter. *Education:* Major in Literature, University of Riga, Latvia. *Appointment:* member of Editorial Staff, Latvian newspaper, Jaunakas Zinas, Riga, 1936–40. *Publications:* (Poetry), Balades, 1947; Nakts uguni, 1953; Skumja pase, 1961; (short stories) Dveselu glabeji, 1959; Torni Daugava, 1964; Zvaigzne egles zara, 1968; (Novels) Rigas gimnaristi, 1939; Slazda, 1952; Rozu gaitenis, 1958; Melnas avis, 1958; Fazudusa paaudze, 1959; Drupu republika, 1960; Tiltu atjaunotaji, 1962; Antins Amerika mekle ligavu, 1963; Antins Amerika cinas ar sievu un trimdu, 1967; Antins debesis makla latviasus, 1970; Milestibas maize, 1971; Lallu meisters Engelis, 1976; Leopolds Maurs atzistas, 1978; Septini saulrieta, 1980; (Essay) Tuvos un talos ciemos, 1977. *Contributor to:* Weekly Journal, Atputa, Riga, 1934–40; Weekly column in, Laiks, (Latvian Newspaper), Brooklyn, New York, 1960–75. *Honours:* Award from American Latvian Association Cultural Foundation for book of short stories, Dveselu glabeji, 1960; Award from Gopper Foundation for book, Torni Deugave, 1964; For Book of Essays from Raisters F, 1977. *Membership:* International PEN Latvian Centre, Stockholm, Sweden. *Address:* 49 S Passaic Avenue, Catham, NJ 07928, USA.

ZENOFON, Fonda, b. 31 Aug. 1953, Greece. Freelance Writer; Poet; Editor; Publisher. *Publications:* Editor, Brunswick Poetry Workshop Newsletter, 1972–79; Ode to a Child: Poetry Anthology, 1980; Matilda Literary & Arts Magazine, 1980–; The Wedding, 1980; Poetry Naked Wasp, 1981; Fly Dirt, 1981; Indepenence Voice, 1978; Books, Love Verse & Other Poems, 1974; Change, 1980; Anvil of Literature, 1982; etc; TV and radio appearances. *Contributor to:* numerous professional journals, magazines and newspapers including The Brunswick Senteniel; The Age; The New York Times of Australia; Australian Book Review; Melbourne Times; Brave New World; Access; Learning Exchange. *Honours include:* Recipient, numerous honours and awards, Honorary Poet Laureate, City of Brunswick, 1983; 1 of Top 50 Poets invited to 1st Poets' Festival in Australia, 1976; various commissions. *Address:* 7 Mountfield Street, Brunswick, Victoria 3056, Australia.

ZERMAN, Melvyn Bernard, b. 10 July 1930, New York City, USA. Sales Manager. m. Mariam Baron, 14 Sep. 1952 (deceased 9 Jan. 1985), 2 sons, 1 daughter. *Education:* BA, University of Michigan; MA, Columbia University. *Publications:* Call the Final Witness, 1977; Beyond a Reasonable Doubt, 1981; Taking on the Press, 1986. *Honour:* Freedom Foundation Award for Beyond a Reasonable Doubt, 1981. *Membership:* Authors Guild.

Address: 110-37 68th Drive, Forest Hills, NY 11375, USA.

ZETTERSTROM, Carl Bertil Erik, b. 23 June 1950, Stockholm, Sweden. Penman; Playwright. 1 daughter. *Publications:* Why Do You Not Repair Your Roof, Klosterhage?, 1968; Nilsson, The Bench and the Pavilion, 1975; Carl Z in Arbetaren, 1982. *Contributor to:* Expressen; Aftonbladet; Columnist, Dagens Nyheter, Arbetaren, 1972–. *Memberships:* Swedish Writers Union; Swedish Union of Playwrights; Pen. *Address:* Dagens Nyheter, 105 15 Stockholm, Sweden.

ZIEGLER, Avis Bosshart, b. 13 Mar. 1931, New York City, USA. Management and Development Consultant; Writer. m. (1) Richard Allan Bosshart (dec. 1965), 1 son, 1 daughter, (2) John G Ziegler, 1969 (div. 1980), 1 son, 1 daughter. *Education:* Purdue University, 1947–48; Writer's Programme, State University Iowa, 1949–50; B Education with honours, National College, Evanston, Illinois, 1959–63; Postgraduate, Northwestern University, 1964–65. *Literary Appointments:* Copywriter, Fletcher Richards Advertisement Agency, New York City, 1948–49; Author, Staff Editor, Scientific Associates, Chicago, 1965–68; Consultant Management and Development, Writer, Professional Systems Design, Fort Lauderdale, 1968–. *Publications include:* Doctor's Administrative Program, 8 book series, 1977–82; Curriculum materials; Air Pressure, editor, 1965. *Memberships include:* American Association for the Advancement of Science; Association Educational Communications and Technology; National League American PEN Women. *Address:* 2955 Northeast 60th Street, Fort Lauderdale, FL 33308, USA.

ZILLIACUS, Clas Robert, b. 26 May 1943, Mariehamn, Finland. University Teacher; Critic; Translator. m. Mona Margareta Vogt, 3 Nov. 1963, Vasda, Finland, 1 daughter. *Education:* PhD, Abo Akademi, Finland, 1976. *Publications:* Beckett and Broadcasting, 1976; Gruppeteater i Norden (Co-author), 1981; Tidningshuvud och tidningshjarta, 1981; Hamlet, 1983; Oponionens tryck (with H Knif), 1985. *Contributions to:* Comparative Drama; Comparative Literature; Entre; Finsk Tidskrift; Maske und Kothurn; Modern Drama; Moderna sprak; Nya Argus, etc. *Honour:* State Prize for Hamlet, Translation, 1984. *Memberships:* Svenska litteratursallskapet i Finland: Allmanna prisnamnden (awards committee), 1970–72, litteraturvetenskapliga namnden (literary studies committee), 1983–; Statens biblioteksersattningsnamnd (Ministry of Education library refund board), 1982–; Member, Finlands svenska forfattareforening; Suomalaisen kirjallisuuden seura. *Address:* Litteraturvetenskapliga institutionen, Abo Akademi, 20500 Abo, Finland.

ZIMMERMAN, David, b. 10 Aug. 1934. Chicago, Illinois, USA. Writer. m. Veva Hampton, 12 Oct. 1967, New York City, 2 sons. *Education:* AB cum laude, Brandeis University; Graduate work, University of Paris, France. *Literary Appointments:* Instructor (part-time) City College of New York Department of English, 1972–73; Adjunct Professor, Columbia University Graduate School of Journalism, 1981–. *Pubications:* Rh, The Intimate History of a Disease & its Conquest, 1973; To Save a Bird in Peril, 1975; The essential Guide to Nonprescription Drugs, 1983; Doctors Anti-Breast Cancer Diet, co-author, 1984. *Contributons to:* Monthly medical column, Ladies Home Journal, 1967–80; Feature articles, New York Times Magazine, Smithsonian, Science 83, Audubon, Natural History, Mosaic, National Wildlife, Womans Day, Glamour, Good Housekeeping, Consumer reports, etc. *Honours:* Christopher Award, nonfiction, 1975; Award for Excellence, American Medical Writers Association, 1973; Research Grants, World Wildlife Fund, 1973; Fund for Investigative Journalism, 1979; Council for the Advancement of Science Writers, 1980. *Memberships:* President 1973–74, American Society of Journalists & Authors; Treasurer 1982, National Association of Science Writers. *Literary Agent:* Connie Clausen.

Address: c/o Connie Clausen, 250 East 87th Street, New York, NY 10128, USA.

ZIMROTH, Evan, b. 24 Feb. 1943, Philadelphia, Pennsylvania, USA. Poet; Professor of English. m. Henry Wollman, 29 Oct. 1977, 2 daughters. *Education:* BA, Barnard College, USA, 1965; PhD, Columbia University, 1972. *Literary Appointments:* Associate Professor of English, Queens College, City University of New York, since 1972; Maitre-Assistant, Université de Paris VIII, 1975–76. *Publications:* Giselle Considers Her Future. *Contributor to:* Poetry; The Sewanee Review; The Hudson Review; The Little Magazine; Pequod; Women's Studies; Woodstock Poetry Review; Beloit Poetry Journal; Poésie Vincennes, (Paris); Dremples, (Amsterdam); numerous anthologies. *Literary Awards:* CUNY Translation Grant: The Poetry of Else Lasker-Schüler. *Memberships:* Poets and Writers; American Poetry Society. *Address:* Department of English, Queens College CUNY, Flushing, NY 11367, USA.

ZINKIN, Nathalie Taya, b. 23 Sep. 1918, Zurich. Journalist/Author. m. Maurice Zinkin, 1 May 1945, London, 1 son. *Education:* BSc, Research Fellowship in Biochemistry. *Literary Appointments:* Chief Correspondent, Economist and Manchester Guardian for India, 1950–60; Chief Correspondent in India for Le Monde, 1955–60. *Publications:* India Changes 1958; Rishi 1960; Rishi Returns 1961; Castle Today 1962; Life of Ghandi 1965, US 1966, paperback 1983; Reporting India 1962; India 1964; (in the world series); India 1965 (in the new nations and peoples series); Britain and India (with Maurice Zinkin) 1964; Challenges in India 1966; India and Her Neighbours 1967; The Faithful Parrot 1967; Tales Told Round the World 1968; The Heartland of Asia 1971; Odious Child (autobiography) 1971; Weeds Grow Fast (autobiography) 1973; Write Right 1980. *Contributions to:* Fodor's Guidebook on India and Penguin's Handbook on Asia. *Contributions to:* Sunday Telegraph; The Times; Sunday Times. *Literary Agent:* David Rodrigues. *Address:* 6, Kensington Court Gardens, Kensington Court Place, London W8 5QE, England.

ZINNES, Harriet, b. Massachusetts, USA. Professor of English; Poet; Fiction Writer. m. Irving I Zinnes, (dec), 24 Sep. 1943, New York, 1 son, 1 daughter. *Education:* BA, Hunter College, 1939; MA, Brooklyn College, 1944; PhD, New York University, 1953. *Literary Appointments:* Member, National Book Critics Circle; Professor of English, Queens College, City University of New York, 1962–; Art Critic, Pictures on Exhibit, 1971–82; Visiting Professor, American Literature, University of Geneva, Switzerland, 1969; Book critic, Weekly Tribune, Switzerland, 1969–70; Associate Editor, Harpers Bazaar, 1944–46. *Publications:* An Eye for an I, poems, 1966; I Wanted to See Something Flying, poems, 1976; Entropisms, prose poems, 1978; Ezra Pound & the Visual Arts, Editor, 1980; Book of Ten, poems, 1981. *Contributions to:* New York Times Sunday Book Review; The Nation; New Leader; Chelsea; Parnassus; Southern Review; Carleton Miscellany; Centennial Review; Poetry; etc. *Honours:* Resident Fellowships, MacDowell Colony, 1972–77, Yaddo, 1978–81, Virginia Centre for Creative Arts, 1975–84. ACLS Grant, 1978; CUNY Creative Writing Summer Fellowships, 1979, 1981. *Memberships:* Translation Committee, PEN American Centre; Academy of American Poets; Poetry Society of America; National Book Critics Circle. *Address:* Department of English, Queens College of the CUNY, Flushing, NY 11367, USA.

ZIPP, Paula Mitchell, b. 19 Jan. 1952, Barbourville, Kentucky, USA. Manager, Documentation; Publications Engineer; Romance Writer; Technical Writer. m. Alan S Zipp, 19 Aug. 1971, Barbourville, Kentucky, 1 son. *Education:* BA, English, University of Maryland, 1973; Postgraduate work in Systems Management, University of Southern California, 1984; MGA, University of Maryland, 1986. *Literary Appointments:* Historical Romance Book Editor Romantic Times, 1985–; Manager, Documentation, Martin Marietto Data Systems, 1985–; Executive Editor HaKol (The Voice),

1974–78; Medical Editor, The Doctor's Voice and The Waistline, 1977–78; Vice-Chairman, 1982, Recorder, 1983, Chairman, 1984 of Editorial Board for The Vitro Technical Journal. *Contributor to:* Romantic Times; The Vitro Technical Journal; The Doctor's Voice; Fiction Writer's Monthly; The Waistline; HaKol. *Honours:* Various awards of International Society for Technical Communication. *Memberships:* Senior Member, Society for Technical Communication; Society for Scholarly Publishing; American Medical Writers Association: Romance Writers of America; Washinton Romance Writers. *Address:* 2425 White Horse Lane, Silver Spring, MD 20906, USA.

ZIVADIN, Steven, b. 20 Nov. 1908. Retired University Lecturer; Writer; Painter. *Education:* Lycee de Nice, Real-Gymn, Zagreb and Belgrade, Yugoslavia; Graduate, Law and Economics, University of Paris, France; Doctor of Civil Law, University of Belgrade. *Appointments Include:* Assistant Professor, Faculty of Subotica, University of Belgrade. *Publications:* The Anag-Rhyme, innovation, 1974; Metre, Rhyme and Freedom, 1975–76; Techniques in Surrealist Poetry, 1976–77; A Study and Anthology of the Ana-Rhyme, 1978; Biology of Nature. 1978; The Species and Biorbis, 1978. *Contributions to:* L'Impossible, Bilingual; Nadrealisam DIO; Le Surrealisme ASDLR (Letter to Salvador Dali; Pennine Platform; True Thomas; Orbis; Pall Mall Quarterly; Phoenix Special Supplement, reprints and translations in various books and periodicals. Main innovations include: The Plural Automatic text; Poetry of the Imaginery (Contents and others); the Ana-Rhyme (non-chiming rhyme), in minor tonality; The Schoenberg verse and the Poem with Cadenza. *Memberships:* Fellow, International Poetry Society; Museum for Modern Art, Oxford, England; Oxford Union Society; Yugoslavian French Circle (Founder and Honorary Secretary). *Address:* Arthur Garrard House, 288 Iffley Road, Oxford OX4 4AE, England.

ZOBEL, Louise Purwin, b. 10 Jan. 1922, Laredo TX, USA. Writer; Lecturer; Teacher. m. Dr Jerome Fremont Zobel, 14 Nov. 1943, San Francisco CA, 1 son, 3 daughters. *Education:* BA, Journalism, 1943, MA, Communication, 1976, Stanford University. *Literary Appointments:* Journalist, United Press Bureau, San Francisco, 1943; Editor, Illustrated Service and News Broadcasts, rewrite, Freelance Magazine writer, over 250 publications, 1942–45, 1959–; Teacher of Writing, Foothill Community College, 1969–, Lecturer on Writing, Travel and Historical Subjects, 1959–; Editorial Assistant, Bulletin of Association of College Unions, International 1972–73; Cruise Enrichment Lecturer and Writing Teacher, Royal Viking Lines, 1974; Teacher of Writing, De Anza Community College, 1975–; Instructor in Journalism, San Jose State University, 1976–, University of California, Santa Cruz, University of California, Santa Barbara. *Publications:* The Travel Writer's Handbook, 1980; Let's Have Fun in Japan, 1983. *Contributor to:* Over 150 magazines and journals including; House Beautiful; Writer; Writer's Digest; Coronet; Parents' Magazine; American Home; Lady's Circle; Going Places; Los Angeles Times; Off Duty; Weight Watcher's Magazine; Northwest Today; New England Review; etc. *Honours:* Phi Beta Kappa, Sigma Delta Chi Award for Scholarship, 1943; Prize, Writers' Digest National Article Contest, 1967; First Prize, American Association of University Women National Juvenile Fiction Contest, 1969; Prize, Armed Forces' Writers League National Essay Contest, 1972; Prize, Writers' Digest National Article Contest, 1975; Prize, National Writers' Club Contest, 1976. *Memberships:* California Writers' Club; National League of American Pen Women; American Association of University Women; Stanford Alumni; Theta Sigma Phi; National Writers' Club; American Society of Journalists and Authors; Travel Journalists' Guild; Authors' Guild; Auxiliary, Santa Clara County Medical Society. *Address:* 877 Northampton Drive, Palo Alto, CA 94303, USA.

ZOHN, Harry, b. 21 Nov. 1923, Vienna, Austria. University Professor. *Education:* BA, Suffolk University,

1946; MEd, Clark University, 1947; MA, 1949, PhD, 1952, Harvard University; Honorary LittD, Suffolk University, 1976. *Publications:* The World is a Comedy: A Kurt Tucholsky Anthology, 1957; Wiener Juden in der deutschen Literatur, 1964; Men of Dialogue: Martin Buber and Albrecht Goes, 1969; Karl Kraus, 1971; Der farbenvolle Untergang, 1971; Half-Truths and One-and-a-Half Truths: Aphorisms of Karl Kraus, 1976; In These Great Times: A Karl Kraus Reader, 1976; Juedisches Erbe in der oesterreichischen Literatur, 1985. Translations: works by Theodor Herzl; Walter Benjamin; Walter Toman; Marianne Weber; Karl Kraus; Kurt Tucholsky; Jacob Burckhardt and others. *Contributions to:* Several international literary reviews. *Honours:* Officer Cross, Order of Merit, Federal Republic of Germany, 1960; Cross of Honor for Science and Art, Austrian Republic, 1984. *Address:* Brandeis University, Waltham, MA 02154, USA.

ZOLA, Irving Kenneth, b. 24 Jan. 1935, Boston, Massachusetts, USA. Sociology Educator. m. Judy Norsigian, 23 Oct. 1981, Watertown, 1 daughter, 1 son and 1 daughter from previous marriage. *Education:* BA, Harvard College, 1956; PhD, Social Relations, Harvard University, 1962. *Publications:* Disabling Professions, with Ivan Illich and others, 1977, Dutch and Italian versions, 1978, Spanish, 1981; Missing Pieces, 1982, Dutch version forthcoming; Ordinary Lives, 1982; Independent Living for Physically Disabled People, with Nancy Crewe, 1983; Socio-Medical Inquiries, 1983. *Contributions to:* Numerous professional journals and magazines including: Journal of Gerontology; Social Problems; Journal of Medical Education; Medical Care; Medicine; American Sociology Review; Social Science and Medicine; Together, columnist, 1980–; Medecene et Societe Less Annees; Disability Studies Quarterly. Contributions to numerous books including: A New Way of Life for the Handicapped, 1983; Psychological and Social Impact of Physical Disability, 1984, Numerous reviews and conference participant. *Honours:* Mary E Switzer Scholar, 1983; Culture and Symptoms, designated a Citation Classic in Current Contents, 1983. *Address:* Department of Sociology, Brandeis University, Waltham, MA 02254, USA.

ZOLKIEWSKI, Stefan, b. 9 Dec. 1911, Warsaw, Poland. University Professor. *Education:* PhD, Poland. *Publications include:* Spor o Mickiewicza, 1952; Kultura i polityka, 1958; Perspektywy literatury XXu, 1960; O kulturze Polski Ludowej, 1964; Kultura a semiotika, 1969; Kultura literacka 1918–1932, 1974; Kultura, sociologia semiotyka literacka, 1979; La cultura letteraria, Semiotica e letteraturlogia, 1982. *Contributions to:* Kuznica; Studia sociologiczhe; Pamietnik literacki; Polityka; Studia semiotycne; Semiotica; Informations sur les sciences sociales, UNESCO and others. *Honours:* State Prizes, 1953, 64. *Memberships:* Polish Academy of Science; Polish Semiotics Society; Society of Polish Men of Letters; PEN. *Address:* Aleja Roz 6-14, Warsaw 00556, Poland.

ZOOK, Amy Jo, b. 25 Apr. 1937, Glen Ellyn, Illinois, USA. College Instructor. m. Samuel J Zook Junior, 15 July 1972, 2 sons, 1 daughter (all by previous marriage). *Education:* BA, Wittenberg University, Springfield, Ohio, 1969; MA, West Virginia University, 1981. Presently studying for PhD at West Virginia University. *Literary Appointments:* Writer (formerly Poet) in the Schools for Ohio Council, 1977–. *Publications:* Echoes of England (poetry), 1975; A Sonnet Sampler, 1979, reprinted 1981; A New Page (poetry), 1979, reprinted and revised 1984; Two chapters in The Study and Writing of Poetry, Editor, W Hackleman, 1983. *Contributions:* Cornfield Review; The Lyric; Gryphon; Kentucky Poetry Review; Descant; Mississippi Valley Review; Bluegrass Literare Review; Pteranodon; Pudding; Windless Orchard; Great Lakes Review; Encore; Pirot; The Villager; Christian Science Monitor; Voices International; The Liguorian. *Honours:* in 1984: 1st and 3rd Prizes, Ohio Poetry Day; 2nd Prize, Springdale Poets; Leitch Prize, The Lyric; 3rd Prize, Indiana; 3rd Prize, Georgia; 1st Prize, VWG Contest; 3rd Prize, Tennessee; 1st Prize, Tennessee; 1st Prize, West

Virginia; 1st and 2nd Prizes, Morgantown; 3rd Prize, Kentucky; 2nd and 3rd Prizes, Pascagoula; 2nd Prize, South Dakota, also 16 Honorable mentions. *Memberships:* National Federation of State Poetry Societies (contest chairman); Verse Writers Guild of Ohio (twice President); National League of American Pen Women; Central Ohio Branch); Ohio Das Assocation (Contest Chairman); World Poetry Society. *Address:* 3520 State Route 56, Mechanicsburg, OH 43044, USA.

ZUCKERMAN, Marilyn, b. 26 Mar. 1925, New York City, New York, USA. Writer; Teacher. divorced, 2 sons, 1 daughter. *Education:* BA, Sarah Lawrence College; MA, Goddard College. *Literary Appointments:* Poet in Residence, New Hampshire Council on the Arts, 1975–76, Massachusetts Foundation for Arts and Humanities, 1976–79. *Publications:* Personal Effects, with other poets, 1976; Monday Morning Movie, 1981. *Contributions to:* New York Quarterly; Sunbury; Little Magazine; Hanging Loose; The Real Paper; Greenhouse; Connections, and others. *Honours:* Panelist, Massachussetts Arts and Humanities Foundation, 1975; Officer of the Board, Cummington Commun. of the Arts, 1978–79; Syndicated Fiction Award, PEN, 1985. *Address:* 153 Medford Street, Arlington, MA 02174, USA.

ZUCKERMAN, Matthew Ian Stanley, b. 7 Nov. 1956, Berlin, Federal Republic of Germany. Teacher; Writer; Editor. m. Mieko Kitazume, 28 Apr. 1984, Tokyo, Japan, 1 daughter. *Publications:* Okinawa By Road, 1985; Book-Rate, 1985. *Contributions to:* Various publications. *Membership:* Tokyo English Literature Society. *Address:* Toshima-ku, Ikebukuro Honcho 3 31 14, Ikebukuro No 2 Hill Heim 207, Tokyo 170, Japan.

ZUEHLSDORFF, Volkmar J A F M, b. 9 Dec. 1912, Finow, Germany. Diplomat and Author. *Education:* Law and Political Science, University of Berlin, Germany and University of Innsbruck, Austria; Dr iur.utr, University of Innsbruck, 1936. Postgraduate studies Vienna and London, 1936–37. *Publications:* Deutschlands Schicksal, 1957; Verteidigung des Westens, (with Prince Hubertus zu Loewenstein), 1960; NATO: The Defense of the West, 1963, 1975; Sunthon Phu's Endlose Trauer, 1983; Wenn vom Tau der Reis erwacht, 1984. Contributor, Atem des Mittelmeers, 1961; Contributor, Thailand Handbook, 1980; Contributor to: Das Papsttum, 1982; Contributor to, Grosse Gestalten des Glaubens, 1983; Die Grossen des Glaubens, 1985. *Contributor to:* Various newspapers etc. German Federal Republic, USA, Canada and Switzerland. Translated: Klaus Wenk, Phali Teachers; The Young, from German and Thai to English, 1980. *Memberships include:* Honorary Freier Deutscher Autorenverband (Bd MBr, 1979); Deutscher Autorenrat; Deutscher Journalistenverband; Speaker, Literary Section, Deutscher, Kulturvat, 1985; Siam Society. *Address:* Lahn Strasse 50, D–5300, Bonn 2, Federal Republic of Germany.

ZUSPAN, Frederick Paul, b. 20 Jan. 1922, Ohio, USA. Professor, Doctor. m. Mary Jane Cox, 23 Nov. 1943, Ohio, 1 son, 2 daughters. *Education:* BA, 1947, MD, 1951 , Ohio State University, Columbus, Ohio, USA; Internship, 1951–52, Department of Obstetrics and Gynaecology, 1952–54, Ohio State University, Case Reserve, University of the North-West, Cleveland, Ohio, 1954–56; Oglebay Fellow of Reproductive Biology, Western Reserve, 1958–60; Professor & Chairman, Department of Obstetrics & Gynaegology, Medical College, Augusta, Georgia, 1960–66; J B Delee Professor & Chairman, Department of Obstetrics and Gynaecology, University of Chicago, 1966–75; Professor & Chairman, Department of Obstetrics and Gynaecology, Ohio State University, 1974–; R Meiling Professor, 1984. *Literary Appointments:* Founding Editor, Journal of Reproductive Medicine, 1967; Editor, American Journal of Obstetrics & Gynaecology, 1969–; Editor, Contemporary Obstetrics & Gynaecology, Monograph Series, 1970–83; Editor, Journal of Clinical & Experimental Hypertension in Pregnancy, 1982; Editor, Reproductive Medicine Series, 1982–. *Major Publications:* Handbook of Obstetrics (with Quilligan), 1981; Operative Obstetrics (with Quilligan), 1982, Drug Therapy in Obstetrics & Gynaecology (with Rayburn), 1982; Clinical Procedures in Obstetrics & Gynaecology, 1983–84; on editorial Boards of 4 other journals. *Contributor to:* Numerous professional Journals with more than 200 original scientific articles. *Honours:* South Atlantic Foundation Research Prize, 1960; Armine Award, Lund, Sweden, 1978. *Address:* Department of Obstetrics & Gynaecology, Ohio State University, Columbus, OH 43210, USA.

APPENDIX 1

PSEUDONYMS OF AUTHORS AND WRITERS

The following constitutes a list of pen names of all those included in the biographical section with cross-reference to the name under which the entry appears.

Aad—Deleuran, Aage
Anna Aaron—Selden, Neil Roy
Abercrombie, V. T.—Abercrombie, Virginia Townsend
Ada—Jafarey, Aziz Jahan
Adams, Jolene—Harper, Olivia
Adams, Leonie—Troy, Leonie Fuller Adams
Adams, Lowell—Joseph, James
Adams, Loyce—Adams, Lillian Loyce Adams
Adrian, Frances—Polland, Madeleine Angela
Ads—Adsofte, Flemming Krone Haugsted
Adytum, James—Curl, James Stevens
Agrawal, Suren—S. P. Agrawal
Ahern, Tom—Ahern, Thomas Francis
Ahnstrom D. N.—Ahnstrom, Doris Newell
Airlie, Catherine—MacLeod, Jean Sutherland
Ajibade, Yemi—Ajibade, Adeyemi Olanrewaju
Aka, Jackie Lewis—Lewis, Jacqueline Rose (Guccione)
Akhtar, Hoshiarpuri—Akhtar, Hoshiarpuri
Alanagh, Patricia—Rosenfield, Patricia Byrne
Albatross, Nowicka—Auderska, Halina
Alden, James—Burton James Myers
Aldobrandini, Carlo—Wall, Bengt Verner
Aldyne, Nathan—McDowell, Michael McEachern
Alexander, Justin—Smith, Rev. Robert Dickie
Alexander, Taylor—Burke, A. E. Richard
Alexeyeva, Lydia—Ivannikoff, Lydia
Alexie, Angela—Talias, Angela
Aliki—Brandenburg, Aliki
Allen, Alastair—Mason, Stanley
Allen, Peter—Underwood, Peter
Allyson, June—Hornbaker, Alice J.
Alma, Rio—Almario, Virgilio S.
Ames, Leslie—Rigoni, Orlando Joseph
Anderson, Ella—MacLeod, Ellen Jane
Anderson, Maggie—Anderson, Margaret Anna
Anderson, Torsten—Sohre, Helmut
Anderson, Walt—Anderson, Walter Truett
Andrews, Sylvester—Spingarn, Lawrence Perreira
Andy—Anderson, Alfred George
Angus, Tom—Powell, Geoffrey Stewart
Appel-Dichler—Appel, Maria Magdalena Helene Eugenia
Arana, Nelly Cattarossi—Cattarossi Arana, Nelinda Maria
Archer, S.—Walker, Stella Archer

Arno, Marcel—Criton (Plato) Tomazos
Arnold, Douglas—Arnold, Harry John Philip
Arnold, Margot—Cook, Petronelle Marguerite Mary
Arnold, Marie-Madeleine—Arnold-Gulikers, Marie Madelein
Arnott, Anne—Arnott, Margaret Anne
Ashby, Nora—Africano, Lillian
Ashlandonian—Chamberlain, Kent Clair
Ashleigh ('Ash')—Scharf, Lauren Ileene Barnett
Ansell, Thomas—Ansell, Sydney Thomas
Astley, Elizabeth—Caughey, John
Astolat, John—Haigh, Jack

Bailey, Paul—Bailey, Peter Harry
Baldwin, Jean—Jolliffe, Lee Baldwin
Baldwin, Marjorie—Baldwin, Bertha Marjorie
Baloti—Lawrence, D. Baloti
Bannister, Sally—Pratt, James Norwood
Banovitch, Michael—Banner, Bob
Barnes, R. G.—Barnes, Richard Gordon
Barr, Densil—Buttrey, Douglas Norton
Barr, Pat—Barr, Patricia Miriam
Barth, Jason—Bartholomew, Paul Jason
Bassermann, Lujo—Schreiber, Hermann Otto Ludwig
Bauer-Patitz, Dolores—Patitz, Dolores R.
Bayliss, Timothy—Baybars, Taner
Beaumont, Kathleen—MacKenzie, Jean Kathleen
Becker, Klaus—Koch, Kurt E.
Beckford, Louisa—Howard, Theresa Lizbeth
Beckworth, Lillian—Beckwith-Comber, Lillian
Bedoya, Fausto—Jirgens, Karl Edward
Behrens-Giegl, Erna—Behrens, Erna (Sylvia J)
Belsen, Patricia—Thevoz, Jacqueline
Bemister—Barrett, Harry Bemister
Benedetti, Quint—Benedetti, Quentin J.
Benn, Matthew—Siegal, Benjamin
Beresford—Hamburger, Ann Ellen
Berg, Rilla—France, Thelma Edith Minnie
Berge, H. C. Ten—Berge, Hans Cornelis Ten
Berkhot, Aster—Van Den Burgh, Lodewyk Paulina
Berlez, R. M.—Adams, Wilfried, M. G.
Bern, Bobb—Balthazar, Robert, Louis Marie
Bernard, Robert—Martin, Robert Bernard
Bernardo—Bernard Alan Aaron
Bernlef, Henk—Marsman, Hendrik Jan
Bev—Byers-Pevitts, Beverley

Bi, El—Biberger, Erich Ludwig
Bickerich, Gerhard—Goebel-Schilling,
    Gerhard
Billzinko, Bill—McConnell, William Tate
Bis—Schenkel, Barbara Carolina
Bishop, Morchard—Stoner, Oliver
Bisignani, J. D.—Bisignani, Joseph, Daniel
Black, Gavin—Wynd, Oswald
Black, Kitty—Black, Dorothy
Black, Matte—Bedard, Patrick Joseph
Blacklin, Malcolm—Chambers, Aidan
Blade, Alexander—Swain, Dwight Vreeland
Blair, Mark—Silva, David B.
Blake, Jennifer—Maxwell, Patricia Anne
Blayn, Robert—Morzfeld, Erwin Wilhelm
Blair, Harriet—Greene, Freda Hannah
Blight, Rose—Greer, Germaine
Blum, Rick—Blum, Richard A.
Blyth, John—Hibbs, John Alfred Blyth
Bociany, Kosy I.—Marzecki, Longin Walter
Boesche-Zacharow, Tilly—Boesche,
    Mathilde
Bogart, Steve—Feely, Terence John
Bolton, Deric—Bolton, Frederic James
Bor, Vane—Zivadin, Steven
Borel, Helene—Hegeler, Sten
Borg,- Elmar—Aerts, Huil Maria
Bortin, V. G.—Bortin, Virginia
Boschmans, Jan—de Bosscher, Lucien
    Stanislas
Bough, Lee—Huser, Laverne (Verne) C.
Bower, Alison—Beckett, Gillian
Brabazon, James—Seth-Smith, Leslie James
Bracha—Stadtler, Bea
Bradley, James—Ball, John Bradley
Brainbeau, J. C.—Lemon, George Edward
Bratt, Ronald—Brattman, Steven Ronald
Bregenz—Bergel, Hans
Brendall, Edith—Bertin, Eddy C.
Brett, Val—Barrett, Charles Peter
Brisco, Patty—Matthews, Patricia Anne
Brisson, Ferdinand—Landsburgh, Werner
Britt, George—Sealey, Leonard George
    William
Britton, Dorothy—Bouchier, Lady Isabella
    D. G.
Brock, Gavin—Lindsay, John Maurice
Brodie—Easton, Thomas James
Brodie, Wilfred—Wellesley-Cole, Robert
    Benjamin Ageh
Brown, Neva—Arnot, Michelle
Brown, Olivia—Caldecott, Moyra
Brown, Peter L.—Lancaster-Brown, Peter
Bruller, Jean—Vercors, Jean
Bryer, Robin—Bryer, Alastair Robin
    Mornington
Buckley, Fiona—Anand, Valerie May
    Florence
Burden, Jack—Lockhart, Kim Lawrence
Burfield, Eva—Ebbett, Frances Eva
Burton, Thomas—Longstreet, Stephen
Butler, Nathan—Sohl, Jerry
Butt, Anna Adams Theresa—Adams, Anna
    Theresa
Buttaci, Sal St John—Buttaci, Salvatore M.

Byola, Uga da—Bolay, Karl H.

Cab—Brunila, Kai Daniel
Cade, Alexander—Methold, Kenneth
Cailliau, Phil—Cailliau, Philippe (Jules Erna)
Caine—Vercammen, Kenneth Albert
Cairo, Jon—Romano, Deane Louis
Cairns, Patrick—Mulgrue, George Edward
Calder, Lyn—Calmenson, Stephanie Lyn
Calvin, Henry—Hanley, Clifford
Campbell, Jim—Campbell, James Howard
Campbell, Judith—Pares, Marion Stapylton
Cannon, Ravenna—Mayhar, Ardath
    (Frances)
Carette, Louis—Marceau, Felicien
Carrigan, Sean—Bennett, John (Frederic)
Carfax, Catherine—Fairburn, Eleanor M.
Cariolanus—McMillan, James
Carroll, Mary—Bagley, Mary Carol
Case, L. L.—Lewin, Leonard C.
Cecht, Mac—O'Ceirin, Cyril
C'Halan, Reun ar—Garland, Rene
Chagnan—Assiniwi, Bernard
Chalmers, Allen—Upward, Edward Falaise
Chance, Sara—Clary, Sydney Ann
Chance, Stephen—Turner, Philip William
Chandler, Laurel—Holder, Nancy L.
Chapelle, Stavaux de la—Stavaux, Michel
Chaplan, San—Boone, Gene
Chard, Judy—Chard, Dorothy Doreen
Cherrill, Jack—Paxton, John
Chibeau, Edmond—Chibeau, Edmond Victor
    Peter
Chrisholm, Boris—Mackillop, James John
Christopher, Matt—Christopher, Matthew F.
Chub, Dmytro—Nytczenko, Emytro
Church, Peter—Nuttall, Jeff
Church, Suzanne—Bates, Susannah Vacella
    (Church)
Cinderella—Erichsen, Eli Store
Ciro, Rona—Cirone, Bettina
Clare, Ellen—Sinclair, Olga Ellen
Clare, Helen—Blair, Pauline Hunter
Clark, Clark C—Baker, Samm Sinclair
Clarkson, Helen—McCloy Dresser, Helen
    Worrell Clarkson
Cleary, Polly Chase—Cleary, Marion E.
Clifton, Robin Michelle—Clifton, Merritt
    Robin
Cline, Beverly Fink—Cline, Beverly Marilyn
Clinton, D.—Clinton, Lloyd DeWitt
Cody, Kate—Coffman, Kimberly Ann
Cody, James P.—Rohrbach, Peter Thomas
Cohan, Tony—Cohan, Anthony Robert
Cole, W.—Kulski, Wladyslaw Wszebor
Colley, Kenneth—Dyba, Kenneth Walter
Collier, Margaret—Taylor, Margaret Stewart
Collins, Michael—Lynds, Dennis
Colt, Clem—Nye, Nelson
Commonwealth, Mr.—Smith, Arnold
    Cantwell
Conde, Bruce—Conde, Abdurrahman Bruce
    Alfronso, Prince de Bourdon de
Conner, Rearden—Conner, Patrick Rearden
Connor, Tony—Connor, John Anthony

Conradi—Conradi-Bleibtreu, Ellen
Contay—Taylor, Walter Harold
Conway, James—Longmate, Norman
    Richard
Cook, Lyn—Waddell, Evelyn Margaret
Cooper, William—Hoff, Harry Summerfield
Copeland, Ann—Furtwangler, Virginia W.
Cormac, James—Pettifer, James Milward
Cory, Ray—Marshall, Melvin
Cosgrove, Rachel—Payes, Rachel Cosgrove
Cosolaro, Barbara—Shields, Barbara
Cotes, Peter—Boulting, Sydney
Court, Wesli—Turco, Lewis (Putnam)
Coutinho, Edilberto—Coutinho, Jose
    Edilberto
Cox-Johnson-, Ann Loreille—Sanders, Ann
    Loreille
Craig, Jasmine—Cresswell, Jasmine
    Rosemary
Cricket, for Haiku—Faiers, Christopher
    Fordham
Cripps, Joy Beaudette—Cripps, Joyce
Croman, Dorothy Young—Rosenberg,
    Dorothy Louise
Cunning, Alfred—Holliday, D.
Curlah, Curt—Hall, Gerald L.
Curling, Audrey—Clark, Marie Catherine
    Audrey
Currie, Bob—Currie, Robert Frank
Curtis, George—Freemantle, Michael Harold
Curtis, Will—Nunn, William Curtis
Cysi, Chuck—Gysi, Charles L. III.

Danbury, Richard S. III.—Olmsted, Robert
    Walsh
Daniela—Gioseffi, Dorothy
Daubier, Louis—Dupont, Louis Jules Joseph
Daunt Neto, Ricardo—Daunt Neto, Ricardo
    Gumbleton
D'Avrigny, France—La Tousche D'Avrigny,
    de (Baronne) Francoise Anne
Davis, Burke—Davis (Walter) Burke
Davies, Christie—Davies, John Christopher
    Hughes
Davis, J. Madison—Davis, James Madison,
    Jr.
Davys, Sarah—Manning, Rosemary Joy
Deacon, Richard—McCormick, (George)
    Donald (King)
Dee, Sherry—Flournoy, Sheryl Diane Hines
Deeps, Frederick—Speed, Frederick Maurice
deKoven, D. M.—deKoven, Don
Demske, Dick—Demske, Richard John
Dennett, Joann Temple—Dennett, Joann
    Taylor Temple
Deriex—Piguet, Suzanne
Derry—Jeffares, Alexander Norman
Devin, Marius—Landau, Edwin Maria
Devonshire, Kercheval—Alexander, Charles
    Robert
De Vrieze, Gerda—de Vrieze, Gerda Spaens
Dezsery, Andras—Dezsery, Endre Istvan
Diamond, Jack—Silver, Abraham Jack
Dick—Singleton, Richard Fred
Dick—Weaver, Richard L. II

Dierickx, Jos—Vinks, Adrian Jos.
Dillon, Patrick—Lewis, Robert William
Digby (UK)—Adams, Howard Digby
Dixon, Paige—Corcoran, Barbara
Dobkin, Kaye—Hamel Dobkin, Kathleen L.
Doc—Temple (Dr.) Wayne C(alhoun)
Dolman, Margaret—Haenen, Paul
Dominic, Mary—Parker, Marian Dominica
    Hope (Sister Mary Dominic of the
    Cross)
Don—Groves, Dr. Donald G.
Don—O'Reilly, Donald Edmund
Don—Thornton, Donald Ray
Donovan, Nellie—Hair, Nellie Eileen
    Donovan
Donovan, Rhoda—Yerburgh, Rhoda Carol
    Goldberg
Dor-Doroslovac, Milutin.-
    Dorizzi, Irma—Christen-Dorizzi, Irma
Douglas, Russ—Day, Richard Somers
Dowski, Lee Van—Lewandowski, Herbert
Doyle, Mike—Doyle (Charles) Desmond
Drake, Kimbal—Gallagher, Rachel Mary
Drake, W. Raymond—Drake, Walter
    Raymond
Drojine, N. A.—Christiaens, Andre
Droste, Lotte—Brugmann-Eberhardt, Lotte
Dubois, Henri—MacLean, Charles Peter
    Bruce
Dubois, Rochelle Holt—Holt, Rochelle Lynn
Dunsing, Dee—Mowery, Dorothy May

Ebner, Jeannie—Ebner-Allinger, Jeannie
Eddy, R. U.—Allman, Edwin Christian
Eden, Laura—Harrison, Claire Ellen
Edler von Dewidrow, Karl—Mundstock, Karl
Edmonds, Ann—Welch, Ann Courtenay
Edwards, Lee—Behme, Robert Lee
Edwards, Ron—Edwards, Ronald George
Eisenberg, Phyllis Rose—Eisenberg, Phyllis
Elg, Stefan—Van Over, Raymond
Elvesmere, Rose—Penn, Emily Josephine
Emmott, Bill—Emmott, William John
Engle, Eloise—Paananen, Eloise K.
Ensor, David—Ensor, Alick Charles Davidson
Ephraim, Ben—Chamiel, Haim Itzchak
Erd—Herrgard, Elin
Ernest—Salcedo, Ernesto Abao
Erkshine, Rosalind—Longrigg, Roger Erskine
Es, Johan Frank—Spiessens, Raymond,
    Francois Philomene
Esten, Elizabeth—Nilsen, Mary Ylvisaker
Evans, Bennett—Berger, Ivan Bennett
Evans, Ewart—Evans, George Ewart

Fabrizius, Peter—Fabry, Joseph Benedikt
Faire, Zabrina—Stevenson, Florence
Farah, Amin—Munro, John Murchison
Farely, Alison—Poland, Dorothy Elizabeth
    Hayward
Farrant, Elizabeth—Reardon, Janet Elizabeth
    Mauk
Feikeme, Feike—Manfred, Frederick Feikema
Felsen, Juana Von—Lemp, Liselotte
    (Annemarie)

Ferguson, Liz—Poole, Mildred Ferguson
Fernandez, Happy—Fernandez, Glady Vivian
  Craven
Field, Baker S.—Walsh, Steve
Finn, Mary B.—Finn, Mary Beavers
Finnegan, Joan—Mackenzie, Helen Joan
Finow, Hans-Achim.—Zuehlsdorff, Volkmar
Firestone, Tom—Newcomb, Duane
Firooze, Frank—Colaabavala, Firooze
  Darashaw
Fiske, Tarleton—Bloch, Robert
Fitzgerald, Julia—Watson, Julia
Fleetwood, Frank—Fleetwood, Frances
Fontana, Tom—Fontana, Thomas Michael
Forrester, Helen—Bhatia, Jamunadevi
Foster, Charles—Turner, Bernard Charles
  Arthur
Foxx, Jack—Pronzini, Bill
Frank—Tonogbanua, Francisco G.
Frank, Helene—Vautier-Frank, Ghislaine
Fraser, Jane—Pilcher, Rosamunde
Frazier, Charlotte—Frazier, Anitra
Freienmuth Ilse—von Helms McElroy—
  McElroy, Ilse Editha
French, Christine—Clark, Christine May
Frost, Paul—Castle, Anthony Percy
Fyson, J. G.—Fyson, Jenny Grace

Gaio, Gualtiero Malde—Servadio, Gaia
  Cecilia Metella
Garrard, Christopher—Milton, John R.
Garrick, Andrew—Simmonds, Samuel
  (Andrew Samuel Garriock)
Gaye, Pamela—Gay, Pamela
Genie—Ellison, Eugenia Irene Adams
George, Jonathan—Theiner, George Frederic
Glende, Mary Helen—Deer, Helen Glende
Gibson, James—Long, Edward Gerald
  Hanslip
Gillar, Fred—Vandenbrouck, Arthur Alfred
  Julien
Giles, Kris—Nielsen, Helen Berniece
Gillette, Bob—Shaw, Bynum Gillette
Gilmour, Jane—Shales, Melissa Jane
Goodard, Hazel Firth—Goodard, Hazel Idella
  Firth
Goliard, Roy—Shipley, Joseph Twadell
Goodwin, Eugene D.—Kaye, Marvin Nathan
Goodwin, Gene—Goodwin, H. Eugene
Gotama—Bisscondoyal, Basdeo
Graham, David—Wright (Evan) Wilbur
Graham, Vanessa—Fraser, Anthea Mary
Granite, Tony—Politella, Dario
Grant, C. D.—Grant, Claude DeWitt
Grant, Ross—Westergaard, Ross Grant
Gray, Brenda—MacKinlay, Leila Antoinette
  Sterling
Grayson, Laura—Wilson, Barbara
Green, Cliff—Green, Clifford
Greene, Bob—Everett Robert Greene
Greene, Charles E. Jr.—Cooper, John
  Charles
Greene, Julia—Marlow, Joyce Mary
Gregor, Eric—Aura, Erkki Olavi
Grenzer, Walter Dixi—König, Josef Walker

Grey, Ireland—Elisa, Victoria Ireland Elisa-
  Grey
Griffiths, Grace—Griffiths, Edith Grace
  Chalmers
Grimes, Nikki—Grimes, Naomi
Guinness, Bryan—Guinness, Bryan Walter
  (Lord Moyne)
Gustas, Aldona—Holmsten, Aldona

H20—Hoogland, Claes Abraham
Hadley-Garcia, George—Hadleigh, Boze
Hagen, Martin S.—Pahlow, Mannfried Otto
  Siegfried
Hale, Miss K.—Hale (Mrs. McClean)
  Kathleen
Halleran, Dorothy Wilder—Halleran, Dorothy
  Eleanor Wilder
Hallgarten, S. F.—Hallgarten, Siegfried
  Solomon "Fritz"
Halliday, Ena—Baumgarten, Sylvia (Rosen)
Hancock, Lyn—Hancock, Beryl Lynette
Handy, Nixeon Civille—Handy, Mary Nixeon
  Civille
Hanmer, Davina—Courtney, Nicholas Piers
Harding, George—Raubenheimer, George
  Harding
Harding, Patrick—Premont, Henri
Hardy, Jason—Oxley, William
Harri, William—Sirola, Harri Erkki William
Harris, Bob—Harris, Robert Stone
Harries, Joan—Katsarakis, Joan
Harris, Kenneth—Harris, David Kenneth
Harris, Robert—Harris, Robert von
  Dassanowsky
Harris, Thistle Y.—Stead, Thistle Yolette
Hart, R. W.—Ferneyhough, Roger Edmund
Harte, Marjorie—McEvoy, Marjorie
Harte, Samantha—Hart, Sandra Lynn
  (Housby)
Harvey, Lyndall—Chesterfield-Evans, Janet
  Lyndall
Havil, Anthony—Philipp, Elliott Elias
Haynes, Renee—Tickell, Renee O.
Heale, Jay—Heale, Jeremy Peter Wingfield
Healey, Brooke—Burton, Albert
Heath, Monica—Fitzgerald, Arlene Janiece
Hebden, Mark—Harris, John
Heimberg, Marilyn Markham—Ross, Marilyn
Herald, Kathleen—Peyton, Kathleen Wendy
Herckenrode, Willem Van—Haeven, Paul
Herrmann, Taffy—Herrmann, Dorothy
Hesse, Jean—Hessie, Bettie Jean
Hester, M. L.—Hester, Martin L.
Hewitt, Ben—Mitchell, Adrian
Heyer, Maureen—Korp, Maureen Elizabeth
Heynen, Jim—Heynen, James Alvin
Hicks, Betty Brown—Hicks, Alice Louise
Higgins, Jimmy—Tidler, Charles Lewis
Highland, Monica—See, Carolyn
Highland, Monica—See, Lisa Lenine
Hill, Niki—Hill, Nicola Mary
Hoggard, James—Hoggard, James Martin
Hoffman, E.—Price, Edgar Hoffman
Hon Member for X—de Chair, Somerset
Hoover, H. M.—Hoover, Helen Mary

Hoover, Ralph—Spike, Paul Robert
Horneman, Anton—Hyypia, Jorma
Horwood, Gay—Gibson, Sue G.
Houtland, Maria—Demedts, Gabriëelle-
    Maria
Howard, Colin—Shaw, Howard
Howells, Roscoe—Howells, William Herbert
    Roscoe
Hisia, Hsiaw—Liu, Wu-chi
Hubbell, Patricia—Hornstein, Patricia
Hudson, Harrison—Condon, George, H.
Hughes, Frank—Bird, Paul Francis Hughes
Hugo, Grant—Cable, Sir James
Hugrun—Kristjansdottir, Filippa, S.
Humphrey, Jenny—Humphrey, Jennifer
    Margaret
Humphyrs, Geoffrey—Humphrys, Leslie
    George
Hunt, Francesca—Holland, Isabelle Christian
Hunt, Frederick—Kuhner, Herbert

Ian—Madsen, Christian
Imo, Nell—Otambo, Mary Emily Inda
Ireland, Doreen—Lord, Doreen Mildred
    Douglas
Irwin, Kip—Bursk, Christopher
Ishmael—Hart, Joseph Patrick

Jabez—Nicol, Eric Patrick
Jabry—Brillant, Jacques
Jack—Bales, James Edward
Jacks, Oliver—Royce, Kenneth
Jackson, Elaine—Freeman, Gillian
Jackson, R. Eugene—Jackson, Richard
    Eugene
Jackson, J. P.—Atkins, Arthur Harold
Jacobsen, Ulf—Frøydarlund, Jan-Anker
Jacques, Marie—Brown, Sister Marie James
    O. P.
Jaffa, George—Wallace-Clarke, George
James, Edwin—Gunn, James Ewin
Jammu—Kanerva, Erkki Olavi
Janus—Buchanan, Robert Angus
Jasiemczyk, Janusz—Poray-Biernacki,
    Janusz
Jay—Bunyan, Hector
Jay—Thornton, John William, Jr.
Jerome, Roman—Biesiadecki, Roman J.
Jerry—Van Diver, Gerald R.
Joe—Dill, William Joseph
Johns, Michael—Chittleburgh, Michael John
Johnson, Dick—Johnson, James Richard
Johnson, Jenny—Johnson, Jennifer Hilary
Johnson, Mike—Sharkey, Jack
Johnson, Oliver—Wilcock, John
Jones, Alison—Gyger, Alison Isabel
Jones, D. Gareth—Jones, David Gareth
Jones, Joanna—Burke, John Frederick
Jones, John L.—Jones, John Llewelyn
Jones, R. P.—Jones, Richard Preston
Jonsson, Jonna—Bergman, Ellen Anna
Jordan, Lee—Scholefield, Alan
Jrl, Jørrich—Lund, Jørgen, Richard
Judapress, Simone—Press, Simone Naomi
    Juda
Juge, J. P.—Richter, Hans Peter

Kachel, Zeev—Kachel, Zeev Zew Wolf
Kaipainen, Anu—Kaipainen, Auve Helina
Kalamu—Roskam, Karel Lodewyk
Kaplan, L. Jay—Kaplan, Lois
Kaplan, Sunny Jay—Kaplan, Lois
Karlowna, E.—Leobner-Felski, Erika
Karniewski, Janusz—Wittlin, Thaddeus
Kaviraj—Dowden, George
Kaye, Philip B.—Adams, Alger LeRoy
Kelly, Guy—Moore, Nicholas
Kennedy, X. J.—Kennedy, Joseph Charles
Kenward—Chesterman, Jean
Kern, Canyon—Raborg, Frederick Ashton, Jr.
Kersten, P. J.—Brooks, Patricia K.
Kess—Kessler, Kaye Warren
Khan, Hakim—Cohen, Ira
Kiekeboe—Merhottein, Walter T. E.
Kim—Cardell, Margaret Timothea
Kimbro, Harriet—Kofalk, Harriet
King-Smith, Dick—King-Smith, Ronald
    Gordon
Kinsey, Elizabeth—Clymer, Eleanor
Kiri—Sanders Lewis, H.
Kjp—Prytz, Kjeld Jan
Kobayshi, Chris—Tagami, Marshal L.
Koningsberger, Hans—Koning, Hans
Kope-Rivka—Koplewicz, Rebecca
Kor, Buma—Kor, Billa Dickson Buma
Kovarik, Bill—Kovarik, William Joseph
Krait, Paul—Hedden, Jay W.
Krantz, D.—Izban, Samuel
Krispe, Ralph—Krispe, Randel (Ralph)
KSK—Keys, Kerry Shawn
Kubly, Nic—Kubly, Herbert Oswald
Kulik, Boles—Costley, Bill (William Kirkwood
    Jr.)
Kusikiven, Äija—Hemminki, Heikki Veli Matti
Kwan, William—Kwan, William Chao-Yu

Ladd, Emilie—Cullen, Lee Stowell
Ladd, Veronica—Claypool-Miner, Jane
Lance, Dorothea—Latz, Dorothy L.
Lan-Chan—Lee, Hun
Landecker, Lewis—Rosenthal, Edwin Stanley
Lane, Naunton—Moss, Robert Alfred
Lane, M. Travis—Lane, M. Travis (Millicent
    Elizabeth Travis)
Lang, Elizabeth—Dean, Nancy
Lang, Elmy—Lang-Dillenburger, Elmy
Lang, Matthew—Marowittz, Charles
Lantz, Fran—Latnz, Francess Lin
Laredo, L.—McKeown, Lorraine Laredo
Larrowe 'Lash'—Larrowe, Charles P.
Laski, Marghanita—Howard, Marghanik
Later, C. U.—Hoolmqvist, Nils (Okar Anders)
Lauder, Phyllis—Lauder, Phyllis Anna Lynn
Laura, Judith—Willis, Judith Laura Levine
Lauren, Linda—Bunce, Linda Susan
Lawson, Michael—Ryder, Michael Lawson
Lawrence, Linda—Hunt, Linda (Christensen)
Lear, Peter—Lovesey, Peter
Lee, Brad—Slattery, Bradley
Lefort, Suzanne-Jules—Lefort, Suzanne
Lehmann-Brune—Lehmann, Marlies
Lenny—Lipton, Leonard Lenny

Leonhard, Leo—Leonhardt, Siegmund
LeShawney, Trischelle K.—Graham, Teresa R.
Leslie, A. L.—Lazarus, A(rnold) Leslie
Lester, Mark—Russell, Martin James
Lewis, D. F.—Burke, Martyn John
Lewis, Francine—Wells, Helen
Lewis, Ted—Lewis, Theodore Gyle
Lima, Robert—Lima, Robert F. Jr.
Lindsay, John—Ladell, John Lindsay
Litsey, Sarah—Ford, Sarah Litsey
Livingston, Carole—Stuart, Carole
Livingston, Nancy—Foster, Janet
Logan, Jake—Rifkin, Shepard
Lois, Carol—Fallows, Carolyn Lois
Lomosia, Andrew—Stern, Jay Benjamin
Loomis, Dennis—Shelton, William Roy
Loosley, William Robert—Langford, David
Lorenz, Sarah E.—Winston, Sarah
Lorimer, Scat—Fuentes, Martha Frances Ayers
Lorrimer, Claire—Clark, Patricia Denise
Lorts, J. E.—Lorts, Jack E.
Lovell, Marc—McShane, Mark
Lund, James—Stonehouse, John Thomson
Luellen, Valentina—Polley, Judith Anne
Lynn—Kern-Foxworth, Dr. Marilyn
Lynton, Ann—Rayner, Claire Berenice

MacAdam, Ian—Adamson, Iain
MacLean, Jonathan—Wheatcroft, Andrew Jonathan MacLean
MacNair, John—Whitcomb, Philip Wright
MacNeil, Duncan—McCutchan, Philip Donald
McCammon, Kay—Pritchard, Hilary Kathleen
McCarty, Norma—Crandall, Norma Rand
McDaniel, Evelyn—Bryan, Evelyn McDaniel Frazier
McElroy, Lee—Kelton, Elmer Stephen
McGinnis, T. J.—McGinnis, Terry Jack
McKenzie, Thomas—Reilly, Robert Thomas
McLaughlin, William—McLaughlin, William DeWitt
McLendon, Gloria H.—Houston-McLendon, Gloria Sue
McMorrow, Tom—McMorrow, Thomas Evers
McNeill, Janet—Alexander, Janet
McPhail, Tom—McPhail, Thomas Lawrence
McPherson, James Alan—McPherson, James Allen

Ma, Fei—Marr, William W.
Macer-Story, E.—Macer-Story, Eugenia
Mackenzie, R. Alec—Mackenzie, Richard Alexander
Mackenzie, Alec—Mackenzie, Richard Alexander
Mackworth, Cecily—Mackworth, Cecily
Magus, Carolus—Wise, Charles Conrad
Mahler, Werner—Spillemaeckers, Werner Lodewijk
Majo—Maurer, Joseph
Mallet, Marilu—Mallet, Marilu Marie Louise

Malpott, Virgule—Ghnassia, Maurice Jean-Henri
Mallory, Fawne—McCrohan, Donna Marie
Maltby, Gillian—Bryce-Smith, Gillian
Mann, Dorothy—Harman, Jeanne Perkins
Mann, Josephine—Pullein-Thompson, Josephine Mary Wedderburn
Mansfield, John—Bunting, John Reginald
Mantel—Kusche, Lothar
March, John—Baly, Lindsay Gordon
Mardie—Munzer, Martha E.
Maritz—Maritz, Magdalena Petronella
Marko, Katherine McGlade—Marko, Katherine Dolores
Marriott, Thomas—Barling, Thomas F. R.
Marsh, Jean—Marshall, Evelyn
Marshall, James Vance—Payne, Donald Gordon
Martin, Bud—Martin, George Thomas Jr.
Martin, Joe—Martin, Joseph Hirsch
Martin-Morris, Ed.—Morris, William Edward
Martineau, Frank—Martineau, Francis Edward
Maruna, Annikki—Aaltonen, Ilta Annikki Tyyne
Marx, Woody K.—Sharland, Michael Reginald
Maska—Szuprowicz, Bohdan Olgierd
Mason, Howard—Worsfold, David Howard
Mason, Ted—Mason, Theodore Charles
Matthews, Ellen—Bache, Ellyn
Matthews, Jack—Matthews, John Harold
Matu—Matuszenski, Reinhard
Maurice, Roger—Asselineau, Roger Maurice
Maya, Tristan—Maton, Jean
Maynard, Nan—Maynard, Nancy Kathleen Brazier
Maz—Harris, Ian Richard
Meadows, Stephen—Stephenson, Raymond Meadows
Meidinger-Geise, Inge—Meidinger, Ingeborg Lucie
Melville, Anne—Potter, Margaret
Melville, Laurie—McKean, John Maule Laurie
Mercer, Brad—Spence, Donald P.
Merlin, David—Moreau, David Merlin
Merritt, E. B.—Waddington, Miriam Dworkin
Merritt, T. E.—Pinckard, Terri Ellen
Messiers, Nicole de—Spurney, Nicole
Meunier-Bourg de la Roche, Alfred—Muller-Felsenburg, Alfred
Michaels, Barbara—Mertz, Barbara Gross
Michaels, Christopher—Dalrymple, Byron William
Middleton, O. E.—Middleton, Osman Edwards
Mieskivi, Kaarina—Jokinen, Ulla Kaarina Vellamo
Mikkola, Marja-Leena—Pirinen, Marja-Leena
Milan, Angel—Lynn, Mary Elizabeth
Miles, Richard—Perreau-Saussine, Gerald
Miller, Margaret—Dale, Margaret Jessy
Milne, Alexander Antony—Milne, Antony Alexander

Mitchell, Don—Mitchell, Donald Earl
Mitchell, Elizabeth (Kenya)—Chappell, Barbara Elizabeth
Mitchell, K. L.—Lamb, Elizabeth Searle
Mitchell, Paula—Zipp, Paula M.
Mitchell, Ray—Mitchell, Raymond Walker
Montardit, Th.G.—Montardit, Teresa Grifoll
Moolson, Melusa—Solomon, Samuel
Moore, Marna—Reynolds, (Marjorie) Moira Davison
Moosrainer, Lorenz—Merkle, Ludwig
Morckhoven, Paul van—Pauwels, Lode Jozef
More, Glen—Allan, Roger Glenmor
Morgan, Louise—Morgan, Helen Louise
Morgan, Helen Tudor—Morgan, Helen Louise
Morgan-Jones, Jonathan—Docherty, John
Moriarty, J.—Kelly Tim
Morisot, Simone—Sylvester, Doreen Rosalie Mammott
Morris, Claude—Ilmer, Walter
Morris, James—Morris, Jan
Mortimer, Leslie—Sartori, Eva Maria
Morton, Harry—Morton, Henry Albert
Mosberger, Catherine—Mosberger, Katharina
Moskowitz, Rhina P.—Espaillat, Rhina Polonia
Moult, Ted—Moult, Edward Walker
Mountbatten, Richard—Wallmann, Jeffrey M(iner)
Moyo, Rusununguko—Tsodzo, Thompson Kumbirai
Mudiarasn—Durairaj, Kaviarasu
Mueller, John—Muenzer, Paul John
Muizniece, Sarma—Muiznieks, Sarma Gundega
Mullick, Woomesh—Mallik, Umesh Charan
Muni, Narad—Anand, Mulkraj
Murphy, Pat—Murphy, Emmett Jefferson
Murti, K. V. S.—Murti, Kotikalapudi Venkata Suryanarayana

Nash, Simon—Chapman, Raymond
Nada—Ligi
Naiche, Victoria—Ben-Ari, Dani
Nalle—Valtiala, Kaarle-Juhani Bertel
Nanushka—Whitcomb, Nan
Nastau, John—Latta, Richard John
Nathan, Leobard—Nathan, Edward Leonard
Nauroy, Rene de—Le Clere, Rene
Naval, Frederik—Brustat, Fritz
Neal, Berniece Roer—Neal, Berniece Marie
Neri, Felipe—Junquera-Huergo Y Torres, Felipe Neri
Nelson, R. F.—Nelson, Ray Faraday
Nelson, Ray—Nelson, Ray Faraday
Nevin, Evelyn C.—Ferguson, Evelyn Cook
Newberry, E. G.—Muir, Kenneth
Nic—Dymott, Roderick
Nicolson, Angus—MacNeacail, Aonghas
Nilak, Robert—Kalin, Robert
Nilak, Trebor—Kalin, Robert
Nitzsche, Jane Chance—Chance Jane

Noble, Nicholas R.—Cole, Eugene Roger
Nomar, Benjamin, Ono—Reece, Benny Ramon
Norcross, John—Conray, John Wesley (Jack)
Norman, Yvonne—Seely, Norma Yvonne
Norton, Bram—Norton, Jay Bramesco
Nott, Barry—Hurren, Bernard Jon
Nuraini—Sim, Katharine Phyllis
Nylund, Sjostedt—Nylund-Karlsson, Harriet Linnea

Obiak, Marcel—Debroey, Marcel
O'Brien, Katharine—O'Brien, Katharine Elizabeth
October, John—Portway, Christopher
O'Grady, Rohan—Skinner, June Margaret O'Grady
Ohan—Barba, Harry
Olivares, Tomas—Oliver, Covey Thomas
Ombudsman—Bauwens, Marcel Francois Maximilien
Onlooker—Parsons, Edward
Orlier, Blaise—Sylvestre, Jean Guy
Opfermann, H. C.—Opfermann, Hans-Carl
Orga, Ates—Orga, Hüsnü Ates, D'arcy
Osmond, A. E.—Shinkman, Elizabeth Benn
Ostrich, Kevin—Oberrecht, George Kenneth (Kenn)
Overy, Claire May—Bass, Clara May
Owen, Dilys—Gater, Dilys
Owen, Luri—Owen, Maude Lurline

Padfield, Peter—Padfield, Peter Lawrence Notton
Press, Page—Lyles, Donald
Page, P. K.—Irwin, Patricia Kathleen
Page, P. K.—Page, Patricia Kathleen
Page, Vicki—Avey, Ruby Doreen
Pallister, Jan—Pallister, Janis L.
Palmer, Lynn—Palmer, Pamela Lynn
Palued—Oeyen, Edith Clothildis
Panno V. V.—Thomas, Michael Charles
Parker, Kay Grayman—Parker, Catherine E.
Paris, Hilary—Doling, Hilary
Patrick, Robert—O'Connor, Robert Patrick
Parthasarathy, Rahoula ('Froggy')—Miller, Robinder Rahoula
Pasionaria—Ibarruri, Dolores
Pater, Elias—Friedman, Jacob Horace
Patey-Grabowska—Grabowska-Steffen, Alicja Wanda
Pavey, Don—Pavey, Donald Adair
Pazolski—Passes, Alan
PBP—Buchwald-Pelc, Paulina Maria
P. C.—Hodgell, Patricia Christine
Pearce, Philippa—Christie, Ann Philippa
Pearce, A. Philippa—Christie, Ann Philippa
Pearl, Erik—Elman, Richard
Pecos, Bill—Sherman, William David
Peebles, Anne—Galloway, Priscilla
Peel, Wallis—Peel, Hazel Mary
Pegas, Daren—De Pages, Andre Denis
Pell, Jay—Collins, Robert George
Penena-Guitte—Penen, Virginie-Marguerite

Penfold, Nita—Raquet, Bonita Susan Penfold
Penn, Mrs.—Street, Lucie
Pennant, Edmund—Zaslow, Edmund
Pereira, Teresinka—Pereira, Teresinha
Perrachon, Alix G.—Perrachon, Alix Gudjin
Pervin, Alice—Anneliese
"Peter"—Reilly, Noel Marcus Prowse
Peters, Edmund—Nelson (Edwin) P.
Peterson, Casey—Peterson, Kenneth Curtis, Jr.
Phelps, Joy Eleanor—Friggin, Joy Eleanor Griffin Fogleman Phelps
Phoenice, J.—Hutchinson, Juliet Mary Fox
PHS—Gordon, Angela
Plummer, J. B.—Basmajian, Shaunt (Shant)
Piano, Celeste—Lykiard, Alexis Constantine
Pickard, Tom—Pickard, Thomas Mariner
Piguet, Marie-Jose—Piguet-Knight, Marie-Jose
Pinoak, Justine W.—Prosser, Harold Lee
Piraianu, Alexandru—Mitru, Alexandru
Plunkett, James—Kelly, James Plunkett
Polking, Kirk—Polking, Dorothy
Pomfret, John—Townsend, J.
Poole, Josephine—Helyar, Jane Penelope Josephine
Pope, Christina—St. Jacques, Elizabeth Joyce Gloria
Portal, Ellis—Powe, Bruce Allen
Porter, Bern—Porter, Bernard Harden
Positano, Rico di—Leihr, Heinz Fritz Siegfried
Potter, Simon—Jarrett, Dennis Evan
Powell, Neil—Innes, Brian
Power, Victor—Power, Patrick Victor
Poyer, Joe—Poyer, Joseph
Prieto, Mariana—Beeching-Prieto, Marian Train
Prince Hal—Gutzin, Harold H.
Pullein-Thompson, Christine—Popescu, Christine
Pullein-Thompson, Diana—Farr, Diana
Puupalikka—Pylkkonen-Suomi, Maila Annikki.

Qimson, S. Zin—Kim, Soon Jin
Quick, Orville—Wood, Tom J.
Quindt, Diethelm Pierre—Lanczkowski, Cl.

Raase, Gosta Olof—Lindholm, Gosta, Olof Ferdinand
Rae, Doris—Rae, Margaret Doris
Radley, Sheila—Robinson, Sheila Mary
Raki—Maple, Gordon Extra
Ramsay, Jay—Campbell, Ramsey
Ran—Hall, Rand
Rana, Christina—Rana-Bengtsson, Frida Christina
Randall, Rona—Shambrook, Rona
Ranjan, Sri—Bose, Dakshina Ranjan
Raworth, Tom—Raworth, Thomas Moore
Ray, Irene—Sutton, Margaret Rachel Irene
Raymond, Mary—Heathcott, Mary
Read, Miss—Saint, Dora Jessie

Reaves, Robert Lee—Oswald, Roy Lee
Reed, Lawrence—Reday, Ladislaw
Reeves, Joyce—Gard, Joyce
Remolif, Charles—Shere, Charles
Reubeni, Meir—Faerber, Meir Marcell
Revell, Jack—Revell, John Robert Stephen
Reynolds, Anne—Steinke, Ann E.
Reynolds, Elizabeth—Steinke, Ann E.
Reynolds, John—Whitlock, Ralph
Reynolds, Madge—Whitlock, Ralph
Rhodas—Rhodas, Virginia
Rice, Jim—Rice, James William Jr.
Richards, Michael—Langworth, Richard Michael
Richards, Steve—Strehlow, Loretta Jean
Richmond, Roe—Richmond, Roaldus Frederick
Ridgway, Judy—Ridgway, Judith Anne
Ridley, Jasper—Ridley, Jasper Godwin
Rigelhof, T. F.—Rigelhof, Terrance Frederick
Rikki—Ducornet, Erica
Roar, Robert A.—Grimshaw, James Albert
Robert the Phymer—Williams, Alan Moray
Roberts, Len—Roberts, Leonard Robert
Robles, Wystan—Espino, Federico Junior
Rock, Richard—Mainprize, Donald Charles
Rogers, Mary Polito—Polito, Mary Elaine
Romun, Isak—Bennett, Gordon Clowe James Joseph
Rook, Pearl Newton—Rook, Pearl Lucille Newton
Roos, Murphre—Mele, Jim
Rose, Lysbeth—Cohen, Lysbeth Rose
Ross, Angus—Giggal, Kenneth
Ross, Dave—Ross, David Hugh
Ross, Marilyn—Ross, William Edward Daniel
Ross, Clarissa—Ross, William Edward Daniel
Roth, June—Roth, June Doris Spiewak
Rouve, Pierre—Unalieff, Peter
Rovin, Alex—Russo, Albert
Rud—Kofoed, Rud
Rudder, Virginia L.—Long, Virginia Love
Royce, Kenneth—Gandleu, Kenneth Royce
R. T.—Smith, Rodney Theodore
Rycon, Elizabeth Cloberry—Savery, Constance Winifred
Rys—Susilo, Richard Yani

Saddler, Allen—Richards, Ronald Charles William
Saint-Gil, Philippe—Gillet, Philippe
Sam—Snape, Christopher Paul
Sanchez, Lavinia—Elmslie, Kenward
Sanders, Winston P.—Anderson, Poul William
Sanford, Geraldine A. J.—Sanford, Geraldine Agnes Jones
Santos, Helen—Griffiths, Helen
Savalvio, Leo—Webberley, Maxwellyn Grant
Savage, Catharine—Brosman, Catharine
Savion, Thom—Savino, Thomas
Scarlett, Susan—Streatfield, Mary Noel
Schei, Veneto—Hyams, Jay
Schoonover, Amy Jo. (Miss)—Zook, Amy Jo

Schofield, Paul—Tubb, E(dwin) C(harles)
Schwemer-Uhlhorn, Erna—Schwemer, Erna Anna Helene
Scott, Douglas—Clew, Jeffrey Robert
Scott, Elizabeth Austin—Scott, Elizabeth Patricia
Scott, John—Jmoynihan, John Dominic
Scott, Jud—Ware, Clyde
Seabright, Idris—St. Clair, Margaret
Seagull, Frank—Hamley, Ernest Basil
Searls, Hank—Searls, Henry (Hank) H. Jr.,
Sebastian, Margaret—Gladstone, Arthur M.
Seed, Jenny—Seed, Cecile Eugenie
Sefton, Catharine—Waddell, Martin
Sennachie, Donald—Whyte, Donald
Seppings, Joan—Webster, Joan Katherine
Seppings Webster, Joan—Webster, Joan Katherine
Seys, Raf—Weys, Rafael Jozef
Shambaugh, Joan—Shambaugh, Joan Dibble
Shambaugh, Joan Dibble—Shambaugh, Joan Dibble
Sharp, Hal—Sharp, Harold Wilson
Sharpe, Tom—Sharpe, Thomas Ridley
Sheldon, Walt—Sheldon, Walter James
Sheikh—Sallah, Tijan, M.
Shelston, Mark—Boyd Maunsell, Nevill Francis Wray
Shero—Bozarslan, Mehmet Emin
Sherrin, Ned—Sherrin, Edward George
Sherry, Sylvia—Sherry, Dulcie Sylvia
Sherwood, Michael—Weathers, Philip Joseph
Shibasaki, Sosuke—Civasaqui, Jose
Shibukawa, Gyo—Yamasaki, Takeo Gyo
Shields, Mike—Shields, Michael Joseph
Shih-po Chin—Ginsburg, Philip Eliot
Shuford, Gene—Shuford, Cecil Eugene
Shura, Mary Francis—Craig, Mary Francis
Sichel, Marion—Cassin-Scott, Marion Doret
Sihti, Arton, Reiska—Kythohonka, Arto Olavi
Sikora, Mieczyslaw Stefan—Rey, Michael Stephan
Silitch, Clarissa Mac Veagh—Silitch, Clarissa Silene MacVeagh
Silvio, David—da Silva, Joao
Simon, Robert—Musto, Gordon Barry
Simon, Ted—Simon, Edward John
Simpson, Epy—Simpson, Ervin Peter Young
Slater, Lydia Pasternak—Slater, Lydia Elizabeth
Slocombe, Joan—Slocombe Bouchon, Joan Tamara
Small, Mary Vivian—Bonine, Vivian Way
Smith, A. C. H.—Smith, Anthony Charles
Smith, Dave—Smith, David Jeddie
Smith, Frederick E.—Smith, Frederick Escreet
Smith Harry—Smith, H(orace) Bernard
Smith Ralph—Smith, H(orace) Bernard
Smith, Tom—Smith, Thomas Henry
Snow, Lucy—Aubert, Rosemary Proe
Snowdon, Mary Bewley—Baigent, Beryl
Spalt, Karl Heinz G.—Spalding, Keith
Spartan, J.—Goldkorn, Isaac

Speedie-Pask, Michael—Pask, Gordon Andrew Speedie
Spencer, Philip—Kramer, Aaron
St. George, Edith—Delatush, Edith
St. Denis, Michael George—Koehler, Isabel Winifred
St. James, Andrew—Stern, James Andrew
Stankiewicz, Michal—Bystrzycki, Przemystaw
Stark, Joshua—Olsen, Theodore Victor
Stanley, Ian—Zuckerman, Mattew Ian Stanley
Steel, Byron—Steegmuller, Francis
Stern, Ellen Norman—Stern, Ellen Norman
Stevens, R. L.—Hoch, Edward D.
Stevens, Robert Tyler—Staples, Reginald Thomas
Stewart, Jim—Stewart, James Alexander
Stewart, Michael—Stewart, Robert Michael Maitland (Lord Stewart of Fulham)
Stirling, Jessica—Rae, Hugh Crauford
Stocks, Bryan—Stocks, John Bryan
Stott, Mary—Stott, Charlotte Mary
Stranger, Joyce—Wilson, Joyce Muriel
Strong, Milt—Strong, Milton V.
Stroud, Kandy—Stroud, Andrea Diane
Stuart, Frederick—Tomlin, Eric Walter Frederick
Stuart, V. A.—Stuart, Vivian Alex (ne Finlay)
Stuart, Vivian—Stuart, Vivian Alex (ne Finlay)
Stuart Long, William—Stuart, Vivian Alex (ne Finlay)
Summers, Essie—Flett, Ethel Snelson
Summers, Rowena—Saunders, Jean
Sundowner—Pike, Glenville
Sutherland, Elizabeth—Marshall, Elizabeth Margaret
Svenningsen, Paul F.—Svenningsen, Poul Fløe
Swerfgeest, Frans—De Cnodder, Remi Frans Jozef
Sylvester, Philip—Worner, Philip Arthur Incledon
Sysman—Mansfield, Charles
S. Z.—Zaveri, Shantilal Mansukhlal
Szymanski, Richard—Symanski, Richard

Tabard, Peter—Blake, Leslie James
Tabor, B. Lyle—Tabor, Bruce Lyle
Tambuzi, JiTu—Byrd, Odell Richard
Taylor, L. A.—Taylor, Laurie Aylma
Ted—Holmberg, Theodore
Templeton, Robert—Smith, Rodney Robert Templeton
Terry, Margaret—Dunnahoox, Terry
Thilakam, Neela—Padmanabhan, Neela
Thompson, J. J.—Thompson, Jesse Jackson
Thorne, Nicola—Ellerbeck, Rosemary Anne L'Estrange
Thornton, Burgess—Ballou, H. B.
Tibber, Robert—Friedman, Rosemary
Tilton, Rafael—Tilton, Madonna Elaine
Tim—Hays, Howard H.
Timber Fred—Reimers, Emil

Timotesus—Toyryla, Timo Sakari
Titleman, M.—Tamari, Moshe
Tivoli, Adam—Berry, Jim
Tobias-Turner, Bessye—Tobias-Turner, Bessye
Tolan—Thomas, Paul
Tollas, Tibor—Kecskesi, Tibor
Tombo—Harr, Lorraine Ellis
Tondury, Marie—Roten, Iris von
Tony—Bove, Anthony
Totten, Solange—Totten, Caroline V.
Tracy, Silver—Sexauer, Arwin Garellick
Tracy, Susan—Marino, Carolyn Fitch
Traips, Janis—Noritis, Rudolfs-Pauls
Tramontanus—Lempp, Karl Ferdinand
Tremaine, Carol—Berry, Joan Carol
Tremayne, Peter—Ellis, Peter Berresford
Trent, Brenda—Himrod, Brenda Lee
Tresillian, Richard—Royston Ellis
Travers, Kenneth—Hutchin, Kenneth Charles
Treu, Konrad—Sturmthal, Adolf (Fox)
Trevor, Edward—Skelton, Peter
Tulasi—Paniker, Ayyappa
Turkel, Judi K.—Kesselman-Turkel, Judi
Turner, Mary—Lambot, Isobel Mary
Turner, Sheila—Rowbotham, Sheila

Uma—Aaltonen, Ulla-Maija
Underwood, Michael—Evelyn, John Michael
Unthank, Tessa—Nelson-Humphries, Tessa
Ute, Mohan—Milton, David Q.

Vaal, Anna de—Ladell, Norah Monica
Vala, Erkki — Vala, Erik August Waldemar
Valencak, Hannelore—Mayer, Hannelore
Valles, Marc—Sales, Joan
Vanity—Crouch, Annette S.
Van Ness, Lika—Sullivan, Eleanor Regis
Van Puthen, Geert—Soete, Gerard Andre
Vance, Jack—Vance, John Holbrook
Vaughan, Vera—Vaughan Bowden, Vera
Vejvoda, Jaroslav—Marek, Jaroslav
Vermeulen, John—Vermeulen, Johan
Veryan, Patricia—Bannister, Patricia Valeria
Vesey, Paul—Allen, Samuel Washington
Vetch, M.—Schappes,Morris Urman
Vial, Gion—Deplazes, Gion
Vinayak—Gokak, Vinayak
Vincent, William Ray—Heitzmann, William Ray
Viret, Margaret—Viret, Margaret Mary-Buchanan
Vivier, Jean-Paul—Duvivier, Jean-Paul

Wade, Candice—Whelchel, Sandra Jane
Wagenvoorde, H. Van—Regin, Deric Wagenvoort
Walbrook, Louise—Templeton, Edith
Waldschratt—Speidel, Michael P.
Wales, Nym—Snow, Helen Foster
Walker, J.—Crawford, John Richard
Wallace, E.—Wallace-Carter, Evelyn Clara
Wally—Sims, Watson Shedrick
Wanjila, Redge Tatanka—Laubin, Reginald Karl

Ward, John—Tigges, John
Ware, Wallace—Karp, David
Warner, Ken—Warner, Kenneth Wilson, Jr.
Wastewin, Wiyaka—Laubin, Gladys Winifred
Watkins, Mervyn—Williams, Malcolm David
Watt, Donald Cameron—Cameron-Watt, Donald
Watts, Irene N.—Watts, Irene Naemi
Wayne, Joseph—Overholser, Wayne D.
Webb, Ron—Webb, Sharon Lynn
Weiheng, Mei—Mair, Victor Henry
Well, Alan Stewart—Sewart, Alan
Welles, Alyssa—Berger, Nomi
West, Anthony C.—West, Cathcart Anthony Muir
Westgate, John—Bloomfield, Anthony John Westgate
Weston, Marian—Lakritz, Esther nee Himmelman
Weston, William—Milsom, Charles Henry
Whitbread, Elizabeth—Barrett, Helen Elizabeth-Anne
White, Margaret Rossiter—Thiele, Margaret
White, Scott—Bairden, Andrew White
White, Steve—McGarvey, Robert
Whiteside, Tom—Whiteside, Thomas C.
Whitewood, Simone—Whyte, Barbara Birkbeck
Whitten, Les—Whitten, Leslie Hunter
Whittle, Tyler—Tyler-Whittle, Michael
Wideen, L. M.—Wideen, Lennart Mauritz
Wides—Schutter, Willy Alfons Jan De
Wilks, Mike—Wilks, Michael Thomas
Williams, Jo Paula—Watson, Jerine P.
Williams, Ursula Moray—John, Ursula Moray
Wilmet, Casey—Tattersall, Laura Catherine Mary
Wilson, Gina—Wilson, Georgina Marion
Wilson, John C.—Morrow, Felix
Wilson, Norma—Wilson, Norma Jean Clark
Wilson, D. Ray—Wilson, Delbert Ray
Wilson, R. V.—Vivian, Robert W. (Bob)
Wilson, Sue—Wilson, Sarah Elizabeth Turpin
Winans, A. D.—Winans, Allan Davis
Winkler, Kees—Winkler, Cornelis
Wolfe, Elizabeth—Lederer, Paul Joseph
Wood, Pat—Baxter, Patricia Edith Wilson
Wood, Tessa—Toner, Barbara
Wood, Ursula—Vaughan Williams, Ursula
Woods, H. G.—Bush, George Franklin
Woodstock Jones—Woods, Eddie
Woolf, F. X. (with Janet Hamilton)—Engel, Howard
Wordsmith, James A.—Hanf, James Alphonso
Worley, Stella—Johnson, Stella Gertrude
Worth, James—Worthington-Williams, Michael James
Worth, Margaret—Strickland, Margot Teresa
Wostall, Nina—Misselwitz, Anna
Wyndham, Esther—Lutyens, Mary

X, Laura—Orthwein, Laura Rand
Xawery—Truchanowski, Kazimierz

Yaffe, Alan—Yorinks, Arthur
Yale, Kathleen Betsko—Betsko, Kathleen
    Selina
Yale, Kathleen—Betsko, Kathleen Selina
Yair, Ish—Shtern, Israel Hersh
Young, Carrie—Young, Ahdele Carrine
Young, Ellin Dodge—Dodge, Ellin
Young, Elizabeth—Kennet (Lady) Elizabeth
Young, Patrick—Young, Patrick Grant
Ysreal, Elie-Pierre—Renaud (Ernest)
    Jacques

Z Carl—Zetterström, Carl Bertil Erik
ZŁK—Zolkiewski, Stefan
Zacharias, Lee—Zacharias, Lela Ann
Zaidys, Chantier—Gaida-Gaidamavicius,
    Pranas
Zaphire—Peter Adrian Steele
Zimmerman, Robert Allen—Dylan, Bob
Zongpu—Feng, Zhong pu
Zurawiec, Mateusz—Lichniak, Zygmunt

APPENDIX 2

LITERARY AGENTS

The following list of agents does not claim to be exhaustive although every effort has been made to make it as comprehensive as possible.

In all instances, authors are advised to send preliminary letters to agents before submitting manuscripts.

U.K. AGENTS

ADAMASTOR PRESS & LITERARY AGENCY LTD.
6 Somerton Road
London NW2
Contact: Sydney Clouts or Marjorie Clouts
Handles full-length, non-fiction books.

ALPHA BOOK AGENCY
Boyden End
260 Hayes Lane
Kenley
Surrey CR2 5EG
Contact: P H Hargreaves
Educational MSS only.

ANGLO-GERMAN LITERARY AGENCY
87 Upper Selsdon Road
South Croydon
Surrey CR2 0DP
Contact: Gordon or Walburg Fielden
Specializes in works written in German as well as English. Handles all types of full-length work for book publication, particularly in the fields of natural history and information books for children.

STEPHEN ASKE
Wildacre
The Warren
Ashtead
Surrey KT21 2SL
Contact: A S Knight
Accepts full-length and short MSS. Handles theatre, films, television and sound broadcasting.

THE AUTHORS' ALLIANCE
64 The Dean
Alresford
Hampshire
Contact: Mrs. Deborah Greenep
Does not accept short stories or articles.

ROGER BARNETT ASSOCIATES
143 Holborn
London EC1N 2NJ
Contact: Roger Barnett
Accepts full-length and short MSS.

BOLT & WATSON LIMITED
8-12 Old Queen Street
London SW1
Contact: David Bolt or Sheila Watson
Accepts full-length and short MSS. Handles translations, theatre, films, television and sound broadcasting.

CURTIS BROWN ACADEMIC LTD.
1 Craven Hill
London W2 3EP
Contact: Andrew Best or Frances Kelly
Represents specialist and educational academic writers.

CURTIS BROWN LIMITED
1 Craven Hill, London, W2 3EP
Contact: Graham Watson, Chairman, or Peter Grose, Managing Director
Represents book and short story writers throughout the world.

CURTIS BROWN ACADEMIC LTD.
1 Craven Hill
London W2 3EP
Contact: Michael Shaw or Alastair Maclean
Specializes in authors writing professional or student books for the college and university markets but also handles works of general non-fiction and school books.

CHRISTOPHER BUSBY LIMITED
44 Great Russell Street
London WC1 3PA
Contact: C R Busby
Does not handle stage plays, unsolicited short stories and articles, poetry, or unsolicited television scripts.

JOHN CADELL LIMITED
2 Southwood Lane
London N6 5EE
Contact: John Cadell
Considers writing for the theatre, television and radio only.

CAMPBELL THOMSON AND McLAUGHLIN LIMITED
31 Newington Green
London N16 9PU
Contact: Christine Campbell Thomson, John McLaughlin, Hal Cheetham or John Parker
Accepts full-length and short MSS.

C AND B (THEATRE)
Calder & Boyars Limited
Publishers, 18 Brewer Street
London W1R 4AS
Contact: J M Calder, Marion Boyars or Michael Hayes
Handles the sale of dramatic rights to amateur

and professional theatre companies, radio, television and film.

E J CARNELL LITERARY AGENCY
Rowneybury Bungalow
Sawbridgeworth
Old Harlow
Essex CH20 2EX
Contact: Leslie Flood
Specializes in science fiction.

JONATHAN CLOWES LIMITED
19 Jeffrey's Place
London NW1 9PP
Contact: Jonathan Clowes, Ann Evans, Donald Carroll or Enyd Clowes
Handles theatre, films, television, and sound broadcasting.

ELSPETH COCHRANE AGENCY
1 The Pavement
London SW4 0HY
Contact: Miss Elspeth Cochrane
Handles writers of theatre, films, television and sound broadcasting script writers and all publishing rights.

ROSICA COLIN LIMITED
1 Clareville Grove Mews
London SW7 5AH
Contact: Rosica Colin or Joanna Marston
Specializes in general publishing, original MSS, theatre and foreign rights but handles all types of MSS except poetry and newspaper articles.

DONALD COPEMAN LIMITED
52 Bloomsbury Street
London WC1B 3QT
Contact: Donald Copeman or L G Turney

RUPERT CREW LIMITED
King's Mews
Gray's Inn Road
London WC1N 2JA
Contact: D Montgomery for non-fiction, S Russell for fiction
Offers world representation to feature and fiction writers.

DALZELL DURBRIDGE AUTHORS LIMITED
see Harvey Unna and Stephen Durbridge Ltd.

FELIX DE WOLFE
1 Robert Street
Adelphi
London WC2N 6BH
Contact: Felix de Wolfe
Represents playwrights, dramatists, non-fiction writers relating to the entertainment profession and screenwriters.

ENGLISH THEATRE GUILD LIMITED
5A South Side
Clapham Common

London SW4 7AA
Contact: Joan Ling

JOHN FARQUHARSON LIMITED (1919)
Bell House
Bell Yard
London WC2A 2JU
Contact: Innes Rose, George Greenfield or Vanessa Holt
Full length general fiction and non-fiction works. All rights handled with special emphasis on overseas markets.

FILM RIGHTS LIMITED
113-117 Wardour Street
London W1
Contact: John E Hunter, D. M. Sims, Maurice Lambert or Laurence Fitch
Handles theatre, films, television and sound broadcasting.

LAURENCE FITCH LIMITED
113-117 Wardour Street
London W1V 4EH
Contact: Laurence Fitch
Handles all type of MSS except poetry.

FRASER AND DUNLOP SCRIPTS LIMITED/ROBIN DALTON ASSOCIATES LIMITED
91 Regent Street
London W1R 8RU
Contact: Kenneth Ewing, Mark Lucas, Richard Wakeley or Timothy Corrie
Represents writers, producers and directors in television, theatre, films, publishing (fiction, non-fiction and children's) and radio.

J F GIBSON'S LITERARY AGENCY
PO Box 173
London SW3
Contact: J F Gibson
Handles full-length fiction and non-fiction for adults and children.

ERIC GLASS LIMITED
28 Berkeley Square
London W1X 6HD
Contact: Eric Glass or Janet Crowley
Specializes in screen, stage and TV plays as well as fiction and non-fiction books.

CLIVE GOODWIN ASSOCIATES
12 Upper Addison Gardens
London W14 8AP
Represents the first class writers in England for television, film and theatre.

ELAINE GREENE LIMITED
31 Newington Green
Islington
London N16 9PU
Contact: Elaine Greene, Ilsa Yardley
Does not handle plays, original film scripts or poetry. Will handle articles and short stories written by existing clients only.

ROBERT HARBEN LITERARY AGENT
3 Church Vale
London N2 9PD
Contact: Robert Harben
Representative of Publishers for The Netherlands and English and American agents. Interested in placing top class German books on history, sociology, etc. in England.

ALEC HARRISON AND ASSOCIATES
International Press Centre,
Shoe Lane
London EC4A 3JB
Contact: Alec Harrison
Specializes in non-fiction works ranging from the educational to the autobiographical.

A M HEATH AND COMPANY LIMITED
40-42 William IV Street
London WC2N 4DD
Contact: Mark Hamilton, Chairman and Managing Director
Interested in work of new and established writers. Handles theatre, films, television and sound broadcasting and accepts full-length and short MSS.

DAVID HIGHAM ASSOCIATES LIMITED
5-8 Lower John Street
Golden Square
London W1R 4HA
Contact: David Higham, Bruce Hunter, Jacqueline Korn, John Rush
Represents every kind of writer and provides authors with a complete service throughout the world. Deals with all rights.

HUGHES MASSIE LIMITED
31 Southampton Row
London WC1B 5HL
Contact: Edmund Cork, N E Cork, J E Lunn or P E Cork
Interested in theatre, films, television, sound broadcasting and translations. Full-length and short MSS.

INTERCONTINENTAL LITERARY AGENCY
10 Buckingham Street
London WC2
Contact: Anthony Gornall
Only handles translation rights on behalf of partners in London and New York.

INTERNATIONAL COPYRIGHT BUREAU LIMITED
26 Charing Cross Road
London WC2H 0DG
Specializes in radio and television plays, films and fiction books.

INTERNATIONAL CREATIVE MANAGEMENT LTD
22 Grafton Street
London W1
Contact: Laurence Evans

PETER JANSON-SMITH LIMITED
31 Newington Green
London N16 9PU
See Campbell Thomson & McLaughlin Ltd. of which it is a subsidiary.

JOHN JOHNSON
Clerkenwell House
45-47 Clerkenwell Green
London EC1R 0HT
Contact: Andrew Hewson or Anna Cooper
Handles plays, television and radio scripts and poetry. Does not handle journalism nor unsolicited articles for the press. Particularly interested in educational and school textbooks and the work of new writers.

IRENE JOSEPHY
35 Craven Street
Strand
London WC2N 5NG

CHARLES LAVELL LIMITED
176 Wardour Street
London W1V 3AA
Contact: Carl or Kay Routledge
No specialities.

LE DAIN MANAGEMENT
92 North Road
Highgate
London N6 4AA
Contact: Yvonne Le Dain
Handles plays for theatre, film, television and sound broadcasting.

HOPE LERESCHE & SAYLE
11 Jubilee Place
London SW3 3TE
Contact: Tessa Sayle, Drama: Dawn Arnall
Handles full-length fiction and non-fiction MSS plays, films, television and sound broadcasting.

LLOYD-GEORGE AND COWARD
20 Richmond Crescent
London N1
Contact: B G Coward
Does not handle plays, poetry, science or technical books.

LONDON INDEPENDENT BOOKS LIMITED
1A Montagu Mews North
London W1H 1AJ
Contact: Sydney Box, Carolyn Whitaker or Patrick Whitaker
Does not handle children's books.

LONDON MANAGEMENT
235-241 Regent Street
London W1A 2JT
Contact: Herbert van Thal
Handles all MSS except poetry.

MACNAUGHTON LOWE REPRESENTA-TION LTD.
194 Old Brompton Road
London SW5 0AS
Contact: Robin Lowe or Patricia MacNaughton
Confines activities to dramatists in all media. Handles film, TV and stage rights but not concerned with publishing rights.

BLANCHE MARVIN
21A St John's Wood High Street
London NW8
Theatre, film, T.V., radio, books, video.

P B MAYER
Literary Agency Department
37A Church Road
Wimbledon
London SW19 5DQ
Acts as a literary agent between publishers not as an independent agent for authors.

MAURICE MICHAEL
Partridge Green
Horsham
Sussex
Contact: M A Michael or P K Michael
Scandinavian, Polish, German and French language books.

RICHARD MILNE LIMITED
28 Makepeace Avenue
Highgate
London N6
Contact: R M Sharples or K N Sharples
Handles film scripts, television and stage plays as well as a limited amount of book MSS.

WILLIAM MORRIS AGENCY (UK) LIMITED
147-149 Wardour Street
London W1
Contact: Robert W Shapiro
Interested in theatre, film and television scripts.

DEBORAH OWEN LIMITED
78 Narrow Street
Limehouse
London E14 8BP
Contact: Deborah Owen
Does not handle plays.

MARK PATERSON & ASSOCIATES
11-12 West Stockwell Street
Colchester CO1 1BN
Specializes in psychological and psychiatric books as well as children's books. Does not accept short stories or articles.

THE PENMAN LITERARY AGENCY
175 Pall Mall
Leigh-on-Sea
Essex SS9 1RE
Contact: Leonard G Stubbs, FRSA
Handles full-length MSS, novels, theatre, films, television and sound broadcasting.

A D PETERS AND COMPANY LIMITED
10 Buckingham Street
London WC2N 6BU
Contact: Michael Sissons, Anthony Jones or Pat Kavanagh
Represents novelists, writers for film, television and radio, all categories of general non-fiction and academic authors. No children's books or foreign language material.

LAURENCE POLLINGER LIMITED
18 Maddox Street
Mayfair
London W1R 0EU
Contact: Gerald J Pollinger, Margaret Pepper, Juliet Burton
Does not handle original film stories, poetry, freelance journalistic articles or children's books.

MURRAY POLLINGER
4 Garrick Street
London WC2 9BH
Contact: Murray Pollinger
Does not handle poetry, plays, journalism technical or academic books.
Progressive Management
11 Blenheim Street
London W1Y 0LG
Contact: Neil Landor or Diane Landor.

RADALA AND ASSOCIATES
17 Avenue Mansions
Finchley Road
London NW3 7AX
Contact: Richard Gollner or Istvan Siklos
Mainly represent East European writers.

MARGARET RAMSAY LIMITED
14A Goodwin's Court
St Martin's Lane
London WC2N 4LL
Contact: Margaret Ramsay
Represents writers for theatre, television films and radio only.

DEBORAH ROGERS LIMITED
5-11 Mortimer Street
London W1N 7RH
Contact: Deborah Rogers, Ann Warnford-Davis or Patricia White
Accepts all types of MSS.

KAY ROUTLEDGE ASSOCIATES
176 Wardour Street
London W1V 3AA
Contact: Mrs. Kay Routledge
Handles fiction written by professional women writers.

PATRICK SEALE BOOKS LIMITED
2 Motcomb Street
Belgrave Square
London SW1X 8JU
Contact: Patrick Seale, Jane Blackstock or Mary Bruton

Handles biography, memoirs, general non-fiction, politics, crafts, art and general fiction.

ANTHONY SHEIL ASSOCIATES LIMITED
2-3 Morwell Street
London WC1B 3AR
Contact: Anthony Sheil, Giles Gordon or Gill Coleridge
Interested in all types of MSS.

RICHARD SCOTT SIMON LIMITED
32 College Cross
London N1 1PR
Contact: Richard Scott Simon
Does not handle plays, poetry, children's and technical books.

SPOKESMEN
1 Craven Hill
London W2 3EP
Contact: Sheila Lemon, Peter Murphy or Richard Odgers
Represents playwrights film and television script writers and directors.

ABNER STEIN
43 Albany Mansions
Albert Bridge Road
London SW11 4PG
Contact: Abner Stein
Will consider any type of MS.

THE STRATHMORE LITERARY AGENCY
145 Park Road
London NW8
No specialities.

UNITED WRITERS
Trevail Mill
Zennor
St. Ives
Cornwall
Contact: Sydney Sheppard
Handles fiction, non-fiction, romantic fiction and serial stories for women's magazines.

HARVEY UNNA AND STEPHEN DURBRIDGE LTD.
14 Beaumont Mews
Marylebone High Street
London W1N 4HE
Contact: Harvey Unna, Stephen Durbridge or Nina Froud
Specializes in dramatic works for all media but also handles book MSS.

DR. JAN VAN LOEWEN LIMITED
81-83 Shaftesbury Avenue
London W1V 8BX
Contact: Dr. Jan Van Loewen, Michael Imison, Elisabeth Van Loewen, Katherine Gould
Handles full-length fiction and general MSS theatre, films, television and sound broadcasting.

LORNA VESTEY
33 Dryburgh
London SW15
Contact: Mrs. Lorna Vestey
Deals with full-length works of all sorts including fiction, non-fiction, children's books, drama and poetry.

MARGERY VOSPER LIMITED
Suite 8, 26 Charing Cross Road
London WC2H 0DG
Specializes in plays and film scripts as well as material for sound broadcasting and television.

WALKER LITERARY AGENCY
199 Hampermill Lane
Oxhey
Watford
Hertfordshire WD1 4PJ
Contact: Samuel Walker or Emily Kathleen Walker
Interested in literary works of all kinds with the exception of short topical articles, poetry and stories for juveniles.

J C WALLS LITERARY SERVICE
37 Henley Grove
Henleaze
Bristol BS9 4EQ
Contact: J C Walls
Interested in all types of book length material for criticism, revision and market advice.

A P WATT AND SON
26/28 Bedford Row
London WC1R 4HL
Contact: Hilary Rubinstein
Interested in all types of full-length MSS except plays, short stories or poetry.

WINANT TOWERS LIMITED
14 Clifford's Inn
London EC4A 1DA
Contact: Ursula R Winant
Does not handle plays.

CHARLOTTE WOLFERS
3 Regent Square
London WCL

U.S.A. AGENTS

ACKERMAN SCI-FI AGENCY
2495 Glendower Avenue
Hollywood
California 90027
USA
Contact: Forrest J Ackerman
Specializes in science fiction and mystery.

BRET ADAMS LIMITED
36 East 61st Street
New York
NY 10021
USA

Contact: Mr. Charles Hunt, Head of Literary Department
A full service agency handling all aspects of writing.

ADAMS, RAY & ROSENBERG
9200 Sunset Boulevard
Penthouse 25
Los Angeles
CA 90069
USA
Contact: Mr. Rick Ray
Represents writers, producers and directors, plus the works of a great many novelists and playwrights in the motion picture and television industries.

MAXWELL ALEY ASSOCIATES
145 East 35th Street
New York
NY 10016
USA
Contact: Mrs. Ruth Aley

AMERICAN PLAY COMPANY INCORPORATED
19 W 44th Street
New York
NY 10036
USA
Contact: Sheldon Abend, President

AM-RUS LITERARY AGENCY
25 West 43rd Street
New York
NY 10036
USA
Contact: Leah Siegel
Represents Soviet authors in the USA including writers of children's and adults' books, fiction, non-fiction as well as dramatists.

AUTHOR AID ASSOCIATES
340 E 52nd Street
New York
NY 10022
USA

AUTHORS & DRAMATISTS AGENCY INC.
116 W 72nd Street
Suite 15A
New York
NY 10023
USA

JULIAN BACH LITERARY AGENCY INC.
747 Third Avenue
New York
NY 10017
USA
Contact: Miss Wendy Weil

VIRGINIA BARBER
44 Greenwich Avenue
New York

NY 10011
USA

SCOTT BARTLETT ASSOCIATES
3 East 65th Street
New York
NY 10021
USA

MAXIMILIAN BECKER
115 East 82nd Street
New York
NY 10028
USA

BILL BERGER ASSOCIATES INC.
444 E 58th Street
New York
NY 10022
USA

LOIS BERMAN
250 W 57th Street
New York
NY 10019
USA

BLASSINGAME, MCCAULEY & WOOD
60 East 42nd Street
New York
NY 10017
USA

BLOOM, BECKETT, LEVY & SHORR
8816 Burton-Way
Beverly Hills
CA 90211
USA
Contact: Mel Bloom

GEORGES BORCHARDT INC.
136 E 57th Street
New York
NY 10022
USA
Contact: Georges Borchardt
Represent both fiction and non-fiction writers, only take on new clients recommended by authors already represented by the agency. Unsolicited MSS not considered.

BRANDT AND BRANDT
1501 Broadway
New York
NY 10036
USA

HELEN BRANN AGENCY
14 Sutton Place
New York
NY 10022
USA

JOHN BROCKMAN ASSOCIATES
200 W 57th Street
New York

NY 10016
USA

CURTIS BROWN LIMITED
575 Madison Avenue
New York
NY 10022
USA
Contact: Perry H Knowlton, Miss Martha Winston or Miss Emilie Jacobson

JAMES BROWN ASSOCIATES INC.
25 W 43rd Street
New York
NY 10036
USA
Contact: James Oliver Brown, David Stewart Hull, John Ware
Do not represent poetry, plays, screenplays, articles, short stories or juvenile books unless they are written by long-standing clients with published books to their credit.

NED BROWN INCORPORATED
407 North Maple Drive
Box 5020
Beverly Hills
CA 90210
USA
Contact: Ned Brown
Literary and Dramatic Agent NY Office: Lorna Brown, PO Box 2082 Grand Central Station, New York, NY 10017, USA

JANE JORDAN BROWNE MULTI MEDIA PRODUCT DEVELOPMENT INC.
410 S Michigan Avenue
Suite 724
Chicago
IL 60605
USA

BRUNNER/MAZEL
19 Union Square West
New York
NY 10003
USA

KNOX BURGER ASSOCIATES LIMITED
39½ Washington Square South
New York
NY 10012
USA
Contact: Knox Burger

SHIRLEY BURKE, LITERARY REPRESEN-TATIVE
370 East 76th Street
Suite B 704
New York
NY 10021
USA
Contact: Miss Shirley Burke
Interested in fiction and non-fiction, in MS only. Query first. Enclose s.a.e. No dramatists, writers of children's stories.

RUTH CANTOR
156 Fifth Avenue
New York
NY 10010
USA
Contact: Ruth Cantor
Specialize in children's books but also handles general trade books, fiction and non-fiction, on the adult level. Not interested however in plays, screenplays, TV scripts, poetry, magazine material, articles or short stories.

COLLIER ASSOCIATES
280 Madison Avenue
New York
NY 10016
USA
Contact: Lisa Collier
Handles general fiction and non-fiction books. No screen plays, poetry or short stories.

THE COLLINS AGENCY
41 Sunswick Lane
Westhampton Beach
New York
NY 11978
USA
Contact: Thomas P Collins
Handles fiction and non-fiction books as well as plays, films and television material.

CRITICS ASSOCIATED
4457 Straight Line Pike
Richmond
IN 47374
USA
Contact: Joseph E Longstreth

RICHARD CURTIS
156 E 52 Street
New York
NY 10022
USA

JOHN CUSHMAN ASSOCIATES INCOR-PORATED
25 West 43rd Street
New York
NY 10036
USA
Contact: John Cushman or Jane W. Wilson

JOAN DAVES LITERARY AGENCY
59 E 54th Street
New York
NY 10022
USA
Contact: Joan Daves or Ruth Soika
Trade books, fiction and non-fiction.

MISS ANITA DIAMANT
51 East 42nd Street
New York
NY 10017
USA
Handles fiction and non-fiction books, TV, films.

CANDIDA DONADIO AND ASSOCIATES INC.
111 West 57th Street
New York
NY 10019
USA
Contact: Miss Candida Donadio

ANN ELMO AGENCY INCORPORATED
60E 42nd Street
New York
NY 10017
USA
Contact: Ann Elmo
Handles all types of commercial writing for the adult and juvenile markets, fiction and non-fiction in all lengths. Also covers the play, television and movie markets.

HANNS FISCHER, LITERARY AGENCY
2332 West Farwell Avenue
Chicago
IL 60659
USA

MISS FRIEDA FISHBEIN
353 West 57th Street
New York
NY 10019
USA
Contact: Ms. Janice Fishbein
Handles plays, books, screen plays and television scripts.

BARTHOLD FLES LITERARY AGENCY
507 Fifth Avenue
New York
NY 10017
USA
Contact: Miss Vikki Power
Interested in adult and juvenile fiction and non-fiction.

THE FOLEY AGENCY
34 East 38th Street
New York
NY 10016
USA
Contact: Joseph Foley, Joan Foley or Minnie Foley
Fiction and non-fiction books plus limited magazine material.

THE FOX CHASE AGENCY INCORPORATED
419 E 57th Street
New York
NY 10022
USA
Contact: A L Hart or J Hart

HAROLD FREEDMAN BRANDT AND BRANDT DRAMATIC DEPARTMENT, INCORPORATED
1501 Broadway
New York
NY 10036
USA

SAMUEL FRENCH INCORPORATED
25 West 45th Street
New York
NY 10036
USA
Authors' Agent, and sub-agent dealing with other agents. Play scripts, books on the theatre and all other related subjects.

JAY GARON-BROOKE ASSOCIATES INC.
415 Central Park West
New York
NY 10025
USA
Represented in England by Abner Stein
43 Albany Mansions
Albert Bridge Road
London SW11 4PG
UK
Contact: Jay Garon
Literary and dramatic agency.

MAX GARTENBERG
15 West 44th Street
New York
NY 10036
USA
Adult fiction and non-fiction. Write before submitting.

LARNEY GOODKIND
180 E 11 Street
New York
NY 1003
USA
Contact: Mrs. Karen Rose Goodkind

GRAHAM AGENCY
317 West 45th Street
New York
NY 10036
USA
Contact: Earl Graham
Represents dramatists almost exclusively.

SANFORD J GREENBURGER ASSOCIATES INC.
825 Third Avenue
New York
NY 10022
USA
Contact: Heidi Lange or Peter Skolnik

BLANCHE C GREGORY INC.
2 Tudor City Place
New York
NY 10017
USA

REECE HALSEY AGENCY
8733 Sunset Boulevard
Los Angeles
CA 90069
USA

MITCHELL J HAMILBURG AGENCY
292 S La Cienega Blvd.
Suite 212
Beverly Hills
CA 90211
USA

SHIRLEY HECTOR AND ASSOCIATES
29 West 46th Street
New York
NY 10036
USA
Contact: Roy Gilbert
Represents authors and publishers. No reading charge. Handles fiction and non-fiction including subsidiary rights.

HOLUB AND ASSOCIATES
5 Glen Oaks Avenue
Summit
NJ 07801
USA
Contact: William Holub
Specialize in religious material aimed at general and specialized (clergy and religious) audiences. No fiction or children's books.

ILA INTERNATIONAL LITERARY AGENCY
305 East 75th Street
New York
NY 10021
USA
Correspondence to Operating Headquarters
I 18015 Terzorio IM Italy
Contact: Tomas D W Friedmann or Miss Ingeborg Grundmann
Primarily works between publishers in the sale of foreign language rights, co-productions etc. Want only popular and best selling works, series of books rather than individual volumes. Prefer non-fiction to fiction.

INTERNATIONAL CREATIVE MANAGEMENT
40 W 57th Street
New York
NY 10019 and 8899 Beverly Boulevard
Los Angeles
CA 90048
USA
Literary and Dramatic Agents 775207.

INTERNATIONAL LITERARY AGENTS LIMITED
9255 Sunset Blvd.
Suite 501
Los Angeles
CA 90069
USA
Contact: Ms. Peri Winkler, President

ALEX JACKINSON
55 West 42nd Street
New York
NY 10036
USA

VIRGINIA KIDD LITERARY AGENTS
538 E Harford Street
Milford
PA 18337
USA

VIRGINIA KIDD WITH JAMES ALLEN AND BETH BLISH LITERARY AGENTS
538 E Harford ST.
Milford
PA 18337
USA
1 Sheridan Square, New York, NY 10014
Contact: Virginia Kidd or James Allen
Specializes in speculative fiction but handles all the popular genres as well as mainstream fiction and non-fiction. Has affiliates in countries world-wide.

BERTHA KLAUSNER INTERNATIONAL LITERARY AGENCY INC.
71 Park Avenue
New York
NY 10016
USA
Contact: Bertha Klausner
Handles adult and juvenile fiction and non-finction books, plays, television and motion picture scripts.

LUCY KROLL AGENCY
390 West End Avenue
New York
NY 10024
USA
Contact: Lucy Kroll/Kathe Telingator
Represents writers of full-length fiction, non-fiction and drama. Does not accept unsolicited MSS and does not handle short stories, poetry, children's literature or other specialized work.

PHOEBE LARMORE
44 Greenwich Avenue
New York
NY 10011
USA

MICHAEL LARSEN/ELIZABETH POMADA LITERARY AGENTS
1029 Jones St.
San Francisco
CA 94109
USA
Contact: Elizabeth Pomada
Handles adult and juvenile, fiction and non-fiction, trade books.

IRVING PAUL LAZAR
211 South Beverly Drive
Beverly Drive
Beverly Hills
CA 90212
USA
1 66th Street
New York

NY 10021
Contact: Irving Lazar
Represents writers for theatre and motion pictures.

LENNIGER LITERARY AGENCY INC.
437 Fifth Avenue
New York
NY 10016
USA
Contact: August Lenniger or Grace Lenniger
Handles teenage and juvenile fiction and non-fiction books and magazine articles.

ROBERT LESCHER
155 East 71st Street
New York
NY 10021
USA
Contact: Ms. Susan Lescher

PATRICIA LEWIS/INGRID HALLEN
450 Seventh Avenue
Room 602
New York
NY 10001
USA

ROBERT LEWIS
500 Fifth Avenue
New York
NY 10036
USA

THE STERLING LORD AGENCY INC.
660 Madison Avenue
New York
NY 10021
USA
Contact: Sterling Lord or Helen Brann

DONALD MACCAMPBELL INC.
12 East 41st Street
New York
NY 10017
USA
Contact: Donald MacCampbell, President, Kathleen MacCampbell, Vice President or Maureen Moran, Editor
Handles adult books only.

GERARD MCCAULEY AGENCY INC.
209 56th St. (I-E) New York
NY 10022
USA
Contact: Gerard F McCauley
Specializes in non-fiction but does not handle juveniles.

KIRBY MCCAULEY
60 E 42nd St.
New York
NY 10017
USA
Contact: Kirby McCauley

Handles all types of commercial writing but special emphasis on genre fiction (mysteries, science fiction fantasy), and biographies. Full length books only, unless by special arrangement.

MCINTOSH & OTIS INC.
475 Fifth Avenue
New York NY 10017
USA
Contact: Patricia Myrer.

MCINTOSH, MCKEE AND DODDS INC.
22 East 40th Street
New York
NY 10016
USA

JANET WILKENS MANUS
145 E 52nd Street
Suite 904
New York
NY 10022
USA

BETTY MARKS
176 East 77 Street
New York
NY 10021
USA
Handles adult and juvenile fiction and non-fiction books as well as magazine articles.

ELAINE MARKSON
44 Greenwich Avenue
New York
NY 10011
USA
Contact: Elaine Markson or Jeannette Kosauth.

MISS ELISABETH MARTON
96 Fifth Avenue
New York
NY 10011
USA
Contact: Mrs. Jo Ann Burbank.

HAROLD MATSON COMPANY INC.
276 Fifth Avenue
Suite 1105
New York
NY 10001
USA
Contact: Ben Camardi

TONI MENDEZ INC.
140 East 56th Street
New York
NY 10022
USA

SCOTT MEREDITH LITERARY AGENCY INC.
845 Third Avenue
New York

NY 10022
USA
Contact: Jonathan Silverman/William T Haas
Handles general fiction and non-fiction books
and magazines, juveniles, plays, TV scripts,
motion picture rights and properties.

MRS. TONI MILFORD
50 East 86th Street
New York
NY 10028
USA

ROBERT P MILLS LIMITED
156 East 52nd Street
New York
NY 10022
USA
Contact: Bob Mills
Handles a wide variety of general fiction and
non-fiction but does not represent dramatists.

HOWARD MORREPARK
444E 82nd Street
New York
NY 10028
USA
Book length material only.

WILLIAM MORRIS AGENCY
151 El Camino,
Beverly Hills
CA 90212
USA
435 North Michigan Avenue
Chicago
IL 60611
1350 Avenue of the Americas
New York
NY 10019
USA

HENRY MORRISON INC.
58 West 10th
New York
NY 10011. USA
Contact: Henry Morrison
Represents novelists and screenwriters.

MARVIN MOSS
9200 Sunset Boulevard
Suite 601
Los Angeles
CA 90069
USA
Contact: Marvin Moss
Mainly represents writers for the motion
picture and television industries.

CHARLES NEIGHBORS INC.
240 Waverly Place
New York
NY 10011
USA

B K NELSON LITERARY AGENCY
10 E 39th Street

New York
NY 10016
USA
Contact: Bonita K Nelson

ELLEN NEUWALD INC.
905 West End Avenue
New York
NY 10025
USA
Contact: Ellen Neuwald
Represents playwrights as well as fiction and
non-fiction writers.

HAROLD OBER ASSOCIATES INC.
40 East 49th Street
New York
NY 10017
USA
Contact: Dorothy Olding

DOROTHEA OPPENHEIMER
866 United Nations Plaza
New York
NY 10017
USA
Contact: Dorothea Oppenheimer
Represents writers of adult fiction and non-
fiction.

MISS EVELYN OPPENHEIMER
7929 Meadow Park Drive
Apt. 201
Dallas
TX 75230
USA
Handles fiction and non-fiction adult books.

OTTE COMPANY
9 Goden Street
Belmont
MA 02178
USA
Contact: June H & L David Otte

PARK AVENUE LITERARY AGENCY
See Collier Associates

RAY PEEKNER LITERARY AGENCY
2625 North 36th Street
Milwaukee
WI 53210
USA
Contact: Ray Puecher
Handles booklengths, fiction and non-fiction,
adult and juvenile. No poetry, plays, juvenile
picture books or unsolicited MSS.

MARJORIE PETERS AND PIERRE LONG
5744 South Harper Avenue
Chicago
IL 60637
USA
Contact: Pierre Long
Represents poets, short story writers, novel-
ists, playwrights and article/essay writers.

PHOENIX LITERARY AGENCY INC.
150 E 74th Street
New York
NY 10021
USA
Contact: Robert Dattila.

ARTHUR PINE ASSOCIATES INC.
1780 Broadway
New York
NY 10019
USA
Contact: Arthur Pine
General fiction and non-fiction books.

SIDNEY E PORCELAIN AGENCY
Box J
Rocky Hill
NJ 08553
USA
Fiction, non-fiction, and juvenile books, short stories and articles television plays. Query first with s.a.s.e.

PORTER, DIERKS & PORTER-LENT
215 W Ohio Street
Chicago
IL 60610
USA

AARON M PRIEST LITERARY AGENCY
15 E 40th Street
New York
NY 10016
USA

SUSAN ANN PROTTER
Suite 1408
110 West 40th Street
New York
NY 10018
USA
Contact: Susan Ann Protter
Handles writers of both fiction, and non-fiction for adults only also photojournalism.

**RAINES & RAINES AUTHORS'
REPRESENTATIVES**
475 Fifth Avenue
New York
NY 10017
USA
Contact: Joan or Theron Raines
Handle all fields.

PAUL R REYNOLDS INC.
12 E 41st Street
New York
NY 10017
USA

FLORA ROBERTS INC.
65 East 55th Street
New York
NY 10022
USA

MARIE RODELL-FRANCES COLLIN LITERARY AGENCY
156 E 52nd Street
Suite 605
New York
NY 10022
USA
Contact: John Meyer
No unsolicited MSS.

JANE ROTROSEN
318 E 51st Street
New York
NY 10022
USA
Contact: Don Cleary
Handles fiction and non-fiction books as well as material for television and motion pictures.

RUSSELL VOLKENING, INC.
551 Fifth Avenue
New York
NY 10017
USA
Contact: Timothy Seldes or Harriet Wasserman

GLORIA SAFIER INC.
667 Madison Avenue
New York
NY 10021
USA

JOHN SCHAFFNER LITERARY AGENCY
425 East 51st Street
New York
NY 10022
USA
Contact: John Schaffner or Victor Chapin
Handles fiction and non-fiction books as well as magazine material. Does not deal with dramatic material.

JANE SCHWENGER
Box 5992
Grand Central Station
New York
NY 10017
USA

RITA SCOTT INC./MARJE FIELDS
165 West 46th ST.
New York
NY 10036
USA
Contact: Ray Powers
Represents fiction and non-fiction book writers as well as juveniles.

SELIGMANN AND COLIER
280 Madison Avenue
New York
NY 10016
USA
Contact: James F Seligmann or Oscar Collier.

EVELYN SINGER AGENCY
P.O. Box 594
White Plains
New York
NY 10602
USA
Contact: Evelyn Singer
Represents adult and juvenile fiction and non-fiction. No poetry, plays, film or T.V. material.

ELYSE SOMMER INC.
Box E 962 Allen Lane
Woodmere
New York
NY 11598
USA
Specialises in non-fiction, how-to-do-it books.

PHILIP G SPITZER
111-25 76th Avenue
Forest Hills
New York
NY 11375
USA
Contact: Philip G Spitzer

RENEE SPODHEIM ASSOCIATES
698 West End Avenue
New York
NY 10025
USA
No specialities.

STEPPING STONE LITERARY AGENCY INC.
59 West 71st Street
New York Suite 9B
NY 10023
USA
Contact: S. J. FREYMANN

LARRY STERNIG LITERARY AGENCY
742 Robertson Street
Milwaukee
WI 53213
USA
Contact: Larry Sternig
Handles professional writers who turn out a wide variety of books, articles & short stories.

TONI STRASSMAN
130 East 18th Street 7-D
New York
NY 10003
USA
No new clients accepted.

GUNTHER STUHLMANN
PO Box 276
Becket
MA 01223
USA
Contact: Ms. Barbara Ward
Handles books, both fiction and non-fiction, juveniles, as well as all subsidiary rights to same, including foreign, motion picture and television. No plays, poetry or short fiction accepted.

H N SWANSON INC.
8523 Sunset Boulevard
Los Angeles
CA 90069
USA
Contact: B F Kamsler
Serves the motion picture and television industries. Represents dramatists, with main thrust being fiction, and authors for the magazine & general book market.

ROSLYN TARG LITERARY AGENCY INC.
250 West 57th Street
New York
NY 10019
USA

MADELINE E UNGER ASSOCIATES INC.
15 E 26th Street
New York
NY 10010
USA

J H VAN DAELE
225 East 57th Street
New York
NY 10022
USA
Contact: Jacqueline H Van Daele
Handles only psychiatrically orientated books, including all behavioural sciences aimed at the popular market. New clients obtained through recommendation only.

WALLACE, AND SHEIL INC.
177 E 70 Street
New York
NY 10021
USA

JAMES A WARREN ASSOCIATES
7317 Haskell Ave. Suite 108
Van Nuys
CA 91406
USA
Contact: James A Warren, Barbara Thorburn, Frank Bisignano.
Does not handle poetry.

A WATKINS INC.
77 Park Avenue
New York
NY 10016
USA
Contact: Armitage Watkins, Miss Peggy Caulfield, Mrs. Patricia Rochefort or Mrs. Gloria C Loomis.
Handles fiction, non-fiction and children's book properties.

W B AGENCY
575 Madison Avenue
New York

NY 10022
USA

LEW WEITZMAN AND ASSOCIATES
9171 Wilshire Boulevard Suite 427
Beverly Hills
CA 90210
USA
Contact: Lew Weitzman
Represents writers for the motion picture and
television industries.

WENDER AND ASSOCIATES INC.
30 East 60th Street Room 902
New York
NY 10022
USA
Contact: Phyllis B Wender

MARY YOST ASSOCIATES
75 E 55th Street
New York
NY 10022
USA
Contact: Miss Mary Yost

ZIEGLER ASSOCIATES INC.
9255 Sunset Boulevard Apt. 1222
Los Angeles
CA 90069
USA
Represents authors, writers, producers, and
directors.

AGENTS OTHER THAN U.K. OR U.S.A.

Argentina

INTERNATIONAL EDITORS COMPANY
Avenida Cabildo 1156
Buenos Aires

LAWRENCE SMITH
Avenida de los Incas 3110
Buenos Aires 1426
Argentine Republic
World Book, Serial and Stage Rights in
Spanish and Portuguese.

Australia

DOROTHY BLEWETT ASSOCIATES
50 View Hill Crescent,
Eltham
Victoria 3095

CURTIS BROWN (AUSTRALIA) PTY. LTD.
86 William Street
Paddington
Sydney
New South Wales 2021

Contact: Tim Curnow
Handles book-length fiction, non-fiction and
educational works, stage plays, radio, TV and
film scripts and short stories.

CHARTER BOOKS PTY. LTD
Foveaux House
63 Foveaux Street
Surry Hills
New South Wales 2101
Contact: Bruce Semler, Malcolm Newel or
Donald McLean
Especially interested in educational books and
information type books including historical,
natural science, geographical and political.
Documentary-fiction also welcomed.

HAMPTON PRESS FEATURES SYNDICATE
5 Dick Street
Henley
New South Wales 2111

YAFFA SYNDICATE PTY. LTD
432-436 Elizabeth Street
Surry Hills
New South Wales 2020

Austria

COPRO INTERNATIONAL
Verlagsgesellschaft mbH
A-1134 Vienna
Biraghigasse 30

Belgium

AGENCE BELGE DES GRANDS EDITIONS
110-116 Ave. Louise B 1050 Brussels

A VAN HAGELAND LITERARY AGENCY
Blutsdelle 10
B 1641 Alsemberg
Contact: Albert van Hageland
Specialities include science fiction, supernatural, horror and anthologies. Features and
magazine material not requested. Handles
international transactions and all kinds of
printed popular literature for Dutch language
rights.

INTERNATIONAL LITERAIR AGENTSCHAP
Blankenbergestraat 23
9000 Gent
Contact: Dr. Hugo Tomme

Brazil

DR. J E BLOCH
Rua Oscar Freire 416

Ap. 83
01426 Sao Paulo
Contact: Dr. J E Block or Mrs. Karin Schindler
Interested in all Brazilian authors' works
Portuguese rights for the world or for Brazil
only.

Bulgaria

JUSAUTOR-COPYRIGHT AGENCY
7 Levski St.
Sofia
The agency promotes literary, dramatic, musical, scientific and other works by Bulgarian authors, supplies information, grants options, and in the capacity of the exclusive representative of the Bulgarian authors negotiates and makes the contracts with foreign publishers and other foreign users of their works. The agency acts as an intermediary between foreign authors, publishers and agencies and Bulgarian users of their works.
Contact: Director General Mrs. Y Markova

Czechoslovakia

DILIA-THEATRICAL AND LITERARY AGENCY
Vysehradska 28
PO Box 34
12824 Prague 2
Contact: Mr. Robert Jurak
Activity is limited to the Czech Socialist Republic. Protects the authors rights of all dramatic and other works, of theatre, radio and film and television plays, and works connected with them, including their musical and graphic parts.

LITA-SLOVENSKA LITERARNA AGENTURA
ulica Cs Armady 37/111 894 20 Bratislava
Contact: Mr. Matej András
Represents all authors living in Slovakia including dramatists, writers of children's books, non-fiction and fiction writers, authors of musico-dramatic works etc.

Denmark

R P ADAM
Brede Bovej 31 DK 2800 Lyngby
Copenhagen.

A/S BOOKMAN
12 Fiolstraede
DK 1171 Copenhagen K
Contact: Ib. H. Lauritzen
Handles British, American, French and Italian authors rights in Scandinavia.

GEORG JUELNER
Smøgen 1
DK 3480
Fredensburg

EDITH KILERICH
Fiolstraede 12
DK 1171 Copenhagen K

PREBEN KLEIN
PO Box 50
DK 3200
Helsinge

ALBRECHT LEONHARDT APS LITERARY AGENCY
35 Studiestraede
DK 1455 Copenhagen K

SVEND MONDRUP INTERNATIONAL LITERARY AGENCY
Holbegsgade 20
DK 1057 Copenhagen K

NORDISKA TEATER
Førlaget/Edition Wilhelm Hansen
Gothersgade 9-11
DK 1123 Copenhagen K
Play agents representing authors of plays, children's plays, musicals for stage, radio and TV.

CARL STRAKOSCH AND OLAF NORDGREEN
Nyhavn 5
DK 1051 Copenhagen K

Finland

WERNER SODERSTROM
Osakeyhtio (WSOY)
Pl. 222 Bulevardi 12
SF-00121 Helsinki

France

AGENCE HOFFMAN
77 Boulevard Saint-Michel
75005 Paris
Contact: Boris or Georges Hoffman or Madame Merrily de Douhet
Represents American, British and German agents and publishers for French volume translation sales, television (French language) and motion picture contracts, and negotiations worldwide translation rights for a limited number of authors represented directly by the agency.

ALICE BAYON
113 Boulevard Saint-Germain
Paris

JEAN-PIERRE BOSCQ
65 rue de Fauborg Saint-Honoré
75008 Paris

WILLIAM ASPENWALL BRADLEY
18 Quai de Béthune
Paris 4
Contact: Mrs. W A Bradley

BUREAU LITTERAIRE INTERNATIONAL MARGUERITE SCIALTIEL
14 Rue Chanoinesse
75004 Paris
Contact: Geneviève Ulmann
Represents writers of all sorts of books as well as theatrical works.

MME FRANÇOISE GERMAIN
8 Rue de la Paix
75002 Paris

MADAME MICHELLE LAPAUTRE
6 rue Jean Carriers
75007 Paris
Contact: Michelle Lepautre
Represents American, English and Israeli publishers and agents for the sale of French translation rights.

MCKEE AND MOUCHE
16 rue du Regard
75006 Paris
Contact: Douglas McKee or Madame Donine Mouche
Handles only French translation rights in material published in the USA or in the UK.

IRMGARD MATTHIAS-PAUL ESTIENNE AGENTS LITTÉRAIRES
27 rue de Dragon
75006 Paris

LA NOUVELLE AGENCE
7 rue Corneille
75006 Paris
Contact: Mme. Mary Kling

JANINE QUET BUREAU LITTÉRAIRE
20 rue de la Michodière
75002 Paris

AGENCE STRASSOVA
4 rue Git-le-Coeur
75006 Paris
Contact: Greta Strassova
No restrictions.

LE TELESCOPE, AGENCE LITTÉRAIRE
10 rue Mayet
75006 Paris

MME. ELLEN WRIGHT
20 rue Jacob
75006 Paris
French Rights Representative.

Germany

BÜRÖ FÜR URHEBERRECHTE
DDR 108 Berlin
Clara Zetkinstr. 105
Handles all agreements with individuals and firms outside the DDR.

AGENCE HOFFMAN
D 8000 München 40 Seestrasse 6
Contact: Frau Dagmar Henne
Handles negotiations of German translation rights.

WINFRIED BLUTH LITERARY AGENCY
5630 Remscheid
Augustinusstr. 43

BUCHAGENTUR MUNCHEN
Maria-Eich-Str. 54b
8032 Gräfelfing
Contact: Dr. Hanns Martin Elster

FRALIT
D2000 Hamburg 13, Brahmsallee 29/1
Contact: Fritz Kurt Albrecht
Handles all publishing material except economics, law, medicine and technical MSS

GUSTAV GREVE LITERARISCHE AGENTUR
1000 Berlin 12
Fasanenstr. 15

GEISENHEYNER AND CRONE, INTERNATIONAL LITERARY AGENTS
D 7000 Stuttgart 1
Gymnasiumstrasse 31B
Handles German and foreign literary rights.

DAGMAR HENNE
8000 Munich 40
Seestr. 6

HANS HERMANN HAGEDORN
Erikastr. 142
2000 Hamburg 20

INTERLITA-LITERATURAGENTUR PETER VILIMEK GmbH
15 Postf. 150210
Pavlsborner Str. 90
1000 Berlin 31
Contact: Peter Vilimek

INTERNATIONAL LITERARY AGENCY
D 2000 Hamburg 39
Zesenstr. 16

KARL LUDWIG LEONHARDT
Literarische Agentur
An der Alster 22
2000 Hamburg 1

ROSE M MEERVEIN
D 1000 Berlin 33
Reuterpfad 6-8

MÜNCHNER VERLAGSBÜRO HORST HO-
DEMACHER-AXEL POLDNER
8000 Munich 19
Barellistrasse 7

AXEL POLDNER
D 8000 Munich 21
Rauheckstr. 11

THOMAS SCHLUCK LITERARY AGENCY
Hinter der Worth 12
D 3008 Garbsen 9

WILFRIED TH. SIEBER
D 4973 Viotho 2
Im Konigsfeld 5
Interested in science fiction and speculative
literature.

SKANDINAVIA VERLAG
D 1000 Berlin 12
Knesebeckstrasse 100
Contact: Marianne Weno or Michael Günther
Represents most of the modern Scandinavian
dramatists for the German speaking countries.

HERTA WEBER-STUMFOHL
Literarisches Büro
Waldpromenade 32
8035 Gauting
Contact: Herta Weber-Stumfohl
Translates and handles translations from Swe-
dish into German.

Greece

ANGLO-HELLENIC AGENCY
5 Koumpari Str.
Kolonaki Square
Athens 138
Represents Greek Authors

Hungary

ARTISJUS, AGENCY FOR LITERATURE,
THEATRE AND MUSIC
Vörösmartg ter 1
Postafiok 67
H 1364 Budapest
Contact: Mrs. Vera Acs or Mrs. Sarolta Révész.
Represents all authors and copyright owners
resident in Hungary, acts as intermediary in
the conclusion of agreements between foreign
copyright holders and Hungarian publishers.

Iceland

SVEINBJÖRN JONSSON
PO Box 438
Reykjavik

Handles general fiction and non-fiction books,
and magazines, plays, radio and TV scripts.

India

KUNNUPARAMPIL P PUNNOOSE
Jaffe Publishing Management Service
Kurichy 686549
Contact: Kunnuparampil P Punnoose, Kot-
tayam Dist., India.

Israel

BAR-DAVID LITERARY AGENCY
PO Box 1104
Tel Aviv
Contact: Abraham Mor
Represents authors, publishers and agents in
Israel from all over the world.

BOOK PUBLISHERS ASSOCIATION OF
ISRAEL
International Promotion and Literary Rights
Dept.
29 Carlebach Street PO Box 20123
Tel Aviv

MOADIM-PLAY PUBLISHERS AND LITER-
ARY AGENTS
144 Hayarkon Street
63 451 Tel Aviv
Contact: Manfred Geis
Represents almost all foreign plays translated
into Hebrew and produced by Israeli theatres.
Specializes in guarding the performing rights
of Israeli and foreign plays vis a vis producers
and theatres abroad and the Israeli theatres
respectively.

Italy

AGENZIA LETTERARIA INTERNAZIONALE
Via Manzoni 41
1-20121 Milan

MARIA-PIA D'ARBORIO
Viale Tiziano 5
Rome

URSULA CAPUTO
Via Pisacane 25, 1-20129 Milan

DIAS AGENZIA LETTERARIA
Via Nicotera 7
00195 Rome

EULAMA SA
Europäisch-Lateinamerikanische Verlagsa-
gentur, Via Torino 135
1-00184 Rome

Contact: Lic. phil. Harald Kahnemann, Director

Primarily a publishers' agency but does handle the rights of a few authors. Open to all fields of literary works and handles all language areas of the world with a particular stress in Europe and Latin America.

WILLIAM MORRIS ORGANIZATION SPA
Via Nomentana 60
1-00161 Rome

NATOLI AND STEFAN LITERARY AGENCY
Galleria Buenos Aires 14
1-20124 Milan

RIZZOLI
via Rizzoli 2
1-20132 Milan.

Japan

ORION PRESS INTERNATIONAL LITERARY AGENCY
1-55 Kanda-Jimbocho
Chiyoda-ku Tokyo 101
Contact: Jintaro Takano.

CHARLES E TUTTLE COMPANY INC.
1-2-6 Suido
Bunkyo-ku
Tokyo 112

Kenya

AFRICAN EDUCATIONAL REPRESEN-TATIVES
PO Box 20521
Nairobi.

Netherlands

GRETA BAARS-JELGERSMA AUTEURS-BUREAU
Den Heuvel 73 6881 VD Velp GLD
Specialities: International Co-printing of illustrated books, translations from Scandinavian languages, book production.

ALEXANDER GANS LITERAIR AGENT
Witte de Withstraat 20
Noordwijk Aan Zee
Contact: Alexander Gans
Represents mainly English and American literary agents as well as Belgium and Dutch rights.

INTERNATIONAL BUREAU VOOR AU-TEURSRECHT BV
Goudestein 1
2352 JX Leiderdorp
Contact: Hans Keuls

INTERNATIONAL LITERATUUR BUREAU
Koninginneweg 2A
1217 KW Hilversum
Contact: Hein or Menno Kohn
Specializes in placing authors' rights in Holland and throughout the world.

PRINS AND PRINS LITERARY AGENTS
de Lairessestraat 6
PO Box 5400 Amsterdam 1007

Norway

EMBLA LITERARY AGENCY -now Pat Shaw Associates
Fredbosvel 61
N 1370 Asker
Handles fiction, non-fiction children's books, theatre, radio and television.

CARLOTA FRAHM LITERARY AGENCY
Valkyriegaten M
Postboks 5385
Majorstva
Oslo 3
Contact: Carlota Frahm or Suzanne Palme.

HANNA-KIRSTI KOCH LITERARY AGENCY
POB 3043
Oslo 2
Contact: Mr Eilif Koch
All round literary agent handling books, articles and short stories for weekly magazines.

Poland

AGENCJA AUTORSKA sp.z.o.o.
ul Hipoteczna 2
00-950 Warsaw
Contact: Wladyslaw Jakubowski, Manager
Polish copyrights, foreign contracts, information.

Portugal

ILIDIO DA FONSECA MATOS
Rue De S Bernardo 68-3
Lisbon 2
Handles the book rights of properties received from publishers and literary agents in USA and UK.

Singapore

CHOPMEN ENTERPRISES
428-29 Katong Shopping Centre (4th Floor)
Singapore 15.

South Africa

THE INTERNATIONAL PRESS AGENCY
(Pty) Ltd.
PO Box 682
Cape Town 8000
Contact: Ursula A Barnett
London Office: Mrs. Shelley Power
International Press Centre
Shoe Lane
London
Sub-agents for British and American literary
agents.

Spain

A.C.E.R.
Bolonia 5
Madrid 28
Contact: Mr. Marcel Laignoux
Represents mainly German and French Publishers for the exclusive handling of Spanish
and Portuguese world rights of all books
published by them in the field of documents,
essays, novels, non-fiction, psychology, sociology, human sciences and theology.

AGENCIE LITERARIA CARMEN BALCELLA
Diagonal 580
Barcelona 21
Contact: Magdalena Oliver.

**ANDRES DE KRAMER, AGENCIA LITER-
ARIA**
Castello 30
Madrid 1

INTERNATIONAL EDITIONS, S.A.
Rambla de Cataluna 39
Barcelona 7

**JOSÉ MOYA AND UTE KÖRNER DE MOYA-
LITERARY AGENCY**
Ronda Guinardo 32 5° 5a
Barcelona 08025
Contact: José Moya or Ute Körner de Moya
Represents foreign publishers, agents and
authors for the Spanish speaking territory and
Spanish authors throughout the world.

**UNIVERSITAS-AGENCIA LITERARIA JU-
LIO F YANEZ**
c/o Marco Aurelio, 5, 5°, 3a
Barcelona 6
Contact: Mr. or Mrs. J F Yanez
Particularly devoted to fiction and non-fiction
subjects such as biographies, history, topical
features, technology, sociology, etc.

Sweden

ARLECCHINO TEATERFÖRLAG
Gränsvägen 14
S-131 71 Nacka.

D RICHARD BOWEN
Post Box 30037
S-200 61 Malmo 30
Contact: D Richard Bowen
Agent for translations and licensed editions of
books. Handles titles translated into European
languages in particular.

GÖSTA DAHL AND SON AB
Aladdinsvägen 145-161 38 Bromma.

LENA I GEDIN
Linnegatan 38
114 47 Stockholm.

**FOLMER HANSEN, BUREAU LITTERAIRE
INTERNATIONAL**
Gerd Widestedt-Ericsson
Lundag 4
171 63 Solna
Theatre Agent.

NORDISKA
Teaterförlaget/Edition Wilhelm Hansen
Norrlandsgatan 16
111 43 Stockholm
Play agents representing authors of plays,
children's plays and musicals for the stage,
radio and television.

LENNART SANE AGENCY
Hollanderplan 9
S-292 00 Karlshama
Contact: Lennart Sane
Represents Scandinavian authors worldwide
and a great number of American, British and
French authors, agents and publishers in
Scandinavia, Germany and Holland. Interest-
ed in fiction, non-fiction as well as children's
books.

TEATERFÖRLAG ARVID ENGLIND AB
Karlavägen 56
Box 5124
102 43 Stockholm 5
Contact: Christer Englind
Represents drama writers, both domestic and
foreign.

Switzerland

GESELLSCHAFT FÜR VERLAGSWERTE
GmbH
Hafenstr. 38, 8380 Kreuzlingen.

DR. RUTH LIEPMAN
Maienburgweg 23
8044 Zürich.

LINDER AG
Postfach
8039 Zürich
Does not represent authors directly.

LITPRESS
Rudlf Streit and Company
Amtshausgasschen 3
3011 Bern

MOHRBOOKS
Klosbachstrasse 110
8030 Zürich
Contact: Rainer Heumann
No specialities.

NEUE PRESSE AGENTUR (NPA)
Haus am Herterberg
Haldenstrasse 5
CH-8500
Frauenfeld-Herten
Contact: René Marti
Handles novels, light entertainment and exclusive articles including popular scientific works, medical articles and reports.

Turkey

NURCHIHAN KESIM LITERARY AGENCY
Head Office Basinköy
Ahmet Ihsan Blok 6
Istanbul
Branch Office Nuruosmaniye Caddesi No. 8/3
Cagaloglu
Istanbul
Handles books, newspaper serials, part works, syndicated material, merchandising rights, cartoons, strips. Represents American, English, German authors and companies.

HÜR YAYIN VE TICARET
Gemai Nadir Sokak 7
Cagaloglu
Istanbul

ONK COPYRIGHT AGENCY
POB 983
Istanbul
Contact: Osman N Karaca
Only agency which represents Turkish writers. Official representative of the Turkish Playwrights' Society. Deals with books, serials, plays, TV programmes as the representative of many foreign firms.

USSR

THE COPYRIGHT AGENCY OF THE USSR/ VAAP
6a Bolshaya Bronnaya
K-104 Moscow 103104
Contact: B Pankin, Chairman of the Board or Y Zharov, Vice-Chairman
Ensures the protection of the rights of Soviet and foreign authors in scientific, literary and artistic works when they are used in the territory of the USSR, and the rights of Soviet authors in their works when they are used abroad.

Yugoslavia

JUGOSLOVENSKA AUTORSKA AGENCIJA
Majke Jevrosime 38
Belgrade.

APPENDIX 3

LITERARY SOCIETIES

These are listed as follows:

International Literary Societies
Literary Societies in the UK and Republic of Ireland
Literary and Poetry Societies of the USA
Literary Societies other than in the UK, Republic of Ireland and USA

Please note that while every effort has been made to include as many societies and organizations as possible, the editors acknowledge that the following lists are by no means exhaustive. Many societies are organized and administered by unpaid individuals from their own homes; not only do the addresses of secretaries change frequently, therefore, but these are difficult to trace.

Secretaries of societies which have yet to be listed are consequently urged to send details for publication in future editions of the INTERNATIONAL AUTHORS AND WRITERS WHO'S WHO to the editors at the following address:

The International Authors and Writers Who's Who,
International Biographical Centre,
Cambridge CB2 3QP, England

The friendly co-operation of the listed societies is gratefully acknowledged; the future assistance of others is cordially invited.

INTERNATIONAL LITERARY SOCIETIES

CENTRO STUDI E SCAMBI INTERNAZIONALI
Casella Postale N. 537, Rome 00100, Italy.

THE COSMOSYNTHESIS LEAGUE
GPO Box 2108-S Melbourne, Victoria, Australia 3001.

THE INTERNATIONAL ACADEMY OF POETS
(see The World Literary Academy)

THE INTERNATIONAL GUILD OF CONTEMPORARY BARDS
GPO Box 2108-S Melbourne, Victoria, Australia 3001.

INTERNATIONAL P.E.N.
Headquarters—Glebe House, 62/63 Glebe Place, Chelsea, London SW3 5JB, England.

International Centres:

AUSTRALIA (Melbourne)
17-1 Domain Park
193 Domain Road
South Yarra
Victoria
Australia

AUSTRALIA (Sydney)
No. 14 Illeroy Avenue
Killara 2071
N.S.W.
Australia

AUSTRIA
Concordia Haus
Bankgasse 8, Vienna 1
Austria

BANGLADESH
Jahangirnagar University
119-B Dhanmondi R.A.
Road No. 2
Dacca, Bangladesh

BELGIUM (French)
Le Bel-Air
76 Av. du 11 Novembre
Boite 7
1040 Bruxelles
Belgium

BOLIVIA
Casilla 149
La Paz, Bolivia

BRAZIL (Rio de Janeiro)
P.E.N. Clube do Brasil
Praia do Flamengo 172-11°
Rio de Janeiro 20.00
Brazil

BRAZIL (São Paulo)
Caixa Postal 1574
São Paulo 01000
Brazil

BULGARIA
Rue Anghel Kantchev 5
Sofia
Bulgaria

CANADA
5040 Grand Blvd.
Montreal, Que H3X 3S2
Canada

CATALONIA
5 Lyndewode Road
Cambridge
England

COLOMBIA
Carrera 20 No. 58-77
Bogota
Colombia

CZECHOSLOVAKIA
U. Rajske Zahrady 1839/1B
Prague 3
Czechoslovakia

DENMARK
Vindrose Publishers
Nybrogade 14
DK 1203 Copenhagen
Denmark

EGYPT
104 Kast El- Eini St.
Cairo
Egypt

ENGLAND
62/63 Glebe Place
London SW3 5JB
England

ESTONIA
3 Pinnacle Ridge Road
Farmington
CT 06032
USA

FINLAND
Suuri Suomalainen Kirjakerho
Köydenpunojankatu 2
00180 Helsinki 18
Finland

FRANCE
Maison Internationale des P.E.N. Clubs
6 rue Françoise Miron
Paris IV
France

GERMAN DEMOCRATIC REPUBLIC
Friedrichstr. 194/199
108 Berlin
German Democratic Republic

GERMAN FEDERAL REPUBLIC
Sandstr. 10
61 Darmstadt
German Federal Republic

GERMAN SPEAKING WRITERS ABROAD
315 Upper Richmond Road
London SW15 6ST
England

GREECE
60a Rue Skoufa
Athens 144
Greece

HONG KONG (Chinese Centre)
Victoria Park Mansion
15th Floor, Flat A
Paterson Street
Hong Kong

HONG KONG (English Centre)
Box 1528
Kowloon Central Post Office
Hong Kong

HUNGARY
Võrõs Marty ter 1
Budapest H-1051
Hungary

ICELAND
Solheimar 23
Reykjavik
Iceland

INDIA
40 New Marine Lines
Bombay 20BR
India

IRAN
Iran P.E.N. Centre
Avenue Pahlavi
34th Street, No. 9
Tehran 16
Iran

IRELAND (Dublin)
Chilham House
Rathfarnham Village
Dublin 14
Ireland

ISRAEL
19 Shmaryahu Lewine Street
Jerusalem
Israel

ITALY
via Muzio Clementi 64
Rome 00193
Italy

IVORY COAST
B.P. 1718 Abidjan
Ivory Coast

JAMAICA
Department of English
University of the West Indies
Mona
Kingston 7
Jamaica

JAPAN
The Japan P.E.N. Club
Room 265 Shyuwa Akasaka RH
9-1-7 Akasaka
Tokyo 107
Japan

JORDAN
PO Box 1514
Amman
Jordan

KOREA
163 Ankuk-dong
Jongno-ku
Seoul
Korea

LANGUE D'OC
4 rue Déparcieux
30 Nimes
Gard
France

LATVIA
Box 498
S-101 31 Stockholm 1
Sweden

LEBANON
12 Avenue Madame Curie
Beirut
Lebanon

MEXICO
Filomeno Mata 8
Mexico 1, DF

NETHERLANDS
Wevelaan 39
Utrecht
Netherlands

NEW ZEALAND
PO Box 2283
Wellington
New Zealand

NORWAY
2829 Ø Snertingdal
Norway

PHILIPPINES
Solidaridad Publishing House
531 Padre Faura
Ermita
Manilla
Philippines

POLAND
Polish P.E.N. Centre
Palac Kultury i Nauki
Warsaw
Poland

PORTUGAL
Rua do Loreto, 13-2°
Lisbon
Portugal

PUERTO RICO
Apartado 4692
San Juan
Puerto Rico 0093

ROMANIA
Calea Victoriei 115
Bucharest
Romania

SCOTLAND
18 Crown Terrace
Glasgow G12 9ES

SENEGAL
President of the Republic of Senegal
Dakar
Senegal

SOUTH AFRICA (Cape Town)
Apartment C
2 Scott Road E
Claremont
Cape
South Africa

SRI LANKA
37/1 Thimbirigasyaya
Colombo 5
Sri Lanka

SWEDEN
A/B P.A. Norstedt & Söner
Box 2052
S-103 12, Stockholm
Sweden

SWITZERLAND (Basel)
Morgartenring 168
4054 Basel
Switzerland

SWITZERLAND (Italian Romansch)
Casa Basilio
Via Signor in Croce 12
CH 6612 Asconia
Switzerland

SWITZERLAND (Suisse Romande)
Les Armillaires
Praz-Berthoud 25
1010 Lausanne
Switzerland

TAIPEI CHINESE CENTRE
PO Box 13-25
277 Roosevelt Ave. Sec. 3
Taipei
Taiwan

THAILAND
56/21-22 Rama I Road
Bangkok 5
Thailand

TURKEY
Cagaloglu Yokuso 40
Istanbul
Turkey

UNITED STATES (American Centre)
American P.E.N. Centre
47 Fifth Avenue
New York
NY 10003
USA

UNITED STATES (Hawaii)
Depta. of Asian Studies
Seton Hall University
So. Orange
NJ 07079
USA

UNITED STATES (Los Angeles)
Box 144
Encino
CA 91316
USA

VIETNAM
107 Doan-Thi-Diem
Ho Chi Minh City
Vietnam

WRITERS IN EXILE (Germany)
Hamburg 20
Alendrothsweg 65
1 D-2000
German Federal Republic

WRITERS IN EXILE (London)
6 Gordon Avenue
London SW14
England

WRITERS IN EXILE (New York)
3 Mountain View Drive
New Milford
CT 06776
USA

WRITERS IN EXILE (Paris)
6 rue du Pont-de-Lodi
Paris IV
France

YIDDISH
66-66 Thornton Place
Rego Park
NY 11374
USA

YUGOSLAVIA (Croatian)
Solovljeva 22/IV
Zagreb
Yugoslavia

YUGOSLAVIA (Macedonian)
P.E.N. Clob Centre Skopje
Str. Maksim Gorki No. 18
91000 Skopje
Yugoslavia

YUGOSLAVIA (Serbian)
Francuska br. 7
Belgrade
Yugoslavia

YUGOSLAVIA (Slovene)
Tomsiceva 12
Ljubljana
Yugoslavia

ZIMBABWE
4 Avonfriars
Oxford Road
Avondale
Salisbury
Zimbabwe

THE INTERNATIONAL WRITER'S GUILD AND SOCIETY OF NEW AUTHORS
Rose House, Youlgrave, Bakewell, Derbyshire, England

THE WORLD LITERARY ACADEMY
International Biographical Centre, Cambridge CB2 3QP, England
(see APPENDIX 6 for full details)

THE WORLD POETRY SOCIETY INTERCONTINENTAL
General Secretariat Headquarters, 208 W Latimer Avenue, Campbell, CA 950008, USA

LITERARY SOCIETIES IN THE UK AND REPUBLIC OF IRELAND

ABERDEEN LITERARY SOCIETY
54 Tillydrone Ave., Aberdeen, AB2 2TN. Scotland.

ALEXANDER BURNS CLUB
126 Middleton Street, Alexandria, Dumbarton, Scotland.

ANON
131 Ridge Road, Sutton, Surrey.

APOLLO SOCIETY
16 Eccleston Square, London, SW1.

ARTS COUNCIL OF GREAT BRITAIN
Literature Department, 105 Piccadilly, London, W1V 0AU.

ARTS COUNCIL OF NORTHERN IRELAND
181a Stranmills Road, Belfast, BT9 5DU. Northern Ireland.

ARVON FOUNDATION LTD.
Totleigh Barton, Sheepwash, Beaworthy, Devon.

ATTINGHAM WRITERS
9 Meadow View Road, Whitchurch, Shropshire.

THE BARROW POETS
70 Parliament Hill, London, NW3 2TJ.

THE BIRMINGHAM CENTRAL LITERARY ASSOCIATION
"Crossmeads", Vicarage Hill, Tamworth-in-Arden, Warwickshire.

BIRMINGHAM POETRY CENTRE
158 Long Nuke Road, Northfield, Birmingham, B31.

BLACKHEATH POETRY SOCIETY
37 Blackheath Park, London, SE3.

BLACKPOOL WRITERS' CIRCLE
3 Ashfield Road, Bispham, Blackpool, FY2 0DH.

BOURNEMOUTH WRITERS' CIRCLE
51 Salisbury Road, Fordingbridge, Hants.

BRADFORD WRITERS' CIRCLE
38 Grove House Road, Bolton Road, Bradford 2, Yorks.

BRENTWOOD WRITERS' CIRCLE
5 Chestnut Grove, Brentwood, Essex.

CALDER VALLEY POETS
3 Callis Wood Bottom, Charlestown, Hebden Bridge, HX7 6PY. Yorks.

THE CAMDEN POETRY GROUP
7 Netherhall Gardens, London, NW3 5RN.

CARDIFF ARTS CENTRE
Market Road, Canton, Cardiff, Wales.

CARDIFF WRITERS' CIRCLE
20 West Rise, Llanishen, Cardiff, Wales.

CENTRE 17 (The Walthamstow Poetry Group)
Chingford Community Centre, Friday Hill, Chingford, London, E4.

CHICHESTER POETS CO-OPERATIVE
4 Little Breach, Chichester.

THE COOL WEB
4a Colinette Road, London SW15 and 122 Lincoln Avenue, Twickenham, Middlesex.

COSMIC CONTROL:PADIHAM SINK
1 Spring Bank, Salesbury, Blackburn, BB1 9EU. Lancs.

COUNTESTHORPE COMMUNITY COLLEGE POETRY WORKSHOP
15 Orange Street, South Wigston, Leicester.

COVENTRY WRITERS' GROUP
38 Biggin Hall Crescent, Coventry.

DERBY POETRY SOCIETY
5 Park Grove. Derby, DE3 1HE.

DUMBARTON BURNS CLUB
111 Brucehill Road, Dumbarton, Scotland.

THE DUNEDIN SOCIETY
104 Hill Street, Glasgow, Scotland.

EALING WRITERS CIRCLE
17 Barn Close, Northolt, Middlesex.

EAST ANGLIAN WRITERS
Artilda, The Street, Dilham, North Walsham, Norfolk.

EAST MIDLANDS ARTS ASSOCIATION
1 Frederick Street, Loughborough, Leicestershire. LE11 3BH.

EDINBURGH POETRY CLUB
15 Lennox Street, Edinburgh, 4.

EIGHTEEN NINTIES SOCIETY
3 Kemplay Road, London, NW3 1TA.

THE ENGLISH ASSOCIATION
1 Priory Gardens, London, W4 1TT.

ESSEX POETRY AND PROSE SOCIETY
The Lodge, Great Ruffins, Wickham Bishops, Witham, Essex.

FRENCH CULTURAL SERVICES-FRENCH POETRY LIBRARY
1 Kildare Street, Dublin 2, Repub. of Ireland.

FYLDE POETS
41 Ormont Avenue, Cleveleys, Nr. Blackpool, Lancs.

GOETHE INSTITUTE-GERMAN POETRY LIBRARY
37 Merrion Square, Dublin 2, Repub. of Ireland

GOSPORT WRITERS GROUP
8 Bury Hall Lane, Gosport.

GREENWICH POETRY SOCIETY
52 Dallin Road, London, SE18 3NX.

THE GWENT POETRY SOCIETY
107 St. Julian's Road, Newport, Mon. Wales.

HAROLD HIKINS FAMOUS MERSEYSIDE ARTS ASSOCIATION POETRY CIRCUS
14 Harringay Ave., Liverpool, L18 1JE.

HAVANT ARTS COUNCIL
Brambledene, New Cut, Havant Road, Hayling Island.

HUMBERSIDE THEATRE AND ARTS CENTRE
Spring Street, Hull, HU2 8RW.

INNER CIRCLE POETRY/MEDIA GROUP
4 Nowell Place, Almondbury, Huddersfield, HD5 8PB.

INSTITUTE OF CONTEMPORARY ARTS LTD.
Nash House, 12 Carlton House Terrace, London, SW1Y 5AH.

INTERNATIONAL SOCIETY OF LITERATURE
20 Skipton Road, Ilkley, Yorkshire.

IRISH ACADEMY OF LETTERS
"Elstow," Knapton Road, Dun Laoghaire, Co. Dublin, Repub. of Ireland.

IRISH ARTS COUNCIL
70 Merrion Square, Dublin 2, Repub. of Ireland.

JARROW AND HEBBURN POETRY GROUP
31 Burn Heads Road, Hebburn, Co. Durham.

KEATS-SHELLEY MEMORIAL ASSOCIATION
Keats House, Keats Grove, Hampstead, London, NW3 2RR.

KENT AND SUSSEX POETRY SOCIETY
40 St. James' Road, Tunbridge Wells.

KILMARNOCK BURNS CLUB
Mid Gartocharn Farm, Gartocharn, By Alexandria, Dunbartonshire. Scotland.

LANCASHIRE AUTHORS' ASSOCIATION
"Sea Winds", 22 Lune View, Knott End on Sea, Fylde Coast, Lancs. FY6 0AG.

THE LANCASHIRE POETRY ASSOCIATION
Kintore Drive, Great Sankey, Warrington, Lancs.

LEICESTER POETRY SOCIETY
15 Orange Street, South Wigston, Leicester.

LEICESTER WRITERS CLUB
36 Westfield Road, Leicester, LE3 6HT.

LINCOLNSHIRE AND HUMBERSIDE ARTS
St. Hugh's, Newport, Lincoln, LN1 3DN. (Regional Arts Ass).

LITERARY SOCIETY OF THE CITY LIT
Stukeley Street, Drury Lane, Lincoln, WC2B 5LJ.

LONDON WRITER CIRCLE
308 Lewisham Road, London, SE13 7PA.

LUTON ARTS COUNCIL
200 Barton Road, Luton, Beds.

LUTON WRITERS' GUILD
96 Kinross Crescent, Luton, Beds.

MALVERN POETRY CIRCLE
Davenham Close, Worcester.

MANCHESTER POETRY CENTRE
The University, Manchester, M13 9PL.

MERSEYSIDE ARTS ASSOCIATION
6 Bluecoat Chambers, School Lane, Liverpool, LI3 BX.

NEW RICHMOND POETRY GROUP
19 Grove Terrace, Teddington, Middlesex.

1970's POETS GROUP
Rose Vale, 40 Robin Hood Lane, Walderslade, Chatham, Kent.

NORTH WALES ARTS ASSOCIATION
10 Wellfield House, Bangor, Gwynedd. LL57 1ER. Wales.

NORTH WEST ARTS ASSOCIATION
12 Harter Street, Manchester, M1 6HY.

NOTTINGHAM POETRY SOCIETY
82 Kentwood Road, Sneiton Dale, Nottingham.

NOTTINGHAM WRITERS CLUB
52 Hilton Road, Mapperley, Nottingham.

OSWESTRY WRITERS
Rock House, Kinnerley, Oswestry, Shropshire.

OXFORD POETRY GROUP
35 Blenheim Drive, Oxford, OX2 8DJ.

OXFORD WRITERS' CIRCLE
10 Lucas Place, Meadow Lane, Iffley, Oxford.

PATRICK KAVANAGH SOCIETY
c/o Farmlink Ltd., Bluebell, Dublin 12, Repub. of Ireland.

THE PENMAM CLUB
175 Pall Mall, Leigh-on-Sea, Essex SS9 1RE.

PENNINE POETS
Fairfield, Victoria Road, Morley, Leeds.

PENTAMETERS POETRY CIRCLE
57 Belsize Avenue, Hampstead, London, NW3.

THE POETRY BOOK SOCIETY LTD
21 Earls Court Square, London SW5 9DE.

POETRY IN MOTION
37 Salisbury Road, Barnett, Herts.

THE POETRY LOVERS' FELLOWSHIP
Clee Saint Margaret, via Craven Arms, S. Shropshire. SY7 9DT.

POETRY ONE
86 Marshalls Drive, Romford, Essex. RM1 4JS.

THE POETRY SOCIETY
21 Earls Court Square, London SW5 9DE.

The following are Poetry Societies outside London

UNITED KINGDOM
Guildford and West Surrey Centre, 14 Bushbridge Lane, Godalming, Surrey.

Nottinghamshire Centre 82 Kentwood Road, Sneiton Dale, Nottingham.

Suffolk Centre 'Doggers', Copdock, Ipswich, Suffolk. 1P8 3JF.

U.S.A.
Eastern Centre 1270 Fifth Ave. 2F, New York, NY 10029, U.S.A.

Chicago Centre 569 North Laramie Ave, Chicago, IL, U.S.A.

CANADA
Nova Scotia Centre 9 Mayo Street, Armdale, Nova Scotia, Canada.

INDIA
Hyderabad Centre 'Shangrila', 8-2-584 Jubilee Hills, Road No. 9, Hyderabad-34, AP India.

THE POETRY SOCIETY OF CHELTENHAM
245 Cirencester Road, Charlton Kings, Cheltenham, Glos.

POETRY SOCIETY, TRINITY AND ALL SAINTS COLLEGES
Brownberrie Lane, Horsforth, Leeds, LS18 5HD.

POETRY TRIANGLE
33 Grangecliffe Gardens, London, SE25 6SY.

POETRY WORKSHOP
6 Balmoral Road, Bristol, BS7 9AZ.

PORTSMOUTH POETRY SOCIETY
256 Powerscourt Road, Portsmouth, PO2 7JR.

PRESTON POETS' SOCIETY
8 Whitefield Road E., Penwortham, Preston, Lancs.

RICHMOND HILL LITERARY SOCIETY
5 Kinross Road, Talbot Woods, Bournemouth, Hants.

RICHMOND POETRY GROUP
72 Heathfield South, Twickenham, Middlesex.

RICHMOND WRITERS' CIRCLE
c/o Adult College, Parkshot, Richmond, Surrey.

ROYAL SOCIETY OF LITERATURE
1 Hyde Park Gardens, London, W2 2LT.

SALISBURY POETRY CIRCLE
57 Bouveria Avenue, Salisbury.

THE SALTIRE SOCIETY
13 Atholl Crescent, Edinburgh, EH3 8HA. Scotland.—Administrator Miss K. Austin.

SCAFFOLD
The Old Bakery, Woolpit, Suffolk.

SCOTTISH ARTS
24 Rutland Square, Edinburgh, EH1 2BW. Scotland.

THE SCOTTISH ARTS COUNCIL
19 Charlotte Square, Edinburgh, EH2 4DF. Scotland.

SCOTTISH ASSOCIATION FOR THE SPEAKING OF VERSE
22 Craigmont Avenue North, Edinburgh, EH12 8DF. Scotland.

THE MARGARET ST. MUSE
Birmingham and Midland Institute, Margaret St., Birmingham, B3 3BS.

THE SHAKESPEARE BIRTHPLACE TRUST
The Shakespeare Centre, Stratford-upon-Avon.

SHORTLANDS POETRY CIRCLE
Flat 7, High Gables, 1 Scotts Avenue, Shortlands, Bromley, Kent. BR2 0NB.

SHREWSBURY POETRY CIRCLE
41 St. John's Hill, Shrewsbury, SY1 1JQ.

THE SOCIETY OF AUSTRALIAN WRITERS
Australia House, Strand, London, WC2B 4LA.

THE SOCIETY OF AUTHORS
84 Drayton Gardens, London, SW10 9SB.

SOCIETY OF CIVIL SERVICE AUTHORS
17 Abbotsford Road, Goodmayes, Ilford, Essex.

SOLIHULL WRITERS' WORKSHOP
The Manor House, Solihull, Warwicks.

SOUTH EAST ARTS ASSOCIATION
As of June '86
10 Mount Ephraim, Tunbridge Wells, Kent TN4 8AS.

SOUTH EAST WALES ARTS ASSOCIATION
Victoria Street, Cwmbran, Gwent. NP44 3YT.

SOUTHERN ARTS ASSOCIATION
19 Southgate Street, Winchester, SO23 9DQ.

SOUTH WESTERN ARTS ASSOCIATION
23 Southernhay East, Exeter, Devon.

SPECTRO GALLERY
18 Station Road, Whitley Bay, Northumberland.

STRATFORD-UPON-AVON POETRY FESTIVAL
See The Shakespeare Birthplace Trust.

SUFFOLK POETRY SOCIETY
'Doggers', Copdock, Ipswich, 1P8 3JF.

SUNDERLAND ARTS CENTRE
17 Grance Terrace, Stockton Road, Sunderland.

SURREY POETRY CENTRE (Guildford & Wey Poets)
4, The Mount, Leatherhead, Surrey.

SWANSEA AND DISTRICT WRITERS' CIRCLE
932 Carmarthen Road, Fforestfach, Swansea, SA5 4AB. Wales.

TORBAY POETRY CENTRE
Church Style, Bovey Tracey, Newton Abbot, Devon.

THE TRANSLATORS ASSOCIATION
84 Drayton Gardens, London, SW10 9SD.

THE UMBRELLA CLUB
Tudor House, 14 Spon Street, Coventry, CV1 3BA.

VER POETS
61 & 63 Chiswell Green Lane, St. Albans, Herts.

THE WALTHAMSTOW POETRY GROUP
See Centre 17.

THE WELSH ARTS COUNCIL
Holst House, 9 Museum Place, Cardiff, CF1 3NX. Wales.

THE WEST COUNTRY WRITERS' ASSOCIATION
The Dene, The Street, Aldermaston, Berks.

WEST MIDLAND ARTS
Brunswick Terrace, Stafford. ST16 IB2.

WEST WALES ASSOCIATION FOR THE ARTS
Dark Gate, Red Street, Carmarthen. Wales.

WIGAN POETS
18 Sycamore Avenue, Golborne, Nr. Warrington, Lancs.

WINCHESTER POETRY CIRCLE
8 Taplings Road, Weeke, Winchester.

WINCHESTER WRITERS' CIRCLE
65 Greenhill Road, Winchester, SO22 SEA.

WORCESTER WRITERS' CIRCLE
15 Lynn Close, Leigh Sinton, Nr. Malvern, Worcs.

THE WRITERS
35 Rundell Crescent, London, NW4 3BS.

YORK POETRY SOCIETY
7 Monkstray, Stockton Lane, York.

YORKSHIRE ARTS ASSOCIATION
Glyde House, Glydegate, Bradford, Yorkshire. BD5 0BQ.

THE YORKSHIRE DIALECT SOCIETY
Fieldhead House, West Street, Hoyland, Barnsley, S74 9AG.

YR ACADEMI GYMREIG: ENGLISH LANGUAGE SECTION
4th Floor, Cory Building, Bute St., Cardiff, CF1 6QP. Wales.

YR ACADEMI GYMREIG: WELSH LANGUAGE SECTION
Tŷ Mount Stuart, Sgwâr Mount Stuart, Caerdydd, CF1 6DQ. Wales.

LITERARY AND POETRY SOCIETIES OF THE USA

Listed below are
(a) Literary societies within the United States of America other than societies which are members of the National Federation of State Poetry Societies, and
(b) Members of the National Federation of State Poetry Societies.

(a) Literary Societies of the USA

AKRON POETRY SOCIETY
4623 Provens Drive, Akron, OH 44319.

AMERICAN JUNIOR POETRY SOCIETY
Renee Gate, Rt. 6, Main Street, Laurie Road, Peekskill, NY 10566.

AMERICAN POETRY LEAGUE
10419 Audrey Drive, Sun City, AZ

AMERICAN POETS FELLOWSHIPS SOCIETY
902 10th Street, Charleqton, IL 61920.

ARKANSAS WRITERS' CONFERENCE
510 East Street, Benton, AR 72015.

AUSTIN POETRY SOCIETY
See Poetry Society of Texas—Austin Chapter.

BERGEN POETS
197 Delmar Avenue, Glen Rock, AR 07452.

BRAILLE POETS GUILD
148 Washington Street, Tanton, MA.

BREAD LOAF WRITERS' CONFERENCE
Middlebury College, Middlebury, VT 05753.

BROOKLYN POETRY CIRCLE
61 Pierrepont Street, Brooklyn, NY 11201.

CALIFORNIA FEDERATION OF CHAPARRAL POETS
1422 Ashland Avenue, Claremont, CA 91711.

CALIFORNIA FEDERATION OF CHAPARRAL POETS—APOLLO CHAPTER
13361 El Dorado, 201H Seal Beach, CA.

Colonial Apts. No. 2, East Garden Lane, Fairmont, WV 26554.

FEDERAL POETS OF WASHINGTON, D.C.
District of Colombia Chapter of National Federation of State Poetry Societies,
5321 Willard Avenue, Chevy Chase, MD 20815.

FLORIDA STATE POETRY SOCIETY, INC.
1110 North Venetian Drive, Miami Beach, FL 33139.

FORT LAUDERDALE POETRY WORKSHOP
5307 NE 32nd Avenue, Fort Lauderdale, FL 33308.

GANSVOORT PIER POETS
Gansvoort Street & West St. Pier, New York, NY 10014.

GEN STATE WRITERS GUILD
1702 N. 23rd, Boise, ID 83702.

GEORGIA WRITERS ASSOCIATION, INC.
18 Collier Road, NW, Atlanta, GA 30309.

THE GREATER CINCINNATI WRITERS LEAGUE
2413 Ohio Avenue, Cincinnati, OH 45219.

HAIKU SOCIETY OF AMERICA
Japan House, 333 East 47th Street, New York, NY 10017.

IDAHO POETS' AND WRITERS' GUILD
317 6th Street, Idaho Falls, ID 83401.

IDAHO STATE POETRY SOCIETY
Homedale, ID 83628.

THE INA COOLBRITH CIRCLE
Room 401, Marines' Memorial Building, San Francisco, CA

INKY TRAILS POETS
Inky Trails Publication, Route No. 2, Box 2028, Nampa, ID 83651.

INTERNATIONAL CULTURAL POETRY & EFFICIENCY SOCIETY
13604 Summer Hill Drive, Phoenix, MD 21131.

INTERNATIONAL POETRY FORUM
4400 Forbes Avenue, Pittsburgh, PA 51213.

INTERNATIONAL POETS' SHRINE
1060 N. St. Andrews Place, Hollywood, CA 90038.

INTERNATIONAL WRITING PROGRAM
The University of Iowa, Iowa City, Iowa 52240.

IOWA POETRY ASSOCIATION
208 South Church Street, Leon, 1A 50144.

IOWA POETRY DAY ASSOCIATION
2614 East Avenue NE, Cedar Rapids, IA.

KANSAS AUTHORS CLUB
Marymount College, Salina, KS 67401.

KOKOMO POETRY CIRCLE
1418 West Jefferson Street, Kokomo, IN 46901.

LAKELAND POETRY WORKSHOP
810 East Bella Vista, Apt. 203, Lakeland, FL 33801.

LARAMORE RADER POETRY GROUP
3170 Gifford Lane, Miami, FL 33133.

LEAGUE OF MINNESOTA POETS
4425 West 7th St., Duluth, MN 55807.

LONG ISLAND WRITERS
30 Skidmore Place, Valley Stream, NY 11581.

THE MACDOWELL COLONY, INC.
100 High St., Peterborough, NH 03458.

MAINE POETRY DAY ASSOCIATION
P.O. Box 143, Yarmouth, ME 04096.

MANUSCRIPT CLUB OF LOS ANGELES
1100 South Ninth Street, Alhambra, CA 91801.

MIDWEST FEDERATION OF CHAPARRAL POETS
3447 S. Garfield Avenue, Minneapolis, MN 55408.

MIDWEST FEDERATION OF CHAPARRAL POETS—MINNESOTA CHAPTER
3447 S. Garfield Avenue, Minneapolis, MN 55408.

MISSISSIPPI POETRY SOCIETY
542 W. Galatin St., Hazlehurst, MS 39083.

MODERN POETRY ASSOCIATION
601 S Morgan St., PO Box 4348 Chicago, IL 60680.

MORGANTOWN POETRY SOCIETY
101 Jones Avenue, Morgantown, WV 26505.

NATIONAL LEAGUE OF AMERICAN PEN WOMEN, INC.
1300 17th Street, NW, Washington, DC 20036.

NATIONAL LEAGUE OF AMERICAN PEN WOMEN—ARIZONA STATE
2505 Paul Place, Prescott, AZ 86301.

NATIONAL LEAGUE OF AMERICAN PEN WOMEN—POETRY WORKSHOP OF CORAL-GABLES BRANCH
1100 Sorolla Avenue, Coral Gables, FL 33134.

NATIONAL LEAGUE OF AMERICAN PEN WOMEN—MATTOON (ILLINOIS) BRANCH
902 10th Street, Charleston, IL 61920.

NATIONAL LEAGUE OF AMERICAN PEN WOMEN—NEW MEXICO CHAPTER
1140 Alameda Road, NW, Albuquerque, NM 87107.

NATIONAL POETRY DAY COMMITTEE, INC.
1110 North Venetian Drive, Miami Beach, FL 33139.

THE NEW ENGLAND POETRY CIRCUIT
See Connecticut Poetry Circuit and Northern New England Poetry Circuit.

THE NEW ENGLAND POETRY CLUB
43A Joy Street, Boston, MA 02114.

NEW JERSEY POETRY SOCIETY, INC.—DELAWARE VALLEY POETS CHAPTER
11 Alexander St., Princeton, NJ 08540.

NEW JERSEY POETRY SOCIETY, INC.—LEAVES OF GRASS CHAPTER
519 Jacksonville Road, Mt. Holly, NJ 08060.

NEW JERSEY POETRY SOCIETY, INC.—MUSCONETCONG CHAPTER

THE NEW ORLEANS POETRY FORUM
3404 Louisiana Avenue Pkwy., New Orleans, LA 70125 and 828 Lesseps Street, New Orleans, LA 70117.

THE NEW YORK POETRY FORUM
The New York Poetry Forum Inc., P.O. Box 855, Madison Square Station, 149 East 23rd Street, New York, NY 10010.

NEW YORK POETS COOPERATIVE
14 Morton Street, New York, NY 10014.

NORTH CAROLINA POETRY CIRCUIT
Laurinburg, NC 28372.

NORTH CAROLINA POETRY SOCIETY
Dept. of Business Administration University of North Carolina, Chapel Hill, NC.

NORTHWEST CONNECTICUT VISITING POETS PROGRAM
Falls Village, CT 06031.

THE NORTHWEST POETRY CIRCUIT
Division of Continuing Education, University of Oregon, 1736 Moss Street, Eugene, OR 97403.

OHIO POETS ASSOCIATION
RD 4, Box 131, Ashland, OH 44805.

OVERSEAS CHINESE POETS CLUB
54 Catherne St., 15J, New York, NY.

OZARK WRITERS & ARTISTS GUILD
1110 Valley View Drive, Fayetteville, AR 72701.

PAN
PO Box 24C45, Los Angles, CA 90024.

PASADENA WRITERS' CLUB
5403 Bartlett Avenue, San Gabriel, CA 91776.

PENN LAUREL POETS OF PHILADELPHIA
27 W. Mt. Pleasant Avenue, Philadelphia, PA 19119.

THE PENROCK WRITERS
424 McKinley Street, Waupon, WI 53963.

PHILADELPHIA Y POETRY CENTER
401 South Broad Street, Philadelphia, PA 19417.

PHILLIS WHEATLEY LITERARY CLUB
21 Enfield Avenue, Montclair, NJ 07645.

POETRY AND PHILOSOPHY GROUP
1762 Albany Street, Schenectady, NY 12304.

THE POETRY CENTER, SAN FRANCISCO STATE UNIVERSITY
1600 Holloway Avenue, San Francisco, CA 94132.

THE POETRY CENTER, 92nd STREET YM—YWHA
92nd Street YM—YWHA, Lexington Avenue at 92nd Street, New York, NY 10028.

POETRY CIRCUIT OF OHIO
Department of English, Kenyon College, Gambier OH 43022.

POETRY CLUB
PO Box 279, Clinton, AR 72031.

POETRY FELLOWSHIP OF MAINE
Thayer Village, Apt. 38, Waterville, ME 04901.

POETRY FORUM
633 Wood Street, Vineland, NJ 08360.

POETRY SOCIETY OF ALASKA, INC.
Box 433, Juneau, AK 99801.

THE POETRY SOCIETY OF AMERICA
15 Gramercy Park South, New York, NY 10003.

POETRY SOCIETY OF BEDFORD
Route 5, Bedford, VA 24523.

POETRY SOCIETY OF GEORGIA
65 Cronwell Road, Savannah, GA 31404.

POETRY SOCIETY OF SOUTH CAROLINA
The Citadel, Charleston, SC 29409.

THE POETRY SOCIETY OF SOUTHERN CALIFORNIA
338 N. Kenmore Avenue, Los Angeles, CA 90004.

POETRY SOCIETY OF TEXAS—AUSTIN CHAPTER
Ambassador Apartments, No. 316, 407 W. 18th Street, Austin, TX 78701.

POETRY SOCIETY OF VIRGINIA
5000 E. Seminary Avenue, Richmond, VA 23227.

POETRY WORKSHOP OF THE LYNCHBURG WOMAN'S CLUB
Apartments, Rivermont Avenue, Lynchburg, VA 24503.

POETRY WORKSHOP OF THE STATE UNIVERSITY OF IOWA
University of Iowa, Iowa City, IA 52240.

POETS AND PATRONS, INC.
4205 Madison Avenue, Brookfield, IL 60513.

POETS AND WRITERS, INC.
201 West 54 Street, New York, NY 10019.

POETS' CLUB OF CHICAGO
1628 W. Touhy Avenue, Chicago, IL 60626.

POETS OF PARNASSUS (founded 1976)
625 Holly St., Ashland, OR 97520.

POETS STUDY CLUB
302 N. 3rd Street, Marshall, IL 62441.

POETS TAPE EXCHANGE
109 Twin Oak Drive, Lynchburg, VA 24502.

PURCHASE POETS CLUB
Mid-Continent Bible College, 502 N. 15th Street, Mayfield, KY 42066.

RIDGE POETRY ASSOCIATION
Fedhaven, Lake Wales, FL 33853.

RIMERS OF TUCSON, ARIZONA
2246 East Mabel Street, Tucson, AZ 85719.

THE ROCHESTER POETRY SOCIETY
155 S. Main Street, Fairport, NY 14450

ROCHESTER WORLD POETRY DAY COMMITTEE
PO Box 1101, Rochester, NY 14603.

ROUND TABLE POETS OF FORT SMITH
6510 Meadowcliff, Fort Smith, AR 72901.

ST. LOUIS POETRY CENTER
223 Tiffen Street, St. Louis, MO 63135.

ST. PETERSBURG POETRY ASSOCIATION
775 123rd Avenue, Treasure Island, FL 33706.

SHELLEY SOCIETY OF NEW YORK
221 East 28th Street, New York, NY 10016.

THE SOCIETY MIDLAND AUTHORS
205 N. Mayflower, Lake Forest, IL 60045.

SOUTH AND WEST, INC.
2601 South Phoenix, Fort Smith, AR 72901.

SOUTHWEST MICHIGAN WRITERS SOCIETY
706 Pipestone, Benton Harbor, MI.

SPOKESMAN POETS
Department of English, Loras College, Dubuque, IA 52001.

STATE POETRY SOCIETY OF IOWA
Box 218, Plainfield, IA 50660.

STATEN ISLAND POETRY SOCIETY
25 Washington Place, Staten Island, NY 10302.

TENNESSEE POETRY CIRCUIT
The University of Tennessee, Chattanooga, TN 37401.

TEXAS COUNCIL FOR THE PROMOTION OF POETRY
3936 Colgate Street, Dallas, TX 75225.

UNIVERSITY OF ARIZONA POETRY CENTER
1086 North Highland Avenue, Tucson, AZ 85719.

VACHEL LINDSAY ASSOCIATION
502 S. State St., Springfield, IL 62704.

VERDIGRIS VALLEY WRITERS
213 W. Locust, Independence, KS 67301.

WASHINGTON STATE POETRY FOUNDATION, Inc.
5727 35th NE, Seattle, WA 98105.

WAUSAU POETRY SOCIETY AND DELAWARE WRITERS, INC.
905 South 6th Avenue, Wausau, WI 54401.

WILMINTON POETRY SOCIETY AND DELAWARE WRITERS, INC.
PO Box 1005, Wilmington DE 19899.

WISCONSIN ARTS FOUNDATION AND COUNCIL
PO Box 90191, Milwaukee, WI 53202.

WISCONSIN REGIONAL WRITERS ASSOCIATION
Box 146, Rhinelander, WI 54501.

WORLD POETRY DAY
27 W. Mt. Pleasant Avenue, Philadelphia, PA 19119.

WORLD POETRY SOCIETY INTERCONTINENTAL
208 W. Latimer Avenue, Campbell, CA 95008.

WORLD POETS RESOURCE CENTER, INC.
1270 5th Avenue, New York, NY 10029.

WRITERS ASSOCIATION OF THE ITHACA AREA
106 E. State Street, Ithaca, NY 14850.

WRITERS' FORUM OF VIRGINIA COMMONWEALTH UNIVERSITY
Virginia Commonwealth University, 910 W. Franklin Street, Richmond, VA 23220.

YUKUHARU HAIKU SOCIETY—AMERICAN DIVISION
208 W. Latimer Avenue, Campbell, CA 95008.

(b) Members of the National Federation of State Poetry Societies, Inc.

ALABAMA STATE POETRY SOCIETY
1247 Westmoreland Avenue, Montgomery, AL 36106.

ARIZONA STATE POETRY SOCIETY
3171 No. 48th St., Phoenix, AZ 85018.

POETS' ROUNDTABLE OF ARKANSAS
305 Johnston St., Little Rock, AR 72205.

CALIFORNIA STATE POETRY SOCIETY
PO Box 61297, Sunnyvale, CA 94088.

POETRY SOCIETY OF COLORADO
2695 Eudroa St., Denver, CO 80207.

CONNECTICUT STATE POETRY ASSOCIATION
4 Rice Road, Broad Brook, CT 06016.

FIRST STATE WRITERS OF DELAWARE
6 Marley Road, Penn Acres, New Castle, DE 19720.

DISTRICT OF COLUMBIA—FEDERAL POETS OF WASHINGTON, DC
4500 Chesapeake St., NW, Washington, DC 20016.

FLORIDA STATE POETS ASSOCIATION
92 Clairmont Avenue, Debarry, FL 32713.

HAWAII WRITERS' CLUB
2522 Makiki Heights, Honolulu, HI 96822.

ILLINOIS STATE POETRY SOCIETY
Box 32, Rt. 1, Eureka, IL 61530.

INDIANA STATE FEDERATION OF POETRY CLUBS
402 E. Main St., Swayzee, IN 46896.

IOWA POETRY ASSOCIATION
509 North 16th, Marshalltown, IA 50158.

KENTUCKY STATE POETRY SOCIETY
Rt. 2, Olive Hill, KY 41164.

LOUISIANA STATE POETRY SOCIETY
2319 S. Carrollton Avenue, New Orleans, LA 70118.

MARYLAND STATE POETRY SOCIETY
5821 Swarthmore Drive, College Park, MD 20740.

MASSACHUSETTS STATE POETRY SOCIETY
4 Russett Land, Winchester, MA 01890.

POETRY SOCIETY OF MICHIGAN
3061 Country Club Drive, Muskegon, MI 49441.

MISSISSIPPI STATE POETRY SOCIETY
1104 Monroe St., Apt. A., Vicksburg, MS 39180.

NEBRASKA POETRY ASSOCIATION
6419 Parker St., Omaha, NE 68104.

NEVADA POETRY SOCIETY
McCarran Ranch, via Sparks, NV 89431.

NEW JERSEY POETRY SOCIETY
6 Park Avenue, Mine Hill, Dover, NJ 07801.

NEW MEXICO STATE POETRY SOCIETY
8901 W. Frontage, NE, No. 235, Albuquerque, NM 87113.

NEW YORK POETRY FORUM
PO Box 855, Madison Square Station, 149 East 23rd Street, New York, NY 10010.

NORTH CAROLINA POETRY SOCIETY
2342 New Bern Avenue, Raleigh, NC 27610.

VERSE WRITERS' GUILD OF OHIO
2500 W. Granville Road, Worthington, OH 43085.

POETRY SOCIETY OF OKLAHOMA
1732 NW 28th, Oklahoma City, OK 731060.

OREGON STATE POETRY ASSOCIATION
Echo Bend Drive, Roseburg, OR 97470.

PENNSYLVANIA POETRY SOCIETY, INC.
10 Cherry Lane, Wynnewood, PA 19096.

RHODE ISLAND STATE POETRY SOCIETY
37 Park Avenue, Edgewood, RI 02905.

SOUTH DAKOTA STATE POETRY SOCIETY
909 E. 34th St., Sioux Falls, SD 57105.

POETRY SOCIETY OF TENNESSEE
375A Ridgemont, Memphis, TN 38128.

POETRY SOCIETY OF TEXAS
1424 Highland Road, Dallas, TX 75218.

UTAH STATE POETRY SOCIETY, INC.
1115 Paterson, Ogden, UT 84403.

WEST VIRGINIA POETRY SOCIETY
4101 Venable Avenue, SE Charleston, WV 25304.

WISCONSIN FELLOWSHIP OF POETS
1104 Church St., Rib Lake, WI 54470.

LITERARY SOCIETIES OTHER THAN IN THE U.K., REPUBLIC OF IRELAND AND U.S.A.

AFRICA

CAMEROON
Association Nationale des Poètes et Ecrivains Camerounais, B.P. 2180, Yaounde-Messa, Cameroon.

GHANA
Creative Writers Association, The National Organizer, c/o Institute of African Studies, University of Ghana, Legon-Accra, Ghana.

Ghana Association of Writers, P.O. Box 4414, Accra, Ghana.

National Association of Writers, The Arts Council of Ghana, P.O. Box 2738, Accra, Ghana. Writers Forum, c/o S.R.C. Office, University of Ghana, Legon-Accra, Ghana.

REPUBLIC OF SOUTH AFRICA
The South African Poetry Society, c/o The Institute for the Study of English in Africa, Grahamstown, Rhodes University, Grahamstown 6140, South Africa.

SUDAN
National Council for Culture, Ministry of Culture and Information, Khartoum, Sudan.

ASIA

REPUBLIC OF CHINA
Chinese Poets Association, P.O. Box 58508, Taipei.

Chinese Writers' and Artists' Association, Apt. 3, 17 Lane 390, Tun Hwa South Road, Taipei.

Chun Jen Poetry Association, 27 Han Kou Street, Sec. 2, Taipei.

Ying Ming Poetry Association, 24-2 Alley 32, Lane 417, Sungshan Road, Taipei.

HONG KONG
Sun Lui Poetry Association, 1U7 Sai Yeung Choi Street, 9/P Flat C, Kowloon, Hong Kong.

INDIA
World Poetry Society Intercontinental, 3 Venkatesan St., Madras—17.

INDONESIA
Dewan Kesenian Jakarta (The Arts Council of Jakarta), Jalan Cikini Raya 73, Jakarta, Indonesia.

Paguyuban Pengarang Sastra Sunda. c/o "Pustaka Jaya" Jalan Banteng 37, Bandung, Yayasan Indonesia "Horison." Jalan Gereja Theresia 47, Jakarta.

ISRAEL
Hebrew Writers Association, 18 Hirshenberg St., Tel Aviv, Israel.

The Kibbutzs' Authors Association, Kibbutz Mizra, Israel.

JAPAN
Japan Yukuharu Haiku Society. American Address 1020 S. 8th St., Jan Jose, CA 95112, USA.

MALAYSIA
The Sirius Poetry Society, U-31 Theatre Street, Bidor, Perak, Malaysia.

PAKISTAN
National Book Centre of Pakistan, 1 Montgomery Road, Lahore, Pakistan.

Pakistan Writers' Guild, 16/B Sindhi Muslim Housing Society, Karachi-3, Pakistan.

Sindhi Adabi Board, Hyderabad (Sind), Pakistan.

SAUDI ARABIA
Higher Council for Sciences, Literature and Arts, Ministry of Education, Riyadh, Saudi Arabia.

AUSTRALIA AND NEW ZEALAND

Australian Literature Society, c/o 221 Clarendon Street, South Melbourne 3205.

Australian Society of Authors, 24 Alfred St., Milsons Point, NSW 2061.

Australian Writers' Workshop, 31 Salkeld Street, Tarragindi, Queensland 4121.

Children's Book Council of Australia (Canberra), 27 Waller Crescent, Campbell, 2601 A.C.T.

Fellowship of Australian Writers, 27 Waller Crescent, Campbell 2601, A.C.T.

Canberra: 50 Booroondara Street, Reed, A.C.T. 2601.

New South Wales: 2/2 Holbrook Avenue, Kirribilli, N.S.W. 2061.

Queensland: 14 Kanumbra Street, Coorparoo, Queensland 4151 and Wellington Road, Red Hill, Queensland 4059.

South Australia: 122 Osmond Terrace, Norwood, South Australia 5067.

Tasmania: 11 Fowler Street, Montrose, Tasmania 7010.

Tasmania-Launceston Regional: Private Mail Bag 77, Launceston, Tasmania 7250.

Tasmania-North Regional: Box 464 P.O., Burnie 7320.

Victoria: 1/317 Barkers Road, Kew, Victoria 3101.

Victoria-Geelong Regional: 41 Shackleton Street, Belmont, Victoria 3216.

Victoria-North Central Regional: 15 Coomboona Street, Shepparton, Victoria 3630.

Victoria-Western Districts Regional: 17 Sedgwick Street, Hamilton 3300, Victoria.

Western Australia: c/o Tom Collins House, 9 Servetus Street, Swanbourne, Western Australia 6010.

Western Australia-Albany Regional: P.O. Box 310 Albany, Western Australia 6330.

Western Australia-Geraldton Regional: 151 Brede Street, Geraldton 6530.

Hervey Bay Writers' Workshop: 47 Truro Street, Torquay, Queensland 4657.

New Zealand Women Writers Society, 75 Hall Crescent, Lower Hutt, New Zealand.

The Poetry Society of Australia, Box 110, George Street North Sydney, N.S.W. 2001.

Toowoomba Ladies' Literary Society, 3 Kent Street, Queensland 4350.

CANADA

Canadian Authors' Association, 24 Ryerson Avenue, Toronto, Ontario M5T 2P3.

Full Tide (Vancouver Poetry Society), 2964 West 8th Avenue, Vancouver 8, British Columbia.

League of Canadian Poets, 106 Avenue Road, Toronto, Ontario, M5R 2H2.

Nova Scotia Centre of the Poetry Society, 1327 Dresden Row, Halifax, Nova Scotia.

Saskatchewan poetry Society, 201 2500 Victoria Avenue, Regina, Saskatchewan.

Scotian Pen Guild, P.O. Box 173, Dartmouth, Nova Scotia, B2Y 3Y3.

The Wilson MacDonald Poetry Society of Canada, 66 Burnaby Blvd., Toronto 12, Ontario.

CENTRAL AND SOUTH AMERICA

ARGENTINA
Sociedad Argentina de Escritores, Mexico 524, Buenos Aires, Argentina.

ECUADOR
Casa de la Cultura Ecuatoriana, Avenida 6 de Diciembre 332, Quito, Ecuador.

Club Femenino de Cultura, Manabi 309, Quito, Ecuador.

MEXICO
Centro Mexicano de Escritoires A.C., Valle Arizpe 18, Mexico D.F.

PERU
Centro Peruano del PEN Club Internacional, 694, Jesús Mariá, Lima, Peru.

Instituto Nacional de Cultura, 390 Ancash, Lima, Peru.

EUROPE

AUSTRIA
Osterreichische Gesellschaft Fur Literatur, Palais Wilczek, Herrengasse 5, 1010 Vienna, Austria.

BELGIUM
Association des Ecrivans Belges, 150 Chaussée de Wavre, 1050 Brussels, Belgium.

Association Royale Des Ecrivains Wallons, Rue de la Carrière 41, Kockelberg, 1080 Brussels, Belgium.

Centre International D'Etudes Poétiques, Boulevard de l'Empereur 4, 1000 Brussels, Belgium.

Maison Internationale de la Poesie, 147 Chaussée de Haecht, B 1030 Brussels, Belgium.

BULGARIA
The Union of Bulgarian Writers, 'Angel Kantchev' Street, No. 5, Sofia, Bulgaria.

DENMARK
Dansk Forfatterforening (Danish Authors Society), Nyhavn 21, 1051 Copenhagen K, Denmark.

Danske Dramatikers Forbund, Klosterstraede 24, Copenhagen K, Denmark.

FINLAND
Finlands Svenska Forfattareforening (Association of Swedo-Finnish Authors), Runebergsgatin 32 C 27, 00100 Helsinki 10, Finland.

Lounais Suomen Kirjailijat r.y., Eerikinkatu 1 A 26, 20110 Turku 10 Finland.

Suomen Kirjailijalitto (Association of Finnish Authors), Runegerginkatu 32 C 28, 00100 Helsinki 10, Finland.

Svenska Osterbottens Litteraturforening, Pedersespl. 12, 68 620 Jakobstad 2, Finland.

FRANCE
Club des Poetes, 30 rue de Bourgogne, 75 Paris 7e, France.

Fondation Victor Hugo, 8 rue du Sergent Maginot, 75016 Paris, France.

Société des Gens de Lettres, Hotel De Massa, 38 rue du Faubourg-Saint-Jacques, 75 Paris 14e, France.

Société des Poètes Francais, 38 rue du Faubourg-Saint-Jacques, 75 Paris 14e, France.

Syndicat des Ecrivains, 38 rue du Faubourg-Saint-Jacques, 75 Paris 14e, France.

Union des Ecrivains, 6 Passage Charles Dallery, 75 Paris Ile, France.

GERMAN FEDERAL REPUBLIC
Der Tukan-Kreis Intn. literarische Gesellschaft, 8000 Munich 40, Moosacherstr. 47, German Federal Republic.

Deutsche Akademie für Sprache und Dichtung, 6100 Darmstadt, Alexandraweg 23, German Federal Republic.

Deutscher Autoren-Verband e. V., 3000 Hannover, Sophienstr. 2, German Federal Republic.

Gesellschaft fur deutsche Sprache e. V., 6200 Wiesbaden, Taunusstr. 11, German Federal Republic.

Interessengemeinschaft deutschsprachiger Autoren e. V., 415 Krefeld-Holterhöfe, Am Rotforn 7, German Federal Republic.

Literary Union, Petersbergstrasse 82, D-66 Saarbrucken 6, German Federal Republic.

P.E.N.-Zentrum, Sanstr 10, D-6100 Darmstadt, German Federal Republic.

Verband deutscher Schriftsteller (VS) in der Industriegewerkschaft Druck und Papier, friedrichstrasse 15, D-7000 Stuttgart, German Federal Republic.

Verband deutscher Schriftsteller (VS) in Hamburg e. V., 2000 Hamburg 1, Glockengiesserwall 2, German Federal Republic.

HUNGARY
Magyar Irók Szövetsége (Union of Hungarian Writers), Budapest VI, Bajza Utca 18, Hungary.

ICELAND
Félag islenzkra rithöfunda, Olduslód 3, Hafnarfjodur, Iceland.

Rithöfundafélag Islands, Vonarstraeti 12, Reykjavik, Iceland.

ITALY
Sindacato Nazionale Scrittori (Writers' Union), via Basento 52 D Rome, Italy.

GRAND DUCHY OF LUXEMBOURG
Institut grand-ducal, Section des Arts et Lettres, 19 Cote d'Eich, Luxembourg, Grand Duchy of Luxembourg.

Lochness-Verlag Luxemburger Autoren, 17 rue J.P. Koenig, Luxembourg, Grand Duchy of Luxembourg.

Société des Ecrivains Luxembourgeois de Langue Francaise, 10 rue de l'abbé Lemire, Luxembourg, Grand Duchy of Luxembourg.

THE NETHERLANDS
Maatschappij der Nederlandse Letterkunde, Universiteitsbibliotheck, Rapenburg 70-74, 2311 EZ Leiden, The Netherlands.

NORWAY
Den Norske Forfatterfoening (The Norwegian Authors' Union), Rådhusgata 7, 0103, Oslo 1, Norway.

POLAND
Agencja Autorska (Authors' Agency Ltd.), 00-950 Warsaw, ul, Hipoteczna 2, Poland.

Zwiazek Literatow Polskich (Polish Writers' Association), Warsaw, Krakowskie Przedmiescie 87/89, Poland.

PORTUGAL
Academia das Ciências de Lisboa, Rua de Academia das Ciências, Lisbon, Portugal.

Associacão Portuguesa de Escritores, Rua do Loreto, 13-2°, Lisbon, Portugal.

Instituto de Cultura Portuguesa, Rua D. João V, 30-Lisbon, Portugal.

Sociedade Portuguesa de Autores, Av. Duque, 31-1098 Lisbon, Portugal.

ROMANIA
The Writers Union of the Socialist Republic of Romania, Calea Victoriei 115, Bucarest, Romania.

SPAIN
Sociedad General de Autores de Espana, Fernando VI, 4, Madrid 4, Apartado 484, Spain.

SWEDEN
Sveriges Forfattarforbund, Box 5252, 102 45 Stockholm 5, Sweden.

SWITZERLAND
Schweizer Autorengruppe Olten, Siedlung Halen 43, CH 3037 Stuckishaus, Swtizerland.

Schweizerischer Schriftsteller-Verband. Kirchgasse 25, 8001 Zurich, Switzerland.

U.S.S.R.
Union of Soviet Writers, ul. Vorovskogo 52, Moscow, U.S.S.R.

Yugoslavia
Szvez Knjizevnika Jugoslavije, 11000 Belgrade, Lalić Francuska br 7, Yugoslavia.

APPENDIX 4

POETS LAUREATE OF THE UNITED KINGDOM

The title of Poet Laureate in England was conferred back as far as the 17th century in the form of a pension which specifically recognized the poet's services to the Crown. The laureateship has become the reward for eminence in poetry and is recognized as a Royal office to be filled when vacant.

The following is a list of the Poets Laureate of the United Kingdom from the date of inception of that honour.

Samuel Daniel—1599
Ben Jonson—1619
Sir William D'Avenant—1637
John Dryden—1670
Thomas Shadwell—1688
Nahum Tate—1692
Nicholas Rowe—1715
Rev. Laurence Eusden—1718
Colley Cibber—1730
William Whitehead—1757
Rev. Thomas Warton—1785
Henry James Pye—1790
Robert Southey—1813
William Wordsworth—1843
Lord Tennyson—1850
Alfred Austin—1896
Robert Bridges—1913
John Masefield—1930
Cecil Day-Lewis—1967
Sir John Betjeman—1972
Edward (Ted) Hughes—1984

APPENDIX 5

OXFORD PROFESSORSHIP OF POETRY

The Professorship of Poetry was established in 1508 from funds left by Henry Birkhead who was a scholar of Trinity College, Oxford, from 1635, and a Fellow of All Souls College from 1638-57.

The Professor's appointment procedure is totally unlike that for other professorships. Appointments are made by panels of nine people including specialists in the subject of the professorship. Convocation, consisting of all the holders of the degree of M.A. from Oxford University, then elects the Professor. In order to vote for the Professorship it is necessary to attend in person at Oxford and give one's vote to the Vice-Chancellor or his representative.

By way of duties, the Professor, by statute, has to deliver a public lecture each term. The position carries a small salary for the five year term of office.

The following is a list of holders of the Professorship of Poetry from the date of the chair's inception. Only in recent times has the Professor been primarily a poet so the list contains many purely professorial names.

Joseph Trapp	1708-18
Thomas Warton	1718-28
Joseph Spence	1728-38
John Whitfield	1738-41
Robert Lowth	1741-51
William Hawkins	1751-56
Thomas Warton	1756-66
Benjamin Wheeler	1766-76
John Randolph	1776-83
Robert Holmes	1783-93
James Hurdis	1793-1802
Edward Copleston	1802-12
John Josias Conybeare	1812-21
Henry Hart Milman	1821-31
John Keble	1831-42
James Garbett	1842-52
Thomas Legh Claughton	1852-57
Mathew Arnold	1857-67
Sir Francis Hastings Charles Doyle	1867-77
John Campbell Shairp	1877-85
Francis Turner Palgrave	1885-95
William John Courthope	1895-1900
Andrew Cecil Bradley	1901-06
John William Mackail	1906-11
Sir Thomas Herbet Warren	1911-16
William Paton Ker	1920-23
Heathcote William Garrod	1923-28
Ernest de Selincourt	1928-33
George Gordon	1933-38
Adam Fox	1938-43
Sir Cecil Maurice Bowra	1946-51
Cecil Day-Lewis	1951-55
Wystan Hugh Auden	1956-61
Robert Ranke Graves	1961-66
Edmund Charles Blunden	1966-68
Roy Broadbent Fuller	1968-73
John Barrington Wain	1973-78
Henry John Franklin Jones	1979-84
Peter Chad Tigar Levi	1984-

Vacancies occurred from 1917-19 and from 1944-45.

APPENDIX 6

THE WORLD LITERARY ACADEMY

In 1976 the International Biographical Centre of Cambridge, England, the publishers of the INTERNATIONAL AUTHORS AND WRITERS WHO'S WHO and the INTERNATIONAL WHO'S WHO IN POETRY, decided to set up the International Academy of Poets to bring together poets throughout the world and to bring attention to their work. Invitations to take up Fellowship of the Academy were sent out to selected poets and within a few months 217 had been appointed as Founder Fellows. Annual and Life Fellowships have been granted to many additional applicants since December 1976 and as the Academy grew in size a quarterly magazine was distributed without charge to all Fellows who also received priority invitations to attend the annual International Congresses of the International Biographical Centre. Beginning with the Fourth IBC International Congress in London in July 1977 Fellows held their own closed sessions and poetry readings.

To celebrate the Silver Jubilee of the International Biographical Centre in 1985 it was decided to extend the fellowship of the IAP and incorporate this organization into a new WORLD LITERARY ACADEMY, into which writers of all disciplines and interests would be welcomed. Already journalists, novelists, academic writers and others have applied for Fellowship and invitations to join them have been sent to those listed in this Edition of the INTERNATIONAL AUTHORS AND WRITERS WHO'S WHO.

Each Fellow receives a Fellowship Card, a Diploma of Fellowship, and a subscription to the IBC Magazine which includes a reviews and news section for writers. Fellows may take discounts when ordering books from the International Biographical Centre and receive priority invitations to attend IBC International Congresses at reduced rates. Fellows who pay an annual subscription may use the letters 'FWLA' after their name; those who have paid a once-only fee for life use 'LFWLA'.

Fees (at April 1986) are:
    Entrance Fee: US $37.50 or £20.00 Sterling and either
    Annual Subscription: US $42.50 or £25.00 Sterling
    Thre-Years' Subscription: US $112.50 or £65.00 Sterling
    or
    Once-Only Life Subscription: US $412.50 or £250.00 Sterling.

    (The Academy reserve the right to increase fees at future dates).

Those who wish to take up Fellowship of THE WORLD LITERARY ACADEMY may write for an application form and further information to:

The World Literary Academy,
International Biographical Centre,
Cambridge, CB2 3QP. England

DIRECTORY OF
FELLOWS OF THE WORLD LITERARY ACADEMY

The following have taken up or confirmed Fellowship of the Academy since its foundation in 1985:

LIFE FELLOWS

Bartholomew, Dr. Paul J. (Life Fellow)
6 Drakes Bay, Corona Del Mar, CA 92625, USA

Batal, Mr. A.R. (Life Fellow)
Hannibal T & T Co, P.O. Box 4088, Damascus, Syria

Buckingham-White, Mrs. M.E. (Life Fellow)
136½ A. Alessandro, Hemet, CA 02343, USA

Civasaqui, Mr. Jose (Life Fellow)
Honcho 2-12-11, Ikebukuro, Toshima-ku, Tokyo 170, Japan

Cohen, Mr. Irwin (Life Fellow)
372 Central Park Avenue, Apt 2K, Scarsdale, NY 10583, USA

Cripps, Mrs. Joy Beaùdette (Life Fellow)
3 Mill Street, Aspendale 3195, Australia

Dow, Mrs. Marguerite Ruth (Life Fellow)
52 First Avenue, Apt 2, Ottawa, Ontario, Canada

Friedman, Mr. Elias (Life Fellow)
"Stella Maris' Monastery, P.O. Box 9047, 31090 Haifa, Israel

Gonzalez, Mr. Anson J. (Life Fellow)
P.O. Box 3254, Diego Martin, Trinidad & Tobago, W.I.

Harris, Louise M. (Life Fellow)
395 Angell Street, Apt 111, Providence, RI 02906, USA

Kabadi, Mr. Dwarakanath H. (Life Fellow)
21 Gopalakrishna, Swamy Temple Street, Chickpet Cross, Bangalore 560 053, S. India

Kahn, Ms. Faith-Hope (Life Fellow)
213-16-85th Avenue, Hollis Hills, NY 11427-1324, USA

Koch, Prof. Dr. Kurt E. (Life Fellow)
D-6955 Aglasterhausen, Germany

La Claustra, Dr. Vera B. (Life Fellow)
P.O. Box 2715, La Grande, Oregon 97850, USA

Landers, Dr. Vernette T. (Life Fellow)
P.O. Box 3839, Landers, CA 92285, USA

Mark, Mr. Paul J. (Life Fellow)
Buchholzstrasse 119, CH-8053 Zurich, Switzerland

Scharndorff, Prof. Werner (Life Fellow)
Hellbrunnerstrasse 7a/IV/21, A-5020 Salzburg, Austria

Sen, Prof. Dr. M.K. (Life Fellow)
Flat No N-4, Tarabag, Burdwan 713104, India

Sexauer, Dr. Arwin F.B. Garellick (Life Fellow)
La Casa de Paz-Dewey Street, Richford, VT 05476, USA

Sharp, Mrs. S. Laverna J. (Life Fellow)
Boite Postale 668, Conakry, Guinea, West Africa

Suzuki, Mrs. T. Chizu (Life Fellow)
1-31-16 Denenchofu, Otaku, Tokyo, Japan

Swede, Mr. George (Life Fellow)
Psychology Dept., Ryerson Polyt. Inst., 50 Gould St, Toronto, Ontario, Canada

Towne, Dr. Dorothea Alice III (Life Fellow)
East 508 Eaton Avenue, Spokane, Washington 99218, USA

Urhman, Miss Celia (Life Fellow)
1655 Flatbush Avenue, Apt C2010, Brooklyn, NY 11210, USA

Urhman, Miss Esther (Life Fellow)
1655 Flatbush Avenue, Brooklyn, NY 11210, USA

Urry, Dr. Vern William (Life Fellow)
3301 Accolade Drive, Clinton, Maryland 20735, USA

Wilkinson, Rosemary, R.C. (Life Fellow)
1239 Bernal Avenue, Burlingame, CA 94010, USA

Wolanin, Dr. Sophie Mae (Life Fellow)
1608 Lafayette Road, Pittsburgh, PA 15221, USA

ANNUAL FELLOWS

Akavia, Mrs. Mirjam (Annual Fellow)
Refidim Str. 4/a, Tel-Aviv 69982, Israel

Amor, Mrs. Anne Clark (Annual Fellow)
16 Parkfields Avenue, London, NW9 7PE, England

Amster, Mr. S.M. (Annual Fellow)
3 Montifiore Street, Petah-Tiquvah, Israel

Arrowsmith, Mrs. Judith Mary (Annual Fellow)
3 Strathalmond Park, Edinburgh, EH4 8AJ, Scotland

Ashe, Mr. John Harold (Annual Fellow)
P.O. Box 1601, Townsville, Queensland 8401, Australia

Bagg, Mr. Charles, E. (Annual Fellow)
Little Broomfield, Broomfield Hill, Great Missenden, Bucks, England.

Baker, Mrs. Lillian (Annual Fellow)
15237 Chanera Avenue, Gardena, CA 90249, USA

Barcock, Mr. George (Annual Fellow)
430 Bay Street NE, Apt 904, St Petersburg, FL 33701, USA

Bassir, Prof. Olumbe (Annual Fellow)
P.O. Box 4021, University of Ibadan, Ibadan, Nigeria

Batarse, Mr. Guillermo F. (Annual Fellow)
Calle Durango No. 319 Oriente, Gomez Palacio, Durango, Mexico

Bemberg, Mr. Georges (Annual Fellow)
20 Rue du Dragon, Paris, 75006, France

Bera, Dr. Sudhir (Annual Fellow)
Flat No. 2, Esplande Mansions, Calcutta 700001, India

Biro, Dr. Yvette (Annual Fellow)
2 Washington Square Village No 8-I, New York, NY 10012, USA

Blake, Mr. Leslie Bamford James (Annual Fellow)
4 Anton Court, Karingal, Victoria, 3199, Australia

Blank, Mr. Franklin (Annual Fellow)
5477 Cedonia Avenue, Baltimore, MD 21206, USA

Bowden, Mrs. Vera Vaughen (Annual Fellow)
Saffierhorst 200 2592GN, The Hague, Netherlands

Brown, Mrs. Marel (Annual Fellow)
1983 N. Decatur Rd NE, Atlanta, Georgia 30307, USA

Brulotte, Dr. Gaetan (Annual Fellow)
82 Des Casernes, Trois-Rivieres, Quebec, Canada

Caldwell, Prof. Stratton F. (Annual Fellow)
80 North Kanan Road, Agoura, CA 91301, USA

Cattarossi Arana, Prof. Nelida M (Annual Fellow)
Av. Gutierrez 650-4° piso, Dept 29 (5500), Mendoz R, Argentina

Chapelle, Mr. M. Stavaux de la (Annual Fellow)
Closeoles Chenes 64, 1170 Bruxelles, Belgium

Chiarelotto, Mr. Antonio (Annual Fellow)
16 Via Giacomelli, 31100 Treviso, Italy

Christensen, Ms. V.A. (Annual Fellow)
7 Idle Day Drive, Centerport, NY 11712, USA

Corder, Mr. George Edward (Annual Fellow)
P.O. Box 1723, Hollywood, CA 90078, USA

Cucin, Dr. Robert L. (Annual Fellow)
8 East 62nd Street, New York, NY 10021, USA

Cunningham, Mr. Clifford Joseph (Annual Fellow)
250 Frederick Street, Apt 1707, Kitchener, Ontario, Canada

Crobaugh, Ms. Emma (Annual Fellow)
Seagate of Highland 821-C, 3300 S Ocean Blvd., Highland Beach, FL 33431, USA

Davis, Mr. Orville K. (Annual Fellow)
P.O. Box 1427, Ruston, Louisiana 71270, USA

Del Valle, Ms. Helen C. (Annual Fellow)
P.O. Box 958, Chicago, IL 60690, USA

Dilks, Mrs. John H. (Annual Fellow)
394 Carlton Place, Exton, PA 19341, USA

Dodge, Miss Ellin (Annual Fellow)
4216 W. Missouri, Phoenix, AZ 85019, USA

England, Mr. Gerald (Annual Fellow)
23 Gambrel Bank Road, Ashton-under-Lyne, Lancashire OL6 8TN, England

Fergus, Dr. Patricia M. (Annual Fellow)
510 Groveland Avenue, Minneapolis, MN 55403, USA

Foster, Mrs. Linda N. (Annual Fellow)
427 W. PEre Marquette, Big Rapids, MI 49307, USA

Foque, Prof. Richard (Annual Fellow)
'Hortside', Bruinstraat 14, B-2418 Lille, Belgium

Frøydarlund, Prof. Dr. Jan Anker (Annual Fellow)
P.O. Box 28, 3701 Skien, Norway

Fuentes Blanco, Maria de los Reyes (Annual Fellow)
Apartado de correos 94, 41080 Sevilla, Spain

Fukuda, Miss Haruko (Annual Fellow)
'Creems', Wissington, Nayland, Nr. Colchester, Essex, England

Gilchrist, Mr. Martyn W. (Annual Fellow)
22 Fernhill Road, New Milton, Hants. BH25 55Z, England

Gillespie, Mr. Lyall Leslie (Annual Fellow)
"Lynora", 18 Ferdinand Street, Campbell, ACT 2601, Australia

Goff, Mr. Richard Martin (Annual Fellow)
8 Corkscrew Hill, West Wickham, Kent, BR4 9BB, England

Gragsin, Mr. José Valliente (Annual Fellow)
104 Collins Avenue, Baltimore, Maryland 21229, USA

Green, Dr. Rose B. (Annual Fellow)
308 Manor Road, Philadelphia, PA 19128, USA

Greene, Ms. Freda (Annual Fellow)
6624 Newcastle Avenue, Reseda, CA 91335, USA

Grossie, Mrs. Patricia Ann (Annual Fellow)
1890 Northcliffe Loop N., Columbus, Ohio 43229, USA

Hanton, Mr. E. Michael (Annual Fellow)
P.O. Box 872, Chico, CA 95927, USA

Heald, Dr. Bruce Day (Annual Fellow)
Box 1052, Meredith, New Hampshire 03253, USA

Horswell-Chambers, Ms. Margaret (Annual Fellow)
P.O. Box 1263, La Marque, TX 77568, USA

Hutchins, Mrs. Myldred Flanigan (Annual Fellow)
413 Princeton Way NE, Atlanta, GA 30307, USA

Iglesias, Prof. Dr. José F. Moratinos (Annual Fellow)
C/Av Aguilera 48 2°d, 03006 Alicante, Spain

Johnsen, Mr. Kjell (Annual Fellow)
Skigardveien 43, 0681 Oslo, Norway

Johnson, Miss. A. Pauline (Annual Fellow)
76 Rue Laural, Hull, Quebec, Canada

Jones, Prof. David Gareth (Annual Fellow)
Dept of Anatomy, University of Otago, P.O. Box 913, Dunedin, New Zealand

Kiddell, Rev. Sidney George (Annual Fellow)
The Church Court, Kettlestone, Fakenham, Norfolk, England

Kikkawa, Prof. Jun'ichi (Annual Fellow)
5-23 2-chome Kunokidai, Tondabayashi City, Osaka, Japan

Kisjokai, Mrs. Erzsebet (Annual Fellow)
Tesselschade laan 6, NL 1217 Hilversum, The Netherlands

Klemettinen, Mr. Yrhó (Annual Fellow)
Kaislatie 11 L 43, 90160 Oulu, Finland

Knibb, Mrs. Shirley M. (Annual Fellow)
80 Auckland Road, Potters Bar, Herts. England

Kwan, Mr. William Chao-Yu (Annual Fellow)
Tappan Oaks, 12 Carol Lane, Tappan, NY 10983, USA

Lee, Mr. Brad (Annual Fellow)
Box 8, Forest Hills, NY 11375, USA

Lee, Mr. Kuei-Shien (Annual Fellow)
Room 705, Asia Enterprisecenter, No. 600 Minchuan East Road, Taipei, Taiwan ROC

Limet, Ms. Elisabeth (Annual Fellow)
4444 Sherbrooke, Apt 201, Westmount, Montreal, Quebec, Canada

Lindholm, Dr. Gosta O. Ferdinand (Annual Fellow)
Parivaljakonkuja 4 A 13, 00410 Helsinki 41, Finland

List, Mrs. Anneliese (Annual Fellow)
Fúnfbronn 26, 8545 Spalt, German Federal Republic

Loebner-Felski, Mrs. Erika (Annual Fellow)
D-8262 Altoetting, P.O. Box 132, German Federal Republic

Loewen, Dr. Walter (Annual Fellow)
Kampstrasse 91 D, D-3000 Hannover 61, German Federal Republic

McCoin, Dr. Jack M. (Annual Fellow)
310-B Kiowa Street, Leavenworth, Kansas 66048, USA

McCromack, Mr. Kenneth A. (Annual Fellow)
6 Nuthurst, Sutton Coldfield, West Midlands, England

McCudden, J.P., Mrs. M.L. (Annual Fellow)
14/31 Churchill Crescent, Concord, N.S.W. 2137, Sydney, Australia

McElroy, Mrs. Ilse Ireienmuth von Helms (Annual Fellow)
P.O. Box 363, Comfort, TX 78013, USA

McLaren, Dr. Peter Lawrence (Annual Fellow)
116 North Bishop Avenue, Oxford, OH,, USA

Mackay, Mr. A.M. (Annual Fellow)
RMB 217 Rose Valley Road, Gerringong, NSW 2534, Australia

Malin, Dr. H.G. (Annual Fellow)
c/o Veterans Admin. Medical Center, Chief Podiatric Section, Martinsburg, W. VA 25401, USA

Manaf, Dr. Mohammed Z. (Annual Fellow)
Hampstead Lodge, P.O. Box 1052, Jalan Semangat, Petaling, Jaya, Malaysia

Mannes, Mrs. Totte (Annual Fellow)
Moreto 10, 28014 Madrid, Spain

Martin, Mr. Ernest Walter (Annual Fellow)
Editha Cottage, Black Torrington, Beaworthy, Devon, England

Martin, Dr. Gerald (Annual Fellow)
70 Des Ormeaux, Ville Ile Perrot, Quebec, Canada

Mavrommatis, Mr. F.S. (Annual Fellow)
10 Alimedontos Str., GR-113 63, Kipseli, Athens, Greece

Maxwell-Mahon, Prof. William Dundas (Annual Fellow)
Dept. of English, University of Pretoria, Hillcrest 0083, Pretoria, S. Africa

Mishra, Dr. Raghu Nath (Annual Fellow)
Dept. of Electrical Engineering, College of Tech., GBPUAT Pant Nagar Dist., Nainital UP 263 145, India

Morris, Mr. William E. (Annual Fellow)
50 Harvey Street, Tauranga, Bay of Plenty, New Zealand

Moses Jr, Prof. Elbert R. (Annual Fellow)
2001 Rocky Dells Dr, Prescott, AZ 86301, USA

Muesing-Ellwood, Mrs. Edith E. (Annual Fellow)
128 Dean Street, Apt 1, Brooklyn, NY 11201, USA

Nnolim, Prof. Charles E. (Annual Fellow)
Dept. of English Studies, University of Port Harcourt, Port Harcourt, Nigera

Noritis, Mr. R.P. (Annual Fellow)
159 Goldhawk Trail, Scarborough, Ontario, Canada

Novelli, Florence (Annual Fellow)
18A Gloucester Street, Clifton Village, Clifton, Bristol, England

Orsi, Mrs. Gloria M. (Annual Fellow)
P.O. Box 5013, Santa Ana, CA 92704, USA

Pages, André de (Annual Fellow)
P.O. Box 596, Saint-Eustache, Quebec, Canada

Pampel, Mrs. Martha Maria (Annual Fellow)
Lortzingstr. 9 (3423), Bad Sachsa, German Federal Republic

Paratte, Dr. Prof. Henri-Dominique (Annual Fellow)
Box 298, Acadia University, Wolfville, Nova Scotia, Canada

Parson, Dr. Erwin Randolph (Annual Fellow)
316 Pemaco Lane, Uniondale, NY 11553, USA

Pearce, Mr. Francis J.C. (Annual Fellow)
'Trees', 7 Cosanes Park, Perrmarworthal, Truro, Cornwall, England

Persson, Prof. Dr. Bertil (Annual Fellow)
P.O. Box 7048, S-171 07 Solne, Sweden

Pritchard, Ms. Hilary K. (Annual Fellow)
University of California School of Dentistry, Restorative Dentistry D-3212, 707 Pamassus Avenue, San Francisco, CA 94143, USA

Quartey, Mr. Fred R. (Annual Fellow)
State Insurance Corporation of Ghana, Life Division, P.O. Box 2363, Accra, Ghana

Rein, Mr. Karl Carolus Hilding Gabrial (Annual Fellow)
Kopingsvagen 25B, 02700 Grankulla, Finland

Roth, Frederic Hull (Annual Fellow)
20661 Avalon Drive, Rocky River, OH 44116, USA

Rzepecki, Ms. Renata Dawidowicz (Annual Fellow)
2363 Poland, Hamtramck, Michigan 48212, USA

Schmidt, Mr. Frank H. (Annual Fellow)
29 First Avenue, Klemzig, South Australia 5087, Australia

Scott, Ms. Elizabeth Patricia (Annual Fellow)
24 Martins Walk, Muswell Hill, London N10 1JT, England

Sethuraman, Dr. A.R. (Annual Fellow)
18 Second Main Road, Madras 600 061, Nanganallur, India

Shankaran, Dr. T.S. (Annual Fellow)
N. 16-D Sri Ramaprasada 37th Cross Jayanagar, 8th Block, Jayanagar, Bangalore 82560082, India

Sim, Mrs. Katherine (Annual Fellow)
Pencarrey, Llanybydder, Dyfed, Wales. UK

Sirola, Mr. Harri Erkki William (Annual Fellow)
Jaakarinkatu 5 B 3, 00150 Helsinki, Finland

Snellgrove, Mr. Laurence Ernest (Annual Fellow)
23 Harvest Hill, East Grinstead, W. Sussex, England

Snodgrass, Miss Ann (Annual Fellow)
1121 1st Avenue, No 3, Salt Lake City, Utah 84103, USA

Snowden, Mr. Alan (Annual Fellow)
5 Folkington Corner, Woodside Park, Finchley, London, England

Stamp-Chevalley, Mr. Roger (Annual Fellow)
'Au Verger', 1812 Rivaz, Canton Vaud, Suisse, Switzerland

Starling, Dr. Lirrel (Annual Fellow)
P.O. Box 307, San Andreas, CA 95249, USA

Starr, Mrs. Joan Elizabeth (Annual Fellow)
'Arakoon', Via Tenterfield, N.S.W. 2372, Australia

Steele, Mr. Peter Adrian (Annual Fellow)
101A Quedgeley Court Park, Greenhill Drive, Tuffley, Gloucs., England

Stone, Prof. Lowell (Annual Fellow)
Conquistador 7-107, Stuart, FL 33494, USA

Strom-Paikin, Prof. Joyce (Annual Fellow)
6112 NW 1st Street, Margate, FL 33063, USA

Stuart, Miss Vivian (Annual Fellow)
461 Malton Road, York, YO3 9TH, England

Subhas, Ms. Jeannette Spavieri (Annual Fellow)
1210 Grouse Drive, Pittsburgh, PA 15243, USA

Sutton, Mrs. Bridie (Annual Fellow)
22 Irving Place, Blackburn, Lancs, England

Tamari, Mr. Moshe (Annual Fellow)
P.O. Box 21488, Tel-Aviv 61214, Israel

Tapia, Dr. John (Annual Fellow)
326 S. Mt. Vernon Avenue, Prescott, AZ 86301, USA

Tatelbaum, Ms. Brenda Loew (Annual Fellow)
367 Brush Hill Road, Milton, MA 02186, USA

Taylor, Mr. Walter Harold (Annual Fellow)
19 Lawson Street, Hawthorn East, Victoria 2123, Australia

Thiagarajan, Dr. K. (Annual Fellow)
8 Warren Road, RR Flat 17-E, Mylapore 600 004, India

Thomas, Dr. Grace Fern (Annual Fellow)
2001 La Jolla Court, Modesto, CA 95350, USA

Tigges, Mr. John Thomas (Annual Fellow)
P.O. Box 902, Dubuque, IA 52004-0902, USA

Tisch, Prof. Dr. Johannes (Annual Fellow)
1 Cedar Court, Sandy Bay, Tasmania 7005, Australia

Torres, Dr. Rafael A. Gonzalez (Annual Fellow)
Box 22525 URP Sta., University of Puerto Rico, Rio Piedras, Puerto Rico 00931

Truck, Le Comte Robert-Paul (Annual Fellow)
"Varouna", 49 Rue de Lhomel, 62600 Berck-Plage, France

Twum, Michael Kyei (Annual Fellow)
P.O. Box 48, London SW17 0HF, England

Voinvich, Vladimir (Annual Fellow)
Hans Carossa Strasse 5, 8035 Stockdorf, German Federal Republic

Wade, Mr. Graham (Annual Fellow)
34 Holmwood Avenue, Leeds, LS6 4NJ, West Yorkshire, England

Whaling, Rev. Dr. Frank (Annual Fellow)
29 Ormidale Terrace, Edinburgh, Scotland

Whitehouse, Dr. Jack Edward (Annual Fellow)
16619 Graystone Avenue, Artesia, CA 90701, USA

Whyte, Mrs. Barbara (Annual Fellow)
45 Verbena Road, Birkdale, Auckland 10, New Zealand

Williams, Mr. Malcolm David (Annual Fellow)
58 Oxbutts Park, Woodmancote, Cheltenham, Gloucs., England

Willings, Dr. D.R. (Annual Fellow)
11 Windsor Park, Kings Lynn, Norfolk, England

Zuspan, Dr. Frederick (Annual Fellow)
2400 Coventry Road, Columbus, Ohio 43221, USA

The following were Fellows of the International Academy of Poets and have yet to confirm their Fellowship of the new World Literary Academy:

Ahsan, Professor Syed Ali (Founder Fellow)
60/1 Bashiruddin Road, North Whanmondi, Dacca 5, Bangladesh

Altabe, Mr. David (Fellow)
421 West Olive Street, Long Beach, NY 11561, USA

Alurista (Fellow)
3967-F Miramar Street, La Jolla, CA 92037, USA

Andrews, Mr. James D. (Fellow)
P.O. Box 4641, Baltimore, MD 21212, USA

Annoh, Mr. Godfried Kwesi (Founder Fellow)
Public Relations Officer, Bank for Housing and Construction, Box M1, Accra, Ghana

Anyidoho, Mr. Kofi (Founder Fellow)
Akuafo Hall, University of Ghana, Legon, Ghana

Argow, Sylvia (Founder Fellow)
2150 Wallace Avenue, Bronx, NY 10453, USA

Arnold, Mr. Colin A.E. (Founder Fellow)
Shady Side, Winford Road, Winford, Nr. Sandown, Isle of Wight, PO36 0JX, UK

Bailey, Mr. Gordon (Fellow)
32, Frederick Road, Edgbaston, Birmingham, B15 1JN, UK

Bailey, Lela L. Brooks (Fellow)
342 Jacobs Drive, Morgantown, West Virginia 26505, USA

Baldwin, Bertha Marjorie (Founder Fellow)
Old School Cottage, Forest Road, Colgate, Horsham, Sussex, UK

Baldwin, Mrs. Mary (Fellow)
Little Meadow, Edgton, Craven Arms, Shropshire, UK

Baldwin, Mary Newton (Founder Fellow)
59, Fairway Drive, Ormond Beach, Florida 32074, USA

Baltzell, Mrs. Virginia (Fellow)
115 Blakeney Street, Stephenville, TX 76401, USA

Barnes, Mr. Jim W. (Founder Fellow)
918 Pine Street, Macon, Missouri 63552, USA

Baucom, Margaret Dean (Founder Fellow)
710 South Hayne Street, Monroe, NC 28110, USA

Beauregard-Bezou, Marion (Fellow)
4529 Western, Detroit, MI 48210, USA

Beckman, Mr. Erik (Founder Fellow)
Prastmon 2319, S-870 52 Nyland, Sweden

Beissel, Mr. Henry (Founder Fellow)
English Department, Concordia University, 1455 de Maisonneuve, West Montreal, Canada H3G 1MS

Bellegarde, Ida R. (Fellow)
2720 No. Hutchinson Street, Pine Bluff, AR 71602, USA.

Betanzos-Santos, Professor Manuel (Fellow)
P.O. Box 262, Victoria Station, Montreal, Quebec, Canada H3Z 2V5

Blankner, Dr. Frederika (Founder Fellow)
Hotel des Artistes, One West 67th Street, New York, NY 10023, USA

Blumenkron, Carmen (Founder Fellow)
Avenue San Francisco No. 609, Colonia Del Valle, Mexico 12, D.F. Mexico

Bogue, Lucile Maxfield (Founder Fellow)
2611 Brooks, El Cerrito, CA 94530, USA

Bolay, Dr. Karl (Life Fellow)
PL 844 Flundrarps Bostalle, S-260 40 Viken, Sweden

Bonnette, Mrs. Jeanne DeLamarter (Founder Fellow)
6801 Ina Drive NE Albuquerque, NM 87109, USA

Boswell, Mrs. Winthrop P. (Fellow)
835 Black Mountain Road, Hillsborough, CA 94010, USA

Botelho, Mr. Eugene G.E. (Fellow)
P.O. Box 2188, Leucadia, CA 92024, USA

Bowman, Mrs. Elton N. (Founder Fellow)
3521 Eastridge Drive, Fort Worth, TX 76117, USA

Boyadjian, Mrs. Knarig (Fellow)
2924 Saint George Street, Los Angeles, CA 90027, USA

Brandt, Mr. Edward R. (Founder Fellow)
167 Bedford Street SE, Minneapolis, MN 55414, USA

Braz, Mr. Joao (Fellow)
Portimao, Algarve, Portugal

Brisk, Mrs. Rita (Founder Fellow)
40 Broadway, Cheadle, Cheshire, UK

Brown, Rita Mae (Founder Fellow)
401 Marlboro Street, Boston, MA 02115, USA

Bryant, Sylvia Leigh (Fellow)
Route 5 Box 498A, Madison Height's VA 24572, USA

Brzostowska, Janina (Founder Fellow)
J. Dabrowskiego 75m. 113, 02-586 Warsaw, Poland

Bulli, Dr. H.C. (Fellow)
H-1, Jangpura Extension, New Delhi 110 014, India

Buonocore, Dr. Michaelina (Founder Fellow)
2141 Cotona Avenue, (Bldg 2, Apt. 13G), Bronx, NY 10457, USA

Burnett, Mr. Alfred David (Founder Fellow)
33 Hastings Avenue, Merry Oaks, Durham, DH1 3QK, UK

Burrell, Evelyn Patterson (Founder Fellow)
3721 Gwynn Oak Avenue, Baltimore, MD 21207, USA

Byrd, Mr. Richard O. (Fellow)
Tambuzi Publications, UPO 3443, Kingston, NY 12401, USA

Cacciatore, Mr. Edoardo (Founder Fellow)
Largo Cristina di Svezia 12, 00165 Roma, Italy

Cameron Mrs. Bella (Founder Fellow)
Flat 2, 22 York Road, St. Annes-on-Sea, Lancs. FY8 1HP, UK

Canellos, Mr. George (Founder Fellow)
Mousson and Laskou, 20 Str., Psychico, Athens, Greece

Cannon, M. Minerva (Founder Fellow)
9120 SW 32nd Street, Miami, FL 33165, USA

Carpenter, Miss Margaret H. (Fellow)
1032 Cambridge Crescent, Norfolk, VA 23508, USA

Carrier, Dr. Warren (Founder Fellow)
Chancellor's Office, University of Wisconsin-Platteville, Platteville, WI 53818, USA

Carter, Marian (Founder Fellow)
44 Hollins Grove Street, Darwen, Lancs, BB3 1HG, UK

Catala, Mr. Rafael E. (Fellow)
RD 1, Box 356, Baptist Church Road, Hampton, NJ 08827, USA

Chadwell, Pearl (Founder Fellow)
RD No. 1, Karns City, PA 16041, USA

Chamberlain, Mr. Kent Clair (Founder Fellow)
625 Holly Street Ashland, Jackson County, OR 97520, USA

Chamiel, Dr. Haim Itzchak (Founder Fellow)
7 Fichman Street, Jerusalem, Israel

Chan, Mr. Stephen (Fellow)
P.O. Box 30190, Lusaka, Zambia

Chand, H.S.H. Prince (Fellow)
Chirayu Rajani, 256 Don Kaeo 3, Mae Rim, Chiengmai, Thailand

Chin Lin, Reverend John L. (Fellow)
123 Q Block 211, Boon Lay Place, Singapore 2264

Church, Mr. Avery Grenfell (Fellow)
351 Azalea Road, Apt. B-28, Mobile, AL 36609, USA

Clayton, Fay Marie (Life Fellow)
43 Messines Road, Karori, Wellington, New Zealand

Cleary, Dr. Marion E. (Fellow)
3 Lovers Lane, Groton, MA 01450, USA

Clemmons, Mr. Vincent Burton (Fellow)
2138 E. 76th Street, Chicago, IL 60649, USA

Cline, Mr. Charles (Founder Fellow)
9866 S. Westnedge Avenue, Kalamazoo, MI 49002, USA

Clitheroe, Mr. Frederic (Fellow)
6 St. Edmunds Avenue, Newcastle, Staffs, ST5 0AB, UK

Cole, Mr. Eddie Lou (Founder Fellow)
1841 Garden Highway, Sacramento, CA 95833, USA

Comaish, Mr. Peter William (Fellow)
48 Cherry Tree Walk, Beckenham, Kent, BR3 3PQ, UK

Conley, Mr. Robert J. (Founder Fellow)
721 Burlington, Billings, MT 59101, USA

Connellan, Mary (Founder Fellow)
105 Mathoura Road, Toorak, Victoria 3142, Australia

Coppone, Professor Filadelfio (Fellow)
Via del Falcetto N. 59/E, 95121-Catania, Italy

Correas de Zapata, Maria C. (Fellow)
128 Waverly Place, Mountain View, CA 94040, USA

Cox, Professor Joseph M.A. (Founder Fellow)
Tilden Towers 11, 801 Tilden Street, Bronx, NY 10467, USA

Cramer, Eila Johanna (Fellow)
Ignacio Esteva 20 B 405, Col San Miguel Chapultepec, Mexico 18, D.F.

Cullingford, Mrs. Ada Sophia (Founder Fellow)
7 Beeches, Oxford Road, Sutton Scotney, Nr. Winchester, Hants. SO21 3JW, UK

Currell, Mr. Ronald Gordon (Founder Fellow)
2113 Madison Avenue, Redwood City, CA 94061, USA

Cutbush, Mr. Andrew S.B. (Fellow)
62 North Road, Highgate Village, London, N6 4AA, UK

Darby, Miss Edith M. (Founder Fellow)
210 Cedarcrest Avenue, Pleasantville, NJ 08232, USA

Dawson, Mrs. Susan H. (Fellow)
245 Albert Hart Dr., Baton Rouge, LA 70808, USA

Day, Audrey (Founder Fellow)
"Redvers", 127 Queen Mary Avenue, Cleethorpes, South Humberside, UK

Dayton, Irene Catherine Glossenger (Founder Life Fellow)
Pine Stone, 209 S. Hillandale Drive, E. Flat Rock, NC 28726, USA

De Bolt, Dr. William Walter (Founder Fellow)
Trenton, NB 69044, USA

Deleski, Mrs. G.R. (Fellow)
6910 East Rutgers Place, Tucson, Arizona, USA

DeLisa, Dr. Emilia (Fellow)
Renee Gate Rt. 6, P.O. Box 378, Mohegan Lake, NY 10547, USA

De Mesne, Mr. Eugene F.P.C. (Founder Fellow)
Triple P Publications, Box 8776, Boston, MA 02114, USA

Densford, Edna (Fellow)
17736 Hatteras Street, Encino, CA 91316, USA

Desich, Helen Cynthia (Founder Fellow)
22 East 22nd Street, Apt. 209, Minneapolis, MN 55404, USA

De Souza, Judge Robert (Fellow)
Assagao, Goa, India

De Villasenor, Laura Agatha Wells (Founder Fellow)
Reyna 73, San Angel, Mexico, 20 D.F., Mexico

Dewhirst, Mr. Brian John (Founder Fellow)
250 West Barnes Lane, New Malden, Surrey, KT3 6LU

Dickson, Mr. Robert C. (Founder Fellow)
907 Columbia Avenue, North Bergen, NJ 07047, USA

Diener, Mary E. (Founder Fellow)
c/o Diener & Associates Inc., P.O. Box 12052, Research Triangle Park, NC 27709, USA

Dor, Mr. Moshe (Founder Fellow)
Embassy of Israel, 2 Palace Green, London, W8 4QB, UK

Doyle, Mr. Charles (Founder Fellow)
759 Helvetia Crescent, Victoria B.C., Canada

Dryman, Mr. John W. (Founder Fellow)
30 Burford Road, Salisbury, Wiltshire, UK

Dyer, Roberta Coldren (Founder Fellow)
1325 Manchester Road, Wheaton, IL 60187, USA

Eaton, Mrs. Howard Lucy Ellen (Founder Fellow)
101 8th Avenue, North, Castlegar, B.C., Canada V1N 1M7

Edwardes, Mr. Peter Ivan (Fellow)
51 Kingston Crescent, North End, Portsmouth, Hants., UK

Ee, Mr. Tiang Hong (Founder Fellow)
30 Stoddart Way, Bateman, Western Australia 6153, Australia

Eisenberg, Mr. William David (Founder Fellow)
5380 Old Berwick Road, Bloomsburg, PA 17815, USA

Emms, Josepha Murray (Founder Fellow)
205 South Huntington Avenue, Jamaica Plain, Boston, MA 02130, USA

Fargason, Ina May (Founder Fellow)
2202 Sunset, Snyder, TX 79549, USA

Farquhar, Betty M. (Fellow)
P.O. Box 127, Marion, TX 78124, USA

Farran, Commander Don Wilson (Fellow)
124 Main Street, Rowan, IA 50470, USA

Farthing-Owens, Mrs. Alberta (Fellow)
P.O. Box 48, Woodland, ME 04694, USA

Faust, Dr. Naomi F. (Fellow)
112-01 175th Street, Jamaica, NY 11433, USA

Florian, Mr. Tibor (Founder Fellow)
3 Mountain View Drive, New Milford, CT 06776, USA

Flynn, Mr. John Joseph (Founder Fellow)
788 Rowanville, Kildare, Co. Kildare, Ireland

Fountain, Helen Van Alstyne (Founder Fellow)
23-B Maryland Avenue, Cedar Glen Lakes, Whiting, NJ 08759, USA

Foxe, Dr. Arthur N. (Fellow)
9 East 67th Street, New York City, NY 10021, USA

Francis, Miss Mabel A. (Life Fellow)
100 Leyland Road, Southport, Merseyside, PR9 0NJ, UK

Friedman, Mr. Jacob H. (Founder Life Fellow)
"Stella Maris" Monastry, P.O. Box 9047, Haifa 31090, Israel

Gapert, Werner H. (Life Fellow)
Ranheckstr. 11, 8000 Munich 21, German Federal Republic

Garden, Mr. David Kennedy (Founder Fellow)
10 Pitairlie Road, Mid Craigie, Dundee, Scotland, UK

Garrett, Mrs. Florence R. (Fellow)
Hut Hill Road, Bridgewater, CT 06752, USA

Gaumond, Mary Rockefeller (Founder Fellow)
12115 Foxhill Lane, Bowie, MD 20715, USA

George, Professor Emergy Edward (Founder Fellow)
1485 Maywood, Ann Arbor, MI 48103, USA

Giammarino, Mr. Jaye (Founder Fellow)
P.O. Box 209, Coatesville, PA 19320, USA

Gibson, Mr. Peter Sean (Fellow)
58 Church Avenue, Kircubbin, Newtownards, Co. Down, N. Ireland, UK

Gilburt, Mr. Samuel Gale (Founder Fellow)
6751 181st Street, Fresh Meadows, NY 11365, USA

Gill, Mr. Stephen (Fellow)
Box 1641, Cornwall, Ontario, Canada K6H 5V6

Glassberg, Gwendolyn Revilda Kroman Darling (Founder Fellow)
1119 Carolina Avenue, West Chester, PA 19380, USA

Glassbury, Betty Blanc (Founder Fellow)
150 West 55th Street, New York, NY 10019, USA

Glazebrook, Mr. Christopher J (Fellow)
294 Birchfield Road East, Northampton, NN3 2SY, UK

Goldkorn, Mr. Isaac (Fellow)
122 Clanton Park Road, Downsview, Ontario, Canada M3H 2E5

Goldthorpe, Mrs. Ruth (Founder Fellow)
8 Cynthia Street, Para Hills, South Australia 5096, Australia

Gordon, Mrs. Guanetta Stewart (Founder Fellow)
12238 Riviera Drive, Sun City, AZ 85351, USA

Grace, Mr. Dorman J. (Founder Fellow)
10 West Main Street, P.O. Box 352, Palmyra, PA 17078, USA

Gray, Reverend Leonard Benjamin (Founder Fellow)
Morning Glory Bungalow, 17 Johnson Road, Saugur, MA 01906, USA

Greeff, Mrs. Adele M.B. (Founder Fellow)
Dune Road, P.O. Box 1526, Long Island, NY 11959, USA

Gress, Esther (Fellow)
Ny Strandvej 27, 3050 Humlebaek, Denmark

Gugl, Mr. Wolfgang D. (Fellow)
Am Freigarten 12/IV/15, A-8020 Graz, Austria

Haddad, Mr. Qassim (Fellow)
c/o Bahrain Litterateurs & Writers Ass., P.O. Box 1010, Bahrain

Hall, Alice Clay (Founder Life Fellow)
109 Saddletree Road, San Antonio, TX 78231, USA

Hall, Inez Jean (Fellow)
1733 W. 38th Street, Anderson, IN 46013, USA

Halverson, Mr. Lloyd B. (Founder Fellow)
1306 West Main, Medford, OR 97501, USA

Hammer, Dr. Lillian (Founder Fellow)
15 Elmwood Street, Albany, NY 12203, USA

Hanf, Mr. James A. (Fellow)
P.O. Box 374, Bremerton, WA 98310, USA

Harpster, Rev, Dr. V. Aileen (Fellow)
International Research Institute, 5623 North 16th Street, Omaha, NE 68110, USA

Harvey, Margie Ballard (Founder Fellow)
205 Waert Street, Seagoville, TX 75159, USA

Hasbrouck, Patricia Marie (Founder Fellow)
2807 E. Binkley No. 205, Dallas, TX 75205, USA

High, Mr. Graham John (Founder Fellow)
13 Witham Road, Isleworth, Middlesex, TW7 4AJ, UK

Hill, Hyacinthe (Founder Fellow)
166 Hathorne Avenue, Yonkers, NY 10705, USA

Hobsbaum, Hannah (Founder Fellow)
64 Lilyville Road, London, SW6, UK

Hoeft, Mr. Robert Dean (Founder Fellow)
916 S.E. Byers Avenue, Pendleton, OR 97801, USA

Holden, Mrs. W. Sprague (Fellow)
28150 Westbrook Court, Farmington Hills, MI 48018, USA

Holman, Ottilie Ann (Founder Fellow)
58-25 74 Street, Elmhurst, NY 11373, USA

Holmberg, Margit (Founder Fellow)
Drakenbergsgatan 12, 41269 Göteborg, Sweden

Homan, Agnes Jones (Founder Fellow)
3170 Gifford Lane, Coconut Grove, FL 33133, USA

Hoole, Margaret Mary (Founder Fellow)
Thornley Villa, 213 Crook Lane, Winsford, Cheshire, CW7 3EG, UK

Hope, Mrs. Thelma P. (Fellow)
440 Santa Ana Ave., Newport Beach, CA 92663, USA

Horiuchi, Mrs. Amy (Fellow)
Apt. No. 3203, 5-13-29 Arajuku, Kawagoe, Saitama (350), Japan

Horn, Dr. Don Louis (Fellow)
P.O. Box 670, Punta Gorda, FL 33950, USA

Hunter, Mrs. Sarah Ann (Founder Fellow)
24 Top Street, Greenacres, Oldham, Lancs. OL4 2DR, UK

Hurst, Mr. Charles J. (Fellow)
Seestrasse 34, 8703 Erlenbach, Zurich, Switzerland

Husain, Mr. Syed Akbar (Founder Fellow)
162F/3 Pechs, Karachi, Pakistan

Hwang, Mrs. Seong E. (Fellow)
81-192 Ssang Moon, 2 Dong, Do Bong Ku, Korea

Ireland, Thelma (Founder Fellow)
25 Smithbridge Park, Reno, NV 89502, USA

Ivanisevic, Mr. Drago (Founder Fellow)
41000 Zagreb, Bogoviceva 1/VIII, Yugoslavia

Jack, Sheila Beryl (Founder Fellow)
"Longacre", Wrockwardine, Nr. Telford, Shropshire, UK

Jekeley, Mr. Zoltan (Founder Fellow)
1023 Budapest, Frankel-ut 23, Hungary

Johannessen, Mr. Matthias (Founder Fellow)
c/o Morgumbladid, Reykjavik, Iceland

Johnson, Mr. Avah (Fellow)
2009 Kirby Road, McLean, VA 22101, USA

Johnston, Mr. George (Founder Fellow)
RR 1, Athelstan, Quebec, Canada JOS 1AO

Jones, Juanita B. (Fellow)
288 E Marshall Blvd., San Bernardino, CA 92404, USA

Jungling, Mr. Otto (Founder Fellow)
Vordere Muhlstrasse 12, 7320 Goppingen-Faurndau, German Federal Republic

Kagame, Alexis (Founder Fellow)
B.P. 62, Butare, Rwanda

Kagan, Dr. Elieser (Founder Fellow)
29 Homa Umigdal Street, Kiryat Haim, 26264, Israel

Kakugawa, Mr. Frances Hideko (Founder Fellow)
2649 Varsity Place, Apartment 208, Honolulu, HI 96814, USA

Kaplan, Lois Jay (Fellow)
616 Lenwood Dr., Anniston, AL 36201, USA

Karlstedt-Saarsen, Karin Marie (Founder Fellow)
Ringvagen 10 V, S-11726 Stockholm, Sweden

Kastel, Daisylea Carl (Founder Fellow)
Bay Shore Road, Wittman, MD 21676, USA

Katz, Mrs. Susan A. (Fellow)
12 Timothy Court, Monsey, NY 10952, USA

Kazem, Dr. Ismail (Fellow)
Kwakkerbergweg 59,6523 ML Nymegen, The Netherlands

Keithley, Mr. George (Founder Fellow)
1302 Sunset Avenue, Chico, CA 95926, USA

Kendall, Alice B. (Founder Fellow)
2105 West Forest Lane, Ahaheim, CA 92804, USA

King, Janet Byers (Fellow)
1760 Beechwood Blvd., Pittsburgh, PA 15217, USA

Kingery, Lionel B. (Fellow)
4821 Buckingham, Detroit, MI 48224, USA

Kirby, Mrs. Patricia P. (Fellow)
3907 Club Drive NE, Atlanta, GA 30319, USA

Kirkup, Professor James (Founder Fellow)
BM-Box 2780, London WC1V 6XX, UK

Kishan, Mr. J. Gopal (Fellow)
5-10-29/A, Behind I.H.P. Co., Ellammagutta, Nizamabad, A.P. 50300L, India

Kivimaa, Professor Kaarlo Arvi (Founder Fellow)
00150 Helsinki 15, Sepankatu 15B, Finland

Kiya-Hinidza, Mr. Richard (Fellow)
University of Ghana, Legon, Ghana

Konnyu, Mr. Leslie (Founder Fellow)
5410 Kerth Road, St. Louis, MO 63128, USA

Konopka, Baron Feliks I.L. (Fellow)
ul. Krupnicza 8/2 31-123 Kradow, Poland

Kramer, Mr. Aaron (Founder Fellow)
96 Van Bomel Blvd., Oakdale, NY 11769, USA

Kress-Fricke, Regine I.J.D. (Founder Fellow)
Kronenstrasse 9, 75 Karlsruhe, German Federal Republic

Kukubajaska, Maria D. (Fellow)
91000 Skopje, Yugoslavia

Kulkarni, Dr. Hemant (Fellow)
1510 East 1100 North, Logan, UT 84321, USA

Kunkel, Pearle Tannery (Founder Fellow)
8525 S.E. 21st Avenue, Portland, OR 97202, USA

Kurz, Dr. Carl Heinz (Fellow)
Pappelhof, D 3406 Bovenden, German Federal Republic

Lam, Dr. Yan-Chiu L.H.D. (Founder Fellow)
107 Sai Yeung Choi Street, (9th Floor, Flat C), Kowloon, Hong Kong

Landers, Blanche B. (Founder Fellow)
P.O. Box 412, Fredericksburg, TX 78624, USA

Lane, Mr. John Thoddens (Founder Fellow)
Ballinrea Road, Carrigaline, Co. Cork, Ireland

Lane, Mary Louisa (Founder Fellow)
65 McPherson Street, Horsham, Victoria 3400, Australia

Lang, Professor Helmer (Founder Fellow)
S-26007 Hjarnarp, Sweden

Lappalainen, Mr. Kauko Kalevi (Founder Fellow)
132 1/2 West 13th Avenue, Emporia, KS 66801, USA

Latz, Dr. Dorothy L. (Fellow)
P.O. Box 265, New Rochelle, NY 10801, USA

Lawson, Helen J. (Fellow)
56 Old Mill Lane, West Hartford, CT 06107, USA

Lee, Mr. Hun (Fellow)
150 Mt. Whitney Ct., San Rafael, CA 94903, USA

Lee, Joyce I. (Fellow)
5 Morrison Street, Hawthorn 3122, Melbourne, Australia

Lesztak, Sara Marie (Fellow)
c/o P.O. Box 1723, Hope, British Columbia, Canada UOX 1LO

Liebknecht, Miss Henrietta (Founder Fellow)
2126 Village Drive, Apartment 6, Louisville, KY 40205, USA

Lin, Mr. Ching-Chyuan (Fellow)
No. 93 Yan Ping Road, Syh Gou Chuen, Wan Lan Shiang, Ping Tung, Taiwan, Republic of China

Lin, Professor Jong-teh (Fellow)
185-6 Nan-men Road, Tainan 700, Taiwan

Lindsley, Dr. Mary F. (Vice-Chancellor)
13361 El Dorado, 201 H Seal Beach, CA 90740, USA

Llewellyn, Mr. David William Alun (Founder Fellow)
52 Silchester Park, Glengeary, Dun Laoghaire, Co. Dublin, Ireland

Lomasney, Eileen Mary (Founder Fellow)
29B Windy Hill, Ballston Lake, NY 12019, USA

LuTour, Mr. Lou (Honorary Life Fellow)
1270 Fifth Avenue, New York, NY 10029, USA

Lyon, Mabelle A. (Founder Fellow)
8801 N. 17th Avenue, Phoenix, AZ 85021, USA

McElwain, Mr. Daniel B. (Founder Fellow)
2909 Beau Lane, Fairfax, VA 22030, USA

McFarlane, Col. Roy Livingstone Clare (Founder Fellow)
4 Lemon Close, Kingston 8, Jamaica, West Indies

McGaughey, Florence Helen (Founder Fellow)
136 South 25th Street, Terre Haute, IN 47803, USA

McGaughy, Mary Stallard (Founder Fellow)
4931 Pershing, Forth Worth, TX 76107, USA

McKerrow, Marjorie Jean (Fellow)
655 Esplanade, Urangan, Queensland, Australia

McKinney, Judith A.W. (Founder Fellow)
c/o Post Office, Braidwood, N.S.W. 2622, Australia

McNeil, Mr. Neil (Founder Fellow)
76 Hawthorn Road, Cumbernauld, Glasgow, G67 3LY, UK

McNeil, Dee Dee (Founder Fellow)
P.O. Box 2039, Altadena, CA 91001, USA

McWhorter, Mr. Bright Jasper (Founder Fellow)
Box 19, Route 1, Walkersville, WV 26447, USA

Mahapatra, Mr. Sitakant (Founder Fellow)
Homi Bhabha Fellow, Qrs. No. 5, Type VII, Bhubanswar 751001, Orissa, India

Mainone, Mr. Robert F. (Life Fellow)
Route 3, Box 485, Delton, MI 49046, USA

Makar, Dr. Boshra H. (Founder Fellow)
410 Fairmount Avenue, Jersey City, NJ 07306, USA

Matthyssen, Mr. Joannes (Founder Fellow)
Cedarlaan 4, B 2610, Wilrjik, Belgium

Meinke, Mr. Peter (Founder Fellow)
Director, Writing Workshop, Eckard College, St. Petersburg, FL 33733, USA

Menon, Dr. Rabindranath (Fellow)
Eonchakkal House, Trivandrum 695008, Kerala State, India

Menzel, Mr. Roderich (Founder Fellow)
Haushofer Str. 3, Munchen 81, German Federal Republic

Mercer, Betty D. (Fellow)
1422 New Street, Muskegon, MI 49442, USA

Michael-Titus, Dr. Constantin (Founder Fellow)
44 Howard Road, Upminster, RM14 2UF, UK

Michaels, Pearl D.B. (Founder Life Fellow)
7004 Blvd. East, Gutterberg, NJ 07093, USA

Min-Hwa, Dr. Chen (First Vice-Chancellor)
Pension Costa Rica Inn, P.O. Box 10282, San Jose, Costa Rica

Miner, Mrs. Virgina Scott (Founder Fellow)
30 N. Buffalo Street, Warsaw, IN 46580, USA

Misakowski, Mr. Stanislaw (Fellow)
ul. Marchlewskiego 1 B m. 52, 76-200 Sluspsk, Poland

Moland, Mrs. Ruby Louise (Fellow)
Box 417, Shelburne, Nova Scotia, Canada

Morales, Golide Peal Laden (Founder Life Fellow)
1340 College View Drive, Apartment No. 3, Monterey Park, CA 91754, USA

Morey, Mr. Frederick Lotharo (Founder Fellow)
4508 38th Street, Brentwood, MD 20722, USA

Mukherji, Mr. Brittendu K. (Fellow)
43 Vivekanand Marg, Allahabad (U.P.), Pin 211003, India

Murphy, Mary Elizabeth (Founder Fellow)
3948 Oak, Kansas City, MO 64111, USA

Murray, Mrs. S. (Fellow)
13 Fern Avenue, Lorne, Victoria 3232, Australia

Murti, Dr. Kotikalapudi Venkata Suryanarayana (Founder Fellow)
Lecturer in English, 27-4-42 Main Road, Visakhapatnam - 530 002 India

Myers, Dr. Mary Athena (Fellow)
3427 Denson Place, Charlotte, NC 28215, USA

Naik, Mr. Balwant G. (Fellow)
48 Shackleton Road, Southall, Middlesex, UK

Nanji, Mr. Salim S.N. (Founder Fellow)
11 Devonshire Road, Palmers Green, London, N13 4QU, UK

Napier, Mr. Lenox Scott (Founder Fellow)
Los Arcos, Mojacar, Almeria, Spain

Nartsissov, Mr. Boris (Fellow)
6213 Garretson Street, Burke, VA 22015, USA

Narula, Mr. Subhash (Founder Fellow)
35 DoubleStoreyed Bldgs., New Rajinder Nargar, New Delhi 110060, India

Neale, Dr. Dorothea (Vice-Chancellor)
3064 Albany Crescent, Apartment 54, New York, NY 10463, USA

Negalha, Mr. Jonas (Fellow)
Caixa Postal 7244, 01000 Sao Paula, Brazil

Neilson, Dr. Philip (Fellow)
Dept. of Communications, Queensland Institute of Technology, George Street, Brisbane, 4001, Australia

Nelson, Mr. Charles L. (Fellow)
P.O. Box 57, Caledonia, MS 39740, USA

Nelson, Mrs. Vera Joyce (Founder Fellow)
5558 SE Aldercrest Lane, Milwaukie, OR 97222, USA

Nikolai, Lorraine C. (Founder Fellow)
701 Humboldt Avenue, Wausau, Wisconsin 54401, USA

Noe, Bessie Wherry (Founder Fellow)
226 Naples Terrace, Bronx, New York, NY 10463, USA

North, Professor Eleanor Beryl (Founder Fellow)
204 East Hamilton Avenue, State College, PA 16801, USA

O'Brien, Katharine Elizabeth (Founder Fellow)
130 Hartley Street, Portland, ME 04103, USA

Offen, Mr. Yehuda (Founder Fellow)
8 Gazit Street, Tel-Aviv 69271, Israel

Okeke, Mr. Uchefuna (Founder Fellow)
Department of Fine & Applied Art, University of Nigeria, Nsukka, Nigeria

Okulski-Schmid, Diane Rose (Founder Fellow)
111 St Marks Place, No. 4, New York, NY 10009, USA

Osterlund, Mr. Steven (Fellow)
2024 Revere Road, Akron, OH 44313, USA

Oswald, Mr. Roy Lee (Fellow)
4396 Wares Ferry Road, Montgomery AL 36109, USA

Painton, Mr. Ivan E. (Fellow)
Studio of Fine Arts, C.S.R. Orion Road, Fairview, OK 73737, USA

Palmer, Pastor Jack H. (Fellow)
P.O. Box 111, Liberty, PA 16930, USA

Pappas, Neva J. (Founder Fellow)
Route 1 Box C29, Mammoth Spring, AR 72554, USA

Parks, Mr. Gerald B. (Fellow)
Via S. Michele 43, 34124 Trieste, Italy

Pastor, Miss Lucille E. (Fellow)
94 Ledgeside Avenue, Waterbury, CT 06708, USA

Patel, Mr. Yogesh (Founder Fellow)
Co-Editor Skylark, 50 Coniston Gardens, London, NW9, UK

Paterson, Mrs. Evangeline (Fellow)
2 Stoneygate Avenue, Leicester, LE2 3HE, UK

Peden, Mr. David S. (Fellow)
137 S. Broad Street, Grove City, PA 16127, USA

Petrik, Mr. Peter (Fellow)
419 West 17th Street, 22A, New York, NY 10011, USA

Pierce, Mr. Ben W. (Fellow)
491 South Kalispell Wy, Aurora, CO 80017, USA

Pintyre, Mrs. Carolyn A. (Fellow)
3396 Brunswick Pike, Princeton, NJ 08540, USA

Pluck, Dr. Derek J. (Fellow)
28 Barnsfold, Fulwood, Preston, Lancs. PR2 3FU, UK

Porter, Mr. Bern (Fellow)
22 Salmond Road, Belfast, ME 04915, USA

Posse, Mr. M.E. Echenique (Founder Fellow)
Lavalleja 1321, DPTO 19, Cofico, 5.000 Cordoba, Argentina

Poulsen, Mr. Ezra James (Founder Fellow)
587 First Avenue, Salt Lake City, Utah, USA

Quintana, Mr. Jose (Life Fellow)
Poligono Residencial Cruz de Piedra, c/o/ F. Manuel Blanco 1.6.D, Las Palmas, Canary Islands

Ransemar, Mr. Erik (Fellow)
Hoksigen 26, 144 00 Ronninge, Sweden

Ratliff, Dr. Gerald Lee (Fellow)
Department of Theatre, Montclair State College, Upper Montclair, NJ 07043, USA

Rees, Ennis (Founder Fellow)
English Department, University of South Carolina, Columbia, SC 29208, USA

Riddell, Mrs. C. Homer (Fellow)
51 Kingston Crescent, North End, Portsmouth, Hants. UK

Riley, Mr. Cyril Leslie (Founder Fellow)
20 Skipton Road, Ilkley, Yorkshire, UK

Rodrigues, Mr. Louis J. (Fellow)
c/Granja 30-32, 1°, 2°, Barcelona 24, Spain

Roney, Alice Mann (Founder Fellow)
1105 Georgina Avenue, Santa Monica, CA 90402, USA

Rook, Pearl Newton (Founder Fellow)
126 Williams Street, Newark, NY 14513, USA

Rosenbaum, Sylvia Portugal (Founder Fellow)
10 Heritage Court, Valley Stream, Long Island, NY 11581, USA

Rosner, Martin C. (Founder Fellow)
234 Vivian Court, Paramus, NJ 07652, USA

Rottiers, Mr. Arthur-Kamiel (Founder Fellow)
Rubenstraat 88, B2510-Mortsel, Belgium

Rudge, Mary R. (Fellow)
532 Haight Avenue, Alameda, CA 94501, USA

Ruggier, Mr. Joseph (Fellow)
c/o 2310 Mahon Avenue, Nr. Vancouver, British Columbia, Canada V7M 2V2

Saha, Mr. Subhas C. (Founder Fellow)
43/B Nandarem Sen Street, Calcutta 700005, India

Schmidt, Mr. Eberhard (Founder Fellow)
Tannenweg 1, D-6682 Ottweiler 1, German Federal Republic

Schrader, Margarete M.E. (Fellow)
Emmastr. 6, 4790 Paderborn, German Federal Republic

Schuck, Marjorie Massey (Founder Fellow)
8245 26th Avenue N, St. Petersburg, FL 33710, USA

Segal, Helen Gertrude (Founder Fellow)
7 Dunbar Street, Yeoville, Johannesburg 2001, South Africa

Setterberg, Ruth Elizabeth (Founder Fellow)
770 Boylston, Boston, Massachusetts 02199, USA

Setterlind, Mr. Bo Alf Ingemar (Founder Life Fellow)
Ekegarden, S-15200, Strangnas, Sweden

Settle, Patricia Claire Peters (Founder Fellow)
104 Bay Ridge Avenue, Brooklyn, NY 11220, USA

Shalom, Mr. Shin (Founder Fellow)
P.O. Box 6095, Haifa 31060, Israel

Shannon, Mrs. Elsie June (Fellow)
Route 4 Box 21, Stephenville, TX 76401, USA

Sharma, Mr. Har Prasad (Fellow)
SD-660, DIZ Area, Gold Marker, New Delhi-110001, India

Sheftel, Mr. Harry B. (Founder Fellow)
5813 3rd Place NW, Washington DC20011, USA

Shepherd, Barbara K. (Fellow)
Route 1 Box 81, Solon, 1A 52333, USA

Shu-Shun, Mr. Dai (Fellow)
2572 Lenox Road E-2, Atlanta, GA 30324, USA

Siano, Mary Martha (Founder Fellow)
37 Shore Haven Park Road, Hazlet, NJ 07730, USA

Silverman, Mr. Hirsch I. (Founder Fellow)
47 East 33rd Street, Bayonne, NJ 07002, USA

Smith, Mr. Michael (Fellow)
11 Arkley Court, Springfield Park, Holyport, Nr. Maidenhead, Berkshire, UK

Slappey, Mary McGowan (Founder Fellow)
4500 Chesapeake Street NW

Sliwinski, Mr. Wincenty P. (Fellow)
4/78 Tatrzanska Street, 00-742 Warsaw, Poland

Slonim, Ruth (Founder Fellow)
Dept. of English, Washington State University, Pullman, WA 99164, USA

Smeltzer, Mary S. (Fellow)
8102 Tavenor, Houston, TX 77075, USA

Smith, Dolleta Jean (Fellow)
Route 2 Box 32, Wayside Acres, Parkersburg, WV 26101, USA

Smith, Mr. Jared (Founder Fellow)
9 Bursley Place, White Plains, NY 10605, USA

Smith, Margery (Founder Fellow)
12 Springfield Crescent, Horsham, Sussex RH12 2PP, UK

Smith, Mr. Vivian Brian (Founder Fellow)
19 McLeod, Mosman, N.S.W. 2088, Australia

Smithdas, Mr. Robert Joseph (Founder Life Fellow)
Apartment 1-C, 225 1st Street, Mineola, NY 11501, USA

Sop, Mr. Nikola (Founder Fellow)
Vocarska 90 4100 Zagreb, Yugoslavia

Sowden, Miss Myrtle V. (Fellow)
44 Ebbisham Road, Worcester Park, Surrey, KT4 8NE, UK

Spain, Jane Spalding
2012 W Calle Placida, Tucson, AZ 85705, USA

Spain, Miss Mary (Fellow)
Flat 6, 67 Gloucester Terrace, London, W2, UK

Speer, Mr. Robert Louis (Founder Fellow)
715 North 14 Street, Fort Smith, AR 72901, USA

Srinivasan, Miss Banumathi (Fellow)
38 Second Main Road, Kasturbanagar, Adyar, Madras 600 020, S. India

Stahl, Virginia Elizabeth McDaniel (Founder Fellow)
Route 1, Woodsfield, OH 43793, USA

Stallard, Mr. Bernard B. (Founder Fellow)
P.O. Box 1645, Middlesboro, KY 40965, USA

Stone, Mr. Lloyd (Founder Fellow)
1335-101 Wilder Avenue, Honolulu, HI 96822, USA

Storey, Mr. Edward (Founder Fellow)
18 Eastfield Grove, Peterborough, Cambs. PE1 4BB, UK

Strong, Eithne (Founder Fellow)
17 Eaton Square, Monkstown, Co. Dublin, Ireland

Stuart, Alice V. (Founder Fellow)
57 Newington Road, Edinburgh, EH9 1QW, Scotland, UK

Sutton, Mr. Louide Weibert (Founder Fellow)
203 S. Bosse Avenue, Evansville, IN 47712, USA

Swartz, Mrs. Roberta Teale (Founder Fellow)
6 Haven Road, Wellesley, MA 02181, USA

Swetman, Mr. Glenn R. (Fellow)
638 Fairway Drive, Thibodaux, LA 70301, USA

Tacderas, Rev. Father Joseph (Founder Fellow)
St. Marianne's Church, 7922 South Passons Blvd., Pico Rivera, CA 90660, USA

Tait, Cornelia Damian (Founder Fellow)
10 Armour Road, Hatboro, PA 19040, USA

Taylor, Mr. Michael John (Founder Fellow)
Fishertown Craft Centre, 47/49 Shore Street, Cromarty, Ross & Cromarty, Scotland, UK

Telemaque, Mr. Harold M. (Founder Fellow)
Bungalow 11, No. 22 Road, Fyybad, Trinidad, West Indies

Thomae, Mrs. Betty Jane (Founder Fellow)
1008 Hardesty Place West, Columbus, OH 43204, USACR

Thomas, Stellera Marie A. (Founder Fellow)
3705 Tulsa Way, Apartment E, Fort Worth, TX 76107, USA

Thompson, Mrs. Esther Lee Johnson (Founder Fellow)
200 South Chandler Drive, Fort Worth, TX 76111, USA

Thorburn, Mr. James Alexander (Founder Fellow)
Box 739, English Department, Southeastern Louisiana University, Hammond, LA 70401, USA

Tierney, Margaret A. (Fellow)
Grange Clare, Kilmeague, Naas, Co. Kildare, Eire

Tschernek, Mr. Viktor (Founder Fellow)
Hoeppergang 14, D-3250 Hameln, German Federal Republic

Tunstall, Velma (Founder Fellow)
928 Third Place, Upland, CA 91786, USA

Turkay, Mr. Osman (Fellow)
22 Avenue Mansions, FInchley Road, London, NW3 7AX, UK

Turmeau, Constance E. (Founder Fellow)
31 Myln Meadow, Stock, Ingatestone, Essex, CM4 9NE, UK

Tuthill, Stacy Evelyn Johnson (Founder Life Fellow)
5821 Swarthmore Drive, College Park, MD 20740, USA

Vanson, Mr. Frederic (Vice-Chancellor)
24 Morley Grove, Harlow, Essex, UK

Van Ijzer, Meta (Life Fellow)
Soendastraat 30a, 2585 The Hague, Netherlands

Varma, Monika (Founder Fellow)
c/o Mr. S. Varma, C-34 Pamposh Enclave, New Delhi 110048, India

Vitoritto, Elvira Wamza (Founder Fellow)
P.O. Box 7116, West Trenton, NJ 08628, USA

Von Spakovsky, Dr. Anatol (Founder Fellow)
10020 Hampshire Drive S.E., Huntsville, AL 35803, USA

Walker, Mrs. Ida C. (Fellow)
P.O. Box 28, Hot Springs, AR 71901, USA

Waltman-Harmon, Nadine (Fellow)
1204 N.E. Ninth Street, Bend, OR 97701, USA

Wansbrough, Mr. David J. (Fellow)
18 The Links, Leura, N.S.W. 2781, Australia

Ward, Mary B. (Founder Fellow)
512 S. 55th Street, Birmingham, AL 35212, USA

Warren, Mr. James E. (Fellow)
544 Deering Road NW, Atlanta, GA 30309, USA

Webb, Ethel (Founder Fellow)
7 Auckland Way, Cottesloe, Western Australia 6011, Australia

Weber, Hulda (Founder Fellow)
915 West End Avenue, Apartment 5D, New York, NY 10025, USA

Weinbaum Eleanor Perlstein (Founder Life Fellow)
1215 Beaumont Savings Building, Beaumont, TX 77701, USA

Whitby, Julie L. (Fellow)
10 Old Square, Lincoln's Inn, London, WC2 3SU, UK

Wiley, Mrs. Vivian (Fellow)
374 Broadway, Paintsville, KY 41240, USA

Williams, Mr. Alan Moray (Honorary Life Fellow)
Postbox 4 3450 Allerod, Denmark

Williams, Florence (Founder Fellow)
20 Barnfield, Hemel Hempstead, Herts. HP3 9QH, UK

Winchell, Mr. Wallace (Founder Fellow)
P.O. Box 1046, Manchester, CT 06040, USA

Winful, Mr. Emmanuel A. (Life Fellow)
c/o African Development Bank, B.P. 1387, Abidjan 01, Ivory Coast, West Africa

Winkler, Mr. Manfred (Founder Fellow)
Balirar Street 7, Jerusalem, Kiriat Jowel, Israel

Woodall, Dr. Stella (Vice-Chancellor)
P.O. Box 253, Junction, TX 76849, USA

Woods, Mrs. Barbara (Fellow)
5 Rene Drive, Spencerport, NY 14559, USA

Wright, Mr. John M. (Fellow)
10/49 Osborne Road, Manly, N.S.W. 2095, Australia

Zaimof, Mr. Gueni G. (Fellow)
7386 Calle Real 30, Goleta, CA 93117, USA

Zeliff, Dr. Viola T. (Fellow)
2025 S.E. 17th Street, Pomfano Beach, FL 33062, USA

Zola, Marion (Founder Fellow)
999 N. Doheny Drive, Los Angeles, CA 90069, USA